BIOGRAPHY AND GENEALOGY MASTER INDEX 1995

ISSN 0730-1316

Gale Biographical Index Series
Number 1

BIOGRAPHY AND GENEALOGY MASTER INDEX

1995

A consolidated index to more than 455,000 biographical sketches in over 90 current and retrospective biographical dictionaries

Barbara McNeil, Editor

Gale Research Inc.

An International Thomson Publishing Company

Editor: Barbara McNeil

Associate Editors: Karen D. Kaus, Catherine A. Coulson, Brian Escamilla, Julie K. Karmazin, Terrance W. Peck, Geri J. Speace, Kelly L. Sprague

Assistant Editors: Aileen Collins, Sheryl Eichstaedt, Christopher M. McKenzie

Senior Editor: Peter M. Gareffa

Manager, Technical Support Services: Theresa Rocklin

Programmer: Ida M. Wright

Data Entry Supervisor: Benita Spight

Data Entry Group Leader: Gwendolyn Tucker

Data Entry Associates: LySandra C. Davis, Civie Ann Green

Production Director: Mary Beth Trimper

Production Assistant: Catherine Kemp

Art Director: Cynthia Baldwin

Desktop Publisher/Typesetter : C.J. Jonik

While every effort has been made to ensure the reliability of the information presented in this publication, Gale Research Inc. does not guarantee the accuracy of the data contained herein. Gale accepts no payment for listing; and inclusion in the publication of any organization, agency, institution, publication, service, or individual does not imply endorsement of the editors or publisher. Errors brought to the attention of the publisher and verified to the satisfaction of the publisher will be corrected in future editions.

Data from Marquis Who's Who publications has been licensed from Marquis Who's Who. "Marquis Who's Who" is a registered trademark of Reed Reference Publishing. All rights reserved. *BGMI* is an independent publication of Gale Research Inc. It has not been published or approved by Marquis Who's Who.

∞™ The paper used in this publication meets the minimum requirements of American National Standard for Information Sciences—Permanence Paper for Printed Library Materials. ANSI Z39.48-1984.

♻ This book is printed on recycled paper that meets Environmental Protection Agency standards.

Library of Congress Catalog Number 82-15700
ISBN 0-8103-8599-6
ISSN 0730-1316

Printed in the United States of America

Published simultaneously in the United Kingdom
by Gale Research International Limited
(An affiliated company of Gale Research Inc.)

Gale Research Inc., an International Thomson Publishing Company.

I(T)P™

ITP logo is a trademark under license.

The Gale Biographical Index Series

Biography and Genealogy Master Index
Second Edition, Supplements and Annual Volumes
(GBIS Number 1)

Children's Authors and Illustrators
Fourth Edition
(GBIS Number 2)

Author Biographies Master Index

(GBIS Number 3)

Journalist Biographies Master Index
(GBIS Number 4)

Performing Arts Biography Master Index
Second Edition
(GBIS Number 5)

Writers for Young Adults: Biographies Master Index

(GBIS Number 6)

Historical Biographical Dictionaries Master Index
(GBIS Number 7)

Twentieth-Century Author Biographies Master Index
(GBIS Number 8)

Artist Biographies Master Index
(GBIS Number 9)

Business Biography Master Index
(GBIS Number 10)

Abridged Biography and Genealogy Master Index
(GBIS Number 11)

Contents

Introduction

Biography and Genealogy Master Index 1995 is the fourteenth in a series of annual updates to the *Biography and Genealogy Master Index (BGMI)* base volumes published in 1981. Containing more than 455,000 citations, *BGMI 1995* provides an index to 135 volumes and editions of over 90 biographical dictionaries, including new editions of sources previously indexed as well as new titles. With the publication of *BGMI 1995*, the total number of biographical sketches indexed by the *BGMI* base set and its fourteen updates exceeds 9.7 million. The chart at the conclusion of this introduction provides further details on *BGMI* publications already available and those planned for the future.

Concept and Scope

BGMI is a unique index that enables the user to determine which edition(s) of which publication to consult for biographical information. Almost as helpful, if there is no listing for a given individual in *BGMI* it reveals that there is no listing for that individual in any of the sources indexed. In cases where *BGMI* shows multiple listings for the same person, the user is able either to choose which source is the most convenient or to locate multiple sketches to compare and expand information furnished by a single listing.

Biographical sources indexed in *BGMI* are of several different types: 1) biographical dictionaries and who's whos, which supply information on a number of individuals; 2) subject encyclopedias, which include some biographical entries; 3) volumes of literary criticism, which may contain only a limited amount of biographical information but give critical surveys of a writer's works; and 4) indexes, which do not provide immediate information but refer the user to a body of information elsewhere. *BGMI* indexes only reference books containing multiple biographies; it does not index periodicals or books of biography about only one individual.

Sources indexed by *BGMI* cover both living and deceased persons from every field of activity and from all areas of the world. (Names from myth or legend and literary characters are not indexed.) The sources are predominantly current, readily available, "standard" reference books (for example, the Marquis Who's Who series); however, *BGMI* also includes important retrospective sources and general subject sources that cover both contemporary and noncontemporary people.

Although the majority of the sources indexed in *BGMI* covers individuals in the United States, this index also includes sources that cover individuals in foreign countries in such titles as *The Dictionary of National Biography* (Great Britain), *Dictionary of Canadian Biography*, and *Who's Who in the World*.

BGMI 1995, for example, indexes general works, both current and retrospective *(Current Biography, The New York Times Biographical Service, Who Was Who in America)*. Also included are sources on special subject areas such as literature *(The Bloomsbury Guide to Women's Literature, A Directory of American Poets and Fiction Writers, The Encyclopedia of Science Fiction, Writers Directory)*, music *(Contemporary Musicians, The New Grove Dictionary of Opera)*, and entertainment *(Contemporary Theatre, Film, and Television; International Dictionary of Films and Filmmakers; International Motion Picture Almanac; Who's Who in Hollywood)*. Other subject areas covered in *BGMI 1995* include science, law and politics, ethnic and special interest groups, business, art, religion, social issues, and sports.

How to Read a Citation

Each citation in *BGMI* gives the person's name followed by the years of birth and/or death as found in the source book. If a source has indicated that the dates may not be accurate, the questionable date(s) are preceded by a *c.* (circa) or followed by a question mark. When the source gives flourished dates rather than birth or death dates, this is indicated in *BGMI* by the abbreviation *fl.* Centuries are indicated with

the abbreviation *cent*. If there is no year of birth, the death date is preceded by a lower case *d*. The codes for the books indexed follow the dates.

Walsh, William 1512?-1577 *DcNaB*
Youll, Henry fl. c. 1600- *Baker 92*
Sokoine, Edward d1984 *NewYTBS 84*

References to names that are identical in spelling and dates have been consolidated under a single name and date entry, as in the example below for *Bernard Goodwin*. When a name appears in more than one edition or volume of an indexed work, the title code for the book is given only once and is followed by the various codes for the editions in which the name appears.

Goodwin, Bernard 1907- *IntMPA 81, -82, -84,*
WhoAm 80, -82, -84, WhoWor 82

Another feature of the *BGMI* updates is the portrait indicator. If the source has a portrait or photograph of the person, this is indicated by the abbreviation *[port]* after the source code.

Daniel, C William 1925- *WhoCan 84 [port]*

A list of the works indexed in *BGMI 1995*, and the codes used to refer to them, is printed on the endsheets. Complete bibliographic citations to the titles indexed follow this introduction.

Editorial Practices

All names in an indexed work are included in *BGMI*. There is no need to consult the work itself if the name being researched is not found, since it is editorial policy to index every name in a particular book. Names that are not listed in the sources selected for indexing are not added to *BGMI*.

Many source books differ in their method of alphabetizing names; therefore, some names may have an alphabetic position in a source book different from their position in this index. Names are alphabetized in *BGMI* letter-by-letter.

John, Terry
Johncock, Gordon
John-Sandy, Rene Emanuel

Delasa, Jose M
De las Heras, Gonzalo
Delavigne, Casimir
De La Warr, Earl

Names appear in *BGMI* exactly as they are listed in the source books; no attempt has been made to determine whether names with similar spellings and dates refer to the same individual, or to add dates if they are known but are not listed in the source. With a file consisting of millions of names, it is not possible to edit each name thoroughly and still publish on a timely basis. Therefore, several listings for the same individual may sometimes be found:

Bellman, Richard 1920- *ConAu 12NR*
Bellman, Richard 1920-1984 *ConAu 112*
Bellman, Richard E 1920- *WhoAm 84*
Bellman, Richard Ernest 1920- *WhoFrS 84*

Despite the variations in the form of the name, it is apparent that the same person is referred to in the above citations. The existence of such variations can be of importance to anyone attempting to determine biographical details about an individual.

In a very few cases, extremely long names have been shortened because of typesetting limitations. For example: *Robertson, Alexander Thomas Parke Anthony Cecil* would be shortened to:

Robertson, Alexander Thomas Parke A

It is believed that such editing will not affect the usefulness of individual entries.

Research Aids

Researchers will need to look under all possible listings for a name, especially in the cases of:

1. Names with prefixes or suffixes:

> **Angeles,** Victoria De Los
> **De Los Angeles,** Victoria
> **Los Angeles,** Victoria De

2. Compound surnames which may be entered in sources under either part of the surname:

> **Garcia Lorca,** Federico
> **Lorca,** Federico Garcia
>
> **Benary-Isbert,** Margot
> **Isbert,** Margot Benary-

3. Chinese names which may be entered in sources in direct or inverted order:

> **Chiang,** Kai-Shek
> **Kai-Shek,** Chiang

Or which may be listed by the Pinyin spelling:

> **Hsiang,** Chung-Hua
> **Xiang,** Zhonghua

4. Names transliterated in the sources from non-Roman alphabets:

> **Amelko,** Nikolai Nikolayevich
> **Amelko,** Nikolay Nikolayevich
> **Amel'ko,** Nikolay Nikolayevich

5. Pseudonyms, noms de plume, and stage names:

> **Clemens,** Samuel Langhorne
> **Twain,** Mark
>
> **Crosby,** Bing
> **Crosby,** Harry Lillis

6. Names which may be entered in the sources both under the full name and either initials or part of the name:

> **Eliot,** T S
> **Eliot,** Thomas Stearns
>
> **Welles,** George Orson
> **Welles,** Orson

To further aid research, cross-references are included in *BGMI* when significant biographical information on an individual is included within the biographical sketch of another person or group. For example, if information on Mike Love appears in a biographical dictionary under the entry for Brian Wilson, a cross-reference will appear in *BGMI:*

> **Love,** Mike 1941- *See* Wilson, Brian 1942- *Baker 92*

In addition, all cross-references appearing in indexed publications have been retained in *BGMI* as regular citations, e.g., *Morris, Julian SEE West, Morris* would appear in *BGMI* as *Morris, Julian* followed by the source code.

Available in Electronic Formats

The data base used to create *BGMI* and its updates is also available in a microfiche edition called *Bio-Base,* on-line through DIALOG Information Services, Inc. as *Biography Master Index (BMI),* and on CD-ROM

as *BGMI CD-ROM*. The chart below outlines the relationships, in existing and future publications, between the *BGMI* hardcover annual updates and cumulations, and the microfiche, on-line, and CD-ROM formats. *BGMI* is also available for licensing on magnetic tape or diskette in a fielded format. Either the complete data base or a custom selection of entries may be ordered.

YEAR OF PUBLICATION	HARDCOVER		MICROFICHE	ELECTRONIC
1980-81	Biography and Genealogy Master Index, 2nd ed.			
1982	BGMI 1981-82 Supplement			
1983	BGMI 1983 Supplement			**ON-LINE** Entire data base is in DIALOG BMI File 287 (updated annually)
1984	BGMI 1984 Supplement			
1985	BGMI 1985	BGMI 1981-85 Cumulation		
1986	BGMI 1986			
1987	BGMI 1987			
1988	BGMI 1988			
1989	BGMI 1989			
1990	BGMI 1990	BGMI 1986-90 Cumulation		**CD-ROM** Entire data base is available as *BGMI CD-ROM* (updated annually)
1991	BGMI 1991			
1992	BGMI 1992			
1993	BGMI 1993		Bio-Base 1995 Master Cumulation (Supersedes all previous editions)	
1994	BGMI 1994			
1995	BGMI 1995	BGMI 1991-95 Cumulation		

Suggestions Are Welcome

Additional sources will be indexed in future publications as their availability and usefulness become known. The editor welcomes suggestions for additional works which could be indexed, or any other comments and suggestions.

Bibliographic Key to Source Codes

Code	Book Indexed
AfrAmG	*African American Generals and Flag Officers.* Biographies of over 120 blacks in the United States military. By Walter L. Hawkins. Jefferson, NC: McFarland & Co., 1993.
AfrAmAl 6	*The African-American Almanac.* Sixth edition. Detroit: Gale Research, 1994. Formerly published as *The Negro Almanac.* Use the Index to locate biographies.
AmCulL	*American Cultural Leaders.* From colonial times to the present. By Justin Harmon et al. Santa Barbara, CA: ABC-Clio, 1993.
AmRev	*The American Revolution, 1775-1783.* An encyclopedia. Two volumes. Edited by Richard L. Blanco. New York: Garland Publishing, 1993.
AmSocL	*American Social Leaders.* By William McGuire and Leslie Wheeler. Santa Barbara, CA: ABC-Clio, 1993.
AnObit 1992	*The Annual Obituary. 1992.* Detroit: St. James Press, 1993. Use the "Alphabetical Index of Entrants" to locate biographies.
AstEnc	*The Astrology Encyclopedia.* By James R. Lewis. Detroit: Gale Research, 1994. Use the Index at the back of the book to locate entries.
Au&Arts	*Authors & Artists for Young Adults.* Detroit: Gale Research, 1993-1994. *Au&Arts 11* Volume 11; 1993. *Au&Arts 12* Volume 12; 1994.
BasBi	*Basketball Biographies.* 434 U.S. players, coaches and contributors to the game, 1891-1990. By Martin Taragano. Jefferson, NC: McFarland & Co., 1991.
BlkWr 2	*Black Writers.* A selection of sketches from *Contemporary Authors.* Second edition. Detroit: Gale Research, 1994.
BlmGEL	*The Bloomsbury Guide to English Literature.* The new authority on English literature. Edited by Marion Wynne-Davies. New York: Prentice Hall General Reference, 1990. Originally published in hardcover as the *Prentice Hall Guide to English Literature.* Biographies begin on page 295.

BlmGWL	*The Bloomsbury Guide to Women's Literature.* Edited by Claire Buck. New York: Prentice Hall General Reference, 1992. Biographies begin on page 247.
BuCMET	*Bud Collins' Modern Encyclopedia of Tennis.* Edited by Bud Collins and Zander Hollander. Detroit: Gale Research, 1994. Use the Index to locate biographies.
ChlLR	*Children's Literature Review.* Excerpts from reviews, criticism, and commentary on books for children and young people. Detroit: Gale Research, 1993-1994.

ChlLR 30	Volume 30; 1993.
ChlLR 31	Volume 31; 1994.
ChlLR 32	Volume 32; 1994.

ClMLC	*Classical and Medieval Literature Criticism.* Excerpts from criticism of the works of world authors from classical antiquity through the fourteenth century, from the first appraisals to current evaluations. Detroit: Gale Research, 1993-1994.

ClMLC 11	Volume 11; 1993.
ClMLC 12	Volume 12; 1994.

CngDr 93	*Congressional Directory.* 103d Congress, 1993-1994. Washington, DC: United States Government Printing Office, 1993. Use the "Name Index" to locate entries.
ConAu	*Contemporary Authors.* A bio-bibliographical guide to current writers in fiction, general nonfiction, poetry, journalism, drama, motion pictures, television, and other fields. Detroit: Gale Research, 1993-1994.

ConAu 140	Volume 140; 1993.
ConAu 141	Volume 141; 1994.
ConAu 142	Volume 142; 1994.

ConAu	*Contemporary Authors, Autobiography Series.* Detroit: Gale Research, 1994.

ConAu 18AS	Volume 18.
ConAu 19AS	Volume 19.

ConAu	*Contemporary Authors, New Revision Series.* A bio-bibliographical guide to current writers in fiction, general nonfiction, poetry, journalism, drama, motion pictures, television, and other fields. Detroit: Gale Research, 1994.

ConAu 41NR	Volume 41.
ConAu 42NR	Volume 42.
ConAu 43NR	Volume 43.

ConBlB	*Contemporary Black Biography.* Profiles from the international black community. Detroit: Gale Research, 1994.

ConBlB 5	Volume 5.
ConBlB 6	Volume 6.

ConDr 93	*Contemporary Dramatists.* Fifth edition. Edited by K.A. Berney. London: St. James Press, 1993.
ConLC	*Contemporary Literary Criticism.* The year in fiction, poetry, drama, and world literature and the year's new authors, prizewinners, obituaries, and outstanding literary events. Detroit: Gale Research, 1993-1994.

ConLC 76	Volume 76: Yearbook 1992; 1993. Use the "Cumulative Author Index" to locate entries.
ConLC 77	Volume 77; 1993.
ConLC 78	Volume 78; 1994.
ConLC 79	Volume 79; 1994.
ConLC 80	Volume 80; 1994.
ConLC 81	Volume 81: Yearbook 1993; 1994. Use the "Cumulative Author Index" to locate entries.

ConMus   *Contemporary Musicians*. Profiles of the people in music. Detroit: Gale Research, 1994.

        ConMus 10   Volume 10.
        ConMus 11   Volume 11.

ConTFT 11   *Contemporary Theatre, Film, and Television*. A biographical guide featuring performers, directors, writers, producers, designers, managers, choreographers, technicians, composers, executives, dancers, and critics in the United States and Great Britain. Volume 11. Detroit: Gale Research, 1994. Earlier editions published as *Who's Who in the Theatre*.

ConWorW 93   *Contemporary World Writers*. Second edition. Edited by Tracy Chevalier. Contemporary Writers of the English Language Series. Detroit: St. James Press, 1993. First edition published as *Contemporary Foreign-Language Writers*.

CurBio 93   *Current Biography Yearbook. 1993*. New York: H.W. Wilson Co., 1993.

        CurBio 93N   Obituary section located in the back of the volume.

DcAmReB 2   *Dictionary of American Religious Biography*. Second edition. By Henry Warner Bowden. Westport, CT: Greenwood Press, 1993.

DcLB   *Dictionary of Literary Biography*. Detroit: Gale Research, 1993-1994.

        DcLB 129   Volume 129: *Nineteenth-Century German Writers, 1841-1900*. Edited by James Hardin and Sicgfricd Mcws; 1993.

        DcLB 130   Volume 130: *American Short-Story Writers since World War II*. Edited by Patrick Meanor; 1993.

        DcLB 131   Volume 131: *Seventeenth-Century British Nondramatic Poets*. Third Series. Edited by M. Thomas Hester; 1993.

        DcLB 132   Volume 132: *Sixteenth-Century British Nondramatic Writers*. First Series. Edited by David A. Richardson; 1993.

        DcLB 133   Volume 133: *Nineteenth-Century German Writers to 1840*. Edited by James Hardin and Siegfried Mews; 1993.

        DcLB 134   Volume 134: *Twentieth-Century Spanish Poets*. Second Series. Edited by Jerry Phillips Winfield; 1994.

        DcLB 135   Volume 135: *British Short-Fiction Writers, 1880-1914: The Realist Tradition*. Edited by William B. Thesing; 1994.

        DcLB 136   Volume 136: *Sixteenth-Century British Nondramatic Writers*. Second Series. Edited by David A. Richardson; 1994.

        DcLB 137   Volume 137: *American Magazine Journalists, 1900-1960*. Second Series. Edited by Sam G. Riley; 1994.

        DcLB 138   Volume 138: *German Writers and Works of the High Middle Ages: 1170-1280*. Edited by James Hardin and Will Hasty; 1994.

        DcLB 139   Volume 139: *British Short-Fiction Writers, 1945-1980*. Edited by Dean Baldwin; 1994.

        DcLB 140   Volume 140: *American Book-Collectors and Bibliographers*. First Series. Edited by Joseph Rosenblum; 1994.

        DcLB 141   Volume 141: *British Children's Writers, 1880-1914*. Edited by Laura M. Zaidman; 1994.

DcLB	*Dictionary of Literary Biography, Yearbook. 1993 Yearbook.* Edited by James W. Hipp. Detroit: Gale Research, 1994.

    DcLB Y93   Use the Table of Contents to locate entries.
    DcLB Y93N   Obituaries section begins on page 261.

DcNaB MP	*The Dictionary of National Biography. Missing Persons.* Edited by C. S. Nicholls. Oxford: Oxford University Press, 1993.
DrAPF 93	*A Directory of American Poets and Fiction Writers.* Names and addresses of contemporary poets and fiction writers whose work has been published in the United States. 1993-1994 edition. New York: Poets & Writers, 1992. Use the Index to locate listings.
DramC 4	*Drama Criticism.* Criticism of the most significant and widely studied dramatic works from all the world's literature. Volume 4. Detroit: Gale Research, 1994.
EncABHB 9	*Encyclopedia of American Business History and Biography. Iron and Steel in the Twentieth Century.* Edited by Bruce E. Seely. New York: Facts on File, 1994.
EncDeaf	*The Encyclopedia of Deafness and Hearing Disorders.* By Carol Turkington and Allen E. Sussman. New York: Facts on File, 1992.
EncEth	*Encyclopedia of Ethics.* Two volumes. Edited by Lawrence C. Becker and Charlotte B. Becker. New York: Garland Publishing, 1992.
EncNAR	*The Encyclopedia of Native American Religions.* By Arlene Hirschfelder and Paulette Molin. New York: Facts on File, 1992.
EncSPD	*The Encyclopedia of Schizophrenia and the Psychotic Disorders.* By Richard Noll. New York: Facts on File, 1992.
EncSF 93	*The Encyclopedia of Science Fiction.* Edited by John Clute and Peter Nicholls. New York: St. Martin's Press, 1993.
EnvEnc	*Environmental Encyclopedia.* First edition. Detroit: Gale Research, 1994.
GayLL	*Gay & Lesbian Literature.* Detroit: St. James Press, 1994.
GuFrLit 2	*Guide to French Literature.* Beginnings to 1789. By Anthony Levi. Detroit: St. James Press, 1994.
HispLC	*Hispanic Literature Criticism.* Two volumes. Detroit: Gale Research, 1994.
HisWorL	*Historic World Leaders.* Five volumes. Edited by Anne Commire. Detroit: Gale Research, 1994. Use the "Biographies in *Historic World Leaders*" Index at the back of Volume 5 to locate biographies.
HisDcKW	*Historical Dictionary of the Korean War.* Edited by James I. Matray. New York: Greenwood Press, 1991.
HorFD	*Horror Film Directors, 1931-1990.* By Dennis Fischer. Jefferson, NC: McFarland & Co., 1991. Use the Table of Contents to locate entries.

IntDcB   *International Dictionary of Ballet.* Two volumes. Edited by Martha Bremser. Detroit: St. James Press, 1993.

IntDcF 2-4   *The International Dictionary of Films and Filmmakers.* Second edition. Volume 4: *Writers and Production Artists.* Edited by Samantha Cook. Detroit: St. James Press, 1993.

IntDcT 2   *International Dictionary of Theatre.* Volume 2: *Playwrights.* Edited by Mark Hawkins-Dady. Detroit: St. James Press, 1994.

IntMPA   *International Motion Picture Almanac.* 1994 edition. New York: Quigley Publishing Co., 1994.

        IntMPA 94   Biographies are found in the "Who's Who in Motion Pictures and Television" section. The listings are identical to those found in the *International Television and Video Almanac.*

        IntMPA 94N   Listings are located in the Obituaries section.

IntWW 93   *The International Who's Who.* 57th edition, 1993-1994. London: Europa Publications, 1993. Distributed by Gale Research, Detroit.

        IntWW 93N   Obituary section is located at the front of the volume.

LitC   *Literature Criticism from 1400 to 1800.* Excerpts from criticism of the works of fifteenth-, sixteenth-, seventeenth-, and eighteenth-century novelists, poets, playwrights, philosophers, and other creative writers, from the first published critical appraisals to current evaluations. Detroit: Gale Research, 1993-1994.

        LitC 22   Volume 22; 1993.
        LitC 23   Volume 23; 1994.
        LitC 24   Volume 24; 1994.

LngBDD   *Longman Biographical Directory of Decision-Makers in Russia and the Successor States.* Edited by Martin McCauley. Harlow, Essex, England: Longman Current Affairs, 1993. Distributed by Gale Research, Detroit.

ModArCr 4   *Modern Arts Criticism.* A biographical and critical guide to painters, sculptors, photographers, and architects from the beginning of the modern era to the present. Volume 4. Detroit: Gale Research, 1994.

NewGrDO   *The New Grove Dictionary of Opera.* Four volumes. Edited by Stanley Sadie. London: Macmillan Press; New York: Grove's Dictionaries of Music, 1992.

New YTBS 93   *The New York Times Biographical Service.* A compilation of current biographical information of general interest. Volume 24, Numbers 1-12. Ann Arbor, MI: University Microfilms International, 1993.

        Use the annual Index to locate biographies.

News   *Newsmakers.* The people behind today's headlines. Detroit: Gale Research, 1993-1994.Issues prior to 1988, Issue 2, were published as *Contemporary Newsmakers.*

        News 93   1993 Cumulation; 1993.
        News 93-3   1993, Issue 3; 1993.
        News 94-1   1994, Issue 1; 1994.
        News 94-2   1994, Issue 2; 1994.

        Use the "Cumulative Newsmaker Index" to locate entries. Biographies in each quarterly issue can also be located in the annual cumulation.

NinCLC   *Nineteenth-Century Literature Criticism.* Excerpts from criticism of the works of novelists, poets, playwrights, short story writers, philosophers, and other creative writers who died between 1800 and 1899, from the first published critical appraisals to current evaluations. Detroit: Gale Research, 1993-1994.

　　　　　NinCLC 40　　Volume 40; 1993. Contains no biographies.
　　　　　NinCLC 41　　Volume 41; 1994.
　　　　　NinCLC 42　　Volume 42; 1994.
　　　　　NinCLC 43　　Volume 43; 1994.

NobelP 91   *Nobel Prize Winners.* Supplement 1987-1991. Edited by Paula McGuire. New York: H.W. Wilson Co., 1992.

　　　　　NobelP 91N　　"Nobel Prize Winners Who Have Died since 1986" section appears on page 25.

PoeCrit   *Poetry Criticism.* Excerpts from criticism of the works of the most significant and widely studied poets of world literature. Detroit: Gale Research, 1994.

　　　　　PoeCrit 7　　Volume 7.
　　　　　PoeCrit 8　　Volume 8.

ProFbHF   *The Pro Football Hall of Fame.* Players, coaches, team owners and league officials, 1963-1991. By Denis J. Harrington. Jefferson, NC: McFarland & Co., 1991.

　　　　　Use the Index to locate entries.

RfGShF   *Reference Guide to Short Fiction.* Edited by Noelle Watson. Detroit: St. James Press, 1994.

ShSCr   *Short Story Criticism.* Excerpts from criticism of the works of short fiction writers. Detroit: Gale Research, 1993-1994.

　　　　　ShSCr 12　　Volume 12; 1993.
　　　　　ShSCr 13　　Volume 13; 1993.
　　　　　ShSCr 14　　Volume 14; 1994.

SmATA   *Something about the Author.* Facts and pictures about authors and illustrators of books for young people. Detroit: Gale Research, 1993-1994.

　　　　　SmATA 74　　Volume 74; 1993.
　　　　　SmATA 75　　Volume 75; 1994.
　　　　　SmATA 76　　Volume 76; 1994.
　　　　　SmATA 77　　Volume 77; 1994.

SmATA   *Something about the Author, Autobiography Series.* Detroit: Gale Research, 1994.

　　　　　SmATA 17AS　　Volume 17.
　　　　　SmATA 18AS　　Volume 18.

TwCLC   *Twentieth-Century Literary Criticism.* Excerpts from criticism of the works of novelists, poets, playwrights, short story writers, and other creative writers who lived between 1900 and 1960, from the first published critical appraisals to current evaluations. Detroit: Gale Research, 1993-1994.

　　　　　TwCLC 49　　Volume 49; 1993.
　　　　　TwCLC 50　　Volume 50; 1993. Contains no biographies.
　　　　　TwCLC 51　　Volume 51; 1994.
　　　　　TwCLC 52　　Volume 52; 1994.
　　　　　TwCLC 53　　Volume 53; 1994.

TwCYAW   *Twentieth-Century Young Adult Writers.* First edition. Twentieth-Century
                  Writers Series. Detroit: St. James Press, 1994.

WhAm 10   *Who Was Who in America.* Volume 10, 1989-1993. New Providence, NJ:
                  Marquis Who's Who, 1993.

WhAmRev   *Who Was Who in the American Revolution.* New York: Facts on File, 1993.

WhWE   *Who Was Who in World Exploration.* By Carl Waldman and Alan Wexler. New
                  York: Facts on File, 1992.

Who 94   *Who's Who.* An annual biographical dictionary. 146th Year of Issue, 1994. New
                  York: St. Martin's Press, 1994.

                      Who 94N   Obituary section.
                      Who 94R   The Royal Family section.

WhoAm 94   *Who's Who in America.* 48th edition, 1994. New Providence, NJ: Marquis
                  Who's Who, 1993.

WhoAmA 93   *Who's Who in American Art.* 20th edition, 1993-1994. New Providence, NJ:
                  R.R. Bowker, 1993.

                      WhoAmA 93N   The Necrology begins on page 1455.

WhoAmL 94   *Who's Who in American Law.* Eighth edition, 1994-1995. New Providence, NJ:
                  Marquis Who's Who, 1994.

WhoAmP 93   *Who's Who in American Politics.* 14th edition, 1993-1994. Two volumes. New
                  Providence, NJ: R.R. Bowker, 1993.

                      Use the Index to locate biographies.

WhoAsA 94   *Who's Who among Asian Americans.* 1994-1995 edition. Detroit: Gale Research,
                  1994.

                      WhoAsA 94N   The Obituaries section is located in the back of the
                                     volume.

WhoBlA 94   *Who's Who among Black Americans.* Eighth edition, 1994/1995. Detroit: Gale
                  Research, 1994.

                      WhoBlA 94N   The Obituaries section is located in the back of the
                                     volume.

WhoCom   *Who's Who in Comedy.* Comedians, comics, and clowns from vaudeville to
                  today's stand-ups. By Ronald L. Smith. New York: Facts on File, 1992.

WhoFI 94   *Who's Who in Finance and Industry.* 28th edition, 1994-1995. New Providence,
                  NJ: Marquis Who's Who, 1993.

WhoHisp 94   *Who's Who among Hispanic Americans.* Third edition, 1994-1995. Detroit: Gale
                  Research, 1994.

                      WhoHisp 94N   The Obituaries section begins on page 887.

WhoHol 92   *Who's Who in Hollywood.* The largest cast of international film personalities
                  ever assembled. Two volumes. By David Ragan. New York: Facts on File,
                  1992.

WhoIns 94   *Who's Who in Insurance.* 1994 edition. Englewood, NJ: Underwriter Printing & Publishing Co., 1994.

WhoMW 93   *Who's Who in the Midwest.* 24th edition, 1994-1995. New Providence, NJ: Marquis Who's Who, 1994.

WhoPRCh 91   *Who's Who in the People's Republic of China.* Third edition. Two volumes. By Wolfgang Bartke. Munich and New York: K.G. Saur, 1991.

WhoScEn 94   *Who's Who in Science and Engineering.* Second edition, 1994-1995. New Providence, NJ: Marquis Who's Who, 1994.

WhoWest 94   *Who's Who in the West.* 24th edition, 1994-1995. New Providence, NJ: Marquis Who's Who, 1993.

WhoWomW 91   *Who's Who of Women in World Politics.* First edition. New York: Bowker-Saur, 1991.

WomPubS   *Women Public Speakers in the United States, 1800-1925.* A bio-critical sourcebook. Edited by Karlyn Kohrs Campbell. Westport, CT: Greenwood Press, 1993.

WorESoc   *The World Encyclopedia of Soccer.* Detroit: Gale Research, 1994.
               Biographies are located in the "Who's Who in Soccer" section which begins on page 49.

WorInv   *World of Invention.* History's most significant inventions and the people behind them. Detroit: Gale Research, 1994.

WorScD   *World of Scientific Discovery.* Scientific milestones and the people who made them possible. Detroit: Gale Research, 1994.

WrDr 94   *The Writers Directory.* 11th edition, 1994-1996. Detroit: St. James Press, 1994.
               WrDr 94N   The Obituaries section is located in the back of the volume.

BIOGRAPHY AND GENEALOGY MASTER INDEX 1995

A

Aabel, Hauk d1961 *WhoHol 92*
Aach, Herb 1923-1985 *WhoAmA 93N*
Aadahl, Jorg 1937- *WhoAm 94, WhoFI 94, WhoWest 94*
Aadland, Beverly 1942- *WhoHol 92*
Aadland, Donald Ingvald 1936- *WhoAm 94*
Aadnesen, Christopher 1948- *WhoMW 93*
Aafedt, Ole 1929- *WhoAmP 93*
Aagaard, George Nelson 1913- *WhoAm 94*
Aaker, Lee 1943- *WhoHol 92*
Aaker, Peggy Ann 1945- *WhoFI 94*
Aakvaag, Torvild 1927- *IntWW 93*
Aalfs, Janet E. *DrAPF 93*
Aalto, Madeleine *WhoWest 94*
Aalund, Suzy 1932- *WhoAmA 93*
Aames, Angela d1988 *WhoHol 92*
Aames, Willie 1960- *IntMPA 94, WhoHol 92*
Aamodt, Gary *WhoAmP 93*
Aamodt, Ludvig Jerry 1937- *WhoMW 93*
Aamodt, Roger Louis 1941- *WhoAm 94*
Aandy, K. d1980 *WhoHol 92*
Aanerud, Melvin Bernard 1943- *WhoMW 93*
Aanestad, Jonathan Robert 1954- *WhoMW 93*
Aaraas, Hans Tandberg 1919- *IntWW 93*
Aardema, Verna 1911- *WrDr 94*
Aarnes, Asbjorn Sigurd 1923- *IntWW 93*
Aaron *BlmGEL*
Aaron, Allen Harold 1932- *WhoAm 94, WhoAmL 94*
Aaron, Barbara Diane 1957- *WhoAmL 94*
Aaron, Benjamin 1915- *WhoAm 94, WhoAmL 94*
Aaron, Bertram Donald 1922- *WhoFI 94*
Aaron, Betsy 1938- *WhoAm 94*
Aaron, Betty *WhoAmP 93*
Aaron, Bud 1927- *WhoWest 94*
Aaron, Chester 1923- *SmATA 74 [port], WrDr 94*
Aaron, Evelyn (Wilhelmina) Keisler *WhoAmA 93*
Aaron, Frank W., Jr. 1942- *WhoIns 94*
Aaron, Hank 1934- *AfrAmAl 6 [port], ConBlB 5 [port], WhoAm 94*
Aaron, Henry Jacob 1936- *WhoAm 94, WhoAmP 94*
Aaron, Henry Louis 1934- *WhoBlA 94*
Aaron, Howard *DrAPF 93*
Aaron, Howard Berton 1939- *WhoMW 93*
Aaron, James E. 1927- *WrDr 94*
Aaron, Jean-Jacques 1939- *WhoScEn 94*
Aaron, Jonathan *DrAPF 93*
Aaron, Kenneth Ellyot 1948- *WhoAm 94, WhoAmL 94*
Aaron, M. Robert 1922- *WhoAm 94*
Aaron, Marcus, II 1929- *WhoAm 94*
Aaron, Michael 1959- *WhoAmL 94*
Aaron, Neal C. 1940- *WhoIns 94*
Aaron, Paul *IntMPA 94, WhoAm 94*
Aaron, Marion Roger S. 1942- *WhoAm 94*
Aaron, Roy H. 1929- *IntMPA 94*
Aaron, Roy Henry 1929- *WhoAm 94, WhoAmL 94*
Aaron, Shirley Mae 1935- *WhoWest 94*
Aaron of Lincoln d1186 *DcNaB MP*
Aaronovitch, Sam 1919- *WrDr 94*
Aarons, George 1896-1980 *WhoAmA 93N*
Aarons-Holder, Charmaine Michele 1959- *WhoAmL 94*

Aaronson, David Ernest 1940- *WhoAm 94, WhoAmL 94*
Aaronson, Graham Raphael 1944- *Who 94*
Aaronson, Irving d1963 *WhoHol 92*
Aaronson, Joel P. 1946- *WhoAm 94, WhoAmL 94*
Aaronson, Robert Jay 1942- *WhoAm 94*
Aars, Rallin James 1941- *WhoFI 94*
Aarsleff, Hans *WhoAm 94*
Aarsvold, Ole *WhoAmP 93*
Aas, Lynn W. *WhoAmP 93*
Aasand, Hardin Levine 1958- *WhoMW 93*
Aase, Jon Morton 1936- *WhoWest 94*
Aasen, Eugene Nels 1952- *WhoWest 94*
Aasen, John d1938 *WhoHol 92*
Aasen, Lawrence Obert 1922- *WhoAm 94*
Aaslestad, Halvor Gunerius 1937- *WhoAm 94*
A B, Orlando 1946- *WhoHisp 94*
Abad, Pacita 1946- *WhoAmA 93*
Abadi, Fritzie *WhoAmA 93*
Abadi, Fritzie 1915- *WhoAm 94*
Abady, Josephine Rose 1949- *WhoMW 93*
Abaijah, Josephine *WhoWomW 91*
Abajian, Henry Krikor 1909- *WhoScEn 94*
Abakanowicz, Magdalena 1930- *IntWW 93*
Abalakin, Viktor Kuz'mich 1930- *WhoScEn 94*
Abalkin, Leonid Ivanovich 1930- *IntWW 93, LoBiDrD*
Aballi, Arturo José, Jr. 1944- *WhoHisp 94*
Abalos, David T. 1939- *WhoHisp 94*
Abalos, Delma J. 1953- *WhoHisp 94*
Abalos, Ted Quinto 1930- *WhoScEn 94*
Abanero, Jose Nelito Talavera 1960- *WhoScEn 94*
Abany, Albert Charles 1921- *WhoAmA 93*
Abarbanel, Henry Don Isaac 1943- *WhoScEn 94*
Abarbanel, Judith Edna 1956- *WhoWest 94*
Abarbanel, Lina d1963 *WhoHol 92*
Abarbanel, Sam X. 1914- *IntMPA 94*
Abarquez-Delacruz, Prosy 1952- *WhoAsA 94*
Abartis, C. *DrAPF 93*
Abashidze, Grigori Grigol Grigorievich 1913- *IntWW 93*
Abashidze, Irakliy Vissarionovich d1992 *IntWW 93N*
Abatantuono, Diego *WhoHol 92*
Abate, Catherine M. 1947- *WhoAmP 93*
Abate, Ernest Nicholas 1943- *WhoAmP 93*
Abate, John E. 1931- *WhoScEn 94*
Abate, Joseph Francis 1946- *WhoAmP 93*
Abate, Kenneth 1944- *WhoMW 93*
Abate, Ralph Francis 1945- *WhoScEn 94*
Abatemarco, Michael J. 1947- *WhoAm 94*
Abaunza, Donald Richard 1945- *WhoAmL 94*
Abaza, Mohamed Maher 1930- *IntWW 93*
Abazis, Theodora Dimitrios 1950- *WhoFI 94*
Abba, Marta d1988 *WhoHol 92*
Abbadia, Luigia 1821-1896 *NewGrDO*
Abbado, Claudio 1933- *IntWW 93, NewGrDO, Who 94, WhoAm 94*

Abbagnaro, Louis Anthony 1942- *WhoAm 94*
Abbas, I 1571-1629 *HisWorL [port]*
Abbas, Hector d1942 *WhoHol 92*
Abbas, K. A. 1914-1987 *IntDcF 2-4*
Abbas, Khwaja Ahmad 1914- *WrDr 94*
Abbas, Mian M. 1933- *WhoAsA 94*
Abbas, Sherkoh A. 1963- *WhoMW 93*
Abbasabadi, Alireza 1950- *WhoMW 93*
Abbaschian, Reza 1944- *WhoScEn 94*
Abbasi, Tariq Afzal 1946- *WhoMW 93, WhoScEn 94*
Abbate, Carolyn 1955- *NewGrDO*
Abbate, Paul J. 1919- *WhoAmP 93*
Abbate, Paul S. 1884-1972 *WhoAmA 93N*
Abbate, Peter J., Jr. 1949- *WhoAmP 93*
Abbatini, Antonio Maria 1595-1679? *NewGrDO*
Abbe, Charles d1932 *WhoHol 92*
Abbe, Cleveland 1838-1916 *WorInv*
Abbe, Colman 1932- *WhoAm 94, WhoFI 94*
Abbe, Elfriede Martha *WhoAm 94, WhoAmA 93*
Abbe, Ernst 1840-1905 *WorInv*
Abbe, George Bancroft 1911-1989 *WhAm 10*
Abbe, Jack Yutaka d1977 *WhoHol 92*
Abbe, Kathryn McLaughlin 1919- *ConAu 142*
Abbell, Samuel 1925-1969 *WhoAmA 93N*
Abbensetts, Michael 1938- *ConDr 93, WrDr 94*
Abberley, John J. 1916- *WhoAm 94*
Abbett, Robert Kennedy 1926- *WhoAmA 93*
Abbey, David J. 1951- *WhoAmL 94*
Abbey, Edward 1927-1989 *ConAu 41NR, EncSF 93, EnvEnc*
Abbey, George Marshall 1933- *WhoAm 94, WhoAmL 94*
Abbey, Leland Russell 1945- *WhoScEn 94*
Abbey, May d1952 *WhoHol 92*
Abbey, Merrill R. 1905- *WhoAm 94*
Abbey, Scott Gerson 1951- *WhoAm 94, WhoFI 94*
Abbey, Steven Heaslet 1960- *WhoMW 93*
Abbiati, Franco 1898-1981 *NewGrDO*
Abbitt, Watkins Moorman, Jr. 1944- *WhoAmP 93*
Abbondanzo, Susan Jane 1962- *WhoScEn 94*
Abbot, Edith d1964 *WhoAmA 93N*
Abbot, Edward Pierce 1958- *WhoAmL 94*
Abbot, Francis Ellingwood 1836-1903 *DcAmReB 2*
Abbot, Quincy Sewall 1932- *WhoAm 94*
Abbot, Rick 1931-1992 *WrDr 94N*
Abbott, Albert (Francis) 1913- *Who 94*
Abbott, Alfreda Helen 1931- *WhoAmP 93*
Abbott, Alice 1916- *WrDr 94*
Abbott, Barbara S. 1930- *WhoAmP 93*
Abbott, Barry A. 1950- *WhoAm 94, WhoAmL 94*
Abbott, Berenice 1898-1991 *WhAm 10*
Abbott, Betty Lorraine 1923- *WhoAmP 93*
Abbott, Bob *WhoAmP 93*
Abbott, Bob 1932- *WhoAm 94, WhoAmL 94, WhoMW 93*
Abbott, Bruce *WhoHol 92*
Abbott, Bud d1974 *WhoHol 92*
Abbott, Bud 1895-1974
  See Abbott and Costello WhoCom

Abbott, Carl John 1944- *WhoAm 94*
Abbott, Carol Sue 1938- *WhoMW 93*
Abbott, Charles Favour, Jr. 1937- *WhoAmL 94, WhoFI 94*
Abbott, Charles Homer 1909- *WhAm 10*
Abbott, Cris Pye 1951- *WhoFI 94*
Abbott, Curtis Jeffrey, Jr. 1951- *WhoAmL 94*
Abbott, David Farrington 1953- *WhoAmL 94, WhoFI 94*
Abbott, David Henry 1936- *WhoAm 94*
Abbott, David Thomas 1952- *WhoMW 93*
Abbott, Diahnne 1945- *WhoHol 92*
Abbott, Diane Julie 1953- *Who 94, WhoWomW 91*
Abbott, Dorothy d1968 *WhoHol 92*
Abbott, Douglas Eugene 1934- *WhoAm 94*
Abbott, Edward Leroy 1930- *WhoAm 94*
Abbott, Edwin A(bbott) 1839-1926 *EncSF 93*
Abbott, Emma 1850-1891 *NewGrDO*
Abbott, Ernest Monroe 1931- *WhoFI 94*
Abbott, Frances Victoria 1956- *WhoAmP 93*
Abbott, Frank d1957 *WhoHol 92*
Abbott, Frank Curtis 1920- *WhoWest 94*
Abbott, Frank Harry 1919- *WhoAm 94*
Abbott, Gayle Elizabeth 1954- *WhoFI 94*
Abbott, George 1887- *WhoAm 94*
Abbott, George (Francis) 1889- *ConDr 93*
Abbott, George Francis 1887- *AmCulL [port]*
Abbott, George Melvin 1959- *WhoAmP 93*
Abbott, Gregory *WhoBlA 94*
Abbott, Gregory d1981 *WhoHol 92*
Abbott, Gypsy d1952 *WhoHol 92*
Abbott, Henry Larcom 1831-1927 *WhWE [port]*
Abbott, Hirschel Theron, Jr. 1942- *WhoAmL 94*
Abbott, Isabella Aiona 1919- *WhoAm 94, WhoScEn 94*
Abbott, J. Carl 1936- *WhoAm 94*
Abbott, James Alan 1928- *Who 94*
Abbott, James Samuel 1918- *WhoFI 94, WhoMW 93*
Abbott, James W. *WhoAmP 93*
Abbott, Jim 1967- *WhoAm 94*
Abbott, John 1905- *WhoHol 92*
Abbott, John Billington 1941- *WhoFI 94*
Abbott, John D. 1957- *WhoHol 92*
Abbott, John Evans d1952 *WhoAmA 93N*
Abbott, John Patrick 1930- *WrDr 94*
Abbott, John Rodger 1933- *WhoScEn 94, WhoWest 94*
Abbott, John Sheldon 1926- *WhoAm 94*
Abbott, Keith *DrAPF 93*
Abbott, Lawrence E. 1944- *WhoAmL 94*
Abbott, Lee K. *DrAPF 93*
Abbott, Lee K. 1947- *DcLB 130 [port]*
Abbott, Loretta *WhoBlA 94*
Abbott, Lyman 1835-1922 *DcAmReB 2*
Abbott, Marion d1937 *WhoHol 92*
Abbott, Marlene Louise 1935- *WhoWest 94*
Abbott, Mary Elaine 1922- *WhoMW 93*
Abbott, Melanie Beth 1951- *WhoAmL 94*
Abbott, Mitchell Edward 1950- *WhoAm 94*
Abbott, Morris Percy 1922- *Who 94*
Abbott, Nancy Ann d1964 *WhoHol 92*
Abbott, Pamela 1947- *WrDr 94*

Abbott, Patti Marie 1942- *WhoWest 94*
Abbott, Peter Charles 1942- *Who 94*
Abbott, Philip *WhoAm 94*
Abbott, Philip 1923- *WhoHol 92*
Abbott, Preston Sargent 1922- *WhoAm 94*
Abbott, R(obert) Tucker 1919- *WrDr 94*
Abbott, Ralph Edwin 1940- *WhoFI 94*
Abbott, Rebecca Phillips 1950- *WhoAm 94*
Abbott, Regina A. 1950- *WhoScEn 94*
Abbott, Richard 1899- *WhoHol 92*
Abbott, Richard Allen 1943- *WhoWest 94*
Abbott, Robert Carl 1955- *WhoFI 94, WhoWest 94*
Abbott, Robert S. 1870-1940 *AfrAmAl 6*
Abbott, Robert Tucker 1919- *WhoAm 94*
Abbott, Roderick Evelyn 1938- *Who 94*
Abbott, Ronald William 1917- *Who 94*
Abbott, Russell J. 1942- *WhoWest 94*
Abbott, S. L. 1924- *WhoAmP 93*
Abbott, Stephanie Lynn 1934- *WhoWest 94*
Abbott, Stephen *DrAPF 93*
Abbott, Susan Marie 1956- *WhoMW 93*
Abbott, Thomas Benjamin *WhoAm 94*
Abbott, Tommy d1987 *WhoHol 92*
Abbott, William H. *DrAPF 93*
Abbott, William Thomas 1938- *WhoFI 94*
Abbott, Wilton Robert 1916- *WhoAm 94*
Abbott and Costello *WhoCom [port]*
Abboud, A. Robert 1929- *IntWW 93*
Abboud, Alfred Robert 1929- *WhoAm 94*
Abboud, Ann Creelman 1952- *WhoAm 94, WhoAmL 94*
Abboud, Christopher W. 1956- *WhoAmP 93*
Abboud, Christopher William 1956- *WhoMW 93*
Abboud, Francois Mitry 1931- *WhoAm 94, WhoScEn 94*
Abboud, Joseph M. 1950- *WhoAm 94*
Abbrecht, Peter Herman 1930- *WhoAm 94*
Abbrescia, Joeseph Leonard 1936- *WhoAmA 93*
Abbruzzese, Albert Vincent, Jr. 1950-1989 *WhAm 10*
Abbruzzese, Carlo Enrico 1923- *WhoWest 94*
Abbruzzese, Dave *See* Pearl Jam *News 94-2*
Abbruzzese, Orlando Louis 1922- *WhoAmP 93*
Abcarian, Herand 1941- *WhoAm 94*
Abcarian, Michael V. 1952- *WhoAmL 94*
Abdallah, Abdelwaheb 1940- *Who 94*
Abdallah, Mahmoud M. 1948- *WhoIns 94*
Abdallah, Michael Joseph 1952- *WhoIns 94*
Abd Al-Qader 1807-1883 *HisWorL [port]*
Abd-al-Rahman, III 891-961 *HisWorL*
Abd Al-Wasi, Abdul Wahhab Ahmad 1929- *IntWW 93*
Abdela, Angelo Solomon 1942- *WhoAm 94, WhoFI 94*
Abdela, Jack Samuel Ronald 1913- *Who 94*
'Abdel 'Aziz, Malak 1923- *BlmGWL*
Abdel-Ghany, Mohamed 1940- *WhoAm 94*
Abdelhak, Sherif Samy 1946- *WhoAm 94, WhoScEn 94*
Abdel Halim Abu-Ghazala, Mohamed 1930- *IntWW 93*
Abdelhamied, Kadry A. 1954- *WhoScEn 94*
Abdel-Khalik, Ahmed Rashad 1940- *WhoAm 94*
Abdel-Khalik, Said Ibrahim 1948- *WhoAm 94*
Abdell, Douglas 1947- *WhoAmA 93*
Abdellah, Faye Glenn *IntWW 93*
Abdellah, Faye Glenn 1919- *WhoAm 94, WhoScEn 94*
Abdellaoui, Aissa 1941- *IntWW 93*
Abdel-Malek, Anouar I. 1924- *IntWW 93*
Abdel Meguid, Ahmed Esmat 1923- *IntWW 93*
Abdelnoor, Alexander Michael 1941- *WhoScEn 94*
Abdelnour, Ziad Khalil 1961- *WhoFI 94*
Abdel-Rahman, Aisha *IntWW 93*
Abdel-Rahman, Mohamed 1941- *WhoScEn 94*
Abdelrahman, Talaat Ahmad Mohammad 1940- *WhoFI 94*
Abdelsayed, Gabriel d1993 *NewYTBS 93*
Abdelsayed, Wafeek Hakim 1958- *WhoFI 94*
Abdel Wahab, Mohamed Mahmoud F. 1932- *IntWW 93*
Abderamane, Halidi *IntWW 93*
Abdessalam, Belaid 1928- *IntWW 93*
Abdnor, E. James 1923- *WhoAmP 93*
Abdnor, James 1923- *IntWW 93*
Abdo, Nicholas S. 1964- *WhoAmL 94*
Abdoo, Frederick F. 1919- *WhoIns 94*
Abdoo, Richard A. 1944- *WhoFI 94*
Abdou, Nabih I. 1934- *WhoAm 94*
Abdoun, Amin Magzoub 1930- *IntWW 93*
Abdrashitov, Vadim Yusupovich 1945- *IntWW 93*
Abdul, Abdul Shaheed 1952- *WhoScEn 94*
Abdul, Corinna Gay 1961- *WhoScEn 94, WhoWest 94*
Abdul, Paula 1962- *IntWW 93, WhoHol 92*
Abdul, Paula Julie 1963- *WhoAm 94*
Abdul, Raoul 1929- *WhoBlA 94*
Abdulah, Frank 1928- *IntWW 93*
Abdulah, Frank Owen 1928- *Who 94*
Abdulai, Yesufu Seyyid Momoh 1940- *IntWW 93*
Abdulatipov, Ramazan Gadzhimuradovich 1946- *LoBiDrD*
Abdul Aziz, Mahmood 1935- *Who 94*
Abdu'l-Baha 1844-1921 *DcAmReB 2*
Abdulgani, Roeslan 1914- *IntWW 93*
Abdul-Ghani, Abdulaziz 1939- *IntWW 93*
Abdul Hamid, II 1842-1918 *HisWorL [port]*
Abdul-Hamid, Ismail 1950- *WhoBlA 94*
Abdul-Jabbar, Kareem 1947- *AfrAmAl 6, BasBi, BlkWr 2, WhoAm 94, WhoBlA 94, WhoHol 92, WhoWest 94*
Abdul Jamil Rais, Tan Sri Dato' 1912- *Who 94*
Abdul-Kabir, Jamal 1941- *WhoBlA 94*
Abdulkareem, Ameen 1938- *WhoFI 94*
Abdulla, Mohamed 1937- *WhoScEn 94*
Abdullah, Anna *WhoWomW 91*
Abdullah, Farooq 1937- *IntWW 93*
Abdullah, Larry Burley 1947- *WhoBlA 94*
Abdullah, Tariq Husam 1941- *WhoBlA 94*
Abdullah bin Ali, Datuk 1922- *Who 94*
Abdullah Bin Mohd Salleh, Tan Sri 1926- *IntWW 93*
Abdullah Ibn Abdul Aziz, H.R.H. Crown Prince 1921- *IntWW 93*
Abdulla Osman Daar, Aden 1908- *IntWW 93*
Abdul Latif, Haji Java bin 1939- *IntWW 93*
Abdullojanov, Abdumalik *IntWW 93*
Abdul-Malik, Ahmed H. 1927- *WhoBlA 94*
Abdul-Malik, Ibrahim *WhoBlA 94*
Abdulov, Osip d1953 *WhoHol 92*
Abdul-Rahman, Tahira Sadiqa 1947- *WhoBlA 94*
Abdy, Valentine (Robert Duff) 1937- *Who 94*
Abe, Benjamin Omara A. 1943- *WhoBlA 94*
Abe, Fumio *IntWW 93*
Abe, Gregory 1954- *WhoWest 94*
Abe, Kobo d1993 *IntWW 93N*
Abe, Kobo 1924-1993 *ConAu 140, ConLC 81 [port], CurBio 93N, EncSF 93, NewYTBS 93 [port]*
Abe, Makoto 1961- *WhoAsA 94*
Abe, Shintaro 1924-1991 *WhAm 10*
Abe, Yoshihiro 1935- *WhoScEn 94*
a'Bear, Howard 1914- *WrDr 94*
Abebe, Ruby 1949- *WhoBlA 94*
Abebe, Teshome 1949- *WhoBlA 94*
Abedon, Stephen Tobias 1961- *WhoWest 94*
Abegg, Eugene 1897- *WhAm 10*
Abegg, Martin G. 1925- *WhoAm 94*
Abekawa, Sumio 1947- *IntWW 93*
Abel, Alfred d1937 *WhoHol 92*
Abel, Andrew Bruce 1952- *WhoAm 94*
Abel, Ashley Bryan 1960- *WhoAmL 94*
Abel, Carlos Alberto 1930- *WhoAm 94, WhoHisp 94*
Abel, Edward William 1931- *IntWW 93, Who 94*
Abel, Elie 1920- *WhoAm 94, WrDr 94*
Abel, Francis Lee 1931- *WhoAm 94*
Abel, Frederick 1827-1902 *WorInv*
Abel, Gene Paul 1941- *WhoFI 94*
Abel, Harold 1926- *WhoAm 94*
Abel, Ilse d1959 *WhoHol 92*
Abel, Iorwith Wilbur 1908-1987 *EncABHB 9 [port]*
Abel, John Jacob *WorInv*
Abel, John Jacob 1857-1938 *WorScD*
Abel, Jonathan Stuart 1960- *WhoWest 94*
Abel, Kenneth Arthur 1926- *Who 94*
Abel, Larry Allen 1949- *WhoMW 93*
Abel, Mark C. 1950- *WhoAmP 93*
Abel, Mary *WhoAmP 93*
Abel, Mary Ellen Kathryn 1949- *WhoMW 93*
Abel, Michael J. *WhoAmP 93*
Abel, Myer 1904- *WhoAmA 93N*
Abel, Niels Henrik 1802-1829 *WorScD*
Abel, R(ichard) Cox *EncSF 93*
Abel, Ray 1911- *WhoAm 94*
Abel, Ray 1914- *WhoAmA 93*
Abel, Renaul N. 1940- *WhoBlA 94*
Abel, Reuben 1911- *WhoAm 94, WrDr 94*
Abel, Richard L. 1941- *WrDr 94*
Abel, Robert Berger 1926- *WhoAm 94*
Abel, Robert H. *DrAPF 93*
Abel, Roger Lee 1943- *Who 94*
Abel, Ronald Dean 1935- *WhoMW 93*
Abel, Sandra Fraley 1965- *WhoAmL 94*
Abel, Theodore 1896- *WhAm 10*
Abel, Ulrich Rainer 1952- *WhoScEn 94*
Abel, Walter d1987 *WhoHol 92*
Abel, Willard Edward 1906- *WhAm 10*
Abela, George Samih 1950- *WhoScEn 94*
Abela, Wistin 1933- *IntWW 93*
Abelar, David 1932- *WhoHisp 94*
Abelard, Peter 1079-1142 *BlmGEL, ClMLC 11 [port], EncEth*
Abele, David Francis 1964- *WhoAmL 94*
Abele, Robert Christopher 1958- *WhoAmL 94, WhoMW 93*
Abeles, Charles Calvert 1929- *WhoAm 94*
Abeles, Edward d1919 *WhoHol 92*
Abeles, James David 1916- *WhoAm 94*
Abeles, Kim Victoria 1952- *WhoAmA 93, WhoWest 94*
Abeles, Norman 1928- *WhoAm 94*
Abeles, (Emil Herbert) Peter 1924- *Who 94*
Abeles, Robert Heinz 1926- *WhoAm 94*
Abeles, Sigmund 1934- *WhoAmA 93*
Abeles, Sigmund M. 1934- *WhoAm 94*
Abeles, Theodore Lillien 1934- *WhoAm 94*
Abelew, Alan *WhoHol 92*
Abel-Grippo, Julie Jacelyn 1961- *WhoMW 93*
Abel Horowitz, Michelle Susan 1950- *WhoMW 93*
Abelite, Jahnis John 1950- *WhoAmL 94*
Abell, Anthony (Foster) 1906- *Who 94*
Abell, Creed W. 1934- *WhoAm 94*
Abell, (John) David 1942- *Who 94*
Abell, David Robert 1934- *WhoAm 94*
Abell, Erwin Marshall 1962- *WhoFI 94*
Abell, John Norman 1931- *Who 94*
Abell, Millicent Demmin 1934- *WhoAm 94*
Abell, Murray Richardson 1920- *WhoAm 94*
Abell, Nancy L. 1950- *WhoAmL 94*
Abell, Paul Irving 1923- *WhoAm 94*
Abell, Richard Bender 1943- *WhoAm 94, WhoAmL 94*
Abell, Sally Danna 1956- *WhoFI 94*
Abell, Thomas Henry 1909- *WhoAm 94*
Abell, Walter Halsey 1897-1956 *WhoAmA 93N*
Abell, William Shepherdson, Jr. 1943- *WhoAmL 94*
Abella, Alex 1950- *WhoHisp 94, WhoWest 94*
Abella, Isaac David 1934- *WhoScEn 94*
Abella, Joseph Francisco 1943- *WhoMW 93*
Abella, Marisela Carlota 1943- *WhoFI 94*
Abella, Olga 1958- *WhoHisp 94*
Abelle, Patsy Caples 1935- *WhoAmL 94*
Abello, Oscar J. *WhoHisp 94*
Abelman, Arthur F. 1933- *WhoAmL 94*
Abelman, Henry Moss 1953- *WhoAmL 94*
Abelmann, William Weldon 1915- *WhoWest 94*
Abelov, Stephen Lawrence 1923- *WhoAm 94, WhoFI 94, WhoMW 93*
Abels, Robert Frederick 1926- *WhoWest 94*
Abel-Smith, Brian 1926- *Who 94, WrDr 94*
Abel Smith, Henriette Alice 1914- *Who 94*
Abel Smith, Henry d1993 *Who 94N*
Abel Smith, Richard Francis 1933- *Who 94*
Abelson, Alan 1925- *WhoAm 94*
Abelson, Herbert Traub 1941- *WhoAm 94*
Abelson, Philip Hauge 1913- *IntWW 93, WhoAm 94, WhoScEn 94, WorScD*
Abelson, Raziel (Alter) 1921- *WrDr 94*
Abelson, Robert Paul 1928- *WhoAm 94*
Abelt, Ralph William 1929- *WhoAm 94*
Abely, Joseph Francis, II 1952- *WhoFI 94*
Abend, Joshua C. 1924- *WhoWest 94*
Abend, Sheldon 1929- *IntMPA 94*
Abendana, Isaac d1699 *DcNaB MP*
Abendana, Jacob c. 1630-1685 *DcNaB MP*
Abendroth, Douglas William 1952- *WhoAmL 94*
Abendroth, Irene 1872-1932 *NewGrDO*
Abendroth, Kent Allen 1943- *WhoWest 94*
Abendroth, Reinhard Paul 1931- *WhoScEn 94*
Aber, Geoffrey Michael 1928- *Who 94*
Aber, Ita 1932- *WhoAmA 93*
Aber, Susan Ward 1955- *WhoMW 93*
Aberbach, David 1953- *IntWW 93, WrDr 94*
Aberbach, Joel David 1940- *WhoWest 94*
Aberconway, Baron 1913- *Who 94*
Aberconway, Baron 1913- *IntWW 93*
Abercorn, Duke of 1934- *Who 94*
Abercrombie, James 1732-1775 *AmRev*
Abercrombie, Joe Wayne 1956- *WhoWest 94*
Abercrombie, Neil 1938- *CngDr 93, WhoAm 94, WhoAmP 93, WhoWest 94*
Abercrombie, Paul D. *WhoAmP 93*
Abercrombie, Robert 1740-1827 *AmRev*
Abercrombie, Robert James 1898- *Who 94*
Abercrombie, Stanley 1935- *WhoAm 94*
Abercrombie, Virginia T. *DrAPF 93*
Abercromby, Ian George 1925- *Who 94*
Abercromby, James d1775 *WhAmRev*
Abercromby, James 1706-1781 *WhAmRev*
Abercromby, Ralph 1734-1801 *WhAmRev*
Abercromby, Robert 1740-1827 *WhAmRev*
Abercrumbie, Paul Eric 1948- *WhoBlA 94*
Aberdare, Baron 1919- *Who 94*
Aberdeen, Bishop of 1934- *Who 94*
Aberdeen, Provost of *Who 94*
Aberdeen And Orkney, Bishop of 1941- *Who 94*
Aberdeen And Orkney, Dean of *Who 94*
Aberdeen And Temair, Marquess of 1920- *Who 94*
Aberdeen And Temair, Marchioness of *Who 94*
Aberdour, Lord 1952- *Who 94*
Aberdour, Master of 1986- *Who 94*
Abere, Andrew Evan 1961- *WhoAm 94*
Aberg, Sivi 1944- *WhoHol 92*
Abergavenny, Marchioness of 1915- *Who 94*
Abergavenny, Marquess of 1914- *Who 94*
Aberkane, Abdelhamid 1945- *IntWW 93*
Aberle, David Friend 1918- *WhoAm 94, WhoWest 94*
Aberle, James Robert 1950- *WhoMW 93*
Abernathy, Catherine Mary 1950- *WhoAmP 93*
Abernathy, Frederick H. 1930- *WhoAm 94*
Abernathy, Harry Hoyle, Jr. 1925- *WhoAmL 94*
Abernathy, Jack Harvey 1911- *WhoAm 94, WhoScEn 94*
Abernathy, James Logan 1941- *WhoAm 94*
Abernathy, James R., II *WhoBlA 94*
Abernathy, Joseph Duncan 1944- *WhoAm 94*
Abernathy, Lee Roy d1993 *NewYTBS 93*
Abernathy, Mabra Glenn 1921-1990 *WhAm 10*
Abernathy, Ralph D. 1926-1990 *AfrAmAl 6 [port]*
Abernathy, Ralph David 1926-1990 *AmSocL [port], WhAm 10*
Abernathy, Ralph David, III 1959- *WhoAmP 93*
Abernathy, Ronald Lee 1950- *WhoBlA 94*
Abernathy, Thomas Edwards, IV 1941- *WhoAmL 94*
Abernethy, Hon. Lord 1938- *Who 94*
Abernethy, David Ford 1958- *WhoAmL 94*
Abernethy, Donald Douglas 1931- *WhoAmP 93*
Abernethy, George Lawrence 1910- *WhoAm 94*
Abernethy, Irene Margaret 1924- *WhoMW 93*
Abernethy, Jack Vernon 1945- *WhoAmP 93*
Abernethy, Pamela Leask 1951- *WhoAmL 94*
Abernethy, Robert John 1940- *WhoAm 94, WhoWest 94*
Abernethy, Ronald Hayes 1948- *WhoWest 94*
Abernethy, Virginia Deane 1934- *WhoScEn 94*
Abernethy, William Leslie 1910- *Who 94*
Abernethy, William S., Jr. 1942- *WhoAmL 94*
Abernethy-Baldwin, Judith Ann 1942- *WhoAmA 93*
Aberson, Leslie Donald 1936- *WhoAm 94*
Abert, Anna Amalie 1906- *NewGrDO*
Abert, Hermann 1871-1927 *NewGrDO*
Abert, James William 1820-1871 *WhWE*
Abert, Johann Joseph 1832-1915 *NewGrDO*
Aberth, William Henry 1933- *WhoScEn 94*
Abetti, Pier Antonio 1921- *WhoAm 94*
Abety, Modesto E. 1951- *WhoHisp 94*
Abeyesundere, Nihal Anton Aelian 1932- *WhoScEn 94*
Abeysundara, Urugamuwe Gamacharige Yasan 1964- *WhoScEn 94*
Abeyta, Frank *WhoHisp 94*
Abeyta, J. A., Jr. 1929- *WhoHisp 94*
Abeyta, Jose R. 1927- *WhoAmP 93*
Abeyta, Jose Reynato 1927- *WhoWest 94*
Abeyta, Samuel James 1943- *WhoHisp 94*
Abhavananda *GayLL*
Abhyankar, Shreeram S. 1930- *WhoAm 94*
Abhyankar, Shreeram Shankar 1930- *WhoAsA 94*

Abi-Ali, Ricky Salim 1940- *WhoFI 94*
Abicair, Shirley 1930- *WhoHol 92*
Abid, Ann B. 1942- *WhoAmA 93*
Abiko, Takashi 1941- *WhoScEn 94*
Abila, Enedina Vejil 1939-1993 *WhoHisp 94N*
Abildgaard, Charles Frederick 1930- *WhoWest 94*
Abildskov, J. A. 1923- *WhoAm 94, WhoScEn 94*
Abinader, Elmaz *DrAPF 93*
Abineri, John 1928- *WhoHol 92*
Abingdon, Earl of *Who 94*
Abingdon, W. L. d1918 *WhoHol 92*
Abinger, Baron 1914- *Who 94*
Abirached, Robert 1930- *IntWW 93*
Abish, Cecile *WhoAm 94, WhoAmA 93*
Abish, Walter *DrAPF 93*
Abish, Walter 1931- *DcLB 130 [port], WrDr 94*
Abishabis fl. 180-?- *EncNAR*
Abisinito, Kiatro Ottao *IntWW 93*
Abkarian, Edward 1951- *WhoFI 94*
Abkowitz, Martin Aaron 1918- *WhAm 10*
Ablad, Bjorn Eric Bertil 1945- *WhoWest 94*
Ablard, Charles David *WhoAm 94*
Ablard, Charles David 1930- *WhoAmP 93*
Able, Edward H. *WhoAm 94*
Able, Warren Walter 1932- *WhoAm 94, WhoFI 94, WhoMW 93*
Able, Will B. d1981 *WhoHol 92*
Able, William F. 1933- *WhoAmP 93*
Ableman, Paul 1927- *ConDr 93, ConTFT 11, EncSF 93, WrDr 94*
Abler, Ronald Francis 1939- *WhoAm 94*
Ables, Charles Robert 1930- *WhoAmL 94, WhoAmP 93*
Ables, Willis Scott 1943- *WhoFI 94*
Ablin, Joanne Marie 1931- *WhoAmP 93*
Ablin, Richard Joel 1940- *WhoAm 94*
Ablon, Arnold Norman 1921- *WhoAm 94, WhoFI 94*
Ablon, Benjamin Manuel 1929- *WhoFI 94*
Ablon, Karen Herrick 1966- *WhoAmL 94*
Ablon, R. Richard *WhoAm 94, WhoFI 94*
Ablon, Ralph E. 1916- *IntWW 93, WhoFI 94*
Ablow, Joseph 1928- *WhoAm 94, WhoAmA 93*
Ablow, Keith Russell 1961- *ConAu 141*
Ablow, Roselyn Karol *WhoAmA 93*
Abma, Kimberly Anderle 1958- *WhoAmL 94*
Abnee, A. Victor 1923- *WhoAm 94*
Abney, Armando J. 1953- *WhoHisp 94*
Abney, Frederick Sherwood 1919- *WhoAm 94*
Abney, Glenda May 1963- *WhoMW 93*
Abney, Joe L. 1941- *WhoAmL 94*
Abney, Robert 1949- *WhoBlA 94*
Abney, William *WhoHol 92*
Abney, Wilson Ray 1947- *WhoAmL 94*
Abney-Hastings *Who 94*
Abo, Ronald K. 1946- *WhoAsA 94*
Aboimov, Ivan Pavlovich 1936- *IntWW 93*
Aboimov, Ivan Petrovich 1936- *LoBiDrD*
Aboites, Vicente 1958- *WhoScEn 94*
Abolafia, Yossi 1944- *ConAu 142*
Abolins, Maris Arvids 1938- *WhoAm 94, WhoMW 93*
Abood, Leo George 1922- *WhoAm 94*
Abood, Mitchell E., Jr. 1921- *WhoAmP 93*
Aboody, Albert Victor 1947- *WhoAm 94*
Aborn, Foster Litchfield 1934- *WhoAm 94*
Aborn, Richard A. 1943- *WhoAmL 94*
Abos, Girolamo 1715-1760 *NewGrDO*
Abott, Bessie 1878-1919 *NewGrDO*
Abourezk, James G. 1931- *IntWW 93, WhoAmP 93*
Abourezk, James G(eorge) 1931- *WrDr 94*
Abou-Samra, Abdul Badi 1954- *WhoScEn 94*
Abou-Seeda, Hassan A. H. 1930- *Who 94*
About, Edmond (Francois Valentin) 1828-1885 *EncSF 93*
Aboville, Francois Marie, Comte d' 1730-1817 *WhAmRev*
Aboyade, Ojetunji 1931- *Who 94*
Aboyne, Earl of 1973- *Who 94*
Abplanalp, Glen Harold 1914- *WhoAm 94*
Abracheff, Ivan 1903-1960 *WhoAmA 93N*
Abragam, Anatole 1914- *IntWW 93*
Abraham, Albert David 1924- *WhoFI 94, WhoWest 94*
Abraham, Andrew 1958- *WhoAmL 94*
Abraham, Ann 1952- *Who 94*
Abraham, Beverly Anne 1931- *WhoMW 93*
Abraham, Carol Jeanne 1949- *WhoAmA 93, WhoWest 94*
Abraham, Claude Kurt 1931- *WrDr 94*
Abraham, E. Spencer 1952- *WhoAmP 93*
Abraham, Edward (Penley) 1913- *Who 94, WrDr 94*
Abraham, Edward Penley 1913- *IntWW 93*
Abraham, F. Murray 1939- *ConTFT 11, IntMPA 94, IntWW 93, WhoHol 92*
Abraham, Fahrid Murray 1939- *WhoAm 94*
Abraham, George 1918- *WhoAm 94, WhoScEn 94*
Abraham, George G. 1906- *WhoAm 94*
Abraham, Gerald (Ernest Heal) 1904-1988 *NewGrDO*
Abraham, Gyorgy 1948- *WhoScEn 94*
Abraham, Henry J. 1921- *WrDr 94*
Abraham, Henry Julian 1921- *WhoAm 94*
Abraham, Irene 1946- *WhoAm 94*
Abraham, Jacob A. 1948- *WhoAm 94, WhoScEn 94*
Abraham, James R. *WhoAmP 93*
Abraham, Jeffery L. 1943- *WhoAmL 94*
Abraham, John 1946- *WhoAsA 94*
Abraham, Karl 1877-1925 *EncSPD*
Abraham, Kenneth Samuel 1946- *WhoAm 94, WhoAmL 94*
Abraham, Lois W. 1933- *WhoAmL 94*
Abraham, (Sutton) Martin (O'Heguerty) 1919- *Who 94*
Abraham, Mary Ann 1955- *WhoWest 94*
Abraham, Mathew M. 1966- *WhoFI 94*
Abraham, Mathews V. 1966- *WhoFI 94*
Abraham, Sinclair Reginald 1951- *WhoBlA 94*
Abraham, Thomas 1948- *WhoAsA 94*
Abraham, Tonson 1948- *WhoMW 93, WhoScEn 94*
Abraham, Victor Elias, Jr. 1935- *WhoHisp 94*
Abraham, Willard 1916- *WrDr 94*
Abraham, Willard B. 1916- *WhoAm 94*
Abraham, William Israel 1919- *WhoWest 94*
Abraham, William John, Jr. 1948- *WhoAm 94, WhoAmL 94*
Abraham, Yohannan 1939- *WhoAm 94*
Abrahams, Allan Rose d1991 *Who 94N*
Abrahams, Andrew Wordsworth 1936- *WhoBlA 94*
Abrahams, Anthony Claud Walter 1923- *Who 94*
Abrahams, Athol Denis 1946- *WhoAm 94*
Abrahams, Gary d1992 *IntMPA 94N*
Abrahams, Gerald Milton 1917- *Who 94*
Abrahams, Ivor 1935- *IntWW 93, Who 94*
Abrahams, Jim 1944- *IntMPA 94*
Abrahams, Johanna L. 1913- *WhoAmP 93*
Abrahams, John Hambleton 1913- *WhoAm 94, WhoIns 94*
Abrahams, Mort *IntMPA 94*
Abrahams, Peter 1919- *WrDr 94*
Abrahams, Robert David 1905- *WhoAm 94*
Abrahams, Robert M. 1948- *WhoAmL 94*
Abrahams, Roger D(avid) 1933- *WrDr 94*
Abrahams, Sidney Cyril 1924- *WhoWest 94*
Abrahams, William *DrAPF 93*
Abrahams, William (Miller) 1919- *ConAu 43NR*
Abrahams, William Miller 1919- *WhoAm 94*
Abrahamsen, David 1903- *WhoAm 94*
Abrahamsen, Egil 1923- *IntWW 93, Who 94*
Abrahamsen, Samuel 1917- *WhoAm 94*
Abrahamson, A. Craig 1954- *WhoAmL 94*
Abrahamson, Barry 1933- *WhoAm 94*
Abrahamson, Bruce Arnold 1925- *WhoAm 94*
Abrahamson, Dean Edwin 1934- *WhoMW 93*
Abrahamson, George R. 1927- *WhoScEn 94*
Abrahamson, James A. 1933- *IntWW 93*
Abrahamson, James Alan 1933- *WhoFI 94, WhoScEn 94*
Abrahamson, James Leonard 1937- *WhoAm 94*
Abrahamson, Mark Courtney 1944- *WhoWest 94*
Abrahamson, Scott David 1959- *WhoScEn 94*
Abrahamson, Shirley Schlanger 1933- *WhoAm 94, WhoAmL 94, WhoAmP 93*
Abrahamson, Vicki Lafer 1953- *WhoAmL 94*
Abrahamsson, Bo Axel 1931- *IntWW 93*
Abram, Donald Eugene 1935- *WhoAm 94, WhoAmL 94, WhoWest 94*
Abram, James Baker, Jr. 1937- *WhoBlA 94*
Abram, Morris Berthold 1918- *WhoAm 94, WhoAmP 93*
Abram, Prudence Beatty 1942- *WhoAm 94, WhoAmL 94*
Abramczuk, Tomasz 1954- *WhoScEn 94*
Abramczyk, Merrie Jo 1955- *WhoMW 93*
Abramis, David Joseph 1955- *WhoAm 94*
Abramoff, Peter 1927- *WhoAm 94*
Abramov, Alexander 1900-1985 *EncSF 93*
Abramov, S(hene'ur) Zalman 1908- *WrDr 94*
Abramov, Sergei 1944- *EncSF 93*
Abramov, Sergei Aleksandrovich 1944- *LoBiDrD*
Abramovitz, Max 1908- *IntWW 93, WhoAm 94*
Abramovitz, Michael John 1939- *WhoAmL 94*
Abramovitz, Moses 1912- *IntWW 93, WhoAm 94, WhoFI 94, WhoWest 94*
Abramowicz, Alfred L. 1919- *WhoAm 94*
Abramowicz, Jacques Sylvain 1948- *WhoScEn 94*
Abramowicz, Janet *WhoAm 94, WhoAmA 93*
Abramowitz, Elkan *NewYTBS 93 [port]*
Abramowitz, George R. 1946- *WhoAmL 94*
Abramowitz, Jerrold 1953- *WhoAmL 94*
Abramowitz, Morton I. 1933- *WhoAmP 93*
Abramowitz, Nathan 1949- *WhoAmL 94*
Abramowitz, Robert Leslie 1950- *WhoAm 94, WhoAmL 94*
Abrams, Alan 1941- *WrDr 94*
Abrams, Alan M. *WhoAmL 94*
Abrams, Barry 1952- *WhoAmL 94*
Abrams, Bernard William 1925- *WhoAm 94*
Abrams, Bertram Alan 1933- *WhoAm 94, WhoAmL 94*
Abrams, Diane Kobisher 1954- *WhoFI 94*
Abrams, Edith Lillian *WhoAmA 93*
Abrams, Edward Marvin 1927- *WhoAm 94*
Abrams, Elliott 1948- *ConAu 140, WhoAm 94, WhoAmP 93*
Abrams, Fredrick Ralph 1928- *WhoWest 94*
Abrams, Gerald David 1932- *WhoAm 94*
Abrams, Harold Eugene 1933- *WhoAm 94*
Abrams, Harry N. 1905-1979 *WhoAmA 93N*
Abrams, Helayne Joan 1937- *WhoWest 94*
Abrams, Herbert E. 1921- *WhoAm 94, WhoAmA 93*
Abrams, Herbert Kerman 1913- *WhoAm 94*
Abrams, Herbert Leroy 1920- *IntWW 93, WhoAm 94*
Abrams, Holly *WhoAmP 93*
Abrams, Hubert J. 1925- *WhoAmP 93*
Abrams, Irwin 1914- *WhoAm 94*
Abrams, Jane Eldora 1940- *WhoAmA 93*
Abrams, Jeanne Esther 1951- *WhoWest 94*
Abrams, Joseph 1936- *WhoFI 94*
Abrams, Joyce Diana 1945- *WhoAmA 93*
Abrams, Jules Clinton *WhoAm 94*
Abrams, Lawrence Jeffrey 1961- *WhoMW 93*
Abrams, Lee Norman 1935- *WhoAm 94*
Abrams, Leigh Jeffrey 1942- *WhoAm 94*
Abrams, Linsey *DrAPF 93*
Abrams, Linsey 1951- *WrDr 94*
Abrams, M(eyer) H(oward) 1912- *WrDr 94*
Abrams, Marc R. 1954- *WhoAm 94*
Abrams, Mark 1906- *WrDr 94*
Abrams, Mark Alexander 1906- *Who 94*
Abrams, Meyer Howard 1912- *WhoAm 94*
Abrams, Michael Ellis 1932- *Who 94*
Abrams, Michael I. 1947- *WhoAmP 93*
Abrams, Muhal Richard 1930- *AfrAmAl 6, WhoAm 94*
Abrams, Nancy 1954- *WhoAmL 94*
Abrams, Norman 1933- *WhoAm 94, WhoAmL 94*
Abrams, Philip 1939- *WhoAmP 93*
Abrams, Richard Brill 1931- *WhoAm 94*
Abrams, Richard Lee 1941- *WhoAm 94, WhoWest 94*
Abrams, Richard M. 1932- *WrDr 94*
Abrams, Robert 1938- *WhoAm 94, WhoAmL 94, WhoAmP 93*
Abrams, Robert Allen 1937- *WhoAm 94*
Abrams, Roberta Busky 1937- *WhoAm 94, WhoFI 94*
Abrams, Roger Ian 1945- *WhoAmL 94*
Abrams, Ronald Lawrence 1952- *WhoAmP 93*
Abrams, Rosalie Silber *WhoAmP 93*
Abrams, Ruth (Davidson) d1986 *WhoAmA 93N*
Abrams, Ruth I. 1930- *WhoAmP 93*
Abrams, Ruth Ida 1930- *WhoAm 94, WhoAmL 94*
Abrams, Sam *DrAPF 93*
Abrams, Samuel K. 1913- *WhoAm 94*
Abrams, Scott Irwin 1959- *WhoScEn 94*
Abrams, Susan Elizabeth 1945- *WhoAm 94*
Abrams, Sylvia Fleck 1942- *WhoMW 93*
Abrams, Talbert 1895- *WhAm 10*
Abrams, Vivien *WhoAm 94*
Abrams, Vivien (Joy) 1946- *WhoAmA 93*
Abrams, Warren Elliott 1928- *WhoAm 94*
Abrams, William Bernard 1922- *WhoAm 94*
Abrams, William F. 1954- *WhoAmL 94*
Abramsky, Alexander 1933- *WhoFI 94*
Abramsky, Jennifer 1946- *Who 94*
Abramson, Albert 1922- *WhoWest 94*
Abramson, Ann 1925- *WhoAmP 93*
Abramson, Arthur Seymour 1925- *WhoAm 94*
Abramson, Burton Ivan 1931- *WhoMW 93*
Abramson, Clarence Allen 1932- *WhoAm 94, WhoAmL 94*
Abramson, Elaine Sandra 1942- *WhoAmA 93*
Abramson, Gil A. 1945- *WhoAmL 94*
Abramson, Hanley Norman 1940- *WhoAm 94*
Abramson, Herbert Francis 1930- *WhoMW 93*
Abramson, Hyman Norman 1926- *WhoAm 94, WhoScEn 94*
Abramson, Ivan, Mrs. d1945 *WhoHol 92*
Abramson, Jack d1993 *NewYTBS 93*
Abramson, Janet Carolyn 1942- *WhoMW 93*
Abramson, Jerry Edwin 1946- *WhoAmP 93*
Abramson, John J., Jr. 1957- *WhoBlA 94*
Abramson, Leonard 1938- *WhoAm 94, WhoFI 94*
Abramson, Mark Joseph 1949- *WhoWest 94*
Abramson, Martin 1921- *WhoAm 94*
Abramson, Mason Harry 1916- *WhoWest 94*
Abramson, Michael A. 1949- *WhoAmP 93*
Abramson, Neal *DrAPF 93*
Abramson, Norman 1932- *WhoAm 94*
Abramson, Paul Robert 1937- *WhoAm 94*
Abramson, Raymond Rue 1951- *WhoAmP 93*
Abramson, Richard L. 1946- *WhoAmL 94*
Abramson, Rochelle Susan 1953- *WhoAm 94*
Abramson, Sara Jane 1945- *WhoAm 94*
Abramson, Sidney 1921- *Who 94*
Abramson, Stephanie W. 1944- *WhoAmL 94*
Abramson, William Edward 1935- *WhoAm 94*
Abrantes, Laure d' 1785-1838 *BlmGWL*
Abranyi, Emil 1882-1970 *NewGrDO*
Abraszewski, Andrzej 1938- *IntWW 93*
Abravanel, Allan Ray 1947- *WhoAm 94, WhoAmL 94, WhoWest 94*
Abravanel, Maurice 1903- *WhoAm 94, WhoWest 94*
Abravanel, Maurice 1903-1993 *NewYTBS 93 [port]*
Abravanel, Maurice (de) 1903- *NewGrDO*
Abrell, Ronald Lane 1934- *WhAm 10*
Abreu, John A. 1944- *WhoHisp 94*
Abreu, Markus Santiago 1961- *WhoWest 94*
Abreu, Pedro M. 1963- *WhoHisp 94*
Abreu, Roberto Daniel 1937- *WhoHisp 94*
Abreu, Zenaida *WhoHisp 94*
Abreu-Páez, Victor Manuel 1956- *WhoHisp 94*
Abrew, Frederick Henry 1937- *WhoFI 94*
Abrikosov, Aleksey Alekseyevich 1928- *IntWW 93*
Abril, Ben 1923- *WhoAmA 93*
Abril, Dorothy d1977 *WhoHol 92*
Abril, Jorge L. 1934- *WhoHisp 94*
Abril, Tony Rodriguez *WhoAmP 93*
Abril, Victoria *IntWW 93, WhoHol 92*
Abril Martoreli, Fernando 1936- *IntWW 93*
Abrohams, Benjamin J. 1944- *WhoAmL 94*
Abron, Lilia A. 1945- *WhoScEn 94*
Abrons, Richard S. *DrAPF 93*
Abrums, John Denise 1923- *WhoScEn 94, WhoWest 94*
Abrunzo, Victor Daniel, Jr. 1946- *WhoWest 94*
Abruzzi, Luigi Amedeo Di Savoia, Duke of The 1873-1933 *WhWE*
Abs, Hermann J. 1901- *IntWW 93*
Absalom, Roger Neil Lewis 1929- *WrDr 94*
Abse, Dannie *DrAPF 93*
Abse, Dannie 1923- *BlmGEL, ConDr 93, IntWW 93, Who 94, WrDr 94*
Abse, David Wilfred 1915- *WhoScEn 94*
Abse, Leo 1917- *Who 94*
Absher, Thomas *DrAPF 93*
Abshire, Alvis John 1942- *WhoAm 94*
Abshire, David Manker 1926- *IntWW 93, WhoAm 94, WhoAmP 93, WrDr 94*
Abston, Dunbar, Jr. 1931- *WhoAm 94*
Abston, Nathaniel, Jr. 1952- *WhoBlA 94*
Abt, Clark Claus 1929- *WhoAm 94*
Abt, Evet Sue Loewen 1952- *WhoAmL 94*
Abt, Jeffrey 1949- *WhoAm 94, WhoAmA 93*
Abt, Ralph Edwin 1960- *WhoAmL 94*
Abt, Sylvia Hedy 1957- *WhoMW 93*

Abts, Daniel Carl 1956- WhoScEn 94
Abts, Gwyneth Hartmann 1923- WhoMW 93
Abts, Henry William 1918- WhoAm 94
Abuba, Ernest 1947- WhoHol 92
Abuba, Ernest Hawkins 1947- WrDr 94
Abubakar, Iya 1934- Who 94
Abu Basha, Hassan 1923- IntWW 93
Abudula Damaola WhoPRCh 91
Abu-Ghazala, Mohamed Abdel Halim IntWW 93
Abu-Jaber, Diana 1959- ConAu 142
Abuladze, Tengiz Yevgenievich 1924- IntWW 93
Abularach, Rodolfo Marco 1933- WhoAmA 93
Abularach, Rodolfo Marco Antonio 1933- WhoAm 94
Abulfaz Elchibei 1938- IntWW 93
Abul-Haj, Suleiman Kahil 1925- WhoWest 94
A-bu-lie-zi Mu-he-mai-ti WhoPRCh 91
Abulizi, Muhemaiti 1920- IntWW 93
Abu-Lughod, Janet Lippman 1928- WhoAm 94
Abumrad, Naji 1945- WhoAm 94
Aburdene, Odeh Felix 1944- WhoAm 94
Aburdene, Patricia 1947?- ConAu 140
Aburgavennie, Frances BlmGWL
Aburish, Said K. 1935- ConAu 140
Abushadi, Mohamed Mahmoud 1913- IntWW 93
Abushama, Sayed El-Rashid Abushama Abdel Mahmoud 1937- Who 94
Abut, Charles C. 1944- WhoAm 94
Abu Taleb, Sufi Hassan 1925- IntWW 93
Abuzakouk, Marai Mohammad 1936- WhoScEn 94
Abzug, Bella S. 1920- WhoAmP 93, WhoWomW 91
Abzug, Bella Savitzky 1920- IntWW 93, WhoAm 94
Abzug, Robert Henry 1945- WrDr 94
Acampora, Andrew Robert 1963- WhoFI 94
Acampora, Anthony Salvator 1946- WhoAm 94
Acampora, Ralph Joseph 1941- WhoAm 94, WhoFI 94
Acar, Yalcin Bekir 1951- WhoAm 94, WhoScEn 94
Accardo, Anthony 1906-1992 AnObit 1992
Accardo, Joseph, Jr. 1938- WhoAmP 93
Accardo, Salvatore 1941- IntWW 93
Accetta, Suzanne Rusconi 1953- WhoAmA 93
Accettola, Albert Bernard 1918- WhoAm 94
Accettura, Guy 1919-1991 WhAm 10
Acciaiuoli, Filippo 1637-1700 NewGrDO
Acciardo, Gregory J. 1957- WhoAmP 93
Accomando, Claire Hsu 1937- ConAu 142
Acconci, Vito 1940- IntWW 93, WhoAmA 93
Acconci, Vito Hannibal 1940- WhoAm 94
Accordino, Frank Joseph 1946- WhoAm 94, WhoFI 94
Accorimboni, Agostino 1739-1818 NewGrDO
Accornero, Harry 1942- WhoAmP 93
Accurso, Catherine Josephine 1955- WhoMW 93
Ace, Goodman d1982 WhoHol 92
Ace, Goodman 1899- WhAm 10
Ace, Goodman 1899-1982 WhoCom
Ace, Jane d1974 WhoHol 92
Ace, Jane 1900-1974 WhoCom
Acebal, Jack Celestino, Jr. 1938- WhoHisp 94
Acebo, Alexander 1927- WhoAmP 93
Acerra, Angelo Thomas 1925-1990 WhAm 10
Acerra, Michele 1937- WhoAm 94, WhoFI 94
Acevedo, Angela de d1644 BlmGWL
Acevedo, Angelique WhoHisp 94
Acevedo, Benjamin WhoHisp 94
Acevedo, Edmund Osvaldo 1960- WhoScEn 94
Acevedo, Eileen L. WhoHisp 94
Acevedo, Gary 1966- WhoHisp 94
Acevedo, George L. 1955- WhoHisp 94
Acevedo, Gerardo 1954- WhoHisp 94
Acevedo, Hector Luis 1947- WhoAm 94
Acevedo, Henry 1937- WhoHisp 94
Acevedo, Jorge Terrazas 1914- WhoHisp 94
Acevedo, Jose Enrique 1939- WhoHisp 94
Acevedo, Juan F. 1961- WhoHisp 94
Acevedo, Julio Eduardo 1931- WhoHisp 94
Acevedo, Louis 1957- WhoFI 94
Acevedo, Luis 1947- WhoAmP 93
Acevedo, Martha Ophelia 1942- WhoHisp 94
Acevedo, Mary Alice WhoHisp 94
Acevedo, Mary Ann 1943- WhoHisp 94
Acevedo, Nelson WhoHisp 94
Acevedo, Ralph Angel 1950- WhoHisp 94
Acevedo, Raydean WhoHisp 94
Acevedo, Sylvester Terrazas 1918- WhoHisp 94
Acevedo Guajardo, Remigio 1863-1911 NewGrDO
Acevedo-Vargas, Luz María 1954- WhoHisp 94
Acevedo Vila, Anibal 1962- WhoAmP 93
Aceves (y Lozano), Rafael 1837-1876 NewGrDO
Aceves, Javier 1955- WhoHisp 94
Aceves, José WhoHisp 94
Achalov, Vladislav Alekseevich 1945- LoBiDrD
Achampong, Francis Kofi 1955- WhoAmL 94
Achar, Narahari B. N. 1939- WhoAsA 94
Achard, Marcel 1899-1974 IntDcF 2-4
Achard de Bonvouloir, Julien 1749-1783 WhAmRev
Achard of St Victor c. 1100-1171 DcNaB MP
Acharya, Harsha 1944- WhoIns 94
Achatz, John 1948- WhoAm 94
Achebe, Chinua 1930- BlmGEL, ConBlB 6 [port], IntWW 93, RfGShF, Who 94, WrDr 94
Achebe, (Albert) Chinua(lumogu) 1930- BlkWr 2
Achee, Roland Joseph 1922- WhoAmL 94
Achen, Dorothy Karen Thompson 1944- WhoWest 94
Achen, Mark Kennedy 1943- WhoWest 94
Achenbach, Jan Drewes 1935- WhoAm 94, WhoScEn 94
Achenbaum, Alvin Allen 1925- WhoAm 94, WhoFI 94
A Cheng 1949- WhoPRCh 91 [port]
Achepohl, Keith Anden 1934- WhoAmA 93
Acheson Who 94
Acheson, Alice Brewen 1936- WhoWest 94
Acheson, Allen Morrow 1926- WhoAm 94
Acheson, Amy J. 1963- WhoAmL 94
Acheson, Clint WhoAmP 93
Acheson, David C(ampion) 1921- WrDr 94
Acheson, David Campion 1921- WhoAm 94
Acheson, Dean 1893-1971 HisWorL
Acheson, Dean G. 1890-1971 HisDcKW
Acheson, (Ernest) Donald 1926- Who 94
Acheson, Edward Goodrich WorInv
Acheson, James WhoAm 94, WhoHol 92
Acheson, Louis Kruzan, Jr. 1926- WhoAm 94
Acheson, Roy Malcolm 1921- Who 94, WhoAm 94
Acheson, Scott Allen 1958- WhoScEn 94
Achgill, Ralph Kenneth 1938- WhoMW 93
Achidi Achu, Simon 1934- IntWW 93
Achille, Jean-Claude 1926- IntWW 93
Achinstein, Asher 1900- WhoAm 94
Achinstein, Peter Jacob 1935- WhoAm 94
Acholonu, Catherine Obianuju BlmGWL
Achonry, Bishop of 1931- Who 94
Achor, Louis Joseph 1948- WhoAm 94
Achord, James Lee 1931- WhoAm 94
Achorn, Robert Comey 1922- WhoAm 94
Achour, Habib 1913- IntWW 93
Achram, Denise Lynn 1954- WhoFI 94
Achstatter, Dorothea Kelly 1959- WhoFI 94
Achte, Emmy (Charlotte) 1850-1924 NewGrDO
Achtel, Robert Andrew 1941- WhoWest 94
Achtenberg, Anya DrAPF 93
Achtenberg, Roberta News 93 [port]
Achtenhagen, Stephen H. 1929- WhoWest 94
Achterberg, Cheryl Lynn 1953- WhoScEn 94
Achterberg, Ernest Reginald 1925- WhoScEn 94
Achterberg, Fritz d1971 WhoHol 92
Achterberg, Gary Jack 1957- WhoMW 93
Achterkirchen, David Martin 1943- WhoAmL 94
Achterman, Gail L. 1949- WhoAmL 94
Achterman, Janet Gibbs 1956- WhoMW 93
Achtert, Walter Scott 1943- WhoAm 94
Acito, Daniel Joseph 1918- WhoAm 94
Ackah, Christian Abraham 1908- WrDr 94
Ackal, Elias, Jr. 1934- WhoAmP 93
Ackell, Edmund Ferris 1925- WhoAm 94
Ackenbom-Kelly, Beatrice Luckenbach 1940- WhoAmL 94
Acker, Alan Scott 1953- WhoAmL 94
Acker, Andrew French, III 1943- WhoMW 93
Acker, Ann 1948- WhoAmL 94
Acker, Daniel R. 1910- WhoBlA 94
Acker, David De Peyster 1921- WhAm 10
Acker, David Seth 1946- WhoAmL 94
Acker, Duane 1931- WhoAmP 93
Acker, Frederick George 1934- WhoAm 94, WhoAmL 94
Acker, Herbert William 1942- WhoAm 94, WhoFI 94
Acker, Jean d1978 WhoHol 92
Acker, Joan Elise Robinson 1924- WhoWest 94
Acker, Joseph Edington 1918- WhoAm 94
Acker, Kathy 1948- BlmGWL, EncSF 93
Acker, Lawrence G. 1950- WhoAm 94, WhoAmL 94
Acker, Martin Herbert 1921- WhoAm 94
Acker, Nathaniel Hull 1927- WhoAm 94
Acker, Raymond Abijah 1932- WhoAm 94
Acker, Robert Flint 1920- WhoAm 94
Acker, Robert Harold 1928- WhoAmP 93, WhoFI 94
Acker, Rodney 1949- WhoAm 94, WhoAmL 94
Acker, Sharon 1935- WhoHol 92
Acker, Verna Helen 1942- WhoMW 93
Acker, William Marsh, Jr. 1927- WhoAm 94, WhoAmL 94, WhoAmP 93
Ackeren, Robert Van 1946- IntWW 93
Ackerley, Barry WhoAm 94, WhoWest 94
Ackerley, J(oe) R(andolph) 1896-1967 GayLL
Ackerley, Joe Randolph 1896-1967 DcNaB MP
Ackerly, Benjamin Clarkson 1942- WhoAm 94, WhoAmL 94
Ackerly, Dana T. 1943- WhoAmL 94
Ackerly, S(amuel) Spafford 1895- WhAm 10
Ackerman, Alan Thomas 1947- WhoAmL 94
Ackerman, Alvin S. 1932- WhoAm 94
Ackerman, Bettye 1928- IntMPA 94, WhoHol 92
Ackerman, Bettye Louise 1928- WhoAm 94
Ackerman, Bruce A. 1945- WhoAmL 94
Ackerman, Diane DrAPF 93
Ackerman, Diane 1948- WrDr 94
Ackerman, Eugene 1920- WhoAm 94
Ackerman, F. Kenneth, Jr. 1939- WhoAm 94
Ackerman, Forrest 1916- WhoHol 92
Ackerman, Forrest J(ames) 1916- EncSF 93
Ackerman, Frank Edward 1933- WhoAmA 93N
Ackerman, Gary Dean 1938- WhoAmP 93
Ackerman, Gary L. 1942- CngDr 93, WhoAm 94, WhoAmP 93
Ackerman, Gerald Martin 1928- WhoAm 94, WhoAmA 93
Ackerman, Harold A. 1928- WhoAm 94, WhoAmL 94
Ackerman, Harry S. 1912-1991 WhAm 10
Ackerman, Helen Page 1912- WhoAm 94
Ackerman, Henry Sweets 1942- WhoAm 94
Ackerman, Jack Rossin 1931- WhoAm 94
Ackerman, James Nils 1912- WhoAm 94
Ackerman, James S. 1919- WhoAmA 93
Ackerman, James S(loss) 1919- WrDr 94
Ackerman, James Sloss 1919- WhoAm 94
Ackerman, Jerry William 1935- WhoFI 94
Ackerman, John C. 1933- WhoAmP 93
Ackerman, John Henry 1925- WhoAm 94
Ackerman, John Robert 1953- WhoFI 94
Ackerman, John Tryon 1941- WhoFI 94, WhoWest 94
Ackerman, Joseph J. H. 1949- WhoAm 94
Ackerman, Kenneth Benjamin 1932- WhoAm 94
Ackerman, Kenneth Edward 1946- WhoAmL 94
Ackerman, Lauren V. d1993 NewYTBS 93 [port]
Ackerman, Lennis Campbell 1917- WhoAm 94
Ackerman, Leslie WhoHol 92
Ackerman, Lillian Alice 1928- WhoWest 94
Ackerman, Linda Diane 1964- WhoFI 94, WhoWest 94
Ackerman, Louise Magaw 1904- WhoMW 93
Ackerman, Mark Robert 1959- WhoWest 94
Ackerman, Marshall 1925- WhoAm 94
Ackerman, Martin S. d1993 NewYTBS 93 [port]
Ackerman, Melvin 1937- WhoAm 94
Ackerman, Noreen Carol 1944- WhoMW 93
Ackerman, Ora Ray 1931- WhoAm 94
Ackerman, Patricia A. 1944- WhoBlA 94
Ackerman, Philip Charles 1944- WhoAm 94, WhoAmL 94, WhoFI 94
Ackerman, Philip M. 1940- WhoAmP 93
Ackerman, Raymond Basil 1922- WhoAm 94
Ackerman, Richard C. 1942- WhoAmP 93
Ackerman, Richard L. 1945- WhoAmL 94
Ackerman, Rick d1974 WhoHol 92
Ackerman, Robert E(dwin) 1928- ConAu 43NR
Ackerman, Robert Wallace 1938- WhoAm 94
Ackerman, Robert Wayne 1942- WhoAmP 93
Ackerman, Rosalie J. 1940- WhoMW 93
Ackerman, Roy Alan 1951- WhoScEn 94
Ackerman, Rudy Schlegel 1933- WhoAmA 93
Ackerman, Sam 1934- WhoAmP 93
Ackerman, Sanford Selig 1932- WhoAm 94
Ackerman, Victoria Mell Laird 1942- WhoMW 93
Ackerman, Walter d1938 WhoHol 92
Ackerman, Wendayne EncSF 93
Ackermann, Georg K. Who 94
Ackermann, John Joseph 1889-1950 WhoAmA 93N
Ackermann, Louise 1813-1890 BlmGWL
Ackermann, Otto 1909-1960 NewGrDO
Ackermann, Russell Albert WhoMW 93
Ackers, Gary Keith 1939- WhoAm 94
Ackers, James George 1935- Who 94
Ackerson, Cathy DrAPF 93
Ackerson, Charles Stanley 1935- WhoMW 93
Ackerson, Duane DrAPF 93
Ackerson, Jeffrey Townsend 1944- WhoAm 94
Ackerson, Jon W. 1943- WhoAmP 93
Ackerson, Nels John 1944- WhoAm 94
Ackert, Terrence William 1946- WhoAmL 94
Ackland, Joss 1928- IntMPA 94, IntWW 93, Who 94, WhoHol 92
Ackland, Len 1944- WhoWest 94
Ackland, Rodney 1908- WhoHol 92
Ackland, Rodney 1908-1991 ConDr 93, WrDr 94N
Ackland, Valentine 1906-1968 BlmGWL
Acklen, Gerald Gill 1907- WhAm 10
Ackles, Janice Vogel WhoWest 94
Ackles, Ken d1986 WhoHol 92
Ackley, Gardner 1915- WhoAmP 93
Ackley, (Hugh) Gardner 1915- IntWW 93
Ackley, Marjorie Rose 1922- WhoWest 94
Ackley, Robert O. 1952- WhoAmL 94, WhoMW 93
Acklie, Duane W. 1931- WhoAmP 93
Acklie, Duane William WhoAm 94, WhoMW 93
Acklie, Phyllis Ann 1933- WhoFI 94, WhoMW 93
Ackman, Lauress V. 1920- WhoAm 94
Ackman, Milton Roy 1932- WhoAm 94
Ackmann, Lowell Eugene 1923- WhoAm 94
Ackner Who 94
Ackner, Baron 1920- Who 94
Ackner, Desmond James Conrad 1920- IntWW 93
Ackoff, Russell Lincoln 1919- WhoAm 94
Ackord, Marie M. 1939- WhoBlA 94
Ackourey, Peter Paul 1954- WhoAm 94
Ackridge, Florence Gateward 1939- WhoBlA 94
Ackrill, John L(loyd) 1921- WrDr 94
Ackrill, John Lloyd 1921- Who 94
Ackroyd, David 1940- WhoHol 92
Ackroyd, John (Robert Whyte) 1932- Who 94
Ackroyd, Norman 1938- IntWW 93, Who 94
Ackroyd, Peter 1949- CurBio 93 [port], EncSF 93, IntWW 93, Who 94, WrDr 94
Ackroyd, Peter (Runham) 1917- WrDr 94
Ackroyd, Peter Runham 1917- Who 94
Ackte, Aino 1876-1944 NewGrDO [port]
Acland, Antony (Arthur) 1930- IntWW 93, Who 94
Acland, (Christopher) Guy (Dyke) 1946- Who 94
Acland, Harriet 1750-1815 WhAmRev
Acland, John (Hugh Bevil) 1928- Who 94
Acland, John Dyke Who 94
Acland, John Dyke d1778 WhAmRev
Acland, Peter Bevil Edward d1993 Who 94N
Aco, Michel fl. 168-?-169-? WhWE
Acob, Norma Denise 1952- WhoWest 94
Acoba, Simeon Rivera, Jr. 1944- WhoAmL 94
Acobe, Fernando 1941- WhoHisp 94
Acomb, Robert Bailey, Jr. 1930- WhoAm 94
Acon, June Kay 1948- WhoBlA 94
Acorace, Joseph John 1935- WhoAmP 93
Acord, Art d1931 WhoHol 92
Acord-Skelton, Barbara Burrows 1928- WhoWest 94
Acorn, Milton 1923- WrDr 94

Acosta, Able 1930- *WhoHisp 94*
Acosta, Alan T. 1952- *WhoHisp 94*
Acosta, Alirio 1933- *WhoHisp 94*
Acosta, Anibal A. 1929- *WhoHisp 94*
Acosta, Antonio A. 1929- *WhoHisp 94*
Acosta, Armando Joel 1956- *WhoHisp 94*
Acosta, Bert 1935- *WhoHisp 94*
Acosta, Carlos Alberto 1957- *WhoHisp 94*
Acosta, Carlos Julis 1939- *WhoHisp 94*
Acosta, Enrique d1949 *WhoHol 92*
Acosta, Heriberto A. 1951- *WhoHisp 94*
Acosta, Ivan M. 1943- *WhoHisp 94*
Acosta, Ivonne *WhoHisp 94*
Acosta, Joel Eleno 1957- *WhoHisp 94*
Acosta, John *WhoHisp 94*
Acosta, Jose De 1539-1600 *WhWE*
Acosta, Joseph 1921- *WhoHisp 94*
Acosta, Juan M. 1961- *WhoHisp 94*
Acosta, Julio Bernard 1927- *WhoAm 94*
Acosta, Lucy 1960- *WhoHisp 94*
Acosta, Lucy G. 1926- *WhoHisp 94*
Acosta, Lydia Maria 1947- *WhoHisp 94*
Acosta, Manuel Gregorio 1921- *WhoAmA 93, WhoHisp 94*
Acosta, Maria Lucy 1943- *WhoHisp 94*
Acosta, Nelia 1945- *WhoHisp 94*
Acosta, Nelson John 1947- *WhoScEn 94, WhoWest 94*
Acosta, Norma A. 1958- *WhoHisp 94*
Acosta, Pamela Ann 1955- *WhoWest 94*
Acosta, Patricia 1961- *WhoWest 94*
Acosta, Ralph 1934- *WhoAmP 93, WhoHisp 94*
Acosta, Raymond L. 1925- *WhoHisp 94*
Acosta, Raymond Luis 1925- *WhoAm 94, WhoAmL 94*
Acosta, Ricardo A. 1945- *WhoHisp 94*
Acosta, Rudolfo d1974 *WhoHol 92*
Acosta, Ruth Ann *WhoHisp 94*
Acosta, Socorro O. 1934- *WhoWomW 91*
Acosta, Valentín 1933- *WhoHisp 94**
Acosta-Belen, Edna 1948- *WhoHisp 94*
Acosta-Colón, Marie *WhoHisp 94*
Acosta de Samper, Soledad 1833-1903 *BlmGWL*
Acosta-Lespier, Luis 1939- *WhoHisp 94*
Acovone, Jay *WhoHol 92*
Acquafresca, Steve 1951- *WhoAmP 93*
Acquafresca, Steven Joseph 1951- *WhoWest 94*
Acquanetta 1920- *WhoHol 92*
Acree, Karen Strother 1956- *WhoFI 94*
Acree, Margaret Louise 1937- *WhoMW 93*
Acree, Michael Coy 1946- *WhoWest 94*
Acree, William B., Jr. 1944- *WhoAmP 93*
Acres, Douglas Ian 1924- *Who 94*
Acrey, Autry 1948- *WhoBlA 94*
Acrivos, Andreas 1928- *WhoScEn 94*
Acs, Joseph Steven 1936- *WhoScEn 94*
Actman, Jane 1949- *WhoHol 92*
Acton, Baron 1941- *Who 94*
Acton, Arlo C. 1933- *WhoAmA 93*
Acton, David 1933- *WhoAm 94*
Acton, David Lawrence 1949- *WhoMW 93*
Acton, Edward McIntosh 1930- *WhoWest 94*
Acton, Emeline 1955- *WhoAmL 94*
Acton, Harold (Mario) 1904- *WrDr 94*
Acton, Harold (Mario Mitchell) 1904- *EncSF 93, Who 94*
Acton, Norman 1918- *WhoAm 94*
Acton, Wallace d1980 *WhoHol 92*
Acton, William Antony d1993 *Who 94N*
Acuff, D. Nicholas 1942- *WhoAmP 93*
Acuff, Eddie d1956 *WhoHol 92*
Acuff, Roy 1903-1992 *AnObit 1992*
Acuff, Roy (Claxton) 1903-1992 *CurBio 93N*
Acuff, Roy Claxton 1903-1992 *WhAm 10*
Acuff, Thomas Aldrich 1936- *WhoFI 94*
Acula, Dr. *EncSF 93*
Acuna, Cristobal De 1597-c. 1676 *WhWE*
Acuna, Dora *BlmGWL*
Acuña, Rodolfo 1932- *WhoHisp 94*
Acworth, Andrew *EncSF 93*
Acworth, Richard Foote 1936- *Who 94*
Acworth, Robert William 1938- *Who 94*
Aczel, Janos D. 1924- *IntWW 93*
Aczel, Janos Dezso 1924- *WhoAm 94*
Aczel, Thomas 1930-1991 *WhAm 10*
Ada, Gordon Leslie 1922- *IntWW 93*
Ada, Joseph Franklin 1943- *WhoAm 94, WhoAmP 93*
Ada, Thomas Castro 1949- *WhoAmP 93*
Adachi, Derek Kasumi 1961- *WhoWest 94*
Adachibara, Akifumi 1924- *IntWW 93*
Adaikan, Ganesan Periannan 1944- *WhoScEn 94*
Adair, Alvis V. 1940- *WhoBlA 94*
Adair, Andrew A. 1933- *WhoBlA 94*
Adair, Brian Campbell 1945- *Who 94*
Adair, Charles, Jr. 1950- *WhoBlA 94*
Adair, Charles E. 1947- *WhoFI 94*
Adair, Charles Robert, Jr. 1914- *WhoAm 94*
Adair, Charles Valloyd 1923- *WhoAm 94*
Adair, Charles Wallace, Jr. 1914- *WhoAmP 93*
Adair, Gerry A. 1940- *WhoAmP 93*
Adair, Jack d1940 *WhoHol 92*
Adair, James d1783 *WhWE*
Adair, James Allen 1929- *WhoWest 94*
Adair, James E. *WhoBlA 94*
Adair, James R(adford) 1923- *WrDr 94*
Adair, Jean d1953 *WhoHol 92*
Adair, Jean R. 1951- *WhoMW 93*
Adair, John d1952 *WhoHol 92*
Adair, John (Eric) 1934- *WrDr 94*
Adair, John Joseph 1941- *WhoAm 94*
Adair, Kenneth 1904- *WhoBlA 94*
Adair, Larry Eugene 1946- *WhoAmP 93*
Adair, Lila McGahee 1947- *WhoScEn 94*
Adair, Red 1915- *WhoAm 94*
Adair, Red (Paul Neal) 1915- *IntWW 93*
Adair, Robert d1954 *WhoHol 92*
Adair, Robert A. 1943- *WhoBlA 94*
Adair, Robert Kemp 1924- *WhoScEn 94, WrDr 94*
Adair, Sidney Arthur 1928- *WhoAmP 93*
Adair, Tom d1993 *NewYTBS 93*
Adair, Wendell Hinton, Jr. 1944- *WhoAm 94, WhoAmL 94*
Adaire, Bruce Bower 1937- *WhoMW 93*
Adál 1947- *WhoHisp 94*
Adalbert, Max d1933 *WhoHol 92*
Adam, Adolphe 1803-1856 *IntDcB [port]*
Adam, Adolphe (Charles) 1803-1856 *NewGrDO*
Adam, Alfred d1982 *WhoHol 92*
Adam, Carrolyne Lee 1944- *WhoMW 93*
Adam, Christopher Eric Forbes 1920- *Who 94*
Adam, Cornel 1915- *WhoAm 94, WhoWest 94*
Adam, Encik Mohamed Adib Haji Mohamed 1941- *IntWW 93*
Adam, Frederic 1904-1984 *NewGrDO*
Adam, Gordon *Who 94*
Adam, (David Stuart) Gordon 1927- *Who 94*
Adam, Gordon Johnston 1934- *Who 94*
Adam, Helen d1993 *NewYTBS 93*
Adam, Jean-Francois d1980 *WhoHol 92*
Adam, Joan *WhoAmP 93*
Adam, John, Jr. 1914- *WhoAm 94*
Adam, Juliette 1836-1936 *BlmGWL*
Adam, Ken *WhoAm 94*
Adam, Ken 1921- *IntDcF 2-4, IntMPA 94, IntWW 93*
Adam, Madge Gertrude 1912- *Who 94*
Adam, Malcolm 1895- *WhAm 10*
Adam, Noelle *WhoHol 92*
Adam, Orval Michael 1930- *WhoAm 94*
Adam, Paul James 1934- *WhoAm 94, WhoFI 94, WhoMW 93*
Adam, Robert 1728-1792 *BlmGEL*
Adam, Robert 1948- *IntWW 93*
Adam, Robert Wilson d1993 *Who 94N*
Adam, Robert Wilson 1923- *IntWW 93*
Adam, Rodney Dean 1954- *WhoWest 94*
Adam, Ronald d1979 *WhoHol 92*
Adam, Stephen Ferenc 1929- *WhoAm 94*
Adam, Steven Jeffrey 1957- *WhoScEn 94*
Adam, Theo 1926- *IntWW 93*
Adam, Theo(dor) 1926- *NewGrDO*
Adam, Thomas Ritchie 1900-1990 *WhAm 10*
Adam, Wallace Burns 1933- *WhoWest 94*
Adamany, David Walter 1936- *WhoAm 94, WhoMW 93*
Adamberger, (Josef) Valentin 1743-1804 *NewGrDO*
Adamczyk, Joseph Roger, Jr. 1955- *WhoAmP 93*
Adam de la Halle c. 1245-c. 1288 *IntDcT 2*
Adame, Leonard 1947- *WhoHisp 94*
Adamec, Christine 1949- *ConAu 141*
Adamec, Joseph Victor 1935- *WhoAm 94*
Adamec, Ludwig W. 1924- *WrDr 94*
Adamek, Charles Andrew 1944- *WhoAm 94, WhoAmL 94*
Adamek, Edward Leo d1988 *WhoHol 92*
Adames, Fermin 1944- *WhoHisp 94*
Adames, Maria 1941- *WhoHisp 94*
Adamez, Alma Carrales 1958- *WhoHisp 94*
Adami, Carl *NewGrDO*
Adami, Edward F. *Who 94*
Adami, Franco 1933- *IntWW 93*
Adami, Giuseppe 1878-1946 *NewGrDO*
Adamian, Gregory Harry 1926- *WhoAm 94*
Adamic, Louis 1899-1951 *AmSocL*
Adamich, Susan Jo Ann 1959- *WhoWest 94*
Adamishin, Anatoly Leonidovich 1934- *IntWW 93, LoBiDrD*
Adamkiewicz, Vincent Witold 1924- *WhoAm 94*
Adamle, Kathleen Nora Duffy 1948- *WhoMW 93*
Adamo, Joseph A. *WhoAmP 93*
Adamo, Kenneth R. 1950- *WhoAm 94*
Adamo, Victor T. 1948- *WhoIns 94*
Adam of Balsham c. 1105-c. 1170 *DcNaB MP*
Adamour, Beth *DrAPF 93*
Adamov, Arthur 1908-1970 *IntDcT 2*
Adamovic, Ivan 1967- *EncSF 93*
Adamovich, Shirley Gray 1927- *WhoAm 94*
Adamovics, Andris 1932- *WhoScEn 94*
Adams, A. John Bertrand 1931- *WhoAm 94*
Adams, Abigail *WhoHol 92*
Adams, Abigail 1744-1818 *WhAmRev*
Adams, Abigail Smith 1744-1818 *AmRev, BlmGWL*
Adams, Afesa M. 1936- *WhoBlA 94*
Adams, Aileen Kirkpatrick 1923- *Who 94*
Adams, Alan Eugene 1939- *WhoMW 93*
Adams, Alan Leonard 1949- *WhoWest 94*
Adams, Albert P. 1942- *WhoAmP 93*
Adams, Albert T. 1950- *WhoAm 94, WhoAmL 94*
Adams, Albert W., Jr. 1948- *WhoBlA 94*
Adams, Albert Willie, Jr. 1948- *WhoAm 94*
Adams, Alec Cecil Stanley 1909- *Who 94*
Adams, Alfred Bernard, Jr. 1920- *WhoScEn 94*
Adams, Alfred G., Jr. 1948- *WhoAmL 94*
Adams, Alfred Gray 1946- *WhoAmL 94*
Adams, Alfred Hugh 1928- *WhoAm 94*
Adams, Algalee Pool 1919- *WhoAm 94*
Adams, Alger LeRoy 1910- *WhoBlA 94*
Adams, Alice *DrAPF 93*
Adams, Alice 1926- *WhoAm 94, WrDr 94*
Adams, Alice 1930- *WhoAm 94, WhoAmA 93*
Adams, Alice Omega 1951- *WhoBlA 94*
Adams, Alvan 1954- *BasBi*
Adams, Alvin P., Jr. *WhoAmP 93*
Adams, Alvin Philip, Jr. 1942- *WhoAm 94*
Adams, Andrew 1736-1797 *WhAmRev*
Adams, Andrew Brian 1968- *WhoFI 94*
Adams, Andrew Joseph 1909- *WhoAm 94*
Adams, Ann Jensen 1949- *WhoMW 93*
Adams, Ann Louise 1934- *WhoWest 94*
Adams, Ann Yutz 1950- *WhoMW 93*
Adams, Anna *DrAPF 93*
Adams, Anne Currin 1942- *WhoBlA 94*
Adams, Ansel 1902-1984 *EnvEnc*
Adams, Ansel Easton 1902-1984 *AmCulL, WhoAmA 93N*
Adams, Anthony John 1953- *WhoAmL 94*
Adams, Anthony Peter 1936- *Who 94*
Adams, Arlin Marvin 1921- *WhoAm 94*
Adams, Armenta Estella 1936- *WhoBlA 94*
Adams, Arvil Van 1943- *WhoAm 94*
Adams, Avery C. 1897-1963 *EncABHB 9*
Adams, Barbara *DrAPF 93*
Adams, Barbara 1951- *WhoAm 94*
Adams, Bart *ConAu 42NR*
Adams, Beejay 1920- *WhoFI 94, WhoMW 93*
Adams, Bernard Charles 1915- *Who 94*
Adams, Bernard LeRoy 1954- *WhoWest 94*
Adams, Bernard Schroder 1928- *WhoAm 94*
Adams, Betsy *DrAPF 93*
Adams, Bett Yates 1942- *WhoAm 94*
Adams, Betty *WhoHol 92*
Adams, Beverly 1945- *WhoHol 92*
Adams, Billie Morris Wright *WhoBlA 94*
Adams, Blake d1913 *WhoHol 92*
Adams, Bobbi 1939- *WhoAmA 93*
Adams, Brady 1945- *WhoAmP 93*
Adams, Brent T. 1948- *WhoAmP 93*
Adams, Brock(man) 1927- *IntWW 93*
Adams, Brockman 1927- *WhoAmP 93*
Adams, Bronte (Jane) 1963- *ConAu 140*
Adams, Brooke 1949- *IntMPA 94, WhoHol 92*
Adams, Bryan 1959- *WhoAm 94*
Adams, Buel Thomas 1933- *WhoAm 94*
Adams, C. Lee 1940- *WhoFI 94*
Adams, Caren 1946- *WrDr 94*
Adams, Carl D. 1934- *WhoAmP 93*
Adams, Carl Douglas 1925- *WhoFI 94*
Adams, Carl Fillmore, Jr. 1950- *WhoFI 94*
Adams, Carl Morgan, Jr. 1940- *WhoFI 94*
Adams, Carl S. *WhoAmP 93*
Adams, Carol J. 1951- *WrDr 94*
Adams, Carol Laurence 1944- *WhoBlA 94*
Adams, Carolyn Loraine 1957- *WhoAmL 94*
Adams, Cary Meredith 1948- *WhoAm 94, WhoAmL 94*
Adams, Casey 1917- *WhoHol 92*
Adams, Catlin *WhoHol 92*
Adams, Catlin 1950- *IntMPA 94*
Adams, Cecil Ray 1948- *WhoBlA 94*
Adams, Celeste Marie 1947- *WhoAmA 93*
Adams, Charles Arthur 1933- *WhAm 10*
Adams, Charles F. 1947- *WhoAmL 94*
Adams, Charles Francis 1910- *IntWW 93*
Adams, Charles Francis 1927- *WhoAm 94*
Adams, Charles Gilchrist 1936- *WhoBlA 94*
Adams, Charles Henry 1918- *WhoAm 94*
Adams, Charles Hubert 1934- *WhoAmP 93*
Adams, Charles Jairus 1917- *WhoAm 94*
Adams, Charles Lynford 1929- *WhoAm 94*
Adams, Charles R. 1834-1900 *NewGrDO*
Adams, Charles R., III 1957- *WhoAmL 94*
Adams, Charles Richard 1927- *WhoWest 94*
Adams, Charles William 1948- *WhoAmL 94*
Adams, Chelsea *DrAPF 93*
Adams, Chester Z. 1908- *WhoScEn 94*
Adams, (Charles) Christian (Wilfred) 1939- *Who 94*
Adams, Christopher Steve, Jr. 1930- *WhoAm 94*
Adams, Chuck 1919- *WrDr 94*
Adams, Claire d1978 *WhoHol 92*
Adams, Clarence Lancelot, Jr. *WhoBlA 94*
Adams, Claudette Coleman 1952- *WhoBlA 94*
Adams, Clinton 1918- *WhoAm 94, WhoAmA 93, WhoWest 94*
Adams, Curtis N. 1931- *WhoBlA 94*
Adams, Daniel 1930- *WrDr 94*
Adams, Daniel Fenton 1922- *WhoAm 94*
Adams, Daniel Lee 1936- *WhoAm 94*
Adams, David *WhoHol 92*
Adams, David, Jr. 1927- *WhoBlA 94*
Adams, David Bachrach 1939- *WhoAm 94*
Adams, David Bennion 1945- *WhoWest 94*
Adams, David Christopher 1967- *WhoWest 94*
Adams, David Dean *WhoFI 94*
Adams, David Huntington 1942- *WhoAmL 94*
Adams, David John 1949- *WhoWest 94*
Adams, David M. 1942- *WhoAmP 93*
Adams, David Parrish 1958- *WhoScEn 94*
Adams, Deanna Sue Duncan 1942- *WhoWest 94*
Adams, Deborah *DrAPF 93*
Adams, Dee Briane 1942- *WhoScEn 94*
Adams, Dennis Paul 1948- *WhoAm 94, WhoAmA 93*
Adams, Denny Eugene 1950- *WhoAmL 94*
Adams, Diana *WhoHol 92*
Adams, Diana d1993 *NewYTBS 93 [port]*
Adams, Diana 1926-1993 *CurBio 93N IntDcB [port]*
Adams, Dolly Desselle *WhoBlA 94*
Adams, Dolph O. 1939- *WhoScEn 94*
Adams, Don 1925- *WrDr 94*
Adams, Don 1926- *IntMPA 94, WhoCom, WhoHol 92*
Adams, Don L. 1927- *WhoBlA 94*
Adams, Don M. *WhoAmL 94*
Adams, Don W. 1935- *WhoAmP 93*
Adams, Donald 1928- *NewGrDO*
Adams, Donald E. 1938- *WhoScEn 94*
Adams, Donald Edward 1964- *WhoScEn 94*
Adams, Donald Scott 1960- *WhoScEn 94*
Adams, Dorothy d1988 *WhoHol 92*
Adams, Douglas 1952- *CurBio 93 [port], WhoAm 94*
Adams, Douglas (Noel) 1952- *EncSF 93, IntWW 93, WrDr 94*
Adams, Douglas Noel 1952- *Who 94*
Adams, Douglass Franklin 1935- *WhoAm 94*
Adams, Duncan Dartrey 1925- *WhoScEn 94*
Adams, Eadie d1983 *WhoHol 92*
Adams, Earl Leonard, III 1953- *WhoBlA 94*
Adams, Earl William, Jr. 1937- *WhoAm 94*
Adams, Earle Myles 1942- *WhoScEn 94*
Adams, Edie 1927- *IntMPA 94*
Adams, Edie 1929- *WhoHol 92*
Adams, Edith d1957 *WhoHol 92*
Adams, Edmund John 1938- *WhoAm 94, WhoFI 94*
Adams, Edward A. 1963- *WhoAmL 94*
Adams, Edward B. 1939- *WhoBlA 94*
Adams, Edward Robert 1943- *WhoBlA 94*
Adams, Edward Thomas 1933- *WhoAm 94*
Adams, Edwin Melville 1914- *WhoAm 94*
Adams, Elaine Parker 1940- *WhoBlA 94*
Adams, Elizabeth *DrAPF 93*
Adams, Elizabeth Herrington 1947- *WhoMW 93*
Adams, Elizabeth Spencer 1957- *WhoAmL 94*
Adams, Ernest Charles 1926- *WrDr 94*
Adams, Ernest Clarence, Jr. 1925- *WhoMW 93*
Adams, Ernest Victor 1920- *Who 94*
Adams, Ernie d1947 *WhoHol 92*
Adams, Eugene Bruce 1953- *WhoBlA 94*
Adams, Eugene William 1920- *WhoBlA 94*

Adams, Eva Bertrand d1991 *WhAm 10*
Adams, Eva Garza 1943- *WhoHisp 94*
Adams, Eva W. 1928- *WhoBlA 94*
Adams, Evangeline 1868-1932 *AstEnc*
Adams, Evelyne Hall d1993 *NewYTBS 93*
Adams, Everett Merle 1920- *WhoAm 94*
Adams, F. Gerard 1929- *WhoAm 94*
Adams, Faneuil 1898- *WhAm 10*
Adams, Frances Grant, II 1955- *WhoAmL 94*
Adams, Frances Sale d1969 *WhoHol 92*
Adams, Frank Alexander 1907- *Who 94*
Adams, Franklin P. d1960 *WhoHol 92*
Adams, Frederick Baldwin, Jr. 1910- *Who 94*
Adams, Frederick G. 1931- *WhoBlA 94*
Adams, Frederick Upham 1859-1921 *EncSF 93*
Adams, G. Rollie 1941- *WhoAm 94*
Adams, Gail Hayes 1944- *WhoAm 94*
Adams, George Bell 1930- *WhoAm 94*
Adams, George Drayton 1915- *WhoAmP 93*
Adams, George Harold 1926- *WhoAm 94*
Adams, George Wallace 1962- *WhoBlA 94*
Adams, Gerald 1948- *News 94-1 [port]*
Adams, Gerald Drayson *IntMPA 94*
Adams, Gerald Edward 1930- *Who 94*
Adams, Gerald Robert 1946- *WhoAm 94*
Adams, Glen Cameron 1912- *WhoWest 94*
Adams, Glenda *DrAPF 93*
Adams, Glenda 1939- *BlmGWL, WrDr 94*
Adams, Gordon *WhoAmP 93*
Adams, Greg F. 1950- *WhoAmL 94*
Adams, Gregory Albert 1958- *WhoBlA 94*
Adams, Gregory Burke 1948- *WhoAm 94, WhoAmL 94*
Adams, Gregory Keith 1958- *WhoBlA 94*
Adams, Hall, Jr. 1933- *WhoAm 94*
Adams, Hank M. 1956- *WhoAmA 93*
Adams, Hannah 1755-1831 *BlmGWL, DcAmReB 2*
Adams, Harold *DrAPF 93*
Adams, Harold Lynn 1939- *WhoAm 94*
Adams, Harriet Chalmers 1875-1937 *WhWE*
Adams, Harriet S(tratemeyer) 1892-1982 *EncSF 93*
Adams, Harroll 1925- *WhoAmP 93*
Adams, Hazard 1926- *WrDr 94*
Adams, Hazard Simeon 1926- *WhoAm 94*
Adams, Henry 1838-1918 *TwCLC 52*
Adams, Henry 1949- *WhoAm 94, WhoAmA 93, WrDr 94*
Adams, Henry Brooks 1838-1918 *AmCulL*
Adams, Herbert C. F. 1953- *WhoAmP 93*
Adams, Herbert Ryan 1932- *WhoAm 94*
Adams, Hervey Cadwallader 1903- *Who 94*
Adams, Howard *WhoAmP 93*
Adams, Howard d1936 *WhoHol 92*
Adams, Howard Glen 1940- *WhoBlA 94*
Adams, Hunter *EncSF 93*
Adams, Iola 1910- *WhoAmP 93*
Adams, Irene *Who 94*
Adams, J. Allen 1932- *WhoAmP 93*
Adams, Jack *EncSF 93*
Adams, Jack 1952- *WhoFI 94, WhoWest 94*
Adams, Jackie W., Sr. 1927- *WhoBlA 94*
Adams, Jad 1954- *ConAu 142*
Adams, James *Who 94*
Adams, (Albert) James 1915- *Who 94*
Adams, (William) James 1932- *IntWW 93, Who 94*
Adams, James Alfred 1949- *WhoScEn 94*
Adams, James Blackburn 1926- *WhoAm 94*
Adams, James Charles 1949- *WhoAmL 94*
Adams, James David 1954- *WhoWest 94*
Adams, James Derek 1962- *WhoScEn 94*
Adams, James E. 1944- *WhoAm 94*
Adams, James Edward 1898- *WhAm 10*
Adams, James Edward, II 1950- *WhoMW 93*
Adams, James F(rederick) 1927- *WrDr 94*
Adams, James Frederick 1927- *WhoAm 94, WhoWest 94*
Adams, James Henry 1957- *WhoScEn 94*
Adams, James Jay 1955- *WhoWest 94*
Adams, James Lee 1953- *WhoScEn 94*
Adams, James Louis 1928- *WhoAm 94*
Adams, James Luther 1901- *WhoAm 94*
Adams, James Malcolm 1954- *WhoBlA 94*
Adams, James Mills 1936- *WhoAm 94, WhoFI 94, WhoScEn 94*
Adams, James Noel 1943- *Who 94*
Adams, James R. 1939- *WhoAm 94, WhoFI 94*
Adams, James Robert 1946- *WhoMW 93*
Adams, James Russell 1945- *WhoWest 94*
Adams, James Thomas 1930- *WhoAm 94*
Adams, James William 1921- *WhoMW 93, WhoScEn 94*
Adams, James Wilson 1928- *WhoAm 94*
Adams, Jane Feathergill 1957- *WhoFI 94*
Adams, Janet *WhoAmP 93*
Adams, Jason *WhoHol 92*
Adams, Jay H. 1937- *WhoAmA 93*
Adams, Jean Ruth 1928- *WhoAm 94*
Adams, Jean Tucker *WhoBlA 94*
Adams, Jeanette *DrAPF 93*
Adams, Jeb Stuart *WhoHol 92*
Adams, Jeff d1967 *WhoHol 92*
Adams, Jeffrey Howard 1966- *WhoMW 93*
Adams, Jeffrey P. 1951- *WhoAmL 94*
Adams, Jennifer 1948- *Who 94*
Adams, Jill 1930- *WhoHol 92*
Adams, Jimmie d1933 *WhoHol 92*
Adams, Jimmie Vick 1936- *WhoAm 94, WhoWest 94*
Adams, Jo-Ann Marie 1949- *WhoWest 94*
Adams, Jody Ann 1960- *WhoMW 93*
Adams, Joey 1911- *WhoAm 94, WhoCom [port], WhoHol 92*
Adams, John *EncSF 93*
Adams, John 1735-1826 *AmRev, HisWorL [port], WhAmRev [port]*
Adams, John (Coolidge) 1947- *NewGrDO*
Adams, John Allan Stewart 1926-1992 *WhAm 10*
Adams, John Andrew 1946- *WhoFI 94*
Adams, John Anthony 1944- *WrDr 94*
Adams, John Brett 1940- *WhoFI 94*
Adams, John Buchanan, Jr. 1948- *WhoAm 94*
Adams, John C. 1939- *WhoFI 94*
Adams, John Carter, Jr. 1936- *WhoFI 94*
Adams, John Couch 1819-1892 *WorScD [port]*
Adams, John Crawford *Who 94*
Adams, John David Vessot 1934- *WhoAm 94, WhoFI 94*
Adams, John Douglas Richard 1940- *Who 94*
Adams, John Evi 1937-1989 *WhAm 10*
Adams, John Ewart 1952- *WhoScEn 94*
Adams, John F. 1950- *WhoAmL 94*
Adams, John Francis, Jr. 1936- *WhoAm 94*
Adams, John Hamilton 1936- *WhoAm 94*
Adams, John Hanly 1918- *WhoAm 94*
Adams, John Harold 1918- *Who 94*
Adams, John Hurst 1929- *WhoAm 94, WhoBlA 94*
Adams, John Jillson 1934- *WhoAm 94*
Adams, John Joseph 1916-1989 *WhAm 10*
Adams, John Kenneth 1915- *Who 94*
Adams, John M. 1950- *WhoAm 94, WhoWest 94*
Adams, John Marshall 1930- *WhoAm 94*
Adams, John Michael 1947- *WhoAmA 93*
Adams, John Nicholas William B. *Who 94*
Adams, John Oscar 1937- *WhoBlA 94*
Adams, John Phillips, Jr. 1920- *WhoWest 94*
Adams, John Powers 1938- *WhoAm 94*
Adams, John Quincy 1767-1848 *HisWorL [port]*
Adams, John Quincy, III 1945- *WhoAm 94*
Adams, John R. 1900- *WhoAm 94*
Adams, John Richard 1918- *WhoAm 94*
Adams, John Robert 1938- *WhoAm 94*
Adams, John Roderick Seton 1936- *Who 94*
Adams, John Shepard 1961- *WhoWest 94*
Adams, John Stephen 1938- *WhoAm 94, WhoMW 93*
Adams, Jon Michael 1956- *WhoWest 94*
Adams, Jonathan S(eth) 1961- *ConAu 141*
Adams, Joseph Brian 1961- *WhoScEn 94*
Adams, Joseph Keith 1949- *WhoAmL 94*
Adams, Joseph Lee, Jr. 1944- *WhoAmP 93, WhoBlA 94*
Adams, Joseph Peter 1907- *WhoAm 94*
Adams, Julia Davis d1993 *NewYTBS 93*
Adams, Julian 1919- *WrDr 94*
Adams, Julie 1926- *IntMPA 94, WhoHol 92*
Adams, Katharine Odell 1954- *WhoFI 94*
Adams, Katherine 1948- *Who 94*
Adams, Katherine 1952- *WhoBlA 94*
Adams, Kathleen Marie 1957- *WhoMW 93*
Adams, Kathryn d1959 *WhoHol 92*
Adams, Kattie Johnson 1938- *WhoBlA 94*
Adams, Kenneth Francis 1946- *WhoAm 94*
Adams, Kenneth Galt 1920- *Who 94*
Adams, Kenneth Marvin 1958- *WhoAmL 94*
Adams, Kenneth Menzies 1922- *WrDr 94*
Adams, Kent J. *WhoAmP 93*
Adams, L. Jerold 1939- *WhoMW 93*
Adams, Lane W. d1993 *NewYTBS 93*
Adams, Larry Dell 1963- *WhoScEn 94*
Adams, Larry J. 1949- *WhoAmP 93*
Adams, Laura Ann 1959- *WhoMW 93*
Adams, Laurie 1941- *WrDr 94*
Adams, Lawrence C. 1950- *WhoAmL 94*
Adams, (Moulton) Lee 1922-1971 *WhoAmA 93N*
Adams, Lee Stephen 1949- *WhoAm 94, WhoAmL 94, WhoMW 93*
Adams, Lehman D. 1925- *WhoBlA 94*
Adams, Leon Ashby, III 1951- *WhoWest 94*
Adams, Leon David 1905- *WhoAm 94*
Adams, Leonard Joseph 1954- *WhoFI 94*
Adams, Leonie 1899-1988 *WhAm 10*
Adams, Leslie d1934 *WhoHol 92*
Adams, Leslie 1930- *WrDr 94*
Adams, Leslie 1932- *WhoBlA 94*
Adams, Leslie Bunn, Jr. 1932- *WhoAm 94*
Adams, Lewis Drummond 1939- *Who 94*
Adams, Lillian Louise T. 1929- *WhoBlA 94*
Adams, Lionel d1952 *WhoHol 92*
Adams, Lisa Kay 1955- *WhoAmA 93*
Adams, Loretta H. 1940- *WhoHisp 94*
Adams, Louis J.A. *EncSF 93*
Adams, Lucinda Williams 1937- *WhoBlA 94*
Adams, Lucretia McKey 1932- *WhoAmP 93*
Adams, Lynne *WhoHol 92*
Adams, M. Elizabeth 1906- *WhoBlA 94*
Adams, M. June 1952- *WhoAmL 94*
Adams, Mac 1943- *WhoAmA 93*
Adams, Margaret Bernice 1936- *WhoAm 94*
Adams, Margaret Boroughs d1965 *WhoAmA 93N*
Adams, Marilyn Jager 1948- *WrDr 94*
Adams, Mark 1925- *WhoAm 94, WhoAmA 93, WhoWest 94*
Adams, Mark Lynn 1951- *WhoAmP 93*
Adams, Marla 1938- *WhoHol 92*
Adams, Martin P. 1956- *WhoBlA 94*
Adams, Marvin 1912- *WhoAmP 93*
Adams, Mary d1973 *WhoHol 92*
Adams, Mary B. *WhoAmP 93*
Adams, Mason 1917- *WhoHol 92*
Adams, Mason 1919- *IntMPA 94*
Adams, Maud 1945- *IntMPA 94, WhoHol 92*
Adams, Michael 1963- *BasBi, WhoAm 94, WhoBlA 94*
Adams, Michael Curtis 1953- *WhoWest 94*
Adams, Michael Ellis 1951- *WhoMW 93*
Adams, Michael Evelyn 1920- *WrDr 94*
Adams, Michael F. 1948- *WhoAm 94*
Adams, Michael John 1945- *WhoAmL 94, WhoMW 93*
Adams, Michael Keith 1934- *Who 94*
Adams, Nancy R. *WhoScEn 94*
Adams, Neal 1941- *EncSF 93*
Adams, Neile 1934- *WhoHol 92*
Adams, Nelson Eddy 1945- *WhoBlA 94*
Adams, Nick d1968 *WhoHol 92*
Adams, Norman 1927- *IntWW 93*
Adams, Norman (Edward Albert) 1927- *Who 94*
Adams, Norman Ilsley, Jr. 1895-1985 *WhAm 10*
Adams, Norman Joseph 1930- *WhoWest 94*
Adams, Norman Joseph 1933- *WhoFI 94*
Adams, Oleta *WhoBlA 94*
Adams, Onie H. Powers 1907- *WhoScEn 94*
Adams, Oscar W., Jr. 1925- *WhoAmP 93, WhoBlA 94*
Adams, Oscar William, Jr. 1925- *WhoAm 94, WhoAmL 94*
Adams, Pamela Crippen *EncSF 93*
Adams, Pat 1928- *WhoAm 94, WhoAmA 93*
Adams, Paul Allison 1940- *WhoScEn 94*
Adams, Paul Ancil 1937- *WhoAm 94, WhoAmP 93*
Adams, Paul Brown 1929- *WhoBlA 94*
Adams, Paul Douglas 1942- *WhoWest 94*
Adams, Paul G. 1945- *WhoAm 94, WhoFI 94*
Adams, Paul Lincoln 1908-1990 *WhAm 10*
Adams, Paul Stuart 1957- *WhoMW 93*
Adams, Paul Winfrey 1913- *WhoAm 94*
Adams, Pauline Gordon 1922- *WhoMW 93*
Adams, Payton F. 1930- *WhoAm 94, WhoFI 94*
Adams, Peggy Hoffman 1936- *WhoAmP 93*
Adams, Perry Ronald 1921- *WhoAm 94*
Adams, Peter d1987 *WhoHol 92*
Adams, Peter David 1937- *WhoAm 94*
Adams, Peter Frederick *WhoAm 94*
Adams, Phelps Haviland 1902-1991 *WhAm 10*
Adams, Philip 1905- *WhoWest 94*
Adams, Philip (George Doyne) 1915- *Who 94*
Adams, Philip George Doyne 1915- *IntWW 93*
Adams, Philip J. *WhoAmP 93*
Adams, Philip James 1920- *WhoWest 94*
Adams, Phoebe 1953- *WhoAmA 93*
Adams, Phoebe-Lou 1918- *WhoAm 94*
Adams, Quinton Douglas 1919- *WhoBlA 94*
Adams, Ralph Wyatt, Sr. 1915- *WhoAm 94, WhoAmL 94*
Adams, Ranald Trevor, Jr. 1925- *WhoAm 94*
Adams, Raymond Edward 1933- *WhoAm 94*
Adams, Raymond William 1898- *WhAm 10*
Adams, Rebecca P. 1953- *WhoAmL 94*
Adams, Richard (George) 1920- *TwCYAW, WrDr 94*
Adams, Richard Arthur 1951- *WhoWest 94*
Adams, Richard Borlase 1921- *Who 94*
Adams, Richard Donald 1909- *WhAm 10*
Adams, Richard Edward 1936- *WhAm 10*
Adams, Richard George 1920- *IntWW 93, Who 94, WhoAm 94*
Adams, Richard John Moreton G. *Who 94*
Adams, Richard Lynnden 1943- *WhoAmP 93*
Adams, Richard Maxwell 1938- *WhoAm 94, WhoWest 94*
Adams, Richard Melvin, Jr. 1951- *WhoBlA 94*
Adams, Richard Towsley 1921- *WhoAm 94*
Adams, Rick Alan 1956- *WhoWest 94*
Adams, Robert 1906- *WhoHol 92*
Adams, (Franklin) Robert 1932-1990 *EncSF 93*
Adams, Robert B. 1933- *AfrAmG [port]*
Adams, Robert Edward 1941- *WhoAm 94, WhoScEn 94*
Adams, Robert Granville 1927- *WhoWest 94*
Adams, Robert Henry 1937- *WhoMW 93*
Adams, Robert Hickman 1937- *WhoAmA 93*
Adams, Robert Hugo 1943- *WhoAm 94, WhoBlA 94*
Adams, Robert Joe 1935- *WhoMW 93*
Adams, Robert M. 1955- *WhoAmL 94*
Adams, Robert Martin 1915- *WrDr 94*
Adams, Robert McCormick 1926- *WhoAm 94, WhoAmA 93*
Adams, Robert McCormick, Jr. 1926- *IntWW 93, WrDr 94*
Adams, Robert Merrihew 1937- *WrDr 94*
Adams, Robert Richard 1965- *WhoHisp 94*
Adams, Robert Thomas 1913- *WhoBlA 94*
Adams, Robert Walker 1950- *WhoAmL 94*
Adams, Robert Waugh, Jr. 1936- *WhoAm 94*
Adams, Ron 1934- *WhoAmP 93*
Adams, Ronald, Jr. 1958- *WhoBlA 94*
Adams, Ronald Emerson 1943- *WhoAm 94*
Adams, Ronnie H. 1956- *WhoFI 94*
Adams, Roscoe H. 1941- *WhoBlA 94*
Adams, Roy M. 1940- *WhoAm 94, WhoAmL 94*
Adams, Royce W. 1938- *WhoAmP 93*
Adams, Russell Baird 1910- *WhoAm 94*
Adams, Russell Francis 1955- *WhoWest 94*
Adams, Russell Lee 1930- *WhoBlA 94*
Adams, Russell Stanley, Jr. 1926- *WhoMW 93*
Adams, Ruth Salzman 1923- *WhoAm 94*
Adams, Ruthie M. 1934- *WhoAmP 93*
Adams, Salvatore Charles 1934- *WhoAmL 94, WhoFI 94*
Adams, Sam d1958 *WhoHol 92*
Adams, Samuel 1722-1803 *AmRev, HisWorL [port], WhAmRev [port]*
Adams, Samuel Clifford, Jr. 1920- *WhoBlA 94*
Adams, Samuel Franklin 1958- *WhoAmL 94*
Adams, Samuel Hopkins 1871-1958 *EncSF 93*
Adams, Samuel Levi, Sr. 1926- *WhoBlA 94*
Adams, Sarah Flower 1805-1848 *BlmGWL*
Adams, Sarah Virginia 1955- *WhoWest 94*
Adams, Scott Leslie 1955- *WhoFI 94*
Adams, Sheila Mary 1947- *WhoBlA 94*
Adams, Sid 1910- *WhoAmP 93*
Adams, Stanley d1977 *WhoHol 92*
Adams, Stanley 1907- *WhoAm 94*
Adams, Stefon Lee 1963- *WhoBlA 94*
Adams, Stella d1961 *WhoHol 92*
Adams, Stephen Thornton 1945- *WhoAmL 94*
Adams, Steve 1951- *WhoAmP 93*
Adams, Suzanne 1872-1953 *NewGrDO*
Adams, T. Patton 1943- *WhoAmP 93, WhoBlA 94*
Adams, Taggart D. 1941- *WhoAm 94, WhoAmL 94*
Adams, Ted (Richard) d1973 *WhoHol 92*

Adiele, Moses Nkwachukwu 1951- *WhoBlA 94*
Adik, Stephen Peter 1943- *WhoAm 94, WhoFI 94, WhoMW 93*
Adikes, John 1894- *WhAm 10*
Adikes, Park Thomas 1931- *WhoAm 94, WhoFI 94*
Adin, Oris Lyle d1972 *WhoHol 92*
Adini, Ada 1855-1924 *NewGrDO*
Adinoff, Bryon Harlen 1953- *WhoScEn 94*
Adireksarn, Pramara 1914- *IntWW 93*
Adisa, Opal Palmer *DrAPF 93*
Adisa, Opal Palmer 1954- *BlmGWL*
Adiseshiah, Malcolm Sathianathan 1910- *IntWW 93, Who 94*
Adisman, Irwin Kenneth 1919- *WhoAm 94*
Adix, Vern 1912- *WhoHol 92*
Adjamah, Kokouvi Michel 1942- *WhoScEn 94*
Adjani, Isabelle 1955- *IntMPA 94, IntWW 93, WhoHol 92*
Adjei, Alex Asiedu 1955- *WhoScEn 94*
Adkerson, Donya Lynn 1959- *WhoMW 93*
Adkins, Arthur William Hope 1929- *WhoAm 94, WrDr 94*
Adkins, Barry W. 1954- *WhoAmL 94*
Adkins, Ben Frank 1938- *WhoWest 94*
Adkins, Betty A. 1934- *WhoAmP 93, WhoMW 93*
Adkins, Cecelia Nabrit 1923- *WhoBlA 94*
Adkins, Claudia K. 1933- *WhoAm 94*
Adkins, David *WhoAmP 93*
Adkins, David Jay 1961- *WhoMW 93*
Adkins, Edward Cleland 1926- *WhoAm 94, WhoAmL 94*
Adkins, Edward James 1947- *WhoAm 94, WhoAmL 94*
Adkins, George Young, Jr. 1923- *WhoAmP 93*
Adkins, Gregory D. 1941- *WhoAm 94*
Adkins, Iona W. 1925- *WhoBlA 94*
Adkins, James Calhoun 1915- *WhoAmP 93*
Adkins, Jeanne M. 1949- *WhoAmP 93*
Adkins, John Earl Jr., Jr. 1937- *WhoAm 94*
Adkins, Leroy J. 1933- *WhoBlA 94*
Adkins, M. Douglas 1936- *WhoAm 94*
Adkins, Robert H. 1945- *WhoAmL 94*
Adkins, Rocky 1959- *WhoAmP 93*
Adkins, Steve B. 1948- *WhoAmP 93*
Adkins, Terry R. 1953- *WhoAmA 93*
Adkins, W. T. 1934- *WhoAmL 94*
Adkins, William H., II *WhoAmP 93*
Adkinson, Brian Lee 1959- *WhoFI 94*
Adkison, Harold Christopher 1963- *WhoFI 94*
Adkison, Kathleen (Gemberling) *WhoAmA 93*
Adkisson, David C. *WhoAmP 93*
Adkisson, Perry Lee 1929- *IntWW 93, WhoAm 94*
Adkisson, Tommy 1949- *WhoAmP 93*
Adlai, Richard Salvatore *WhoWest 94*
Adlard, Edward Joseph 1951- *WhoFI 94*
Adlard, Mark 1932- *EncSF 93, WrDr 94*
Adler, Aaron 1914- *WhoAm 94*
Adler, Allen 1946- *IntMPA 94*
Adler, Allen A. 1916-1964 *EncSF 93*
Adler, Arthur M., Jr. 1917- *WhoAm 94*
Adler, Benjamin 1903-1990 *WhAm 10*
Adler, Bill *WhoHol 92*
Adler, Bob d1987 *WhoHol 92*
Adler, Brigitte 1944- *WhoWomW 91*
Adler, C. S. *DrAPF 93*
Adler, C(arole) S(chwerdtfeger) 1932- *TwCYAW, WrDr 94*
Adler, Carol *DrAPF 93*
Adler, Celia d1979 *WhoHol 92*
Adler, Charles Spencer 1941- *WhoAm 94, WhoWest 94*
Adler, Cyrus 1863-1940 *DcAmReB 2*
Adler, Daniel Joseph 1954- *WhoAmL 94*
Adler, David Avram 1947- *WhoAm 94*
Adler, David Neil 1955- *WhoAmL 94*
Adler, Donald James, Jr. 1958- *WhoWest 94*
Adler, Douglas B. 1952- *WhoAm 94*
Adler, Douglas Ochs 1952- *WhoAmL 94*
Adler, Earl 1932- *WhoIns 94*
Adler, Edward Andrew Koeppel 1948- *WhoAmL 94*
Adler, Ernest E. 1950- *WhoAmP 93*
Adler, Erwin Ellery 1941- *WhoAm 94, WhoAmL 94, WhoFI 94, WhoWest 94*
Adler, Eugene Victor 1947- *WhoScEn 94*
Adler, Felix d1960 *WhoHol 92*
Adler, Felix 1851-1933 *DcAmReB 2*
Adler, Frances d1964 *WhoHol 92*
Adler, Frances Payne *DrAPF 93*
Adler, Fred Peter 1925- *WhoAm 94*
Adler, Freda Schaffer 1934- *WhoAm 94*
Adler, Frederick Richard 1925- *WhoAm 94*
Adler, Frederick Russell 1963- *WhoScEn 94*
Adler, George Fritz Werner 1926- *Who 94*
Adler, Gerald 1924- *WhoAm 94*
Adler, Guido *WhoHisp 94*
Adler, Guido 1855-1941 *NewGrDO*
Adler, Harry d1944 *WhoHol 92*
Adler, Helmut E. 1920- *WrDr 94*
Adler, Howard 1943- *WhoAmP 93*
Adler, Howard, Jr. 1925- *WhoAm 94*
Adler, Howard Bruce 1951- *WhoAm 94*
Adler, Ilya 1945- *WhoHisp 94*
Adler, Ira 1940- *WhoFI 94*
Adler, Ira Jay 1942- *WhoAm 94, WhoAmL 94*
Adler, Jacob Henry 1919- *WhoMW 93, WrDr 94*
Adler, Jacob P. d1926 *WhoHol 92*
Adler, James Barron 1932- *WhoAm 94*
Adler, Jay d1978 *WhoHol 92*
Adler, Jeffrey S(cott) 1957- *ConAu 141*
Adler, Joel A. 1946- *WhoAm 94, WhoAmL 94*
Adler, John Herbert 1959- *WhoAmP 93*
Adler, John William, Jr. 1936- *WhoAmL 94*
Adler, Julius *WhoHol 92*
Adler, Julius 1930- *IntWW 93, WhoAm 94*
Adler, Karl Paul 1939- *WhoAm 94*
Adler, Kraig Kerr 1940- *WhoAm 94*
Adler, Kurt 1907- *WhAm 10*
Adler, Kurt Herbert 1905-1988 *NewGrDO*
Adler, Larry 1914- *IntWW 93, Who 94, WhoHol 92*
Adler, Larry 1938- *WhoAm 94*
Adler, Laurel Ann 1948- *WhoWest 94*
Adler, Lawrence 1923- *WhoAm 94*
Adler, Lee 1926- *WhoAm 94*
Adler, Lee 1934- *WhoAmA 93*
Adler, Louise DeCarl 1945- *WhoAmL 94*
Adler, Luther d1984 *WhoHol 92*
Adler, Mark 1959- *WhoWest 94*
Adler, Marnie *DrAPF 93*
Adler, Martin 1934- *WhoIns 94*
Adler, Matt 1967- *WhoHol 92*
Adler, Michael Alan 1941- *WhoFI 94*
Adler, Michael I. 1949- *WhoAmL 94*
Adler, Michael S. 1943- *WhoAm 94*
Adler, Michael William 1939- *Who 94*
Adler, Mortimer J(erome) 1902- *WrDr 94*
Adler, Mortimer Jerome 1902- *WhoAm 94*
Adler, Myril 1920- *WhoAmA 93*
Adler, Nadia C. 1945- *WhoAmL 94*
Adler, Naomi Samuel 1931- *WhoMW 93*
Adler, Norman Abner 1909-1989 *WhAm 10*
Adler, Patricia Ann 1951- *WhoWest 94*
Adler, Peggy 1942- *WhoFI 94*
Adler, Peter Herman 1899-1990 *NewGrDO*
Adler, Philip 1925- *WhoAm 94*
Adler, Phillip E. 1942- *WhoAmL 94*
Adler, Renata *DrAPF 93*
Adler, Renata 1938- *WrDr 94*
Adler, Richard 1921- *WhoAm 94*
Adler, Richard Gregg 1943- *WhoFI 94*
Adler, Richard Howard 1955- *WhoAmL 94*
Adler, Robert 1913- *WhoAm 94*
Adler, Robert L. 1947- *WhoAmL 94*
Adler, Robert Martin 1943- *WhoAm 94, WhoAmL 94*
Adler, Ruth Gratt *WhoFI 94*
Adler, Samuel (Hans) 1928- *NewGrDO*
Adler, Samuel (Marcus) 1898-1979 *WhoAmA 93N*
Adler, Samuel Hans 1928- *WhoAm 94*
Adler, Sarah d1953 *WhoHol 92*
Adler, Seymour Jack 1930- *WhoMW 93*
Adler, Sherman 1928- *WhoAm 94*
Adler, Stella 1901-1992 *AnObit 1992*
Adler, Stella 1902- *WhoHol 92*
Adler, Stella 1902-1992 *CurBio 93N*
Adler, Stephen Fred 1930- *WhoAm 94*
Adler, Stephen Louis 1939- *WhoAm 94, WhoScEn 94*
Adler, Steven Valentine 1947- *WhoWest 94*
Adler, Thomas Gresham 1945- *WhoAmL 94*
Adler, Thomas Peter 1943- *WhoMW 93*
Adler, Thomas William 1940- *WhoMW 93*
Adler, Warren 1927- *WhoAm 94, WrDr 94*
Adlercreutz, (Carl) Herman (Thomas) 1932- *IntWW 93*
Adley, Robert d1993 *NewYTBS 93*
Adley, Robert James d1993 *Who 94N*
Adley, Robert R. 1947- *WhoAmP 93*
Adlgasser, Anton Cajetan 1729-1777 *NewGrDO*
Adlon, Louis d1947 *WhoHol 92*
Adlon, Percy 1935- *IntMPA 94*
Adlow, Dorothy d1964 *WhoAmA 93N*
Adlum, John 1759-1836 *WhAmRev*
Admani, (Abdul) Karim 1937- *Who 94*
Admire, Ben H. 1949- *WhoAm 94, WhoAmL 94*
'Adnan, Etel 1925- *BlmGWL*
Adney, James Richard 1946- *WhoScEn 94*
Adni, Daniel 1951- *IntWW 93*
Ado, Andrey Dmitriyevich 1909- *IntWW 93*
Adoff, Arnold 1935- *TwCYAW, WrDr 94*
Adolf, Mary McGinley 1955- *WhoMW 93*
Adolfati, Andrea 1721?-1760 *NewGrDO*
Adolfi, John G. d1933 *WhoHol 92*
Adolfo 1933- *IntWW 93, WhoAm 94, WhoHisp 94*
Adolph, Dale Dennis 1948- *WhoWest 94*
Adolph, Gerald Stephen 1953- *WhoBlA 94*
Adolph, Jose B. *EncSF 93*
Adolph, Mary Rosenquist 1949- *WhoFI 94, WhoWest 94*
Adolph, Robert J. 1927- *WhoAm 94*
Adolph, William F., Jr. 1949- *WhoAmP 93*
Adolphe, Bruce 1955- *NewGrDO*
Adom, Edwin Nii Amalai 1941- *WhoBlA 94, WhoScEn 94*
Adomian, George 1922- *WhoAm 94*
Adonis *ConWorW 93*
Adoor, Gopalakrishnan 1941- *IntWW 93*
Adoree, Renee d1933 *WhoHol 92*
Adorf, Mario 1930- *WhoHol 92*
Adorjan, Carol M. *DrAPF 93*
Adorjan, Julius Joe 1938- *WhoAm 94, WhoFI 94*
Adorno, Henry N. 1947- *WhoAmL 94*
Adorno, Theodor W(iesengrund) 1903-1969 *NewGrDO*
Adouki, Martin 1942- *IntWW 93*
Adoum, Mahamat Ali 1947- *IntWW 93*
Adreon, Harry Barnes 1929- *WhoAm 94*
Adri *WhoAm 94*
Adrian *Who 94*
Adrian, Baron 1927- *Who 94*
Adrian, (Gilbert) 1903-1959 *IntDcF 2-4 [port]*
Adrian, Arthur Allen 1906- *WrDr 94*
Adrian, Barbara 1931- *WhoAm 94, WhoAmA 93*
Adrian, Charles Raymond 1922- *WhoAm 94*
Adrian, Dawn Penni 1945- *WhoAmL 94*
Adrian, Donna Jean 1940- *WhoAm 94*
Adrian, Edgar Douglas 1889-1977 *WorScD*
Adrian, Frances 1918- *WrDr 94*
Adrian, Hal L. 1934- *WhoIns 94*
Adrian, Iris 1913- *IntMPA 94, WhoHol 92*
Adrian, James d1981 *WhoHol 92*
Adrian, Max d1973 *WhoHol 92*
Adrian, Richard Hume 1927- *IntWW 93*
Adriance, Anne Altmaier 1957- *WhoAm 94*
Adrianopoli, Barbara Catherine 1943- *WhoMW 93*
Adrien, J.F.M.L. *Who 94*
Adrienne, Jean *WhoHol 92*
Adrine, Ronald Bruce 1947- *WhoBlA 94*
Adrine-Robinson, Kenyette 1951- *WhoMW 93*
Adrov, Aleksei Nikolaevich 1946- *LoBiDrD*
Adshead, Mary *Who 94*
Adsit, John Michael 1961- *WhoWest 94*
Adu, Helen Folasade 1959- *WhoAm 94*
Adubato, Michael F. d1993 *NewYTBS 93*
Adubato, Richard Adam 1937- *WhoAm 94*
Aduddle, Larry Steven 1946- *WhoMW 93*
Adunis 1930- *ConWorW 93*
Advadze, Valerian Sergeevich 1930- *LoBiDrD*
Advadze, Valerian Sergeyevich 1930- *IntWW 93*
Advani, Lal K. 1927- *IntWW 93*
Advani, Sunder *WhoScEn 94*
Advani, Suresh Gopaldas 1959- *WhoAsA 94*
Advincula, Marietta Magsaysay 1939- *WhoMW 93*
Ady, Richard Norman 1931- *WhoWest 94*
Adye, John (Anthony) 1939- *Who 94*
Adye, Tim *EncSF 93*
Adyebo, George *IntWW 93*
Adyrkhayeva, Svetlana Dzantemirovna 1938- *IntWW 93*
Adzhubei, Aleksei I. d1993 *NewYTBS 93*
Adzhubei, Aleksei I(vanovich) 1924-1993 *CurBio 93N*
Adzick, Shirley Rae 1957- *WhoMW 93*
A.E. 1867-1935 *EncSF 93*
Aebersold, Robert Neil 1935- *WhoAm 94*
Aebi, Ernst Walter 1938- *WhoAmA 93*
Aebi, Fred M. 1941- *WhoAmL 94*
Aebi, Imogene McDonough 1933- *WhoMW 93*
Aedelers, Etta Palm d' 1743- *BlmGWL*
Aein, Joseph Morris 1936- *WhoAm 94*
Aelflaed, Abbess of Whitby fl. 8th cent.- *BlmGWL*
Aelfric c. 955-c. 1020 *BlmGEL*
Aelmore, Donald K. 1952- *WhoMW 93*
Aelvoet, Magda 1944- *WhoWomW 91*
Aeppli, Oswald 1916- *IntWW 93*
Aerni, Russell W. 1929- *WhoAmP 93*
Aery, Shaila Rosalie 1938- *WhoAm 94*
Aerynog 1922- *WrDr 94*
Aesara fl. 4th cent.BC- *BlmGWL*
Aeschbacher, Steven John 1960- *WhoAmL 94*
Aeschliman, Lea H. 1943- *WhoAmP 93*
Aeschliman, Roger Timothy 1960- *WhoMW 93*
Aeschylus 525BC-456BC *BlmGEL, ClMLC 11 [port], IntDcT 2 [port], NewGrDO*
Aesop fl. 6th cent.BC- *BlmGEL*
A Family Doctor 1908- *WrDr 94*
Afanasev, Yury Nikolaevich 1934- *LoBiDrD*
Afanasevsky, Nikolai Nikolaevich 1940- *LoBiDrD*
Afanasiev, Yuri Nikolaevich 1934- *IntWW 93*
Afanasiyev, Viktor Grigorevich 1922- *IntWW 93*
Afanasiyevsky, Nikolai Nikolayevich 1940- *IntWW 93*
Afanas'yev, Nikolay Yakovlevich 1820?-1898 *NewGrDO*
af Ekenstam, Adolf W. 1932- *WhoScEn 94*
Afewerki, Issaias 1945- *IntWW 93*
Affabee, Eric *SmATA 76, TwCYAW*
Affandi, Achmad 1927- *IntWW 93*
Affaticati, Giuseppe Eugenio 1932- *WhoScEn 94*
Affeldt, John Ellsworth 1918- *WhoAm 94*
Affleck, Edmund 1723?-1788 *WhAmRev*
Affleck, Ian Keith 1952- *WhoScEn 94*
Affleck, James G. 1923- *IntWW 93*
Affleck, Julie Karleen 1944- *WhoWest 94*
Affleck, Marilyn 1932- *WhoAm 94*
Affleck, Philip 1726-1799 *WhAmRev*
Affleck, Raymond Tait 1922-1989 *WhAm 10*
Affleck-Asch, William Christopher Seth 1960- *WhoWest 94*
Afflerbach, Roy C., II 1945- *WhoAm 94*
Afflerbach, Roy Carl, II 1945- *WhoAmP 93*
Affre, Agustarello 1858-1931 *NewGrDO*
Affron, Charles 1935- *WrDr 94*
Affronti, Lewis Francis 1928- *WhoAm 94*
Afield, Walter Edward 1935- *WhoAm 94*
Afifi, Adel Kassim 1930- *WhoAm 94*
Aflatooni, Arfa 1955- *WhoWest 94*
Afonso, Yves *WhoHol 92*
Afra, Tybee d1982 *WhoHol 92*
Afrah, Hussein Kulmia 1920- *IntWW 93*
Afraid-of-Bears fl. 19th cent.- *EncNAR*
Africa, Thomas W. 1927- *WrDr 94*
Africano, Nicholas 1948- *WhoAm 94*
Africanus, Leo *WhWE*
Africk, Jack 1928- *WhoAm 94, WhoFI 94*
Afrique d1961 *WhoHol 92*
Afsari, Khosrow 1941- *WhoWest 94*
Afsarmanesh, Hamideh 1953- *WhoFI 94, WhoScEn 94, WhoWest 94*
Afsary, Cyrus 1940- *WhoAmA 93, WhoWest 94*
Aftel, Mandy *DrAPF 93*
Afterman, Allen 1941-1992 *WrDr 94N*
Aftoora, Patricia Joan 1940- *WhoAm 94*
Af Ugglas, Margaretha 1939- *WhoWomW 91*
Afzal, Mohammad 1949- *WhoScEn 94*
Agabian, Nina Martha 1945- *WhoAm 94*
Agache, Alexandru 1955- *NewGrDO*
Agadati, Baruch d1976 *WhoHol 92*
Agafonov, Valentin Alekseevich 1935- *LoBiDrD*
Agai, Irene d1950 *WhoHol 92*
Aga Khan, H. H. Prince Karim, IV 1936- *IntWW 93*
Aga Khan, Karim, IV, His Highness Prince 1936- *Who 94*
Aga Khan, Sadruddin 1933- *IntWW 93*
Aga Khan, Sadruddin, Prince 1933- *Who 94*
Agam, Yaacov 1928- *IntWW 93*
Agana, Venecia B. *WhoWomW 91*
Aganbegyan, Abel Gezevich 1932- *IntWW 93, LoBiDrD*
Aganoor Pompilj, Vittoria 1855-1910 *BlmGWL*
Aga-Oglu, Mehmet 1896-1948 *WhoAmA 93N*
Agapiou, John Stylianos 1955- *WhoFI 94*
Agapito, J. F. T. *WhoScEn 94*
Agar *Who 94*
Agar, Eunice Jane 1934- *WhoAmA 93*
Agar, Jane d1948 *WhoHol 92*
Agar, John 1921- *IntMPA 94, WhoHol 92*
Agar, John Russell, Jr. 1949- *WhoScEn 94*
Agard, Emma Estornel *WhoAm 94*
Agard, H. E. *ConAu 42NR*
Agard, John *WrDr 94*
Agarwal, Arun Kumar 1944- *WhoAsA 94*

Agarwal, Duli Chand 1950- *WhoScEn 94*
Agarwal, Girish Chandra 1930- *IntWW 93*
Agarwal, Gyan Chand 1940- *WhoAm 94, WhoAsA 94, WhoMW 93*
Agarwal, Neeraj 1955- *WhoScEn 94*
Agarwal, Pradeep K. 1953- *WhoFI 94*
Agarwal, Ramesh Chandra 1946- *WhoAm 94*
Agarwal, Ramesh Kumar 1947- *WhoAsA 94, WhoMW 93*
Agarwal, Sanjay Krishna 1965- *WhoScEn 94*
Agarwal, Suman Kumar 1945- *WhoMW 93*
Agarwala, Vinod Shanker 1939- *WhoAsA 94*
Agasar, Ronald Joseph 1946- *WhoFI 94*
Agassi, Andre 1970- *BuCMET, IntWW 93*
Agassi, Andre Kirk 1970- *WhoAm 94*
Agassi, Joseph 1927- *ConAu 41NR*
Agassiz, Jean Louis Rodolphe 1807-1873 *AmSocL, WorScD [port]*
Agata, Burton C. 1928- *WhoAm 94, WhoAmL 94*
Agate, May 1892- *WhoHol 92*
Agate, Robert M. 1936- *WhoFI 94*
Agatstein, Richard 1952- *WhoIns 94*
Agazzari, Agostino 1579?-1641? *NewGrDO*
Agba, Emmanuel Ikechukwu 1960- *WhoScEn 94*
Agbetsiafa, Douglas Kofi *WhoMW 93*
Age and Scarpelli *IntDcF 2-4*
Agee, Bob R. 1938- *WhoAm 94*
Agee, Bobby L. 1949- *WhoBlA 94*
Agee, David Anthony 1949- *WhoWest 94*
Agee, George Steven 1952- *WhoAmP 93*
Agee, James d1955 *WhoHol 92*
Agee, James G. *WhoAmP 93*
Agee, Joel *DrAPF 93*
Agee, Jonis *DrAPF 93*
Agee, Philip 1935- *WrDr 94*
Agee, Thomas Lee 1964- *WhoBlA 94*
Agee, Warren Kendall 1916- *WhoAm 94*
Agee, William C. 1936- *WhoAmA 93*
Agee, William J. 1938- *WhoAm 94, WhoFI 94, WhoWest 94*
Agee, William McReynolds 1938- *IntWW 93*
Ager, Derek Victor 1923-1993 *ConAu 140, WrDr 94N*
Ager, Kenneth Gordon 1920- *Who 94*
Agerbek, Sven 1926- *WhoFI 94, WhoWest 94*
Agersborg, Helmer Pareli K. 1928- *WhoAm 94*
Agerwala, Tilak Krishna Mahesh 1950- *WhoAm 94*
Aggarwal, Anil K. 1947- *WhoAsA 94*
Aggarwal, Bharat Bhushan 1950- *WhoAsA 94*
Aggarwal, Ishwar D. 1945- *WhoAsA 94*
Aggarwal, Jagdishkumar Keshoram 1936- *WhoAm 94, WhoScEn 94*
Aggarwal, Lalit Kumar 1944- *WhoAsA 94*
Aggarwal, Manmohan D. 1947- *WhoAsA 94*
Aggarwal, Raj 1947- *WhoAsA 94*
Aggarwal, Rajesh 1959- *WhoAsA 94*
Aggarwal, Roshan Lal 1937- *WhoAsA 94*
Aggarwal, Sundar Lal 1922- *WhoAm 94*
Agger, James H. 1936- *WhoAm 94, WhoAmL 94*
Agghazy, Karoly 1855-1918 *NewGrDO*
Aggrey, O. Rudolph 1926- *WhoBlA 94*
Aggrey, Orison Rudolph 1926- *WhoAm 94*
Aghajanian, George Kevork 1932- *WhoAm 94*
Aghajanian, John Gregory 1947- *WhoScEn 94*
Aghayan, Ray 1934- *ConTFT 11*
Aghazadeh, Fereydoun 1948- *WhoAm 94*
Aghill, Gordon *EncSF 93*
Aghiorgoussis, Maximos Demetrios 1935- *WhoAm 94*
Agid, Steven Jay 1952- *WhoScEn 94*
Agid, Susan Randolph 1941- *WhoAmL 94*
Agin, Charles 1954- *WhoIns 94*
Aginian, Diana Carol 1944- *WhoMW 93*
Agisim, Philip 1919- *WhoAm 94*
Aglen, Francis Arthur 1869-1932 *DcNaB MP*
Agler, David 1947- *WhoWest 94*
Agler, Larry E. 1947- *WhoIns 94*
Agler, Vickie 1946- *WhoAmP 93*
Agler, Vickie Lyn 1946- *WhoWest 94*
Aglietta, Maria Adelaide 1940- *IntWW 93, WhoWomW 91*
Aglionby, Francis John 1932- *Who 94*
Agnar Thordarson *ConWorW 93*
Agnelli, Giovanni 1921- *IntWW 93, Who 94, WhoAm 94*
Agnelli, Salvatore 1817-1874 *NewGrDO*
Agnelli, Susanna 1922- *WhoWomW 91*
Agnelli, Umberto 1934- *IntWW 93*
Agnes, Prioress fl. 12th cent.- *BlmGWL*
Agnes, St. *BlmGEL*
Agnesi, Luigi 1833-1875 *NewGrDO*
Agnesi-Pinottini, Maria Teresa 1720-1795 *NewGrDO*
Agness, Kent E. 1950- *WhoAm 94, WhoAmL 94*
Agnew, (John) Anthony Stuart d1993 *Who 94N*
Agnew, Dan F. 1944- *WhoIns 94*
Agnew, David M. 1945- *WhoAm 94, WhoAmL 94*
Agnew, Edward Charles, Jr. 1939- *WhoFI 94, WhoWest 94*
Agnew, Ellen Schall 1958- *WhoAmA 93*
Agnew, Franklin Ernest, III 1934- *WhoAm 94, WhoFI 94*
Agnew, Godfrey *Who 94*
Agnew, (William) Godfrey 1913- *Who 94*
Agnew, Harold Melvin 1921- *IntWW 93, WhoAm 94, WhoScEn 94*
Agnew, James Lambert 1944- *WhoMW 93*
Agnew, John c. 1727-1812 *WhAmRev*
Agnew, Jonathan Geoffrey William 1941- *IntWW 93, Who 94*
Agnew, Keith *Who 94*
Agnew, (George) Keith 1918- *Who 94*
Agnew, Morland Herbert Julian 1943- *IntWW 93*
Agnew, Peter Graeme 1914- *Who 94*
Agnew, Peter Tomlin 1948- *WhoAm 94, WhoFI 94*
Agnew, Robert d1983 *WhoHol 92*
Agnew, Robert Dana 1937- *WhoWest 94*
Agnew, Rudolph Ion Joseph 1934- *IntWW 93, Who 94*
Agnew, Spiro T(heodore) 1918- *WrDr 94*
Agnew, Spiro Theodore 1918- *IntWW 93, Who 94, WhoAm 94*
Agnew, Stair d1821 *WhAmRev*
Agnew, Stanley Clarke 1926- *Who 94*
Agnew, Theodore Lee, Jr. 1916- *WhoAm 94*
Agnew, Thomas Edward 1950- *WhoWest 94*
Agnew, William Harold 1920- *WhoFI 94*
Agnew Of Lochnaw, Crispin Hamlyn 1944- *Who 94*
Agnew-Somerville, Quentin (Charles Somerville) 1929- *Who 94*
Agnich, Fred Joseph 1913- *WhoAmP 93*
Agnich, Richard John 1943- *WhoAm 94, WhoAmL 94, WhoAmP 93, WhoFI 94*
Agnihotri, Newal K. 1941- *WhoAsA 94*
Agno, John G. 1940- *WhoAm 94, WhoMW 93*
Agnoli, Bruno 1911- *WhoAmP 93*
Agnon, S.Y. 1888-1970 *RfGShF*
Agnos, Art 1938- *WhoAmP 93*
Ago, Roberto 1907- *IntWW 93*
Agocs, Stephen F. 1928- *WhoAmL 94, WhoFI 94*
Agogino, George Allen 1920- *WhoAm 94, WhoWest 94*
Agoglu, 'Adalet 1929- *BlmGWL*
Agonia, Barbara Ann 1934- *WhoWest 94*
Agonia, Robert James 1938- *WhoHisp 94*
Agonito, Rosemary 1937- *WrDr 94*
Agopoff, Agop Minass d1983 *WhoAmA 93N*
Agorastos, Theodoros 1951- *WhoScEn 94*
Agosin, Marjorie 1955- *BlmGWL, WhoHisp 94*
Agosin, Moises Kankolsky 1922- *WhoAm 94*
Agosta, Steven S. 1942- *WhoAmL 94*
Agosta, Vito 1923- *WhoAm 94*
Agosta, William Carleton 1933- *WhoAm 94*
Agostinelli(-Quiroli), Adelina 1882-1954 *NewGrDO*
Agostinelli, Robert Francesco 1953- *WhoAm 94*
Agostini, Giuseppe 1874-1951 *NewGrDO*
Agostini, Peter 1913- *WhoAmA 93*
Agostini, Peter 1913-1993 *NewYTBS 93 [port]*
Agostini, Pietro Simone c. 1635-1680 *NewGrDO*
Agostini, Wanda E. 1927- *WhoAmP 93*
Agostino, Michael N. 1968- *WhoWest 94*
Agosto, Edwin 1956- *WhoHisp 94*
Agoston, Max Karl 1941- *WhoWest 94*
Agrait, Fernando E. *WhoHisp 94*
Agran, Larry *WhoAmP 93*
Agran, Raymond Daniel 1957- *WhoAmL 94*
Agranat, Simon d1992 *IntWW 93N*
Agranoff, Bernard William 1926- *WhoAm 94, WhoMW 93, WhoScEn 94*
Agranoff, Gerald Neal 1946- *WhoAmL 94*
Agras, William Stewart 1929- *WhoAm 94*
Agrawal, Anup 1958- *WhoFI 94*
Agrawal, Brijmohan 1938- *WhoAsA 94*
Agrawal, Chandra Mauli 1959- *WhoScEn 94*
Agrawal, Dharma Prakash 1945- *WhoAm 94, WhoAsA 94*
Agrawal, Divyakant 1958- *WhoWest 94*
Agrawal, Harish Chandra *WhoAm 94*
Agrawal, Krishna Chandra 1937- *WhoAm 94, WhoAsA 94*
Agrawal, Prabhu Lal 1926- *IntWW 93*
Agrawal, Pradeep K. 1954- *WhoAsA 94*
Agrawal, Vimal Kumar 1962- *WhoScEn 94*
Agrawal, Vishwani Deo 1943- *WhoAm 94*
Agrawala, Surendra Kumar 1929- *IntWW 93*
Agrawala, Vasudeva Sharan 1904- *IntWW 93*
Agraz-Guerena, Jorge *WhoHisp 94*
Agre, James Courtland 1950- *WhoMW 93*
Agreda, Maria de 1602-1665 *BlmGWL*
Agreda, Victor Hugo 1953- *WhoHisp 94*
Agren, Janet 1950- *WhoHol 92*
Agres, Stuart J. 1945- *WhoAm 94*
Agresti, Edward d1971 *WhoHol 92*
Agresti, Jack Joseph 1937- *WhoFI 94, WhoWest 94*
Agresto, John *WhoAm 94*
Agri, Jonathan Seth 1961- *WhoFI 94*
Agria, John Joseph 1938- *WhoAm 94*
Agria, Mary A. 1941- *WhoMW 93*
Agricola, Benedetta Emilia 1722-1780 *NewGrDO*
Agricola, Gnaeus Julius c. 37-93 *WhWE*
Agricola, Johann Friedrich 1720-1774 *NewGrDO*
Agricola, Johann Paul 1638?-1697 *NewGrDO*
Agrios, George Nicholas 1936- *WhoAm 94, WhoScEn 94*
Agrippina the Younger 15-59 *HisWorL [port]*
Agrippina the Younger d60 *BlmGWL [port]*
Agrons, Bernard Z. 1922- *WhoAmP 93*
Agruss, Neil Stuart 1939- *WhoMW 93, WhoScEn 94*
Agsten, Melinda A. 1950- *WhoAmL 94*
Agt, Andries A. M. van 1931- *IntWW 93*
Agthe, Dale Robert 1953- *WhoWest 94*
Agthe, Rosa *NewGrDO*
Aguayo, Albert Juan *WhoAm 94*
Aguayo, José 1941- *WhoHisp 94, WhoWest 94*
Aguayo, Patricia 1962- *WhoHisp 94*
Aguayo-Rodriguez, Luis A. 1950- *WhoHisp 94*
Agudelo, Rodrigo *WhoHisp 94*
Agudelo Botero, Orlando 1946- *WhoHisp 94*
Aguero, Bidal 1949- *WhoHisp 94*
Aguero, Joseph Edward 1946- *WhoHisp 94*
Aguero, Kathleen *DrAPF 93*
Aguero, Ramon *WhoHisp 94*
Agüeros, Jack 1934- *WhoHisp 94*
Aguerre, Fernando *WhoHisp 94*
Aguerre, Santiago *WhoHisp 94*
Aguglia, Mimi d1970 *WhoHol 92*
Aguiar, Adam Martin 1929- *WhoAm 94, WhoScEn 94*
Aguiar, Antone Souza, Jr. 1930- *WhoAmP 93*
Aguiar, Fred *WhoAmP 93*
Aguiar, Maria Manuela Aguiar Dias Moreira 1942- *WhoWomW 91*
Aguiar, Yvette M. 1959- *WhoHisp 94*
Aguiari, Lucrezia 1743-1783 *NewGrDO*
Aguiar-Velez, Deborah 1955- *WhoHisp 94*
Aguila, Pancho *DrAPF 93*
Aguilar, Adolfo *WhoHisp 94*
Aguilar, Angel A. 1951- *WhoHisp 94*
Aguilar, Antonio, Jr. *WhoHol 92*
Aguilar, Carlos A. 1943- *WhoHisp 94*
Aguilar, Eduardo E., Sr. 1940- *WhoHisp 94*
Aguilar, Eleanor Garcia *WhoHisp 94*
Aguilar, Ernest Arthur 1942- *WhoHisp 94*
Aguilar, Ernest I. J. *WhoHisp 94*
Aguilar, Francis Joseph 1932- *WhoHisp 94*
Aguilar, George A. 1930- *WhoHisp 94*
Aguilar, Grace 1816-1847 *BlmGWL*
Aguilar, Irma G. 1947- *WhoHisp 94*
Aguilar, John L. 1934- *WhoHisp 94*
Aguilar, Jose Luis 1944- *WhoHisp 94*
Aguilar, Karen 1952- *WhoHisp 94*
Aguilar, Larry 1949- *WhoHisp 94*
Aguilar, Lillian I. *WhoHisp 94*
Aguilar, Louis A. 1953- *WhoHisp 94*
Aguilar, Luis 1949- *WhoHisp 94*
Aguilar, Manuel Jesus 1952- *WhoHisp 94*
Aguilar, Marcus d1960 *WhoHol 92*
Aguilar, Margaret Hope 1951- *WhoWest 94*
Aguilar, Mario 1948- *WhoHisp 94*
Aguilar, Mario Roberto 1952- *WhoHisp 94*
Aguilar, Octavio M. 1931- *WhoHisp 94*
Aguilar, Pat L. 1950- *WhoHisp 94*
Aguilar, Raul Abraham 1954- *WhoWest 94*
Aguilar, Raul Alfonso 1950- *WhoHisp 94*
Aguilar, Richard 1955- *WhoHisp 94*
Aguilar, Robert *WhoHisp 94*
Aguilar, Robert P. *WhoHisp 94*
Aguilar, Robert P. 1931- *WhoAm 94, WhoAmL 94, WhoWest 94*
Aguilar, Rodolfo Jesus 1936- *WhoHisp 94*
Aguilar, Steven, Jr. 1949- *WhoHisp 94*
Aguilar, Tony 1928- *WhoHol 92*
Aguilar-Breedlove, Linda 1947- *WhoMW 93*
Aguilar Mawdsley, Andres 1924- *IntWW 93*
Aguilar-Melantzón, Ricardo 1947- *WhoHisp 94*
Aguilera, Donna Conant *WhoAm 94, WhoWest 94*
Aguilera, Elisa J. *WhoHisp 94*
Aguilera, Gloria Patricia 1959- *WhoFI 94*
Aguilera, Hector 1949- *WhoHisp 94*
Aguilera, Jorge 1962- *WhoScEn 94*
Aguilera, Juan Miguel *EncSF 93*
Aguilera, Julio G. 1956- *WhoHisp 94*
Aguilera, Renato J. 1957- *WhoHisp 94*
Aguilera, Richard Warren 1961- *WhoAm 94*
Aguilera, Rick 1961- *WhoHisp 94*
Aguilera, Rubén 1952- *WhoHisp 94*
Aguilera, Salvador, Jr. 1955- *WhoHisp 94*
Aguilera, Xavier E. 1948- *WhoHisp 94*
Aguillón, Pablo R., Jr. 1945- *WhoHisp 94*
Aguiló, Adolfo 1928- *WhoHisp 94*
Aguiló-Zambrana, Juan M. 1933- *WhoHisp 94*
Aguiña, Mary Elizabeth 1954- *WhoHisp 94*
Aguinsky, Richard Daniel 1958- *WhoFI 94, WhoWest 94*
Aguirre, Alejandro *WhoHisp 94*
Aguirre, Alicia Carmen 1955- *WhoHisp 94*
Aguirre, Benigno E. 1947- *WhoHisp 94*
Aguirre, Carlos Llerena 1952- *WhoHisp 94*
Aguirre, Doris Carolina 1959- *WhoHisp 94*
Aguirre, Edmundo Soto 1926- *WhoHisp 94*
Aguirre, Edward *WhoHisp 94*
Aguirre, Eugene William *WhoHisp 94*
Aguirre, Francisco *WhoHisp 94*
Aguirre, Gabriel Eloy 1935- *WhoHisp 94*
Aguirre, Henry John 1931- *WhoHisp 94*
Aguirre, Horacio *WhoHisp 94*
Aguirre, Jesse 1944- *WhoHisp 94*
Aguirre, John 1924- *WhoHisp 94*
Aguirre, Jose Luis 1961- *WhoHisp 94*
Aguirre, Linda *WhoHisp 94*
Aguirre, Linda G. 1951- *WhoAmP 93*
Aguirre, Lope De c. 1510-1561 *WhWE*
Aguirre, Marcelino O. *Who 94*
Aguirre, Mark 1959- *BasBi, WhoBlA 94, WhoHisp 94*
Aguirre, Marta Lucia 1963- *WhoHisp 94*
Aguirre, Martin 1948- *WhoHisp 94*
Aguirre, Michael Jules 1949- *WhoHisp 94*
Aguirre, Mirta 1912- *BlmGWL*
Aguirre, Rafael Angel, Jr. 1925- *WhoHisp 94*
Aguirre, Raul Ernesto 1955- *WhoHisp 94*
Aguirre, Robert D. 1961- *WhoHisp 94*
Aguirre, Vukoslav Eneas 1941- *WhoHisp 94*
Aguirre Lizaola, Avelino de 1838-1901 *NewGrDO*
Aguirre-Molina, Marilyn 1948- *WhoHisp 94*
Aguirre-Sacasa, Francisco Xavier 1944- *WhoHisp 94*
Aguolu, Christian Chukwunedu 1940- *ConAu 42NR, WrDr 94*
Aguon, John P. 1944- *WhoAmP 93*
Aguon, Katherine Bordallo 1931- *WhoAmP 93*
Agurs, Donald Steele 1947- *WhoBlA 94*
Agurto, Martin 1952- *WhoWest 94*
Agus, Zalman S. 1941- *WhoAm 94*
Agusta, Benjamin J. 1931- *WhoAm 94*
Agusti, Filiberto 1953- *WhoAm 94*
Agustini, Delmira 1886-1914 *BlmGWL*
Agustsson, Helgi 1941- *IntWW 93, Who 94*
Agutter, Jennifer Ann 1952- *Who 94*
Agutter, Jenny 1952- *IntMPA 94, IntWW 93, WhoHol 92, WrDr 94*
Aguzzi-Barbagli, Danilo Lorenzo 1924- *WhoWest 94*
Agypt, Ronald G. 1956- *WhoIns 94*
Ahad, Rafiul 1950- *WhoWest 94*
Ahalt, Arthur Montraville 1942- *WhoAmL 94*
Ahart, Jan Fredrick 1941- *WhoAm 94*
Ahart, Thomas I. 1938- *WhoBlA 94*
Ah-Chuen, Moi Lin Jean Etienne d1992 *Who 94N*
Ahde, Matti Allan 1945- *IntWW 93*
Ahearn, James 1931- *WhoAm 94*
Ahearn, John 1951- *WhoAmA 93*
Ahearn, John Francis, Jr. 1921- *WhoAm 94*

Ahearn, John Stephen 1944- *WhoAm 94*
Ahearn, Patricia Jean 1936- *WhoAmL 94*
Ahearn, Robert John 1961- *WhoAmL 94*
Ahearn, Theresa Mary 1951- *WhoWomW 91*
Ahearn, Vincent Paul 1896- *WhAm 10*
Ahearne, Douglas 1968- *WhoAmP 93*
Ahearne, John Francis 1934- *WhoAm 94, WhoAmP 93, WhoScEn 94*
Ahearne, Stephen James 1939- *Who 94*
Ahearne, Thomas d1969 *WhoHol 92*
Ahern, Arleen Fleming 1922- *WhoWest 94*
Ahern, Bertie 1951- *IntWW 93, Who 94*
Ahern, Eugene 1896-1960 *WhoAmA 93N*
Ahern, Gladys d1983 *WhoHol 92*
Ahern, Janet Mary 1961- *WhoAmL 94*
Ahern, Jay Thomas 1936- *WhoAmL 94*
Ahern, Jerry 1946- *EncSF 93*
Ahern, John Edward 1921- *WhoScEn 94*
Ahern, John J. 1911- *Who 94*
Ahern, John Joseph 1942- *WhoAm 94*
Ahern, Lassie Lou *WhoHol 92*
Ahern, Michael James 1951- *WhoAmL 94*
Ahern, Michael John 1942- *IntWW 93, Who 94*
Ahern, Patrick V. 1919- *WhoAm 94*
Ahern, Paul L., Jr. 1950- *WhoAmL 94*
Ahern, Richard Favor 1912- *WhoAmP 93*
Ahern, Sharon A. *EncSF 93*
Ahern, Thomas Joseph, Jr. 1936- *WhoAmL 94*
Ahern, Tom *DrAPF 93*
Ahern, Veronica Mary 1946- *WhoAm 94*
Ahern, Wilbert Harrell 1942- *WhoMW 93*
Ahern, Will d1983 *WhoHol 92*
Aherne, Brian d1986 *WhoHol 92*
Aherne, Maureen d1979 *WhoHol 92*
Aherne, Pat d1970 *WhoHol 92*
Ahl, Alwynelle Self 1941- *WhoAm 94*
Ahl, David Howard 1939- *WhoAm 94*
Ahl, Henry C. *WhoAmA 93*
Ahl, Stephen L. 1950- *WhoAmL 94*
Ahlander, Leslie Judd *WhoAmA 93*
Ahlberg, Allan 1938- *WrDr 94*
Ahlberg, John Harold 1927- *WhoAm 94*
Ahlberg, Kurt M. 1952- *WhoAmL 94*
Ahlbrandt, Calvin Dale 1940- *WhoMW 93*
Ahlburg, Kaj 1959- *WhoFI 94*
Ahlefeld, Charlotte Elisabeth Sophie Louise Wilhelmine von 1781-1849 *BlmGWL*
Ahlefeldt, Maria Theresia 1755-1823 *NewGrDO*
Ahlem, Lloyd Harold 1929- *WhoAm 94*
Ahlen, John William, III 1947- *WhoAm 94*
Ahlenius, William Matheson 1934- *WhoAm 94, WhoAmL 94*
Ahlers, Anny d1933 *WhoHol 92*
Ahlers, B. Orwin 1926- *WhoAm 94*
Ahlers, Dorothy M. 1931- *WhoAmP 93*
Ahlers, Glen-Peter, Sr. 1955- *WhoAmL 94*
Ahlers, Guenter 1934- *WhoAm 94, WhoWest 94*
Ahlers, Rolf Willi 1936- *WhoAm 94*
Ahlersmeyer, Matthieu 1896-1979 *NewGrDO*
Ahlfors, Lars Valerian 1907- *IntWW 93*
Ahlgren, Gibson-Taylor 1940- *WhoWest 94*
Ahlgren, Madelyn T. 1915- *WhoAmP 93*
Ahlgren, Roy B. 1927- *WhoAmA 93*
Ahlm, Philip d1954 *WhoHol 92*
Ahlmark, Per 1939- *IntWW 93*
Ahlokoba, Aissa *WhoWomW 91*
Ahlquist, David Alan 1951- *WhoMW 93*
Ahlquist, Jon *WorScD*
Ahlquist, Paul Gerald 1954- *WhoAm 94*
Ahlschwede, Arthur Martin 1914- *WhoAm 94*
Ahlsen, Leopold 1927- *IntWW 93*
Ahlsted, David R. 1943- *WhoAmA 93*
Ahlstedt, Borje *WhoHol 92*
Ahlstrand, Charles Thomas 1942- *WhoWest 94*
Ahlstrom, David 1927- *NewGrDO*
Ahlstrom, John Keith 1942- *WhoWest 94*
Ahlstrom, Krister Harry 1940- *IntWW 93*
Ahlstrom, Michael Joseph 1953- *WhoAmL 94*
Ahlstrom, Olof 1756-1835 *NewGrDO*
Ahlstrom, Ronald Gustin 1922- *WhoAm 94, WhoAmA 93*
Ahlswede, Ann 1928- *WrDr 94*
Ahluwalia, Balwant S. 1932- *WhoAsA 94*
Ahluwalia, Brij Mohan Singh 1939- *WhoAsA 94*
Ahluwalia, Daljit Singh 1932- *WhoAsA 94*
Ahluwalia, Dharam Vir 1952- *WhoScEn 94*
Ahluwalia, Harjit Singh 1934- *WhoAsA 94, WhoWest 94*
Ahluwalia, Rashpal S. 1946- *WhoAsA 94*
Ahlvers, Carol A. 1951- *WhoAm 94*
Ahlvin, Richard Glen 1919- *WhoScEn 94*
Ahmad, Abdul Ajib bin 1947- *IntWW 93*
Ahmad, Anwar 1945- *WhoMW 93*
Ahmad, Awang Mohammed Yussof 1944- *IntWW 93*
Ahmad, Imad-Ad-Dean *WhoAmP 93*
Ahmad, Jadwaa 1935- *WhoBlA 94*
Ahmad, Jameel 1941- *WhoAsA 94, WhoScEn 94*
Ahmad, Kabir Uddin 1934- *WhoAm 94*
Ahmad, Khalil 1950- *WhoScEn 94*
Ahmad, Khurshid 1934- *Who 94*
Ahmad, Nafees 1959- *WhoMW 93*
Ahmad, Salahuddin 1954- *WhoScEn 94*
Ahmad, Shaheen 1960- *WhoMW 93*
Ahmad, Shair 1935- *WhoAm 94*
Ahmadieh, Aziz 1930- *WhoAm 94*
Ahmadinejad, Behrouz 1967- *WhoScEn 94*
Ahmadjian, Mark 1951- *WhoScEn 94*
Ahmann, James H. d1993 *NewYTBS 93*
Ahmann, John Stanley 1921- *WhoAm 94*
Ahmann, Mathew Hall 1931- *WhoAm 94*
Ahmed, A. Razzaque 1948- *WhoAsA 94*
Ahmed, Abu 1949- *WhoScEn 94*
Ahmed, Akbar S(alahudin) 1943- *ConAu 141*
Ahmed, Atiq Rahman 1955- *WhoAmL 94*
Ahmed, Fakhruddin 1931- *IntWW 93*
Ahmed, Fayza d1983 *WhoHol 92*
Ahmed, Haroon 1936- *Who 94*
Ahmed, Hassan Juma 1942- *WhoScEn 94*
Ahmed, Imthyas Abdul 1958- *WhoScEn 94*
Ahmed, Iqbal 1951- *WhoScEn 94, WhoWest 94*
Ahmed, Javed 1960- *WhoFI 94*
Ahmed, Kazem Uddin 1948- *WhoScEn 94*
Ahmed, Kazi Zafar 1940- *IntWW 93*
Ahmed, Khalil 1934- *WhoAm 94*
Ahmed, Khandakar Moshtaque 1918- *IntWW 93*
Ahmed, Kyle *WhoAm 94*
Ahmed, Leila 1940- *ConAu 140*
Ahmed, Mohamed el-Baghir 1927- *IntWW 93*
Ahmed, Moudud 1940- *IntWW 93*
Ahmed, Nasim 1927- *IntWW 93*
Ahmed, Osman 1956- *WhoScEn 94*
Ahmed, S. Basheer 1934- *WhoScEn 94*
Ahmed, Shaikh Sultan 1937- *WhoAsA 94*
Ahmed, Wase U. 1931- *WhoAsA 94*
Ahmed, Wase Uddin 1931- *WhoMW 93*
Ahmeti, Vilson 1951- *IntWW 93*
Ahn, Don C. 1937- *WhoAmA 93*
Ahn, Ho-Sam 1940- *WhoAsA 94*
Ahn, Jaehoon 1941- *WhoAsA 94*
Ahn, Philip d1978 *WhoHol 92*
Ahn, Steve Fitzgerald 1933- *WhoAsA 94*
Ahna, Pauline de *NewGrDO*
Ahneman, Patricia Mae, Jr. 1951- *WhoAm 94*
Ahnsjo, Claes Hakan 1942- *NewGrDO*
Aho, Esko Tapani 1954- *IntWW 93*
Aho, Paul William 1950- *WhoFI 94*
'Aho, Siaosi Taimani 1939- *Who 94*
Ahomadegbe, Justin Tometin 1917- *IntWW 93*
Ahonen, Erkki *EncSF 93*
Ahoyo, Veronique *WhoWomW 91*
Ahr, George W. 1904-1993 *NewYTBS 93*
Ahrari, M. E. 1945- *WhoAm 94*
Ahrenberg, Henning d1951 *WhoHol 92*
Ahrends, Peter 1933- *IntWW 93, Who 94*
Ahrendt, Christine *WhoAmA 93*
Ahrendt, Mary E. 1940- *WhoAmA 93*
Ahrens, Carolyn 1959- *WhoAmL 94*
Ahrens, Douglas Thorson 1966- *WhoFI 94*
Ahrens, Edward Hamblin, Jr. 1915- *WhoAm 94*
Ahrens, Erick Karl Frederick 1949- *WhoWest 94*
Ahrens, Ernst H. 1929- *WhoWest 94*
Ahrens, Franklin Alfred 1936- *WhoAm 94, WhoMW 93*
Ahrens, Frederick G. 1915- *WhoAmP 93*
Ahrens, Hanno D. 1954- *WhoAmA 93*
Ahrens, Joseph 1904- *IntWW 93*
Ahrens, Kent *WhoAm 94, WhoAmA 93*
Ahrens, Mary Ann Painovich 1942- *WhoFI 94, WhoMW 93*
Ahrens, Michael Henry 1945- *WhoAm 94, WhoAmL 94*
Ahrens, Pam 1945- *WhoAmP 93*
Ahrens, Richard A. 1950- *WhoAmL 94*
Ahrens, Thomas H. 1919- *WhoAm 94*
Ahrens, William Henry 1925- *WhoAm 94*
Ahrensfeld, Thomas Frederick 1923- *WhoAm 94, WhoAmL 94*
Ahrland, Karin Margareta 1931- *IntWW 93*
Ahronovitch, Yuri (George) 1932- *IntWW 93*
Ahrweiler, Helene 1926- *IntWW 93*
Ahsanullah, Omar Faruk 1964- *WhoScEn 94, WhoWest 94*
Ahsen, Akhter 1931- *WrDr 94*
Ahtchi-Ali, Badreddine 1956- *WhoScEn 94*
Ahuja, Anil 1943- *WhoScEn 94*
Ahuja, Jagdish Chand 1927- *WhoAm 94*
Ahuja, Satinder 1933- *WhoAsA 94*
Ahumada, Martin Miguel 1954- *WhoHisp 94*
Ahuruonye, Hyacinth Chidi 1961- *WhoFI 94*
Ahysen, Harry Joseph 1928- *WhoAmA 93*
Ai *DrAPF 93*
Aibel, Howard James 1929- *IntWW 93, WhoAm 94, WhoAmL 94, WhoFI 94*
Aiblinger, Johann Kaspar 1779-1867 *NewGrDO*
Aichinger, Ilse 1921- *BlmGWL, ConWorW 93, IntWW 93, RfGShF*
Aida, Takefumi 1937- *IntWW 93*
Aida, Yukio *IntWW 93*
Aidar, Nelson 1953- *WhoScEn 94*
Aidekman, Alex 1915-1990 *WhAm 10*
Aidid, Mohammed Farah 1934- *NewYTBS 93 [port]*
Aidinoff, Merton Bernard 1929- *WhoAm 94*
Aidlen, Jerome 1935-1986 *WhoAmA 93N*
Aidman, Barton Terry 1947- *WhoFI 94*
Aidman, Charles 1925- *WhoHol 92*
Aidoo, Ama Ata *IntWW 93*
Aidoo, Ama Ata 1942- *BlmGWL [port]*
Aidoo, (Christina) Ama Ata 1942- *ConDr 93, IntDcT 2, WrDr 94*
Aidun, Cyrus Khodarahm *WhoScEn 94*
Aiello, Danny 1933- *IntMPA 94, WhoHol 92*
Aiello, Danny 1936- *WhoAm 94*
Aiello, Frank Mario 1943- *WhoAmL 94*
Aiello, Gennaro C. 1953- *WhoFI 94*
Aiello, Louis Peter 1932- *WhoWest 94*
Aiello, Neno Joseph 1928- *WhoWest 94*
Aiello, Pietro 1939- *WhoScEn 94*
Aiello, Rick 1955- *WhoHol 92*
Aiello-Contessa, Angela Marie 1954- *WhoAm 94*
Aigamaua, Avegalio P. *WhoAmP 93*
Aigen, Betsy Paula 1938- *WhoAm 94*
Aigner, Dennis John 1937- *WhoAm 94*
Aigner, Herbert John 1929- *WhoAmP 93*
Aigner, Lucien 1901- *WhoAmA 93*
Aigner, Lucien L. 1901- *WhoAm 94*
Aigrain, Pierre Raoul Roger 1924- *IntWW 93*
Aihara, Kazuyuki 1954- *WhoScEn 94*
Aika, Ken-ichi 1942- *WhoScEn 94*
Aikawa, Jerry Kazuo 1921- *WhoAm 94, WhoAsA 94, WhoScEn 94, WhoWest 94*
Aikawa, Masamichi 1931- *WhoAm 94*
Aiken, Charles 1872-1965 *WhoAmA 93N*
Aiken, Conrad (Potter) 1889-1973 *RfGShF*
Aiken, Elaine 1931- *WhoHol 92*
Aiken, Howard H. 1900-1973 *WorInv*
Aiken, J. David 1950- *WhoAmL 94*
Aiken, Joan 1924- *BlmGWL*
Aiken, Joan (Delano) *EncSF 93*
Aiken, Joan (Delano) 1924- *TwCYAW, WrDr 94*
Aiken, Joan Delano 1924- *Who 94*
Aiken, John (Alexander Carlisle) 1921- *Who 94*
Aiken, John (Kempton) 1913-1990 *EncSF 93*
Aiken, John Wallace 1947- *WhoWest 94*
Aiken, Lewis R(oscoe), Jr. 1931- *WrDr 94*
Aiken, Lewis Roscoe, Jr. 1931- *WhoAm 94*
Aiken, Linda H. 1943- *IntWW 93, WrDr 94*
Aiken, Linda Harman 1943- *WhoAm 94*
Aiken, Michael Thomas 1932- *WhoAm 94, WhoMW 93*
Aiken, Patricia 1922- *WhoAmP 93*
Aiken, Phil Lund 1924- *WhoWest 94*
Aiken, Robert McCutchen 1930- *WhoAm 94*
Aiken, V. Fred 1938- *WhoAmP 93*
Aiken, William 1934- *WhoAm 94, WhoBlA 94*
Aiken, William A. 1934- *WhoAmA 93*
Aiken, William David 1923- *WhAm 10*
Aikens, Alexander E., III 1949- *WhoBlA 94*
Aikens, Chester Alfronza 1951- *WhoBlA 94*
Aikens, Clyde Melvin 1938- *WhoAm 94, WhoWest 94*
Aikens, Joan D. 1928- *WhoAmP 93*
Aikens, Joan Deacon *WhoAm 94*
Aikens, Martha Brunette 1949- *WhoAm 94*
Aikens, Richard John Pearson 1948- *Who 94*
Aikens, Willie Mays 1954- *WhoBlA 94*
Aikens-Young, Linda Lee 1950- *WhoBlA 94*
Aikin, A. M., III 1946- *WhoAmP 93*
Aikin, Jim 1948- *EncSF 93*
Aikin, Lucy 1781-1864 *BlmGWL*
Aikin, Olga Lindholm 1934- *Who 94*
Aikins, Douglas B. 1950- *WhoAmL 94*
Aikins, Lincoln James 1898- *WhAm 10*
Aikins-Afful, Nathaniel Akumanyi 1935- *WhoBlA 94*
Aikman, Albert Edward 1922- *WhoAmL 94, WhoFI 94*
Aikman, Carol Chidester 1943- *WhoMW 93*
Aikman, Colin Campbell 1919- *Who 94*
Aikman, Rosalie H. *WhoAmP 93*
Aikman, Troy 1966- *News 94-2 [port], WhoAm 94*
Aikman, William Francis 1945- *WhoFI 94*
Aiksnoras, Peter J. 1917- *WhoAmP 93*
Ailes, Roger Eugene 1940- *WhoAm 94*
Ailesbury, Marquess of 1926- *Who 94*
Ailey, Alvin d1989 *WhoHol 92*
Ailey, Alvin c. 1931-1989 *AmCulL [port], ConTFT 11, WhAm 10*
Ailey, Alvin 1931-1991 *AfrAmAl 6*
Ailloni-Charas, Dan 1930- *WhoAm 94*
Ailloni-Charas, Miriam Clara 1935- *WhoScEn 94*
Ailor, Karen Tana 1943- *WhoWest 94*
Ailsa, Marquess of 1925- *Who 94*
Ailshie, Roger Allen 1962- *WhoWest 94*
Aimaiti Wajiti *WhoPRCh 91*
Aimee, Anouk 1932- *IntMPA 94, IntWW 93, WhoHol 92*
Aimee, Joyce 1930- *WhoAm 94*
Aimon, Pamphile-Leopold-Francois 1779-1866 *NewGrDO*
Aimone, Jon Carlin 1941- *WhoAmL 94*
Aimos, Raymond d1944 *WhoHol 92*
Aimuc de Castelnou fl. 13th cent.- *BlmGWL*
Ain, Sanford King 1947- *WhoAmL 94*
Ainbinder, Seymour 1928- *WhAm 10*
Ainge, Danny 1959- *BasBi*
Ainger, Nicholas Richard 1949- *Who 94*
Aini, Mohsen Ahmed al- 1932- *IntWW 93*
Ainley, Anthony 1937- *WhoHol 92*
Ainley, David Geoffrey 1924- *Who 94*
Ainley, Henry d1945 *WhoHol 92*
Ainley, Richard d1967 *WhoHol 92*
Aino, Koichiro 1928- *IntWW 93*
Ainsbury, Ray *EncSF 93*
Ainscow, Robert Morrison 1936- *Who 94*
Ainslee, Mary *WhoHol 92*
Ainsley, Norman d1948 *WhoHol 92*
Ainsley, Stuart Martin 1956- *WhoWest 94*
Ainslie, John 1745-1828 *DcNaB MP*
Ainslie, Michael Lewis 1943- *WhoAm 94, WhoFI 94*
Ainslie, Paul Joseph 1953- *WhoMW 93*
Ainslie, Peter 1867-1934 *DcAmReB 2*
Ainsworth, Cupid d1961 *WhoHol 92*
Ainsworth, David *Who 94*
Ainsworth, (Thomas) David 1926- *Who 94*
Ainsworth, David Vincent 1940- *WhoAmL 94, WhoWest 94*
Ainsworth, (Mervyn) John 1947- *Who 94*
Ainsworth, John H. 1940- *WhoAmP 93*
Ainsworth, Louis Lynde 1947- *WhoAmL 94*
Ainsworth, Mary D(insmore) Salter 1913- *WrDr 94*
Ainsworth, Mary Dinsmore Salter 1913- *WhoAm 94*
Ainsworth, Patricia 1932- *WrDr 94*
Ainsworth, Peter Michael 1956- *Who 94*
Ainsworth, Robert William 1952- *Who 94*
Ainsworth, Sidney d1922 *WhoHol 92*
Ainsworth, William Harrison 1805-1882 *BlmGEL*
Ainsworthy, Ray *EncSF 93*
Ai Qing 1908- *WhoPRCh 91 [port]*
Ai Qing 1910- *IntWW 93*
Airall, Angela Maureen 1954- *WhoBlA 94*
Airall, Guillermo Evers 1919- *WhoBlA 94*
Airall, Zoila Erlinda 1951- *WhoBlA 94*
Airaudi, Richard Allan 1947- *WhoWest 94*
Aird, Alastair (Sturgis) 1931- *Who 94*
Aird, Catherine 1930- *WrDr 94*
Aird, Holly *WhoHol 92*
Aird, (George) John 1940- *Who 94*
Aird, John Black 1923- *WhoAm 94*
Aird, Robert Burns 1903- *WhoScEn 94*
Airedale, Baron 1915- *Who 94*
Aires, Randolf H. 1935- *WhoFI 94*
Airey, David Lawrence 1935- *Who 94*
Airey, Dawn Elizabeth 1960- *Who 94*
Airey, Lawrence 1926- *IntWW 93, Who 94*
Airey, W. Jonathan 1944- *WhoAmL 94*
Airey of Abingdon, Baroness d1992 *Who 94N*
Airey of Abingdon, Baroness 1919- *WhoWomW 91*
Airhart, Ted *WhoHol 92*
Airkyan, Paruir Arshavirovich 1949- *IntWW 93*
Airlie, Countess of 1933- *Who 94*
Airlie, Earl of 1926- *Who 94*
Airlie, Catherine 1908- *WrDr 94*
Airlie, David George Patrick Coke Ogilvy, Earl of 1926- *IntWW 93*
Airola, Paavo d1983 *WhoAmA 93N*

Ai Rongfu *WhoPRCh 91*
Airst, Malcolm Jeffrey 1957- *WhoScEn 94*
Airy, Christopher (John) 1934- *Who 94*
Airy, William W. 1954- *WhoWest 94*
Aisenberg, Irwin Morton 1925- *WhoAm 94, WhoAmL 94*
Aisenberg, Michele K. 1924- *WhoAmP 93*
Aisenberg, Nadya 1928- *WrDr 94*
Aisenbrey, John C. 1947- *WhoAmL 94*
Aisenbrey, Stuart Keith 1942- *WhoAm 94*
Aisenson, David Judea 1924- *WhoAmL 94*
Aisha 1942- *BlmGWL*
Aisher, Owen (Arthur) 1900- *Who 94*
Aisher, Owen Arthur d1993 *Who 94N*
Aisin Ghiorroh Pujie 1907- *IntWW 93*
Aisin Ghiorroh Pu Jie 1908- *WhoPRCh 91 [port]*
Aisin Ghiorroh Puzuo 1918- *IntWW 93, WhoPRCh 91 [port]*
Aislabie, Benjamin 1774-1842 *DcNaB MP*
Aisner, Joseph 1944- *WhoAm 94, WhoScEn 94*
Aisner, Mark 1910- *WhoScEn 94*
Aissatou, Yaou *WhoWomW 91*
Aisse, Charlotte Elisabeth Aicha 1694?-1733 *BlmGWL*
Aistars, John 1938- *WhoAmA 93*
Aita, Carolyn Rubin 1943- *WhoAm 94, WhoMW 93*
Aitay, Victor *WhoAm 94*
Aitchison, Anne Catherine 1939- *WhoMW 93*
Aitchison, Charles (Walter de Lancey) 1951- *Who 94*
Aitchison, Craigie 1926- *IntWW 93*
Aitchison, Craigie (Ronald John) 1926- *Who 94*
Aitchison, Ian J(ohnston) R(hind) 1936- *WrDr 94*
Aitchison, Jean Margaret 1938- *Who 94*
Aitchison, June Rosemary *Who 94*
Aitchison, Peggy d1990 *WhoHol 92*
Aitken *Who 94*
Aitken, Christopher Charles 1957- *WhoFI 94*
Aitken, Donald Hector 1925- *IntWW 93*
Aitken, Hugh 1924- *NewGrDO*
Aitken, Hugh (George Jeffrey) 1922- *WrDr 94*
Aitken, Ian Levack 1927- *Who 94*
Aitken, John 1839-1919 *DcNaB MP*
Aitken, John Eakin, Jr. 1941- *WhoWest 94*
Aitken, Jonathan William Patrick 1942- *Who 94*
Aitken, Maria 1945- *WhoHol 92*
Aitken, Maria Penelope Katharine 1945- *Who 94*
Aitken, Martin Jim 1922- *IntWW 93, Who 94*
Aitken, Philip Martin 1902- *WhoAmL 94*
Aitken, Robert (Baker) 1917- *WrDr 94*
Aitken, Robert (Stevenson) 1929- *Who 94*
Aitken, Robert Stevenson 1901- *IntWW 93*
Aitken, Spottiswoode d1933 *WhoHol 92*
Aitken, Thomas Dean 1939- *WhoAm 94, WhoAmL 94*
Aitken, William Inglis 1896- *WhAm 10*
Aitkens, Michael *WhoHol 92*
Aitkin, Donald Alexander 1947- *Who 94*
Aitmatov, Chingiz (Torekulovich) 1928- *ConWorW 93, EncSF 93, RfGShF*
Aitmatov, Chingiz Torekulovich 1928- *IntWW 93*
Aiuto, Russell 1934- *WhoAm 94*
Ai Wu 1904- *WhoPRCh 91 [port]*
Ai-xin Jue-luo Pu-jie *WhoPRCh 91*
Aizawa, Hideyuki *IntWW 93*
Aizawa, Keio 1927- *WhoScEn 94*
Aizawa, Masuo 1942- *WhoScEn 94*
Aizenman, Michael 1945- *WhoScEn 94*
Ai Zhisheng 1928- *IntWW 93*
Ai Zhisheng 1929- *WhoPRCh 91 [port]*
Ai Zhongxin *WhoPRCh 91*
Ai Zhongxin 1931- *IntWW 93*
Ajalat, Sol Peter 1932- *WhoAmL 94*
Ajawara, Augustus Chiedozie 1953- *WhoWest 94*
Ajay, Abe 1919- *WhoAm 94, WhoAmA 93*
Ajaye, Franklyn 1949- *WhoHol 92*
Ajayi, Jacob Festus Ade 1929- *IntWW 93, Who 94*
Ajello, Carl Richard 1932- *WhoAmP 93*
Ajello, Edith H. 1944- *WhoAmP 93*
Ajemian, Robert Myron 1925- *WhoAm 94*
A Jia *WhoPRCh 91 [port]*
Ajibola, Bola 1934- *IntWW 93*
Ajifu, Ralph K. 1926- *WhoAmP 93*
Ajmani, Jagdish Chand 1930- *IntWW 93*
Ajmera, Kishore Tarachand 1941- *WhoScEn 94*
Ajmera, Pratul Kumar 1945- *WhoScEn 94*
Ajmera, Pravin V. *WhoAm 94*
Ajootian, Khosrov 1891-1958 *WhoAmA 93N*
Ajzen, Daniel 1950- *WhoHisp 94*
Ajzenberg-Selove, Fay 1926- *WhoAm 94*
Akabusi, Kriss 1958- *IntWW 93*
Akaev, Askar Akaevich 1944- *LoBiDrD*
Akagawa, Jiro 1948- *IntWW 93*
Akahoshi, Steve *WhoHol 92*
Akaka, Daniel K. 1924- *CngDr 93*
Akaka, Daniel Kahikina 1924- *IntWW 93, WhoAm 94, WhoAmP 93, WhoAsA 94, WhoWest 94*
Akaka, Ellen L. *WhoWest 94*
Akalaitis, Joanne 1932- *IntWW 93*
Akalaitis, JoAnne 1937- *ConDr 93, CurBio 93 [port], WhoAm 94*
Akalin, Roberta Ann 1945- *WhoMW 93*
Akama, Yoshihiro 1916- *IntWW 93*
Akamu, Nina 1955- *WhoAmA 93*
Akar, John J. d1975 *WhoHol 92*
Akar, John J(oseph) 1927-1975 *BlkWr 2*
Akard, Sarah Ann 1958- *WhoMW 93*
Akasaka, Richard Y. *WhoHisp 94*
Akasaki, Toshiro 1925- *WhoAm 94*
Akashi, Toshio 1915- *IntWW 93*
Akashi, Yasushi 1931- *IntWW 93*
Akasofu, Syun-Ichi 1930- *WhoAm 94, WhoScEn 94, WhoWest 94*
Akatani, Genichi 1917- *IntWW 93*
Akau, Ronald Leialoha 1955- *WhoWest 94*
Akawie, Thomas Frank 1935- *WhoAmA 93*
Akay, Adnan *WhoScEn 94*
Akayev, Askar 1944- *IntWW 93*
Akbar 1542-1605 *HisWorL [port]*
Akbar, Na'im 1944- *WhoBlA 94*
Akbar, Sheikh Ali 1955- *WhoScEn 94*
Akbarian, S.R. 1953- *WhoWest 94*
Akbulut, Yildirim 1935- *IntWW 93*
Akcasu, Ahmet Ziyaeddin 1924- *WhoAm 94, WhoMW 93*
Ake, H. Worth 1923- *WhoIns 94*
Ake, Jeffrey James 1958- *WhoFI 94*
Ake, John *WhoAmA 93*
Ake, John Notley 1941- *WhoAm 94*
Ake, Simeon 1932- *IntWW 93*
Aked, Muriel d1955 *WhoHol 92*
Akeel, Hadi Abu 1938- *WhoFI 94*
Akehurst, John (Bryan) 1930- *Who 94*
Akel, Ollie James 1933- *WhoScEn 94*
Akella, Jagannadham 1937- *WhoWest 94*
Akello, Grace *BlmGWL*
Akemu Jiafuer *WhoPRCh 91*
Akenhead, Robert 1949- *Who 94*
Akenside, Mark 1721-1770 *BlmGEL*
Akenson, Donald Harman 1941- *IntWW 93, WhoAm 94*
Aker, George Edwin 1937- *WhoFI 94*
Akera, Tai 1932- *WhoAm 94*
Akerlof, Carl William 1938- *WhoAm 94*
Akerlof, George Arthur 1940- *Who 94*
Akerlow, Charles W. 1940- *WhoAmP 93*
Akerman, (Knut Lennart) Alf 1923- *IntWW 93*
Akers, Adela 1933- *WhoAmA 93*
Akers, Alan Burt *EncSF 93*
Akers, Alan Burt 1914- *WrDr 94*
Akers, Andra *WhoHol 92*
Akers, CathayAnne Marie 1952- *WhoFI 94*
Akers, David Paul 1943- *WhoFI 94*
Akers, Deborah Rowley 1949- *WhoAmL 94*
Akers, Ellery *DrAPF 93*
Akers, Floyd *EncSF 93*
Akers, Gary 1951- *WhoAmA 93*
Akers, John Fellows 1934- *IntWW 93, Who 94, WhoAm 94, WhoFI 94*
Akers, Karen 1945- *WhoHol 92*
Akers, Ottie Clay 1949- *WhoAmL 94*
Akers, Samuel Lee 1943- *WhoAmL 94*
Akers, Sheldon Buckingham, Jr. 1926- *WhoAm 94*
Akers, Steve Roy 1952- *WhoAm 94, WhoAmL 94*
Akers, Tom, Jr. 1919- *WhoAm 94*
Akers, William Walter 1922- *WhoAm 94*
Akers-Douglas *Who 94*
Akers-Jones, David 1927- *IntWW 93, Who 94*
Akerson, Alan W. *WhoAm 94, WhoFI 94*
Akerson, Daniel Francis 1948- *WhoAm 94, WhoFI 94*
Akerson, Dorothy S. 1945- *WhoMW 93*
Akert, Konrad 1919- *IntWW 93*
Akeson, Sonja Berta Maria Hammarberg 1926-1977 *BlmGWL*
Akeson, Wayne Henry 1928- *WhoAm 94*
Akesson, Norman Berndt 1914- *WhoAm 94, WhoScEn 94*
Akhanton, Askia *DrAPF 93*
Akhenaten c. 1385BC-1350BC *HisWorL [port]*
Akhmadov, Khusein Saidaminovich 1950- *LoBiDrD*
Akhmadulina, Bella 1937- *ConWorW 93, IntWW 93*
Akhmadulina, Izabella Akhatovna 1937- *BlmGWL*
Akhmatova, Anna 1889-1966 *BlmGWL*
Akhmedov, Khan 1936- *LoBiDrD*
Akhmedov, Khan A. 1936- *IntWW 93*
Akhmedov, Rustam Urmanovich 1943- *LoBiDrD*
Akhmetaliev, Amangeldy Akhmetolimovich 1937- *LoBiDrD*
Akhtar, Muhammad 1933- *IntWW 93, Who 94*
Akhter, Mohammad Nasir 1944- *WhoAm 94*
Akhund, Iqbal Ahmad 1924- *IntWW 93*
Akhurst, Daphne 1903-1933 *BuCMET*
Aki, James Hajime 1936- *WhoAmP 93*
Aki, Keiiti 1930- *IntWW 93, WhoAm 94, WhoAsA 94*
Aki, Tanuki *EncSF 93*
Akiba, Lorraine Hiroko 1956- *WhoAmL 94, WhoWest 94*
Akihito 1933- *IntWW 93*
Akihito, HM the Emperor of Japan 1933- *Who 94*
Akil, Husein Avicenna 1956- *WhoScEn 94*
Akilandam, Perungalur Vaithialingam 1922- *IntWW 93*
Akima, Hiroshi 1925- *WhoWest 94*
Akimoff, Nicolai d1968 *WhoHol 92*
Akimoto Matsuyo 1911- *BlmGWL*
Akin, Billy Larue 1933- *WhoIns 94*
Akin, Cavit 1931- *WhoMW 93*
Akin, Ewen M., Jr. 1930- *WhoBlA 94*
Akin, Gulten 1933- *BlmGWL*
Akin, Gwen 1950- *WhoAmA 93*
Akin, Henry David 1900- *WhoAm 94*
Akin, John Stephen 1945- *WhoFI 94*
Akin, Lewis E. 1937- *WhoAm 94, WhoFI 94*
Akin, Rick Dale 1958- *WhoAmL 94*
Akin, Steven P. 1945- *WhoAm 94, WhoFI 94*
Akin, Timothy Robert 1949- *WhoFI 94*
Akin, W. Todd 1947- *WhoAmP 93*
Akinaka, Asa Masayoshi 1938- *WhoAm 94*
Akinkugbe, Oladipo Olujimi 1933- *Who 94*
Akinkugbe, Oladipo Olujimi Atobase of Ife 1933- *IntWW 93*
Akinmusuru, Joseph Olugbenga 1948- *WhoScEn 94*
Akins, Allen Clinton 1919- *WhoBlA 94*
Akins, Chip 1952- *WhoWest 94*
Akins, Claude 1918- *IntMPA 94*
Akins, Claude 1926- *WhoHol 92*
Akins, Ellen *DrAPF 93, WrDr 94*
Akins, Future Renee 1950- *WhoAmA 93*
Akins, George Charles 1917- *WhoFI 94, WhoWest 94*
Akins, Jacqueline Van Auken 1960- *WhoMW 93*
Akins, James E. 1926- *IntWW 93*
Akins, Kelly 1952- *WhoAmL 94*
Akins, Vaughn Edward 1934- *WhoFI 94*
Akins, Zane Vernon 1940- *WhoAm 94*
Akins, Zoe 1886-1958 *IntDcF 2-4 [port]*
Akira, Yeiri 1928- *IntWW 93*
Akiwumi, Viki *DrAPF 93*
Akiya, Einosuke 1930- *IntWW 93*
Akiyama, Carol Lynn 1946- *WhoWest 94*
Akiyama, Kazuyoshi 1941- *WhoAm 94*
Akiyama, Masayasu 1937- *WhoScEn 94*
Akiyoshi, Mike M. 1940- *WhoAsA 94*
Akiyoshi, Toshiko 1929- *WhoAm 94*
Akkad, Sargon Of *WhWE*
Akkapeddi, Prasad Rao 1943- *WhoAsA 94*
Akkara, Joseph Augustine 1938- *WhoScEn 94*
Akkermann, Schaia 1928- *WhoScEn 94*
Aklestad, Gary C. 1934- *WhoAmP 93*
Aklilu, Tesfaye 1944- *WhoBlA 94*
Akmakjian, Alan P. *DrAPF 93*
Akmakjian, Sam 1957- *WhoMW 93*
Akman, Jerome P. 1944- *WhoAmL 94*
Akoi, Robert, Jr. 1953- *WhoWest 94*
Akos, Francis 1922- *WhoAm 94*
Akpan, Edward 1952- *WhoScEn 94*
Akporode Clark, B. 1934- *IntWW 93*
Akram, Wasim *IntWW 93*
Akridge, John Edward, III 1946- *WhoAm 94, WhoFI 94*
Akridge, Paul Bai 1952- *WhoBlA 94*
Akrigg, George Philip Vernon *WrDr 94*
Akrita, Silva *WhoWomW 91*
Akritidis, Nicolaos 1935- *IntWW 93*
Aks, Patricia 1926- *WrDr 94*
Akselrad, David Martin 1959- *WhoFI 94*
Akselsson, Kjell Roland 1940- *WhoScEn 94*
Aksen, Gerald 1930- *WhoAm 94*
Aksenov, Vasilii (Pavlovich) 1932- *ConWorW 93*
Aksin, Mustafa 1931- *IntWW 93*
Aksoy, Ercument Galip 1952- *WhoWest 94*
Akst, Harry d1963 *WhoHol 92*
Akston, James *WhoAmA 93N*
Aksu, Abdulkadir 1944- *IntWW 93*
Aksyonov, Vasiliy Pavlovich 1932- *IntWW 93*
Aksyonov, Vasily *ConWorW 93*
Aksyonov, Vassily (Pavlovich) 1932- *EncSF 93*
Aksyonov, Vassily Pavlovich 1932- *WhoAm 94*
Aksyuchits, Viktor Vladimirovich 1949- *IntWW 93, LoBiDrD*
Akue, Sokewoe *WhoWomW 91*
Akuoko Sarpong, Nana *WhoWomW 91*
Akurgal, Ekrem 1911- *IntWW 93*
Akutagawa, Donald 1923- *WhoAm 94, WhoWest 94*
Akutagawa, Hiroshi d1981 *WhoHol 92*
Akutagawa, Ryunosuke 1892-1927 *RfGShF*
Akutagawa, Yasushi 1925-1989 *NewGrDO*
Akuzum, Ilhan 1947- *IntWW 93*
Akwei, Richard Maximilian 1923- *IntWW 93*
Akyol, Avni 1931- *IntWW 93*
Akyol, Turkan *WhoWomW 91*
Alaan, Mansour *WhoBlA 94*
Alabaster, William 1568-1640 *DcLB 132 [port]*
al-'Adawiyya, Rabi'a dc. 802 *BlmGWL*
Aladjem, Silvio 1928- *WhoAm 94*
Aladro, Gerardo 1949- *WhoHisp 94*
Al-Afaleq, Eljazi 1956- *WhoScEn 94*
Alafouzo, Antonia 1952- *WhoFI 94*
Alagic, Suad 1946- *WhoScEn 94*
Alaimo, Anthony A. 1920- *WhoAm 94*
Alaimo, Simone c. 1952- *NewGrDO*
Alain, Marie-Claire 1926- *IntWW 93*
Alaix, Emperatriz 1949- *WhoHisp 94*
al-'Akhyaliyya, Layla dc. 700 *BlmGWL*
Alala, Joseph Basil, Jr. 1933- *WhoAm 94*
Alaleona, Domenico (Ottavio Felice Gaspare Maria) 1881-1928 *NewGrDO*
Alali, A. Odasuo 1957- *ConAu 140*
Alam, Juan Shamsul 1946- *WhoHisp 94*
Alameda, Lawrence G. *WhoHisp 94*
Alameda, Russell Raymond, Jr. 1945- *WhoWest 94*
Alami, Saad al-Din Jalal al- d1993 *NewYTBS 93*
Alami, Sa'd Eddin 1911- *IntWW 93*
Alami, Said Eddin d1993 *IntWW 93N*
Alamia, Richard Rene 1946- *WhoAmP 93*
Alamilla, Maclovio David 1942- *WhoHisp 94*
Al-Amin, Jamil Abdullah 1943- *ConBlB 6 [port], WhoBlA 94*
Alamo, Rafael 1952- *WhoHisp 94*
Alamuddin, Najib Salim 1909- *IntWW 93*
Alan, Hervey 1910-1982 *NewGrDO*
Alan, Jay 1907-1965 *WhoAmA 93N*
Alanbrooke, Viscount 1932- *Who 94*
Aland, Robert H. 1940- *WhoAm 94*
Alan Dale, Fletcher 1954- *WhoWest 94*
Alanen, Arnold Robert 1941- *WhoMW 93*
Alaniz, Arnoldo Rene 1957- *WhoHisp 94*
Alaniz, Johnny Segura 1929- *WhoHisp 94*
Alaniz, Joseph J. 1956- *WhoHisp 94*
Alaniz, Miguel José Castañeda 1944- *WhoHisp 94, WhoWest 94*
Alaniz, Robert Manuel 1957- *WhoHisp 94*
Alaniz, Salvador, Sr. *WhoHisp 94*
Alaniz, Valente, Jr. 1952- *WhoHisp 94*
Alaniz, Vicente A. 1945- *WhoHisp 94*
Alanko, Matti Lauri Juhani 1935- *WhoScEn 94*
Alanova, Kyra d1965 *WhoHol 92*
Alanson, Edward 1747-1823 *DcNaB MP*
Alarcon, Alan F. 1948- *WhoHisp 94*
Alarcon, Arthur L. *WhoAmP 93*
Alarcon, Arthur Lawrence 1925- *WhoAm 94, WhoAmL 94, WhoHisp 94, WhoWest 94*
Alarcón, Francisco X. 1954- *WhoHisp 94*
Alarcon, Francisco Xavier 1954- *WhoWest 94*
Alarcón, Graciela Solis 1942- *WhoHisp 94*
Alarcón, Guillermo Gerardo 1960- *WhoHisp 94*
Alarcon, Hernando De fl. 154-?- *WhWE*
Alarcon, Juan Ruiz de *IntDcT 2*
Alarcón, Justo S. 1930- *WhoHisp 94*
Alarcon, Minella Clutario 1948- *WhoScEn 94*
Alarcón, Norma *WhoHisp 94*
Alarcon, Raul, Jr. *WhoHisp 94*
Alarcon, Renato D. 1942- *WhoHisp 94*
Alarcon, Richard Anthony 1953- *WhoHisp 94*
Alarcon, Rogelio Alfonso 1926- *WhoScEn 94*
Alarcon, Terry Quentin 1948- *WhoAmL 94*
Alarcon De Quesada, Ricardo 1937- *IntWW 93*
Alarcon Mantilla, Luis Fernando 1951- *IntWW 93*
Alari, Steven K. 1957- *WhoAmP 93*

Alarid, Albert Joseph 1948- *WhoAmL 94, WhoWest 94*
Alarid, Albert Joseph, III 1948- *WhoHisp 94*
Alarid, Frank 1950- *WhoHisp 94*
Alarid, Jake Ignacio 1934- *WhoHisp 94*
Alarid, Michael *WhoAmP 93, WhoHisp 94*
Alarie, Pierrette (Marguerite) 1921- *NewGrDO*
Alario, John A. 1943- *WhoAm 94*
Alario, John A., Jr. 1943- *WhoAmP 93*
Alaskey, Joe *WhoHol 92*
Alatas, Ali 1932- *IntWW 93*
Alatas, Syed Hussein 1928- *IntWW 93*
Alatis, James Efstathios 1926- *WhoAm 94*
Alatorre, Richard 1943- *WhoAmP 93, WhoHisp 94*
al-Attar, Najah *WhoWomW 91*
Alatzas, George 1940- *WhoFI 94*
Alaupovic, Alexandra V. 1921- *WhoAmA 93*
Alaupovic, Petar 1923- *WhoScEn 94*
Alaya, Flavia 1935- *WrDr 94*
Alayeto, George I. 1926- *WhoFI 94*
Alayrac, Nicolas-Marie d' *NewGrDO*
Al-Azm, Sadik J. *WrDr 94*
Alazraki, Jaime 1934- *WhoAm 94, WhoHisp 94, WrDr 94*
Alba, Armando R. *WhoHisp 94*
Alba, Camilo Benjamin 1956- *WhoMW 93*
Alba, Jesus, H.R.H., the Duke of 1934- *IntWW 93*
Alba, Maria 1905?- *WhoHol 92*
Alba, Nanina 1915?-1968 *BlkWr 2, ConAu 141*
Alba, Ray *WhoHisp 94*
Alba, Victor 1916- *WrDr 94*
Alba-Buffill, Elio 1930- *WhoFI 94, WhoHisp 94*
Albacete, Manuel Joseph 1939- *WhoMW 93*
Albacete Carreira, Alfonso 1950- *IntWW 93*
Albach, Carl Rudolph 1907- *WhoScEn 94*
Albach, Horst 1931- *WhoScEn 94*
Albach-Retty, Rolf d1967 *WhoHol 92*
Albach-Retty, Rosa d1980 *WhoHol 92*
Albagli, Louise Martha 1954- *WhoScEn 94*
Albala, David Mois 1955- *WhoMW 93, WhoScEn 94*
Albam, Manny 1922- *WhoBlA 94*
Alban, Genevieve Novicky 1919- *WhoAm 94*
Alban, Manuel Ernesto, Sr. 1940- *WhoHisp 94*
Alban, Roger Charles 1948- *WhoFI 94, WhoMW 93*
Albanese, (Egide-Joseph-Ignace-)Antoine 1729-1800 *NewGrDO*
Albanese, Donald Joseph 1937- *WhoAmP 93*
Albanese, Francesco 1912- *NewGrDO*
Albanese, Gerard, Jr. 1952- *WhoIns 94*
Albanese, Licia 1913- *NewGrDO, WhoAm 94, WhoHol 92*
Albanese, Rosemarie Ann 1942- *WhoAmP 93*
Albanese, Sal F. 1949- *WhoAmP 93*
Albanese, Vannie Thomas 1941- *WhoFI 94*
Albanese, Vincent Michael 1926- *WhoAmP 93*
Albanese Morella, Constance 1901- *WhoWomW 91*
Albanesi, Meggi d1923 *WhoHol 92*
Albañez, Marguerite A. 1939- *WhoHisp 94*
Albani, Emma (Marie Louise Cecile) 1847-1930 *NewGrDO [port]*
Albani, Suzanne Beardsley 1943- *WhoAm 94*
Albanis, Triadafillos Athanasios 1956- *WhoScEn 94*
Albano, Alfonso M. 1939- *WhoAsA 94*
Albano, Andres, Jr. 1941- *WhoFI 94, WhoWest 94*
Albano, Ippolito d' *NewGrDO*
Albano, Patrick Louis 1947- *WhoAmA 93*
Albano, Peter 1940?- *EncSF 93*
Albano, Salvatore 1935- *WhoAmP 93*
Albany, George Martin 1945- *WhoIns 94*
Albany, James 1935- *WrDr 94*
Albarella, Joan *DrAPF 93*
Albarelli, Luigi fl. 1692-1706 *NewGrDO*
Albarn, Keith 1939- *WrDr 94*
Albaugh, Fred William 1913- *WhoAm 94*
Albaugh, John Charles 1938- *WhoAm 94*
Albaugh, Kevin Bruce 1958- *WhoScEn 94*
Albaum, Gerald Sherwin 1933- *WhoWest 94*
Al-Bayati, 'Abdal-Wahhab *ConWorW 93*
Al-Bayati, Mohammed A. Sultan 1951- *WhoWest 94*
Albeck, Andy 1921- *IntMPA 94*
Albeck, Karen Kay 1948- *WhoAmP 93*
Albeck, Stan 1931- *BasBi*
Albee, Arden Leroy 1928- *WhoAm 94, WhoScEn 94, WhoWest 94*
Albee, Edward *NewYTBS 93 [port]*
Albee, Edward 1928- *Who 94*
Albee, Edward (Franklin) 1928- *WrDr 94*
Albee, Edward (Franklin, III) 1928- *ConDr 93, GayLL, IntDcT 2*
Albee, Edward Franklin 1928- *AmCulL, IntWW 93, WhoAm 94*
Albee, George Wilson 1921- *WhoAm 94*
Albee, Percy F. 1885-1959 *WhoAmA 93N*
Albemarle, Countess of 1909- *Who 94*
Albemarle, Earl of 1965- *Who 94*
Albenda, David 1936- *WhoAm 94, WhoAmL 94*
Albeniz, Isaac (Manuel Francisco) 1860-1909 *NewGrDO*
Alber, Phillip George 1948- *WhoAmL 94*
Alberding, Charles Howard 1901-1989 *WhAm 10*
Alberg, Mildred Freed 1921- *WhoAm 94*
Alberg, Somer d1977 *WhoHol 92*
Alberg, Tom Austin 1940- *WhoAm 94, WhoAmL 94, WhoFI 94*
Alberga, Alta W. *WhoAmA 93*
Alberga, Alta Wheat *WhoAm 94*
Alberger, William Relph 1945- *WhoAm 94, WhoAmL 94, WhoAmP 93*
Alberghetti, Anna Maria 1936- *IntMPA 94, WhoHol 92*
Albergo, Horace Maurice 1932- *WhoAm 94*
Alberici, Aureliana 1941- *WhoWomW 91*
Alberici, Gabriel J. 1909- *WhoFI 94*
Alberni, Luis d1962 *WhoHol 92*
Albero, Richard Lewis 1945- *WhoAm 94*
Alberoni, Sherry 1946- *WhoHol 92*
Albers, Anni 1899- *WhoAm 94, WhoAmA 93*
Albers, Charles Edgar 1940- *WhoAm 94*
Albers, Glenda Tay 1962- *WhoMW 93*
Albers, Hans d1960 *WhoHol 92*
Albers, Hans 1925- *IntWW 93*
Albers, Henri 1866-1925 *NewGrDO*
Albers, James Arthur 1941- *WhoScEn 94*
Albers, John E. 1926- *WhoIns 94*
Albers, John Richard 1931- *WhoAm 94, WhoFI 94*
Albers, Josef 1888-1976 *WhoAmA 93N*
Albers, Sheryl K. 1954- *WhoAmP 93*
Albers, Thomas O. 1943- *WhoAmL 94*
Albers, William Marion 1932- *WhoFI 94*
Albersheim, Peter 1934- *WhoAm 94*
Albert, Monsieur 1787-1865 *IntDcB [port]*
Albert, I 1875-1934 *HisWorL [port]*
Albert, Alan Dale 1956- *WhoAmL 94*
Albert, Alexis (Francois) 1904- *Who 94*
Albert, Calvin 1918- *IntWW 93, WhoAm 94, WhoAmA 93*
Albert, Carl (Bert) 1908- *Who 94, WrDr 94*
Albert, Carl Bert 1908- *IntWW 93, WhoAmP 93*
Albert, Carlos d1980 *WhoHol 92*
Albert, Caterina 1869-1966 *BlmGWL*
Albert, Charles Gregory 1955- *WhoAmL 94, WhoBlA 94*
Albert, Dan d1919 *WhoHol 92*
Albert, Daniel Myron 1936- *WhoAm 94, WhoMW 93*
Albert, Donnie Ray 1950- *WhoBlA 94*
Albert, Eddie 1908- *IntMPA 94, WhoAm 94, WhoHol 92*
Albert, Edward 1951- *IntMPA 94, WhoAm 94, WhoHisp 94, WhoHol 92*
Albert, Elsie d1981 *WhoHol 92*
Albert, Eugen (Francis Charles) d' 1864-1932 *NewGrDO*
Albert, Frank A. 1938- *WhoAmP 93*
Albert, Fred 1957- *ConAu 140*
Albert, Gerald 1917- *WhoAm 94, WhoScEn 94*
Albert, Gregory Charles 1953- *WhoMW 93*
Albert, Hans 1921- *ConAu 141*
Albert, Harry Francis 1935- *WhoFI 94*
Albert, Janyce Louise 1932- *WhoFI 94, WhoMW 93*
Albert, Jeffrey B. 1946- *WhoAm 94, WhoAmL 94*
Albert, Lois Eldora Wilson 1938- *WhoAm 94*
Albert, Marie-Madeleine Bonafous d' fl. 18th cent.- *BlmGWL*
Albert, Marv 1943- *WhoAm 94*
Albert, Marvin H. *WrDr 94*
Albert, Michael L. 1938- *WhoMW 93*
Albert, Michael Robert 1946- *WhoWest 94*
Albert, Milton John 1917- *WhoScEn 94*
Albert, Mimi *DrAPF 93*
Albert, Neale Malcolm 1937- *WhoAm 94*
Albert, Otis William 1909- *WhoAmP 93*
Albert, Robert Alan 1933- *WhoAm 94*
Albert, Robert Bertrand 1932- *WhoFI 94*
Albert, Ronald L., Jr. 1963- *WhoAmL 94*
Albert, Rory Judd 1952- *WhoAm 94, WhoAmL 94*
Albert, Roy Ernest 1924- *WhoAm 94, WhoScEn 94*
Albert, Samuel *DrAPF 93*
Albert, Stephen F. 1950- *WhoWest 94*
Albert, Stephen Joel 1941-1992 *AnObit 1992*
Albert, Steven W. 1946- *WhoAmL 94*
Albert, Susan Wittig 1940- *WhoAm 94*
Albert, Theodor C. 1953- *WhoAmL 94*
Albert, Theodore Merton 1927- *WhoAm 94*
Albert, William Charles 1941- *WhoWest 94*
Alberta, Mark Edward 1950- *WhoAm 94*
Albertarelli, Francesco fl. 18th cent.- *NewGrDO*
Albertazzi, Emma 1814?-1847 *NewGrDO*
Albertazzi, Mario 1920-1991 *WhoAmA 93N*
Alberthal, Lester M., Jr. 1944- *WhoAm 94, WhoFI 94, WhoScEn 94*
Alberti (Merello), Rafael 1902- *ConWorW 93*
Alberti, Daniel E. 1949- *WhoAmL 94*
Alberti, Domenico c. 1710-1746 *NewGrDO*
Alberti, Donald Wesley 1950- *WhoAmA 93*
Alberti, Fritz d1954 *WhoHol 92*
Alberti, Guido *WhoHol 92*
Alberti, Johanna 1940- *WrDr 94*
Alberti, Kurt George Matthew Mayer 1937- *Who 94*
Alberti, Peter William 1934- *WhoAm 94*
Alberti, Salomon 1540-1600 *EncDeaf*
Alberti, Thomas James 1950- *WhoMW 93*
Albertini, Giuliano fl. 1701-1738 *NewGrDO*
Albertini, Joachim 1748-1812 *NewGrDO*
Albertini, Richard Joseph 1935- *WhoScEn 94*
Albertini, William Oliver 1943- *WhoFI 94*
Albert of Saxe-Coburg-Gotha 1819-1861 *BlmGEL*
Alberts, Allison Christine 1960- *WhoScEn 94*
Alberts, Barry S. 1946- *WhoAmL 94*
Alberts, Benita Fay 1966- *WhoFI 94*
Alberts, Bruce Michael 1938- *WhoScEn 94*
Alberts, David 1946- *WhoWest 94*
Alberts, Harold 1920- *WhoAmL 94*
Alberts, Irwin N. d1991 *WhAm 10*
Alberts, James Joseph 1943- *WhoAm 94, WhoScEn 94*
Alberts, Marion Edward 1923- *WhoAm 94*
Alberts, Richard Harold 1941- *WhoMW 93*
Alberts, Robert Carman 1907- *WhoAm 94, WrDr 94*
Albertsen, Harold Lawrence 1931- *WhoWest 94*
Albertson, Arthur d1926 *WhoHol 92*
Albertson, Bradley LeRoy 1955- *WhoMW 93*
Albertson, Charles Woodrow 1932- *WhoAmP 93*
Albertson, Frank d1964 *WhoHol 92*
Albertson, Fred Woodward 1908- *WhoAm 94*
Albertson, Grace *WhoHol 92*
Albertson, Jack d1981 *WhoHol 92*
Albertson, Jack 1910-1981 *WhoCom*
Albertson, Joseph A. d1993 *NewYTBS 93*
Albertson, Lillian d1962 *WhoHol 92*
Albertson, Mabel d1982 *WhoHol 92*
Albertson, Merle d1981 *WhoHol 92*
Albertson, Robert Bernard 1946- *WhoAm 94*
Albertson, Terry L. 1946- *WhoAm 94*
Albertson, Vernon Duane 1928- *WhoAm 94*
Albertson, Wallace Thomson 1924- *WhoAmP 93*
Albertsson, Per-Ake 1930- *IntWW 93*
Alberty, Michael Charles 1959- *WhoAmL 94*
Alberty, Robert Arnold 1921- *IntWW 93, WhoAm 94, WhoScEn 94*
Albertyn, Charles Henry 1928- *Who 94*
Albertz, Heinrich d1993 *NewYTBS 93*
Albertz, Heinrich 1915- *IntWW 93*
Albery, John *Who 94*
Albery, Tim 1952- *NewGrDO, Who 94*
Albery, Wyndham John 1936- *IntWW 93, Who 94*
Albicocco, Gabriel Jean Fernand Joseph 1936- *IntWW 93*
Albietz, Judith Kammins 1948- *WhoAmL 94*
Albiin, Elsy *WhoHol 92*
Albin, Barry Todd 1952- *WhoAm 94*
Albin, Leon 1925- *WhoAmP 93*
Albin, Leslie Owens 1940- *WhoScEn 94*
Albin, Randy Clark 1957- *WhoWest 94*
Albin, Thomas James 1952- *WhoAmL 94*
Albinger, William J., Jr. 1945- *WhoIns 94*
Albini, Srecko 1869-1933 *NewGrDO*
Albino, George Robert 1929- *WhoAm 94*
Albino, Judith E. N. *WhoWest 94*
Albinoni, Tomaso Giovanni 1671-1751 *NewGrDO*
Albinski, Henry Stephen 1931- *WrDr 94*
Albir, Carlos E. *WhoHisp 94*
Al-Biruni 973- *AstEnc*
Albohn, Arthur R. *WhoAmP 93*
Albom, Mitch 1958- *WrDr 94*
Albom, Mitch (David) 1958- *ConAu 140*
Albone, Eric Stephen 1940- *WhoScEn 94*
Alboni, Marietta 1826-1894 *NewGrDO [port]*
Albornoz, Fernando 1950- *WhoHisp 94*
Albornoz-Ruiz, Jose M. 1933- *WhoHisp 94*
Alborough, Jez 1959- *WrDr 94*
Albosta, Donald J. 1925- *WhoAmP 93*
Albrecht, Albert Pearson 1920- *WhoAm 94, WhoScEn 94, WhoWest 94*
Albrecht, Alexander Joseph 1946- *WhoWest 94*
Albrecht, Allan James 1927- *WhoFI 94, WhoScEn 94*
Albrecht, Arthur John 1931- *WhoAm 94, WhoFI 94*
Albrecht, Duane Taylor 1927- *WhoAm 94, WhoWest 94*
Albrecht, Edward Daniel 1937- *WhoAm 94, WhoMW 93*
Albrecht, Ernst Carl Julius 1930- *IntWW 93*
Albrecht, Felix Robert 1926- *WhoAm 94*
Albrecht, Frederick Ivan 1917- *WhoFI 94*
Albrecht, Frederick Steven 1949- *WhoAm 94, WhoMW 93*
Albrecht, Gerd 1935- *NewGrDO*
Albrecht, Helmut Heinrich 1955- *WhoScEn 94*
Albrecht, Johann Friedrich Ernst *EncSF 93*
Albrecht, Kay Montgomery 1949- *WhoAm 94*
Albrecht, Kenneth John 1933- *WhoAmP 93*
Albrecht, Laura *DrAPF 93*
Albrecht, Laura Elizabeth 1967- *WhoMW 93*
Albrecht, Mark Jennings 1950- *WhoAm 94*
Albrecht, Mary Dickson 1930- *WhoAmA 93*
Albrecht, Maureen Ann 1952- *WhoWest 94*
Albrecht, Nadene Ardis 1933- *WhoMW 93*
Albrecht, Paul Abraham 1922- *WhoAm 94*
Albrecht, Peter Leffingwell 1930- *WhoAm 94*
Albrecht, Ralph Gerhart 1896- *WhAm 10*
Albrecht, Richard Lawrence 1938- *WhoAmL 94*
Albrecht, Richard Raymond 1932- *WhoAm 94*
Albrecht, Robert Downing 1931- *WhoAm 94*
Albrecht, Ronald Frank 1937- *WhoAm 94*
Albrecht, Ronald Lewis 1935- *WhoFI 94*
Albrecht, Sophie 1757-1840 *BlmGWL*
Albrecht, Sterling Jean 1937- *WhoAm 94*
Albrecht, Suellen 1945- *WhoAmP 93*
Albrecht, Theodore John 1945- *WhoMW 93*
Albrecht, Thomas W. 1954- *WhoAmL 94*
Albrecht, William Price 1935- *WhoAm 94, WhoAmP 93, WhoFI 94*
Albret, Jeanne d', III 1528-1572 *BlmGWL*
Albrethsen, Adrian Edysel 1929- *WhoScEn 94*
Albright, Adam Emory 1862-1957 *WhoAmA 93N*
Albright, Archie Earl, Jr. 1920- *WhoAm 94*
Albright, Arthur 1811-1900 *DcNaB MP*
Albright, Boyce Singleton 1924- *WhoAm 94*
Albright, D. Erik 1965- *WhoAmL 94*
Albright, Dale Lewis 1933- *WhoAmP 93*
Albright, David Foxwell 1932- *WhoAm 94*
Albright, Deborah Elaine 1958- *WhoMW 93, WhoScEn 94*
Albright, Douglas Eaton 1948- *WhoAmL 94*
Albright, Elaine McClay 1946- *WhoAm 94*
Albright, George 1956- *WhoAmP 93*
Albright, George Franklin, Jr. 1952- *WhoAmL 94*
Albright, George Mark 1955- *WhoAmL 94*
Albright, Gerald Anthony 1957- *WhoBlA 94*
Albright, Hardie d1975 *WhoHol 92*
Albright, Harry Wesley, Jr. 1925- *WhoAm 94*
Albright, Henry J. d1951 *WhoAmA 93N*

Albright, Hugh Norton 1928- WhoAm 94
Albright, Ivan Le Lorraine 1897-1983 WhoAmA 93N
Albright, Jack Lawrence 1930- WhoAm 94
Albright, Jacob 1759-1808 DcAmReB 2
Albright, John Rupp 1937- WhoAm 94
Albright, Joseph Paul 1938- WhoAmP 93
Albright, Justin W. 1908- WhoAm 94
Albright, Kay Dale 1957- WhoMW 93
Albright, Kristine Carol 1956- WhoAmL 94
Albright, Lois 1904- WhoAm 94, WhoWest 94
Albright, Lola 1925- IntMPA 94, WhoHol 92
Albright, Lovelia Fried 1934- WhoFI 94
Albright, Lyle Frederick 1921- WhoAm 94
Albright, Madeleine 1937- WhoAm 94
Albright, Madeleine K. WhoAmP 93
Albright, Madeleine Korbel IntWW 93
Albright, Madeleine Korbel 1937- Who 94
Albright, Malvin Marr 1897- WhoAmA 93
Albright, Ralph N., Jr. 1942- WhoAmL 94
Albright, Ray C. 1934- WhoAmP 93
Albright, Raymond Jacob 1929- WhoAm 94
Albright, Robert, Jr. 1944- WhoBlA 94
Albright, Robert E. WhoAmP 93
Albright, Robert James 1941- WhoWest 94
Albright, Terrill D. 1938- WhoAm 94, WhoAmL 94
Albright, Thomas 1935- WhoAmA 93N
Albright, Thomas A. 1956- WhoAmL 94
Albright, Thomas E. 1950- WhoAmL 94
Albright, Townsend Shaul 1942- WhoAm 94
Albright, Wally, Jr. 1925- WhoHol 92
Albright, Warren Edward 1937- WhoAm 94
Albright, William Alexander, Jr. 1957- WhoWest 94
Albright, William Dudley, Jr. 1949- WhoBlA 94
Albright, William Foxwell 1891-1971 DcAmReB 2
Albrinck, James Louis 1943- WhoMW 93
Albritton, Claude Carroll, Jr. 1913-1988 WhAm 10
Albritton, Daniel L. 1936- WhoScEn 94
Albritton, Gayle Edward 1939- WhoScEn 94
Albritton, Robert Sanford 1914- WhoAm 94
Albritton, William Harold, III 1936- WhoAm 94, WhoAmL 94, WhoAmP 93
Albritton, William Harold, IV 1960- WhoAmL 94, WhoFI 94
Albritton, William Hoyle 1942- WhoAm 94
Albritton, William Leonard 1941- WhoAm 94
Albrizio, Francesco 1947- WhoScEn 94
Albro-Schaad, Kathryn Jeanne 1946- WhoMW 93
Albrow, Desmond 1925- Who 94
Albu, Austen Harry 1903- Who 94
Albu, George 1944- Who 94
Albu, Marie Who 94
Album, Jerald Lewis 1947- WhoAmL 94
Albuquerque, Afonso D' 1453-1515 WhWE
Albuquerque, Lita 1946- WhoAm 94, WhoAmA 93
Albuzzi, Ottavio c. 1720-1766? NewGrDO
Alby, Pierre 1921- IntWW 93
Albyn, Richard Keith 1927- WhoAm 94
Alcaide, Chris WhoHol 92
Alcaide, Mario d1971 WhoHol 92
Alcaide, Tomaz (de Aquino Carmelo) 1901-1967 NewGrDO
Alcaine, Jose Luis 1938- IntMPA 94
Alcala, Dick 1950- WhoHisp 94
Alcala, Dora G. 1937- WhoHisp 94
Alcala, Jose Ramon 1940- WhoHisp 94
Alcala, Luis A., Jr. 1943- WhoHisp 94
Alcalá Fonseca, Josefina 1951- WhoHisp 94
Alcalay, Albert S. 1917- WhoAm 94, WhoAmA 93
Alcalde, Miguel ConAu 42NR
Alcantar, Gerald J. 1946- WhoHisp 94
Alcantar, Joe 1947- WhoHisp 94
Alcantara, Larry James 1947- WhoAsA 94
Alcantara, Theo 1941- WhoAm 94
Alcaraz, Javier 1930- WhoHisp 94
Alcaraz Figueroa, Estanislao 1918- WhoAm 94
Alcayaga, Luciala Godoy BlkWr 2
Alcayaga, Lucila Godoy BlmGWL
Alcazar, Antonio 1965- WhoScEn 94
Alcazar-Sabathié, José A. 1959- WhoHisp 94
Alcedo, Richard 1951- WhoHisp 94
Alcedo, Thomas James 1949- WhoHisp 94
Alchevs'ky, Ivan Olexiyovych 1876-1917 NewGrDO
Alchouron, Guillermo E. 1933- IntWW 93
Alcindor, Lew 1947- WhoBlA 94
Alcindor, (Ferdinand) Lew(is) BlkWr 2
Alcipe BlmGWL
Alcivar, Michael Luis 1943- WhoHisp 94
Alcocer, Robert J. 1933- WhoHisp 94, WhoIns 94
Alcocer, Victor d1984 WhoHol 92
Alcock, Charles Benjamin 1923- WhoAm 94
Alcock, Charles William 1842-1907 WorESoc
Alcock, Douglas d1970 WhoHol 92
Alcock, Leslie 1925- Who 94
Alcock, (Robert James) Michael 1936- Who 94
Alcock, Tammy Marie 1963- WhoAmL 94
Alcock, Vivien 1924- ConAu 41NR, SmATA 76 [port]
Alcock, Vivien (Dolores) 1924- TwCYAW
Alcock, Vivien (Dolores) 1926- WrDr 94
Alcoforado, Mariana 1640-1723 BlmGWL
Alcon, Emilio S. 1926- WhoAmP 93
Alcon, Manuel Benjamin, Jr. 1926- WhoHisp 94
Alconada Aramburu, Carlos Roman Santiago 1920- IntWW 93
Alcopley, L. 1910-1992 WhoAmA 93N
Alcoriza, Luis 1920-1992 IntDcF 2-4
Alcorn, Andrew 1955- WhoAmL 94
Alcorn, Daniel S. 1955- WhoAmP 93
Alcorn, David Stewart 1923- WhoAm 94
Alcorn, George Bennett 1910- WhoWest 94
Alcorn, George E. WorInv
Alcorn, Gordon Dee 1907- WhoAm 94
Alcorn, Howard Wells 1901-1992 WhAm 10
Alcorn, Hugh Meade, Jr. 1907- WhAm 10
Alcorn, Stanley Marcus 1926- WhoAm 94
Alcorn, Wendell Bertram, Jr. 1939- WhoAm 94, WhoAmL 94
Alcorta, Gloria 1915- BlmGWL
Alcosser, Sandra DrAPF 93
Alcosser, Sandra (B.) 1944- ConAu 142
Alcott, Amos Bronson 1799-1888 AmSocL
Alcott, Amy Strum 1956- WhoAm 94
Alcott, James Arthur 1930- WhoAm 94
Alcott, John 1931-1986 IntDcF 2-4
Alcott, Kitty May 1923- WhoAmP 93
Alcott, Louisa May 1832-1888 AmCulL, BlmGWL, TwCYAW
Alcott, Mark Howard 1939- WhoAm 94
Alcovar, Pierre d1954 WhoHol 92
Alda, Alan 1936- IntMPA 94, IntWW 93, WhoAm 94, WhoCom, WhoHol 92
Alda, Anthony 1957- WhoHol 92
Alda, Frances d1952 WhoHol 92
Alda, Frances (Jeanne) 1879-1952 NewGrDO
Alda, Robert d1986 WhoHol 92
Alda, Rutanya 1942- WhoHol 92
Aldaco, Roberto Flores 1938- WhoHisp 94
Aldag, Jerome Marvin 1929- WhoMW 93
Aldag, Ramon John 1945- WhoAm 94
Aldam, Jeffery Heaton 1922- Who 94
Aldama, Benjamin, Jr. 1957- WhoHisp 94
Aldan, Daisy DrAPF 93
Aldan, Tomas Benavente 1945- WhoFI 94
Aldana, Antonio, Jr. WhoHisp 94
Aldana, Carl 1936- WhoAmA 93
Aldana, Carl 1938- WhoHisp 94, WhoWest 94
Aldani, Lino EncSF 93
Aldan Oqir WhoPRCh 91 [port]
Aldave, Barbara Bader 1938- WhoAm 94
Alday, John Hane 1964- WhoScEn 94
Alday, Paul Stackhouse, Jr. 1930- WhoScEn 94
Aldcroft, Derek Howard 1936- WrDr 94
Aldea, Patricia 1947- WhoAm 94
Aldecoa, Josefina R. 1926- BlmGWL
Aldemir, Tunc 1947- WhoMW 93, WhoScEn 94
Alden, Betty d1948 WhoHol 92
Alden, Christopher 1949- NewGrDO
Alden, David 1949- NewGrDO
Alden, David Wills 1948- WhoAm 94
Alden, Douglas William 1912- WhoAm 94
Alden, Eric M. 1950- WhoAmP 93
Alden, Gary Wade 1951- WhoAmA 93
Alden, Ginger WhoHol 92
Alden, Ichabod 1739-1778 WhAmRev
Alden, Ingemar Bengt 1943- WhoScEn 94
Alden, Joan DrAPF 93
Alden, Joan d1968 WhoHol 92
Alden, John Richard 1908- WrDr 94
Alden, Lester d1956 WhoHol 92
Alden, Mary d1946 WhoHol 92
Alden, Newton C. d1953 WhoHol 92
Alden, Norman 1924- WhoHol 92
Alden, Paulette Bates DrAPF 93
Alden, Richard WhoAmA 93
Alden, Richard d1982 WhoHol 92
Alden, Robert Comer 1957- WhoAmL 94
Alden, Steven Michael 1945- WhoAm 94, WhoAmL 94
Alden, Sue 1926- WrDr 94
Alden, Todd 1963- WhoAmA 93
Alden, Vernon Roger 1923- WhoAm 94
Aldenham And Hunsdon Of Hunsdon, Baron 1948- Who 94
Aldenhoff, Bernd 1908-1959 NewGrDO
Aldenhoff, Siegfried A. 1941- WhoMW 93
Alder, Berni Julian 1925- IntWW 93, WhoAm 94, WhoScEn 94
Alder, Douglas Dexter 1932- WhoWest 94
Alder, Henry Ludwig 1922- WhoAm 94, WhoWest 94
Alder, Lucette Who 94
Alder, Mary Ann d1952 WhoAmA 93N
Alder, Michael 1928- Who 94
Alderete, Frank J. WhoHisp 94
Alderete, John Fernando, Jr. 1950- WhoHisp 94
Alderete, Joseph Frank 1920- WhoAm 94, WhoScEn 94
Alderete, Rosemary 1947- WhoHisp 94
Alderete, Sam Albert 1941- WhoHisp 94
Alderette, Robert 1943- WhoWest 94
Alderfer, Clayton Paul 1940- WhoAm 94
Alderman, Bissell 1912- WhoAm 94
Alderman, Charles Wayne 1950- WhoAm 94
Alderman, Eugene Wayne 1936- WhoFI 94
Alderman, Gill 1941- EncSF 93
Alderman, James E. 1936- WhoAmP 93
Alderman, John d1987 WhoHol 92
Alderman, Mark Louis 1952- WhoAmL 94
Alderman, Minnis Amelia 1928- WhoAm 94, WhoFI 94, WhoScEn 94, WhoWest 94
Alderman, Richard Mark 1947- WhoAm 94
Alderman, Robert K. I. 1942- WhoAmP 93
Alderman, Thomas Ray 1948- WhoAmP 93
Alderman, Walter Arthur, Jr. 1945- WhoFI 94
Alderman, William F. 1945- WhoAmL 94
Alders, Hans 1942- IntWW 93
Alderslade, Richard 1947- Who 94
Alderson, Brian Wouldhave 1930- Who 94
Alderson, Brooke WhoHol 92
Alderson, Daphne Elizabeth Who 94
Alderson, Erville d1957 WhoHol 92
Alderson, James Michael 1947- WhoWest 94
Alderson, John WhoHol 92
Alderson, John Cottingham 1922- Who 94
Alderson, Margaret Hanne 1959- Who 94
Alderson, Margaret Northrop 1936- WhoAm 94
Alderson, Richard Lynn 1947- WhoAm 94, WhoWest 94
Alderson, Sue Ann 1940- WrDr 94
Alderson, William Thomas 1926- WhoAm 94
Alderton, John 1940- Who 94, WhoHol 92
Aldighieri, Gottardo 1824-1906 NewGrDO
Aldighieri, Maria Spezia- 1828-1907 NewGrDO
Alding, Peter 1926- WrDr 94
Aldington, 1st Baron 1914- IntWW 93
Aldington, Baron 1914- Who 94
Aldisert, Ruggero John 1919- WhoAm 94, WhoAmL 94
Aldiss, Brian 1925- BlmGEL
Aldiss, Brian (Wilson) 1925- WrDr 94
Aldiss, Brian W(ilson) 1925- EncSF 93
Aldiss, Brian Wilson 1925- IntWW 93, Who 94, WhoAm 94
Aldo, G. R. 1902-1953 IntDcF 2-4
Aldo-Benson, Marlene Ann 1939- WhoAm 94
Aldock, John Douglas 1942- WhoAmL 94
Aldon, Adair TwCYAW
Aldon, Howard GayLL
Aldon, Mari 1929- WhoHol 92
Aldoori, Walid Hamid 1953- WhoScEn 94
Aldous, Charles 1943- Who 94
Aldous, Duane Leo 1930- WhoWest 94
Aldous, Joan WhoAm 94
Aldous, Lucette 1938- Who 94
Aldous, William 1936- Who 94
Aldred, Brian Gordon 1951- Who 94
Aldred, Michelle Margaret 1967- WhoMW 93
Aldredge, James Earl 1939- WhoBlA 94
Aldredge, Ralph Curtis, III 1964- WhoScEn 94
Aldredge, Theoni V. 1932- ConTFT 11, IntMPA 94
Aldredge, Theoni Vachliotis 1932- WhoAm 94
Aldredge, Tom 1928- WhoHol 92
Aldrete, Joaquin Salcedo 1936- WhoHisp 94
Aldrete, Lori Johnson 1946- WhoWest 94
Aldrich, Alexander 1928- WhoAm 94, WhoAmL 94
Aldrich, Ann TwCYAW
Aldrich, Ann 1927- WhoAm 94, WhoAmL 94, WhoMW 93
Aldrich, Bailey 1907- WhoAm 94
Aldrich, Bess Streeter 1881-1954 BlmGWL
Aldrich, Daniel Eugene 1954- WhoWest 94
Aldrich, Daniel Gaskill, Jr. 1918-1990 WhAm 10
Aldrich, David d1985 WhoHol 92
Aldrich, David Lawrence 1948- WhoWest 94
Aldrich, Duane Cannon 1943- WhoAmL 94
Aldrich, Frank Nathan 1923- WhoAm 94, WhoFI 94
Aldrich, Franklin Dalton 1929- WhoAm 94
Aldrich, Fred d1979 WhoHol 92
Aldrich, Frederick Cecil 1924- WhoAmP 93
Aldrich, Hulbert Stratton 1907- IntWW 93
Aldrich, J. Winthrop 1944- WhoWest 94
Aldrich, John Herbert 1947- WhoAm 94
Aldrich, Jonathan DrAPF 93
Aldrich, Larry 1906- WhoAmA 93
Aldrich, Lovell Weld 1942- WhoAmL 94
Aldrich, Mariska d1965 WhoHol 92
Aldrich, Michael Paul 1957- WhoFI 94
Aldrich, Michael Ray 1942- WhoWest 94
Aldrich, Nancy Armstrong 1925- WhoAm 94, WhoScEn 94
Aldrich, Nelson W(ilmarth), Jr. 1935- ConAu 141
Aldrich, Patricia Anne Richardson 1926- WhoAm 94
Aldrich, Ralph Edward 1940- WhoAm 94
Aldrich, Richard John 1925- WhoAm 94
Aldrich, Richard Orth 1921- WhoAm 94
Aldrich, Robert Adams 1924- WhoAm 94
Aldrich, Robert Anderson 1917- WhoAm 94
Aldrich, Robert Keith 1954- WhoMW 93
Aldrich, Spaulding Ross 1932- WhoAmP 93
Aldrich, Stephen Charles 1941- WhoAmL 94
Aldrich, Thomas Albert 1923- WhoAm 94
Aldrich, Thomas Bailey 1836-1907 EncSF 93
Aldrich, Thomas Lawrence 1948- WhoAm 94
Aldrich, William C. 1932- WhoIns 94
Aldridge, A. Owen 1915- WrDr 94
Aldridge, Adele DrAPF 93
Aldridge, Alfred d1934 WhoHol 92
Aldridge, Alfred Owen 1915- WhoAm 94
Aldridge, Arleen Rash 1949- WhoHisp 94
Aldridge, Charles Ray 1946- WhoFI 94
Aldridge, Claude Michael 1950- WhoMW 93
Aldridge, Daniel 1960- WhoScEn 94
Aldridge, Delores P(atricia) BlkWr 2, ConAu 142
Aldridge, Delores Patricia WhoBlA 94
Aldridge, Donald O'Neal 1932- WhoAm 94, WhoWest 94
Aldridge, Donald Ray 1937- WhoAmP 93
Aldridge, Edward C., Jr. 1938- WhoAm 94, WhoScEn 94
Aldridge, Frederick Jesse 1915- Who 94
Aldridge, Gordon James 1916- WrDr 94
Aldridge, Ira c. 1807-1867 AfrAmAl 6
Aldridge, (Harold Edward) James 1918- IntWW 93, TwCYAW, Who 94, WrDr 94
Aldridge, John 1943- WhoAmL 94
Aldridge, John Frederick Lewis 1926- Who 94
Aldridge, John W(atson) 1922- WrDr 94
Aldridge, John Watson 1922- WhoAm 94
Aldridge, Karen Beth 1952- WhoBlA 94
Aldridge, Kay 1917- WhoHol 92
Aldridge, Mark Donald 1960- WhoFI 94
Aldridge, Melvin Dayne 1941- WhoAm 94, WhoFI 94
Aldridge, Michael 1920- WhoHol 92
Aldridge, Michael William ffolliott 1920- Who 94
Aldridge, Noel Henry 1924- WhoWest 94
Aldridge, Ron WhoAmP 93
Aldridge, Trevor Martin 1933- Who 94
Aldriedge, Jean DrAPF 93
Aldrin, Buzz 1930- CurBio 93 [port], IntWW 93, Who 94, WhoAm 94, WhoScEn 94
Aldrin, Edwin E(ugene) Who 94
Aldrin, Edwin Eugene 1896- WhAm 10
Aldroubi, Akram 1958- WhoScEn 94
Aldrovandini, Giuseppe Antonio Vincenzo 1671-1707 NewGrDO
Alducin, Don Jorge 1941- WhoHisp 94
Aldwinckle, Eric 1909-1980 WhoAmA 93N
Aldyne, Nathan 1950- WrDr 94
Ale, Talavou S. 1952- WhoAmP 93
Aleandro, Norma WhoHisp 94
Aleandro, Norma 1936- IntMPA 94

Aleandro, Norma 1940- *WhoHol 92*
Alebua, Ezekiel *IntWW 93*
Aleck, Ghazey H., II 1961- *WhoAmP 93*
Alegi, Peter Claude 1935- *WhoAm 94*
Alegria, Claribel 1924- *BlmGWL, ConWorW 93*
Alegria, Fernando 1918- *WhoHisp 94*
Alegria, Frank Anthony, Jr. 1957- *WhoHisp 94*
Alegria, Isabel L. 1951- *WhoHisp 94*
Alegría, Ricardo E. 1921- *WhoHisp 94*
Alegria, Richard Manuel 1944- *WhoAmP 93*
Alegria-Ortega, Idsa E. 1945- *WhoHisp 94*
Aleixo, Theodore J., Jr. 1942- *WhoAmP 93*
Alejandro, Aaron Enrique 1966- *WhoHisp 94*
Alejandro, Esteban 1911- *WhoHisp 94*
Alejandro, Miguel 1958- *WhoHol 92*
Alejandro, Reynaldo Gamboa 1947- *WhoAsA 94*
Alekan, Henri 1909- *IntDcF 2-4*
Alekin, Boris d1942 *WhoHol 92*
Alekman, Stanley Lawrence 1938- *WhoAm 94, WhoScEn 94*
Aleksander, Igor 1937- *Who 94*
Aleksandr, Archbishop of Dmitrov 1941- *IntWW 93*
Aleksandrov, Aleksandr Danilovich 1912- *IntWW 93*
Aleksandrov, Aleksandr Pavlovich 1943- *IntWW 93*
Aleksandrov, Anatoliy Petrovich 1903- *IntWW 93*
Aleksandrov, Leonid Naumovitsh 1923- *WhoScEn 94*
Alekseev, Anatoly Alekseevich 1950- *LoBiDrD*
Alekseev, Sergei Sergeevich 1924- *LoBiDrD*
Alekseeva, Lidiia Alekseevna 1909- *BlmGWL*
Alekseyev, Dmitri Konstantinovich 1947- *IntWW 93*
Aleksi, II, Patriarch 1929- *LoBiDrD*
Aleksiy 1929- *IntWW 93*
Alemán, George 1944- *WhoHisp 94*
Aleman, Hector E. 1936- *WhoHisp 94*
Aleman, Joe, III 1963- *WhoHisp 94*
Aleman, John Cary 1952- *WhoHisp 94*
Aleman, Julio *WhoHol 92*
Alemán, Narciso L. 1946- *WhoHisp 94*
Alemán, Victor 1946- *WhoHisp 94*
Alemán-Gómez, José Alberto 1961- *WhoHisp 94*
Alemann, Roberto Teodoro 1922- *IntWW 93*
Alemany, Carlos Bernardo d1993 *NewYTBS 93*
Alemany I Roca, Joaquima 1942- *WhoWomW 91*
Alemar, Evelyn T. 1943- *WhoHisp 94*
Alembert, Jean-Baptiste le Rond d' 1717-1783 *GuFrLit 2*
Alembert, Jean le Rond D' 1717-1783 *WorScD*
Alencon, Marguerite d' *GuFrLit 2*
Alenier, Karren LaLonde *DrAPF 93*
Alenikov, Vladimir 1948- *WhoWest 94*
Alentova, Vera *WhoHol 92*
Aleo, Joseph John 1925- *WhoAm 94*
Aleong, Aki *WhoHol 92*
Alepoudelis, Odysseus *ConWorW 93, Who 94*
Aler, John 1949- *NewGrDO*
Aleramo, Sibilla 1876-1960 *BlmGWL*
Alerme, Andre d1960 *WhoHol 92*
Alers, Jose Oscar 1933- *WhoHisp 94*
Alers, Juan M. 1943- *WhoHisp 94*
Ales, Michael Raymond 1958- *WhoFI 94*
Alesana, Tofilau Eti *IntWW 93*
Aleschus, Justine Lawrence 1925- *WhoFI 94*
Aleshire, Joan *DrAPF 93*
Aleshire, Richard Joe 1947- *WhoMW 93*
Alesi, James S. *WhoAmP 93*
Alesia, James Henry 1934- *WhoAm 94, WhoAmL 94*
Alesio, Vena Beth 1954- *WhoMW 93*
Alessandri, Felice 1747-1798 *NewGrDO*
Alessandroni, Venan Joseph 1915- *WhoAm 94*
Alessi, Keith Ernest 1954- *WhoFI 94*
Aletter, Frank 1926- *WhoHol 92*
Alevizos, Susan Bamberger 1936- *WhoAm 94*
Alevizos, Theodore G. 1926- *WhoAm 94*
Alevizos, Thomas J. 1961- *WhoAmP 93, WhoMW 93*
Alevy, Daniel I. 1929- *WhoWest 94*
Alewel, Teresa Fine 1962- *WhoMW 93*
Alewijn, Abraham 1664-1721 *NewGrDO*
Alewine, James William 1930- *WhoFI 94*
Alex, Gary Benninger 1941- *WhoAm 94*
Alex, Gregory K. 1948- *WhoBlA 94*
Alexa, William E. 1941- *WhoAmP 93*
Alexander *Who 94*
Alexander, Viscount *Who 94*
Alexander, I 1777-1825 *HisWorL [port]*
Alexander, II 1818-1881 *HisWorL [port]*
Alexander, A. L. d1967 *WhoHol 92*
Alexander, A. Melvin 1943- *WhoBlA 94*
Alexander, Adele Logan 1938- *ConAu 142*
Alexander, Alan 1943- *Who 94*
Alexander, Albert Geoffrey 1932- *Who 94*
Alexander, Albert George, Jr. 1929- *WhoAmP 93, WhoFI 94*
Alexander, Alec Peter 1923- *WhoAm 94*
Alexander, Alex d1977 *WhoHol 92*
Alexander, Alex (Sandor) 1916- *IntWW 93*
Alexander, Alexander Sandor 1916- *Who 94*
Alexander, Allen D. 1940- *WhoIns 94*
Alexander, Alma Duncan 1939- *WhoBlA 94*
Alexander, Andrew *WhoMW 93*
Alexander, Andrew Clive 1935- *Who 94*
Alexander, Andrew Lamar 1940- *IntWW 93, WhoAm 94*
Alexander, Andrew Nelson 1948- *WhoFI 94*
Alexander, Anthony George Laurence 1938- *Who 94*
Alexander, Anthony K. 1951- *WhoAmA 93*
Alexander, Anthony Victor 1928- *Who 94*
Alexander, Archibald 1772-1851 *DcAmReB 2*
Alexander, Archie 1887-1958 *AfrAmAl 6*
Alexander, Arthur 1940-1993 *NewYTBS 93*
Alexander, Avery 1911- *WhoBlA 94*
Alexander, Avery C. 1910- *WhoAmP 93*
Alexander, Barbara Leah Shapiro 1943- *WhoMW 93*
Alexander, Barbara Toll 1948- *WhoAm 94*
Alexander, Barton 1951- *WhoWest 94*
Alexander, Ben d1969 *WhoHol 92*
Alexander, Ben B. 1920- *WhoAmP 93*
Alexander, Benjamin Harold 1921- *WhoAm 94, WhoBlA 94*
Alexander, Bettina Lawton 1954- *WhoAm 94*
Alexander, Beverly Moore 1947- *WhoScEn 94*
Alexander, Bill 1910- *WrDr 94*
Alexander, Bill 1948- *ConTFT 11, Who 94*
Alexander, Brooke 1937- *IntWW 93*
Alexander, Bruce Donald 1943- *WhoAm 94*
Alexander, Bruce Edward 1951- *WhoAmL 94*
Alexander, Byron Allen 1952- *WhoScEn 94*
Alexander, C. Alex 1935- *WhoAm 94*
Alexander, Carl Albert 1928- *WhoAm 94, WhoScEn 94*
Alexander, Carlos 1915- *NewGrDO*
Alexander, Caroline 1956- *WrDr 94*
Alexander, Catharine Coleman 1934- *WhoWest 94*
Alexander, Cecil Abraham 1918- *WhoAm 94*
Alexander, Charles Fred, Jr. 1957- *WhoBlA 94*
Alexander, Charles G(undry) 1923- *Who 94*
Alexander, Charles Thomas 1928- *WhoAm 94*
Alexander, Charlotte *DrAPF 93*
Alexander, Cherian *Who 94*
Alexander, (Padinjarethalakal) Cherian 1921- *IntWW 93*
Alexander, (Padinjarethalakkal) Cherian 1921- *Who 94*
Alexander, Cheryl Lee 1946- *WhoFI 94*
Alexander, Christina Lillian 1942- *WhoScEn 94*
Alexander, Christine 1893-1975 *WhoAmA 93N*
Alexander, Christopher 1936- *IntWW 93, WrDr 94*
Alexander, Claire d1927 *WhoHol 92*
Alexander, Clifford 1933- *AfrAmAl 6*
Alexander, Clifford Joseph 1943- *WhoAm 94, WhoAmL 94*
Alexander, Clifford L. 1933- *IntWW 93*
Alexander, Clifford L., Jr. 1933- *WhoAm 94, WhoAmP 93, WhoBlA 94*
Alexander, Clyde 1946- *WhoAmP 93*
Alexander, Colleen Shirley 1926- *WhoAmP 93*
Alexander, Constantine 1941- *WhoAm 94*
Alexander, Cornelia *WhoBlA 94*
Alexander, Dale Edward 1962- *WhoScEn 94*
Alexander, David *EncSF 93, Who 94*
Alexander, (John) David 1932- *Who 94*
Alexander, David Cleon, III 1941- *WhoAm 94, WhoAmL 94*
Alexander, David Crichton 1926- *Who 94*
Alexander, David M(ichael) 1945- *EncSF 93*
Alexander, David T. 1946- *WhoAmL 94*
Alexander, Dawn Criket 1960- *WhoBlA 94*
Alexander, DeAngelo Heath 1966- *WhoBlA 94*
Alexander, Debra M. 1955- *WhoAmL 94*
Alexander, Denise *WhoHol 92*
Alexander, Diana Valdez 1963- *WhoHisp 94*
Alexander, Diane Marie 1945- *WhoAm 94*
Alexander, Donald 1937- *WhoBlA 94*
Alexander, Donald Crichton 1921- *IntWW 93, WhoAm 94*
Alexander, Donna *WrDr 94*
Alexander, Dorothy Dexter 1929- *WhoBlA 94*
Alexander, Douglas 1936- *Who 94*
Alexander, Drew W. 1948- *WhoBlA 94*
Alexander, Drury Blakeley 1924- *WhoAm 94*
Alexander, Duane Frederick 1940- *WhoAm 94, WhoScEn 94*
Alexander, Eben, Jr. 1913- *WhoAm 94*
Alexander, Edmund Brooke 1937- *WhoAmA 93*
Alexander, Edward d1964 *WhoHol 92*
Alexander, Edward Cleve 1943- *WhoBlA 94*
Alexander, Edward Russell 1928- *WhoAm 94*
Alexander, Elizabeth *WhoHol 92*
Alexander, Elizabeth 1962- *WhoMW 93, WrDr 94*
Alexander, Erika 1970- *WhoHol 92*
Alexander, Errol D. 1941- *WhoBlA 94*
Alexander, Estella Conwill 1949- *BlkWr 2, WhoBlA 94*
Alexander, Ethel 1925- *WhoAmP 93*
Alexander, F. S. Jack 1930- *WhoBlA 94*
Alexander, Fernande Gardner 1910- *WhoAm 94*
Alexander, Floyce *DrAPF 93*
Alexander, Floyce 1938- *WrDr 94*
Alexander, Floyce Milton 1938- *WhoMW 93*
Alexander, Frances F. *WhoAmP 93*
Alexander, Frank d1937 *WhoHol 92*
Alexander, Frank Lyon 1939- *WhoAm 94*
Alexander, Frank Spruill 1952- *WhoAmL 94*
Alexander, Fred 1880-1969 *BuCMET*
Alexander, Fred Calvin, Jr. 1931- *WhoAm 94, WhoAmL 94*
Alexander, Fritz W., II *WhoAmP 93*
Alexander, Fritz W., II 1926- *WhoBlA 94*
Alexander, Gary 1941- *WrDr 94*
Alexander, Gary R. 1942- *WhoAmP 93*
Alexander, Georg d1945 *WhoHol 92*
Alexander, George d1918 *WhoHol 92*
Alexander, George David *WhoWest 94*
Alexander, George Jonathon 1931- *WhoAm 94, WhoWest 94*
Alexander, Gerard d1962 *WhoHol 92*
Alexander, Gregory Stewart 1948- *WhoAm 94*
Alexander, Harold 1940- *WhoAm 94, WhoScEn 94*
Alexander, Harold Campbell 1920- *WhoFI 94*
Alexander, Harold Edwin, Jr. 1949- *WhoWest 94*
Alexander, Harry Toussaint 1924- *WhoBlA 94*
Alexander, Henry Alan 1953- *WhoWest 94*
Alexander, Henry G., Jr. 1949- *WhoAmL 94*
Alexander, Henry Lee 1949- *WhoFI 94*
Alexander, Herbert E. 1927- *WhoAm 94*
Alexander, Horace M., Jr. 1942- *WhoFI 94*
Alexander, Hubbard Lindsay 1939- *WhoBlA 94*
Alexander, Ian Douglas Gavin 1941- *Who 94*
Alexander, J. B. 1926- *WhoAmP 93*
Alexander, Jack Dudley, III 1962- *WhoWest 94*
Alexander, James d1961 *WhoHol 92*
Alexander, James, Jr. 1945- *WhoBlA 94*
Alexander, James Arthur 1953- *WhoBlA 94*
Alexander, James B(radun) 1831- *EncSF 93*
Alexander, James Brett 1948- *WhoBlA 94*
Alexander, James Eckert 1913- *WhoAm 94*
Alexander, James Marshall, Jr. 1921- *WhoAm 94*
Alexander, James Max 1948- *WhoAmP 93*
Alexander, James Patrick 1944- *WhoAm 94, WhoAmL 94*
Alexander, James W. 1916- *WhoBlA 94*
Alexander, James Wesley 1934- *WhoAm 94, WhoMW 93*
Alexander, Jamie *WhoHol 92*
Alexander, Jane *NewYTBS 93 [port]*
Alexander, Jane 1939- *IntMPA 94, News 94-2 [port], WhoAm 94, WhoHol 92*
Alexander, Jane Marietta 1929- *WhoAmP 93*
Alexander, Janet d1961 *WhoHol 92*
Alexander, Jason 1959- *IntMPA 94, WhoAm 94, WhoHol 92*
Alexander, Jason c. 1962- *News 93-3 [port]*
Alexander, Jeff 1953- *WhoAmP 93*
Alexander, Jeffery Brian 1963- *WhoMW 93*
Alexander, Jeffrey *WhoMW 93*
Alexander, Jessie Durrell 1919- *WhoAmP 93*
Alexander, Jim R. 1946- *WhoAmP 93*
Alexander, Joan *DrAPF 93*
Alexander, John d1951 *WhoHol 92*
Alexander, John d1982 *WhoHol 92*
Alexander, John 1923-1990 *NewGrDO*
Alexander, John Anthony 1962- *WhoAmP 93*
Alexander, John Charles 1915- *WhoScEn 94, WhoWest 94*
Alexander, John Charles 1943- *WhoAm 94*
Alexander, John David, Jr. 1932- *WhoAm 94, WhoWest 94*
Alexander, John Davis, Sr. 1899- *WhAm 10*
Alexander, John E. 1945- *WhoAmA 93*
Alexander, John Frank 1952-1991 *WhAm 10*
Alexander, John Heald 1904- *WhAm 10*
Alexander, John Healy 1942- *WhoWest 94*
Alexander, John J. 1940- *WhoAm 94*
Alexander, John J., Jr. 1935- *WhoAm 94*
Alexander, John Johnston, III 1958- *WhoMW 93*
Alexander, John Macmillan, Jr. 1931- *WhoAm 94*
Alexander, John Malcolm 1921- *Who 94*
Alexander, John Robert 1936- *WhoScEn 94*
Alexander, John Stanley 1944- *WhoBlA 94*
Alexander, John Thorndike 1940- *WhoAm 94, WrDr 94*
Alexander, John Wesley, Jr. 1938- *WhoBlA 94*
Alexander, Johnnie Wilbert 1928- *WhoBlA 94*
Alexander, Jonathan 1947- *WhoScEn 94*
Alexander, Jonathan James Graham 1935- *IntWW 93, Who 94*
Alexander, Joseph Edward 1948- *WhoMW 93*
Alexander, Joseph Kunkle, Jr. 1940- *WhoAm 94, WhoScEn 94*
Alexander, Joseph Lee 1929- *WhoBlA 94*
Alexander, Josephine *WhoBlA 94*
Alexander, Joyce London *WhoBlA 94*
Alexander, Joyce Mary 1927- *WhoAm 94*
Alexander, Judd Harris 1925- *WhoAm 94*
Alexander, Judith 1932- *WhoAmA 93*
Alexander, Judith Ann 1940- *WhoAm 94*
Alexander, Karl *DrAPF 93*
Alexander, Karl 1944- *WrDr 94*
Alexander, Katharine Violet 1934- *WhoAmL 94*
Alexander, Katherine d1981 *WhoHol 92*
Alexander, Keith Milton 1951- *WhoAmL 94*
Alexander, Kelly Miller, Jr. 1948- *WhoBlA 94*
Alexander, Kenneth (John Wilson) 1922- *Who 94*
Alexander, Kenneth Lewis 1924- *WhoAm 94, WhoAmA 93*
Alexander, Kenneth Sidney 1958- *WhoWest 94*
Alexander, Kerry Duane 1935- *WhoAmL 94*
Alexander, L(ouis) G(eorge) 1932- *ConAu 42NR*
Alexander, Lamar 1940- *WhoAm 94, WhoAmP 93*
Alexander, Laurence Benedict 1959- *WhoBlA 94*
Alexander, Lawrence Junior, II 1961- *WhoMW 93*
Alexander, Lawrence R. *WhoAmP 93*
Alexander, Lee 1927- *WhoAmP 93*
Alexander, Lenora Cole 1935- *WhoBlA 94*
Alexander, Lewis McElwain 1921- *WhoAm 94*
Alexander, Lilla d1968 *WhoHol 92*
Alexander, Lindsay *Who 94*
Alexander, (John) Lindsay 1920- *IntWW 93, Who 94*
Alexander, Lloyd (Chudley) 1924- *TwCYAW, WrDr 94*
Alexander, Lloyd Chudley 1924- *WhoAm 94*
Alexander, Lois d1968 *WhoHol 92*
Alexander, Louis 1917-1990 *WhAm 10*
Alexander, Louis 1954- *WhoHisp 94*

Alexander, Louis Alex 1950- *WhoAmL 94*
Alexander, Louis G., Sr. 1910- *WhoBlA 94*
Alexander, Louis George 1932- *WrDr 94*
Alexander, Lydia Lewis 1938- *WhoBlA 94*
Alexander, Lynn 1938- *WhoAm 94*
Alexander, M(ichael) J(oseph) 1941- *WrDr 94*
Alexander, Mara d1965 *WhoHol 92*
Alexander, Marcellus Winston, Jr. 1951- *WhoBlA 94*
Alexander, Margaret Ames 1916- *WhoAmA 93*
Alexander, Margaret Walker 1915- *WhoBlA 94*
Alexander, Marjorie Anne 1928- *WhoMW 93*
Alexander, Martha *WhoAmP 93*
Alexander, Martha Sue 1945- *WhoAm 94*
Alexander, Martin 1930- *WhoAm 94, WhoScEn 94*
Alexander, Mary Elsie 1947- *WhoAmL 94*
Alexander, Max *WhoHol 92*
Alexander, (Robert) McNeill 1934- *Who 94*
Alexander, (Robert) McNeill Alexander 1934- *WrDr 94*
Alexander, Meena *DrAPF 93*
Alexander, Meena 1951- *BlmGWL, WrDr 94*
Alexander, Melvin Taylor 1949- *WhoScEn 94*
Alexander, Mervin Franklin 1938- *WhoBlA 94*
Alexander, Mervyn Alban Newman *Who 94*
Alexander, Michael (O'Donel Bjarne) 1936- *Who 94*
Alexander, Michael Charles 1920- *Who 94*
Alexander, Michael K. 1961- *WhoWest 94*
Alexander, Michael Lee 1959- *WhoAm 94*
Alexander, Michael O'Donel Bjarne 1936- *IntWW 93*
Alexander, Miles Jordan 1931- *WhoAm 94*
Alexander, Milton Otho 1923- *WhoAmP 93*
Alexander, Muriel d1975 *WhoHol 92*
Alexander, Myrl E. d1993 *NewYTBS 93 [port]*
Alexander, Nancy Jeanne 1939- *WhoScEn 94*
Alexander, Neil Kenton, Jr. 1953- *WhoAm 94*
Alexander, Norman (Stanley) *Who 94*
Alexander, Norman E. 1914- *WhoAm 94, WhoFI 94*
Alexander, Norman James 1909- *WhoAm 94*
Alexander, Orin V. 1924- *WhoAmP 93*
Alexander, Otis Douglas 1949- *WhoBlA 94*
Alexander, Pamela *DrAPF 93*
Alexander, Pamela Gayle 1952- *WhoBlA 94*
Alexander, Patricia Ross 1955- *WhoFI 94*
Alexander, Patrick Byron 1950- *WhoAm 94*
Alexander, Patrick Desmond William C. *Who 94*
Alexander, Patrick James 1926- *WrDr 94*
Alexander, Paul Crayton 1946- *WhoBlA 94*
Alexander, Paul Donald 1934- *Who 94*
Alexander, Peter 1939- *WhoAmA 93*
Alexander, Peter Houston 1939- *WhoAm 94*
Alexander, Preston Paul, Jr. 1952- *WhoBlA 94*
Alexander, Ralph *IntMPA 94*
Alexander, Ralph William, Jr. 1941- *WhoAm 94, WhoMW 93*
Alexander, Ric *BlkWr 2, ConAu 42NR*
Alexander, Richard d1989 *WhoHol 92*
Alexander, Richard 1944- *WhoAmL 94*
Alexander, Richard C. 1935- *AfrAmG*
Alexander, Richard Elmont 1924- *WhoAmL 94, WhoMW 93*
Alexander, Richard John 1948- *WhoAmL 94*
Alexander, Richard L. 1947- *WhoAmL 94*
Alexander, Richard Thain 1934- *Who 94*
Alexander, Robb Smith, Jr. 1955- *WhoWest 94*
Alexander, Robert 1739?-1805 *WhAmRev*
Alexander, Robert 1923- *WrDr 94*
Alexander, Robert C. 1947- *WhoAm 94, WhoAmL 94*
Alexander, Robert Darwood 1944- *WhoAmP 93*
Alexander, Robert Earl 1939- *WhoAm 94*
Alexander, Robert I. 1913- *WhoBlA 94*
Alexander, Robert J(ackson) 1918- *WrDr 94*
Alexander, Robert Jackson 1918- *WhoAm 94, WhoFI 94*
Alexander, Robert Love d1993 *Who 94N*
Alexander, Robert McNeill 1934- *IntWW 93*
Alexander, Robert Seymour 1923- *WhoAmA 93*
Alexander, Robert W(illiams) 1905-1980 *EncSF 93*
Alexander, Roberta 1949- *AfrAmAl 6 [port], NewGrDO*
Alexander, Robin 1950- *WhoBlA 94*
Alexander, Rod 1920- *WhoHol 92*
Alexander, Rodney 1946- *WhoAmP 93*
Alexander, Roger Brian 1944- *WhoFI 94*
Alexander, Ronald Algernon 1950- *WhoBlA 94*
Alexander, Roosevelt Maurice 1941- *WhoBlA 94*
Alexander, Rosa M. 1928- *WhoBlA 94*
Alexander, Rosemary Elizabeth 1926- *WhoAm 94*
Alexander, Ross d1937 *WhoHol 92*
Alexander, Roy 1928- *ConAu 42NR*
Alexander, Roy 1930- *WhoAm 94*
Alexander, Samuel Allen, Jr. 1938- *WhoAm 94, WhoFI 94*
Alexander, Samuel Craighead 1930- *WhoAm 94*
Alexander, Samuel P. *WhoHisp 94*
Alexander, Sander Peter 1929- *WhoAm 94*
Alexander, Sara d1927 *WhoHol 92*
Alexander, Scott Kevin 1954- *WhoAmP 93*
Alexander, Shana 1925- *WhoAm 94, WrDr 94*
Alexander, Sidney H., Jr. 1919- *WhoBlA 94*
Alexander, Stephen Winthrop 1941- *WhoMW 93*
Alexander, Steve 1944- *WhoFI 94*
Alexander, Sue 1933- *WrDr 94*
Alexander, Susan Greig 1930- *WhoAmP 93*
Alexander, Suzanne d1975 *WhoHol 92*
Alexander, Terence 1923- *WhoHol 92*
Alexander, Terrance Glenn 1954- *WhoMW 93*
Alexander, Tessa Elizabeth 1954- *WhoWest 94*
Alexander, Theodore Martin, Sr. 1909- *WhoBlA 94*
Alexander, Theodore Thomas, Jr. 1937- *WhoBlA 94*
Alexander, Theodore William, III 1945- *WhoFI 94*
Alexander, Theron *WhoAm 94, WhoScEn 94, WhoWest 94*
Alexander, Thomas Benjamin 1918- *WhoAm 94*
Alexander, Thomas C. 1956- *WhoAmP 93*
Alexander, Thomas Glen 1935- *WhoAm 94*
Alexander, Thomas John 1940- *Who 94*
Alexander, Thomas Stern 1951- *WhoMW 93*
Alexander, Tice d1993 *NewYTBS 93*
Alexander, Tim c. 1965- *See* Primus *ConMus 11*
Alexander, Todd Raymond 1959- *WhoMW 93*
Alexander, Vera 1932- *WhoAm 94*
Alexander, Victor Joe 1969- *WhoBlA 94*
Alexander, Victor Theodore 1956- *WhoFI 94*
Alexander, Vikky M. 1959- *WhoAmA 93*
Alexander, W(alter) Boyd 1898- *WhAm 10*
Alexander, Walter Gilbert, II 1922- *WhoBlA 94*
Alexander, Walter Ronald 1931- *Who 94*
Alexander, Wardine Towers 1955- *WhoBlA 94*
Alexander, Warren Dornell 1921- *WhoBlA 94*
Alexander, Warren Perry 1962- *WhoMW 93*
Alexander, Wayne Andrew 1951- *WhoScEn 94*
Alexander, Wick *WhoAmA 93*
Alexander, William 1567-1640 *BlmGEL*
Alexander, William 1726-1783 *AmRev, WhAmRev [port]*
Alexander, William B. 1921- *WhoAmP 93*
Alexander, William Brooks 1921- *WhoAm 94*
Alexander, William Cameron, II 1938- *WhoIns 94*
Alexander, William Carter 1937- *WhoAm 94*
Alexander, William D., III 1911- *WhoAm 94*
Alexander, William G. 1951- *WhoAmP 93*
Alexander, William Gemmell 1918- *Who 94*
Alexander, William H. 1930- *WhoAmP 93, WhoBlA 94*
Alexander, William Henry 1902- *WhoAm 94*
Alexander, William Henry 1930- *WhoAm 94*
Alexander, William Herbert 1941- *WhoAm 94*
Alexander, William M., Jr. 1928- *WhoBlA 94*
Alexander, William Nelson, II 1944- *WhoAmP 93*
Alexander, William Olin 1939- *WhoAm 94*
Alexander, William Patterson 1893- *WhAm 10*
Alexander, William Powell 1934- *WhoAm 94*
Alexander, William Robert 1967- *WhoScEn 94*
Alexander, William V., Jr. 1934- *WhoAmP 93*
Alexander, Willie *WhoBlA 94*
Alexander, Zachary Paul 1955- *WhoAmL 94*
Alexander-Bridges, Maria Carmalita 1952- *WhoScEn 94*
Alexander-Greene, Grace George 1918- *WhoAmA 93*
Alexander Karadjordjevic, H.R.H. Crown Prince of Yugoslavia 1945- *IntWW 93*
Alexander of Ballochmyle, Claud Hagart- 1927- *Who 94*
Alexander of Potterhill, Baron d1993 *Who 94N*
Alexander, of Potterhill, Baron 1905- *WrDr 94*
Alexander of Stainby d1238 *DcNaB MP*
Alexander Of Tunis, Earl 1935- *Who 94*
Alexander Of Weedon, Baron 1936- *IntWW 93, Who 94*
Alexander-Sinclair of Freswick, David Boyd 1927- *Who 94*
Alexanderson, Ernst Frederik Werner 1878-1975 *WorInv*
Alexanderson, Gerald L(ee) 1933- *ConAu 42NR*
Alexanderson, Gerald Lee 1933- *WhoAm 94*
Alexander the Great 356BC-323BC *BlmGEL*
Alexander the Great, III 356BC-323BC *HisWorL [port]*
Alexander the Mason fl. 1235-1257 *DcNaB MP*
Alexander-Whiting, Harriett 1947- *WhoBlA 94*
Alexandra, H.R.H. Princess *IntWW 93*
Alexandra, Princess 1936- *Who 94R*
Alexandra, Queen 1921-1993 *NewYTBS 93 [port]*
Alexandra, Tiana *WhoHol 92*
Alexandra The Great 356BC-323BC *WhWE [port]*
Alexandre, Charles-Guillaume c. 1735-1787? *NewGrDO*
Alexandre, Gilbert Fernand A.E. 1944- *WhoScEn 94*
Alexandre, Journel 1931- *WhoBlA 94*
Alexandre, Rene d1914 *WhoHol 92*
Alexandre, Roland d1956 *WhoHol 92*
Alexandris, Efstathios (Stathis) *IntWW 93*
Alexandroff, Mirron 1923- *WhoAm 94, WhoMW 93*
Alexandropoulos, Nikolaos 1934- *WhoScEn 94*
Alexandrov *IntWW 93*
Alexandrov, Anatoly Nikolayevich 1888-1982 *NewGrDO*
Alexanian, Raymond 1932- *WhoAm 94*
Alexeff, Igor 1931- *WhoAm 94*
Alexeieff, Alexander 1901-1979 *IntDcF 2-4*
Alexenberg, Mel 1937- *WhoAm 94, WhoAmA 93*
Alexeyev *IntWW 93*
Alexiadis, George 1911- *IntWW 93*
Alexick, David Francis 1942- *WhoAmA 93*
Alexiou, Elli 1898- *BlmGWL*
Alexiou, Margaret Beatrice 1939- *WhoAm 94*
Alexis, Austin *DrAPF 93*
Alexis, Carlton Peter 1929- *WhoBlA 94*
Alexis, Demetrios d1973 *WhoHol 92*
Alexis, Doris Virginia 1921- *WhoBlA 94*
Alexis, Francis 1947- *IntWW 93*
Alexis, Geraldine M. 1948- *WhoAm 94, WhoAmL 94*
Alexis, Laura 1964- *WhoHol 92*
Alexis, Marcus 1932- *WhoBlA 94*
Alexis, Marcus L., II 1959- *WhoFI 94*
Alexis, Willibald 1798-1871 *DcLB 133 [port]*
Alexis Master, The fl. 1125- *DcNaB MP*
Alexis of Piedmont c. 1471-1565 *EncSPD*
Alexopoulos, Helene *WhoAm 94*
Aley, Charles R. 1956- *WhoAmL 94, WhoFI 94*
Alf, Martha Joanne 1930- *WhoAmA 93*
Alfange, Dean 1897-1989 *WhAm 10*
Alfange, Dean, Jr. 1930- *WhoAm 94*
Alfano, Angel 1940- *WhoAmA 93*
Alfano, Blaise F. *WhoHisp 94*
Alfano, Blaise Francis 1923- *WhoAm 94*
Alfano, Charles Thomas, Sr. 1920- *WhoAm 94*
Alfano, Franco 1875-1954 *NewGrDO*
Alfano, Michael Charles 1947- *WhoAm 94, WhoScEn 94*
Alfano, Salvatore T. 1950- *WhoAmL 94*
Alfaro, Andreu 1929- *IntWW 93*
Alfaro, Armando Joffroy 1950- *WhoWest 94*
Alfaro, Armando Joffroy, Jr. 1950- *WhoHisp 94*
Alfaro, Felix Benjamin 1939- *WhoWest 94*
Alfaro, Ricardo 1961- *WhoHisp 94*
Alfaro-Garcia, Rafael 1941- *WhoHisp 94*
Alfaro-Lopez, Maria G. *WhoHisp 94*
Alfau, Felipe 1902- *WhoHisp 94*
Al Fayed, Mohamed 1933- *Who 94*
Alfers, Gerald Junior 1931- *WhoAm 94*
Alfers, Stephen Douglas 1945- *WhoAm 94, WhoAmL 94*
Alfert, Peter Wayne 1953- *WhoAmL 94*
Alff, Gregory Norman 1948- *WhoFI 94*
Alfidi, Ralph Joseph 1932- *WhoAm 94*
Alfidja, Abderrahmane 1942- *IntWW 93*
Alfieri, Lisa Gwyneth 1967- *WhoAm 94*
Alfieri, Vittorio 1749-1803 *IntDcT 2 [port]*
Alfiero, Giuseppe 1630-1665 *NewGrDO*
Alfiero, Salvatore Harry 1937- *WhoAm 94, WhoFI 94*
Alfini, James Joseph 1943- *WhoAmL 94*
Alfon, Estrella 1917-1982 *BlmGWL*
Alfonseca, Manuel 1946- *WhoScEn 94*
Alfonsi, William E. 1923- *WhoMW 93, WhoScEn 94*
Alfonsin, Raul Ricardo 1927- *Who 94*
Alfonsina *BlmGWL*
Alfonsin Foulkes, Raul 1926- *IntWW 93*
Alfonso, X 1221-1284 *HisWorL [port]*
Alfonso, Antonio Escolar 1943- *WhoAm 94*
Alfonso, Carlos *WhoHisp 94*
Alfonso, Eduardo C. *WhoHisp 94*
Alfonso, Elisa J. 1955- *WhoHisp 94*
Alfonso, Kristian *WhoHisp 94*
Alfonso, Marco 1954- *WhoHisp 94*
Alfonso, Pedro 1948- *WhoBlA 94*
Alfonso, Ricardo Manuel 1959- *WhoFI 94*
Alfonso, Robert John 1928- *WhoAm 94*
Alfonso, Roberta Jean *WhoMW 93*
Alford, Andrew 1904-1992 *WhAm 10*
Alford, B(ernard) W(illiam) E(rnest) 1937- *WrDr 94*
Alford, Bobby Ray 1932- *WhoAm 94*
Alford, Brenda 1947- *WhoBlA 94*
Alford, C(harles) Fred(erick) 1947- *WrDr 94*
Alford, Cheryl Purdin 1953- *WhoAmP 93*
Alford, Dallas L., Jr. *WhoAmP 93*
Alford, Dean 1953- *WhoAmP 93*
Alford, Donald Sutton 1950- *WhoAmP 93*
Alford, Duncan Earl 1963- *WhoAmL 94*
Alford, Edna 1947- *BlmGWL*
Alford, Edward c. 1565-c. 1631 *DcNaB MP*
Alford, Francis c. 1565-c. 1631 *DcNaB MP*
Alford, Geary Simmons 1945- *WhoAm 94*
Alford, Gloria K. 1928- *WhoAmA 93*
Alford, Haile Lorraine 1949- *WhoBlA 94*
Alford, J. Keith 1941- *WhoFI 94*
Alford, Jane Marie 1950- *WhoMW 93*
Alford, Joan Franz 1940- *WhoFI 94*
Alford, John Richard 1919- *Who 94*
Alford, John William 1912- *WhoAm 94*
Alford, Joseph Savage, Jr. 1943- *WhoScEn 94*
Alford, Kenneth J. 1930- *WhoAmP 93*
Alford, Margaret Suzanne 1953- *WhoAm 94*
Alford, Neill Herbert, Jr. 1919- *WhoAm 94, WhoAmL 94, WrDr 94*
Alford, Newell Gilder, Jr. 1920- *WhoAm 94*
Alford, Paul Legare 1930- *WhoAm 94*
Alford, Richard Harding 1943- *Who 94*
Alford, Robert Ross 1928- *WhoAm 94*
Alford, Sandra Elaine 1944- *WhoMW 93*
Alford, Thomas Earl 1935- *WhoAm 94, WhoBlA 94*
Alford, Walter Helion 1938- *WhoAm 94, WhoAmL 94, WhoFI 94*
Alford, William Parker 1927- *WhoAm 94*
Alford, Yvonne Marie 1936- *WhoAmP 93*
Alfred, King 849-899 *BlmGEL*
Alfred, Dewitt C., Jr. 1937- *WhoBlA 94*
Alfred, James Jourdan 1933- *WhoAmP 93*
Alfred, Karl Sverre 1917- *WhoAm 94*
Alfred, Lindbergh Davis 1948- *WhoWest 94*
Alfred, (Arnold) Montague 1925- *Who 94*
Alfred, Rayfield 1939- *WhoBlA 94*
Alfred, Stephen J. 1934- *WhoAmP 93*
Alfred, Stephen Jay 1934- *WhoAm 94*
Alfred, William 1922- *ConDr 93, WhoAm 94, WrDr 94*
Alfredsson, Mats Lennart 1946- *WhoScEn 94*

Allen, Adrienne 1907- *WhoHol 92*
Allen, Alex B. 1919- *WrDr 94*
Allen, Alex James, Jr. 1934- *WhoBlA 94*
Allen, Alexander J. 1916- *WhoBlA 94*
Allen, Alfred d1947 *WhoHol 92*
Allen, Alice Catherine Towsley 1924- *WhoAm 94*
Allen, Andrew 1740-1825 *WhAmRev*
Allen, Andrew A. 1921- *WhoBlA 94*
Allen, Anita Ford *WhoBlA 94*
Allen, Anna Foster 1901- *WhoAm 94*
Allen, Anna Marie 1955- *WhoMW 93*
Allen, Anthony John 1939- *Who 94*
Allen, Anthony Kenway 1917- *Who 94*
Allen, Arly Harrison 1938- *WhoMW 93*
Allen, Arnold Millman 1924- *Who 94*
Allen, Arthur d1947 *WhoHol 92*
Allen, Arthur D. d1949 *WhoAmA 93N*
Allen, Audrey Ann 1938- *WhoMW 93*
Allen, Barbara *WhoAmP 93*
Allen, Barbara Jo d1974 *WhoHol 92*
Allen, Barclay d1966 *WhoHol 92*
Allen, Barry Morgan 1939- *WhoFI 94*
Allen, Belle *WhoAm 94, WhoFI 94*
Allen, Ben Robert 1925- *WhoAmP 93*
Allen, Benjamin Curtis 1930- *WhoMW 93*
Allen, Benjamin P., III 1942- *WhoBlA 94*
Allen, Bernestine 1944- *WhoBlA 94*
Allen, Betsy *TwCYAW*
Allen, Bettie Jean 1926- *WhoBlA 94*
Allen, Betty *WhoAm 94, WhoBlA 94*
Allen, Betty (Louise) 1930- *NewGrDO*
Allen, Betty Lou 1930- *AfrAmAl 6*
Allen, Beulah Ream 1897- *WhAm 10*
Allen, Bill *WhoHol 92*
Allen, Billy R. 1945- *WhoBlA 94*
Allen, Blair Sidney 1952- *WhoBlA 94*
Allen, Bob d1989 *WhoHol 92*
Allen, Bob 1961- *SmATA 76 [port]*
Allen, Bob L. 1945- *WhoAmP 93*
Allen, Bonnie Lynn 1957- *WhoWest 94*
Allen, Brenda Foster 1947- *WhoBlA 94*
Allen, Browning E., Jr. 1925- *WhoBlA 94*
Allen, Bruce 1959- *WhoMW 93*
Allen, Bruce S. 1951- *WhoAmP 93*
Allen, Bruce Templeton 1938- *WhoAm 94*
Allen, Bruce Wayne 1953- *WhoAmA 93*
Allen, Burkley 1958- *WhoScEn 94*
Allen, Byron 1961- *ConTFT 11, WhoBlA 94*
Allen, Carol M. *WhoAmP 93*
Allen, Carol Ward *WhoBlA 94*
Allen, Carrol V. 1934- *WhoAmP 93*
Allen, Catherine MacDonald 1949- *WhoAmA 93*
Allen, Chad 1974- *WhoHol 92*
Allen, Charles Claybourne 1935- *WhoBlA 94*
Allen, Charles Curtis 1886-1950 *WhoAmA 93N*
Allen, Charles E. 1931- *WhoBlA 94*
Allen, Charles E., Jr. *WhoAmP 93*
Allen, Charles Edward 1947- *WhoBlA 94*
Allen, Charles Eugene 1939- *WhoAm 94, WhoMW 93, WhoScEn 94*
Allen, Charles H. *WhoAmP 93*
Allen, Charles Joseph, II 1917- *WhoAm 94*
Allen, Charles Lamb 1957- *Who 94*
Allen, Charles Lewis 1946- *WhoIns 94*
Allen, Charles Mengel 1916- *WhoAm 94, WhoAmL 94*
Allen, Charles Richard 1926- *WhoAm 94, WhoFI 94*
Allen, Charles William 1912- *WhoAm 94*
Allen, Charles William 1932- *WhoAm 94*
Allen, Charlotte Vale 1941- *BlmGWL, WrDr 94*
Allen, Chesney d1982 *WhoHol 92*
Allen, Chet d1984 *WhoHol 92*
Allen, Chris(topher) d1955 *WhoHol 92*
Allen, Christopher James 1964- *WhoWest 94*
Allen, Chuck *WhoAm 94, WhoWest 94*
Allen, Clarence Canning 1897-1989 *WhoAmA 93N*
Allen, Clarence Roderic 1925- *WhoAm 94*
Allen, Claxton Edmonds, III 1944- *WhoFI 94*
Allen, Clayton Hamilton 1918- *WhoScEn 94*
Allen, Clifford d1989 *WhoHol 92*
Allen, Clive Victor 1935- *WhoAm 94, WhoAmL 94, WhoFI 94*
Allen, Clyde Cecil 1943- *WhoBlA 94*
Allen, Colin Mervyn Gordon 1929- *Who 94*
Allen, Constance Olleen 1923- *WhoWest 94*
Allen, Constance Olleen Webb 1923- *WhoAmA 93*
Allen, Corey 1934- *IntMPA 94, WhoHol 92*
Allen, Craig Adams 1941- *WhoAmP 93*
Allen, D. Scott 1953- *WhoWest 94*
Allen, Dana Raymond 1953- *WhoWest 94*
Allen, Darryl Frank 1943- *WhoAm 94, WhoFI 94*
Allen, Dave d1955 *WhoHol 92*
Allen, David 1919- *WhAm 10*
Allen, David 1933- *Who 94*
Allen, David Charles 1944- *WhoWest 94*
Allen, David Christopher 1933- *WhoFI 94*
Allen, David Donald 1931- *WhoAm 94*
Allen, David Fairchild 1936- *WhoFI 94*
Allen, David Harlow 1930- *WhoWest 94*
Allen, David James 1935- *WhoAm 94, WhoAmL 94*
Allen, David Murray 1946- *WhoAmL 94*
Allen, David Russell 1942- *WhoAm 94*
Allen, David Woodroffe 1944- *WhoFI 94, WhoScEn 94*
Allen, Dayton 1919- *IntMPA 94, WhoCom*
Allen, Dean Ellis 1950- *WhoWest 94*
Allen, Debbie *WhoAm 94*
Allen, Debbie 1949- *WhoHol 92*
Allen, Debbie 1950- *AfrAmAl 6 [port], IntMPA 94, WhoBlA 94*
Allen, Deborah *DrAPF 93*
Allen, Deborah Colleen 1950- *WhoAmP 93*
Allen, Dede 1924- *IntMPA 94*
Allen, Dede 1925- *IntDcF 2-4*
Allen, Delmas James 1937- *WhoAm 94*
Allen, DeMetrice Michealle 1958- *WhoBlA 94*
Allen, Deryck Norman de Garrs 1918- *Who 94*
Allen, Dick *DrAPF 93*
Allen, Dick 1938- *WhoAmP 93*
Allen, Dick 1939- *WrDr 94*
Allen, Diogenes 1932- *WhoAm 94, WrDr 94*
Allen, Don Lee 1934- *WhoAm 94*
Allen, Donald Clinton 1931- *WhoAm 94*
Allen, Donald George 1930- *Who 94*
Allen, Donald Phillip 1928- *WhoWest 94*
Allen, Donald Vail 1928- *WhoAm 94, WhoFI 94, WhoWest 94*
Allen, Donald Wayne 1936- *WhoWest 94*
Allen, Doris 1936- *WhoAmP 93, WhoWest 94*
Allen, Dorothy d1970 *WhoHol 92*
Allen, Douglas Albert Vivian *IntWW 93*
Allen, Douglas Bruce 1955- *WhoWest 94*
Allen, Dozier T., Jr. 1931- *WhoAmP 93, WhoBlA 94*
Allen, Drew 1918- *WhoHol 92*
Allen, Duane David 1943- *WhoAm 94*
Allen, Duane Edward 1932- *WhoFI 94*
Allen, Duff Shederic, Jr. 1928- *WhoScEn 94*
Allen, Durward L(eon) 1910- *WrDr 94*
Allen, Durward Leon 1910- *WhoAm 94, WhoMW 93*
Allen, E. H. d1942 *WhoHol 92*
Allen, Edda Lynne 1932- *WhoAmA 93*
Allen, Eddie Dale *WhoFI 94*
Allen, Edgar Burns 1929- *WhoWest 94*
Allen, Edna Rowery 1938- *WhoBlA 94*
Allen, Edward *DrAPF 93*
Allen, Edward Jones 1898- *WhAm 10*
Allen, Edward Raymond 1913- *WhoWest 94*
Allen, Edwin 1919- *WrDr 94*
Allen, Elbert E. 1921- *WhoBlA 94*
Allen, Elias c. 1588-1653 *DcNaB MP*
Allen, Elizabeth 1934- *WhoHol 92*
Allen, Eric 1916- *WrDr 94*
Allen, Eric Andre 1965- *WhoAm 94*
Allen, Ernest, Sr. 1932- *WhoAmP 93*
Allen, Ernest Eugene 1946- *WhoAm 94*
Allen, Ernest Marvin, III 1949- *WhoAmL 94*
Allen, Estelle d1970 *WhoHol 92*
Allen, Esther Louisa 1912- *WhoBlA 94*
Allen, Ethan d1940 *WhoHol 92*
Allen, Ethan d1993 *NewYTBS 93*
Allen, Ethan 1738-1789 *AmRev, DcAmReB 2, HisWorL [port], WhAmRev*
Allen, Ethan (Nathan) 1904-1993 *CurBio 93N*
Allen, Ethan Burdette, III 1954- *WhoAmL 94*
Allen, Eugene, Jr. 1937- *WhoBlA 94*
Allen, Eugene Murray 1916- *WhoAm 94*
Allen, F.M. 1856-1937 *EncSF 93*
Allen, Fergus Hamilton 1921- *Who 94*
Allen, Frances Elizabeth 1932- *WhoAm 94*
Allen, Frances Michael 1939- *WhoFI 94*
Allen, Francis c. 1583-1658 *DcNaB MP*
Allen, Francis A. 1919- *WrDr 94*
Allen, Francis Andrew 1933- *Who 94*
Allen, Frank Carroll 1913- *WhoAm 94*
Allen, Frank Clinton, Jr. 1933- *WhoAm 94, WhoAmL 94*
Allen, Frank Graham 1920- *Who 94*
Allen, Fred d1956 *WhoHol 92*
Allen, Fred 1894-1956 *WhoCom*
Allen, Fred Cary 1917- *WhoAm 94*
Allen, Frederic W. 1926- *WhoAm 94, WhoAmL 94, WhoAmP 93*
Allen, Frederick Graham 1923- *WhoScEn 94*
Allen, Frederick Lewis 1890-1954 *DcLB 137 [port]*
Allen, Frederick Warner 1947- *WhoAm 94*
Allen, G. M. *WhoAmP 93*
Allen, Gail Cooper 1960- *WhoWest 94*
Allen, Garland Edward 1936- *WhoAm 94*
Allen, Gary Curtiss 1939- *WhoAm 94*
Allen, Gary James 1944- *IntWW 93, Who 94*
Allen, Gay Wilson 1903- *WrDr 94*
Allen, Geoffrey 1928- *IntWW 93, Who 94*
Allen, George 1922-1990 *WhAm 10*
Allen, George 1952- *WhoAm 94*
Allen, George 1955- *WhoBlA 94*
Allen, George B. d1993 *NewYTBS 93*
Allen, George Felix 1952- *WhoAmP 93*
Allen, George Howard 1914- *WhoAm 94*
Allen, George James 1944- *WhoAm 94*
Allen, George Louis 1910- *WhoBlA 94*
Allen, George Mitchell 1932- *WhoBlA 94*
Allen, George Sewell 1942- *WhoAm 94*
Allen, George Venable, Jr. 1935- *WhoAm 94*
Allen, George W. 1937- *WhoAm 94*
Allen, Georgia *WhoHol 92*
Allen, Geri 1957- *ConMus 10 [port]*
Allen, Gilbert *DrAPF 93*
Allen, Gina *WhoAm 94*
Allen, Gina 1918- *ConAu 43NR*
Allen, Gladstone Wesley 1915- *WhoBlA 94*
Allen, Gloria Marie *WhoBlA 94*
Allen, Gordon 1945- *WhoAmP 93*
Allen, Gordon E. *WhoAm 94, WhoFI 94*
Allen, Grace 1905- *WrDr 94*
Allen, Gracie d1964 *WhoHol 92*
Allen, Graham William 1953- *Who 94*
Allen, (Charles) Grant (Blairfindie) 1848-1899 *EncSF 93*
Allen, Griffin Marion, Jr. 1966- *WhoMW 93*
Allen, Hamish McEwan 1920- *Who 94*
Allen, Hannah (Archer) *BlmGWL*
Allen, (Harvey) Harold 1912- *WhoAmA 93*
Allen, Harriette Louise 1943- *WhoBlA 94*
Allen, Harry d1951 *WhoHol 92*
Allen, Harry Cranbrook 1917- *Who 94, WrDr 94*
Allen, Harry Roger 1933- *WhoAmL 94*
Allen, Heath Ledward 1927- *WhoAm 94*
Allen, Heather Wild 1959- *WhoWest 94*
Allen, Henry Joseph 1931- *WhoFI 94*
Allen, Henry Robinson 1809-1876 *NewGrDO*
Allen, Henry Sermones, Jr. 1947- *WhoAmL 94*
Allen, Henry Tureman 1859-1930 *WhWE*
Allen, Henry Wesley 1927- *WhoScEn 94*
Allen, Henry Wilson 1912- *WrDr 94*
Allen, Henry Wilson 1912-1991 *EncSF 93*
Allen, Herbert 1907- *WhAm 10*
Allen, Herbert 1908- *WhoAm 94, WhoFI 94*
Allen, Herbert Ellis 1939- *WhoAm 94*
Allen, Herbert J. 1922- *WhoBlA 94*
Allen, Hilary P. 1911- *WhoAmP 93*
Allen, Hilda d1986 *WhoHol 92*
Allen, Howard Norman 1936- *WhoWest 94*
Allen, Howard Pfeiffer 1925- *WhoAm 94, WhoWest 94*
Allen, Howard Wilson 1931- *WhoMW 93*
Allen, Ingrid Victoria 1932- *Who 94*
Allen, Ira 1751-1814 *WhAmRev*
Allen, Irwin d1991 *WhAm 10*
Allen, Irwin 1916-1991 *EncSF 93*
Allen, Isaac d1806 *WhAmRev*
Allen, Ivan, Jr. 1911- *WhoAm 94*
Allen, J(oseph) Garrott 1912-1992 *WhAm 10*
Allen, Jack d1961 *WhoHol 92*
Allen, Jack 1907- *WhoHol 92*
Allen, Jacob Benjamin, III 1927- *WhoBlA 94*
Allen, Jacque *WhoAmP 93*
Allen, James d1777 *WhAmRev*
Allen, James 1938- *WhoAmP 93*
Allen, James, Jr. *WhoBlA 94*
Allen, James B. *DrAPF 93*
Allen, James Edward 1943- *WhoAmP 93*
Allen, James H. 1934- *WhoBlA 94*
Allen, James Harmon, Jr. 1948- *WhoScEn 94*
Allen, James Henry 1935- *WhoAm 94, WhoAmL 94*
Allen, James L. 1936- *WhoScEn 94*
Allen, James Lee 1952- *WhoAm 94*
Allen, James Lovic, Jr. 1929- *WhoAm 94*
Allen, James Madison 1944- *WhoAm 94, WhoScEn 94*
Allen, James Norman, Jr. 1958- *WhoMW 93*
Allen, James R. 1925-1992 *WhAm 10*
Allen, James Samuel 1941- *WhoAm 94*
Allen, James Trinton 1924- *WhoBlA 94*
Allen, Jane d1970 *WhoHol 92*
Allen, Jane Addams *WhoAmA 93*
Allen, Jane Elizabeth 1945- *WhoBlA 94*
Allen, Jane Mengel 1888-1952 *WhoAmA 93N*
Allen, Janet Louise 1935- *WhoMW 93*
Allen, Janet Rosemary 1936- *Who 94*
Allen, Jay Frederic 1950- *WhoMW 93*
Allen, Jay Presson 1922- *IntDcF 2-4, IntMPA 94, WhoAm 94*
Allen, Jeanette Mary 1958- *WhoWest 94*
Allen, Jeanie Untersinger 1963- *WhoWest 94*
Allen, Jeffrey Dee 1957- *WhoFI 94*
Allen, Jeffrey Michael 1948- *WhoAm 94, WhoAmL 94*
Allen, Jeffrey Rodgers 1953- *WhoAmL 94*
Allen, Jere Hardy 1944- *WhoAmA 93*
Allen, Jerry Pat 1932- *WhoScEn 94*
Allen, Jesse 1936- *WhoAmA 93*
Allen, Jesse Owen, III 1938- *WhoAm 94, WhoFI 94*
Allen, Jill Pelletier 1955- *WhoAmL 94*
Allen, Jim *WhoAmP 93*
Allen, Joan 1956- *IntMPA 94, WhoHol 92*
Allen, Joanna Cowan 1951- *WhoAmL 94*
Allen, Joe d1955 *WhoHol 92*
Allen, Joe B. 1943- *WhoAmL 94*
Allen, Joe Bailey, III 1951- *WhoAmL 94*
Allen, Johannes 1916-1973 *EncSF 93*
Allen, John d1778 *WhAmRev*
Allen, John Anthony 1926- *Who 94*
Allen, John David 1957- *WhoWest 94*
Allen, John E(lliston) 1921- *WrDr 94*
Allen, John Edward 1932- *Who 94*
Allen, John Frank 1908- *IntWW 93, Who 94*
Allen, John Geoffrey Robyn 1923- *Who 94*
Allen, John Henry 1938- *WhoBlA 94*
Allen, John Hunter *Who 94*
Allen, John Jay 1932- *WrDr 94*
Allen, John Joseph, Jr. 1899- *WhoAmP 93*
Allen, John Kelsey 1950- *WhoWest 94*
Allen, John Logan 1941- *WhoAm 94*
Allen, John Loyd 1931- *WhoAm 94*
Allen, John Neville 1922- *WhoAmP 93*
Allen, John Piers 1912- *Who 94*
Allen, John Robert Lawrence 1932- *IntWW 93, Who 94*
Allen, John Rybolt L. 1926- *WhoScEn 94*
Allen, John Thomas, Jr. 1935- *WhoAmL 94, WhoFI 94*
Allen, John Walter 1928- *IntWW 93*
Allen, Jonathan Dean 1956- *WhoScEn 94*
Allen, Jonelle 1950- *WhoHol 92*
Allen, Jose R. 1951- *WhoAm 94*
Allen, Joseph d1917 *WhoHol 92*
Allen, Joseph, Sr. d1952 *WhoHol 92*
Allen, Joseph, Jr. d1962 *WhoHol 92*
Allen, Joseph B., Jr. 1914- *WhoAmP 93*
Allen, Joseph D., III 1945- *WhoIns 94*
Allen, Joseph Dulles 1945- *WhoAmL 94*
Allen, Joseph Henry 1916- *WhoAm 94*
Allen, Joseph Stanley 1898- *Who 94*
Allen, Joyce Smith 1939- *WhoMW 93*
Allen, Judith *WhoHol 92*
Allen, Judith Elaine 1942- *WhoAmL 94*
Allen, Judith S. 1956- *WhoAmA 93*
Allen, Julian Myrick, Jr. 1956- *WhoFI 94*
Allen, Junius 1898-1962 *WhoAmA 93N*
Allen, Kaola 1952- *WhoAmA 93*
Allen, Karen 1951- *IntMPA 94, WhoHol 92*
Allen, Karen Jane 1951- *WhoAm 94*
Allen, Katherine Yarnell 1925- *WhAm 10*
Allen, Kathryn Adams Lloyd 1943- *WhoAmL 94*
Allen, Kay-Dawn Gable 1961- *WhoAmL 94*
Allen, Kenneth *Who 94*
Allen, Kenneth d1976 *WhoHol 92*
Allen, (William) Kenneth (Gwynne) 1907- *Who 94*
Allen, Kenneth Dale 1939- *WhoAm 94, WhoAmL 94*
Allen, Kenneth William 1923- *Who 94*
Allen, L(ouis) David 1940- *WrDr 94*
Allen, Lana Sue 1958- *WhoMW 93*
Allen, Larry Rollar 1937- *WhoFI 94*
Allen, Laura Jean *WrDr 94*
Allen, Laurie Catherine 1948- *WhoAm 94*
Allen, Lawrence David, Jr. 1952- *WhoFI 94*
Allen, Layman Edward 1927- *WhoMW 93*
Allen, Leatrice Delorice 1948- *WhoMW 93, WhoScEn 94*
Allen, Lee 1927- *WhoAmP 93*
Allen, Lee Harrison 1924- *WhoAm 94, WhoFI 94*
Allen, Lee Norcross 1926- *WhoAm 94*
Allen, Leilani Eleanor 1949- *WhoFI 94, WhoMW 93*
Allen, Leon Arthur, Jr. 1933- *WhoAm 94*
Allen, Leonard Brown 1932- *WhoMW 93*
Allen, Leslie 1935- *WhoScEn 94*
Allen, Leslie 1958- *WhoAmL 94*
Allen, Lester d1949 *WhoHol 92*
Allen, Levi *AmRev*

Allen, Lew, Jr. 1925- *IntWW 93, WhoAm 94, WhoWest 94*
Allen, Lewis 1905- *IntMPA 94*
Allen, Lewis M. 1922- *IntMPA 94*
Allen, Linda Graves 1959- *WhoMW 93*
Allen, Linda Kay 1944- *WhoWest 94*
Allen, Lisa Brenner 1958- *WhoMW 93*
Allen, Lois Arlene Height 1932- *WhoMW 93*
Allen, Loretta B. *WhoAmA 93*
Allen, Louis 1922- *WrDr 94*
Allen, Louis Alexander 1917- *WhoAm 94*
Allen, Lyle Wallace 1924- *WhoAm 94*
Allen, Malcolm d1993 *NewYTBS 93*
Allen, Marcus 1924- *WhoBlA 94*
Allen, Marcus 1960- *WhoAm 94, WhoBlA 94, WhoMW 93, WhoWest 94*
Allen, Margo 1894-1988 *WhoAmA 93N*
Allen, Marilyn Myers Pool 1934- *WhoAm 94*
Allen, Marion H., III 1945- *WhoAmL 94*
Allen, Mark Echalaz 1917- *Who 94*
Allen, Marshall Bonner, Jr. 1927- *WhoScEn 94*
Allen, Martin 1918- *WhoMW 93*
Allen, Marty 1922- *WhoHol 92*
See Also Allen and Rossi *WhoCom*
Allen, Mary 1951- *Who 94*
Allen, Mary Stockbridge 1869-1949 *WhoAmA 93N*
Allen, Maryon Pittman *WhoAmP 93*
Allen, Maryon Pittman 1925- *WhoAm 94*
Allen, Matthew d1845 *EncSPD*
Allen, Matthew Arnold 1930- *WhoAm 94*
Allen, Maude d1956 *WhoHol 92*
Allen, Maude Pierce d1960 *WhoHol 92*
Allen, Maurice Bartelle, Jr. 1926- *WhoAm 94*
Allen, Maxine Bogues 1942- *WhoBlA 94*
Allen, Mel 1913- *IntMPA 94*
Allen, Merle Maeser, Jr. 1932- *WhoAm 94*
Allen, Merrill James 1945- *WhoScEn 94, WhoWest 94*
Allen, Michael A. 1951- *WhoAmL 94*
Allen, Michael Graham 1950- *WhoAm 94*
Allen, Michael John Bridgman 1941- *WhoAm 94*
Allen, Michael Lewis 1937- *WhoAm 94*
Allen, Michael Robert 1945- *WhoWest 94*
Allen, Michael W. 1948- *WhoAm 94*
Allen, Michael Wayne 1958- *WhoWest 94*
Allen, Mildred Mesch *WhoHisp 94*
Allen, Minerva *DrAPF 93*
Allen, Minnie Louise 1956- *WhoBlA 94*
Allen, Monty Dean 1965- *WhoMW 93*
Allen, Monty Kemp 1952- *WhoFI 94*
Allen, Nancy 1950- *IntMPA 94, WhoHol 92*
Allen, Nancy Schuster 1948- *WhoAm 94, WhoAmA 93*
Allen, Nelson Robert 1932- *WhoAmP 93*
Allen, Newton Perkins 1922- *WhoAm 94, WhoAmL 94*
Allen, Nicholas Eugene 1907- *WhoAm 94*
Allen, Nina Stromgren 1935- *WhoScEn 94*
Allen, Norman *Who 94*
Allen, (Harold) Norman (Gwynne) 1912- *Who 94*
Allen, Norman Lynn 1934- *WhoMW 93*
Allen, Ottis Eugene, Jr. 1953- *WhoBlA 94*
Allen, Pamela Kay 1934- *BlmGWL*
Allen, Pamela Suzanne DeCamp 1959- *WhoMW 93*
Allen, Patrick 1927- *WhoHol 92*
Allen, Patrick Michael 1962- *WhoWest 94*
Allen, Paul *WhoWest 94*
Allen, Paul Alfred 1948- *WhoAmL 94*
Allen, Paul C. 1952- *WhoScEn 94*
Allen, Paul Howard 1954- *WhoFI 94*
Allen, Paula Gunn *DrAPF 93*
Allen, Paula Gunn 1939- *BlmGWL, GayLL, WrDr 94*
Allen, Penelope *WhoHol 92*
Allen, Penny 1947- *WhoWest 94*
Allen, Percival 1917- *IntWW 93, Who 94*
Allen, Percy, II 1941- *WhoAm 94, WhoBlA 94*
Allen, Peter 1944-1992 *AnObit 1992, ConMus 11 [port], ConTFT 11*
Allen, Peter (Austin Philip Jermyn) 1929- *Who 94*
Allen, Peter (Christopher) 1905- *WrDr 94*
Allen, Peter Ackerman 1940- *WhoAm 94*
Allen, Peter Christopher d1993 *IntWW 93N, Who 94N*
Allen, Peter William 1938- *Who 94*
Allen, Philip 1939- *WhoHol 92*
Allen, Philip C. 1936- *WhoBlA 94*
Allen, Philip Michael 1956- *WhoMW 93*
Allen, Phillip E. 1931- *WhoAm 94, WhoFI 94*
Allen, Phillip R. 1939- *ConTFT 11*
Allen, Phillip Stephen 1952- *WhoAmL 94, WhoFI 94*
Allen, Phog 1885- *BasBi*
Allen, Phylicia *WhoHol 92*
Allen, Phyllis d1938 *WhoHol 92*
Allen, Pinney L. 1953- *WhoAmL 94*
Allen, R. G. d1981 *WhoHol 92*
Allen, R(eginald) L(ancelot) M(ountford) 1909- *WrDr 94*
Allen, Rae 1927- *WhoHol 92*
Allen, Ralph 1926- *WhoAmA 93*
Allen, Ralph Dean 1941- *WhoAm 94*
Allen, Ralph G. 1934- *ConTFT 11*
Allen, Ralph Gilmore 1934- *WhoAm 94*
Allen, Rand L. 1946- *WhoAmL 94*
Allen, Randall W. 1950- *WhoMW 93*
Allen, Randy Lee 1946- *WhoAm 94*
Allen, Ray 1950- *WhoAmP 93*
Allen, Raymond H. 1960- *WhoMW 93*
Allen, Rex 1922- *IntMPA 94, WhoHol 92*
Allen, Rex Whitaker 1914- *WhoAm 94*
Allen, Rhouis Eric 1964- *WhoScEn 94*
Allen, Ricca d1949 *WhoHol 92*
Allen, Richard 1760-1831 *AfrAmAl 6, AmSocL, DcAmReB 2*
Allen, Richard 1937- *WhoWest 94*
Allen, Richard (Hugh Sedley) 1903- *Who 94*
Allen, (Philip) Richard (Hernaman) 1949- *Who 94*
Allen, Richard Allison 1945- *WhoAmL 94*
Allen, Richard Blose 1919- *WhoAm 94, WhoAmL 94*
Allen, Richard C. 1926- *WhoAm 94*
Allen, Richard Charles 1939- *WhoAm 94*
Allen, Richard Dean 1935- *WhoWest 94*
Allen, Richard Edward 1946- *WhoMW 93*
Allen, Richard Eugene 1938- *WhoWest 94*
Allen, Richard G. 1946- *WhoAmL 94*
Allen, Richard Garrett 1923- *WhoAm 94*
Allen, Richard Ian Gordon 1944- *Who 94*
Allen, Richard Marlow 1940- *WhoAm 94, WhoAmL 94*
Allen, Richard Stanley 1939- *WhoAm 94*
Allen, Richard V. 1936- *IntWW 93*
Allen, Richard Vincent 1936- *WhoAm 94*
Allen, Richie 1942- *WhoBlA 94*
Allen, Rick 1941- *WhoWest 94*
Allen, Robert *DrAPF 93*
Allen, Robert 1906- *WhoHol 92*
Allen, Robert Barton 1950- *WhoAm 94*
Allen, Robert C(lyde) 1950- *ConAu 41NR*
Allen, Robert Dee 1928- *WhoAm 94, WhoAmL 94*
Allen, Robert E. 1937- *WhoIns 94*
Allen, Robert English 1945- *WhoFI 94*
Allen, Robert Eugene 1935- *WhoAm 94, WhoFI 94*
Allen, Robert Eugene Barton 1940- *WhoAmL 94, WhoFI 94, WhoWest 94*
Allen, Robert Hugh 1924- *WhoAm 94*
Allen, Robert L. 1942- *WhoBlA 94*
Allen, Robert S. 1931- *WhoAmP 93*
Allen, Robert Shaw 1931- *WhoAmL 94*
Allen, Robert Smith 1924- *WhoAm 94*
Allen, Roberta *DrAPF 93*
Allen, Roberta 1945- *WhoAmA 93*
Allen, Roberta L. 1945- *WhoAm 94*
Allen, Rocelia J. 1924- *WhoAm 94*
Allen, Roger Kay 1951- *WhoWest 94*
Allen, Roger MacBride 1957- *EncSF 93*
Allen, Roger Williams 1897-1990 *WhAm 10*
Allen, Ronald d1991 *WhoHol 92*
Allen, Ronald Carl 1953- *WhoWest 94*
Allen, Ronald Duane 1946- *WhoMW 93*
Allen, Ronald James 1956- *WhoAmL 94*
Allen, Ronald John 1940- *WhoAm 94*
Allen, Ronald Royce 1930- *WhoAm 94*
Allen, Ronald W. 1941- *WhoAm 94, WhoFI 94*
Allen, Rose d1977 *WhoHol 92*
Allen, Roy Leon 1950- *WhoAmP 93*
Allen, Roy O., Jr. 1921-1992 *WhAm 10*
Allen, Roy Verl 1933- *WhoWest 94*
Allen, Russell G. 1946- *WhoAmL 94*
Allen, Russell Plowman 1951- *WhoAm 94, WhoWest 94*
Allen, Ryne Cunliffe 1962- *WhoScEn 94*
Allen, S. Monique Nicole 1964- *WhoBlA 94*
Allen, Sally Lyman 1926- *WhoAm 94*
Allen, Sally Rothfus 1941- *WhoWest 94*
Allen, Sam d1934 *WhoHol 92*
Allen, Sam Raymond 1953- *WhoWest 94*
Allen, Samuel W. *DrAPF 93*
Allen, Samuel Washington 1917- *WhoBlA 94*
Allen, Sanford 1939- *WhoBlA 94*
Allen, Sarah A. *BlkWr 2, ConAu 141*
Allen, Scott 1933- *WhoWest 94*
Allen, Sebastian Gerald 1964- *WhoMW 93*
Allen, Seth d1986 *WhoHol 92*
Allen, Sheila 1932- *WhoHol 92*
Allen, Sheila Rosalynd 1942- *WrDr 94*
Allen, Shirley Jeanne 1941- *WhoBlA 94*
Allen, Sian Barbara 1946- *WhoHol 92*
Allen, Sonia *WhoHisp 94*
Allen, Stanley M. 1941- *WhoBlA 94*
Allen, Stephen D. 1953- *WhoWest 94*
Allen, Stephen Dean 1943- *WhoAm 94, WhoMW 93, WhoScEn 94*
Allen, Stephen Louis 1956- *WhoScEn 94*
Allen, Stephen Valentine Patrick William 1921- *WhoAm 94*
Allen, Steve 1921- *IntMPA 94, WhoCom [port], WhoHol 92, WrDr 94*
Allen, Steven A. 1949- *WhoAmL 94*
Allen, Steven Joe 1956- *WhoAmP 93*
Allen, Steven Paul 1958- *WhoScEn 94*
Allen, Stuart 1943- *WhoFI 94*
Allen, Sture 1928- *IntWW 93*
Allen, Susan Au 1946- *WhoAsA 94*
Allen, Susan D. 1944- *WhoAmP 93*
Allen, Susan Macall 1944- *WhoWest 94*
Allen, T. Diener *DrAPF 93*
Allen, Terrell Allison, III 1959- *WhoBlA 94*
Allen, Terry 1943- *WhoAmA 93*
Allen, Terry Devereux 1930- *WhoAm 94*
Allen, Theodore Earl 1939- *WhoFI 94*
Allen, Theodore John 1960- *WhoMW 93*
Allen, Theresa Ohotnicky 1948- *WhoAm 94*
Allen, Thomas *WhoAmP 93*
Allen, Thomas d1684 *EncSPD*
Allen, Thomas 1944- *IntWW 93, Who 94*
Allen, Thomas (Boaz) 1944- *NewGrDO*
Allen, Thomas Atherton 1949- *WhoAm 94*
Allen, Thomas Draper 1926- *WhoAm 94, WhoAmL 94*
Allen, Thomas E. 1919- *WhoAm 94, WhoScEn 94*
Allen, Thomas G. 1945- *WhoBlA 94*
Allen, Thomas John 1931- *WhoAm 94*
Allen, Thomas Lavern 1947- *WhoWest 94*
Allen, Thomas Oscar 1914-1989 *WhAm 10*
Allen, Tim *WhoAm 94*
Allen, Timothy Andrew 1955- *WhoAm 94*
Allen, Timothy Burbank 1956- *WhoWest 94*
Allen, Toby 1941- *WhoAm 94*
Allen, Todd 1960- *WhoHol 92*
Allen, Tom, Jr. 1927- *WhoAmA 93*
Allen, Tom L. *WhoAmP 93*
Allen, Toni K. 1940- *WhoAm 94, WhoAmL 94*
Allen, Ty W. 1961- *WhoBlA 94*
Allen, Van Sizar 1926- *WhoBlA 94*
Allen, Vera d1987 *WhoHol 92*
Allen, Viola d1948 *WhoHol 92*
Allen, W. George 1936- *WhoBlA 94*
Allen, W(illiam) Stannard 1913- *WrDr 94*
Allen, Walter (Ernest) 1911- *WrDr 94*
Allen, Walter Brown 1946- *WhoMW 93*
Allen, Walter Ernest 1911- *IntWW 93, Who 94*
Allen, Walter John Gardener 1916- *Who 94*
Allen, Walter R. 1930- *WhoBlA 94*
Allen, Warren Carlyle, Jr. 1942- *WhoMW 93*
Allen, Wayne W. 1936- *WhoAm 94, WhoFI 94*
Allen, Wendell 1947- *WhoBlA 94*
Allen, Wilbur Coleman 1925- *WhoAmL 94*
Allen, Willard C. 1940- *WhoAmP 93*
Allen, William *DrAPF 93*
Allen, William (Guilford) 1932- *Who 94*
Allen, William (the Elder) c. 1704-1780 *WhAmRev*
Allen, William (the Younger) *WhAmRev*
Allen, William Alexander 1914- *Who 94*
Allen, William Anthony 1949- *Who 94*
Allen, William Barclay 1944- *WhoAmP 93, WhoBlA 94*
Allen, William Bland, III 1947- *WhoAmP 93*
Allen, William Cecil 1919- *WhoAm 94, WhoMW 93, WhoScEn 94*
Allen, William Clifford 1937- *IntWW 93*
Allen, William Dale 1938- *WhoAm 94, WhoMW 93*
Allen, William Duncan 1906- *WhoBlA 94*
Allen, William Frederick, Jr. 1919- *WhoAm 94, WhoFI 94*
Allen, William Hayes 1926- *WhoAm 94*
Allen, William Henry 1917- *WhoBlA 94*
Allen, William J. 1945- *WhoAmA 93*
Allen, William Maurice 1931- *Who 94*
Allen, William Oscar 1923- *WhoBlA 94*
Allen, William Richard 1924- *WhoAm 94*
Allen, William Riley 1953- *WhoAmL 94*
Allen, William Sheridan 1932- *WhoAm 94, WrDr 94*
Allen, William Sidney 1918- *IntWW 93, Who 94*
Allen, Willie B. 1921- *WhoBlA 94*
Allen, Winston Earle 1933- *WhoBlA 94*
Allen, Woody *NewYTBS 93*
Allen, Woody 1935- *AmCulL, IntMPA 94, IntWW 93, News 94-1 [port], Who 94, WhoAm 94, WhoCom [port], WhoHol 92, WrDr 94*
Allen and Rossi *WhoCom*
Allenbaugh, G. Eric 1944- *WhoWest 94*
Allen-Bouska, Rebecca Auk 1961- *WhoMW 93*
Allenby *Who 94*
Allenby, Viscount 1931- *Who 94*
Allenby, Edmund H. H. 1861-1936 *HisWorL [port]*
Allenby, Frank d1953 *WhoHol 92*
Allenby, (David Howard) Nicholas 1909- *Who 94*
Allenby, Peggy d1966 *WhoHol 92*
Allenby, Thomas d1933 *WhoHol 92*
Allendale, Viscount 1922- *Who 94*
Allende, Fernando 1954- *WhoHol 92*
Allende, Isabel 1942- *BlmGWL [port], ConWorW 93, HispLC [port], IntWW 93, WhoHisp 94*
Allende, Jorge Eduardo 1934- *IntWW 93, WhoScEn 94*
Allende, Myriam Zahydee 1951- *WhoHisp 94*
Allende, Salvador 1908-1973 *HisWorL [port]*
Allender, John Roland 1950- *WhoAm 94, WhoAmL 94*
Allendorf, Peter F. *WhoAmP 93*
Allen-Jones, John Ernest 1909- *Who 94*
Allen-Jones, Patricia Ann 1958- *WhoBlA 94*
Allen-Noble, Rosie Elizabeth 1938- *WhoBlA 94*
Allen Of Abbeydale, Baron 1912- *Who 94*
Allen-Rasheed, Jamal Randy 1953- *WhoBlA 94*
Allenstein, Leland Carl 1925- *WhoAm 94*
Allensworth, Dorothy Alice 1907- *WhoAm 94*
Allentuck, Marcia Epstein 1928- *WhoAmA 93*
Aller, Lawrence Hugh 1913- *IntWW 93, WhoAm 94, WrDr 94*
Aller, Margo Friedel 1938- *WhoAm 94*
Aller, Ronald G. 1937- *WhoIns 94*
Aller, Wayne Kendall 1933- *WhoAm 94*
Allera, Edward John 1946- *WhoAm 94*
Allerheiligen, Robert Paul 1944- *WhoWest 94*
Allers, Franz 1905- *WhoAm 94*
Allers, Marlene Elaine 1931- *WhoAmL 94, WhoFI 94, WhoMW 93*
Allerslev Jensen, Erik 1911- *IntWW 93*
Allerton, Helen d1959 *WhoHol 92*
Allerton, John Stephen 1926- *WhoAm 94*
Allerton, Marie d1951 *WhoHol 92*
Allerton, Richard Christopher 1935- *Who 94*
Allerton, Samuel Ellsworth 1933- *WhoScEn 94*
Allery, Kenneth Edward 1925- *WhoAm 94, WhoWest 94*
Alles, J. A. *WhoAm 94, WhoFI 94*
Alles, Rodney Neal, Sr. 1950- *WhoScEn 94*
Allest, Frederic Jean Pierre d' 1940- *IntWW 93*
Allestad, Elaine Kinsey 1950- *WhoAmP 93*
Alletzhauser, Albert J. 1960- *WrDr 94*
Alleva, John James 1928- *WhoScEn 94*
Alley, Alphonse 1930- *IntWW 93*
Alley, Ben d1970 *WhoHol 92*
Alley, Douglas Wayne 1951- *WhoAmP 93*
Alley, E. Roberts 1938- *WhoScEn 94*
Alley, Frederick Don 1940- *WhoAm 94*
Alley, Henry Melton *DrAPF 93*
Alley, James Pinckney, Jr. 1942- *WhoAm 94*
Alley, Kirstie *IntWW 93*
Alley, Kirstie 1951- *WhoHol 92*
Alley, Kirstie 1955- *IntMPA 94, WhoAm 94*
Alley, Marcus M. *WhoScEn 94*
Alley, Robert S. 1932- *WrDr 94*
Alley, Ronald Edgar 1926- *Who 94*
Alley, Thomas 1946- *WhoAmP 93*
Alley, Wayne Edward 1932- *WhoAm 94, WhoAmL 94*
Alley, William J. 1929- *IntWW 93*
Alley, William Jack 1929- *WhoAm 94, WhoFI 94, WhoIns 94*
Alleyn, Edward 1566-1626 *BlmGEL*
Alleyne, Edward D. 1928- *WhoBlA 94*
Alleyne, George (Allanmore Ogarren) 1932- *Who 94*
Alleyne, John *WhoAm 94*
Alleyne, John (Olpherts Campbell) 1928- *Who 94*
Alleyne, Mervyn C. 1933- *WrDr 94*
Alleyne, Selwyn Eugene 1930- *Who 94*
Allford, David 1927- *Who 94*
Allfrey, Phyllis Shand 1915-1986 *BlmGWL*
Allgaier, Allison E. 1965- *WhoWest 94*
Allgaier, Glen Robert 1940- *WhoScEn 94*
Allgeyer, David Alan 1953- *WhoAmL 94*
Allgeyer, Edward J. *WhoAmP 93*
Allgeyer, Glen Owen 1925- *WhoMW 93*
Allgood, Charles Henry 1923- *WhoAmA 93*

Allgood, Clarence William 1902-1991 *WhAm 10*
Allgood, Jimmy Eugene 1955- *WhoMW 93*
Allgood, Sara d1950 *WhoHol 92*
Allgood, Thomas Forrest 1928- *WhoAmP 93*
Allgower, Eugene Leo 1935- *WhoWest 94*
Allgyer, Robert Earl 1944- *WhoAm 94, WhoFI 94, WhoMW 93*
Allhoff, Fred 1904-1988 *EncSF 93*
Allhusen, Christian Augustus Henry 1806-1890 *DcNaB MP*
Allhusen, Derek Swithin 1914- *Who 94*
Alli, Richard James, Sr. 1932- *WhoFI 94, WhoMW 93, WhoScEn 94*
Alliali, Camille Zahakro 1926- *IntWW 93*
Alliance, David 1932- *IntWW 93, Who 94*
Allibone, T(homas) E(dward) 1903- *WrDr 94*
Allibone, Thomas Edward 1903- *IntWW 93, Who 94*
Allie, Daniel John 1959- *WhoAmP 93*
Alligham, Garry 1898- *EncSF 93*
Alligood, Douglass Lacy 1934- *WhoBlA 94*
Alligood, Lola Jane Lurvey 1947- *WhoAmP 93*
Allik, Michael 1935- *WhoAm 94*
Alliker, Stanford Arnold 1946- *WhoAm 94*
Allimadi, E. Otema 1929- *IntWW 93*
Allin, George 1933- *Who 94*
Allin, John Maury 1921- *WhoAm 94*
Allin, Norman 1884-1973 *NewGrDO*
Allin, Robert Cameron 1938- *WhoWest 94*
Allin, Thomas Banbury 1949- *WhoAm 94*
Alling, Charles Booth, Jr. 1921- *WhoAm 94*
Alling, Charles Calvin, III 1923- *WhoAm 94*
Alling, Clarence (Edgar) 1933- *WhoAmA 93*
Alling, Janet D. 1939- *WhoAmA 93*
Alling, Norman Larrabee 1930- *WhoAm 94*
Allinger, Norman Louis 1928- *WhoAm 94, WhoScEn 94*
Allingham, Margery Louise 1904-1966 *BlmGWL*
Allington, James Richard 1933- *WhoFI 94*
Allington, Robert William 1935- *WhoMW 93*
Allinson, A. Edward 1934- *WhoAm 94*
Allinson, Gary Dean 1942- *WhoAm 94*
Allinson, Leonard *Who 94*
Allinson, (Walter) Leonard 1926- *Who 94*
Allinson, Walter Leonard 1926- *IntWW 93*
Allio, Robert John 1931- *WhoAm 94, WhoFI 94*
Alliot-Marie, Michele Yvette Marie-Therese 1946- *WhoWomW 91*
Alliott, John (Downes) 1932- *Who 94*
Allis, Samuel, Jr. 1805-1883 *EncNAR*
Allison, A(ntony) F(rancis) 1916- *WrDr 94*
Allison, B. R. 1915- *WhAm 10*
Allison, Beverly Gray 1924- *WhoAm 94*
Allison, Bonnie J. *WhoAmP 93*
Allison, Brian George 1933- *Who 94*
Allison, Cecil Wayne 1930- *WhoFI 94*
Allison, Charles Freeman 1933- *WhoFI 94*
Allison, Charles H. 1956- *WhoFI 94*
Allison, Christopher FitzSimons 1927- *WhoAm 94*
Allison, Davey d1993 *NewYTBS 93 [port]*
Allison, David Bradley 1963- *WhoScEn 94*
Allison, David C. 1924- *WhoAmP 93*
Allison, David Lord 1942- *WhoWest 94*
Allison, Dennis 1932- *Who 94*
Allison, Dorothy *DrAPF 93*
Allison, Dorothy 1949- *ConLC 78 [port]*
Allison, Dorothy (E.) 1949- *GayLL*
Allison, Dorothy E. 1949- *ConAu 140*
Allison, Dwight Leonard, Jr. 1929- *WhoAm 94*
Allison, E. Lavonia Ingram *WhoAmP 93*
Allison, E. M. A. 1947- *WrDr 94*
Allison, Elisabeth Kovacs 1946- *WhoAm 94, WhoFI 94*
Allison, Eric W(illiam) 1947- *WrDr 94*
Allison, Ferdinand V., Jr. 1923- *WhoBlA 94*
Allison, Fran d1989 *WhAm 10*
Allison, Frank *WhoBlA 94*
Allison, Gay 1943- *BlmGWL*
Allison, Grace 1946- *WhoAmL 94*
Allison, Graham Tillett, Jr. 1940- *WhoAm 94*
Allison, Henry E(dward) 1937- *WrDr 94*
Allison, Herbert Monroe, Jr. 1943- *WhoAm 94, WhoFI 94*
Allison, Irl 1896- *WhAm 10*
Allison, James Claybrooke, II 1942- *WhoAm 94*
Allison, James G. 1955- *WhoAmL 94*
Allison, James Purney 1947- *WhoAmL 94, WhoAmP 93*
Allison, James Richard, Jr. 1924- *WhoAm 94*
Allison, Joel Tribble 1948- *WhoAm 94*
Allison, John 1919- *Who 94*
Allison, John Andrew, IV 1948- *WhoAm 94, WhoFI 94*
Allison, John M. 1905-1978 *HisDcKW*
Allison, John McComb 1901- *WhoScEn 94*
Allison, John Robert 1945- *WhoAmL 94*
Allison, John Robert 1948- *WhoAm 94, WhoAmL 94*
Allison, John Shakespeare 1943- *Who 94*
Allison, Keith *WhoHol 92*
Allison, Laird Burl 1917- *WhoFI 94, WhoWest 94*
Allison, Lodowick 1948- *WhoAm 94*
Allison, May d1989 *WhoHol 92*
Allison, Merita Ann *WhoAmP 93*
Allison, Merle Lee 1948- *WhoScEn 94*
Allison, Nancy Louise 1951- *WhoMW 93*
Allison, Pamela Claire 1947- *WhoMW 93*
Allison, Patrick *WhAmRev*
Allison, Paul Judson 1926- *WhoAmL 94*
Allison, Paul W. 1946- *WhoAmL 94*
Allison, R(ichard) Bruce 1949- *WrDr 94*
Allison, Richard Clark 1924- *IntWW 93, WhoAm 94, WhoAmL 94*
Allison, Robert Arthur 1937- *WhoAm 94*
Allison, Robert James, Jr. 1939- *WhoAm 94, WhoFI 94*
Allison, Roderick Stuart 1936- *Who 94*
Allison, Ronald William Paul 1932- *Who 94*
Allison, Samuel Dudleston 1911- *WhoWest 94*
Allison, Sandra Diane Arthur 1950- *WhoAmP 93*
Allison, Sandy Diane *WhoMW 93*
Allison, Sherard Falkner d1993 *Who 94N*
Allison, Sherard Falkner 1907- *IntWW 93*
Allison, Stephen Galender 1952- *WhoFI 94*
Allison, Stephen Philip 1947- *WhoAm 94, WhoAmL 94*
Allison, Steve d1969 *WhoHol 92*
Allison, Thomas Howard 1948- *WhoAmL 94*
Allison, Thomas Jay 1959- *WhoWest 94*
Allison, Tomilea 1934- *WhoAmP 93*
Allison, W. Anthony 1926- *WhoBlA 94*
Allison, William Robert 1941- *WhoWest 94*
Allison, William Thomas, III 1966- *WhoMW 93*
Allison, Wilmer 1904-1977 *BuCMET*
Alliss, Peter 1931- *Who 94*
Allister, Claud d1970 *WhoHol 92*
Alliton, Vaughn 1966- *WhoFI 94*
Allman, Bruce M. 1943- *WhoAmL 94*
Allman, Clesson Dale 1952- *WhoWest 94*
Allman, Elvia *WhoHol 92*
Allman, Gregg 1947- *WhoAm 94*
Allman, John *DrAPF 93*
Allman, John Morgan 1943- *WhoAm 94*
Allman, Margo 1933- *WhoAmA 93*
Allman, Marian Isabel 1946-1992 *WhoBlA 94N*
Allman, Mark C. 1958- *WhoScEn 94*
Allman, Ray Francis d1978 *WhoHol 92*
Allman, Robert 1927- *NewGrDO*
Allman, Sheldon 1924- *WhoHol 92*
Allmand, Linda Faith 1937- *WhoAm 94*
Allmand, W. Warren 1932- *WhoAm 94*
Allman-Ward, Michele Ann 1950- *WhoAm 94*
Allmaras, Lorraine *WhoAmP 93*
Allmendinger, Paul Florin 1922- *WhoAm 94*
Allmon, Clinton 1941- *WhoHol 92*
Allmon, Rebecca Lea 1956- *WhoMW 93*
Allmon, Sue Ann 1960- *WhoMW 93*
Allmond, Charles 1931- *WhoAmA 93*
Allner, Walter H. 1909- *WhoAmA 93*
Allner, Walter Heinz 1909- *WhoAm 94*
Allnutt, Alvin Howard 1932- *WhoWest 94*
Allnutt, Ian Peter 1917- *Who 94*
Allnutt, Robert Frederick 1935- *WhoAm 94, WhoAmP 93*
Allnutt, Wendy 1946- *WhoHol 92*
Allocco, Barbara 1946- *WhoMW 93*
Allott, Ann 1940- *WhoAmL 94*
Allott, Antony Nicolas 1924- *Who 94*
Allott, Kenneth 1912-1973 *EncSF 93*
Allott, Molly Greenwood 1918- *Who 94*
Allott, Robin Michael 1926- *Who 94*
Allouache, Merzak 1944- *IntWW 93*
Allouez, Claude Jean 1622-1689 *EncNAR, WhWE*
Alloway, Anne Maureen Schubert 1954- *WhoAm 94*
Alloway, Lawrence 1927-1990 *WhoAmA 93N*
Alloway, Robert Malcombe 1944- *WhoAm 94*
Allport, Arthur *EncSF 93*
Allport, Denis Ivor 1922- *Who 94*
Allran, Austin M. 1951- *WhoAmP 93*
Allred, Allen D. 1947- *WhoAmL 94*
Allred, C. Keith *WhoAm 94, WhoAmL 94, WhoWest 94*
Allred, Cary Dale 1947- *WhoAmP 93*
Allred, Daniel M. 1945- *WhoAmL 94*
Allred, Eugene Lyle 1949- *WhoWest 94*
Allred, Evan Leigh 1929-1991 *WhAm 10*
Allred, Gloria Rachel 1941- *WhoAmP 93*
Allred, John Caldwell 1926- *WhoAm 94*
Allred, Michael Sylvester 1945- *WhoAm 94, WhoAmP 93*
Allrich, M. Louise Barco 1947- *WhoAmA 93*
Allsbrook, Ogden Olmstead, Jr. 1940- *WhoFI 94, WhoScEn 94*
Allsep, Larry Michael, Jr. 1958- *WhoAmL 94*
Allshouse, John 1951- *WhoAm 94*
Allshouse, Merle Frederick 1935- *WhoAm 94*
Allsman, Paul T. 1898- *WhAm 10*
Allsop, Peter Henry Bruce 1924- *Who 94*
Allsopp *Who 94*
Allsopp, Bruce *Who 94*
Allsopp, (Harold) Bruce 1912- *Who 94, WrDr 94*
Allsopp, Charles (Henry) 1940- *Who 94*
Allston, Thomas Gray, III 1954- *WhoBlA 94*
Allstot, David James 1947- *WhoScEn 94*
Allswang, John Myers 1937- *WhoAm 94, WhoWest 94*
Alltmont, Jack Marks 1947- *WhoAmL 94*
Allum, Geoffrey Michael 1957- *WhoAm 94*
Allum, Sarah Elizabeth Royle *Who 94*
Allumbaugh, Byron *WhoWest 94*
Allumbaugh, James 1941- *WhoAmA 93*
Allums, Victor Anthony 1959- *WhoAmL 94*
Allward, Maurice (Frank) 1923- *WrDr 94*
Allwell, Stephen S. 1906- *WhoAmA 93N*
Allwin, Pernilla 1971- *WhoHol 92*
Allwood, James Lio 1923- *WhoMW 93*
Allworth, Edward A(lfred) 1920- *ConAu 43NR*
Allworth, Frank d1935 *WhoHol 92*
Allwyn, Astrid d1978 *WhoHol 92*
Ally, Akbar F. 1943- *WhoBlA 94*
Allyn, Alyce d1976 *WhoHol 92*
Allyn, Compton 1925- *WhoMW 93*
Allyn, Jerri 1952- *WhoAmA 93*
Allyn, Richard B. 1942- *WhoAmL 94*
Allyn, William Finch 1935- *WhoAm 94*
Allyson, June 1917- *IntMPA 94, WhoHol 92*
Allyson, Kym 1929- *WrDr 94*
Alm, John Richard 1946- *WhoAm 94*
Alm, Richard Sanford 1921- *WhoAm 94*
Alm, Roger Russell 1945- *WhoMW 93, WhoScEn 94*
Almada, Filipa de *BlmGWL*
Almader, Minnie 1957- *WhoHisp 94*
Almagest *AstEnc*
Al-Maghut, Muhammad *ConWorW 93*
Almagro, Diego De c. 1478-1538 *WhWE*
Almaguer, Henry, Jr. 1947- *WhoHisp 94*
Almaguer, Tomás 1948- *WhoHisp 94*
Almaguer-Marino, Maria Elena 1968- *WhoHisp 94*
Al-Maktum, Rashid Ibn Said 1914- *WhAm 10*
al-Mala'ika, Nazik 1923-1992 *BlmGWL*
Almaleh, Lawrence Jay 1952- *WhoMW 93*
Alman, Emily Arnow 1922- *WhoAmL 94*
Alman, Ted Irwin 1946- *WhoScEn 94*
Almand, James Frederick 1948- *WhoAmP 93*
Almansi, Guido 1931- *WrDr 94*
Al-Mansour, Khalid Abdullah 1936- *WhoFI 94*
Almanza-Lumpkin, Carlota *WhoHisp 94*
Al-Marayati, Abid A(min) 1931- *WrDr 94*
Almario, Thelma Z. 1933- *WhoWomW 91*
Al-Mashat, Mohamed Sadiq 1930- *Who 94*
Almasi, George Stanley *WhoAm 94*
Al-Mateen, Cheryl Singleton 1959- *WhoBlA 94*
Al-Mateen, Kevin Bakeer 1958- *WhoBlA 94*
Almazan, Aurea Malabag 1944- *WhoScEn 94*
Almazan, Humberto *WhoHol 92*
Almazan, James A. 1935- *WhoHisp 94*
Alme, Kent Frederick 1963- *WhoFI 94*
Almedingen, E.M. 1898-1971 *EncSF 93*
Almeida, Alfred 1931- *WhoAmP 93*
Almeida, Antonio *WhoHisp 94*
Almeida, Antonio (Jacques) de 1928- *NewGrDO*
Almeida, Francisco Antonio de c. 1702-1755? *NewGrDO*
Almeida, Francisco De 1450-1510 *WhWE*
Almeida, Julia Lopes de 1862-1934 *BlmGWL*
Almeida, Laurindo 1917- *WhoAm 94, WhoHol 92*
Almeida, Lourenco De d1508 *WhWE*
Almeida, Richard J. 1942- *WhoFI 94*
Almeida, Yolanda R. 1945- *WhoHisp 94*
Almeida Garrett, Joao Baptista da Silva Leitao *IntDcT 2*
Almeida Merino, Adalberto 1916- *WhoAm 94*
Almeida Mota, Joao Pedro 1744-c. 1817 *NewGrDO*
Almen, Louis Theodore 1925- *WhoAm 94*
Almen, Lowell Gordon 1941- *WhoAm 94*
Almenara, Juan Ramon 1933- *WhoHisp 94*
Almendarez, Bob 1952- *WhoHisp 94*
Almendro, Jaime 1952- *WhoHisp 94*
Almendros, Nestor 1930-1992 *AnObit 1992, ConAu 142, IntDcF 2-4 [port], WhAm 10*
Alment, (Edward) Anthony (John) 1922- *Who 94*
Almeraz, Ricardo 1940- *WhoHisp 94*
Almes, June 1934- *WhoAm 94*
Almeyda Medina, Clodomiro 1923- *IntWW 93*
Almgren, Herbert Philip 1916- *WhoAm 94*
Almgren, Peter Eric 1948- *WhoWest 94*
Almirante, Luigi d1963 *WhoHol 92*
Almlie, Curt *WhoAmP 93*
Almodovar, Norma Jean 1951- *ConAu 142*
Almodovar, Pedro 1951- *IntMPA 94, IntWW 93*
Almog, Ruth 1936- *BlmGWL*
Al-Mohawes, Nasser Abdullah 1951- *WhoScEn 94*
Almon, Bert *DrAPF 93*
Almon, Reneau Pearson 1937- *WhoAm 94, WhoAmL 94, WhoAmP 93*
Almon, William Joseph 1932- *WhoFI 94*
Almond, Carl Herman 1926- *WhoAm 94*
Almond, David R. *WhoAm 94, WhoAmL 94, WhoFI 94*
Almond, Edward M. 1892-1979 *HisDcKW*
Almond, Gabriel A(braham) 1911- *WrDr 94*
Almond, Gabriel Abraham 1911- *IntWW 93, WhoAm 94*
Almond, Gary Robert 1958- *WhoFI 94*
Almond, Joan 1934- *WhoFI 94*
Almond, Lincoln C. 1936- *WhoAm 94*
Almond, Matthew John 1960- *WhoScEn 94*
Almond, Michael Allen 1949- *WhoAmL 94*
Almond, Paul 1931- *IntMPA 94, WhoAm 94, WhoAmA 93*
Almond, Thomas Clive 1939- *Who 94*
Almonte, Patricia Killelea 1952- *WhoWest 94*
Almony, Robert Allen, Jr. 1945- *WhoAm 94, WhoMW 93*
Almquist, Don 1929- *WhoAm 94*
Almquist, Donald John 1933- *WhoAm 94, WhoScEn 94*
Almquist, Herman James 1903- *WhoWest 94*
Almqvist, Carl Jonas Love 1793-1866 *NinCLC 42 [port]*
Almunia Amann, Joaquin 1948- *IntWW 93*
Almy, Frank Atwood 1900-1956 *WhoAmA 93N*
Almy, Linda L. 1948- *WhoAmP 93*
Almy, Mary Gould 1735-1808 *BlmGWL, WhAmRev*
Almy, Max 1948- *WhoAmA 93*
Almy, R. Christopher 1949- *WhoAmP 93*
Almy, Thomas Pattison 1915- *WhoAm 94*
Alnasrawi, Abbas *ConAu 140*
Al-Nimr, Nabih 1931- *Who 94*
Aloe, Paul Hubschman 1957- *WhoAmL 94*
Aloff, Mindy *DrAPF 93*
Aloff, Mindy 1947- *WhoAm 94, WrDr 94*
Al-Ohali, Khalid Suliman 1964- *WhoScEn 94*
Aloimonos, Yiannis John 1957- *WhoScEn 94*
Alomar, Roberto 1968- *WhoBlA 94, WhoHisp 94*
Alomar, Roberto Velazquez 1968- *WhoAm 94*
Alomar, Sandy 1943- *WhoBlA 94, WhoHisp 94*
Alomar, Sandy, Jr. 1966- *WhoAm 94, WhoBlA 94, WhoHisp 94, WhoMW 93*
Alomar-Hamza, Daisy 1940- *WhoHisp 94*
Aloneftis, Andreas P. 1945- *IntWW 93*
Aloni, Shulamit 1929- *IntWW 93*
Aloni, Shumalit 1929- *WhoWomW 91*
Alonso (Lopez), Francisco 1887-1948 *NewGrDO*
Alonso, Alberto d1967 *WhoHol 92*
Alonso, Alicia 1921- *IntDcB [port]*
Alonso, Antonio Enrique 1924- *WhoAmL 94*
Alonso, Antonio Jorge 1950- *WhoHisp 94*

Alonso, Carmen de 1909- *BlmGWL*
Alonso, Cecilia Holtz 1948- *WhoHisp 94*
Alonso, Danilo *WhoHisp 94*
Alonso, Deana 1958- *WhoHisp 94*
Alonso, Dora 1910- *BlmGWL*
Alonso, Francisco Manuel 1943- *WhoHisp 94*
Alonso, Irma T. de 1941- *WhoHisp 94*
Alonso, Jose Ramon 1941- *WhoScEn 94*
Alonso, Julio d1955 *WhoHol 92*
Alonso, Manrique Domingo 1910- *WhoHisp 94*
Alonso, Manuel 1895-1984 *BuCMET*
Alonso, Maria Conchita 1956- *WhoHol 92*
Alonso, Maria Conchita 1957- *IntMPA 94, WhoHisp 94*
Alonso, Miguel Angel 1930- *WhoHisp 94*
Alonso, Miriam *WhoHisp 94*
Alonso, Noah 1925- *WhoHisp 94*
Alonso, Odon *WhoAm 94*
Alonso, Rafael Alonso *WhoHisp 94*
Alonso, Rafael Alonso 1939- *WhoAmP 93*
Alonso, Santos, Sr. *WhoHisp 94*
Alonso, Silvia Teresita 1941- *WhoHisp 94*
Alonso, Virgil 1941- *WhoHisp 94*
Alonso, William 1933- *WhoAm 94*
Alonso-Alonso, Rafael *WhoAmL 94*
Alonso-Fernandez, Jose Ramon 1946- *WhoScEn 94*
Alonso-Mendoza, Emilio 1954- *WhoHisp 94*
Alonso-Valls, Fidel 1944- *WhoHisp 94*
Alonzi, Loreto Peter 1951- *WhoFI 94, WhoMW 93*
Alonzo, Angelo Anthony 1941- *WhoHisp 94*
Alonzo, Gregory Nelson 1962- *WhoMW 93*
Alonzo, John 1934- *IntDcF 2-4*
Alonzo, John A. 1934- *IntMPA 94*
Alonzo, John A. 1936- *WhoHisp 94*
Alonzo, Martin Vincent 1931- *WhoAm 94*
Alonzo, R. Gregory 1954- *WhoWest 94*
Alonzo, Ralph Edward 1950- *WhoHisp 94*
Alonzo, Roberto R. 1956- *WhoAmP 93, WhoHisp 94*
Aloot, Mariano Daniel 1947- *WhoWest 94*
Alorna, Marquesa de 1750-1839? *BlmGWL*
Alos, Concha 1922- *BlmGWL*
Alost, Robert Allen 1935- *WhoAm 94*
Alota, Ruben Villaruel 1952- *WhoAsA 94*
Alou, Felipe Rojas 1935- *WhoAm 94, WhoHisp 94*
Alou, Jesus Maria Rojas 1942- *WhoHisp 94*
Alou, Matty 1938- *WhoHisp 94*
Alou, Moises 1966- *WhoHisp 94*
Alouani, Mebarek 1958- *WhoScEn 94*
Aloupis, Angela Z. 1943- *WhoAmP 93*
Alpa, Guido Peter 1947- *WhoAm 94*
Alpar, Gitta 1900?- *WhoHol 92*
Alpar, Gitta 1903- *NewGrDO*
Alpaugh, David *DrAPF 93*
Alpaugh, Walter G. 1921- *WhoIns 94*
Alpen, Edward Lewis 1922- *WhoAm 94, WhoScEn 94*
Alpen-Whiteside, Dale 1942- *WhoAmA 93*
Alper, Anne Elizabeth 1942- *WhoAm 94, WhoScEn 94*
Alper, Howard 1941- *IntWW 93, WhoAm 94*
Alper, Jerome Milton 1914- *WhoAm 94*
Alper, Joel Richard 1938- *WhoFI 94*
Alper, Jonathan Louis 1950- *WhAm 10*
Alper, Merlin Lionel 1932- *WhoAm 94*
Alperin, Irwin Ephraim 1925- *WhoAm 94, WhoFI 94*
Alperin, Joseph D. 1943- *WhoAmL 94*
Alpern, Andrew 1938- *WhoAm 94*
Alpern, Mathew 1920- *WhoAm 94*
Alpern, Merry B. *WhoAmA 93*
Alpern, Robert Zellman 1928- *WhoAm 94*
Alperovitz, Gar 1936- *WhoAm 94*
Alpers, Antony 1919- *WrDr 94*
Alpers, Christian 1959- *WhoFI 94*
Alpers, David Hershel 1935- *WhoAm 94, WhoMW 93*
Alpers, Edward Alter 1941- *WhoAm 94*
Alpers, Hans Joachim 1943- *EncSF 93*
Alpers, John Hardesty, Jr. 1939- *WhoFI 94, WhoWest 94*
Alpers, Robert Christopher 1949- *WhoWest 94*
Alperstein, Arthur Stuart 1940- *WhoAmP 93*
Alperstein, Donald Wayne 1951- *WhoWest 94*
Alperstein, Pearl 1927- *WhoAmP 93*
Alpert, Ann Sharon 1938- *WhoFI 94*
Alpert, Barry Mark 1941- *WhoFI 94*
Alpert, Bill 1934- *WhoAmA 93*
Alpert, Burt Morris 1926- *WhoWest 94*
Alpert, Cathryn *DrAPF 93*
Alpert, Deirdre 1945- *WhoAmP 93*
Alpert, George 1898- *WhAm 10*
Alpert, George 1922- *WhoAmA 93*
Alpert, Gordon Myles 1944- *WhoAm 94, WhoAmL 94*
Alpert, Herb 1935- *IntWW 93, WhoAm 94, WhoHol 92*
Alpert, Herb 1937- *ConMus 11 [port]*
Alpert, Hollis 1916- *WhoAm 94, WrDr 94*
Alpert, Janet Anne 1946- *WhoAm 94*
Alpert, Joel Jacobs 1930- *WhoAm 94*
Alpert, Jonathan Louis 1945- *WhoAmL 94*
Alpert, Joseph Stephen 1942- *IntWW 93, WhoAm 94*
Alpert, Marc Stephen 1944- *WhoAm 94*
Alpert, Mark Ira 1942- *WhoAm 94*
Alpert, Michael Edward 1942- *WhoAm 94, WhoAmL 94*
Alpert, Natalie Boyle 1923- *WhoMW 93*
Alpert, Norman 1921- *WhoAm 94*
Alpert, Norman Joseph 1931- *WhoAm 94*
Alpert, Richard Henry 1947- *WhoAmA 93*
Alpert, Rochelle D. 1950- *WhoAmL 94*
Alpert, Seymour 1918- *WhoAm 94*
Alpert, Warren 1920- *WhoAm 94, WhoScEn 94*
Alpha, Karen *DrAPF 93*
Alphand, Herve 1907- *IntWW 93, Who 94*
Alphandery, Edmond Gerard 1943- *Who 94*
alpher, m c *DrAPF 93*
Alpher, Ralph Asher 1921- *WhoAm 94, WhoScEn 94*
Alpher, Victor Seth 1954- *WhoScEn 94*
Alphin, Vance 1947- *WhoAmP 93*
Alphonso Karkala, John B. 1923- *WrDr 94*
Alpiar, Hal 1941- *WhoFI 94*
Alport *Who 94*
Alport, Baron 1912- *Who 94*
Alport, Cuthbert James McCall 1912- *IntWW 93*
Alport, of Colchester, Baron 1912- *WrDr 94*
Alprin, William Samuel 1939- *WhoFI 94*
Alps, Glen Earl 1914- *WhoAm 94, WhoAmA 93, WhoWest 94*
Alptemocin, Ahmet Kurtcebe 1940- *IntWW 93*
Al-Qadi, Imad Lutfi 1962- *WhoScEn 94*
Al-Qaraguli, Wahbi Abdul Razaq Fattah 1929- *Who 94*
Al-Qazzaz, Ayad 1941- *WhoWest 94*
Alquier, Jacqueline Lucienne 1947- *WhoWomW 91*
Alquilar, Maria 1935- *WhoAmA 93*
Alquist, Alfred E. *WhoWest 94*
Alquist, Alfred E. 1908- *WhoAmP 93*
Alquist, Lewis 1946- *WhoAmA 93*
Alquist, Lewis Russell 1946- *WhoWest 94*
Alric, Catherine *WhoHol 92*
Al Saadi, Abdul Amir 1935- *WhoMW 93*
Al-Sabah, Shaikh Saud Nasir 1944- *Who 94*
al-Sabah, Su'ad 1942- *BlmGWL*
Al Sabbagh, Salman Abdul Wahab 1932- *Who 94*
Alsace, Gene d1967 *WhoHol 92*
Al-Sa'dawi, Nawal *ConWorW 93*
Alsadi, Akeel 1936- *WhoFI 94*
Alsaker, Elwood Cecil 1924-1989 *WhAm 10*
Alsaker, Robert John 1945- *WhoWest 94*
Al-Salihi, Azmi Shafeeq 1934- *Who 94*
Al-Salqan, Yahya Yousef 1962- *WhoMW 93, WhoScEn 94*
al-Samman, Ghada 1942- *BlmGWL*
Alsandor, Jude 1938- *WhoBlA 94*
Al-Sari, Ahmad Mohammad 1947- *WhoFI 94, WhoScEn 94*
Alsbach-Zoellner, Shirley Ruth 1940- *WhoMW 93*
Alsberg, Dietrich Anselm 1917- *WhoAm 94*
Alsbro, Donald Edgar 1940- *WhoMW 93*
Alsbrook, James Eldridge 1913- *WhoMW 93*
Alschuler, Albert W. 1948- *WhoAm 94, WhoAmL 94*
Alschuler, Fred H. 1949- *WhoAmL 94*
Alschuler, George Arthur 1935- *WhoAmL 94, WhoWest 94*
Alschuler, Sam 1913- *WhoAm 94*
Alsdorf, James William 1913-1990 *WhAm 10*
Alsen, Elsa d1975 *WhoHol 92*
Alsen, Elsa 1880-1975 *NewGrDO*
Alsen, Herbert 1906-1978 *NewGrDO*
Al Shakar, Karim Ebrahim 1945- *Who 94*
Alsharif, Naser Zaki 1960- *WhoScEn 94*
Al-Shawi, Hisham Ibrahim 1931- *Who 94*
Al-Shaykh, Hanan *ConWorW 93*
al-Shaykh, Hanan 1945- *BlmGWL*
Alsobrook, Henry Bernis, Jr. 1930- *WhoAm 94*
Alsobrook, Henry Herman 1917- *WhoAmP 93*
Alsop, Donald Douglas 1927- *WhoAm 94, WhoAmL 94, WhoMW 93*
Alsop, Jack 1951- *WhoAmP 93*
Alsop, John 1724-1794 *WhAmRev*
Alsop, Joseph Wright 1910- *WrDr 94*
Alsop, Joseph Wright, Jr. 1910- *WhAm 10*
Alsop, Roger Clark 1957- *WhoWest 94*
Alsop, Will *IntWW 93*
Alsop, William Allen 1947- *Who 94*
Alspach, Brian Roger 1938- *WhoWest 94*
Alspach, Donald Stuart 1944- *WhoWest 94*
Alspach, Donn E. 1931- *WhoMW 93*
Alspach, Philip Halliday 1923- *WhoAm 94, WhoWest 94*
Alspaugh, Dale William 1932- *WhoAm 94, WhoMW 93*
Alspaugh, Robert Odo *WhoAm 94*
Alstadt, Lynn Jeffery 1951- *WhoAm 94, WhoAmL 94*
Alstadt, William Robert 1916- *WhoAmP 93*
Alster, Frank G. 1919- *WhoAmL 94*
Alston, Alex Armstrong, Jr. 1936- *WhoAmL 94*
Alston, Betty Bruner 1933- *WhoBlA 94*
Alston, Casco, Jr. 1923- *WhoBlA 94*
Alston, Charles 1907-1972 *AfrAmAl 6*
Alston, Charles Henry 1907-1977 *WhoAmA 93N*
Alston, Cheryl Ann 1946- *WhoFI 94*
Alston, Floyd William 1925- *WhoBlA 94*
Alston, Gerald 1951- *WhoBlA 94*
Alston, Gerald W. 1939- *WhoAmL 94*
Alston, Gilbert C. 1931- *WhoBlA 94*
Alston, Harry L. 1914- *WhoBlA 94*
Alston, J(oseph) Leo 1917- *Who 94*
Alston, James L. 1947- *WhoBlA 94*
Alston, John Alistair 1937- *Who 94*
Alston, Kathy Diane 1958- *WhoBlA 94*
Alston, Lela 1942- *WhoAmP 93, WhoWest 94*
Alston, Philip 1950- *ConAu 140*
Alston, Rex *Who 94*
Alston, Rex 1901- *WrDr 94*
Alston, (Arthur) Rex 1901- *Who 94*
Alston, Richard John William 1948- *Who 94*
Alston, Robert John 1938- *IntWW 93, Who 94*
Alston, Roberta Theresa 1923- *WhoWest 94*
Alston, Robin (Carfrae) 1933- *WrDr 94*
Alston, Robin Carfrae 1933- *Who 94*
Alston, Shirley 1941- *See* Shirelles, The *ConMus 11*
Alston, Steven Gail 1953- *WhoScEn 94*
Alston, Tracey Daniel 1961- *WhoBlA 94*
Alston, William Payne 1921- *WhoAm 94*
Alston-Roberts-West, George Arthur *Who 94*
Alstrup, Carl d1942 *WhoHol 92*
Alsup, James M. 1950- *WhoAmL 94*
Alsup, William 1945- *WhoAmL 94*
Al-Suwaidi, Salem Mohammed 1956- *WhoFI 94*
Alt, Betty Sowers 1931- *WrDr 94*
Alt, Carol 1960- *WhoHol 92*
Alt, James D. 1951- *WhoAmL 94*
Alt, James Edward 1946- *WhoAm 94*
Alt, John 1962- *WhoAm 94*
Alta *DrAPF 93*
Altabe, Joan Augusta Berg 1935- *WhoAm 94*
Altabef, Peter Anthony 1959- *WhoAmL 94*
Al-Tajir, Mohamed Mahdi 1931- *Who 94*
Altalib, Omar Hisham 1967- *WhoMW 93*
Altamirano, Anibal Alberto 1954- *WhoScEn 94*
Altamirano, Ben D. *WhoAmP 93*
Altamirano, Ben D. 1930- *WhoHisp 94, WhoWest 94*
Altamirano, Salvador H. 1947- *WhoHisp 94*
Altamura, Michael Victor 1923- *WhoScEn 94, WhoWest 94*
Altan, Taylan 1938- *WhoAm 94, WhoFI 94, WhoScEn 94*
Altangerel, Bat-Ochiryn 1934- *IntWW 93*
Al'tani, Ippolit (Karlovich) 1846-1919 *NewGrDO*
Altavilla, Randolph Joseph 1953- *WhoFI 94*
Altavista, Juan Carlos d1989 *WhoHol 92*
al-Taymuriyya, 'Aisha 'Esmat 1840-1902 *BlmGWL*
Altbach, Philip 1941- *WhoAm 94*
Altbach, Philip G. 1941- *IntWW 93*
Altchuler, Steven Ira 1951- *WhoMW 93*
Altekruse, Joan Morrissey 1928- *WhoAm 94*
Alten, Frank d1988 *WhoHol 92*
Alten, Jerry *WhoAmA 93*
Altenburger, Gene Paul 1966- *WhoMW 93*
Alter, Blanche Pearl 1941- *WhoScEn 94*
Alter, David 1923- *WhoAm 94*
Alter, Dennis *WhoAm 94, WhoFI 94*
Alter, Edward T. 1941- *WhoAm 94, WhoAmP 93, WhoWest 94*
Alter, Eleanor Breitel 1938- *WhoAm 94*
Alter, Gerald L. 1910- *WhoAm 94, WhoFI 94*
Alter, Harvey 1932- *WhoAm 94*
Alter, Jean Victor 1925- *WhoAm 94*
Alter, Joanne Hammerman 1927- *WhoAmP 93*
Alter, Jonathan Hammerman 1957- *WhoAm 94*
Alter, Judy 1938- *WrDr 94*
Alter, Lottie d1924 *WhoHol 92*
Alter, Milton 1929- *WhoAm 94*
Alter, Nelson Tobias 1926- *WhoFI 94*
Alter, Peter M. 1947- *WhoAmL 94*
Alter, Robert B. 1935- *WhoAm 94, WrDr 94*
Alter, Robert J. 1951- *WhoAmL 94*
Alter, Susan D. 1942- *WhoAmP 93*
Alter, Tom 1950- *WhoHol 92*
Alter, William 1944- *WhoAmP 93*
Alterman, Dean N. 1960- *WhoAmL 94, WhoWest 94*
Alterman, Eric Ross 1960- *WhoWest 94*
Alterman, Irwin Michael 1941- *WhoAm 94*
Alterman, Joseph George 1919- *IntMPA 94*
Alterman, Leonard Mayer 1943- *WhoAmL 94*
Altermann, Tony 1940- *WhoAmA 93*
Altermatt, Paul Barry 1930- *WhoAm 94*
Altersitz, Janet Kinahan 1951- *WhoWest 94*
Altes, Frederik Korthals 1931- *IntWW 93*
Altfeld, Merwin Richard 1913- *WhoAmA 93*
Altfeld, Sheldon Isaac 1937- *WhoAm 94*
Altfest, Lewis Jay 1940- *WhoFI 94*
Altgeld, John Peter 1847-1902 *AmSocL [port]*
Altham, John 1585-1640 *EncNAR*
Altham, John 1589-1640 *DcAmReB 2*
Althaus, David Steven 1945- *WhoFI 94*
Althaus, Keith *DrAPF 93*
Althaus, Nigel (Frederick) 1929- *Who 94*
Althaus, William John 1948- *WhoAmP 93*
Althaver, Lambert Ewing 1931- *WhoAm 94*
Altheimer, Alan J. 1903- *WhoAm 94*
Altheimer, Alan Milton 1940- *WhoFI 94, WhoMW 93*
Altheimer, Brian P. 1956- *WhoWest 94*
Alther, Lisa 1944- *WrDr 94*
Althoff, Charles d1962 *WhoHol 92*
Althoff, James L. 1928- *WhoMW 93*
Althouse, Earl d1971 *WhoHol 92*
Althouse, Paul (Shearer) 1899-1954 *NewGrDO*
Althusser, Louis 1918- *BlmGEL*
Altick, Leslie L. *WhoAm 94*
Altick, Richard Daniel 1915- *WrDr 94*
Altier, William John 1935- *WhoFI 94*
Altieri, Peter Louis 1955- *WhoAmL 94*
Altimari, Frank X. 1928- *WhoAm 94, WhoAmL 94, WhoAmP 93*
Alting, Leo Larsen 1939- *WhoScEn 94*
Altinkaya, Cengiz 1949- *IntWW 93*
Altizer, Nell *DrAPF 93*
Altkorn, Robert Ira *WhoMW 93*
Altman, Adele Rosenhain 1924- *WhoWest 94*
Altman, Arnold David 1917- *WhoAm 94*
Altman, David 1954- *WhoAmL 94*
Altman, David Wayne 1951- *WhoScEn 94*
Altman, Dennis 1943- *GayLL, WrDr 94*
Altman, Edith 1931- *WhoAmA 93*
Altman, Edward Ira 1941- *WhoAm 94*
Altman, Ellen 1936- *WhoAm 94*
Altman, Frances (Evelyn) 1937- *WrDr 94*
Altman, Harold 1924- *WhoAmA 93*
Altman, Irwin 1930- *WhoAm 94, WhoWest 94*
Altman, Irwin M. d1993 *NewYTBS 93*
Altman, Jack *WhoWest 94*
Altman, James 1939- *WhoFI 94*
Altman, James Eston 1938- *WhoAmP 93*
Altman, Jeff 1951- *WhoCom*
Altman, Jeffrey 1951- *WhoHol 92*
Altman, Jeffrey Paul 1949- *WhoAm 94, WhoAmL 94*
Altman, John 1944- *Who 94*
Altman, Joseph 1925- *WhoAm 94*
Altman, Lawrence Kimball 1937- *WhoAm 94*
Altman, Leo Sidney 1911- *WhoAm 94*
Altman, Lionel Phillips *Who 94*
Altman, Louis 1933- *WhoAm 94, WhoAmL 94*
Altman, Milton Hubert 1917- *WhoAm 94*
Altman, Morton Irving 1942- *WhoWest 94*
Altman, Ray H. 1943- *WhoAmP 93*
Altman, Richard Shotz 1963- *WhoAmL 94*
Altman, Robert *EncSF 93*
Altman, Robert 1925- *ConAu 43NR, IntMPA 94, IntWW 93, Who 94*
Altman, Robert 1949- *WhoAmL 94*

Altman, Robert B. 1925- WhoAm 94
Altman, Robert Lee 1935- WhoAm 94
Altman, Robert Linwood WhoAmP 93
Altman, Roger C. 1947- WhoAm 94, WhoFI 94
Altman, Roger Charles 1946- NewYTBS 93 [port]
Altman, Roy Peter 1934- WhoAm 94
Altman, Samuel Pinover 1921- WhoScEn 94
Altman, Seymour 1929- WhoMW 93
Altman, Sheldon 1934- WhoAm 94
Altman, Sheldon 1937- WhoWest 94
Altman, Sidney 1939- NobelP 91 [port], WhoAm 94, WhoScEn 94
Altman, Stuart H. 1942- WhoAmL 94
Altman, Stuart Harold 1937- IntWW 93, WhoAm 94
Altman, William Carl 1957- WhoFI 94
Altman, William Kean 1944- WhoAmL 94
Altmann, Henry S. 1946- WhoAmA 93
Altmann, Jeanne WhoScEn 94
Altmann, Stuart Allen 1930- WhoAm 94
Altmayer, Jay P. 1915- WhoAmA 93
Altmeyer, Jeannine (Theresa) 1948- NewGrDO
Altmiller, John Connell 1936- WhoAmL 94
Altner, Peter Christian 1932- WhoAm 94
Altobello, Daniel Joseph 1941- WhoAm 94
Altobello, Henry D. 1907- WhoAmP 93
Altomari, Mark G. 1947- WhoMW 93, WhoScEn 94
Alton, Ann Leslie 1945- WhoAm 94, WhoAmL 94, WhoFI 94, WhoMW 93
Alton, Bruce Taylor 1939- WhoAm 94
Alton, Cecil Claude 1943- WhoScEn 94
Alton, Colleen Edna 1959- WhoWest 94
Alton, David Patrick 1951- Who 94
Alton, Elaine Vivian 1925- WhoAm 94
Alton, Euan Beresford Seaton 1919- Who 94
Alton, Howard Robert, Jr. 1927- WhoAmL 94
Alton, John 1901- IntDcF 2-4
Alton, Robert d1957 WhoHol 92
Alton, Robert 1906-1957 IntDcF 2-4
Altonji, Joseph Bernard 1957- WhoFI 94
Altov, Genrikh 1926- EncSF 93
Altreuter, William Carlin 1957- WhoAmL 94
Altrincham, Barony of 1934- Who 94
Altrobrandino, Giuseppe Antonio Vincenzo NewGrDO
Altrock, Richard Charles 1940- WhoAm 94
Altschaeffl, Adolph George 1930- WhoAm 94
Altscher, Harold 1947- WhoAmL 94
Altschuh, Gregory William 1946- WhoAmL 94
Altschul, Aaron Mayer 1914- WhoAm 94
Altschul, Alfred Samuel 1939- WhoAm 94
Altschul, Arthur G. 1920- WhoAmA 93
Altschul, Arthur Goodhart 1920- WhoAm 94
Altschul, David Edwin 1947- WhoWest 94
Altschul, Donald Scott 1951- WhoAmL 94
Altschul, Michael F. 1949- WhoAmL 94
Altschul, Stanford Marvin 1936- WhoAmL 94
Altschuler, David Edward 1952- WhoFI 94
Altshiller, Arthur Leonard 1942- WhoScEn 94, WhoWest 94
Altshuler, Alan Anthony 1936- WhoAm 94
Altshuler, David Thomas 1961- WhoScEn 94
Altshuler, Robert Michael 1949- WhoMW 93
Altshuller, Dmitry Alexander 1961- WhoMW 93
Altura, Bella T. WhoScEn 94
Altura, Burton Myron 1936- WhoAm 94, WhoScEn 94
Altuvia, Magen 1956- WhoFI 94
Altwegg, Patricia Ann 1945- WhoMW 93
Altwerger, Libby 1921- WhoAmA 93
Al-Ubaidi, Muthar Radif 1945- WhoMW 93
Aluise, Timothy John 1956- WhoAm 94, WhoAmL 94
Alukal, Varghese George 1945- WhoMW 93
Aluko, T(imothy) M(ofolorunso) 1918- WrDr 94
Alukonis, David J. 1961- WhoAmP 93
Alum, Manuel d1993 NewYTBS 93 [port]
Alum, Manuel Antonio 1943-1993 WhoHisp 94N
Alum, Roland Armando, Jr. WhoHisp 94
Alumbaugh, JoAnn McCalla 1952- WhoAm 94
Alun-Jones, (John) Derek 1933- Who 94
Alured, John 1607-1651 DcNaB MP
Alurista DrAPF 93
Alurista 1947- WhoAm 94, WhoHisp 94
al-Uthman, Layla 1945- BlmGWL
Alutto, Joseph Anthony 1941- WhoAm 94, WhoFI 94, WhoMW 93
Alva, Dinker 1933- IntWW 93
Alva, Luigi 1927- NewGrDO
Alva, Margaret 1942- WhoWomW 91
Alva Castro, Luis IntWW 93
Alvar BlmGWL
Alvarado, Alfredo 1931- WhoHisp 94
Alvarado, Alfredo Javier 1965- WhoAmL 94
Alvarado, Angela 1968- WhoHol 92
Alvarado, Audrey Ramona 1952- WhoHisp 94
Alvarado, Blanca WhoHisp 94
Alvarado, Crox d1984 WhoHol 92
Alvarado, Don d1967 WhoHol 92
Alvarado, Esteban P. 1962- WhoHisp 94
Alvarado, Hernan Carlos 1947- WhoHisp 94
Alvarado, Hernando De fl. 154-?- WhWE [port]
Alvarado, John Charles 1959- WhoHisp 94
Alvarado, Juan Manuel 1938- WhoHisp 94
Alvarado, Leo, Jr. 1939- WhoAmP 93
Alvarado, Linda G. WhoHisp 94
Alvarado, Paul Henry 1939- WhoHisp 94
Alvarado, Pedro De c. 1485-1541 WhWE
Alvarado, Raul, Jr. 1946- WhoHisp 94
Alvarado, Ricardo Raphael 1927- WhoAm 94, WhoHisp 94
Alvarado, Richard A. 1943- WhoHisp 94
Alvarado, Ruben B. 1941- WhoHisp 94
Alvarado, Sam P. 1930- WhoHisp 94
Alvarado, Sully JF WhoHisp 94
Alvarado, Susan E. 1954- WhoHisp 94
Alvarado, Trini 1967- IntMPA 94, WhoHisp 94, WhoHol 92
Alvarado, Yolanda 1943- WhoAm 94, WhoMW 93
Alvarado, Yolanda H. 1943- WhoHisp 94
Alvaré, Helen WhoHisp 94
Alvares, Alvito P. 1935- WhoAsA 94
Alvares, Eduardo 1947- NewGrDO
Alvarez, A(lfred) 1929- WrDr 94
Alvarez, Adolfo 1931- WhoAmP 93
Alvarez, Adolfo, Jr. 1958- WhoAmL 94
Alvarez, Aida 1949- WhoHisp 94
Alvarez, Albert 1861-1933 NewGrDO
Alvarez, Alfred 1929- Who 94
Alvarez, Anne Maino 1941- WhoHisp 94
Alvarez, Antonia V. 1951- WhoHisp 94
Alvarez, Antonio WhoHisp 94
Alvarez, Avelino 1934- WhoHisp 94
Alvarez, Barry 1947- WhoHisp 94
Alvarez, Bob WhoHisp 94
Alvarez, Candida 1955- WhoAmA 93
Alvarez, César L. WhoHisp 94
Alvarez, Cesar L. 1947- WhoAmL 94
Alvarez, Daniel, Sr. 1924- WhoHisp 94
Alvarez, David 1931- WhoHisp 94
Alvarez, Donald Luz 1943- WhoFI 94
Alvarez, Eduardo 1951- WhoHisp 94
Alvarez, Eduardo J. 1935- WhoHisp 94
Alvarez, Eduardo Jorge 1945- WhoHisp 94
Alvarez, Eduardo T. 1930- WhoHisp 94
Alvarez, Elvis WhoHisp 94
Alvarez, Everett, Jr. 1937- WhoHisp 94
Alvarez, F. Dennis 1945- WhoHisp 94
Alvarez, Felix Augusto 1954- WhoHisp 94
Alvarez, Ferdinand Chat, Jr. 1944- WhoHisp 94
Alvarez, Fernando 1935- WhoHisp 94
Alvarez, Francisco Alvarez 1957- WhoHisp 94
Alvarez, Frank D. WhoHisp 94
Alvarez, Fred T. 1937- WhoHisp 94
Alvarez, Fred W. 1949- WhoHisp 94
Alvarez, Guillermo A. 1950- WhoScEn 94
Alvarez, Hector Justo 1938- WhoHisp 94
Alvarez, Javier P. 1951- WhoHisp 94
Alvarez, Jeronimo WhoHisp 94
Alvarez, John ConAu 141, EncSF 93, SmATA 76
Alvarez, Jorge DrAPF 93
Alvarez, Jorge 1936- WhoHisp 94
Alvarez, José 1944- WhoHisp 94
Alvarez, Jose, Jr. 1952- WhoHisp 94
Alvarez, Jose Armando 1949- WhoFI 94
Alvarez, José B. 1949- WhoHisp 94
Alvarez, José José 1951- WhoHisp 94
Alvarez, Jose M. WhoHisp 94
Alvarez, Jose O. 1947- WhoHisp 94
Alvarez, Jose Roberto 1955- WhoFI 94
Alvarez, Juan Holquin 1944- WhoHisp 94
Alvarez, Juan Rafael 1956- WhoHisp 94
Alvarez, Julia DrAPF 93, WhoHisp 94
Alvarez, Julio E. WhoHisp 94
Alvarez, Lili de 1905- BuCMET
Alvarez, Linda WhoHisp 94
Alvarez, Lizette Ann 1964- WhoHisp 94
Alvarez, Luis d1986 WhoHol 92
Alvarez, Luis 1911- WorScD [port]
Alvarez, Luis W. d1988 NobelP 91N
Alvarez, Luis Walter 1911-1988 WorInv
Alvarez, Lynne DrAPF 93
Alvarez, Manuel 1794-1856 WhWE
Alvarez, Manuel Antonio, Sr. 1933- WhoHisp 94
Alvarez, Manuel G., Jr. WhoHisp 94
Alvarez, Marguerite d' NewGrDO
Alvarez, Maria Elena 1947- WhoHisp 94
Alvarez, Maria Elena 1954- WhoHisp 94
Alvarez, Mario 1937- WhoHisp 94
Alvarez, Mario Roberto 1913- IntWW 93
Alvarez, Martin WhoHisp 94
Alvarez, Matt, Jr. 1935- WhoAmP 93
Alvarez, Mercedes WhoHisp 94
Alvarez, Michael John 1949- WhoHisp 94
Alvarez, Ofelia Amparo 1958- WhoHisp 94
Alvarez, Pablo 1964- WhoScEn 94
Alvarez, Paul Hubert 1942- WhoAm 94, WhoFI 94
Alvarez, Pedro M. 1948- WhoHisp 94
Alvarez, Praxedes Eduardo 1958- WhoHisp 94
Alvarez, Ralph WhoHisp 94
Alvarez, Ramon A. 1937- WhoHisp 94
Alvarez, Richard G. WhoHisp 94
Alvarez, Richard S. 1947- WhoHisp 94
Alvarez, Robert Smyth 1912- WhoAm 94
Alvarez, Rodolfo 1936- WhoAm 94, WhoAmP 93, WhoHisp 94
Alvarez, Roman WhoHisp 94
Alvarez, Ronald Julian 1935- WhoHisp 94
Alvarez, Rosa M. 1929- WhoHisp 94
Alvarez, Sarah Lynn 1953- WhoHisp 94
Alvarez, Sofia d1985 WhoHol 92
Alvarez, Stephen Walter 1952- WhoHisp 94
Alvarez, Steven Grant 1955- WhoHisp 94
Alvarez, Thomas 1948- WhoFI 94, WhoMW 93
Alvarez, Walter 1940- WorScD
Alvarez, Wilson 1970- WhoHisp 94
Alvarez-Altman, Grace de Jesus 1926- WhoHisp 94
Alvarez Alvarez, Jose Luis 1930- IntWW 93
Alvarez Armellino, Gregorio Conrado 1925- IntWW 93
Alvarez Bischoff, Ana Maria 1953- WhoHisp 94
Alvarez Bravo, Manuel NewYTBS 93 [port]
Alvarez-Breckenridge, Carmen 1951- WhoHisp 94
Alvarez-Cervela, Jose Maria 1922- WhoAmA 93
Alvarez de la Campa, Alberto 1929- WhoHisp 94
Alvarez de Toledo, Luisa Isabel 1936- BlmGWL
Alvarez-Glasman, Arnold M. WhoHisp 94
Alvarez-Gomez, Ramon 1926- WhoHisp 94
Alvarez-González, José Julián 1952- WhoHisp 94
Alvarez-Lehman, Amalia 1946- WhoHisp 94
Alvarez-Pont, Victor 1949- WhoHisp 94
Alvarez-Recio, Emilio, Jr. 1938- WhoHisp 94
Alvarez Rendueles, Jose Ramon 1940- IntWW 93, WhoFI 94
Alvarez Rios, Maria 1919- BlmGWL
Alvarez Walker, Juan O. 1933- WhoHisp 94
Alvarino De Leira, Angeles 1916- WhoAm 94
Alvary, Lorenzo 1909- WhoAm 94
Alvary, Max(imilian) 1856-1898 NewGrDO
Alvear, Cecilia Estela WhoHisp 94
Alveranga, Glanvin L. 1928- WhoBlA 94
Alverio, Daisy M. 1958- WhoHisp 94
Alverio, Diane WhoHisp 94
Alvernaz, Bil. 1947- WhoWest 94
Alverson, Ben Earl 1940- WhoFI 94
Alverson, Dale Clark 1945- WhoWest 94
Alverson, William H. 1933- WhoAm 94
Alverson, William March 1956- WhoAmP 93
Alves, Arlene Rene 1958- WhoAmL 94
Alves, Colin 1930- Who 94
Alves, Laura 1922- WhoHol 92
Alves, Luis Fernando WhoHol 92
Alves, Manuel John 1929- WhoMW 93
Alves, Stephen D. WhoAmP 93
Alves, William L., Jr. 1935- WhoAmP 93
Alves Da Cunha, Jose Maria d1956 WhoHol 92
Alvey, John 1925- IntWW 93, Who 94
Alvey, Wilbur L. 1912- WhoAmP 93
Alvi, Zahoor Mohem 1942- WhoAm 94
Alviani, Joseph D. 1945- WhoAmL 94
Alvidrez, Richard F. 1943- WhoHisp 94
Alvillar, Ricardo Ernesto 1954- WhoHisp 94
Alvin, Dave See X ConMus 11
Alvin, John 1917- IntMPA 94, WhoHol 92
Alvina, Anicee 1953- WhoHol 92
Alvine, Robert 1938- WhoAm 94, WhoFI 94
Alving, Amy Elsa 1962- WhoScEn 94
Alvingham, Baron 1926- Who 94
Alvirez, David 1936- WhoHisp 94
Alvirez, Hortensia Maria 1944- WhoHisp 94
Alvis, Jerry Shumate, Sr. 1934- WhoAmL 94
Alvis, Ralph Edward 1938- WhoMW 93
Alviso, Edward F. 1963- WhoHisp 94
Alvord, Joel Barnes 1938- WhoAm 94, WhoFI 94
Alvord, Muriel d1960 WhoAmA 93N
Alwan, Abeer Abdul-Hussain 1959- WhoScEn 94
Alwan, Ameen DrAPF 93
Alwan, Georgia DrAPF 93
Alwan, Hamia 1930- IntWW 93
Alway, Richard F. 1950- WhoAmL 94
Alway, Robert Hamilton 1912-1990 WhAm 10
Alwin, Jerry Lee 1942- WhoAmP 93
Alworth, Lance ProFbHF [port]
Alworth, Sandra Ann 1947- WhoAm 94
Alworth, Thomas J. 1940- WhoAmL 94
Alwyn, William 1905-1985 IntDcF 2-4 [port]
Alyab'yev, Alexander Alexandrovich 1787-1851 NewGrDO
Al Yasiri, Kahtan Abbass 1939- WhoAm 94
Alyff, Mrs. NewGrDO
Alyn, Glen 1913- WhoHol 92
Alyn, Kirk 1910- WhoHol 92
Alzado, Lyle WhoHol 92
Alzado, Lyle 1949-1992 AnObit 1992
Alzado, Lyle Martin 1949-1992 WhAm 10
Álzaga, Florinda 1930- WhoHisp 94
Alzamora, Carlos 1926- IntWW 93
al-Zayyat, Latifa 1923- BlmGWL
Alzheimer, Alois 1864-1915 EncSPD
Alzmann, Walter d1980 WhoHol 92
Alzofon, Julia 1954- WhoScEn 94
Al-Zubaidi, Ali Abdul Jabbar 1952- WhoScEn 94
Al-Zubaidi, Amer Aziz 1945- WhoAm 94, WhoScEn 94
Amabile, George DrAPF 93
Amabile, George 1936- WrDr 94
Amabile, John Louis 1934- WhoAm 94
Amabile, Michael John 1968- WhoScEn 94
Amacher, Richard Earl 1917- WhoAm 94
Amachi, Shigeru d1985 WhoHol 92
Amad, Hani Subhi al- 1938- IntWW 93
Amadei, Filippo fl. 1690-1730 NewGrDO
Amadeo, Jose H. 1928- WhoAm 94
Amadeo, Lindsay Laughlin 1963- WhoMW 93
Amadeo, Myrna Passalacqua WhoAmP 93
Amadi, Elechi 1934- WrDr 94
Amadiume, Ifi BlmGWL
Amado, Honey Kessler 1949- WhoAmL 94
Amado, Jesse V. 1951- WhoAmA 93
Amado, Jorge 1912- HispLC [port], IntWW 93
Amado, Jorge (Fazenda Auricidia) 1912- ConWorW 93
Amado, Patricia Ann 1960- WhoWest 94
Amado, Ralph David 1932- WhoHisp 94, WhoScEn 94
Amador, Albert, III 1936- WhoHisp 94
Amador, Antonio Candia 1943- WhoHisp 94
Amador, Antonio Lucas 1948- WhoHisp 94
Amador, Armando Gerardo 1953- WhoMW 93, WhoScEn 94
Amador, Dora 1948- WhoHisp 94
Amador, John Paul, Sr. 1945- WhoHisp 94
Amador, Jose Manuel 1938- WhoScEn 94
Amador, Michael George Sanchez 1936- WhoHisp 94
Amador, Raysa Elena 1949- WhoHisp 94
Amador, Richard S. WhoHisp 94
Amador, Rose Ann 1949- WhoHisp 94
Amadori, Giovanni NewGrDO
Amaker, Norman Carey 1935- WhoBlA 94, WhoMW 93
Amalfi, Frederick Anthony 1950- WhoWest 94
Amalia, Narcisa 1852-1924 BlmGWL
Amaltitano, Lelia WhoAmA 93
Aman, Alfred Charles, Jr. 1945- WhoAm 94
Aman, George Matthias, III 1930- WhoAm 94
Aman, Joseph Patrick 1957- WhoMW 93
Aman, Karl E. 1928- IntWW 93
Aman, Mohammed M. 1940- WhoBlA 94
Aman, Mohammed Mohammed 1940- WhoAm 94
Aman, Reinhold Albert 1936- WhoAm 94, WhoWest 94

Amandry, Pierre 1912- *IntWW 93*
Amann, Betty d1990 *WhoHol 92*
Amann, Charles Albert 1926- *WhoAm 94*
Amann, James A. 1956- *WhoAmP 93*
Amann, Peter Henry 1927- *WhoAm 94*
Amano, Jun 1948- *WhoFI 94*
Amano, Kosei 1905- *IntWW 93*
Amano, Taka 1950- *WhoAmA 93*
Amanova, Maral Bazarovna *WhoWomW 91*
Amantacha 1610?-c. 1636 *EncNAR*
Amanuddin, Syed *DrAPF 93*
Amaon, Gary P. 1945- *WhoAmL 94*
Amara, Lucine 1927- *NewGrDO, WhoAm 94*
Amaral, Annelle C. 1948- *WhoHisp 94*
Amaral, Annelle Claire 1948- *WhoAmP 93*
Amaral, Joseph Ferreira 1955- *WhoAm 94, WhoScEn 94*
Amaral, Pedro *WhoHisp 94*
Amaral, Rich 1962- *WhoHisp 94*
Amarat, Issariyaporn Chulajata 1961- *WhoWest 94*
Amarel, Saul 1928- *WhoAm 94*
Amari, John E. 1948- *WhoAmP 93*
Amarilio, Joseph Daniel 1952- *WhoAmL 94*
Amarilios, John Alexander 1958- *WhoFI 94*
Amarilis fl. 17th cent.- *BlmGWL*
Amaro, Hortensia *WhoHisp 94*
Amaro, Ruben 1936- *WhoBlA 94, WhoHisp 94*
Amaro, Ruben, Jr. 1965- *WhoHisp 94*
Amarotico, Joseph Anthony 1931- *WhoAmA 93N*
Amason, Alvin Eli 1948- *WhoAmA 93*
Amatangelo, Nicholas S. 1935- *WhoFI 94, WhoMW 93*
Amateau, Maurice Francis 1935- *WhoScEn 94*
Amateau, Micaela *WhoAmA 93*
Amateau, Rod 1927- *IntMPA 94*
Amateis, Edmond Romulus 1897-1981 *WhoAmA 93N*
Amathila, Libertine 1940- *WhoWomW 91*
Amatniek, Sara 1922- *WhoAmA 93*
Amato, Carol Joy 1944- *WhoWest 94*
Amato, Frank Charles 1941- *WhoWest 94*
Amato, Giuliano 1938- *CurBio 93 [port], IntWW 93*
Amato, Giuseppe d1964 *WhoHol 92*
Amato, Isabella Antonia 1942- *WhoAm 94*
Amato, Joseph A. 1938- *WhoMW 93*
Amato, Michele 1945- *WhoAmA 93*
Amato, Pasquale d1942 *WhoHol 92*
Amato, Pasquale 1878-1942 *NewGrDO*
Amato, Vincent Anthony 1925- *WhoAmP 93*
Amato, Vincent Edward 1962- *WhoScEn 94*
Amato, Vincent Vito 1929- *WhoAm 94*
Amato, (Epifanio) Vincenzo 1629-1670 *NewGrDO*
Amatori, Michael Louis 1951- *WhoWest 94*
Amatos, Barbara Hansen 1944- *WhoMW 93*
Amawi, Mohammad Sa'di 1946- *WhoMW 93*
Amaya, Abel *WhoHisp 94*
Amaya, Armando 1935- *WhoAmA 93*
Amaya, Carmen d1963 *WhoHol 92*
Amaya, Jorge 1954- *WhoHisp 94*
Amaya, Manuel Enrique 1953- *WhoHisp 94*
Amaya, Maria Alvarez 1955- *WhoHisp 94*
Ambach, Dwight Russell 1931- *WhoAm 94*
Ambach, Gordon Mac Kay 1934- *WhoAm 94*
Ambani, Dhirubhai 1932- *IntWW 93*
Ambardekar, Raj 1941- *WhoAm 94*
Ambartsumian, Victor 1908- *Who 94*
Ambartsumov, Evgeny Arshakovich 1929- *LoBiDrD*
Ambartsumov, Yevgeniy Arshakovich 1929- *IntWW 93*
Ambartsumyan, Sergey Aleksandrovich 1922- *IntWW 93*
Ambartsumyan, Victor Amazaspovich 1908- *IntWW 93*
Ambasz, Emilio 1943- *WhoHisp 94*
Ambeau, Karen M. 1956- *WhoBlA 94*
Amber, Douglas George 1956- *WhoAmL 94*
Amberg, Raymond Michael 1895- *WhAm 10*
Amberg, Richard Hiller, Jr. 1942- *WhoAm 94*
Amberg, Stanley Louis 1934- *WhoAmL 94*
Amberg, Thomas Law 1948- *WhoAm 94, WhoFI 94*
Amberger, Johann Christoph 1963- *WhoFI 94*
Amberley, Viscount 1968- *Who 94*
Amberley, Richard 1916- *WrDr 94*
Amberson, Grace D. 1894-1957 *WhoAmA 93N*
Amberson, James Burns, IV 1951- *WhoFI 94*
Ambert, Alba N. *DrAPF 93*
Ambia *BlmGWL*
Ambirajan, Srinivasa 1936- *WrDr 94*
Ambler, Bruce Melville 1939- *WhoFI 94*
Ambler, David Samuel 1954- *WhoFI 94*
Ambler, Eric 1909- *IntWW 93, Who 94, WhoAm 94, WrDr 94*
Ambler, Ernest 1923- *WhoAm 94*
Ambler, John Doss 1934- *Who 94*
Ambler, John Richard 1934- *WhoWest 94*
Ambler, Joss d1959 *WhoHol 92*
Ambler, Judith Fitts 1959- *WhoAmL 94*
Ambler, Marjane 1948- *WrDr 94*
Ambler, Mary Cary fl. 1770- *BlmGWL*
Ambler, Robert B. 1927- *WhoAmP 93*
Ambo, George Somboba 1925- *Who 94*
Amboise, Chevalier d' *WhAmRev*
Ambraseys, Nicholas 1929- *IntWW 93, Who 94*
Ambre, John Joseph 1937- *WhoMW 93*
Ambriere, Francis 1907- *IntWW 93*
Ambro, Jerome A. d1993 *NewYTBS 93 [port]*
Ambroggio, Luis Alberto 1945- *WhoHisp 94*
Ambrogietti, Giuseppe 1780-1833? *NewGrDO*
Ambros, Vladimir 1890-1956 *NewGrDO*
Ambrosch, Joseph Karl 1759-1822 *NewGrDO*
Ambrose, Alice 1906- *WrDr 94*
Ambrose, Ashley *WhoBlA 94*
Ambrose, Charles Edward 1922- *WhoAmA 93*
Ambrose, Charles Stuart 1951- *WhoFI 94*
Ambrose, Daniel Michael 1955- *WhoAm 94*
Ambrose, Edmund Jack 1914- *Who 94*
Ambrose, Ethel L. 1930- *WhoBlA 94*
Ambrose, Gerald A. 1947- *WhoAm 94*
Ambrose, Helen d1966 *WhoHol 92*
Ambrose, James R. 1922- *WhoAmP 93*
Ambrose, James Richard 1922- *WhoAm 94*
Ambrose, James Walter Davy d1992 *Who 94N*
Ambrose, Joseph Vincent, Jr. 1929- *WhoAm 94*
Ambrose, Myles Joseph 1926- *WhoAm 94, WhoAmL 94, WhoAmP 93*
Ambrose, Robert Micheal 1960- *WhoScEn 94*
Ambrose, Samuel Sheridan, Jr. 1923- *WhoAm 94*
Ambrose, Stephen (Edward) 1936- *WrDr 94*
Ambrose, Stephen E(dward) 1936- *ConAu 43NR*
Ambrose, Stephen Edward 1936- *WhoAm 94*
Ambrose, Thomas Cleary 1932- *WhoFI 94, WhoWest 94*
Ambrose, Tommy W. 1926- *WhoAm 94*
Ambrosi, Gustinus 1893-1975 *EncDeaf*
Ambrosini, Lynne Denise 1953- *WhoMW 93*
Ambrosino, Ralph Thomas, Jr. 1940- *WhoAm 94*
Ambrosio, Gabriel M. 1938- *WhoAmP 93*
Ambrosio, Giacomo d' *NewGrDO*
Ambrosius, Margery Marzahn 1942- *WhoMW 93*
Ambrosius, Mark Ralph 1951- *WhoAm 94, WhoMW 93*
Ambrozic, Aloysius Matthew *Who 94*
Ambrozic, Aloysius Matthew 1930- *WhoAm 94*
Ambrus, Clara Maria 1924- *WhoAm 94*
Ambrus, Julian L. 1924- *WhoAm 94*
Ambrusko, John Stephen 1913- *WhoScEn 94*
Ambs, Todd Lawrence 1958- *WhoMW 93*
Ambuel, Bruce Howard 1952- *WhoMW 93*
Ambur, Damodar Reddy 1947- *WhoAm 94, WhoScEn 94*
Ambush, Robert C. *WhoBlA 94*
Amcher, Jeannie Webb 1953- *WhoFI 94*
Amdahl, Byrdelle John 1934- *WhoAm 94*
Amdahl, Douglas Kenneth 1919- *WhoAm 94, WhoAmL 94*
Amdahl, Gene Myron 1922- *WhoAm 94, WhoWest 94*
Amdahl, Myron 1948- *WhoAmP 93*
Amdahl, Timothy Henning 1955- *WhoAmP 93*
Amdall, William John 1953- *WhoAm 94, WhoFI 94*
Amdur, Eli N. 1947- *WhoFI 94*
Amdur, Martin Bennett 1942- *WhoAm 94, WhoAmL 94*
Ameche, Don 1908- *IntMPA 94, WhoAm 94, WhoHol 92*
Ameche, Don 1908-1993 *NewYTBS 93 [port], News 94-2*
Ameche, Jim d1983 *WhoHol 92*
Ameen, Mark *DrAPF 93*
Ameling, Elly 1938- *IntWW 93, WhoAm 94*
Amelio, Gilbert Frank 1943- *WhoAm 94, WhoWest 94*
Amell, Samuel 1948- *WhoHisp 94*
Amemiya, Chris Tsuyoshi 1959- *WhoScEn 94*
Amemiya, Kenjie 1958- *WhoScEn 94*
Amemiya, Ronald Yoshihiko 1940- *WhoAmP 93*
Amemiya, Takeshi 1935- *WhoAm 94, WhoWest 94*
Amen, Irving 1918- *WhoAm 94, WhoAmA 93*
Amend, Eugene Michael 1950- *WhoAmA 93*
Amend, James Michael 1942- *WhoAmL 94*
Amend, John R(obert) 1938- *WrDr 94*
Amend, William John Conrad, Jr. 1941- *WhoAm 94*
Amende, Lynn Meridith 1950- *WhoAm 94*
Amendola, Giuseppe c. 1750-1808 *NewGrDO*
Amendt, Marilyn Joan 1928- *WhoMW 93*
Amendt, Rudolph d1987 *WhoHol 92*
Amenoff, Gregory 1948- *WhoAmA 93*
Ament, Don 1942- *WhoAmP 93*
Ament, F. Thomas 1937- *WhoMW 93*
Ament, Jeff
See Pearl Jam *News 94-2*
Ament, Richard 1919- *WhoAm 94*
Ament, Richard Rand 1950- *WhoMW 93*
Amenta, Peter Sebastian 1927- *WhoAm 94*
Amer, Kenneth Benjamin 1924- *WhoWest 94*
Amer, Magid Hashim 1941- *WhoScEn 94*
Amer, Nicholas 1928- *WhoHol 92*
Amer, Patrick Joseph 1937- *WhoAmL 94*
Amerasinghe, Chittharanjan Felix 1933- *IntWW 93*
America, Juana de *BlmGWL*
America, Paul 1944- *WhoHol 92*
Americus, Bruce Alfred 1946- *WhoAmL 94*
Amerine, Anne Follette 1950- *WhoFI 94*
Amerine, Maynard Andrew 1911- *WhoAm 94, WhoScEn 94*
Ameringer, Charles D. 1926- *WhoAm 94*
Amerman, John Ellis 1944- *WhoAm 94, WhoAmL 94*
Amerman, John W. 1932- *WhoAm 94, WhoFI 94, WhoWest 94*
Amerman, Monique Gabrielle 1934- *WhoWest 94*
Amero, Jane A. 1941- *WhoAmP 93*
Amero, Sally Ann 1952- *WhoScEn 94*
Amerson, Lucius Davenport 1933- *WhoAmP 93*
Amerson, Tammy *WhoHol 92*
Amery *Who 94*
Amery, Carl *EncSF 93, IntWW 93*
Amery, Colin Robert 1944- *Who 94*
Amery, John 1912-1945 *DcNaB MP*
Amery Of Lustleigh, Baron 1919- *IntWW 93, Who 94, WrDr 94*
Ames, Adelbert, III 1921- *WhoAm 94*
Ames, Adrienne d1947 *WhoHol 92*
Ames, Allyson *WhoHol 92*
Ames, Arthur Forbes 1906-1975 *WhoAmA 93N*
Ames, Bruce N. 1928- *CurBio 93 [port]*
Ames, Bruce Nathan 1928- *IntWW 93, WhoAm 94, WhoScEn 94, WhoWest 94*
Ames, Christopher Norman 1953- *WhoAmL 94*
Ames, Clinton *EncSF 93*
Ames, Craig L. 1944- *WhoAm 94*
Ames, Damaris 1944- *WhoAm 94, WhoFI 94*
Ames, Delano L. 1906- *WrDr 94*
Ames, Donald Paul 1922- *WhoAm 94*
Ames, Edward Scribner 1870-1958 *DcAmReB 2*
Ames, Felicia 1914- *WrDr 94*
Ames, Frank Anthony 1942- *WhoAm 94*
Ames, G. Ronald 1939- *WhoIns 94*
Ames, George Joseph 1917- *WhoAm 94*
Ames, George Ronald 1939- *WhoAm 94*
Ames, Gerald d1933 *WhoHol 92*
Ames, Gerald 1906-1993 *ConAu 140, SmATA 74 [port]*
Ames, James Barr 1911- *WhoAm 94, WhoAmL 94*
Ames, Jane Irene 1950- *WhoMW 93*
Ames, Jessie Daniel 1883-1972 *AmSocL*
Ames, Jimmy d1965 *WhoHol 92*
Ames, Jimmy Ray 1951- *WhoAm 94*
Ames, John Hersh 1943- *WhoFI 94*
Ames, John William 1946- *WhoAmL 94*
Ames, Lawrence Coffin, Jr. 1925- *WhoWest 94*
Ames, Lee Judah 1921- *WhoAmA 93*
Ames, Leon d1993 *NewYTBS 93 [port]*
Ames, Leon 1903- *IntMPA 94, WhoHol 92*
Ames, Lionel *WhoHol 92*
Ames, Louis B. 1918- *IntMPA 94*
Ames, Louise Bates 1908- *WhoAm 94*
Ames, Marc L. 1943- *WhoAmL 94, WhoFI 94*
Ames, Michael d1972 *WhoHol 92*
Ames, Michael McClean 1933- *IntWW 93, WhoAm 94, WhoWest 94*
Ames, Mildred 1919- *EncSF 93*
Ames, Norma Harriet 1920- *WhoWest 94*
Ames, Oakes 1931- *WhoAm 94*
Ames, Percy d1936 *WhoHol 92*
Ames, Polly Scribner 1908- *WhoAmA 93*
Ames, Preston d1983 *IntDcF 2-4*
Ames, Rachel 1922- *WrDr 94*
Ames, Rachel 1929- *WhoHol 92*
Ames, Rachel (Sarah) *Who 94*
Ames, Ramsay 1921- *WhoHol 92*
Ames, Robert d1931 *WhoHol 92*
Ames, Robert Arthur 1925- *WhoAm 94*
Ames, Robert Forbes 1930- *WhoAm 94*
Ames, Robert San 1919- *WhoAm 94*
Ames, Rosemary 1912?- *WhoHol 92*
Ames, Steven Reede 1951- *WhoFI 94*
Ames, Sylvester 1947- *WhoMW 93*
Ames, Thomas-Robert Howland 1930- *WhoFI 94*
Ames, W. Allen, Jr. 1946- *WhoAmL 94*
Ames, William Clark 1950- *WhoWest 94*
Ames, William Eugene 1923- *WhoAmP 93*
Ames, William Francis 1926- *WhoAm 94*
Ames, Wilmer C. d1993 *WhoBlA 94N*
Ames, Wilmer C., Jr. d1993 *NewYTBS 93*
Amess, David Anthony Andrew 1952- *Who 94*
Amestoy, Jeffrey L. 1946- *WhoAmP 93*
Amestoy, Jeffrey Lee 1946- *WhoAm 94, WhoAmL 94*
Ames-Urie, Patricia Yvonne 1946- *WhoWest 94*
Ametistov, Earnest Mikhailovich 1935- *LoBiDrD*
Amey, Earle Bartley 1942- *WhoScEn 94*
Amey, Lorne James 1940- *WhoAm 94*
Amey, William Greenville 1918- *WhoAm 94*
Amézaga, Alfred M., Jr. *WhoHisp 94*
Amezcua, Robert 1951- *WhoHisp 94*
Amezquita, Jesusa Maria 1958- *WhoHisp 94*
Amft, Robert 1916- *WhoAmA 93*
Amgott, Gordon Lee 1948- *WhoFI 94*
Amherst, Earl d1993 *Who 94N*
Amherst, Jeffrey d1815 *WhAmRev*
Amherst, Jeffrey 1717-1797 *AmRev, WhAmRev [port]*
Amherst Of Hackney, Baron 1940- *Who 94*
Amhowitz, Harris J. 1934- *WhoAm 94, WhoAmL 94, WhoFI 94*
Amichai, Yehuda 1924- *ConWorW 93*
Amicis, Anna Lucia de *NewGrDO*
Amick, Carol Campbell *WhoAmP 93*
Amick, Charles L. 1916- *WhoScEn 94*
Amick, Madchen 1970- *WhoHol 92*
Amick, Ollie C. 1920- *WhoAmP 93*
Amick, S. Eugene 1936- *WhoScEn 94*
Amick, Steven Hammond 1947- *WhoAmP 93*
Amico, Charles William 1942- *WhoFI 94, WhoWest 94*
Amico, David Michael 1951- *WhoAmA 93, WhoWest 94*
Amico, Fedele d' *NewGrDO*
Amiconi, Jacopo 1682-1752 *NewGrDO*
Amidei, Ronald Lee 1961- *WhoAmL 94*
Amidei, Sergio 1904-1981 *IntDcF 2-4*
Amidon, Eleanor H. 1929- *WhoAmP 93*
Amidon, Richard Elkins 1927- *WhoAmP 93*
Amidon, Roger Lyman 1938- *WhoAm 94*
Amidon, Stephen 1959- *WrDr 94*
Amidou (Souad) *WhoHol 92*
Amiel, David 1938- *WhoScEn 94, WhoWest 94*
Amiel, Jon *IntMPA 94*
Amies, Alex Phillip 1967- *WhoScEn 94*
Amies, (Edwin) Hardy 1909- *IntWW 93, Who 94*
Amieva, Marta Zenaida 1945- *WhoFI 94*
Amiji, Hatim M. 1939- *WhoBlA 94*
Amin, Adibah *BlmGWL*
Amin, Angela Regina Heinzen Helou 1953- *WhoWomW 91*
Amin, Karima 1947- *WhoBlA 94*
Amin, Khalida Adibah binti Haji 1936- *BlmGWL*
Amin, Mahmoud 1920- *IntWW 93*
Amin, Mirza Ruhul 1922- *IntWW 93*
Amin, Mostafa 1914- *IntWW 93*
Amin, Samir 1931- *IntWW 93*
Amin Dada, Idi 1925- *IntWW 93*
Amini, Ali d1992 *IntWW 93N*
Amini, Ali 1905-1992 *AnObit 1992*
Amini, Bijan Khajehnouri 1943- *WhoFI 94*

Amino, Leo 1911-1989 *WhAm 10, WhoAmA 93N*
Amino, Nobuyuki 1940- *WhoScEn 94*
Aminoff, Judith 1947- *WhoAmA 93*
Amioka, Wallace Shuzo 1914- *WhoFI 94, WhoWest 94*
Amiot, David Bruce 1947- *WhoFI 94*
Amir, Nawal *WhoWomW 91*
Amirikia, Hassan 1937- *WhoMW 93*
Amir Machmud, Lieut.-Gen. 1923- *IntWW 93*
Amir-Moez, Ali Reza 1919- *WhoScEn 94*
Amirouche, Farid M. L. 1954- *WhoMW 93*
Amirov, Fikret (Meshadi Jamil') 1922-1984 *NewGrDO*
Amis, Kingsley 1922- *BlmGEL, DcLB 139 [port], IntWW 93, Who 94, WhoAm 94*
Amis, Kingsley (William) 1922- *EncSF 93, WrDr 94*
Amis, Martin 1949- *BlmGEL [port]*
Amis, Martin (Louis) 1949- *EncSF 93, WrDr 94*
Amis, Martin Louis 1949- *IntWW 93, Who 94*
Amis, Suzy 1961- *WhoHol 92*
Amis, Suzy 1962- *IntMPA 94*
Amish, Keith Warren 1923- *WhoAm 94*
Amiss, Charles R. 1932- *WhoMW 93*
Amistad, Glenn Repiedad 1955- *WhoWest 94*
Amit, Meir 1921- *IntWW 93*
Amitsur, Shimshon Avraham 1921- *IntWW 93*
Amkraut, Alynne 1953- *ConTFT 11*
Amladi, Prasad Ganesh 1941- *WhoFI 94, WhoMW 93, WhoScEn 94*
Amling, Frederick 1926- *WhoAm 94, WrDr 94*
Amlot, Roy Douglas 1942- *Who 94*
Amman, Elizabeth Jean 1941- *WhoMW 93*
Amman, John Charles 1935- *WhoAm 94*
Amman, Robert J. 1938- *WhoFI 94*
Ammann, Jean-Christophe *WhoAm 94*
Ammann, Lillian Ann Nicholson 1946- *WhoFI 94*
Ammann, Thomas d1993 *NewYTBS 93*
Ammar, Mohamed Ali 1937- *IntWW 93*
Ammar, Raymond George 1932- *WhoAm 94, WhoMW 93*
Ammar, Reda Anwar 1950- *WhoScEn 94*
Ammarell, John Samuel 1920- *WhoAm 94*
Ammarell, Scott William 1960- *WhoAmL 94*
Amme, Robert C. 1930- *WhoWest 94*
Ammer, Christine (Parker) 1931- *WrDr 94*
Ammer, William 1919- *WhoAmL 94, WhoMW 93*
Ammeraal, Robert Neal 1936- *WhoFI 94, WhoMW 93*
Ammerman, Calvin P. 1924- *WhoWest 94*
Ammerman, James Harry, II 1951- *WhoAmL 94*
Ammerman, Joseph S. 1924- *WhoAmP 93*
Ammerman, Robert Ray 1927- *WhoAm 94*
Ammeson, Charles F. 1953- *WhoAmL 94*
Ammirati, Ralph *WhoAm 94*
Ammon, Alicia d1980 *WhoHol 92*
Ammon, Gunter Karl-Johannes 1918- *IntWW 93*
Ammon, Harry 1917- *WhoAm 94*
Ammons, A. R. *DrAPF 93*
Ammons, A(rchie) R(andolph) 1926- *WrDr 94*
Ammons, Archie Randolph 1926- *WhoAm 94*
Ammons, Barbara E. 1937- *WhoMW 93*
Ammons, Edsel Albert 1924- *WhoAm 94, WhoBlA 94*
Ammons, Robert Bruce 1920- *WhoAm 94*
Amneus, D. A. 1919- *WhoAm 94*
Amon, Arthur Howard, Jr. 1927- *WhoAm 94*
Amon, Carol Bagley 1946- *WhoAm 94, WhoAmL 94*
Amon, Cristina Hortensia 1956- *WhoScEn 94*
Amon, William Frederick, Jr. 1922- *WhoAm 94*
Amondson, Neil Arthur 1954- *WhoAmP 93*
Amon Parisi, Cristina Hortensia 1956- *WhoAm 94*
Amonson, Johanne Leslie 1949- *WhoAmL 94*
Amonte, Anthony Lewis 1970- *WhoAm 94*
Amontons, Guillaume 1666-1705 *WorInv*
Amoore, Frederick Andrew 1913- *Who 94*
Amor, Christine *WhoHol 92*
Amor, Guadalupe 1920- *BlmGWL*
Amor, Simeon, Jr. 1924- *WhoWest 94*
Amorello, Matthew J. *WhoAmP 93*
Amorevoli, Angelo (Maria) 1716-1798 *NewGrDO*
Amornmarn, Lina *WhoScEn 94*
Amoros, Sandy 1930-1992 *AnObit 1992*
Amoroso, Marie Dorothy 1924- *WhoScEn 94*
Amortegui, Antonio J. 1930- *WhoHisp 94*
Amory *Who 94*
Amory, Claudia *WhoAmA 93*
Amory, Cleveland 1917- *EnvEnc [port], WhoAm 94, WrDr 94*
Amory, Katherine 1731-1777 *BlmGWL*
Amory, Reginald L. 1936- *WhoBlA 94*
Amory, Robert, Jr. 1915-1989 *WhAm 10*
Amory, Roger d1322 *DcNaB MP*
Amory, Thomas Carhart 1933- *WhoAm 94, WhoFI 94, WhoWest 94*
Amos, Alan Thomas 1952- *Who 94*
Amos, Archie L., Jr. 1947- *WhoAmP 93*
Amos, Barbara Mary D. *Who 94*
Amos, Betty Ann 1948- *WhoMW 93*
Amos, Charles Clinton 1940- *WhoFI 94*
Amos, Daniel Paul 1951- *WhoAm 94, WhoFI 94*
Amos, Dennis B. 1923- *WhoAm 94, WhoScEn 94*
Amos, Emma 1938- *WhoAmA 93*
Amos, Ethel S. *WhoBlA 94*
Amos, Eugene P. *WhoAmP 93*
Amos, Francis John Clarke 1924- *Who 94*
Amos, George Henry, III 1959- *WhoWest 94*
Amos, Harton Douglas 1943- *WhoIns 94*
Amos, James H., Jr. 1946- *WhoFI 94, WrDr 94*
Amos, James Lysle 1929- *WhoAm 94*
Amos, John 1940- *WhoHol 92*
Amos, John 1941- *IntMPA 94, WhoAm 94*
Amos, John Beverly 1924- *WhAm 10*
Amos, Kent B. 1944- *WhoBlA 94*
Amos, Larry C. 1935- *WhoBlA 94*
Amos, Oris Elizabeth Carter *WhoBlA 94*
Amos, Paul Denver 1951- *WhoWest 94*
Amos, Paul Shelby 1926- *WhoAm 94, WhoFI 94*
Amos, Valerie 1954- *Who 94*
Amos, Wally 1937- *AfrAmAl 6 [port], WhoBlA 94*
Amos and Andy *WhoCom, WhoHol 92*
Amosov, N(icolai Mikhailovitch) 1913- *EncSF 93*
Amoss, Berthe 1925- *WhoAmA 93*
Amoss, W. James, Jr. 1924- *WhoFI 94*
Amoss, William H. 1936- *WhoAmP 93*
Amotz, Dan Ben d1989 *WhoHol 92*
Amour, Jan'ette Alice 1957- *WhoMW 93*
Amouzadeh, Hamid R. *WhoScEn 94*
Amouzegar, Jamshid 1923- *IntWW 93*
Amoyal, Pierre Alain Wilfred 1949- *IntWW 93*
Amparado, Keith D. 1952- *WhoFI 94*
Ampel, Leon Louis 1936- *WhoAm 94*
Ampere, Andre Marie *WorInv*
Ampere, Andre Marie 1775-1836 *WorScD [port]*
Amphavannasouk, Eng 1935- *WhoAsA 94*
Ampleforth, Abbot of *Who 94*
Ampon, Felicismo 1920- *BuCMET*
Ampthill, Baron 1921- *Who 94*
Ampudia-Whitt, Robert, III 1930- *WhoFI 94*
Ampy, Franklin R. 1936- *WhoBlA 94*
Amr, Asad Tamer 1941- *WhoScEn 94*
Amram, David (Werner) 1930- *NewGrDO*
Amram, David Werner 1930- *WhoAm 94*
Amram, Philip Werner 1900-1990 *WhAm 10*
Amrane, Djamila 1941- *BlmGWL*
Amrein, Robert Stephen 1954- *WhoAmL 94*
Amrhein, John Kilian 1938- *WhoAm 94*
Amri Sued, Ismail 1942- *IntWW 93*
Amritanand, Joseph 1917- *IntWW 93, Who 94*
Amritraj, Anand 1952- *BuCMET*
Amritraj, Ashok 1957- *BuCMET*
Amritraj, Vijay 1953- *BuCMET*
Amrouche, Fadhma Ait Mansur 1882-1967 *BlmGWL*
Amrouche, Marie-Louise (Taos) 1913-1976 *BlmGWL*
Amschler, James Ralph 1943- *WhoAmL 94*
Amsden, Floyd T. 1913- *WhoAmA 93N*
Amsden, Ted Thomas 1950- *WhoAm 94, WhoAmL 94*
Amsei, Abram 1922- *WhoAm 94*
Amsel, Robert Gary 1957- *WhoAmL 94*
Amspoker, James Mack 1926- *WhoAm 94*
Amstadter, Laurence 1922- *WhoAm 94*
Amster, Linda Evelyn 1938- *WhoAm 94*
Amster, Sally d1988 *WhoAmA 93N*
Amsterdam, Anthony Guy 1935- *WhoAm 94*
Amsterdam, Jay D. 1949- *WhoScEn 94*
Amsterdam, Mark Lemle 1944- *WhoAmL 94*
Amsterdam, Morey 1912- *WhoCom*
Amsterdam, Morey 1914- *IntMPA 94, WhoHol 92*
Amstutz, Daniel Gordon 1932- *WhoAm 94*
Amstutz, Harold Emerson 1919- *WhoAm 94*
Amstutz, Ronald D. *WhoAmP 93*
Amstuz, Dennis Gordon 1951- *WhoMW 93*
Amte, Baba *IntWW 93*
Amtoft-Nielsen, Joan Theresa 1940- *WhoScEn 94*
A Mu 1942- *WhoPRCh 91 [port]*
A-mu-dong Ni-ya-zi *WhoPRCh 91*
Amudun Niyaz *WhoPRCh 91 [port]*
Amudun Niyaz 1932- *IntWW 93*
Amuedo, Jerry 1937- *WhoHisp 94*
Amuedo, Mark Gerard 1937- *WhoHisp 94*
Amundsen, Roald Engelbregt Gravning 1872-1928 *WhWE [port]*
Amundson, Clyde Howard 1927- *WhoAm 94, WhoScEn 94*
Amundson, Duane Melvin 1925- *WhoFI 94, WhoMW 93*
Amundson, Eva Donalda 1911- *WhoWest 94*
Amundson, Merle Edward 1936- *WhoScEn 94*
Amundson, Neal Russell 1916- *WhoAm 94*
Amundson, Robert A. *WhoAm 94, WhoAmL 94*
Amundson, Robert A. 1938- *WhoAmP 93*
Amur-Umarjee, Shashi Gururaj 1955- *WhoWest 94*
Amusia, Miron Ya 1934- *WhoScEn 94*
Amwell, Baron 1943- *Who 94*
Amy, Dennis Oldrieve 1932- *Who 94*
Amy, Jonathan Weekes 1923- *WhoAm 94*
Amylon, Kenneth L. 1948- *WhoIns 94*
Amylon, Michael David 1950- *WhoAm 94*
Amy-Moreno de Toro, Angel Alberto 1945- *WhoHisp 94*
Amyot, Leopold Henri 1930- *Who 94*
Amyot, Rene 1926- *Who 94*
Amyx, Darrell Arlynn 1911- *WhoAm 94*
Amyx, Leon Kirkman 1908- *WhoAmA 93*
An, Myoung Hee 1958- *WhoAsA 94*
An, Nack Young 1936- *WhoAsA 94*
Ana-Alicia *WhoHisp 94*
Ana-Alicia 1957- *WhoHol 92*
Anabara, Semyon fl. 170-?- *WhWE*
Anacker, John William 1960- *WhoAmA 93*
Anaebonam, Aloysius Onyeabo 1955- *WhoScEn 94*
Anagnost, Themis John 1913- *WhoMW 93*
Anagnostaki, Loula 1940- *BlmGWL*
Anagnostopoulos, Stavros Aristidou 1946- *WhoScEn 94*
Analla, Isabel d1958 *WhoHol 92*
'Anan dc. 846 *BlmGWL*
Anand, A. Angela *WhoAsA 94*
Anand, Bal Krishan 1917- *IntWW 93*
Anand, Charanjit S. 1956- *WhoAsA 94*
Anand, Mulk Raj 1905- *IntWW 93, RfGShF, WrDr 94*
Anand, Rajen S. 1937- *WhoAm 94*
Anand, Rajen S. 1939- *WhoAsA 94*
Anand, Rakesh 1955- *WhoAsA 94*
Anand, Satish Chandra 1930- *WhoAsA 94*
Anand, Suresh Chandra 1931- *WhoAm 94, WhoScEn 94, WhoWest 94*
Anand, Yogindra Nath 1939- *WhoMW 93*
Anandan, Munisamy 1939- *WhoScEn 94*
Anandan, Munisamy 1940- *WhoAsA 94*
Anand Panyarachun *IntWW 93*
Anania, George *EncSF 93*
Anania, Michael (Angelo) 1939- *WrDr 94*
Anania, Michael A. *DrAPF 93*
Anania, William Christian 1958- *WhoScEn 94*
Ananiashvili, Nina 1963- *IntWW 93*
Ananiashvili, Nina 1964- *IntDcB [port]*
Ananta Toer, Pramoedya *IntWW 93*
Ananth, Jambur 1932- *WhoAm 94*
Ananyev, Anatoliy Andreyevich 1925- *IntWW 93*
Anaple, Elsie Mae 1932- *WhoMW 93*
Anaporte-Easton, Jean *DrAPF 93*
Anargyros, Spero 1915- *WhoAm 94, WhoAmA 93*
Anas, Julianne Kay 1941- *WhoMW 93, WhoScEn 94*
Anast, David George 1955- *WhoWest 94*
Anastanio, Anthony J. *WhoIns 94*
Anastas, Peter *DrAPF 93*
Anastas, Terrence Joseph 1958- *WhoAmL 94*
Anastasatu, Constantin 1917- *IntWW 93*
Anastasi, Anne 1908- *WhoAm 94*
Anastasi, Richard Joseph 1951- *WhoFI 94*
Anastasi, William (Joseph) 1933- *WhoAmA 93*
Anastasi, William Joseph 1933- *WhoAm 94*
Anastasia, Lawrence J. *WhoAmP 93*
Anastasio, James 1930- *WhoIns 94*
Anastasio, Thomas Joseph 1958- *WhoMW 93, WhoScEn 94*
Anastasiou, Clifford (John) 1929- *WrDr 94*
Anastos, Rosemary Park 1907- *WhoAm 94*
Anati, Emmanuel 1930- *WrDr 94*
Anatol, Karl W. E. *WhoAm 94*
Anawalt, Patricia Rieff 1924- *WhoAm 94, WhoWest 94*
Anawangmani, Simon c. 1808-1891 *EncNAR*
Anawati, Joseph Soliman 1941- *WhoWest 94*
Anaya, Gabriel 1937- *WhoAmP 93*
Anaya, George, Jr. 1964- *WhoHisp 94*
Anaya, M. Steven 1956- *WhoAmP 93*
Anaya, Mary *WhoHisp 94*
Anaya, Richard Alfred, Jr. 1932- *WhoAm 94*
Anaya, Rudolfo 1937- *HispLC [port]*
Anaya, Rudolfo A. *DrAPF 93*
Anaya, Rudolfo A. 1937- *WhoHisp 94*
Anaya, Rudolfo A(lfonso) 1937- *WrDr 94*
Anaya, Toney 1941- *WhoAmP 93, WhoHisp 94*
Anbar, Michael 1927- *WhoAm 94, WhoScEn 94*
Anbari, Abdul-Amir al- 1934- *IntWW 93*
Anbinder, Paul 1940- *WhoAmA 93*
Anbinder, Tyler (Gregory) 1962- *ConAu 141*
Anburey, Thomas *WhAmRev*
Ancelet, Barry Jean 1951- *WrDr 94*
Ancell, Judith Anne 1943- *WhoWest 94*
Ancelot, Marguerite 1792-1875 *BlmGWL*
Ances, I. George 1935- *WhoAm 94, WhoScEn 94*
Ancetti, Carlo Guido 1933- *WhoFI 94*
Anchell, Melvin 1919- *WhoWest 94*
An Chengxin 1939- *WhoPRCh 91 [port]*
Ancheta, Caesar Paul 1947- *WhoScEn 94*
Anchevsky, Igor Georgievich 1957- *LoBiDrD*
Anchlia, Than Mal 1918- *WhoFI 94*
Anchondo, Daniel 1946- *WhoAmP 93*
Anchorena, Manuel de 1933- *Who 94*
Ancira, Ernesto, Jr. 1944- *WhoHisp 94*
Ancira, Oscar, Sr. *WhoHisp 94*
Ancira, Oscar, Jr. *WhoHisp 94*
Ancker-Johnson, Betsy 1927- *WhoFI 94*
Ancoli-Israel, Sonia 1951- *WhoWest 94*
Ancona, Barry 1948- *WhoAm 94*
Ancona, George 1929- *SmATA 18AS [port], WrDr 94*
Ancona, George Ephraim 1929- *WhoAm 94, WhoWest 94*
Ancona, Mario 1860-1931 *NewGrDO*
Anconina, Richard *WhoHol 92*
Ancram, Earl of 1945- *Who 94*
And, Miekal *DrAPF 93*
Andagoya, Pascual De c. 1495-1548 *WhWE*
Andal, Dean *WhoAmP 93*
Andalafte, Edward Ziegler 1935- *WhoMW 93*
Andary, Thomas Joseph 1942- *WhoWest 94*
Anday, Rosette 1903-1977 *NewGrDO*
Andell, Nancy 1953- *WhoAmA 93*
Andelson, Robert V. 1931- *WrDr 94*
Andelson, Robert Vernon 1931- *WhoAm 94*
Anden, Mathew d1985 *WhoHol 92*
Andenaes, Johannes 1912- *IntWW 93*
Ander, Aloys 1817-1864 *NewGrDO*
Andera, Leonard E. 1934- *WhoAmP 93*
Anderberg, Edward Clarence 1918-1992 *WhAm 10*
Anderberg, Judy Ruth 1945- *WhoAmL 94*
Anderberg, Robert John 1967- *WhoWest 94*
Anderberg, Roy Anthony 1921- *WhoWest 94*
Andere, Jacqueline *WhoHol 92*
Anderegg, George Francis, Jr. 1937- *WhoAm 94*
Anderer, Joseph Henry 1924- *WhoAm 94*
Anderer, Mark J. 1957- *WhoFI 94*
Andergast, Maria 1912- *WhoHol 92*
Anderhalter, Oliver Frank 1922- *WhoAm 94*
an der Heiden, Wulf-Uwe 1942- *WhoScEn 94*
Anderl, Stephen 1910- *WhAm 10*
Anderluh, John Russell 1934- *WhoFI 94*
Anderman, George Gibbs 1926- *WhoWest 94*
Anderman, Irving Ingersoll 1918- *WhoScEn 94*
Anderman, Janusz 1949- *ConAu 142*
Anders, Claudia Dee 1951- *WhoMW 93*
Anders, Dan Raney 1933- *WhoAmL 94*
Anders, Edward 1926- *IntWW 93*
Anders, George Charles 1957- *WhoFI 94*
Anders, Glenn d1981 *WhoHol 92*
Anders, Hendrik c. 1657-1714 *NewGrDO*
Anders, Irene d1988 *WhoHol 92*

Anders, Jerrold Paul 1953- *WhoAm 94*
Anders, Leslie 1922- *WrDr 94*
Anders, Luana 1940- *WhoHol 92*
Anders, Mardellya Mary 1918- *WhoAmP 93*
Anders, Max *NewGrDO*
Anders, Merry 1933- *WhoHol 92*
Anders, Patricia Lee 1948- *WhoWest 94*
Anders, Peter 1908-1954 *NewGrDO*
Anders, Rex 1928- *WrDr 94*
Anders, Richard H. 1925- *WhoBlA 94*
Anders, Robert Joseph 1956- *WhoMW 93*
Anders, Robert Lee 1947- *WhoWest 94*
Anders, Rudolph *WhoHol 92*
Anders, Shirley B. *DrAPF 93*
Anders, William Alison 1933- *IntWW 93, WhoAm 94, WhoFI 94, WhoScEn 94, WhoWest 94*
Andersdatter, Karla M. *DrAPF 93*
Andersen, Alice Klopstad 1912- *WhoAmP 93*
Andersen, Anders 1912- *IntWW 93*
Andersen, Andreas Storrs 1908-1974 *WhoAmA 93N*
Andersen, Anthony L. 1935- *WhoAm 94, WhoFI 94*
Andersen, Burton Robert 1932- *WhoAm 94*
Andersen, Carol Ann 1946- *WhoWest 94*
Andersen, Dale V. *WhoAmP 93*
Andersen, Daniel Johannes 1909- *WhoAm 94*
Andersen, David R. L. 1957- *WhoAmA 93*
Andersen, David Roger 1959- *WhoMW 93*
Andersen, Dennis O. 1941- *WhoMW 93*
Andersen, Donald Edward 1923- *WhoAm 94*
Andersen, Doris Evelyn 1923- *WhoFI 94, WhoWest 94*
Andersen, Elmer Lee 1909- *WhoAm 94, WhoFI 94, WhoMW 93*
Andersen, Else Winther 1941- *WhoWomW 91*
Andersen, Ernest Christopher 1909- *WhoAmL 94, WhoWest 94*
Andersen, Frank 1953- *IntDcB*
Andersen, Hanne 1939- *WhoWomW 91*
Andersen, Hans Christian *EncSF 93*
Andersen, Hans Christian 1805-1875 *BlmGEL, NewGrDO, RfGShF*
Andersen, Hans Christian 1941- *WhoAm 94, WhoScEn 94*
Andersen, Hans George 1919- *IntWW 93*
Andersen, Harold Wayne 1923- *WhoAm 94, WhoMW 93*
Andersen, Harry Edward 1906- *WhoFI 94, WhoMW 93*
Andersen, Henning 1934- *WhoAm 94*
Andersen, Ib 1954- *IntDcB [port], IntWW 93*
Andersen, Iva *WhoHol 92*
Andersen, James A. 1924- *WhoAm 94, WhoAmL 94, WhoAmP 93, WhoWest 94*
Andersen, Kenneth Benjamin 1905- *WhoAm 94*
Andersen, Kenneth Eldon 1933- *WhoAm 94*
Andersen, Kent Tucker 1942- *WhoAm 94, WhoFI 94*
Andersen, Laird Bryce 1928- *WhoAm 94*
Andersen, Leif (Werner) 1925- *WhoAmA 93*
Andersen, Leif Percival 1951- *WhoScEn 94*
Andersen, Leonard Christian 1911- *WhoMW 93*
Andersen, Luba 1945- *WhoMW 93*
Andersen, Ludwig 1883-1978 *NewGrDO*
Andersen, Michael Paul 1946- *WhoWest 94*
Andersen, Mogens 1916- *IntWW 93*
Andersen, Morten 1960- *WhoAm 94*
Andersen, Niels Hjorth 1943- *WhoAm 94*
Andersen, Richard Arnold 1946- *WhoAm 94*
Andersen, Richard Esten 1957- *WhoAmL 94*
Andersen, Robert Allen 1936- *WhoAm 94*
Andersen, Ronald Max 1939- *IntWW 93, WhoAm 94*
Andersen, Sheree Hilton 1954- *WhoWest 94*
Andersen, Svend 1915- *IntWW 93*
Andersen, Theodore Selmer 1944- *WhoScEn 94*
Andersen, Torben Brender 1954- *WhoScEn 94, WhoWest 94*
Andersen, Torkild 1934- *IntWW 93*
Andersen, Valdemar Jens 1919- *Who 94*
Andersen, Wayne R. 1945- *WhoAm 94, WhoAmL 94, WhoMW 93*
Andersen, Wayne Vesti 1930- *WhoAmA 93*
Andersen, Willem Hendrik Jan 1941- *WhoWest 94*
Andersland, Orlando Baldwin 1929- *WhoAm 94, WhoScEn 94*
Anderson *Who 94*
Anderson, Abbie H. 1928- *WhoBlA 94*
Anderson, Adelaide Mary 1863-1936 *DcNaB MP*
Anderson, Adrienne *EncSF 93*
Anderson, Al H., Jr. 1942- *WhoBlA 94*
Anderson, Alan, Jr. 1943- *WrDr 94*
Anderson, Alan Julian 1953- *WhoScEn 94*
Anderson, Alan Lee 1955- *WhoMW 93*
Anderson, Alan Marshall 1955- *WhoAmL 94*
Anderson, Alan R. 1935- *WhoFI 94*
Anderson, Alan Reinold 1949- *WhoFI 94*
Anderson, Albert D. d1993 *NewYTBS 93*
Anderson, Albert Esten 1921- *WhoAm 94*
Anderson, Albert Sydney 1940- *WhoAmL 94*
Anderson, Aldon J. 1917- *WhoAm 94, WhoWest 94*
Anderson, Alfred Anthony 1961- *WhoBlA 94*
Anderson, Alfred Charles 1943- *WhoAmP 93*
Anderson, Alfred Oliver 1928- *WhoFI 94, WhoScEn 94*
Anderson, Alice Marie 1931- *WhoWest 94*
Anderson, Alistair Andrew Gibson 1927- *Who 94*
Anderson, Allan Crosby 1932- *WhoAm 94*
Anderson, Alun Mark 1948- *Who 94*
Anderson, Alvin E. 1943- *WhoIns 94*
Anderson, Amel 1936- *WhoBlA 94*
Anderson, Amelia Veronica 1947- *WhoBlA 94*
Anderson, Andrew Herbert 1928- *WhoAm 94*
Anderson, Andy *EncSF 93*
Anderson, Angelique Layton 1962- *WhoAmL 94*
Anderson, Angry *WhoHol 92*
Anderson, Ann 1952- *WhoAmP 93, WhoWest 94*
Anderson, Annelise Graebner 1938- *WhoAm 94, WhoFI 94*
Anderson, Ansel Cochran 1933- *WhoMW 93*
Anderson, Anthony John 1938- *Who 94*
Anderson, Arlen Keith 1956- *WhoFI 94*
Anderson, Arnett Artis 1931- *WhoBlA 94*
Anderson, Arnold C. 1919- *WhoAmP 93*
Anderson, Arnold Stuart 1934-1991 *WhAm 10*
Anderson, Arthur Allan 1939- *WhoAm 94*
Anderson, Arthur G., Jr. 1918- *WhoAm 94*
Anderson, Arthur George 1926- *WhoAm 94*
Anderson, Arthur Irvin 1951- *WhoAm 94, WhoAmL 94*
Anderson, Arthur John Ritchie (Iain) 1933- *Who 94*
Anderson, Arthur N. 1912- *WhoAm 94*
Anderson, Arthur Rodney 1930- *WhoMW 93*
Anderson, Arthur Roland 1910- *WhoAm 94, WhoWest 94*
Anderson, Arthur Salzner 1923- *WhoAm 94, WhoWest 94*
Anderson, Arvid 1921- *WhoAmL 94*
Anderson, Aubrey Lee 1940- *WhoAm 94*
Anderson, Audley d1966 *WhoHol 92*
Anderson, Austin Gilman *WhoAm 94, WhoFI 94*
Anderson, Austin Gothard 1931- *WhoAm 94, WhoAmL 94*
Anderson, Avis Olivia 1949- *WhoBlA 94*
Anderson, Barbara 1926- *BlmGWL*
Anderson, Barbara Jenkins 1928- *WhoBlA 94*
Anderson, Barbara Louise *WhoBlA 94*
Anderson, Barbara Louise 1933- *WhoWest 94*
Anderson, Barbara McComas 1950- *WhoAm 94*
Anderson, Barbara Smith 1932- *WhoAmP 93*
Anderson, Barry Lynn 1951- *WhoMW 93*
Anderson, Basil Douglas 1942- *WhoMW 93*
Anderson, Benard Harold 1935- *WhoAm 94*
Anderson, Benjamin Stratman, Jr. 1936- *WhoBlA 94*
Anderson, Bernard E. *WhoBlA 94, WhoFI 94*
Anderson, Bernard Joseph 1942- *WhoAmP 93*
Anderson, Beth *DrAPF 93*
Anderson, Beth 1950- *NewGrDO*
Anderson, Betty Keller 1951- *WhoBlA 94*
Anderson, Betty Radford 1954- *WhoAmP 93*
Anderson, Beverly Jean 1940- *Who 94*
Anderson, Bill 1941- *WhoAmA 93*
Anderson, Bob 1932- *WhoAmP 93, WhoMW 93*
Anderson, Bob 1943- *WhoAm 94*
Anderson, Brad J. 1924- *WhoAmA 93*
Anderson, Bradford 1952- *WhoAmL 94*
Anderson, Bradford William 1956- *WhoFI 94, WhoWest 94*
Anderson, Bradley Clark 1961- *WhoWest 94*
Anderson, Bradley Jay 1924- *WhoAm 94*
Anderson, Brenda Jean 1961- *WhoScEn 94*
Anderson, Brian David Outram 1941- *Who 94*
Anderson, Brian L. 1952- *WhoIns 94*
Anderson, Bror Ernest 1914- *WhoScEn 94*
Anderson, Bruce A. 1948- *WhoAmA 93*
Anderson, Bruce Carl 1949- *WhoWest 94*
Anderson, Bruce E. *WhoAmP 93*
Anderson, Bruce James 1940- *WhoAmA 93*
Anderson, Bruce John 1943- *WhoAm 94, WhoMW 93*
Anderson, Bruce MacLeod 1956- *WhoWest 94*
Anderson, Bruce Morgan 1941- *WhoScEn 94, WhoWest 94*
Anderson, Bruce Nils 1939- *WhoWest 94*
Anderson, Bryan N. 1955- *WhoBlA 94*
Anderson, Bryan Sanfred 1961- *WhoMW 93*
Anderson, Buist Murfee 1904- *WhoAm 94*
Anderson, Byron F. 1953- *WhoAmP 93*
Anderson, Byron Floyd 1953- *WhoWest 94*
Anderson, C. E. d1956 *WhoHol 92*
Anderson, C. Leonard 1946- *WhoWest 94*
Anderson, C. Wilson, Jr. 1939- *WhoMW 93*
Anderson, Calvin B. 1948- *WhoAmP 93*
Anderson, Campbell McCheyne 1941- *IntWW 93, Who 94*
Anderson, Carey Laine, Jr. 1950- *WhoBlA 94*
Anderson, Carl 1945- *WhoHol 92*
Anderson, Carl Albert 1951- *WhoAmP 93*
Anderson, Carl D. d1991 *NobelP 91N*
Anderson, Carl D. 1930- *WhoAmP 93*
Anderson, Carl David 1905-1991 *WhAm 10, WorScD*
Anderson, Carl Edward 1939- *WhoBlA 94*
Anderson, Carl Edwin 1934- *WhoBlA 94*
Anderson, Carl F., III 1966- *WhoAmP 93*
Anderson, Carl John 1952- *WhoMW 93*
Anderson, Carl Thomas 1865-1948 *WhoAmA 93N*
Anderson, Carl West 1935- *WhoAmL 94*
Anderson, Carla Lee 1930- *WhoMW 93*
Anderson, Carlton Leon 1942- *WhoBlA 94*
Anderson, Carol Ann 1957- *WhoAmP 93*
Anderson, Carol Byrd 1941- *WhoBlA 94*
Anderson, Carol Lee 1943- *WhoFI 94, WhoMW 93*
Anderson, Carol Leslie 1963- *WhoMW 93*
Anderson, Carol McMillan 1938- *WhoAm 94, WhoAmL 94*
Anderson, Carol Ruth 1926- *WhoWest 94*
Anderson, Carole Ann 1938- *WhoAm 94*
Anderson, Carole Lewis 1944- *WhoAm 94*
Anderson, Carolyn Jennings 1913- *WhoAm 94*
Anderson, Carolyn Joyce 1947- *WhoFI 94, WhoMW 93*
Anderson, Carson Anthony 1951- *WhoWest 94*
Anderson, Cat d1981 *WhoHol 92*
Anderson, Cathy Ellen 1953- *WhoMW 93*
Anderson, Cathy Jean 1953- *WhoMW 93*
Anderson, Charles *WhoAmP 93*
Anderson, Charles Alfred 1902-1990 *WhAm 10*
Anderson, Charles Arnold 1907- *WhAm 10*
Anderson, Charles Arthur 1917- *WhoAm 94*
Anderson, Charles Bernard 1938- *WhoAm 94*
Anderson, Charles D. *WhoMW 93*
Anderson, Charles Henry 1951- *WhoAm 94*
Anderson, Charles Hill 1930- *WhoAmL 94*
Anderson, Charles Joseph 1947- *WhoMW 93*
Anderson, Charles Lee 1961- *WhoFI 94*
Anderson, Charles Michael 1944- *WhoWest 94*
Anderson, Charles Roberts 1902- *WhoAm 94*
Anderson, Charles Ross 1937- *WhoFI 94, WhoScEn 94, WhoWest 94*
Anderson, Charles S. 1930- *WhoAm 94*
Anderson, Charles William 1934- *WhoAm 94*
Anderson, Chester 1932- *WrDr 94*
Anderson, Chester (Valentine John) 1932-1991 *EncSF 93*
Anderson, Chester Grant 1923- *WhoAm 94*
Anderson, Chester R. 1912- *WhoBlA 94*
Anderson, Christine Lee 1963- *WhoScEn 94*
Anderson, Christine Marlene 1947- *WhoAm 94, WhoScEn 94*
Anderson, Christopher 1944- *IntWW 93*
Anderson, Christopher James 1950- *WhoAm 94*
Anderson, Claire d1964 *WhoHol 92*
Anderson, Clifton Einar 1923- *WhoWest 94*
Anderson, Clyde Bailey 1934- *WhoMW 93*
Anderson, Colin 1904- *EncSF 93*
Anderson, Courtney *Who 94*
Anderson, Courtney 1906- *WrDr 94*
Anderson, (Charles) Courtney 1916- *Who 94*
Anderson, Craig James 1952- *WhoWest 94*
Anderson, Craig Knute 1953- *WhoFI 94*
Anderson, Curtis Stovall 1949- *WhoAmP 93*
Anderson, Cynthia Finkbeiner Sjoberg 1949- *WhoAm 94, WhoMW 93*
Anderson, D. G. *WhoAmP 93*
Anderson, Dale 1933- *WhoAm 94, WhoFI 94*
Anderson, Dale Arden 1936- *WhoAm 94*
Anderson, Dale C. 1953- *WhoMW 93*
Anderson, Dale Gene 1935- *WhoMW 93*
Anderson, Dale Kenneth 1922- *WhoAm 94*
Anderson, Dallas d1934 *WhoHol 92*
Anderson, Damon Ernest 1946- *WhoAmL 94*
Anderson, Dan Richard 1924- *WhoAmP 93*
Anderson, Dana Alan 1945- *WhoWest 94*
Anderson, Dana DeWitt 1948- *WhoWest 94*
Anderson, Daniel David 1964- *WhoFI 94*
Anderson, Daniel Erwin 1928- *WhoMW 93*
Anderson, Daniel J. 1945- *WhoAmA 93*
Anderson, Daniel L. 1968- *WhoAmP 93*
Anderson, Daphne 1922- *WhoHol 92*
Anderson, Darlene Yvonne 1953- *WhoWest 94*
Anderson, Darrell Edward 1932- *WhoAm 94*
Anderson, Daryl *WhoAm 94*
Anderson, Daryl 1954- *WhoHol 92*
Anderson, David *EncSF 93, WhoAmP 93*
Anderson, David 1919- *Who 94*
Anderson, David 1935- *WhoAmA 93*
Anderson, David 1937- *IntWW 93, WhoAm 94*
Anderson, David 1952- *WrDr 94*
Anderson, David A. 1941- *WhoAm 94, WhoAmL 94*
Anderson, David Alan 1955- *WhoAmL 94*
Anderson, David Atlas 1930- *WhoBlA 94*
Anderson, David Bowen 1948- *WhoAmL 94*
Anderson, David Boyd 1942- *WhoAmL 94*
Anderson, David C. 1931- *WhoAmA 93*
Anderson, David Charles 1931- *WhoWest 94*
Anderson, David Colville 1916- *Who 94*
Anderson, David Cord 1948- *WhoFI 94*
Anderson, David Daniel 1924- *WhoAm 94, WhoMW 93, WrDr 94*
Anderson, David E. *WhoAm 94, WhoWest 94*
Anderson, David Elliott 1964- *WhoWest 94*
Anderson, David Franklin 1926- *WhoIns 94*
Anderson, David Gary 1963- *WhoMW 93*
Anderson, David Gaskill, Jr. 1945- *WhoMW 93*
Anderson, David Heywood 1937- *Who 94*
Anderson, David Langley 1944- *WhoFI 94*
Anderson, David Lawrence 1934- *WhoMW 93*
Anderson, David Lawrence 1948- *WhoAm 94, WhoAmL 94*
Anderson, David Lloyd 1935- *WhoAm 94*
Anderson, David Melvin 1944- *WhoWest 94*
Anderson, David Munro 1937- *Who 94*
Anderson, David Paul 1946- *WhoAmA 93*
Anderson, David Poole 1929- *WhoAm 94*
Anderson, David Prewitt 1934- *WhoAm 94, WhoScEn 94*
Anderson, David Roy 1962- *WhoAmL 94*
Anderson, David Trevor 1938- *WhoAm 94*
Anderson, David Turpeau 1942- *WhoAm 94, WhoBlA 94*
Anderson, David William 1929- *Who 94*
Anderson, Davin Charles 1955- *WhoMW 93*
Anderson, Dean W. 1927- *WhoAmP 93*
Anderson, Dean William 1946- *WhoAm 94*
Anderson, Declan John 1920- *Who 94*
Anderson, Del Marie 1937- *WhoBlA 94*
Anderson, Dennis Keith 1956- *WhoMW 93*

Anderson, Dennis Lester 1949- *WhoWest 94*
Anderson, Dewey 1897- *WhAm 10*
Anderson, Digby Carter 1944- *Who 94*
Anderson, Don 1943- *WhoAmP 93*
Anderson, Don L. 1933- *IntWW 93*
Anderson, Don Lynn 1933- *WhoAm 94, WhoScEn 94*
Anderson, Donald 1939- *Who 94*
Anderson, Donald Bernard 1919- *WhoAm 94, WhoWest 94*
Anderson, Donald Edward 1938- *WhoBlA 94*
Anderson, Donald Gordon Marcus 1937- *WhoAm 94*
Anderson, Donald H. d1986 *WhoHol 92*
Anderson, Donald K., Jr. 1922- *WrDr 94*
Anderson, Donald Kennedy, Jr. 1922- *WhoAm 94*
Anderson, Donald L. 1932- *WhoBlA 94*
Anderson, Donald Lloyd 1921- *WhoWest 94*
Anderson, Donald Mark 1948- *WhoScEn 94*
Anderson, Donald Meredith 1928- *WhoAm 94*
Anderson, Donald Morgan 1930- *WhoAm 94, WhoScEn 94*
Anderson, Donald Myers *WhoAmA 93*
Anderson, Donald Norton, Jr. 1928- *WhoScEn 94, WhoWest 94*
Anderson, Donald Paul 1930- *WhoAm 94*
Anderson, Donald Thomas 1931- *IntWW 93, Who 94, WhoScEn 94*
Anderson, Donald Thomas, Jr. 1937- *WhoMW 93, WhoScEn 94*
Anderson, Donald W. 1943- *WhoAm 94*
Anderson, Donna 1925- *ConTFT 11*
Anderson, Donna 1939- *WhoHol 92*
Anderson, Donna K. 1935- *ConAu 142*
Anderson, Donna Kay 1935- *WhoAm 94*
Anderson, Donnald K. 1942- *CngDr 93*
Anderson, Doreatha Madison 1943- *WhoBlA 94*
Anderson, Doris 1921- *BlmGWL*
Anderson, Doris Ehlinger 1926- *WhoAmL 94*
Anderson, Doris J. 1933- *WhoBlA 94*
Anderson, Dorothy Fisher 1924- *WhoWest 94*
Anderson, Dorothy Jean 1926- *WhoMW 93*
Anderson, Dorrine Ann Petersen 1923- *WhoMW 93*
Anderson, Doug 1954- *WhoAmA 93*
Anderson, Douglas Charles 1934- *WhoMW 93*
Anderson, Douglas Leavon 1939- *WhoAmP 93*
Anderson, Douglas Richard 1938- *WhoAm 94*
Anderson, Douglas Scranton Hesley 1929- *WhoFI 94*
Anderson, Douglas Warren 1950- *WhoScEn 94*
Anderson, Douglas Williams 1932- *WhoAmL 94*
Anderson, Dusty *WhoHol 92*
Anderson, Duwayne Marlo 1927- *WhoAm 94, WhoScEn 94*
Anderson, E. Clive 1947- *WhoAm 94, WhoAmL 94*
Anderson, E. Karl 1931- *WhoAm 94*
Anderson, E. Riley *WhoAmP 93*
Anderson, Earl L. 1935- *WhoAmP 93*
Anderson, Eddie d1977 *WhoHol 92*
Anderson, Eddie 1905-1977 *WhoCom*
Anderson, Eddie 1906-1977 *AfrAmAl 6 [port]*
Anderson, Edgar L. 1931- *WhoBlA 94*
Anderson, Edgar R., Jr. 1940- *WhoAm 94*
Anderson, Edith Helen 1927- *WhoAm 94*
Anderson, Edward d1943 *WhoHol 92*
Anderson, Edward Frederick 1932- *WhoAm 94*
Anderson, Edward Riley 1932- *WhoAm 94, WhoAmL 94*
Anderson, Edward V. 1953- *WhoAm 94, WhoWest 94*
Anderson, Edwyna G. 1930- *WhoBlA 94*
Anderson, Eileen Ruth 1928- *WhoAmP 93*
Anderson, Eleanor M. 1928- *WhoAmP 93*
Anderson, Eli H. 1955- *WhoAmP 93*
Anderson, Elijah 1943- *ConAu 140*
Anderson, Elizabeth Helen Lathrop 1931- *WhoMW 93*
Anderson, Elizabeth M. *WhoBlA 94*
Anderson, Ella *WrDr 94*
Anderson, Ella L. 1917- *WhoBlA 94*
Anderson, Ellen R. 1959- *WhoAmP 93*
Anderson, Ellen Ruth 1959- *WhoMW 93*
Anderson, Ellis Bernard 1926- *WhoAm 94*
Anderson, Elmer Ebert 1922- *WhoAm 94*
Anderson, Eloise B. McMorris *WhoBlA 94*
Anderson, Enoch 1753-1824 *WhAmRev*
Anderson, Ephraim Saul 1911- *Who 94*
Anderson, Eric *Who 94*
Anderson, (William) Eric (Kinloch) 1936- *Who 94*
Anderson, Eric Anthony 1946- *WhoFI 94*
Anderson, Eric Scott 1949- *WhoAm 94, WhoAmL 94*
Anderson, Eric Severin 1943- *WhoAm 94, WhoAmL 94*
Anderson, Eric William 1923- *WhoAm 94*
Anderson, Erland *DrAPF 93*
Anderson, Ernest *WhoHol 92*
Anderson, Ernest Leroy 1910-1988 *WhAm 10*
Anderson, Ernest Washington 1922- *WhoAm 94*
Anderson, Ethel Avara *WhoFI 94*
Anderson, Eugene *Who 94, WhoAmP 93*
Anderson, Eugene 1944- *WhoBlA 94*
Anderson, (Clarence) Eugene 1938- *Who 94*
Anderson, Eugene David 1951- *WhoFI 94*
Anderson, Eugene Robert 1927- *WhoAm 94*
Anderson, Evans Leland 1914- *WhoWest 94*
Anderson, Eve *WhoHol 92*
Anderson, Ferguson *Who 94*
Anderson, (William) Ferguson 1914- *Who 94, WrDr 94*
Anderson, Flavia 1910- *WrDr 94*
Anderson, Fletcher Neal 1930- *WhoAm 94*
Anderson, Florence d1962 *WhoHol 92*
Anderson, Forrest Howard 1913-1989 *WhAm 10*
Anderson, Frances Swem 1913- *WhoMW 93, WhoScEn 94*
Anderson, Frederic Simon B. 1953- *WhoScEn 94*
Anderson, Frederick J. 1912- *WhoAmP 93*
Anderson, Frederick Randolph, Jr. 1941- *WhoAm 94, WhoAmL 94*
Anderson, Freedolph Deryl 1933- *WhoScEn 94*
Anderson, G. M. d1971 *WhoHol 92*
Anderson, Gary Alan 1955- *WhoScEn 94*
Anderson, Gary Arlen 1953- *WhoMW 93, WhoScEn 94*
Anderson, Gary Dean 1947- *WhoAm 94*
Anderson, Gary K. *WhoAmP 93*
Anderson, Gary Wayne 1961- *WhoBlA 94*
Anderson, Gary William 1951- *WhoAm 94*
Anderson, Gene d1965 *WhoHol 92*
Anderson, Geoffrey Allen 1947- *WhoAm 94, WhoAmL 94, WhoMW 93*
Anderson, George d1948 *WhoHol 92*
Anderson, George c. 1875- *EncNAR*
Anderson, George 1921- *WhoAm 94*
Anderson, George, Jr. 1906-1992 *AnObit 1992*
Anderson, George A. 1923- *WhoBlA 94*
Anderson, George Allan 1930- *WhoWest 94*
Anderson, George Edward 1938- *WhoWest 94*
Anderson, George Harding 1931- *WhoAm 94*
Anderson, George Joseph 1960- *WhoAmL 94*
Anderson, George Kenneth 1946- *WhoAm 94*
Anderson, George Lee 1934- *WhoAm 94*
Anderson, George Ross, Jr. 1929- *WhoAm 94, WhoAmL 94*
Anderson, George W. 1934- *WhoFI 94*
Anderson, George Walter 1932-1992 *WhAm 10*
Anderson, George Wishart 1913- *IntWW 93, Who 94*
Anderson, Gerald 1939- *WhoAmP 93*
Anderson, Gerald Edwin 1931- *WhoAm 94, WhoFI 94*
Anderson, Gerald Leslie 1940- *WhoAm 94, WhoFI 94*
Anderson, Gerald Verne 1931- *WhoWest 94*
Anderson, Geraldine Louise 1941- *WhoMW 93, WhoScEn 94*
Anderson, Gerry 1929- *EncSF 93, IntMPA 94, IntWW 93*
Anderson, Gidske d1993 *NewYTBS 93*
Anderson, Girard F. 1932- *WhoFI 94*
Anderson, Gladys Peppers *WhoBlA 94*
Anderson, Glen Clark 1944- *WhoWest 94*
Anderson, Glen H. 1938- *WhoAmP 93*
Anderson, Glen Robert 1952- *WhoMW 93*
Anderson, Glenn Elwood 1914- *WhoAm 94*
Anderson, Glenn M. 1913- *WhoAmP 93*
Anderson, Glenn Richard 1940- *WhoAmP 93*
Anderson, Gloria L. 1938- *WhoBlA 94*
Anderson, Gloria Long 1938- *WhoScEn 94*
Anderson, Gordon A. 1924- *WhoAmP 93*
Anderson, Gordon Alexander 1931- *Who 94*
Anderson, Gordon Earl 1940- *WhoWest 94*
Anderson, Gordon MacKenzie 1932- *WhoScEn 94*
Anderson, Grace Merle 1923-1989 *WhAm 10*
Anderson, Grady Lee 1931- *WhoBlA 94*
Anderson, Grant Allan 1963- *WhoWest 94*
Anderson, Granville Scott 1947- *WhoBlA 94*
Anderson, Gregg I. 1949- *WhoAm 94, WhoAmL 94*
Anderson, Gregory 1946- *WrDr 94*
Anderson, Gregory Joseph 1944- *WhoAm 94*
Anderson, Gregory Martin 1959- *WhoScEn 94*
Anderson, Gregory Shane 1947- *WhoFI 94*
Anderson, Gregory Wayne 1964- *WhoBlA 94*
Anderson, Gunnar Donald 1927- *WhoAmA 93*
Anderson, Guy *WhoHol 92*
Anderson, Guy Irving 1906- *WhoAmA 93*
Anderson, Guy W., Jr. 1943- *WhoAmL 94*
Anderson, Gwen Odegaard 1930- *WhoAmP 93*
Anderson, H(ector) John 1915- *Who 94*
Anderson, Harold 1907- *BasBi*
Anderson, Harold 1939- *WhoBlA 94*
Anderson, Harold Albert 1908- *WhoAm 94*
Anderson, Harold H(omer) 1897- *WhAm 10*
Anderson, Harold J. 1909- *WhoAmL 94*
Anderson, Harold Lloyd 1927- *WhoAmL 94*
Anderson, Harold Paul 1946- *WhoWest 94*
Anderson, Harrison Clarke 1932- *WhoAm 94*
Anderson, Harry 1952- *IntMPA 94*
Anderson, Harry Alan 1945- *WhoIns 94*
Anderson, Harry Frederick, Jr. 1927- *WhoAm 94*
Anderson, Harry Robert 1927- *WhoFI 94*
Anderson, Harry S. 1945- *WhoAmL 94*
Anderson, Harvey Gregg 1953- *WhoFI 94*
Anderson, Helen Louise 1941- *WhoBlA 94*
Anderson, Henry Earl 1950- *WhoMW 93*
Anderson, Henry J. *WhoIns 94*
Anderson, Henry L(ee Norman) 1934- *BlkWr 2, ConAu 142*
Anderson, Henry L. N. 1934- *WhoBlA 94*
Anderson, Henry Lee Norman 1934- *WhoWest 94*
Anderson, Herbert 1917- *WhoHol 92*
Anderson, Herbert H. 1920- *WhoAm 94, WhoAmL 94*
Anderson, Herschel Vincent 1932- *WhoAm 94, WhoWest 94*
Anderson, Holly Geis 1946- *WhoFI 94, WhoScEn 94, WhoWest 94*
Anderson, Howard Benjamin 1903- *WhoAmA 93N*
Anderson, Howard Clevenger 1910- *WhAm 10*
Anderson, Howard D. 1936- *WhoBlA 94*
Anderson, Howard N. 1929- *WhoIns 94*
Anderson, Howard Palmer 1915- *WhoAmP 93*
Anderson, Hubert, Jr. *WhoBlA 94*
Anderson, Hugh 1920- *Who 94*
Anderson, Iain *Who 94*
Anderson, Iris Anita 1930- *WhoWest 94*
Anderson, Irvin Neal 1923- *WhoAmP 93*
Anderson, Ivan Delos 1915-1991 *WhAm 10, WhoAmA 93N*
Anderson, Ivan Verner, Jr. 1939- *WhoAm 94*
Anderson, Ivie d1949 *WhoHol 92*
Anderson, Ivy I. 1957- *WhoBlA 94*
Anderson, J. Blaine 1922-1988 *WhAm 10*
Anderson, J. Morris 1936- *WhoBlA 94*
Anderson, J. Robert 1937- *WhoFI 94*
Anderson, J. Trent 1939- *WhoAm 94, WhoAmL 94*
Anderson, J. Wayne 1947- *IntMPA 94*
Anderson, Jack *DrAPF 93*
Anderson, Jack (Northman) 1922- *WrDr 94*
Anderson, Jack Joe 1928- *WhoWest 94*
Anderson, Jack Northman 1922- *WhoAm 94*
Anderson, Jack Oland 1921- *WhoAm 94*
Anderson, Jack Roy 1925- *WhoAm 94, WhoScEn 94*
Anderson, Jacqueline Jones 1935- *WhoBlA 94*
Anderson, James *WrDr 94*
Anderson, James d1953 *WhoHol 92*
Anderson, James d1969 *WhoHol 92*
Anderson, James Alan 1948- *WhoBlA 94*
Anderson, James Alfred 1940- *WhoAm 94*
Anderson, James Arthur 1935- *WhoAm 94*
Anderson, James Burton 1943- *WhoFI 94*
Anderson, James Doig 1940- *WhoAm 94*
Anderson, James Donald 1935- *WhoMW 93*
Anderson, James Frazer Gillan 1929- *Who 94*
Anderson, James Frederick 1927- *WhoAm 94*
Anderson, James G. 1936- *WrDr 94*
Anderson, James George 1936- *WhoAm 94*
Anderson, James Gerard 1944- *WhoAm 94*
Anderson, James Gilbert *WhoScEn 94*
Anderson, James Henry 1926- *WhoScEn 94*
Anderson, James Hilbert 1908- *WhoFI 94*
Anderson, James Keith 1924- *WhoAm 94*
Anderson, James L. 1943- *WhoIns 94*
Anderson, James Maxwell 1888-1959 *AmCulL*
Anderson, James Michael 1944- *WhoWest 94*
Anderson, James Michael 1948- *WhoAmL 94*
Anderson, James Milton 1941- *WhoAm 94, WhoAmL 94*
Anderson, James P. 1929- *WhoAmA 93*
Anderson, James R., Jr. 1922- *WhoBlA 94*
Anderson, James Thomas 1939- *WhoFI 94*
Anderson, James William, III 1937- *WhoAm 94*
Anderson, Jan Lee 1937- *WhoAmP 93*
Anderson, Janeen Drene Williams 1964- *WhoWest 94*
Anderson, Janelle Marie 1954- *WhoFI 94*
Anderson, Janet 1949- *Who 94*
Anderson, Janet A. 1934- *ConAu 140*
Anderson, Janet Alm 1952- *WhoWest 94*
Anderson, Janet Elisabeth Pettit 1929- *WhoWest 94*
Anderson, Janice Linn 1943- *WhoFI 94*
Anderson, Jay LaMar 1931- *WhoScEn 94*
Anderson, Jay Rosamond 1953- *WhoBlA 94*
Anderson, Jean *DrAPF 93*
Anderson, Jean 1908- *WhoHol 92*
Anderson, Jean Blanche 1940- *WhoWest 94*
Anderson, Jeff Gordon 1965- *WhoFI 94*
Anderson, Jeffrey L. 1958- *WhoAmP 93*
Anderson, Jeffrey Lance 1944- *WhoScEn 94*
Anderson, Jeffrey Lynn 1955- *WhoMW 93*
Anderson, Jeffrey R. *NewYTBS 93 [port]*
Anderson, Jerald Clayton 1934- *WhoAmP 93*
Anderson, Jeremy Radcliffe 1921-1982 *WhoAmA 93N*
Anderson, Jerry Allen 1947- *WhoFI 94*
Anderson, Jerry Maynard 1933- *WhoAm 94*
Anderson, Jerry William, Jr. 1926- *WhoFI 94, WhoMW 93, WhoScEn 94*
Anderson, Jervis (B.) 1936- *BlkWr 2, ConAu 141*
Anderson, Jesse Lemond 1966- *WhoBlA 94*
Anderson, Jessica *BlmGWL*
Anderson, Jessica (Margaret) *WrDr 94*
Anderson, Jim 1895-1960 *BuCMET*
Anderson, Jim 1937- *WrDr 94*
Anderson, Joe Lewis, Sr. 1948- *WhoBlA 94*
Anderson, John 1909- *WrDr 94*
Anderson, John 1921- *Who 94*
Anderson, John 1922- *WhoHol 92*
Anderson, John 1936- *Who 94*
Anderson, John 1950- *WhoAmP 93*
Anderson, John (Evelyn) 1916- *Who 94*
Anderson, John (Muir) 1914- *Who 94*
Anderson, John A. 1937- *WhoBlA 94*
Anderson, John Albert 1943- *WhoWest 94*
Anderson, John Allan Dalrymple 1926- *Who 94*
Anderson, John Ansel 1903- *WhoAm 94*
Anderson, John Anthony 1945- *IntWW 93*
Anderson, John B. 1922- *WhoAmP 93*
Anderson, John B(ayard) 1922- *WrDr 94*
Anderson, John Bailey 1945- *WhoAm 94, WhoScEn 94*
Anderson, John Bayard 1922- *IntWW 93, WhoAm 94*
Anderson, John C., Jr. 1917- *WhoBlA 94*
Anderson, John David 1926- *WhoAm 94*
Anderson, John David, Jr. 1937- *WhoAm 94*
Anderson, John E. 1943- *WhoBlA 94*
Anderson, John Edward 1927- *WhoAm 94*
Anderson, John Erling 1929- *WhoAm 94*
Anderson, John Filmore 1942- *WhoIns 94*
Anderson, John Firth 1928- *WhoAm 94*
Anderson, John Foster 1956- *WhoAmL 94*
Anderson, John Gaston 1922- *WhoAm 94*
Anderson, John Graeme 1927- *Who 94*
Anderson, John H., Jr. 1916- *WhoAmP 93*
Anderson, John Henry 1936- *WhoAmP 93*
Anderson, John Hope 1912- *WhoAmP 93*

Anderson, John Huxley Fordyce 1945- *Who 94*
Anderson, John Kinloch 1924- *Who 94*
Anderson, John Leonard 1927- *WhoFI 94*
Anderson, John Leonard 1945- *WhoAm 94*
Anderson, John M. *Who 94*
Anderson, John MacKenzie d1993 *NewYTBS 93*
Anderson, John MacKenzie 1938- *WhoAmL 94*
Anderson, John Melvin 1946- *WhoAmP 93*
Anderson, John Mueller 1914- *WhoAm 94*
Anderson, John Murray 1926- *WhoAm 94*
Anderson, John Neil 1922- *Who 94*
Anderson, John Quentin 1951- *WhoAm 94, WhoFI 94*
Anderson, John R. 1941- *WhoAm 94, WhoFI 94*
Anderson, John Richard 1931- *WhoAm 94, WhoWest 94*
Anderson, John Robert 1928- *WhoAm 94*
Anderson, John Robert 1936- *WhoAm 94, WhoFI 94*
Anderson, John Robert 1947- *WhoAm 94*
Anderson, John Roland, II 1942- *WhoMW 93*
Anderson, John Roy 1919- *WhoScEn 94*
Anderson, John Russell 1918- *Who 94*
Anderson, John S. 1928- *WhoAmA 93*
Anderson, John Thomas 1930- *WhoAm 94*
Anderson, John Tracy 1928- *WhoMW 93*
Anderson, John Weir 1928- *WhoAm 94*
Anderson, John Whiting 1934- *WhoAm 94*
Anderson, John William 1934- *WhoAmP 93*
Anderson, Jon *DrAPF 93*
Anderson, Jon (Victor) 1940- *WrDr 94*
Anderson, Jon David 1952- *WhoAm 94, WhoAmL 94*
Anderson, Jon Mac 1937- *WhoAm 94*
Anderson, Jon Stephen 1936- *WhoAm 94*
Anderson, Jon Timothy 1953- *WhoAmL 94*
Anderson, Jonpatrick Schuyler 1951- *WhoWest 94*
Anderson, Joseph Andrew, Jr. 1921- *WhoAm 94*
Anderson, Joseph F. 1921- *WhoBlA 94*
Anderson, Joseph F., Jr. 1949- *WhoAmP 93*
Anderson, Joseph Fletcher, Jr. 1949- *WhoAm 94, WhoAmL 94*
Anderson, Joseph Norman 1926- *WhoAm 94*
Anderson, Joseph Walter 1945- *WhoAmL 94*
Anderson, Josephine *Who 94*
Anderson, Josephine Margaret 1959- *WhoWest 94*
Anderson, Judith 1898- *WhoHol 92*
Anderson, Judith 1898-1992 *AnObit 1992*
Anderson, Judith Helena 1940- *WhoAm 94, WhoMW 93*
Anderson, Judson Truett 1933- *WhoWest 94*
Anderson, Julian *DrAPF 93*
Anderson, Julian Anthony 1938- *Who 94*
Anderson, June *IntWW 93*
Anderson, June 1952- *NewGrDO*
Anderson, Kare 1950- *ConAu 142*
Anderson, Karen *EncSF 93*
Anderson, Karen (Kruse) 1932- *WrDr 94*
Anderson, Karl Elmo 1940- *WhoScEn 94*
Anderson, Karl Richard 1917- *WhoFI 94, WhoWest 94*
Anderson, Karl Stephen 1933- *WhoMW 93*
Anderson, Kathleen Gay 1950- *WhoAmL 94, WhoWest 94*
Anderson, Kathleen Wiley 1932- *WhoBlA 94*
Anderson, Keith 1917- *WhoAm 94*
Anderson, Keith Russell 1955- *WhoAmP 93*
Anderson, Kelly Elizabeth 1957- *WhoWest 94*
Anderson, Ken *DrAPF 93*
Anderson, Ken d1993 *NewYTBS 93*
Anderson, Kenneth Edmund 1950- *WhoAmA 93*
Anderson, Kenneth Edward 1943- *WhoFI 94*
Anderson, Kenneth Edwin 1931- *WhoScEn 94*
Anderson, Kenneth Jeffery 1954- *WhoFI 94, WhoWest 94*
Anderson, Kenneth L. 1939-1990 *WhoAmA 93N*
Anderson, Kenneth Norman 1921- *WhoAm 94, WrDr 94*
Anderson, Kenneth Patrick 1966- *WhoFI 94*
Anderson, Kenneth Richard 1936- *WhoBlA 94*
Anderson, Kenneth Wayne 1940- *WhoAmL 94*
Anderson, Kenning Meredith 1933- *WhoMW 93*
Anderson, Kenny 1970- *WhoBlA 94*
Anderson, Kent Taylor 1953- *WhoAm 94, WhoAmL 94, WhoFI 94*
Anderson, Kernie L. 1940- *WhoBlA 94*
Anderson, Kevin 1960- *IntMPA 94, WhoHol 92*
Anderson, Kevin (Victor) 1912- *Who 94*
Anderson, Kevin J(ames) 1962- *EncSF 93, SmATA 74 [port]*
Anderson, Kim Elizabeth 1960- *WhoFI 94, WhoMW 93*
Anderson, Kimball Richard 1952- *WhoAm 94, WhoAmL 94*
Anderson, Kinsey A. 1926- *WhoAm 94*
Anderson, Kirk 1965- *ConAu 140*
Anderson, Kurt M. 1953- *WhoAmP 93*
Anderson, Larry Ernest 1943- *WhoWest 94*
Anderson, Laurence Alexis 1940- *WhoAm 94*
Anderson, Lauretta Mae 1936- *WhoMW 93*
Anderson, Laurie 1947- *IntWW 93, WhoAm 94, WhoAmA 93, WhoHol 92*
Anderson, LaVerne Eric 1922- *WhoAm 94*
Anderson, Lawrence d1939 *WhoHol 92*
Anderson, Lawrence Bernhart 1906- *WhoAm 94*
Anderson, Lawrence Keith 1935- *WhoAm 94, WhoWest 94*
Anderson, Lawrence Leslie, Jr. 1930- *WhoAm 94*
Anderson, Lea E. 1954- *WhoAmL 94*
Anderson, Lee Roger 1945- *WhoAm 94*
Anderson, Lee Stratton 1925- *WhoAm 94*
Anderson, Lennart 1928- *WhoAm 94, WhoAmA 93*
Anderson, Leo E. 1902- *WhoAm 94*
Anderson, Leon H. 1928- *WhoBlA 94*
Anderson, Leona *WhoHol 92*
Anderson, Leonard 1945- *WhoAmP 93*
Anderson, Leonard Gustave 1919- *WhoAm 94*
Anderson, Lewis Daniel 1930- *WhoAm 94*
Anderson, Linda 1949- *BlmGWL*
Anderson, Linda Cook 1943- *WhoAmP 93*
Anderson, Lindsay 1923- *IntMPA 94, WhoHol 92*
Anderson, Lindsay (Gordon) 1923- *Who 94*
Anderson, Lindsay Gordon 1923- *IntWW 93*
Anderson, Lloyd Lee 1933- *WhoAm 94, WhoMW 93, WhoScEn 94*
Anderson, Lloyd Vincent 1943- *WhoAmL 94, WhoWest 94*
Anderson, Lois D. 1929- *WhoMW 93*
Anderson, Loni 1946- *IntMPA 94*
Anderson, Loni 1947- *WhoHol 92*
Anderson, Loni Kaye 1946- *WhoAm 94*
Anderson, Loren D. *WhoAmP 93*
Anderson, Lori *DrAPF 93*
Anderson, Louie 1952- *WhoHol 92*
Anderson, Louis Wilmer, Jr. 1933- *WhoAm 94*
Anderson, Louise Eleanor 1934- *WhoAm 94*
Anderson, Louise Payne, . 1923- *WhoBlA 94*
Anderson, Louise Stout 1952- *WhoWest 94*
Anderson, Lyle Arthur 1931- *WhoAm 94*
Anderson, Lyle R. 1955- *WhoAmP 93*
Anderson, Lyman Frank 1926- *WhoAmP 93*
Anderson, Lyman M. d1993 *NewYTBS 93*
Anderson, Lynda K. *WhoBlA 94*
Anderson, Lynn 1947- *WhoAm 94*
Anderson, Mabel M. 1924- *WhoAmP 93*
Anderson, Madeline *WhoBlA 94*
Anderson, Maggie *DrAPF 93*
Anderson, Mal 1935- *BuCMET*
Anderson, Malachi *WhoAmP 93*
Anderson, Malcolm 1934- *WrDr 94*
Anderson, Marc Richard 1954- *WhoWest 94*
Anderson, Marcellus J., Sr. 1908- *WhoBlA 94*
Anderson, Margaret *BlmGWL*
Anderson, Margaret d1922 *WhoHol 92*
Anderson, Margaret 1930- *WhoHol 92*
Anderson, Margaret Allyn 1922- *WhoWest 94*
Anderson, Margaret Ellen 1941- *WhoAm 94*
Anderson, Margaret Pomeroy 1943- *WhoAmA 93*
Anderson, Marian d1993 *IntWW 93N, Who 94N*
Anderson, Marian 1897-1993 *CurBio 93N, NewYTBS 93 [port]*
Anderson, Marian 1899- *NewGrDO*
Anderson, Marian 1902- *IntWW 93*
Anderson, Marian 1902-1993 *AfrAmAl 6 [port], AmCulL [port], WhoBlA 94N*
Anderson, Marilyn Nelle 1942- *WhoWest 94*
Anderson, Marion 1897-1993 *News 93*
Anderson, Marion Cornelius 1926- *WhoAm 94*
Anderson, Marjorie *WhoBlA 94*
Anderson, Mark *DrAPF 93*
Anderson, Mark Alexander 1953- *WhoAmL 94, WhoWest 94*
Anderson, Mark Edward 1957- *WhoScEn 94*
Anderson, Mark Eugene 1952- *WhoFI 94, WhoWest 94*
Anderson, Mark Joseph 1966- *WhoMW 93*
Anderson, Mark Robert 1948- *WhoAmA 93*
Anderson, Mark Robert 1951- *WhoWest 94*
Anderson, Mark T. 1953- *WhoFI 94*
Anderson, Martin Carl 1936- *WhoAm 94, WhoAmP 93, WhoScEn 94, WhoWest 94*
Anderson, Marva Jean 1945- *WhoBlA 94*
Anderson, Mary d1940 *WhoHol 92*
Anderson, Mary 1872-1964 *EncSF 93*
Anderson, Mary 1922- *WhoHol 92*
Anderson, Mary Ann 1939- *WhoAm 94, WhoMW 93*
Anderson, Mary Ann 1946- *WhoWest 94*
Anderson, Mary Elizabeth *WhoBlA 94*
Anderson, Mary Ellen 1964- *WhoFI 94*
Anderson, Mary Jane 1935- *WhoAm 94*
Anderson, Mary Leigh 1956- *WhoAm 94*
Anderson, Mary Lou 1949- *WhoMW 93*
Anderson, Mary M. 1919- *WrDr 94*
Anderson, Mary Mackenzie *Who 94*
Anderson, Mary Margaret 1932- *Who 94*
Anderson, Mary R. 1937- *WhoWest 94*
Anderson, Matthew James 1962- *WhoFI 94*
Anderson, Matthew Smith 1922- *IntWW 93, WrDr 94*
Anderson, Max Elliot 1946- *WhoMW 93*
Anderson, Maxwell 1888-1959 *IntDcT 2*
Anderson, Maxwell L. 1956- *WhoAmA 93*
Anderson, McKenny Willis 1943- *WhoAmP 93*
Anderson, Mel 1928- *WhoAm 94*
Anderson, Melissa Sue 1962- *IntMPA 94, WhoHol 92*
Anderson, Melody 1954- *WhoHol 92*
Anderson, Melvern 1929- *WhoIns 94*
Anderson, Merlyn Dean 1941- *WhoMW 93*
Anderson, Michael *DrAPF 93*
Anderson, Michael 1920- *IntMPA 94, IntWW 93*
Anderson, Michael 1942- *Who 94*
Anderson, Michael, Jr. 1943- *IntMPA 94, WhoHol 92*
Anderson, Michael Falconer 1947- *WrDr 94*
Anderson, Michael George 1951- *WhoWest 94*
Anderson, Michael Joseph 1920- *WhoAm 94*
Anderson, Michael L. 1958- *WhoAm 94*
Anderson, Michael Robert 1953- *WhoWest 94*
Anderson, Michael Wayne 1942- *WhoBlA 94*
Anderson, Michelle Renee 1961- *WhoMW 93*
Anderson, Mignon d1983 *WhoHol 92*
Anderson, Mignon Holland *DrAPF 93*
Anderson, Milada Filko 1922- *WhoFI 94*
Anderson, Mildred White 1922- *WhoWest 94*
Anderson, Milton Andrew 1927- *WhoMW 93*
Anderson, Milton Henry 1919- *WhoAm 94*
Anderson, Mitchell 1963- *WhoWest 94*
Anderson, Monroe 1947- *WhoBlA 94*
Anderson, Morris *WhoAmP 93*
Anderson, Moses B. *WhoBlA 94*
Anderson, N. Christian, III 1950- *WhoAm 94, WhoWest 94*
Anderson, Nathalie F. *DrAPF 93*
Anderson, Neal 1964- *WhoAm 94, WhoMW 93*
Anderson, Ned, Sr. 1943- *WhoAm 94, WhoWest 94*
Anderson, Neil (Dudley) 1927- *Who 94*
Anderson, Nels A., Jr. 1939- *WhoAmP 93*
Anderson, Nicholas Charles 1953- *WhoBlA 94*
Anderson, Nick 1968- *WhoBlA 94*
Anderson, Nils, Jr. 1914- *WhoAm 94*
Anderson, Norma V. 1932- *WhoAmP 93*
Anderson, Norman *Who 94*
Anderson, Norman 1932- *WhoAmP 93*
Anderson, (James) Norman (Dalrymple) 1908- *IntWW 93, Who 94, WrDr 94*
Anderson, Norman Dean 1928- *ConAu 42NR*
Anderson, Norman G(ulden) 1913- *WrDr 94*
Anderson, Oddie 1937- *WhoBlA 94*
Anderson, Odin Waldemar 1914- *IntWW 93, WhoAm 94, WrDr 94*
Anderson, Olive M(ary) 1915- *ConAu 42NR*
Anderson, Olive Ruth 1926- *IntWW 93, WrDr 94*
Anderson, Oliver Duncan 1940- *WhoAm 94*
Anderson, Oliver John 1928- *WhoFI 94*
Anderson, Olof W. *EncSF 93*
Anderson, Ora Sterling 1931- *WhoBlA 94*
Anderson, Orvil Roger 1937- *WhoAm 94*
Anderson, Owen Raymond 1919- *WhoAm 94*
Anderson, P. Christian 1951- *WhoAmL 94*
Anderson, Pamela Boyette 1957- *WhoScEn 94*
Anderson, Patricia Ann 1944- *WhoMW 93*
Anderson, Patricia Francis 1956- *WhoMW 93*
Anderson, Patricia Hebert 1945- *WhoBlA 94*
Anderson, Patricia Joyce 1941- *WhoMW 93*
Anderson, Patricia Sue 1940- *WhoAmP 93*
Anderson, Patrick Mores 1954- *WhoAmL 94*
Anderson, Paul 1963- *WhoScEn 94*
Anderson, Paul Edward 1921- *WhoAm 94*
Anderson, Paul Irving 1935- *WhoAm 94, WhoFI 94*
Anderson, Paul Jacques 1958- *WhoAmL 94*
Anderson, Paul James 1959- *Who 94*
Anderson, Paul Maurice 1926- *WhoAm 94*
Anderson, Paul Milton 1945- *WhoFI 94*
Anderson, Paul N(athaniel) 1898- *WhAm 10*
Anderson, Paul Nathaniel 1937- *WhoWest 94*
Anderson, Paul R. d1993 *NewYTBS 93 [port]*
Anderson, Paul Simon 1943- *WhoMW 93*
Anderson, Paula Lee 1953- *WhoMW 93*
Anderson, Pearl G. 1950- *WhoBlA 94*
Anderson, Peer LaFollette 1944- *WhoAm 94, WhoAmL 94*
Anderson, Peggy 1938- *WrDr 94*
Anderson, Perry L. *WhoBlA 94*
Anderson, Perry William 1959- *WhoMW 93*
Anderson, Peter 1942- *ConTFT 11*
Anderson, Peter David 1940- *WhoAmP 93*
Anderson, Peter Glennie 1954- *WhoScEn 94*
Anderson, Peter Joseph 1951- *WhoAm 94*
Anderson, Peter MacArthur 1937- *WhoAm 94*
Anderson, Peter Rudge 1960- *WhoAmL 94*
Anderson, Phelps 1951- *WhoAmP 93*
Anderson, Philip Sidney 1935- *WhoAm 94, WhoAmL 94*
Anderson, Philip Vernon 1928- *WhoMW 93*
Anderson, Philip W. 1923- *IntWW 93*
Anderson, Philip Warren 1923- *Who 94, WhoAm 94, WhoScEn 94*
Anderson, Phyllis Reinhold 1936- *WhoMW 93*
Anderson, Polly Gordon 1934- *WhoWest 94*
Anderson, Poul *DrAPF 93*
Anderson, Poul 1926- *WrDr 94*
Anderson, Poul (William) 1926- *EncSF 93*
Anderson, Poul William 1926- *WhoAm 94*
Anderson, Priscilla B. 1935- *WhoAmP 93*
Anderson, Quentin 1912- *WhoAm 94, WrDr 94*
Anderson, R. Lanier, III *WhoAmP 93*
Anderson, R. Quintus 1930- *WhoAm 94, WhoFI 94*
Anderson, Rachael Keller 1938- *WhoAm 94*
Anderson, Rachel 1943- *SmATA 18AS [port], WrDr 94*
Anderson, Ralph *WhoAmP 93*
Anderson, Ray C. 1934- *WhoAm 94, WhoFI 94*
Anderson, Ray Thomas 1936- *Who 94*
Anderson, Raymond Francis, Jr. 1962- *WhoFI 94*
Anderson, Raymond Hartwell, Jr. 1932- *WhoScEn 94, WhoWest 94*
Anderson, Rebecca Cogwell 1948- *WhoScEn 94*
Anderson, Reginald 1921- *Who 94*
Anderson, Reid Bryce 1949- *WhoAm 94*
Anderson, Reuben V. 1942- *WhoAm 94, WhoAmP 93*
Anderson, Reuben Vincent 1942- *WhoBlA 94*

Anderson, Rex Herbert, Jr. 1954- *WhoFI 94*
Anderson, Richard 1926- *IntMPA 94, WhoHol 92*
Anderson, Richard C. 1929- *WhoFI 94*
Anderson, Richard Carl 1928- *WhoAm 94*
Anderson, Richard Charleton 1947- *WhoMW 93*
Anderson, Richard D. 1965- *WhoAmL 94*
Anderson, Richard Dean 1950- *IntMPA 94, WhoAm 94, WhoHol 92*
Anderson, Richard Edmund 1938- *WhoAm 94*
Anderson, Richard Ellsworth 1935- *WhoMW 93*
Anderson, Richard Ernest 1926- *WhoWest 94*
Anderson, Richard Ernest 1945- *WhoWest 94*
Anderson, Richard Gordon 1949- *WhoFI 94*
Anderson, Richard Lloyd 1926- *WrDr 94*
Anderson, Richard Loree 1915- *WhoAm 94*
Anderson, Richard Louis 1927- *WhoAm 94*
Anderson, Richard M. 1949- *WhoAmP 93*
Anderson, Richard McLemore 1930- *WhoScEn 94*
Anderson, Richard Norman 1926- *WhoAm 94, WhoWest 94*
Anderson, Richard Paul 1929- *WhoAm 94, WhoMW 93*
Anderson, Richard Paul 1946- *WhoAmP 93*
Anderson, Richard Powell 1934- *WhoAm 94*
Anderson, Richard R. 1944- *WhoAmP 93*
Anderson, Richard Roy 1941- *WhoFI 94*
Anderson, Richard Vernon 1946- *WhoScEn 94*
Anderson, Richard William *WhoMW 93*
Anderson, Richard William 1919- *WhoAm 94*
Anderson, Rick Gary 1941- *WhoAm 94, WhoWest 94*
Anderson, Robbin Gail 1964- *WhoMW 93*
Anderson, Robert 1920- *IntWW 93, WhoAm 94, WhoWest 94*
Anderson, Robert 1922- *WhoAmP 93*
Anderson, Robert 1944- *WhoAm 94, WhoFI 94, WhoScEn 94, WhoWest 94*
Anderson, Robert (Woodruff) 1917- *ConDr 93, IntDcT 2, Who 94, WrDr 94*
Anderson, Robert Alan 1957- *WhoAmL 94*
Anderson, Robert Alexander 1894- *WhAm 10*
Anderson, Robert Alexander 1946- *WhoAmA 93*
Anderson, Robert B. 1950- *WhoAm 94, WhoAmL 94*
Anderson, Robert Bernerd 1910-1989 *WhAm 10*
Anderson, Robert Bruce 1946- *WhoWest 94*
Anderson, Robert Bruce 1956- *WhoAmL 94*
Anderson, Robert Dennis 1947- *WhoAm 94, WhoAmL 94*
Anderson, Robert Ernest 1926- *WhoWest 94*
Anderson, Robert Floyd 1938- *WhoWest 94*
Anderson, Robert Geoffrey William 1944- *IntWW 93, Who 94*
Anderson, Robert Gregg 1928- *WhoAm 94*
Anderson, Robert H. 1924- *WhoMW 93*
Anderson, Robert Helms 1939- *WhoAm 94*
Anderson, Robert Henry 1918- *WhoAm 94*
Anderson, Robert Henry 1942- *Who 94*
Anderson, Robert James 1943- *WhoMW 93*
Anderson, Robert K. 1935- *WhoAm 94*
Anderson, Robert L. 1940- *WhoBlA 94*
Anderson, Robert Lanier, III 1936- *WhoAm 94, WhoAmL 94*
Anderson, Robert Lewis *WhoAmP 93*
Anderson, Robert Marshall 1933- *WhoMW 93*
Anderson, Robert Morris, Jr. 1939- *WhoAm 94*
Anderson, Robert Nils 1936- *WhoWest 94*
Anderson, Robert Orville 1917- *IntWW 93, WhoAm 94, WhoAmP 93, WhoWest 94*
Anderson, Robert Raymond 1945- *WhoAmA 93*
Anderson, Robert Rowand 1834-1921 *DcNaB MP*
Anderson, Robert T. 1945- *WhoAmP 93*
Anderson, Robert Theodore 1934- *WhoAm 94*
Anderson, Robert Wayne 1951- *WhoWest 94*
Anderson, Robert Woodruff 1917- *WhoAm 94*
Anderson, Roberta 1942- *ConAu 42NR, WrDr 94*
Anderson, Roberta Joan 1943- *WhoAm 94*
Anderson, Rodney 1931- *WhoAmP 93*
Anderson, Roger Clark 1941- *WhoScEn 94*
Anderson, Roger E. 1921- *IntWW 93, WhoAm 94*
Anderson, Roland C. 1944- *WhoAmL 94*
Anderson, Rolph Ely 1936- *WhoAm 94*
Anderson, Ron *WhoAm 94*
Anderson, Ron Joe 1946- *WhoAm 94*
Anderson, Rona 1928- *WhoHol 92*
Anderson, Ronald A. 1944- *WhoAmP 93*
Anderson, Ronald Delaine 1937- *WhoAm 94*
Anderson, Ronald Edward 1948- *WhoBlA 94*
Anderson, Ronald G. 1930- *WhoMW 93*
Anderson, Ronald G. 1949- *WhoAmP 93*
Anderson, Ronald Gene 1958- *WhoBlA 94*
Anderson, Ronald Gordon 1948- *WhoIns 94*
Anderson, Ronald Truman 1933- *WhoIns 94*
Anderson, Roscoe Odell Dale 1913- *WhoWest 94*
Anderson, Ross Barrett 1951- *WhoFI 94*
Anderson, Ross Carl 1951- *WhoAmL 94, WhoWest 94*
Anderson, Ross Cornelius 1951- *WhoAmA 93*
Anderson, Ross Sherwood 1951- *WhoAm 94*
Anderson, Roy Alan 1949- *WhoScEn 94*
Anderson, Roy Arnold 1920- *IntWW 93, Who 94*
Anderson, Roy Everett 1918- *WhoAm 94, WhoScEn 94*
Anderson, Roy Malcolm 1947- *IntWW 93, Who 94*
Anderson, Roy Ryden 1920- *WhoAm 94*
Anderson, Royal John 1914- *WhoFI 94, WhoWest 94*
Anderson, Rudolph J., Jr. 1924- *WhoAm 94*
Anderson, Russell Karl, Jr. 1943- *WhoScEn 94*
Anderson, Russell Lloyd 1907- *WhoBlA 94*
Anderson, Ruth Bluford 1921- *WhoBlA 94*
Anderson, Ruth Carrington 1915- *WhoMW 93*
Anderson, S. A. 1935- *WhoBlA 94*
Anderson, Sally J. 1942- *WhoAmA 93*
Anderson, Sally Jane 1942- *WhoWest 94*
Anderson, Sam 1923- *WhoHol 92*
Anderson, Samuel Wentworth 1929- *WhoScEn 94*
Anderson, Sandra Florence 1948- *WhoMW 93*
Anderson, Sandra Jo 1951- *WhoAm 94*
Anderson, Sarah A. *WhoBlA 94*
Anderson, Sarah Jane 1943- *WhoAmL 94*
Anderson, Scott David 1957- *WhoAm 94, WhoWest 94*
Anderson, Scott Robbins 1940- *WhoAm 94, WhoMW 93*
Anderson, Sharon Louise 1948- *WhoMW 93*
Anderson, Sherwood (Berton) 1876-1941 *RfGShF*
Anderson, Sherwood Berton 1876-1941 *AmCulL*
Anderson, Shiell 1961- *WhoAmP 93*
Anderson, Sigurd 1904-1990 *WhAm 10*
Anderson, Sparky 1934- *WhoAm 94, WhoMW 93*
Anderson, Stanford Owen 1934- *WhoAm 94*
Anderson, Stanley Edward, Jr. 1940- *WhoWest 94*
Anderson, Stanton Dean 1940- *WhoAm 94*
Anderson, Stefan Stolen 1934- *WhoAm 94*
Anderson, Stephen Francis 1950- *WhoMW 93*
Anderson, Stephen Hale 1932- *WhoAm 94, WhoAmL 94, WhoAmP 93, WhoWest 94*
Anderson, Stephen J. 1949- *WhoAmP 93*
Anderson, Stephen Mills 1946- *WhoFI 94*
Anderson, Stephen Thomas 1949- *WhoScEn 94*
Anderson, Steven R. 1952- *WhoAmL 94*
Anderson, Susan Blalock 1953- *WhoAmL 94*
Anderson, Susan Carol 1945- *WhoAmP 93*
Anderson, Susan Lou 1947- *WhoAm 94*
Anderson, Susan Lynne 1964- *WhoWest 94*
Anderson, Susan Stuebing 1951- *WhoAm 94*
Anderson, Sydney 1927- *WhoAm 94*
Anderson, Sylvia *IntMPA 94*
See Also Anderson, Gerry 1929- *EncSF 93*
Anderson, Sylvia 1938- *NewGrDO*
Anderson, Talmadge 1932- *WhoBlA 94*
Anderson, Ted *WhoAmP 93*
Anderson, Tempest 1846-1913 *DcNaB MP*
Anderson, Teresa *DrAPF 93*
Anderson, Terrill Gordon 1952- *WhoAmP 93*
Anderson, Terry *NewYTBS 93 [port]*
Anderson, Terry Marlene 1954- *WhoScEn 94*
Anderson, Theodore Carl 1960- *WhoAmL 94*
Anderson, Theodore Robert 1949- *WhoFI 94, WhoScEn 94*
Anderson, Theodore Wellington 1941- *WhoFI 94*
Anderson, Theodore Wilbur 1918- *IntWW 93, WhoAm 94*
Anderson, Thomas *WhoHol 92*
Anderson, Thomas B., Jr. 1942- *WhoAmL 94*
Anderson, Thomas Caryl 1944- *WhoFI 94*
Anderson, Thomas Dunaway 1912- *WhoAm 94*
Anderson, Thomas Edward 1947- *WhoFI 94*
Anderson, Thomas F(oxen) 1911-1991 *WhAm 10*
Anderson, Thomas J. 1910- *WhoAm 94*
Anderson, Thomas Jefferson 1919- *WhoAmP 93*
Anderson, Thomas Jefferson 1928- *AfrAmAl 6, WhoBlA 94*
Anderson, Thomas Jefferson, Jr. 1928- *WhoAm 94*
Anderson, Thomas Kemp, Jr. 1926- *WhoAm 94*
Anderson, Thomas Leif *WhoWest 94*
Anderson, Thomas Leighton 1895- *WhAm 10*
Anderson, Thomas Patrick 1934- *WhoAm 94*
Anderson, Thomas Willman 1950- *WhoAm 94*
Anderson, Timothy B. 1951- *WhoAmL 94*
Anderson, Timothy Christopher 1950- *WhoAm 94*
Anderson, Timothy Lee 1969- *WhoScEn 94*
Anderson, Tom H. 1946- *WhoAmP 93*
Anderson, Tony 1947- *WhoBlA 94*
Anderson, Totton James 1909-1992 *WhAm 10*
Anderson, Troy 1948- *WhoAmA 93*
Anderson, Veanne Nixon 1955- *WhoMW 93*
Anderson, Velma Lucille 1918- *WhoAmP 93*
Anderson, Verner J. 1925- *WhoAmP 93*
Anderson, Vernon E(llsworth) 1908- *WrDr 94*
Anderson, Vic, Jr. 1942- *WhoAmL 94*
Anderson, Victor Charles 1922- *WhoScEn 94*
Anderson, Vinton Randolph *WhoAm 94, WhoMW 93*
Anderson, Vinton Randolph 1927- *WhoBlA 94*
Anderson, Violette d19th cent. *AfrAmAl 6*
Anderson, W. E. 1949- *WhoAmP 93*
Anderson, W. French 1936- *WhoAm 94*
Anderson, W. Townsend 1934- *WhoAmP 93*
Anderson, Walter Charles 1910- *Who 94*
Anderson, Walter Dixon 1932- *WhoAm 94*
Anderson, Walter Herman 1944- *WhoAm 94*
Anderson, Wanni W. 1937- *WhoAsA 94*
Anderson, Warner d1976 *WhoHol 92*
Anderson, Warren Harold 1925- *WhoAmA 93*
Anderson, Warren M. 1921- *IntWW 93*
Anderson, Warren Mattice 1915- *WhoAm 94, WhoAmL 94, WhoAmP 93*
Anderson, Wayne Arthur 1938- *WhoAm 94, WhoScEn 94*
Anderson, Wayne Carl 1935- *WhoAm 94*
Anderson, Wayne H. 1936- *WhoAmP 93*
Anderson, Wayne R. 1945- *WhoAmL 94*
Anderson, Wendell R. 1933- *WhoAmP 93*
Anderson, Wendell Richard 1933- *IntWW 93*
Anderson, Whitney T. 1931- *WhoAmP 93*
Anderson, William 1923- *WhoWest 94*
Anderson, William A. 1921- *WhoBlA 94*
Anderson, William A. 1937- *WhoBlA 94*
Anderson, William Albion, Jr. 1939- *WhoAm 94*
Anderson, William Augustus 1942- *WhoAmL 94*
Anderson, William Banks, Jr. 1931- *WhoAm 94*
Anderson, William Bert 1938- *WhoAm 94*
Anderson, William C. *DrAPF 93*
Anderson, William C(harles) 1920- *EncSF 93*
Anderson, William Carl 1943- *WhoAm 94, WhoScEn 94*
Anderson, William Carl 1958- *WhoAmL 94*
Anderson, William Cornelius, III 1947- *WhoAm 94, WhoAmL 94*
Anderson, William Edward 1922- *WhoAm 94*
Anderson, William H. 1911- *IntMPA 94*
Anderson, William Henry 1940- *WhoAm 94*
Anderson, William Hopple 1926- *WhoAm 94*
Anderson, William J. 1949- *WhoAmL 94*
Anderson, William L(ouis) 1941- *WrDr 94*
Anderson, William R. *WhoScEn 94*
Anderson, William R. 1921- *IntWW 93*
Anderson, William Ray 1928- *WhoAmP 93*
Anderson, William Robert 1921- *WhoAm 94*
Anderson, William Robert 1950- *WhoScEn 94*
Anderson, William Scovil 1927- *WhoAm 94, WhoWest 94*
Anderson, William Summers 1919- *IntWW 93*
Anderson, William Thomas 1936- *WhoAmA 93*
Anderson, Willie Lee, Jr. 1965- *WhoBlA 94*
Anderson, Willie Lloyd 1967- *WhoBlA 94*
Anderson, Winslow 1917- *WhoAmA 93*
Anderson, Wyatt Wheaton 1939- *WhoAm 94*
Anderson-Coons, Susan *DrAPF 93*
Anderson Growe, Joan 1935- *WhoWomW 91*
Anderson-Imbert, Enrique 1910- *IntWW 93, WhoAm 94*
Anderson Janniere, Iona Lucille 1919- *WhoBlA 94*
Anderson Long, Dee 1939- *WhoWomW 91*
Anderson-Pimes, Carol 1948- *WhoWest 94*
Anderson-Tanner, Frederick T., Jr. 1937- *WhoBlA 94*
Anders-Richards, Donald 1928- *WrDr 94*
Anderssen, Anton 1960- *WhoHisp 94*
Andersson, Alfhild Marianne 1942- *WhoWomW 91*
Andersson, Bibi 1935- *IntMPA 94, IntWW 93, WhoHol 92*
Andersson, Borje 1930- *IntWW 93*
Andersson, Claes 1937- *IntWW 93*
Andersson, Craig Remington 1937- *WhoAm 94*
Andersson, Einar 1909-1989 *NewGrDO*
Andersson, Georg 1936- *IntWW 93*
Andersson, Harriet 1932- *IntWW 93, WhoHol 92*
Andersson, Laila 1941- *NewGrDO*
Andersson, Leif Christer Leander 1944- *IntWW 93*
Andersson, Leif Per Roland 1923- *WhoFI 94*
Andersson, Sten 1923- *IntWW 93*
Andersson, Stig Ingvar 1945- *WhoScEn 94*
Andersson, Tommy Evert 1956- *WhoScEn 94*
Andersson, Ulf Goran Christer 1960- *WhoScEn 94*
Andert, Jeffrey Norman 1950- *WhoMW 93*
Anderton, Bob 1941- *WhoAmP 93*
Anderton, Brian Henry 1945- *Who 94*
Anderton, James *Who 94*
Anderton, James 1904- *Who 94*
Anderton, (Cyril) James 1932- *Who 94*
Anderton, James Franklin, IV 1943- *WhoFI 94, WhoMW 93*
Andes, Charles Lovett 1930- *WhoAm 94, WhoScEn 94*
Andes, G. Thomas 1942- *WhoAm 94*
Andes, Keith 1920- *IntMPA 94, WhoHol 92*
Andes, Mary Vivienne 1950- *WhoMW 93*
Andewelt, Roger B. *WhoAm 94, WhoAmL 94*
Andewelt, Roger B. 1946- *CngDr 93*
Andich, Bruce Robert 1945- *WhoWest 94*
Anding, Charles R. 1928- *WhoAmP 93*
Andino, Mario A. 1936- *WhoHisp 94*
Andino, Tiburcio Carias 1876-1969 *HisWorL*
Andis, Michael D. 1954- *WhoScEn 94*
Andler, Donald Andrew 1938- *WhoAm 94*
Ando, Koichi 1950- *WhoAsA 94*
Ando, Salvatore 1945- *IntWW 93*
Ando, Shigeru 1929- *WhoScEn 94*
Ando, Tadao 1941- *WhoAm 94*
Ando, Takashi 1937- *WhoScEn 94*

Andolfati, Pietro c. 1755-c. 1829 *NewGrDO*
Andolina, Lawrence J. 1948- *WhoAmL 94*
Andolsek, Charles Merrick 1947- *WhoFI 94*
Andolsek, Ludwig J. 1910- *WhoAm 94*
Andolsen, Alan Anthony 1943- *WhoAm 94*
Andom, R. 1869-1920 *EncSF 93*
Andor, Paul *WhoHol 92*
Andora, Anthony Dominick 1930- *WhoAmP 93*
Andorfer, Donald Joseph 1937- *WhoAm 94*
Andorka, Frank Henry 1946- *WhoAm 94, WhoAmL 94*
Andorn, Anne Cramer 1947- *WhoMW 93*
Andosca, Robert George 1967- *WhoScEn 94*
Andover, Viscount 1974- *Who 94*
Andra, Fern d1974 *WhoHol 92*
Andrada, Wilmer Vigilia 1948- *WhoAsA 94*
Andrade, Alfredo Rolando 1932- *WhoHisp 94*
Andrade, Antonio De c. 158-?-1634 *WhWE*
Andrade, Augusto A. 1952- *WhoHisp 94*
Andrade, Billy *WhoHisp 94*
Andrade, Bruno 1947- *WhoAmA 93*
Andrade, C. Roberto 1925- *WhoHisp 94*
Andrade, Carolyn Marie *WhoAmP 93*
Andrade, Edna *WhoAm 94*
Andrade, Edna Wright 1917- *WhoAmA 93*
Andrade, Francisco Alvaro Conceicao 1943- *WhoScEn 94*
Andrade, Francisco d' *NewGrDO*
Andrade, Frank John 1939- *WhoFI 94*
Andrade, Franklin Gabriel 1937- *WhoHisp 94*
Andrade, James C. 1953- *WhoHisp 94*
Andrade, Joe Russell 1947- *WhoWest 94*
Andrade, Jorge 1922-1984 *IntDcT 2*
Andrade, Jorge 1951- *WhoHisp 94*
Andrade, Jose Leandro 1901-1957 *WorESoc*
Andrade, Juan, Jr. 1947- *WhoHisp 94*
Andrade, Marcel Charles 1940- *WhoHisp 94*
Andrade, Mary Juana 1943- *WhoHisp 94*
Andrade, Nancy Lee 1937- *WhoWest 94*
Andrade, Rafael Gustavo 1964- *WhoHisp 94*
Andrade, Stephen Paul 1952- *WhoHisp 94*
Andrade-Gordon, Patricia 1956- *WhoScEn 94*
Andrakovich, Christina Diane 1966- *WhoMW 93*
Andrasfalvy, Bertalan 1931- *IntWW 93*
Andrasic, Stanley 1953- *WhoWest 94*
Andrasick, James Stephen 1944- *WhoAm 94, WhoFI 94*
Andrassy, Timothy Francis 1948- *WhoAm 94*
Andrauskas, Donna Marie 1960- *WhoMW 93*
Andre, Alix *EncSF 93*
Andre, Carl 1935- *IntWW 93, WhoAm 94, WhoAmA 93*
Andre, Carl Pierre d1972 *WhoHol 92*
Andre, Carol *WhoHol 92*
Andre, Curt A. 1953- *WhoWest 94*
Andre, David Jules 1942- *WhoAmL 94*
Andre, E. J. d1984 *WhoHol 92*
Andre, Gaby d1972 *WhoHol 92*
Andre, Gwili d1959 *WhoHol 92*
Andre, Harvie 1940- *IntWW 93, WhoAm 94*
Andre, James H. 1929- *WhoAmP 93*
Andre, Jerry P. 1940- *WhoAmP 93*
Andre, Johann 1741-1799 *NewGrDO*
Andre, John 1750-1780 *AmRev*
Andre, John 1751-1780 *WhAmRev [port]*
Andre, Judith 1941- *ConAu 140*
Andre, Kenneth B., Jr. 1933- *WhoIns 94*
Andre, L. Aumund 1916- *WhoMW 93*
Andre, Lona 1915- *WhoHol 92*
Andre, Maurice 1933- *IntWW 93*
Andre, Michael *DrAPF 93*
Andre, Michael 1946- *WhoAm 94, WrDr 94*
Andre, Michael Paul 1951- *WhoWest 94*
Andre, Michel d1987 *WhoHol 92*
Andre, Michele Marie Claude 1947- *WhoWomW 91*
Andre, Monya d1981 *WhoHol 92*
Andre, Pamela Q. J. 1942- *WhoAm 94*
Andre, Paul Dean 1928- *WhoAm 94*
Andre, Rae 1946- *WhoAm 94, WhoFI 94*
Andrea, Elfreda C. 1924- *WhoAmP 93*
Andrea, Joseph F. 1927- *WhoAmP 93*
Andrea, Marianne *DrAPF 93*
Andrea, Mario Iacobucci 1917- *WhoScEn 94*
Andreacchi, Grace *DrAPF 93*
Andreae, Volkmar 1879-1962 *NewGrDO*
Andreae-Jones, William Pearce 1942- *Who 94*
Andreano, Ralph Louis 1929- *WhoAm 94*
Andreas, Dwayne Orville 1918- *WhoAm 94, WhoFI 94, WhoMW 93*
Andreas, Jurgen *EncSF 93*
Andreas, Luke d1988 *WhoHol 92*
Andreas, Michael Dwayne 1948- *WhoAm 94, WhoFI 94*
Andreas, Stacy Marie 1964- *WhoAmL 94*
Andreas Capellanus fl. 1175- *BlmGEL*
Andreasen, Arman C. 1937- *WhoIns 94*
Andreasen, James H. 1931- *WhoAmP 93*
Andreasen, James Hallis 1931- *WhoAmL 94, WhoMW 93*
Andreasen, Nancy Coover *WhoAm 94, WhoScEn 94*
Andreasen, Niels-Erik Albinus 1941- *WhoAm 94*
Andreasen, Steven W. 1948- *WhoAmL 94*
Andreason, John Christian 1924- *WhoAm 94*
Andreas-Salome, Lou 1861-1937 *BlmGWL*
Andreassen, Karl 1918- *WrDr 94*
Andreassen, Poul 1928- *WhoFI 94*
Andree, Salomon August 1854-1897 *WhWE*
Andreeff, Starr *WhoHol 92*
Andreev, Aleksandr Fyodorovich 1939- *IntWW 93*
Andreev, Vacheslav Mikchaylovitch 1941- *WhoScEn 94*
Andreeva, Nina Aleksandrovna 1938- *LoBiDrD*
Andrei, Frederic *WhoHol 92*
Andrei, Stefan 1931- *IntWW 93*
Andreichenko, Natalia *WhoHol 92*
Andreini, Giovanni Battista 1579?-1654 *NewGrDO*
Andreini, Virginia 1583-1630? *NewGrDO*
Andreissen, David *EncSF 93*
Andrejevic, Milet 1925-1989 *WhAm 10, WhoAmA 93N*
Andrejew, Andre 1887-1966 *IntDcF 2-4*
Andren, Anders 1939- *IntWW 93*
Andren, Carl-Gustaf 1922- *IntWW 93*
Andreoff, Christopher Andon 1947- *WhoAmL 94, WhoFI 94, WhoMW 93*
Andreoli, Kathleen Gainor 1935- *IntWW 93, WhoAm 94*
Andreoli, Peter Donald 1919- *WhoAmL 94*
Andreoli, Thomas Eugene 1935- *WhoAm 94*
Andreoni, Giovanni Battista d1797 *NewGrDO*
Andreopoulos, Spyros George 1929- *WhoWest 94*
Andreos, George Philip 1935- *WhoAmL 94*
Andreotti, Giulio 1919- *IntWW 93, Who 94*
Andreotti, Raymond Edward 1940- *WhoScEn 94*
Andreozzi, Gaetano 1755-1826 *NewGrDO*
Andreozzi, Marie Tina 1937- *WhoFI 94*
Andres, Glenn Merle 1941- *WhoAmA 93*
Andres, Prentice Lee 1939- *WhoIns 94*
Andres, Reubin 1923- *WhoAm 94*
Andres, Ronald Paul 1938- *WhoAm 94*
Andresen, Bjorn 1955- *WhoHol 92*
Andresen, Graciela Vazquez 1952- *WhoMW 93*
Andresen, Ivar (Frithiof) 1896-1940 *NewGrDO*
Andresen, Julie Tetel *ConAu 42NR*
Andresen, Malcolm 1917- *WhoAmL 94*
Andresen, Mark Nils 1957- *WhoScEn 94*
Andresen, Norman Arnold 1943- *WhoMW 93*
Andresen, Sophia de Mello Breyner 1919- *BlmGWL*
Andreski, Stanislav Leonard 1919- *Who 94, WrDr 94*
Andreson, Laura F. 1902- *WhoAmA 93*
Andress, Geneva Oak 1923- *WhoAmP 93*
Andress, Ursula 1936- *IntMPA 94, WhoHol 92*
Andretta, Gage 1941- *WhoAmL 94*
Andretti, John 1963- *WhoAm 94*
Andretti, Mario Gabriele 1940- *IntWW 93, WhoAm 94*
Andretti, Michael Mario 1962- *WhoAm 94*
Andreu, Blanca *BlmGWL*
Andreu, Blanca 1959- *DcLB 134 [port]*
Andreu-Garcia, Jose A. 1937- *WhoAmP 93*
Andreu-Garcia, Jose Antonio *WhoAmL 94*
Andréu-García, José Antonio 1937- *WhoHisp 94*
Andreuzzi, Denis 1931- *WhoAm 94*
Andrew, Christopher M(aurice) 1941- *WrDr 94*
Andrew, Christopher Maurice 1941- *Who 94*
Andrew, Christopher Robert 1963- *IntWW 93*
Andrew, Colin 1934- *Who 94*
Andrew, David Neville 1934- *WhoAmA 93*
Andrew, Edward Raymond 1921- *IntWW 93, Who 94, WhoAm 94, WrDr 94*
Andrew, Frederick James 1942- *WhoAm 94*
Andrew, Gwen 1922- *WhoAm 94*
Andrew, Herbert Henry 1928- *Who 94*
Andrew, James Osgood 1794-1871 *DcAmReB 2*
Andrew, Jane Hayes 1947- *WhoAm 94, WhoWest 94*
Andrew, John-Christian 1952- *WhoWest 94*
Andrew, John Henry 1936- *WhoAm 94, WhoAmL 94*
Andrew, John Wallace 1946- *WhoScEn 94*
Andrew, Joseph Jerald 1960- *WhoAmL 94*
Andrew, Joseph Maree *BlkWr 2, ConAu 142*
Andrew, Karen Jean 1955- *WhoMW 93*
Andrew, Kenneth L. 1919- *WhoAm 94*
Andrew, Kevin Darrell 1959- *WhoFI 94*
Andrew, Lucius Archibald David, III 1938- *WhoAm 94, WhoFI 94*
Andrew, Ludmilla *IntWW 93*
Andrew, Mark Henry 1954- *WhoMW 93*
Andrew, Prudence 1924- *WrDr 94*
Andrew, Ralph K. 1943- *WhoAmP 93*
Andrew, Robert (John) 1928- *Who 94*
Andrew, Seymour L. 1948- *WhoIns 94*
Andrew, Sydney Percy Smith 1926- *IntWW 93, Who 94*
Andrew, Sylvia Rodriguez 1953- *WhoHisp 94*
Andrewartha, Herbert George 1907-1992 *WrDr 94N*
Andrewes, Lancelot 1555-1626 *BlmGEL*
Andrewes, Thomas d1659 *DcNaB MP*
Andrew of St Victor c. 1110-1175 *DcNaB MP*
Andrews, Adelia Smith 1914- *WhoBlA 94*
Andrews, Adolphus 1943- *WhoBlA 94*
Andrews, Adora d1956 *WhoHol 92*
Andrews, Albert O'Beirne, Jr. 1939- *WhoAm 94, WhoAmL 94, WhoMW 93*
Andrews, Alfred Lyle 1941- *WhoFI 94*
Andrews, Andrew Edward 1942- *WhoWest 94*
Andrews, Angus Percy 1937- *WhoScEn 94*
Andrews, Ann d1986 *WhoHol 92*
Andrews, Anthony 1948- *IntMPA 94, IntWW 93, WhoAm 94, WhoHol 92*
Andrews, Anthony Darwin, Jr. 1964- *WhoAmP 93*
Andrews, Archie Moulton 1919- *WhoAm 94*
Andrews, Arkansas Slim *WhoHol 92*
Andrews, Barry *WhoHol 92*
See Also XTC *ConMus 10*
Andrews, Ben d1981 *WhoHol 92*
Andrews, Benny 1930- *AfrAmAl 6, WhoAm 94, WhoAmA 93, WhoBlA 94*
Andrews, Bert 1929-1993 *NewYTBS 93 [port]*
Andrews, Bert J. 1929-1993 *WhoBlA 94N*
Andrews, Bethlehem Kottes 1936- *WhoScEn 94*
Andrews, Billy Franklin 1932- *WhoAm 94*
Andrews, Brad Francis 1949- *WhoAm 94*
Andrews, Bruce *DrAPF 93*
Andrews, Bruce 1948- *WrDr 94*
Andrews, Candace Lou 1957- *WhoWest 94*
Andrews, Carl R. 1926- *WhoBlA 94*
Andrews, Carolyn Fraser 1951- *WhoAm 94*
Andrews, Carolyn P. 1941- *WhoMW 93*
Andrews, Charleen Kohl 1925- *WhoAmA 93*
Andrews, Charles Beresford Eaton B. *Who 94*
Andrews, Charles Forrest 1956- *WhoMW 93*
Andrews, Charles Rolland 1930- *WhoAm 94*
Andrews, Christina 1944- *WhoAmL 94*
Andrews, Clara Padilla *WhoHisp 94*
Andrews, Clarence Adelbert 1912- *WhoAm 94, WrDr 94*
Andrews, Colin 1946- *WrDr 94*
Andrews, Colman Robert 1945- *WhoWest 94*
Andrews, Craig S. 1952- *WhoAmL 94*
Andrews, Curtis D., Jr. 1960- *WhoAmP 93*
Andrews, Cyril Blythe 1901- *WhoBlA 94*
Andrews, Dana d1992 *IntMPA 94N*
Andrews, Dana 1909- *WhoHol 92*
Andrews, Dana 1909-1992 *AnObit 1992, ConTFT 11*
Andrews, (Carver) Dana 1909-1992 *CurBio 93N*
Andrews, David 1935- *IntWW 93, Who 94*
Andrews, David 1952- *WhoHol 92*
Andrews, David Charles 1950- *WhoScEn 94*
Andrews, David Henry 1933- *WhoAm 94*
Andrews, David Ralph 1942- *WhoAm 94, WhoAmL 94*
Andrews, David Roger Griffith 1933- *IntWW 93, Who 94*
Andrews, Derek (Henry) 1933- *Who 94*
Andrews, Dormer (George) 1919- *Who 94*
Andrews, E. Lee 1935- *WhoFI 94*
Andrews, Edgar Harold 1932- *WrDr 94*
Andrews, Edward d1985 *WhoHol 92*
Andrews, Edwin C. 1956- *WhoAmA 93*
Andrews, Eleanor De Ling 1934- *WhoMW 93*
Andrews, Elmer 1948- *WrDr 94*
Andrews, Emanuel Carl 1956- *WhoBlA 94*
Andrews, Emmett Lynn 1954- *WhoMW 93*
Andrews, Evelyn F. 1958- *WhoAmL 94*
Andrews, Felicia *EncSF 93*
Andrews, Frank Lewis 1950- *WhoAm 94*
Andrews, Frazier L. 1933- *WhoBlA 94*
Andrews, Fred Charles 1924- *WhoAm 94*
Andrews, Frederick B. 1922- *WhoAmP 93*
Andrews, Frederick Franck 1938- *WhoAm 94*
Andrews, Frederick Newcomb 1914- *WhoAm 94*
Andrews, Garth E. 1943- *WhoWest 94*
Andrews, Gary Blaylock *WhoAmP 93*
Andrews, Gary Blaylock 1946- *WhoAm 94, WhoAmL 94*
Andrews, George Eyre 1938- *WhoAm 94*
Andrews, George Lewis Williams 1910- *Who 94*
Andrews, George Reid 1951- *ConAu 141*
Andrews, Gerald Bruce 1937- *WhoAm 94*
Andrews, Glen K. 1948- *WhoScEn 94*
Andrews, Glenn 1909- *WhoAm 94*
Andrews, Gloria Maxine 1927- *WhoMW 93*
Andrews, Gordon Clark 1941- *WhoAm 94*
Andrews, Harold Marcus E. *Who 94*
Andrews, Harry d1989 *WhoHol 92*
Andrews, Harvey Wellington 1928- *WhoScEn 94*
Andrews, Henry Nathaniel, Jr. 1910- *IntWW 93, WhoAm 94*
Andrews, Holdt 1946- *WhoFI 94*
Andrews, Hunter Booker 1921- *WhoAmP 93*
Andrews, Ike Franklin 1925- *WhoAmP 93*
Andrews, J. David 1933- *WhoAm 94*
Andrews, J(ames) S(ydney) 1934- *WrDr 94*
Andrews, James E. 1943- *WhoBlA 94*
Andrews, James Edgar 1928- *WhoAm 94*
Andrews, James Edward 1948- *WhoBlA 94*
Andrews, James F. 1918- *WhoBlA 94*
Andrews, James Roland Blake F. *Who 94*
Andrews, James Rowland 1941- *WhoAm 94*
Andrews, James V., Jr. 1930- *WhoAm 94*
Andrews, James Whitmore, Jr. 1950- *WhoWest 94*
Andrews, Jim 1934- *WrDr 94*
Andrews, John 1746-1813 *WhAmRev*
Andrews, John 1936- *WrDr 94*
Andrews, John Albert 1935- *Who 94*
Andrews, John Frank 1930- *WhoAm 94*
Andrews, John Frank 1942- *WhoAm 94*
Andrews, John Gerard 1960- *WhoMW 93*
Andrews, John Hamilton 1933- *IntWW 93*
Andrews, John Hayward 1919- *Who 94*
Andrews, John Henry 1939- *WrDr 94*
Andrews, John Hobart McLean 1926- *WhoAm 94*
Andrews, John Kneeland 1920- *WhoWest 94*
Andrews, John Malcolm 1936- *ConAu 41NR*
Andrews, John Miller 1871-1956 *DcNaB MP*
Andrews, John Robert 1942- *Who 94*
Andrews, John Stewart 1919- *WhoAm 94*
Andrews, John T., Jr. 1941- *WhoIns 94*
Andrews, Judis R. 1941- *WhoBlA 94*
Andrews, Judy Coker 1940- *WhoScEn 94*
Andrews, Julie 1935- *IntMPA 94, IntWW 93, WhoAm 94, WhoHol 92*
Andrews, Julie (Elizabeth) 1935- *Who 94, WrDr 94*
Andrews, Keith William *EncSF 93*
Andrews, Kenneth Raymond 1921- *IntWW 93, Who 94*
Andrews, Kenneth Richmond 1916- *WhoAm 94*
Andrews, Kevin Paul 1965- *WhoScEn 94*
Andrews, Kim 1939- *WhoAmA 93*
Andrews, La Verne d1967 *WhoHol 92*
Andrews, Lavone D. 1912- *WhoAm 94*
Andrews, Lawrence 1964- *WhoAmA 93*
Andrews, Lawrence Donald 1960- *WhoFI 94*
Andrews, Lawrence James 1920- *WhoAm 94*
Andrews, Lois d1968 *WhoHol 92*

Andrews, Lucilla (Mathew) 1919- *WrDr 94*
Andrews, Lyman 1938- *WrDr 94*
Andrews, M(aurice) Nell 1894- *WhAm 10*
Andrews, Maidie d1986 *WhoHol 92*
Andrews, Malachi 1933- *WhoBlA 94*
Andrews, Mari 1955- *WhoAmA 93*
Andrews, Mark 1926- *IntWW 93, WhoAmP 93*
Andrews, Mark Anthony William 1959- *WhoScEn 94*
Andrews, Mark J. 1949- *WhoAmP 93*
Andrews, Mark Joseph 1944- *WhoAm 94, WhoAmL 94*
Andrews, Mary Ella 1935- *WhoMW 93*
Andrews, Mary Eloise Okeson 1923- *WhoAmP 93*
Andrews, Mason C. *WhoAmP 93*
Andrews, Mason Cooke 1919- *WhoAm 94*
Andrews, Maxene 1918- & Andrews, Patti 1920- *WhoHol 92*
Andrews, Maxine Ramseur *WhoBlA 94*
Andrews, Michael *DrAPF 93*
Andrews, Michael A. 1944- *CngDr 93*
Andrews, Michael Allen 1944- *WhoAm 94, WhoAmP 93*
Andrews, Michael Frank 1916- *WhoAmA 93*
Andrews, Nancy *DrAPF 93*
Andrews, Nancy d1989 *WhoHol 92*
Andrews, Nelson Montgomery 1951- *WhoBlA 94*
Andrews, Oakley V. 1940- *WhoAm 94*
Andrews, Patrick E. 1936- *WrDr 94*
Andrews, Patti 1920-
See Andrews, Maxene 1918- & Andrews, Patti 1920- *WhoHol 92*
Andrews, Patti 1920- *WhoHol 92*
Andrews, Peter J. *WhoAmP 93*
Andrews, Peter John 1946- *Who 94*
Andrews, Phillip 1963- *WhoBlA 94*
Andrews, Rawle 1926- *WhoBlA 94*
Andrews, Rawle, Jr. 1965- *WhoAmL 94*
Andrews, Raymond *DrAPF 93*
Andrews, Raymond 1934- *AfrAmAl 6*
Andrews, Raymond 1934-1991 *BlkWr 2, ConAu 42NR, WhoBlA 94N*
Andrews, Raymond Denzil Anthony 1925- *Who 94*
Andrews, Richard Gibson 1955- *WhoAmL 94*
Andrews, Richard Nigel Lyon 1944- *WhoAm 94*
Andrews, Richard Otis 1949- *WhoAm 94, WhoWest 94*
Andrews, Richard Vincent 1932- *WhoAm 94, WhoMW 93*
Andrews, Robert *WhoHol 92*
Andrews, Robert E. *WhoAmP 93*
Andrews, Robert E. 1957- *CngDr 93, WhoAm 94*
Andrews, Robert Frederick 1927- *WhoAm 94*
Andrews, Robert Graham M. *Who 94*
Andrews, Robert Taylor 1920- *WhoAmP 93*
Andrews, Rodney D., Jr. d1993 *NewYTBS 93*
Andrews, Sally May 1956- *WhoScEn 94*
Andrews, Sharony S. *WhoBlA 94*
Andrews, Stanley d1969 *WhoHol 92*
Andrews, Stuart Morrison 1932- *Who 94*
Andrews, Susan Beth 1948- *WhoMW 93*
Andrews, Sybil 1898- *WhoAmA 93*
Andrews, Thelma 1904-1989 *WhAm 10*
Andrews, Theodora Anne 1921- *WhoMW 93*
Andrews, Thomas H. *WhoAmP 93*
Andrews, Thomas H. 1953- *CngDr 93, WhoAm 94*
Andrews, Tige 1924- *WhoHol 92*
Andrews, Tina 1954- *WhoHol 92*
Andrews, Tod d1972 *WhoHol 92*
Andrews, V(irginia) C(leo) d1986 *TwCYAW*
Andrews, W. Thomas 1941- *WhoAmP 93*
Andrews, Wallace Henry 1943- *WhoScEn 94*
Andrews, Wendy *SmATA 74*
Andrews, Wendy 1928- *WrDr 94*
Andrews, Willard Douglas 1926- *WhoAm 94*
Andrews, William Cooke 1924- *WhoAm 94*
Andrews, William Denys Cathcart 1931- *Who 94*
Andrews, William Eugene 1943- *WhoAm 94*
Andrews, William Frederick 1931- *WhoAm 94*
Andrews, William G. *WhoAmL 94*
Andrews, William G. 1930- *SmATA 74*
Andrews, William Henry 1919- *WhoBlA 94*
Andrews, William L., Sr. 1955- *WhoBlA 94*
Andrews, William L(eake) 1946- *WrDr 94*
Andrews, William Leake 1946- *WhoAm 94*
Andrews, William Mitchell 1946- *WhoWest 94*
Andrews, William Parker, Jr. 1949- *WhoAm 94, WhoAmL 94*
Andrews, William Phillip 1938- *WhoBlA 94*
Andrews, William S. 1949- *WhoAm 94*
Andrews, William Scott 1955- *WhoFI 94*
Andrews, William Shankland 1925- *WhoAmL 94*
Andrews, Wright Harleston, Jr. 1947- *WhoAmL 94*
Andrex d1989 *WhoHol 92*
Andreyanova, Elena 1819-1857 *IntDcB [port]*
Andreyev, Boris 1915- *WhoHol 92*
Andreyev, Leonid Nikolayevich 1871-1919 *IntDcT 2*
Andreyev, Stepan fl. 176-?- *WhWE*
Andreyev, Vladimir Alekseyevich 1930- *IntWW 93*
Andreyeva, Victoria *DrAPF 93*
Andreyor, Yvette d1962 *WhoHol 92*
Andrezel, Pierre *BlmGWL*
Andrezeski, Anthony B. 1947- *WhoAmP 93*
Andri, John 1951- *WhoMW 93*
Andriacchi, Dominic Francis 1943- *WhoAmL 94*
Andriani, Marino N. 1947- *WhoFI 94*
Andrias, Richard Thompson 1943- *WhoAmL 94*
Andriashev, Anatoliy Petrovich 1910- *IntWW 93*
Andric, Ivo 1892-1975 *ConAu 43NR, RfGShF*
Andrie, Eugene Steven 1914- *WhoWest 94*
Andriessen, Franciscus H. J. J. 1929- *IntWW 93*
Andriessen, Frans 1929- *Who 94*
Andriessen, Hendrik 1892-1981 *NewGrDO*
Andriessen, Jacobus Eije 1928- *IntWW 93*
Andriessen, Louis 1939- *NewGrDO*
Andriessen, Pelagie *NewGrDO*
Andrieu, Rene Gabriel 1920- *IntWW 93*
Andring, Ronald Paul 1953- *WhoWest 94*
Andringa, Calvin Bruce 1941- *WhoAm 94*
Andriola, Rocco F. 1958- *WhoAmL 94*
Andriole, Stephen John 1949- *WhoAm 94*
Andriot, Poupee d1988 *WhoHol 92*
Andrisani, John Anthony 1949- *WhoAm 94*
Andrisani, Paul Joseph 1946- *WhoFI 94*
Andrist, John M. 1931- *WhoAmP 93, WhoMW 93*
Andritzky, Frank William 1947- *WhoAmL 94*
Andritzky, Joseph George 1947- *WhoAmL 94*
Andriulli, Robert 1948- *WhoAmA 93*
Andrle, William James, Jr. 1960- *WhoMW 93*
Androla, Ron *DrAPF 93*
Andronica, James *WhoHol 92*
Andronikos, Manolis 1919-1992 *AnObit 1992*
Andropov, Yuri 1914-1984 *HisWorL [port]*
Andros, Hazel Laverne 1939- *WhoMW 93*
Andros, James Harry 1955- *WhoAmL 94*
Andros, Phil *GayLL*
Andros, Stephen John 1955- *WhoWest 94*
Androsch, Hannes 1938- *IntWW 93*
Androsky, Carol *WhoHol 92*
Androus, Melvin D. 1925- *WhoAmP 93*
Androutsellis-Theotokis, Paul 1939- *WhoScEn 94*
Androutsopoulos, Adamantios 1919- *IntWW 93*
Androvaskaya, Olga d1975 *WhoHol 92*
Andrunache, Emilia *WhoWomW 91*
Andrus, Alan Richard 1943- *WhoWest 94*
Andrus, Cecil D. 1931- *IntWW 93, WhoAmP 93*
Andrus, Cecil Dale 1931- *WhoAm 94, WhoWest 94*
Andrus, Donald R. *WhoFI 94*
Andrus, Francis Sedley 1915- *Who 94*
Andrus, Gerald Louis 1904- *WhoAm 94*
Andrus, Hyrum Leslie 1924- *WrDr 94*
Andrus, James Roman 1907- *WhoAmA 93*
Andrus, Roger Douglas 1945- *WhoAm 94, WhoAmL 94*
Andrus, Vance Robert 1947- *WhoAmP 93*
Andrus, Winfield Scott 1938- *WhoScEn 94*
Andry, Keith Anthony 1960- *WhoAmA 93*
Andry, Steven Craig 1959- *WhoScEn 94*
Andrzejewski, Chester, Jr. 1953- *WhoScEn 94*
Andrzejewski, Pat 1953- *WhoAm 94*
Andujar, Carlos A. 1966- *WhoHisp 94*
Andujar, Joaquin 1952- *WhoBlA 94, WhoHisp 94*
Andzhaparidze, Georgiy Andreyevich 1943- *IntWW 93*
Anees, Munawar Ahmad 1948- *WrDr 94*
Anel, Alberto 1963- *WhoScEn 94*
Anelay, Richard Alfred 1946- *Who 94*
Anell, Lars Evert Roland 1941- *IntWW 93*
Anelli, Angelo 1761-1820 *NewGrDO*
Anema, Durlynn Carol 1935- *WhoWest 94*
Anemone *WhoHol 92*
Anestin, Victor *EncSF 93*
Anestos, Harry Peter 1917- *WhoAmL 94*
Anet, Claude 1868-1931 *EncSF 93*
Aneziris, Charilaos N. 1961- *WhoAm 94*
An Fengshi *WhoPRCh 91*
Anfimov, Nikolai 1935- *WhoScEn 94*
Anfinsen, Christian Boehmer 1916- *IntWW 93, Who 94, WhoAm 94, WhoScEn 94*
Anfinson, Thomas Elmer 1941- *WhoAm 94*
Anfom, Emmanuel E. *Who 94*
Anfossi, Pasquale 1727-1797 *NewGrDO*
Anfosso, Christian Lorenz 1963- *WhoScEn 94*
Ang, Alfredo Hua-Sing 1930- *WhoAm 94*
Ang, Charles C. 1927- *WhoAsA 94*
Ang, Jit Fu 1962- *WhoMW 93*
An Gang *WhoPRCh 91*
Angarola, Robert Thomas 1945- *WhoAm 94*
Angel, Allen Robert 1942- *WhoFI 94*
Angel, Armando Carlos 1940- *WhoHisp 94, WhoWest 94*
Angel, Arthur Ronald 1948- *WhoAm 94*
Angel, Aubie 1935- *WhoAm 94, WhoScEn 94*
Angel, D. Richard 1940- *WhoFI 94*
Angel, Dennis 1947- *WhoAmL 94*
Angel, Frank, Jr. 1914- *WhoHisp 94*
Angel, Gerald Bernard Nathaniel Aylmer 1937- *Who 94*
Angel, Heather d1986 *WhoHol 92*
Angel, Heather 1941- *Who 94, WrDr 94*
Angel, Heather Hazel 1941- *IntWW 93*
Angel, James Roger Prior 1941- *Who 94, WhoAm 94, WhoScEn 94*
Angel, James Terrance 1945- *WhoAm 94*
Angel, Joe 1949- *WhoHisp 94*
Angel, John 1881-1960 *WhoAmA 93N*
Angel, José Vicente González, Jr. 1959- *WhoHisp 94*
Angel, Larry David 1957- *WhoFI 94*
Angel, Marie 1953- *NewGrDO*
Angel, Ralph *DrAPF 93*
Angel, Steven Michael 1950- *WhoAmL 94*
Angel, Vanessa 1963- *WhoHol 92*
Angela, June 1959- *ConTFT 11*
Angelakos, Diogenes James 1919- *WhoAm 94*
Angelakos, Evangelos Theodorou 1929- *WhoAm 94*
Angele, Alfred Robert 1940- *WhoWest 94*
Angeleri, Lucy *DrAPF 93*
Angeles, Peter Adam 1931- *WhoWest 94*
Angeles, Victoria de los *Who 94*
Angeli, Pier d1971 *WhoHol 92*
Angelica, Norma d1962 *WhoHol 92*
Angelici, Robert J. 1937- *WhoAm 94*
Angelides, Demosthenes Constantinos 1947- *WhoScEn 94*
Angelides, Philip N. *WhoAmP 93*
Angelini, Arnaldo M. 1909- *IntWW 93*
Angelini, Giovanni Andrea *NewGrDO*
Angelini, John Michael 1921- *WhoAmA 93*
Angelis, Michael *WhoHol 92*
Angelis, Nazzareno de *NewGrDO*
Angelis, Paul *WhoHol 92*
Angell, Charles Marshall 1946- *WhoIns 94*
Angell, Christopher C. 1944- *WhoAmL 94*
Angell, Edgar O. *WhoBlA 94*
Angell, Israel 1740-1832 *WhAmRev*
Angell, James Browne 1924- *WhoAm 94, WhoScEn 94*
Angell, James Waterhouse 1898- *WhAm 10*
Angell, Jean *WhoAmP 93*
Angell, Judie 1937- *Au&Arts 11 [port]*
Angell, Karol 1950- *WhoAm 94*
Angell, Mary Faith 1938- *WhoAm 94, WhoAmL 94*
Angell, Philip A., Jr. 1936- *WhoAmP 93*
Angell, Richard Bradshaw 1918- *WhoAm 94*
Angell, Roger *DrAPF 93*
Angell, Roger 1920- *WhoAm 94, WrDr 94*
Angell, Tony 1940- *WhoAmA 93*
Angell, Wayne D. 1930- *IntWW 93, WhoAmP 93*
Angell, Wayne D. 1939- *WhoAm 94, WhoFI 94*
Angell-James, John 1901- *Who 94*
Angelo, Christopher Edmond 1949- *WhoAmL 94*
Angelo, Domenick Michael 1925-1976 *WhoAmA 93N*
Angelo, Emidio 1903- *WhoAmA 93N*
Angelo, Ernest, Jr. 1934- *WhoAmP 93*
Angelo, Gayle-Jean 1951- *WhoScEn 94*
Angelo, James M. 1961- *WhoAmP 93*
Angelo, Jean d1933 *WhoHol 92*
Angelo, Michael Arnold 1944- *WhoScEn 94*
Angelo, Percy L. 1945- *WhoAm 94, WhoAmL 94*
Angelo, Steven V. 1952- *WhoAmP 93*
Angeloch, Robert 1922- *WhoAmA 93*
Angeloff, Dann V. 1935- *WhoAm 94*
Angeloni, Luana 1952- *WhoWomW 91*
Angelopoulos, Theo 1936- *ConTFT 11, IntWW 93*
Angelotti, Richard H. 1944- *WhoAm 94, WhoScEn 94*
Angelou, Maya *DrAPF 93*
Angelou, Maya 1928- *AfrAmAl 6 [port], BlkWr 2, BlmGWL [port], ConAu 42NR, ConLC 77 [port], IntWW 93, NewYTBS 93 [port], News 93 [port], TwCYAW, WhoAm 94, WhoBlA 94, WrDr 94*
Angelov, George Angel 1925- *WhoWest 94*
Angeloz, Eduardo Cesar 1931- *IntWW 93*
Angelus, Muriel 1909- *WhoHol 92*
Angenot, Marc 1941- *IntWW 93*
Anger, David A. W. 1963- *WhoAmP 93*
Anger, Jane *BlmGWL*
Anger, Jane fl. 1589- *DcLB 136*
Anger, Kenneth 1932- *WhoHol 92*
Anger, Robert Michael 1957- *WhoFI 94*
Angerer, Margit 1903-1978 *NewGrDO*
Angerer, Paul 1927- *IntWW 93*
Angeri, Anna D' *NewGrDO*
Angermayer, Stephen Bruce 1962- *WhoAmL 94*
Angermeier, Ingo 1950- *WhoAm 94*
Angermuller, Rudolph 1940- *NewGrDO*
Angers, Avril *IntMPA 94*
Angers, Avril 1922- *WhoHol 92*
Angerville, Edwin Duvanel 1961- *WhoFI 94*
Angevin, Robert Perkins Brown 1963- *WhoWest 94*
Anghaie, Samim 1949- *WhoAm 94, WhoScEn 94*
Anghelaki-Rooke, Katerina 1939- *BlmGWL, ConWorW 93*
Anghelopoulos, Yannis 1881-1943 *NewGrDO*
Anghileri, Leopoldo Jose 1928- *WhoScEn 94*
Angier, Natalie Marie 1958- *WhoAm 94*
Angino, Ernest Edward 1932- *WhoAm 94*
Angino, Richard Carmen 1940- *WhoAmL 94*
Angiola, Maria Angiosa *NewGrDO*
Angiolillo, Glenn J. 1953- *WhoAmL 94*
Angiolini, Enzo d1993 *NewYTBS 93*
Angiolini, (Domenico Maria) Gasparo 1731-1803 *NewGrDO*
Angiolini, Gaspero 1731-1803 *IntDcB*
Angione, Howard Francis 1940- *WhoAm 94*
Anglace, John Francis, Jr. 1931- *WhoAmP 93*
Anglada, Jay Alfred 1939- *WhoAm 94*
Anglada, Maria Angels 1930- *BlmGWL*
Anglade, Jean 1915- *ConAu 43NR*
Anglade, Jean-Hugues 1955- *WhoHol 92*
Angland, Joseph 1949- *WhoAmL 94*
Angle, John Charles 1923- *WhoAm 94*
Angle, John Edwin 1931- *WhoAm 94*
Angle, Lisa Alison 1953- *WhoWest 94*
Angle, Margaret Susan 1948- *WhoAmL 94, WhoFI 94*
Angle, Richard Warner, Jr. 1941- *WhoAm 94*
Angle, Roger R. *DrAPF 93*
Anglemire, Kenneth Norton *WhoAm 94, WhoWest 94*
Anglemyer, Roma Kathleen 1932- *WhoMW 93*
Anglen, Reginald Charles 1952- *WhoBlA 94*
Angles, Amalia 1827-1859 *NewGrDO*
Anglesey, Marchioness of 1924- *Who 94*
Anglesey, Marquess of 1922- *Who 94, WrDr 94*
Anglesi, Domenico c. 1610-1669 *NewGrDO*
Anglesio, Franco J. 1943- *WhoAm 94, WhoFI 94, WhoWest 94*
Anglim, Philip 1953- *WhoHol 92*
Anglin, Betty Lockhart 1937- *WhoAmA 93*
Anglin, Douglas (George) 1923- *Who 94*
Anglin, Douglas G(eorge) 1923- *WrDr 94*
Anglin, Eric Jack 1923- *Who 94*
Anglin, Linda Tannert 1941- *WhoMW 93*
Anglin, Michael Williams 1946- *WhoAm 94, WhoAmL 94*
Anglo, Margaret Mary *Who 94*
Anglund, Joan Walsh 1926- *WrDr 94*
Angoff, William H. d1993 *NewYTBS 93*
Angold, Edit d1971 *WhoHol 92*
Angold, Michael (J.) *WrDr 94*
Angood, Donald John 1931- *WhoMW 93*
Angora, Anne Louise 1947- *WhoWest 94*

Anthony, James R(aymond) 1922- NewGrDO
Anthony, Jeffrey Conrad 1949- WhoBlA 94
Anthony, Joan Caton 1939- WhoAmL 94
Anthony, John J. d1970 WhoHol 92
Anthony, John Peter 1941- WhoWest 94
Anthony, Joseph d1993 NewYTBS 93 [port]
Anthony, Joseph 1912- WhoHol 92
Anthony, Julian Danford, Jr. 1935- WhoAm 94
Anthony, Kizhake Valiaveedu 1928- WhoMW 93
Anthony, Lawrence Kenneth 1934- WhoAmA 93
Anthony, Leander Aldrich 1917- WhoBlA 94
Anthony, Lysette 1963- WhoHol 92
Anthony, (Henry) Mark 1817-1886 DcNaB MP
Anthony, Michael 1916- WhoHol 92
Anthony, Michael 1930- BlkWr 2, ConAu 18AS [port], -43NR, WrDr 94
Anthony, Michael Francis 1950- WhoAm 94, WhoAmL 94
Anthony, Michael Thomas 1959- WhoAm 94
Anthony, Peter 1926- WrDr 94
Anthony, Peter 1958- WhoAmA 93
Anthony, Philip Levern 1935- WhoAmP 93
Anthony, Piers 1934- Au&Arts 11 [port], EncSF 93, TwCYAW, WhoAm 94, WrDr 94
Anthony, Ray 1922- WhoHol 92
Anthony, Robert Armstrong 1931- WhoAm 94, WhoAmL 94
Anthony, Robert Holland 1948- WhoAm 94, WhoFI 94
Anthony, Robert Newton 1916- WhoAm 94
Anthony, Ronald Desmond 1925- Who 94
Anthony, Sheila Foster 1940- WhoAmP 93
Anthony, Susan B. 1820-1906 HisWorL [port], WomPubS
Anthony, Susan Brownell 1820-1906 AmSocL [port], BlmGWL
Anthony, Thomas Dale 1952- WhoAm 94, WhoAmL 94
Anthony, Thomas Richard 1941- WhoAm 94, WhoScEn 94
Anthony, Tony 1937- WhoHol 92
Anthony, Tony 1939- IntMPA 94
Anthony, Vernice Davis 1945- WhoMW 93
Anthony, Virginia Quinn Bausch 1945- WhoAm 94
Anthony, Vivian Stanley 1938- Who 94
Anthony, Wendell 1950- WhoBlA 94
Anthony, William Graham 1934- WhoAm 94, WhoAmA 93
Anthony, William Philip 1943- WhoAm 94
Anthony-Perez, Bobbie M. 1923- WhoBlA 94
Anthrax ConMus 11 [port]
Antia, Kersey H. 1936- WhoFI 94
Antich, Rose Ann WhoAmP 93, WhoMW 93
Antico, Tristan 1923- IntWW 93, Who 94
Antier, Marie 1687-1747 NewGrDO
Antill, John (Henry) 1904-1986 NewGrDO
Antilla, Susan 1954- WhoAm 94
Antille, Rosemarie 1949- WhoWomW 91
Antin, David DrAPF 93
Antin, David 1932- WhoAm 94, WrDr 94
Antin, David A. 1932- WhoAmA 93
Antin, Eleanor DrAPF 93
Antin, Eleanor 1935- WhoAmA 93
Antine, Gertrude d1974 WhoHol 92
Antinori, Luigi fl. 1719-1734 NewGrDO
Antioco, John F. WhoAm 94, WhoFI 94, WhoWest 94
Antipa, Gregory Alexis 1941- WhoAm 94, WhoWest 94
Antipas, Constantine George 1962- WhoFI 94
Antisdel, Louis Willard 1925- WhoAmP 93
Antle, Charles Edward 1930- WhoAm 94
Antler DrAPF 93
Antler, Morton 1928- WhoAm 94
Antman, Stuart Sheldon 1939- WhoAm 94
Antoch, Zdenek Vincent 1943- WhoScEn 94, WhoWest 94
Antokal, Gale 1951- WhoAmA 93
Antokoletz, Elliott Maxim 1942- WhoAm 94
Antol, Joseph James 1947- WhoAmA 93
Antolovich, Stephen Dale WhoScEn 94
Anton, Alexander Elder 1922- Who 94
Anton, David 1958- WhoAmL 94
Anton, Frank A. 1949- WhoAm 94
Anton, Frank Leland 1930- WhoFI 94, WhoMW 93
Anton, Frederick W., III 1934- WhoIns 94
Anton, Harvey 1923- WhoAm 94, WhoFI 94
Anton, Ioan 1924- IntWW 93
Anton, James 1914- WhoAmP 93
Anton, Jim A. 1951- WhoAmP 93
Anton, John M. 1947- WhoAmL 94
Anton, Ludwig 1872- EncSF 93
Anton, Mace Damon 1961- WhoFI 94
Anton, Nicholas Guy 1906-1992 WhAm 10
Anton (Clemens Theodor) of Saxony 1755-1836 NewGrDO
Anton, Ronald David 1933- WhoAmL 94
Anton, Susan 1950- IntMPA 94, WhoHol 92
Anton, Thomas 1931- WhoAm 94
Anton, Thomas Julius 1934- WhoAm 94
Anton, Walter Foster 1936- WhoScEn 94
Anton, William WhoHisp 94
Anton, William R. WhoAm 94, WhoWest 94
Antonacci, Anna Caterina 1961- NewGrDO
Antonacci, Anthony Eugene 1949- WhoFI 94, WhoMW 93, WhoScEn 94
Antonacci, Greg WhoHol 92
Antonaccio, Mario Americo 1930- WhoFI 94
Antonakakis, Dimitris 1933- IntWW 93
Antonakakis, Suzana Maria 1935- IntWW 93
Antonakos, Stephen 1926- WhoAm 94, WhoAmA 93
Antonanzas Perez-Egea, Juan Miguel 1932- IntWW 93
Antonazzi, Frank J., Jr. DrAPF 93
Antone, Nahil Peter 1952- WhoAmL 94
Antone, Steve 1921- WhoAmP 93, WhoWest 94
Antonell, Walter John 1934- WhoAm 94
Antonelli, Daniel Salvatore 1952- WhoAm 94
Antonelli, H.E. Cardinal Ferdinando Giuseppe 1896- IntWW 93
Antonelli, Laura 1944- WhoHol 92
Antonen, James William 1948- WhoMW 93
Antonetti, Richard P. WhoAmP 93
Antoni, Antonio d' 1801-1859 NewGrDO
Antoniades, Harry Nicholas 1923- WhoAm 94
Antoniadis, Dimitri Alexander 1947- WhoAm 94
Antonic, James Paul 1943- WhoFI 94
Antonicek, Theophil 1937- NewGrDO
Antonicello, Nicholas J., Jr. 1960- WhoAmP 93
Antonini, Christina WhoHol 92
Antonini, Joseph E. 1941- WhoAm 94, WhoFI 94
Antonini, Michael Joseph 1946- WhoWest 94
Antoninus 1912- WhoAm 94
Antoninus, Brother 1912- WrDr 94
Antonio Who 94
Antonio 1921- IntWW 93
Antonio 1922- WhoHol 92
Antonio, James Frederic 1939- WhoAmP 93
Antonio, Lou IntMPA 94
Antonio, Lou 1934- WhoHol 92
Antonioni, Michelangelo 1912- CurBio 93 [port], IntWW 93, Who 94
Antonioni, Michelangelo 1913- IntMPA 94
Antonioni, Robert WhoAmP 93
Antoniono, James Richard 1945- WhoAmP 93
Antoniou, Andreas 1938- WhoAm 94
Antoniou, Lucy D. 1929- WhoAm 94
Antoniou, Panayotis A. 1962- WhoScEn 94
Antoniou, Theodore 1935- NewGrDO
Antonoff, Gary L. 1936- WhoAm 94
Antonoff, Steven Ross 1948- WhoAm 94
Antonov, Alexander d1962 WhoHol 92
Antonov, Guryan Vasilevich 1903- LoBiDrD
Antonov, Sergei Petrovich 1915- IntWW 93
Antonov, Viktor Ivanovych 1935- LoBiDrD
Antonova, Irina Aleksandrovna 1922- IntWW 93
Antonovich, Michael Dennis WhoAmP 93
Antonovich, Michael Dennis 1939- WhoWest 94
Antonovici, Constantin 1911- WhoAmA 93
Antonowsky, Marvin 1929- IntMPA 94
Antons, Pauline Marie 1926- WhoMW 93, WhoScEn 94
Antonsen, Elmer Harold 1929- WhoAm 94
Antonson, Joan Margaret 1951- WhoWest 94
Antonucci, John WhoAm 94
Antonuccio, Joseph Albert 1932- WhoAm 94
Antonutti, Omero WhoHol 92
Antony, P. J. d1979 WhoHol 92
Antony, Scott 1950- WhoHol 92
Antoon, A(lfred) J(oseph) 1944-1992 WhAm 10
Antos, Jan fl. 1772-1792 NewGrDO
Antosz, John Michael 1958- WhoAmL 94
Antoun, Annette Agnes 1927- WhoAm 94
Antreasian, Garo Zareh 1922- WhoAm 94, WhoAmA 93, WhoWest 94
Antremont, Marie-Henriette-Anne Payan Delestang, Marquise d' 1746-1802 BlmGWL
Antrim, Earl of 1935- Who 94
Antrim, Craig Keith 1942- WhoAm 94, WhoAmA 93
Antrim, Donald A. 1947- WhoAmL 94
Antrim, Harry d1967 WhoHol 92
Antrim, Minnie Faye 1916- WhoFI 94
Antrobus, John EncSF 93
Antrobus, John 1933- ConDr 93, WrDr 94
Antrobus, Philip Coutts 1908- Who 94
Anttila, Samuel David 1942- WhoScEn 94
Anttila, Sirkka-Liisa 1943- WhoWomW 91
Antunes, Carlos Lemos 1951- WhoScEn 94
Antunez, Ellis Lewis 1950- WhoHisp 94
Antuofermo, Vito 1954- WhoHol 92
Antupit, Samuel Nathaniel 1932- WhoAm 94
Antzelevitch, Charles 1951- WhoScEn 94
Antzis, David S. 1953- WhoAmL 94
Anudurayimu Litifu 1923- WhoPRCh 91 [port]
Anuszkiewicz, Richard Joseph 1930- IntWW 93, WhoAm 94, WhoAmA 93
Anuta, Karl Frederick 1935- WhoWest 94
Anuta, Michael Joseph 1901- WhoAmL 94, WhoMW 93
Anutta, Lucile Jamison 1943- WhoFI 94
Anuzis, Saul 1959- WhoAmP 93
Anvaripour, M. A. 1935- WhoAm 94
Anvil, Christopher EncSF 93, WrDr 94
Anwar, Gabrielle 1969- WhoHol 92
Anwar, Mohamed Samih 1924- Who 94
Anwyl, Shirley Anne Who 94
Anwyl-Davies, Marcus John 1923- Who 94
An Yanfeng 1963- WhoPRCh 91 [port]
Anyanwu, Chukwukre 1943 WhoFI 94, WhoScEn 94
Anyaoku, Eleazar Chukwuemeka 1933- IntWW 93, Who 94
Anyidoho, Kofi 1947- WrDr 94
An Yifu WhoPRCh 91 [port]
Anyte fl. 4th cent.BC- BlmGWL
An Yutao WhoPRCh 91 [port]
Anza, Juan Bautista De 1735-1788 WhWE
Anzaldi, James Anthony 1950- WhoAmP 93
Anzaldua, Gloria (Evanjelina) 1942- GayLL
Anzaldua, Gloria E. BlmGWL, DrAPF 93, WhoHisp 94
Anzalone, Filippa Elizabeth 1953- WhoAmL 94
Anzel, Sanford Harold 1929- WhoAm 94
Anzengruber, Ludwig 1839-1889 DcLB 129 [port]
Anzeveno, Frank J., Jr. 1958- WhoAmP 93
An Zhendong 1930- IntWW 93
An Zhendong 1931- WhoPRCh 91 [port]
An Zhiwen 1919 IntWW 93, WhoPRCh 91
Anzia, Joan Meyer 1950- WhoMW 93
An Zijie 1911- WhoPRCh 91 [port]
Aoki, Brenda Jean 1953- WhoAsA 94
Aoki, Carole I. WhoAmA 93
Aoki, Guy Miki 1962- WhoAsA 94
Aoki, Haruo 1930- WhoAsA 94
Aoki, Ichiro 1935- WhoScEn 94
Aoki, John H. 1931- WhoAm 94, WhoFI 94, WhoWest 94
Aoki, Junjiro 1910- WhoScEn 94
Aoki, Kathryn Kiku 1960- WhoAsA 94
Aoki, Keizo 1941- WhoScEn 94
Aoki, Masamitsu 1945- WhoScEn 94
Aoki, Masanao 1931- WhoWest 94
Aoki, Rocky 1940- WhoAsA 94
Aoki, Thomas T. 1940- WhoAsA 94
Aoki, Tsura d1961 WhoHol 92
Aoki Yayohi 1927- BlmGWL
Aono, Isamu 1944- WhoAsA 94
Aonuma, Tatsuo 1933- WhoScEn 94
Aotearoa, Bishop of 1928- Who 94
Aouchal, Leila 1937- BlmGWL
Aoude, Ibrahim Georges 1945- WhoWest 94
Aoun, Michel 1935- IntWW 93
Aoyama, Calvin Takeo 1942- WhoAsA 94
Aoyama, Hiroyuki 1932- WhoAm 94, WhoScEn 94
Aoyama, Yasutaka Barron 1962- WhoAsA 94
Apang, Gegong 1945- IntWW 93
Aparicio, Frances R. 1955- WhoHisp 94
Aparicio, Frances Rivera 1955- WhoMW 93
Aparicio, Luis Ernesto Montiel 1934- WhoHisp 94
Apatoff, Michael John 1955- WhoAm 94, WhoWest 94
Apcel, Melissa Anne 1951- WhoAm 94
Apea, Joseph Bennet Kyeremateng 1932- WhoBlA 94
A-pei A-wang Jin-mei WhoPRCh 91
A-pei-Cai-tan Zhuo-jia WhoPRCh 91
Apel, Barbara Jean 1935- WhoAmA 93
Apel, Hans Eberhard 1932- IntWW 93, Who 94
Apel, John Paul 1932- WhoScEn 94
Apel, John Ralph 1930- WhoAm 94
Apel, Myrna L. 1942- WhoFI 94, WhoMW 93
Apelian, Diran 1945- WhoAm 94, WhoScEn 94
Apelian, Virginia Matosian 1934- WhoScEn 94
Apell, David August von 1754-1832 NewGrDO
Apeloig, Yitzhak 1944- WhoScEn 94
Apes, William 1798- EncNAR
Apess, William 1798- EncNAR
Apfel, Edwin R. 1934- IntMPA 94
Apfel, Gary 1952- WhoAm 94, WhoAmL 94, WhoWest 94
Apfel, Jerome B. 1929- WhoAm 94
Apfel, Kenneth S. WhoAmP 93
Apfel, Kenneth S. 1948- WhoAm 94
Apfel, Oscar d1938 WhoHol 92
Apfel, Robert Edmund 1943- WhoAm 94
Apfelbaum, Marc Jeffrey 1955- WhoAmL 94
Apfelbeck, Ute 1943- WhoWomW 91
Apgar, Barbara Sue 1943- WhoMW 93
Apgar, David Allen 1945- WhoWest 94
Apgar, Jean E. 1949- WhoAmA 93
Apgar, Mahlon, IV 1941- WhoAm 94
Apgar, Nicolas Adam 1918- WhoAmA 93
Apicella, David Bruce 1954- WhoAm 94
ApIvor, Denis 1916- NewGrDO
Apker, Burton Marcellus, Jr. 1924- WhoWest 94
Apking, William Tappan 1933- WhoAmP 93
Aplan, Frank Fulton 1923- WhoAm 94, WhoScEn 94
Apley, Alan Graham 1914- Who 94
Aplon, Boris WhoHol 92
Aplon, Roger DrAPF 93
Apo, Peter K. 1938- WhoAmP 93
Apodaca, Aliana 1954- WhoHisp 94
Apodaca, Clara R. 1934- WhoHisp 94
Apodaca, Dennis Ray 1956- WhoHisp 94
Apodaca, Ed C. 1941- WhoHisp 94
Apodaca, Edward James 1948- WhoHisp 94
Apodaca, Esteban Corral 1952- WhoHisp 94
Apodaca, Francisco A. 1935- WhoHisp 94
Apodaca, Frank B. 1962- WhoHisp 94
Apodaca, James Max 1948- WhoHisp 94
Apodaca, Jerry 1934- WhoAmP 93, WhoHisp 94
Apodaca, Larry G. 1955- WhoHisp 94
Apodaca, Robert Anthony 1964- WhoWest 94
Apodaca, Rosa Elodia 1944- WhoHisp 94
Apodaca, Rudy S. DrAPF 93
Apodaca, Rudy S. 1939- WhoHisp 94
Apodaca, Rudy Samuel 1939- WhoAmL 94, WhoWest 94
Apodaca, Victor D., Jr. 1958- WhoHisp 94
Apodaca, Victor G., Jr. 1940- WhoHisp 94
Apolinsky, Stephen Douglas 1961- WhoAmL 94
Apollinaire, Guillaume 1880-1918 IntDcT 2, PoeCrit 7 [port], TwCLC 51 [port]
Apollon, Dave d1972 WhoHol 92
Apolloni, Giovanni Filippo c. 1635-1688 NewGrDO
Apolloni, Giuseppe 1822-1889 NewGrDO
Apolloni, Salvatore c. 1704- NewGrDO
Apollonius of Perga c. 262BC-190BC WorScD
Apone, Carl Anthony 1923- WhoAm 94
Aponte, Angelo J. 1946- WhoHisp 94
Aponte, Antonio 1957- WhoHisp 94
Aponte, Carmen Iris 1951- WhoHisp 94
Aponte, Christopher Bennedettey 1950- WhoWest 94
Aponte, Humberto 1924- WhoAmP 93
Aponte, Jose WhoAmP 93
Aponte, Julio 1945- WhoMW 93
Aponte, Leonardo 1934- WhoHisp 94
Aponte, Luis, Cardinal 1922- WhoHisp 94
Aponte, Mari Carmen 1946- WhoHisp 94
Aponte, Maria A. 1955- WhoHisp 94
Aponte, Nestor H. 1948- WhoAmP 93
Aponte, Néstor S. 1948- WhoHisp 94
Aponte, Philip 1936- WhoHisp 94
Aponte-Lebrón, Nilda I. 1944- WhoHisp 94

Aponte Martinez, Luis 1922- IntWW 93
Aponte Martinez, Luis Cardinal 1922- WhoAm 94
Aponte-Merced, Luis Antonio 1946- WhoHisp 94
Aponte Perez, Francisco 1928- WhoAmP 93
Apostle, Christos Nicholas 1935- WhoScEn 94
Apostle, Hippocrates George 1910-1990 WhAm 10
Apostolakis, James John 1942- WhoAm 94
Apostolides, Alex EncSF 93
Apostolides, Anthony Demetrios WhoMW 93, WhoScEn 94
Apostolou, Yannis 1860?-1905 NewGrDO
App, Timothy 1947- WhoAmA 93
Appachana, Anjana BlmGWL
Appel, Alfred 1906- WhoAm 94
Appel, Alfred, Jr. 1934- WrDr 94
Appel, Allan DrAPF 93
Appel, Allan F. 1946- WhoFI 94
Appel, Allen 1946?- EncSF 93
Appel, Andre 1921- IntWW 93
Appel, Anna d1963 WhoHol 92
Appel, Benjamin 1907-1977 EncSF 93
Appel, Bernard Sidney 1932- WhoAm 94
Appel, Dori DrAPF 93
Appel, Eric A. 1945- WhoAmA 93
Appel, Jacob J. 1940- WhoWest 94
Appel, Joanne Sciortino 1958- WhoFI 94
Appel, John J. 1921- WhoAm 94
Appel, Judith Ann 1939- WhoWest 94
Appel, Karel 1921- WhoAmA 93
Appel, Karel Christian 1921- IntWW 93, Who 94, WhoAm 94
Appel, Keith Kenneth 1934- WhoAmA 93
Appel, Kenneth Ellmaker 1896- WhAm 10
Appel, Kenneth I. 1932- WhoAm 94
Appel, Nina S. 1936- WhoAm 94, WhoAmL 94
Appel, Robert Eugene 1958- WhoAmL 94
Appel, Sam d1947 WhoHol 92
Appel, Stanley Hersh 1933- WhoScEn 94
Appel, Susan Kay 1946- WhoMW 93
Appel, Thelma 1940- WhoAmA 93
Appel, Wallace Henry 1925- WhoAm 94
Appel, William Frank 1924- WhoAm 94
Appelbaum, Bruce David 1957- WhoScEn 94, WhoWest 94
Appelbaum, Jeffrey R. 1952- WhoAmL 94
Appelbaum, Joel Alan 1941- WhoAm 94
Appelbaum, Matthew Aron 1951- WhoWest 94
Appelbaum, Michael Arthur 1945- WhoAm 94
Appelbaum, Paul Stuart 1951- WhoAm 94
Appelbaum, Robert Donald 1929- WhoMW 93
Appeldorn, Francis R. 1935- WhoAm 94
Appelfeld, Aharon 1932- ConWorW 93, RfGShF, WrDr 94
Appelhof, Ruth A. 1945- WhoAmA 93
Appelhof, Ruth Stevens 1945- WhoAm 94
Appell, George Nathan 1926- WhoScEn 94
Appell, Louise Sophia 1930- WhoAm 94
Appelman, Evan Hugh 1935- WhoAm 94
Appelman, Mary Goold 1926- WhoAmP 93
Appelson, Herbert J. 1937- WhoAmA 93
Appelson, Wallace Bertrand 1930- WhoAm 94, WhoMW 93
Appelwick, Marlin J. WhoAmP 93
Appenzell, Anthony 1912- WrDr 94
Appenzeller, Otto 1927- WhoAm 94, WhoWest 94
Appere, Guy 1923- ConAu 41NR
Apperson, Bernard James 1956- WhoAmL 94
Apperson, Jack Alfonso 1934- WhoAm 94
Apperson, Jean 1934- WhoAm 94, WhoMW 93
Apperson, Jeffrey A. 1954- WhoAmL 94
Appert, Nicolas Francois 1750?-1841 WorInv
Appert, Richard Henry 1940- WhoFI 94
Appia, Adolphe (Francois) 1862-1928 NewGrDO
Appiah, (K.) anthony 1954- BlkWr 2, ConAu 140
Appiah, Peggy 1921- WrDr 94
Appier, Kevin 1967- WhoAm 94, WhoMW 93
Appl, Fredric Carl 1932- WhoAm 94
Applbaum, Ronald Lee 1943- WhoAm 94
Apple, B. Nixon 1924- WhoAm 94
Apple, Daina Dravnieks 1944- WhoFI 94
Apple, Daniel Bryce 1951- WhoWest 94
Apple, David Joseph 1941- WhoAm 94, WhoScEn 94
Apple, Ed 1932- WhoAmP 93
Apple, Jacki DrAPF 93, WhoAmA 93
Apple, James Glenn 1937- WhoAmL 94
Apple, John Boyd 1935- WhoAm 94
Apple, Lowell D. 1928- WhoAmP 93
Apple, Martin Allen 1938- WhoFI 94
Apple, Max DrAPF 93
Apple, Max 1941- DcLB 130 [port]
Apple, Max (Isaac) 1941- WrDr 94
Apple, Max Isaac 1941- WhoAm 94
Apple, R. W., Jr. 1934- CurBio 93 [port]
Apple, Raymond Walter, Jr. 1934- WhoAm 94
Apple, Steven Anthony 1954- WhoWest 94
Applebaum, Charles 1947- WhoAmL 94
Applebaum, Edward Leon 1940- WhoAm 94
Applebaum, Emanuel d1993 NewYTBS 93
Applebaum, Harvey Milton 1937- WhoAm 94, WhoAmL 94
Applebaum, Louis 1918- WhoAm 94
Applebaum, Martin A. 1960- WhoFI 94
Applebaum, Michael Murray 1958- WhoAmL 94
Applebaum, Stuart S. 1949- WhoAm 94
Applebee, William Robert 1936- WhoAm 94
Appleberry, James Bruce 1938- WhoAm 94
Appleberry, Walter Thomas 1926- WhoWest 94
Applebroog, Ida 1929- WhoAmA 93
Appleby, Basil WhoHol 92
Appleby, Brian John 1930- Who 94
Appleby, Charlie L., Jr. WhoAmP 93
Appleby, Daniel Bart 1954- WhoAmA 93
Appleby, Dorothy d1990 WhoHol 92
Appleby, Douglas Edward Surtees 1929- Who 94
Appleby, (Lesley) Elizabeth 1942- Who 94
Appleby, John 1840-1917 WorInv
Appleby, Joyce Oldham 1929- WhoAm 94
Appleby, Ken 1953- EncSF 93
Appleby, Malcolm Arthur 1946- Who 94
Appleby, Raphael 1931- Who 94
Appleby, Richard Franklin Who 94
Appleby, Robert 1913- Who 94
Appleby-Young, Sadye Pearl 1927- WhoBlA 94
Appleford, John Widman 1938- WhoAmP 93
Applegarth, Paul Vollmer 1946- WhoAm 94
Applegarth, Robert 1834-1924 DcNaB MP
Applegarth, Ronald Wilbert 1934- WhoScEn 94
Applegate, Albert Augustus 1928- WhoAmP 93
Applegate, Arthur David 1965- WhoWest 94
Applegate, Christina 1972- WhoHol 92
Applegate, Donald Jay 1944- WhoFI 94
Applegate, Douglas 1928- CngDr 93, WhoAm 94, WhoAmP 93, WhoMW 93
Applegate, Eddie 1935- WhoHol 92
Applegate, Hazel d1959 WhoHol 92
Applegate, James 1923- WrDr 94
Applegate, James L. 1931- WhoAmP 93
Applegate, Jesse 1811-1888 WhWE
Applegate, Karl Edwin 1923- WhoAmL 94
Applegate, Malcolm W. 1936- WhoAm 94
Applegate, Minerva Irons 1939- WhoAm 94
Applegate, Randall Glenn 1948- WhoMW 93
Applegate, Stephen S. 1942- WhoMW 93
Applegate, William E., III 1942- WhoAmL 94, WhoAmP 93
Applegate, William Joseph 1946- WhoMW 93
Applegath, Augustus 1788-1871 DcNaB MP
Appleman, David Earl 1943- WhoAmA 93
Appleman, M(arjorie) H. 1928- ConAu 43NR
Appleman, Margie ConAu 43NR
Appleman, Marjorie DrAPF 93, WhoAm 94
Appleman, Philip DrAPF 93
Appleman, Philip 1926- ConAu 18AS [port], WhoAm 94
Appleman, Philip (Dean) 1926- WrDr 94
Applequist, Virgil H. 1947- WhoIns 94
Appler, Thomas L. 1943- WhoAm 94, WhoAmL 94
Appler, Walter d1956 WhoHol 92
Appleton, Arthur Ivar 1915- WhoAm 94, WhoMW 93
Appleton, Clevette Wilma WhoBlA 94
Appleton, Donald 1894-1989 WhAm 10
Appleton, Edward Victor 1892-1965 WorScD
Appleton, Elaine 1942- WhoWest 94
Appleton, George d1993 Who 94N
Appleton, George 1902- IntWW 93
Appleton, James Robert 1937- WhoAm 94, WhoWest 94
Appleton, John Fortnam 1946- Who 94
Appleton, John Roper 1938- Who 94
Appleton, Joseph Hayne 1927- WhoAm 94
Appleton, Myra 1934- WhoAm 94
Appleton, Peter Arthur 1941- WhoWest 94
Appleton, R. O., Jr. 1945- WhoAm 94
Appleton, Sarah DrAPF 93
Appleton, Sheldon Lee 1933- WrDr 94
Appleton, Victor EncSF 93
Appleton, Victor 1926- WrDr 94
Appleton, Victor 1949- WrDr 94
Applewhaite, Leon B. 1927- WhoBlA 94
Applewhite, Eric Leon d1973 WhoHol 92
Applewhite, Francine Laura 1962- WhoAmL 94
Applewhite, James DrAPF 93
Appley, Lawrence A. 1904- WhoAm 94
Appley, Mortimer Herbert 1921- WhoAm 94
Appleyard, Bryan (Edward) 1951- ConAu 141
Appleyard, David Frank 1939- WhoAm 94
Appleyard, Leonard Vincent 1938- Who 94
Appleyard, Raymond (Kenelm) 1922- Who 94
Appleyard, Raymond K. 1922- IntWW 93
Appleyard, William James 1935- Who 94
Appollonia WhoHol 92
Apps, Jerold Willard 1934- WhoMW 93
Aprahamian, Felix 1914- IntWW 93
Aprahamian, Vahe Apraham 1934- WhoMW 93
Aprea, John WhoHol 92
ap Rees, Thomas 1930- Who 94
Apreleva, Elena Ivanovna 1846-1923 BlmGWL
Aprigliano, Louis Francis 1950- WhoScEn 94
April, Lewis Benjamin 1949- WhoAmL 94
April, Rand Scott 1951- WhoAm 94
Aprile, Giuseppe 1732-1813 NewGrDO
Aprill, Arnold DrAPF 93
Aprille, Thomas Joseph, Jr. 1943- WhoAm 94
Aprison, Morris Herman 1923- WhoAm 94
ap Robert, Hywel Wyn Jones 1923- Who 94
Apruzzese, Vincent John 1928- WhoAm 94, WhoAmL 94
Apruzzi, Gene 1934- WhoAm 94, WhoFI 94
Apryska, Ales (Alaksandravic) 1941- LoBiDrD
Apsley, Lord 1961- Who 94
Apstein, Barbara Frances Holt 1942- WhoAm 94
Apstein, Theodore 1918- WrDr 94
Apt, Charles 1933- WhoAmA 93
Apt, Denise C. 1929- WhoAmP 93
Apt, Kenneth Ellis 1945- WhoWest 94
Apt, Leonard 1922- WhoAm 94
Apt, Lesley Ann 1946- WhoAmL 94
Apted, Michael 1941- IntMPA 94, IntWW 93, WhoHol 92
Apted, Michael D. 1941- WhoAm 94
Aptekar, Ken 1950- WhoAmA 93
Apter, David Ernest 1924- WhoAm 94, WrDr 94
Apter, Michael John 1939- WrDr 94
Apter, Nathaniel Stanley 1913- WhoScEn 94
Apter, T(erri) E 1949- WrDr 94
Apteryx ConAu 41NR
Aptheker, Bettina 1944- WrDr 94
Aptheker, Bettina Fay 1944- WhoWest 94
Aptheker, Herbert 1915- WhoAm 94
Apthomas, Ifan 1917- WrDr 94
Apthorp, John Dorrington 1935- Who 94
Apuron, Anthony Sablan 1945- WhoWest 94
Apuzzo, Gloria Isabel 1935- WhoFI 94
Apyan, Roseanne Lucille 1949- WhoWest 94
Aquila, Evelyn J. 1932- WhoAmP 93
Aquila, Francis Joseph 1957- WhoAmP 93
Aquilanti, Francesco fl. 1719-1742 NewGrDO
Aquilecchia, Giovanni 1923- Who 94
Aquilino, Daniel 1924- WhoAm 94
Aquilino, Thomas J., Jr. 1939- CngDr 93
Aquilino, Thomas Joseph, Jr. 1939- WhoAm 94, WhoAmL 94
Aquinas EncEth
Aquinas, Thomas c. 1225-1274 BlmGEL
Aquino, Carlos Alberto 1960- WhoHisp 94
Aquino, (Maria) Corazon 1933- IntWW 93
Aquino, Corazon C. 1933- WhoWomW 91
Aquino, Edmundo 1939- WhoAmA 93
Aquino, Felix John 1952- WhoAm 94
Aquino, Humberto 1947- WhoAmA 93, WhoHisp 94
Aquino, Joseph Mario 1947- WhoScEn 94
Aquino, Luis 1965- WhoHisp 94
Aquino, Maria Corazon Cojuangco 1933- Who 94
Aquino, Robert Joseph 1957- WhoFI 94
Aquino-Oreta, Teresa 1944- WhoWomW 91
Arabe, Michael Don 1947- WhoWest 94
Arabia, Paul 1938- WhoAmL 94, WhoMW 93
Arabian, Armand 1934- WhoAm 94, WhoAmL 94, WhoWest 94
Arabian, Armand A. 1934- WhoAmP 93
Arabia Rojas, José A. 1952- WhoHisp 94
Arabie, Phipps 1948- WhoAm 94
Arabiej, Lidzija (Lvouna) 1925- LoBiDrD
Arabyan, Ara 1953- WhoScEn 94
Arad, Nava 1938- WhoWomW 91
Arad, Yael NewYTBS 93 [port]
Arader, Harry Frederick, Jr. 1953- WhoMW 93
Arader, Walter Graham 1920- WhoAm 94
Arado, John J. 1942- WhoAmL 94
Arafat, Yasir NewYTBS 93
Arafat, Yasser 1929- IntWW 93
Aragall (y Garriga), Giacomo 1939- NewGrDO
Arago, Dominique-Francois-Jean 1786-1853 WorScD
Arago, Jacques 1790-1855 WhWE
Aragon, Arlene Bernice 1954- WhoHisp 94
Aragón, Bill John 1946- WhoHisp 94
Aragón, Carla Y. 1955- WhoHisp 94
Aragon, Ernest WhoHisp 94
Aragon, Janice Lynn 1954- WhoWest 94
Aragon, Jeff Paul 1962- WhoHisp 94
Aragon, Jesse d1988 WhoHol 92
Aragón, John A. 1930- WhoHisp 94
Aragon, Joseph M. WhoHisp 94
Aragon, Juan 1947- WhoHisp 94
Aragon, Manny WhoHisp 94
Aragon, Manny M. WhoAmP 93
Aragon, Rafael De Jesus 1938- WhoHisp 94
Aragón, Sergio Ramiro 1949- WhoHisp 94
Aragona, D'Tullia 1510-1556 BlmGWL
Arai, Ikuo 1934- Who 94
Arai, Masami 1953- ConAu 140
Arai, Tomie 1949- WhoAsA 94
Araia, Francesco 1709-1770 NewGrDO
Arain, Shafiq 1933- Who 94
Araiz, Joseph Michael 1961- WhoFI 94
Araiza, Daniel John 1952- WhoHisp 94
Araiza, Francisco 1950- IntWW 93, NewGrDO, WhoAm 94
Arakaki, Dennis Akira 1947- WhoAmP 93
Arakaki, Wayne S. 1932- WhoIns 94
Arakawa, (Shusaku) 1936- WhoAmA 93
Arakawa, Edward Takashi 1929- WhoAsA 94
Arakawa, Kasumi 1926- WhoAm 94, WhoAsA 94, WhoMW 93, WhoScEn 94
Arakawa, Minoru WhoAsA 94
Araki, Hiroshi 1949- WhoScEn 94
Araki, James Tomomasa 1925- WrDr 94
Araki, Minoru S. WhoAsA 94
Araki, Takaharu 1929- WhoScEn 94
Araki, Takeo 1934- WhoAm 94, WhoScEn 94
Araki, Yoshiro 1921- IntWW 93
Arakishvili, Dimitri Ignat'yevich 1873-1953 NewGrDO
Aral, Mustafa Mehmet 1945- WhoScEn 94
Arambewela, Lakshmi Sriyani Rajapakse 1946- WhoScEn 94
Aramburo, Sophie Watts 1931- WhoBlA 94
Aramburu, Albert 1934- WhoHisp 94
Aramburu, John Richard 1945- WhoAmL 94
Arams, Frank Robert 1925- WhoAm 94
Aran, Alberto Joaquin 1954- WhoHisp 94
Aran, Fernando Santiago 1957- WhoAmL 94
Arana, Helen DrAPF 93
Arana, Lucrecia 1871-1927 NewGrDO
Arana, Suelena M. 1958- WhoHisp 94
Arana, Thomas WhoHol 92
Arana, Victor M. WhoHisp 94
Arana Osorio, Carlos Manuel 1918- IntWW 93
Aranas, Maria Elena Lizares 1937- WhoMW 93
Aranbarri, Ricardo 1959- WhoHisp 94
Aranda, Benjamin, III 1940- WhoHisp 94
Aranda, Jess Robert 1949- WhoHisp 94
Aranda, Kathryn 1945- WhoAmP 93
Aranda, Miguel Angel 1939- WhoAm 94
Aranda, Thomas, Jr. 1934- WhoAmP 93
Arangi-Lombardi, Giannina 1891-1951 NewGrDO
Arangio-Ruiz, Gaetano 1919- IntWW 93
Arangno, Deborah Catherine 1956- WhoAm 94
Arango, Angel EncSF 93
Arango, Anthony Glenn 1945- WhoFI 94
Arango, Deborah Ann 1964- WhoHisp 94
Arango, Emilio 1927- WhoAmL 94
Arango, H. Humberto 1944- WhoHisp 94
Arango, J. A. WhoHisp 94
Arango, Jorge Sanin 1916- WhoAm 94

Arango, Jose O. 1957- WhoAmP 93
Arango, Richard Steven 1953- WhoScEn 94
Aranoff, Daniel 1944- WhoFI 94
Aranow, Peter Jones 1946- WhoAm 94
Aranson, Michael J. 1944- WhoAm 94
Arant, Eugene Wesley 1920- WhoAm 94
Arant, Patricia 1930- WhoAm 94
Arante, Al WhoHisp 94
Arantes, Jose Carlos 1955- WhoScEn 94
Arantes do Nascimento, Edson 1940- WhoAm 94
Aranzadi Martinez, Jose Claudio 1946- IntWW 93
Araoz, Daniel L. 1930- WhoHisp 94
Araoz, Daniel Leon 1930- WhoAm 94
Arapov, Boris Aleksandrovich d1992 IntWW 93N
Arapov, Boris Alexandrovich 1905-1992 NewGrDO
Arashi, Kanjuro d1980 WhoHol 92
Arashi, Qadi Abdul Karim al- IntWW 93
Araskog, Rand Vincent 1931- IntWW 93, WhoAm 94, WhoFI 94
Arasmith, Neil H. 1930- WhoAmP 93
Arasse, Jenny WhoHol 92
Arata, Louis Kenneth 1952- WhoMW 93
Arau, Alfonso WhoHol 92
Araujo, Jess J., Sr. 1947- WhoHisp 94
Araujo, Joao Gomes de NewGrDO
Araujo, Julius C. 1926- WhoHisp 94
Araujo, Marcio Santos Silva 1946- WhoScEn 94
Araujo, Norman 1933- WhoBlA 94
Araujo Sales, Eugenio de 1920- IntWW 93
Arauz, Carlos G. 1949- WhoHisp 94
Arauz, Carlos Gaspar 1949- WhoWest 94
Aravas, Nikolaos 1957- WhoScEn 94
Araya, Tom 1962- See Slayer ConMus 10
Araz, Nezihe 1922- BlmGWL
Arbatov, Georgiy Arkadyevich 1923- IntWW 93
Arbatov, Georgy Arkadevich 1923- LoBiDrD
Arbeau, Thionot 1520-1595 IntDcB
Arbeid, Murray 1935- IntWW 93
Arbeit, Robert David 1947- WhoScEn 94
Arbeli-Almozlino, Shoshana 1926- IntWW 93
Arbeli-Almozlino, Soshana 1929- WhoWomW 91
Arbell, Lucy 1882-1947 NewGrDO
Arbenina, Stella d1976 WhoHol 92
Arbenz, Andrew Edward WhoFI 94
Arber, Werner Who 94
Arber, Werner 1929- IntWW 93, WhoAm 94, WhoScEn 94, WorScD
Arberry, Morse, Jr. 1953- WhoAmP 93, WhoBlA 94
Arbes, Jakub EncSF 93
Arbess, Daniel Jay 1961- WhoAmL 94
Arbetman, Jeffrey Farrell 1941- WhoAmL 94
Arbhabhirama, Anat 1938- IntWW 93
Arbib, John A. 1924- WhoFI 94
Arbib, Michael Anthony 1940- WhoAm 94
Arbin, Astrid Valborg 1942- WhoScEn 94
Arbit, Beryl Ellen 1949- WhoAmL 94
Arbit, Bruce 1954- WhoAm 94
Arbit, Terry Steven 1958- WhoAmL 94
Arbitell, Michelle Renee 1962- WhoScEn 94
Arbiter, Andrew Richard 1958 WhoFI 94
Arbitman, Kahren J. 1948- WhoAmA 93
Arbogast, Zollie O., Jr. 1929-1989 WhAm 10
Arboleda, Gustavo 1951- WhoHisp 94
Arboleya, Carlos Jose 1929- WhoHisp 94
Arbor, Jane WrDr 94
Arbour, Alger 1932- WhoAm 94
Arbuckle, Andrew d1939 WhoHol 92
Arbuckle, Charles E. WhoBlA 94
Arbuckle, Fatty 1887-1933 WhoCom
Arbuckle, J. Gordon 1942- WhoAm 94
Arbuckle, James d1921 WhoHol 92
Arbuckle, John Finley, Jr. 1938- WhoBlA 94
Arbuckle, Kurt 1949- WhoAmL 94
Arbuckle, Maclyn d1931 WhoHol 92
Arbuckle, Minta Durfee d1975 WhoHol 92
Arbuckle, Pamela Susan 1955- WhoBlA 94
Arbuckle, Philip Wayne 1954- WhoMW 93
Arbuckle, Ronald Lee, Sr. 1945- WhoBlA 94
Arbuckle, Roscoe d1933 WhoHol 92
Arbulu, Agustin 1928- WhoHisp 94
Arbulu, Agustin Victor 1949- WhoAmL 94, WhoHisp 94
Arbulu, Maria Azucena 1956- WhoHisp 94
Arbulu Galliani, Guillermo IntWW 93
Arburtha, Leodies U. 1923- WhoBlA 94
Arbury, Guy d1972 WhoHol 92
Arbus, Alan 1918- WhoHol 92
Arbus, Diane 1923-1971 AmCulL
Arbuthnot, Andrew Robert Coghill 1926- Who 94
Arbuthnot, Harriett 1793-1834 DcNaB MP
Arbuthnot, James Norwich 1952- Who 94
Arbuthnot, John 1667-1735 BlmGEL
Arbuthnot, Keith Robert Charles 1951- Who 94
Arbuthnot, Mariot 1711-1794 AmRev
Arbuthnot, Marriot 1711-1794 WhAmRev [port]
Arbuthnot, Robert Murray 1936- WhoAmL 94
Arbuthnot, William (Reierson) 1950- Who 94
Arbuthnott Who 94
Arbuthnott, Master of 1950- Who 94
Arbuthnott, Viscount of 1924- Who 94
Arbuthnott, Hugh James 1936- Who 94
Arbuthnott, John Peebles 1939- Who 94
Arbuthnott, Robert 1936- Who 94
Arbuzov, Alexei Nikolaievich 1908-1986 IntDcT 2
Arbuzov, Boris Aleksandrovich d1991 IntWW 93N
Arbuzov, Valery Petrovich 1939- LoBiDrD
Arca, Giuseppe 1949- WhoScEn 94
Arca, Paolo 1953- NewGrDO
Arcade, Penny 1950- WhoHol 92
Arcadi, John Albert 1924- WhoAm 94, WhoWest 94
Arcadipane, Angelo Vincent 1941- WhoAm 94, WhoAmL 94
Arcais, Francesco d' NewGrDO
Arcand, Denys 1941- IntMPA 94, IntWW 93, WrDr 94
Arcand, Gabriel WhoHol 92
Arcara, Flavia d1937 WhoHol 92
Arcara, James Paul 1934- WhoAm 94, WhoFI 94
Arcara, Richard Joseph 1940- WhoAm 94, WhoAmL 94
Arcari, Ralph Donato 1943- WhoAm 94
Arcaro, Eddie 1916- WhoAm 94
Arcaro, Harold Conrad, Jr. 1935- WhoAm 94
Arcaya, Ignacio 1939- Who 94
Arce, A. Anthony 1923- WhoAm 94, WhoHisp 94
Arce, Carlos H. WhoHisp 94
Arce, Cecilia 1954- WhoHisp 94
Arce, Jose Antonio 1948- WhoHisp 94
Arce, Jose Martinez 1952- WhoHisp 94
Arce, Ligia A. WhoHisp 94
Arce, Miguel Luis 1951- WhoHisp 94
Arce, Pedro Edgardo 1952- WhoScEn 94
Arce, Phillip William 1937- WhoAm 94
Arce, Rafael 1944- WhoHisp 94
Arce, Rose Marie 1964- WhoHisp 94
Arce Bello, Jane WhoHisp 94
Arce-Cacho, Eric Amaury 1940- WhoScEn 94
Arce-Larreta, Jorge J. 1939- WhoHisp 94
Arceneaux, Jean 1951- WrDr 94
Arceneaux, Paul Oliver, Jr. 1936- WhoFI 94
Arceneaux, William 1941- WhoAm 94
Arceo, Liwayway 1924- BlmGWL
Arceo, Thelma Llave 1956- WhoScEn 94
Arceri, Joyce Ann 1963- WhoMW 93
Arch, E.L. 1922- EncSF 93
Arch, John d1825 EncNAR
Arch, Michael Alexis 1951- WhoAmL 94
Archabal, Nina Marchetti 1940- WhoAm 94, WhoMW 93
Archainbaud, George d1959 WhoHol 92
Archambault, Mademoiselle c. 1724- BlmGWL
Archambault, Bennett WhoAm 94
Archambault, John WrDr 94
Archambault, Louis 1915- WhoAm 94, WhoAmA 93
Archambeau, Charles Bruce 1933- WhoScEn 94
Archambeau, John Orin 1925- WhoAm 94
Archard, Bernard 1916- WhoHol 92
Archard, Douglas Bruce 1937- WhoAm 94
Archdale, Alexander WhoHol 92
Archdale, Edward (Folmer) 1921- Who 94
Archdeacon, John Robert 1919- WhoWest 94
Archdeacon, Joseph George 1940- WhoFI 94
Archer Who 94
Archer, Albert 1915- Who 94
Archer, Anne IntMPA 94
Archer, Anne 1947- WhoHol 92
Archer, Anne 1949- WhoAm 94
Archer, Barbara WhoHol 92
Archer, Barbara Callery 1954- WhoFI 94
Archer, Bill 1928- CngDr 93
Archer, Bruce Who 94
Archer, (Leonard) Bruce 1922- Who 94
Archer, Bruce F. 1950- WhoMW 93
Archer, C. Russell 1918- WhoAm 94
Archer, Carl Marion 1920- WhoAmP 93, WhoFI 94
Archer, Chalmers, Jr. 1938- BlkWr 2, WhoBlA 94
Archer, Chris James 1948- WhoWest 94
Archer, Cynthia 1953- WhoAmA 93
Archer, Dennis Wayne NewYTBS 93 [port]
Archer, Dennis Wayne 1942- WhoAm 94, WhoAmL 94, WhoAmP 93, WhoBlA 94, WhoMW 93
Archer, Dorothy Bryant 1919- WhoAmA 93N
Archer, Douglas Robert 1948- WhoWest 94
Archer, Ellen M. 1946- WhoMW 93
Archer, Eugene d1973 WhoHol 92
Archer, Eva P. WhoBlA 94
Archer, Frank Joseph 1912- Who 94
Archer, Fred 1915- WrDr 94
Archer, Frederick Scott WorInv
Archer, Gleason Leonard, Jr. 1916- WrDr 94
Archer, Glenn LeRoy 1929- CngDr 93
Archer, Glenn LeRoy, Jr. 1929- WhoAm 94, WhoAmL 94, WhoAmP 93
Archer, Graham Robertson 1939- Who 94
Archer, Gregory Alan 1957- WhoScEn 94
Archer, Harry Randall 1947- WhoWest 94
Archer, Hugh Morris 1916- WhoFI 94
Archer, Ian W. 1960- WrDr 94
Archer, J. Thomas 1954- WhoAmL 94
Archer, James Elson 1922- WhoAm 94
Archer, James G. 1936- WhoAm 94
Archer, Jean Mary 1932- Who 94
Archer, Jeffrey NewYTBS 93 [port]
Archer, Jeffrey (Howard) 1940- WrDr 94
Archer, Jeffrey Howard 1940- WhoAm 94
Archer, John Who 94
Archer, John dc. 1639 DcNaB MP
Archer, John 1741-1810 WhAmRev
Archer, John 1915- IntMPA 94, WhoHol 92
Archer, (Arthur) John 1924- Who 94
Archer, John Francis Ashweek 1925- Who 94
Archer, John Hall 1914- WrDr 94
Archer, John Norman 1921- Who 94
Archer, John Stuart 1943- Who 94
Archer, Juanita A. 1934- WhoBlA 94
Archer, Jules 1915- WrDr 94
Archer, Julian Pratt Waterman 1938- WhoMW 93
Archer, Kathleen Frances 1955- WhoAm 94
Archer, Keith (Allan) 1955- WrDr 94
Archer, Lee EncSF 93
Archer, Leonie (Jane) 1955- WrDr 94
Archer, Louis d1922 WhoHol 92
Archer, Maria 1905- BlmGWL
Archer, Mary Doreen 1944- Who 94
Archer, Mildred (Agnes) 1911- WrDr 94
Archer, Mildred Agnes 1911- Who 94
Archer, Neill 1961- NewGrDO
Archer, Nuala DrAPF 93
Archer, Richard A. 1927- WhoIns 94
Archer, Richard Earl 1945- WhoFI 94
Archer, Richard Joseph 1922- WhoAm 94
Archer, Robert M. 1943- WhoAmL 94
Archer, Ron EncSF 93
Archer, Ron 1938- WrDr 94
Archer, Ronald Dean 1932- WhoAm 94
Archer, Ronald Walter 1929- IntWW 93
Archer, Stephen Hunt 1928- WhoAm 94, WhoFI 94, WhoWest 94
Archer, Stephen Murphy 1934- WhoAm 94
Archer, Steven Ronald 1953- WhoScEn 94
Archer, Susie Coleman 1946- WhoBlA 94
Archer, Sydney 1917- WhoAm 94
Archer, Thomas John 1927- WhoScEn 94
Archer, Van Henry, Jr. 1940- WhoAmP 93
Archer, Violet Balestreri 1913- WhoAm 94
Archer, William Reynolds, Jr. 1928- WhoAm 94, WhoAmP 93
Archerd, Army WhoAm 94, WhoWest 94
Archerd, Army 1922- IntMPA 94
Archerd, Army 1923- WhoHol 92
Archerd, Selma WhoHol 92
Archer Of Sandwell, Baron 1926- Who 94
Archer of Sandwell, Lord 1926- WrDr 94
Archer Of Weston-Super-Mare, Baron 1940- IntWW 93, Who 94
Archer Of Weston-Super-Mare, Lady Who 94
Archette, Guy EncSF 93
Archetto, Paul H. 1960- WhoAmP 93
Archibald, Baron of Who 94
Archibald, Arnold Adams 1905-1980 EncABHB 9
Archibald, B. Milele 1945- WhoBlA 94
Archibald, Charles Arnold 1936- WhoMW 93
Archibald, David William 1953- WhoScEn 94
Archibald, Douglas 1919- ConTFT 11
Archibald, (Rupert) Douglas 1919- ConDr 93
Archibald, E. McDuff 1945- WhoAmL 94
Archibald, Francis X. 1931- WhoAmP 93
Archibald, Fred John 1922- WhoFI 94
Archibald, Frederick Ratcliffe 1905- WhoScEn 94
Archibald, George Christopher 1926- IntWW 93, Who 94
Archibald, James David 1950- WhoScEn 94
Archibald, James Kenway 1949- WhoAm 94, WhoAmL 94
Archibald, Jeanne S. 1951- WhoAmL 94
Archibald, Liliana 1928- Who 94
Archibald, Munro Who 94
Archibald, (Harry) Munro 1915- Who 94
Archibald, Nate 1948- BasBi, WhoBlA 94
Archibald, Nolan D. 1943- WhoAm 94, WhoFI 94
Archibald, Rae William 1941- WhoWest 94
Archibald, Reginald Mac Gregor 1910- WhoAm 94
Archie, Cornell B., Jr. 1948- WhoBlA 94
Archie, James Lee 1922- WhoBlA 94
Archie, Robert L., Jr. 1944- WhoAmL 94
Archie, Shirley Franklin 1944- WhoBlA 94
Archie-Hudson, Marguerite WhoAmP 93
Archilei, Vittoria 1550-162-? NewGrDO
Archimedes 3rd cent.BC- BlmGEL
Archimedes 287BC-212BC WorInv, WorScD [port]
Archipenko, Alexander 1887-1964 WhoAmA 93N
Archuleta, Adelmo E. 1950- WhoHisp 94
Archuleta, Alfonso Luis 1931- WhoHisp 94
Archuleta, Celestino E. WhoHisp 94
Archuleta, Isaac Rivera 1933- WhoHisp 94
Archuleta, Katherine Lorraine 1947- WhoHisp 94
Archuleta, Laura Lynn 1962- WhoMW 93
Archuleta, Nancy E. 1945- WhoHisp 94
Archuleta, Ralph J. 1947- WhoHisp 94
Archuleta, Rudolph Alonzo 1950- WhoHisp 94
Archuleta, Steve A. 1951- WhoHisp 94
Archuleta, Teresa Ann 1957- WhoHisp 94
Archway, Charles D. 1954- WhoAm 94
Arcieri, Sandy Lee 1955- WhoMW 93
Arciga, Joseph 1930- WhoHisp 94
Arcilesi, Vincent J. 1932- WhoAmA 93
Arcilesi, Vincent Jasper 1932- WhoAm 94
Arciniaga, Robert WhoHisp 94
Arciniega, Ricardo Jesus 1939- WhoHisp 94
Arciniega, Tomas A. 1937- WhoHisp 94
Arciniega, Tomas Abel 1937- WhoAm 94, WhoWest 94
Arciniegas, German 1900- IntWW 93
Arcino, Manuel Dagan 1941- WhoScEn 94
Arcis, Francois-Joseph d' NewGrDO
Arcoleo, Antonio fl. 1685-1690 NewGrDO
Arcomano, Cathryn WhoAmA 93
Arcomano, Joseph Peter 1924-1987 WhAm 10
Arconville, Genevieve Charlotte D' WorScD
Arcos, Cresencio S. WhoAmP 93
Arcos, Cresencio S. 1943- WhoAm 94
Arcos, Cresencio S., Jr. 1943- WhoHisp 94
Arctic, Bishop of The 1936- Who 94
Arculus, Ronald 1923- IntWW 93, Who 94
Arcuri, Edward Louis, III 1943- WhoAmP 93
Arcuri, Mary Anne 1947- WhoAmP 93
Arcy, Paul d' NewGrDO
Ard, Ben Neal, Jr. 1922- WrDr 94
Ard, Harold Jacob 1940- WhoAm 94
Ard, Saradell 1920- WhoAmA 93
Ardagh And Clonmacnoise, Bishop of 1935- Who 94
Ardai, Charles 1969- WrDr 94
Ardans, Alexander Andrew 1941- WhoAm 94
Ardant, Fanny 1949- IntMPA 94
Ardant, Fanny 1951- WhoHol 92
Ardash, Garin 1963- WhoScEn 94
Ardeberg, Arne Lennart 1940- IntWW 93
Ardee, Lord 1941- Who 94
Ardell, Franklyn d1969 WhoHol 92
Ardell, Lillian d1950 WhoHol 92
Ardelli, Norberto d1972 WhoHol 92
Arden, Alice Lloyd d1981 WhoHol 92
Arden, Andrew Paul Russel 1948- Who 94
Arden, Bruce Wesley 1927- WhoAm 94, WhoScEn 94
Arden, Donald Seymour 1916- Who 94
Arden, Edwin d1918 WhoHol 92
Arden, Eugene 1923- WhoAm 94
Arden, Eve d1990 WhoHol 92
Arden, Eve 1912-1990 WhAm 10, WhoCom
Arden, Hunter WhoHol 92

Arden, Jane *ConDr 93*
Arden, Jane d1981 *WhoHol 92*
Arden, John 1930- *BlmGEL, ConDr 93, IntDcT 2 [port], IntWW 93, Who 94, WrDr 94*
Arden, Mary (Howarth) 1947- *Who 94*
Arden, Robert 1921- *WhoHol 92*
Arden, Sherry W. 1930- *WhoAm 94*
Arden, Toni *WhoHol 92*
Arden, William 1924- *WrDr 94*
Arderiu, Clementina 1899- *BlmGWL*
Arderius (y Bardan), Francisco (de) 1836-1886 *NewGrDO*
Ardery, Joseph Lord 1947- *WhoAmL 94*
Ardery, Joseph Lord Tweedy 1947- *WhoAm 94*
Ardery, Philip Pendleton 1914- *WhoAm 94*
Ardia, Stephen Vincent 1941- *WhoAm 94*
Ardies, Tom 1931- *WrDr 94*
Ardigan, Art d1960 *WhoHol 92*
Ardin, Milagros E. *WhoHisp 94*
Arditi, Luigi 1822-1903 *NewGrDO*
Arditi, Pierre *WhoHol 92*
Arditti, Fred D. 1939- *WhoAm 94*
Arditto, Gino *WhoHol 92*
Ardizzone, Edward 1900-1979 *WhoAmA 93N*
Ardizzone, Tony *DrAPF 93*
Ardley, Harry Mountcastle 1926- *WhoWest 94*
Ardoin, John Louis 1935- *WhoAm 94*
Ardoin, Richard A. 1947- *WhoAmL 94*
Ardolino, Emile *IntMPA 94, WhoAm 94*
Ardolino, Emile d1993 *NewYTBS 93 [port]*
Ardov, E. *BlmGWL*
Ardrey, Robert 1908-1980 *ConDr 93, EncSF 93*
Ardrey, Ross James 1943- *WhoWest 94*
Ardrey, Saundra Curry 1953- *WhoBlA 94*
Ardrey, Stephanie Dionne 1965- *WhoWest 94*
Ardwick, Baron 1910- *IntWW 93, Who 94*
Ardzinba, Vladislav 1945- *LoBiDrD*
Ardzinba, Vladislav Grigoriyvich 1945- *IntWW 93*
Area, Ronald Gilbert 1945- *WhoAm 94*
Areeda, Phillip 1930- *WhoAm 94, WhoAmL 94, WrDr 94*
Areen, Gordon E. 1918- *WhoAm 94*
Areen, Judith Carol 1944- *WhoAmL 94*
Aref, Abdul Rahman Mohammed 1916- *IntWW 93*
Aref, Hassan 1950- *WhoScEn 94*
Arefece, Antonio *NewGrDO*
Aregood, Richard Lloyd 1942- *WhoAm 94*
Areheart, Gary Alan 1956- *WhoFI 94*
Areias, John Rusty 1949- *WhoWest 94*
Areias, Rusty 1949- *WhoAmP 93*
Areilza, Jose Maria de 1909- *IntWW 93*
Arekapudi, Kumar Vijaya Vasantha 1957- *WhoFI 94, WhoMW 93*
Arekapudi, Vijayalakshmi 1948- *WhoMW 93*
Arel, Bulent 1919-1990 *WhAm 10*
Arel, Maurice Louis 1937- *WhoAmP 93*
Arellanes, Audrey Spencer 1920- *WhoAmA 93, WhoWest 94*
Arellano, Agustin R. 1947- *WhoHisp 94*
Arellano, Albert E. *WhoHisp 94*
Arellano, Alfredo 1948- *WhoHisp 94*
Arellano, C. Rolando 1945- *WhoHisp 94*
Arellano, George R. 1933- *WhoHisp 94*
Arellano, Ignacio 1928- *WhoAm 94*
Arellano, Javier 1956- *WhoHisp 94*
Arellano, Jose M. 1944- *WhoHisp 94*
Arellano, Luis *WhoHisp 94*
Arellano, Oswaldo Lopez 1921- *HisWorL*
Arellano, Silvia *WhoHisp 94*
Arem, Lawrence Jay 1950- *WhoAmL 94*
Arena, Alan Joseph 1950- *WhoWest 94*
Arena, Albert A. 1929- *WhoAm 94*
Arena, Blaise Joseph 1948- *WhoScEn 94*
Arena, Giuseppe 1713-1784 *NewGrDO*
Arena, M. Scott 1946- *WhoAm 94*
Arena, Maurizio d1979 *WhoHol 92*
Arena, Nick Frank 1939- *WhoAm 94*
Arena, Ramona Mary *WhoAmL 94*
Arena, Rodolfo d1980 *WhoHol 92*
Arena, Salvatore F. 1937- *WhoAmP 93*
Arenal, Julie *WhoAm 94*
Arenal, Julie 1942- *WhoHisp 94*
Arenas, Andrea-Teresa 1951- *WhoHisp 94*
Arenas, Fernando George, Jr. 1937- *WhoHisp 94*
Arenas, Marion *DrAPF 93*
Arenas, Reinaldo 1943-1990 *HispLC [port]*
Arenas, Rosa M. *DrAPF 93*
Arenberg, Jonathan William 1961- *WhoWest 94*
Arenberg, Julius Theodore, Jr. 1923- *WhoAm 94*
Arencibia, Demetrio A. 1960- *WhoHisp 94*
Arend, Robert Lee 1944- *WhoWest 94*
Arendall, Douglas T. 1945- *WhoAmL 94*
Arendarski, Andrzej 1949- *IntWW 93*
Arendrup, Edith 1846-1934 *DcNaB MP*
Arends, Mark Paul 1966- *WhoWest 94*
Arends, Robert Allan 1939- *WhoMW 93*
Arends, Stuart 1950- *WhoAmA 93*
Arends, Wendell Leonard 1922- *WhoMW 93*
Arendt, Hannah 1906-1975 *AmSocL, BlmGWL, EncEth*
Areno, Lois *WhoHol 92*
Arenowitz, Albert Harold 1925- *WhoAm 94, WhoWest 94*
Arens, Moshe 1925- *IntWW 93*
Arensky, Anton Stepanovich 1861-1906 *NewGrDO*
Arenson, Barbara Levine 1947- *WhoWest 94*
Arenson, Donald Lewis 1926- *WhoMW 93*
Arenson, Gregory K. 1949- *WhoAm 94, WhoAmL 94*
Arenson, Karen Wattel 1949- *WhoAm 94*
Arenstein, Robert David 1947- *WhoAmL 94*
Arent, Albert Ezra 1911- *WhoAm 94*
Arent, Lorene Lucille 1927- *WhoMW 93*
Arentz, Andrew Albert 1928- *WhoFI 94*
Arentz, Dick 1935- *WhoWest 94*
Arentzen, Charles 1919- *WhoWest 94*
Areola, Armando d1978 *WhoHol 92*
Areskog, Donald Clinton 1926- *WhoScEn 94*
Arespacochaga Y Felipe, Juan de 1920- *IntWW 93*
Aresty, Jeffrey M. 1951- *WhoAmL 94*
Aresty, Joel M. 1949- *WhoAm 94, WhoAmL 94*
Arete fl. 5th cent.BC- *BlmGWL*
Aretino, Pietro 1492-1556 *BlmGEL, IntDcT 2*
Arett, Buddy d1985 *WhoHol 92*
Arevalo, Alfred Daniel 1947- *WhoHisp 94*
Arevalo, Henrietta Martinez 1949- *WhoHisp 94*
Arévalo, Jorge Enrique 1940- *WhoHisp 94*
Arevalo, Ricardo Vidal 1949- *WhoHisp 94*
Arevalo, Robert Carl 1942- *WhoMW 93*
Arevalo, Rodolfo 1946- *WhoHisp 94*
Arey, Patrick Kane 1947- *WhoAm 94*
Arey, Wayne d1937 *WhoHol 92*
Arfa, Harvey Z. 1945- *WhoAmL 94*
Arfmann, Dennis Leon 1951- *WhoAmP 93*
Argabright, Melvin Scott 1927- *WhoMW 93*
Argall, Charles G. *WhoAmA 93N*
Argall, David G. 1958- *WhoAmP 93*
Argan, Giulio Carlo d1992 *IntWW 93N*
Argana, Luis Maria *IntWW 93*
Argand, Aime *WorInv*
Argand, Jean Robert 1768-1822 *WorScD*
Argast, Scott Frederick 1956- *WhoMW 93*
Argenbright, Ed *WhoAmP 93*
Argent, Eric William 1923- *Who 94*
Argent, Malcolm 1935- *Who 94*
Argent, Maurice d1981 *WhoHol 92*
Argenta, Nancy (Maureen Herbison) 1957- *NewGrDO*
Argenteri, Laetitia 1950- *WhoWest 94*
Argenti, Bonaventura 1620?-1697 *NewGrDO*
Argentina, Bishop of 1935- *Who 94*
Argento, Dario 1940- *HorFD [port], IntDcF 2-4*
Argento, Dario 1943- *IntMPA 94*
Argento, Dominick 1927- *NewGrDO, WhoAm 94*
Argento, Vittorio Karl 1937- *WhoScEn 94*
Argerich, Martha 1941- *IntWW 93*
Argeris, George John 1931- *WhoAmL 94, WhoWest 94*
Argeros, Anthony George 1964- *WhoAmL 94*
Argetsinger, J. C. *WhoAmP 93*
Arghezi, Tudor 1880-1967 *ConLC 80*
Argibay, Jorge Luis 1953- *WhoScEn 94*
Argirion, Michael 1940- *WhoAm 94*
Argiro, Vinny *WhoHol 92*
Argiz, Antonio L. 1952- *WhoHisp 94*
Argo, Ellen *DrAPF 93*
Argo, Robert Eugene, Jr. 1923- *WhoAmP 93*
Argo, Victor *WhoHol 92*
Argo, William Frank 1951- *WhoFI 94*
Argon, Ali Suphi 1930- *WhoAm 94*
Argov, Shlomo 1929- *Who 94*
Argow, Keith Angevin 1936- *WhoAm 94*
Argow, Sylvia *DrAPF 93*
Argrette, Joseph 1931- *WhoBlA 94*
Argudin, Bernardo M. *WhoHisp 94*
Argue, David *WhoHol 92*
Argue, Douglas *WhoAmA 93*
Argue, Jim, Jr. 1951- *WhoAmP 93*
Argue, John Clifford 1932- *WhoAm 94, WhoWest 94*
Arguelles, Ivan *DrAPF 93*
Arguelles, John A. *WhoAmP 93*
Arguelles, John A. 1927- *WhoHisp 94*
Arguello, Alexis 1952- *WhoHisp 94*
Arguello, Benjamin W. 1961- *WhoHisp 94*
Arguello, Roberto J. T., Sr. 1932- *WhoHisp 94*
Arguello, Roberto Jose 1955- *WhoHisp 94*
Arguello, Stella Villarreal 1959- *WhoHisp 94*
Argueta, Manlio *IntWW 93*
Argueta, Manlio 1935- *ConWorW 93*
Argueta Antillon, Jose Luis 1932- *IntWW 93*
Arguijo, Conrad V. *WhoHisp 94*
Argun, Fatima Hatice 1959- *WhoAm 94*
Argyle, Michael 1925- *WrDr 94*
Argyle, Michael Victor 1915- *Who 94*
Argyle, Pearl d1947 *WhoHol 92*
Argyle, Pearl 1910-1947 *IntDcB [port]*
Argyll, Duke of 1937- *Who 94*
Argyll And The Isles, Bishop of 1935- *Who 94*
Argyll And The Isles, Bishop of 1940- *Who 94*
Argyll And The Isles, Dean of *Who 94*
Argyll And The Isles, Provosts in *Who 94*
Argyris, Chris 1923- *WhoAm 94*
Argyris, George T. 1946- *WhoAmL 94*
Argyris, John 1913- *WrDr 94*
Argyris, John 1916- *IntWW 93, Who 94*
Argyros, George L. *WhoAm 94, WhoFI 94*
Arhar, Joseph Ronald 1964- *WhoScEn 94*
Ari, Bakuji 1922- *IntWW 93*
Ari, Mark *DrAPF 93*
Arian, Jacqueline *DrAPF 93*
Ariane 1963- *WhoHol 92*
Ariarajah, Wesley 1941- *IntWW 93*
Arias, Abelardo Antonio 1954- *WhoHisp 94*
Arias, Alejandro Antonio 1959- *WhoHisp 94*
Arias, Alex 1967- *WhoHisp 94*
Arias, Anna Maria 1960- *WhoHisp 94*
Arias, Armando Antonio, Jr. 1953- *WhoHisp 94*
Arias, Ernesto G. 1943- *WhoHisp 94*
Arias, Ileana 1956- *WhoHisp 94*
Arias, Irwin Monroe 1926- *WhoAm 94*
Arias, Jimmy 1964- *WhoAm 94*
Arias, Pedro Luis 1959- *WhoScEn 94*
Arias, Rafael 1937- *WhoHisp 94*
Arias, Ramon H. 1943- *WhoHisp 94*
Arias, Raquel *WhoHisp 94*
Arias, Rita C. *WhoHisp 94*
Arias, Ron *DrAPF 93*
Arias, Ron 1941- *HispLC [port]*
Arias, Ronald F. 1941- *WhoHisp 94*
Arias, Steve 1944- *WhoHisp 94*
Arias, Victor, Jr. 1956- *WhoHisp 94*
Arias, Victor R., Jr. 1936- *WhoHisp 94*
Arias, William E. 1945- *WhoHisp 94*
Arias E., Ricardo M. d1993 *IntWW 93N*
Arias E., Ricardo M. 1912- *IntWW 93*
Arias Espinosa, Ricardo M. d1993 *NewYTBS 93*
Arias-Misson, Alain *DrAPF 93*
Arias-Misson, Alain 1939- *WhoAmA 93*
Arias-Misson, Nela 1925- *WhoAmA 93, WhoHisp 94*
Arias-Salgado Y Montalvo, Fernando 1938- *IntWW 93, Who 94*
Arias Sanchez, Oscar 1940- *IntWW 93, NobelP 91 [port], Who 94*
Arias Stella, Javier 1924- *IntWW 93*
Arico, Anthony V., Jr. 1936- *WhoAmP 93*
Aridas, Chris 1947- *ConAu 42NR*
Aridjis, Homero 1940- *ConWorW 93*
Aridor, Yoram 1933- *IntWW 93*
Arie, Raffaele 1922-1988 *NewGrDO*
Arie, Thomas Harry David 1933- *IntWW 93, Who 94*
Arieff, Allen Ives 1938- *WhoScEn 94*
Ariel, Brigitte 1955- *WhoHol 92*
Arieli, Adi 1947- *WhoWest 94*
Arienzo, Marco d' *NewGrDO*
Arienzo, Nicola d' *NewGrDO*
Arieti, Silvano 1914-1981 *EncSPD*
Arif, Shoaib 1950- *WhoAsA 94*
Arifin, Bustanil 1925- *IntWW 93*
Arifin, Bustanul 1963- *WhoMW 93*
Arifin, Sjahabuddin 1928- *Who 94*
Arigoni, Duilio 1928- *IntWW 93*
Arigoni, Giovanni Giacomo *NewGrDO*
Arikawa, Hiroo 1926- *WhoFI 94*
Arikawa, Norman *WhoAsA 94*
Arikpo, Okoi 1916- *IntWW 93*
Arima, Akito 1930- *IntWW 93, WhoScEn 94*
Arimondi, Vittorio 1861-1928 *NewGrDO*
Arimoto, Richard 1952- *WhoScEn 94*
Arimura, Akira 1923- *WhoAsA 94, WhoScEn 94*
Arinbasarova, Natalia *WhoHol 92*
Arinin, Aleksandr Nikolaevich 1955- *LoBiDrD*
Arinze, Francis A. 1932- *IntWW 93*
Ario, Joel Scott 1953- *WhoWest 94*
Arion, Douglas Norman 1957- *WhoWest 94*
Ariosti, Attilio (Malachia) 1666-1729 *NewGrDO*
Ariosto, Ludovico *EncSF 93*
Ariosto, Ludovico 1474-1533 *BlmGEL, IntDcT 2 [port], NewGrDO*
Aris, Aung San Suu Kyi *Who 94*
Aris, Ben 1937- *WhoHol 92*
Aris, John Bernard Benedict 1934- *Who 94*
Aris, Rutherford 1929- *WhoAm 94*
Arisman, Ruth Kathleen 1942- *WhoScEn 94*
Arison, Barbara J. 1952- *WhoAm 94, WhoAmL 94*
Arison, Micky 1949- *WhoFI 94*
Ariss, Bruce (Wallace) 1911- *EncSF 93*
Ariss, David William 1939- *WhoWest 94*
Ariss, Herbert Joshua 1918- *WhoAmA 93*
Ariss, Margot (Joan Phillips) 1929- *WhoAmA 93*
Aristedes the Just fl. 6th cent.BC- *BlmGEL*
Aristide, Jean Bertrand *IntWW 93*
Aristide, Jean-Bertrand 1953- *ConBlB 6 [port]*
Aristodama *BlmGWL*
Aristodemou, Loucas Elias 1946- *WhoScEn 94*
Aristophanes 457?BC-c. 385BC *IntDcT 2 [port]*
Aristophanes c. 450BC-c. 385BC *NewGrDO*
Aristophanes c. 448BC-c. 380BC *BlmGEL*
Aristotle 384BC-324BC *EncDeaf*
Aristotle 384BC-322BC *BlmGEL, EncEth, WorScD [port]*
Arita, George Shiro 1940- *WhoAm 94, WhoWest 94*
Ariturk, Haluk 1949- *WhoIns 94*
Aritzeta, Margarida 1953- *BlmGWL*
Ariyoshi, George Ryoichi 1926- *IntWW 93, WhoAm 94, WhoAmP 93, WhoWest 94*
Ariyoshi, Toshihiko 1930- *WhoScEn 94*
Ariyoshi Sawako 1931-1984 *BlmGWL*
Ariza, Ramon Enrique 1951- *WhoHisp 94*
Ariza, Yasumi 1927- *WhoAsA 94*
Arizin, Paul 1928- *BasBi*
Arizpe, Lourdes 1946- *WhoScEn 94*
Arjas, Elja 1943- *WhoScEn 94*
Arje, Daniel d1993 *NewYTBS 93*
Arjona Perez, Marta Maria 1923- *IntWW 93*
Ark, Billie D. 1924- *WhoAmP 93*
Arkadan, Abdul-Rahman Ahmad 1956- *WhoScEn 94*
Arkansaw, Tim 1925- *WhoBlA 94*
Arkas, Mykola Mykolayovych 1852?-1909 *NewGrDO*
Arkebauer, Jerry James 1941- *WhoMW 93*
Arkell, David 1913- *ConAu 142*
Arkell, John Hardy 1939- *Who 94*
Arkell, John Heward 1909- *Who 94*
Arkenberg, Amy Rosalie 1943- *WhoMW 93*
Arkes, Hadley P. *WhoAm 94*
Arkfeld, Leo 1912- *Who 94*
Arkhipova, Irina (Konstantinovna) 1925- *NewGrDO*
Arkhipova, Irina Konstantinovna 1925- *IntWW 93*
Arkhurst, Joyce Cooper 1921- *WhoBlA 94*
Arkie The Woodchopper d1981 *WhoHol 92*
Arkilic, Galip Mehmet 1920- *WhoAm 94, WhoScEn 94*
Arkin, Adam 1956- *WhoHol 92*
Arkin, Alan 1934- *ConTFT 11, IntMPA 94, WhoCom, WhoHol 92*
Arkin, Alan Wolf 1934- *IntWW 93, WhoAm 94*
Arkin, Angela R. 1959- *WhoAmL 94*
Arkin, David d1991 *WhoHol 92*
Arkin, Frieda *DrAPF 93*
Arkin, Gerald Franklin 1942- *WhoScEn 94*
Arkin, J. Gordon 1946- *WhoAmL 94*
Arkin, Joseph 1923- *WhoScEn 94*
Arkin, Marcus 1926- *WrDr 94*
Arkin, Matthew 1961- *WhoHol 92*
Arkin, Michael Barry 1941- *WhoAm 94*
Arkin, Stanley Herbert 1932- *WhoFI 94*
Arking, Jonathan Jacob 1966- *WhoMW 93*
Arking, Linda *DrAPF 93*
Arking, Lucille Musser 1936- *WhoMW 93*
Arkles, Barry Charles 1949- *WhoAm 94*
Arkley, Arthur James 1919- *WrDr 94*
Arklin, Henry 1928- *WhoAmP 93*
Arkoff, Samuel Z. *IntMPA 94*
Arkoff, Samuel Z. 1918- *WhoAm 94*
Arkor, Andre d' *NewGrDO*
Arkowitz, Martin Arthur 1935- *WhoAm 94*
Arkus, Leon A. 1915- *WhoAmA 93*
Arkus, Leon Anthony 1915- *WhoAm 94*
Arkush, Allan 1948- *IntMPA 94*

Arkush, Ralph David 1940- *WhoMW 93*
Arkuss, Neil Philip 1945- *WhoAm 94, WhoAmL 94*
Arkwright, Richard 1732-1792 *WorInv*
Arky, Ronald Alfred 1929- *WhoAm 94*
Arlberg, (Georg Efraim) Fritz 1830-1896 *NewGrDO*
Arledge, Charles Stone 1935- *WhoAm 94*
Arledge, G. Edward 1943- *WhoAmL 94*
Arledge, John d1947 *WhoHol 92*
Arledge, Roone 1931- *IntMPA 94, WhoAm 94, WhoFI 94*
Arlen, Betty d1966 *WhoHol 92*
Arlen, Elizabeth *WhoHol 92*
Arlen, Harold 1905-1986 *AmCulL*
Arlen, Jennifer Hall 1959- *WhoAmL 94*
Arlen, Judith d1968 *WhoHol 92*
Arlen, Mark Dale 1959- *WhoFI 94*
Arlen, Michael 1895-1956 *EncSF 93*
Arlen, Michael J. 1930- *WhoAm 94, WrDr 94*
Arlen, Richard d1976 *WhoHol 92*
Arlen, Roxanne d1989 *WhoHol 92*
Arlen, Stephen (Walter) 1913-1972 *NewGrDO*
Arlene, Herbert *WhoAmP 93*
Arlene, Herbert 1917- *WhoBlA 94*
Arletty 1898- *WhoHol 92*
Arletty 1898-1992 *AnObit 1992*
Arlidge, John Walter 1933- *WhoAm 94*
Arling, Arthur E. 1906- *IntMPA 94*
Arling, Bryan Jeremy 1944- *WhoScEn 94*
Arling, Joyce 1911- *WhoHol 92*
Arlinghaus, Edward James 1925- *WhoAm 94*
Arlinghaus, Sandra Judith Lach 1943- *WhoMW 93*
Arlinghaus, William Charles 1944- *WhoMW 93, WhoScEn 94*
Arliss, Dimitra 1932- *WhoHol 92*
Arliss, Florence d1950 *WhoHol 92*
Arliss, George d1946 *WhoHol 92*
Arliss, Pam *WhoHol 92*
Arlman, Paul 1946- *IntWW 93*
Arlook, Ira Arthur 1943- *WhoAm 94*
Arlook, Theodore David 1910- *WhoMW 93, WhoScEn 94*
Arloro, Julie Ann 1968- *WhoFI 94*
Arlott, John 1914-1991 *WrDr 94N*
Arlow, Allan Joseph 1944- *WhoAm 94, WhoMW 93*
Arlow, Arnold Jack 1933- *WhoAm 94*
Arlow, Jacob A. 1912- *WhoAm 94*
Arlt, Gustave Otto 1895- *WhAm 10*
Arlt, Lewis 1949- *WhoHol 92*
Arlt, Roberto 1900-1942 *HispLC [port], IntDcT 2*
Arlt, William H. 1868- *WhoAmA 93N*
Armacost, Michael H. 1937- *WhoAmP 93*
Armacost, Michael Hayden 1937- *IntWW 93, WhoAm 94*
Armacost, Peter Hayden 1935- *WhoAm 94*
Armacost, Samuel Henry 1939- *IntWW 93*
Armagh, Archbishop of 1917- *Who 94*
Armagh, Archbishop of 1937- *Who 94*
Armagh, Dean of *Who 94*
Armagost, Elsa Gafvert *WhoFI 94, WhoMW 93*
Armah, Ayi Kwei 1939- *WrDr 94*
Armajani, Siah 1939- *WhoAmA 93*
Armaly, Mansour Farid 1927- *WhoAm 94*
Arman 1928- *WhoAmA 93*
Arman, Ara 1930- *WhoAm 94*
Arman, Armand Pierre 1928- *WhoAm 94*
Arman, Dianne *WhoMW 93*
Armand, Mlle fl. 1704-1707 *NewGrDO*
Armand, Charles Tuffin 1750-1793 *WhAmRev*
Armand, Patrick *WhoAm 94*
Armand, Teddy V. d1947 *WhoHol 92*
Armani, Frank Henry 1927- *WhoAmP 93*
Armani, Giorgio 1934- *IntWW 93, WhoAm 94*
Armanios, Erian Abdelmessih 1950- *WhoScEn 94*
Armantrout, Rae *DrAPF 93*
Armas, Jose *DrAPF 93, WhoHisp 94*
Armas, Maureen V. *WhoHisp 94*
Armas, Tony 1953- *WhoHisp 94*
Armatrading, Joan 1950- *IntWW 93*
Armbrecht, Michael Ray 1967- *WhoMW 93*
Armbrecht, William Henry, III 1929- *WhoAm 94, WhoAmL 94*
Armbrister, Andrew Jackson, II 1948- *WhoMW 93*
Armbrister, Cyril d1966 *WhoHol 92*
Armbrister, Kenneth 1941- *WhoAmP 93*
Armbrust, David B. 1947- *WhoAmL 94*
Armbruster, Barbara Louise 1952- *WhoScEn 94*
Armbruster, Walter Joseph 1940- *WhoAm 94, WhoScEn 94*
Arme, Christopher 1939- *Who 94*
Armellino, Michael Ralph 1940- *WhoAm 94, WhoFI 94*
Armen, Kay 1920?- *WhoHol 92*
Armenante, Piero M. 1953- *WhoScEn 94*
Armendaris, Alex d1992 *WhoHisp 94N*
Armendáriz, David Esteban 1950- *WhoHisp 94*
Armendariz, Debra M. 1960- *WhoHisp 94*
Armendariz, Guadalupe M. 1943- *WhoHisp 94*
Armendariz, Lorenzo 1957- *WhoHisp 94*
Armendariz, Luis S. 1943- *WhoHisp 94*
Armendariz, Pedro d1963 *WhoHol 92*
Armendariz, Pedro, (Jr.) *WhoHol 92*
Armendariz, Robert L. *WhoHisp 94*
Armendariz, Tony *WhoHisp 94*
Armendariz, Victor Manuel 1945- *WhoHisp 94*
Armengod, Ramon d1976 *WhoHol 92*
Armeniades, Constantine D. 1936- *WhoScEn 94*
Armenta, A. E. *WhoHisp 94*
Armenti, Joseph Rocco 1950- *WhoAmL 94*
Armentieres, Peronnelle d' c. 1340- *BlmGWL*
Armentrout, Steven Alexander 1933- *WhoAm 94, WhoWest 94*
Armer, Sondra Audin *DrAPF 93*
Armes, Jay J. *WhoHisp 94*
Armes, Roy 1937- *WrDr 94*
Armes, Walter Scott 1939- *WhoMW 93*
Armesto, Eladio, III 1957- *WhoHisp 94*
Armesto-Garcia, Eladio 1936- *WhoAmP 93*
Armetta, Henry d1945 *WhoHol 92*
Armey, Dick 1940- *CngDr 93*
Armey, Douglas Richard 1948- *WhoWest 94*
Armey, Richard Keith 1940- *WhoAm 94, WhoAmP 93*
Armfield, Diana Maxwell 1920- *Who 94*
Armgardt, Charles Anthony 1958- *WhoAmL 94*
Armida 1913- *WhoHol 92*
Armidale, Bishop of 1934- *Who 94*
Armijo, Alan B. 1951- *WhoHisp 94*
Armijo, Arthur d1993 *NewYTBS 93*
Armijo, David C. 1916- *WhoHisp 94*
Armijo, Dennis 1940- *WhoHisp 94*
Armijo, Frances P. 1947- *WhoAmP 93*
Armijo, Jacqulyn Doris 1938- *WhoWest 94*
Armijo, John Joe 1954- *WhoHisp 94*
Armijo, Richard R. *DrAPF 93*
Armiñana, Ruben 1947- *WhoHisp 94, WhoWest 94*
Armistead, Milton 1947- *WhoBlA 94*
Armistead, Moss William, III 1915- *WhoAm 94*
Armistead, Parkes 1893- *WhAm 10*
Armistead, Thomas Boyd, III 1918- *WhoAm 94*
Armistead, Willis William 1916- *WhoAm 94*
Armitage, Barri *DrAPF 93*
Armitage, Buford d1978 *WhoHol 92*
Armitage, Carinthia Urbanette 1954- *WhoWest 94*
Armitage, David M. 1950- *WhoAmL 94*
Armitage, Edward 1917- *Who 94*
Armitage, Ella Sophia 1841-1931 *DcNaB MP*
Armitage, Frank 1948- *WrDr 94*
Armitage, Geoffrey Thomas Alexander 1917- *Who 94*
Armitage, Graham *WhoHol 92*
Armitage, Henry St. John Basil 1924- *Who 94*
Armitage, Jenifer *WhoHol 92*
Armitage, John Vernon 1932- *Who 94*
Armitage, Karole 1954- *WhoAm 94*
Armitage, Kenneth 1916- *IntWW 93, Who 94*
Armitage, (William) Kenneth *Who 94*
Armitage, Kenneth Barclay 1925- *WhoAm 94, WhoScEn 94*
Armitage, Michael 1930- *ConAu 41NR*
Armitage, Michael (John) 1930- *Who 94*
Armitage, Pauline d1926 *WhoHol 92*
Armitage, Peter 1924- *Who 94*
Armitage, Robert Allen 1948- *WhoAmL 94*
Armitage, Robert Ernest 1926-1989 *WhAm 10*
Armitage, Ronda (Jacqueline) 1943- *WrDr 94*
Armitage, Simon 1963- *WrDr 94*
Armitage, Thomas Edward 1946- *WhoMW 93*
Armitage, Walter d1953 *WhoHol 92*
Armocida, Patricia Anne 1956- *WhoFI 94*
Armold, Judith Ann 1945- *WhoAmL 94*
Armon, Norma 1937- *WhoHisp 94*
Armontel, Roland d1980 *WhoHol 92*
Armor, David J. 1938- *WhoAm 94*
Armor, James Burton 1926-1992 *WhAm 10*
Armor, John N. 1944- *WhoScEn 94*
Armour, Christopher E. 1959- *WhoBlA 94*
Armour, David Edward Ponton 1921- *WhoAm 94*
Armour, George Porter 1921- *WhoAmL 94*
Armour, Gordon Charles 1929- *WhoWest 94*
Armour, James Lott 1938- *WhoAm 94, WhoAmL 94*
Armour, Laurance Hearne, Jr. 1923- *WhoAm 94*
Armour, Lawrence A. 1935- *WhoAm 94*
Armour, Mary Nicol Neill 1902- *Who 94*
Armour, Rebecca Agatha 1846-1891 *BlmGWL*
Armour, Richard (Willard) 1906-1989 *WhAm 10*
Arms, Brewster Lee 1925- *WhoAm 94*
Arms, Richard Woodworth, Jr. 1935- *WhoWest 94*
Arms, Russell *WhoHol 92*
Arms, Suzanne 1944- *WrDr 94*
Armson, John Moss 1939- *Who 94*
Armson, Simon *Who 94*
Armson, (Frederick) Simon (Arden) 1948- *Who 94*
Armstead, Chapelle M. 1926- *WhoBlA 94*
Armstead, David M. *WhoAmP 93*
Armstead, Robert Louis 1936- *WhoWest 94*
Armstead, Ron E. 1947- *WhoBlA 94*
Armstead, Wilbert Edward, Jr. 1934- *WhoBlA 94*
Armster-Worrill, Cynthia Denise 1960- *WhoBlA 94*
Armstrong *Who 94*
Armstrong, Alan Gordon 1937- *Who 94*
Armstrong, Alexandra 1939- *ConAu 142, WhoAm 94*
Armstrong, Almetta *WhoAmP 93*
Armstrong, Alun 1946- *WhoHol 92*
Armstrong, Andrew (Clarence Francis) 1907- *Who 94*
Armstrong, Andrew Thurman 1935- *WhoScEn 94*
Armstrong, Anna Dawn 1943- *WhoWest 94*
Armstrong, Anne Legendre 1927- *IntWW 93, Who 94, WhoAm 94, WhoAmP 93*
Armstrong, Anthony 1897-1976 *EncSF 93*
Armstrong, Arthur Hilary 1909- *Who 94*
Armstrong, B. J. 1967- *WhoBlA 94*
Armstrong, Barbara Betty 1935- *WhoFI 94*
Armstrong, Bess 1953- *IntMPA 94, WhoHol 92*
Armstrong, Bill Howard 1926- *WhoAmA 93*
Armstrong, Billy d1924 *WhoHol 92*
Armstrong, Bridget *WhoHol 92*
Armstrong, Bruce A. 1944- *WhoAmL 94*
Armstrong, Bruce Charles 1965- *WhoAm 94*
Armstrong, Byron Eugene 1927- *WhoMW 93*
Armstrong, C. Michael 1938- *WhoAm 94, WhoFI 94*
Armstrong, C. Torrence 1945- *WhoAm 94*
Armstrong, Carl Hines 1926- *WhoAm 94*
Armstrong, Carol *WhoAmA 93*
Armstrong, Carol Hallow 1943- *WhoAmP 93*
Armstrong, Charles G. 1942- *WhoAm 94*
Armstrong, Charles Lester 1958- *WhoMW 93*
Armstrong, Charles P. 1951- *WhoIns 94*
Armstrong, Charles Wicksteed 1871- *EncSF 93*
Armstrong, Clyde d1937 *WhoHol 92*
Armstrong, Connie Charles 1925- *WhoAmP 93*
Armstrong, Crowell *WhoAmP 93*
Armstrong, Curtis 1953- *WhoHol 92*
Armstrong, Daniel Wayne 1949- *WhoAm 94, WhoMW 93*
Armstrong, David *WhoBlA 94*
Armstrong, David 1941- *WhoAmP 93*
Armstrong, David Andrew 1940- *WhoAm 94*
Armstrong, David Anthony 1930- *WhoAm 94*
Armstrong, David J. 1931- *WhoAm 94, WhoAmL 94*
Armstrong, David John 1947- *IntWW 93*
Armstrong, David M. 1965- *WhoAmP 93*
Armstrong, David Malet 1926- *IntWW 93, WrDr 94*
Armstrong, David Michael 1944- *WhoWest 94*
Armstrong, David William 1954- *WhoScEn 94*
Armstrong, Deane 1934- *WhoAmP 93*
Armstrong, Dickwin Dill 1934- *WhoAm 94, WhoWest 94*
Armstrong, Donald Arthur 1957- *WhoAmP 93*
Armstrong, Donald Budd, Jr. 1915-1990 *WhAm 10*
Armstrong, Douglas 1941- *WhoScEn 94*
Armstrong, Edward Allworthy 1900-1978 *DcNaB MP*
Armstrong, Edward Bradford, Jr. 1928- *WhoScEn 94*
Armstrong, Edward Gabriel 1897- *WhAm 10*
Armstrong, Edwin Alan 1950- *WhoAmL 94*
Armstrong, Edwin Howard 1890-1954 *WorInv*
Armstrong, Edwin Richard 1921- *WhoAm 94*
Armstrong, Elizabeth Neilson 1952- *WhoAm 94*
Armstrong, Elmer Franklin 1931- *WhoMW 93, WhoScEn 94*
Armstrong, Ernest 1915- *Who 94*
Armstrong, Ernest McAlpine 1945- *Who 94*
Armstrong, Ernest W., Sr. 1915- *WhoBlA 94*
Armstrong, Evelyn Walker *WhoBlA 94*
Armstrong, Frank 1920- *WhoAmP 93*
Armstrong, Frank William 1931- *Who 94*
Armstrong, Fredric Michael 1942- *WhoAm 94, WhoWest 94*
Armstrong, Gary Alan 1960- *WhoAmL 94*
Armstrong, Gene Lee 1922- *WhoAm 94, WhoFI 94, WhoScEn 94, WhoWest 94*
Armstrong, Geoffrey *EncSF 93*
Armstrong, Geoffrey 1928- *WhoAmA 93*
Armstrong, George Robert 1898- *WhAm 10*
Armstrong, Gerald Carver 1934- *WhoScEn 94*
Armstrong, Gibson Edward 1943- *WhoAmP 93*
Armstrong, Gillian 1950- *IntMPA 94*
Armstrong, Glenn Garnett 1916- *WhoWest 94*
Armstrong, Gordon 1937- *IntMPA 94*
Armstrong, Gregory Timon 1933- *WhoAm 94*
Armstrong, Harriet Jane 1930- *WhoAmP 93*
Armstrong, Hart Reid 1912- *WhoMW 93*
Armstrong, Henry d1988 *WhoHol 92*
Armstrong, Henry 1912-1988 *AfrAmAl 6 [port]*
Armstrong, Henry Conner 1925- *WhoAm 94*
Armstrong, Herbert W. 1892-1986 *ConAu 142*
Armstrong, Hilary Jane 1945- *Who 94, WhoWomW 91*
Armstrong, Hugh *WhoHol 92*
Armstrong, J. Gaylord 1939- *WhoAmL 94*
Armstrong, J. Niel 1907- *WhoBlA 94*
Armstrong, Jack *Who 94*
Armstrong, Jack Gilliland 1929- *WhoAm 94, WhoAmL 94*
Armstrong, Jack Lee 1947- *WhoFI 94*
Armstrong, James d1973 *WhoHol 92*
Armstrong, James 1748-1828 *WhAmRev*
Armstrong, James 1924- *WhoAm 94*
Armstrong, James Franklin *WhoAm 94*
Armstrong, James Louden, III 1932- *WhoAm 94, WhoAmL 94*
Armstrong, James Sinclair 1915- *WhoAm 94, WhoAmL 94*
Armstrong, James Wray 1950- *WhoAm 94*
Armstrong, Jane Botsford *WhoAm 94*
Armstrong, Jane Botsford 1921- *WhoAmA 93*
Armstrong, Jay John 1953- *WhoAmP 93*
Armstrong, Jeannette *BlmGWL*
Armstrong, Jennifer 1961- *SmATA 77 [port]*
Armstrong, Jim L. *WhoAmP 93*
Armstrong, Joan Bernard *WhoBlA 94*
Armstrong, Joanne Marie 1956- *WhoScEn 94*
Armstrong, Joe E. 1947- *WhoAmL 94*
Armstrong, John d1987 *WhoHol 92*
Armstrong, John d1992 *Who 94N*
Armstrong, John 1709-1779 *BlmGEL*
Armstrong, John 1755-1816 *WhAmRev*
Armstrong, John, Sr. c. 1717-1795 *AmRev, WhAmRev*
Armstrong, John, Jr. 1758-1843 *WhAmRev [port]*
Armstrong, John Alexander 1922- *WhoAm 94, WrDr 94*
Armstrong, John Allan 1934- *WhoAm 94*
Armstrong, John Archibald 1917- *Who 94*
Armstrong, John Kenaston 1929- *WhoAm 94*
Armstrong, John Kremer 1934- *WhoAm 94, WhoAmL 94*
Armstrong, Joseph E. 1956- *WhoAmP 93*
Armstrong, Judith (Mary) 1935- *WrDr 94*
Armstrong, Judith Ann 1946- *WhoWest 94*
Armstrong, Karan 1941- *NewGrDO*
Armstrong, Keith Bernard 1931- *WhoScEn 94*

Armstrong, Kenneth 1949- *WhoAmL 94, WhoWest 94*
Armstrong, Kenneth 1955- *WhoAmL 94*
Armstrong, Kevin William 1958- *WhoMW 93*
Armstrong, Lilian Hardin 1898-1971 *AfrAmAl 6*
Armstrong, Lloyd, Jr. 1940- *WhoAm 94*
Armstrong, Louis d1971 *WhoHol 92*
Armstrong, Louis c. 1898-1971 *AmCulL*
Armstrong, Louis 1901-1971 *AfrAmAl 6*
Armstrong, Margaret Teague 1956- *WhoAmL 94*
Armstrong, Marguerite d1973 *WhoHol 92*
Armstrong, Martha (Allen) 1935- *WhoAmA 93*
Armstrong, Mary (Elizabeth) Willems 1957- *WrDr 94*
Armstrong, Matthew Jordan, Jr. 1955- *WhoBlA 94*
Armstrong, Michael (Allan) 1956- *EncSF 93*
Armstrong, Michael C. 1939- *WhoFI 94, WhoWest 94*
Armstrong, Michael David 1955- *WhoFI 94*
Armstrong, Michael Francis 1932- *WhoAm 94*
Armstrong, Michael Robert 1943- *WhoMW 93*
Armstrong, Moe 1944- *WhoWest 94*
Armstrong, Nancy 1924- *WrDr 94*
Armstrong, Nancy L. 1948- *WhoAm 94*
Armstrong, Neal Earl 1941- *WhoAm 94*
Armstrong, Neil A. 1930- *IntWW 93, Who 94, WhoAm 94, WhoScEn 94*
Armstrong, Nelson 1950- *WhoBlA 94*
Armstrong, Nelson William, Jr. 1941- *WhoAm 94*
Armstrong, Oliver Wendell 1919- *WhoAm 94*
Armstrong, Orville 1929- *WhoAm 94, WhoAmL 94, WhoWest 94*
Armstrong, Owen Thomas 1923- *WhoAmL 94*
Armstrong, Paul Richard 1948- *WhoMW 93*
Armstrong, Peter Brownell 1939- *WhoScEn 94*
Armstrong, Philip B(rownell) 1898- *WhAm 10*
Armstrong, Phillip Dale 1943- *WhoAmL 94, WhoFI 94*
Armstrong, R. G. 1917- *WhoHol 92*
Armstrong, R. L. d1978 *WhoHol 92*
Armstrong, Reginald Donald, II 1958- *WhoBlA 94*
Armstrong, Richard 1943- *NewGrDO, Who 94*
Armstrong, Richard A. 1935- *WhoFI 94*
Armstrong, Richard B(yron) 1956- *WrDr 94*
Armstrong, Richard Burke 1924- *WhoAm 94*
Armstrong, Richard Lee 1937- *WhAm 10*
Armstrong, Richard LeRoy 1953- *WhoAmL 94*
Armstrong, Richard Scott 1942- *WhoScEn 94*
Armstrong, Richard Stoll 1924- *WhoAm 94*
Armstrong, Richard W. 1936- *WhoAmP 93*
Armstrong, Richard William 1932- *WhoFI 94*
Armstrong, Robert d1973 *WhoHol 92*
Armstrong, Robert Arnold 1928- *WhoAm 94*
Armstrong, Robert Baker 1914- *WhoAm 94*
Armstrong, Robert Dean 1923- *WhoWest 94*
Armstrong, Robert Don 1928- *WhoScEn 94*
Armstrong, Robert George 1913- *Who 94*
Armstrong, Robert Landis 1932- *WhoAmP 93*
Armstrong, Robert Laurence 1926- *WrDr 94*
Armstrong, Robert Stillman 1949- *WhoWest 94*
Armstrong, Robin Louis 1935- *IntWW 93, WhoAm 94, WhoScEn 94*
Armstrong, Rodney 1923- *WhoAm 94*
Armstrong, Roger Joseph 1917- *WhoAmA 93*
Armstrong, Samuel Chapman 1839-1893 *AmSocL [port], DcAmReB 2*
Armstrong, Samuel E., Jr. 1933- *WhoAmP 93*
Armstrong, Saundra Brown 1947- *WhoAm 94, WhoAmL 94, WhoWest 94*
Armstrong, Seth 1941- *WhoAmP 93*
Armstrong, Sheila Ann 1942- *IntWW 93, Who 94*
Armstrong, Stephen Wales 1943- *WhoAm 94, WhoAmL 94*
Armstrong, Susan Carol 1952- *WhoAmL 94*
Armstrong, T.I.F. *EncSF 93*
Armstrong, Terence Edward 1920- *Who 94*
Armstrong, Theodore Morelock 1939- *WhoAm 94, WhoFI 94*
Armstrong, Thomas Errol 1959- *WhoAmP 93*
Armstrong, Thomas Henry Wait 1898- *IntWW 93, Who 94*
Armstrong, Thomas Newton, III 1932- *WhoAm 94, WhoAmA 93*
Armstrong, Todd 1939- *WhoHol 92*
Armstrong, Tommy Gene 1941- *WhoAmP 93*
Armstrong, Vickie *WhoAmP 93*
Armstrong, Victoria Elizabeth 1950- *WhoAmL 94*
Armstrong, Wallace Dowan, Jr. 1926- *WhoWest 94*
Armstrong, Walter 1948- *WhoBlA 94*
Armstrong, Walter Preston, Jr. 1916- *WhoAm 94, WhoAmL 94*
Armstrong, Ward Lynn 1956- *WhoAmP 93*
Armstrong, Warren Bruce 1933- *WhoAm 94, WhoMW 93*
Armstrong, Will d1943 *WhoHol 92*
Armstrong, William d1952 *WhoHol 92*
Armstrong, William H(oward) 1914- *TwCYAW, WrDr 94*
Armstrong, William Henry 1943- *WhoAm 94, WhoAmL 94*
Armstrong, William L. 1937- *WhoAmP 93*
Armstrong, William Warren 1935- *WhoAm 94*
Armstrong Gibbs, Cecil *NewGrDO*
Armstrong-Jones *Who 94*
Armstrong-Jones, Antony (Charles Robert) 1930- *ConAu 43NR*
Armstrong Jones, Tony *ConAu 43NR*
Armstrong Of Ilminster, Baron 1927- *IntWW 93, Who 94*
Armytage, David George 1929- *Who 94*
Armytage, Lisa *WhoHol 92*
Armytage, (John) Martin 1933- *Who 94*
Armytage, W(alter) H(arry) G(reen) 1915- *EncSF 93*
Armytage, Walter Harry Green 1915- *Who 94*
Arn, Kenneth Dale 1921- *WhoAm 94, WhoMW 93, WhoScEn 94*
Arna, Lissi d1964 *WhoHol 92*
Arnaboldi, Cristoforo c. 1750-1798? *NewGrDO*
Arnaboldi, Patrizia 1946- *WhoWomW 91*
Arnade, Charles W. 1927- *WrDr 94*
Arnal, Michel Philippe 1955- *WhoScEn 94*
Arnall, Ellis (Gibbs) 1907-1992 *CurBio 93N*
Arnall, Ellis Gibbs 1907- *IntMPA 94*
Arnall, Joseph Henry 1947- *WhoAmP 93*
Arnall, Julia 1931- *WhoHol 92*
Arnason, Barry Gilbert Wyatt 1933- *WhoScEn 94*
Arnason, Eleanor (Atwood) 1942- *EncSF 93*
Arnason, H. Harvard 1909-1986 *WhoAmA 93N*
Arnason, Jon Yard 1946- *WhoAmL 94*
Arnason, Tomas 1923- *IntWW 93*
Arnatt, John 1917- *WhoHol 92*
Arnaud, Angelique 1799-1884 *BlmGWL*
Arnaud, Claude d1991 *IntWW 93N*
Arnaud, Claude Donald, Jr. 1929- *WhoAm 94*
Arnaud, Francois 1721-1784 *NewGrDO*
Arnaud, G.-J. *EncSF 93*
Arnaud, Jean-Loup 1942- *IntWW 93*
Arnaud, Yvonne d1958 *WhoHol 92*
Arnauld, Agnes 1593-1671 *BlmGWL*
Arnauld, Jacqueline Marie Angelique 1591-1661 *BlmGWL*
Arnault, Bernard 1949- *IntWW 93*
Arnault, Bernard Jean 1949- *WhoAm 94*
Arnault, Ronald J. 1943- *WhoAm 94, WhoFI 94*
Arnaz, Desi d1986 *WhoHol 92*
Arnaz, Desi 1917-1986 *WhoCom*
Arnaz, Desi, Jr. 1953- *IntMPA 94, WhoHisp 94, WhoHol 92*
Arnaz, Lucie 1951- *IntMPA 94, WhoHisp 94, WhoHol 92*
Arnberg, Robert Lewis 1945- *WhoAm 94*
Arnberger, H. Bennett 1953- *WhoAmL 94*
Arndt, Bruce Allen 1956- *WhoScEn 94*
Arndt, Elizabeth Moore 1920- *WhoAmP 93*
Arndt, Heinz Wolfgang 1915- *IntWW 93, WrDr 94*
Arndt, Janet S. 1947- *WhoAmP 93*
Arndt, Joan Marie 1945- *WhoMW 93*
Arndt, Julie Anne Preuss 1968- *WhoScEn 94*
Arndt, Karl (John Richard) 1903- *WrDr 94*
Arndt, Kenneth Alfred 1936- *WhoAm 94*
Arndt, Kenneth Eugene 1933- *WhoAm 94, WhoFI 94*
Arndt, Mary Jo 1933- *WhoAmP 93, WhoWomW 91*
Arndt, Michael Paul 1930- *WhoWest 94*
Arndt, Nancy Yvonne 1938- *WhoAm 94*
Arndt, Norbert Karl Erhard 1960- *WhoScEn 94*
Arndt, Richard T. 1928- *WhoAm 94*
Arndt, Roger Edward Anthony 1935- *WhoAm 94, WhoMW 93, WhoScEn 94*
Arndt, Ulrich W. 1924- *IntWW 93*
Arndt, Ulrich Wolfgang 1924- *Who 94*
Arndt, Walter Werner 1916- *WhoAm 94*
Arndt-Ober, Margarethe 1885-1971 *NewGrDO*
Arne, Mrs. *NewGrDO*
Arne, Kenneth George 1942- *WhoWest 94*
Arne, Michael c. 1740-1786 *NewGrDO*
Arne, Peter d1983 *WhoHol 92*
Arne, Susanna Maria *NewGrDO*
Arne, Thomas Augustine 1710-1778 *NewGrDO*
Arnedo Orbananos, Miguel Angel 1944- *IntWW 93*
Arnell, Gordon Edwin 1935- *WhoFI 94*
Arnell, Peter 1918- *IntMPA 94*
Arnell, Richard Anthony 1938- *WhoAm 94, WhoMW 93*
Arnell, Richard Anthony Sayer 1917- *IntWW 93, Who 94*
Arnell, Robert Edward 1941- *WhoWest 94*
Arnell, Walter James William 1924- *WhoAm 94, WhoWest 94*
Arnelle, Hugh Jesse 1933- *WhoBlA 94*
Arnesen, Deborah Arnie 1953- *WhoAmP 93*
Arnesen, Mark R. 1952- *WhoAmL 94*
Arneson, Gary A. 1948- *WhoIns 94*
Arneson, George Stephen 1925- *WhoAm 94*
Arneson, Harold Elias Grant 1925- *WhoScEn 94*
Arneson, James Herman 1952- *WhoAmL 94*
Arneson, Robert 1930- *WhoAmA 93N*
Arneson, Robert Carston 1930-1992 *WhAm 10*
Arneson, Wendell H. 1946- *WhoAmA 93*
Arness, James 1923- *IntMPA 94, WhoHol 92*
Arness, John Palmer 1927- *WhoAm 94*
Arnest, Bernard 1917-1986 *WhoAmA 93N*
Arnett, Carroll *DrAPF 93*
Arnett, Carroll D. 1946- *WhoMW 93*
Arnett, Edward McCollin 1922- *WhoScEn 94*
Arnett, Foster Deaver 1920- *WhoAm 94*
Arnett, Harold Edward 1931- *WhoAm 94*
Arnett, Jack *EncSF 93*
Arnett, James Edward 1912- *WhoFI 94, WhoMW 93*
Arnett, James Edward, II 1955- *WhoFI 94*
Arnett, James William 1949- *WhoFI 94*
Arnett, Louise Eva 1945- *WhoMW 93*
Arnett, Peter *IntWW 93*
Arnett, Peter 1934- *ConTFT 11, WhoAm 94*
Arnett, Warren Grant 1923- *WhoAm 94*
Arnette, Dorothy Deanna 1942- *WhoBlA 94*
Arnette, Jeannetta *WhoHol 92*
Arnette, Robert *EncSF 93*
Arnette, Walter Gregory, Jr. 1947- *WhoAmP 93*
Arney, James 1934- *WrDr 94*
Arney, Rex Odeli 1940- *WhoAmP 93*
Arney, William Ray 1950- *ConAu 43NR, WhoWest 94*
Arnez, Nancy L. 1928- *WhoBlA 94*
Arnez, Nancy Levi 1928- *WhoAm 94*
Arngrim, Stefan 1955- *WhoHol 92*
Arnhart, Larry Eugene 1949- *WhoMW 93*
Arnheim, Gus d1955 *WhoHol 92*
Arnheim, Rudolf 1904- *WhoAmA 93, WrDr 94*
Arnheim, Valy d1950 *WhoHol 92*
Arnhoff, Franklyn Nathaniel 1926- *WhoAm 94*
Arnhold, Henry H. 1921- *WhoFI 94*
Arnholm, Ronald Fisher 1939- *WhoAmA 93*
Arniches (y Barrera), Carlos 1866-1943 *NewGrDO*
Arnick, John Stephen 1933- *WhoAmP 93*
Arnim, Bettina von 1785-1859 *BlmGWL*
Arning, Bill A. 1960- *WhoAmA 93*
Arning, John Fredrick 1925- *WhoAm 94, WhoAmL 94*
Arnitz, Rick 1949- *WhoAmA 93*
Arnizaut de Mattos, Ana Beatriz 1959- *WhoScEn 94*
Arno, Daniel James 1950- *WhoAmL 94*
Arno, Elroy *EncSF 93*
Arno, Nelly *WhoHol 92*
Arno, Peter d1968 *WhoHol 92*
Arno, Peter 1904-1968 *WhoAmA 93N*
Arno, Sig d1975 *WhoHol 92*
Arnof, Ian 1939- *WhoAm 94, WhoFI 94*
Arnoff, E. Leonard 1922- *WhAm 10*
Arnold, A(lbert) James, Jr. 1939- *WrDr 94*
Arnold, Adrian K. 1932- *WhoAmP 93*
Arnold, Alton A., Jr. 1932- *WhoBlA 94*
Arnold, Alva Lee C. 1919- *WhoAmP 93*
Arnold, Armin 1931- *IntWW 93*
Arnold, Arnold F. 1929- *WrDr 94*
Arnold, Arthur Palmer 1946- *WhoScEn 94*
Arnold, Arthur Z. 1898- *WhAm 10*
Arnold, Barbara Eileen 1924- *WhoAmP 93*
Arnold, Barbara Jeanne 1950- *WhoMW 93*
Arnold, Benedict 1741-1801 *AmRev, HisWorL [port], WhAmRev [port]*
Arnold, Bettina 1961- *WhoMW 93*
Arnold, Betty d1985 *WhoHol 92*
Arnold, Betty Ann 1948- *WhoMW 93*
Arnold, Beverly Sue 1949- *WhoMW 93*
Arnold, Billy L. 1926- *WhoAmP 93*
Arnold, Bob *DrAPF 93*
Arnold, Bob 1943- *WhoAmP 93*
Arnold, Cecile d1931 *WhoHol 92*
Arnold, Charles Burle, Jr. 1934- *WhoAm 94*
Arnold, Clarence Edward, Jr. 1944- *WhoBlA 94*
Arnold, Clifford Delos 1920- *WhoAmP 93*
Arnold, Craig Anthony 1965- *WhoAmL 94*
Arnold, Craig C. 1945- *WhoFI 94*
Arnold, Daniel W. 1951- *WhoIns 94*
Arnold, Danny 1925- *IntMPA 94, WhoHol 92*
Arnold, Daryl 1924- *WhoAmP 93*
Arnold, David 1946- *WhoBlA 94*
Arnold, David (J.) 1946- *WrDr 94*
Arnold, David Alan 1946- *WhoMW 93*
Arnold, David Burton 1939- *WhoAm 94*
Arnold, David Dean 1958- *WhoScEn 94*
Arnold, David Paul 1942- *WhoMW 93*
Arnold, David Walker 1936- *WhoAm 94*
Arnold, Dennis B. 1950- *WhoAm 94, WhoAmL 94*
Arnold, Dennis Paul 1951- *WhoFI 94*
Arnold, Dianne Ekberg 1944- *WhoAm 94*
Arnold, Don *WhoAmP 93*
Arnold, Donald Smith 1920- *WhoScEn 94*
Arnold, Douglas Norman 1954- *WhoAm 94*
Arnold, Duane Wade-Hampton 1953- *WhoAm 94*
Arnold, Ed 1943- *WhoAmP 93*
Arnold, Eddy 1918- *ConMus 10 [port], IntMPA 94, WhoAm 94, WhoHol 92*
Arnold, Edmund Clarence 1913- *WrDr 94*
Arnold, Edward d1956 *WhoHol 92*
Arnold, Edward Henry 1939- *WhoAm 94*
Arnold, Edwin Lester 1857-1935 *EncSF 93*
Arnold, Elizabeth *NewGrDO*
Arnold, Emily *DrAPF 93*
Arnold, Emily 1939- *SmATA 76 [port]*
Arnold, Ethel N. 1924- *WhoBlA 94*
Arnold, Everett John 1932-1989 *WhAm 10*
Arnold, Florence M. 1900- *WhoAmA 93*
Arnold, Frank Byrd 1952- *WhoFI 94*
Arnold, Frank Edward 1914-1987 *EncSF 93*
Arnold, G. Dewey, Jr. 1925- *WhoAm 94, WhoFI 94*
Arnold, Gary Howard 1942- *WhoAm 94*
Arnold, Gene *WhoAmP 93*
Arnold, George Feversham 1914- *Who 94*
Arnold, Gertrud d1931 *WhoHol 92*
Arnold, Glynis *Who 94*
Arnold, Gordon Thomas 1960- *WhoAmL 94*
Arnold, Grace d1979 *WhoHol 92*
Arnold, Guy 1932- *WrDr 94*
Arnold, Gyorgy 1781-1848 *NewGrDO*
Arnold, H(arry) J(ohn) P(hilip) (Douglas) 1932- *WrDr 94*
Arnold, Hans Redlef 1923- *IntWW 93*
Arnold, Harriet Amelia Chapman 1937- *WhoBlA 94*
Arnold, Haskell N., Jr. 1945- *WhoBlA 94*
Arnold, Helen E. 1924- *WhoBlA 94*
Arnold, Helen Elizabeth 1924- *WhoMW 93*
Arnold, Helen T. 1927- *WhoAmP 93*
Arnold, Henri *WhoAm 94*
Arnold, Herbert Anton 1935- *WhoAm 94*
Arnold, Hilda F. 1935- *WhoAm 94*
Arnold, Jack *WhoAmA 93, WhoHol 92*
Arnold, Jack 1916-1982 *AnObit 1992*
Arnold, Jack 1916-1992 *EncSF 93*
Arnold, Jack Waldo 1935- *WhoScEn 94*
Arnold, Jacqueline Clements 1923- *WhoMW 93*
Arnold, Jacques Arnold 1947- *Who 94*
Arnold, James Keith 1959- *WhoAmP 93*
Arnold, James R. 1923- *IntWW 93*
Arnold, James Richard 1923- *WhoAm 94, WhoWest 94*

Ascanio, Pam 1950- *ConAu 142*
Asch, Arthur Louis 1941- *WhoAm 94*
Asch, David Kent 1958- *WhoScEn 94*
Asch, Frank 1946- *WrDr 94*
Asch, Marc 1946- *WhoAmP 93*
Asch, Nolan E. 1949- *WhoIns 94*
Asch, Susan McClellan 1945- *WhoMW 93*
Aschaffenburg, Walter Eugene 1927- *WhoAm 94, WhoWest 94*
Ascham, Margaret Howe 1535?-1590 *BlmGWL*
Ascham, Roger 1515-1568 *BlmGEL*
Aschauer, Charles Joseph, Jr. 1928- *WhoAm 94*
Asche, Oscar d1936 *WhoHol 92*
Aschen, Sharon Ruth 1948- *WhoMW 93*
Aschenborn, Hans Jurgen 1920-1986 *WhAm 10*
Aschenbrener, Carol Ann 1944- *WhoMW 93*
Aschenbrenner, Frank Aloysious 1924- *WhoFI 94, WhoScEn 94, WhoWest 94*
Aschenbrenner, John E. 1949- *WhoIns 94*
Aschenbrenner, Karl 1911-1988 *WhAm 10*
Ascher, Anton d1928 *WhoHol 92*
Ascher, Carol *DrAPF 93*
Ascher, David Mark 1952- *WhoAmL 94*
Ascher, Eugene *EncSF 93*
Ascher, James John 1928- *WhoAm 94, WhoFI 94, WhoMW 93*
Ascher, Maria Louise *ConAu 140*
Ascher, Mary *WhoAmA 93N*
Ascher, Robert 1931- *WhoAm 94*
Ascher, Sheila *DrAPF 93*
Ascherl, Jack 1937- *WhoAmP 93*
Ascherson, (Charles) Neal 1932- *Who 94, WrDr 94*
Aschheim, Joseph 1930- *WhoAm 94*
Aschieri, Catterina c. 1720-1755? *NewGrDO*
Aschleman, James Allan 1944- *WhoAm 94*
Aschliman, Pat Tanner 1944- *WhoWest 94*
Aschoff, Jurgen Walter Ludwig 1913- *IntWW 93*
Ascian 1943- *WhoAmA 93*
Ascione, Frank Joseph 1946- *WhoMW 93*
Ascot, Hazel 1928- *WhoHol 92*
Aseer, Ghulam Nabi 1940- *WhoFI 94*
Aselage, Susan Seabury 1954- *WhoMW 93*
Asen, Shel F. 1937- *WhoAm 94*
Asencio, Diego C. 1931- *WhoAm 94, WhoHisp 94*
Asenjo, Florencio González 1926- *WhoHisp 94*
Asfa Wossen Haile Sellassie, Merd Azmatch 1916- *Who 94*
Asfoury, Zakaria Mohammed 1921- *WhoScEn 94*
Asgill, Charles 1762?-1823 *WhAmRev*
Asgrimsson, Halldor 1947- *IntWW 93*
Ash, Alan 1908- *EncSF 93*
Ash, Arty d1954 *WhoHol 92*
Ash, Brian 1936- *EncSF 93*
Ash, Brian Maxwell 1941- *Who 94*
Ash, Eric (Albert) 1928- *Who 94*
Ash, Eric Albert 1928- *IntWW 93*
Ash, Fenton *EncSF 93*
Ash, Gordon d1929 *WhoHol 92*
Ash, J. Marshall 1940- *WhoAm 94*
Ash, James Lee, Jr. 1945- *WhoAm 94*
Ash, James Mathew 1958- *WhoWest 94*
Ash, Jerry d1953 *WhoHol 92*
Ash, John 1948- *WrDr 94*
Ash, Leslie *WhoHol 92*
Ash, Major McKinley, Jr. 1921- *WhoAm 94, WhoScEn 94*
Ash, Mary Kay Wagner *WhoAm 94, WhoFI 94*
Ash, Maurice Anthony 1917- *Who 94*
Ash, Mitchell Graham 1948- *WhoMW 93*
Ash, Philip 1917- *WhoAm 94, WhoScEn 94*
Ash, Raymond 1928- *Who 94*
Ash, Rene 1939- *IntMPA 94*
Ash, Richard Larry 1959- *WhoBlA 94*
Ash, Rosemary Ann 1946- *WhoMW 93*
Ash, Roy L. 1918- *WhoAmP 93*
Ash, Roy Lawrence 1918- *IntWW 93, WhoAm 94*
Ash, Russell d1974 *WhoHol 92*
Ash, Russell (John) 1946- *WrDr 94*
Ash, Sam d1951 *WhoHol 92*
Ash, Susan Joy 1952- *WhoMW 93*
Ash, Thomas Phillip 1949- *WhoMW 93*
Ash, Walter Brinker 1932- *WhoAmL 94, WhoWest 94*
Ash, Walter William Hector 1906- *Who 94*
Ash, William Franklin 1917- *WrDr 94*
Ash, William Noel 1921- *Who 94*
Ashabranner, Brent (Kenneth) 1921- *TwCYAW*
Ashabranner, Melissa 1950- *WrDr 94*
Ashadawi, Ahmed Ali 1939- *WhoFI 94*
Ashamalla, Medhat Guirguis 1942- *WhoAm 94*
Ashanti, Baron James *DrAPF 93*
Ashbach, David Laurence 1942- *WhoMW 93*
Ashbach, Robert O. 1916- *WhoAmP 93*
Ashbacher, Charles David 1954- *WhoMW 93, WhoScEn 94*
Ashbaugh, Dennis John 1946- *WhoAmA 93*
Ashbaugh, John Harvey 1897- *WhAm 10*
Ashbaugh, Scott Gregory 1968- *WhoScEn 94*
Ashbee, Paul 1918- *Who 94*
Ashbery, John *DrAPF 93*
Ashbery, John 1927- *ConLC 77 [port]*
Ashbery, John (Lawrence) 1927- *GayLL, WrDr 94*
Ashbery, John Lawrence 1927- *AmCulL, IntWW 93, WhoAm 94, WhoAmA 93*
Ashbolt, Allan (Campbell) 1921- *WrDr 94*
Ashbourne, Baron 1933- *Who 94*
Ashbridge, Elizabeth 1713-1755 *BlmGWL*
Ashbrook, Viscount 1905- *Who 94*
Ashbrook, Dana 1967- *WhoHol 92*
Ashbrook, Daphne *WhoHol 92*
Ashbrook, Fern Paulette 1943- *WhoMW 93*
Ashbrook, James Barbour 1925- *WhoAm 94, WrDr 94*
Ashbrook, Kate Jessie 1955- *Who 94*
Ashbrook, William (Sinclair) 1922- *NewGrDO*
Ashbrook, William Sinclair, Jr. 1922- *WhoAm 94*
Ashburn, Anderson 1919- *WhoAm 94*
Ashburn, Mark Edmund 1946- *WhoAmL 94*
Ashburn, Vivian Diane 1949- *WhoBlA 94*
Ashburne, Lydia Eudora d1992 *WhoBlA 94N*
Ashburner, Michael 1942- *Who 94*
Ashburnham, Denny Reginald 1916- *Who 94*
Ashburton, Baron 1928- *IntWW 93, Who 94*
Ashby, Baron d1992 *IntWW 93N, Who 94N*
Ashby (of Brandon, Suffolk), Baron 1904- *WrDr 94*
Ashby, Bradford Scott 1963- *WhoMW 93*
Ashby, Carl 1914- *WhoAmA 93*
Ashby, Christopher Thomas 1965- *WhoFI 94*
Ashby, Cliff 1919- *WrDr 94*
Ashby, Clifford Charles 1925- *WhoAm 94*
Ashby, David Glynn 1940- *Who 94*
Ashby, Donald Wayne, Jr. 1926- *WhoAm 94*
Ashby, Dorothy J. 1932- *WhoBlA 94*
Ashby, Eric 1904- *WrDr 94*
Ashby, Ernestine Arnold 1928- *WhoBlA 94*
Ashby, Eugene Christopher 1930- *WhoScEn 94*
Ashby, Francis Dalton 1920- *Who 94*
Ashby, Godfrey William Ernest Candler 1930- *Who 94*
Ashby, Gwynneth Margaret 1922- *WrDr 94*
Ashby, Hugh C(linton) 1934-1991 *WhAm 10*
Ashby, Jack Lane 1911-1990 *WhAm 10*
Ashby, John Forsythe 1929- *WhoAm 94*
Ashby, Laura Lee 1954- *WhoWest 94*
Ashby, Lisa Scherry 1963- *WhoMW 93*
Ashby, Lucius Antoine 1944- *WhoBlA 94*
Ashby, Lucius Antone 1944- *WhoWest 94*
Ashby, Michael Farries 1935- *IntWW 93, Who 94, WhoScEn 94*
Ashby, Philip H(arrison) 1916- *WrDr 94*
Ashby, Reginald W. *WhoBlA 94*
Ashby, Richard James, Jr. 1944- *WhoAm 94*
Ashby, Robert Samuel 1916-1989 *WhAm 10*
Ashby, Roger Arthur 1940- *WhoAm 94, WhoFI 94*
Ashby, Willis Gatch 1955- *WhoFI 94*
Ashcom, John M. 1945- *WhoFI 94*
Ashcombe, Baron 1924- *Who 94*
Ashcraft, Clarence William 1938- *WhoFI 94*
Ashcraft, David Lee 1946- *WhoAm 94*
Ashcraft, Elizabeth Eva 1957- *WhoAmL 94*
Ashcraft, Eve 1963- *WhoAmA 93*
Ashcraft, Percy C., II 1957- *WhoAmP 93*
Ashcroft, David 1920- *Who 94*
Ashcroft, James Geoffrey 1928- *Who 94*
Ashcroft, John *IntWW 93*
Ashcroft, John David 1942- *WhoAmP 93*
Ashcroft, John Kevin 1948- *Who 94*
Ashcroft, Lawrence 1901- *Who 94*
Ashcroft, Neil William 1938- *WhoAm 94*
Ashcroft, Peggy 1907-1991 *WhAm 10, WhoHol 92*
Ashcroft, Philip Giles 1926- *Who 94*
Ashcroft, Richard Carter 1942- *WhoMW 93*
Ashcroft, Richard Thomas 1934- *WhoWest 94*
Ashdown, Franklin Donald 1942- *WhoWest 94*
Ashdown, Jeremy John Durham 1941- *Who 94*
Ashdown, Jeremy John Durham (Paddy) 1941- *IntWW 93*
Ashdown, Philomena Saldanha 1958- *WhoAmL 94*
Ashe, Andrew Munro 1959- *WhoWest 94*
Ashe, Arthur 1943-1993 *AfrAmAl 6 [port], BuCMET [port], CurBio 93N, NewYTBS 93 [port], News 93-3*
Ashe, Arthur (R., Jr.) 1943-1993 *WrDr 94N*
Ashe, Arthur (Robert, Jr.) 1943-1993 *BlkWr 2, ConAu 42NR*
Ashe, Arthur James, III 1940- *WhoAm 94*
Ashe, Arthur R., Jr. 1943-1993 *WhoBlA 94N*
Ashe, Arthur Robert d1993 *IntWW 93N*
Ashe, Bernard Flemming 1936- *WhoAm 94, WhoAmL 94*
Ashe, Derick (Rosslyn) 1919- *Who 94*
Ashe, Derick Rosslyn 1919- *IntWW 93*
Ashe, Geoffrey Thomas 1923- *WrDr 94*
Ashe, Gordon *EncSF 93*
Ashe, James S. 1947- *WhoAm 94*
Ashe, John 1720-1781 *WhAmRev*
Ashe, John 1725-1781 *AmRev*
Ashe, John Baptista 1748-1802 *WhAmRev*
Ashe, John Herman 1944- *WhoWest 94*
Ashe, Kathleen B. 1946- *WhoAmP 93*
Ashe, Mary Ann *ConAu 43NR*
Ashe, Oliver Richard 1933- *WhoFI 94*
Ashe, Robert Lawrence, Jr. 1940- *WhoAm 94, WhoAmL 94*
Ashe, Samuel 1725-1813 *WhAmRev*
Ashe, Victor Henderson 1945- *WhoAm 94, WhoAmP 93*
Ashe, Warren d1947 *WhoHol 92*
Ashear, Linda *DrAPF 93*
Ashe Lincoln, Fredman *Who 94*
Ashen, Philip 1915- *WhoScEn 94*
Ashenden, William Joseph 1957- *WhoWest 94*
Ashendorf, Linda *WhoAmP 93*
Ashenfelter, David Louis 1948- *WhoAm 94*
Ashenfelter, Orley Clark 1942- *WhoAm 94*
Ashenhurst, Francis Ernest 1933- *Who 94*
Asher, Aaron *WhoAm 94*
Asher, Bernard Harry 1936- *Who 94*
Asher, Betty Turner 1944- *WhoAm 94, WhoMW 93*
Asher, David 1946- *WhoIns 94*
Asher, Donna Thompson 1933- *WhoMW 93*
Asher, Elise *WhoAmA 93*
Asher, Eugene Leon 1929- *WhAm 10*
Asher, Frederick 1915- *WhoAm 94*
Asher, Frederick M. 1941- *WhoAmA 93*
Asher, Garland Parker 1944- *WhoAm 94*
Asher, James Edward 1931- *WhoWest 94*
Asher, James Michael 1949- *WhoAm 94*
Asher, Jane 1946- *IntMPA 94, IntWW 93, Who 94, WhoHol 92, WrDr 94*
Asher, Jefferson William, Jr. 1924- *WhoWest 94*
Asher, John Alexander 1921- *WrDr 94*
Asher, Kathleen May 1932- *WhoAmP 93*
Asher, Lila Oliver *WhoAmA 93*
Asher, Lila Oliver 1921- *WhoAm 94*
Asher, Max d1957 *WhoHol 92*
Asher, Michael 1943- *WhoAmA 93*
Asher, Miriam 1938- *WrDr 94*
Asher, Robert B. 1937- *WhoAmP 93*
Asher, Sandy 1942- *TwCYAW*
Asherson, Renee 1920- *WhoHol 92*
Ashford, Anita Rhea 1950- *WhoMW 93*
Ashford, Brad 1949- *WhoAmP 93*
Ashford, Clinton Rutledge 1925- *WhoAm 94*
Ashford, Daisy 1881-1972 *BlmGWL*
Ashford, Douglas Elliott 1928- *WhoAm 94*
Ashford, Evelyn *WhoAm 94, WhoWest 94*
Ashford, Evelyn 1957- *WhoBlA 94*
Ashford, George Allen 1940- *WhoFI 94*
Ashford, George Francis 1911- *Who 94*
Ashford, George R. 1952- *WhoAmL 94*
Ashford, Jeffrey 1926- *WrDr 94*
Ashford, L. Jerome 1937- *WhoBlA 94*
Ashford, Laplois 1935- *WhoBlA 94*
Ashford, Nicholas 1943- & Simpson, Valerie 1948- *AfrAmAl 6*
Ashford, Nicholas 1943- *WhoBlA 94*
Ashford, Nicholas Askounes 1938- *WhoScEn 94*
Ashford, Percival Leonard 1927- *Who 94*
Ashford, Reginald *Who 94*
Ashford, (Albert) Reginald 1914- *Who 94*
Ashford, Robert Louis 1938- *WhoScEn 94*
Ashford, Ronald 1932- *Who 94*
Ashford, Ronald Gordon 1931- *Who 94*
Ashford, William Stanton 1924- *Who 94*
Ashforth, Albert C. 1893- *WhAm 10*
Ashgriz, Nasser 1957- *WhoAm 94*
Ashhurst-Watson, Carmen *WhoBlA 94*
Ashida, Jun 1930- *IntWW 93*
Ashihara, Yoshinobu 1918- *IntWW 93*
Ashikaga Takauji 1305-1358 *HisWorL [port]*
Ashinoff, Reid L. 1949- *WhoAm 94, WhoAmL 94*
Ashiotis, Costas 1908- *Who 94*
Ashjian, Mesrob 1941- *WhoAm 94*
Ashken, Kenneth Richard 1945- *Who 94*
Ashkenas, Irving Louis 1916- *WhoAm 94*
Ashkenasi, Shmuel 1941- *IntWW 93*
Ashkenazi, Josef 1944- *WhoScEn 94*
Ashkenazy, Vladimir 1937- *IntWW 93, Who 94*
Ashkenazy, Vladimir Davidovich 1937- *WhoAm 94*
Ashkin, Ronald Evan 1957- *WhoFI 94, WhoMW 93*
Ashkinazy, Larry Robert 1952- *WhoAm 94*
Ashland, Calvin Kolle 1933- *WhoAm 94, WhoAmL 94, WhoWest 94*
Ashler, Philip Frederic 1914- *WhoAm 94, WhoAmP 93, WhoScEn 94*
Ashley *Who 94*
Ashley, Lord 1977- *Who 94*
Ashley, Arthur d1970 *WhoHol 92*
Ashley, Barbara d1978 *WhoHol 92*
Ashley, Bernard 1935- *TwCYAW, WrDr 94*
Ashley, Bernard (Albert) 1926- *Who 94*
Ashley, Beulah d1965 *WhoHol 92*
Ashley, Cedric 1936- *Who 94*
Ashley, Corlanders 1951- *WhoBlA 94*
Ashley, Darlene Joy 1945- *WhoAm 94*
Ashley, Edward 1904- *WhoHol 92*
Ashley, Elizabeth 1939- *IntMPA 94, WhoHol 92*
Ashley, Elizabeth 1941- *WhoAm 94*
Ashley, Ella Jane 1941- *WhoScEn 94*
Ashley, Fletcher 1926- *WhoAm 94*
Ashley, Francis Paul 1942- *Who 94*
Ashley, Franklin *DrAPF 93*
Ashley, Franklin Bascom 1942- *WhoAm 94*
Ashley, Fred *EncSF 93*
Ashley, Herbert d1958 *WhoHol 92*
Ashley, Holt 1923- *WhoAm 94, WhoScEn 94*
Ashley, Iris 1910- *WhoHol 92*
Ashley, Jack 1922- *WrDr 94*
Ashley, James MacGregor 1941- *WhoFI 94*
Ashley, James Robert 1927- *WhoAm 94*
Ashley, James Wheeler 1923- *WhoAm 94*
Ashley, Jennifer *WhoHol 92*
Ashley, John 1934- *IntMPA 94*
Ashley, John 1935- *WhoHol 92*
Ashley, John M., Jr. *WhoAmP 93*
Ashley, Kevin Edward 1958- *WhoScEn 94*
Ashley, Kimberly Danette 1968- *WhoAmL 94*
Ashley, Lane J. 1952- *WhoAmL 94*
Ashley, Lawrence Atwell, Jr. 1929- *WhoAm 94*
Ashley, Leonard R(aymond) N(elligan) 1928- *WrDr 94*
Ashley, Leonard Raymond Nelligan 1928- *WhoAm 94*
Ashley, Lillard Governor 1909- *WhoBlA 94*
Ashley, Lynn 1920- *WhoMW 93*
Ashley, Maurice 1907- *WrDr 94*
Ashley, Maurice Percy 1907- *Who 94*
Ashley, Merrill *WhoAm 94*
Ashley, Merrill 1950- *IntDcB [port]*
Ashley, Michael Harold 1956- *WhoWest 94*
Ashley, Mike 1948- *EncSF 93*
Ashley, Ona Christine 1954- *WhoMW 93*
Ashley, Paula Claire 1939- *WhoWest 94*
Ashley, Renee *DrAPF 93*
Ashley, Robert 1953- *WhoAmP 93*
Ashley, Robert (Reynolds) 1930- *NewGrDO*
Ashley, Robert Paul, Jr. 1915- *WhoAm 94*
Ashley, Rosalind Minor 1923- *WhoWest 94*
Ashley, Sharon Anita 1948- *WhoAm 94, WhoScEn 94, WhoWest 94*
Ashley, Thomas Ludlow 1923- *WhoAmP 93*
Ashley, Wendy Z. 1942- *AstEnc*
Ashley, William Henry c. 1778-1838 *WhWE*
Ashley, William Hilton, Jr. 1954- *WhoScEn 94*
Ashley, William J. 1955- *WhoIns 94*
Ashley-Cooper *Who 94*
Ashley-Cooper, Anthony 1801-1885 *HisWorL [port]*
Ashley-Farrand, Margalo 1944- *WhoAmL 94, WhoWest 94*
Ashley Harris, Dolores B. *WhoBlA 94*

Ashley-Miller, Michael 1930- Who 94
Ashley Of Stoke, Baron 1922- Who 94
Ashley-Smith, Jonathan 1946- Who 94
Ashliman, Joseph Lyle, Jr. 1927-
WhoFI 94
Ashlock, Jesse d1976 WhoHol 92
Ashman, Howard (Elliott) 1950- WrDr 94
Ashman, Mike (Vincent Crocker) 1950-
NewGrDO
Ashman, William Alfred, Jr. 1954-
WhoWest 94
Ashmann, Jon 1950- WhoAm 94
Ashmead, Allez Morrill 1916-
WhoScEn 94, WhoWest 94
Ashmead, Harve DeWayne 1944-
WhoScEn 94, WhoWest 94
Ashmead, John, Jr. 1917-1992 WhAm 10
Ashmole, (Harold) David 1949- Who 94
Ashmore, Alick 1920- Who 94
Ashmore, Andrea Lynn 1954- WhoBlA 94
Ashmore, Edward (Beckwith) 1919-
IntWW 93, Who 94
Ashmore, Peter (William Beckwith) 1921-
Who 94
Ashmore, Philip George 1916- Who 94
Ashmore, Robert Thomas 1904-1989
WhAm 10
Ashmore, Robert W. 1940- WhoAmL 94
Ashmore, Robert Winston 1955-
WhoScEn 94
Ashmos, Curtis R. 1952- WhoAmL 94
Ashmus, Keith Allen 1949- WhoAm 94,
WhoAmL 94
Ashnault, Paul O. WhoAmP 93
Ashrafi, Mukhtar 1912-1975 NewGrDO
Ashrawi, Hanan IntWW 93
Ashtal, Abdalla Saleh al- 1940- IntWW 93
Ashtekar, Abhay Vasant 1949-
WhoAsA 94
Ashton Who 94
Ashton, Baron 1842-1930 DcNaB MP
Ashton, Alan C. WhoAm 94, WhoFI 94,
WhoWest 94
Ashton, Ann 1929- WrDr 94
Ashton, Anthony Southcliffe 1916-
Who 94
Ashton, Arthur Benner 1941-
WhoWest 94
Ashton, Barry d1978 WhoHol 92
Ashton, Bruce Leland 1945- WhoAmL 94
Ashton, David John 1921- WhoAm 94
Ashton, Dore WhoAm 94, WhoAmA 93,
WrDr 94
Ashton, Dorrit d1936 WhoHol 92
Ashton, Elizabeth WrDr 94
Ashton, Elizabeth Ann 1947- WhoMW 93
Ashton, Ethel V. d1975 WhoAmA 93N
Ashton, Francis Leslie 1904- EncSF 93
Ashton, Frederick d1988 WhoHol 92
Ashton, Frederick 1904-1988
IntDcB [port]
Ashton, Frederick (William Malandaine)
1904-1988 NewGrDO
Ashton, Geoffrey Cyril 1925- WhoAm 94
Ashton, George Arthur 1921- Who 94
Ashton, Gerald 1931- WhoWest 94
Ashton, Harris John 1932- WhoFI 94
Ashton, Herbert d1960 WhoHol 92
Ashton, John IntMPA 94, WhoHol 92
Ashton, John Felton 1929- Who 94
Ashton, John Peter 1945- WhoWest 94
Ashton, John Russell 1925- Who 94
Ashton, Joseph William 1933- Who 94
Ashton, Kenneth Bruce 1925- Who 94
Ashton, Leonard (James) 1915- Who 94
Ashton, Mal Stanhope 1878-1976
WhoAmA 93N
Ashton, Mark Randolph 1955-
WhoAmL 94, WhoAmP 93
Ashton, Marvin EncSF 93
Ashton, Mary Madonna WhoAm 94
Ashton, Norman (Henry) 1913- Who 94
Ashton, Norman Henry 1913- IntWW 93
Ashton, P. J. 1935- WhoFI 94
Ashton, Patrick Thomas 1916- Who 94
Ashton, Rick James 1945- WhoWest 94
Ashton, Robert 1924- Who 94, WrDr 94
Ashton, Robert W. 1937- WhoAmL 94,
WhoAmL 94
Ashton, Roy 1928- Who 94
Ashton, Ruth Mary 1939- Who 94
Ashton, Sylvia d1940 WhoHol 92
Ashton, Thomas Walsh 1929- WhoFI 94
Ashton, Vera d1965 WhoHol 92
Ashton, Vivian Christina R. 1910-
WhoBlA 94
Ashton, William Michael Allingham
1936- Who 94
Ashton, Winifred BlmGWL
Ashton-Griffiths, Roger WhoHol 92
Ashton Of Hyde, Baron 1926- Who 94
Ashton-Warner, Sylvia Constance
1908-1984 BlmGWL
Ashtown, Baron 1916- Who 94
'Ashur, Radwa 1946- BlmGWL
Ashurbanipal c. 700BC-626BC
HisWorL [port]

Ashwood, Andrew Mark 1957-
WhoWest 94
Ashworth, Alan A. 1929- WhoWest 94
Ashworth, Andrew John 1947- Who 94
Ashworth, Brent Ferrin 1949-
WhoAmL 94, WhoFI 94
Ashworth, Geoffrey Hugh 1950-
WhoIns 94
Ashworth, Graham William 1935-
Who 94
Ashworth, Herbert 1910- Who 94
Ashworth, Ian Edward 1930- Who 94
Ashworth, James Louis 1906- Who 94
Ashworth, John d1993 NewYTBS 93
Ashworth, John Blackwood 1910- Who 94
Ashworth, John Lawrence 1934-
WhoAm 94
Ashworth, John Michael 1938-
IntWW 93, Who 94
Ashworth, Kenneth Hayden 1932-
WhoAm 94
Ashworth, Lawrence Nelson 1942-
WhoFI 94
Ashworth, Peter Anthony Frank 1935-
Who 94
Ashworth, Piers 1931- Who 94
Ashworth, Richard Goodspeed 1926-
WhoAm 94
Ashworth, Ronald Broughton 1945-
WhoAm 94, WhoFI 94
Ashworth, (Lewis) William 1942-
WrDr 94
Asia, Daniel Isaac 1953- WhoWest 94
Asif Nawaz, General d1993
NewYTBS 93 [port]
Asihene, Emmanuel V. 1937-
WhoAmA 93
Asimakopulos, Athanasios 1930-
IntWW 93
Asimov, Isaac 1920-1990 WhAm 10
Asimov, Isaac 1920-1992 AnObit 1992,
ConLC 76 [port], EncSF 93,
SmATA 74 [port], TwCYAW, WrDr 94N
Asimov, Janet (Opal Jeppson) 1926-
EncSF 93
Asimov, Janet Jeppson 1926- WrDr 94
Asimov, Stanley 1929- WhoAm 94
Asinof, Eliot 1919- WrDr 94
Asinor, Freddie Andrew 1955- WhoBlA 94
Asioli, Bonifazio 1769-1832 NewGrDO
Asip, Patricia Victoria WhoHisp 94
Asiroglu, Vahap 1916- Who 94
"Ask", Upendranath 1910- ConWorW 93
Askalonov, Artur Aleksandrovich 1940-
LoBiDrD
Askam, Earl d1940 WhoHol 92
Askan, Harry d1934 WhoHol 92
Askan, Perry d1961 WhoHol 92
Askanas-Engel, Valerie 1937- WhoAm 94
Askari, Emilia Shirin 1959- WhoMW 93
Aske, Conan 1912- Who 94
Askeland, Kari Elizabeth 1968-
WhoMW 93
Askenazy, Mischa 1888-1961
WhoAmA 93N
Asker, James Robert 1952- WhoScEn 94
Askevold, David 1940- WhoAmA 93
Askew (Kyme), Anne 1521-1546
BlmGWL
Askew, Anne c. 1521-1546
DcLB 136 [port]
Askew, Barry Reginald William 1936-
Who 94
Askew, Bob E. 1942- WhoIns 94
Askew, Bonny Lamar 1955- WhoBlA 94
Askew, Bryan 1930- Who 94
Askew, Emil Boyd 1941- WhoIns 94
Askew, Homer L. 1913-' WhoAmP 93
Askew, John Marjoribanks Eskdale 1908-
Who 94
Askew, Luke WhoHol 92
Askew, Pamela WhoAmA 93
Askew, Reginald James Albert 1928-
Who 94
Askew, Reubin O'D 1928- WhoAmP 93
Askew, Reubin O'Donovan 1928-
IntWW 93, WhoAm 94
Askew, Rilla DrAPF 93
Askew, Roger L. 1931- WhoBlA 94
Askew, Thomas A(delbert), Jr. 1931-
WrDr 94
Askew, Thomas Rendall 1955-
WhoScEn 94
Askew, William Earl 1943- WhoScEn 94
Askey, Arthur d1982 WhoHol 92
Askey, Richard Allen 1933- WhoAm 94,
WhoScEn 94
Askey, William Hartman 1919-
WhoAm 94, WhoWest 94
Askin, Elisa Mullenix 1953- WhoIns 94
Askin, Leon 1907- WhoAm 94,
WhoHol 92
Askin, Richard Henry, Jr. 1947-
WhoAm 94, WhoWest 94
Askin, Walter Miller 1929- WhoAm 94,
WhoAmA 93
Askinosie, Michael Shawn 1961-
WhoAmL 94

Askins, Arthur James 1944- WhoFI 94
Askins, Harry R. 1946- WhoAmP 93
Askins, Keith WhoBlA 94
Askins, Knox Winfred 1937- WhoAmL 94
Askman, Tom K. 1941- WhoAmA 93
Askonas, Brigitte Alice 1923- IntWW 93,
Who 94
Askwith, Betty Ellen 1909- Who 94
Askwith, Robin 1950- WhoHol 92
Aslakhanov, Aslanbek Akhmedovich
1942- LoBiDrD
Aslam, Muhammed Javed 1938-
WhoScEn 94
Aslam, Nasim Mohammed 1946-
WhoAsA 94
Aslan, Gregoire d1982 WhoHol 92
Aslan, Raoul d1958 WhoHol 92
Aslanov, Nikolay d1944 WhoHol 92
Aslaoui, Leila WhoWomW 91
Aslet, Clive William 1955- Who 94
Aslin, M. M. 1947- WhoAm 94
Asling, Clarence Willet 1913- WhoAm 94
Asling, Nils Gunnar 1927- IntWW 93
Asma, Thomas M. WhoBlA 94
Asmar, Alice WhoAmA 93
Asmar, Charles Edmond 1958-
WhoScEn 94
Asmar, Mark Abdon 1945- WhoAmL 94
Asmodi, Herbert 1923- IntWW 93
Asmonas, Vladas 1910- WhoWest 94
Asmus, John Fredrich 1937- WhoAm 94
Asmussen, Jes, Jr. 1938- WhoMW 93,
WhoScEn 94
Asner, Edward 1929- IntMPA 94,
WhoAm 94, WhoHol 92
Asner, Marie A. DrAPF 93
Asnes, Marvin Arthur 1928-1987
WhAm 10
Asnin, Scott EncSF 93
Aso, Kaji WhoAmA 93
Asom, Moses T. 1958- WhoBlA 94
Asoma, Tadashi 1923- WhoAmA 93
Asomoza, Rene 1948- WhoScEn 94
Asp, Eero Rafael 1922- IntWW 93
Asp, William George 1943- WhoAm 94
Aspa, Mario 1797-1868 NewGrDO
Aspasia fl. 5th cent.BC- BlmGWL
Aspaturian, Vernon Varazdat 1922-
WhoAm 94
Aspbury, Herbert Francis 1944-
WhoAm 94
Aspdin, Joseph 1778-1855 DcNaB MP
Aspe, Pedro 1950- WhoAm 94
Aspe Armella, Pedro 1950- IntWW 93,
WhoFI 94
Aspel, Michael 1957- IntMPA 94
Aspel, Michael Terence 1933- Who 94
Aspell, Amy Suzanne 1942- WhoAmA 93
Aspell, Gerald Laycock 1915- Who 94
Aspen, Marvin Edward 1934- WhoAm 94,
WhoAmL 94, WhoMW 93
Aspenberg, Gary DrAPF 93
Aspenquid dc. 1682 EncNAR
Aspenstrom, (Karl) Werner 1918-
ConWorW 93
Asper, Israel Harold 1932- IntWW 93,
WhoAm 94, WhoFI 94
Aspero, Benedict Vincent 1940-
WhoAm 94, WhoAmL 94
Aspero, Stephen M. 1947- WhoAmL 94
Asphaug, Rolf Gunnar 1958-
WhoAmL 94
Aspin, Les 1938- IntWW 93, WhoAm 94,
WhoAmP 93
Aspin, Norman 1922- Who 94
Aspinall, John Audley Frederick
1851-1937 DcNaB MP
Aspinall, John Victor 1926- Who 94
Aspinall, Owen Stewart 1927-
WhoAmP 93
Aspinall, Wilfred 1942- Who 94
Aspinwall, Jack Heywood 1933- Who 94
Aspinwall, Richard 1932- WhoFI 94
Aspinwall, William 1743-1823 WhAmRev
Aspiotou, Koula 1946- WhoFI 94
Asplin, Edward William 1922- WhoAm 94
Asplmayr, Franz 1728-1786 NewGrDO
Asplund, Bronwyn Lorraine 1947-
WhoAm 94
Aspnes, David Erik 1939- WhoAm 94
Aspray, Rodney George 1934- Who 94
Asprey, Robert Brown 1923- WrDr 94
Asprin, Robert (Lynn) 1946- WhoAm 94
Asprin, Robert Lynn 1946- EncSF 93
Aspuru, Carlos M. 1936- WhoHisp 94
Aspuru, Eugenio WhoHisp 94
Asquith Who 94
Asquith, Viscount 1952- Who 94
Asquith, Harry W., Jr. 1952- WhoAmL 94
Asquith, Mary d1942 WhoHol 92
Asquith, Ronald H. 1932- WhoFI 94
Assad, Hafiz al- 1928- IntWW 93
Assad, Nassir El-Din El- 1923- IntWW 93
Assael, Henry 1935- WhoAm 94
Assael, Michael 1949- WhoAmL 94,
WhoFI 94
Assalone, John Richard 1942-
WhoAmP 93

Assanis, Dennis N. 1959- WhoAm 94,
WhoScEn 94
Assante, Armand 1949- ConTFT 11,
IntMPA 94, WhoAm 94, WhoHol 92
Assante, Katharine DrAPF 93
Assarian, Gary Steven 1952- WhoMW 93
Assatly, Richard d1993
NewYTBS 93 [port]
Asscher, (Adolf) William 1931- Who 94
Asselin, Don Thomas 1954- WhoMW 93
Asselin, John Thomas 1951- WhoAmL 94
Asselin, Martial 1924- WhoAm 94
Asselin, Robert Paul 1956- WhoAmP 93
Assenmacher, Ivan 1927- IntWW 93
Assennato, Vincent Thomas 1950-
WhoIns 94
Asseyev, Tamara IntMPA 94
Assheton Who 94
Assing, Ottilie 1819-1884 BlmGWL
Assink, Brent E. 1955- WhoAm 94
Assmann, David Oswald 1952-
WhoWest 94
Asson, Thomas Henry 1933- WhoFI 94
Ast, Dieter Gerhard 1939- WhoScEn 94
Ast, Pat 1941- WhoHol 92
Astacio, Julio Ernesto 1932- IntWW 93
Astacio, Pedro 1969- WhoHisp 94
Astafev, Mikhail Georgevich 1946-
LoBiDrD
Astafiev, Viktor Petrovich 1924-
IntWW 93
Astaire, Adele d1981 WhoHol 92
Astaire, Fred d1987 WhoHol 92
Astaire, Fred 1899-1987 AmCulL [port]
Astaire, Jarvis Joseph 1923- Who 94
Astala, Heli Hellevi 1937- WhoWomW 91
Astalos, Lynn Makoto 1962- WhoFI 94
Astangov, Mikhail d1965 WhoHol 92
Astar, Ben WhoHol 92
Astarita, Gennaro c. 1745-c. 1803
NewGrDO
Astbury, Alan 1934- Who 94
Astell, Mary 1666-1731 BlmGEL,
BlmGWL
Asthagiri, Rajappa Krishnamachari
1946- WhoMW 93
Asther, Nils d1981 WhoHol 92
Asti, Adrianna WhoHol 92
Asti, Alison Louise 1954- WhoAmL 94
Astigarraga, Jose Ignacio 1953-
WhoAm 94
Astill, Bernard Douglas 1925-
WhoScEn 94
Astill, Kenneth Norman 1923-
WhoAm 94
Astill, Michael John 1938- Who 94
Astin, Alexander William 1932-
WhoAm 94
Astin, John 1930- IntMPA 94, WhoCom,
WhoHol 92
Astin, John Allen 1930- WhoAm 94
Astin, Patty Duke WhoHol 92
Astin, Sean 1971- IntMPA 94, WhoHol 92
Astington, John Harold 1945- WhoAm 94
Astle, Gary Clark 1961- WhoFI 94
Astle, John C. 1943- WhoAmP 93
Astley Who 94
Astley, Eugene Roy 1926- WhoWest 94
Astley, Francis Jacob Dugdale 1908-
Who 94
Astley, Neil 1953- WrDr 94
Astley, Philip Sinton 1943- Who 94
Astley, Thea 1925- BlmGWL
Astley, Thea (Beatrice May) 1925-
ConAu 43NR, WrDr 94
Astley-Bell, Rita Duis WhoAmA 93
Astling, Alistair Vivian 1943- Who 94
Astman, Barbara Ann 1950- WhoAm 94,
WhoAmA 93
Astol, Paco d1962 WhoHol 92
Aston, Archdeacon of Who 94
Aston, Bishop Suffragan of 1939- Who 94
Aston, Francis William 1877-1945
WorScD
Aston, Harold (George) 1923- Who 94
Aston, James William 1911- IntWW 93,
WhoAm 94
Aston, Louise 1814-1871 BlmGWL
Aston, Miriam WhoAmA 93
Aston, Peter George 1938- Who 94
Aston, William (John) 1916- Who 94
Astor Who 94
Astor, Viscount 1951- Who 94
Astor, Brooke WhoAm 94
Astor, (Francis) David (Langhorne) 1912-
Who 94
Astor, (Francis) David Langhorne 1912-
IntWW 93
Astor, David Waldorf 1943- Who 94
Astor, Frank Charles 1927- WhoHisp 94
Astor, Gerald WrDr 94
Astor, Gertrude 1887-1977 WhoHol 92
Astor, Hugh Waldorf 1920- Who 94
Astor, John (Jacob) 1918- Who 94
Astor, John Jacob 1763-1848
WhWE [port]
Astor, John Jacob 1864-1912 EncSF 93
Astor, Junie d1967 WhoHol 92

Atlas, John Wesley 1941- WhoBlA 94
Atlas, Laurence David 1957- WhoAmL 94
Atlas, Liane Wiener WhoFI 94
Atlas, Morris 1926- WhoAmP 93
Atlas, Nancy Friedman 1949-
WhoAmL 94
Atlas, Nava 1955- WhoAmA 93
Atlas, Ronald M. 1946- WhoScEn 94
Atlas, Scott Jerome 1950- WhoAm 94,
WhoAmL 94
Atlasov, Vladimir Vasilyevich d1711
WhWE
Atlee, Emilie Des 1915- WhoAmA 93
Atlee, Frank V. 1940- WhoFI 94
Atlee, John Light, III 1941- WhoMW 93,
WhoScEn 94
Atlee, Samuel 1739-1786 WhAmRev
Atlee, William Augustus 1942-
WhoAmL 94
Atluri, Satya Nadham 1945- WhoAm 94,
WhoScEn 94
Atluru, Durgaprasadarao 1949-
WhoScEn 94
Atmar, Ann d1966 WhoHol 92
Atobe, Yasuzo 1926- WhoAm 94
Atoji, Masao 1925- WhoAsA 94,
WhoMW 93
Atomcracker, Buzz-Bolt EncSF 93
Atossa fl. 6th cent.BC- BlmGWL
Atrash, Muhammad al- 1934- IntWW 93
Atresio Geonuntino NewGrDO
Atreya, Arvind 1954- WhoScEn 94
Atreya, Sushil Kumar 1946- WhoAm 94
Atoumi, Ikuko 1940 WhoFI 94
Attali, Bernard 1943- IntWW 93
Attali, Jacques 1943- IntWW 93, Who 94
Attalla, Albert 1931- WhoScEn 94
Attallah, Naim Ibrahim 1931- IntWW 93,
Who 94
Attanasio, A(lfred) A(ngelo) 1951-
EncSF 93
Attanasio, John Baptist 1954-
WhoMW 93
Attanasio, Salvator d1993 NewYTBS 93
Attao, Jesus Torres WhoAmP 93
'Attar, Samar 1940- BlmGWL
Attardo, Lewis Charles 1950- WhoFI 94
Attas, Haydar Abu Bakr al- IntWW 93
Attassi, Louai 1926- IntWW 93
Attaway, David Henry 1938-
WhoScEn 94
Attaway, John David 1929- WhoBlA 94
Attaway, Ruth d1987 WhoHol 92
Attaway, William (Alexander) 1911-1986
BlkWr 2
Atteberry, William Duane 1920-
WhoAm 94
Attebery, Louie Wayne 1927- WhoAm 94,
WhoWest 94
Attebury, Janice Marie 1954- WhoFI 94
Attebury, William Hugh 1929- WhoFI 94
Attee, Joyce Valerie Jungclas 1926-
WhoMW 93
Attenborough Who 94
Attenborough, Baron 1923- Who 94
Attenborough, David 1926- IntMPA 94
Attenborough, David (Frederick) 1926-
Who 94
Attenborough, David (Frederick), Sir
1926- WrDr 94
Attenborough, David Frederick 1926-
IntWW 93
Attenborough, John Philip 1901- Who 94
Attenborough, Peter John 1938- Who 94
Attenborough, Philip John 1936-
IntWW 93, Who 94
Attenborough, Richard 1923- WhoAm 94,
WhoHol 92
Attenborough, Richard (Samuel)
IntMPA 94
Attenborough, Richard (Samuel) 1923-
IntWW 93
Atterberg, Douglas Keith 1945-
WhoMW 93
Atterberg, Kurt (Magnus) 1887-1974
NewGrDO
Atterberry, Richard Lyle 1953-
WhoMW 93
Atterbury, Malcolm 1907- WhoHol 92
Atterbury, Robert Rennie, III 1937-
WhoAmL 94, WhoFI 94
Atterley, Joseph 1775-1861 EncSF 93
Attermeier, Fredric Joseph 1946-
WhoAmL 94
Attersee 1942- IntWW 93
Atterton, David Valentine 1927- Who 94
Attewell, Brian 1939- Who 94
Atteya, Ahmad Mamdouh 1923-
IntWW 93
Atthill, Robin 1912- WrDr 94
Attia, Gilles S. 1949- WhoAmL 94
Atticus 109BC-32BC BlmGEL
Attie, Dotty 1938- WhoAmA 93
Attig, John Clare 1936- WhoWest 94
Attila d453 BlmGEL
Attila c. 370-453 HisWorL [port]
Attinger, Ernst Otto 1922- WhoAm 94
Attix, Frank Herbert 1925- WhoAm 94

Attiyeh, Richard Eugene 1937-
WhoAm 94
Attlee Who 94
Attlee, Earl 1956- Who 94
Attlee, Clement R. 1883-1967 HisDcKW
Attlee, Donald Laurence 1922- Who 94
Attles, Alvin WhoBlA 94
Attles, Alvin 1936- BasBi
Attles, Joseph d1990 WhoHol 92
Attles, LeRoy 1966- WhoScEn 94
Attoe, Wayne Osborne 1940- WhoAm 94
Attoh, Samuel Aryeetey 1956-
WhoMW 93
Attolico, Giacomo 1928- IntWW 93
Attridge, Elizabeth Ann Johnston 1934-
Who 94
Attridge, Richard Byron 1933- WhoAm 94
Attucks, Crispus c. 1723-1770 AfrAmAl 6,
WhAmRev
Attwood, David Thomas 1941-
WhoAm 94, WhoScEn 94
Attwood, James Albert 1927-1989
WhAm 10
Attwood, James Dewitt 1956- WhoMW 93
Attwood, Stephen S(tanley) 1897-
WhAm 10
Attwood, Thomas 1765-1838 NewGrDO
Attwood, Thomas Jaymril 1931- Who 94
Attwood, William 1919-1989 WhAm 10
Attygalle, Don Sepala 1921- IntWW 93,
Who 94
Atutis, Bernard P. 1933- WhoScEn 94
Atwater, Barry d1978 WhoHol 92
Atwater, Edith d1986 WhoHol 92
Atwater, Horace Brewster, Jr. 1931-
IntWW 93, WhoAm 94, WhoFI 94,
WhoMW 93
Atwater, James David 1928- WhoAm 94
Atwater, Julie Demers 1945- WhoWest 94
Atwater, N. William 1934- WhoFI 94
Atwater, P(hyllis) M. H. 1937- WrDr 94
Atwater, Stephen Dennis 1966-
WhoAm 94, WhoBlA 94, WhoWest 94
Atwater, Tanya Maria 1942- WhoScEn 94
Atwater, Verne Stafford 1920- WhoAm 94
Atwater, William E., III 1948-
WhoAmL 94
Atwater, William Felix 1945- WhoAm 94
Atwell, Allen 1925- WhoAmA 93
Atwell, Charles Emmert 1950-
WhoAmL 94
Atwell, Constance Woodruff 1942-
WhoAm 94
Atwell, Eleanor C. 1936- WhoAmP 93
Atwell, Grace d1952 WhoHol 92
Atwell, John (William) 1911- Who 94
Atwell, Margaret Ann 1949- WhoAm 94
Atwell, Mary WhoAmL 94
Atwell, Robert Herron 1931- WhoAm 94
Atwell, Roy d1962 WhoHol 92
Atwill, (Milton) John (Napier) 1926-
Who 94
Atwill, Lionel d1946 WhoHol 92
Atwill, William Henry, Jr. 1956-
WhoAmL 94
Atwong, Matthew Kok Lun 1950-
WhoScEn 94
Atwood, Barry Thomas 1940- Who 94
Atwood, Diana Field 1946- WhoFI 94
Atwood, Donald Jesse, Jr. 1924-
WhoAm 94
Atwood, Donald Keith 1933- WhoAm 94
Atwood, Edward Charles 1922-
WhoAm 94
Atwood, Edward Wilson 1897- WhAm 10
Atwood, Genevieve 1946- WhoAm 94,
WhoAmP 93
Atwood, Harold Leslie 1937- WhoAm 94
Atwood, Hollye Stolz 1945- WhoAm 94,
WhoAmL 94
Atwood, J. Brian 1942- WhoAmP 93
Atwood, James R. 1944- WhoAm 94,
WhoAmL 94
Atwood, Jeffrey Nelson 1950- WhoFI 94
Atwood, John Brian 1942- WhoAm 94
Atwood, John Leland 1904- IntWW 93
Atwood, John Rawson 1946- WhoAmP 93
Atwood, Kelly Palmer 1946- WhoWest 94
Atwood, Margaret DrAPF 93
Atwood, Margaret 1939-
Au&Arts 12 [port], BlmGEL [port],
IntWW 93, PoeCrit 8 [port], Who 94,
WrDr 94
Atwood, Margaret (Eleanor) 1939-
EncSF 93, RfGShF, TwCYAW
Atwood, Margaret Eleanor 1939-
BlmGWL [port], WhoAm 94
Atwood, Mary Sanford 1935- WhoWest 94
Atwood, Raymond Percival, Jr. 1952-
WhoAmL 94
Atwood, Robert Bruce 1907- WhoAm 94,
WhoWest 94
Atwood, Sam EncSF 93
Atwood, Theodore 1925- WhoScEn 94
Atwood, William 1927-1991 WhAm 10
Atwood, William G(oodson) 1932-
ConAu 142

Atwood Pinardi, Brenda 1941-
WhoAmA 93
Atzmon, Michael 1956- WhoMW 93
Atzmon, Moshe 1931- IntWW 93
Au, Andrew T. 1964- WhoAsA 94
Au, Calvin K. 1948- WhoAsA 94
Au, Chi-Kwan 1946- WhoAsA 94
Au, Leo Yuin 1949- WhoAsA 94
Au, Mary Wai-Yin WhoWest 94
Au, Matthew Kam-Yuen 1964- WhoFI 94
Au, Patrick Siu-Kee 1941- WhoAsA 94
Au, Tung 1923- WhoAm 94, WhoAsA 94
Au, Wilkie Wai Kee 1944- WhoAsA 94
Aubee, Caleb Babatunde 1942- Who 94
Auber, Brigitte WhoHol 92
Auber, Daniel-Francois-Esprit 1782-1871
NewGrDO
Auberger, Bernard 1937- IntWW 93
Auberjonois, Rene 1940- IntMPA 94,
WhoHol 92
Auberjonois, Rene Murat 1940-
WhoAm 94
Aubert, Allan Charles 1957- WhoScEn 94
Aubert, Alvin DrAPF 93
Aubert, Alvin 1930- WrDr 94
Aubert, Alvin Bernard 1930- WhoBlA 94
Aubert, Constance 1803- BlmGWL
Aubert, Jacques 1689-1753 NewGrDO
Aubert, Jeanne BlmGWL
Aubert, Lenore 1920- WhoHol 92
Aubert, Louis d1943 WhoHol 92
Aubert, Louis(-Francois-Marie)
1877-1968 NewGrDO
Aubert, Maurice 1924- IntWW 93
Aubert, Pierre 1927- IntWW 93
Aubery, Joseph 1673-1755 EncNAR
Aubespin, Mervin R. 1937- WhoBlA 94
Aubespine, Madeleine de 1546-1596
BlmGWL
Aubigne, Theodore Agrippa d' 1552-1630
GuFrLit 2
Aubin, Barbara 1928- WhoAmA 93
Aubin, Richard Thomas, II 1946-
WhoWest 94
Aubin, Tony (Louis Alexandre)
1907-1981 NewGrDO
Aubke, Friedhelm 1932- WhoAm 94
Aubouin, Jean Armand 1928- IntWW 93
Aubrey, Anne 1937- WhoHol 92
Aubrey, Elizabeth 1951- WhoMW 93
Aubrey, Frank 1840-1927 EncSF 93
Aubrey, Georges d1975 WhoHol 92
Aubrey, James 1947- WhoHol 92
Aubrey, James T., Jr. 1918- IntMPA 94
Aubrey, Jean 1935- WhoHol 92
Aubrey, Jimmie d1983 WhoHol 92
Aubrey, John 1626-1697 BlmGEL
Aubrey, John Melbourn 1921- Who 94
Aubrey, Karen 1945- WhoAmL 94
Aubrey, Roger Frederick 1929-
WhoAm 94
Aubrey, Skye 1945- WhoHol 92
Aubrey, Will d1958 WhoHol 92
Aubrey-Fletcher Who 94
Aubrey-Fletcher, Henry (Egerton) 1945-
Who 94
Aubry, Cecile 1928- IntWW 93
Aubry, Cecile 1929- WhoHol 92
Aubry, Eugene Edwards 1935- WhoAm 94
Aubry, Genevieve 1928- WhoWomW 91
Aubry, Jeffrion L. WhoAmP 93
Aubry, Marie c. 1656-1704 NewGrDO
Aubry, Martine 1950- WhoWomW 91
Aubry, Martine Louise Marie 1950-
IntWW 93
Aubuchon, Jacques WhoHol 92
Aubuchon, Joseph Ramey 1944-
WhoAmL 94
Auburn, Joy d1932 WhoHol 92
Auburn, Norman Paul 1905- WhoAm 94
Aubut, Marcel 1948- WhoAm 94
Auch, Walter Edward 1921- WhoAm 94
Auchincloss, Kenneth 1937- WhoAm 94
Auchincloss, Louis DrAPF 93
Auchincloss, Louis (Stanton) 1917-
WrDr 94
Auchincloss, Louis Stanton 1917-
IntWW 93, WhoAm 94, WhoAm 94
Auchincloss, Peter Eric 1960-
WhoScEn 94
Auchmuthy, Robert d1788 WhAmRev
Auchmuty, Samuel c. 1758-1822
WhAmRev
Auchter, John R. 1922- WhoAmP 93
Auciello, Anthony Andrew 1956-
WhoMW 93
Auciello, Orlando Hector 1945-
WhoScEn 94
Auckerman, Raymond A. 1944-
WhoIns 94
Auckland, Archdeacon of Who 94
Auckland, Assistant Bishop of Who 94
Auckland, Baron 1926- Who 94
Auckland, Bishop of 1937- Who 94
Auckland, Bishop of 1938- Who 94
Auckland, Lord WhAmRev
Auclair, Alphonse Felix 1924-
WhoAmP 93

Auclair, Michel d1988 WhoHol 92
Auclert, Hubertine 1848-1914 BlmGWL
AuCoin, Les 1942- WhoAm 94,
WhoAmP 93
Aucott, George William 1934- IntWW 93
Aucutt, Ronald David 1945- WhoAm 94,
WhoAmL 94
Audain, Linz 1959- WhoBlA 94
Auden, W. H. 1907-1973 BlmGEL
Auden, W(ystan) H(ugh) 1907-1973
ConDr 93, GayLL, IntDcT 2, NewGrDO
Auden, Wystan Hugh 1907-1973 AmCulL
Auderska, Halina 1904- IntWW 93
Audet, David Maurice 1951- WhoAmL 94
Audet, Henri 1918- WhoAm 94
Audet, Leonard 1932- WhoAm 94
Audet, Paul Andre 1923- WhoAm 94
Audet, Rene 1920- WhoAm 94
Audette, Anna Held WhoAmA 93
Audia, Christina 1941- WhoAm 94
Audiard, Michel 1920-1985 IntDcF 2-4
Audiberti, Jacques 1899-1965 IntDcT 2
Audin, Lindsay Peter 1946- WhoScEn 94
Audinot, Nicolas-Medard 1732-1801
NewGrDO
Audland, Christopher (John) 1926-
Who 94
Audley, Baron 1914- Who 94
Audley, Barbara Marie 1940- WhoMW 93
Audley, (George) Bernard 1924- Who 94
Audley, Eleanor WhoHol 92
Audley, Hugh, Earl of Gloucester c.
1291-1347 DcNaB MP
Audley, Maxine 1923- WhoHol 92
Audley, Robert John 1928- Who 94
Audley-Charles, Michael Geoffrey 1935-
Who 94
Audo, Martine WhoHol 92
Audouard, Olympe 1830-1890 BlmGWL
Audoux, Marguerite 1863-1937 BlmGWL
Audrain, Paul Andre Marie 1945-
IntWW 93
Audran, Edmond d1951 WhoHol 92
Audran, Edmond 1840-1901 NewGrDO
Audran, Stephane IntWW 93
Audran, Stephane 1933- WhoHol 92
Audran, Stephane Louise 1932- WhoHol 92
Audu, Ishaya Shu'aibu 1927- Who 94
Audubon, John James 1785-1851
EnvEnc [port], WhWE [port]
Audus, Leslie John 1911- Who 94,
WrDr 94
Auel, Jean 1936- BlmGWL
Auel, Jean M. DrAPF 93
Auel, Jean M(arie) 1936- EncSF 93,
WrDr 94
Auel, Jean Marie 1936- WhoAm 94
Auen, Michael H. 1946- WhoAm 94
Auen, Signe d1966 WhoHol 92
Auenbrugger, Joseph Leopold 1722-1809
NewGrDO
Auer, Arthur Irwin, II 1958- WhoMW 93
Auer, Benedict LeRoy 1939- WhoWest 94
Auer, Delmar L. 1929- WhoAmP 93
Auer, Florence d1962 WhoHol 92
Auer, J. P. 1953- WhoAmP 93
Auer, James M(atthew) 1928- WrDr 94
Auer, James Matthew 1928- WhoAm 94,
WhoAmA 93
Auer, John d1975 WhoHol 92
Auer, Karl 1858-1929 WorInv
Auer, Martin 1951- SmATA 77
Auer, Mischa d1967 WhoHol 92
Auer, Ron 1950- WhoAmP 93
Auerbach, Alan Jeffrey 1951- WhoAm 94
Auerbach, Artie d1957 WhoHol 92
Auerbach, Berthold 1812-1882
DcLB 133 [port]
Auerbach, Bob Shipley 1919- WhoAmP 93
Auerbach, Boris 1931- WhoAm 94
Auerbach, Bradford Carlton 1957-
WhoWest 94
Auerbach, Bryan Neil 1946- WhoWest 94
Auerbach, Carl Abraham 1915-
WhoAm 94
Auerbach, Charlotte 1899- IntWW 93,
Who 94
Auerbach, Ernest Sigmund 1936-
WhoAm 94, WhoAmL 94, WhoFI 94
Auerbach, Evaline Jones 1943-
WhoWest 94
Auerbach, Frank 1931- IntWW 93,
WhoAmA 93
Auerbach, Frank Helmuth 1931- Who 94
Auerbach, Heine d1916 WhoHol 92
Auerbach, Jonathan Louis 1942-
WhoFI 94
Auerbach, Joseph 1916- WhoAm 94,
WhoAmL 94
Auerbach, Leon d1984 WhoHol 92
Auerbach, Marshall Jay 1932- WhoAm 94,
WhoAmL 94, WhoFI 94
Auerbach, Michael Howard 1943-
WhoAm 94
Auerbach, Norbert T. 1923- IntMPA 94
Auerbach, Norman E. d1993
NewYTBS 93 [port]
Auerbach, Paul Ira 1932- WhoAmL 94

Auerbach, Philip Gary 1932- *WhoAmL 94*
Auerbach, Red 1917- *BasBi, WhoAm 94, WrDr 94*
Auerbach, Robert 1929- *WhoMW 93*
Auerbach, Robert 1947- *WhoFI 94*
Auerbach, Seymour 1929- *WhoAm 94*
Auerbach, Stanley Irving 1921- *IntWW 93, WhoAm 94, WhoScEn 94*
Auerbach, Stuart Charles 1935- *WhoAm 94*
Auerbach, William 1914- *WhoAm 94*
Auerbacher, Peter 1950- *WhoScEn 94*
Auerbach-Levy, William 1889-1964 *WhoAmA 93N*
Auerback, Alfred 1915- *WhoAm 94*
Auerback, Sandra Jean 1946- *WhoWest 94*
Auernheimer, Leonardo 1936- *WhoHisp 94*
Aufdenkamp, Jo Ann 1926- *WhoMW 93*
Aufderheide, Arthur Carl 1922- *WhoMW 93*
Auffant, James Robert 1949- *WhoHisp 94*
Aufses, Arthur Harold, Jr. 1926- *WhoAm 94*
Aufzien, Alan L. *WhoAm 94*
Aug, Edna d1938 *WhoHol 92*
Aug, Ellen W. *DrAPF 93*
Aug, Jonathan Vincent 1946- *WhoAm 94, WhoAmL 94*
Aug, Stephen M. 1936- *WhoAm 94*
Augelli, John Pat 1921- *WhoAm 94*
Augello, William Joseph 1926- *WhoAm 94*
Augenbraum, Harold 1953- *ConAu 142*
Augenstein, Bruno W. 1923- *WhoAm 94*
Augenstein, Vincent Eugene 1943- *WhoMW 93*
Auger, Arleen 1939- *IntWW 93, NewGrDO*
Auger, Arleen 1939-1993 *CurBio 93N, NewYTBS 93 [port]*
Auger, Claudine 1942- *WhoHol 92*
Auger, David J. *WhoAm 94*
Auger, Harvey J. 1947- *WhoFI 94*
Auger, Pierre Victor 1899- *IntWW 93, Who 94*
Auger, Simone *WhoAm 94*
Augerson, William Sinclair 1927- *WhoScEn 94*
Aughenbaugh, Karl Richard 1936- *WhoAmL 94*
Aughenbaugh, Nolan Blaine 1928- *WhoScEn 94*
Aughtry, Dewette Candy 1959- *WhoAmL 94*
Augier, (Guillaume-Victor-) Emile 1820-1889 *IntDcT 2 [port]*
Augmon, Stacey Orlando 1968- *WhoBlA 94*
Augsburger, Aaron Donald 1925- *WhoAm 94*
Augsburger, John Bird 1934- *WhoAmP 93*
Augsburger, Lisa Marie 1962- *WhoMW 93*
Augsburger, Robert Ray 1926- *WhoWest 94*
Augspurger, Gregory Paul 1955- *WhoMW 93*
Augstein, Rudolf 1923- *IntWW 93*
Augur, Marilyn Hussman 1938- *WhoFI 94*
August, Bille 1948- *IntMPA 94, IntWW 93, WhoAm 94*
August, Edwin d1964 *WhoHol 92*
August, Hal d1918 *WhoHol 92*
August, Jan d1976 *WhoHol 92*
August, Joseph H. 1890-1947 *IntDcF 2-4 [port]*
August, Paul Rudolph 1966- *WhoAmP 93*
August, Robert Olin 1921- *WhoAm 94*
August, Robert William 1944- *WhoMW 93*
August, Rudolf 1926- *WhoAm 94, WhoScEn 94*
Auguste, Yves L. *IntWW 93*
Augustin, William d1934 *WhoHol 92*
Augustine, Saint 354-430 *EncEth*
Augustine, Alan M. *WhoAmP 93*
Augustine, Brian Howard 1968- *WhoScEn 94*
Augustine, Fennis Lincoln 1932- *Who 94*
Augustine, Jane *DrAPF 93*
Augustine, Jerome Samuel 1928- *WhoAm 94*
Augustine, John 1938- *WhoFI 94*
Augustine, Kathy M. 1956- *WhoAmP 93*
Augustine, Kathy Marie 1956- *WhoWest 94*
Augustine, Margret L. 1953- *WhoScEn 94*
Augustine, Mary 1896- *WhAm 10*
Augustine, Mildred 1905- *WrDr 94*
Augustine, Norman Ralph 1935- *WhoAm 94, WhoFI 94, WhoScEn 94*
Augustine of Hippo 354-430 *HisWorL [port]*
Augustini, Pietro Simone *NewGrDO*
Augusto, Antonio C. 1937- *WhoHisp 94*
Augusto, Carl Robert 1946- *WhoAm 94*
Augustus 63BC-14AD *HisWorL [port]*
Augustus, Albert, Jr. *EncSF 93*
Augustus, Franklin J. P. 1950- *WhoBlA 94*
Augustyn, Frank Joseph 1953- *WhoAm 94*
Auker, David *WhoHol 92*
Aukerman, James Vance 1948- *WhoAmP 93*
Aukin, David 1942- *IntWW 93, Who 94*
Aukland, Duncan Dayton 1954- *WhoAmL 94*
Aulakh, Kay *WhoAsA 94*
Aulas, Marie-Christine 1945- *WhoWomW 91*
Aulbach, George Louis 1925- *WhoAm 94*
Auld, Aggie d1983 *WhoHol 92*
Auld, Alasdair Alpin 1930- *Who 94*
Auld, Albert Michael 1943- *WhoBlA 94*
Auld, Bernie Dyson 1958- *WhoScEn 94*
Auld, Bertram Alexander 1922- *WhoAm 94*
Auld, Frank 1923- *WhoAm 94*
Auld, Georgie d1990 *WhoHol 92*
Auld, John H. 1940- *WhoAmP 93*
Auld, Lorna Bergeson 1944- *WhoAmP 93*
Auld, Margaret Gibson 1932- *Who 94*
Auld, Robert Henry, Jr. 1942- *WhoScEn 94*
Auld, Robin Ernest 1937- *Who 94*
Auld, Rose A. 1946- *WhoBlA 94*
Auldjo, John 1805-1886 *DcNaB MP*
Auld-Louie, Margaret Elizabeth 1958- *WhoWest 94*
Auletta, Joan Miglorisi 1940- *WhoFI 94*
Auletta, Pietro c. 1698-1771 *NewGrDO*
Aulich, James 1952- *WrDr 94*
Aulie, Richard Paul 1926- *WhoMW 93*
Aulin, Ewa 1949- *WhoHol 92*
Aulitzky, Herbert 1922- *WhoScEn 94*
Aulnoy, Marie-Catherine Le Jumel de Barneville, Comtesse d' 1650?-1705 *BlmGWL*
Aulson, Patrick J. 1951- *WhoIns 94*
Ault, Addison 1933- *WhoMW 93*
Ault, George *WhoAmA 93N*
Ault, George Copeland 1891-1948 *WhoAmA 93N*
Ault, Hugh Joseph 1940- *WhoAm 94*
Ault, James Andrew 1953- *WhoAmL 94*
Ault, James Mase 1918- *WhoAm 94*
Ault, James William 1926- *WhoAm 94*
Ault, Marie d1951 *WhoHol 92*
Ault, Phillip H. 1914- *WhoWest 94*
Ault, Thomas Jefferson, III 1911- *WhoFI 94*
Ault, Wendy L. *WhoAmP 93*
Aultman, William Robert 1953- *WhoWest 94*
Aumale, Christian d' 1918- *IntWW 93*
Aumand, Ernest James, III *WhoWest 94*
Aumbry, Alan *ConAu 43NR, EncSF 93*
Aumer, Jean-Louis 1774?-1833 *IntDcB*
Aumoeualogo, Muafono *WhoAmP 93*
Aumont, Jean Pierre 1909- *IntMPA 94, WhoHol 92*
Aumont, Jean-Pierre 1911- *IntWW 93, WhoAm 94*
Aumont, Michel *WhoHol 92*
Aumont, Tina 1946- *WhoHol 92*
Aune, Leif Jorgen 1925- *IntWW 93*
Aune, R. Benjamin 1946- *WhoMW 93*
Aung San Suu Kyi *IntWW 93*
Aung San Suu Kyi 1945- *NobelP 91 [port], Who 94, WhoWomW 91*
Aunis, Dominique 1948- *WhoScEn 94*
Aunon, Jorge Ignacio 1942- *WhoHisp 94*
Aupaumut, Hendrick 1757-1830 *EncNAR*
Auping, Michael G. 1949- *WhoAm 94*
Auping, Michael Graham 1949- *WhoAmA 93*
Aupperle, Eric Max 1935- *WhoScEn 94*
Aura, Matti Ilmari 1943- *IntWW 93*
Aurand, Calvin W., Jr. 1930- *WhoAm 94, WhoFI 94*
Aurand, Charles Henry, Jr. 1932- *WhoAm 94, WhoWest 94*
Aurand, Douglas R. 1941- *WhoAmP 93*
Aurangzeb 1618-1707 *HisWorL [port]*
Aurbach, Gerald Donald 1927-1991 *WhAm 10*
Aurbach, Herbert Alexander 1924- *WhoAm 94*
Aureli, Aurelio fl. 1652-1708 *NewGrDO*
Aureli, Diana Margherita fl. 1691-1696 *NewGrDO*
Aurelius, George M. 1911- *IntMPA 94*
Aurell, John Karl 1935- *WhoAm 94*
Aurenche, Jean 1904-1992 *IntDcF 2-4*
Auribeau, Alexandre Hesmivy D' d1794 *WhWE*
Auric, Georges 1899-1983 *IntDcF 2-4, NewGrDO*
Auriemma, Louis Francis 1937- *WhoAm 94, WhoFI 94*
Auriemmo, Frank J., Jr. 1942- *WhoIns 94*
Auriemmo, Frank Joseph, Jr. 1942- *WhoAm 94*
Aurilia, Antonio 1942- *WhoScEn 94*
Aurin, Robert James 1943- *WhoAm 94*
Auringer, Amos Lewis 1963- *WhoWest 94*
Aurisicchio, Antonio c. 1710-1781 *NewGrDO*
Aurner, Robert Ray 1898- *WhoAm 94, WhoWest 94*
Aurner, Robert Ray, II 1927- *WhoFI 94, WhoScEn 94*
Aurnhammer, Thomas Walter 1958- *WhoWest 94*
Auroux, Jean 1942- *IntWW 93*
Aurrecoechea, Rafael 1962- *WhoHisp 94*
Ausbrooks, Beth Nelson 1930- *WhoBlA 94*
Ausby, Ellsworth Augustus 1942- *WhoAm 94, WhoAmA 93, WhoBlA 94*
Ausensi, Manuel 1919- *NewGrDO*
Ausere, Joe Morris 1929- *WhoAm 94*
Auses, John Paul 1949- *WhoScEn 94*
Aushev, Ruslan Sultanovich 1954- *LoBiDrD*
Auslander, Edith S. *WhoHisp 94*
Auslander, Jay Stuart *DrAPF 93*
Auslander, Jay Stuart 1964- *WhoAmL 94*
Auslander, Rose 1901-1988 *BlmGWL*
Auslander, Steven Lawrence 1959- *WhoAm 94*
Ausman, Jon Michael 1953- *WhoAmP 93*
Ausman, Robert K. 1933- *WhoAm 94*
Ausnehmer, John Edward 1954- *WhoAmL 94*
Auspitz, Jack C. 1942- *WhoAmL 94*
Auspitz, Josiah Lee 1941- *WhoAmP 93*
Aussem, Cilly 1909-1963 *BuCMET*
Aust, Anthony Ivall 1942- *Who 94*
Aust, Joe Bradley 1926- *WhoAm 94*
Aust, Steven Douglas 1938- *WhoAm 94*
Austad, Eric David 1944- *WhoMW 93*
Austad, Oscar *WhoMW 93*
Austad, Randall John 1956- *WhoAmP 93*
Austad, Tore 1935- *IntWW 93*
Austad, Vigdis 1954- *WhoAm 94*
Austell, Edward Callaway 1937- *WhoAm 94*
Austen, Hallie Iglehart 1947- *WhoWest 94*
Austen, Jane 1775-1817 *BlmGEL, BlmGWL*
Austen, K(arl) Frank 1928- *IntWW 93*
Austen, Karl Frank 1928- *WhoAm 94*
Austen, Leslie d1924 *WhoHol 92*
Austen, Ralph A. 1937- *WhoAm 94*
Austen, Shelli 1954- *WhoWest 94*
Austen, William Gerald 1930- *WhoAm 94*
Austen-Smith, Roy (David) 1924- *Who 94*
Auster, Lawrence Scott 1947- *WhoIns 94*
Auster, Paul *DrAPF 93*
Auster, Paul 1947- *EncSF 93, WhoAm 94, WrDr 94*
Austerberry, Sidney Denham 1908- *Who 94*
Austermann, Kurt 1937- *WhoWest 94*
Austgen, Robert Joseph 1932- *WrDr 94*
Austick, David 1920- *Who 94*
Austill, Allen 1927- *WhoAm 94*
Austin, Alan K. 1948- *WhoAmL 94*
Austin, Albert d1953 *WhoHol 92*
Austin, Ann Sheree 1960- *WhoAmL 94*
Austin, Arthur Donald, II 1932- *WhoAm 94*
Austin, Barbara Jean *WhoAmA 93*
Austin, Berit Synnove 1938- *WhoFI 94*
Austin, Bobby William 1944- *WhoBlA 94*
Austin, Brian Patrick 1938- *Who 94*
Austin, Bunny 1906- *BuCMET*
Austin, Carl Fulton, Sr. 1932- *WhoWest 94*
Austin, Carroll Eugene 1923- *WhoMW 93*
Austin, Catherine Brannelly 1955- *WhoAmL 94*
Austin, Cedric Ronald Jonah 1912- *WrDr 94*
Austin, Charles d1944 *WhoHol 92*
Austin, Charles Edwin 1928- *WhoAm 94*
Austin, Charles John 1934- *WhoAm 94*
Austin, Charles Louis 1948- *WhoScEn 94*
Austin, Charlotte 1933- *WhoHol 92*
Austin, Colin Francois Lloyd 1941- *IntWW 93, Who 94*
Austin, Colin Russell 1914- *Who 94*
Austin, Dan 1967- *WhoAmP 93*
Austin, Daniel Lynn 1952- *WhoWest 94*
Austin, Daniel William 1949- *WhoAmL 94*
Austin, Darrel 1907- *WhoAm 94, WhoAmA 93*
Austin, David Fletcher 1927- *WhoWest 94*
Austin, David Mayo 1923- *WhoAm 94*
Austin, Donald Thomas 1955- *WhoFI 94*
Austin, Doris Jean *DrAPF 93*
Austin, Dorothy Mayover 1931- *WhoFI 94*
Austin, E. V. *DrAPF 93*
Austin, Ed *WhoAmP 93*
Austin, Edith *WhoAmP 93*
Austin, Edwin A. d1937 *WhoHol 92*
Austin, Elizabeth c. 1800-1835? *NewGrDO*
Austin, Ellen Jane *WhoAmP 93*
Austin, Ernest Augustus 1932- *WhoBlA 94*
Austin, F(rederick) Britten 1885-1941 *EncSF 93*
Austin, Frank d1954 *WhoHol 92*
Austin, Frank 1933- *WhoBlA 94*
Austin, Frank Hutches, Jr. 1924- *WhoScEn 94*
Austin, Frederic 1872-1952 *NewGrDO*
Austin, Gary F. 1954- *WhoFI 94*
Austin, Gene d1972 *WhoHol 92*
Austin, George Bernard 1931- *Who 94*
Austin, George Lynn 1944- *WhoScEn 94*
Austin, Gerald Grant 1937- *WhoAm 94, WhoFI 94*
Austin, Grace Baliunas 1940- *WhoAm 94*
Austin, Harry Gregory 1936- *WhoAm 94, WhoAmL 94*
Austin, Harry Guiden 1917- *WhoAm 94*
Austin, Henry Wilfred 1906- *WrDr 94*
Austin, Inez J. *WhoScEn 94*
Austin, Isaac Edward 1969- *WhoBlA 94*
Austin, Jacob 1932- *Who 94, WhoAm 94*
Austin, James Albert 1931- *WhoScEn 94, WhoWest 94*
Austin, James Bliss 1904- *EncABHB 9*
Austin, James Howard, Jr. 1951- *WhoFI 94*
Austin, James P. 1900- *WhoBlA 94*
Austin, Janyth Yvonne 1958- *WhoBlA 94*
Austin, Jeanie Reed 1933- *WhoAmP 93*
Austin, Jere d1927 *WhoHol 92*
Austin, Jerry d1976 *WhoHol 92*
Austin, Jesse Hinnant, III 1954- *WhoAmL 94*
Austin, Jim 1957- *WrDr 94*
Austin, Jo-Anne 1925- *WhoAmA 93N*
Austin, Joan 1903- *BuCMET*
Austin, Johanna d1944 *WhoHol 92*
Austin, John David 1936- *WhoAm 94*
Austin, John DeLong 1935- *WhoAmL 94*
Austin, John Michael *Who 94*
Austin, John Norman 1937- *WhoAm 94*
Austin, Jonathan Loring 1748-1826 *WhAmRev*
Austin, Joyce Phillips 1923- *WhoBlA 94*
Austin, Karen *WhoHol 92*
Austin, L. Kathleen 1949- *WhoWest 94*
Austin, Larry 1930- *WhoFI 94*
Austin, Lemuel, Jr. *WhoAmP 93*
Austin, Lisa Susan Coleman 1963- *WhoScEn 94*
Austin, Lloyd James 1915- *Who 94*
Austin, Lois d1957 *WhoHol 92*
Austin, M(ichel) M(ervyn) 1943- *WrDr 94*
Austin, Margaret Elizabeth 1933- *WhoWomW 91*
Austin, Marshall Edward 1957- *WhoFI 94*
Austin, Mary 1864-1934 *BlmGWL*
Austin, Mary Jane 1935- *WhoBlA 94*
Austin, Max Eugene 1933- *WhoAm 94*
Austin, Michael (Trescawen) 1927- *Who 94*
Austin, Mike Gerard 1954- *WhoAmP 93*
Austin, Page Insley 1942- *WhoAmL 94*
Austin, Pamela 1942- *WhoHol 92*
Austin, Pat 1937- *WhoAmA 93*
Austin, Patti 1948- *WhoBlA 94*
Austin, Paul Thomas 1943- *WhoMW 93*
Austin, Penelope *DrAPF 93*
Austin, Peter (Murray) 1921- *Who 94*
Austin, Phil *WhoCom*
Austin, Phil 1910- *WhoAmA 93*
Austin, Philip Edward 1942- *WhoAm 94*
Austin, Ralph Leroy 1929- *WhoScEn 94*
Austin, Randolph Lee 1940- *WhoAm 94*
Austin, Ray 1932- *ConTFT 11, IntMPA 94*
Austin, Raymond Darrel 1953- *WhoAmL 94*
Austin, Richard *EncSF 93*
Austin, Richard 1926- *WrDr 94*
Austin, Richard H. 1913- *WhoAm 94, WhoAmP 93, WhoBlA 94, WhoMW 93*
Austin, Richard William 1931- *WhoAm 94, WhoAmL 94*
Austin, Robert B. 1940- *WhoAm 94*
Austin, Robert Brendon 1956- *WhoScEn 94*
Austin, Robert Clarke 1931- *WhoAm 94, WhoWest 94*
Austin, Robert Eugene, Jr. 1937- *WhoAm 94, WhoAmL 94, WhoFI 94*
Austin, Roger (Mark) 1940- *Who 94*
Austin, Ronald Ralph 1933- *WhoAmL 94*
Austin, Russell Anderson, Jr. 1930- *WhoAmP 93*
Austin, Sam M. 1933- *WhoAm 94, WhoScEn 94*
Austin, Sarah Short 1933- *WhoBlA 94*
Austin, Spencer Peter 1909- *WhoAm 94*
Austin, Sue A. *DrAPF 93*
Austin, Summer (Francis) 1888-1981 *NewGrDO*
Austin, T. Edward 1926- *WhoAm 94*
Austin, Teri 1959- *WhoHol 92*
Austin, Terry *WhoHol 92*
Austin, Timothy *WhoAm 94*
Austin, Tom Noell 1916- *WhoAm 94*
Austin, Tracy *NewYTBS 93 [port]*

Austin, Tracy 1962- BuCMET
Austin, Warren R. 1877-1962 HisDcKW
Austin, William d1975 WhoHol 92
Austin, William Lamont 1915- WhoAm 94
Austin, William W. 1920- WrDr 94
Austin-Lazarus, Phyllis Chappell 1962- WhoWest 94
Austin-Nuhfer, Olive H. 1933- WhoAmA 93
Austin-Smith, Michael Gerard 1944- Who 94
Austin-Walker, John Eric 1944- Who 94
Auston, David Henry 1940- WhoAm 94
Austral, Florence 1894-1968 NewGrDO
Australia, Primate of Who 94
Australia, North-West, Bishop of 1938- Who 94
Austregesilo De Athayde, Belarmino Maria 1898- IntWW 93
Austrian, Neil R. 1940- WhoAm 94
Austrian, Robert 1916- IntWW 93, WhoAm 94, WhoScEn 94
Austwick, Kenneth 1927- Who 94
Ausubel, Sheva 1896-1957 WhoAmA 93N
Autant-Lara, Claude IntMPA 94
Autant-Lara, Claude 1901- IntWW 93
Autele, Faofamo WhoAmP 93
Auten, David Charles 1938- WhoAm 94
Auten, Dean Garland 1937- WhoAmP 93
Auten, Donald R. 1946- WhoAmL 94
Auten, John Harold 1922- WhoAm 94
Autenreith, Ferdinand 1772-1835 EncSPD
Antera, Michael Edward 1938- WhoAm 94, WhoFI 94
Auteuil, Daniel WhoHol 92
Auteuil, Daniel 1950- IntMPA 94
Auth, Robert R. 1926- WhoAmA 93
Auth, Robert Ralph 1926- WhoWest 94
Auth, Susan Handler 1939- WhoAmA 93
Auth, Tony 1942- WhoAm 94
Auth, Tony, Jr. 1942- WhoAmA 93
Authement, Louis Gerard 1964- WhoAmL 94
Autin, Ernest Anthony, II 1957- WhoAm 94
Autio, (A) Rudy 1926- WhoAmA 93
Autobee, George 1949- WhoHisp 94
Autolitano, Astrid 1938- WhoAm 94, WhoFI 94, WhoHisp 94
Autori, Franco 1903-1990 WhAm 10
Autrey, Henry Edward 1952- WhoAmL 94
Autrey, Robert Luis 1932- WhoFI 94
Autrum, Hansjochem 1907- IntWW 93
Autry, Alan WhoHol 92
Autry, Carolyn 1940- WhoAm 94, WhoAmA 93
Autry, Gene 1907- IntMPA 94, WhoAm 94, WhoFI 94, WhoHol 92, WhoWest 94
Autry, James A(rthur) 1933- WrDr 94
Autry, Robert F. 1940- WhoAm 94, WhoFI 94
Autton, Norman (William James) 1920- WrDr 94
Auty, Richard Mossop 1920- Who 94
Auvenshine, William R. 1937- WhoAm 94
Auvil, Kenneth William 1925- WhoAmA 93
Auvinen, Thomas Roger 1939- WhoIns 94
Auvray, Jean-Claude 1942- NewGrDO
Auwarter, Franklin Paul 1934- WhoAm 94
Auwers, Stanley John 1923- WhoAm 94
Auwerx, Johan Henri 1958- WhoScEn 94
Auxentios 1953- WhoAm 94
Auza, Enrique Alfredo 1942- WhoHisp 94
Ava, Frau d1127 BlmGWL
Avakian, John WhoAmA 93
Avakoff, Joseph Carnegie 1936- WhoWest 94
Avalier, Don d1973 WhoHol 92
Avalle-Arce, Juan Bautista 1927- WhoAm 94
Avallone, Anthony Francis 1926- WhoAmL 94
Avallone, Anthony Vincent 1947- WhoAmP 93
Avallone, Lawrence Joseph 1949- WhoAmL 94
Avallone, Michael (Angelo), Jr. 1924- EncSF 93
Avallone, Michael (Angelo, Jr.) 1924- WrDr 94
Avallone, Michael Angelo 1924- WhoAm 94
Avalon, Frankie 1939- WhoHol 92
Avalon, Frankie 1940- IntMPA 94, WhoAm 94
Avalon, Phillip 1945- WhoHol 92
Avalos, Andy Anthony 1956- WhoHisp 94
Avalos, Luis 1954- WhoHol 92
Avalos, Martin Eduardo 1959- WhoHisp 94
Avant, David Alonzo, Jr. 1919- WhoAm 94
Avant, David Louis 1943- WhoAmP 93
Avant, Grady, Jr. 1932- WhoAm 94, WhoAmL 94
Avant, Robert Frank 1937- WhoAm 94
Avants, Beecher WhoAmP 93
Avara, R. Charles 1932- WhoAmP 93
Avasthi, Kokila Pradeep 1946- WhoMW 93
Avasthi, Ram Bandhu 1941- WhoScEn 94
Avdeyeva, Larisa (Ivanovna) 1925- NewGrDO
Avebury, Baron 1928- Who 94
Avebury, Lady 1934- Who 94
Aved, Barry 1943- WhoFI 94
Avedian, Leonard V. 1934- WhoWest 94
Avedis, Howard WrDr 94
Avedisian, Armen G. 1926- WhoAm 94
Avedisian, Edward 1936- WhoAm 94, WhoAmA 93
Avedon, Barry 1941- WhoAmA 93
Avedon, Doe 1928- IntMPA 94, WhoHol 92
Avedon, Richard 1923- IntWW 93, WhoAm 94, WhoAmA 93, WrDr 94
Avelar, Carlos WhoHisp 94
Aveline, Claude 1901- IntWW 93
Aveling, Alan John 1928- Who 94
Aveling, Hugh ConAu 140
Aveling, J(ohn) C(edric) H(ugh) 1917-1993 ConAu 140, WrDr 94N
Avellaneda, La BlmGWL
Avellino, Bernard Joseph 1937- WhoAmP 93
Aven, Petr Olegovich 1955- LoBiDrD
Aven, Piotr Olegovich 1955- IntWW 93
Avendaño, Fausto 1941- WhoHisp 94
Avendano, Tania 1963- WhoScEn 94
Avendt, Raymond Joseph, III 1948- WhoFI 94
Avenell, William d1976 WhoHol 92
Avenel-Navara, Cheryl Ann 1947- WhoMW 93
Aveni, Virginia Lee 1933- WhoAmP 93
Avenna, Paul Robert 1943- WhoHisp 94
Avenson, Donald Dean 1944- WhoAmP 93
Avent, Anthony WhoBlA 94
Avent, Edwin Vernon 1962- WhoBlA 94
Avent, Jacques Myron 1940- WhoBlA 94
Averara, Diana Margherita NewGrDO
Averara, Pietro d' d1720 NewGrDO
Averbach, Benjamin L. 1919- WhoAmP 93
Averback, Hy 1925- IntMPA 94
Averbakh, Yury Lvovich 1922- LoBiDrD
Averbuch, Ilan 1953- WhoAmA 93
Averbuck, Clayton C. 1950- WhoAmL 94
Averch, Harvey Allan 1935- WhoAm 94
Averill, Barry William 1938- WhoMW 93
Averill, Bruce Alan 1948- WhoAm 94, WhoScEn 94
Averill, Esther (Holden) 1902- WrDr 94
Averill, James Reed 1935- WhoAm 94
Averill, Lloyd James, Jr. 1923- WhoAm 94
Averill, Marilyn 1946- WhoAmL 94, WhoWest 94
Averill, Thomas Fox DrAPF 93
Averitt, Kip 1954- WhoAmP 93
Averitt, Richard Garland, III 1945- WhoFI 94
Aversa, Dolores Sejda 1932- WhoFI 94
Avery, Alan Douglas 1953- WhoAmL 94
Avery, Anne Forster 1938- WhoMW 93
Avery, Bruce Edward 1949- WhoAmL 94
Avery, Bryce David 1965- WhoWest 94
Avery, Cameron Scott 1938- WhoAm 94
Avery, Charles d1926 WhoHol 92
Avery, Charles 1938- WhoBlA 94
Avery, Charles Carrington 1933- WhoScEn 94
Avery, Dennis T. 1946- WhoAmP 93
Avery, Dennis Teel 1936- WhoMW 93
Avery, Donald Hills 1937- WhoAm 94
Avery, Ed Blandford 1931- WhoAmP 93
Avery, Emerson Roy, Jr. 1954- WhoAmL 94
Avery, Eugene d1975 WhoHol 92
Avery, Frances 1910- WhoAmA 93
Avery, George Allen 1931- WhoAm 94
Avery, Gerald Kenneth 1953- WhoMW 93
Avery, Gillian (Elise) 1926- SmATA 75 [port], WrDr 94
Avery, Gillian Elise 1926- Who 94
Avery, Gordon Bennett 1931- WhoAm 94
Avery, Graham John Lloyd 1943- Who 94
Avery, Herbert B. 1933- WhoBlA 94
Avery, James WhoBlA 94, WhoHol 92
Avery, James Knuckey 1921- WhoAm 94
Avery, James Royle 1925- Who 94
Avery, James S. 1923- WhoBlA 94
Avery, James Stephen 1923- WhoAm 94
Avery, James Thomas, III 1945- WhoAmL 94
Avery, Jan Mariann 1959- WhoFI 94
Avery, Jeromye Lee 1949- WhoBlA 94
Avery, John Ernest 1940- Who 94
Avery, Louis King 1951- WhoFI 94
Avery, Luther James 1923- WhoAm 94, WhoAmL 94
Avery, Margaret WhoHol 92
Avery, Mary Ellen 1927- IntWW 93, WhoAm 94, WhoScEn 94
Avery, Michael T. 1952- WhoAmP 93
Avery, Milton 1893-1965 WhoAmA 93N
Avery, Myrtilla d1959 WhoAmA 93N
Avery, Oswald Theodore 1877-1955 WorScD
Avery, Patricia d1973 WhoHol 92
Avery, Percy Leonard 1915- Who 94
Avery, Phyllis 1924- WhoHol 92
Avery, Ralph Hillyer 1906-1976 WhoAmA 93N
Avery, Richard EncSF 93
Avery, Richard Eugene 1935- WhoWest 94
Avery, Robert Dean 1944- WhoAm 94
Avery, Roger Webster 1938- WhoAmL 94
Avery, Roy Who 94
Avery, Stephen Goodrich 1938- WhoAmP 93
Avery, Steven Thomas 1970- WhoAm 94
Avery, Susan Kathryn 1950- WhoAm 94, WhoScEn 94, WhoWest 94
Avery, Tex 1907-1980 IntDcF 2-4
Avery, Tol d1973 WhoHol 92
Avery, Val WhoHol 92
Avery, Waddell 1928- WhoBlA 94
Avery, William Barton 1946- WhoMW 93
Avery, William Harold 1943- WhoAmL 94
Avery, William Henry 1911- WhoAmP 93
Avery, William Hinckley 1912- IntWW 93, WhoAm 94
Avery, William Joseph 1940- WhoAm 94, WhoFI 94
Avery Jones, Francis 1910- Who 94
Avery Jones, John Francis 1940- Who 94
Averyt, Gayle Owen 1933- WhoAm 94, WhoFI 94, WhoIns 94
Avgousti, Marios 1966- WhoScEn 94
Avi ConAu 42NR
Avi 1937- TwCYAW, WhoAm 94, WrDr 94
Aviado, Domingo M. 1924- WhoAm 94, WhoAsA 94
Avian, Bob 1937- WhoAm 94
Avice, Edwige 1945- IntWW 93, WhoWomW 91
Avidom (Mahler-Kalkstein), Menahem 1908- IntWW 93
Avidom, Menahem 1908- NewGrDO
Aviel, Jo Ann B. Fagot 1942- WhoWest 94
Avil, Richard D., Jr. 1948- WhoAm 94, WhoAmL 94
Avila, Arthur Julian 1917- WhoMW 93
Avila, Carlos Francisco 1925- WhoHisp 94
Avila, David A. 1953- WhoHisp 94
Avila, Eduardo E. 1948- WhoHisp 94
Avila, Edward J. 1943- WhoHisp 94
Avila, Eli Narciso 1959- WhoHisp 94
Avila, Elza S. 1931- WhoHisp 94
Avila, Fernando Bastos de 1918- IntWW 93
Avila, Humberto Nuño 1954- WhoHisp 94
Avila, Joaquin G. 1948- WhoHisp 94
Avila, Joe Martinez 1937- WhoHisp 94
Avila, John WhoHisp 94
Avila, Juan Marcos 1959- WhoHisp 94
Avila, Pablo 1949- WhoHisp 94
Avila, Pedro Arias De c. 1442-1531 WhWE
Avila, Philip Gerard 1956- WhoHisp 94
Avila, Rafael Urbano 1930- WhoHisp 94
Avila, Ralph 1957- WhoHisp 94
Avila, Raul 1959- WhoHisp 94, WhoWest 94
Avila, Vernon L. 1941- WhoHisp 94
Avila, William Thaddeus 1954- WhoAmL 94
Avildsen, John G. 1935- IntMPA 94
Avildsen, John Guilbert 1935- WhoAm 94
Aviles, Arthur 1963- WhoHisp 94
Aviles, Brian Andrew 1959- WhoHisp 94
Aviles, Carmelo Anibal, Sr. 1932- WhoHisp 94
Aviles, Christopher B. 1957- WhoHisp 94
Avilés, Juan 1905- WhoHisp 94
Aviles, Juan Carlos 1957- WhoHisp 94
Aviles, Patricio Ubaldo 1951- WhoHisp 94
Avilés, Pedro WhoHisp 94
Aviles, Pedro Menendez De WhWE
Aviles, Rick 1956- WhoHol 92
Aviles, Rosemarie 1957- WhoHisp 94
Avilés Cordero, Leonor 1941- WhoHisp 94
Avilova, Lidiia Alekseevna 1864?-1943 BlmGWL
Avina-Rhodes, Nina Alvarado 1944- WhoFI 94
Avineri, Shlomo 1933- IntWW 93
Avinoff, Andrey 1884-1948 WhoAmA 93N
Avino Pepls, Joaquin WhoHisp 94
Avis, Deborah Kah 1959- WhoAmL 94
Avis, Robert Grier 1931- WhoAm 94
Avise, John Charles 1948- WhoAm 94
Avison, David 1937- WhoAm 94, WhoAmA 93
Avison, Margaret 1918- BlmGWL
Avissar, Yael Julia 1946- WhoScEn 94
Avitabile, George P. WhoAmP 93
Aviv, David Gordon 1928- WhoScEn 94
Aviv, Jonathan Enoch 1960- WhoScEn 94
Avlon-Daphnis, Helen Basilea 1932- WhoAmA 93
Avlonitis, Vassilis WhoHol 92
Avner, Brett Kim 1949- WhoMW 93
Avner, Yehuda 1928- IntWW 93, Who 94
Avnet, John Benjamin 1933- WhoWest 94
Avnet, Jon 1949- ConTFT 11, IntMPA 94
Avnet, Pearl d1987 WhoHol 92
Avni, Abraham 1921- WrDr 94
Avni, Haim 1930- WrDr 94
Avogadro, Amedeo 1776-1856 WorScD [port]
Avoglio, Christina Maria fl. 1727-1746 NewGrDO
Avolio, John 1958- WhoScEn 94
Avolio, Wendy Freedman 1953- WhoWest 94
Avon, Roger WhoHol 92
Avon, Violet d1984 WhoHol 92
Avon Comedy Four WhoCom
Avondano, Pedro Antonio 1714-1782 NewGrDO
Avonde, Richard WhoHol 92
Avonside, Lady 1917- Who 94
Avonside, Rt. Hon. Lord 1914- Who 94
Avos, Girolamo NewGrDO
Avossa, Giuseppe 1708-1796 NewGrDO
Avouris, Phaedon 1945- WhoScEn 94
Avram, Henriette Davidson 1919- WhoAm 94
Avramides, Anita 1952- WrDr 94
Avramis, Tom Peter 1955- WhoWest 94
Avramovic, Dragoslav 1919- WrDr 94
Avramovich, Michael Paul 1952- WhoFI 94
Avranches, Henry of d1262? DcNaB MP
Avrett, John Glenn 1929- WhoAm 94
Avril, Jack Joseph 1932- WhoWest 94
Avril, Pierre 1930- IntWW 93
Avril, Prosper IntWW 93
Avrit, Richard Calvin 1932- WhoAm 94
Avshalomov, Aaron 1894-1965 NewGrDO
Avtsyn, Aleksandr Pavlovich 1908- IntWW 93
Avveduto, Saverio 1924- IntWW 93
Awad, Marie Elizabeth 1954- WhoMW 93
Awad, Muhammad Hadi 1934- IntWW 93, Who 94
Awadallah, Babikir 1917- IntWW 93
Awais, George Musa 1929- WhoAm 94
Awak, Shehu 1932- Who 94
Awakuni, Gene I. WhoAsA 94
Awalt, Elizabeth Grace 1956- WhoAmA 93
Awalt, Francis Gloyd 1895- WhAm 10
Awan, Ahmad Noor 1942- WhoScEn 94
Awan, Ghulam Mustafa 1940- WhoScEn 94
Awdry, Christopher Vere 1940- WrDr 94
Awdry, Daniel (Edmund) 1924- Who 94
Awdry, W(ilbert) V(ere) 1911- WrDr 94
Awdry, Wilbert Vere 1911- Who 94
Awerbuch, Shimon 1946- WhoFI 94, WhoScEn 94
Awkard, Julita Castro 1929- WhoBlA 94
Awl, Charlotte Jane 1935- WhoMW 93
Awl, William EncSPD
Awolowo, Obafemi Awo 1909-1987 BlkWr 2
Awoonor, Kofi DrAPF 93
Awoonor, Kofi 1935- WrDr 94
Awoonor, Kofi (Nyidevu) 1935- BlkWr 2, ConAu 42NR
Awoonor, Kofi Nyidevu 1935- IntWW 93
Awoonor-Williams, George BlkWr 2, ConAu 42NR
Awramik, Stanley Michael 1946- WhoAm 94
Awret, Irene 1921- WrDr 94
Awschalom, David Daniel 1956- WhoScEn 94
Awtrey, Dennis 1948- BasBi
Awtrey, Jim L. 1943- WhoAm 94
Ax, Emanuel 1949- WhoAm 94
Axam, John Arthur 1930- WhoAm 94, WhoBlA 94
Axdahl, Evelyn Irene 1929- WhoAmP 93, WhoWomW 91
Axe, Albert R., Jr. 1954- WhoAmL 94
Axe, Harry d1955 WhoHol 92
Axe, John Randolph 1938- WhoAm 94
Axel, Bernard 1946- WhoFI 94
Axel, Gabriel 1918- IntMPA 94
Axel, Leon 1947- WhoScEn 94
Axel-Lute, Paul 1945- WhoAmL 94
Axelman, Arthur 1944- IntMPA 94
Axelrad, Irving Irmas 1915- WhoAm 94
Axelrad, Stephen 1943- WhoWest 94
Axelrod, Arnold Mark 1943- WhoFI 94
Axelrod, Bernadette Bonner 1963- WhoMW 93

Azumano, George Ichiro 1918-
  WhoAsA 94, WhoWest 94
Azumaya, Goro 1920- *WhoAsA 94*
Azus, Louis 1936- *WhoIns 94*
Azuz, David 1942- *WhoAmA 93*
Azzali, Augusto 1863-1907 *NewGrDO*
Azzara, Candice 1947- *WhoHol 92*
Azzarello, Russell J. 1942- *WhoAmP 93*
Azzato, Louis E. 1930- *IntWW 93*
Azzato, Louis Enrico 1930- *WhoAm 94,*
  WhoFI 94
Azzi, Daniel W. 1966- *WhoScEn 94*
Azziz, Ricardo 1958- *WhoHisp 94*
Azzolina, Joseph 1926- *WhoAmP 93*
Azzolini, Caterina fl. 1700-1708
  NewGrDO
Azzopardi, Marc Antoine 1940-
  WhoScEn 94
Azzouni, Jody *DrAPF 93*

B

B(eck), Rosemarie *WhoAmA 93*
Ba, Babacar 1930- *IntWW 93*
Ba, Mariama 1929-1981 *BlkWr 2, BlmGWL, ConAu 141*
Ba, Sy Maimouna *WhoWomW 91*
Baab, William Eugene 1929- *WhoMW 93*
Baack, Dennis 1946- *WhoAmP 93*
Baack, Dennis G. 1946- *WhoAm 94, WhoMW 93*
Baack, John Edward 1936- *WhoAm 94*
Baade, Paul T. 1940- *WhoAmP 93*
Baade, Wilhelm Heinrich Walter 1893-1960 *WorScD*
Baal, Karin 1940- *WhoHol 92*
Baalman, Robert Joseph 1939- *WhoScEn 94*
Baantjer, Albert Cornelis 1923- *ConAu 141*
Baaqee, Susanne Inez 1952- *WhoBlA 94*
Baar, James A. 1929- *WhoAm 94, WhoFI 94*
Baar, John Greenfield, II 1952- *WhoMW 93*
Baars, Bernard Joseph 1946- *WhoWest 94*
Baarsma, William Henry 1942- *WhoAmP 93*
Baarveld-Schlaman, E.M.P. *WhoWomW 91*
Baas, Jacquelynn 1948- *WhoAm 94, WhoAmA 93, WhoWest 94*
Baas, R. Ryan 1963- *WhoMW 93*
Baatz, Leroy Michael 1951- *WhoMW 93*
Baba, Corneliu 1906- *IntWW 93*
Baba, Encik Abdul Ghafar Bin 1925- *IntWW 93*
Baba, Isamu 1923- *WhoFI 94*
Baba, Marietta Lynn 1949- *WhoAm 94, WhoWW 93*
Baba, Thomas Frank 1957- *WhoFI 94*
Baba, Yoshinobu 1958- *WhoScEn 94*
Babadzhan, Ramz 1921- *IntWW 93*
Babangida, Ibrahim 1941- *IntWW 93*
Babar, Raza Ali 1947- *WhoFI 94*
Babar the Conqueror 1483-1530 *HisWorL [port]*
Babauta, Juan N. 1953- *WhoAmP 93*
Babauta, Juan Nekai 1953- *WhoAm 94*
Babayans, Emil 1951- *WhoFI 94, WhoWest 94*
Babayev, Agadzhan 1929- *IntWW 93*
Babb, Albert Leslie 1925- *IntWW 93, WhoAm 94*
Babb, Alvin Charles 1932- *WhoFI 94*
Babb, Billie Margaret 1918- *WhoAmP 93*
Babb, Donald Lynn 1953- *WhoAmL 94*
Babb, Dorothy *WhoHol 92*
Babb, Douglas *WhoAmL 94*
Babb, Frank Edward 1932- *WhoAm 94*
Babb, Harold 1926- *WhoAm 94*
Babb, Julius Wistar, III 1946- *WhoAm 94*
Babb, Lawrence Alan *WhoAm 94*
Babb, Michael Paul 1944- *WhoAm 94*
Babb, Ralph Wheeler, Jr. 1949- *WhoAm 94*
Babb, Sanora 1907- *WrDr 94*
Babb, Valerie (Melissa) 1955- *BlkWr 2, ConAu 142*
Babb, Valerie M. 1955- *WhoBlA 94*
Babb, Wylie Sherrill 1940- *WhoAm 94*
Babbage, Charles 1791-1871 *WorInv*
Babbage, Charles 1792-1871 *EncSF 93*
Babbage, Robert 1951- *WhoAmP 93*
Babbage, Robert A. *WhoAm 94*

Babbage, Stuart Barton 1916- *WrDr 94*
Babbage, Wilfred *WhoHol 92*
Babbel, David Frederick 1949- *WhoAm 94*
Babbi, Gregorio (Lorenzo) 1708-1768 *NewGrDO*
Babbie, Leon F. 1926- *WhoAmP 93*
Babbin, Jed Lloyd 1950- *WhoAm 94, WhoAmL 94*
Babbini, Matteo 1754-1816 *NewGrDO*
Babbit, Bruce 1938- *IntWW 93*
Babbit, Harold W. 1941- *WhoAmL 94*
Babbitt, Bruce *NewYTBS 93 [port]*
Babbitt, Bruce 1938- *CngDr 93, News 94-1 [port]*
Babbitt, Bruce E. 1938- *WhoAmP 93*
Babbitt, Bruce Edward 1938- *WhoAm 94*
Babbitt, Gary D. 1946- *WhoAmL 94*
Babbitt, Harriett C. 1947- *WhoAmP 93*
Babbitt, Harry *WhoHol 92*
Babbitt, Milton Bryon 1916- *AmCulL*
Babbitt, Milton Byron 1916- *IntWW 93, WhoAm 94*
Babbitt, Natalie 1932- *WrDr 94*
Babbitt, Orrin d1941 *WhoHol 92*
Babbitt, Samuel Fisher 1929- *WhoAm 94*
Babbs, Junious C., Sr. 1924- *WhoBlA 94*
Babbush, Howard Edward 1941- *WhoAmP 94*
Babby, Ellen Reisman 1950- *WhoAm 94*
Babby, Lon S. 1951- *WhoAmL 94*
Babchuk, Nicholas 1922- *WhoAm 94*
Babcock, Barbara *WhoHol 92*
Babcock, Barbara Allen 1938- *WhoAm 94, WhoAmL 94*
Babcock, Carmel Ann 1929- *WhoAmP 93*
Babcock, Charles Luther 1924- *WhoAm 94*
Babcock, Charles Lynde, IV 1949- *WhoAm 94, WhoAmL 94*
Babcock, Charles Witten, Jr. 1941- *WhoAmL 94, WhoMW 93*
Babcock, Daniel Lawrence 1930- *WhoAm 94*
Babcock, Edward C. *WhAm 10*
Babcock, Elkanah Andrew 1941- *WhoScEn 94*
Babcock, Gerald Thomas 1946- *WhoAm 94*
Babcock, Horace 1912- *WhoAm 94, WhoWest 94*
Babcock, Horace W. 1912- *IntWW 93, WhoScEn 94*
Babcock, Horace Welcome 1912- *Who 94*
Babcock, Jack Emerson 1915- *WhoAm 94*
Babcock, Janice Beatrice 1942- *WhoFI 94, WhoMW 93, WhoScEn 94*
Babcock, Jeff Charles 1960- *WhoFI 94*
Babcock, Jo 1954- *WhoAmA 93*
Babcock, Karen Kay Shook 1941- *WhoMW 93*
Babcock, Keith Moss 1951- *WhoAmL 94*
Babcock, Lewis Thornton 1943- *WhoAm 94, WhoAmL 94, WhoWest 94*
Babcock, Lyndon Ross, Jr. 1934- *WhoAm 94*
Babcock, Michael Ward 1944- *WhoAm 94, WhoFI 94, WhoMW 93, WhoScEn 94*
Babcock, Patrick Gerard 1962- *WhoMW 93*
Babcock, Peter Heartz 1949- *WhoAm 94*

Babcock, Robert Evans 1943- *WhoAm 94, WhoAmL 94*
Babcock, Rufus 1798-1875 *DcAmReB 2*
Babcock, Stephen Lee 1939- *WhoAmL 94*
Babcock, Theodore d1930 *WhoHol 92*
Babcock, Warner King 1951- *WhoFI 94*
Babcock, Wendell Keith 1925- *WhoMW 93*
Babe, Thomas 1941- *ConDr 93, WrDr 94*
Babej, Peter 1963- *WhoAmL 94*
Babel, Henry Wolfgang 1933- *WhoWest 94*
Babel, Isaak (Emmanuilovich) 1894-1941 *RfGShF*
Babel, Robert Richard 1950- *WhoFI 94*
Babenco, Hector 1946- *IntMPA 94*
Babenko, Hector 1946- *IntWW 93*
Babenko, Vladimir Dmitrievich 1931- *LoBiDrD*
Baber, Alice 1928-1982 *WhoAmA 93N*
Baber, Asa *DrAPF 93*
Baber, Asa 1936- *ConAu 140*
Baber, Bruce W. 1955- *WhoAmL 94*
Baber, Ceola Ross 1950- *WhoBlA 94*
Baber, Ernest George 1924- *Who 94*
Baber, Lucky Larry 1949- *WhoBlA 94*
Baber, Wilbur H., Jr. 1926- *WhoAmL 94, WhoFI 94*
Babero, Andras F. 1955- *WhoHisp 94*
Babero, Bert Bell 1918- *WhoBlA 94*
Babiarz, John Edward 1915- *WhoAmP 93*
Babich, Michael Wayne 1945- *WhoAm 94*
Babicky, Charlotte L. *DrAPF 93*
Babics, Antal d1992 *IntWW 93N*
Babicz, William Matthew 1950- *WhoFI 94*
Babikian, George H. *WhoFI 94*
Babikian, Khatchik Diran 1924- *IntWW 93*
Babilee, Jean 1923- *IntDcB [port]*
Babilonia, Ana J. *WhoHisp 94*
Babin, Claude Hunter 1924- *WhoAm 94*
Babin, Mara L. 1950- *WhoAm 94, WhoAmL 94*
Babin, Richard Weyrd 1942- *WhoAm 94*
Babin, Steven Michael 1954- *WhoScEn 94*
Babin, Victor d1972 *WhoHol 92*
Babin, William Albert, Jr. 1929- *WhoAmP 93*
Babineau, Anne Serzan 1951- *WhoAm 94*
Babineau, Margaret Louise 1947- *WhoMW 93*
Babinec, Gehl P. *WhoFI 94*
Babinec, George Frederick 1957- *WhoWest 94*
Babington, Anthony Patrick 1920- *Who 94, WrDr 94*
Babington, Charles Martin, III 1944- *WhoAm 94*
Babington, Robert John 1920- *Who 94*
Babington, William 1944- *Who 94*
Babington-Browne, Gillian Brenda 1949- *Who 94*
Babington Smith, Constance 1912- *WrDr 94*
Babior, Daniel 1953- *WhoAmA 93*
Babits, Mihaly 1883-1941 *EncSF 93*
Babiuc, Victor 1938- *IntWW 93*
Babiuch, Edward 1927- *IntWW 93*
Babiuk, Lorne Alan 1946- *WhoScEn 94*
Babjak, Richard Steven, Jr. 1963- *WhoMW 93*

Babler, Wayne E. 1915- *WhoAm 94, WhoAmL 94*
Babler, Wayne E., Jr. 1942- *WhoAm 94, WhoAmL 94*
Bablitch, William A. 1941- *WhoAm 94, WhoAmL 94, WhoAmP 93*
Babois, Marguerite-Victoire 1760-1839 *BlmGWL*
Babson, David Leveau 1911- *WhoAm 94*
Babson, Irving K. 1936- *WhoAm 94, WhoFI 94*
Babson, Marian *WrDr 94*
Babson, Marshall B. 1945- *WhoAmL 94*
Babson, Stephen E. 1950- *WhoAmL 94*
Babst, Dean Voris 1921- *WhoWest 94*
Babst, James A. 1949- *WhoAmL 94*
Babu, Suresh Chandra 1961- *WhoFI 94*
Babula, William 1943- *WhoAm 94, WhoWest 94*
Babun, Teo Abraham 1948- *WhoFI 94*
Baburin, Sergey Nikolaevich 1959- *IntWW 93*
Baby Charlie Spafford d1935 *WhoHol 92*
Baby Early Gehrig d1982 *WhoHol 92*
Baby Jane *WhoHol 92*
Baby Le Roy 1932- *WhoHol 92*
Baby Marie *WhoHol 92*
Baby Peggy 1917- *WhoHol 92*
Baby Sandy 1938- *WhoHol 92*
Baby Sunshine d1917 *WhoHol 92*
Baca, Augustine Christobal 1944- *WhoHisp 94*
Baca, Bernal C. 1952- *WhoHisp 94*
Baca, Bettie 1943- *WhoHisp 94*
Baca, Dorothy M. *WhoHisp 94*
Baca, Elmo L. 1953- *WhoHisp 94*
Baca, E. Shirley *WhoAmP 93*
Baca, Fernie 1939- *WhoHisp 94*
Baca, Geraldine Tomasita 1962- *WhoHisp 94*
Baca, Gloria Yvonne 1957- *WhoHisp 94*
Baca, Guy A. 1936- *WhoHisp 94*
Baca, Jim R. 1945- *WhoAmP 93, WhoHisp 94*
Baca, Jimmy Santiago 1952- *HispLC [port], WhoBlA 94, WhoHisp 94*
Baca, Joe *WhoAmP 93*
Baca, Joe 1947- *WhoHisp 94*
Baca, Jose J. *WhoHisp 94*
Baca, Joseph F. 1936- *WhoAmP 93*
Baca, Joseph Francis 1936- *WhoAm 94, WhoAmL 94, WhoHisp 94, WhoWest 94*
Baca, Joseph P. *WhoHisp 94*
Baca, Judith *WhoHisp 94*
Baca, Lee F., Jr. 1944- *WhoHisp 94*
Baca, M. Carlota 1943- *WhoWest 94*
Baca, Maria A. *WhoHisp 94*
Baca, Mary Lou *WhoHisp 94*
Baca, Milton L. *WhoHisp 94*
Baca, Oswald G. 1942- *WhoHisp 94*
Baca, Patricia V. *WhoAmP 93*
Baca, Paul Anthony 1965- *WhoWest 94*
Baca, Polly B. 1941- *WhoHisp 94*
Baca, Richard 1942- *WhoHisp 94*
Baca, Robert T. *WhoHisp 94*
Baca, Rowena Joyce *WhoHisp 94*
Baca, Ruben Albert 1936- *WhoHisp 94*
Baca, Sacramento Henry, Jr. 1939- *WhoHisp 94*
Baca, Samuel Valdez 1949- *WhoHisp 94*
Baca, Steven Michael 1950- *WhoHisp 94*
Baca, Ted Paul 1941- *WhoHisp 94*
Baca, Theresa Marie 1950- *WhoHisp 94*

Baca, Virginia G. 1933- *WhoHisp 94*
Baca, Wilfred Ruben 1940- *WhoHisp 94*
Baca-Barragan, Polly 1941- *WhoAmP 93*
Bacall, Lauren 1924- *IntMPA 94, IntWW 93, WhoAm 94, WhoHol 92, WrDr 94*
Bacaloglu, Radu 1937- *WhoScEn 94*
Bacani, Nicanor-Guglielmo Vila 1947- *WhoScEn 94*
Bacarella, Flavia *WhoAmA 93*
Bacarisse, Salvador 1898-1963 *NewGrDO*
Baca Zinn, Maxine 1942- *WhoHisp 94*
Baccaloni, Salvatore d1969 *WhoHol 92*
Baccaloni, Salvatore 1900-1969 *NewGrDO [port]*
Baccelli, Giovanna c. 1753-1801 *IntDcB [port]*
Bacchiocchi, Norman d1978 *WhoHol 92*
Bacchus, James L. 1949- *WhoAm 94*
Bacchus, Jim 1949- *CngDr 93, WhoAmP 93*
Baccigaluppi, Roger John 1934- *WhoAm 94, WhoWest 94*
Baccini, Laurance Ellis 1945- *WhoAm 94, WhoAmL 94*
Baccouche, Hedi 1930- *IntWW 93*
Baccus, Janet Glee 1933- *WhoWest 94*
Baccus-Lobel, Shirley Ann 1945- *WhoAmL 94*
Bacevicius, John Anthony, V 1953- *WhoMW 93*
Bacewicz, Grazyna 1909-1969 *NewGrDO*
Bach, Alice (Hendricks) 1942- *TwCYAW*
Bach, Arthur James 1929- *WhoAm 94*
Bach, Barbara 1950- *WhoHol 92*
Bach, Catherine 1954- *IntMPA 94, WhoHol 92*
Bach, Dirk 1939- *WhoAmA 93*
Bach, George Leland 1915- *WhoAm 94*
Bach, Gunther 1928- *WhoScEn 94*
Bach, Jan (Morris) 1937- *NewGrDO*
Bach, Jan Morris 1937- *WhoAm 94*
Bach, Johann Christian 1735-1782 *DcNaB MP, NewGrDO*
Bach, John *WhoHol 92*
Bach, Lars 1934- *WhoScEn 94*
Bach, Laurence 1947- *WhoAmA 93*
Bach, Marcus 1906- *WhoAm 94*
Bach, Martin Wayne 1940- *WhoWest 94*
Bach, Michael Klaus 1931- *WhoMW 93*
Bach, Otto Karl 1909-1990 *WhoAmA 93N*
Bach, P. D. Q. *NewGrDO*
Bach, Reginald d1941 *WhoHol 92*
Bach, Richard 1936- *WrDr 94*
Bach, Richard D. 1934- *WhoAm 94*
Bach, Richard David 1936- *WhoAm 94*
Bach, Richard F. 1887-1968 *WhoAmA 93N*
Bach, Sabine *WhoHol 92*
Bach, Scott Lawrence 1962- *WhoAmL 94*
Bach, Stephan Bruno Heinrich 1959- *WhoScEn 94*
Bach, Steve Crawford 1921- *WhoAm 94*
Bach, Steven 1940- *ConAu 141*
Bacha, Edmar Lisboa 1942- *IntWW 93*
Bachand, Stephen E. 1938- *WhoFI 94*
Bacharach, Burt 1928- *IntMPA 94*
Bacharach, Burt 1929- *WhoAm 94*
Bacharach, Melvin Lewis 1924- *WhoAm 94*
Bachardy, Don 1934- *WhoAmA 93*
Bachas, Leonidas Gregory 1958- *WhoScEn 94*
Bache, Andrew Philip Foley 1939- *Who 94*
Bache, Douglas Albert 1951- *WhoAmP 93*
Bache, Ellyn *DrAPF 93*
Bache, Ellyn 1942- *WrDr 94*
Bache, Richard 1737-1811 *WhAmRev*
Bache, Theodore Stephen 1936- *WhoAm 94*
Bachel, Larry F. 1949- *WhoIns 94*
Bachelder, Jon Paul 1942- *WhoAmL 94*
Bachelder, Joseph Elmer, III 1932- *WhoAm 94*
Bachelet, Alfred 1864-1944 *NewGrDO*
Bachelor, Stephanie 1920- *WhoHol 92*
Bachelot-Narquin, Roselyne 1946- *WhoWomW 91*
Bachenberg, Steven Kurt 1947- *WhoFI 94*
Bachenheimer, Ralph James 1928- *WhoFI 94*
Bacher, Ali 1942- *IntWW 93*
Bacher, Ingeborg 1937- *WhoWomW 91*
Bacher, Judith St. George 1946- *WhoAm 94, WhoFI 94*
Bacher, Robert Fox 1905- *IntWW 93*
Bacher, Rosalie Wride 1925- *WhoWest 94*
Bacheracht, Terese von 1804-1852 *BlmGWL*
Bachert, Hildegard Gina 1921- *WhoAmA 93*
Bachert, Robert Frederic 1932- *WhoMW 93*
Bachi, Roberto 1909- *IntWW 93*
Bachicha, Joseph A. *WhoHisp 94*
Bachicha, Joseph Alfred *WhoMW 93, WhoScEn 94*
Bachicha, Willie A. 1952- *WhoHisp 94*
Bachilor, John c. 1615-1674 *DcNaB MP*
Bachini, Robert F. 1933- *WhoAmP 93*
Bachinski, Walter Joseph 1939- *WhoAmA 93*
Bachkosky, John M. 1939- *WhoScEn 94*
Bachli, Ronald W. 1940- *WhoAmL 94*
Bachman, Arthur 1947- *WhoAm 94*
Bachman, Brian Richard 1945- *WhoWest 94*
Bachman, Carol Christine 1959- *WhoFI 94*
Bachman, Clifford Albert 1958- *WhoScEn 94*
Bachman, David Christian 1934- *WhoAm 94*
Bachman, George 1933- *WhoAm 94*
Bachman, Henry Lee 1930- *WhoAm 94*
Bachman, Ilse 1924- *WhoAmP 93*
Bachman, James Vernon 1946- *WhoMW 93*
Bachman, John W(alter) 1916- *WrDr 94*
Bachman, Katharine Elizabeth 1953- *WhoAm 94*
Bachman, Kenneth Leroy, Jr. 1943- *WhoAmL 94*
Bachman, Leonard 1925- *WhoAm 94*
Bachman, Nathan Dulaney, IV 1935- *WhoAm 94*
Bachman, Neal Kenyon 1950- *WhoMW 93*
Bachman, Richard *EncSF 93, TwCYAW*
Bachman, Richard 1947- *WrDr 94*
Bachman, Robert Jay 1945- *WhoAmL 94*
Bachman, Ronald Elwood 1942- *WhoMW 93*
Bachman, Walter Crawford 1911-1991 *WhAm 10*
Bachmann, Albert Edward 1917- *WhoFI 94*
Bachmann, Donna Grace 1948- *WhoMW 93*
Bachmann, Fedor Wolfgang 1927- *WhoScEn 94*
Bachmann, Hermann 1869-1937 *NewGrDO*
Bachmann, Ingeborg 1926-1973 *BlmGWL [port], NewGrDO*
Bachmann, John William 1938- *WhoAm 94, WhoFI 94*
Bachmann, Richard Arthur 1944- *WhoAm 94*
Bachmann, Richard H. 1953- *WhoAmL 94*
Bachmeyer, Robert Wesley 1915- *WhoAm 94*
Bachmeyer, Thomas John 1942- *WhoScEn 94*
Bachner, Edward F., III 1945- *WhoMW 93*
Bacho, Norris V. 1954- *WhoAsA 94*
Bacho, Peter *WhoAsA 94*
Bachrach, Anne Jameson 1919- *WhoAmP 93*
Bachrach, Bradford K. 1910-1992 *WhAm 10*
Bachrach, Charles Lewis 1946- *WhoAm 94*
Bachrach, George *WhoAmP 93*
Bachrach, George J. 1948- *WhoAmL 94*
Bachrach, Howard L. 1920- *IntWW 93, WhoAm 94*
Bachrach, Ira Nathaniel 1938- *WhoAm 94*
Bachrach, Nancy 1948- *WhoAm 94*
Bachrach, Peter 1918- *WrDr 94*
Bachschmidt, (Johann) Anton (Adam) 1728-1797 *NewGrDO*
Bachtel, Ann Elizabeth 1928- *WhoWest 94*
Bachur, Nicholas Robert, Sr. 1933- *WhoAm 94*
Bachus, Benson Floyd 1917- *WhoFI 94, WhoScEn 94, WhoWest 94*
Bachus, Blaine Louis 1954- *WhoScEn 94*
Bachus, Marie Darsey 1940- *WhoBlA 94*
Bachus, Spencer *WhoAmP 93*
Bachus, Spencer 1947- *CngDr 93*
Bachus, Spencer 1948- *WhoAm 94*
Bachus, Walter Otis 1926- *WhoAm 94*
Bachus, William Earl 1940- *WhoAmP 93*
Bachynski, Morrel Paul 1930- *IntWW 93, WhoAm 94*
Bach-y-Rita, Paul 1934- *WhoAm 94*
Bacigalupa, Andrea 1923- *WhoAmA 93, WhoWest 94*
Bacigalupi, Louis d1966 *WhoHol 92*
Bacigalupo, Charles Anthony 1934- *WhoAm 94, WhoFI 94*
Bacino, Kathy E. 1940- *WhoAmP 93*
Back, George 1796-1878 *WhWE*
Back, Kathleen *Who 94*
Back, Kenneth John Campbell 1925- *Who 94*
Back, Leon B. 1912- *IntMPA 94*
Back, Patrick 1917- *Who 94*
Back, Paul d1993 *NewYTBS 93*
Back, Robert Wyatt 1936- *WhoFI 94, WhoMW 93*
Back, Sven-Erik 1919- *NewGrDO*
Backas, James Jacob 1926- *WhoAm 94*
Backberg, Bruce Allen 1948- *WhoAm 94*
Backe, John David 1932- *IntWW 93, WhoAm 94*
Backe, Pamela Renee 1955- *WhoWest 94*
Backenroth-Ohsako, Gunnel Anne Maj 1951- *WhoScEn 94*
Backenstoss, Henry Brightbill 1912- *WhoFI 94, WhoScEn 94*
Backer, Brian 1957- *WhoHol 92*
Backer, Bruce Everett 1955- *WhoWest 94*
Backer, David F. 1940- *WhoFI 94*
Backer, Gracia Yancy 1950- *WhoAmP 93*
Backer, Mary Barbara 1931- *WhoMW 93*
Backer, Matthias Henry, Jr. 1926- *WhoAm 94*
Backer, Michael A. 1944- *WhoAmL 94*
Backer, Terrance E. *WhoAmP 93*
Backer, William Montague 1926- *WhoAm 94, WhoFI 94*
Backes, Alice *WhoHol 92*
Backes, David James 1957- *WhoMW 93*
Backes, Frank d1923 *WhoHol 92*
Backes, Joan 1950- *WhoMW 93*
Backes, Richard J. 1925- *WhoAmP 93*
Backett, Edward Maurice 1916- *Who 94*
Backhaus, Ralph Andrew 1951- *WhoWest 94*
Backherms, Kathryn Anne 1955- *WhoMW 93*
Backhouse, David Miles 1939- *Who 94*
Backhouse, Jonathan 1907- *Who 94*
Backhouse, Jonathan Roger 1939- *Who 94*
Backhouse, Roger Bainbridge 1938- *Who 94*
Backis, Robert Joseph 1949- *WhoAm 94*
Backlinie, Susan 1947- *WhoHol 92*
Backlund, Gordon 1940- *WhoAmP 93*
Backlund, Ralph Theodore 1918- *WhoAm 94*
Backman, Ari Ismo 1961- *WhoScEn 94*
Backman, Gerald Stephen 1938- *WhoAm 94, WhoAmL 94*
Backman, Jack H. 1922- *WhoAmP 93*
Backof, Mary Elizabeth 1956- *WhoFI 94*
Backstrom, Don 1941- *WhoBlA 94*
Backstrom, James W. 1942- *WhoAmL 94*
Backstrom, Lathrop Gustaf 1895- *WhAm 10*
Backstrom, William M. 1954- *WhoAmL 94*
Backus, Bertha Gilman 1946- *WhoAmP 93*
Backus, Bradley 1950- *WhoBlA 94*
Backus, Charles Edward 1937- *WhoScEn 94, WhoWest 94*
Backus, Elaine Athene 1956- *WhoScEn 94*
Backus, George d1939 *WhoHol 92*
Backus, George Edward 1930- *IntWW 93, WhoAm 94, WrDr 94*
Backus, Georgia d1983 *WhoHol 92*
Backus, Henny c. 1918- *WhoHol 92*
Backus, Isaac 1724-1806 *DcAmReB 2, WhAmRev*
Backus, Jan 1947- *WhoAmP 93*
Backus, Jim d1989 *WhoHol 92*
Backus, Jim 1913-1989 *WhAm 10, WhoCom*
Backus, John 1924- *IntWW 93, WhoAm 94, WhoScEn 94*
Backus, John King 1925- *WhoAm 94*
Backus, Richard 1945- *WhoHol 92*
Backus, Robert Coburn 1913- *WhoScEn 94*
Backus, Standish, Jr. 1910-1989 *WhoAmA 93N*
Backus, (D.) William 1926- *WrDr 94*
Backvall, Jan-Erling 1947- *WhoScEn 94*
Baclanova, Olga d1974 *WhoHol 92*
Bacoate, Matthew, Jr. 1931- *WhoBlA 94*
Bacon, Baroness *WhoWomW 91*
Bacon, Baroness d1993 *Who 94N*
Bacon, Albert S. 1942- *WhoBlA 94*
Bacon, Anne Cooke 1528-1610 *BlmGWL*
Bacon, Barbara Crumpler 1943- *WhoBlA 94*
Bacon, Brett Kermit 1947- *WhoAm 94, WhoAmL 94*
Bacon, Carter Smith, Jr. 1950- *WhoAmL 94*
Bacon, Charlotte Meade *WhoBlA 94*
Bacon, David d1943 *WhoHol 92*
Bacon, David L. 1944- *WhoAmL 94*
Bacon, David Walter 1935- *WhoAm 94*
Bacon, Deanna Maria 1943- *WhoMW 93*
Bacon, Donald C(onrad) 1935- *WrDr 94*
Bacon, Donald Conrad 1935- *WhoAm 94*
Bacon, Donald Howard 1953- *WhoAmL 94*
Bacon, Edmund N(orwood) 1910- *WrDr 94*
Bacon, Edmund Norwood 1910- *IntWW 93, WhoAm 94*
Bacon, Edward Alsted 1897- *WhAm 10*
Bacon, Ernst 1898-1990 *WhAm 10*
Bacon, Faith d1956 *WhoHol 92*
Bacon, Francis 1561-1626 *AstEnc, BlmGEL, EncSF 93, EnvEnc [port]*
Bacon, Francis 1909-1992 *AnObit 1992, WhAm 10*
Bacon, Francis Thomas d1992 *IntWW 93N*
Bacon, Frank d1922 *WhoHol 92*
Bacon, George Edgar 1932- *WhoAm 94*
Bacon, George Edward 1917- *Who 94, WrDr 94*
Bacon, George Hughes 1935- *WhoFI 94*
Bacon, Gloria Jackson 1937- *WhoBlA 94*
Bacon, Irving d1965 *WhoHol 92*
Bacon, J. Raymond 1906- *WhAm 10*
Bacon, James *WhoHol 92*
Bacon, James Chauncey, Jr. 1946- *WhoMW 93*
Bacon, James Edmund 1931- *WhoAm 94*
Bacon, Jennifer Gille 1949- *WhoAmL 94*
Bacon, Jennifer Helen 1945- *Who 94*
Bacon, John 1738-1820 *WhAmRev*
Bacon, John Stuart 1959- *WhoScEn 94*
Bacon, Kevin 1958- *IntMPA 94, WhoAm 94, WhoHol 92*
Bacon, Lawrence E. 1938- *WhoIns 94*
Bacon, Leonard 1802-1881 *DcAmReB 2*
Bacon, Leonard Anthony 1931- *WhoFI 94, WhoHisp 94, WhoWest 94*
Bacon, Lloyd d1955 *WhoHol 92*
Bacon, Louis Albert 1921- *WhoAm 94*
Bacon, Mai d1981 *WhoHol 92*
Bacon, Margaret *WrDr 94*
Bacon, Martha Brantley 1938- *WhoFI 94*
Bacon, Max d1969 *WhoHol 92*
Bacon, Nicholas c. 1510-1579 *DcLB 132 [port]*
Bacon, Nicholas (Hickman Ponsonby) 1953- *Who 94*
Bacon, Paul 1907- *IntWW 93*
Bacon, Paul Caldwell 1945- *WhoAm 94, WhoFI 94, WhoWest 94*
Bacon, Peggy 1895-1987 *WhoAmA 93N*
Bacon, Peter James 1941- *Who 94*
Bacon, Phillip 1922- *WhoAm 94*
Bacon, R(onald) L(eonard) 1924- *WrDr 94*
Bacon, Randall C. 1937- *WhoBlA 94*
Bacon, Randall Clyde 1937- *WhoWest 94*
Bacon, Reba Broyles 1908- *WhoAmP 93*
Bacon, Robert *DrAPF 93*
Bacon, Robert Elwin 1934- *WhoFI 94*
Bacon, Robert John, Jr. 1948- *WhoBlA 94*
Bacon, Rod d1948 *WhoHol 92*
Bacon, Roger 1210?-c. 1291 *BlmGEL*
Bacon, Roxana C. 1943- *WhoAm 94, WhoAmL 94*
Bacon, Selden D(askam) 1909-1992 *CurBio 93N*
Bacon, Sidney (Charles) 1919- *Who 94*
Bacon, Sylvia 1931- *WhoAm 94, WhoAmL 94*
Bacon, Vicky Lee 1950- *WhoFI 94, WhoScEn 94, WhoWest 94*
Bacon, Wallace Alger 1914- *WhoAm 94, WhoWest 94*
Bacon, Walter *EncSF 93*
Bacon, Walter Scott d1973 *WhoHol 92*
Bacon, Warren H. 1923- *WhoBlA 94*
Bacon, William Francis 1956- *WhoAmL 94*
Bacon, William Louis 1936- *WhoBlA 94*
Bacot, Henry Parrott 1941- *WhoAmA 93*
Bacot, John Carter 1933- *WhoAm 94, WhoFI 94*
Bacot, Marie 1942- *WhoFI 94*
Bacque, Odon Lessley, Jr. 1944- *WhoAmP 93*
Bacquier, Gabriel 1924- *IntWW 93*
Bacquier, Gabriel (-Augustin-Raymond-Theodore-Louis) 1924- *NewGrDO*
Bacri, Jean-Pierre *WhoHol 92*
Bacs, Ludovic 1930- *IntWW 93*
Bacus, Terrence Lee 1944- *WhoMW 93*
Baczek, Peter Gerard 1945- *WhoAmA 93*
Baczko, Joseph R. 1946- *WhoAm 94, WhoFI 94*
Baczko, Ludwig von 1756-1823 *NewGrDO*
Bada, Angelo 1876-1941 *NewGrDO*
Badai 1930- *IntWW 93, WhoPRCh 91 [port]*
Badal, Daniel Walter 1912- *WhoAm 94*
Badalamenti, Anthony 1940- *WhoMW 93*
Badalamenti, Fred 1935- *WhoAmA 93*
Badamhaamb, Her Excellency Ch. *WhoWomW 91*
Badanes, Menke 1906-1991 *WrDr 94N*
Badani, Abdulla 1955- *WhoIns 94*
Badash, Lawrence 1934- *WhoAm 94*
Badawi, Abdel Halim 1930- *IntWW 93*
Badawi, Abdullah Bin Haj 1939- *IntWW 93*
Badawi, Mohamed Mustafa 1925- *WrDr 94*
Badcock, Christopher Robert 1946- *WrDr 94*
Badcock, John Michael Watson 1922- *Who 94*
Baddam, Benjamin fl. 1720-1742 *DcNaB MP*

Baddeley, Alan David 1934- *Who 94*
Baddeley, Angela d1976 *WhoHol 92*
Baddeley, Herbert 1872-1931 *BuCMET*
Baddeley, Hermione d1986 *WhoHol 92*
Baddeley, John (Wolsey Beresford) 1938- *Who 94*
Baddeley, Sophia 1745?-1786 *NewGrDO*
Baddeley, Wilfred 1872-1929 *BuCMET*
Baddeley, William Pye 1914- *Who 94*
Baddiley, James 1918- *IntWW 93, Who 94*
Baddour, Philip A., Jr. *WhoAmP 93*
Baddour, Raymond Frederick 1925- *WhoAm 94*
Bade, Phillip C. 1951- *WhoMW 93*
Badea, Christian 1947- *NewGrDO*
Badeau, Marcel Raymond 1961- *WhoFI 94*
Badeau, Roger R. 1936- *WhoAmP 93*
Badeer, Henry Sarkis 1915- *WhoAm 94, WhoScEn 94*
Badel, Alan d1982 *WhoHol 92*
Badel, Julie 1946- *WhoAm 94, WhoAmL 94*
Badel, Sarah 1943- *WhoHol 92*
Baden, Alan P. 1947- *WhoAmL 94*
Baden, (Edwin) John 1928- *Who 94*
Baden, Michael M. 1934- *WhoScEn 94*
Baden, Mowry T. 1936- *WhoAmA 93*
Baden, Robert Charles 1942- *WhoAm 94*
Badeni, June 1925- *WrDr 94*
Badenoch, George E. 1941- *WhoAmL 94*
Badenoch, (Ian) James (Forster) 1945- *Who 94*
Badenoch, John 1920- *Who 94*
Baden-Powell *Who 94*
Baden-Powell, Baron 1936- *Who 94*
Baden-Powell, Lady 1936- *Who 94*
Baden-Powell, Robert d1941 *WhoHol 92*
Baden-Semper, Nina 1945- *WhoHol 92*
Bader, Barbara Carol Joanis 1945- *WhoWest 94*
Bader, Charles W. 1940- *WhoAmP 93*
Bader, Eliot Mark 1961- *WhoAmL 94*
Bader, Eugene William 1946- *WhoMW 93*
Bader, Franz 1903- *WhoAm 94, WhoAmA 93*
Bader, Gregory Vincent 1948- *WhoAmL 94*
Bader, Izaak Walton 1922- *WhoAmL 94*
Bader, John Merwin 1919- *WhoAm 94*
Bader, Keith Bryan 1956- *WhoScEn 94*
Bader, Kenneth Leroy 1934- *WhoMW 93*
Bader, Michael Haley 1929- *WhoAm 94*
Bader, Robert Smith 1925- *WhoAm 94*
Bader, Samuel David 1947- *WhoMW 93*
Bader, W. Reece 1941- *WhoAm 94, WhoAmL 94*
Bader, William Alan 1964- *WhoScEn 94*
Bader, William Banks 1931- *WhoAm 94*
Bader-Hendricks, Patricia Ann 1947- *WhoMW 93*
Badertscher, David Glen 1935- *WhoAm 94, WhoAmL 94*
Badertscher, Doris Rae 1935- *WhoMW 93*
Badertscher, Mark Allen 1964- *WhoMW 93*
Badescu, Dinu 1904- *NewGrDO*
Badetti, Rolando Emilio 1947- *WhoScEn 94*
Badge, Peter Gilmour Noto 1931- *Who 94*
Badge, Thomas *WhAmRev*
Badger, Anthony John 1947- *Who 94*
Badger, Brenda Joyce 1950- *WhoBlA 94*
Badger, Charles H. 1917- *WhoAm 94*
Badger, David Harry 1931- *WhoAm 94, WhoAmL 94*
Badger, Geoffrey Malcolm 1916- *IntWW 93, Who 94*
Badger, Lloyd, Jr. 1950- *WhoBlA 94*
Badger, Pat c. 1967- *See* Extreme *ConMus 10*
Badger, Richard Mclean 1896- *WhAm 10*
Badgerow, John Nicholas 1951- *WhoAmL 94*
Badgett, Edward 1935- *WhoBlA 94*
Badgett, Lee Douglas 1939- *WhoAm 94*
Badgett, Rick 1953- *WhoAmP 93*
Badgley, Delores Romélia 1963- *WhoHisp 94*
Badgley, Frank d1955 *WhoHol 92*
Badgley, Helen d1977 *WhoHol 92*
Badgley, John Herbert 1930- *WrDr 94*
Badgley, John Roy 1922- *WhoScEn 94, WhoWest 94*
Badgley, Judeth Birdwell 1954- *WhoWest 94*
Badgley, Marie Minor Curry 1926- *WhoAm 94*
Badgley, Theodore McBride 1925- *WhoAm 94*
Badgley, William S. 1930- *WhoAm 94, WhoFI 94*
Badgro, Morris *ProFbHF*
Badham, Douglas George 1914- *Who 94*
Badham, John 1939- *EncSF 93, IntMPA 94*
Badham, John MacDonald 1939- *WhoAm 94*
Badham, Leonard 1923- *Who 94*
Badham, Mary 1952- *WhoHol 92*
Badham, Robert E. 1929- *WhoAm 94, WhoWest 94*
Badham, Robert Edward 1929- *WhoAmP 93*
Badia, Carlo Agostino 1672-1738 *NewGrDO*
Badia, Leopold d1976 *WhoHol 92*
Badiali, Cesare c. 1803-1865 *NewGrDO*
Badian, Ernst 1925- *IntWW 93, Who 94, WhoAm 94, WrDr 94*
Badias, Maria Elena 1959- *WhoHisp 94*
Badie, Ronald Peter 1942- *WhoAm 94*
Badikian, Beatriz 1951- *WhoHisp 94*
Badillo, Herman 1929- *WhoAmP 93, WhoHisp 94*
Badillo-Martinez, Diana 1946- *WhoHisp 94*
Badinger, Michael Albert 1954- *WhoScEn 94*
Badings, Henk 1907- *IntWW 93*
Badings, Henk 1907-1987 *NewGrDO*
Badini, Carlo Francesco fl. 1770-1793 *NewGrDO*
Badini, Ernesto 1876-1937 *NewGrDO*
Badinter, Elisabeth 1944- *BlmGWL*
Badinter, Robert 1928- *IntWW 93*
Badish, Kenneth Michael 1951- *WhoWest 94*
Badiyi, Reza S. 1930?- *ConTFT 11*
Badler, Jane *WhoHol 92*
Badlesmere, Bartholomew c. 1275-1322 *DcNaB MP*
Badley, Bernard William David 1933- *WhoAm 94*
Badner, Barry 1937- *WhoFI 94*
Badner, Mino 1940-1978 *WhoAmA 93N*
Bado, Kenneth Steve 1941- *WhoFI 94, WhoMW 93*
Badoaro, Giacomo 1602-1654 *NewGrDO*
Badolati, Louis d1968 *WhoHol 92*
Badolato, Dominic J. *WhoAmP 93*
Badombe, Betty *WhoWomW 91*
Bado-Santana, Eduardo 1950- *WhoHisp 94*
Badovinus, Wayne L. 1943- *WhoFI 94*
Badoyen, Dean Andrew 1968- *WhoWest 94*
Badr, Liana 1952- *BlmGWL*
Badr, Mostafa Zaki 1950- *WhoMW 93*
Badra, Robert George 1933- *WhoMW 93*
Badran, Mudar 1934- *IntWW 93*
Badretdinov, Nil Karamovich 1936- *LoBiDrD*
Badstuebner, Hans Alexander 1916- *WhoWest 94*
Badura, Carl Werner 1937- *WhoFI 94*
Badura-Skoda, Eva 1929- *NewGrDO*
Badura-Skoda, Paul 1927- *IntWW 93, WhoAm 94*
Badzian, Andrzej Ryszard 1938- *WhoScEn 94*
Badzio, Yurii Vasylovych 1936- *LoBiDrD*
Bae, Ben Hee Chan 1939- *WhoScEn 94*
Bae, Frank S. H. 1941- *WhoAmL 94*
Baechle, James Joseph 1932- *WhoAm 94, WhoAmL 94*
Baechler, Bruce Andrew 1955- *WhoAmP 93*
Baechler, Donald 1956- *WhoAmA 93*
Baechtold, Robert Louis 1937- *WhoAmL 94*
Baedeker, Karl 1801-1859 *BlmGEL*
Baeder, Donald Lee 1925- *WhoAm 94*
Baeder, John 1938- *WhoAmA 93*
Baeder, John Alan 1938- *WhoAm 94*
Baehr, Anne Ruth Ediger *DrAPF 93*
Baehr, Karl Joseph 1959- *WhoWest 94*
Baek, Se-Min 1943- *WhoScEn 94*
Baekeland, Leo 1863-1944 *WorInv [port]*
Baelz, Peter Richard 1923- *Who 94*
Baen, Jim 1943- *EncSF 93*
Baena, Robert B. 1930- *WhoHisp 94*
Baena, Scott Louis 1949- *WhoAm 94, WhoAmL 94*
Baender, Margaret Woodruff 1921- *WhoWest 94*
Baer, Albert Max 1905- *WhoAm 94*
Baer, Andrew Rudolf 1946- *WhoAm 94*
Baer, Ben Kayser 1926- *WhoAm 94*
Baer, Benjamin Franklin 1918-1991 *WhAm 10*
Baer, Buddy d1986 *WhoHol 92*
Baer, Bugs d1969 *WhoHol 92*
Baer, Byron M. 1929- *WhoAmP 93*
Baer, Elizabeth Roberts 1946- *WhoMW 93*
Baer, Eric 1932- *WhoAm 94*
Baer, Francis Shaw 1893- *WhAm 10*
Baer, George Martin 1936- *WhoAm 94*
Baer, Henry 1930- *WhoAm 94*
Baer, Jack Mervyn Frank 1924- *Who 94*
Baer, Jerome I. 1936- *WhoIns 94*
Baer, Jo 1929- *WhoAm 94, WhoAmA 93*
Baer, Jo Webb 1936- *WhoAmP 93*
Baer, John 1925- *WhoHol 92*
Baer, John Richard Frederick 1941- *WhoAm 94, WhoAmL 94, WhoMW 93*
Baer, Joseph Winslow 1917- *WhoAm 94*
Baer, Karl Ernst von 1792-1876 *WorScD*
Baer, Kenneth Peter 1930- *WhoAm 94*
Baer, Ledolph 1929- *WhoScEn 94*
Baer, Luke 1950- *WhoAmL 94*
Baer, Marc H. 1953- *WhoAmL 94*
Baer, Martha Lynn 1939- *WhoAm 94*
Baer, Max d1959 *WhoHol 92*
Baer, Max, Jr. 1937- *WhoHol 92*
Baer, Michael Alan 1943- *WhoAm 94*
Baer, Morley 1916- *WhoAmA 93*
Baer, Norbert Sebastian 1938- *WhoAm 94, WhoAmA 93*
Baer, Olaf 1957- *IntWW 93*
Baer, Parley *WhoHol 92*
Baer, Ralph August 1933- *WhoAm 94*
Baer, Richard Myron 1928- *WhoFI 94*
Baer, Robert J. 1937- *WhoAm 94, WhoFI 94*
Baer, Robert Jacob 1924- *WhoAm 94*
Baer, Rod *WhoAmA 93*
Baer, Rudolf Lewis 1910- *WhoAm 94, WhoScEn 94*
Baer, Stephen Cooper 1938- *WhoScEn 94*
Baer, Thomas James 1927- *WhoAm 94*
Baer, Timothy Robert 1951- *WhoAmP 93*
Baer, Werner 1931- *WhoAm 94*
Baer, William Bruce 1938- *WhoWest 94*
Baer, William Harold 1947- *WhoFI 94*
Baer, William J. 1950- *WhoAmL 94*
Baerg, Harry John 1909- *WrDr 94*
Baerg, Richard Henry 1937- *WhoAm 94, WhoScEn 94*
Baerga, Carlos 1968- *WhoHisp 94*
Baerga, Carlos Obed Ortiz 1968- *WhoAm 94, WhoMW 93*
Baerlein, Anthony *EncSF 93*
Baerlein, Richard Edgar 1915- *Who 94*
Baermann, Donna Lee Roth 1939- *WhoMW 93*
Baernstein, Albert, II 1941- *WhoAm 94*
Baerwald, Hans H. 1927- *WrDr 94*
Baerwald, John Edward 1925- *WhoAm 94*
Baesch, John Francis 1944- *WhoFI 94*
Baesel, Stuart Oliver 1925- *WhoAm 94*
Baesler, Scotty *WhoAm 94*
Baesler, Scotty 1941- *CngDr 93, WhoAmP 93*
Baety, Edward L. 1944- *WhoBlA 94*
Baetz, Albert Lewis 1938- *WhoMW 93*
Baetz, W. Timothy 1944- *WhoAm 94, WhoAmL 94*
Baetzel, Tracey Alene 1954- *WhoMW 93*
Baetzhold, Howard George 1923- *WhoAm 94*
Baeumer, Max Lorenz *WhoAm 94*
Baeyens, August 1895-1966 *NewGrDO*
Baeyer, Adolf Johann Friedrich Wilhelm von 1835-1917 *WorScD*
Baeyer, Adolf Von 1835-1917 *WorInv*
Baez, Albert Vinicio 1912- *WhoHisp 94*
Baez, Joan 1941- *IntWW 93, WhoHol 92*
Baez, Joan Chandos 1941- *WhoAm 94, WhoHisp 94, WhoWest 94*
Báez, Josefina E. *WhoHisp 94*
Baez, Julio A. 1954- *WhoHisp 94*
Báez, Luis 1948- *WhoHisp 94*
Baez, Manuel 1941- *WhoAm 94, WhoFI 94*
Baez, Mary Belinda 1955- *WhoHisp 94*
Baez, Ramon J. 1938- *WhoHisp 94*
Baeza, Abelardo 1944- *WhoHisp 94*
Baeza, Mario Leon 1951- *WhoAm 94, WhoAmL 94*
Báez Báez, Edith María 1961- *WhoHisp 94*
Báezconde-Garbanati, Lourdes A. 1955- *WhoHisp 94*
Baffes, Thomas Gus 1923- *WhoAm 94*
Baffico, Paul Anthony 1946- *WhoFI 94*
Baffin, William c. 1584-1622 *WhWE*
Bafile, Corrado 1903- *IntWW 93*
Bafile, Corrado Cardinal 1903- *WhoAm 94*
Baganz, Lorraine Pauleen 1939- *WhoMW 93*
Bagarry, Alexander Anthony, III 1949- *WhoWest 94*
Bagasao, Paula Y. *WhoAsA 94*
Bagasra, Omar 1948- *WhoAsA 94*
Bagaza, Jean-Baptiste 1946- *IntWW 93*
Bagbeni Adeito Nzengeya 1941- *IntWW 93*
Bagby, Daniel Gordon 1941- *WhoAm 94*
Bagby, Frederick Lair, Jr. 1920- *WhoAm 94*
Bagby, Joseph Rigsby 1935- *WhoFI 94*
Bagby, Myron Rex 1944- *WhoFI 94*
Bagby, Rachel L 1956- *WhoBlA 94*
Bagby, Thomas Richard 1950- *WhoAm 94*
Bagby, William Rardin 1910- *WhoAmL 94*
Bagchi, Amalendu 1946- *WhoScEn 94*
Bagchi, Amiya Kumar 1936- *IntWW 93*
Bagchi, Kallol Kumar 1951- *WhoScEn 94*
Bagdad, William d1975 *WhoHol 92*
Bagdasarian, Andranik 1935- *WhoWest 94*
Bagdasarian, Carol *WhoHol 92*
Bagdasarian, Ross d1972 *WhoHol 92*
Bagdikian, Ben Haig 1920- *WhoAm 94, WhoWest 94, WrDr 94*
Bagdonas, Kathy Joann 1953- *WhoAm 94, WhoAmL 94*
Bagehot, Walter 1826-1877 *BlmGEL*
Bageris, John 1924- *WhoAm 94, WhoAmA 93*
Bagert, Bernard J., Jr. 1944- *WhoAmP 93*
Bagg, Robert *DrAPF 93*
Bagg, Robert Ely 1935- *ConAu 42NR, WhoAm 94*
Bagga, K. Jay Singh 1952- *WhoAsA 94*
Bagge, Carl Elmer 1927- *WhoAm 94*
Bagge, (John) Jeremy (Picton) 1945- *Who 94*
Bagge, Michael Charles 1950- *WhoAm 94, WhoAmL 94*
Bagger, Richard H. 1960- *WhoAmP 93*
Baggerly, John Lynwood 1956- *WhoScEn 94*
Baggerly, Leo Lon 1928- *WhoWest 94*
Bagget, Dave d1959 *WhoHol 92*
Baggett, Donnis Gene 1952- *WhoAm 94*
Baggett, James Alex 1932- *WhoAmP 93*
Baggett, Kelsea Kindrick 1937- *WhoWest 94*
Baggett, Lynne d1960 *WhoHol 92*
Baggett, Rebecca *DrAPF 93*
Baggett, W. Mike 1946- *WhoAm 94, WhoAmL 94*
Baggett, William Carter, Jr. 1946- *WhoAmA 93*
Baggetta, Vincent *WhoHol 92*
Baggett Boozer, Linda Dianne 1956- *WhoAmL 94*
Baggio, Roberto 1967- *WorESoc*
Baggio, Sebastiano d1993 *IntWW 93N*
Baggio, Sebastiano 1913- *IntWW 93*
Baggio, Sebastiano 1913-1993 *NewYTBS 93*
Baggish, Joy 1950- *WhoWest 94*
Baggley, Charles David Aubrey 1923- *Who 94*
Baggott, King d1948 *WhoHol 92*
Baggott, Thomas McCann 1943- *WhoAmL 94*
Baghai, Nina Lucille 1954- *WhoScEn 94*
Baghdadi, Maroun d1993 *NewYTBS 93*
Baghzouz, Yahia 1956- *WhoWest 94*
Bagier, Gordon Alexander Thomas 1924- *Who 94*
Bagley, Amy Lynn 1971- *WhoAmP 93*
Bagley, Brian G. 1934- *WhoAm 94, WhoMW 93, WhoScEn 94*
Bagley, Charles F. 1944- *WhoAmL 94*
Bagley, Cherie Albertha 1954- *WhoMW 93*
Bagley, Colleen 1954- *WhoFI 94*
Bagley, Constance Elizabeth 1952- *WhoAmL 94, WhoFI 94, WhoWest 94*
Bagley, Floyd Caldwell 1922- *WhoAmP 93*
Bagley, Gregory P. 1930- *WhoBlA 94*
Bagley, H. Michael 1955- *WhoAmL 94*
Bagley, John 1960- *WhoBlA 94*
Bagley, John Joseph 1908-1989 *WrDr 94N*
Bagley, John Neff 1944- *WhoWest 94*
Bagley, Margaret Ann 1944- *WhoAmP 93*
Bagley, Mary Carol 1958- *WhoAm 94, WhoMW 93*
Bagley, Peter B. E. 1935- *WhoBlA 94*
Bagley, Philip Joseph, III 1941- *WhoAm 94, WhoAmL 94*
Bagley, Richard Marshall 1927- *WhoAmP 93*
Bagley, Robert Waller 1921- *WhoAm 94*
Bagley, Sam d1968 *WhoHol 92*
Bagley, Stanley B. 1935- *WhoBlA 94*
Bagley, Taffy D. 1949- *WhoAmL 94*
Bagley, Thomas Steven 1952- *WhoMW 93*
Bagley, William Charles 1956- *WhoMW 93*
Bagley, William Thompson 1928- *WhoAm 94*
Bagli, Vincent Joseph 1925- *WhoAm 94*
Baglin, Richard John 1942- *Who 94*
Baglini, Norman A. 1942- *WhoIns 94*
Baglio, Vincent Paul 1960- *WhoFI 94, WhoScEn 94*
Baglioni, Antonio fl. 1780-1790 *NewGrDO*
Baglioni, Bruna 1947- *NewGrDO*
Baglioni, Clementina fl. 1753-1788 *NewGrDO*
Baglioni, Francesco fl. 1729-1762 *NewGrDO*
Baglioni, Giovanna fl. 1752-1770 *NewGrDO*
Baglioni Family *NewGrDO*
Bagliore, Virginia *DrAPF 93*

Bagnal, Charles Wilson, Jr. 1957- WhoFI 94
Bagnal, Harry Stroman 1928- WhoAmP 93
Bagnall, Anthony John Crowther 1945- Who 94
Bagnall, Graham Edward 1948- WhoAm 94
Bagnall, Kenneth Reginald 1927- Who 94
Bagnall, Nigel (Thomas) 1927- IntWW 93, Who 94, WrDr 94
Bagnall, R.D. 1945- EncSF 93
Bagnall, Richard Maurice 1917- Who 94
Bagnall, Roger Shaler 1947- WhoAm 94
Bagnariol, John A. 1932- WhoAmP 93
Bagnell, Louis Herbert WhoFI 94
Bagneris, Dennis R., Sr. 1948- WhoAmP 93
Bagni, John d1954 WhoHol 92
Bagno, Carlo WhoHol 92
Bagnold, Enid 1889-1981 BlmGWL
Bagnold, Enid 1962-1981 ConDr 93
Bagnolesi, Anna Maria Antonia fl. 1726-1743 NewGrDO
Bagnoli, Vincent James, Jr. 1952- WhoAm 94
Bagot Who 94
Bagot, Baron 1914- Who 94
Bagot, Drew N. 1948- WhoAmL 94
Bagri, Durgadas S. 1942- WhoWest 94
Bagri, Raj 1930- IntWW 93
Bagrier, Frank William 1947- WhoFI 94
Bagrodia, Shriram 1952- WhoScEn 94
Bagrov, Mykola Vasylovych 1937- LoBiDrD
Bagrov, Nikolai Vassilievich 1937- IntWW 93
Bagryana, Elisaveta 1893-1991 BlmGWL
Bagshaw, Bradley Holmes 1953- WhoAmL 94
Bagshaw, Joseph Charles 1943- WhoAm 94
Bagshaw, Malcolm A. 1925- WhoAm 94
Bagshawe, Kenneth Dawson 1925- IntWW 93, Who 94
Baguer, Carlos 1768-1808 NewGrDO
Bagwell, Kathleen Kay 1951- WhoScEn 94
Bagwell, Louis Lee 1947- WhoAm 94
Bagwill, John Williams, Jr. 1930- WhoAm 94
Baha, Daniel Scott 1955- WhoWest 94
Bahadur, Birendra 1949- WhoAm 94, WhoScEn 94
Bahadur, Chance 1942- WhoAm 94
Bahadur, Khawaja Ali 1930- WhoScEn 94
Bahadur, Raj 1912- IntWW 93
Bahadur K.C., Kaisher 1907- IntWW 93
Bahal, Surendra Mohan 1935- WhoAsA 94
Bahar, Ezekiel 1933- WhoAm 94
Baharna, Husain Mohammad al- 1932- IntWW 93
Bahash, Robert J. 1945- WhoAm 94, WhoFI 94
Bahati, Amirh DrAPF 93
Bahc, Mo 1957- WhoAmA 93
Bahcall, John Norris 1934- IntWW 93, WhoAm 94
Bahcall, Neta Assaf 1942- WhoScEn 94
Bahl, Franklin EncSF 93
Bahl, Kamlesh 1956- Who 94
Bahl, Om Parkash 1927- WhoAsA 94
Bahler, Beth DrAPF 93
Bahler, Brent Norman 1953- WhoAmP 93
Bahler, Gary M. WhoAmL 94
Bahlman, Dudley Ward Rhodes 1923- WhoAm 94
Bahlman, William Thorne, Jr. 1920- WhoAm 94
Bahlmann, David William 1939- WhoAm 94
Bahlo, Peter 1959- WhoWest 94
Bahls, Gene Charles 1929- WhoAm 94, WhoFI 94
Bahls, Steven Carl 1954- WhoAmL 94
Bahm, Archie J(ohn) 1907- WrDr 94
Bahm, Archie John 1907- WhoAm 94
Bahmer, Robert H. 1904-1990 WhAm 10
Bahn, Monsieur c. 1700-1726? NewGrDO
Bahn, Gilbert Schuyler 1922- WhoScEn 94, WhoWest 94
Bahn, Roma d1975 WhoHol 92
Bahnak, John J., Jr. 1947- WhoAmL 94
Bahner, Carl Tabb 1908- WhoAm 94
Bahner, Thomas Maxfield 1933- WhoAm 94, WhoAmL 94
Bahnini, Hadj M'Hammed 1914- IntWW 93
Bahniuk, Eugene 1926- WhoAm 94
Bahniuk, Frank Theodore 1937- WhoAm 94
Bahnson, Agnew H., Jr. 1915-c. 1964 EncSF 93
Bahr, Alice Harrison 1946- WhoAm 94
Bahr, Conrad Charles, III 1938- WhoAm 94
Bahr, Donald Walter 1927- WhoAm 94
Bahr, Egon 1922- IntWW 93
Bahr, Ehrhard 1932- WhoAm 94, WhoWest 94, WrDr 94
Bahr, Howard Miner 1938- WhoAm 94, WhoWest 94
Bahr, Janice Mary 1935- WhoScEn 94
Bahr, Jerome 1909- WrDr 94
Bahr, Lauren S. 1944- WhoAm 94
Bahr, Mark A. 1952- WhoFI 94
Bahr, Mary 1946- WrDr 94
Bahr, Morton 1926- WhoAm 94, WhoFI 94
Bahr, Richard George 1954- WhoWest 94
Bahr, Robert 1940- WrDr 94
Bahr, Sheila Kay 1956- WhoMW 93
Bahrawy, Ramsey A. 1954- WhoAmL 94
Bahre, Thomas E. 1943- WhoAmP 93
Bahrenburg, D. Claeys 1947- WhoAm 94
Bahr-Mildenburg, Anna 1872-1947 NewGrDO [port]
Bahti, Mark Tomas 1950- WhoWest 94
Bai, Er-Wei 1951- WhoMW 93
Bai, Gohar d1985 WhoHol 92
Bai, Qingcai 1932- WhoPRCh 91 [port]
Bai, Rubing 1906- WhoPRCh 91
Bai, Shen Hum 1932- WhoAsA 94
Bai, Sungchul Charles 1954- WhoScEn 94
Bai, Taeil Albert 1945- WhoAsA 94, WhoScEn 94
Bai, Wei 1894- BlmGWL
Baiardi, John Charles 1918- WhoAm 94
Baica, Malvina Florica 1942- WhoMW 93
Bai Dongcai WhoPRCh 91 [port]
Bai Enpei WhoPRCh 91
Baier, Augusto Carlos 1941- WhoScEn 94
Baier, Edward John 1925- WhoAm 94
Baier, George Patrick 1945- WhoAm 94
Baier, Kurt E. M. 1917- EncEth
Baier, Max A. 1953- WhoMW 93
Baier, Ronald Anton 1943- WhoFI 94
Baif, Jean-Antoine de 1532-1589 GuFrLit 2
Bai Fengxi 1934- BlmGWL, WhoPRCh 91 [port]
Baigell, Matthew 1933- WrDr 94
Bai Hua 1930- IntWW 93, WhoPRCh 91 [port]
Bai Hualing 1928- WhoPRCh 91 [port]
Bai Jiefu 1921- WhoPRCh 91 [port]
Bai Jingzhong WhoPRCh 91
Bai Jingzhou 1947- WhoPRCh 91
Bai Jinian 1926- IntWW 93, WhoPRCh 91 [port]
Bai Junqing 1925- WhoPRCh 91 [port]
Baikalov, Igor A. 1961- WhoWest 94
Baikie, William Balfour 1825-1864 WhWE
Bail, Chuck WhoHol 92
Bail, Joe Paul 1925- WhoAm 94
Bail, Murray 1941- WrDr 94
Bail, Philip Milo 1898- WhAm 10
Bailar, Barbara Ann 1935- WhoAm 94
Bailar, Benjamin Franklin 1934- IntWW 93, WhoAm 94
Bailar, John Christian, III 1932- WhoAm 94, WhoScEn 94
Baile, Clifton A. 1940- WhoScEn 94
Bailer, Bonnie Lynn 1946- WhoAmL 94, WhoBlA 94
Bailer, Kermit Gamaliel 1921- WhoBlA 94
Bailes, Alyson Judith Kirtley 1949- Who 94
Bailes, Dale Alan DrAPF 93
Bailey Who 94
Bailey, A. Peter 1938- WhoBlA 94
Bailey, A. Richard 1946- WhoAmL 94
Bailey, Abigail Abbott 1746-1815 BlmGWL
Bailey, Adrienne Yvonne 1944- WhoBlA 94
Bailey, Agnes Jackson 1931- WhoBlA 94
Bailey, Alan (Marshall) 1931- Who 94
Bailey, Alan J. WhoFI 94
Bailey, Albert d1952 WhoHol 92
Bailey, Alex Stuart 1952- WhoWest 94
Bailey, Alice A. 1880-1949 AstEnc
Bailey, Allen Jackson 1931- Who 94
Bailey, Amos Purnell 1918- WhoAm 94
Bailey, Andrew Dewey, Jr. 1942- WhoAm 94, WhoFI 94
Bailey, Andrew J(ackson) 1840-1927 EncSF 93
Bailey, Ann 1936- WhoAmP 93
Bailey, Anna Warner 1758-1851 WhAmRev
Bailey, Anne 1742-1825 AmRev
Bailey, Annie L. 1918- WhoAmP 93
Bailey, Anthony 1933- WrDr 94
Bailey, Antoinette M. 1949- WhoBlA 94
Bailey, Arthur WhoBlA 94
Bailey, Arthur Emery 1953- WhoScEn 94
Bailey, Arthur L. 1946- WhoAmL 94
Bailey, Barbara Ann 1928- WhoAmA 93
Bailey, Barry Stone 1952- WhoAmA 93
Bailey, Benny Ray 1944- WhoAmP 93
Bailey, Bert d1953 WhoHol 92
Bailey, Beth L. 1957- ConAu 142
Bailey, Bill d1978 WhoHol 92
Bailey, Bill 1910- WhoHol 92
Bailey, Billy Wayne, Jr. 1957- WhoAmP 93
Bailey, Bob Carl 1935- WhoBlA 94
Bailey, Brenda Marie 1940- WhoFI 94
Bailey, Brian (Harry) 1923- Who 94
Bailey, Brian Dennis 1952- WhoWest 94
Bailey, Byron J. 1934- WhoAm 94
Bailey, Calvin 1909- WhoBlA 94
Bailey, Carol Bray WhoAmP 93
Bailey, Cecil Dewitt 1921- WhoAm 94
Bailey, Charles-James Nice 1926- WhoWest 94
Bailey, Charles Lyle 1934- WhoAm 94
Bailey, Charles Philamore d1993 NewYTBS 93 [port]
Bailey, Charles R. 1929- WhoAmP 93
Bailey, Charles Stanley 1949- WhoAm 94
Bailey, Charles W(aldo) 1929- EncSF 93
Bailey, Charles Waldo, (II) 1929- WrDr 94
Bailey, Charles Waldo, II 1929- WhoAm 94
Bailey, Charles William 1932- WhoFI 94, WhoMW 93
Bailey, Chauncey Wendell, Jr. 1949- WhoBlA 94
Bailey, Chip 1944- WhoAmP 93
Bailey, Clarence Walter 1933- WhoBlA 94
Bailey, Clark T. 1932-1978 WhoAmA 93N
Bailey, Claude d1950 WhoHol 92
Bailey, Clayton George 1939- WhoAmA 93, WhoWest 94
Bailey, Cliff WhoAmP 93
Bailey, Curtis Darnell 1954- WhoBlA 94
Bailey, D(avid) R. Shackleton 1917- WrDr 94
Bailey, D(avid) R(oy) Shackleton 1917- IntWW 93, Who 94
Bailey, Daniel Allen 1953- WhoAm 94, WhoAmL 94
Bailey, Daniel Joseph, III 1959- WhoAmL 94
Bailey, D'Army 1941- WhoBlA 94
Bailey, Daryl Wayne 1957- WhoAmL 94
Bailey, David WhoHol 92
Bailey, David 1938- IntWW 93, Who 94
Bailey, David Emmett 1942- WhoAmP 93
Bailey, David Nelson 1945- WhoAm 94
Bailey, David Roy Shackleton 1917- WhoAm 94
Bailey, Debra Sue 1953- WhoAm 94
Bailey, Dennis 1931- Who 94
Bailey, Dennis B. EncSF 93
Bailey, Derrick Thomas Louis 1918- Who 94
Bailey, Desmond Patrick 1907- Who 94
Bailey, Didi Giselle 1948- WhoBlA 94
Bailey, Don 1945- WhoAmP 93
Bailey, Don Matthew 1946- WhoScEn 94
Bailey, Donald Coleman 1901-1985 DcNaB MP
Bailey, Donald Lee 1960- WhoAmL 94
Bailey, Donn Fritz 1932- WhoBlA 94
Bailey, Doris Jones 1927- WhoBlA 94
Bailey, Doug 1951- WhoAmP 93
Bailey, Douglas Kent 1949- WhoWest 94
Bailey, Dudley 1918- WhoAm 94
Bailey, Dudley Graham 1924- Who 94
Bailey, Duwain 1957- WhoBlA 94
Bailey, E. H. 1876-1959 AstEnc
Bailey, Elizabeth Ellery 1938- WhoAm 94
Bailey, Eric 1913- Who 94
Bailey, Eugene Ridgeway 1938- WhoBlA 94
Bailey, Exine Margaret Anderson 1922- WhoAm 94, WhoWest 94
Bailey, F(rancis) Lee 1933- WrDr 94
Bailey, Francis c. 1735-1815 WhAmRev
Bailey, Francis Lee 1933- WhoAm 94, WhoAmL 94
Bailey, Frank I., Jr. 1936- WhoAmP 93
Bailey, Frankie d1953 WhoHol 92
Bailey, Fred Coolidge 1925- WhoAm 94
Bailey, (John) Frederick, (II) 1946- WrDr 94
Bailey, Frederick Eugene, Jr. 1927-1991 WhAm 10
Bailey, Frederick George 1924- WrDr 94
Bailey, Fredric L. 1935- WhoAmP 93
Bailey, G. W. WhoHol 92
Bailey, George 1946- WhoFI 94
Bailey, George Gilbert 1913-1989 WhAm 10
Bailey, George Hampton 1937- WhoAmP 93
Bailey, George Rufus 1925- WhoAmP 93
Bailey, George Screven 1951- WhoAm 94, WhoAmL 94
Bailey, Gilbert E. 1933- WhoAmP 93
Bailey, Glenn Martin 1956- WhoWest 94
Bailey, Glenn Waldemar 1925- WhoAm 94, WhoFI 94
Bailey, Gordon (Keith) 1936- WrDr 94
Bailey, Gracie Massenberg 1936- WhoBlA 94
Bailey, Gregory Wayne 1952- WhoAmL 94
Bailey, Guy Vernie 1929- WhoFI 94
Bailey, Harley Evan 1915- WhoAmP 93
Bailey, Harold 1914- Who 94
Bailey, Harold 1946- WhoBlA 94
Bailey, Harold (Walter) 1899- Who 94
Bailey, Harold Stevens, Jr. 1922- WhoAm 94
Bailey, Harold Walter 1899- IntWW 93
Bailey, Harry WhoAmP 93
Bailey, Harry d1954 WhoHol 92
Bailey, Harry A., Jr. 1932- WhoBlA 94
Bailey, Harry Augustine, Jr. 1932- WhoAm 94
Bailey, Harvey Alan 1937- WhoWest 94
Bailey, Helen McShane 1916- WhoAm 94
Bailey, Henry John, III 1916- WhoAm 94
Bailey, Herbert Smith, Jr. 1921- WhoAm 94
Bailey, Hilary 1936- EncSF 93
Bailey, Howland Haskell 1912- WhoWest 94
Bailey, Hugh Coleman 1929- WhoAm 94
Bailey, Ian James 1957- WhoWest 94
Bailey, Irving Widmer, II 1941- WhoAm 94, WhoFI 94
Bailey, J. Chalmers Da Costa 1931- WhoAmP 93
Bailey, J. Hugh 1936- WhoIns 94
Bailey, J(ames) O(sler) 1903-1979 EncSF 93
Bailey, J. R. d1985 WhoHol 92
Bailey, Jack d1980 WhoHol 92
Bailey, Jack Arthur 1930- Who 94
Bailey, Jack Blendon 1925-1989 WhAm 10
Bailey, Jacqueline 1961- WhoBlA 94
Bailey, James Allen 1934- WhoWest 94
Bailey, James J. 1944- WhoAmP 93
Bailey, James Martin 1929- WhoAm 94
Bailey, James Russell 1935- WhoIns 94
Bailey, James W. 1922- WhoBlA 94
Bailey, Jane DrAPF 93
Bailey, Janet Dee 1946- WhoAm 94
Bailey, Jann L. M. 1952- WhoAmA 93
Bailey, Jerry Dean 1950- WhoBlA 94
Bailey, Jerry Lynn 1948- WhoFI 94
Bailey, Jerry Wayne 1948- WhoWest 94
Bailey, Jessica Margolin 1962- WhoWest 94
Bailey, Jewell R. 1920- WhoAmP 93
Bailey, Jim WhoHol 92
Bailey, Joel Furness 1913- WhoAm 94
Bailey, John Who 94
Bailey, John d1989 WhoHol 92
Bailey, John 1942- IntMPA 94, WhoAm 94
Bailey, (William) John (Joseph) 1940- Who 94
Bailey, John Bilsland 1928- Who 94
Bailey, John Everett Creighton 1905- Who 94
Bailey, John H., III 1945- WhoAmL 94
Bailey, John M., III 1942- WhoIns 94
Bailey, John Martin 1928- WhoAm 94
Bailey, John Maxwell 1927- WhoAm 94
Bailey, John Milton 1925- WhoAm 94
Bailey, John Preston 1951- WhoAmP 93
Bailey, John Turner 1926- WhoAm 94
Bailey, Jonathan Sansbury Who 94
Bailey, Joseph Alexander, II 1935- WhoBlA 94
Bailey, K. Ronald 1947- WhoAmL 94
Bailey, K. William 1946- WhoAmL 94
Bailey, Karen Miller 1956- WhoMW 93
Bailey, Katherine Christine 1952- WhoWest 94
Bailey, Kathleen WhoHol 92
Bailey, Keith E. 1942- WhoFI 94
Bailey, Kenneth Elvin 1946- WhoAmP 93
Bailey, Kenneth Kyle 1923- WhoAm 94
Bailey, Kent Joseph 1956- WhoFI 94
Bailey, Kerry Douglas 1950- WhoWest 94
Bailey, Kevin E. 1951- WhoAmP 93
Bailey, Kristen 1952- WhoAmL 94, WhoMW 93
Bailey, Larrie 1934- WhoAm 94, WhoAmP 93
Bailey, Lawrence R., Sr. 1918- WhoBlA 94
Bailey, Lawrence Randolph, Sr. 1918- WhoAm 94, WhoAmL 94
Bailey, Lee WhoBlA 94
Bailey, Lee 1926- WrDr 94
Bailey, Leonard Lee 1942- WhoAm 94, WhoScEn 94, WhoWest 94
Bailey, Linda F. 1951- WhoBlA 94
Bailey, Lucille Marie 1945- WhoMW 93
Bailey, Marcia Mead 1947- WhoAmA 93
Bailey, Mark William 1945- WhoScEn 94
Bailey, Marshall Lee 1927- WhoAmP 93
Bailey, Martin 1947- WrDr 94
Bailey, Michael John 1953- WhoWest 94
Bailey, Michael Keith 1956- WhoAmL 94
Bailey, Michael Wayne 1947- WhoMW 93
Bailey, Mildred d1951 WhoHol 92
Bailey, Mildred T. 1920- WhoBlA 94
Bailey, Mona Humphries 1932- WhoBlA 94
Bailey, Myrtle Lucille 1954- WhoBlA 94

Bailey, Norman (Alishan) 1931- *WrDr 94*
Bailey, Norman (Stanley) 1933- *NewGrDO*
Bailey, Norman Alishan 1931- *WhoFI 94, WhoScEn 94*
Bailey, Norman Stanley 1933- *IntWW 93, Who 94*
Bailey, Orville Taylor 1909- *WhoAm 94*
Bailey, Oscar 1925- *WhoAmA 93*
Bailey, Patricia L. 1936- *WhoAmP 93*
Bailey, Patricia Price 1937- *WhoAm 94*
Bailey, Patrick Edward Robert 1925- *Who 94*
Bailey, Paul 1937- *IntWW 93, Who 94, WrDr 94*
Bailey, Paul (Dayton) 1906-1987 *EncSF 93*
Bailey, Pearl d1990 *WhoHol 92*
Bailey, Pearl 1918-1990 *AfrAmAl 6, WhAm 10*
Bailey, Pearl (Mae) 1918-1990 *BlkWr 2, ConAu 42NR*
Bailey, Philip Sigmon 1916- *WhoAm 94*
Bailey, Philip Sigmon, Jr. 1943- *WhoAm 94, WhoWest 94*
Bailey, Phyllis Ann 1957- *WhoBlA 94*
Bailey, Polly d1952 *WhoHol 92*
Bailey, R. Wendell 1940- *WhoAmP 93*
Bailey, Randall Charles 1947- *WhoBlA 94*
Bailey, Raymond d1980 *WhoHol 92*
Bailey, Reeve Maclaren 1911- *WhoAm 94*
Bailey, Reginald Bertram 1916- *Who 94*
Bailey, Richard (John) 1923- *Who 94*
Bailey, Richard Briggs 1926- *WhoAm 94*
Bailey, Richard H. 1940- *WhoAmA 93*
Bailey, Richard Weld 1939- *WhoAm 94*
Bailey, Robert d1983 *WhoHol 92*
Bailey, Robert, Jr. 1945- *WhoAm 94*
Bailey, Robert B., III 1929- *WhoBlA 94*
Bailey, Robert C. 1936- *WhoAm 94, WhoWest 94*
Bailey, Robert Earl 1938- *WhoMW 93*
Bailey, Robert Elliott 1932- *WhoAm 94*
Bailey, Robert Roy 1948- *WhoWest 94*
Bailey, Robert Short 1931- *WhoAm 94, WhoMW 93*
Bailey, Robert W. 1944- *WhoIns 94*
Bailey, Robert William 1944- *WhoAm 94*
Bailey, Robin 1919- *ConTFT 11, IntMPA 94, WhoHol 92*
Bailey, Ronald Bruce 1934- *WhoWest 94*
Bailey, Ronald C. *WhoAmP 93*
Bailey, Ronald W. 1938- *WhoBlA 94*
Bailey, Ronald William 1917- *Who 94*
Bailey, Samuel, Jr. 1940- *WhoAm 94*
Bailey, Scott Arthur 1947- *WhoFI 94*
Bailey, Shane 1971- *WhoHol 92*
Bailey, Sherwood d1987 *WhoHol 92*
Bailey, Sheryl K. 1958- *WhoBlA 94*
Bailey, Stacey Dwayne 1960- *WhoBlA 94*
Bailey, Stanley (Ernest) 1926- *Who 94*
Bailey, Steven Scott 1948- *WhoFI 94*
Bailey, Susan Carol 1954- *WhoMW 93*
Bailey, T. Wayne 1935- *WhoAmP 93*
Bailey, Thomas *WhoAmP 93*
Bailey, Thomas Aubrey 1912- *Who 94*
Bailey, Thomas Charles 1948- *WhoAmL 94*
Bailey, Thomas David 1897- *WhAm 10*
Bailey, Thomas Edward 1947- *WhoAm 94*
Bailey, Thomas Everett 1936- *WhoScEn 94, WhoWest 94*
Bailey, Thurl Lee 1961- *WhoBlA 94*
Bailey, Timothy James 1949- *WhoFI 94*
Bailey, Vicky A. *WhoAmP 93*
Bailey, Virginia Ellen *WhoAmA 93*
Bailey, Virginia Hurt 1937- *WhoWest 94*
Bailey, W. Edward 1944- *WhoAmL 94*
Bailey, Weltman D., Sr. 1927- *WhoBlA 94*
Bailey, Wilford Sherrill 1921- *WhoAm 94*
Bailey, Wilfrid 1910- *Who 94*
Bailey, William 1930- *WhoAmA 93*
Bailey, William Alvin 1934- *WhoAm 94, WhoMW 93*
Bailey, William H. *WhoBlA 94*
Bailey, William Harrison 1930- *WhoAm 94*
Bailey, William John 1921-1989 *WhAm 10*
Bailey, William Nathan 1955- *WhoScEn 94*
Bailey, William Norton d1962 *WhoHol 92*
Bailey, William O. 1926- *WhoAm 94, WhoFI 94*
Bailey, William R. 1935- *WhoBlA 94*
Bailey, William Ralph 1937- *WhoWest 94*
Bailey, William W. 1948- *WhoAmP 93*
Bailey, Worth 1908-1980 *WhoAmA 93N*
Bailey-Carman, Susan Marie 1948- *WhoMW 93*
Bailhache, Philip Martin 1946- *Who 94*
Bailhe, Jacques Pierre 1952- *WhoFI 94, WhoWest 94*
Bai Lichen 1941- *IntWW 93, WhoPRCh 91 [port]*
Bailie, Robin John 1937- *Who 94*
Bailin, David 1954- *WhoAmA 93*
Bailin, George *DrAPF 93*
Bailin, Hella 1915- *WhoAmA 93*
Baillargeon, Paule *WhoHol 92*
Baillarger, Jules 1809-1890 *EncSPD*
Baille, David L. *WhoScEn 94*
Baille, Hugh 1890-1966 *HisDcKW*
Baillie *Who 94*
Baillie, Alastair Turner 1932- *Who 94*
Baillie, Alexander Charles, Jr. 1939- *WhoAm 94*
Baillie, Allan 1943- *TwCYAW*
Baillie, Allan (Stuart) 1943- *ConAu 42NR*
Baillie, Charles Douglas 1918- *WhoAm 94*
Baillie, Gawaine George Hope 1934- *Who 94*
Baillie, Glenn Herbert 1928- *WhoMW 93*
Baillie, Ian Fowler 1921- *Who 94*
Baillie, James Leonard 1942- *WhoAm 94, WhoAmL 94*
Baillie, Joanna 1762-1851 *BlmGEL, BlmGWL*
Baillie, John 1944- *Who 94*
Baillie, Patricia Ann 1952- *WhoWest 94*
Baillie, Priscilla Woods 1935- *WhoAm 94*
Baillie, William James Laidlaw 1923- *Who 94*
Baillie-David, Sonja Kirsteen 1961- *WhoMW 93*
Baillie-Hamilton *Who 94*
Baillieu *Who 94*
Baillieu, Baron 1950- *Who 94*
Baillieu, Colin Clive 1930- *Who 94*
Baillieul, John Brouard 1945- *WhoAm 94*
Baillio, O. Dallas, Jr. 1940- *WhoAm 94*
Baillou, Luigi de c. 1735-c. 1809 *NewGrDO*
Bailly, Henri-Claude Albert 1946- *WhoAm 94*
Bailly, Jean Paul Marie Henri 1921- *IntWW 93*
Bailon, Gilbert Herculano 1959- *WhoHisp 94*
Bailón, Roberto 1938- *WhoHisp 94*
Bai Lutang *WhoPRCh 91*
Baily, Alfred Ewing 1925- *WhoAm 94*
Baily, Douglas B. 1937- *WhoAmP 93*
Baily, Douglas Boyd 1937- *WhoAm 94, WhoAmL 94, WhoWest 94*
Baily, Everett Minnich 1938- *WhoWest 94*
Baily, George Donald d1927 *WhoHol 92*
Baily, John T. 1944- *WhoIns 94*
Baily, Nathan A. 1920- *WrDr 94*
Baily, Nathan Ariel 1920- *WhoAm 94*
Bailyn, Bernard 1922- *IntWW 93, WhoAm 94, WrDr 94*
Baiman, Gail 1938- *WhoFI 94*
Baimbridge, Gloria Ann 1946- *WhoWest 94*
Bai Meiqing 1931- *WhoPRCh 91 [port]*
Bain, Andrew David 1936- *Who 94*
Bain, Barbara 1934- *WhoHol 92*
Bain, C. Randall 1934- *WhoAm 94, WhoAmL 94*
Bain, Charles Robert 1926- *WhoAmP 93*
Bain, Conrad 1923- *WhoHol 92*
Bain, Conrad Stafford 1923- *WhoAm 94*
Bain, David Haward 1949- *ConAu 141*
Bain, Donald K. 1935- *WhoAmP 93*
Bain, Donald Knight 1935- *WhoAm 94*
Bain, Douglas John 1924- *Who 94*
Bain, Edgar Collins 1891-1971 *EncABHB 9*
Bain, Erlin 1950- *WhoBlA 94*
Bain, George Sayers 1939 *Who 94*
Bain, George William 1901-1991 *WhAm 10*
Bain, Iain Andrew 1949- *Who 94*
Bain, James Arthur 1918- *WhoAm 94*
Bain, James William 1949- *WhoAmL 94*
Bain, John *Who 94*
Bain, (Kenneth) John 1939- *Who 94*
Bain, John Taylor 1912- *Who 94*
Bain, Josie Gray *WhoBlA 94*
Bain, Kenneth (Ross) 1923- *WrDr 94*
Bain, Lawrence David 1950- *WhoMW 93*
Bain, Lilian Pherne 1873- *WhoAmA 93N*
Bain, Linda Valerie 1947- *WhoBlA 94, WhoFI 94*
Bain, Margaret Anne *Who 94*
Bain, Mary Anderson 1911- *WhoAmP 93*
Bain, Neville Clifford 1940- *Who 94*
Bain, Raymone Kaye 1954- *WhoBlA 94*
Bain, Robert Addison 1932- *WhoAm 94*
Bain, Sherry 1947- *WhoHol 92*
Bain, Travis Whitsett, II 1934- *WhoAm 94*
Bain, Walt 1932- *WhoAmP 93*
Bain, Wilfred Conwell 1908- *NewGrDO, WhoAm 94*
Bain, William Donald, Jr. 1925- *WhoAm 94*
Bain, William James 1896-1985 *WhAm 10*
Bain, William James, Jr. 1930- *WhoAm 94*
Bainbridge, Beryl 1933- *BlmGEL [port]*
Bainbridge, Beryl 1934- *BlmGWL, IntWW 93, Who 94*
Bainbridge, Beryl (Margaret) 1934- *WrDr 94*
Bainbridge, Cyril 1928- *Who 94*
Bainbridge, Dona Bardelli 1953- *WhoFI 94*
Bainbridge, Elizabeth 1930- *NewGrDO*
Bainbridge, Frederick Freeman, III 1927- *WhoAm 94*
Bainbridge, Hazel 1911- *WhoHol 92*
Bainbridge, Henry d1993 *Who 94N*
Bainbridge, John 1913- *WrDr 94*
Bainbridge, John 1913-1992 *WhAm 10*
Bainbridge, John Seaman 1915- *WhoAmL 94*
Bainbridge, Kenneth Tompkins 1904- *IntWW 93, WhoAm 94*
Bainbridge, Russell Benjamin, Jr. 1945- *WhoFI 94*
Bainbridge, Stephen Mark 1958- *WhoAmL 94*
Bainbridge, William d1931 *WhoHol 92*
Baine, Herman 1940- *WhoBlA 94*
Baine, Jeff 1928- *WrDr 94*
Baine, Kevin T. 1949- *WhoAmL 94*
Bainer, Philip La Vern 1931- *WhoAm 94*
Bainer, Roy 1902-1990 *WhAm 10*
Baines, Amelia d1987 *WhoHol 92*
Baines, Anthony Cuthbert 1912- *Who 94*
Baines, Beulah d1930 *WhoHol 92*
Baines, George G. *Who 94*
Baines, Harold Douglas 1959- *WhoBlA 94*
Baines, Harold Douglass 1959- *WhoAm 94*
Baines, Henry T. *WhoBlA 94*
Baines, John Robert 1946- *Who 94*
Baines, Sherry *WhoHol 92*
Baines, Tyrone Randolph 1943- *WhoBlA 94*
Bainma Dandzin 1931- *WhoPRCh 91 [port]*
Bains, Elizabeth Miller 1943- *WhoScEn 94*
Bains, Harrison MacKellar, Jr. 1943- *WhoAm 94*
Bains, Lawrence Arthur 1920- *Who 94*
Bains, Lee Edmundson 1912- *WhoAm 94*
Bains, Leslie Elizabeth 1943- *WhoAm 94*
Bains, Linda Jane 1956- *WhoWest 94*
Bains, Malcolm Arnold 1921- *Who 94*
Bainter, Fay d1968 *WhoHol 92*
Bainter, M. Juanita 1919- *WhoAmP 93*
Bainter, Stan 1931- *WhoAmP 93*
Bainton, Donald J. 1931- *WhoAm 94, WhoFI 94*
Bainton, Dorothy Ford 1933- *WhoAm 94, WhoWest 94*
Bainton, Edgar (Leslie) 1880-1956 *NewGrDO*
Bainton, John Joseph 1947- *WhoAm 94, WhoAmL 94*
Bainton, Roland Herbert 1894-1984 *DcAmReB 2*
Bainum, Duke 1952- *WhoAmP 93*
Bainum, Peter Montgomery 1938- *WhoAm 94, WhoScEn 94*
Bainum, Stewart, Jr. 1946- *WhoAmP 93*
Bainum, Stewart William, Jr. 1946- *WhoFI 94*
Bainun Binti Mohd Ali, Raja Permaisuri Agong Tunku *WhoWomW 91*
Baio, Jimmy 1962- *WhoHol 92*
Baio, Scott 1959- *WhoHol 92*
Baio, Scott 1961- *IntMPA 94*
Bai Qingcai 1932- *IntWW 93*
Bair, Bruce B. 1928- *WhoAmL 94*
Bair, Deirdre 1935- *WrDr 94*
Bair, Edward Jay 1922- *WhoAm 94*
Bair, Gary Eugene 1950- *WhoAmL 94*
Bair, Myrna Lynn 1940- *WhoAmP 93*
Bair, Patrick *EncSF 93*
Bair, Robert Rippel 1925- *WhoAm 94*
Bair, Royden Stanley 1924- *WhoAm 94*
Bair, Sheila Colleen 1954- *WhoAm 94, WhoFI 94*
Bair, Stewart d1977 *WhoHol 92*
Bair, Teri Lynn 1958- *WhoAmL 94*
Bair, William Alois 1931- *WhoScEn 94*
Bair, William J. 1924- *WhoAm 94, WhoScEn 94*
Bairam, Erkin Ibrahim 1958- *WhoScEn 94*
Baird, Alan C. 1951- *WhoWest 94*
Baird, Ansie *DrAPF 93*
Baird, Anthony *Who 94*
Baird, (Eric) Anthony (Bamber) 1920- *Who 94*
Baird, Antony *WhoHol 92*
Baird, Bobbie d1937 *WhoHol 92*
Baird, Bruce Allen 1948- *WhoAm 94, WhoAmL 94*
Baird, Charles Bruce 1935- *WhoAmL 94*
Baird, Charles Fitz 1922- *Who 94, WhoAm 94*
Baird, Clay P. *WhoAmP 93*
Baird, David Charles 1912- *Who 94*
Baird, David Leach, Jr. 1945- *WhoAm 94*
Baird, David Tennent 1935- *Who 94*
Baird, Delpha 1930- *WhoWest 94*
Baird, Delpha A. 1930- *WhoAmP 93*
Baird, Dorothea d1933 *WhoHol 92*
Baird, Douglas Gordon 1953- *WhoAm 94*
Baird, Dugald Euan 1937- *IntWW 93, WhoAm 94, WhoFI 94*
Baird, Edward Rouzie, Jr. 1936- *WhoAm 94*
Baird, Eugenie d1988 *WhoHol 92*
Baird, Gordon Prentiss 1950- *WhoAm 94*
Baird, Harry *WhoHol 92*
Baird, Haynes Wallace 1943- *WhoScEn 94*
Baird, Irene 1901-1981 *BlmGWL*
Baird, J. Ernest 1944- *WhoWest 94*
Baird, J. Ernie 1944- *WhoAmP 93*
Baird, James 1943- *WhoAmL 94*
Baird, James (Parlane) 1915- *Who 94*
Baird, James Abington 1926- *WhoAm 94*
Baird, James Hewson 1944- *Who 94*
Baird, James L. 1947- *WhoFI 94*
Baird, James Richard Gardiner 1913- *Who 94*
Baird, James Vernon 1953- *WhoAmL 94*
Baird, Jeanne *WhoHol 92*
Baird, John Absalom, Jr. 1918- *WhoAm 94*
Baird, John Alexander 1937- *Who 94*
Baird, John Jeffers 1921- *WhoWest 94*
Baird, John Logie 1888-1946 *WorInv [port]*
Baird, Joseph Armstrong, (Jr.) 1922-1992 *ConAu 142*
Baird, Joseph Armstrong, Jr. 1922- *WhoAmA 93*
Baird, Joyce Elizabeth Leslie 1929- *Who 94*
Baird, Julianne 1952- *NewGrDO*
Baird, Keith E. 1923- *WhoBlA 94*
Baird, Kenneth William 1950- *Who 94*
Baird, Leah d1971 *WhoHol 92*
Baird, Lourdes G. *WhoAm 94, WhoWest 94*
Baird, Lourdes G. 1935- *WhoAmL 94, WhoHisp 94*
Baird, Mellon Campbell, Jr. 1931- *WhoAm 94*
Baird, Patricia Ann *WhoAm 94*
Baird, Paul Theodore 1944- *WhoAmP 93*
Baird, Perry James 1951- *WhoAm 94*
Baird, Phillip A. 1923- *WhoMW 93*
Baird, Robert 1798-1863 *DcAmReB 2*
Baird, Robert Dahlen 1933- *WhoAm 94*
Baird, Robert Dean 1933- *WhoMW 93*
Baird, Robert Lawrence 1942- *WhoAmL 94*
Baird, Robert Malcolm 1937- *WhoAm 94*
Baird, Robert R. 1929- *WhoIns 94*
Baird, Robert Royce 1929- *WhoAmL 94*
Baird, Robert S. 1944- *WhoAmL 94*
Baird, Roger Allen 1914- *WhoAm 94*
Baird, Ronald 1930- *Who 94*
Baird, Rosemarie Annette 1956- *WhoScEn 94*
Baird, Russell Miller 1916- *WhoAm 94*
Baird, Russell N(orman) 1922- *WrDr 94*
Baird, S. L. *WhoHol 92*
Baird, Sandra L. 1940- *WhoAmP 93*
Baird, Sharon *WhoHol 92*
Baird, Stewart d1947 *WhoHol 92*
Baird, Susan 1940- *Who 94*
Baird, Tadeusz 1928-1981 *NewGrDO*
Baird, Thomas (Henry Eustace) 1924- *Who 94*
Baird, Thomas Bryan, Jr. 1931- *WhoAmL 94*
Baird, Thomas Terence 1916- *Who 94*
Baird, William 1927- *Who 94*
Baird, William McKenzie 1944- *WhoAm 94, WhoScEn 94*
Baird, Zoe 1952- *WhoAm 94, WhoAmL 94*
Baird Anstine, Anna 1924- *WhoWomW 91*
Baird Whittlesey, Eunice *WhoWomW 91*
Bairnsfather, Bruce d1959 *WhoHol 92*
Bairsto, Peter (Edward) 1926- *Who 94*
Bairstow, John 1930- *Who 94*
Bairstow, Richard Raymond 1917- *WhoAmL 94*
Baisch, Steven Dale 1955- *WhoMW 93, WhoScEn 94*
Baisden, Eleanor Marguerite 1935- *WhoFI 94, WhoMW 93*
Bai Shangwu 1928- *IntWW 93, WhoPRCh 91 [port]*
Bai Shi 1927- *WhoPRCh 91 [port]*
Bai Shiming 1954- *WhoPRCh 91 [port]*
Bai Shoumian *WhoPRCh 91*
Bai Shouyi 1909- *IntWW 93*
Bai Shouyi, Djamal al-Din 1909- *WhoPRCh 91 [port]*
Bai Shuxiang 1939- *WhoPRCh 91 [port]*
Bai Shuxiang, Miss 1939- *IntWW 93*
Baisley, Charles William 1930- *WhoAmL 94*
Baisley, Robert William 1923- *WhoAm 94*

Baisman, Margarita Alejo 1945- WhoFI 94
Bai-ta-yi WhoPRCh 91
Bai Tongshuo WhoPRCh 91
Baity, Gail Owens 1952- WhoBlA 94
Baity, John Cooley 1933- WhoAm 94
Baitz, Jon Robin 1961- WrDr 94
Baitz, Jon Robin 1964- ConDr 93
Baitzel, Gregory Wilson 1955- WhoFI 94
Bai Xueshi 1915- IntWW 93, WhoPRCh 91 [port]
Bai Yang WhoPRCh 91
Bai Yang 1920- IntWW 93, WhoPRCh 91 [port]
Baizan, Gabriel WhoHisp 94
Baizer, Eric DrAPF 93
Baizerman, Saul 1889-1957 WhoAmA 93N
Bai Zhimin 1918- WhoPRCh 91 [port]
Bai Zuoguang 1933- WhoPRCh 91 [port]
Bajaj, Harjit Singh 1956- WhoAsA 94
Bajaj, Rahul 1938- IntWW 93
Bajaria, Hans Jamnadas 1943- WhoMW 93
Bajefsky, Robert D. 1943- WhoAmL 94
Bajek, Frank Michael 1950- WhoFI 94
Bajic, Isidor 1878-1915 NewGrDO
Ba Jin 1904?- ConWorW 93, IntWW 93, WhoPRCh 91 [port]
Bajla, Jan EncSF 93
Bajoie, Diana E. 1948- WhoAmP 93, WhoWomW 91
Bajor, Gizi d1951 WhoHol 92
Bajor, James Henry 1953- WhoMW 93
Bajorek, Christopher Henry 1943- WhoAm 94
Bajos, Orlando L. WhoHisp 94
Bajpai, Girja S. 1891-1954 HisDcKW
Bajpai, Pramod Kumar 1951- WhoScEn 94
Bajpai, Praphulla Kumar 1936- WhoAsA 94
Bajpai, Rajendra Kumari 1925- IntWW 93, WhoWomW 91
Bajpai, Rakesh Kumar 1950- WhoAsA 94
Bajt, Aleksander 1921- IntWW 93
Bajzer, William Xavier 1940- WhoMW 93
Bak, Chan Soo 1936- WhoAsA 94
Bak, David John 1950- WhoAm 94
Bak, Martin Joseph 1947- WhoScEn 94
Bakal, Carl 1918- WhoAm 94
Bakala, Bretislav 1897-1958 NewGrDO
Bakalar, John Stephen 1948- WhoAm 94
Bakalian, Alexander Edward 1957- WhoScEn 94
Bakaluba, Jane J. BlmGWL
Bakaly, Charles G., Jr. 1927- WhoAmP 93
Bakaly, Charles George, Jr. 1927- WhoAm 94
Bakalyan, Richard WhoHol 92
Bakanowsky, Louis J. 1930- WhoAmA 93
Bakatin, Vadim Viktorovich 1937- IntWW 93, LoBiDrD
Bakaty, Mike 1936- WhoAmA 93
Bakay, Louis 1917- WhoAm 94
Bakay, Roy Arpad Earle 1949- WhoAm 94, WhoScEn 94
Bakeman, Carol Ann 1934- WhoWest 94
Baker, Adolph 1917- WhoAm 94
Baker, Al 1956- WhoBlA 94
Baker, Alan 1939- IntWW 93, Who 94, WrDr 94
Baker, Alex Anthony 1922- Who 94
Baker, Alexander Shelley d1992 Who 94N
Baker, Almina Rogers 1923- WhoAmP 93
Baker, Althea 1949- WhoBlA 94
Baker, Alton Fletcher, Jr. 1919- WhoAm 94, WhoWest 94
Baker, Alton Wesley 1912-1992 WhAm 10
Baker, Amanda Sirmon 1934- WhoAm 94
Baker, Andrew Hartill 1948- WhoAm 94
Baker, Andrew Zachariah 1919- WhoAmP 93
Baker, Anita 1958- AfrAmAl 6 [port], WhoAm 94, WhoBlA 94
Baker, Anita Diane 1955- WhoAmL 94, WhoFI 94
Baker, Ann Maureen Who 94
Baker, Anthony Baxter 1923- Who 94
Baker, Anthony Castelli 1921- Who 94
Baker, Art d1966 WhoHol 92
Baker, Arthur John 1928- Who 94
Baker, Arthur John 1942- WhoFI 94, WhoMW 93
Baker, Avery Dean 1935- WhoIns 94
Baker, Barry WhoMW 93
Baker, Bart 1915- WhoAmP 93
Baker, Belle d1957 WhoHol 92
Baker, Benjamin Joseph 1954- WhoAmL 94
Baker, Benny 1907- WhoHol 92
Baker, Bernard Robert, II 1915- WhoAm 94
Baker, Beverly Poole 1944- WhoBlA 94
Baker, Bill d1993 NewYTBS 93
Baker, Bill 1940- CngDr 93
Baker, Blanche 1956- IntMPA 94, WhoHol 92
Baker, Bob d1975 WhoHol 92
Baker, Bonnie 1917- WhoHol 92
Baker, Boyd Odell 1961- WhoAmP 93
Baker, Bridget Downey 1955- WhoWest 94
Baker, Bruce Edward 1937- WhoScEn 94
Baker, Bruce J. 1954- WhoAmL 94
Baker, Bruce Jay 1954- WhoAmL 94, WhoMW 93
Baker, Bruce S. WhoScEn 94
Baker, C. C. WhoBlA 94
Baker, C(hristopher) J(ohn) 1948- WrDr 94
Baker, C. Ray WhoAmP 93
Baker, Calvin Daniel, Jr. 1949- WhoAmL 94
Baker, Cameron 1937- WhoAm 94, WhoAmL 94, WhoFI 94, WhoWest 94
Baker, Carl Gwin 1920- WhoScEn 94
Baker, Carl Leroy 1943- WhoAm 94, WhoAmL 94
Baker, Carleton Harold 1930- WhoAm 94
Baker, Carol DrAPF 93
Baker, Carol Ann 1958- WhoMW 93
Baker, Carolyn Ann 1936- WhoScEn 94
Baker, Carroll 1931- ConAu 142, IntMPA 94, IntWW 93, WhoHol 92
Baker, Carroll G. 1944- WhoMW 93
Baker, Cecil John 1915- Who 94
Baker, Charles A. Who 94
Baker, Charles DeWitt 1932- WhoAm 94, WhoWest 94
Baker, Charles Duane WhoAmP 93
Baker, Charles Duane 1928- WhoAm 94
Baker, Charles Edwin 1902-1971 WhoAmA 93N
Baker, Charles Ernest 1946- WhoAm 94, WhoFI 94
Baker, Charles H. 1951- WhoScEn 94
Baker, Charles Porter 1941- WhoAmL 94
Baker, Charles Ray 1932- WhoAm 94
Baker, Charles Stewart 1959- WhoAmL 94
Baker, Charles Wayne 1940- WhoAmP 93
Baker, Christopher Paul 1938- Who 94
Baker, Clarence Albert, Sr. 1919- WhoFI 94, WhoMW 93
Baker, Claude Douglas 1944- WhoMW 93
Baker, Clive Andrew 1946- WhoIns 94
Baker, Constance H. 1948- WhoAmL 94
Baker, Cornelia Draves 1929- WhoAmA 93
Baker, Cornelius O. AfrAmG
Baker, D. James WhoScEn 94
Baker, Dale Eugene 1930- WhoScEn 94
Baker, Dan d1939 WhoHol 92
Baker, Danial Edwin 1955- WhoWest 94
Baker, Daniel Richard 1932- WhoFI 94
Baker, Darrius Gene 1946- WhoIns 94
Baker, Darryl Brent 1955- WhoBlA 94
Baker, Dave E. 1943- WhoBlA 94
Baker, David DrAPF 93
Baker, David d1981 WhoHol 92
Baker, David A. 1951- WhoAm 94, WhoAmL 94
Baker, David Arthur 1941- WhoFI 94
Baker, David B. 1936- WhoScEn 94
Baker, David Bigelow 1946- WhoMW 93
Baker, David Brian 1955- WhoMW 93
Baker, David Guy 1947- WhoAmL 94
Baker, David Harris 1955- WhoAm 94
Baker, David Hiram 1939- WhoAm 94, WhoMW 93
Baker, David Nathaniel, Jr. 1931- AfrAmAl 6, WhoBlA 94
Baker, David Remember 1932- WhoAm 94, WhoAmL 94
Baker, David S. 1937- WhoAm 94, WhoAmL 94
Baker, Deane 1925- WhoMW 93
Baker, Deborah Ann 1956- WhoWest 94
Baker, Delbert Wayne 1953- WhoBlA 94
Baker, Denys Marie 1948- WhoWest 94
Baker, Derek Who 94
Baker, (Leonard Graham) Derek 1931- Who 94
Baker, Dexter Farrington 1927- WhoAm 94
Baker, Diane 1938- IntMPA 94, WhoHol 92
Baker, Dina Gustin WhoAmA 93
Baker, Don M. 1932- WhoIns 94
Baker, Don Robert 1933- WhoWest 94
Baker, Donald 1929- WhoAm 94, WhoAmL 94, WhoMW 93
Baker, Donald Gardner 1923- WhoAm 94
Baker, Donald James 1937- WhoAm 94, WhoScEn 94
Baker, Donald Matthew 1925- WhoAmP 93
Baker, Donald P. 1947- WhoAmL 94
Baker, Donald Parks 1932- WhoAm 94
Baker, Donald Scott 1939- WhoAm 94
Baker, Donald W. DrAPF 93
Baker, Douglas Robert Pelham 1929- Who 94
Baker, Dusty 1949- WhoAm 94, WhoBlA 94, WhoWest 94
Baker, Dylan 1958- WhoHol 92
Baker, E. Lamar 1915- WhoAmP 93
Baker, Earl M. 1940- WhoAmP 93
Baker, Earl Russel, II 1950- WhoFI 94
Baker, Ed DrAPF 93
Baker, Eddie d1968 WhoHol 92
Baker, Edward George 1908- WhoScEn 94
Baker, Edward Kevin 1948- WhoAm 94
Baker, Edward L. 1946- WhoAm 94
Baker, Edward Martin 1941- WhoAm 94
Baker, Edwin Clarence 1925- WhoIns 94
Baker, Edwin Herbert 1934- WhoAm 94
Baker, Edwin Moody 1923- WhoAm 94, WhoWest 94
Baker, Edwin Stuart 1944- WhoWest 94
Baker, Elaine WhoHol 92
Baker, Elizabeth 1941- WhoAmP 93
Baker, Elizabeth C. WhoAmA 93
Baker, Elizabeth Calhoun WhoAm 94
Baker, Elizabeth Margaret 1945- Who 94
Baker, Elizabeth N. 1933- WhoAmP 93
Baker, Ella 1902-1986 ConBlB 5 [port]
Baker, Ella Jo 1903-1986 AmSocL
Baker, Ella Josephine 1903-1986 AfrAmAl 6
Baker, Elliott 1922- WrDr 94
Baker, Elmer Elias, Jr. 1922- WhoAm 94
Baker, Elsie d1971 WhoHol 92
Baker, Eric Edward 1933- WhoAm 94
Baker, Ernest Waldo, Jr. 1926- WhoAm 94, WhoFI 94, WhoMW 93
Baker, Eugene 1938- WhoBlA 94
Baker, Eugene Ames 1928- WhoAmA 93N
Baker, Eugene Manigault 1951- WhoWest 94
Baker, Falcon (O., Jr.) 1916- WrDr 94
Baker, Fay WhoHol 92
Baker, Florence c. 1841-1918 WhWE
Baker, Floyd d1943 WhoHol 92
Baker, Floyd Edward 1920- WhoBlA 94
Baker, Floyd Wilmer 1927- WhoAm 94
Baker, Francis Edward N. Who 94
Baker, Francis Eustace 1933- Who 94
Baker, Frank d1963 WhoHol 92
Baker, Frank d1980 WhoHol 92
Baker, Frank 1910- WrDr 94
Baker, Fred Greentree 1950- WhoWest 94
Baker, Frederick John 1941- WhoAm 94
Baker, Frederick Milton, Jr. 1949- WhoAm 94, WhoAmL 94
Baker, Frederick Waller 1949- WhoIns 94
Baker, Gail Dyer 1954- WhoAmL 94
Baker, Garrison Buford 1955- WhoAmP 93
Baker, Gene Stewart 1937- WhoAmP 93
Baker, Geoffrey 1925- Who 94
Baker, Geoffrey Hunter 1916- Who 94
Baker, George d1976 WhoHol 92
Baker, George 1929- WhoHol 92
Baker, George 1931- IntMPA 94
Baker, George Allen, Jr. 1932- WhoAm 94
Baker, George Chisholm 1918- WhoAm 94
Baker, George H. 1919- WhoAmP 93
Baker, George Harold, III 1949- WhoScEn 94
Baker, George P. 1931- WhoAmA 93
Baker, George Pierce 1903- IntWW 93
Baker, George Russell 1956- WhoWest 94
Baker, George William 1917- Who 94
Baker, Gertrude Margaret 1894- WhAm 10
Baker, Gilbert Jens 1946- WhoMW 93
Baker, Gladys Corvera 1950- WhoHisp 94
Baker, Gladys Elizabeth 1908- WhoWest 94
Baker, Gloria Ann 1939- WhoMW 93
Baker, Gordon (P.) 1938- WrDr 94
Baker, Gordon Meldrum 1941- Who 94
Baker, Gregory D. 1948- WhoBlA 94
Baker, Gregory Richard 1947- WhoMW 93, WhoScEn 94
Baker, Gwendolyn Calvert 1931- WhoBlA 94
Baker, Harlan Robert 1947- WhoAmP 93
Baker, Harold Albert 1929- WhoAm 94, WhoAmL 94, WhoMW 93
Baker, Harold Cecil 1954- WhoFI 94
Baker, Helen Doyle Peil 1943- WhoFI 94
Baker, Helen Marie 1946- WhoScEn 94
Baker, Henry Judd WhoHol 92
Baker, Henry S., Jr. 1926- WhoAm 94
Baker, Henry W., Sr. 1937- WhoBlA 94
Baker, Herbert Geoffrey 1941- WhoWest 94
Baker, Herbert George 1920- WhoScEn 94, WhoWest 94
Baker, Herman 1926- WhoAm 94
Baker, Hollis MacLure 1916- WhoAm 94
Baker, Houston A., Jr. 1943- BlkWr 2, ConAu 42NR, ConBlB 6 [port], WhoBlA 94
Baker, Houston Alfred, Jr. 1943- WrDr 94
Baker, Howard H., Jr. 1925- WhoAmP 93
Baker, Howard Henry, Jr. 1925- IntWW 93, Who 94, WhoAm 94
Baker, Hugh D(avid) R(oberts) 1937- WrDr 94
Baker, Hylda d1986 WhoHol 92
Baker, Ian Helstrip 1927- Who 94
Baker, Ian Michael 1947- Who 94
Baker, Ira Lee 1914- WhoAm 94
Baker, Ivor Who 94
Baker, (Allan) Ivor 1908- Who 94
Baker, J. A., II WhoIns 94
Baker, J. A., II 1944- WhoAm 94
Baker, Jack Sherman 1920- WhoAm 94
Baker, James 1818-1898 WhWE
Baker, James A., III 1930- WhoAmP 93
Baker, James Addison 1930- Who 94
Baker, James Addison, III 1930- IntWW 93, WhoAm 94, WhoAmL 94
Baker, James Allan 1942- WhoAm 94
Baker, James Barnes 1933- WhoAm 94
Baker, James Burnell 1930- WhoScEn 94
Baker, James E. 1935- WhoBlA 94
Baker, James Edward Sproul 1912- WhoAm 94, WhoAmL 94, WhoMW 93
Baker, James Edyrn 1951- WhoAmL 94
Baker, James Estes 1935- WhoAm 94, WhoAmP 93
Baker, James Gilbert 1914- WhoAm 94, WhoScEn 94
Baker, James Glen 1938- WhoAmL 94
Baker, James Kendrick 1931- WhoAm 94, WhoFI 94
Baker, James Reginald 1945- WhoScEn 94
Baker, James Rupert 1925- WrDr 94
Baker, James W. 1926- WrDr 94
Baker, Jane Elaine 1923- WhoAmP 93, WhoWest 94
Baker, Jane Marie 1958- WhoWest 94
Baker, Janet 1933- IntWW 93
Baker, Janet (Abbott) 1933- NewGrDO, Who 94
Baker, Jay WhoHol 92
Baker, Jean Harvey 1933- WhoAm 94
Baker, Jean Mary 1944- WhoAm 94
Baker, Jeanette Sledge 1947- WhoWest 94
Baker, Jeannie 1950- WrDr 94
Baker, Jennifer 1946- & Baker, Susan 1946- WhoHol 92
Baker, Jill Withrow 1942- WhoAmA 93
Baker, Joby 1934- WhoHol 92
Baker, Joe 1946- WhoAmA 93
Baker, Joe Don 1936- IntMPA 94, WhoAm 94, WhoHol 92
Baker, Joe M., Jr. 1927- WhoAmP 93
Baker, John WhoHol 92
Baker, John A. 1939- WhoIns 94
Baker, John Alexander 1927- WhoAm 94
Baker, John Arnold 1925- Who 94
Baker, John Austin 1928- IntWW 93, Who 94
Baker, John B. Who 94
Baker, John Burkett 1931- Who 94
Baker, John Coalter 1953- WhoFI 94
Baker, John Daniel, II 1948- WhoFI 94
Baker, John E. 1954- WhoMW 93, WhoScEn 94
Baker, John Edward 1917- WhoAmP 93
Baker, John Hamilton 1944- IntWW 93, Who 94
Baker, John Martin 1944- WhoAmP 93
Baker, John Milnes 1932- WhoAm 94
Baker, John R. 1943- WhoAmL 94
Baker, John Russell 1926- WhoAm 94, WhoFI 94
Baker, John Stevenson 1931- WhoAm 94, WhoMW 93, WhoScEn 94
Baker, John William 1937- IntWW 93, Who 94
Baker, Joni Elizabeth 1959- WhoAmP 93
Baker, Joseph Edmond 1940- WhoAmP 93
Baker, Joseph Roderick, III 1947- WhoWest 94
Baker, Josephine d1975 WhoHol 92
Baker, Josephine 1906- ConMus 10 [port]
Baker, Josephine 1906-1975 AfrAmAl 6 [port]
Baker, Joy d1993 NewYTBS 93
Baker, Joyce Irene 1929- WhoAmP 93
Baker, Judith Ann 1953- WhoAm 94
Baker, June Frankland DrAPF 93
Baker, Kathleen Ann 1935- WhoWest 94
Baker, Kathy 1950- IntMPA 94
Baker, Kathy 1951- WhoHol 92
Baker, Kathy Whitton 1950- WhoAm 94
Baker, Keith Lorden 1931- WhoWest 94
Baker, Keith Michael 1938- WhoAm 94, WhoWest 94
Baker, Ken WhoAmP 93
Baker, Ken 1947- WhoAmP 93
Baker, Kendall L. 1942- WhoAm 94, WhoMW 93
Baker, Kenneth 1946- WhoAmA 93
Baker, Kenneth (Wilfred) 1934- IntWW 93, Who 94
Baker, Kenneth Albert 1946- WhoAm 94
Baker, Kenneth L. 1952- WhoWest 94
Baker, Kenny WhoHol 92
Baker, Kenny d1985 WhoHol 92
Baker, Kent Alfred 1948- WhoWest 94
Baker, Kent Steven 1945- WhoAmP 93

Balanoff, Clement 1953- WhoAmP 93
Balanoff, Miriam D. WhoAmP 93
Balantzow, Robert Sheldon 1940- WhoMW 93
Balaras, Constantinos Agelou 1962- WhoScEn 94
Balard, Antoine Jerome 1802-1876 WorScD
Balart, Luis A. 1948- WhoHisp 94
Balas, Irene 1928- WhoAmA 93
Balasa, Mark Edward 1958- WhoFI 94
Balasanian, Sergey Artem'yevich 1902-1982 NewGrDO
Balash, Jeffrey Linke 1948- WhoWest 94
Balaski, Belinda WhoHol 92
Balasko, Josiane WhoHol 92
Balassa, Bela 1928- WrDr 94
Balassa, Bela 1928-1991 WhAm 10
Balassa, Ivan 1917- IntWW 93
Balassa, Leslie Ladislaus 1903-1992 WhAm 10
Balassa, Sandor 1935- IntWW 93, NewGrDO
Balasubramanian, Aiylam Subramaniaier 1937- WhoScEn 94
Balasubramanian, Krishna 1945- WhoScEn 94
Balasuriya, Stanislaus Tissa 1924- IntWW 93
Balatsky, Alexander Vasilievitch 1961- WhoScEn 94
Balay, Felicie 1940- WhoAmA 93
Balay, Robert Elmore 1930- WhoAm 94
Balayan, Roman Gurgenovich 1941- IntWW 93
Balaye, Simone 1925- IntWW 93
Balazs, Artur Krzysztof 1952- IntWW 93
Balazs, Bela 1884-1949 IntDcF 2-4, NewGrDO
Balazs, Eva H. 1915- IntWW 93
Balazs, Louis Attila Peter 1937- WhoMW 93
Balazs, Mary DrAPF 93
Balbach, George Charles 1931- WhoMW 93
Balbach, Stanley Byron 1919- WhoAm 94
Balbi, Giovan Battista fl. 1636-1657 NewGrDO
Balbilla fl. 2nd cent.- BlmGWL
Balbin, Julius DrAPF 93
Balbin, Julius 1917- WhoAm 94
Balbo, Ceccarelli Laura 1933- WhoWomW 91
Balboa, Marcelo WhoHisp 94
Balboa, Richard Mario 1936- WhoHisp 94
Balboa, Vasco Nunez De 1475-1519 WhWE [port]
Balboni, Michael A. L. 1959- WhoAmP 93
Balcarres, Alexander Lindsay, Earl of 1752-1825 WhAmRev
Balcazar, Jose Luis 1959- WhoScEn 94
Balcazar-Monzon, Gustavo 1927- Who 94
Balcer, Charles Louis 1921- WhoAm 94
Balcerowicz, Leszek 1947- IntWW 93
Balcerzak, Marion John 1933- WhoScEn 94
Balcerzak, Stanley Paul 1930- WhoAm 94, WhoScEn 94
Balcerzak-Dyer, Judith Geneva 1949- WhoWest 94
Balch, Charles M. 1942- WhoAm 94
Balch, Emily Greene 1867-1961 AmSocL
Balch, Frank 1880-1937 EncSF 93
Balch, Glenn McClain, Jr. 1937- WhoAm 94, WhoWest 94
Balch, Glenn O. 1902-1989 WhAm 10
Balch, Joe d1967 WhoHol 92
Balch, Pamela Mae 1950- WhoWest 94
Balch, Ralph Elias 1934- WhoFI 94
Balch, Samuel Eason 1919- WhoAm 94
Balchin, John Alfred 1914- Who 94
Balchin, Nigel (Marlin) 1908-1970 EncSF 93
Balchin, Robert (George Alexander) 1942- Who 94
Balchin, William George Victor 1916- Who 94, WrDr 94
Balciar, Gerald George 1942- WhoAmA 93, WhoWest 94
Balcom, Gloria Darleen 1939- WhoFI 94, WhoWest 94
Balcom, Orville 1937- WhoWest 94
Balcomb, M. Michelle 1927- WhoWest 94
Balcombe, Frederick James 1911- Who 94
Balcombe, John Who 94
Balcombe, (Alfred) John 1925- Who 94
Balcon, Jill 1925- WhoHol 92
Balcon, Michael 1896-1977 IntDcF 2-4
Balcon, Raphael 1936- Who 94
Bald, William c. 1789-1857 DcNaB MP
Balda, Juan Carlos 1956- WhoHisp 94
Baldacci, John E. WhoAmP 93
Baldanello, Emilio d1952 WhoHol 92
Baldasaro, P. Michael 1948- WhoAm 94
Baldassano, Corinne Leslie 1950- WhoAm 94
Baldassari, Benedetto fl. 1708-1725 NewGrDO
Baldassari, Jeffrey John 1963- WhoAmL 94, WhoFI 94, WhoMW 93
Baldassari, Robert Gene 1949- WhoFI 94
Baldassaro, Lawrence Anthony 1943- WhoMW 93
Baldauf, Kent Edward 1943- WhoAmL 94
Baldaya, Alfonso Gonclaves fl. 143-?- WhWE
Balder, James Ellsworth WhoMW 93
Balderacchi, Arthur Eugene 1937- WhoAmA 93
Balderas, Robert Mario 1938- WhoHisp 94
Balderrama, Fernando Hiriart WhoAm 94, WhoFI 94
Balderrama, Fred WhoHisp 94
Balderrama, Sylvia Ramirez 1952- WhoHisp 94
Balderson, Margaret 1935- WrDr 94
Balderston, Frederick E(mery) 1923- WrDr 94
Balderston, Jean DrAPF 93
Balderston, John L. 1889-1954 IntDcF 2-4
Balderston, Thomas William 1941- WhoFI 94
Balderston, William, III 1927- WhoAm 94
Balderstone, James (Schofield) 1921- Who 94
Balderstone, James Schofield 1921- IntWW 93
Baldeschwieler, John Dickson 1933- IntWW 93, WhoAm 94, WhoScEn 94
Baldessari, John Anthony 1931- WhoAm 94, WhoAmA 93
Baldi, Antonio fl. 1722-1735 NewGrDO
Baldi, Robert Otjen 1949- WhoAmL 94
Baldin, Aleksandr Mikhailovich 1926- IntWW 93
Balding, Bruce Edward 1931- WhoFI 94
Balding, Rebecca WhoHol 92
Baldini, Lucrezia 1700?-1733 NewGrDO
Baldisseri, Marie Rosanne 1955- WhoAm 94
Baldizar, Barbara J. 1947- WhoAmP 93
Baldo, George Jesse 1952- WhoScEn 94
Baldock, Bobby R. WhoAmP 93
Baldock, Bobby Ray 1936- WhoAm 94, WhoAmL 94, WhoWest 94
Baldock, Brian Ford 1934- Who 94
Baldock, John Markham 1915- Who 94
Baldock, Lionel Trevor 1936- Who 94
Baldock, (Richard) Stephen 1944- Who 94
Baldon, Cleo 1927- WhoWest 94
Baldonado, Ardelina Albano WhoAsA 94
Baldonado, Arthur WhoHisp 94
Baldonado, George WhoHisp 94
Baldonado, Lisa 1937- WhoHisp 94
Baldonado, Michael WhoHisp 94
Baldoz, Gerald L. 1948- WhoAsA 94
Baldra, Chuck d1949 WhoHol 92
Baldree, Phyllis Anne 1954- WhoFI 94
Baldrey, Keith (Donald) 1958- WrDr 94
Baldridge, Charlene DrAPF 93
Baldridge, Judy Jean 1942- WhoMW 93
Baldridge, Mark S. 1946- WhoAmA 93
Baldridge, Robert Crary 1921- WhoAm 94
Baldrige, Letitia WhoAm 94
Baldry, Antony Brian 1950- Who 94
Baldry, Harold Caparne 1907-1991 WrDr 94N
Baldry, Jack Thomas 1911- Who 94
Baldry, Tony Who 94
Balducci, Carolyn DrAPF 93
Balducci, Marina 1758?-1784? NewGrDO
Balducci, Richard J. 1942- WhoAmP 93
Balducci, Stephen Watts 1950- WhoFI 94
Baldursson, Sigtryggur See Sugarcubes, The ConMus 10
Baldus, Alvin J. 1926- WhoAmP 93
Baldwin Who 94
Baldwin, A. Quillian, Jr. WhoAmP 93
Baldwin, Abraham 1754-1807 WhAmRev
Baldwin, Adam 1962- IntMPA 94, WhoHol 92
Baldwin, Alan Charles 1948- Who 94
Baldwin, Alec 1958- IntMPA 94, WhoAm 94, WhoHol 92
Baldwin, Allan Oliver 1948- WhoMW 93
Baldwin, Anne Norris 1938- WrDr 94
Baldwin, Anthony Blair 1928- WhoFI 94
Baldwin, Arthur Dwight, Jr. 1938- WhoAm 94
Baldwin, Bee EncSF 93
Baldwin, Benjamin d1993 NewYTBS 93 [port]
Baldwin, Betty Jo 1925- WhoFI 94, WhoScEn 94, WhoWest 94
Baldwin, Bill WhoHol 92
Baldwin, Bill d1982 WhoHol 92
Baldwin, Bill 1935- EncSF 93
Baldwin, Brent Winfield 1952- WhoAmL 94
Baldwin, Calvin Benham, Jr. 1925- WhoAm 94
Baldwin, Carolyn H. WhoBlA 94
Baldwin, Carolyn Whitmore 1932- WhoAmL 94
Baldwin, Carrie Marie 1965- WhoWest 94
Baldwin, Charlene Marie 1946- WhoWest 94
Baldwin, Charles Carroll, Jr. 1956- WhoIns 94
Baldwin, Charles F. d1993 NewYTBS 93
Baldwin, Clarence Jones, Jr. 1929- WhoAm 94
Baldwin, Cynthia A. 1945- WhoBlA 94
Baldwin, Daniel Flanagan 1965- WhoScEn 94
Baldwin, David Arthur 1936- Who 94
Baldwin, David E. 1936- WhoScEn 94
Baldwin, David Rawson 1923- WhoAm 94
Baldwin, David Shepard 1921- WhoAm 94
Baldwin, DeWitt Clair d1993 NewYTBS 93
Baldwin, DeWitt Clair, Jr. 1922- WhoAm 94
Baldwin, Dick WhoHol 92
Baldwin, Douglas Parks 1936- WhoAmP 93
Baldwin, Edwin Steedman 1932- WhoAm 94
Baldwin, Elaine Marshall 1947- WhoAmP 93
Baldwin, Everett Newton 1932- WhoAm 94
Baldwin, Frank Bruce, III 1939- WhoAm 94
Baldwin, Gary Lee 1943- WhoAm 94
Baldwin, Garza, Jr. 1921- WhoAm 94
Baldwin, George Clifton 1921- Who 94
Baldwin, George Curriden 1917- WhoAm 94
Baldwin, George Koehler 1919- WhoMW 93
Baldwin, George Michael 1960- WhoScEn 94
Baldwin, George R. 1934- WhoBlA 94
Baldwin, Gerald Erwin 1950- WhoWest 94
Baldwin, Gerald Lee 1946- WhoAmL 94
Baldwin, Gladys Jane 1924- WhoWest 94
Baldwin, Gordon Brewster 1929- WhoAm 94, WhoAmL 94
Baldwin, Gordon C(ortis) 1908- WrDr 94
Baldwin, Grant Kermit 1953- WhoFI 94, WhoWest 94
Baldwin, Gregory Alan 1946- WhoAm 94
Baldwin, Hanson W. 1903- HisDcKW
Baldwin, Hanson Weightman 1903-1991 WhAm 10
Baldwin, Harold Fletcher 1923- WhoAmA 93
Baldwin, Harry, II WhoAmA 93N
Baldwin, Henry Furlong 1932- WhoAm 94, WhoFI 94
Baldwin, Irene S. 1939- WhoFI 94, WhoMW 93
Baldwin, J. Michael 1947- WhoAmL 94
Baldwin, Jack Edward 1938- IntWW 93, Who 94
Baldwin, Jack Norman 1919-1989 WhAm 10
Baldwin, James 1924-1987 AfrAmAl 6 [port]
Baldwin, James (Arthur) 1924-1987 ConDr 93, GayLL, RfGShF, TwCYAW
Baldwin, James Arthur 1924-1987 AmCulL [port]
Baldwin, James William 1923- WhoAm 94
Baldwin, Janice Murphy 1926- WhoAmL 94, WhoMW 93
Baldwin, Jeduthan 1730-1788 AmRev
Baldwin, Jeduthan 1732-1788 WhAmRev
Baldwin, Jeffrey Kenton 1954- WhoAmL 94, WhoAmP 93, WhoMW 93
Baldwin, Jerome Charles 1941- WhoAmP 93
Baldwin, John d1969 WhoHol 92
Baldwin, John 1922-1987 WhoAmA 93N
Baldwin, John 1923- Who 94
Baldwin, John 1954- WhoAmL 94
Baldwin, John Ashby, Jr. 1933- WhoAm 94
Baldwin, John Chandler 1945- WhoAm 94, WhoAmL 94
Baldwin, John Charles 1948- WhoAm 94, WhoScEn 94
Baldwin, John David 1941- WhoAm 94, WhoWest 94
Baldwin, John Evan 1931- Who 94
Baldwin, John H. 1913- WhoBlA 94
Baldwin, John Wesley 1929- WhoAm 94
Baldwin, Judy WhoHol 92
Baldwin, Judy 1942- WhoMW 93
Baldwin, Leona B. 1934- WhoFI 94
Baldwin, Lewis V. 1949- WhoBlA 94, WrDr 94
Baldwin, Lionel Vernon 1932- WhoWest 94
Baldwin, Loammi 1740-1807 WhAmRev
Baldwin, Louis J. WhoBlA 94
Baldwin, Lynne Maury 1949- WhoAmL 94
Baldwin, Mary Karen 1965- WhoMW 93
Baldwin, Matthias 1795-1866 WorInv
Baldwin, Merl EncSF 93
Baldwin, Michael WhoHol 92
Baldwin, Mitchell Cardell 1958- WhoBlA 94
Baldwin, Muriel Frances WhoAmA 93N
Baldwin, Neil DrAPF 93
Baldwin, Neil 1947- WrDr 94
Baldwin, Nigel Bruce 1941- Who 94
Baldwin, Olivia McNair 1943- WhoBlA 94
Baldwin, Paul Clay 1914-1990 WhAm 10
Baldwin, Peter ConTFT 11, WhoHol 92
Baldwin, Peter 1951- IntWW 93
Baldwin, Peter (Robert) 1922- Who 94
Baldwin, Peter Alan Charles 1927- Who 94
Baldwin, Peter Arthur 1932- WhoAm 94
Baldwin, Phillip B. 1924- CngDr 93
Baldwin, Ransom Leland 1935- WhoAm 94, WhoScEn 94
Baldwin, Richard Eugene 1940- WhoWest 94
Baldwin, Richard Wood 1920- WhoAmA 93
Baldwin, Robert 1912?- WhoHol 92
Baldwin, Robert Edward 1924- WhoAm 94
Baldwin, Robert Frederick, Jr. 1939- WhoAm 94
Baldwin, Robert Lesh 1927- WhoAm 94
Baldwin, Robert Roy 1920- IntWW 93
Baldwin, Roger N. 1950- WhoAmA 93
Baldwin, Roger Nash 1884-1981 AmSocL [port]
Baldwin, Russell W. 1933- WhoAmA 93
Baldwin, Shaun McFarland 1954- WhoAmL 94
Baldwin, Stanley 1867-1947 HisWorL [port]
Baldwin, Stephen 1966- WhoHol 92
Baldwin, Susan Olin 1954- WhoAmL 94, WhoMW 93
Baldwin, Tammy 1962- WhoAmP 93
Baldwin, Thomas 1750-1820 DcNaB MP
Baldwin, Thomas Richard 1945- WhoAm 94
Baldwin, Velma Neville Wilson 1918- WhoFI 94
Baldwin, Walter d1977 WhoHol 92
Baldwin, Wendy Harmer 1945- WhoAm 94, WhoScEn 94
Baldwin, Wilhelmina F. 1923- WhoBlA 94
Baldwin, William WhoAm 94
Baldwin, William c. 1515-1563 DcLB 132
Baldwin, William 1963- IntMPA 94, WhoHol 92
Baldwin, William A. 1949- WhoHisp 94
Baldwin, William David 1939- WhoIns 94
Baldwin, William E. 1948- WhoAmP 93
Baldwin, William Howard 1916- WhoAm 94
Baldwin, William Russell 1926- WhoAm 94
Baldwin Of Bewdley, Earl 1938- Who 94
Baldy, Anderson Lacy, III 1960- WhoAmL 94
Baldyga, Leonard J. 1932- WhoAm 94
Bale, Christian 1974- IntMPA 94, WhoHol 92
Bale, Don 1937- WrDr 94
Bale, James Franklin, Jr. 1949- WhoMW 93
Bale, John 1495-1563 BlmGEL, DcLB 132
Bale, Joy DrAPF 93
Bale, Steven Charles 1957- WhoWest 94
Baleja, James Donald 1961- WhoScEn 94
Balenda, Carla WhoHol 92
Balerini, Francesco NewGrDO
Bales, Edward Wagner 1939- WhoMW 93
Bales, J. 1946- WhoAmA 93
Bales, Jerry F. WhoAmP 93
Bales, Jewel 1928- WhoAmA 93
Bales, John Foster, III 1940- WhoAm 94
Bales, Kenneth Frederick 1931- Who 94
Bales, Kent Roslyn 1936- WhoAm 94
Bales, Kevin 1952- ConAu 140
Bales, Richard Henry Horner 1915- WhoAm 94
Bales, Robert Freed 1916- WhoAm 94
Bales, Ronald C. 1938- WhoAm 94
Bales, Royal Eugene 1934- WhoAm 94
Balestra, Chester Lee 1943- WhoScEn 94
Balestre, Jean-Marie 1921- IntWW 93
Balestrero, Gregory 1947- WhoAm 94
Balestri, John 1947- WhoAmP 93
Balestrino, Charles Joseph 1941- WhoAm 94
Balettie, Roger Eugene 1964- WhoScEn 94
Balevski, Angel Tonchev 1910- IntWW 93
Baley, Jerry Joseph 1947- WhoMW 93
Balfa, Dewey 1927-1992 AnObit 1992
Balfe, Alan 1956- WhoScEn 94
Balfe, Michael William 1808-1870 NewGrDO
Balfe, Richard Andrew 1944- Who 94
Balfort, Neil EncSF 93
Balfour Who 94
Balfour, Earl of 1925- Who 94

Balfour, Betty 1903- *WhoHol 92*
Balfour, Dale Elliman 1941- *WhoAmP 93*
Balfour, Danny Lee 1955- *WhoMW 93*
Balfour, David Mathers 1910- *Who 94*
Balfour, Don 1957- *WhoAmP 93*
Balfour, George Ian Mackintosh 1912- *Who 94*
Balfour, Henry Hallowell, Jr. 1940- *WhoAm 94*
Balfour, Hugh Maxwell 1933- *Who 94*
Balfour, Jean *Who 94*
Balfour, (Elizabeth) Jean 1927- *Who 94*
Balfour, John Charles 1919- *Who 94*
Balfour, Katharine d1990 *WhoHol 92*
Balfour, Lorna d1932 *WhoHol 92*
Balfour, Mark Robin 1927- *Who 94*
Balfour, Michael 1918- *WhoHol 92*
Balfour, Michael (Leonard Graham) 1908- *WrDr 94*
Balfour, Michael John 1925- *Who 94*
Balfour, Nancy 1911- *Who 94*
Balfour, Neil Roxburgh 1944- *Who 94*
Balfour, Nisbet 1743-1832 *WhAmRev*
Balfour, Nisbet 1793-1832 *AmRev*
Balfour, Peter Edward Gerald 1921- *Who 94*
Balfour, Raymond Lewis 1923- *Who 94*
Balfour, Reginald James 1928- *WhoAm 94*
Balfour, Richard Creighton 1916- *Who 94*
Balfour, Robert George Victor FitzGeorge *Who 94*
Balfour, William d1964 *WhoHol 92*
Balfour Of Burleigh, Lady 1945- *Who 94*
Balfour Of Burleigh, Lord 1927- *Who 94*
Balfour Of Inchrye, Baron 1924- *Who 94*
Balfour-Paul, (Hugh) Glencairn 1917- *Who 94*
Balgeman, Richard Vernon 1929- *WhoMW 93*
Balgonie, Lord 1954- *Who 94*
Balguy, John 1686-1748 *EncEth*
Balhaus, Carl d1968 *WhoHol 92*
Bali, Vyjayanthimala 1933- *WhoWomW 91*
Balian, Lorna 1929- *WrDr 94*
Balick, Helen Shaffer *WhoAm 94, WhoAmL 94*
Balickas, Vincas 1904- *IntWW 93*
Balieff, Nikita d1936 *WhoHol 92*
Baliga, Bantval Jayant 1948- *WhoAm 94, WhoScEn 94*
Baliga, Jayant 1948- *WhoAsA 94*
Balikov, Henry R. 1946- *WhoAmL 94, WhoFI 94*
Baliles, Gerald L. 1940- *WhoAm 94, WhoAmL 94, WhoAmP 93*
Balin, Ina d1990 *WhoHol 92*
Balin, Marty 1942- *WhoAm 94*
Balin, Mireille d1968 *WhoHol 92*
Balino *NewGrDO*
Balint, Enid 1903- *WrDr 94*
Balint, Eszter 1966- *WhoHol 92*
Balint, Joseph Philip 1948- *WhoWest 94*
Balis, Moses Earl 1921- *WhoAm 94*
Balk, Alfred William 1930- *WhoAm 94*
Balk, Christianne *DrAPF 93*
Balk, Fairuza 1974?- *ConTFT 11*
Balk, Fairuza 1975- *WhoHol 92*
Balka, Don Stephen 1946- *WhoMW 93*
Balka, Sigmund Ronell 1935- *WhoAm 94, WhoAmL 94*
Balkan, Kenneth J. 1948- *WhoAmL 94*
Balkcom, Ralph J. *WhoAmP 93*
Balke, Victor H. 1931- *WhoAm 94, WhoMW 93*
Balkema, Alan 1948- *WhoMW 93*
Balkin, Ruth Goldring 1951- *WhoAmL 94*
Balkind, Alvin Louis 1921- *WhoAmA 93*
Balkins, Almon James, III 1952- *WhoAmL 94*
Balkwill, Bryan (Havell) 1922- *NewGrDO*
Balkwill, Bryan Havell 1922- *Who 94*
Ball, Alfred (Henry Wynne) 1921- *Who 94*
Ball, Angela *DrAPF 93*
Ball, Angela 1952- *WrDr 94*
Ball, Anne H. 1939- *WhoAm 94*
Ball, Anthony George 1934- *Who 94*
Ball, Ardella Patricia 1932- *WhoAm 94*
Ball, Armand Baer 1930- *WhoAm 94*
Ball, Arthur Beresford 1923- *Who 94*
Ball, Blair Evan 1954- *WhoFI 94*
Ball, Blair M 1957- *WhoWest 94*
Ball, Bobby *WhoHol 92*
Ball, Brenda Louise 1951- *WhoMW 93*
Ball, Brian N(eville) 1932- *EncSF 93*
Ball, C(harles) Olin 1893- *WhAm 10*
Ball, Carroll Raybourne 1925- *WhoAm 94*
Ball, Charles (Irwin) 1924- *Who 94*
Ball, Charles Elihue 1924- *WhoAm 94*
Ball, Christopher (John Elinger) 1935- *Who 94*
Ball, Christopher John Elinger 1935- *IntWW 93*
Ball, Christopher John Watkins 1939- *Who 94*
Ball, Claire Melvin, Jr. 1941- *WhoAmP 93*
Ball, Clarence M., Jr. 1949- *WhoBlA 94*
Ball, Corinne 1953- *WhoAmL 94*
Ball, Darrell Wayne 1960- *WhoMW 93*
Ball, David Warren 1962- *WhoMW 93*
Ball, Denis William 1928- *Who 94*
Ball, Donald Edmon 1942- *WhoWest 94*
Ball, Donald Lewis 1922- *WhoAm 94*
Ball, Donald Lincoln 1932- *WhoMW 93*
Ball, Douglas Schelling 1920- *WhoAm 94*
Ball, Drexel Bernard 1948- *WhoBlA 94*
Ball, Edna Marion 1944- *WhoScEn 94*
Ball, Edward R. *WhoAmA 93*
Ball, Eric Clinton 1966- *WhoBlA 94*
Ball, Frank Jervey 1919- *WhoAm 94*
Ball, G. Thomas 1947- *WhoAm 94, WhoAmL 94*
Ball, George (Wildman) 1909- *WrDr 94*
Ball, George Carl 1921- *WhoAm 94*
Ball, George L. *WhoFI 94*
Ball, George Wildman 1909- *IntWW 93, WhoAm 94, WhoAmP 93*
Ball, Guy David 1953- *WhoWest 94*
Ball, Harold William 1926- *Who 94*
Ball, Howard Guy 1930- *WhoAm 94*
Ball, J. Donald, III 1957- *WhoWest 94*
Ball, James *IntWW 93, Who 94*
Ball, (Robert) James 1933- *IntWW 93, Who 94*
Ball, James Herington 1942- *WhoAmL 94, WhoFI 94, WhoWest 94*
Ball, James M. 1949- *WhoAmL 94*
Ball, James William 1942- *WhoFI 94*
Ball, Jane *WhoHol 92*
Ball, Jane Lee 1930- *WhoBlA 94*
Ball, Jay N. 1957- *WhoFI 94*
Ball, Jennifer (M. V.) 1958- *WrDr 94*
Ball, Jerry Lee 1964- *WhoAm 94, WhoBlA 94, WhoMW 93*
Ball, Jo-Anne Moreland 1930- *WhoWest 94*
Ball, John d1381 *BlmGEL*
Ball, John (Dudley, Jr.) 1911-1988 *EncSF 93*
Ball, John A. 1928- *WhoFI 94*
Ball, John Calvin, Sr. 1924- *WhoBlA 94*
Ball, John Fleming 1930- *WhoAm 94*
Ball, John Geoffrey 1916- *Who 94*
Ball, John Hanstein 1919- *WhoAm 94*
Ball, John Macleod 1948- *Who 94*
Ball, John Paul 1946- *WhoAm 94*
Ball, John Robert 1944- *WhoAm 94*
Ball, Jon Winston 1954- *WhoWest 94*
Ball, Joseph H. d1993 *NewYTBS 93 [port]*
Ball, Karen Elaine 1947- *WhoWest 94*
Ball, Karen Fisher 1958- *WhoWest 94*
Ball, Karen Susan 1947- *WhoAmP 93*
Ball, Kay Atkinson 1949- *WhoMW 93*
Ball, Kenneth Leon 1932- *WhoMW 93*
Ball, Lawrence 1933- *WhoWest 94*
Ball, Lewis Edwin, II 1931- *WhoAm 94*
Ball, Lillian 1955- *WhoAmA 93*
Ball, Louis Alvin 1921- *WhoMW 93*
Ball, Louis Oliver, Jr. 1929- *WhoAm 94*
Ball, Lucille d1989 *WhoHol 92*
Ball, Lucille 1911-1989 *WhAm 10, WhoCom [port]*
Ball, Lyle V. 1909- *WhoAmA 93*
Ball, M. Isabel 1929- *WhoAm 94*
Ball, Markham 1934- *WhoAm 94*
Ball, Michael Ray 1950- *WhoMW 93*
Ball, Michael Thomas *Who 94*
Ball, Nelson 1942- *WrDr 94*
Ball, Nicholas 1946- *WhoHol 92*
Ball, Owen Keith, Jr. 1950- *WhoAmL 94*
Ball, Patricia Ann 1941- *WhoMW 93*
Ball, Peter Edward 1959- *WhoAmL 94*
Ball, Peter John 1932- *Who 94*
Ball, Peter William 1930- *Who 94*
Ball, Rex Harrison 1943- *WhoAmP 93*
Ball, Rex Martin 1934- *WhoAm 94*
Ball, Richard E. 1918- *WhoBlA 94*
Ball, Robert Bates, Sr. *WhoAmP 93*
Ball, Robert Edwin 1935- *WhoWest 94*
Ball, Robert Kenneth, II 1937- *WhoAmL 94*
Ball, Robert L. 1936- *WhoIns 94*
Ball, Robert M. 1914- *WhoAm 94*
Ball, Robert Michael 1952- *WhoAm 94*
Ball, Roger 1961- *WhoBlA 94*
Ball, Roger Alford 1944- *WhoAmP 93*
Ball, Roy Orville 1945- *WhoFI 94*
Ball, Sheri Beth 1963- *WhoFI 94*
Ball, Stuart 1956- *WrDr 94*
Ball, Sue *WhoAmP 93*
Ball, Susan 1947- *WhoAm 94*
Ball, Susan L. 1947- *WhoAmA 93*
Ball, Suzan d1955 *WhoHol 92*
Ball, Vincent 1924- *WhoHol 92*
Ball, Virginia B. *WhoMW 93*
Ball, Walter N. 1930- *WhoAmA 93*
Ball, Wilfred R. 1932- *WhoBlA 94*
Ball, William 1923- *WhoAm 94, WhoAmP 93*
Ball, William 1931- *IntWW 93*
Ball, William 1931-1991 *WhAm 10*
Ball, William Batten 1928- *WhoBlA 94*
Ball, William Bentley 1916- *WhoAm 94*
Ball, William Ernest 1930- *WhoAm 94*
Ball, William James 1910- *WhoMW 93, WhoScEn 94*
Ball, William James, Jr. 1942- *WhoScEn 94*
Ball, William Kenneth 1927- *WhoAm 94*
Ball, William L. 1948- *WhoAmP 93*
Ball, William Paul 1913- *WhoScEn 94, WhoWest 94*
Balla, Bulcsu 1934- *WhoFI 94, WhoMW 93*
Balladur, Edouard 1929- *IntWW 93, Who 94*
Ballal, Dilip Ramchandra 1946- *WhoScEn 94*
Ballal, S. K. 1938- *WhoAmP 93*
Ballam, Joseph 1917- *WhoAm 94*
Ballam, Michael Lynn 1951- *WhoWest 94*
Ballam, Samuel Humes, Jr. 1919- *WhoAm 94*
Ballance, Frank Winston, Jr. 1942- *WhoAmP 93, WhoBlA 94*
Ballanfant, Kathleen Gamber 1945- *WhoFI 94*
Ballantine, Carl 1922- *WhoHol 92*
Ballantine, Caroline *WhoMW 93*
Ballantine, E. J. d1968 *WhoHol 92*
Ballantine, (David) Grant 1941- *Who 94*
Ballantine, Ian 1916- *IntWW 93, WhoAm 94*
Ballantine, John Tilden 1931- *WhoAmL 94*
Ballantine, Mary Keith 1926- *WhoAmP 93*
Ballantine, Morley Cowles 1925- *WhoAm 94, WhoWest 94*
Ballantyne, Catherine Turk 1912- *WhoAmA 93*
Ballantyne, John (Chalmers) 1917- *WrDr 94*
Ballantyne, Joseph Merrill *WhoAm 94, WhoScEn 94*
Ballantyne, Michael Alan 1945- *WhoAm 94, WhoWest 94*
Ballantyne, Nell d1959 *WhoHol 92*
Ballantyne, Paul 1909- *WhoHol 92*
Ballantyne, Reginald Malcolm 1943- *WhoAm 94*
Ballantyne, Richard L. 1939- *WhoFI 94*
Ballantyne, Richard Lee 1939- *WhoAmL 94*
Ballantyne, Richard Van 1955- *WhoFI 94*
Ballantyne, Robert Jadwin 1925- *WhoAm 94*
Ballantyne, Sheila *DrAPF 93*
Ballarat, Bishop of 1936- *Who 94*
Ballarat, Bishop of, (RC) 1930- *Who 94*
Ballard, Alden G. *WhoAmP 93*
Ballard, Allen Butler, Jr. 1930- *WhoBlA 94*
Ballard, Barbara W. *WhoAmP 93*
Ballard, Billy Ray 1940- *WhoBlA 94*
Ballard, Billy Ward 1925- *WhoAmP 93*
Ballard, Bruce Laine 1939- *WhoBlA 94*
Ballard, Carroll 1937- *IntMPA 94*
Ballard, Charles Alan *WhoAm 94*
Ballard, Clark Tilton, Jr. 1941- *WhoWest 94*
Ballard, Claude Mark, Jr. 1929- *WhoAm 94*
Ballard, Clifford Frederick 1910- *Who 94*
Ballard, Clyde 1936- *WhoAmP 93*
Ballard, David Eugene 1949- *WhoAm 94*
Ballard, Eddie 1929- *WhoAmP 93*
Ballard, Edna Wheeler 1886-1971 *DcAmReB 2*
Ballard, Edward Brooks 1906- *WhoAm 94*
Ballard, Edward Goodwin 1910-1989 *WhAm 10*
Ballard, Edward Hunter 1900- *WhoBlA 94*
Ballard, Edward Parke 1916- *WhoAmP 93*
Ballard, Elmer d1947 *WhoHol 92*
Ballard, Florence d1976 *WhoHol 92*
Ballard, Frederic Lyman, Jr. 1941- *WhoAm 94*
Ballard, Gerald Porter 1936- *WhoMW 93*
Ballard, Guy Warren 1878-1939 *DcAmReB 2*
Ballard, Harold Edwin 1903-1990 *WhAm 10*
Ballard, Harold Stanley 1927- *WhoBlA 94*
Ballard, J. G. *DrAPF 93*
Ballard, J. G. 1930- *BlmGEL*
Ballard, J(ames) G(raham) 1930- *EncSF 93, RfGShF, WrDr 94*
Ballard, James Graham 1930- *IntWW 93, Who 94, WhoAm 94*
Ballard, James M., Jr. 1938- *WhoBlA 94*
Ballard, Jane Elizabeth 1947- *WhoWest 94*
Ballard, Janet Jones 1930- *WhoBlA 94*
Ballard, Joe Nathan 1942- *AfrAmG [port]*
Ballard, John David 1936- *WhoIns 94*
Ballard, John Frederick 1943- *Who 94*
Ballard, John Houston, III 1944- *WhoIns 94*
Ballard, John Stuart 1922- *WhoAm 94, WhoAmP 93*
Ballard, John William, Jr. 1922- *WhoAm 94*
Ballard, Kathryn W. 1930- *WhoBlA 94*
Ballard, Kaye 1926- *IntMPA 94, WhoHol 92*
Ballard, Larry Coleman 1935- *WhoAm 94, WhoIns 94*
Ballard, Lockett Ford, Jr. 1946- *WhoAmA 93*
Ballard, Louis Wayne 1931- *WhoAm 94*
Ballard, Lowell Douglas 1933- *WhoFI 94, WhoScEn 94*
Ballard, Lucien 1908-1988 *IntDcF 2-4*
Ballard, Lucinda d1993 *NewYTBS 93 [port]*
Ballard, Martha Moore 1735-1812 *BlmGWL*
Ballard, Mary Melinda 1957- *WhoAm 94*
Ballard, Melvin Russell, Jr. 1928- *WhoWest 94*
Ballard, Michael Eugene 1953- *WhoAmL 94*
Ballard, Myrtle Ethel 1930- *WhoBlA 94*
Ballard, Rand Alexander 1955- *WhoFI 94*
Ballard, Richard Owen 1962- *WhoScEn 94*
Ballard, Robert Duane 1942- *WhoAm 94, WhoScEn 94*
Ballard, Robert Eugene, Jr. 1943- *WhoFI 94*
Ballard, Ronald Alfred 1925- *Who 94*
Ballard, Ronald Lee 1947- *WhoAm 94, WhoAmL 94*
Ballard, Stanley Sumner 1908- *WhoAm 94*
Ballard, Walter W. 1928- *WhoBlA 94*
Ballard, William Donaldson 1927- *WhoAmP 93*
Ballard, William F. R. 1905-1993 *NewYTBS 93*
Ballard, William Ralph 1926- *WhoWest 94*
Ballasiotes, Ida *WhoAmP 93*
Ballas-Traynor, Lucía Verónica 1964- *WhoHisp 94*
Ballati, Deborah S. 1950- *WhoAmL 94*
Ballato, Anthony Thomas 1960- *WhoAmL 94*
Ballbach, John Daniel 1942- *WhoAmL 94*
Ballbach, Philip Thornton 1939- *WhoMW 93*
Balle, Francis 1939- *IntWW 93*
Balledux, Pierre d1976 *WhoHol 92*
Balleisen, Donald Herbert 1924- *WhoAmL 94*
Ballem, John Bishop 1925- *WhoAm 94*
Ballengee, James McMorrow 1923- *WhoAm 94*
Ballenger, Cass 1926- *CngDr 93*
Ballenger, Hurley Rene 1946- *WhoFI 94, WhoMW 93, WhoScEn 94*
Ballenger, Thomas Cass 1926- *WhoAm 94, WhoAmP 93*
Ballentine, J. Gregory 1948- *WhoAm 94*
Ballentine, Krim Menelik 1936- *WhoAmP 93, WhoBlA 94*
Ballentine, Lee Kenney 1954- *WhoFI 94, WhoWest 94*
Ballentine, Paula Fiscal 1950- *WhoWest 94*
Ballentine, Roger S. 1963- *WhoAmL 94*
Ballentine, Rosalie Simmonds *WhoAmP 93*
Ballentyne, Donald Francis 1929- *Who 94*
Balleny, John c. 1770-c. 1843 *DcNaB MP*
Ballerini, Francesco fl. 1680-1717 *NewGrDO*
Balles, John Joseph 1921- *WhoAm 94*
Ballestero, Manuel 1937- *WhoHisp 94*
Ballesteros, David 1933- *WhoHisp 94, WhoWest 94*
Ballesteros, Frank Trujillo 1948- *WhoHisp 94*
Ballesteros, Hugo 1923- *WhoHisp 94*
Ballesteros, Juventino Ray, Jr. 1953- *WhoAm 94*
Ballesteros, Mario Alberto 1952- *WhoHisp 94*
Ballesteros, Severiano 1957- *Who 94, WhoAm 94*
Ballesteros de Gaibrois, Mercedes 1913- *BlmGWL*
Ballesteros Sota, Severiano 1957- *IntWW 93*
Ballestrero, Anastasio Alberto 1913- *IntWW 93*
Balletbo I Puig, Anna Maria 1943- *WhoWomW 91*
Ballew, Charles William 1931- *WhoAm 94*
Ballew, David Wayne 1940- *WhoAm 94*
Ballew, Frederick Keith 1938- *WhoAmP 93*
Ballew, Glenn L. 1948- *WhoIns 94*
Ballew, Nellie Hester 1914- *WhoAm 94*
Ballew, Smith d1984 *WhoHol 92*
Ballhaus, Michael 1935- *IntMPA 94*
Ballhaus, Michael 1942- *IntDcF 2-4*
Ballhaus, William Francis, Jr. 1945- *WhoWest 94*
Balliett, Gene 1931- *WhoAm 94*
Balliett, John William 1947- *WhoFI 94*

Balliett, Whitney 1926- *WhoAm 94, WrDr 94*
Ballin, (Reubina) Ann 1932- *Who 94*
Ballin, Ernst Hirsch *IntWW 93*
Ballin, Hugo 1879-1956 *WhoAmA 93N*
Ballin, Mabel d1958 *WhoHol 92*
Ballin, William Christopher 1927- *WhoAm 94*
Balling, Michael 1866-1925 *NewGrDO*
Ballingall, James McLean, III 1955- *WhoScEn 94*
Ballinger, Bill S. *EncSF 93*
Ballinger, Charles Edwin 1935- *WhoWest 94*
Ballinger, Charles Kenneth 1950- *WhoWest 94*
Ballinger, James K. 1949- *WhoAmA 93, WhoWest 94*
Ballinger, James N. 1914- *WhoAmP 93*
Ballinger, John 1860-1933 *DcNaB MP*
Ballinger, Philip Albert 1957- *WhoWest 94*
Ballinger, Ruth Ann 1960- *WhoWest 94*
Ballinger, W.A. *EncSF 93*
Ballinger, Walter Francis 1925- *WhoAm 94*
Ballinger, William S(anborn) 1912-1980 *EncSF 93*
Ballista, Gigi (Luigi) d1980 *WhoHol 92*
Ballman, Donald Karl 1910-1989 *WhAm 10*
Ballman, Gary Edward 1948- *WhoMW 93*
Ballmer, Ray Wayne 1926- *IntWW 93*
Ballod, Martin Charles 1950- *WhoScEn 94*
Ballon, Claude c. 1671-1744 *IntDcB [port]*
Ballon, Edward Mahler 1925- *WhoAm 94*
Ballot, Alissa E. 1955- *WhoAmL 94*
Ballot, Charles Joseph, Jr. 1930- *WhoMW 93*
Ballou, Adin Augustus 1803-1890 *DcAmReB 2*
Ballou, Anne MacDougall *WhoAmA 93*
Ballou, Charles Herbert 1945- *WhoFI 94*
Ballou, Christopher Aaron 1963- *WhoScEn 94*
Ballou, Clinton Edward 1923- *IntWW 93*
Ballou, Hosea 1771-1852 *DcAmReB 2*
Ballou, Kenneth Walter 1930- *WhoAm 94*
Ballou, Marion d1939 *WhoHol 92*
Ballou, Mark *WhoHol 92*
Ballou, Paul Holton 1897- *WhAm 10*
Ballou, Richard A. 1945- *WhoAmP 93*
Balloue, John Edward 1948- *WhoWest 94*
Balloun, Joseph Eugene 1929- *WhoAm 94, WhoAmL 94*
Ballowe, James *DrAPF 93*
Ballowe, James 1933- *WhoAm 94*
Balls, Alastair Gordon 1944- *Who 94*
Ball-Sundine, Sandra Jean 1963- *WhoWest 94*
Ballweber, Hettie Lou 1944- *WhoScEn 94*
Ballweg, Ernest Carl 1944- *WhoMW 93*
Ballweg, Larry Veneard 1944- *WhoAmP 93*
Ballweg, Mitchell Joseph 1958- *WhoAmL 94*
Bally, Albert W. *WhoScEn 94*
Bally, Laurent Marie Joseph 1943- *WhoScEn 94*
Balmaceda, Margarita S. 1933- *WhoAmA 93*
Balmain, Keith George 1933- *WhoAm 94*
Balmain, Rollo d1920 *WhoHol 92*
Balmann, Michael Jay 1965- *WhoFI 94*
Balmaseda, Elizabeth R. 1959- *WhoHisp 94*
Balmaseda, Liz 1959- *WhoAm 94*
Balmer, David Gregory 1962- *WhoAmP 93*
Balmer, Edwin 1883-1959 *EncSF 93*
Balmer, Horace Dalton, Sr. 1939- *WhoBlA 94*
Balmer, James Walter 1948- *WhoAm 94*
Balmer, Jean-Francois *WhoHol 92*
Balmer, Joseph (Reginald) 1899- *Who 94*
Balmer, Thomas Ancil 1952- *WhoAmL 94*
Balmer, Thomas James 1913- *WhAm 10*
Balmforth, Anthony James 1926- *Who 94*
Balniel, Lord 1958- *Who 94*
Balochino, Carlo 1770-1850 *NewGrDO*
Balodis, Janis 1950- *ConTFT 11*
Balodis, Janis (Maris) 1950- *ConDr 93, WrDr 94*
Baloff, Nicholas 1937- *WhoAm 94*
Balog, B. E. *DrAPF 93*
Balog, James Dennis 1952- *WhoAm 94, WhoWest 94*
Balog, Michael 1946- *WhoAmA 93N*
Balog, Richard Thomas 1951- *WhoFI 94*
Balog, Rita Jean 1930- *WhoMW 93*
Balogun, Kolawole 1926- *IntWW 93*
Baloian, James C. *DrAPF 93*
Balon, Claude c. 1671-1744 *IntDcB [port]*
Balon, Richard 1951- *WhoMW 93*
Balonick, Bruce H. 1948- *WhoAmL 94*
Balonon, Peter M. 1945- *WhoHisp 94*
Balossi, John 1931- *WhoAmA 93*
Balota, D(avid) A. 1954- *WrDr 94*
Balotti, R. Franklin 1942- *WhoAmL 94*
Baloun, John Charles 1934- *WhoAm 94*
Baloun, Rosemary Ann 1945- *WhoMW 93*
Balousek, John B. *WhoAm 94, WhoFI 94*
Balow, Irving Henry 1927- *WhoAm 94*
Balows, Albert 1921- *WhoAm 94*
Baloyra, Enrique Antonio 1942- *WhoHisp 94*
Balpetre, Antoine d1963 *WhoHol 92*
Balsai, Istvan 1947- *IntWW 93*
Balsam, Martin 1919- *IntMPA 94, WhoHol 92*
Balsam, Martin Henry 1919- *IntWW 93, WhoAm 94*
Balsam, Talia 1960- *WhoHol 92*
Balsan, Allison *WhoHol 92*
Balsan, Humbert *WhoHol 92*
Balsara, Poras Tehmurasp 1961- *WhoScEn 94*
Balschi, James Alvin 1950- *WhoScEn 94*
Balsdon, (John Percy Vyvian) Dacre 1901-1977 *EncSF 93*
Balseiro, José Agustín 1900- *WhoHisp 94*
Balseiro Gonzalez, Manuel 1940- *WhoFI 94*
Balsemao, Francisco Pinto *IntWW 93*
Balser, Ewald d1978 *WhoHol 92*
Balser, Walter Thomas 1925- *WhoAmP 93*
Balsham, Adam of c. 1105-c. 1170 *DcNaB MP*
Balshi, Philip John *WhoAm 94*
Balsiger, David Wayne 1945- *WhoAm 94, WhoWest 94*
Balslev, Lisbeth 1945- *NewGrDO*
Balsley, Ben Burton 1932- *WhoWest 94*
Balsley, Howard Lloyd 1913- *WhoAm 94, WhoScEn 94*
Balsley, Irol Whitmore 1912-1989 *WhAm 10*
Balsley, John Gerald 1944- *WhoAmA 93*
Balsley, Philip E. 1939- *See* Statler Brothers, The *WhoHol 92*
Balsley, Philip Elwood 1939- *WhoAm 94*
Balson, John Bruce 1941- *WhoAm 94*
Balstad, Jan 1937- *IntWW 93*
Balston, Antony Francis 1939- *Who 94*
Balswick, Jack Orville *WrDr 94*
Balswick, Judith K. 1939- *WrDr 94*
Balsys, Eduardas 1919-1984 *NewGrDO*
Baltacioglu, Mehmet Necip 1954- *WhoScEn 94*
Baltake, Joe *WhoAm 94, WhoWest 94*
Baltazar, Eulalio 1925- *WrDr 94*
Baltazar, Romulo Flores 1941- *WhoScEn 94*
Baltazzi, Evan Serge 1921- *WhoAm 94*
Balter, Alan *WhoAm 94, WhoMW 93*
Balter, Robert Brandon 1925-1982 *WhAm 10*
Balthaser, James Harvey 1954- *WhoAmL 94*
Balthaser, Linda Irene 1939- *WhoMW 93*
Balthazard, Mark Joseph 1957- *WhoAmL 94*
Balthis, Bill W. 1939- *WhoAmP 93*
Balthrop, Carmen Arlen 1948- *NewGrDO*
Balthrope, Jacqueline Morehead *WhoBlA 94*
Balthus *IntWW 93*
Baltich, Linda Kaase 1956- *WhoWest 94*
Baltierra, Ronald J. *WhoHisp 94*
Baltimore, Baron 1606-1675 *DcNaB MP*
Baltimore, David 1938- *IntWW 93, Who 94, WhoAm 94, WhoScEn 94, WorScD*
Baltimore, J. *SmATA 74*
Baltimore, Mary 1920- *WrDr 94*
Baltimore, Richard Lewis, III 1947- *WhoAm 94, WhoBlA 94*
Baltimore, Roslyn Lois 1942- *WhoBlA 94*
Baltin, Eduard Dmitrievich 1936- *LoBiDrD*
Baltl, Hermann Josef 1918- *IntWW 93*
Baltodano, Guiselle 1944- *WhoHisp 94*
Balton, Kirkwood R. 1935- *WhoBlA 94*
Balton, Nancy Crain 1935- *WhoAmP 93*
Baltrusitis, Arleane 1951- *WhoHisp 94*
Baltsa, Agnes *IntWW 93*
Baltsa, Agnes 1944- *NewGrDO*
Baltz, Lewis 1945- *WhoAm 94, WhoAmA 93*
Baltz, Richard Arthur 1959- *WhoScEn 94*
Baltz, Richard Jay 1952- *WhoAm 94*
Baltz, Walter F. 1938- *WhoAmP 93*
Baltzell, Deborah d1981 *WhoHol 92*
Baltzell, Edward Digby 1915- *WhoAm 94*
Baltzer, Kimberly Lenore 1964- *WhoMW 93*
Balukas, Jean 1959- *WhoAm 94*
Balunas, Robert John 1947- *WhoFI 94*
Balunek, Peter Matthew 1968- *WhoFI 94*
Baluni, Alice 1945- *WhoWest 94*
Balut, George Samuel 1955- *WhoMW 93*
Balutin, Jacques *WhoHol 92*
Balve, Beba Carmen 1931- *WhoScEn 94*
Balverde-Sanchez, Laura *WhoHisp 94*
Baly, Hilda 1966- *WhoHisp 94*
Balyo, John Gabriel 1920- *WhoWest 94*
Balyozov, Rumen 1949- *NewGrDO*
Balz, Douglas Charles 1943- *WhoAm 94*
Balza, John Joseph 1949- *WhoWest 94*
Balzac, Honore de 1799-1850 *BlmGEL, EncSF 93, RfGShF*
Balzac, Jean-Louis Guez de 1597-1654 *GuFrLit 2*
Balzekas, Stanley, Jr. 1924- *WhoAm 94, WhoMW 93*
Balzer, Craig James 1963- *WhoMW 93*
Balzer, Giorgio 1940- *WhoIns 94*
Balzhiser, Richard Earl 1932- *WhoAm 94, WhoScEn 94, WhoWest 94*
Bam, Foster 1927- *WhoAm 94*
Bamattre, Martha d1970 *WhoHol 92*
Bamba, George 1951- *WhoAmP 93*
Bamba, Joseph George 1951- *WhoAm 94, WhoWest 94*
Bambace, Robert Shelly 1930- *WhoAm 94, WhoAmL 94*
Bambacus, John N. 1945- *WhoAmP 93*
Bambara, Toni Cade *DrAPF 93*
Bambara, Toni Cade 1939- *BlkWr 2, BlmGWL, RfGShF, WhoBlA 94*
Bamber, George *DrAPF 93*
Bamber, George 1932- *EncSF 93*
Bamber, Judie 1961- *WhoAmA 93*
Bamber, Kathleen Elizabeth 1968- *WhoMW 93*
Bamberg, Harold Rolf 1923- *Who 94*
Bamberg, Louis M. 1940- *WhoFI 94*
Bamberger, Carlos 1944- *WhoHisp 94*
Bamberger, David 1940- *WhoAm 94, WhoMW 93*
Bamberger, David Harned 1942- *WhoAmL 94*
Bamberger, Gerald Francis 1920- *WhoAm 94*
Bamberger, Joseph Alexander 1927- *WhoScEn 94*
Bamberger, Michael (F.) 1960- *WrDr 94*
Bamberger, Michael Albert 1936- *WhoAm 94, WhoAmL 94*
Bamberger, Richard H. 1945- *WhoAm 94, WhoAmL 94*
Bamberger, Ronald Joseph 1942- *WhoAmL 94*
Bambini, Eustachio 1697-1770 *NewGrDO*
Bambini, Felice c. 1743-1787? *NewGrDO*
Bamborough, John Bernard 1921- *Who 94*
Bambrick, James Alan 1946- *WhoIns 94*
Bambrick, James Joseph 1917- *WhoAm 94, WhoMW 93*
Bambrough, John Renford 1926- *WhoAm 94*
Bamburg, James Robert 1943- *WhoAm 94, WhoScEn 94*
Bambury, Johnny d1960 *WhoHol 92*
Bambury, Ronald Edward 1932- *WhoScEn 94*
Bame, Samuel Jarvis, Jr. 1924- *WhoAm 94*
Bamfield, Clifford 1922- *Who 94*
Bamford, Alan George 1930- *Who 94*
Bamford, Anthony (Paul) 1945- *Who 94*
Bamford, Brian Reginald 1932- *WrDr 94*
Bamford, Clement Henry 1912- *IntWW 93, Who 94*
Bamford, Donald Lawrence 1957- *WhoScEn 94*
Bamford, Joseph Cyril 1916- *Who 94*
Bamford, Louis Neville Jules 1932- *Who 94*
Bamford, Nigel Simon 1960- *WhoWest 94*
Bampfylde *Who 94*
Bampton, James William 1909- *WhoAm 94*
Bampton, Rose (Elizabeth) 1908- *NewGrDO*
Ban, Sadayuki 1949- *WhoScEn 94*
Ban, Stephen Dennis 1940- *WhoAm 94*
Ban, Thomas Arthur 1929- *WrDr 94*
Ban, Woodrow William 1947- *WhoMW 93*
Banach, Art John 1931- *WhoFI 94, WhoMW 93*
Banada-Tan, Leticia 1950- *WhoAsA 94*
Banakar, Umesh Virupaksh 1956- *WhoAsA 94*
Bañales, Frank 1945- *WhoHisp 94*
Bañales, Irma 1956- *WhoHisp 94*
Banales, J. Manuel 1950- *WhoHisp 94*
Banana, Anna 1940- *WhoAmA 93*
Banana, Canaan Sodindo 1936- *IntWW 93*
Banana, Sodindo 1936- *Who 94*
Banas, Anne 1948- *WhoAmA 93*
Banas, Christine Leslie 1951- *WhoAm 94, WhoAmL 94*
Banas, Emil Mike 1921- *WhoScEn 94, WhoWest 94*
Banas, John *WhoHol 92*
Banas, John Stanley 1955- *WhoMW 93*
Banas, Richard Frederick 1948- *WhoFI 94*
Banaschewski, Bernhard 1926- *WhoAm 94*
Banasiak, Anthony Richard 1970- *WhoMW 93*
Banasik, Robert Casmer 1942- *WhoFI 94, WhoMW 93*
Banaszak, John Dennis 1945- *WhoMW 93*
Banaszynski, Jacqueline Marie 1952- *WhoMW 93*
Banaugh, Robert Peter 1922- *WhoAm 94, WhoWest 94*
Banba, George *WhoAmP 93*
Banbi, Hamdi El 1935- *IntWW 93*
Banbury *Who 94*
Banbury, Frith *Who 94*
Banbury, Frith 1912- *WhoHol 92*
Banbury, (Frederick Harold) Frith 1912- *IntWW 93, Who 94*
Banbury, Larry Francis 1935- *WhoFI 94*
Banbury, Philip 1914- *WrDr 94*
Banbury Of Southam, Baron 1953- *Who 94*
Banchoff, Thomas Francis 1938- *WhoAm 94*
Banchs, Jaime 1946- *WhoHisp 94*
Bancroft *Who 94*
Bancroft, Baron 1922- *Who 94*
Bancroft, Alexander Clerihew 1938- *WhoAm 94*
Bancroft, Anne 1923- *WrDr 94*
Bancroft, Anne 1931- *IntMPA 94, IntWW 93, WhoAm 94, WhoHol 92*
Bancroft, Bradford *WhoHol 92*
Bancroft, Bruce Richard 1940- *WhoAm 94*
Bancroft, Charles d1969 *WhoHol 92*
Bancroft, Charles E. 1935- *WhoIns 94*
Bancroft, Edward 1744-1820 *WhAmRev*
Bancroft, Elizabeth Abercrombie 1947- *WhoAm 94, WhoFI 94*
Bancroft, Francis *BlmGWL*
Bancroft, George d1956 *WhoHol 92*
Bancroft, George 1800-1891 *AmSocL*
Bancroft, George Michael 1942- *WhoAm 94, WhoScEn 94*
Bancroft, Harding Foster 1910-1992 *WhAm 10*
Bancroft, Hubert Howe 1832-1918 *DcLB 140 [port]*
Bancroft, James Ramsey 1919- *WhoAm 94*
Bancroft, Laura *EncSF 93*
Bancroft, Margaret Armstrong 1938- *WhoAm 94, WhoAmL 94*
Bancroft, Paul, III 1930- *WhoAm 94, WhoFI 94*
Bancroft, Paul Marshall 1954- *WhoIns 94*
Bancroft, Richard Anderson 1918- *WhoBlA 94*
Bancroft, Simon Powell 1953- *WhoIns 94*
Band, Albert 1924- *IntMPA 94*
Band, Charles 1951- *IntMPA 94*
Band, Charles 1952- *EncSF 93*
Band, David 1942- *Who 94, WhoAm 94*
Band, David Moshe 1947- *WhoAmA 93*
Band, Henretta Trent 1932- *WhoMW 93*
Band, Jordan Clifford 1923- *WhoMW 93*
Band, Robert Murray Niven 1919- *Who 94*
Band, Thomas Mollison 1934- *Who 94*
Banda, Aleke Kadonaphani 1939- *IntWW 93*
Banda, Hastings Kamuzu 1898?- *ConBlB 6 [port]*
Banda, Hastings Kamuzu 1905- *Who 94*
Banda, Hastings Kamuzu 1906- *IntWW 93*
Bandar, Bassem Mansour 1964- *WhoFI 94*
Bandaranaike, Sirimavo, Mrs. 1916- *Who 94*
Bandaranaike, Sirimavo R.D. 1916- *WhoWomW 91*
Bandaranaike, Sirimavo Ratwatte Dias 1916- *IntWW 93*
Bandar Ibn Sultan Ibn Abdulaziz Al-Saud 1949- *IntWW 93*
Bande, Andrés 1944- *WhoHisp 94*
Bandeen, Robert Angus 1930- *IntWW 93, WhoAm 94*
Bandeen, William Reid 1926- *WhoAm 94*
Bandeira, Alda *WhoWomW 91*
Bandeira De Mello, Lydio Machado 1901- *IntWW 93*
Bandel, David Brian 1951- *WhoFI 94*
Bandel, Lennon Raymond 1906- *WhoAmA 93*
Bandemer, Norman John 1949- *WhoFI 94*
Bander, Edward Julius 1923- *WhoAmL 94*
Bander, Myron 1937- *WhoAm 94*
Bander, Norman Robert *WhoFI 94*
Bander, Thomas Samuel 1924- *WhoMW 93*
Banderali, Davidde 1789-1849 *NewGrDO*
Banderas, Antonio 1960- *IntMPA 94, WhoHol 92*
Banderas, Antonio 1961- *WhoHisp 94*

Bandes, Susan Jane 1951- *WhoAm 94, WhoAmA 93*
Bandier, Martin *WhoAm 94*
Bandiere, Richard Charles 1943- *WhoAm 94*
Bandler, Faith 1918- *BlmGWL*
Bandler, John William 1941- *IntWW 93, WhoAm 94*
Bando, Amit 1957- *WhoFI 94*
Bando, Thelma Preyer 1919- *WhoBlA 94*
Bandong, Paul Anthony 1956- *WhoFI 94, WhoWest 94*
Bandopadhyaya, Amitava 1957- *WhoFI 94, WhoScEn 94*
Bandow, Douglas Leighton 1957- *WhoAmP 93*
Bandrowski-Sas, Aleksander 1860-1913 *NewGrDO*
Bandstra, Richard 1950- *WhoAmP 93*
Bandt, Paul Douglas 1938- *WhoWest 94*
Bandura, Albert 1925- *WhoAm 94, WrDr 94*
Bandurraga, Peter Louis 1944- *WhoWest 94*
Bandurski, Bruce Lord 1940- *WhoScEn 94*
Bandy, Amanda 1944- *WhoAmP 93*
Bandy, Gary 1944- *WhoAmA 93*
Bandy, James 1950- *WhoAmL 94*
Bandy, Mary Lea 1943- *IntMPA 94, WhoAm 94, WhoAmA 93*
Bandy, Riley Thomas, Sr. 1920- *WhoBlA 94*
Bandy, Ron F. 1936- *WhoAmA 93*
Bandy, William Thomas, Jr. 1903-1989 *WhAm 10*
Bandy-Hedden, Irene Gesa 1940- *WhoMW 93*
Bane, Charles Arthur 1913- *WhoAm 94*
Bane, Holly *WhoHol 92*
Bane, Keith James 1939- *WhoFI 94*
Bane, Margo Ewing 1949- *WhoAmP 93*
Banegas, Estevan Brown 1941- *WhoFI 94, WhoScEn 94*
Baner, Sandra Mae 1960- *WhoAmL 94*
Banerjee 1939- *WhoAm 94*
Banerjee, (Bimal) 1939- *WhoAmA 93*
Banerjee, Ajoy Kumar 1945- *WhoScEn 94*
Banerjee, Amiya Kumar 1936- *WhoAm 94, WhoAsA 94, WhoMW 93, WhoScEn 94*
Banerjee, Bejoy Kumar 1931- *WhoScEn 94*
Banerjee, Chandra Madhab 1932- *WhoAsA 94*
Banerjee, Debasish 1951- *WhoAsA 94*
Banerjee, Jayanta Kumar 1941- *WhoAsA 94*
Banerjee, Mukul R. 1937- *WhoAsA 94*
Banerjee, Pranab Kumar 1961- *WhoWest 94*
Banerjee, Prashant 1962- *WhoMW 93, WhoScEn 94*
Banerjee, Prithviraj 1960- *WhoAsA 94*
Banerjee, Samarendranath 1932- *WhoAm 94, WhoMW 93, WhoScEn 94*
Banerjee, Sanjay K. 1958- *WhoAsA 94*
Banerji, Asoka Nath 1917- *IntWW 93*
Banerji, Ranan Bihari 1928- *WhoAm 94, WhoAsA 94*
Banes, Lisa 1955- *WhoHol 92*
Baness, Jerome Alex 1936- *WhoAmP 93*
Banet, Charles Henry 1922- *WhoAm 94*
Banet, D. Beatrice *WhoAmP 93*
Banevich, Sergey 1941- *NewGrDO*
Baney, Joan Blazer d1990 *WhoHol 92*
Baney, John Edward 1934- *WhoAm 94*
Baney, Ralph Ramoutar 1929- *WhoAmA 93*
Baney, Richard Neil 1937- *WhoFI 94, WhoScEn 94*
Baney, Vera 1930- *WhoAmA 93*
Banfelder, Robert Joseph *DrAPF 93*
Banffy, Miklos 1874-1950 *NewGrDO*
Banfield, A(lexander) W(illiam) Frank 1918- *WrDr 94*
Banfield, Anne L. 1925- *WhoBlA 94*
Banfield, David John 1933- *Who 94*
Banfield, Edison H. 1924- *WhoBlA 94*
Banfield, Edward Christie 1916- *WhoAm 94*
Banfield, William Gethin 1920- *WhoScEn 94*
Bang, Joy *WhoHol 92*
Bang, Otto T., Jr. 1931- *WhoAmP 93*
Bangaru, Babu Rajendra Prasad 1947- *WhoWest 94*
Bangdiwala, Ishver Surchand 1922- *WhoAm 94*
Bangel, Herbert K. 1928- *WhoAmL 94*
Bangemann, Martin 1934- *IntWW 93, Who 94*
Bangert, Colette Stuebe 1934- *WhoAmA 93*
Bangerter, Hans Ernst 1924- *IntWW 93*
Bangerter, Jack M. 1925- *WhoAmP 93*
Bangerter, Norman H. 1933- *WhoAmP 93*
Bangerter, Norman Howard 1933- *IntWW 93, WhoAm 94*
Bangham, Alec Douglas 1921- *Who 94*
Bangham, Robert Arthur 1942- *WhoWest 94*
Banghart, William 1948- *WhoAmP 93*
Bangiola, Paul 1923- *WhoAmL 94*
Bangle, Richard Morris 1941- *WhoWest 94*
Bangor, Bishop of 1947- *Who 94*
Bangor, Dean of *Who 94*
Bangor, Viscount d1993 *Who 94N*
Bangor, Viscount 1948- *Who 94*
Bangs, Allan Philip 1930- *WhoScEn 94*
Bangs, Carol Jane *DrAPF 93*
Bangs, Cate 1951- *WhoWest 94*
Bangs, Frank Kendrick 1914- *WhoAm 94*
Bangs, John Kendrick 1862-1922 *EncSF 93*
Bangs, John Kendrick 1920- *WhoAm 94*
Bangs, John Wesley, III 1941- *WhoWest 94*
Bangs, Jonathan 1943- *WhoAmL 94*
Bangs, Nathan 1778-1862 *DcAmReB 2*
Bangs, Richard Johnston 1950- *WhoFI 94*
Bangs, Will Johnston 1923- *WhoAm 94*
Bangsund, Edward Lee 1935- *WhoAm 94, WhoWest 94*
Banham, Belinda Joan *Who 94*
Banham, John (Michael Middlecott) 1940- *Who 94*
Banham, John Michael Middlecott 1940- *IntWW 93*
Banharn Silpaarcha, Nai 1932- *IntWW 93*
Baniak, Sheila Mary 1953- *WhoMW 93*
Banik, Niranjan Chandra-Dutta 1946- *WhoScEn 94*
Banik, Sambhu Nath 1935- *WhoAm 94, WhoAsA 94*
Banionis, Donatis *WhoHol 92*
Banis, Robert Joseph 1943- *WhoFI 94, WhoMW 93*
Bani-Sadr, Abolhasan 1933- *IntWW 93*
Banister, George R. 1950- *WhoAmP 93*
Banister, John 1734-1788 *WhAmRev*
Banister, Manly (Miles) 1914- *EncSF 93*
Banister, Stephen Michael Alvin 1918- *Who 94*
Banjanin, Tom 1942- *WhoAmP 93*
Banjerjee, Victor 1946- *IntMPA 94*
Ban Jieyu c. 48BC-c. 6BC *BlmGWL*
Banjo, Ladipo Ayodeji 1934- *IntWW 93*
Banjoko, Alimi Ajimon 1954- *WhoFI 94*
Bank, Jonathan F. 1943- *WhoAm 94*
Bank, Malvin E. 1930- *WhoAm 94*
Bank, Steven Barry 1939- *WhoAm 94*
Bankard, Robert Joseph 1963- *WhoFI 94*
Banker, Gilbert Stephen 1931- *WhoAm 94*
Banker, James R. 1938- *WrDr 94*
Banker, Nancy Sirmay 1944- *WhoWest 94*
Banker, Stephen M. 1952- *WhoAm 94*
Bankert, Pamela Beryl 1954- *WhoAmL 94*
Bankes, Lyn 1941- *WhoAmP 93*
Bankes, Lyn R. 1941- *WhoMW 93*
Bankett, Paula Regina 1959- *WhoWest 94*
Bankett, William Daniel 1930- *WhoBlA 94*
Bankewaka, Anna Danuta *WhoWomW 91*
Bankhead, Patricia Ann 1947- *WhoBlA 94*
Bankhead, Tallulah d1968 *WhoHol 92*
Bankhead, William G. 1941- *WhoAmP 93*
Bankhurst, Arthur Dale 1937- *WhoWest 94*
Bankoff, Joseph R. 1945- *WhoAmL 94*
Bankoff, Seymour George 1921- *WhoAm 94, WhoMW 93*
Bankole, Edward O. 1956- *WhoFI 94*
Bankole, Timothy 1920?- *BlkWr 2*
Bankowski, Lawrence 1931- *WhoAm 94*
Banks *Who 94*
Banks, Baron 1918- *Who 94*
Banks, Alan George 1911- *Who 94*
Banks, Albert Victor, Jr. 1956- *WhoAm 94*
Banks, Allan R. 1948- *WhoAmA 93*
Banks, Allen *WhoAm 94, WhoFI 94*
Banks, Anna Delceina 1952- *WhoFI 94*
Banks, Anne Johnson 1924- *WhoAmA 93*
Banks, Arthur C., Jr. 1915- *WhoBlA 94*
Banks, Arthur Sparrow 1926- *WhoAm 94*
Banks, Barbara *DrAPF 93*
Banks, Beatrice 1936- *WhoBlA 94*
Banks, Bettie Sheppard 1933- *WhoAm 94*
Banks, Bradley Carter 1952- *WhoAmP 93*
Banks, Bruce A. 1942- *WhoScEn 94*
Banks, Carl 1962- *WhoBlA 94*
Banks, Carl A. 1903- *WhoBlA 94*
Banks, Carlton Luther 1958- *WhoBlA 94*
Banks, Caroline Giles 1944- *WhoMW 93*
Banks, Caroline Long 1940- *WhoBlA 94*
Banks, Carolyn *DrAPF 93*
Banks, Carolyn Long 1940- *WhoAmP 93*
Banks, Cecil J. 1947- *WhoBlA 94*
Banks, Charlie 1931- *WhoBlA 94*
Banks, Cherry Ann McGee 1945- *WhoWest 94*
Banks, Chip 1959- *WhoBlA 94*
Banks, Colin 1932- *Who 94*
Banks, David *Who 94*
Banks, (Arthur) David 1948- *Who 94*
Banks, David Russell 1937- *WhoAm 94, WhoFI 94*
Banks, Dennis James 1932- *AmSocL*
Banks, Dwayne Martin 1961- *WhoBlA 94*
Banks, Earle S. *WhoAmP 93*
Banks, Ellen *WhoAmA 93, WhoBlA 94*
Banks, Ephraim 1918- *WhoAm 94, WhoScEn 94*
Banks, Eric Kendall 1955- *WhoAmL 94*
Banks, Ernest 1931- *WhoAm 94, WhoWest 94*
Banks, Ernie 1931- *WhoBlA 94*
Banks, Frank David 1933- *Who 94*
Banks, Fred L., Jr. 1942- *WhoBlA 94*
Banks, Fred Lee, Jr. 1942- *WhoAmL 94, WhoAmP 93*
Banks, Garnie 1932- *WhoBlA 94*
Banks, Gene 1959- *WhoBlA 94*
Banks, Gillian Theresa 1933- *Who 94*
Banks, Gordon 1937- *WorESoc [port]*
Banks, Gordon 1958- *WhoBlA 94*
Banks, Haywood Elliott 1922- *WhoBlA 94*
Banks, Henry H. 1921- *WhoAm 94*
Banks, Henry Stephen 1920- *WhoFI 94*
Banks, Iain M(enzies) 1954- *EncSF 93*
Banks, Iola Kelley 1935- *WhoAmP 93*
Banks, Isabella 1821-1887 *BlmGWL*
Banks, J. B. 1926- *WhoAmP 93*
Banks, J. B. 1934- *WhoBlA 94*
Banks, James Albert 1941- *WhoAm 94, WhoBlA 94, WrDr 94*
Banks, James Barber 1951- *WhoAm 94*
Banks, James Daniel 1947- *WhoScEn 94*
Banks, Jerry L. 1943- *WhoBlA 94*
Banks, Jessie 1921- *WhoAmP 93*
Banks, John *WhAmRev*
Banks, John 1627-1699 *DcNaB MP*
Banks, John 1920- *Who 94*
Banks, John Houston 1911- *WhoAm 94*
Banks, John T. 1947- *WhoIns 94*
Banks, Jonathan 1947- *WhoHol 92*
Banks, Joseph 1743-1820 *WhWE [port]*
Banks, Joseph Eugene 1908- *WhoAm 94*
Banks, Joyce P. 1930- *WhoBlA 94*
Banks, June Skinner 1936- *WhoBlA 94*
Banks, Karl Marvin 1949- *WhoAmP 93*
Banks, Kenneth E. 1943- *WhoBlA 94*
Banks, Laura N. 1921- *WhoBlA 94*
Banks, Leslie d1952 *WhoHol 92*
Banks, Loubertha May *WhoBlA 94*
Banks, Louis d1993 *NewYTBS 93*
Banks, Lynne Reid *BlmGWL*
Banks, Lynne Reid 1929- *Who 94*
Banks, Manley E. 1913- *WhoBlA 94*
Banks, Margaret Amelia 1928- *WhoAmL 94*
Banks, Marguerita C. 1946- *WhoBlA 94*
Banks, Marshall D. 1940- *WhoBlA 94*
Banks, Matthew Richard William 1961- *Who 94*
Banks, Melinda Bruce 1955- *WhoAmL 94*
Banks, Michael A. 1945- *WhoAm 94*
Banks, Michael A. 1951- *EncSF 93*
Banks, Monty d1950 *WhoHol 92*
Banks, Patricia 1949- *WhoBlA 94*
Banks, Paul Edward 1938- *WhoFI 94*
Banks, Perry d1934 *WhoHol 92*
Banks, Perry L. 1955- *WhoBlA 94*
Banks, Peter Louis 1938- *WhoAmP 93*
Banks, Peter Morgan 1937- *WhoAm 94, WhoScEn 94*
Banks, Philip Alan 1952- *WhoWest 94*
Banks, Priscilla Sneed 1941- *WhoBlA 94*
Banks, Rela 1933- *WhoAm 94*
Banks, Richard Alford 1902- *Who 94*
Banks, Richard Edward 1960- *WhoBlA 94*
Banks, Richard L. 1930- *WhoBlA 94*
Banks, Robert Earl 1929- *WhoScEn 94*
Banks, Robert George 1937- *Who 94*
Banks, Robert J. 1928- *WhoAm 94, WhoMW 93*
Banks, Robert Louis 1921-1989 *WhAm 10*
Banks, Robert Sherwood 1934- *WhoAm 94*
Banks, Roland Fitzgerald, Jr. 1932- *WhoAm 94*
Banks, Ronald 1951- *WhoBlA 94*
Banks, Ronald Eric *WhoScEn 94*
Banks, Ronald Trenton 1947- *WhoBlA 94*
Banks, Russell *DrAPF 93*
Banks, Russell 1919- *WhoAm 94, WhoFI 94, WhoScEn 94*
Banks, Russell 1940- *DcLB 130 [port]*
Banks, Russell (Earl) 1940- *WrDr 94*
Banks, Saundra Elizabeth 1948- *WhoBlA 94*
Banks, Sharon P. 1942- *WhoBlA 94*
Banks, Stanley E. *DrAPF 93*
Banks, Tazewell 1932- *WhoBlA 94*
Banks, Terry Michael 1947- *WhoBlA 94*
Banks, Tony *Who 94*
Banks, Virginia 1920-1985 *WhoAmA 93N*
Banks, Waldo R., Sr. 1928- *WhoBlA 94*
Banks, William Hartley 1909- *Who 94*
Banks, William J. P. 1949- *WhoAmP 93*
Banks, William Jasper, Jr. 1944- *WhoBlA 94*
Banks, William Maron, III 1943- *WhoBlA 94*
Banks, Willie Anthony 1969- *WhoBlA 94*
Bankson, Douglas Henneck 1920- *WhoWest 94*
Bankson, Jacob *WhAmRev*
Bankston, Archie M. 1937- *WhoBlA 94*
Bankston, Archie Moore, Jr. 1937- *WhoAm 94*
Bankston, Charles E. *WhoBlA 94*
Bankston, Gene Clifton 1924- *WhoAm 94*
Bankston, Jesse H. 1907- *WhoAmP 93*
Bankston, Larry S. 1951- *WhoAmP 93*
Bankston, Mary Gay 1952- *WhoWest 94*
Banks-Williams, Lula 1947- *WhoBlA 94*
Banky, Vilma 1903- *WhoHol 92*
Ban-ma Dan-zeng *WhoPRCh 91*
Bannan, C. Forrest 1946- *WhoAmL 94*
Bannan, Jan Gumprecht 1931- *WhoWest 94*
Bannard, Walter Darby 1934- *WhoAm 94, WhoAmA 93*
Bannasch, Gerald John 1945- *WhoMW 93*
Bannatyne, Jack 1927- *WrDr 94*
Banneker, Benjamin 1731-1806 *AfrAmAl 6, WorInv*
Bannen, Carol 1951- *WhoAmL 94*
Bannen, Ian 1928- *IntMPA 94, IntWW 93, WhoHol 92*
Bannen, John T. 1951- *WhoAm 94*
Bannenberg, Jon 1929- *Who 94*
Banner, Angela 1923- *WrDr 94*
Banner, Bob 1921- *IntMPA 94, WhoAm 94*
Banner, Franklin Coleman 1895- *WhAm 10*
Banner, James J. 1921- *WhoAmP 93*
Banner, Jill d1982 *WhoHol 92*
Banner, John d1973 *WhoHol 92*
Banner, Josephina *Who 94*
Banner, Larry Shyres 1936- *WhoWest 94*
Banner, Mark Thomas 1950- *WhoAmL 94*
Banner, Melvin Edward 1914- *WhoBlA 94*
Banner, Stephen Edward 1938- *WhoAm 94, WhoFI 94*
Banner, Steve *WhoHol 92*
Banner, William Augustus 1915- *WhoBlA 94*
Bannerjee, Victor 1946- *WhoHol 92*
Bannerman, Celia 1946- *WhoHol 92*
Bannerman, David (Gordon) 1935- *Who 94*
Bannerman, Gene *EncSF 93*
Bannerman, Helen 1862-1946 *DcLB 141 [port]*
Bannerman, John Anthony 1947- *WhoAmL 94*
Bannerman, Margaret d1976 *WhoHol 92*
Bannerman-Richter, Gabriel 1931- *WhoBlA 94*
Bannes, Stephen William 1958- *WhoMW 93*
Bannigan, Eugene F. 1941- *WhoAmL 94*
Banning, Beatrice Harper 1885- *WhoAmA 93N*
Banning, Jack (John Peck), Jr. 1939- *WhoAmA 93*
Banning, Oakley M., Jr. *WhoAmP 93*
Banning, Ronald Ray 1960- *WhoScEn 94*
Bannister, Alan *WhoBlA 94*
Bannister, Charles 1741-1804
See Bannister Family *NewGrDO*
Bannister, Charles E. 1939- *WhoAmP 93*
Bannister, Edward Mitchell 1828-1901 *AfrAmAl 6, WhoAmA 93N*
Bannister, Elizabeth c. 1757-1849
See Bannister Family *NewGrDO*
Bannister, Geoffrey 1945- *WhoAm 94, WhoMW 93*
Bannister, Harry d1961 *WhoHol 92*
Bannister, Jo *EncSF 93*
Bannister, John 1760-1836
See Bannister Family *NewGrDO*
Bannister, Joseph Anthony 1952- *WhoWest 94*
Bannister, Kenneth 1960- *WhoBlA 94*
Bannister, Lance Terry 1954- *WhoScEn 94*
Bannister, Lee Kenneth 1939- *WhoWest 94*
Bannister, (Richard) Matthew 1957- *Who 94*
Bannister, Pati 1929- *WhoAmA 93*
Bannister, Patricia Brown *WhoAmA 93*
Bannister, Reggie *WhoHol 92*
Bannister, Robert Corwin, Jr. 1935- *WhoAm 94*
Bannister, Roger (Gilbert) 1929- *Who 94*
Bannister, Roger (Gilbert), Sir 1929- *WrDr 94*
Bannister, Roger G. 1929- *IntWW 93*
Bannister, Shala Mills 1962- *WhoMW 93*
Bannister, Wes 1936- *WhoAmP 93*
Bannister Family *NewGrDO*
Bannock, Graham 1932- *WrDr 94*

Bannon, Ann 1932- *GayLL*
Bannon, Ann c. 1937- *BlmGWL*
Bannon, Gary Anthony 1954- *WhoScEn 94*
Bannon, George 1925- *WhoFI 94, WhoScEn 94*
Bannon, Jack 1940- *WhoHol 92*
Bannon, Jim 1911- *WhoHol 92*
Bannon, John Charles *IntWW 93*
Bannon, John Kernan 1916- *Who 94*
Bannon, Mark *EncSF 93*
Bannon, Peter 1921- *WrDr 94*
Bannon, William F. 1952- *WhoAmL 94*
Banoff, Harry 1915- *WhoWest 94*
Banoff, Sheldon Irwin 1949- *WhoAm 94, WhoAmL 94*
Banos, Jose Luis 1918- *WhoAmL 94*
Baños-Milton, Margarita 1952- *WhoHisp 94*
Banotti, Mary 1939- *WhoWomW 91*
Banoun, Raymond 1945- *WhoAmL 94*
Banovetz, James Michael 1937- *WhoMW 93*
Banovic, Zlatko Josip 1951- *WhoFI 94*
Banowetz, Joseph Murray 1934- *WhoAm 94*
Bansak, Stephen A., Jr. 1939- *WhoAm 94, WhoFI 94*
Bansal, Narottam Prasad 1946- *WhoScEn 94*
Bansal, Satish Kumar 1960- *WhoScEn 94*
Bansal, Vipul K. 1959- *ConAu 142*
Banschbach, Valerie Suzanne 1964- *WhoScEn 94*
Banse, Karl 1929- *WhoAm 94*
Banse, Robert Lee 1927- *WhoAm 94*
Bansemer, Roger L. 1948- *WhoAmA 93*
Banshchikov, Gennady Ivanovich 1943- *NewGrDO*
Bansod, Pradeep Narayan 1951- *WhoFI 94*
Banstetter, Robert J. 1940- *WhoAmL 94*
Banta, Henry David 1938- *WhoAm 94*
Banta, James Joseph 1950- *WhoFI 94*
Banta, Merle Henry 1932- *WhoAm 94, WhoFI 94*
Banta, Richard Stuart 1951- *WhoFI 94*
Banta, Robert Mason 1946- *WhoWest 94*
Bantel, Linda 1943- *WhoAmA 93*
Bantel, Linda Mae 1943- *WhoAm 94*
Banther, Michael Robert 1957- *WhoWest 94*
Banti, Anna 1895-1985 *BlmGWL*
Banti, Brigida Giorgi c. 1756-1806 *NewGrDO*
Banting, Frederick Grant 1891-1941 *WorScD [port]*
Bantle, John Albert, II 1946- *WhoAm 94*
Bantle, Louis Francis 1928- *WhoAm 94, WhoFI 94*
Bantock, Geoffrey Herman 1914- *Who 94, WrDr 94*
Bantock, Granville 1868-1946 *NewGrDO*
Bantock, John Leonard 1927- *Who 94*
Bantock, Leedham d1928 *WhoHol 92*
Bantock, Nick 1950?- *ConAu 142*
Banton, Michael Parker 1926- *Who 94*
Banton, Stephen Chandler *WhoMW 93*
Banton, Stephen Chandler 1947- *WhoAmP 93*
Banton, Travis 1894-1958 *IntDcF 2-4 [port]*
Banton, William C., II 1922- *AfrAmG [port], WhoBlA 94*
Bantry, Bryan 1956- *WhoAm 94, WhoFI 94*
Bantz, Bruce William 1949- *WhoFI 94*
Bañuelas, Arturo 1949- *WhoHisp 94*
Banuelos, Betty Lou 1930- *WhoWest 94*
Bañuelos, Rodrigo 1954- *WhoHisp 94*
Bañuelos, Romana Acosta 1925- *WhoHisp 94*
Banuk, Ronald Edward 1944- *WhoScEn 94, WhoWest 94*
Banvard, Fifi d1962 *WhoHol 92*
Banville, Debra Lee 1959- *WhoScEn 94*
Banville, John *IntWW 93*
Banville, John 1945- *WrDr 94*
Banwart, George Junior 1926- *WhoAm 94*
Banwart, Wayne Lee 1948- *WhoAm 94, WhoMW 93*
Banwell, Derick Frank 1919- *Who 94*
Banwell, Martin Gerhardt 1954- *WhoScEn 94*
Banyasz, Rezso 1931- *Who 94*
Banz, George 1928- *WhoAmA 93*
Banzer, Cindy 1947- *WhoAmP 93*
Banzer Suarez, Hugo 1926- *IntWW 93*
Banzhaf, Clayton Harris 1917-1990 *WhAm 10*
Banzhaf, John F., III 1940- *WhoAm 94*
Ban Zhao 52?-125 *BlmGWL*
Bao, Joseph Yue-Se 1937- *WhoScEn 94, WhoWest 94*
Bao, Katherine Sung 1920- *WhoWest 94*
Bao, Zhenlei 1963- *WhoScEn 94*
Bao Chuan 1942- *BlmGWL*
Bao Chuan 1943- *WhoPRCh 91 [port]*
Bao Hanchen *WhoPRCh 91*
Bao Keming 1932- *WhoPRCh 91 [port]*
Bao Tong *WhoPRCh 91*
Bao Wenkui 1915- *WhoPRCh 91 [port]*
Bao Wenkui 1916- *IntWW 93*
Bao Yishan 1923- *WhoPRCh 91*
Bao Yongkang 1934- *WhoPRCh 91*
Bao Yujun 1942- *WhoPRCh 91 [port]*
Bao Yushan 1928- *WhoPRCh 91 [port]*
Bao Zhongmou *WhoPRCh 91*
Bao Zunxin *WhoPRCh 91*
Bapatla, Krishna M. *WhoAsA 94*
Bappoo, Sheilabai *WhoWomW 91*
Bappoo, Sheilabai 1947- *IntWW 93*
Bapst, Sarah 1950- *WhoAmA 93*
Baptist, Allwyn J. 1943- *WhoAm 94*
Baptist, Errol Christopher 1945- *WhoMW 93*
Baptist, James Noel 1930- *WhoScEn 94*
Baptist, R. Hernekin *BlmGWL*
Baptist, Sylvia Evelyn 1944- *WhoMW 93*
Baptista, Carlos d1950 *WhoHol 92*
Baptista, Howard 1930- *WhoBlA 94*
Baptista, Luis Felipe 1941- *WhoWest 94*
Baptista, Pedro Joao fl. 180-?- *WhWE*
Baptiste, Hansom Prentice, Jr. 1939- *WhoBlA 94*
Baptiste, Jacquelyn D. 1948- *WhoBlA 94*
Baptiste, Kim E. 1950- *WhoAmL 94*
Baptiste, Thomas 1936- *WhoHol 92*
Baqai, Uddin Ahmad 1945- *WhoWest 94*
Baquet, Charles R., III 1941- *WhoAmP 93*
Baquet, Dean Paul 1956- *WhoMW 93*
Baquet, Edward, Sr. d1993 *NewYTBS 93*
Bar, Jacques Jean Louis 1921- *IntMPA 94*
Bar, Olaf 1957- *NewGrDO*
Bar, Robert S. 1943- *WhoScEn 94*
Bara, Fausto *WhoHol 92*
Bara, Jean Marc 1946- *WhoAm 94*
Bara, John V. 1926- *WhoAmP 93*
Bara, Nina d1990 *WhoHol 92*
Bara, Theda d1955 *WhoHol 92*
Barab, Marvin 1927- *WhoWest 94*
Barab, Nira *WhoHol 92*
Barab, Ronald E. 1952- *WhoAmL 94*
Barab, Seymour 1921- *NewGrDO*
Barabanov, Vladimir Aleksandrovich 1951- *LoBiDrD*
Barabanov, Yevgeniy Viktorovich 1943- *IntWW 93*
Barabas, Gabor 1948- *WrDr 94*
Barabas, Sari 1918- *NewGrDO*
Barabas, Silvio *WhoAm 94*
Barabas, SuzAnne 1949- *WrDr 94*
Barabtarlo, Gennady Alexis 1949- *WhoMW 93*
Barach, Philip G. 1930- *WhoFI 94*
Baracks, Barbara *DrAPF 93*
Barad, Jill 1951- *News 94-2 [port]*
Barad, Jill Elikann 1951- *WhoAm 94, WhoFI 94, WhoWest 94*
Barad, Judith Adrian 1949- *WhoMW 93*
Baraga, Frederick 1797-1868 *EncNAR*
Baragiola, Raul Antonio 1945- *WhoScEn 94*
Baragrey, John d1975 *WhoHol 92*
Baragwanath, Albert Kingsmill 1917- *WhoAm 94*
Barajas, Charles 1944- *WhoHisp 94*
Barajas, Gil Cuevas 1952- *WhoHisp 94*
Barajas, Richard 1953- *WhoHisp 94*
Barak, Ehud 1942- *IntWW 93*
Barak, Ronald S. 1943- *WhoAmL 94*
Baraka, Amiri *DrAPF 93*
Baraka, Amiri 1934- *BlkWr 2, ConDr 93, WhoAm 94*
Baraka, (Imamu) Amiri 1934- *IntDcT 2*
Baraka, Imamu Amiri 1934- *AfrAmAl 6, AmCulL, WhoBlA 94, WrDr 94*
Baraka, Larry *WhoBlA 94*
Barakat, Nayel 1922- *IntWW 93*
Barakat, Russell G. 1940- *WhoAmP 93*
Barakat, Samir F. 1954- *WhoAm 94, WhoFI 94*
Baraket, Edmund S., Jr. 1947- *WhoFI 94*
Baram, Tallie Zeev 1951- *WhoWest 94*
Baram, Uzi 1937- *IntWW 93*
Baran, Jan Witold 1948- *WhoAm 94, WhoAmL 94*
Baran, William Lee 1943- *WhoAm 94, WhoFI 94*
Barañano, Carlos, Sr. 1935- *WhoHisp 94*
Baranco, Beverly Victor, Jr. *WhoBlA 94*
Baranco, Gordon S. 1948- *WhoBlA 94*
Baranco, Gregory T. *WhoBlA 94*
Baranco, Raphael Alvin 1932- *WhoBlA 94*
Baranczak, Stanislaw *DrAPF 93*
Baranczak, Stanislaw 1946- *ConWorW 93*
Barandas, Ana Euridice de *BlmGWL*
Barandes, Robert 1947- *WhoAm 94*
Baranek, Paul Peter 1914- *WhoWest 94*
Baranik, Rudolf 1920- *WhoAm 94, WhoAmA 93*
Barannikov, Viktor Pavlovich 1940- *IntWW 93, LoBiDrD*
Baranoff, Mort 1923-1978 *WhoAmA 93N*
Baranov, Alexandr Andreevich 1747-1819 *WhWE [port]*
Baranovic, Kresimir 1894-1975 *NewGrDO*
Baranow, Joan *DrAPF 93*
Baranowski, Edwin Michael 1947- *WhoAm 94, WhoAmL 94, WhoMW 93*
Baranowski, Frank Paul 1921- *WhoAm 94*
Baranowski, Paul Joseph 1950- *WhoScEn 94*
Baranowski, Shelley Osmun 1946- *WhoMW 93*
Baranowski, Tom 1946- *WhoAm 94*
Baranskaia, Natal'ia Vladimirovna 1908- *BlmGWL*
Baranski, Christine 1952- *ConTFT 11, WhoHol 92*
Baranski, Joan Sullivan 1933- *WhoAm 94*
Barany, George 1955- *WhoMW 93*
Barany, James Walter 1930- *WhoAm 94, WhoMW 93*
Barany, Kate 1929- *WhoAm 94*
Barany, Michael 1921- *WhoMW 93*
Barany, Nancy 1960- *WhoMW 93*
Barasch, Clarence Sylvan 1912- *WhoAm 94*
Barasch, Frances K. 1928- *WrDr 94*
Barasch, Lynne 1939- *SmATA 74 [port]*
Barasch, Mal Livingston 1929- *WhoAm 94, WhoAmL 94*
Barasch, Max d1966 *WhoHol 92*
Barash, Anthony Harlan 1943- *WhoAm 94*
Barash, David Philip 1946- *WhoAm 94*
Barash, Olivia 1965- *WhoHol 92*
Barash, Paul George 1942- *WhoAm 94*
Barash, Samuel T. 1921- *WrDr 94*
Barassi, Dario 1940- *WhoScEn 94*
Barat, Kahar 1950- *WhoAsA 94*
Barath, Peter 1946- *WhoWest 94*
Baratta, Pietro fl. 1723-1741 *NewGrDO*
Baratz, Morton Sachs 1923- *WhoAm 94*
Baray, Enrique *WhoHisp 94*
Barayon, Ramon Sender *DrAPF 93*
Barazani, Morris 1924- *WhoAmA 93*
Barb, Cynthia Marie 1962- *WhoMW 93*
Barba, Carl John, Jr. 1946- *WhoFI 94*
Barba, Carlos 1935- *WhoHisp 94*
Barba, Evans Michael 1950- *WhoScEn 94*
Barba, Harry *DrAPF 93*
Barba, Harry 1922- *WhoAm 94, WrDr 94*
Barba, John 1950- *WhoHisp 94*
Barba, Philip S(tanley) 1895- *WhAm 10*
Barba, Ralph N. *WhoHisp 94*
Barba, Raymond Felix 1923- *WhoHisp 94*
Barba, Sharon *DrAPF 93*
Barba, Thomas Milton 1954- *WhoAmL 94*
Barbachano, Fernando G. R. 1926- *WhoFI 94*
Barback, Ronald Henry 1919- *Who 94*
Barbadoro, Paul J. 1955- *WhoAm 94, WhoAmL 94*
Barbagallo, Ralph A. 1942- *WhoAmL 94*
Barbagelata, Robert Dominic 1925- *WhoAm 94*
Barbaia, Domenico 1778?-1841 *NewGrDO*
Barbakow, Jeffery C. 1944- *WhoAm 94, WhoFI 94*
Barbalas, Lorina Cheng 1958- *WhoScEn 94*
Barbalet, Margaret 1949- *SmATA 77 [port]*
Barban, Arnold Melvin 1932- *WhoAm 94*
Barbanel, Jack Allen 1950- *WhoAmL 94*
Barbanell, Alexander Stanley 1930- *WhoFI 94*
Barbanell, Frank d1959 *WhoHol 92*
Barbano, Frances Elizabeth 1944- *WhoWest 94*
Barbara, Agatha 1923- *IntWW 93, Who 94*
Barbara, Paola d1989 *WhoHol 92*
Barbaran, Francisco Ramon 1960- *WhoScEn 94*
Barbareschi, Luca *WhoHol 92*
Barbarese, J. T. *DrAPF 93*
Barbarese, J. T. 1948- *WrDr 94*
Barbarich, Stanley Joseph 1945- *WhoWest 94*
Barbarito, Luigi 1922- *Who 94*
Barbaro, Frank J. 1927- *WhoAmP 93*
Barbaro, Frank Pasquale 1943- *WhoAmP 93*
Barbaro, Ronald D. 1931- *WhoAm 94, WhoFI 94*
Barbarosh, Milton Harvey 1955- *WhoFI 94*
Barbarossa, Theodore C. 1906-1992 *WhoAmA 93N*
Barbarow, Thomas Steven 1951- *WhoAm 94*
Barbarula, John Matthew 1953- *WhoAmL 94*
Barbary, James *EncSF 93*
Barbas, Stephen Michael 1954- *WhoAmL 94*
Barbash, Fred 1945- *WhoAm 94*
Barbash, Joseph 1921- *WhoAm 94*
Barbat, Alex Horia 1947- *WhoScEn 94*
Barbat, Percy d1965 *WhoHol 92*
Barbatano, Salvatore A. 1947- *WhoAmL 94*
Barbatis, Calypso 1946- *WhoScEn 94*
Barbato, Joseph Allen 1944- *WhoScEn 94*
Barbato, Silvio *WhoAm 94*
Barbauld, Anna Laetitia 1743-1824 *BlmGEL*
Barbauld, Anna Laetitia (Aikin) 1743-1825 *BlmGWL*
Barbault, Andre 1921- *AstEnc*
Barbe, Betty Catherine 1930- *WhoFI 94, WhoMW 93*
Barbe, David Franklin 1939- *WhoAm 94*
Barbe, Walter Burke 1926- *WhoAm 94*
Barbeau, Adrienne 1946- *WhoHol 92*
Barbeau, Adrienne 1947- *IntMPA 94*
Barbeau, Jean 1945- *IntDcT 2*
Barbeau, Marcel (Christian) 1925- *WhoAmA 93*
Barbee, Allen Cromwell 1910- *WhoAmP 93*
Barbee, Bobby H., Sr. 1927- *WhoAmP 93*
Barbee, Elizabeth Joann 1940- *WhoWest 94*
Barbee, George E. L. 1943- *WhoAm 94, WhoFI 94*
Barbee, Jack d1981 *WhoHol 92*
Barbee, Joe Ed 1934- *WhoAmL 94, WhoScEn 94, WhoWest 94*
Barbee, Linton E. 1938- *WhoAm 94*
Barbee, Lloyd Augustus 1925- *WhoAm 94, WhoAmL 94, WhoAmP 93, WhoBlA 94*
Barbee, Phillips *EncSF 93*
Barbee, Phyllis May 1930- *WhoAmP 93*
Barbee, Rob 1940- *WhoAmA 93*
Barbee, Robert Thomas 1921- *WhoAmA 93*
Barbee, Robert Wayne 1956- *WhoScEn 94*
Barbee, Victor 1954- *WhoAm 94*
Barbeito, Nelson 1946- *WhoHisp 94*
Barbe-Marbois, Francois, Marquis de 1745-1837 *WhAmRev*
Barbenel, Joseph Cyril 1937- *IntWW 93*
Barbeosch, William Peter 1954- *WhoAmL 94*
Barber *Who 94*
Barber, Baron 1920- *Who 94*
Barber, Albert W. 1930- *WhoAmP 93*
Barber, Andrew Bollons 1909- *WhoAm 94*
Barber, Ann McDonald 1951- *WhoScEn 94*
Barber, Anthony Perrinot Lysberg 1920- *IntWW 93*
Barber, Arthur Whiting 1926- *WhoAm 94*
Barber, Barry 1945- *WhoFI 94*
Barber, Ben Bernard Andrew 1944- *WhoAm 94*
Barber, Benjamin R(eynolds) 1939- *WrDr 94*
Barber, Benjamn R. *DrAPF 93*
Barber, Bruce Alistair 1950- *WhoAmA 93*
Barber, Charles Edward 1939- *WhoAm 94, WhoFI 94*
Barber, Charles Finch 1917- *WhoAm 94*
Barber, Charles Laurence 1915- *WrDr 94*
Barber, Charles Turner 1941- *WhoAm 94, WhoMW 93*
Barber, Chris *Who 94*
Barber, (Donald) Chris(topher) 1930- *Who 94*
Barber, Clarence Lyle 1917- *IntWW 93, WhoAm 94, WhoWest 94*
Barber, Cynthia 1939- *WhoAmA 93*
Barber, Daniel Rowland 1948- *WhoMW 93*
Barber, Earl Eugene 1939- *WhoMW 93*
Barber, Edmund Amaral, Jr. 1916- *WhoScEn 94*
Barber, Edward Bruce 1937- *WhoFI 94, WhoMW 93*
Barber, Edward J. 1958- *WhoAmP 93*
Barber, Edwin B. 1927- *WhoIns 94*
Barber, Ellen *WhoHol 92*
Barber, (Edward Hamilton) Esler d1991 *Who 94N*
Barber, Frances 1957- *IntMPA 94, WhoHol 92*
Barber, Francis 1751-1783 *WhAmRev*
Barber, Frank 1923- *Who 94*
Barber, Frank David, III 1956- *WhoAmL 94*
Barber, Giles Gaudard 1930- *Who 94*
Barber, Glynis *WhoHol 92*
Barber, Hargrow Dexter 1956- *WhoBlA 94*
Barber, Herbert Bradford 1943- *WhoWest 94*
Barber, James 1940- *Who 94*
Barber, James Alden 1934- *WhoAm 94*
Barber, James David 1921- *WhoAmP 93*
Barber, James David 1930- *WhoAm 94, WrDr 94*
Barber, James P. 1944- *WhoAmL 94*
Barber, James Peden 1931- *Who 94*
Barber, James W. 1936- *WhoBlA 94*
Barber, Janice Denise 1952- *WhoBlA 94*

Barber, Jean Marie 1929- *WhoMW 93*
Barber, Jerry Randel 1940- *WhoAm 94*
Barber, Jesse B., Jr. 1924- *WhoBlA 94*
Barber, John 1675-1741 *DcNaB MP*
Barber, John 1898-1965 *WhoAmA 93N*
Barber, John (Douglass) 1944- *WrDr 94*
Barber, John L. *Who 94*
Barber, John Merrell 1935- *WhoAm 94*
Barber, John Norman Romney *Who 94*
Barber, John Norman Romney 1919- *IntWW 93*
Barber, Kathleen Ann Starks 1950- *WhoWest 94*
Barber, Kathleen Lucas 1924- *WhoAmP 93*
Barber, Kimberly Lisanby 1955- *WhoMW 93*
Barber, Linda Lee 1937- *WhoAmP 93*
Barber, Lloyd Ingram 1932- *IntWW 93, WhoAm 94*
Barber, Marsha 1946- *WhoMW 93*
Barber, Muriel V. d1971 *WhoAmA 93N*
Barber, Nicholas Charles Faithorn 1940- *Who 94*
Barber, Orion Metcalf, II 1935- *WhoAm 94*
Barber, Paul (Thomas) 1941- *WrDr 94*
Barber, Paul D. *WhoAmP 93*
Barber, Paul Everard *Who 94*
Barber, Philip Judd 1951- *WhoAmA 93*
Barber, Phillip Mark 1944- *WhoAmL 94*
Barber, Putnam 1940- *WhoWest 94*
Barber, Rahe Darlynn 1944- *WhoAmP 93*
Barber, Red *ConAu 141*
Barber, Red 1908-1992 *AnObit 1992, CurBio 93N, WhAm 10*
Barber, Richard (William) 1941- *WrDr 94*
Barber, Richard A. 1911- *WhoAmL 94*
Barber, Robert A., Jr. 1949- *WhoAmP 93*
Barber, Robert Charles 1936- *WhoAm 94*
Barber, Ronald *WhoAmA 93*
Barber, Russell Brooks Butler 1934- *WhoAm 94*
Barber, Sam 1943- *WhoAmA 93*
Barber, Samuel 1910-1981 *AmCulL, NewGrDO*
Barber, Stanley Arthur 1921- *WhoAm 94*
Barber, Stephan Allen 1950- *WhoAm 94*
Barber, Susan Carrol 1952- *WhoScEn 94*
Barber, Theodore Francis 1931- *WhoFI 94, WhoWest 94*
Barber, Thomas King 1923- *WhoAm 94*
Barber, Trevor Wing 1943- *Who 94*
Barber, Walter Lanier 1908-1992 *ConAu 141*
Barber, William, Jr. 1942- *WhoBlA 94*
Barber, William (Francis) 1905- *Who 94*
Barber, William Joseph 1925- *Who 94*
Barbera, Joe *WhoAmA 93*
Barbera, Joseph *WhoAm 94*
Barbera, Joseph 1905- *See* Hanna, William 1910- *IntDcF 2-4*
Barbera, Joseph R. 1911- *IntMPA 94*
Barbera, Ross William 1950- *WhoAmA 93*
Barbera, Vincent Joseph 1956- *WhoAmP 93*
Barbera Guillem, Emilio 1946- *IntWW 93*
Barber Dickerson, Ornetta M. 1949- *WhoBlA 94*
Barberena, Eduardo J. 1957- *WhoHisp 94*
Barberi, Robert Obed 1945- *WhoAm 94*
Barberia, Richard A. 1944- *WhoAmP 93*
Barberina, La 1721-1799 *IntDcB [port]*
Barberini, Urbano 1962- *WhoHol 92*
Barberini Family *NewGrDO*
Barberis, Dorothy Watkeys 1918- *WhoAmA 93*
Barberis, Grace H. 1932- *WhoAmP 93*
Barberis, Mansi 1899-1986 *NewGrDO*
Barberis, Pierre Georges 1942- *IntWW 93*
Barbero, Giulio John 1923- *WhoScEn 94*
Barbero, Jose Alfredo 1950- *WhoScEn 94*
Barber Of Tewkesbury, Baron *Who 94*
Barbet, Pierre 1925- *EncSF 93*
Barbette d1973 *WhoHol 92*
Barbezat, Eugene LaVar 1936- *WhoWest 94*
Barbi, Josef Walter 1949- *WhoMW 93, WhoScEn 94*
Barbian, David 1949- *WhoFI 94*
Barbier, (Henri-)Auguste 1805-1882 *NewGrDO*
Barbier, George d1945 *WhoHol 92*
Barbier, Jane c. 1692-1757 *NewGrDO*
Barbier, Jules 1825-1901 *NewGrDO*
Barbier, Marie-Anne 1670-1745 *BlmGWL, NewGrDO*
Barbier, Rene (Auguste Ernest) 1890-1981 *NewGrDO*
Barbieri, Antonio fl. 1720-1743 *NewGrDO*
Barbieri, Arthur Robert 1926- *WhoFI 94*
Barbieri, Carlo Emanuele 1822-1867 *NewGrDO*
Barbieri, Christopher George 1941- *WhoAm 94*
Barbieri, David Arthur 1930- *WhoWest 94*
Barbieri, Enrique 1959- *WhoHisp 94*
Barbieri, Fedora 1919- *IntWW 93*
Barbieri, Fedora 1920- *NewGrDO*
Barbieri, Francisco Asenjo 1823-1894 *NewGrDO*
Barbieri, Giovan Domenico c. 1674-c. 1740 *NewGrDO*
Barbieri, Margaret Elizabeth 1947- *Who 94*
Barbieri, Ronald Francis 1947- *WhoWest 94*
Barbieri, Tagliavini Silvia 1938- *WhoWomW 91*
Barbieri-Nini, Marianna 1818-1887 *NewGrDO*
Barbieri-Webb, M. E., Mrs. 1947- *Who 94*
Barbirolli, John 1899-1970 *NewGrDO*
Barbo, Dorothy Marie 1932- *WhoAm 94*
Barboni, Paola *WhoHol 92*
Barbor, John Howard 1952- *WhoAmL 94*
Barbosa, Pedro, III 1944- *WhoHisp 94*
Barbosa-Canovas, Gustavo Victor 1949- *WhoHisp 94*
Barbot, Ivan 1937- *IntWW 93*
Barbot, Joseph-Theodore-Desire 1824-1879 *NewGrDO*
Barbour, Alan G. 1933- *IntMPA 94*
Barbour, Alton Bradford 1933- *WhoWest 94*
Barbour, Arthur J. 1926- *WhoAmA 93*
Barbour, Billy Michael 1953- *WhoFI 94*
Barbour, Charlene 1949- *WhoFI 94*
Barbour, Claude Marie 1935- *WhoMW 93*
Barbour, Dave d1965 *WhoHol 92*
Barbour, David A. *WhoFI 94*
Barbour, David A. 1948- *WhoAmL 94*
Barbour, Douglas 1940- *WrDr 94*
Barbour, Douglas (Fleming) 1940- *EncSF 93*
Barbour, Edwin d1914 *WhoHol 92*
Barbour, Eric S. 1966- *WhoScEn 94*
Barbour, Haley Reeves 1947- *WhoAmP 93*
Barbour, Hugh (Stewart) 1921- *WrDr 94*
Barbour, Hugh Revell 1929- *WhoAm 94*
Barbour, John c. 1320-1395 *BlmGEL*
Barbour, Joyce d1977 *WhoHol 92*
Barbour, Julian B. 1937- *WrDr 94*
Barbour, Larry Gregory 1950- *WhoAmL 94*
Barbour, Louise Yvonne Devoley *WhoMW 93*
Barbour, Malcolm 1934- *IntMPA 94*
Barbour, Michael George 1942- *WhoAm 94*
Barbour, Oliver d1968 *WhoHol 92*
Barbour, Patricia Jeanne *WhoAmP 93*
Barbour, Robert Alexander Stewart 1921- *IntWW 93, Who 94*
Barbour, Robert Charles 1935- *WhoScEn 94*
Barbour, Robert G. 1947- *WhoHisp 94*
Barbour, William H., Jr. 1941- *WhoAmL 94*
Barbour, William Rinehart, Jr. 1922- *WhoAm 94*
Barbour, Williams H., Jr. 1941- *WhoAm 94*
Barboza, Anthony 1944- *WhoAm 94, WhoAmA 93*
Barboza, Mario G. *Who 94*
Barboza, Steven Alan 1952- *WhoBlA 94*
Barbre, John H. 1934- *WhoIns 94*
Barbulescu, Romulus *EncSF 93*
Barbusse, Henri 1874-1935 *EncSF 93*
Barbut, Erol 1940- *WhoWest 94*
Barbuy, Beatriz 1950- *WhoScEn 94*
Barca, George Gino 1937- *WhoAm 94, WhoFI 94, WhoWest 94*
Barca, Kathleen 1946- *WhoFI 94, WhoWest 94*
Barca, Peter 1955- *CngDr 93*
Barca, Peter William 1955- *WhoAm 94, WhoAmP 93, WhoMW 93*
Barcal, Anne 1965- *WhoFI 94*
Barcan, Stephen Emanuel 1942- *WhoAm 94*
Barcella, Ernest Lawrence, Jr. 1945- *WhoAmL 94*
Barcelo, Alvaro 1952- *WhoHisp 94*
Barcelo, Elia *EncSF 93*
Barcelo, John James, III 1940- *WhoAm 94*
Barcelo, Miquel 1948- *EncSF 93*
Barcelona, Charles B. *WhoFI 94*
Barcena, Catalina d1978 *WhoHol 92*
Barcenas, Jude Ramon Legaspi 1956- *WhoFI 94*
Barcey, Harold Edward Dean 1949- *WhoFI 94, WhoMW 93*
Barchet, Stephen 1932- *WhoAm 94*
Barchi, Robert Lawrence 1946- *WhoAm 94, WhoScEn 94*
Barchuk, Vasily Vasilevich 1941- *LoBiDrD*
Barchuk, Vasily Vasilievich 1941- *IntWW 93*
Barcia, James A. 1952- *CngDr 93, WhoAm 94, WhoAmP 93, WhoMW 93*
Barckley, Robert Eugene 1922- *WhoAm 94*
Barclay, Alan 1910- *EncSF 93*
Barclay, Alexander c. 1475-1552 *DcLB 132*
Barclay, Bill *EncSF 93*
Barclay, Bill 1939- *WrDr 94*
Barclay, Carl Archie 1922- *WhoBlA 94*
Barclay, Christopher Francis Robert 1919- *Who 94*
Barclay, Colville Herbert Sanford 1913- *Who 94*
Barclay, David d1969 *WhoHol 92*
Barclay, David 1682-1769 *DcNaB MP*
Barclay, David 1729-1809 *DcNaB MP*
Barclay, David 1934- *IntWW 93*
Barclay, David Ronald 1932- *WhoBlA 94*
Barclay, Don d1975 *WhoHol 92*
Barclay, Frederick 1934- *IntWW 93*
Barclay, Gabriel *EncSF 93*
Barclay, Hugh Douglas 1932- *WhoAm 94, WhoAmL 94*
Barclay, Hugh Maben 1927- *Who 94*
Barclay, James fl. 1774- *DcNaB MP*
Barclay, James Christopher 1945- *Who 94*
Barclay, James Patrick 1948- *WhoFI 94*
Barclay, James Ralph 1926- *WhoAm 94*
Barclay, Jeffrey Lee 1956- *WhoMW 93*
Barclay, John d1978 *WhoHol 92*
Barclay, John Alistair 1933- *Who 94*
Barclay, John Allen 1951- *WhoWest 94*
Barclay, Lawrence V. *WhoBlA 94*
Barclay, Peter (Maurice) 1926- *Who 94*
Barclay, Richard L. 1937- *WhoAmP 93*
Barclay, Robert, Jr. 1928- *WhoScEn 94*
Barclay, Robin Marie 1956- *WhoBlA 94*
Barclay, Roderick (Edward) 1909- *Who 94*
Barclay, Roderick Edward 1909- *IntWW 93*
Barclay, Stanton Dewitt 1899- *WhoScEn 94*
Barclay, Thomas 1753-1830 *WhAmRev*
Barclay, Yvonne Fay *Who 94*
Barclift, William C., III 1949- *WhoAm 94*
Barco, Virgilio 1921- *IntWW 93*
Barcroft, Henry 1904- *IntWW 93, Who 94*
Barcroft, Roy d1969 *WhoHol 92*
Barcus, Benjamin Franklin 1960- *WhoAmL 94, WhoWest 94*
Barcus, Gilbert Martin 1937- *WhoFI 94*
Barcus, James Edgar 1938- *WhoAm 94*
Barcus, Mary Evelyn 1938- *WhoMW 93*
Barcus, Robert Alan 1947- *WhoMW 93*
Barcus, Robert Gene 1937- *WhoMW 93*
Barcza, David Kenneth 1946- *WhoFI 94*
Bard, Allen J. 1933- *IntWW 93*
Bard, Allen Joseph 1933- *WhoAm 94, WhoScEn 94*
Bard, Basil Joseph Asher 1914- *Who 94*
Bard, Ben d1974 *WhoHol 92*
Bard, Gayle *WhoAmA 93*
Bard, Joellen 1942- *WhoAmA 93*
Bard, John Franklin 1941- *WhoAm 94*
Bard, Jonathan Adam 1958- *WhoScEn 94*
Bard, Jonathan F. 1946- *WhoScEn 94*
Bard, Katharine d1983 *WhoHol 92*
Bard, Maria d1944 *WhoHol 92*
Bard, Richard H. 1947- *WhoAm 94*
Barda, Jean Francis 1940- *WhoScEn 94*
Bardach, Joan Lucile 1919- *WhoAm 94*
Bardach, Sheldon Gilbert 1937- *WhoAm 94, WhoWest 94*
Bardack, Paul Roitman 1953- *WhoAm 94*
Bardacke, Paul G. 1944- *WhoAmP 93*
Bardacke, Paul Gregory 1944- *WhoAm 94*
Bardaglio, Wrexie Lainson 1946- *WhoAmP 93*
Bardagy, Robert A. 1939- *WhoFI 94*
Bardanouve, Francis 1917- *WhoAmP 93*
Bardari, Giuseppe 1817-1861 *NewGrDO*
Bardasz, Ewa Alice *WhoAm 94*
Bardazzi, Peter 1943- *WhoAm 94, WhoAmA 93*
Barde, Digambar Krushnaji 1940- *WhoScEn 94*
Bardeen, John d1991 *NobelP 91N*
Bardeen, John 1908- *WorScD*
Bardeen, John 1908-1991 *WhAm 10, WorInv*
Bardeen, William Leonard 1938- *WhoAm 94*
Bardell, Paul Harold, Jr. 1935- *WhoScEn 94*
Barden, Don H. 1943- *WhoAm 94, WhoBlA 94, WhoFI 94*
Barden, John Allan 1936- *WhoAm 94*
Barden, Kenneth Eugene 1955- *WhoAmL 94*
Barden, Laing 1931- *Who 94*
Barden, Robert Christopher 1954- *WhoMW 93, WhoScEn 94*
Barden, Thomas E(arl) 1946- *WrDr 94*
Barder, Brian (Leon) 1934- *Who 94*
Barder, Brian Leon 1934- *IntWW 93*
Bardette, Trevor d1977 *WhoHol 92*
Bardgett, Mark Edward 1964- *WhoMW 93*
Bardi, Giovanni de' 1534-1612 *NewGrDO*
Bardi, Pietro Maria 1900- *ConAu 42NR*
Bardin, Clyde Wayne 1934- *WhoAm 94, WhoScEn 94*
Bardin, David J. 1933- *WhoAm 94*
Bardin, Jesse Redwin 1923- *WhoAmA 93*
Bardini, Adolfo 1915- *IntWW 93*
Bardini, Aleksander 1913- *IntWW 93*
Bardins, Kathryn Ballowe 1952- *WhoMW 93*
Bardis, Panos D. 1924- *IntWW 93, WrDr 94*
Bardis, Panos Demetrios 1924- *WhoAm 94, WhoMW 93*
Bardo, John William 1948- *WhoAm 94*
Bardol, Daniel *WhoHol 92*
Bardole, Betty Jean 1932- *WhoMW 93*
Bardolph, Richard 1915- *WhoAm 94*
Bardon, Diane Marie 1949- *WhoWest 94*
Bardon, Henry 1923-1991 *NewGrDO*
Bardon, Jack Irving 1925- *WhoAm 94*
Bardon, Marcel 1927- *WhoAm 94*
Bardonnet, Daniel 1931- *IntWW 93*
Bardos, Denes Istvan 1938- *WhoAm 94*
Bardos, Thomas Joseph 1915- *WhoAm 94*
Bardot, Brigitte 1934- *IntMPA 94, IntWW 93, WhoHol 92*
Bardsley, Andrew Tromlow 1927- *Who 94*
Bardsley, Elizabeth S. 1931- *WhoAmP 93*
Bardwell, Leland 1928- *BlmGWL*
Bardwell, Rufus B., III 1937- *WhoBlA 94*
Bardwick, David Alan 1950- *WhoWest 94*
Bardwick, Judith M(arcia) 1933- *WrDr 94*
Bardwick, Judith Marcia 1933- *WhoAm 94*
Bardwil, Joseph Anthony 1928- *WhoAm 94*
Bardyguine, Patricia Wilde 1928- *WhoAm 94*
Bare, B. Bruce 1942- *WhoWest 94*
Bare, Bruce 1914- *WhoAm 94*
Bare, Donald Richard 1931- *WhoAmP 93*
Bare, Joseph Edward, Jr. 1923- *WhoAm 94*
Bare, Lois Kieffaber 1942- *WhoMW 93*
Bare, Richard L. *IntMPA 94*
Bare, Robert Joseph 1935- *WhoAm 94*
Bared, Jose *WhoHisp 94*
Barefield, Eddie d1991 *WhoHol 92*
Barefield, Morris 1939- *WhoBlA 94*
Barefield, Ollie Delores 1930- *WhoBlA 94*
Barefield, Thomas A. *WhoIns 94*
Barefoot, JoAnn S. 1949- *WhoFI 94*
Bareham, Lindsey 1948- *ConAu 140*
Bareham, Terence 1937- *WrDr 94*
Bareiss, Erwin Hans 1922- *WhoAm 94*
Bareiss, Philip C. 1949- *WhoAmA 93*
Bareiss, Walter 1919- *WhoAmA 93*
Barela, Alfredo David 1950- *WhoHisp 94*
Barela, Alicia Irene 1943- *WhoHisp 94*
Barela, Arthur *WhoHisp 94*
Barela, Bertha Cicci 1913- *WhoWest 94*
Barela, Esmerlindo Jaramillo 1948- *WhoWest 94*
Barela, George Larry 1948- *WhoHisp 94*
Barela, Henry T. *WhoHisp 94*
Barela, Jonathan Lewis 1960- *WhoAmL 94*
Barela, Linel G. 1947- *WhoHisp 94*
Barell, Martin C. d1993 *NewYTBS 93 [port]*
Baren, Harvey M. 1931- *IntMPA 94*
Barenberg, Sumner 1945- *WhoAm 94*
Barenboim, Daniel 1942- *IntWW 93, NewGrDO, Who 94, WhoAm 94*
Barengo, Robert R. 1941- *WhoAmP 93*
Barenholtz, Ben 1935- *IntMPA 94*
Barenis, Pat Peaster 1951- *WhoWest 94*
Barenklau, Keith Edward 1931- *WhoAm 94*
Barents, Brian Edward 1944- *WhoAm 94, WhoFI 94, WhoMW 93*
Barents, Willem d1597 *WhWE*
Barer, Sol Joseph 1947- *WhoScEn 94*
Bares, Allen R. 1936- *WhoAmP 93*
Bares, William G. 1941- *WhoAm 94, WhoFI 94, WhoScEn 94*
Baresi, Franco 1960- *WorESoc*
Baret, Jeanne c. 1740-c. 1788 *WhWE*
Baretski, Charles Allan 1918- *WhoAm 94, WhoFI 94*
Barfett, Thomas 1916- *Who 94*
Barfield, Bourdon Rea 1926- *WhoFI 94*
Barfield, Clementine 1950- *WhoBlA 94*
Barfield, Deborah Denise 1963- *WhoBlA 94*
Barfield, Gilbert Allen 1933- *WhoAmL 94*
Barfield, H. Lee, II 1946- *WhoAmL 94*
Barfield, Jesse Lee 1959- *WhoBlA 94*
Barfield, John E. *WhoBlA 94*
Barfield, Leila Millford 1923- *WhoBlA 94*
Barfield, Liston 1945- *WhoAmP 93*
Barfield, Owen 1898- *WrDr 94*
Barfield, (Arthur) Owen 1898- *EncSF 93*
Barfield, Quay F. 1912- *WhoBlA 94*
Barfield, Robert F. 1933- *WhoAm 94*
Barfield, Rufus L. 1929- *WhoBlA 94*

Barfield, Thomas Harwell 1917- *WhAm 10*
Barfield, Walter David 1928- *WhoScEn 94*
Barfoot, Fisher 1929- *WhoAmP 93*
Barfoot, Joan 1946- *BlmGWL*
Barford, Cherie 1960- *BlmGWL*
Barford, George, IV 1940- *WhoAm 94, WhoAmL 94*
Barford, Lee Alton 1961- *WhoWest 94*
Barford, Ralph MacKenzie 1929- *WhoAm 94*
Barg, Barbara *DrAPF 93*
Bargabos, Sheree Lynn 1955- *WhoWest 94*
Bargar, Robert Sellstrom 1919- *WhoAm 94*
Bargas, Joe G., Sr. 1927- *WhoHisp 94*
Barge, Gillian 1940- *WhoHol 92*
Barge, Jeffrey Thomas 1957- *WhoWest 94*
Barge, Richmond Mason 1949- *WhoAmL 94*
Bargellini, Pier Luigi 1914- *WhoAm 94*
Bargen, Walter *DrAPF 93*
Barger, Abraham Clifford 1917- *WhoAm 94*
Barger, Carl *WhoAm 94*
Barger, Catherine Harden 1954- *WhoAmP 93*
Barger, Cecil Edwin 1917- *WhoAm 94*
Barger, Darrell Lee 1946- *WhoAmL 94*
Barger, Harold 1907-1989 *WhAm 10*
Barger, James Daniel 1917- *WhoAm 94, WhoWest 94*
Barger, James Edwin 1934- *WhoAm 94, WhoScEn 94*
Barger, Kathleen Carson 1948- *WhoAmL 94*
Barger, Maurice W., Jr. 1931- *WhoIns 94*
Barger, Ralph 1923- *WhoAmP 93*
Barger, Richard Wilson 1934- *WhoAm 94*
Barger, Richards D. 1928- *WhoIns 94*
Barger, Stephen Richard 1950- *WhoWest 94*
Barger, Vernon Duane 1938- *WhoAm 94*
Barger, William James 1944- *WhoAm 94*
Bargeron, Emory E. 1927- *WhoAmP 93*
Bargfrede, James Allen 1928- *WhoAmL 94, WhoFI 94*
Barghini, Sandra Jean 1951- *WhoWest 94*
Barghoorn, Frederick C. 1911-1991 *WrDr 94N*
Bargielski, Zbigniew 1937- *NewGrDO*
Bargmann, Valentine 1908-1989 *WhAm 10*
Bargone, Frederic Charles Pierre Edouard *EncSF 93*
Bargreen, Melinda Lueth 1947- *WhoAm 94, WhoWest 94*
Barham, Blaine Michael 1955- *WhoFI 94*
Barham, Charles C. *WhoAmP 93*
Barham, Charles Dewey, Jr. 1930- *WhoAm 94, WhoFI 94*
Barham, Mack Elwin 1924- *WhoAm 94*
Barham, Patte *WhoAm 94*
Barham, Robert Edward 1942- *WhoWest 94*
Barham, Warren S. 1919- *WhoScEn 94*
Barham, Wilbur Stectson 1955- *WhoBlA 94*
Barham Hill, Brenda Marie 1948- *WhoWest 94*
Bari, Lynn d1989 *WhoHol 92*
Bari, Susan Phillips 1945- *WhoAmP 93*
Barial, Ellen V. *WhoAmL 94*
Bariani, Didier 1943- *IntWW 93*
Barich, Bill 1943- *WrDr 94*
Barich, Dewey Frederick 1911- *WhoAm 94*
Bariff, Martin Louis 1944- *WhoMW 93*
Barik, Sudhakar 1949- *WhoAm 94*
Baril, Ofier L(udger) 1898- *WhAm 10*
Barile, Andrew J. 1942- *WhoIns 94*
Barilich, Thomas Anthony 1955- *WhoFI 94, WhoMW 93*
Barilli-Patti, Caterina Chiesa *NewGrDO*
Barine, Arvede 1840-1908 *BlmGWL*
Baring *Who 94*
Baring, Arnulf Martin 1932- *IntWW 93*
Baring, John 1863-1929 *DcNaB MP*
Baring, John (Francis) 1947- *Who 94*
Baring, John Francis Harcourt *IntWW 93*
Baring, Nicholas Hugo 1934- *Who 94*
Baring, Norah 1907- *WhoHol 92*
Baring, Peter 1935- *Who 94*
Baring, Rose (Gwendolen Louisa) 1909- *Who 94*
Baringer, Richard E. 1921-1980 *WhoAmA 93N*
Barisas, Bernard George, Jr. 1945- *WhoWest 94*
Barish, Evelyn 1935- *WrDr 94*
Barish, George 1938- *WhoAmL 94*
Barish, Jonas A. 1922- *WrDr 94*
Barish, Jonas Alexander 1922- *WhoAm 94, WhoWest 94*
Barish, Keith *IntMPA 94*
Barison, Ferdinando *EncSPD*
Barist, Jeffrey A. 1941- *WhoAm 94, WhoAmL 94*
Baritz, Loren 1928- *WhoAm 94*
Barjacoba, Pedro 1934- *WhoHisp 94*
Barjavel, Rene 1911-1985 *EncSF 93*
Bark, Dennis L(aistner) 1942- *ConAu 41NR*
Bark, Evelyn Elizabeth Patricia d1993 *Who 94N*
Barkan, Alexander Elias 1909-1990 *WhAm 10*
Barkan, Joanne *SmATA 77 [port]*
Barkan, Joel David 1941- *WhoAm 94*
Barkan, Philip 1925- *WhoAm 94*
Barkan, Stanley H. *DrAPF 93*
Barkauskas, Antanas Stase 1917- *IntWW 93*
Barke, (James) Allen 1903- *WhAm 10*
Barkeley, Norman A. *IntWW 93*
Barkemeijer de Wit, Jeanne Sandra 1955- *WhoAm 94*
Barken, Bernard Allen 1924- *WhoAmL 94, WhoMW 93*
Barker *Who 94*
Barker, A. L. 1918- *DcLB 139 [port]*
Barker, A(udrey) L(illian) 1918- *WrDr 94*
Barker, Adella d1930 *WhoHol 92*
Barker, Al C. 1941- *WhoAmA 93*
Barker, Albert Winslow 1874-1947 *WhoAmA 93N*
Barker, Allen Vaughan 1937- *WhoAmP 93*
Barker, Alwyn (Bowman) 1900- *Who 94*
Barker, Andrew (Dennison) 1943- *WrDr 94*
Barker, Anne Judith *Who 94*
Barker, Anthony d1993 *NewYTBS 93*
Barker, Anthony 1944- *Who 94*
Barker, Arthur Vincent 1911- *Who 94*
Barker, Audrey Lilian 1918- *Who 94*
Barker, Barbara 1938- *WhoMW 93*
Barker, Barry 1929- *Who 94*
Barker, Bill d1981 *WhoHol 92*
Barker, Bob *IntMPA 94*
Barker, Bradley d1951 *WhoHol 92*
Barker, Brian John 1945- *Who 94*
Barker, Charles *WhoAm 94*
Barker, Charles Albro 1904-1993 *ConAu 142*
Barker, Charles Thomas 1946- *WhoAmL 94*
Barker, Clarence Austin 1911- *WhoAm 94*
Barker, Clayton Guinard *WhoWest 94*
Barker, Clayton Robert, III 1957- *WhoFI 94*
Barker, Clifford Conder 1926- *Who 94*
Barker, Clive *HorFD [port]*
Barker, Clive 1952- *IntMPA 94, WhoAm 94, WrDr 94*
Barker, Clyde Frederick 1932- *WhoAm 94, WhoScEn 94*
Barker, Colin 1926- *Who 94*
Barker, Corinne d1928 *WhoHol 92*
Barker, D.A. *EncSF 93*
Barker, Daniel Stephen 1934- *WhoAm 94*
Barker, Daphne *WhoHol 92*
Barker, David 1932- *Who 94*
Barker, David (Faubert) 1922- *Who 94*
Barker, David J. P. 1938- *WrDr 94*
Barker, Dee H. 1921- *WhoScEn 94*
Barker, Dennis (Malcolm) 1929- *WrDr 94*
Barker, Dorothy Jean 1929- *WhoAmP 93*
Barker, Douglas H. 1947- *WhoAmL 94*
Barker, Douglas Wayne 1952- *WhoFI 94*
Barker, Earl Middleton, Jr. 1944- *WhoAmL 94*
Barker, Ed *WhoAmP 93*
Barker, Edmund William 1920- *IntWW 93*
Barker, Edward 1909- *Who 94*
Barker, Edwin Bogue 1954- *WhoAm 94*
Barker, Eileen (Vartan) 1938- *WrDr 94*
Barker, Emmett Wilson, Jr. 1937- *WhoAm 94*
Barker, Eric d1990 *WhoHol 92*
Barker, Felix 1917- *WrDr 94*
Barker, Florence d1913 *WhoHol 92*
Barker, Garry *DrAPF 93*
Barker, Garry 1943- *ConAu 140, WrDr 94*
Barker, Gary Leland 1942- *WhoMW 93*
Barker, George (Granville) 1913-1991 *WrDr 94N*
Barker, George Granville 1913- *BlmGEL*
Barker, George Granville 1913-1991 *WhAm 10*
Barker, Graeme William Walter 1946- *Who 94*
Barker, Harley Granville *IntDcT 2*
Barker, Harold 1919- *Who 94*
Barker, Harold Grant 1917- *WhoAm 94*
Barker, Harold Kenneth 1922- *WhoAm 94*
Barker, Harry Heaton 1898- *Who 94*
Barker, Horace Albert 1907- *IntWW 93, WhoAm 94*
Barker, Howard 1946- *BlmGEL, ConDr 93, IntDcT 2 [port], Who 94, WrDr 94*
Barker, James Edward, Jr. 1936- *WhoWest 94*
Barker, James Joseph 1922- *WhoWest 94*
Barker, James McClure 1934- *WhoAmP 93*
Barker, James Montgomery 1941- *WhoFI 94*
Barker, James Nelson 1784-1858 *IntDcT 2*
Barker, James Peter 1935- *WhoAmP 93*
Barker, James Rex 1935- *WhoAm 94*
Barker, Jane 1652-1727? *BlmGWL, DcLB 131, DcNaB MP*
Barker, Jeffrey Dillon 1959- *WhoWest 94*
Barker, Jess 1912- *WhoHol 92*
Barker, Jim L. 1935- *WhoAmP 93*
Barker, John Francis Holroyd 1925- *Who 94*
Barker, John Lindsay 1910- *Who 94*
Barker, John M. 1916- *WhoAmP 93*
Barker, John Michael Adrian 1932- *Who 94*
Barker, John Perronet 1930- *Who 94*
Barker, John Phillip 1933- *WhoFI 94*
Barker, John William 1954- *WhoWest 94*
Barker, Judy 1941- *WhoAm 94*
Barker, Keith 1947- *WrDr 94*
Barker, Keith Rene 1928- *WhoFI 94, WhoMW 93*
Barker, Kenneth 1934- *Who 94*
Barker, Kenneth Neil 1937- *WhoAm 94*
Barker, Larry Lee 1941- *WhoAm 94*
Barker, Laurenn Russell 1945- *WhoAm 94*
Barker, Lee Dickinson 1943- *WhoAmL 94*
Barker, Leslie Paxton 1901-1990 *WhAm 10*
Barker, Lex d1973 *WhoHol 92*
Barker, Linda Gail 1948- *WhoFI 94*
Barker, Linda K. *WhoAmP 93*
Barker, Llyle James, Jr. 1932- *WhoAm 94*
Barker, Maggie d1993 *NewYTBS 93*
Barker, Mary-Anne 1831-1911 *BlmGWL*
Barker, Mary Katherine 1921- *WhoMW 93*
Barker, Michael Dean 1960- *WhoScEn 94*
Barker, Michael W. 1954- *IntMPA 94*
Barker, Mildred *DrAPF 93*
Barker, Nancie Lynne 1942- *WhoWest 94*
Barker, Nancy Lepard 1936- *WhoAm 94, WhoMW 93*
Barker, Nicola 1966- *ConAu 141*
Barker, Nicolas (John) 1932- *ConAu 43NR*
Barker, Nicolas John 1932- *Who 94*
Barker, Pat 1943- *BlmGWL [port]*
Barker, Pat(ricia) 1943- *WrDr 94*
Barker, Paul *See* Ministry *ConMus 10*
Barker, Paul 1935- *Who 94*
Barker, Pauline J. 1930- *WhoBlA 94*
Barker, Peter Keefe 1948- *WhoAm 94, WhoFI 94*
Barker, Peter William 1928- *Who 94*
Barker, Philip 1929- *WrDr 94*
Barker, Phillip *WhoHol 92*
Barker, Richard Canfield 1935- *WhoFI 94*
Barker, Richard Clark 1926- *WhoAm 94*
Barker, Richard Gordon 1937- *WhoAm 94*
Barker, Richard Philip 1939- *Who 94*
Barker, Robert 1928- *WhoScEn 94*
Barker, Robert Jeffery 1946- *WhoWest 94*
Barker, Robert William *WhoAm 94*
Barker, Ronald Hugh 1915- *Who 94*
Barker, Ronnie 1929- *Who 94, WhoHol 92*
Barker, Roy Edwin 1925- *WhoAmP 93*
Barker, Samuel Booth 1912- *WhoAm 94*
Barker, Sandra Mills 1958- *WhoFI 94*
Barker, Sarah Evans 1943- *WhoAm 94, WhoAmL 94*
Barker, Stephen L. 1950- *WhoAmL 94*
Barker, Stephen Richards 1955- *WhoFI 94*
Barker, Susan Vera *Who 94*
Barker, Theodore Cardwell 1923- *Who 94, WrDr 94*
Barker, Thomas Carl 1931- *WhoAm 94*
Barker, Thomas Christopher 1928- *Who 94*
Barker, Thomas Watson, Jr. 1944- *WhoAm 94*
Barker, Timothy Gwynne 1940- *Who 94*
Barker, Timothy T. 1948- *WhoBlA 94*
Barker, Tom 1943- *WhoAmP 93*
Barker, Trevor 1935- *Who 94*
Barker, Virgil 1890-1964 *WhoAmA 93N*
Barker, W. Gardner 1913-1990 *WhAm 10*
Barker, Walter Lee 1928- *WhoAm 94*
Barker, Walter William, Jr. 1921- *WhoAm 94, WhoAmA 93*
Barker, Wende 1951- *WhoAmP 93*
Barker, Wendy *DrAPF 93*
Barker, Wiley Franklin 1919- *WhoWest 94*
Barker, William c. 1520-c. 1576 *DcLB 132*
Barker, William 1909-1992 *AnObit 1992*
Barker, William Alfred 1919- *WhoAm 94*
Barker, William Clyde 1931- *WhoWest 94*
Barker, William Daniel 1926- *WhoAm 94*
Barker, William H. *WhoAmP 93*
Barker, William Thomas 1947- *WhoAm 94, WhoAmL 94*
Barker, Willie G., Jr. 1937- *WhoAm 94*
Barkett, Diane DeMichele *DrAPF 93*
Barkett, Rosemary 1939- *WhoAm 94, WhoAmL 94, WhoAmP 93, WhoHisp 94*
Barkett, Steve 1950- *IntMPA 94*
Barkhaus, Paul Edward 1949- *WhoMW 93*
Barkhausen, David N. 1950- *WhoAmP 93*
Barkhordar, Parviz *WhoWest 94*
Barkhorn, Henry Charles, III 1949- *WhoAm 94*
Barkhoudarian, Sarkis 1938- *WhoWest 94*
Barkhuus, Arne 1906- *WhoAm 94*
Barkin, Carol 1944- *WrDr 94*
Barkin, Ellen 1954- *IntMPA 94*
Barkin, Ellen 1955- *IntWW 93, WhoAm 94*
Barkin, Ellen 1959- *WhoHol 92*
Barkin, Jill 1939- *WrDr 94*
Barkin, Martin 1936- *WhoAm 94*
Barkin, Marvin E. 1933- *WhoAm 94*
Barkin, Richard Bruce 1952- *WhoAmL 94*
Barkin, Robert Allan 1939- *WhoAm 94*
Barkin, Roger Michael 1944- *WhoAm 94*
Barkin, Solomon 1907- *WhoAm 94*
Barking, Anonymous Nun of fl. 1163- *BlmGWL*
Barking, Area Bishop of 1936- *Who 94*
Barkis, Marvin William 1943- *WhoAmP 93*
Barkla, Charles Glover 1877-1944 *WorScD*
Barklem, Jill 1951- *ChlLR 31 [port]*
Barkley, Alben William, II 1944- *WhoAmP 93*
Barkley, Brian Evan 1945- *WhoAm 94*
Barkley, Charles 1963- *BasBi [port], ConBlB 5 [port]*
Barkley, Charles Wade 1963- *WhoAm 94, WhoBlA 94, WhoWest 94*
Barkley, Drew S. *WhoIns 94*
Barkley, Ivan *WhoAm 94*
Barkley, John Montieth 1910- *Who 94*
Barkley, Joseph Richard 1942- *WhoFI 94*
Barkley, Linda Kay 1953- *WhoScEn 94*
Barkley, Lucille 1925- *WhoHol 92*
Barkley, Mark E. 1932- *WhoBlA 94*
Barkley, Paul C. d1993 *NewYTBS 93*
Barkley, Paul Haley, Jr. 1937- *WhoAm 94*
Barkley, Richard C. 1932- *IntWW 93, WhoAmP 93*
Barkley, Richard Clark 1932- *WhoAm 94*
Barkley, Rufus, Jr. 1949- *WhoBlA 94*
Barkley, Theodore Mitchell 1934- *WhoAm 94, WhoScEn 94*
Barkley, Thierry Vincent 1955- *WhoAmL 94, WhoWest 94*
Barkley, William Donald 1941- *WhoAm 94*
Barkman, Annette Shaulis 1948- *WhoFI 94*
Barkman, Gary William 1962- *WhoFI 94*
Barkman, Jon Albert 1947- *WhoAmL 94*
Barkoff, Rupert Mitchell 1948- *WhoAm 94, WhoAmL 94*
Barkofske, Francis Lee 1939- *WhoAm 94*
Barkova, Anna Aleksandrovna 1901-1976 *BlmGWL*
Barkow, Al 1932- *WrDr 94*
Barks, Coleman *DrAPF 93*
Barks, Coleman Bryan 1937- *WrDr 94*
Barks, Horace Bushnell 1921- *WhoMW 93*
Barks, Ronald Edward 1938- *WhoWest 94*
Barksdale, Charles Madsen 1947- *WhoMW 93*
Barksdale, Clarence Caulfield 1932- *WhoAm 94*
Barksdale, Don d1993 *NewYTBS 93 [port]*
Barksdale, Don 1929- *BasBi*
Barksdale, Donald Argee 1923-1993 *WhoBlA 94N*
Barksdale, Hudson L. 1907- *WhoBlA 94*
Barksdale, Leonard N., III 1948- *WhoBlA 94*
Barksdale, Mary Frances 1934- *WhoBlA 94*
Barksdale, Rhesa H. 1944- *WhoAmP 93*
Barksdale, Rhesa Hawkins 1944- *WhoAm 94, WhoAmL 94*
Barksdale, Richard Dillon 1938- *WhoAm 94*
Barksdale, Richard Kenneth 1915- *WhoBlA 94*
Barksdale Hall, Roland C. 1960- *WhoBlA 94*
Barkshire, John *Who 94*
Barkshire, Robert Hugh 1909- *Who 94*
Barkshire, Robert Renny St. John 1935- *Who 94*

Barkstall, Vernon L. 1929- *WhoBlA 94*
Barkum, Jerome Phillip 1950- *WhoBlA 94*
Barkun, Michael 1938- *WrDr 94*
Barkus, Mariona Marcia 1948- *WhoAmA 93*
Barkworth, John (Edmond) 1858-1929 *NewGrDO*
Barkworth, Peter 1929- *WhoHol 92*
Barkworth, Peter Wynn 1929- *Who 94*
Barlach, Ernst (Heinrich) 1870-1938 *IntDcT 2*
Barlas, Julie Sandall 1944- *WhoAm 94*
Barlay, Stephen 1930- *WrDr 94*
Barlett, Donald L. 1936- *WhoAm 94*
Barletta, Joseph Francis 1936- *WhoAm 94*
Barletta, Naomi Lockwood *DrAPF 93*
Barletta, Nicolas Ardito 1938- *IntWW 93*
Bar-Lev, Haim 1924- *IntWW 93*
Bar-Levav, Doron Mordecai 1954- *WhoAmL 94*
Barley, Barbara Ann 1954- *WhoMW 93*
Barley, George McKim, Jr. 1934- *WhoFI 94*
Barley, John Alvin 1940- *WhoAmL 94*
Barley, John E. 1945- *WhoAmP 93*
Barley, Vernon 1934- *WhoAmP 93*
Barliant, Ronald 1945- *WhoAm 94, WhoAmL 94*
Barlich, Jack F. 1922- *WhoAmP 93*
Barline, John 1946- *WhoAm 94*
Barling, Gerald Edward 1949- *Who 94*
Barloco, Gerard H. 1944- *WhoIns 94*
Barlog, Boleslaw 1906- *IntWW 93*
Barloga, Viola H. 1890- *WhoAmA 93N*
Barlow, Anne Louise 1925- *WhoAm 94*
Barlow, Charles Franklin 1923- *WhoAm 94*
Barlow, Christopher Hilaro 1929- *Who 94*
Barlow, Clark W. 1938- *WhoAm 94, WhoFI 94*
Barlow, David Hearnshaw 1949- *Who 94*
Barlow, David John 1937- *Who 94*
Barlow, David Michael Rigby 1936- *Who 94*
Barlow, Deborah Lynn 1958- *WhoAmA 93*
Barlow, Donald Spiers Monteagle 1905- *Who 94*
Barlow, Edward Dawson 1938- *WhoAmP 93*
Barlow, Frank 1911- *Who 94, WrDr 94*
Barlow, Frank 1930- *Who 94*
Barlow, Frank John 1914- *WhoAm 94, WhoFI 94, WhoMW 93*
Barlow, Franklin Sackett 1912- *WhoMW 93*
Barlow, George *DrAPF 93*
Barlow, George Francis 1939- *Who 94*
Barlow, Harold d1993 *NewYTBS 93*
Barlow, Haven J. 1922- *WhoAmP 93, WhoWest 94*
Barlow, Horace Basil 1921- *Who 94, WhoScEn 94*
Barlow, James 1921-1973 *EncSF 93*
Barlow, James William 1826-1913 *EncSF 93*
Barlow, Jim B. 1936- *WhoAm 94*
Barlow, Joel 1908- *WhoAm 94*
Barlow, Joel William 1942- *WhoAm 94, WhoScEn 94*
Barlow, John (Alfred) 1924-1991 *WrDr 94N*
Barlow, John (Kemp) 1934- *Who 94*
Barlow, Joyce Krutick 1946- *WhoAmL 94*
Barlow, Kenneth James 1932- *WhoAm 94*
Barlow, Kent Michael 1935- *WhoScEn 94*
Barlow, Loren Call 1926- *WhoWest 94*
Barlow, Lou
See Dinosaur Jr. *ConMus 10*
Barlow, Maude 1947- *WrDr 94*
Barlow, Nadine Gail 1958- *WhoScEn 94*
Barlow, Pat *WhoHol 92*
Barlow, Patrick 1947- *Who 94*
Barlow, R(euel) R(ichard) 1894- *WhAm 10*
Barlow, Reginald d1943 *WhoHol 92*
Barlow, Robert Dudley 1954- *WhoScEn 94*
Barlow, Ronald S. 1936- *ConAu 142*
Barlow, Roy Oxspring 1927- *Who 94*
Barlow, Samuel L(atham) M(itchell) 1892-1982 *NewGrDO*
Barlow, Tani E. 1950- *WrDr 94*
Barlow, Thomas (Erasmus) 1914- *Who 94*
Barlow, Thomas James 1922- *IntWW 93*
Barlow, Thomas Martin 1935- *WhoWest 94*
Barlow, Thomas Reed 1952- *WhoMW 93*
Barlow, Tom *WhoAmP 93*
Barlow, Tom 1940- *CngDr 93*
Barlow, Tom 1941- *WhoAm 94*
Barlow, Walter Greenwood 1917- *WhoAm 94*
Barlow, Wilfred 1915-1991 *WrDr 94N*
Barlow, William *Who 94*
Barlow, William 1924- *IntWW 93*
Barlow, (George) William 1924- *Who 94*
Barlow, William B. 1943- *WhoBlA 94*
Barlow, William Edward 1917- *WhoAm 94*
Barlow, William K. 1936- *WhoAmP 93*
Barlow, William Pusey, Jr. 1934- *WhoAm 94, WhoFI 94, WhoWest 94*
Barlowe, Raleigh 1914- *WrDr 94*
Barlowe, Wayne Douglas 1958- *EncSF 93, WrDr 94*
Barltrop, Robert 1922- *WrDr 94*
Barltrop, Roger Arnold Rowlandson 1930- *IntWW 93, Who 94*
Barlund, Kaj-Ole Johannes 1945- *IntWW 93*
Barmack, Neal Herbert 1942- *WhoScEn 94*
Barman, Robert John *WhoWest 94*
Barman, Susan Marie 1949- *WhoMW 93*
Barmann, Bernard Charles, Sr. 1932- *WhoAmL 94, WhoWest 94*
Barmann, Lawrence (Francis) 1932- *WrDr 94*
Barmann, Lawrence Francis 1932- *WhoAm 94*
Barme, Geremie 1954- *WrDr 94*
Barmen, Stewart B. 1940- *WhoAm 94*
Barmettler, Joseph John 1933- *WhoAmL 94*
Barmeyer, John R. 1946- *WhoIns 94*
Barmore, Gregory Terhune 1941- *WhoAm 94*
Barna, Ed *DrAPF 93*
Barna, Kenneth James 1954- *WhoMW 93*
Barna, Lillian Carattini 1929- *WhoWest 94*
Barna, Steven M. 1943- *WhoAmL 94*
Barna, Tibor 1919- *Who 94*
Barnabas, Mathews Mar 1924- *WhoAsA 94*
Barnabe, Bruno 1905- *WhoHol 92*
Barnabeo, Susan Patricia 1960- *WhoAmL 94*
Barnabo, Guglielmo d1954 *WhoHol 92*
Barnaby, Charles Frank 1927- *IntWW 93, WrDr 94*
Barnala, Surjit Singh 1925- *IntWW 93*
Barnao, Jack *ConAu 141*
Barnard, Baron 1923- *Who 94*
Barnard, Allen Donald 1944- *WhoAmL 94*
Barnard, Ann Watson 1930- *WhoMW 93*
Barnard, Anne 1750-1825 *BlmGWL*
Barnard, Annette Williamson 1948- *WhoWest 94*
Barnard, Aurora Caro 1908- *WhoAmP 93*
Barnard, Christaan (Neethling) 1922- *WrDr 94*
Barnard, Christiaan 1922- *WorInv*
Barnard, Christiaan Neethling 1922- *IntWW 93, Who 94*
Barnard, Clare Amundson 1927- *WhoAmP 93*
Barnard, Druie Douglas, Jr. 1922- *WhoAm 94, WhoAmP 93*
Barnard, Eric Albert 1927- *IntWW 93, Who 94*
Barnard, Ernest Edward Peter 1927- *Who 94*
Barnard, Frederick Augusta 1743-1830 *DcNaB MP*
Barnard, Frederick Mechner 1921- *WrDr 94*
Barnard, George (Edward) 1907- *Who 94*
Barnard, George Alfred 1915- *Who 94*
Barnard, George Smith *WhoAmL 94*
Barnard, H. B. *WhoAmP 93*
Barnard, Henry 1811-1900 *AmSocL*
Barnard, Ivor d1953 *WhoHol 92*
Barnard, John 1709-1784 *DcNaB MP*
Barnard, John 1932- *WhoMW 93*
Barnard, John Michael 1936- *Who 94*
Barnard, Joseph (Brian) 1928- *Who 94*
Barnard, Joseph Edwin 1868-1949 *DcNaB MP*
Barnard, Kathleen Rainwater 1927-1991 *WhAm 10*
Barnard, Kurt 1927- *WhoAm 94*
Barnard, Lance Herbert 1919- *IntWW 93, Who 94*
Barnard, Lukas Daniel 1949- *IntWW 93*
Barnard, Mae d1948 *WhoHol 92*
Barnard, Marjorie 1897-1987 *BlmGWL*
Barnard, Marjorie Faith *EncSF 93*
Barnard, Mary *DrAPF 93*
Barnard, Maxwell Kay 1946- *WhoScEn 94*
Barnard, Michael Dana 1946- *WhoAm 94, WhoWest 94*
Barnard, Morton John 1905- *WhoAmL 94*
Barnard, Peter Deane 1932- *WhoScEn 94*
Barnard, Rob(ert E.) 1949- *WhoAmA 93*
Barnard, Robert 1936- *WrDr 94*
Barnard, Robert C. 1913- *WhoAmL 94*
Barnard, Robert N. 1947- *WhoAm 94*
Barnard, Rollin Dwight 1922- *WhoAm 94, WhoFI 94, WhoWest 94*
Barnard, Scott Henry 1943- *WhoAm 94*
Barnard, Sheri S. 1937- *WhoAm 94, WhoAmP 93*
Barnard, Susan Muller 1935- *WhoAm 94*
Barnard, Thomas *Who 94*
Barnard, (Arthur) Thomas 1893- *Who 94*
Barnard, Thomas Harvie 1939- *WhoAm 94*
Barnard, Walther M. 1937- *WhoAm 94*
Barnard, William Calvert 1914- *WhoAm 94, WhoWest 94*
Barnard, William Howard, Jr. 1945- *WhoScEn 94*
Barnard, William Marion 1949- *WhoScEn 94, WhoWest 94*
Barnard-Bailey, Wanda Arlene 1962- *WhoBlA 94*
Barnard-Eldershaw, M. *EncSF 93*
Barncastle, Delia Garcia 1925- *WhoAmP 93*
Barndorff-Nielsen, Ole Eiler 1935- *IntWW 93*
Barne, George c. 1500-1558 *DcNaB MP*
Barne, Leo *EncSF 93*
Barne, Nicholas Michael Lancelot 1943- *Who 94*
Barnea, Uri N. 1943- *WhoWest 94*
Barnebey, Kenneth Alan 1931- *WhoAm 94*
Barnebey, Malcolm 1927- *WhoAmP 93*
Barnebey, Mark Patrick 1957- *WhoAmL 94*
Barneby, Henry Habington 1909- *Who 94*
Barnell, Nora Ely d1933 *WhoHol 92*
Barner, Annabel Monroe 1925- *WhoMW 93*
Barner, Bruce Monroe 1951- *WhoAm 94, WhoMW 93*
Barner, Jennifer Caitlin 1962- *WhoMW 93*
Barnes *Who 94*
Barnes, A. James 1942- *WhoAm 94, WhoAmP 93*
Barnes, Adrian Francis Patrick 1943- *Who 94*
Barnes, Alan Robert 1927- *Who 94*
Barnes, Albert 1789-1870 *DcAmReB 2*
Barnes, Andre LaMont 1957- *WhoAm 94*
Barnes, Andrew Earl 1939- *WhoAm 94*
Barnes, Anne Craig 1932- *WhoAmP 93*
Barnes, Anne T. 1940- *WhoBlA 94*
Barnes, Anthony Hugh 1931- *Who 94*
Barnes, Arthur Hewitt, III 1959- *WhoMW 93*
Barnes, Arthur K(elvin) 1911-1969 *EncSF 93*
Barnes, Audra Guyton 1921- *WhoWest 94*
Barnes, B. Jack 1934- *WhoFI 94*
Barnes, Barnabe c. 1571-1609 *DcLB 132*
Barnes, Barry K. d1965 *WhoHol 92*
Barnes, Benjamin Shields, Jr. 1919- *WhoAm 94*
Barnes, Benny 1951- *WhoBlA 94*
Barnes, Bernard Ellis 1931- *WhoFI 94*
Barnes, Betty Rae 1932- *WhoScEn 94*
Barnes, Binnie 1905- *WhoHol 92*
Barnes, Bobbe Morse 1945- *WhoFI 94*
Barnes, Boisey O. 1943- *WhoBlA 94*
Barnes, Burton V(erne) 1930- *WrDr 94*
Barnes, Carla Leddy 1938- *WhoMW 93*
Barnes, Carlyle Fuller 1924- *WhoAm 94*
Barnes, Carole D. 1935- *WhoAmA 93*
Barnes, Cathy Lynn 1952- *WhoMW 93*
Barnes, Charles Ahrens 1938- *WhoAmP 93*
Barnes, Charles Andrew 1921- *WhoAm 94*
Barnes, Charles D. 1935- *WhoAm 94, WhoScEn 94*
Barnes, Charles Winfred 1934- *WhoAm 94*
Barnes, Charlotte Mary Sanford 1818-1863 *BlmGWL*
Barnes, Christopher J(ohn) 1942- *WrDr 94*
Barnes, Christopher John Andrew 1944- *Who 94*
Barnes, Christopher Richard 1940- *IntWW 93, WhoAm 94*
Barnes, Clemens H. 1944- *WhoAmL 94*
Barnes, Cliff 1940- *WhoAmA 93*
Barnes, Clive (Alexander) 1927- *WrDr 94*
Barnes, Clive Alexander 1927- *IntWW 93, Who 94, WhoAm 94*
Barnes, Constance Ingalls 1903- *WhoMW 93*
Barnes, Craig Martin 1949- *WhoFI 94*
Barnes, Curt 1943- *WhoAmA 93*
Barnes, Cyril Arthur 1926- *Who 94*
Barnes, Daniel Sennett 1924- *Who 94*
Barnes, David *Who 94*
Barnes, David 1943- *WhoAmP 93*
Barnes, (James) David (Francis) 1936- *Who 94*
Barnes, David Benton *WhoScEn 94*
Barnes, David K., Jr. 1944- *WhoAmL 94*
Barnes, David Robert, Jr. 1952- *WhoWest 94*
Barnes, Delorise Creecy 1947- *WhoBlA 94*
Barnes, Denis Tat *WhoFI 94*
Barnes, Dennis Norman 1940- *WhoAm 94*
Barnes, Diane 1961- *WhoBlA 94*
Barnes, Djuna 1892-1982 *BlmGWL [port], ConDr 93, GayLL*
Barnes, Don B. 1924- *WhoAmP 93*
Barnes, Donald Frederic 1914- *WhoIns 94*
Barnes, Donald Gayle 1940- *WhoAm 94*
Barnes, Donald L. 1943- *WhoIns 94*
Barnes, Donald Michael 1943- *WhoAm 94, WhoAmL 94*
Barnes, Donald Winfree 1943- *WhoAm 94*
Barnes, Douglas 1927- *ConAu 41NR, WrDr 94*
Barnes, Duncan 1935- *WhoAm 94*
Barnes, Edward Campbell 1928- *Who 94*
Barnes, Edward F. *WrDr 94*
Barnes, Edward Larrabee 1915- *IntWW 93, WhoAm 94, WhoAmA 93*
Barnes, Edwin Ronald 1935- *Who 94*
Barnes, Eric Charles 1924- *Who 94*
Barnes, Ernest Eugene, Jr. 1938- *WhoBlA 94*
Barnes, Eugene M. 1931- *WhoBlA 94*
Barnes, Fannie Burrell *WhoBlA 94*
Barnes, Florence d1975 *WhoHol 92*
Barnes, Francis M., III 1918- *WhoAmP 93*
Barnes, Francis Walter Ibbetson 1914- *Who 94*
Barnes, Frank d1940 *WhoHol 92*
Barnes, Frank Stephenson 1932- *WhoAm 94, WhoScEn 94*
Barnes, Gary H. 1949- *WhoAmL 94*
Barnes, Geoffrey K. 1945- *WhoAm 94, WhoAmL 94*
Barnes, Geoffrey Thomas 1932- *Who 94*
Barnes, George d1949 *WhoHol 92*
Barnes, George S. 1893-1953 *IntDcF 2-4*
Barnes, George William 1927- *WhoAm 94*
Barnes, Gerald R. 1945- *WhoWest 94*
Barnes, Gerald Richard 1945- *WhoHisp 94*
Barnes, Gloria Johnson 1957- *WhoAmL 94*
Barnes, Grant Alan 1932- *WhoAm 94*
Barnes, Harold 1936- *Who 94*
Barnes, Harry G., Jr. 1926- *WhoAm 94*
Barnes, Harry George, Jr. 1926- *WhoAmP 93*
Barnes, Henson Perrymoore 1934- *WhoAmP 93*
Barnes, Herman Verdain 1935- *WhoAm 94, WhoMW 93*
Barnes, Hershell Louis, Jr. 1943- *WhoAm 94, WhoAmL 94*
Barnes, Howard G. 1913- *WhoAm 94*
Barnes, Hubert Lloyd 1928- *WhoAm 94, WhoScEn 94*
Barnes, Ingrid Victoria *Who 94*
Barnes, Iraline G. *WhoBlA 94*
Barnes, Isabel Janet 1936- *WhoAm 94*
Barnes, J. H. d1925 *WhoHol 92*
Barnes, Jack Henry 1943- *Who 94*
Barnes, Jack Whittier 1940- *WhoAm 94*
Barnes, James A. 1951- *WhoAmP 93*
Barnes, James Byron 1942- *WhoMW 93*
Barnes, James E. 1934- *WhoAm 94, WhoFI 94*
Barnes, James Edwin d1991 *Who 94N*
Barnes, James Frederick 1932- *Who 94*
Barnes, James Garland, Jr. 1940- *WhoAm 94*
Barnes, James George 1908- *Who 94*
Barnes, James J. 1931- *WrDr 94*
Barnes, James John 1931- *WhoAm 94*
Barnes, James Milton 1923- *WhoAm 94*
Barnes, James Neil 1944- *WhoAmL 94*
Barnes, James Thomas, Jr. 1958- *WhoAm 94*
Barnes, Jane *DrAPF 93*
Barnes, Jane M. 1926- *WhoAmP 93*
Barnes, Jeffrey Alan 1961- *WhoMW 93*
Barnes, Jerry 1931- *WhoAmP 93*
Barnes, Jhane Elizabeth 1954- *WhoAm 94*
Barnes, Jim *DrAPF 93*
Barnes, Jim 1956- *WhoWest 94*
Barnes, Joanna 1934- *WhoAm 94, WhoHol 92, WhoWest 94*
Barnes, John 1957- *EncSF 93*
Barnes, (Ernest) John (Ward) d1992 *IntWW 93N*
Barnes, John Alfred 1930- *Who 94*
Barnes, John Arundel 1918- *IntWW 93, Who 94, WrDr 94*
Barnes, John B., Sr. 1922- *WhoBlA 94*
Barnes, John Breasted 1926- *WhoAmL 94*
Barnes, John Fayette 1930- *WhoWest 94*
Barnes, John J. 1924- *WhoIns 94*
Barnes, John Maurice 1931- *WhoScEn 94*
Barnes, John Stanley, Jr. 1931- *WhoAmP 93*
Barnes, Johnnie *WhoBlA 94*
Barnes, Johnny *WhoHol 92*
Barnes, Jonathan 1942- *Who 94, WrDr 94*
Barnes, Joseph Harry George 1930- *Who 94*
Barnes, Joseph J. 1952- *WhoAmL 94*
Barnes, Joseph Nathan 1950- *WhoBlA 94*
Barnes, Josephine *Who 94*

Barnes, (Alice) Josephine (Mary Taylor) 1912- *IntWW 93, Who 94, WrDr 94*
Barnes, Julian 1946- *BlmGEL, DcLB Y93 [port]*
Barnes, Julian (Patrick) 1946- *EncSF 93, IntWW 93, WrDr 94*
Barnes, Julian Patrick 1946- *Who 94*
Barnes, Justus D. d1946 *WhoHol 92*
Barnes, Kate *DrAPF 93*
Barnes, Kathleen Adele 1955- *WhoWest 94*
Barnes, Kenneth 1922- *Who 94*
Barnes, Kenneth James 1930- *Who 94*
Barnes, Kevin J. 1952- *WhoWest 94*
Barnes, Kitt 1946- *WhoAmA 93*
Barnes, Lahna Harris 1947- *WhoFI 94, WhoMW 93*
Barnes, Lee 1933- *WhoAmP 93*
Barnes, Linda (Joyce Appelblatt) 1949- *WrDr 94*
Barnes, Louie Burton, III 1948- *WhoAm 94, WhoAmL 94*
Barnes, Loutricia 1953- *WrDr 94*
Barnes, Mabel d1935 *WhoHol 92*
Barnes, Mae 1907- *WhoHol 92*
Barnes, Margo 1947- *WhoAmA 93*
Barnes, Mark James 1957- *WhoAm 94*
Barnes, Mark Richard Purcell *Who 94*
Barnes, Marshall Hayes, II 1937- *WhoMW 93*
Barnes, Martin G. 1948- *WhoBlA 94*
Barnes, Martin McRae 1920- *WhoAm 94*
Barnes, Matthew Molena, Jr. 1933- *WhoBlA 94*
Barnes, Melver Raymond 1917- *WhoScEn 94*
Barnes, Melvyn Peter Keith 1942- *Who 94*
Barnes, Michael *Who 94*
Barnes, (David) Michael (William) 1943- *Who 94*
Barnes, Michael Cecil John 1932- *Who 94*
Barnes, Michael Darr 1943- *WhoAm 94, WhoAmL 94, WhoAmP 93*
Barnes, Michael Keith 1942- *WhoWest 94*
Barnes, Michael Patrick 1940- *Who 94*
Barnes, Milton *WhoBlA 94*
Barnes, Molly 1936- *WhoAmA 93*
Barnes, Myra Edwards 1933- *EncSF 93*
Barnes, N. Kurt 1947- *WhoBlA 94*
Barnes, Nancy *DrAPF 93*
Barnes, Norman Frank 1939- *WhoAm 94*
Barnes, Nyle G. 1938- *WhoAmL 94*
Barnes, Paul Douglas 1946- *WhoBlA 94*
Barnes, Paul McClung 1914- *WhoAm 94*
Barnes, Paul Randall 1943- *WhoScEn 94*
Barnes, Peter 1931- *ConDr 93, IntDcT 2, Who 94, WrDr 94*
Barnes, Peter 1940- *WhoFI 94*
Barnes, Peter Crain 1935- *WhoMW 93*
Barnes, Peter John 1947- *WhoScEn 94*
Barnes, Peter Robert 1921- *Who 94*
Barnes, Peter William 1939- *WhoWest 94*
Barnes, Priscilla 1954- *WhoHol 92*
Barnes, Ramona L. 1938- *WhoAmP 93*
Barnes, Raymond Edward 1950- *WhoWest 94*
Barnes, Richard *DrAPF 93*
Barnes, Richard George 1922- *WhoAm 94, WhoMW 93*
Barnes, Richard Gordon 1932- *WhoAm 94*
Barnes, Richard O. 1921- *WhoAmP 93*
Barnes, Richard Walter 1943- *WhoAmP 93*
Barnes, Robert E. 1927- *WhoFI 94*
Barnes, Robert E. 1933- *WhoWest 94*
Barnes, Robert F. 1933- *WhoAm 94, WhoMW 93, WhoScEn 94*
Barnes, Robert Goodwin 1914- *WhoAm 94*
Barnes, Robert Henry 1921- *IntWW 93, WhoWest 94*
Barnes, Robert M. 1934- *WhoAmA 93*
Barnes, Robert Merton 1934- *WhoAm 94*
Barnes, Robert Sandford 1924- *Who 94*
Barnes, Robert Vertreese, Jr. 1946- *WhoAm 94*
Barnes, Robin Dawn 1960- *WhoBlA 94*
Barnes, Roger Anthony 1937- *Who 94*
Barnes, Roland 1907- *Who 94*
Barnes, Ronald Francis 1942- *WhoScEn 94*
Barnes, (Keith) Rory *EncSF 93*
Barnes, Rosemary Lois 1946- *WhoMW 93*
Barnes, Rosemary Susan 1946- *Who 94*
Barnes, Rosie Susan 1946- *WhoWomW 91*
Barnes, Roy E. 1948- *WhoAmP 93*
Barnes, Rudolph Counts 1917- *WhoAmL 94*
Barnes, Russell C. 1897-1989 *WhAm 10*
Barnes, Samuel Henry 1931- *WhoAm 94, WrDr 94*
Barnes, Samuel Lee 1941- *WhoMW 93*
Barnes, Sandra Henley 1943- *WhoAm 94, WhoFI 94*
Barnes, Shirley Elizabeth 1938- *WhoAm 94*
Barnes, Simon 1951- *WrDr 94*
Barnes, Stan Oscar 1961- *WhoAmP 93*
Barnes, Stephanie *DrAPF 93*
Barnes, Stephen Darryl 1953- *WhoBlA 94*
Barnes, Stephen Paul 1957- *WhoFI 94*
Barnes, Steven (Emory) 1952- *EncSF 93, WrDr 94*
Barnes, Steven Lee 1950- *WhoMW 93*
Barnes, Susan *WhoHol 92*
Barnes, Susan L. *WhoAmL 94*
Barnes, T. Roy d1937 *WhoHol 92*
Barnes, Theodore William 1950- *WhoAmL 94*
Barnes, Thomas 1936- *WhoBlA 94*
Barnes, Thomas Aaron, Sr. 1928- *WhoAmP 93, WhoWest 94*
Barnes, Thomas G. 1930- *WhoAm 94*
Barnes, Thomas John 1943- *WhoAm 94*
Barnes, Thomas Joseph 1930- *WhoAm 94*
Barnes, Thomas V. 1936- *WhoAmP 93*
Barnes, Tim *DrAPF 93*
Barnes, Timothy Paul 1944- *Who 94*
Barnes, V. L. d1949 *WhoHol 92*
Barnes, Valerie Elizabeth 1954- *WhoWest 94*
Barnes, Vanessa Summers *WhoAmP 93*
Barnes, Virgil Everett, II 1935- *WhoAm 94, WhoMW 93*
Barnes, Vivian Leigh 1946- *WhoBlA 94*
Barnes, W. D. *DrAPF 93*
Barnes, Wallace 1926- *WhoAm 94, WhoFI 94*
Barnes, Wallace Ray 1928- *WhoAm 94*
Barnes, Walter *WhoHol 92*
Barnes, Wesley Edward 1937- *WhoAm 94*
Barnes, William 1801-1886 *BlmGEL*
Barnes, William Anderson 1944- *WhoWest 94*
Barnes, William David 1946- *WhoAmA 93*
Barnes, William Henry 1944- *WhoFI 94*
Barnes, William L. 1936- *WhoBlA 94*
Barnes, William Oliver, Jr. 1922- *WhoAm 94*
Barnes, Willie R. 1931- *WhoAm 94, WhoAmL 94, WhoBlA 94*
Barnes, Wilson Edward 1938- *WhoBlA 94*
Barnes, Wilson King 1907- *WhoAm 94*
Barnes, Zane Edison 1921- *WhoAm 94*
Barnes-Brown, Peter Newton 1948- *WhoAmL 94*
Barnes-Bruce, Mary Hanford *WhoMW 93*
Barnes-Linklater, Karen Sue 1953- *WhoMW 93*
Barness, Amnon Shemaya 1924- *WhoAm 94*
Barness, Lewis Abraham 1921- *WhoAm 94, WhoScEn 94*
Bar-Ness, Yeheskel 1932- *WhoAm 94, WhoScEn 94*
Barnes-Svarney, Patricia L(ou) 1953- *WrDr 94*
Barnet, Boris d1965 *WhoHol 92*
Barnet, Charlie 1913-1991 *WhoHol 92*
Barnet, Richard Jackson 1929- *WhoAm 94*
Barnet, Robert Joseph 1929- *WhoAm 94, WhoWest 94*
Barnet, Sylvan 1926- *WhoAm 94*
Barnet, Will 1911- *WhoAm 94, WhoAmA 93*
Barnett *Who 94*
Barnett, Baron 1923- *IntWW 93, Who 94*
Barnett, Alfreda W. Duster 1904- *WhoBlA 94*
Barnett, Alva P. 1947- *WhoBlA 94*
Barnett, Arthur Doak 1921- *WhoAm 94, WrDr 94*
Barnett, Benjamin Lewis, Jr. 1926- *WhoAm 94*
Barnett, Bernard 1920- *WhoAm 94*
Barnett, Betty G. 1947- *WhoMW 93*
Barnett, Bill H. *WhoAmP 93*
Barnett, Bill Marvin 1931- *WhoAm 94, WhoFI 94*
Barnett, Carol Lee 1955- *WhoMW 93*
Barnett, Charles d1929 *WhoHol 92*
Barnett, Charles E. *WhoAmL 94, WhoFI 94*
Barnett, Charlie 1954- *WhoHol 92*
Barnett, Chester d1947 *WhoHol 92*
Barnett, Christopher Andrew 1953- *Who 94*
Barnett, Christopher John Anthony 1936- *Who 94*
Barnett, Colin Michael 1929- *Who 94*
Barnett, Correlli (Douglas) 1927- *Who 94, WrDr 94*
Barnett, Correlli Douglas 1927- *IntWW 93*
Barnett, Crawford Fannin, Jr. 1938- *WhoAm 94, WhoFI 94, WhoScEn 94*
Barnett, David Austin 1945- *WhoAmL 94*
Barnett, David Hughes 1947- *WhoWest 94*
Barnett, David J. 1946- *WhoAmA 93*
Barnett, Denis Hensley Fulton d1992 *Who 94N*
Barnett, DeVitt D. *WhoAmL 94*
Barnett, Dick 1936- *BasBi*
Barnett, Don Marvin 1940- *WhoAmL 94*
Barnett, Earl D. *WhoAmA 93*
Barnett, Edward William 1933- *WhoAm 94, WhoAmL 94*
Barnett, Edward Willis 1922-1987 *WhoAmA 93N*
Barnett, Elizabeth Hale 1940- *WhoFI 94*
Barnett, Emily 1947- *WhoAmA 93*
Barnett, Ethel S. 1929- *WhoBlA 94*
Barnett, Etta Moten 1901- *WhoBlA 94*
Barnett, Evelyn Brooks 1945- *WhoBlA 94*
Barnett, Frank R. d1993 *NewYTBS 93*
Barnett, Fred Lee, Jr. 1966- *WhoBlA 94*
Barnett, Garry Lee 1939- *WhoMW 93*
Barnett, Gary Allen 1959- *WhoFI 94*
Barnett, Geoffrey Grant Fulton 1943- *Who 94*
Barnett, George Leonard 1915- *WrDr 94*
Barnett, Griff d1958 *WhoHol 92*
Barnett, Helmut 1946- *WhoAmA 93*
Barnett, Henry Joseph Macaulay 1922- *WhoScEn 94*
Barnett, Henry Lewis 1914- *WhoAm 94*
Barnett, Henry William 1927- *WhoAmP 93*
Barnett, Herbert P. 1910-1972 *WhoAmA 93N*
Barnett, Howard Albert 1920- *WhoAm 94*
Barnett, Ida B. Wells 1864-1931 *AfrAmAl 6*
Barnett, Jacalyn F. 1952- *WhoAmL 94*
Barnett, Jahnae Harper 1946- *WhoAm 94*
Barnett, James Wallace 1930- *WhoAm 94*
Barnett, Jana Ruth 1952- *WhoIns 94*
Barnett, Jenifer W. *Who 94*
Barnett, Jeremy John 1941- *Who 94*
Barnett, Jim C. *WhoAmP 93*
Barnett, John 1802-1890 *NewGrDO*
Barnett, John Bernard 1934- *WhoMW 93*
Barnett, John H. 1942- *WhoAm 94*
Barnett, Jonathan 1937- *WhoAm 94*
Barnett, Joseph Anthony 1931- *Who 94*
Barnett, Joseph W. 1929- *WhoAmP 93*
Barnett, Judith Anne 1938- *WhoAmP 93*
Barnett, Kenneth Thomas 1921- *Who 94*
Barnett, Lena Sue 1959- *WhoAmL 94*
Barnett, Leonard (Palin) 1919- *WrDr 94*
Barnett, Lester Alfred 1915- *WhoAm 94*
Barnett, Margaret Edwina 1949- *WhoMW 93*
Barnett, Marguerite Ross 1942-1992 *AnObit 1992, WhAm 10, WhoBlA 94N*
Barnett, Marilyn 1934- *WhoFI 94*
Barnett, Marilyn Doan 1934- *WhoMW 93*
Barnett, Mark Andrew 1950- *WhoFI 94*
Barnett, Mark W. 1954- *WhoAmP 93*
Barnett, Mark William 1954- *WhoAm 94, WhoAmL 94, WhoMW 93*
Barnett, Martha Walters 1947- *WhoAm 94, WhoAmL 94*
Barnett, Michael 1949- *WhoAmP 93*
Barnett, Michael James 1948- *WhoAmL 94*
Barnett, Mickey Dee 1951- *WhoAmP 93*
Barnett, Nate d1988 *WhoHol 92*
Barnett, Nicholas John 1940- *Who 94*
Barnett, O. M. *WhoAmP 93*
Barnett, Oliver (Charles) 1907- *Who 94*
Barnett, Paul (Le Page) 1949- *EncSF 93*
Barnett, Paul Anthony 1962- *WhoMW 93*
Barnett, Paul William 1935- *Who 94*
Barnett, Peter John 1944- *WhoAm 94*
Barnett, Peter Leonard 1930- *IntWW 93*
Barnett, Peter Ralph 1951- *WhoFI 94, WhoScEn 94*
Barnett, Ralph Lipsey 1933- *WhoAm 94*
Barnett, Richard Blair 1927- *WhoAm 94*
Barnett, Richard Chambers 1932- *WhoAm 94*
Barnett, Robert 1927- *WrDr 94*
Barnett, Robert 1938- *WhoBlA 94*
Barnett, Robert Bruce 1946- *WhoAmL 94*
Barnett, Robert Glenn 1933- *WhoAm 94, WhoAmL 94*
Barnett, Robert James 1925- *WhoAm 94*
Barnett, Robert L. 1940- *WhoAm 94, WhoFI 94*
Barnett, Robert Neal 1947- *WhoScEn 94*
Barnett, Robert Warren 1911- *WhoAm 94*
Barnett, Ronald David 1943- *WhoAm 94*
Barnett, Roy N. d1993 *NewYTBS 93*
Barnett, S(amuel) Anthony 1915- *WrDr 94*
Barnett, Samuel *WhoAm 94*
Barnett, Samuel B. 1931- *WhoBlA 94*
Barnett, Stanley Kendall 1953- *WhoAmP 93*
Barnett, Susanne La Mar 1946- *WhoMW 93*
Barnett, Teddy 1948- *WhoBlA 94*
Barnett, Thomas Buchanan 1919- *WhoAm 94*
Barnett, Tim P. *WhoScEn 94*
Barnett, Vince d1977 *WhoHol 92*
Barnett, Vincent MacDowell, Jr. 1913- *WhoAm 94*
Barnett, Vivian Endicott 1944- *WhoAm 94, WhoAmA 93*
Barnett, Walter Michael 1903- *WhoAm 94*
Barnett, William 1917- *WhoBlA 94*
Barnett, William Allen 1941- *WhoFI 94*
Barnett, William Arnold 1941- *WhoAm 94*
Barnett, William Bill 1943- *WhoAmL 94*
Barnett, William Evans 1937- *Who 94*
Barnette, Curtis Handley 1935- *WhoAm 94, WhoAmL 94, WhoFI 94*
Barnette, Dennis Arthur 1941- *WhoAm 94*
Barnette, James Thomas, Jr. 1959- *WhoFI 94*
Barnette, Martha 1957- *WrDr 94*
Barnevik, Percy 1941- *Who 94*
Barnevik, Percy Nils 1941- *IntWW 93, WhoAm 94, WhoFI 94*
Barnewall *Who 94*
Barnewall, Gordon Gouverneur 1924- *WhoAm 94*
Barnewall, Reginald Robert 1924- *Who 94*
Barney, Alan 1945- *WhoAm 94*
Barney, Bob 1942- *WhoAmP 93*
Barney, Charles Lester 1925- *WhoAm 94*
Barney, Charles Richard 1935- *WhoAm 94*
Barney, Clarence Lyle 1934- *WhoBlA 94*
Barney, Duane R. 1956- *WhoMW 93*
Barney, Jay d1985 *WhoHol 92*
Barney, John Stewart 1868-1925 *EncSF 93*
Barney, Joshua 1759-1818 *AmRev, WhAmRev*
Barney, Kline Porter, Jr. 1934- *WhoWest 94*
Barney, Lawrence Davis 1906-1989 *WhAm 10*
Barney, Lemuel Jackson 1945- *WhoBlA 94*
Barney, Maginal Wright d1966 *WhoAmA 93N*
Barney, Mary Margaret 1917- *WhoAmP 93*
Barney, Michael E. 1947- *WhoAmL 94*
Barney, Natalie 1876-1972 *BlmGWL*
Barney, Natalie (Clifford) 1876-1972 *GayLL*
Barney, Steven Matthew 1943- *WhoAm 94, WhoFI 94, WhoMW 93*
Barney, Thomas McNamee 1938- *WhoAm 94*
Barney, William Joshua, Jr. 1911-1991 *WhAm 10*
Barney, Willie J. 1927- *WhoBlA 94*
Barnfield, Richard 1574-1627 *BlmGEL*
Barnhard, Sherwood Arthur 1921- *WhoFI 94*
Barnhardt, James Harper 1913- *WhoFI 94*
Barnhardt, Robert Alexander 1937- *WhoAm 94, WhoScEn 94*
Barnhardt, Zeb Elonzo, Jr. 1941- *WhoAm 94, WhoAmL 94*
Barnhart, Beverly Homyak 1929- *WhoAmP 93, WhoFI 94*
Barnhart, Beverly Jean 1954- *WhoAm 94*
Barnhart, Charles Elmer 1923- *WhoAm 94*
Barnhart, Clarence Lewis d1993 *NewYTBS 93 [port]*
Barnhart, Clarence Lewis 1900- *WhoAm 94*
Barnhart, David Allan 1961- *WhoWest 94*
Barnhart, Forrest Gregory 1951- *WhoAmL 94*
Barnhart, Jo Anne B. 1950- *WhoAm 94*
Barnhart, Richard A. 1953- *WhoAmL 94*
Barnhart, Terry Eugene 1955- *WhoMW 93*
Barnhart, Timothy Coleman 1956- *WhoAmP 93*
Barnhart, Timothy V. 1947- *WhoAmP 93*
Barnhart, William Rupp 1903-1989 *WhAm 10*
Barnhill, Charles Joseph, Jr. 1943- *WhoAm 94*
Barnhill, David Stan 1949- *WhoAmL 94*
Barnhill, Donald Earl 1951- *WhoAmL 94*
Barnhill, Georgia Brady 1944- *WhoAmA 93*
Barnhill, Helen Iphigenia 1937- *WhoBlA 94*
Barnhill, Henry Grady, Jr. 1930- *WhoAm 94, WhoAmL 94*
Barnhill, Howard Clinton *WhoAmP 93*
Barnhill, Howard Eugene 1923- *WhoAm 94*
Barnhill, Leonard Almontia 1955- *WhoMW 93*
Barnhill, Robert E. 1939- *WhoWest 94*
Barnholdt, Terry Joseph 1954- *WhoAmL 94, WhoFI 94*
Barnholtz, Barry 1945- *IntMPA 94*
Barnhorst, Leo 1924- *BasBi*
Barnhouse, Lillian May Palmer 1918- *WhoMW 93*
Barnicle, Thomas William 1954- *WhoMW 93*

Barnidge, Mary Shen *DrAPF 93*
Barnidge, Thomas Howard 1948- *WhoAm 94*
Barnie, John 1941- *WrDr 94*
Barnley, George c. 1817- *EncNAR*
Barnouw, Erik 1908- *WrDr 94*
Barns, Justine 1925- *WhoAmP 93*
Barns, Suzanne Falter *ConAu 141*
Barnstaple, Archdeacon of *Who 94*
Barnston, Betsy Hahn 1935- *WhoFI 94*
Barnstone, Aliki *DrAPF 93*
Barnstone, Willis *DrAPF 93*
Barnstone, Willis 1927- *WhoAm 94*
Barnum, George d1937 *WhoHol 92*
Barnum, Jeanne Schubert 1950- *WhoAmL 94*
Barnum, John Wallace 1928- *WhoAm 94, WhoAmP 93*
Barnum, Mary Ann Mook 1946- *WhoScEn 94*
Barnum, Mel Bloyce 1949- *WhoFI 94*
Barnum, Paul Frederick 1951- *WhoWest 94*
Barnum, Phineas Taylor 1810-1891 *AmCulL, BlmGEL*
Barnum, William Douglas 1946- *WhoFI 94*
Barnum, William Laird 1916- *WhoAm 94, WhoWest 94*
Barnum, William Milo 1927- *WhoAm 94*
Barnwell, David Ray 1953- *WhoFI 94, WhoWest 94*
Barnwell, Franklin Hershel 1937- *WhoAm 94*
Barnwell, Henry Lee 1934- *WhoBlA 94*
Barnwell, John L. 1922- *WhoAmA 93*
Barnwell, Ray Ervin, Sr. 1945- *WhoAm 94*
Barnwell, Robert 1761-1814 *WhAmRev*
Barnwell, Thomas Pinkney, III 1943- *WhoAm 94*
Barnwell, William (Curtis) 1943- *EncSF 93, WrDr 94*
Baro, Agnes Louise 1942- *WhoMW 93*
Baró, Robert Aristides 1948- *WhoHisp 94*
Barocas, Ralph David 1949- *WhoHisp 94*
Barocci, Robert Louis 1942- *WhoAm 94*
Baroff, George Stanley 1924- *WhoAm 94*
Baroff, Lynn Elliott 1949- *WhoWest 94*
Baroja, Pio 1872-1956 *HispLC [port]*
Barolini, Helen *DrAPF 93*
Barolsky, Paul 1941- *WhoAm 94*
Baron, Alan d1993 *NewYTBS 93*
Baron, Alexander *Who 94*
Baron, (Joseph) Alexander 1917- *Who 94*
Baron, Alma Fay S. 1923- *WhoAm 94*
Baron, Barbara Ann 1950- *WhoMW 93*
Baron, Carolyn 1940- *IntWW 93, WhoAm 94*
Baron, Charles Hillel 1936- *WhoAm 94*
Baron, David *ConTFT 11*
Baron, David Alan 1951- *WhoMW 93*
Baron, David Hume 1964- *WhoScEn 94*
Baron, Denis Neville 1924- *WrDr 94*
Baron, Devorah 1887-1956 *BlmGWL*
Baron, Dick d1977 *WhoHol 92*
Baron, Franklin Andrew 1923- *IntWW 93*
Baron, Franklin Andrew Merrifield 1923- *Who 94*
Baron, Frederick David 1947- *WhoAm 94*
Baron, Gino Victor 1948- *WhoScEn 94*
Baron, Hazen Jay 1934- *WhoScEn 94*
Baron, Jean-Jacques 1909- *IntWW 93*
Baron, Jeffrey 1942- *WhoAm 94*
Baron, John Herschel 1936- *WhoAm 94*
Baron, Judson Richard 1924- *WhoAm 94*
Baron, Linda Michelle *DrAPF 93*
Baron, Lita *WhoHol 92*
Baron, Martin Raymond 1922- *WhoAm 94*
Baron, Mary *DrAPF 93*
Baron, Melvin Leon 1927- *WhoAm 94*
Baron, Michael Alan 1949- *WhoMW 93*
Baron, Mitchell Neal 1947- *WhoAm 94, WhoAmL 94*
Baron, Myrna 1934- *WhoWest 94*
Baron, Naomi S(usan) 1946- *ConAu 140*
Baron, Neville A. 1933- *WhoBlA 94*
Baron, Othello *EncSF 93*
Baron, Richard Albert 1940- *WhoMW 93*
Baron, Richard Stephen 1956- *WhoAmL 94*
Baron, Robert Alan 1943- *WhoAm 94*
Baron, Robert Charles 1934- *WhoWest 94*
Baron, Salo Wittmayer 1895-1989 *WhAm 10*
Baron, Samuel 1925- *WhoAm 94*
Baron, Samuel 1928- *WhoAm 94*
Baron, Samuel Haskell 1921- *WhoAm 94*
Baron, Sandy 1938- *WhoHol 92*
Baron, Seymour 1923- *WhoAm 94*
Baron, Sheldon 1934- *WhoAm 94*
Baron, Suze *DrAPF 93*
Baron, Theodore 1928- *WhoAm 94*
Baron, Thomas *Who 94*
Baron, Wendy 1937- *WrDr 94*
Baron, (Ora) Wendy 1937- *Who 94*
Barona, Andrés, Jr. 1945- *WhoHisp 94*
Baroncelli, Jacques d1951 *WhoHol 92*
Baron Crespo, Enrique 1944- *IntWW 93*
Baron Crespo, Enrique Carlos 1944- *Who 94*
Barondes, Anita 1950- *WhoAmL 94*
Barondes, Samuel Herbert 1933- *WhoScEn 94*
Barondess, Barbara 1907- *WhoHol 92*
Barondess, Jeremiah Abraham 1924- *WhoAm 94*
Barone, Anita *WhoHol 92*
Barone, Constance M. 1956- *WhoMW 93*
Barone, Dennis *DrAPF 93*
Barone, Donald Anthony 1948- *WhoAm 94*
Barone, James Patrick 1956- *WhoAmP 93*
Barone, John Anthony 1924- *WhoAm 94*
Barone, Michael D. 1944- *WhoAm 94*
Barone, Michele Hope 1963- *WhoAmL 94*
Barone, Patricia *DrAPF 93*
Barone, Robert Paul 1937- *WhoFI 94*
Barone, Rose Marie Pace 1920- *WhoAm 94*
Barone, Sandra M. 1946- *WhoAmP 93*
Barone, Thomas Anthony 1946- *WhoAm 94*
Baroness, The *NewGrDO*
Baroni, Leonora *NewGrDO*
Baronian, Maureen Murphy 1934- *WhoAmP 93*
Baroni-Kaestner, Mary Ann 1953- *WhoMW 93*
Baronova, Irina 1919- *IntDcB [port], WhoHol 92*
Barons, Richard Irwin 1946- *WhoAmA 93*
Barooah, Dev Kanta 1914- *IntWW 93*
Baroody, Benjamin C. 1946- *WhoAmP 93*
Baroody, Michael Elias 1946- *WhoAm 94, WhoAmP 93*
Baroody, William J., Jr. 1937- *WhoAmP 93*
Barooshian, Martin 1929- *WhoAmA 93*
Barosky, Bertha Elizabeth 1929- *WhoAmP 93*
Barot, Navnit Manilal 1944- *WhoAsA 94*
Baroudy, Bahige Mourad 1950- *WhoFI 94*
Baroux, Lucien d1968 *WhoHol 92*
Barowitz, Elliott 1936- *WhoAmA 93*
Barpal, Isaac Ruben 1940- *WhoAm 94, WhoScEn 94*
Barquet, Jesús José 1953- *WhoHisp 94*
Barquin, Ramon Carlos 1942- *WhoAm 94, WhoHisp 94*
Barquist, Charles S. 1953- *WhoAmL 94*
Barr, A. W. Cleeve 1910- *Who 94*
Barr, Alfred Hamilton, Jr. 1902-1981 *WhoAmA 93N*
Barr, Allan 1890-1959 *WhoAmA 93N*
Barr, Allan Ralph 1926- *WhoWest 94*
Barr, Alwyn 1938- *WrDr 94*
Barr, Amelia Edith Huddleston 1831-1919 *BlmGWL*
Barr, Andrew 1961- *WrDr 94*
Barr, Anthony 1921- *IntMPA 94*
Barr, Bryon d1966 *WhoHol 92*
Barr, Burt 1938- *WhoAmA 93*
Barr, Burton S. *WhoAmP 93*
Barr, Carlos Harvey 1936- *WhoAmL 94*
Barr, Charlene Russell 1943- *WhoAmP 93*
Barr, Charles Francis 1950- *WhoIns 94*
Barr, D. Daniel 1943- *WhoAmL 94*
Barr, David 1925- *Who 94*
Barr, David Charles 1950- *WhoAm 94, WhoFI 94*
Barr, David G. 1895-1970 *HisDcKW*
Barr, David John 1939- *WhoAm 94, WhoAmA 93*
Barr, Densil *WrDr 94*
Barr, Densil Neve 1918- *EncSF 93*
Barr, Dixie 1934- *WhoMW 93*
Barr, Donald 1921- *EncSF 93*
Barr, Donald Roy 1938- *WhoAm 94*
Barr, Doug 1949- *WhoHol 92*
Barr, Douglas *WhoHol 92*
Barr, Douglas N. 1947- *WhoAm 94, WhoAmL 94*
Barr, George 1937- *EncSF 93*
Barr, Ginger 1947- *WhoAmP 93, WhoMW 93*
Barr, Harry Edwin 1941- *WhoAmL 94*
Barr, Howard Raymond 1910- *WhoAm 94*
Barr, Ian 1927- *Who 94*
Barr, Ida d1967 *WhoHol 92*
Barr, Irwin Robert 1920- *WhoAm 94*
Barr, Jacob Dexter 1944- *WhoAm 94*
Barr, James 1924- *IntWW 93, Who 94, WrDr 94*
Barr, James George 1951- *WhoFI 94*
Barr, James Houston, III 1941- *WhoAmL 94*
Barr, James Norman 1940- *WhoAmL 94*
Barr, Jean-Marc 1960- *WhoHol 92*
Barr, Jeanne d1967 *WhoHol 92*
Barr, Jene *ConAu 42NR*
Barr, John Alexander James Pooler 1939- *Who 94*
Barr, John Baldwin 1932- *WhoAm 94*
Barr, John Douglas, II 1963- *WhoAmP 93*
Barr, John Michael 1957- *WhoFI 94*
Barr, John Robert 1936- *WhoAm 94, WhoAmP 93*
Barr, John Tilman, IV 1948- *WhoWest 94*
Barr, John Wallace 1929- *WhoFI 94*
Barr, Jon Michael 1938- *WhoAm 94*
Barr, Joseph Walker 1918- *IntWW 93, WhoAm 94*
Barr, Julia *WhoHol 92*
Barr, Kenneth Glen 1941- *Who 94*
Barr, Leonard d1980 *WhoHol 92*
Barr, LeRoy 1936- *WhoBlA 94*
Barr, Lewis T. 1942- *WhoAmL 94*
Barr, Marlene Joy 1935- *WhoMW 93*
Barr, Martin 1925- *WhoAm 94*
Barr, Marylin Lytle *DrAPF 93*
Barr, Michael Blanton 1948- *WhoAm 94, WhoAmL 94*
Barr, Michael Charles 1947- *WhoAm 94, WhoFI 94*
Barr, Morris Alfred 1922- *IntWW 93*
Barr, Murray Llewellyn 1908- *IntWW 93, Who 94, WhoAm 94, WorScD*
Barr, Norman 1908- *WhoAmA 93*
Barr, Patricia (Miriam) 1934- *WrDr 94*
Barr, Patrick d1985 *WhoHol 92*
Barr, Reginald Alfred 1920- *Who 94*
Barr, Richard Gary 1956- *WhoMW 93*
Barr, Robert 1850-1912 *EncSF 93*
Barr, Robert Alfred, Jr. 1934- *WhoAm 94*
Barr, Robert Dale 1939- *WhoAm 94*
Barr, Robert Edward 1956- *WhoFI 94*
Barr, Roger 1921- *WhoAmA 93*
Barr, Roger Terry 1921- *WhoAm 94*
Barr, Roseanne *IntWW 93, WhoCom*
Barr, Roseanne 1952- *WhoHol 92*
Barr, Sanford Lee 1952- *WhoMW 93*
Barr, Scott 1916- *WhoAmP 93*
Barr, Stringfellow 1897- *WhAm 10*
Barr, Sue 1942- *WhoAmP 93*
Barr, Thomas Delbert 1931- *WhoAm 94, WhoAmL 94*
Barr, Tina *DrAPF 93*
Barr, Tyrone C. *EncSF 93*
Barr, William Greig 1917- *Who 94*
Barr, William Pelham *WhoAmP 93*
Barr, William Pelham 1950- *IntWW 93, WhoAm 94, WhoAmL 94*
Barrack, William Sample, Jr. 1929- *Who 94, WhoAm 94, WhoFI 94*
Barraclough, Jack T. 1927- *WhoAmP 93*
Barraclough, John 1918- *Who 94*
Barraclough, Kenneth (James Priestley) 1907- *Who 94*
Barraclough, William George 1935- *WhoAm 94*
Barraco, I. Robin Anthony 1945- *WhoMW 93*
Barra de Llanos, Ema de la 1861-1947 *BlmGWL*
Barraga, Thomas Francis 1943- *WhoAmP 93*
Barragan, Charles J., III 1958- *WhoWest 94*
Barragan, Miguel F. *WhoHisp 94*
Barragan, Napoleon *WhoHisp 94*
Barragan, Nina *DrAPF 93*
Barragry, Mary Ann 1948- *WhoMW 93*
Barral, Carlos 1928-1989 *DcLB 134 [port]*
Barrales, Ruben 1962- *WhoHisp 94*
Barrall, James D. C. 1950- *WhoAm 94, WhoAmL 94*
Barrall, Raymond Charles 1930- *WhoMW 93*
Barran, David Haven 1912- *IntWW 93, Who 94*
Barran, John (Napoleon Ruthven) 1934- *Who 94*
Barranco, Maria *WhoHol 92*
Barranco, Sam Christopher 1938- *WhoScEn 94*
Barranger, M(illy Hilliard) S(later) 1937- *WrDr 94*
Barrantes, Denny Manny 1948- *WhoScEn 94*
Barrantes, Francisco Jose 1944- *WhoScEn 94*
Barrar, Annette Knight 1939- *WhoAm 94*
Barras, Jacques Melchoir Saint-Laurent dc. 1800 *AmRev*
Barras, Jonetta Rose *DrAPF 93*
Barras, Louis, Comte de dc. 1800 *WhAmRev [port]*
Barrass, Gordon Stephen 1940- *Who 94*
Barrass, Stanley Russell 1926- *WhoWest 94*
Barrat, Robert d1970 *WhoHol 92*
Barratt, Cynthia Louise 1953- *WhoAm 94*
Barratt, Eric George 1938- *WhoFI 94*
Barratt, Ernest Stoelting 1925- *WhoAm 94*
Barratt, Francis Russell 1924- *Who 94*
Barratt, Gilbert Alexander 1930- *Who 94*
Barratt, Herbert George Harold 1905- *Who 94*
Barratt, Lawrence Arthur 1927- *Who 94*
Barratt, Michael Fieldhouse 1928- *Who 94*
Barratt, Michael George 1927- *Who 94*
Barratt, Raymond William 1920- *WhoAm 94*
Barratt, Richard (Stanley) 1928- *Who 94*
Barratt, Robin Alexander 1945- *Who 94*
Barratt, Thomas Keating 1927- *WhoWest 94*
Barratt-Boyes, Brian (Gerald) 1924- *Who 94*
Barratt-Boyes, Brian Gerald 1924- *IntWW 93*
Barratt Brown, Michael 1918- *WrDr 94*
Barraud, Henry 1900- *IntWW 93, NewGrDO*
Barrault, Jean-Louis 1910- *IntWW 93, Who 94, WhoHol 92*
Barrault, Marie-Christine 1944- *IntMPA 94, WhoHol 92*
Barrax, Gerald *DrAPF 93*
Barrax, Gerald William 1933- *BlkWr 2*
Barraza, Rosaleo N. 1947- *WhoHisp 94*
Barraza, Santa C. 1951- *WhoHisp 94*
Barraza, Viola Y. 1951- *WhoHisp 94*
Barre, Charles 1950- *WhoFI 94*
Barre, Isaac 1726-1802 *WhAmRev [port]*
Barre, Laura Kohlman 1931- *WhoAmP 93*
Barre, Raymond 1924- *IntWW 93, Who 94*
Barre, Steven Craig 1959- *WhoAmL 94*
Barreas Arrechea, Ricardo Alfredo 1934- *IntWW 93*
Barreda, Antonio 1942- *WhoHisp 94*
Barredo, Eduardo *EncSF 93*
Barreira, Brian Ernest 1958- *WhoAmL 94*
Barreiro, Bruno A., Jr. 1965- *WhoAmP 93*
Barreiro, Eliezer Jesus 1947- *WhoScEn 94*
Barreiro, José 1948- *WhoHisp 94*
Barreiro, Luis G. d1947 *WhoHol 92*
Barrell, Anthony Charles 1933- *Who 94*
Barrell, Bill 1932- *WhoAmA 93*
Barren, Bruce Willard 1942- *WhoAm 94, WhoFI 94*
Barren, Charles 1913- *EncSF 93*
Barren, Jean VanAken 1917- *WhoAmP 93*
Barreno, Maria Isabel 1939- *BlmGWL*
Barrer, Richard Maling 1910- *IntWW 93, Who 94*
Barrera (Saavedra), Tomas 1870-1938 *NewGrDO*
Barrera, Alfonso 1954- *WhoHisp 94*
Barrera, Elvira Puig 1943- *WhoAm 94, WhoFI 94*
Barrera, Ernest C. 1950- *WhoHisp 94*
Barrera, Fabricio, Jr. 1940- *WhoHisp 94*
Barrera, Felix N. 1936- *WhoHisp 94*
Barrera, Frank A. d1993 *NewYTBS 93 [port]*
Barrera, Giulia 1942- *NewGrDO*
Barrera, Guillermo José 1927- *WhoHisp 94*
Barrera, Manuel 1943- *WhoAm 94*
Barrera, Manuel, Jr. 1943- *WhoHisp 94*
Barrera, Mario 1939- *WhoHisp 94*
Barrera, Ralph A. 1959- *WhoHisp 94*
Barrera, Rodolfo Luis 1938- *WhoAmP 93*
Barrera, Ruben Rivera 1939- *WhoFI 94*
Barrera, Victor T. 1939- *WhoHisp 94*
Barrera Lombana, Jose Pablo 1956- *WhoHisp 94*
Barreras, Amelita Manoto 1954- *WhoFI 94*
Barreras, Raymond Domingo 1949- *WhoHisp 94*
Barreras del Rio, Petra *WhoHisp 94*
Barreres, Domingo 1941- *WhoAmA 93*
Barrero, Nestor 1956- *WhoAmL 94*
Barrero, Richard E. 1959- *WhoFI 94*
Barres, Madeleine d1978 *WhoHol 92*
Barresi, Dorothy *DrAPF 93*
Barret, Maxwell P. 1944- *WhoAmL 94*
Barreto, Charlton Bodenberg 1968- *WhoWest 94*
Barreto, Eduardo 1957- *WhoHisp 94*
Barreto, Hector 1935- *WhoHisp 94*
Barreto, Martin O. 1957- *WhoHisp 94*
Barreto, Pedro d1943 *WhoHol 92*
Barrett, Alan Hildreth 1927-1991 *WhAm 10*
Barrett, Andrea *DrAPF 93*
Barrett, Andrew *WhoAm 94, WhoFI 94*
Barrett, Angela (Jane) 1955- *SmATA 75*
Barrett, Anne Therese 1957- *WhoMW 93*
Barrett, Anthony A(rthur) 1941- *WrDr 94*
Barrett, Barbara McConnell 1950- *WhoAm 94, WhoWest 94*
Barrett, Beatrice Helene 1928- *WhoAm 94*
Barrett, Bernard Morris, Jr. 1944- *WhoScEn 94*
Barrett, Bill 1929- *CngDr 93*
Barrett, Bill 1934- *WhoAm 94, WhoAmA 93*
Barrett, Bruce Edward 1955- *WhoAmL 94*
Barrett, Bruce Richard 1939- *WhoAm 94, WhoWest 94*
Barrett, Carol *DrAPF 93*
Barrett, Charles Kingsley 1917- *IntWW 93, Who 94, WrDr 94*
Barrett, Colleen Crotty 1944- *WhoAm 94*

Barrett, Craig R. 1939- WhoAm 94, WhoFI 94, WhoWest 94
Barrett, David 1930- IntWW 93, Who 94
Barrett, David A. 1950- WhoAmL 94
Barrett, David Eugene 1955- WhoAmL 94
Barrett, David L. WhoFI 94
Barrett, David William S. Who 94
Barrett, Denis Everett 1911- Who 94
Barrett, Dennis WhoAmP 93
Barrett, Dennis Charles T. Who 94
Barrett, Donald John 1927- WhoWest 94
Barrett, Doug 1957- WhoMW 93
Barrett, Edith d1977 WhoHol 92
Barrett, Edmond Fox 1928- Who 94
Barrett, Edward d1977 WhoHol 92
Barrett, Edward Ware 1910-1989 WhAm 10
Barrett, Edythe Hart 1915- WhoMW 93
Barrett, Elizabeth BlmGWL
Barrett, Ernest 1917- Who 94
Barrett, Ethel WrDr 94
Barrett, Eugene J. 1946- WhoAm 94, WhoScEn 94
Barrett, Evan Donald 1945- WhoAmP 93
Barrett, Frank Joseph 1932- WhoAm 94
Barrett, Gentry d1956 WhoHol 92
Barrett, Geoffrey John 1928- EncSF 93, WrDr 94
Barrett, George Edward 1927- WhoAmL 94
Barrett, Gregory Lawrence 1952- WhoScEn 94
Barrett, H. Stanford 1909-1970 WhoAmA 93N
Barrett, Helen Mary 1965- WhoAmL 94
Barrett, Herbert 1873-1943 BuCMET
Barrett, Herbert 1910- WhoAm 94
Barrett, Iris Louise Killian 1962- WhoBlA 94
Barrett, Izadore 1926- WhoAm 94
Barrett, Jack Wheeler 1912- Who 94
Barrett, James A. 1932- WhoBlA 94
Barrett, James E. 1922- WhoAm 94, WhoAmL 94, WhoWest 94
Barrett, James Edward 1942- WhoScEn 94
Barrett, James Edward, Jr. 1929- WhoAm 94
Barrett, James Joseph 1956- WhoWest 94
Barrett, James Lee 1929-1989 WhAm 10
Barrett, James P. 1936- WhoAm 94
Barrett, James Peter 1924- WhoWest 94
Barrett, James Robert 1950- WhoMW 93
Barrett, James Thomas 1927- WhoAm 94, WhoMW 93
Barrett, Jamie WhoHol 92
Barrett, Jan Elasky 1963- WhoMW 93
Barrett, Jane d1969 WhoHol 92
Barrett, Jane Hayes 1947- WhoAm 94, WhoAmL 94
Barrett, Jeffrey Scott 1949- WhoMW 93
Barrett, John WhoHol 92
Barrett, John, III 1947- WhoAmP 93
Barrett, John Adams 1937- WhoAm 94, WhoAmL 94
Barrett, John Anthony 1942- WhoAm 94
Barrett, John Charles Allanson 1943- Who 94
Barrett, John Edward 1931- Who 94
Barrett, John Eugene, Jr. 1949- WhoAm 94
Barrett, John F. 1949- WhoIns 94
Barrett, John G(ilchrist) 1921- WrDr 94
Barrett, John Henry 1913- WrDr 94
Barrett, John James, Jr. 1948- WhoAm 94, WhoAmL 94
Barrett, John Patrick, Jr. 1956- WhoFI 94
Barrett, John Richard 1928- WhoAmL 94
Barrett, Joseph Michael 1934- WhoAm 94
Barrett, Judi 1941- WrDr 94
Barrett, Judith 1914- WhoHol 92
Barrett, Karen Fox 1949- WhoAm 94
Barrett, Kim Elaine 1958- WhoWest 94
Barrett, Larry Leon 1940- WhoWest 94
Barrett, Laurence Irwin 1935- WhoAm 94
Barrett, Laurinda WhoHol 92
Barrett, Leni Mancuso WhoAmA 93
Barrett, Lenore Hardy 1934- WhoAmP 93, WhoWest 94
Barrett, Lida Kittrell 1927- WhoAm 94
Barrett, Linda L. 1948- WhoFI 94
Barrett, (Eseoghene) Lindsay 1941- BlkWr 2
Barrett, Loretta Anne 1941- WhoAm 94
Barrett, Lynne DrAPF 93
Barrett, Majel 1932- WhoHol 92
Barrett, Marilyn Woody 1949- WhoFI 94
Barrett, Marvin DrAPF 93
Barrett, Mary Lou 1941- WhoAmP 93
Barrett, Matthew Anderson 1947- WhoBlA 94
Barrett, Matthew W. 1944- IntWW 93, WhoAm 94
Barrett, Michael Who 94
Barrett, (Arthur) Michael 1932- Who 94
Barrett, Michael Henry 1932- WhoAm 94
Barrett, Michael J. 1948- WhoAmP 93
Barrett, Michael John 1954- WhoScEn 94
Barrett, Michael Wayne 1955- WhoScEn 94
Barrett, Minnette d1964 WhoHol 92
Barrett, Nancy WhoHol 92
Barrett, Nancy Smith 1942- WhoAm 94, WrDr 94
Barrett, Neal, Jr. WrDr 94
Barrett, Neal, Jr. 1929- EncSF 93
Barrett, O'Neill, Jr. 1929- WhoAm 94
Barrett, Pat d1959 WhoHol 92
Barrett, Phillip Heston 1943- WhoAmL 94
Barrett, Ray d1973 WhoHol 92
Barrett, Ray 1926- WhoHol 92
Barrett, Raymond Walter 1933- WhoMW 93
Barrett, Reginald Haughton 1942- WhoWest 94
Barrett, Richard David 1931- WhoAm 94
Barrett, Richard H. 1930- WhoAmP 93
Barrett, Richard Hewins 1949- WhoWest 94
Barrett, Richard James 1948- WhoFI 94
Barrett, Richard O. 1923- WhoBlA 94
Barrett, Robert Daker 1945- WhoWest 94
Barrett, Robert Dumas 1903- WhoAmA 93N
Barrett, Robert F. 1942- WhoAmL 94
Barrett, Robert John, Jr. 1917- WhoAm 94
Barrett, Robert Matthew 1948- WhoAmL 94, WhoWest 94
Barrett, Robert S., IV WhoAmP 93
Barrett, Robert South, IV 1927- WhoAm 94
Barrett, Roger d1968 WhoHol 92
Barrett, Roger Watson 1915- WhoAm 94
Barrett, Rona 1936- IntMPA 94, WhoHol 92
Barrett, Ronald Keith 1948- WhoBlA 94
Barrett, Ronald Martin 1965- WhoScEn 94
Barrett, S. Barre 1936- WhoAm 94
Barrett, Sheila Ann 1966- WhoWest 94
Barrett, Sheila Marie 1967- WhoMW 93
Barrett, Sherman L. 1945- WhoBlA 94
Barrett, Stephen (Jeremy) 1931- Who 94
Barrett, Stephen W. 1956- WhoIns 94
Barrett, Susan Patricia 1948- WhoAmP 93
Barrett, Sweet Emma d1983 WhoHol 92
Barrett, Terry R. 1944- WhoAmL 94
Barrett, Theresa Jean 1967- WhoMW 93
Barrett, Thomas Joseph 1934- WhoFI 94
Barrett, Thomas Joseph 1948- WhoAmL 94
Barrett, Thomas Leon Francis 1938- WhoFI 94
Barrett, Thomas M. 1953- CngDr 93, WhoAmP 93, WhoMW 93
Barrett, Thomas M. 1954- WhoAm 94
Barrett, Thomas Marshall 1955- WhoFI 94
Barrett, Thomas R. 1927- WhoAmA 93
Barrett, Thomas Weeks 1902-1947 WhoAmA 93N
Barrett, Tom Hans 1930- IntWW 93
Barrett, Tomi WhoHol 92
Barrett, Tony d1974 WhoHol 92
Barrett, Walter Carlin, Jr. 1947- WhoBlA 94
Barrett, William C. 1913- WhoAm 94
Barrett, William Christopher 1913-1992 AnObit 1992
Barrett, William E. 1929- WhoAm 94, WhoAmP 93, WhoMW 93
Barrett, William E(dmund) 1900-1986 EncSF 93
Barrett, William H. 1946- WhoAm 94
Barrett, William Joel 1939- WhoAm 94, WhoFI 94
Barrett, William L. D. 1938- WhoAmL 94
Barrett, William O. 1945- WhoAmA 93
Barrett, William Owen 1945- WhoAm 94, WhoWest 94
Barrett, William Spencer 1914- Who 94
Barrett-Bryson, Debbie 1957- WhoMW 93
Barrett-Connor, Elizabeth Louise 1935- WhoAm 94
Barrette, Jean 1946- WhoScEn 94
Barrett-Lennard, Hugh (Dacre) 1917- Who 94
Barretton, Grandall EncSF 93
Barri, Mario d1963 WhoHol 92
Barrick, Gary Wayne 1949- WhoAmL 94
Barrick, William Henry 1916- WhoAm 94
Barrie, Alexander 1923- WrDr 94
Barrie, Amanda 1939- WhoHol 92
Barrie, Barbara 1931- IntMPA 94, WhoHol 92
Barrie, Barbara Ann 1931- WhoAm 94
Barrie, (Charles) David (Ogilvy) 1953- Who 94
Barrie, Dennis Ray 1947- WhoAmA 93
Barrie, Elaine 1916- WhoHol 92
Barrie, Erwin S. 1886-1983 WhoAmA 93N
Barrie, George Napier 1940- IntWW 93
Barrie, Herbert 1927- Who 94
Barrie, J. M. 1860-1937 DcLB 141 [port]
Barrie, J(ames) M(atthew) 1860-1937 IntDcT 2 [port]
Barrie, James M. d1937 WhoHol 92
Barrie, James Matthew 1869-1937 BlmGEL
Barrie, John d1980 WhoHol 92
Barrie, John Paul 1947- WhoAm 94, WhoAmL 94
Barrie, Mona d1964 WhoHol 92
Barrie, Nigel d1971 WhoHol 92
Barrie, Robert 1927- WhoAm 94
Barrie, Scott d1993 NewYTBS 93 [port]
Barrie, Susan WrDr 94
Barrie, Wendy d1978 WhoHol 92
Barrientos, Ben 1946- WhoAmP 93
Barrientos, Gahona Omar 1940- WhoMW 93
Barrientos, Gonzalo 1941- WhoAmP 93, WhoHisp 94
Barrientos, Julian Adolph WhoHisp 94
Barrientos, Maria 1884-1946 NewGrDO
Barrientos, Raúl Ernesto 1942- WhoHisp 94
Barrientos, Robert John 1953- WhoFI 94
Barrier, Edgar d1964 WhoHol 92
Barrier, Ernestine d1989 WhoHol 92
Barrier, Maurice WhoHol 92
Barriera, Iris D. 1944- WhoHisp 94
Barriger, John Walker, IV 1927- WhoFI 94, WhoMW 93
Barringer, Barry d1938 WhoHol 92
Barringer, John Paul 1903- WhoAm 94
Barringer, Leland David 1943- WhoAm 94
Barringer, Ned d1976 WhoHol 92
Barringer, Paul Brandon, II 1930- WhoAm 94
Barringer, Philip E. 1916- WhoAm 94
Barringer, Russell Newton 1903- WhoAmP 93
Barringer, Thomas Lawson 1940- WhoAmP 93
Barringer, William H. 1948- WhoAmL 94
Barrington, Alexander (Fitzwilliam Croker) 1909- Who 94
Barrington, Bruce David 1942- WhoFI 94
Barrington, Herbert d1933 WhoHol 92
Barrington, James Henry 1952- Who 94
Barrington, Judith DrAPF 93
Barrington, Leonard Barry 1925- WhoMW 93
Barrington, Michael EncSF 93
Barrington, Michael d1988 WhoHol 92
Barrington, Nicholas (John) 1934- Who 94
Barrington, Nicholas John 1934- IntWW 93
Barrington, Rodney Craig 1953- WhoMW 93
Barrington, Rutland d1922 WhoHol 92
Barrington, Rutland 1853-1922 NewGrDO
Barrington, Samuel 1729-1800 WhAmRev
Barrington, Thomas Joseph 1916- WrDr 94
Barrington, William Wildman 1717-1793 WhAmRev
Barrington-Carlson, Sharyn Marie 1946- WhoMW 93
Barrington-Ward, Simon Who 94
Barrington-Ward, Simon 1930- IntWW 93
Barrio, Guilmo 1939- WhoHisp 94
Barrio, Jorge Raul 1941- WhoAm 94
Barrio, Raymond DrAPF 93
Barrio, Raymond 1921- WhoAm 94, WhoAmA 93, WhoHisp 94, WrDr 94
Barrio, Tony 1933- WhoHisp 94
Barrio-Garay, Jose Luis 1932- WhoAmA 93
Barrionuevo Pena, Jose 1942- IntWW 93
Barrios, Alfred Angel 1933- WhoHisp 94, WhoWest 94
Barrios, Benny Perez 1925- WhoAmA 93
Barrios, Larry, Jr. 1929- WhoHisp 94
Barrios, Zulma X. 1943- WhoHisp 94
Barrios de Chamorro, Violeta 1939- IntWW 93
Barris, Chuck WrDr 94
Barris, Chuck 1929- WhoHol 92
Barris, Harry d1962 WhoHol 92
Barriscale, Bessie d1965 WhoHol 92
Barritt, Evelyn Ruth Berryman 1929- WhoAm 94
Barritt, Gordon Emerson 1920- Who 94
Barriuso, Frank Raymond 1958- WhoMW 93
Barrnett, Russell Joffree 1920-1989 WhAm 10
Barro, Gregory John 1957- WhoAmP 93
Barro, Mary Helen 1938- WhoHisp 94, WhoWest 94
Barro, Robert Joseph 1944- WhoAm 94
Barroilhet, Paul(-Bernard) 1810-1871 NewGrDO
Barron, Almen Leo 1926- WhoAm 94
Barron, Arthur Ray 1934- IntMPA 94
Barron, Barbara Marilyn 1937- WhoAm 94
Barron, Baynes d1982 WhoHol 92
Barron, Bernie Garcia 1956- WhoHisp 94
Barron, Brian Munro 1940- Who 94
Barron, Bryton 1898- WhAm 10
Barron, Caroline 1958- WhoWest 94
Barron, Charles Elliott 1928- WhoAm 94
Barron, Charles Joel 1952- WhoMW 93
Barron, Charles Thomas 1950- WhoScEn 94
Barron, Clemente 1943- WhoHisp 94
Barron, D(onald) G(abriel) 1922- EncSF 93
Barron, David Henry 1953- WhoAmP 93
Barron, Dempsey James 1922- WhoAmP 93
Barron, Dennis H. 1940- WhoAm 94
Barron, Derek Donald 1929- IntWW 93, Who 94
Barron, Donald (James) 1921- Who 94
Barron, Donald James 1921- IntWW 93
Barron, Ernesto Alvarez 1946- WhoHisp 94
Barron, Francis Patrick 1951- WhoAm 94, WhoAmL 94
Barron, Frank WhoHol 92
Barron, Fred ConAu 41NR
Barron, Harold Sheldon 1936- WhoAm 94, WhoAmL 94, WhoFI 94
Barron, Howard Robert 1930- WhoAm 94
Barron, Iann Marchant 1936- Who 94
Barron, Ilona Eleanor 1929- WhoMW 93
Barron, James 1740-1787 AmRev, WhAmRev
Barron, James Turman 1954- WhoAm 94
Barron, Jerome Aure 1933- WhoAm 94, WhoAmL 94
Barron, John 1920- WhoHol 92
Barron, John C. WhoAmL 94
Barron, John Penrose 1934- IntWW 93, Who 94
Barron, Keith 1934- WhoHol 92
Barron, Keith Douglas 1956- WhoFI 94
Barron, Kevin John 1946- Who 94
Barron, Larry R. 1953- WhoAmL 94
Barron, Louis 1919-1990 WhAm 10
Barron, Lowell Ray 1942- WhoAmP 93
Barron, Marcus d1944 WhoHol 92
Barron, Martin George 1963- WhoWest 94
Barron, Myra Hymovich 1938- WhoAmL 94
Barron, (Richard) Neil 1934- EncSF 93
Barrón, Nelda L. 1964- WhoHisp 94
Barron, (Arthur) Oswald 1868-1939 DcNaB MP
Barron, Pamela Gursky 1943- WhoFI 94
Barron, Patrick Harold Falkiner 1911- Who 94
Barron, Peggy Pennisi 1958- WhoFI 94
Barron, Pepe 1937- WhoHisp 94
Barron, Purificacion C. 1932- WhoAsA 94
Barron, Randall Franklin 1936- WhoAm 94
Barron, Reginald WhoBlA 94
Barron, Richard Edward 1940- Who 94
Barron, (Thomas) Robert 1918- Who 94
Barron, Roberta 1940- WhoFI 94, WhoMW 93
Barron, Ronald Michael 1948- WhoScEn 94
Barron, Ros 1933- WhoAm 94, WhoAmA 93
Barron, Russell J. 1946- WhoAm 94
Barron, Stephanie 1950- WhoWest 94
Barron, Susan 1940- WhoAm 94, WhoScEn 94
Barron, Thomas 1949- WhoAmA 93
Barron, Wendell WhoBlA 94
Barron, William 1805-1891 DcNaB MP
Barrons, John Lawson 1932- Who 94
Barros, Dana Bruce 1967- WhoBlA 94
Barros, Henry 1960- WhoHisp 94
Barros, Teresa Leitao de BlmGWL
Barroso, Maria Alice 1926- BlmGWL
Barroux, Lucien d1968 WhoHol 92
Barrow, Arthur Ray 1959- WhoScEn 94
Barrow, Bernard d1993 NewYTBS 93
Barrow, Bernard 1927- ConTFT 11, WhoHol 92
Barrow, Bernard Gibbs 1937- WhoAmP 93
Barrow, Charles Herbert 1930- WhoAm 94
Barrow, Charles Wallace 1921- WhoAm 94
Barrow, Denise 1943- WhoBlA 94
Barrow, Frank Pearson, Jr. 1928- WhoAm 94
Barrow, G(eoffrey) W(allis) S(teuart) 1924- WrDr 94
Barrow, Geoffrey Ridley 1944- WhoMW 93
Barrow, Geoffrey Wallis Steuart 1924- Who 94
Barrow, Jocelyn (Anita) 1929- Who 94
Barrow, John 1764-1848 WhWE

Barrow, John D(avid) 1952- *WrDr 94*
Barrow, John Frederick 1918- *Who 94*
Barrow, John J. 1955- *WhoAmL 94*
Barrow, John Jenkins 1955- *WhoAmP 93*
Barrow, Kenneth 1945-1993 *ConAu 142*
Barrow, Lionel Ceon, Jr. 1926- *WhoAm 94, WhoBlA 94*
Barrow, Marilyn *GayLL*
Barrow, Mark Steven 1958- *WhoAmL 94*
Barrow, Michael Ernest 1932- *Who 94*
Barrow, Nita *Who 94, WhoWomW 91*
Barrow, (Ruth) Nita 1916- *Who 94*
Barrow, Richard John Uniacke 1933- *Who 94*
Barrow, Robert Earl 1930- *WhoAm 94*
Barrow, Robin (St. Clair) 1944- *WrDr 94*
Barrow, Ruth Nita *IntWW 93*
Barrow, Ruth Nita 1916- *WhoAm 94*
Barrow, Simon William 1942- *Who 94*
Barrow, Thomas Davies 1924- *WhoAm 94, WhoFI 94, WhoScEn 94*
Barrow, Thomas Francis 1938- *WhoAm 94, WhoAmA 93, WhoWest 94*
Barrow, Thomas Joe 1949- *WhoBlA 94*
Barrow, Ursula Helen 1955- *IntWW 93*
Barrow, William David, III 1955- *WhoMW 93*
Barrow, Willie T. 1924- *WhoBlA 94*
Barrowclough, Anthony (Richard) 1924- *Who 94*
Barrowclough, Anthony Richard 1924- *IntWW 93*
Barrowman, Mike *WhoAm 94*
Barrows, Anita *DrAPF 93*
Barrows, Bryan H., III 1952- *WhoBlA 94*
Barrows, Dan *WhoHol 92*
Barrows, Frank David *WhoAmP 93*
Barrows, Henry A. d1945 *WhoHol 92*
Barrows, James O. d1925 *WhoHol 92*
Barrows, Joseph Howard 1950- *WhoAmP 93*
Barrows, Richard Lee 1945- *WhoAm 94*
Barrows, Robert Guy 1926- *WhoWest 94*
Barrows, Robert L. 1948- *WhoAmL 94*
Barrows, Ronald Thomas 1954- *WhoAmL 94*
Barr-Sharrar, Beryl *WhoAmA 93*
Barrull, Agustin 1933- *WhoHisp 94*
Barrus, John Evan 1954- *WhoWest 94*
Barry, Allan Ronald 1945- *WhoFI 94*
Barry, Anne Meredith 1932- *WhoAmA 93*
Barry, Bert 1954- *WhoMW 93*
Barry, Brenda Elizabeth 1950- *WhoScEn 94*
Barry, Brian Michael 1936- *IntWW 93, Who 94*
Barry, Carole Joyce 1933- *WhoWest 94*
Barry, Christopher John 1947- *WhoAm 94*
Barry, Colman James 1921- *WhoAm 94*
Barry, Daniel 1928- *Who 94*
Barry, Dave *NewYTBS 93 [port], WhoAm 94*
Barry, Dave 1919- *WhoHol 92*
Barry, Dave 1947- *WrDr 94*
Barry, David Andrew 1941- *WhoAmL 94*
Barry, David Earl 1945- *WhoAm 94, WhoAmL 94*
Barry, David N., III *WhoFI 94*
Barry, David Walter 1943- *WhoScEn 94*
Barry, Desmond Thomas, Jr. 1945- *WhoAm 94, WhoAmL 94*
Barry, Don d1980 *WhoHol 92*
Barry, Donald Lee 1953- *WhoFI 94*
Barry, Edward *Who 94*
Barry, (Lawrence) Edward (Anthony Tress) 1939- *Who 94*
Barry, Edward Louis 1951- *WhoAmL 94*
Barry, Edward Norman 1920- *Who 94*
Barry, Edward William 1937- *IntWW 93, WhoAm 94*
Barry, Elizabeth 1658-1713 *BlmGEL*
Barry, Francis Julian, Jr. 1949- *WhoAm 94, WhoAmL 94*
Barry, Gene 1919- *IntMPA 94, WhoAm 94*
Barry, Gene 1921- *WhoHol 92*
Barry, Gerald 1952- *NewGrDO*
Barry, Henry Ford 1923- *WhoWest 94*
Barry, Herbert, III 1930- *ConAu 43NR, WhoAm 94*
Barry, Hilary D. *WhoAmP 93*
Barry, Hugh Collis 1912- *WrDr 94*
Barry, Ivor *WhoHol 92*
Barry, J. J. d1990 *WhoHol 92*
Barry, Jack *DrAPF 93*
Barry, Jack d1984 *WhoHol 92*
Barry, James Edward 1938- *Who 94*
Barry, James Michael 1956- *WhoWest 94*
Barry, James P. 1918- *WrDr 94*
Barry, James Paul 1953- *WhoWest 94*
Barry, James Potvin 1918- *WhoAm 94, WhoMW 93*
Barry, James Russell 1960- *WhoAmL 94*
Barry, Jan *DrAPF 93*
Barry, Jane 1925- *WrDr 94*
Barry, Janet Gail 1938- *WhoAmP 93*
Barry, Joan d1989 *WhoHol 92*
Barry, Joe d1974 *WhoHol 92*
Barry, John *WhoHol 92*
Barry, John 1745-1803 *AmRev, WhAmRev [port]*
Barry, John 1933- *ConTFT 11, IntDcF 2-4, IntMPA 94, IntWW 93*
Barry, John J. *WhoAm 94, WhoFI 94*
Barry, John J. 1940- *WhoAmL 94*
Barry, John Kevin 1925- *WhoAm 94*
Barry, John Reagan 1921- *WhoAm 94*
Barry, John Willard 1934- *WhoWest 94*
Barry, Jonathan B. 1945- *WhoAmP 93*
Barry, Lynda *WhoAm 94*
Barry, Lynda 1956- *WrDr 94*
Barry, Margaret Stuart 1927- *WrDr 94*
Barry, Marion S., Jr. 1936- *WhoAmP 93*
Barry, Marion Shepilov, Jr. 1936- *IntWW 93, WhoAm 94, WhoBlA 94*
Barry, Mary Alice 1928- *WhoAm 94*
Barry, Maryanne Trump 1937- *WhoAm 94, WhoAmL 94*
Barry, Michael Thomas 1945- *WhoAmP 93*
Barry, Michaela Marie 1960- *WhoAmL 94*
Barry, Mike 1939- *WrDr 94*
Barry, Miranda Robbins 1951- *ConTFT 11*
Barry, Neill 1965- *WhoHol 92*
Barry, Norman J., Jr. 1950- *WhoAm 94, WhoAmL 94*
Barry, P(atricia) S(teepee) 1926- *ConAu 140*
Barry, Patricia *WhoHol 92*
Barry, Patricia Pound 1941- *WhoAm 94*
Barry, (Noel) Patrick 1917- *Who 94*
Barry, Patrick Alan 1953- *WhoAmL 94*
Barry, Paul *WhoHol 92*
Barry, Peter 1928- *IntWW 93, Who 94*
Barry, Philip 1896-1949 *IntDcT 2*
Barry, Philip M. 1938- *WhoAmP 93*
Barry, Philip Semple 1923- *WhoAm 94*
Barry, Philip Stuart M. *Who 94*
Barry, Ray *EncSF 93*
Barry, Ray J. 1939- *WhoHol 92*
Barry, Richard Francis 1917- *WhoAm 94*
Barry, Richard Francis, III 1943- *WhoAm 94*
Barry, Richard Hugh 1908- *Who 94*
Barry, Richard William 1934- *WhoScEn 94*
Barry, Rick 1944- *BasBi, WhoAm 94, WhoWest 94*
Barry, Robert E. 1931- *WhoAmA 93*
Barry, Robert Everett 1931- *WrDr 94*
Barry, Robert L. 1934- *WhoAmP 93*
Barry, Robert Louis 1934- *WhoAm 94*
Barry, Robert Thomas 1936- *WhoAmA 93*
Barry, Roger Graham 1935- *WhoAm 94*
Barry, Sheila Anne *WrDr 94*
Barry, Spranger 1717?-1777 *BlmGEL*
Barry, Steve 1956- *WhoAmA 93*
Barry, Thomas Corcoran 1944- *WhoAm 94*
Barry, Thomas Hubert 1918- *WhoAm 94*
Barry, Thomas Joseph 1955- *WhoAmL 94*
Barry, Thomas M. 1949- *WhoAm 94, WhoFI 94*
Barry, Thomas Wayne 1950- *WhoMW 93*
Barry, Tom d1931 *WhoHol 92*
Barry, Tony *WhoHol 92*
Barry, Viola d1964 *WhoHol 92*
Barry, Vivian 1938- *WhoAmP 93*
Barry, Warren E. 1933- *WhoAmP 93*
Barry, Wesley 1906- *WhoHol 92*
Barry, William Garrett, III 1955- *WhoAm 94*
Barry, William H., Jr. 1930- *WhoAmL 94*
Barry, William Logan 1926- *WhoAmP 93*
Barry, William M. 1959- *WhoAmP 93*
Barry, William Parke 1940- *WhoAm 94*
Barrye, Emily d1957 *WhoHol 92*
Barrymoe, Ethel 1879-1959 *AmCulL*
Barrymore, Deborah 1963- *WhoHol 92*
Barrymore, Diana d1960 *WhoHol 92*
Barrymore, Drew *NewYTBS 93 [port]*
Barrymore, Drew 1975- *IntMPA 94, WhoHol 92*
Barrymore, Ethel d1959 *WhoHol 92*
Barrymore, Eugene d1984 *WhoHol 92*
Barrymore, John d1942 *WhoHol 92*
Barrymore, John 1882-1942 *AmCulL*
Barrymore, John Blyth 1954- *WhoHol 92*
Barrymore, John Drew 1932- *IntMPA 94*
Barrymore, John Drew, Jr. 1932- *WhoHol 92*
Barrymore, Lionel d1954 *WhoHol 92*
Barrymore, Lionel 1878-1954 *AmCulL*
Barrymore, William d1979 *WhoHol 92*
Barr Young, Gavin Neil 1939- *Who 94*
Bars, Itzhak 1943- *WhoWest 94*
Bars, Ivars John 1954- *WhoAmL 94*
Barsacq, Leon 1906-1969 *IntDcF 2-4*
Barsalona, Frank Samuel 1938- *WhoAm 94, WhoFI 94*
Barsalou, Yves 1932- *IntWW 93*
Barsam, Rene d1956 *WhoHol 92*
Barsamian, John Albert 1934- *WhoAmL 94*
Barsamian, Khajag Sarkis 1951- *WhoAm 94*
Barsan, Richard Emil 1945- *WhoWest 94*
Barsan, Robert Blake 1948- *WhoMW 93*
Barsano, Ron 1945- *WhoAmA 93*
Barsch, Wulf Erich 1943- *WhoAmA 93*
Barschall, Henry Herman 1915- *IntWW 93, WhoAm 94*
Barschel, Hans J. 1912- *WhoAmA 93*
Bar-Schwab, Muri 1947- *WhoWomW 91*
Barsdate, Mary Kathryn 1933- *WhoWest 94*
Barselou, Paul Edgar 1922- *WhoAm 94*
Barsh, Harry Edward, Jr. 1930- *WhoAmL 94*
Barshai, Rudolf Borisovich 1924- *IntWW 93, WhoAm 94*
Barshak, Edward Joel 1924- *WhoAmL 94*
Barshefsky, Charlene *WhoAmL 94*
Barshop, Samuel Edwin 1929- *WhoAm 94, WhoFI 94*
Barsi, Judith d1988 *WhoHol 92*
Barsi, Louis Michael 1941- *WhoFI 94*
Barsis, Edwin Howard 1940- *WhoWest 94*
Barski, Aleksander *NewGrDO*
Barskiy, Vladimir G. d1936 *WhoHol 92*
Barsky, Bernard *WhoAm 94*
Barsky, Leona Lynn 1958- *WhoAmL 94*
Barsky, Martin 1927- *WhoWest 94*
Barsness, Richard Webster 1935- *WhoAm 94*
Barsom, Valerie *WhoAmP 93*
Barsova, Valeriya Vladimirovna 1892-1967 *NewGrDO*
Barst, Fran *DrAPF 93*
Barstow, Josephine (Clare) 1940- *NewGrDO*
Barstow, Josephine Clare 1940- *IntWW 93, Who 94*
Barstow, Leon ElRoy 1940- *WhoWest 94*
Barstow, Stan 1928- *BlmGEL, DcLB 139 [port], Who 94*
Barstow, Stan(ley) 1928- *WrDr 94*
Bart, A. S. *Who 94*
Bart, Edward 1917- *WhoIns 94*
Bart, Jan d1971 *WhoHol 92*
Bart, Jill *DrAPF 93*
Bart, Lionel 1930- *IntWW 93, Who 94, WhoAm 94, WrDr 94*
Bart, Peter 1932- *IntMPA 94, WrDr 94*
Bart, Peter Benton 1932- *WhoAm 94*
Bart, Polly Turner 1944- *WhoAm 94*
Barta, Dorothy Elaine 1924- *WhoAmA 93*
Barta, Frank Rudolph, Sr. 1913- *WhoAm 94*
Barta, James Joseph 1940- *WhoAm 94, WhoAmL 94*
Barta, James Omer 1931- *WhoAm 94*
Barta, Josef c. 1746-1787 *NewGrDO*
Barta, Sharyn Levine 1952- *WhoWest 94*
Barta, Suzann 1956- *WhoMW 93*
Bartali, Antonio *NewGrDO*
Bartalini, C. Richard 1931- *WhoAm 94*
Bartay, Andras 1799-1854 *NewGrDO*
Barteau, John Frank 1928- *WhoAm 94*
Bartee, Darrell H. *DrAPF 93*
Bartee, Stephen William 1950- *WhoFI 94*
Bartee, Thomas Creson 1926- *WhoAm 94*
Bartek, Edward J. 1921- *WrDr 94*
Bartek, Gordon Luke 1925- *WhoScEn 94*
Bartek, Tom 1932- *WhoAmA 93*
Bartel, Arthur Gabriel 1934- *WhoWest 94*
Bartel, Eddie d1991 *WhoHol 92*
Bartel, Fred Frank 1917- *WhoAm 94*
Bartel, Harry Edward 1942- *WhoAmL 94*
Bartel, Paul *WhoHol 92*
Bartel, Paul 1938- *IntMPA 94*
Bartell, Anne *Who 94*
Bartell, George William d1993 *Who 94N*
Bartell, Gerald Aaron 1914-1990 *WhAm 10*
Bartell, Jeffrey Bruce 1943- *WhoAm 94, WhoAmL 94*
Bartell, Lawrence Sims 1923- *WhoAm 94*
Bartell, Richard d1967 *WhoHol 92*
Bartelle, Talmadge Louis *WhoBlA 94*
Bartels, Brian Desmond 1957- *WhoFI 94*
Bartels, Bruce Michael 1946- *WhoAm 94*
Bartels, Gerald Lee 1931- *WhoAm 94*
Bartels, Jean Ellen 1949- *WhoMW 93*
Bartels, Joachim Conrad 1938- *WhoFI 94*
Bartels, John Ries 1897- *WhoAm 94, WhoAmL 94*
Bartels, Juergen E. 1940- *WhoFI 94*
Bartels, Keith B. 1949- *WhoMW 93*
Bartels, Louis John d1932 *WhoHol 92*
Bartels, Millard 1905- *WhoAm 94*
Bartels, Phyllis Elaine 1930- *WhoAmA 93*
Bartels, Stanley Leonard 1927- *WhoAm 94*
Bartelski, Leslaw 1920- *IntWW 93*
Bartelsmeyer, Karl Louis 1941- *WhoFI 94*
Bartelstone, Rona Sue 1951- *WhoAm 94*
Bartelstone, Steven David 1947- *WhoAm 94*
Bartelt, Robert Louis, Jr. 1949- *WhoMW 93*
Bartemeier, Lee H(enry) 1895- *WhAm 10*
Bartenfelder, A. Joseph 1957- *WhoAmP 93*
Bartenstein, Louis 1946- *WhoIns 94*
Barter, James T. 1930- *WhoScEn 94*
Barter, John William, III 1946- *WhoAm 94*
Barter, Judith A. 1951- *WhoAmA 93*
Barter, Nicholas Arthur Beamish 1940- *Who 94*
Barter, Robert Henry 1913- *WhoAm 94*
Bartet, Julia d1941 *WhoHol 92*
Bartfield, Lewis Alan 1953- *WhoMW 93*
Barth, Alvin Ludwig, Jr. 1936- *WhoAmP 93*
Barth, Andrew Francis 1961- *WhoFI 94*
Barth, Belle d1971 *WhoHol 92*
Barth, Belle 1911-1971 *WhoCom*
Barth, Carolyn Lou 1936- *WhoScEn 94*
Barth, Charles Fredrik 1935- *WhoMW 93*
Barth, Charles John 1942- *WhoAmA 93*
Barth, David Keck 1943- *WhoAm 94*
Barth, David Victor 1942- *WhoScEn 94, WhoWest 94*
Barth, Delbert Sylvester 1925- *WhoAm 94, WhoScEn 94*
Barth, Earl E. 1901-1990 *WhAm 10*
Barth, Ed *WhoHol 92*
Barth, Elmer Ernest 1922- *WhoAm 94*
Barth, Else M. 1928- *IntWW 93*
Barth, Ernest 1926- *WhAm 10*
Barth, Frances 1946- *WhoAmA 93*
Barth, Frances D. 1946- *WhoAm 94*
Barth, (Thomas) Fredrik (Weybye) 1928- *IntWW 93*
Barth, Heinrich 1821-1865 *WhWE*
Barth, J(ohn) Robert 1931- *WrDr 94*
Barth, Jack Alexander 1946- *WhoAmA 93*
Barth, James Richard 1943- *WhoAm 94*
Barth, John *DrAPF 93*
Barth, John 1930- *IntWW 93*
Barth, John (Simmons) 1930- *EncSF 93, RfGShF, WrDr 94*
Barth, John Robert 1931- *WhoAm 94*
Barth, John Simmons 1930- *AmCulL [port], WhoAm 94*
Barth, Mark Harold 1951- *WhoAm 94, WhoAmL 94*
Barth, Markus 1915- *WrDr 94*
Barth, Max 1907- *WhoAm 94*
Barth, Michael Carl 1941- *WhoAm 94*
Barth, Norman Kenneth 1933- *WhoAm 94*
Barth, Richard 1931- *WhoAm 94*
Barth, Richard 1943- *WrDr 94*
Barth, Roger Vincent 1938- *WhoAm 94*
Barth, Rolf Frederick 1937- *WhoAm 94*
Barth, Steve 1964- *WhoAmP 93*
Barth, Tami Sue 1962- *WhoMW 93*
Barth, Timothy D. 1959- *WhoAmP 93*
Barth, Uta 1958- *WhoAmA 93*
Bartha, Denes 1908- *IntWW 93*
Bartha, Tibor 1912- *IntWW 93*
Barthe, Adrien (Grat-Norbert) 1828-1898 *NewGrDO*
Barthe, Richmond 1901-1989 *AfrAmAl 6 [port], WhoAmA 93N*
Bartheld, Thomas McCann 1957- *WhoAmL 94*
Barthelemon, Mrs. *NewGrDO*
Barthelemon, Francois Hippolyte 1741-1808 *NewGrDO*
Barthelemy, Sidney John 1942- *AfrAmAl 6 [port], WhoAm 94, WhoAmP 93, WhoBlA 94*
Barthelmas, Ned Kelton 1927- *WhoAm 94, WhoMW 93*
Barthelme, Donald 1907- *WhoAm 94*
Barthelme, Donald 1931-1989 *RfGShF, WhAm 10*
Barthelme, Donald 1933-1989 *EncSF 93*
Barthelme, Frederick 1943- *WrDr 94*
Barthelme, Steve(n) 1947- *WrDr 94*
Barthelmeh, Hans Adolf 1923- *IntWW 93*
Barthelmess, Richard d1963 *WhoHol 92*
Barthes, Roland 1915-1980 *BlmGEL*
Barthes, Roland (Gerard) 1915- *WrDr 94*
Barthold, Aubin K. 1945- *WhoAmL 94*
Barthold, Clementine B. 1921- *WhoAmL 94, WhoMW 93*
Barthold, Lionel Olav 1926- *WhoAm 94*
Bartholdson, John Robert 1944- *WhoAm 94*
Bartholet, Elizabeth 1940- *ConAu 141, WhoAm 94, WhoAmL 94*
Bartholet, Elizabeth Ives *WhoAmA 93*
Bartholin, Thomas 1616-1680 *WorScD*
Bartholomaus, Derek Charles 1969- *WhoMW 93*
Bartholomay, William C. 1928- *WhoAm 94, WhoFI 94, WhoIns 94*
Bartholome, Peter William 1893- *WhAm 10*
Bartholome, William Gibson 1944- *WhoMW 93*
Bartholomeusz, Dennis 1930- *WrDr 94*
Bartholomew, Agnes d1955 *WhoHol 92*
Bartholomew, Arthur Peck, Jr. 1918- *WhoAm 94, WhoFI 94*

Bartholomew, Barbara 1941- *EncSF 93*
Bartholomew, David John 1931- *Who 94*
Bartholomew, Donald Dekle 1929- *WhoFI 94, WhoMW 93, WhoScEn 94*
Bartholomew, Freddie 1924- *WhoHol 92*
Bartholomew, Freddie 1924-1992 *AnObit 1992*
Bartholomew, George Adelbert 1919- *WhoAm 94*
Bartholomew, Gilbert Alfred 1922- *WhoAm 94*
Bartholomew, Grant Newman 1952- *WhoWest 94*
Bartholomew, James 1950- *WrDr 94*
Bartholomew, Jean 1922-1991 *WrDr 94N*
Bartholomew, Jerri Lee 1958- *WhoWest 94*
Bartholomew, Lloyd Gibson 1921- *WhoAm 94*
Bartholomew, Reginald 1936- *IntWW 93, WhoAm 94, WhoAmP 93*
Bartholomew, Richard Alan 1958- *WhoMW 93*
Bartholomew, Richard William 1954- *WhoScEn 94*
Bartholomew, Summer 1955- *WhoHol 92*
Bartholomew, William Lee 1950- *WhoMW 93*
Bartholow, Steven Alan 1948- *WhoAmL 94*
Barth-Wehrenalp, Gerhard 1920- *WhoAm 94*
Barthwell, Jack Clinton, III 1950- *WhoBlA 94*
Bartilucci, Andrew Joseph 1922- *WhoAm 94*
Bartizal, Robert George 1932- *WhoAm 94*
Bartkowech, R. *DrAPF 93*
Bartkowiak, Andrzej 1950- *IntMPA 94*
Bartkowski, Eugene H. 1934- *WhoIns 94*
Bartkowski, William Patrick 1951- *WhoFI 94*
Bartkus, Edward Alfred 1957- *WhoWest 94*
Bartkus, Richard Anthony 1931- *WhoAm 94*
Bartkus, Robert Edward 1946- *WhoAmL 94*
Bartkus, Thomas Edward 1947- *WhoMW 93*
Bartky, Ian Robertson 1934- *WhoScEn 94*
Bartl, Frederick J. *WhoAm 94*
Bartlam, Dorothy 1908- *WhoHol 92*
Bartle, Annette Gruber *WhoAm 94*
Bartle, Dorothy Budd 1924- *WhoAmA 93*
Bartle, Emery Warness 1943- *WhoAm 94, WhoAmL 94*
Bartle, Harvey, III 1941- *WhoAm 94, WhoAmL 94*
Bartle, Robert Gardner 1927- *WhoAm 94*
Bartle, Ronald David 1929- *Who 94*
Bartleet, David Henry 1929- *Who 94*
Bartles-Smith, Douglas Leslie 1937- *Who 94*
Bartlett, Alan Claymore 1934- *WhoWest 94*
Bartlett, Alex 1937- *WhoAm 94, WhoMW 93*
Bartlett, Alice Brand 1950- *WhoMW 93*
Bartlett, Allen Lyman, Jr. 1929- *WhoAm 94*
Bartlett, Andrew Vincent Bramwell 1952- *Who 94*
Bartlett, Arthur Eugene 1933- *WhoAm 94, WhoFI 94*
Bartlett, Barry Thomas 1952- *WhoAmA 93*
Bartlett, Bennie 1927- *WhoHol 92*
See Also East Side Kids *WhoCom*
Bartlett, Bonnie 1929- *WhoHol 92*
Bartlett, Boyd C. 1925- *IntWW 93*
Bartlett, Bruce R(eeves) 1951- *WrDr 94*
Bartlett, Bruce Reeves 1951- *WhoAm 94*
Bartlett, Byron E. 1931- *WhoMW 93*
Bartlett, Cal *WhoHol 92*
Bartlett, Charles *Who 94*
Bartlett, (Harold) Charles 1921- *Who 94*
Bartlett, Charles Leffingwell 1921- *WhoAm 94*
Bartlett, Christopher E. 1944- *WhoAmA 93*
Bartlett, Christopher John 1931- *WrDr 94*
Bartlett, Clifford d1936 *WhoHol 92*
Bartlett, Clifford Adams, Jr. 1937- *WhoAm 94, WhoAmL 94*
Bartlett, Cody Blake 1939- *WhoAm 94*
Bartlett, D. Brook 1937- *WhoAm 94, WhoAmL 94, WhoMW 93*
Bartlett, Dana 1882-1957 *WhoAmA 93N*
Bartlett, David Carson 1944- *WhoAmP 93, WhoWest 94*
Bartlett, David Farnham 1938- *WhoAm 94*
Bartlett, Dede Thompson 1943- *WhoAm 94*
Bartlett, Desmond William 1931- *WhoAm 94*
Bartlett, Elise d1944 *WhoHol 92*
Bartlett, Elizabeth *DrAPF 93*
Bartlett, Elizabeth 1924- *WrDr 94*
Bartlett, Elizabeth Easton 1937- *WhoScEn 94*
Bartlett, Elizabeth Susan 1927- *WhoAm 94*
Bartlett, Elsa Jaffe 1935- *WhoScEn 94*
Bartlett, Eric Bruce 1959- *WhoMW 93*
Bartlett, Eric George 1920- *ConAu 41NR, WrDr 94*
Bartlett, Fred Michael Pearce 1957- *WhoScEn 94*
Bartlett, Fred Stewart 1905-1988 *WhoAmA 93N*
Bartlett, Gene Ebert 1910-1989 *WhAm 10*
Bartlett, George Robert 1944- *Who 94*
Bartlett, George Shepstone 1931- *IntWW 93*
Bartlett, Gerald Lloyd 1939- *WhoMW 93*
Bartlett, Gordon E. 1926- *WhoAmP 93*
Bartlett, Hall d1993 *NewYTBS 93 [port]*
Bartlett, Hall 1925- *IntMPA 94*
Bartlett, Hall 1929- *WhoAm 94, WhoFI 94, WhoWest 94*
Bartlett, Henry Francis 1916- *Who 94*
Bartlett, James Lowell, III 1945- *WhoAm 94*
Bartlett, James Williams 1926- *WhoAm 94*
Bartlett, James Wilson, III 1946- *WhoAm 94, WhoAmL 94*
Bartlett, Jeffrey Stanton 1962- *WhoScEn 94*
Bartlett, Jennifer 1941- *IntWW 93*
Bartlett, Jennifer Losch 1941- *WhoAm 94, WhoAmA 93, WrDr 94*
Bartlett, Joe 1926- *WhoAmP 93*
Bartlett, John (Hardington) 1938- *Who 94*
Bartlett, John B. 1938- *WhoAmL 94*
Bartlett, John Bruen 1941- *WhoAm 94*
Bartlett, John Laurence 1942- *WhoAm 94, WhoAmL 94*
Bartlett, John Leonard 1926- *Who 94*
Bartlett, John Vernon 1927- *IntWW 93, Who 94*
Bartlett, John Wesley 1935- *WhoAm 94*
Bartlett, Joseph Warren 1933- *WhoAm 94*
Bartlett, Josiah 1729-1795 *AmRev, WhAmRev*
Bartlett, Lee *DrAPF 93*
Bartlett, Leonard Lee 1930- *WhoAm 94*
Bartlett, Lynn Conant 1921- *WhoAm 94*
Bartlett, Margaret Paige 1940- *WhoMW 93*
Bartlett, Martine 1925- *WhoHol 92*
Bartlett, Mary d1789 *BlmGWL*
Bartlett, Mary 1940- *WhoAmP 93*
Bartlett, Maurice Stevenson 1910- *Who 94*
Bartlett, Michael 1903- *WhoHol 92*
Bartlett, Michael John 1943- *WhoAm 94, WhoAmL 94*
Bartlett, Michael R. 1948- *WhoIns 94*
Bartlett, Neil 1932- *IntWW 93, Who 94, WhoAm 94, WhoWest 94*
Bartlett, Neil 1958- *ConDr 93, GayLL*
Bartlett, Oliver Richard 1945- *WhoAmP 93*
Bartlett, Paul Dana, Jr. 1919- *WhoAm 94, WhoMW 93*
Bartlett, Paul Doughty 1907- *IntWW 93, WhoAm 94, WhoScEn 94*
Bartlett, Peter Greenough 1930- *WhoFI 94, WhoMW 93, WhoScEn 94*
Bartlett, Randolph W. 1954- *WhoScEn 94*
Bartlett, Richard 1935- *WhoAm 94*
Bartlett, Richard James 1926- *WhoAm 94*
Bartlett, Richard Wrelton 1939- *WhoWest 94*
Bartlett, Richmond Jay 1927- *WhoAm 94*
Bartlett, Robert John 1950- *WhoAm 94*
Bartlett, Robert Perry, Jr. 1938- *WhoAm 94*
Bartlett, Robert Watkins 1933- *WhoAm 94, WhoScEn 94, WhoWest 94*
Bartlett, Robert Webster 1922-1979 *WhoAmA 93N*
Bartlett, Robert William 1941- *WhoAmL 94, WhoMW 93*
Bartlett, Roger Danforth 1949- *WhoMW 93*
Bartlett, Roscoe *WhoAmP 93*
Bartlett, Roscoe 1926- *WhoAm 94*
Bartlett, Roscoe G. 1926- *CngDr 93*
Bartlett, Ruhl Jacob 1897- *WhAm 10*
Bartlett, Sarah 1955- *ConAu 140*
Bartlett, Scott 1943-1990 *WhoAmA 93N*
Bartlett, Shirley Anne 1933- *WhoMW 93*
Bartlett, Steve 1947- *WhoAm 94, WhoAmP 93*
Bartlett, Steven Thade 1962- *WhoWest 94*
Bartlett, Sue 1947- *WhoAmP 93*
Bartlett, Susan J. 1946- *WhoAmP 93*
Bartlett, Thomas c. 1490-1555 *DcNaB MP*
Bartlett, Thomas Alva 1930- *WhoAm 94, WhoWest 94*
Bartlett, Thomas F. 1918- *WhoFI 94*
Bartlett, Thomas Henry 1931- *WhoWest 94*
Bartlett, Vernon (Oldfield) 1894-1983 *EncSF 93*
Bartlett, Walter E. 1928- *WhoAm 94, WhoMW 93*
Bartlett, William McGillivray 1932- *WhoAm 94*
Bartlett, William S., Jr. 1930- *WhoAmP 93*
Bartlett Diaz, Manuel 1936- *IntWW 93*
Bartlette, Donald Lloyd 1939- *WhoMW 93*
Bartley, Brian Scott 1969- *WhoAmP 93*
Bartley, Burnett Graham, Jr. 1924- *WhoAm 94*
Bartley, David Michael 1935- *WhoAmP 93*
Bartley, Diana Esther Pelaez Rivera 1940- *WhoMW 93*
Bartley, John C. *WhoAmP 93*
Bartley, Lester Maylon 1945- *WhoFI 94*
Bartley, Murray Hill 1933- *WhoWest 94*
Bartley, Opelene 1924- *WhoWest 94*
Bartley, Robert LeRoy 1937- *WhoAm 94, WhoFI 94*
Bartley, Roger David 1945- *WhoWest 94*
Bartley, Sherry P. 1942- *WhoAmL 94*
Bartley, Talmadge O. 1920- *WhoBlA 94*
Bartley, Thomas Lee 1942- *WhoScEn 94*
Bartley, William Raymond 1944- *WhoBlA 94*
Bartling, John Bram, Jr. 1957- *WhoFI 94*
Bartling, Judd Quenton 1936- *WhoWest 94*
Bartling, Theodore Charles 1922- *WhoAm 94*
Bartling, Wayne Earl *WhoAmP 93*
Bartlit, Fred Holcomb, Jr. 1932- *WhoAm 94*
Bartlo, Sam D. 1919- *WhoAm 94*
Bartman, John Gaylord 1950- *WhoMW 93*
Bartman, Robert E. *WhoAm 94*
Bartnick, Harry William 1950- *WhoAmA 93*
Bartnicki, Stanley Thomas 1933- *WhoAmL 94*
Bartnicki-Garcia, Salomon 1935- *WhoAm 94*
Bartnik, Jerry C. 1943- *WhoAmP 93*
Bartnikas, Ray 1936- *WhoAm 94*
Bartnoff, Judith 1949- *WhoAm 94, WhoAmL 94*
Barto, Charles O., Jr. 1946- *WhoAmL 94*
Barto, Morris L. 1948- *WhoIns 94*
Bartocha, Bodo 1928- *WhoAm 94*
Bartoe, Otto Edwin, Jr. 1927- *WhoAm 94*
Bartok, Bela 1881-1945 *IntDcB*
Bartok, Bela (Viktor Janos) 1881-1945 *NewGrDO*
Bartok, Eva 1926- *WhoHol 92*
Bartok, William 1930- *WhoAm 94*
Bartol, Ernest Thomas 1946- *WhoAmL 94, WhoFI 94*
Bartol, George E., III 1921- *WhAm 10*
Bartol, Walter W. 1931- *WhoWest 94*
Bartold, Norman *WhoHol 92*
Bartoletti, Bruno 1926- *NewGrDO, WhoAm 94*
Bartoletti, Karen J. 1948- *WhoAmL 94*
Bartoli, Cecilia *NewYTBS 93 [port]*
Bartoli, Cecilia 1966- *NewGrDO, News 94-1 [port]*
Bartoli, Cecilia 1967- *WhoAm 94*
Bartoli, Diane S. 1938- *WhoFI 94*
Bartoli, Renato Pompeo 1946- *WhoWest 94*
Bartolini, Anthony Louis 1931- *WhoAm 94*
Bartolini, Kathleen Barry 1947- *WhoAmP 93*
Bartolini, Robert Alfred 1942- *WhoAm 94*
Bartolo, Adolph Marion 1929- *WhoAm 94, WhoFI 94*
Bartolo, Donna M. 1941- *WhoAm 94, WhoFI 94, WhoScEn 94*
Bartolome, Joseph S. 1939- *WhoFI 94*
Bartolome de Roxas, Juan *ConAu 41NR*
Bartolone, Joseph Francis, Sr. 1929- *WhoAm 94*
Bartolozzi, Bruno 1911-1980 *NewGrDO*
Bartolozzi, James Joseph 1954- *WhoAmL 94*
Bartolucci, Luis A. 1946- *WhoHisp 94*
Barton, Alan Joel 1938- *WhoAm 94*
Barton, Alan Raymond 1925- *WhAm 10*
Barton, Allen Hoisington 1924- *WhoAm 94*
Barton, Ann Elizabeth 1923- *WhoFI 94, WhoWest 94*
Barton, Anne *Who 94*
Barton, Anne 1933- *IntWW 93*
Barton, (Barbara) Anne 1933- *Who 94*
Barton, Bernard Alan, Jr. 1948- *WhoAm 94, WhoAmL 94*
Barton, Buzz d1980 *WhoHol 92*
Barton, C. Robert 1926- *WhoAm 94*
Barton, Carl P. 1916- *WhoAm 94*
Barton, Charles d1981 *WhoHol 92*
Barton, Clara 1821-1912 *DcAmReB 2, HisWorL [port], WomPubS*
Barton, Clarissa Harlowe 1821-1912 *AmSocL [port]*
Barton, Cole 1946- *WhoScEn 94*
Barton, David Knox 1927- *WhoAm 94*
Barton, David M. 1939- *WhoWest 94*
Barton, Derek Harold Richard 1918- *IntWW 93, Who 94, WhoAm 94, WhoScEn 94*
Barton, Dora d1966 *WhoHol 92*
Barton, Eric Walter 1928- *Who 94*
Barton, Erle *EncSF 93*
Barton, Erle 1935- *WrDr 94*
Barton, Ernesto F. 1930- *WhoHisp 94*
Barton, Erwin W. 1931- *WhoAmP 93*
Barton, Evan Mansfield 1903- *WhoAm 94*
Barton, Francis Christopher 1916- *Who 94*
Barton, Frederick 1949- *WhoAmP 93*
Barton, Fredrick *DrAPF 93*
Barton, Fredrick (Preston) 1948- *ConAu 43NR*
Barton, Gail Melinda 1937- *WhoAm 94*
Barton, George C. d1955 *WhoHol 92*
Barton, Georgie Read *WhoAmA 93*
Barton, Gerald Gaylord 1931- *WhoFI 94*
Barton, Gerald Lee 1934- *WhoAm 94*
Barton, Grant Ennes 1940- *WhoWest 94*
Barton, Greg *WhoAm 94*
Barton, Henry David 1944- *WhoScEn 94*
Barton, Homer d1935 *WhoHol 92*
Barton, Jacqueline K. 1952- *WhoAm 94*
Barton, James *EncSF 93*
Barton, James d1962 *WhoHol 92*
Barton, James 1938- *WrDr 94*
Barton, James Cary 1940- *WhoAmL 94*
Barton, James Clifton 1925- *WhoAmL 94*
Barton, James Clyde, Jr. 1945- *WhoScEn 94*
Barton, James Miller 1942- *WhoAm 94*
Barton, Janice Sweeny 1939- *WhoMW 93*
Barton, Jay 1922- *WhoAm 94*
Barton, Jean Marie 1945- *WhoAm 94*
Barton, Jerry O'Donnell 1947- *WhoAm 94*
Barton, Jill(ian) 1940- *SmATA 75 [port]*
Barton, Joan d1977 *WhoHol 92*
Barton, Joan Chi-Hung Lo 1944- *WhoFI 94*
Barton, Joe d1937 *WhoHol 92*
Barton, Joe 1949- *CngDr 93*
Barton, Joe Linus 1949- *WhoAm 94, WhoAmP 93*
Barton, John 1789-1852 *DcNaB MP*
Barton, John 1946- *WhoIns 94*
Barton, John 1948- *Who 94*
Barton, John Bernard Adie 1928- *IntWW 93, Who 94*
Barton, John Greenwood *Who 94*
Barton, (Charles) John Greenwood 1936 *Who 94*
Barton, John Hays 1936- *WhoAm 94*
Barton, John Murray 1921- *WhoAmA 93*
Barton, Jon 1938- *WrDr 94*
Barton, Larry d1990 *WhoHol 92*
Barton, Laurence 1956- *WhoWest 94*
Barton, Lee *EncSF 93*
Barton, Lee 1935- *WrDr 94*
Barton, Lewis 1940- *WhoAm 94, WhoFI 94*
Barton, Lyndon O'Dowd *WhoScEn 94*
Barton, Margaret *Who 94N*
Barton, Margaret 1926- *WhoHol 92*
Barton, Mark Quayle 1928- *WhoAm 94, WhoScEn 94*
Barton, Mary d1970 *WhoHol 92*
Barton, Meta Packard 1928- *WhoAm 94, WhoScEn 94*
Barton, Nelda Ann Lambert 1929- *WhoAm 94, WhoAmP 93*
Barton, Nick 1944- *WhoScEn 94*
Barton, Otis *WorInv*
Barton, Paul Booth, Jr. 1930- *WhoAm 94*
Barton, Peter Richard, III 1950- *WhoAm 94, WhoWest 94*
Barton, Phyllis Settecase 1934- *WhoAmA 93*
Barton, Raymond Oscar, III 1949- *WhoFI 94*
Barton, Rhonda L. 1966- *WhoBlA 94*
Barton, Robert L., Jr. 1943- *WhoAmL 94*
Barton, Roger 1945- *Who 94*
Barton, Russell William 1923- *WhoAm 94, WhoScEn 94*
Barton, S.W. *EncSF 93*
Barton, Samuel *EncSF 93*
Barton, Stanley Faulkner 1927- *WhoAm 94*
Barton, Stephen Howard 1951- *WhoWest 94*
Barton, Terry Charlene 1949- *WhoAm 94*
Barton, Thomas Jackson 1940- *WhoAm 94*
Barton, Thomas L. 1942- *WhoAmL 94*
Barton, Thomas O. 1950- *WhoAmL 94*

Barton, Thomas Pennant 1803-1869 DcLB 140 [port]
Barton, Timothy Winton 1938- WhoAmL 94
Barton, (Samuel) Wayne 1944- WrDr 94
Barton, Wayne Darrell 1961- WhoBlA 94
Barton, William 1740-1831 AmRev
Barton, William 1748-1831 WhAmRev [port]
Barton, William Arnold 1948- WhoAmL 94
Barton, William Blackburn 1899- WhoAm 94
Barton, William Elliott 1956- WhoScEn 94
Barton, William Henry, II 1921- WhoWest 94
Barton, William L. 1939- WhoAmP 93
Barton, William R(enald, III) 1950- EncSF 93
Barton, William Russell 1925- WhoAm 94
Barton, William Thomas 1933- WhoAmP 93
Barton-Chapple, Dorothy Who 94
Bartoo, Richard Kieth 1938- WhoScEn 94
Bartos, Jerry WhoAmP 93
Bartos, Jerry Garland 1933- WhoFI 94
Bartosch, Charles d1967 WhoHol 92
Bartosek, Karel 1930- IntWW 93
Bartosic, Florian 1926- WhoAm 94
Bartosik, Josef C. 1917- Who 94
Bartoszcze, Roman Boleslaw 1946- IntWW 93
Bartov, Omer 1954- WrDr 94
Bartow, Gene 1931- BasBi
Bartow, Jerome E. WhoIns 94
Bartow, Jerome Edward WhoBlA 94
Bartow, Randy David 1951- WhoAm 94
Bartow, Thomas Mack 1949- WhoAm 94
Bartram, Gus d1951 WhoHol 92
Bartram, John 1699-1777 WhWE
Bartram, Ralph Herbert 1929- WhoAm 94
Bartram, William 1739-1823 WhWE [port]
Bartruff, Robert David 1927- WhoAmP 93
Bartsch, David Leo 1953- WhoScEn 94
Bartsch, Dirk-Uwe Guenther 1965- WhoScEn 94
Bartscherer, Joseph 1954- WhoAmA 93
Barttelot, Brian Walter de Stopham 1941- Who 94
Bartter, Brit Jeffrey 1949- WhoAm 94, WhoFI 94, WhoMW 93
Bartter, Martha Ann 1932- WhoMW 93
Bartunek, James Scott 1962- WhoMW 93
Bartunek, Joseph Wenceslaus 1924- WhoAm 94, WhoAmL 94
Bartunek, Robert Richard 1914- WhoAm 94
Bartunek, Robert Richard, Jr. 1946- WhoAmL 94
Barturen Duenas 1936- IntWW 93
Bartus, Raymond Thomas 1947- WhoAm 94
Bartusis, Constance DrAPF 93
Bartusis, Mark Charles 1953- WhoMW 93
Bart-Williams, Gaston 1938- BlkWr 2
Barty, Billy 1925- WhoHol 92
Barty, Jack d1943 WhoHol 92
Bartz, Albert 1933- WrDr 94
Bartz, David John 1955- WhoAmL 94
Bartz, James Ross 1942- WhoAmA 93
Bartz, Mary Russo WhoAm 94
Bartz, Merlin E. 1961- WhoAmP 93
Barucci, Piero 1933- IntWW 93
Baruch, Anne WhoAmA 93
Baruch, Eduard 1907- WhoAm 94
Baruch, Hurd 1937- WhoAm 94
Baruch, Jordan Jay 1923- WhoAm 94
Baruch, Ralph M. 1923- IntMPA 94, WhoAm 94
Baruch, Ruth-Marion Evelyn 1922- WhoAmA 93, WhoWest 94
Barun, Kenneth Lee 1948- WhoMW 93
Barusch, Lawrence Roos 1949- WhoAmL 94
Barusch, Ronald Charles 1953- WhoAm 94
Barut, Asim Orhan 1926- WhoAm 94, WhoWest 94
Barve, Kumar P. 1958- WhoAmP 93, WhoAsA 94
Barville, Rebecca Penelope 1936- WhoWest 94
Barwell, Cindy Ann 1957- WhoAmL 94
Barwell, David John Frank 1938- Who 94
Barwick, David Robert 1927- Who 94
Barwick, Garfield (Edward John) 1903- Who 94
Barwick, Garfield Edward John 1903- IntWW 93
Barwick, Jane Cook 1954- WhoAmL 94
Barwick, JoAnn R. WhoAm 94
Barwick, Plato Collins, Jr. 1937- WhoAmP 93
Barwig, Regis Norbert James 1932- WhoAm 94
Barwin, Thomas William 1954- WhoMW 93
Barwood, Frances WhoAmP 93
Barwood, Hal IntMPA 94
Barwood, Lee DrAPF 93
Bary, Alfred von 1873-1926 NewGrDO
Bary, Leon d1954 WhoHol 92
Barykova, Anna Pavlovna 1839-1893 BlmGWL
Baryshnikov, Mikhail 1948- IntDcB [port], IntMPA 94, IntWW 93, Who 94, WhoAm 94, WhoHol 92
Baryshnikov, Mikhail (Nikolayevich) 1948- WrDr 94
Barz, Diane G. WhoAmP 93
Barz, Richard L. 1955- WhoScEn 94
Barza, Harold A. 1952- WhoAm 94, WhoAmL 94
Barzdukas, Robert Charles 1944- WhoWest 94
Barzel, Amnon 1935- IntWW 93
Barzel, Rainer 1924- IntWW 93
Barzel, Rainer C. 1924- Who 94
Barzelay, Douglas E. WhoAmL 94
Barzelay, Walter Moshe 1914- WrDr 94
Barzell, Wolfe d1969 WhoHol 92
Barzey, Raymond Clifford, II WhoBlA 94
Barzilai, Miriam Eva 1952- WhoMW 93
Barzilay, Isaac Eisenstein 1915- WhoAm 94
Barzman, Ben 1912- WrDr 94
Barzman, Ben 1912-1989 EncSF 93
Barzman, Ben Frank 1910-1989 WhAm 10
Barzun, Jacques 1907- IntWW 93, Who 94, WhoAm 94, WhoAmA 93, WrDr 94
Barzune, Dolores 1939- WhoHisp 94
Basabarajeswari, S.M.T. 1928- WhoWomW 91
Basaldella, Afro 1912- IntWW 93
Basang 1937- IntWW 93
Basang 1938- WhoPRCh 91 [port]
Basappa, Shivanand 1954- WhoScEn 94
Basar, Ronald John 1950- WhoScEn 94
Basar, Sukufe Nihal 1896-1973 BlmGWL
Basar, Tamer 1946- WhoAm 94
Basar, Tangul Unerdem 1951- WhoScEn 94
Basaraba, Gary WhoHol 92
Basarah, Saleh 1928- Who 94
Basaran, Osman A. 1956- WhoScEn 94
Basargin, Grigory Gavrilovich dc. 1853 WhWE
Basart, John Philip 1938- WhoAm 94
Basavanhally, Nagesh Ramamoorthy 1952- WhoScEn 94
Basbas, Monte George 1921- WhoAmL 94
Bascaran, Ermogene Imleghi NewGrDO
Basch, Buddy 1922- IntMPA 94
Basch, David WhoAm 94, WhoFI 94
Basch, Ernst d1980 WhoHol 92
Basch, Felix d1944 WhoHol 92
Basch, Michael Franz WrDr 94
Basch, Michael Franz 1929- WhoScEn 94
Basch, Paul Frederick 1933- WhoAm 94
Basci, Joseph Ronald 1948- WhoAmP 93
Bascom, C. Perry 1936- WhoAm 94
Bascom, Earl W. 1906- WhoAmA 93
Bascom, Earl Wesley 1906- WhoAm 94, WhoWest 94
Bascom, Harold A(dolphus) 1951- WrDr 94
Bascom, John G. 1943- WhoAm 94, WhoFI 94
Bascom, Lester William 1954- WhoFI 94
Bascom, Perry Bagnall 1924- WhoAm 94
Bascom, Ruth F. 1926- WhoAmP 93
Bascom, Willard Newell 1916- WhoAm 94, WhoScEn 94
Bascombe, Ronald D. DrAPF 93
Basconcillo, Lindy 1943- WhoWest 94
Bascope, Marisa 1958- WhoAmL 94
Bas Csatary, Laszlo Kalman 1923- WhoScEn 94
Basden, Barbara Holz 1940- WhoWest 94
Basden, Cameron WhoAm 94
Base, Graeme (Rowland) 1958- WrDr 94
Base, Graeme Rowland 1958- WhoAm 94
Basefsky, Stuart Mark 1949- WhoAmL 94
Baseggio, Lorenzo c. 1660-1715? NewGrDO
Basehart, Jackie WhoHol 92
Basehart, Richard d1984 WhoHol 92
Basehead ConMus 11 [port]
Basel, Edward Douglas 1947- WhoAmL 94
Basel, Frances Rita 1933- WhoMW 93
Baseleon, Michael d1986 WhoHol 92
Baselitz, Georg 1938- IntWW 93
Baselt, Randall Clint 1944- WhoAm 94, WhoScEn 94
Baserga, Renato Luigi 1925- WhoAm 94
Baserva, Guillermo WhoHisp 94
Basevi, Abramo 1818-1885 NewGrDO
Basevi, Giorgio 1938- IntWW 93
Basevi, James 1890-1943 IntDcF 2-4
Basey, Glen Robert 1942- WhoAm 94
Basey, Ovetta T. 1920- WhoBlA 94
Basford, James Orlando 1931- WhoFI 94, WhoMW 93
Basford, Madaline Lee d1974 WhoHol 92
Basford, Robert Eugene 1923- WhoAm 94
Basford, (Stanley) Ronald 1932- IntWW 93
Bash, Charles Dayton 1949- WhoAmL 94
Bash, Frank N(ess) 1937- WrDr 94
Bash, Frank Ness 1937- WhoAm 94, WhoScEn 94
Bash, James Francis 1925- WhoAm 94
Bash, Philip Edwin 1921- WhoAm 94
Bash, Roy 1949- WhoAmL 94
Bash, Yigal Amir 1938- WhoAm 94
Basham, Brian Arthur 1943- Who 94
Basham, Debra Ann 1960- WhoAm 94
Basham, Terry 1953- WhoAmP 93
Basham-Tooker, Janet Brooks 1919- WhoAm 94, WhoScEn 94
Bashara, Nicolas Mitchell 1917- WhoMW 93
Basharmal, Khodaidad 1945- IntWW 93
Bashashkin, Anatoly Vasilevich 1924- LoBiDrD
Bashaw, Matthew Charles 1963- WhoScEn 94
Bashe, Gilbert Gregg 1954- WhoAm 94
Bashe, Philip (Scott) 1954- WrDr 94
Basher, Mick See X ConMus 11
Bashford, Humphrey John Charles 1920- Who 94
Bashford, James Adney, Jr. 1948- WhoScEn 94
Bashful, Emmett W. 1917- WhoBlA 94
Bashias, Norman Jack 1962- WhoScEn 94
Bashinski, Leonard C. 1943- WhoIns 94
Bashir, Nabil Ahmad 1954- WhoScEn 94
Bashir, Naheed 1937- WhoWest 94
Bashir, Omar Hassan Ahmad al- IntWW 93
Bashiri, Iraj 1940- WhoMW 93
Bashkin, Lloyd Scott 1951- WhoFI 94
Bashkirtseff, Marie 1858-1884 BlmGWL
Bashkirtseva, Mariia Konstantinovna BlmGWL
Bashkow, Theodore Robert 1921- WhoAm 94
Bashmakov, Lev Polievktovich 1938- LoBiDrD
Bashmakov, Pyotr fl. 175-?- WhWE
Bashmet, Yuri Abramovich 1953- IntWW 93
Bashook, Philip G. 1943- WhoAm 94
Bashor, John W. 1926- WhoAmA 93
Bashore, George Willis 1934- WhoAm 94
Bashwiner, Steven Lacelle 1941- WhoAm 94, WhoAmL 94
Basich, Bob WhoAmP 93
Basichis, Gordon Allen 1947- WhoWest 94
Basie, Count d1984 WhoHol 92
Basie, William 1904-1984 AfrAmAl 6 [port]
Basil, II 957-1025 HisWorL [port]
Basil, Douglas Constantine 1923- WhoAm 94
Basil, Otto 1901-1983 EncSF 93
Basil, Toni 1948- WhoHol 92
Basil, de, Colonel IntDcB
Basile, Adriana c. 1590-c. 1640 NewGrDO
Basile, Joseph John, Jr. 1952- WhoAmL 94
Basile, Louis d1984 WhoHol 92
Basile, Marjory G. 1941- WhoAmL 94
Basile, Michael 1948- WhoAm 94
Basile, Neal Fahr 1944- WhoAm 94
Basile, Paul Louis, Jr. 1945- WhoAm 94, WhoAmL 94, WhoFI 94, WhoWest 94
Basile, Richard Emanuel 1921- WhoAm 94
Basile, Thomas Paul 1935- WhoFI 94
Basili, Basilio 1803-c. 1895 NewGrDO
Basili, Francesco 1767-1850 NewGrDO
Basilides, Maria 1886-1946 NewGrDO
Basilier, Erik Nils 1947- WhoScEn 94
Basilio, Eleanor Vasco 1961- WhoWest 94
Basilone, Peter J. 1920- WhoAmP 93
Basin, Efim Vladimirovich 1940- LoBiDrD
Basing, Baron 1939- Who 94
Basinger, Jeanine (Deyling) 1936- WrDr 94
Basinger, Kim 1953- IntMPA 94, IntWW 93, WhoAm 94, WhoHol 92
Basinger, Richard Lee 1941- WhoAmL 94, WhoWest 94
Basinger, William Daniel 1952- WhoScEn 94
Basingstoke, Archdeacon of Who 94
Basingstoke, Bishop Suffragan of Who 94
Basinski, Anthony Joseph 1947- WhoAm 94, WhoAmL 94
Basinski, Michael DrAPF 93
Basinski, Zbigniew Stanislaw 1928- IntWW 93, Who 94, WhoAm 94
Basiola, Mario 1892-1965 NewGrDO
Basir, Ismail 1927- IntWW 93
Baska, James Louis 1927- WhoAm 94
Baskcomb, A. W. d1939 WhoHol 92
Baskcomb, Betty WhoHol 92
Baskcomb, John 1916- WhoHol 92
Baskcomb, Lawrence d1962 WhoHol 92
Baske, C. Alan 1927- WhoFI 94, WhoMW 93
Basken, Reginald C. 1937- WhoAm 94
Basker, Robin Michael 1936- Who 94
Baskervill, Charles Thornton 1953- WhoAmL 94
Baskerville, Charles 1896- WhAm 10, WhoAmA 93
Baskerville, Charles Alexander 1928- WhoAm 94, WhoBlA 94, WhoScEn 94
Baskerville, Pearl 1929- WhoBlA 94
Baskerville, Penelope Anne 1946- WhoBlA 94
Baskerville, Randolph 1949- WhoBlA 94
Baskerville, Samuel J., Jr. 1933- WhoBlA 94
Baskervyle-Glegg, John 1940- Who 94
Baskett, James d1948 WhoHol 92
Baskett, Jason Wells 1953- WhoWest 94
Baskett, Kenneth Gerald 1942- WhoBlA 94
Baskett, Thomas Sebree 1916- WhoAm 94
Baskette, Ernest E., Jr. 1944- WhoBlA 94
Baskette, F. Kenneth, Jr. 1940- WhoAmP 93
Baskette, Roger DuVal, Sr. 1924- WhoAmL 94
Baskharone, Erian Aziz 1947- WhoScEn 94
Baskin, Andrew Lewis 1951- WhoBlA 94
Baskin, Charles Richard 1926- WhoFI 94
Baskin, Clarence L. 1927- WhoBlA 94
Baskin, David Stuart 1952- WhoAm 94
Baskin, Leland Burleson 1952- WhoAm 94
Baskin, Leonard 1922- WhoAm 94, WhoAmA 93
Baskin, Ronald Joseph 1935- WhoAm 94
Baskin, Scott David 1953- WhoAm 94, WhoAmL 94
Baskin, Stuart J. 1950- WhoAm 94
Baskin, Stuart Jay 1950- WhoAmL 94
Baskin, William Maxwell, Sr. 1921- WhoAmL 94
Baskin, Yvonne E. 1951- WhoBlA 94
Baskind, Stephen L. 1950- WhoAmL 94
Baskins, Lewis C. 1932- WhoBlA 94
Basler, John Michell 1926- WhoWest 94
Basler, Marianne WhoHol 92
Basler, Richard Alan 1939- WhoWest 94
Basler, Sabra DrAPF 93
Basler, Thomas G. 1940- WhoAm 94
Basmajian, John Varoujan 1921- WhoAm 94, WhoScEn 94
Basmajian, Walter 1922- WhoAmP 93
Basmeson, Gustavo Adolfo 1952- WhoHisp 94
Basnight, Arvin Odell 1915- WhoScEn 94
Basnight, Marc 1947- WhoAmP 93
Basolo, Fred 1920- IntWW 93, WhoAm 94, WhoMW 93, WhoScEn 94
Bason, George R., Jr. 1954- WhoAmL 94
Basora, Adrian A. 1938- WhoAmP 93
Basov, Emelyan c. 1705-c. 1765 WhWE
Basov, Nicolai G. WorInv
Basov, Nikolai Gennadievich 1922- IntWW 93, Who 94, WhoScEn 94
Basque, David 1927- WhoAmP 93
Basquette, Lina 1907- WhoHol 92
Basquiat, Jean-Michel 1960-1988 AfrAmAl 6, ConBlB 5 [port]
Basquiat, Jean Michel 1961-1988 WhoAmA 93N
Basquin, Kit (Mary Smyth) 1941- WhoAmA 93
Basri, Gibor Broitman 1951- WhoBlA 94
Bass Who 94
Bass, Alfie d1987 WhoHol 92
Bass, Alice Cabaniss DrAPF 93
Bass, Arthur C. d1993 NewYTBS 93 [port]
Bass, Barbara DeJong 1946- WhoAm 94
Bass, Bernard M(orris) 1925- WrDr 94
Bass, Bob WhoAm 94
Bass, Bobby WhoHol 92
Bass, Bryan Geoffrey 1934- Who 94
Bass, Carol Sue 1940- WhoAm 94
Bass, Charles Foster 1952- WhoAmP 93
Bass, Charles Morris 1949- WhoFI 94
Bass, David Arle, Jr. 1957- WhoFI 94
Bass, David Jason 1954- WhoWest 94
Bass, David Loren 1943- WhoAmA 93
Bass, Dorothy Ussery DrAPF 93
Bass, Edwin Warner 1941- WhoAmL 94
Bass, Ellen DrAPF 93
Bass, Floyd L. 1921- WhoBlA 94
Bass, Gail I. 1949- WhoMW 93
Bass, George 1771-c. 1803 WhWE
Bass, George Fletcher 1932- WhoAm 94, WhoScEn 94
Bass, Harold Neal 1939- WhoAm 94
Bass, Harry Godfrey Mitchell 1914- Who 94
Bass, Herbert H. 1929- WhoBlA 94

Bass, Howard 1923- WrDr 94
Bass, Hyman 1932- WhoAm 94
Bass, Jack 1934- WrDr 94
Bass, James Albert, Jr. 1933- WhoFI 94
Bass, James Gifford 1936- WhoFI 94
Bass, James Orin 1910- WhoAm 94
Bass, James Willis 1930- WhoWest 94
Bass, Joel 1942- WhoAmA 93
Bass, Joel Leonard 1942- WhoAm 94
Bass, Johanna d1970 WhoAmA 93N
Bass, John 1891-1978 WhoAmA 93N
Bass, John A. 1949- WhoAmP 93
Bass, John F. 1926- WhoAmP 93
Bass, John Fred 1941- WhoAm 94
Bass, Joseph Frank 1938- WhoBlA 94
Bass, Judy 1946- WhoAmA 93
Bass, Kenneth Carrington, III 1944- WhoAm 94, WhoAmL 94, WhoAmP 93
Bass, Kevin Charles 1959- WhoBlA 94
Bass, Kingsley B., Jr. BlkWr 2
Bass, Lawrence M. 1952- WhoAmL 94
Bass, Leonard Channing 1941- WhoBlA 94
Bass, Mark David 1961- WhoFI 94
Bass, Marshall Brent WhoBlA 94
Bass, Max S. 1940- WhoFI 94
Bass, Melinda Aikins 1940- WhoAmL 94
Bass, Michael 1939- WhoAm 94
Bass, Mikhail 1948- WhoScEn 94
Bass, Milton DrAPF 93
Bass, Nancy Agnes 1937- WhoFI 94
Bass, Norman Herbert 1936- WhoAm 94
Bass, Paul 1928- WhoAm 94
Bass, Paul Eric 1925- Who 94
Bass, Perkins 1912- WhoAmP 93
Bass, Perry Richardson 1914- WhoAm 94, WhoFI 94
Bass, Richard Samuel 1938- WhoWest 94
Bass, Rick 1958- ConLC 79 [port]
Bass, Robert Olin 1917- WhoAm 94
Bass, Robert P., Jr. 1923- WhoAmP 93
Bass, Robert Thrane 1949- WhoAmP 93
Bass, Ronald WhoAm 94, WhoWest 94
Bass, Ross 1917-1992? NewYTBS 93
Bass, Ross F., Jr. 1946- WhoAmL 94
Bass, Ruth 1938- WhoAmA 93
Bass, Saul 1920- IntDcF 2-4, IntMPA 94, WhoAm 94
Bass, Steven Craig 1943- WhoMW 93
Bass, T.J. 1932- EncSF 93, WrDr 94
Bass, Thomas A. 1951- WrDr 94
Bass, Thomas David 1956- WhoScEn 94
Bassani, Giorgio 1916- ConWorW 93, IntWW 93
Bassani, Giovanni Battista c. 1657-1716 NewGrDO
Bassani, Giuseppe Franco 1929- IntWW 93
Bassano, C. Louis 1942- WhoAmP 93
Bassard, Yvonne Brooks 1937- WhoBlA 94
Basseches, Robert Treinis 1934- WhoAmL 94
Bassen, Ned H. 1948- WhoAmL 94
Bassen, Ned Henry 1948- WhoAm 94
Basserman, Albert d1952 WhoHol 92
Basserman, Else d1961 WhoHol 92
Basset, Bryan Ronald 1932- Who 94
Basset, Elizabeth 1908- Who 94
Basset, Gene 1927- WhoAmA 93
Basset, Mary Roper fl. 1544-1572 BlmGWL
Bassett, Alice Cook 1925- WhoAmP 93
Bassett, Angela WhoBlA 94
Bassett, Angela 1958- IntMPA 94, WhoAm 94
Bassett, Angela 1959?- ConBlB 6 [port]
Bassett, Anne S. EncSPD
Bassett, Arthur Ray 1935- WhoWest 94
Bassett, Barbara Wies 1939- WhoAm 94, WhoWest 94
Bassett, Charles Andrew Loockerman 1924- WhoAm 94, WhoScEn 94
Bassett, Charles Walker 1932- WhoAm 94
Bassett, Dennis 1947- WhoBlA 94
Bassett, Douglas Anthony 1927- Who 94
Bassett, Edward Powers 1929- WhoAm 94
Bassett, Elizabeth Ewing 1937- WhoAm 94
Bassett, H. Ellsworth d1943 WhoHol 92
Bassett, Harold Lawrence 1934- WhoMW 93
Bassett, Harry Hood 1917- WhAm 10
Bassett, Henry Gordon 1924- WhoWest 94
Bassett, J. Thomas 1945- WhoAmL 94
Bassett, Joel Eric 1944- WhoAm 94, WhoAmL 94
Bassett, John Walden, Jr. 1938- WhoAmL 94
Bassett, Joseph M. 1948- WhoFI 94
Bassett, Lawrence C 1931- WhoAm 94
Bassett, Leland Kinsey 1945- WhoMW 93, WhoScEn 94
Bassett, Leslie Raymond 1923- WhoAm 94
Bassett, Linda IntMPA 94, WhoHol 92
Bassett, Michail Edward Rainton 1938- IntWW 93
Bassett, Nigel F. Who 94
Bassett, Peter Q. WhoAm 94, WhoAmL 94
Bassett, Richard 1745-1815 WhAmRev
Bassett, Robert Cochem 1911- WhoAm 94, WhoMW 93
Bassett, Robert Ross, Jr. 1920- WhoFI 94
Bassett, Russell d1918 WhoHol 92
Bassett, Steve WhoHol 92
Bassett, Tina WhoAm 94, WhoFI 94
Bassett, William Akers 1931- WhoAm 94
Bassett, Woodson William, Jr. 1926- WhoAm 94
Bassett Cross, Alistair Robert Sinclair 1944- Who 94
Bassetti, Fred Forde 1917- WhoAm 94
Bassey, Shirley 1937- IntWW 93
Bassford, Daniel Joseph 1949- WhoMW 93
Bassham, Genevieve Prieto 1939- WhoHisp 94
Bassi, Amedeo 1874-1949 NewGrDO
Bassi, Joseph Arthur 1951- WhoScEn 94
Bassi, Luigi 1766-1825 NewGrDO
Bassi Montanari, Franca 1956- WhoWomW 91
Bassin, Joan 1938- WhoAmA 93
Bassin, Jules 1914- WhoAm 94
Bassingthwaighte, James Bucklin 1929- WhoAm 94
Bassingthwaighte, Keith 1943- Who 94
Bassini, Achille de NewGrDO
Bassiouny, Mohamed Abdel-Aziz 1937- IntWW 93
Bassis, Michael Steven 1944- WhoAm 94
Bassist, Donald Herbert 1923- WhoAm 94, WhoWest 94
Bassler, John Peter WhoAm 94
Bassler, Robert Covey 1935- WhoAm 94
Bassler, William G. 1938- WhoAm 94, WhoAmL 94
Bassman, Robert Stuart 1947- WhoAm 94, WhoAmL 94
Bassnett, Peter James 1933- WhoAm 94
Basso, Alberto 1931- NewGrDO
Basso, Keith H(amilton) 1940- WrDr 94
Basso, Keith Hamilton 1940- WhoAm 94
Bassole, Bazomboue Leandre 1946- IntWW 93
Bassuk, Richard 1941- WhoAm 94
Bast, Albert John, III 1948- WhoScEn 94
Bast, James Louis 1936- WhoAm 94
Bast, Ray Roger 1925- WhoAm 94
Bast, Richard John 1952- WhoMW 93
Bast, Robert Clinton, Jr. 1943- WhoAm 94, WhoScEn 94
Bast, Rose Ann 1934- WhoMW 93
Bast, William DeForrest 1957- WhoMW 93
Basta, Alan James 1960- WhoFI 94
Basta, Joseph C. 1947- WhoAmL 94
Bastable, Bernard 1936- WrDr 94
Bastarache, Julie Rico 1957- WhoHisp 94
Bastardi, Marilyn Patricia 1945- WhoFI 94
Bastedo, Alexandra 1946- WhoHol 92
Bastedo, Ralph Walter 1953- WhoAm 94
Bastedo, Wayne Webster 1948- WhoAmL 94
Basti, Juli 1957- IntWW 93
Bastiaans, Glenn John 1947- WhoScEn 94
Bastiaanse, Gerard C. 1935- WhoAm 94, WhoAmL 94
Bastian, Bertha d1949 WhoHol 92
Bastian, Bruce Wayne 1948- WhoAm 94, WhoWest 94
Bastian, Donald Noel 1925- WhoAm 94
Bastian, Gert d1992 IntWW 93N
Bastian, Henry Charlton 1837-1915 DcNaB MP
Bastian, James Harold 1927- WhoAm 94
Bastian, Janelle Annette 1955- WhoWest 94
Bastian, Linda 1940- WhoAmA 93
Bastian, Valerie Joy 1964- WhoMW 93
Bastianelli, Ann Irene 1956- WhoMW 93
Bastianini, Ettore 1922-1967 NewGrDO
Bastid, Suzanne 1906- IntWW 93
Bastida, Daniel 1954- WhoScEn 94
Bastida, Elena Beck 1950- WhoHisp 94
Bastidas, Rodrigo De 1460-1526 WhWE
Bastide, Francois-Regis 1926- IntWW 93
Bastidos, Hugo A. WhoHisp 94
Bastien, Christopher Paul 1958- WhoAmL 94
Bastien, Joseph William 1935- WhoAm 94
Bastien, Robert Edward 1952- WhoAmL 94
Bastin, Charles d1989 WhoHol 92
Bastin, Gary C. 1950- WhoAmP 93
Bastin, John Andrew 1929- Who 94
Bastin, Jules 1933- NewGrDO
Basto, La Donna Joan 1933- WhoMW 93
Bastoky, Bruce Michael 1953- WhoFI 94, WhoMW 93
Bastón, Elvira 1944- WhoHisp 94
Baston, Jack d1970 WhoHol 92
Bastoni, Steve WhoHol 92
Bastos, Augusto Roa ConWorW 93
Basu, Asish Ranjan 1944- WhoAm 94
Basu, Asit Prakas 1937- WhoAm 94, WhoAsA 94
Basu, Janet Else 1947- WhoScEn 94
Basu, Jyoti 1914- IntWW 93
Basu, Prithwish 1956- WhoScEn 94
Basu, Prodyot Kumar 1939- WhoScEn 94
Basu, Rajat Subhra WhoAm 94
Basu, Sutapa 1957- WhoAsA 94
Basulto, Maria 1949- WhoHisp 94
Basye, Paul Edmond 1901- WhAm 10
Baszak, Bernard Frank 1958- WhoFI 94
Baszny, Jozef d1862? NewGrDO
Bata, Rudolph Andrew, Jr. 1947- WhoAmL 94
Bata, Thomas John 1914- IntWW 93
Batagaev, Aleksei Nikolaevich 1950- LoBiDrD
Bataille, Emmanuelle WhoHol 92
Bataille, Jacques Albert 1926- WhoBlA 94
Bataille, Sylvie 1912- WhoHol 92
Bataillon, Joseph Francis 1949- WhoAmP 93
Batakov, Anton fl. 1780-179-? WhWE
Batalden, Paul Bennett 1941- WhoAm 94
Batalla, Pedro Ramon 1950- WhoFI 94
Batalov, Aleksey Vladimirovich 1928- IntWW 93
Batalov, Alexei 1928- WhoHol 92
Batalov, Nikolai d1937 WhoHol 92
Batarse, Anthony Abraham, Jr. 1933- WhoHisp 94, WhoWest 94
Batarsé, Elizabeth Carina 1935- WhoHisp 94
Batastini, Armando Emilio, Jr. 1930- WhoAmP 93
Batayneh, Ghassan Jason Rizek 1960- WhoFI 94
Batbayar, Bat-Erdeniin 1955- IntWW 93, WhoScEn 94
Batbedat, Jean 1926- IntWW 93
Batcha, George 1928- WhoFI 94, WhoMW 93, WhoScEn 94
Batcheff, Pierre d1932 WhoHol 92
Batchelder, Alice M. WhoAmP 93
Batchelder, Alice M. 1944- WhoAm 94, WhoAmL 94, WhoMW 93
Batchelder, Anne Stuart 1920- WhoAm 94, WhoMW 93
Batchelder, Samuel Lawrence, Jr. 1932- WhoAm 94
Batchelder, William F. WhoAmP 93
Batchelder, William F. 1926- WhoAm 94, WhoAmL 94
Batchelder, William George 1942- WhoAmP 93
Batchelder, William George, III 1942- WhoMW 93
Batchelor, Anthony John 1944- WhoAmA 93
Batchelor, Anthony Stephen 1948- WhoScEn 94
Batchelor, Asbury Collins 1929- WhoBlA 94
Batchelor, Barrington de Vere 1928- WhoAm 94
Batchelor, Barry Lee 1952- WhoScEn 94
Batchelor, Betsey Ann 1952- WhoAmA 93
Batchelor, Bill 1949- WhoScEn 94
Batchelor, Clarence Daniel 1888-1977 WhoAmA 93N
Batchelor, David 1943- WrDr 94
Batchelor, George Keith 1920- IntWW 93, Who 94, WrDr 94
Batchelor, Ian Gordon d1986 WhoHol 92
Batchelor, Ivor (Ralph Campbell) 1916- Who 94
Batchelor, James Kent 1934- WhoWest 94
Batchelor, John 1942- WrDr 94
Batchelor, John Calvin 1948- EncSF 93, WrDr 94
Batchelor, Joseph Brooklyn, Jr. 1922- WhoAm 94, WhoScEn 94
Batchelor, Joy 1914-
See Halas, John 1912- IntDcF 2-4
Batchelor, (John) Richard 1931- Who 94
Batchman, John Clifford 1944- WhoMW 93
Batdorf, Samuel Burbridge 1914- WhoAm 94, WhoScEn 94, WhoWest 94
Bate, Anthony 1929- WhoHol 92
Bate, Brian R. 1940- WhoScEn 94
Bate, David (Lindsay) 1916- Who 94
Bate, (Walter) Edwin 1901- Who 94
Bate, Jennifer Lucy 1944- IntWW 93
Bate, Jonathan 1958- WrDr 94
Bate, Judith Ellen 1934- WhoAm 94
Bate, Natalie WhoHol 92
Bate, Norman Arthur 1916-1980 WhoAmA 93N
Bate, Robert Brettell 1782-1847 DcNaB MP
Bate, Walter Jackson 1918- Who 94, WhoAm 94, WrDr 94
Bate, William 1920- Who 94
Bate, William Joseph, Jr. 1934- WhoAmP 93
Bately, Janet Margaret 1932- Who 94
Bateman, Ann Creighton 1943- WhoWest 94
Bateman, Cecil (Joseph) 1910- Who 94
Bateman, David Alfred 1946- WhoAmL 94
Bateman, Dottye Jane Spencer WhoFI 94
Bateman, Frank B(race) 1897- WhAm 10
Bateman, Fred Willom 1916- WhoAm 94
Bateman, Geoffrey (Hirst) 1906- Who 94
Bateman, Giles Hirst Litton 1944- WhoAm 94
Bateman, Herbert H. 1928- CngDr 93
Bateman, Herbert Harvell 1928- WhoAm 94, WhoAmP 93
Bateman, Jason 1969- IntMPA 94, WhoHol 92
Bateman, Jeanne Naegele 1954- WhoFI 94
Bateman, Jessie d1940 WhoHol 92
Bateman, John Jay 1931- WhoAm 94
Bateman, John L. 1953- WhoWest 94
Bateman, John Roger 1927- WhoAm 94
Bateman, Justine 1966- IntMPA 94, WhoHol 92
Bateman, Leslie Clifford 1915- IntWW 93, Who 94
Bateman, Mary-Rose Christine 1935- Who 94
Bateman, Michael Allen 1952- WhoBlA 94
Bateman, Paul Terence 1946- Who 94
Bateman, Paul Trevier 1919- WhoAm 94
Bateman, Paul William 1937- WhoAm 94
Bateman, Philip L. 1952- WhoAmL 94
Bateman, Ralph (Melton) 1910- IntWW 93, Who 94
Bateman, Raymond Henry 1927- WhoAmP 93
Bateman, Richard George Saumarez La T. Who 94
Bateman, Richard Montague 1943- Who 94
Bateman, Robert (Moyes Carruthers) 1922-1973 EncSF 93
Bateman, Robert Earl, II 1958- WhoWest 94
Bateman, Robert Edwin 1923- WhoScEn 94, WhoWest 94
Bateman, Robert McLellan 1930- IntWW 93, WhoAm 94, WhoAmA 93
Bateman, Rocklin WhoAmP 93
Bateman, Ronald C. 1947- WhoAmA 93
Bateman, Ronald Rao 1947- WhoWest 94
Bateman, Samuel T., Jr. 1936- WhoAmP 93
Bateman, Stephen c. 1510-1584 DcLB 136
Bateman, Thomas Robert 1944- WhoAm 94
Bateman, Veda Mae 1921- WhoAm 94
Bateman, Victory d1926 WhoHol 92
Bateman, William Maxwell 1920- WhoAm 94
Bateman, Zillah d1970 WhoHol 92
Batenburg, Andries 1922- IntWW 93
Bates Who 94
Bates, Alan 1934- IntMPA 94, IntWW 93, WhoAm 94, WhoHol 92
Bates, Alan (Arthur) 1934- Who 94
Bates, Albert Jr., IV 1961- WhoAmL 94
Bates, Alfred 1944- Who 94
Bates, Alonzo W. 1939- WhoBlA 94
Bates, Ann WhAmRev
Bates, Arthenia J. BlkWr 2
Bates, Arthur Verdi 1916- WhoBlA 94
Bates, Barbara d1969 WhoHol 92
Bates, Barbara Ann WhoBlA 94
Bates, Baron Kent 1934- WhoAm 94
Bates, Bart S. 1963- WhoAmP 93
Bates, Betty F. 1931- WhoAmP 93
Bates, Beverly Bailey 1938- WhoAmL 94
Bates, Bill d1978 WhoHol 92
Bates, Blanchard W. d1993 NewYTBS 93
Bates, Blanche d1941 WhoHol 92
Bates, Carol 1895- WhoAmA 93N
Bates, Charles Carpenter 1918- WhoAm 94
Bates, Charles Emerson 1946- WhoWest 94
Bates, Charles Turner 1932- WhoAm 94
Bates, Charles Walter 1953- WhoFI 94, WhoWest 94
Bates, Clayton Wilson, Jr. 1932- WhoBlA 94
Bates, Craig D. 1952- ConAu 140
Bates, Craig Dana 1952- WhoWest 94
Bates, Daisy WhoBlA 94
Bates, Daisy 1863-1951 BlmGWL
Bates, Daisy Lee Gatson 1920- AfrAmAl 6 [port]
Bates, Dallas Kelvin 1949- WhoMW 93
Bates, David 1952- WhoAm 94, WhoAmA 93
Bates, David (Robert) 1916- Who 94
Bates, David E. 1941- WhoAmP 93
Bates, David Frank 1928- Who 94
Bates, David Martin 1934- WhoAm 94, WhoScEn 94

Bates, David Quentin, Jr. 1951- *WhoAm 94*
Bates, David Robert 1916- *IntWW 93*
Bates, David Vincent 1922- *WhoAm 94*
Bates, Dawson *Who 94*
Bates, (John) Dawson 1921- *Who 94*
Bates, Don 1939- *WhoAm 94*
Bates, Donald Lloyd 1932- *WhoWest 94*
Bates, Dwight Lee 1943- *WhoWest 94*
Bates, E. William, II 1955- *WhoAmL 94*
Bates, Edward Brill 1919- *WhoAm 94*
Bates, Edward Lawrence 1948- *WhoMW 93*
Bates, Eric 1908- *Who 94*
Bates, Ernest Alphonso 1936- *WhoBlA 94*
Bates, Florence d1954 *WhoHol 92*
Bates, Geoffrey Voltelin 1921- *Who 94*
Bates, George Edmonds 1933- *WhoWest 94*
Bates, George William 1940- *WhoAm 94*
Bates, Gerald Earl 1933- *WhoAm 94*
Bates, Gladys Edgerly 1896- *WhoAm 94, WhoAmA 93*
Bates, Gordon *Who 94*
Bates, Grace Kamp 1917- *WhoWest 94*
Bates, Granville d1940 *WhoHol 92*
Bates, H(erbert) E(rnest) 1905-1974 *RfGShF*
Bates, Harry 1900-1981 *EncSF 93*
Bates, Henry Walter 1825-1892 *WhWE [port]*
Bates, J. Douglas 1946- *ConAu 142*
Bates, James 1926- *WrDr 94*
Bates, James Earl 1923- *WhoAm 94*
Bates, James Leonard 1919- *WhoAm 94*
Bates, James P. M. *Who 94*
Bates, Jeanne *WhoHol 92*
Bates, Jeffrey C. 1949- *WhoAm 94*
Bates, Jeffrey Wayne 1958- *WhoAmL 94*
Bates, Jim 1941- *WhoAmP 93*
Bates, John Bertram 1914- *WhoAm 94*
Bates, John Burnham 1918- *WhoAm 94*
Bates, John Burnham, Jr. 1948- *WhoAmL 94*
Bates, John Cecil, Jr. 1936- *WhoAm 94, WhoAmL 94*
Bates, John David d1992 *Who 94N*
Bates, John Gerald Higgs 1936- *Who 94*
Bates, John Loren 1898- *WhAm 10*
Bates, John Robert 1947- *WhoMW 93*
Bates, Judith Louise 1944- *WhoMW 93*
Bates, Kathryn d1964 *WhoHol 92*
Bates, Kathy 1948- *IntMPA 94, IntWW 93, WhoAm 94, WhoHol 92*
Bates, Kenneth 1895-1973 *WhoAmA 93N*
Bates, Kenneth Francis 1904- *WhoAmA 93*
Bates, Kenneth Norris 1949- *WhoWest 94*
Bates, Kermit Francis, Jr. 1936- *WhoAmP 93*
Bates, Lawrence Fulcher 1954- *WhoAmL 94*
Bates, Lawson d1975 *WhoHol 92*
Bates, Leo James 1944- *WhoAmA 93*
Bates, Les d1930 *WhoHol 92*
Bates, Lionel Ray, Sr. 1955- *WhoBlA 94*
Bates, Louise d1972 *WhoHol 92*
Bates, Louise Rebecca 1932- *WhoBlA 94*
Bates, Lura Wheeler 1932- *WhoFI 94*
Bates, Malcolm Rowland 1934- *WhoAm 94*
Bates, Maxwell Bennett 1906-1980 *WhoAmA 93N*
Bates, Michael *WhoAm 94*
Bates, Michael d1978 *WhoHol 92*
Bates, Michael Walton 1961- *Who 94*
Bates, Milton J. 1945- *WhoMW 93*
Bates, Nathaniel Rubin 1931- *WhoAmP 93, WhoBlA 94*
Bates, Paul Spencer 1940- *Who 94*
Bates, Percy 1932- *WhoBlA 94*
Bates, Peter Edward Gascoigne 1924- *Who 94*
Bates, Ralph d1991 *WhoHol 92*
Bates, Ralph 1899- *Who 94*
Bates, Reitta Ione 1924- *WhoMW 93*
Bates, Richard Mather 1932- *WhoAm 94*
Bates, Richard Warden 1929- *WhoAmL 94*
Bates, Robert E., Jr. 1934- *WhoBlA 94*
Bates, Robert Hinrichs 1942- *WhoAm 94*
Bates, Robert Searle 1928- *WhoMW 93*
Bates, Scott *DrAPF 93*
Bates, Scott D. *WhoAmP 93*
Bates, Sharon Ann 1958- *WhoScEn 94*
Bates, Stephen Cuyler 1948- *WhoScEn 94*
Bates, Stewart Taverner 1926- *Who 94*
Bates, Sturgis Goodwin, III 1937- *WhoAmP 93*
Bates, Thorpe d1958 *WhoHol 92*
Bates, Timothy 1950- *WhoAmP 93*
Bates, Timothy Dexter 1948- *WhoAmP 93*
Bates, Tom d1930 *WhoHol 92*
Bates, Tom 1938- *WhoAmP 93*
Bates, Valentino Travis 1955- *WhoBlA 94*
Bates, Walter 1760-1842 *WhAmRev*
Bates, Walter Alan 1925- *WhoAm 94*
Bates, William, III 1949- *WhoAm 94, WhoAmL 94*
Bates, William Hubert 1926- *WhoAm 94, WhoAmL 94*
Bates, William J. 1952- *WhoBlA 94*
Bates, William Lawrence 1957- *WhoScEn 94*
Bates, William Stanley d1993 *Who 94N*
Bates, Willie Earl 1940- *WhoBlA 94*
Batesky, Richard Philip, Jr. 1963- *WhoMW 93*
Bateson *Who 94*
Bateson, Andrew James 1925- *Who 94*
Bateson, Gregory 1904-1985 *EncSPD*
Bateson, John Swinburne 1942- *Who 94*
Bateson, Mary Catherine 1939- *WhoAm 94, WhoScEn 94*
Bateson, (Paul) Patrick (Gordon) 1938- *Who 94*
Bateson, Paul Patrick Gordon 1938- *IntWW 93*
Bateson, Timothy 1926- *WhoHol 92*
Bateson, William 1861-1926 *WorScD*
Bates-Parker, Linda 1944- *WhoBlA 94*
Bates-Silva, Mary Louise 1930- *WhoAm 94*
Batey, Douglas Leo 1947- *WhoAmL 94*
Bath, Archdeacon of *Who 94*
Bath, Marquess of 1932- *Who 94*
Bath, Marquis of *WhAmRev*
Bath, Alan Alfred 1924- *Who 94*
Bath, Patricia E. 1942- *WhoBlA 94*
Bath, Peter Donald Henry 1952- *WhoAm 94*
Bath and Wells, Bishop of 1936- *Who 94*
Bathen, Karl Hans 1934- *WhoAm 94*
Bather, Paul Charles 1947- *WhoAmP 93, WhoBlA 94*
Bathersby, John Alexius *Who 94*
Bathey, Balakrishnan R. 1940- *WhoScEn 94*
Bathias, Claude 1938- *WhoScEn 94*
Bathiat, Leonie (Arletty) d1992 *IntWW 93N*
Bathina, Harinath Babu 1940- *WhoMW 93, WhoScEn 94*
Batho, James *Who 94*
Batho, (Walter) James (Scott) 1925- *Who 94*
Batho, Peter (Ghislain) 1939- *Who 94*
Bathon, Thomas Neil 1961- *WhoFI 94*
Bathori, Jane 1877-1970 *NewGrDO*
Bathurst *Who 94*
Bathurst, Earl 1927- *Who 94*
Bathurst (NSW), Bishop of 1942- *Who 94*
Bathurst, (David) Benjamin 1936- *IntWW 93, Who 94*
Bathurst, Bill *DrAPF 93*
Bathurst, Frederick Peter Methuen Hervey- 1903- *Who 94*
Bathurst, Henry, Earl of 1714-1794 *WhAmRev*
Bathurst, Joan Caroline *Who 94*
Bathurst, Maurice (Edward) 1913- *Who 94*
Bathurst Norman, George Alfred 1939- *Who 94*
Bathy, Anna 1901-1962 *NewGrDO*
Batie, Franklin d1949 *WhoHol 92*
Batiffol, Henri 1905- *IntWW 93*
Batignani, Laurie A. 1953- *WhoAm 94*
Batine, Rafael 1947- *WhoBlA 94*
Batinkoff, Randall 1968- *WhoHol 92*
Batista, Alberto Victor 1963- *WhoAmL 94, WhoHisp 94*
Batista, Duane R. 1934- *WhoAm 94, WhoAmL 94*
Batista, Fulgencio 1901-1973 *HisWorL [port]*
Batista, George *WhoHisp 94*
Batista, John Veloso 1934- *WhoAm 94, WhoFI 94*
Batista, Juan Carlos 1957- *WhoHisp 94*
Batista, Juan E. 1936- *WhoHisp 94*
Batista, Kenneth 1952- *WhoAmA 93*
Batista, León Félix 1964- *WhoHisp 94*
Batista, Santiago 1931- *WhoHisp 94*
Batista Gastón, Melchor Ignacio 1944- *WhoHisp 94*
Batista-Wales, Maria del Carmen 1960- *WhoHisp 94*
Batiste, Edna E. 1931- *WhoBlA 94*
Batiste, Kim 1968- *WhoBlA 94*
Batiste, Mary Virginia 1925- *WhoBlA 94*
Batiste, Robert Joseph 1950- *WhoFI 94*
Batiste, Spencer Lee 1945- *Who 94*
Batistin *NewGrDO*
Batiuk, Thomas Martin 1947- *WhoAm 94, WhoWest 94*
Batiza, Paul M. 1948- *WhoAmL 94*
Batiz Campbell, Enrique 1942- *IntWW 93*
Batjer, Cameron McVicar 1919- *WhoAmP 93*
Batka, Richard 1868-1922 *NewGrDO*
Batki, John *DrAPF 93*
Batkin, Bruce David 1953- *WhoFI 94*
Batkin, Sanford Lewis 1923- *WhoFI 94*
Batko, Blaise Joseph 1961- *WhoAmA 93*
Batla, Raymond John, Jr. 1947- *WhoAm 94, WhoAmL 94, WhoFI 94*
Batley, Dorothy 1902- *WhoHol 92*
Batley, Ernest G. d1917 *WhoHol 92*
Batley, John Geoffrey 1930- *Who 94*
Batlin, Robert Alfred 1930- *WhoAm 94*
Batliner, Gerard 1928- *IntWW 93*
Batlivala, Robert Bomi D. 1940- *WhoFI 94, WhoMW 93, WhoScEn 94*
Batlle, Daniel Campi 1950- *WhoScEn 94*
Batlle, Jose 1856-1929 *HisWorL [port]*
Batlogg, Bertram 1950- *WhoScEn 94*
Bat-Miriam, Yocheved 1901-1980 *BlmGWL*
Batmunh, Jambyn 1926- *IntWW 93*
Batoff, Jeffrey Steven 1958- *WhoAmL 94*
Bator, Francis Michel 1925- *WhoAm 94*
Bators, Stiv d1990 *WhoHol 92*
Batory, Ronald Louis 1950- *WhoAm 94, WhoFI 94, WhoMW 93*
Batra, Prem Parkash 1936- *WhoMW 93*
Batra, Rajeev *WhoAsA 94*
Batra, Ravi 1943- *WhoAsA 94*
Batra, Romesh Chander 1947- *WhoAsA 94, WhoMW 93*
Batres, Eduardo *WhoAm 94*
Batsakis, John George 1929- *WhoAm 94*
Batscha, Robert Michael 1945- *WhoAm 94*
Bat-Shachar, Hannah 1944- *BlmGWL*
Batson, Blair Everett 1920- *WhoAm 94*
Batson, David Warren 1956- *WhoAmL 94*
Batson, Raymond Milner 1931- *WhoWest 94*
Batson, Richard Neal 1941- *WhoAm 94, WhoAmL 94*
Batson, Ruth Marion *WhoBlA 94*
Batson, Susan Catherine 1957- *WhoScEn 94*
Batsukh, Damdinsurengiin 1952- *IntWW 93*
Batt, Alyse Schwartz 1960- *WhoFI 94*
Batt, David L. 1934- *WhoAmP 93*
Batt, John Paul 1952- *WhoAm 94, WhoAmL 94*
Batt, Miles Girard 1933- *WhoAmA 93*
Batt, Neil Leonard Charles 1937- *IntWW 93*
Batt, Nick 1952- *WhoAm 94, WhoAmL 94, WhoFI 94, WhoMW 93*
Batt, Philip E. *WhoAmP 93*
Batt, Robert E. 1933- *WhoAmP 93*
Battaglia, Adolfo 1930- *IntWW 93*
Battaglia, Anthony *WhoHol 92*
Battaglia, Anthony Sylvester 1927- *WhoAm 94*
Battaglia, Basil Richard 1935- *WhoAmP 93*
Battaglia, David P. *WhoAmP 93*
Battaglia, Franco 1953- *WhoScEn 94*
Battaglia, Frederick Camillo 1932- *WhoAm 94*
Battaglia, Lynne Ann *WhoAmL 94*
Battaglia, Michael Salvatore 1944- *WhoAm 94*
Battaglia, Pasquale M. 1905-1959 *WhoAmA 93N*
Battaglia, Paul A. 1947- *WhoAmL 94*
Battaglia, Philip Maher 1935- *WhoAm 94*
Battaglia, Richard Anthony 1955- *WhoWest 94*
Battaglia, Rik *WhoHol 92*
Battaglia, Robert Kenneth 1939- *WhoWest 94*
Battaglia, William P. 1950- *WhoAmL 94*
Battaglini, Frank Paul 1944- *WhoAm 94*
Battaille, Charles (Amable) 1822-1872 *NewGrDO*
Battat, Emile A. 1938- *WhoAm 94*
Batteast, Margaret W. 1904- *WhoBlA 94*
Batteast, Robert V. 1931- *WhoBlA 94*
Batten, Alan Henry 1933- *IntWW 93, WhoAm 94*
Batten, Anne K. 1932- *WhoAmP 93*
Batten, Frank 1927- *WhoAm 94*
Batten, Grace Ruth 1943- *WhoBlA 94*
Batten, James Knox 1936- *IntWW 93, WhoAm 94, WhoFI 94*
Batten, James William 1919- *WrDr 94*
Batten, John (Charles) 1924- *Who 94*
Batten, John Charles 1924- *IntWW 93*
Batten, Mark Wilfrid d1993 *Who 94N*
Batten, Michael Ellsworth 1940- *WhoAm 94*
Batten, Stephen Duval 1945- *Who 94*
Batten, T(homas) R(eginald) 1904- *WrDr 94*
Batten, Tony 1935- *WhoBlA 94*
Batten, William Milfred 1909- *IntWW 93, WhoAm 94*
Battenfield, Jackie 1950- *WhoAmA 93*
Battenhouse, Roy W(esley) 1912- *WrDr 94*
Battenhouse, Roy Wesley 1912- *WhoAm 94*
Batterberry, Shawn Norman 1960- *WhoMW 93*
Batterbury, Paul Tracy Shepherd 1934- *Who 94*
Batterman, Boris William 1930- *WhoAm 94, WhoScEn 94*
Batterman, Robert Coleman 1911- *WhoWest 94*
Batterman, Steven Charles 1937- *WhoAm 94, WhoScEn 94*
Battersby, Alan (Rushton) 1925- *Who 94*
Battersby, Alan Rushton 1925- *IntWW 93*
Battersby, Christine 1946- *WrDr 94*
Battersby, Harold Ronald 1922- *WhoAm 94*
Battersby, James Lyons, Jr. 1936- *WhoAm 94*
Battersby, Robert Christopher 1924- *Who 94*
Battershell, James Robert, Jr. 1954- *WhoMW 93*
Batterson, Earl d1972 *WhoHol 92*
Batterson, J. Robert 1937- *WhoIns 94*
Batterson, James Robert, Sr. 1937- *WhoMW 93*
Battestin, Martin Carey 1930- *WhoAm 94, WrDr 94*
Battey, Charles W. 1932- *WhoFI 94, WhoWest 94*
Battey, David Ray 1953- *WhoAmL 94*
Battey, Richard Howard 1929- *WhoAm 94, WhoAmL 94, WhoMW 93*
Battey, Thomas C. 1828-1897 *EncNAR*
Battie, David 1942- *WrDr 94*
Battie, William 1703-1776 *EncSPD*
Battier, Robert d1946 *WhoHol 92*
Batties, Paul Terry 1941- *WhoBlA 94*
Battin, Cynthia Ann 1957- *WhoWest 94*
Battin, James Franklin 1925- *WhoAm 94, WhoAmL 94, WhoWest 94*
Battin, M. Pabst *DrAPF 93*
Battin, Richard Horace 1925- *WhoAm 94*
Battin, Wendy *DrAPF 93*
Battino, Rubin 1931- *WhoAm 94*
Battis, David Gregory 1945- *WhoAm 94, WhoAmL 94*
Battiscombe, Christopher Charles Richard 1940- *Who 94*
Battiscombe, Georgina 1905- *WrDr 94*
Battiscombe, (Esther) Georgina 1905- *Who 94*
Battishill, Anthony (Michael William) 1937- *Who 94*
Battishill, Jonathan 1738-1801 *NewGrDO*
Battison, John Henry 1915- *WhoAm 94*
Battista, Jerry Joseph 1950- *WhoScEn 94*
Battista, Lloyd *WhoHol 92*
Battista, Miriam d1980 *WhoHol 92*
Battista, Orlando Aloysius 1917- *IntWW 93, WhoAm 94*
Battista, Robert James 1939- *WhoAm 94*
Battistelli, Joseph John 1930- *WhoScEn 94*
Battisti, Carlo d1977 *WhoHol 92*
Battisti, Frank Joseph 1922- *WhoAm 94, WhoAmL 94, WhoMW 93*
Battisti, Oreste Guerino 1951- *WhoScEn 94*
Battisti, Paul Oreste 1922- *WhoAm 94*
Battistini, Mattia 1856-1928 *NewGrDO [port]*
Battisto, Jack Richard 1922- *WhoMW 93*
Battisto, Joseph W. 1931- *WhoAmP 93*
Battjes, Carl Robert 1929- *WhoWest 94*
Battle, Allen Overton, Jr. 1927- *WhoAm 94*
Battle, Bernard J., Sr. 1927- *WhoBlA 94*
Battle, Charles E. 1953- *WhoBlA 94*
Battle, Dennis Frank Orlando 1942- *Who 94*
Battle, Edward Gene 1931- *WhoWest 94*
Battle, Emery Alford, Jr. 1947- *WhoFI 94*
Battle, Frank Vincent, Jr. 1942- *WhoAm 94, WhoAmL 94*
Battle, Gloria Jean 1950- *WhoBlA 94*
Battle, Hinton 1956- *ConTFT 11*
Battle, Jacqueline 1962- *WhoBlA 94*
Battle, Jean Allen 1914- *WhoAm 94*
Battle, Joe David 1958- *WhoMW 93*
Battle, Joe Turner 1941- *WhoBlA 94*
Battle, John Dominic 1951- *Who 94*
Battle, John Sidney 1962- *WhoBlA 94*
Battle, Joseph F. 1937- *WhoAmP 93*
Battle, Kathleen *IntWW 93*
Battle, Kathleen 1948- *AfrAmAl 6 [port], NewGrDO, WhoBlA 94*
Battle, Kathleen Deanna 1948- *WhoAm 94*
Battle, Kenny 1964- *WhoBlA 94*
Battle, Leonard Carroll 1929- *WhoAmL 94*
Battle, Lucius D. 1918- *WhoAmP 93*
Battle, Lucius Durham 1918- *IntWW 93, WhoAm 94*
Battle, Mark G. 1924- *WhoBlA 94*
Battle, Mark Garvey 1924- *WhoAm 94*
Battle, Maurice Tazwell 1926- *WhoBlA 94*
Battle, Thomas Cornell 1946- *WhoBlA 94*
Battle, Thomas Howard 1950- *WhoWest 94*

Battle, Thomas Peyton 1942- *WhoAm 94, WhoAmL 94, WhoFI 94*
Battle, Timothy Joseph 1953- *WhoAmL 94*
Battle, Turner Charles, III 1926- *WhoBlA 94*
Battle, William R. 1924- *WhoIns 94*
Battle, William Rainey 1924- *WhoAm 94*
Battle, William Robert 1927- *WhoAm 94*
Battles, Cliff d1981 *ProFbHF*
Battles, Gary Dennis 1950- *WhoWest 94*
Battles, Marjorie 1952- *WhoAmP 93*
Battles, Marjorie Ann d1987 *WhoHol 92*
Battles, Michaele Snyder 1942- *WhoAmL 94*
Battles, Ronald Lee 1948- *WhoAmL 94, WhoWest 94*
Battles, Roxy Edith 1921- *WhoAm 94*
Battocchi, Ronald Silvio 1947- *WhoAmL 94*
Battocletti, Joseph Henry 1925- *WhoAm 94*
Batton, Desire-Alexandre 1798-1855 *NewGrDO*
Battram, Richard L. 1934- *WhoAm 94*
Batts, H. Lewis, Jr. 1922- *WhoMW 93*
Batts, Michael Stanley 1929- *WhoAm 94, WhoWest 94*
Batts, Terry Milburn 1914- *WhoBlA 94*
Batts, Thomas fl. 167-?- *WhWE*
Batts, Warren Leighton 1932- *IntWW 93, WhoAm 94, WhoFI 94*
Battu, Marie 1838-1888 *NewGrDO*
Battuta, Abu Abd-Allah Muhammad Ibn *WhWE*
Batty, Archibald d1961 *WhoHol 92*
Batty, Byron A. 1941- *WhoAmP 93*
Batty, Christina Agnes Lillian *Who 94*
Batty, E. Jerome 1945- *WhoAm 94, WhoAmL 94*
Batty, Hugh Kenworthy *WhoWest 94*
Batty, J. Michael 1945- *WhoAm 94, WhoScEn 94*
Batty, Peter 1931- *IntMPA 94*
Batty, Peter Wright 1931- *Who 94*
Batty, William (Bradshaw) 1913- *IntWW 93, Who 94*
Batu Bagan 1924- *WhoPRCh 91 [port]*
Ba-tu Ba-gen *WhoPRCh 91*
Batu Bagen 1924- *IntWW 93*
Bat-Uul, Erdeniin 1957- *IntWW 93*
Baty, Ace 1944- *WhoAmP 93*
Bat-Yisrael, Shulamith *DrAPF 93*
Batzel, Roger Elwood 1921- *WhoAm 94, WhoScEn 94*
Batzer, Mark Andrew 1961- *WhoScEn 94*
Batzer, R. Kirk 1915- *WhoAm 94*
Batzli, George Oliver 1936- *WhoAm 94, WhoMW 93*
Batzli, Terrence Raymond 1946- *WhoAm 94, WhoAmL 94*
Bauch, Thomas Jay 1943- *WhoAm 94, WhoAmL 94, WhoFI 94, WhoWest 94*
Bauchau, Patrick *WhoHol 92*
Bauchspiess, Karl Rudolf 1955- *WhoScEn 94*
Baucin, Escolastico d1965 *WhoHol 92*
Baucom, Earl d1981 *WhoHol 92*
Baucom, Sidney George 1930- *WhoAm 94*
Baucum, William Emmett, Jr. 1945- *WhoAm 94*
Baucus, Max 1941- *CngDr 93, IntWW 93, WhoAmP 93*
Baucus, Max S. 1941- *WhoAm 94, WhoWest 94*
Baudelaire, Charles 1821-1867 *BlmGEL*
Baudendistel, Daniel *WhoAm 94*
Bauder, Kenneth F. 1946- *WhoMW 93*
Bauder, Marianna 1943- *WhoAm 94*
Baudin, Ginette d1971 *WhoHol 92*
Baudin, Nicolas 1754-1803 *WhWE*
Baudler, Betty Ann 1953- *WhoMW 93*
Baudler, Bryan John 1940- *WhoAmL 94*
Baudo, Serge 1927- *IntWW 93, NewGrDO*
Baudoin, Peter 1946- *WhoFI 94*
Baudot-Puente, Gregorio 1884-1938 *NewGrDO*
Baudouin, I 1930- *IntWW 93*
Baudouin, I, King of Belgium 1930-1993 *CurBio 93N, NewYTBS 93 [port]*
Baudouin, Jean-Louis 1938- *IntWW 93*
Baudrier, Jaqueline 1922- *IntWW 93*
Baudrillard, Jean 1929- *CurBio 93 [port]*
Baudron, Antoine Laurent 1742-1834 *NewGrDO*
Bauduit, Harold S. 1930- *WhoBlA 94*
Baue, Arthur Edward 1929- *WhoAm 94, WhoMW 93*
Bauer *Who 94*
Bauer, Baron 1915- *IntWW 93, Who 94*
Bauer, Albert N., Jr. 1928- *WhoAmP 93*
Bauer, Arthur Adolph 1925- *WhoMW 93*
Bauer, August Robert, Jr. 1928- *WhoAm 94, WhoScEn 94, WhoWest 94*
Bauer, Belinda 1951- *WhoHol 92*
Bauer, Bernard Oswald 1957- *WhoWest 94*
Bauer, Bruce Richard 1944- *WhoAm 94*
Bauer, Bruno 1809-1882 *DcLB 133 [port]*
Bauer, Burnett Calix 1916- *WhoAmP 93*
Bauer, Burnett Patrick 1944- *WhoAmP 93*
Bauer, Caroline Feller *WhoAm 94*
Bauer, Caroline Feller 1935- *WrDr 94*
Bauer, Chris Michael 1948- *WhoAm 94*
Bauer, Dale Robert 1928- *WhAm 10*
Bauer, David d1973 *WhoHol 92*
Bauer, David Patrick 1961- *WhoFI 94*
Bauer, Douglas *DrAPF 93*
Bauer, Douglas F. 1942- *WhoAm 94*
Bauer, Earl William 1934- *WhoWest 94*
Bauer, Elaine Louise 1949- *WhoAm 94*
Bauer, Ernst Georg 1928- *WhoScEn 94*
Bauer, Erwin A. 1919- *CurBio 93 [port]*
Bauer, Esperanza d1954 *WhoHol 92*
Bauer, Eugene Andrew 1942- *WhoScEn 94*
Bauer, Ferdinand Lucas 1760-1826 *WhWE*
Bauer, Frederick Christian 1927- *WhoAm 94*
Bauer, Gary Lee 1946- *WhoAm 94*
Bauer, George 1925- *WhoAm 94*
Bauer, George W. 1931- *WhoAm 94*
Bauer, Gerard Joseph 1954- *WhoFI 94*
Bauer, Grace *DrAPF 93*
Bauer, Harold d1951 *WhoHol 92*
Bauer, Harry d1941 *WhoHol 92*
Bauer, Henry Hermann 1931- *WhoAm 94*
Bauer, Henry Leland 1928- *WhoWest 94*
Bauer, Herbert 1910- *WhoWest 94*
Bauer, Jean Marie 1958- *WhoFI 94*
Bauer, Jerome Leo, Jr. 1938- *WhoWest 94*
Bauer, Logan Probst 1940- *WhoWest 94*
Bauer, Lois Darlene 1938- *WhoAmP 93*
Bauer, Louis Edward 1937- *WhoWest 94*
Bauer, Ludwig 1908- *IntWW 93*
Bauer, Marilyn Schluterman 1950- *WhoMW 93*
Bauer, Marion Dane 1938- *TwCYAW, WhoAm 94*
Bauer, Max William 1957- *WhoWest 94*
Bauer, Michael Anthony 1948- *WhoScEn 94*
Bauer, Michelle *WhoHol 92*
Bauer, Nyles Jason 1961- *WhoWest 94*
Bauer, Otto Frank 1931- *WhoAm 94*
Bauer, Paul David 1943- *WhoAm 94*
Bauer, Peggy 1932- *CurBio 93 [port]*
Bauer, Peter Thomas 1915- *WrDr 94*
Bauer, Ralph Glenn 1925- *WhoAm 94*
Bauer, Ralph Leroy 1925- *WhoWest 94*
Bauer, Randy Mark 1946- *WhoWest 94*
Bauer, Raymond Gale 1934- *WhoFI 94*
Bauer, Richard *WhoHol 92*
Bauer, Richard Carlton 1944- *WhoAm 94*
Bauer, Robert Albert 1910- *WhoAm 94*
Bauer, Rodney Charles 1949- *WhoMW 93*
Bauer, Roger Duane 1932- *WhoAm 94*
Bauer, Rosemarie 1944- *WhoWomW 91*
Bauer, Ruth Kruse 1956- *WhoAmA 93*
Bauer, Stephen Walter 1960- *WhoAmL 94*
Bauer, Steven *DrAPF 93*
Bauer, Steven 1956- *IntMPA 94, WhoHisp 94, WhoHol 92*
Bauer, Steven Michael 1949- *WhoScEn 94, WhoWest 94*
Bauer, Terry Layne 1956- *WhoMW 93*
Bauer, Theodore Henry 1943- *WhoScEn 94*
Bauer, Theodore James 1909- *WhoAm 94*
Bauer, Tricia *DrAPF 93*
Bauer, Victor John 1935- *WhoAm 94, WhoScEn 94*
Bauer, Walter E(mil) 1897- *WhAm 10*
Bauer, William J. 1926- *WhoAmP 93*
Bauer, William Joseph 1926- *WhoAm 94, WhoAmL 94, WhoMW 93*
Bauer, Yehuda 1926- *WrDr 94*
Bauerlein, Mark (Weightman) 1959- *ConAu 141*
Bauerly, Jerry J. 1943- *WhoAmP 93*
Bauerly, Ronald John 1953- *WhoFI 94, WhoMW 93*
Bauermeister, Mathilde 1849-1926 *NewGrDO*
Bauers, John Allen 1950- *WhoWest 94*
Bauer-Schoof, Vicki Marie 1960- *WhoMW 93*
Bauersfeld, Carl Frederick 1916- *WhoAm 94*
Bauer-Tomich, Faith E. 1957- *WhoMW 93*
Bauge, Andre 1892-1966 *NewGrDO*
Bauge, Cynthia Wise 1943- *WhoFI 94*
Baugh, Charles Milton 1931- *WhoAm 94, WhoScEn 94*
Baugh, Florence Ellen 1935- *WhoBlA 94*
Baugh, James Edward 1941- *WhoBlA 94*
Baugh, Jerry Phelps 1933- *WhoAmL 94*
Baugh, John 1949- *WhoFI 94*
Baugh, John Frank 1916- *WhoAm 94, WhoFI 94*
Baugh, John Trevor 1932- *Who 94*
Baugh, Joyce Ann 1959- *WhoBlA 94*
Baugh, Kenneth Lee O'Neil 1941- *IntWW 93*
Baugh, L. Darrell 1930- *WhoFI 94, WhoWest 94*
Baugh, Lynnette 1949- *WhoBlA 94*
Baugh, Robert Franklin 1942- *WhoWest 94*
Baugh, Sammy *ProFbHF [port]*
Baugh, Slingin' Sammy 1914- *WhoHol 92*
Baugh, Wilbur E. 1927- *WhoAmP 93*
Baughan, Blanche Edith 1870-1958 *BlmGWL*
Baughan, Julian James 1944- *Who 94*
Baughan, Peter Edward 1934- *WrDr 94*
Baughcum, Steven Lee 1950- *WhoWest 94*
Baughen, Michael Alfred *Who 94*
Baugher, Forrest *WhoAmP 93*
Baugher, Gary Lee 1942- *WhoAmP 93*
Baugher, Peter V. 1948- *WhoAm 94*
Baughman, Ann Louise 1942- *WhoMW 93*
Baughman, Fred Hubbard 1926- *WhoAm 94*
Baughman, George Fechtig 1915- *WhoAm 94*
Baughman, George Washington 1911- *WhoScEn 94*
Baughman, J. Ross 1953- *WhoAm 94*
Baughman, James L(ewis) 1952- *ConAu 41NR*
Baughman, John Thomas 1943- *WhoScEn 94*
Baughman, Jon A. 1942- *WhoAm 94, WhoAmL 94*
Baughman, Leonora Knoblock 1956- *WhoAmL 94*
Baughman, Robert J. 1937- *WhoAmP 93*
Baughman, Robert Patrick 1938- *WhoAm 94, WhoAmL 94*
Baughman, Ronald Carl 1945- *WhoMW 93*
Baughman, Russell George 1946- *WhoMW 93*
Baughman, Susan S. 1934- *WhoAm 94*
Baughman, William H., Jr. 1949- *WhoAmL 94*
Baughn, Alfred Fairhurst 1912- *WhoAmL 94, WhoWest 94*
Baughn, William Hubert 1918- *WhoAm 94, WhoWest 94*
Bauguess, Milt *WhoIns 94*
Bauhof, Rudolf 1902-1989 *WhAm 10*
Bauhs, Marian Sayles 1928- *WhoAmP 93*
Bauknecht, Sharon Mary 1947- *WhoAmP 93*
Bauknight, Clarence Brock 1936- *WhoAm 94*
Baukol, Ronald Oliver 1937- *WhoAm 94*
Bauldock, Gerald 1957- *WhoBlA 94*
Bauler, William d1962 *WhoHol 92*
Baulieu, Etienne Emile 1926- *IntWW 93, WhoScEn 94*
Baum, Axel Helmuth 1930- *WhoAm 94*
Baum, Bernard H. 1926- *WrDr 94*
Baum, Bernard Helmut 1926- *WhoAm 94, WhoMW 93*
Baum, Bernard Rene 1937- *IntWW 93, WhoScEn 94*
Baum, Carl Edward 1940- *WhoAm 94, WhoScEn 94, WhoWest 94*
Baum, (John) David 1940- *Who 94*
Baum, David Roy 1946- *WhoAm 94*
Baum, Derek Michael 1935- *WhoWest 94*
Baum, Dirk Sawyers 1956- *WhoWest 94*
Baum, Don 1922- *WhoAmA 93*
Baum, Dwight Crouse 1912- *WhoAm 94*
Baum, Eleanor 1940- *WhoAm 94*
Baum, Elmer d1993 *NewYTBS 93*
Baum, Friedrich d1777 *WhAmRev*
Baum, Hank *WhoAmA 93*
Baum, Harry d1974 *WhoHol 92*
Baum, Herbert 1912-1942 *HisWorL*
Baum, Herbert Merrill 1936- *WhoAm 94*
Baum, Howard Barry 1952- *WhoScEn 94*
Baum, Janet Suzanne 1944- *WhoScEn 94*
Baum, Jayne H. 1954- *WhoAmA 93*
Baum, Joan 1937- *WrDr 94*
Baum, John 1927- *WhoAm 94*
Baum, John Frederick 1956- *WhoAmL 94*
Baum, Jonathan Edward 1960- *WhoMW 93*
Baum, Joseph Herman 1927- *WhoAm 94*
Baum, Jules Leonard 1931- *WhoAm 94*
Baum, Kerry Robert 1939- *WhoWest 94*
Baum, Kurt 1900-1989 *NewGrDO*
Baum, L(yman) Frank 1856-1919 *EncSF 93*
Baum, Lal d1987 *WhoHol 92*
Baum, Lawrence Stephen 1938- *WhoScEn 94*
Baum, Lester Jerome 1928- *WhoAmP 93*
Baum, Louis 1948- *WrDr 94*
Baum, Marilyn Ruth 1939- *WhoAmA 93*
Baum, Martin 1924- *IntMPA 94*
Baum, Michael 1937- *Who 94*
Baum, Michael E. 1952- *WhoAmL 94*
Baum, Michael Lin 1952- *WhoAmL 94*
Baum, Michael Scott 1952- *WhoAm 94*
Baum, Paul Frank 1936- *WhoScEn 94*
Baum, Peter Alan 1947- *WhoAmL 94*
Baum, Peter Samuel 1944- *WhoScEn 94*
Baum, Phyllis Gardner 1930- *WhoWest 94*
Baum, Ray 1955- *WhoAmP 93*
Baum, Richard Theodore 1919- *WhoAm 94, WhoFI 94, WhoScEn 94*
Baum, Sherry Liss *WhoAmP 93*
Baum, Stanley 1929- *WhoAm 94*
Baum, Stanley M. 1944- *WhoAmL 94*
Baum, Stefi Alison 1958- *WhoScEn 94*
Baum, Vicki 1888-1960 *BlmGWL*
Baum, Warren C. 1922- *IntWW 93*
Baum, Werner A. 1923- *WhoAm 94*
Baum, William Alvin 1924- *WhoAm 94*
Baum, William Wakefield 1926- *IntWW 93*
Bauman, Art d1993 *NewYTBS 93*
Bauman, Carl J.D. 1947- *WhoAmL 94*
Bauman, Carl James 1953- *WhoMW 93*
Bauman, Clyde Allen 1953- *WhoMW 93*
Bauman, Dale Elton 1942- *WhoAm 94, WhoScEn 94*
Bauman, David Wayne 1966- *WhoFI 94*
Bauman, Earl William 1916- *WhoFI 94, WhoWest 94*
Bauman, Frederick Carl 1952- *WhoAmL 94*
Bauman, George Duncan 1912- *WhoAm 94*
Bauman, George Fredrick 1920- *WhoAmP 93*
Bauman, Jan Georgius Josef 1950- *WhoScEn 94*
Bauman, Janina (G.) 1926- *WrDr 94*
Bauman, Jeffrey Allen 1955- *WhoWest 94*
Bauman, John Andrew 1921- *WhoAm 94, WhoAmL 94*
Bauman, John Duane 1930- *WhoAm 94, WhoAmL 94, WhoMW 93*
Bauman, John E., Jr. 1933- *WhoAm 94*
Bauman, Judith C. *WhoAmP 93*
Bauman, M. Garrett *DrAPF 93*
Bauman, Martin Harold 1929- *WhoAm 94, WhoFI 94*
Bauman, Natan 1945- *WhoScEn 94*
Bauman, Raquel 1948- *WhoHisp 94*
Bauman, Richard 1940- *WhoAm 94*
Bauman, Richard Arnold 1924- *WhoAm 94*
Bauman, Robert D. 1940- *WhoIns 94*
Bauman, Robert David 1940- *WhoAmL 94*
Bauman, Robert Gene 1945- *WhoMW 93*
Bauman, Robert Patten 1931- *IntWW 93, Who 94*
Bauman, Robert Poe 1928- *WhoAm 94*
Bauman, Sebastian 1739-1803 *WhAmRev*
Bauman, Stephen A. 1935- *WhoAmL 94*
Bauman, Susan Joan Mayer 1945- *WhoMW 93*
Bauman, Thomas (Allen) 1948- *NewGrDO*
Bauman, William Winter 1961- *WhoWest 94*
Bauman, Zygmunt 1925- *IntWW 93, WrDr 94*
Bauman Eisenstadt, Pauline 1938- *WhoWomW 91*
Baumann, Alan Frederic 1947- *WhoFI 94*
Baumann, Carol Edler 1932- *WrDr 94*
Baumann, Carol Kay 1946- *WhoMW 93*
Baumann, Daniel E. 1937- *WhoAm 94, WhoMW 93*
Baumann, Edward Robert 1921- *WhoAm 94*
Baumann, Frederick 1930- *WhoWest 94*
Baumann, Gary Joseph 1949- *WhoAm 94*
Baumann, Gary N. 1941- *WhoIns 94*
Baumann, Gregory William 1947- *WhoMW 93*
Baumann, Herbert Karl Wilhelm 1925- *IntWW 93*
Baumann, James L. 1931- *WhoAmP 93*
Baumann, Julian Henry, Jr. 1943- *WhoAmL 94*
Baumann, Karl H. *WhoAm 94, WhoFI 94*
Baumann, Marion Muns 1928- *WhoAmP 93*
Baumann, Oskar 1864-1899 *WhWE*
Baumann, Ramona Ann 1955- *WhoFI 94*
Baumann, Richard Charles 1935- *WhoWest 94*
Baumann, Richard Gordon 1938- *WhoAm 94*
Baumann, Robert Jay 1940- *WhoAm 94*
Baumann, Theodore Robert 1932- *WhoScEn 94, WhoWest 94*
Baumann-Tobien, Emmy d1961 *WhoHol 92*
Baumbach, Harold 1904- *WhoAm 94*
Baumbach, Harold 1905- *WhoAmA 93*
Baumbach, Jonathan *DrAPF 93*
Baumbach, Jonathan 1933- *WrDr 94*
Baumber, Michael (Leslie) 1935- *WrDr 94*
Baumberger, Charles Henry 1941- *WhoAmL 94*
Baumberger, Martha Kail 1913- *WhoAm 94*
Baume, Madame de la 17th cent.- *BlmGWL*

Baume, Hal L. 1951- WhoAm 94
Baumeister, Michel F. 1945- WhoAmL 94
Baumeister, Richard Thomas, Jr. 1961- WhoFI 94
Baumel, Herbert 1919- WhoAm 94
Baumel, Jacques 1918- IntWW 93
Baumel, Judith DrAPF 93
Baumer, Beverly Belle 1926- WhoAm 94
Baumer, Franklin L. 1913-1990 WhAm 10
Baumer, Gertrud 1873-1954 BlmGWL
Baumer, Jacques d1951 WhoHol 92
Baumert, Paulette Jean 1951- WhoFI 94
Baumgaertel, Marc Warren WhoWest 94
Baumgaertner, William G. 1947- WhoAm 94
Baumgardner, James Lewis 1938- WhoAm 94
Baumgardner, John Ellwood, Jr. 1951- WhoAm 94, WhoAmL 94
Baumgardt, Arden Charles 1941- WhoIns 94, WhoMW 93
Baumgardt, Billy Ray 1933- WhoAm 94, WhoScEn 94
Baumgart, James R. 1938- WhoAmP 93
Baumgart, Norbert K. 1931- WhoAm 94
Baumgartel, Howard J., Jr. 1920- WhoAm 94
Baumgarten, Alice Marie 1939- WhoMW 93
Baumgarten, Craig 1949- IntMPA 94
Baumgarten, Elias 1945- WhoMW 93
Baumgarten, Herbert Joseph 1935- WhoAmL 94, WhoFI 94
Baumgarten, Jon A. 1942- WhoAm 94, WhoAmL 94
Baumgarten, Karl Friedrich c. 1740-1824 NewGrDO
Baumgarten, Paul Anthony 1934- WhoAm 94
Baumgarten, Ronald Joseph 1935- WhoMW 93
Baumgarten, Sidney 1933- WhoAm 94, WhoAmL 94
Baumgarten, Willard Frederick, Jr. 1943- WhoWest 94
Baumgartner, Anton Edward 1948- WhoWest 94
Baumgartner, Bruce O. 1942- WhoAm 94, WhoAmL 94
Baumgartner, Donald Lawrence 1954- WhoScEn 94
Baumgartner, Ferdinand 1931- IntWW 93
Baumgartner, Frederic Joseph 1945- WhoAm 94
Baumgartner, James Earl 1943- WhoAm 94, WhoScEn 94
Baumgartner, James H., Jr. 1943- WhoAmL 94
Baumgartner, John F. 1947- WhoAmP 93
Baumgartner, John H. 1936- WhoAm 94
Baumgartner, Joy Ann 1946- WhoMW 93
Baumgartner, Leona 1902-1991 WhAm 10
Baumgartner, Rena V. 1934- WhoAmP 93
Baumgartner, Reuben Albert 1912- WhoMW 93
Baumgartner, Warren W. 1894-1963 WhoAmA 93N
Baumgartner, William Hans, Jr. 1955- WhoAm 94
Baumhart, Raymond Charles 1923- WhoAm 94
Baumhefner, Clarence Herman 1912- WhoAm 94
Baumhefner, Robert Walter 1948- WhoScEn 94
Baumhoff, Walter Henry 1937- WhoWest 94
Baumhover, Beverly Anne 1941- WhoMW 93
Baumkel, Mark S. 1951- WhoAmL 94
Bauml, Franz Heinrich 1926- WhoAm 94
Baumlin, Ursula 1938- WhoWomW 91
Baumol, William J. 1922- WrDr 94
Baumol, William Jack 1922- IntWW 93, WhoAm 94
Baumrin, Bernard Stefan Herbert 1934- WhoAm 94
Baumrind, Diana 1927- WhoAm 94, WhoWest 94
Baumrukova, Nasta WhoWomW 91
Bauner, Ruth Elizabeth WhoMW 93
Baur, Charles Wayne 1967- WhoMW 93
Baur, Christopher Frank 1942- Who 94
Baur, Elizabeth 1948- WhoHol 92
Baur, Harry d1943 WhoHol 92
Baur, Jean DrAPF 93
Baur, John Edward 1922- WrDr 94
Baur, Margrit 1937- BlmGWL
Baur, Robert F. 1945- WhoAmP 93
Baur, Werner Heinz 1931- WhoAm 94, WhoScEn 94
Baurle, Thomas Dean 1960- WhoMW 93
Baurmeister, Carl Leopold 1734-1803 WhAmRev
Baus, Herbert Michael 1914- WhoFI 94, WrDr 94
Bausani, Alessandro 1921-1988 ConAu 43NR
Bausch, James John 1936- WhoAm 94
Bausch, James Michael 1944- WhoAmL 94
Bausch, Janet Jean 1942- WhoAmL 94
Bausch, Michael George 1949- WhoMW 93
Bausch, Pina 1940- ConTFT 11
Bausch, Richard DrAPF 93
Bausch, Richard 1945- DcLB 130 [port], WrDr 94
Bausch, Richard (Carl) 1945- ConAu 43NR
Bauschard, Richard Bach 1944- WhoMW 93
Bausell, R. Barker, Jr. WhoScEn 94
Bausewein, Kaspar 1838-1903 NewGrDO
Bausher, Verne Charles WhoAm 94, WhoFI 94
Bausman, Dennis Charles 1949- WhoFI 94
Baussnern, Waldemar von 1866-1931 NewGrDO
Baustian, Robert Frederick 1921- WhoAm 94
Bauthumley, Jacob 1613-c. 1685 DcNaB MP
Bautier, Robert-Henri 1922- IntWW 93
Bautista, Abraham Parana 1952- WhoScEn 94
Bautista, Anthony Hernandez 1955- WhoWest 94
Bautista, Lualhati 1946- BlmGWL
Bautista, Manny Hector, Jr. 1958- WhoHisp 94
Bautista, Pilar 1958- WhoHisp 94
Bautista, Renato Go 1934- WhoScEn 94
Bautista, Veltisezar Bal 1933- WhoAsA 94
Bautz, Gordon Thomas 1942- WhoScEn 94
Bautz, Jeffrey Emerson 1966- WhoMW 93
Bautz, Laura Patricia 1940- WhoAm 94
Bauza, Mario d1993 NewYTBS 93 [port]
Bauzá, Mario 1911-1993 WhoHisp 94N
Bava, Gordon M. WhoAmL 94
Bava, Lamberto 1944- HorFD
Bava, Mario 1914-1980 HorFD [port]
Bavadra, Adi Kuini Teimumu Vuikaba 1949- IntWW 93
Bavaria, Albrecht Luitpold Ferdinand Michael, Duke of 1905- IntWW 93
Bavasi, Peter Joseph 1942- WhoAm 94
Bave, William Harold, Jr. 1948- WhoAmL 94
Baver, Roy Lane 1942- WhoMW 93
Bavero, Ronald Joseph 1950- WhoAmL 94
Baversjo, Charlotte Elizabeth 1959- WhoWest 94
Baverstock, Donald Leighton 1924- Who 94
Bavicchi, Robert Ferris 1957- WhoScEn 94
Bavier, Frances d1989 WhoHol 92
Baviera, Il NewGrDO
Bavin, Alfred Robert Walter 1917- Who 94
Bavin, Timothy John Who 94
Bavin, Timothy John 1935- IntWW 93
Bavinger, Eugene Allen 1919- WhoAmA 93
Bavis, Karen Ann 1962- WhoFI 94
Bavly, Dan (Abraham) 1929- WrDr 94
Bawa, Mohendra S. 1931- WhoAsA 94
Bawcutt, Priscilla (June) 1931- ConAu 141
Bawden, Charles Roskelly 1924- Who 94
Bawden, D. Lee d1993 NewYTBS 93
Bawden, David George 1949- WhoMW 93
Bawden, Garth Lawry 1939- WhoAm 94, WhoWest 94
Bawden, James Wyatt 1930- WhoAm 94
Bawden, Nina 1925- TwCYAW
Bawden, Nina (Mary) 1925- WrDr 94
Bawden, Nina Mary 1925- IntWW 93, Who 94, WhoAm 94
Bawn, Cecil Edwin Henry 1908- Who 94
Bawoyeu, Jean Alingue IntWW 93
Bawr, Alexandrine de 1773-1860 BlmGWL
Bawtree, David Kenneth 1937- Who 94
Bax, Martin 1933- EncSF 93
Bax, Martin (Charles Owen) 1933- WrDr 94
Bax, Roger 1908- WrDr 94
Bax, Simon Tristan 1959- WhoAm 94
Baxandall, David Kighley d1992 Who 94N
Baxandall, Michael David Kighley 1933- IntWW 93, Who 94
Baxendale, James Edward 1940- WhoIns 94
Baxendale, Joseph 1785-1872 DcNaB MP
Baxendale, Presiley Lamorna 1951- Who 94
Baxendale, Simone Marie 1958- WhoFI 94
Baxendell, Peter (Brian) 1925- Who 94
Baxendell, Peter Brian 1925- IntWW 93, WhoAm 94
Baxevanos, Peter 1908-1982 NewGrDO
Baxley, Barbara d1990 WhoHol 92
Baxley, Jack d1950 WhoHol 92
Baxley, John Michael 1956- WhoAmP 93
Baxley, William J. 1941- WhoAmP 93
Baxt, David WhoHol 92
Baxt, George 1923- WrDr 94
Baxter(-Wright), Keith (Stanley) 1935- WrDr 94
Baxter, Alan d1976 WhoHol 92
Baxter, Albert James, II 1935- WhoBlA 94
Baxter, Anne d1985 WhoHol 92
Baxter, Annie Maria 1816-1905 BlmGWL
Baxter, Arthur Pearce 1943- WhoAm 94
Baxter, Barry d1922 WhoHol 92
Baxter, Belgium Nathan 1921- WhoBlA 94
Baxter, Beryl 1926- WhoHol 92
Baxter, Billy d1936 WhoHol 92
Baxter, Billy 1926- IntMPA 94
Baxter, Bonnie Jean 1946- WhoAmA 93
Baxter, Brian WrDr 94
Baxter, Bruce Osborne 1945- WhoAm 94
Baxter, Carla Louise Chaney 1955- WhoMW 93
Baxter, Carol Cairns 1940- WhoWest 94
Baxter, Cecil William, Jr. 1923- WhoAm 94
Baxter, Charles DrAPF 93
Baxter, Charles 1947- ConLC 78 [port], DcLB 130 [port]
Baxter, Charles F., Jr. 1959- WhoBlA 94
Baxter, Christina Ann 1947- Who 94
Baxter, Clive WhoHol 92
Baxter, Craig 1929- WrDr 94
Baxter, Cynthia WhoHol 92
Baxter, Donald William 1926- WhoAm 94
Baxter, Douglas W. 1949- WhoAmA 93
Baxter, Duby Yvonne 1953- WhoWest 94
Baxter, E. R., III DrAPF 93
Baxter, Edward L. 1945- WhoAmL 94
Baxter, Elaine 1933- WhoAm 94, WhoMW 93
Baxter, Elaine Bland 1933- WhoAmP 93
Baxter, Ellen NewYTBS 93 [port]
Baxter, George d1976 WhoHol 92
Baxter, George 1804-1867 DcNaB MP
Baxter, Glen 1944- IntWW 93
Baxter, Gregory H.A. 1953- WhoFI 94
Baxter, Harry Stevens 1915- WhoAm 94
Baxter, Harry Youngs 1930- WhoAmP 93
Baxter, Howard H. 1931- WhoAmL 94
Baxter, Iain 1936- WhoAmA 93
Baxter, Ian Stuart 1937- Who 94
Baxter, James H., III 1945- WhoAmL 94
Baxter, James K(eir) 1926-1972 ConDr 93
Baxter, James Phinney, III 1893- WhAm 10
Baxter, James William, III 1931- WhoAm 94
Baxter, Jane 1909- WhoHol 92
Baxter, Jimmy d1969 WhoHol 92
Baxter, John 1918- WrDr 94
Baxter, John 1939- EncSF 93, WrDr 94
Baxter, John Darling 1940- WhoAm 94, WhoScEn 94
Baxter, John Lawson 1939- Who 94
Baxter, John Lincoln, Jr. 1920- WhoAm 94
Baxter, John Walter 1917- Who 94
Baxter, Joseph Diedrich 1937- WhoScEn 94
Baxter, Keith 1933- IntMPA 94, WhoHol 92
Baxter, Kevin Victor 1957- WhoWest 94
Baxter, Lawrence Gerald 1952- WhoAmL 94
Baxter, Lora d1955 WhoHol 92
Baxter, Loran Richard 1953- WhoScEn 94
Baxter, Marvin 1940- WhoAmP 93
Baxter, Marvin R. 1940- WhoAm 94, WhoAmL 94, WhoWest 94
Baxter, Mary Ann 1956- WhoMW 93
Baxter, Maurice Glen 1920- WhoAm 94
Baxter, Meredith 1947- IntMPA 94, WhoAm 94, WhoHol 92
Baxter, Meriwether Lewis, Jr. 1914- WhoScEn 94
Baxter, Murdoch Scott 1944- Who 94
Baxter, Pat Ann 1929- WhoWest 94
Baxter, Paula Adell 1954- WhoAmA 93
Baxter, Randolph 1946- WhoAmL 94
Baxter, Raoul 1950- WhoFI 94
Baxter, Ray 1952- WhoAmP 93
Baxter, Raymond Frederic 1922- Who 94
Baxter, Reginald Robert 1925- WhoAm 94
Baxter, Richard 1615-1691 BlmGEL
Baxter, Richard Brian 1927- WhoAm 94
Baxter, Robert Hampton, III 1931- WhoAm 94
Baxter, Rodney James 1940- IntWW 93, Who 94
Baxter, Roger George 1940- Who 94
Baxter, Ronald James 1952- WhoWest 94
Baxter, Sarah Elizabeth 1931- WhoAmP 93
Baxter, Stanley 1928- IntMPA 94, WhoHol 92
Baxter, Stephen (M.) 1957- EncSF 93
Baxter, Stephen Bartow 1929- WhoAm 94
Baxter, Terry Lawrence 1945- WhoAm 94
Baxter, Turner Butler 1922- WhoFI 94
Baxter, Violet WhoAmA 93
Baxter, Walter 1915- Who 94
Baxter, Warner d1951 WhoHol 92
Baxter, Wendy Marie 1952- WhoBlA 94
Baxter, William 1929- WhoAmP 93
Baxter, William Francis 1929- WhoAm 94
Baxter, William MacNeil 1923- WhoAm 94
Baxter, William T. 1906- Who 94
Baxter, William T(hreipland) 1906- WrDr 94
Bay, Austin 1951- WrDr 94
Bay, Ben WhoAmP 93
Bay, Catherine Marie WhoFI 94
Bay, Cynthia Ruth 1947- WhoMW 93
Bay, Frances WhoHol 92
Bay, John Cantrell 1929- WhoAm 94
Bay, Niels 1947- WhoScEn 94
Bay, Richard Anthony 1948- WhoWest 94
Bay, Rick WhoAm 94
Bay, Ronald Hampton 1948- WhoIns 94
Bay, Susan Louise 1946- WhoMW 93
Bay, Tom d1933 WhoHol 92
Bay, William Robert 1953- WhoAm 94
Bayandin, Lev Sergeevich 1942- LoBiDrD
Bayard, Alton Ernest, III 1952- WhoAm 94
Bayard, Franck 1917- WhoBlA 94
Bayard, Jean-Francois-Alfred 1796-1853 NewGrDO
Bayard, John B. 1738-1807 WhAmRev
Bayarski, Edward Leo 1950- WhoFI 94
Bayati, 'Abdal-Wahhab al- ConWorW 93
Baybars, Taner 1936- WrDr 94
Baybayan, Ronald Alan 1946- WhoAmL 94
Baybutt, Arlene Evans 1921- WhoAmP 93
Bayda, Edward Dmytro 1931- Who 94, WhoAm 94, WhoWest 94
Baye, Lawrence James J. 1933- WhoBlA 94
Baye, Nathalie 1948- IntWW 93, WhoHol 92
Bayefsky, Aba 1923- WhoAmA 93
Bayer, Arlyne WhoAmA 93
Bayer, Arthur Craig 1946- WhoScEn 94
Bayer, Gary Richard 1941- WhoAm 94
Bayer, Herbert 1900- WhoAmA 93N
Bayer, Janice Ilene 1966- WhoScEn 94
Bayer, Jeffrey Joshua 1942-1983 WhoAmA 93N
Bayer, Joel Laurence 1963- WhoMW 93
Bayer, Margret Helene Janssen 1931- WhoAm 94
Bayer, Oswald 1939- IntWW 93
Bayer, Patricia 1952- ConAu 141
Bayer, Valerie Townsend 1924- ConAu 141
Bayer, William 1939- WrDr 94
Bayer, William Martin 1930- WhoAm 94
Bayero, Alhaji Ado 1930- IntWW 93
Bayes, Gene d1966 WhoHol 92
Bayes, James R.W. 1950- WhoAmL 94
Bayes, Kyle David 1935- WhoScEn 94
Bayes, Ronald H. DrAPF 93
Bayes, Thomas 1701?-1761 DcNaB MP
Bayev, Aleksandr Aleksandrovich 1904- IntWW 93
Bayfield, Anthony Michael 1946- Who 94
Bayh, Birch 1928- WhoAmP 93
Bayh, Birch Evans, Jr. 1928- IntWW 93, WhoAm 94
Bayh, Evan 1955- IntWW 93, WhoAm 94, WhoAmP 93, WhoMW 93
Bayi, Filbert 1953- IntWW 93
Baykam, Bedri 1957- IntWW 93
Baykara, Zeyyad 1918- IntWW 93
Bayko, Emil Thomas 1947- WhoAm 94, WhoAmL 94
Baykut, Mehmet Gokhan 1954- WhoScEn 94
Bayldon, Geoffrey 1924- WhoHol 92
Bayle, Generes Dufour 1933- WhoFI 94
Bayle, Pierre 1647-1706 GuFrLit 2
Baylen, Joseph O. 1920- WhoAm 94, WrDr 94
Bayler, Terence 1930- WhoHol 92
Bayles, Deborah Lynn 1966- WhoAmL 94
Bayles, Donald Hamilton, Jr. 1949- WhoAmL 94
Bayles, Samuel Heagan 1910- WhoAm 94
Bayless, Charles Edward 1942- WhoAm 94, WhoFI 94
Bayless, James Leavell, Jr. 1952- WhoAmP 93
Bayless, Jerry Roger 1937- WhoMW 93
Bayless, Paul Clifton 1935- WhoBlA 94
Bayless, Raymond 1920- WhoAmA 93
Bayless, Romaine Belle 1945- WhoMW 93
Bayless, Theodore Morris 1931- WhoAm 94

Bayless, Timothy 1936- *WrDr 94*
Baylet, Jean-Michel 1946- *IntWW 93*
Bayley, Barrington J(ohn) 1937- *ConAu 43NR, EncSF 93*
Bayley, Barrington John 1937- *WrDr 94*
Bayley, Christopher T. 1938- *WhoAm 94, WhoFI 94*
Bayley, Eleanor d1976 *WhoHol 92*
Bayley, Gordon Vernon 1920- *Who 94*
Bayley, Hilda d1971 *WhoHol 92*
Bayley, Hugh 1952- *Who 94*
Bayley, Iris *Who 94*
Bayley, James Roosevelt 1814-1877 *DcAmReB 2*
Bayley, John *WhoAmP 93*
Bayley, John (Oliver) 1925- *WrDr 94*
Bayley, John Oliver 1925- *IntWW 93, Who 94*
Bayley, Nicola Mary 1949- *Who 94*
Bayley, Oscar Stewart Morris 1926- *Who 94*
Bayley, Peter (Charles) 1921- *WrDr 94*
Bayley, Peter Charles 1921- *Who 94*
Bayley, Peter James 1944- *Who 94*
Bayley, Richard 1745-1801 *WhAmRev*
Bayley, Stephen 1951- *IntWW 93, WrDr 94*
Bayley, Stephen Paul 1951- *Who 94*
Bayliff, Brad 1959- *WhoAmP 93*
Bayliff, W. Lane d1938 *WhoHol 92*
Baylin, Frank 1947- *WhoWest 94*
Baylin, Lee 1943- *WhoAmL 94*
Baylinson, A. S. 1882-1950 *WhoAmA 93N*
Baylis, Clifford Henry 1915- *Who 94*
Baylis, John 1946- *WrDr 94*
Baylis, Lilian 1874-1937 *IntDcB*
Baylis, Lilian (Mary) 1874-1937 *NewGrDO*
Baylis, Robert Goodwin 1925- *Who 94*
Baylis, Robert Montague 1938- *WhoAm 94, WhoFI 94*
Baylis, William Thomas 1952- *WhoScEn 94*
Bayliss, Frederic Joseph 1926- *Who 94*
Bayliss, George 1931- *WhoAmA 93*
Bayliss, George Vincent 1931- *WhoAm 94*
Bayliss, John 1934- *Who 94*
Bayliss, Larry Dale 1940- *WhoAm 94*
Bayliss, Noel (Stanley) 1906- *Who 94*
Bayliss, Noel Stanley 1906- *IntWW 93*
Bayliss, Peter *WhoHol 92*
Bayliss, Richard (Ian Samuel) 1917- *Who 94*
Bayliss, Richard Ian Samuel 1917- *IntWW 93*
Bayliss, Valerie June 1944- *Who 94*
Bayliss, William Maddock 1860-1924 *WorScD*
Baylor, Denis Aristide 1940- *WhoAm 94, WhoScEn 94*
Baylor, Don 1949- *ConBlB 6 [port]*
Baylor, Don Edward 1949- *WhoAm 94, WhoBlA 94*
Baylor, Elgin 1934- *AfrAmAl 6, BasBi, WhoBlA 94*
Baylor, Elgin Gay 1934- *WhoAm 94, WhoWest 94*
Baylor, George 1752-1784 *WhAmRev*
Baylor, Hal *WhoHol 92*
Baylor, Hugh Murray 1913-1992 *WhAm 10*
Baylor, Jill Stein 1954- *WhoScEn 94*
Baylor, John Patrick 1952- *WhoScEn 94*
Baylor, Sandra Johnson 1960- *WhoScEn 94*
Baylor, Solomon 1922- *WhoBlA 94*
Baylos, Zelma U. *WhoAmA 93N*
Bayly, Ada *BlmGWL*
Bayly, Christopher Alan 1945- *Who 94*
Bayly, John Henry, Jr. 1944- *WhoAm 94, WhoAmL 94*
Bayly, Patrick (Uniacke) 1914- *Who 94*
Baym, Gordon Alan 1935- *IntWW 93, WhoAm 94, WhoMW 93, WhoScEn 94*
Baym, Nina 1936- *WhoAm 94*
Baynard, Ed 1940- *WhoAmA 93*
Baynard, Ernest Cornish, III 1944- *WhoAm 94, WhoAmL 94*
Bayne, Beverly d1982 *WhoHol 92*
Bayne, Brian Leicester 1938- *Who 94*
Bayne, Charles Lee, Jr. 1963- *WhoWest 94*
Bayne, David Cowan 1918- *WhoAm 94*
Bayne, Henry G. 1925- *WhoBlA 94*
Bayne, J. Phillip 1929- *WhoAm 94*
Bayne, James Elwood 1940- *WhoAm 94, WhoFI 94*
Bayne, James Wilmer 1925- *WhoAm 94, WhoScEn 94*
Bayne, John *Who 94*
Bayne, Nicholas (Peter) 1937- *Who 94, WrDr 94*
Bayne, Nicholas Peter 1937- *IntWW 93*
Bayne-Powell, Robert Lane 1910- *Who 94*
Baynes, John (Christopher Malcolm) 1928- *Who 94*
Baynes, John (Christopher Malcolm), Sir 1928- *WrDr 94*
Baynes, Kenneth R(ichard) 1954- *ConAu 141*
Baynes, Pauline Diana 1922- *Who 94*
Baynes, Thomas Edward, Jr. 1940- *WhoAm 94, WhoAmL 94*
Baynham, Alexander Christopher 1935- *Who 94*
Baynham, Henry Wellesley Forster 1933- *WrDr 94*
Baynham, John William 1929- *Who 94*
Baynton, Barbara 1857-1929 *BlmGWL*
Baynton, Barbara (Lawrence) 1857-1929 *RfGShF*
Baynton, Edward c. 1495-1544 *DcNaB MP*
Bayo, Eduardo 1954- *WhoHisp 94, WhoWest 94*
Bayod, Florinda 1942- *WhoHisp 94*
Bays, Eric *Who 94*
Bays, Eric 1932- *WhoAm 94, WhoWest 94*
Bays, John Theophanis 1947- *WhoAm 94*
Bays, Karl Dean 1933-1989 *WhAm 10*
Bayse, Elinor Louise 1944- *WhoMW 93*
Bayseitova, Kulyash (Gul'bakhram) Zhasimovna 1912-1957 *NewGrDO*
Baysinger, Stephen Michael 1954- *WhoScEn 94*
Bayster, R. Jeffrey 1953- *WhoAmL 94*
Bayt, Robert Louis 1940- *WhoAm 94, WhoAmL 94*
Bayton, John 1930- *Who 94*
Bayulken, Umit Haluk 1921- *IntWW 93, Who 94*
Bayya, Shyam Sundar 1964- *WhoScEn 94*
Bazaine, Jean 1904- *IntWW 93*
Bazalgette, Derek Willoughby 1924- *Who 94*
Bazan, Alfonso M. *WhoHisp 94*
Bazán, Carlos, Jr. 1922- *WhoHisp 94*
Bazan, Elias, Jr. 1943- *WhoHisp 94*
Bazan, Jose Luis 1946- *WhoHisp 94*
Bazan-Figueras, Patricia 1957- *WhoHisp 94*
Bazant, Zdenek Pavel 1937- *WhoMW 93*
Bazargan, Mehdi 1907- *IntWW 93*
Bazarova, Roza Atamuradovna 1933- *WhoWomW 91*
Baz-Dresch, Felix R. 1938- *WhoFI 94*
Bazela, Jean Ann 1947- *WhoAm 94, WhoMW 93*
Bazelon, David L. 1909-1993 *NewYTBS 93 [port]*
Bazelon, David L(ionel) 1909-1993 *CurBio 93N*
Bazerman, Steven Howard 1940- *WhoAm 94, WhoAmL 94*
Ba Zhongtan *WhoPRCh 91*
Bazil, Ronald 1937- *WhoBlA 94*
Bazile, Leo *WhoBlA 94*
Bazin, Francois (Emmanuel-Joseph) 1816-1878 *NewGrDO*
Bazin, Germain Rene Michel d1990 *WhAm 10*
Bazin, Herve *IntWW 93*
Bazin, Marc Louis 1932- *IntWW 93*
Bazin, Nancy Topping 1934- *WhoAm 94*
Bazincourt, Thomas de, Mademoiselle fl. 18th cent.- *BlmGWL*
Bazinet, James Richard *WhoAmP 93*
Baziotes, William 1912-1963 *WhoAmA 93N*
Bazlen, Brigid d1989 *WhoHol 92*
Bazler, Frank Ellis 1930- *WhoAmL 94*
Bazley, Colin Frederick *Who 94*
Bazley, Thomas Stafford 1907- *Who 94*
Bazluke, Francine Tilewick 1954- *WhoAmL 94*
Bazylewicz-Murtha, Rosemary 1947- *WhoMW 93*
Bazzani, Francesco Maria c. 1650-c. 1700 *NewGrDO*
Bazzaz, Fakhri A. 1933- *WhoAm 94, WhoScEn 94*
Bazzazieh, Nader 1947- *WhoScEn 94*
Bazzini, Antonio 1818-1897 *NewGrDO*
Bea, Carlos Tiburcio 1934- *WhoHisp 94*
Beach *Who 94*
Beach, Amy Marcy 1867-1944 *NewGrDO*
Beach, Amy Marcy Cheney 1867-1944 *AmCulL*
Beach, Ann 1938- *WhoHol 92*
Beach, Arthur O'Neal 1945- *WhoAmL 94, WhoFI 94, WhoWest 94*
Beach, Arthur Thomas 1920- *WhoScEn 94*
Beach, Barbara Purse 1947- *WhoAmL 94*
Beach, Brandon d1974 *WhoHol 92*
Beach, Charles Addison 1945- *WhoAmL 94*
Beach, Charles Robert 1959- *WhoAmL 94*
Beach, Corra d1963 *WhoHol 92*
Beach, Daniel Robert 1943- *WhoMW 93*
Beach, David Duncan 1918- *WhoMW 93, WhoScEn 94*
Beach, Douglas Ryder 1948- *WhoAmL 94*
Beach, Edward L. *DrAPF 93*
Beach, Edward L. 1918- *WrDr 94*
Beach, Edward Latimer 1918- *WhoAm 94*
Beach, Franklin Ford 1925- *WhoFI 94*
Beach, Guy d1952 *WhoHol 92*
Beach, (William Gerald) Hugh 1923- *Who 94*
Beach, John dc. 1776 *WhAmRev*
Beach, John Arthur 1932- *WhoAm 94, WhoAmL 94*
Beach, John Parsons 1877-1953 *NewGrDO*
Beach, Lani Leroy 1944- *WhoAm 94*
Beach, Lee Roy 1936- *WhoAm 94, WhoWest 94*
Beach, Lynn *EncSF 93, SmATA 76*
Beach, Mary *DrAPF 93*
Beach, Michael *WhoHol 92*
Beach, Mildred A. 1924- *WhoAmP 93*
Beach, Milo C. *WhoAm 94*
Beach, Morrison H. 1917- *IntWW 93*
Beach, Robert C. 1935- *WhoAmP 93*
Beach, Robert Mark 1957- *WhoScEn 94*
Beach, Robert Oliver, II 1932- *WhoAm 94*
Beach, Roger C. 1936- *WhoFI 94, WhoWest 94*
Beach, Sammie Clair, Jr. 1948- *WhoMW 93*
Beach, Stephen Holbrook 1915- *WhoAmL 94*
Beach, Theo O. 1921- *WhoAmP 93*
Beach, Walter Eggert 1934- *WhoAm 94*
Beach, Walter G., II *WhoBlA 94*
Beach, Warren 1914- *WhoAmA 93*
Beach, William Vincent 1903- *Who 94*
Beacham, Arthur 1913- *Who 94*
Beacham, Dorothy Ann 1957- *WhoScEn 94*
Beacham, Richard C. 1946- *ConAu 141*
Beacham, Stephanie 1947- *WhoHol 92*
Beachcomber *EncSF 93*
Beachcroft, Nina 1931- *WrDr 94*
Beachem, Constance 1921- *WhoBlA 94*
Beachley, Michael Charles 1940- *WhoAm 94*
Beachley, Norman Henry 1933- *WhoAm 94*
Beachner, Louis d1986 *WhoHol 92*
Beachum, Sharon Garrison 1953- *WhoAmA 93*
Beachy, Rosemarie Scanlan 1958- *WhoFI 94*
Beachy, William R. 1948- *WhoAmP 93*
Beaconsfield, Lord *BlmGEL*
Beadell, Len 1923- *WrDr 94*
Beadle, Alfred Newman 1927- *WhoAm 94*
Beadle, Charles Wilson 1930- *WhoAm 94*
Beadle, George W. d1989 *NobelP 91N*
Beadle, George Wells 1903-1989 *WhAm 10, WorScD*
Beadle, John Grant 1932- *WhoAm 94*
Beadle, Sue M. 1944- *WhoAmP 93*
Beadles, Anthony Hugh 1940- *Who 94*
Beadles, Jon David 1956- *WhoMW 93*
Beadleston, Alfred N. 1912- *WhoAmP 93*
Beadleston, William L. 1938- *WhoAmA 93*
Beagle, E. Hampton d1990 *WhoHol 92*
Beagle, Gail Joyce 1935- *WhoAmP 93*
Beagle, John Gordon 1943- *WhoWest 94*
Beagle, Peter S. *DrAPF 93*
Beagle, Peter S(oyer) 1939- *TwCYAW, WrDr 94*
Beagle, Peter Soyer 1939- *WhoAm 94*
Beagle, Scott Robert 1952- *WhoFI 94*
Beagley, Thomas Lorne 1919- *Who 94*
Beagrie, George Simpson 1925- *WhoAm 94, WhoWest 94*
Beahler, John Leroy 1930- *WhoAm 94*
Beahrs, Oliver Howard 1914- *WhoAm 94, WhoMW 93, WhoScEn 94*
Beaird, Barbara *WhoHol 92*
Beaird, Betty 1939- *ConTFT 11*
Beaird, Charles T. 1922- *WhoAm 94*
Beaird, Daniel R. 1944- *WhoAmP 93*
Beaird, James Ralph 1925- *WhoAm 94*
Beak, Peter Andrew 1936- *WhoAm 94, WhoScEn 94*
Beake, John *WhoAm 94, WhoWest 94*
Beakley, George Carroll, Jr. 1922- *WhoAm 94*
Beakley, Robert Paul 1946- *WhoAmL 94*
Beal, Andrew Allen 1953- *WhoWest 94*
Beal, Anthony Ridley 1925- *Who 94*
Beal, Bernard *WhoBlA 94*
Beal, Bob 1949- *WrDr 94*
Beal, Dallas Knight 1926- *WhoAm 94*
Beal, Frank d1934 *WhoHol 92*
Beal, Graham William John 1947- *WhoAm 94, WhoAmA 93, WhoMW 93*
Beal, Gregory John 1942- *WhoAmP 93*
Beal, Ilene *WhoAm 94*
Beal, Jack 1931- *WhoAm 94, WhoAmA 93*
Beal, Jacqueline Jean 1960- *WhoBlA 94*
Beal, John 1909- *ConTFT 11, IntMPA 94, WhoAm 94, WhoHol 92*
Beal, John M. 1915- *WhoAm 94*
Beal, M. Allan d1993 *NewYTBS 93*
Beal, M. F. *DrAPF 93*
Beal, Mack 1924- *WhoAmA 93*
Beal, Merrill David 1926- *WhoAm 94*
Beal, Michael McNulty 1959- *WhoAmL 94*
Beal, Myron Clarence 1920- *WhoAm 94*
Beal, Norman Eugene 1943- *WhoAmL 94*
Beal, Orville E. d1993 *NewYTBS 93 [port]*
Beal, Peter George 1944- *Who 94*
Beal, Polly W. 1942- *WhoAmP 93*
Beal, Reynolds 1867-1951 *WhoAmA 93N*
Beal, Robert George *Who 94*
Beal, Robert Lawrence 1941- *WhoAm 94, WhoFI 94*
Beal, Royal d1969 *WhoHol 92*
Beal, Scott d1973 *WhoHol 92*
Beal, Valette Irene 1936- *WhoMW 93*
Beal, Wesley Arnold, Jr. 1946- *WhoAmP 93*
Beal Bagneris, Michele Christine 1959- *WhoBlA 94*
Beale, Anthony John 1932- *Who 94*
Beale, Arthur C. 1940- *WhoAmA 93*
Beale, Betty *WhoAm 94*
Beale, Charles Willing 1845-1932 *EncSF 93*
Beale, Christopher William 1947- *WhoAm 94*
Beale, David A. 1949- *WhoAmL 94*
Beale, Edward *Who 94*
Beale, (Thomas) Edward 1904- *Who 94*
Beale, Edward Fitzgerald 1822-1893 *WhWE [port]*
Beale, Geoffrey Herbert 1913- *IntWW 93, Who 94*
Beale, Georgia Robison 1905- *WhoFI 94*
Beale, Guy Otis 1944- *WhoScEn 94*
Beale, Josiah Edward Michael 1928- *Who 94*
Beale, Kenneth d1979 *WhoHol 92*
Beale, Larry D. 1949- *WhoBlA 94*
Beale, Michael Addis 1940- *WhoAmL 94*
Beale, Paul (Christian) 1933- *WrDr 94*
Beale, Peter (John) 1934- *Who 94*
Beale, Robert Lyndon 1936- *WhoAmL 94*
Beale, Sara Sun 1949- *WhoAmL 94*
Beale, Thomas J. 1940- *WhoAmL 94*
Beale, Walter M., Jr. 1945- *WhoAmL 94*
Beale, William Francis 1908-1992 *AnObit 1992*
Beale, William Taylor 1928- *WhoScEn 94*
Bealer, Jonathan Miles 1946- *WhoWest 94*
Beales, D(erek) E(dward) D(awson) 1931- *WrDr 94*
Beales, Derek Edward Dawson 1931- *IntWW 93, Who 94*
Beales, Peter Leslie 1936- *Who 94*
Beales, Valerie 1915- *SmATA 74 [port]*
Bealey, Frank (William) 1922- *WrDr 94*
Bealey, Frank William 1922- *Who 94*
Bealke, Linn Hemingway 1944- *WhoAm 94*
Beall, Burtch W., Jr. 1925- *WhoAm 94*
Beall, Charles M. 1920- *WhoAmP 93*
Beall, Charles Porter 1924- *WhoWest 94*
Beall, Cynthia 1949- *WhoAm 94, WhoMW 93*
Beall, Dennis Ray 1929- *WhoAm 94, WhoAmA 93, WhoWest 94*
Beall, DeWitt Talmadge 1940- *WhoWest 94*
Beall, Donald Ray 1938- *IntWW 93, WhoAm 94, WhoFI 94, WhoWest 94*
Beall, Frank Carroll 1933- *WhoWest 94*
Beall, George 1937- *WhoAm 94, WhoAmL 94*
Beall, George Halsey 1935- *WhoScEn 94*
Beall, Ingrid Lillehei 1926- *WhoAm 94*
Beall, J. Glenn, Jr. 1927- *WhoAmP 93*
Beall, James Crichton 1942- *WhoWest 94*
Beall, James Howard 1945- *WhoScEn 94*
Beall, Joanna 1935- *WhoAmA 93*
Beall, Karen Friedmann *WhoAmA 93*
Beall, Lawrence Anthony 1961- *WhoAmL 94*
Beall, Lester Thomas 1902-1969 *WhoAmA 93N*
Beall, Robert Joseph 1943- *WhoAm 94, WhoScEn 94*
Beall, Robert Matthews, II 1943- *WhoAm 94*
Beall, Russell G. 1922- *WhoAmP 93*
Beall, Samuel E., III 1950- *WhoFI 94*
Beall, Sandra *WhoHol 92*
Beall, Ware Thompson, Jr. 1940- *WhoMW 93*
Beallor, Fran 1957- *WhoAmA 93*
Bealmer, William 1919- *WhoAmA 93*
Beals, Jennifer 1963- *IntMPA 94, WhoAm 94, WhoHol 92*
Beals, John D(avid) 1896- *WhAm 10*
Beals, Loren Alan 1933- *WhoAm 94*
Beals, Nancy Farwell 1938- *WhoAmP 93*
Beals, Paul Archer 1924- *WhoMW 93*
Beals, Ralph Everett 1936- *WhoAm 94*
Beals, Vaughn Le Roy, Jr. 1928- *WhoAm 94, WhoFI 94*
Beam, Alex 1954- *WrDr 94*
Beam, Alvin d1989 *WhoHol 92*
Beam, C. Arlen 1930- *WhoAmP 93*

Beam, Clarence Arlen 1930- WhoAm 94, WhoAmL 94, WhoMW 93
Beam, Frank Letts 1942- WhoFI 94
Beam, Jacob D. d1993 NewYTBS 93
Beam, Jacob D(yneley) 1908-1993 CurBio 93N
Beam, Jacob Dyneley d1993 Who 94N
Beam, James C. 1933- WhoAm 94
Beam, James Harold 1934- WhoAmP 93
Beam, Jeffery DrAPF 93
Beam, Jerry Edward 1947- WhoMW 93, WhoScEn 94
Beam, John Scott 1944- WhoAmP 93
Beam, Joline Landry WhoAmP 93
Beam, Lillian Kennedy 1924- WhoBlA 94
Beam, Mary Todd 1931- WhoAmA 93
Beam, Patricia Hosang 1954- WhoMW 93
Beam, Philip Conway 1910- WhoAmA 93
Beam, Robert Garrett 1958- WhoFI 94
Beam, Robert Thompson 1919- WhoAm 94
Beam, William Washington, III 1960- WhoFI 94, WhoScEn 94, WhoWest 94
Beaman, Jack 1924- WhoAmP 93
Beaman, John David 1965- WhoWest 94
Beaman, Joyce Proctor 1931- WrDr 94
Beaman, Margarine Gaynell WhoFI 94
Beaman, Mark T. 1954- WhoAmL 94
Beaman, Peter Hays 1945- WhoAm 94
Beaman, William Charles 1945- WhoAm 94, WhoAmL 94, WhoWest 94
Beame, Abraham David 1906- IntWW 93, WhoAmP 93
Beament, Harold 1898- WhoAmA 93N
Beament, James (William Longman) 1921- IntWW 93, Who 94
Beament, Thomas Harold 1941- WhoAm 94
Beament, Tib (Thomas Harold) 1941- WhoAmA 93
Beamer, Brenda Jane 1945- WhoMW 93
Beamer, Janet Gries 1965- WhoMW 93
Beamer, Lesa Jean 1963- WhoScEn 94
Beamer, Sarah Armbrister 1959- WhoFI 94
Beamer-Patton, June Elizabeth 1944- WhoWest 94
Beamish, Adrian John 1939- Who 94
Beamish, Cecil Howard 1915- Who 94
Beamish, Frank d1921 WhoHol 92
Beamon, Arthur L. 1942- WhoBlA 94
Beamon, Launa Rae 1955- WhoWest 94
Beamon, Reginald Glenn 1951- WhoAmP 93
Beamon, Teresa Kristine Nkenge Zola 1954- WhoBlA 94
Beamont, Roland Prosper 1920- Who 94
Bean, Alan LaVern 1932- WhoAm 94
Bean, Andrew James 1964- WhoAmL 94
Bean, Basil 1931- Who 94
Bean, Bennett 1941- WhoAm 94, WhoAmA 93
Bean, Bobby Gene 1951- WhoBlA 94
Bean, Bourne 1922- WhoAm 94
Bean, Bruce Winfield 1941- WhoAm 94
Bean, Carl Norman, Jr. 1954- WhoMW 93
Bean, Charles Palmer 1923- WhoAm 94
Bean, Donna Rae 1950- WhoWest 94
Bean, Edwin Temple, Jr. 1926- WhoAm 94, WhoAmL 94
Bean, Elizabeth Harriman 1923- WhoAmP 93
Bean, Frank Dawson 1942- WhoAm 94
Bean, George Washington 1831-1897 EncNAR
Bean, Hugh (Cecil) 1929- Who 94
Bean, Jacob 1923- WhAm 10
Bean, James H. 1934- WhoAmL 94
Bean, James L., Jr. 1932- WhoAmP 93
Bean, James Woolson, Jr. 1947- WhoWest 94
Bean, Joan P. 1933- WhoAm 94
Bean, John David 1947- WhoIns 94
Bean, John Victor 1925- Who 94
Bean, Leonard 1914- Who 94
Bean, Marisa Who 94
Bean, Maurice Darrow 1928- WhoAm 94
Bean, Norman EncSF 93
Bean, Orson 1926- WhoCom
Bean, Orson 1928- IntMPA 94, WhoHol 92
Bean, Oscar Belmont 1923- WhoAmP 93
Bean, Pamela B. 1942- WhoAmP 93
Bean, Ron 1938- WhoAmP 93
Bean, Scott W. WhoAm 94
Bean, Sean WhoHol 92
Bean, Sean 1958- IntMPA 94
Bean, Stephen Michael 1953- WhoAmP 93
Bean, Walter Dempsey 1912- WhoBlA 94
Bean, William James 1933- WhoWest 94
Beane, Dorothea Annette 1952- WhoBlA 94
Beane, J. D. 1963- WhoAmP 93
Beane, Jerry Lynn 1944- WhoAm 94, WhoAmL 94
Beane, Patricia Jean 1944- WhoBlA 94
Beane, Reginald d1985 WhoHol 92
Beane, Robert Hubert 1947- WhoBlA 94
Beans, Charles Raymond 1962- WhoAmL 94
Beans, Doanld Ring 1953- WhoWest 94
Bear, Bullen 1933- WrDr 94
Bear, Dinah 1951- WhoAm 94, WhoAmL 94
Bear, Donald 1905-1952 WhoAmA 93N
Bear, Donald 1945- WhoFI 94
Bear, Greg 1951- EncSF 93
Bear, Greg(ory Dale) 1951- WrDr 94
Bear, Gregory Dale 1951- WhoAm 94, WhoWest 94
Bear, Herbert Stanley, Jr. 1929- WhoWest 94
Bear, James B. 1941- WhoAmL 94
Bear, Jeffrey Warren 1945- WhoWest 94
Bear, Larry Alan 1928- WhoAm 94, WhoAmL 94, WhoFI 94
Bear, Leslie William 1911- Who 94
Bear, Marcelle L. 1917- WhoAmA 93
Bear, Mary d1972 WhoHol 92
Bear, William Edward 1931- WhoWest 94
Bearak, Corey Becker 1955- WhoAmL 94
Bearb, Michael Edwin 1956- WhoScEn 94
Bearce, Jeana Dale WhoAm 94
Bearce, Jeana Dale 1929- WhoAmA 93
Bearce, Winfield Hutchinson, Jr. 1937- WhoAm 94
Beard, Allan Geoffrey 1919- Who 94
Beard, Andrew J. 1849-1941 WorInv
Beard, Andrew Jackson c. 1850-1910 AfrAmAl 6
Beard, Anson McCook, Jr. 1936- WhoFI 94
Beard, Butch 1946- BasBi
Beard, Charles Austin 1874-1948 AmSocL
Beard, Charles Julian 1943- WhoAm 94, WhoAmL 94, WhoBlA 94
Beard, Charles Stephen 1952- WhoFI 94, WhoMW 93
Beard, Constance Rachelle 1949- WhoWest 94
Beard, Daniel Perry 1943- WhoAmP 93
Beard, Derek 1930- Who 94
Beard, Elizabeth Letitia 1932- WhoAm 94
Beard, Elmer 1937- WhoAmP 93
Beard, Eugene WhoAm 94
Beard, Geoffrey 1929- WrDr 94
Beard, George Plummer, Jr. 1921- WhoAmP 93
Beard, Hazel WhoAm 94, WhoAmP 93
Beard, Israel 1932- WhoBlA 94
Beard, James d1985 WhoHol 92
Beard, James Franklin 1919-1989 WhAm 10
Beard, James William, Jr. 1941- WhoBlA 94
Beard, Janet Marie 1930- WhoAm 94
Beard, Joan Mardelle 1942- WhoMW 93
Beard, John c. 1717-1791 NewGrDO
Beard, John Edwards 1932- WhoAm 94
Beard, Joseph James 1933- WhoAm 94
Beard, Kenneth Van Kirke 1937- WhoMW 93
Beard, Leo Roy 1917- WhoAm 94
Beard, Lillian McLean WhoBlA 94
Beard, Malcolm E. 1919- WhoAmP 93
Beard, Marion L. Patterson WhoAmA 93N
Beard, Martin Luther 1926- WhoBlA 94
Beard, Mary Ritter 1876-1958 AmSocL
Beard, Matthew d1981 WhoHol 92
Beard, Melvin Charles 1935-1985 WhoBlA 94N
Beard, Michael Carl 1956- WhoMW 93
Beard, Michael Kenneth 1941- WhoAm 94
Beard, Montgomery, Jr. 1932- WhoBlA 94
Beard, Nigel Who 94
Beard, (Christopher) Nigel 1936- Who 94
Beard, Patrick 1947- WhoAmP 93
Beard, R. D. 1923- WhoAmP 93
Beard, R. T., III 1947- WhoAmL 94
Beard, Ralph 1927- BasBi
Beard, Richard Elliott 1928- WhoAmA 93
Beard, Richard Leonard 1909- WhoAm 94
Beard, Richard William 1931- Who 94
Beard, Robert Douglas 1961- WhoScEn 94
Beard, Rodney Allen 1961- WhoAmL 94
Beard, Rodney Rau 1911- WhoAm 94
Beard, Ronald Stratton 1939- WhoAm 94
Beard, Stanley WhoHol 92
Beard, Stymie WhoCom
Beard, Thomas Lee 1955- WhoAm 94
Beard, Virginia H. 1941- WhoBlA 94
Beard, William Kelly 1898-1990 WhAm 10
Bearden, Carl Lee 1956- WhoMW 93
Bearden, James Hudson 1933- WhoAm 94
Bearden, Mike R. 1948- WhoAmP 93
Bearden, Patricia Ann 1942- WhoAm 94
Bearden, Romare 1914-1988 AfrAmAl 6
Bearden, Thomas Edward 1958- WhoFI 94
Beardmore, Alexander Francis 1931- Who 94
Beardmore, Dorothy WhoAm 94
Beardmore, Harvey Ernest 1921- WhoAm 94
Beardmore, John Alec 1930- Who 94
Beards, Paul Francis Richmond 1916- Who 94
Beardslee, William Armitage 1916- WhoAm 94
Beardsley, Alice 1925- WhoHol 92
Beardsley, Aubrey 1872-1898 BlmGEL
Beardsley, Barbara H. 1945- WhoAmA 93
Beardsley, Charles Mitchell 1921- WhoFI 94, WhoIns 94
Beardsley, Charles William 1939- WhoAm 94
Beardsley, George Peter 1940- WhoAm 94
Beardsley, James H., II 1945- WhoAmP 93
Beardsley, John Ray 1937- WhoFI 94
Beardsley, Lisa Marie 1958- WhoMW 93
Beardsley, Robert Eugene 1923- WhoAm 94
Beardsley, Theodore S., Jr. 1930- WrDr 94
Beardsley, Theodore Sterling, Jr. 1930- WhoAm 94
Beardsworth, Simon John 1929- Who 94
Beare, Bruce Riley 1942- WhoAm 94
Beare, Gene Kerwin 1915- WhoAm 94
Beare, Robin Lyell Blin 1922- Who 94
Beare, Stuart Newton 1936- Who 94
Bearer, Cynthia Frances 1950- WhoScEn 94
Beare-Rogers, Joyce Louise 1927- WhoAm 94
Bearg, David Warren 1948- WhoFI 94
Bearley, William Leon 1938- WhoWest 94
Bearman, Toni Carbo 1942- WhoAm 94
Bearmon, Lee WhoFI 94
Bearn, Alexander Gordon 1923- IntWW 93, Who 94, WhoAm 94
Bearne, Guy 1908- Who 94
Bearnson, William R. 1961- WhoScEn 94
Bearss, Edwin Cole 1923- WhoAm 94
Bearss, Joyce C. 1930- WhoAmP 93
Bearsted, Viscount 1911- Who 94
Bearstler, Wayne Alan 1959- WhoMW 93
Beart, Emmanuelle 1965- IntMPA 94, WhoHol 92
Beart, Guy 1930- IntWW 93
Bear-Track c. 1790-c. 1880 EncNAR
Bearwald, Jean Haynes 1924- WhoFI 94, WhoWest 94
Beary, John Francis, III 1946- WhoAm 94
Beary, Lori Knauss 1958- WhoAmP 93
Beary, Shirley Lorraine 1928- WhoAm 94
Beasing, David Bryan 1962- WhoMW 93
Beasley, Alice Margaret 1945- WhoBlA 94
Beasley, Anne Vickers 1917- WhoBlA 94
Beasley, Annie Ruth 1928- WhoBlA 94
Beasley, Arch Adam, III 1966- WhoFI 94
Beasley, Arlene A. 1943- WhoBlA 94
Beasley, Barbara Starin 1955- WhoAm 94
Beasley, Bea Cassandra 1942- WhoFI 94
Beasley, Bruce 1939- WhoAmA 93
Beasley, Bruce Miller 1939- WhoAm 94, WhoWest 94
Beasley, Cecil Ackmond, Jr. 1911- WhoAm 94
Beasley, Charles Alfred 1934- WhoScEn 94
Beasley, Cloyd Orris, Jr. 1933- WhoAm 94
Beasley, Daniel L. 1910- WhoBlA 94
Beasley, David Muldrow 1957- WhoAmP 93
Beasley, Edward, III WhoBlA 94
Beasley, Ernest William, Jr. 1924- WhoScEn 94
Beasley, Eula Daniel 1958- WhoBlA 94
Beasley, J. Lamar 1936- WhoAmP 93
Beasley, James Edwin 1926- WhoAmL 94
Beasley, James George WhoMW 93
Beasley, James W., Jr. 1943- WhoAm 94, WhoAmL 94
Beasley, Jesse C. 1929- WhoBlA 94
Beasley, Jim Sanders 1936- WhoAm 94
Beasley, John P. WhoAmP 93
Beasley, John T. Who 94
Beasley, Kim Allen 1952- WhoFI 94
Beasley, Lois Rene 1960- WhoAmL 94
Beasley, Malcolm Roy 1940- WhoAm 94, WhoScEn 94
Beasley, Mary Catherine 1922- WhoAm 94
Beasley, Maurine 1936- ConAu 42NR
Beasley, Michael Charles 1924- Who 94
Beasley, Modena James 1934- WhoAm 94
Beasley, Neal Alan 1951- WhoMW 93
Beasley, Oscar Homer 1925- WhoAmL 94
Beasley, Paul Lee 1950- WhoBlA 94
Beasley, Robert Palmer WhoAm 94
Beasley, Robert Scott 1949- WhoAm 94, WhoFI 94
Beasley, Ruth 1942- WrDr 94
Beasley, Ulysses Christian, Jr. 1928- WhoBlA 94
Beasley, Val Richard 1948- WhoMW 93
Beasley, Victor Mario 1956- WhoBlA 94
Beasley, William De Ford 1929- WhoFI 94
Beasley, William Gerald 1919- Who 94, WrDr 94
Beasley, William Howard, III 1946-1990 WhAm 10
Beasley, William Michael 1951- WhoAmL 94
Beasley, William Rex 1934- WhoAm 94
Beasley-Murray, George Raymond 1916- Who 94, WrDr 94
Beasley-Murray, Paul 1944- Who 94
Beason, Amos Theodore 1940- WhoAm 94
Beason, Donald Ray 1943- WhoAmA 93
Beason, Doug 1953- EncSF 93
Beason, Kenneth Garrett 1942- WhoBlA 94
Beason, Margaret Eva 1933- WhoAmP 93
Beason, Nina d1929 WhoHol 92
Beastall, John Sale 1941- Who 94
Beath, Warren Newton 1951- WrDr 94
Beathard, Bobby 1937- WhoAm 94, WhoWest 94
Beatie, Russel Harrison, Jr. 1938- WhoAmL 94
Beatles, The WhoHol 92
Beato, Maritza 1949- WhoHisp 94
Beaton, Cecil 1904-1980 IntDcF 2-4
Beaton, James Duncan 1930- WhoScEn 94
Beaton, James Wallace 1943- Who 94
Beaton, Lyle Glen 1935- WhoMW 93
Beaton, Mary Louise d1961 WhoHol 92
Beaton, Nancy C. 1955- WhoAmP 93
Beaton, Norman WhoHol 92
Beaton, Roy Howard 1916- WhoAm 94
Beatrice de Romans fl. 13th cent.- BlmGWL
Beatrice of Kent BlmGWL
Beatrix, Queen of the Netherlands 1938- IntWW 93, WhoWomW 91
Beatson, Jack 1948- Who 94
Beattie, Alexander (Craig) 1912- Who 94
Beattie, Ann DrAPF 93
Beattie, Ann 1947- BlmGWL, RfGShF, WhoAm 94, WrDr 94
Beattie, Anthony Who 94
Beattie, (George) Anthony 1944- Who 94
Beattie, Arthur James 1914- Who 94
Beattie, Charles Kenneth 1923- WhoAmP 93
Beattie, Charles Noel 1912- Who 94
Beattie, Charles Robert, III 1948- WhoAmL 94
Beattie, Dame Heather Who 94
Beattie, David 1938- Who 94
Beattie, David (Stuart) 1924- Who 94
Beattie, David Stuart 1924- IntWW 93
Beattie, Diana Scott 1934- WhoAm 94
Beattie, Donald A. 1929- WhoAm 94, WhoScEn 94
Beattie, Edward James 1918- WhoAm 94
Beattie, George 1919- WhoAm 94, WhoAmA 93
Beattie, George Chapin 1919- WhoWest 94
Beattie, James 1735-1803 BlmGEL
Beattie, James Raymond 1935- WhoAmL 94
Beattie, Janet Holtzman 1927- WhoAm 94
Beattie, Lane 1951- WhoAmP 93
Beattie, Melody (Lynn) 1948- ConAu 141
Beattie, Nora Maureen 1925- WhoAm 94
Beattie, Pamela Marie Pash 1944- WhoFI 94
Beattie, Richard Irwin 1939- WhoAmL 94
Beattie, Ted Arthur 1945- WhoAm 94
Beattie, Thomas Brunton 1924- Who 94
Beattie, William John Hunt Montgomery d1993 Who 94N
Beatty, Earl 1946- Who 94
Beatty, Andrew Hyland 1964- WhoAmL 94
Beatty, Charles Eugene, Sr. 1909- WhoBlA 94
Beatty, Clyde d1965 WhoHol 92
Beatty, David F. 1941- WhoAmL 94
Beatty, David Lawrence 1952- WhoAmP 93
Beatty, Donald W. 1952- WhoAmP 93
Beatty, Frances 1940- WhoMW 93
Beatty, Frances Fielding Lewis 1948- WhoAmA 93
Beatty, George d1971 WhoHol 92
Beatty, Haradon 1940- WhoAmL 94
Beatty, Hugh Tyrrell 1939- WhoWest 94
Beatty, Jack J. 1945- WhoAm 94
Beatty, James D. WhoAmP 93
Beatty, John 1749-1826 WhAmRev
Beatty, John Cabeen, Jr. 1919- WhoAm 94
Beatty, John Lee 1948- WhoAm 94
Beatty, John Townsend, Jr. 1936- WhoFI 94
Beatty, Joseph Robert 1944- WhoAmL 94
Beatty, Kenneth Orion, Jr. 1913- WhoAm 94
Beatty, Linda L. 1942- WhoAmP 93

Beatty, Martha Nell 1933- *WhoWest 94*
Beatty, Martin Clarke *WhoBlA 94*
Beatty, May d1945 *WhoHol 92*
Beatty, Michael Alexander *WhoAmP 93*
Beatty, Michael L. 1947- *WhoAm 94, WhoAmL 94, WhoFI 94*
Beatty, Ned 1937- *IntMPA 94, WhoAm 94, WhoHol 92*
Beatty, Otto, Jr. *WhoAmP 93*
Beatty, Otto, Jr. 1940- *WhoBlA 94*
Beatty, Ozell Kakaskus 1921- *WhoBlA 94*
Beatty, Patricia 1922-1991 *WrDr 94N*
Beatty, Patricia Jean d1991 *WhAm 10*
Beatty, Pearl 1935- *WhoBlA 94*
Beatty, Perrin 1950- *IntWW 93*
Beatty, (Henry) Perrin 1950- *Who 94*
Beatty, Richard Scrivener 1934- *WhoAm 94*
Beatty, Robert 1909- *WhoHol 92*
Beatty, Robert L. 1939- *WhoBlA 94*
Beatty, Samuel Alston 1923- *WhoAmP 93*
Beatty, Warren 1937- *ConTFT 11, IntMPA 94, IntWW 93, WhoAm 94, WhoHol 92*
Beatty, William Kaye 1926- *WhoAm 94*
Beatty, William Louis 1925- *WhoAm 94, WhoAmL 94, WhoMW 93*
Beatty, Zelmo 1939- *BasBi*
Beatty-Brown, Florence R. 1912- *WhoBlA 94*
Beatty-Kingston, William 1837-1900 *NewGrDO*
Beatus Of Valcavado fl. 77-?- *WhWE*
Beaty, Betty (Smith) 1919- *WrDr 94*
Beaty, (Arthur) David 1919- *WrDr 94*
Beaty, Ernest Albert 1898- *WhAm 10*
Beaty, Harry Nelson 1932- *WhoAm 94*
Beaty, John Thurston, Jr. 1944- *WhoFI 94*
Beaty, Narlin Bennet 1950- *WhoFI 94*
Beaty, Orren, Jr. 1919- *WhoAm 94*
Beaty, Paul Richard 1946- *WhoWest 94*
Beaty, Rufus F. 1958- *WhoAmL 94*
Beau, Heine d1987 *WhoHol 92*
Beaubien, Anne Kathleen 1947- *WhoAm 94*
Beaubien, George H. 1937- *WhoBlA 94*
Beaubien, Julien d1947 *WhoHol 92*
Beaubien, Philippe de Gaspe, II 1928- *WhoAm 94*
Beauchamp, Christopher Radstock Proctor- 1935- *Who 94*
Beauchamp, Gary Fay 1951- *WhoAmL 94*
Beauchamp, Gary Keith 1943- *WhoScEn 94*
Beauchamp, George 1933- *WhoAmA 93*
Beauchamp, Jack *WhoAmP 93*
Beauchamp, Jacques 1948- *WhoAm 94*
Beauchamp, James Harry 1942- *WhoAmL 94*
Beauchamp, Jeffery Oliver 1943- *WhoScEn 94*
Beauchamp, Jerry J. 1932- *WhoAmP 93*
Beauchamp, Jesse Lee 1942- *WhoScEn 94*
Beauchamp, Kathleen Mansfield *GayLL*
Beauchamp, Kenneth 1939- *WrDr 94*
Beauchamp, Martha Jean 1956- *WhoMW 93*
Beauchamp, Patrick L. *WhoBlA 94*
Beauchamp, Pierre 1631-c. 1705 *IntDcB*
Beauchamp, Pierre 1943- *WhoAm 94*
Beauchamp, Robert 1923- *WhoAmA 93*
Beauchamps, Pierre 1631-c. 1705 *IntDcB, NewGrDO*
Beauchesne, Wilfred P. 1923- *WhoAmP 93*
Beauclerk *Who 94*
Beaudeau, Marie-Claude 1937- *WhoWomW 91*
Beau de Rochas, Alphonse *WorInv*
Beaudet, Louise d1947 *WhoHol 92*
Beaudet, Robert Arthur 1935- *WhoWest 94*
Beaudette, Robert Lee 1943- *WhoMW 93*
Beaudine, William d1970 *WhoHol 92*
Beaudoin, Andre Eugene 1920- *WhoAmA 93*
Beaudoin, Francois 1951- *WhoAm 94*
Beaudoin, Gerald-A. 1929- *IntWW 93*
Beaudoin, Gerald-Armand 1929- *WhoAm 94*
Beaudoin, Kenneth L. *DrAPF 93*
Beaudoin, Laurent 1938- *WhoAm 94, WhoFI 94*
Beaudoin, Marcel C. 1932- *WhoFI 94*
Beaudoin, Monica 1937- *WhoAmP 93*
Beaudoin, Robert Lawrence 1933- *WhoFI 94, WhoMW 93*
Beaudouin, David *DrAPF 93*
Beaudreau, David Eugene 1929- *WhoAm 94*
Beaudreau, Louise F. 1928- *WhoAmP 93*
Beaudry, Alice Marie 1947- *WhoMW 93*
Beaudry, Donald Arthur 1929- *WhoAmL 94*
Beaudry, Janis Stonier 1956- *WhoWest 94*
Beaufait, Frederick William 1936- *WhoAm 94*
Beauford, Fred 1940- *WhoBlA 94*
Beaufort, Duke of 1928- *Who 94*
Beaufort, Margaret 1443-1509 *BlmGWL [port], HisWorL [port]*
Beaugrand, Leontine 1842-1925 *IntDcB [port]*
Beaugrand, Michel 1945- *WhoScEn 94*
Beauharnais, Marie-Anne-Francoise Mouchard, Comtesse de 1737-1813 *BlmGWL*
Beaujeu-Garnier, Jacqueline 1917- *IntWW 93*
Beaujon, Paul 1900-1969 *EncSF 93*
Beaujoyeulx, Balthasar de c. 1535-c. 1587 *IntDcB*
Beaujoyeux, Balthasar de c. 1535-c. 1587 *IntDcB*
Beaulac, Willard L. 1899-1990 *WhAm 10*
Beaulieu, Edith S. 1937- *WhoAmP 93*
Beaulieu, Hyacinthe 1916- *WhoAmP 93*
Beaulieu, Jacques Alexandre 1932- *WhoAm 94, WhoScEn 94*
Beaulieu, Jon P. 1937- *WhoAmP 93*
Beauman, Katharine (Burgoyne) Bentley *WrDr 94*
Beauman, Sally 1944- *WrDr 94*
Beaumarchais, Pierre-Augustin (Caron de) 1732-1799 *NewGrDO*
Beaumarchais, Pierre-Augustin Caron de 1732-1799 *AmRev, DramC 4 [port], GuFrLit 2, IntDcT 2, WhAmRev*
Beaumavielle, Francois d1688 *NewGrDO*
Beaumer, Madame de d1766 *BlmGWL*
Beaumesnil, Henriette Adelaide Villard de 1748-1813 *NewGrDO*
Beaumier, Sarah Ellen 1955- *WhoFI 94*
Beaumont *Who 94*
Beaumont, Agnes 1652-1720 *DcNaB MP*
Beaumont, Bill *Who 94*
Beaumont, Charles d1967 *WhoHol 92*
Beaumont, Charles 1929-1967 *EncSF 93*
Beaumont, Christopher *Who 94*
Beaumont, (Herbert) Christopher 1912- *Who 94*
Beaumont, Christopher Hubert 1926- *Who 94*
Beaumont, David Colin Baskcomb 1942- *Who 94*
Beaumont, Diana d1964 *WhoHol 92*
Beaumont, Donald A. 1935- *WhoAm 94*
Beaumont, Enid Franklin 1930- *WhoAm 94*
Beaumont, Etienne de *IntDcB*
Beaumont, Francis 1584-1616 *BlmGEL, IntDcT 2*
Beaumont, George Howland Francis 1924- *Who 94*
Beaumont, Harry d1966 *WhoHol 92*
Beaumont, Henry c. 1280-1340 *DcNaB MP*
Beaumont, Hugh d1982 *WhoHol 92*
Beaumont, Jeanne *DrAPF 93*
Beaumont, John Richard 1957- *Who 94*
Beaumont, Kathryn 1938- *WhoHol 92*
Beaumont, Lucy d1937 *WhoHol 92*
Beaumont, (John) Michael 1927- *Who 94*
Beaumont, Mona *WhoAmA 93, WhoWest 94*
Beaumont, Nellie d1938 *WhoHol 92*
Beaumont, Nicholas *Who 94*
Beaumont, (Edward) Nicholas (Canning) 1929- *Who 94*
Beaumont, Pamela Jo 1944- *WhoAm 94*
Beaumont, Peter John Luther 1944- *Who 94*
Beaumont, Richard Ashton 1912- *Who 94*
Beaumont, Richard Austin 1925- *WhoAm 94*
Beaumont, Roberta Rodriquez 1957- *WhoHisp 94*
Beaumont, Roger *EncSF 93*
Beaumont, Susan 1936- *WhoHol 92*
Beaumont, Vertee d1934 *WhoHol 92*
Beaumont, Victor d1977 *WhoHol 92*
Beaumont, William 1785-1853 *WorScD [port]*
Beaumont, William Anderson 1924- *Who 94*
Beaumont, William Blackledge 1952- *Who 94*
Beaumont-Dark, Anthony (Michael) 1932- *Who 94*
Beaumont Of Whitley, Baron 1928- *Who 94*
Beaune, Michel *WhoHol 92*
Beaupain, Elaine Shapiro 1949- *WhoAm 94, WhoScEn 94*
Beaupeurt, Joseph Eugene 1912- *WhoWest 94*
Beaupre, Roland O. 1931- *WhoAmP 93*
Beauregard, Erving E. 1920- *ConAu 43NR*
Beaurepaire, Beryl (Edith) 1923- *Who 94*
Beaurepaire, Ian Francis 1922- *Who 94*
Beaurepaire, Quesnay de *WhAmRev*
Beausay, Thomas Jeffery 1962- *WhoAmL 94*
Beausoleil, Beau *DrAPF 93*
Beautemps-Beaupre, Charles-Francois 1766-1854 *WhWE*
Beauvain d'Althenheim, Gabrielle 1814-1886 *BlmGWL*
Beauvais, Edward R. 1936- *WhoFI 94*
Beauvau, Princesse de 1729- *BlmGWL*
Beauvoir *EncEth*
Beauvoir, Simone de *BlmGEL*
Beauvoir, Simone (Lucie Ernestine Marie) de 1908-1986 *RfGShF*
Beavan *Who 94*
Beaven, John Lewis 1930- *Who 94*
Beaven, Peter Jamieson 1925- *IntWW 93*
Beaven, Thornton Ray 1937- *WhoScEn 94*
Beaven, Winton Henry 1915- *WhoAm 94*
Beaver, Bonnie Veryle 1944- *WhoAm 94*
Beaver, Bruce (Victor) 1928- *WrDr 94*
Beaver, Charles A. J. 1952- *WhoAmL 94*
Beaver, Charles R. *WhoMW 93*
Beaver, Frank Eugene 1938- *WhoAm 94*
Beaver, Howard Oscar, Jr. 1925- *WhoAm 94*
Beaver, James N., Jr. *ConTFT 11*
Beaver, Jim 1950- *ConTFT 11, WhoHol 92*
Beaver, Joseph T., Jr. 1922- *WhoBlA 94*
Beaver, (Jack) Patrick 1923- *WrDr 94*
Beaver, Paul 1953- *WrDr 94*
Beaver, Paul Chester 1905- *WhoAm 94*
Beaver, William Henry 1940- *WhoAm 94*
Beaverbrook, Baron 1951- *Who 94*
Beavers, Alvin Herman 1913- *WhoAm 94*
Beavers, Ellington McHenry 1916- *WhoAm 94*
Beavers, John Parrish 1947- *WhoAmL 94*
Beavers, Louise d1962 *WhoHol 92*
Beavers, Nathan Howard, Jr. 1928- *WhoBlA 94*
Beavers, Peggy Jones 1946- *WhoBlA 94*
Beavers, Robert M., Jr. 1944- *WhoBlA 94*
Beavers, Roy L. 1930- *WhoScEn 94*
Beavers, William *WhoAmP 93*
Beaverson, Lowell V. 1933- *WhoMW 93*
Beavis, Ivan 1926- *WhoHol 92*
Beavis, Michael (Gordon) 1929- *Who 94*
Beazer, Brian Cyril 1935- *Who 94*
Beazley, Christopher John Pridham 1952- *Who 94*
Beazley, Hamilton Scott 1943- *WhoAm 94*
Beazley, Kim Christian 1948- *IntWW 93, Who 94*
Beazley, Peter George 1922- *Who 94*
Beban, Gary Joseph 1946- *WhoAm 94*
Beban, George d1928 *WhoHol 92*
Bebber, Donna Gaye 1956- *WhoWest 94*
Bebbington, D(avid) W(illiam) 1949- *WrDr 94*
Bebear, Claude 1935- *IntWW 93*
Bebel-Gisler, Dany *BlmGWL*
Beber, Robert H. 1933- *WhoAm 94, WhoAmL 94, WhoFI 94*
Bebler, Ales 1907-1981 *HisDcKW*
Bebout, Eli D. 1946- *WhoAmP 93*
Bebout, Eli Daniel 1946- *WhoWest 94*
Bebout, John William 1898- *WhAm 10*
Becan, Daniel Joseph 1932- *WhoAmP 93*
Becaud, Gilbert 1927- *WhoHol 92*
Beccaria, Cesare (Bonesana), marchesi di 1738-1794 *EncEth*
Beccarina, La *NewGrDO*
Beccary, Madame fl. 18th cent.- *BlmGWL*
Becchetti, Frederick Daniel 1943- *WhoMW 93*
Becchetti, John Joseph 1935- *WhoWest 94*
Becchetti, Rita J. Haedel 1946- *WhoMW 93*
Becchi, Ada 1937- *WhoWomW 91*
Becerra, Abel 1936- *WhoHisp 94*
Becerra, Felipe Edgardo 1958- *WhoHisp 94*
Becerra, Francisco 1932- *WhoHisp 94*
Becerra, Francisco J., Jr. 1961- *WhoHisp 94*
Becerra, Jose E. 1953- *WhoHisp 94*
Becerra, Rosina M. 1939- *WhoHisp 94*
Becerra, Xavier 1958- *CngDr 93, WhoAm 94, WhoAmP 93, WhoHisp 94, WhoWest 94*
Becerra Barney, Manuel Francisco 1951- *IntWW 93*
Bech, Douglas York 1945- *WhoAm 94, WhoAmL 94*
Bech, Lili d1939 *WhoHol 92*
Bechac, A. Denis 1939- *WhoAmP 93*
Bechara, Jose A., Jr. 1944- *WhoHisp 94*
Bechdolt, Jack 1884-1954 *EncSF 93*
Bechel, Diane Lynn 1964- *WhoMW 93*
Becher, Andrew Clifford 1946- *WhoAm 94, WhoAmL 94, WhoMW 93*
Becher, John C. d1986 *WhoHol 92*
Becher, Paul Eugene 1947- *WhoAm 94*
Becher, Paul Ronald 1934- *WhoAm 94*
Becher, William Don 1929- *WhoAm 94*
Becher, William Fane Wrixon- 1915- *Who 94*
Becherer, Deborah Zorn 1958- *WhoMW 93*
Becherer, Hans Walter 1935- *IntWW 93, WhoAm 94, WhoFI 94, WhoMW 93*
Becherer, Richard John 1951- *WhoScEn 94*
Bechert, Heinz 1932- *IntWW 93*
Béchervaise, John Mayston 1910- *WrDr 94*
Bechet, Sidney 1897-1959 *AfrAmAl 6*
Bechet, Sidney Joseph 1897-1959 *AmCulL*
Bechi, Gino d1993 *NewYTBS 93*
Bechi, Gino 1913- *NewGrDO*
Bechily, Maria Concepción 1949- *WhoHisp 94*
Bechina, Melvin Jeremiah 1945- *WhoMW 93*
Bechko, P(eggy) A(nne) 1950- *WrDr 94*
Bechler, Ronald Jerry 1943- *WhoScEn 94*
Bechman, Charles Edward 1922- *WhoAmP 93*
Becht, Hermann 1939- *NewGrDO*
Becht, Paul Frederick 1937- *WhoAmP 93*
Bechtel, Donald Bruce 1949- *WhoScEn 94*
Bechtel, James M. 1941- *WhoMW 93*
Bechtel, Riley Peart *WhoAm 94, WhoFI 94, WhoWest 94*
Bechtel, Stephen Davison 1900-1989 *WhAm 10*
Bechtel, Stephen Davison, Jr. 1925- *WhoAm 94, WhoScEn 94, WhoWest 94*
Bechtel, Stephen E. *WhoScEn 94*
Bechtel, Steven Craig 1958- *WhoAmL 94*
Bechtel, Thomas Shawn 1962- *WhoAmL 94*
Bechtel, William d1930 *WhoHol 92*
Bechtel, William, Mrs. *WhoHol 92*
Bechtelheimer, Robert Russell 1932- *WhoWest 94*
Bechtholdt, Henry Wilbert 1933- *WhoAm 94, WhoMW 93*
Bechtle, C. Ronald 1924- *WhoAmA 93*
Bechtle, Louis Charles 1927- *WhoAm 94, WhoAmL 94*
Bechtle, Perry Stevens 1926- *WhoAm 94*
Bechtle, Robert Alan 1932- *WhoAm 94, WhoAmA 93, WhoWest 94*
Bechtol, William Milton 1931- *WhoAm 94*
Bechtold, Timohty V. 1953- *WhoIns 94*
Becich, Raymond Brice 1945- *WhoAm 94*
Beck, Aaron Temkin 1921- *WhoAm 94, WhoScEn 94*
Beck, Abe Jack 1914- *WhoAm 94*
Beck, Adrian Robert 1932- *WhoAm 94*
Beck, Albert 1928- *WhoAm 94*
Beck, Alexander J. 1926- *IntMPA 94*
Beck, Anatole 1930- *WhoAm 94*
Beck, Andrew James 1948- *WhoAmL 94, WhoFI 94*
Beck, Anna Nadine 1922- *WhoMW 93*
Beck, Arnold Hugh William *Who 94*
Beck, Art *DrAPF 93*
Beck, Arthello, Jr. 1941- *WhoBlA 94*
Beck, Barbara Jean 1956- *WhoMW 93*
Beck, Beatrix Marie 1914- *IntWW 93*
Beck, Billy *WhoHol 92*
Beck, Brian Edgar 1933- *IntWW 93, Who 94*
Beck, Brian Joseph 1941- *WhoFI 94*
Beck, Christopher *EncSF 93*
Beck, Clark E. 1929- *WhoBlA 94*
Beck, Clifford Wallace 1908- *WhoAmP 93*
Beck, Clive 1937- *Who 94*
Beck, Conrad 1901- *IntWW 93*
Beck, Curt Peter 1953- *WhoAmL 94*
Beck, Curt Werner 1927- *WhoAm 94*
Beck, Danny d1959 *WhoHol 92*
Beck, Dave 1894-1993 *NewYTBS 93*
Beck, David Paul 1944- *WhoScEn 94*
Beck, Dennis L. 1947- *WhoAmL 94*
Beck, Doreen 1935- *WhoAmA 93*
Beck, Dorothy Fahs *WhoAm 94*
Beck, Dwight Marion 1893- *WhAm 10*
Beck, Earl Ray 1916- *WhoAm 94, WrDr 94*
Beck, Edgar (Charles) 1911- *IntWW 93, Who 94*
Beck, Edward William 1944- *WhoAm 94*
Beck, Frances Josephine Mottey 1918- *WhoMW 93*
Beck, Frances Patricia 1937- *ConTFT 11*
Beck, Franz Ignaz 1734-1809 *NewGrDO*
Beck, Gary 1939- *WhoAmP 93*
Beck, Gary Jerome 1943- *WhoMW 93*
Beck, George William 1921- *WhoAm 94*
Beck, H. Thomas *WhoFI 94*
Beck, Hans 1861-1952 *IntDcB [port]*
Beck, Hershell P. 1940- *WhoBlA 94*
Beck, Jackson *IntMPA 94*
Beck, Jacque Carey 1964- *WhoFI 94*
Beck, James d1973 *WhoHol 92*
Beck, James 1930- *WhoAmA 93, WrDr 94*
Beck, James M. 1917- *WhoAmP 93*
Beck, Jan Scott 1955- *WhoAm 94, WhoAmL 94*
Beck, Jean Marie 1938- *WhoMW 93*
Beck, Jeff 1944- *See* Yardbirds, The *ConMus 10*
Beck, Jeffrey Haines 1949- *WhoAmL 94*
Beck, Jenny 1974- *WhoHol 92*
Beck, Jerome Joseph 1957- *WhoWest 94*

Beck, Joan Wagner 1923- *WhoAm 94*
Beck, Joe Eugene 1947- *WhoAm 94*
Beck, Johann Nepomuk 1827-1904 *NewGrDO*
Beck, John *WhoAmP 93*
Beck, John d1993 *NewYTBS 93*
Beck, John 1943- *IntMPA 94*
Beck, John 1953- *WhoHol 92*
Beck, (James Henry) John 1920- *Who 94*
Beck, John Albert 1925- *WhoAmL 94*
Beck, John C. 1924- *IntWW 93*
Beck, John Christen 1959- *WhoWest 94*
Beck, John Christian 1924- *WhoAm 94*
Beck, John G. 1925- *WhoIns 94*
Beck, John Robert 1953- *WhoAm 94, WhoWest 94*
Beck, John Robert, Jr. 1952- *WhoAm 94, WhoFI 94*
Beck, John Roland 1929- *WhoScEn 94, WhoWest 94*
Beck, Joseph M. 1943- *WhoAmL 94*
Beck, Julian d1985 *WhoHol 92*
Beck, K(athrine) K(ristine) 1950- *ConAu 142*
Beck, Keith Lindell 1946- *WhoWest 94*
Beck, Kenneth David 1932- *WhoAm 94*
Beck, Kimberly 1956- *WhoHol 92*
Beck, Kirsten Lee 1961- *WhoMW 93*
Beck, Lewis Alfred 1919- *WhoWest 94*
Beck, Lewis White 1913- *WrDr 94*
Beck, Lily Adams d1931 *BlmGWL*
Beck, Linda Louise 1960- *WhoMW 93*
Beck, Lois Grant 1944- *WhoAm 94, WhoScEn 94*
Beck, Lonnie Lee 1942- *WhoAmA 93*
Beck, Lowell R. 1934- *WhoIns 94*
Beck, Ludwig 1880-1944 *HisWorL*
Beck, Margaret Elizabeth 1929- *WhoMW 93*
Beck, Margit *WhoAm 94, WhoAmA 93*
Beck, Marilyn *WhoHol 92*
Beck, Marilyn Mohr 1928- *WhoAm 94, WhoWest 94*
Beck, Martha Ann 1938- *WhoAmA 93*
Beck, Martin *WhoHol 92*
Beck, Marvin *WhoHol 92*
Beck, Mary Constance 1946- *WhoAm 94*
Beck, Mary Jean 1934- *WhoAmP 93*
Beck, Mary L. (Giraudo) 1924- *WrDr 94*
Beck, Mary McLean 1946- *WhoMW 93*
Beck, Mat *WhoAm 94*
Beck, Maxine Louise 1917- *WhoWest 94*
Beck, Michael 1948- *WhoHol 92*
Beck, Michael 1949- *IntMPA 94*
Beck, Mike 1947- *WhoFI 94*
Beck, Morris 1927- *WhoScEn 94*
Beck, Neva Ann 1941- *WhoMW 93*
Beck, Noelle 1968- *WhoHol 92*
Beck, Paul Adams 1908- *WhoAm 94, WhoMW 93*
Beck, Paul Allen 1944- *WhoAm 94, WhoMW 93*
Beck, Paul Augustine 1936- *WhoAmL 94*
Beck, Philip *Who 94*
Beck, (Edgar) Philip 1934- *Who 94*
Beck, Philip S. 1951- *WhoAm 94*
Beck, Phyllis Whitman *WhoAmL 94*
Beck, Raymond Edward 1939- *WhoAmP 93*
Beck, Richard A. 1933- *WhoAmP 93*
Beck, Richard P. 1943- *WhoAmL 94*
Beck, Richard R. 1930- *WhoIns 94*
Beck, Robert A. 1925- *IntWW 93, WhoIns 94*
Beck, Robert Alfred 1920- *WhoAm 94*
Beck, Robert Arthur 1925- *WhoAm 94*
Beck, Robert Holmes 1918-1991 *WhAm 10*
Beck, Robert Lee 1921- *WhoMW 93*
Beck, Robert Louis 1938- *WhoAm 94*
Beck, Robert N. 1928- *WhoScEn 94*
Beck, Robert Randall 1940- *WhoFI 94*
Beck, Rod *WhoAmP 93*
Beck, Rodney Roy 1968- *WhoAm 94, WhoWest 94*
Beck, Rosemarie 1924- *WhoAm 94*
Beck, Roswell Nathaniel *WhoBlA 94*
Beck, Samuel Jacob 1896- *EncSPD*
Beck, Saul L. 1928- *WhoBlA 94*
Beck, Simone Simca 1904-1991 *WhAm 10*
Beck, Stanley Dwight 1919- *WhoAm 94*
Beck, Stanton Phillip 1961- *WhoAmL 94*
Beck, Swanson *Who 94*
Beck, (John) Swanson 1928- *Who 94*
Beck, (Richard) Theodore 1905- *Who 94*
Beck, Theresa 1953- *WhoAmA 93*
Beck, Thomas 1909- *WhoHol 92*
Beck, Thomas Arthur, III 1929- *WhoBlA 94*
Beck, Thomas Davis 1943- *WhoWest 94*
Beck, Thomas Edwin 1946- *WhoWest 94*
Beck, Timothy Daniel 1953- *WhoWest 94*
Beck, Tom 1939- *WhoAmP 93*
Beck, Vernon David 1949- *WhoScEn 94*
Beck, Vincent d1984 *WhoHol 92*
Beck, Warren Albert 1918- *WrDr 94*
Beck, William G. 1954- *WhoAmL 94*
Beck, William Harold, Jr. 1928- *WhoAmL 94, WhoFI 94*
Beck, William Samson 1923- *WhoAm 94*
Becke, Shirley Cameron 1917- *Who 94*
Becke, William Hugh Adamson 1916- *Who 94*
Beckedorff, David Lawrence 1940- *WhoAm 94*
Beckel, Charles Leroy 1928- *WhoAm 94, WhoWest 94*
Beckel, Graham *WhoHol 92*
Beckelhymer, (Paul) Hunter 1919- *WrDr 94*
Beckemeier, Edward A. 1925- *WhoIns 94*
Becken, Bradford Albert 1924- *WhoAm 94*
Beckenbauer, Franz 1945- *IntWW 93, WorESoc [port]*
Beckenstein, Myron 1938- *WhoAm 94*
Becker, Adolph Eric 1925- *WhoBlA 94*
Becker, Alan S. 1946- *WhoAmL 94*
Becker, Arlene 1948- *WhoAmP 93*
Becker, Barbara 1945- *WhoMW 93*
Becker, Betsy 1939- *WhoAm 94*
Becker, Bettie 1918- *WhoAmA 93*
Becker, Bettie Geraldine 1918- *WhoAm 94, WhoMW 93*
Becker, Boris 1967- *IntWW 93, WhoAm 94*
Becker, Boris 1968- *BuCMET [port]*
Becker, Boris William 1939- *WhoAm 94*
Becker, Brooks 1931- *WhoScEn 94*
Becker, Bruce Carl, II 1948- *WhoMW 93, WhoScEn 94*
Becker, Bruce Douglas 1959- *WhoFI 94*
Becker, Carl Johan 1915- *IntWW 93*
Becker, Carol *DrAPF 93*
Becker, Charles J. *WhoAmP 93*
Becker, Charles McVey 1937- *WhoFI 94*
Becker, David 1937- *WhoAmA 93*
Becker, David Mandel 1935- *WhoAm 94*
Becker, Deborah *WhoIns 94*
Becker, Desiree *WhoHol 92*
Becker, Dismas Paul 1936- *WhoAmP 93*
Becker, Don Crandall 1933- *WhoAm 94*
Becker, Donald Eugene 1923- *WhoAm 94*
Becker, Douglas Wesley 1950- *WhoAmL 94*
Becker, Dwight Lowell 1918- *WhoAm 94*
Becker, Ed d1981 *WhoHol 92*
Becker, Edward A. 1938- *WhoAm 94, WhoFI 94*
Becker, Edward R. *WhoAmP 93*
Becker, Edward Roy 1933- *WhoAm 94, WhoAmL 94*
Becker, Edwin Demuth 1930- *WhoAm 94*
Becker, Elizabeth 1947- *ConAu 141*
Becker, Eugene E. *WhoIns 94*
Becker, Fred Paul 1926- *WhoWest 94*
Becker, Fred Ronald 1937- *WhoAm 94*
Becker, Frederic Kenneth 1935- *WhoAm 94*
Becker, Frederick Fenimore 1931- *WhoAm 94, WhoScEn 94*
Becker, Gail Roselyn 1942- *WhoAm 94*
Becker, Gary S. d1930 *CurBio 93 [port]*
Becker, Gary S. 1930- *WrDr 94*
Becker, Gary Stanley 1930- *IntWW 93, Who 94, WhoAm 94, WhoFI 94, WhoMW 93, WhoScEn 94*
Becker, George Joseph 1908-1989 *WhAm 10*
Becker, Gerald Arthur 1941- *WhoMW 93*
Becker, Gert 1933- *IntWW 93*
Becker, Gregory R. *WhoAmP 93*
Becker, Harold *IntMPA 94*
Becker, Heinz 1922- *NewGrDO*
Becker, Herbert P. 1920- *WhoScEn 94*
Becker, Howard S(aul) 1928- *WrDr 94*
Becker, Isidore A. 1926- *IntWW 93, WhoAm 94*
Becker, Ivan Endre 1929- *WhoAm 94*
Becker, Jacques d1960 *WhoHol 92*
Becker, James William 1942- *WhoAmL 94, WhoFI 94*
Becker, Jillian 1932- *BlmGWL*
Becker, JoAnn Elizabeth 1948- *WhoAm 94*
Becker, Johanna Lucille 1921- *WhoAmA 93*
Becker, John J(oseph) 1886-1961 *NewGrDO*
Becker, John Lionel, Jr. 1956- *WhoWest 94*
Becker, Joseph 1887-1966 *EncABHB 9 [port]*
Becker, Joseph 1923- *WhoAm 94*
Becker, Juliette 1938- *WhoScEn 94*
Becker, Jurek 1937- *ConWorW 93, IntWW 93*
Becker, Jurgen 1932- *IntWW 93*
Becker, Karl Martin 1943- *WhoAm 94, WhoAmL 94*
Becker, Kevin Lynn 1959- *WhoMW 93*
Becker, Lanson 1941- *WhoMW 93*
Becker, Larry Keith 1948- *WhoIns 94*
Becker, Larry Wayne 1946- *WhoWest 94*
Becker, Leslee *DrAPF 93*
Becker, Lewis Charles *WhoScEn 94*
Becker, Lillie Elaine 1950- *WhoWest 94*
Becker, Linda Sue 1954- *WhoMW 93*
Becker, Lucille Frackman 1929- *WrDr 94*
Becker, Marie G. 1955- *WhoHisp 94*
Becker, Marshall Hilford 1940- *WhoAm 94*
Becker, Marvin Burton 1922- *WhoAm 94*
Becker, Mary Julia 1928- *WhoMW 93*
Becker, Mary Louise *WhoAm 94*
Becker, Mayer Gil 1951- *WhoFI 94*
Becker, Michael 1948- *WhoWest 94*
Becker, Michael Lewis 1940- *WhoAm 94*
Becker, Michael Richard 1945- *WhoAmL 94*
Becker, Murray Leonard 1933- *WhoFI 94*
Becker, Naomi d1974 *WhoAmA 93N*
Becker, Natalie Rose *WhoAmA 93*
Becker, Norman Otto 1918- *WhAm 10*
Becker, Patricia Winifred *WhoAmL 94, WhoFI 94*
Becker, Paul Joseph 1953- *WhoIns 94*
Becker, Philip d1975 *WhoHol 92*
Becker, Quinn Henderson 1930- *WhoAm 94*
Becker, Ralph Edward 1931- *WhoAm 94*
Becker, Ralph Elihu 1907- *WhoAm 94, WhoAmL 94*
Becker, Ralph Leonard 1927- *WhoMW 93*
Becker, Renee Lyn 1960- *WhoMW 93*
Becker, Rex Louis 1913- *WhoAm 94*
Becker, Richard Charles 1931- *WhoAm 94*
Becker, Richard Stanley 1934- *WhoAm 94*
Becker, Richard Thomas 1935- *WhoAmL 94*
Becker, Robert A. 1920- *WhoAm 94*
Becker, Robert Allen 1942- *WhoMW 93*
Becker, Robert Cappel 1941- *WhoAm 94*
Becker, Robert Clarence 1927- *WhoAm 94*
Becker, Robert Jerome 1922- *WhoAm 94, WhoMW 93*
Becker, Robert Joseph 1946- *WhoMW 93*
Becker, Robert M. 1948- *WhoAmL 94*
Becker, Robert Otto 1923- *WhoAm 94*
Becker, Robert Richard 1923- *WhoAm 94*
Becker, Robin *DrAPF 93*
Becker, Roger Vern 1947- *WhoWest 94*
Becker, Samuel Leo 1923- *WhoMW 93*
Becker, Seymour 1924- *WhoScEn 94*
Becker, Stanley R. *WhoAm 94, WhoFI 94, WhoWest 94*
Becker, Stephen *DrAPF 93*
Becker, Stephen (David) 1927- *WrDr 94*
Becker, Stephen A. 1944- *WhoAmL 94*
Becker, Stephen Arnold 1951- *WhoAm 94*
Becker, Susan Kaplan 1948- *WhoFI 94*
Becker, Terry 1930- *WhoHol 92*
Becker, Theodor d1952 *WhoHol 92*
Becker, Theodore Michaelson 1949- *WhoAmL 94*
Becker, Therese *DrAPF 93*
Becker, Thomas Bain 1944- *WhoAm 94, WhoAmL 94*
Becker, Tony 1965- *WhoHol 92*
Becker, Uwe Eugen 1947- *WhoScEn 94*
Becker, Vaneta G. 1949- *WhoAmP 93*
Becker, Virginia Grafton 1951- *WhoScEn 94*
Becker, Walter *WhoAm 94*
Becker, Walter Heinrich 1939- *WhoMW 93*
Becker, Wesley Clemence 1928- *WhoAm 94*
Becker, William Adolph 1933- *WhoFI 94*
Becker, William Albert 1930- *WhoMW 93*
Becker, William Watters 1943- *WhoAm 94, WhoAmL 94*
Becker-Inglau, Ingrid 1946- *WhoWomW 91*
Beckerman, Nancy Greyson *WhoAmA 93*
Beckerman, Paul 1948- *ConAu 141*
Beckerman, Robert Cy 1946- *WhoScEn 94*
Beckerman, Wilfred 1925- *Who 94, WrDr 94*
Beckers, William Kurt 1900-1989 *WhAm 10*
Beckers-de-Bruijn, Ria 1938- *WhoWomW 91*
Becker-Slaton, Nellie Frances 1921- *WhoBlA 94*
Becket, Thomas 1118?-1170 *BlmGEL, HisWorL [port]*
Beckett *Who 94*
Beckett, Arnold Heyworth 1920- *Who 94*
Beckett, Bradley Arthur 1953- *WhoAmP 93*
Beckett, Bruce Probart 1924- *Who 94*
Beckett, Charles Campbell 1912- *WhoBlA 94*
Beckett, Denis Arthur 1917- *Who 94*
Beckett, Edwin Horace Alexander 1937- *Who 94*
Beckett, Evette Olga 1956- *WhoBlA 94*
Beckett, Grace 1912- *WhoFI 94, WhoMW 93*
Beckett, Guy d1973 *WhoHol 92*
Beckett, James Camlin 1912- *Who 94*
Beckett, John Angus 1916- *WhoAm 94*
Beckett, John Douglas 1938- *WhoAm 94*
Beckett, Justin F. 1963- *WhoBlA 94*
Beckett, Margaret 1943- *WhoWomW 91*
Beckett, Margaret M. 1943- *Who 94*
Beckett, Margaret Mary 1943- *IntWW 93*
Beckett, Martyn Gervase 1918- *Who 94*
Beckett, Mary 1926- *BlmGWL*
Beckett, Ray Herbert, Jr. 1928- *WhoWest 94*
Beckett, Richard Gervase 1944- *Who 94*
Beckett, Samuel d1989 *NobelP 91N*
Beckett, Samuel 1906-1989 *BlmGEL [port], WhAm 10*
Beckett, Samuel (Barclay) 1906-1989 *ConDr 93, IntDcT 2 [port], RfGShF*
Beckett, Scotty d1968 *WhoHol 92*
Beckett, Sydney A. 1943- *WhoBlA 94*
Beckett, Terence (Norman) 1923- *IntWW 93, Who 94*
Beckett, Theodore Charles 1929- *WhoAm 94, WhoAmL 94*
Beckett, Theodore Cornwall 1952- *WhoAmL 94, WhoFI 94, WhoMW 93*
Beckett, William Cartwright 1929- *Who 94*
Beckett, William H. M. 1940- *WhoAmL 94*
Beckett, William Wade 1928- *WhoAm 94*
Beckett-Rinker, Peggy *WhoAmP 93*
Beckey, Sylvia Louise 1946- *WhoAm 94, WhoAmL 94*
Beckford, William 1759-1844 *BlmGEL*
Beck-Gaden, Hanns d1956 *WhoHol 92*
Beckham, Barry (Earl) 1944- *WrDr 94*
Beckham, Barry Earl 1944- *WhoBlA 94*
Beckham, Edgar Frederick 1933- *WhoAm 94, WhoBlA 94*
Beckham, Walter Hull, III 1948- *WhoAmL 94*
Beckham, William Arthur 1927- *WhoAm 94*
Beckham, William J., Jr. 1940- *WhoBlA 94*
Beckhard, Ellie *WhoAmA 93*
Beckhard, Herbert 1926- *WhoAm 94*
Beckhusen, Eric Herman 1922- *WhoScEn 94*
Beckingham, Charles Fraser 1914- *IntWW 93, Who 94, WrDr 94*
Beckinsale, Richard d1979 *WhoHol 92*
Beckinsale, Robert Percy 1908- *WrDr 94*
Beckjord, Eric Stephen 1929- *WhoAm 94, WhoScEn 94*
Becklake, (Ernest) John (Stephen) 1943- *Who 94*
Becklake, Margaret Rigsby 1922- *WhoAm 94*
Beckler, David Zander 1918- *WhoAm 94, WhoScEn 94*
Beckler, Richard William 1940- *WhoAm 94, WhoAmL 94*
Beckles, Benita Harris 1950- *WhoBlA 94*
Beckles Willson, Robina (Elizabeth) 1930- *ConAu 43NR*
Beckley, Beatrice 1885- *WhoHol 92*
Beckley, Bill 1946- *WhoAmA 93*
Beckley, David Lenard 1946- *WhoAm 94, WhoBlA 94*
Beckley, Donald K. 1916- *WhoAm 94*
Beckley, John 1757-1807 *WhAmRev*
Beckley, Michael John 1942- *WhoAm 94, WhoFI 94*
Beckley, Robert Mark 1934- *WhoMW 93*
Beckley, Tony d1980 *WhoHol 92*
Beckman, Arnold Orville 1900- *WhoScEn 94, WhoWest 94*
Beckman, Bradley Tobin 1960- *WhoAmL 94*
Beckman, Donald 1932- *WhoAm 94, WhoAmL 94*
Beckman, Donald A. 1947- *WhoScEn 94*
Beckman, Douglas Gary 1944- *WhoAm 94, WhoAmL 94*
Beckman, Ericka 1951- *WhoAm 94, WhoAmA 93*
Beckman, Ernestine Elizabeth 1930- *WhoAmP 93*
Beckman, Gail M(cKnight) 1938- *WrDr 94*
Beckman, Gail McKnight 1938- *WhoAm 94, WhoAmL 94*
Beckman, Henry 1925- *WhoHol 92*
Beckman, Hester Finke *WhoAm 94*
Beckman, James Wallace Bim 1936- *WhoFI 94, WhoScEn 94, WhoWest 94*
Beckman, John Coyle 1919- *WhoWest 94*
Beckman, Johnny 1898- *BasBi*
Beckman, Joseph Alfred 1937- *WhoAm 94, WhoScEn 94*
Beckman, Judith 1951- *WhoAm 94*
Beckman, Judith Kalb 1940- *WhoAm 94*
Beckman, Kenneth Oren 1948- *WhoWest 94*
Beckman, Melissa Ann 1964- *WhoMW 93*
Beckman, Michael David 1932- *Who 94*
Beckman, Paul *DrAPF 93*

Beckman, Ronald Melvin 1938- *WhoMW 93*
Beckman, Tracy L. 1945- *WhoAmP 93*
Beckmann, Jane Miluna 1935- *WhoWest 94*
Beckmann, John 1960- *WhoAmA 93*
Beckmann, Jon Michael 1936- *WhoAm 94, WhoWest 94*
Beckmann, Judith 1935- *NewGrDO*
Beckmann, Petr 1924- *WhoAm 94*
Beckmann, Robert Dean, Jr. 1941- *WhoMW 93*
Beckmeyer, Dwight Clarence 1962- *WhoWest 94*
Beckmeyer, Henry Ernest 1939- *WhoMW 93, WhoScEn 94*
Becknell, William c. 1790-1865 *WhWE*
Beckner, Donald Lee 1939- *WhoAm 94, WhoAmL 94*
Beckner, Jeffery Edward 1960- *WhoMW 93*
Beck-Oberdorf, Marieluise 1952- *WhoWomW 91*
Becks, Ronald Arthur 1953- *WhoWest 94*
Beckstead, Lucy 1920- *WhoAmP 93*
Beckum, Leonard Charles 1937- *WhoAm 94*
Beck-von-Peccoz, Stephen George Wolfgang 1933- *WhoWest 94*
Beckwith, Athelstan Laurence Johnson 1930- *IntWW 93, Who 94*
Beckwith, Barbara Jean 1948- *WhoAm 94*
Beckwith, Burnham Putnam 1904- *WrDr 94*
Beckwith, Catherine S. 1958- *WhoMW 93, WhoScEn 94*
Beckwith, Charles Emilio 1917- *WhoAm 94*
Beckwith, Christopher Irving 1945- *WhoAm 94*
Beckwith, David E. 1928- *WhoAm 94*
Beckwith, Edward Griffin 1818-1881 *WhWE*
Beckwith, Edward Jay 1949- *WhoAm 94, WhoAmL 94*
Beckwith, Geoffrey Clifton 1958- *WhoAmP 93*
Beckwith, George 1753-1823 *WhAmRev*
Beckwith, Herbert L. 1903- *WhoAm 94*
Beckwith, James 1907- *WhoAmA 93N*
Beckwith, John 1927- *NewGrDO, WhoAm 94*
Beckwith, John Adams 1942- *WhoMW 93*
Beckwith, John Charles 1941- *WhoFI 94*
Beckwith, John Gordon 1918- *WrDr 94*
Beckwith, John Lionel 1947- *Who 94*
Beckwith, Lewis Daniel 1948- *WhoAm 94, WhoAmL 94*
Beckwith, Lillian 1916- *WrDr 94*
Beckwith, Maxine Marie 1939- *WhoMW 93*
Beckwith, Merle Ray *DrAPF 93*
Beckwith, Peter Michael 1945- *Who 94*
Beckwith, Reginald d1965 *WhoHol 92*
Beckwith, Rodney Fisk 1935- *WhoAm 94, WhoFI 94*
Beckwith, Ronald Lee 1935- *WhoAm 94*
Beckwith, Sandra Shank 1943- *WhoAm 94, WhoAmL 94, WhoMW 93*
Beckwith, William *WhoHol 92*
Beckwith, William Hunter 1896- *WhoAm 94*
Beckworth, Lindley Gary, Jr. 1943- *WhoAmL 94*
Beckwourth, James Pierson 1798-1866 *AfrAmAl 6 [port]*
Beckwourth, James Pierson c. 1800-c. 1866 *WhWE*
Becnel, Philip Alfred, III 1942- *WhoAmL 94*
Becofsky, Arthur Luke 1950- *WhoAm 94*
Becon, Thomas c. 1512-1567 *DcLB 136 [port]*
Becote, Fohliette W. 1958- *WhoBlA 94*
Becque, Henry (-Francois) 1837-1899 *IntDcT 2*
Becquerel, Alexandre-Edmond 1820-1891 *WorInv*
Becquerel, Antoine Henri 1852-1908 *WorScD*
Bective, Earl of 1959- *Who 94*
Becton, Henry Prentiss, Jr. 1943- *WhoAm 94*
Becton, Julius W., Jr. 1926- *AfrAmG [port]*
Becton, Julius Wesley, Jr. 1926- *WhoAm 94, WhoAmP 93, WhoBlA 94*
Becton, Rudolph 1930- *WhoBlA 94*
Becton, Sharvell *WhoBlA 94*
Becuwe, Ivan Gerard 1967- *WhoScEn 94*
Becwar, George d1970 *WhoHol 92*
Bedapudi, Prakash 1966- *WhoScEn 94*
Bedard, Patrick Joseph 1941- *WhoAm 94*
Bedau, Hugo Adam 1926- *ConAu 41NR, WhoAm 94, WrDr 94*
Beday, Eugene d1975 *WhoHol 92*
Bedbrook, Jack Harry 1924- *Who 94*
Beddall, David 1948- *IntWW 93*
Beddall, Hugh Richard Muir 1922- *Who 94*
Beddall, Thomas Henry 1922- *WhoAm 94*
Beddard, Nicholas Elliot 1934- *Who 94*
Beddingfield, Edward C. *WhoBlA 94*
Beddington, Charles Richard 1911- *Who 94*
Beddoe, Don 1903-1991 *WhoHol 92*
Beddoes, John Geoffrey Genior d1993 *Who 94N*
Beddoes, Thomas Lovell 1803-1849 *BlmGEL*
Beddome, John MacDonald 1930- *IntWW 93*
Beddow, David Pierce 1943- *WhoAm 94*
Beddow, Jean T. *WhoAmP 93*
Beddow, Thomas John 1914- *WhoAm 94*
Bede 673-735 *BlmGEL*
Bedeaux, Dick 1941- *WhoScEn 94*
Bedeian, Arthur George 1946- *WhoAm 94*
Bedelia, Bonnie 1946- *IntMPA 94*
Bedelia, Bonnie 1948- *WhoAm 94, WhoHol 92*
Bedell, Berkley Warren 1921- *WhoAmP 93*
Bedell, Frederick Delano 1934- *WhoBlA 94*
Bedell, George Chester 1928- *WhoAm 94*
Bedell, George Noble 1922- *WhoAm 94*
Bedell, Harriet M. 1875- *EncNAR*
Bedell, Kenneth Berkley 1947- *WhoAm 94*
Bedell, Ralph Clairon *IntWW 93N*
Bedell, Richard Munro 1958- *WhoFI 94*
Bedells, Phyllis 1893-1985 *IntDcB [port]*
Bedenis, Kay Floranne *WhoMW 93*
Bederka, Stephen Edward 1930- *WhoWest 94*
Bederson, Benjamin 1921- *WhoAm 94*
Bedesky, Michael J. 1966- *WhoAmL 94*
Bedford, Archdeacon of *Who 94*
Bedford, Bishop Suffragan of *Who 94*
Bedford, Duke of 1917- *Who 94*
Bedford, Alfred William 1920- *Who 94*
Bedford, Anthony John 1943- *WhoScEn 94*
Bedford, Brian 1935- *ConTFT 11, WhoAm 94, WhoHol 92*
Bedford, Clay Patrick, Sr. 1903-1991 *WhAm 10*
Bedford, Daniel Ross 1945- *WhoAm 94, WhoAmL 94*
Bedford, David 1937- *IntWW 93, Who 94*
Bedford, Gunning 1742-1797 *WhAmRev*
Bedford, Gunning, Jr. 1747-1812 *WhAmRev*
Bedford, Harry d1939 *WhoHol 92*
Bedford, Henry Frederick 1931- *WrDr 94*
Bedford, Jean 1946- *BlmGWL*
Bedford, John *EncSF 93*
Bedford, Keith Wilson 1945- *WhoScEn 94*
Bedford, Lyman D. 1942- *WhoAm 94*
Bedford, Norton Moore 1916- *WhoAm 94*
Bedford, Patrick *WhoHol 92*
Bedford, Roger, Jr. 1956- *WhoAmP 93*
Bedford, Simi 1942- *BlmGWL*
Bedford, Steuart (John Rudolf) 1939- *NewGrDO*
Bedford, Steuart John Rudolf 1939- *IntWW 93, Who 94*
Bedford, Sybille 1911- *BlmGWL, Who 94, WrDr 94*
Bedford, William 1963- *WhoBlA 94*
Bedford-Jones, H(enry James O'Brien) 1887-1949 *EncSF 93*
Bedford-Lloyd, John *WhoHol 92*
Bedi, Bishan Singh 1946- *IntWW 93*
Bedi, Kabir 1945- *WhoHol 92*
Bedi, Rahul 1941- *WhoFI 94*
Bedi, Sandeep 1966- *WhoAsA 94*
Bediako, Kwabena Asare *BlkWr 2*
Bedinger, George M. 1756-1843 *WhAmRev*
Bedingfeld *Who 94*
Bedingfield, Christopher Ohl Macredie 1935- *Who 94*
Bedingfield, Mary Dolorosa 1939- *WhoAmL 94*
Bedini, Domenico c. 1745-1795? *NewGrDO*
Bedini, Silvio A. 1917- *WhoAm 94, WrDr 94*
Bedjaoui, Mohammed 1929- *IntWW 93*
Bedke, Ernest Alford 1934- *WhoAm 94*
Bedke, Kathryn Lynn 1951- *WhoAmL 94*
Bednall, James Andrew 1954- *WhoAmL 94*
Bednar, Carolyn Diane 1953- *WhoMW 93*
Bednar, Charles Sokol 1930- *WhoAm 94*
Bednar, Joseph J. 1943- *WhoFI 94*
Bednar, Michael John 1942- *WhoAm 94*
Bednar, Richard John 1931- *WhoAmL 94*
Bednar, Rudy Gerard 1951- *WhoAm 94*
Bednarek, Alexander Robert 1933- *WhoAm 94*
Bednarek, Jana Maria 1934- *WhoAm 94*
Bednarek, Stanley Michael 1904- *WhoAmP 93*
Bednarik, Chuck *ProFbHF [port]*
Bednarz, James C. *WhoScEn 94*
Bednarz, Paul Robert 1950- *WhoIns 94*
Bednarz, Susan Clare 1955- *WhoMW 93*
Bedner, Mark Allen 1948- *WhoFI 94*
Bednorz, George 1950- *IntWW 93*
Bednorz, J. Georg 1950- *NobelP 91 [port], Who 94, WhoScEn 94, WorScD*
Bedore, Michael Paul 1956- *WhoFI 94, WhoWest 94*
Bedos, Guy *WhoHol 92*
Bedott, Widow *BlmGWL*
Bedoun, Eddie Amad 1958- *WhoMW 93*
Bedoya, Alfonso d1957 *WhoHol 92*
Bedoya, Consuelo *WhoHisp 94*
Bedoya, Luis 1939- *WhoHisp 94*
Bedoya, Michael Julian 1945- *WhoScEn 94*
Bedoya, Roberto Eligio 1951- *WhoHisp 94*
Bedoya Velez, Luis 1920- *IntWW 93*
Bedregal, Yolanda 1916- *BlmGWL*
Bedrick, Bernice 1916- *WhoScEn 94*
Bedrick, Jeffrey Keith 1960- *WhoWest 94*
Bedrick, Melvin Leonard 1932- *WhoAm 94*
Bedrij, Orest J. 1933- *WhoScEn 94*
Bedrosian, Edward 1922- *WhoAm 94*
Bedrosian, Edward Robert 1932- *WhoAm 94*
Bedrosian, John C. 1934- *WhoAm 94, WhoFI 94*
Bedrossian, Robert Haig 1924- *WhoAmP 93*
Bedser, Alec Victor 1918- *IntWW 93, Who 94*
Bedsole, Ann Smith 1930- *WhoAmP 93*
Bedsworth, O. Diane 1942- *WhoFI 94*
Bedyngham, John 1422?-1459? *DcNaB MP*
Bee, Adeline Mary 1954- *WhoAmP 93*
Bee, Clair 1900-1983 *BasBi*
Bee, Keith 1965- *WhoAmP 93*
Bee, Linda Jane 1947- *WhoMW 93*
Bee, Martin Joseph 1951- *WhoMW 93*
Bee, Molly 1939- *WhoHol 92*
Bee, Robert Norman 1925- *WhoAm 94*
Bee, Ronald J. 1955- *ConAu 140*
Bee, Steven Robert 1963- *WhoMW 93*
Bee, Thomas 1725-1812 *WhAmRev*
Beebe, B. F. 1922- *WrDr 94*
Beebe, B(urdette) F(aye) 1920- *WrDr 94*
Beebe, Charles William *WorInv*
Beebe, Cora Prifold 1937- *WhoAm 94*
Beebe, George Hollis 1910-1990 *WhAm 10*
Beebe, John Eldridge 1923- *WhoAm 94*
Beebe, Leo Clair 1917- *WhoAm 94*
Beebe, Mary Livingstone 1940- *WhoAmA 93*
Beebe, Mike 1946- *WhoAmP 93*
Beebe, Ralph K. 1932- *WrDr 94*
Beebe, Raymond Mark 1942- *WhoAm 94*
Beebe, Richard Townsend 1902- *WhoAm 94*
Beebe, Robert Gardner 1915- *WhoWest 94*
Beebe, Robert Park 1909-1988 *WhAm 10*
Beebe, Robert R. 1928- *WhoWest 94*
Beebe, Sandra E. 1934- *WhoWest 94*
Beebee, Chris *EncSF 93*
Beebe Tarantelli, Carole Jane 1942- *WhoWomW 91*
Beeby, Bruce 1923- *WhoHol 92*
Beeby, Clarence Edward 1902- *IntWW 93, Who 94, WrDr 94*
Beeby, George Harry 1902- *Who 94*
Beeby, Kenneth Jack 1936- *WhoAm 94, WhoAmL 94*
Beeby, Thomas H. *WhoAm 94*
Beeby, Thomas Hall 1941- *IntWW 93*
Beech, H. R(eginald) 1925- *WrDr 94*
Beech, Harvey Elliott 1924- *WhoBlA 94*
Beech, Johnny Gale 1954- *WhoAmL 94*
Beech, Keyes 1913-1990 *WhAm 10*
Beech, Olive A. d1993 *NewYTBS 93 [port]*
Beech, Olive Ann (Mellor) 1903-1993 *CurBio 93N*
Beech, Patrick Mervyn d1993 *Who 94N*
Beecham, Jeremy Hugh 1944- *Who 94*
Beecham, John Stratford Roland 1942- *Who 94*
Beecham, Thomas d1961 *WhoHol 92*
Beecham, Thomas 1879-1961 *NewGrDO*
Beecher, Catharine 1800-1878 *AmSocL, BlmGWL*
Beecher, Christopher William Ward 1948- *WhoMW 93*
Beecher, Donald A(llen) 1942- *WrDr 94*
Beecher, Earl William 1942- *WhoFI 94*
Beecher, Edward 1803-1895 *DcAmReB 2*
Beecher, Graciela F. 1927- *WhoHisp 94*
Beecher, Henry Ward 1813-1887 *AmSocL [port], DcAmReB 2*
Beecher, Janet d1955 *WhoHol 92*
Beecher, Lyman 1775-1863 *AmSocL, DcAmReB 2*
Beecher, Stephen Clinton 1954- *WhoScEn 94*
Beecher, William John 1914- *WhoAm 94*
Beecher, William Manuel 1933- *WhoAm 94*
Beechey, Frederick William 1796-1856 *WhWE*
Beeching, Charles Train, Jr. 1930- *WhoAm 94*
Beeching, Jack 1922- *EncSF 93*
Beecke, (Notger) Ignaz (Franz) von 1733-1803 *NewGrDO*
Beeckman, Isaac 1588-1637 *WorScD*
Beecroft, David 1956- *WhoHol 92*
Beecroft, John 1790-1854 *DcNaB MP*
Beecroft, Victor d1958 *WhoHol 92*
Beed, David James 1945- *WhoFI 94, WhoIns 94*
Beeder, David Charles 1930- *WhoAm 94*
Beedham, Brian James 1928- *Who 94*
Beeding, Francis *EncSF 93*
Beedle, Lynn Simpson 1917- *WhoAm 94*
Beedles, William LeRoy 1948- *WhoAm 94*
Bee Gees, The *WhoHol 92*
Beeghly, Charles Milton 1908- *EncABHB 9 [port]*
Beehan, Cathy *WhoAm 94*
Beehler, Bruce McPherson 1951- *WhoScEn 94*
Beeke, Joel Robert 1952- *WhoAm 94*
Beekley, Clare Hutton 1940- *WhoFI 94*
Beekley, Cynthia Xanthopoulos 1940- *WhoMW 93*
Beekman, Allan 1913- *WrDr 94*
Beekman, Carol Tschannen *WhoWest 94*
Beekman, Eunice Kay 1950- *WhoMW 93*
Beekman, Robert Lee 1945- *WhoFI 94*
Beekman, Robert Struthers d1993 *NewYTBS 93*
Beeler, Donald Daryl 1935- *WhoAm 94, WhoMW 93*
Beeler, Joe (Neil) 1931- *WhoAmA 93*
Beeler, Laurel Daniels 1961- *WhoWest 94*
Beeler, R. Scott 1954- *WhoAmL 94*
Beeler, Thomas Joseph 1933- *WhoAm 94, WhoAmL 94*
Beeler, Virgil L. 1931- *WhoAm 94*
Beeley, Harold 1909- *IntWW 93, Who 94*
Beelke, Ralph G. 1917- *WhoAmA 93N*
Beelner, Ken Phillip 1936- *WhoAmL 94*
Beem, Jack Darrel 1931- *WhoAm 94*
Beem, John Kelly 1942- *WhoAm 94, WhoMW 93, WhoScEn 94*
Beeman, Carol Ann *DrAPF 93*
Beeman, Curt Pletcher 1944- *WhoScEn 94*
Beeman, John Sanders 1945- *WhoMW 93*
Beeman, Malinda 1949- *WhoAmA 93*
Beeman, Richard E. 1945- *WhoAm 94*
Beeman, Richard Roy 1942- *WhoAm 94*
Beeman, Robin *DrAPF 93*
Beemer, Elvin Homer 1919- *WhoAmP 93*
Beemster, Joseph Robert 1941- *WhoFI 94*
Been, Hans Henrik 1949- *WhoFI 94, WhoWest 94*
Been, Michael *WhoHol 92*
Beene, Geoffrey 1927- *IntWW 93, WhoAm 94*
Beene, Kirk D. 1967- *WhoScEn 94*
Beenen, Richard 1953- *WhoAmA 93*
Beeners, Wilbert John 1921- *WhoAm 94*
Beenstock, Michael 1946- *Who 94*
Beeny, Christopher 1941- *WhoHol 92*
Beer, Alan Earl 1937- *WhoAm 94*
Beer, Angelika 1957- *WhoWomW 91*
Beer, Barrett Lynn 1936- *WhoAm 94*
Beer, Clara Louise Johnson 1918- *WhoAm 94*
Beer, Gillian (Patricia Kempster) 1935- *ConAu 142, WrDr 94*
Beer, Gillian Patricia Kempster 1935- *Who 94*
Beer, Ian David Stafford 1931- *Who 94*
Beer, Jacqueline 1932- *WhoHol 92*
Beer, James Edmund 1931- *Who 94*
Beer, Janos Miklos 1923- *Who 94, WhoAm 94*
Beer, Jeanette Mary Scott *WhoAm 94*
Beer, John Bernard 1926- *Who 94*
Beer, Joseph Ernest 1959- *WhoWest 94*
Beer, Kenneth John 1932- *WhoAmA 93*
Beer, Louis Delamare 1945- *WhoAmL 94*
Beer, Michael 1926- *WhoAm 94*
Beer, Otto F. 1910- *IntWW 93*
Beer, Pamela Jill Porr 1941- *WhoMW 93*
Beer, Patricia 1924- *BlmGEL, BlmGWL, Who 94, WrDr 94*
Beer, Peter George 1941- *Who 94*
Beer, Peter Hill 1928- *WhoAm 94, WhoAmL 94*
Beer, Ralph (Robert) 1947- *WrDr 94*
Beer, Reinhard 1935- *WhoAm 94*
Beer, Samuel (Hutchinson) 1911- *WrDr 94*
Beer, Stafford *Who 94*
Beer, Stafford 1926- *WrDr 94*
Beer, (Anthony) Stafford 1926- *Who 94*
Beer, Walter R., Jr. 1926- *WhoAmP 93*
Beerbohm, Max 1872-1956 *BlmGEL*
Beerbower, Cynthia Gibson 1949- *WhoAm 94, WhoAmL 94*

Beerbower, John Edwin 1948- *WhoAmL 94*
Beere, Peter *EncSF 93*
Beering, John George 1936- *WhoFI 94*
Beering, Steven Claus 1932- *IntWW 93, WhoAm 94, WhoMW 93*
Beerline, Kurt Alan 1960- *WhoMW 93*
Beerling, John William 1937- *Who 94*
Beerman, Henry F. 1950- *WhoAmL 94*
Beerman, Herbert 1926- *WhoAmA 93*
Beerman, Miriam *WhoAm 94, WhoAmA 93*
Beermann, Allen J. 1940- *WhoAm 94, WhoMW 93*
Beermann, Allen Jay 1940- *WhoAmP 93*
Beermann Kappaladonna, Judith Countesa Ana 1945- *WhoFI 94*
Beernink, Darrell W. 1937- *WhoIns 94*
Beers, Bruce James 1942- *WhoFI 94*
Beers, Burton F(loyd) 1927- *ConAu 41NR*
Beers, Burton Floyd 1927- *WrDr 94*
Beers, Charlotte Lenore 1935- *WhoAm 94, WhoFI 94*
Beers, Clifford W. 1876-1943 *EncSPD*
Beers, Darrell 1927- *WhoAmP 93*
Beers, Donald Osborne 1949- *WhoAmL 94*
Beers, Ethel Lynn 1827-1879 *BlmGWL*
Beers, Fannie d1951 *WhoHol 92*
Beers, Francine *WhoHol 92*
Beers, Franklin Arthur *WhAm 10*
Beers, Fred C. d1946 *WhoHol 92*
Beers, Greg *WhoAmP 93*
Beers, Jack *WhoHol 92*
Beers, Mark H. 1954- *ConAu 140*
Beers, Orvas E. 1918- *WhoAmL 94, WhoAmP 93*
Beers, Paul Graham 1957- *WhoAmL 94*
Beers, Robert Wilson 1947- *WhoAmP 93*
Beers, Victor Gilbert 1928- *WhoAm 94*
Beers, William O. d1992 *IntWW 93N*
Beers, William O. 1914-1992 *WhAm 10*
Beer-Walbrunn, Anton 1864-1929 *NewGrDO*
Beery, Art 1930- *WhoAmA 93*
Beery, Dwight Beecher 1937- *WhoMW 93*
Beery, Mary *WrDr 94*
Beery, Noah 1913- *WhoHol 92*
Beery, Noah, Sr. d1946 *WhoHol 92*
Beery, Rhonda Gail 1967- *WhoMW 93*
Beery, Rita d1986 *WhoHol 92*
Beery, Wallace d1949 *WhoHol 92*
Beese, J. Carter, Jr. 1956- *WhoAm 94, WhoAmL 94, WhoFI 94*
Beese, P.J. 1946- *EncSF 93*
Beesel, J. Carter, Jr. 1956- *WhoAmP 93*
Beesemyer, Fritz Timothy 1952- *WhoWest 94*
Beesley, David 1938- *WhoWest 94*
Beesley, David 1947- *WhoAmP 93*
Beesley, Horace Brent 1946- *WhoAm 94*
Beesley, Ian Blake 1942- *Who 94*
Beesley, Michael Edwin 1924- *Who 94*
Beesley, Peter Frederick Barton 1943- *Who 94*
Beesley, Richard Clarence 1922- *WhoAmL 94*
Beesley, Walter Wade, Jr. 1948- *WhoAmP 93*
Beeson, Diane *DrAPF 93*
Beeson, Jack (Hamilton) 1921- *NewGrDO*
Beeson, Jack Hamilton 1921- *WhoAm 94*
Beeson, Paul Bruce 1908- *Who 94, WhoAm 94*
Beeson, Trevor Randall 1926- *Who 94, WrDr 94*
Beeston, Alfred Felix Landon 1911- *Who 94*
Beeston, Joseph Mack 1918- *WhoWest 94*
Beetham, Bruce Craig 1936- *IntWW 93*
Beetham, Geoffrey Howard 1933- *Who 94*
Beetham, Michael (James) 1923- *Who 94*
Beetham, Roger Campbell 1937- *Who 94*
Beetham, Stanley Williams 1933- *WhoAm 94, WhoFI 94, WhoWest 94*
Beethoven, Ludwig van 1770-1827 *EncDeaf, NewGrDO*
Beeton, Mrs. 1836-1865 *BlmGEL*
Beeton, Alfred Merle 1927- *WhoAm 94, WhoScEn 94*
Beeton, David Christopher 1939- *Who 94*
Beeton, Isabella Mary 1836-1865 *DcNaB MP*
Beets, F. Lee 1922- *WhoMW 93*
Beets, Freeman Haley 1919- *WhoAm 94*
Beetz, Carl Hugo 1911-1974 *WhoAmA 93N*
Beetz, Jean 1927- *WhAm 10*
Beetz, Justice Jean *IntWW 93N*
Beever, James William, III 1955- *WhoScEn 94*
Beever, Lisa Britt-Dodd 1960- *WhoScEn 94*
Beever, William Herbert 1952- *WhoScEn 94*
Beevers, Harry 1924- *IntWW 93, WhoAm 94, WhoWest 94*
Beevor, Antony Romer 1940- *Who 94*
Beevor, Miles 1900- *Who 94*
Beevor, Thomas Agnew 1929- *Who 94*
Beezer, Robert Arnold 1958- *WhoWest 94*
Beezer, Robert R. *WhoAmP 93*
Beezer, Robert Renaut 1928- *WhoAm 94, WhoAmL 94, WhoWest 94*
Beezhold, Donald Harry 1955- *WhoScEn 94*
Beezley, Frederick Ernest 1921- *Who 94*
Beezley, Linda *WhoAmP 93*
Beezley, Linda D. *WhoWest 94*
Beezley, William M. 1917- *WhoAmP 93*
Befera, Mary Rose 1963- *WhoMW 93*
Beffa, Jean-Louis Guy Henri 1941- *IntWW 93, Who 94*
Beffroy de Reigny, Louis-Abel 1757-1811 *NewGrDO*
Befort, Alois George, Jr. 1927- *WhoAmP 93*
BeFoure, Jeannine Marie 1923- *WhoFI 94*
Beg, Mirza Abdul Baoi 1934-1990 *WhAm 10*
Beg, Mirza Aslam 1931- *IntWW 93*
Beg, Mirza Umair 1946- *WhoScEn 94*
Begalka, Timothy Paul 1960- *WhoMW 93*
Begam, Robert G. 1928- *WhoAmP 93*
Begam, Robert George 1928- *WhoAm 94, WhoAmL 94*
Begando, Joseph Sheridan 1921- *WhoAm 94*
Begbie, (Edward) Harold 1871-1929 *EncSF 93*
Begell, William 1928- *WhoAm 94*
Begelman, Mitchell C. *WhoAm 94, WhoScEn 94*
Begeman, Myron Louis 1893- *WhAm 10*
Begenisich, Ted Bert *WhoScEn 94*
Begg, Alexander Charles 1912- *WrDr 94*
Begg, Gordon d1954 *WhoHol 92*
Begg, Heather 1932- *NewGrDO*
Begg, John Alfred 1903-1974 *WhoAmA 93N*
Begg, Neil (Colquhoun) 1915- *Who 94*
Begg, Neil (Colquhoun), Sir 1915- *WrDr 94*
Begg, Robert William 1922- *Who 94*
Begg, Varyl (Cargill) 1908- *Who 94*
Beggan, John Francis 1935- *WhoAm 94, WhoAmL 94*
Beggerly, Clay Evans 1956- *WhoMW 93*
Beggs, Bill 1950- *WhoFI 94*
Beggs, David 1909- *WrDr 94*
Beggs, Harry Mark 1941- *WhoAmL 94, WhoWest 94*
Beggs, James Harry 1940- *WhoScEn 94*
Beggs, James Montgomery 1926- *IntWW 93, WhoAm 94, WhoAmP 93*
Beggs, Joe Edward 1946- *WhoAmP 93*
Beggs, Lee d1943 *WhoHol 92*
Beggs, Lyman M., III *WhoAm 94, WhoFI 94, WhoMW 93*
Beggs, Malcolm Lee d1956 *WhoHol 92*
Beggs, Roy 1936- *Who 94*
Beggs, Thomas Montague 1899-1990 *WhoAmA 93N*
Beghe, Jason *WhoHol 92*
Beghe, Renato 1933- *CngDr 93, WhoAm 94, WhoAmL 94*
Beghini, Victor Gene 1934- *WhoAm 94, WhoFI 94*
Begich, Joseph R. 1930- *WhoAmP 93*
Begichev, Nikifor Alekseyevich 1874-1927 *WhWE*
Begin, Menachem d1992 *NobelP 91N*
Begin, Menachem 1913-1992 *AnObit 1992, HisWorL [port], WhAm 10*
Begin, Roger Normand 1952- *WhoAmP 93*
Beginin, Igor 1931- *WhoAmA 93*
Beglarian, Grant 1927- *WhoAm 94*
Begle, Douglas Pierce 1958- *WhoScEn 94*
Begleiter, Henri 1935- *WhoScEn 94*
Begleiter, Martin David 1945- *WhoAmL 94*
Begley, Anthony Martin 1966- *WhoScEn 94*
Begley, Charles M. 1927- *WhoAmP 93*
Begley, Ed d1970 *WhoHol 92*
Begley, Ed, Jr. 1949- *ConTFT 11, IntMPA 94, WhoAm 94, WhoHol 92*
Begley, J. 1947- *WhoAmA 93*
Begley, Jack 1934- *WhoAmP 93*
Begley, Jeanne F. 1930- *WhoAmP 93*
Begley, Kim 1952- *NewGrDO*
Begley, Louis *NewYTBS 93 [port]*
Begley, Louis 1933- *ConAu 140, WhoAm 94, WhoAmL 94*
Begley, Michael Joseph 1909- *WhoAm 94*
Begley, Wayne E. 1937- *WhoAmA 93*
Beglin, Edward W., Jr. 1934- *WhoAmL 94*
Begnis, Giuseppe de 1793-1849 *NewGrDO*
Begouen, Max *EncSF 93*
Begougne De Juniac, Gontran 1908- *IntWW 93*
Begovich, Nicholas Anthony 1921- *WhoAm 94*
Begrez, Pierre (Ignace) 1787-1863 *NewGrDO*
Beguin, Bernard 1923- *IntWW 93*
Beguine Anonyme, La fl. 13th cent.- *BlmGWL*
Begun, Semi Joseph 1905- *WhoAm 94*
Beh, Warren Albert, Jr. 1932- *WhoFI 94*
Beha, James Joseph 1916- *WhoAm 94*
Behaim, Martin c. 1436-1506 *WhWE*
Behan, Brendan 1923-1964 *BlmGEL, ConLC 79 [port]*
Behan, Brendan (Francis) 1923- *IntDcT 2 [port]*
Behan, John 1944- *WhoAmP 93*
Behar, David Albert 1958- *WhoWest 94*
Behar, Joy *WhoHol 92*
Behar, Robert *WhoHisp 94*
Beharrell, Steven Roderic 1944- *WhoAm 94*
Beharriell, Frederick John 1918- *WhoAm 94*
Behbehani, Abbas M. 1925- *WhoAm 94*
Behbehanian, Mahin Fazeli *WhoScEn 94*
Beheler, Laura *DrAPF 93*
Behl, Charanjit R. 1950- *WhoScEn 94*
Behl, Wishvender K. 1935- *WhoAsA 94*
Behl, Wolfgang 1918- *WhoAm 94, WhoAmA 93*
Behlar, Patricia Ann 1939- *WhoMW 93*
Behle, William Harroun 1909- *WrDr 94*
Behlen, Charles *DrAPF 93*
Behler, Diana Ipsen *WhoAm 94*
Behler, Ernst Heitmar 1928- *WhoWest 94*
Behling, Charles Frederick 1940- *WhoAm 94*
Behling, Paul Lawrence 1948- *WhoAmL 94*
Behlke, Charles Edward 1926- *WhoAm 94*
Behlmer, Rudy H., Jr. 1926- *WhoWest 94*
Behm, Dennis Arthur 1947- *WhoScEn 94*
Behm, Forrest Edwin 1919- *WhoAm 94, WhoFI 94*
Behm, John Robert 1953- *WhoMW 93*
Behm, Mark Edward 1945- *WhoFI 94*
Behn, Aphra 1640-1689 *BlmGEL, BlmGWL, DcLB 131 [port], DramC 4 [port], IntDcT 2 [port]*
Behn, Harry 1898-1973 *TwCYAW*
Behn, Noel 1928- *WrDr 94*
Behn, Robert Dietrich 1941- *WhoAmP 93*
Behn, Robin *DrAPF 93*
Behne, Edmond Rowlands 1906- *Who 94*
Behner, Elton Dale 1952- *WhoMW 93*
Behney, Charles Augustus, Jr. 1929- *WhoWest 94*
Behning, Robert W. 1954- *WhoAmP 93*
Behnke, Bruce Ivan 1944- *WhoFI 94*
Behnke, Carl Gilbert 1945- *WhoAm 94*
Behnke, Elizabeth Doelker 1926- *WhoMW 93*
Behnke, Erica Jean 1957- *WhoMW 93, WhoScEn 94*
Behnke, James Ralph 1943- *WhoScEn 94*
Behnke, Joe Martin 1950- *WhoWest 94*
Behnke, Leigh 1946- *WhoAmA 93*
Behnke, Marylou 1950- *WhoAm 94*
Behnke, Richard Frederick 1939- *WhoFI 94*
Behnke, Roy Herbert 1921- *WhoAm 94, WhoScEn 94*
Behnke, Wallace Blanchard, Jr. 1926- *WhoAm 94*
Behnke, William Alfred 1924- *WhoAm 94*
Behounek, Frantisek *EncSF 93*
Behr, Edward 1926- *WrDr 94*
Behr, Edward (Samuel) 1926- *ConAu 42NR*
Behr, Karl 1885-1949 *BuCMET*
Behr, Lawrence Van Der Poel 1940- *WhoAmP 93*
Behr, Marion Ray 1939- *WhoAm 94*
Behr, Norman Isaac 1922- *Who 94*
Behr, Omri M. *WhoAm 94*
Behr, Richard Henry 1942- *WhoAm 94*
Behr, Tom *WhoAmP 93*
Behren, Roy Douglas 1960- *WhoAmL 94*
Behrenbruch, William David 1946- *WhoWest 94*
Behrend, Donald Fraser 1931- *WhoAm 94, WhoWest 94*
Behrend, Frank Ludwig 1938- *WhoMW 93*
Behrend, Fritz 1889-1972 *NewGrDO*
Behrend, George (Henry Sandham) 1922- *WrDr 94*
Behrend, Hilde 1917- *IntWW 93*
Behrend, William Louis 1923- *WhoAm 94, WhoScEn 94*
Behrends, Ralph Eugene 1926-1990 *WhAm 10*
Behrendt, David Frogner 1935- *WhoAm 94, WhoMW 93*
Behrendt, John Charles 1932- *WhoAm 94*
Behrendt, John Thomas 1945- *WhoAm 94*
Behrens, Ahn *DrAPF 93*
Behrens, Bernard *WhoHol 92*
Behrens, Diane R. 1941- *WhoMW 93*
Behrens, Frank d1986 *WhoHol 92*
Behrens, Hildegard *IntWW 93*
Behrens, Hildegard 1937- *NewGrDO, WhoAm 94*
Behrens, Jack 1935- *NewGrDO*
Behrens, John C. 1933- *WrDr 94*
Behrens, June Adelle 1925- *WhoWest 94*
Behrens, Katia 1942- *BlmGWL*
Behrens, Mary 1942- *WhoAmP 93*
Behrens, Mary Snyder 1957- *WhoAmA 93*
Behrens, Peter 1868-1940 *ModArCr 4 [port]*
Behrens, Richard John 1946- *WhoFI 94*
Behrens, Roy R. 1946- *WhoAmA 93*
Behrens, Rudolph 1953- *WhoScEn 94*
Behrens, Thomas A. 1957- *WhoAmP 93*
Behrens, William 1906- *WhoHol 92*
Behring, Emil von 1854-1917 *WorScD*
Behring, Kenneth E. 1928- *WhoAm 94, WhoWest 94*
Behringer, John W. 1938- *WhoAmL 94*
Behrle, Franklin Charles 1922- *WhoAm 94*
Behrle, Fred d1941 *WhoHol 92*
Behrman, Edward Joseph 1930- *WhoAm 94, WhoScEn 94*
Behrman, Elizabeth Colden 1958- *WhoMW 93*
Behrman, Harold Richard 1939- *WhoAm 94*
Behrman, Jack Newton 1922- *WhoAm 94, WhoScEn 94, WrDr 94*
Behrman, Jere Richard 1940- *WhoAm 94*
Behrman, Myron M. 1906- *WhoAm 94*
Behrman, Richard Elliot 1931- *IntWW 93, WhoAm 94*
Behrman, S. N. 1893-1973 *IntDcF 2-4*
Behrman, S(amuel) N(athaniel) 1893-1973 *ConDr 93, IntDcT 2*
Behrmann, Joan Metzner *WhoAm 94*
Behrmann, Serge T. 1937- *WhoBlA 94*
Behrnd-Klodt, Menzi Louise 1953- *WhoAmL 94*
Behrs, Patti *WhoHol 92*
Behrstock, Julian Robert 1916- *WhoAm 94*
Behymer, Ruby Jo 1940- *WhoAm 94*
Beichman, Arnold 1913- *WhoAm 94, WhoWest 94*
Beickel, Sharon Lynne 1943- *WhoWest 94*
Beickler, Ferdinand 1922- *IntWW 93*
Bei Dao 1949- *ConWorW 93, WhoPRCh 91 [port]*
Beidel, Deborah Casamassa 1955- *WhoScEn 94*
Beideman, Ronald Paul 1926- *WhoMW 93*
Beider, Andrew Michael 1951- *WhoMW 93*
Beidleman, Richard Gooch 1923- *WhoScEn 94*
Beidler, Marsha Wolf 1948- *WhoAm 94, WhoAmL 94*
Beidler, Peter Grant 1940- *WhoAm 94*
Beier, Friedrich-Karl 1926- *IntWW 93*
Beierwaltes, William Henry 1916- *WhoAm 94, WhoMW 93, WhoScEn 94*
Beig, Maria 1920- *BlmGWL*
Beigel, Allan 1940- *WhoAm 94*
Beighey, Lawrence Jerome 1938- *WhoAm 94*
Beighle, Douglas Paul 1932- *WhoAm 94, WhoAmL 94*
Beighley, David Glenn 1951- *WhoMW 93*
Beight, Janice Marie 1947- *WhoMW 93*
Beighton, Leonard John Hobhouse 1934- *Who 94*
Beigie, Carl Emerson 1940- *WhoAm 94*
Beigl, William 1950- *WhoAm 94, WhoMW 93*
Beigler, Jerome Sallan 1916- *WhoMW 93*
Beihl, Frederick 1932- *WhoAm 94*
Beijerinck, Martinus Willem 1851-1931 *WorScD*
Beik, Mostafa Ali-Akbar 1958- *WhoScEn 94*
Beil, Charles A. d1976 *WhoAmA 93N*
Beil, Marshall Howard 1946- *WhoAmL 94*
Beilby, Alvin Lester 1932- *WhoAm 94, WhoWest 94*
Beilby, Vangie d1958 *WhoHol 92*
Beilenson, Anthony C. 1932- *CngDr 93, WhoAmP 93*
Beilenson, Anthony Charles 1932- *WhoAm 94, WhoWest 94*
Beilin, Howard *WhoAmA 93*
Beilke, Irma 1904-1989 *NewGrDO*
Beill, Alfred 1931- *Who 94*
Beim, David Odell 1940- *WhoAm 94*
Beim, Helen 1943- *WhoWomW 91*
Beim, Norman *WhoAm 94*
Beim, Norman 1923- *WhoHol 92*
Beiman, Elliott 1935- *WhoScEn 94*
Beimborn, Ronald Vernon 1945- *WhoMW 93*
Beimer, Michael Richard 1947- *WhoMW 93*
Beims, Harold Scott 1939- *WhoMW 93*
Beinecke, Candace Krugman 1946- *WhoAm 94, WhoAmL 94*

Beinecke, Frederick William 1943- *WhoAm 94*
Beinecke, William S. 1914- *WhoAm 94*
Beinecke, William Sperry 1914- *IntWW 93*
Beineix, Jean-Jacques 1946- *IntWW 93*
Beineke, Lowell Wayne 1939- *WhoAm 94, WhoScEn 94*
Beiner, Ronald 1953- *ConAu 42NR*
Beinhocker, Gilbert David 1932- *WhoAm 94, WhoFI 94*
Beining, Guy R. *DrAPF 93*
Beins, Bernard Charles 1950- *WhoScEn 94*
Beir, Fred d1980 *WhoHol 92*
Beirer, Hans 1911- *NewGrDO*
Beirne, Bill 1941- *WhoAmA 93*
Beirne, Danielle Ululani *WhoAmP 93*
Beirne, Kathleen Walsh 1945- *WhoAmL 94*
Beirne, Kenneth Joseph 1946- *WhoAm 94*
Beirne, Martin Douglas 1944- *WhoAmL 94*
Beirne, Michael d1983 *WhoHol 92*
Beiro, Sara Margaret 1963- *WhoAmL 94*
Beise, S. Clark 1898-1989 *WhAm 10*
Beisecker, Analee Elizabeth 1943- *WhoMW 93*
Beisel, Daniel Cunningham 1916- *WhoAm 94*
Beisenov, Sayat Dyusenbaievich 1940- *LoBiDrD*
Beiser, Gerald J. 1930- *WhoFI 94*
Beiser, Helen Ruth 1914- *WhoAm 94*
Bei Shizhang 1903- *IntWW 93, WhoPRCh 91 [port]*
Beishon, (Ronald) John 1930- *Who 94*
Beisner, John Herbert 1953- *WhoAm 94*
Beisner, Robert L. 1936- *WrDr 94*
Beissel, Henry (Eric) 1929- *WrDr 94*
Beissel, Johann Conrad 1690-1768 *DcAmReB 2*
Beisser, Judith Kay 1946- *WhoMW 93*
Beisswenger, Harry Louis, Jr. 1935- *WhoFI 94*
Beistline, Earl Hoover 1916- *WhoAm 94*
Beiswanger, Gary Lee 1938- *WhoAmL 94*
Beiswanger, George W. d1993 *NewYTBS 93*
Beit, Alfred Lane 1903- *Who 94*
Beit-Arie, Malachi 1937- *IntWW 93*
Beitelspacher, Ronald J. 1945- *WhoAmP 93*
Beith, Alan (James) 1943- *Who 94*
Beith, John 1914- *Who 94*
Beith, John William 1909- *Who 94*
Beitia, Sally A. 1957- *WhoAmP 93*
Beitler, J. Paul 1945- *WhoAm 94, WhoFI 94, WhoMW 93*
Beitler, Stephen Seth 1956- *WhoMW 93, WhoScEn 94*
Beittel, Adam Daniel 1898- *WhAm 10*
Beitz, Berthold 1913- *IntWW 93*
Beitz, Michael B. 1942- *WhoAmP 93*
Beitzel, George B. 1928- *WhoAm 94*
Beizer, Richard L. 1942- *WhoAmL 94*
Beizer, Robert A. 1939- *WhoAm 94*
Beja, Morris 1935- *WhoAm 94, WrDr 94*
Bejan, Adrian 1948- *WhoScEn 94*
Bejarano, Carmen 1944- *WhoHisp 94*
Bejarano, Richard Xavier, Sr. 1950- *WhoHisp 94*
Bejart, Maurice 1927- *ConTFT 11, IntDcB [port]*
Bejart, Maurice (Jean) 1927- *IntWW 93, Who 94*
Bejczy, Antal Karoly 1930- *WhoAm 94*
Bejerano, Maya 1949- *BlmGWL*
Bejnar, Thaddeus Putnam 1948- *WhoAmL 94*
Bekaroglu, Ozer 1933- *WhoScEn 94*
Bekavac, Nancy Yavor 1947- *WhoAm 94, WhoWest 94*
Beke, Kata *WhoWomW 91*
Bekederemo, J.P. Clark *ConDr 93*
Bekefi, George 1925- *WhoAm 94*
Bekemeyer, Dennis Lee 1943- *WhoAm 94*
Beker, Gisela *WhoAmA 93*
Beker, Henry Joseph 1951- *Who 94*
Bekerdomo, J. P. Clark *IntDcT 2*
Bekesi, Julis George 1931- *WhoScEn 94*
Bekesi, Laszlo 1942- *IntWW 93*
Bekesy, Georg von *WorInv*
Bekesy, Georg von 1899-1972 *EncDeaf, WorScD*
Beketov, Pyotr fl. 162-?-166-? *WhWE*
Bekey, George Albert 1928- *WhoAm 94, WhoWest 94*
Bekey, Shirley White *WhoWest 94*
Bekhtereva, Natalya Petrovna 1924- *IntWW 93*
Beki, Gabriella *WhoWomW 91*
Bekir, Nagwa Esmat 1944- *WhoWest 94*
Bekkedahl, Brad Douglas 1957- *WhoMW 93*
Bekken, James Malcolm 1948- *WhoMW 93*
Bekken, Robert John 1951- *WhoAmL 94*
Bekker, (Max) Paul (Eugen) 1882-1937 *NewGrDO*
Bekku, Sadao 1922- *NewGrDO*
Bekman, Paul David 1946- *WhoAmL 94*
Bekoe, Daniel Adzei 1928- *Who 94*
Bekovich-Cherkassky, Alexandr dc. 1717 *WhWE*
Beksics, Gusztav *EncSF 93*
Bela, Nicholas d1963 *WhoHol 92*
Bela, Richard José *WhoHisp 94*
Belack, Doris *WhoHol 92*
Belafonte, Gina 1961- *WhoHol 92*
Belafonte, Harry *NewYTBS 93 [port]*
Belafonte, Harry 1927- *AfrAmAl 6, IntMPA 94, IntWW 93, WhoAm 94, WhoBlA 94, WhoHol 92*
Belafonte, Shari 1954- *IntMPA 94, WhoBlA 94, WhoHol 92*
Belag, Andrea 1951- *WhoAmA 93*
Belaga, Julie D. *WhoAmP 93*
Belaga, M. W. 1929- *WhoAmP 93*
Belagaje, Rama M. 1942- *WhoMW 93, WhoScEn 94*
Belaire, Joel Alfred 1941- *WhoFI 94*
Belak, Michael James 1961- *WhoFI 94*
Belamaric, Miro 1935- *NewGrDO*
Belan, Albert V. 1930- *WhoAmP 93*
Belancourt, Dunet Francois 1928- *WhoBlA 94*
Belanger, David Martin *WhoAmL 94*
Belanger, Gerard 1940- *IntWW 93, WhoAm 94*
Belanger, Michel 1929- *IntWW 93*
Belanger, Michel Ferdinand 1929- *WhoFI 94*
Belanger, Pierre Rolland 1937- *WhoAm 94, WhoScEn 94*
Belanger, Robert Eugene 1958- *WhoAmL 94*
Belanger, Ronald Joseph 1939- *WhoAmP 93*
Belanger, Ronald Louis 1955- *WhoScEn 94*
Belanger, William Joseph 1925- *WhoAm 94*
Belanger, William V., Jr. 1928- *WhoAmP 93*
Belanov, Igor Ivanovich 1960- *LoBiDrD*
Belarbi, Abdeldjelil 1959- *WhoScEn 94*
Belardi, Fred 1942- *WhoAmP 93*
Belardo De O'Neal, Lilliana 1944- *WhoAmP 93, WhoBlA 94*
Belasco, Arthur d1979 *WhoHol 92*
Belasco, David d1931 *WhoHol 92*
Belasco, David 1853-1931 *AmCulL [port], NewGrDO*
Belasco, Genevieve d1956 *WhoHol 92*
Belasco, Leon d1988 *WhoHol 92*
Belasco, Simon 1918- *WhoAm 94*
Belasco, Walter d1939 *WhoHol 92*
Belatti, Richard G. *WhoAmP 93*
Belau, Jane Carol Gullickson 1934- *WhoFI 94*
Belaunde Terry, Fernando 1913- *IntWW 93*
Belay, Stephen Joseph 1958- *WhoAmL 94*
Belayev, A. *EncSF 93*
Belbis, Manuel Emuslan 1941- *WhoAsA 94*
Belcampo *EncSF 93*
Belcastro, Patrick Frank 1920- *WhoAm 94, WhoMW 93*
Belch, Charles Henry 1938- *WhoAmP 93*
Belch, (Alexander) Ross 1920- *Who 94*
Belchak, Frank Robert 1943- *WhoMW 93*
Belcher, Alice d1939 *WhoHol 92*
Belcher, Charles d1943 *WhoHol 92*
Belcher, David Christopher 1961- *WhoMW 93*
Belcher, Dennis Irl 1951- *WhoAm 94, WhoAmL 94*
Belcher, Donald David 1938- *WhoFI 94*
Belcher, Edward 1799-1877 *WhWE*
Belcher, Frank d1947 *WhoHol 92*
Belcher, George 1941- *WhoAmA 93*
Belcher, Hilda 1881-1963 *WhoAmA 93N*
Belcher, Jennifer M. 1944- *WhoAmP 93, WhoWomW 91*
Belcher, John Cheslow 1920-1990 *WhAm 10*
Belcher, John Christopher 1951- *WhoAmL 94*
Belcher, John Rashleigh 1917- *Who 94*
Belcher, La Jeune 1960- *WhoMW 93*
Belcher, Leon H. 1930- *WhoBlA 94*
Belcher, Lewis, Jr. 1931- *WhoBlA 94*
Belcher, Louis D. 1939- *WhoAmP 93*
Belcher, Louis David 1939- *WhoAm 94*
Belcher, Margaret L. 1922- *WhoBlA 94*
Belcher, Nathaniel L. 1929- *WhoBlA 94*
Belcher, Nathaniel Lee 1929- *WhoAmL 94*
Belcher, Ronald Anthony 1950- *WhoScEn 94*
Belcher, Ronald Harry 1916- *Who 94*
Belcher, Taylor Garrison 1920- *WhoAmP 93*
Belcher, Taylor Garrison 1920-1990 *WhAm 10*
Belcher, William Walter, Jr. 1943- *WhoWest 94*
Belchior, Murillo 1913- *IntWW 93*
Belcourt, Emile 1926- *NewGrDO*
Belcourt, Mignonne L. 1945- *WhoFI 94*
Belcourt, Norma Elizabeth *Who 94*
Beldam, Asplan 1841-1912 *DcNaB MP*
Beldam, (Alexander) Roy (Asplan) 1925- *Who 94*
Belde, Cameluta *WhoWomW 91*
Belden, David (Corderoy) 1949- *EncSF 93*
Belden, David Leigh 1935- *WhoAm 94, WhoFI 94, WhoScEn 94*
Belden, H. Reginald 1907- *WhoAmL 94*
Belden, Richard O. 1934- *WhoAmP 93*
Belding, Melvin Earl 1938- *WhoWest 94*
Belding, William Anson 1944- *WhoScEn 94*
Beldock, Donald Travis 1934- *WhoAm 94*
Beldock, Myron 1929- *WhoAm 94, WhoAmL 94*
Beldon, Sanford T. 1932- *WhoAm 94*
Belefant, Arthur 1927- *WhoScEn 94*
Belen, Frederick Christopher 1913- *WhoAm 94*
Belet, Jacques Henry, III 1948- *WhoAm 94*
Belew, Adrian *WhoAm 94*
Belew, David Lee 1931- *WhoAm 94*
Belew, David Owen, Jr. 1920- *WhoAm 94*
Belew, Joe Duncan 1949- *WhoAmP 93*
Belew, John Seymour 1920- *WhoAm 94*
Belfanti, Robert Edward, Jr. 1948- *WhoAmP 93*
Belfast, Dean of *Who 94*
Belfast, Earl of 1952- *Who 94*
Belfer, Arthur B. d1993 *NewYTBS 93*
Belfer, Hal B. *IntMPA 94*
Belfield, Judy *DrAPF 93*
Belfield, Kevin Donald 1960- *WhoScEn 94*
Belfield, Richard d1940 *WhoHol 92*
Belford, Barbara 1935- *WrDr 94*
Belford, Christine 1949- *WhoHol 92*
Belford, Richard David 1945- *WhoAm 94*
Belford, Virginia Helen Wisdom 1948- *WhoMW 93*
Belford, William Wiess 1897- *WhAm 10*
Belfore, Lee Alyn, II 1960- *WhoMW 93*
Belfort-Chalat, Jacqueline 1930- *WhoAmA 93*
Belfour, Ed 1965- *WhoAm 94, WhoMW 93*
Belfrage, Bruce d1974 *WhoHol 92*
Belgau, Robert Joseph 1960- *WhoScEn 94*
Bel Geddes, Barbara 1922- *IntMPA 94, WhoHol 92*
Bel Geddes, Joan *WhoAm 94*
Bel Geddes, Norman 1893-1958 *NewGrDO, WhoAmA 93N*
Belgium, I, King Baudouin of *IntWW 93*
Belgrade, Miles Jay 1952- *WhoMW 93*
Belgrader, Phillip 1961- *WhoScEn 94*
Belgrave, Cynthia *WhoHol 92*
Belgrave, Valerie *BlmGWL*
Belham, David Ernest 1914- *Who 94*
Belhaven, Master of 1953- *Who 94*
Belhaven and Stenton, Lord 1927- *Who 94*
Belhomme, Hypolite 1854-1923 *NewGrDO*
Beliaev, Alexander *EncSF 93*
Belian, Garabed *WhoAmA 93*
Belian, Isabelle *WhoAmA 93*
Beliard, Jean 1919- *IntWW 93*
Beliayev, Alexander *EncSF 93*
Belich, James 1927- *Who 94*
Belich, John Patrick, Sr. 1938- *WhoAm 94*
Belichick, Bill *WhoAm 94, WhoMW 93*
Beligan, Radu 1918- *IntWW 93*
Belille, Ronald 1947- *WhoWest 94*
Belin, Carl A., Jr. 1934- *WhoAmP 93*
Belin, David William 1928- *WhoAm 94, WhoAmL 94, WhoFI 94*
Belin, Gaspard d'Andelot 1918- *WhoAm 94*
Belin, Jacob Chapman 1914- *WhoAm 94*
Belin, Roger 1916- *IntWW 93*
Belinfante, Johan Gijsbertus Frederik 1940- *WhoAm 94*
Beling, Helen 1914- *WhoAm 94, WhoAmA 93*
Belinger, Harry Robert 1927- *WhoAm 94*
Belinoff, Deanne *WhoAmA 93*
Belinski, William J. 1950- *WhoIns 94*
Belisani Buini, Cecilia fl. 1716-1767 *NewGrDO*
Belisle, Denton 1948- *Who 94*
Belisle, Gilles 1923- *WhoAm 94*
Belita 1923- *WhoHol 92*
Belitt, Ben *DrAPF 93*
Belitt, Ben 1911- *WhoAm 94, WrDr 94*
Belitz, Paul Edward 1951- *WhoAm 94*
Beliveau, Jean-Guy Lionel 1946- *WhoScEn 94*
Beliveau, John Austin 1961- *WhoFI 94*
Beliveau, Severin Matthew 1938- *WhoAmP 93*
Beljan, John Richard 1930- *WhoAm 94, WhoWest 94*
Belk, Irwin 1922- *WhoFI 94*
Belk, John Blanton 1925- *WhoAm 94, WhoWest 94*
Belk, Keith E. 1961- *WhoScEn 94*
Belk, Thomas Milburn 1925- *WhoAm 94, WhoFI 94*
Belka, Kevin Lee 1949- *WhoScEn 94*
Belkaid, Aboubakr 1934- *IntWW 93*
Belkaoui, Ahmed R. *ConAu 140*
Belkin, Boris David 1948- *WhoAm 94*
Belkin, Keith Ellis 1951- *WhoAmL 94*
Belkin, Lisa 1960- *ConAu 141*
Belkin, Michael 1941- *WhoScEn 94*
Belkind-Gerson, Jaime 1964- *WhoScEn 94*
Belknap, Jeremy 1744-1798 *WhAmRev*
Belknap, Jerry P. 1917- *WhoAmL 94*
Belknap, John Corbould 1946- *WhoAm 94*
Belknap, Kathy Andre 1954- *WhoWest 94*
Belknap, Michael H. P. 1940- *WhoFI 94*
Belknap, Morris B. d1952 *WhoAmA 93N*
Belknap, Norton 1925- *WhoAm 94*
Belknap, Robert Ernest, III 1938- *WhoFI 94*
Belknap, Robert L. 1929- *WrDr 94*
Belknap, Robert Lamont 1929- *WhoAm 94*
Belkov, Meredith Ann 1939- *WhoAm 94*
Bell, A. Jean 1926- *WhoAmP 93*
Bell, Acton *BlmGWL*
Bell, Aileen Marie 1964- *WhoAmL 94*
Bell, Alan 1954- *WhoWest 94*
Bell, Alan Scott 1942- *Who 94*
Bell, Albert A., Jr. 1945- *ConAu 142*
Bell, Alberta Saffell 1944- *WhoBlA 94*
Bell, Alexander Gilmour 1933- *Who 94*
Bell, Alexander Graham 1847-1922 *EncDeaf, WorInv*
Bell, Alistair Macready 1913- *WhoAmA 93*
Bell, Alistair Watson 1930- *Who 94*
Bell, Allan Craig 1959- *WhoAmL 94*
Bell, Allen Andrew, Jr. 1951- *WhoAmL 94*
Bell, Alphonzo 1914- *WhoAmP 93*
Bell, Andrew Montgomery 1940- *Who 94*
Bell, Andy 1965- *See* Erasure *ConMus 11*
Bell, Ann 1939- *WhoHol 92*
Bell, Anthony Dewitt 1964- *WhoBlA 94*
Bell, Archibald Angus 1923- *Who 94*
Bell, Arnold d1988 *WhoHol 92*
Bell, Arthur *Who 94*
Bell, (Ernest) Arthur 1926- *IntWW 93, Who 94*
Bell, Bernard Iddings 1886-1958 *DcAmReB 2*
Bell, Bert d1959 *ProFbHF [port]*
Bell, Bobby *ProFbHF*
Bell, Bradley J. 1952- *WhoAm 94*
Bell, Brian d1982 *WhoHol 92*
Bell, Brian Mayes 1940- *WhoAmL 94*
Bell, Brigitte Schmidt 1948- *WhoAmL 94*
Bell, Bryan 1918- *WhoFI 94*
Bell, Carl Compton 1947- *WhoBlA 94*
Bell, Carmela Leone 1960- *WhoAmL 94*
Bell, Carol Willsey 1939- *WhoAm 94*
Bell, Carolyn Shaw 1920- *WhoAm 94*
Bell, Catherine 1905- *WrDr 94*
Bell, Catherine Elisabeth 1951- *Who 94*
Bell, Charles 1774-1842 *WorScD*
Bell, Charles Eugene, Jr. 1932- *WhoFI 94, WhoMW 93, WhoScEn 94*
Bell, Charles G(reenleaf) 1916- *WrDr 94*
Bell, Charles Greenleaf *DrAPF 93*
Bell, Charles Ray 1941- *WhoAm 94*
Bell, Charles Robert, Jr. 1930- *WhoAm 94*
Bell, Charles S. 1935- *WhoAmA 93*
Bell, Charles Smith 1934- *WhoBlA 94*
Bell, Charolette Renee 1949- *WhoWest 94*
Bell, Chester Gordon 1934- *WhoAm 94, WhoScEn 94, WhoWest 94*
Bell, Clara Ellen 1934- *WhoBlA 94*
Bell, Clare (Louise) 1952- *EncSF 93*
Bell, Clare Louise 1952- *WhoAm 94*
Bell, Clarence Deshong 1914- *WhoAmP 93*
Bell, Clarence E. 1912- *WhoAmP 93*
Bell, Clark Wayne 1951- *WhoAm 94*
Bell, Clyde Roberts 1931- *WhoAm 94*
Bell, Coca (Mary Catlett) 1924- *WhoAmA 93*
Bell, Corinne Reed 1943- *WhoScEn 94*
Bell, Currer *BlmGWL*
Bell, Cyril Felix 1942- *WhoAmP 93*
Bell, Daniel 1919- *WhoAm 94, WrDr 94*
Bell, Daniel Carroll 1940- *WhoWest 94*
Bell, Daniel Long, Jr. 1929- *WhoAm 94, WhoAmL 94*
Bell, Darryl Stephen 1945- *WhoAm 94, WhoAmL 94*
Bell, David Arthur 1943- *WhoAm 94, WhoFI 94*

Bell, David Charles Maurice 1946- *Who 94*
Bell, David Curtis 1953- *WhoMW 93*
Bell, David Elliott 1919- *IntWW 93*
Bell, David Eugene 1944- *WhoFI 94*
Bell, David Lee 1953- *WhoWest 94*
Bell, Denise Louise 1967- *WhoWest 94*
Bell, Dennis Arthur 1934- *WhoAmL 94*
Bell, Dennis Philip 1948- *WhoBlA 94*
Bell, Derek Nathaniel 1968- *WhoBlA 94*
Bell, Derrick 1930- *ConBlB 6 [port]*
Bell, Derrick A. 1930- *CurBio 93 [port]*
Bell, Derrick Albert 1930- *WhoAm 94*
Bell, Derrick Albert, Jr. 1930- *AfrAmAl 6, BlkWr 2, WhoBlA 94*
Bell, Diana Lynne 1952- *WhoBlA 94*
Bell, Digby d1917 *WhoHol 92*
Bell, Don Wayne 1945- *WhoWest 94*
Bell, Donald Allen 1938- *WhoAmA 93*
Bell, Donald Atkinson 1941- *Who 94*
Bell, Donald L. *Who 94*
Bell, Donald Munro 1934- *Who 94*
Bell, Donald Robert 1928- *WhoWest 94*
Bell, Donald William 1936- *WhoWest 94*
Bell, Doris E. 1938- *WhoBlA 94*
Bell, Douglas Maurice d1993 *Who 94N*
Bell, Dozier 1957- *WhoAmA 93*
Bell, Drucilla Emma 1951- *WhoAmL 94*
Bell, Edith Alice 1919- *Who 94*
Bell, Edna Talbert 1944- *WhoBlA 94*
Bell, Edward 1949- *Who 94*
Bell, Edward Francis 1930- *WhoFI 94*
Bell, Edwin Graham 1939- *WhoAmP 93*
Bell, Eldrin A. *WhoBlA 94*
Bell, Ellis *BlmGWL*
Bell, Elmer A. 1941- *WhoBlA 94*
Bell, Eric Temple *EncSF 93*
Bell, Ernest Lorne, III 1926- *WhoAm 94*
Bell, Eudorus N. *DcAmReB 2*
Bell, Everett Thomas 1909- *WhoBlA 94*
Bell, Ewart *Who 94*
Bell, (William) Ewart 1924- *Who 94*
Bell, Felix C. 1936- *WhoBlA 94*
Bell, Forest Stirling *DrAPF 93*
Bell, Frances Louise 1926- *WhoAm 94, WhoScEn 94*
Bell, Frank d1992 *Who 94N*
Bell, Frank 1905- *WrDr 94*
Bell, Frank Ouray, Jr. 1940- *WhoAm 94*
Bell, Franklin R. 1943- *WhoAmP 93*
Bell, Gail Marie 1951 *WhoFI 94*
Bell, Gaston d1963 *WhoHol 92*
Bell, Gawain (Westray) 1909- *Who 94, WrDr 94*
Bell, Genevieve d1951 *WhoHol 92*
Bell, Geoffrey Lakin 1939- *IntWW 93, Who 94*
Bell, George *WhoBlA 94*
Bell, George 1959- *WhoHisp 94*
Bell, George Antonio 1959- *WhoAm 94, WhoBlA 94, WhoMW 93*
Bell, George Douglas Hutton d1993 *Who 94N*
Bell, George Edwin 1923- *WhoAm 94*
Bell, George Irving 1926- *WhoAm 94*
Bell, George O. d1969 *WhoHol 92*
Bell, Gertrude Margaret 1868-1926 *WhWE*
Bell, Glenn Belanga 1959- *WhoFI 94*
Bell, Gregory Joseph 1948- *WhoAmP 93*
Bell, Gregory Knox 1960- *WhoFI 94*
Bell, Gregory Leon 1962- *WhoBlA 94*
Bell, Griffin B. 1918- *Who 94, WhoAm 94, WhoAmP 93*
Bell, Griffin B., Jr. 1944- *WhoAmL 94*
Bell, Guy Davies 1933- *Who 94*
Bell, H. B. 1938- *WhoBlA 94*
Bell, Haney Hardy, III 1944- *WhoAm 94*
Bell, Hank d1950 *WhoHol 92*
Bell, Harold Kevin 1939- *WhoBlA 94*
Bell, Harry Edward 1947- *WhoMW 93*
Bell, Harry Fullerton, Jr. 1954- *WhoAmL 94*
Bell, Hayley *WhoHol 92*
Bell, Helen Cherry 1937- *WhoScEn 94*
Bell, Henry 1647-1711 *DcNaB MP*
Bell, Henry Marsh, Jr. 1928- *WhoAm 94*
Bell, Herbert Aubrey Frederick 1921- *WhoAm 94*
Bell, Hilton S. 1942- *WhoAmL 94*
Bell, Houston Lesher, Jr. 1944- *WhoAm 94*
Bell, Howard Earl 1934- *WhoFI 94*
Bell, Howard Eugene 1920- *WhoBlA 94*
Bell, Howard Wesley, Jr. 1948- *WhoMW 93*
Bell, Hubert Julius, Jr. 1942- *WhoAmL 94*
Bell, Hubert Thomas, Jr. 1942- *WhoBlA 94*
Bell, Ian Wright 1913- *Who 94*
Bell, Ivan d1977 *WhoHol 92*
Bell, J. A. Gordon 1929- *WhoAm 94, WhoFI 94*
Bell, J. Allen 1946- *WhoFI 94*
Bell, J. Brandon, II 1958- *WhoAmP 93*
Bell, James d1973 *WhoHol 92*
Bell, James A. *WhoBlA 94*
Bell, James Bacon 1952- *WhoFI 94*
Bell, James Edward 1926- *WhoBlA 94*
Bell, James Edward 1941- *WrDr 94*
Bell, James Frederick 1914- *WhoAm 94*
Bell, James Frederick 1922- *WhoAm 94, WhoAmL 94*
Bell, James H. 1916- *WhoBlA 94*
Bell, James Halsey 1939- *WhoAm 94, WhoAmL 94*
Bell, James Kenton 1937- *WrDr 94*
Bell, James L., Jr. 1921- *WhoBlA 94*
Bell, James M. *WhoAmA 93*
Bell, James Milton 1921- *WhoAm 94, WhoBlA 94, WhoScEn 94*
Bell, James Scott *DrAPF 93*
Bell, James Steven 1914- *Who 94*
Bell, Janet Sharon 1947- *WhoBlA 94*
Bell, Jason Cameron 1963- *WhoMW 93*
Bell, Jay Stuart 1965- *WhoAm 94*
Bell, Jeannette Lois 1941- *WhoAmP 93, WhoWomW 91*
Bell, Jeannie *WhoHol 92*
Bell, Jeanny *WhoHol 92*
Bell, Jeffrey Donald 1956- *WhoAm 94*
Bell, Jerome Albert 1940- *WhoScEn 94*
Bell, Jerry *WhoAm 94, WhoMW 93*
Bell, Jerry Arch, Jr. 1951- *WhoAmL 94*
Bell, Jimmy 1944- *WhoBlA 94*
Bell, Jocelyn *Who 94, WorScD*
Bell, Joe W. *WhoAmP 93*
Bell, John 1940- *WhoHol 92*
Bell, John Alexander Gordon 1929- *IntWW 93*
Bell, John Alton 1958- *WhoAmL 94*
Bell, John Anthony 1924- *Who 94*
Bell, John Franklin 1945- *WhoAmL 94*
Bell, John Irving 1952- *Who 94*
Bell, John Lowthian 1960- *Who 94*
Bell, John Milton 1922- *IntWW 93, WhoAm 94*
Bell, John Stewart 1928-1990 *WhAm 10*
Bell, John William 1946- *WhoAmL 94*
Bell, John Wright 1925- *WhoAmL 94*
Bell, Jonathan Robert 1947- *WhoAm 94, WhoAmL 94*
Bell, Joseph 1837-1911 *DcNaB MP*
Bell, Joseph Curtis 1933- *WhoBlA 94*
Bell, Joseph Denis Milburn 1920- *Who 94*
Bell, Joseph Ernest, II 1941- *WhoAmP 93*
Bell, Joseph James *WhoAmP 93*
Bell, Joseph James 1947- *WhoAmL 94, WhoWest 94*
Bell, Joseph N. 1948- *WhoBlA 94*
Bell, Joshua 1967- *IntWW 93*
Bell, Joy *WhoHol 92*
Bell, Juanita 1923- *WhoAmP 93*
Bell, Kathleen Myra 1920- *Who 94*
Bell, Kathryn Leise 1942- *WhoAmA 93*
Bell, Katie Roberson 1936- *WhoAm 94, WhoBlA 94*
Bell, Kenneth John 1930- *WhoAm 94*
Bell, Kenneth M. 1941- *WhoBlA 94*
Bell, Larry Stuart 1939- *WhoAm 94, WhoAmA 93, WhoWest 94*
Bell, Laura Jeane 1922- *WhoMW 93, WhoScEn 94*
Bell, Lawrence F. 1958- *WhoBlA 94*
Bell, Lawrence R. 1941- *WhoIns 94*
Bell, Lee Phillip *WhoAm 94*
Bell, Leo S. 1913- *WhoWest 94*
Bell, Leon 1930- *WhoBlA 94*
Bell, Leroy Crawford 1932- *AfrAmG [port]*
Bell, Leslie d1962 *WhoHol 92*
Bell, Leslie Gladstone 1919- *Who 94*
Bell, Lilian A. 1943- *WhoAmA 93*
Bell, Linda Beteet 1947- *WhoMW 93*
Bell, Louis 1946- *WhoAmL 94*
Bell, Madison Smartt *DrAPF 93*
Bell, Madison Smartt 1957- *WrDr 94*
Bell, Marian Whieldon *WhoAmP 93*
Bell, Marie d1985 *WhoHol 92*
Bell, Marie 1946- *WhoAmP 93*
Bell, Marilyn Lenora 1943- *WhoBlA 94*
Bell, Marjorie *WhoHol 92*
Bell, Marshall *WhoHol 92*
Bell, Martha Jane 1943- *WhoAmP 93*
Bell, Martha Lue 1945- *WhoBlA 94*
Bell, Martin 1938- *Who 94*
Bell, Martin Allen 1951- *WhoAm 94, WhoFI 94*
Bell, Martin George Henry 1935- *Who 94*
Bell, Martin J. 1937- *WhoAmP 93*
Bell, Marvin *DrAPF 93*
Bell, Marvin (Hartley) 1937- *WrDr 94*
Bell, Mary Catherine 1946- *WhoAmA 93*
Bell, Mary E. Beniteau 1937- *WhoFI 94*
Bell, Mary L. *WhoBlA 94*
Bell, Maxine T. 1931- *WhoAmP 93*
Bell, Maxine Toolson 1931- *WhoWest 94*
Bell, Melvyn Clarence 1944- *WhoBlA 94*
Bell, Michael *WhoHol 92*
Bell, Michael John Vincent 1941- *Who 94*
Bell, Michael S. *DrAPF 93*
Bell, Michael Steven 1946- *WhoAmA 93*
Bell, Mildred Bailey 1928- *WhoAmL 94, WhoFI 94*
Bell, Monta d1958 *WhoHol 92*
Bell, Napoleon A. 1927- *WhoBlA 94*
Bell, Nathan James 1946- *WhoAmP 93*
Bell, Neil 1887-1964 *EncSF 93*
Bell, Norman Francis 1948- *WhoWest 94*
Bell, Norman Howard 1931- *WhoAm 94*
Bell, Normand W. 1930- *WhoIns 94*
Bell, Olin Nile 1939- *WhoAm 94*
Bell, P. Jackson 1941- *WhoAm 94, WhoFI 94*
Bell, Paul, Jr. 1921- *WhoBlA 94*
Bell, Paul A. *WhoAmP 93*
Bell, Peter Mayo 1934- *WhoAm 94, WhoScEn 94*
Bell, Peter Robert 1920- *Who 94*
Bell, Peter Robert Frank 1938- *Who 94*
Bell, Philip Michael 1942- *WhoAmA 93*
Bell, Philip Wilkes 1924- *WhoAm 94*
Bell, Phillip Michael 1942- *WhoAm 94*
Bell, Quentin (Claudian Stephen) 1910- *Who 94, WrDr 94*
Bell, R. Murray *WhoAmA 93*
Bell, Rachel *WhoHol 92*
Bell, Raleigh Berton 1915- *WhoBlA 94*
Bell, Ralph d1936 *WhoHol 92*
Bell, Ralph S. 1934- *ConBlB 5 [port]*
Bell, Raymond *IntWW 93, Who 94*
Bell, (George) Raymond 1916- *Who 94*
Bell, Raymond M(artin) 1907- *WrDr 94*
Bell, Regina Jean *WhoMW 93*
Bell, Reva Pearl 1925- *WhoBlA 94*
Bell, Rex d1962 *WhoHol 92*
Bell, Rex, Jr. *WhoHol 92*
Bell, Richard 1920- *WhoAmP 93*
Bell, Richard Chevalier 1928- *WhoAm 94*
Bell, Richard Eugene 1934- *WhoAm 94*
Bell, Richard F. 1944- *WhoAm 94*
Bell, Richard G. 1947- *WhoAmL 94*
Bell, Ricky *WhoBlA 94*
Bell, Robert Charles 1917- *WrDr 94*
Bell, Robert Collins 1912- *WhoAmL 94, WhoFI 94*
Bell, Robert Donald Murray 1916- *Who 94*
Bell, Robert Edward *IntWW 93N*
Bell, Robert Edward d1992 *Who 94N*
Bell, Robert Edward 1918- *WhAm 10*
Bell, Robert Eugene 1914- *WhoAm 94, WrDr 94*
Bell, Robert G. 1947- *WhoAm 94*
Bell, Robert Holmes 1944- *WhoAm 94, WhoAmL 94, WhoMW 93*
Bell, Robert Hudson 1929- *WhoAmP 93*
Bell, Robert J. 1947- *WhoAmL 94*
Bell, Robert L. 1934- *WhoBlA 94*
Bell, Robert M. 1943- *WhoAmL 94, WhoAmP 93*
Bell, Robert Mack 1943- *WhoBlA 94*
Bell, Robert Maurice 1944- *WhoAm 94*
Bell, Robert Morrall 1936- *WhoAmL 94*
Bell, Robert Paul 1918-1992 *WhAm 10*
Bell, Robert Vaughn 1924- *WrDr 94*
Bell, Robert Wesley 1918- *WhoBlA 94*
Bell, Robert William 1938- *WhoAmL 94*
Bell, Robin 1945- *WrDr 94*
Bell, Rodger 1939- *Who 94*
Bell, Rodney d1968 *WhoHol 92*
Bell, Roger 1947- *WrDr 94*
Bell, Ronald Leslie 1929- *Who 94*
Bell, Ronald Percy 1907- *IntWW 93, Who 94*
Bell, Rosalind 1938- *WhoFI 94*
Bell, Rosalind Nanette 1958- *WhoBlA 94*
Bell, Roseann P. 1945- *BlkWr 2, WhoBlA 94*
Bell, Roseanne 1946- *WhoAm 94*
Bell, Rouzeberry 1934- *WhoBlA 94*
Bell, S. Aaron 1924- *WhoBlA 94*
Bell, Samuel H. 1925- *WhoAm 94, WhoAmL 94, WhoMW 93*
Bell, Samuel P., III 1939- *WhoAmP 93*
Bell, Sandra Elizabeth 1957- *WhoFI 94*
Bell, Sandra Watson 1955- *WhoBlA 94*
Bell, Scott *Who 94*
Bell, (Alexander) Scott 1941- *Who 94*
Bell, Sharon Kaye 1943- *WhoFI 94, WhoWest 94*
Bell, Sheila Trice 1949- *WhoBlA 94*
Bell, Spencer d1935 *WhoHol 92*
Bell, Stanley Marvin 1943- *WhoMW 93*
Bell, Stephen Martin 1946- *WhoAmL 94*
Bell, Stephen Robert 1942- *WhoAm 94, WhoAmL 94*
Bell, Stephen Scott 1935- *WhoAm 94*
Bell, Steve 1951- *WhoAmP 93*
Bell, Steven Scott 1948- *WhoAmL 94*
Bell, Stoughton 1923- *WhoAm 94*
Bell, Stuart 1938- *Who 94*
Bell, Susan J. 1948- *WhoAmP 93*
Bell, Susan Jane 1946- *WhoMW 93*
Bell, T. Knox 1942- *WhoAmL 94*
Bell, Temma 1945- *WhoAmA 93*
Bell, Terrel H. 1921- *WhoAmP 93*
Bell, Terrel Howard 1921- *IntWW 93, WhoAm 94*
Bell, Theodore Augustus 1946- *WhoAm 94, WhoFI 94*
Bell, Theodore Joshua, II 1961- *WhoBlA 94*
Bell, Theron J. 1931- *WhoBlA 94*
Bell, Thom R. 1943- *WhoBlA 94*
Bell, Thomas Devereaux, Jr. 1949- *WhoAm 94*
Bell, Thomas Eugene 1945- *WhoScEn 94*
Bell, Thomas Mimms 1959- *WhoFI 94*
Bell, Thomas Rowe 1928- *WhoAm 94*
Bell, Thornton *EncSF 93*
Bell, Thorton 1935- *WrDr 94*
Bell, Tim John Leigh 1941- *IntWW 93*
Bell, Timothy Alexander 1942- *WhoAmP 93*
Bell, Timothy John Leigh 1941- *Who 94*
Bell, Todd Anthony 1958- *WhoBlA 94*
Bell, Tom 1932- *IntMPA 94, WhoHol 92*
Bell, Tom, Jr. 1941- *WhoBlA 94*
Bell, Tommy Lee, III 1948- *WhoBlA 94*
Bell, Travers J., Sr. *WhoBlA 94*
Bell, Trenton Grandville 1924- *WhoBlA 94*
Bell, Trevor *Who 94*
Bell, Trevor 1930- *WhoAmA 93*
Bell, (Charles) Trevor 1927- *Who 94*
Bell, Troy Nathan 1962- *WhoAmL 94*
Bell, Vanessa *WhoHol 92*
Bell, Vera 1906- *BlmGWL*
Bell, Victory 1934- *WhoAmP 93, WhoBlA 94*
Bell, W(illiam) H(enry) 1873-1946 *NewGrDO*
Bell, W. James 1929- *WhoFI 94*
Bell, Walter (Fancourt) 1909- *Who 94*
Bell, Warren, Jr. 1951- *WhoBlA 94*
Bell, Wayne Steven 1954- *WhoAm 94, WhoAmL 94, WhoWest 94*
Bell, Wendell 1924- *WhoAm 94*
Bell, Whitfield Jenks, Jr. 1914- *WhoAm 94*
Bell, Wilfred Joseph 1927- *WhoAmP 93*
Bell, Wilhemenia 1954- *WhoBlA 94*
Bell, William A. *WhoBlA 94*
Bell, William Archibald Ottley Juxon 1919- *Who 94*
Bell, William Augustus, II 1917- *WhoBlA 94*
Bell, William Bradshaw 1935- *Who 94*
Bell, William Charles 1945- *WhoBlA 94*
Bell, William David 1951- *WhoMW 93*
Bell, William Edwin 1926- *IntWW 93, Who 94*
Bell, William Fletcher 1929- *WhoAmP 93*
Bell, William H. D. M. *Who 94*
Bell, William Hall 1951- *WhoAmL 94*
Bell, William Henry 1926-1988 *WhAm 10*
Bell, William Henry, Jr. 1918- *WhoAm 94*
Bell, William Jack 1915- *WhoAm 94*
Bell, William Jerry 1934- *WhoBlA 94*
Bell, William Joseph 1939- *WhoAm 94, WhoFI 94*
Bell, William Lewis 1919- *Who 94*
Bell, William Mathew, Jr. 1955- *WhoAmL 94*
Bell, William McKinley 1926- *WhoBlA 94*
Bell, William Rupert Graham 1920- *Who 94*
Bell, William Vaughn 1941- *WhoBlA 94*
Bell, William Woodward 1938- *WhoAmL 94*
Bell, Wilson Townsend 1934- *WhoMW 93*
Bell, Winston Alonzo 1930- *WhoBlA 94*
Bell, Yolanda Maria 1949- *WhoBlA 94*
Bell, Yvonne Lola 1953- *WhoBlA 94*
Bella, Eugene Alan 1953- *WhoMW 93*
Bella, Jan Levoslav 1843-1936 *NewGrDO*
Bella, Salvatore Joseph 1919- *WhoAm 94*
Bella, Vincent J. 1927- *WhoAmP 93*
Bellack, Alan Scott 1944- *WhoAm 94*
Bellack, Daniel Willard 1941- *WhoAm 94*
Bellacosa, Joseph W. 1937- *WhoAm 94, WhoAmL 94, WhoAmP 93*
Belladonna, Joey
See Anthrax *ConMus 11*
Bellah, Robert N(eelly) 1927- *WrDr 94*
Bellah, Robert Neelly 1927- *WhoAm 94, WhoWest 94*
Bellaiche, Charles Roger 1955- *WhoScEn 94*
Bellairs, Angus d'Albini 1918-1990 *WrDr 94N*
Bellairs, John 1938-1991 *WrDr 94N*
Bellais, William F. 1934- *WhoMW 93*
Bellak, Adolf d1955 *WhoHol 92*
Bellak, John George 1930- *Who 94*
Bellak, Leopold 1916- *WhoAm 94*
Bellamy, Albert John 1915- *Who 94*
Bellamy, Alexander (William) 1909- *Who 94*
Bellamy, Angela Robinson 1952- *WhoBlA 94*
Bellamy, Audrey Virginia 1931- *WhoAmP 93*
Bellamy, Bill C. 1949- *WhoAmP 93*
Bellamy, Calvin Edward 1942- *WhoAm 94*
Bellamy, Carol 1942- *NewYTBS 93 [port], WhoAmP 93*
Bellamy, Christopher William 1946- *IntWW 93, Who 94*

Beltz, Charles Robert 1913- *WhoAm 94*
Beltz, Fred Wallace, III 1949- *WhoFI 94*
Beltz, Herbert Allison 1926- *WhoAm 94*
Beltz, William Albert 1929- *WhoAm 94*
Beltzer, Herman Martin 1927- *WhoAm 94*
Belushi, James 1954- *IntMPA 94, WhoAm 94, WhoHol 92*
Belushi, John d1982 *WhoHol 92*
Belushi, John 1949-1982 *WhoCom*
Belval, Jules-Bernard 1819-1876 *NewGrDO*
Belval, Paul Norman 1962- *WhoAmL 94*
Belvaux, Lucas 1961- *WhoHol 92*
Belville, Scott Robert 1952- *WhoAmA 93*
Belvin, B. Frank 1914- *EncNAR*
Belwin, Anna d1924 *WhoHol 92*
Belyaev, Alexander (Romanovich) 1884-1942? *EncSF 93*
Belyaev, Evgeny Nikolaevich 1937- *LoBiDrD*
Belyakov, Aleksandr Semenovich 1945- *LoBiDrD*
Belyakov, Rostislav Appollonovich 1919- *IntWW 93*
Belyayev, Albert Andreyevich 1928- *IntWW 93*
Belyayev, Spartak Timofeyevich 1923- *IntWW 93*
Belyew, Paul Lawrence 1913- *WhoAmP 93*
Belykh, Yury Vasilevich 1941- *LoBiDrD*
Belytschko, Ted Bohdan 1943- *WhoAm 94*
Belz, Carl Irvin 1937- *WhoAmA 93*
Belz, Mark 1943- *WhoAm 94, WhoMW 93*
Belz, Stephen Robert 1953- *WhoFI 94*
Belzberg, Brent Stanley 1951- *WhoAm 94, WhoFI 94*
Belzberg, Samuel 1928- *WhoAm 94, WhoFI 94, WhoWest 94*
Belzer, Alan 1932- *WhoAm 94, WhoFI 94*
Belzer, Ellen J. 1951- *WhoMW 93*
Belzer, Folkert Oene 1930- *WhoAm 94*
Belzer, Irvin V. 1948- *WhoAmL 94*
Belzer, Richard 1944- *WhoHol 92*
Beman, Deane Randolph 1938- *WhoAm 94*
Beman, Lynn Susan 1942- *WhoAmA 93*
Bemben, Michael George 1956- *WhoScEn 94*
Bemberg, Herman 1859?-1931 *NewGrDO*
Bemberis, Ivars 1941- *WhoFI 94*
Bembery, Chester Allen, Jr. 1955- *WhoBlA 94*
Bembo, Antonia fl. 1690-1710 *NewGrDO*
Bembridge, John Anthony 1937- *WhoAm 94, WhoMW 93*
Bemelmans, Ludwig 1898-1963 *WhoAmA 93N*
Bement, Arden Lee, Jr. 1932- *WhoAm 94, WhoMW 93, WhoScEn 94*
Bemis, Hal Lawall 1912- *WhoAm 94, WhoFI 94*
Bemis, James Ernest Sanford 1954- *WhoWest 94*
Bemis, James R(osborough) 1898- *WhAm 10*
Bemis, Lawrence Perry 1949- *WhoAm 94*
Bemis, Mary 1961- *WhoAm 94*
Bemis, Waldo Edmund d1951 *WhoAmA 93N*
Bemmann, Hans *EncSF 93*
Bemo, John fl. 19th cent.- *EncNAR*
Bempong, Maxwell A. 1938- *WhoBlA 94*
Ben (Haim), Myriem 1928- *BlmGWL*
Benabdeljalil, Mohamed-Mehdi 1930- *Who 94*
Benacerraf, Baruj 1920- *IntWW 93, Who 94, WhoAm 94, WhoScEn 94, WorScD*
Benacerraf, Paul 1931- *WhoAm 94*
Benach, Sharon Ann 1944- *WhoWest 94*
Benachenhou, Mouroud 1938- *IntWW 93*
Benackova, Gabriela 1944- *NewGrDO*
Benade, Leo Edward 1916- *WhoAm 94*
Benaderet, Bea d1968 *WhoHol 92*
Benak, James Donald 1954- *WhoAmL 94*
Benaki-Psarouda, Anna 1934- *WhoWomW 91*
Benalcazar, Sebastian De c. 1479-1551 *WhWE*
Benamati, Dennis Charles 1948- *WhoAmL 94*
Ben-Ami, Jacob d1977 *WhoHol 92*
Ben Amor, Ismail 1937- *WhoScEn 94*
Benanav, Gary G. 1945- *WhoAm 94, WhoFI 94*
Benander, Carl D. 1941- *ConAu 141, SmATA 74 [port]*
Benante, Charlie *See* Anthrax *ConMus 11*
Benard, Andre Pierre Jacques 1922- *IntWW 93, Who 94*
Benard, Raymond d1976 *WhoHol 92*
Benarde, Melvin Albert 1924- *WrDr 94*
Ben-Ari, Raikin d1968 *WhoHol 92*
Benario, Herbert William 1929- *WhoAm 94*
Benarroch, Heather Mary *Who 94*
Ben-Asher, Joseph Zalman 1955- *WhoScEn 94*
Ben-Asher, M. David 1931- *WhoWest 94*
Benassi, August Louis 1942- *WhoAmL 94*
Benassi, John M. 1948- *WhoAmL 94*
Benassi, Memo d1957 *WhoHol 92*
Benassy, Jean-Pascal 1948- *IntWW 93, WhoScEn 94*
Benasutti, Marion 1908-1992 *WrDr 94N*
Benatar, Leo 1930- *WhoAm 94*
Benatar, Pat 1953- *WhoAm 94, WhoHol 92*
Benatzky, Ralph 1884-1957 *NewGrDO*
Benaud, Richard 1930- *IntWW 93, Who 94*
Benaud, Richie 1930- *WrDr 94*
Benavente, Diego Tenorio 1959- *WhoAmP 93*
Benavente, Luis Arriola 1939- *WhoAmP 93*
Benavente, Luis Cepeda 1948- *WhoAmP 93*
Benavente y Martinez, Jacinto 1866-1954 *IntDcT 2*
Benavides, Alonso De 1580-1636 *EncNAR*
Benavides, Alonzo De fl. 162-?- *WhWE*
Benavides, Escobar 1920- *IntWW 93*
Benavides, Fortunato P. *WhoHisp 94*
Benavides, George Henry 1944- *WhoHisp 94*
Benavides, Jaime Miguel 1923- *WhoScEn 94*
Benavides, Jesse *WhoHisp 94*
Benavides, Luis Jordan 1949- *WhoFI 94*
Benavides, Norma *WhoHisp 94*
Benavides, Pedro *WhoHisp 94*
Benavides, Raul Falcon 1950- *WhoHisp 94*
Benavides, Steven Mel 1963- *WhoHisp 94*
Benavides, Thomas R. *WhoHisp 94*
Benavides, Tom R. 1939- *WhoWest 94*
Benavides, Tomas R. 1939- *WhoAmP 93*
Benavides, Tony 1937- *WhoHisp 94*
Benavides, Vida 1964- *WhoAsA 94*
Benavidez, Celina G. *WhoHisp 94*
Benavidez, Celina Garcia 1954- *WhoAmP 93, WhoWest 94*
Benavidez, Frank Gregory 1927- *WhoHisp 94*
Benavidez, Jose Modesto 1941- *WhoHisp 94*
Benavidez, Michael D. 1959- *WhoHisp 94*
Benavidez, Roy Perez 1935- *WhoHisp 94*
Benavidez, Troy Kenneth 1967- *WhoHisp 94*
Benawa, Abdul Raouf 1913- *IntWW 93*
Ben Bella, Mohammed 1916- *IntWW 93*
Benben, Brian *WhoHol 92*
Benbenek, Janeen Louise 1969- *WhoMW 93*
Benberg, John Edwin 1961- *WhoMW 93*
Benberry, Cuesta Ray 1923- *WhoAm 94, WhoMW 93*
Benbow, Camilla Persson 1956- *WhoAm 94*
Benbow, Charles Clarence 1929- *WhoAm 94*
Benbow, John Robert 1931- *WhoAm 94*
Benbow, Richard Addison 1949- *WhoWest 94*
Bence-Jones, Mark 1930- *WrDr 94*
Bench, Dan A. 1934- *WhoIns 94*
Bench, John Rees 1927- *WhoWest 94*
Bench, Johnny (Lee) 1947- *WrDr 94*
Bench, Johnny Lee 1947- *WhoAm 94, WhoMW 93*
Bench, Russell W. 1950- *WhoAmL 94*
Benchik, Edward John 1938- *WhoMW 93*
Benchimol, Alberto 1932- *WhoWest 94*
Benchley, Nathaniel (Goddard) 1915-1981 *TwCYAW*
Benchley, Peter (Bradford) 1940- *WrDr 94*
Benchley, Peter Bradford 1940- *WhoAm 94*
Benchley, Robert d1945 *WhoHol 92*
Benchley, Robert 1889-1945 *IntDcF 2-4 [port], WhoCom*
Benchoff, James Martin 1927- *WhoAm 94*
Bencke, Ronald Lee 1940- *WhoFI 94*
Bencomo, Yolanda Elinora 1937- *WhoHisp 94*
Benda, Ernst 1925- *IntWW 93*
Benda, Friedrich (Wilhelm Heinrich) 1745-1814 *See* Benda Family *NewGrDO*
Benda, Friedrich Ludwig 1752-1792 *See* Benda Family *NewGrDO*
Benda, Georg (Anton) 1722-1795 *See* Benda Family *NewGrDO*
Benda, Helena d1986 *WhoHol 92*
Benda, Vaclav 1946- *IntWW 93*
Benda, W. T. d1948 *WhoHol 92*
Benda, W. T. 1891-1948 *WhoAmA 93N*
Benda Family *NewGrDO*
Bendall, David Vere 1920- *Who 94*
Bendall, Eve Rosemarie Duffield 1927- *Who 94*
Bendall, James W. 1945- *WhoAmL 94*
Bendall, Vivian Walter Hough 1938- *Who 94*
Bendall, Wilfred (Ellington) 1850-1920 *NewGrDO*
Ben Daniel, David Jacob 1931- *WhoAm 94*
Ben-David, Zadok 1949- *IntWW 93*
Bendayan, Amador d1989 *WhoHol 92*
Bendazzi, Luigia 1827?-1901 *NewGrDO*
Bendelac, Roger Emile 1956- *WhoFI 94*
Bendelius, Arthur George 1936- *WhoAm 94*
Bendell, Don *DrAPF 93*
Bendell, Donald Ray 1947- *WhoAm 94, WhoWest 94*
Bendell, Marilyn 1921- *WhoAmA 93*
Bender, Angela Marie 1967- *WhoMW 93*
Bender, Arnold 1918- *WrDr 94*
Bender, Arnold Eric 1918- *IntWW 93, Who 94*
Bender, Barbara A. 1939- *WhoBlA 94*
Bender, Bert Arthur 1938- *WhoWest 94*
Bender, Betty Wion 1925- *WhoAm 94*
Bender, Beverly Sterl 1918- *WhoAmA 93*
Bender, Bill 1919- *WhoAmA 93, WhoWest 94*
Bender, Bob George 1925- *WhoWest 94*
Bender, Brian Geoffrey 1949- *Who 94*
Bender, Bruce F. 1949- *WhoAm 94*
Bender, Byron Wilbur 1929- *WhoAm 94*
Bender, Carl Martin 1943- *WhoAm 94, WhoMW 93*
Bender, Charles Christian 1936- *WhoAm 94*
Bender, Charles William 1935- *WhoAm 94*
Bender, Coleman Coalport 1921- *WhoWest 94*
Bender, Darrell G. *WhoAmP 93*
Bender, David Michael 1952- *WhoMW 93*
Bender, David Ray 1942- *WhoAm 94*
Bender, Douglas Ray 1953- *WhoBlA 94, WhoFI 94*
Bender, Edward Trotter 1916- *WhoAmP 93*
Bender, Erwin Rader 1930- *WhoWest 94*
Bender, Erwin Rader, Jr. 1956- *WhoScEn 94*
Bender, Frank Norcross 1920- *WhoWest 94*
Bender, Gary Nedrow 1940- *WhoAm 94*
Bender, Graham I. 1939- *WhoAm 94*
Bender, Harold 1910- *WhoFI 94*
Bender, Harold Stauffer 1897-1962 *DcAmReB 2*
Bender, Harvey A. 1933- *WhoScEn 94*
Bender, Harvey W., Jr. 1933- *WhoAm 94*
Bender, Heinz H. 1909-1993 *NewYTBS 93*
Bender, Jack *WhoHol 92*
Bender, James Frederick 1905- *WhoAm 94*
Bender, Janet Pines 1934- *WhoMW 93*
Bender, John R. 1938- *WhoAmP 93*
Bender, Larry Wayne 1942- *WhoMW 93*
Bender, May 1921- *WhoAmA 93*
Bender, Michael David 1942- *WhoScEn 94*
Bender, Pattie Sue 1950- *WhoAmP 93*
Bender, Paul 1875-1947 *NewGrDO*
Bender, Paul Edward 1951- *WhoAm 94, WhoAmL 94*
Bender, Ralph Edward 1910-1990 *WhAm 10*
Bender, Richard 1930- *WhoAm 94*
Bender, Rick S. 1949- *WhoAmP 93*
Bender, Rita Levant 1942- *WhoAmL 94*
Bender, Robert 1936- *WhoAmP 93*
Bender, Ronald Andrew 1946- *WhoAmL 94*
Bender, Ross Thomas 1929- *WhoAm 94*
Bender, Russell d1969 *WhoHol 92*
Bender, Thomas 1944- *WhoAm 94, WrDr 94*
Bender, Timothy Arthur 1956- *WhoMW 93*
Bender, Todd K. 1936- *WrDr 94*
Bender, Victoria 1950- *WhoAmL 94*
Bender, Virginia Best 1945- *WhoMW 93*
Benderman, Harvey *WhoAmP 93*
Bendernagel, James F., Jr. 1951- *WhoAm 94*
Bendersky, Pamela May H. *Who 94*
Benderson, Bruce *DrAPF 93*
Bendetsen, Karl R. 1907-1989 *HisDcKW*
Bendetsen, Karl Robin 1907-1989 *WhAm 10*
Bendick, Robert 1917- *IntMPA 94*
Bendig, William Charles 1927- *WhoAm 94*
Bendiner, Robert 1909- *WhoAm 94, WrDr 94*
Benditt, Earl Philip 1916- *IntWW 93*
Benditt, Theodore Matthew 1940- *WhoAm 94*
Bendix, Doreen d1931 *WhoHol 92*
Bendix, Frances *DrAPF 93*
Bendix, Helen Irene 1952- *WhoAm 94*
Bendix, Linda Ann 1951- *WhoMW 93*
Bendix, Reinhard 1916-1991 *WrDr 94N*
Bendix, Richard Charles 1948- *WhoWest 94*
Bendix, William d1964 *WhoHol 92*
Bendix, William 1906-1964 *WhoCom*
Bendix, William Emanuel 1935- *WhoAm 94*
Bendixen, Arturo 1950- *WhoHisp 94*
Bendixen, Henrik Holt 1923- *WhoAm 94, WhoScEn 94*
Bendixen, Sergio 1948- *WhoAmP 93*
Bendixson, Terence 1934- *WrDr 94*
Bendjedid, Chadli *IntWW 93*
Bendl, Karel 1838-1897 *NewGrDO*
Bendler, Salomon 1683-1724 *NewGrDO*
Bendow, Wilhelm d1950 *WhoHol 92*
Bendrihem, Elliott 1948- *WhoAm 94*
Bene, Adriana Ferrarese del *NewGrDO*
Benedek, Elissa Leah 1936- *WhoMW 93*
Benedek, George Bernard 1928- *WhoScEn 94*
Benedek, John Joseph 1949- *WhoMW 93*
Beneden, Edouard van 1846-1910 *WorScD*
Benedetta 1899-1977 *BlmGWL*
Benedetti, David *DrAPF 93*
Benedetti, Joseph Benedict 1929- *WhoAmP 93*
Benedetti, Mario 1920- *IntWW 93*
Benedetti, Michele 1778-1828? *NewGrDO*
Benedetti, Robert L. 1939- *ConTFT 11*
Benedetti, Thomas Joseph 1947- *WhoAm 94*
Benedetto, Anthony Dominick 1926- *WhoAm 94*
Benedetto, M. William 1941- *WhoAm 94*
Benedetto, William Arthur 1949- *WhoFI 94*
Benedick, Richard Elliot 1935- *WhoAm 94*
Benedict, Al 1929- *WhoAmP 93*
Benedict, Audrey DeLella 1951- *WhoScEn 94*
Benedict, Bill *WhoCom*
Benedict, Billy 1917- *WhoHol 92*
Benedict, Brooks d1968 *WhoHol 92*
Benedict, Burton 1923- *WhoAm 94, WhoWest 94*
Benedict, Cleve 1935- *WhoAmP 93*
Benedict, Dirk 1945- *IntMPA 94, WhoHol 92*
Benedict, Elinor *DrAPF 93*
Benedict, Elizabeth 1954- *WrDr 94*
Benedict, Gary Francis 1954- *WhoWest 94*
Benedict, Helen *DrAPF 93*
Benedict, Helen 1952- *ConAu 140*
Benedict, James Edward 1946- *WhoAmL 94*
Benedict, James Nelson 1949- *WhoAm 94, WhoAmL 94*
Benedict, Jean d1943 *WhoHol 92*
Benedict, Jeffrey Dean 1961- *WhoScEn 94*
Benedict, Julius 1804-1885 *NewGrDO*
Benedict, Kent 1941- *WhoWest 94*
Benedict, Kingsley d1951 *WhoHol 92*
Benedict, Lawrence *WhoHol 92*
Benedict, Linda Sherk 1945- *WhoAm 94*
Benedict, Manson 1907- *WhoAm 94*
Benedict, Paul 1938- *IntMPA 94, WhoHol 92*
Benedict, Philip (Joseph) 1949- *WrDr 94*
Benedict, Rex (Arthur) 1920- *WrDr 94*
Benedict, Richard d1984 *WhoHol 92*
Benedict, Robert C. 1951- *WhoIns 94*
Benedict, Ruth Fulton 1887-1948 *AmSocL*
Benedict, Samuel S. 1930- *WhoAm 94, WhoFI 94*
Benedict, Steve 1948- *WhoAmP 93*
Benedict, William 1917- *See* East Side Kids *WhoCom*
Benedict-Jones, Linda 1947- *WhoAmA 93*
Benedicto, Roberto S. 1917- *IntWW 93*
Benedict of Nursia c. 480-c. 547 *HisWorL [port]*
Benedictsson, Vicotria 1850-1888 *BlmGWL*
Benedictus, David (Henry) 1938- *WrDr 94*
Benedictus, David Henry 1938- *Who 94*
Benedikt, Michael *DrAPF 93*
Benedikt, Michael 1935- *WhoAm 94, WhoAmA 93, WrDr 94*
Benediktsson, Einar 1931- *IntWW 93, Who 94*
Benefield, Curtis J. 1945- *WhoAmL 94*
Benefield, Jeniefer Len 1957- *WhoScEn 94*
Benefield, Jimmy W. 1941- *WhoAmP 93*
Benefield, Michael Maurice, Jr. 1968- *WhoBlA 94*
Beneke, Sarah Emblen 1924- *WhoAmP 93*
Ben-Eli, Michael Uri 1943- *WhoAm 94*
Ben-Eliezer, Benjamin 1936- *IntWW 93*
Ben Elissar, Eliahu 1932- *IntWW 93*
Benelli, Antonio (Pellegrino) 1771-1830 *NewGrDO*

Benelli, Sem 1877-1949 NewGrDO
Benelli, Ugo 1935- NewGrDO
Benenson, Abram Salmon 1914-
WhoWest 94
Benenson, Claire Berger WhoFI 94
Benenson, David Maurice 1927-
WhoAm 94
Benenson, Edward Hartley 1914-
WhoAm 94, WhoAmA 93
Benenson, James, Jr. 1936- WhoAm 94
Benenson, Mark Keith 1929- WhoAm 94
Benenson, Walter 1936- WhoAm 94
Benerito, Ruth Rogan 1916- WhoAm 94
Benes, Andrew Charles 1967- WhoAm 94,
WhoWest 94
Benes, Barton Lidice 1942- WhoAmA 93
Benes, Juraj 1940- NewGrDO
Benes, Norman Stanley 1921-
WhoWest 94
Benes, Solomon 1925- WhoScEn 94
Benesch, Otto 1896-1964 WhoAmA 93N
Benesch, Ruth Erica 1925- WhoAm 94
Benesch, William Milton 1922-
WhoAm 94
Benet, Brenda d1982 WhoHol 92
Benet, John fl. 1415-1450 DcNaB MP
Benet, Juan 1927-1992 AnObit 1992
Benet, Juan 1927-1992 NewYTBS 93
Benet, Leslie Zachary 1937- WhoAm 94,
WhoScEn 94
Benet, Stephen Vincent 1898-1943
EncSF 93, RfGShF
Benet, Thomas Carr 1926- WhoAm 94
Benetatos, George Gerasimos 1945-
WhoAmL 94
Benetschik, Hannes 1960- WhoScEn 94
Benetton, Luciano 1935- Who 94
Benevenia, Michael A. 1956- WhoIns 94
Benevides, Alfredo WhoHisp 94
Benezet, Anthony 1713-1784 DcAmReB 2
Benezet, Louis Tomlinson 1915-
WhoAm 94
Benezra, Neal 1953- ConAu 141,
WhoAm 94
Benfenati, Emilio 1954- WhoScEn 94
Benfer, David William 1946- WhoAm 94
Benfer, James Elmer, III 1954-
WhoAmL 94
Benfey, Otto Theodor 1925- WhoAm 94
Benfield, Ann Kolb 1946- WhoAmL 94
Benfield, John Richard 1931- WhoAm 94
Benfield, Marion Wilson, Jr. 1932-
WhoAm 94
Benflis, Ali 1944- IntWW 93
Benforado, David M. 1925- WhoAm 94
Benford, Clare E. 1939- WhoBlA 94
Benford, Gregory 1941- EncSF 93
Benford, Gregory (Albert) 1941- WrDr 94
Benford, Gregory Albert 1941- WhoAm 94
Benford, Harry Bell 1917- WhoAm 94
Benford, Norman J. 1938- WhoAm 94
Benfreha, Ahmed 1940- IntWW 93
Benge, Sarah d1954 WhoHol 92
Benge, Wilson d1955 WhoHol 92
Bengelloun, Ahmed Majid 1927-
IntWW 93
Bengelsdorf, Irving Swem 1922-
WhoAm 94
Benghiat, Jacques 1955- WhoWest 94
Benghiat, Russell 1948- WhoMW 93
Bengis, Ingrid DrAPF 93
Bengisu, Murat 1963- WhoWest 94
Benglia, Habib d1961 WhoHol 92
Benglis, Lynda 1941- WhoAm 94,
WhoAmA 93
Bengough, Piers (Henry George) 1929-
Who 94
Bengson, Stuart A. 1943- WhoWest 94
Bengston, Billy Al 1934- IntWW 93,
WhoAm 94, WhoAmA 93
Bengtson, David DrAPF 93
Bengtson, Esther G. 1927- WhoAmP 93
Bengtson, Gaylynn Snider 1957-
WhoWest 94
Bengtson, Larry Edwin 1939- WhoAmP 93
Bengtson, Roger Dean 1941- WhoAm 94
Bengtson, Vern L. 1941- WrDr 94
Bengtz, Ture 1907-1973 WhoAmA 93N
Ben-Gurion, David 1886-1973
HisWorL [port]
Bengzon, Cesar 1896- IntWW 93
Ben Haddou, Halima BlmGWL
Ben-Haim, Tsipi 1951- WhoAmA 93
Ben-Haim, Zigi 1945- WhoAm 94,
WhoAmA 93
Benham, Dorothy d1956 WhoHol 92
Benham, Ethyle Cook d1949 WhoHol 92
Benham, Harry d1969 WhoHol 92
Benham, Isabel Hamilton 1909-
WhoAm 94
Benham, James Mason 1935- WhoAm 94
Benham, John d1981 WhoHol 92
Benham, Lee Kenneth 1940- WhoAm 94
Benham, Leland d1976 WhoHol 92
Benham, Lelia 1945- WhoMW 93
Benham, Linda Sue 1954- WhoMW 93,
WhoScEn 94
Benham, Pamela J. 1947- WhoAmA 93

Benham, Paul B., III 1946- WhoAmL 94
Benham, Philip Owen, Jr. 1944-
WhoMW 93
Benham, Robert WhoAm 94, WhoAmL 94
Benham, Robert 1946- WhoAmP 93,
WhoBlA 94
Benham, Robert Charles 1913-
WhoAmA 93
Benhamouda, Boualem 1933- IntWW 93
Benhima, Mohamed 1924- IntWW 93
Beni, Gerardo 1946- WhoAm 94,
WhoScEn 94
Beni, John Joseph 1932- WhoAm 94
Benichou, Jacques 1922- IntWW 93
Benichou, Marcel 1931- IntWW 93
Benichou, Pascal WhoAm 94
Benidickson, Agnes WhoAm 94,
WhoScEn 94
Benigni, Domenico 1596-1653 NewGrDO
Benigni, Pietro Paolo fl. 1670-1707
NewGrDO
Benigni, Roberto 1952- WhoHol 92
Benigno, Thomas Daniel 1954-
WhoAmL 94, WhoFI 94
Benincori, Angelo Mario 1779-1821
NewGrDO
Benini 1941- WhoAmA 93
Benini, Anna fl. 1784-1791 NewGrDO
Benirschke, Kurt 1924- WhoAm 94,
WhoWest 94
Benislawska, Konstancja 1747-1806
BlmGWL
Benitez, Carlos Humberto 1967-
WhoHisp 94
Benitez, Celeste WhoHisp 94
Benitez, Daniel 1940- WhoHisp 94
Benitez, Horacio A., Jr. 1943-
WhoHisp 94
Benitez, Isidro Basa 1927- WhoScEn 94
Benitez, Margarita WhoHisp 94
Benitez, Pedro Luis 1948- WhoHisp 94
Benitez, Ruben A. 1928- WhoHisp 94
Benitez-de-Avila, Crucita 1938-
WhoHisp 94
Benitez-Hodge, Grissel Minerva 1950-
WhoHisp 94
Benito, Louis d1993 NewYTBS 93
Benjamin, Albert, III 1904- WhoAm 94
Benjamin, Alice 1936- WhoAmA 93
Benjamin, Arthur 1893-1960 NewGrDO
Benjamin, Arthur, Jr. 1938- WhoBlA 94
Benjamin, Ben E. 1941- WhoAm 94,
WhoAmL 94
Benjamin, Benoit 1964- WhoBlA 94
Benjamin, Bernard 1910- Who 94
Benjamin, Bezaleel Solomon 1938-
WhoAm 94
Benjamin, Brooke Who 94
Benjamin, (Thomas) Brooke 1929-
IntWW 93, Who 94
Benjamin, Christopher 1934- WhoHol 92
Benjamin, David ConAu 41NR
Benjamin, David Joel, III 1947-
WhoAm 94, WhoAmL 94
Benjamin, David Peter 1962- WhoAmL 94
Benjamin, Donald F. 1925- WhoBlA 94
Benjamin, Donald S. 1938- WhoBlA 94
Benjamin, Edward A. 1938- WhoAm 94
Benjamin, Edward Bernard, Jr. 1923-
WhoAm 94, WhoAmL 94
Benjamin, Ernst 1937- WhoAm 94
Benjamin, George David 1933-
WhoAm 94
Benjamin, George William John 1960-
IntWW 93, Who 94
Benjamin, Harold (Raymond Wayne)
1893- WhAm 10
Benjamin, Harvey E. 1941- WhoAm 94
Benjamin, Irb 1946- WhoAmP 93
Benjamin, James Cover 1952- WhoAm 94,
WhoFI 94, WhoMW 93
Benjamin, Janice Yukon 1951-
WhoMW 93
Benjamin, Jeff 1945- WhoAm 94,
WhoAmL 94
Benjamin, Jeffrey Royce 1954-
WhoWest 94
Benjamin, Jim d1978 WhoHol 92
Benjamin, Joseph Kevin 1964-
WhoAmL 94
Benjamin, Karen Jean 1951- WhoWest 94
Benjamin, Karl Stanley 1925- WhoAm 94,
WhoAmA 93, WhoWest 94
Benjamin, Kathleen Kelly ConAu 140
Benjamin, Keith Edward 1943-
WhoScEn 94
Benjamin, Lloyd William, III 1944-
WhoAmA 93
Benjamin, Lorna Smith 1934- WhoAm 94,
WhoWest 94
Benjamin, Louis 1922- Who 94
Benjamin, Louis Henry 1955-
WhoAmL 94
Benjamin, Monica G. 1947- WhoBlA 94

Benjamin, P. J. 1951- WhoHol 92
Benjamin, Paul WhoHol 92
Benjamin, Pauline Who 94
Benjamin, Ralph 1922- Who 94
Benjamin, Richard 1938- WhoHol 92
Benjamin, Richard 1939- IntMPA 94
Benjamin, Robert Spiers 1917- WhoAm 94
Benjamin, Ronald 1941- WhoBlA 94
Benjamin, Rose Mary 1933- WhoBlA 94
Benjamin, Ruth DrAPF 93
Benjamin, Stephen Alfred 1939-
WhoScEn 94
Benjamin, Theodore Simon 1926-
WhoAm 94
Benjamin, Tritobia Hayes 1944-
WhoBlA 94
Benjamin, Vernon Henry 1949-
WhoAmP 93
Benjamin, Wayne Ronald 1953-
WhoAmL 94
Benjamin, William Chase 1947-
WhoAm 94
Benjamine, Elbert 1882-1951 AstEnc
Benjamin Of Tudela d1173 WhWE
Benjamins, Joyce Ann 1941- WhoMW 93,
WhoScEn 94
Ben Jelloun, Tahar 1944- ConWorW 93,
IntWW 93
Benjenk, Munir P. 1924- IntWW 93
ben-Jochannan, Yosef 1918- BlkWr 2
Benka, Richard William 1947-
WhoAm 94
Benkard, James W. B. 1937- WhoAm 94
Benke, Paul Arthur 1921- WhoAm 94
Benker, Hans Otto 1942- WhoScEn 94
Benkert, Joseph Philip, Jr. 1958-
WhoAmL 94
Benkert, Paul James, Jr. 1956-
WhoAmL 94
Benkhoff, Fita d1967 WhoHol 92
Benkin, Isaac David 1935- WhoAm 94
Benko, James John 1943- WhoMW 93,
WhoScEn 94
Benlon, Lisa L. 1953- WhoAmP 93
Benmaati, Nadir 1944- IntWW 93
Benmark, Leslie Ann 1944- WhoAm 94,
WhoScEn 94
Ben-Menachem, Yoram 1934- WhoAm 94
Benn, Anthony 1912- Who 94
Benn, Ben 1884-1983 WhoAmA 93N
Benn, Douglas Frank 1936- WhoFI 94
Benn, Edward 1922- Who 94
Benn, Edward Glanvill 1905- Who 94
Benn, Jonathan WhoAm 94
Benn, (James) Jonathan 1933- Who 94
Benn, June 1930- WrDr 94
Benn, Theodore Alexander 1918-
WhoAm 94
Benn, Timothy John 1936- Who 94
Benn, Tony 1925- IntWW 93, Who 94,
WrDr 94
Bennack, Donald Lloyd 1962-
WhoAmL 94
Bennack, Frank Anthony, Jr. 1933-
IntWW 93, WhoAm 94, WhoFI 94
Bennane, Michael J. 1945- WhoAmP 93
Bennani, Ben DrAPF 93
Ben-Natan, Asher 1921- IntWW 93
Benne, Kenneth Dean 1908-1992
WrDr 94N
Bennedsen, Dorte 1938- WhoWomW 91
Bennent, Ann WhoHol 92
Bennent, David 1966- WhoHol 92
Bennent, Heinz 1921- WhoHol 92
Benner, Craig Michael 1963- WhoMW 93
Benner, Dorothy Spurlock 1938-
WhoWest 94
Benner, Martha Lee 1951- WhoMW 93
Benner, Nolan Paul 1893- WhAm 10
Benner, Patrick 1923- Who 94
Benner, Richard Edward, Jr. 1932-
WhoAm 94
Benner, Ronald Allen, Jr. 1966-
WhoScEn 94
Benner, Yale d1952 WhoHol 92
Ben-Ner, Yitzhak EncSF 93
Bennet Who 94
Bennet, Abraham 1749-1799 DcNaB MP
Bennet, Douglas J., Jr. 1938- IntWW 93
Bennet, Douglas Joseph, Jr. 1938-
WhoAm 94, WhoAmP 93
Bennet, Glin 1927- WrDr 94
Bennet, Henry Grey 1777-1836
DcNaB MP
Bennet, Hugh Hammond 1881-1960
EnvEnc
Bennet, John 1715-1759 DcNaB MP
Bennet, Robert Ames 1870-1954
EncSF 93
Bennet, Spencer Gordon d1987
WhoHol 92
Bennet, William Samuel, II 1952-
WhoWest 94
Bennett, Al WhoBlA 94
Bennett, Alan 1934- ConDr 93,
ConLC 77 [port], IntDcT 2, IntMPA 94,
IntWW 93, Who 94, WrDr 94
Bennett, Alan Jerome 1941- WhoAm 94

Bennett, Albert Farrell 1944- WhoAm 94,
WhoScEn 94
Bennett, Albert Joseph 1913- Who 94
Bennett, (Frederick Onslow) Alexander
(Godwyn) d1993 Who 94N
Bennett, Alexander Elliot 1940-
WhoAm 94, WhoAmL 94
Bennett, Alfred Gordon 1901-1962
EncSF 93
Bennett, Alfred Rosling 1850-1928
DcNaB MP
Bennett, Alma d1958 WhoHol 92
Bennett, Andrea WhoAmP 93
Bennett, Andrew Francis 1939- Who 94
Bennett, Andrew John 1942- Who 94
Bennett, Anna Maria Evans c. 1750-1808
BlmGWL
Bennett, Arnold 1867-1931 BlmGEL,
DcLB 135 [port]
Bennett, Arthur 1862-1931 EncSF 93
Bennett, Arthur T. 1933- WhoBlA 94
Bennett, Barbara d1958 WhoHol 92
Bennett, Barbara Esther 1953- WhoFI 94
Bennett, Belle d1932 WhoHol 92
Bennett, Bessye Warren 1938- WhoBlA 94
Bennett, Betty T. WhoAm 94
Bennett, Billie d1951 WhoHol 92
Bennett, Billy d1942 WhoHol 92
Bennett, Bob 1933- IntWW 93
Bennett, Bobby 1944- WhoBlA 94
Bennett, Boyd d1983 WhoHol 92
Bennett, Bradford Carl 1953- WhoWest 94
Bennett, Brian Erland 1942- WhoAmL 94
Bennett, Brian O'Leary 1955- WhoAm 94,
WhoFI 94, WhoScEn 94, WhoWest 94
Bennett, Bruce DrAPF 93
Bennett, Bruce 1909- IntMPA 94,
WhoHol 92
Bennett, Bruce Anthony 1950-
WhoScEn 94
Bennett, Bruce David 1948- WhoWest 94
Bennett, Bruce Michael 1941-
WhoWest 94
Bennett, Bruce W. 1930- WhoAm 94,
WhoFI 94, WhoScEn 94, WhoMW 93
Bennett, Bruce Webb 1948- WhoWest 94
Bennett, C. Leonard 1939- WhoAm 94
Bennett, Caleb P. 1758-1836 WhAmRev
Bennett, Carl 1920- WhoAm 94
Bennett, Carl D(ouglas) 1917- ConAu 140
Bennett, Carl McGhie 1933- WhoWest 94
Bennett, Carol Elizabeth 1951- WhoAm 94
Bennett, Carol Weaver 1944- WhoFI 94
Bennett, Charles d1925 WhoHol 92
Bennett, Charles d1943 WhoHol 92
Bennett, Charles 1899- IntDcF 2-4,
IntMPA 94
Bennett, Charles (Moihi) 1913- Who 94
Bennett, Charles E. 1910- WhoAmP 93
Bennett, Charles Edward 1910-
WhoAm 94
Bennett, Charles Franklin, Jr. 1926-
WhoAm 94
Bennett, Charles James, Jr. 1956-
WhoBlA 94
Bennett, Charles John Michael 1906-
Who 94
Bennett, Charles Leo 1920- WhoAm 94
Bennett, Charles Leon 1951- WhoWest 94
Bennett, Charles Moihi To Arawaka
1913- IntWW 93
Bennett, Charles Turner 1932-
WhoAm 94, WhoWest 94
Bennett, Charles William, Jr. 1962-
WhoWest 94
Bennett, Christine Lora 1948- WhoAm 94
Bennett, Claire Richardson 1928-
WhoAm 94
Bennett, Clarence Edwin 1902-1990
WhAm 10
Bennett, Collin B. 1931- WhoBlA 94
Bennett, Constance d1965 WhoHol 92
Bennett, Cornelius 1965- WhoAm 94
Bennett, Courtney Ajaye 1959-
WhoBlA 94
Bennett, Curtis Owen 1954- WhoScEn 94
Bennett, Daina T. WhoBlA 94
Bennett, Dave 1930- WhoAmL 94
Bennett, David E. 1944- WhoAmL 94
Bennett, Deborah Minor 1951-
WhoBlA 94
Bennett, Debra Quinette 1958-
WhoBlA 94
Bennett, Dee 1935- WhoAmP 93
Bennett, Delores WhoBlA 94
Bennett, Denzil Page, II 1963-
WhoMW 93
Bennett, Dianne 1942- WhoAmL 94
Bennett, Don Bemco 1916- WhoAmA 93
Bennett, Donald Dalton 1936- WhoFI 94
Bennett, Dorothea 1929-1990 WhAm 10
Bennett, Douglas 1955- WhoWest 94
Bennett, Douglas Carleton 1946-
WhoAm 94
Bennett, Douglas Marshall 1947-
WhoFI 94
Bennett, Dwight 1916- WrDr 94
Bennett, Edmond d1986 WhoHol 92

Bennett, Edmund C. 1942- *WhoAmL 94*
Bennett, Edna d1976 *WhoHol 92*
Bennett, Edward *Who 94*
Bennett, (Albert) Edward 1931- *Who 94*
Bennett, Edward Henry 1917- *WhoFI 94*
Bennett, Edward Herbert, Jr. 1915- *WhoAm 94*
Bennett, Edward J. 1925- *WhoAmP 93*
Bennett, Edward J. 1937- *WhoAmP 93*
Bennett, Edward James 1941- *WhoAm 94, WhoAmL 94, WhoFI 94*
Bennett, Edward M. 1927- *WrDr 94*
Bennett, Edward Moore 1927- *WhoAm 94*
Bennett, Edward Nevill 1936- *WhoAm 94, WhoFI 94*
Bennett, ElDean 1928- *WhoAm 94*
Bennett, Elizabeth *WhoHol 92*
Bennett, Elizabeth 1948- *WrDr 94*
Bennett, Elizabeth Deare 1910- *WrDr 94*
Bennett, Elmer Frank 1917-1989 *WhAm 10*
Bennett, Emmett Leslie 1918- *IntWW 93*
Bennett, Enid d1969 *WhoHol 92*
Bennett, Eric Ransom 1942- *WhoMW 93*
Bennett, Erik Peter 1928- *Who 94*
Bennett, Ernest Walter 1921- *WrDr 94*
Bennett, Eugene F. 1923- *WhoIns 94*
Bennett, Faith 1908- *WhoHol 92*
Bennett, Fran *WhoHol 92*
Bennett, Frank d1957 *WhoHol 92*
Bennett, Frank Cantelo, Jr. 1930- *WhoAm 94*
Bennett, Fred Gilbert 1946- *WhoAmL 94*
Bennett, Fred Lawrence 1939- *WhoAm 94, WhoWest 94*
Bennett, Frederic (Mackarness) 1918- *Who 94*
Bennett, Frederick Onslow Alexander Godwyn 1913- *IntWW 93*
Bennett, Gary L. *DrAPF 93*
Bennett, Gary Lee 1940- *WhoAm 94*
Bennett, Gary Paul 1941- *WhoAm 94*
Bennett, George Frederick 1911- *WhoAm 94*
Bennett, George P. 1927- *WhoBlA 94*
Bennett, Georgette 1946- *WhoAm 94*
Bennett, Gordon C. *DrAPF 93*
Bennett, Gray Weston 1960- *WhoAmL 94*
Bennett, Grover Bryce 1921- *WhoAm 94*
Bennett, H. O. 1928- *WrDr 94*
Bennett, Hal *DrAPF 93*
Bennett, Hal (Zina) 1936- *WrDr 94*
Bennett, Harold d1981 *WhoHol 92*
Bennett, Harold Clark 1924- *WhoAm 94*
Bennett, Harry 1895-1990 *WhAm 10*
Bennett, Harry Graham 1921- *Who 94*
Bennett, Harry Louis 1923- *WhoAm 94*
Bennett, Harve 1930- *IntMPA 94, WhoAm 94*
Bennett, Herbert Branin 1948- *WhoAmL 94*
Bennett, Hollis Haukum, Jr. 1959- *WhoFI 94*
Bennett, Hubert 1909- *Who 94*
Bennett, Hugh Peter Derwyn 1943- *Who 94*
Bennett, Hywel 1944- *IntMPA 94, IntWW 93, WhoHol 92*
Bennett, Hywel Thomas 1944- *Who 94*
Bennett, Imogene d1961 *WhoHol 92*
Bennett, Ivan Loveridge, Jr. 1922-1990 *WhAm 10*
Bennett, J. William 1935- *WhoAmL 94*
Bennett, Jack Franklin 1924- *IntWW 93, WhoAm 94*
Bennett, Jacqueline Beekman 1946- *WhoWest 94*
Bennett, James Austin 1915- *WhoAm 94*
Bennett, James Chester 1932- *WhoWest 94*
Bennett, James Edward 1925- *WhoAm 94*
Bennett, James Jefferson 1920- *WhoAm 94*
Bennett, James Patrick 1950- *WhoAm 94, WhoAmL 94*
Bennett, James Patrick 1957- *WhoFI 94*
Bennett, James Richard 1932- *WrDr 94*
Bennett, James Ronald 1940- *WhoAmP 93*
Bennett, James T. 1942- *WhoAm 94*
Bennett, Jamie 1948- *WhoAmA 93*
Bennett, Janet Huff 1932- *WhoWest 94*
Bennett, Jay 1912- *ConAu 42NR, TwCYAW*
Bennett, Jay Brett 1961- *WhoScEn 94*
Bennett, Jay D. 1952- *WhoAm 94, WhoAmL 94*
Bennett, Jean Louise McPherson 1930- *WhoAm 94*
Bennett, Jeffrey 1962- *WhoAmL 94*
Bennett, Jeffrey Stephen 1963- *WhoFI 94*
Bennett, Jennifer Lewis 1958- *WhoFI 94*
Bennett, Jill d1990 *WhoHol 92*
Bennett, Jim 1921- *WhoAm 94*
Bennett, Joan d1990 *WhoHol 92*
Bennett, Joan 1910-1990 *WhAm 10*
Bennett, Joan S. 1941- *WrDr 94*
Bennett, Joan Wennstrom 1942- *WhoAm 94*
Bennett, Joe Claude 1933- *WhoAm 94*
Bennett, Joel Herbert 1936- *WhoAm 94*
Bennett, Joel P. 1946- *WhoAmL 94*
Bennett, John *DrAPF 93*
Bennett, John 1912- *Who 94, WhoAmP 93*
Bennett, John 1928- *WhoHol 92*
Bennett, John (Frederic) 1920-1991 *WrDr 94N*
Bennett, John (Mokonuiarangi) 1912- *Who 94*
Bennett, John A. 1937- *WhoAmL 94, WhoWest 94*
Bennett, John A. 1950- *WhoAmL 94*
Bennett, John Drew d1944 *WhoHol 92*
Bennett, John E. 1941- *WhoAm 94, WhoAmP 93*
Bennett, John Edwin 1943- *WhoMW 93*
Bennett, John F. 1933- *WhoAmP 93*
Bennett, John Joseph 1923- *WhoAm 94*
Bennett, John K. 1955- *WhoAmL 94*
Bennett, John M. *DrAPF 93*
Bennett, John M. 1942- *WhoAmA 93*
Bennett, John M(ichael) 1942- *ConAu 41NR, WrDr 94*
Bennett, John Morrison 1933- *WhoAm 94*
Bennett, John O. 1948- *WhoAmP 93*
Bennett, John Richard 1952- *WhoFI 94*
Bennett, John Roscoe 1922- *WhoAm 94*
Bennett, John Thomas 1921- *WhoAmP 93*
Bennett, Jonathan David 1954- *WhoAmL 94*
Bennett, Joseph d1931 *WhoHol 92*
Bennett, Josiah Whitney 1916-1992 *WhAm 10*
Bennett, Julie 1943- *WhoHol 92*
Bennett, June Newton 1926- *WhoWest 94*
Bennett, Kathryn d1978 *WhoHol 92*
Bennett, Keith 1956- *WhoBlA 94*
Bennett, Keith L. *WhoIns 94*
Bennett, Kenneth A(lan) 1935- *WrDr 94*
Bennett, Kenneth Alan 1935- *WhoAm 94*
Bennett, Laurie Edward 1919- *WhoAmP 93*
Bennett, Lawrence Allen 1923- *WhoAm 94, WhoWest 94*
Bennett, Lawrence E. 1923- *WhoAmP 93*
Bennett, Lawrence Herman 1930- *WhoAm 94*
Bennett, Lee d1954 *WhoHol 92*
Bennett, Lerone, Jr. 1928- *BlkWr 2, ConBlB 5 [port], WhoAm 94, WhoBlA 94*
Bennett, Leslie R. 1948- *WhoAmL 94*
Bennett, Leslie Robert 1918- *WhoWest 94*
Bennett, Lewis Tilton, Jr. 1940- *WhoWest 94*
Bennett, Lois 1933- *WhoFI 94*
Bennett, Louis Lowell 1909-1991 *WhAm 10*
Bennett, Louise 1919- *WrDr 94*
Bennett, Louise (Simone) 1919- *BlkWr 2*
Bennett, Louise Simone 1919- *BlmGWL*
Bennett, Maisha B. H. 1948- *WhoBlA 94*
Bennett, Manu Augustus 1916- *Who 94*
Bennett, Marcia J(oanne) 1945- *EncSF 93*
Bennett, Margaret Airola 1950- *WhoMW 93*
Bennett, Margaret Ethel Booker 1923- *WhoAm 94*
Bennett, Margot 1912-1980 *EncSF 93*
Bennett, Marion D. 1936- *WhoBlA 94*
Bennett, Marion T. 1914- *CngDr 93, WhoAmP 93*
Bennett, Marion Tinsley 1914- *WhoAm 94, WhoAmL 94*
Bennett, Marjorie d1982 *WhoHol 92*
Bennett, Marshall Goodloe 1943- *WhoAmP 93*
Bennett, Marta Dawn 1953- *WhoWest 94*
Bennett, Martin Arthur 1935- *WhoScEn 94*
Bennett, Mary Elizabeth 1949- *WhoAm 94, WhoAmL 94*
Bennett, Mary Letitia Somerville 1913- *Who 94*
Bennett, Matt d1991 *WhoHol 92*
Bennett, Maxwell Richard 1939- *IntWW 93*
Bennett, Maybelle Taylor 1949- *WhoBlA 94*
Bennett, Meg *WhoHol 92*
Bennett, Michael B. 1942- *WhoAmP 93*
Bennett, Michael Vander Laan 1931- *IntWW 93*
Bennett, Michael William 1947- *WhoWest 94*
Bennett, Mickey d1950 *WhoHol 92*
Bennett, Miriam Frances 1928- *WhoAm 94*
Bennett, Nancy McCullough 1942- *WhoAmL 94*
Bennett, Neville 1937- *ConAu 41NR, WrDr 94*
Bennett, Neville Hough 1934- *WhoWest 94*
Bennett, Nicholas Jerome 1949- *Who 94*
Bennett, Norman *WhoHol 92*
Bennett, Ovell Francis 1929- *WhoScEn 94*
Bennett, Pamela Gale 1938- *WhoMW 93*
Bennett, Patricia A. *WhoBlA 94*
Bennett, Patricia W. 1953- *WhoBlA 94*
Bennett, Patrick 1924- *Who 94*
Bennett, Paul *DrAPF 93*
Bennett, Paul Edward 1947- *WhoAm 94, WhoAmL 94*
Bennett, Paul Frederick 1949- *WhoAmL 94*
Bennett, Paul Grover 1940- *WhoFI 94*
Bennett, Paul Lester 1946- *WhoWest 94*
Bennett, Peter d1990 *WhoHol 92*
Bennett, Peter 1960- *WhoAmL 94*
Bennett, Peter Brian 1931- *WhoAm 94, WhoScEn 94*
Bennett, Peter Dunne 1933- *WhoAm 94*
Bennett, Peter Ward *Who 94*
Bennett, Philip Hugh Penberthy 1919- *Who 94*
Bennett, Phillip (Harvey) 1928- *Who 94*
Bennett, Philomene Dosek 1935- *WhoAmA 93*
Bennett, Rafael *WhoHol 92*
Bennett, Rainey 1907- *WhoAmA 93*
Bennett, Ralph Culver d1959 *WhoHol 92*
Bennett, Ralph Featherstone 1923- *Who 94*
Bennett, Ray d1957 *WhoHol 92*
Bennett, Raymond Clayton Watson 1939- *Who 94*
Bennett, Reginald (Frederick Brittain) 1911- *Who 94*
Bennett, Reynold 1918- *WhoAm 94*
Bennett, Richard d1944 *WhoHol 92*
Bennett, Richard Alan 1963- *WhoAmP 93*
Bennett, Richard Carl 1933- *WhoMW 93*
Bennett, Richard Clement W. *Who 94*
Bennett, Richard Edwin 1943- *WhoFI 94*
Bennett, Richard Joseph 1917- *WhoAm 94*
Bennett, Richard M. *EncSF 93*
Bennett, Richard Rodney 1936- *IntWW 93, NewGrDO, Who 94*
Bennett, Richard Taylor 1936- *WhoFI 94*
Bennett, Richard Thomas 1930- *WhoAm 94*
Bennett, Richard Thomas 1939- *WhoAmL 94*
Bennett, Rick 1948- *WhoAmP 93*
Bennett, Robert *WhoAmP 93*
Bennett, Robert 1933- *WhoAm 94, WhoWest 94*
Bennett, Robert A. 1933- *WhoBlA 94*
Bennett, Robert D. 1928- *WhoAmP 93*
Bennett, Robert E., Jr. 1944- *WhoAmL 94*
Bennett, Robert F. 1933- *CngDr 93*
Bennett, Robert Frederick 1927- *IntWW 93, WhoAm 94, WhoAmL 94, WhoAmP 93*
Bennett, Robert John 1941- *WhoAm 94*
Bennett, Robert John 1948- *Who 94*
Bennett, Robert Louis 1925- *WhoWest 94*
Bennett, Robert Menzies 1926- *WhoAm 94, WhoFI 94*
Bennett, Robert Pierce 1949- *WhoAmL 94*
Bennett, Robert Royce 1926- *WhoAm 94*
Bennett, Robert Russell 1894- *WhAm 10*
Bennett, Robert Russell 1894-1981 *NewGrDO*
Bennett, Robert Stephen 1939- *WhoAm 94*
Bennett, Robert Thomas 1939- *WhoAmP 93*
Bennett, Robert William 1941- *WhoAmL 94*
Bennett, Roberta *WhoHol 92*
Bennett, Robin 1934- *Who 94*
Bennett, Ronald (Wilfred Murdoch) 1930- *Who 94*
Bennett, Ronald Alistair 1922- *Who 94*
Bennett, Ronald Thomas 1944- *WhoAm 94, WhoWest 94*
Bennett, Ronan 1956- *ConAu 142*
Bennett, Roy Frederick 1928- *IntWW 93*
Bennett, Roy Grissell 1917- *Who 94*
Bennett, Russell Odbert 1915- *WhoAm 94*
Bennett, Ruth M. 1899-1960 *WhoAmA 93N*
Bennett, Sally *DrAPF 93*
Bennett, Saul 1936- *WhoAm 94, WhoFI 94*
Bennett, Scott Boyce 1939- *WhoAm 94*
Bennett, Shelley M. 1947- *WrDr 94*
Bennett, Shirley M. 1936- *WhoAmP 93*
Bennett, Sidney Kimball (Wynn) 1892-195-? *AstEnc*
Bennett, Sidney Suzanne Forester 1957- *WhoAmL 94*
Bennett, Stanley T. 1947- *WhoAmP 93*
Bennett, Stephen Christopher 1956- *WhoScEn 94*
Bennett, Steven Alan 1953- *WhoAmL 94, WhoFI 94*
Bennett, Ted d1941 *WhoHol 92*
Bennett, Thomas E. 1929- *WhoFI 94*
Bennett, Thomas Gray 1946- *WhoFI 94*
Bennett, Thomas LeRoy, Jr. 1942- *WhoAm 94*
Bennett, Thomas Mitchell 1945- *WhoMW 93*
Bennett, Thomas Peter 1937- *WhoAm 94, WhoScEn 94*
Bennett, Thompson 1912- *WhoAmL 94*
Bennett, Tony 1926- *WhoAm 94, WhoHol 92*
Bennett, Tony L. 1940- *WhoAmP 93*
Bennett, Virginia Vogelsang 1927- *WhoFI 94*
Bennett, Vivienne d1978 *WhoHol 92*
Bennett, W. W., Jr. 1940- *WhoAmP 93*
Bennett, Wallace F. *WhoAmP 93*
Bennett, Wallace F. 1898-1993 *NewYTBS 93 [port]*
Bennett, Walter Scott, Jr. 1929- *WhoWest 94*
Bennett, Wayne 1927- *WhoAmP 93*
Bennett, Wilda d1967 *WhoHol 92*
Bennett, William *WhoAm 94*
Bennett, William Andrew 1963- *WhoWest 94*
Bennett, William Donald 1939- *WhoBlA 94*
Bennett, William G. 1924- *WhoFI 94*
Bennett, William J. 1943- *WhoAmP 93*
Bennett, William John d1991 *Who 94N*
Bennett, William John 1943- *IntWW 93*
Bennett, William Michael 1938- *WhoAm 94*
Bennett, William Paul, Jr. 1942- *WhoWest 94*
Bennett, William Ralph 1933- *WhoAmP 93*
Bennett, William Ralph, Jr. 1930- *WhoAm 94*
Bennett, William Richards 1932- *IntWW 93, Who 94*
Bennett, William Ronald 1935- *WhoBlA 94*
Bennett, William Tapley, Jr. 1917- *IntWW 93, WhoAmP 93*
Bennett, Winslow Wood 1925- *WhoAm 94*
Bennett, Winston George, III 1965- *WhoBlA 94*
Bennett-Alexander, Dawn DeJuana 1951- *WhoBlA 94*
Bennette, Connie E. 1951- *WhoBlA 94*
Bennett-England, Rodney (Charles) 1936- *WrDr 94*
Bennett-Kastor, Tina L. 1954- *WhoMW 93*
Bennett McNall Lockwood, Belva 1830-1917 *WomPubS*
Bennetts, James William 1955- *WhoMW 93*
Bennewitt, Loi Dene 1946- *WhoWest 94*
Benney, Adrian Gerald Sallis 1930- *IntWW 93*
Benney, Douglas Mabley 1922- *WhoAm 94, WhoFI 94*
Benney, (Adrian) Gerald (Sallis) 1930- *Who 94*
Benney, Robert *WhoAmA 93*
Benni, Stefano 1947- *EncSF 93*
Bennici, Andrea 1942- *WhoScEn 94*
Benning, Emma Bowman 1928- *WhoBlA 94*
Benning, Joseph Francis, Jr. 1922- *WhoAm 94*
Benninger, Edward C., Jr. 1942- *WhoAm 94, WhoFI 94*
Bennington, Leslie Orville, Jr. 1946- *WhoWest 94*
Bennington, Ronald Kent 1936- *WhoAm 94*
Bennington, William Jay 1939- *WhoAm 94*
Bennion, Bruce Carver 1941- *WhoWest 94*
Bennion, Francis Alan Roscoe 1923- *Who 94*
Bennion, John Edwin 1949- *WhoWest 94*
Bennion, John Stradling 1954- *WhoScEn 94*
Bennion, John Warren *WhoWest 94*
Bennion, Joseph W. 1952- *WhoAmA 93*
Bennis, Warren 1925- *WrDr 94*
Bennis, Warren Gameliel 1925- *WhoAm 94, WhoWest 94*
Bennison, Allan Parnell 1918- *WhoScEn 94*
Bennison, Louis d1929 *WhoHol 92*
Bennitt, Mortimer Wilmot 1910- *Who 94*
Bennoit, Joseph d1925 *WhoHol 92*
Bennon, Saul 1914- *WhoAm 94*
Benny, Jack d1974 *WhoHol 92*
Benny, Jack 1894-1977 *WhoCom [port]*
Benny, Sandra 1944- *WhoAmA 93*
Beno, Carolyn Elizabeth 1953- *WhoWest 94*
Beno, John Richardson 1931- *WhoAmP 93*
Beno-Clark, Candice Lynn 1951- *WhoFI 94*

Benton, Fletcher 1931- *WhoAm 94, WhoAmA 93, WhoWest 94*
Benton, George A. 1933- *WhoBlA 94*
Benton, George Stock 1917- *WhoAm 94*
Benton, Gladys Gay 1906- *WhoWest 94*
Benton, Homer Grabill 1926- *WhoWest 94*
Benton, Ishmael Claud 1920- *WhoAmP 93*
Benton, Jack Mitchell 1941- *WhoFI 94*
Benton, James Wilbert, Jr. 1944- *WhoBlA 94*
Benton, Jerome *WhoHol 92*
Benton, Joseph Edward 1933- *Who 94*
Benton, Juanita 1959- *WhoBlA 94*
Benton, Kenneth (Carter) 1909- *WrDr 94*
Benton, Kenneth Carter 1909- *Who 94*
Benton, Lee F. 1944- *WhoAmL 94*
Benton, Lee Rimes 1951- *WhoAmL 94*
Benton, Leonard D. 1939- *WhoBlA 94*
Benton, Luther 1947- *WhoBlA 94*
Benton, Margaret Peake d1975 *WhoAmA 93N*
Benton, Marjorie Craig 1933- *WhoAmP 93*
Benton, Martin d1976 *WhoHol 92*
Benton, Mary Anne 1952- *WhoWest 94*
Benton, Nelkane O. 1935- *WhoBlA 94*
Benton, Nicholas 1926- *WhoAm 94*
Benton, Peter Faulkner 1934- *IntWW 93, Who 94*
Benton, Peter Montgomery 1948- *WhoScEn 94*
Benton, Philip Eglin, Jr. 1928- *WhoAm 94, WhoFI 94*
Benton, Richardson D. 1914- *WhoAmP 93*
Benton, Robert 1932- *IntMPA 94, WhoAm 94*
Benton, Robert Austin, Jr. 1921- *WhoAm 94*
Benton, Robert Dean 1929- *WhoAm 94*
Benton, Robert Wilmer 1931- *WhoWest 94*
Benton, Stephen Richard 1952- *WhoScEn 94*
Benton, Steve d1976 *WhoHol 92*
Benton, Stuart Raymond 1965- *WhoFI 94*
Benton, Susanne *WhoHol 92*
Benton, Suzanne E. 1936- *WhoAmA 93*
Benton, Thomas Hart 1889-1975 *AmCulL, WhoAmA 93N*
Benton, Thomas Iden 1946- *WhoAmP 93*
Benton, W. Duane 1950- *WhoAm 94, WhoAmL 94*
Benton, William 1900-1973 *WhoAmA 93N*
Benton, William Pettigrew 1923- *WhoAm 94*
Benton-Borghi, Beatrice Hope 1946- *WhoMW 93*
Benton Jones, Simon W. F. *Who 94*
Bentov, Mirtala *WhoAmA 93*
Ben-Tovim, Atarah 1940- *Who 94*
Ben Tre, Howard 1949- *WhoAm 94*
Ben Tre, Howard B. 1949- *WhoAmA 93*
Bentsen, Kenneth Edward 1926- *WhoAm 94*
Bentsen, Lloyd 1921- *CurBio 93 [port], News 93-3 [port], WhoAm 94, WhoFI 94*
Bentsen, Lloyd Millard 1921- *WhoAmP 93*
Bentsen, Lloyd Millard, Jr. 1921- *IntWW 93, Who 94*
Bentz, Bryan Lloyd 1953- *WhoScEn 94*
Bentz, Dale Monroe 1919- *WhoAm 94*
Bentz, Frederick Jacob 1922- *WhoAm 94*
Bentz, Harry Donald 1931- *WhoAmA 93*
Bentz, John d1950 *WhoAmA 93N*
Bentz, Melitta *WorInv*
Bentz, Warren Worthington 1926- *WhoAm 94, WhoAmL 94*
Bentz, William Frederick 1940- *WhoAm 94*
Bentzen, Richard D. 1953- *WhoAmL 94*
Bentzin, Charles Gilbert 1932- *WhoIns 94*
Bentzon, Niels Viggo 1919- *IntWW 93, NewGrDO*
Bentzon, Therese 1840-1907 *BlmGWL*
Benucci, Francesco c. 1745-1824 *NewGrDO*
Benussi, Femi 1948- *WhoHol 92*
Benveniste, Asa 1925- *WrDr 94*
Benveniste, Daniel Stephen 1954- *WhoWest 94*
Benveniste, Jacob 1921- *WhoAm 94*
Benveniste, Rachelle *DrAPF 93*
Ben-Veniste, Richard 1943- *WhoAm 94, WhoAmL 94*
Benvenuti, Tomaso 1838-1906 *NewGrDO*
Benvenuto, Elio 1914- *WhoAmA 93*
Benvenuto, Emil Vincent 1931- *WhoAmP 93*
Benvenuto, Giorgio 1937- *IntWW 93*
Benvenuto, Sergio, Sr. 1930- *WhoHisp 94*
Benvenuto Nichele, Virginia Alison 1959- *WhoHisp 94*
Benvenutti, Peter J. 1949- *WhoAm 94, WhoAmL 94*
Benway, Joseph Calise 1949- *WhoAm 94, WhoFI 94*
Beny, Roloff 1924- *WhoAmA 93N*
Benya, Anton 1912- *IntWW 93*
Benya, Rosemarie Ann 1942- *WhoAm 94*
Ben-Yaacov, Gideon 1941- *WhoScEn 94*
Ben-Yaacov, Miriam *DrAPF 93*
Benyard, William B., Jr. 1948- *WhoBlA 94*
Ben-Yehuda, Hemda 1873-1951 *BlmGWL*
Benyei, Candace Reed 1946- *WhoAm 94*
Benyo, Richard Stephen 1946- *WhoAm 94, WhoWest 94*
Benyon, Thomas Yates 1942- *Who 94*
Benyon, William Richard 1930- *Who 94*
Ben-Yoseph, Yoav 1941- *WhoMW 93*
Ben-Yossef, Avraham d1980 *WhoHol 92*
Benz, Donald Ray 1950- *WhoMW 93, WhoScEn 94*
Benz, Edward John 1923- *WhoAm 94*
Benz, George Albert 1926- *WhoAm 94*
Benz, Harry R. 1937- *WhoAm 94, WhoFI 94*
Benz, Joan Ryder 1948- *WhoMW 93*
Benz, Karl Friedrich 1844-1929 *WorInv [port]*
Benz, Lee R. d1984 *WhoAmA 93N*
Benz, Mary Patricia 1951- *WhoAmL 94*
Benz, Philip John 1955- *WhoMW 93*
Benz, Robert Daniel 1947- *WhoScEn 94*
Benz, Samuel Paul 1962- *WhoScEn 94*
Benz, William J. 1954- *WhoAmL 94*
Benz, William Robert 1931- *WhoAmP 93*
Benza, Ronald Joseph 1952- *WhoAm 94*
Benzak, Louis Richard 1939- *WhoFI 94*
Benzer, Jim Kevin 1967- *WhoFI 94*
Benzer, Seymour 1921- *IntWW 93, WhoAm 94, WhoScEn 94, WhoWest 94*
Benzi, Roberto 1937- *IntWW 93*
Benzie, William 1930- *WrDr 94*
Benzil, Philip Stanley 1933- *WhoAmP 93*
Benzing, David Warren 1953- *WhoWest 94*
Benzinger, Raymond Burdette 1938- *WhoAm 94*
Benzle, Curtis Munhall 1949- *WhoAm 94, WhoAmA 93, WhoMW 93*
Benzoni, Julie 1920- *BlmGWL*
Benzor-Cox, Betty *WhoHisp 94*
Ben-Zvi, Phillip Norman 1942- *WhoFI 94, WhoIns 94*
Beolco, Angelo *IntDcT 2*
Bepko, Gerald Lewis 1940- *WhoAm 94, WhoAmL 94, WhoMW 93*
Bequette, Doris Elaine 1934- *WhoMW 93*
Beracha, Barry Harris 1942- *WhoAm 94*
Beradino, John 1917- *WhoHol 92*
Berain, Jean 1640-1711 *NewGrDO*
Berain, Jesse S. 1928- *WhoAmP 93*
Berall, Frank Stewart 1929- *WhoAm 94, WhoAmL 94*
Beran, Denis Carl 1935- *WhoAm 94*
Beran, Rudolf Jaroslav Vaclav 1943- *WhoAm 94, WhoWest 94*
Beranek, Leo Leroy 1914- *WhoAm 94, WhoScEn 94*
Beranger, Andre d1973 *WhoHol 92*
Berangere, Mme. d1928 *WhoHol 92*
Berard, Andre 1940- *WhoAm 94, WhoFI 94*
Berard, Christian 1902-1949 *IntDcB*
Berard, Christian(-Jacques) 1902-1949 *NewGrDO*
Berard, Jean-Antoine 1710-1772 *NewGrDO*
Berardesco, Michael Richard 1951- *WhoFI 94*
Berardi, Ronald Joseph 1944- *WhoFI 94*
Berbary, Maurice Shehadeh 1923- *WhoAm 94, WhoScEn 94*
Berbenich, William Alfred 1961- *WhoScEn 94*
Berber, Adi 1915- *WhoHol 92*
Berberet, Grace Margaret 1915- *WhoAmP 93*
Berberich, George Edward, Jr. *WhoWest 94*
Berberich, Lois Ann 1944- *WhoMW 93*
Berberova, Nina 1901-1993 *NewYTBS 93*
Berberova, Nina (Nikolaevna) 1901-1993 *ConAu 142*
Berberova, Nina Nikolaevna 1901- *BlmGWL*
Berbie, Jane 1934- *NewGrDO*
Berbrich, Joan D. 1925- *WrDr 94*
Bercaw, Donald C. 1930- *WhoAmP 93*
Bercaw, John Edward 1944- *WhoScEn 94*
Bercel, Nicholas Anthony 1911- *WhoScEn 94*
Berch, Rebecca White 1955- *WhoAmL 94*
Berchem, Robert Lee, Sr. 1941- *WhoAmL 94*
Berchten, Rachel *DrAPF 93*
Berck, Judith 1960- *ConAu 142, SmATA 75 [port]*
Berclaz, Theodore M. 1949- *WhoScEn 94*
Bercovici, Luca *WhoHol 92*
Bercovici, Martin William 1942- *WhoAmL 94*
Bercovitch, Hanna Margareta 1934- *WhoAm 94*
Bercovitch, Sacvan 1933- *WhoAm 94*
Bercq, Alexis Claude 1960- *WhoWest 94*
Berczi, Andrew Stephen 1934- *WhoAm 94*
Berd, Morris 1914- *WhoAmA 93*
Berdahl, Robert Max 1937- *WhoAm 94*
Berdanier, Carolyn Dawson 1936- *WhoAm 94*
Berdell, James Russell 1944- *WhoWest 94*
Berdennikov, Grigory Vitalievich 1950- *IntWW 93*
Berdick, Leonard Stanley 1938- *WhoFI 94*
Berdine, Richard Alan 1963- *WhoMW 93*
Berdon, Robert I. *WhoAmP 93*
Berdon, Robert Irwin 1929- *WhoAm 94, WhoAmL 94*
Berdrow, Stanton K. 1928- *WhoWest 94*
Berdy, Gregg Jonathan 1957- *WhoMW 93*
Bere, James Frederick 1922- *WhoFI 94*
Bere, Rennie Montague 1907- *WrDr 94*
Beregan, Nicolo 1627-1713 *NewGrDO*
Beregi, Oscar d1965 *WhoHol 92*
Beregi, Oscar, Jr. d1976 *WhoHol 92*
Beregovoy, Georgiy Timofeyevich 1921- *IntWW 93*
Beregovoy, Pierre d1993 *Who 94N*
Beregovoy, Pierre 1925- *CurBio 93 [port]*
Beregovoy, Pierre 1925-1993 *CurBio 93N*
Beregovoy, Pierre Eugene d1993 *IntWW 93N*
Beregovoy, Pierre Eugene 1925- *IntWW 93*
Berek, Jonathan Samuel 1948- *WhoWest 94*
Berek, Peter 1940- *WhoAm 94*
Berella, Henry *WhoHisp 94*
Berelson, Philip P. 1943- *WhoAmL 94*
Beren, Stanley O. 1920- *WhoAmA 93*
Berenato, Mark Anthony 1958- *WhoAmL 94*
Berenberg, William 1915- *WhoAm 94*
Berend, T. Ivan 1930- *IntWW 93*
Berenda, Ruth W. *WhoAm 94*
Berendes, Heinz Werner 1925- *WhoAm 94*
Berendi, Erlinda Bayaua 1947- *WhoMW 93*
Berendonck, Gerd 1924- *IntWW 93*
Berendsen, Carl A. 1890-1973 *HisDcKW*
Berendt, Rachel d1957 *WhoHol 92*
Berendt, Robert Tryon 1939- *WhoAmL 94, WhoMW 93*
Berendzen, Richard 1938- *WhoAm 94*
Berenger, Paul Raymond 1945- *IntWW 93*
Berenger, Tom 1950- *IntMPA 94, IntWW 93, WhoAm 94, WhoHol 92*
Berenguer, Amanda 1912- *BlmGWL*
Berenguer, Elba F. 1940- *WhoHisp 94*
Berenguer, Juan Bautista 1954- *WhoHisp 94*
Berens, Harold *WhoHol 92*
Berens, (Johann) Hermann 1826-1880 *NewGrDO*
Berens, Mark H. 1928- *WhoIns 94*
Berens, Mark Harry 1928- *WhoAm 94*
Berens, Randolph Lee 1943- *WhoScEn 94*
Berens, Rodney Bristol 1945- *WhoAm 94, WhoFI 94*
Berens, William Joseph 1952- *WhoAm 94, WhoAmL 94*
Berensohn, Roger 1933- *WhoHisp 94*
Berenson, Abe d1977 *WhoHol 92*
Berenson, Bernard 1865-1959 *WhoAmA 93N*
Berenson, Berry *WhoHol 92*
Berenson, Gerald Sanders 1922- *WhoAm 94, WhoScEn 94*
Berenson, Marisa 1947- *IntMPA 94, WhoHol 92*
Berenson, Robert Leonard 1939- *WhoAm 94, WhoFI 94*
Berenson, William Keith 1954- *WhoAmL 94*
Berenstadt, Gaetano c. 1690-1735 *NewGrDO*
Berenstain, Janice 1923- *WhoAm 94*
Berenstain, Stanley 1923- *WhoAm 94*
Berens-Totenohl, Josefa 1891-1969 *BlmGWL*
Berentsen, Kurtis George 1953- *WhoAm 94*
Berenzweig, Jack Charles 1942- *WhoAmL 94*
Berenzy, Alix 1957- *WrDr 94*
Bereola, Enitan Olu 1947- *WhoBlA 94*
Beres, Joel Edward 1961- *WhoScEn 94*
Beres, Michael John 1950- *WhoMW 93*
Beres, Milan 1936- *WhoScEn 94*
Beresford *Who 94*
Beresford, Anne 1929- *BlmGWL, WrDr 94*
Beresford, Bruce 1940- *CurBio 93 [port], IntMPA 94, IntWW 93, WhoAm 94*
Beresford, Douglas Lincoln 1956- *WhoAmL 94*
Beresford, Elisabeth *WrDr 94*
Beresford, Evelyn d1959 *WhoHol 92*
Beresford, Harry d1944 *WhoHol 92*
Beresford, J(ohn) D(avys) 1873-1947 *EncSF 93*
Beresford, Leigh *EncSF 93*
Beresford, Leslie 1891?-1937? *EncSF 93*
Beresford, Maurice (Warwick) 1920- *WrDr 94*
Beresford, Maurice Warwick 1920- *Who 94*
Beresford, Meg 1937- *IntWW 93, Who 94*
Beresford, (Alexander) Paul 1946- *Who 94*
Beresford, Richard 1755-1803 *WhAmRev*
Beresford, Richard 1930- *WhoAmL 94*
Beresford, William Marcus Joseph 1798-1883 *DcNaB MP*
Beresford-Howe, Constance 1922- *BlmGWL*
Beresford-Howe, Constance (Elizabeth) 1922- *WrDr 94*
Beresford-Peirse, Henry Grant de la Poer 1933- *Who 94*
Beresford-West, Michael Charles 1928- *Who 94*
Beresik, Gregory Allan 1949- *WhoFI 94*
Beresovsky, Boris Vadimovich 1969- *IntWW 93*
Bereston, Eugene Sydney 1914- *WhoAm 94*
Berestovoi, Vladimir Ivanovich 1948- *LoBiDrD*
Berestynski, Adam S. 1927- *WhoWest 94*
Beretta, Amy 1964- *WhoAmL 94*
Beretta, Giordano Bruno 1951- *WhoFI 94, WhoScEn 94, WhoWest 94*
Beretz, Paul Basil 1938- *WhoWest 94*
Bereuter, Doug 1939- *CngDr 93*
Bereuter, Douglas K. 1939- *WhoAmP 93*
Bereuter, Douglas Kent 1939- *WhoAm 94, WhoMW 93*
Berezin, Tanya 1941- *WhoAm 94*
Bereznoff, Gregory Michael 1951- *WhoAmL 94*
Berezovsky, Maxim Sozontovich 1745-1777 *NewGrDO*
Berfield, Sue Ellen 1949- *WhoWest 94*
Berg, A. Scott 1949- *WrDr 94*
Berg, Adrian 1929- *IntWW 93, Who 94*
Berg, Alban (Maria Johannes) 1885-1935 *NewGrDO*
Berg, Albert Frederick 1930- *WhoFI 94*
Berg, Arthur Paul 1940- *WhoAmL 94*
Berg, Barbara Best 1931- *WhoFI 94*
Berg, Bernard 1931- *IntWW 93*
Berg, Bernd Albert 1949- *WhoScEn 94*
Berg, Carolyn Nourse 1938- *WhoWest 94*
Berg, Charles A. 1927- *WhoAmP 93*
Berg, Charles Ramirez 1947- *WhoHisp 94*
Berg, Christian 1944- *IntWW 93*
Berg, Clyde Clarence 1936- *WhoScEn 94*
Berg, Daniel 1929- *WhoAm 94*
Berg, Dave 1920-1993 *WrDr 94N*
Berg, Dave 1948- *WhoWest 94*
Berg, David 1920- *WhoAm 94*
Berg, David Howard 1942- *WhoAm 94*
Berg, Dean Michael 1968- *WhoScEn 94*
Berg, Dick *IntMPA 94*
Berg, Donald James 1935- *WhoMW 93*
Berg, Eivinn 1931- *IntWW 93*
Berg, Eric Wilhelm 1921- *WhoAmP 93*
Berg, Ericson 1942- *WhoAm 94*
Berg, Evelynne Marie *WhoMW 93*
Berg, George G. 1919- *WhoScEn 94*
Berg, Gerald Brett 1950- *WhoAmL 94*
Berg, Gertrude d1966 *WhoHol 92*
Berg, Gertrude 1899-1966 *WhoCom*
Berg, Gordon 1927- *WhoAmP 93*
Berg, Gordon Hercher 1937- *WhoFI 94*
Berg, Hans Fredrik 1936- *WhoAmL 94*
Berg, Harry K. 1943- *WhoAmP 93*
Berg, Helen MacDuffee 1932- *WhoWest 94*
Berg, Howard C. 1934- *WhoAm 94*
Berg, Ira David 1931- *WhoMW 93*
Berg, Irwin August 1913- *WhoAm 94*
Berg, Ivar Elis, Jr. 1929- *WhoScEn 94*
Berg, James A. *WhoAmP 93*
Berg, Jan Mikael 1928- *WhoScEn 94*
Berg, Jean Horton Lutz 1913- *WhoAm 94*
Berg, Jeff 1947- *IntMPA 94*
Berg, Jeffrey Scott 1955- *WhoMW 93*
Berg, Jeffrey Spencer 1947- *WhoAm 94*
Berg, Jeremy M. *WhoScEn 94*
Berg, John J. *Who 94*
Berg, John Paul 1920- *WhoFI 94*
Berg, John Richard 1932- *WhoAm 94*
Berg, Jonathan Albert 1943- *WhoFI 94*
Berg, Josef 1927-1971 *NewGrDO*
Berg, Kimberly *DrAPF 93*
Berg, Knut 1925- *IntWW 93*
Berg, Lawrence Andrew 1937- *WhoMW 93*
Berg, Leila 1917- *WrDr 94*
Berg, Leonard 1927- *WhoAm 94*
Berg, Lillian Douglas 1925- *WhoScEn 94*
Berg, Lloyd 1914- *WhoAm 94*
Berg, Marie Majella 1916- *WhoAm 94*

Berg, Mary Jaylene 1950- WhoMW 93, WhoScEn 94
Berg, Merril 1928- WhoAm 94
Berg, Mona Lea 1935- WhoAmA 93
Berg, Nancy 1931- WhoHol 92
Berg, (Carl) Natanael 1879-1957 NewGrDO
Berg, Norman Alf 1918- WhoAm 94
Berg, Norman Asplund 1930- WhoAm 94
Berg, Paul 1926- IntWW 93, Who 94, WhoAm 94, WhoScEn 94, WhoWest 94, WorScD
Berg, Paul Edward 1941- WhoFI 94
Berg, Peter 1962- WhoHol 92
Berg, Phil 1902- WhoAmA 93N
Berg, Richard Archie 1917- WhoWest 94
Berg, Rick A. 1959- WhoAmP 93
Berg, Rick Alan 1959- WhoMW 93
Berg, Robert Charles 1944- WhoWest 94
Berg, Robert Lewis 1918- WhoAm 94
Berg, Robert Michael 1950- WhoFI 94
Berg, Robert Raymond 1924- WhoAm 94, WhoScEn 94
Berg, Roy Torgny 1927- WhoAm 94
Berg, Sandra 1947- WhoAmP 93
Berg, Siri WhoAmA 93
Berg, Stanton Oneal 1928- WhoAm 94, WhoFI 94, WhoMW 93, WhoScEn 94
Berg, Stephen DrAPF 93
Berg, Stephen 1934- WrDr 94
Berg, Stephen Warren 1948- WhoFI 94
Berg, Stina d1930 WhoHol 92
Berg, Thomas 1914- WhoAm 94
Berg, Thomas Kenneth 1940- WhoAm 94
Berg, Thomas Sidney 1952- WhoAmL 94
Berg, Tom 1943- WhoAmA 93, WhoWest 94
Berg, Virginia Marie 1932- WhoAmP 93
Berg, Virginia Seymour 1948- WhoMW 93
Berg, W. Robert 1932- WhoAm 94, WhoFI 94
Berg, Warren Stanley 1922- WhoAm 94
Berg, William James 1942- WhoAm 94
Bergalli Gozzi, Luisa 1703-1779 BlmGWL
Bergamini, Eduardo Whitaker 1944- WhoScEn 94
Bergamo, Ron 1943- WhoAm 94, WhoWest 94
Bergan, Edmund Paul, Jr. 1950- WhoAmL 94, WhoFI 94
Bergan, John Jerome 1927- WhoAm 94
Bergan, Philip James 1938- WhoAmL 94
Bergan, William Luke 1939- WhoAm 94
Bergansky, Suzanne M. WhoAmP 93
Bergant, Paul R. 1946- WhoAm 94, WhoFI 94
Bergantz, Arthur 1944- WhoMW 93
Berganza (Vargas), Teresa 1935- NewGrDO
Berganza, Teresa WhoHol 92
Berganza, Teresa 1935- IntWW 93
Berganza, Teresa 1957- Who 94
Berganza Vargas, Teresa 1935- WhoAm 94
Bergau, Frank Conrad 1926- WhoFI 94
Bergdall, Obera Jean 1929- WhoAmP 93
Berge, Carol DrAPF 93
Berge, Carol 1928- WhoAm 94, WhoWest 94, WrDr 94
Berge, Dorothy Alphena 1923- WhoAmA 93
Berge, Gunnar 1940- IntWW 93
Berge, H(ans) C(ornelis) ten 1938- ConWorW 93
Berge, Henry 1908- WhoAmA 93
Berge, Kenneth George 1926- WhoAm 94
Berge, Paul Morton 1937- WhoAm 94
Berge, Pierre 1930- WhoAm 94
Berge, Pierre Vital Georges 1930- IntWW 93
Bergel, Richard 1935- WhoFI 94
Berge-Lavigne, Maryse 1941- WhoWomW 91
Bergeman, George William 1946- WhoScEn 94
Bergemann, Susan C. 1956- WhoAmL 94
Bergemont, Albert Michel 1953- WhoWest 94
Bergen, Candice 1946- ConAu 142, IntMPA 94, WhoAm 94, WhoHol 92, WrDr 94
Bergen, Candice Patricia 1946- IntWW 93
Bergen, Christopher Brooke 1949- WhoWest 94
Bergen, D. Thomas 1930- WhoAm 94, WhoAmA 93, WhoFI 94
Bergen, Daniel Patrick 1935- WhoAm 94
Bergen, Edgar d1978 WhoHol 92
Bergen, Edgar 1903-1978 WhoCom
Bergen, Frances WhoHol 92
Bergen, G. S. Peter 1936- WhoAm 94
Bergen, Jerry WhoHol 92
Bergen, John Axel Von 1939- WhoAmA 93
Bergen, John Donald 1942- WhoAm 94, WhoFI 94
Bergen, Kenneth William 1911- WhoAm 94
Bergen, Margarita 1946- WhoHisp 94
Bergen, Martha Steagall 1954- WhoMW 93
Bergen, Polly 1930- IntMPA 94, WhoHol 92
Bergen, Robert Ludlum, Jr. 1929- WhoScEn 94
Bergen, Sidney L. 1922- WhoAmA 93
Bergen, Stanley Silvers, Jr. 1929- WhoAm 94
Bergen, Thomas Joseph 1913-1992 WhAm 10
Bergen, Veritas Leo BlmGWL
Bergen, Werner Gerhard 1943- WhoAm 94
Bergen, William Benjamin 1915- IntWW 93
Bergendoff, Conrad John Immanuel 1895- WhoAm 94
Bergendoff, Robert Perry 1935- WhoMW 93
Bergenfeld, Nathan DrAPF 93
Bergenn, James Walter 1954- WhoAmL 94
Bergenstrom, Stig Gullmar 1909- IntWW 93
Berger, Alan I. 1933- WhoAmL 94
Berger, Allan Sidney 1931- WhoAm 94
Berger, Andre d1977 WhoHol 92
Berger, Andrew L. 1946- WhoAm 94, WhoFI 94
Berger, Arthur A(sa) 1933- WrDr 94
Berger, Arthur Victor 1912- WhoAm 94
Berger, Barbara (Helen) 1945- SmATA 77 [port]
Berger, Bennett Maurice 1926- WhoAm 94
Berger, Bernard Ben 1912- WhoAm 94
Berger, Brigitte (M. L.) 1928- WrDr 94
Berger, Bruce DrAPF 93
Berger, Bruce 1938- WrDr 94
Berger, Bruce 1944- WhoAm 94
Berger, Bruce Warren 1942- WhoScEn 94
Berger, Burman Aaron 1963- WhoAmL 94
Berger, Cary J. A. 1963- WhoAmL 94
Berger, Charles Lee 1947- WhoAmL 94
Berger, Charles Martin 1936- WhoAm 94, WhoFI 94
Berger, Charles W. 1936- WhoAmP 93
Berger, Curtis Jay 1926- WhoAm 94, WhoAmL 94
Berger, Daniel O. 1945- WhoAmL 94
Berger, David 1912- WhoAm 94, WhoAmL 94
Berger, David Joseph 1954- WhoAmP 93
Berger, Diane Klein 1946- WhoWest 94
Berger, Edmond Louis 1939- WhoAm 94, WhoMW 93
Berger, Eric 1906- WhoAm 94
Berger, Erna d1990 WhoHol 92
Berger, Erna 1900-1990 NewGrDO
Berger, Eugenia Hepworth 1925- WhoWest 94
Berger, Evelyn Miller 1896- WhAm 10
Berger, Francine Ellis 1949- WhoAm 94
Berger, Frank Milan 1913- WhoAm 94
Berger, Frank Stanley 1939- WhoAm 94, WhoFI 94
Berger, Frederick Jerome 1916- WhoScEn 94
Berger, Fredericka 1932- WrDr 94
Berger, George 1936- WhoAm 94, WhoAmL 94
Berger, George John 1944- WhoAmL 94
Berger, Gilda 1935- WrDr 94
Berger, Glenn Wayne 1945- WhoWest 94
Berger, Gottfried O. 1924- WhoIns 94
Berger, Gustav d1958 WhoHol 92
Berger, Gustav A. 1920- WhoAmA 93
Berger, Harold 1925- WhoAm 94, WhoAmL 94, WhoFI 94
Berger, Harold 1926- WhoAm 94
Berger, Harold D. 1921- WhoAmP 93
Berger, Harvey James 1950- WhoAm 94
Berger, Helmut 1942- IntWW 93
Berger, Helmut 1943- IntMPA 94
Berger, Helmut 1944- WhoHol 92
Berger, Herbert 1909- WhoAm 94, WhoScEn 94
Berger, Howard Martin 1927- WhoWest 94
Berger, James Charles 1941- WhoFI 94
Berger, Jason 1924- WhoAm 94, WhoAmA 93
Berger, Jay Vari 1944- WhoWest 94
Berger, Jerry Allen 1943- WhoAm 94, WhoAmA 93, WhoMW 93
Berger, John 1926- BlmGEL, IntWW 93, Who 94
Berger, John (Peter) 1926- WrDr 94
Berger, John Milton 1943- WhoWest 94
Berger, John Torrey, Jr. 1938- WhoAm 94
Berger, Joseph WhoAm 94
Berger, Kenneth Walter 1924- WhoAm 94
Berger, L. E. WhoAmP 93
Berger, Lawrence Douglas 1947- WhoAm 94, WhoAmL 94
Berger, Lawrence Howard 1947- WhoAm 94, WhoAmL 94
Berger, Leland Roger 1956- WhoAmL 94, WhoWest 94
Berger, Leo WhoAmP 93
Berger, Lev Isaac 1929- WhoAm 94
Berger, Martin Edgar 1942- WhoMW 93
Berger, Maurice 1956- WhoAmA 93
Berger, Mel WhoHol 92
Berger, Melvin 1927- ChlLR 32 [port]
Berger, Melvin Gerald 1943- WhoAmL 94
Berger, Meyer 1912- WhoAmP 93
Berger, Michael Edward 1945- WhoFI 94
Berger, Mitchell Wayne 1956- WhoAmL 94
Berger, Murry P. 1926- WhoAm 94
Berger, Neal Jeffrey 1952- WhoAmP 93
Berger, Newell James, Jr. 1926- WhoFI 94, WhoWest 94
Berger, Nicole d1967 WhoHol 92
Berger, Oscar 1901- WhoAm 94, WhoAmA 93
Berger, Pat 1948- WhoAmA 93
Berger, Pat Patricia Eve 1929- WhoWest 94
Berger, Patricia Wilson 1926- WhoAm 94
Berger, Paul Eric 1948- WhoAm 94, WhoAmA 93, WhoWest 94
Berger, Pearl 1943- WhoAm 94
Berger, Peter (Egerton Capel) 1925- Who 94
Berger, Philip Jeffrey 1943- WhoAm 94
Berger, Philip Raymond 1924- WhoFI 94
Berger, Raoul 1901- WhoAm 94
Berger, Richard L. 1939- IntMPA 94
Berger, Richard Laurence 1939- WhoAm 94
Berger, Robert Bertram 1924- WhoAm 94, WhoAmL 94
Berger, Robert Glenn 1954- WhoAmL 94
Berger, Robert Lewis 1925- WhoAm 94
Berger, Robert Michael 1942- WhoAm 94
Berger, Roberta 1941- WhoFI 94
Berger, Rudolf 1874-1915 NewGrDO
Berger, Samuel R. WhoAmP 93
Berger, Sandra Christine Q. 1948- WhoAmA 93
Berger, Sanford Jason 1926- WhoAm 94
Berger, Senta 1941- WhoHol 92
Berger, Seymour Maurice 1928- WhoAm 94
Berger, Stanley Allan 1934- WhoAm 94
Berger, Stephen 1939- WhoAm 94, WhoFI 94
Berger, Steven R. 1945- WhoAmL 94
Berger, Suzanne 1939- WhoAm 94
Berger, Suzanne E. DrAPF 93
Berger, Thomas (Louis) 1924- EncSF 93, WrDr 94
Berger, Thomas Gerald 1955- WhoMW 93
Berger, Thomas Jan 1952- WhoAm 94
Berger, Thomas Louis 1924- IntWW 93, WhoAm 94
Berger, Timothy John 1948- WhoMW 93
Berger, Toby 1940- WhoAm 94
Berger, Wilhelm Georg 1929- IntWW 93
Berger, William 1928- WhoHol 92
Berger, William Ernest 1918- WhoAm 94
Berger, William Merriam Bart 1925- WhoFI 94
Berger, Wolfgang H. 1937- WhoWest 94
Berger, Yves 1936- EncSF 93
Bergerac, Jacques 1927- IntMPA 94, WhoHol 92
Bergere, Carleton Mallory 1919- WhoMW 93
Bergere, Clifford Wendell, Jr. 1945- WhoAmL 94
Bergere, Dorothy d1979 WhoHol 92
Bergere, Lee 1923- WhoHol 92
Bergere, Ouida d1974 WhoHol 92
Bergere, Valerie d1938 WhoHol 92
Bergeron, Andre Louis 1922- IntWW 93
Bergeron, Arthur W(illiam), Jr. 1946- ConAu 141
Bergeron, Belvin Francis 1924- WhoAmP 93
Bergeron, C. Patrick 1955- WhoAmP 93
Bergeron, Charles Edward 1945- WhoFI 94
Bergeron, Clifton George 1925- WhoAm 94
Bergeron, Jeffrey David 1953- WhoAm 94, WhoMW 93
Bergeron, Louis E. 1934- WhoIns 94
Bergeron, Lucien G. 1933- WhoAmP 93
Bergeron, Normand R. 1927- WhoAmP 93
Bergeron, R. Thomas 1931- WhoAm 94
Bergeron, Robert J. 1938- WhoAmP 93
Bergeron, Scott Malcolm 1962- WhoFI 94
Bergersen, Baldwin 1914- NewGrDO
Bergersen, Fraser John 1929- IntWW 93, Who 94
Bergerson, David Raymond 1939- WhoAm 94, WhoAmL 94, WhoFI 94
Bergerson, J. Steven 1942- WhoAmL 94, WhoFI 94
Bergerson, Stephen Richard 1945- WhoAm 94, WhoAmL 94
Bergerud, Eric M. 1948- ConAu 141
Berges, Emily Trafford DrAPF 93
Berges, Emily Trafford 1937- WrDr 94
Bergeson, John Henning 1919- WhoWest 94
Bergeson, Marian WhoWest 94
Bergeson, Marian 1927- WhoAmP 93
Bergeson, Scott 1938- WhoFI 94
Berget, Grete Anni 1954- IntWW 93
Bergethon, Kaare Roald 1918- WhoAm 94
Bergevin, Louis W. 1922- WhoAmP 93
Bergey, Earle K(ulp) 1901-1952 EncSF 93
Bergez, Craig Martin 1963- WhoAmL 94
Bergfeld, John Albert 1938- WhoMW 93
Bergfeld, Wilma Fowler 1938- WhoMW 93
Bergfield, Barbara Komie 1945- WhoMW 93
Bergfield, Gene Raymond 1951- WhoScEn 94
Berggol'ts, Ol'ga Fedorovna 1910-1975 BlmGWL
Berggren, Bo Erik Gunnar 1936- IntWW 93
Berggren, Dick 1942- WhoAm 94
Berggren, Jerry Lee 1948- WhoMW 93
Berggren, Paulette Therese 1939- WhoMW 93
Berggren, Ronald Bernard 1931- WhoAm 94
Berggren, Terry K. 1958- WhoMW 93
Berggren, Thage 1932- WhoScEn 94
Berggren, Thommy 1937- IntWW 93, WhoHol 92
Berggren, William Alfred 1931- WhoAm 94, WhoScEn 94
Berggruen, John Henry 1943- WhoAm 94, WhoAmA 93
Bergh, Birger 1935- IntWW 93
Bergh, David Morgan 1947- WhoWest 94
Berghahn, Volker R. 1938- WrDr 94
Berghash, Mark W. 1935- WhoAm 94, WhoAmA 93
Berghash, Rachel DrAPF 93
Berghaus, Ruth 1927- IntWW 93, NewGrDO
Berghoefer, Beulah d1973 WhoHol 92
Berghoefer, Fred George 1921- WhoAmP 93
Berghof, Herbert d1990 WhoHol 92
Berghof, Herbert 1909-1990 WhAm 10
Berghofer-Weichner, Mathilde WhoWomW 91
Berghoff, John C., Jr. 1941- WhoAm 94
Berghold, Joseph Philip 1938- WhoAm 94
Bergholtz, Norbert F. 1944- WhoAm 94, WhoAmL 94
Bergholz, David 1938- WhoAm 94
Bergholz, George Frederick 1963- WhoMW 93
Bergholz, Ol'ga Fedorovna 1910-1975 BlmGWL
Bergholz, Richard Cady 1917- WhoAm 94
Berghuser, Hugo (Erich) 1935- Who 94
Bergia, Roger Merle 1937- WhoMW 93
Bergin, Allen Eric 1934- WhoAm 94, WhoWest 94
Bergin, Daniel Timothy 1930- WhoAm 94
Bergin, Edward Daniel 1943- WhoAmP 93
Bergin, John Francis 1924- WhoAm 94, WhoFI 94
Bergin, Patrick 1954- WhoHol 92
Bergin, Thomas Francis 1924- WhoAm 94, WhoAmL 94
Berg-Johnson, Karen Ann 1959- WhoMW 93
Bergkamp, Dennis 1969- WorESoc
Bergkamp, Lucas 1961- WhoAmL 94
Bergland, Martha 1945- WrDr 94
Bergland, Robert Selmer 1928- IntWW 93
Berglas, Frank E. 1940- WhoIns 94
Berglas, Steven 1949- ConAu 142
Bergleitner, George Charles, Jr. 1935- WhoAm 94, WhoFI 94
Bergles, Arthur Edward 1935- WhoAm 94, WhoScEn 94
Berglin, Linda 1944- WhoMW 93, WhoWomW 91
Berglin, Linda L. 1944- WhoAmP 93
Berglund, Carl Neil 1938- WhoAm 94
Berglund, Erik d1965 WhoHol 92
Berglund, Joel (Ingemar) 1903-1985 NewGrDO
Berglund, Paavo Allan Engelbert 1929- IntWW 93
Berglund, Robin G. 1945- WhoAm 94
Bergman, Alan IntMPA 94, WhoAm 94
Bergman, Alan 1925- WhoHol 92
Bergman, Andrew 1945?- ConTFT 11, IntMPA 94
Bergman, Anna 1949- WhoHol 92

Bergman, Bruce Jeffrey 1944- *WhoAmL 94, WhoFI 94*
Bergman, Carla Elaine 1962- *WhoScEn 94*
Bergman, Charles Carroll 1932- *WhoWest 94*
Bergman, Daniel Alan 1952- *WhoAmL 94*
Bergman, David *DrAPF 93*
Bergman, Denise *DrAPF 93*
Bergman, Ellen 1942- *WhoAmP 93*
Bergman, Ernest L. 1922- *WhoAm 94*
Bergman, Eugene 1930- *WrDr 94*
Bergman, Garrett Edward 1946- *WhoFI 94*
Bergman, George Mark 1943- *WhoAm 94*
Bergman, Harlan W. 1932- *WhoIns 94*
Bergman, Harry 1912- *WhoAm 94*
Bergman, Henri d1917 *WhoHol 92*
Bergman, Henry d1946 *WhoHol 92*
Bergman, Hermas John 1926- *WhoAm 94*
Bergman, Hjalmar (Frederick Elgerus) 1883-1931 *IntDcT 2*
Bergman, Ingmar *Who 94*
Bergman, Ingmar 1918- *IntMPA 94, IntWW 93, WhoAm 94*
Bergman, (Ernst) Ingmar 1918- *ConWorW 93, NewGrDO, Who 94*
Bergman, Ingrid d1982 *WhoHol 92*
Bergman, Ingrid 1915-1982 *AmCulL*
Bergman, Joel *WhoHol 92*
Bergman, John H. 1943- *WhoMW 93*
Bergman, Klaus 1931- *WhoAm 94, WhoFI 94*
Bergman, Lawrence Alan 1944- *WhoScEn 94*
Bergman, Marilyn *IntMPA 94*
Bergman, Marilyn Keith *WhoAm 94*
Bergman, Mats *WhoHol 92*
Bergman, Nancy Palm 1938- *WhoAm 94*
Bergman, Richard Isaac 1934- *WhoAm 94*
Bergman, Robert Aaron 1928- *WhoWest 94*
Bergman, Robert George 1942- *WhoAm 94, WhoScEn 94*
Bergman, Robert P. 1945- *WhoAmA 93*
Bergman, Robert Paul 1945- *WhoAm 94*
Bergman, Sandahl *WhoHol 92*
Bergman, Stephenie Jane 1946- *IntWW 93*
Bergman, Terrie 1942- *WhoWest 94*
Bergmann, Barbara Rose 1927- *IntWW 93, WhoAm 94*
Bergmann, Charles Arnold 1938- *WhoWest 94*
Bergmann, Felix 1908- *IntWW 93*
Bergmann, Fred Heinz 1928- *WhoAm 94*
Bergmann, Fred Warren 1948- *WhoFI 94*
Bergmann, Fredrick Louis 1916- *WhoAm 94*
Bergmann, Martin *WhoHol 92*
Bergmann, Peter George 1949- *WhoAm 94, WhoAmL 94*
Bergmann, Richard Ronald 1935- *WhoAm 94*
Bergner, Elisabeth d1986 *WhoHol 92*
Bergner, Lanny Michael 1952- *WhoAmA 93*
Bergner, Mark 1963- *WhoMW 93*
Bergo, Conrad Hunter 1943- *WhoScEn 94*
Bergo, Edward Arthur 1938- *WhoWest 94*
Bergofsky, Edward Harold d1993 *NewYTBS 93*
Bergold, Harry E., Jr. 1931- *WhoAmP 93*
Bergold, Harry Earl, Jr. 1931- *WhoAm 94*
Bergold, Orm 1925- *WhoScEn 94*
Bergonia, Raymond David 1951- *WhoAm 94*
Bergonzi, Bernard 1929- *Who 94, WrDr 94*
Bergonzi, Carlo 1924- *IntWW 93, NewGrDO, WhoAm 94*
Bergonzi, Frank Michael 1945- *WhoFI 94*
Bergquist, Barry Darril 1945- *WhoAmP 93*
Bergquist, Gene Alfred 1927- *WhoMW 93*
Bergquist, Gordon Neil 1932- *WhoAm 94*
Bergquist, Jon David 1951- *WhoMW 93*
Bergquist, Patricia Rose 1933- *IntWW 93*
Bergreen, Laurence 1950- *WrDr 94*
Bergreen, Laurence R. 1950- *ConAu 42NR*
Berg-Ridenour, Sherryl Lee 1963- *WhoWest 94*
Bergrun, Norman Riley 1921- *WhoScEn 94*
Bergs, William F. 1947- *WhoIns 94*
Bergsagel, Ernest 1955- *WhoAmP 93*
Bergsagel, John Dagfinn 1928- *IntWW 93*
Bergsma, Daniel 1909- *WhoAm 94*
Bergsma, William (Laurence) 1921- *NewGrDO*
Bergsma, William Laurence 1921- *WhoAm 94, WhoWest 94*
Bergsmark, Edwin Martin 1941- *WhoAm 94, WhoMW 93*
Bergsoe, Vilhelm *EncSF 93*
Bergson, Abram 1914- *IntWW 93, WhoAm 94, WhoFI 94, WrDr 94*
Bergson, Brian 1964- *WhoAmP 93*
Bergson, Henry Paul 1942- *WhoFI 94*
Bergson, Maria *WhoAm 94*
Bergstein, Daniel Gerard 1943- *WhoAm 94, WhoAmL 94*
Bergstein, Eleanor *DrAPF 93*
Bergstein, Harry Benjamin 1916- *WhoAm 94*
Bergsteiner, Harald 1944- *WhoScEn 94*
Bergsten, C. Fred 1941- *WhoAm 94, WhoAmP 93*
Bergstrand, Wilton Everet 1909- *WhoAm 94*
Bergstresser, Marta *EncSF 93*
Bergstrom, Betty Howard 1931- *WhoMW 93*
Bergstrom, Carl Philip 1957- *WhoMW 93*
Bergstrom, Dedric Waldemar 1919- *WhoAm 94*
Bergstrom, Edith Harrod *WhoAmA 93*
Bergstrom, Edith Harrod 1941- *WhoWest 94*
Bergstrom, Elaine 1946- *WhoAmP 93*
Bergstrom, K. Sune D. 1916- *WhoScEn 94*
Bergstrom, Kristin M. 1948- *WhoAmL 94*
Bergstrom, Lars 1935- *IntWW 93*
Bergstrom, Nathan Hough 1895- *WhAm 10*
Bergstrom, Richard Norman 1921- *WhoAm 94*
Bergstrom, Robert William 1918- *WhoAm 94, WhoAmL 94*
Bergstrom, Rolf Olof Bernhard 1934- *WhoFI 94*
Bergstrom, Sten Rudolf 1934- *WhoScEn 94*
Bergstrom, Stig Magnus 1935- *WhoAm 94*
Bergstrom, Sune 1916- *Who 94*
Bergsund, Richard T. 1927- *WhoIns 94*
Bergt, (Christian Gottlob) August 1771-1837 *NewGrDO*
Berguland, William d1958 *WhoHol 92*
Bergus, Donald Clayton 1920- *WhoAmP 93*
Berguson, Robert Jenkins 1944- *WhoAmA 93*
Berhang, Mattie *WhoAmA 93*
Berhard, Richard J., Mrs. *WhoAmA 93N*
Berhe, Annette Toney *WhoBlA 94*
Beria, Lavrenti 1899-1953 *HisWorL [port]*
Beric, Berislav 1927- *IntWW 93*
Berick, James Herschel 1933- *WhoAm 94*
Bering, Vitus Jonassen 1681-1741 *WhWE*
Beringer, Esme d1972 *WhoHol 92*
Beringer, John Evelyn 1944- *Who 94*
Beringer, Stuart Marshall 1923- *WhoAm 94*
Beringer, William Ernst 1928- *WhoAm 94*
Beringhaus, Kerry Lee 1950- *WhoAmL 94*
Berini, Mario d1993 *NewYTBS 93*
Berinstein, William Paul 1935- *WhoFI 94*
Berio, Luciano 1925- *IntWW 93, NewGrDO, WhoAm 94*
Berio, Luciano 1977- *Who 94*
Beriosoff, Nicholas 1906- *IntDcB [port]*
Beriosova, Svetlana 1932- *IntDcB [port], IntWW 93*
Beriozoff, Nicholas 1906- *IntDcB [port]*
Beriozova, Svetlana 1932- *Who 94*
Berisavljevic, Zivan 1935- *Who 94*
Berisha, Sali 1944- *IntWW 93*
Beristain, Leopoldo d1948 *WhoHol 92*
Beristain, Luis d1962 *WhoHol 92*
Beritich, Michael Lester 1960- *WhoWest 94*
Berk, Alan S. 1934- *WhoAm 94*
Berk, Allen Joel 1940- *WhoAm 94*
Berk, Ann E. *WhoAm 94*
Berk, Harlan Joseph 1942- *WhoMW 93*
Berk, Howard 1926- *EncSF 93*
Berk, Jack Edward *WhoAm 94*
Berk, James Lawrence, II 1960- *WhoFI 94*
Berk, Jeremiah E. 1941- *WhoAm 94*
Berk, Kenneth Nathan 1938- *WhoMW 93*
Berk, Paul David 1938- *WhoAm 94*
Berk, Peggy Faith 1951- *WhoFI 94*
Berk, Sara d1975 *WhoHol 92*
Berk, Steven Lee 1949- *WhoAm 94*
Berke, Amy Turner 1942- *WhoMW 93*
Berke, Ed *WhoHol 92*
Berke, Judith A. *DrAPF 93*
Berke, Nancy *DrAPF 93*
Berke, Roberta 1943- *ConAu 43NR*
Berkel, Charles John 1925- *WhoFI 94, WhoMW 93*
Berkeley, Baron 1939- *Who 94*
Berkeley, Baroness d1992 *Who 94N*
Berkeley, Alan J. 1942- *WhoAmL 94*
Berkeley, Arthur d1962 *WhoHol 92*
Berkeley, Ballard d1988 *WhoHol 92*
Berkeley, Bernard 1923- *WhoMW 93*
Berkeley, Busby d1976 *WhoHol 92*
Berkeley, Charles, Earl of Falmouth 1630-1665 *DcNaB MP*
Berkeley, Edmund 1912- *WrDr 94*
Berkeley, Frederic George 1919- *Who 94*
Berkeley, George 1685-1753 *BlmGEL*
Berkeley, Gertrude d1946 *WhoHol 92*
Berkeley, Humphry John 1926- *Who 94*
Berkeley, Jill Brenda 1950- *WhoAmL 94*
Berkeley, Lennox (Randal Francis) 1903-1989 *NewGrDO*
Berkeley, Marvin H. 1922- *WhoAm 94*
Berkeley, Michael Fitzhardinge 1948- *IntWW 93, Who 94*
Berkeley, Norbonne *WhAmRev*
Berkeley, Sara 1967- *BlmGWL*
Berkeley, Xander *WhoHol 92*
Berkeley Milne, Alexander *Who 94*
Berkelman, Karl 1933- *WhoAm 94, WhoScEn 94*
Berkelman, Thomas Roger 1949- *WhoAmP 93*
Berkenhout, John c. 1730-1801 *WhAmRev*
Berkenkamp, Fred Julius 1925- *WhoAm 94*
Berkenstadt, James Allan 1956- *WhoMW 93*
Berkery, Dermot Joseph 1964- *WhoFI 94*
Berkery, Michael John 1945- *WhoAm 94*
Berkes, Howard 1954- *WhoAm 94*
Berkes, John d1951 *WhoHol 92*
Berkes, Leslie John 1946- *WhoWest 94*
Berkes, Milton 1924- *WhoAmP 93*
Berkey, Jonathan P. 1959- *ConAu 140*
Berkhemer-Credaire, Betsy 1947- *WhoAm 94*
Berkhouwer, Cornelis 1919- *Who 94*
Berking, Max 1917- *WhoAmP 93*
Berklavs, Eduards 1914- *IntWW 93*
Berkley, Burton 1934- *WhoAmL 94*
Berkley, Constance E. *DrAPF 93*
Berkley, Constance Elaine 1931- *WhoBlA 94*
Berkley, E. Carolan 1950- *WhoAm 94*
Berkley, Eugene Bertram 1923- *WhoAm 94*
Berkley, Gary L. 1943- *WhoAm 94*
Berkley, James Donald 1950- *WhoAm 94*
Berkley, Peter Lee 1939- *WhoAm 94*
Berkley, Richard 1931- *WhoAmP 93*
Berkley, Robert John 1933- *WhoWest 94*
Berkley, Stephen Mark 1944- *WhoAm 94, WhoFI 94, WhoWest 94*
Berkley, Thomas Lucius 1915- *WhoBlA 94*
Berkley, William R. 1945- *WhoIns 94*
Berkley, William Robert 1945- *WhoAm 94, WhoFI 94*
Berkman, Aaron 1900-1991 *WhoAmA 93N*
Berkman, Claire Fleet 1942- *WhoMW 93*
Berkman, Craig Lamont 1941- *WhoAmP 93*
Berkman, Harold William 1926- *WhoAm 94*
Berkman, Jack Neville 1905- *WhoAm 94, WhoFI 94*
Berkman, Lillian *WhoAm 94, WhoAmA 93*
Berkman, Marsha Lee *DrAPF 93*
Berkman, Marshall L. 1936- *WhoAm 94*
Berkman, Michael G. 1917- *WhoAm 94*
Berkman, Richard Lyle 1946- *WhoAm 94, WhoAmL 94*
Berkman, Susan C. Josephs 1953- *WhoWest 94*
Berkman, Sylvia *DrAPF 93*
Berkman, William Roger 1928- *WhoAm 94, WhoAmL 94*
Berkner, Klaus Hans 1938- *WhoAm 94*
Berko, Ferenc 1916- *WhoAm 94, WhoAmA 93*
Berko, Stephan 1924-1991 *WhAm 10*
Berkoff, Charles Edward 1932- *WhoAm 94*
Berkoff, David *WhoAm 94*
Berkoff, Marshall Richard 1937- *WhoAm 94*
Berkoff, Steven 1937- *ConDr 93, IntDcT 2 [port], IntMPA 94, IntWW 93, Who 94, WhoHol 92*
Berkoff, Steven 1939- *WrDr 94*
Berkon, Martin 1932- *WhoAmA 93*
Berkos, Christy S. 1926- *WhoAmP 93*
Berkovec, Jiri 1922- *NewGrDO*
Berkovich, Gary A. 1935- *WhoAm 94*
Berkovitch, Boris S. 1921- *WhoAm 94*
Berkovitz, Jay R. 1951- *WrDr 94*
Berkow, David Willard 1957- *WhoFI 94*
Berkow, Ira Harvey 1940- *WhoAm 94*
Berkowitz, Bernard Joseph 1945- *WhoAmL 94*
Berkowitz, Bernard Solomon 1930- *WhoAm 94*
Berkowitz, David J. 1941- *WhoAmP 93*
Berkowitz, Emily Sue 1954- *WhoFI 94*
Berkowitz, Gerald Zarach 1932- *WhoAmL 94*
Berkowitz, Henry 1857-1924 *DcAmReB 2*
Berkowitz, Henry 1933- *WhoAmA 93*
Berkowitz, Jonathan Mark *DrAPF 93*
Berkowitz, Joseph 1930- *WhoMW 93*
Berkowitz, Lawrence M. 1941- *WhoAm 94*
Berkowitz, Leonard 1926- *WhoAm 94*
Berkowitz, Michael 1959- *WhoMW 93*
Berkowitz, Michael H. *WhoIns 94*
Berkowitz, Michael Harold 1942- *WhoAm 94*
Berkowitz, Monroe 1919- *WrDr 94*
Berkowitz, Paul 1948- *WhoAmL 94*
Berkowitz, Philip Joseph 1965- *WhoAmL 94*
Berkowitz, Roger M. 1944- *WhoAmA 93*
Berkowitz, Terry *WhoAmA 93*
Berkowitz, William R(obby) 1939- *ConAu 43NR*
Berkshire, Archdeacon of *Who 94*
Berkshire, Steven David 1947- *WhoWest 94*
Berkson, Bill *DrAPF 93*
Berkson, Bill 1939- *WhoAmA 93, WrDr 94*
Berkson, Burton Martin 1939- *WhoWest 94*
Berkson, David Mayer 1934- *Who 94*
Berkson, Jacob Benjamin 1925- *WhoAmL 94*
Berkson, Robert Gary 1939- *WhoFI 94*
Berkson, William Craig 1939- *WhoWest 94*
Berkstresser, Jerry William 1934- *WhoAmL 94*
Berkus, David William 1941- *WhoWest 94*
Berkwitt, George Joseph 1921- *WhoAm 94*
Berl, Joseph M. 1942- *WhoAm 94, WhoAmL 94*
Berlack, Evan Raden 1934- *WhoAm 94*
Berlad, Abraham Leon 1921- *WhoWest 94*
Berlage, Gai Ingham 1943- *WhoAm 94*
Berland, Abel Edward 1915- *WhoAm 94*
Berland, David I. 1947- *WhoMW 93*
Berland, Howard *DrAPF 93*
Berland, James Fred 1943- *WhoAm 94*
Berland, Karen Ina 1947- *WhoAm 94*
Berlandier, Jean-Louis c. 1805-1851 *WhWE*
Berlanga, David, Jr. 1943- *WhoHisp 94*
Berlanga, Hugo 1948- *WhoAmP 93, WhoHisp 94*
Berlant, Anthony 1941- *WhoAm 94*
Berlant, Tony 1941- *WhoAmA 93*
Berlat, William Leonard 1937- *WhoAmL 94*
Berle, Beatrice Bishop 1902-1993 *ConAu 141, NewYTBS 93*
Berle, Gustav 1920- *ConAu 140*
Berle, Jack d1985 *WhoHol 92*
Berle, Milton 1908- *IntMPA 94, WhoAm 94, WhoCom [port], WhoHol 92*
Berle, Peter Adolf Augustus 1937- *WhoAm 94, WhoAmL 94, WhoScEn 94*
Berleant, Arnold 1932- *WhoAm 94*
Berlekamp, Elwyn Ralph 1940- *WhoAm 94*
Berlepsch, Emilie von 1755-1830 *BlmGWL*
Berlew, Frank Kingston 1930- *WhoAm 94*
Berley, Andre d1936 *WhoHol 92*
Berley, David Richard 1942- *WhoAmL 94*
Berliet, Paul 1918- *IntWW 93*
Berlin, Alan Daniel 1939- *WhoAm 94, WhoAmL 94, WhoFI 94*
Berlin, Andrew Mark *WhoAm 94*
Berlin, Beatrice Winn 1922- *WhoAm 94, WhoAmA 93*
Berlin, Byron Sanford 1921- *WhoMW 93*
Berlin, Charles I. 1933- *WhoScEn 94*
Berlin, Don R. 1898- *WhAm 10*
Berlin, Emily 1947- *WhoAm 94, WhoAmL 94*
Berlin, Fred Saul 1941- *WhoAm 94*
Berlin, Howard Richard 1935- *WhoAm 94, WhoFI 94*
Berlin, Irving d1989 *WhoHol 92*
Berlin, Irving 1888-1989 *AmCulL [port], IntDcF 2-4, NewGrDO, WhAm 10*
Berlin, Isaiah 1909- *IntWW 93, Who 94*
Berlin, Isaiah, Sir 1909- *WrDr 94*
Berlin, Jeannie 1949- *WhoHol 92*
Berlin, Jordan Stuart 1952- *WhoAm 94, WhoFI 94*
Berlin, Kenneth 1947- *WhoAm 94*
Berlin, Kenneth Darrell 1933- *WhoAm 94*
Berlin, Lorna Chumley 1938- *WhoAm 94*
Berlin, Lucia 1936- *DcLB 130 [port]*
Berlin, Mark A. 1944- *WhoAmL 94*
Berlin, Meredith Rise 1955- *WhoAm 94*
Berlin, Norman B. 1954- *WhoAmL 94*
Berlin, Richard Barnard, Jr. 1948- *WhoFI 94*
Berlin, Stanton Henry 1934- *WhoAm 94*
Berlin, Steven Benjamin 1949- *WhoAm 94*
Berlin, Steven Ritt 1944- *WhoAm 94, WhoFI 94*
Berlind, Bruce *DrAPF 93*
Berlind, Bruce Peter 1926- *WhoAm 94*
Berlind, Robert 1938- *WhoAmA 93*
Berlind, Robert Elliot 1938- *WhoAm 94*
Berlind, Roger Stuart 1930- *WhoAm 94*
Berline, James H. 1946- *WhoAm 94*
Berliner, Allen Irwin 1947- *WhoAm 94*
Berliner, Emile 1851-1929 *WorInv*

Berliner, Ernst 1915- *WhoAm 94*
Berliner, Hans Jack 1929- *WhoAm 94, WhoScEn 94*
Berliner, Henry A., Jr. 1934- *WhoAmP 93*
Berliner, Herman Albert 1944- *WhoAm 94*
Berliner, Joseph Scholom 1921- *WhoAm 94*
Berliner, Lawrence 1941- *WhoMW 93*
Berliner, Martin d1966 *WhoHol 92*
Berliner, Patricia Mary 1946- *WhoAm 94*
Berliner, Robert W. 1915- *IntWW 93*
Berliner, Robert W., Jr. 1945- *WhoAmL 94, WhoMW 93*
Berliner, Robert William 1915- *WhoAm 94*
Berliner, Ruth Shirley 1928- *WhoAm 94, WhoFI 94*
Berliner, William Michael 1923- *WhoAm 94, WhoFI 94*
Berling, John George 1934- *WhoAm 94*
Berlinger, Warren 1937- *IntMPA 94, WhoAm 94, WhoHol 92*
Berlins, Marcel Joseph 1941- *Who 94*
Berlioz, Georges Louis 1943- *WhoAmL 94, WhoFI 94*
Berlioz, (Louis-)Hector 1803-1869 *NewGrDO*
Berlo, Robert Christopher 1941- *WhoWest 94*
Berlow, Robert Alan 1947- *WhoAm 94*
Berlowitz Tarrant, Laurence 1934- *WhoAm 94*
Berlusconi, Silvio 1936- *IntWW 93*
Berlyn, Ivan d1934 *WhoHol 92*
Berlyn, Michael (Steven) 1949- *EncSF 93*
Berlyn, Sheldon 1929- *WhoAmA 93*
Berman, Aaron 1922- *WhoAmA 93*
Berman, Alan 1925- *WhoAm 94*
Berman, Alexander Leonid 1960- *WhoMW 93*
Berman, Allan 1940- *WhoAm 94*
Berman, Ariane R. 1937- *WhoAm 94, WhoAmA 93*
Berman, Arthur Leonard 1935- *WhoAmP 93, WhoMW 93*
Berman, Arthur Malcolm 1935- *WhoAm 94*
Berman, Barbara P. 1938- *WhoAmP 93*
Berman, Barnett 1922- *WhoAm 94*
Berman, Barry David 1937- *WhoAm 94*
Berman, Baruch 1925- *WhoWest 94*
Berman, Bennett I. 1918- *WhoAm 94*
Berman, Bernard 1920- *WhoAmA 93*
Berman, Bruce *WhoAm 94, WhoFI 94*
Berman, Bruce Judson 1946- *WhoAm 94, WhoAmL 94*
Berman, Carol 1923- *WhoAmP 93*
Berman, Cassia *DrAPF 93*
Berman, Claire 1936- *WrDr 94*
Berman, Constance Ann Hoffman *WhoMW 93*
Berman, Daniel Katzel 1954- *WhoFI 94, WhoWest 94*
Berman, Daniel Lewis 1934- *WhoAm 94*
Berman, David 1934- *WhoAm 94, WhoAmL 94*
Berman, David 1942- *WrDr 94*
Berman, David Allan 1950- *WhoFI 94*
Berman, Edward David 1941- *Who 94*
Berman, Edward Henry 1940- *WhoAm 94*
Berman, Eleanore 1928- *WhoAm 94, WhoAmA 93, WhoWest 94*
Berman, Eli 1960- *WhoFI 94*
Berman, Elihu H. 1922- *WhoAmL 94*
Berman, Ellen Mercil Trew 1946- *WhoAmA 93*
Berman, Eugene 1899-1972 *NewGrDO, WhoAmA 93N*
Berman, Franklin Delow 1939- *Who 94*
Berman, Fred J. 1926- *WhoAmA 93*
Berman, Fred Jean 1926- *WhoAm 94*
Berman, Greta W. *WhoAmA 93*
Berman, Henry Stephen 1942- *WhoAmL 94*
Berman, Herbert E. 1933- *WhoAmP 93*
Berman, Howard Allen 1949- *WhoAm 94, WhoMW 93*
Berman, Howard James 1945- *WhoAm 94*
Berman, Howard L. 1941- *CngDr 93, WhoAmP 93*
Berman, Howard Lawrence 1941- *WhoAm 94, WhoWest 94*
Berman, Jeffrey 1945- *WrDr 94*
Berman, Joanna *WhoAm 94*
Berman, John Arthur 1932- *WhoAmP 93*
Berman, Joshua Mordecai 1938- *WhoAm 94, WhoAmL 94*
Berman, Judith Gabriella 1957- *WhoMW 93*
Berman, Julius 1935- *WhoAm 94*
Berman, Kenneth R. 1952- *WhoAmL 94*
Berman, Laura 1953- *WhoAm 94*
Berman, Lawrence Sam 1928- *Who 94*
Berman, Lazar 1930- *WhoAm 94*
Berman, Leo 1917- *WhoMW 93*
Berman, Lewis Paul 1937- *WhoAm 94*
Berman, Linda Fran 1952- *WhoAmL 94*
Berman, Louise Marguerite 1928- *WhoAm 94*
Berman, Malcolm Frank 1941- *WhoAm 94*
Berman, Marcelo Samuel 1945- *WhoAm 94, WhoScEn 94*
Berman, Mark Laurence 1940- *WhoWest 94*
Berman, Marlene Oscar 1939- *WhoAm 94, WhoScEn 94*
Berman, Marshall Fox 1939- *WhoAm 94*
Berman, Marshall Howard 1940- *WhoAm 94*
Berman, Maxine 1946- *WhoAmP 93*
Berman, Mervyn Clive 1934- *WhoScEn 94*
Berman, Michael Alan 1965- *WhoAmL 94*
Berman, Michael Allan 1957- *WhoScEn 94*
Berman, Milton 1924- *WhoAm 94*
Berman, Mira 1928- *WhoAm 94*
Berman, Mitch 1956- *WrDr 94*
Berman, Mona S. 1925- *WhoAm 94*
Berman, Monty M. 1912- *IntMPA 94*
Berman, Muriel Mallin *WhoAm 94*
Berman, Muriel Mallin 1924- *WhoAmA 93*
Berman, Myles Lee 1954- *WhoAmL 94*
Berman, Neil Sheldon 1933- *WhoAm 94, WhoScEn 94*
Berman, Pandro S. 1905- *IntDcF 2-4, IntMPA 94*
Berman, Paul J. 1951- *WhoAm 94, WhoAmL 94*
Berman, Philip I. 1915- *WhoAm 94, WhoAmA 93*
Berman, Philip M. 1934- *WhoAmL 94*
Berman, Rhoda Gelfond *DrAPF 93*
Berman, Richard Angel 1945- *WhoAm 94*
Berman, Richard Bruce 1951- *WhoAmL 94*
Berman, Richard L. d1993 *NewYTBS 93*
Berman, Richard Miles 1943- *WhoAm 94, WhoAmL 94*
Berman, Robert S. 1932- *WhoAm 94*
Berman, Ronald Charles 1949- *WhoAmL 94*
Berman, Rosalind *WhoAmP 93*
Berman, Sanford 1933- *WrDr 94*
Berman, Saul J. 1946- *WhoWest 94*
Berman, Shelley 1926- *WhoCom, WhoHol 92*
Berman, Sidney 1908- *WhoAm 94*
Berman, Simeon Moses 1935- *WhoAm 94*
Berman, Sonny d1947 *WhoHol 92*
Berman, Stanley 1934- *WhoFI 94*
Berman, Stanley Miles 1947- *WhoFI 94*
Berman, Steve William 1954- *WhoAmL 94, WhoWest 94*
Berman, Steven H. 1952- *IntMPA 94*
Berman, Steven Joel 1950- *WhoFI 94*
Berman, Steven Mark 1949- *WhoWest 94*
Berman, Steven Richard 1947- *WhoFI 94, WhoWest 94*
Berman, Susan *WhoHol 92*
Berman, Tony 1933- *WhoAmL 94*
Berman, Vivian 1928- *WhoAmA 93*
Berman, William H. 1936- *WhoAm 94, WhoFI 94*
Berman, Yitzhak 1913- *IntWW 93*
Berman, Zeke *WhoAmA 93*
Bermange, Barry 1933- *ConDr 93, ConTFT 11, WrDr 94*
Berman-Hammer, Susan 1950- *WhoFI 94, WhoMW 93*
Bermann, George Alan 1945- *WhoAm 94*
Bermant, Chaim (Icyk) 1929- *WrDr 94*
Bermant, Chaim Icyk 1929- *Who 94*
Bermant, David W. 1919- *WhoAmA 93*
Bermant, George Wilson 1926- *WhoAm 94, WhoAmL 94*
Bermas, Stephen 1925- *WhoAm 94, WhoAmL 94*
Bermello, Willy A. *WhoHisp 94*
Bermeo, Nancy 1951- *WrDr 94*
Bermingham, Ann 1948- *WhoAmA 93*
Bermingham, Debra Pandell 1953- *WhoAmA 93*
Bermingham, Gerald Edward 1940- *Who 94*
Bermingham, John C. 1920- *WhoAmA 93*
Bermingham, Joseph Daniel 1938- *WhoAmL 94*
Bermingham, Peter *WhoWest 94*
Bermingham, Peter 1937- *WhoAmA 93*
Bermingham, Richard P. 1939- *WhoFI 94*
Bermuda, Bishop of 1934- *Who 94*
Bermudez, Diana *WhoHisp 94*
Bermudez, Eugenia M. *WhoAmA 93*
Bermudez, Eugenia M. 1932- *WhoAm 94*
Bermúdez, Gloria 1930- *WhoHisp 94*
Bermudez, Jesse 1943- *WhoHisp 94*
Bermudez, Jorge Alberto 1951- *WhoFI 94*
Bermudez, Jose Ygnacio 1922- *WhoAmA 93*
Bermudez, Juan 1941- *WhoHisp 94*
Bermudez, Luis A. 1953- *WhoAmA 93*
Bermudez, Manuel Enrique 1957- *WhoHisp 94*
Bermudez Colom, Helcias Daniel 1947- *WhoHisp 94*
Bern, Howard Alan 1920- *IntWW 93, WhoAm 94*
Bern, Lars A. V. 1942- *IntWW 93*
Bern, Marc Jay 1950- *WhoAmL 94*
Bern, Murray Morris 1944- *WhoScEn 94*
Bern, Ronald Lawrence 1936- *WhoAm 94, WhoFI 94*
Bern, Victoria 1908-1992 *ConLC 76 [port]*
Bernabe, Amalia d1983 *WhoHol 92*
Bernabé, Teresa 1970- *WhoHisp 94*
Bernabei, Giuseppe Antonio 1649?-1732 *NewGrDO*
Bernabei, Vincenzo 1660-1736? *See* Bernabei, Giuseppe Antonio 1649?-1732 *NewGrDO*
Bernabel, Ettore 1921- *IntWW 93*
Bernabo-Brea, Luigi 1910- *IntWW 93*
Bernabucci, John R., Jr. 1930- *WhoAmP 93*
Bernacchi, Antonio Maria 1685-1756 *NewGrDO [port]*
Bernacchi, Guy A. 1941- *WhoMW 93*
Bernacchi, Richard Lloyd 1938- *WhoAm 94*
Bernadotte, (Gustaf) Lennart (Nicolaus Paul) 1909- *IntWW 93*
Bernadotte, Sigvard Oscar Fredrik 1907- *IntWW 93*
Bernal, Armando, Jr. *WhoHisp 94*
Bernal, Emilia 1884-1964 *BlmGWL*
Bernal, Ernesto M. 1938- *WhoHisp 94*
Bernal, Gilbert J., Jr. 1950- *WhoAmL 94*
Bernal, Harriet Jean Daniels 1931- *WhoWest 94*
Bernal, Henrietta *WhoHisp 94*
Bernal, Ignacio 1910- *WhAm 10*
Bernal, Ivan 1931- *WhoHisp 94*
Bernal, Jesus Rodriguez 1953- *WhoHisp 94*
Bernal, Joe J. 1927- *WhoAmP 93*
Bernal, Louis Carlos 1941- *WhoAmA 93*
Bernal, Lynda Evelyn 1959- *WhoWest 94*
Bernal, Margarita Solano 1954- *WhoHisp 94*
Bernal, Martha E. 1931- *WhoHisp 94*
Bernal, Mike *WhoHisp 94*
Bernal, Philip Vincent 1944- *WhoHisp 94*
Bernal, Robert d1973 *WhoHol 92*
Bernal Jimenez, Miguel 1910-1956 *NewGrDO*
Bernal-Pereira, Waldo 1934- *Who 94*
Bernal y del Rio, Victor 1917- *WhoHisp 94*
Bernard, Al d1949 *WhoHol 92*
Bernard, Alexander 1952- *WhoWest 94*
Bernard, Andre 1956- *WrDr 94*
Bernard, April *DrAPF 93*
Bernard, April 1956- *WrDr 94*
Bernard, Barney d1924 *WhoHol 92*
Bernard, Barry d1978 *WhoHol 92*
Bernard, Bryce Allison 1960- *WhoWest 94*
Bernard, Canute Clive 1924- *WhoBlA 94*
Bernard, Carl d1972 *WhoHol 92*
Bernard, Catherine 1662-1712 *BlmGWL*
Bernard, Cathy S. 1949- *WhoFI 94*
Bernard, Christopher *DrAPF 93*
Bernard, Claire Marie Anne 1947- *IntWW 93*
Bernard, Claude 1813-1878 *WorScD*
Bernard, Crystal 1959- *WhoHol 92*
Bernard, Dale Anthony 1959- *WhoAmL 94*
Bernard, Dallas (Edmund) 1926- *Who 94*
Bernard, David A. 1945- *WhoFI 94*
Bernard, David Edwin 1913- *WhoAmA 93*
Bernard, David George 1921- *WhoAm 94*
Bernard, Dennis Orrin 1944- *WhoAm 94*
Bernard, Dick d1925 *WhoHol 92*
Bernard, Donald Ray 1932- *WhoAmL 94, WhoFI 94*
Bernard, Donald Ray 1936- *WhoAmP 93*
Bernard, Dorothy d1955 *WhoHol 92*
Bernard, Ed *WhoHol 92*
Bernard, Eddie Nolan 1946- *WhoAm 94, WhoScEn 94, WhoWest 94*
Bernard, Francis 1712-1779 *WhAmRev*
Bernard, Frank Charles 1908- *WhoAm 94, WhoAmL 94, WhoMW 93*
Bernard, H. Russell 1940- *WhoAm 94*
Bernard, Harold O. 1938- *WhoBlA 94*
Bernard, Harry d1940 *WhoHol 92*
Bernard, Henry 1912- *IntWW 93*
Bernard, Herbert Fritz 1957- *WhoScEn 94*
Bernard, Jacques Niels 1938- *WhoFI 94*
Bernard, James 1925- *IntDcF 2-4*
Bernard, James William 1937- *WhoAm 94, WhoFI 94, WhoWest 94*
Bernard, Jami 1956- *WhoAm 94*
Bernard, Jason *WhoHol 92*
Bernard, Jeffrey Joseph 1932- *Who 94*
Bernard, Joan Constance 1918- *Who 94*
Bernard, Joan Kovalic 1948- *WhoAmL 94*
Bernard, John 1883- *EncSF 93*
Bernard, John Marley 1941- *WhoAm 94, WhoAmL 94*
Bernard, John P. 1958- *WhoScEn 94*
Bernard, Kenneth *DrAPF 93*
Bernard, Kenneth 1930- *ConDr 93, WhoAm 94, WrDr 94*
Bernard, Lewis W. *WhoAm 94*
Bernard, Louis Joseph 1925- *WhoAm 94, WhoBlA 94*
Bernard, Lowell Francis 1931- *WhoAm 94*
Bernard, Lucien 1913- *IntWW 93*
Bernard, Marcel 1914- *BuCMET*
Bernard, Marvin A. 1934- *IntMPA 94*
Bernard, Mary E. 1908- *WhoAmP 93*
Bernard, Michael Anthony 1937- *WrDr 94*
Bernard, Michael Mark 1926- *WhoAmL 94*
Bernard, Michelle Denise 1963- *WhoAmL 94, WhoBlA 94*
Bernard, Nesta Hyacinth *WhoBlA 94*
Bernard, Oliver 1925- *WrDr 94*
Bernard, Oliver Percy 1881-1939 *DcNaB MP*
Bernard, Paul d1958 *WhoHol 92*
Bernard, Paul T. 1951- *WhoAmP 93*
Bernard, Peter d1960 *WhoHol 92*
Bernard, Peter Alan 1936- *WhoAmL 94, WhoWest 94*
Bernard, Pierre-Joseph 1708-1775 *NewGrDO*
Bernard, Rafe *EncSF 93*
Bernard, Raymond d1977 *WhoHol 92*
Bernard, Richard Lawson 1926- *WhoAm 94*
Bernard, Richard Phillip 1950- *WhoAm 94*
Bernard, Rita d1988 *WhoHol 92*
Bernard, Robert 1918- *WrDr 94*
Bernard, Ronald Allan 1953- *WhoScEn 94*
Bernard, Sam d1927 *WhoHol 92*
Bernard, Sam d1950 *WhoHol 92*
Bernard, Sharon Elaine 1943- *WhoAmL 94, WhoBlA 94, WhoMW 93*
Bernard, Thelma Rene *WhoWest 94*
Bernard, Viola Wertheim 1907- *WhoAm 94*
Bernard, Walter *WhoAm 94*
Bernardez, Gary Christopher 1963- *WhoWest 94*
Bernardez, Teresa 1931- *WhoHisp 94*
Bernardi, Ernani *WhoAmP 93*
Bernardi, Francesco *NewGrDO*
Bernardi, Herschel d1986 *WhoHol 92*
Bernardi, Jack *WhoHol 92*
Bernardi, James Edward 1946- *WhoMW 93*
Bernardi, John Lawrence, Jr. 1944- *WhoAm 94*
Bernardi, Mario 1930- *NewGrDO, WhoAm 94, WhoWest 94*
Bernardi, Nerio d1971 *WhoHol 92*
Bernardi, Theodore C. 1903-1990 *WhAm 10*
Bernardin, Joseph L. 1928- *IntWW 93*
Bernardin, Joseph Louis Cardinal 1928- *WhoAm 94, WhoMW 93*
Bernardin de Saint-Pierre, Jacques-Henri 1737-1814 *GuFrLit 2*
Bernardini, Isa 1943- *WhoAm 94*
Bernardini, Joe 1937- *WrDr 94*
Bernardini, Marcello 1730?-1799? *NewGrDO*
Bernardini, Orestes 1880-1957 *WhoAmA 93N*
Bernardo, Everett d1992 *WhoHisp 94N*
Bernardo, Jose Raul 1938- *WhoHisp 94*
Bernardo, Thomas Paul 1963- *WhoMW 93*
Bernard of Clairvaux 1090-1153 *HisWorL [port]*
Bernardon *NewGrDO*
Bernardone, Jeffrey John 1958- *WhoScEn 94*
Bernardoni, Pietro Antonio 1672-1714 *NewGrDO*
Bernard-Stevens, David L. 1951- *WhoAmP 93*
Bernasconi, Andrea 1706-1784 *NewGrDO*
Bernasconi, Anna Maria 1945- *WhoWomW 91*
Bernasconi, Antonia c. 1741-1803? *NewGrDO*
Bernasconi, Christian 1946- *WhoScEn 94*
Bernat, Eugene 1896- *WhAm 10*
Bernath, Otto Nicolaus 1932- *WhoMW 93*
Bernatowicz, Felix Jan Brzozowski 1920- *WhoFI 94, WhoScEn 94*
Bernatowicz, Frank Allen 1954- *WhoAm 94, WhoFI 94, WhoMW 93*
Bernau, Bill 1964- *WhoAmP 93*
Bernau, George (B.) 1945- *EncSF 93*
Bernau, Simon John 1937- *WhoAm 94*
Bernauer, Richard Martin 1957- *WhoMW 93*
Bernauer, Rudolf 1880-1953 *NewGrDO*
Bernay, Betti *WhoAmA 93*
Bernay, Betti 1926- *WhoAm 94*

Bernays, Anne *DrAPF 93*
Bernays, Anne Fleischman 1930- *WhoAm 94*
Bernays, Edward L. 1891- *WhoAm 94, WrDr 94*
Bernays, Peter Michael 1918- *WhoScEn 94*
Bernazard, Tony 1956- *WhoHisp 94*
Bernbach, John Lincoln 1944- *WhoAm 94, WhoFI 94*
Bernbaum, Gerald 1936- *Who 94*
Bernberg, Bruce Arthur 1943- *WhoAm 94*
Bernberg, Michael Nathan 1953- *WhoMW 93*
Berndt, Jerry W. 1943- *WhoAm 94, WhoAmA 93*
Berndt, Joan Gassaway 1936- *WhoMW 93*
Berndt, Jule F. *WhoAmP 93*
Berndt, Rexer 1920-1991 *WhAm 10*
Berndt, Robert J. 1918- *WhoAmP 93*
Berndt, Ronald Murray 1916- *WrDr 94*
Berndt, Walter 1900-1979 *WhoAmA 93N*
Berndt, William F. 1956- *WhoAmP 93*
Berne, Bruce J. 1940- *WhoAm 94*
Berne, Robert Matthew 1918- *IntWW 93, WhoAm 94*
Berne, Stanley *DrAPF 93*
Bernea, Horia Mihai 1938- *IntWW 93*
Berneche, Jerry Douglas 1932- *WhoAmA 93*
Bernee, Andrea Lorel 1960- *WhoWest 94*
Berneis, Kenneth Stanley 1951- *WhoMW 93*
Bernelle, Agnes *WhoHol 92*
Berner, David Leo 1938- *WhoMW 93*
Berner, Frederic George, Jr. 1943- *WhoAm 94, WhoAmL 94*
Berner, Gary *WhoAmP 93*
Berner, Jeff *DrAPF 93*
Berner, Leo De Witte, Jr. 1922- *WhoAm 94*
Berner, Norman Arthur 1910-1991 *WhAm 10*
Berner, Peter 1924- *IntWW 93*
Berner, Robert Arbuckle 1935- *WhoAm 94*
Berner, Robert Frank 1917- *WhoAm 94*
Berner, Robert Lee, Jr. 1931- *WhoAm 94*
Berner, T. Roland 1909-1990 *WhAm 10*
Bernerd, Elliott 1945- *Who 94*
Berners, Barony 1929- *Who 94*
Berners, Lord 1883-1950 *NewGrDO*
Berners, Edgar Hubert 1898- *WhAm 10*
Bernes, Julyans fl. 15th cent.- *BlmGWL*
Bernes, Mark d1969 *WhoHol 92*
Bernette, Sheila 1941- *WhoHol 92*
Berney, Bertram S. 1884- *WhoAmA 93N*
Berney, Joseph Henry 1932- *WhoAm 94*
Berney, Julian (Reedham Stuart) 1952- *Who 94*
Berney, Robert Edward 1932- *WhoWest 94*
Bernfeld, Peter Harry William 1912- *WhoAm 94*
Bernfield, Merton Ronald 1938- *WhoAm 94*
Bernhagen, John Joseph 1934- *WhoAmP 93*
Bernhagen, Lillian Flickinger 1916- *WhoAm 94*
Bernham, John Albert 1933- *WhoWest 94*
Bernhard, Alexander Alfred 1936- *WhoAm 94, WhoAmL 94*
Bernhard, Berl *WhoAm 94, WhoFI 94*
Bernhard, Berl 1929- *WhoAm 94, WhoAmL 94*
Bernhard, Gosta d1986 *WhoHol 92*
Bernhard, Harvey 1924- *IntMPA 94, WhoAm 94*
Bernhard, Herbert Ashley 1927- *WhoAm 94, WhoAmL 94*
Bernhard, Jon Casper 1961- *WhoWest 94*
Bernhard, Linda Anne 1947- *WhoMW 93*
Bernhard, Michael Ian 1944- *WhoScEn 94*
Bernhard, Robert Arthur 1928- *WhoAm 94*
Bernhard, Ruth 1905- *WhoAmA 93*
Bernhard, Sandra 1955- *IntMPA 94, WhoAm 94, WhoCom, WhoHol 92*
Bernhard, Thomas 1931-1989 *IntDcT 2 [port]*
Bernhard, William Francis 1924- *WhoAm 94*
Bernhardi, Sopie 1775-1833 *BlmGWL*
Bernhard Leopold Frederik Everhard J., H.R.H. Prince *IntWW 93*
Bernhardt, Arthur Dieter 1937- *WhoAm 94, WhoFI 94*
Bernhardt, Herbert Nelson *WhoAm 94*
Bernhardt, Jean Louise 1961- *WhoMW 93*
Bernhardt, John Bowman 1929- *WhoAm 94*
Bernhardt, Melvin *WhoAm 94*
Bernhardt, Michael Howard 1937- *WhoAmP 93*
Bernhardt, Peter 1943- *WhoAmL 94*
Bernhardt, Randy John 1962- *WhoMW 93*
Bernhardt, Robert *WhoAm 94, WhoWest 94*
Bernhardt, Roger 1934- *WhoAmL 94, WhoWest 94*
Bernhardt, Russ d1978 *WhoHol 92*
Bernhardt, Sarah d1923 *WhoHol 92*
Bernhardt-Kabisch, Ernest Karl-Heinz 1934- *WhoMW 93*
Bernheim, Elinor Kridel 1907-1992 *WhAm 10*
Bernheim, Stephanie Hammerschlag *WhoAmA 93*
Bernheimer, Alan *DrAPF 93*
Bernheimer, Charles 1942- *WrDr 94*
Bernheimer, Martin 1936- *NewGrDO, WhoAm 94, WhoWest 94*
Bern Heimer, Richard 1907-1958 *WhoAmA 93N*
Bernhoft, Franklin Otto *WhoWest 94*
Berni, Betty Catherine 1942- *WhoWest 94*
Bernicat, Firmin 1843-1883 *NewGrDO*
Bernick, David M. 1954- *WhoAm 94, WhoAmL 94*
Bernick, Howard Barry 1952- *WhoAm 94, WhoFI 94*
Bernie, Ben d1943 *WhoHol 92*
Bernie, Dick d1971 *WhoHol 92*
Bernier, Alexis 1956- *WrDr 94*
Bernier, George Matthew, Jr. 1934- *WhoAm 94*
Bernier, John Marshall 1965- *WhoFI 94*
Bernier, Paul-Emile 1911- *WhoWest 94*
Bernieri, Frank John 1961- *WhoScEn 94, WhoWest 94*
Bernikow, Louise *DrAPF 93*
Bernikow, Louise 1940- *WrDr 94*
Bernikow, Piedad A. *WhoAmL 94*
Berning, Gerald Louis 1965- *WhoFI 94*
Berning, Larry D. 1940- *WhoAm 94, WhoAmL 94*
Berninger, Virginia Wise 1946- *WhoWest 94*
Berninghaus, Oscar E. 1874-1952 *WhoAmA 93N*
Bernini, Carlo *IntWW 93*
Bernius, Mark T. 1957- *WhoScEn 94*
Bernius, Robert Charles 1946- *WhoAm 94, WhoAmL 94*
Bernlohr, Robert William 1933- *WhoAm 94*
Bernocco Garzanti, Luigina 1922- *WhoWomW 91*
Bernoco, Domenico 1935- *WhoScEn 94, WhoWest 94*
Bernoudy, James Logan 1919- *WhoBlA 94*
Bernoudy, Jane d1972 *WhoHol 92*
Bernoulli, Daniel 1700-1782 *WorScD*
Bernoulli, Jacques *WorScD*
Bernoulli, Jakob 1654-1705 *WorScD*
Bernoulli, Jean *WorScD*
Bernoulli, Johann *WorScD*
Bernoulli, Johann 1667-1748 *WorScD*
Berns, Donald Sheldon 1934- *WhoScEn 94*
Berns, Kenneth I. 1938- *IntWW 93*
Berns, Kenneth Ira 1938- *WhoAm 94, WhoScEn 94*
Berns, Michael W. 1942- *WhoScEn 94*
Berns, Pamela Kari 1947- *WhoAmA 93*
Berns, Peter Vernon 1956- *WhoAmL 94*
Berns, Philip Allan 1933- *WhoAmL 94*
Berns, Sheldon 1932- *WhoAmL 94*
Berns, Walter Fred 1919- *WhoAm 94*
Bernsen, Corbin 1954- *IntMPA 94, WhoHol 92*
Bernsen, Harold John 1936- *WhoAm 94*
Bernson, Hall *WhoAmP 93*
Bernstam, Mikhail S. 1943- *WrDr 94*
Bernstein, Baron d1993 *IntWW 93N, Who 94N*
Bernstein, Baron 1899- *IntWW 93*
Bernstein, Lord d1993 *NewYTBS 93*
Bernstein, Aaron 1904- *WhoFI 94*
Bernstein, Alan Arthur 1944- *WhoAm 94, WhoFI 94*
Bernstein, Alexander 1936- *Who 94*
Bernstein, Anne Elayne 1937- *WhoAm 94*
Bernstein, Armyan *IntMPA 94*
Bernstein, Arthur Harold 1925- *WhoFI 94*
Bernstein, Barton Jannen 1936- *WrDr 94*
Bernstein, Basil (Bernard) 1924- *WrDr 94*
Bernstein, Basil Bernard 1924- *Who 94*
Bernstein, Benjamin D. 1907- *WhoAmA 93*
Bernstein, Bernard 1915- *WhoScEn 94*
Bernstein, Bernard 1929- *WhoAm 94*
Bernstein, Blanche d1993 *NewYTBS 93 [port]*
Bernstein, Blanche 1912-1993 *ConAu 140*
Bernstein, Bob *IntMPA 94*
Bernstein, Bruce Lawrence 1956- *WhoWest 94*
Bernstein, Burton *DrAPF 93*
Bernstein, Burton 1932- *WrDr 94*
Bernstein, Carl 1944- *IntWW 93, WhoAm 94, WrDr 94*
Bernstein, Caryl Salomon 1933- *WhoAmL 94, WhoFI 94*
Bernstein, Charles *DrAPF 93*
Bernstein, Charles 1943- *ConTFT 11*
Bernstein, Charles 1950- *WrDr 94*
Bernstein, Charles Gerald 1939- *WhoAmL 94*
Bernstein, Charles Marc 1952- *WhoWest 94*
Bernstein, Daniel Lewis 1937- *WhoAm 94*
Bernstein, David 1910-1988 *WhAm 10*
Bernstein, David Allan 1952- *WhoFI 94*
Bernstein, Donald Chester 1942- *WhoAm 94*
Bernstein, Donald Scott 1953- *WhoAmL 94*
Bernstein, Edward I. 1917- *WhoAmA 93*
Bernstein, Edwin S. 1930- *WhoAm 94, WhoAmL 94*
Bernstein, Elliot Louis 1934- *WhoAm 94*
Bernstein, Elliot Roy 1941- *WhoAm 94, WhoScEn 94*
Bernstein, Elmer 1922- *ConTFT 11, IntDcF 2-4, IntMPA 94, WhoAm 94, WhoHol 92*
Bernstein, Emil Steven 1946- *WhoAm 94*
Bernstein, Eric Martin 1957- *WhoAmL 94*
Bernstein, Eugene Felix 1930- *WhoAm 94*
Bernstein, Eugene Merle 1931- *WhoAm 94*
Bernstein, Eva 1871-1958 *WhoAmA 93N*
Bernstein, Eva Gould 1918- *WhoMW 93*
Bernstein, Florence Henderson 1934- *WhoAm 94*
Bernstein, George *DrAPF 93*
Bernstein, George L. 1932- *WhoAm 94*
Bernstein, Gerald 1917- *WhoAmA 93*
Bernstein, Gerald William 1947- *WhoWest 94*
Bernstein, Gerda Meyer *WhoAmA 93*
Bernstein, H. Bruce 1943- *WhoAm 94, WhoAmL 94, WhoFI 94*
Bernstein, Harold Seth 1959- *WhoScEn 94*
Bernstein, Harris 1934- *WhoWest 94*
Bernstein, Harvey Michael 1945- *WhoAm 94*
Bernstein, Hilda 1915- *BlmGWL, WrDr 94*
Bernstein, Howard L. 1943- *WhoAm 94, WhoAmL 94*
Bernstein, I. Leonard 1924- *WhoAm 94, WhoMW 93*
Bernstein, Ingeborg 1931- *Who 94*
Bernstein, Ingrid *ConWorW 93*
Bernstein, Ira Borah 1924- *WhoAm 94*
Bernstein, Irving 1921- *WhoAm 94*
Bernstein, Irving Melvin 1938- *WhoAm 94*
Bernstein, Isadore Abraham 1919- *WhoAm 94, WhoMW 93*
Bernstein, Jack B. 1937- *IntMPA 94*
Bernstein, Jamie 1952- *WhoHol 92*
Bernstein, Jane *DrAPF 93*
Bernstein, Jay 1927- *WhoAm 94*
Bernstein, Jay 1937- *IntMPA 94*
Bernstein, Jay Harold 1962- *WhoAmL 94*
Bernstein, Jay S. 1942- *WhoAmP 93*
Bernstein, Jeffrey Alan 1959- *WhoMW 93*
Bernstein, Jeremy 1929- *WhoScEn 94*
Bernstein, Jeremy Marshall 1952- *WhoAmL 94*
Bernstein, Jonathan 1951- *WhoWest 94*
Bernstein, Joseph 1930- *WhoAmL 94, WhoFI 94*
Bernstein, Judith 1942- *WhoAmA 93*
Bernstein, Kenneth Alan 1956- *WhoAmL 94*
Bernstein, Larry Howard 1941- *WhoScEn 94*
Bernstein, Laurel 1945- *WhoAm 94*
Bernstein, Lawrence 1940- *WhoAm 94*
Bernstein, Leonard d1990 *WhoHol 92*
Bernstein, Leonard 1918-1990 *AmCulL, ConTFT 11, IntDcB [port], NewGrDO, WhAm 10*
Bernstein, Leroy G. *WhoAmP 93*
Bernstein, Lester 1920- *WhoAm 94*
Bernstein, Lewis Sol 1950- *WhoAmL 94*
Bernstein, Lisa *DrAPF 93*
Bernstein, Lori Robin 1958- *WhoScEn 94*
Bernstein, Louis 1927- *WhoAm 94*
Bernstein, Margaret Esther 1959- *WhoBlA 94*
Bernstein, Mark D. *WhoMW 93*
Bernstein, Marver Hillel 1919-1990 *WhAm 10*
Bernstein, Merton Clay 1923- *WhoAm 94, WhoAmL 94*
Bernstein, Mitchell Harris 1949- *WhoAm 94*
Bernstein, Paul 1927- *WhoAm 94*
Bernstein, Paul Murray 1929-1990 *WhAm 10*
Bernstein, Richard Allen 1946- *WhoAm 94, WhoFI 94*
Bernstein, Richard Barry 1923-1990 *WhAm 10*
Bernstein, Richard Kent 1929- *WhoAmL 94*
Bernstein, Robert 1920- *WhoAm 94*
Bernstein, Robert Jay 1948- *WhoAmL 94*
Bernstein, Robert Louis 1923- *IntWW 93, WhoAm 94*
Bernstein, Robert Steven 1954- *WhoAmL 94*
Bernstein, Roger Joel 1952- *WhoAmL 94*
Bernstein, Ronald Harold 1918- *Who 94*
Bernstein, Saralinda 1951- *WhoAmA 93*
Bernstein, Sheldon 1927- *WhoScEn 94*
Bernstein, Sidney Ralph d1993 *NewYTBS 93 [port]*
Bernstein, Sol 1927- *WhoAm 94, WhoScEn 94, WhoWest 94*
Bernstein, Stanley Joseph *WhoAm 94*
Bernstein, Stuart 1919- *WhoAmL 94*
Bernstein, Stuart Neil 1964- *WhoFI 94*
Bernstein, Susan Lisa 1965- *WhoWest 94*
Bernstein, Susan Powell 1938- *WhoAm 94*
Bernstein, Sylvia 1914-1990 *WhoAmA 93N*
Bernstein, Ted S. 1959- *WhoMW 93*
Bernstein, Theresa *WhoAm 94, WhoAmA 93*
Bernstein, Walter 1919- *IntMPA 94*
Bernstein, William 1933- *IntMPA 94, WhoFI 94*
Bernstein, William Joseph 1945- *WhoAmA 93*
Bernstein, William Robert 1947- *WhoFI 94*
Bernstein, Zalman C. *WhoFI 94*
Bernstine, Daniel O. 1947- *WhoBlA 94*
Bernstine, Daniel O'Neal 1947- *WhoAm 94, WhoAmL 94*
Bernstine, Rod Earl 1965- *WhoBlA 94*
Bernstorf, Betty James 1925- *WhoAmP 93*
Bernt, Benno Anthony 1931- *WhoAm 94, WhoFI 94*
Bernthal, Eric L. 1946- *WhoAmL 94*
Bernthal, Frederick M. 1943- *WhoAmP 93*
Bernthal, Frederick Michael 1943- *WhoAm 94, WhoScEn 94*
Bernthal, Frederick W. 1928- *WhoAm 94, WhoFI 94*
Bernthal, Harold George 1928- *WhoAm 94*
Bernt Hazzard, Charlotte Irene 1953- *WhoMW 93*
Bernthsen, Solveig Jenny *WhoHol 92*
Berntsen, Denis A. 1947- *WhoAmL 94*
Berntson, Gary Glen 1945- *WhoScEn 94*
Bero, Robert John 1965- *WhoMW 93*
Bero, Ronald Arthur 1935- *WhoAm 94*
Berol, Emile Albert d1993 *NewYTBS 93*
Berolzheimer, Karl 1932- *WhoAm 94, WhoAmL 94, WhoFI 94*
Beron, Alberto 1940- *WhoWest 94*
Beron, Gail Laskey 1943- *WhoMW 93*
Beroul fl. 1190- *BlmGEL*
Berov, Lyuben *IntWW 93*
Beroza, Allen H. 1949- *WhoAmL 94*
Berquez, Gerard Paul 1945- *WhoScEn 94*
Berquist, Goodwin 1930- *WhoMW 93*
Berr, Doris *WhoHol 92*
Berr, Georges d1942 *WhoHol 92*
Berra, P. Bruce 1935- *WhoAm 94*
Berra, Paul M. 1925- *WhoAmP 93*
Berra, Robert Louis 1924- *WhoAm 94*
Berra, Tim Martin 1943- *WhoMW 93*
Berra, Yogi 1925- *WhoAm 94*
Berragan, Gerald Brian 1933- *Who 94*
Berre, Andre Dieudonne 1940- *WhoScEn 94*
Berrell, George d1933 *WhoHol 92*
Berres, Terrence Robert 1950- *WhoAmL 94*
Berresford, Susan Vail 1943- *WhoAm 94*
Berresford, Virginia 1902- *WhoAmA 93*
Berrey, Robert Forrest 1939- *WhoAm 94*
Berrey, Robert Wilson, III 1929- *WhoAmL 94, WhoMW 93*
Berri, (Claude) 1934- *IntWW 93*
Berri, Claude 1934- *IntMPA 94, WhoHol 92*
Berri, Nabih 1939- *IntWW 93*
Berrian, Brenda F. *BlmGWL*
Berriau, Simone d1984 *WhoHol 92*
Berriault, Gina 1926- *DcLB 130 [port]*
Berridge, Elizabeth 1962- *WhoHol 92*
Berridge, George Bradford 1928- *WhoAm 94, WhoAmL 94*
Berridge, Gina Gail 1955- *WhoMW 93*
Berridge, Marc Sheldon 1954- *WhoScEn 94*
Berridge, Michael John 1938- *Who 94*
Berridge, (Donald) Roy 1922- *Who 94*
Berridge, Thomas E. 1946- *WhoIns 94*
Berridge, William Arthur 1893- *WhAm 10*
Berrie, Russell 1933- *WhoAm 94*
Berriedale, Lord 1981- *Who 94*
Berrien, James Stuart 1952- *WhoAm 94*
Berrier, David Jewell 1934- *WhoWest 94*
Berrigan, Daniel *DrAPF 93*
Berrigan, Daniel 1921- *ConAu 43NR*
Berrigan, Daniel J. 1921- *WhoHol 92, WrDr 94*

Berrigan, Patrick Joseph 1933- WhoAmL 94
Berrill, Kenneth 1920- IntWW 93, Who 94
Berrill, Norman John 1903- IntWW 93, Who 94, WhoAm 94, WrDr 94
Berriman, David 1928- Who 94
Berring, Robert Charles, Jr. 1949- WhoAmL 94
Berrington, Craig Anthony 1943- WhoAmL 94
Berrington, Hugh Bayard 1928- WrDr 94
Berrio, Antonio De c. 1520-1597 WhWE
Berrios, Angel O. 1940- WhoAmP 93
Berrios, Javier 1961- WhoScEn 94
Berrios, Joseph 1952- WhoAmP 93, WhoHisp 94
Berrios Cuadrado, José Diego 1934- WhoHisp 94
Berrios de Santos, Elsa I. WhoHisp 94
Berrios Martinez, Ruben WhoAmP 93
Berriozábal, Manuel Phillip 1931- WhoHisp 94
Berriozabal, Maria Antonietta 1941- WhoAmP 93, WhoHisp 94
Berritt, Harold Edward 1936- WhoAmL 94
Berroa, Billy WhoHisp 94
Berroa, Jorge 1938- NewGrDO
Berry Who 94
Berry, Abel 1921- WhoHisp 94
Berry, Adrian 1937- EncSF 93
Berry, Adrian M. 1937- WrDr 94
Berry, Alan M. 1944- WhoAm 94, WhoAmL 94
Berry, Albert G. 1933- WhoBlA 94
Berry, Aline d1967 WhoHol 92
Berry, Ann Roper 1934- WhoAm 94
Berry, Anthony Arthur 1915- Who 94
Berry, Archie Paul 1935- WhoBlA 94
Berry, Art, Sr. d1945 WhoHol 92
Berry, Barbara 1937- WrDr 94
Berry, Benjamin Donaldson 1939- WhoBlA 94
Berry, Beverly A. 1939- WhoMW 93
Berry, Bill WhoAm 94
Berry, Brewton 1901- WhoAm 94
Berry, Brian J. 1958- WhoAmP 93
Berry, Brian Joe Lobley 1934- IntWW 93, WhoAm 94, WrDr 94
Berry, Bryan 1930-1955 EncSF 93
Berry, Buford Preston 1935- WhoAm 94
Berry, Carolyn 1930- WhoAmA 93
Berry, Charlene Armstrong 1932- WhoAmL 94
Berry, Charlene Helen 1947- WhoMW 93
Berry, Charles Edward Anderson c. 1926- AmCulL
Berry, Charles Eugene 1950- WhoAmP 93, WhoWest 94
Berry, Charles Gordon 1950- WhoAm 94, WhoAmL 94
Berry, Charles L. 1943- WhoAmL 94
Berry, Charles Oscar 1907- WhoAm 94
Berry, Charles Richard 1948- WhoAmL 94, WhoWest 94
Berry, Cherie Killian WhoAmP 93
Berry, Chester Ridlon 1919- WhoScEn 94
Berry, Chuck 1926- AfrAmAl 6 [port], IntWW 93, WhoAm 94, WhoBlA 94, WhoHol 92
Berry, Cicely 1926- WrDr 94
Berry, Cicely Frances 1926- Who 94
Berry, Coburn Dewees, IV 1951- WhoAmL 94
Berry, Colin Leonard 1937- Who 94
Berry, D. C. DrAPF 93
Berry, Dan C. WhoAmP 93
Berry, David J. 1944- WhoAm 94
Berry, Dean Lester 1935- WhoAm 94
Berry, Deborah 1961- WhoWest 94
Berry, Don 1932- WrDr 94
Berry, Earl A., Jr. 1942- WhoAmL 94
Berry, Edgar P. d1993 NewYTBS 93
Berry, Edna Janet 1917- WhoAm 94
Berry, Edward DeJarnette 1949- WhoAmP 93
Berry, Edward Henry 1945- WhoFI 94
Berry, Edwin X. 1935- WhoWest 94
Berry, Eliot DrAPF 93
Berry, Eric 1913- WhoHol 92
Berry, Faith 1939- WrDr 94
Berry, Francis 1915- Who 94, WrDr 94
Berry, Fraser Who 94
Berry, (Robert Edward) Fraser 1926- Who 94
Berry, Frederick E. 1949- WhoAmP 93
Berry, Frederick Joseph 1940- WhoBlA 94
Berry, Glenn 1929- WhoAmA 93
Berry, Gordon L. WhoBlA 94
Berry, Guy Curtis 1935- WhoAm 94
Berry, Halle 1968- ConTFT 11
Berry, Halle M. WhoBlA 94
Berry, Henry Gordon 1940- WhoMW 93
Berry, Howard K., Jr. 1931- WhoAmL 94
Berry, J. Edward 1945- WhoMW 93
Berry, Jack K. 1930- WhoAmL 94
Berry, James d1969 WhoHol 92
Berry, James 1924- BlmGEL, WrDr 94
Berry, James 1925- WrDr 94
Berry, James Christopher 1960- WhoMW 93
Berry, James Frederick 1927- WhoAm 94
Berry, James Frederick 1947- WhoAmL 94
Berry, James R. EncSF 93
Berry, James W., Jr. 1949- WhoAmL 94
Berry, James William 1931- Who 94
Berry, Janice Rae 1937- WhoWest 94
Berry, Janis Marie 1949- WhoAm 94, WhoAmL 94
Berry, Jay 1950- WhoBlA 94
Berry, Joe Wilkes 1938- WhoAm 94
Berry, John DrAPF 93
Berry, John 1907- Who 94
Berry, John 1917- ConTFT 11, IntMPA 94, WhoHol 92
Berry, John Charles 1938- WhoWest 94
Berry, John Coltrin 1937- WhoAm 94, WhoFI 94
Berry, John Douglas 1944- WhoFI 94
Berry, John E. d1993 NewYTBS 93
Berry, John Fredrick 1955- WhoAmL 94
Berry, John Ray WhoMW 93
Berry, John Stevens 1938- WrDr 94
Berry, John VanderHorst 1957- WhoFI 94
Berry, John Widdup 1939- WhoAm 94
Berry, John Willard 1947- WhoAm 94
Berry, Jonas GayLL
Berry, Joni Ingram 1953- WhoScEn 94
Berry, Joseph John 1946- WhoFI 94
Berry, Joy (Wilt) 1944- WrDr 94
Berry, Joyce Charlotte 1937- WhoAm 94
Berry, Jules d1951 WhoHol 92
Berry, Julianne Elward 1946- WhoAm 94
Berry, Ken WhoHol 92
Berry, Ken 1933- IntMPA 94
Berry, Kim Lamar 1956- WhoScEn 94
Berry, L. Michael 1937- IntWW 93
Berry, Ladricca Price 1950- WhoMW 93
Berry, Latin 1967- WhoBlA 94
Berry, Laurie Ann 1954- WhoMW 93
Berry, Lee Roy, Jr. 1943- WhoBlA 94
Berry, Lemuel, Jr. 1946- WhoAm 94, WhoBlA 94
Berry, Leonidas H. 1902- WhoBlA 94
Berry, Leonidas Harris 1902- WhoAm 94
Berry, LeRoy 1920- WhoBlA 94
Berry, Lisbon C., Jr. 1922- WhoBlA 94
Berry, Loren Curtis 1912- WhoFI 94
Berry, Lorraine L. 1949- WhoAmP 93
Berry, Louise Spaulding 1927- WhoAmP 93
Berry, Mady d1965 WhoHol 92
Berry, Margaret Loree 1927- WhoAmP 93
Berry, Mary Frances 1938- AfrAmAl 6 [port], WhoBlA 94
Berry, Mary Tom 1924- WhoAm 94
Berry, Max Nathan 1935- WhoAmL 94, WhoAmP 93
Berry, Michael James 1947- WhoAm 94, WhoScEn 94
Berry, Michael Victor 1941- Who 94
Berry, Michael Wayne 1959- WhoMW 93
Berry, Nancy Michaels 1928- WhoAm 94
Berry, Nicholas (William) 1942- Who 94
Berry, Noah, Jr. 1916- IntMPA 94
Berry, Nyas d1951 WhoHol 92
Berry, Ondra Lamon 1958- WhoBlA 94
Berry, Patricia d1928 WhoHol 92
Berry, Paul 1919- WrDr 94
Berry, Paul Lawrence 1944- WhoBlA 94
Berry, Peter Austin 1935- Who 94
Berry, Peter Fremantle 1944- Who 94
Berry, Philip Alfonso 1950- WhoBlA 94
Berry, Phillip Reid 1950- WhoMW 93
Berry, Phillip Samuel 1937- WhoAmL 94, WhoWest 94
Berry, Priscilla 1946- WhoAm 94
Berry, Raymond ProFbHF [port]
Berry, Raymond J. WhoHol 92
Berry, Richard WhoHol 92
Berry, Richard Chisholm 1928- WhAm 10
Berry, Richard Douglas 1926- WhoAm 94
Berry, Richard Lewis 1946- WhoAm 94
Berry, Richard Morgan 1945- WhoAmL 94
Berry, Richard Stephen 1931- IntWW 93, WhoAm 94, WhoMW 93, WhoScEn 94
Berry, Robert 1943- WhoMW 93
Berry, Robert Bass 1948- WhoFI 94
Berry, Robert James 1934- Who 94
Berry, Robert Langley Page 1918- Who 94
Berry, Robert Vaughan 1933- WhoAm 94
Berry, Robert Worth 1926- WhoAm 94, WhoAmL 94, WhoFI 94, WhoWest 94
Berry, Rodney T. 1948- WhoAmP 93
Berry, Roger Julian 1935- Who 94
Berry, Roger Leslie 1948- Who 94
Berry, Ron 1920- WrDr 94
Berry, Ronald 1917- Who 94
Berry, Sarah WhoHol 92
Berry, Scyld Who 94
Berry, Scyld 1954- WrDr 94
Berry, (Anthony) Scyld (Ivens) 1954- Who 94
Berry, Shirley Nichols 1930- WhoMW 93
Berry, Sidney Bryan 1926- WhoAm 94
Berry, Simon Who 94
Berry, (Roger) Simon 1948- Who 94
Berry, Stephen Ames 1947- EncSF 93
Berry, Stephen Joseph 1948- WhoAm 94
Berry, Theodore M. 1905- WhoBlA 94
Berry, Thomas 1914- WrDr 94
Berry, Thomas Clayton 1948- WhoWest 94
Berry, Thomas Eugene 1923- WhoAmL 94
Berry, Thomas Henry S. Who 94
Berry, Thomas Joseph 1925- WhoAm 94
Berry, Thomas Robert 1931- WhoAm 94
Berry, Virgil Jennings, Jr. 1928- WhoAm 94
Berry, W. H. d1951 WhoHol 92
Berry, Wallace Taft 1928- WrDr 94N
Berry, Walter 1929- IntWW 93, NewGrDO, WhoAm 94
Berry, Weldon H. WhoBlA 94
Berry, Wendell 1934- EnvEnc, IntWW 93, WhoAm 94
Berry, Wendell (Erdman) 1934- WrDr 94
Berry, Wendell E. DrAPF 93
Berry, William Augustus 1933- WhoAmA 93
Berry, William Benjamin Newell 1931- WhoAm 94, WhoScEn 94
Berry, William Bernard 1931- WhoScEn 94
Berry, William David 1926-1979 WhoAmA 93N
Berry, William Fouts 1943- WhoMW 93
Berry, William Lee 1935- WhoAm 94
Berry, William Martin 1920- WhoAm 94, WhoFI 94, WhoMW 93
Berry, William W., Jr. 1946- WhoAmL 94
Berry, William Wells 1917- WhoAm 94, WhoAmL 94
Berry, William Willis 1932- WhoAm 94, WhoFI 94
Berry-Caban, Cristobal S. 1953- WhoHisp 94
Berryessa, Richard Greaves 1947- WhoWest 94
Berryhill, Henry Lee, Jr. 1921- WhoAm 94
Berryhill, Michael DrAPF 93
Berryhill, Stuart Randall 1951- WhoWest 94
Berryman, Clifford Kennedy 1869-1949 WhoAmA 93N
Berryman, Donald Carroll 1934- WhoWest 94
Berryman, Dorothee WhoHol 92
Berryman, Jerome Causin 1810-1906 EncNAR
Berryman, Jim 1947- WhoAmP 93
Berryman, John 1914-1972 AmCulL
Berryman, John c. 1919-1988 EncSF 93
Berryman, Macon M. 1908- WhoBlA 94
Berryman, Matilene S. WhoBlA 94
Berryman, Michael WhoHol 92
Berryman, Richard Byron 1932- WhoAm 94
Berryman, Thomas Harrison 1943- WhoMW 93
Bers, Donald Martin 1953- WhoMW 93
Bers, Lipman d1993 NewYTBS 93 [port]
Bers, Lipman 1914- IntWW 93
Bersa, Blagoje 1873-1934 NewGrDO
Berscheid, Ellen S. 1936- WhoAm 94, WhoMW 93
Berscheidt, Joanne Marie 1944- WhoAmL 94
Berselli, Matteo fl. 1708-1721 NewGrDO
Bersenov, Ivan d1951 WhoHol 92
Bersentes, Nafsika J. 1931- WhoAmA 93
Bersh, Philip Joseph 1921- WhoAm 94
Bershad, Andrew David 1955- WhoAmL 94
Bershad, David L. 1942- WhoAmA 93
Bershad, Jack R. 1930- WhoAm 94, WhoAmL 94
Bershad, Neil Jeremy 1937- WhoAm 94
Bershadsky, Luba 1916- WrDr 94
Bersianik, Louky 1930- BlmGWL
Bersin, Alan Douglas 1946- WhoAmL 94
Bersoff, Donald Neil 1939- WhoAm 94, WhoAmL 94
Berson, Eliot Lawrence 1937- WhoAm 94, WhoScEn 94
Berson, Jerome Abraham 1924- IntWW 93, WhoAm 94, WhoScEn 94
Berson, Mark Ira 1943- WhoAmL 94
Berson, Norman S. 1926- WhoAmP 93
Bersoux, Henri Robert 1959- WhoFI 94
Berssenbrugge, Mei-mei 1947- WhoAsA 94
Berstein, Irving Aaron 1926- WhoAm 94, WhoScEn 94
Bersticker, Albert Charles 1934- WhoAm 94, WhoFI 94
Bersu, Edward Thorwald 1946- WhoMW 93
Bert, Charles Wesley 1929- WhoAm 94, WhoScEn 94
Bert, Norman Allen 1942- WhoWest 94
Berta, Joseph Michel 1940- WhoAm 94
Bertagnolli, Leslie DrAPF 93
Bertain, George Joseph, Jr. 1929- WhoAm 94, WhoAmL 94, WhoWest 94
Bertalan, Frank Joseph 1914- WhoWest 94
Bertali, Antonio 1605-1669 NewGrDO
Bertani, Dante G. 1931- WhoAmP 93
Bertati, Giovanni 1735-c. 1815 NewGrDO
Bertch, Karen Elizabeth 1958- WhoMW 93
Berte, Neal Richard 1940- WhoAm 94
Bertea, Hyla Holmes 1940- WhoWest 94
Berteau, David John 1949- WhoAm 94
Bertele, William 1935- WhoScEn 94
Bertelle, Jeanne T. 1947- WhoAm 94
Bertelsen, Mark A. 1944- WhoAmL 94
Bertelsen, Richard A. d1993 NewYTBS 93
Bertelsen, Thomas Elwood, Jr. 1940- WhoAm 94
Bertelsman, William Odis 1936- WhoAm 94, WhoAmL 94
Bertero, James B. 1939- WhoAmL 94
Bertero, Vitelmo Victorio WhoAm 94, WhoWest 94
Bertheau, Cesar Jordan 1897- WhAm 10
Bertheau, Julien WhoHol 92
Berthelemy, Jean-Simon 1743-1811 NewGrDO
Berthelet, Arthur d1949 WhoHol 92
Berthelet, Thomas c. 1490-1555 DcNaB MP
Berthelier, Jean-Francois (Philibert) 1830-1888 NewGrDO
Berthelot, Pierre Eugene Marcelin 1827-1907 WorScD
Berthelot, Pierre Eugene Marcellin 1827-1907 WorInv
Berthelot, Yves M. 1937- IntWW 93
Berthelsdorf, Siegfried 1911- WhoAm 94, WhoWest 94
Berthelsen, Asger 1928- IntWW 93
Berthelsen, John Robert 1954- WhoAm 94, WhoMW 93
Berthelsen, Marilyn A. 1929- WhoAmP 93
Berthelson, Larry d1993 NewYTBS 93
Bertheroy, Jean BlmGWL
Berthgyth fl. 8th cent.?- BlmGWL
Berthier, Jean-Ferdinand 1803-1886 EncDeaf
Berthier, Louis-Alexandre 1753-1815 AmRev, WhAmRev
Berthoff, Rowland Tappan 1921- WhoAm 94
Berthoin, Georges Paul 1925- IntWW 93, Who 94
Berthold, Dennis Alfred 1942- WhoAm 94
Berthold, John William, III 1945- WhoMW 93
Berthold, Richard M(artin) 1946- WrDr 94
Bertholf, Neilson Allan, Jr. 1933- WhoAm 94
Bertholf, Roger Lloyd 1955- WhoScEn 94
Berthollet, Claude Louis WorInv
Berthollet, Claude Louis 1748-1822 WorScD
Berthon, Stephen (Ferrier) 1922- Who 94
Berthot, Jake 1939- WhoAm 94, WhoAmA 93
Berthoud, Jacques Alexandre 1935- Who 94
Berthoud, Kenneth H., Jr. 1928- WhoBlA 94
Berthoud, Martin (Seymour) 1931- Who 94
Berthouex, Paul Mac 1940- WhoAm 94, WhoMW 93, WhoScEn 94
Berti, Arturo Luis 1912- WhoScEn 94
Berti, Dehl WhoHol 92
Berti, Luciano 1922- IntWW 93
Berti, Marina 1925- WhoHol 92
Bertie Who 94
Bertie, John Robert 1923- WhoAmL 94
Bertin, Eddy EncSF 93
Bertin, Jack 1904-1963 EncSF 93
Bertin, John Joseph 1938- WhoAm 94
Bertin, Louise(-Angelique) 1805-1877 NewGrDO
Bertin, Pierre d1984 WhoHol 92
Bertin, Roland WhoHol 92
Bertin de la Doue, Toussaint c. 1680-1743 NewGrDO
Bertinelli, Valerie 1960- IntMPA 94, WhoAm 94, WhoHol 92
Bertini, Catherine 1950- IntWW 93
Bertini, Francesca d1985 WhoHol 92
Bertini, Gary 1927- NewGrDO
Bertino, Frank Christen 1938- WhoWest 94
Bertino, Joseph Rocco 1930- WhoAm 94, WhoScEn 94
Bertinotti(-Radicati), Teresa 1776-1854 NewGrDO
Bertinuson, Teresalee WhoAmP 93
Bertish, Suzanne WhoHol 92

Beton, John Allen 1950- *WhoFI 94*
Betow, Gary L. 1954- *WhoAmL 94*
Betrone, Annibale d1950 *WhoHol 92*
Betrozoff, John W. *WhoAmP 93*
Betsch, Madeline *WhoAm 94*
Betsch, Reinhold 1945- *WhoFI 94*
Betsinger, Peggy Ann 1939- *WhoMW 93*
Bett, Michael 1935- *Who 94*
Betta, Mary Beth 1961- *WhoScEn 94*
Bettac, Robert Edward 1949- *WhoAmL 94*
Bettauer, Hugo *EncSF 93*
Bettelheim, Bruno 1903-1990 *AmSocL, ConLC 79 [port], WhAm 10*
Bettelheim, Charles 1913- *IntWW 93*
Bettelheim, Eric Christopher 1952- *WhoAmL 94*
Bettencourt, Lawrence J. *WhoAmP 93*
Bettencourt, Nuno c. 1966- *See* Extreme *ConMus 10*
Bettencourt Santos, Humberto 1940- *IntWW 93*
Bettendorf, Emmy 1895-1963 *NewGrDO*
Bettendorf, James Bernard 1933- *WhoMW 93*
Bettenhausen, Brad Lee 1958- *WhoFI 94, WhoMW 93*
Bettenhausen, Elizabeth Ann 1942- *WhoAm 94*
Better, Cathy Drinkwater *DrAPF 93*
Better, William Joel 1951- *WhoWest 94*
Betteridge, Anne 1926- *WrDr 94*
Betteridge, Elizabeth Ann 1932- *WhoMW 93*
Betteridge, Lois Etherington 1928- *WhoAmA 93*
Bettermann, Hilda 1942- *WhoAmP 93*
Betterton, Mary 1637-1712 *BlmGEL*
Betterton, Thomas 1635-1710 *BlmGEL, NewGrDO*
Bettey, J(oseph) H(arold) 1932- *WrDr 94*
Bettger, Lyle 1915- *IntMPA 94, WhoHol 92*
Betti, John Anso 1931- *WhoAm 94*
Betti, Laura *WhoHol 92*
Betti, Raimondo 1959- *WhoScEn 94*
Betti, Ugo 1892-1953 *IntDcT 2*
Bettinelli, Bruno 1913- *NewGrDO*
Bettinger, James Richard 1947- *WhoWest 94*
Bettinger, Jeffrie Allen 1954- *WhoScEn 94*
Bettinghaus, Erwin Paul 1930- *WhoAm 94*
Bettinson, Brenda 1929- *WhoAmA 93*
Bettiol, Marie E. 1943- *WhoWest 94*
Bettis, Anne Katherine 1949- *WhoBlA 94*
Bettis, Denise Reed 1955- *WhoWest 94*
Bettis, Frank d1977 *WhoHol 92*
Bettis, John Gregory 1946- *WhoWest 94*
Bettis, Valerie d1982 *WhoHol 92*
Bettison, Cynthia Ann 1958- *WhoWest 94*
Bettison, James *WhoAmA 93*
Bettisworth, Robert H. *WhoAmP 93*
Bettler, Janet Louise Bell 1940- *WhoMW 93*
Bettles, Robert *WhoHol 92*
Bettley, F(rancis) Ray 1909- *Who 94*
Bettman, Gary Bruce 1952- *WhoAm 94*
Bettman, James Ross 1943- *WhoAm 94*
Bettman, Maur *DrAPF 93*
Bettmann, Otto Ludwig 1903- *WhoAm 94, WhoAmA 93*
Betton, George d1969 *WhoHol 92*
Bettoni, Vincenzo 1881-1954 *NewGrDO*
Bettridge, Ben 1952- *WhoAmP 93*
Bettridge, John Bryan 1932- *Who 94*
Betts, Alan Keith 1945- *WhoScEn 94*
Betts, Alan Osborn 1927- *Who 94*
Betts, Austin Wortham 1912- *WhoAm 94*
Betts, Barbara Lang 1926- *WhoAmL 94, WhoWest 94*
Betts, Barbara Stoke 1924- *WhoWest 94*
Betts, Bert A. 1923- *WhoAm 94*
Betts, Burr Joseph 1945- *WhoScEn 94*
Betts, Charles Valentine 1942- *Who 94*
Betts, Clive James Charles 1950- *Who 94*
Betts, Dicky 1943- *WhoAm 94*
Betts, Donald Drysdale 1929- *IntWW 93*
Betts, Doris *DrAPF 93*
Betts, Doris June Waugh 1932- *WhoAm 94*
Betts, Douglas Norman 1932- *WhoScEn 94*
Betts, Edward 1920- *WhoAm 94*
Betts, Edward Howard 1920- *WhoAmA 93*
Betts, Floyd O. 1915- *WhoAmP 93*
Betts, Henry Brognard 1928- *WhoAm 94*
Betts, Isaac Franklin 1897- *WhAm 10*
Betts, Jack *WhoHol 92*
Betts, Jackson E. d1993 *NewYTBS 93 [port]*
Betts, James Gordon 1954- *WhoScEn 94*
Betts, James T. 1943- *WhoAmL 94*
Betts, James William, Jr. 1923- *WhoFI 94, WhoWest 94*
Betts, Jane d1976 *WhoHol 92*
Betts, Kirk Howard 1951- *WhoAmL 94*
Betts, Leah Warrington 1932- *WhoAmP 93*
Betts, Lily Edna Minerva *Who 94*
Betts, Louis 1873-1961 *WhoAmA 93N*
Betts, M. Roger 1944- *WhoMW 93*
Betts, Michael J. 1955- *WhoAmL 94*
Betts, Raymond Frederick 1925- *WrDr 94*
Betts, Robert Budd 1922-1989 *WhAm 10*
Betts, Robert Budd, Jr. 1956- *WhoAmP 93*
Betts, Robert Ian 1943- *WhoAm 94, WhoAmL 94*
Betts, Sheri Elaine 1958- *WhoBlA 94*
Betts, Stanley Woodley 1912- *Who 94*
Betts, Stephen *Who 94*
Betts, (Charles) Stephen 1919- *Who 94*
Betts, Warren R. 1929- *WhoAm 94*
Betts, William d1929 *WhoHol 92*
Betts, William Wilson, Jr. 1926- *WrDr 94*
Betty, L(ewis) Stafford 1942- *ConAu 42NR*
Betty, Lewis Stafford 1942- *WhoWest 94*
Betty, Warren Randall 1931- *WhoBlA 94*
Bettys, Joseph d1782 *WhAmRev*
Betuel, Jonathan *IntMPA 94*
Betunada, Rosco Julio 1949- *WhoWest 94*
Betz, Carl d1978 *WhoHol 92*
Betz, Charles W. 1922- *WhoAm 94*
Betz, Don 1946- *WhoAmP 93*
Betz, Eugene William 1921- *WhoAm 94*
Betz, Frank Herbert, III 1933- *WhoAmP 93*
Betz, Franz 1835-1900 *NewGrDO*
Betz, Hans Dieter 1931- *ConAu 41NR, WhoAm 94, WhoMW 93*
Betz, Kevin Thomas 1961- *WhoMW 93*
Betz, Matthew d1938 *WhoHol 92*
Betz, Norman L. 1938- *WhoScEn 94*
Betz, Pauline 1919- *BuCMET [port]*
Betz, Ronald Philip 1933- *WhoMW 93*
Betz, Valerie P. 1933- *WhoAmP 93*
Betza, Barbara Ann 1955- *WhoWest 94*
Betzig, Laura L. 1953- *WhoMW 93*
Betzler, Daniel Joseph 1957- *WhoMW 93*
Betzold, Don 1950- *WhoAmP 93*
Betzold, Donald R. 1950- *WhoMW 93*
Betzold, Paul Frederick, Jr. 1943- *WhoAm 94*
Beube, Frank Edward 1904- *WhoScEn 94*
Beuc, Rudolph, Jr. 1931- *WhoMW 93*
Beuchert, Edward William 1937- *WhoAm 94*
Beuerlein, Juliana 1921- *WhoAm 94*
Beuerman, Donald Roy 1928- *WhoAm 94*
Beugen, Joan Beth 1943- *WhoMW 93*
Beugen, Robert Joel 1938- *WhoMW 93*
Beugnot, Bernard Andre Henri 1932- *WhoAm 94*
Beuke, Vernon Lee 1941- *WhoAm 94*
Beukema, John Frederick 1947- *WhoAm 94, WhoAmL 94*
Beukes, Wiets Daniel 1927- *IntWW 93*
Beum, Robert *DrAPF 93*
Beumel, Wilford J. 1935- *WhoAm 94, WhoWest 94*
Beumer, Richard Eugene 1938- *WhoAm 94, WhoFI 94*
Beumler, Henry Weber 1913- *WhoAmL 94*
Beus, Stanley Spencer 1930- *WhoWest 94*
Beusch, Gladys Jeanette 1937- *WhoFI 94*
Beuter, Richard William 1942- *WhoMW 93*
Beuther, Friedrich Christian 1777-1856 *NewGrDO*
Beutler, Arthur Julius 1924- *WhoMW 93*
Beutler, August fl. 175-?- *WhWE*
Beutler, Christopher John 1944- *WhoAmP 93*
Beutler, Earl Bryan 1954- *WhoWest 94*
Beutler, Ernest 1928- *IntWW 93, WhoAm 94, WhoWest 94*
Beutler, Frederick Joseph 1926- *WhoAm 94, WhoMW 93*
Beutler, Larry Edward 1941- *WhoScEn 94*
Beutler, Maja 1936- *BlmGWL*
Beutler, Margarete 1876-1949 *BlmGWL*
Beutler, Randy L. 1961- *WhoAmP 93*
Beutner, Roger Earl 1930- *WhoAm 94, WhoFI 94*
Beuttenmuller, Rudolf William 1953- *WhoAmL 94*
Beutter, Robert Charles 1935- *WhoAmP 93*
Beuve-Mery, Hubert 1902-1989 *WhAm 10*
Beuzekom, Richard A. 1940- *WhoWest 94*
Bevan, Alistair *EncSF 93*
Bevan, Aneurin 1897-1960 *HisDcKW*
Bevan, Billy d1957 *WhoHol 92*
Bevan, Charles Albert, Jr. 1944- *WhoAm 94*
Bevan, Christopher Martin 1923- *Who 94*
Bevan, (Andrew) David Gilory 1928- *Who 94*
Bevan, David Gilroy *Who 94*
Bevan, Donald Edward 1921- *WhoAm 94*
Bevan, Edward John 1856-1921 *WorInv*
Bevan, Gloria (Isabel) 1911- *WrDr 94*
Bevan, Hugh Keith 1922- *Who 94*
Bevan, James (Stuart) 1930- *WrDr 94*
Bevan, (Edward) John 1856-1921 *DcNaB MP*
Bevan, John Penry Vaughan 1947- *Who 94*
Bevan, John Stuart 1935- *Who 94*
Bevan, Julian *Who 94*
Bevan, (Edward) Julian 1940- *Who 94*
Bevan, Kenneth Graham 1898- *Who 94*
Bevan, Martyn Evan E. *Who 94*
Bevan, Michael John 1945- *Who 94*
Bevan, Nicolas 1942- *Who 94*
Bevan, Peter Gilroy 1922- *Who 94*
Bevan, Richard Justin William 1922- *Who 94*
Bevan, Richard Thomas 1914- *Who 94*
Bevan, Robert Lewis 1928- *WhoAm 94, WhoAmL 94, WhoFI 94*
Bevan, Timothy (Hugh) 1927- *Who 94*
Bevan, Timothy Hugh 1927- *IntWW 93*
Bevan, Timothy Michael 1931- *Who 94*
Bevan, Walter Harold 1916- *Who 94*
Bevan, William 1922- *IntWW 93, WhoAm 94*
Bevan, William, III 1945- *WhoAm 94, WhoAmL 94*
Bevani, Alexander d1938 *WhoHol 92*
Bevans, Clem d1963 *WhoHol 92*
Bevans, Margaret Van Doren d1993 *NewYTBS 93*
Bevans, Philippa d1968 *WhoHol 92*
Bevel, James Luther 1936- *WhoBlA 94*
Beven, Thomas D. 1898- *WhAm 10*
Bever, Christopher Theodore 1919- *WhoAm 94*
Bever, Robert Lynn 1953- *WhoAmL 94, WhoAmP 93*
Beverage, Harold Henry d1993 *NewYTBS 93*
Beverett, Andrew Jackson 1917- *WhoAm 94, WhoFI 94, WhoWest 94*
Beveridge, Albert Jeremiah, III 1935- *WhoAm 94*
Beveridge, Crawford William 1945- *Who 94*
Beveridge, Gordon Smith Grieve 1933- *IntWW 93, Who 94*
Beveridge, James MacDonald Richardson 1912- *WhoAm 94*
Beveridge, John Caldwell 1937- *Who 94*
Beveridge, Karl J. 1945- *WhoAmA 93*
Beveridge, Terrance James 1945- *WhoAm 94*
Beveridge, William (Ian Beardmore) 1908- *WrDr 94*
Beveridge, William Ian Beardmore 1908- *Who 94*
Beverley, Barrington *EncSF 93*
Beverley, Henry (York La Roche) 1935- *Who 94*
Beverley, Jane Taylor 1918- *WhoAm 94, WhoMW 93*
Beverley, Nick *WhoAm 94, WhoWest 94*
Beverley, Tranzana *WhoHol 92*
Beverloo, Cornelis Van 1922- *IntWW 93*
Beverly, Alan Craig 1951- *WhoWest 94*
Beverly, Benjamin Franklin 1938- *WhoBlA 94*
Beverly, Creigs C. 1942- *WhoBlA 94*
Beverly, Frankie *WhoBlA 94*
Beverly, Nick *WhoWest 94*
Beverly, Patty Libby 1954- *WhoFI 94*
Beverly, Robert E., III 1948- *WhoMW 93*
Beverly, Robert Graham 1925- *WhoAmP 93, WhoWest 94*
Beverly, Theria M. 1931- *WhoWest 94*
Beverly, William C., Jr. 1943- *WhoBlA 94*
Bevers, William Leon 1945- *WhoAmP 93*
Beverton, Raymond John Heaphy 1922- *IntWW 93, Who 94*
Be Vier, William A. 1927- *WhoMW 93*
Bevignani, Enrico 1841-1903 *NewGrDO*
Bevilacqua, Anthony Joseph Cardinal 1923- *WhoAm 94*
Bevilacqua, Cristina 1962- *WhoWomW 91*
Bevilacqua, Don *WhoHisp 94*
Bevilacqua, Francis J. 1923- *WhoAmP 93*
Bevilacqua, Gabriel Louis Ignati 1948- *WhoAm 94*
Bevilacqua, John J. 1948- *WhoAmP 93*
Bevilacqua, Joseph A. 1918-1989 *WhAm 10*
Bevilacqua, Louis J. 1948- *WhoAmL 94*
Bevill, Tom 1921- *CngDr 93, WhoAm 94, WhoAmP 93*
Beville, Hugh M., Jr. 1908- *IntMPA 94*
Beville, Norborne P., Jr. 1941- *WhoAmP 93*
Bevin, Ernest 1881-1951 *HisDcKW*
Bevington, David Martin 1931- *WhoAm 94, WhoMW 93*
Bevington, Edmund Milton 1928- *WhoAm 94*
Bevington, Eric Raymond 1914- *Who 94*
Bevington, Gary Loyd 1944- *WhoMW 93*
Bevins, Anthony John 1942- *Who 94*
Bevins, Burke d1967 *WhoHol 92*
Bevins, John Reginald 1908- *Who 94*
Bevins, Kenneth Milton 1918- *Who 94*
Bevins, Leslie *WhoHol 92*
Bevins, Mabel d1916 *WhoHol 92*
Bevins, Robert Jackson 1928- *WhoFI 94, WhoScEn 94*
Bevis, H(erbert) U(rlin) 1902- *EncSF 93*
Bevis, James Wayne 1934- *WhoAm 94, WhoMW 93*
Bevis, Joseph C. 1910-1990 *WhAm 10*
Bevis, Leslie *WhoHol 92*
Bevlin, Marjorie Elliott 1917- *WhoAmA 93*
Bewes, Richard 1934- *WrDr 94*
Bewes, Richard Thomas 1934- *Who 94*
Bewes, Rodney 1937- *WhoHol 92*
Bewick, Herbert 1911- *Who 94*
Bewick, John Arters 1937- *WhoAm 94*
Bewick Colby, Clara 1840-1916 *WomPubS*
Bewicke-Copley *Who 94*
Bewkes, E. Garrett, III 1951- *WhoAm 94*
Bewkes, Eugene Garrett 1895- *WhAm 10*
Bewkes, Eugene Garrett, Jr. 1926- *WhoAm 94*
Bewkes, Jeff *WhoAm 94, WhoFI 94*
Bewley, David Charles 1942- *WhoFI 94*
Bewley, Edward de Beauvoir 1931- *Who 94*
Bewley, Harrison James 1957- *WhoWest 94*
Bewley, Joe L. *WhoAmP 93*
Bewley, John Derek 1943- *WhoAm 94*
Bewley, Judy Baker 1942- *WhoAmP 93*
Bewley, Loyal Vivian 1898- *WhAm 10*
Bewley, Thomas Henry 1926- *IntWW 93, Who 94*
Bexon, Roger 1926- *IntWW 93, Who 94*
Bey, Gwendolyn Konigsberg 1954- *WhoAm 94*
Bey, Turhan 1920- *WhoHol 92*
Bey, Turhan 1921- *IntMPA 94*
Beyala, Calixte *BlmGWL*
Beyard, Thomas Blaine 1955- *WhoAmP 93*
Beye, Holly *DrAPF 93*
Beyea, Louise Michele 1958- *WhoMW 93*
Beyene, Wendemagegnehu Tsegaye 1963- *WhoScEn 94*
Beyer, Aaron Jay 1946- *WhoAmL 94*
Beyer, Charles d1953 *WhoHol 92*
Beyer, Charlotte Bishop 1947- *WhoFI 94*
Beyer, Donald S., Jr. *WhoAmP 93*
Beyer, Donald Sternoff, Jr. 1950- *WhoAm 94*
Beyer, Emil E., Jr. 1929- *WhoAmP 93*
Beyer, Erik 1936- *WhoAmP 93*
Beyer, Frank Michael 1928- *IntWW 93*
Beyer, Gene *WhoAmP 93*
Beyer, Gordon Robert 1930- *WhoAm 94*
Beyer, Jane Magdalyn 1959- *WhoMW 93*
Beyer, Jennifer Elmer 1963- *WhoAmL 94*
Beyer, Karen Ann 1942- *WhoMW 93*
Beyer, Karl Henry, Jr. 1914- *WhoAm 94*
Beyer, Landon Edward 1949- *WhoMW 93*
Beyer, Lee 1948- *WhoAmP 93*
Beyer, Lee Dixie 1944- *WhoMW 93*
Beyer, Lee Louis 1948- *WhoWest 94*
Beyer, Paul J., III 1950- *SmATA 74 [port]*
Beyer, Paul K. 1943- *WhoIns 94*
Beyer, Richard G. *DrAPF 93*
Beyer, Robert Edward 1928- *WhoMW 93*
Beyer, Robert Thomas 1920- *WhoAm 94*
Beyer, Ruth A. 1955- *WhoAmL 94*
Beyer, Sonya von Zitzewitz 1931- *WhoFI 94*
Beyer, Stanley C. 1943- *WhoAmL 94*
Beyer, Steven J. 1951- *WhoAmA 93*
Beyer, Troy 1964- *WhoBlA 94*
Beyer, Troy 1965- *WhoHol 92*
Beyer, Uwe d1993 *NewYTBS 93*
Beyer, W(illiam) G(ray) *EncSF 93*
Beyer, Wayne Cartwright 1946- *WhoAmL 94*
Beyer, Werner W(illiam) 1911- *WrDr 94*
Beyerchen, Alan Duane 1945- *WhoMW 93*
Beyerlein, Douglas Craig 1950- *WhoWest 94*
Beyer-Mears, Annette 1941- *WhoAm 94, WhoScEn 94*
Beyers, Catherine Meyer 1947- *WhoMW 93*
Beyers, Patricia Joan *WhoMW 93*
Beyers, Robert West 1931- *WhoWest 94*
Beyers, William Bjorn 1940- *WhoAm 94, WhoWest 94*
Beyersdorf, Marguerite Mulloy 1922- *WhoAm 94*
Beyfus, Drusilla *WrDr 94*
Beyfus, Drusilla Norman *Who 94*
Beylkin, Gregory 1953- *WhoScEn 94, WhoWest 94*
Beyman, Jonathan Eric 1955- *WhoAm 94, WhoFI 94*
Beymer, Richard 1939- *IntMPA 94, WhoHol 92*
Beynon, Ernest Geoffrey 1926- *Who 94*

Beynon, Francis Marion 1884-1951 BlmGWL
Beynon, Granville Who 94
Beynon, (William John) Granville 1914- IntWW 93, Who 94
Beynon, Huw 1942- WrDr 94
Beynon, John EncSF 93
Beynon, John David Emrys 1939- IntWW 93, Who 94
Beynon, John Herbert 1923- IntWW 93, Who 94
Beynon, Timothy George 1939- Who 94
Beyron, Einar (Oscar) 1901-1979 NewGrDO
Beyrouty, Craig A. WhoScEn 94
Beyster, John Robert 1924- WhoAm 94, WhoFI 94, WhoScEn 94
Beytagh, Francis Xavier, Jr. 1935- WhoAm 94
Beytagh-Maldonado, Guillermo José 1957- WhoHisp 94
Beytin, Kenneth Alan 1952- WhoAm 94
Bezace, Didier WhoHol 92
Bezahler, Donald Jay 1932- WhoAm 94, WhoAmL 94
Bezanson, Keith Arthur 1941- WhoAm 94
Bezanson, Philip (Thomas) 1916-1975 NewGrDO
Bezanson, Thomas Edward 1945- WhoAm 94, WhoAmL 94
Bezar, Gilbert Edward 1930- WhoAm 94
Bezazian, Paul D. 1906-1988 WhAm 10
Bezdek, Hugo Frank 1936- WhoAm 94, WhoScEn 94
Bezer, David Leon 1943- WhoWest 94
Bezerra, Zila 1945- WhoWomW 91
Bezkorovainy, Anatoly 1935- WhoMW 93
Bezman, Victor H. 1941- WhoAm 94, WhoAmL 94
Bezoari, Massimo Daniel 1952- WhoScEn 94
Bezombes, Roger 1913- IntWW 93
Bezos, Beatriz M. 1958- WhoHisp 94
Bezucha, Robert Joseph 1940- WhoAm 94
Bezursik, Edward Anthony, Jr. 1951- WhoFI 94
Bezzone, Albert Paul 1931- WhoAm 94
Bezzulo, Ted d1979 WhoHol 92
Bhabha, J. J. 1914- IntWW 93
Bhada, Rohinton Khurshed 1935- WhoAsA 94, WhoWest 94
Bhada, Yezdi Khurshed 1940- WhoFI 94
Bhagaloo, Roy 1945- WhoAmP 93
Bhagat, Ashok Kumar 1942- WhoScEn 94
Bhagat, Bali Ram 1922- IntWW 93
Bhagat, Goberdhan 1928- WrDr 94
Bhagat, H. K. L. IntWW 93
Bhagat, Hitesh Rameshchandra 1961- WhoAsA 94
Bhagat, Nazir A. 1944- WhoAsA 94
Bhagat, Phiroz Maneck 1948- WhoScEn 94
Bhagat, Surinder Kumar 1935- WhoAm 94
Bhagavatula, Vijayakumar 1953- WhoAsA 94
Bhagwan, Sudhir 1942- WhoFI 94, WhoScEn 94, WhoWest 94
Bhagwati, Prafulla Chandra 1921- IntWW 93
Bhajan Lal, Chaudhri 1930- IntWW 93
Bhaktiprana, Pravrajika 1922- WhoWest 94
Bhalla, Deepak Kumar 1946- WhoScEn 94, WhoWest 94
Bhalla, Vipan Kumar 1945- WhoAsA 94
Bhalodkar, Narendra Chandrakant 1948- WhoAm 94
Bhambhani, Kanta 1947- WhoMW 93
Bhamidipaty, Kameswara Rao 1955- WhoWest 94
Bhandari, Anil Kumar 1953- WhoWest 94
Bhandari, Arvind 1950- WhoAm 94
Bhandari, Mannu 1931- BlmGWL
Bhandari, Sanjiv 1959- WhoAsA 94
Bhandarkar, Suhas D. 1964- WhoAsA 94
Bhanu, Bir 1951- WhoAm 94, WhoWest 94
Bhapkar, Vasant P. 1931- WhoAsA 94
Bharaj, Satinder Singh 1965- WhoMW 93
Bharati, Agehananda 1923-1991 WhAm 10, WrDr 94N
Bhargava, Ashok 1943- WhoAm 94, WhoAsA 94
Bhargava, Hemendra Nath 1942- WhoMW 93
Bhargava, Pushpa Mittra 1958- IntWW 93
Bhargava, Rakesh Kumar 1953- WhoFI 94
Bhargava, Rameshwar Nath 1939- WhoAm 94
Bharghava, Vijay WhoScEn 94
Bharti, Dharmvir 1926- ConWorW 93
Bhartia, Prakash 1944- WhoAm 94
Bhaskar 1930- WhoHol 92
Bhaskar, Krishan Nath 1945- Who 94
Bhaskar, Ramamoorthi 1951- WhoScEn 94
Bhaskar, Surindar Nath 1923- WhoAsA 94
Bhat, Bal Krishen 1940- WhoScEn 94, WhoWest 94
Bhat, Hari Krishen 1954- WhoScEn 94
Bhat, K. Ramachandra 1941- WhoAsA 94
Bhat, Shankar U. 1955- WhoAsA 94
Bhathena, Sam Jehangirji 1936- WhoAsA 94
Bhatia, Deepak Hazarilal 1953- WhoScEn 94
Bhatia, Jamunadevi 1919- WrDr 94
Bhatia, June 1919- WrDr 94
Bhatia, Peter K. 1953- WhoAm 94, WhoWest 94
Bhatia, Prem Narain 1911- IntWW 93
Bhatia, Ramesh 1944- WhoAsA 94
Bhatia, Salim A. L. 1950- WhoAsA 94
Bhatia, Sharmila 1964- WhoAsA 94
Bhatia, Tej K. 1945- WhoAsA 94
Bhatnagar, Deepak 1949- WhoAsA 94
Bhatnagar, Kunwar P. 1934- WhoAsA 94
Bhatnagar, Yogendra Mohan 1945- WhoAsA 94
Bhatt, Gita 1945- WhoAsA 94
Bhatt, Gunvant R. 1942- WhoAsA 94
Bhatt, Jagdish J. 1939- WhoAsA 94
Bhatt, Jagdish J(eyshanker) 1939- WrDr 94
Bhatt, Kiran Chandrakant 1940- WhoAsA 94
Bhattacharjee, Jnanendra Kumar 1936- WhoAsA 94
Bhattacharya, Basu 1936- IntWW 93
Bhattacharya, Pallab Kumar 1949- WhoScEn 94
Bhattacharya, Prabir 1948- WhoMW 93
Bhattacharya, Pradeep Kumar 1940- WhoAsA 94
Bhattacharya, Purna 1946- WhoAsA 94
Bhattacharya, Rabi Sankar 1948- WhoAsA 94
Bhattacharya, Utpal 1958- WhoMW 93
Bhattacharya-Chatterjee, Malaya 1946- WhoAm 94
Bhattacharyya, Ashim Kumar 1936- WhoAsA 94
Bhattacharyya, Birendra Kumar 1924- IntWW 93
Bhattacharyya, Gouri Kanta 1940- WhoAsA 94
Bhattacharyya, Shankar P. 1946- WhoAsA 94
Bhattacharyya, Shankar Prashad 1946- WhoAm 94
Bhattacharyya, Sushantha Kumar 1940- Who 94
Bhattacherjee, Parimal 1937- WhoScEn 94
Bhattarai, Krishna Prasad 1924- IntWW 93
Bhatti, Iftikhar Hamid 1929- WhoMW 93, WhoScEn 94
Bhatti, Neeloo 1955- WhoScEn 94
Bhatti, Rashid A. WhoAsA 94
Bhaumik, Mani Lal 1932- WhoAm 94
Bhavaraju, Murty Parabrahma 1940- WhoAm 94
Bhavnani, Pratap Gagumal 1914- WhoAsA 94
Bhavsar, Natvar 1934- IntWW 93
Bhavsar, Natvar Prahladji 1934- WhoAm 94, WhoAmA 93
Bhayani, Kiran Lilachand 1944- WhoScEn 94, WhoWest 94
Bhichai Rattakul, Nai 1926- IntWW 93
Bhide, Amar 1955- WrDr 94
Bhide, Dan Bhagwatprasad Dinkar 1964- WhoScEn 94
Bhogilal, Pratap 1916- IntWW 93
Bhojwani, Ram J. 1942- WhoAsA 94
Bhore, Jay Narayan 1915- WhoMW 93
Bhote, Keki R. 1925- ConAu 142
Bhown, Ajit Singh 1934- WhoAsA 94
Bhugra, Bindu 1963- WhoScEn 94
Bhuiyan, Rabia 1944- IntWW 93
Bhumibol Adulyadej 1927- IntWW 93
Bhunia, Arun Kumar 1960- WhoScEn 94
Bhushan, Bharat 1949- WhoMW 93, WhoScEn 94
Bhushan, Shanti 1925- IntWW 93
Bhutani, Tony 1939- WhoWest 94
Bhutto, Begum Nusrat 1934- IntWW 93, WhoWomW 91
Bhutto, Benazir 1953- IntWW 93, Who 94, WhoWomW 91, WrDr 94
Bhuyan, Bijoy Kumar 1930- WhoAsA 94
Biafore, Gabriel J. WhoAmP 93
Biagas, Edward D. 1948- WhoBlA 94
Biaggi, Girolamo Alessandro 1819-1897 NewGrDO
Biaggi, Mario 1917- IntWW 93
Biagi, L.D. EncSF 93
Biagi, Richard Charles 1925- WhoAm 94
Biagi, Shirley Anne 1944- WhoWest 94
Bial, Raymond 1948- SmATA 76 [port]
Biala, Janice 1903- WhoAm 94, WhoAmA 93
Bialas, Gunter 1907- NewGrDO
Bialczak, Carole 1943- WhoAmP 93
Bialek, Alvin 1929- WhoFI 94
Bialer, Seweryn 1926- WhoAm 94
Bialik, Mayim 1975- News 93-3 [port]
Bialkin, Kenneth Jules 1929- WhoAm 94, WhoAmL 94
Bialo, Kenneth Marc 1946- WhoAm 94, WhoAmL 94
Bialobroda, Anna 1946- WhoAmA 93
Bialy, Harvey DrAPF 93
Biancheri, Boris 1930- IntWW 93, Who 94
Bianchetti, Suzanne d1936 WhoHol 92
Bianchi, Al 1932- BasBi
Bianchi, Angelantonio 1962- WhoAmL 94
Bianchi, Antonio c. 1710-1772? NewGrDO
Bianchi, Antonio 1758-1817? NewGrDO
Bianchi, Carmine Paul 1927- WhoAm 94
Bianchi, Charles Paul 1945- WhoFI 94
Bianchi, Daniela 1942- WhoHol 92
Bianchi, David Wayne 1950- WhoAmL 94
Bianchi, Don 1938- WhoAmP 93
Bianchi, Donald Ernest 1933- WhoAm 94
Bianchi, Eugene Carl 1930- WrDr 94
Bianchi, (Giuseppe) Francesco c. 1752-1810 NewGrDO
Bianchi, Giuseppe fl. 1637-1663 NewGrDO
Bianchi, Icilio William, Jr. WhoAmP 93
Bianchi, Marianna c. 1735-1790? NewGrDO
Bianchi, Richard A. 1940- WhoIns 94
Bianchi, Robert George 1925- WhoMW 93
Bianchi, Tancredi IntWW 93
Bianchi, Ted J., Jr. 1940- WhoIns 94
Bianchi, Thomas Stephen 1956- WhoScEn 94
Bianchine, Joseph Raymond 1929- WhoAm 94, WhoScEn 94
Bianchini, Angela 1921- BlmGWL
Bianchini, Robert V. 1940- WhoAmP 93
Bianchino, Bernard Anthony 1948- WhoAm 94, WhoAmL 94
Bian Chunguang WhoPRCh 91
Bian Chunguang 1925- IntWW 93
Biancini, Angelo 1911- IntWW 93
Biancini, Ferrucio d1955 WhoHol 92
Bianco, Anthony 1953- WrDr 94
Bianco, Anthony Joseph, III 1953- WhoAm 94
Bianco, Don Christopher 1947- WhoMW 93
Bianco, Ernesto d1977 WhoHol 92
Bianco, Gerardo 1931- IntWW 93
Bianco, Jean-Louis 1943- IntWW 93
Bianco, Joseph Paul, Jr. 1936- WhoAm 94
Bianco, Michael Fabius Patrick 1940- WhoWest 94
Bianco, Nicole Ann 1949- WhoWest 94
Bianco, Phillip, Jr. 1939- WhoAmP 93
Bianco, Sal C. 1944- WhoAmP 93
Bianco, William A. 1946- WhoAmL 94
Biancolini(-Rodriguez), Marietta 1846-1905 NewGrDO
Biancolli, Louis 1907-1992 WhAm 10
Bianconi, Lorenzo (Gennaro) 1946- NewGrDO
Bianculli, Joseph Leo 1953- WhoFI 94
Bian Guoqiang 1958- WhoPRCh 91 [port]
Bi'anki c. 1835- EncNAR
Bian Yaowu 1936- WhoPRCh 91 [port]
Bian Zhilin 1910- WhoPRCh 91 [port]
Biard, James Robert 1931- WhoAm 94
Biard, Pierre 1567?-1622 EncNAR
Bias, Dana G. 1959- WhoAmL 94
Biasin, Gian-Paolo 1933- WhoWest 94, WrDr 94
Biasone, Danny 1914- BasBi
Biassey, Earle Lambert 1920- WhoBlA 94
Biava, Luis WhoAm 94
Biba, Gjela Marku WhoWomW 91
Bibalo, Antonio 1922- NewGrDO
Bibart, Richard L. 1942- WhoAm 94, WhoAmL 94
Bibas, Frank Percy 1917- IntMPA 94
Bibb, Daniel Roland 1951- WhoFI 94
Bibb, James Richard 1952- WhoMW 93
Bibb, Julian Lee 1951- WhoAmL 94
Bibb, Leon WhoHol 92
Bibb, Rose Anne 1965- WhoMW 93
Bibb, T. Clifford 1938- WhoBlA 94
Bibbo, James V., Jr. 1919- WhoAmP 93
Bibbo, Marluce 1939- WhoAm 94
Bibbs, Janice Denise 1958- WhoBlA 94
Bibbs, Lona Carol 1948- WhoMW 93
Bibby, Benjamin Who 94
Bibby, (John) Benjamin 1929- Who 94
Bibby, Deirdre L. 1951- WhoBlA 94
Bibby, Derek (James) 1922- Who 94
Bibby, Douglas Martin 1946- WhoAm 94
Bibby, James John 1947- WhoMW 93
Bibby, John E. 1920- WhoAmP 93
Bibby, John Franklin 1934- WhoAmP 93
Bibel, Debra Jan 1945- WhoAm 94
Biber, Heinrich Ignaz Franz von 1644-1704 NewGrDO
Biberman, Abner d1977 WhoHol 92
Biberman, Edward 1904-1986 WhoAmA 93N
Biberman, Lucien Morton 1919- WhoAm 94
Biberstein, Ernst Ludwig 1922- WhoAm 94
Biberti, Leopold d1969 WhoHol 92
Bibiena NewGrDO
Bibikov, Maria WhoHol 92
Bible, Frances (L.) 1927- NewGrDO
Bible, Frances Lillian WhoAm 94, WhoWest 94
Bibler, Todd Douglas 1952- WhoWest 94
Biblo, Mary 1927- WhoBlA 94
Biblow, Charlotte 1952- WhoAmL 94
Bibring, Yoram 1957- WhoFI 94
Biby, Edward d1952 WhoHol 92
Bican, Josef 1913- WorESoc
Bicat, Tony 1945- WrDr 94
Bice, Clare 1909-1976 WhoAmA 93N
Bice, Jean Annette 1946- WhoAmL 94
Bice, Michael David 1956- WhoFI 94
Bice, Robert d1968 WhoHol 92
Bice, Scott Haas 1943- WhoAm 94, WhoAmL 94, WhoWest 94
Bicehouse, Henry James 1943- WhoScEn 94
Bicerano, Jozef 1952- WhoMW 93
Bicester, Baron 1932- Who 94
Bich, Baron Marcel 1914- IntWW 93
Bicha, Karel Denis 1937- WhoAm 94
Bichachi, Olga Victoria 1952- WhoHisp 94
Bichard, Michael G. 1947- Who 94
Bichat, Marie Francois Xavier WorScD
Bicheldei, Kaadur-Ool Alekseevich 1950- LoBiDrD
Bicigo, David Paul 1956- WhoMW 93
Bick, David Greer 1953- WhoAm 94, WhoFI 94, WhoMW 93
Bick, Jerry 1923- IntMPA 94
Bick, Katherine Livingstone 1932- WhoAm 94, WhoScEn 94
Bick, Kenneth Roland 1955- WhoAmL 94
Bick, Martin James M. Who 94
Bick, Robert Steven 1961- WhoAmL 94
Bickart, David O. 1944- WhoAm 94, WhoAmL 94
Bickart, Theodore Albert 1935- WhoAm 94
Bickel, Bertram Watkins 1925- WhoFI 94
Bickel, David Robert 1944- WhoAmL 94
Bickel, Floyd Gilbert, III 1944- WhoFI 94
Bickel, George d1941 WhoHol 92
Bickel, Henry Joseph 1929- WhoAm 94
Bickel, Herbert Jacob, Jr. 1930- WhoAm 94
Bickel, John Frederick 1928- WhoScEn 94
Bickel, John W., II 1948- WhoAmL 94
Bickel, Lennard 1923- WrDr 94
Bickel, Nancy Kramer 1941- WhoWest 94
Bickel, Peter John 1940- WhoAm 94, WhoScEn 94
Bickel, Stephen Douglas 1939- WhoAm 94, WhoFI 94, WhoIns 94
Bickel, Sue 1944- WhoMW 93
Bickel, Warren Kurt 1956- WhoScEn 94
Bickelhaupt, David Lynn 1929- WhoIns 94
Bickerman, Hylan A. d1993 NewYTBS 93
Bickers, David Rinsey 1941- WhoAm 94
Bickers, Richard (Leslie) Townshend 1917- ConAu 42NR
Bickersons, The WhoCom
Bickerstaff(e), Isaac (John) 1733-c. 1808 IntDcT 2
Bickerstaff, Bernard Tyrone, Sr. 1943- WhoBlA 94
Bickerstaff, Bernie Lavelle 1944- WhoAm 94, WhoWest 94
Bickerstaff, Edwin Robert 1920- WrDr 94
Bickerstaff, Isaac (John) 1733-1808? NewGrDO
Bickerstaff, Patsy Anne DrAPF 93
Bickersteth, John Monier 1921- Who 94
Bickerton, Frank Donald 1917- Who 94
Bickerton, John Thorburn 1930- WhoAm 94, WhoFI 94
Bickford, Allen WhoHol 92
Bickford, Andrew Thomas 1952- WhoAm 94
Bickford, Charlene Nora 1944- WhoAmP 93
Bickford, Charles d1967 WhoHol 92
Bickford, Christopher Penny 1943- WhoAm 94
Bickford, David 1953- WrDr 94
Bickford, Drucilla 1925- WhoAmP 93
Bickford, Gary WhoAmP 93
Bickford, George 1901- WhoAmA 93
Bickford, George Percival 1901-1991 WhAm 10
Bickford, James David Prydeaux 1940- Who 94

BICKFORD 94 Biography and Genealogy Master Index 1995

Bickford, James Gordon 1928- *WhoAm 94*
Bickford, Jewelle Wooten 1941- *WhoAm 94, WhoFI 94*
Bickford, John Van Buren 1934-1991 *WhAm 10*
Bickford, William 1774-1834 *DcNaB MP*
Bickford Smith, John Roger 1915- *Who 94*
Bickham, Jack M. 1930- *WrDr 94*
Bickham, Jack M(iles) 1930- *EncSF 93*
Bickham, Jim David, Jr. 1962- *WhoAmL 94*
Bickham, L. B. 1923- *WhoBlA 94*
Bickham, Noel 1919- *WhoAmP 93*
Bickle, Marianne Claudia 1958- *WhoWest 94*
Bickley, Gary Steven 1953- *WhoAmA 93*
Bickley, Tony d1976 *WhoHol 92*
Bickmore, J. Grant 1916- *WhoAm 94*
Bicknell, Brian Keith 1957- *WhoMW 93*
Bicknell, Christine Betty 1919- *Who 94*
Bicknell, Claud 1910- *Who 94*
Bicknell, Gioconda *Who 94*
Bicknell, Joseph McCall 1933- *WhoAm 94*
Bicknell, Nadyne C. 1935- *WhoWest 94*
Bicknell, Nadyne Cooke 1935- *WhoAmP 93*
Bicknell, Robert C. 1929- *WhoAmP 93*
Bickner, Bruce Pierce 1943- *WhoAm 94*
Bicks, David Peter 1933- *WhoAm 94*
Bickwit, Leonard, Jr. 1940- *WhoAmL 94*
Bidard-Reydet, Danielle Louise 1939- *WhoWomW 91*
Bidart, Frank 1939- *ConAu 140, WrDr 94*
Bidart de Satulsky, Gay-Darlene *WhoHisp 94*
Biddinger, Paul Williams 1953- *WhoAm 94*
Biddington, William Robert 1925- *WhoAm 94*
Biddison, Jack Michael 1954- *WhoMW 93*
Biddiss, Michael Denis 1942- *IntWW 93, WrDr 94*
Biddle, Adrian *WhoAm 94*
Biddle, Albert George Wilkinson, III 1961- *WhoFI 94*
Biddle, Anthony Joseph Drexel, III 1948- *WhoFI 94*
Biddle, Bruce Jesse 1928- *WhoAm 94, WrDr 94*
Biddle, C. Thomas, Jr. 1947- *WhoAmL 94*
Biddle, Daniel R. *WhoAm 94*
Biddle, David 1944- *WhoScEn 94*
Biddle, Donald Ray 1936- *WhoFI 94, WhoScEn 94, WhoWest 94*
Biddle, Doris Jean 1955- *WhoMW 93*
Biddle, Edward 1738-1779 *WhAmRev*
Biddle, Flora Miller *WhoAm 94*
Biddle, George 1885-1973 *WhoAmA 93N*
Biddle, Jack, III *WhoAmP 93*
Biddle, James 1929- *WhoAmA 93*
Biddle, Jane Lammert 1926- *WhoAmP 93*
Biddle, Kenneth Allen 1952- *WhoFI 94*
Biddle, Livingston Ludlow, Jr. 1918- *WhoAm 94, WhoAmA 93*
Biddle, Martin 1937- *IntWW 93, Who 94*
Biddle, Nicholas 1750-1778 *AmRev, WhAmRev [port]*
Biddle, Owen 1754-1806 *AmRev*
Biddle, Stanton F. 1943- *WhoBlA 94*
Biddle, Stanton Fields 1943- *WhoAm 94*
Biddle, Timothy Maurice 1940- *WhoAm 94, WhoAmL 94, WhoFI 94*
Biddle, Wayne *DrAPF 93*
Biddulph *Who 94*
Biddulph, Baron 1959- *Who 94*
Biddulph, Constance *Who 94*
Biddulph, Ian D'Olier 1940- *Who 94*
Biddy, Ernest C., Jr. 1945- *WhoIns 94*
Biddy, Fred Douglas 1932- *WhoAmP 93*
Bide, Austin (Ernest) 1915- *IntWW 93, Who 94*
Bideau, Edwin H., III *WhoAmP 93*
Bideau, Jean-Luc 1940- *WhoHol 92*
Bidelman, William Pendry 1918- *WhoAm 94, WhoMW 93*
Biden, Joseph R., Jr. 1942- *CngDr 93*
Biden, Joseph Robinette, Jr. 1942- *IntWW 93, WhoAm 94, WhoAmP 93*
Bidera, Giovanni Emanuele 1784-1858 *NewGrDO*
Biderman, Donna Lynne 1963- *WhoAmL 94*
Biderman, Mark Charles 1945- *WhoAm 94, WhoFI 94*
Biderman, Sumiko 1924- *WhoAmP 93*
Bidez, Earle Felton 1897- *WhAm 10*
Bidgood, John Claude 1914- *Who 94*
Bidlack, Russell Eugene 1920- *WhoAm 94*
Bidlack, Wayne Ross 1944- *WhoMW 93*
Bidlo, Mike 1953- *WhoAmA 93*
Bidstrup, (Patricia) Lesley 1916- *Who 94*
Bidwell, Arline M. 1914- *WhoAmP 93*
Bidwell, Arline M. 1940- *WhoWomW 91*
Bidwell, Charles Edward 1932- *IntWW 93, WhoAm 94*
Bidwell, Charles W., Sr. d1947 *ProFbHF*
Bidwell, Hugh (Charles Philip) 1934- *Who 94*
Bidwell, Hugh Charles Philip 1934- *IntWW 93*
Bidwell, James Truman, Jr. 1934- *WhoAm 94, WhoAmL 94*
Bidwell, Roger Grafton Shelford 1927- *IntWW 93, WhoAm 94*
Bidwell, Sydney James 1917- *Who 94*
Bidwell, Watson 1904- *WhoAmA 93N*
Bidwick, Albert Joseph, III 1957- *WhoFI 94*
Bidwill, William V. *WhoAm 94, WhoWest 94*
Bie, Helen *WhoAmP 93, WhoWomW 91*
Bie, James Edward 1927- *WhoWest 94*
Biebel, Curt Fred, Jr. 1947- *WhoMW 93*
Biebel, Franklin M. 1908-1966 *WhoAmA 93N*
Biebel, Frederick K. 1926- *WhoAmP 93*
Biebel, Paul P., Jr. 1942- *WhoAm 94*
Biebel, Paul Philip, Jr. 1942- *WhoAmL 94*
Bieber, Elinore Maria Korow 1934- *WhoAmA 93*
Bieber, Frederick Robert 1950- *WhoScEn 94*
Bieber, Konrad (F.) 1916- *ConAu 141*
Bieber, Lynn 1928- *WhoWest 94*
Bieber, Margarete 1880-1978 *WhoAmA 93N*
Bieber, Owen F. 1929- *IntWW 93, WhoAm 94, WhoFI 94*
Bieber, Sander M. 1950- *WhoAm 94, WhoAmL 94*
Bieber-Meek, Susan Kay 1951- *WhoAmL 94*
Biebrach, Rudolf d1938 *WhoHol 92*
Biebuyck, Daniel P. 1925- *WrDr 94*
Biebuyck, Daniel Prosper 1925- *WhoAm 94*
Biebuyck, Julien Francois 1935- *WhoAm 94*
Biechlin, Robert R., Jr. 1950- *WhoAmL 94*
Bieck, Robert Barton, Jr. 1952- *WhoAm 94, WhoAmL 94*
Biedenbender, Gerhard Harold 1940- *WhoMW 93*
Biedenharn, Lawrence C., Jr. 1922- *WhoAm 94*
Biedenkop, Kurt Hans 1930- *IntWW 93*
Bieder, Richard Allan 1940- *WhoAmL 94*
Biederman, Barron Zachary *WhoAm 94*
Biederman, Charles (Karel Joseph) 1906- *WhoAmA 93*
Biederman, Charles Joseph 1906- *WhoAm 94*
Biederman, Donald Ellis 1934- *WhoAm 94, WhoAmL 94, WhoWest 94*
Biederman, Edwin Williams, Jr. 1930- *WhoScEn 94*
Biederman, James Mark 1947- *WhoAmA 93*
Biederman, Jerry H. 1946- *WhoAmL 94*
Biederman, Marcia *DrAPF 93*
Biederman, Robert W. 1952- *WhoAmL 94*
Biederman, Ronald R. 1938- *WhoAm 94*
Biedler, June L. 1925- *WhoScEn 94*
Biedron, Theodore John 1946- *WhoAm 94*
Biegel, Eileen Mae 1937- *WhoMW 93*
Biegel, Paul 1925- *SmATA 18AS [port]*
Biegen, Elaine Ruth 1939- *WhoScEn 94*
Bieging, David Arthur 1949- *WhoAmP 93*
Bieging, I. Thomas 1943- *WhoAmL 94*
Biegler, David W. 1946- *WhoAm 94, WhoFI 94*
Biegler, Louis W. 1914- *WhoIns 94*
Biego, Paolo fl. 1682-1714 *NewGrDO*
Biehl, Amy c. 1967-1993 *News 94-1*
Biehl, Cathleen Shaughnessy 1952- *WhoAmL 94*
Biehl, Charlotta Dorothea 1731-1788 *BlmGWL*
Biehl, Francis Walter 1928- *WhoMW 93*
Biehl, Michael M. 1951- *WhoAm 94*
Biehn, Michael 1956- *WhoHol 92*
Biehn, Michael 1957- *IntMPA 94*
Biek, Richard William 1931- *WhoMW 93*
Bieke, James Robert 1945- *WhoAmL 94*
Bielawski, Alan P. 1953- *WhoAm 94*
Bielawski, Anthony *WhoAmP 93*
Bielby, Gregory John 1955- *WhoScEn 94*
Biele, Hugh Irving 1942- *WhoAm 94, WhoAmL 94*
Bielecki, Jan Krzysztof 1951- *IntWW 93*
Bielefeldt, Catherine C. *WhoMW 93*
Bielenstein, Hans Henrik August 1920- *WhoAm 94*
Bieler, Andre 1896-1989 *WhAm 10*
Bieler, Andre Charles 1896-1989 *WhoAmA 93N*
Bieler, Charles Linford 1935- *WhoAm 94*
Bieler, Manfred 1934- *IntWW 94*
Bieler, Rudiger 1955- *WhoScEn 94*
Bieler, Ted Andre 1938- *WhoAmA 93*
Bieliauskas, Vytautas Joseph 1920- *WhoAm 94*
Bielinski, Daniel Walter 1961- *WhoFI 94*
Bielinski, Peter Anthony 1948- *WhoAmL 94*
Bielke, Patricia Anne 1949- *WhoMW 93*
Bielory, Abraham Melvin 1946- *WhoAmL 94*
Bielski, Alison (Joy Prosser) 1925- *WrDr 94*
Bieluch, William Charles 1918- *WhoAm 94, WhoAmL 94*
Biemann, Klaus 1926- *WhoAm 94*
Biembiel, Aleh Andrejevic 1939- *LoBiDrD*
Biemesderfer, Daniel L(uke) 1894- *WhAm 10*
Biemiller, Carl L(udwig, Jr.) 1912-1979 *EncSF 93*
Bien, Clark David 1953- *WhoAmL 94*
Bien, Darl Dean 1940- *WhoWest 94*
Bien, Joseph Julius 1936- *WhoAm 94*
Bien, Peter A. 1930- *WrDr 94*
Bien, Peter Adolph 1930- *WhoAm 94*
Bien-Austerman, Sue Ellen 1950- *WhoMW 93*
Bienemann, Charles Edward, Jr. 1941- *WhoAmL 94*
Bienen, Leigh Buchanan *DrAPF 93*
Bienen, Leigh Buchanan 1938- *WhoAmL 94*
Bienenstock, Arthur Irwin 1935- *WhoAm 94, WhoScEn 94*
Bienenstock, John 1936- *WhoAm 94, WhoScEn 94*
Bienenstock, Martin J. 1952- *WhoAm 94*
Bienes, Nicholas Peter 1952- *WrDr 94*
Bienhoff, Dallas Gene 1952- *WhoScEn 94*
Bieniawski, Zdzislaw Tadeusz 1936- *WhoAm 94, WhoScEn 94*
Bienkowska, Alicja *WhoWomW 91*
Biensfeldt, Paul d1933 *WhoHol 92*
Bienvenu, Robert Charles 1922- *WhoWest 94*
Bienville, Jean-Baptiste Le Moyne, Sieur De 1680-1768 *WhWE [port]*
Bienz, Darrel Rudolph 1926- *WhoAm 94*
Bier, Jesse 1925- *WhoWest 94*
Bier, John Leo 1936- *WhoIns 94*
Bierbauer, Charles 1942- *WhoAm 94*
Bierbaum, J. Armin 1924- *WhoAm 94*
Bierbaum, Janith Marie 1927- *WhoAm 94, WhoWest 94*
Bierbaum, Paul Martin, Jr. 1946- *WhoAmL 94, WhoWest 94*
Bierbaum, Philip James 1942- *WhoAm 94*
Bierbower, Austin 1844-1913 *EncSF 93*
Bierbower, James J. 1923- *WhoAmL 94*
Bierbower, Mark Butler 1951- *WhoAmL 94*
Bierce, Ambrose (Gwinett) 1842-c. 1914 *EncSF 93*
Bierce, Ambrose (Gwinnet) 1842-1914 *RfGShF*
Bierce, James Malcolm 1931- *WhoAmL 94*
Bierdeman, Brenda Lee 1954- *WhoMW 93*
Bierds, Linda *DrAPF 93*
Bierdz, Thom *WhoHol 92*
Bierey, Gottlob Benedict 1772-1840 *NewGrDO*
Biergaum, Gretchen 1942- *WhoAm 94*
Bierhorst, John 1936- *WrDr 94*
Bieri, Ramon *WhoHol 92*
Bierich, Marcus 1926- *IntWW 93, Who 94*
Bierig, Jack R. 1947- *WhoAm 94, WhoAmL 94*
Bierkoe, George Olaf 1895- *WhAm 10*
Bierley, John Charles 1936- *WhoAm 94*
Bierley, Paul Edmund 1926- *WhoAm 94*
Bierly, Edward J. 1920- *WhoAmA 93*
Bierly, Eugene Wendell 1931- *WhoAm 94*
Bierly, Richard A. 1946- *WhoAm 94*
Bierman, Charles Warren 1924- *WhoAm 94, WhoWest 94*
Bierman, Edwin Lawrence 1930- *WhoAm 94, WhoWest 94*
Bierman, Everett E. *WhoAmP 93*
Bierman, George William 1925- *WhoAm 94*
Bierman, Irene A. *WhoAmA 93*
Bierman, James Norman 1945- *WhoAm 94, WhoAmL 94*
Bierman, Mary Jo *WhoAmP 93*
Bierman, Philip Jay 1955- *WhoScEn 94*
Bierman, Samuel 1902-1978 *WhoAmA 93N*
Bierman, Steven M. 1952- *WhoAm 94*
Biermann, Wallace Wayne 1932- *WhoMW 93*
Biermann, Wolf 1936- *ConWorW 93*
Biernacki-Poray, Wlad Otton 1924- *WhoFI 94*
Biernat, Joseph Paul 1956- *WhoAmP 93*
Bierring, Ole 1926- *IntWW 93*
Biers, William Richard 1938- *WhoMW 93*
Bierschbach, Doug *WhoAmP 93*
Bierschwale, Bryan Walter 1950- *WhoAmP 93*
Bierstadt, Albert 1830-1902 *AmCulL [port]*
Bierstedt, Peter Richard 1943- *WhoAm 94, WhoWest 94*
Bierstedt, Robert 1913- *WhoAm 94*
Bierwirth, John Cocks 1924- *IntWW 93, WhoAm 94*
Biery, Evelyn Hudson 1946- *WhoAm 94, WhoAmL 94*
Biesdorf, Heinz Bernard 1924- *WhoAm 94*
Biesecker, John Morris 1945- *WhoMW 93*
Biesel, David B. 1931- *ConAu 140*
Biesel, David Barrie 1931- *WhoAm 94*
Biesel, Diane Jane 1934- *WhoAm 94*
Biesele, John Julius 1918- *WhoAm 94, WhoScEn 94*
Biesemeyer, Marilyn Jean 1931- *WhoMW 93*
Bieser, Irvin Gruen 1902-1989 *WhAm 10*
Biesheuvel, Barend Willem 1920- *IntWW 93*
Bieshu, Mariya Lukyanovna 1934- *IntWW 93*
Biesinger, John William, III 1949- *WhoAmL 94*
Biesiot, Patricia Marie 1950- *WhoScEn 94*
Biess, Barbara Dziedzic 1963- *WhoMW 93*
Biestek, John Paul 1935- *WhoAmL 94, WhoMW 93*
Bieterman, Michael Brady 1952- *WhoWest 94*
Bietz, Elmer A. *WhoAmP 93*
Biever, Robert Henry 1931- *WhoFI 94*
Biever, Violet S. 1911- *WhoAmP 93*
Biewen, Robert L. *WhoAm 94*
Biezup, John Thomas 1929- *WhoAm 94*
Biferie, Dan, Jr. 1950- *WhoAmA 93*
Biffen, John 1930- *IntWW 93*
Biffen, (William) John 1930- *Who 94*
Biffi, Giacomo 1928- *IntWW 93*
Biffle, Richard Lee, III 1949- *WhoWest 94*
Biffot, Laurent Marie 1925- *IntWW 93*
Bifoss, R. Ben 1953- *WhoMW 93*
Big, Guy d1978 *WhoHol 92*
Big, Susan Nagy 1946- *WhoFI 94*
Bigard, Barney d1980 *WhoHol 92*
Bigari, Francesco fl. 1766-1771 *NewGrDO*
Bigart, Homer 1907-1991 *WhAm 10*
Bigas, Johnny 1929- *WhoHisp 94*
Bigatti, Michael Marshall 1962- *WhoWest 94*
Bigbee, John Franklin, Jr. 1934- *WhoAmP 93*
Bigbie, John Taylor 1923- *WhoAm 94*
Bigbie, Scott Woodson 1946- *WhoFI 94, WhoWest 94*
Bigbie, Wanda Louise 1944- *WhoWest 94*
Bigby Young, Betty 1930- *WhoBlA 94*
Bigda, Rudolph A. 1916- *WhoFI 94*
Big Daddy Kane 1968- *WhoBlA 94*
Big Day, William c. 1891- *EncNAR*
Big Eagle, Duane *DrAPF 93*
Bigeleisen, Jacob 1919- *IntWW 93, WhoAm 94, WhoScEn 94*
Bigelow, Albert Smith d1993 *NewYTBS 93 [port]*
Bigelow, Anita (Anne Edwige Lourie) 1946- *WhoAmA 93*
Bigelow, Bruce C. 1946- *WhoAmL 94*
Bigelow, Charles Cross 1928- *WhoAm 94*
Bigelow, Daniel James 1935- *WhoFI 94, WhoMW 93*
Bigelow, David Skinner, III 1931- *WhoAm 94, WhoFI 94*
Bigelow, Donald Nevius 1918- *WhoAm 94*
Bigelow, Erastus Brigham 1814-1879 *WorInv*
Bigelow, Frank d1916 *WhoHol 92*
Bigelow, Kathryn 1951- *IntMPA 94*
Bigelow, Margaret Elizabeth Barr 1923- *WhoAm 94*
Bigelow, Martha Mitchell 1921- *WhoAm 94*
Bigelow, Michael *WhoAm 94*
Bigelow, Robert Clayton 1940- *WhoAmA 93*
Bigelow, Robert P. 1927- *WhoAm 94*
Bigelow, Timothy 1739-1790 *WhAmRev*
Bigelow, Victoria Lee 1948- *WhoMW 93*
Bigelow, W. T. 1929- *WhoBlA 94*
Bigelow-Lourie, Anne Edwige 1946- *WhoAm 94*
Bigg, Dort Sharon 1930- *WhoAmP 93*
Biggam, Robin Adair 1938- *IntWW 93, Who 94*
Biggar, (Walter) Andrew 1915- *Who 94*
Biggar, Barry P. 1952- *WhoAm 94, WhoAmL 94*
Biggar, Laura d1935 *WhoHol 92*
Biggar, Robert M., Jr. 1960- *WhoMW 93*
Biggart, (Thomas) Norman 1930- *Who 94*
Biggart, Waddell Alexander 1935- *WhoAmL 94*
Bigge, Morris L(ee) 1908- *WrDr 94*
Bigger, John P. 1934- *WhoAm 94*
Bigger, John Thomas, Jr. 1935- *WhoAm 94*
Bigger, Michael D. 1937- *WhoAmA 93*

Bigger, Richard Andrew, Jr. 1937- *WhoAmL 94*
Biggers, John 1924- *AfrAmAl 6*
Biggers, John Thomas 1924- *WhoAmA 93*
Biggers, Neal Brooks, Jr. 1935- *WhoAm 94, WhoAmL 94*
Biggers, Samuel Loring, Jr. 1935- *WhoBlA 94*
Biggers, William Joseph 1928- *WhoAm 94*
Biggerstaff, Myra 1905- *WhoAmA 93*
Biggerstaff, Randy Lee 1951- *WhoFI 94, WhoMW 93, WhoScEn 94*
Biggert, Judith Borg 1937- *WhoMW 93*
Biggert, Judy *WhoAmP 93*
Biggins, Christopher 1948- *WhoHol 92*
Biggins, Robert A. 1946- *WhoAmP 93*
Biggle, Lloyd, Jr. 1923- *EncSF 93, WrDr 94*
Biggles, Richard Robert 1946- *WhoAm 94*
Biggs *Who 94*
Biggs, Arlene *DrAPF 93*
Biggs, Arthur Edward 1930- *WhoAm 94*
Biggs, Barry Hugh 1935- *WhoAm 94*
Biggs, Barton Michael 1932- *WhoAm 94, WhoFI 94*
Biggs, Cynthia DeMari 1953- *WhoBlA 94*
Biggs, Donald Anthony 1936- *WhoAm 94*
Biggs, Geoffrey William Roger 1938- *Who 94*
Biggs, Hugh Lawry 1904- *WhoAm 94*
Biggs, J. O. 1925- *WhoAm 94*
Biggs, Janet 1959- *WhoAmA 93*
Biggs, Jeremy Hunt 1935- *WhoAm 94*
Biggs, Joel Gilson, Jr. 1947- *WhoWest 94*
Biggs, John 1933- *Who 94*
Biggs, John Burville 1934- *WrDr 94*
Biggs, John H. 1936- *WhoIns 94*
Biggs, John Herron 1936- *WhoAm 94, WhoFI 94*
Biggs, Jon Allen 1953- *WhoMW 93*
Biggs, Julie Hayward 1946- *WhoAmL 94*
Biggs, Leonard Lee 1945- *WhoMW 93*
Biggs, Lewis 1952- *Who 94*
Biggs, Margaret Key *DrAPF 93*
Biggs, Michael Worthington 1911- *Who 94*
Biggs, Norman (Parris) 1907- *Who 94*
Biggs, Norman Parris 1907- *IntWW 93*
Biggs, Peter Martin 1926- *IntWW 93, Who 94*
Biggs, R.G. 1935- *WhoWest 94*
Biggs, Richard Lee 1949- *WhoBlA 94*
Biggs, Robert Dale 1934- *WhoAm 94*
Biggs, Shirley Ann 1938- *WhoBlA 94*
Biggs, Thomas Jones 1912- *WhoAm 94*
Biggs, Thomas Wylie 1950- *WhoWest 94*
Biggs, William 1916- *WhoHol 92*
Biggy, Mary Virginia 1924- *WhoAm 94*
Bigham *Who 94*
Bigham, Reta Lacy 1949- *WhoBlA 94*
Bigham, William J. 1949- *WhoAm 94*
Bigiani, Albertino Roberto 1959- *WhoScEn 94*
Bigioni, Neil Robert 1964- *WhoAmL 94*
Bigler, Erin David 1949- *WhoWest 94*
Bigler, Glade S. 1928- *WhoAmL 94*
Bigler, Harold Edwin, Jr. 1931- *WhoAm 94*
Bigler, Wesley Dean 1955- *WhoFI 94*
Bigler, William Norman 1937- *WhoScEn 94*
Bigley, George Arthur 1898- *WhAm 10*
Bigley, Nancy Jane 1932- *WhoAm 94, WhoMW 93*
Bigley, William Joseph, Jr. 1924- *WhoFI 94, WhoScEn 94*
Bigliani, Gabriele 1952- *WhoWest 94*
Biglieri, Edward George 1925- *WhoAm 94*
Bigman, Anton W. 1929- *WhoAm 94, WhoAmL 94*
Big Mike
 See Geto Boys, The *ConMus 11*
Bignall, John Reginald 1913- *Who 94*
Bignone, Reynaldo Benito 1928- *IntWW 93*
Bigonzi, Giuseppe fl. 1707-1724 *NewGrDO*
Bigos, Stanley James 1946- *WhoWest 94*
Bigot, Eugene 1888-1965 *NewGrDO*
Big Road, Mark fl. 195-?- *EncNAR*
Bigsby, C(hristopher) W(illiam) E(dgar) 1941- *WrDr 94*
Biguenet, John *DrAPF 93*
Bigus, Edward Lowell 1958- *WhoAmL 94*
Bigus, Lawrence Weaver 1955- *WhoAmL 94*
Bihalji-Merin, Oto 1904- *IntWW 93*
Bi Hao 1927- *WhoPRCh 91 [port]*
Bihary, Joyce 1950- *WhoAm 94, WhoAmL 94*
Bihldorff, John Pearson 1945- *WhoAm 94*
Bihler, Penny Harter *DrAPF 93*
Bi Jilong *WhoPRCh 91 [port]*
Bijlani, Chandur Kishinchand 1943- *WhoAsA 94*
Bijns, Anna 1493-1575 *BlmGWL*
Bijou, Rachelle *DrAPF 93*
Bijou, Sidney William 1908- *WhoAm 94*
Bijur, Peter I. *WhoAm 94, WhoFI 94*
Bijur, Peter Isaac 1942- *Who 94*
Bikales, Norbert M. 1929- *WhoScEn 94*
Bikales, Norman Allen 1935- *WhoAm 94, WhoAmL 94*
Bikel, Ofra *NewYTBS 93 [port]*
Bikel, Theodore 1924- *WhoAm 94, WhoHol 92*
Bikin, Bruce Harlan 1948- *WhoAmL 94*
Bikkal, Cecilia G. 1954- *WhoHisp 94*
Biklen, Paul 1915- *WhoAm 94*
Bilal, Enki 1951- *EncSF 93*
Bilancia, Oreste d1945 *WhoHol 92*
Bilandic, M. 1923- *WhoAmP 93*
Bilandic, Michael A. 1923- *WhoAm 94, WhoAmL 94, WhoMW 93*
Bilaniuk, Larissa Tetiana 1941- *WhoAm 94*
Bilaniuk, Oleksa Myron 1926- *WhoAm 94*
Bilash, Olexander Ivanovych 1931- *NewGrDO*
Bilbao, Francisco Ernesto 1933- *WhoHisp 94*
Bilbao, Maria Antonieta 1950- *WhoHisp 94*
Bilbo, Claude V., Jr. 1941- *WhoAmP 93*
Bilbray, James H. 1938- *CngDr 93*
Bilbray, James Hubert 1938- *WhoAm 94, WhoAmP 93, WhoWest 94*
Bilbro, Griff Luhrs 1948- *WhoScEn 94*
Bilbrook, Lydia d1990 *WhoHol 92*
Bilby, Bruce Alexander 1922- *IntWW 93, Who 94*
Bilby, Curt 1960- *WhoFI 94, WhoScEn 94*
Bilby, Kenneth W. 1918- *IntMPA 94*
Bilby, Richard Mansfield 1931- *WhoAm 94, WhoAmL 94, WhoWest 94*
Bilchik, Gary B. 1945- *WhoAm 94*
Bild, Frank 1911- *WhoAmP 93*
Bilda, Barbara *WhoWomW 91*
Bilder, James Gerard 1958- *WhoMW 93*
Bilder, Lawrence 1923- *WhoAmL 94*
Bilderback, Diane Elizabeth 1951- *WhoWest 94*
Bilderdijk, Willem 1756-1831 *EncSF 93*
Bildersee, Robert Alan 1942- *WhoAm 94, WhoAmL 94*
Bildt, Carl 1949- *CurBio 93 [port], IntWW 93*
Bildt, Paul d1957 *WhoHol 92*
Bilecki, Ronald Allan 1942- *WhoFI 94*
Bilello, John Charles 1938- *WhoAm 94, WhoScEn 94*
Bilenkin, Dmitri (Aleksandrovich) 1933-1987 *EncSF 93*
Biles, John Alexander 1923- *WhoAm 94, WhoScEn 94*
Biles, Robert Erle 1942- *WhoAm 94*
Biletnikoff, Fred *ProFbHF [port]*
Bilett, Jane Louise 1944- *WhoScEn 94*
Bileydi, Sumer 1936- *WhoAm 94*
Bilezikjian, Edward Andrew 1950- *WhoWest 94*
Bilge, Ali Suat 1921- *IntWW 93*
Bilger, Bruce R. 1952- *WhoAmL 94*
Bilgrami, Akeel 1950- *ConAu 140*
Bilgrav-Nielsen, Jens 1936- *IntWW 93*
Bilheimer, Robert Sperry 1917- *IntWW 93*
Bilhorn, William W. 1930- *WhoAm 94*
Bilimoria, Karl Dhunjishaw 1960- *WhoScEn 94, WhoWest 94*
Bilinsky, Yaroslav 1932- *WhoAm 94, WhoScEn 94*
Bilirakis, Michael 1930- *CngDr 93, WhoAm 94, WhoAmP 93*
Bilisoly, Roger Sessa 1963- *WhoScEn 94*
Biljetina, Richard 1947- *WhoScEn 94*
Bilka, Paul Joseph 1919- *WhoAm 94*
Bill, (Edward) Geoffrey (Watson) 1924- *Who 94*
Bill, James A(lban) 1939- *WrDr 94*
Bill, Mary Fournier 1925- *WhoMW 93*
Bill, Max 1908- *IntWW 93*
Bill, Raffles d1940 *WhoHol 92*
Bill, Richard Allen 1943- *WhoFI 94*
Bill, Stephen 1948- *ConDr 93*
Bill, Tony 1940- *IntMPA 94, WhoAm 94, WhoHol 92*
Billadello, Joseph John 1952- *WhoMW 93*
Billage, Judith 1949- *WhoAmL 94*
Billard, William Thomas 1946- *WhoFI 94, WhoMW 93*
Billardiere, Jacques-Julien Houtou De La *WhWE*
Billatos, Samir Botros 1954- *WhoFI 94*
Billau, Robin Louise 1951- *WhoFI 94*
Billaud, Bernard 1942- *IntWW 93*
Billauer, Barbara Pfeffer 1951- *WhoAm 94, WhoAmL 94*
Billcliffe, Roger (George) 1946- *WrDr 94*
Billeaud, Manning Francis 1927- *WhoScEn 94*
Billeci, Andre George 1933- *WhoAm 94, WhoAmA 93*
Biller, Henry Burt 1940- *WhoAm 94*
Biller, Hugh Frederick 1934- *WhoAm 94*
Biller, Joel Wilson 1929- *WhoAm 94, WhoAmL 94*
Biller, Leslie Stuart 1948- *WhoAm 94, WhoFI 94*
Biller, Morris 1915- *WhoAm 94*
Billera, Louis Joseph 1943- *WhoScEn 94*
Billesbach, David Paul 1956- *WhoMW 93*
Billeskov-Jansen, Frederik Julius 1907- *IntWW 93*
Billet, Bret Lee 1962- *WhoMW 93*
Billetdoux, Raphaele 1951- *BlmGWL*
Billett, Don(ald) *WhoHol 92*
Billett, Paul Rodney 1921- *Who 94*
Billheimer, Stephanie Dana 1955- *WhoWest 94*
Billia, Darlene A. 1948- *WhoAm 94*
Billian, Cathey R. *WhoAm 94, WhoAmA 93*
Billias, George Athan 1919- *WhoAm 94, WrDr 94*
Billias, Stephen *EncSF 93*
Billie, Josie c. 1887- *EncNAR*
Billig, Erwin H. 1927- *WhoFI 94*
Billig, Etel Jewel 1932- *WhoMW 93*
Billig, Frederick Stucky 1933- *WhoScEn 94*
Billig, Robert Emmanuel 1946- *WhoScEn 94*
Billig, Thomas Clifford 1930- *WhoAm 94*
Billimoria, Eddie d1981 *WhoHol 92*
Billing, Graham (John) 1936- *WrDr 94*
Billing, Noel Pemberton 1881-1948 *DcNaB MP*
Billingham, Rupert Everett 1921- *IntWW 93, Who 94, WhoAm 94, WhoScEn 94*
Billings, Benjamin d1923 *WhoHol 92*
Billings, Brian Lee 1957- *WhoAmP 93*
Billings, Charles Edgar 1929- *WhoAm 94, WhoMW 93*
Billings, Charles R. 1944- *WhoAmL 94*
Billings, Cora Marie, Sister 1939- *WhoBlA 94*
Billings, Donald Franklin 1957- *WhoAm 94*
Billings, Earl William 1945- *WhoBlA 94*
Billings, Edward Robert 1913- *WhoAm 94*
Billings, Elmo d1964 *WhoHol 92*
Billings, Franklin S., Jr. 1922- *WhoAmP 93*
Billings, Franklin Swift, Jr. 1922- *WhoAm 94, WhoAmL 94*
Billings, George A. d1934 *WhoHol 92*
Billings, Harold Wayne 1931- *WhoAm 94*
Billings, Harry d1944 *WhoHol 92*
Billings, Henry 1901-1987 *WhoAmA 93N*
Billings, James G. 1942- *WhoAmL 94*
Billings, John Shaw 1898-1975 *DcLB 137 [port]*
Billings, Joseph c. 1758-1806 *WhWE*
Billings, Judith *WhoAm 94, WhoWest 94*
Billings, Judith A. 1939- *WhoAmP 93*
Billings, Leon *WhoAmP 93*
Billings, Linda 1951- *WhoScEn 94*
Billings, Marland Pratt 1902- *WhoAm 94*
Billings, Matthew Breck 1963- *WhoMW 93*
Billings, Patricia Anne 1943- *WhoFI 94*
Billings, Peggy Marie 1928- *WhoAm 94*
Billings, Peter, Jr. 1945- *WhoAmP 93*
Billings, Richard Whitten 1924- *WhoFI 94*
Billings, Robert Northrop 1947- *WhoIns 94*
Billings, Ted d1947 *WhoHol 92*
Billings, Thomas Neal 1931- *WhoFI 94, WhoScEn 94, WhoWest 94*
Billings, William Dwight 1910- *WhoAm 94, WhoScEn 94*
Billings, William Howard 1921- *WhAm 10*
Billingslea, Charles 1914-1989 *WhAm 10*
Billingslea, Edgar D. 1910- *WhoBlA 94*
Billingslea, Monroe L. 1933- *WhoBlA 94*
Billingsley, Andrew 1926- *BlkWr 2, WhoBlA 94*
Billingsley, Barbara *WhoHol 92*
Billingsley, Charles Edward 1933- *WhoAm 94*
Billingsley, David Stuart 1929- *WhoScEn 94*
Billingsley, Jennifer *WhoHol 92*
Billingsley, Lance William 1940- *WhoAmP 93*
Billingsley, Orzell, Jr. 1924- *WhoBlA 94*
Billingsley, Peter 1972- *WhoHol 92*
Billingsley, Ray C. 1957- *WhoBlA 94*
Billingsley, Robert Thaine 1954- *WhoAmL 94*
Billingsley, William Scott 1963- *WhoFI 94*
Billington, Brian John 1939- *Who 94*
Billington, Clyde, Jr. 1934- *WhoBlA 94*
Billington, David P(erkins) 1927- *WrDr 94*
Billington, David Perkins 1927- *WhoAm 94*
Billington, Elizabeth 1765?-1818 *NewGrDO*
Billington, Francelia d1934 *WhoHol 92*
Billington, James H(adley) 1929- *WrDr 94*
Billington, James Hadley 1929- *IntWW 93, Who 94, WhoAm 94*
Billington, Kevin 1934- *IntWW 93, Who 94*
Billington, Michael 1939- *Who 94, WhoHol 92, WrDr 94*
Billington, Peter James 1948- *WhoWest 94*
Billington, Rachel 1942- *WrDr 94*
Billington, Rachel (Mary) 1942- *Who 94*
Billington, Ray(mond John) 1930- *WrDr 94*
Billinson, George David 1954- *WhoAm 94*
Billinton, Roy 1935- *WhoAm 94, WhoWest 94*
Billion, John J. 1939- *WhoAmP 93*
Billion, John Joseph 1939- *WhoMW 93*
Billiot, John Alvas 1933- *WhoAmP 93*
Billiter, Freda Delorous 1937- *WhoMW 93*
Billiter, William Overton, Jr. 1934- *WhoAm 94*
Billman, Irwin Edward 1940- *WhoAm 94*
Billmeyer, Fred W., Jr. 1919- *WrDr 94*
Billmeyer, Fred Wallace, Jr. 1919- *WhoScEn 94*
Billmyer, John Edward 1912- *WhoAmA 93*
Billopp, Christopher 1737-1827 *WhAmRev*
Billops, Camille 1933- *AfrAmAl 6*
Billops, Camille J. 1933- *WhoBlA 94*
Billot, Barbara Kathleen 1920- *Who 94*
Billotte, Pierre d1992 *IntWW 93N*
Billotte, Pierre 1906-1992 *AnObit 1992*
Billow, Andrew, Jr. *WhoAmP 93*
Bills, Johnny Bernard 1949- *WhoBlA 94*
Bills, Linda 1943- *WhoAmA 93*
Bills, Mitchell 1950- *WhoAmA 93*
Bills, Robert Howard 1944- *WhoAm 94*
Billups, Florence W. 1921- *WhoBlA 94*
Billups, Mattie Lou 1935- *WhoBlA 94*
Billups, Myles E., Sr. 1926- *WhoBlA 94*
Billups, Norman Fredrick 1934- *WhoAm 94*
Billups, Rufus L. 1928- *AfrAmG [port]*
Billy, George John 1940- *WhoAm 94*
Billy, Little d1967 *WhoHol 92*
Bilney, Gordon 1939- *IntWW 93*
Bilodeau, John Lowell 1941- *WhoScEn 94*
Bilofsky, Howard Steven 1943- *WhoScEn 94*
Bilon, Michael d1983 *WhoHol 92*
Bilott, Robert Alan 1965- *WhoAmL 94*
Bilotti, Salvatore F. 1879-1953 *WhoAmA 93N*
Bilotti-Stark, Kathryn Elizabeth 1950- *WhoWest 94*
Bilous, Priscilla Haley *WhoAmA 93*
Bilow, Sharon Swarsensky 1953- *WhoAmL 94*
Bilow, Steven Craig 1960- *WhoWest 94*
Bilpuch, Edward George 1927- *WhoAm 94, WhoScEn 94*
Bilslend, Marcy Jean 1968- *WhoFI 94*
Bilson, Bruce 1928- *ConTFT 11, IntMPA 94*
Bilt, Peter van der 1936-1983 *NewGrDO*
Biltonen, Rodney Lincoln 1937- *WhoAm 94*
Biltz, Jim 1947- *WhoMW 93*
Bilyeu, Byron Lee 1936- *WhoAmP 93*
Bilyeu, Charles Edward 1917- *WhoAmP 93*
Bilzin, Brian L. 1945- *WhoAmL 94*
Bimboni, Alberto 1882-1960 *NewGrDO*
Bimrose, Arthur Sylvanus, Jr. 1912- *WhoAmA 93*
Bimson, Carl Alfred 1900- *WhoAm 94, WhoWest 94*
Bina, Cyrus 1946- *ConAu 140*
Bina, Melvin Joseph 1931- *WhoWest 94*
Binai, Paul Freye 1932- *WhoAmA 93*
Binaisa, Godfrey Lukwongwa 1920- *IntWW 93*
Bincer, Adam Marian 1930- *WhoAm 94*
Binchy, Maeve 1940- *BlmGWL, IntWW 93, Who 94, WrDr 94*
Binder, Alvin M. d1993 *NewYTBS 93 [port]*
Binder, Amy Finn 1955- *WhoAm 94, WhoFI 94*
Binder, Carl 1816-1860 *NewGrDO*
Binder, David Franklin 1935- *WhoAm 94, WhoAmL 94, WhoFI 94*
Binder, Eando *EncSF 93*
Binder, Earl Andrew *EncSF 93*
Binder, Erwin 1934- *WhoAmA 93, WhoWest 94*
Binder, Gordon M. 1935- *WhoWest 94*
Binder, Herbert R. 1937- *WhoAm 94, WhoFI 94*
Binder, Jack *EncSF 93*

Binder, James Kauffman 1920- WhoWest 94
Binder, John 1930- WhoMW 93
Binder, Kurt 1944- WhoScEn 94
Binder, Leonard James 1926- WhoAm 94
Binder, Lucy Simpson 1937- WhoAm 94
Binder, Madeline Dotti 1942- WhoMW 93
Binder, Matthew J. 1917- WhoAmP 93
Binder, Otto O. EncSF 93
Binder, Paul NewYTBS 93 [port]
Binder, Richard Allen 1937- WhoAm 94
Binder, Rima Kasuba 1939- WhoMW 93
Binder, Robert Lawrence 1951- WhoAm 94
Binder, Steve IntMPA 94
Binder, Sybille d1962 WhoHol 92
Binder, Theodor 1919- IntWW 93
Binder, Wendy C. 1948- WhoAmL 94
Bindernagel, Gertrud 1894-1932 NewGrDO
Bindi, Rosaria 1951- WhoWomW 91
Binding, Gunther 1936- IntWW 93
Bindler, Paul Lawrence 1951- WhoAmL 94
Bindley, William Edward 1940- WhoAm 94, WhoFI 94, WhoMW 93
Binegar, Gwendolyn Ann 1924- WhoWest 94
Bines, Harvey Ernest 1941- WhoAm 94, WhoAmL 94
Binet, Betsey Jan 1953- WhoWest 94
Binford, Gregory Glenn 1948- WhoAm 94, WhoAmL 94
Binford, Henry C. 1944- WhoBlA 94
Binford, Jesse Stone, Jr. 1928- WhoAm 94
Binford, Laurence C. 1935- WrDr 94
Binford, Lewis R(oberts) 1930- WrDr 94
Bing, Alexander 1878-1959 WhoAmA 93N
Bing, Anthony Grayum 1935- WhoMW 93
Bing, Dave 1943- AfrAmAl 6 [port], BasBi, WhoBlA 94
Bing, Gus d1967 WhoHol 92
Bing, Herman d1947 WhoHol 92
Bing, Inigo Geoffrey 1944- Who 94
Bing, John Howard 1939- WhoMW 93
Bing, Jon EncSF 93
Bing, Leon 1950- ConAu 140
Bing, Ralph Sol 1917- WhoWest 94
Bing, Richard McPhail 1950- WhoAmL 94
Bing, Rubell M. 1938- WhoBlA 94
Bing, Rudolf 1902- IntWW 93, NewGrDO
Bing, Rudolf (Franz Joseph) 1902- Who 94
Bingaman, Anne K. NewYTBS 93 [port]
Bingaman, Anne Kovacovich 1943- WhoAmL 94
Bingaman, Jeff 1943- CngDr 93, IntWW 93, WhoAm 94, WhoAmP 93, WhoWest 94
Binger, Glenn H. 1931- WhoAmP 93
Binger, Louis-Gustav 1856-1936 WhWE
Binger, Wilson Valentine 1917- WhoAm 94
Bingham Who 94
Bingham, Lord 1967- Who 94
Bingham, Alice 1936- WhoAmA 93
Bingham, Arthur E. 1906- WhoBlA 94
Bingham, Bruce Bryan 1948- WhoAm 94
Bingham, Caroline 1938- WrDr 94
Bingham, Caroline Margery Conyers 1938- Who 94
Bingham, Carter 1920- EncSF 93
Bingham, Cecil d1925 WhoHol 92
Bingham, Charles W. 1933- WhoFI 94
Bingham, Charlotte 1942- WrDr 94
Bingham, Charlotte Mary Therese 1942- Who 94
Bingham, Christopher 1937- WhoAm 94, WhoMW 93
Bingham, Curtis Harry 1898- WhAm 10
Bingham, Donna Guydon 1961- WhoBlA 94
Bingham, Edwin Theodore 1936- WhoAm 94
Bingham, Eula 1929- WhoAm 94
Bingham, George Barry, Jr. 1933- WhoAm 94
Bingham, George Caleb 1811-1879 AmCulL
Bingham, Harry Payne, Mrs. WhoAmA 93
Bingham, Hiram 1789-1869 DcAmReB 2
Bingham, J. Peter WhoScEn 94
Bingham, Jinsie Scott 1935- WhoAm 94, WhoMW 93
Bingham, John 1930- IntWW 93, Who 94
Bingham, June Rossbach 1919- WrDr 94
Bingham, Leslie d1945 WhoHol 92
Bingham, Lois A. 1913- WhoAmA 93
Bingham, Max Who 94
Bingham, (Eardley) Max 1927- Who 94
Bingham, Nelson Preston 1925- WhoAmP 93
Bingham, Paris Edward, Jr. 1957- WhoScEn 94, WhoWest 94
Bingham, Rebecca Josephine 1928- WhoBlA 94
Bingham, Richard Donnelly 1937- WhoAm 94, WhoMW 93
Bingham, Robert Frederick 1962- WhoFI 94, WhoWest 94
Bingham, S. J. d1962 WhoHol 92
Bingham, Sallie DrAPF 93
Bingham, Sallie 1937- WrDr 94
Bingham, Thomas (Henry) 1933- IntWW 93, Who 94
Bingham, Timothy W. 1945- WhoAmL 94
Bingham, Walter D. 1921- WhoAm 94
Bingham, William 1752-1804 WhAmRev
Bingham, William Brian 1943- WhoFI 94
Bingham, William H. 1943- WhoAmL 94
Bingley, Clive (Hamilton) 1936- WrDr 94
Bingley, D. E. ConAu 42NR
Bingley, David Ernest 1920-1985 ConAu 42NR
Bingley, Edward J. 1934- WhoIns 94
Bingley, Juliet Martin 1925- Who 94
Bingman, Bradlee Ann 1959- WhoMW 93
Bingman, Charles Franklin 1929- WhoFI 94
Bingman, Terrence Lee 1948- WhoAm 94
Bing Xin WhoPRCh 91
Bing Xin 1900- BlmGWL
Bini, Carlo c. 1944- NewGrDO
Bini, Dante Natale 1932- WhoScEn 94, WhoWest 94
Binicki, Stanislav 1872-1942 NewGrDO
Binienda, John Joseph, Sr. 1947- WhoAmP 93
Bining, Avtar Singh 1955- WhoWest 94
Binion, Beatrice Marie 1958- WhoMW 93
Binion, Rudolph 1927- WrDr 94
Binkerd, Gordon Ware 1916- WhoAm 94
Binkert, Alvin John 1910- WhoAm 94
Binkert, Pius 1923- IntWW 93
Binkley, Joan Vivian 1933- WhoWest 94
Binkley, Johne 1953- WhoAmP 93
Binkley, Luther John 1925- WrDr 94
Binkley, Margaret Ann 1941- WhoMW 93
Binkley, Marguerite Hall 1926- WhoAmP 93
Binkley, Nicholas Burns 1945- WhoAm 94, WhoFI 94, WhoWest 94
Binkley, Olin Trivette 1908- WhoAm 94
Binkley, Thomas (Eden) 1931- WrDr 94
Binkowski, Edward Stephan 1948- WhoAm 94
Binkowski, Johannes Aloysius Joseph 1908- IntWW 93
Binks, Les
See Judas Priest ConMus 10
Binks, Rebecca Anne 1955- WhoFI 94, WhoMW 93
Binks, Ronald C. 1934- WhoAmA 93
Binney, Constance 1900- WhoHol 92
Binney, David H. 1952- WhoAmL 94
Binney, Faire d1957 WhoHol 92
Binney, H(arry) A(ugustus) Roy 1907- Who 94
Binney, James Jeffrey 1950- WhoScEn 94
Binney, Marcus Hugh Crofton Who 94
Binney, Robert Harry 1945- WhoAm 94
Binnie, David Stark 1922- Who 94
Binnie, Nancy Catherine 1937- WhoWest 94
Binnig, Gerd WorInv
Binnig, Gerd 1947- IntWW 93
Binnig, Gerd Karl 1947- Who 94, WhoAm 94, WhoScEn 94
Binning, Lord 1985- Who 94
Binning, Bertram Charles 1909-1976 WhoAmA 93N
Binning, Gene Barton 1953- WhoFI 94
Binning, J. Boyd 1944- WhoAmL 94
Binning, John Harlan 1923- WhoIns 94
Binning, Kenneth George Henry 1928- Who 94
Binning, William Charles 1944- WhoAmP 93
Binnion, John Edward 1918- WhoAm 94, WhoAmP 93
Binns, David John 1929- Who 94
Binns, Edward d1990 WhoHol 92
Binns, Geoffrey John 1930- Who 94
Binns, George d1918 WhoHol 92
Binns, Jack Robert 1933- WhoAmP 93
Binns, James Edward 1931- WhoAm 94
Binns, James W. 1946- WhoFI 94
Binns, Malcolm 1936- IntWW 93, Who 94
Binns, Michael Ferrers Elliott 1923- WrDr 94
Binns, St. John 1914- Who 94
Binns, Silas Odell 1920- WhoBlA 94
Binns, Susan May 1948- Who 94
Binns, Walter Gordon, Jr. 1929- WhoAm 94, WhoFI 94
Binns, Walter Robert 1940- WhoScEn 94
Binns, William Arthur 1925- WhoMW 93, WhoScEn 94
Binnuna, Khanatta 1940- BlmGWL
Binny, John Anthony Francis 1911- Who 94
Binoche, Juliette IntWW 93
Binoche, Juliette 1965- WhoHol 92
Bins, Milton 1934- WhoBlA 94
Bins, Patricia 1930- BlmGWL
Binsfeld, Connie B. 1924- WhoAmP 93
Binsfeld, Connie Berube 1924- WhoAm 94, WhoMW 93
Binsfield, Craig Thomas 1961- WhoFI 94
Binstock, Robert Henry 1935- WhoAm 94
Binswanger, Frank G., Jr. 1928- WhoAm 94, WhoFI 94
Binswanger, John K. 1932- WhoFI 94
Bintley, David 1957- IntDcB [port]
Bintley, David Julian 1957- Who 94
Bintliff, Barbara Ann 1953- WhoAmL 94
bin Yeop, Abdul Aziz 1916- Who 94
Binyon, Michael (Roger) 1944- ConAu 142
Binzen, Peter (Husted) 1922- WrDr 94
Binzen, Peter Husted 1922- WhoAm 94
Biobaku, Saburi Oladeni 1918- IntWW 93, Who 94
Bioke Malabo, Cristino Seriche IntWW 93
Biolchini, Gregory Phillip 1948- WhoAmA 93
Biolchini, Robert Fredrick 1939- WhoAm 94, WhoAmL 94, WhoFI 94
Biondi, Christine A. 1952- WhoAmP 93
Biondi, Frank J., Jr. 1945- IntMPA 94, WhoAm 94, WhoFI 94
Biondi, Lawrence 1938- WhoAm 94, WhoMW 93
Biondi, Manfred Anthony 1924- WhoAm 94
Biondi, Matt WhoAm 94
Biondo, Dino Dominick 1958- WhoMW 93
Biondo, Michael Thomas 1928- WhoAm 94
Biondo, Raymond Vitus 1936- WhoScEn 94
Bioni, Antonio 1698-1739 NewGrDO
Biorn, David Olaf 1942- WhoAm 94
Biot, Jean Baptiste 1774-1862 WorScD
Bioy Casares, Adolfo 1914- ConAu 43NR, ConWorW 93, EncSF 93, HispLC [port], IntWW 93, RfGShF
Bippes, Bernece 1918- WhoAmP 93
Bippus, David Paul 1949- WhoAm 94, WhoFI 94, WhoMW 93
Bippus, Leon Dale 1936- WhoFI 94
Bir, Michelle Marie 1965- WhoMW 93
Biradavolu, Kaleswara Rao 1956- WhoAsA 94
Biran, Yoav 1939- Who 94
Birath, John F., Jr. 1946- WhoAmL 94
Biraud, Maurice d1982 WhoHol 92
Birbari, Adil Elias 1933- WhoScEn 94
Birch, Albert Francis 1903-1992 WhAm 10
Birch, Alexander Hope 1913- Who 94
Birch, Anthony Harold 1924- Who 94, WrDr 94
Birch, Arthur John 1915- IntWW 93, Who 94
Birch, Bryan John 1931- IntWW 93, Who 94
Birch, Clifford Wadsworth, Jr. 1920- WhoAmP 93
Birch, David William 1913- WhoFI 94
Birch, Dennis Arthur 1925- Who 94
Birch, Edward Elton 1938- WhoWest 94
Birch, Eugenius 1818-1884 DcNaB MP
Birch, Frank d1956 WhoHol 92
Birch, Frank Stanley Heath 1939- Who 94
Birch, Jack Willard 1915- WhoAm 94
Birch, Jean Gordon 1921- WhoAmP 93
Birch, Jim Hunter 1957- WhoAmL 94
Birch, John 1745-1815 EncSPD
Birch, John (Allan) 1935- Who 94
Birch, John A. 1943- WhoAmP 93
Birch, John Anthony 1929- Who 94
Birch, L. Charles 1918- IntWW 93
Birch, Murray Patrick 1953- WhoAm 94
Birch, Paul d1969 WhoHol 92
Birch, Peter Gibbs 1937- Who 94
Birch, Philip Thomas 1927- Who 94
Birch, Reginald 1914- Who 94
Birch, Robert Edward Thomas 1917- Who 94
Birch, Robin Arthur 1939- Who 94
Birch, Roger 1930- Who 94
Birch, Stanley F., Jr. WhoAmP 93
Birch, Stanley Francis, Jr. 1945- WhoAm 94, WhoAmL 94
Birch, V. Lane 1954- WhoMW 93
Birch, William 1925- Who 94
Birch, William (Francis) 1934- Who 94
Birch, William Dunham, Jr. 1940- WhoAm 94
Birch, Willie M. 1942- WhoAmA 93
Birch, Wyrley d1959 WhoHol 92
Birchall, (James) Derek 1930- Who 94
Birchall, James Derek 1930- IntWW 93
Birchall, Linda Grimes 1947- WhoAmL 94
Birchansky, Leo 1887-1949 WhoAmA 93N
Birchby, Kenneth Lee 1915- WhoAm 94, WhoFI 94
Birch-Connery, Michele Anne DrAPF 93
Birchem, Regina 1938- WhoAm 94
Birchenough, (John) Michael 1923- Who 94
Bircher, Edgar Allen 1934- WhoAm 94, WhoAmL 94
Birchette, William Ashby, III 1942- WhoBlA 94
Birchette-Pierce, Cheryl L. 1945- WhoBlA 94
Birchfield, John Kermit, Jr. 1940- WhoAm 94, WhoAmL 94
Birchill, Isabella NewGrDO
Birchmeier, James Robert 1960- WhoAmL 94
Birch-Pfeiffer, Charlotte 1800-1868 BlmGWL
Birck, Michael John 1938- WhoAm 94
Birckett, Anna Belle WhoAmA 93
Bird, Adrian Peter 1947- Who 94
Bird, Agnes Thornton 1921- WhoAm 94, WhoAmL 94, WhoAmP 93
Bird, Allen Williamson, II 1943- WhoAmL 94
Bird, Anthony Peter 1931- Who 94
Bird, Bille 1908- WhoHol 92
Bird, Caroline 1915- WhoAm 94, WrDr 94
Bird, Charles Albert 1947- WhoAmL 94, WhoWest 94
Bird, Charles Coleman 1945- WhoAm 94, WhoAmL 94
Bird, Cordwainer EncSF 93
Bird, Daniel Chambers, Jr. 1947- WhoAm 94
Bird, Daniel Woodrow, Jr. 1938- WhoAmP 93
Bird, David 1945- WhoAmP 93
Bird, Deborah Kay 1950- WhoWest 94
Bird, Dennis Leslie 1930- WrDr 94
Bird, Edward Dennis 1926- WhoAm 94
Bird, Francis Marion, Jr. 1938- WhoAmL 94
Bird, George Richard 1942- WhoMW 93
Bird, Glenn V. 1949- WhoAmP 93
Bird, Harrie Waldo, Jr. 1917- WhoAm 94, WhoMW 93, WhoScEn 94
Bird, Harry H. 1933- WhoAm 94
Bird, Hector Ramon 1939- WhoHisp 94
Bird, Henry WhAmRev
Bird, James Gurth 1909- Who 94
Bird, James Harold 1923- WrDr 94
Bird, Joann T. 1949- WhoAmP 93
Bird, John 1936- WhoHol 92
Bird, John 1941- WrDr 94
Bird, John Adams 1937- WhoAm 94
Bird, John Alfred William Who 94
Bird, John Commons 1922- WhoAmL 94
Bird, John Eric 1958- WhoWest 94
Bird, John Malcolm 1931- WhoAm 94
Bird, John T. WhoAmP 93
Bird, Kendal Sue 1964- WhoAmL 94
Bird, L. Raymond 1914- WhoFI 94
Bird, Larry 1956- BasBi
Bird, Larry Joe 1956- WhoAm 94
Bird, Laurie d1979 WhoHol 92
Bird, Lesley Ann 1963- WhoWest 94
Bird, Mary Lynne Miller 1934- WhoAm 94, WhoScEn 94
Bird, Matthew Alexius 1957- WhoMW 93
Bird, Michael C. 1939- WhoAmP 93
Bird, Michael James 1935- Who 94
Bird, Michael Larry 1949- WhoAmP 93
Bird, Mynah WhoHol 92
Bird, Norman 1919- WhoHol 92
Bird, Patricia Coleen 1953- WhoWest 94
Bird, Pete d1981 WhoHol 92
Bird, Peter 1951- WhoAm 94
Bird, Phillip Craig 1947- WhoMW 93
Bird, Randall Charles 1949- WhoWest 94
Bird, Richard Who 94
Bird, Richard 1895- WhoHol 92
Bird, Richard 1938- WrDr 94
Bird, Richard 1950- Who 94
Bird, (Colin) Richard (Bateman) 1933- Who 94
Bird, Richard (Geoffrey Chapman) 1935- Who 94
Bird, Richard Herries 1932- Who 94
Bird, Robert Byron 1924- WhoAm 94, WhoMW 93
Bird, Robert Wilson 1918- WhoAm 94
Bird, Ronald Charles 1936- WhoAmP 93
Bird, Rose Elizabeth 1936- WhoAm 94, WhoAmP 93
Bird, Stephen C. 1939- WhoAmP 93
Bird, Vere Cornwall 1910- Who 94
Bird, Vere Cornwall, Sr. 1909- IntWW 93
Bird, Wendell Raleigh 1954- WhoAmL 94
Bird, Whitworth F. 1932- WhoIns 94
Bird, William Henry Fleming 1896-1971 EncSF 93
Bird, William Russell 1898- WhAm 10
Birdlebough, Harold 1928- WhoWest 94
Birdman, Jerome Moseley 1930- WhoAm 94
Birdoff, David C. 1945- WhoAmL 94
Birdsall, Arthur Anthony 1947- WhoMW 93
Birdsall, Blair 1907- WhoAm 94
Birdsall, Byron 1937- WhoAmA 93

Birdsall, Charles Kennedy 1925- WhoAm 94
Birdsall, David Lee 1954- WhoWest 94
Birdsall, Derek Walter 1934- Who 94
Birdsall, Doris 1915- Who 94
Birdsall, Jesse WhoHol 92
Birdsall, William Forest 1937- WhoAm 94
Birdsell, Sandra 1942- BlmGWL, WrDr 94
Birdsey, Anna Campas 1949- WhoAm 94
Birdseye, Clarence 1886-1956 WorInv
Birdseye, Tom 1951- WrDr 94
Birdsong, George Yancy 1939- WhoAm 94
Birdsong, Jimmy 1925- WhoAmP 93
Birdsong, Kenneth Wilson 1927- WhoAmP 93
Birdsong, Otis 1955- BasBi
Birdsong, William Herbert, Jr. 1918- WhoAm 94
Birdwell, James Edwin, Jr. 1924- WhoAm 94
Birdwhistell, Ray L. 1918- WhoAm 94
Bird-Wilson, Harold Arthur Cooper 1919- Who 94
Birdwood Who 94
Birdwood, Baron 1938- Who 94
Birdzell, Samuel Henry 1916- WhoAm 94
Bireline, George Lee 1923- WhoAmA 93
Birell, Tala d1959 WhoHol 92
Biren, David Robert 1937- WhoFI 94
Birenbaum, Barbara 1941- WrDr 94
Birenbaum, Cynthia WhoAmA 93
Birenbaum, William M. 1923- WhoAm 94, WrDr 94
Birendra Bir Bikram Shah Dev, King of Nepal 1945- IntWW 93
Birewar, Deepak Baburao 1962- WhoScEn 94
Birgbauer, Bruce D. 1942- WhoAmL 94
Birge, Robert Richards 1946- WhoAm 94, WhoScEn 94
Birgel, Willy d1974 WhoHol 92
Birgeneau, Robert Joseph 1942- WhoAm 94
Birgitta av Vadstena 1303-1373 BlmGWL
Birido, Omer Yousif 1939- IntWW 93
Birimisa, George 1924- ConDr 93
Birincioglu, Ahmet Ihsan 1923- IntWW 93
Biringer, Paul Peter 1924- WhoAm 94
Birk Who 94
Birk, Baroness Who 94, WhoWomW 91
Birk, Jim WhoFI 94
Birk, John R. 1951- WhoAm 94
Birk, Robert Eugene 1926- WhoAm 94
Birk, Roger Emil 1930- IntWW 93
Birk, Sharon Anastasia 1937- WhoAm 94
Birkby, Walter Hudson 1931- WhoWest 94
Birke, Adolf Mattias 1939- IntWW 93
Birkedal-Hansen, Henning WhoScEn 94
Birkeland, Arthur C. 1904- WhoAmP 93
Birkeland, Bryan Collier 1951- WhoAm 94
Birkeland, Kristian Olaf Bernhard 1867-1917 WorInv
Birkelbach, Albert Ottmar 1927- WhoAm 94
Birkelund, John Peter 1930- WhoAm 94, WhoFI 94
Birkelund, Palle 1912- IntWW 93
Birkenhead, Bishop Suffragan of 1946- Who 94
Birkenhead, Earl of 1907-1975 DcNaB MP
Birkenhead, Thomas Bruce 1931- WhoAm 94
Birkenkamp, Dean Frederick 1956- WhoAm 94
Birkenstein, Lillian Ray 1900-1988 WhAm 10
Birkenstock, James Warren 1912- WhoAm 94
Birkerts, Gunnar 1925- IntWW 93, WhoAm 94
Birkerts, Sven 1951- WrDr 94
Birkett Who 94
Birkett, Baron 1929- Who 94
Birkett, Cynthia Anne 1960- WhoMW 93
Birkett, Peter Vidler 1948- Who 94
Birkett, Viva d1934 WhoHol 92
Birkhead, Guthrie Sweeney, Jr. 1920- WhoAm 94
Birkhead, John Andrew 1954- WhoWest 94
Birkhoff, Garrett 1911- IntWW 93, WhoAm 94, WrDr 94
Birkhoff, Neil Vincent 1955- WhoAmL 94
Birkholz, Raymond James 1936- WhoAm 94, WhoMW 93
Birkin, Andrew (Timothy) 1945- ConAu 41NR
Birkin, Derek Who 94
Birkin, Derek 1929- IntWW 93
Birkin, (John) Derek 1929- Who 94
Birkin, Jane 1946- IntMPA 94
Birkin, Jane 1947- WhoHol 92
Birkin, John (Christian William) 1953- Who 94
Birkin, Morton 1919- WhoAmA 93N
Birkinbine, John, II 1930- WhoAm 94, WhoWest 94
Birkinbine, John L., Jr. 1946- WhoAmP 93
Birkinshaw, John Howard 1894- Who 94
Birkland, Bryan Collier 1951- WhoAmL 94
Birkmaier, Robert David 1955- WhoAmL 94
Birkmyre, Archibald 1923- Who 94
Birks, Jack 1920- IntWW 93, Who 94
Birks, John William 1946- WhoScEn 94
Birks, Michael 1920- Who 94
Birks, Neil 1935- WhoAm 94
Birks, Peter Brian Herrenden 1941- Who 94
Birk-Updyke, Dawn Marie 1963- WhoScEn 94
Birky, John Edward 1934- WhoAm 94
Birla, Basant Kumar 1921- IntWW 93
Birla, Ganga Prasad 1922- IntWW 93
Birle, James Robb 1936- WhoAm 94
Birleffi, Lynn 1944- WhoAmP 93
Birley, Anthony Addison 1920- Who 94
Birley, Cindy Sue 1959- WhoAmL 94
Birley, Derek 1926- Who 94
Birley, Eric 1906- Who 94
Birley, James Leatham Tennant 1928- Who 94
Birley, Michael Pellew 1920- Who 94
Birley, Susan Joyce Who 94
Birman, Joseph Leon 1927- WhoAm 94, WhoScEn 94
Birman, Victor Mark 1950- WhoScEn 94
Birmele, Raymond Elsworth 1948- WhoMW 93
Birmelin, A. Robert 1933- WhoAmA 93
Birmelin, August Robert 1933- WhoAm 94
Birmelin, Jerry WhoAmP 93
Birmingham, Archbishop of 1929- Who 94
Birmingham, Archdeacon of Who 94
Birmingham, Auxiliary Bishop of Who 94
Birmingham, Bishop of 1936- Who 94
Birmingham, Provost of Who 94
Birmingham, Alan 1943- WhoAmL 94
Birmingham, Bascom Wayne 1925- WhoAm 94
Birmingham, Maisie 1914- WrDr 94
Birmingham, Mary Irene 1926- WhoAmP 93
Birmingham, Paul A. 1937- IntMPA 94
Birmingham, Richard Francis 1949- WhoAmL 94
Birmingham, Richard Gregory 1929- WhoAm 94
Birmingham, Richard Joseph 1953- WhoAm 94, WhoAmL 94
Birmingham, Stephen 1931- WhoAm 94, WrDr 94
Birmingham, Thomas Edward 1951- WhoFI 94, WhoWest 94
Birmingham, Thomas F. 1949- WhoAmP 93
Birmingham, Walter (Barr) 1913- WrDr 94
Birmingham, William Joseph 1923- WhoAmL 94, WhoMW 93
Birn, Donald S. 1937- WrDr 94
Birn, Raymond Francis 1935- WhoAm 94, WrDr 94
Birnbach, Martin 1929- WrDr 94
Birnbaum, Dara WhoAmA 93
Birnbaum, Donald Howard 1946- WhoAmL 94
Birnbaum, Edward Lester 1939- WhoAm 94
Birnbaum, Eleazar 1929- WhoAm 94
Birnbaum, Henrik 1925- WhoAm 94
Birnbaum, Henry 1917- WhoAm 94
Birnbaum, Howard Kent 1932- WhoAm 94
Birnbaum, Irwin Morton 1935- WhoAm 94, WhoAmL 94
Birnbaum, Jerome WhoScEn 94
Birnbaum, Joel M. 1938- WhoFI 94
Birnbaum, Julian R. 1948- WhoAmL 94
Birnbaum, Linda D. 1937- WhoAmL 94
Birnbaum, Malcolm A. d1993 NewYTBS 93
Birnbaum, Michael Henry 1946- WhoWest 94
Birnbaum, Michael Ian 1947- Who 94
Birnbaum, Robert 1936- WhoAm 94
Birnbaum, Robert Jack 1927- WhoAm 94
Birnbaum, Robert L. 1943- WhoAmL 94
Birnbaum, Roger ConTFT 11
Birnbaum, Sheila L. 1940- WhoAm 94
Birnbaum, Stephen Norman 1937-1991 WhAm 10
Birnbaum, Stevan Allen 1943- WhoFI 94, WhoWest 94
Birne, Kenneth Andrew 1956- WhoAmL 94
Birne, Robert Eric 1959- WhoAmL 94
Birney, Alice Lotvin 1938- WrDr 94
Birney, Brenda 1950- WhoAmP 93
Birney, David 1939- WhoHol 92
Birney, David 1940- IntMPA 94
Birney, Earle 1904- IntWW 93, WrDr 94
Birney, James Gillespie 1792-1857 DcAmReB 2
Birney, Meredith Baxter WhoHol 92
Birney, Reed 1954- WhoHol 92
Birney, Robert Charles 1925- WhoAm 94
Birnhak, Sandra Jean 1945- WhoFI 94
Birnholz, Jason Cordell 1942- WhoAm 94
Birnie, Daryl Elmer 1933- WhoFI 94
Birnkrant, Henry Joseph 1955- WhoAmL 94
Birnkrant, Sherwin Maurice 1927- WhoAmL 94
Birns, Mark Theodore 1949- WhoAm 94
Birnstiel, Charles WhoAm 94
Birnstiel, Max Luciano 1933- IntWW 93
Biro, Georg WorInv
Biro, Ladislao WorInv
Biro, Lajos 1880-1948 IntDcF 2-4
Biro, Laszlo 1929- WhoAm 94
Biro, Val 1921- WrDr 94
Biroc, Joseph 1903- IntDcF 2-4
Biroc, Joseph F. 1900- IntMPA 94
Biron, Duc de WhAmRev
Biron, Christine Anne 1951- WhoScEn 94
Biron, Thomas E. 1946- WhoAmL 94
Birr, Larry Gale 1954- WhoMW 93
Birr, Martin James 1960- WhoFI 94
Birr, Timothy Blane 1953- WhoWest 94
Birrell, Anne (Margaret) WrDr 94
Birrell, James Drake 1933- IntWW 93, Who 94
Birrell, James Peter 1928- WrDr 94
Birren, James Emmett 1918- WhoAm 94
Birren, Jeffrey Emmett 1951- WhoAmL 94
Birrer, Holli Ileen 1954- WhoMW 93
Birschel, Dee Baltzer 1947- WhoMW 93
Birse, Peter Malcolm 1942- Who 94
Birsh, Arthur Thomas 1932- WhoAm 94
Birstein, Ann DrAPF 93
Birstein, Ann 1927- WrDr 94
Birstein, Seymour Joseph 1927- WhoFI 94
Birt, John 1944- IntWW 93, Who 94
Birt, Kay B. 1924- WhoAmP 93
Birt, Lindsay Michael 1932- IntWW 93
Birt, (Lindsay) Michael 1932- Who 94
Birt, Walter Arthur 1915- WhoAmP 93
Birt, William Raymond 1911- Who 94
Birtcher, Normand Harold 1955- WhoWest 94
Birtel, Frank Thomas 1932- WhoAm 94
Birtha, Becky DrAPF 93
Birtha, Becky 1948- BlkWr 2, ConAu 142, GayLL
Birtha, Jessie M. 1920- WhoBlA 94
Birts, Peter William 1946- Who 94
Birtwistle, Archibald Cull 1927- Who 94
Birtwistle, Harrison 1934- IntWW 93, NewGrDO, Who 94
Birx, Donald L. 1952- WhoFI 94
Biryukov, Nikolai Vasilevich 1944- LoBiDrD
Biryukov, Vladimir Afanasevich 1933- LoBiDrD
Bis, Hippolyte-Louis-Florent 1789-1855 NewGrDO
Bisamunyu, Jeanette WhoMW 93
Bisamunyu, Jeanette 1959- WhoBlA 94
Bisanz, Richard M. 1945- WhoAmL 94
Bisbee, Dave 1946- WhoAmP 93
Bisbee, Gerald Elftman, Jr. 1942- WhoAm 94, WhoFI 94
Bisby, Mark Ainley 1946- WhoAm 94
Biscaccianti, Eliza 1824-1896 NewGrDO
Biscardi, Chester 1948- WhoAm 94
Bischof, Merriem Lanova WhoAm 94
Bischoff, Bernhard IntWW 93N
Bischoff, David Canby 1930- WhoAm 94
Bischoff, David F(rederick) 1951- WrDr 94
Bischoff, David F(redrick) 1951- EncSF 93
Bischoff, Douglas K. 1944- WhoAmL 94
Bischoff, Elmer 1916-1991 WhAm 10, WhoAmA 93N
Bischoff, Janet E. WhoMW 93
Bischoff, Joyce Arlene 1938- WhoFI 94, WhoScEn 94
Bischoff, Kenneth Bruce 1936- WhoAm 94, WhoScEn 94
Bischoff, Robert John 1941- WhoAmP 93, WhoMW 93
Bischoff, Susan Ann 1951- WhoAm 94
Bischoff, Winfried Franz Wilhelm 1941- IntWW 93, Who 94, WhoAm 94
Biscoe, Alec Julian T. Who 94
Biscoe, John d1848 WhWE
Biscoe, John 1794-1843 DcNaB MP
Biscoe, Timothy John 1932- Who 94
Biscone, Joseph Gregory 1950- WhoWest 94
Biscot, Georges d1944 WhoHol 92
Bisel, Harry Ferree 1918- WhoAm 94
Bisel, Jane Ferree 1955- WhoMW 93
Bisenius, Stephen William 1947- WhoAmP 93
Bisgaard, Edward Lawrence, Jr. 1946- WhoFI 94, WhoWest 94
Bisgard, Gerald Edwin 1937- WhoAm 94
Bisgard, James Dewey 1898-1975 WhoAmA 93N
Bisgyer, Barbara G. (Cohn) 1933- WhoAmA 93
Bish, David Lee 1952- WhoScEn 94
Bish, Milan D. 1929- WhoAmP 93
Bish, Milan David 1929- WhoAm 94
Bish, Robert Leonard 1941- WhoScEn 94
Bish, Tedi Lori 1956- WhoAm 94
Bish, William Howard 1957- WhoWest 94
Bishar, John Joseph, Jr. 1950- WhoAm 94, WhoAmL 94
Bishara, Abdulla Yacoub 1936- IntWW 93
Bishara, Amin Tawadros 1944- WhoScEn 94
Bishara, Samir Edward 1935- WhoAm 94
Bisher, Ilmar 1930- IntWW 93
Bisher, James Furman 1918- WhoAm 94
Bishin, William Robert 1939- WhoAmL 94
Bishku, Michael Barry 1953- WhoMW 93
Bishop Who 94
Bishop, Al 1925- WhoAmP 93
Bishop, Alan Henry 1929- Who 94
Bishop, Alfred d1928 WhoHol 92
Bishop, Alfred A. 1923- WhoBlA 94
Bishop, Alfred Chilton, Jr. 1942- WhoAmL 94
Bishop, Andre 1948- WhoAm 94
Bishop, Ann d1948 WhoHol 92
Bishop, Anna 1810-1884 NewGrDO
Bishop, Arthur Clive 1930- Who 94
Bishop, Barbara Lee 1938- WhoAmA 93N
Bishop, Barney Tipton, III 1951- WhoAmP 93, WhoFI 94
Bishop, Barry Chapman 1932- WhoAm 94
Bishop, Barry K. 1942- WhoAmL 94
Bishop, Ben 1923- WhoAmA 93
Bishop, Benjamin Pierce 1953- WhoWest 94
Bishop, Betty Josephine 1947- WhoFI 94, WhoWest 94
Bishop, Beverly Petterson 1922- WhoAm 94
Bishop, Bronwyn Kathleen 1942- WhoWomW 91
Bishop, Bryan Edwards 1945- WhoAm 94, WhoAmL 94
Bishop, Budd Harris 1936- WhoAm 94, WhoAmA 93
Bishop, C. Diane 1943- WhoAm 94, WhoAmP 93, WhoWest 94
Bishop, Calvin Thomas 1929- WhoAm 94
Bishop, Carla Jo 1950- WhoAmL 94
Bishop, Carolyn Benkert 1939- WhoWest 94
Bishop, Cecil 1930- WhoBlA 94
Bishop, Charles Dean 1937- WhoAmP 93
Bishop, Charles E. 1930- WhoIns 94
Bishop, Charles Edwin 1921- WhoAm 94
Bishop, Charles Joseph 1941- WhoAm 94
Bishop, Charles Landon 1938- WhoAm 94
Bishop, Chester d1937 WhoHol 92
Bishop, Christine Faith 1958- WhoAmP 93
Bishop, Claire Huchet 1898-1993 WrDr 94N
Bishop, Claire Huchet 1899?-1993 ConAu 140, SmATA 74
Bishop, Clare Huchet d1993 NewYTBS 93
Bishop, Clarence 1959- WhoBlA 94
Bishop, Claude Titus 1925- WhoAm 94
Bishop, Clifford Leofric Purdy 1908- Who 94
Bishop, David Fulton 1937- WhoAm 94
Bishop, David Hugh Langler 1937- Who 94
Bishop, David John 1951- WhoScEn 94
Bishop, David Nolan 1940- WhoFI 94, WhoScEn 94
Bishop, David Rudolph 1924- WhoBlA 94
Bishop, David T. 1929- WhoAmP 93
Bishop, Donald GayLL
Bishop, Donald Francis 1897- WhAm 10
Bishop, Edna Noe 1912- WhoAmP 93
Bishop, Edward 1942- WhoHol 92
Bishop, Elizabeth 1911-1979 AmCulL, BlmGWL
Bishop, Elizabeth Shreve 1951- WhoMW 93
Bishop, Ernest Merrill 1927- WhoWest 94
Bishop, Fayette d1927 WhoHol 92
Bishop, Frank Hamilton 1944- WhoAmL 94
Bishop, Frederick (Arthur) 1915- Who 94
Bishop, Gene Herbert 1930- WhoAm 94
Bishop, George d1668 DcNaB MP
Bishop, George (Sidney) 1913- Who 94
Bishop, George Archibald GayLL
Bishop, George Franklin 1942- WhoAm 94

Bishop, George Robert 1927- Who 94
Bishop, George Sidney 1913- IntWW 93
Bishop, Gordon Bruce 1938- WhoAm 94
Bishop, Harry Craden 1921- WhoAm 94
Bishop, Henry R(owley) 1786-1855 NewGrDO
Bishop, Howard Stuart 1938- WhoAm 94
Bishop, Isabella Bird 1831-1904 BlmGWL
Bishop, Isabella Lucy Bird 1831-1904 WhWE
Bishop, Ivan D. 1940- WhoIns 94
Bishop, J. Michael 1936- NobelP 91 [port]
Bishop, Jacqueline K. 1955- WhoAmA 93
Bishop, James 1927- WhoAmA 93
Bishop, James, Jr. 1930- WhoBlA 94
Bishop, James A. 1922- WhoAm 94
Bishop, James Allen 1950- WhoWest 94
Bishop, James Drew 1929- IntWW 93, Who 94, WrDr 94
Bishop, James Francis 1937- WhoFI 94
Bishop, James Francis 1940- WhoMW 93
Bishop, James Joseph 1936- WhoAm 94
Bishop, James Keough 1938- IntWW 93
Bishop, Jay Lyman 1932- WhoWest 94
Bishop, Jeffrey Britton 1949- WhoAmA 93
Bishop, Jerold 1936- WhoAmA 93
Bishop, Jerry E. 1931- ConAu 142
Bishop, Jim DrAPF 93
Bishop, Joey 1918- WhoAm 94, WhoCom, WhoHol 92
Bishop, John Edward 1935- Who 94
Bishop, John H. 1896- WhAm 10
Bishop, John J., Jr. 1927- WhoAmP 93
Bishop, John Joseph 1948- WhoAmP 93
Bishop, John Michael 1936- IntWW 93, WhoAm 94, WhoScEn 94, WhoWest 94
Bishop, (Margaret) Joyce d1993 Who 94N
Bishop, Joyce Ann 1935- WhoMW 93
Bishop, Julie 1914- WhoHol 92
Bishop, Katherine L. 1952- WhoAmL 94
Bishop, Kathryn Elizabeth 1945- WhoAm 94
Bishop, Kelly 1944- WhoHol 92
Bishop, Larry WhoHol 92
Bishop, Leo Kenneth 1911- WhoAm 94
Bishop, Louise 1933- WhoAmP 93
Bishop, Louise Williams 1933- WhoAm 94
Bishop, Luther Doyle 1921- WhoAm 94
Bishop, Malcolm Leslie 1944- Who 94
Bishop, Marjorie Cutler WhoAmA 93
Bishop, Mary Kathryn 1935- WhoAmP 93
Bishop, Matthew EncSF 93
Bishop, Michael Who 94
Bishop, Michael 1945- EncSF 93, WrDr 94
Bishop, Michael (David) 1942- Who 94
Bishop, (John) Michael 1936- Who 94
Bishop, Michael Daryl 1945- WhoAm 94
Bishop, Michael William 1941- Who 94
Bishop, Morian Hoover 1896- WhAm 10
Bishop, Nancy Ventress Rider 1920- WhoMW 93
Bishop, Oliver Richard 1928- WhoFI 94, WhoMW 93
Bishop, Patrick 1952- WrDr 94
Bishop, Paul D. 1944- WhoAmL 94
Bishop, Paul Edward 1940- WhoAm 94
Bishop, Peter Orlebar 1917- IntWW 93, Who 94
Bishop, Philippe Charles 1964- WhoWest 94
Bishop, R. Doak 1950- WhoAm 94, WhoAmL 94
Bishop, Rand DrAPF 93
Bishop, Randall Warren 1958- WhoFI 94
Bishop, Raymond Holmes, Jr. 1925- WhoAm 94
Bishop, Richard d1956 WhoHol 92
Bishop, Richard Evett 1897-1975 WhoAmA 93N
Bishop, Robert 1938- WrDr 94
Bishop, Robert 1938-1991 WhAm 10
Bishop, Robert Calvin 1943- WhoAm 94
Bishop, Robert Charles 1929- WhoWest 94
Bishop, Robert Charles 1938-1991 WhoAmA 93N
Bishop, Robert Harold 1957- WhoScEn 94
Bishop, Robert Lyle 1916- WhoAm 94
Bishop, Robert Milton 1921- WhoAm 94
Bishop, Robert Whitsitt 1949- WhoAmL 94
Bishop, Robert William 1951- WhoAmP 93
Bishop, Ronald L. 1949- WhoBlA 94
Bishop, Roy Lovitt 1939- WhoAm 94
Bishop, Ruth Ann 1942- WhoMW 93
Bishop, Samuel P. WrDr 94
Bishop, Sanford 1947- CngDr 93
Bishop, Sanford, Jr. 1947- WhoAm 94
Bishop, Sanford D., Jr 1947- WhoBlA 94
Bishop, Sanford Dixon, Jr. 1947- WhoAmP 93
Bishop, Sherre Whitney 1958- WhoBlA 94
Bishop, Sid Glenwood 1923- WhoFI 94
Bishop, Sidney Willard 1926- WhoAm 94, WhoIns 94
Bishop, Stanley Victor 1916- Who 94
Bishop, Stephen Who 94
Bishop, Stephen 1952- WhoAm 94
Bishop, Stephen Hurst 1936- WhoMW 93
Bishop, Steven C. WhoMW 93
Bishop, Sue 1953- WhoFI 94
Bishop, Sue Marquis 1939- WhoAm 94
Bishop, Susan Katharine 1946- WhoFI 94
Bishop, Terence Alan Martyn 1907- Who 94
Bishop, Thomas A. 1955- WhoAmP 93
Bishop, Thomas Ray 1925- WhoScEn 94
Bishop, Thomas Walter 1929- WhoAm 94
Bishop, Tilman M. 1933- WhoAmP 93
Bishop, Tilman Malcolm 1933- WhoWest 94
Bishop, Verissa Rene 1954- WhoBlA 94
Bishop, Walton Burrell 1917- WhoScEn 94
Bishop, Warner Bader 1918- WhoAm 94
Bishop, Wayne Staton 1937- WhoAm 94
Bishop, Wendy DrAPF 93
Bishop, Wesdon d1993 NewYTBS 93
Bishop, William d1959 WhoHol 92
Bishop, William Paul 1956- WhoFI 94
Bishop, William Peter 1940- WhoAm 94
Bishop, William Squire 1947- WhoAm 94, WhoFI 94
Bishop, William Wade 1939- WhoAm 94
Bishop-Kovacevich, Stephen Who 94
Bishop-Kovacevich, Stephen 1940- IntWW 93
Bishopric, Karl 1925- WhoAm 94
Bisignani, Giovanni 1946- IntWW 93
Bisignano, Tony 1952- WhoAmP 93
Bisio, Richard David 1948- WhoAmL 94
Biskind, Edward Ian 1952- WhoMW 93
Bisley, Steve WhoHol 92
Bismarck, Klaus von 1912- IntWW 93
Bismarck, Otto von 1815-1898 DcLB 129 [port], HisWorL [port]
Bismarck-Nasr, Maher Nasr 1940- WhoScEn 94
Bisnar, Miguel Chiong 1953- WhoScEn 94
Bisno, Alison Peck 1955- WhoAm 94, WhoFI 94
Bisnow, Mark (C.) 1952- WrDr 94
Bisoglio, Val 1926- WhoHol 92
Bison, Barbara Scott 1948- WhoAmL 94
Bispham, David (Scull) 1857-1921 NewGrDO
Bispham, Frank L. 1924- WhoBlA 94
Bisping, Bruce Henry 1953- WhoAm 94
Bisping, Herbert Joseph 1941- WhoMW 93
Bisquert (Prado), Prospero 1881-1959 NewGrDO
Biss, Ellen Graf DrAPF 93
Bissada, Nabil Kaddis 1938- WhoScEn 94
Bissat, Bahaeddine 1923- IntWW 93
Bissell, A. Keith 1941- WhoAmP 93
Bissell, Allen Morris 1935- WhoFI 94
Bissell, Anna WorInv
Bissell, Betty Dickson 1932- WhoAm 94
Bissell, Brent John 1950- WhoMW 93
Bissell, Charles Overman 1908- WhoAmA 93
Bissell, Claude T(homas) 1916- IntWW 93
Bissell, Claude Thomas 1916- Who 94
Bissell, Frances Mary 1946- Who 94
Bissell, George Arthur 1927- WhoAm 94
Bissell, Israel WhAmRev
Bissell, James D. 1951- ConTFT 11
Bissell, James Dougal, III 1951- WhoAm 94
Bissell, Jean Galloway 1936-1990 WhAm 10
Bissell, John Howard 1935- WhoAm 94, WhoMW 93
Bissell, John W. 1940- WhoAm 94, WhoAmL 94
Bissell, LeClair 1928- WrDr 94
Bissell, Melville WorInv
Bissell, Michael Gilbert 1947- WhoWest 94
Bissell, Mina Jahan 1940- WhoAm 94
Bissell, Patrick 1957-1987 IntDcB
Bissell, Phil 1926- WhoAm 94, WhoAmA 93
Bissell, Richard Etter 1946- WhoAm 94, WhoAmP 93
Bissell, Richard Mervin, Jr. 1909- WhoAm 94
Bissell, Whit 1909- WhoHol 92
Bissen-Nobriga, Sheron Leihuanani 1958- WhoWest 94
Bissert, Ellen Marie DrAPF 93
Bisset, Davies W., Jr. 1930- WhoIns 94
Bisset, Donald WhoHol 92
Bisset, Donald 1910- WrDr 94
Bisset, Jacqueline 1944- IntMPA 94, IntWW 93, WhoHol 92
Bisset, Jacqueline 1946- WhoAm 94
Bissett, Barbara Anne 1950- WhoMW 93
bissett, bill 1939- ConAu 19AS [port], WrDr 94
Bissett, Phil WhoAmP 93
Bissett, Terry Lee 1949- WhoMW 93
Bissette, Samuel Delk 1921- WhoAmA 93
Bissette, Winston Louis, Jr. 1943- WhoAm 94, WhoAmP 93
Bissex, Walter Earl 1950- WhoAm 94
Bissinger, Frederick Lewis 1911- IntWW 93, WhoAm 94
Bissinger, H(arry) G(erard) 1954- WrDr 94
Bissinger, H(arry) G(erard, III) 1954- ConAu 140
Bissinger, Harry Gerard 1954- WhoAm 94
Bissinger, Mark Christian 1957- WhoAmL 94
Bissler, Richard Thomas 1953- WhoMW 93
Bisson, Claude 1931- Who 94, WhoAm 94
Bisson, Edmond Emile 1916- WhoAm 94, WhoMW 93
Bisson, Gordon (Ellis) 1918- Who 94
Bisson, Jean-Pierre WhoHol 92
Bisson, Terry (Ballantine) 1942- EncSF 93
Bisson, Thomas Noel 1931- IntWW 93
Bissoondath, Neil (Devindra) 1955- WrDr 94
Bissoondoyal, Basdeo 1906- WrDr 94
Bista, Kirti Nidhi 1927- IntWW 93
Bistagne, Emile d1950 WhoHol 92
Bistany, Diane V. 1930- WhoIns 94
Bistline, F. Walter, Jr. 1950- WhoAm 94
Bistline, Stephen 1921- WhoAm 94, WhoAmL 94, WhoAmP 93, WhoWest 94
Biswas, Abdul Rahman IntWW 93
Biswas, Anil 1914- IntDcF 2-4
Biswas, Dipak R. 1949- WhoAsA 94
Biswas, Nripendra Nath 1930- WhoAsA 94
Biswas, Prosanto K. 1934- WhoBlA 94
Biswas, Renuka 1928- WhoAsA 94
Biszick, Doris A. M. 1963- WhoAm 94, WhoFI 94
Bisztyga, Jan 1933- Who 94
Bita, Lili DrAPF 93
Bitan, Giora Yoav 1954- WhoAm 94
Bitat, Rabah 1925- IntWW 93
Bitensky, Susan Helen 1948- WhoAmL 94
Bitetti, Ernesto G. 1943- WhoMW 93
Bitner, David I. 1948- WhoAmP 93
Bitner, Harry 1916- WhoAmL 94
Bitner, Jerri Lynne 1951- WhoFI 94
Bitner, John Howard 1940- WhoAm 94, WhoAmL 94
Bitner, John William 1948- WhoFI 94
Bitner, William Lawrence, III 1931- WhoAm 94
Bitondo, Domenic 1925- WhoAm 94
Bitov, Andrei (Georgievich) 1937- ConAu 142
Bitov, Andrei Georgevich 1937- IntWW 93
Bitsch, Hans-Ullrich 1946- IntWW 93
Bitsch-Larsen, Lars Kristian 1945- WhoScEn 94
Bittari, Zoubida 1937- BlmGWL
Bittenbender, Brad James 1948- WhoScEn 94, WhoWest 94
Bitter, Frank Gordon 1943- WhoFI 94
Bitter, John 1909- WhoAm 94
Bitterman, Mary G. F. 1944- WhoAmP 93
Bitterman, Melvin Lee 1938- WhoFI 94, WhoWest 94
Bitterman, Morton Edward 1921- WhoAm 94, WhoWest 94
Bitters, Conrad Lee 1946- WhoWest 94
Bitterwolf, Thomas Edwin 1947- WhoWest 94
Bittker, David WhoAm 94
Bittle, Edgar H. 1942- WhoAmL 94
Bittle, Harley Earnest 1937- WhoAmP 93
Bittle, Russell Harry 1938- WhoAmP 93
Bittleman, Arnold I. 1933- WhoAmA 93N
Bittleman, Dolores Dembus 1931- WhoAmA 93
Bittman, James Michael 1936- WhoFI 94
Bittman, William Omar 1931- WhoAm 94
Bittner, Carl S. 1903- WhoAm 94
Bittner, Hans Oskar 1905- WhoAmA 93
Bittner, Jack d1993 NewYTBS 93
Bittner, Julius 1874-1939 NewGrDO
Bittner, Marvin Joel 1950- WhoMW 93
Bittner, Ronald Joseph 1954- WhoScEn 94
Bittner, Van A. 1885-1949 EncABHB 9
Bittner, William d1918 WhoHol 92
Bitton-Jackson, Livia E(lvira) 1931- WrDr 94
Bitton-Schwartz, Denise 1963- WhoWest 94
Bitts, Todd Michael 1946- WhoAm 94
Bitzegaio, Harold James 1921- WhoAmL 94
Bitzer, Billy 1872-1944 IntDcF 2-4 [port]
Bitzer, Donald Lester 1934- WhoAm 94
Bivens, Dave 1925- WhoAmP 93
Bivens, Donald Wayne 1952- WhoAmL 94
Bivens, Lynette Kupka 1950- WhoMW 93
Bivens, Ruben 1950- WhoMW 93
Bivens, Shelia Reneea 1954- WhoBlA 94
Bivens, Stephen Dale 1946- WhoAmP 93
Bivins, Edward Byron 1929- WhoBlA 94
Bivins, Ollie B., Jr. 1923- WhoBlA 94
Bivins, Susan Steinbach 1941- WhoWest 94
Bivins, Teel 1947- WhoAmP 93
Bivona, John Vincent 1941- WhoAmL 94
Bixby, Allan Barton 1936- WhoAm 94, WhoFI 94
Bixby, Bill d1993 NewYTBS 93 [port]
Bixby, Bill 1934- IntMPA 94, WhoAm 94, WhoHol 92
Bixby, Bill 1934-1993 News 94-2
Bixby, Brian Dale 1952- WhoAmL 94
Bixby, Frank Lyman 1928- WhoAm 94
Bixby, Harold Glenn 1903- WhoAm 94
Bixby, (Drexel) Jerome (Lewis) 1923- EncSF 93
Bixby, Joseph Reynolds 1925- WhoIns 94
Bixby, Mark Ellis 1955- WhoScEn 94
Bixby, R. Burdell 1914-1991 WhAm 10
Bixby, Robert DrAPF 93
Bixby, Walter E. 1932- WhoAm 94, WhoIns 94
Bi Xizhen 1930- WhoPRCh 91 [port]
Bixler, David 1929- WhoAm 94
Bixler, David Loren 1948- WhoMW 93
Bixler, Denise WhoHol 92
Bixler, John Mourer 1927- WhoAmL 94
Bixler, Joseph H. 1945- WhoIns 94
Bixler, Otto Chauncey 1916- WhoWest 94
Bixler-Márquez, Dennis J. 1945- WhoHisp 94
Biya, Paul 1933- IntWW 93
Bi Ye 1916- WhoPRCh 91 [port]
Bizar, Irving 1932- WhoAm 94, WhoAmL 94
Bizet, Georges (Alexandre Cesar Leopold) 1838-1875 NewGrDO
Bizinsky, (Hyman) Robert 1915-1982 WhAm 10
Biz Markie 1964- ConMus 10 [port]
Bizub, Dawn Deborah 1961- WhoFI 94
Bizub, Johanna Catherine 1957- WhoAmL 94
Bizzari, Janice Carol 1939- WhoAm 94
Bizzaro, Patrick DrAPF 93
Bizzell, Bobby Gene 1940- WhoAm 94
Bizzell, Kinchen Carey 1954- WhoAmL 94
Bizzi, Emilio 1933- WhoAm 94
Bizzigotti, George Ora 1957- WhoScEn 94
Bjarkman, Peter C(hristian) 1941- WrDr 94
Bjarme, Brynjolf ConAu 141
Bjarnason, Gudmundur 1944- IntWW 93
Bjarnason, Matthias 1921- IntWW 93
Bjarnason, Sigurdur 1915- Who 94
Bjarni Herjulfsson WhWE
Bjartveit, Eleonore 1924- IntWW 93
Bjartveit, Erna Eleonore 1924- WhoWomW 91
Bjazic, Mladen EncSF 93
Bjelinski, Bruno 1909- NewGrDO
Bjelke-Petersen, Florence Isabel 1920- WhoWomW 91
Bjelke-Petersen, Johannes 1911- IntWW 93, Who 94
Bjelland, Harley LeRoy 1926- WhoWest 94
Bjercke, Alf Richard 1921- WhoFI 94
Bjergo, Allen Clifford 1935- WhoWest 94
Bjerkaas, Carlton Lee 1948- WhoMW 93
Bjerke, Alan 1961- WhoAmP 93
Bjerke, Bruce Terry 1950- WhoAmL 94
Bjerke, Harold William 1940- WhoFI 94
Bjerke, Robert Keith 1941- WhoScEn 94
Bjerknes, Jacob Aall Bonnevie 1897-1975 WorScD
Bjerknes, Michael Leif 1956- WhoAm 94
Bjerknes, Vilhelm Frimann Koren 1862-1951 WorScD
Bjerregaard, Ritt Jytte 1941- WhoWomW 91
Bjerve, Petter Jakob 1913- IntWW 93
Bjoerk, Christina 1938- WrDr 94
Bjoerling, Rolf d1993 NewYTBS 93
Bjoner, Ingrid 1927- NewGrDO
Bjontegard, Arthur Martin, Jr. 1938- WhoAm 94
Bjoraker, Walter Thomas 1920- WhoAm 94
Bjorck, Anders 1944- IntWW 93
Bjorck, Jeffrey Paul 1960- WhoScEn 94
Bjorge, Gary J(ohn) 1940- WrDr 94
Bjorhovde, Reidar 1941- WhoAm 94
Bjork, Anita 1923- IntWW 93, WhoHol 92
Bjork, Gordon Carl 1935- WhoAm 94
Bjork, Philip Reese 1940- WhoAm 94
Bjork, Robert Allen 1939- WhoAm 94
Bjork, Robert David, Jr. 1946- WhoAmL 94

Blevins, Dale Glenn 1943- *WhoAm 94, WhoMW 93*
Blevins, Donn Irving *DrAPF 93*
Blevins, Gary Lynn 1941- *WhoAm 94, WhoFI 94*
Blevins, James Richard 1934- *WhoAmA 93*
Blevins, Jeffrey Alexander 1955- *WhoAmL 94*
Blevins, Leslie W. 1939- *WhoMW 93*
Blevins, Michael 1960- *WhoHol 92*
Blevins, Patricia M. *WhoAmP 93*
Blevins, Robert d1977 *WhoHol 92*
Blevins, Walter, Jr. 1950- *WhoAmP 93*
Blevins, Willard Ahart 1949- *WhoWest 94*
Blevins, William Edward 1927- *WhoAm 94*
Blewett, John Paul 1910- *WhoAm 94, WhoScEn 94*
Blewett, Neal 1933- *IntWW 93*
Blewett, Robert Noall 1915- *WhoAm 94*
Blewitt, George Augustine 1937- *WhoAm 94*
Blewitt, Jonathan 1782-1853 *NewGrDO*
Blewitt, Shane (Gabriel Basil) 1935- *Who 94*
Bley, Ann 1954- *WhoMW 93*
Bley, Carla Borg 1938- *IntWW 93, WhoAm 94*
Bley, Kenneth B. 1939- *WhoAmL 94*
Bley, Walter Henry, Jr. 1955- *WhoAmL 94*
Bleyl, Robert Lingren 1936- *WhoWest 94*
Bleyle, John A. 1944- *WhoIns 94*
Bleznick, Donald William 1924- *WhoAm 94*
Blezzard, Judith 1944- *WrDr 94*
Blicher, Bert 1943- *WhoAm 94*
Blick, Benny George 1943- *WhoAmP 93*
Blick, Newton d1965 *WhoHol 92*
Blickensderfer, Peter William 1932- *WhoMW 93*
Blickensderfer, Tom 1957- *WhoAmP 93*
Blickenstaff, Danny Jay 1946- *WhoFI 94*
Blickwede, Donald Johnson 1920- *WhoAm 94*
Blide, Bernard Leroy 1926- *WhoFI 94*
Bliek, Eldon Maurice 1945- *WhoMW 93*
Bliek, James David 1947- *WhoMW 93*
Blier, Bernard d1989 *WhoHol 92*
Blier, Bertrand 1939- *IntMPA 94, IntWW 93*
Bliesner, James Douglas 1945- *WhoWest 94*
Blige, Mary J. *WhoBlA 94*
Bligh *Who 94*
Bligh, Aurora *DrAPF 93*
Bligh, Catto, Mrs. d1926 *WhoHol 92*
Bligh, William 1754-1817 *HisWorL [port], WhWE [port]*
Blight, John 1913- *WrDr 94*
Blijstra, Rein *EncSF 93*
Bliley, Linda M. 1958- *WhoFI 94*
Bliley, Thomas J., Jr. 1932- *CngDr 93, WhoAmP 93*
Bliley, Thomas Jerome, Jr. 1932- *WhoAm 94*
Blim, Richard Don 1927- *IntWW 93, WhoAm 94, WhoMW 93*
Blin, Roger d1983 *WhoHol 92*
Blind, Eric d1916 *WhoHol 92*
Blind, Mathilde 1841-1896 *BlmGWL*
Blind, William Charles 1911- *WhoAm 94, WhoAmL 94*
Blinder, Abe Lionel 1909- *WhoAm 94*
Blinder, Alan S(tuart) 1945- *WrDr 94*
Blinder, Alan Stuart 1945- *WhoAm 94, WhoFI 94*
Blinder, Albert Allan 1925- *WhoAmL 94*
Blinder, Janet 1953- *WhoWest 94*
Blinder, Martin S. 1946- *WhoAm 94, WhoAmA 93, WhoWest 94*
Blinder, Richard Lewis 1935- *WhoAm 94*
Blinder, Seymour Michael 1932- *WhoAm 94*
Blinderman, Barry Robert 1952- *WhoAmA 93*
Blinderman, Charles 1930- *WrDr 94*
Blinken, Alan *WhoAmP 93*
Blinken, Donald 1925- *WhoAm 94*
Blinken, Robert James 1929- *WhoAm 94*
Blinks, John Rogers 1931- *WhoAm 94*
Blinks, Lawrence Rogers 1900-1989 *WhAm 10*
Blinn, Beatrice d1979 *WhoHol 92*
Blinn, Benjamin d1941 *WhoHol 92*
Blinn, Genevieve d1956 *WhoHol 92*
Blinn, Gilbert Eugene 1938- *WhoAm 94*
Blinn, Holbrook d1928 *WhoHol 92*
Blinn, John Randolph 1943- *WhoAmL 94*
Blinn, Johna 1928- *WhoAm 94*
Blinn, Keith Wayne 1917-1990 *WhAm 10*
Blinn, S. David 1945- *WhoAmL 94*
Blinnikov, Sergei Petrovich 1945- *LoBiDrD*
Blin-Stoyle, Roger John 1924- *IntWW 93, Who 94*
Blischke, Wallace Robert 1934- *WhoWest 94*
Blish, Eugene Sylvester 1912- *WhoWest 94*
Blish, James (Benjamin) 1921-1975 *EncSF 93*
Blish, John Harwood 1937- *WhoAmL 94*
Blishen, Anthony Owen 1932- *Who 94*
Blishen, Edward 1920- *Who 94, WrDr 94*
Bliss, Anthony A(ddison) 1913-1991 *NewGrDO*
Bliss, Anthony Addison 1913-1991 *WhAm 10*
Bliss, Arthur 1891-1975 *IntDcB*
Bliss, Arthur (Drummond) 1891-1975 *NewGrDO*
Bliss, Barbara Allen 1919- *WhoMW 93*
Bliss, Bruce James 1935- *WhoAmP 93*
Bliss, Caroline *WhoHol 92*
Bliss, Christopher John Emile 1940- *Who 94*
Bliss, Corinne Demas *DrAPF 93*
Bliss, Daniel 1740-1806 *WhAmRev*
Bliss, David James 1942- *WhoAm 94*
Bliss, Donald Tiffany, Jr. 1941- *WhoAm 94, WhoAmL 94*
Bliss, Edwin C(rosby) 1923- *WrDr 94*
Bliss, Edwin Crosby 1923- *WhoWest 94*
Bliss, John Cordeux 1914- *Who 94*
Bliss, John William Michael 1941- *IntWW 93*
Bliss, Lawrence Carroll 1929- *WhoAm 94*
Bliss, Lela d1980 *WhoHol 92*
Bliss, Lowell Scott 1912- *WhoAmP 93*
Bliss, Nancy Ellen 1945- *WhoMW 93*
Bliss, Reginald *EncSF 93*
Bliss, Richard M. 1937- *WhoIns 94*
Bliss, Robert Harms 1940- *WhoAm 94*
Bliss, Robert Landers 1907- *WhoAmP 93*
Bliss, Robert Lewis 1921- *WhoAm 94*
Bliss, Robert Woods 1875-1962 *WhoAmA 93N*
Bliss, Robert Woods, Mrs. d1969 *WhoAmA 93N*
Bliss, Ronald Glenn 1943- *WhoAm 94, WhoAmL 94*
Bliss, S. W. *DrAPF 93*
Bliss, William Dwight Porter 1856-1926 *DcAmReB 2*
Bliss, William Stanley, Jr. 1932- *WhoAm 94*
Blissett, William 1921- *IntWW 93*
Blissett, William Frank 1921- *WhoAm 94*
Blistein, Elmer M. d1993 *NewYTBS 93*
Blistein, Elmer M(ilton) 1920-1993 *ConAu 142*
Blitch, Iris F(aircloth) 1912-1993 *CurBio 93N*
Blitch, Iris Faircloth d1993 *NewYTBS 93*
Blitch, James Buchanan 1923- *WhoAm 94*
Blitch, Peg 1928- *WhoAmP 93*
Blitch, Stephen G. 1947- *WhoAmL 94*
Blitman, Howard Norton 1926- *WhoAm 94*
Blitz, Daniel 1920- *WhoFI 94*
Blitz, Mark 1946- *WhoAmP 93*
Blitz, Stephen M. 1941- *WhoAm 94, WhoAmL 94*
Blitzer, Andrew 1946- *WhoAm 94, WhoScEn 94*
Blitzer, Charles 1927- *WhoAm 94*
Blitzer, Wolf 1948- *WrDr 94*
Blitzstein, Marc 1905-1964 *NewGrDO*
Blitz-Weisz, Sally 1954- *WhoWest 94*
Bliven, Bruce 1889-1977 *DcLB 137 [port]*
Bliven, Bruce, Jr. 1916- *WhoAm 94*
Bliven, Naomi 1925- *WhoAm 94*
Blivess, Michael P. 1947- *WhoIns 94*
Bliwas, Philip R. 1920- *WhoFI 94*
Bliwas, Ronald Lee 1942- *WhoAm 94*
Bliwise, Lester Martin 1945- *WhoAm 94, WhoAmL 94*
Blix, Glen Garry 1944- *WhoWest 94*
Blix, Hans 1928- *Who 94*
Blix, Hans Martin 1928- *IntWW 93, WhoScEn 94*
Blixen, Karen *RfGShF*
Blixen, Karen 1885-1962 *BlmGWL [port]*
Blixt, Roy Elof 1915- *WhoAmL 94, WhoMW 93*
Bliznakov, Emile George 1926- *WhoAm 94*
Bliznakov, Milka Tcherneva 1927- *WhoAm 94*
Blizzard, Alan 1939- *WhoAm 94, WhoAmA 93*
Blobel, Gunter 1936- *WhoAm 94*
Bloch, Alan Neil 1932- *WhoAm 94, WhoAmL 94*
Bloch, Albert 1882-1961 *WhoAmA 93N*
Bloch, Alice *DrAPF 93*
Bloch, Andre 1873-1960 *NewGrDO*
Bloch, Andrea Lynn 1952- *WhoAm 94, WhoMW 93*
Bloch, Antoine 1938- *WhoScEn 94*
Bloch, Augustyn (Hipolit) 1929- *NewGrDO*
Bloch, Bernard *WhoHol 92*
Bloch, Chana *DrAPF 93*
Bloch, Dan 1943- *ConAu 140*
Bloch, E. Maurice d1989 *WhoAmA 93N*
Bloch, Edward Henry 1914- *WhoScEn 94*
Bloch, Erich 1925- *WhoAm 94, WhoScEn 94*
Bloch, Ernest 1880-1959 *NewGrDO*
Bloch, Felix 1905- *WorScD*
Bloch, Henry Wollman 1922- *WhoAm 94, WhoFI 94*
Bloch, Herman Samuel 1912-1990 *WhAm 10*
Bloch, James Phillips 1946- *WhoScEn 94*
Bloch, Jeff(rey W.) 1959- *WrDr 94*
Bloch, Julia Chang 1942- *WhoAm 94, WhoAsA 94*
Bloch, Julius 1888-1966 *WhoAmA 93N*
Bloch, Konrad 1912- *IntWW 93*
Bloch, Konrad E. 1912- *Who 94*
Bloch, Konrad Emil *WorScD*
Bloch, Konrad Emil 1912- *WhoAm 94, WhoScEn 94*
Bloch, Kurt Julius 1929- *WhoAm 94*
Bloch, Lucienne S. *DrAPF 93*
Bloch, Marie Halun 1910- *WrDr 94*
Bloch, Martin B. 1935- *WhoAm 94*
Bloch, Maurice Emile Felix 1939- *Who 94*
Bloch, Merle Florence *Who 94*
Bloch, Milton Joseph 1937- *WhoAmA 93*
Bloch, Paul 1939- *WhoAm 94*
Bloch, Paul David 1953- *WhoMW 93*
Bloch, Randal Sue 1949- *WhoAmL 94*
Bloch, Ray E. 1894- *WhAm 10*
Bloch, Raymond 1914- *IntWW 93*
Bloch, Richard Isaac 1943- *WhoAm 94*
Bloch, Robert *DrAPF 93*
Bloch, Robert 1917- *EncSF 93, IntMPA 94, WrDr 94*
Bloch, Robert Albert 1917- *WhoAm 94*
Bloch, Robert Wagner 1928- *WhoFI 94*
Bloch, Sandra A. 1954- *WhoAmL 94*
Bloch, Scotty *ConTFT 11*
Bloch, Stanley E. 1942- *WhoAmL 94*
Bloch, Stuart Fulton 1933- *WhoAmP 93*
Bloch, Stuart Marshall 1942- *WhoAmL 94*
Bloch, Thomas Morton 1954- *WhoAm 94, WhoFI 94*
Bloch-Laine, Francois 1912- *IntWW 93*
Blochwitz, Hans Peter 1949- *NewGrDO*
Block, Adam Johnstone Cheyne 1908- *Who 94*
Block, Adolph 1906-1978 *WhoAmA 93N*
Block, Adriaen fl. 160-?- *WhWE*
Block, Alan Jay 1938- *WhoAm 94*
Block, Alan Peter 1964- *WhoWest 94*
Block, Allan *DrAPF 93*
Block, Allan James 1954- *WhoAm 94, WhoMW 93*
Block, Allan Martin 1942- *WhoMW 93*
Block, Amanda Roth 1912- *WhoAm 94, WhoAmA 93*
Block, Arthur Lee 1949- *WhoMW 93*
Block, Barbara Ann 1958- *WhoScEn 94*
Block, Bruce T. 1953- *WhoAmL 94*
Block, Carolyn B. 1942- *WhoBlA 94*
Block, Carolyn Rebecca 1943- *WhoMW 93*
Block, David Arthur Kennedy William 1908- *Who 94*
Block, David Greenberg 1936- *Who 94*
Block, Dennis Jeffery 1942- *WhoAm 94, WhoAmL 94*
Block, Edward Martel 1927- *WhoAm 94*
Block, Emil Nathaniel, Jr. 1930- *WhoAm 94*
Block, Eric 1942- *WhoAm 94*
Block, Ethel Lasher 1919- *WhoAmP 93*
Block, Francesca (Lia) 1962- *WrDr 94*
Block, Francesca Lia 1962- *TwCYAW*
Block, Franklin L. 1936- *WhoAmP 93*
Block, Frederick Henry 1909- *WhoAmL 94*
Block, Gary Michael 1961- *WhoAmL 94*
Block, Gay (S.) 1942- *WhoAmA 93*
Block, Gene David 1948- *WhoAm 94*
Block, George Edward 1926- *WhoAm 94*
Block, Haskell Mayer 1923- *WhoAm 94*
Block, Herbert Lawrence 1909- *AmSocL, IntWW 93, WhoAm 94*
Block, Isaac Edward 1924- *WhoAm 94*
Block, Jack 1924- *WhoScEn 94*
Block, James A. 1940- *WhoAm 94*
Block, James Harold 1945- *WhoWest 94*
Block, Janet Leven *WhoMW 93*
Block, Jerome D. 1948- *WhoHisp 94*
Block, Jesse d1983 *WhoHol 92*
Block, John Douglas 1948- *WhoAm 94*
Block, John R. 1935- *WhoAmP 93*
Block, John Robinson 1954- *WhoAm 94, WhoMW 93*
Block, John Rusling 1935- *IntWW 93, WhoAm 94*
Block, Joseph L. 1902-1992 *EncABHB 9 [port]*
Block, Joseph L(eopold) 1902-1992 *CurBio 93N*
Block, Jules Richard 1930- *WhoAm 94*
Block, Julia Chang 1942- *WhoAmP 93*
Block, Larry 1943- *WhoHol 92*
Block, Lawrence *DrAPF 93*
Block, Lawrence 1938- *WhoAm 94, WrDr 94*
Block, Leonard Nathan 1911- *WhoAm 94, WhoFI 94*
Block, Leopold E. 1869-1952 *EncABHB 9*
Block, Leslie S. *WhoBlA 94*
Block, Lynne Wood 1943- *WhoFI 94*
Block, Martin d1967 *WhoHol 92*
Block, Marvin Avram 1903-1989 *WhAm 10*
Block, Marylaine 1943- *WhoMW 93*
Block, Melvin August 1921- *WhoAm 94*
Block, Michael I. 1956- *WhoIns 94*
Block, Michael Kent 1942- *WhoAm 94, WhoWest 94*
Block, Mitchell Stern 1953- *WhoAmL 94*
Block, Murray Harold 1924- *WhoAm 94*
Block, Neal Jay 1942- *WhoAm 94, WhoAmL 94*
Block, Ned 1942- *WhoAm 94*
Block, Ned Joel 1942- *IntWW 93*
Block, Nelson Richard 1951- *WhoAmL 94*
Block, Pamela Jo 1947- *WhoFI 94*
Block, Philip D. 1871-1942 *EncABHB 9*
Block, Philip D., Jr. 1906-1981 *EncABHB 9*
Block, Philip Dee, III 1937- *WhoAm 94*
Block, Richard Atten *WhoScEn 94*
Block, Richard Earl 1931- *WhoAm 94*
Block, Richard H. 1951- *WhoAm 94*
Block, Richard Raphael 1938- *WhoAmL 94*
Block, Robert Charles 1929- *WhoAm 94*
Block, Robert I. 1951- *WhoMW 93, WhoScEn 94*
Block, Robert Jackson 1922- *WhoAm 94*
Block, Ruth 1930- *WhoAm 94*
Block, S. Lester 1917- *WhoAm 94*
Block, Seymour Stanton 1918- *WhoAm 94*
Block, Stanley Marlin 1922- *WhoAm 94*
Block, Thomas H(arris) 1945- *EncSF 93, WrDr 94*
Block, Virginia Schaffer 1946- *WhoAmA 93*
Block, Walter *WhoWest 94*
Block, Willard 1930- *IntMPA 94*
Block, William 1915- *WhoAm 94*
Block, William Karl, Jr. 1944- *WhoAm 94, WhoMW 93*
Block, William Kenneth 1950- *WhoAmL 94, WhoFI 94*
Block, Zenas 1916- *WhoAm 94*
Blocker, Dan d1972 *WhoHol 92*
Blocker, Dirk 1957- *WhoHol 92*
Blocker, Helen Powell 1923- *WhoBlA 94*
Blocker, Mark Bruce 1964- *WhoAmL 94*
Blocker, Robert Lewis 1946- *WhoWest 94*
Blockinger, James Anson 1945- *WhoMW 93*
Blocksma, Mary 1942- *WrDr 94*
Blocksom, Rita Verlene Haynes 1952- *WhoMW 93*
Blockson, Charles L. 1933- *WhoBlA 94*
Blockson, Charles L(eRoy) 1933- *BlkWr 2, ConAu 141*
Blockton, Gilbert B. 1953- *WhoAmL 94*
Blockx, Jan 1851-1912 *NewGrDO*
Blodek, Vilem 1834-1874 *NewGrDO*
Blodgett, Anne Washington 1940- *WhoAmA 93*
Blodgett, Edmund Walton 1908- *WhoAmA 93N*
Blodgett, Elsie Grace 1921- *WhoFI 94, WhoWest 94*
Blodgett, Forrest Clinton 1927- *WhoFI 94, WhoScEn 94, WhoWest 94*
Blodgett, Frank Caleb 1927- *WhoAm 94, WhoFI 94*
Blodgett, Gary B. *WhoAmP 93*
Blodgett, Geoffrey Thomas 1931- *WhoMW 93*
Blodgett, George Winslow 1888- *WhoAmA 93N*
Blodgett, Julian Robert 1919- *WhoWest 94*
Blodgett, Katherine Burr 1898-1979 *WorInv*
Blodgett, Michael 1940- *WhoHol 92*
Blodgett, Omer William 1917- *WhoAm 94*
Blodgett, Ralph Hamilton 1905-1988 *WhAm 10*
Blodgett, Stephen Sargent 1944- *WhoAmP 93*
Blodgett, Todd Alan 1960- *WhoFI 94*
Blodgett, Warren Terrell 1923- *WhoAm 94*
Blodgett, William Arthur 1937- *WhoAm 94*
Bloede, Victor Carl 1917- *WhoAm 94, WhoAmL 94, WhoWest 94*
Bloede, Victor Gustav 1920- *WhoAm 94*
Bloedel, Lawrence Hotch Kiss 1902-1976 *WhoAmA 93N*
Bloembergen, Nicolaas 1920- *IntWW 93, Who 94, WhoAm 94, WhoScEn 94, WrDr 94*

Bloemer, Rosemary Celeste 1930- *WhoFI 94, WhoMW 93*
Bloemfontein, Bishop of 1932- *Who 94*
Bloemsma, Marco Paul 1924- *WhoAm 94, WhoFI 94*
Bloes, Richard K. 1951- *WhoAmA 93*
Bloesch, Donald George 1928- *WrDr 94*
Blofeld, John Christopher Calthorpe 1932- *Who 94*
Blois, Charles (Nicholas Gervase) 1939- *Who 94*
Blois, Marsden S(cott), Jr. 1919- *WrDr 94*
Blok, Alexander Alexandrovich 1880-1921 *IntDcT 2*
Blok, Bobbi Helene 1953- *WhoAmP 93*
Blokh, Alexandre 1923- *Who 94*
Blokhin, Nikolay Nikolayevich 1912- *IntWW 93*
Blokhin, Oleg 1952- *WorESoc*
Blokhin, Oleg Vladimirovich 1952- *LoBiDrD*
Blokhin, Oleg Vladimirovich 1953- *IntWW 93*
Bloland, Paul Anson 1923- *WhoAm 94*
Blom, Daniel Charles 1919- *WhoAm 94, WhoAmL 94, WhoIns 94*
Blom, Donald Edwin 1942- *WhoFI 94*
Blom, Eric Walter 1888-1959 *DcNaB MP*
Blom, Gaston Eugene 1920- *WhoAm 94*
Blom, Gertrude d1993 *NewYTBS 93*
Blomain, Karen *DrAPF 93*
Blomberg, Goran Ernst Daniel 1941- *WhoMW 93*
Blom-Cooper, Louis (Jacques) 1926- *Who 94*
Blom-Cooper, Louis Jacques 1926- *IntWW 93*
Blomdahl, Eric Charles 1965- *WhoFI 94*
Blomdahl, Karl-Birger 1916-1968 *NewGrDO*
Blomdahl, Sonja 1952- *WhoAmA 93*
Blomefield, (Thomas) Charles (Peregrine) 1948- *Who 94*
Blomer, Philip Joseph 1948- *WhoAmL 94*
Blomfield, Adelaide *DrAPF 93*
Blomfield, Derek d1964 *WhoHol 92*
Blomfield, John Reginald d1992 *Who 94N*
Blomgren, Bruce Holmes 1945- *WhoAm 94*
Blomhoff, Rune 1955- *WhoScEn 94*
Blomingdale, Arthur Lee, Jr. 1930- *WhoIns 94*
Blomme, Jeannine 1936- *WhoWomW 91*
Blommel, Scot Anthony 1966- *WhoScEn 94*
Blomquist, Carl Arthur 1947- *WhoFI 94, WhoWest 94*
Blomquist, Carl Gunnar 1931- *WhoAm 94*
Blomquist, Dian 1940- *WhoAmP 93*
Blomquist, Glenn C. 1945- *WhoFI 94*
Blomquist, Jane Ann 1958- *WhoMW 93*
Blomquist, Michael Allen 1953- *WhoScEn 94*
Blomquist, Robert Oscar 1930- *WhoAm 94*
Blomquist, Thomas Melville 1957- *WhoWest 94*
Blomquist, William Kenneth 1945- *WhoAmL 94*
Blomquist-Stanbery, Ruth Ellen 1949- *WhoMW 93*
Blomqvist, Leif 1937- *Who 94*
Blomstedt, Henrik Lennart 1921- *IntWW 93*
Blomstedt, Herbert Thorson 1927- *IntWW 93, WhoAm 94, WhoWest 94*
Blond, Irwin E. 1945- *WhoAmL 94*
Blondal, Patricia 1926-1959 *BlmGWL*
Blondeau, Jacques Patrick Adrien 1944- *WhoIns 94*
Blondel, Jean (Fernand Pierre) 1929- *WrDr 94*
Blondel, Jean Fernand Pierre 1929- *Who 94*
Blondell, Gloria d1986 *WhoHol 92*
Blondell, Joan d1979 *WhoHol 92*
Blondy, Michel 1675-1739 *IntDcB*
Blood, Adele d1936 *WhoHol 92*
Blood, Archer Kent 1923- *WhoAm 94*
Blood, Bindon 1920- *Who 94*
Blood, Edward Linford 1945- *WhoAm 94*
Blood, Ernest A. 1872-1955 *BasBi*
Blood, Marilyn Kay 1942- *WhoMW 93*
Blood, Marje *WrDr 94*
Bloodstone, John *EncSF 93*
Bloodsworth-Thomason, Linda 1947- *IntMPA 94*
Bloodworth, Albert William Franklin 1935- *WhoAm 94, WhoAmL 94*
Bloodworth, Darryl M. 1942- *WhoAmL 94*
Bloodworth, J. M. Bartow, Jr. 1925- *WhoAm 94, WhoMW 93*
Bloodworth, Thomas L. 1953- *WhoAmL 94*
Bloodworth, Timothy 1736-1814 *WhAmRev*
Bloodworth, William Andrew, Jr. 1942- *WhoAm 94*
Bloodworth-Thomason, Linda 1947- *CurBio 93 [port], News 94-1 [port]*
Bloodworth-Thomason, Linda 1948- *WhoAm 94*
Bloom, Alan 1945- *WhoAm 94*
Bloom, Alan Arthur 1930- *WhoScEn 94*
Bloom, Alfred Howard 1946- *WhoAm 94*
Bloom, Allan d1992 *IntWW 93N*
Bloom, Allan 1930-1992 *AnObit 1992, WhAm 10*
Bloom, Allan (David) 1930-1992 *WrDr 94N*
Bloom, Andre Borisovich *Who 94*
Bloom, Arnold Sanford 1942- *WhoAm 94*
Bloom, Barbara 1951- *WhoAmA 93*
Bloom, Barry Malcolm 1928- *WhoAm 94, WhoFI 94*
Bloom, Benjamin S. 1913- *WhoAm 94*
Bloom, Beth Francine 1962- *WhoAmL 94*
Bloom, Brian d1984 *WhoHol 92*
Bloom, Bryan Scott 1955- *WhoFI 94*
Bloom, Charles 1940- *Who 94*
Bloom, Christopher Arthur 1951- *WhoAm 94, WhoAmL 94*
Bloom, Claire 1931- *ConTFT 11, IntMPA 94, IntWW 93, Who 94, WhoAm 94, WhoHol 92*
Bloom, Clive 1953- *WrDr 94*
Bloom, David I. 1954- *WhoAm 94, WhoAmL 94*
Bloom, David Ronald 1943- *WhoAm 94*
Bloom, Debby Lee Whitehill 1955- *WhoMW 93*
Bloom, Diane 1942- *WhoMW 93*
Bloom, Donald Eugene 1944- *WhoIns 94*
Bloom, Donald S. 1932- *WhoAmA 93*
Bloom, Edith Salvin 1917- *WhoAmA 93*
Bloom, Edward A(lan) 1914- *WrDr 94*
Bloom, Edward Alan 1914- *WhoAm 94*
Bloom, Edward D. 1944- *WhoAmL 94*
Bloom, Edwin John, Jr. 1931- *WhoAm 94*
Bloom, Elaine 1937- *WhoAmP 93*
Bloom, Floyd Elliott 1936- *WhoAm 94, WhoWest 94*
Bloom, Frank 1937- *WhoAm 94*
Bloom, G(eorge) Cromarty d1992 *Who 94N*
Bloom, George d1989 *WhoHol 92*
Bloom, Harold 1930- *BlmGEL, EncSF 93, IntWW 93, WhoAm 94, WrDr 94*
Bloom, Harold Edward 1946- *WhoFI 94*
Bloom, Herschel M. 1943- *WhoAmL 94*
Bloom, Howard Martin 1951- *WhoAm 94*
Bloom, Hyman 1913- *WhoAm 94, WhoAmA 93*
Bloom, J. J. d1981 *WhoHol 92*
Bloom, Jack Sandler 1957- *WhoFI 94*
Bloom, James Armin 1952- *WhoAmP 93*
Bloom, James E. 1958- *WhoMW 93*
Bloom, James Edward 1941- *WhoAm 94, WhoFI 94, WhoMW 93*
Bloom, James W. 1960- *WhoFI 94*
Bloom, Janet *DrAPF 93*
Bloom, Jeffrey Brian 1953- *WhoAmP 93*
Bloom, Jessie L. 1933- *WhoAmP 93*
Bloom, Joel N. 1925- *WhoAm 94*
Bloom, John 1935- *ConTFT 11*
Bloom, John Porter 1924- *WhoAm 94*
Bloom, John Scott 1946- *WhoAmP 93*
Bloom, Jolene Rae 1951- *WhoAmP 93*
Bloom, Jordan L. 1943- *WhoAmL 94*
Bloom, Lary 1943- *WhoAm 94*
Bloom, Lawrence S. 1943- *WhoAmP 93*
Bloom, Lawrence Stephen 1930- *WhoAm 94*
Bloom, Lee Hurley 1919- *WhoAm 94*
Bloom, Lindsay 1952- *WhoHol 92*
Bloom, Lynn (Marie Zimmerman) 1934- *WrDr 94*
Bloom, Mark David 1953- *WhoAmL 94*
Bloom, Martha 1951- *WhoAmA 93*
Bloom, Michael Anthony 1947- *WhoAm 94, WhoAmL 94*
Bloom, Michael Eugene 1947- *WhoFI 94*
Bloom, Murray Teigh 1916- *WhoAm 94, WrDr 94*
Bloom, Myer 1928- *IntWW 93, WhoAm 94*
Bloom, Robert Avrum 1930- *WhoAmL 94*
Bloom, Rodney Merlin 1933- *WhoAm 94*
Bloom, Ronald d1993 *Who 94N*
Bloom, Samuel W. 1921- *WrDr 94*
Bloom, Sherman 1934- *WhoAm 94*
Bloom, Stephen Joel 1936- *WhoAm 94*
Bloom, Stephen Michael 1948- *WhoAm 94, WhoAmL 94, WhoWest 94*
Bloom, Steven D. 1943- *WhoAmL 94*
Bloom, Steven Paul 1944- *WhoAmP 93*
Bloom, Susan 1951- *WhoAm 94*
Bloom, Valerie 1956- *BlmGWL*
Bloom, Verna 1939- *IntMPA 94, WhoHol 92*
Bloom, Wallace 1916- *WhoScEn 94*
Bloom, William James 1947- *WhoFI 94*
Bloom, William Millard 1925- *WhoScEn 94*
Bloomberg, Avril Renee 1967- *WhoFI 94*
Bloomberg, Coe Arthur 1943- *WhoAmL 94*
Bloomberg, Edward S. 1947- *WhoAmL 94*
Bloomberg, Marty 1938- *WhoWest 94*
Bloomberg, Mitchell R. 1949- *WhoAmL 94*
Bloomberg, Morris Jacob 1930- *WhoAmL 94*
Bloomberg, Robert Joseph 1947- *WhoWest 94*
Bloomberg, Warner, Jr. 1926- *WhoAm 94*
Bloomer, Amelia Jenks 1818-1894 *AmSocL [port]*
Bloomer, Harold Franklin, Jr. 1933- *WhoAm 94, WhoAmL 94*
Bloomer, John H. 1930- *WhoAmP 93*
Bloomer, Robert A. 1921- *WhoAmP 93*
Bloomer, Stephen J. 1947- *IntMPA 94*
Bloomer, William Arthur 1933- *WhoWest 94*
Bloomfield, Arthur Irving 1914- *WhoAm 94*
Bloomfield, Barry (Cambray) 1931- *WrDr 94*
Bloomfield, Barry Cambray 1931- *Who 94*
Bloomfield, Clara Derber 1942- *WhoAm 94*
Bloomfield, Coleman *WhoIns 94*
Bloomfield, Coleman 1926- *WhoAm 94, WhoFI 94*
Bloomfield, Daniel Kermit 1926- *WhoAm 94*
Bloomfield, Jordan Jay 1930- *WhoWest 94*
Bloomfield, Joseph 1753-1823 *WhAmRev*
Bloomfield, Keith Martin 1951- *WhoFI 94*
Bloomfield, Kenneth Percy 1931- *IntWW 93, Who 94*
Bloomfield, Lincoln P(almer) 1920- *WrDr 94*
Bloomfield, Lincoln Palmer 1920- *WhoAm 94*
Bloomfield, Lisa Diane 1951- *WhoAmA 93*
Bloomfield, Louis J. 1936- *WhoIns 94*
Bloomfield, Mary Sue 1940- *WhoAmL 94*
Bloomfield, Maureen *DrAPF 93*
Bloomfield, Maxwell Herron, III 1931- *WhoAm 94*
Bloomfield, Michael d1981 *WhoHol 92*
Bloomfield, Peter 1946- *WhoAm 94*
Bloomfield, Randall D. 1923- *WhoBlA 94*
Bloomfield, Richard J. 1927- *WhoAm 94*
Bloomfield, Sally Ward 1943- *WhoAmL 94*
Bloomfield, Suzanne 1934- *WhoAmA 93*
Bloomfield, Victor Alfred 1938- *WhoAm 94*
Bloomgarden, Judith Mary 1942- *WhoAmA 93*
Bloomgarden, Kathy Finn 1949- *WhoAm 94, WhoFI 94*
Bloomingdale, Arthur Lee, Jr. 1930- *WhoFI 94*
Bloomquist, Dennis Howard 1942- *WhoAmL 94*
Bloomquist, Edward Robert 1924- *WhoWest 94*
Bloomquist, Eunice I. 1940- *WhoAm 94*
Bloomquist, Gloria Jean 1950- *WhoMW 93*
Bloomquist, Kenneth Gene 1931- *WhoAm 94*
Bloomquist, Rodney Gordon 1943- *WhoWest 94*
Bloomwell, Arthur Eugene 1933- *WhoFI 94*
Bloor, David 1937- *Who 94*
Blore, Eric d1959 *WhoHol 92*
Blore, William Harold 1940- *WhoMW 93*
Blos, Joan 1928- *WrDr 94*
Blos, Joan W. 1928- *WhoAm 94*
Blos, Joan W(insor) 1928- *TwCYAW*
Blos, Peter W. 1908-1986 *WhoAmA 93N*
Bloser, Dieter 1944- *WhoMW 93*
Bloskas, John D. 1928- *WhoFI 94*
Bloss, George F., III 1950- *WhoAmL 94*
Blosse, Richard Hely L. *Who 94*
Blosser, Henry Gabriel 1928- *WhoAm 94, WhoScEn 94*
Blosser, Nicholas 1958- *WhoAmA 93*
Blosser, Patricia Ellen 1931- *WhoAm 94*
Blossman, Alfred Rhody, Jr. 1931- *WhoAm 94*
Blossom, Charles N. 1935- *WhoIns 94*
Blossom, Laurel *DrAPF 93*
Blossom, Neal William 1961- *WhoScEn 94*
Blossom, Roberts *WhoHol 92*
Blot, Jean *Who 94*
Blot, Thomas *EncSF 93*
Blotkamp, Robert 1956- *WhoAmP 93*
Blotner, Joseph 1923- *WrDr 94*
Blotner, Joseph Leo 1923- *WhoAm 94*
Blotner, Norman David 1918- *WhoAm 94*
Blotnick, Srully (D.) 1941- *WrDr 94*
Blotzer, Timothy Robert 1952- *WhoWest 94*
Blouch, Timothy Craig 1954- *WhoFI 94*
Blouet, Olwyn M(ary) 1948- *WrDr 94*
Blough, Carman George 1895- *WhAm 10*
Blough, Donald S. 1929- *WhoAm 94*
Blough, Roger M. 1904-1985 *EncABHB 9 [port]*
Blough, Roy 1901- *WhoAm 94*
Blouin, Georges Henri 1921- *IntWW 93*
Blouin, Rose Louise 1948- *WhoBlA 94*
Blouke, Milton Baker 1946- *WhoWest 94*
Blount, Alice McDaniel 1942- *WhoScEn 94*
Blount, Ben B., Jr. *WhoFI 94*
Blount, Bertie Kennedy 1907- *Who 94*
Blount, Charles, Jr. 1897- *WhAm 10*
Blount, Charlotte Renee 1952- *WhoBlA 94*
Blount, Clarence W. 1921- *WhoAmP 93, WhoBlA 94*
Blount, Don H. 1929- *WhoAm 94*
Blount, Evelyn 1942- *WhoAm 94*
Blount, Harry Neil 1944- *WhoWest 94*
Blount, James L. d1973 *WhoHol 92*
Blount, Joseph Lamar 1946- *WhoAmP 93*
Blount, Julius A. 1926- *WhoAmP 93*
Blount, Larry Elisha 1950- *WhoBlA 94*
Blount, Lisa *IntMPA 94, WhoHol 92*
Blount, Mel *ProFbHF*
Blount, Melvin Cornell 1948- *WhoBlA 94*
Blount, Michael Eugene 1949- *WhoAm 94, WhoAmL 94, WhoMW 93*
Blount, Nancy Munjiovi *WhoAmL 94*
Blount, Robert Grier 1938- *WhoAm 94, WhoFI 94*
Blount, Robert Haddock 1922- *WhoAm 94*
Blount, Roy, Jr. 1941- *WrDr 94*
Blount, Stanley Freeman 1929- *WhoAm 94*
Blount, Thomas 1759-1812 *WhAmRev*
Blount, Walter (Edward Alpin) 1917- *Who 94*
Blount, Wilbur Clanton 1929- *WhoBlA 94*
Blount, William *WhoAmP 93*
Blount, William 1749-1800 *WhAmRev*
Blount, William Allan 1954- *WhoAm 94, WhoAmP 93*
Blount, William Houston 1922- *WhoAm 94*
Blount, Winton Malcolm, Jr. 1921- *WhoAm 94, WhoFI 94*
Blount, Winton Malcolm, III 1943- *WhoAm 94, WhoFI 94*
Blount-Porter, David 1947- *WhoWest 94*
Bloustein, Edward J. 1925-1989 *WhAm 10*
Blout, Elkan R(ogers) 1919- *IntWW 93*
Blout, Elkan Rogers 1919- *WhoAm 94, WhoScEn 94*
Blovits, Larry John 1936- *WhoAmA 93*
Blow, David Mervyn 1931- *IntWW 93, Who 94*
Blow, George 1928- *WhoAm 94*
Blow, John 1649-1708 *NewGrDO*
Blow, John Needham 1905- *WhoWest 94*
Blow, Joyce 1929- *Who 94*
Blow, Michael 1930- *WrDr 94*
Blow, Sandra 1925- *IntWW 93, Who 94*
Blow, Sarah Parsons 1921- *WhoBlA 94*
Blower, David Harrison 1901-1976 *WhoAmA 93N*
Blowers, Anthony John 1926- *Who 94*
Blowers, George Kindrick 1945- *WhoMW 93*
Blowers, Sampson Salter 1742-1842 *WhAmRev*
Blowsnake, Sam 1875- *EncNAR*
Bloxom, Donna Raye 1957- *WhoAmP 93*
Bloxom, Robert Spurgeon 1937- *WhoAmP 93*
Bloy, Francis Eric Irving 1904- *Who 94*
Bloyd, Beverly 1952- *WhoMW 93*
Bloyd, Stephen Roy 1953- *WhoWest 94*
Blubaugh, Danny Jay 1955- *WhoWest 94*
Bluck, Duncan Robert Yorke 1927- *Who 94*
Bludman, Peter 1953- *WhoAmL 94*
Bludman, Sidney Arnold 1927- *WhoAm 94*
Bludson-Francis, Vernett Michelle 1951- *WhoBlA 94*
Blue, Ben d1975 *WhoHol 92*
Blue, Buddy 1957- *WhoWest 94*
Blue, Daniel T., Jr. 1949- *WhoAmP 93*
Blue, Daniel Terry, Jr. 1949- *WhoBlA 94*
Blue, David d1982 *WhoHol 92*
Blue, James Guthrie 1920- *WhoWest 94*
Blue, James Monroe 1941- *WhoAmL 94*
Blue, James R., Sr. 1939- *WhoAmP 93*
Blue, Jean d1972 *WhoHol 92*
Blue, Jeffrey Kenneth 1956- *WhoScEn 94*
Blue, John A. 1943- *WhoAmL 94*
Blue, Joseph Edward 1936- *WhoScEn 94*
Blue, Katherine Mary 1938- *WhoAmP 93*
Blue, Lionel 1930- *Who 94*
Blue, Marian *DrAPF 93*
Blue, Monte d1963 *WhoHol 92*
Blue, Patt 1945- *WhoAmA 93*
Blue, Reginald C. 1942- *WhoMW 93, WhoScEn 94*
Blue, Richard Arthur 1936- *WhoMW 93*

Blue, Sherwood 1905- *WhoAmL 94*
Blue, Steven Joshua 1945- *WhoWest 94*
Blue, Timothy David 1953- *WhoAmL 94*
Blue, Vida, Jr. 1949- *WhoBlA 94*
Blue, Zachary *SmATA 76, TwCYAW*
Blue Bird, James c. 1889- *EncNAR*
Bluechel, Alan 1924- *WhoWest 94*
Bluechel, Alan Joseph 1924- *WhoAmP 93*
Blue Cloud, Peter *DrAPF 93*
Bluefarb, Samuel Mitchell 1912- *WhoAm 94*
Blue Man Group *WhoAmA 93*
Bluemle, Lewis William, Jr. 1921- *WhoAm 94*
Bluemle, Paul Edward 1926- *WhoWest 94*
Bluemle, Robert Louis 1933- *WhoAm 94, WhoAmL 94*
Bluestein, Edwin A., Jr. 1930- *WhoAm 94, WhoAmL 94*
Bluestein, Harold Alan 1948- *WhoWest 94*
Bluestein, Paul Harold 1923- *WhoAm 94, WhoFI 94, WhoMW 93*
Bluestein, Venus Weller 1933- *WhoAm 94*
Bluestone, Andrew Lavoott 1951- *WhoAmL 94*
Bluestone, Hugh Lawrence 1948- *WhoAm 94*
Bluestone, Irving 1917- *WhoAmP 93*
Bluestone, Stanton J. 1944- *WhoFI 94*
Bluett, Thomas Byron, Sr. 1931- *WhoMW 93*
Bluette, Isa d1939 *WhoHol 92*
Bluford, Grady L. 1930- *WhoBlA 94*
Bluford, Guion Stewart, Jr. 1942- *AfrAmAl 6, WhoAm 94, WhoBlA 94*
Bluglass, Robert Saul 1930- *Who 94*
Bluh, Bonnie *DrAPF 93*
Bluher, Grigory 1960- *WhoScEn 94*
Bluhm, Barbara Jean 1925- *WhoAm 94*
Bluhm, Heinz 1907- *WhoAm 94, WrDr 94*
Bluhm, Myron Dean 1934- *WhoMW 93*
Bluhm, Neil Gary 1938- *WhoMW 93*
Bluhm, Norman 1920- *WhoAm 94*
Bluhm, Norman 1921- *WhoAmA 93*
Bluhm, Terry Lee 1947- *WhoScEn 94*
Bluhm, Walter d1976 *WhoHol 92*
Bluhm, William Theodore 1923- *WhoAm 94*
Bluitt, Karen 1957- *WhoFI 94, WhoScEn 94*
Blum, Albert A. 1924- *WrDr 94*
Blum, Andrea 1950- *WhoAmA 93*
Blum, Arthur 1926- *WhoAm 94*
Blum, Barbara Bennett 1930- *WhoAmP 93*
Blum, Barbara Davis *WhoAm 94*
Blum, Barry 1940- *WhoWest 94*
Blum, Bradley Joseph 1969- *WhoMW 93*
Blum, David Arthur 1962- *WhoWest 94*
Blum, Deborah *WhoWest 94*
Blum, Eleanor Goodfriend 1940- *WhoAmP 93*
Blum, Etta *DrAPF 93*
Blum, Fred Andrew 1939- *WhoAm 94, WhoWest 94*
Blum, Gerald Harris 1932- *WhoFI 94*
Blum, Gerald Henry 1926- *WhoAm 94*
Blum, Gerald Saul 1922- *WhoAm 94*
Blum, Gregory Lee 1960- *WhoScEn 94*
Blum, Harry N. 1932- *IntMPA 94*
Blum, Helaine Dorothy *WhoAmA 93*
Blum, Israel 1947- *WhoAmL 94*
Blum, Jacob Joseph 1926- *WhoAm 94*
Blum, James Arnold 1942- *WhoFI 94, WhoIns 94*
Blum, Jeffrey Stuart 1947- *WhoAmL 94*
Blum, Jerome d1993 *NewYTBS 93*
Blum, Jerome 1913- *WrDr 94*
Blum, Jerome 1913-1993 *ConAu 141*
Blum, John Alan 1933- *WhoAm 94, WhoWest 94*
Blum, John Curtis 1915- *WhoAm 94*
Blum, John Fredrick 1955- *WhoFI 94*
Blum, John Morton 1921- *WhoAm 94*
Blum, June 1939- *WhoAmA 93*
Blum, Klara 1904- *BlmGWL*
Blum, Lawrence Philip 1917- *WhoAm 94*
Blum, Leon 1872-1950 *HisWorL [port]*
Blum, Louise A. *DrAPF 93*
Blum, Marc Paul 1942- *WhoAmL 94*
Blum, Mark *WhoHol 92*
Blum, Mark 1950- *IntMPA 94*
Blum, Michael David 1958- *WhoHisp 94*
Blum, Michael Stephen 1939- *WhoAm 94, WhoFI 94*
Blum, Norbert 1935- *IntWW 93*
Blum, Norman Allen 1932- *WhoScEn 94*
Blum, Patricia Rae 1948- *WhoMW 93*
Blum, Peter 1950- *WhoFI 94*
Blum, Ralph 1932- *EncSF 93*
Blum, Rene 1878-1942 *IntDcB [port]*
Blum, Richard Hosmer Adams 1927- *WhoAm 94*
Blum, Richard Joseph 1946- *WhoAm 94*
Blum, Robert Allan 1938- *WhoAm 94*
Blum, Robert Edward 1899- *WhoAm 94*
Blum, Robert M. 1954- *WhoAmL 94*
Blum, Sam d1945 *WhoHol 92*
Blum, Seymour L. 1925- *WhoAm 94*
Blum, Vicky Jolene 1951- *WhoMW 93*
Blum, Virgil Clarence 1913-1990 *WhAm 10*
Blum, Walter J. 1918- *WhoAm 94*
Blum, William L. 1952- *WhoAmP 93*
Blum, William Lee 1920- *WhoAm 94*
Blum, Yehuda Z. 1931- *IntWW 93*
Blumberg, Arnold 1925- *WrDr 94*
Blumberg, Avrom Aaron 1928- *WhoAm 94*
Blumberg, Barbara Griffiths 1920- *WhoAmA 93*
Blumberg, Barbara Salmanson 1927- *WhoFI 94*
Blumberg, Baruch Samuel 1925- *IntWW 93, Who 94, WhoAm 94, WhoScEn 94*
Blumberg, Benjamin Mautner 1942- *WhoScEn 94*
Blumberg, David 1925- *WhoAm 94*
Blumberg, David Russell 1956- *WhoAmP 93*
Blumberg, Donald Freed 1935- *WhoAm 94*
Blumberg, Edward Robert 1951- *WhoAmL 94, WhoFI 94*
Blumberg, Gerald 1911- *WhoAm 94*
Blumberg, Herbert Haskell 1941- *WhoScEn 94*
Blumberg, Herbert Kurt 1925- *WhoAm 94*
Blumberg, Irving d1993 *NewYTBS 93*
Blumberg, John Philip 1949- *WhoAmL 94*
Blumberg, Mark Stuart 1924- *WhoAm 94*
Blumberg, Nathaniel Bernard 1922- *WhoAm 94, WhoWest 94*
Blumberg, Patricia Helene 1956- *WhoAmL 94*
Blumberg, Peter Steven 1944- *WhoFI 94*
Blumberg, Phillip Irvin 1919- *WhoAm 94, WhoAmL 94, WrDr 94*
Blumberg, Rhoda 1917- *WrDr 94*
Blumberg, Robert Lee 1942- *WhoWest 94*
Blumberg, Ron *WhoAmA 93*
Blumberg, Stanley A. 1912- *WrDr 94*
Blumberg, Yuli 1894-1964 *WhoAmA 93N*
Blume, Basil Westwood 1965- *WhoWest 94*
Blume, Gary Ray 1954- *WhoAmL 94*
Blume, Harvey 1946- *ConAu 141*
Blume, Heinrich 1788-1856 *NewGrDO*
Blume, Horst Karl 1927- *WhoScEn 94*
Blume, Jack Paul 1915- *WhoAm 94*
Blume, James Beryl 1941- *WhoWest 94*
Blume, James Donald 1950- *WhoAmL 94*
Blume, John August 1909- *WhoAm 94, WhoScEn 94*
Blume, Judy 1938- *BlmGWL, TwCYAW, WrDr 94*
Blume, Judy Sussman 1938- *WhoAm 94*
Blume, Lawrence Dayton 1948- *WhoAm 94, WhoAmL 94*
Blume, Marshall Edward 1941- *WhoAm 94, WhoFI 94*
Blume, Martin 1932- *WhoAm 94*
Blume, Norbert L. 1922- *WhoAmP 93*
Blume, Paul Chiappe 1929- *WhoAmL 94, WhoMW 93*
Blume, Peter d1992 *IntWW 93N*
Blume, Peter 1906-1992 *CurBio 93N, WhAm 10, WhoAmA 93N*
Blume, Peter Frederick 1946- *WhoAm 94*
Blumel, Joseph Carlton 1928- *WhoAm 94*
Blumen, Ian Gregg 1965- *WhoFI 94*
Blumenfeld, Alan *WhoHol 92*
Blumenfeld, Alfred Morton 1919- *WhoAm 94*
Blumenfeld, Charles Raban 1944- *WhoAm 94*
Blumenfeld, Eli 1933- *WhoAmL 94*
Blumenfeld, F. Yorick 1932- *EncSF 93*
Blumenfeld, Felix (Mikhaylovich) 1863-1931 *NewGrDO*
Blumenfeld, Harold 1923- *NewGrDO*
Blumenfeld, Jeffrey 1948- *WhoAmL 94*
Blumenfeld, Seth David 1940- *WhoAm 94, WhoFI 94*
Blumenfeld, Sue Deborah 1952- *WhoAm 94*
Blumenkrantz, Steven Jay 1946- *WhoAmL 94*
Blumenkranz, Steven 1943- *WhoFI 94*
Blumenreich, Julia *DrAPF 93*
Blumenreich, Martin Sigvart 1949- *WhoScEn 94*
Blumenschein, Ernest Leonard 1874-1960 *WhoAmA 93N*
Blumenschein, Mary Greene 1869-1958 *WhoAmA 93N*
Blumenshine, Gary Baker 1944- *WhoMW 93*
Blumenshine, Mahlon 1928- *WhoMW 93*
Blumenson, Martin 1918- *WrDr 94*
Blumenstock, David Albert 1927- *WhoAm 94*
Blumenthal, Andre 1904-1989 *WhAm 10*
Blumenthal, Charles S. 1924- *WhoAmP 93*
Blumenthal, David A. 1945- *WhoAm 94, WhoAmL 94*
Blumenthal, David Mark 1956- *WhoAmL 94*
Blumenthal, Fritz 1913- *WhoAm 94, WhoAmA 93*
Blumenthal, Gary Howard 1954- *WhoAmP 93*
Blumenthal, Gerda Renee 1923- *WrDr 94*
Blumenthal, Harold Jay 1926- *WhoAm 94*
Blumenthal, Herman Bertram 1916- *WhoAm 94*
Blumenthal, Howard J. 1952- *WrDr 94*
Blumenthal, Jeffrey Michael 1960- *WhoAmL 94*
Blumenthal, Marcia *DrAPF 93*
Blumenthal, Margaret M. 1905- *WhoAmA 93*
Blumenthal, Marian 1933- *AstEnc*
Blumenthal, Michael C. *DrAPF 93*
Blumenthal, Richard *WhoAm 94, WhoAmL 94, WhoAmP 93*
Blumenthal, Richard Cary 1951- *WhoWest 94*
Blumenthal, Ronnie 1944- *WhoAmL 94*
Blumenthal, Rosa Lee *WhoAmP 93*
Blumenthal, Sid *ConAu 142*
Blumenthal, Sidney 1909- *WhoAm 94*
Blumenthal, Sidney 1909-1990 *WhAm 10*
Blumenthal, Sidney 1948- *ConAu 142, WrDr 94*
Blumenthal, Thomas Michael 1951- *WhoAmL 94*
Blumenthal, W. Michael 1926- *WhoAmP 93*
Blumenthal, W(erner) Michael 1926- *IntWW 93, Who 94*
Blumenthal, Werner Michael 1926- *WhoAm 94*
Blumenthal, William 1955- *WhoAmL 94*
Blumenthal-Tamarina, Maria d1938 *WhoHol 92*
Blumer, Frederick Elwin 1933- *WhoAm 94*
Blumer, Rodney *NewGrDO*
Blumer, Rodney Milnes 1936- *Who 94*
Blumfield, Clifford William 1922- *Who 94*
Blumgart, Herrman L(udwig) 1895- *WhAm 10*
Blumgart, Leslie Harold 1931- *IntWW 93, Who 94*
Blumhardt, Jon Howard 1951- *WhoWest 94*
Bluming, Avrum Zvi 1940- *WhoWest 94*
Bluming, Sidney David 1944- *WhoAmL 94*
Blumkin, Linda Ruth 1944- *WhoAm 94, WhoAmL 94*
Blumlein, Alan Dower 1903-1942 *DcNaB MP*
Blumlein, Michael 1948- *EncSF 93*
Blumm, Michael Charles 1950- *WhoWest 94*
Blummer, Kathleen Ann 1945- *WhoWest 94*
Blumner, Rudolf d1945 *WhoHol 92*
Blumofe, Robert F. *IntMPA 94*
Blumofe, Robert Fulton *WhoAm 94*
Blumrich, Josef Franz 1913- *WhoScEn 94, WhoWest 94*
Blumrich, Stephen 1941- *WhoAmA 93*
Blumrosen, Alfred William 1928- *WhoAmL 94*
Blumrosen, Ruth Gerber 1927- *WhoAmL 94*
Blumstein, Alfred 1930- *WhoAm 94*
Blumstein, Allan 1937- *WhoAm 94*
Blumstein, Edward 1933- *WhoAmL 94*
Blumstein, James Franklin 1945- *WhoAm 94*
Blumstein, Renee J. 1957- *WhoAm 94*
Blumstein, William A. 1948- *WhoAm 94, WhoFI 94*
Blunck, Lawrence Paul 1956- *WhoAmL 94*
Blunck, Lilo 1942- *WhoWomW 91*
Blundell, Daphne Mary 1916- *Who 94*
Blundell, (Walter) Derek (George) 1929- *WrDr 94*
Blundell, Derek John 1933- *Who 94*
Blundell, Graeme 1945- *WhoHol 92*
Blundell, Michael d1993 *IntWW 93N, Who 94N*
Blundell, Richard William 1952- *Who 94*
Blundell, Thomas Leon 1942- *IntWW 93, Who 94, WhoScEn 94*
Blundell, William Edward 1934- *WhoAm 94*
Blundell, William Richard Charles 1927- *WhoAm 94*
Blunden, Caroline 1948- *WrDr 94*
Blunden, Edmund 1896-1974 *BlmGEL*
Blunden, George 1922- *IntWW 93, Who 94*
Blunden, Philip (Overington) 1922- *Who 94*
Blunk, Forrest Stewart 1913- *WhoAm 94*
Blunkett, David 1947- *IntWW 93, Who 94*
Blunt, Anne Isabella 1837-1917 *WhWE*
Blunt, Charles William 1951- *IntWW 93, Who 94*
Blunt, David John 1944- *Who 94*
Blunt, David Richard Reginald Harvey 1938- *Who 94*
Blunt, Don 1906- *WrDr 94*
Blunt, Erin *WhoHol 92*
Blunt, Gabrielle *WhoHol 92*
Blunt, Leroy 1921- *WhoAmP 93*
Blunt, Madelyne Bowen *WhoBlA 94*
Blunt, Peter 1923- *Who 94*
Blunt, Peter Howe 1945- *WhoAmL 94, WhoFI 94, WhoWest 94*
Blunt, Raymond Stewart 1943- *WhoAmP 93*
Blunt, Robert Matteson 1916- *WhoWest 94*
Blunt, Roger Reckling 1930- *AfrAmG [port], WhoBlA 94*
Blunt, Roy D. 1950- *WhoAmP 93*
Blunt, Wilfrid Scawen 1840-1922 *WhWE*
Blunthal, John *WhoHol 92*
Blush, Steven Michael 1948- *WhoScEn 94*
Blust, Larry D. 1943- *WhoAmL 94*
Blute, James Francis, III 1944- *WhoWest 94*
Blute, Peter I. 1956- *CngDr 93, WhoAm 94, WhoAmP 93*
Bluteau, Lothaire *WhoHol 92*
Bluth, B. J. 1934- *WhoAm 94*
Bluth, Don 1938- *IntMPA 94*
Bluthardt, Edward Earl 1916- *WhoAmP 93*
Bluting, Edward 1925- *WrDr 94*
Blutstein, Harvey M. 1927- *WhoIns 94*
Blutter, Joan Wernick 1929- *WhoAm 94*
Bly, Belden G., Jr. *WhoAmP 93*
Bly, Belden Gerald, Jr. 1914- *WhoAmL 94*
Bly, Carol *DrAPF 93*
Bly, Charles Albert 1952- *WhoFI 94, WhoScEn 94*
Bly, David Alan 1953- *WhoWest 94*
Bly, Herbert Arthur 1929- *WhoAm 94*
Bly, James Charles, Jr. 1952- *WhoFI 94*
Bly, James L. 1959- *WhoFI 94*
Bly, Nellie 1867-1922 *BlmGWL, EncSPD*
Bly, Robert *DrAPF 93*
Bly, Robert 1926- *CurBio 93 [port], IntWW 93*
Bly, Robert (Elwood) 1926- *ConAu 41NR, WrDr 94*
Bly, Robert Elwood 1926- *WhoAm 94*
Bly, William J. *DrAPF 93*
Blyden, Edward Wilmot 1832-1912 *AfrAmAl 6 [port]*
Blyden, Larry d1975 *WhoHol 92*
Blydenburgh, Jeffrey Lewis 1948- *WhoMW 93*
Blye, Cecil A., Sr. 1927- *WhoBlA 94*
Blye, Douglas William Alfred 1924- *Who 94*
Blye, Maggie *WhoHol 92*
Blyler, Allison Lee 1966- *SmATA 74 [port]*
Blyler, William Edward 1936- *WhoAmL 94*
Blyma, Franz Xaver 1770-c. 1812 *NewGrDO*
Blynn, Guy Marc 1945- *WhoAm 94, WhoAmL 94*
Blystone, Robert Vernon 1943- *WhoAm 94*
Blystone, Stanley d1956 *WhoHol 92*
Blyth, Baron 1931- *Who 94*
Blyth, (Geoffrey) Alan 1929- *NewGrDO*
Blyth, Alan Geoffrey 1929- *WrDr 94*
Blyth, Ann 1928- *IntMPA 94, WhoHol 92*
Blyth, Ann Marie 1949- *WhoMW 93*
Blyth, Charles 1940- *Who 94*
Blyth, Chay 1940- *WrDr 94*
Blyth, James 1864-1933 *EncSF 93*
Blyth, James 1940- *IntWW 93, Who 94*
Blyth, John *ConAu 41NR*
Blyth, John 1925- *WrDr 94*
Blyth, John Douglas Morrison 1924- *Who 94*
Blyth, John E. 1931- *WhoAmL 94*
Blyth, Michael Leslie 1950- *WhoAm 94*
Blyth, Myrna Greenstein 1939- *WhoAm 94*
Blythe, Betty d1972 *WhoHol 92*
Blythe, James David, II 1940- *WhoAmL 94*
Blythe, James Forbes 1917- *Who 94*
Blythe, James Granville 1938- *WhoMW 93*
Blythe, John 1921- *WhoHol 92*
Blythe, Mark Andrew 1943- *Who 94*
Blythe, Peter 1934- *WhoHol 92*
Blythe, Rex Arnold 1928- *Who 94*
Blythe, Ronald (George) 1922- *WrDr 94*
Blythe, Ronald George 1922- *Who 94*
Blythe, William Jackson, Jr. 1935- *WhoAmP 93*
Blythe, William LeGette, II 1957- *WhoAm 94*

Blyton, Enid 1897-1968 *BlmGWL, ChlLR 31 [port]*
Bninski, Roman A. 1946- *WhoAmL 94*
Bo, Armando d1981 *WhoHol 92*
Bo, Jorgen 1919- *IntWW 93*
Boa, Bruce *WhoHol 92*
Boadicea d61 *BlmGEL*
Boado, Ruben Jose 1955- *WhoScEn 94, WhoWest 94*
Boag, John Wilson 1911- *Who 94*
Boag, Thomas Johnson 1922- *WhoAm 94*
Boags, Charles D. 1929- *WhoBlA 94*
Boak, Ruth Alice 1906- *WhoAm 94*
Boal, Dean 1931- *WhoAm 94*
Boal, (John) Graham 1943- *Who 94*
Boal, Marcia Anne Riley 1944- *WhoMW 93*
Boal, Peter Cadbury 1965- *WhoAm 94*
Boal, Sara Metzner 1896-1979 *WhoAmA 93N*
Boalch, Donald Howard 1914- *WrDr 94*
Boam, Thomas Anthony 1932- *Who 94*
Boan, Bobby Jack 1945- *WhoAm 94*
Boan, William D. 1949- *WhoAmP 93*
Boand, Charles Wilbur 1908- *WhoAmL 94, WhoFI 94*
Board, Dwaine 1956- *WhoBlA 94*
Board, Dwight Vernon 1944- *WhoAmL 94*
Board, Joseph Breckinridge 1931- *WhoAmP 93*
Board, Joseph Breckinridge, Jr. 1931- *WhoAm 94*
Board, Warren Lee 1942- *WhoAm 94*
Boardley, Curtestine May 1943- *WhoBlA 94*
Boardman *Who 94*
Boardman, Baron 1919- *IntWW 93, Who 94*
Boardman, Barrington 1933- *WrDr 94*
Boardman, Claude d1928 *WhoHol 92*
Boardman, David *WhoAm 94*
Boardman, Deborah *WhoAmA 93*
Boardman, Eleanor 1898- *WhoHol 92*
Boardman, Elijah 1760-1823 *WhAmRev*
Boardman, Eunice 1926- *WhoAm 94*
Boardman, Fon W(yman), Jr. 1911- *WrDr 94*
Boardman, Gregory Dale 1950- *WhoScEn 94*
Boardman, Harold 1907- *Who 94*
Boardman, Harold Frederick, Jr. 1939- *WhoAm 94, WhoAmL 94*
Boardman, James Paul 1957- *WhoAmL 94*
Boardman, John 1927- *Who 94*
Boardman, John, Sir 1927- *WrDr 94*
Boardman, John Michael 1938- *WhoAm 94*
Boardman, Kay Irene 1939- *WhoWest 94*
Boardman, Kenneth (Ormrod) 1914- *Who 94*
Boardman, Linda Irene 1948- *WhoFI 94*
Boardman, Mark Seymour 1958- *WhoAmL 94*
Boardman, Michael Neil 1942- *WhoAmL 94*
Boardman, Nell d1968 *WhoAmA 93N*
Boardman, Norman Keith 1926- *IntWW 93, Who 94*
Boardman, Richard John 1940- *WhoAmL 94*
Boardman, Robert A. 1947- *WhoAmL 94*
Boardman, Robert Emmett 1932- *WhoAmP 93*
Boardman, Rosanne Virginia 1946- *WhoScEn 94, WhoWest 94*
Boardman, Seymour 1921- *WhoAm 94, WhoAmA 93*
Boardman, Thelma Hubbard d1978 *WhoHol 92*
Boardman, Tom 1930- *EncSF 93*
Boardman, True d1918 *WhoHol 92*
Boardman, True 1909- *WhoHol 92*
Boardman, Virginia True d1971 *WhoHol 92*
Boardman, William Penniman 1941- *WhoAm 94*
Boarini, Edward James 1949- *WhoWest 94*
Boarman, Gerald Jude 1940- *WhoFI 94*
Boarman, Patrick Madigan 1922- *WhoAm 94, WhoWest 94*
Boas, Anna d1975 *WhoHol 92*
Boas, Frances Cullman d1993 *NewYTBS 93*
Boas, Franz 1858-1942 *AmSocL*
Boas, Robert Sanford 1923-1992 *WhAm 10*
Boas, Roger 1921- *WhoAm 94*
Boasberg, Leonard W. 1923- *WhoAm 94*
Boase, Frederic 1843-1916 *DcNaB MP*
Boase, Martin 1932- *IntWW 93, Who 94*
Boast, Molly Shryer 1948- *WhoAmL 94*
Boast, Philip 1952- *WrDr 94*
Boast, Warren Benefield 1909- *WhAm 10*
Boat, Ronald Allen 1947- *WhoFI 94, WhoWest 94*
Boat, Thomas Frederick 1939- *WhoAm 94*
Boateng, Ernest Amano 1920- *IntWW 93, Who 94*
Boateng, Paul Yaw 1951- *Who 94*
Boatman, Dennis LeRoy 1952- *WhoWest 94*
Boatman, Michael *WhoHol 92*
Boatner, Haydon L. 1900-1977 *HisDcKW*
Boatner, Roy Alton 1941- *WhoAmP 93*
Boatright, James Francis 1933- *WhoAm 94*
Boatright, Joanna Morson 1958- *WhoFI 94*
Boatwright, Charlotte Jeanne 1937- *WhoFI 94*
Boatwright, Daniel E. 1930- *WhoAmP 93*
Boatwright, Joseph Weldon 1949- *WhoBlA 94*
Boatwright, M. Tracy 1942- *WhoAmP 93*
Boatwright, Mary H. 1920- *WhoAmP 93*
Boatwright, Purvis James, Jr. 1927-1991 *WhAm 10*
Boatwright, Walter James 1957- *WhoFI 94*
Boaz, David Douglas 1953- *WhoAm 94*
Boaz, Doniella 1934- *WhoAm 94*
Boaz, Frank W., III 1956- *WhoFI 94*
Boba, Imre 1919- *WhoAm 94*
Bobak, Bruno Joseph 1923- *WhoAmA 93*
Bob & Bob 1953- *WhoAmA 93*
Bob and Ray *WhoCom [port]*
Bobb, L. Edward 1951- *WhoIns 94*
Bobb, Merrick John 1946- *WhoAmL 94*
Bobb, Richard Allen 1937- *WhoFI 94*
Bobbitt, Archie Newton 1895- *WhAm 10*
Bobbitt, J. Frank 1940- *WhoMW 93*
Bobbitt, James McCue 1930- *WhoAm 94*
Bobbitt, Leroy 1943- *WhoAm 94, WhoAmL 94, WhoBlA 94*
Bobbitt, Max E. 1945- *WhoAm 94, WhoFI 94*
Bobbitt, Philip Chase 1948- *WhoAm 94*
Bobbitt, Ronald Albert 1953- *WhoMW 93*
Bobby, Anne *WhoHol 92*
Bobco, William David, Jr. 1946- *WhoMW 93*
Bobe, Henry Dale 1952- *WhoMW 93*
Bobek, Mark H. 1962- *WhoFI 94*
Bobel, Ronald Emmett 1939- *WhoAmP 93*
Bobenhouse, Nellie Ruth 1936- *WhoMW 93*
Bober, Lawrence Harold 1924- *WhoAm 94*
Boberg, Wayne D. 1952- *WhoAm 94*
Bobescu, Constantin 1899- *NewGrDO*
Bobick, Bruce 1941- *WhoAmA 93*
Bobier, Bill *WhoAmP 93*
Bobino, Rita Florencia 1934- *WhoBlA 94*
Bobinski, George S. 1929- *WrDr 94*
Bobinski, George Sylvan 1929- *WhoAm 94*
Bobisud, Larry Eugene 1940- *WhoAm 94*
Bobleter, Lowell Stanley 1902-1973 *WhoAmA 93N*
Boblett, Mark Anthony 1959- *WhoScEn 94*
Bobo, Anne Roberts 1961- *WhoAmL 94*
Bobo, Jack E. 1924- *WhoIns 94*
Bobo, Jack Edward 1924- *WhoFI 94*
Bobo, James Robert 1923- *WhoAm 94*
Bobo, Melvin 1924- *WhoAm 94*
Bobo, Roscoe Lemual 1912-1992 *WhoBlA 94N*
Bobo, Stephen Todd 1955- *WhoAmL 94*
Bobrick, Steven Aaron 1950- *WhoWest 94*
Bobrick, William David 1955- *WhoAmP 93*
Bobrik, Gunther d1957 *WhoHol 92*
Bobroff, Harold 1920- *WhoAm 94, WhoAmP 93*
Bobroff, Michael J. 1942- *WhoAmL 94*
Bobrofsky, Albert C. 1933- *WhoAmP 93*
Bobrovnikoff, Nicholas Theodore 1896- *WhAm 10*
Bobrow, Alvan Lee 1949- *WhoAmL 94*
Bobrow, Arlene S. 1952- *WhoAmL 94*
Bobrow, Davis Bernard 1936- *WhoAm 94*
Bobrow, Henry Bernard 1924- *WhoAmL 94*
Bobrow, Martin 1938- *Who 94*
Bobrowicz, Yvonne Pacanovsky 1928- *WhoAmA 93*
Bobrowski, Czeslaw 1904- *IntWW 93*
Bobrowsky, Kim Russell 1951- *WhoAmL 94*
Bobry, Howard Hale 1948- *WhoWest 94*
Bobu, Maria *WhoWomW 91*
Bobyshev, Dmitri Vasilevich 1936- *IntWW 93*
Bobzien, H.J., Jr. 1935- *WhoAm 94, WhoMW 93*
Bocaccio *DrAPF 93*
Bocage, Marie-Anne Le Page du 1710-1802 *BlmGWL*
Bocage, Ronald J. 1946- *WhoBlA 94*
Bocan, David E. 1948- *WhoAmL 94*
Bocardo, Claire 1939- *ConAu 141*
Bocca, Julio *WhoAm 94, WhoHisp 94*
Bocca, Julio 1967-1991 *IntDcB [port]*
Boccabadati, Luigia 1800-1850 *NewGrDO*
Boccaccio, Giovanni 1313?-1375 *BlmGEL*
Boccardi, Louis Donald 1937- *WhoAm 94, WhoFI 94*
Boccardi, Michelangelo fl. 1724-1735 *NewGrDO*
Boccardo, Delia *WhoHol 92*
Boccherini, Giovanni Gastone 1742-1798? *NewGrDO*
Boccherini, (Ridolfo) Luigi 1743-1805 *NewGrDO*
Bocchimuzzo, Vincent Louis 1952- *WhoFI 94*
Bocchini, Joseph L., Jr. 1944- *WhoAmP 93*
Bocchini, Suzanne S. 1947- *WhoAmL 94*
Bocchino, Linda Elizabeth 1948- *WhoFI 94*
Boccia, Barbara 1957- *WhoAmL 94*
Boccia, Edward Eugene 1921- *WhoAmA 93*
Boccia, Maria Liboria 1953- *WhoWest 94*
Boccitto, Bonnie L. 1949- *WhoIns 94*
Boccone, Andrew Albert 1945- *WhoAm 94*
Bochak, Grayce 1956- *SmATA 76 [port]*
Bocharov, Dmitry Ivanovich fl. 177-?-179-? *WhWE*
Bocharov, Mikhail Aleksandrovich 1941- *IntWW 93*
Bochco, Steven 1943- *Au&Arts 11 [port], IntMPA 94, WhoAm 94*
Bochenski, Joseph 1902- *IntWW 93*
Bochert, Linda H. 1949- *WhoAmL 94*
Bochicchio-Ausura, Jill Arden 1951- *WhoAm 94*
Bochin, Leonid Arnoldovich 1949- *LoBiDrD*
Bochkarev, Nikolai Gennadievich 1947- *WhoScEn 94*
Bochner, Bruce Scott *WhoScEn 94*
Bochner, Hart 1956- *IntMPA 94, WhoAm 94*
Bochner, Hart 1957- *WhoHol 92*
Bochner, Lloyd 1924- *IntMPA 94, WhoHol 92*
Bochner, Mel 1940- *WhoAm 94, WhoAmA 93*
Bochsa, (Robert) Nicholas Charles 1789-1856 *NewGrDO*
Bock, Angela Marie 1939- *WhoMW 93*
Bock, Bennie W., II 1942- *WhoAmP 93*
Bock, Berta 1857-1945 *NewGrDO*
Bock, Carolyn Ann 1942- *WhoMW 93*
Bock, Claus Victor 1926- *Who 94*
Bock, David Allen 1946- *WhoMW 93*
Bock, Dieter *IntWW 93*
Bock, Dieter 1939- *Who 94*
Bock, Edward John 1916- *IntWW 93, WhoAm 94*
Bock, Fred 1939- *WhoWest 94*
Bock, Frederick *DrAPF 93*
Bock, Frederick d1916 *WhoHol 92*
Bock, Hans 1928- *IntWW 93*
Bock, J. Kathryn 1948- *WhoMW 93*
Bock, Jeffrey William 1950- *WhoWest 94*
Bock, Jerry 1928- *IntWW 93, WhoAm 94*
Bock, Jerry (Lewis) 1928- *NewGrDO*
Bock, Joseph Gerard 1957- *WhoAmP 93, WhoMW 93*
Bock, Joseph Reto 1929- *WhoFI 94*
Bock, Peter Ernest 1948- *WhoAmP 93*
Bock, Philip Karl 1934- *WrDr 94*
Bock, Robert Howard 1932- *WhoAm 94*
Bock, Robert M. 1923-1991 *WhAm 10*
Bock, Russell Samuel 1905- *WhoAm 94, WhoWest 94*
Bock, Walter Joseph 1933- *WhoAm 94*
Bock, William Sauts-Netamux'we 1939- *WhoAmA 93*
Bockelman, John Richard 1925- *WhoAm 94, WhoAmL 94, WhoFI 94, WhoMW 93*
Bockelmann, Rudolf (August Louis Wilhelm) 1892-1958 *NewGrDO*
Bockemuehl, Richard George 1939- *WhoAmP 93*
Bockhoff, Frank James 1928- *WhoAm 94*
Bockhoff, Harry W. 1895- *WhAm 10*
Bockhop, Clarence William 1921- *WhoAm 94, WhoScEn 94*
Bockian, James Bernard 1936- *WhoFI 94*
Bockian, James Bernard 1941- *WhoScEn 94*
Bockius, Thomas John 1968- *WhoScEn 94*
Bockle, Franz *IntWW 93N*
Bocklin von Bocklinsau, Franz Friedrich Siegmund August von 1745-1813 *NewGrDO*
Bockman, Miriam Levine *WhoAmP 93*
Bockman, Robert T. 1946- *WhoAmL 94*
Bockmon, Harthia W. 1932- *WhoAmP 93*
Bock/Pallant, Layeh *DrAPF 93*
Bockris, Victor *DrAPF 93*
Bockserman, Robert Julian 1929- *WhoMW 93, WhoScEn 94*
Bockshorn, Samuel Friedrich *NewGrDO*
Bockstein, Herbert 1943- *WhoAm 94, WhoAmL 94*
Bockus, Henry L. 1894- *WhAm 10*
Bockus, William Ward 1950- *WhoMW 93*
Bockwoldt, Todd Shane 1967- *WhoScEn 94*
Bocock, Frederic Scott 1931- *WhoFI 94*
Bocock, Joseph H. 1954- *WhoAmL 94*
Bocock, Maclin *DrAPF 93*
Bocock, Robert James 1940- *WrDr 94*
Bocour, Leonard d1993 *NewYTBS 93*
Bocour, Leonard 1910- *WhoAmA 93*
Bocuse, Paul 1926- *IntWW 93*
Bocvarov, Spiro 1962- *WhoScEn 94*
Boczar, Jim 1947- *WhoAmP 93*
Boczkaj, Bohdan Karol 1930- *WhoScEn 94*
Bod, Peter Akos 1951- *IntWW 93*
Bod'a, Koloman 1927- *IntWW 93*
Bodack, Leonard J. 1932- *WhoAmP 93*
Bodahl, Larry D. 1947- *WhoAmP 93*
Bodalo, Jose d1985 *WhoHol 92*
Bodansky, Barbara Biber d1993 *NewYTBS 93 [port]*
Bodansky, David 1924- *WhoAm 94*
Bodansky, Robert Lee *WhoAmL 94*
Bodanszky, Miklos 1915- *WhoAm 94, WhoMW 93*
Bodanzky, Artur 1877-1939 *NewGrDO*
Bodard, Lucien Albert 1914- *IntWW 93*
Bodde, William, Jr. 1931- *WhoAm 94, WhoAmP 93*
Bodden, Wendell N. 1930- *WhoBlA 94*
Bodden, William Michael 1929- *WhoAm 94*
Boddey, Martin d1975 *WhoHol 92*
Boddicker, Daniel J. *WhoAmP 93*
Boddie, Algernon Owens 1933- *WhoBlA 94*
Boddie, Arthur Walker 1910- *WhoBlA 94*
Boddie, Daniel W. 1922- *WhoBlA 94*
Boddie, Gwendolyn M. 1957- *WhoBlA 94*
Boddie, James T., Jr. 1931- *AfrAmG [port]*
Boddie, Lewis F., Sr. 1913- *WhoBlA 94*
Boddie, Lewis Franklin 1913- *WhoWest 94*
Boddie, Reginald Alonzo 1959- *WhoAmL 94*
Boddie, William Willis 1945- *WhoMW 93*
Boddiger, George Cyrus 1917- *WhoAm 94*
Boddington, Craig Thornton 1952- *WhoAm 94*
Boddington, Ewart Agnew 1927- *Who 94*
Boddington, Lewis 1907- *Who 94*
Boddu, Veera Mallu 1958- *WhoScEn 94*
Boddy, Jack Richard 1922- *Who 94*
Boddy, James E., Jr. 1946- *WhoAmL 94*
Boddy, Janice 1951- *WrDr 94*
Bode, Barbara *WhoAm 94*
Bode, Carl *DrAPF 93*
Bode, Carl d1993 *NewYTBS 93 [port]*
Bode, Carl 1911-1993 *ConAu 140, WrDr 94N*
Bode, Christoph Albert-Maria 1955- *WhoScEn 94*
Bode, Hannelore 1941- *NewGrDO*
Bode, James Adolph 1938- *WhoAmP 93*
Bode, Janet 1943- *TwCYAW*
Bode, Johann Elert 1747-1826 *WorScD*
Bode, John William 1955- *WhoAmP 93*
Bode, Joyce Scruggs 1953- *WhoAmL 94*
Bode, Lyndon Eugene 1963- *WhoMW 93*
Bode, Ralf *IntMPA 94*
Bode, Ralf D. *ConTFT 11*
Bode, Richard Albert 1931- *WhoAm 94*
Bode, Robert William 1912- *WhoAmA 93*
Bode, Sara Giddings 1935- *WhoMW 93*
Bode, Vaughn (Frederick) 1941-1975 *EncSF 93*
Bode, Walter Albert 1950- *WhoAm 94*
Bodeen, Dewitt d1988 *WhoHol 92*
Bodeen, DeWitt 1908-1988 *IntDcF 2-4*
Bodega y Quadra, Juan Francisco De La 1743-1794 *WhWE*
Bodel, Burman d1969 *WhoHol 92*
Bodel, Jean c. 1165-c. 1210 *IntDcT 2*
Bodelsen, Anders 1937- *ConWorW 93, EncSF 93*
Bodelun, Rogelio 1936- *IntWW 93*
Bodem, Beverly 1940- *WhoAmP 93*
Bodem, Dennis Richard 1937- *WhoAmA 93*
Boden, Deirdre 1940- *WhoWest 94*
Boden, Herman d1985 *WhoHol 92*
Boden, Leonard *Who 94*
Boden, Margaret A(nn) 1936- *WrDr 94*
Boden, Margaret Ann 1936- *IntWW 93, Who 94*
Boden, Thomas Bennion 1915- *Who 94*
Bodenhamer, David J(ackson) 1947- *ConAu 142*
Bodenhamer, David Jackson 1947- *WhoMW 93*
Bodenmann, Linda Arden 1956- *WhoFI 94*
Bodensieck, Ernest Justus 1923- *WhoWest 94*

Bodenstedt, Friedrich von 1819-1892 *DcLB 129 [port]*
Bodenstein, Ira 1954- *WhoAmL 94*
Bodenstein, Robert Quentin 1936- *WhoIns 94*
Boderman, Mary Lou 1953- *WhoWest 94*
Bodett, Thomas Edward 1955- *WhoWest 94*
Bodett, Tom 1955- *WrDr 94*
Bodewitz, Hendrik Wilhelm 1939- *IntWW 93*
Bodey, Bela 1949- *WhoWest 94*
Bodey, David Roderick Lessiter 1947- *Who 94*
Bodey, Gerald Paul 1934- *WhoAm 94*
Bodger *Who 94*
Bodi, Lynn Judith 1962- *WhoAmL 94*
Bodi, Sonia Ellen 1940- *WhoMW 93*
Bodian, David d1992 *IntWW 93N*
Bodian, David 1910-1992 *WhAm 10*
Bodian, Nat G. 1921- *WhoAm 94*
Bodichon, Barbara Leigh Smith 1827-1891 *BlmGWL*
Bodig, Jozsef *WhoWest 94*
Bodiker, Richard W. 1936- *WhoAmP 93*
Bodilly, Jocelyn 1913- *Who 94*
Bodily, Stephen M. 1936- *WhoAmP 93*
Bodin, Felix *EncSF 93*
Bodin, Jean 1529?-1596 *GuFrLit 2*
Bodin, Manfred 1939- *IntWW 93*
Bodin, Paul 1910- *WhoAmA 93*
Bodine, Helen *WhoAmA 93N*
Bodine, James Forney 1921- *WhoAm 94*
Bodine, Janice M. 1937- *WhoAmP 93*
Bodine, Jerry *WhoAmP 93*
Bodine, Laurence 1950- *WhoAm 94, WhoMW 93*
Bodine, Peter Van Nest 1958- *WhoScEn 94*
Bodine, Willis Ramsey, Jr. 1935- *WhoAm 94*
Bodington, Charles E. 1930- *WhoScEn 94*
Bodington, Nancy Hermione 1912- *WrDr 94*
Bodinson, Holt 1941- *WhoWest 94*
Bodisco, Michael Andrew 1941- *WhoWest 94*
Bodkin, Francis Fisher, Jr. 1944- *WhoFI 94*
Bodkin, Henry Grattan, Jr. 1921- *WhoAm 94, WhoAmL 94*
Bodkin, Lawrence Edward 1927- *WhoFI 94, WhoScEn 94*
Bodlaj, Viktor 1928- *WhoScEn 94*
Bodley, Harley Ryan, Jr. 1936- *WhoAm 94*
Bodley, James William 1937- *WhoMW 93*
Bodley, John Edward Courtenay 1853-1925 *DcNaB MP*
Bodman, Richard Stockwell 1938- *WhoAm 94, WhoFI 94*
Bodman, Roger Alan 1952- *WhoAmP 93*
Bodman, Samuel Wright, III 1938- *IntWW 93, WhoAm 94, WhoFI 94*
Bodman-Bustamante, Denise Ann 1951- *WhoWest 94*
Bodmer, Karl 1809-1893 *WhWE [port]*
Bodmer, Walter (Fred) 1936- *Who 94*
Bodmer, Walter (Fred), Sir 1936- *WrDr 94*
Bodmer, Walter Fred 1936- *IntWW 93, WhoScEn 94*
Bodmin, Archdeacon of *Who 94*
Bodnar, John, III 1958- *WhoFI 94*
Bodnar, Peter 1928- *WhoAmA 93*
Bodnar, Peter O. 1945- *WhoAmL 94*
Bodner, Emanuel 1947- *WhoFI 94*
Bodner, Herbert 1948- *WhoAm 94, WhoFI 94*
Bodner, John, Jr. 1927- *WhoAm 94*
Bodner, Randall Wayne 1959- *WhoAmL 94*
Bodney, David Jeremy 1954- *WhoAmL 94, WhoWest 94*
Bodo, Sandor 1920- *WhoAmA 93*
Bodonyi, Richard James 1943- *WhoMW 93*
Bodor, Nicholas Stephen 1939- *WhoScEn 94*
Bodorff, Richard J. 1949- *WhoAmL 94*
Bodovitz, James Philip 1958- *WhoAmL 94*
Bodrick, Leonard Eugene 1953- *WhoBlA 94*
Bodstrom, Lennart 1928- *IntWW 93*
Bodsworth, Fred 1918- *WhoAm 94*
Bodsworth, (Charles) Fred(erick) 1918- *WrDr 94*
Bodtke, Richard *DrAPF 93*
Bodurtha, James H. 1944- *WhoAm 94, WhoAmL 94*
Body, Geoffrey 1929- *WrDr 94*
Body, Richard (Bernard Frank Stewart) 1927- *Who 94*
Bodzy, Glen Alan 1952- *WhoAmL 94*
Boe, Barbara Louise 1935- *WhoMW 93*
Boe, David Stephen 1936- *WhoAm 94*
Boe, Deborah *DrAPF 93*
Boe, Gerard Patrick 1936- *WhoAm 94*
Boe, Jason Douglas 1929-1990 *WhAm 10*
Boe, Myron Timothy 1948- *WhoAmL 94, WhoFI 94*
Boe, Nils A. 1913- *CngDr 93*
Boe, Norman Wallace 1943- *Who 94*
Boe, Roy Asbjorn 1919- *WhoAmA 93N*
Boeck, August de 1865-1937 *NewGrDO*
Boeck, Larry James 1947- *WhoFI 94, WhoWest 94*
Boeckman, Steven Emil 1952- *WhoAmP 93*
Boeddeker, Timothy Mark 1948- *WhoMW 93*
Boede, Marvin J. *WhoAm 94, WhoFI 94*
Boeder, Thomas L. 1944- *WhoAm 94, WhoWest 94*
Boedigheimer, Robert David 1962- *WhoAmL 94*
Boedigheimer, Scott Michael 1966- *WhoMW 93*
Boegner, Jean-Marc 1913- *Who 94*
Boehle, William Randall 1919- *WhoAm 94*
Boehler, Conrad Joseph 1930- *WhoAmP 93*
Boehler, Hans 1884-1961 *WhoAmA 93N*
Boehlert, Sherwood L. 1936- *CngDr 93*
Boehlert, Sherwood Louis 1936- *WhoAm 94, WhoAmP 93*
Boehlke, William Fredrick 1946- *WhoWest 94*
Boehm, Barry William 1935- *WhoScEn 94*
Boehm, David Alfred 1914- *WhoAm 94*
Boehm, Eric Hartzell 1918- *WhoAm 94*
Boehm, Eric Walter Albert 1960- *WhoScEn 94*
Boehm, Felix Hans 1924- *WhoAm 94, WhoWest 94*
Boehm, George A. W. d1993 *NewYTBS 93*
Boehm, Gottfried Karl 1942- *IntWW 93*
Boehm, Gunther 1946- *WhoScEn 94*
Boehm, Herb *EncSF 93*
Boehm, James *WhoAmP 93*
Boehm, John Philip 1683-1749 *DcAmReB 2*
Boehm, Karl 1928- *WhoHol 92*
Boehm, Lawrence Edward 1961- *WhoScEn 94*
Boehm, Martin 1724-1812 *DcAmReB 2*
Boehm, Richard W. 1926- *WhoAmP 93*
Boehm, Robert Foty 1940- *WhoAm 94*
Boehm, Robert Kenneth 1925- *WhoMW 93*
Boehm, Steven Bruce 1954- *WhoAm 94*
Boehm, Theodore Reed 1938- *WhoMW 93*
Boehm, Toni Georgene 1946- *WhoMW 93*
Boehm, Werner William 1913- *WhoAm 94*
Boehme, Wolf B. 1960- *WhoFI 94*
Boehmer, Clifford Bernard 1927- *WhoWest 94*
Boehmer, Gerhard Walter 1935- *IntWW 93*
Boehmer, Konrad 1941- *NewGrDO*
Boehmer, Richard A. 1951- *WhoAmL 94*
Boehmer, Ronald Glenn 1947- *WhoWest 94*
Boehne, Edward George 1940- *WhoAm 94*
Boehnen, Daniel A. 1950- *WhoAmL 94*
Boehnen, David Leo 1946- *WhoAm 94, WhoAmL 94, WhoFI 94*
Boehner, John A. 1949- *CngDr 93, WhoAm 94, WhoMW 93*
Boehner, John Andrew 1949- *WhoAmP 93*
Boehner, Leonard Bruce 1930- *WhoAmL 94*
Boek, Walter Erwin 1923- *WhoAm 94*
Boeke, Chet Lee 1945- *WhoAmP 93*
Boeke, Eugene H., Jr. 1925- *WhoAm 94*
Boekelheide, Virgil Carl 1919- *IntWW 93, WhoAm 94, WhoScEn 94, WhoWest 94*
Boekenheide, Russell William 1930- *WhoAm 94*
Boeker, Paul Harold 1938- *WhoAm 94, WhoAmP 93*
Boell, Edgar John 1906- *WhoAm 94*
Boelter, Philip F. 1943- *WhoAm 94*
Boelter, Philip Floyd 1943- *WhoAmL 94*
Boelz, Thomas Leonard 1935- *WhoMW 93*
Boelzner, Gordon 1937- *WhoAm 94*
Boen, Roger D. 1952- *WhoAmP 93*
Boeniger, Henry R. 1947- *WhoAmP 93*
Boenisch, Peter H. 1927- *IntWW 93*
Boenke, Clyde Allen 1939- *WhoMW 93*
Boenning, Henry Dorr, Jr. 1914- *WhoAm 94*
Boensch, Arthur Cranwell 1933- *WhoAmL 94*
Boepple, Jo-Ann 1935- *WhoMW 93*
Boer, Charles 1939- *WrDr 94*
Boer, F. Peter 1941- *WhoAm 94, WhoFI 94, WhoScEn 94*
Boer, Karl Wolfgang 1936- *WhoScEn 94*
Boer, Ralf Reinhard 1948- *WhoAmL 94*
Boer, Roger Philip 1959- *WhoMW 93*
Boerboom, Jim *WhoAmP 93*
Boerger, James G. 1930- *WhoAmP 93*
Boergers, Mary H. 1946- *WhoAmP 93*
Boerhaave, Hermann 1668-1738 *EncSPD*
Boeri, Renato Raimondo 1922- *WhoScEn 94*
Boerlage, Frans Theodoor 1930- *WhoAm 94*
Boerma, Addeke Hendrik d1992 *IntWW 93N*
Boerma, Henry Roger *WhoScEn 94*
Boerne, Alfred *ConAu 141*
Boerner, Jo M. 1944- *WhoFI 94*
Boerner, Peter 1926- *WhoAm 94*
Boero, Felipe 1884-1958 *NewGrDO*
Boerrigter, Glenn Charles 1932- *WhoAm 94*
Boers, Terry John 1950- *WhoAm 94*
Boersma, Lawrence Allan 1932- *WhoWest 94*
Boersma, Theodore John 1952- *WhoAmL 94*
Boerste, Dean William 1952- *WhoAmP 93*
Boers-Wijnberg, Mieke H.A. 1946- *WhoWomW 91*
Boerum, Simon 1724-1775 *WhAmRev*
Boes, Lawrence William 1935- *WhoAm 94, WhoAmL 94*
Boesak, Allan 1946- *IntWW 93*
Boesch, Francis Theodore 1936- *WhoAm 94*
Boesch, Lawrence Michael 1951- *WhoAmL 94*
Boesche, Philip W. 1946- *WhoAmL 94*
Boeschenstein, Bernice 1906-1951 *WhoAmA 93N*
Boeschenstein, William Wade 1925- *IntWW 93, WhoAm 94, WhoFI 94*
Boese, Alvin William 1910-1986 *WhoAmA 93N*
Boese, Eleanor Jane 1940- *WhoAmP 93*
Boese, Gilbert Karyle 1937- *WhoAm 94*
Boese, John T. 1947- *WhoAm 94, WhoAmL 94*
Boese, Kathleen Carol 1942- *WhoMW 93*
Boese, Mark Alan 1960- *WhoMW 93, WhoScEn 94*
Boese, Robert Alan 1934- *WhoAm 94, WhoScEn 94*
Boesel, Milton Charles, Jr. 1928- *WhoAm 94, WhoFI 94, WhoMW 93*
Boesen, William d1972 *WhoHol 92*
Boesmans, Philippe 1936- *NewGrDO*
Boespflug, John F., Jr. 1944- *WhoAmL 94*
Boethius, Ancius Manlius Torquatus Severinus 475-524 *BlmGEL*
Boetsch, Wolfgang 1938- *IntWW 93*
Boettcher, Armin Schlick 1941- *WhoFI 94*
Boettcher, Frederick Hans Rudolf 1935- *WhoAmP 93*
Boettcher, Harold Paul 1923- *WhoAm 94*
Boettcher, Norbe Birosel 1932- *WhoAm 94*
Boettcher, Richard A. 1926- *WhoFI 94*
Boettcher, Robert Walter 1931- *WhoMW 93*
Boettcher, Wilfried 1929- *IntWW 93*
Boettger, William F. 1945- *WhoWest 94*
Boetticher, Budd 1916- *IntMPA 94*
Boettner, Dorothy Ellen 1917- *WhoAmP 93*
Boetzel, Eric *EncSF 93*
Boeve, Edgar Gene 1929- *WhoAmA 93*
Boevey, Thomas (Michael Blake) C. *Who 94*
Boeynants, Paul Van Den 1919- *IntWW 93*
Boff, Leonardo 1938- *HispLC [port]*
Boff, Leonardo Genezio Darci 1938- *IntWW 93*
Boffa, Giuseppe 1923- *ConAu 140*
Boffetti, Raymond John 1924- *WhoAmP 93*
Bofill, Angela 1954- *WhoBlA 94*
Bofill, Rano Solidum 1942- *WhoScEn 94*
Bofill, Ricardo 1939- *IntWW 93, WhoAm 94*
Bofinger, Helge 1940- *IntWW 93*
Bogaard, William Joseph 1938- *WhoAm 94, WhoAmL 94*
Bogaers, Petrus Clemens Wilhelmus Maria 1924- *IntWW 93*
Bogaert, Lucienne d1983 *WhoHol 92*
Bogan, Elizabeth Chapin 1944- *WhoAm 94*
Bogan, James J. *DrAPF 93*
Bogan, Louise 1897-1970 *BlmGWL*
Bogan, Mary Flair 1948- *WhoFI 94*
Bogar, John A. 1918- *WhoIns 94*
Bogard, Carole Christine *WhoAm 94*
Bogard, David Kenneth 1953- *WhoWest 94*
Bogard, Hazel Zinamon 1925- *WhoBlA 94*
Bogard, Lawrence Joseph *WhoAm 94*
Bogard, Travis (Miller) 1918- *WrDr 94*
Bogarde, Dirk *Who 94*
Bogarde, Dirk 1921- *IntMPA 94, IntWW 93, WhoHol 92, WrDr 94*
Bogard-Reynolds, Christine Elizabeth 1954- *WhoWest 94*
Bogardus, Carl Robert, Jr. 1933- *WhoAm 94*
Bogardus, James 1800-1874 *WorInv*
Bogarin, Rafael 1946- *WhoAmA 93*
Bogart, Ernest F. 1942- *WhoAmL 94*
Bogart, George A. 1933- *WhoAmA 93*
Bogart, Homer Gordon 1922- *WhoAm 94, WhoFI 94*
Bogart, Humphrey d1957 *WhoHol 92*
Bogart, James Edward 1945- *WhoMW 93*
Bogart, John-Paul 1952- *NewGrDO*
Bogart, Keith Charles 1936- *WhoMW 93*
Bogart, Mark Hanks 1950- *WhoWest 94*
Bogart, Michele Helene 1952- *WhoAmA 93*
Bogart, Neil d1982 *WhoHol 92*
Bogart, Paul 1919- *IntMPA 94, WhoAm 94*
Bogart, Richard Jerome 1929- *WhoAmA 93*
Bogart, Robert B. 1944- *WhoAm 94*
Bogart, Wanda Lee 1939- *WhoFI 94, WhoWest 94*
Bogart, William Harry 1931- *WhoAmL 94*
Bogas, Kathleen Laura 1951- *WhoAmL 94*
Bogash, Richard 1922- *WhoAm 94*
Bogati, Peter *EncSF 93*
Bogatiryov, Anatoly Vasil'yevich 1913- *NewGrDO*
Bogda, Esther Jane 1944- *WhoMW 93*
Bogdan, Carolyn Louetta 1941- *WhoFI 94*
Bogdan, James Thomas 1938- *WhoScEn 94, WhoWest 94*
Bogdan, Victor Michael 1933- *WhoAm 94*
Bogdandy, Ludwig von 1930- *IntWW 93*
Bogdanich, Walt 1950- *WhoAm 94*
Bogdanoff, John Lee 1916- *WhoAm 94*
Bogdanor, Vernon 1943- *WrDr 94*
Bogdanor, Vernon Bernard 1943- *Who 94*
Bogdanov, Alexander 1873-1928 *EncSF 93*
Bogdanov, Michael 1938- *IntWW 93, Who 94*
Bogdanov, Nikita Alexeevich 1931- *WhoScEn 94*
Bogdanova, Nadezhda 1836-1897 *IntDcB*
Bogdanov-Berezovsky, Valerian Mikhaylovich 1903-1971 *NewGrDO*
Bogdanovic, Bogomir 1923- *WhoAmA 93*
Bogdanovich, Joseph James 1912- *WhoAm 94, WhoFI 94*
Bogdanovich, Peter 1939- *IntMPA 94, IntWW 93, Who 94, WhoAm 94, WhoHol 92, WrDr 94*
Bogdanow, Alan J. 1947- *WhoAmL 94*
Bogdanowicz-Bindert, Christine Anne 1951- *WhoFI 94*
Bogdasarian, John Robert 1944- *WhoAm 94*
Bogdon, Glendon Joseph 1935- *WhoMW 93*
Bogdonoff, Maurice Lambert 1926- *WhoAm 94, WhoMW 93, WhoScEn 94*
Bogdonoff, Morton David 1925- *WhoAm 94*
Bogdonoff, Seymour Moses 1921- *WhoAm 94, WhoScEn 94*
Bogen, Andrew E. 1941- *WhoAm 94, WhoAmL 94*
Bogen, Don *DrAPF 93*
Bogen, Edward J., Jr. 1944- *WhoAmL 94*
Bogen, Hyman 1924- *ConAu 140*
Bogen, Joseph Elliot 1926- *WhoWest 94*
Bogen, Karen Iris *DrAPF 93*
Bogen, Laurel Ann *DrAPF 93*
Bogen, Nancy *DrAPF 93*
Bogen, Roy Arne 1927- *WhoMW 93*
Bogen, Samuel Adams 1913- *WhoAm 94*
Bogenschneider, Neil E. 1948- *WhoAmP 93*
Bogenschutz, J. David 1944- *WhoAmL 94*
Boger, Dale L. 1953- *WhoAm 94, WhoScEn 94*
Boger, Dan Calvin 1946- *WhoFI 94, WhoScEn 94, WhoWest 94*
Boger, Gilbert Lee 1927- *WhoAmP 93*
Boger, Kenneth Snead 1946- *WhoAmL 94*
Boger, Lawrence Leroy 1923- *WhoAm 94*
Bogert, Frank M. *WhoAmP 93*
Bogert, George Taylor 1920- *WhoAmL 94*
Bogert, Ivan Lathrop 1918- *WhoAm 94*
Boggan, Daniel, Jr. 1945- *WhoBlA 94*
Boggess, Jerry Reid 1944- *WhoAm 94*
Boggess, Thomas Phillip, III 1921- *WhoAm 94, WhoMW 93*
Boggio, Dennis Ray 1953- *WhoWest 94*
Boggio, Giandomenico 1738-1816 *NewGrDO*
Boggio, Miriam A. 1952- *WhoIns 94*
Boggis, Andrew Gurdon 1954- *Who 94*
Boggis, John Graham 1949- *Who 94*
Boggis-Rolfe, Hume 1911- *Who 94*
Boggs, Beth Clemens 1967- *WhoAmL 94*
Boggs, Bill *WhoHol 92*
Boggs, Carl Elwood, Jr. 1937- *WhoWest 94*

Boggs, Corinne Morrison Claiborne 1916- WhoAmP 93
Boggs, Danny J. 1944- WhoAmP 93
Boggs, Danny Julian 1944- WhoAm 94, WhoAmL 94
Boggs, David William 1958- WhoWest 94
Boggs, Francis WhoHol 92
Boggs, Franklin 1914- WhoAmA 93
Boggs, George Edward, Jr. 1946- WhoFI 94, WhoWest 94
Boggs, George Trenholm 1947- WhoAm 94, WhoAmL 94
Boggs, Gil WhoAm 94
Boggs, Jack Aaron 1935- WhoAm 94
Boggs, James 1919- WhoBlA 94
Boggs, James Ernest 1921- WhoAm 94
Boggs, Jean Sutherland 1922- WhoAmA 93
Boggs, John Steven 1960- WhoMW 93
Boggs, John William 1951- WhoMW 93
Boggs, Joseph Dodridge 1921- WhoAm 94, WhoMW 93, WhoScEn 94
Boggs, Judith Roslyn 1939- WhoAmP 93
Boggs, Judith Susan 1946- WhoAmL 94
Boggs, Marion A. 1894- WhAm 10
Boggs, Mayo Mac 1942- WhoAmA 93
Boggs, Nathaniel 1926- WhoBlA 94
Boggs, Ralph Stuart 1917- WhoAm 94
Boggs, Robert J. WhoAmP 93
Boggs, Robert Newell 1930- WhoAm 94
Boggs, Ross, Jr. WhoAmP 93
Boggs, Sam, Jr. 1928- WhoAm 94
Boggs, Steven Eugene 1947- WhoWest 94
Boggs, Thomas Hale, Jr. 1940- WhoAm 94
Boggs, Wade Anthony 1958- WhoAm 94
Boggs, William Brady 1943- WhoFI 94
Boggs, William O. DrAPF 93
Boggs, William S. 1946- WhoAmL 94
Bogguss, Suzy 1956- ConMus 11 [port], WhoAm 94
Boghani, Ashok Balvantrai 1949- WhoFI 94
Boghassian, Skunder 1937- WhoBlA 94
Boghosian, Paula der 1933- WhoScEn 94
Boghosian, Varujan 1926- WhoAmA 93
Boghosian, Varujan Yegan 1926- WhoAm 94
Boghurst, William c. 1631-1685 DcNaB MP
Bogianckino, Massimo 1922- IntWW 93, NewGrDO
Bogie, David Wilson 1946- Who 94
Bogin, Magda DrAPF 93
Bogin, Nina DrAPF 93
Bogina, August, Jr. 1927- WhoAmP 93, WhoMW 93
Boginis, James William 1937- WhoWest 94
Bogle, David Blyth 1903- Who 94
Bogle, Ellen Gray Who 94
Bogle, Ellen Gray 1941- IntWW 93
Bogle, George 1746-1781 WhWE
Bogle, Hugh Andrew 1909- WhoAm 94
Bogle, JoeAnn Rose 1934- WhoFI 94, WhoMW 93
Bogle, Jon 1940- WhoAmA 93
Bogle, Robert W. WhoAm 94, WhoBlA 94
Bogle, Warren ConTFT 11
Bogli, Lina 1858-1941 BlmGWL
Bognanno, Paul E. 1949- WhoIns 94
Bognar, Botond 1944- WhoMW 93
Bognar, Charles Ralph 1926- WhoWest 94
Bognar, Jozsef 1917- IntWW 93
Bogner, Fred Karl 1939- WhoMW 93
Bogner, Willy 1942- IntWW 93
Bogolyubov, Mikhail Nikolayevich 1918- IntWW 93
Bogolyubov, Nikolay Nikolayevich d1992 IntWW 93N
Bogomolny, Richard Joseph 1935- WhoAm 94, WhoFI 94
Bogomolny, Robert Lee 1938- WhoAm 94, WhoAmL 94
Bogomolov, Aleksey Fedorovich 1913- IntWW 93
Bogomolov, Oleg Timofeyevich 1927- IntWW 93
Bogorad, Barbara Ellen WhoScEn 94
Bogorad, Lawrence 1921- IntWW 93, WhoAm 94, WhoScEn 94
Bogorad, Samuel Nathaniel 1917- WhoAm 94
Bogoras, Waldemar EncSF 93
Bogoraz, Vladimir Germanovitch 1865-1936 EncSF 93
Bogosian, Eric 1953- ConDr 93, IntMPA 94, IntWW 93, WhoAm 94, WhoHol 92
Bogosian, Richard W. 1937- WhoAmP 93
Bograd, Sandra Lynn 1958- WhoAmL 94
Bogren, Hugo Gunnar 1933- WhoAm 94, WhoScEn 94
Bogsch, Arpad 1919- IntWW 93, Who 94, WhoAm 94
Bogucka-Skowronska, Anna Teresa WhoWomW 91
Bogue, A. Stevenson 1947- WhoAmL 94
Bogue, Allan G. 1921- WhoAm 94
Bogue, Andrew Wendell 1919- WhoAmL 94
Bogue, Cynthia Marie 1955- WhoMW 93
Bogue, Lucile DrAPF 93
Bogue, Lucile Maxfield 1911- WrDr 94
Bogue, Philip Roberts 1924- WhoAm 94
Bogue, Sean Kenneth 1969- WhoScEn 94
Bogues, Leon Franklin 1926- WhoBlA 94
Bogues, Tyrone 1965- BasBi, WhoBlA 94
Bogus, Carl Thomas 1948- WhoAmL 94
Bogus, Houston, Jr. 1951- WhoBlA 94
Bogus, SDiane DrAPF 93
Bogus, SDiane (Adams) 1946- BlkWr 2, ConAu 141
Bogus, SDiane Adams 1946- WhoBlA 94, WhoWest 94
Bogusky, Alf 1947- WhoAm 94
Boguslavsky, Mark Moiseyevich 1924- IntWW 93
Boguslaw, Robert 1919- WhoAm 94, WrDr 94
Boguslawski, Edward 1940- NewGrDO
Boguslawski, Wojciech 1757-1829 NewGrDO
Bogut, John Carl, Jr. 1961- WhoAmL 94
Bogutz, Jerome Edwin 1935- WhoAm 94, WhoAmL 94
Bogy, David Beauregard 1936- WhoAm 94
Boh, Ivan 1930- WhoAm 94
Bohac, Josef 1929- NewGrDO
Bohan, Marc, 1926- IntWW 93
Bohan, Ruth L. 1946- WhoAmA 93
Bohan, Ruth Louise 1946- WhoMW 93
Bohan, William Joseph 1929- Who 94
Bohanan, David John 1946- WhoFI 94
Bohannan, Joseph Daniel 1941- WhoAmL 94
Bohannan, Jules Kirby 1917- WhoFI 94
Bohannan, Paul (James) 1920- WrDr 94
Bohannan, Paul James 1920- WhoAm 94
Bohannan-Sheppard, Barbara 1950- WhoBlA 94
Bohannon, David D. 1898- WhoAm 94
Bohannon, Marcia Marie 1960- WhoMW 93
Bohannon, Marshall Topping, Jr. 1930- WhoAmL 94
Bohanon, Luther L. 1902- WhoAm 94, WhoAmL 94
Bohanon, Richard Lee 1935- WhoAm 94
Bohanske, Robert Thomas 1953- WhoWest 94
Boharski, William E. 1961- WhoAmP 93
Bohata, Emil Anton 1918- WhoMW 93
Bohay, Heidi 1959- WhoHol 92
Bohen, Barbara E. 1941- WhoAmA 93
Bohen, Frederick M. 1937- WhoAmP 93
Bohi, Douglas Ray 1939- WhoScEn 94
Bohi, Lynn L. 1947- WhoAmP 93
Bohigas Guardiola, Oriol 1925- IntWW 93
Bohigian, Robert J. WhoAmP 93
Bohl, Heinrich Friedrich 1945- IntWW 93
Bohl, Randall Joseph 1962- WhoWest 94
Bohland, Gustav 1897-1959 WhoAmA 93N
Bohlander, Ronald Arthur 1945- WhoFI 94
Bohlau, Helene 1859-1940 BlmGWL
Bohle, Bruce William 1918- WhoAm 94
Bohlen, Bradley Dean 1959- WhoMW 93
Bohlen, Charles E. 1904-1974 HisDcKW
Bohlen, Joe Merl 1919-1989 WhAm 10
Bohlen, Nina 1931- WhoAm 94
Bohlen, Nina (Celestine Eustis) 1931- WhoAmA 93
Bohlender, Hugh Darrow 1951- WhoAmL 94
Bohler, Joseph Stephen 1938- WhoAmA 93
Bohlin, Britt Eva Irene 1956- WhoWomW 91
Bohlin, Carol Fry 1958- WhoWest 94
Bohlin, Gorel Ruth Charlotte 1930- WhoWomW 91
Bohlin, Peter Quarfordt 1937- WhoAm 94
Bohling, William B. 1941- WhoAmL 94
Bohlinger, John C. 1936- WhoAmP 93
Bohling-Philippi, Vicki Dee 1964- WhoMW 93
Bohlke, Ardyce 1943- WhoAmP 93
Bohlken, Deborah Kay 1952- WhoFI 94
Bohlmann, Daniel Robert 1948- WhoAmL 94, WhoWest 94
Bohlmann, Ralph Arthur 1932- WhoAm 94, WhoMW 93
Bohl von Faber, Cecilla 1796-1877 BlmGWL
Bohm, Arno Rudolf 1936- WhoScEn 94
Bohm, David Joseph d1992 Who 94N
Bohm, Henry Victor 1929- WhoAm 94, WhoMW 93
Bohm, Joel Lawrence 1942- WhoAmL 94
Bohm, Johann(es Heinrich) 174-?-1792 NewGrDO
Bohm, Karl 1894-1981 NewGrDO
Bohm, Karl-Heinz Hermann 1923- WhoWest 94
Bohm, Robert Dean 1945- WhoAmL 94
Bohm, Susan Mary 1956- WhoMW 93
Bohman, George Vroom 1908-1989 WhAm 10
Bohman, Verle Rudolph 1924- WhoWest 94
Bohme, Diethard Kurt 1941- WhoAm 94
Bohme, Helmut 1936- IntWW 93
Bohme, Kurt 1908-1989 NewGrDO
Bohmer, David Alan 1947- WhoFI 94
Bohmont, Dale Wendell 1922- WhoAm 94
Bohn, Charlotte Galitz 1930- WhoFI 94, WhoMW 93
Bohn, Dennis Allen 1942- WhoScEn 94, WhoWest 94
Bohn, Hinrich Lorenz 1934- WhoWest 94
Bohn, Horst-Ulrich 1946- WhoScEn 94
Bohn, J(acob) Lloyd 1896- WhAm 10
Bohn, John Augustus, Jr. 1937- WhoAm 94, WhoFI 94
Bohn, Marty d1976 WhoHol 92
Bohn, Merritt d1978 WhoHol 92
Bohn, Paul Bradley 1957- WhoWest 94
Bohn, Ralph Carl 1930- WhoAm 94, WhoWest 94
Bohne, Carl John, Jr. 1916- WhoAm 94
Bohne, Edward Daniel 1956- WhoAmL 94
Bohne, Jeanette Kathryn 1936- WhoMW 93, WhoScEn 94
Bohnen, Blythe 1940- WhoAmA 93
Bohnen, Michael d1965 WhoHol 92
Bohnen, Michael 1887-1965 NewGrDO
Bohnen, Michael J. 1947- WhoAm 94, WhoAmL 94
Bohnen, Roman d1949 WhoHol 92
Bohnenberger, Dale Vincent 1952- WhoWest 94
Bohnenkamp, Leslie George 1943- WhoAmA 93
Bohner, Charles Henry 1927- WhoAm 94
Bohner, Dean Arlington 1929- WhoFI 94
Bohner, Robert Joseph 1934- WhoAmL 94
Bohnert, Betty Louise 1941- WhoMW 93
Bohnert, Herbert 1890-1967 WhoAmA 93N
Bohnert, Thom 1948- WhoAmA 93
Bohnett, William H. 1948- WhoAmL 94
Bohning, Elizabeth Edrop 1915- WhoAm 94
Bohnstedt, Joan Embick 1962- WhoWest 94
Boho, Dan L. 1952- WhoAm 94, WhoAmL 94
Bohor, Bruce Forbes 1932- WhoWest 94
Bohorquez, Fernando Augusto 1945- WhoHisp 94
Bohr, Aage Niels 1922- IntWW 93, Who 94, WhoAm 94, WhoScEn 94
Bohr, Niels Henrik David 1885-1962 WorScD [port]
Bohren, Janet Linderoth WhoMW 93
Bohren, Michael Oscar 1947- WhoAmP 93
Bohrer, Corinne 1959- WhoHol 92
Bohrer, Karl Heinz 1932- IntWW 93
Bohrer, Mark W. 1956- WhoWest 94
Bohrer, Robert Arnold 1949- WhoAmL 94
Bohringer, Richard 1941- WhoHol 92
Bohrk, Gisela 1945- WhoWomW 91
Bohrnsen, Andrew C. 1949- WhoAmL 94
Bohrnstedt, George William 1938- WhoAm 94
Bohrod, Aaron 1907-1992 WhAm 10, WhoAmA 93N
Bohus, William P. d1993 NewYTBS 93
Bohusz-Szyszko, Cicely (Mary Strode) Who 94
Boiardo, Matteomaria 1441?-1494 BlmGEL
Boiarski, Phil DrAPF 93
Boice, Craig Kendall 1952- WhoAm 94, WhoFI 94
Boice, James Montgomery 1938- WrDr 94
Boice, Robert McIntosh, Jr. 1958- WhoFI 94, WhoWest 94
Boice, William H. 1946- WhoAmL 94
Boidevaix, Serge Marie-Germain 1928- IntWW 93
Boieldieu, (Francois-)Adrien 1775-1834 NewGrDO
Boieldieu, (Adrien) Louis (Victor) 1815-1883 NewGrDO
Boies, David 1941- WhoAmL 94
Boies, Wilber H. 1944- WhoAm 94, WhoAmL 94
Boigon, Brian Joseph 1955- WhoAmA 93
Boigon, Howard Lawrence 1946- WhoAmL 94
Boike, Shawn Paul 1964- WhoScEn 94
Boileau, Guy (Francis) 1935- Who 94
Boileau, Nicolas 1636-1711 BlmGEL
Boileau, Oliver Clark, Jr. 1927- IntWW 93, WhoAm 94
Boileau-Despreaux, Nicolas 1636-1711 GuFrLit 2
Boillat, Guy Maurice Georges 1937- WhoScEn 94
Boiman, Donna Rae 1946- WhoMW 93
Boime, Albert Isaac 1933- WhoAm 94
Boio fl. 4th cent.?- BlmGWL
Boireau d1931 WhoHol 92
Bois, Curt 1901- WhoHol 92
Bois, Pierre 1924- WhoAm 94, WhoScEn 94
Boisbaudran, Paul Emile Lecoq de 1836-1912 WorScD
Boisbertrand, Rene Etienne Henri de Vic Gayault de 1746- WhAmRev
Boisdeffre (Neraud le Mouton de), Pierre Jules Marie Raoul 1926- IntWW 93
Boisgilbert, Edmund EncSF 93
Boisjoli, Charlotte WhoHol 92
Boisjoly, Roger Mark 1938- WhoScEn 94
Boismortier, Joseph Bodin de 1689-1755 NewGrDO
Boismortier, Suzanne Bodin de fl. 18th cent.- BlmGWL
Boissard, Janine 1932- TwCYAW
Boisse, Joseph Adonias 1937- WhoAm 94
Boisseau, Jerry Philip 1939- WhoFI 94
Boisseau, Michelle DrAPF 93
Boisseau, Richard Robert 1944- WhoAm 94, WhoAmL 94
Boisset, Caroline 1955- WrDr 94
Boisset, Yves 1939- IntWW 93
Boissier, Martin Scobell 1926- Who 94
Boissier, Roger Humphrey 1930- Who 94
Boissieu Dean De Luigne, Alain Henri Paul Marie-Joseph de 1914- IntWW 93
Boisson, Christine 1957- WhoHol 92
Boisvert, William Andrew 1962- WhoScEn 94
Boitano, Brian NewYTBS 93 [port]
Boitmann, Robert J. WhoAmL 94
Boito, Arrigo 1842-1918 NewGrDO
Boivin, Marie Gillain 1773-1841 WorInv
Boizot, Peter James 1929- Who 94
Bojanic, Ranko 1924- WhoMW 93
Bojarski, Jeanne Frances 1951- WhoMW 93
Bojart Ortega, Rafael 1920- IntWW 93
Bojaxhiu, Agnes Gonxha Who 94
Bok, Dean 1939- WhoAm 94
Bok, Derek 1930- IntWW 93, Who 94, WhoAm 94, WrDr 94
Bok, Hannes 1914-1964 EncSF 93
Bok, Joan T. NewYTBS 93 [port]
Bok, Joan Toland 1929- WhoAm 94
Bok, John Fairfield 1930- WhoAm 94, WhoAmL 94
Bok, Sissela 1934- WhoAm 94, WrDr 94
Bok, Song Hae 1943- WhoScEn 94
Bokaemper, Stefan 1936- WhoAm 94
Bokar, Hal d1990 WhoHol 92
Bokassa, Jean Bedel 1921- IntWW 93
Bokat, Stephen Arthur 1946- WhoAmL 94
Boke, Norman Hill 1913- WhoAm 94
Boker, George Henry 1823-1890 IntDcT 2
Bokhary, Syed Kemal Shah 1947- Who 94
Bokor, Bruce H. 1947- WhoAmL 94
Bokor, Margit 1905-1949 NewGrDO
Bokov, Nikolai Konstantinovich 1945- IntWW 93
Boksay, Istvan Janos Endre 1940- WhoScEn 94
Boksenberg, Alexander 1936- IntWW 93, Who 94
Bol, Manute WhoBlA 94
Bol, Manute 1962- BasBi
Bolaffi, Janice Lerner 1933- WhoAm 94
Bolam, James 1937- WhoHol 92
Bolam, James 1938- Who 94
Bolam, James 1960- IntMPA 94
Bolan, James Russell 1930- WhoWest 94
Bolan, Marc 1947- See T. Rex ConMus 11
Bolan, Richard Stuart 1927- WhoMW 93
Bolan, Robert S. 1941- WhoAm 94
Bolan, Thomas Anthony 1924- WhoAm 94, WhoAmL 94
Boland, Ardney James, Sr. 1920- WhoAmP 93
Boland, Beth Irene Zimmerman 1961- WhoAmL 94
Boland, Bridget 1913-1988 ConDr 93
Boland, Christopher Thomas, II 1915- WhoAm 94
Boland, Eammon WhoHol 92
Boland, Eavan 1944- BlmGWL
Boland, Edward P. 1911- WhoAmP 93
Boland, Gerald Lee 1946- WhoFI 94
Boland, Janet Lang 1924- WhoAm 94
Boland, (Bertram) John 1913-1976 EncSF 93
Boland, John Anthony 1931- Who 94
Boland, Joseph d1987 WhoHol 92
Boland, Lois Walker 1919- WhoScEn 94
Boland, Mary d1965 WhoHol 92
Boland, Michael Joseph 1942- WhoAmP 93
Boland, Paula L. 1940- WhoAmP 93
Boland, Raymond James 1932- WhoAm 94

Boland, Rosalinda Samano 1949- *WhoHisp 94*
Boland, Thomas Aloysius 1896- *WhAm 10*
Boland, Thomas Edwin 1934- *WhoAm 94*
Bolande, Robert Paul 1926- *WhoAm 94*
Bolander, Bruce D. 1951- *WhoAmL 94*
Bolander, Gunhild Anna Maria 1932- *WhoWomW 91*
Bolander, Robert C. *WhoAmP 93*
Bolanos, Alberto Antonio 1962- *WhoHisp 94*
Bolaños, Alvaro Félix 1955- *WhoHisp 94*
Bolaños, Benjamín 1951- *WhoHisp 94*
Bolaños, Jack 1930- *WhoHisp 94*
Bolaños, José M. 1933- *WhoHisp 94*
Bolas, Gerald Douglas 1949- *WhoAm 94, WhoAmA 93, WhoWest 94*
Bolch, Carl Edward, Jr. 1943- *WhoAm 94, WhoFI 94*
Bolcom, William (Elden) 1938- *NewGrDO*
Bolcom, William Elden 1938- *WhoAm 94, WhoMW 93*
Bold, Alan 1943- *WrDr 94*
Bold, Davey d1978 *WhoHol 92*
Bold, Frances Ann 1930- *WhoAm 94*
Boldan, Kelton John 1956- *WhoAm 94, WhoMW 93*
Boldemann, Laci 1921-1969 *NewGrDO*
Bolden, Betty A. 1944- *WhoBlA 94*
Bolden, Buddy 1868-1931 *AfrAmAl 6*
Bolden, Charles E. 1941- *WhoBlA 94*
Bolden, Charles Frank, Jr. 1946- *AfrAmAl 6 [port], WhoBlA 94*
Bolden, Dorothy Lee 1920- *WhoBlA 94*
Bolden, Frank A. 1942- *WhoAm 94*
Bolden, Frank Augustus 1942- *WhoBlA 94*
Bolden, J. Taber, III 1926- *WhoBlA 94*
Bolden, James Lee 1936- *WhoBlA 94*
Bolden, John Henry 1922- *WhoBlA 94*
Bolden, Michael Geronia 1953- *WhoWest 94*
Bolden, Raymond A. 1933- *WhoBlA 94*
Bolden, Theodore E. 1920- *WhoBlA 94*
Bolden, Theodore Edward 1920- *WhoAm 94*
Bolden, Wiley Speights 1918- *WhoBlA 94*
Bolder, Robert d1937 *WhoHol 92*
Boldi, Lana Lorraine 1941- *WhoAmP 93*
Boldi, Massimo *WhoHol 92*
Boldin, Valery Ivanovich 1935- *LoBiDrD*
Bolding, Alene Marsha 1949- *WhoFI 94*
Bolding, Amy (Agnes) 1910- *WrDr 94*
Bolding, F. 1958- *WhoWomW 91*
Bolding, Grady M. 1951- *WhoAmL 94*
Boldizsar, Ivan *EncSF 93*
Boldrey, Edwin Barkley 1906-1988 *WhAm 10*
Boldrey, Edwin Eastland 1941- *WhoWest 94*
Boldridge, George 1947- *WhoBlA 94*
Boldt, David Rhys 1941- *WhoAm 94*
Boldt, Heinz 1923- *WhoScEn 94*
Boldt, Michael Herbert 1950- *WhoAm 94, WhoAmL 94*
Boldt, Oscar Charles 1924- *WhoAm 94, WhoMW 93*
Boldt, Peter 1927- *WhoScEn 94*
Boldt, Richard Charles 1958- *WhoAmL 94*
Bolduc, Dennis R. 1959- *WhoAmP 93*
Bolduc, Ernest Joseph 1924- *WhoAm 94*
Bolduc, J.P. 1939- *IntWW 93, WhoAm 94, WhoFI 94*
Bolduc, James Philip 1949- *WhoAm 94*
Boldyrev, Yury Yurevich 1960- *LoBiDrD*
Bole, Filipe Nagera 1936- *IntWW 93*
Bole, Giles G. 1928- *WhoAm 94*
Boleat, Mark John 1949- *Who 94*
Bolebruch, Jeffrey John 1963- *WhoFI 94, WhoScEn 94*
Bolebruch, John J. 1954- *WhoAm 94, WhoFI 94*
Bolen, Bob 1926- *WhoAm 94, WhoAmP 93*
Bolen, Charles Warren 1923- *WhoAm 94, WhoMW 93*
Bolen, David B. 1923- *WhoAm 94*
Bolen, David B. 1927- *WhoBlA 94*
Bolen, David Benjamin 1923- *WhoAmP 93*
Bolen, Jean Shinoda 1936- *WhoAsA 94*
Bolen, John E. 1953- *WhoAmA 93*
Bolen, Kenneth James 1947- *WhoIns 94*
Bolen, Lynne N. 1954- *WhoAmA 93, WhoWest 94*
Bolen, Terry Lee 1945- *WhoScEn 94, WhoWest 94*
Bolender, Carroll Herdus 1919- *WhoAm 94*
Bolender, James Henry 1937- *WhoAm 94*
Bolender, Todd 1914- *IntDcB [port]*
Bolender, Todd 1919- *WhoAm 94, WhoMW 93*
Bolene, Margaret Rosalie Steele 1923- *WhoAm 94*
Boler, John Alfred 1942- *WhoAmA 93*
Boles, David LaVelle 1937- *WhoAmL 94*
Boles, Deborah Ann 1953- *WhoWest 94*
Boles, Dyek R. 1936- *WhoIns 94*
Boles, Ewing Thomas 1895- *WhAm 10*
Boles, Forrest H. *WhoAm 94*
Boles, Glen *WhoHol 92*
Boles, H. Hampton 1942- *WhoAmL 94*
Boles, Harold Wilson 1915- *WrDr 94*
Boles, Jeffrey Oakley 1961- *WhoScEn 94*
Boles, Jeremy John Fortescue 1932- *Who 94*
Boles, Jim d1977 *WhoHol 92*
Boles, John d1969 *WhoHol 92*
Boles, John Dennis 1925- *Who 94*
Boles, Robert (E.) 1943- *BlkWr 2*
Boles, Roger 1928- *WhoAm 94*
Boleslawski, Richard d1937 *WhoHol 92*
Bolet, Jorge 1914-1990 *WhAm 10*
Boleware, Michael W. 1963- *WhoAmL 94*
Boley, Bruno Adrian 1924- *WhoAm 94, WhoScEn 94*
Boley, Dennis Lynn 1951- *WhoFI 94*
Boley, Donna Jean 1935- *WhoAmP 93*
Boley, John N. 1935- *WhoAm 94*
Boley, Mark S. 1967- *WhoScEn 94*
Boley, May d1963 *WhoHol 92*
Boley Bolaffio, Rita *WhoAm 94*
Boleyn, Anne c. 1507-1536 *BlmGWL*
Bolge, George S. *WhoAmA 93*
Bolger, Heidi A. 1956- *WhoAm 94*
Bolger, James B. 1935- *Who 94*
Bolger, James Brendan 1935- *IntWW 93*
Bolger, Jeanne Marie 1928- *WhoAmP 93*
Bolger, John *WhoHol 92*
Bolger, Ray d1987 *WhoHol 92*
Bolger, Robert Joseph 1922- *WhoFI 94*
Bolger, Timothy Joseph 1955- *WhoFI 94*
Bolger, William Frederick 1923- *WhAm 10*
Bolgiano, Ralph, Jr. 1922- *WhoAm 94*
Bolian, George Clement 1930- *WhoAm 94*
Bolick, Stephanie Corinne 1952- *WhoAmP 93*
Bolie, Victor Wayne 1924- *WhoAm 94, WhoScEn 94*
Boliek, Luther C. 1941- *WhoAm 94, WhoFI 94*
Bolin, (Axel) Bertil 1923- *IntWW 93*
Bolin, Bruce Martin 1950- *WhoAmP 93*
Bolin, Darren Dwayne 1966- *WhoWest 94*
Bolin, Edmund Mike 1944- *WhoScEn 94*
Bolin, Elizabeth Anne 1947- *WhoAmP 93*
Bolin, Jane Matilda 1908- *AfrAmAl 6*
Bolin, Lionel E. 1927- *WhoBlA 94*
Bolin, Richard Luddington 1923- *WhoWest 94*
Bolin, Shannon 1917- *WhoHol 92*
Bolin, Vernon Spencer 1913- *WhoWest 94*
Bolin, Vladimir Dustin 1965- *WhoWest 94*
Bolin, William Harvey 1922- *WhoAm 94*
Bolinder, Robert Donald 1931- *WhoFI 94*
Bolinder, Scott W. 1952- *WhoAm 94*
Bolinder, William H. *WhoIns 94*
Boling, Edward J. 1922- *IntWW 93*
Boling, Edward Joseph 1922- *WhoAm 94*
Boling, Joseph Edward 1942- *WhoAm 94*
Boling, Karen O'Reilly 1961- *WhoWest 94*
Boling, Thomas Edwin 1930- *WhoMW 93*
Bolingbroke, Viscount 1927- *Who 94*
Bolingbroke, Henry 1367-1413 *BlmGEL*
Bolingbroke, Henry St. John 1678-1751 *BlmGEL*
Bolingbroke, Robert A. 1938- *WhoAm 94*
Bolinger, Corbin Eugene 1929- *WhoAm 94*
Bolinger, Dwight Lemerton 1907-1992 *AnObit 1992, WhAm 10, WrDr 94N*
Bolinger, John C., Jr. 1922- *WhoAm 94*
Bolinger, Robert Stevens 1936- *WhoAm 94*
Bolino, August C. 1922- *WrDr 94*
Bolino, John Vincent 1941- *WhoAm 94*
Bolinsky, Joseph Abraham 1917- *WhoAmA 93*
Bolivar, Simon 1783-1830 *HisWorL [port]*
Bolkan, Florinda 1941- *WhoHol 92*
Bolker, Henry Irving 1926- *WhoAm 94*
Bolkiah, Jefri *IntWW 93*
Bolkiah, Mohamed *IntWW 93*
Bolkiah Mu'izzuddin Waddaulah, Muda Hassanal 1946- *IntWW 93*
Bolkow, Ludwig 1912- *IntWW 93*
Boll, Charles Raymond 1920- *WhoAm 94*
Boll, Heinrich (Theodor) 1917-1985 *RfGShF*
Boll, Johannes Anton, Jr. 1959- *WhoMW 93*
Bolla, Robert Irving 1943- *WhoMW 93*
Bollag, Jean-Marc 1935- *WhoAm 94*
Bollan, William 1710-1782 *WhAmRev*
Bolland, Alexander 1950- *Who 94*
Bolland, Brian (John) 1951- *EncSF 93*
Bolland, Edwin 1922- *Who 94*
Bolland, Guy Alfred 1909- *Who 94*
Bolland, John d1993 *Who 94N*
Bolland, Mark William 1964- *Who 94*
Bolland, Michael *Who 94*
Bolland, (David) Michael 1947- *Who 94*
Bollard, Edward George 1920- *IntWW 93*
Bolle, Dale J. 1923- *WhoAmP 93*
Bolle, Donald Martin 1933- *WhoAm 94*
Bolle, Frank Kenneth 1935- *WhoWest 94*
Bollen, Roger 1941- *WhoAm 94*
Bollenbach, Stephen Frasier 1942- *WhoAm 94, WhoFI 94*
Bollenbacher, Herbert Kenneth 1933- *WhoFI 94, WhoMW 93*
Boller, Carole Ann 1941- *WhoMW 93*
Boller, Henry A. 1836-1902 *WhWE*
Boller, Howard Lee 1934- *WhoMW 93*
Boller, Paul F., Jr. 1916- *WrDr 94*
Boller, Paul Franklin, Jr. 1916- *ConAu 41NR*
Boller, Ronald Cecil 1939- *WhoAm 94*
Bollers, Harold (Brodie Smith) 1915- *Who 94*
Bolles, A. Lynn 1949- *WhoBlA 94*
Bolles, Blair 1911-1990 *WhAm 10*
Bolles, Donald Scott 1936- *WhoAmL 94*
Bolles, Edmund Blair 1942- *WrDr 94*
Bolles, Richard Nelson 1927- *WhoAm 94, WrDr 94*
Bolles, Ronald Kent 1948- *WhoWest 94*
Bollet, Alfred Jay 1926- *WhoAm 94*
Bollettieri, Nick 1931- *BuCMET*
Bollich, Charles N. *WhoScEn 94*
Bolliger, Eugene Frederick 1923- *WhoMW 93*
Bollin, Thomas Douglas 1941- *WhoMW 93*
Bolling, Alexander Russell, Jr. 1922- *WhoAm 94*
Bolling, Bruce C. *WhoBlA 94*
Bolling, Carol Nicholson 1952- *WhoBlA 94*
Bolling, Claude 1930- *IntWW 93*
Bolling, Deborah A. 1957- *WhoBlA 94*
Bolling, George Richard, Sr. 1937- *WhoAmP 93*
Bolling, Landrum Rymer 1913- *WhoAm 94*
Bolling, Raynal Cawthorne 1877-1918 *EncABHB 9 [port]*
Bolling, Richard 1916-1991 *WhAm 10*
Bolling, Royal L., Sr. *WhoAmP 93*
Bolling, Tiffany 1947- *WhoHol 92*
Bollinger, Don Mills 1914- *WhoAm 94*
Bollinger, Donald G. 1915- *WhoAmP 93*
Bollinger, Donald T. 1949- *WhoAmP 93*
Bollinger, John Gustave 1935- *WhoScEn 94*
Bollinger, Joni Lynette 1967- *WhoMW 93*
Bollinger, Lee Carroll 1946- *WhoAm 94, WhoAmL 94*
Bollinger, Michael 1954- *WhoMW 93*
Bollinger, Pamela Beemer 1947- *WhoFI 94*
Bollman, James Guy 1951- *WhoMW 93*
Bollman, Mark Brooks, Jr. 1925- *WhoAm 94*
Bollmeier, Emil Wayne 1925-1989 *WhAm 10*
Bollock, Margot *DrAPF 93*
Bollon, Arthur Peter 1942- *WhoAm 94*
Bolls, Imogene L. *DrAPF 93*
Bollum, Frederick James 1927- *WhoAm 94*
Bolm, Adolph 1884-1951 *IntDcB [port]*
Bolman, Pieter Simon Heinrich 1941- *WhoAm 94, WhoFI 94*
Bolnick, Howard J. 1945- *WhoIns 94*
Bolnick, Howard Jeffrey 1945- *WhoAm 94*
Bolnick, Ira 1949- *WhoAmL 94*
Bolo, Jean d1982 *WhoHol 92*
Bolocofsky, David N. 1947- *WhoAmL 94, WhoWest 94*
Bologna, Joseph 1936- *WhoHol 92*
Bologna, Joseph 1938- *IntMPA 94*
Bolognese, Il *NewGrDO*
Bolognese, Domenico 1819-1881 *NewGrDO*
Bolognesi, Dani Paul 1941- *WhoAm 94*
Bolomey, Roger Henry 1918- *WhoAm 94, WhoAmA 93*
Bolon, Albert Eugene 1939- *WhoScEn 94*
Bolon, Brad Newland 1961- *WhoScEn 94*
Bolonchuk, William Walter 1934- *WhoScEn 94*
Bolonkin, Alexander Alexandrovich 1933- *WhoScEn 94*
Bolonkin, Kirill Andrew 1929- *WhoScEn 94*
Bolooki, Hooshang 1937- *WhoAm 94*
Bolotowsky, Ilya 1907-1981 *WhoAmA 93N*
Boloyan, Myron B. 1957- *WhoAmL 94*
Bol'shakov, Nikolay (Arkad'yevich) 1874-1958 *NewGrDO*
Bolster, Archie Milburn 1933- *WhoAm 94*
Bolster, Arthur Stanley, Jr. 1922- *WhoAm 94*
Bolster, Calvin Mathews 1897- *WhAm 10*
Bolster, Jill Elaine 1966- *WhoWest 94*
Bolster, Paul D. 1944- *WhoAmP 93*
Bolster, Sally M. *WhoAmP 93*
Bolsterli, Margaret Jones 1931- *WhoAm 94*
Bolt, Arthur Seymour 1907- *Who 94*
Bolt, Bruce (Alan) 1930- *WrDr 94*
Bolt, Bruce Alan 1930- *WhoAm 94, WhoScEn 94, WhoWest 94*
Bolt, Carol 1941- *BlmGWL, ConDr 93*
Bolt, David Ernest 1921- *Who 94*
Bolt, Eugene Albert, Jr. 1963- *WhoScEn 94*
Bolt, Eunice Mildred DeVries 1926- *WhoMW 93*
Bolt, Michael Gerald 1953- *WhoScEn 94*
Bolt, Richard (Bruce) 1923- *Who 94*
Bolt, Richard Henry 1911- *WhoAm 94*
Bolt, Robert 1924- *BlmGEL, IntMPA 94*
Bolt, Robert (Oxton) 1924- *ConDr 93, IntDcT 2, WrDr 94*
Bolt, Robert Oxton 1924- *IntWW 93*
Bolt, Robert Oxton 1967- *Who 94*
Bolt, Ron 1938- *WhoAmA 93*
Bolt, Thomas *DrAPF 93*
Bolt, Thomas 1959- *WrDr 94*
Bolt, Thomas Alvin Waldrep 1956- *WhoAmL 94, WhoAmP 93*
Boltanski, Christian 1944- *IntWW 93*
Bolte, Amely 1811-1891 *BlmGWL*
Bolte, Brown 1908- *WhoAm 94*
Bolte, Charles L. 1895-1989 *HisDcKW*
Bolter, Eugene 1932- *WhoAm 94, WhoFI 94*
Boltho, Andrea 1939- *ConAu 42NR, WrDr 94*
Bolton, Archdeacon of *Who 94*
Bolton, Baron 1929- *Who 94*
Bolton, Bishop Suffragan of 1934- *Who 94*
Bolton, Ann D. 1930- *WhoAmP 93*
Bolton, Arthur Key 1922- *WhoAmP 93*
Bolton, Arthur Thomas 1864-1945 *DcNaB MP*
Bolton, Charles E. 1841-1901 *EncSF 93*
Bolton, Charles Thomas 1943- *WhoAm 94*
Bolton, David 1932- *Who 94*
Bolton, Earl Clinton 1919- *WhoAm 94, WhoWest 94*
Bolton, Elizabeth *WrDr 94*
Bolton, Eric James 1935- *Who 94*
Bolton, Evelyn *TwCYAW*
Bolton, Evelyn 1928- *WrDr 94*
Bolton, Frederic (Bernard) 1921- *Who 94*
Bolton, Frederick Rolshoven 1896- *WhAm 10*
Bolton, Geoffrey Curgenven 1931- *Who 94*
Bolton, Joe d1986 *WhoHol 92*
Bolton, Johanna M. *EncSF 93*
Bolton, John d1993 *NewYTBS 93*
Bolton, John Eveleigh 1920- *Who 94*
Bolton, John Robert 1948- *WhoAm 94, WhoAmP 93*
Bolton, John Roger 1950- *WhoAm 94*
Bolton, Joseph D. 1948- *WhoAmL 94*
Bolton, Julia Gooden 1940- *WhoScEn 94*
Bolton, Julian Taylor 1949- *WhoBlA 94*
Bolton, Kenneth Albert 1941- *WhoFI 94*
Bolton, Kevin Michael 1951- *WhoFI 94*
Bolton, Linda Burnes *WhoBlA 94*
Bolton, Martha O. 1951- *WhoWest 94*
Bolton, Mason d1780 *AmRev*
Bolton, Merle Ray, Jr. 1943- *WhoScEn 94*
Bolton, Michael *WhoAm 94*
Bolton, Michael 1953- *CurBio 93 [port]*
Bolton, Nancye 1917- *BuCMET*
Bolton, Richard 1956- *WhoAmA 93*
Bolton, Richard M. 1952- *WhoAmL 94*
Bolton, Robert Floyd 1942- *WhoWest 94*
Bolton, Robert Harvey 1908- *WhoAm 94*
Bolton, Robin Jean 1943- *WhoAmA 93*
Bolton, Roger Edwin 1938- *WhoAm 94*
Bolton, Stephen Timothy 1946- *WhoAmL 94*
Bolton, Wanda E. 1914- *WhoBlA 94*
Bolton-Smith, Robin Lee 1941- *WhoAmA 93*
Boltwood, Bertram Borden 1870-1927 *WorScD*
Boltz, Gerald Edmund 1931- *WhoAm 94, WhoAmL 94*
Boltz, Mary Ann 1923- *WhoFI 94*
Boltzmann, Ludwig 1844-1906 *WorScD*
Boly, Jeffrey Elwyn 1942- *WhoAmL 94*
Bolyai, Janos *WorScD*
Bolyard, Lewis d1977 *WhoHol 92*
Bolyard, Robert Delano 1936- *WhoMW 93*
Bolz, Jody *DrAPF 93*
Bolz, Roger William 1914- *WhoScEn 94*
Bolz, Sanford Hegleman 1915-1991 *WhAm 10*
Bolzoni, Giovanni 1841-1919 *NewGrDO*
Boma, John Clement 1961- *WhoMW 93*
Boman, John Harris, Jr. 1910- *WhoAm 94*
Boman, Marc A. 1948- *WhoAm 94*
Boman, Marc Allen 1948- *WhoAmL 94*
Bomani, Paul Lazaro 1925- *IntWW 93*
Bomba, Margaret Ann 1947- *WhoAmL 94*
Bombaciari, Anna *NewGrDO*
Bombal, Maria Luisa 1909-1980 *RfGShF*

Bombal, Maria Luisa 1910-1980 *BlmGWL*
Bombard, Charles Frederick 1944- *WhoAm 94*
Bombard, Lottie Gertrude d1913 *WhoHol 92*
Bombardier, Andre J. R. 1942- *WhoFI 94*
Bombassei Frascani De Vettor, Giorgio 1910- *IntWW 93*
Bombay, Archbishop of 1920- *Who 94*
Bombay, Sidi d1885 *WhWE*
Bombeck, Erma 1927- *WrDr 94*
Bombeck, Erma Louise 1927- *WhoAm 94*
Bombela, Rose Mary 1950- *WhoHisp 94*
Bomberg, David 1890-1957 *DcNaB MP*
Bomberg, Thomas James 1928- *WhoAm 94, WhoWest 94*
Bomberger, Glen R. 1937- *WhoFI 94*
Bomberger, Russell Branson 1934- *WhoAm 94, WhoAmL 94*
Bomchill, Fern C. 1948- *WhoAm 94, WhoAmL 94*
Bomer, Elton 1935- *WhoAmP 93*
Bomers, Henricus J.A. 1936- *IntWW 93*
Bomes, Stephen D. 1948- *WhoAm 94, WhoAmL 94*
Bomford, Nicholas Raymond 1939- *Who 94*
Bomgardner, William Earl 1925- *WhoAm 94*
Bommarito, Peter 1915-1989 *WhAm 10*
Bommelaer, Alain 1947- *WhoAm 94*
Bommer, Minnie L. 1940- *WhoBlA 94*
Bommer, Timothy J. 1940- *WhoAm 94, WhoAmL 94, WhoWest 94*
Bompas, Donald George 1920- *Who 94*
Bompas, William C. 1834-1906 *EncNAR*
Bompey, Stuart Howard 1940- *WhoAm 94*
Bomse, Stephen V. 1944- *WhoAmL 94*
Bon, Christoph Rudolf 1921- *Who 94*
Bon, Michel Marie 1943- *Who 94*
Bon, Rosa Ruvinetti *NewGrDO*
Bona, Christian Maximilian 1937- *WhoScEn 94*
Bona, Frederick Emil 1939- *WhoAm 94*
Bonacci Brunamonti, Maria Alinda 1841-1903 *BlmGWL*
Bonachea, Rolando *WhoHisp 94*
Bonacic, John J. 1942- *WhoAmP 93*
Bonacker, Joyce McGee 1932- *WhoMW 93*
Bonacorsi, Mary Catherine 1949- *WhoAmL 94*
Bonadonna, Gianni 1934- *WhoScEn 94*
Bonaduce, Danny 1959- *WhoHol 92*
Bonahoom, Otto M. 1930- *WhoAmL 94*
Bonaiuto, John A. *WhoAm 94*
Bonakdar, Mojtaba 1959- *WhoScEn 94*
Bonallack, Michael Francis 1934- *Who 94*
Bonallack, Richard (Frank) 1904- *Who 94*
Bonan, Seon Pierre 1917- *WhoAm 94*
Bonanate, Ugo *EncSF 93*
Bonanni, Laudomia 1908- *BlmGWL*
Bonanno, Louie 1961- *IntMPA 94*
Bonanno, Margaret Wander 1950- *EncSF 93*
Bonanno, Robert Henry 1944- *WhoHisp 94*
Bonanova, Fortunio d1969 *WhoHol 92*
Bonapart, Alan David 1930- *WhoAm 94*
Bonaparte, Lois Ann 1941- *WhoBlA 94*
Bonaparte, Norton Nathaniel, Jr. 1953- *WhoBlA 94*
Bonaparte, Tony Hillary 1939- *WhoBlA 94*
Bonar, Albert J. *WhoAmA 93*
Bonar, Herbert Vernon d1993 *Who 94N*
Bonar, Ivan d1988 *WhoHol 92*
Bonar, Lucian George 1934- *WhoAm 94*
Bonasera, Thomas J. 1948- *WhoAmL 94*
Bonate, Peter Lawrence 1964- *WhoScEn 94*
Bonati, Gina Angeline *DrAPF 93*
Bonaventura, Arnaldo 1862-1952 *NewGrDO*
Bonaventura, John M. 1963- *WhoAmP 93*
Bonaventura, Joseph 1942- *WhoAm 94, WhoScEn 94*
Bonaventura, Leo Mark 1945- *WhoMW 93*
Bonavia-Hunt, Henry George 1847-1917 *DcNaB MP*
Bonavita, Jack d1917 *WhoHol 92*
Bonazinga, Marie Therese 1948- *WhoFI 94*
Bonazzi, Elaine Claire *WhoAm 94*
Boncek, Barbara *DrAPF 93*
Boncher, Mary 1946- *WhoMW 93*
Bonchev, Danail Georgiev 1937- *WhoScEn 94*
Bonci, Alessandro 1870-1940 *NewGrDO*
Boncompagni, Elio 1933- *NewGrDO*
Boncourt, Louis-Charles-Adelaide Chamisso de *WhWE*
Bond, Adrienne *DrAPF 93*
Bond, Alan 1938- *IntWW 93, Who 94*
Bond, Alan D. 1945- *WhoBlA 94*
Bond, Alan Maxwell 1946- *IntWW 93*
Bond, Alma H(albert) 1923- *WrDr 94*
Bond, Andrea M. 1950- *WhoAmL 94*
Bond, C(hristopher Godfrey) 1945- *WrDr 94*
Bond, Calhoun 1921- *WhoAm 94*
Bond, Carrie Jacobs d1946 *WhoHol 92*
Bond, Cecil Walton, Jr. 1937- *WhoBlA 94*
Bond, Charles Dailey 1932- *WhoAmP 93*
Bond, Charles Eugene 1930- *WhoAm 94*
Bond, Chris(topher Godfrey) 1945- *ConDr 93*
Bond, Christopher S. 1939- *CngDr 93*
Bond, Christopher Samuel 1939- *IntWW 93, WhoAm 94, WhoAmP 93, WhoMW 93*
Bond, Cornelius Combs, Jr. 1933- *WhoAm 94*
Bond, David d1989 *WhoHol 92*
Bond, Derek 1919- *WhoHol 92*
Bond, Derek 1920- *IntMPA 94*
Bond, (Charles) Derek 1927- *Who 94*
Bond, Dorothy M. 1927- *WhoWest 94*
Bond, Edward 1934- *BlmGEL, ConDr 93, IntWW 93, NewGrDO, Who 94, WrDr 94*
Bond, (Thomas) Edward 1934- *IntDcT 2 [port]*
Bond, Edward Underwood 1959- *WhoWest 94*
Bond, Floyd Alden 1913- *WhoAm 94*
Bond, Ford d1962 *WhoHol 92*
Bond, Frank d1929 *WhoHol 92*
Bond, Gary 1940- *WhoHol 92*
Bond, Gay *WhoHol 92*
Bond, George Clement 1936- *WhoBlA 94*
Bond, Gladys B. 1914- *WhoBlA 94*
Bond, Godfrey William 1925- *Who 94*
Bond, Harold *DrAPF 93*
Bond, Harold 1939- *WrDr 94*
Bond, Henry Mark Garneys 1922- *Who 94*
Bond, Howard H. 1938- *WhoBlA 94*
Bond, J. Harvey *EncSF 93*
Bond, J. Max, Jr. 1935- *WhoAm 94*
Bond, James, III *WhoHol 92*
Bond, James Arthur 1917- *WhoBlA 94*
Bond, James G. 1924- *WhoBlA 94*
Bond, James G. 1944- *WhoBlA 94*
Bond, James Max, Jr. 1935- *WhoBlA 94*
Bond, John 1941- *IntWW 93*
Bond, John Adikes 1955- *WhoAmL 94*
Bond, John Percy, III 1937- *WhoBlA 94*
Bond, John Reed 1912-1990 *WhAm 10*
Bond, John Reginald Hartnell 1941- *Who 94*
Bond, Johnny d1978 *WhoHol 92*
Bond, Jonathan Holbert *WhoAm 94*
Bond, Joseph Francis 1927- *WhAm 10*
Bond, Jules Jerome d1993 *NewYTBS 93*
Bond, Julian 1940- *AfrAmAl 6 [port], AmSocL, HisWorL, IntWW 93, WhoAm 94, WhoAmP 93, WhoBlA 94*
Bond, Kenneth (Raymond Boyden) 1920- *Who 94*
Bond, Kenneth Walter 1947- *WhoAmL 94*
Bond, Leslie Fee 1928- *WhoBlA 94*
Bond, Lillian d1991 *WhoHol 92*
Bond, Linda Jean Bertrand 1959- *WhoWest 94*
Bond, Lloyd 1941- *WhoBlA 94*
Bond, Lora 1917- *WhoMW 93*
Bond, Louis Grant 1947- *WhoBlA 94*
Bond, M. G. 1932- *WhoAmP 93*
Bond, Marsha Ann 1945- *WhoMW 93*
Bond, Maurice Chester 1897- *WhAm 10*
Bond, Michael 1926- *Who 94*
Bond, (Thomas) Michael 1926- *WrDr 94*
Bond, Michael Richard 1936- *Who 94*
Bond, Nancy 1945- *TwCYAW, WrDr 94*
Bond, Nelson Leighton, Jr. 1935- *WhoFI 94, WhoScEn 94*
Bond, Nelson S(lade) 1908- *EncSF 93, WrDr 94*
Bond, Niles W. 1916- *HisDcKW*
Bond, Niles Woodbridge 1916- *WhoAm 94*
Bond, Ollie P. 1925- *WhoBlA 94*
Bond, Oriel Edmund 1911- *WhoAmA 93*
Bond, Peter Danford 1940- *WhoAm 94*
Bond, Raleigh d1989 *WhoHol 92*
Bond, Randall Clay 1953- *WhoScEn 94*
Bond, Raymond d1972 *WhoHol 92*
Bond, Richard Ewing 1953- *WhoAmL 94*
Bond, Richard Lee 1935- *WhoAmP 93, WhoMW 93*
Bond, Richard Milton 1924- *WhoAmP 93*
Bond, Richard N. 1950- *WhoAmP 93*
Bond, Richard Norman 1950- *WhoAm 94*
Bond, Richard Randolph 1927- *WhoAm 94, WhoAmP 93, WhoWest 94*
Bond, Roland S. 1898- *WhoAmA 93N*
Bond, Rudy d1982 *WhoHol 92*
Bond, Ruskin 1934- *RfGShF, WrDr 94*
Bond, Sarah Ann 1955- *WhoAmL 94*
Bond, Sheila 1928- *WhoHol 92*
Bond, Steve 1953- *WhoHol 92*
Bond, Sudie d1984 *WhoHol 92*
Bond, Thomas Alden 1938- *WhoAm 94, WhoWest 94*
Bond, Thomas Moore, Jr. 1930- *WhoWest 94*
Bond, Thomas Richard 1945- *WhoAmL 94*
Bond, Tommy 1927- *WhoHol 92*
Bond, Victoria Ellen 1945- *WhoAm 94*
Bond, Vincent Earl 1947- *WhoWest 94*
Bond, Ward d1960 *WhoHol 92*
Bond, Ward C. 1961- *WhoScEn 94*
Bond, Wilbert, Sr. 1925- *WhoBlA 94*
Bond, William Henry 1915- *WhoAm 94*
Bond, William Jennings, Jr. 1953- *WhoMW 93*
Bond, Zinny Sans 1940- *WhoMW 93*
Bonda, Alva Ted 1917- *WhoMW 93*
Bondarchuk, Natalia *WhoHol 92*
Bondarchuk, Sergei 1920- *WhoHol 92*
Bondarchuk, Sergey Fedorovich 1920- *IntWW 93*
Bondareff, William 1930- *WhoAm 94*
Bondarev, Yuriy Vasiliyevich 1924- *IntWW 93*
Bondarev, Yury Vasilevich 1924- *LoBiDrD*
Bonde, Brian James 1958- *WhoMW 93*
Bonde, Olaf Carl 1927- *WhoAm 94*
Bonde, Peder 1923- *IntWW 93*
Bondevik, Kjell Magne 1947- *IntWW 93*
Bondeville, Emmanuel (Pierre Georges) 1898-1987 *NewGrDO*
Bondhill, Gertrude d1960 *WhoHol 92*
Bondhus, Lee Mark 1939- *WhoFI 94*
Bondi, Bert Roger 1945- *WhoWest 94*
Bondi, Beulah d1981 *WhoHol 92*
Bondi, Enrico 1933- *WhoScEn 94*
Bondi, Gene L. 1913- *WhoAmP 93*
Bondi, Hermann *WorScD*
Bondi, Hermann 1919- *IntWW 93, Who 94*
Bondi, Joseph Charles, Jr. 1936- *WhoAm 94*
Bondi, Kathleen 1952- *WhoMW 93*
Bondi, Michele Neri *NewGrDO*
Bondini, Pasquale 1737?-1789 *NewGrDO*
Bondoc, Rommel 1938- *WhoAmL 94*
Bondon, Jacques (Laurent Jules Desire) 1927- *NewGrDO*
Bond-Owen, Nicholas 1968- *WhoHol 92*
Bonds, Barry 1964- *ConBlB 6 [port], News 93-3 [port]*
Bonds, Barry Lamar 1964- *WhoAm 94, WhoBlA 94, WhoWest 94*
Bonds, Bobby Lee 1946- *WhoBlA 94*
Bonds, John Wilfred, Jr. 1943- *WhoAm 94, WhoAmL 94*
Bonds, Margaret Allison 1913-1972 *AfrAmAl 6*
Bonds, Thyra Verle 1927- *WhoMW 93*
Bondurant, Byron Lee 1925- *WhoScEn 94*
Bondurant, David William 1948- *WhoWest 94*
Bondurant, Emmet Jopling, II 1937- *WhoAm 94*
Bondurant, Stuart 1929- *IntWW 93, WhoAm 94*
Bond-Williams, Noel Ignace 1914- *Who 94*
Bondy, Luc 1948- *NewGrDO*
Bondy, Philip Kramer 1917- *WhoAm 94*
Bondy, Philip Lederer 1910-1990 *WhAm 10*
Bondy, Robert Earl 1895- *WhAm 10*
Bone, Bruce Charles 1928- *WhoAm 94, WhoFI 94*
Bone, Charles 1926- *Who 94*
Bone, Charles W. 1946- *WhoAmL 94*
Bone, Hugh A. 1909- *WrDr 94*
Bone, J(esse) F(ranklin) 1916- *EncSF 93, WrDr 94*
Bone, Janet Witmeyer 1930- *WhoMW 93*
Bone, John Frank Ewan *Who 94*
Bone, Mary *Who 94*
Bone, Quentin 1931- *Who 94*
Bone, Robert Gehlmann 1906-1991 *WhAm 10*
Bone, Robert William 1932- *WhoWest 94*
Bone, Roger Bridgland 1944- *Who 94*
Bone, Roger Conley 1941- *WhoAm 94*
Bone, Thomas Renfrew 1935- *Who 94*
Bone, Winston S. 1932- *WhoBlA 94*
Boneau, C. Alan 1926- *WhoAm 94*
Bonebrake, D. J. 1955- *See X ConMus 11*
Bonee, John Leon, III 1947- *WhoAmL 94*
Bonell, Carlos Antonio 1949- *IntWW 93*
Bonell, Paul Ian 1961- *WhoFI 94*
Bonelli, Joseph Edward 1946- *WhoWest 94*
Bonelli, Richard 1887-1980 *NewGrDO*
Bonelli, William Jeffrey 1958- *WhoAmL 94*
Bonem, Elliott Jeffrey 1953- *WhoScEn 94*
Boner, Donald Leslie 1944- *WhoMW 93*
Boner, Eleanor Katz 1922- *WhoAmL 94*
Boner, Michael Lynn 1953- *WhoMW 93*
Boner, William Hill 1945- *WhoAmP 93*
Bonerz, Peter 1938- *ConTFT 11, WhoAm 94, WhoHol 92*
Bones, Ken *WhoHol 92*
Bones, Ricky 1969- *WhoBlA 94, WhoHisp 94*
Bones, Walter I. 1927- *WhoAmP 93*
Bonesi, Barnaba 1745?-1824 *NewGrDO*
Bonesio, Woodrow Michael 1943- *WhoAm 94, WhoAmL 94*
Bonessa, Dennis R. 1948- *WhoAm 94, WhoAmL 94*
Bonesteel, Michael John 1939- *WhoAm 94, WhoAmL 94*
Bonestell, Chesley 1888-1986 *EncSF 93*
Bonet, Frank Joseph 1937- *WhoAm 94*
Bonet, Guillermo A. 1942- *WhoHisp 94*
Bonet, Jose 1955- *WhoScEn 94*
Bonet, Juan Pablo 1579-1623 *EncDeaf*
Bonet, Lisa 1967- *IntMPA 94, WhoBlA 94, WhoHol 92*
Bonet, Nai *IntMPA 94, WhoHol 92*
Bonet, Pep 1941- *IntWW 93*
Bonett, Emery 1906- *WrDr 94*
Bonett, John 1906- *WrDr 94*
Bonetti, David *WhoAm 94, WhoWest 94*
Bonetti, Lucia fl. 1688-1719 *NewGrDO*
Bonetti, Mattia 1952- *IntWW 93*
Bonevardi, Marcelo 1929- *WhoAmA 93*
Bonewitz, Robert Allen 1943- *WhoScEn 94*
Boney, Guy Thomas Knowles 1944- *Who 94*
Boney, J. Don 1928- *WhoBlA 94*
Boney, Jean Harris *Who 94*
Boney, William Andrew 1933- *WhoFI 94*
Bonfante, Larissa *WhoAm 94*
Bonfatti, Liliana 1931- *WhoHol 92*
Bonfatti Paini, Marisa 1947- *WhoWomW 91*
Bonfield, Andrew Joseph 1924- *WhoWest 94*
Bonfield, Arthur Earl 1936- *WhoAm 94*
Bonfield, Gordon Bradley, III 1951- *WhoMW 93*
Bonfield, Peter Leahy 1944- *IntWW 93, Who 94*
Bonfield, William 1937- *Who 94*
Bonfiglio, Joel David 1958- *WhoAmL 94*
Bonfiglio, Michael 1917- *WhoAm 94*
Bonfiglioli, Kyril *EncSF 93*
Bonforte, Richard James 1940- *WhoAm 94*
Bong, Robert Edward 1954- *WhoMW 93*
Bongard, David L(awrence) 1959- *ConAu 140*
Bongart, Sergei R. d1985 *WhoAmA 93N*
Bongartz, Ferdinand A. 1923- *WhoAmP 93*
Bongartz, Roy 1924- *WhAm 10*
Bongartz, Seth 1954- *WhoAmP 93*
Bonge, Nicholas Jay, Jr. 1954- *WhoWest 94*
Bongers, Paul Nicholas 1943- *Who 94*
Bongiorno, James William 1943- *WhoAm 94*
Bongiorno, John Jacques 1938- *WhoAm 94, WhoFI 94*
Bongiorno, Joseph John, Jr. 1936- *WhoAm 94*
Bongiorno, Laurine Mack 1903-1988 *WhoAmA 93N*
Bongo, Albert-Bernard (Omar) 1935- *IntWW 93*
Bongo, Martin 1940- *IntWW 93*
Bonhag, Thomas Edward 1952- *WhoFI 94*
Bonhag, Wayne Thompson 1945- *WhoFI 94*
Bonham, Antony Lionel Thomas 1916- *Who 94*
Bonham, Barbara 1926- *WrDr 94*
Bonham, Charlie Leonard 1939- *WhoWest 94*
Bonham, Clifford Vernon 1921- *WhoAm 94, WhoWest 94*
Bonham, Francis Robert 1785-1863 *DcNaB MP*
Bonham, Frank 1914-1988 *EncSF 93*
Bonham, Frank 1914-1989 *TwCYAW*
Bonham, George Wolfgang 1924- *WhoAm 94*
Bonham, Harold Florian 1928- *WhoWest 94*
Bonham, John d1980 *WhoHol 92*
Bonham, Nicholas 1948- *Who 94*
Bonham, Robert Logan 1927- *WhoFI 94*
Bonham, Russell Aubrey 1931- *WhoMW 93*
Bonham, Vence L., Jr. *WhoBlA 94*
Bonham Carter *Who 94*
Bonham-Carter, Baron 1922- *Who 94*
Bonham Carter, Helena 1966- *IntMPA 94, IntWW 93, WhoHol 92*
Bonham-Carter, John Arkwright 1915- *Who 94*
Bonham Carter, Raymond Henry 1929- *Who 94*
Bonham Carter, Richard Erskine 1910- *Who 94*
Bonham-Carter, Victor 1913- *Who 94, WrDr 94*

Bonham-Yeaman, Doria 1932- WhoAmL 94
Bonheur, Stella WhoHol 92
Bonhoeffer, Dietrich 1906-1945 HisWorL
Boni, Carmen d1963 WhoHol 92
Boni, Michal 1954- IntWW 93
Bonica, John Joseph 1917- WhoAm 94, WrDr 94
Bonica, John R. 1953- WhoAm 94, WhoAmL 94
Bonicelli, Derito 1918- WhoAmP 93
Bonicelli, Joanne 1951- WhoWest 94
Boniek, Zbigniew 1956- WorESoc
Boniface, Christian Pierre 1962- WhoScEn 94
Boniface, Symona d1950 WhoHol 92
Bonifanti, Alisann Marie 1946- WhoAm 94
Bonifas, Jane Marie 1935- WhoMW 93
Bonifas, Paul WhoHol 92
Bonifield, Eugene 1933- WhoIns 94
Bonifield, William C. 1934- WhoAm 94
Bonilla, Anthony Cruz 1950- WhoHisp 94
Bonilla, Bobby 1963- WhoAm 94, WhoBlA 94, WhoHisp 94
Bonilla, Eduardo WhoHisp 94
Bonilla, Frank WhoHisp 94
Bonilla, Gladys WhoHisp 94
Bonilla, Hector WhoHisp 94
Bonilla, Henry WhoAmP 93
Bonilla, Henry 1954- CngDr 93, WhoAm 94, WhoHisp 94
Bonilla, Julio 1957- WhoHisp 94
Bonilla, Luis Lopez 1956- WhoScEn 94
Bonilla, Maria O. 1952- WhoHisp 94
Bonilla, Mary Ann 1956- WhoHisp 94
Bonilla, Ruben, Jr. WhoHisp 94
Bonilla, Tony 1936- WhoAm 94, WhoHisp 94
Bonilla, Tony 1952- WhoHisp 94
Bonilla, Tony Correa 1940- WhoHisp 94
Bonilla, Victor Orlando 1945- WhoHisp 94
Bonillas, Myrta d1959 WhoHol 92
Bonilla-Santiago, Gloria 1954- WhoHisp 94
Bonin, Bernard 1936- IntWW 93, WhoAm 94
Bonin, Charles 1865-1929 WhWE
Bonin, Paul Joseph 1929- WhoAm 94
Bonington, Chris(tian) 1934- WrDr 94
Bonington, Christian John Storey 1934- IntWW 93, Who 94
Bonini, Aleta M. 1954- WhoAmL 94
Bonini, Julio d1951 WhoHol 92
Bonino, Alfredo 1925-1981 WhoAmA 93N
Bonino, Fernanda 1927- WhoAm 94, WhoAmA 93
Bonino, Mark G. 1951- WhoAm 94, WhoAmL 94
Boninsegna, Celestina 1877-1947 NewGrDO
Boniol, Eddie Eugene 1931- WhoFI 94
Bonior, David E. 1945- CngDr 93, WhoAmP 93
Bonior, David Edward 1945- WhoAm 94, WhoMW 93
Bonis, Laszlo Joseph 1931- WhoScEn 94
Bonis, Novello fl. 1675-1681 NewGrDO
Bonisolli, Franco 1937- NewGrDO
Bonito Oliva, Achille WhoAm 94
Boniventi, Giuseppe 1670?-1727? NewGrDO
Boniver, Margherita 1938- WhoWomW 91
Bonjean, Charles Michael 1936- WhoAm 94
Bon Jovi ConMus 10 [port]
Bon Jovi, Jon 1962- WhoAm 94
See Also Bon Jovi ConMus 10
Bonk, James DrAPF 93
Bonker, Don L. 1937- WhoAmP 93
Bonkovsky, Herbert Lloyd 1941- WhoAm 94
Bonkowski, Ronald L. 1938- WhoAmP 93
Bonkowski, Ronald Lawrence 1938- WhoAm 94, WhoMW 93
Bonlini, Giovanni Carlo 1673-1731 NewGrDO
Bonn, Bernard J., III 1944- WhoAmL 94
Bonn, Ethel May 1925- WhoAm 94
Bonn, Ferdinand d1933 WhoHol 92
Bonn, Ferdinand J. 1943- WhoScEn 94
Bonn, Frank d1944 WhoHol 92
Bonn, Issy d1977 WhoHol 92
Bonn, John R. 1949- WhoAmL 94
Bonn, Paul Verne 1939- WhoAm 94
Bonn, Theodore Hertz 1923- WhoAm 94
Bonn, Walter d1953 WhoHol 92
Bonnafe, Jacques WhoHol 92
Bonnaire, Sandrine WhoHol 92
Bonnar, James King 1885-1961 WhoAmA 93N
Bonnar, John 1934- WhoScEn 94
Bonnar, R. Paul 1948- WhoAmL 94
Bonnard, Mario d1965 WhoHol 92
Bonneau, Frederic Daniel 1962- WhoAm 94
Bonneau, Sarah K. 1951- WhoAmP 93
Bonnefoy, Yves 1923- ConWorW 93
Bonnefoy, Yves Jean 1923- IntWW 93
Bonnell, Bonnie d1964 WhoHol 92
Bonnell, David William 1943- WhoScEn 94
Bonnell, Hettie Hazlett 1898- WhAm 10
Bonnell, John Sutherland 1893-1992 WhAm 10
Bonnell, Lee d1986 WhoHol 92
Bonnell, Paula DrAPF 93
Bonnell, Victoria Eileen 1942- WhoAm 94, WhoWest 94
Bonnelli, Richard d1980 WhoHol 92
Bonner, Alice A. 1941- WhoBlA 94
Bonner, Alice Carol 1948- WhoBlA 94
Bonner, Anthony 1968- WhoBlA 94
Bonner, Arthur 1922- WrDr 94
Bonner, Bertram F. d1993 NewYTBS 93
Bonner, Bester Davis WhoBlA 94
Bonner, Brian 1917- WrDr 94
Bonner, Charles William, III 1928- WhoAm 94
Bonner, David Calhoun 1946- WhoAm 94, WhoScEn 94
Bonner, Della M. 1929- WhoBlA 94
Bonner, Elena Georgievna 1922- LoBiDrD
Bonner, Elena Georgievna 1923- IntWW 93
Bonner, Ellis WhoBlA 94
Bonner, Francis Truesdale 1921- WhoAm 94
Bonner, Frank 1942- WhoHol 92
Bonner, Frederick Ernest 1923- Who 94
Bonner, Herbert Dwight 1942- WhoMW 93
Bonner, Hilton WhoHol 92
Bonner, Isabel d1955 WhoHol 92
Bonner, Jack 1948- WhoAm 94
Bonner, Jack Wilbur, III 1940- WhoAm 94
Bonner, James 1910- IntWW 93
Bonner, Joe d1959 WhoHol 92
Bonner, John Tyler 1920- IntWW 93, WhoAm 94, WrDr 94
Bonner, Jonathan G. WhoAmA 93
Bonner, Joseph Steven 1961- WhoFI 94
Bonner, Margerie d1988 WhoHol 92
Bonner, Marita BlkWr 2, ConAu 142
Bonner, Mary Winstead 1924- WhoBlA 94
Bonner, Michael 1924- WrDr 94
Bonner, Patricia J. 1939- WhoAm 94
Bonner, Paul Max 1934- IntWW 93, Who 94
Bonner, Priscilla 1904- WhoHol 92
Bonner, Robert 1942- WhoAmP 93
Bonner, Robert Cleve 1942- WhoAm 94, WhoAmL 94
Bonner, Robert William 1920- IntWW 93, WhoAm 94
Bonner, Theophulis W. 1917- WhoBlA 94
Bonner, Thomas Neville 1923- WhoAm 94
Bonner, Tony WhoHol 92
Bonner, Walter Joseph 1925- WhoAm 94, WhoAmL 94
Bonner, William WhoHol 92
Bonner, William Andrew 1919- WhoAm 94
Bonner, William Neely, Jr. 1923- WhoAm 94, WhoAmL 94
Bonnes, Charles Andrew 1941- WhoAm 94
Bonneson, Mary Elisabeth 1961- WhoMW 93
Bonnet, Beatriz Alicia 1959- WhoAm 94
Bonnet, C. M. Who 94
Bonnet, Charles 1720-1793 WorScD
Bonnet, Christian 1921- IntWW 93
Bonnet, Felix A. 1955- WhoHisp 94
Bonnet, Henri 1888-1978 HisDcKW
Bonnet, Henri 1934- WhoScEn 94
Bonnet, Juan Amedee 1939- WhoAm 94
Bonnet, Peter Robert Frank 1936- Who 94
Bonnet, Raymond 1931- Who 94
Bonneville, Benjamin Louis Eulalie De 1796-1878 WhWE
Bonneville, Richard Briggs 1942- WhoAm 94
Bonney, Allan L. 1917- WhoAmP 93
Bonney, Barbara 1956- IntWW 93, NewGrDO
Bonney, Donald Ernest 1952- WhoWest 94
Bonney, Gail d1984 WhoHol 92
Bonney, George Louis William 1920- Who 94
Bonney, Hal James, Jr. 1929- WhoAm 94, WhoAmL 94
Bonney, J. Dennis 1930- IntWW 93
Bonney, John Dennis 1930- WhoAm 94, WhoFI 94, WhoWest 94
Bonney, Mary Lucinda 1816-1900 EncNAR
Bonney, Samuel Robert 1943- WhoAm 94
Bonney, Therese 1895-1978 WhoAmA 93N
Bonney, Weston Leonard 1925- WhoAm 94
Bonney, William Lawless 1932- WhoAm 94
Bonnici, Carmelo M. Who 94
Bonnici, Emanuel 1928- IntWW 93
Bonnici, Karmenu Mifsud IntWW 93
Bonnici, Ugo Mifsud IntWW 93
Bonnie, Richard Jeffrey 1945- WhoAm 94
Bonnielizabethoag DrAPF 93
Bonnin, Gertrude Simmons 1876-1938 AmSocL [port]
Bonnington, Vicki Van Velson 1950- WhoAmL 94
Bonnin Julia, Sebastian, III 1951- WhoHisp 94
Bonnivier, B. William WhoFI 94
Bonniwell, Katherine WhoAm 94
Bonno, Giuseppe 1711-1788 NewGrDO
Bonnor, William Bowen 1920- WrDr 94
Bonny, Blaine Milan 1909- WhoWest 94
Bonny, Jack 1939- WhoAmP 93
Bonnycastle, Lawrence Christopher 1907- WhoAm 94
Bonnycastle, Murray C. WhoAmA 93N
Bonnyman, George Gordon 1919- WhoAm 94
Bono 1960- CurBio 93 [port], IntWW 93, WhoAm 94
Bono, Alexander Dominic 1952- WhoAm 94
Bono, Anthony Salvatore Emanuel, II 1946- WhoFI 94, WhoScEn 94
Bono, Gaspare Joseph 1950- WhoAm 94
Bono, Philip 1921- WhoAm 94, WhoScEn 94
Bono, Sonny WhoAmP 93
Bono, Sonny 1935- IntMPA 94, WhoHol 92
Bono, Sonny Salvatore 1935- WhoAm 94, WhoWest 94
Bono, Susie 1953- WhoHol 92
Bonomi, John Gurnee 1923- WhoAm 94, WhoAmL 94
Bonomo, Joe d1978 WhoHol 92
Bononcini, Antonio Maria 1677-1726 NewGrDO
Bononcini, Giovanni 1670-1747 NewGrDO
Bonoris, Athanasios I. 1953- WhoMW 93
Bonosaro, Carol Alessandra 1940- WhoAm 94
Bonsack, Rose Mary Hatem WhoAmP 93
Bonsal, Dudley Baldwin 1906- WhoAm 94, WhoAmL 94
Bonsal, Richard Irving 1920- WhoAm 94, WhoFI 94
Bonsall, Arthur (Wilfred) 1917- Who 94
Bonsall, Crosby (Newell) 1921- WrDr 94
Bonsall, Frank Featherstone 1920- Who 94
Bonsall, Joseph Sloan, Jr. 1948- WhoAm 94
Bonser, David Who 94
Bonser, Quentin 1920- WhoWest 94
Bonser, Stanley Haslam 1916- Who 94
Bonsignore, Joseph John 1920- WhoAm 94, WhoScEn 94
Bonsignore, Michael Robert 1941- WhoFI 94
Bonsky, Jack Alan 1938- WhoAm 94, WhoAmL 94, WhoFI 94
Bonsor, Nicholas (Cosmo) 1942- Who 94
Bonstelle, Helen d1979 WhoHol 92
Bonta, Diana Maria 1950- WhoHisp 94
Bonte, Frederick James 1922- WhoAm 94
Bontempi, Giovanni Andrea 1625-1705 NewGrDO
Bontempo, Daniel 1962- WhoScEn 94
Bontempo, Paul N. 1951- WhoAmP 93
Bontemps, Arna 1902-1973 AfrAmAl 6 [port]
Bontemps, Jacqueline Marie Fonvielle WhoBlA 94
Bonting, Sjoerd Lieuwe 1924- WhoAm 94, WhoScEn 94
Bontly, Thomas DrAPF 93
Bontoyan, Warren Roberts 1932- WhoAm 94
Bonuccelli, Charles Louis 1955- WhoFI 94
Bonus, Holger 1935- WhoScEn 94
Bonutti, Boris Paul 1959- WhoMW 93
Bonventre, Joseph Vincent 1949- WhoAm 94
Bonvillian, William Boone 1947- WhoAm 94
Bonvino, Frank W. 1941- WhoAmL 94
Bonvouloir, Julien Achard de WhAmRev
Bony, Jean V. 1908- Who 94
Bony, Jean Victor 1908- WhoAmA 93
Bonynge, Joan Who 94
Bonynge, Richard 1930- IntWW 93, Who 94, WhoAm 94
Bonynge, Richard (Alan) 1930- NewGrDO
Bonzagni, Vincent Francis 1952- WhoFI 94
Boo, Ben 1925- WhoAmP 93
Boochever, Robert 1917- WhoAm 94, WhoAmL 94, WhoAmP 93, WhoWest 94
Boocock, Sarane Spence 1935- WhoAm 94
Boocock, Stephen William 1948- WhoAmL 94
Boodell, Thomas Joseph, Jr. 1935- WhoAm 94
Boodey, Cecil Webster, Jr. 1931- WhoAm 94
Boodman, H. Citron 1927- WhoAmA 93
Boody, Frederick Parker, Jr. 1949- WhoScEn 94
Boody, Irving Rickerson, Jr. 1917- WhoFI 94
Boody, Janet 1946- WhoAmP 93
Booe, James Marvin 1906- WhoFI 94, WhoMW 93
Boogar, William F. 1893-1958 WhoAmA 93N
Boohaker, Charles Hikel 1964- WhoAmL 94
Booher, Alice Ann 1941- WhoAmL 94
Booher, Charles Forest 1944- WhoAm 94, WhoFI 94, WhoMW 93
Booher, Edward E. 1911-1990 WhAm 10
Booher, Robert Peter Joseph 1947- WhoFI 94
Book, Edward R. 1931- WhoAm 94
Book, Jeffrey S. 1959- WhoAmP 93
Book, John Kenneth 1950- WhoFI 94
Book, Raymond Thomas 1925- WhoAmP 93
Book, Ronald Lee 1952- WhoAmP 93
Book, William Joseph 1942- WhoMW 93
Bookatz, Samuel 1910- WhoAmA 93
Bookbinder, Hyman Harry 1916- WhoAm 94
Bookbinder, Jack 1911-1990 WhAm 10, WhoAmA 93N
Bookchin, Murray 1921- EnvEnc [port], WrDr 94
Booke, Sorrell 1926- WhoHol 92
Booke, Sorrell 1930- IntMPA 94
Booker, Alvin Eugene 1928- WhoFI 94
Booker, Anne M. WhoBlA 94
Booker, Betty DrAPF 93
Booker, Bruce E. WhoIns 94
Booker, Carl Granger, Sr. 1928- WhoBlA 94
Booker, Christopher (John Penrice) 1937- WrDr 94
Booker, Christopher John Penrice 1937- Who 94
Booker, Clifford R. 1926- WhoBlA 94
Booker, Daniel I. 1947- WhoAm 94, WhoAmL 94
Booker, Donald Brandon 1942- WhoFI 94
Booker, Garvall H. 1925- WhoBlA 94
Booker, Gordon Alan 1938- Who 94
Booker, Harry d1924 WhoHol 92
Booker, Henry George 1910-1988 WhAm 10
Booker, Irvin B. WhoBlA 94
Booker, James Avery, Jr. 1936- WhoBlA 94
Booker, James E. 1926- WhoBlA 94
Booker, John, III 1947- WhoBlA 94
Booker, John Franklin 1934- WhoAm 94
Booker, Larry Frank 1950- WhoFI 94
Booker, Lewis Thomas 1929- WhoAm 94, WhoAmL 94
Booker, Michael Eugene 1951- WhoAmP 93
Booker, Nana Laurel 1946- WhoFI 94
Booker, Robert Joseph 1935- WhoBlA 94
Booker, Simeon S. 1918- WhoBlA 94
Booker, Teresa Hillary Clarke 1963- WhoBlA 94
Booker, Thurman D. 1937- WhoBlA 94
Booker, Vaughan P. L. 1942- WhoBlA 94
Booker, Venerable Francis 1920- WhoBlA 94
Booker-Davis, Janet Marie 1954- WhoMW 93
Booker-Milburn, Donald 1940- Who 94
Bookert, Charles C. 1918- WhoBlA 94
Bookhammer, Eugene Donald 1918- WhoAm 94, WhoAmP 93
Bookhardt, Fred Barringer, Jr. 1934- WhoAm 94
Bookholder, Ronald Michael 1943- WhoAmL 94
Bookin, Daniel H. 1951- WhoAm 94, WhoAmL 94
Bookman, George B. 1914- WhoAm 94
Bookman, Mark 1952- WhoAmL 94
Bookman, Philip 1936- WhoAm 94, WhoWest 94
Bookman, Robert 1947- IntMPA 94
Bookout, Jerry 1933- WhoAmP 93
Bookout, John Frank, Jr. 1922- IntWW 93, WhoAm 94
Bookout, Ruth Lorraine 1940- WhoAmP 93
Books, Joy Ann 1937- WhoMW 93
Bookser, Mary Catherine 1945- WhoMW 93
Bookshester, Dennis Steven WhoFI 94
Bookspan, David Israel WhoAmL 94
Bookspan, Michael Lloyd 1929- WhoAm 94

Bookstein, Abraham 1940- *WhoScEn 94*
Bookwalter, Deveren d1987 *WhoHol 92*
Boole, George *WorScD*
Boolell, Satcam 1920- *IntWW 93, Who 94*
Boolootian, Richard Andrew 1927- *WhoWest 94*
Boolos, George Stephen 1940- *IntWW 93, WhoAm 94*
Boomer, Walter Eugene 1938- *WhoAm 94*
Boomershine, Donald Eugene 1931- *WhoAm 94*
Booms, Hans 1924- *IntWW 93*
Boomsliter, Paul Colgan 1915- *WhAm 10*
Boomstra, Sjoerd 1913- *IntWW 93*
Boon, Emilie (Laetitia) 1958- *WrDr 94*
Boon, Eric d1981 *WhoHol 92*
Boon, George Counsell 1927- *Who 94*
Boon, Ina M. 1927- *WhoBlA 94*
Boon, John Trevor 1916- *IntWW 93, Who 94*
Boon, Peter Coleman 1916- *Who 94*
Boon, Robert *WhoHol 92*
Boon, William Robert 1911- *Who 94*
Boone, Alexandria 1947- *WhoBlA 94*
Boone, Ashley A., Jr. 1938- *IntMPA 94*
Boone, Billy Warren 1955- *WhoAm 94, WhoAmL 94*
Boone, Brendon *WhoHol 92*
Boone, Carol Marie 1945- *WhoBlA 94*
Boone, Celia Trimble 1953- *WhoAmL 94*
Boone, Clarence Donald 1939- *WhoBlA 94*
Boone, Clarence Wayne 1931- *WhoBlA 94*
Boone, Clinton Caldwell 1922- *WhoBlA 94*
Boone, Daniel 1734-1820 *AmRev, HisWorL [port], WhAmRev [port], WhWE [port]*
Boone, Daniel Alexander 1955- *WhoMW 93*
Boone, Daniel R. 1927- *WrDr 94*
Boone, David Daniel 1960- *WhoScEn 94*
Boone, Dell d1960 *WhoHol 92*
Boone, Elwood Bernard, Jr. 1943- *WhoBlA 94*
Boone, Eugene Lawrence 1937- *WhoAmP 93*
Boone, Faith Alexis 1960- *WhoMW 93*
Boone, Franklin Delanor Roosevelt, Sr. 1942- *WhoAm 94*
Boone, Frederick Oliver 1941- *WhoBlA 94*
Boone, Harold Thomas 1921- *WhoAm 94*
Boone, J. Sidney, Jr. 1944- *WhoAmL 94*
Boone, J. William 1952- *WhoAm 94*
Boone, James A. 1949- *WhoAmL 94*
Boone, James Virgil 1933- *WhoAm 94, WhoScEn 94*
Boone, Jeffrey Lynn 1951- *WhoWest 94*
Boone, Joy Bale *DrAPF 93*
Boone, Libby *WhoHol 92*
Boone, Lois Ruth 1947- *WhoWest 94*
Boone, Louis Eugene 1941- *WhoAm 94*
Boone, Mark Philip 1951- *WhoWest 94*
Boone, Mary 1951- *WhoAmA 93*
Boone, Michael Mauldin 1941- *WhoAm 94, WhoAmL 94*
Boone, Morell Douglas 1942- *WhoAm 94*
Boone, Norman McKieghan 1947- *WhoWest 94*
Boone, Oliver Kiel 1922- *WhoAm 94*
Boone, Pat 1934- *IntMPA 94, WhoAm 94, WhoHol 92, WrDr 94*
Boone, Randy 1942- *WhoHol 92*
Boone, Raymond Harold 1938- *WhoBlA 94*
Boone, Richard d1981 *WhoHol 92*
Boone, Richard Winston, Sr. 1941- *WhoAmL 94*
Boone, Robert Franklin 1949- *WhoBlA 94*
Boone, Robert Lawrence 1947- *WhoAmP 93*
Boone, Ron 1946- *BasBi*
Boone, Ronald Bruce 1946- *WhoBlA 94*
Boone, Sylvia A. d1993 *NewYTBS 93 [port], WhoBlA 94N*
Boone, Theodore Sebastian 1961- *WhoAmL 94*
Boone, Thomas John 1957- *WhoMW 93, WhoScEn 94*
Boone, Walker *WhoHol 92*
Boone, Willie Belle 1934- *WhoAmP 93*
Boone, Zola Ernest 1937- *WhoBlA 94*
Boonieh, Obi Anthony 1957- *WhoBlA 94*
Boonlua 1911-1982 *BlmGWL*
Boonshaft-Lewis, Hope Judith 1949- *WhoAm 94*
Boonstra, Cornelis 1938- *WhoFI 94*
Boonyachai, Sonthi 1917- *IntWW 93*
Boonzaier, Hugh Murray 1933- *IntWW 93*
Boor, Myron Vernon 1942- *WhoMW 93, WhoScEn 94*
Booraem, Hendrik 1886-1951 *WhoAmA 93N*
Boord, Nicolas (John Charles) 1936- *Who 94*
Boorde, Andrew c. 1490-1549 *DcLB 136 [port]*
Boorman, Charley 1967- *WhoHol 92*
Boorman, Derek 1930- *Who 94*
Boorman, Edwin Roy Pratt 1935- *Who 94*
Boorman, Howard Lyon 1920- *WhoAm 94*
Boorman, John 1933- *IntMPA 94, IntWW 93, WhoAm 94*
Boorman, Katrine 1951- *WhoHol 92*
Boorman, Philip Michael 1939- *WhoAm 94*
Boorman, Roy Slater 1936- *WhoScEn 94*
Boorstein, Beverly Weinger 1941- *WhoAmL 94*
Boorstein, Lucille Paula 1927- *WhoAmL 94*
Boorstin, Daniel J. 1914- *IntWW 93, Who 94, WhoAm 94, WrDr 94*
Boorstin, Daniel Joseph 1914- *WhoAmP 93*
Boorstin, Jon *WrDr 94*
Boorstin, Ruth (Carolyn) F(rankel) 1917- *WrDr 94*
Boortz, Donald L. 1946- *WhoAmL 94*
Boos, Florence Saunders 1943- *WhoMW 93*
Boos, John L. 1946- *WhoAmL 94*
Boose, Jerry Dale 1942- *WhoAmP 93*
Boose, Maryetta Kelsick *DrAPF 93*
Boose, Richard Bradshaw 1928- *WhoScEn 94*
Boosey, John Arthur 1929- *WhoAm 94*
Booskaver, Alexander 1911- *WhAm 10*
Boosler, Elaine 1952- *CurBio 93 [port]*
Boosler, Elayne 1952?- *ConTFT 11*
Boot, Gladys d1964 *WhoHol 92*
Boot, John C. G. 1936- *WrDr 94*
Boote, Alfred Shepard 1929- *WhoAm 94*
Boote, Charles Geoffrey Michael 1909- *Who 94*
Boote, Mary Joyce 1956- *WhoAmP 93*
Boote, Robert Edward 1920- *Who 94*
Booth *Who 94*
Booth, Adrian 1921- *WhoHol 92*
Booth, Alan Shore 1922- *Who 94*
Booth, Albert Edward 1928- *IntWW 93, Who 94*
Booth, Albert Edward, II 1942- *WhoAm 94*
Booth, Andrew Donald 1918- *WhoAm 94*
Booth, Anna Belle 1912- *WhoFI 94*
Booth, Anna Maxine 1917- *WhoAmP 93*
Booth, Anthony 1937- *WhoHol 92*
Booth, Anthony John 1939- *Who 94*
Booth, Anthony Robert 1941- *WhoFI 94*
Booth, Barton 1679?-1733 *BlmGEL*
Booth, Bert 1925- *WhoAmP 93*
Booth, Bill 1935- *WhoAmA 93*
Booth, Brian Geddes 1936- *WhoAm 94*
Booth, Brian George 1942- *Who 94*
Booth, Bronwen *WhoHol 92*
Booth, Cameron 1892-1980 *WhoAmA 93N*
Booth, Charles E. 1947- *WhoBlA 94*
Booth, Charles Leonard 1925- *Who 94*
Booth, Charles Loomis, Jr. 1933- *WhoAm 94*
Booth, Chesley Peter Washburn 1939- *WhoAm 94*
Booth, Christopher (Charles) 1924- *Who 94*
Booth, Clive 1943- *Who 94*
Booth, Connie 1941- *WhoHol 92*
Booth, David Eric 1940- *WhoAmL 94*
Booth, David Herbert d1993 *Who 94N*
Booth, Dot *WhoAmA 93*
Booth, Douglas Alan 1956- *WhoMW 93*
Booth, Douglas Allen 1949- *Who 94*
Booth, Edgar Hirsch 1926- *WhoAm 94*
Booth, Edward 1928- *WrDr 94*
Booth, Edwin 1906- *WrDr 94*
Booth, Edwin Thomas 1833-1893 *AmCulL*
Booth, Edwina d1991 *WhoHol 92*
Booth, Elmer d1915 *WhoHol 92*
Booth, Eric Stuart 1914- *Who 94*
Booth, Evangeline Cory 1865-1950 *DcAmReB 2*
Booth, Forrest 1946- *WhoAmL 94*
Booth, Geoffrey 1939- *WrDr 94*
Booth, George 1926- *WhoAm 94*
Booth, George Geoffrey 1942- *WhoAm 94*
Booth, George Warren 1917- *WhoAm 94, WhoAmA 93*
Booth, Glenna Greene 1928- *WhoAm 94*
Booth, Gordon 1921- *Who 94*
Booth, Gordon Dean, Jr. 1939- *WhoAm 94, WhoAmL 94*
Booth, Gordon J. 1931- *WhoAmP 93*
Booth, Harold Waverly 1934- *WhoAm 94, WhoAmL 94*
Booth, Hartley 1946- *Who 94*
Booth, Helen d1971 *WhoHol 92*
Booth, Henry Scripps 1897- *WhAm 10*
Booth, Herbert Cecil *WorInv*
Booth, Hester 1690?-1773 *BlmGEL*
Booth, I. MacAllister 1931- *IntWW 93*
Booth, Irwin *EncSF 93*
Booth, Israel MacAllister 1931- *WhoAm 94, WhoFI 94*
Booth, James 1914- *Who 94*
Booth, James 1933- *WhoHol 92*
Booth, James Albert 1946- *WhoMW 93*
Booth, Jim 1946- *WhoAmP 93*
Booth, John Antony W. *Who 94*
Booth, John Barton 1937- *Who 94*
Booth, John Dick L. *Who 94*
Booth, John Louis 1933- *WhoFI 94, WhoWest 94*
Booth, John Nicholls 1912- *WhoAm 94*
Booth, John Thomas 1929- *WhoAm 94*
Booth, John Wells 1903- *Who 94*
Booth, Karin 1923- *WhoHol 92*
Booth, Karla Ann Smith 1951- *WhoScEn 94*
Booth, Ken 1943- *WrDr 94*
Booth, Laurence Ogden 1936- *WhoAm 94, WhoAmA 93*
Booth, Lavaughn Venchael 1919- *WhoBlA 94*
Booth, Le-Quita 1946- *WhoBlA 94*
Booth, Margaret 1898- *IntDcF 2-4, IntMPA 94*
Booth, Margaret (Myfanwy Wood) 1933- *Who 94*
Booth, Martin 1944- *WrDr 94*
Booth, Michael Addison John W. *Who 94*
Booth, Mitchell B. 1927- *WhoAm 94*
Booth, Nesdon d1964 *WhoHol 92*
Booth, Nina Mason 1884- *WhoAmA 93N*
Booth, Pat 1942- *WrDr 94*
Booth, Peter John Richard 1949- *Who 94*
Booth, Philip *DrAPF 93*
Booth, Philip 1925- *WhoAm 94, WrDr 94*
Booth, Rachel Zonelle 1936- *WhoAm 94*
Booth, Randolph Lee 1952- *WhoAm 94*
Booth, Richard Earl 1919- *WhoAm 94*
Booth, Richard George William Pitt 1938- *Who 94*
Booth, Richard H. *WhoAm 94, WhoFI 94, WhoIns 94*
Booth, Robert (Camm) 1916- *Who 94*
Booth, Robert Alan 1952- *WhoAmA 93*
Booth, Robert Edmond 1917-1992 *WhAm 10*
Booth, Robert Lee, Jr. 1936- *WhoFI 94*
Booth, Sara Daniel 1964- *WhoMW 93*
Booth, Shirley d1992 *IntMPA 94N*
Booth, Shirley 1898-1992 *AnObit 1992, ConTFT 11*
Booth, Shirley 1899- *IntMPA 94*
Booth, Shirley 1907- *WhoHol 92*
Booth, Shirley 1907-1992 *CurBio 93N*
Booth, Stanley 1942- *WrDr 94*
Booth, Sydney d1937 *WhoHol 92*
Booth, Vernon Edward Hartley *Who 94*
Booth, Wayne C(layson) 1921- *ConAu 43NR*
Booth, Wayne Clayson 1921- *WhoAm 94, WrDr 94*
Booth, Webster d1984 *WhoHol 92*
Booth, William H. 1922- *WhoBlA 94*
Booth, William H. 1947- *WhoAmL 94*
Booth, William James 1939- *Who 94*
Boothby, Brooke (Charles) 1949- *Who 94*
Boothby, Frances fl. 1669- *BlmGWL*
Boothby, Guy (Newell) 1867-1905 *EncSF 93*
Boothby, James M. 1959- *WhoAmP 93*
Boothby, Penelope 1881-1970 *BuCMET*
Boothby, Willard Sands, III 1946- *WhoAm 94, WhoFI 94*
Boothby, William Munger 1918- *WhoAm 94*
Booth Cabot, M(ary Ann) 1942- *WhoAmA 93*
Booth-Clibborn, Stanley Eric Francis 1924- *IntWW 93, Who 94*
Boothe, Jeffrey Ferris 1955- *WhoAmP 93*
Boothe, Leon Estel 1938- *WhoAm 94*
Boothe, Power 1945- *WhoAm 94, WhoAmA 93*
Boothe, Powers 1949- *IntMPA 94, WhoHol 92*
Boothe, Ronald George 1947- *WhoScEn 94*
Boothe, Viva Belle 1893- *WhAm 10*
Boothman, Campbell Lester 1942- *Who 94*
Boothman, Derek Arnold 1932- *Who 94*
Boothman, Nicholas 1941- *Who 94*
Boothroyd, Betty 1929- *IntWW 93, Who 94, WhoWomW 91*
Boothroyd, Geoffrey 1932- *WhoScEn 94*
Boothroyd, Herbert J. 1928- *WhoAm 94*
Bootle, William Augustus 1902- *WhoAm 94*
Bootle-Wilbraham *Who 94*
Booty, John Everitt 1925- *ConAu 43NR, WhoAm 94*
Bootz, Antoine H. 1956- *WhoAmA 93*
Booysen, Peter de Villiers 1930- *IntWW 93*
Booz, Gretchen Arlene 1933- *WhoMW 93*
Booze, Thomas Franklin 1955- *WhoWest 94*
Boozer, Bob 1937- *BasBi*
Boozer, Emerson, Jr. 1943- *WhoBlA 94*
Boozer, F. Vernon 1936- *WhoAmP 93*
Boozer, Howard Rai 1923- *WhoAm 94*
Bopp, Edward Sidney 1930- *WhoAmP 93*
Bopp, Emery 1924- *WhoAmA 93*
Bopp, James, Jr. 1948- *WhoAmL 94*
Boquet, Louis-Rene 1717-1814 *NewGrDO*
Boquist, Ronald Jay 1964- *WhoWest 94*
Bor, Jonathan Steven 1953- *WhoAm 94*
Bor, Walter George 1916- *Who 94*
Bora, Alexander 1916- *WhoWest 94*
Bora, Sunder S. 1938- *WhoAsA 94*
Bora, Sunil K. 1964- *WhoFI 94*
Borah, Brett A. 1950- *WhoWest 94*
Borah, Gregory Louis 1950- *WhoScEn 94*
Borah, Kripanath 1931- *WhoScEn 94*
Borah, Lyn R. 1939- *WhoAmP 93*
Boratto, Caterina 1923- *WhoHol 92*
Borawaka, Marianna *WhoWomW 91*
Borax, Benjamin 1909- *WhoAmA 93*
Boraz, Robert Alan 1951- *WhoMW 93*
Borbon y Battenberg, Juan de d1993 *IntWW 93N*
Borbon Y Battenberg, Juan de 1913- *IntWW 93*
Borbridge, G. *WhoWest 94*
Borch, Kurt Esben 1944- *WhoScEn 94*
Borch, Otto Rose 1921- *IntWW 93*
Borch, Richard Frederic 1941- *WhoAm 94, WhoScEn 94*
Borchard, Perry Lee 1965- *WhoFI 94*
Borchard, William Marshall 1938- *WhoAmL 94*
Borchardt, Frank L. 1938- *WrDr 94*
Borchardt, Paul Douglas 1942- *WhoFI 94*
Borchardt, Ronald Terrance 1944- *WhoAm 94*
Borcherding, Lee Ann 1956- *WhoMW 93*
Borchers, Cornell 1925- *WhoHol 92*
Borchers, Elisabeth 1926- *IntWW 93*
Borchers, Robert Reece 1936- *WhoAm 94, WhoWest 94*
Borchert, Donald Marvin 1934- *WhoAm 94*
Borchert, Jochen 1940- *IntWW 93*
Borchert, John Robert 1918- *WhoAm 94*
Borchert, William P. 1950- *WhoAmL 94*
Borchert, Wolfgang 1921-1947 *IntDcT 2*
Borchgrevink, Carsten Egeberg 1864-1934 *WhWE*
Borcoman, James 1926- *WhoAmA 93*
Borcoman, James Willmott 1926- *WhoAm 94*
Bord, Andre 1922- *IntWW 93*
Borda, Deborah 1949- *WhoAm 94*
Borda, Richard Joseph 1931- *WhoAm 94, WhoWest 94*
Bordaberry Arocena, Juan Maria 1928- *IntWW 93*
Bordallo, Madeleine Mary 1933- *WhoAmP 93*
Bordallo, Ricardo Jerome 1927-1990 *WhAm 10*
Bordao, Rafael *DrAPF 93*
Bordas, Juana *WhoHisp 94*
Bordaz, Robert 1908- *IntWW 93*
Bordeaux, Jean Luc 1937- *WhoAmA 93*
Bordeaux, Joe d1950 *WhoHol 92*
Bordeaux, Tom 1954- *WhoAmP 93*
Bordelon, Scott Lee 1967- *WhoWest 94*
Borden, Christopher, III 1925- *WhoAmP 93*
Borden, David 1937- *WhoAmL 94*
Borden, David M. *WhoAmP 93*
Borden, Eddie d1955 *WhoHol 92*
Borden, Ernest Carleton 1939- *WhoAm 94*
Borden, Eugene d1971 *WhoHol 92*
Borden, Gail 1801-1874 *WorInv*
Borden, Harold F., Jr. 1942- *WhoBlA 94*
Borden, Henry 1901-1989 *WhAm 10*
Borden, John Anthony 1933- *WhoAm 94*
Borden, Lee *BlkWr 2, ConAu 43NR*
Borden, Leigh *BlkWr 2, ConAu 43NR*
Borden, Louise (Walker) 1949- *WrDr 94*
Borden, Lynn 1940- *WhoHol 92*
Borden, Mark G. 1951- *WhoAm 94*
Borden, Mary 1886-1968 *EncSF 93*
Borden, Olive d1947 *WhoHol 92*
Borden, Richard Stanley 1962- *WhoWest 94*
Borden, Robert 1854-1937 *HisWorL [port]*
Borden, Roy Herbert, Jr. 1949- *WhoScEn 94*
Borden, Thomas Allen 1937- *WhoWest 94*
Borden, Weston Thatcher 1943- *WhoAm 94*
Borden, William *DrAPF 93*
Borden, Winston Wendell 1943- *WhoAmP 93*
Border, Allan Robert 1955- *IntWW 93*
Border, Larry 1951- *WhoAmP 93*
Borders, Carol Lee *WhoMW 93*
Borders, Charlie 1948- *WhoAmP 93*
Borders, Florence Edwards 1924- *WhoBlA 94*
Borders, Michael G. 1946- *WhoBlA 94*
Borders, Thomas C. 1948- *WhoAm 94*
Borders, William Alexander 1939- *WhoAm 94*
Borders, William Donald 1913- *WhoAm 94*

Borders, William Holmes d1993 NewYTBS 93
Bordes, Adrienne WhoAmA 93
Bordet, Jules 1870-1961 WorScD
Bordewijk, F. EncSF 93
Bordie, John George 1931- WhoAm 94
Bordier, Primrose 1929- IntWW 93
Bordier, Roger 1923- IntWW 93
Bordiga, Benno 1920- WhoAm 94
Bordley, John Earle d1993 NewYTBS 93
Bordman, Gerald (Martin) 1931- NewGrDO
Bordner, Gregory Wilson 1959- WhoWest 94
Bordogna, Joseph 1933- WhoAm 94, WhoScEn 94
Bordogni, Giulio (Marco) 1789-1856 NewGrDO
Bordon, David E. 1943- WhoAmL 94
Bordoni, Faustina 1697-1781 NewGrDO [port]
Bordoni, Irene d1953 WhoHol 92
Bordow, Robert Alexander 1954- WhoWest 94
Borduas, Paul Emile d1960 WhoAmA 93N
Boreel, Francis (David) 1926- Who 94
Boreham, Arthur John 1925- IntWW 93
Boreham, Hervey of c. 1228-1277 DcNaB MP
Boreham, (Arthur) John 1925- Who 94
Boreham, Leslie Kenneth Edward Who 94
Borek, Gary D. 1953- WhoAmL 94
Borel, Armand 1923- WhoAm 94, WhoScEn 94
Borel, Georges Antoine 1936- WhoScEn 94
Borel, J. F. WorInv
Borel, Jacques 1925- IntWW 93
Borel, Jacques Paul 1927- IntWW 93
Borel, James David 1951- WhoWest 94
Borel, Jean-Francois WorScD
Borel, Petrus 1809-1859 NinCLC 41 [port]
Borel, Richard Wilson 1943- WhoAm 94, WhoFI 94
Borel, Steven James 1947- WhoAmL 94, WhoMW 93
Borell, Louis d1973 WhoHol 92
Borelli, Carla WhoHol 92
Borelli, Francis Joseph 1935- WhoAm 94
Borelli, Lyda d1958 WhoHol 92
Boren, Arthur Rodney 1916- WhoAm 94
Boren, Arthur Rodney, Jr. 1946- WhoAm 94
Boren, Benjamin N. 1909- WhoAm 94
Boren, Bryant C., Jr. 1954- WhoAmL 94
Boren, David L. 1941- CngDr 93, IntWW 93
Boren, David Lyle 1941- WhoAm 94, WhoAmP 93
Boren, Donna 1937- WhoMW 93
Boren, Hollis Grady 1923- WhoAm 94
Boren, James Edgar 1949- WhoAmL 94
Boren, James Erwin 1921-1990 WhoAmA 93N
Boren, Kenneth Ray 1945- WhoScEn 94, WhoWest 94
Boren, Lynda Sue 1941- WhoAm 94
Boren, Thomas Garner 1949- WhoAm 94, WhoFI 94
Boren, William Meredith 1924- WhoAm 94
Borenstein, Abe Isaac 1957- WhoAm 94
Borenstein, Audrey DrAPF 93
Borenstein, Emily DrAPF 93
Borenstein, Emily 1923- WrDr 94
Borenstein, Mark A. 1951- WhoAmL 94
Borenstein, Milton Conrad 1914- WhoAm 94, WhoAmL 94, WhoFI 94
Borenstein, Neil Barry 1962- WhoMW 93
Borenstine, Alvin Jerome 1933- WhoFI 94
Boreo, Emile d1951 WhoHol 92
Borer, Edward Turner 1938- WhoAm 94, WhoFI 94
Borer, Jeffrey Stephen 1945- WhoAm 94
Borer, Mary Cathcart 1906- WrDr 94
Borer, Robert Chamberlain, III 1966- WhoFI 94
Borer-Skov, Londa Lou 1942- WhoAm 94
Boresi, Arthur Peter WhoAm 94, WhoWest 94
Boretti, Giovanni Antonio c. 1640-1672 NewGrDO
Boretz, Benjamin (Aaron) 1934- ConAu 43NR
Boretz, Naomi WhoAmA 93
Borg, Alan Charles Nelson 1942- IntWW 93, Who 94
Borg, Axel Edwin 1953- WhoWest 94
Borg, Bjorn 1956- BuCMET [port], WhoAm 94
Borg, Bjorn Rune 1956- IntWW 93, Who 94
Borg, Dorothy d1993 NewYTBS 93 [port]
Borg, Kim 1919- IntWW 93, NewGrDO
Borg, Lars Goran 1913- IntWW 93
Borg, Malcolm Austin 1938- WhoAm 94
Borg, Parker WhoAm 94
Borg, Parker W. 1939- WhoAmP 93
Borg, Per O. 1943- IntWW 93
Borg, Ruth I. 1934- WhoMW 93
Borg, Sidney Fred 1916- WhoAm 94
Borg, Stefan Lennart 1945- WhoScEn 94
Borg, Susan 1947- WrDr 94
Borg, Sven-Hugo d1981 WhoHol 92
Borg, Veda Ann d1973 WhoHol 92
Borgani, Nick d1987 WhoHol 92
Borgaonkar, Digamber Shankarrao 1932- WhoAm 94, WhoAsA 94
Borgato, Agostino d1939 WhoHol 92
Borgatta, Edgar F. 1924- WhoAm 94
Borgatta, Isabel Case 1922- WhoAmA 93
Borgatta, Marie Lentini 1925- WhoWest 94
Borgatta, Robert Edward 1921- WhoAmA 93
Borgatti, Douglas Richard 1952- WhoScEn 94
Borgatti, Giuseppe 1871-1950 NewGrDO
Borg Costanzi, Edwin J. 1925- Who 94
Borge, Victor 1909- CurBio 93 [port], IntMPA 94, IntWW 93, WhoAm 94, WhoCom [port], WhoHol 92
Borgeaud, Pierre 1934- IntWW 93
Borge Martinez, Tomas 1930- IntWW 93
Borgen, Kjell 1939- IntWW 93
Borgen, Ole Edvard 1925- WhoAm 94
Borgenicht, Grace 1915- WhoAmA 93
Borgenicht, Miriam 1915- WrDr 94
Borger, John Philip 1951- WhoAm 94, WhoAmL 94
Borger, Michael Hinton Ivers 1951- WhoAm 94, WhoMW 93
Borger, Riekele 1929- IntWW 93
Borgerding, Shirley Ruth 1929- WhoAmP 93
Borges, Anibal Vega WhoAmP 93
Borges, Carlos Rego 1939- WhoWest 94
Borges, Dain Edward 1954- WhoHisp 94
Borges, Evelyn 1951- WhoHisp 94
Borges, Francisco L. 1951- WhoAmP 93, WhoBlA 94
Borges, Jacobo 1931- IntWW 93
Borges, Jorge Luis 1899-1986 EncSF 93, HispLC [port], RfGShF
Borges, Juan Roberto 1950- WhoHisp 94
Borges, Lynne MacFarlane 1952- WhoBlA 94
Borges, Max E., Jr. 1942- WhoHisp 94
Borges, Ramon F. 1939- WhoHisp 94
Borges, Thomas William Alfred 1923- Who 94
Borges, William, III 1948- WhoWest 94
Borges, Yamil WhoHol 92
Borgese, Elisabeth Mann 1918- WhoAm 94, WhoScEn 94
Borgese, John A. 1951- WhoAmL 94
Borgese Freschi, Maria 1881-1947 BlmGWL
Borgeson, Earl Charles 1922- WhoAm 94, WhoAmL 94
Borgeson, Ralph Irwin, Jr. 1932- WhoAmP 93
Borgeson, Vernon R. 1920- WhoAmP 93
Borget, Lloyd George 1913- WhoAm 94
Borghardt, P. Bruce 1955- WhoAmL 94
Borghese, Antonio D. R. fl. 18th cent.- NewGrDO
Borghese, Viglione d1957 WhoHol 92
Borghi, Cristiana WhoHol 92
Borghi, Giovanni Battista 1738-1796 NewGrDO
Borghi, Guido Rinaldo 1903-1971 WhoAmA 93N
Borghi-Mamo, Adelaide 1826-1901 NewGrDO
Borgia, John F. 1940- WhoHisp 94
Borgia, Lucrezia 1480-1519 HisWorL [port]
Borgia, Sid 1910- BasBi
Borgia-Aberle, Nina 1955- WhoAmA 93
Borgioli, Armando 1898-1945 NewGrDO
Borgioli, Dino 1891-1960 NewGrDO
Borgiotti, Giorgio Vittorio 1932- WhoAm 94
Borglum, James Lincoln De La Mothe 1912-1986 WhoAmA 93N
Borgman, Bennie 1899- BasBi
Borgman, George Allan 1928- WhoAm 94
Borgman, James Mark 1954- WhoMW 93
Borgman, Jim 1954- WrDr 94
Borgman, Patricia Edna 1948- WhoMW 93
Borgman, Robert Lee 1935- WhoMW 93
Borgmann, Connie Sue 1963- WhoMW 93
Borgnine, Ernest 1917- IntMPA 94, IntWW 93, WhoAm 94
Borgnine, Ernest 1918- WhoHol 92
Borgo, John L. 1949- WhoMW 93
Borgomeo, Pasquale 1933- IntWW 93
Borgos, Stephen John 1941- WhoAm 94
Borgstadt, Elvira 1950- WhoMW 93
Borgstahl, Kaylene Denise 1951- WhoAm 94
Borgstedt, Douglas 1911- WhoAm 94
Borgstedt, Harold Heinrich 1929- WhoAm 94
Borgstrom, Georg Arne 1912-1990 WhAm 10
Borgstrom, Hilda d1953 WhoHol 92
Bori, Lucrezia 1887-1960 NewGrDO
Borich, Michael DrAPF 93
Borie, Bernard Simon, Jr. 1924- WhoScEn 94
Borin, James L. 1944- WhoAmL 94
Boring, Charles Marion 1943- WhoWest 94
Boring, Delbert Franklin 1947- WhoFI 94, WhoMW 93
Boring, Edward d1923 WhoHol 92
Boring, John Wayne 1929- WhoAm 94
Boringdon, Viscount 1956- Who 94
Borinstein, Dennis Ivan 1949- WhoWest 94
Boris EncSF 93
Boris, Anthony d1954 WhoHol 92
Boris, Bessie WhoAmA 93
Boris, Bessie d1993 NewYTBS 93
Boris, Kathleen Vaughan 1947- WhoAmP 93
Boris, Martin DrAPF 93
Boris, Robert 1945- IntMPA 94
Boris, Ruthanna 1918- WhoAm 94
Boris, William O. 1939- WhoAm 94
Borisenko, Vera 1918- NewGrDO
Borisevich, Nikolai Aleksandrovich 1923- IntWW 93
Borish, Elaine WrDr 94
Borisoff, Richard Stuart 1945- WhoAm 94, WhoAmL 94
Borisov, Oleg Ivanovich 1929- IntWW 93
Borisova, Yulia 1925- WhoHol 92
Borisy, Gary G. 1942- WhoScEn 94
Boritt, Gabor Szappanos 1940- WhoAm 94
Borja, Francisco Manglona WhoAmP 93
Borja, Joaquin H. WhoAmP 93
Borja, Mary Ellen Murphy 1942- WhoAmL 94
Borja Cevallos, Rodrigo 1937- IntWW 93
Borjas, George 1950- WhoHisp 94
Borjas, George Jesus 1950- WhoAm 94
Borjon, Robert Patrick 1935- WhoHisp 94
Bork, Alfred 1926- WhoWest 94
Bork, Christopher Edward 1946- WhoMW 93
Bork, Robert H(eron) 1927- WrDr 94
Bork, Robert Heron 1927- IntWW 93, WhoAm 94, WhoAmL 94, WhoAmP 93
Bork, Walter Albert 1927- WhoFI 94
Borkan, William Noah 1956- WhoFI 94
Borker, Wallace Jacob 1919- WhoAmL 94
Borkh, Inge 1917- NewGrDO
Borkh, Inge 1921- IntWW 93
Borko, Harold 1922- WhoAm 94, WrDr 94
Borkovic, David Allen 1950- WhoAm 94, WhoAmL 94
Borkowski, Francis Thomas 1936- WhoAm 94
Borkowski, Vincent 1948- WhoFI 94
Borland, Barbara Dodge d1991 WhAm 10
Borland, Barlowe d1948 WhoHol 92
Borland, Carroll 1914- WhoHol 92
Borland, David Morton 1911- Who 94
Borland, James Barton, Jr. 1945- WhoMW 93
Borland, Kathryn 1916- WrDr 94
Borland, Kathryn Kilby 1916- WhoAm 94
Borland, William K. 1942- WhoIns 94
Borlaug, Allen 1941- WhoAmP 93
Borlaug, Norman E. 1914- EnvEnc [port]
Borlaug, Norman Ernest 1914- IntWW 93, Who 94, WhoAm 94
Borle, Andre Bernard 1930- WhoAm 94
Borleis, Melvin William 1943- WhoFI 94, WhoMW 93
Borley, Lester 1931- Who 94
Borlin, Jean 1893-1930 IntDcB [port]
Borling, John Lorin 1940- WhoAm 94
Borman, Deborah Lynn 1961- WhoMW 93
Borman, Earle Kirkpatrick, Jr. 1930- WhoAm 94
Borman, Frank 1928- IntWW 93, WhoAm 94
Borman, Karen Therese 1960- WhoMW 93
Borman, Paul 1932- WhoFI 94
Bormann, Frederick Herbert 1922- WhoAm 94
Bormann, Maria Benedita Camara de 1853-1895 BlmGWL
Bormolini, Barbara Jean 1962- WhoMW 93
Born, Allen 1933- WhoAm 94, WhoFI 94, WhoScEn 94
Born, Brooksley Elizabeth 1940- WhoAm 94, WhoAmL 94
Born, Claire 1898- NewGrDO
Born, David Omar 1944- WhoScEn 94
Born, Emily Marie 1959- WhoAm 94, WhoMW 93
Born, George H. 1939- WhoScEn 94
Born, Gunthard Karl 1935- WhoScEn 94
Born, Gustav Victor Rudolf 1921- IntWW 93, Who 94
Born, James E. 1934- WhoAmA 93, WhoMW 93
Born, John 1937- WhoAmP 93
Born, Max 1882-1970 WorScD
Born, Samuel Roydon, II 1945- WhoAm 94
Born, Steven Murray 1947- WhoWest 94
Born, Suzanne 1946- WhoAmL 94
Born, Wolfgang 1893-1949 WhoAmA 93N
Bornand, Ruth Chaloux 1901- WhoAm 94
Borne, Allen Helwick, Jr. 1959- WhoAmL 94
Borne, Bonita H. 1953- WhoAm 94
Borne, Keith Michael 1954- WhoAmL 94
Borne, Leon L. 1938- WhoAmP 93
Borne, Mortimer 1902-1987 WhoAmA 93N
Borneman, Ernest 1915- ConAu 41NR
Borneman, John 1952- ConAu 140
Borneman, John Paul 1958- WhoWest 94
Bornemann, Alfred Henry 1908-1991 WhAm 10
Borner, Silvio 1941- IntWW 93
Bornet, Stephen Folwell 1947- WhoAm 94
Bornet, Vaughn Davis 1917- ConAu 42NR, WhoAm 94
Bornewasser, Hans (Johannes Antonius) 1924- IntWW 93
Bornheimer, Allen Millard 1942- WhoAm 94, WhoAmL 94
Bornholdt, Jenny 1960- BlmGWL
Bornholdt, Laura Anna 1919- WhoAm 94
Bornhorst, John Bernard 1942- WhoFI 94
Bornhuetter, Ronald L. 1932- WhoIns 94
Bornino-Glusac, Anna Maria 1946- WhoScEn 94
Bornmann, Carl Malcolm 1936- WhoAm 94, WhoAmL 94
Borns, David James 1950- WhoWest 94
Borns, Harold William, Jr. 1927- WhoAm 94
Borns, Robert Aaron 1935- WhoFI 94, WhoMW 93
Bornstein, Deborah H. 1953- WhoAm 94, WhoAmL 94
Bornstein, Eli 1922- WhoAm 94, WhoAmA 93, WhoWest 94
Bornstein, George 1941- WrDr 94
Bornstein, George Jay 1941- WhoAm 94
Bornstein, Jeffrey Victor 1950- WhoMW 93
Bornstein, Julia WhoAmP 93
Bornstein, Lester Milton 1925- WhoAm 94
Bornstein, Morris 1927- WhoAm 94
Bornstein, Paul 1934- WhoAm 94
Bornstein, Rita 1936- WhoAm 94
Bornstein, Robert Joseph 1937- WhoAm 94
Bornstein, Ronald E. 1945- WhoAmL 94
Borny, Walter Michael 1948- WhoWest 94
Borochoff, (Ida) Sloan 1939- WhoAmA 93
Borock, Herb WhoAmP 93
Borod, Richard Melvin 1933- WhoAm 94, WhoAmL 94
Borod, Ronald Sam 1941- WhoAm 94, WhoAmL 94
Borodale, Viscount 1973- Who 94
Borodin, Alexander Porfir'yevich 1833-1887 NewGrDO
Borodin, George Who 94
Borodin, George 1903- EncSF 93
Borodin, Oleg Petrovich LoBiDrD
Borodinsky, Samuel 1941- IntMPA 94
Borofsky, Jon 1942- WhoAmA 93
Borofsky, Jonathan 1942- WhoAm 94
Borom, Lawrence H. 1937- WhoBlA 94
Boronat, Olimpia 1867-1934 NewGrDO
Boroni, Antonio 1738-1792 NewGrDO
Boros, Ferike d1951 WhoHol 92
Boros, Jerome S. 1926- WhoAm 94
Borosini, Antonio c. 1655-1721? NewGrDO
Borosini, Francesco c. 1690-1747? NewGrDO
Boroskin, Alan 1942- WhoWest 94
Boross, Peter 1928- IntWW 93
Borotra, Jean 1898- BuCMET [port]
Borotra, Jean (Robert) 1898- IntWW 93
Borough, Stephen 1525-1584 WhWE
Borough, William 1536-1599 WhWE
Borovansky, Edouard 1902-1959 IntDcB
Borovik, Artyom 1960- ConAu 141
Borovik-Romanov, Viktor-Andrey Stanislavovich 1920- IntWW 93
Borovkov, Aleksandr Alekseyevich 1931- IntWW 93
Borovoi, Konstantin Natanovich 1948- IntWW 93, LoBiDrD
Borovoy, Marc Allen 1960- WhoMW 93, WhoScEn 94
Borovoy, Roger Stuart 1935- WhoAm 94
Borovski, Conrad 1930- WhoWest 94
Borow, Richard Henry 1935- WhoAm 94
Borowitz, Albert Ira 1930- WhoAm 94

Borowitz, Grace Burchman 1934- *WhoAm 94*
Borowitz, Joseph Leo 1932- *WhoAm 94*
Borowitz, Katherine *WhoHol 92*
Borowitz, Sidney 1918- *WhoAm 94*
Borowski, Jennifer Lucile 1934- *WhoFI 94*
Borowski, Tadeusz 1922-1951 *RfGShF*
Borowsky, Philip 1946- *WhoAm 94*
Borradaile, Hugh Alastair 1907- *Who 94*
Borre, Preudhomme de *WhAmRev*
Borreca, John Peter 1953- *WhoFI 94*
Borrego, Carlos Soares 1948- *WhoScEn 94*
Borrego, Jesus Garcia 1953- *WhoWest 94*
Borrel, Andre 1936- *WhoAm 94, WhoFI 94, WhoWest 94*
Borrell, Anthony J., Jr. 1940- *WhoHisp 94*
Borrell, Tommy Joseph 1946- *WhoHisp 94*
Borrell Fontelles, Jose 1947- *IntWW 93*
Borrelli, Charles 1898- *WhoHol 92*
Borrelli, James Vincent 1962- *WhoMW 93*
Borrelli, Mario 1922- *IntWW 93*
Borrero, Dulce Maria 1883-1945 *BlmGWL*
Borrero, I. Michael *WhoHisp 94*
Borrero, Juana 1877-1896 *BlmGWL*
Borrero-de Jesús, Nydia 1963- *WhoHisp 94*
Borresen, (Aksel Ejnar) Hakon 1876-1954 *NewGrDO*
Borrett, Charles Walter 1916- *Who 94*
Borrett, Louis Albert Frank 1924- *Who 94*
Borrett, Neil Edgar 1940- *Who 94*
Borri, Carlo *NewGrDO*
Borrie, Gordon 1931- *IntWW 93*
Borrie, Gordon (Johnson) 1931- *Who 94*
Borrie, John 1915- *WrDr 94*
Borrie, Wilfred David 1913- *IntWW 93*
Borror, Caywood Joseph 1930- *WhoAmL 94*
Borrow, George Henry 1803-1881 *BlmGEL*
Borrus, Jack 1928- *WhoAm 94*
Borrus, Michael (Glen) 1956- *ConAu 141*
Bors, Linda Jean 1955- *WhoMW 93*
Borsa, Andrew J. 1944- *WhoAmP 93*
Borsari, George Robert, Jr. 1940- *WhoAm 94*
Borsch, Frederick Houk 1935- *WhoAm 94, WhoWest 94*
Borsche, Dieter d1982 *WhoHol 92*
Borschke, Daniel Christopher 1952- *WhoMW 93*
Borsheim, Curtis Allen 1955- *WhoAmL 94*
Borsick, Marlin Lester 1953- *WhoMW 93*
Borski, Robert A. 1948- *CngDr 93, WhoAmP 93*
Borski, Robert Anthony 1948- *WhoAm 94*
Borski, Thomas Anthony 1941- *WhoFI 94*
Borsody, Robert Peter 1937- *WhoAm 94*
Borson, Daniel Benjamin 1946- *WhoScEn 94, WhoWest 94*
Borson, Robert Oliver 1938- *WhoWest 94*
Borson, Roo 1952- *BlmGWL*
Borst, David Wellington 1918- *WhoAm 94*
Borst, John, Jr. 1927- *WhoAm 94, WhoAmL 94*
Borst, Lawrence Marion 1927- *WhoAmP 93*
Borst, Lyle Benjamin 1912- *WhoAm 94, WhoScEn 94*
Borst, Philip Craig 1950- *WhoAmP 93*
Borst, Philip West 1928- *WhoAm 94*
Borst, Piet 1934- *IntWW 93*
Borst, Scott William 1958- *WhoMW 93*
Borst, Terry *DrAPF 93*
Borstein, Elena 1946- *WhoAmA 93*
Borstein, Yetta d1968 *WhoAmA 93N*
Borstelmann, Thomas 1958- *ConAu 142*
Borsten, Rick 1955- *ConAu 140*
Borsting, Jack Raymond 1929- *WhoAm 94, WhoWest 94*
Borteck, Robert D. 1947- *WhoAm 94, WhoAmL 94*
Bortell, Glen *WhoAmP 93*
Borten, Per 1913- *IntWW 93*
Borten, William H. 1935- *WhoAm 94*
Borth, Ray Lynn 1943- *WhoAmL 94*
Borthakur, Dulal 1955- *WhoWest 94*
Borthwick *Who 94*
Borthwick, Lord 1905- *Who 94*
Borthwick, Master of 1940- *Who 94*
Borthwick, J. S. *WrDr 94*
Borthwick, James Ross 1938- *WhoAmL 94*
Borthwick, Jason *Who 94*
Borthwick, (William) Jason (Maxwell) 1910- *Who 94*
Borthwick, John Thomas 1917- *Who 94*
Borthwick, Kenneth W. 1915- *Who 94*
Borthwick, Wm. Harold 1948- *WhoAmL 94*
Bortin, Mortimer M. 1922- *WhoAm 94*
Bortko, Edward Joseph 1929- *WhoMW 93*
Bortle, Mark Robert 1955- *WhoMW 93*
Bortman, David 1938- *WhoAm 94*
Bortner, James Bradley 1958- *WhoScEn 94*
Bortner, Michael E. 1949- *WhoAmP 93*
Bortnyansky, Dmitry Stepanovich 1751-1825 *NewGrDO*
Bortolotti, Mauro 1926- *NewGrDO*
Bortolussi, Michael Richard 1956- *WhoWest 94*
Bortoluzzi, Paolo d1993 *NewYTBS 93 [port]*
Bortoluzzi, Paolo 1938- *IntDcB [port], IntWW 93*
Borton, George Robert 1922- *WhoWest 94*
Borton, John Carter, Jr. 1938- *WhoAm 94*
Borton, Robert Ernest 1942- *WhoAm 94*
Bortz, Daniel 1943- *NewGrDO*
Bortz, Edward Leroy 1896- *WhAm 10*
Bortz, Fred 1944- *ConAu 141, SmATA 74 [port]*
Bortz, Paul Isaac 1937- *WhoAm 94*
Bortz, Phyllis E. 1926- *WhoFI 94*
Boru, Brian c. 941-1014 *HisWorL [port]*
Boruch, Marianne *DrAPF 93*
Boruchowitz, Stephen Alan 1952- *WhoWest 94*
Boruff, John 1910- *WhoHol 92*
Boruff, John David 1930- *WhoMW 93*
Borum, Isabel *WhoAmP 93*
Borum, Regina A. 1938- *WhoBlA 94*
Borum, Rodney Lee 1929- *WhoAm 94, WhoFI 94*
Borum, William Donald 1932- *WhoFI 94*
Borunda, Daniel Manuel 1959- *WhoHisp 94*
Borunda, Ernest *WhoHisp 94*
Borunda, Kathy *WhoHisp 94*
Borunda, Luis G. 1935- *WhoHisp 94*
Borunda, Mario Rene 1952- *WhoHisp 94*
Borunda, Patrick 1947- *WhoWest 94*
Boruszak, James Martin 1930- *WhoMW 93*
Borut, Donald J. 1941- *WhoAm 94*
Borwein, David 1924- *WhoAm 94*
Borwick, Baron 1917- *Who 94*
Bory, Jean-Marc *WhoHol 92*
Boryla, Vince 1927- *BasBi*
Borysewicz, Mary Louise *WhoMW 93*
Borzaga, Marita 1936- *WhoAmP 93*
Borzage, Danny d1975 *WhoHol 92*
Borzage, Frank d1962 *WhoHol 92*
Borzio, Carlo fl. c. 1656-1676 *NewGrDO*
Borzov, Valeriy Filippovich 1949- *IntWW 93*
Borzutzky, Silvia 1946- *WhoHisp 94*
Bos, Annie d1975 *WhoHol 92*
Bos, John Arthur 1933- *WhoScEn 94, WhoWest 94*
Bos, Norman Calvin 1924- *WhoMW 93*
Bosa, Louis 1905-1981 *WhoAmA 93N*
Bosabalian, Luisa 1936- *NewGrDO*
Bosacchi, Bruno 1938- *WhoScEn 94*
Bosakov, Joseph Blagoev 1942- *WhoAm 94*
Bosan, Alonso d1959 *WhoHol 92*
Bosanquet, Helen 1860-1925 *DcNaB MP*
Bosanquet, Nick 1942- *WrDr 94*
Bosart, Lance F. 1942- *WhoAm 94, WhoScEn 94*
Bosbach, Bruno 1932- *WhoScEn 94*
Bos-Beernink, B.F. 1931- *WhoWomW 91*
Boscaglia, Clara *WhoWomW 91*
Boscawen *Who 94*
Boscawen, Frances 1719-1805 *BlmGWL*
Boscawen, Robert Thomas 1923- *Who 94*
Bosch, Brian A. 1959- *WhoAmL 94*
Bosch, Carl 1874-1940 *WorInv*
Bosch, Daniel *DrAPF 93*
Bosch, Guillermo L. 1949- *WhoHisp 94*
Bosch, Henry G(erard) 1914- *WrDr 94*
Bosch, John Albert 1929- *WhoMW 93*
Bosch, Juan 1909- *IntWW 93*
Bosch, Peter Daniel 1958- *WhoAmL 94*
Bosch, Robert August 1861-1942 *WorInv*
Bosch, Robert John, Jr. 1945- *WhoScEn 94*
Bosch, Samuel Henry 1934- *WhoAm 94*
Bosche, Robert Paul, Jr. 1951- *WhoWest 94*
Boschert, Douglas Francis 1921- *WhoAmP 93*
Boschi, Francesca *NewGrDO*
Boschi, Giulia *WhoHol 92*
Boschi, Giuseppe Maria fl. 1698-1744 *NewGrDO*
Boschi, Srdjan 1927- *WhoScEn 94*
Boschulte, Alfred F. 1942- *WhoBlA 94*
Boschulte, Joseph Clement 1931- *WhoBlA 94*
Boschwitz, Rudy 1930- *IntWW 93, WhoAmP 93*
Bosco, Anthony Gerard 1927- *WhoAm 94*
Bosco, Douglas H. 1946- *WhoAmP 93*
Bosco, Giacinto 1905- *IntWW 93*
Bosco, Jay William 1951- *WhoMW 93*
Bosco, Joseph A. 1938- *WhoAmP 93*
Bosco, Maria Angelica 1917- *BlmGWL*
Bosco, Monique 1927- *BlmGWL*
Bosco, Paul D. *WhoScEn 94*
Bosco, Philip 1930- *ConTFT 11, IntMPA 94, WhoHol 92*
Bosco, Philip Michael 1930- *WhoAm 94*
Bosco, Ronald F. 1950- *WhoScEn 94*
Bosco, Wallace *WhoHol 92*
Boscolo, Benjamin Tederick 1961- *WhoAmL 94*
Bose, Ajay Kumar 1925- *WhoScEn 94*
Bose, Amar Gopal 1929- *WhoAm 94, WhoFI 94, WhoScEn 94*
Bose, Animesh 1953- *WhoFI 94, WhoScEn 94*
Bose, Anjan 1946- *WhoAm 94, WhoScEn 94, WhoWest 94*
Bose, Bimal Kumar 1932- *WhoAm 94, WhoAsA 94*
Bose, Carl Ernst Johann von *WhAmRev*
Bose, Hans-Jurgen von 1953- *NewGrDO*
Bose, Joachim d1971 *WhoHol 92*
Bose, Katrick *EncSPD*
Bose, Lucia 1931- *WhoHol 92*
Bose, Miguel 1956- *WhoHol 92*
Bose, Mihir 1947- *Who 94*
Bose, Nirmal Kumar 1940- *WhoAm 94*
Bose, Pratim 1956- *WhoAsA 94*
Bose, Subir Kumar 1931- *WhoAm 94*
Bosee, John Kennard, 4th 1952- *WhoAmL 94*
Boseker, Barbara Jean 1944- *WhoMW 93*
Boselli, Anna 1943- *WhoWomW 91*
Bosello, Anna *NewGrDO*
Boserup, Ester Talke 1910- *IntWW 93*
Bosetti, Hermine 1875-1936 *NewGrDO*
Boshears, Edward E. 1946- *WhoAmP 93*
Boshell, Ada d1924 *WhoHol 92*
Boshell, Buris Raye 1926- *WhoAm 94*
Bosher, John Francis 1929- *IntWW 93*
Boshes, Louis D. 1908- *WhoAm 94*
Boshier, Maureen Louise 1946- *WhoFI 94*
Boshkov, Stefan Hristov 1918- *WhoAm 94, WhoScEn 94*
Boshkov, Stefan Robert 1949- *WhoAm 94, WhoAmL 94*
Boshoff, Carel Willem Hendrik 1927- *IntWW 93*
Bosick, Joseph John, Jr. 1947- *WhoAmL 94*
Bosin, Blackbear 1921-1980 *WhoAmA 93N*
Bosio, Angelo 1955- *WhoScEn 94*
Bosio, Angiolina 1830-1859 *NewGrDO*
Boskey, Bennett 1916- *WhoAm 94*
Boskin, Joseph 1929- *WrDr 94*
Boskin, Michael Jay 1945- *IntWW 93, WhoAm 94, WhoAmP 93*
Boskind, Paul Arthur 1929- *WhoAm 94*
Boskoff, Alvin 1924- *WrDr 94*
Boskovic, Anica 1714-1804 *BlmGWL*
Boskovsky, Willi 1909-1991 *NewGrDO*
Boskowsky, Willy 1909-1991 *WhAm 10*
Bosl, Phillip L. 1945- *WhoAm 94, WhoAmL 94*
Bosland, Chelcie Clayton 1901- *WrDr 94*
Boslaugh, Leslie 1917- *WhoAm 94, WhoAmL 94, WhoAmP 93, WhoMW 93*
Bosley, Daniel Edward 1953- *WhoAmP 93*
Bosley, David Calvin 1959- *WhoScEn 94*
Bosley, Freeman R., Jr. 1954- *WhoAmP 93*
Bosley, Freeman Robertson, Jr. 1954- *WhoBlA 94*
Bosley, John Scott 1943- *WhoAm 94*
Bosley, Keith 1937-1987 *WrDr 94N*
Bosley, Robert Andrew 1964- *WhoMW 93*
Bosley, Thad 1956- *WhoBlA 94*
Bosley, Tom 1927- *IntMPA 94, WhoAm 94, WhoHol 92*
Bosley, Warren Guy 1922- *WhoScEn 94*
Boslow, Edward S., III 1956- *WhoFI 94*
Bosma, Brian Charles 1957- *WhoAmP 93*
Bosma, Charles Edward 1922- *WhoAmP 93*
Bosma, James Frederick 1916- *WhoScEn 94*
Bosma, Janice Mae 1952- *WhoMW 93*
Bosmajian, Haig 1928- *WrDr 94*
Bosmajian, Haig Aram 1928- *WhoAm 94*
Bosman, Herman Charles 1905-1951 *RfGShF, TwCLC 49 [port]*
Bosman, Paul Wray 1929- *WhoWest 94*
Bosman, Richard 1944- *WhoAmA 93*
Bosnak, Robert J. *WhoScEn 94*
Bosniak, Morton Arthur 1929- *WhoAm 94*
Bosomworth, Peter Palliser 1930- *WhoAm 94*
Bosonnet, Paul Graham 1932- *Who 94*
Bosquet, Alain 1919- *IntWW 93*
Bosquez, Jess 1935- *WhoHisp 94*
Bosquez, Juan Manuel 1941- *WhoHisp 94*
Boss, Amelia Helen 1949- *WhoAmL 94*
Boss, Hugh M. 1947- *WhoAmL 94*
Boss, Kenneth Jay 1935- *WhoAm 94*
Boss, Laura *DrAPF 93*
Boss, Lenard Barrett 1960- *WhoAmL 94*
Boss, Michael Alan 1955- *WhoScEn 94*
Boss, Pauline Grossenbacher 1934- *WhoMW 93*
Boss, Russel Wayne 1943- *WhoAm 94*
Boss, Yale d1977 *WhoHol 92*
Bossaller, Harold Dean 1946- *WhoMW 93*
Bossano, Joseph 1939- *Who 94*
Bossano, Joseph J. 1939- *IntWW 93*
Bossanyi, Katalin *WhoWomW 91*
Bossard, Andre 1926- *IntWW 93*
Bossart, William Haines *WhoWest 94*
Bossbach, Shirley Cagle 1941- *WhoAmP 93*
Bosse, Fred Charles 1949- *WhoIns 94*
Bosse, Fred M. 1947- *WhoAmP 93*
Bosse, Harriet d1961 *WhoHol 92*
Bosse, Janet C. *WhoAmA 93*
Bosse, Leigh Dennis 1947- *WhoAmP 93*
Bosse, Malcolm J. *DrAPF 93*
Bosse, Virginia Mae 1927- *WhoAmP 93*
Bosseau, Donald Lee 1936- *WhoAm 94*
Bosselman, Fred Paul 1934- *WhoAm 94, WhoAmL 94*
Bossemeyer, William John, III 1950- *WhoFI 94*
Bossen, David August 1927- *WhoAm 94, WhoWest 94*
Bossen, Wendell John 1933- *WhoAm 94*
Bosserman, Gordon E. 1948- *WhoAmL 94*
Bosserman, Joseph Norwood 1925- *WhoAm 94*
Bosserman, Lorelei 1964- *WhoWest 94*
Bossert, David Edward 1962- *WhoScEn 94*
Bossert, Edythe H. 1908- *WhoAmA 93*
Bossert, Philip Joseph 1944- *WhoFI 94*
Bosses, Stevan J. 1937- *WhoAmL 94*
Bossi, (Rinaldo) Renzo 1883-1965 *NewGrDO*
Bossick, Bernard d1975 *WhoHol 92*
Bossidy, Lawrence Arthur 1935- *IntWW 93, WhoAm 94, WhoFI 94*
Bossie, Robert F. 1942- *WhoAmP 93*
Bossier, Albert Louis, Jr. 1932- *WhoAm 94, WhoFI 94*
Bossmeyer, Glenn David *WhoAmL 94*
Bossom, Clive 1918- *Who 94*
Bosson, Barbara 1940- *WhoHol 92*
Bosson, Bernard 1948- *IntWW 93*
Bosson, Jack, Jr. 1937- *WhoAmA 93*
Bossone, Richard M. 1924- *WrDr 94*
Bossong, Kenneth James 1952- *WhoAmL 94*
Bossuet, Jacques-Benigne 1627-1704 *GuFrLit 2*
Bossy, John Antony 1933- *Who 94*
Bossy, Michael 1957- *WhoAm 94*
Bossy, Michael Joseph Frederick 1929- *Who 94*
Bost, Fred M. 1938- *WhoBlA 94*
Bost, Pierre 1901-1975 *IntDcF 2-4*
Bost, Raymond Morris 1925- *WhoAm 94*
Bost, Thomas Glen 1942- *WhoAm 94, WhoAmL 94, WhoWest 94*
Bostaph, Paul
See Slayer *ConMus 10*
Bostedt, Marina Debellagente *DrAPF 93*
Bostel, Lucas von 1649-1716 *NewGrDO*
Bostelle, Thomas (Theodore) 1921- *WhoAmA 93*
Boster, Constanza Helena G. 1944- *WhoFI 94*
Boster, Davis Eugene 1920- *WhoAmP 93*
Bosterud, Helen 1940- *IntWW 93*
Bostetter, Martin V. B., Jr. 1926- *WhoAm 94, WhoAmL 94*
Bostian, Harry Edward 1933- *WhoAm 94, WhoMW 93*
Bostic, Dorothy d1992 *WhoBlA 94N*
Bostic, Florine 1934- *WhoAm 94*
Bostic, James Edward, Jr. 1947- *WhoBlA 94*
Bostic, Lee H. 1935- *WhoBlA 94*
Bosticco, (Isabel Lucy) Mary *WrDr 94*
Bostick, Charles Dent 1931- *WhoAm 94*
Bostick, George Hale 1944- *WhoAm 94, WhoAmL 94*
Bostick, Henry *WhoAmP 93*
Bostick, Robert L. 1909- *IntMPA 94*
Bostick, William Allison 1913- *WhoAmA 93*
Bostick, William Green, Jr. 1953- *WhoAmL 94*
Bostin, Marvin Jay 1933- *WhoAm 94*
Bostleman, Richard Lee 1944- *WhoAm 94*
Bostock, Barbara 1935- *WhoHol 92*
Bostock, David 1936- *WrDr 94*
Bostock, David John 1948- *Who 94*
Bostock, Donald Ivan 1924- *WrDr 94*
Bostock, Evelyn d1944 *WhoHol 92*
Bostock, James Edward 1917- *Who 94*
Bostock, Peter Geoffrey 1911- *Who 94*
Bostock, Roy Jackson 1940- *WhoAm 94, WhoFI 94*
Boston *ConMus 11 [port], Who 94*
Boston, Baron 1939- *Who 94*
Boston, Anne 1945- *WrDr 94*
Boston, Archie, Jr. 1943- *WhoBlA 94*

Boston, Bernard d1989 *WhoHol 92*
Boston, Betty Lee 1935- *WhoFI 94*
Boston, Betty Roach 1926- *WhoWest 94*
Boston, Bruce 1943- *EncSF 93*
Boston, Charles D. 1928- *WhoAm 94*
Boston, Daryl Lamont 1963- *WhoBlA 94*
Boston, David Merrick 1931- *Who 94*
Boston, Derrick Osmond 1964- *WhoAmL 94*
Boston, Edward Dale 1942- *WhoAm 94*
Boston, Eugene Alfred 1928- *WhoAmP 93*
Boston, Frank D., Jr. 1938- *WhoAmP 93*
Boston, Garry 1936- *WhoAmP 93*
Boston, George David 1923- *WhoBlA 94*
Boston, Horace Oscar 1934- *WhoBlA 94*
Boston, James Robert, Jr. 1958- *WhoAmL 94*
Boston, Jonathan 1957- *ConAu 140*
Boston, L(ucy) M(aria Wood) 1892-1990 *TwCYAW*
Boston, Leona 1914- *WhoAm 94, WhoMW 93*
Boston, Louis Russell 1937- *WhoScEn 94*
Boston, Lucy 1892-1990 *BlmGWL*
Boston, Marcia Ann 1938- *WhoWest 94*
Boston, McKinley, Jr. 1945- *WhoBlA 94*
Boston, Nelroy Buck d1962 *WhoHol 92*
Boston, Ralph 1939- *WhoBlA 94*
Boston, Richard 1938- *Who 94*
Boston, Wallace Ellsworth, Jr. 1954- *WhoFI 94*
Boston, William Clayton 1934- *WhoAmL 94*
Boston Of Faversham, Baron 1930- *Who 94*
Bostrom, Carl Otto 1932- *WhoAm 94, WhoScEn 94*
Bostrom, Curt 1926- *IntWW 93*
Bostrom, Rolf Gustav 1936- *IntWW 93*
Bostwick, Angelina Celeste 1969- *WhoWest 94*
Bostwick, Barry *WhoHol 92*
Bostwick, Barry 1945- *IntMPA 94, WhoAm 94*
Bostwick, Fredrick deBurlo, III 1953- *WhoAmL 94*
Bostwick, Randell A. 1922- *WhoAm 94*
Bostwick, Richard Raymond 1918- *WhoAmL 94*
Bosustow, Nick 1940- *IntMPA 94*
Bosustow, Nick Onslow 1940- *WhoWest 94*
Bosustow, Stephen 1911-1981 *IntDcF 2-4*
Bosustow, Ted 1938- *IntMPA 94*
Bosveld, Jennifer Groce Welch *DrAPF 93*
Bosville Macdonald Of Sleat, Ian Godfrey 1947- *Who 94*
Boswall, (Thomas) Alford H. *Who 94*
Boswall, Jeffery 1931- *IntMPA 94*
Boswell *ConAu 43NR*
Boswell, Alexander (Crawford Simpson) 1928- *Who 94*
Boswell, Annabella 1826-1916 *BlmGWL*
Boswell, Arnita J. *WhoBlA 94*
Boswell, Arthur W. 1909- *WhoBlA 94*
Boswell, Bennie, Jr. 1948- *WhoBlA 94*
Boswell, Christopher 1957- *WhoAmP 93*
Boswell, Christopher Orr 1957- *WhoWest 94*
Boswell, Connee d1976 *WhoHol 92*
Boswell, David E. 1949- *WhoAmP 93*
Boswell, Fred C. 1930- *WhoScEn 94*
Boswell, Gary Taggart 1937- *WhoAm 94*
Boswell, George Marion, Jr. 1920- *WhoFI 94*
Boswell, James 1740-1795 *BlmGEL*
Boswell, James Douglas 1942- *WhoAm 94*
Boswell, John (Eastburn) 1947- *GayLL, WrDr 94*
Boswell, John Howard 1932- *WhoAmL 94*
Boswell, Larry Ray 1940- *WhoMW 93*
Boswell, Leonard L. 1934- *WhoAmP 93, WhoMW 93*
Boswell, Marion Lillard 1923- *WhoAm 94*
Boswell, Martha d1958 *WhoHol 92*
Boswell, Nathalie Spence 1924- *WhoMW 93*
Boswell, Paul P. 1905- *WhoBlA 94*
Boswell, Peyton, Jr. 1904-1950 *WhoAmA 93N*
Boswell, Philip John 1949- *WhoAm 94*
Boswell, Robert *DrAPF 93*
Boswell, Robert 1953- *WrDr 94*
Boswell, Rupert Dean, Jr. 1929- *WhoAm 94*
Boswell, Susan G. 1945- *WhoAmL 94*
Boswell, Thomas Murray 1947- *WhoAm 94*
Boswell, Thomas Wayne 1944- *WhoFI 94*
Boswell, Timothy Eric 1942- *Who 94*
Boswell, Vet d1988 *WhoHol 92*
Boswell, William Douglas 1918- *WhoAmL 94*
Boswell, William Paret 1946- *WhoAmL 94*
Boswood, Anthony Richard 1947- *Who 94*
Bosworth, Brian 1964- *WhoHol 92*
Bosworth, Bruce Leighton 1942- *WhoWest 94*
Bosworth, Bruce Lynn 1943- *WhoWest 94*
Bosworth, Clifford Edmund 1928- *Who 94*
Bosworth, David *DrAPF 93*
Bosworth, Douglas LeRoy 1939- *WhoAm 94, WhoScEn 94*
Bosworth, Hobart d1943 *WhoHol 92*
Bosworth, Jeffrey Willson 1948- *WhoMW 93*
Bosworth, (John) Michael (Worthington) 1921- *Who 94*
Bosworth, Neville (Bruce Alfred) 1918- *Who 94*
Bosworth, Patricia *WhoHol 92*
Bosworth, R(ichard) J(ames) B(oon) 1943- *WrDr 94*
Bosworth, Stephen Warren 1939- *WhoAmP 93*
Bosworth, Thomas Lawrence 1930- *WhoWest 94*
Boszin, Andrew 1923- *WhoAmA 93*
Botan 1945- *BlmGWL*
Botana, William Amadeo 1920- *WhoHisp 94*
Botcher, Scott Allyn 1962- *WhoMW 93*
Boteler, Charlotte *NewGrDO*
Boteler, Wade d1943 *WhoHol 92*
Boteler, William fl. 1640-1660 *DcNaB MP*
Botelho, Bruce M. 1948- *WhoAmP 93*
Botelho, Bruce Manuel 1948- *WhoWest 94*
Botelho, Eugene G. E. *DrAPF 93*
Botelho, Fernanda 1926- *BlmGWL*
Botelho, Joao 1949- *IntWW 93*
Botelho, Robert Gilbert 1948- *WhoScEn 94*
Botelho, Stephen M. *WhoHisp 94*
Botella, Rita Ann 1951- *WhoHisp 94*
Botello, Angel 1913-1986 *WhoAmA 93N*
Botello, John Lynn, Sr. 1953- *WhoHisp 94*
Botello, Jorge Alberto 1969- *WhoHisp 94*
Botello, Michael Steven 1950- *WhoHisp 94*
Botello, Troy James 1953- *WhoWest 94*
Boterf, Check 1934- *WhoAmA 93*
Botero 1932- *IntWW 93*
Botero, Fernando 1932- *WhoAm 94, WhoAmA 93*
Botero Restrepo, Oscar 1933- *IntWW 93*
Botetourt, Norbonne Berkeley, Baron de 1718-1770 *WhAmRev*
Botez, Dan 1948- *WhoAm 94*
Botha, Jan Christoffel Greyling (Stoffel) 1929- *IntWW 93*
Botha, Louis 1862-1919 *HisWorL [port]*
Botha, Matthys (Izak) 1913- *Who 94*
Botha, Matthys Izak 1913- *IntWW 93*
Botha, Pieter Willem 1916- *IntWW 93, Who 94*
Botha, Roelof Frederik 1932- *Who 94*
Botha, Roelof Frederik (Pik) 1932- *IntWW 93*
Botham, Ian Terence 1955- *IntWW 93, Who 94*
Bothe, Robert J. 1951- *WhoAmL 94*
Bothmer, Bernard V. d1993 *NewYTBS 93 [port]*
Bothmer, Bernard V. 1912- *WhoAmA 93*
Bothmer, Dietrich Felix von 1918- *WhoAm 94, WhoAmA 93*
Bothner-By, Aksel Arnold 1921- *WhoAm 94*
Bothroyd, Shirley Ann 1958- *Who 94*
Bothuel, Ethel C. S. 1941- *WhoBlA 94*
Bothwell, Dorr 1902- *WhoAm 94*
Bothwell, John d1967 *WhoHol 92*
Bothwell, John Charles 1926- *Who 94, WhoAm 94*
Bothwell, Thomas Hamilton 1926- *IntWW 93*
Botica, Matthew J. 1951- *WhoAm 94, WhoAmL 94*
Botifoll, Luis J. *WhoHisp 94*
Botimer, Allen Ray 1930- *WhoWest 94*
Botkin, Daniel B. 1937- *WrDr 94*
Botkin, Henry 1896-1983 *WhoAmA 93N*
Botkin, Monty Lane 1951- *WhoFI 94*
Botkin, Perry d1973 *WhoHol 92*
Botley, Calvin 1944- *WhoAm 94, WhoAmL 94*
Botman, Selma 1950- *WrDr 94*
Botos, Katalin *WhoWomW 91*
Botsai, Elmer Eugene 1928- *WhoAm 94*
Botsch, Sharyn 1950- *WhoMW 93*
Botsford, Sara *WhoHol 92*
Botsko, Ronald Joseph 1937- *WhoWest 94*
Botstein, David 1942- *IntWW 93, WhoAm 94, WhoScEn 94*
Botstein, Leon 1946- *WhoAm 94*
Bott, H(arvey) J(ohn) 1933- *WhoAmA 93*
Bott, Harold Sheldon 1933- *WhoAm 94*
Bott, Ian Bernard 1932- *Who 94*
Bott, John 1936- *WhoAmA 93*
Bott, John Charles 1960- *WhoAmP 93*
Bott, Margaret Deats *WhoAmA 93*
Bott, Martin Harold Phillips 1926- *IntWW 93, Who 94*
Bott, Patricia Allen *WhoAmA 93*
Bott, Raoul 1923- *IntWW 93, WhoAm 94, WhoScEn 94*
Bottacchiari, Ugo 1879-1944 *NewGrDO*
Bottai, Bruno 1930- *IntWW 93, Who 94*
Bottar, Anthony Samuel 1950- *WhoAmL 94*
Bottarelli, Giovanni Gualberto fl. 1762-1779 *NewGrDO*
Bottaro, Timothy Shanahan 1958- *WhoAmP 93*
Bottel, Helen 1914- *WrDr 94*
Bottel, Helen Alfea *WhoAm 94, WhoWest 94*
Bottelli, Richard 1937- *WhoAm 94*
Bottenfield, Jack L. *WhoAm 94*
Bottenus, Ralph Edward 1956- *WhoScEn 94*
Botteri, Richard Merlo 1945- *WhoAmP 93*
Bottero, Philippe Bernard 1940- *WhoScEn 94*
Bottesini, Giovanni 1821-1889 *NewGrDO*
Bottger, Lorna Conley 1910- *WhoAmP 93*
Bottger, William Carl, Jr. 1941- *WhoAm 94*
Botti, Aldo E. 1936- *WhoMW 93*
Botti, Richard Charles 1939- *WhoWest 94*
Bottiger, R. Ted 1932- *WhoAmP 93*
Bottiglia, Frank Robert 1946- *WhoFI 94*
Bottiglia, William Filbert 1912- *WhoAm 94*
Bottin, Rob c. 1958- *IntDcF 2-4*
Botting, David Francis Edmund 1937- *Who 94*
Botting, Douglas 1934- *WrDr 94*
Botting, Louise 1939- *Who 94*
Bottini, David M. 1945- *WhoAmA 93*
Bottini, Joseph W. *WhoAmL 94*
Bottini, Reginald Norman 1916- *Who 94*
Bottini, Thomas H. 1943- *WhoAm 94, WhoAmL 94*
Bottis, Hugh P. d1964 *WhoAmA 93N*
Bottjer, David John 1951- *WhoScEn 94*
Bottner, Irving Joseph 1916- *WhoAm 94, WhoFI 94*
Botto De Barros, Adwaldo Cardoso 1925- *IntWW 93, Who 94*
Bottom, Dale Coyle 1932- *WhoAm 94*
Bottomley, Baron 1907- *Who 94*
Bottomley, Lady 1906- *Who 94*
Bottomley, Jacob 1613-c. 1685 *DcNaB MP*
Bottomley, James (Reginald Alfred) 1920- *Who 94*
Bottomley, Peter James 1944- *Who 94*
Bottomley, Roland d1947 *WhoHol 92*
Bottomley, Virginia (Hilda Brunette Maxwell) 1948- *Who 94*
Bottomley, Virginia Hilda Brunette Maxwell 1948- *IntWW 93, WhoWomW 91*
Bottomore, T(homas) B(urton) 1920-1992 *ConAu 140*
Bottomore, Thomas (Burton) 1920-1992 *WrDr 94N*
Bottomore, Tom 1920-1992 *AnObit 1992*
Bottoms, Anthony Edward 1939- *Who 94*
Bottoms, Ben 1960- *WhoHol 92*
Bottoms, David *DrAPF 93*
Bottoms, James A. *WhoHol 92*
Bottoms, John *WhoHol 92*
Bottoms, Joseph 1954- *IntMPA 94, WhoHol 92*
Bottoms, Robert Garvin 1944- *WhoAm 94, WhoMW 93*
Bottoms, Sam 1955- *IntMPA 94, WhoHol 92*
Bottoms, Timothy 1951- *IntMPA 94, WhoHol 92*
Bottoms, William Clay, Jr. 1946- *WhoWest 94*
Bottone, Bonaventura 1950- *NewGrDO*
Bottorff, C. W. 1941- *WhoWest 94*
Bottorff, Dennis C. 1944- *WhoAm 94, WhoFI 94*
Bottorff, James L. 1944- *WhoAmP 93*
Bottrall, Margaret (Florence Saumarez) 1909- *WrDr 94*
Botts, Elizabeth Doris 1956- *WhoMW 93*
Botts, Pamela Jean 1943- *WhoMW 93*
Bottum, Thomas George 1950- *WhoIns 94*
Botturini, Mattia 1752-1797? *NewGrDO*
Botty, Kenneth John 1927- *WhoAm 94*
Botvinnik, Mikhail Moiseyevich 1911- *IntWW 93*
Botvinnik, Mikhail Moisseyevich 1911- *Who 94*
Botwick, Juliet Frances 1928- *WhoFI 94*
Botwin, Michael David 1957- *WhoScEn 94*
Botwinick, Michael 1943- *WhoAm 94, WhoAmA 93*
Botwinick, Moshe Lev 1953- *WhoAm 94*
Botwood, Richard Price 1932- *Who 94*
Botz, Gustav d1932 *WhoHol 92*
Bouabid, Maati 1927- *IntWW 93*
Bouassida, Abdelhafidh 1947- *WhoMW 93*
Boubai, Wilfred Brass 1947- *WhoFI 94, WhoMW 93*
Boubaker, Sidi Mohamed Ould *IntWW 93*
Boubelik, Henry Fredrick, Jr. 1936- *WhoAm 94*
Boucetta, M'Hamed 1925- *IntWW 93*
Bouchard, Benoit 1940- *IntWW 93, WhoAm 94, WhoFI 94*
Bouchard, Constance Brittain 1948- *WhoMW 93*
Bouchard, Craig Thomas 1953- *WhoMW 93*
Bouchard, James Chrysostom 1823-1889 *EncNAR*
Bouchard, James Paul 1961- *WhoMW 93*
Bouchard, Lorne Holland 1913-1978 *WhoAmA 93N*
Bouchard, Michael J. 1956- *WhoAmP 93*
Bouchard, Paul E. 1946- *WhoAmA 93*
Bouchard, Paul Eugene 1946- *WhoWest 94*
Bouchard, Peter T. 1947- *WhoAmP 93*
Bouchard, Philippe Ovide 1932- *WhoMW 93*
Bouchard, Rene Joseph, Jr. 1931- *WhoAmP 93*
Bouchard, Robert F. 1944- *WhoAmL 94*
Bouchard, Thomas Joseph, Jr. 1937- *WhoAm 94*
Bouchard, Velma Mae 1931- *WhoAmP 93*
Bouchardeau, Huguette 1935- *IntWW 93, WhoWomW 91*
Bouche, Louis 1896- *WhAm 10*
Bouche, Louis 1896-1969 *WhoAmA 93N*
Bouche, Rene d1963 *WhoAmA 93N*
Boucher, Anthony 1911-1968 *EncSF 93*
Boucher, Bill *WhoAmP 93*
Boucher, Bill Antonio 1934- *WhoWest 94*
Boucher, Darrell A., Jr. 1944- *WhoScEn 94*
Boucher, David 1951- *WrDr 94*
Boucher, Denise 1935- *BlmGWL*
Boucher, Frederick C. 1946- *WhoAm 94*
Boucher, H. A. *WhoAmP 93*
Boucher, Harold Irving 1906- *WhoAm 94*
Boucher, Henry Joseph 1947- *WhoFI 94*
Boucher, Henry Mason 1907- *WhoAmP 93*
Boucher, Jonathan 1738-1804 *WhAmRev*
Boucher, Joseph William 1951- *WhoAmL 94, WhoFI 94*
Boucher, Laurence James 1938- *WhoAm 94*
Boucher, Laurent J. 1915- *WhoAmP 93*
Boucher, Lionel R. 1931- *WhoAmP 93*
Boucher, Louis Jack 1922- *WhoAm 94*
Boucher, Merle *WhoAmP 93*
Boucher, Rick 1946- *CngDr 93, WhoAmP 93*
Boucher, Sherry *WhoHol 92*
Boucher, Tania Kunsky 1927- *WhoAmA 93*
Boucher, Thomas Owen 1942- *WhoScEn 94*
Boucher, Wayne Irving 1934- *WhoAm 94*
Boucher, William Paul 1930- *WhoAmP 93*
Bouchet, Barbara 1943- *WhoHol 92*
Bouchey, L. Francis 1942- *WhoAm 94*
Bouchey, Myrna *DrAPF 93*
Bouchey, Willis d1977 *WhoHol 92*
Bouchier, Chili 1909- *IntMPA 94, WhoHol 92*
Bouchier, Dorothy *WhoHol 92*
Bouchier, Ian Arthur Dennis 1932- *IntWW 93, Who 94*
Boucicault, Dion 1820-1890 *IntDcT 2, NewGrDO, NinCLC 41 [port]*
Boucicault, Nina d1950 *WhoHol 92*
Bouck, John F. 1941- *WhoAmP 93*
Bouck, Steven Fraser 1957- *WhoFI 94*
Bouckaert, Harm J. G. 1934- *WhoAmA 93*
Boucolon, Maryse *BlkWr 2*
Boucot d1949 *WhoHol 92*
Boucot, Barbara Pierce 1926- *WhoAmP 93*
Boucouvalas, Marcie 1947- *WhoAm 94*
Bouda, David William 1945- *WhoScEn 94*
Boudalia, Nafissa 1948- *BlmGWL*
Boudart, Michel 1924- *IntWW 93, WhoAm 94, WhoScEn 94, WhoWest 94*
Boudet, Jacques *WhoHol 92*
Boudet, Micheline *WhoHol 92*
Boudiaf, Mohammed d1992 *IntWW 93N*
Boudicca c. 26-62 *HisWorL [port]*
Boudin, Jean *DrAPF 93*
Boudin, Leonard B. 1912-1989 *WhAm 10*
Boudin, Michael 1939- *WhoAm 94, WhoAmL 94, WhoAmP 93*
Boudinot, Elias 1740-1821 *AmRev, WhAmRev*
Boudinot, Elias 1802?-1839 *DcAmReB 2, EncNAR*
Boudinot, Frank Douglas 1956- *WhoScEn 94*
Boudoulas, Harisios 1935- *WhoAm 94*
Boudouris, Georges 1919- *IntWW 93*

Boudousquie, Charles 1814-1866 *NewGrDO*
Boudreau, Anne Marie 1959- *WhoAmA 93*
Boudreau, James Lawton 1935- *WhoAm 94*
Boudreau, Jean Claude *DrAPF 93*
Boudreau, Kathryn Lynda Sattler 1947- *WhoWest 94*
Boudreau, Paul J. 1938- *WhoIns 94*
Boudreau, Robert Donald 1931- *WhoAm 94*
Boudreau, Robert James 1950- *WhoMW 93, WhoScEn 94*
Boudreau, Susan Kalmus 1960- *WhoWest 94*
Boudreau, Thomas M. 1951- *WhoAmL 94*
Boudreaux, Jack Lawrence 1960- *WhoAmP 93*
Boudreaux, John 1946- *WhoAm 94*
Boudreaux, Joseph *WhoHol 92*
Boudreaux, Kenneth Justin 1943- *WhoAm 94*
Boudreaux, Paul, Jr. 1953- *WhoAmL 94*
Boudreaux, Warren Louis 1918- *WhoAm 94*
Boueil, Sylvain R. 1952- *WhoIns 94*
Bouer, Judith 1942- *WhoFI 94*
Bouey, Gerald Keith 1920- *IntWW 93*
Bouffar, Zulma (Madeleine) 1841-1909 *NewGrDO*
Bouffard, Andre Denis 1959- *WhoAmL 94*
Bouffard, Paul Henri 1895- *WhAm 10*
Bougainville, Hyacinthe-Yves-Philippe Potentien, Baron De 1782-1846 *WhWE*
Bougainville, Louis-Antoine, Comte De 1729-1811 *WhWE*
Bougainville, Louis Antoine de 1729-1811 *WhAmRev*
Bougalis, Katherine G. 1940- *WhoMW 93*
Bougas, James Andrew 1924- *WhoScEn 94*
Bough, Bradley A. 1958- *WhoAmL 94*
Bough, Francis Joseph 1933- *Who 94*
Boughan, Constance McManus 1951- *WhoAmL 94*
Boughey, John (George Fletcher) 1959- *Who 94*
Boughey, John Fenton C. *Who 94*
Boughey, Lynn Martin 1956- *WhoMW 93*
Boughner, Leslie C. *WhoIns 94*
Boughton, Donald William 1935- *WhoAmP 93*
Boughton, James Murray 1944- *WhoFI 94*
Boughton, Richard 1954- *ConAu 142, SmATA 75 [port]*
Boughton, Robert Ivan, Jr. 1942- *WhoAm 94*
Boughton, Rutland 1878-1960 *NewGrDO*
Boughton, William Hart 1937- *WhoWest 94*
Bougie, Jacques 1947- *WhoAm 94, WhoFI 94*
Bouhoutsos, Jacqueline Cotcher *WhoAm 94, WhoWest 94*
Bouhy, Jacques(-Joseph-Andre) 1848-1929 *NewGrDO*
Bouie, Merceline 1929- *WhoBlA 94*
Bouie, Preston L. 1926- *WhoBlA 94*
Bouie, Simon Pinckney 1939- *WhoBlA 94*
Bouille, Francois Claude Amour, Marquis de 1739-1800 *WhAmRev*
Bouilliant-Linet, Francis Jacques 1932- *WhoFI 94*
Bouillion, Frances Moran 1945- *WhoAmL 94*
Bouilly, Jean-Nicolas 1763-1842 *NewGrDO*
Bouise, Jean d1989 *WhoHol 92*
Bouissac, Paul Antoine 1934- *WhoAm 94*
Bouix, Evelyne *WhoHol 92*
Boujenah, Michael *WhoHol 92*
Boukerrou, Lakhdar 1952- *WhoScEn 94*
Boukidis, Constantine Michael 1959- *WhoAmL 94, WhoWest 94*
Bouknight, J. A., Jr. 1944- *WhoAmL 94*
Bouknight, Reynard Ronald 1946- *WhoBlA 94*
Boulais, Craig Francis 1954- *WhoFI 94*
Boulanger, Daniel 1922- *WhoHol 92*
Boulanger, Debra Ann 1956- *WhoAm 94*
Boulanger, Donald Richard 1944- *WhoAm 94*
Boulanger, Jacques Pierre 1942- *WhoFI 94*
Boulanger, Paul 1905- *IntWW 93*
Boulanger, Philomena M. *WhoAmP 93*
Boulanger, Raymond P. 1944- *WhoAmL 94*
Boulanger, Rodney Edmund 1940- *WhoAm 94*
Bould, Beckett *WhoHol 92*
Boulden, Judith Ann 1948- *WhoAm 94, WhoAmL 94, WhoWest 94*
Boulden, Michael Rowe 1951- *WhoAmL 94*
Boulden, Patrick Timmons 1953- *WhoAmL 94*
Bouldes, Charlene 1945- *WhoBlA 94*
Bouldin, Danny Lee 1953- *WhoWest 94*
Bouldin, Marshall Jones, III 1923- *WhoAmA 93*
Boulding, Elise Marie 1920- *WhoAm 94*
Boulding, Kenneth 1910- *EnvEnc [port]*
Boulding, Kenneth 1910-1993 *NewYTBS 93 [port]*
Boulding, Kenneth E(wart) 1910-1993 *ConAu 140, CurBio 93N*
Boulding, Kenneth Ewart d1993 *IntWW 93N*
Boulding, Kenneth Ewart 1910- *IntWW 93, WrDr 94*
Boulet, Gilles 1926- *Who 94*
Boulet, Jean-Claude 1941- *IntWW 93*
Boulet, Lionel 1919- *WhoAm 94*
Boulet, Roger Henri 1944- *WhoAm 94, WhoWest 94*
Bouley, Richard L. 1938- *WhoAmP 93*
Boulez, Pierre 1925- *IntWW 93, NewGrDO, Who 94, WhoAm 94*
Boulger, Francis William 1913- *WhoAm 94*
Boulger, William Charles 1924- *WhoAmL 94*
Boulian, Charles Joseph 1955- *WhoScEn 94*
Boulind, (Olive) Joan 1912- *Who 94*
Boulle, Pierre 1912- *EncSF 93*
Boulos, Atef Zekry 1945- *WhoScEn 94*
Boulos, Edward Nashed 1941- *WhoFI 94, WhoMW 93, WhoScEn 94*
Boulos, Nadia Ebid 1938- *WhoAm 94*
Boulos, Paul Fares 1963- *WhoAm 94, WhoScEn 94*
Boulos, Rida Wahba 1941- *WhoMW 93*
Boulpaep, Emile Louis J. B. 1938- *WhoAm 94, WhoFI 94*
Boulse, Gerald Lee 1950- *WhoWest 94*
Boult, Adrian d1983 *WhoHol 92*
Boult, Adrian (Cedric) 1889-1983 *NewGrDO*
Boult, S. Kye *EncSF 93*
Boultbee, John Arthur 1943- *WhoAm 94*
Boulter, Beau 1942- *WhoAmP 93*
Boulter, Donald 1926- *Who 94*
Boulter, Patrick Stewart 1927- *Who 94, WhoScEn 94*
Boulter, Rosalyn 1917- *WhoHol 92*
Boulting, Ingrid 1947- *WhoHol 92*
Boulting, Roy 1913- *IntMPA 94, IntWW 93, Who 94*
Boulting, S. A. *Who 94*
Boultinghouse, Marion Craig Bettinger 1930- *WhoAm 94*
Boulton, Christian *Who 94*
Boulton, (Harold Hugh) Christian 1918- *Who 94*
Boulton, Clifford (John) 1930- *Who 94*
Boulton, David 1935- *WrDr 94*
Boulton, Edwin Charles 1928- *WhoAm 94, WhoMW 93*
Boulton, Geoffrey Stewart 1940- *Who 94*
Boulton, Grace 1926- *WhoAmP 93*
Boulton, James T(hompson) 1924- *WrDr 94*
Boulton, James Thompson 1924- *Who 94*
Boulton, Lyndie McHenry *WhoWest 94*
Boulton, Matthew d1962 *WhoHol 92*
Boulton, Matthew 1728-1809 *WorInv*
Boulton, Milo d1989 *WhoHol 92*
Boulton, Peter Henry 1925- *Who 94*
Boulton, Schroeder 1909- *WhoFI 94*
Boulton, William (Whytehead) 1912- *Who 94*
Boulware, Fay D. *WhoBlA 94*
Boulware, Lemuel Ricketts 1895-1990 *WhAm 10*
Boulware, Patricia A. 1949- *WhoBlA 94*
Boulware, Richard Stark 1935- *WhoWest 94*
Boulware, William H. 1949- *WhoBlA 94*
Bouma, J(ohanas) L. *WrDr 94*
Bouma, Johannes 1940- *IntWW 93*
Bouma, John Jacob 1937- *WhoAm 94, WhoAmL 94*
Bouma, Robert Edwin 1938- *WhoAm 94*
Bouman, John K. 1943- *WhoAmL 94*
Boumann, Robert Lyle 1946- *WhoWest 94*
Bounar, Khaled Hosie 1957- *WhoScEn 94*
Boundas, Louise Gooch *WhoAm 94*
Bounds, Mark Allen 1963- *WhoMW 93*
Bounds, Nancy 1928- *WhoMW 93*
Bounds, (Kenneth) Peter 1943- *Who 94*
Bounds, Shelton E. 1929- *WhoAmP 93*
Bounds, Sydney J(ames) 1920- *EncSF 93, WrDr 94*
Bounds, Wallace Mezick, II 1957- *WhoFI 94*
Bounous, Denise Ida 1952- *WhoScEn 94*
Bouquet, Carole 1957- *WhoHol 92*
Bouquet, Francis Lester 1926- *WhoAm 94*
Bouquet, Michel 1926- *WhoHol 92*
Bouquett, Tamara Tunie *WhoHol 92*
Bour, Armand d1945 *WhoHol 92*
Bour, Jean-Antoine 1934- *WhoWest 94*
Bouras, Harry 1931-1990 *WhAm 10*
Bourassa, Alphonse J. 1941- *WhoAmP 93*
Bourassa, Henri 1868-1952 *HisWorL [port]*
Bourassa, Robert 1933- *IntWW 93, Who 94, WhoAm 94*
Bourbault, Jean-Claude *WhoHol 92*
Bourber, Aaf d1974 *WhoHol 92*
Bourbon, Diana d1978 *WhoHol 92*
Bourbon Busset, Jacques Louis Robert Marie de 1912- *IntWW 93*
Bourchier, Arthur d1927 *WhoHol 92*
Bourcicault, Dion *NewGrDO*
Bourdage, James Sevall 1952- *WhoMW 93*
Bourdais de Charbonniere, Eric 1939- *WhoAm 94*
Bourdara, Kelly *WhoWomW 91*
Bourdeau, Bernard N. 1948- *WhoIns 94*
Bourdeau, James Edward 1948- *WhoScEn 94*
Bourdeau, Paul Layman 1955- *WhoAmL 94*
Bourdeau, Paul T. *WhoIns 94*
Bourdeau, Paul Turgeon 1932- *WhoAm 94*
Bourdeau, Philippe 1926- *WhoScEn 94*
Bourdeau, Robert Charles 1931- *WhoAmA 93*
Bourdeaux, Michael Alan 1934- *Who 94, WrDr 94*
Bourdeaux, Norma E. Sanders 1930- *WhoAmP 93*
Bourdelais, Alfred Arthur 1936- *WhoMW 93*
Bourdell, Pierre Van Parys d1966 *WhoAmA 93N*
Bourdet, Claude 1909- *IntWW 93*
Bourdic-Viot, Marie-Henriette Payan de d'Estang de 1746-1802 *BlmGWL*
Bourdieu, Pierre 1930- *IntWW 93*
Bourdillon, Mervyn Leigh 1924- *Who 94*
Bourdillon, Peter John 1941- *Who 94*
Bourdin, Roger 1900-1973 *NewGrDO*
Bourdon, David 1934- *WhoAm 94, WhoAmA 93, WrDr 94*
Bourdon, Derek Conway 1932- *Who 94*
Bourdon, James Brian 1960- *WhoFI 94*
Bourdon, Robert Slayton 1947- *WhoAmA 93*
Bourdonnay, Barbara Elizabeth 1961- *WhoAmL 94*
Boureau, Edouard 1913- *IntWW 93*
Bourekis, James George 1930- *WhoWest 94*
Bouret, Marc Patrick 1953- *WhoAmL 94*
Bourette, Charlotte Rouyer 1714-1784 *BlmGWL*
Bourey, Alan Douglas 1952- *WhoAmL 94*
Bourgaize, Robert G. *WhoAm 94*
Bourgault, Lise *WhoWomW 91*
Bourgault-Ducoudray, Louis (Albert) 1840-1910 *NewGrDO*
Bourgeaud, Nelly *WhoHol 92*
Bourgeois, Adam 1929- *WhoBlA 94*
Bourgeois, Andre Marie Georges 1902- *WhoAm 94*
Bourgeois, Douglas 1951- *WhoAmA 93*
Bourgeois, Louise 1563-1636 *BlmGWL*
Bourgeois, Louise 1911- *News 94-1 [port], WhoAm 94, WhoAmA 93*
Bourgeois, Louyse 1563-1636 *WorScD*
Bourgeois, Thomas-Louis(-Joseph) 1676-1750? *NewGrDO*
Bourges, Herve 1933- *IntWW 93*
Bourges, Yvon 1921- *IntWW 93*
Bourges-Maunoury, Maurice d1993 *IntWW 93N*
Bourgmont, Etienne Veniard, Sieur De 1680-c. 1730 *WhWE*
Bourgoin, David L. 1946- *WhoAmL 94*
Bourgoine, Ella Florence 1935- *WhoAmP 93*
Bourguiba, Habib, Jr. 1927- *IntWW 93*
Bourguiba, Habib Ben Ali 1903- *IntWW 93*
Bourguignon, Erika Eichhorn 1924- *WhoAm 94*
Bourguignon, Francis de 1890-1961 *NewGrDO*
Bourguignon, Philippe Etienne 1948- *WhoFI 94*
Bourham, Mohamed Abdelhay 1944- *WhoScEn 94*
Bouricius, Terry 1954- *WhoAmP 93*
Bourin, Jeanne *BlmGWL*
Bouris, Michael Lee 1942- *WhoIns 94*
Bourjaily, Vance *DrAPF 93*
Bourjaily, Vance 1922- *IntWW 93, WhoAm 94*
Bourjaily, Vance (Nye) 1922- *WrDr 94*
Bourke *Who 94*
Bourke, Christopher John 1926- *Who 94*
Bourke, Fan d1959 *WhoHol 92*
Bourke, Lyle James 1963- *WhoFI 94, WhoScEn 94, WhoWest 94*
Bourke, Martin 1947- *Who 94*
Bourke, Michael *Who 94*
Bourke, Vernon J(oseph) 1907- *WrDr 94*
Bourke, Vernon Joseph 1907- *WhoAm 94*
Bourke, William Oliver 1927- *IntWW 93, WhoAm 94*
Bourliere, Francois (Marie Gabriel) 1913- *IntWW 93*
Bourmeister, Vladimir *IntDcB*
Bourn, James 1917- *Who 94*
Bourn, John (Bryant) 1934- *Who 94*
Bourne, Adeline d1965 *WhoHol 92*
Bourne, Beal Vernon, II 1950- *WhoBlA 94*
Bourne, Carol Elizabeth Mulligan 1948- *WhoScEn 94*
Bourne, Charles Beresford 1921- *IntWW 93*
Bourne, Charles Percy 1931- *WhoAm 94*
Bourne, Daniel *DrAPF 93*
Bourne, Francis Stanley 1919- *WhoAm 94*
Bourne, Frederick John 1937- *Who 94*
Bourne, Gordon Lionel 1921- *Who 94*
Bourne, Hazel d1956 *WhoHol 92*
Bourne, Henry Clark, Jr. 1921- *WhoAm 94*
Bourne, James Gerald 1906- *Who 94*
Bourne, John 1620-1667 *DcNaB MP*
Bourne, John David 1937- *WhoFI 94*
Bourne, Judith Louise 1945- *WhoBlA 94*
Bourne, Kenneth d1992 *IntWW 93N, Who 94N*
Bourne, Kenneth 1930- *WrDr 94*
Bourne, Kenneth 1930-1992 *ConAu 140*
Bourne, Larry Stuart 1939- *IntWW 93, WrDr 94*
Bourne, Larz E. d1993 *NewYTBS 93*
Bourne, Lyle Eugene, Jr. 1932- *WhoAm 94*
Bourne, Margaret Janet 1931- *Who 94*
Bourne, Martha Flowers 1943- *WhoAmL 94*
Bourne, Mary Bonnie Murray 1903- *WhoFI 94*
Bourne, Peter Geoffrey 1939- *WhoAm 94*
Bourne, Philip Walley 1907- *WhAm 10*
Bourne, Ralph W., Jr. 1936- *WhoIns 94*
Bourne, Randolph Silliman 1886-1918 *AmSocL*
Bourne, (Rowland) Richard *Who 94*
Bourne, Russell 1928- *WhoAm 94, WrDr 94*
Bourne, Samuel G. 1916- *WhoAm 94*
Bourne, Vicki Worrall 1954- *WhoWomW 91*
Bourne, Whitney d1988 *WhoHol 92*
Bourne, Wilfrid *Who 94*
Bourne, (John) Wilfrid 1922- *Who 94*
Bourne-Arton, Anthony Temple 1913- *Who 94*
Bourneuf, Philip d1979 *WhoHol 92*
Bournonville, August 1805-1879 *IntDcB*
Bournonville, Auguste (Antoine) 1805-1879 *NewGrDO*
Bourns, Arthur Newcombe 1919- *Who 94*
Bourque, Ann J. 1941- *WhoAmP 93*
Bourque, George J. 1913- *WhoAmP 93*
Bourque, Linda Anne Brookover 1941- *WhoWest 94*
Bourque, Philip John 1922- *WhoAm 94*
Bourque, Ray 1960- *WhoAm 94*
Bourquin, Paul Henry James 1916- *WrDr 94*
Bourret, Marjorie Ann 1925- *WhoWest 94*
Bourseiller, Antoine 1930- *IntWW 93*
Bourton, Cyril Leonard 1916- *Who 94*
Bourvil d1970 *WhoHol 92*
Bousfield, Edward Lloyd 1926- *IntWW 93, WhoAm 94*
Bousquet, Francis 1890-1942 *NewGrDO*
Bousquet, John Frederick 1948- *WhoWest 94*
Bousquet, Thomas Gourrier 1934- *WhoAm 94*
Bousquette, William C. 1936- *WhoAm 94, WhoFI 94*
Boussena, Sadek 1948- *IntWW 93*
Boussenard, Louis 1847-1910 *EncSF 93*
Boussingault, Jean-Baptiste Joseph Dieudonne 1802-1887 *WorScD*
Boustani, Rafic 1942- *ConAu 141*
Boustany, Alfred Frem 1953- *WhoAmL 94*
Boustedt, Christer d1986 *WhoHol 92*
Boutaleb, Abdelhadi 1923- *IntWW 93*
Boutall, Kathleen *WhoHol 92*
Bouteflika, Abdul Aziz 1937- *IntWW 93*
Boutelle, Ann Edwards 1943- *WrDr 94*
Boutelle, Sara Holmes *WhoWest 94*
Boutet de Monvel, M(aurice) 1850?-1913 *ChlLR 32 [port]*
Boutilier, Bradford *WhoAmP 93*
Boutillier, Robert John 1924- *WhoAm 94, WhoFI 94*
Boutin, Bernard Louis 1923- *IntWW 93*
Boutin, Christine 1944- *WhoWomW 91*
Boutin, Peter Rucker 1950- *WhoAmL 94*
Boutis, Tom 1922- *WhoAmA 93*
Bouton, James Alan 1939- *WhoAm 94*
Bouton, Jim 1939- *WhoHol 92*
Boutos, Ioannis 1925- *IntWW 93*
Boutris, Demetrios A. 1961- *WhoAmL 94*
Boutros, Fouad 1920- *IntWW 93*
Boutros Ghali, Boutros 1922- *IntWW 93, Who 94*

Boutross, Denise Marie 1952- WhoAm 94
Boutrous, Victor Nicholas 1962- WhoMW 93
Boutsikaris, Dennis WhoHol 92
Boutte, Alvin J. 1929- WhoBlA 94
Boutte, David Gray 1944- WhoAmL 94, WhoFI 94
Boutte, Ernest John 1943- WhoBlA 94
Boutte, Jean-Luc IntWW 93
Boutwell, Ralph S. 1926- WhoAmP 93
Boutwell, Roswell Knight 1917- WhoAm 94
Boutwell, William T. c. 1803-1890 EncNAR
Bouvard, Francois c. 1683-1760 NewGrDO
Bouvard, Marguerite Guzman DrAPF 93
Bouve, Edward T(racy) EncSF 93
Bouverie Who 94
Bouvier, Helene 1905-1978 NewGrDO
Bouvier, Jacqueline WhoHol 92
Bouvier, John Andre, Jr. 1903-1989 WhAm 10
Bouvier, Marshall Andre 1923- WhoAmL 94, WhoFI 94, WhoWest 94
Bouw, Pieter WhoFI 94
Bouwer, Herman 1927- WhoAm 94, WhoScEn 94
Bouwsma, William James 1923- WhoAm 94
Bouygues, Francis d1993 NewYTBS 93 [port]
Bouygues, Francis Georges 1922- IntWW 93
Bouygues, Martin Pierre Marie 1952- IntWW 93
Bouyoucos, John Vinton 1926- WhoAm 94
Bouzeghoub, Mohamed Tahar 1947- IntWW 93
Bova, Ben 1932- ConAu 18AS [port]
Bova, Ben(jamin William) 1932- EncSF 93, WrDr 94
Bova, Benjamin William 1932- WhoAm 94
Bova, Joe 1941- WhoAmA 93
Bova, Joseph 1924- WhoHol 92
Bova, Michael Anthony 1968- WhoScEn 94
Bova, Tony WhoHol 92
Bova, Vincent Arthur, Jr. 1946- WhoAmL 94
Bovaird, Brendan Peter 1948- WhoAm 94, WhoAmL 94
Bovaird, Davis D(outhett) 1896- WhAm 10
Bovasso, Julie 1930- WhoHol 92, WrDr 94
Bovasso, Julie 1930-1991 ConDr 93
Bovasso, Louis Joseph 1935- WhoAmL 94
Bovay, Harry Elmo, Jr. 1914- WhoAm 94
Bove, John G. 1946- WhoAmL 94
Bove, John Louis 1928- WhoAm 94
Bove, Linda 1945- EncDeaf
Bove, Martin N. 1949- WhoAmP 93
Bove, Marylou Goodman 1958- WhoMW 93
Bove, Nicholas Joseph, Jr. 1952- WhoAmL 94
Bove, Richard 1920- WhoAmA 93
Bovee, Eugene Cleveland 1915- WhoAm 94
Bovee, Terry L. 1946- WhoMW 93
Bovell, Carlton Rowland 1924- WhoAm 94
Bovell, (William) Stewart 1906- Who 94
Boven, Douglas G. 1943- WhoAmL 94
Bovender, Jack Oliver, Jr. 1945- WhoAm 94
Bovender, William C. 1950- WhoAmL 94
Bovenizer, Bruce 1945- WhoIns 94
Bovenizer, Vernon Gordon Fitzell 1908- Who 94
Boveri, Theodor 1862-1915 WorScD
Boverini, Walter John 1925- WhoAmP 93
Boverman, Harold 1927- WhoWest 94
Boves, Joaquin Lorenzo 1949- WhoFI 94
Bovet, Daniel d1992 NobelP 91N
Bovet, Daniel 1907-1992 AnObit 1992, WhAm 10
Bovet, Daniele 1907-1992 WorScD
Bovey, Edmund Charles 1916-1990 WhAm 10
Bovey, Frank Alden 1918- WhoScEn 94
Bovey, John DrAPF 93
Bovey, Leonard 1924- Who 94
Bovey, Philip Henry 1948- Who 94
Bovey, Terry Robinson 1948- WhoScEn 94
Bovier de Fontenelle, Bernard le NewGrDO
Bovin, Aleksandr Yevgeniyevich 1930- IntWW 93
Bovin, Denis Alan 1947- WhoAm 94, WhoFI 94
Bovingdon, George Geil 1934- WhoAmL 94
Bovino, Charles Anthony 1940- WhoFI 94
Bovy, Berthe d1977 WhoHol 92
Bovy, Vina 1900-1983 NewGrDO
Bow, Clara d1965 WhoHol 92

Bow, Simmy d1987 WhoHol 92
Bow, Sing Tze 1924- WhoMW 93, WhoScEn 94
Bowab, John 1933- ConTFT 11
Boward, Joseph Frank 1961- WhoScEn 94
Bowater, Euan David Vansittart 1935- Who 94
Bowater, J(ohn) Vansittart 1918- Who 94
Bowater, Marian 1924- WhoAmA 93
Bowcock, Anne Mary 1956- WhoScEn 94
Bowd, Douglas Gordon 1918- WrDr 94
Bowden Who 94
Bowden, Andrew Who 94
Bowden, Andrew 1930- Who 94
Bowden, (Robert) Andrew 1938- Who 94
Bowden, Bobby 1930- WhoAm 94
Bowden, Denise Lynn 1963- WhoScEn 94
Bowden, Elbert Victor 1924- WhoAm 94
Bowden, Frank Houston 1909- Who 94
Bowden, Gerald Francis 1935- Who 94
Bowden, Gordon Townley 1915- WhoFI 94
Bowden, Henry Elmo 1944- WhoAm 94
Bowden, Henry Lumpkin 1910- WhoAm 94
Bowden, Henry Lumpkin, Jr. 1949- WhoAm 94, WhoAmL 94
Bowden, Howard Kent 1955- WhoFI 94
Bowden, Howard W. 1935- WhoAmP 93
Bowden, Hugh Winslow WhoAmP 93
Bowden, James Alvin 1948- WhoAm 94, WhoFI 94
Bowden, James H. DrAPF 93
Bowden, Jesse Earle 1928- WhoAm 94
Bowden, Jim ConAu 43NR
Bowden, Jim 1923- WrDr 94
Bowden, Logan S. Who 94
Bowden, Marion A. WhoBlA 94
Bowden, Mary W(eatherspoon) 1941- WrDr 94
Bowden, Otis Hearne, II 1928- WhoFI 94
Bowden, Rick 1947- WhoAmP 93
Bowden, Robert D. WhoAmP 93
Bowden, Roland Heywood 1916- WrDr 94
Bowden, Ruth Elizabeth Mary 1915- Who 94
Bowden, Sally Ann 1943- WhoAm 94
Bowden, William Breckenridge 1951- WhoScEn 94
Bowden, William Darsie 1920- WhoAm 94
Bowditch, Ebenezer Francis 1912-1990 WhAm 10
Bowditch, Henry Ingersoll 1808-1892 AmSocL [port]
Bowditch, Hoel Lawrence 1915- WhoFI 94
Bowditch, Nathaniel Rantoul 1932- WhoAm 94
Bowdler, Anthony John 1928- WhoAm 94
Bowdler, Thomas 1754-1825 BlmGEL
Bowdoin, Harriette d1947 WhoAmA 93N
Bowdoin, James 1726-1790 WhAmRev
Bowdoin, Robert E. 1929- WhoBlA 94
Bowdon, Dorris 1916- WhoHol 92
Bowdring, Paul (Edward) 1946- WrDr 94
Bowe, David WhoHol 92
Bowe, David Robert 1955- Who 94
Bowe, Richard Welbourn 1949- WhoAmL 94
Bowe, Riddick 1967- ConBlB 6 [port], WhoBlA 94
Bowe, Riddick Lamont 1967- WhoAm 94
Bowe, Roger Lee 1954- WhoWest 94
Bowe, Rosemarie 1932- WhoHol 92
Bowe, William John 1942- WhoAm 94
Bowell, William David, Sr. 1921- WhoMW 93
Bowen, Anabel Smith 1950- WhoAmP 93
Bowen, 'Asta 1955- WhoWest 94
Bowen, Barbara C(herry) 1937- WrDr 94
Bowen, Barbara Cherry 1937- WhoAm 94
Bowen, Bill d1981 WhoHol 92
Bowen, Billy M. 1935- WhoIns 94
Bowen, Blannie Evans 1953- WhoBlA 94
Bowen, Brenda Lee Matistic 1960- WhoAmL 94
Bowen, Bryan Morris 1932- Who 94
Bowen, Carolyn Elizabeth Cunningham Who 94
Bowen, Clotilde Dent 1923- WhoAm 94, WhoBlA 94, WhoWest 94
Bowen, Constance Lee 1952- WhoAmA 93, WhoWest 94
Bowen, David Aubrey Llewellyn 1924- Who 94
Bowen, David Reece 1932- WhoAmP 93
Bowen, Debra WhoAmP 93
Bowen, Debra Lynn 1955- WhoWest 94
Bowen, Duane Glenn 1935- WhoAmP 93
Bowen, Dudley Hollingsworth, Jr. 1941- WhoAm 94
Bowen, Edward C. 1923- WhoAmP 93
Bowen, Edward Farquharson 1945- Who 94
Bowen, Edwin Anderson 1932- WhoWest 94

Bowen, Elizabeth 1899-1973 BlmGEL, BlmGWL
Bowen, Elizabeth (Dorothea Cole) 1899-1973 GayLL, RfGShF
Bowen, Emma L. 1916- WhoBlA 94
Bowen, Erva J. 1919- WhoBlA 94
Bowen, Esmond John 1922- Who 94
Bowen, Frank 1930- Who 94
Bowen, Geoffrey (Fraser) WhoAm 94
Bowen, George Hamilton, Jr. 1925- WhoAm 94, WhoMW 93
Bowen, Gilbert Willard 1931- WhoMW 93
Bowen, Howard Rothmann 1908-1989 WhAm 10
Bowen, J. Donald 1944- WhoAmL 94
Bowen, J(ean) Donald 1922-1989 WhAm 10
Bowen, James David 1962- WhoWest 94
Bowen, James Ronald 1941- WhoAm 94
Bowen, James Thomas, Jr. 1948- WhoFI 94
Bowen, Jay Scott 1949- WhoAmL 94
Bowen, Jeanne Gay 1946- WhoMW 93
Bowen, Jewell Ray 1934- WhoAm 94, WhoScEn 94
Bowen, John (Griffith) 1924- ConDr 93, EncSF 93, WrDr 94
Bowen, John Griffith 1924- Who 94
Bowen, John Metcalf 1933- WhoAm 94, WhoScEn 94
Bowen, John Richard 1934- WhoAm 94
Bowen, John Wesley Edward, IV 1954- WhoAmL 94
Bowen, John William 1944- WhoAm 94
Bowen, Lawrence 1914- Who 94
Bowen, Lionel Frost 1922- IntWW 93, Who 94
Bowen, Lowell Reed 1931- WhoAm 94
Bowen, M. John, Jr. 1941- WhoAmL 94
Bowen, Mark Edward Mortimer 1958- Who 94
Bowen, Michael WhoHol 92
Bowen, Michael 1951- WrDr 94
Bowen, Michael Anthony 1951- WhoAm 94, WhoAmL 94
Bowen, Michael George Who 94
Bowen, Michael George 1930- IntWW 93
Bowen, Nigel (Hubert) 1911- Who 94
Bowen, Nigel Hubert 1911- IntWW 93
Bowen, Otis R. 1918- WhoAmP 93
Bowen, Otis Ray 1918- IntWW 93
Bowen, Patrick Harvey 1939- WhoAm 94
Bowen, Paul 1951- WhoAmA 93
Bowen, Peggy Lear 1949- WhoAmP 93
Bowen, Peter Geoffrey 1939- WhoWest 94
Bowen, Peter Wilson 1939- WhoFI 94
Bowen, R. William 1953- WhoAmL 94
Bowen, Raymond C. 1934- WhoBlA 94
Bowen, Richard, Jr. 1942- WhoBlA 94
Bowen, Richard Lee 1933- WhoAm 94, WhoWest 94
Bowen, Richard Lee 1935- WhoMW 93
Bowen, Robert Allen 1946- WhoIns 94
Bowen, Robert O. 1920- WrDr 94
Bowen, Robert Sidney 1900-1977 EncSF 93
Bowen, Robert William 1960- WhoFI 94
Bowen, Roderic Who 94
Bowen, (Evan) Roderic 1913- Who 94
Bowen, Roger WhoHol 92
Bowen, Rooney L. 1933- WhoAmP 93
Bowen, Ryan 1968- WhoBlA 94
Bowen, Sandra Dixon 1941- WhoAmP 93
Bowen, Stanley 1910- Who 94
Bowen, Stephen Francis, Jr. 1932- WhoAm 94
Bowen, Stephen George 1944- WhoAm 94
Bowen, Stephen Stewart 1946- WhoAm 94, WhoAmL 94
Bowen, Thomas Edward Ifor L. Who 94
Bowen, Thomas Edwin 1934- WhoAm 94, WhoWest 94
Bowen, Thomas Lee 1965- WhoMW 93
Bowen, Tracey Scott 1961- WhoWest 94
Bowen, W. J. 1922- WhoAm 94, WhoFI 94
Bowen, William (Gordon) 1933- WrDr 94
Bowen, William Augustus 1930- WhoAm 94
Bowen, William F. 1929- WhoAmP 93, WhoBlA 94
Bowen, William G(ordon) 1933- Who 94
Bowen, William Gordon 1933- IntWW 93, WhoAm 94
Bowen, William H. 1933- WhoAm 94
Bowen, William Harvey 1923- WhoAm 94
Bowen, William Henry 1933- WhoScEn 94
Bowen, William Joseph 1934- WhoAm 94, WhoFI 94
Bowen, Zack 1934- WrDr 94
Bowen-Forbes, Jorge C. 1937- WhoAmA 93
Bowens, Johnny Wesley 1946- WhoBlA 94
Bowens, Malick WhoHol 92
Bower, Alexander 1875-1952 WhoAmA 93N
Bower, Allan Maxwell 1936- WhoAm 94, WhoAmL 94, WhoWest 94

Bower, Angus Bruce 1927- WhoWest 94
Bower, Antoinette WhoHol 92
Bower, Barbara Rose 1946- WhoAmP 93
Bower, Beverly Lynne 1951- WhoBlA 94
Bower, Bruce Lester 1933- WhoAm 94
Bower, Christopher James 1957- WhoAm 94
Bower, Dallas 1927- IntMPA 94
Bower, Donald Edward 1920- WhoWest 94
Bower, Fay Louise 1929- WhoMW 93
Bower, Florence Turitz d1993 NewYTBS 93
Bower, G. Kevin 1951- WhoAmP 93
Bower, Gary David 1940- WhoAmA 93
Bower, Glen Landis 1949- WhoAm 94, WhoAmL 94, WhoAmP 93
Bower, Gordon 1932- IntWW 93
Bower, Greg Hollis 1949- WhoWest 94
Bower, Jean Helen 1933- WhoWest 94
Bower, Jean Ramsay 1935- WhoAm 94, WhoAmL 94
Bower, John Joseph 1925- WhoAm 94
Bower, Joseph Lyon 1938- WhoAm 94
Bower, Kathleen Ann 1962- WhoFI 94
Bower, Kenneth Francis 1942- WhoMW 93
Bower, Marvin 1903- WhoAm 94
Bower, Marvin D. 1924- WhoAm 94
Bower, Michael Douglas 1942- Who 94
Bower, Paul George 1933- WhoAm 94, WhoWest 94
Bower, Peter Thomas 1946- WhoFI 94
Bower, Richard James 1939- WhoAm 94
Bower, Richard Stuart 1928- WhoAm 94
Bower, Robert Frederick, Jr. 1940- WhoFI 94
Bower, Robert Hewitt 1949- WhoMW 93
Bower, Robert S. 1917- WhoAmL 94
Bower, Roger DrAPF 93
Bower, Ronald Edward 1944- WhoMW 93
Bower, Ruth Lawther 1917- WhoAm 94, WhoScEn 94
Bower, Sandra Irwin 1946- WhoAm 94
Bower, Stephen Ernest D. Who 94
Bower, Thomas Michael 1952- WhoAmL 94
Bower, Tom WhoHol 92
Bower, Ward Alan 1947- WhoAm 94
Bower, William David 1964- WhoFI 94, WhoWest 94
Bower, Willis Herman 1916- WhoAm 94
Bowerfind, Edgar Sihler, Jr. 1924- WhoAm 94
Bowering, Christine 1936- Who 94
Bowering, George 1938- WrDr 94
Bowering, George Harry 1936- WhoAm 94, WhoWest 94
Bowering, Marilyn 1949- BlmGWL
Bowering, Marilyn (Ruthe) 1949- WrDr 94
Bowering, Michael Ernest 1935- Who 94
Bowerman, Charles Leo 1939- WhoFI 94
Bowerman, David Alexander 1903- Who 94
Bowerman, Richard Henry 1917- WhoAm 94
Bowerman, Richard Whitney 1946- WhoAmL 94
Bowerman, William Wesley, IV 1961- WhoScEn 94
Bowermaster, Jon 1954- SmATA 77 [port]
Bowers, Adele d1992 NewYTBS 93
Bowers, Albert 1930-1990 WhAm 10
Bowers, Allan Dale 1951- WhoFI 94
Bowers, Bathsheba c. 1672-1718 BlmGWL
Bowers, Ben James 1932- WhoAm 94
Bowers, Beth Baker DrAPF 93
Bowers, Bobby Eugene 1933- WhoWest 94
Bowers, Charles R. 1940- WhoAm 94
Bowers, Conrad Paul 1959- WhoScEn 94
Bowers, David A. 1952- WhoAmP 93
Bowers, David Alexander WhoAm 94
Bowers, Dorothy C. WhoAmP 93
Bowers, Douglas Edward 1947- WhoFI 94
Bowers, E. Kenneth 1935- WhoFI 94
Bowers, Edgar 1924- WhoAm 94, WrDr 94
Bowers, Edgar R. 1937- WhoAmP 93
Bowers, Emmett Wadsworth 1926- WhoAm 94
Bowers, Francis Robert 1920- WhoAm 94
Bowers, Fredson Thayer 1905-1991 DcLB 140 [port], WhAm 10
Bowers, Glenn Lee 1921- WhoAm 94
Bowers, Grayson Hunter 1897- WhoFI 94
Bowers, Greg DrAPF 93
Bowers, H. Michael 1948- WhoAmL 94
Bowers, Jack 1947- WhoWest 94
Bowers, James Charles, Jr. 1943- WhoAmL 94
Bowers, James Russell, Jr. 1949- WhoAmL 94
Bowers, James S. 1952- WhoAmP 93
Bowers, John DrAPF 93
Bowers, John d1936 WhoHol 92
Bowers, John 1928- WrDr 94
Bowers, John Waite 1935- WhoAm 94

Bowser, Anita Olga 1920- *WhoAmP 93, WhoMW 93, WhoWomW 91*
Bowser, Benjamin Paul 1946- *WhoBlA 94*
Bowser, Charles d1917 *WhoHol 92*
Bowser, Charles Emanuel 1959- *WhoBlA 94*
Bowser, Eileen 1928- *IntMPA 94*
Bowser, Hamilton Victor, Sr. 1928- *WhoBlA 94*
Bowser, Harry E. 1931- *WhoAmP 93*
Bowser, James A. 1913- *WhoBlA 94*
Bowser, McEva R. 1922- *WhoBlA 94*
Bowser, Robert Dwight 1948- *WhoMW 93*
Bowser, Robert Louis 1935- *WhoBlA 94*
Bowser, Vivian Roy 1926- *WhoBlA 94*
Bowser of Argaty & the King's Lundies, David Stewart 1926- *Who 94*
Bowsher, Charles A. *WhoAmP 93*
Bowsher, Charles Arthur 1931- *WhoAm 94, WhoFI 94*
Bowsher, Laura Kay 1967- *WhoMW 93*
Bowsher, Peter Charles 1935- *Who 94*
Bowtell, Ann Elizabeth 1938- *Who 94*
Bowtell, Elizabeth c. 1650-1697 *BlmGEL*
Bowyer *Who 94*
Bowyer, Charles Stuart 1934- *WhoAm 94, WhoWest 94*
Bowyer, Charles T. 1947- *WhoAmL 94*
Bowyer, Edna L. 1917- *WhoAmP 93*
Bowyer, Gordon Arthur 1923- *Who 94*
Bowyer, Jane Baker 1934- *WhoWest 94*
Bowyer, Mathew Justice 1926- *WrDr 94*
Bowyer, Robert c. 1560-1621 *DcNaB MP*
Bowyer, William 1926- *IntWW 93, Who 94*
Bowyer-Smyth, T. W. *Who 94*
Bowytz, Robert B. 1938- *WhoAm 94*
Box, Barry Glenn 1958- *WhoAm 94, WhoFI 94*
Box, Betty 1920- *IntDcF 2-4 [port]*
Box, Betty Evelyn *IntWW 93*
Box, Betty Evelyn 1949- *Who 94*
Box, Charles 1951- *WhoBlA 94*
Box, Charles E. *WhoAmP 93*
Box, Donald Stewart d1993 *Who 94N*
Box, Dwain D. 1916- *WhoAm 94*
Box, Edgar *GayLL*
Box, Edgar 1925- *WrDr 94*
Box, George Edward Pelham 1919- *Who 94, WhoAm 94*
Box, Glenn 1958- *WhoAmP 93*
Box, James Ellis, Jr. 1931- *WhoAm 94*
Box, John 1920- *IntDcF 2-4*
Box, John Harold 1929- *WhoAm 94*
Box, Michael Edward 1954- *WhoAmP 93*
Box, Muriel 1905-1991 *IntDcF 2-4 [port]*
Box, Thadis Wayne 1929- *WhoAm 94*
Boxall, Barbara Ann *Who 94*
Boxall, Bernard 1906- *Who 94*
Boxall, Richard George 1936- *WhoAm 94*
Boxberg, Christian Ludwig 1670-1729 *NewGrDO*
Box Betty, Obe 1920- *IntMPA 94*
Box Elder c. 1795-1892 *EncNAR*
Boxenhorn, Burton 1928- *WhoScEn 94*
Boxer, Alan (Hunter Cachemaille) 1916- *Who 94*
Boxer, Alan Lee 1935- *WhoWest 94*
Boxer, Alvin B. d1993 *NewYTBS 93*
Boxer, Arabella *WrDr 94*
Boxer, Barbara 1940- *CngDr 93, IntWW 93, WhoAm 94, WhoAmP 93, WhoWest 94, WhoWomW 91*
Boxer, Charles Ian 1926- *Who 94*
Boxer, Charles Ralph 1904- *Who 94*
Boxer, Henry Everard Crichton 1914- *Who 94*
Boxer, Herman d1983 *WhoHol 92*
Boxer, Jerome Harvey 1930- *WhoAm 94, WhoWest 94*
Boxer, John 1909- *WhoHol 92*
Boxer, Leonard 1939- *WhoAm 94*
Boxer, Lester 1935- *WhoWest 94*
Boxer, Richard James 1947- *WhoMW 93*
Boxer, Robert William 1933- *WhoAm 94*
Boxer, Rubin 1927- *WhoAm 94*
Boxer, Stanley (Robert) 1926- *WhoAmA 93*
Boxer, Stanley Robert 1926- *WhoAm 94*
Bo Xicheng *WhoPRCh 91 [port]*
Boxleitner, Bruce 1950- *IntMPA 94, WhoHol 92*
Boxleitner, Warren James 1948- *WhoScEn 94*
Boyack, Alan Dean 1940- *WhoAmL 94*
Boyadzhiev, Khristo Nonev 1948- *WhoMW 93*
Boyajian, Aram *DrAPF 93*
Boyajian, Carole L. 1948- *WhoWest 94*
Boyajian, Jerry 1953- *EncSF 93*
Boyan, Norman J. 1922- *WhoAm 94*
Boyar, Sully 1923- *WhoHol 92*
Boyarchuk, Alexander 1931- *WhoScEn 94*
Boyars, Albert 1924- *IntMPA 94*
Boyarski, Joel I. 1946- *WhoFI 94*
Boyarsky, Benjamin William 1934- *WhoAm 94*
Boyarsky, Rose Eisman 1924- *WhoMW 93*
Boyatt, Thomas D. 1933- *WhoAmP 93*
Boyatt, Thomas David 1933- *WhoAm 94*
Boyce, Alan *WhoHol 92*
Boyce, Allan R. 1943- *WhoFI 94*
Boyce, Bert Roy 1938- *WhoAm 94*
Boyce, Charles N. 1935- *WhoBlA 94*
Boyce, Chris 1943- *EncSF 93*
Boyce, Daniel Hobbs 1953- *WhoFI 94*
Boyce, David Edward 1938- *WhoAm 94*
Boyce, Donald Nelson 1938- *WhoAm 94*
Boyce, Edward Wayne, Jr. 1926- *WhoAm 94*
Boyce, Emily Stewart 1933- *WhoAm 94, WhoFI 94*
Boyce, George d1977 *WhoHol 92*
Boyce, George L. 1942- *WhoAmP 93*
Boyce, Gerald G. 1925- *WhoAm 94, WhoAmA 93*
Boyce, Gerard Robert 1954- *WhoAmL 94*
Boyce, Graham Hugh 1945- *Who 94*
Boyce, Henry Emerson *WhoFI 94*
Boyce, Jack d1923 *WhoHol 92*
Boyce, James 1947- *Who 94*
Boyce, James H. 1922- *WhoAmP 93*
Boyce, John G. 1935- *WhoBlA 94*
Boyce, Joseph Frederick 1926- *Who 94*
Boyce, Joseph Nelson 1937- *WhoAm 94, WhoBlA 94*
Boyce, Kenneth Ingram 1942- *WhoMW 93*
Boyce, Laura E. 1962- *WhoBlA 94*
Boyce, Mark Stephen 1950- *WhoWest 94*
Boyce, Meherwan Phiroz 1942- *WhoScEn 94*
Boyce, Michael Cecil 1943- *Who 94*
Boyce, Michael David 1937- *Who 94*
Boyce, Michael Ross 1947- *WhoFI 94*
Boyce, Peter Bradford 1936- *WhoAm 94, WhoScEn 94*
Boyce, Peter John 1935- *Who 94*
Boyce, Richard 1920- *WhoAmA 93N*
Boyce, Richard Lee 1959- *WhoScEn 94*
Boyce, Robert Abbott 1942- *WhoWest 94*
Boyce, Robert (Charles) Leslie 1962- *Who 94*
Boyce, Ronald Reed 1931- *WhoWest 94*
Boyce, Tracy A. 1969- *WhoBlA 94*
Boyce, Walter Edwin 1918- *Who 94*
Boyce, William 1711-1779 *NewGrDO*
Boyce, William G. 1921-1992 *WhoAmA 93N*
Boyce, William George 1921-1992 *WhAm 10*
Boyce, William M. 1928- *WhoBlA 94*
Boycott, Brian Blundell 1924- *IntWW 93, Who 94*
Boycott, Geoff(rey) 1940- *WrDr 94*
Boycott, Geoffrey 1940- *IntWW 93, Who 94*
Boycott, Rosie *IntWW 93*
Boycott, Rosie 1951- *WrDr 94*
Boyd *Who 94*
Boyd, Ada d1978 *WhoHol 92*
Boyd, Adeline Smith 1910- *WhoMW 93*
Boyd, Alan Conduitt 1926- *WhoAm 94*
Boyd, Alan Martin 1959- *WhoAmL 94*
Boyd, Alan Stephenson 1922- *IntWW 93*
Boyd, Alex *WhoAm 94*
Boyd, Alexander Walter 1934- *Who 94*
Boyd, Allen 1945- *WhoAmP 93*
Boyd, Alvah L. 1948- *WhoAmP 93*
Boyd, Aquilino Edgardo 1921- *IntWW 93*
Boyd, Arthur Bernette, Jr. 1947- *WhoMW 93*
Boyd, Arthur Merric Bloomfield 1920- *IntWW 93, Who 94*
Boyd, Atarah *Who 94*
Boyd, Barbara *WhoAmP 93*
Boyd, Barbara Jean 1954- *WhoBlA 94*
Boyd, Betty d1971 *WhoHol 92*
Boyd, Betty 1924- *WhoAmP 93*
Boyd, Beverley Randolph 1947- *WhoAmL 94*
Boyd, Bill d1977 *WhoHol 92*
Boyd, Blanche McCrary *DrAPF 93*
Boyd, Blanche McCrary 1945- *GayLL*
Boyd, Bradford Bivin 1953- *WhoMW 93*
Boyd, Bruce L. 1938- *WhoIns 94*
Boyd, Bruce Michael 1947- *WhoAm 94*
Boyd, Candy Dawson 1946- *BlkWr 2*
Boyd, Carl 1936- *ConAu 141*
Boyd, Charles Flynn 1938- *WhoBlA 94*
Boyd, Charles Graham 1938- *WhoAm 94*
Boyd, Christopher *Who 94*
Boyd, (Thomas) Christopher 1916- *Who 94*
Boyd, Clarence Elmo 1911- *WhoAm 94*
Boyd, Dan Stewart 1949- *WhoAm 94*
Boyd, David J. 1939- *WhoAm 94*
Boyd, David Milton 1918-1990 *WhAm 10*
Boyd, David Preston 1914-1989 *WhAm 10*
Boyd, David Preston 1943- *WhoFI 94*
Boyd, David William 1941- *WhoAm 94*
Boyd, Dawn Michele 1952- *WhoAm 94*
Boyd, Deborah Ann 1955- *WhoMW 93*
Boyd, Deborah Jean 1949- *WhoAmP 93*
Boyd, Delores Rosetta 1950- *WhoBlA 94*
Boyd, Dennis Galt 1931- *Who 94*
Boyd, Dennis Ray 1959- *WhoBlA 94*
Boyd, Doris Regina 1952- *WhoBlA 94*
Boyd, Dorothy 1907- *WhoHol 92*
Boyd, E. 1903-1974 *WhoAmA 93N*
Boyd, Eddie L. 1939- *WhoBlA 94*
Boyd, Edward Hascal 1934- *WhoWest 94*
Boyd, Edward Lee 1930- *WhoAm 94*
Boyd, Edward Lee 1932- *WhoScEn 94*
Boyd, Elise Stephens 1930-1986 *WhAm 10*
Boyd, Elizabeth fl. 1727-1745 *BlmGWL*
Boyd, Elizabeth French 1905- *WrDr 94*
Boyd, Evelyn Shipps *WhoBlA 94*
Boyd, Felix *EncSF 93*
Boyd, Francis *Who 94*
Boyd, (John) Francis 1910- *Who 94*
Boyd, Francis Virgil 1922- *WhoAm 94*
Boyd, Frolly *WhoIns 94*
Boyd, Gary Delane 1932- *WhoAm 94*
Boyd, Gary Harlow 1936- *WhoWest 94*
Boyd, Gavin d1993 *Who 94N*
Boyd, George Arthur 1928- *WhoBlA 94*
Boyd, George Edward 1911- *WhoAm 94*
Boyd, Gordon McArthur 1946- *WhoFI 94*
Boyd, Greg *DrAPF 93*
Boyd, Guy *WhoHol 92*
Boyd, Harry Dalton 1923- *WhoAm 94, WhoAmL 94*
Boyd, Ian Robertson 1922- *Who 94*
Boyd, James Brown 1937- *WhoAm 94, WhoWest 94*
Boyd, James Edward 1928- *Who 94*
Boyd, James Fleming 1920- *Who 94*
Boyd, James Harold Allen 1951- *WhoAmP 93*
Boyd, James Henderson 1928- *WhoAmA 93*
Boyd, James Preston, Jr. 1929- *WhoAmP 93*
Boyd, James Robert 1946- *WhoAm 94, WhoFI 94*
Boyd, Jan Gan *WhoHol 92*
Boyd, Jimmy 1939- *WhoHol 92*
Boyd, John *Who 94*
Boyd, John d1779 *AmRev*
Boyd, John 1919- *EncSF 93, WrDr 94*
Boyd, (David) John 1935- *Who 94*
Boyd, John (Dixon Ikle) 1936- *Who 94*
Boyd, John A. 1928- *WhoIns 94*
Boyd, John Addison, Jr. 1930- *WhoScEn 94*
Boyd, John David 1939- *WhoAmA 93*
Boyd, John E. 1946- *WhoAm 94, WhoAmL 94*
Boyd, John Garth 1942- *WhoWest 94*
Boyd, John Hamilton 1924- *WhoAm 94*
Boyd, John Howard 1950- *WhoFI 94*
Boyd, John Kent 1910- *WhoAm 94, WhoFI 94*
Boyd, John MacInnes 1933- *Who 94*
Boyd, John Thomas 1927- *WhoAmL 94*
Boyd, Joseph Arthur, Jr 1916- *WhoAm 94, WhoAmP 93*
Boyd, Joseph Aubrey 1921- *IntWW 93, WhoAm 94*
Boyd, Joseph Don 1926- *WhoAm 94*
Boyd, Joseph L. 1947- *WhoBlA 94*
Boyd, Karen White 1936- *WhoAmA 93*
Boyd, Lakin 1946- *WhoAmA 93*
Boyd, Landis Lee 1923- *WhoAm 94, WhoScEn 94*
Boyd, Laura W. 1949- *WhoAmP 93*
Boyd, Leona Potter 1907- *WhoWest 94*
Boyd, Leslie Balfour 1914- *Who 94*
Boyd, Liona Maria *WhoAm 94*
Boyd, Louis Jefferson 1928- *WhoAm 94*
Boyd, Louise Arner 1887-1972 *WhWE*
Boyd, Louise Yvonne 1959- *WhoBlA 94*
Boyd, Lucille I. 1906-1992 *WhoBlA 94N*
Boyd, Malcolm 1923- *GayLL, WhoAm 94, WrDr 94*
Boyd, Marc Adam 1960- *WhoWest 94*
Boyd, Mary d1970 *WhoHol 92*
Boyd, Mary Olert 1930- *WhoAmP 93*
Boyd, Megan *DrAPF 93*
Boyd, Melba Joyce 1950- *WhoBlA 94*
Boyd, Michael 1936- *WhoAmA 93*
Boyd, Michael Alan 1937- *WhoAm 94*
Boyd, Michael Joel 1938- *WhoIns 94*
Boyd, Miller W., Jr. 1934- *WhoBlA 94*
Boyd, Morgan Alistair 1934- *Who 94*
Boyd, Morton *Who 94*
Boyd, (John) Morton 1925- *Who 94*
Boyd, Muriel Isabel Belton 1910- *WhoBlA 94*
Boyd, Nancy *GayLL*
Boyd, Obie Dale 1925- *WhoAmP 93*
Boyd, Paul Milton 1955- *WhoAmL 94*
Boyd, Peter James 1919- *WhoAmL 94*
Boyd, Randall M. 1946- *WhoIns 94*
Boyd, Richard Alfred 1927- *WhoAm 94*
Boyd, Richard Hays 1929- *WhoScEn 94*
Boyd, Richard Henry 1843-1922 *DcAmReB 2*
Boyd, Richard Lyn 1953- *WhoMW 93*
Boyd, Richard Victor 1942- *WhoWest 94*
Boyd, Robert (Lewis Fullarton) 1922- *Who 94*
Boyd, Robert E. 1939- *WhoFI 94*
Boyd, Robert Friend 1927- *WhoAmL 94*
Boyd, Robert Giddings, Jr. 1940- *WhoAm 94*
Boyd, Robert Jamison 1930- *WhoFI 94*
Boyd, Robert John, III 1961- *WhoAmL 94*
Boyd, Robert Lewis Fullarton 1922- *IntWW 93*
Boyd, Robert Nathaniel, III 1928- *WhoBlA 94*
Boyd, Robert Stanley 1927- *Who 94*
Boyd, Robert Wright, III 1945- *WhoAm 94*
Boyd, Rozelle 1934- *WhoAmP 93, WhoBlA 94, WhoMW 93*
Boyd, Rutherford d1951 *WhoAmA 93N*
Boyd, Sam 1910-1993 *NewYTBS 93*
Boyd, Scott T. *WhoWest 94*
Boyd, Shyla *DrAPF 93*
Boyd, Stephen d1977 *WhoHol 92*
Boyd, Stephen Mather 1934- *WhoAm 94*
Boyd, Steven Armen 1956- *WhoScEn 94*
Boyd, Steven Don 1957- *WhoAmL 94*
Boyd, Stewart Craufurd 1943- *Who 94*
Boyd, Stowe 1953- *WhoWest 94*
Boyd, Stuart Robert 1939- *WhoAm 94*
Boyd, Sue Abbott *DrAPF 93*
Boyd, T. B., III 1947- *ConBlB 6 [port]*
Boyd, Tanya *WhoHol 92*
Boyd, Terry A. *WhoBlA 94*
Boyd, Theophilus B., III 1947- *WhoBlA 94*
Boyd, Thomas d1779 *WhAmRev*
Boyd, Thomas 1942- *WhoBlA 94*
Boyd, Thomas Henry 1962- *WhoAmL 94*
Boyd, Thomas James Morrow 1932- *WhoScEn 94*
Boyd, Thomas Marshall 1946- *WhoAm 94, WhoAmL 94*
Boyd, Tom 1928- *WhoAmP 93*
Boyd, Virginia Ann Lewis 1944- *WhoScEn 94*
Boyd, Vivienne (Myra) 1926- *Who 94*
Boyd, W(illiam) Harland 1912- *WrDr 94*
Boyd, Waldo T. 1918- *WrDr 94*
Boyd, Wayne Edwin 1939- *WhoAmP 93*
Boyd, Wilda Mae 1936- *WhoAmP 93*
Boyd, Willard Lee 1927- *WhoAm 94, WhoMW 93*
Boyd, William d1935 *WhoHol 92*
Boyd, William d1972 *WhoHol 92*
Boyd, William 1952- *WrDr 94*
Boyd, William, Jr. 1915- *WhoAm 94*
Boyd, William Andrew Murray 1952- *IntWW 93, Who 94*
Boyd, William Arthur, II 1953- *WhoWest 94*
Boyd, William Beaty 1923- *WhoAm 94*
Boyd, William Harland 1912- *WhoWest 94*
Boyd, William Sprott 1943- *WhoAm 94, WhoAmL 94*
Boyd, William Stewart 1952- *WhoBlA 94*
Boyd-Bell, Karen Denise 1955- *WhoMW 93*
Boyd-Brown, Lena Ernestine 1937- *WhoAm 94*
Boyd-Carpenter, Baron 1908- *Who 94*
Boyd-Carpenter, John (Archibald), Lord 1908- *WrDr 94*
Boyd-Carpenter, John Archibald 1908- *IntWW 93*
Boyd-Carpenter, Thomas (Patrick John) 1938- *Who 94*
Boyd-Clinkscales, Mary Elizabeth 1918- *WhoBlA 94*
Boyde, Patrick 1934- *Who 94*
Boydell, Peter Thomas Sherrington 1920- *Who 94*
Boyden, Alan Arthur 1897-1986 *WhAm 10*
Boyden, Allen Marston 1908- *WhoAm 94*
Boyden, Cary C. 1945- *WhoAmL 94*
Boyden, (Harold) James 1910- *Who 94*
Boyden, Joel Michael 1937- *WhoAm 94*
Boyden, Walter Lincoln 1932- *WhoAm 94*
Boyden, Willard Newhall 1897- *WhAm 10*
Boyd-Foy, Mary Louise 1936- *WhoBlA 94*
Boyd of Merton, Viscount 1939- *IntWW 93, Who 94*
Boydston, James Christopher 1947- *WhoWest 94*
Boye, Frederick Charles 1923- *WhoMW 93*
Boye, Karin 1900-1941 *BlmGWL, EncSF 93*
Boye, Mohamed Mahjoub Ould 1947- *IntWW 93*
Boyea, Earl Alfred, Jr. 1951- *WhoMW 93*
Boy-Ed, Ida 1852-1928 *BlmGWL*
Boyenga, Cindy A. 1957- *WhoMW 93*
Boyer, Andrew Ben 1958- *WhoAmL 94*
Boyer, Calvin James 1939- *WhoAm 94*
Boyer, Carl, III 1937- *WhoWest 94*
Boyer, Chance *WhoHol 92*
Boyer, Charles d1978 *WhoHol 92*

Bracey, Clara T. d1941 WhoHol 92
Bracey, Henry J. 1949- WhoBlA 94
Bracey, John Henry, Jr. 1941- WhoBlA 94
Bracey, Lucius H., Jr. 1939- WhoAmL 94
Bracey, Sidney d1942 WhoHol 92
Bracey, William Rubin 1920- WhoBlA 94
Bracey, Willie Earl 1950- WhoBlA 94
Brach, Paul Henry 1924- WhoAmA 93
Brach, Richard S. 1948- WhoAmL 94
Bracher, George 1909- WhoWest 94
Bracher, Karl Dietrich 1922- IntWW 93
Braches, Ernst 1930- IntWW 93
Brachman, Malcolm K. 1926- WhoFI 94
Brachman, Philip Sigmund 1927- WhoAm 94
Brachman, Richard John, II 1951- WhoFI 94, WhoMW 93
Brachman, Todd Harrison 1959- WhoMW 93
Brachmann, Karoline Louise 1777-1822 BlmGWL
Brachtenbach, Robert F. WhoAmP 93
Brachtenbach, Robert F. 1931- WhoAm 94, WhoAmL 94, WhoWest 94
Brack, O. M., Jr. 1938- WhoAm 94
Brack, Phillip d1979 WhoHol 92
Brack, Reginald Kufeld, Jr. 1937- WhoAm 94
Brack, Rita MacDonald 1918- WhoAmP 93
Brack, Terence John 1938- Who 94
Brack, Vektis EncSF 93
Bracken, Andrew Joseph 1961- WhoAmL 94
Bracken, Charles Herbert 1921- WhoAm 94
Bracken, Chuck Richard 1949- WhoMW 93
Bracken, Eddie 1915- WhoHol 92
Bracken, Eddie 1920- IntMPA 94, WhoAm 94, WhoCom
Bracken, Harry McFarland 1926- WhoAm 94
Bracken, James K. 1952- ConAu 142
Bracken, John P. 1938- WhoAmL 94
Bracken, Kathleen Ann 1947- WhoMW 93
Bracken, Louis Everett 1947- WhoFI 94
Bracken, Peg 1918- WhoAm 94
Bracken, Robert W. 1938- WhoAm 94, WhoFI 94
Brackenbury, Alison 1953- WrDr 94
Brackenbury, Michael Palmer 1930- Who 94
Brackenrich, James D. 1936- WhoAmP 93
Brackenridge, Henry Marie 1786-1871 WhWE
Brackenridge, Hugh Henry 1748-1816 WhAmRev
Brackenridge, Robert L. 1941- WhoAmP 93
Bracker, Virginia Lee d1993 NewYTBS 93
Brackett, Charles 1892-1969 IntDcF 2-4 [port]
Brackett, Colquitt Prater, Jr. 1946- WhoAmL 94
Brackett, Dolli Tingle d1993 NewYTBS 93
Brackett, Douglas Lane 1938- WhoAm 94
Brackett, Edward Boone, III 1936- WhoMW 93, WhoScEn 94
Brackett, Leigh 1915-1978 IntDcF 2-4
Brackett, Leigh (Douglass) 1915-1978 EncSF 93
Brackett, Martin Luther, Jr. 1947- WhoAmL 94
Brackett, Norman E. 1929- WhoAm 94, WhoFI 94
Brackett, Noy E. 1913- WhoAmP 93
Brackett, Peggy Lynn 1953- WhoFI 94
Brackett, Ronald E. 1942- WhoAmL 94
Brackett, Virginia Hemmer 1948- WhoMW 93
Brackley, William Lowell 1919- WhoAm 94
Brackman, Robert 1898-1980 WhoAmA 93N
Brackney, Charles Jackson 1947- WhoAmL 94
Bracy, Michael Blakeslee 1941- WhoAm 94, WhoFI 94
Bracy, Ursula J. 1908- WhoBlA 94
Bracy, Warren D. 1942- WhoAmP 93
Bradbeer, Clive 1933- WhoAm 94
Bradbeer, (John) Derek (Richardson) 1931- IntWW 93, Who 94
Bradberry, Anthony d1987 WhoHol 92
Bradberry, Brent Alan 1939- WhoWest 94
Bradberry, Bruce Martin 1948- WhoWest 94
Bradberry, Richard Paul 1951- WhoBlA 94
Bradbrook, M(uriel) C(lara) 1909-1993 ConAu 141
Bradbrook, Muriel Clara d1993 NewYTBS 93, Who 94N
Bradbrook, Muriel Clara 1909- IntWW 93, WrDr 94
Bradburn, David Denison 1925- WhoAm 94
Bradburn, John 1915- Who 94
Bradburn, Norman M. 1933- WhoAm 94
Bradbury, Baron 1914- Who 94
Bradbury, Anita Jean Who 94
Bradbury, Anthony Vincent 1941- Who 94
Bradbury, Daniel Joseph 1945- WhoAm 94, WhoMW 93
Bradbury, Edgar 1927- Who 94
Bradbury, Edward P. EncSF 93
Bradbury, Edward P. 1939- WrDr 94
Bradbury, Edwin Morton 1933- WhoAm 94, WhoWest 94
Bradbury, Ellen A. 1940- WhoAmA 93
Bradbury, Eric (Blackburn) 1911- Who 94
Bradbury, James, Sr. d1940 WhoHol 92
Bradbury, James, Jr. d1936 WhoHol 92
Bradbury, Jim 1937- ConAu 140
Bradbury, John 1768-1823 WhWE
Bradbury, John Wymond 1960- WhoWest 94
Bradbury, Malcolm 1932- BlmGEL [port]
Bradbury, Malcolm (Stanley) 1932- WrDr 94
Bradbury, Malcolm Stanley 1932- IntWW 93, Who 94
Bradbury, Norris Edwin 1909- WhoAm 94, WhoScEn 94
Bradbury, Ray DrAPF 93
Bradbury, Ray (Douglas) 1920- IntWW 93, RfGShF, TwCYAW, WrDr 94
Bradbury, Ray(mond) (Douglas) 1920- EncSF 93
Bradbury, Ray Douglas 1920- Who 94, WhoAm 94
Bradbury, Robin Mark 1956- WhoFI 94
Bradbury, Saax d1976 WhoHol 92
Bradbury, Thomas Henry 1922- Who 94
Bradbury, William Chapman 1949- WhoAmP 93
Bradbury Reid, Ellen Adele 1940- WhoWest 94
Bradby, David Henry 1942- Who 94
Bradby, Edward Lawrence 1907- Who 94
Braddell, Maurice d1990 WhoHol 92
Braddock, Carol T. 1942- WhoBlA 94
Braddock, Donald Layton 1941- WhoAmL 94
Braddock, Elizabeth Margaret 1899-1970 DcNaB MP
Braddock, John William 1947- WhoScEn 94
Braddock, Marilyn Eugenia 1955- WhoBlA 94
Braddock, Richard S. 1941- WhoAm 94, WhoFI 94
Braddon, Mary Elizabeth 1835-1915 BlmGEL, BlmGWL
Braddon, Russell 1921- EncSF 93, WrDr 94
Braddon, Russell Reading 1921- Who 94
Brademas, John 1927- WhoAm 94, WhoAmP 93
Braden, Bernard d1993 Who 94N
Braden, Bernard 1916- WhoHol 92
Braden, Berwyn Bartow 1928- WhoAm 94
Braden, Brenda Lou 1940- WhoWest 94
Braden, Charles Hosea 1926- WhoAm 94
Braden, David Rice 1924- WhoAm 94
Braden, Dennis DrAPF 93
Braden, Donna R. 1953- WrDr 94
Braden, Efrem Mark 1951- WhoAm 94
Braden, Everette Arnold 1932- WhoBlA 94
Braden, George Walter 1936- WhoWest 94
Braden, Henry E., IV 1944- WhoAmP 93, WhoBlA 94
Braden, Hugh Reginald 1923- Who 94
Braden, James Dale 1934- WhoAm 94, WhoAmP 93
Braden, James Wylie, Jr. 1953- WhoAmL 94
Braden, Joan Kay 1934- WhoAm 94
Braden, John WhoHol 92
Braden, Samuel Edward 1914- WhoAm 94
Braden, Stanton Connell 1960- WhoBlA 94
Braden, Thomas Wardell 1918- WhoAm 94
Braden, Waldo W. 1911-1991 WrDr 94N
Braden, Waldo W. 1911-1992 WhAm 10
Braden, William 1939- IntMPA 94
Braden, William Edward 1919- WhoFI 94
Braden, William Lou 1944- WhoMW 93
Bradfield, Clarence McKinley 1942- WhoBlA 94
Bradfield, Horace Ferguson 1913- WhoBlA 94
Bradfield, John Richard Grenfell 1925- Who 94
Bradfield, Nancy 1913- WrDr 94
Bradfield, Nellie Evangeline 1925- WhoAmP 93
Bradfield, Richard 1896- WhAm 10
Bradfield, Scott (Michael) 1955- EncSF 93
Bradfield, Stephanie Alison 1950- WhoWest 94
Bradford, Archdeacon of Who 94
Bradford, Bishop of 1935- Who 94
Bradford, Earl of 1947- Who 94
Bradford, Mistress BlmGWL
Bradford, Provost of Who 94
Bradford, Alex d1978 WhoHol 92
Bradford, Andrew WhoHol 92
Bradford, Archie J. 1931- WhoBlA 94
Bradford, Arvine M. 1915- WhoBlA 94
Bradford, Barbara Reed 1948- WhoAmL 94
Bradford, Barbara Taylor WhoAm 94
Bradford, Barbara Taylor 1933- BlmGWL, IntWW 93, WrDr 94
Bradford, Carl O. 1932- WhoAm 94, WhoAmL 94
Bradford, Charles Avery d1926 WhoHol 92
Bradford, Charles Edward 1925- WhoBlA 94
Bradford, Charles Lobdell 1936- WhoAm 94, WhoFI 94
Bradford, Christina 1942- WhoAm 94, WhoMW 93
Bradford, David Frantz 1939- WhoAm 94
Bradford, David K. 1953- WhoIns 94
Bradford, David Paul 1955- WhoAmL 94, WhoFI 94, WhoWest 94
Bradford, Dennis Doyle 1945- WhoFI 94
Bradford, Donald Wray 1944- WhoIns 94
Bradford, Edward Alexander Slade 1952- Who 94
Bradford, Elwood Walter 1909- WhoAmP 93
Bradford, Equilla Forrest 1931- WhoBlA 94
Bradford, Eric Watts 1919- Who 94
Bradford, Francis Scott 1898-1961 WhoAmA 93N
Bradford, Garrett Eugene 1970- WhoWest 94
Bradford, Gary C. 1956- WhoBlA 94
Bradford, Georgia Walton 1935- WhoAmP 93
Bradford, Gordon d1993 NewYTBS 93
Bradford, Howard 1919- WhoAm 94, WhoAmA 93, WhoWest 94
Bradford, J.S. EncSF 93
Bradford, James C., Jr. 1933- WhoAm 94, WhoFI 94
Bradford, James Edward 1943- WhoBlA 94
Bradford, Jay 1940- WhoAmP 93
Bradford, John d1983 WhoHol 92
Bradford, John C. 1940- WhoAmP 93
Bradford, John Carroll 1924- WhoAm 94
Bradford, Keith Lynn 1955- WhoAmL 94
Bradford, Lane d1973 WhoHol 92
Bradford, M(elvin) E(ustace) 1934- WrDr 94
Bradford, M(elvin) E(ustace) 1934-1993 ConAu 140
Bradford, Marshall d1971 WhoHol 92
Bradford, Martina Lewis 1952- WhoBlA 94
Bradford, Mary R. 1949- WhoFI 94
Bradford, Matthew C. EncSF 93
Bradford, Melvin E. A. d1993 NewYTBS 93
Bradford, Orcelia Sylvia 1953- WhoMW 93
Bradford, Peter Amory 1942- WhoAm 94, WrDr 94
Bradford, Phillips Verner 1940- WhoScEn 94
Bradford, R(ichard) Knox 1896- WhAm 10
Bradford, Ray 1954- WhoHisp 94
Bradford, Reagan Howard, Jr. 1954- WhoScEn 94
Bradford, Richard WhoHol 92
Bradford, Richard (Roark) 1932- WrDr 94
Bradford, Richard J. 1932- WhoAmP 93
Bradford, Richard Roark 1932- WhoAm 94
Bradford, Robert Edward 1931- WhoAm 94, WhoWest 94
Bradford, Robert Ernest WhoAm 94, WhoFI 94
Bradford, Robert William 1931- WhoWest 94
Bradford, Roy Hamilton 1921- Who 94
Bradford, Susan Kay 1952- WhoScEn 94
Bradford, Thomas 1745-1838 WhAmRev
Bradford, Volta Rowena d1986 WhoHol 92
Bradford, Walter L. DrAPF 93
Bradford, William 1590-1657 DcAmReB 2, HisWorL [port]
Bradford, William (the Elder) 1722-1791 WhAmRev
Bradford, William (the Younger) 1755-1795 WhAmRev
Bradford, William Allen, Jr. 1944- WhoAm 94, WhoAmL 94
Bradford, William Dalton 1931- WhoAm 94
Bradford, William E. 1933- IntWW 93
Bradford, William Edward 1935- WhoFI 94
Bradford, William Hollis, Jr. 1937- WhoAm 94, WhoAmP 93
Bradford-Eaton, Zee 1953- WhoBlA 94
Bradic, Zdravko 1947- WhoScEn 94
Bradie, Peter Richard 1937- WhoAmL 94
Brading, Charles 1935- WhoAmP 93
Brading, Charles Richard 1935- WhoMW 93
Brading, D. A. 1936- WrDr 94
Brading, James Edward, II 1933- WhoAmL 94
Brading, Keith 1917- Who 94
Brading, Stanley Gatewood, Jr. 1954- WhoAmL 94
Bradish, Warren Allen 1937- WhoFI 94
Bradlee, Ben(jamin Crowninshield) 1921- WrDr 94
Bradlee, Benjamin Crowninshield 1921- IntWW 93, WhoAm 94
Bradler, James Edward 1935- WhoAm 94
Bradley, A. C. 1851-1935 BlmGEL
Bradley, Allen 1951- WhoAmP 93
Bradley, Amanda d1916 WhoHol 92
Bradley, Amelia Jane 1947- WhoAmL 94
Bradley, Andrew Thomas, Sr. 1948- WhoBlA 94
Bradley, Anthony Wilfred 1934- Who 94
Bradley, Ardyth DrAPF 93
Bradley, Benjamin Arthur de Burgh 1942- Who 94
Bradley, Betty d1973 WhoHol 92
Bradley, Bill 1921- IntMPA 94
Bradley, Bill 1943- BasBi, CngDr 93, IntWW 93, WhoAm 94, WhoAmL 94, WhoAmP 93
Bradley, Brian Scott 1956- WhoMW 93
Bradley, Buddy 1913- WhoHol 92
Bradley, Burton Gyrth B. Who 94
Bradley, C. William, Jr. 1951- WhoAmL 94
Bradley, Charles H. 1922- WhoAmP 93
Bradley, Charles Harvey, Jr. 1923- WhoAmL 94
Bradley, Charles James, Jr. 1935- WhoAm 94
Bradley, Charles MacArthur 1918- WhoMW 93, WhoScEn 94
Bradley, Charles William 1923- WhoAm 94, WhoScEn 94, WhoWest 94
Bradley, Clarence Walter 1909- WhoAmP 93
Bradley, Clive Who 94
Bradley, Clive 1934- IntWW 93, Who 94
Bradley, (Charles) Clive 1937- Who 94
Bradley, Curley d1985 WhoHol 92
Bradley, Daniel Joseph 1928- IntWW 93, Who 94
Bradley, David DrAPF 93, WhoHol 92
Bradley, David (Henry, Jr.) 1950- WrDr 94
Bradley, David Gilbert 1916-1992 WhAm 10
Bradley, David Hammond 1936- WhoAmP 93
Bradley, David Henry, Jr. 1950- WhoAm 94, WhoBlA 94
Bradley, David John 1937- Who 94
Bradley, David Lee 1950- WhoAmP 93
Bradley, David P(aul) 1954- WhoAmA 93
Bradley, David Quentin 1936- WhoFI 94
Bradley, David R. 1950- WhoIns 94
Bradley, David Rall, Sr. 1917-1988 WhAm 10
Bradley, David Rice 1938- Who 94
Bradley, David Wayne 1959- WhoFI 94
Bradley, Donald A. 1925-1974 AstEnc
Bradley, Donald Charlton 1924- IntWW 93, Who 94
Bradley, Donald Edward 1943- WhoAm 94, WhoAmL 94
Bradley, Dorothy 1920- WhoAmA 93
Bradley, Dorothy 1947- WhoAmP 93
Bradley, Doug WhoHol 92
Bradley, E. Michael 1939- WhoAm 94, WhoAmL 94, WhoFI 94
Bradley, Ed 1941- AfrAmAl 6 [port], IntMPA 94
Bradley, Edgar Leonard 1917- Who 94
Bradley, Edward R. 1941- WhoAm 94, WhoBlA 94
Bradley, Edward William 1927- WhoAm 94
Bradley, Elizabeth Franco 1939- WhoAmL 94
Bradley, Estelle d1990 WhoHol 92
Bradley, F. H. 1846-1924 BlmGEL
Bradley, F(rancis) H(erbert) 1846-1924 EncEth
Bradley, Francine Agnes-Marie 1954- WhoWest 94
Bradley, Francis Xavier 1915- WhoAm 94
Bradley, Fred 1931- WhoAmP 93
Bradley, Frederick W. 1946- WhoAmL 94

Bradley, Frederick Wilcox 1956- *WhoMW 93*
Bradley, George *DrAPF 93*
Bradley, George 1953- *WrDr 94*
Bradley, George H. 1932- *WhoFI 94*
Bradley, Gerald Allen 1927- *WhoAmP 93*
Bradley, Gilbert Francis 1920- *WhoAm 94*
Bradley, Gordon Roy 1921- *WhoAmP 93*
Bradley, Grace 1913- *WhoHol 92*
Bradley, Gwendolyn 1952- *AfrAmAl 6*
Bradley, Harold Whitman 1903-1990 *WhAm 10*
Bradley, Harry d1947 *WhoHol 92*
Bradley, Harry Lynde, Mrs. *WhoAmA 93N*
Bradley, Hilbert L. 1920- *WhoBlA 94*
Bradley, J.F., Jr. 1930- *WhoAm 94*
Bradley, J. Robert 1920- *WhoBlA 94*
Bradley, Jack Carter 1919- *WhoBlA 94*
Bradley, James 1693-1762 *WorScD*
Bradley, James Alexander 1965- *WhoScEn 94, WhoWest 94*
Bradley, James E. 1944- *WrDr 94*
Bradley, James George 1940- *WhoBlA 94*
Bradley, James Howard, Jr. 1936- *WhoBlA 94*
Bradley, James Monroe, Jr. 1934- *WhoBlA 94*
Bradley, James Vandiver 1924- *WrDr 94*
Bradley, Jane *DrAPF 93*
Bradley, Jeb E. 1952- *WhoAmP 93*
Bradley, Jeffrey 1963- *WhoBlA 94*
Bradley, Jesse J., Jr. 1929- *WhoBlA 94*
Bradley, Jessie Mary *WhoBlA 94*
Bradley, John Albertson 1908- *WhoAmP 93*
Bradley, John Andrew 1930- *WhoAm 94*
Bradley, John Daniel, III 1946- *WhoAmP 93*
Bradley, John Edmund 1906- *WhoAm 94*
Bradley, John Floyd 1914- *WhoAmP 93*
Bradley, John H. *WhoHol 92*
Bradley, John Lewis 1917- *WrDr 94*
Bradley, John M. *DrAPF 93*
Bradley, John Michael 1950- *WhoMW 93*
Bradley, John Miller, Jr. 1925- *WhoAm 94*
Bradley, Katherine *BlmGWL*
Bradley, Keith John Charles 1950- *Who 94*
Bradley, Kenneth Daniel 1949- *WhoWest 94*
Bradley, Kevin Joseph 1928- *WhoFI 94*
Bradley, Kim Alexandra 1955- *WhoMW 93*
Bradley, Laurel E. 1952- *WhoAmA 93*
Bradley, Lawrence D., Jr. 1920- *WhoAm 94*
Bradley, Leslie 1907- *WhoHol 92*
Bradley, Lester Eugene 1921- *WhoAm 94*
Bradley, Lisa M. 1951- *WhoAm 94*
Bradley, Lola 1921- *WhoAmP 93*
Bradley, London M., Jr. 1943- *WhoBlA 94*
Bradley, Lovyss d1969 *WhoHol 92*
Bradley, Lynn Louise 1960- *WhoMW 93*
Bradley, M. Louise 1920- *WhoBlA 94*
Bradley, Marilynne Gail 1938- *WhoMW 93*
Bradley, Marion Zimmer 1930- *BlmGWL, EncSF 93, GayLL, TwCYAW, WhoAm 94, WrDr 94*
Bradley, Mark Edmund 1936- *WhoAm 94*
Bradley, Melvin 1938- *WhoAmP 93*
Bradley, Melvin LeRoy 1938- *WhoAm 94, WhoBlA 94*
Bradley, Michael John 1933- *Who 94*
Bradley, Mitchell Hugh 1935- *WhoAm 94*
Bradley, Myra James 1924- *WhoAm 94*
Bradley, Myra James, Sister 1924- *WhoMW 93*
Bradley, Naila d1978 *WhoHol 92*
Bradley, Nolen Eugene, Jr. 1925- *WhoFI 94*
Bradley, Norman Robert 1917-1991 *WhAm 10*
Bradley, Omar N. 1893-1981 *HisDcKW*
Bradley, Patricia Ellen 1951- *WhoAm 94*
Bradley, Patrick Joseph 1954- *WhoMW 93*
Bradley, Paul William 1961- *WhoFI 94*
Bradley, Paula E. 1924- *WhoAmP 93*
Bradley, Peggy Gordon *WhoAmP 93*
Bradley, Peter Edward Moore 1914- *Who 94*
Bradley, Phil Poole 1959- *WhoBlA 94*
Bradley, Philip Tibbs 1938- *WhoAmP 93*
Bradley, Phillip Alden 1954- *WhoAmL 94*
Bradley, R. C. 1929- *WrDr 94*
Bradley, Raymond Joseph 1920- *WhoAm 94, WhoAmL 94*
Bradley, Rebecca Louise 1941- *WhoAmL 94*
Bradley, Richard Alan 1925- *Who 94*
Bradley, Richard Edwin 1926- *WhoAm 94*
Bradley, Richard Gordon, Jr. 1932- *WhoScEn 94*
Bradley, Richard John 1946- *Who 94*
Bradley, Robert Foster 1940- *WhoScEn 94*
Bradley, Robert Lee 1920- *WhoAm 94*
Bradley, Roberta Palm 1947- *WhoBlA 94*
Bradley, Roger Thubron 1936- *Who 94*
Bradley, Roger William 1944- *WhoAmL 94*
Bradley, Ronald Calvin 1915- *WhoAm 94*
Bradley, Ronald James 1943- *WhoAm 94*
Bradley, Ronald Lynn 1958- *WhoFI 94*
Bradley, Russell d1952 *WhoHol 92*
Bradley, Shawn *NewYTBS 93 [port]*
Bradley, Stanley Walter 1927- *Who 94*
Bradley, Stephen 1754-1830 *WhAmRev*
Bradley, Sterling Gaylen 1932- *WhoAm 94, WhoScEn 94*
Bradley, Stewart *WhoHol 92*
Bradley, Stuart *Who 94*
Bradley, (Charles) Stuart 1936- *Who 94*
Bradley, Susan M. *WhoScEn 94*
Bradley, Thomas 1917- *AfrAmAl 6 [port], IntWW 93, WhoAm 94, WhoAmP 93, WhoBlA 94, WhoWest 94*
Bradley, Thomas Andrew 1957- *WhoAm 94*
Bradley, Thomas George 1926- *Who 94*
Bradley, Thomas S. *WhoAmP 93*
Bradley, Todd Arthur 1951- *WhoAmL 94*
Bradley, Truman d1974 *WhoHol 92*
Bradley, Wade Harlow *WhoFI 94, WhoWest 94*
Bradley, Walter D. 1946- *WhoFI 94, WhoWest 94*
Bradley, Walter Dwight 1946- *WhoAmP 93*
Bradley, Walter Lee 1943- *WhoScEn 94*
Bradley, Walter Thomas, Jr. 1925- *WhoBlA 94*
Bradley, Wayne W. 1948- *WhoBlA 94*
Bradley, Wesley Holmes 1922- *WhoAm 94*
Bradley, Will *EncSF 93*
Bradley, Will d1989 *WhoHol 92*
Bradley, William B. 1926- *WhoBlA 94*
Bradley, William Ewart 1910- *Who 94*
Bradley, William Guy 1956- *WhoScEn 94*
Bradley, William H. 1944- *WhoAmL 94*
Bradley, William Steven 1949- *WhoAmA 93, WhoMW 93*
Bradley Goodman, Michael *Who 94*
Bradlow, Basil Arnold 1929- *WhoMW 93*
Bradlow, Frank Rosslyn 1913- *WrDr 94*
Bradlow, Herbert Leon 1924- *WhoScEn 94*
Bradman, Donald (George) 1908- *Who 94*
Bradman, Donald (George), Sir 1908- *WrDr 94*
Bradman, Donald George 1908- *IntWW 93*
Bradman, Godfrey Michael 1936- *IntWW 93, Who 94*
Bradna, Joanne Justice 1952- *WhoMW 93*
Bradna, Olympe 1920- *WhoHol 92*
Bradney, John Robert 1931- *Who 94*
Brado, Michael Wayne 1958- *WhoWest 94*
Bradpiece, Theodore Grant 1965- *WhoWest 94*
Bradshaw, Afton B. *WhoAmP 93*
Bradshaw, Anthony David 1926- *IntWW 93, Who 94*
Bradshaw, Billy Dean 1940- *WhoFI 94, WhoMW 93*
Bradshaw, Carl John 1930- *WhoAm 94, WhoAmL 94, WhoWest 94*
Bradshaw, Carolyn Sue 1935- *WhoMW 93*
Bradshaw, Conrad Allan 1922- *WhoAm 94*
Bradshaw, David *WhoHol 92*
Bradshaw, Doris Marion 1928- *WhoBlA 94*
Bradshaw, Dove 1949- *WhoAmA 93*
Bradshaw, Eugene Barry 1938- *WhoAmL 94*
Bradshaw, Eunice d1973 *WhoHol 92*
Bradshaw, Gerald Haywood 1934- *WhoBlA 94*
Bradshaw, Gillian 1956- *WrDr 94*
Bradshaw, Glenn Raymond 1922- *WhoAmA 93*
Bradshaw, Howard Holt 1937- *WhoAm 94*
Bradshaw, Ira Webb 1929- *WhoFI 94, WhoWest 94*
Bradshaw, James R. 1938- *WhoWest 94*
Bradshaw, Jean Paul, II 1956- *WhoAm 94, WhoAmL 94*
Bradshaw, Jeffrey Mark 1956- *WhoWest 94*
Bradshaw, Joel C. 1946- *WhoAmP 93*
Bradshaw, John E. 1933- *CurBio 93 [port]*
Bradshaw, Kenneth (Anthony) 1922- *Who 94*
Bradshaw, Lawrence A. 1932- *WhoBlA 94*
Bradshaw, Lawrence James 1945- *WhoAmA 93*
Bradshaw, Lillian Moore 1915- *WhoAm 94*
Bradshaw, Lionel d1918 *WhoHol 92*
Bradshaw, Maire 1943- *BlmGWL*
Bradshaw, Martin Clark 1935- *Who 94*
Bradshaw, Mary Fenton 1933- *WhoMW 93*
Bradshaw, Melvin B. 1922-1991 *WhAm 10*
Bradshaw, Michael T. 1945- *WhoAmL 94*
Bradshaw, Murray Charles 1930- *WhoAm 94, WhoWest 94*
Bradshaw, Nanci Marie 1940- *WhoFI 94*
Bradshaw, Peter 1935- *IntWW 93, Who 94, WhoAm 94, WhoScEn 94*
Bradshaw, Ralph Alden 1941- *WhoAm 94, WhoWest 94*
Bradshaw, Richard (Phillip) 1920- *Who 94*
Bradshaw, Richard James 1944- *WhoAm 94*
Bradshaw, Richard Rotherwood 1916- *WhoAm 94*
Bradshaw, Robert George 1915- *WhoAmA 93*
Bradshaw, Robert Wallace, Jr. 1933- *WhoAmP 93*
Bradshaw, Rod Eric 1951- *WhoFI 94*
Bradshaw, Stanley J. 1957- *WhoAm 94, WhoFI 94*
Bradshaw, Terry *ProFbHF [port]*
Bradshaw, Terry 1948- *WhoAm 94, WhoHol 92*
Bradshaw, Walter H., Jr. 1938- *WhoBlA 94*
Bradshaw, Wayne *WhoBlA 94*
Bradshaw, William David 1928- *WhoAm 94, WhoMW 93*
Bradshaw, William Peter 1936- *Who 94*
Bradshaw, William R. 1851-1927 *EncSF 93*
Bradsher, Henry S(t. Amant) 1931- *WrDr 94*
Bradstock, John *WhoAm 94*
Bradstreet, Anne Dudley 1612-1672 *BlmGWL*
Bradstreet, Bernard Francis 1945- *WhoAm 94*
Bradstreet, Simon 1603-1697 *DcNaB MP*
Bradt, Gene Paul 1937- *WhoAmL 94*
Bradt, Hale Van Dorn 1930- *WhoAm 94*
Bradt, Rexford Hale 1908- *WhoMW 93, WhoScEn 94*
Bradunas, Edward Terence 1944- *WhoFI 94*
Bradway, Becky *DrAPF 93*
Bradway, Becky J. 1957- *WhoMW 93*
Bradwell, Area Bishop of 1945- *Who 94*
Bradwell, David 1931- *WhoFI 94*
Bradwell, James 1925- *WrDr 94*
Brady, Adelaide Burks 1926- *WhoAm 94*
Brady, Alexander *WhoAm 94*
Brady, Alice d1939 *WhoHol 92*
Brady, Barbara Dianne 1947- *WhoAmL 94*
Brady, Carl Franklin 1919- *WhoAm 94*
Brady, Carolyn 1937- *WhoAmA 93*
Brady, Carolyn L. 1941- *WhoAmP 93*
Brady, Charles 1926- *WhoAmA 93*
Brady, Charles A. 1945- *WhoBlA 94*
Brady, Colleen Anne 1951- *WhoWest 94*
Brady, Conor 1949- *IntWW 93*
Brady, David D. 1937- *WhoAmP 93*
Brady, Edmund Matthew, Jr. 1941- *WhoAm 94*
Brady, Edwin J. d1942 *WhoHol 92*
Brady, Ernest William 1917- *Who 94*
Brady, Francis J. 1945- *WhoAmL 94*
Brady, Francis R., Jr. 1931- *WhoAmP 93*
Brady, Frank Benton 1914- *WhoAm 94*
Brady, Fred d1961 *WhoHol 92*
Brady, George K(eyports) 1893- *WhAm 10*
Brady, George Moore 1922- *WhoAm 94*
Brady, Harvey Joe 1944- *WhoAmP 93*
Brady, James d1987 *WhoHol 92*
Brady, James Joseph 1936- *WhoAm 94*
Brady, James Joseph 1944- *WhoAmP 93*
Brady, James S. 1944- *IntWW 93, WhoAm 94, WhoAmL 94*
Brady, James Winston 1928- *WhoAm 94*
Brady, Jane Frances 1935- *WhoAm 94*
Brady, Jane Mariette 1955- *WhoWest 94*
Brady, Joan 1939- *ConAu 141*
Brady, John (Mary) 1955- *WrDr 94*
Brady, John David 1956- *WhoAmP 93*
Brady, John E. 1945- *WhoAmL 94*
Brady, John Joseph, Jr. 1923- *WhoAm 94*
Brady, John Patrick, Jr. 1929- *WhoWest 94*
Brady, John Paul 1928- *WhoAm 94*
Brady, Joseph John 1926- *WhoAm 94*
Brady, Joseph Vincent 1922- *WhoAm 94*
Brady, Julio A. 1942- *WhoBlA 94*
Brady, Kathleen *DrAPF 93*
Brady, Kevin 1955- *WhoAmP 93*
Brady, Lawrence Peter 1940- *WhoAmL 94*
Brady, Luther W. 1925- *WhoAmA 93*
Brady, Luther W., Jr. 1925- *WhoAm 94*
Brady, Marie E. d1981 *WhoHol 92*
Brady, Martin R., Jr. 1938- *WhoIns 94*
Brady, Mary Sue 1945- *WhoScEn 94*
Brady, Mathew 1823?-1896 *ModArCr 4 [port]*
Brady, Mathew B. c. 1823-1896 *AmSocL*
Brady, Maureen *DrAPF 93*
Brady, Melvin Michael 1933- *WhoScEn 94*
Brady, (John) Michael 1945- *Who 94*
Brady, Michael Cameron 1957- *WhoFI 94, WhoMW 93*
Brady, Michael J. 1941- *WhoAmL 94*
Brady, Michael Jeff 1941- *WhoAmP 93*
Brady, Nelvia M. 1948- *WhoAm 94, WhoBlA 94*
Brady, Nicholas F. 1930- *IntWW 93*
Brady, Nicholas Frederick 1930- *Who 94, WhoAm 94, WhoAmP 93*
Brady, Nyle C. 1920- *WhoAm 94*
Brady, P. John 1954- *WhoAmL 94*
Brady, Pat d1972 *WhoHol 92*
Brady, Patricia 1943- *WrDr 94*
Brady, Patrick 1933- *WhoAm 94*
Brady, Paul R., III 1952- *WhoAmL 94*
Brady, Philip *DrAPF 93*
Brady, Phillip Donley 1951- *WhoAm 94*
Brady, Richard Alan 1934- *WhoAm 94, WhoAmL 94*
Brady, Robert D. 1946- *WhoAmA 93*
Brady, Robert Eugene 1933- *WhoWest 94*
Brady, Rodney Howard 1933- *WhoAm 94*
Brady, Ronald L. 1944- *WhoFI 94*
Brady, Roscoe O. 1923- *WhoAm 94*
Brady, Roscoe Owen 1923- *IntWW 93, WhoScEn 94*
Brady, Ryder *DrAPF 93*
Brady, Scott d1985 *WhoHol 92*
Brady, Stephen Gerald 1947- *WhoFI 94*
Brady, Terence Joseph 1939- *Who 94*
Brady, Terrence 1939- *WhoHol 92*
Brady, Terrence Joseph 1940- *WhoAmL 94*
Brady, Terrie *WhoAmP 93*
Brady, Thomas Carl 1947- *WhoAmL 94*
Brady, Thomas Denis 1955- *WhoFI 94, WhoWest 94*
Brady, Thomas Michael 1962- *WhoWest 94*
Brady, Upton Birnie 1938- *WhoAm 94*
Brady, Veronica d1964 *WhoHol 92*
Brady, William d1936 *WhoHol 92*
Brady, William E. *WhoAmP 93*
Brady, William Robert 1956- *WhoAmP 93*
Brady, William S. 1938- *WrDr 94*
Brady, Wray Grayson 1918- *WhoAm 94*
Braeden, Eric *IntMPA 94*
Braeden, Eric 1942- *WhoHol 92*
Braein, Edvard Fliflet 1924-1976 *NewGrDO*
Braen, Bernard Benjamin 1928- *WhoAm 94*
Braestrup, Peter 1929- *WhoAm 94*
Braeutigam, Ronald Ray 1947- *WhoFI 94, WhoScEn 94*
Brafford, William Charles 1932- *WhoAm 94, WhoAmL 94*
Brafman, Benjamin 1948- *WhoAmL 94*
Braga, Daniel 1946- *WhoFI 94*
Braga, (Antonio) Francisco 1868-1945 *NewGrDO*
Braga, Gaetano 1829-1907 *NewGrDO*
Braga, Larry Dennis 1948- *WhoFI 94*
Braga, Lucia 1934- *WhoWomW 91*
Braga, Maria Ondina 1932- *BlmGWL*
Braga, Sonia 1950- *IntMPA 94, WhoHol 92*
Bragaglia, Arturo d1962 *WhoHol 92*
Bragagnolo, Julio Alfredo 1941- *WhoScEn 94*
Bragar, Philip Frank 1925- *WhoAmA 93*
Braga Santos, (Jose Manuel) Joly *NewGrDO*
Bragdon, Catherine Creamer 1957- *WhoAmA 93*
Bragdon, Clifford Richardson 1940- *WhoScEn 94*
Bragdon, Paul Errol 1927- *WhoAm 94, WhoWest 94*
Bragenzer, June Anna Ruth Grimm 1923- *WhoMW 93*
Brager, Walter S. 1925- *WhoAm 94*
Bragg, Albert Forsey 1932- *WhoFI 94*
Bragg, Bernard 1928- *EncDeaf*
Bragg, Charles David 1939- *WhoFI 94*
Bragg, Darrell Brent 1933- *WhoWest 94*
Bragg, David Gordon 1933- *WhoAm 94*
Bragg, E. Ann 1935- *WhoAmA 93*
Bragg, Ellis Meredith, Jr. 1947- *WhoAmL 94*
Bragg, Harland W. *WhoAmP 93*
Bragg, Janet Harmon d1993 *WhoBlA 94N*
Bragg, Jay Miller 1950- *WhoAmP 93*
Bragg, Jefferson Davis 1896- *WhAm 10*
Bragg, Jeffrey S. 1949- *WhoIns 94*
Bragg, Jeffrey Steven 1949- *WhoAmP 93*
Bragg, John Mackie 1921- *WhoAm 94*
Bragg, John Thomas 1918- *WhoAmP 93*
Bragg, Joseph L. 1937- *WhoBlA 94*
Bragg, Lawrence D., III 1948- *WhoAmL 94*

Bragg, Melvyn 1939- *ConTFT 11, IntWW 93, Who 94, WrDr 94*
Bragg, Michael Ellis 1947- *WhoAm 94, WhoAmL 94, WhoFI 94, WhoMW 93*
Bragg, Patricia Dunmire 1949- *WhoAmL 94*
Bragg, Richard Christopher 1967- *WhoMW 93*
Bragg, Robert Henry 1919- *WhoBlA 94*
Bragg, Robert Lloyd 1916- *WhoBlA 94*
Bragg, Ruth Gembicki 1943- *SmATA 77 [port]*
Bragg, Stephen Lawrence 1923- *Who 94*
Bragg, William Henry 1862-1942 *WorInv*
Bragg, William Lawrence 1890-1971 *WorInv*
Braggins, Derek Henry 1931- *Who 94*
Braggiotti, Francesca *WhoHol 92*
Braggiotti, Herbert d1984 *WhoHol 92*
Bragin, David Held 1944- *WhoAm 94*
Bragin, Jack S. 1965- *WhoFI 94*
Bragin, Vyacheslav Ivanovich 1939- *LoBiDrD*
Braginsky, Stanislav Iosifovich 1926- *WhoScEn 94*
Bragman, Michael J. 1940- *WhoAmP 93*
Braha, Thomas I. 1947- *WhoAm 94, WhoFI 94*
Braham, Allan (John Witney) 1937- *WrDr 94*
Braham, Allan John Witney 1937- *IntWW 93, Who 94*
Braham, Delphine Doris 1946- *WhoMW 93*
Braham, Harold 1907- *Who 94*
Braham, Harry d1923 *WhoHol 92*
Braham, Horace d1955 *WhoHol 92*
Braham, Jeanne *DrAPF 93*
Braham, John 1774-1856 *NewGrDO*
Braham, John Robert Daniel 1920-1974 *DcNaB MP*
Braham, Lionel d1947 *WhoHol 92*
Braham, Randolph L(ewis) 1922- *ConAu 41NR*
Braham, Randolph Lewis 1922- *WhoAm 94*
Brahe, Tycho 1546-1601 *AstEnc, WorScD*
Brahimi, Abdelhamid 1936- *IntWW 93*
Brahimi, Lakhdar 1934- *Who 94*
Brahm, John 1893-1982 *HorFD [port]*
Brahm, John W. 1936- *WhoAmL 94*
Brahma, Chandra Sekhar 1941- *WhoAm 94, WhoAsA 94*
Brahmananda, Palahally Ramaiya 1926- *IntWW 93, WrDr 94*
Brahmbhatt, Sudhirkumar 1951- *WhoFI 94, WhoScEn 94*
Brahmbhatt, Varsha 1969- *WhoMW 93*
Brahms, Thomas Walter 1945- *WhoAm 94*
Brahs, Stuart J. 1940- *WhoIns 94*
Brahtz, John Frederick Peel 1918- *WhoScEn 94*
Braibant, Guy 1927- *IntWW 93*
Braibanti, Ralph John 1920- *WhoAm 94*
Braid, Malcolm Ross 1947- *WhoScEn 94*
Braida, Louis Benjamin Daniel *WhoScEn 94*
Braide, Robert David 1953- *WhoAm 94*
Braidek, John George *WhoScEn 94*
Braiden, Paul Mayo 1941- *Who 94*
Braiden, Rose Margaret 1922- *WhoWest 94*
Braiden, Rose Margaret J. 1923- *WhoAmA 93*
Braider, Donald 1923-1977 *WhoAmA 93N*
Braidon, Thomas d1950 *WhoHol 92*
Braidwood, Linda Schreiber 1909- *WhoAm 94*
Braidwood, Robert J. 1907- *WhoAm 94*
Braidwood, Robert John 1907- *IntWW 93*
Braidwood, Thomas 1715-1806 *EncDeaf*
Braig, Betty Lou 1931- *WhoAmA 93*
Braiker, Harriet B. 1948- *ConAu 141*
Brail, Richard Kenneth 1940- *WhoAm 94*
Brailes, William de fl. 1230-1260 *DcNaB MP*
Brailey, Troy *WhoAmP 93*
Brailey, Troy 1916- *WhoBlA 94*
Braille, Louis 1809-1852 *WorInv [port]*
Brailsford, Alan David 1930- *WhoMW 93*
Brailsford, Marvin D. 1939- *WhoBlA 94*
Brailsford, Marvin Delano 1939- *AfrAmG [port]*
Brain, Baron 1926- *Who 94*
Brain, Albert Edward Arnold 1917- *Who 94*
Brain, Donald Chester 1917- *WhoIns 94*
Brain, George Bernard 1920- *WhoAm 94*
Brain, J(oy) B(lundell) 1926- *ConAu 41NR*
Brain, Joseph David 1940- *WhoAm 94*
Brain, (Henry) Norman 1907- *Who 94*
Brain, Romney R. 1951- *WhoAmL 94*
Brain, Terence John 1938- *Who 94*
Brainard, Cecilia Manguerra *DrAPF 93*
Brainard, Edward Axdal 1931- *WhoAm 94*
Brainard, James C. 1954- *WhoAmL 94*
Brainard, Jayne Dawson *WhoAm 94*
Brainard, Joe *DrAPF 93*
Brainard, Joe 1942- *WhoAmA 93*
Brainard, Owen 1924- *WhoAmA 93*
Brainard, Paul Henry 1928- *WhoAm 94*
Brainard, William Crittenden 1935- *WhoAm 94*
Braine *Who 94*
Braine, John 1922- *BlmGEL*
Braine, Richard Allix 1900- *Who 94*
Braine of Wheatley, Baron 1914- *Who 94*
Brainerd, David 1718-1747 *DcAmReB 2, EncNAR*
Brainerd, John Calhoun 1934- *WhoWest 94*
Brainin, Norbert 1923- *IntWW 93, Who 94*
Brainin-Rodríguez, Laura 1951- *WhoHisp 94*
Brais, F(rancois) Philippe 1894- *WhAm 10*
Braislin, Gordon Stuart 1901-1990 *WhAm 10*
Braiterman, Thea G. 1927- *WhoAmP 93*
Braithwaite, Bernard Richard 1917- *Who 94*
Braithwaite, Charles Henry 1920- *WhoWest 94*
Braithwaite, Cleantis Esewanu *WhoScEn 94*
Braithwaite, E(dward) R(ichard) 1922- *WrDr 94*
Braithwaite, Eustace Adolphe 1922- *IntWW 93*
Braithwaite, Eustace Edward Adolph Ricardo 1922- *Who 94*
Braithwaite, (Joseph) Franklin (Madders) 1917- *Who 94*
Braithwaite, Gordon L. *WhoBlA 94*
Braithwaite, James Roland 1927- *WhoBlA 94*
Braithwaite, John Michael 1958- *WhoFI 94*
Braithwaite, John Neldon 1957- *WhoAmL 94*
Braithwaite, Joseph Lorne 1941- *WhoAm 94, WhoFI 94*
Braithwaite, Lilian d1948 *WhoHol 92*
Braithwaite, M. Christine 1945- *WhoMW 93*
Braithwaite, Mark Winston 1954- *WhoBlA 94*
Braithwaite, Nicholas (Paul Dallon) 1939- *NewGrDO*
Braithwaite, Rodric (Quentin) 1932- *Who 94*
Braithwaite, Rodric Quentin 1932- *IntWW 93*
Braithwaite, Walt Waldiman 1945- *WhoWest 94*
Braithwaite, (Henry) Warwick 1896-1971 *NewGrDO*
Braithwaite, William Thomas Scatchard 1948- *Who 94*
Braitstein, Marcel 1935- *WhoAmA 93*
Brajder, Antonio 1942- *WhoScEn 94*
Brake, Cecil Clifford 1932- *WhoAm 94*
Brake, Patricia 1942- *WhoHol 92*
Brakeall, Mary Jane 1939- *WhoMW 93*
Brakefield, Charles B. d1993 *NewYTBS 93 [port]*
Brakel, Linda A. Wimer 1950- *WhoScEn 94*
Brakeley, George Archibald, Jr. 1916- *WhoAm 94*
Brakeman, Louis Freeman 1932- *WhoAm 94*
Brakensiek, Jay Clemence 1954- *WhoWest 94*
Braker, William Paul 1926- *WhoAm 94, WhoMW 93, WhoScEn 94*
Brakhage, James Stanley 1933- *WhoAm 94, WhoAmA 93, WhoWest 94*
Brakhage, (James) Stan(ley) 1933- *WrDr 94*
Brakke, Myron Kendall 1921- *IntWW 93, WhoAm 94*
Brakke, P(erry) Michael 1943- *WhoAmA 93*
Brakov, Yergeniy Alekseyevich 1937- *IntWW 93*
Braks, Gerrit J. M. 1933- *IntWW 93*
Braley, Jean *WhoAmA 93*
Bralver, Peter Jeffrey 1943- *WhoWest 94*
Braly, Terrell Alfred 1953- *WhoFI 94*
Bram, Christopher 1952- *GayLL*
Bram, Isabelle Mary Rickey McDonough *WhoMW 93*
Bram, Leon Leonard 1931- *WhoAm 94*
Bramah, Ernest 1868-1942 *DcNaB MP, EncSF 93*
Bramah, Joseph 1748-1814 *WorInv*
Bramall, Baron 1923- *Who 94*
Bramall, (Ernest) Ashley 1916- *Who 94*
Bramall, Edwin (Noel Westby) 1923- *IntWW 93*
Bramall, Margaret Elaine 1916- *Who 94*
Braman, Heather Ruth 1934- *WhoMW 93, WhoScEn 94*
Braman, S. Kristine 1956- *WhoScEn 94*
Braman, Sandra *DrAPF 93*
Bramann, Jorn K(arl) 1938- *ConAu 43NR*
Bramante, A. Donald 1930- *WhoAm 94, WhoAmP 93*
Bramante, Pietro Ottavio 1920- *WhoAm 94*
Brambell, Wilfrid d1985 *WhoHol 92*
Brambila, Art Peralta 1941- *WhoHisp 94*
Brambilla, Giuseppina 1819-1903 *NewGrDO*
Brambilla, Marietta 1807-1875 *NewGrDO*
Brambilla, Teresa 1813-1895 *NewGrDO*
Brambilla Family *NewGrDO*
Brambilla-Ponchielli, Teresa 1845-1921 *NewGrDO*
Bramble, A. V. d1963 *WhoHol 92*
Bramble, Frank P. 1948- *WhoAm 94, WhoFI 94*
Bramble, James Henry 1930- *WhoAm 94, WhoScEn 94*
Bramble, John Myles 1946- *WhoWest 94*
Bramble, Peter W. D. 1945- *WhoBlA 94*
Bramble, Ronald Lee 1937- *WhoAmL 94, WhoFI 94*
Bramblett, Barbara Doyle 1951- *WhoMW 93*
Brame, Gloria G. *DrAPF 93*
Brame, Joseph Robert, III 1942- *WhoAm 94, WhoAmL 94*
Brame, Marillyn A. 1928- *WhoWest 94*
Brame, Walter Melvyn 1946- *WhoBlA 94*
Bramhall, Dorothy *WhoHol 92*
Bramhall, Kib 1933- *WhoAmA 93*
Bramhall, Robert Richard 1927- *WhoAm 94, WhoFI 94*
Bramlet, Roland Charles 1921- *WhoScEn 94*
Bramlett, Betty Jane *WhoAmA 93*
Bramlett, Christopher Lewis 1938- *WhoAm 94*
Bramlett, Lonnie L., Jr. 1943- *WhoMW 93*
Bramlett, Paul Kent 1944- *WhoAmL 94*
Bramlette, David C., III 1939- *WhoAm 94, WhoAmL 94*
Bramley, Flora *WhoHol 92*
Bramley, Paul (Anthony) 1923- *Who 94*
Bramley, Raymond 1891- *WhoHol 92*
Bramley, Russell 1945- *WhoAmP 93*
Bramley, William *WhoHol 92*
Bramly, Serge 1949- *ConAu 142*
Bramma, Harry Wakefield 1936- *Who 94*
Brammer, Forest Evert 1913- *WhoAm 94*
Brammer, Julius 1877-1943? *NewGrDO*
Brammer, Lawrence Martin 1922- *WhoAm 94*
Brammer, Leonard Griffith 1906- *Who 94*
Brammer, Phil 1932- *WhoAmP 93*
Bramnick, Michael Richard 1965- *WhoAmL 94*
Bramnik, Robert Paul 1949- *WhoAm 94*
Bramon, Christopher John 1960- *WhoScEn 94*
Brampton, Edward c. 1440-1508 *DcNaB MP*
Brampton, Sally Jane 1955- *Who 94*
Brams, Joan *WhoAmA 93*
Brams, Marvin Robert 1937- *WhoAm 94*
Brams, Steven John 1940- *WhoAm 94*
Bramson, Leon 1930- *WhoAm 94, WrDr 94*
Bramson, Phyllis Halperin 1941- *WhoAmA 93*
Bramson, Robert Sherman 1938- *WhoAm 94, WhoScEn 94*
Bramwell, Charlotte 1929- *WrDr 94*
Bramwell, Fitzgerald Burton 1945- *WhoBlA 94*
Bramwell, Henry 1919- *WhoAm 94, WhoBlA 94*
Bramwell, Marvel Lynnette 1947- *WhoWest 94*
Bramwell, Patricia Ann 1941- *WhoBlA 94*
Bramwell, Richard Mervyn 1944- *Who 94*
Bran, Edgar Antonio 1934- *WhoHisp 94*
Branagan, James Joseph 1943- *WhoAm 94*
Branagh, Emma *Who 94*
Branagh, Kenneth 1960- *IntMPA 94, IntWW 93, WhoAm 94*
Branagh, Kenneth 1961- *WhoHol 92*
Branagh, Kenneth Charles 1960- *Who 94*
Braña-Lopez, Angel Rafael 1950- *WhoHisp 94*
Branan, Carolyn Benner 1953- *WhoAmL 94*
Branan, James Dale 1939- *WhoMW 93*
Branan, John Maury 1933- *WhoAm 94*
Branca, Andrew Angelo 1950- *WhoScEn 94*
Branca, John Gregory 1950- *WhoAm 94*
Branca, John R. 1924- *WhoAmP 93*
Branca, Vittore (Felice Giovanni) 1913- *IntWW 93*
Brancato, Carolyn Kay 1945- *WhoAm 94*
Brancato, Emanuel Leonard 1914- *WhoAm 94*
Brancato, Leo John 1922- *WhoAm 94*
Brancato, Robin F(idler) 1936- *ChlLR 32 [port], TwCYAW*
Brancel, Ben 1950- *WhoAmP 93*
Branch, Addison A., Sr. 1903- *WhoBlA 94*
Branch, Alan E(dward) 1933- *WrDr 94*
Branch, Andre Jose 1959- *WhoBlA 94*
Branch, B. Lawrence 1937- *WhoBlA 94*
Branch, Bill J. 1932- *WhoAmP 93*
Branch, Charles Henry Hardin 1908-1990 *WhAm 10*
Branch, Clifford 1948- *WhoBlA 94*
Branch, Daniel Hugh 1958- *WhoAmL 94*
Branch, Dorothy L. 1912- *WhoBlA 94*
Branch, Edgar Marquess 1913- *WrDr 94*
Branch, Eldridge Stanley 1906- *WhoBlA 94*
Branch, G. Murray 1914- *WhoBlA 94*
Branch, George 1928- *WhoBlA 94*
Branch, George S. 1948- *WhoAmL 94*
Branch, Geraldine Burton 1908- *WhoBlA 94*
Branch, Harrison 1947- *WhoBlA 94*
Branch, John Curtis 1934- *WhoAm 94, WhoScEn 94*
Branch, Judson B. d1989 *WhAm 10*
Branch, Michael Arthur 1940- *Who 94*
Branch, Otis Linwood 1943- *WhoBlA 94*
Branch, Paul Sheldon, Jr. 1925- *WhoAmP 93*
Branch, Robert Lee 1924- *WhoAm 94*
Branch, Sarah 1938- *WhoHol 92*
Branch, Taylor 1947- *WhoAm 94, WrDr 94*
Branch, Thomas Broughton, III 1936- *WhoAm 94, WhoAmL 94*
Branch, Thomas Harry 1928- *WhoAmP 93*
Branch, Tobie 1927- *WhoAmP 93*
Branch, Turner Williamson 1938- *WhoAmL 94*
Branch, William (Blackwell) 1927- *BlkWr 2*
Branch, William Allan Patrick 1915- *Who 94*
Branch, William Blackwell 1927- *WhoAm 94, WhoBlA 94*
Branch, William McKinley 1918- *WhoBlA 94*
Branchaud, James Howard 1946- *WhoWest 94*
Branche, Derrick *WhoHol 92*
Branche, Gilbert M. 1932- *WhoBlA 94*
Branche, William C., Jr. 1934- *WhoBlA 94*
Branch Simpson, Germaine Gail 1950- *WhoBlA 94*
Branchu, Alexandrine Caroline 1780-1850 *NewGrDO*
Brancker, (John Eustace) Theodore 1909- *Who 94*
Branco, James 1951- *WhoIns 94*
Branco, Joaquim Rafael 1953- *IntWW 93*
Branco, Paulo 1950- *IntDcF 2-4*
Brand *Who 94*
Brand, Alexander George 1918- *Who 94*
Brand, Alice G. *DrAPF 93*
Brand, Charles Macy 1932- *WhoAm 94*
Brand, Charles Peter 1923- *Who 94*
Brand, Christianna *ConAu 43NR*
Brand, David William Robert *Who 94*
Brand, David William Robert Brand 1923- *Who 94*
Brand, Dionne 1953- *BlkWr 2, BlmGWL*
Brand, Dollar 1934- *WhoBlA 94*
Brand, Donald A. 1940- *WhoFI 94*
Brand, Edward Cabell 1923- *WhoAm 94, WhoAmP 93*
Brand, Frank Amery 1924- *WhoFI 94*
Brand, Geoffrey Arthur 1930- *Who 94*
Brand, George Edward, Jr. 1918- *WhoAm 94*
Brand, Gibby *WhoHol 92*
Brand, Grover Junior 1930- *WhoMW 93*
Brand, Jay Lloyd 1959- *WhoWest 94*
Brand, John Charles 1921- *WhoAm 94*
Brand, Joseph Lyon 1936- *WhoAm 94, WhoAmL 94*
Brand, Joshua 1952?- *ConTFT 11*
Brand, Larry Milton 1949- *WhoScEn 94*
Brand, Leonard 1923- *WhoAm 94*
Brand, Leonard Roy 1941- *WhoWest 94*
Brand, Malcolm Leigh 1935- *WhoAmL 94*
Brand, Martha C. 1948- *WhoAmL 94*
Brand, Mary Lou 1934- *WhoWest 94*
Brand, Max 1892-1944 *EncSF 93*
Brand, Max 1896-1980 *NewGrDO*
Brand, Michael *NewGrDO*
Brand, Mona 1915- *BlmGWL, WrDr 94*
Brand, Myles 1942- *WhoAm 94, WhoWest 94*
Brand, Neville 1920- *WhoHol 92*
Brand, Neville 1921-1992 *WhAm 10*
Brand, Oscar 1920- *WhoAm 94, WrDr 94*
Brand, Othal Eugene 1919- *WhoAmP 93*
Brand, Ray Manning 1922-1991 *WhAm 10*

Brand, Steve Aaron 1948- *WhoAm 94, WhoAmL 94, WhoMW 93*
Brand, Stewart 1938- *WhoAm 94*
Brand, Vance Devoe 1931- *WhoAm 94, WhoScEn 94*
Brand, Wayne Leslie 1942- *WhoAmP 93*
Brand, William J. 1958- *WhoAmP 93*
Brandalise, Silvia Regina 1943- *WhoScEn 94*
Brandao, Duarte c. 1440-1508 *DcNaB MP*
Brandao, Fiama Hasse Pais 1938- *BlmGWL*
Brandauer, Frederick Paul 1933- *WhoAm 94*
Brandauer, Klaus Maria 1944- *IntMPA 94, IntWW 93, WhoAm 94, WhoHol 92*
Brandborg, Stewart Monroe 1925- *WhoAm 94*
Brandeis, Louis Dembitz 1856-1941 *AmSocL*
Brandeis, Madeleine d1937 *WhoHol 92*
Brandel, Roland Eric 1938- *WhoAm 94, WhoAmL 94*
Brandell, (Erik) Gunnar 1916- *ConAu 42NR*
Brandell, Sol Richard *WhoScEn 94*
Brandemuehl, David A. 1931- *WhoAmP 93*
Brandemuehl, Jenny Angela 1963- *WhoWest 94*
Branden, Nathaniel 1930- *WrDr 94*
Brandenberg, Aliki 1929- *WrDr 94*
Brandenberg, Aliki (Liacouras) 1929- *SmATA 75 [port]*
Brandenberg, Aliki Liacouras *WhoAmA 93*
Brandenberg, Franz 1932- *SmATA 75 [port], WrDr 94*
Brandenberger, Jacques E. *WorInv*
Brandenburg, Carlos Enrique 1948- *WhoHisp 94*
Brandenburg, Glen Ray 1950- *WhoWest 94*
Brandenburg, John Roger 1941- *WhoAmL 94*
Brandenburg, Richard George 1935- *WhoAm 94*
Brandenburg, Robert Fairchild, Jr. 1938- *WhoAmL 94*
Brandenburgh, Donald Carter 1931- *WhoWest 94*
Brandenstein, Daniel Charles 1943- *WhoAm 94, WhoScEn 94*
Brander, John *DrAPF 93*
Brander, Reynolds A., Jr. 1937- *WhoAmL 94*
Brandes, George *WhoHisp 94*
Brandes, Johann Christian 1735-1799 *NewGrDO*
Brandes, Joseph 1928- *WrDr 94*
Brandes, Lawrence Henry 1924- *Who 94*
Brandes, Norman Scott 1923- *WhoAm 94*
Brandes, Raymond S. 1924- *WhoHisp 94*
Brandes, Raymond Stewart 1924- *WhoAm 94*
Brandes, Stanley Howard 1942- *WhoAm 94, WhoWest 94*
Brandewie, Ray 1940- *WhoAmP 93*
Brandewyne, Rebecca 1955- *WrDr 94*
Brandford, Napoleon, III 1952- *WhoBlA 94*
Brandhorst, Bruce Peter 1944- *WhoScEn 94*
Brandhorst, Wesley Theodore 1933- *WhoAm 94*
Brandi, Jay Thomas 1947- *WhoFI 94*
Brandi, John *DrAPF 93*
Brandi, John 1943- *WrDr 94*
Brandi, Maria Luisa 1953- *WhoScEn 94*
Brandies, Warren 1939- *WhoFI 94*
Brandin, Alf Elvin 1912- *WhoAm 94, WhoFI 94, WhoScEn 94, WhoWest 94*
Brandin, Mark Semple 1950- *WhoAm 94, WhoFI 94*
Brandinger, Jay Jerome 1927- *WhoAm 94*
Brandis, Pamela 1946- *WhoAm 94*
Brandl, Ernest David 1952- *WhoFI 94*
Brandl, John Edward 1937- *WhoAm 94, WhoAmP 93*
Brandle, Anne Marie 1951- *WhoMW 93*
Brandler, Jonathan M. 1946- *WhoAmL 94*
Brandly, Michael Scott 1960- *WhoMW 93*
Brandmeyer, Donald Wayne 1919- *WhoWest 94*
Brandner, Margaret Anne Shaw 1937- *WhoWest 94*
Brando, Jocelyn 1919- *IntMPA 94, WhoHol 92*
Brando, Kevin *WhoHol 92*
Brando, Marlon 1924- *AmCulL, IntMPA 94, IntWW 93, Who 94, WhoHol 92*
Brando, Marlon, Jr. 1924- *WhoAm 94*
Brandolph, Arthur N. 1942- *WhoAmL 94*
Brandom, Charlynn 1953- *WhoWest 94*
Brandon *Who 94*
Brandon, Allen DeWain 1957- *WhoWest 94*
Brandon, Anita Zoe Ann 1962- *WhoFI 94*
Brandon, Arthur Leon 1898- *WhAm 10*
Brandon, Artie d1975 *WhoHol 92*
Brandon, Barbara *WhoBlA 94*
Brandon, Carl Ray 1953- *WhoBlA 94*
Brandon, Clark *WhoHol 92*
Brandon, David *WhoHol 92*
Brandon, David A. 1952- *WhoAm 94, WhoFI 94*
Brandon, Doug 1932- *WhoAmP 93*
Brandon, Edward Bermetz 1931- *WhoAm 94, WhoFI 94*
Brandon, Elvis Denby, III 1954- *WhoFI 94*
Brandon, Francis d1924 *WhoHol 92*
Brandon, Frank *EncSF 93*
Brandon, Henry d1990 *WhoHol 92*
Brandon, Henry d1993 *IntWW 93N, NewYTBS 93*
Brandon, Henry 1916- *IntWW 93*
Brandon, (Oscar) Henry d1993 *Who 94N*
Brandon, (Oscar) Henry 1916- *WrDr 94*
Brandon, (Oscar) Henry 1916-1993 *ConAu 141*
Brandon, James L. *WhoAmP 93*
Brandon, Joan Mack 1930- *WhoAm 94*
Brandon, John *WhoHol 92*
Brandon, Joseph P. 1959- *WhoIns 94*
Brandon, Joyce A(lmeta) 1938- *ConAu 42NR*
Brandon, Kathryn Elizabeth Beck 1916- *WhoWest 94*
Brandon, Lawrence G. 1936- *WhoIns 94*
Brandon, Liane *WhoAm 94*
Brandon, Michael *IntMPA 94, WhoHol 92*
Brandon, Michael 1945- *WhoHol 92*
Brandon, Michael Patrick 1961- *WhoWest 94*
Brandon, Peter d1983 *WhoHol 92*
Brandon, Phyllis Dillaha 1935- *WhoAmP 93*
Brandon, Robert Norton 1952- *WhoScEn 94*
Brandon, Warren Eugene 1916-1977 *WhoAmA 93N*
Brandon-Bravo, Martin Maurice 1932- *Who 94*
Brandon Of Oakbrook, Baron 1920- *IntWW 93, Who 94*
Brandon-Thomas, Amy d1974 *WhoHol 92*
Brandon-Thomas, Jevan d1977 *WhoHol 92*
Brandow, George Everett 1913- *WhoAm 94*
Brandram, Rosina (Moult) 1845-1907 *NewGrDO*
Brandreth, Gyles (Daubeney) 1948- *WrDr 94*
Brandreth, Gyles Daubeney 1948- *Who 94*
Brandrick, David Guy 1932- *Who 94*
Brandrup, Douglas Warren 1940- *WhoAmL 94*
Brands, Allen Jean 1914- *WhoAm 94*
Brands, James Edwin 1937- *WhoAm 94, WhoFI 94*
Brands, X 1927- *WhoHol 92*
Brandsness, David R. 1936- *WhoAm 94*
Brandstetter, Bruce George 1956- *WhoFI 94*
Brandstetter, John 1949- *NewGrDO*
Brandt, Aleksander *NewGrDO*
Brandt, Arthur Francis 1964- *WhoAmL 94*
Brandt, Carl Gunard 1897- *WhAm 10*
Brandt, Charles d1924 *WhoHol 92*
Brandt, Charles Thomas 1959- *WhoFI 94*
Brandt, Cornelis J. 1913- *IntWW 93*
Brandt, David Dean 1947- *WhoMW 93*
Brandt, Di *BlmGWL*
Brandt, Donald Edward 1954- *WhoFI 94*
Brandt, Edward Newman, Jr. 1933- *WhoAm 94*
Brandt, Elizabeth Anne 1945- *WhoWest 94*
Brandt, Elmar 1936- *IntWW 93*
Brandt, Frederick Robert 1936- *WhoAmA 93*
Brandt, Frederick William 1933- *WhoAm 94*
Brandt, George W(illiam) 1920- *WrDr 94*
Brandt, Grace Borgenicht *WhoAmA 93*
Brandt, Grace Borgenicht 1915- *WhoAm 94*
Brandt, Hank *WhoHol 92*
Brandt, Harry 1925- *WhoAm 94*
Brandt, I. Marvin 1942- *WhoFI 94, WhoScEn 94*
Brandt, Ira Kive 1923- *WhoAm 94*
Brandt, J. Michael *WhoMW 93*
Brandt, Janet *WhoHol 92*
Brandt, Jerry 1929- *WhoWest 94*
Brandt, Jo *WhoAmP 93*
Brandt, John Ashworth 1950- *WhoMW 93*
Brandt, John Edward 1946- *WhoMW 93*
Brandt, Kathleen Weil-Garris *WhoAmA 93, WhoScEn 94*
Brandt, Kenneth 1938- *WhoAmP 93*
Brandt, Leslie F 1919- *WrDr 94*
Brandt, Lillian B. 1919- *WhoBlA 94*
Brandt, Louis *WhoHol 92*
Brandt, Louise d1959 *WhoHol 92*
Brandt, Marianne 1842-1921 *NewGrDO*
Brandt, Michael Dean 1950- *WhoFI 94*
Brandt, Nat(han Henry, Jr.) 1929- *WrDr 94*
Brandt, Paul Nicholas 1937- *Who 94*
Brandt, Peter Augustus 1931- *Who 94*
Brandt, Reinhard 1932- *WhoScEn 94*
Brandt, Rex 1914- *WhoAmA 93*
Brandt, Rexford Elson 1914- *WhoAm 94*
Brandt, Richard B. 1910- *EncEth*
Brandt, Richard Booker 1910- *WhoAm 94*
Brandt, Richard E. 1943- *WhoAmL 94*
Brandt, Richard M. 1922- *WrDr 94*
Brandt, Richard Martin 1922- *WhoAm 94*
Brandt, Richard Paul 1927- *IntMPA 94, WhoAm 94*
Brandt, Robert Frederic, III 1946- *WhoAm 94*
Brandt, Susan J. 1952- *WhoAmL 94*
Brandt, Thomas J. 1952- *WhoAmL 94*
Brandt, Victor *WhoHol 92*
Brandt, Warren 1918- *WhoAm 94, WhoAmA 93*
Brandt, Werner W. 1938- *CngDr 93, WhoAmP 93*
Brandt, William Arthur, Jr. 1949- *WhoFI 94, WhoMW 93*
Brandt, William Edmund 1936- *WhoMW 93*
Brandt, William Perry 1953- *WhoAm 94, WhoAmL 94*
Brandt, William S. 1946- *WhoAmL 94*
Brandt, Willy d1992 *IntWW 93N, Who 94N*
Brandt, Willy 1913-1992 *AnObit 1992, HisWorL [port], WhAm 10*
Brandt, Yale M. 1930- *WhoFI 94*
Brandt-Forster, Ellen 1866-1921 *NewGrDO*
Brandus, Nicolae 1935- *IntWW 93*
Brandvold, Lynn Airheart 1940- *WhoWest 94*
Brandwajn, Alexandre 1948- *WhoWest 94*
Brandwein, Larry 1931- *WhoAm 94*
Brandzel, Robert Aaron 1968- *WhoMW 93*
Branegan, James Augustus, III 1950- *WhoAm 94*
Branen, Alfred Larry 1945- *WhoWest 94*
Branfield, John (Charles) 1931- *WrDr 94*
Branflick, Robert Andrew, Jr. 1948- *WhoMW 93*
Branfman, Steven 1953- *WhoAmA 93*
Brangman, H. Alan 1952- *WhoBlA 94*
Branham, Andrew d1980 *WhoHol 92*
Branham, George, III 1962- *WhoBlA 94*
Branham, Ira Edsel 1958- *WhoAmL 94*
Branham, Richard Lacy, Jr. 1943- *WhoScEn 94*
Branham, William Marrion 1909-1965 *DcAmReB 2*
Branic, Carolyn Sue 1957- *WhoMW 93*
Branigan, Craig Wolfe 1951- *WhoAm 94*
Branigan, Keith 1940- *WrDr 94*
Branigan, Laura 1957- *WhoHol 92*
Branigan, Patrick (Francis) 1906- *Who 94*
Branigan, Thomas Patrick 1963- *WhoAmL 94*
Branigin, Roger D., Jr. 1931- *WhoAmL 94*
Branigin, William Joseph 1952- *WhoAm 94*
Branin, Joan Julia 1944- *WhoFI 94, WhoWest 94*
Branitzki, Heinz 1929- *IntWW 93*
Brankamp, Robert George 1961- *WhoScEn 94*
Branker, Julian Michael *WhoBlA 94*
Brankovich, Mark J. 1922- *WhoWest 94*
Brann, Alton Joseph 1941- *WhoAm 94, WhoFI 94, WhoWest 94*
Brann, Donald Treasurer 1929- *WhoMW 93*
Brann, Edward Rommel 1920- *WhoFI 94, WhoMW 93*
Brann, Richard Roland 1943- *WhoAm 94, WhoAmL 94*
Brann, William Norman 1915- *Who 94*
Brann, William Paul 1916- *WhoAm 94*
Brannan, Charles Franklin d1992 *Who 94N*
Brannan, David Lee 1972- *WhoWest 94*
Brannan, Eulie Ross 1928- *WhoAm 94*
Brannan, George W. 1932- *WhoAmP 93*
Brannan, Michael Steven 1946- *WhoScEn 94*
Brannan, Pat White 1930- *WhoAmP 93*
Brannan, Peter Randolph 1960- *WhoAmL 94*
Brannan, Steve J. 1949- *WhoAmP 93*
Brannan, William 1925- *WhoAm 94*
Brannan, William C. 1949- *WhoFI 94*
Brannen, James H., III 1940- *WhoBlA 94*
Brannen, Jeffrey Richard 1945- *WhoAmL 94*
Brannen, John Howard 1949- *WhoAmL 94*
Brannen, Jonathan *DrAPF 93*
Brannen, Julia (M.) 1944- *WrDr 94*
Branner, Robert 1927-1973 *WhoAmA 93N*
Brannian, Ross E. 1925- *WhoAmP 93*
Brannick, Ellen Marie 1934- *WhoFI 94*
Brannigan, James W., Jr. *WhoAmL 94*
Brannigan, Joseph C. *WhoAmP 93*
Brannigan, Owen d1973 *WhoHol 92*
Brannigan, Owen 1908-1973 *NewGrDO*
Brannon, Brian Ray 1944- *WhoAmL 94, WhoWest 94*
Brannon, Carmen 1899-1974 *BlmGWL*
Brannon, Clifton Woodrow, Sr. 1912- *WhoAm 94*
Brannon, Donn *DrAPF 93*
Brannon, Hezzie Raymond, Jr. 1926- *WhoAm 94*
Brannon, James R. 1943- *WhoBlA 94*
Brannon, Judith A. 1948- *WhoIns 94*
Brannon, Lester Travis, Jr. 1926- *WhoAm 94*
Brannon, Max R. *WhoAmP 93*
Brannon, Nancy Ruth 1947- *WhoAmP 93*
Brannon, Winona Eileen 1948- *WhoFI 94*
Brannon-Peppas, Lisa 1962- *WhoAm 94*
Branover, Herman 1931- *WrDr 94*
Brans, Thomas Joseph 1958- *WhoFI 94*
Bransby, Eric James 1916- *WhoAm 94, WhoAmA 93*
Branscomb, Anne Wells 1928- *WhoAm 94, WhoAmL 94*
Branscomb, Harvie 1894- *WhAm 10*
Branscomb, Harvie, Jr. 1922- *WhoAm 94*
Branscomb, Lewis Capers, Jr. 1911- *WhoAm 94*
Branscomb, Lewis McAdory 1926- *IntWW 93, WhoAm 94, WhoScEn 94*
Branscombe, Jean Murray d1993 *NewYTBS 93*
Branscombe, Lily d1970 *WhoHol 92*
Branscombe, Peter (John) 1929- *NewGrDO*
Branscum, Christine Maria 1951- *WhoMW 93*
Branscum, David Lawdon 1958- *WhoAmP 93*
Branscum, Herby, Jr. 1941- *WhoAmP 93*
Branscum, Robbie 1937- *SmATA 17AS [port], TwCYAW*
Bransdorfer, Stephen Christie 1929- *WhoAm 94*
Bransford, Paris 1930- *WhoBlA 94*
Bransford, Stephen 1949- *WrDr 94*
Bransky, Joseph Raymond 1943- *WhoMW 93*
Bransom, (John) Paul 1885-1979 *WhoAmA 93N*
Branson, Albert Harold 1935- *WhoAm 94, WhoAmL 94, WhoWest 94*
Branson, Branley Allan 1929- *WhoAm 94*
Branson, Cecil Robert Peter Charles 1924- *Who 94*
Branson, Dan Earle 1928- *WhoAm 94, WhoMW 93*
Branson, David John 1943- *WhoAm 94, WhoAmL 94*
Branson, Edward James 1918- *Who 94*
Branson, Fredine McBryde 1931- *WhoAmP 93*
Branson, Harley Kenneth 1942- *WhoFI 94*
Branson, Herman Russell 1914- *WhoAm 94, WhoBlA 94*
Branson, Jessie M. *WhoAmP 93*
Branson, Lindley S. 1942- *WhoAmL 94*
Branson, Margaret Aber 1927- *WhoAmP 93*
Branson, Mary Lou 1932- *WhoAm 94*
Branson, Richard 1950- *IntWW 93, WhoFI 94*
Branson, Richard Charles Nicholas 1950- *Who 94*
Branson, William Rainforth 1905- *Who 94*
Branstad, Clifford 1924- *WhoAmP 93*
Branstad, Terry Edward 1946- *IntWW 93, WhoAm 94, WhoAmP 93, WhoMW 93*
Branstetter, Gwendolyn H. *WhoAmA 93*
Branstetter, Olin 1929- *WhoAmP 93*
Branstner, Karl Christian 1931- *WhoMW 93*
Branstool, Charles Eugene 1936- *WhoAm 94, WhoAmP 93*
Brant, Beth *DrAPF 93*
Brant, Colin Trevor 1929- *Who 94*
Brant, Donald B., Jr. 1942- *WhoAmL 94*
Brant, Gerald Allen 1953- *WhoAmP 93*
Brant, Henry 1913- *WhoAm 94*
Brant, Jay E. 1937- *WhoAmL 94*
Brant, Jerome Edward 1946- *WhoAmL 94*
Brant, Jonathan 1947- *WhoAmL 94*
Brant, Joseph 1742-1807 *AmRev, HisWorL [port], WhAmRev [port]*
Brant, Marley 1950- *ConAu 140*
Brant, Molly c. 1735-1796 *WhAmRev*

Brant, Molly c. 1736-1796 *AmRev*
Brant, Sandra *WhoAm 94*
Brantenberg, Gerd 1941- *BlmGWL, ConWorW 93*
Brantford, Aggie 1884- *WhoHol 92*
Brantford, Mickey 1911- *WhoHol 92*
Branthaver, Jan Franklin 1936- *WhoWest 94*
Brantingham, Barney 1932- *WhoAm 94*
Brantingham, Charles Ross 1917- *WhoWest 94*
Brantingham, Patricia Louise 1943- *WhoWest 94*
Brantingham, Paul Jeffrey 1943- *WhoWest 94*
Brantley, Betsy 1955- *WhoHol 92*
Brantley, Bobby Lynn 1948- *WhoAmP 93*
Brantley, Clifford 1968- *WhoBlA 94*
Brantley, Daniel 1944- *WhoBlA 94*
Brantley, Edward J. 1923- *WhoBlA 94*
Brantley, Haskew Hawthorne, Jr. 1922- *WhoAmP 93*
Brantley, John Randolph 1951- *WhoAm 94, WhoAmL 94*
Brantley, Lee Reed 1906- *WhoAm 94*
Brantley, Montague Delano 1919- *WhoBlA 94*
Brantley, Oliver Wiley 1915- *WhoAm 94*
Brantley, Rickey Joe 1958- *WhoAmL 94*
Brantlinger, Frank Herbert 1939- *WhoFI 94*
Brantome, Pierre de Bourdeille, Seigneur de c. 1540-1614 *GuFrLit 2*
Branton, Leo, Jr. 1922- *WhoBlA 94*
Branton, Raymond 1924- *WhoAmP 93*
Branton, William Strobel 1939- *WhoAmP 93*
Brantz, George Murray 1930- *WhoAm 94*
Branum, Paul Monroe, Jr. 1960- *WhoWest 94*
Branum, William Howell 1941- *WhoAm 94*
Branyan, Helen Baird 1927- *WhoMW 93*
Branyan, Robert Lester 1930- *WhoAm 94*
Branzell, Karin (Maria) 1891-1974 *NewGrDO*
Branzeu, Nicolae 1907-1983 *NewGrDO*
Braque, Georges 1882-1963 *ModArCr 4 [port]*
Brar, Gurdarshan Singh 1946- *WhoScEn 94*
Bras, Luisa A. *WhoHisp 94*
Bras, Rafael Luis 1950- *WhoAm 94*
Brasch, Klaus Rainer 1940- *WhoWest 94*
Brasch, Rudolph 1912- *WrDr 94*
Braschi, Nicoletta 1960- *WhoHol 92*
Brascia, John *WhoHol 92*
Brasda, Bernard William 1938- *WhoWest 94*
Brase, David Arthur 1945- *WhoScEn 94*
Brasel, Jo Anne 1934- *WhoAm 94*
Braselman, Lin Emery *WhoAmA 93*
Braseth, John E. 1959- *WhoAmA 93*
Brasey, Henry L. 1937- *WhoBlA 94*
Brasfield, Evans Booker 1932- *WhoAm 94, WhoAmL 94*
Brasfield, J. Hunt 1942- *WhoAmL 94*
Brasfield, James *DrAPF 93*
Brasfield, Rod d1958 *WhoHol 92*
Brash, Alan Anderson 1913- *Who 94*
Brash, Donald Thomas 1940- *IntWW 93*
Brash, Edward *DrAPF 93*
Brash, Robert 1924- *Who 94*
Brashares, William Charles 1939- *WhoAm 94*
Brashear, Berlaind Leander 1934- *WhoBlA 94*
Brashear, Diane Lee 1933- *WhoAm 94, WhoMW 93*
Brashear, Kermit, II 1944- *WhoAmP 93*
Brashear, Philip Whisman 1941- *WhoMW 93*
Brashears, Wilford Session, Jr. 1925- *WhoFI 94*
Brasher, Christopher (William) 1928- *WrDr 94*
Brasher, Christopher William 1928- *Who 94*
Brasher, George Walter 1936- *WhoScEn 94*
Brasher, John Odus 1945- *WhoFI 94*
Brasher, Norman Henry 1922- *WrDr 94*
Brashers, Charles *DrAPF 93*
Brashers, Howard C. *DrAPF 93*
Brashier, Edward Martin 1954- *WhoScEn 94*
Brashier, Philip Charles 1962- *WhoFI 94*
Brashler, William 1947- *WhoAm 94, WrDr 94*
Brasic, Gregory Lee 1961- *WhoMW 93*
Brasier, Steven Paul 1960- *WhoScEn 94*
Brasileira, Floresta Augusta *BlmGWL*
Brasileira, Uma *BlmGWL*
Brasileira Augusta, Madame *BlmGWL*
Brask, Gerald Irving 1927- *WhoScEn 94*
Brasket, Curt Justin 1932- *WhoAm 94*
Brasnett, John 1929- *Who 94*
Brasno, George d1982 *WhoHol 92*
Brasno, Olive *WhoHol 92*
Brass, John 1908- *Who 94*
Brass, Perry *DrAPF 93*
Brass, William 1921- *Who 94*
Brassac, Rene de Bearn, Marquis de fl. 1733-1750 *NewGrDO*
Brassell, Gilbert W. *WhoHisp 94*
Brassell, Roselyn Strauss 1930- *WhoAm 94, WhoWest 94*
Brasselle, Keefe d1981 *WhoHol 92*
Brassens, Georges d1981 *WhoHol 92*
Brasseur, Claude 1936- *IntWW 93, WhoHol 92*
Brasseur, Pierre d1972 *WhoHol 92*
Brassey *Who 94*
Brassey, John Michael 1946- *WhoAmL 94*
Brassey, Peter (Esme) 1907- *Who 94*
Brassey of Apethorpe, Baron 1932- *Who 94*
Brassfield, Eugene Everett 1933- *WhoAmL 94*
Brassfield, Patricia Ann *WhoScEn 94*
Brassil, Jean Ella 1933- *WhoAm 94*
Brasunas, Anton de Sales 1919- *WhoAm 94*
Braswell, Arnold Webb 1925- *WhoAm 94*
Braswell, Charles d1974 *WhoHol 92*
Braswell, James Randall 1926- *WhoScEn 94*
Braswell, Jerry *WhoAmP 93*
Braswell, Louis Erskine 1937- *WhoAm 94*
Braswell, Palmira 1928- *WhoBlA 94*
Braswell, Robert Neil 1932- *WhoAm 94*
Braswell, Thomas Edward, Jr. 1921- *WhoAmP 93*
Brata, Sasthi (Sasthibrata Chakravarti) 1939- *WrDr 94*
Brataas, Nancy Osborn 1928- *WhoAmP 93*
Bratby, Jean Esme Oregon *Who 94*
Bratby, John d1992 *IntWW 93N*
Bratby, John 1928-1992 *AnObit 1992*
Bratby, John R.A. 1928-1992 *WhAm 10*
Bratby, John Randall 1928- *WrDr 94*
Bratcher, Dale 1932- *WhoAmA 93*
Bratcher, Glenn Omer 1935- *WhoMW 93*
Bratcher, Twila Langdon *WhoAm 94, WhoScEn 94*
Braterman, Paul Sydney 1938- *WhoScEn 94*
Bratesman, Stuart, Jr. 1953- *WhoAmP 93*
Brathwaite, Edward (Kamau) 1930- *BlkWr 2*
Brathwaite, Edward Kamau 1930- *BlmGEL, WrDr 94*
Brathwaite, Errol (Freeman) 1929- *WrDr 94*
Brathwaite, Kamau *DrAPF 93*
Brathwaite, Mellissa Annette 1961- *WhoAm 94*
Brathwaite, Nicholas *IntWW 93*
Bratkowski, Andrzej 1936- *IntWW 93*
Bratkowski, Charles J. 1949- *WhoAmP 93*
Bratman, Jude Robert 1961- *WhoAmL 94*
Bratnober, Patricia Ray 1925- *WhoMW 93*
Bratsafolis, Michelle Sokol 1957- *WhoAmL 94*
Bratsburg, Harry 1915- *WhoAm 94*
Bratsch, Steven Gary 1951- *WhoWest 94*
Bratt, Bengt Erik 1922- *WhoAm 94*
Bratt, Byron H. 1952- *WhoAmA 93*
Bratt, Guy Maurice 1920- *Who 94*
Bratt, Nicholas 1948- *WhoAm 94, WhoFI 94*
Brattain, Arlene Jane Clark 1938- *WhoMW 93*
Brattain, Richard Howard 1955- *WhoAmL 94*
Brattain, Walter H. d1987 *NobelP 91N*
Brattain, Walter Houser 1902-1987 *WorInv*
Bratter, Peter 1935- *WhoScEn 94*
Brattin, Gary Dean 1950- *WhoMW 93*
Brattin, Kathleen Ann 1957- *WhoFI 94, WhoMW 93*
Bratton, Christopher 1959- *WhoAmA 93*
Bratton, Howard Calvin 1922- *WhoAm 94, WhoAmL 94, WhoWest 94*
Bratton, J(acqueline) S(usan) 1945- *WrDr 94*
Bratton, Richard Waldo 1933- *WhoAmP 93*
Bratton, William Edward 1919- *WhoFI 94, WhoScEn 94*
Brattstrom, Bayard Holmes 1929- *WhoAm 94*
Bratu, Teodor 1922- *NewGrDO*
Bratza, Nicolas Dusan 1945- *Who 94*
Brau, Charles Allen 1938- *WhoAm 94*
Brauch, Merry Ruth Moore 1920- *WhoAm 94*
Braucher, Jean 1950- *WhoAmL 94, WhoMW 93*
Brauchli, Robert Charles 1945- *WhoAmL 94*
Braucht, La Vere T., Jr. 1929- *WhoIns 94*
Braud, Bert Stephen 1959- *WhoAmL 94*
Braud, Kenneth Warren 1952- *WhoFI 94*
Braude, Ann (Deborah) 1955- *WrDr 94*
Braude, Edwin S. 1927- *WhoAm 94*
Braude, Jacob Morton 1896- *WhAm 10*
Braude, Marvin *WhoAmP 93*
Braude, Michael 1936- *WhoAm 94, WhoFI 94, WhoMW 93*
Braude, Robert Michael 1939- *WhoAm 94*
Braude, Stanton H. 1961- *WhoMW 93*
Braudel, Fernand (Paul) 1902-1985 *ConAu 42NR*
Braudy, Dorothy *WhoAmA 93*
Braudy, Leo 1941- *WrDr 94*
Braudy, Leo Beal 1941- *WhoAm 94*
Brauer, Arik 1929- *IntWW 93*
Brauer, Beth-Ellen *WhoMW 93*
Brauer, Connie Ann 1949- *WhoAmA 93*
Brauer, Donald George 1929- *WhoFI 94, WhoMW 93*
Brauer, Gwendolyn Gail *WhoFI 94*
Brauer, Harrol Andrew, Jr. 1920- *WhoAm 94, WhoFI 94*
Brauer, Jerald C(arl) 1921- *WrDr 94*
Brauer, Jerald Carl 1921- *IntWW 93*
Brauer, John Robert 1943- *WhoScEn 94*
Brauer, Ralph Werner 1921- *WhoAm 94*
Brauer, Rima Lois 1938- *WhoScEn 94*
Brauer, Tiny d1990 *WhoHol 92*
Braugher, Andre 1962- *WhoHol 92*
Brauker, William Charles 1948- *WhoWest 94*
Brault, Adelard Lionel 1909- *WhoAmP 93*
Brault, Gayle Lorain 1944- *WhoWest 94*
Brault, Gerard Joseph 1929- *WhoAm 94*
Brauman, John I. 1937- *IntWW 93, WhoAm 94, WhoScEn 94*
Braumiller, Allen Spooner 1934- *WhoAm 94*
Braun, Madame fl. c. 1725- *NewGrDO*
Braun, Monsieur 1700?-1735? *NewGrDO*
Braun, Alan F. 1957- *WhoWest 94*
Braun, Beverly Wright *WhoAm 94*
Braun, Carl 1886-1960 *NewGrDO*
Braun, Carl 1927- *BasBi*
Braun, Carl P. *WhoAmP 93*
Braun, Carol Moseley 1947- *AfrAmAl 6 [port], IntWW 93*
Braun, Carol Moseley E. 1947- *WhoAmP 93*
Braun, Charles Louis 1937- *WhoAm 94*
Braun, Charles Stuart 1941- *WhoAm 94*
Braun, Craig Allen 1939- *WhoAm 94*
Braun, Daniel Carl 1905- *WhoAm 94*
Braun, David Adlai 1931- *WhoAm 94*
Braun, Edward 1936- *WrDr 94*
Braun, Eunice Hockspeier *WhoMW 93*
Braun, George William 1946- *WhoFI 94*
Braun, Gerry Cole 1948- *WhoWest 94*
Braun, Glenn Robert 1956- *WhoAmL 94*
Braun, Gunter *EncSF 93*
Braun, Hans-Benjamin *WhoScEn 94*
Braun, Harry Jean 1941- *WhoAm 94*
Braun, Helena 1903-1990 *NewGrDO*
Braun, Henry *DrAPF 93*
Braun, Hubert Henry 1924- *WhoMW 93*
Braun, Jeffrey Louis 1946- *WhoAm 94, WhoAmL 94*
Braun, Jerome Irwin 1929- *WhoAm 94, WhoAmL 94, WhoWest 94*
Braun, Johanna *EncSF 93*
Braun, Joseph Carl 1942- *WhoAm 94, WhoMW 93, WhoScEn 94*
Braun, Karl Ferdinand 1850-1918 *WorInv*
Braun, Lilian Jackson *WhoAm 94, WrDr 94*
Braun, Lilian Jackson 1916?- *ConAu 140*
Braun, Lily 1865-1916 *BlmGWL*
Braun, Ludwig 1926- *WhoAm 94*
Braun, Marta (A.) 1946- *ConAu 141*
Braun, Matt(hew) 1932- *WrDr 94*
Braun, Michael Alan 1949- *WhoAm 94*
Braun, Michael Walter 1955- *WhoScEn 94*
Braun, Nancy Lynn 1952- *WhoAmL 94*
Braun, Paul D. 1944- *WhoAmL 94*
Braun, Pinkas 1923- *IntWW 93*
Braun, Reto 1944- *WhoAm 94, WhoFI 94*
Braun, Richard Emil *DrAPF 93*
Braun, Richard Emil 1934- *WrDr 94*
Braun, Richard Lane 1917- *WhoAm 94*
Braun, Richard Lane, II 1948- *WhoAm 94*
Braun, Robert Alexander 1910- *WhoMW 93*
Braun, Robert C. 1945- *WhoAmL 94*
Braun, Robert Clare 1928- *WhoFI 94, WhoMW 93*
Braun, Rodney Otis 1953- *WhoMW 93*
Braun, Stephen Hughes 1942- *WhoWest 94*
Braun, Stephen J. *WhoAmP 93*
Braun, Theodore E. D. 1933- *WhoAm 94*
Braun, Thomas Williams 1953- *WhoAmL 94*
Braun, Tibor 1932- *WhoScEn 94*
Braun, Victor (Conrad) 1935- *NewGrDO*
Braun, Viktor d1971 *WhoHol 92*
Braun, Virginia Mary 1917- *WhoAmP 93*
Braun, Volker 1939- *ConWorW 93, IntDcT 2*
Braun, Wernher von 1912-1977 *WorInv*
Braun, William David 1950- *WhoAm 94, WhoAmL 94*
Braun, William J. 1925- *WhoIns 94*
Braun, William Joseph 1925- *WhoAm 94*
Braun, William Todde 1950- *WhoFI 94*
Braun, Zev *WhoAm 94*
Braunberger, Pierre 1905-1990 *IntDcF 2-4*
Braune, Marga d1974 *WhoHol 92*
Braunegg, George Gwyer 1957- *WhoWest 94*
Braunfels, Michael 1917- *IntWW 93*
Braunfels, Walter 1882-1954 *NewGrDO*
Braungart, Richard Gottfried 1935- *WhoAm 94*
Braun-Moser, Ursula 1937- *WhoWomW 91*
Braunmuller, A(lbert) R(ichard) 1945- *WrDr 94*
Braun-Munk, Eugene Clarence d1993 *NewYTBS 93*
Brauns, Barry *WhoAmP 93*
Braunschweig, Ralph 1928- *WhoMW 93*
Braunschweig-Luneburg, Elisabeth von 1519-1558 *BlmGWL*
Braunschweig-Luneburg, Sibylle Ursula von 1629-1691 *BlmGWL*
Braunschweig-Luneburg, Sophie Elisabeth von 1613-1676 *BlmGWL*
Braunsdorf, James Allen 1938- *WhoMW 93*
Braunsdorf, Paul Raymond 1943- *WhoAm 94, WhoAmL 94*
Braunstein, Daniel Norman 1938- *WhoScEn 94*
Braunstein, George Gregory 1947- *IntMPA 94*
Braunstein, H. Terry (Malikin) 1942- *WhoAmA 93*
Braunstein, Herbert 1926- *WhoAm 94*
Braunstein, Mark Mathew 1951- *WhoAmA 93*
Braunstein, Phillip 1930- *WhoAm 94*
Braunstein, Ruth *WhoAmA 93*
Braunthal, Gerard 1923- *WrDr 94*
Brauntuch, Troy 1954- *WhoAmA 93*
Braunwald, Eugene 1929- *WhoAm 94*
Braus, Harry d1993 *NewYTBS 93*
Brauswetter, Hans d1945 *WhoHol 92*
Braut, Frigga d1974 *WhoHol 92*
Brauth, Marvin Jeffrey 1950- *WhoAm 94*
Brautigam, Hans Otto 1931- *IntWW 93*
Brautigan, Richard 1935-1984 *EncSF 93*
Brauwerman, Suzan Carol 1948- *WhoAmL 94*
Brave, Georgine Frances 1940- *WhoAmL 94*
Braveman, Wayne S. 1953- *WhoAmL 94*
Braver, Samuel W. 1950- *WhoAmL 94*
Braverman, Bart 1946- *WhoHol 92*
Braverman, Charles 1944- *IntMPA 94*
Braverman, Donna 1947- *WhoAmA 93*
Braverman, Donna Caryn 1947- *WhoWest 94*
Braverman, Elliott Kenneth 1935- *WhoAm 94*
Braverman, Herbert Leslie 1947- *WhoAm 94, WhoAmL 94*
Braverman, Irwin Merton 1929- *WhoAm 94*
Braverman, Louise Marcia 1948- *WhoFI 94*
Braverman, Philip 1933- *WhoAm 94*
Braverman, Robert Allen 1940- *WhoWest 94*
Braverman, Robert Jay 1933- *WhoAm 94*
Bravin, Don Alan 1943- *WhoWest 94*
Bravmann, Ludwig 1925- *WhoAm 94, WhoFI 94*
Bravmann, Rene A. 1939- *WhoAmA 93*
Bravnicar, Matija 1897-1977 *NewGrDO*
Bravo, Anthony John 1938- *WhoAm 94*
Bravo, Carlos E. 1959- *WhoHisp 94*
Bravo, Facundo D. 1941- *WhoHisp 94*
Bravo, Jaime d1970 *WhoHol 92*
Bravo, Joseph Javier 1939- *WhoHisp 94*
Bravo, Kenneth A. 1942- *WhoAm 94, WhoAmL 94*
Bravo, Martin Maurice B. *Who 94*
Bravo, Rose Marie 1951- *WhoAm 94, WhoFI 94*
Bravo, Ruben 1913- *WhoHisp 94*
Brawer, Marc Harris 1946- *WhoAmL 94*
Brawley, C. Robert 1944- *WhoAmP 93*
Brawley, Ernest 1937- *WrDr 94*
Brawley, Robert Julius 1937- *WhoAm 94, WhoAmA 93*
Brawn, John P. d1954 *WhoHol 92*
Brawn, Linda Curtis 1947- *WhoAmP 93*
Brawne, Michael 1925- *WrDr 94*
Brawner, Gerald Theodore 1941- *WhoAm 94, WhoAmL 94*
Brawner, Lee Basil 1935- *WhoAm 94*
Brawner, Thomas A. 1945- *WhoMW 93*
Brax, Coleman *EncSF 93*
Braxton, Carter 1736-1797 *WhAmRev*

Braxton, Edward Kenneth 1944- *WhoBlA 94*
Braxton, Harriet E. 1926- *WhoBlA 94*
Braxton, Joanne M(argaret) 1950- *BlkWr 2, ConAu 140*
Braxton, Jodi *BlkWr 2, ConAu 140*
Braxton, John Ledger 1945- *WhoBlA 94*
Braxton, Malva 1905- *WhoAmP 93*
Braxton, Toni *WhoBlA 94*
Braxton, William E. 1878-1932 *WhoAmA 93N*
Bray, Allen Anthony 1949- *WhoWest 94*
Bray, Andrew Malcolm 1962- *WhoScEn 94*
Bray, Andrew William 1959- *WhoAmL 94*
Bray, Anna Eliza 1790-1883 *BlmGWL*
Bray, Arthur Philip 1933- *WhoAm 94*
Bray, Bonnie Anderson 1929- *WhoAm 94*
Bray, Charles William, III 1933- *WhoAm 94*
Bray, Claude A., Jr. 1931- *WhoAmP 93*
Bray, David Charles 1949- *WhoMW 93*
Bray, David Maurice 1941- *WhoAm 94*
Bray, Denis Campbell 1926- *Who 94*
Bray, Donald Claude 1937- *WhoAm 94*
Bray, Elizabeth Ann 1954- *WhoWest 94*
Bray, Frank T. J. 1948- *WhoAmP 93*
Bray, Gail Etheridge 1948- *WhoAmP 93*
Bray, George August 1931- *WhoAm 94*
Bray, Henry de c. 1248-c. 1313 *DcNaB MP*
Bray, J. R. 1879- *IntDcF 2-4*
Bray, James Charles 1948- *WhoFI 94*
Bray, James Houston 1926- *WhoAmP 93*
Bray, Jeffrey Howard 1951- *WhoWest 94*
Bray, Jeremy (William) 1930- *WrDr 94*
Bray, Jeremy William 1930- *Who 94*
Bray, Jessica Kelly 1953- *WhoFI 94*
Bray, Jo Ann Elizabeth 1943- *WhoWest 94*
Bray, Joan 1945- *WhoAmP 93*
Bray, John d1955 *WhoHol 92*
Bray, John 1782-1822 *NewGrDO*
Bray, John 1879-1978 *WhoAmA 93N*
Bray, John Donald 1938- *WhoWest 94*
Bray, John Francis 1809-1897 *EncSF 93*
Bray, John Jefferson 1912- *IntWW 93, Who 94, WrDr 94*
Bray, Kenneth Noel Corbett 1929- *Who 94*
Bray, Lane *WhoAmP 93*
Bray, Laurack Doyle 1949- *WhoAmL 94*
Bray, Merlin Leroy, Jr. 1932- *WhoMW 93*
Bray, Oscar S. 1905- *WhoAm 94*
Bray, Paul Sheldon 1936- *Who 94*
Bray, Philip James 1925- *WhoAm 94*
Bray, Pierce 1924- *WhoAm 94*
Bray, Ralph 1921- *WhoMW 93*
Bray, Richard D. *WhoAmP 93*
Bray, Richard Daniel 1945- *WhoWest 94*
Bray, Richard Winston Atterton 1945- *Who 94*
Bray, Robert d1983 *WhoHol 92*
Bray, Robert Bruce 1924- *WhoAm 94, WhoWest 94*
Bray, Robert C. 1944- *WhoAm 94*
Bray, Stephen d1990 *WhoHol 92*
Bray, Theodor (Charles) 1905- *Who 94*
Bray, Thomas 1656-1730 *DcAmReB 2, EncNAR*
Bray, Thomas J. 1867-1933 *EncABHB 9*
Bray, Thomas Joseph 1941- *WhoAm 94*
Bray, William Harold 1958- *WhoScEn 94*
Bray, William John 1911- *Who 94*
Bray, William Lawrence 1969- *WhoMW 93*
Bray, William Trewartha 1794-1868 *DcNaB MP*
Bray, Winston 1910- *Who 94*
Braybon, (Charmian) Gail 1952- *WrDr 94*
Braybrook, Edward John 1911- *Who 94*
Braybrooke, Baron 1932- *Who 94*
Braybrooke, David 1924- *IntWW 93, WhoAm 94*
Braybrooke, Marcus Christopher Rossi 1938- *Who 94*
Braybrooke, Neville (Patrick Bellairs) 1928- *WrDr 94*
Braybrooke, Neville Patrick Bellairs 1925- *Who 94*
Braye, Baroness 1941- *Who 94*
Brayer, Donald J. 1942- *WhoIns 94*
Brayer, Menachem Mendel 1922- *WhoAm 94*
Brayer, Robert Marvin 1939- *WhoScEn 94*
Brayfield, Celia 1945- *WrDr 94*
Brayfield, George d1968 *WhoHol 92*
Brayman, Harold Halliday 1935- *WhoAmP 93*
Brayman, Kenneth Lewis 1955- *WhoScEn 94*
Braymer, Marguerite Annetta 1911- *WhoAm 94*
Brayne, John d1654 *DcNaB MP*
Brayne, Richard Bolding 1924- *Who 94*
Brayne-Baker, John 1905- *Who 94*
Braynen, Alvin Rudolph d1992 *Who 94N*
Brayne-Nicholls, (Francis) Brian (Price) 1914- *Who 94*
Braynon, Edward J., Jr. 1928- *WhoBlA 94*
Brayshaw, (Alfred) Joseph 1912- *Who 94*
Brayson, Albert Aloysius, II 1953- *WhoFI 94*
Brayton, Lily d1953 *WhoHol 92*
Brayton, Margaret *WhoHol 92*
Brayton, Peter Russell 1950- *WhoScEn 94*
Brayton, Russell Steven 1953- *WhoMW 93*
Braz, Evandro Freitas 1943- *WhoFI 94*
Brazaitis, Thomas Joseph 1940- *WhoAm 94*
Brazauskas, Algirdas-Mikolas Kazevich 1932- *IntWW 93*
Brazauskas, Algirdas Mykolas 1932- *LoBiDrD*
Brazeal, Aurelia E. *WhoAmP 93*
Brazeal, Aurelia E. 1943- *WhoAm 94*
Brazeal, Donna Smith 1947- *WhoAm 94*
Brazealle, Hal d1973 *WhoHol 92*
Brazeau, James Edward 1953- *WhoAmL 94*
Brazeau, Wendell (Phillips) 1910-1974 *WhoAmA 93N*
Brazeir, Thomas J. 1930- *WhoAmP 93*
Brazel, Anthony James 1941- *WhoScEn 94*
Brazell, James Ervin 1926- *WhoAm 94*
Brazell, Karen Woodard 1938- *WhoAm 94*
Brazelton, Frank Alexander 1926- *WhAm 10*
Brazelton, Roy Dale 1941- *WhoAm 94*
Brazelton, T. Berry 1918- *CurBio 93 [port]*
Brazelton, Thomas Berry 1918- *WhoAm 94*
Brazelton, William Thomas 1921- *WhoAm 94*
Braz-Filho, Raimundo 1935- *WhoScEn 94*
Brazier, Don Roland 1921- *WhoAm 94*
Brazier, John Richard 1940- *WhoAmL 94, WhoWest 94*
Brazier, Julian William Hendy 1953- *Who 94*
Brazier, Leslie Ann 1957- *WhoWest 94*
Brazier, Robert G. *WhoFI 94, WhoWest 94*
Brazier, Wesley R. 1917-1991 *WhoBlA 94N*
Brazier, William H. 1922- *WhoBlA 94*
Brazier-Creagh, (Kilner) Rupert 1909- *Who 94*
Brazil, Ernest L. 1943- *WhoBlA 94*
Brazil, Gino T. 1956- *WhoHisp 94*
Brazil, Harold *WhoAmP 93*
Brazil, Harold Edmund 1920- *WhoAm 94*
Brazil, Jeff 1962- *WhoAm 94*
Brazil, John Russell 1946- *WhoAm 94, WhoMW 93*
Brazil, Robert D. 1939- *WhoBlA 94*
Brazil, William Clay 1942- *WhoAmL 94*
Brazile, Robert Lorenzo, Jr. 1953- *WhoBlA 94*
Braziller, George *WhoAm 94*
Brazington, Andrew Paul 1918- *WhoBlA 94*
Brazinsky, Irving 1936- *WhoAm 94*
Brazley, Michael Duwain 1951- *WhoBlA 94*
Brazzeal, Marie *WhoAmP 93*
Brazzi, Lydia d1981 *WhoHol 92*
Brazzi, Rossano 1916- *IntMPA 94, WhoHol 92*
Brdecka, Jiri 1917-1982 *IntDcF 2-4*
Brdicka, Miroslav 1913- *WhoScEn 94*
Brdlik, Carola Emilie 1930- *WhoMW 93*
Brea, Luis C. 1932- *WhoHisp 94*
Breach, Gerald Ernest John 1932- *Who 94*
Breadalbane and Holland, Earl of 1919- *Who 94*
Breaden, Robert William 1937- *Who 94*
Bready, Richard Lawrence 1944- *WhoAm 94, WhoFI 94*
Breaker, Richard Carroll 1926- *WhoWest 94*
Breakfield, Paul Thomas, III 1940- *WhoScEn 94*
Breaks, Sebastian *WhoHol 92*
Breakston, George d1973 *WhoHol 92*
Breakstone, Donald S. 1945- *WhoAm 94, WhoAmL 94*
Breakstone, Robert Albert 1938- *WhoAm 94, WhoScEn 94*
Breakwell, Glynis M(arie) 1952- *WrDr 94*
B-Real c. 1970- *See* Cypress Hill *ConMus 11*
Brealey, Richard Arthur 1936- *Who 94*
Bream, Julian 1933- *IntWW 93, Who 94, WhoAm 94*
Breamer, Sylvia d1943 *WhoHol 92*
Breard, L. Christopher 1954- *WhoAmL 94*
Breare, William Robert Ackrill d1993 *Who 94N*
Brearley, Christopher John Scott 1943- *Who 94*
Brearley, David 1745-1790 *WhAmRev*
Brearley, Harry 1871-1948 *DcNaB MP*
Brearley, John Michael 1942- *IntWW 93*
Brearley, (John) Michael 1942- *Who 94*
Brearley, Mike (John Michael) 1942- *WrDr 94*
Brears, Peter C. D. 1944- *WrDr 94*
Brears, Peter Charles David 1944- *Who 94*
Breasher, Philip M. 1941- *WhoWest 94*
Breasure, Rebecca Ann *WhoAmP 93*
Breathed, Berkeley 1957- *WhoAm 94*
Breathitt, Edward Thompson, Jr. 1924- *WhoAm 94, WhoAmP 93*
Breathnach, Aodán S. 1922- *WrDr 94*
Breault, Theodore Edward 1938- *WhoAmL 94*
Breaux, Billie J. *WhoAmP 93*
Breaux, John 1944- *CngDr 93*
Breaux, John B. 1944- *IntWW 93, WhoAm 94, WhoAmP 93*
Breaux, Melvin C. 1940- *WhoAmL 94*
Breaux, Michael Joseph 1949- *WhoAmL 94*
Breaux, Paul Joseph 1942- *WhoAmL 94*
Breay, James H. 1945- *WhoAmL 94*
Breazeale, Mack Alfred 1930- *WhoAm 94, WhoScEn 94*
Brebbia, Carlos Alberto 1948- *WhoScEn 94*
Brebbia, John Henry 1932- *WhoAm 94*
Brebeuf, Jean De 1593-1649 *EncNAR, WhWE*
Brebner, Winston 1924?- *EncSF 93*
Brebrick, Robert Frank 1925- *WhoMW 93*
Brechbill, Susan Reynolds 1943- *WhoAmL 94, WhoWest 94*
Brecher, Armin G. 1942- *WhoAm 94, WhoAmL 94*
Brecher, Arthur Seymour 1928- *WhoAm 94*
Brecher, Bernd 1932- *WhoFI 94*
Brecher, Edward Moritz 1911-1989 *WhAm 10*
Brecher, Egon d1946 *WhoHol 92*
Brecher, Ephraim Fred 1931- *WhoScEn 94*
Brecher, Gustav 1879-1940 *NewGrDO*
Brecher, Irving 1914- *IntMPA 94*
Brecher, Irving 1923- *WhoAm 94*
Brecher, Kenneth 1943- *WhoAm 94, WhoScEn 94*
Brecher, Michael 1925- *IntWW 93, WhoAm 94, WrDr 94*
Brecher, Samuel 1897-1982 *WhoAmA 93N*
Brechin, Bishop of 1932- *Who 94*
Brechin, Dean of *Who 94*
Brechin, Garry David 1944- *WhoWest 94*
Brecht, Bertolt 1898-1956 *BlmGEL, IntDcT 2 [port]*
Brecht, Bertolt (Eugen Friedrich) 1898-1956 *NewGrDO*
Brecht, George 1926- *WhoAmA 93*
Brecht, Warren Frederick 1932- *WhoAm 94*
Breck, Allen du Pont 1914- *WhoAm 94*
Breck, Edward J. d1993 *NewYTBS 93 [port]*
Breck, Henry C(ushman) 1893- *WhAm 10*
Breck, Howard Rolland 1912- *WhoAm 94*
Breck, James Edward 1946- *WhoMW 93, WhoScEn 94*
Breck, James Lloyd 1818-1876 *DcAmReB 2, EncNAR*
Breck, Katherine Anne 1964- *WhoScEn 94*
Breck, Peter 1929- *WhoHol 92*
Brecke, Barry John 1947- *WhoScEn 94*
Breckel, Alvina Hefeli 1948- *WhoMW 93*
Breckenfelder, Lynn E. 1964- *WhoMW 93*
Breckenridge, Adam (Carlyle) 1916- *WrDr 94*
Breckenridge, Alasdair Muir 1937- *IntWW 93, Who 94*
Breckenridge, Bruce M. 1929- *WhoAmA 93*
Breckenridge, Franklin E. *WhoBlA 94*
Breckenridge, Jackie B. 1941- *WhoBlA 94*
Breckenridge, James D. 1926-1982 *WhoAmA 93N*
Breckenridge, Jill *DrAPF 93*
Breckenridge, John L. 1913- *WhoBlA 94*
Brecker, Jeffrey Ross 1953- *WhoAmL 94*
Brecker, Manfred 1927- *WhoAm 94*
Breckinridge, Flint 1960- *WhoAmP 93*
Breckinridge, James Bernard 1939- *WhoAm 94*
Breckman, James d1967 *WhoHol 92*
Breckner, Gary d1945 *WhoHol 92*
Breckner, William John, Jr. 1933- *WhoAm 94, WhoWest 94*
Brecknock, Earl of 1965- *Who 94*
Brecknock, John 1937- *NewGrDO*
Breckon, Donald John 1939- *WhoAm 94*
Brecon, Dean of *Who 94*
Breda, Malcolm J. 1934- *WhoBlA 94*
Breda, Roberta 1952- *WhoWomW 91*
Bredar, Marcia Ann 1953- *WhoMW 93*
Breddan, Joe 1950- *WhoWest 94*
Brede, Andrew Douglas 1953- *WhoScEn 94, WhoWest 94*
Bredehoft, Elaine Charlson 1958- *WhoAmL 94*
Bredehoft, John Michael 1958- *WhoAmL 94*
Bredemeier, Kenneth Herbert 1945- *WhoAm 94*
Bredemeyer, Reiner 1929- *NewGrDO*
Breder, Hans Dieter 1935- *WhoAmA 93*
Bredesen, Philip N. *WhoAmP 93*
Bredesen, Philip Norman 1943- *WhoAm 94*
Bredeson, Dean Kardell 1921- *WhoFI 94*
Bredfeldt, John Creighton 1947- *WhoFI 94*
Brediceanu, Tiberiu 1877-1968 *NewGrDO*
Bredin, Frederique 1956- *WhoWomW 91*
Bredin, Frederique Marie Denise Colette 1956- *IntWW 93*
Bredin, Humphrey Edgar Nicholson 1916- *Who 94*
Bredin, James John 1924- *Who 94*
Bredin, John Bruce 1914- *WhoAm 94*
Bredlow, Tom 1938- *WhoAmA 93*
Bredsdorff, Elias 1912- *IntWW 93*
Bredsdorff, Elias Lunn 1912- *WrDr 94*
Bredt, Charles Franklin 1952- *WhoMW 93*
Bree, Germaine 1907- *IntWW 93, WrDr 94*
Bree, Marlin Duane 1933- *WhoMW 93*
Breece, Del d1977 *WhoHol 92*
Breece, Robert William, Jr. 1942- *WhoAm 94*
Breed, Allen Forbes 1920- *WhoAm 94*
Breed, Charles Ayars 1927- *WhoAmA 93*
Breed, Charles N., Jr. d1993 *NewYTBS 93*
Breed, Eileen Judith 1945- *WhoMW 93*
Breed, Helen Illick 1925- *WhoAm 94*
Breed, Nathaniel P., Jr. 1937- *WhoAmL 94*
Breed, Ria 1944- *WhoAm 94*
Breeden, Carolyn Sullivan 1943- *WhoAm 94*
Breeden, Chris David 1955- *WhoMW 93*
Breeden, David *DrAPF 93, WhoAm 94*
Breeden, Edward Lebbaeus, Jr. 1905-1990 *WhAm 10*
Breeden, James Pleasant 1934- *WhoBlA 94*
Breeden, John d1977 *WhoHol 92*
Breeden, Rex Earl 1920- *WhoAm 94, WhoMW 93*
Breeden, Richard 1949- *IntWW 93*
Breeden, Richard C. *WhoAmP 93*
Breeding, Carl L. 1932- *WhoBlA 94*
Breeding, Carl Wayne 1954- *WhoAmL 94*
Breeding, David C. 1952- *WhoFI 94*
Breeding, Larry d1982 *WhoHol 92*
Breedlove, Jimmie Dale, Jr. 1958- *WhoMW 93*
Breedlove, Keith R. *WhoAmP 93*
Breedlove, Michael M. 1940- *WhoAmP 93*
Breedlove, Nancy Jean Free 1960- *WhoMW 93*
Breedlove, S. Marc 1954- *WhoWest 94*
Breeland, Floyd *WhoAmP 93*
Breeland, Kevin Mark 1957- *WhoWest 94*
Breen, Bobby 1927- *WhoHol 92*
Breen, David Hart 1960- *WhoAmL 94*
Breen, F. Glenn 1912- *WhoAm 94*
Breen, Geoffrey Brian 1944- *Who 94*
Breen, Harry d1918 *WhoHol 92*
Breen, Harry Frederick, Jr. 1930- *WhoAmA 93*
Breen, James M. 1943- *WhoAmL 94*
Breen, John Edward 1932- *WhoAm 94, WhoScEn 94*
Breen, John Francis 1929- *WhoAm 94*
Breen, John Gerald 1934- *WhoAm 94, WhoFI 94*
Breen, John Wakefield 1945- *WhoMW 93*
Breen, Jon L(inn) 1943- *WrDr 94*
Breen, Margaret d1960 *WhoHol 92*
Breen, Marie (Freda) 1902- *Who 94*
Breen, Thomas Albert 1956- *WhoAm 94, WhoFI 94, WhoWest 94*
Breen, Thomas John 1948- *WhoAm 94*
Breen, Timothy Hall 1942- *WhoAm 94*
Breene, Roger J. 1954- *WhoAmL 94*
Breer, Robert 1926- *IntDcF 2-4 [port]*
Breer, Robert C. 1926- *WhoAmA 93*
Brees, Eugene Wilson, II 1950- *WhoAm 94, WhoAmL 94*
Breese, Edmund d1936 *WhoHol 92*
Breese, Frank Chandler, III 1944- *WhoAm 94*
Breese, Gerald (William) 1912- *WrDr 94*
Breese, John Allen 1951- *WhoFI 94, WhoScEn 94*
Breeskin, Adelyn Dohme 1896-1986 *WhoAmA 93N*
Breeze, Alastair Jon 1934- *Who 94*
Breeze, David John 1944- *Who 94*

Breeze, Jean Binta 1956- *BlmGWL*
Breeze, Lou d1969 *WhoHol 92*
Breeze, William Hancock 1923- *WhoAm 94, WhoIns 94*
Breezley, Roger Lee 1938- *WhoAm 94, WhoFI 94, WhoWest 94*
Breffeilh, Louis Andrew 1913- *WhoAm 94*
Brega, Charles Franklin 1933- *WhoAm 94*
Bregel, Yuri 1925- *WhoMW 93*
Breger, Brian *DrAPF 93*
Breger, Dave 1908-1970 *WhoAmA 93N*
Breger, Dwayne Steven 1957- *WhoScEn 94*
Breger, Marshall J. 1946- *WhoAm 94*
Breger, Marshall Jordan 1946- *WhoAmP 93*
Breggin, Peter (Roger) 1936- *EncSF 93*
Breggin, Peter Roger 1936- *WhoAm 94*
Breglio, John F. 1946- *WhoAm 94, WhoAmL 94*
Bregman, Howard 1949- *WhoAmL 94*
Bregman, Jacob I. 1923- *WhoAmP 93*
Bregman, Jacob Israel 1923- *WhoAm 94*
Bregman, Jacqueline De Oliveira 1961- *WhoAmL 94*
Bregman, Jenn Swenson 1960- *WhoWest 94*
Bregman, Martin 1931- *IntMPA 94, WhoAm 94*
Bregman, Sandra Kaye 1947- *WhoAmL 94*
Bregman, Tracey E. *WhoHol 92*
Bregou, Christian Robert 1941- *IntWW 93*
Bregvadze, Nani Georgevna 1938- *IntWW 93*
Brehant De Galinee, Rene De c. 1645-1678 *WhWE*
Brehaut, Charles Henry 1938- *WhoFI 94*
Brehl, James William *WhoAmL 94*
Brehm, Frederick Carl 1930- *WhoFI 94*
Brehm, Jack Williams 1928- *WhoScEn 94*
Brehm, Sharon Stephens 1945- *WhoAm 94*
Brehm, Victoria Louise 1947- *WhoMW 93*
Brehm, William Allen, Jr. 1945- *WhoMW 93*
Brehme, Hans (Ludwig Wilhelm) 1904-1957 *NewGrDO*
Brehony, John Albert Noel 1936- *Who 94*
Breidegam, DeLight Edgar, Jr. 1926- *WhoAm 94*
Breidenbach, Cherie Elizabeth 1952- *WhoAmL 94*
Breidenbach, Francis Anthony 1930- *WhoAm 94*
Breidenbach, Rowland William 1935- *WhoAm 94*
Breidenthal, Robert Edward 1951- *WhoWest 94*
Breiger, Elaine *WhoAmA 93*
Breihan, Erwin Robert 1918- *WhoAm 94*
Breil, David Allen 1938- *WhoScEn 94*
Breil, Joseph Carl 1870-1926 *NewGrDO*
Breimayer, Joseph Frederick 1942- *WhoAm 94*
Breimyer, Harold F 1914- *WrDr 94*
Breimyer, Harold Frederick 1914- *WhoAm 94, WhoMW 93*
Breinburg, Petronella 1927- *ChILR 31 [port]*
Breiner, Richard Harry 1935- *WhoWest 94*
Breiner, Rosemary 1937- *WhoHisp 94, WhoWest 94*
Breiner, Sander James 1925- *WhoMW 93*
Breiner, Sheldon 1936- *WhoScEn 94*
Breines, Paul 1941- *WrDr 94*
Breines, Simon 1906- *WhoAm 94*
Breinin, Goodwin M. 1918- *WhoAm 94*
Breinin, Raymond 1910- *WhoAm 94, WhoAmA 93*
Breipohl, Walter Eugene 1953- *WhoMW 93*
Breisach, Ernst A. 1923- *WhoAm 94, WhoMW 93*
Breiseth, Christopher Neri 1936- *WhoAm 94*
Breit, Alice Evelyn 1922- *WhoAmP 93*
Breit, Jeffrey A. 1955- *WhoAmP 93*
Breit, Jeffrey Arnold 1955- *WhoAmL 94*
Breit, Luke *DrAPF 93*
Breitbach, Tim Richard 1958- *WhoFI 94*
Breitbart, Barbara Renee *WhoWest 94*
Breitberg, Freddie 1947- *WhoFI 94*
Breitel, Charles D. 1908-1991 *WhAm 10*
Breitenbach, Allan Joseph 1949- *WhoScEn 94*
Breitenbach, Edgar 1903-1977 *WhoAmA 93N*
Breitenbach, Mary Louise McGraw 1936- *WhoAm 94, WhoWest 94*
Breitenbach, Thomas George 1947- *WhoAm 94, WhoMW 93*
Breitenbach, William John 1936- *WhoAmA 93*
Breitenecker, Rudiger 1929- *WhoAm 94*
Breitenfeld, Frederick, Jr. 1931- *WhoAm 94*
Breitenstein, Peter Frederic 1938- *WhoAmL 94*
Breithaupt, Erwin M. 1920- *WhoAmA 93*
Breithaupt, Henry C. 1947- *WhoAmL 94*
Breitling, Peter M. 1943- *WhoAmL 94*
Breitman, Joseph B. 1952- *WhoScEn 94*
Breitmeyer, Alan Norman 1924- *Who 94*
Breitmeyer, Jo Anne 1947- *WhoAm 94, WhoFI 94*
Breitnauer, Paul J. 1939- *WhoIns 94*
Breitrose, Henry S. 1936- *WhoAm 94*
Breitsameter, Frank John 1919- *WhoScEn 94*
Breitschwerdt, Werner 1927- *IntWW 93*
Breitweiser, James Russell 1936- *WhoFI 94, WhoWest 94*
Breitwieser, Charles John 1910- *WhoAm 94*
Brejcha, Vernon Lee 1942- *WhoAmA 93*
Brejean-Silver, Georgette 1870-1951? *NewGrDO*
Brekhovskikh, Leonid Maksimovich 1917- *IntWW 93*
Brekke, Gail Louise 1949- *WhoMW 93*
Brekke, Joanne J. *WhoAmP 93*
Brekke, Kris 1954- *WhoAmP 93*
Brekke, Lola M. 1931- *WhoAmP 93*
Brel, Jacques d1978 *WhoHol 92*
Breland, Albert Edward, Jr. 1939- *WhoWest 94*
Breland, H. Terrell *WhoAmP 93*
Breland, Hunter Mansfield 1933- *WhoScEn 94*
Breland, Mark *WhoHol 92*
Breland, Rupert Earl 1935- *WhoAmP 93*
Brelis, Matthew Dean Burns 1957- *WhoAm 94*
Brelsford, Gates Grissom 1950- *WhoFI 94*
Brem, Beppo d1990 *WhoHol 92*
Brem, Robert John 1958- *WhoWest 94*
Brem, Thomas Hamilton 1910-1990 *WhAm 10*
Brema, Marie 1856-1925 *NewGrDO*
Breman, Jan 1936- *IntWW 93*
Breman, Joseph Eliot 1945- *WhoAm 94*
Brembeck, Winston Lamont 1912- *WhoAm 94*
Bremberg, Ginger *WhoAmP 93*
Bremby, Roderick LeMar 1960- *WhoBlA 94*
Bremen, Lennie d1986 *WhoHol 92*
Bremen, Ronald David 1950- *WhoAmL 94*
Brement, Marshall 1932- *WhoAmP 93*
Bremer, Alfonso M. 1939- *WhoScEn 94*
Bremer, Charles E. 1941- *WhoBlA 94*
Bremer, Donald Duane 1934- *WhoWest 94*
Bremer, Fredrika 1801-1865 *BlmGWL*
Bremer, James Patrick 1949- *WhoMW 93*
Bremer, Joanna Charles 1947- *WhoMW 93*
Bremer, John M. 1947- *WhoAmL 94*
Bremer, Jon 1928- *IntWW 93*
Bremer, L. Paul 1941- *WhoAmP 93*
Bremer, Lucille 1923- *WhoHol 92*
Bremer, Marlene S. *WhoAmA 93*
Bremer, Richard H. 1948- *WhoFI 94*
Bremer, Victor John 1943- *WhoMW 93*
Bremerman, Michael Vance 1954- *WhoScEn 94*
Bremner, Bruce Barton 1939- *WhoAm 94*
Bremner, D. Roger 1937- *WhoAmP 93*
Bremner, John McColl 1922- *WhoAm 94, WhoMW 93, WhoScEn 94*
Bremridge, John (Henry) 1925- *Who 94*
Bremridge, John Henry 1925- *IntWW 93*
Brems, David Paul 1950- *WhoWest 94*
Brems, Hans J 1915- *WrDr 94*
Brems, Hans Julius 1915- *WhoAm 94*
Bremser, George, Jr. 1928- *WhoAm 94, WhoWest 94*
Bremser, Ray *DrAPF 93*
Bremser, Ray 1934- *WrDr 94*
Brenaa, Hans 1910-1988 *IntDcB*
Brenan, Denis V. 1937- *WhoAm 94*
Brenchley, Jean Elnora 1944- *WhoAm 94, WhoScEn 94*
Brenchley, Thomas Frank 1918- *IntWW 93, Who 94*
"Brenda" d1952 *WhoHol 92*
Brendan, Saint c. 484-c. 578 *WhWE*
Brendel, Alfred 1931- *IntWW 93, Who 94, WhoAm 94*
Brendel, Bettina *WhoAmA 93*
Brendel, El d1964 *WhoHol 92*
Brendel, John S. 1951- *WhoAmL 94*
Brendel, Karl Franz 1811-1868 *NewGrDO*
Brendel, Klaus 1933- *WhoAm 94*
Brendel, Neal R. 1954- *WhoAmL 94*
Brendel, Otto J. 1901-1973 *WhoAmA 93N*
Brendel, Wolfgang 1947- *NewGrDO*
Brenden, Byron Byrne 1927- *WhoScEn 94*
Brenden, John C., II 1941- *WhoAmP 93*
Brendle, Kenneth Lee *WhoIns 94*
Brendler, (Frans Fredric) Eduard 1800-1831 *NewGrDO*
Brendlinger, LeRoy R. 1918- *WhoAm 94*
Brendon, Piers 1940- *WrDr 94*
Brendon, Rupert Timothy Rundle 1943- *WhoAm 94*
Brendsel, Leland C. *WhoAm 94, WhoFI 94*
Brendtro, Larry Kay 1940- *WhoAm 94*
Breneisen, Albert J. 1934- *WhoAmL 94*
Breneman, David Worthy 1940- *WhoAm 94*
Breneman, Debra Lynn 1955- *WhoMW 93*
Breneman, Diane Marie 1965- *WhoAmL 94*
Breneman, Gerald Myers 1924-1990 *WhAm 10*
Breneman, Suzanne 1960- *WhoMW 93*
Breneman, Tom d1948 *WhoHol 92*
Breneman, William Dudley 1943- *WhoAmL 94*
Breneman, William Raymond 1907-1992 *WhAm 10*
Brenenstuhl, Henry Brent 1963- *WhoAmL 94*
Brener, Roland 1942- *WhoAmA 93*
Brenerman, David H. 1951- *WhoAmP 93*
Brengel, Fred Lenhardt 1923- *WhoAm 94, WhoFI 94*
Brengelman, Fred(erick Henry) 1928- *WrDr 94*
Brengk, Ernest d1961 *WhoHol 92*
Brengle, Samuel Logan 1860-1936 *DcAmReB 2*
Brengle, Thomas Alan 1952- *WhoWest 94*
Brenikov, Paul 1921- *Who 94*
Breningstall, Galen Natley 1951- *WhoMW 93*
Brenker, Thomas Clarkson 1944- *WhoAm 94*
Brenlin, George d1986 *WhoHol 92*
Brenna, Guglielmo 1806?-1882? *NewGrDO*
Brennan, Ann Herlevich 1956- *WhoScEn 94*
Brennan, Anthony John Edward 1927- *Who 94*
Brennan, Archibald Orr *Who 94*
Brennan, Barbara Jane 1936- *WhoWest 94*
Brennan, Barney d1938 *WhoHol 92*
Brennan, Bernard Francis 1938- *WhoAm 94, WhoFI 94*
Brennan, Brian John 1918- *Who 94*
Brennan, Carey M. 1948- *WhoAm 94*
Brennan, Carol 1934- *ConAu 142*
Brennan, Cecelia Jean 1965- *WhoFI 94*
Brennan, Charles Martin, III 1942- *WhoAm 94*
Brennan, Ciaran Brendan 1944- *WhoFI 94, WhoWest 94*
Brennan, Daniel Edward, Jr. 1942- *WhoAmL 94*
Brennan, Daniel Joseph 1942- *Who 94*
Brennan, Daniel L. 1943- *WhoAm 94, WhoFI 94*
Brennan, David Leo 1931- *WhoAm 94, WhoMW 93*
Brennan, Denis d1983 *WhoHol 92*
Brennan, Donald P. 1940- *WhoFI 94*
Brennan, Donald P. 1941- *WhoAm 94, WhoFI 94*
Brennan, Donna Lesley 1945- *WhoAm 94*
Brennan, Doris Alene 1920- *WhoAmP 93*
Brennan, Edward 1915- *WhoAmP 93*
Brennan, Edward A. 1934- *IntWW 93, Who 94, WhoAm 94, WhoFI 94, WhoMW 93*
Brennan, Eileen 1935- *IntMPA 94, WhoHol 92*
Brennan, Eileen Regina 1935- *WhoAm 94*
Brennan, Fanny *WhoAmA 93*
Brennan, Francis Edwin 1910- *WhoAmA 93*
Brennan, Francis Patrick 1917- *WhoAm 94*
Brennan, Francis W. 1919- *WhoAm 94, WhoAmL 94*
Brennan, Frank *WhoHol 92*
Brennan, George Gerard 1931- *WhoScEn 94*
Brennan, (Francis) Gerard 1928- *Who 94*
Brennan, Henry Higginson 1932- *WhoAm 94*
Brennan, J. Michael 1939- *WhoAmL 94*
Brennan, James F. 1952- *WhoAmP 93*
Brennan, James G. 1927- *WhoAm 94*
Brennan, Jay d1961 *WhoHol 92*
Brennan, Jay 1882-1961
See Savoy and Brennan *WhoCom*
Brennan, Jerry Michael 1944- *WhoWest 94*
Brennan, Joan Stevenson 1933- *WhoAm 94, WhoAmL 94, WhoWest 94*
Brennan, John A., Jr. 1945- *WhoAmP 93*
Brennan, John Edward 1928- *WhoAm 94*
Brennan, John Joseph 1958- *WhoAmL 94*
Brennan, John Merritt 1935- *WhoAm 94*
Brennan, John V. 1934- *WhoIns 94*
Brennan, Johnny d1940 *WhoHol 92*
Brennan, Joseph d1940 *WhoHol 92*
Brennan, Joseph Edward 1934- *WhoAmP 93*
Brennan, Joseph Fancis Xavier 1939- *WhoIns 94*
Brennan, Joseph Gerard 1910- *WhoAm 94*
Brennan, Joseph Patrick, Jr. 1944- *WhoAmL 94*
Brennan, Judith Ann Slocombe 1951- *WhoMW 93*
Brennan, Lawrence Edward 1927- *WhoAm 94*
Brennan, Leo Joseph, Jr. 1930- *WhoAm 94*
Brennan, Leonard Alfred 1957- *WhoScEn 94*
Brennan, Louise Smith 1922- *WhoAmP 93*
Brennan, Maeve *DrAPF 93*
Brennan, Martin A. 1946- *WhoIns 94*
Brennan, Mary 1954- *WhoAmP 93*
Brennan, Maryann 1946- *WhoFI 94*
Brennan, Matthew *DrAPF 93*
Brennan, Matthew Cannon 1955- *WhoMW 93*
Brennan, Maureen A. 1949- *WhoAm 94*
Brennan, Michael *WhoAmP 93*
Brennan, Michael 1912- *WhoHol 92*
Brennan, Murray Frederick 1940- *WhoAm 94*
Brennan, Neil F 1923- *WrDr 94*
Brennan, Nizette 1950- *WhoAmA 93*
Brennan, Norma Jean 1939- *WhoFI 94*
Brennan, Patrick Francis 1931- *WhoAm 94*
Brennan, Patrick Thomas 1952- *WhoAm 94*
Brennan, Paul Joseph 1920- *WhoAm 94*
Brennan, Richard E. 1941- *WhoAmL 94*
Brennan, Richard J. 1936- *WhoAm 94*
Brennan, Richard Snyder 1938- *WhoAm 94, WhoAmL 94*
Brennan, Robert d1940 *WhoHol 92*
Brennan, Robert Bryan 1941- *WhoFI 94*
Brennan, Robert J. *WhoFI 94*
Brennan, Robert J. 1949- *WhoAmL 94*
Brennan, Robert Lawrence 1944- *WhoAm 94*
Brennan, Robert Walter 1934- *WhoMW 93*
Brennan, Seamus 1948- *IntWW 93*
Brennan, Sean Michael 1954- *WhoScEn 94*
Brennan, T. Casey 1948- *WhoAm 94, WhoMW 93*
Brennan, Terrence Michael 1947- *WhoAm 94*
Brennan, Thomas Emmett 1929- *WhoAm 94*
Brennan, Thomas George, Jr. 1953- *WhoScEn 94*
Brennan, Thomas John 1923- *WhoFI 94*
Brennan, Timothy Louis 1957- *WhoAmP 93*
Brennan, Timothy William 1951- *WhoAm 94*
Brennan, Tom *WhoHol 92*
Brennan, Vincent Terrance 1949- *WhoMW 93*
Brennan, Walter d1974 *WhoHol 92*
Brennan, William Bernard, Jr. 1931- *WhoAm 94*
Brennan, William J., Jr. 1906- *CngDr 93*
Brennan, William J., III 1933- *WhoAmL 94*
Brennan, William Joseph 1928- *WhoAm 94*
Brennan, William Joseph 1958- *WhoAmL 94*
Brennan, William Joseph, Jr. 1906- *IntWW 93, Who 94, WhoAm 94, WhoAmL 94, WhoAmP 93*
Brennan, William R., Jr. d1993 *NewYTBS 93*
Brennecke, Allen Eugene 1937- *WhoAm 94, WhoAmL 94*
Brenneis, Gerd 1936- *NewGrDO*
Brenneise, Geraldine Ungerecht 1932- *WhoMW 93*
Brenneman, Delbert Jay 1950- *WhoAm 94*
Brenneman, Helen Good 1925- *WrDr 94*
Brenneman, Hugh Warren, Jr. 1945- *WhoAm 94, WhoAmL 94, WhoMW 93*
Brenneman, John David 1942- *WhoAmP 93*
Brenneman, Richard James 1946- *WhoWest 94*
Brenneman, Russell Langdon 1928- *WhoAmL 94*
Brenneman, Sharon Kay 1949- *WhoMW 93*
Brennen, Christopher E. *WhoScEn 94*
Brennen, Claire d1977 *WhoHol 92*
Brennen, Patrick Wayne 1940- *WhoAm 94*
Brennen, Stephen Alfred *WhoAm 94*
Brennen, Steven Russell 1953- *WhoWest 94*

Brennen, William Elbert 1930- *WhoFI 94*
Brenner, Albert 1926- *ConTFT 11, WhoAm 94*
Brenner, Alfred Ephraim 1931- *WhoAm 94*
Brenner, Amy Rebecca 1958- *WhoScEn 94*
Brenner, Arnold S. 1937- *WhoFI 94*
Brenner, Barbara (Johnes) 1925- *SmATA 76 [port]*
Brenner, Barry Morton 1937- *WhoAm 94, WhoScEn 94*
Brenner, Brian Raymond 1960- *WhoScEn 94*
Brenner, Daniel L. 1951- *WhoWest 94*
Brenner, Daniel Leon 1904- *WhoAm 94*
Brenner, David 1945- *WhoAm 94, WhoCom, WhoHol 92, WrDr 94*
Brenner, David McCaskie 1957- *WhoMW 93*
Brenner, Dean Elliott 1949- *WhoMW 93*
Brenner, Donald Robert 1936- *WhoAm 94, WhoFI 94*
Brenner, Dori *WhoHol 92*
Brenner, Edgar H. 1930- *WhoAm 94, WhoAmL 94*
Brenner, Edward John 1923-1992 *WhAm 10*
Brenner, Egon 1925- *WhoAm 94*
Brenner, Erma 1911- *WhoAm 94*
Brenner, Frank 1927- *WhoAm 94*
Brenner, Frederic James 1936- *WhoAm 94*
Brenner, George Marvin 1943- *WhoScEn 94*
Brenner, Gita Kedar Voivodas 1942- *WhoAm 94*
Brenner, Henry 1914- *WhoAm 94*
Brenner, Howard 1929- *WhoAm 94*
Brenner, Howard Martin 1933- *WhoAm 94*
Brenner, James d1993 *NewYTBS 93*
Brenner, Janet Maybin Walker *WhoAmL 94*
Brenner, Joseph 1918- *IntMPA 94*
Brenner, Marshall Leib 1933- *WhoAmL 94*
Brenner, Maurice *WhoHol 92*
Brenner, Paul R. 1942- *WhoAmL 94*
Brenner, Rena Claudy *WhoFI 94*
Brenner, Reuven 1947- *ConAu 142*
Brenner, Ronald John 1933- *WhoAm 94*
Brenner, Saul Daniel 1962- *WhoAmL 94*
Brenner, Shore Hodge 1949- *WhoAmA 93N*
Brenner, Summer *DrAPF 93*
Brenner, Susan Woolf 1947- *WhoAmL 94*
Brenner, Sydney 1927- *IntWW 93, Who 94, WhoScEn 94*
Brenner, Thomas Edward 1955- *WhoAmL 94*
Brenner, William Edward 1936- *WhoAm 94*
Brenner, William Irwin 1943- *WhoWest 94*
Brenner, Yehojachin Simon 1926- *WrDr 94*
Brennert, Alan (Michael) 1954- *EncSF 93*
Brenno, Vonnie Mei-Lin 1950- *WhoAmA 93*
Brenny, Mary Clare 1950- *WhoMW 93*
Brenon, Herbert d1958 *WhoHol 92*
Brenon, John Gene 1948- *WhoAmL 94*
Brenon, Juliet d1978 *WhoHol 92*
Brenson, Theodore 1893-1959 *WhoAmA 93N*
Brenson, Verdel Lee 1925- *WhoBlA 94*
Brent, Anne Marie 1926- *WhoAmP 93*
Brent, Charlotte d1802 *NewGrDO*
Brent, David L. 1929- *WhoBlA 94*
Brent, Eve 1930- *WhoHol 92*
Brent, Evelyn d1975 *WhoHol 92*
Brent, George d1979 *WhoHol 92*
Brent, Ira Martin 1944- *WhoWest 94*
Brent, Leslie 1925- *Who 94*
Brent, Lynton d1981 *WhoHol 92*
Brent, Madeleine 1920- *WrDr 94*
Brent, Michael Leon 1936- *Who 94*
Brent, Paul Leslie 1916- *WhoAm 94*
Brent, Paul M. 1960- *WhoAmL 94*
Brent, Richard Peirce 1946- *IntWW 93*
Brent, Richard Samuel 1949- *WhoWest 94*
Brent, Robert Leonard 1927- *WhoAm 94, WhoScEn 94*
Brent, Romney d1976 *WhoHol 92*
Brent, Ruth Stumpe 1951- *WhoMW 93*
Brenta, Gaston 1902-1969 *NewGrDO*
Brentano, Clemens (Wenzeslaus Maria) 1778-1842 *NewGrDO*
Brentano, Franz Clemens 1838-1917 *EncEth*
Brentford, Viscount 1933- *Who 94*
Brentlinger, Paul Smith 1927- *WhoAm 94, WhoFI 94*
Brentlinger, William Brock 1926- *WhoAm 94*
Brent of Bin Bin *BlmGWL*
Brenton, Howard 1942- *BlmGEL, ConDr 93, IntDcT 2 [port], IntWW 93, Who 94, WrDr 94*
Brenton, Marianne 1933- *WhoAmP 93*
Brents, Barbara Gayle 1957- *WhoWest 94*
Brentwood, Bishop of 1936- *Who 94*
Brenz, Gary Jay 1945- *WhoMW 93*
Breon, Edmund d1951 *WhoHol 92*
Brepoels, Frederika 1955- *WhoWomW 91*
Brereton, Donald 1945- *Who 94*
Brereton, Giles John 1958- *WhoScEn 94*
Brereton, Sandra Joy 1960- *WhoScEn 94*
Brereton, Tyrone d1939 *WhoHol 92*
Bres, Philip Wayne 1950- *WhoWest 94*
Bresani, Federico Fernando 1945- *WhoAm 94, WhoFI 94*
Brescher, John B., Jr. 1947- *WhoAmL 94*
Breschi, Karen Lee 1941- *WhoAmA 93*
Brescia, Michael Joseph 1933- *WhoAm 94*
Bresee, James Collins 1925- *WhoAm 94*
Bresgen, Cesar 1913-1988 *NewGrDO*
Breshears, Gerry Everett 1947- *WhoWest 94*
Breshkovsky, Catherine 1844-1934 *HisWorL [port]*
Bresilienne, Une *BlmGWL*
Bresina-Hawkins, Donald Charles 1954- *WhoFI 94*
Bresis, Vilnis-Edvins 1938- *IntWW 93*
Breske, Roger M. 1938- *WhoAmP 93*
Bresky, H. Harry 1925- *WhoFI 94*
Breslau, Howard Louis 1964- *WhoFI 94*
Breslau, Neil Art 1947- *WhoScEn 94*
Breslauer, George William 1946- *WhoAm 94, WhoWest 94*
Breslauer, Suzanne Eisen 1938- *WhoMW 93*
Breslauer, Thelma 1926- *WhoAm 94, WhoAmL 94*
Bresler, Boris 1918- *WhoAm 94*
Bresler, Charles Sheldon 1927- *WhoAm 94*
Bresler, Mark Irwin 1953- *WhoAm 94*
Bresler, Martin I. 1931- *WhoAm 94*
Breslin, Eric Robert 1957- *WhoAmL 94*
Breslin, George M(ontgomery) 1895- *WhAm 10*
Breslin, Jimmy 1929- *WhoAm 94*
Breslin, Jimmy 1930- *WhoHol 92, WrDr 94*
Breslin, Kevin *WhoHol 92*
Breslin, Michael Edward 1937- *WhoAmL 94*
Breslin, Patricia *WhoHol 92*
Breslin, Patricia 1959- *WhoAmL 94*
Breslin, Peg McDonnell 1946- *WhoAmP 93*
Breslin, Richard David 1937- *WhoAm 94*
Breslin, Thomas Peter 1949- *WhoAmL 94*
Breslin, Thomas Raymond 1944- *WhoFI 94*
Breslin, Wynn 1932- *WhoAmA 93*
Breslow, Jan Leslie 1943- *WhoScEn 94*
Breslow, Jerome Wilfred 1934- *WhoAm 94*
Breslow, John 1949- *WhoAmP 93*
Breslow, Lester 1915- *IntWW 93, WhoAm 94*
Breslow, Maurice (A.) 1935- *WrDr 94*
Breslow, Michael *DrAPF 93*
Breslow, Norman Edward 1941- *WhoAm 94, WhoWest 94*
Breslow, Ronald Charles 1931- *IntWW 93, WhoAm 94, WhoScEn 94*
Bresnahan, Arthur Stephen 1944- *WhoAmL 94*
Bresnahan, David Parsons 1930- *WhoIns 94*
Bresnahan, James Francis 1926- *WhoAm 94*
Bresnahan, James Patrick 1954- *WhoWest 94*
Bresnahan, Pamela Anne 1954- *WhoAmL 94*
Bresnick, Sidney Ralph 1932- *WhoAmL 94*
Bress, Michael E. 1933- *WhoAm 94*
Bressan, Paul Louis 1947- *WhoAm 94, WhoAmL 94*
Bressand, Friedrich Christian c. 1670-1699 *NewGrDO*
Bressani, Francesco-Gioseppe 1612-1672 *WhWE*
Bressani, Ricardo 1926- *IntWW 93*
Bressart, Felix d1949 *WhoHol 92*
Bressers, Daniel Joseph 1956- *WhoScEn 94*
Bressi, Betty *DrAPF 93, WhoAmA 93*
Bresslaw, Bernard 1933- *WhoHol 92*
Bressler, Arnold Nacht 1949- *WhoAmL 94*
Bressler, Barry Evan 1947- *WhoAmL 94*
Bressler, Bernard 1928- *WhoAm 94*
Bressler, Marcus N. *WhoScEn 94*
Bressler, Steven L. 1951- *WhoAm 94*
Bressman, David L. 1951- *WhoAmL 94*
Bresson, Robert 1901- *IntWW 93, Who 94*
Bresson, Robert 1907- *IntMPA 94*
Bressor, Gary T. 1950- *WhoAmP 93*
Bressoud, David M(arius) 1950- *ConAu 141*
Brest, Albert N. 1928- *WhoAm 94*
Brest, Martin 1951- *IntMPA 94, WhoAm 94*
Brest, Paul A. 1940- *WhoAm 94, WhoAmL 94, WhoWest 94*
Brestoff, Richard *WhoHol 92*
Bretan, Barbara 1953- *WhoAmL 94*
Bretan, Nicolae 1887-1968 *NewGrDO*
Bretas, Ana Lins dos Guimaraes Peixoto *BlmGWL*
Breternitz, Cory Dale 1955- *WhoWest 94*
Breth, Andrea 1952- *IntWW 93*
Bretherton, Di 1943- *WhoWomW 91*
Bretherton, James Russell 1943- *Who 94*
Bretnor, Reginald 1911-1992 *WrDr 94N*
Bretnor, (Alfred) Reginald 1911-1992 *EncSF 93*
Bretoi, Remus Nicolae 1925- *WhoWest 94*
Breton (y Hernandez), Tomas 1850-1923 *NewGrDO*
Breton, Albert 1929- *WrDr 94*
Breton, Albert A. 1929- *WhoAm 94*
Breton, Andre 1896-1966 *BlmGEL*
Breton, Nicholas 1545?-1626? *BlmGEL*
Breton, Nicholas c. 1555-c. 1626 *DcLB 136*
Bretones, Reynaldo 1936- *WhoHisp 94*
Bretos, Miguel A. 1943- *WhoHisp 94*
Bretsch, Carey Lane 1958- *WhoScEn 94*
Bretscher, Barbara Mary Frances *Who 94*
Bretscher, Mark Steven 1940- *IntWW 93, Who 94*
Bretschneider, Ann Margery 1934- *WhoAm 94*
Brett *Who 94*
Brett, Arthur Cushman, Jr. 1928- *WhoAm 94, WhoFI 94*
Brett, Barbara Jeanne *WhoAm 94*
Brett, Charles 1941- *NewGrDO*
Brett, Charles (Edward Bainbridge) 1928- *Who 94*
Brett, Cliff *WhoAm 94, WhoScEn 94*
Brett, Donna W(hitson) 1947- *WrDr 94*
Brett, Edward T(racy) 1944- *WrDr 94*
Brett, George Howard 1953- *WhoAm 94, WhoMW 93*
Brett, George Wendell 1912- *WhoAm 94*
Brett, Ingrid *WhoHol 92*
Brett, James T. *WhoAmP 93*
Brett, Jan (Churchill) 1949- *ConAu 41NR*
Brett, Jan Churchill 1949- *WhoAm 94*
Brett, Jay Elliot 1931- *WhoAmP 93*
Brett, Jeremy 1933- *IntMPA 94*
Brett, Jeremy 1935- *Who 94, WhoHol 92*
Brett, John Alfred 1915- *Who 94*
Brett, Leo *EncSF 93*
Brett, Leo 1935- *WrDr 94*
Brett, Lionel *Who 94*
Brett, Lionel (Gordon Baliol) 1913- *WrDr 94*
Brett, Michael 1923- *WrDr 94*
Brett, Michael 1928- *WrDr 94*
Brett, Michael John Lee 1939- *Who 94*
Brett, Nancy *WhoAmA 93*
Brett, Peter *DrAPF 93*
Brett, Raymond Laurence 1917- *Who 94, WrDr 94*
Brett, Richard John 1921- *WhoMW 93*
Brett, Richard John 1947- *Who 94*
Brett, Robin 1935- *WhoAm 94*
Brett, Rosalind *WrDr 94*
Brett, Simon (Anthony Lee) 1945- *WrDr 94*
Brett, Simon Anthony Lee 1945- *Who 94*
Brett, Stephen M. *WhoAm 94, WhoFI 94*
Brett, Stephen Noel 1946- *WhoIns 94*
Brett, Thomas Rutherford 1931- *WhoAm 94, WhoAmL 94*
Brett, Timothy Andrew 1953- *WhoAmP 93*
Brett, Tybe Ann 1954- *WhoAmL 94*
Brett, William Henry 1942- *Who 94*
Brettell, Richard R(obson) 1949- *WrDr 94*
Brettell, Richard Robson 1949- *WhoAm 94, WhoAmA 93*
Bretten, George Rex 1942- *Who 94*
Bretthauer, Erich Walter 1937- *WhoAm 94*
Bretting, Peter Konrad 1953- *WhoMW 93*
Brett-Major, Lin 1943- *WhoAmL 94*
Bretton, Henry L. 1916- *WhoAm 94*
Bretty, Beatrice d1982 *WhoHol 92*
Bretz, Ronald James 1951- *WhoAmL 94, WhoMW 93*
Bretz, Thurman Wilbur 1934- *WhoAm 94, WhoFI 94*
Bretz, William Franklin 1937- *WhoMW 93*
Bretzfelder, Deborah May 1932- *WhoAm 94*
Bretzke, Virginia Louise 1963- *WhoScEn 94*
Bretzmann, Gary L. 1939- *WhoAmP 93*
Bretzner, Christoph Friedrich 1748-1807 *NewGrDO*
Breu, George 1954- *WhoMW 93*
Breuel, Birgit 1937- *IntWW 93*
Breuer, Hans 1868-1929 *NewGrDO*
Breuer, Lee *WhoAm 94*
Breuer, Lee 1937- *ConDr 93*
Breuer, Lee 1939- *WrDr 94*
Breuer, Melvin Allen 1938- *WhoAm 94, WhoWest 94*
Breuer, Miles J(ohn) 1889-1947 *EncSF 93*
Breuer, Rolf E. *IntWW 93*
Breuer, Ronald Karl, Sr. 1945- *WhoFI 94*
Breuer, Siegfried d1954 *WhoHol 92*
Breuer, Stephen Ernest 1936- *WhoWest 94*
Breuer Baculis, Diana Ruth 1949- *WhoMW 93*
Breuker, John 1938- *WhoMW 93*
Breum, Arlene Adair 1936- *WhoAmP 93*
Breunig, H. Latham 1910- *EncDeaf*
Breunig, Robert Henry 1926- *WhoWest 94*
Breuning, Stephan von 1774-1827 *NewGrDO*
Breuninger, Tyrone 1939- *WhoAm 94*
Breval, Lucienne 1869-1935 *NewGrDO*
Brevard, Sidney Adair, III 1929- *WhoFI 94*
Breverman, Harvey 1934- *WhoAm 94, WhoAmA 93*
Brevig, Eric *WhoAm 94*
Brevignon, Jean-Pierre 1948- *WhoScEn 94*
Brevik, J. Albert 1920- *WhoAm 94*
Breville, Pierre (Eugene Onfroy) de 1861-1949 *NewGrDO*
Brevorka, Peter J. 1943- *WhoAmL 94*
Brew, David Alan 1930- *WhoWest 94*
Brew, (Osborne Henry) Kwesi 1928- *BlkWr 2, ConAu 142*
Brew, O. H. Kwesi 1928- *WrDr 94*
Brew, Richard Maddock 1930- *Who 94*
Brew, William Robert 1941- *WhoAm 94*
Breward, Ian 1934- *WrDr 94*
Brewbaker, James Lynn 1926- *WhoWest 94*
Brewer, Albert Preston 1928- *WhoAm 94, WhoAmP 93*
Brewer, Alvin L. 1946- *WhoBlA 94*
Brewer, Arnold, Jr. *WhoAmP 93*
Brewer, Bessie Marsh 1883-1952 *WhoAmA 93N*
Brewer, Bruce 1944- *NewGrDO*
Brewer, Carey 1927- *WhoAm 94*
Brewer, Curtis 1925- *WhoBlA 94*
Brewer, David Madison 1953- *WhoAmL 94, WhoFI 94*
Brewer, David Meredith 1934- *WhoAm 94*
Brewer, Deborah Lynn 1963- *WhoAmL 94*
Brewer, Derek Stanley 1923- *IntWW 93, Who 94*
Brewer, Douglas James 1954- *WhoMW 93*
Brewer, Edward Eugene 1925-1992 *WhAm 10*
Brewer, Garry D(wight) 1941- *WrDr 94*
Brewer, George Eugene Francis 1909- *WhoAm 94, WhoMW 93*
Brewer, George Maxted Kenneth 1930- *Who 94*
Brewer, Harper, Jr. 1937- *WhoAmP 93*
Brewer, James A., Sr. 1931- *WhoBlA 94*
Brewer, James Lawrence 1951- *WhoAmL 94*
Brewer, Janice Kay 1944- *WhoAmP 93, WhoWest 94, WhoWomW 91*
Brewer, John *Who 94*
Brewer, John Charles 1947- *WhoAm 94*
Brewer, John D(avid) 1951- *WrDr 94*
Brewer, John Thomas 1938- *WhoWest 94*
Brewer, Judy Daughtry 1945- *WhoAm 94*
Brewer, Kenneth W. *DrAPF 93*
Brewer, Leo 1919- *IntWW 93, WhoAm 94*
Brewer, Leslie G. 1945- *WhoAm 94*
Brewer, Lewis Gordon 1946- *WhoAmL 94*
Brewer, Monte d1942 *WhoHol 92*
Brewer, Moses 1947- *WhoBlA 94*
Brewer, Nathan Ronald 1904- *WhoAm 94*
Brewer, Oliver Gordon, Jr. 1936- *WhoAm 94*
Brewer, Richard George 1928- *IntWW 93, WhoAm 94*
Brewer, Richard Lynn 1953- *WhoMW 93*
Brewer, Robert Franklin 1927- *WhoWest 94*
Brewer, Robert Neal 1924- *WhoAm 94, WhoFI 94*
Brewer, Robert S., Jr. 1946- *WhoAmL 94*
Brewer, Ronald James 1950- *WhoAmP 93*
Brewer, Rose Marie 1947- *WhoBlA 94, WhoMW 93*
Brewer, Roy Edward 1949- *WhoAmL 94, WhoWest 94*
Brewer, Sheryl Denise 1958- *WhoWest 94*
Brewer, Soila Padilla 1942- *WhoHisp 94*
Brewer, Stanley R. 1937- *WhoAm 94*

Brewer, Stephen Michael 1948- *WhoAmP 93*
Brewer, Teresa 1931- *WhoHol 92*
Brewer, Thomas Bowman 1932- *WhoAm 94, WhoWest 94*
Brewer, Thomas J. 1946- *WhoAmL 94*
Brewer, Webster L. 1935- *WhoBlA 94*
Brewer, William A., III 1952- *WhoAmL 94*
Brewer, William Dixon 1936- *WhoAm 94, WhoFI 94*
Brewer, William Dodd 1922- *WhoAm 94, WhoAmP 93*
Brewer-Mangum, Ernestine Tywanna 1936- *WhoBlA 94*
Brewington, Donald Eugene 1954- *WhoBlA 94*
Brewington, Marion Vernon 1902-1974 *WhoAmA 93N*
Brewington, Rudolph W. 1946- *WhoBlA 94*
Brewington, Thomas E., Jr. 1943- *WhoBlA 94*
Brewster, Albert James, III 1931- *WhoFI 94*
Brewster, Benjamin 1907- *WrDr 94*
Brewster, Bill 1941- *CngDr 93*
Brewster, Bill K. 1941- *WhoAm 94, WhoAmP 93*
Brewster, Caleb *WhAmRev*
Brewster, Carol 1929- *WhoHol 92*
Brewster, Carroll Worcester 1936- *WhoAm 94*
Brewster, Christopher Ralph 1950- *WhoAmL 94*
Brewster, Clark Otto 1956- *WhoAmL 94*
Brewster, David 1781-1868 *WorInv, WorScD*
Brewster, Diane *WhoHol 92*
Brewster, Donald B. d1993 *NewYTBS 93*
Brewster, Donald William 1930- *WhoAmP 93*
Brewster, Elizabeth 1922- *BlmGWL*
Brewster, Elizabeth (Winifred) 1922- *WrDr 94*
Brewster, Elizabeth Winifred 1922- *WhoAm 94*
Brewster, Eva 1922- *WrDr 94*
Brewster, Gerry Leiper *WhoAmP 93*
Brewster, Gloria 1918- *WhoHol 92*
Brewster, Gregory Bush 1959- *WhoMW 93*
Brewster, James Henry 1922- *WhoAm 94*
Brewster, John, Jr. 1766-1854 *EncDeaf*
Brewster, Luther George 1942- *WhoBlA 94*
Brewster, Margaret *WhoHol 92*
Brewster, Martha Wadsworth fl. 1725-1757 *BlmGWL*
Brewster, Michael 1946- *WhoAmA 93*
Brewster, Nadine Pinnell 1916- *WhoAmP 93*
Brewster, Robert Charles 1921- *WhoAm 94, WhoAmP 93*
Brewster, Robert Gene 1938- *WhoAm 94*
Brewster, Rudi Milton 1932- *WhoAm 94, WhoAmL 94, WhoWest 94*
Brewster, William 1560-1644 *DcAmReB 2*
Brewster, (Elsie) Yvonne 1938- *Who 94*
Brewster-Jones, (Josiah) Hooper 1887-1949 *NewGrDO*
Brewton, Butler E. 1935- *WhoBlA 94*
Brewton, John E. 1898- *WhAm 10*
Brewton, Maia 1977- *WhoHol 92*
Brey, James Arnold 1950- *WhoMW 93*
Brey, William Edward 1932- *WhoFI 94*
Breyer, Hiltrud 1957- *WhoWomW 91*
Breyer, Maggie d1931 *WhoHol 92*
Breyer, Norman Nathan 1921- *WhoAm 94*
Breyer, Stephen G. *WhoAmP 93*
Breyer, Stephen Gerald 1938- *WhoAm 94, WhoAmL 94*
Breyfogle, Stacey Mitchell Jonasz 1966- *WhoMW 93*
Breymann, Heinrich Christoph d1777 *WhAmRev*
Breymann, Heinrich Christoph von d1777 *AmRev*
Breytenbach, Breyten *NewYTBS 93 [port]*
Breytenbach, Breyten 1939- *ConWorW 93*
Breytspraak, John, Jr. 1929- *WhoFI 94*
Brezene, George S. 1946- *WhoMW 93*
Brezenoff, Stanley 1937- *WhoAm 94*
Brezhnev, Leonid 1906-1982 *HisWorL [port]*
Brezhnev, Yuriy Leonidovich 1933- *IntWW 93*
Brezinski, Darlene Rita 1941- *WhoMW 93*
Brezinsky, Helene 1950- *WhoAm 94, WhoAmL 94*
Brezis, Haim 1944- *IntWW 93*
Breznahan, Tom *WhoHol 92*
Breznay, Deborah B. 1943- *WhoAmL 94*
Breznitz, Shlomo 1936- *ConAu 140*
Brezovec, Paul John 1957- *WhoScEn 94*
Brezzo, Steven Louis *WhoAmA 93*
Brezzo, Steven Louis 1949- *WhoAm 94, WhoWest 94*
Brialy, Jean-Claude 1933- *IntMPA 94, IntWW 93, WhoHol 92*
Brian, Alexis Morgan, Jr. 1928- *WhoAmL 94*
Brian, Brad D. 1952- *WhoAmL 94*
Brian, David d1993 *IntMPA 94N, NewYTBS 93 [port]*
Brian, David 1914- *WhoHol 92*
Brian, Donald d1948 *WhoHol 92*
Brian, Frank 1923- *BasBi*
Brian, Havergal 1876-1972 *NewGrDO*
Brian, John Garfield, III 1946- *WhoAmL 94*
Brian, Mary 1908- *WhoHol 92*
Brian, Pierre Leonce Thibaut 1930- *WhoAm 94*
Brian, Tom 1948- *WhoAmP 93*
Briani, Francesco fl. 1709-1710 *NewGrDO*
Briansky, Rita Prezament 1925- *WhoAmA 93*
Briant, (Bernard) Christian d1993 *Who 94N*
Briant, Clyde Leonard 1948- *WhoAm 94*
Briant, Roy d1927 *WhoHol 92*
Briant, Shane 1946- *WhoHol 92*
Briante, Nicholas Michael 1937- *WhoIns 94*
Brianza, Carlotta 1867-c. 1935 *IntDcB*
Briarton, Grendel *EncSF 93*
Briarton, Grendel 1911-1992 *WrDr 94N*
Briault, Eric William Henry 1911- *Who 94*
Bricall, Josep M. 1936- *IntWW 93*
Briccetti, Joan Therese 1948- *WhoAm 94*
Brice, Ashbel Green 1915-1988 *WhAm 10*
Brice, Carol (Lovette Hawkins) 1918-1985 *NewGrDO*
Brice, Derrick d1987 *WhoHol 92*
Brice, Eric John 1917- *Who 94*
Brice, Eugene Clay 1929- *WhoBlA 94*
Brice, Fanny d1951 *WhoHol 92*
Brice, Fanny 1891-1951 *WhoCom*
Brice, Forney Stevenson, Jr. 1945- *WhoFI 94*
Brice, Geoffrey James Barrington Groves 1938- *Who 94*
Brice, James John 1925- *WhoAm 94*
Brice, John R. 1956- *WhoAm 94*
Brice, Monte d1962 *WhoHol 92*
Brice, Nuala *Who 94*
Brice, (Ann) Nuala 1937- *Who 94*
Brice, Percy A., Jr. 1923- *WhoBlA 94*
Brice, Roger Thomas 1948- *WhoAm 94, WhoAmL 94*
Brice, Rosetta d1935 *WhoHol 92*
Brice, Tom *WhoAmP 93*
Brice, Tom Luther 1965- *WhoWest 94*
Brice, W. Robins 1945- *WhoAmL 94*
Brice, William 1921- *WhoAmA 93*
Briche, Adelaide-Edmee Prevost de la 1755-1844 *BlmGWL*
Brichford, Maynard Jay 1926- *WhoAm 94*
Brichta, Paul 1931- *WhoFI 94*
Brichto, Sidney 1936- *Who 94*
Brick, Barrett Lee 1954- *WhoAmL 94*
Brick, Cary R. 1945- *WhoAmP 93*
Brick, David Joseph 1947- *WhoIns 94*
Brick, Donald Bernard 1927- *WhoAm 94*
Brick, Steven A. *WhoAm 94, WhoAmL 94*
Brickell, Beth 1941- *WhoHol 92*
Brickell, Charles Hennessey, Jr. 1935- *WhoAm 94, WhoScEn 94*
Brickell, Christopher David 1932- *Who 94*
Brickell, Edward Ernest, Jr. 1926- *WhoAm 94*
Bricken, Barry Irwin 1943- *WhoAm 94*
Bricken, Meredith Stephanie 1946- *WhoWest 94*
Bricken, William Marion 1945- *WhoWest 94*
Bricker, Betty d1954 *WhoHol 92*
Bricker, Dale Eugene, Sr. 1925- *WhoAmP 93*
Bricker, Donald Lee 1935- *WhoAm 94*
Bricker, Gerald Wayne 1947- *WhoMW 93*
Bricker, Harvey Miller 1940- *WhoAm 94*
Bricker, Neal S. 1927- *IntWW 93*
Bricker, Ruth 1930- *WhoWest 94*
Bricker, Seymour Murray 1924- *WhoAm 94, WhoWest 94*
Bricker, Victoria Reifler 1940- *WhoAm 94*
Bricker, William Rudolph 1923- *WhoAm 94*
Brickert, Carlton d1943 *WhoHol 92*
Brickey, James Allan 1965- *WhoScEn 94*
Brickey, James Nelson 1942- *WhoAmL 94*
Brickey, Kathleen Fitzgerald 1944- *WhoAm 94*
Brickfield, Cyril Francis 1919- *WhoAm 94*
Brickhouse, John B. 1916- *WhoAm 94*
Bricklebank, Peter *DrAPF 93*
Brickler, John Weise 1944- *WhoAmL 94*
Brickley, David Guy 1944- *WhoAmP 93*
Brickley, James H. 1928- *WhoAmL 94, WhoAmP 93, WhoMW 93*
Brickley, Richard Agar 1925- *WhoAm 94*
Bricklin, Mark Harris 1939- *WhoAm 94*
Bricklin, Patricia Ellen 1932- *WhoAm 94*
Brickman, Marshall *WhoAm 94*
Brickman, Marshall 1941- *IntMPA 94*
Brickman, Morley 1924- *WhoFI 94*
Brickman, Paul *IntMPA 94*
Brickman, Ravelle 1936- *WhoAm 94*
Brickner, Gerald Bernard 1938- *WhoMW 93*
Brickner, Ralph Gregg 1951- *WhoWest 94*
Brickner, Richard P. *DrAPF 93*
Brickson, Richard Alan 1948- *WhoAm 94, WhoFI 94*
Bricktop d1984 *WhoHol 92*
Brickus, John W. 1919- *WhoBlA 94*
Brickwedde, Ferdinand Graft 1903-1989 *WhAm 10*
Brickwood, Basil (Greame) 1923- *Who 94*
Brickwood, Susan Callaghan 1946- *WhoAmL 94*
Bricusse, Leslie 1931- *IntMPA 94*
Bride, Robert Fairbanks 1953- *WhoFI 94, WhoWest 94*
Bridegam, Willis Edward, Jr. 1935- *WhoAm 94*
Briden, James Christopher 1938- *Who 94*
Bridenbaugh, Carl 1903-1992 *WhAm 10*
Bridenbaugh, Peter Reese 1940- *WhoFI 94, WhoScEn 94*
Bridenbaugh, Phillip Owen 1932- *WhoAm 94*
Bridenstine, Eugene *WhoAmP 93*
Bridewell, David Alexander 1909- *WhoAmL 94, WhoMW 93*
Bridge *Who 94*
Bridge, Al d1957 *WhoHol 92*
Bridge, Andrew *WhoAm 94*
Bridge, Antony Cyprian 1914- *Who 94*
Bridge, Frank 1879-1941 *NewGrDO*
Bridge, John 1755-1834 *DcNaB MP*
Bridge, John 1915- *Who 94*
Bridge, Keith James 1929- *Who 94*
Bridge, Loie d1974 *WhoHol 92*
Bridge, Ronald George Blacker 1932- *Who 94*
Bridge, Thomas Peter 1945- *WhoScEn 94*
Bridgeford, Gary James 1947- *WhoMW 93*
Bridgeford, William 1894-1971 *HisDcKW*
Bridgeforth, Arthur Mac, Jr. 1965- *WhoBlA 94*
Bridgeforth, Barbara 1943- *WhoBlA 94*
Bridgeland, James Ralph, Jr. 1929- *WhoAm 94*
Bridgeman *Who 94*
Bridgeman, Viscount 1930- *Who 94*
Bridgeman, David Marsh 1943- *WhoScEn 94*
Bridgeman, Donald Earl 1939- *WhoBlA 94*
Bridgeman, June 1932- *Who 94*
Bridgeman, Junior 1953- *BasBi, WhoBlA 94*
Bridgeman, Michael *Who 94*
Bridgeman, (John) Michael 1931- *Who 94*
Bridgeman, Richard *EncSF 93*
Bridgeman, William Clive 1864-1935 *DcNaB MP*
Bridge of Harwich, Baron 1917- *Who 94*
Bridger, Adam *ConAu 42NR*
Bridger, Baldwin, Jr. 1928- *WhoAm 94*
Bridger, Bub 1924- *BlmGWL*
Bridger, Gordon Frederick 1932- *Who 94*
Bridger, James 1804-1881 *WhWE [port]*
Bridger, Pearl 1912- *Who 94*
Bridger, Wagner H. 1928- *WhoAm 94*
Bridger, William Aitken 1941- *WhoAm 94*
Bridgers, Sue Ellen *DrAPF 93*
Bridgers, Sue Ellen 1942- *TwCYAW*
Bridgers, Sue Ellen (Hunsucker) 1942- *WrDr 94*
Bridgers, William Frank 1932- *WhoAm 94*
Bridges, Baron 1927- *IntWW 93, Who 94*
Bridges, Alan 1927- *IntMPA 94, IntWW 93*
Bridges, Alan Lynn *WhoAm 94*
Bridges, Alfred Bryant Renton 1901-1990 *AmSocL*
Bridges, Alvin Leroy 1925- *WhoBlA 94*
Bridges, B. Ried 1927- *WhoAm 94*
Bridges, Beau 1941- *IntMPA 94, WhoAm 94, WhoHol 92*
Bridges, Ben 1958- *WrDr 94*
Bridges, Beryl Clarke 1941- *WhoAm 94*
Bridges, Bill 1939- *BasBi, WhoBlA 94*
Bridges, Brian 1937- *Who 94*
Bridges, Cecil David 1933- *WhoMW 93*
Bridges, David Manning 1936- *WhoAm 94, WhoAmL 94*
Bridges, Dewi Morris *Who 94*
Bridges, Edwin Clifford 1945- *WhoAm 94*
Bridges, Edwin Maxwell 1934- *WhoWest 94*
Bridges, Gailen Wayne 1933- *WhoAmL 94*
Bridges, Harry 1901-1990 *WhAm 10*
Bridges, Jack Edgar 1925- *WhoAm 94*
Bridges, James d1993 *IntMPA 94N, NewYTBS 93 [port]*
Bridges, James 1936- *WhoHol 92*
Bridges, James 1936-1993 *ConAu 141*
Bridges, James R. 1943- *WhoAm 94, WhoFI 94*
Bridges, James Sibley 1913- *WhoAmP 93*
Bridges, James Wilfrid 1938- *Who 94*
Bridges, James Wilson 1935- *WhoBlA 94*
Bridges, Jeff *NewYTBS 93 [port]*
Bridges, Jeff 1949- *IntMPA 94, IntWW 93, WhoHol 92*
Bridges, Jeff 1951- *WhoAm 94*
Bridges, John d1973 *WhoHol 92*
Bridges, Lee *DrAPF 93*
Bridges, Leon 1932- *WhoAm 94, WhoBlA 94*
Bridges, Les *DrAPF 93*
Bridges, Lloyd *WhoAm 94*
Bridges, Lloyd 1913- *ConTFT 11, IntMPA 94, WhoHol 92*
Bridges, Lucille W. 1923- *WhoBlA 94*
Bridges, Mary (Patricia) 1930- *Who 94*
Bridges, Peter Scott 1932- *WhoAmP 93*
Bridges, Peter Sydney Godfrey 1925- *Who 94*
Bridges, Phillip (Rodney) 1922- *Who 94*
Bridges, Phillip Rodney 1922- *IntWW 93*
Bridges, Robert d1988 *WhoHol 92*
Bridges, Robert Lysle 1909- *WhoAm 94*
Bridges, Robert McSteen 1914- *WhoWest 94*
Bridges, Robert Seymour 1844-1930 *BlmGEL*
Bridges, Rochelle Marie 1954- *WhoBlA 94*
Bridges, Roy Dubard, Jr. 1943- *WhoAm 94, WhoWest 94*
Bridges, T(homas) C(harles) 1868-1944 *EncSF 93*
Bridges, Todd 1965- *WhoHol 92*
Bridges, Webster E., Jr. 1933- *WhoAmP 93*
Bridges, William Bruce 1934- *WhoAm 94, WhoWest 94*
Bridges-Adams, John Nicholas William 1930- *Who 94*
Bridges-Adams, William 1889-1965 *BlmGEL*
Bridget of Sweden *BlmGWL*
Bridgett-Chisolm, Karen 1956- *WhoBlA 94*
Bridgewater, Albert Louis 1941- *WhoAm 94, WhoBlA 94*
Bridgewater, Allan 1936- *Who 94*
Bridgewater, Bentley Powell Conyers 1911- *Who 94*
Bridgewater, Dee Dee *WhoHol 92*
Bridgewater, Herbert Jeremiah, Jr. 1942- *WhoAm 94, WhoBlA 94*
Bridgewater, Nancy 1940- *WhoAmP 93*
Bridgewater, Paul *WhoBlA 94*
Bridgforth, Robert Moore, Jr. 1918- *WhoAm 94, WhoFI 94, WhoScEn 94, WhoWest 94*
Bridgland, Milton Deane 1922- *Who 94*
Bridgman, Elizabeth Klein *WhoMW 93*
Bridgman, George Ross 1947- *WhoAm 94, WhoAmL 94*
Bridgman, James Campbell 1950- *WhoWest 94*
Bridgman, Laura Dewey 1829-1889 *EncDeaf*
Bridgman, Percy *WorScD*
Bridgman, Percy 1882-1961 *WorInv*
Bridgman, Thomas Francis 1933- *WhoAm 94*
Bridgwater, John 1938- *Who 94*
Bridie, James 1888-1951 *BlmGEL, IntDcT 2*
Bridle, Gordon Walter 1923- *Who 94*
Bridle, Ronald Jarman 1930- *Who 94*
Bridport, Viscount 1948- *Who 94*
Bridston, Paul Joseph 1928- *WhoAm 94, WhoFI 94*
Bridwell, Herbert H. 1928- *WhoBlA 94*
Bridwell, Naidyne Brown 1924- *WhoWest 94*
Bridwell, Norman Ray 1928- *WrDr 94*
Bridwell, Robert Kennedy 1943- *WhoAm 94, WhoAmL 94*
Bridwell, Robert Leslie 1940- *WhoAm 94*
Bridwell, Wilburn Fowler 1933- *WhoWest 94*
Bridwell-Jones, Margaret *DrAPF 93*
Brieant, Charles La Monte 1923- *WhoAm 94, WhoAmL 94*
Brief, Henry 1924- *WhoAm 94*
Briegel, Geoffrey Michael Olver 1923- *Who 94*
Briegel, Wolfgang Carl 1626-1712 *NewGrDO*
Brieger, Gert Henry 1932- *WhoAm 94*
Brieger, Gottfried 1935- *WhoMW 93*
Brieger, Stephen Gustave 1935- *WhoWest 94*
Briegs, David Michael 1965- *WhoFI 94*
Briehl, Marie H. d1993 *NewYTBS 93*
Brien, Alan 1925- *Who 94*

Brien, Albert George 1940- WhoAmP 93
Brien, Lois Ann 1928- WhoWest 94
Brien, Marilyn Biggs 1938- WhoAmP 93
Brier, Bonnie Susan 1950- WhoAmL 94
Brier, Helene 1924- WhoAmA 93
Brier, Jack H. 1946- WhoAmP 93
Brierley, Bert d1978 WhoHol 92
Brierley, Christopher Wadsworth 1929- Who 94
Brierley, James Alan 1938- WhoAm 94, WhoWest 94
Brierley, John David 1918- Who 94
Brierley, John E. C. 1936- WhoAm 94
Brierley, Richard Greer 1915- WhoWest 94
Brierley, Ronald (Alfred) 1937- Who 94
Brierley, Ronald Alfred 1937- IntWW 93
Brierley, Zachry d1993 Who 94N
Brierly, Joseph Edward 1939- WhoMW 93
Brierly, Keppel 1909- WhoWest 94
Brierre, Maurice d1959 WhoHol 92
Brierre de Boismont, Alexander 1798-1881 EncSPD
Briers, Richard 1934- WhoHol 92
Briers, Richard David 1934- IntWW 93, Who 94
Brierton, Cheryl Lynn 1947- WhoAmL 94
Brierton, Robert Sylvester 1948- WhoAmL 94
Briesmeister, Richard Arthur 1942- WhoScEn 94, WhoWest 94
Briess, Roger Charles 1937- WhoAm 94
Brieux, Bernard WhoHol 92
Brieux, Eugene 1858-1932 IntDcT 2
Brieve-Martin, Ila Corrinna 1939- WhoBlA 94
Brigantti-Hughes, Mary Ann WhoHisp 94
Brigden, Richard Nevius 1939- WhoAm 94
Brigden, Wallace 1916- Who 94
Briggerman, Steven Leslie 1943- WhoAm 94
Briggins, Charles E. 1930- WhoBlA 94
Briggle, William James 1925- WhoAm 94
Briggs, Baron 1921- Who 94
Briggs, Alan Leonard 1942- WhoAm 94, WhoAmL 94
Briggs, Asa 1921- IntWW 93, WrDr 94
Briggs, Austin 1808-1973 WhoAmA 93N
Briggs, Berta N. 1884-1976 WhoAmA 93N
Briggs, Charles d1985 WhoHol 92
Briggs, Charles Augustus 1841-1913 DcAmReB 2
Briggs, Clarence E., III 1960- WrDr 94
Briggs, Cynthia Anne 1950- WhoMW 93
Briggs, David Griffith 1932- WhoScEn 94
Briggs, Dean Winfield 1953- WhoWest 94
Briggs, Dinus Marshall 1940- WhoWest 94
Briggs, Donald d1986 WhoHol 92
Briggs, Eddie 1949- WhoAm 94, WhoAmP 93
Briggs, Edward Samuel 1926- WhoAm 94, WhoWest 94
Briggs, Ellis O. 1899-1976 HisDcKW
Briggs, Ernest 1923-1984 WhoAmA 93N
Briggs, Everett Ellis 1934- WhoAm 94, WhoAmP 93
Briggs, Frank P. 1894- WhAm 10
Briggs, Geoffrey Gould d1993 Who 94N
Briggs, Geoffrey Hugh 1926- WhoAm 94
Briggs, George Cardell 1910- Who 94
Briggs, George Madison 1927- WhoAm 94, WhoScEn 94
Briggs, Greg WhoBlA 94
Briggs, Harlan d1952 WhoHol 92
Briggs, Harold Melvin 1904- WhoAm 94
Briggs, Henry 1561-1630 WorScD
Briggs, Henry Payson, Jr. 1932- WhoMW 93
Briggs, Herbert Whittaker 1900-1990 WhAm 10
Briggs, Isabel Diana Who 94
Briggs, James Henry, II 1953- WhoWest 94
Briggs, Janet Marie Louise 1951- WhoMW 93
Briggs, Jean Audrey 1943- WhoAm 94
Briggs, Jeffrey Lawrence 1943- WhoScEn 94
Briggs, Joe Bob 1959- WrDr 94
Briggs, John Who 94
Briggs, John 1945- WrDr 94
Briggs, (Peter) John 1928- Who 94
Briggs, John DeQuedville, III 1943- WhoAmL 94
Briggs, John Gurney, Jr. 1916-1990 WhAm 10
Briggs, John Mancel, III 1942- WhoAmL 94
Briggs, John Porter 1953- WhoFI 94
Briggs, Johnny 1935- WhoHol 92
Briggs, Kenneth 1934- WrDr 94
Briggs, Lamar A. 1935- WhoAmA 93
Briggs, Leslie Ray 1944- WhoMW 93
Briggs, Lloyd Clark 1942- WhoIns 94
Briggs, Marjorie Crowder 1946- WhoAm 94, WhoAmL 94
Briggs, Matt d1962 WhoHol 92
Briggs, Morton Winfield 1915- WhoAm 94
Briggs, Oscar d1928 WhoHol 92
Briggs, Patrick David 1940- Who 94
Briggs, Paul Wellington 1922- WhoFI 94
Briggs, Peter Who 94
Briggs, (Michael) Peter 1944- Who 94
Briggs, Peter S. 1946- WhoAmA 93
Briggs, Peter Stromme 1946- WhoAm 94
Briggs, Philip 1928- WhoAm 94
Briggs, Philip James 1938- WhoAm 94
Briggs, Philip Terry 1934- WhoAm 94
Briggs, Raymond (Redvers) 1934- EncSF 93, WrDr 94
Briggs, Raymond Redvers 1934- IntWW 93, Who 94
Briggs, Robert Henry 1937- WhoMW 93
Briggs, Robert Nathan 1946- WhoWest 94
Briggs, Robert Peter 1903- WhoAm 94
Briggs, Robert Stephen 1949- WhoIns 94
Briggs, Rodney Arthur 1923- WhoAm 94, WhoScEn 94
Briggs, Sherwood Gilmour 1936- WhoFI 94
Briggs, Shirley Ann 1918- WhoAm 94
Briggs, Susan Shadinger 1941- WhoAm 94, WhoAmL 94
Briggs, Taylor Rastrick 1933- WhoAm 94
Briggs, Thomas Vallack 1906- Who 94
Briggs, Tony WhoBlA 94
Briggs, Tracey Wong 1961- WhoAsA 94
Briggs, Vernon Mason, Jr. 1937- WhoAm 94
Briggs, Ward W(right), Jr. 1945- WrDr 94
Briggs, William Benajah 1922- WhoAm 94
Briggs, William Egbert 1925- WhoAm 94
Briggs, Winslow Russell 1928- IntWW 93, WhoAm 94, WhoScEn 94, WhoWest 94
Briggs-Graves, Anasa WhoBlA 94
Briggum, Sue Marie 1950- WhoAmL 94
Brigham, Amariah 1798-1848 EncSPD
Brigham, Besmilr DrAPF 93
Brigham, Elizabeth Anne 1952- WhoFI 94
Brigham, Jerry Powell 1947- WhoAmP 93
Brigham, John Allen, Jr. 1942- WhoWest 94
Brigham, John Carl 1942- WhoScEn 94
Brigham, Ralph Allen 1949- WhoWest 94
Brigham, Samuel Townsend Jack, III 1939- WhoAmL 94
Brigham, William Everett 1929- WhoAm 94
Brighouse, Harold 1882-1958 IntDcT 2
Brighouse, Timothy Robert Peter 1940- Who 94
Bright, Al(fred Lee) 1940- WhoAmA 93
Bright, Alfred Lee 1940- WhoBlA 94
Bright, Barney 1927- WhoAmA 93
Bright, Colin Charles 1948- Who 94
Bright, Craig Bartley 1931- WhoAm 94
Bright, David Forbes 1942- WhoAm 94
Bright, Donald Bolton 1930- WhoWest 94
Bright, E. Shippen 1956- WhoAmP 93
Bright, Freda 1929- WrDr 94
Bright, Gerald 1923- WhoAm 94, WhoAmL 94
Bright, Graham Frank James 1942- Who 94
Bright, Harold Frederick 1913- WhoAm 94
Bright, Herbert L., Sr. 1941- WhoBlA 94
Bright, Jean Marie 1915- WhoBlA 94
Bright, John 1811-1889 HisWorL
Bright, Joseph Coleman 1942- WhoAm 94, WhoAmL 94
Bright, Joseph Converse 1940- WhoAmL 94
Bright, Keith 1931- IntWW 93
Bright, Louvenia Dorsey 1941- WhoAmP 93
Bright, Margaret 1918- WhoAm 94
Bright, Marilyn Agnes 1946- WhoFI 94
Bright, Mildred d1967 WhoHol 92
Bright, Myron H. 1919- WhoAm 94, WhoAmL 94, WhoMW 93, WrDr 94
Bright, Richard IntMPA 94, WhoHol 92
Bright, Richard S. 1936- IntMPA 94
Bright, Stanley J. 1940- WhoAm 94, WhoFI 94
Bright, Thomas Lynn 1948- WhoAmL 94
Bright, Willard Mead 1914- WhoAm 94
Bright, William Oliver 1928- WhoAm 94
Bright, Willie S. 1934- WhoBlA 94
Brightbill, David John 1942- WhoAmP 93
Brightling, Peter Henry Miller 1921- Who 94
Brightman, Baron 1911- Who 94
Brightman, Carol WhoAm 94
Brightman, Edgar Sheffield 1884-1953 DcAmReB 2
Brightman, John Anson 1911- IntWW 93
Brightman, Robert Lloyd 1920- WhoAm 94
Brightman, Sarah WhoAm 94
Brightmire, Paul William 1924- WhoAm 94
Brighton, Albert d1911 WhoHol 92
Brighton, Carl Theodore 1931- WhoAm 94
Brighton, Catherine 1943- WrDr 94
Brighton, Gerald David 1920- WhoAm 94
Brighton, Howard 1925- WhoFI 94
Brighton, John Austin 1934- WhoScEn 94
Brighton, Peter 1933- Who 94
Brighton, Sue d1983 WhoHol 92
Brightwell, Walter 1919- WhoAmA 93
Brighty, (Anthony) David 1939- Who 94
Brigman, James Gemeny 1965- WhoScEn 94
Brignone, Lilla d1984 WhoHol 92
Brigstocke, David Hugh Charles 1953- WhoAm 94, WhoFI 94
Brigstocke, John Richard 1945- Who 94
Brigstoke, Baroness 1929- Who 94
Brijalba, Rufus, Jr. WhoHisp 94
Brijbhushan, Jamila 1918- WrDr 94
Briles, David Elwood 1945- WhoScEn 94
Briles, John Christopher 1963- WhoScEn 94
Briles, Margaret Stevenson 1925- WhoAmL 94
Briley, David Wesley 1952- WhoWest 94
Briley, Greg 1965- WhoBlA 94
Brilioth, Helge 1931- NewGrDO
Brill, A. Bertrand 1928- WhoAm 94
Brill, Alan Richard 1942- WhoAm 94, WhoFI 94, WhoMW 93
Brill, Alida 1949- ConAu 142
Brill, Arthur Sylvan 1927- WhoAm 94
Brill, Donald Maxim 1922- WhoMW 93
Brill, Ernie DrAPF 93
Brill, Fran 1946- WhoHol 92
Brill, Glenn 1949- WhoAmA 93
Brill, Henry 1906-1990 WhAm 10
Brill, James Lathrop 1951- WhoAm 94, WhoWest 94
Brill, Joel Victor 1956- WhoWest 94
Brill, Kathy Diane Mitchell 1950- WhoMW 93
Brill, Lesley 1943- WhoAm 94
Brill, Marlene Targ 1945- SmATA 77 [port]
Brill, Marty WhoHol 92
Brill, Newton Clyde, Jr. 1936- WhoAmP 93
Brill, Patti d1963 WhoHol 92
Brill, Ralph David 1944- WhoAm 94
Brill, Ronald Mitchel 1943- WhoFI 94
Brill, Steven Charles 1953- WhoAm 94, WhoAmL 94
Brill, Stuart 1948- WhoFI 94
Brill, Winston Jonas 1939- WhoAm 94, WhoMW 93
Brill, Yvonne Claeys 1924- WhoAm 94
Brillantes, Hermogenes Bilgera 1944- WhoAsA 94
Brill-Edwards, Harry Walter 1941- WhoAm 94, WhoFI 94
Brillembourg, Gustavo E. d1993 NewYTBS 93
Brilliant, Alan 1936- WrDr 94
Brilliant, Fredda Who 94
Brilliant, Howard Michael 1945- WhoMW 93
Brilliant, Richard 1929- WhoAm 94, WhoAmA 93, WrDr 94
Brilliant, Robert Lee 1948- WhoAm 94
Brillinger, David Ross 1937- IntWW 93, WhoAm 94
Brillstein, Bernie 1931- IntMPA 94
Briloff, Abraham Jacob 1917- WhoAm 94
Brim, Armand Eugene 1930- WhoAm 94
Brim, Orville G., Jr. 1923- IntWW 93
Brim, Orville Gilbert, Jr. 1923- WhoAm 94
Brimacombe, James Keith 1943- WhoAm 94, WhoScEn 94
Brimacombe, John Stuart 1935- Who 94
Brimberg, Robert H. d1993 NewYTBS 93
Brimble, Alan 1930- WhoAm 94
Brimelow, Baron 1915- Who 94
Brimelow, Peter 1947- WhoAm 94, WrDr 94
Brimelow, Thomas 1915- IntWW 93
Brimer, Kenneth Kimberlin, Jr. 1945- WhoAmP 93
Brimer, Philip G. 1950- WhoIns 94
Brimhall, Dennis C. 1948- WhoAm 94
Brimhall, George H., Jr. 1947- WhoAm 94
Brimley, Wilford 1934- IntMPA 94, WhoAm 94, WhoHol 92
Brimm, Charles Edwin 1924- WhoBlA 94
Brimmer, Andrew F. 1926- WhoBlA 94
Brimmer, Andrew Felton 1926- IntWW 93
Brimmer, Clarence Addison 1922- WhoAm 94, WhoAmL 94, WhoWest 94
Brin, David 1950- WrDr 94
Brin, (Glen) David 1950- EncSF 93
Brin, Herb DrAPF 93
Brin, Royal Henry, Jr. 1919- WhoAm 94
Brinberg, Herbert Raphael 1926- WhoAm 94
Brinck, Keith 1955- WhoScEn 94
Brinckerhoff, Burt 1936- ConTFT 11, WhoHol 92
Brinckerhoff, Richard Charles 1931- WhoAm 94
Brinckman, Donald Wesley 1931- WhoAm 94, WhoFI 94
Brinckman, Elsie d1950 WhoHol 92
Brinckman, Frederick Edward, Jr. 1928- WhoScEn 94
Brinckman, Theodore (George Roderick) 1932- Who 94
Brind, (Arthur) Henry 1927- Who 94
Brind, Peter Holmes Walter 1912- Who 94
Brind, Tessa WhoHol 92
Brindamour, Jean-Louis Edmond, II 1933- WhoWest 94
Brind'Amour, Rod Jean 1970- WhoAm 94
Brindel, June Rachuy DrAPF 93
Brindle, Ian 1943- Who 94
Brindle, Michael John 1952- Who 94
Brindley, Giles Skey 1926- IntWW 93, Who 94
Brindley, Joseph Warren, II 1945- WhoAmP 93
Brindley, Madge d1968 WhoHol 92
Brine, John Alfred Seymour 1926- WhoScEn 94
Brinegar, Claude Stout 1926- WhoAm 94, WhoFI 94, WhoScEn 94, WhoWest 94
Brinegar, Don Eugene 1929- WhoWest 94
Brinegar, Elizabeth Anne 1949- WhoMW 93
Brinegar, Elizabeth Anne 1953- WhoWest 94
Brinegar, Paul 1925- WhoHol 92
Brinek, Gertrude 1952- WhoWomW 91
Briner, Joseph Lee 1964- WhoMW 93
Briner, Pamela Joan 1950- WhoFI 94, WhoWest 94
Briner, Wayne Edward 1959- WhoMW 93
Briner, William Watson 1928- WhoMW 93
Brines, Francisco 1932- DcLB 134 [port]
Bring, Karl Elmer 1959- WhoAmL 94, WhoWest 94
Bring, Murray H. 1935- WhoAmL 94
Bringhurst, Robert DrAPF 93
Bringhurst, Robert 1946- WrDr 94
Brings, Lawrence Martin 1897- WhoAm 94
Brings, Virginia Natalie 1932- WhoAmP 93
Bringsvaerd, Tor Age EncSF 93
Bringuier, Jean-Claude 1925- WrDr 94
Brinig, Myron d1991 WhAm 10
Brink, Andre 1935- WrDr 94
Brink, Andre Philippus 1935- IntWW 93, Who 94
Brink, Andries Jacob 1923- IntWW 93
Brink, Benjamin McAlester 1952- WhoFI 94
Brink, Carol Ryrie 1895-1981 ChlLR 30 [port]
Brink, Charles Oscar 1907- Who 94
Brink, Charles Patrick 1955- WhoAmL 94
Brink, David F. 1946- WhoFI 94
Brink, David Maurice 1930- IntWW 93, Who 94
Brink, David Ryrie 1919- WhoAm 94
Brink, Frank, Jr. 1910- IntWW 93, WhoAm 94
Brink, Gerald R. 1938- WhoAm 94
Brink, John William 1945- WhoFI 94
Brink, Marion Francis 1932- WhoAm 94, WhoMW 93
Brink, Richard Edward 1923- WhoAm 94
Brink, William P. 1916- WhoAm 94
Brinkema, Leonie Milhomme 1944- WhoAm 94, WhoAmL 94
Brinker, Connie Juge 1928- WhoWest 94
Brinker, Ervin Raymond 1946- WhoMW 93
Brinker, John Henry 1914-1991 WhAm 10
Brinker, Nancy (Goodman) 1946- WrDr 94
Brinker, Thomas Michael 1933- WhoAm 94, WhoFI 94
Brinkerhoff, Dericksen Morgan 1921- WhoAmA 93
Brinkerhoff, Lorin C. 1929- WhoScEn 94
Brinkerhoff, Peter John 1945- WhoAm 94, WhoFI 94
Brinkerhoff, Richard Noel 1930- WhoAmP 93
Brinkerhoff, Tom J. 1939- WhoAm 94, WhoMW 93
Brinkhaus, Armand Joseph 1935- WhoAmP 93
Brinkhous, Kenneth Merle 1908- IntWW 93, WhoAm 94, WhoScEn 94
Brinkhues, Josef 1913- IntWW 93
Brinkley, Alan 1949- WrDr 94
Brinkley, Carl Edward 1948- WhoIns 94

Brinkley, Charles Alexander 1929- *WhoAm 94*
Brinkley, Charles H., Sr. 1942- *WhoBlA 94*
Brinkley, Christie 1954- *WhoHol 92*
Brinkley, David 1920- *IntMPA 94, IntWW 93, WhoAm 94*
Brinkley, Donald R. 1937- *WhoAm 94, WhoFI 94*
Brinkley, Elise Hoffman 1922- *WhoAm 94*
Brinkley, Fred Sinclair, Jr. 1938- *WhoAm 94*
Brinkley, Jack Thomas 1930- *WhoAm 94, WhoAmP 93*
Brinkley, James Wellons 1937- *WhoAm 94, WhoFI 94*
Brinkley, James Wiley 1935- *WhoMW 93*
Brinkley, Joseph Willard 1926- *WhoAm 94*
Brinkley, Norman, Jr. 1931- *WhoBlA 94*
Brinkley, Stanley Alan 1950- *WhoAmP 93*
Brinkley, William Clark d1993 *NewYTBS 93 [port]*
Brinkley, William Clark 1917- *WhoAm 94*
Brinkley, William John 1925- *WhoMW 93*
Brinkman, Allan 1948- *WhoIns 94*
Brinkman, Bernard J. *WhoAmP 93*
Brinkman, Bo *WhoHol 92*
Brinkman, Dale Thomas 1952- *WhoAmL 94*
Brinkman, Dennis William 1950- *WhoMW 93*
Brinkman, Elmer Paul 1946- *WhoMW 93*
Brinkman, Herbert Charles 1926- *WhoAmL 94*
Brinkman, John Anthony 1934- *WhoAm 94*
Brinkman, Joyce Elaine 1944- *WhoAmP 93, WhoMW 93*
Brinkman, Karen Elaine 1950- *WhoAm 94*
Brinkman, Leonard Cornelis (Eelco) 1948- *IntWW 93*
Brinkman, Paul Delbert 1937- *WhoAm 94*
Brinkman, Richard J. 1930- *WhoFI 94*
Brinkman, William Frank 1938- *WhoAm 94*
Brinkmann, Robert Joseph 1950- *WhoAmL 94*
Brinkmann, Uwe K. d1993 *NewYTBS 93*
Brinkmeier, Alan James 1954- *WhoAmL 94*
Brinley, Charles d1946 *WhoHol 92*
Brinley, Daniel Putnam 1879-1963 *WhoAmA 93N*
Brinley, Floyd John, Jr. 1930- *WhoScEn 94*
Brinley, George, Jr. 1817-1875 *DcLB 140 [port]*
Brinley, Maryann B(ucknum) 1949- *WrDr 94*
Brinley Jones, Robert *Who 94*
Brinn, Chauncey J. 1932- *WhoBlA 94*
Brinnin, John Malcolm 1916- *IntWW 93, WhoAm 94, WrDr 94*
Brinning, Nancy Gillespie 1927- *WhoAm 94*
Brinsfield, Shirley D. 1922- *WhoAm 94*
Brinsley, John Harrington 1933- *WhoAm 94*
Brinsmade, Lyon Louis 1924- *WhoAm 94, WhoAmL 94*
Brinsmead, H(esba) F(ay) 1922- *WrDr 94*
Brinsmead, Hesba 1922- *BlmGWL*
Brinson, Gay Creswell, Jr. 1925- *WhoAm 94, WhoAmL 94*
Brinson, Harold Thomas 1930- *WhoAm 94*
Brinson, Robert Maddox 1940- *WhoAmL 94*
Brinster, Kenneth Joseph 1953- *WhoWest 94*
Brinster, Ralph Lawrence 1932- *WhoAm 94*
Brint, Armand *DrAPF 93*
Brint, Michael (E.) 1955- *ConAu 140*
Brinton, Donald Eugene 1927- *WhoAmP 93*
Brinton, Henry 1901-1977 *EncSF 93*
Brinton, Margo Ann 1945- *WhoAm 94*
Brinton, Richard Kirk 1946- *WhoWest 94*
Brinton, Timothy Denis 1929- *Who 94*
Brinton, William David 1952- *WhoAmL 94*
Brion, Francoise 1934- *WhoHol 92*
Briones, David Francisco 1944- *WhoHisp 94*
Briones, Ellen Margaret 1962- *WhoAmL 94*
Briones, Robert A. *WhoHisp 94*
Brioschi, Anton 1855-1920 *NewGrDO*
Brioschi, Carlo 1826-1895 *NewGrDO*
Brioschi, Giuseppe 1802-1858 *NewGrDO*
Brioschi Family *NewGrDO*
Brisbane, Archbishop of 1935- *Who 94*
Brisbane, Archbishop of 1936- *Who 94*
Brisbane, Assistant Bishop of *Who 94*
Brisbane, Arthur d1936 *WhoHol 92*
Brisbane, Samuel Chester 1914- *WhoBlA 94*
Brisbin, Robert Edward 1946- *WhoWest 94*
Brisby, Stewart *DrAPF 93*
Brisco, Donald Gilfrid 1920- *Who 94*
Brisco, P. A. 1927- *WrDr 94*
Brisco, Patty 1927- *WrDr 94*
Brisco, Rodney E. *WhoHisp 94*
Brisco, Valerie 1960- *WhoAm 94*
Briscoe, Brian Anthony 1945- *Who 94*
Briscoe, Carl E. 1924- *AfrAmG [port]*
Briscoe, Edward Gans 1937- *WhoBlA 94*
Briscoe, Glenn *WhoAmP 93*
Briscoe, Hattie Ruth Elam 1916- *WhoBlA 94*
Briscoe, Jack Clayton 1920- *WhoAm 94, WhoAmL 94*
Briscoe, (John) James 1951- *Who 94*
Briscoe, James E. 1942- *WhoAmP 93*
Briscoe, John 1948- *WhoAmL 94, WhoWest 94*
Briscoe, John Frederick, Jr. 1952- *WhoWest 94*
Briscoe, John Hanson 1934- *WhoAm 94, WhoAmP 93*
Briscoe, John Leigh Charlton d1993 *Who 94N*
Briscoe, Keith G. 1933- *WhoAm 94*
Briscoe, Leonard E. 1940- *WhoBlA 94*
Briscoe, Lottie d1950 *WhoHol 92*
Briscoe, Marianne Grier 1945- *WhoWest 94*
Briscoe, Melbourne G. 1941- *WhoScEn 94*
Briscoe, Ralph Owen 1927- *WhoAm 94*
Briscoe, Sidney Edward, Jr. 1929- *WhoBlA 94*
Briscoe, Terry Lee 1948- *WhoFI 94*
Briscoe, Thomas F. 1910-1992 *WhoBlA 94N*
Brisco-Hooks, Valerie 1960- *WhoBlA 94*
Brise *Who 94*
Brisebois, Danielle 1969- *WhoHol 92*
Brisebois, Marcel 1933- *WhoAm 94*
Brisendine-St. Germaine, Pamela G. 1947- *WhoMW 93*
Briseño, Alexander E. 1949- *WhoHisp 94*
Briseño, Fernando Antonio 1967- *WhoHisp 94*
Briseno, Francisco P. *WhoHisp 94*
Brisepierre, Paulette Louise Fernande Mireille 1917- *WhoWomW 91*
Brisker, John 1947- *BasBi*
Brisker, Lawrence 1934- *WhoBlA 94*
Brisker, Steven 1949- *WhoBlA 94*
Briskin, Donald Phillip 1955- *WhoScEn 94*
Briskin, Jacqueline 1927- *WrDr 94*
Briskin, Mae *DrAPF 93*
Briskin, Mae 1924- *WrDr 94*
Briskin, Mort 1919- *IntMPA 94*
Briskin, Robert K. 1945- *WhoAmL 94*
Briskman, Louis J. *WhoAmL 94*
Briskman, Robert David 1932- *WhoAm 94*
Brisolara, Ashton 1924- *WhoAm 94*
Brison, Kenneth E. 1939- *WhoAmP 93*
Brison, William Stanley 1929- *Who 94*
Brissac, Virginia d1979 *WhoHol 92*
Brissenden, Alan (Theo) 1932- *WrDr 94*
Brissenden-Bennett, Jo Ann 1943- *WhoWest 94*
Brissey, Ruben Marion 1923- *WhoAm 94*
Brissie, Eugene Field, Jr. 1949- *WhoAm 94*
Brissman, Bernard Gustave 1919- *WhoAm 94*
Brisson, Carl d1958 *WhoHol 92*
Brisson, Elsa Ramirez 1954- *WhoHisp 94*
Brisson, Pat 1951- *WrDr 94*
Bristah, Pamela Jean 1956- *WhoAm 94*
Brister, Bill H. 1930- *WhoAm 94*
Brister, Donald Wayne 1949- *WhoScEn 94*
Brister, John W. 1944- *WhoAmL 94*
Brister, Richard 1915- *WrDr 94*
Brister, Robert S. d1945 *WhoHol 92*
Brister, Stuart MacDonald 1963- *WhoFI 94*
Brister, William Arthur Francis 1925- *Who 94*
Bristley, Calvin Wesley, Jr. 1926- *WhoAmP 93*
Bristol, Archdeacon of *Who 94*
Bristol, Bishop of *IntWW 93*
Bristol, Bishop of 1936- *Who 94*
Bristol, Dean of *Who 94*
Bristol, Marquess of 1954- *Who 94*
Bristol, Arlen A. 1952- *WhoAmL 94*
Bristol, David *DrAPF 93*
Bristol, Kent 1941- *WhoMW 93*
Bristol, Norman 1924- *WhoAm 94*
Bristol, Stanley David 1948- *WhoScEn 94*
Bristow, Alan Edgar 1923- *Who 94*
Bristow, Allan Mercer 1951- *WhoAm 94*
Bristow, Clinton, Jr. 1949- *WhoBlA 94*
Bristow, David Ian 1931- *WhoAm 94*
Bristow, Gary Thomas 1952- *WhoFI 94*
Bristow, George Frederick 1825-1898 *NewGrDO*
Bristow, Julian Paul Gregory 1961- *WhoScEn 94*
Bristow, Lucille May 1937- *WhoAmP 93*
Bristow, Peter (Henry Rowley) 1913- *Who 94*
Bristow, Preston Abner, Jr. 1926- *WhoScEn 94*
Bristow, Richard Wilson 1946- *WhoFI 94*
Bristow, Robert James 1935- *WhoAmP 93*
Bristow, Robert O'Neil 1926- *WhoAm 94, WrDr 94*
Bristow, Tom *WhoAmP 93*
Bristow, Walter James, Jr. 1924- *WhoAmL 94*
Bristow, William Arthur 1937- *WhoAmA 93*
Brisville, Jean-Claude Gabriel 1922- *IntWW 93*
Britain, Dan *EncSF 93*
Britain, Dan 1927- *WrDr 94*
Britain, Ian (Michael) 1948- *WrDr 94*
Britain, James Edward 1950- *WhoAmL 94*
Britain, Radie 1908- *NewGrDO, WhoAm 94*
Brite, Jane Fassett *WhoAmA 93*
Brite, Poppy Z. 1967- *ConAu 141*
Britell, Peter Stuart 1940- *WhoAm 94*
Britnell, Charlie *WhoAmP 93*
Britnell, R(ichard) H. 1944- *ConAu 142*
Britneva, Maria *WhoHol 92*
Brito, Aristeo 1942- *WhoHisp 94*
Brito, Christi L. 1955- *WhoAmP 93*
Brito, Dagobert Llanos 1941- *WhoAm 94, WhoHisp 94*
Brito, John Solomon 1945- *WhoHisp 94*
Brito, Jose Manuel 1948- *WhoHisp 94*
Brito, Maria 1947- *WhoAmA 93*
Brito, Maria C. 1947- *WhoHisp 94*
Brito, Silvia E. 1933- *WhoHisp 94*
Brito Cruz, Carlos Henrique 1956- *WhoScEn 94*
Britschgi, Brenton Carl 1935- *WhoAmP 93*
Britsky, Nicholas 1913- *WhoAmA 93*
Britt, Alan *DrAPF 93*
Britt, Charles Robin 1942- *WhoAmP 93*
Britt, Chester Olen 1920- *WhoScEn 94*
Britt, Clifford Calvin 1948- *WhoAmP 93*
Britt, David Van Buren 1937- *WhoAm 94, WhoFI 94*
Britt, Earl Thomas 1940- *WhoAm 94*
Britt, Elton d1972 *WhoHol 92*
Britt, Glenn Alan 1949- *WhoAm 94, WhoFI 94*
Britt, Harold C. 1934- *WhoScEn 94*
Britt, Henry Middleton 1919- *WhoAm 94, WhoAmL 94, WhoAmP 93*
Britt, Horace d1971 *WhoHol 92*
Britt, James Thomas 1904- *WhoAm 94*
Britt, John Roy 1937- *WhoAm 94*
Britt, Katrina *WrDr 94*
Britt, Maisha Dorrah *WhoFI 94*
Britt, May 1936- *WhoHol 92*
Britt, Melendy *WhoHol 92*
Britt, Nancy G. 1947- *WhoAm 94*
Britt, Nelson Clark 1944- *WhoAmA 93*
Britt, Paul D., Jr. 1951- *WhoBlA 94*
Britt, Ronald Leroy 1935- *WhoMW 93*
Britt, Sam Glenn 1940- *WhoAmA 93*
Britt, Stanford R. 1944- *WhoFI 94*
Britt, Susan Fagen 1947- *WhoAmL 94*
Britt, W. Earl 1932- *WhoAm 94, WhoAmL 94*
Brittain, Alfred, III 1922- *IntWW 93*
Brittain, Bill *DrAPF 93, SmATA 76*
Brittain, Bradley Bernard, Jr. 1948- *WhoBlA 94*
Brittain, Clive Edward 1933- *Who 94*
Brittain, Jack Oliver 1928- *WhoAmL 94, WhoAmP 93*
Brittain, James Edward 1931- *WhoAm 94*
Brittain, Jeffrey Charles 1949- *WhoWest 94*
Brittain, Miller G. d1968 *WhoAmA 93N*
Brittain, Ronald d1981 *WhoHol 92*
Brittain, Ross 1951- *WhoAm 94*
Brittain, Vera 1893-1970 *BlmGWL*
Brittain, William 1930- *WrDr 94*
Brittain, William (E.) 1930- *SmATA 76 [port]*
Brittan, Leon 1939- *IntWW 93, Who 94*
Brittan, Samuel 1933- *IntWW 93, Who 94, WrDr 94*
Brittany, Morgan 1951- *IntMPA 94, WhoHol 92*
Britten, Alan Edward Marsh 1938- *Who 94*
Britten, (Edward) Benjamin 1913-1976 *NewGrDO [port]*
Britten, Craig Eric 1946- *WhoWest 94*
Britten, Enid d1993 *NewYTBS 93*
Britten, George Vallette 1909- *Who 94*
Britten, Gerald 1930- *WhoAmP 93*
Britten, Gerald Hallbeck 1930- *WhoAm 94*
Britten, Rae Gordon 1920- *Who 94*
Britten, Robert Wallace Tudor 1922- *Who 94*
Britten, Roy John 1919- *IntWW 93, WhoAm 94*
Britten, William Harry 1921- *WhoMW 93*
Brittenden, (Charles) Arthur 1924- *Who 94*
Brittenham, Raymond Lee 1916- *WhoAm 94*
Brittigan, Robert Lee 1942- *WhoAmL 94*
Brittin, Norman Aylsworth 1906- *WrDr 94*
Brittingham, Geoffrey (Hugh) 1959- *SmATA 76 [port]*
Brittingham, James Calvin 1942- *WhoScEn 94*
Britton, Aileen d1986 *WhoHol 92*
Britton, Albert B., Jr. 1922- *WhoBlA 94*
Britton, Andrew James Christie 1940- *Who 94*
Britton, Barbara d1980 *WhoHol 92*
Britton, Boyd Reinert 1947- *WhoWest 94*
Britton, Carla Boden 1941- *WhoMW 93*
Britton, Clarold Lawrence 1932- *WhoAm 94, WhoAmL 94*
Britton, Dane Blackmour 1952- *WhoMW 93*
Britton, Daniel Robert 1949- *WhoAmA 93*
Britton, David 1945- *EncSF 93*
Britton, Denis (King) 1920- *WrDr 94*
Britton, Denis King 1920- *Who 94*
Britton, Dennis A. 1940- *WhoAm 94, WhoMW 93*
Britton, Donald W. 1948- *WhoAm 94*
Britton, Edna d1960 *WhoHol 92*
Britton, Edward (Louis) 1909- *Who 94*
Britton, Elizabeth 1930- *WhoBlA 94*
Britton, Erwin Adelbert 1915- *WhoAm 94*
Britton, Ethel d1972 *WhoHol 92*
Britton, Florence 1910- *WhoHol 92*
Britton, Harry 1879-1958 *WhoAmA 93N*
Britton, James, II 1915-1983 *WhoAmA 93N*
Britton, John Edgar 1921- *WhoAmL 94*
Britton, John H., Jr. 1937- *WhoBlA 94*
Britton, John William 1936- *Who 94*
Britton, Julia *WhoHol 92*
Britton, Katherine Lela Quainton 1960- *WhoAmL 94*
Britton, Keith d1970 *WhoHol 92*
Britton, Laurence George 1951- *WhoScEn 94*
Britton, Lionel (Erskine Nimmo) 1887-1971 *EncSF 93*
Britton, Mark Walter 1960- *WhoMW 93*
Britton, Mary Kay 1939- *WhoWest 94*
Britton, Melvin Creed, Jr. 1935- *WhoAm 94*
Britton, Milt d1948 *WhoHol 92*
Britton, Mozelle d1953 *WhoHol 92*
Britton, Nellie Hutin d1965 *WhoHol 92*
Britton, Pamela d1974 *WhoHol 92*
Britton, Paul John James 1949- *Who 94*
Britton, Robert Austin 1946- *WhoAm 94*
Britton, Sandra Loucille Mary 1948- *WhoWest 94*
Britton, Theodore R., Jr. 1925- *WhoBlA 94*
Britton, Theodore Roosevelt, Jr. 1925- *WhoAmP 93*
Britton, Thomas Warren, Jr. 1944- *WhoWest 94*
Britton, Tony 1924- *IntMPA 94, WhoHol 92*
Britz, Diane Edward 1952- *WhoFI 94*
Britz, Jack 1930- *Who 94*
Britz, Lewis 1933- *Who 94*
Brivio, Giuseppe Ferdinando dc. 1758 *NewGrDO*
Brix, Herman *WhoHol 92*
Brixey, John Clark 1904-1989 *WhAm 10*
Brixey, Loretta Sanchez 1960- *WhoWest 94*
Brixworth, Bishop Suffragan of 1935- *Who 94*
Brizgys, Vincentas 1903-1992 *WhAm 10*
Brizius, Janice Jane 1935- *WhoMW 93*
Brizzolara, Charles Anthony 1929- *WhoAm 94*
Brkanovic, Ivan 1906-1987 *NewGrDO*
Brlic-Mazuranic, Ivana 1874-1938 *BlmGWL*
Broach, S. Elizabeth *WhoBlA 94*
Broackes, Nigel 1934- *IntWW 93, Who 94*
Broad, Andrea Rosenbaum 1951- *WhoAmL 94*
Broad, Eli 1933- *WhoAm 94, WhoAmA 93, WhoFI 94, WhoWest 94*
Broadbent, Amalia Sayo Castillo 1956- *WhoFI 94*
Broadbent, Andrew George 1963- *Who 94*
Broadbent, Donald (Eric) 1926- *WrDr 94*
Broadbent, Donald Eric d1993 *IntWW 93N, Who 94N*
Broadbent, Donald Eric 1926- *IntWW 93*
Broadbent, Edward Granville 1923- *IntWW 93, Who 94*
Broadbent, Ewen d1993 *Who 94N*

Broadbent, Hyrum Smith 1920- WhoWest 94
Broadbent, Jeffrey Praed 1944- WhoMW 93
Broadbent, John Edward 1936- IntWW 93
Broadbent, (John) Michael 1927- Who 94
Broadbent, Miles Anthony Le Messurier 1980- Who 94
Broadbent, Simon Hope 1942- Who 94
Broadbent, Thomas Valentine 1935- WhoAm 94
Broadbridge, Baron 1938- Who 94
Broadd, Harry Andrew 1910- WhoAmA 93N
Broaddus, Robert Lewis 1935- WhoAm 94
Broaddus, William WhoAmP 93
Broadfield, Aubrey Alfred (Alan) 1910- WrDr 94
Broadfoot, Albert Lyle 1930- WhoAm 94
Broadfoot, Elma J. WhoAmP 93
Broadhead, James Lowell 1935- WhoAm 94, WhoFI 94
Broadhead, Ronald Frigon 1955- WhoWest 94
Broadhurst, Arthur J. WhoAmP 93
Broadhurst, Austin 1917- WhoAm 94
Broadhurst, Austin, Jr. 1947- WhoFI 94
Broadhurst, George d1952 WhoHol 92
Broadhurst, Jerome Anthony 1945- WhoAm 94
Broadhurst, Norman Neil 1946- WhoAm 94, WhoFI 94, WhoWest 94
Broadhurst, Sir Harry 1905- Who 94
Broadley, Edward d1947 WhoHol 92
Broadley, Hugh T. 1922- WhoAmA 93
Broadley, John Kenneth Elliott 1936- Who 94
Broadnax, David IntMPA 94
Broadnax, David 1943- WhoHol 92
Broadnax, Madison 1914- WhoBlA 94
Broadnax, Melvin F. 1929- WhoBlA 94
Broadnax, Walter Doyce 1944- WhoBlA 94
Broadus, Clyde R. d1991 WhoBlA 94N
Broadus, James Matthew 1947- WhoScEn 94
Broadus, John Albert 1827-1895 DcAmReB 2
Broadwater, Douglas Dwight 1944- WhoAm 94, WhoAmL 94
Broadwater, James E. 1945- WhoAm 94
Broadwater, Tommie, Jr. 1942- WhoAmP 93, WhoBlA 94
Broadway, Judith Lee 1935- WhoAmP 93
Broadway, Nancy Ruth 1946- WhoAm 94
Broadwell, Charles E. 1931- WhoScEn 94
Broadwell, Milton Edward 1938- WhoFI 94, WhoScEn 94
Broadwin, Joseph Louis 1930- WhoAm 94, WhoAmL 94
Broady, Earl Clifford 1904-1992 WhoBlA 94N
Broady, K(nute) O(scar) 1898- WhAm 10
Broback, Art WhoAmP 93
Brobeck, John R. 1914- IntWW 93
Brobeck, John Raymond 1914- WhoAm 94
Brobeck, Stephen James 1944- WhoAm 94
Brobyn, Robert John Frederick 1938- WhoAmL 94
Broca, Laurent Antoine 1928- WhoScEn 94, WhoWest 94
Broca, Pierre Paul 1824-1880 WorScD [port]
Brocas, Viscount 1950- Who 94
Brocato, Joseph Myron 1917- WhoAm 94
Brocchi, Giovanni Battista fl. 1776-1807 NewGrDO
Brocchini, Ronald Gene 1929- WhoAm 94
Brocco, Peter WhoHol 92
Broccoli, Albert 1909- IntMPA 94
Broccoli, Albert Romolo 1909- IntWW 93, WhoAm 94
Broch, Harald Beyer 1944- WrDr 94
Brochand, Christian Pierre 1935- IntWW 93
Brochard, Jean d1972 WhoHol 92
Brocheler, John 1945- NewGrDO
Broches, Aron 1914- IntWW 93, WhoAm 94
Brochet, Anne WhoHol 92
Brochet, Sophie WhoHol 92
Brochu, Claude Renaud WhoAm 94
Brock Who 94
Brock, Alice May 1941- WhoAm 94
Brock, Annette WhoBlA 94
Brock, Betty (Carter) 1923- WrDr 94
Brock, Charles Lawrence 1943- WhoAm 94, WhoAmL 94, WhoFI 94
Brock, Charles Marquis 1941- WhoAmL 94, WhoFI 94, WhoMW 93
Brock, Charles Michael 1952- WhoWest 94
Brock, Dan Willets 1937- WhoAm 94
Brock, David A. WhoAmP 93
Brock, David Allen 1936- WhoAm 94, WhoAmL 94
Brock, David George 1945- WhoAmL 94
Brock, Dee Sala 1930- WhoAm 94
Brock, Delia 1944- WrDr 94
Brock, Edwin 1927- WrDr 94
Brock, Eleanor (Hope) 1921- WrDr 94
Brock, George d1942 WhoHol 92
Brock, Gerald 1932- WhoBlA 94
Brock, Gerald Wayne 1948- WhoAm 94
Brock, Harry Blackwell, Jr. 1926- WhoAm 94
Brock, Heinie d1989 WhoHol 92
Brock, Horace Rhea 1927- WhoAm 94
Brock, James Daniel 1916- WhoAm 94
Brock, James Melmuth 1944- WhoScEn 94
Brock, James Robert 1944- WhoAm 94
Brock, James Rush 1931- WhoAm 94
Brock, James Sidney 1913- WhoAm 94
Brock, James Wilson 1919- WhoWest 94
Brock, John 1932- WhoAmP 93
Brock, John H. 1937- WhoAmP 93
Brock, Karena Diane 1942- WhoAm 94
Brock, Lila Mae 1915- WhoBlA 94
Brock, Lonnie Rex 1950- WhoWest 94
Brock, Louis Clark 1939- WhoAm 94, WhoBlA 94
Brock, Margaret Martin WhoAmP 93
Brock, Mary Anne 1932- WhoAm 94, WhoScEn 94
Brock, Michael (George) 1920- WrDr 94
Brock, Michael George 1920- Who 94
Brock, Mitchell 1927- WhoAm 94
Brock, Paul Warrington 1928- WhoAm 94, WhoAmL 94
Brock, Peter de Beauvoir 1920- WrDr 94
Brock, Phil WhoHol 92
Brock, Randall DrAPF 93
Brock, Ray Leonard, Jr. 1922- WhoAmP 93
Brock, Richard Thomas 1947- WhoFI 94
Brock, Robert Lee 1924- WhoAm 94, WhoAmP 93, WhoFI 94
Brock, Robert W. 1936- WhoAmA 93
Brock, Rose GayLL
Brock, Rose 1923- WrDr 94
Brock, Sebastian Paul 1938- Who 94
Brock, Stanley d1991 WhoHol 92
Brock, Stanley M. 1950- WhoAmL 94
Brock, Thomas Dale 1926- WhoAm 94
Brock, Thomas F. 1950- WhoMW 93
Brock, Thomas Gregory 1954- WhoScEn 94
Brock, Van K. DrAPF 93
Brock, William Allen, III 1941- WhoAm 94
Brock, William Emerson 1930- IntWW 93, WhoAm 94
Brock, William Emerson, III 1930- WhoAmP 93
Brock, William George 1928- WhoAm 94
Brock, William Hodson 1936- WrDr 94
Brock, William Ranulf 1916- IntWW 93, Who 94, WrDr 94
Brocka, Bruce 1959- WhoMW 93
Brocka, M. Suzanne 1960- WhoFI 94
Brockbank, Gary H. WhoAmP 93
Brockbank, Harrison d1947 WhoHol 92
Brockbank, John Myles 1921- Who 94
Brockbank, Tyrrell Who 94
Brockbank, (James) Tyrrell 1920- Who 94
Brock-Broido, Lucie DrAPF 93
Brockelbank, William John 1895- WhAm 10
Brockelman, Michael D. 1939- WhoAmP 93
Brockenbrough, Edwin Chamberlayne 1930- WhoWest 94
Brockenbrough, Henry Watkins 1923- WhoAm 94
Brocket, Baron 1952- Who 94
Brockett, Charles A. 1937- WhoBlA 94
Brockett, John Henry, Jr. 1915-1992 WhoBlA 94N
Brockett, Oscar Gross 1923- WhoAm 94, WrDr 94
Brockett, Peter Charles 1946- WhoAm 94
Brockett, Ralph Grover 1954- WhoAm 94
Brockett, Roger Ware 1938- WhoAm 94
Brockey, Harold d1991 WhAm 10
Brockfeld, Russell G. 1926- WhoAmP 93
Brockhaus, Robert Herold, Sr. 1940- WhoFI 94, WhoMW 93
Brockhoff, Klaus K.L. 1939- WhoScEn 94
Brockholes, Michael John F. Who 94
Brockhouse, Bertram Neville 1918- Who 94
Brockington, Benjamin 1933- WhoBlA 94
Brockington, Colin Fraser 1903- Who 94
Brockington, Donald Leslie 1929- WhoAm 94
Brockington, Donella P. 1952- WhoBlA 94
Brockington, Eugene Alfonzo 1931- WhoBlA 94
Brockington, Howard Burnell 1922- WhoAm 94
Brockington, Ian Fraser 1935- IntWW 93
Brockish, Robert Francis 1931- WhoWest 94
Brocklebank, Aubrey (Thomas) 1952- Who 94
Brocklebank-Fowler, Christopher 1934- Who 94
Brocklehurst, Arthur Evers 1905- Who 94
Brocklehurst, John Charles 1924- Who 94
Brocklehurst, Robert James 1899- Who 94
Brocklesby, David William 1929- Who 94
Brockley, Fenton EncSF 93
Brockman, David Dean 1922- WhoMW 93
Brockman, Estes David 1937- WhoAmL 94
Brockman, John J. 1946- IntMPA 94
Brockman, John St. Leger 1928- Who 94
Brockman, Michael 1938- IntMPA 94
Brockman, Peter 1938- WhoAmP 93
Brockman, Rita Jo 1955- WhoWest 94
Brockman, Ronald 1909- Who 94
Brockman, Rosalie Ortega WhoHisp 94
Brockman, Ted S. WhoIns 94
Brockman, Terry James 1955- WhoAmL 94
Brockman, Wayne Edward 1968- WhoWest 94
Brockmann, William Frank 1942- WhoAm 94
Brockmeier, Kristina Crittenberger 1953- WhoAm 94
Brockmeier, Louis Berry 1949- WhoMW 93
Brockmeier, Matthew George 1955- WhoMW 93
Brockmeier, Norman Frederick 1937- WhoMW 93
Brocks, Eric Randy 1946- WhoScEn 94
Brocksmith, James G., Jr. 1942- WhoAm 94
Brocksmith, Roy WhoHol 92
Brocksome, Brent 1946- WhoAmP 93
Brocks-Shedd, Virgia Lee 1943- WhoBlA 94
Brockway, David Hunt 1943- WhoAm 94, WhoAmL 94
Brockway, Duncan 1932- WhoAm 94
Brockway, (Archibald) Fenner 1888-1988 EncSF 93
Brockway, George Pond 1915- WhoAm 94
Brockway, Merrill LaMonte 1923- WhoAm 94
Brockway, William Robert 1924- WhoAm 94
Brockwell, Charles Wilbur, Jr. 1937- WhoAm 94
Brockwell, Gladys d1929 WhoHol 92
Brod, Catherine Marie 1959- WhoMW 93
Brod, Max d1959 WhoHol 92
Brod, Max 1884-1968 NewGrDO
Brod, Morton Shlevin 1926- WhoAm 94
Brod, Stanford 1932- WhoAm 94, WhoAmA 93
Broda, Betty Lorraine 1932- WhoAmP 93
Broda, Michael Vincent 1955- WhoFI 94
Broda, Rafael Jan 1944- WhoScEn 94
Brodbeck, Charles Richard 1949- WhoAmL 94
Brodbeck, William Jan 1944- WhoMW 93
Brodber, Erna 1936- BlmGWL
Brodber, Erna (May) 1940- BlkWr 2
Brode, David B. 1946- WhoAm 94, WhoMW 93
Brode, Marvin Jay 1931- WhoAm 94, WhoAmL 94, WhoAmP 93
Brode, Patrick 1950- WrDr 94
Brodecki, Joseph Michael 1946- WhoFI 94
Brodel, Joan WhoHol 92
Brodel, Mary 1917- WhoHol 92
Broder, Bill DrAPF 93
Broder, Christopher Charles 1961- WhoScEn 94
Broder, David Salzer 1929- WhoAm 94
Broder, Douglas Fisher 1948- WhoAm 94
Broder, Ernst-Gunther 1927- IntWW 93, Who 94
Broder, Irvin 1930- WhoScEn 94
Broder, Joe Arnold 1939- WhoAmP 93
Broder, Patricia Janis 1935- WhoAm 94, WhoAmA 93
Broder, Robert M. 1946- WhoAmL 94
Broder, Samuel WhoAm 94, WhoScEn 94
Broder, Sherry Phyllis 1948- WhoAmL 94
Broderick, Anthony James 1943- WhoAm 94
Broderick, Carlfred Bartholomew 1932- WhoAm 94
Broderick, Damien 1944- WrDr 94
Broderick, Damien (Francis) 1944- EncSF 93
Broderick, Dennis John WhoAmL 94
Broderick, Donald Leland 1928- WhoScEn 94, WhoWest 94
Broderick, Edward M., III 1947- WhoIns 94
Broderick, Edward Michael, III 1947- WhoWest 94
Broderick, Glen Reid 1943- WhoWest 94
Broderick, Harold Christian 1925- WhoWest 94
Broderick, Helen d1959 WhoHol 92
Broderick, Herbert Reginald, III 1945- WhoAmA 93
Broderick, James d1982 WhoHol 92
Broderick, James Allen 1939- WhoAmA 93
Broderick, John Caruthers 1926- WhoAm 94
Broderick, Johnny d1977 WhoHol 92
Broderick, Judith Ann 1943- WhoMW 93
Broderick, Matthew 1962- ConTFT 11, IntMPA 94, IntWW 93, WhoAm 94, WhoHol 92
Broderick, Patricia Ann WhoAmL 94
Broderick, Raymond Joseph 1914- WhoAm 94, WhoAmL 94
Broderick, Richard James 1921- WhoFI 94
Broderick, Terry 1945- WhoIns 94
Broderick, Terry Richard 1946- WhoAm 94
Broderick, Vincent Lyons 1920- WhoAm 94, WhoAmL 94
Brodersen, Arthur James 1939- WhoAm 94
Broderson, Morris 1928- WhoAmA 93
Broderson, Robert 1920- WhoAmA 93
Brodeur, Alfred L. 1948- WhoAmP 93
Brodeur, Alphonse Toner 1902- WhoAm 94
Brodeur, Armand Edward 1922- WhoAm 94
Brodeur, Catherine R. WhoAmA 93
Brodeur, Paul (Adrian, Jr.) 1931- WrDr 94
Brodeur, Richard Dennis 1953- WhoFI 94
Brodhead, Daniel 1736-1809 AmRev, WhAmRev
Brodhead, David Crawmer 1934- WhoAm 94, WhoAmL 94, WhoFI 94
Brodhead, Quita WhoAmA 93
Brodhead, William McNulty 1941- WhoAm 94, WhoAmP 93
Brodian, Laura 1947- WhoAm 94
Brodie, Agnes Hahn 1924-1992 WhoAmA 93N
Brodie, Alan David 1960- WhoWest 94
Brodie, Benjamin David Ross 1925- Who 94
Brodie, Buster d1948 WhoHol 92
Brodie, Colin Alexander 1929- Who 94
Brodie, Don 1899- WhoHol 92
Brodie, Donald Gibbs 1938- WhoAm 94
Brodie, Elizabeth Who 94
Brodie, Gandy 1924-1975 WhoAmA 93N
Brodie, Harlow Keith Hammond 1939- IntWW 93, WhoAm 94
Brodie, Howard 1915- WhoAm 94, WhoWest 94
Brodie, James Kennedy 1947- WhoAmP 93
Brodie, James William 1920- IntWW 93
Brodie, Jan Lois 1947- WhoAmL 94
Brodie, M. J. 1936- WhoAm 94
Brodie, Norman 1920- WhoAm 94
Brodie, Philip Hope 1950- Who 94
Brodie, Regis Conrad 1942- WhoAmA 93
Brodie, Robert 1938- Who 94
Brodie, Stanley Eric 1930- Who 94
Brodie, Steve 1919- WhoHol 92
Brodie, Thomas d1993 Who 94N
Brodie-Hall, Laurence (Charles) 1910- Who 94
Brodie Of Brodie, (Montagu) Ninian (Alexander) 1912- Who 94
Brodine, Charles Edward 1925- WhoAm 94
Brodka, Mark A. 1956- WhoAmL 94
Brodkey, Donald 1910- WhoAmP 93
Brodkey, Harold DrAPF 93, NewYTBS 93 [port]
Brodkey, Harold 1930- DcLB 130 [port], WrDr 94
Brodkey, Harold Roy 1930- WhoAm 94
Brodkey, Robert Stanley 1928- WhoAm 94, WhoMW 93
Brodkin, Roger Harrison 1932- WhoScEn 94
Brodl, Mark Raymond 1959- WhoScEn 94
Brodl, Raymond Frank 1924- WhoAm 94
Brodman, Estelle 1914- WhoAm 94
Brodnax, Margaret O'Bryan 1932- WhoAm 94
Brodney, Oscar 1906- IntMPA 94
Brodniewicz, Teresa Maria 1949- WhoScEn 94
Brodoway, Barbara A. 1959- WhoAmL 94
Brodribb, (Arthur) Gerald (Norcott) 1915- WrDr 94
Brodrick Who 94
Brodrick, James Ray 1948- WhoScEn 94
Brodrick, Michael John Lee 1941- Who 94
Brodrick, Nancy Ann 1944- WhoMW 93
Brodshaug, Jackie WhoAmP 93
Brodskii, Iosif (Alexandrovich) 1940- ConWorW 93

Brodsky, Allen 1928- *WhoScEn 94*
Brodsky, Arthur James 1946- *WhoAmL 94*
Brodsky, David M. 1943- *WhoAm 94, WhoAmL 94*
Brodsky, Donald W. 1948- *WhoAmL 94*
Brodsky, Eugene V. 1946- *WhoAmA 93*
Brodsky, Frank 1933- *WhoFI 94*
Brodsky, Harry 1908- *WhoAmA 93*
Brodsky, Irwin Abel 1910- *WhoAm 94*
Brodsky, Jack 1932- *IntMPA 94*
Brodsky, Joseph *ConWorW 93*
Brodsky, Joseph 1940- *NobelP 91 [port]*
Brodsky, Joseph (Iosif Alexandrovich) 1940- *WrDr 94*
Brodsky, Joseph Aleksandrovich 1940- *IntWW 93*
Brodsky, Joseph Alexandrovich 1940- *Who 94, WhoAm 94*
Brodsky, Judith Kapstein 1933- *WhoAmA 93*
Brodsky, Julian A. 1933- *WhoAm 94, WhoFI 94*
Brodsky, Marc Herbert 1938- *WhoAm 94*
Brodsky, Michael Mark 1948- *ConAu 41NR*
Brodsky, Philip Hyman 1942- *WhoAm 94*
Brodsky, Richard Eugene 1946- *WhoAm 94*
Brodsky, Richard Louis 1946- *WhoAmP 93*
Brodsky, Robert Fox 1925- *WhoAm 94*
Brodsky, Robert Jay 1939- *WhoFI 94*
Brodsky, Samuel 1912- *WhoAm 94*
Brodsky, Stan 1925- *WhoAmA 93*
Brodsky, Stanley Martin 1924- *WhoScEn 94*
Brodsky, William J. 1944- *WhoAm 94, WhoFI 94, WhoMW 93*
Brodt, Burton Pardee 1931- *WhoScEn 94*
Brodus, Tex d1986 *WhoHol 92*
Brody, Aaron Leo 1930- *WhoAm 94*
Brody, Alan Jeffrey 1952- *WhoAm 94, WhoFI 94*
Brody, Alexander 1933- *IntWW 93, WhoAm 94*
Brody, Alfred Walter 1920- *WhoAm 94*
Brody, Anita Blumstein 1935- *WhoAm 94, WhoAmL 94*
Brody, Ann d1944 *WhoHol 92*
Brody, Arthur 1920- *WhoAm 94, WhoWest 94*
Brody, Arthur William 1943- *WhoAmA 93*
Brody, Baruch Alter 1943- *WhoScEn 94*
Brody, Bernard B. 1922- *WhoAm 94*
Brody, Blanche *WhoAmA 93*
Brody, Carol Z. 1941- *WhoAmA 93*
Brody, David 1930- *WhoWest 94*
Brody, David Allan 1916- *WhoAmL 94*
Brody, David Andrew 1953- *WhoAmL 94*
Brody, Eugene B. 1921- *WhoAm 94*
Brody, Eugene David 1931- *WhoAm 94*
Brody, Harold 1923- *WhoAm 94*
Brody, Harry *DrAPF 93*
Brody, Jacob Allan 1931- *WhoAm 94*
Brody, Jacob Jerome 1929- *WhoAmA 93*
Brody, Jacqueline 1932- *WhoAm 94, WhoAmA 93*
Brody, James Patrick 1920- *WhoAm 94*
Brody, Jane E(llen) 1941- *WrDr 94*
Brody, Jane Ellen 1941- *IntWW 93, WhoAm 94*
Brody, Jean *DrAPF 93*
Brody, Jeffrey M. 1953- *WhoWest 94*
Brody, Kenneth D. *WhoAmP 93*
Brody, Kenneth David 1943- *WhoAm 94, WhoFI 94*
Brody, Lawrence 1942- *WhoAm 94, WhoAmL 94, WhoMW 93*
Brody, Leslie *DrAPF 93*
Brody, Morton *WhoAmP 93*
Brody, Morton Aaron 1933- *WhoAm 94, WhoAmL 94*
Brody, Myron Roy 1940- *WhoAmA 93*
Brody, Richard Eric 1947- *WhoAm 94, WhoAmL 94*
Brody, Robert 1948- *WhoMW 93*
Brody, Ruth 1917- *WhoAmA 93*
Brody, Samuel Mandell 1926-1992 *WhAm 10*
Brody, Saul Nathaniel 1938- *WhoAm 94*
Brody, Sigmund A. 1941- *WhoIns 94*
Brody, Theodore Meyer 1920- *WhoAm 94*
Brody-Watts, Stella 1939- *WhoWest 94*
Broecker, Eugene William 1931- *WhoAm 94*
Broecker, Wallace S. 1931- *WhoScEn 94*
Broedling, Laurie Adele 1945- *WhoAm 94*
Broeg, Bob 1918- *WhoAm 94*
Broeker, John Milton 1940- *WhoAmL 94*
Broekhuysen, Martin *DrAPF 93*
Broeksmit, Peter Stillman *WhoMW 93*
Broer, Lawrence R(ichard) 1938- *WrDr 94*
Broer, Matthijs Meno 1956- *WhoScEn 94*
Broer, Roger L. 1945- *WhoAmA 93, WhoWest 94*
Broering, Naomi Cordero 1929- *WhoAm 94*
Broers, Alec Nigel 1938- *IntWW 93, Who 94*
Broers, J. Terry 1939- *WhoFI 94*
Broers, Kimberly Ann 1956- *WhoMW 93*
Broestl, Mary Katherine 1954- *WhoMW 93*
Brof, Janet *DrAPF 93*
Brofman, Lance Mark 1949- *WhoAm 94, WhoFI 94*
Brofman, Woody 1935- *WhoAm 94*
Brog, David 1933- *WhoAm 94*
Brog, Terrence Kenyon 1957- *WhoWest 94*
Brog, Tov Binyamin 1960- *WhoScEn 94*
Brogan, Elise 1921- *WrDr 94*
Brogan, Harry d1977 *WhoHol 92*
Brogan, Howard Oakley *WhoAm 94*
Brogan, James 1926- *WrDr 94*
Brogan, Mervyn (Francis) 1915- *Who 94*
Brogan, Ron d1989 *WhoHol 92*
Brogan-Werntz, Bonnie Bailey 1941- *WhoMW 93*
Brogden, Stephen Richard 1948- *WhoWest 94*
Brogdon, Byron Gilliam 1929- *WhoAm 94*
Brogdon, Joan Lee 1951- *WhoMW 93*
Brogger, Suzanne 1944- *BlmGWL, ConWorW 93*
Broggi, Michael Joseph 1942- *WhoFI 94*
Brogi, Caterina fl. 1737-1758 *NewGrDO*
Brogliatti, Barbara Spencer 1946- *WhoAm 94, WhoWest 94*
Broglie, Louis de d1987 *NobelP 91N*
Broglie, Louis Victor de 1892-1987 *WorScD*
Brogoitti, Robert A. 1920- *WhoAmP 93*
Brogunier, Claude Rowland 1960- *WhoScEn 94*
Brohman, Mark Allen 1963- *WhoAmL 94*
Brohon, Jacqueline-Aimee 1731-1778 *BlmGWL*
Broich, William John, Jr. 1952- *WhoFI 94*
Broide, Mace Irwin 1924- *WhoAm 94*
Broido, Arnold Peace 1920- *WhoAm 94*
Broido, Lucy 1924- *WhoAmA 93*
Broiles, Steven Anthony 1940- *WhoAm 94*
Broili, Robert Howard 1942- *WhoAmL 94*
Broin, Thayne Leo 1922- *WhoWest 94*
Broinowski, John Herbert 1911- *Who 94*
Broitman, Selwyn Arthur 1931- *WhoAm 94*
Brojanac, Rosaline Rose 1924- *WhoAmP 93*
Brok, Laurence del c. 1210-1274 *DcNaB MP*
Brokaw, A. L. *WhoAm 94*
Brokaw, Beth Fletcher 1955- *WhoWest 94*
Brokaw, Carol Ann 1946- *WhoBlA 94*
Brokaw, Cary 1951- *ConTFT 11, IntMPA 94*
Brokaw, Charles d1975 *WhoHol 92*
Brokaw, Charles Jacob 1934- *WhoScEn 94*
Brokaw, Clifford Vail, III 1928- *WhoAm 94*
Brokaw, Jim *WhoAmP 93*
Brokaw, Kathryn Louise Zimmer 1946- *WhoMW 93*
Brokaw, Norman R. 1927- *IntMPA 94*
Brokaw, Norman Robert 1927- *WhoAm 94, WhoFI 94, WhoWest 94*
Brokaw, Thomas John 1940- *IntWW 93, WhoAm 94*
Brokaw, Tom 1940- *IntMPA 94*
Broke *Who 94*
Broke, George Robin Straton 1946- *Who 94*
Broke, Robert Straton 1913- *Who 94*
Broker, Karin 1950- *WhoAmA 93*
Brokke, Catherine Juliet 1926- *WhoMW 93*
Brokke, Darwin Ray 1955- *WhoMW 93*
Brolick, Henry John 1944- *WhoFI 94*
Brolin, James *WhoAm 94*
Brolin, James 1940- *IntMPA 94, WhoHol 92*
Brolin, Josh 1968- *WhoHol 92*
Broll, Norbert 1947- *WhoScEn 94*
Brom, Libor 1923- *WhoAm 94*
Brom, Robert H. 1938- *WhoAm 94, WhoWest 94*
Broman, David Alan 1952- *WhoMW 93*
Broman, Keith Leroy 1922- *WhoAm 94*
Bromberg, Alan Robert 1928- *WhoAmL 94*
Bromberg, Barbara Schwartz 1941- *WhoAm 94*
Bromberg, Faith 1919-1990 *WhoAmA 93N*
Bromberg, Frank Wallace, Jr. 1955- *WhoAmP 93*
Bromberg, Henri Louie, Jr. 1911- *WhoAm 94*
Bromberg, J. Edward d1951 *WhoHol 92*
Bromberg, John E. 1946- *WhoAm 94*
Bromberg, Myron James 1934- *WhoAm 94, WhoAmL 94*
Bromberg, Robert 1921- *WhoAm 94*
Bromberg, Robert Sheldon 1935- *WhoAm 94*
Bromberg, Stephen Aaron 1930- *WhoAm 94*
Bromberg, Walter 1900- *WhoAm 94*
Bromberger, Frederick Sigmund 1918- *WhoWest 94*
Brombert, Victor (Henri) 1923- *WrDr 94*
Brombert, Victor Henri 1923- *WhoAm 94*
Brome, Richard c. 1590-1652 *IntDcT 2 [port]*
Brome, Richard 1590-1653 *BlmGEL*
Brome, Robert Harrison 1911- *WhoAm 94*
Brome, Thomas Reed 1942- *WhoAm 94, WhoAmL 94*
Brome, Vincent *Who 94, WrDr 94*
Bromeland, Andrew Allan 1948- *WhoAmP 93*
Bromell, Henry *DrAPF 93*
Bromell, Henry 1947- *WrDr 94*
Bromer, Lewis William 1942- *WhoMW 93*
Bromery, Keith Marcel 1948- *WhoBlA 94*
Bromery, Randolph Wilson 1926- *WhoAm 94, WhoBlA 94, WhoScEn 94*
Bromet, Jean (Lena Annette) *Who 94*
Bromfield, Donald Coleman 1893- *WhAm 10*
Bromfield, John 1922- *WhoHol 92*
Bromfield, Valri *WhoHol 92*
Bromhead, David M. 1960- *IntMPA 94*
Bromhead, Edward Thomas Ffrench 1789-1855 *DcNaB MP*
Bromhead, John Desmond Gonville 1939- *Who 94*
Bromhead, Peter Alexander 1919- *WrDr 94*
Bromige, David *DrAPF 93*
Bromige, David (Mansfield) 1933- *WrDr 94*
Bromige, Iris (Amy Edna) 1910- *WrDr 94*
Bromiley, Dorothy 1935- *WhoHol 92*
Bromiley, Geoffrey William 1915- *WrDr 94*
Bromilow, Peter 1933- *WhoHol 92*
Bromke, Adam 1928- *WrDr 94*
Bromley, Archdeacon of *Who 94*
Bromley, Daniel Wood 1940- *WhoAm 94*
Bromley, David Allan 1926- *IntWW 93, WhoAm 94, WhoScEn 94*
Bromley, Dennis Karl 1940- *WhoAm 94*
Bromley, Ernest W. *WhoHisp 94*
Bromley, Lance Lee 1920- *Who 94*
Bromley, Leonard John 1929- *Who 94*
Bromley, Peter Mann 1922- *Who 94*
Bromley, Richard 1944- *WhoAm 94, WhoAmL 94*
Bromley, Rupert Charles 1936- *Who 94*
Bromley, Sheila 1911- *WhoHol 92*
Bromley, Sydney d1987 *WhoHol 92*
Bromley, Wayne Leon, Jr. 1951- *WhoAm 94*
Bromley-Davenport, Arthur d1946 *WhoHol 92*
Bromley-Davenport, William Arthur 1935- *Who 94*
Bromm, Curt 1945- *WhoAmP 93*
Bromm, Frederick Whittemore 1953- *WhoAmL 94*
Bromm, Hal *WhoAmA 93*
Bromm, Robert Dale 1950- *WhoWest 94*
Brommer, Gerald F. 1927- *WhoAmA 93*
Brommer, Gerald Frederick 1927- *WhoWest 94*
Bromsen, Maury Austin 1919- *WhoAm 94*
Bromund, Cal E. 1903-1979 *WhoAmA 93N*
Bromwell, Thomas L. 1949- *WhoAmP 93*
Bromwich, Jack 1918- *BuCMET*
Bromwich, Michael 1941- *Who 94*
Bron, Anthony John 1936- *Who 94*
Bron, Eleanor *Who 94*
Bron, Eleanor 1934- *IntMPA 94, WhoHol 92*
Bron, Guillermo 1951- *WhoHisp 94*
Bron, Walter Ernest 1930- *WhoWest 94*
Bronaugh, Edwin Lee 1932- *WhoAm 94, WhoScEn 94*
Brondfield, Jerome 1913- *IntMPA 94*
Brondo, Robert Stanley 1951- *WhoAm 94*
Brondsted, Mogens 1918- *IntWW 93*
Broneer, Oscar T. 1894-1992 *AnObit 1992*
Broner, E. M. *DrAPF 93*
Broner, E(sther) M(asserman) 1930- *WrDr 94*
Broner, Mathew 1924- *WhoAmA 93*
Broner, Robert 1922- *WhoAmA 93*
Bronescombe, Walter c. 1220-1280 *DcNaB MP*
Bronesky, Joseph J. 1947- *WhoAmL 94*
Bronfenbrenner, Urie 1917- *IntWW 93, WhoAm 94*
Bronfin, Fred 1918- *WhoAmL 94*
Bronfman, Allan 1895- *WhAm 10*
Bronfman, Charles Rosner 1931- *IntWW 93, WhoAm 94, WhoFI 94*
Bronfman, Edgar M. *WhoAm 94*
Bronfman, Edgar M. 1929- *IntWW 93*
Bronfman, Edgar Miles 1929- *Who 94, WhoAm 94, WhoFI 94*
Bronfman, Peter Frederick 1929- *WhoAm 94*
Brong, Gerald Russell 1939- *WhoWest 94*
Bronger, Jerry 1935- *WhoAmP 93*
Bronhill, June 1930- *NewGrDO*
Broniarek, Zygmunt 1925- *IntWW 93*
Bronis, Stephen J. 1947- *WhoAmL 94*
Bronk, Daniel A. 1963- *WhoAmL 94*
Bronk, William *DrAPF 93*
Bronk, William 1918- *WhoAm 94, WrDr 94*
Bronkema, Frederick Hollander 1934- *WhoAm 94*
Bronner, Edwin Blaine 1920- *WhoAm 94, WrDr 94*
Bronner, Ethan (Samuel) 1954- *ConAu 140*
Bronner, Ethan Samuel 1954- *WhoAm 94*
Bronner, Felix 1921- *WhoAm 94*
Bronner, Georg 1667-1720 *NewGrDO*
Bronner, Nathaniel, Sr. *WhoBlA 94*
Bronner, Nathaniel H., Sr. d1993 *NewYTBS 93*
Bronsart, Ingeborg (Lena) von 1840-1913 *NewGrDO*
Bronsdon, Melinda Ann 1940- *WhoAm 94*
Bronsgeest, Cornelis 1878-1957 *NewGrDO*
Bronshvag, Vivian *WhoAmP 93*
Bronskaya, Eugenia 1882-1953 *NewGrDO*
Bronson, A. A. 1946- *WhoAmA 93*
Bronson, Betty d1971 *WhoHol 92*
Bronson, Charles *WhoAm 94*
Bronson, Charles 1920- *WhoHol 92*
Bronson, Charles 1921- *IntMPA 94*
Bronson, Charles 1922- *IntWW 93*
Bronson, Clark Everice 1939- *WhoAmA 93*
Bronson, Franklin H. 1932- *WhoAm 94*
Bronson, Fred James 1935- *WhoBlA 94*
Bronson, Gwendolyn T. 1937- *WhoAmP 93*
Bronson, Irlo Overstreet, Jr. 1936- *WhoAmP 93*
Bronson, Kenneth 1934- *WhoAmL 94*
Bronson, Kenneth Caldean 1933- *WhoAm 94*
Bronson, Lillian 1902- *WhoHol 92*
Bronson, Oswald P., Sr. 1927- *WhoBlA 94*
Bronson, Oswald Perry 1927- *WhoAm 94*
Bronson, Patricia Ann 1931-1989 *WhAm 10*
Bronson, Peter Robert 1948- *WhoAmL 94*
Bronstein, Alvin J. 1928- *WhoAm 94, WhoAmL 94*
Bronstein, Arthur J. 1914- *WhoAm 94, WhoWest 94, WrDr 94*
Bronstein, Glen Max 1960- *WhoAmL 94*
Bronstein, Lynne *DrAPF 93*
Bronstein, Richard J. 1949- *WhoAm 94, WhoAmL 94*
Bronston, Samuel 1908- *IntMPA 94, IntWW 93*
Bronswick, Leonard 1933- *WhoMW 93*
Bronte, Anne 1820-1849 *BlmGEL [port], BlmGWL [port]*
Bronte, Charlotte 1816-1855 *BlmGEL [port], BlmGWL [port]*
Bronte, Emily 1818-1848 *BlmGEL [port], BlmGWL [port], PoeCrit 8 [port]*
Bronz, Lois Gougis Taplin 1927- *WhoBlA 94*
Bronzan, Bruce 1947- *WhoAmP 93*
Bronzino, Joseph D. 1937- *WrDr 94*
Bronzino, Joseph Daniel 1937- *WhoAm 94, WhoScEn 94*
Bronzo, Mark Peter 1960- *WhoIns 94*
Broocks, Linda 1950- *WhoAmL 94*
Brook, Adrian G. 1924- *IntWW 93*
Brook, Adrian Gibbs 1924- *WhoAm 94*
Brook, Alexander 1898-1980 *WhoAmA 93N*
Brook, Allen d1962 *WhoHol 92*
Brook, Anthony Donald 1936- *Who 94*
Brook, Claudio *WhoHol 92*
Brook, Clive d1974 *WhoHol 92*
Brook, David 1932- *WrDr 94*
Brook, David Conway Grant 1935- *Who 94*
Brook, David William 1936- *WhoAm 94*
Brook, Donna *DrAPF 93*
Brook, Faith 1922- *WhoHol 92*
Brook, Gary Fred 1961- *WhoFI 94*
Brook, Helen 1907- *Who 94*
Brook, Irina 1962- *WhoHol 92*
Brook, John Michael 1934- *Who 94*
Brook, Judith Suzanne 1939- *WhoScEn 94*
Brook, Leopold 1912- *Who 94*
Brook, Lesley 1916- *WhoHol 92*
Brook, Lyndon 1926- *WhoHol 92*
Brook, Peter 1925- *BlmGEL, IntMPA 94*
Brook, Peter (Stephan Paul) 1925- *NewGrDO*
Brook, Peter Stephen Paul 1925- *IntWW 93, Who 94*

Brook, Ralph Ellis *Who 94*
Brook, Richard John 1938- *Who 94*
Brook, Robert *Who 94*
Brook, (Gerald) Robert 1928- *Who 94*
Brook, Robert H. 1943- *IntWW 93*
Brook, Robert Henry 1943- *WhoAm 94*
Brook, Robin 1908- *Who 94*
Brook, Robin (Ralph Ellis) 1908- *IntWW 93*
Brook, Susan G. 1949- *WhoMW 93*
Brook, Timothy (James) 1951- *ConAu 140*
Brook, Victor John, Jr. 1946- *WhoAmL 94*
Brook, William Edward d1993 *Who 94N*
Brook, Winston Rollins 1931- *WhoWest 94*
Brookbank, John Warren 1927- *WhoWest 94*
Brooke *Who 94*
Brooke, Lord 1957- *Who 94*
Brooke, Alistair Weston 1947- *Who 94*
Brooke, Arthur Caffin 1919- *Who 94*
Brooke, Avery Rogers 1923- *WhoAm 94*
Brooke, Bryan Nicholas 1915- *Who 94, WrDr 94*
Brooke, Charles Patrick 1914- *WhoWest 94*
Brooke, Charles Vyner 1874-1963 *DcNaB MP*
Brooke, Charlotte d1793 *BlmGWL*
Brooke, Christopher N. L. 1927- *WrDr 94*
Brooke, Christopher N(ugent) L(awrence) 1927- *ConAu 42NR*
Brooke, Christopher Nugent Lawrence 1927- *IntWW 93, Who 94*
Brooke, Claude d1933 *WhoHol 92*
Brooke, Clifford d1951 *WhoHol 92*
Brooke, Clive 1942- *Who 94*
Brooke, David Stopford 1931- *WhoAm 94, WhoAmA 93*
Brooke, Edna Mae 1923- *WhoFI 94, WhoWest 94*
Brooke, Edward W. 1919- *AfrAmAl 6 [port]*
Brooke, Edward William 1919- *IntWW 93, WhoAm 94, WhoAmL 94, WhoAmP 93, WhoBlA 94*
Brooke, Frances 1724-1789 *BlmGWL*
Brooke, Francis (George Windham) 1963- *Who 94*
Brooke, Francis John, III 1929- *WhoAm 94*
Brooke, Francis Taliaferro 1763-1851 *WhAmRev*
Brooke, Gregory Michael 1964- *WhoMW 93*
Brooke, Henry 1903-1984 *DcNaB MP*
Brooke, Henry 1936- *Who 94*
Brooke, Henry William 1772?-1842 *DcNaB MP*
Brooke, Hillary 1914- *WhoHol 92*
Brooke, (Bernard) Jocelyn 1908-1966 *EncSF 93*
Brooke, John L. 1953- *ConAu 140*
Brooke, Keith 1966- *EncSF 93*
Brooke, L. Leslie 1862-1940 *DcLB 141 [port]*
Brooke, Michael d1978 *WhoHol 92*
Brooke, Myra d1944 *WhoHol 92*
Brooke, Paul 1944- *WhoHol 92*
Brooke, Paul Alan 1945- *WhoAm 94, WhoFI 94*
Brooke, Pegan 1950- *WhoAmA 93*
Brooke, Peter 1934- *IntWW 93*
Brooke, Peter Leonard 1934- *Who 94*
Brooke, Ralph d1963 *WhoHol 92*
Brooke, Ralph Ian 1934- *WhoAm 94, WhoScEn 94*
Brooke, Richard, Jr. 1926- *WhoIns 94*
Brooke, Richard (Neville) 1915- *Who 94*
Brooke, Robert Larry 1949- *WhoAmL 94*
Brooke, Rodney George 1939- *Who 94*
Brooke, Roger *Who 94*
Brooke, (Christopher) Roger (Ettrick) 1931- *Who 94*
Brooke, Rupert 1887-1915 *BlmGEL*
Brooke, Tal 1945- *WhoWest 94*
Brooke, Tyler d1943 *WhoHol 92*
Brooke, Van Dyke d1921 *WhoHol 92*
Brooke, Vivian M. 1943- *WhoAmP 93*
Brooke, Walter d1986 *WhoHol 92*
Brooke, William J. 1946- *WrDr 94*
Brookeborough, Viscount 1952- *Who 94*
Brooke-Little, John (Philip Brooke) 1927- *WrDr 94*
Brooke-Little, John Philip Brooke 1927- *Who 94*
Brooke of Ystradfellte, Baroness 1908- *Who 94, WhoWomW 91*
Brooker, Alan Bernard 1931- *Who 94*
Brooker, George M. d1993 *NewYTBS 93 [port]*
Brooker, Jeff Zeigler 1941- *WhoScEn 94*
Brooker, Jewel Spears 1940- *WrDr 94*
Brooker, Moe Albert 1940- *WhoBlA 94*
Brooker, Norton William, Jr. 1944- *WhoAmL 94*
Brooker, Robert Elton 1905- *IntWW 93, WhoAm 94*
Brooker, Rosalind Poll 1928- *WhoAmP 93*
Brooker, Thomas Kimball 1939- *WhoAm 94, WhoFI 94, WhoMW 93*
Brooker, Tom d1929 *WhoHol 92*
Brooke-Rose, Christine *Who 94, WrDr 94*
Brooke-Rose, Christine 1923- *BlmGWL, EncSF 93*
Brooke-Rose, Christine 1926- *BlmGEL*
Brookes, Baron 1909- *Who 94*
Brookes, Beata 1931- *Who 94*
Brookes, Bernard L. 1950- *WhoBlA 94*
Brookes, Jacqueline 1930- *WhoHol 92*
Brookes, James Robert 1941- *Who 94*
Brookes, John 1933- *Who 94*
Brookes, Norman 1877-1968 *BuCMET [port]*
Brookes, Olwen d1976 *WhoHol 92*
Brookes, Pamela 1922- *WrDr 94*
Brookes, Peter C. *Who 94*
Brookes, Raymond Percival 1909- *IntWW 93*
Brookes, Valentine 1913- *WhoAm 94, WhoAmL 94, WhoWest 94*
Brookes, Wilfred (Deakin) 1906- *Who 94*
Brooke-Taylor, Tim 1940- *WhoHol 92*
Brooke Turner, Alan 1926- *Who 94*
Brookey, Brian Kent 1965- *WhoAmL 94*
Brookhouse, Christopher *DrAPF 93*
Brooking, Patrick Guy 1937- *Who 94*
Brooking, Trevor David 1948- *Who 94*
Brookins, Dolores 1948- *WhoBlA 94*
Brookins, H. Hartford 1925- *WhoBlA 94*
Brookins, Howard B. 1932- *WhoAmP 93*
Brookins, Howard B., Sr. 1932- *WhoBlA 94*
Brookins, Jacob Boden 1935- *WhoAmA 93*
Brook-Jones, Elwyn d1962 *WhoHol 92*
Brookler, Kenneth Haskell 1938- *WhoScEn 94*
Brookman, Anthony Raymond 1922- *WhoAm 94, WhoAmL 94, WhoFI 94, WhoWest 94*
Brookman, Eileen B. 1921- *WhoAmP 93*
Brookman, Marc D. 1942- *WhoAmL 94*
Brookner, Anita *Who 94, WhoAm 94*
Brookner, Anita 1928- *BlmGEL [port], IntWW 93, WrDr 94*
Brookner, Anita 1938- *BlmGWL*
Brookner, Eli 1931- *WhoAm 94*
Brookner, Jackie 1945- *WhoAmA 93*
Brookover, Thomas Wilbur 1944- *WhoAmL 94*
Brookover, Wilbur B. 1911- *WrDr 94*
Brook-Partridge, Bernard 1927- *Who 94*
Brooks *Who 94*
Brooks, A. Russell 1906- *WhoBlA 94, WrDr 94*
Brooks, Alan d1936 *WhoHol 92*
Brooks, Alan 1935- *Who 94*
Brooks, (John) Alan 1931- *WhoAmA 93*
Brooks, Albert 1947- *IntMPA 94, WhoAm 94, WhoCom, WhoHol 92*
Brooks, Alison Anne 1954- *WhoAmL 94, WhoWest 94*
Brooks, Alison Lesley 1958- *WhoWest 94*
Brooks, Alvin Lee 1932- *WhoBlA 94*
Brooks, Andree Aelion 1937- *WhoAm 94*
Brooks, Andree (Nicole) Aelion 1937- *WrDr 94*
Brooks, Annabel *WhoHol 92*
Brooks, Arkles Clarence, Jr. 1943- *WhoBlA 94*
Brooks, Arthur V. N. 1936- *WhoAm 94*
Brooks, Avery *WhoBlA 94*
Brooks, Babert Vincent 1926- *WhoAm 94*
Brooks, Barbara E. d1993 *NewYTBS 93*
Brooks, Ben *DrAPF 93*
Brooks, Bernard E. 1935- *WhoBlA 94*
Brooks, Bernard W. 1939- *WhoBlA 94*
Brooks, Beverly 1933- *WhoHol 92*
Brooks, Bradford Oldham 1951- *WhoWest 94*
Brooks, Brian Shedd 1945- *WhoMW 93*
Brooks, Bruce 1950- *TwCYAW*
Brooks, Bruce Delos 1950- *WhoAm 94*
Brooks, Bruce W. 1948- *WhoAmA 93*
Brooks, Carl 1949- *WhoBlA 94*
Brooks, Carol Lorraine 1955- *WhoBlA 94*
Brooks, Carolyn Branch 1946- *WhoBlA 94*
Brooks, Chandler McCuskey 1905-1989 *WhAm 10*
Brooks, Charles Irving 1944- *WhoScEn 94*
Brooks, Charlotte Kendrick 1918- *WhoBlA 94*
Brooks, Chet Edward 1935- *WhoAmP 93*
Brooks, Christine D. *WhoBlA 94*
Brooks, Claude *WhoHol 92*
Brooks, Claudia Marie 1952- *WhoAmL 94*
Brooks, Cleanth 1906- *IntWW 93, Who 94, WhoAm 94, WrDr 94*
Brooks, Clifton Rowland 1925- *WhoHisp 94*
Brooks, Clyde Henry 1941- *WhoBlA 94*
Brooks, Craig Martin 1955- *WhoAmL 94*
Brooks, Curtis Randall 1955- *WhoFI 94*
Brooks, Daisy M. Anderson *WhoBlA 94*
Brooks, Dana D. 1951- *WhoAm 94*
Brooks, Dana DeMarco 1951- *WhoBlA 94*
Brooks, Daniel Townley 1941- *WhoAm 94*
Brooks, David 1756-1838 *WhAmRev*
Brooks, David (Gordon) 1953- *ConAu 140*
Brooks, David Allen *WhoHol 92*
Brooks, David Barry 1934- *WhoAm 94*
Brooks, David William 1901- *WhoAm 94*
Brooks, Debra Lee 1952- *WhoMW 93*
Brooks, Delores J. 1944- *WhoMW 93*
Brooks, Delores Jean 1944- *WhoBlA 94*
Brooks, Diana D. 1950- *WhoAm 94*
Brooks, Dick *IntMPA 94*
Brooks, Dolores Ann 1931- *WhoAmP 93*
Brooks, Don Locellus 1953- *WhoBlA 94*
Brooks, Donna Staples 1946- *WhoAmP 93*
Brooks, Doris F. *WhoAmP 93*
Brooks, Doris Jean 1955- *WhoWest 94*
Brooks, Douglas 1928- *Who 94*
Brooks, Douglas Lee 1916- *WhoScEn 94*
Brooks, Dunbar 1950- *WhoBlA 94*
Brooks, E. R. 1937- *WhoAm 94, WhoFI 94*
Brooks, Eda Helen d1993 *NewYTBS 93*
Brooks, Edward 1942- *WhoAm 94, WhoFI 94*
Brooks, Edward Howard 1921- *WhoAm 94, WhoWest 94*
Brooks, Edward Pennell 1895- *WhAm 10*
Brooks, Edwin 1929- *Who 94, WrDr 94*
Brooks, Ellen *WhoAmA 93*
Brooks, Elmer T. 1932- *AfrAmG [port]*
Brooks, Eric Arthur Swatton 1907- *Who 94*
Brooks, Foster 1912- *WhoCom, WhoHol 92*
Brooks, Francis Gerard *Who 94*
Brooks, Francis K. 1943- *WhoAmP 93*
Brooks, Frank B. *WhoBlA 94*
Brooks, Frank Pickering 1920-1991 *WhAm 10*
Brooks, Frederick Phillips, Jr. 1931- *WhoAm 94*
Brooks, Garth 1962- *WhoAm 94*
Brooks, Gary 1934- *WhoAm 94, WhoFI 94*
Brooks, Gary Allen 1946- *WhoAmP 93*
Brooks, Gene 1936- *WhoAm 94*
Brooks, Gene C. *WhoAmL 94*
Brooks, Gene Edward 1931- *WhoAm 94, WhoAmL 94, WhoMW 93*
Brooks, George *WhoAmP 93*
Brooks, George E., Jr. 1933- *WrDr 94*
Brooks, George M. *AfrAmG*
Brooks, Geraldine d1977 *WhoHol 92*
Brooks, Geraldine 1955- *WhoAm 94*
Brooks, Gilbert 1934- *WhoBlA 94*
Brooks, Gladys Sinclair 1914- *WhoMW 93*
Brooks, Glenn Allen 1960- *WhoWest 94*
Brooks, Glenn Ellis 1931- *WhoAm 94*
Brooks, Gwendolyn *DrAPF 93*
Brooks, Gwendolyn 1917- *AfrAmAl 6 [port], BlkWr 2, BlmGWL, IntWW 93, PoeCrit 7 [port], WhoAm 94, WhoBlA 94, WhoMW 93, WrDr 94*
Brooks, H. Allen 1925- *WhoAm 94*
Brooks, H(arold) Allen 1925- *WhoAmA 93, WrDr 94*
Brooks, Hadda 1916- *WhoHol 92*
Brooks, Hank d1925 *WhoHol 92*
Brooks, Harold W. 1948- *WhoBlA 94*
Brooks, Harry A. *WhoAmA 93*
Brooks, Harry W., Jr. 1928- *WhoBlA 94*
Brooks, Harry William, Jr. 1928- *AfrAmG [port]*
Brooks, Harvey 1915- *IntWW 93*
Brooks, Hazel 1924- *WhoHol 92*
Brooks, Henri E. *WhoAmP 93*
Brooks, Henry Marcellus 1942- *WhoBlA 94*
Brooks, Hildy *WhoHol 92*
Brooks, Howard Stanley 1958- *WhoAmL 94*
Brooks, Hubie 1956- *WhoBlA 94*
Brooks, Hunter O. 1929- *WhoBlA 94*
Brooks, Iris *WhoHol 92*
Brooks, Jack 1922- *CngDr 93, WhoAmP 93*
Brooks, Jack Bascom 1922- *WhoAm 94*
Brooks, James *DrAPF 93*
Brooks, James 1906-1992 *AnObit 1992, WhAm 10, WhoAmA 93N*
Brooks, James C., Jr. 1945- *WhoIns 94*
Brooks, James Elwood 1925- *WhoAm 94, WhoScEn 94*
Brooks, James Joe, III 1948- *WhoFI 94*
Brooks, James L. 1940- *IntMPA 94, WhoAm 94*
Brooks, James O'Neil 1922- *WhoBlA 94*
Brooks, James Robert 1958- *WhoBlA 94*
Brooks, James Sprague 1925- *WhoAm 94, WhoWest 94*
Brooks, Janice Willena 1946- *WhoBlA 94*
Brooks, Jeanne 1946- *WrDr 94*
Brooks, Jeremy 1926- *WrDr 94*
Brooks, Jerome Bernard 1932- *WhoAm 94*
Brooks, Jerry Claude 1936- *WhoFI 94*
Brooks, Jess Lee d1944 *WhoHol 92*
Brooks, Joae Graham 1926- *WhoAm 94*
Brooks, Joe 1938- *WhoHol 92*
Brooks, Joel *WhoHol 92*
Brooks, John 1752-1825 *WhAmRev*
Brooks, John 1920-1993 *NewYTBS 93 [port], WrDr 94N*
Brooks, John (Nixon) 1920-1993 *ConAu 142*
Brooks, John Ashton 1928- *Who 94*
Brooks, John C. *WhoAmP 93*
Brooks, John Edward 1923- *WhoAm 94*
Brooks, John H. 1935- *WhoAmA 93*
Brooks, John Robinson 1918- *WhoAm 94*
Brooks, John Samuel Joseph 1948- *WhoScEn 94*
Brooks, John White 1936- *WhoAm 94*
Brooks, Joseph *IntMPA 94*
Brooks, Josephine 1934- *WhoAmP 93*
Brooks, Joyce Julianna 1931- *WhoMW 93*
Brooks, Julie Anne 1945- *WhoAm 94, WhoFI 94*
Brooks, Karl B. 1956- *WhoAmP 93*
Brooks, Keefe Alan 1954- *WhoAmL 94*
Brooks, Keith 1923- *WhoAm 94*
Brooks, Kenneth Thomas 1956- *WhoAmL 94*
Brooks, Kent Fagegren 1947- *WhoMW 93*
Brooks, Kevin 1969- *WhoBlA 94*
Brooks, Kevin P. 1944- *WhoIns 94*
Brooks, Kix 1955- *WhoAm 94*
Brooks, Kristina Marie 1949- *WhoWest 94*
Brooks, Laura Kasley d1974 *WhoHol 92*
Brooks, Leo Austin 1932- *AfrAmG [port], WhoBlA 94*
Brooks, Leslie 1922- *WhoHol 92*
Brooks, Leslie James 1916- *Who 94*
Brooks, Lester 1924- *ConAu 42NR*
Brooks, Lewis William, Jr. 1944- *WhoAmP 93*
Brooks, Lloyd William, Jr. 1949- *WhoScEn 94*
Brooks, Lorenzo 1942- *WhoAm 94*
Brooks, Lorimer Page 1917- *WhoAm 94*
Brooks, Louise d1985 *WhoHol 92*
Brooks, Louise Cherry 1906- *WhoAmA 93*
Brooks, Maggie 1951- *WrDr 94*
Brooks, Marc Benjamin 1966- *WhoScEn 94*
Brooks, Marcellus 1941- *WhoBlA 94*
Brooks, Maria Gowen c. 1794-1845 *BlmGWL*
Brooks, Marion Jackson 1920- *WhoBlA 94*
Brooks, Marsha Storper 1951- *WhoAmL 94*
Brooks, Martha *WrDr 94*
Brooks, Mary Elizabeth *WhoAmP 93*
Brooks, Maurice Edward 1922- *WhoAm 94*
Brooks, Mel 1926- *IntMPA 94, IntWW 93, Who 94, WhoAm 94, WhoCom [port], WhoHol 92*
Brooks, Michael Paul 1937- *WhoAm 94*
Brooks, Monica Marie 1964- *WhoFI 94*
Brooks, Morris Jackson, Jr. 1954- *WhoAmP 93*
Brooks, Nicholas Peter 1941- *Who 94*
Brooks, Norman Leon 1932- *WhoBlA 94*
Brooks, Norward J. 1934- *WhoBlA 94*
Brooks, Patricia d1993 *NewYTBS 93 [port]*
Brooks, Patricia 1937- *NewGrDO*
Brooks, Patrick, Jr. 1944- *WhoBlA 94*
Brooks, Patrick William 1943- *WhoAmL 94*
Brooks, Paul *WhoHol 92*
Brooks, Paul 1909- *WrDr 94*
Brooks, Pauline d1967 *WhoHol 92*
Brooks, Peter Newman 1931- *WrDr 94*
Brooks, Peter Preston 1938- *WhoAm 94*
Brooks, Peter T. *WhoAmP 93*
Brooks, Peter Wright 1920- *WrDr 94*
Brooks, Philip Russell 1938- *WhoScEn 94*
Brooks, Phillip Daniel 1946- *WhoBlA 94*
Brooks, Phillips 1835-1893 *DcAmReB 2*
Brooks, Phyllis 1914- *WhoHol 92*
Brooks, R. Daniel 1946- *WhoIns 94*
Brooks, Rand 1918- *WhoHol 92*
Brooks, Randi *WhoHol 92*
Brooks, Randy *WhoHol 92*
Brooks, Randy d1967 *WhoHol 92*
Brooks, Ray 1939- *WhoHol 92*
Brooks, Richard *WhoBlA 94, WhoHol 92*
Brooks, Richard 1912-1992 *AnObit 1992, WhAm 10, WrDr 94N*
Brooks, Richard Dickinson 1944- *WhoAm 94*
Brooks, Richard Leonard 1934- *WhoBlA 94*
Brooks, Richard M. 1962- *WhoScEn 94*
Brooks, Richard Mallon 1928- *WhoFI 94*
Brooks, Robert 1922- *WhoAmA 93*
Brooks, Robert Alexander 1944- *WhoFI 94*
Brooks, Robert Earl, Jr. 1956- *WhoAmP 93*

Brouwenstyn, Gerarda *IntWW 93*
Brouwer, Arie R. d1993 *NewYTBS 93 [port]*
Brouwer, Luitzen Egbertus Jan 1881-1966 *WorScD*
Brouwer, Peter 1945- *WhoHol 92*
Brovarski, Edward Joseph 1943- *WhoAm 94*
Broverman, Robert Lee 1931- *WhoAmP 93*
Brovold, Frederick Norman 1939- *WhoScEn 94*
Browaldh, Tore 1917- *IntWW 93, Who 94*
Browde, Anatole 1925- *WhoAm 94*
Browder, Anne Elna 1935- *WhoBlA 94*
Browder, Catherine *DrAPF 93*
Browder, Felix Earl 1927- *IntWW 93, WhoAm 94, WhoScEn 94*
Browder, Glen 1943- *CngDr 93*
Browder, John Glen 1943- *WhoAm 94, WhoAmP 93*
Browdy, Alvin 1917- *WhoAm 94*
Browdy, Joseph Eugene 1937- *WhoAm 94, WhoAmL 94*
Browdy, Michelle H. 1964- *WhoAmL 94*
Brower, Charles Nelson 1935- *WhoAm 94, WhoAmL 94*
Brower, David Ross 1912- *EnvEnc [port], WhoAm 94, WhoWest 94, WrDr 94*
Brower, Forrest Allen 1930- *WhoAm 94*
Brower, James Calvin 1914- *WhoMW 93*
Brower, John E. 1949- *WhoAmL 94*
Brower, Kenneth 1944- *WrDr 94*
Brower, Kent Everett 1946- *WhoAm 94*
Brower, Michael Chadbourne 1960- *WhoScEn 94*
Brower, Millicent *DrAPF 93*
Brower, Myron Riggs 1949- *WhoFI 94, WhoWest 94*
Brower, Otto d1946 *WhoHol 92*
Brower, Robert d1934 *WhoHol 92*
Brower, Robert Clark 1896- *WhAm 10*
Brower, Tom d1937 *WhoHol 92*
Browes, Pauline A. *WhoWomW 91*
Browman, David Ludvig 1941- *WhoAm 94*
Brown, A. David 1942- *WhoBlA 94*
Brown, A(rthur) I(vor) Parry 1908- *Who 94*
Brown, A. J. d1978 *WhoHol 92*
Brown, A. Sue 1946- *WhoBlA 94*
Brown, Aaron Clifton, Jr. 1940- *WhoAm 94, WhoAmL 94*
Brown, Aaron Donald 1954- *WhoWest 94*
Brown, Abbott Louis 1943- *WhoAm 94*
Brown, Abner Bertrand 1942- *WhoBlA 94*
Brown, Ada d1950 *WhoHol 92*
Brown, Ada Katherine 1927- *WhoAmP 93*
Brown, Adrian Worley 1928- *WhoFI 94*
Brown, Adrienne Jean 1950- *WhoAm 94*
Brown, Agnes Marie 1933- *WhoBlA 94*
Brown, Alan Anthony 1936- *WhoFI 94*
Brown, Alan Charlton 1929- *WhoAm 94, WhoScEn 94*
Brown, Alan Crawford 1956- *WhoAmL 94, WhoMW 93*
Brown, Alan James 1921- *Who 94*
Brown, Alan Johnson 1951- *WhoScEn 94*
Brown, Alan M., Jr. *WhoAmA 93*
Brown, Alan Thomas 1928- *Who 94*
Brown, Alan Winthrop 1934- *Who 94*
Brown, Alanna Kathleen 1944- *WhoWest 94*
Brown, Albert C. 1918- *WhoAmP 93*
Brown, Albert Jacob 1914- *WhoAm 94*
Brown, Albert Joseph, Jr. 1934- *WhoAm 94*
Brown, Albert Theodore, Jr. 1942- *WhoAmL 94*
Brown, Alec (John Charles) 1900-1962 *EncSF 93*
Brown, Alex 1913- *WhoBlA 94*
Brown, Alexander Claude 1931- *IntWW 93*
Brown, Alexander Cosens Lindsay 1920- *Who 94*
Brown, Alexander Crosby, Jr. 1936- *WhoWest 94*
Brown, Alexander Crum 1838-1922 *DcNaB MP*
Brown, Alexander Douglas G. *Who 94*
Brown, Alfie Parham d1988 *WhoHol 92*
Brown, Alfred d1978 *WhoHol 92*
Brown, Alfred 1931- *WhoWest 94*
Brown, Alfred Peter 1943- *WhoMW 93*
Brown, Alice 1857-1948 *BlmGWL*
Brown, Alice Dalton 1939- *WhoAmA 93*
Brown, Allen 1919- *WhoAmL 94*
Brown, Allen (Stanley) 1911- *Who 94*
Brown, Allen Webster 1908-1990 *WhAm 10*
Brown, Allyn Stephens 1916- *WhoFI 94*
Brown, Alson W. 1922- *WhoAmP 93*
Brown, Alvin Montero 1924- *WhoBlA 94*
Brown, Alyce Doss *WhoBlA 94*
Brown, Amelda *WhoHol 92*
Brown, Amelia 1868-1979 *EncNAR*
Brown, Amos Cleophilus 1941- *WhoBlA 94*
Brown, Andre L. 1966- *WhoBlA 94*
Brown, Andrew J. 1922- *WhoBlA 94*
Brown, Angela *WhoHol 92*
Brown, Angela Yvette 1964- *WhoBlA 94*
Brown, Angeline 1931- *WhoAm 94*
Brown, Ann c. 1759-1784 *NewGrDO*
Brown, Ann Carol 1946- *WhoFI 94*
Brown, Ann Catherine 1935- *WhoAm 94*
Brown, Ann L. 1964- *WhoBlA 94*
Brown, Anna 1747-1810 *BlmGWL*
Brown, Anne *WhoHol 92*
Brown, Annie Gibson 1944- *WhoBlA 94*
Brown, Anthony B. 1922- *WhoWest 94*
Brown, Anthony P. 1926- *WhoAm 94*
Brown, Anthony Vincent 1961- *WhoBlA 94*
Brown, Antoinette 1825-1921 *HisWorL*
Brown, Archibald Haworth 1938- *Who 94, WrDr 94*
Brown, Arnold 1913- *Who 94*
Brown, Arnold 1939- *WhoAm 94*
Brown, Arnold E. 1932- *WhoBlA 94*
Brown, Arnold Harris 1930- *WhoMW 93*
Brown, Arnold Lanehart, Jr. 1926- *WhoAm 94*
Brown, Arnold M. *WhoAmP 93*
Brown, Arthur 1922- *WhAm 10*
Brown, Arthur 1940- *WhoAm 94, WhoWest 94*
Brown, Arthur Carl, Jr. 1915- *WhoWest 94*
Brown, Arthur Durrant 1926- *Who 94*
Brown, Arthur Edmon, Jr. 1929- *WhoAm 94*
Brown, Arthur Edward 1945- *WhoScEn 94*
Brown, Arthur Godfrey Kilner 1915- *Who 94*
Brown, Arthur Huntingdon 1895- *WhAm 10*
Brown, Arthur Joseph 1914- *IntWW 93, Who 94*
Brown, Arthur Thomas 1900- *WhoAm 94*
Brown, Arthur William, Jr. 1939- *WhoAm 94*
Brown, Arvin Bragin 1940- *WhoAm 94*
Brown, Atlanta Thomas 1931- *WhoBlA 94*
Brown, Aubrey Neblett, Jr. 1908- *WhoAm 94*
Brown, Audrey Alexandra 1904- *BlmGWL*
Brown, Austin Cary 1959- *WhoFI 94*
Brown, Autry 1924- *WhoMW 93*
Brown, B. Peter 1922- *WhoIns 94*
Brown, B. R. 1932- *WhoAm 94, WhoFI 94*
Brown, Bachman Storch, Jr. 1926- *WhoAmP 93*
Brown, Bailey 1917- *WhoAm 94, WhoAmL 94*
Brown, Banks 1952- *WhoAm 94*
Brown, Barbara d1975 *WhoHol 92*
Brown, Barbara Ann 1949- *WhoBlA 94*
Brown, Barbara Berish 1946- *WhoAm 94, WhoAmL 94*
Brown, Barbara D. 1929- *WhoAmP 93*
Brown, Barbara Eddy 1924- *WhoAmP 93*
Brown, Barbara J. *WhoBlA 94*
Brown, Barbara Jeanne 1941- *WhoAm 94*
Brown, Barbara Mahone 1944- *WhoBlA 94*
Brown, Barbara S. 1951- *WhoScEn 94*
Brown, Barbara Willis 1952- *WhoMW 93*
Brown, Barri Anne 1961- *WhoBlA 94*
Brown, Barry *Who 94*
Brown, Barry d1978 *WhoHol 92*
Brown, Barry 1939- *WhoAm 94*
Brown, Barry 1942- *WhoAm 94*
Brown, (James) Barry (Conway) 1937- *Who 94*
Brown, Barry Stephen 1951- *WhoAmL 94*
Brown, Bart A., Jr. 1933- *WhoAm 94, WhoFI 94, WhoWest 94*
Brown, Barton 1924- *WhoAm 94*
Brown, Basil W. 1927- *WhoAmP 93*
Brown, Beatrice 1917- *WhoAm 94*
Brown, Beatrice S. 1950- *WhoBlA 94*
Brown, Ben 1941- *WhoAmP 93*
Brown, Ben Hill, Jr. 1914-1989 *WhAm 10*
Brown, Ben Maurice 1943- *WhoWest 94*
Brown, Benjamin 1756-1831 *WhAmRev*
Brown, Benjamin A. 1943- *WhoAm 94*
Brown, Benjamin Andrew 1933- *WhoAm 94*
Brown, Benjamin Leonard 1929- *WhoBlA 94*
Brown, Bennett Alexander 1929- *WhoAm 94, WhoFI 94*
Brown, Bernard E(dward) 1925- *WrDr 94*
Brown, Bernice Baynes 1935- *WhoBlA 94*
Brown, Bernice H. 1907- *WhoBlA 94*
Brown, Berton d1978 *WhoHol 92*
Brown, Beryl P. *Who 94*
Brown, Beth Ann 1966- *WhoAmL 94*
Brown, Betty Ann 1949- *WhoAmA 93*
Brown, Betty Louise 1942- *WhoMW 93*
Brown, Bettye Jean 1955- *WhoBlA 94*
Brown, Beulah Louise 1917- *WhoMW 93*
Brown, Beverly J. *DrAPF 93*
Brown, Blair 1948- *IntMPA 94, WhoHol 92*
Brown, Blair Alan 1948- *WhoAmP 93*
Brown, Blanche Lenn 1895- *WhoAmP 93*
Brown, Blanche R. 1915- *WrDr 94*
Brown, Bob M. 1937- *WhoAmP 93*
Brown, Bob Oliver 1929- *WhoFI 94, WhoMW 93*
Brown, Bobby 1966- *AfrAmAl 6, WhoBlA 94*
Brown, Bonnie Louise 1942- *WhoAmP 93*
Brown, Bonnie Maryetta 1953- *WhoAmL 94*
Brown, Booker T. 1950- *WhoBlA 94*
Brown, Bowman 1941- *WhoAmL 94*
Brown, Boyd Alex 1948- *WhoMW 93*
Brown, Brendan F. 1898- *WhAm 10*
Brown, Bret Kelly 1963- *WhoMW 93*
Brown, Brewster Warren 1947- *WhoAmP 93*
Brown, Brian 1911-1958 *WhoAmA 93N*
Brown, Brian (Thomas) 1934- *Who 94*
Brown, Brian A. 1952- *WhoBlA 94*
Brown, Brice Norman 1945- *WhoAm 94*
Brown, Britt 1927- *WhoAm 94*
Brown, Brook Bennett 1951- *WhoAmL 94*
Brown, Bruce Claire 1944- *WhoMW 93*
Brown, Bruce Harding 1954- *WhoMW 93*
Brown, Bruce Leonard 1941- *WhoAm 94*
Brown, Bruce Macdonald 1930- *Who 94*
Brown, Bruce Maitland 1947- *WhoAm 94*
Brown, Bruce Robert 1938- *WhoAmA 93*
Brown, Bryan 1947- *IntMPA 94, WhoHol 92*
Brown, Buck 1936- *WhoBlA 94*
Brown, Burnell V. 1925- *WhoBlA 94*
Brown, Buster Jack 1944- *WhoAmP 93*
Brown, Byrd R. 1929- *WhoBlA 94*
Brown, Byron William 1958- *WhoBlA 94*
Brown, Byron William, Jr. 1930- *WhoAm 94, WhoWest 94*
Brown, C. E. 1938- *WhoIns 94*
Brown, C. Harold 1931- *WhoAm 94*
Brown, C. Stuart *WhoAmP 93*
Brown, C. W. *WhoAmA 93*
Brown, Calvin Anderson, Jr. 1931- *WhoBlA 94*
Brown, Cameron 1914- *WhoAm 94, WhoMW 93*
Brown, Candace 1950- *WhoAm 94, WhoMW 93*
Brown, Candy Ann *WhoHol 92*
Brown, Carl Anthony 1930- *WhoBlA 94*
Brown, Carl Williamson 1944- *WhoWest 94*
Brown, Carlotta Love 1964- *WhoAmL 94*
Brown, Carlyle d1964 *WhoAmA 93N*
Brown, Carol Ann 1952- *WhoBlA 94*
Brown, Carol Elizabeth 1950- *WhoWest 94*
Brown, Carol K. *WhoAmA 93*
Brown, Carolyn M. 1948- *WhoBlA 94*
Brown, Carolyn Marie 1957- *WhoAmL 94*
Brown, Carolyn P. 1923- *WhoAm 94*
Brown, Carolyn Smith 1946- *WhoAm 94, WhoWest 94*
Brown, Carroll 1928- *WhoAm 94*
Brown, Carroll Elizabeth 1942- *WhoBlA 94*
Brown, Carter *EncSF 93, Who 94*
Brown, (John) Carter 1934- *Who 94*
Brown, Cassandra d1981 *WhoHol 92*
Brown, Cathey Ann 1954- *WhoWest 94*
Brown, Cecil *DrAPF 93*
Brown, Cedric Harold 1935- *Who 94*
Brown, Cee Scott 1952- *WhoAmA 93*
Brown, Chamberlain d1955 *WhoHol 92*
Brown, Channing T. 1929- *WhoAmP 93*
Brown, Charles 1951- *WhoAmP 93*
Brown, Charles D. d1948 *WhoHol 92*
Brown, Charles Daniel 1927- *WhoAm 94*
Brown, Charles Dargie 1927- *Who 94*
Brown, Charles Dodgson 1928- *WhoAm 94*
Brown, Charles Durward 1930- *WhoScEn 94*
Brown, Charles Earl 1919- *WhoAm 94, WhoAmL 94*
Brown, Charles Edward 1948- *WhoBlA 94*
Brown, Charles Foster, III 1947- *WhoFI 94*
Brown, Charles Frederick Richmond 1902- *Who 94*
Brown, Charles Freeman 1914- *WhoAm 94*
Brown, Charles G., III 1950- *WhoAmP 93*
Brown, Charles Harrison 1941- *WhoMW 93*
Brown, Charles Irving 1932- *WhoWest 94*
Brown, Charles N(ikki) 1937- *EncSF 93*
Brown, Charles Stuart 1918- *WhoAm 94*
Brown, Charles Sumner 1937- *WhoBlA 94*
Brown, Charles Vertis, Jr. 1943- *WhoAmP 93*
Brown, Charlie 1938- *WhoAmP 93, WhoBlA 94*
Brown, Charlotte *WhoAmA 93*
Brown, Charlotte Vestal 1942- *WhoAmA 93*
Brown, Chauncey I., Jr. 1928- *WhoBlA 94*
Brown, Chelsea 1943- *WhoHol 92*
Brown, Chester 1960?- *EncSF 93*
Brown, Chris 1961- *WhoBlA 94*
Brown, Chris A. 1962- *WhoIns 94*
Brown, Christina Hambley *Who 94*
Brown, Christopher 1938- *Who 94*
Brown, Christopher 1951- *WhoAmA 93*
Brown, Christopher C. 1938- *WhoBlA 94*
Brown, Christopher David 1944- *Who 94*
Brown, Christopher Patrick 1951- *WhoFI 94*
Brown, Christopher Paul Hadley 1948- *Who 94*
Brown, Clancy *IntMPA 94*
Brown, Clancy 1958- *WhoHol 92*
Brown, Clarence 1924- *ConMus 11 [port]*
Brown, Clarence J. 1927- *WhoAmP 93*
Brown, Clarence William 1933- *WhoBlA 94*
Brown, Clarice Ernestine 1929- *WhoBlA 94*
Brown, Clark S. *WhoBlA 94*
Brown, Clark Samuel 1911- *WhoAmP 93*
Brown, Clark Tait 1935- *WhoWest 94*
Brown, Claude *DrAPF 93*
Brown, Claude 1937- *AfrAmAl 6*
Brown, Claudell, Jr. 1949- *WhoBlA 94*
Brown, Cliff *WhoAmP 93*
Brown, Clifford 1930-1956 *AfrAmAl 6*
Brown, Clifford Anthony 1951- *WhoBlA 94*
Brown, Clifton George 1959- *WhoBlA 94*
Brown, Colin Wegand 1949- *WhoAm 94*
Brown, Conella Coulter 1925- *WhoBlA 94*
Brown, Connell Jean 1924- *WhoAm 94*
Brown, Connie Yates 1947- *WhoFI 94*
Brown, Constance Charlene 1939- *WhoBlA 94*
Brown, Constance George *WhoAmA 93*
Brown, Constance M. 1953- *WhoFI 94*
Brown, Constance Young 1933- *WhoBlA 94*
Brown, Corrick *WhoWest 94*
Brown, Corrine 1946- *CngDr 93, WhoAm 94, WhoAmP 93, WhoBlA 94*
Brown, Costello L. 1942- *WhoBlA 94*
Brown, Courtney C. 1904-1990 *WhAm 10*
Brown, Courtney Coleridge 1924- *WhoBlA 94*
Brown, Craig Vincent 1943- *WhoBlA 94*
Brown, Craig William 1953- *WhoScEn 94*
Brown, Curtis *WhoHol 92*
Brown, Curtis Carnegie, Jr. 1951- *WhoBlA 94*
Brown, Cynthia Jane 1948- *WhoWest 94*
Brown, Cynthia Lynn 1957- *WhoMW 93*
Brown, Cyril James 1904- *Who 94*
Brown, D. Joan *WhoBlA 94*
Brown, Dale Duward 1935- *WhoAm 94*
Brown, Dale Marius 1931- *WhoAm 94*
Brown, Dale Patrick 1947- *WhoAm 94*
Brown, Dale Robert 1967- *WhoWest 94*
Brown, Dale W. 1926- *WrDr 94*
Brown, Dale Weaver 1926- *WhoAm 94*
Brown, Dallas C., Jr. 1932- *WhoBlA 94*
Brown, Dallas Coverdale, Jr. 1932- *AfrAmG [port], WhoAm 94*
Brown, Dan R. 1948- *WhoAmL 94*
Brown, Daniel 1946- *WhoAmA 93, WhoFI 94, WhoMW 93*
Brown, Daniel Allen 1944- *WhoAm 94, WhoAmL 94*
Brown, Daniel Joseph 1941- *WhoMW 93*
Brown, Daniel McGillivray 1923- *Who 94*
Brown, Daniel Putnam, Jr. 1943- *WhoAmL 94*
Brown, Daniel Russell *GayLL*
Brown, Daniel Warren 1930- *WhoWest 94*
Brown, Darryl Newton 1944- *WhoAmP 93*
Brown, Dave 1948- *WhoAmP 93*
Brown, Dave Steven 1953- *WhoBlA 94*
Brown, David d1993 *Who 94N*
Brown, David 1904- *IntWW 93*
Brown, David 1916- *IntMPA 94, WhoAm 94*
Brown, David 1917- *WhoAm 94*
Brown, David (Worthington) 1927- *Who 94*
Brown, David A. 1945- *WhoFI 94*
Brown, David Alan 1942- *WhoAmA 93*
Brown, David Anthony 1936- *Who 94*
Brown, David Arthur 1929- *IntWW 93*
Brown, David Clifford 1929- *Who 94*
Brown, David Edwin 1923- *WhoMW 93, WhoScEn 94*
Brown, David Emerson 1926- *WhoAmP 93*
Brown, David Eugene 1938- *WhoBlA 94*
Brown, David Eugene 1941- *WhoWest 94*
Brown, David Grant 1936- *WhoAm 94*
Brown, David John Bowes 1925- *Who 94*
Brown, David Julian 1943- *WhoAm 94*
Brown, David K. *Who 94*
Brown, David K. 1936- *WhoAmP 93*

Brown, David Lee 1957- *WhoAmA 93*
Brown, David Lewis 1952- *WhoAmL 94*
Brown, David M. 1935- *WhoAm 94, WhoMW 93*
Brown, David Millard 1918- *WhoAmP 93*
Brown, David Nelson 1940- *WhoAm 94, WhoAmL 94*
Brown, David Randolph 1923- *WhoAm 94*
Brown, David Robert 1954- *WhoMW 93*
Brown, David Rodney H. *Who 94*
Brown, David Ronald 1939- *WhoAmL 94*
Brown, David Rupert 1934- *WhoAm 94*
Brown, David Springer 1915- *WhoAm 94*
Brown, David W. 1955- *WhoAmL 94*
Brown, David Warfield 1937- *WhoAm 94*
Brown, David William 1948- *Who 94*
Brown, Dawn Michele 1965- *WhoFI 94*
Brown, Dean Alan 1938- *WhoAmL 94*
Brown, Dean Naomi 1944- *WhoWest 94*
Brown, Deaver 1943- *WhoFI 94*
Brown, Debra Wood 1951- *WhoAmP 93*
Brown, Debria M. 1936- *WhoBlA 94*
Brown, Dee 1968- *WhoBlA 94*
Brown, Dee (Alexander) 1908- *WrDr 94*
Brown, Dee Alexander 1908- *WhoAm 94, WhoWest 94*
Brown, Deidra Marie 1967- *WhoMW 93*
Brown, Delores Elaine 1945- *WhoBlA 94*
Brown, Deloris A. *WhoBlA 94*
Brown, Delwin (Wray) 1935- *WrDr 94*
Brown, Deming Bronson 1919- *WhoAm 94*
Brown, Denise Lebreton *Who 94*
Brown, Denise Scott 1931- *IntWW 93, WhoAm 94*
Brown, Denise Sharon 1957- *WhoBlA 94*
Brown, Dennis Taylor 1941- *WhoScEn 94*
Brown, Dennison Robert 1934- *WhoAm 94*
Brown, Denys Downing 1918- *Who 94*
Brown, Derrick H. *Who 94*
Brown, Diana *DrAPF 93*
Brown, Diana Johnson 1951- *WhoBlA 94*
Brown, Diane 1947- *WhoAmA 93*
Brown, Dock M. *WhoAmP 93*
Brown, Donald Arthur 1929- *WhoAm 94, WhoFI 94*
Brown, Donald David 1931- *IntWW 93, WhoAm 94, WhoScEn 94*
Brown, Donald Douglas 1931- *WhoAm 94*
Brown, Donald James, Jr. 1948- *WhoAm 94, WhoAmL 94*
Brown, Donald James, Jr. 1955- *WhoFI 94*
Brown, Donald Jerould 1926- *WhoWest 94*
Brown, Donald Linn 1946- *WhoFI 94*
Brown, Donald R., Sr. 1939- *WhoBlA 94*
Brown, Donald Ray 1935- *WhoAm 94*
Brown, Donald Robert 1945- *WhoAm 94*
Brown, Donald S. 1928- *IntWW 93*
Brown, Donald Wesley 1953- *WhoAm 94*
Brown, Doreen Leah Hurwitz 1927- *WhoFI 94*
Brown, Dorothy Lavania 1919- *WhoBlA 94*
Brown, Doug Randall 1951- *WhoFI 94*
Brown, Douglas (Denison) 1917- *Who 94*
Brown, Douglas (Dunlop) 1931- *Who 94*
Brown, Drew Bundini d1987 *WhoHol 92*
Brown, Dudley Earl, Jr. 1928- *WhoAm 94, WhoAmP 93*
Brown, Dwayne Marc 1962- *WhoBlA 94*
Brown, Dwier 1959- *WhoHol 92*
Brown, E. Lynn 1936- *WhoAm 94*
Brown, Earl Kent 1925- *WhoAm 94*
Brown, Earle 1926- *WhoAm 94*
Brown, Earle Palmer 1922- *WhoAm 94, WhoFI 94*
Brown, Eddie C. 1940- *WhoBlA 94*
Brown, Eddie F. 1945- *WhoAm 94*
Brown, Edgar Cary 1916- *WhoAm 94*
Brown, Edgar Henry, Jr. 1926- *WhoAm 94*
Brown, Edith 1935- *WhoAm 94, WhoMW 93*
Brown, Edith Rae 1942- *WhoAmA 93*
Brown, Edmund Gerald 1905- *WhoAm 94*
Brown, Edmund Gerald, Jr. 1938- *IntWW 93, Who 94, WhoAm 94, WhoAmP 93, WhoWest 94*
Brown, Edmund Gerald (Pat) 1905- *IntWW 93*
Brown, Edward James 1909-1991 *WhAm 10*
Brown, Edward James 1937- *WhoFI 94, WhoScEn 94*
Brown, Edward Lynn 1936- *WhoBlA 94*
Brown, Edward Maurice 1909- *WhoAm 94, WhoMW 93*
Brown, Edward Randolph 1933- *WhoAm 94*
Brown, Edward Sherman 1940- *WhoFI 94*
Brown, Edwin C., Jr. 1935- *WhoBlA 94*
Brown, Edwin S. 1942- *WhoAmL 94*
Brown, Edwin Thomas 1938- *Who 94*
Brown, Edwin Wilson, Jr. 1926- *WhoAm 94*
Brown, Effie Mayhan Jones 1922- *WhoBlA 94*
Brown, Elaine *NewYTBS 93 [port]*
Brown, Elaine 1943- *BlkWr 2, ConAu 142*
Brown, Elaine Teresa 1956- *WhoMW 93*
Brown, Eli Matthew 1923- *WhoAm 94*
Brown, Elisabeth Potts 1939- *WrDr 94*
Brown, Eliza d1896 *BlmGWL*
Brown, Elizabeth *DrAPF 93, Who 94*
Brown, Elizabeth Ann 1918- *WhoAm 94*
Brown, Elizabeth Brown 1753-1812 *BlmGWL*
Brown, Elizabeth Crichton *WhoAmP 93*
Brown, Elizabeth Eleanor 1921- *WhoScEn 94*
Brown, Elizabeth Ruth 1946- *WhoScEn 94*
Brown, Ella Mae *WhoHol 92*
Brown, Ellen Rochelle 1949- *WhoBlA 94*
Brown, Elliott Rowe 1955- *WhoScEn 94*
Brown, Ellsworth Howard 1943- *WhoAm 94*
Brown, Elona M. 1917- *WhoAmP 93*
Brown, Elvin J. 1922- *WhoAm 94*
Brown, Elzie Lee 1914- *WhoFI 94*
Brown, Emma Jean Mitchell 1939- *WhoBlA 94*
Brown, Emmett Earl 1932- *WhoBlA 94*
Brown, Ephraim Taylor, Jr. 1920- *WhoAm 94*
Brown, Eric 1960- *EncSF 93*
Brown, Eric 1965- *WhoHol 92*
Brown, Eric Herbert 1922- *Who 94*
Brown, Eric Melrose 1919- *Who 94*
Brown, Eric Vandyke, Jr. 1940- *WhoAm 94*
Brown, Esther Lucile 1920-1990 *WhAm 10*
Brown, Eugene Francis 1940- *WhoScEn 94*
Brown, Eula Mae Bruce 1909- *WhoFI 94*
Brown, Evelyn 1930- *WhoBlA 94*
Brown, Evelyn Drewery 1935- *WhoBlA 94*
Brown, Everett d1953 *WhoHol 92*
Brown, Everett W. 1912- *WhoAmP 93*
Brown, Ewart F., Jr. 1946- *WhoBlA 94*
Brown, Faith Gideon 1942- *WhoFI 94*
Brown, Fannie E. Garrett 1924- *WhoBlA 94*
Brown, Firman Hewitt, Jr. 1926- *WhoAm 94*
Brown, Floyd A. 1930- *WhoBlA 94*
Brown, Frances Susan 1956- *WhoScEn 94*
Brown, Franchot A. 1943- *WhoBlA 94*
Brown, Francis Cabell, Jr. 1936- *WhoAm 94*
Brown, Francis Robert 1914- *WhoAm 94*
Brown, Frank 1935- *WhoAm 94, WhoBlA 94*
Brown, Frank Beverly, IV 1945- *WhoAmL 94*
Brown, Frank Eugene, Jr. 1941- *WhoAm 94*
Brown, Frank London 1927-1962 *BlkWr 2, ConAu 141*
Brown, Frankie Mae 1953- *WhoMW 93*
Brown, Fred 1925- *IntWW 93, Who 94*
Brown, Fred 1948- *BasBi*
Brown, Fred Elmore 1913- *WhoAm 94*
Brown, Freddiemae Eugenia 1928- *WhoBlA 94*
Brown, Frederic Emil 1943- *WhoAmP 93*
Brown, Frederic Joseph 1934- *WhoAm 94*
Brown, Frederic Milton 1946- *WhoAmP 93*
Brown, Frederick 1948- *WhoAmL 94*
Brown, Frederick Calvin 1924- *WhoAm 94, WhoFI 94, WhoWest 94*
Brown, Frederick Douglas 1929- *WhoFI 94*
Brown, Frederick G. 1932- *WrDr 94*
Brown, Frederick Gramm 1932- *WhoAm 94*
Brown, Frederick H. 1927- *WhoIns 94*
Brown, Frederick Harold 1927- *WhoAm 94, WhoFI 94*
Brown, Frederick James 1927- *WhoAm 94, WhoFI 94*
Brown, Frederick James 1945- *WhoAmA 93*
Brown, Frederick Lee 1940- *WhoAm 94, WhoMW 93*
Brown, Frederick Raymond 1912- *WhoFI 94*
Brown, Frederick Wilhelm 1955- *WhoFI 94*
Brown, Fredric (William) 1906-1972 *EncSF 93*
Brown, Freezell, Jr. 1957- *WhoMW 93*
Brown, G. Steven 1947- *WhoAmP 93*
Brown, Gail 1943- *WhoHol 92*
Brown, Garrett Edward, Jr. 1943- *WhoAm 94, WhoAmL 94*
Brown, Garrett M. *WhoHol 92*
Brown, Gary Elson 1948- *WhoAmL 94*
Brown, Gary Hugh 1941- *WhoAmA 93*
Brown, Gary Ross 1947- *WhoAm 94, WhoAmL 94, WhoWest 94*
Brown, Gary Sandy 1940- *WhoAm 94*
Brown, Gary W. 1944- *WhoBlA 94*
Brown, Gary Wayne 1942- *WhoAm 94, WhoAmL 94*
Brown, Gates 1939- *WhoBlA 94*
Brown, Gavin 1942- *IntWW 93*
Brown, Gay West 1953- *WhoWest 94*
Brown, Gene W. 1936- *WhoAm 94*
Brown, Geoffrey E. *Who 94*
Brown, Geoffrey Harold 1930- *Who 94*
Brown, Geoffrey Robert C. *Who 94*
Brown, Georg Stanford 1943- *IntMPA 94, WhoHol 92*
Brown, George (Noel) 1942- *Who 94*
Brown, George Arthur d1993 *NewYTBS 93*
Brown, George Arthur 1922- *Who 94*
Brown, George E., Jr. 1920- *CngDr 93*
Brown, (Cedric Wilfred) George E. *Who 94*
Brown, George Edward, Jr. 1920- *WhoAm 94, WhoAmP 93, WhoScEn 94, WhoWest 94*
Brown, George F. 1922- *WhoAmP 93*
Brown, George Frame d1979 *WhoHol 92*
Brown, George Frederick William d1991 *Who 94N*
Brown, George Hardin 1931- *WhoWest 94*
Brown, George Hay 1910- *WhoAm 94*
Brown, George Henry, Jr. 1939- *WhoBlA 94*
Brown, George Houston 1916- *WhoBlA 94*
Brown, George L. 1926- *WhoBlA 94*
Brown, George Leslie 1926- *WhoAm 94*
Brown, George Mackay 1921- *DcLB 139 [port], RfGShF, Who 94, WrDr 94*
Brown, George Milton 1948- *WhoAmP 93*
Brown, George Philip 1920- *WhoBlA 94*
Brown, George Stephen 1945- *WhoAm 94, WhoWest 94*
Brown, George William 1930- *Who 94*
Brown, Georgia 1933- *WhoHol 92*
Brown, Georgia 1933-1992 *AnObit 1992*
Brown, Georgia L. 1948- *WhoHisp 94*
Brown, Georgia R. d1993 *WhoBlA 94N*
Brown, Georgia W. 1934- *WhoBlA 94*
Brown, Georgia Watts 1934- *WhoAm 94*
Brown, Gerald Curtis 1942- *WhoAm 94*
Brown, Gerald Edward 1926- *WhoScEn 94*
Brown, Geraldine 1945- *WhoScEn 94*
Brown, Geraldine Reed 1947- *WhoAm 94*
Brown, Gerviece Hortense 1940- *WhoAm 94*
Brown, Gilbert David, III 1949- *WhoBlA 94*
Brown, Giles Tyler 1916- *WhoAm 94*
Brown, Gillian *WhoAmA 93*
Brown, Gillian 1937- *Who 94*
Brown, Gillian (Gerda) 1923- *Who 94*
Brown, Glen *DrAPF 93*
Brown, Glenn Arthur 1953- *WhoBlA 94*
Brown, Glenn E. 1943- *WhoAmP 93*
Brown, Glenn Robbins, Jr. 1930- *WhoAm 94*
Brown, Glenn Willard 1918- *WhoBlA 94*
Brown, Glenn William, Jr. 1955- *WhoAm 94, WhoAmL 94, WhoFI 94*
Brown, Gloria Campos 1954- *WhoHisp 94*
Brown, Godfrey Norman 1926- *Who 94*
Brown, Gordon *Who 94, WhoAmP 93*
Brown, (James) Gordon 1951- *IntWW 93, Who 94*
Brown, Gordon Marshall 1934- *WhoMW 93*
Brown, Gordon Stewart 1936- *WhoAm 94*
Brown, Gordon William 1928- *WhoAmL 94*
Brown, Grady 1944- *WhoAmP 93*
Brown, Grant C. *WhoAmP 93*
Brown, Greggory Lee 1953- *WhoBlA 94*
Brown, Gregory K. 1951- *WhoAm 94, WhoAmL 94*
Brown, Gregory Michael 1934- *WhoAm 94*
Brown, Gregory Neil 1938- *WhoAm 94*
Brown, H. Douglas 1941- *WhoWest 94*
Brown, H. Emmett 1897- *WhAm 10*
Brown, H. Jackson, Jr. 1940- *ConAu 140*
Brown, H(oward) Mayer d1993 *Who 94N*
Brown, H. Rap 1943- *HisWorL [port], WhoBlA 94*
Brown, H. Rap (Jamil Abdullah Al-Amin) 1943- *AfrAmAl 6 [port]*
Brown, H. William 1933- *WhoScEn 94, WhoWest 94*
Brown, H. William 1938- *WhoAm 94*
Brown, Hal M. 1942- *WhoAmL 94*
Brown, Halbert d1942 *WhoHol 92*
Brown, Hank 1940- *CngDr 93, IntWW 93, WhoAm 94, WhoAmP 93, WhoWest 94*
Brown, Hannah M. 1939- *WhoBlA 94*
Brown, Harcourt 1900-1990 *ConAu 141*
Brown, Harold 1927- *IntWW 93, Who 94, WhoAm 94, WhoAmP 93, WhoScEn 94*
Brown, Harold Arthur Neville 1914- *Who 94*
Brown, Harold C., Jr. 1932- *WhoAmP 93*
Brown, Harold James 1911- *Who 94*
Brown, Harold MacVane 1940- *WhoAm 94, WhoAmL 94*
Brown, Harriet *DrAPF 93, WhoAmP 93*
Brown, Harriett Baltimore 1911- *WhoBlA 94*
Brown, Harris Robert 1950- *WhoFI 94*
Brown, Harrison (Scott) 1917-1986 *EncSF 93*
Brown, Harry d1966 *WhoHol 92*
Brown, Harry Joe 1892-1972 *IntDcF 2-4*
Brown, Harry Lester 1924- *WhoWest 94*
Brown, Hazel Evelyn 1940- *WhoBlA 94*
Brown, Headley Adolphus *IntWW 93*
Brown, Helen Avis 1934- *WhoAmP 93*
Brown, Helen Bennett 1902- *WhoAm 94*
Brown, Helen Gurley *IntWW 93, NewYTBS 93 [port]*
Brown, Helen Gurley 1922- *AmSocL [port], WhoAm 94, WrDr 94*
Brown, Helen W. d1974 *WhoHol 92*
Brown, Henry 1907- *WhoScEn 94*
Brown, Henry Bedinger Rust 1926- *WhoAm 94*
Brown, Henry E., Jr. 1935- *WhoAmP 93*
Brown, Henry H. *WhoBlA 94*
Brown, Henry Phelps *Who 94*
Brown, (Ernest) Henry Phelps 1906- *IntWW 93, Who 94*
Brown, (Ernest) Henry Phelps, Sir 1906- *WrDr 94*
Brown, Henry Thomas C. *Who 94*
Brown, Herbert C. 1912- *WrDr 94*
Brown, Herbert Charles 1912- *IntWW 93, Who 94, WhoAm 94, WhoMW 93, WhoScEn 94*
Brown, Herbert R. 1940- *WhoBlA 94*
Brown, Herbert Russell 1931- *WhoAm 94, WhoAmL 94, WhoAmP 93*
Brown, Herman 1922- *WhoBlA 94*
Brown, Herman Cubbage 1925- *WhoAmP 93*
Brown, Hermione Kopp 1915- *WhoAm 94, WhoAmL 94, WhoWest 94*
Brown, Herschel J. d1993 *NewYTBS 93*
Brown, Hezekiah 1923- *WhoBlA 94*
Brown, Hilton 1938- *WhoAmA 93*
Brown, Himan 1910- *IntMPA 94*
Brown, Hobson *WhoAm 94, WhoFI 94*
Brown, Hobson, Jr. 1942- *WhoAm 94, WhoFI 94*
Brown, Horace d1972 *WhoHol 92*
Brown, Howard Bernard 1924- *WhoAm 94*
Brown, Howard C. 1921- *WhoAm 94*
Brown, Howard Mayer d1993 *NewYTBS 93*
Brown, Howard Mayer 1930- *NewGrDO, WrDr 94*
Brown, Howard Mayer 1930-1993 *ConAu 140*
Brown, Howard V(achel) 1878-1945 *EncSF 93*
Brown, Hoyt C. 1920- *WhoBlA 94*
Brown, Hubie 1933- *BasBi*
Brown, Hugh Dunbar 1919- *Who 94*
Brown, Ian James Morris 1945- *Who 94*
Brown, Idalyn Stoll *WhoWest 94*
Brown, Iona 1941- *WhoAm 94, WhoWest 94*
Brown, Ira Bernard 1927- *WhoFI 94, WhoScEn 94*
Brown, Irma Hunter 1939- *WhoAmP 93*
Brown, Irma Jean 1948- *WhoBlA 94*
Brown, J. Calvin 1896- *WhAm 10*
Brown, J. E. 1940- *WhoAmP 93*
Brown, J. Martin 1941- *WhoScEn 94*
Brown, J(oseph) P(aul) S(ummers) 1930- *WrDr 94*
Brown, J. W. *DrAPF 93*
Brown, J. Willcox 1915- *WhoAmP 93*
Brown, Jack 1927- *WhoAm 94*
Brown, Jack A. *WhoAmP 93*
Brown, Jack Chapler 1919- *WhoAmL 94*
Brown, Jack Cole 1930- *WhoAm 94*
Brown, Jack Delbert 1954- *WhoWest 94*
Brown, Jack Edward 1927- *WhoAm 94*
Brown, Jack Ernest 1914- *WhoAm 94*
Brown, Jack H. 1939- *WhoAm 94, WhoWest 94*
Brown, Jack Harold Upton 1918- *WhoAm 94, WhoScEn 94*
Brown, Jack Wyman 1922- *WhoAm 94*
Brown, Jacqueline D. 1957- *WhoBlA 94*
Brown, James *DrAPF 93, WhoAmA 93*
Brown, James 1920- *WhoHol 92*
Brown, James 1925- *Who 94*
Brown, James 1928- *IntWW 93, Who 94, WhoAm 94*
Brown, James 1933- *AfrAmAl 6 [port], WhoHol 92*
Brown, James 1934- *WhoBlA 94*
Brown, James Alexander 1914- *Who 94*
Brown, James Allison 1934- *WhoMW 93, WhoScEn 94*
Brown, James Andrew 1914- *WhoAm 94*
Brown, James Barrow 1932- *WhoAm 94*
Brown, James Benton 1945- *WhoAmL 94*

Brown, James Briggs 1922- WhoAm 94
Brown, James Bruce 1964- WhoFI 94
Brown, James C. 1936- WhoAmP 93
Brown, James Carrington, III 1939- WhoWest 94
Brown, James Chandler 1947- WhoWest 94
Brown, James Channing 1944- WhoFI 94
Brown, James Cooke 1921- EncSF 93, WhoWest 94
Brown, James Douglas 1934- WhoScEn 94
Brown, James E. 1923- WhoBlA 94
Brown, James Edward 1939- WhoAmP 93
Brown, James Elliott 1947- WhoAmL 94
Brown, James Eugene, III 1942- WhoScEn 94
Brown, James Gerard, Jr. 1946- WhoMW 93
Brown, James H. 1935- WhoBlA 94
Brown, James H., Jr. 1940- WhoAm 94
Brown, James Harold 1961- WhoWest 94
Brown, James Harry 1941- WhoMW 93
Brown, James Harvey 1924- WhoBlA 94
Brown, James Harvey 1936- WhoAm 94, WhoScEn 94
Brown, James Harvey 1940- WhoAmP 93
Brown, James Hyatt 1937- WhoAmP 93
Brown, James I. 1908- WrDr 94
Brown, James Jeffrey 1960- WhoAmL 94
Brown, James Joseph 1928- WhoAm 94
Brown, James K. 1942- WhoAmL 94
Brown, James Kenneth 1937- WhoScEn 94
Brown, James Knight 1929- WhoAm 94, WhoAmL 94
Brown, James Marion 1952- WhoBlA 94
Brown, James Marston 1950- WhoAmL 94
Brown, James Monroe 1928- WhoAmP 93, WhoBlA 94
Brown, James Monroe, III 1917- WhoAm 94, WhoAmA 93
Brown, James Montgomery 1921- WhoMW 93
Brown, James Robert 1930- WhoAm 94
Brown, James Scott 1945- WhoAmL 94
Brown, James Shelly 1945- WhoAm 94, WhoAmL 94
Brown, James Thompson, Jr. 1935- WhoAm 94, WhoFI 94
Brown, James Ward 1934- WhoAm 94, WhoMW 93
Brown, James William 1944- WhoFI 94
Brown, J'Amy Maroney 1945- WhoWest 94
Brown, Jan W. 1942- WhoAmP 93
Brown, Jane G. 1941- WhoAm 94
Brown, Janet WhoHol 92
Brown, Janet McNalley 1960- WhoFI 94
Brown, Janice 1935- WhoWest 94
Brown, Jared WhoAm 94
Brown, Jared Allen 1936- ConAu 142
Brown, Jarvis Ardel 1967- WhoBlA 94
Brown, Jason Walter 1938- WhoAm 94, WhoScEn 94
Brown, Jasper C., Jr. 1946- WhoBlA 94
Brown, Jay Norman 1956- WhoMW 93
Brown, Jay Wright 1945- WhoAm 94, WhoFI 94, WhoScEn 94
Brown, Jean Bodfish d1993 NewYTBS 93
Brown, Jean Rae 1956- WhoAmL 94
Brown, Jean William 1928- WhoAm 94
Brown, Jeffrey Douglas 1951- WhoMW 93
Brown, Jeffrey LeMonte 1961- WhoBlA 94
Brown, Jeffrey M. 1962- WhoAmP 93
Brown, Jeffrey Monet 1953- WhoAmL 94
Brown, Jennifer S. H. 1940- WrDr 94
Brown, Jeremy Earle 1946- WhoAm 94, WhoFI 94
Brown, Jeremy James 1954- WhoIns 94
Brown, Jerome 1965-1992 WhoBlA 94N
Brown, Jerrold Stanley 1953- WhoAmL 94
Brown, Jerry Who 94
Brown, Jerry 1938- WhoAm 94, WhoWest 94
Brown, Jerry Anthony 1939- WhoMW 93
Brown, Jerry Earl 1940- EncSF 93
Brown, Jerry Milford 1938- WhoScEn 94
Brown, Jerry William 1925- WhoAm 94
Brown, Jesse IntWW 93, WhoBlA 94
Brown, Jesse 1944- CngDr 93, ConBlB 6 [port], CurBio 93 [port], WhoAmP 93
Brown, Jesse L. 1926-1950 AfrAmAl 6
Brown, Jewelle Harbin 1921- WhoAmP 93
Brown, Jim ProFbHF [port]
Brown, Jim 1935- WhoHol 92
Brown, Jim 1936- AfrAmAl 6, IntMPA 94, WhoAm 94, WhoBlA 94
Brown, Joan P. WhoBlA 94
Brown, Joe 1930- Who 94
Brown, Joe 1932- WhoAmP 93
Brown, Joe 1941- WhoHol 92
Brown, Joe, Jr. WhoHol 92
Brown, Joe Blackburn 1940- WhoAm 94, WhoAmL 94
Brown, Joe E. d1973 WhoHol 92
Brown, Joe E. 1892-1973 WhoCom
Brown, Joe Ellis 1933- WhoAmP 93
Brown, Joeanna Hurston 1939- WhoBlA 94
Brown, Joel W. 1964- WhoAmP 93
Brown, John d1957 WhoHol 92
Brown, John fl. 1480-1500 DcNaB MP
Brown, John 1736-1803 WhAmRev
Brown, John 1744-1780 WhAmRev
Brown, John 1800-1859 AmSocL [port], HisWorL [port]
Brown, John 1826-1883 DcNaB MP
Brown, John 1923- Who 94
Brown, John 1931- Who 94
Brown, John (Douglas Keith) 1913- Who 94
Brown, John (Gilbert Newton) 1916- Who 94
Brown, John Allin 1947- WhoMW 93
Brown, John Andrew 1945- WhoBlA 94
Brown, John B. Who 94
Brown, John Baker, Jr. 1947- WhoBlA 94
Brown, John C. 1921- WhoIns 94
Brown, John C. 1952- WhoAmP 93
Brown, John C., Jr. 1939- WhoBlA 94
Brown, John Canvin 1938- IntWW 93
Brown, John Carter 1934- WhoAm 94, WhoAmA 93
Brown, John David 1957- WhoScEn 94
Brown, John E. 1948- WhoBlA 94
Brown, John Edward Who 94
Brown, John Edward 1936- WhoAm 94
Brown, John Edward 1939- WhoAm 94, WhoMW 93
Brown, John Fred 1941- WhoAm 94, WhoFI 94
Brown, John Gilbert Newton 1916- IntWW 93
Brown, John Hall 1910- WhoAmA 93
Brown, John Hampton 1945- WhoAm 94
Brown, John J. 1946- WhoMW 93
Brown, John Joseph 1931- IntWW 93
Brown, John L. 1952- WhoAmP 93
Brown, John Lawrence, Jr. 1925- WhoAm 94
Brown, John Lott 1924- WhoAm 94
Brown, John M. 1924- WhoFI 94
Brown, John MacMillan EncSF 93
Brown, John Mitchell, Sr. 1929- AfrAmG, WhoBlA 94
Brown, John Moulder 1931- WhoHol 92
Brown, John O. 1934- WhoAm 94, WhoMW 93
Brown, John Ollis 1922- WhoBlA 94
Brown, John Ollis Langford, Jr. 1946- WhoWest 94
Brown, John Patrick 1925- WhoAm 94
Brown, John R. d1993 NewYTBS 93
Brown, John Robert 1935- WhoFI 94
Brown, John Robert 1943- WhoMW 93
Brown, John Robert 1947- WhoAm 94
Brown, John Robert 1948- WhoAmL 94
Brown, John Russell 1923- Who 94, WrDr 94
Brown, John Scott 1930- WhoBlA 94
Brown, John Thomas 1948- WhoAmL 94
Brown, John Walter 1918- WhoAmP 93
Brown, John Walter 1939- WhoAmP 93
Brown, John William 1913- WhoAmP 93
Brown, John William 1922- WhoFI 94
Brown, John Y., Jr. 1933- WhoAmP 93
Brown, John Young EncSF 93
Brown, Johnny WhoHol 92
Brown, Johnny Mac WhoBlA 94
Brown, Johnny Mack WhoMW 93
Brown, Johnny Mack d1974 WhoHol 92
Brown, Jonathan 1939- WhoAm 94, WhoAmA 93
Brown, Jonathan (Mayer) 1939- WrDr 94
Brown, Jophery Clifford WhoHol 92
Brown, Joseph 1733-1785 WhAmRev
Brown, Joseph 1909- WhoAmA 93N
Brown, Joseph A. 1926- WhoAm 94
Brown, Joseph Clifton 1908- WhoBlA 94
Brown, Joseph Davidson, Sr. 1929- WhoBlA 94
Brown, Joseph E. 1951- WhoAmP 93
Brown, Joseph Gordon 1927- WhoAm 94
Brown, Joseph L. d1982 WhoHol 92
Brown, Joseph Lawler 1921- Who 94
Brown, Joseph Lee 1959- WhoAmL 94
Brown, Joseph Samuel 1943- WhoBlA 94
Brown, Josephine d1976 WhoHol 92
Brown, Joyce 1937- WhoBlA 94
Brown, Joyce F. 1946- WhoBlA 94
Brown, Judith Anne 1941- WhoAmL 94
Brown, Judith C(ora) WrDr 94
Brown, Judith Gwyn 1933-1992 WhoAmA 93N
Brown, Judith Margaret 1944- Who 94
Brown, Judith Olans 1941- WhoAm 94
Brown, Judy WhoHol 92
Brown, Julie 1949- WhoAsA 94
Brown, Julie 1958- WhoHol 92
Brown, Julie M. 1935- WhoAmP 93
Brown, Julius J. 1907- WhoBlA 94
Brown, Julius Ray 1940- WhoBlA 94
Brown, June 1923- WhoAm 94
Brown, June Gibbs 1933- WhoAm 94, WhoAmP 93
Brown, June Gottlieb 1932- WhoAmA 93
Brown, June P. Who 94
Brown, Jurutha 1950- WhoBlA 94
Brown, Justine Thomas 1938- WhoBlA 94
Brown, Karen F. 1951- WhoBlA 94
Brown, Karen Howard 1945- WhoMW 93
Brown, Karen Kennedy 1947- WhoAm 94, WhoAmL 94
Brown, Karen M. 1954- WhoMW 93
Brown, Karl 1895- WhAm 10
Brown, Karl 1897-1990 IntDcF 2-4
Brown, Kate 1960- WhoAmP 93
Brown, Kathie 1947- WhoMW 93
Brown, Kathleen WhoAm 94, WhoAmP 93, WhoWest 94
Brown, Kathleen 1945- NewYTBS 93 [port]
Brown, Kay 1948- WhoAmP 93
Brown, Kay 1950- WhoAmP 93
Brown, Keith 1933- WhoAm 94
Brown, Keith 1943- WhoFI 94
Brown, Keith Lapham 1925- WhoAm 94, WhoAmP 93, WhoWest 94
Brown, Kelly d1981 WhoHol 92
Brown, Kenneth C. 1923- WhoAmP 93
Brown, Kenneth Charles 1952- WhoAm 94, WhoFI 94
Brown, Kenneth Edward 1946- WhoBlA 94
Brown, Kenneth Gerald 1944- WhoScEn 94
Brown, Kenneth H. DrAPF 93
Brown, Kenneth H. 1936- ConDr 93, WrDr 94
Brown, Kenneth L. 1936- WhoAm 94
Brown, Kenneth Lee 1933- WhoMW 93
Brown, Kenneth Lee 1936- WhoAmP 93
Brown, Kenneth Lloyd 1927- WhoAm 94
Brown, Kenneth Ray 1936- WhoAm 94
Brown, Kenneth Russell 1939- WhoMW 93
Brown, Kenneth S. 1917- WhoBlA 94
Brown, Kent Louis, Sr. 1916- WhoAm 94
Brown, Kent Louis, Jr. 1943- WhoAm 94
Brown, Kent Newville 1944- WhoAm 94
Brown, Kermit 1939- WhoHol 92
Brown, Kevin 1959- WhoAmP 93
Brown, Kevin 1965- WhoAm 94
Brown, Kevin Michael 1948- WhoFI 94
Brown, Kimberly Ann 1964- WhoAmL 94
Brown, Kris Harold 1954- WhoMW 93
Brown, L. Ed 1937- WhoAmP 93
Brown, L(ionel) Neville 1923- Who 94
Brown, Lana M. 1954- WhoAmP 93
Brown, Lanita WhoBlA 94
Brown, LaRita Early Dawn Ma-Ka-Lani 1937- WhoFI 94
Brown, Larry 1940- BasBi [port]
Brown, Larry 1942- WhoAmA 93
Brown, (William) Larry 1951- WrDr 94
Brown, Larry T. 1947- WhoBlA 94
Brown, Laurence Ambrose 1907- Who 94
Brown, Laurence David 1926- WhoAm 94, WhoMW 93
Brown, Laurie Mark 1923- WhoAm 94, WhoMW 93
Brown, Lawrence d1972 WhoHol 92
Brown, Lawrence d1988 WhoHol 92
Brown, Lawrence Alan 1935- WhoMW 93
Brown, Lawrence E. 1947- WhoBlA 94
Brown, Lawrence Haas 1934- WhoAm 94
Brown, Lawrence Harvey 1940- WhoAm 94, WhoMW 93
Brown, Lawrence Michael 1936- IntWW 93, Who 94
Brown, Lawrence Raymond, Jr. 1928- WhoAm 94
Brown, Lawrie 1949- WhoAmA 93
Brown, Leander A. 1959- WhoBlA 94
Brown, Leanna 1935- WhoAmP 93, WhoWomW 91
Brown, Lee d1957 WhoHol 92
Brown, Lee P. WhoAmP 93
Brown, Lee Patrick 1937- WhoAm 94, WhoBlA 94
Brown, Leland 1914- WrDr 94
Brown, Leland R. 1928- WhoAmP 93
Brown, Leo C., Jr. 1942- WhoBlA 94
Brown, Leo Dale 1948- WhoScEn 94
Brown, Leon Carl 1928- WhoAm 94
Brown, LeRoy 1936- WhoBlA 94
Brown, Leroy Bradford 1929- WhoBlA 94
Brown, Leroy J. H. 1912- WhoBlA 94
Brown, LeRoy Ronald 1949- WhoBlA 94
Brown, Leroy Thomas 1922- WhoBlA 94
Brown, Les WhoBlA 94
Brown, Les 1912- WhoHol 92
Brown, Les 1926- WhoWest 94
Brown, Les 1928- WhoAm 94
Brown, Les 1945- ConBlB 5 [port]
Brown, Leslie 1902- Who 94
Brown, Leslie Edwin 1898- WhAm 10
Brown, Leslie F. Who 94
Brown, Leslie Wilfrid 1912- Who 94
Brown, Lester J. 1942- WhoBlA 94
Brown, Lester R. 1934- CurBio 93 [port], EnvEnc [port]
Brown, Lester R(ussell) 1934- WrDr 94
Brown, Lester Russell 1934- WhoAm 94
Brown, Lettie June 1927- WhoAmP 93
Brown, Lew WhoHol 92
Brown, Lewis Arnold 1931- WhoAm 94
Brown, Lewis Frank 1929- WhoAmL 94, WhoBlA 94, WhoWest 94
Brown, Lewis Nathan 1953- WhoAmL 94
Brown, Lewis W. 1921- WhoAmP 93
Brown, Lillian Eriksen 1921- WhoWest 94
Brown, Lillie Richard 1946- WhoBlA 94
Brown, Linda A. DrAPF 93
Brown, Linda Jenkins 1946- WhoBlA 94
Brown, Linda Joan 1941- WhoScEn 94
Brown, LindaJean DrAPF 93
Brown, Lisa Claire 1954- WhoAmL 94
Brown, Lisa J. WhoAmP 93
Brown, Llewellyn Don 1945- WhoBlA 94
Brown, Lloyd 1938- WhoBlA 94
Brown, Lloyd L(ouis) 1913- BlkWr 2
Brown, Lloyd Odom, Sr. 1928-1993 WhoBlA 94N
Brown, Lois Heffington 1940- WhoFI 94
Brown, Lomas, Jr. 1963- WhoAm 94, WhoBlA 94, WhoMW 93
Brown, Lorene Byron 1933- WhoAm 94
Brown, Loretta Ann Port 1945- WhoAm 94
Brown, Lori Lipman 1958- WhoAmP 93
Brown, Lorraine d1987 WhoHol 92
Brown, Louis WhoHol 92
Brown, Louis 1929- WhoScEn 94
Brown, Louis Morris 1909- WhoAm 94
Brown, Louis Sylvester 1930- WhoBlA 94
Brown, Lowell Severt 1934- WhoAm 94
Brown, Lucille M. WhoBlA 94
Brown, Lyn Mikel ConAu 140
Brown, Lyn Stephen 1952- WhoAm 94
Brown, Lynette Ralya 1926- WhoAm 94, WhoMW 93
Brown, Mabel Estle 1907- WhoMW 93
Brown, Majornetta Alexander 1962- WhoMW 93
Brown, Malcolm Who 94
Brown, (George) Malcolm 1925- IntWW 93, Who 94
Brown, Malcolm McCleod 1931- WhoBlA 94
Brown, Marc 1946- WrDr 94
Brown, Marcia 1918- WrDr 94
Brown, Marcia Joan 1918- WhoAm 94
Brown, Margaret 1867- BlmGWL
Brown, Margaret 1910-1952 WhoAmA 93N
Brown, Margaret A. 1954- WhoAmL 94
Brown, Margaret Ruth Anderson 1944- WhoAmP 93
Brown, Margery (Wheeler) BlkWr 2
Brown, Margery Wheeler WhoBlA 94
Brown, Marion B. 1913- WhoAmA 93
Brown, Marion Lipscomb, Jr. 1925- WhoAm 94
Brown, Mark Ransom 1959- WhoFI 94
Brown, Mark S. 1951- WhoAmP 93
Brown, Mark Steven 1955- WhoScEn 94, WhoWest 94
Brown, Mark Terrill 1953- WhoWest 94
Brown, Mark Thomas 1956- WhoWest 94
Brown, Marsha J. 1949- WhoBlA 94
Brown, Marshall Carson 1918- WhoBlA 94
Brown, Martha Taylor 1922- WhoAmP 93
Brown, Martin 1949- Who 94
Brown, Martin Christopher 1951- WhoAmP 93
Brown, Martin Parks 1914- WhAm 10
Brown, Martin Raymond 1954- WhoAm 94
Brown, Martin Robert 1959- WhoAmL 94
Brown, Marva Y. 1936- WhoBlA 94
Brown, Marvin Lee 1926- WhoScEn 94
Brown, Marvin S. 1935- WhoAm 94
Brown, Mary Boykin 1942- WhoBlA 94
Brown, Mary C. 1935- WhoAmP 93, WhoMW 93
Brown, Mary Carolyn 1934- WhoAmP 93
Brown, Mary Eleanor 1906- WhoAm 94
Brown, Mary Elizabeth 1932- WhoBlA 94
Brown, Mary Ellen 1939- ConAu 41NR
Brown, Mary Helen 1958- WhoWest 94
Brown, Mary Katherine 1948- WhoBlA 94
Brown, Mary Lee 1923- WhoBlA 94
Brown, Mary Rachel WhoAmA 93
Brown, Mary SuAnn 1942- WhoMW 93
Brown, Mary Ward 1917- WrDr 94
Brown, Mason C. 1945- WhoAmL 94
Brown, Matthew 1905- WhoAm 94
Brown, Mattie R. 1901- WhoBlA 94
Brown, Max Who 94
Brown, Maxine J. Childress 1943- WhoBlA 94
Brown, (Cyril) Maxwell Palmer 1914- Who 94
Brown, Melville d1938 WhoHol 92
Brown, Melvin Edward DrAPF 93

Brown, Melvin F. 1935- *WhoAm 94, WhoFI 94*
Brown, Melvin R. 1938- *WhoAmP 93*
Brown, Meredith M. 1940- *WhoAm 94*
Brown, Merle *WhoAmP 93*
Brown, Merlyn Louis 1954- *WhoAmP 93*
Brown, Mervyn 1923- *Who 94*
Brown, Merwin L. 1944- *WhoWest 94*
Brown, Michael *Who 94*
Brown, Michael d1993 *Who 94N*
Brown, Michael 1943- *WhoAm 94*
Brown, (John) Michael 1929- *Who 94*
Brown, Michael Arthur 1938- *WhoAm 94, WhoAmL 94*
Brown, Michael David 1948- *WhoWest 94*
Brown, Michael Dean 1955- *WhoMW 93*
Brown, Michael DeWayne 1954- *WhoAmL 94, WhoBlA 94, WhoWest 94*
Brown, Michael Douglas 1948- *WrDr 94*
Brown, Michael Eugene 1952- *WhoAmL 94*
Brown, Michael F(obes) 1950- *ConAu 142*
Brown, Michael John Douglas 1936- *Who 94*
Brown, Michael L. 1958- *WhoMW 93*
Brown, Michael Neil 1946- *WhoAmL 94*
Brown, Michael R. 1938- *WhoAm 94, WhoAmL 94*
Brown, Michael Rene Warneford 1915- *Who 94*
Brown, Michael Richard 1959- *WhoMW 93*
Brown, Michael Robert 1960- *WhoFI 94*
Brown, Michael Russell 1951- *Who 94*
Brown, Michael Stuart 1941- *IntWW 93, Who 94, WhoAm 94, WhoScEn 94*
Brown, Mike *WhoAm 94, WhoMW 93*
Brown, Milbert Orlando 1956- *WhoBlA 94*
Brown, Milton F. 1943- *WhoBlA 94*
Brown, Milton Wolf 1911- *WhoAm 94, WhoAmA 93*
Brown, Mitch *WhoHol 92*
Brown, Montague 1931- *WhoAm 94*
Brown, Montforte *WhAmRev*
Brown, Morgan d1961 *WhoHol 92*
Brown, Morgan Cornelius 1916- *WhoBlA 94*
Brown, Morris 1928- *WhoAm 94*
Brown, Morris Jonathan 1951- *Who 94*
Brown, Morse L. 1943- *WhoBlA 94*
Brown, Mortimer 1924- *WhoBlA 94*
Brown, Morton B. 1941- *WhoAm 94*
Brown, Morton Paul 1937- *WhoAm 94, WhoAmL 94*
Brown, Moses 1738-1836 *WhAmRev*
Brown, Murray 1929- *WrDr 94*
Brown, Naaman d1988 *WhoHol 92*
Brown, Nacio Herb 1896-1964 *IntDcF 2-4*
Brown, Nancy Cofield 1932- *WhoBlA 94*
Brown, Nancy Diane 1961- *WhoWest 94*
Brown, Nancy J. 1942- *WhoMW 93*
Brown, Nancy Joyce 1942- *WhoAmP 93, WhoWomW 91*
Brown, Nancy McIntire 1965- *WhoMW 93*
Brown, Neal Mullan 1959- *WhoAmL 94*
Brown, Nicholas 1729-1791 *WhAmRev*
Brown, Nicholas 1932- *WhoAm 94*
Brown, Nicholas Hugh 1950- *Who 94*
Brown, Noah, Jr. 1925- *WhoBlA 94*
Brown, Norman A. 1938- *WhoAm 94*
Brown, Norman Donald 1935- *WhoAm 94*
Brown, Norman E. 1935- *WhoBlA 94*
Brown, Norman Jack 1934- *WhoAmL 94*
Brown, Norman James 1942- *WhoFI 94*
Brown, Norman Wesley 1931- *IntWW 93, WhoFI 94*
Brown, Ola M. 1941- *WhoBlA 94*
Brown, Olen Ray 1935- *WhoAm 94, WhoMW 93, WhoScEn 94*
Brown, Olivia *WhoBlA 94, WhoHol 92*
Brown, Ollie Dawkins 1941- *WhoAm 94*
Brown, Omer Forrest, II 1947- *WhoAm 94, WhoAmL 94*
Brown, Oral Lee 1945- *WhoBlA 94*
Brown, Oscar, Jr. 1926- *WhoAm 94*
Brown, Otha N., Jr. 1931- *WhoBlA 94*
Brown, Otha Nathaniel, Jr. 1931- *WhoAmP 93*
Brown, Owsley, II 1942- *WhoAm 94*
Brown, Palmer 1919- *WrDr 94*
Brown, Pamela d1975 *WhoHol 92*
Brown, Pamela Wedd 1928- *WhoAmA 93*
Brown, Pat Crawford *WhoHol 92*
Brown, Patricia *Who 94*
Brown, (Marion) Patricia 1927- *Who 94*
Brown, Patricia Anne 1947- *WhoWest 94*
Brown, Patricia B. 1939- *WhoAmP 93*
Brown, Patricia Fortini 1936- *WrDr 94*
Brown, Patricia Griffith 1953- *WhoAmL 94*
Brown, Patricia Irene *WhoAmL 94*
Brown, Patricia Lynn 1954- *WhoWest 94*
Brown, Patricia Mary 1945- *WhoFI 94, WhoMW 93*
Brown, Patricia Memingwa 1946- *WhoMW 93*
Brown, Patrick *Who 94*
Brown, (Austen) Patrick 1940- *Who 94*
Brown, Paul d1991 *ProFbHF [port]*
Brown, Paul 1893-1958 *WhoAmA 93N*
Brown, Paul 1908-1991 *WhAm 10*
Brown, Paul, Jr. 1926- *WhoBlA 94*
Brown, Paul A. 1938- *WhoAm 94*
Brown, Paul B. 1942- *WhoScEn 94*
Brown, Paul Bradley 1912- *WhoAm 94*
Brown, Paul D. 1901- *WhoBlA 94*
Brown, Paul E. X. 1910- *WhoBlA 94*
Brown, Paul Edmondson 1915- *WhoAmL 94, WhoMW 93*
Brown, Paul Fremont 1921- *WhoWest 94*
Brown, Paul G. 1942- *Who 94*
Brown, Paul Handy 1948- *WhoAmL 94*
Brown, Paul Howard 1906-1990 *WhAm 10*
Brown, Paul L. 1919- *WhoBlA 94*
Brown, Paul Leighton 1959- *WhoScEn 94*
Brown, Paul M. 1938- *WhoAm 94*
Brown, Paul Meredith 1954- *WhoAmL 94*
Brown, Paul Neeley 1926- *WhoAm 94, WhoAmL 94*
Brown, Paul Neil 1942- *WhoAmP 93*
Brown, Paul Sherman 1921- *WhoAmL 94, WhoMW 93*
Brown, Paul W. 1915- *WhoAm 94*
Brown, Paul Wayne 1944- *WhoMW 93*
Brown, Paula Evie *WhoBlA 94*
Brown, Paulette 1951- *WhoAm 94*
Brown, Peggy Ann 1934- *WhoAmA 93*
Brown, Peter 1935- *WhoHol 92*
Brown, (Albert) Peter (Graeme) d1993 *Who 94N*
Brown, Peter (Robert Lamont) 1935- *WrDr 94*
Brown, Peter C. 1940- *WhoAmA 93*
Brown, Peter C(urrell) 1940?- *EncSF 93*
Brown, Peter Douglas 1925- *WrDr 94*
Brown, Peter Duke 1948- *WhoAm 94*
Brown, Peter Gilbert 1940- *WhoAm 94*
Brown, Peter Harrison 1943- *WhoWest 94*
Brown, Peter Megargee 1922- *WhoAm 94, WhoAmL 94*
Brown, Peter Robert *WhoAm 94*
Brown, Peter Robert Lamont 1935- *Who 94*
Brown, Peter Stewart 1951- *WhoAm 94*
Brown, Peter Thomson 1948- *WhoAmA 93*
Brown, Peter W. 1944- *WhoAm 94, WhoAmL 94*
Brown, Peter Wilfred Henry 1941- *Who 94*
Brown, Phil d1973 *WhoHol 92*
Brown, Philip Albert 1949- *WhoAm 94, WhoAmL 94*
Brown, Philip Anthony Russell 1924- *Who 94*
Brown, Philip Carlton 1947- *WhoMW 93*
Brown, Philip Edward 1952- *WhoMW 93*
Brown, Philip Rayfield, III 1917- *WhoBlA 94*
Brown, Phillip Edward 1927- *WhoAmL 94*
Brown, Polly Sarah 1952- *WhoWest 94*
Brown, Preston 1936- *WhoAm 94*
Brown, Priscilla 1957- *WhoBlA 94*
Brown, Quincalee 1939- *WhoAm 94*
Brown, R.E. 1944- *WhoFI 94*
Brown, R(ichard) H(arvey) 1940- *WrDr 94*
Brown, Rachel 1898- *WorScD*
Brown, Ralph d1990 *WhoHol 92*
Brown, Ralph 1928- *Who 94*
Brown, Ralph 1931- *Who 94*
Brown, Ralph H. 1919- *WhoBlA 94*
Brown, Ralph Kilner 1909- *Who 94*
Brown, Ralph R. 1944- *WhoAmP 93*
Brown, Ralph Sawyer, Jr. 1931- *WhoAm 94*
Brown, Randall Emory 1917- *WhoWest 94*
Brown, Randy 1968- *WhoBlA 94*
Brown, Randy Lee 1963- *WhoScEn 94, WhoWest 94*
Brown, Ray 1926- *AfrAmAl 6*
Brown, Ray Kent 1924- *WhoAm 94*
Brown, Raymond *Who 94*
Brown, Raymond d1939 *WhoHol 92*
Brown, Raymond 1928- *Who 94*
Brown, (Robert) Raymond 1936- *Who 94*
Brown, Raymond George 1924- *WrDr 94*
Brown, Raymond Madison 1949- *WhoBlA 94*
Brown, Reb *WhoHol 92*
Brown, Rebecca *DrAPF 93*
Brown, Reed, Jr. d1962 *WhoHol 92*
Brown, Reginald Royce, Sr. 1946- *WhoBlA 94*
Brown, Reuben *WhAmRev*
Brown, Rex Jay 1938- *WhoAmP 93*
Brown, Reynold 1917- *WhoAmA 93*
Brown, Rhett Delford 1924-1988 *WhAm 10*
Brown, Rhoderick Edmiston 1953- *WhoMW 93*
Brown, Rhonda Rochelle 1956- *WhoScEn 94*
Brown, Rich *EncSF 93*
Brown, Richard Allen, IV 1959- *WhoWest 94*
Brown, Richard Arthur *WhoAmP 93*
Brown, Richard C. 1937- *WhoAm 94, WhoAmP 93*
Brown, Richard E. 1946- *WrDr 94*
Brown, Richard Earl 1922- *WhoBlA 94*
Brown, Richard F. 1916-1979 *WhoAmA 93N*
Brown, Richard George 1945- *Who 94*
Brown, Richard Harris 1947- *WhoAm 94, WhoFI 94*
Brown, Richard Holbrook 1927- *WhoAm 94*
Brown, Richard Kevin 1956- *WhoAmL 94*
Brown, Richard L. 1938- *WhoIns 94*
Brown, Richard Laurence 1962- *WhoAm 94, WhoFI 94*
Brown, Richard Lawrence 1932- *WhoAmL 94, WhoMW 93*
Brown, Richard Lee 1925- *WhoAm 94*
Brown, Richard M. d1964 *WhoAmA 93N*
Brown, Richard M. 1940- *WhoBlA 94*
Brown, Richard M. 1942- *WhoWest 94*
Brown, Richard Malcolm, Jr. 1939- *WhoScEn 94*
Brown, Richard Osborne 1930- *WhoBlA 94*
Brown, Richard P., Jr. 1920- *WhoAm 94*
Brown, Rita Mae *DrAPF 93*
Brown, Rita Mae 1944- *BlmGWL [port], ConLC 79 [port], GayLL, WhoAm 94, WrDr 94*
Brown, Robert *WhoAmP 93*
Brown, Robert 1744-1823 *WhAmRev*
Brown, Robert 1773-1858 *WhWE, WorScD*
Brown, Robert 1908- *Who 94*
Brown, Robert 1918- *WhoHol 92*
Brown, Robert 1931- *WhoAm 94, WhoFI 94*
Brown, Robert 1933- *IntWW 93*
Brown, Robert 1943- *Who 94*
Brown, Robert, Jr. 1936- *WhoBlA 94*
Brown, Robert Alan 1930- *WhoAm 94*
Brown, Robert Alan 1943- *WhoAm 94*
Brown, Robert Arthur 1951- *WhoAm 94, WhoScEn 94*
Brown, Robert B. 1955- *WhoAmP 93*
Brown, Robert Burnett 1942- *Who 94*
Brown, Robert C. *Who 94*
Brown, Robert Carroll 1948- *WhoAmL 94*
Brown, Robert Cephas, Sr. 1925- *WhoBlA 94*
Brown, Robert Clarence 1948- *WhoAmL 94*
Brown, Robert Crofton 1921- *Who 94*
Brown, Robert Dale 1917- *WhoAmP 93*
Brown, Robert Delford 1930- *WhoAm 94, WhoAmA 93*
Brown, Robert Edward *DrAPF 93*
Brown, Robert Ellis 1945- *WhoAm 94*
Brown, Robert Frederick 1944- *WhoFI 94*
Brown, Robert Freeman 1935- *WhoWest 94*
Brown, Robert G. 1956- *WhoAmL 94*
Brown, Robert G(oodell) 1923- *WrDr 94*
Brown, Robert Glencairn 1930- *Who 94*
Brown, Robert Glenn 1940- *WhoAm 94*
Brown, Robert Goodell 1923- *WhoAm 94*
Brown, Robert Griffith 1941- *WhoScEn 94*
Brown, Robert Grover 1926- *WhoAm 94, WhoScEn 94*
Brown, Robert Hanbury 1916- *IntWW 93, Who 94*
Brown, Robert Harold 1921- *WhoAm 94, WhoWest 94*
Brown, Robert Henry 1915- *WhoWest 94*
Brown, Robert Henry 1926- *WhoAmP 93*
Brown, Robert Horatio 1917- *WhoAm 94*
Brown, Robert J., III 1919- *WhoBlA 94*
Brown, Robert James 1935- *WhoIns 94*
Brown, Robert James Sidford 1924- *WhoScEn 94*
Brown, Robert Joe 1935- *WhoBlA 94*
Brown, Robert John 1935- *WhoAmP 93*
Brown, Robert Joseph 1929- *WhoAmP 93*
Brown, Robert Joseph 1947- *WhoAmP 93*
Brown, Robert K. 1942- *WhoAmA 93*
Brown, Robert L 1921- *WrDr 94*
Brown, Robert L. 1941- *WhoAmP 93*
Brown, Robert L. 1947- *WhoAmP 93*
Brown, Robert Laidlaw 1941- *WhoAm 94, WhoAmL 94*
Brown, Robert Lee 1908- *WhoAm 94*
Brown, Robert Lee 1947- *WhoBlA 94*
Brown, Robert Lee 1960- *WhoBlA 94*
Brown, Robert Lyle 1920- *WhoAm 94*
Brown, Robert McAfee 1920- *IntWW 93, WhoAm 94, WrDr 94*
Brown, Robert Mott, III 1947- *WhoFI 94*
Brown, Robert N. *ConTFT 11*
Brown, Robert Ross Buchanan 1909- *Who 94*
Brown, Robert Saville 1914- *Who 94*
Brown, Robert Utting 1912- *WhoAm 94*
Brown, Robert Wallace 1925- *WhoAm 94*
Brown, Robert Wayne 1942- *WhoAm 94, WhoAmL 94*
Brown, Robert William 1924- *WhoAm 94*
Brown, Robin R. *WhoBlA 94*
Brown, Roderick 1952- *WhoBlA 94*
Brown, Rodger L., Jr. 1955- *WhoBlA 94*
Brown, Rodney Jay 1948- *WhoWest 94*
Brown, Rodney Lee 1956- *WhoAmL 94*
Brown, Rodney W. *WhoBlA 94*
Brown, Roger 1941- *WhoAmA 93*
Brown, Roger 1942- *BasBi*
Brown, Roger A. 1946- *WhoWest 94*
Brown, Roger John 1947- *Who 94*
Brown, Roger William 1925- *IntWW 93, WhoAm 94, WrDr 94*
Brown, Roger William 1940- *WhoMW 93*
Brown, Roland George MacCormack 1924- *Who 94*
Brown, Roland O. 1929- *WhoBlA 94*
Brown, Ron 1941- *ConBlB 5 [port]*
Brown, Ron James 1961- *WhoBlA 94*
Brown, Ronald 1926- *Who 94*
Brown, Ronald 1930- *WhoAm 94, WhoFI 94*
Brown, Ronald 1933- *WhoAm 94*
Brown, Ronald 1940- *Who 94*
Brown, Ronald Alan 1950- *WhoFI 94*
Brown, Ronald Drayton 1927- *IntWW 93*
Brown, Ronald Edward 1952- *WhoBlA 94*
Brown, Ronald H. 1941- *AfrAmAl 6 [port], CngDr 93, WhoAmP 93, WhoBlA 94*
Brown, Ronald Harmon 1941- *WhoAm 94, WhoAmL 94, WhoFI 94*
Brown, Ronald Lee 1946- *WhoAmL 94*
Brown, Ronald Malcolm 1938- *WhoWest 94*
Brown, Ronald Osborne 1941- *WhoFI 94*
Brown, Ronald Paul 1938- *WhoBlA 94*
Brown, Ronald William 1917- *Who 94*
Brown, Ronald William 1921- *Who 94*
Brown, Ronnie Jeffrey 1953- *WhoScEn 94*
Brown, Roosevelt *ProFbHF [port]*
Brown, Roosevelt H., Jr. 1932- *WhoBlA 94*
Brown, Roscoe C., Jr. 1922- *WhoBlA 94*
Brown, Rose Denise *WhoBlA 94*
Brown, Rosel George 1926-1967 *EncSF 93*
Brown, Rosellen *DrAPF 93*
Brown, Rosellen 1939- *WrDr 94*
Brown, Roswell 1910- *WrDr 94*
Brown, Rowine Hayes 1913- *WhoAm 94*
Brown, Rowland Chauncey Widrig 1923- *WhoAm 94*
Brown, Rowland Percival 1933- *Who 94*
Brown, Roy 1879-1956 *WhoAmA 93N*
Brown, Roy Dudley 1916- *Who 94*
Brown, Roy Hershel 1924- *WhoBlA 94*
Brown, Roy S.F. *Who 94*
Brown, Ruby Edmonia 1943- *WhoBlA 94*
Brown, Rubye Golsby 1923- *WhoAmP 93, WhoBlA 94*
Brown, Rudolph Valentino, Jr. 1953- *WhoWest 94*
Brown, Russ d1964 *WhoHol 92*
Brown, Russell *Who 94*
Brown, Russell G. 1958- *WhoAmP 93*
Brown, Russell M. 1929- *WhoAmP 93*
Brown, Ruth 1928- *ConTFT 11, WhoAm 94, WhoHol 92*
Brown, Samuel Allen 1951- *WhoAmP 93*
Brown, Samuel Franklin, Jr. 1921- *WhoBlA 94*
Brown, Samuel Joseph, Jr. 1941- *WhoAm 94, WhoFI 94, WhoScEn 94*
Brown, Samuel Preston 1913- *WhoAm 94*
Brown, Sandra 1948- *WrDr 94*
Brown, Sandra Elaine 1961- *WhoMW 93*
Brown, Sandra Jane 1937- *WhoMW 93*
Brown, Sandra Jean 1936- *WhoAm 94*
Brown, Sandra Lee 1943- *WhoMW 93*
Brown, Sandra Louise Palmer *WhoFI 94*
Brown, Sanford Donald 1952- *WhoAmL 94*
Brown, Sara Lou 1942- *WhoAm 94, WhoFI 94*
Brown, Sarah E. 1936- *WhoAmL 94*
Brown, Sarah Elizabeth 1943- *Who 94*
Brown, Sarah S. 1932- *WhoAmP 93*
Brown, Scott McLean 1945- *WhoFI 94*
Brown, Scott Sinclair 1956- *WhoFI 94*
Brown, Scott Wilson 1952- *WhoScEn 94*
Brown, Sedley d1928 *WhoHol 92*
Brown, Serena Marie 1951- *WhoMW 93, WhoScEn 94*
Brown, Seymour R. 1924- *WhoAm 94*
Brown, Seymour William 1914- *WhoAm 94*
Brown, Seyom 1933- *WhoAm 94*
Brown, Sharon Gail 1941- *WhoFI 94, WhoMW 93*
Brown, Sharon Marjorie Revels 1938- *WhoBlA 94*
Brown, Shelly Rae 1955- *WhoAmL 94*
Brown, Shepherd Spencer Neville, Jr. 1954- *WhoFI 94*
Brown, Sherman L. 1943- *WhoBlA 94*
Brown, Sherrod 1952- *CngDr 93, WhoMW 93*

Brown, Sherrod Campbell 1952- *WhoAm 94, WhoAmP 93*
Brown, Shirley 1952- *WhoAmP 93*
Brown, Shirley Ann Vining *WhoBlA 94*
Brown, Shirley Anne 1955- *WhoWest 94*
Brown, Sidney DeVere 1925- *WhoAm 94*
Brown, Sidonie Dossin 1947- *WhoMW 93*
Brown, Simon Denis 1937- *Who 94*
Brown, Simon F. 1952- *WhoBlA 94*
Brown, Spencer 1909- *WrDr 94*
Brown, Spencer Hunter 1928- *WhoAm 94, WhoMW 93*
Brown, Spencer L. 1954- *WhoWest 94*
Brown, Stanley *Who 94*
Brown, (Frederick Herbert) Stanley 1910- *Who 94*
Brown, Stanley Donovan 1933- *WhoBlA 94*
Brown, Stephanie Diane 1944- *WhoWest 94*
Brown, Stephen *Who 94*
Brown, Stephen 1924- *Who 94*
Brown, (Arthur James) Stephen 1906- *Who 94*
Brown, Stephen D. 1949- *WhoAm 94, WhoAmL 94*
Brown, Stephen David Reid 1945- *Who 94*
Brown, Stephen Edward 1949- *WhoAmL 94*
Brown, Stephen H. 1927- *WhoBlA 94*
Brown, Stephen Ira 1938- *WhoAm 94*
Brown, Stephen Landesman 1938- *WhoAm 94, WhoFI 94*
Brown, Stephen Lawrence 1937- *WhoScEn 94*
Brown, Stephen Lee 1937- *WhoAm 94, WhoFI 94*
Brown, Stephen Smiley 1952- *WhoAmL 94*
Brown, Stephen Thomas 1947- *WhoAm 94, WhoAmL 94*
Brown, Stephen Wayne 1950- *WhoAm 94*
Brown, Steve 1960- *WhoBlA 94*
Brown, Steven Brien 1952- *WhoWest 94*
Brown, Steven Day, Jr. 1965- *WhoAmP 93*
Brown, Steven Edward 1951- *WhoAm 94*
Brown, Steven Ford *DrAPF 93*
Brown, Steven Spencer 1948- *WhoAmL 94*
Brown, Stewart 1951- *WrDr 94*
Brown, Stratton Shartel 1923- *WhoAm 94*
Brown, Stuart Christopher 1950- *Who 94*
Brown, Stuart I. 1933- *WhoAm 94*
Brown, Suzanne Goldman 1929- *WhoAmA 93*
Brown, Suzanne Wiley 1938- *WhoMW 93*
Brown, Sydney d1979 *WhoHol 92*
Brown, Tally d1989 *WhoHol 92*
Brown, Ted Leon, Jr. 1956- *WhoFI 94*
Brown, Terence 1944- *ConAu 41NR, WrDr 94*
Brown, Terence Michael 1941- *WhoAm 94, WhoMW 93*
Brown, Teresa E. 1953- *WhoAmP 93*
Brown, Terrence Charles 1949- *WhoAm 94*
Brown, Terry Wayne 1950- *WhoAmP 93*
Brown, Theodore E., Jr. 1960- *WhoAmP 93*
Brown, Theodore Lawrence 1928- *WhoAm 94, WhoScEn 94*
Brown, Theodore M 1925- *WrDr 94*
Brown, Theodore Morey 1925- *WhoAm 94*
Brown, Theodore Roosevelt d1979 *WhoHol 92*
Brown, Theophile Waldorf 1925- *WhoBlA 94*
Brown, Theophilus 1919- *WhoAmA 93*
Brown, Thomas *WhAmRev*
Brown, Thomas 1750-1825 *AmRev*
Brown, Thomas 1915- *Who 94*
Brown, Thomas Allan 1942- *WhoIns 94*
Brown, Thomas Andrew 1932- *WhoAm 94*
Brown, Thomas Andrew 1958- *WhoAmL 94*
Brown, Thomas Archer 1917- *WhoWest 94*
Brown, Thomas B. 1927- *WhoAm 94*
Brown, Thomas C., Jr. 1945- *WhoAm 94, WhoAmL 94*
Brown, Thomas Daniel 1959- *WhoAmL 94*
Brown, Thomas Edison, Jr. 1952- *WhoBlA 94*
Brown, Thomas Edward 1967- *WhoScEn 94*
Brown, Thomas Elzie, Jr. 1929- *WhoAmP 93*
Brown, Thomas Harold 1930- *WhoWest 94*
Brown, Thomas Huntington 1945- *WhoAm 94*
Brown, Thomas J. 1949- *WhoFI 94*
Brown, Thomas Loyd 1951- *WhoAmP 93*
Brown, Thomas McPherson 1906-1989 *WhAm 10*
Brown, Thomas Philip, III 1931- *WhoAm 94, WhoAmL 94*
Brown, Thomas Raymond 1947- *WhoWest 94*
Brown, Thomas Walter Falconer 1901- *Who 94*
Brown, Timothy *WhoHol 92*
Brown, Timothy Charles 1950- *WhoFI 94*
Brown, Timothy Dale 1962- *WhoAmL 94*
Brown, Timothy Donell 1966- *WhoAm 94, WhoBlA 94, WhoWest 94*
Brown, Timothy L. 1940- *WhoIns 94*
Brown, Tina *NewYTBS 93 [port]*
Brown, Tina 1953- *IntWW 93, Who 94, WhoAm 94*
Brown, Tod David 1936- *WhoAm 94, WhoWest 94*
Brown, Tom d1990 *WhoHol 92*
Brown, Tom C. 1933- *WhoAmP 93*
Brown, Tommie F. *WhoAmP 93*
Brown, Tommie Florence 1934- *WhoBlA 94*
Brown, Tony 1933- *AfrAmAl 6, WhoBlA 94*
Brown, Tony 1960- *WhoBlA 94*
Brown, Trevor Ernest 1939- *WhoScEn 94*
Brown, Trisha *IntWW 93*
Brown, Trisha 1936- *WhoAm 94*
Brown, Troy d1944 *WhoHol 92*
Brown, Troy Anderson, Jr. 1934- *WhoAm 94*
Brown, Troy R. 1944- *WhoAm 94, WhoAmL 94*
Brown, Tyrone W. 1940- *WhoBlA 94*
Brown, Valerie Dee 1962- *WhoAmL 94*
Brown, Valerie K. 1945- *WhoAmP 93*
Brown, Vanessa 1928- *WhoHol 92*
Brown, Vernon E. 1943- *WhoBlA 94*
Brown, Vernon Ray 1959- *WhoMW 93*
Brown, Vicki Lee 1954- *WhoScEn 94*
Brown, Vinson 1912-1991 *WrDr 94N*
Brown, Virdin C. 1941- *WhoAmP 93*
Brown, Virgil E., Jr. *WhoBlA 94*
Brown, Vivian *Who 94*
Brown, Vivian d1987 *WhoHol 92*
Brown, (Harold) Vivian (Bigley) 1945- *Who 94*
Brown, W(illiam) Glanville 1907- *Who 94*
Brown, W. Michael *WhoAm 94, WhoFI 94*
Brown, Wade H. 1940- *WhoWest 94*
Brown, Wally d1961 *WhoHol 92*
Brown, Wally 1898-1961
See Brown and Carney *WhoCom*
Brown, Walston Shepard 1908- *WhoAm 94*
Brown, Walter A. 1905-1964 *BasBi*
Brown, Walter Creighton 1913- *WhoScEn 94, WhoWest 94*
Brown, Walter E. 1931- *WhoBlA 94*
Brown, Walter Franklin 1952- *WhoWest 94*
Brown, Walter Frederick 1926- *WhoAmP 93, WhoWest 94*
Brown, Walter Lyons 1924- *WhoAm 94*
Brown, Walter Redvers John 1925- *WhoScEn 94*
Brown, Walter Taylor 1943- *WhoAm 94, WhoAmL 94*
Brown, Walter V. 1915- *WhoAmP 93*
Brown, Warren Aloysius 1948- *WhoBlA 94*
Brown, Warren Charles 1944- *WhoFI 94*
Brown, Warren Henry, Jr. 1905- *WhoBlA 94*
Brown, Warren Joseph 1924- *WhoAm 94, WhoScEn 94*
Brown, Warren Shelburne, Jr. 1944- *WhoWest 94*
Brown, Wendell Blane 1945- *WhoAmP 93*
Brown, Wenzel 1912- *EncSF 93*
Brown, Wesley 1945- *BlkWr 2*
Brown, Wesley Anthony 1927- *WhoBlA 94*
Brown, Wesley Ernest 1907- *WhoAm 94, WhoAmL 94, WhoMW 93*
Brown, Willard L. 1911- *WhoBlA 94*
Brown, Willet Henry 1905- *WhoAm 94*
Brown, William 1752-1792 *WhAmRev*
Brown, William 1929- *IntMPA 94, Who 94*
Brown, William, Jr. 1935- *WhoBlA 94*
Brown, William A. 1930- *WhoAmP 93*
Brown, William A. 1957- *WhoAmL 94*
Brown, William Adams 1865-1943 *DcAmReB 2*
Brown, William Arthur 1945- *Who 94*
Brown, William B.P. *Who 94*
Brown, William Charles Langdon 1931- *IntWW 93, Who 94*
Brown, William Christopher 1928- *Who 94*
Brown, William Clifford 1911- *WhoAm 94*
Brown, William Crawford 1925- *WhoBlA 94*
Brown, William Crews 1920- *WhoBlA 94*
Brown, William E., Jr. 1927- *AfrAmG [port]*
Brown, William Eden T. *Who 94*
Brown, William Edwin 1934- *WhoWest 94*
Brown, William Ernest 1922- *WhoAm 94*
Brown, William Ernest 1929- *WhoWest 94*
Brown, William Ernest 1939- *WhoFI 94*
Brown, William F. 1900- *WhoBlA 94*
Brown, William F. 1904-1990 *WhAm 10*
Brown, William Ferdinand 1928- *WhoAm 94*
Brown, William Gardner 1942- *WhoAm 94, WhoAmL 94, WhoMW 93*
Brown, William H. 1929-1985 *WhoBlA 94N*
Brown, William H. 1935- *WhoBlA 94*
Brown, William H., III 1928- *WhoBlA 94*
Brown, William Henry Charles 1939- *WhoAmL 94*
Brown, William Hill, III 1928- *WhoAm 94, WhoAmL 94*
Brown, William Holmes 1929- *WhoAm 94, WhoAmP 93*
Brown, William Houston 1941- *WhoAm 94, WhoAmL 94*
Brown, William J. 1917- *WhoBlA 94*
Brown, William J. 1951- *WhoAmL 94*
Brown, William K. 1947- *WhoAmL 94*
Brown, William L. 1922- *WhoAm 94, WhoFI 94*
Brown, William Lacy 1913-1991 *WhAm 10*
Brown, William Lee 1946- *WhoMW 93*
Brown, William Lee Lyons, Jr. 1936- *WhoAm 94, WhoFI 94*
Brown, William Lewis 1926- *WhoFI 94*
Brown, William M. 1942- *WhoIns 94*
Brown, William Martyn 1914- *Who 94*
Brown, William McKinley, Jr. 1926- *WhoBlA 94*
Brown, William Melvin, Jr. 1934- *WhoBlA 94*
Brown, William Oscar 1915- *WhoWest 94*
Brown, William Paul 1919- *WhoAm 94*
Brown, William R. 1939- *WhoAm 94, WhoIns 94*
Brown, William Randall 1913- *WhoAm 94*
Brown, William Robert 1926- *WhoAm 94*
Brown, William Rocky, III 1955- *WhoBlA 94*
Brown, William Samuel, Jr. 1940- *WhoScEn 94*
Brown, William T. 1929- *WhoBlA 94*
Brown, William T. 1947- *WhoBlA 94*
Brown, William Thacher 1947- *WhoAm 94*
Brown, William Wells 1815-1884 *AfrAmAl 6*
Brown, Willie *ProFbHF, WhoBlA 94*
Brown, Willie B. 1940- *WhoAmP 93, WhoBlA 94*
Brown, Willie L. 1932- *WhoBlA 94*
Brown, Willie L., Jr. 1934- *WhoAmP 93, WhoBlA 94*
Brown, Willie Lewis, Jr. 1934- *WhoAm 94*
Brown, Willis, Jr. 1924- *WhoBlA 94*
Brown, Willis Donald 1929- *WhoAmP 93*
Brown, Wood, III 1936- *WhoAm 94*
Brown, Woodrow Martin 1944- *WhoAmP 93*
Brown, Yolanda 1946- *WhoBlA 94*
Brown, Yvonne Margaret Rose 1940- *WhoWest 94*
Brown, Zack 1949- *ConTFT 11*
Brown, Zania Faye 1954- *WhoMW 93*
Brown, Zora Kramer 1949- *WhoBlA 94*
Brown and Carney *WhoCom*
Brownawell, Woodrow Dale 1942- *WhoAm 94*
Brownback, Henry Oliver 1950- *WhoMW 93*
Brown Blackwell, Antoinette 1825-1921 *WomPubS*
Brown-Cochrane, Andrea Kane 1962- *WhoFI 94*
Browne *Who 94*
Browne, Aidan Francis 1955- *WhoAmL 94*
Browne, Aldis Jerome, Jr. 1912- *WhoMW 93*
Browne, Andrew Harold 1923- *Who 94*
Browne, Anthony (Edward Tudor) 1946- *WrDr 94*
Browne, Anthony Arthur Duncan M. *Who 94*
Browne, Barbara *DrAPF 93*
Browne, Bernard Peter Francis K. *Who 94*
Browne, Betty d1923 *WhoHol 92*
Browne, Bothwell d1947 *WhoHol 92*
Browne, Brooks Halsey 1949- *WhoAm 94*
Browne, C. Willing, III 1939- *WhoAmL 94*
Browne, Charles Duncan Alfred 1922- *Who 94*
Browne, Charles Idol 1922- *WhoAm 94*
Browne, Cicely *WhoHol 92*
Browne, Coral 1913-1991 *WhoHol 92*
Browne, Cornelius Payne 1923- *WhoAm 94*
Browne, Denis George *Who 94*
Browne, Denis John Wolko 1892-1967 *DcNaB MP*
Browne, Desmond John Michael 1947- *Who 94*
Browne, Diana Gayle 1924- *WhoAm 94*
Browne, Dik 1917-1989 *WhAm 10*
Browne, Donald Roger 1934- *WhoAm 94*
Browne, E. John P. 1948- *IntWW 93*
Browne, Earle d1944 *WhoHol 92*
Browne, Edmund John Phillip 1948- *WhoAm 94*
Browne, Ernest C., Jr. 1925- *WhoBlA 94*
Browne, F. Sedgwick 1942- *WhoAm 94, WhoAmL 94*
Browne, Frances 1816-1879 *DcNaB MP*
Browne, George Byron 1907-1961 *WhoAmA 93N*
Browne, George D. d1993 *NewYTBS 93 [port]*
Browne, George Sheldon *EncSF 93*
Browne, Gerald Austin *WrDr 94*
Browne, Gerald Michael 1943- *WhoAm 94*
Browne, Gillian Brenda B. *Who 94*
Browne, H. Monroe 1917- *WhoAmP 93*
Browne, Harry 1933- *WrDr 94*
Browne, Henry 1918- *WrDr 94*
Browne, Howard 1908- *EncSF 93, WrDr 94*
Browne, Irene d1965 *WhoHol 92*
Browne, Jackson *WhoAm 94*
Browne, James Clayton 1935- *WhoScEn 94*
Browne, Jeffrey Francis 1944- *WhoAm 94*
Browne, Jerry d1980 *WhoHol 92*
Browne, Jerry 1966- *WhoBlA 94*
Browne, John *Who 94*
Browne, John c. 1590-1651 *DcNaB MP*
Browne, John c. 1608-1691 *DcNaB MP*
Browne, (Edmund) John (Phillip) 1948- *Who 94*
Browne, John Anthony 1948- *Who 94*
Browne, John Charles 1942- *WhoAm 94*
Browne, John Ernest Douglas Delavalette 1938- *Who 94*
Browne, John Philip Ravenscroft 1937- *Who 94*
Browne, John Robinson 1914- *WhoAm 94*
Browne, Joseph Peter 1929- *WhoWest 94*
Browne, Kale *WhoHol 92*
Browne, Kathie *WhoHol 92*
Browne, Kingsbury 1922- *WhoAm 94*
Browne, Laidman d1961 *WhoHol 92*
Browne, Lee F. 1922- *WhoBlA 94*
Browne, Leslie 1957- *WhoAm 94*
Browne, Leslie 1958- *IntDcB, WhoHol 92*
Browne, Leslie M. 1948- *WhoAmL 94*
Browne, Lucile d1976 *WhoHol 92*
Browne, Malcolm Wilde 1931- *WhoAm 94*
Browne, Maria de Felicidade do Couto 1797?-1861 *BlmGWL*
Browne, Marjorie Lee 1942- *AfrAmAl 6*
Browne, Marmaduke E(dmonstone) 1843?-1917? *NewGrDO*
Browne, Mary Anita *WhoAm 94*
Browne, Mary K. 1891-1971 *BuCMET*
Browne, Mary Stephanie 1963- *WhoWest 94*
Browne, Mervyn Ernest 1916- *Who 94*
Browne, Michael Dennis *DrAPF 93*
Browne, Michael Dennis 1940- *WhoAm 94, WrDr 94*
Browne, Michael Leon 1946- *WhoAm 94, WhoAmL 94*
Browne, Millard Child 1915- *WhoAm 94*
Browne, Montfort d1785 *AmRev*
Browne, Morgan Trew 1919- *WhoAm 94*
Browne, Moyra (Blanche Madeleine) 1918- *Who 94*
Browne, Nicholas Walker 1947- *Who 94*
Browne, Patrick (Reginald Evelyn) 1907- *Who 94*
Browne, Percy Basil 1923- *Who 94*
Browne, Peter K. *Who 94*
Browne, Ray 1938- *WhoFI 94*
Browne, Ray Broadus 1922- *WhoAm 94*
Browne, Reno d1991 *WhoHol 92*
Browne, Richard Cullen 1938- *WhoAm 94, WhoAmL 94*
Browne, Richard Harold 1946- *WhoScEn 94*
Browne, Robert M. 1926- *WhoAmA 93*
Browne, Robert Span 1924- *WhoAm 94, WhoBlA 94*
Browne, Robert William M. *Who 94*
Browne, Roscoe Lee 1925- *ConTFT 11, IntMPA 94, WhoBlA 94, WhoHol 92*
Browne, Sam d1972 *WhoHol 92*
Browne, Sandra 1947- *NewGrDO*
Browne, Sheila Jeanne 1924- *Who 94*
Browne, Stanhope Stryker 1931- *WhoAm 94*
Browne, Steven Emery 1950- *WhoWest 94*
Browne, Syd J. 1907- *WhoAmA 93*
Browne, Therese Marie 1966- *WhoMW 93*
Browne, Thomas d1825 *WhAmRev*
Browne, Thomas 1605-1682 *BlmGEL*
Browne, Thomas L. 1949- *WhoAmL 94*
Browne, Vincent J. 1917- *WhoBlA 94*

Browne, Vincent Jefferson, Jr. 1953- WhoBlA 94
Browne, Vivian E. 1929- WhoAmA 93, WhoBlA 94
Browne, W. Graham d1937 WhoHol 92
Browne, Walter Shawn 1949- WhoAm 94, WhoWest 94
Browne, William 1591-1643 BlmGEL
Browne, William 1737-1802 WhAmRev
Browne, William Bitner 1914- WhoAm 94
Browne, William James 1940- WhoFI 94
Browne, William Samuel 1932- WhoAmP 93
Browne-Cave, Robert C. Who 94
Brownell, Barbara WhoHol 92
Brownell, Blaine Allison 1942- WhoAm 94
Brownell, Carlton Kearns, III 1964- WhoAmL 94
Brownell, David Paul 1944- WhoAm 94
Brownell, David Wheaton 1941- WhoAm 94
Brownell, Edwin Rowland 1924- WhoAm 94, WhoFI 94
Brownell, Gordon Lee 1922- WhoAm 94
Brownell, Herbert 1904- IntWW 93, WhoAmP 93
Brownell, Jeff Allen 1953- WhoWest 94
Brownell, John Arnold 1924- WhoAm 94
Brownell, Robert Harrie 1938- WhoMW 93
Brownell, Samuel Miller 1900-1990 WhAm 10
Brownell, Thomas F. WhoAmP 93
Brownell, Thomas M. 1953- WhoAmL 94
Browne-Miller, Angela 1952- WrDr 94
Browner, Carol WhoAm 94, WhoAmP 93, WhoScEn 94
Browner, Carol 1955- EnvEnc [port]
Browner, Carol 1956- IntWW 93
Browner, Carol M. 1955- News 94-1 [port]
Browner, Joey Matthew 1960- WhoBlA 94
Browner, Julius Harvey 1930- WhoAmL 94
Browner, Ross 1954- WhoBlA 94
Brownett, Thelma Denyer 1924- WhoAmA 93
Browne-Wilkinson 1930- IntWW 93
Browne-Wilkinson, Baron 1930- Who 94
Brownfield, Mathew Dale 1957- WhoAmL 94
Brown-Foster, Arnita Christine 1950- WhoAmL 94
Brown-Francisco, Teresa Elaine 1960- WhoBlA 94
Brown-Guillory, Elizabeth 1954- WhoBlA 94
Brownhill, Bud H. 1941- WhoFI 94, WhoWest 94
Brownhill, Harold WhoAmA 93N
Brownhill, Toni Robeck 1946- WhoMW 93
Browning, Alan d1979 WhoHol 92
Browning, Angela Frances 1946- Who 94
Browning, Burt Oliver 1957- WhoScEn 94
Browning, Charles Benton 1931- WhoAm 94, WhoScEn 94
Browning, Chauncey H., Jr. 1934- WhoAmP 93
Browning, Christopher R(obert) 1944- WrDr 94
Browning, Colin Arrott 1935- WhoAm 94
Browning, Colleen 1929- WhoAmA 93
Browning, Craig EncSF 93
Browning, Daniel Dwight 1921- WhoAm 94
Browning, David Gunter 1937- WhoScEn 94
Browning, Deborah Lea 1955- WhoAmL 94
Browning, Dixie Burrus 1930- WhoAmA 93, WrDr 94
Browning, Don 1934- WrDr 94
Browning, Don Spencer 1934- WhoAm 94
Browning, Edmond L. 1929- IntWW 93
Browning, Edmond Lee WhoAm 94
Browning, Edmond Lee 1929- Who 94
Browning, Elizabeth Barrett 1806-1861 BlmGEL [port], BlmGWL
Browning, Frank Milton 1897- WhAm 10
Browning, G. Wesley 1868-1951 WhoAmA 93N
Browning, Galen B. 1923- WhoAmP 93
Browning, George Victor Who 94
Browning, Grainger 1917- WhoBlA 94
Browning, Grayson Douglas 1929- WhoAm 94
Browning, Henry Prentice 1911- WhoAm 94
Browning, Ian Andrew 1941- Who 94
Browning, Iben 1918-1991 WhAm 10
Browning, James Alexander 1922- WhoAm 94
Browning, James Franklin 1923- WhoAm 94
Browning, James Louis, Jr. 1932- WhoAmL 94
Browning, James R. WhoAmP 93
Browning, James Robert 1918- WhoAm 94, WhoAmL 94, WhoWest 94
Browning, Jean NewGrDO
Browning, Jesse Harrison 1935- WhoWest 94
Browning, John NewYTBS 93 [port]
Browning, John 1855-1926 WorInv
Browning, John 1933- WhoAm 94
Browning, John S. EncSF 93
Browning, Kaye 1933- WhoAmP 93
Browning, Keith Anthony 1938- IntWW 93, Who 94
Browning, Kirk 1921- IntMPA 94
Browning, Kurt WhoAm 94
Browning, Mark Daniel 1946- WhoAmA 93
Browning, Norma Lee 1914- WhoAm 94
Browning, Peter Who 94
Browning, (David) Peter (James) 1927- Who 94
Browning, Peter Crane 1941- WhoAm 94, WhoFI 94
Browning, R. Stephen 1940- WhoAmL 94
Browning, Reed S. 1938- WhoAm 94
Browning, Rex Alan 1930- Who 94
Browning, Richard 1952- WhoAmP 93
Browning, Richard Arlen 1941- WhoAm 94
Browning, Ricou 1930- WhoHol 92
Browning, Robert 1812-1889 BlmGEL
Browning, Robert 1914- IntWW 93, Who 94, WrDr 94
Browning, Robert Masters 1912- WhoAm 94
Browning, Roderick Hanson 1925- WhoAm 94
Browning, Ronald Kenneth 1934- WhoScEn 94
Browning, Sarah Louise 1952- WhoAmP 93
Browning, Tod d1962 WhoHol 92
Browning, Tod 1882-1962 ConAu 141, HorFD [port]
Browning, Wilfrid (Robert Francis) 1918- WrDr 94
Browning, Wilfrid Robert Francis 1918- Who 94
Browning, William Docker 1931- WhoAm 94, WhoAmL 94, WhoWest 94
Browning, William E. d1930 WhoHol 92
Browning, William Elgar, Jr. 1923- WhoScEn 94
Brownjohn, Alan (Charles) 1931- EncSF 93, WrDr 94
Brown Knable, Bobbie Margaret 1936- WhoBlA 94
Brownlee, Christene 1955- WhoAmP 93
Brownlee, David B(ruce) 1951- WrDr 94
Brownlee, Dennis J. WhoBlA 94
Brownlee, Donald Eugene, II 1943- WhoAm 94
Brownlee, Frank d1948 WhoHol 92
Brownlee, George 1911- IntWW 93, Who 94
Brownlee, George Gow 1942- Who 94
Brownlee, Geraldine Daniels WhoBlA 94
Brownlee, Jack M. 1940- WhoBlA 94
Brownlee, John (Donald Mackenzie) 1901-1969 NewGrDO
Brownlee, Judith Marilyn 1940- WhoAm 94
Brownlee, Lester Harrison-Pierce MacDougall 1915- WhoBlA 94
Brownlee, Paula Pimlott 1934- WhoAm 94
Brownlee, Richard Smith 1918- WhAm 10
Brownlee, Robert Calvin 1922- WhoAm 94
Brownlee, Robert Hammel 1951- WhoAm 94, WhoAmL 94
Brownlee, Thomas Marshall 1926- WhoAm 94
Brownlee, Vivian Aplin 1946- WhoBlA 94
Brownlee, Wilson Elliot, Jr. 1941- WhoAm 94, WhoWest 94
Brownlee, Wyatt China 1909- WhoBlA 94
Brownley, John Forrest 1942- WhoFI 94
Brownlie, Albert Dempster 1932- IntWW 93, Who 94
Brownlie, Deborah Louise 1955- WhoAmP 93
Brownlie, Ian 1932- IntWW 93, Who 94, WrDr 94
Brownlow, Baron 1936- Who 94
Brownlow, Bertrand 1929- Who 94
Brownlow, Frank Walsh 1934- WhoAm 94
Brownlow, James Hilton 1925- Who 94
Brownlow, James Scott 1926- WhoMW 93
Brownlow, Kevin 1938- IntMPA 94, IntWW 93, Who 94, WrDr 94
Brownlow, William Stephen 1921- Who 94
Brownmiller, Susan 1935- AmSocL, WrDr 94
Brown-Nash, JoAhn Weaver 1935- WhoBlA 94
Brownridge, J. Paul 1945- WhoBlA 94
Brownrigg, John Clinton 1948- WhoAmL 94
Brownrigg, Nicholas (Gawen) 1932- Who 94
Brownrigg, Philip Henry Akerman 1911- Who 94
Brownrigg, Walter Grant 1940- WhoAm 94
Brownson, Charles DrAPF 93
Brownson, E. Ramona Lidstone Brady 1930- WhoMW 93
Brownson, Jacques Calmon 1923- WhoAm 94
Brownson, Nathan 1742-1796 WhAmRev
Brownson, Orestes Augustus 1803-1876 DcAmReB 2
Brownson, William Clarence 1928- WhoAm 94
Brownstein, Alan P. 1944- WhoAm 94
Brownstein, Andrew Richard 1953- WhoAmL 94
Brownstein, Barbara Lavin 1931- WhoAm 94
Brownstein, Martin Herbert 1935- WhoAm 94
Brownstein, Michael DrAPF 93
Brownstein, Michael 1943- WrDr 94
Brownstein, Michael Z. 1947- WhoAmL 94
Brownstein, Philip Nathan 1917- WhoAm 94
Brownstein, Richard Joseph 1930- WhoAmL 94
Brownstein, Ronald Jay 1958- WhoWest 94
Brownstein-Santiago, Cheryl WhoHisp 94
Brown-Stigger, Alberta Mae 1932- WhoWest 94
Brownstone, Hugh Michael 1957- WhoFI 94
Brownstone, Paul Lotan 1923- WhoAm 94
Brown-Waite, Virginia 1943- WhoAmP 93
Brown Wolf, Coleen Joyce 1951- WhoMW 93
Brownwood, David Owen 1935- WhoAm 94, WhoAmL 94, WhoFI 94
Brown-Wright, Marjorie 1935- WhoBlA 94
Browse, Lillian Gertrude Who 94
Browse, Norman Leslie 1931- Who 94
Broxmeyer, Hal Edward 1944- WhoScEn 94
Broxon, Mildred Downey EncSF 93
Broxon, Mildred Downey 1944- WrDr 94
Broxterman, Janice Creagh 1940- WhoFI 94
Broydrick, Bill B. 1948- WhoAmP 93
Broyhill, James T. 1927- WhoAmP 93
Broyhill, Roy Franklin 1919- WhoMW 93
Broyles, Donald Lee 1966- WhoFI 94
Broyles, Gladys Benites 1959- WhoMW 93
Broyles, Michael Lee 1942- WhoScEn 94
Broyles, Robert WhoHol 92
Broyles, Susan Irene 1949- WhoAmL 94
Broyles, Thomas Edwin 1951- WhoAm 94
Broyles, William Dodson, Jr. 1944- IntWW 93, WhoAm 94
Broyles-Williams, Maxine WhoBlA 94
Brozek, Josef 1913- WhoAm 94
Brozek, Richard Carl 1953- WhoFI 94
Brozman, Tina L. 1952- WhoAm 94, WhoAmL 94
Brsozowska, Anna WhoWomW 91
Bru (Albinana), Enrique 1873-1951 NewGrDO
Bru, Isabel c. 1870- NewGrDO
Bru, Myriam WhoHol 92
Brubacher, John Seller 1898- WhAm 10
Brubaker, Charles William 1926- WhoAm 94
Brubaker, Connie Colleen 1953- WhoMW 93
Brubaker, Crawford Francis, Jr. 1924- WhoAm 94, WhoWest 94
Brubaker, Harold J. 1946- WhoAmP 93
Brubaker, Jack 1944- WhoAmA 93
Brubaker, James Clark 1947- WhoMW 93
Brubaker, James D. 1937- IntMPA 94
Brubaker, James Edward 1935- WhoFI 94
Brubaker, Janice Aleeda 1930- WhoMW 93
Brubaker, John E. 1941- WhoAm 94, WhoFI 94, WhoWest 94
Brubaker, Karen Sue 1953- WhoFI 94
Brubaker, Lauren Edgar 1914- WhoAm 94
Brubaker, Robert WhoHol 92
Brubaker, Robert Loring 1947- WhoAm 94
Brubaker, Robert Paul 1934- WhoAm 94
Brubaker, Robert Robinson 1933- WhoMW 93
Brubeck, Anne Elizabeth Denton 1918- WhoMW 93
Brubeck, Dave 1920- CurBio 93 [port]
Brubeck, David Warren 1920- IntWW 93, Who 94, WhoAm 94
Bruccoli, Matthew J. 1931- WrDr 94
Bruccoli, Matthew Joseph 1931- WhoAm 94
Bruce Who 94
Bruce, Lord 1961- Who 94
Bruce, Agnes Marie 1910- WhoAmP 93
Bruce, Amos Jerry, Jr. 1942- WhoAm 94
Bruce, Antoinette Johnson 1917- WhoBlA 94
Bruce, Belle d1960 WhoHol 92
Bruce, Betty d1974 WhoHol 92
Bruce, Beverly d1925 WhoHol 92
Bruce, Beverly Joan 1927- WhoAmP 93
Bruce, Blanche K. 1841-1898 AfrAmAl 6 [port]
Bruce, Brenda 1918- WhoHol 92
Bruce, Brenda 1922- IntMPA 94
Bruce, Carol 1919- WhoHol 92
Bruce, Carol 1954- WhoWest 94
Bruce, Carol Pitt 1941- WhoBlA 94
Bruce, Christopher 1945- IntDcB [port], Who 94
Bruce, Clifford d1919 WhoHol 92
Bruce, Danny Monroe 1950- WhoAmP 93
Bruce, David d1976 WhoHol 92
Bruce, David 1855-1931 WorScD [port]
Bruce, David 1927- Who 94
Bruce, David Lionel 1933- WhoAm 94
Bruce, Debra M. DrAPF 93
Bruce, Dickson Davies, Jr. 1946- WhoWest 94, WrDr 94
Bruce, Edgar K. d1971 WhoHol 92
Bruce, Estel Edward 1938- WhoAm 94, WhoAmL 94
Bruce, Eve WhoHol 92
Bruce, F(rederick) F(yvie) 1910-1990 ConAu 41NR
Bruce, George 1909- WrDr 94
Bruce, George John Done 1930- Who 94
Bruce, George Walter, Jr. 1958- WhoMW 93
Bruce, (William) Harry 1934- SmATA 77 [port]
Bruce, Hervey (James Hugh) 1952- Who 94
Bruce, Ian Cameron 1947- Who 94
Bruce, Ian Waugh 1945- Who 94
Bruce, Jackson Martin, Jr. 1931- WhoAm 94
Bruce, James 1730-1794 WhWE
Bruce, James C. 1929- WhoBlA 94
Bruce, James Donald 1936- WhoAm 94
Bruce, James Edmond 1927- WhoAmP 93
Bruce, James Edmund 1920- WhoAm 94
Bruce, James Michael Edward 1927- Who 94
Bruce, James Thomas, III 1947- WhoAm 94
Bruce, Jill Renee 1956- WhoMW 93
Bruce, John Allen 1934- WhoWest 94
Bruce, John Foster 1940- WhoAm 94, WhoAmL 94
Bruce, John Irvin 1929- WhoBlA 94
Bruce, Kate d1946 WhoHol 92
Bruce, Katharine Fenn 1925- WhoAmP 93
Bruce, Kenneth E. 1921- WhoBlA 94
Bruce, Lennart DrAPF 93
Bruce, Lennart 1919- WrDr 94
Bruce, Lenny d1966 WhoHol 92
Bruce, Lenny 1925-1966 WhoCom [port]
Bruce, Linda Culligan 1957- WhoAmL 94
Bruce, Louis Rooks 1906-1989 WhAm 10
Bruce, Malcolm Gray 1944- Who 94
Bruce, Martha Elena Aguilar 1946- WhoHisp 94
Bruce, Marvin Ernest 1928- WhoAm 94, WhoFI 94
Bruce, Mary Grant 1878-1958 BlmGWL
Bruce, Michael Ian 1926- Who 94
Bruce, (Francis) Michael Ian Who 94
Bruce, Michael Stewart Rae Who 94
Bruce, Nadine Cecile 1942- WhoAm 94
Bruce, Neal Douglas 1969- WhoFI 94
Bruce, (Frank) Neely 1944- NewGrDO
Bruce, Nigel d1953 WhoHol 92
Bruce, Paul d1971 WhoHol 92
Bruce, Paul Love 1933- WhoAmP 93
Bruce, Preston, Jr. 1936- WhoBlA 94
Bruce, Robert WhoHol 92
Bruce, Robert 1274-1329 HisWorL [port]
Bruce, Robert Douglas 1941- WhoScEn 94
Bruce, Robert James 1937- WhoAm 94
Bruce, Robert Kirk 1942- WhoWest 94
Bruce, Robert Nigel (Beresford Dalrymple) 1907- Who 94
Bruce, Robert Rockwell 1944- WhoAm 94, WhoAmL 94
Bruce, Robert the fl. 1306-1320 BlmGEL
Bruce, Robert Thomas 1950- WhoAm 94, WhoFI 94
Bruce, Robert Vance 1923- WhoAm 94
Bruce, Shelley 1965- WhoHol 92
Bruce, Terry L. 1944- WhoAmP 93
Bruce, Thomas Allen 1930- WhoAm 94
Bruce, Thomas Edward 1937- WhoWest 94
Bruce, Tonie Edgar d1966 WhoHol 92
Bruce, Tony d1937 WhoHol 92
Bruce, Victoria Geraldine 1953- Who 94
Bruce, Virginia d1982 WhoHol 92

Bruce, Wesley Bernard 1959- *WhoMW 93*
Bruce, Willa Marie 1938- *WhoMW 93*
Bruce, William David 1928- *WhoIns 94*
Bruce, William Robert 1929- *WhoAm 94*
Bruce, William Spiers 1867-1921 *WhWE*
Bruce-Gardner, Douglas (Bruce) 1917- *Who 94*
Bruce Lockhart, John Macgregor 1914- *Who 94*
Bruce Lockhart, Logie 1921- *Who 94*
Bruce Lockhart, Robin 1920- *WrDr 94*
Bruce-Mitford, Rupert Leo Scott 1914- *Who 94*
Bruce-Novoa *DrAPF 93*
Bruce-Novoa 1944- *ConAu 18AS [port]*
Bruce-Novoa, Juan 1944- *WhoHisp 94*
Bruce Of Donington, Baron 1912- *Who 94*
Bruch, Carol Sophie 1941- *WhoAm 94*
Bruch, Delores Ruth 1934- *WhoAm 94*
Bruch, John Clarence, Jr. 1940- *WhoWest 94*
Bruch, Max (Christian Friedrich) 1838-1920 *NewGrDO*
Bruch, Thomas James 1959- *WhoFI 94*
Bruchac, Joseph 1942- *WrDr 94*
Bruchac, Joseph E., III *DrAPF 93*
Bruchal, Richard Symeon 1937- *WhoAmP 93*
Bruchesi, Jean 1901- *IntWW 93*
Bruci, Rudolf 1917- *NewGrDO*
Bruck, Bella d1982 *WhoHol 92*
Bruck, Charles 1911- *NewGrDO*
Bruck, Connie 1946- *ConAu 140*
Bruck, Ferdinand Frederick 1921- *WhoAm 94*
Bruck, Glenn R. 1956- *WhoWest 94*
Bruck, Hermann Alexander 1905- *IntWW 93, Who 94*
Bruck, James Alvin 1947- *WhoScEn 94*
Bruck, Jean Francois Julien *IntWW 93N*
Bruck, Karl d1987 *WhoHol 92*
Bruck, Natalie Renee 1967- *WhoWest 94*
Bruck, Nicholas 1932- *WhoFI 94*
Bruck, Phoebe Ann Mason 1928- *WhoAm 94*
Bruck, Stephen Desiderius 1927- *WhoAm 94*
Bruckart, Walter E. 1937- *WhoFI 94*
Brucken, Eleanor Elizabeth 1929- *WhoAm 94*
Brucken, Lois Gilbert 1936- *WhoMW 93*
Brucken, Nancy Elizabeth 1961- *WhoMW 93*
Brucken, Robert Matthew 1934- *WhoAm 94*
Bruckenstein, Stanley 1927- *WhoAm 94*
Brucker, Edmund 1912- *WhoAmA 93*
Brucker, Eric 1941- *WhoAm 94*
Brucker, Gregory 1948- *WhoFI 94*
Brucker, Wilber Marion 1926- *WhoAm 94*
Bruckheimer, Jerry *IntMPA 94, WhoAm 94*
Bruckman, Betty *WhoAmP 93*
Bruckman, Clyde 1894-1955 *IntDcF 2-4 [port]*
Bruckmann, Donald John 1929- *WhoAm 94*
Bruckmann, Gerhart 1932- *IntWW 93*
Bruckmann, Mark F. 1950- *WhoAm 94*
Bruckner, Christine 1921- *BlmGWL, IntWW 93*
Bruckner, D. J. R. 1933- *WrDr 94*
Bruckner, Karl 1906- *EncSF 93*
Bruckner, William J. 1944- *WhoAmL 94*
Bruckner, Winfried *EncSF 93*
Brucks, William Charles 1956- *WhoFI 94*
Brudenell-Bruce *Who 94*
Bruder, George Frederick 1938- *WhoAm 94*
Bruder, Harold Jacob 1930- *WhoAm 94, WhoAmA 93*
Bruder, Judith *DrAPF 93*
Bruder, Kevin Michael 1968- *WhoMW 93*
Bruder, William Paul 1946- *WhoAm 94*
Bruderlin, Beat Dominik 1955- *WhoWest 94*
Bruderman, Robert William 1951- *WhoFI 94*
Brudner, Harvey Jerome 1931- *WhoAm 94*
Brudner, Helen Gross *WhoAm 94*
Brudno, Barbara 1941- *WhoWest 94*
Brudvig, Glenn Lowell 1931- *WhoAm 94*
Brueck, Christa Anita 1899- *BlmGWL*
Brueckheimer, William Rogers 1921- *WhoAm 94*
Brueckner, Keith Allan 1924- *IntWW 93, WhoAm 94*
Brueckner, Robert Davis 1935- *WhoFI 94*
Bruegel, David Robert 1953- *WhoAm 94, WhoAmL 94, WhoMW 93*
Bruegmann, Robert 1948- *WhoMW 93*
Bruel, Iris Barbara 1933- *WhoAm 94*
Bruel, Jean-Marc Andre 1936- *IntWW 93*
Bruel, Patrick *WhoHol 92*
Bruemmer, Fred 1929- *WhoAm 94, WrDr 94*
Bruen, David D. 1929- *WhoAmP 93*
Bruen, James A. 1943- *WhoAmL 94*
Bruen, John Dermot 1930- *WhoAm 94*
Bruene, Warren Benz 1916- *WhoAm 94*
Bruening, Richard Patrick 1939- *WhoAm 94, WhoAmL 94*
Bruening, Robert John 1939- *WhoScEn 94*
Bruenn, Howard Gerald 1905- *WhoAm 94*
Bruenn, Ronald Sherman 1940- *WhoWest 94*
Bruer, John Thomas 1949- *WhoMW 93*
Brues, Alice Mossie 1913- *WhoScEn 94*
Brueschke, Erich Edward 1933- *WhoAm 94*
Bruesewitz, Lynn Joy 1952- *WhoMW 93*
Bruesewitz-Lopinto, Gail Cecelia 1956- *WhoFI 94*
Brueske, Patrick Jeremy 1964- *WhoMW 93*
Bruess, Charles Edward 1938- *WhoAm 94*
Bruetsch, Walter L. 1896- *WhAm 10*
Bruett, Till Arthur 1938- *WhoAm 94*
Bruey, Alfred J. *DrAPF 93*
Brufsky, Allen David 1939- *WhoAmL 94*
Brugaletta, John J. *DrAPF 93*
Brugam, Richard Blair 1946- *WhoMW 93*
Bruggeman, George d1967 *WhoHol 92*
Bruggeman, Lewis LeRoy 1941- *WhoWest 94*
Bruggeman, Terrance John 1946- *WhoAm 94*
Bruggemann, Kurt 1908- *NewGrDO*
Bruggen, Carry van 1881-1932 *BlmGWL*
Bruggen, Frans 1934- *Who 94*
Brugger, Ernst 1914- *IntWW 93*
Brugger, George Albert 1941- *WhoAm 94*
Brugger, Paul Raymond 1942- *WhoWest 94*
Bruggink, Eric G. 1949- *CngDr 93, WhoAm 94, WhoAmL 94*
Bruggink, Herman 1946- *WhoAm 94*
Brugler, Alan Robert 1954- *WhoMW 93*
Brugmans, Hendrik 1906- *IntWW 93*
Brugnatelli, Bruno Ercole 1935- *WhoAm 94*
Brugnon, Jacques 1895-1978 *BuCMET*
Brugnoni, John J. 1935- *WhoMW 93*
Bruhl, Carl Richard Ernst Theodor 1925- *IntWW 93*
Bruhn, Erik d1986 *WhoHol 92*
Bruhn, Erik 1928-1986 *IntDcB [port]*
Bruhn, Hans-Juergen 1940- *WhoFI 94*
Bruhn, Hjalmar Diehl 1907- *WhoScEn 94*
Bruhn, John Glyndon 1934- *WhoAm 94*
Bruhn, Michael Vernon 1956- *WhoFI 94*
Bruin, John *BlkWr 2, ConAu 42NR*
Bruin, John 1924- *WhoBlA 94, WrDr 94*
Bruinsma, Theodore August 1921- *WhoAm 94*
Bruinsma, Tim C. 1947- *WhoAmL 94*
Bruinvels, Peter Nigel Edward 1950- *Who 94*
Brukner, Ira Beryl *DrAPF 93*
Bruland, Raymond Velause 1917- *WhoWest 94*
Brulc, Lillian G. *WhoAmA 93*
Brule, Andre d1953 *WhoHol 92*
Brule, Etienne c. 1592-1633 *WhWE*
Bruley, Duane Frederick 1933- *WhoAm 94*
Brull, Eugene Edwin, Jr. 1940- *WhoWest 94*
Brull, Ignaz 1846-1907 *NewGrDO*
Brullo, Robert Angelo 1948- *WhoMW 93*
Brulte, Jim *WhoAmP 93*
Brum, Brenda Kay 1954- *WhoAmP 93*
Brumage, Edward d1945 *WhoHol 92*
Brumaghim, Paul 1926- *WhoMW 93*
Brumagne, Fernand (Maximilien Napoleon) 1887-1939 *NewGrDO*
Brumback, Charles Tiedtke 1928- *IntWW 93, WhoAm 94, WhoFI 94, WhoMW 93*
Brumback, Clarence Landen 1914- *WhoAm 94*
Brumback, Gary Bruce 1935- *WhoScEn 94*
Brumback-Henry, Sarah Elizabeth 1948- *WhoAm 94*
Brumbaugh, Granville Martin 1901-1992 *WhAm 10*
Brumbaugh, John A., Jr. 1927- *WhoFI 94*
Brumbaugh, John Maynard 1927- *WhoAm 94*
Brumbaugh, Philip S. 1932- *WhoScEn 94*
Brumbaugh, Robert Dan, Jr. *WhoAm 94*
Brumbaugh, Robert S(herrick) 1918- *WrDr 94*
Brumbaugh, Roland John 1940- *WhoAm 94, WhoAmL 94, WhoWest 94*
Brumberg, G. David 1939- *WhoAm 94*
Brumby, Colin (James) 1933- *NewGrDO*
Brumer, Miriam 1939- *WhoAmA 93*
Brumer, Paul William 1945- *WhoScEn 94*
Brumer, Shulamith 1924- *WhoAmA 93*
Brumfiel, Elizabeth Margarethe 1945- *WhoMW 93*
Brumfield, John Richard 1934- *WhoAmA 93*
Brumfit, Christopher John 1940- *Who 94*
Brumgardt, John Raymond 1946- *WhoAm 94*
Brumley, David Lee 1949- *WhoAm 94*
Brumm, Douglas Bruce 1940- *WhoMW 93*
Brumm, James Earl 1942- *WhoAm 94, WhoFI 94*
Brumm, Paul Michael 1947- *WhoAm 94, WhoFI 94*
Brummel, Fred B. *WhoAmP 93*
Brummel, Marilyn Reeder 1926- *WhoAmA 93*
Brummel, Mark Joseph 1933- *WhoAm 94*
Brummels, J. V. *DrAPF 93, EncSF 93*
Brummer, Carole Jean 1947- *WhoMW 93*
Brummer, Chauncey Eugene 1948- *WhoBlA 94*
Brummer, Richard H. 1942- *WhoAmP 93*
Brummer, Robert Craig 1945- *WhoAm 94*
Brummet, John *DrAPF 93*
Brummet, Richard Lee 1921- *WhoAm 94*
Brummet, Shauna Renea 1955- *WhoMW 93*
Brummett, Claudia Mae 1927- *WhoAmP 93*
Brummett, Robert Eddie 1934- *WhoAm 94, WhoWest 94*
Brumsickle, Bill *WhoAmP 93*
Brun, Edmond Antoine 1898- *WhAm 10*
Brun, Friederike Sophie Christiane 1765-1835 *BlmGWL*
Brun, Herbert 1918- *WhoAm 94*
Brun, Judy Kay *WhoWest 94*
Brun, Kim Eric 1947- *WhoWest 94*
Brun, Margaret Ann Charlene 1945- *WhoWest 94*
Brun, Marie-Marguerite de Maison-Forte 1713-1794 *BlmGWL*
Brun, Roy Louis 1953- *WhoAmP 93*
Bruna, Dick 1927- *SmATA 76 [port], Who 94*
Brunacini, Alan Vincent 1937- *WhoWest 94*
Brunale, Vito John 1925- *WhoAm 94, WhoFI 94, WhoScEn 94*
Brundage, Avery 1887-1975 *WhoAmA 93N*
Brundage, Cory 1947- *WhoAmL 94*
Brundage, Gertrude Barnes 1941- *WhoScEn 94*
Brundage, Howard Denton 1923- *IntWW 93*
Brundage, James A. 1929- *WrDr 94*
Brundage, John Denton 1919-1989 *WhAm 10*
Brundage, Margaret (Johnson) 1900-1976 *EncSF 93*
Brundage, Mathilde d1939 *WhoHol 92*
Brundage, Russell Archibald 1929- *WhoAm 94*
Brundage, Susan 1949- *WhoAm 94*
Brundage, Susan Lounsbury 1949- *WhoAmA 93*
Brundage, W(illiam) Fitzhugh 1959- *ConAu 142*
Brundidge, Nancy Corinne 1920- *WhoBlA 94*
Brundige, Robert W., Jr. 1944- *WhoAm 94, WhoAmL 94*
Brundin, Bo 1937- *WhoHol 92*
Brundin, Brian Jon 1939- *WhoWest 94*
Brundin, Clark Lannerdahl 1931- *IntWW 93, Who 94*
Brundrett, George Lee, Jr. 1921- *WhoAm 94*
Brundtland, Gro Harlem 1939- *EnvEnc [port], IntWW 93, Who 94, WhoWomW 91*
Brundy, Stanley Dwayne 1967- *WhoBlA 94*
Brune, David Hamilton 1930- *WhoAm 94*
Brune, Goldie Esther 1912- *WhoAmP 93*
Bruneau, (Louis Charles Bonaventure) Alfred 1857-1934 *NewGrDO*
Bruneau, Angus A. 1935- *WhoScEn 94*
Bruneau, Bill 1948- *WhoWest 94*
Bruneau, Charles Emile, Jr. 1942- *WhoAmP 93*
Bruneau, Kittie 1929- *WhoAmA 93*
Brunei, Sultan of *Who 94*
IntWW 93
Brunel, Adrian d1958 *WhoHol 92*
Brunel, Isambard Kingdom 1806-1859 *WorInv [port]*
Brunel, Marc Isambard 1769-1849 *WorInv*
Brunell, Frank Octave 1939- *WhoMW 93*
Brunell, Jonathan 1955- *WhoAm 94*
Brunell, Philip A. 1931- *WhoAm 94*
Brunell, Richard Howard 1916- *WhoAmA 93*
Brunelle, Eugene John, Jr. 1932- *WhoScEn 94*
Brunelle, Robert Joseph 1957- *WhoFI 94*
Brunelle, Robert L. 1924- *WhoAm 94*
Brunello, Rosanne 1960- *WhoFI 94, WhoWest 94*
Bruner, Charles Hughes 1948- *WhoAmP 93*
Bruner, Charlotte Hughes 1917- *WhoAm 94*
Bruner, Cindy Hull 1949- *WhoWest 94*
Bruner, Edward M. 1924- *WhoAm 94*
Bruner, Janet M. 1949- *WhoScEn 94*
Bruner, Jerome S(eymour) 1915- *WrDr 94*
Bruner, Jerome Seymour 1915- *IntWW 93, Who 94*
Bruner, Joseph 1872-1957 *AmSocL*
Bruner, Louise Katherine 1910- *WhoAmA 93*
Bruner, Mabel D. 1916- *WhoAmP 93*
Bruner, Millie *WhoAmP 93*
Bruner, Philip Lane 1939- *WhoAm 94, WhoAmL 94*
Bruner, Robert B. 1933- *WhoAm 94*
Bruner, Stephen C. 1941- *WhoAm 94, WhoAmL 94*
Bruner, Tom 1945- *WhoAm 94*
Bruner, Van B., Jr. 1931- *WhoBlA 94*
Bruner, Vincent Michael 1957- *WhoAmP 93*
Bruner, William Gwathmey, III 1951- *WhoAmL 94, WhoFI 94*
Bruner, William Wallace 1920- *WhAm 10*
Brunet, Marta 1897-1967 *BlmGWL*
Brunett, William Daniel 1942- *WhoMW 93*
Brunetta, Renato 1950- *IntWW 93*
Brunette, Fritzi d1943 *WhoHol 92*
Brunetti, Antonio 1767?-1845? *NewGrDO*
Brunetti, Argentina *WhoHol 92*
Brunetti, Giovan Gualberto 1706-1787 *NewGrDO*
Brunetti, Melvin T. *WhoAmP 93*
Brunetti, Melvin T. 1933- *WhoAm 94, WhoAmL 94, WhoWest 94*
Brunetti, Miro d1966 *WhoHol 92*
Brunetto, Frank 1921- *WhoScEn 94*
Brungard, Martin Alan *WhoScEn 94*
Brunger, Axel Thomas 1956- *WhoScEn 94*
Brungot, Catherine V. 1922- *WhoAmP 93*
Brungot, George Oliver Robert 1923- *WhoFI 94*
Brungraber, Louis Edward 1926- *WhoScEn 94*
Brunhart, Hans 1945- *IntWW 93*
Bruni, Antonio Bartolomeo 1757-1821 *NewGrDO*
Bruni, Domenico Luigi 1758-1821 *NewGrDO*
Bruni, John Richard 1951- *WhoWest 94*
Bruni, Stephen Thomas 1949- *WhoAm 94*
Bruni, Umberto 1914- *WhoAmA 93*
Brunie, Charles Henry 1930- *WhoAm 94*
Brunig, Robert Arthur 1946- *WhoAmL 94*
Bruning, David Hall 1952- *WhoMW 93*
Bruning, Elfriede 1910- *BlmGWL*
Bruning, James Leon 1938- *WhoAm 94*
Bruning, Janet Ann 1942- *WhoWest 94*
Bruni-Sakraischik, Claudio Alberico 1926- *IntWW 93*
Brunius, Jacques d1967 *WhoHol 92*
Brunius, John d1937 *WhoHol 92*
Brunius, Pauline d1954 *WhoHol 92*
Brunk, Gary Powell 1950- *WhoMW 93*
Brunk, Gunter William 1934- *WhoWest 94*
Brunk, Max Edwin 1914- *WhoAm 94*
Brunk, Randall Jay 1955- *WhoFI 94*
Brunk, Samuel Frederick 1932- *WhoAm 94, WhoMW 93, WhoScEn 94*
Brunk, William Edward 1928- *WhoAm 94*
Brunken, Gerald Walter, Sr. 1938- *WhoFI 94, WhoMW 93*
Brunkhorst, Bob 1965- *WhoAmP 93*
Brunkhorst, Bob John 1965- *WhoMW 93*
Brunkus, Richard Allen 1950- *WhoAmA 93*
Brunn, Anke 1942- *WhoWomW 91*
Brunn, David Kevin 1956- *WhoWest 94*
Brunnell, Joseph d1943 *WhoHol 92*
Brunner, Charlotte Marie 1956- *WhoMW 93*
Brunner, Earl Chester, Jr. 1924- *WhoWest 94*
Brunner, Eldon John 1923- *WhoMW 93*
Brunner, Gary Michael 1955- *WhoMW 93*
Brunner, George Matthew 1925- *WhoAm 94*
Brunner, Gordon Francis 1938- *WhoAm 94, WhoMW 93*
Brunner, Guido 1930- *IntWW 93, Who 94*
Brunner, John (K. H.) 1934- *WrDr 94*
Brunner, John (Kilian Houston) 1934- *EncSF 93*
Brunner, John Henry Kilian 1927- *Who 94*
Brunner, John Tomlinson 1842-1919 *DcNaB MP*
Brunner, Julia *WhoAmA 93*
Brunner, Karl 1916-1989 *WhAm 10*
Brunner, Lillian Sholtis *WhoAm 94*

Brunner, Marguerite Ashworth 1913- WrDr 94
Brunner, Mary Martinez 1945- WhoMW 93
Brunner, Norman James 1942- WhoWest 94
Brunner, Robert Francis 1938- WhoAm 94
Brunner, Thomas 1821-1874 WhWE
Brunner, Thomas William 1945- WhoAm 94, WhoAmL 94
Brunner, Vernon Anthony 1940- WhoFI 94
Brunngraber, Eric Henry 1957- WhoFI 94
Brunngraber, Rudolf 1901-1960 EncSF 93
Brunni, Conni M. 1961- WhoWest 94
Brunning, David Wilfrid 1943- Who 94
Bruno, Angelo J. 1922-1991 WhAm 10
Bruno, Anthony J. 1929- WhoFI 94
Bruno, David James 1947- WhoAmL 94
Bruno, Frank d1945 WhoHol 92
Bruno, Franklin Roy 1961- IntWW 93
Bruno, George C. 1942- WhoAmP 93
Bruno, Grace Angelia 1935- WhoFI 94
Bruno, Harold Robinson, Jr. 1928- WhoAm 94
Bruno, James C. 1943- WhoAmL 94
Bruno, Joe d1977 WhoHol 92
Bruno, Joseph WhoAmP 93
Bruno, Joseph L. 1929- WhoAmP 93
Bruno, Joseph S. 1914- WhoFI 94
Bruno, Judyth Ann 1944- WhoWest 94
Bruno, Kim Gordon 1955- WhoAmL 94
Bruno, Michael 1932- IntWW 93
Bruno, Michael B. 1948- WhoBlA 94
Bruno, Michael Stephen 1958- WhoScEn 94
Bruno, Nicholas Joseph 1938- WhoFI 94
Bruno, Phillip A. WhoAmA 93
Bruno, Ronald G. 1952- WhoAm 94, WhoFI 94
Bruno, Santo M. WhoAmA 93
Bruno, Teresa Puckett 1961- WhoAmL 94
Bruno, Thomas Carl 1963- WhoAmL 94
Bruno, Vincent J. 1926- WhoAmA 93
Bruno, Vincent James 1933- WhoAmP 93
Bruno, Vincent John 1926- WhoAm 94
Brunot, Andre d1973 WhoHol 92
Brunow, Gordon Peter 1926- WhoAmL 94
Bruns, Billy Lee 1925- WhoMW 93, WhoScEn 94
Bruns, Edna d1960 WhoHol 92
Bruns, Frederick R., Jr. 1913-1979 WhoAmA 93N
Bruns, Gerald L. 1938- WhoAm 94
Bruns, Gerald Thomas 1931- WhoMW 93
Bruns, Julia d1927 WhoHol 92
Bruns, Mark Robert 1952- WhoFI 94, WhoMW 93
Bruns, Michael Willi Erich 1945- WhoScEn 94
Bruns, Nicolaus, Jr. 1926- WhoAm 94, WhoAmL 94
Bruns, Patricia Jane 1925- WhoAmP 93
Bruns, Philip WhoHol 92
Bruns, Robert Frederick, Jr. 1950- WhoMW 93
Bruns, Tom 1931- WhoAmP 93
Bruns, William John, Jr. 1935- WhoAm 94, WrDr 94
Brunschwig, Jacques 1929- IntWW 93
Brunsdale, Anne E. WhoAmP 93
Brunsdale, Anne E. 1923- WhoAm 94
Brunsden, Denys 1936- Who 94
Brunsdon, Norman Keith 1930- Who 94
Brunsen, William Henry 1940- WhoWest 94
Brunskill, Muriel d1980 WhoHol 92
Brunskill, Ronald William 1929- Who 94, WrDr 94
Brunson, Adriel 1949- WhoWest 94
Brunson, Alfred 1793-1882 EncNAR
Brunson, Burlie Allen 1945- WhoAm 94
Brunson, David 1929- WhoBlA 94
Brunson, Debora Bradley 1952- WhoBlA 94
Brunson, Dorothy Edwards 1938- WhoAm 94, WhoBlA 94
Brunson, Frank 1957- WhoBlA 94
Brunson, Hugh Ellis 1927- WhoAmL 94
Brunson, Ida Lucille 1936- WhoMW 93
Brunson, Jack E. 1956- WhoIns 94
Brunson, Jack Rushing 1928- WhoIns 94
Brunson, Joel Garrett 1923- WhoAm 94, WhoScEn 94
Brunson, John Soles 1934- WhoAmL 94, WhoFI 94
Brunson, Michael John 1940- Who 94
Brunson, William Reeder 1895- WhAm 10
Brunst-May, Lois 1944- WhoMW 93
Brunstrom, Gerald Ray 1929- WhoScEn 94
Brunsvic NewGrDO
Brunsvig, Per 1917- IntWW 93
Brunsvold, Brian Garrett 1938- WhoAm 94, WhoAmL 94
Brunsvold, Joel Dean 1942- WhoAmP 93
Brunswick 1805-1859 NewGrDO
Brunswick, Tonja JoAnn 1961- WhoMW 93
Brunt, Harry Herman, Jr. 1921- WhoAm 94
Brunt, Manly Yates, Jr. 1926- WhoAm 94
Brunt, Peter Astbury 1917- IntWW 93, Who 94
Brunt, Peter William 1936- Who 94
Brunt, Samuel EncSF 93
Brunt, Samuel Jay 1961- WhoBlA 94
Bruntisfield, Baron d1993 Who 94N
Bruntisfield, Baron 1921- Who 94
Brunton, Garland Lewis d1975 WhoHol 92
Brunton, Gordon (Charles) 1921- Who 94
Brunton, Gordon Charles 1921- IntWW 93
Brunton, Lauder Who 94
Brunton, (Edward Francis) Lauder 1916- Who 94
Brunton, Paul D. 1944- WhoAmP 93
Brunton, Paul Edward 1922- WhoAm 94
Brunton, William d1965 WhoHol 92
Brunvand, Dana Kari 1964- WhoWest 94
Brus, Gunter 1938- WhoAmA 93
Brus, Wlodzimierz 1921- Who 94
Brusa, Douglas Peter 1958- WhoScEn 94
Brusa, (Giovanni) Francesco c. 1700-1768? NewGrDO
Brusati, Franco d1993 NewYTBS 93 [port]
Brusca, Jack d1993 NewYTBS 93
Brusca, Jack 1939- WhoAmA 93
Brusca, Richard C. 1945- WhoAm 94, WhoScEn 94
Brusca, Robert Andrew 1950- WhoFI 94
Bruscantini, Sesto 1919- NewGrDO
Brusch, John Lynch 1943- WhoScEn 94
Brusewitz, Gerald Henry 1942- WhoAm 94, WhoScEn 94
Brush, B. Joseph, Jr. WhoAmP 93
Brush, Carey Wentworth 1920- WhoAm 94
Brush, Charles Francis WorInv
Brush, Charles Francis 1923- WhoAm 94
Brush, Clinton E., III 1911- WhoAm 94
Brush, Craig Balcombe 1930- WhoAm 94
Brush, George W. 1921- WhoAm 94
Brush, Gloria (Elizabeth) Defilipps 1947- WhoAmA 93
Brush, Leif 1932- WhoAmA 93
Brush, Louis Frederick 1946- WhoAmL 94
Brush, Lucien Munson, Jr. 1929- WhoAm 94
Brush, Peter Norman 1944- WhoAm 94
Brush, Richard Frank 1930- WhoFI 94
Brush, Thomas DrAPF 93
Brusilovsky, Yevgeny Grigor'yevich 1905-1981 NewGrDO
Brusilow, Saul 1927- WhoAm 94
Bruski, Paul Steven 1949- WhoMW 93
Bruski-Maus, Betty Jean 1927- WhoWest 94
Bruskin, Grisha Brouskine Grigori 1945- IntWW 93
Bruski-Naus, Betty Jean 1927- WhoAmP 93
Bruskotter, Eric WhoHol 92
Brusky, Linda L. 1948- WhoMW 93
Bruson, Renato 1936- NewGrDO
Brussaard, Gerrit 1942- WhoScEn 94
Brussard, Peter Frans 1938- WhoWest 94
Brusse, James A. 1934- WhoHisp 94
Brusseau, Mark Lewis 1958- WhoScEn 94, WhoWest 94
Brussel-Smith, Bernard 1914-1989 WhAm 10, WhoAmA 93N
Brussolo, Serge EncSF 93
Brust, David 1935- WhoWest 94
Brust, John Calvin Morrison 1936- WhoScEn 94
Brust, Robert Gustave 1945- WhoAmA 93
Brust, Steven (Karl Zoltan) 1955- EncSF 93
Brustad, Orin Daniel 1941- WhoAm 94, WhoAmL 94
Brustad, Tor 1926- IntWW 93
Brustein, Abram Isaac 1946- WhoFI 94
Brustein, Lawrence 1936- WhoAm 94
Brustein, Robert 1927- IntWW 93, WrDr 94
Brustein, Robert Sanford 1927- WhoAm 94
Brustlein, Daniel 1904- WhoAmA 93
Brustowicz, Paul M. 1944- WhoIns 94
Brute de Remur, Simon William Gabriel 1799-1839 DcAmReB 2
Brutlag, Rodney Sheldon 1938- WhoAm 94
Bruton, Bertram A. 1931- WhoBlA 94
Bruton, Charles R. 1946- WhoAmL 94
Bruton, Eric (Moore) 1915- WrDr 94
Bruton, James DeWitt, Jr. 1908- WhoAm 94
Bruton, John (Gerard) 1947- Who 94
Bruton, John Gerard 1947- IntWW 93
Bruton, John Macaulay 1937- WhoAm 94
Bruton, Marvin Dwayne 1945- WhoAmP 93
Brutosky, Mary Veronica 1932- WhoAmA 93, WhoWest 94
Brutting, Thomas Charles 1954- WhoWest 94
Brutus, Dennis 1924- BlkWr 2, ConAu 42NR, IntWW 93
Brutus, Dennis (Vincent) 1924- WrDr 94
Brutus, Dennis Vincent 1924- WhoAm 94, WhoBlA 94
Brutvan, Cheryl Ann 1955- WhoAm 94
Bruyas, Jacques 1635-1712 WhWE
Bruyere, Gaby d1978 WhoHol 92
Bruyere, Harold Joseph, Jr. 1947- WhoWest 94
Bruyn, Henry Bicker 1918- WhoAm 94
Bruyr, Jose 1889-1980 NewGrDO
Bruzda, Francis Joseph 1935- WhoAm 94
Bruzdowicz, Joanna 1943- NewGrDO
Bruzelius, Nils Johan Axel 1947- WhoAm 94
Bruzs, Boris Olgerd 1933- WhoAm 94
Bry, Edith 1898-1992 WhoAmA 93N
Bry, Jeffrey Allen 1949- WhoMW 93
Bry, Pierre Francois 1950- WhoScEn 94
Bryan, A. Bradford, Jr. WhoFI 94
Bryan, Adelbert M. 1943- WhoAmP 93, WhoBlA 94
Bryan, Albert V., Jr. 1926- WhoAmL 94
Bryan, Alonzo Jay 1917- WhoWest 94
Bryan, Arthur 1923- IntWW 93, Who 94
Bryan, Arthur Q. d1959 WhoHol 92
Bryan, Ashley F. 1923- BlkWr 2, ConAu 43NR
Bryan, Barbara Day 1927- WhoAm 94
Bryan, Barry Richard 1930- WhoAm 94
Bryan, Billie Marie 1932- WhoAm 94
Bryan, Bobby Harold 1949- WhoFI 94
Bryan, C. Clark 1910- WhoIns 94
Bryan, C. D. B. DrAPF 93
Bryan, Caroline Elizabeth 1951- WhoWest 94
Bryan, Carter Byrd 1945- WhoIns 94
Bryan, Christopher 1935- ConAu 43NR
Bryan, Clarice 1923- WhoBlA 94
Bryan, Clifton A. 1930- WhoAmP 93
Bryan, Colgan Hobson 1909- WhoAm 94
Bryan, Courtlandt Dixon Barnes 1936- WhoAm 94
Bryan, Curtis WhoBlA 94
Bryan, Curtis France 1896- WhAm 10
Bryan, Cynthia Joan 1953- WhoMW 93
Bryan, David c. 1962- See Bon Jovi ConMus 10
Bryan, David Alan 1946- WhoMW 93
Bryan, David Everett, Jr. 1947- WhoBlA 94
Bryan, David Merle 1921- WhoFI 94
Bryan, David Tennant 1906- WhoAm 94
Bryan, Dennis L. 1945- WhoFI 94
Bryan, Donald P. d1981 WhoHol 92
Bryan, Dora 1923- WhoHol 92
Bryan, Dora 1924- IntMPA 94, Who 94
Bryan, Ferald Joseph 1958- WhoMW 93
Bryan, Flize A. WhoBlA 94
Bryan, Ford R. 1912- WrDr 94
Bryan, George d1969 WhoHol 92
Bryan, George 1731-1791 WhAmRev
Bryan, Gerald Jackson 1921- Who 94
Bryan, Gordon Redman, Jr. 1928- WhoWest 94
Bryan, Harris Leden, Sr. 1935- WhoAmP 93
Bryan, Harrison 1923- WrDr 94
Bryan, Hayden Gitt 1945- WhoAmP 93
Bryan, Hayes Richard 1937- WhoScEn 94
Bryan, Henry Clark, Jr. 1930- WhoAm 94
Bryan, Henry Collier 1941- WhoScEn 94
Bryan, Hob 1952- WhoAmP 93
Bryan, Howard F. 1942- WhoAmP 93
Bryan, J(oseph), III 1904-1993 ConAu 141
Bryan, Jack L. 1942- WhoAmA 93
Bryan, Jacob F., IV 1943- WhoIns 94
Bryan, James E., Jr. 1948- WhoAmP 93
Bryan, James Lee 1936- WhoAm 94
Bryan, James Perry, Jr. 1940- WhoFI 94
Bryan, James Spencer 1944- WhoAmL 94
Bryan, James Timothy 1967- WhoMW 93
Bryan, Jane 1918- WhoHol 92
Bryan, Jean Marie Wehmueller 1964- WhoMW 93
Bryan, Jesse A. 1939- WhoBlA 94
Bryan, Joan Marie 1963- WhoMW 93
Bryan, John Henry 1936- IntWW 93, WhoAm 94, WhoFI 94, WhoMW 93
Bryan, John Leland 1926- WhoAm 94, WhoScEn 94
Bryan, John Rodney 1953- WhoFI 94, WhoWest 94
Bryan, John Stewart, III 1938- WhoAm 94, WhoFI 94
Bryan, Joseph, III d1993 NewYTBS 93
Bryan, Joseph McKinley 1896- WhoAm 94
Bryan, L. L. 1920- WhoAmP 93
Bryan, Lawrence Dow 1945- WhoAm 94
Bryan, Margaret 1929- Who 94
Bryan, Monk 1914- WhoAm 94
Bryan, Norman E. 1947- WhoMW 93
Bryan, Paul (Elmore Oliver) 1913- Who 94
Bryan, Paul Robey, Jr. WhoAm 94
Bryan, Raymond Guy 1961- WhoScEn 94
Bryan, Richard H. 1937- CngDr 93, IntWW 93, WhoAm 94, WhoAmP 93, WhoWest 94
Bryan, Richard Ray 1932- WhoAm 94, WhoFI 94
Bryan, Robert Armistead 1926- WhoAm 94
Bryan, Robert Fessler 1913- WhoAm 94, WhoFI 94
Bryan, Robert J. 1934- WhoAm 94, WhoAmL 94, WhoWest 94
Bryan, Robert Patrick 1926- Who 94
Bryan, Robert Russell 1943- WhoAmL 94
Bryan, Rosemarie Luise 1951- WhoAmL 94
Bryan, Roy DrAPF 93
Bryan, Sharon Ann WhoAmL 94, WhoWest 94
Bryan, Shirley Winifred 1916- WhoMW 93
Bryan, Spencer Maurice 1962- WhoScEn 94
Bryan, Thomas Lynn 1935- WhoAm 94, WhoAmL 94
Bryan, Wayne WhoMW 93
Bryan, Wilhelmus B(ogart), Jr. 1898- WhAm 10
Bryan, William F., III 1943- WhoIns 94
Bryan, William Jennings 1860-1925 DcAmReB 2, HisWorL [port]
Bryan, William Royal 1932- WhoAm 94
Bryans, Anne (Margaret) 1909- Who 94
Bryans, Christopher Loren 1955- WhoWest 94
Bryans, John Armond 1925- WhoAmA 93
Bryans, John Thomas 1924- WhoAm 94
Bryans, Richard W. 1931- WhoAmL 94
Bryans, Tom 1920- Who 94
Bryant, Adrian EncSF 93
Bryant, Alan Willard 1940- WhoFI 94, WhoWest 94
Bryant, Albert AfrAmG [port]
Bryant, Alvin 1937- AfrAmG [port]
Bryant, Andrea Pair 1942- WhoBlA 94
Bryant, Andrew Daniel 1929- WhoBlA 94
Bryant, Anne Lincoln 1949- WhoAm 94
Bryant, Anthony 1963- WhoBlA 94
Bryant, Anxious E. 1938- WhoBlA 94
Bryant, Arthur H. 1954- WhoAm 94
Bryant, Arthur Herbert, II 1942- WhoAm 94
Bryant, Arthur L. 1934- WhoIns 94
Bryant, Barbara Everitt 1926- WhoAm 94
Bryant, Benjamin 1905- Who 94
Bryant, Bertha Estelle 1927- WhoAm 94
Bryant, Betty Jane 1926- WhoMW 93
Bryant, Beulah d1988 WhoHol 92
Bryant, Beverley Brown 1942- WhoAmP 93
Bryant, Britain Hamilton 1940- WhoAmP 93
Bryant, Carl Paul 1941- WhoAmL 94
Bryant, Carol Lee 1946- WhoWest 94
Bryant, Castell Vaughn WhoBlA 94
Bryant, Cecil Farris 1914- WhoAm 94, WhoAmP 93
Bryant, Celia Mae Small 1913- WhoAm 94
Bryant, Charles d1948 WhoHol 92
Bryant, Charles Austin, IV 1946- WhoAm 94
Bryant, Charles R. 1959- WhoAmP 93
Bryant, Christopher Who 94
Bryant, (Alan) Christopher 1923- Who 94
Bryant, Clarence 1928- WhoBlA 94
Bryant, Clarence W. 1931- WhoBlA 94
Bryant, Clifton Dow 1932- WhoAm 94, WhoScEn 94
Bryant, Clovis WhoAmP 93
Bryant, Connie L. 1936- WhoBlA 94
Bryant, Cunningham C. 1921- AfrAmG [port], WhoBlA 94
Bryant, David John 1931- Who 94
Bryant, David Michael Arton 1942- Who 94
Bryant, Delores Hall E. 1935- WhoBlA 94
Bryant, Denis William 1918- Who 94
Bryant, Derek Thomas 1933- Who 94
Bryant, Don Estes 1917- WhoWest 94
Bryant, Donald Ashley 1950- WhoScEn 94
Bryant, Donald Loudon 1908- WhoAm 94, WhoFI 94
Bryant, Donald Loyd 1919- WhoAm 94
Bryant, Donnie L. 1942- WhoBlA 94
Bryant, Dorothy 1930- ConAu 41NR
Bryant, Dorothy (Calvetti) 1930- WrDr 94
Bryant, Douglas Wallace 1913- IntWW 93, WhoAm 94
Bryant, Edward DrAPF 93
Bryant, Edward (Arnot) 1948- ConAu 141

Bryant, Edward (Winslow), (Jr.) 1945- *WrDr 94*
Bryant, Edward (Winslow, Jr.) 1945- *EncSF 93*
Bryant, Edward Albert 1928- *WhoAmA 93*
Bryant, Edward Clark 1915- *WhoAm 94*
Bryant, Edward Joe, III 1947- *WhoBlA 94*
Bryant, Edward Kendall 1902-1991 *WhAm 10*
Bryant, Faye B. 1937- *WhoBlA 94*
Bryant, Flossie Byrd 1907- *WhoAmP 93*
Bryant, Franklyn *WhoBlA 94*
Bryant, Fred Boyd 1952- *WhoScEn 94*
Bryant, Garry Eugene 1954- *WhoWest 94*
Bryant, Gary Allen 1951- *WhoAmL 94*
Bryant, Gary Lee 1943- *WhoWest 94*
Bryant, Gay 1945- *WhoAm 94, WrDr 94*
Bryant, Glenn E. *WhoAmP 93*
Bryant, Greyham Frank 1931- *Who 94*
Bryant, Henry C. 1915- *WhoBlA 94*
Bryant, Hilda Marie 1928- *WhoWest 94*
Bryant, Hubert Hale 1931- *WhoAm 94 WhoBlA 94*
Bryant, Hurley Douglas, Jr. 1944- *WhoWest 94*
Bryant, Ira Houston, III 1942- *WhoAmL 94*
Bryant, Isaac Rutledge 1914- *WhoBlA 94*
Bryant, Jack Kendall 1925- *WhoWest 94*
Bryant, James 1950- *WhoMW 93*
Bryant, James Bruce 1961- *WhoAmL 94*
Bryant, James Harold 1942- *WhoFI 94*
Bryant, James Sears 1953- *WhoAmP 93*
Bryant, James W. 1922- *WhoBlA 94*
Bryant, James Wesley 1921- *WhoAm 94*
Bryant, Jeff Dwight 1960- *WhoBlA 94*
Bryant, Jenkins, Jr. *WhoAmP 93, WhoBlA 94*
Bryant, Jerome Benjamin 1916- *WhoBlA 94*
Bryant, Jerry Doyle 1947- *WhoAmP 93*
Bryant, Jesse A. 1922- *WhoBlA 94*
Bryant, Jo Elizabeth 1937- *WhoAmP 93*
Bryant, John d1989 *WhoHol 92*
Bryant, John 1943- *WhoFI 94*
Bryant, John 1947- *CngDr 93*
Bryant, John Bradbury 1947- *WhoAm 94*
Bryant, John G. 1944- *WhoBlA 94*
Bryant, John Richard 1943- *WhoBlA 94*
Bryant, John S. 1947- *WhoAmL 94*
Bryant, John Wiley 1947- *WhoAm 94, WhoAmP 93*
Bryant, John William, Jr. 1957- *WhoAmP 93*
Bryant, Joseph Allen, Jr. 1919- *WhoAm 94, WrDr 94*
Bryant, Josephine Harriet 1947- *WhoAm 94*
Bryant, Judith Marie 1942- *Who 94*
Bryant, Karen Worstell 1942- *WhoFI 94*
Bryant, Kathryn Ann 1949- *WhoBlA 94*
Bryant, Keith Lynn, Jr. 1937- *WhoAm 94*
Bryant, Kelvin LeRoy 1960- *WhoBlA 94*
Bryant, Larry Michael 1946- *WhoScEn 94*
Bryant, Laura Militzer 1955- *WhoAmA 93*
Bryant, Leon Serle 1949- *WhoBlA 94*
Bryant, Lester R. 1930- *WhoAm 94*
Bryant, Linda Goode 1949- *WhoAmA 93*
Bryant, Margaret M. d1993 *NewYTBS 93*
Bryant, Margaret M. 1900-1993 *ConAu 141*
Bryant, Marguerite d1951 *WhoHol 92*
Bryant, Marie d1978 *WhoHol 92*
Bryant, Mark 1965- *WhoBlA 94*
Bryant, Martha J. 1949- *WhoAm 94*
Bryant, Marvin Pierce 1925- *WhoAm 94*
Bryant, Michael 1928- *IntWW 93, WhoHol 92*
Bryant, Michael Dennis 1928- *Who 94*
Bryant, N. Z., Jr. 1949- *WhoBlA 94*
Bryant, Nana d1955 *WhoHol 92*
Bryant, Napoleon Adebola, Jr. 1929- *WhoBlA 94*
Bryant, Neil R. 1948- *WhoAmP 93*
Bryant, Olen L. 1927- *WhoAmA 93*
Bryant, Oscar Sims, Jr. 1920- *WhoAm 94*
Bryant, Peter *EncSF 93*
Bryant, Peter Elwood *Who 94*
Bryant, Peter George Francis 1932- *Who 94*
Bryant, Peter James 1944- *WhoScEn 94*
Bryant, Phil *WhoAmP 93*
Bryant, Preston 1938- *WhoBlA 94*
Bryant, R. Kelly, Jr. 1917- *WhoBlA 94*
Bryant, Randal Everitt 1952- *WhoAm 94*
Bryant, Reece L(awrence) 1898- *WhAm 10*
Bryant, Regina Lynn 1950- *WhoBlA 94*
Bryant, Richard Charles 1908- *Who 94*
Bryant, Richard Todd 1952- *WhoAmL 94*
Bryant, Robert E. 1910- *WhoBlA 94*
Bryant, Robert Edward 1931- *WhoBlA 94*
Bryant, Robert Harry 1925- *WrDr 94*
Bryant, Robert Leamon 1953- *WhoScEn 94*
Bryant, Robert Parker 1922- *WhoAm 94*
Bryant, Robin d1976 *WhoHol 92*
Bryant, Russell Philip, Jr. 1949- *WhoBlA 94*
Bryant, Ruth Alyne 1924- *WhoAm 94*
Bryant, Susan Lynn Zuhl 1960- *WhoMW 93*
Bryant, T. J. 1934- *WhoBlA 94*
Bryant, Tamara Thompson *WhoAmA 93*
Bryant, Teresena Wise 1940- *WhoBlA 94*
Bryant, Thomas 1938- *Who 94*
Bryant, Thomas Edward 1936- *IntWW 93*
Bryant, Thos Lee 1943- *WhoAm 94*
Bryant, Vaughn Motley, Jr. 1940- *WhoAm 94*
Bryant, Wayne R. 1947- *ConBlB 6 [port], WhoBlA 94*
Bryant, Wayne Richard 1947- *WhoAmP 93*
Bryant, Wendy Sims 1967- *WhoScEn 94*
Bryant, Willa Coward 1919- *WhoBlA 94*
Bryant, William *WhoHol 92*
Bryant, William Arnett, Jr. 1942- *WhoBlA 94*
Bryant, William Benson 1911- *CngDr 93, WhoBlA 94*
Bryant, William Cullen 1794-1878 *AmSocL*
Bryant, William Gover 1923- *WhoMW 93*
Bryant, William H. 1933- *WhoAm 94, WhoFI 94*
Bryant, William Henry, Jr. 1963- *WhoBlA 94*
Bryant, William Jesse 1935- *WhoBlA 94*
Bryant, William M. *WhoAmP 93*
Bryant, William R., Jr. 1938- *WhoAmP 93*
Bryant, William Robert, Jr. 1938- *WhoMW 93*
Bryant, Willie d1964 *WhoHol 92*
Bryant, Winston 1938- *WhoAm 94, WhoAmL 94, WhoAmP 93*
Bryant-Mitchell, Ruth Harriet 1943- *WhoBlA 94*
Bryant-Reid, Johanne 1949- *WhoBlA 94*
Bryant-VanDerAa, Carolyn Joyce 1962- *WhoMW 93*
Bryar, Claudia *WhoHol 92*
Bryar, Paul 1910- *WhoHol 92*
Bryars, Donald Leonard 1929- *Who 94*
Bryars, Gavin 1943- *NewGrDO*
Bryars, (Richard) Gavin 1943- *IntWW 93*
Bryars, John Desmond 1928- *Who 94*
Bryce *Who 94*
Bryce, Eileen Ann 1953- *WhoAmA 93*
Bryce, Gabe Robb 1921- *Who 94*
Bryce, Gordon *Who 94*
Bryce, Gordon 1943- *Who 94*
Bryce, (William) Gordon 1913- *Who 94*
Bryce, Herrington J. *WhoBlA 94, WhoFI 94*
Bryce, Jabez Leslie *Who 94*
Bryce, Mark Adams 1953- *WhoAmA 93*
Bryce, Scott *WhoHol 92*
Bryce, William Delf 1932- *WhoAmL 94*
Bryceland, Yvonne *WhoHol 92*
Bryceland, Yvonne 1924-1992 *AnObit 1992*
Bryce-Laporte, Roy Simon 1933- *WhoBlA 94*
Brycelea, Clifford 1953- *WhoAmA 93*
Bryce-Smith, Derek 1926- *Who 94*
Brychel, Rudolph Myron 1934- *WhoScEn 94, WhoWest 94*
Bryde, June *WhoHol 92*
Bryden, David John 1943- *Who 94*
Bryden, John (Herbert) 1943- *WrDr 94*
Bryden, William Campbell Rough 1942- *Who 94*
Brydges, Harford Jones 1774-1829 *WhWE*
Brydges, Thomas Eugene 1942- *WhoAmL 94*
Brydon, Donald James 1922- *WhoAm 94*
Brydon, Harold Wesley 1923- *WhoAm 94, WhoFI 94, WhoScEn 94, WhoWest 94*
Brydon, Ruth Vickery 1930- *WhoWest 94*
Bryenton, Gary L. 1939- *WhoAm 94*
Bryer, Anthony Applemore Mornington 1937- *Who 94*
Bryer, David Ronald William 1944- *Who 94*
Bryfonski, Dedria Anne 1947- *WhoAm 94*
Bryhan, Anthony James 1945- *WhoScEn 94*
Bryher 1894-1983 *GayLL*
Bryher, (Annie Winifred Ellerman) 1894-1983 *BlmGWL*
Brymer, Jack 1915- *IntWW 93, Who 94*
Brynelson, Floyd A. 1914- *WhoAmL 94*
Bryngdahl, Olof 1933- *IntWW 93*
Bryngelson, Jim 1941- *WhoWest 94*
Brynielsson, Harry Anders Bertil 1914- *IntWW 93*
Brynildson, John Edward 1943- *WhoMW 93*
Brynn, Edward Paul 1942- *WhoAm 94*
Brynner, Yul d1985 *WhoHol 92*
Bryon, Kathleen 1922- *IntMPA 94*
Bryskin, Boris David 1941- *WhoMW 93*
Bryson, Betty *WhoHol 92*
Bryson, Bill 1951?- *ConAu 142*
Bryson, Brady Oliver 1915- *WhoAm 94*
Bryson, Bruce Alan Randy 1946- *WhoWest 94*
Bryson, Cheryl Blackwell *WhoAm 94, WhoAmL 94*
Bryson, Cheryl Blackwell 1950- *WhoBlA 94*
Bryson, Dorothy Printup 1894- *WhoWest 94*
Bryson, Gary Spath 1943- *WhoAm 94, WhoWest 94*
Bryson, (James) Graeme 1913- *Who 94*
Bryson, James d1935 *WhoHol 92*
Bryson, John 1923- *WrDr 94*
Bryson, John (Noel) 1935- *ConAu 142*
Bryson, John E. 1943- *WhoAm 94, WhoFI 94, WhoWest 94*
Bryson, Keith 1951- *WhoScEn 94*
Bryson, Kenneth Donald 1924- *WhoAm 94*
Bryson, Larry Arthur 1948- *WhoMW 93*
Bryson, Lindsay (Sutherland) 1925- *Who 94*
Bryson, Lindsay Sutherland 1925- *IntWW 93*
Bryson, Peabo 1951- *ConMus 11 [port], WhoBlA 94*
Bryson, Ralph J. 1922- *WhoBlA 94*
Bryson, Reid Allen 1920- *WhoAm 94*
Bryson, Seymour L. 1937- *WhoBlA 94*
Bryson, Vern Elrick 1920- *WhoScEn 94*
Bryson, Winifred d1987 *WhoHol 92*
Bryt, Albert 1913- *WhoScEn 94*
Brzana, Stanislaus Joseph 1917- *WhoAm 94*
Brzezinski, Elaine Victoria 1964- *WhoAmL 94*
Brzezinski, Zbigniew 1928- *WhoAm 94, WhoAmP 93, WrDr 94*
Brzezinski, Zbigniew K. 1928- *IntWW 93*
Brzezinski, Zbigniew K(azimierz) 1928- *ConAu 41NR*
Brzoska, Michael Jerome 1940- *WhoFI 94*
Brzosko, Jan Stefan 1939- *WhoScEn 94*
Brzowski, Josef 1803-1888 *NewGrDO*
Brzozowski, Richard Joseph 1932- *WhoAmA 93*
Brzustowicz, John Cing-Mars 1957- *WhoAmL 94*
Brzustowicz, Richard John 1917- *WhoAm 94, WhoScEn 94*
Brzustowicz, Stanislaw Henry 1919- *WhoAm 94*
Bschorr, Paul Joseph 1941- *WhoAm 94*
Bua, Nicholas John 1925- *WhoAm 94*
Bub, Alexander David 1949- *WhoMW 93, WhoScEn 94*
Buba, Joy Flinsch 1904- *WhoAmA 93*
Bubash, James Edward 1945- *WhoScEn 94*
Bubash, Patricia Jane *WhoMW 93*
Bubb, Brian David 1962- *WhoWest 94*
Bubb, Harry Geiple 1924- *WhoWest 94*
Bubb, Henry Agnew 1907-1989 *WhAm 10*
Bubba, Joseph L. 1938- *WhoAmP 93*
Bubbles, John 1902-1986 *AfrAmAl 6*
Bube, Richard H 1927- *WrDr 94*
Bube, Richard Howard 1927- *WhoAm 94*
Bubeck, Roy R. 1946- *WhoIns 94*
Bubenzer, Gary Dean 1940- *WhoAm 94*
Buber, (Mordekhai) Martin 1878-1965 *EncEth*
Bubier, Ellen Stewart 1962- *WhoAm 94*
Bubka, Sergey Nazarovich 1963- *IntWW 93*
Bublys, Algimantas Vladas 1941- *WhoAm 94*
Bubna, Shashi K. 1944- *WhoFI 94*
Bubrick, George Joseph 1947- *WhoAm 94*
Bubrick, Melvin Phillip 1944- *WhoMW 93*
Bubriski, Kevin E. 1954- *WhoAmA 93*
Bubriski, Kevin Ernest 1954- *WhoAm 94*
Bubulka, Grace Marie 1951- *WhoWest 94*
Bubwith, Nicholas c. 1355-1424 *DcNaB MP*
Buc, Nancy Lillian 1944- *WhoAm 94, WhoAmL 94*
Bucalossi, Pietro 1905- *IntWW 93*
Bucceleni, Giovanni *NewGrDO*
Buccella, William Victor 1943- *WhoAm 94, WhoAmL 94, WhoFI 94*
Buccellati, Giorgio 1937- *WhoWest 94*
Buccello, Henry Louis 1920- *WhoAm 94*
Bucchi, Valentino 1916-1976 *NewGrDO*
Bucchieri, Peter Charles 1955- *WhoFI 94*
Bucci, Anthony J. 1925- *WhoAmP 93*
Bucci, Elaine Theresa 1957- *WhoAmP 93*
Bucci, Flavio *WhoHol 92*
Bucci, Mark 1924- *NewGrDO*
Bucci, Maurizio 1923- *IntWW 93*
Bucci, Raymond 1938- *WhoFI 94*
Bucci, Thomas *WhoAmP 93*
Buccieri, M. Elaine 1960- *WhoAmL 94*
Buccigrossi, David Eric 1956- *WhoWest 94*
Buccini, Frank John 1959- *WhoScEn 94*
Buccino, Alphonse 1931- *WhoAm 94*
Buccino, Ernest John, Jr. 1945- *WhoAmL 94*
Buccino, Salvatore George 1933- *WhoAm 94*
Buccleuch, Duke of 1923- *Who 94*
Buccleuch and Queensberry, Duke of 1923- *IntWW 93*
Bucco, Martin 1929- *WhoWest 94*
Buccola, Guy d1962 *WhoHol 92*
Bucerius, (Karl Anton Martin) Gerd 1906- *IntWW 93*
Bucge fl. 8th cent.- *BlmGWL*
Buch, Gary 1954- *WhoAmA 93*
Buch, René Augusto 1925- *WhoHisp 94*
Buch, Richard Alan 1959- *WhoFI 94*
Buch, Robert E. 1946- *WhoAmL 94*
Bucha, Edward Richard 1954- *WhoFI 94*
Buchachenko, Anatoliy Leonidovich 1935- *IntWW 93*
Buchalter, Stuart David 1937- *WhoAm 94*
Buchan *Who 94*
Buchan, Earl of 1930- *Who 94*
Buchan, Alan Bradley 1936- *WhoAm 94*
Buchan, Anna *BlmGWL*
Buchan, Cynthia 1949- *NewGrDO*
Buchan, David 1790-1845 *WhWE*
Buchan, Douglas Charles 1936- *WhoFI 94*
Buchan, Eric Ancrum 1907- *Who 94*
Buchan, Hamish Noble 1944- *WhoAm 94*
Buchan, James 1916- *WrDr 94*
Buchan, Jane O'Neil *WhoWomW 91*
Buchan, Janey 1926- *Who 94*
Buchan, John 1912- *Who 94*
Buchan, Jonathan Edward, Jr. 1950- *WhoAm 94*
Buchan, Ronald Forbes 1915- *WhoAm 94, WhoScEn 94*
Buchan, Stevenson 1907- *Who 94*
Buchan, Thomas Johnston *Who 94*
Buchan, Tom 1931- *WrDr 94*
Buchanan, Andrew George 1937- *Who 94*
Buchanan, Angela Marie 1948- *WhoAmP 93*
Buchanan, B. Merritt, Jr. 1948- *WhoFI 94*
Buchanan, Bruce, II 1945- *WhoAm 94*
Buchanan, Bryce John 1965- *WhoWest 94*
Buchanan, Buck d1992 *WhoBlA 94N*
Buchanan, C. Cleave, Jr. 1945- *WhoAmL 94*
Buchanan, Charles Alexander James L. *Who 94*
Buchanan, Charles Franklin 1936- *WhoAmP 93*
Buchanan, Colin (Douglas) 1907- *Who 94*
Buchanan, Colin (Ogilvie) 1934- *WrDr 94*
Buchanan, Colin Douglas 1907- *IntWW 93*
Buchanan, Colin Ogilvie 1934- *Who 94*
Buchanan, Daniel Harvey 1923- *WhoAm 94*
Buchanan, Debra Ann 1956- *WhoAm 94*
Buchanan, Dennis *Who 94*
Buchanan, (Ranald) Dennis 1932- *Who 94*
Buchanan, Dennis Michael 1945- *WhoAm 94*
Buchanan, Diane Kay 1960- *WhoScEn 94*
Buchanan, Dodds Ireton 1931- *WhoAm 94*
Buchanan, Edgar d1979 *WhoHol 92*
Buchanan, Edna *WhoAm 94*
Buchanan, Edna (Rydzik) 1939- *WrDr 94*
Buchanan, Ellery Rives 1950- *WhoAm 94*
Buchanan, Eric 1932- *Who 94*
Buchanan, George 1506-1582 *BlmGEL, DcLB 132 [port]*
Buchanan, George Duncan *Who 94*
Buchanan, George Duncan 1935- *IntWW 93*
Buchanan, Ian *WhoHol 92*
Buchanan, Isobel 1954- *IntWW 93, NewGrDO*
Buchanan, Isobel Wilson 1954- *Who 94*
Buchanan, J. Robert 1928- *IntWW 93*
Buchanan, J. Vincent Marino 1951- *WhoAmL 94*
Buchanan, J. W. *WhoAmP 93*
Buchanan, Jack d1957 *WhoHol 92*
Buchanan, James A. d1993 *NewYTBS 93*
Buchanan, James David 1929- *WrDr 94*
Buchanan, James J 1925- *WrDr 94*
Buchanan, James Junkin 1925- *WhoAm 94*
Buchanan, James King 1935- *WhoMW 93*
Buchanan, James M 1919- *WrDr 94*
Buchanan, James McGill 1919- *IntWW 93, Who 94, WhoAm 94, WhoFI 94*
Buchanan, Jerry 1936-1992 *WhoAmA 93N*
Buchanan, John 1924- *WhoAmP 93*
Buchanan, John David 1916- *Who 94*
Buchanan, John Dewey, Jr. 1933- *WhoAmL 94*
Buchanan, John Donald 1927- *WhoAm 94*
Buchanan, John Edward, Jr. 1953- *WhoAmA 93*
Buchanan, John Grant 1926- *WhoScEn 94*

Buchanan, John Hall, Jr. 1928- *WhoAmP 93*
Buchanan, John M. *Who 94*
Buchanan, John Machlin 1917- *IntWW 93, WhoAm 94, WhoScEn 94*
Buchanan, John MacLennan 1931- *IntWW 93, WhoAm 94, WhoAmL 94*
Buchanan, John Murdoch 1897- *WhAm 10*
Buchanan, John Robert 1928- *WhoAm 94*
Buchanan, Junious *ProFbHF [port]*
Buchanan, Larry 1924- *HorFD*
Buchanan, Laura *ConAu 41NR*
Buchanan, Lee Ann 1955- *WhoAm 94, WhoFI 94*
Buchanan, Marie 1922- *WrDr 94*
Buchanan, Mary Estill 1934- *WhoAmP 93*
Buchanan, Meg d1970 *WhoHol 92*
Buchanan, Michael A. 1949- *WhoAmP 93*
Buchanan, Miles *WhoHol 92*
Buchanan, Nancy 1946- *WhoAmA 93*
Buchanan, Otis 1951- *WhoBlA 94*
Buchanan, Patrick Joseph 1938- *IntWW 93, WhoAm 94, WhoAmP 93*
Buchanan, Paul D. 1938- *WhoAmP 93*
Buchanan, Peter (William) 1925- *Who 94*
Buchanan, Peter McEachin 1935- *WhoAm 94*
Buchanan, Richard 1912- *Who 94*
Buchanan, Richard Allen 1951- *WhoAm 94*
Buchanan, Richard Kent 1951- *WhoFI 94, WhoMW 93*
Buchanan, Richard Lee 1947- *WhoAmL 94*
Buchanan, Robert Alexander 1932- *WhoAm 94*
Buchanan, Robert Angus 1930- *Who 94, WhoAm 94, WrDr 94*
Buchanan, Robert Campbell 1940- *WhoAm 94*
Buchanan, Robert Edgar 1919- *WhoAm 94*
Buchanan, Robert Fulton 1955- *WhoAm 94*
Buchanan, Robert James 1963- *WhoAmL 94*
Buchanan, Robert Lee, Jr. 1951- *WhoAm 94, WhoAmL 94*
Buchanan, Robert McLeod 1932- *WhoAm 94, WhoAmL 94*
Buchanan, Robert Michael 1953- *WhoMW 93*
Buchanan, Robert Taylor 1944- *WhoAm 94*
Buchanan, Robert Williams 1848-1901 *EncSF 93*
Buchanan, Robert Wilson 1930- *Who 94*
Buchanan, Sidney Arnold 1932- *WhoAmA 93*
Buchanan, Stuart d1974 *WhoHol 92*
Buchanan, Susan Shaver 1954- *WhoFI 94*
Buchanan, Teri Bailey 1946- *WhoFI 94, WhoWest 94*
Buchanan, Thomas 1744-1815 *WhAmRev*
Buchanan, Thomas Steven 1958- *WhoMW 93*
Buchanan, Walter Woolwine 1941- *WhoMW 93*
Buchanan, William Hobart, Jr. 1937- *WhoAm 94, WhoFI 94*
Buchanan, William Jennings 1948- *WhoAmL 94*
Buchanan, William Murray 1935- *WhoFI 94, WhoMW 93*
Buchanan, William Walter 1927- *WhoAm 94*
Buchanan-Dunlop, Richard 1919- *Who 94*
Buchanan-Jardine, A.R.J. *Who 94*
Buchan-Hepburn, (John) Alastair (Trant Kidd) 1931- *Who 94*
Buchan Of Auchmacoy, David William Sinclair 1929- *Who 94*
Buchardo, Carlos Lopez *NewGrDO*
Bucharoff, Simon 1881-1955 *NewGrDO*
Buchbinder, Darrell Bruce 1946- *WhoAmL 94*
Buchbinder-Green, Barbara Joyce 1944- *WhoMW 93*
Buchdahl, Gerd 1914- *WrDr 94*
Bucheger, Ronald R. 1948- *WhoWest 94*
Bucheister, Patt 1942- *WrDr 94*
Buchele, Wesley Fisher 1920- *WhoAm 94, WhoScEn 94*
Buchen, John Gustave 1920- *WhoAm 94*
Buchenrot, Stephen R. 1948- *WhoAmL 94*
Buchenroth, Stephen Richard 1948- *WhoAm 94, WhoAmL 94*
Bucher, Bernard Jean-Marie 1962- *WhoScEn 94*
Bucher, Francois 1927- *WhoAmA 93, WrDr 94*
Bucher, Gail Phillips 1941- *WhoScEn 94*
Bucher, George Scott 1942- *WhoIns 94*
Bucher, Jeffrey Martin 1933- *WhoAm 94*
Bucher, John Henry 1939- *WhoAm 94*
Bucher, Julian R. 1942- *WhoMW 93*
Bucher, Ronald Eugene 1959- *WhoAmL 94*
Bucherre-Frazier, Veronique 1951- *WhoAm 94, WhoFI 94*
Buchheim, Lothar-Gunther 1918- *IntWW 93*
Buchheit, Teresa Clare 1962- *WhoAmL 94*
Buchhofer, Monsieur fl. c. 1725- *NewGrDO*
Buchholz, Brian Scott 1961- *WhoFI 94*
Buchholz, Christopher 1962- *WhoHol 92*
Buchholz, Donald Alden 1929- *WhoAm 94*
Buchholz, Edward J. 1948- *WhoAm 94*
Buchholz, Horst 1933- *IntMPA 94, WhoHol 92*
Buchholz, Jeffrey Carl 1947- *WhoMW 93*
Buchholz, John Nicholas 1956- *WhoWest 94*
Buchholz, Richard 1964- *WhoScEn 94*
Buchholz, Sheri Rae 1962- *WhoFI 94*
Buchholz, William James 1945- *WhoFI 94*
Buchi, George H. 1921- *IntWW 93*
Buchi, George Hermann 1921- *WhoScEn 94*
Buchi, Mark Keith 1951- *WhoAm 94*
Buchignani, Leo Joseph 1922- *WhoAm 94*
Buchin, Irving D. 1920-1989 *WhAm 10*
Buchin, Stanley Ira 1931- *WhoAm 94, WhoFI 94*
Buchinskaia, Nadezhda Aleksandrovna *BlmGWL*
Buchinsky, Charles *WhoAm 94, WhoHol 92*
Buchko, Aaron Anthony 1956- *WhoMW 93*
Buchler, Justus 1914-1991 *WhAm 10*
Buchman, Arles *WhoAmA 93*
Buchman, Elwood 1923- *WhoAm 94*
Buchman, Frank Nathan Daniel 1878-1961 *DcAmReB 2*
Buchman, Heather Rebecca 1965- *WhoAm 94*
Buchman, James Wallace 1948- *WhoAmA 93*
Buchman, Kenneth William 1956- *WhoAmL 94*
Buchman, Marion *DrAPF 93, WhoAm 94*
Buchman, Mark Edward 1937- *WhoAm 94*
Buchman, Matthew Lieber 1958- *WhoWest 94*
Buchman, Seth Barry 1955- *WhoAmL 94*
Buchman, Sidney 1902-1975 *IntDcF 2-4*
Buchmann, Alan Paul 1934- *WhoAm 94, WhoAmP 93*
Buchmeyer, Jerry 1933- *WhoAm 94, WhoAmL 94*
Buchner, Eberhart 1939- *NewGrDO*
Buchner, Eduard 1860-1917 *WorScD*
Buchner, Georg 1813-1837 *DcLB 133 [port], IntDcT 2, NewGrDO, RfGShF*
Buchner, Luise 1821-1877 *BlmGWL*
Bucholtz, Alan Howard 1937- *WhoAmL 94*
Bucholtz, Harold Ronald 1952- *WhoAm 94*
Buchsbaum, Harvey William 1935- *WhoWest 94*
Buchsbaum, Peter A. 1945- *WhoAm 94*
Buchsbaum, Solomon J. d1993 *IntWW 93N, NewYTBS 93 [port]*
Buchsbaum, Solomon J. 1929- *IntWW 93*
Buchsieb, Walter Charles 1929- *WhoMW 93*
Buchta, Edmund 1928- *WhoWest 94*
Buchter, Jonathan F. 1949- *WhoAmL 94*
Buchter, Thomas 1949- *WhoAm 94*
Buchthal, David Charles 1943- *WhoMW 93*
Buchthal, Fritz 1907- *IntWW 93*
Buchthal, Hugo 1909- *Who 94*
Buchthal, Hugo H. 1909- *IntWW 93*
Buchwald, Art 1925- *IntWW 93, Who 94, WhoAm 94, WrDr 94*
Buchwald, Caryl Edward 1937- *WhoAm 94*
Buchwald, Don David 1944- *WhoAmL 94*
Buchwald, Elias 1924- *WhoAm 94*
Buchwald, Emilie *DrAPF 93*
Buchwald, Emilie Daisy 1935- *WhoMW 93*
Buchwald, Henry 1932- *WhoAm 94*
Buchwald, Howard 1964- *WhoAmA 93*
Buchwald, Martyn Jerel 1942- *WhoAm 94*
Buchwald, Naomi Reice 1944- *WhoAm 94, WhoAmL 94*
Buchwald, Nathaniel Avrom 1925- *WhoAm 94*
Buchwalter, Stephen L. 1947- *WhoScEn 94*
Buchy, G. James 1940- *WhoAmP 93*
Bucinell, Ronald Blaise 1958- *WhoScEn 94*
Bucio, Paz Guadalupe 1942- *WhoHisp 94*
Buck, Adele d1912 *WhoHol 92*
Buck, Alan Charles 1931- *WhoWest 94*
Buck, Albert Charles d1992 *Who 94N*
Buck, Alfred Andreas 1921- *WhoAm 94*
Buck, (Philip) Antony (Fyson) 1928- *Who 94*
Buck, Carl Nelson 1952- *WhoWest 94*
Buck, Carol Kathleen 1925- *WhoAm 94*
Buck, Christian Brevoort Zabriskie 1914- *WhoFI 94, WhoScEn 94, WhoWest 94*
Buck, Craig 1952- *ConAu 141*
Buck, David d1989 *WhoHol 92*
Buck, David Douglass 1949- *WhoAmL 94*
Buck, Donald Tirrell 1931- *WhoAm 94*
Buck, Douglas Earl 1936- *WhoScEn 94*
Buck, Dudley 1839-1909 *NewGrDO*
Buck, Earl Chris 1947- *WhoMW 93*
Buck, Earl Wayne 1939- *WhoMW 93*
Buck, Ford d1955 *WhoHol 92*
Buck, Frank d1950 *WhoHol 92*
Buck, Frank F. 1943- *WhoAmP 93*
Buck, Gregory Allen 1951- *WhoScEn 94*
Buck, Gurdon Hall 1936- *WhoAm 94, WhoAmL 94*
Buck, Harry M 1921- *WrDr 94*
Buck, Heather 1926- *BlmGWL*
Buck, Inez d1957 *WhoHol 92*
Buck, Ivory M., Jr. 1928- *WhoBlA 94*
Buck, Jack *WhoAm 94*
Buck, James E. *WhoAm 94, WhoFI 94*
Buck, James Michael 1967- *WhoMW 93*
Buck, John 1946- *WhoAmA 93*
Buck, John Bonner 1912- *WhoAm 94*
Buck, Judith Brooks 1949- *WhoBlA 94*
Buck, Jules 1917- *IntMPA 94*
Buck, Kathleen Ann 1948- *WhoAm 94*
Buck, Kenneth William 1938- *Who 94*
Buck, Lawrence Paul 1944- *WhoAm 94*
Buck, Lawrence Richard 1953- *WhoWest 94*
Buck, Lee Albert 1923- *WhoAm 94*
Buck, Linda Dee 1946- *WhoWest 94*
Buck, Louise Zierdt 1919- *WhoAm 94*
Buck, Lynn *DrAPF 93*
Buck, M. Scott 1966- *WhoScEn 94*
Buck, Margaret Waring 1910- *WrDr 94*
Buck, Nell Roy d1962 *WhoHol 92*
Buck, Pearl S. 1892-1973 *BlmGWL*
Buck, Pearl Sydenstricker 1892-1973 *AmCulL [port]*
Buck, Peter *WhoAm 94*
Buck, Porge 1931- *WhoAmA 93*
Buck, Richard d1948 *WhoHol 92*
Buck, Richard D. 1903-1977 *WhoAmA 93N*
Buck, Richard Forde 1921- *WhoScEn 94*
Buck, Robert Follette 1917- *WhoAm 94*
Buck, Robert Treat, Jr. 1939- *WhoAm 94, WhoAmA 93*
Buck, Rosemary Alice 1953- *WhoMW 93*
Buck, Susan J. 1947- *ConAu 141*
Buck, Thomas Bryant, III 1938- *WhoAmP 93*
Buck, Thomas Randolph 1930- *WhoAm 94, WhoAmL 94*
Buck, Vernon Ashley, Jr. 1920- *WhoBlA 94*
Buck, Vince 1968- *WhoBlA 94*
Buck, William Boyd 1933- *WhoAm 94*
Buck, William Fraser, II 1944- *WhoAm 94*
Buckalew, Judith Adele 1947- *WhoAm 94*
Buck and Bubbles *WhoHol 92*
Buckardt, Everett L. *WhoFI 94*
Buckaway, Catherine M(argaret) 1919- *WrDr 94*
Buckaway, William Allen, Jr. 1934- *WhoAmL 94*
Buckelew, Joseph Earl 1929- *WhoAmP 93*
Buckelew, Robin Browne 1947- *WhoScEn 94*
Buckels, Marvin Wayne 1929- *WhoAm 94*
Buckely, Lord 1906-1960 *WhoCom*
Buckeridge, Anthony 1912- *WrDr 94*
Buckhalter, Emerson R. 1954- *WhoBlA 94*
Buckhanan, Dorothy Wilson 1958- *WhoBlA 94*
Buckholts, Claudia *DrAPF 93*
Buckhurst, Lord 1979- *Who 94*
Buckingham, Archdeacon of *Who 94*
Buckingham, Amyand David 1930- *IntWW 93, Who 94*
Buckingham, Edwin John, III 1947- *WhoAm 94*
Buckingham, Harold Canute, Jr. 1930- *WhoAm 94*
Buckingham, Hugh Fletcher 1932- *Who 94*
Buckingham, Lindsey 1949- *WhoAm 94*
Buckingham, Michael John 1943- *WhoAm 94, WhoScEn 94, WhoWest 94*
Buckingham, Nancy 1919- *WrDr 94*
Buckingham, Nancy 1924- *WrDr 94*
Buckingham, Richard Arthur 1911- *Who 94*
Buckingham, Richard G. 1947- *WhoAmL 94*
Buckingham, Richard John 1945- *WhoWest 94*
Buckingham, Ulisa Diane 1955- *WhoMW 93*
Buckingham, Vivian Leona 1925- *WhoAmP 93*
Buckingham, W. Bruce 1955- *WhoAmP 93*
Buckingham, Yvonne *WhoHol 92*
Buckinghamshire, Earl of 1944- *Who 94*
Buckius, Richard O. 1950- *WhoScEn 94*
Buckland, Charles Smillie 1934- *WhoAm 94*
Buckland, David John 1949- *IntWW 93*
Buckland, Michael Keeble 1941- *WhoAm 94*
Buckland, Peter Graham 1938- *WhoScEn 94*
Buckland, Roger Basil 1942- *WhoAm 94, WhoScEn 94*
Buckland, Ronald John Denys Eden 1920- *Who 94*
Buckland, Ross 1942- *Who 94*
Buckland, Veda d1941 *WhoHol 92*
Buckland, Wilfred 1866-1946 *IntDcF 2-4*
Buckland, William 1784-1856 *WorScD*
Buckle, Denys Herbert Vintcent 1902- *Who 94*
Buckle, Edward Gilbert 1926- *Who 94*
Buckle, Frederick Tarifero 1949- *WhoAm 94*
Buckle, Richard *Who 94*
Buckle, (Christopher) Richard (Sandford) 1916- *IntWW 93, Who 94, WrDr 94*
Buckle, Wayne Ford 1916- *WhoAmP 93*
Buckler, Beatrice 1933- *WhoAm 94*
Buckler, Hugh d1936 *WhoHol 92*
Buckler, John d1936 *WhoHol 92*
Buckler, Sheldon A. 1931- *WhoAm 94*
Buckler, William Earl 1924-1990 *WhAm 10*
Buckles, Ann *WhoHol 92*
Buckles, Robert Edwin 1917- *WhoAm 94*
Buckles, Robert Howard 1932- *WhoAm 94*
Buckles, Stephen Gary 1943- *WhoAm 94*
Bucklew, Neil S. 1940- *WhoAm 94*
Buckley *Who 94*
Buckley, Ann E. 1954- *WhoAmL 94*
Buckley, Anna Patricia 1924- *WhoAmP 93*
Buckley, Anthony James Henthorne 1934- *Who 94*
Buckley, Arthur Ralph 1951- *WhoMW 93*
Buckley, Betty 1947- *IntMPA 94, WhoHol 92*
Buckley, Betty Bob 1925- *WhoAm 94*
Buckley, Betty Lynn 1947- *WhoAm 94*
Buckley, C. Fitzergerald, III 1918- *WhoAmP 93*
Buckley, Cecelia Anne 1940- *WhoAmP 93*
Buckley, Charles Robinson, III 1942- *WhoAmL 94*
Buckley, Cheryl Rae 1947- *WhoMW 93*
Buckley, Christopher *DrAPF 93*
Buckley, Christopher Henry, Jr. 1940- *WhoAm 94, WhoAmL 94*
Buckley, Daniel Jerome 1949- *WhoAm 94, WhoAmL 94*
Buckley, David Whitaker 1951- *WhoWest 94*
Buckley, Denys (Burton) 1906- *Who 94*
Buckley, Donald 1955- *IntMPA 94*
Buckley, Emerson 1916-1989 *WhAm 10*
Buckley, Eric Joseph 1920- *Who 94*
Buckley, Esther Gonzalez-Arroyo 1948- *WhoAmP 93, WhoHisp 94*
Buckley, Eugene *WhoAm 94, WhoFI 94*
Buckley, Floyd d1956 *WhoHol 92*
Buckley, Francis Joseph 1928- *WrDr 94*
Buckley, Frank Wilson 1914- *WhoAm 94*
Buckley, Frederick Jean 1923- *WhoAmL 94*
Buckley, Gail Lumet 1937- *BlkWr 2, ConAu 142, WhoBlA 94*
Buckley, George Eric 1916- *Who 94*
Buckley, Hal d1986 *WhoHol 92*
Buckley, Horace Lawson 1941- *WhoAmP 93*
Buckley, J. Stephen 1942- *WhoAm 94*
Buckley, James 1944- *Who 94*
Buckley, James Arthur 1917- *Who 94*
Buckley, James L. 1923- *WhoAmP 93*
Buckley, James Lane 1923- *CngDr 93, IntWW 93, WhoAm 94, WhoAmL 94*
Buckley, James Sartwelle 1954- *WhoMW 93*
Buckley, Jeremiah Stephen 1944- *WhoAm 94, WhoAmL 94*
Buckley, Jerome Hamilton 1917- *WhoAm 94*
Buckley, Joanie Louise 1952- *WhoMW 93*
Buckley, John (William) 1913- *Who 94*
Buckley, John Joseph 1929- *WhoAmP 93*
Buckley, John Joseph 1930- *WhoMW 93*
Buckley, John Joseph, Jr. 1944- *WhoAm 94*
Buckley, John Joseph, Jr. 1947- *WhoAmL 94*
Buckley, John Leo 1920- *WhoScEn 94*
Buckley, John Michael 1891-1958 *WhoAmA 93N*

Buckley, Joseph Paul 1924- WhoAm 94
Buckley, Joseph Paul, III 1949- WhoAm 94
Buckley, Joseph W. 1943- WhoAm 94
Buckley, Kathleen EncSF 93
Buckley, Kathleen McKenna 1956- WhoFI 94
Buckley, Kay d1982 WhoHol 92
Buckley, Keith 1941- WhoHol 92
Buckley, Kevin 1941?- ConAu 140
Buckley, Lisa Louise 1958- WhoFI 94
Buckley, Loren G. 1943- WhoFI 94
Buckley, Martin Christopher Burton 1936- Who 94
Buckley, Mary L. WhoAmA 93
Buckley, Michael Edward 1950- WhoAmL 94
Buckley, Michael Francis 1943- WhoAm 94, WhoAmL 94
Buckley, Michael Sydney 1939- Who 94
Buckley, Mike Clifford 1944- WhoAm 94, WhoAmL 94
Buckley, Page Scott 1918- WhoAm 94
Buckley, Paul Richard 1935- WhoFI 94
Buckley, Peter Neville 1942- Who 94
Buckley, Priscilla Langford 1921- WhoAm 94
Buckley, Raymond Carl, II 1959- WhoAmP 93
Buckley, Rebecca Hatcher 1933- WhoAm 94, WhoScEn 94
Buckley, Richard d1960 WhoHol 92
Buckley, (Peter) Richard 1928- Who 94
Buckley, Richard Bennett 1942- WhoFI 94
Buckley, Richard Edward 1953- WhoAm 94
Buckley, Robert Paul 1947- WhoAm 94
Buckley, Roger (John) 1939- Who 94
Buckley, Samuel Olliphant, III 1947- WhoAm 94
Buckley, Sheridan John 1930- WhoAmL 94
Buckley, Stephen 1944- IntWW 93
Buckley, Thomas 1932- WrDr 94
Buckley, Thomas Hugh 1932- WhoAm 94
Buckley, Trevor d1993 Who 94N
Buckley, Virginia Laura 1929- WhoAm 94
Buckley, William Edwin 1937- WhoIns 94
Buckley, William Elmhirst 1913- WhoAm 94
Buckley, William F., Jr. 1925- DcLB 137 [port]
Buckley, William F(rank), Jr. 1925- WrDr 94
Buckley, William Frank, Jr. 1925- AmSocL, IntWW 93, WhoAm 94, WhoAmP 93
Buckley, William Kemmis 1921- Who 94
Buckley, William Randolph 1957- WhoWest 94
Bucklin, Donald Thomas 1938- WhoAm 94, WhoAmL 94
Bucklin, Kenneth Duane 1939- WhoFI 94
Bucklin, Leonard Herbert 1933- WhoAmL 94
Bucklin, Louis Pierre 1928- WhoWest 94
Bucklo, Elaine Edwards 1944- WhoAm 94
Buckman, Frederick W. WhoFI 94
Buckman, Gregory Paul 1966- WhoFI 94
Buckman, Harley Royal 1907- WhoFI 94
Buckman, James Edward 1944- WhoAmL 94
Buckman, James F. WhoWest 94
Buckman, Karel Welch 1962- WhoMW 93
Buckman, Melvin Joseph 1930- WhoAmL 94
Buckman, Peter (Michael Amiel) 1941- WrDr 94
Buckman, Robert Henry 1937- WhoAm 94
Buckman, Rosina 1881-1948 NewGrDO
Buckman, Thomas Richard 1923- WhoAm 94
Buckmaster, Viscount 1921- Who 94
Buckmaster, Cuthbert Harold Septimus 1903- Who 94
Buckmore, Alvah Clarence, Jr. 1944- WhoAm 94, WhoFI 94, WhoScEn 94
Bucknall, Barbara Jane 1933- WrDr 94
Bucknall, Malcolm Roderick 1935- WhoAmA 93
Bucknam, James Romeo 1911- WhoAm 94
Bucknam, Mary Olivia Caswell 1914- WhoAm 94
Buckner, Bradnor EncSF 93
Buckner, Edwin R. 1914-1985 WhoBlA 94N
Buckner, Elmer La Mar 1922- WhoAm 94
Buckner, Fred Lynn 1932- WhoAm 94, WhoFI 94
Buckner, Gail M. 1950- WhoAmP 93
Buckner, Harry Benjamin 1970- WhoScEn 94
Buckner, Iris Bernell 1952- WhoBlA 94
Buckner, James L. 1934- WhoBlA 94
Buckner, James Lee 1940- WhoScEn 94
Buckner, James Lowell 1934- WhoAm 94
Buckner, John Hugh 1919- WhoAm 94
Buckner, John Kendrick 1936- WhoScEn 94
Buckner, John Knowles 1936- WhoAm 94
Buckner, Kay Lamoreux 1935- WhoAmA 93
Buckner, Mary Alice 1948- WhoBlA 94
Buckner, Parris WhoHol 92
Buckner, Paul Eugene 1933- WhoAmA 93
Buckner, Philip Franklin 1930- WhoAm 94, WhoWest 94
Buckner, Quinn 1954- BasBi, WhoAm 94, WhoBlA 94
Buckner, Robert 1906- IntDcF 2-4
Buckner, Robert H. 1906- IntMPA 94
Buckner, Sally DrAPF 93
Buckner, William Claiborne 1926- WhoMW 93
Buckner, William Pat, Jr. 1929- WhoBlA 94
Buckney, Edward L. 1929- WhoBlA 94
Bucknill, John Charles 1817-1897 EncSPD
Bucko, Buck d1962 WhoHol 92
Bucko, John Joseph 1937- WhoAm 94
Bucko, Roy d1954 WhoHol 92
Buckridee, Patricia Ilona 1960- WhoFI 94
Bucks, Charles Alan 1927- WhoAm 94
Bucksbaum, Martin 1920- WhoAm 94, WhoFI 94
Bucksbaum, Matthew 1926- WhoAm 94, WhoFI 94
Bucksbaum, Philip Howard 1953- WhoScEn 94
Buckson, Toni Yvonne 1949- WhoBlA 94
Buckstein, Mark 1939- IntWW 93
Buckstein, Mark Aaron 1939- WhoAm 94, WhoAmL 94
Buckstone, J. C. d1924 WhoHol 92
Buckstone, Rowland d1922 WhoHol 92
Buckton, Raymond William 1922- Who 94
Buckvar, Felice DrAPF 93
Buckwalter, Ronald Lawrence 1936- WhoAm 94, WhoAmL 94
Buckwell, Allan Edgar 1947- Who 94
Buckwell, Lloyd John 1955- WhoMW 93
Buckwitz, Harry d1987 WhoHol 92
Buckwold, Victor Ephraim 1964- WhoWest 94
Buckworth, Gerald Allan 1940- WhoAmP 93
Buco, Stephen W. 1943- WhoAmP 93
Bucur, John Charles 1925- WhoAm 94
Bucy, J. Fred 1928- WhoAm 94
Bucy, John L., Jr. 1953- WhoFI 94
Bucy, Richard Snowden 1935- WhoAm 94, WhoWest 94
Buczacki, Stefan Tadeusz 1945- Who 94
Buczak, Douglas Chester 1949- WhoMW 93
Buczko, Thaddeus 1926- WhoAmP 93
Buczko, Thaddeus Joseph 1926- WhoAmL 94
Buczkowski, Joseph James 1957- WhoFI 94
Buczynski, Walter 1933- NewGrDO
Buda, Aleks 1910- WhoScEn 94
Budagher, John A. 1946- WhoAmP 93
Budai, Livia 1950- NewGrDO
Budak, Mary Kay WhoAmP 93, WhoWomW 91
Budalur, Thyagarajan Subbanarayan 1929- WhoAm 94, WhoScEn 94
Buday, Helen 1963- WhoHol 92
Budbill, David DrAPF 93
Budbill, David 1940- WrDr 94
Budd, Alan Peter 1937- IntWW 93, Who 94
Budd, Bernard Wilfred 1912- Who 94
Budd, Colin Richard 1945- Who 94
Budd, Dan S. 1927- WhoAmP 93
Budd, David Glenn 1934- WhoAmL 94
Budd, Edward H. 1933- WhoIns 94
Budd, Edward Hey 1933- WhoAm 94, WhoFI 94
Budd, Elaine 1923- WhoMW 93
Budd, Henry c. 1812-1875 EncNAR
Budd, Hugh Christopher Who 94
Budd, Jim WhoMW 93
Budd, John H. 1938- WhoIns 94
Budd, John Henry 1908- WhoAm 94
Budd, Julie 1954- WhoHol 92
Budd, Louis John 1921- WhoAm 94
Budd, Martin L. 1940- WhoAmL 94
Budd, Richard Wade 1934- WhoAm 94
Budd, Robert Wesley 1956- WhoWest 94
Budd, Roy d1993 NewYTBS 93
Budd, Wayne Anthony WhoBlA 94
Buddee, Paul Edgar 1913- WrDr 94
Budden, Julian (Medforth) 1924- NewGrDO, WrDr 94
Budden, Julian Medforth 1924- Who 94
Budden, Kenneth George 1915- IntWW 93, Who 94
Buddenberg, Hellmuth 1924- IntWW 93
Buddenbohm, Harold William 1959- WhoWest 94
Buddha 6th cent.BC- EncEth
Buddhadassa Bhikkhu d1993 NewYTBS 93
Buddicom, William Barber 1816-1887 DcNaB MP
Budding, Robert August 1956- WhoFI 94
Buddington, Patricia Arrington 1950- WhoScEn 94
Bude, Guillaume 1468-1540 GuFrLit 2
Budelman, Robert Burns, Jr. 1937- WhoAmL 94
Budelmann, Bernd Ulrich 1942- WhoScEn 94
Buden, David 1930- WhoScEn 94
Budenholzer, Roland Anthony 1912- WhoAm 94, WhoScEn 94
Budenz, Julia DrAPF 93
Budge, Don 1916- BuCMET [port]
Budge, (John) Donald 1915- IntWW 93
Budge, Hamer Harold 1910- WhoAm 94, WhoAmP 93
Budge, Hamilton Whithed 1928- WhoAm 94
Budge, Ian 1936- WrDr 94
Budge, Reed William 1921- WhoAmP 93
Budgen, Nicholas William 1937- Who 94
Budiansky, Bernard 1925- WhoAm 94
Budig, Gene Arthur 1939- WhoAm 94, WhoMW 93
Budinger, Charles Jude 1940- WhoFI 94, WhoMW 93
Budinger, Frederick Charles 1936- WhoScEn 94
Budinger, Thomas Francis 1932- WhoScEn 94
Budington, William Stone 1919- WhoAm 94
Budinski, Kenneth Gerard 1939- WhoScEn 94
Budish, Armond David 1953- WhoAmL 94
Budke, Camilla Eunice 1928- WhoMW 93
Budke, Charles Henry 1924- WhoAm 94
Budkevics, Girts Janis 1952- WhoFI 94
Budlong, Jack d1941 WhoHol 92
Budman, Charles Avrom 1963- WhoScEn 94
Budnick, Ernest Joseph 1948- WhoFI 94
Budnick, Thomas Peter 1947- WhoScEn 94
Budnitz, Arron Edward 1949- WhoAmL 94
Budnitz, Mark Elliott 1944- WhoAmL 94
Budny, James Charles 1948- WhoMW 93
Budny, Virginia 1944- WhoAmA 93
Budow, Harry Scott 1961- WhoFI 94
Budowski, Gerardo 1925- IntWW 93
Budrevics, Alexander 1925- WhoAm 94
Budries, David 1953- ConTFT 11
Budry, John Francis 1966- WhoMW 93
Budrys, Algis 1931- EncSF 93, WrDr 94
Budrys, Grace 1943- WhoMW 93
Bu-duo-ji WhoPRCh 91
Budwani, Ramesh Nebhandas 1940- WhoFI 94, WhoScEn 94
Budy, Andrea Hollander DrAPF 93
Budyka, Betty L. 1953- WhoMW 93
Budzak, Kathryn Sue 1940- WhoMW 93
Budzinski, James Edward 1953- WhoWest 94
Budzinsky, Armin Alexander 1942- WhoAm 94, WhoFI 94
Bue, Carl Olaf, Jr. 1922- WhoAm 94
Buechel, William Benjamin 1926- WhoAmL 94
Buechlein, Daniel Mark 1938- WhoAm 94, WhoMW 93
Buechler, Bradley Bruce 1948- WhoAm 94
Buechler, Jean Ann 1945- WhoMW 93
Buechler, John Carl HorFD
Buechler, Melanie Kay 1966- WhoWest 94
Buechner, Carl Frederick 1926- WhoAm 94
Buechner, Frederick DrAPF 93
Buechner, (Carl) Frederick 1926- WrDr 94
Buechner, Howard Albert 1919- WhoAm 94
Buechner, John C. WhoWest 94
Buechner, John William 1940- WhoAmP 93
Buechner, Robert William 1947- WhoAmL 94
Buechner, Thomas Scharman 1926- WhoAm 94, WhoAmA 93
Buecker, Robert 1935- WhoAmA 93
Buegeler, Barbara Stephanie 1945- WhoFI 94
Buehler, Arthur d1962 WhoHol 92
Buehler, Bernice Alice 1904- WhoMW 93
Buehler, Calvin A. 1896- WhAm 10
Buehler, J. Frank 1919- WhoAmP 93
Buehler, John Wilson 1950- WhoAmL 94
Buehler, Marilyn Kay Hasz 1946- WhoWest 94
Buehrer, Elaine Emilie 1929- WhoMW 93
Buehring, Gertrude Case 1940- WhoWest 94
Buel, James Wes 1937- WhoFI 94, WhoWest 94
Buel, Kenean d1948 WhoHol 92
Buel, Richard Van Wyck, Jr. 1933- WhoAm 94
Bueler, William Merwin 1934- WrDr 94
Buell, Abel 1742-1822 WhAmRev
Buell, Barbara Hayes 1942- WhoAmL 94
Buell, Bruce Temple 1932- WhoAm 94
Buell, Carmen D. WhoAmP 93
Buell, Frederick (Henderson) 1942- WrDr 94
Buell, Frederick Henderson DrAPF 93
Buell, Lawrence Ingalls 1939- WhoAm 94
Buell, Lawrence Lee 1934- WhoAmP 93, WhoMW 93
Buell, Marjorie Henderson 1904-1993 NewYTBS 93
Buell, Robert C. 1931- WhoAmP 93
Buell, Rodd Russell 1946- WhoAmL 94
Buell, Thomas Allan 1931- WhoAm 94, WhoFI 94
Buell, Victor P 1914- WrDr 94
Buell, Victor Paul 1914- WhoAm 94
Buell, William Ackerman 1925- WhoAm 94
Buelow, Edward Heller, Jr. 1940- WhoAmP 93
Buelow, George J(ohn) 1929- NewGrDO
Buelow, George John 1929- WhoAm 94
Buenker, John David 1937- WhoMW 93
Bueno, Antonio De Padua Jose Maria 1942- Who 94
Bueno, Julián L. 1942- WhoHisp 94
Bueno, Maria 1939- BuCMET [port]
Buente, David T. 1946- WhoAm 94
Buenz, John Buechler 1933- WhoAm 94
Buenzli, William Lewis 1912- WhoAmL 94
Buergenthal, Thomas 1934- WhoAm 94, WhoAmL 94
Buerger, David Bernard 1909- WhoAm 94, WhoAmL 94
Buerger, Janet E. 1946- WhoAmA 93
Buerger, Jim 1940- WhoAmP 93
Buerk, Donald Gene 1946- WhoScEn 94
Buerk, Michael Duncan 1946- Who 94
Buerki, Robert Armin 1939- WhoMW 93
Buerkle, Jack Vincent 1923- WhoAm 94
Buerman, Gunther K. 1943- WhoAmL 94
Buero Vallejo, Antonio 1916- ConWorW 93, IntDcT 2, IntWW 93
Bueschel, David Alan 1942- WhoAm 94, WhoFI 94
Bueschel, Richard Martin 1926- WhoMW 93
Bueschel, Thomas A. 1952- WhoAmL 94
Bueschen, Anton Joslyn 1940- WhoAm 94, WhoScEn 94
Buescher, Adolph Dolph Ernst 1922- WhoAm 94
Buescher, Adolph Ernst 1922- WhoScEn 94
Buescher, Stephen L. 1944- WhoAm 94, WhoAmL 94
Buescher, Thomas Paul 1949- WhoMW 93
Buesing, Farah Lea 1942- WhoMW 93
Buesing, Mary Donai 1931- WhoMW 93
Buesinger, Ronald Ernest 1933- WhoAm 94
Buesseler, John Aure 1919- WhoAm 94
Buesser, Frederick Gustavus, III 1941- WhoAm 94
Buesser, William Ronal 1944- WhoAmL 94
Buessing, Marjorie B. 1950- WhoAmP 93
Buesst, Aylmer 1883-1970 NewGrDO
Buestrin, Mary F. 1939- WhoAmP 93
Buetel, Jack d1989 WhoHol 92
Bueter, Larry Urban 1946- WhoMW 93
Buethe, Neal Thomas 1958- WhoAmL 94
Buetow, Dennis Edward 1932- WhoAm 94, WhoMW 93
Buettner, Carol Ann 1948- WhoAmP 93, WhoMW 93
Buettner, Joyce Margueritte 1937- WhoAmP 93
Buettner, Kenneth Louis 1950- WhoAmL 94
Buettner, Lispeth Ann 1948- WhoMW 93
Buettner, Michael Lewis 1957- WhoFI 94
Buettner-Janusch, John 1924-1992 AnObit 1992
Bufalino, Gesualdo 1920- ConWorW 93
Bufano, Vincent 1951- WhoHol 92
Bufe, Gina Marie 1965- WhoMW 93
Buff, Conrad 1886-1975 WhoAmA 93N
Buff, Frank Paul 1924- WhoAm 94
Buffalo Bill, Jr. 1961- WhoHol 92
Buffenstein, Daryl R. 1951- WhoAmL 94
Buffery, Judith 1943- EncSF 93
Buffery, Kate WhoHol 92
Buffet, Bernard 1928- IntWW 93, Who 94
Buffet, Marguerite d1680 BlmGWL
Buffet, Pierre 1946- WhoScEn 94

Buffett, George D. *WhoAmP 93*
Buffett, Jimmy 1946- *ConAu 141, SmATA 76 [port], WhoAm 94*
Buffett, Warren *IntWW 93*
Buffett, Warren Edward 1930- *WhoAm 94, WhoFI 94*
Buffington, Dennis Elvin 1944- *WhoAm 94, WhoScEn 94*
Buffington, Eugene J. 1863-1937 *EncABHB 9 [port]*
Buffington, Francis Stephan 1916-1989 *WhAm 10*
Buffington, Gary Lee Roy 1946- *WhoFI 94, WhoScEn 94, WhoWest 94*
Buffington, J. Larry 1953- *WhoAmP 93*
Buffington, Lamont E. 1950- *WhoAmL 94*
Buffington, Linda Brice 1936- *WhoWest 94*
Buffington, Nancy Catherine 1939- *WhoWest 94*
Buffington, Sam 1960- *WhoHol 92*
Buffkins, Archie Lee 1934- *WhoAm 94*
Buffmire, Judy Ann 1929- *WhoAmP 93, WhoWest 94*
Buffon, Charles Edward 1939- *WhoAm 94*
Buffon, Georges-Louis Leclerc, comte de 1707-1788 *GuFrLit 2, WorScD*
Buffone, Charles Joseph 1919- *WhoAmP 93*
Buffong, Eric Arnold 1951- *WhoBlA 94*
Bufford, Edward Eugene 1935- *WhoBlA 94*
Bufford, Samuel Lawrence 1943- *WhoAm 94, WhoAmL 94, WhoWest 94*
Bufi, Ylli *IntWW 93*
Bufis, Paul *DrAPF 93*
Bufka, John Andrew 1958- *WhoMW 93*
Bufman, Zev 1930- *WhoAm 94, WhoHol 92*
Buford, Abraham 1749-1833 *WhAmRev*
Buford, Floyd Moye, Jr. 1957- *WhoAmP 93*
Buford, Jack William 1912- *WhoFI 94*
Buford, James Henry 1944- *WhoBlA 94*
Buford, Robert Pegram 1925- *WhoAmL 94*
Buford, Sharnia 1939- *WhoBlA 94*
Buford, Tom 1949- *WhoAmP 93*
Buford, William Holmes 1954- *Who 94*
Buford, William P. 1936- *WhoBlA 94*
Bufton, Sydney Osborne d1993 *Who 94N*
Bugajski, Joseph Michael 1951- *WhoMW 93*
Bugarinovic, Melanija 1905-1986 *NewGrDO*
Bugatto, B. John 1934- *WhoAmP 93*
Bugbee-Jackson, Joan 1941- *WhoAm 94, WhoAmA 93, WhoWest 94*
Bugdaev, Ilya Erdnievich 1938- *LoBiDrD*
Bugeja, Michael J. *DrAPF 93*
Bugeja, Raymond 1956- *IntWW 93*
Bugel, Joe 1940- *WhoAm 94, WhoWest 94*
Bugen, David Henry 1948- *WhoFI 94*
Bugental, James F(rederick) T(homas) 1915- *WrDr 94*
Bugg, Charles Basil 1942- *WhoAm 94*
Bugg, Charles Edward 1941- *WhoAm 94, WhoScEn 94*
Bugg, George Wendell 1935- *WhoBlA 94*
Bugg, James Nelson 1904- *WhoBlA 94*
Bugg, Mayme Carol 1945- *WhoBlA 94*
Bugg, Robert 1941- *WhoAmP 93, WhoBlA 94*
Bugg, William J. 1939- *WhoIns 94*
Bugg, William Joseph, Jr. 1939- *WhoAm 94*
Buggage, Cynthia Marie 1958- *WhoBlA 94*
Buggan, Constantine *WhoAm 94*
Bugge, Lawrence John 1936- *WhoAm 94*
Bugge Fougner, Else 1944- *IntWW 93, WhoWomW 91*
Buggey, Lesley JoAnne 1938- *WhoMW 93*
Buggie, Frederick Denman 1929- *WhoFI 94*
Buggie, Stephen Edward 1946- *WhoScEn 94*
Buggs, Charles Wesley 1906-1991 *WhoBlA 94N*
Buggs, George *DrAPF 93*
Buggs, James 1925- *WhoBlA 94*
Bugh, Gary Howard 1940- *WhoMW 93*
Bugher, Mark *WhoMW 93*
Bugher, Mark D. *WhoAmP 93*
Bugher, Robert Dean 1925- *WhoAm 94*
Bugielski, Robert J. 1947- *WhoAmP 93*
Bugliarello, George 1927- *WhoAm 94*
Bugliosi, Vincent T. 1934- *WhoAm 94*
Bugno, Walter Thomas 1942- *WhoScEn 94*
Bugos, Joseph V. *WhoAm 94, WhoFI 94*
Bugotu, Francis 1937- *Who 94*
Bugul, Ken 1948- *BlmGWL*
Buhac, Hrvoje Joseph 1938- *WhoScEn 94*
Buhagiar, Marion 1932- *ConAu 141, WhoAm 94*
Buhari, Muhammadu 1942- *IntWW 93*
Buhe 1926- *WhoPRCh 91 [port]*
Bu He (Yun Shuguang) 1926- *IntWW 93*
Buhks, Ephraim 1949- *WhoScEn 94*
Buhl, Lloyd Frank 1918- *WhoAmP 93*
Buhler, Jill Lorie 1945- *WhoAm 94, WhoFI 94, WhoWest 94*
Buhler, Luis Paltenghe 1953- *WhoWest 94*
Buhler, Phillip Arthur 1962- *WhoAmL 94*
Buhler, Richard d1925 *WhoHol 92*
Buhler, Richard Gerhard 1946- *WhoWest 94*
Buhler, Winfried 1929- *IntWW 93*
Buhlmann, Michael Richard 1960- *WhoWest 94*
Buhner, Byron Bevis 1950- *WhoMW 93*
Buhr, Florence D. 1933- *WhoAmP 93, WhoMW 93*
Buhr, Glenn 1930- *WhoAmP 93*
Buhrer, Esther 1926- *WhoWomW 91*
Buhrer, Heiner Georg 1943- *WhoScEn 94*
Buhrfeind, Susan Marie 1968- *WhoMW 93*
Buhrow, William Carl 1934- *WhoAm 94*
Buhs, Stephen William 1952- *WhoFI 94*
Buhsmer, John Henry 1932- *WhoAm 94*
Bu-Hulaiga, Mohammed-Ihsan Ali 1956- *WhoScEn 94*
Bui, James 1961- *WhoScEn 94*
Bui, Khoi Tien 1937- *WhoAm 94*
Bui, Philip Phu-Van 1955- *WhoWest 94*
Bui, Ty Van 1959- *WhoMW 93*
Buice, Bonnie Carl 1932- *WhoAmL 94*
Buick, Fred J.R. 1951- *WhoScEn 94*
Buickerood, James Gerard 1951- *WhoMW 93*
Buidang, George 1924- *WhoWest 94*
Buie, James Randall 1953- *WhoWest 94*
Buie, Sampson, Jr. 1929- *WhoBlA 94*
Buie, T. Dan 1941- *WhoAmP 93*
Buijnsters, Piet J. 1933- *IntWW 93*
Builder, J. Lindsay, Jr. 1943- *WhoAmL 94*
Buini, Cecilia Belisani *NewGrDO*
Buini, Giuseppe Maria 1687-1739 *NewGrDO*
Buini, Matteo fl. 1748-1749 *NewGrDO*
Buira, Ariel 1940- *IntWW 93*
Buis, Jeffrey 1968- *WhoAmP 93*
Buis, Thomas Paul 1952- *WhoAmP 93*
Buist, Jean Mackerley 1919- *WhoAm 94*
Buist, John Latto Farquharson 1930- *Who 94*
Buist, Richardson 1921- *WhoAm 94*
Buitenhuis, Peter M 1925- *WrDr 94*
Buitenhuis, Peter Martinus 1925- *WhoAm 94*
Buiter, Willem Hendrik 1949- *IntWW 93, Who 94, WhoAm 94*
Buitrago, Flor Maria 1955- *WhoHisp 94*
Buitrago, Rudy G. 1951- *WhoHisp 94*
Buitrago, Walter 1935- *WhoHisp 94*
Buitron-Oliver, Diana 1946- *WhoAmA 93*
Bujac, Gregorie Wayne 1946- *WhoAm 94*
Bujak, Zbigniew 1954- *IntWW 93*
Bujake, John Edward, Jr. 1933- *WhoAm 94*
Bujanda, Moises Arturo 1958- *WhoHisp 94*
Bujese, Arlene 1938- *WhoAmA 93*
Bujnowski, Joel A. 1949- *WhoAmA 93*
Bujold, Genevieve 1941- *WhoHol 92*
Bujold, Genevieve 1942- *ConTFT 11, IntMPA 94, IntWW 93*
Bujold, Lois McMaster 1949- *EncSF 93*
Bujold, Tyrone Patrick 1937- *WhoAm 94*
Bujones, Fernando *WhoHol 92*
Bujones, Fernando 1955- *IntDcB [port], IntWW 93, WhoHisp 94*
Bujones, Fernando Calleiro 1955- *WhoAm 94*
Buka, Donald 1921- *WhoHol 92*
Bukantz, Samuel Charles 1911- *WhoAm 94*
Bukar, Margaret Witty 1950- *WhoMW 93*
Bukata, Aniela *WhoWomW 91*
Buker, Robert Hutchinson, Sr. 1928- *WhoAm 94*
Bukewaka, Anna Teresa *WhoWomW 91*
Bukey, Evan Burr 1940- *WrDr 94*
Bukhgolts, Ivan Dmitryevich fl. 170-?- *WhWE*
Buki, Dennis Gabor 1945- *WhoAmL 94*
Buki, Zoltan 1929- *WhoAmA 93*
Bukiet, Melvin Jules *DrAPF 93*
Buklarewicz, Paul Joseph 1949- *WhoWest 94*
Bukonda, Ngoyi K. Zacharie 1951- *WhoScEn 94*
Bukovac, Daniel 1952- *WhoAmL 94, WhoMW 93*
Bukovac, Martin J. 1929- *IntWW 93*
Bukovac, Martin John 1929- *WhoAm 94*
Bukovnik, Gary 1947- *WhoAmA 93*
Bukovnik, Gary A. 1947- *WhoWest 94*
Bukovsky, Vladimir Konstantinovich 1942- *IntWW 93*
Bukowinski, Mark Stefan Tadeusz 1946- *WhoWest 94*
Bukowski, Arthur F. 1905-1989 *WhAm 10*
Bukowski, Charles *DrAPF 93*
Bukowski, Charles 1920- *DcLB 130 [port], WhoAm 94, WrDr 94*
Bukowski, Daniel Joseph 1963- *WhoMW 93*
Bukowski, Elaine Louise 1949- *WhoAm 94*
Bukowski, Gary L. 1951- *WhoAmP 93*
Bukowski, Horst Norbert 1960- *WhoHisp 94*
Bukowski, James Bernard 1944- *WhoWest 94*
Bukowski, Jeffrey David 1965- *WhoWest 94*
Bukowski, Robert John 1957- *WhoFI 94*
Bukreev, Yury Dmitrievich 1941- *LoBiDrD*
Bukry, John David 1941- *WhoAm 94, WhoScEn 94, WhoWest 94*
Buksa, Mykolas 1869-1953 *NewGrDO*
Buktenica, Ray *WhoHol 92*
Buky, Dorottya *WhoWomW 91*
Bula, Raymond J. 1927- *WhoAm 94*
Bulakhov, Pavel Petrovich 1824-1875 *NewGrDO*
Bulatovic, Momir 1928- *IntWW 93*
Bulatovic, Vukoje 1927- *IntWW 93*
Bulbank, Israel 1934- *WhoHisp 94*
Bulbulian, Arthur H. 1900- *WhoAm 94*
Buldakov, Gennadiy Nikanorovich 1924- *IntWW 93*
Buldrini, George James *WhoAmL 94*
Bulen, Lawrence Keith 1926- *WhoAmP 93*
Bulfield, Peter William 1930- *Who 94*
Bulfinch, Hannah Apthorp 1768-1841 *BlmGWL*
Bulgak, Vladimir Borisovich 1941- *LoBiDrD, WhoScEn 94*
Bulgakov, Leo d1948 *WhoHol 92*
Bulgakov, Mikhail 1891-1940 *EncSF 93*
Bulgakov, Mikhail (Afanasevich) 1891-1940 *IntDcT 2, RfGShF*
Bulgakov, Mikhail Afanas'yevich 1891-1940 *NewGrDO*
Bulganin, Nikolai 1895-1975 *HisWorL [port]*
Bulgarelli-Benti, Maria Anna *NewGrDO*
Bulgarian State Female Vocal Choir, The *ConMus 10 [port]*
Bulgatz, Jim 1962- *WhoFI 94*
Bulger, Anthony Clare 1912- *Who 94*
Bulger, Brian Wegg 1951- *WhoAm 94, WhoAmL 94*
Bulger, Dennis Bernard 1938- *WhoAm 94*
Bulger, Lucille O. 1912- *WhoBlA 94*
Bulger, Raymonde Albertine 1921- *WhoMW 93*
Bulger, Roger James 1933- *IntWW 93*
Bulger, Tom *WhoAmP 93*
Bulger, William M. *WhoAmP 93*
Bulgren, William Gerald 1937- *WhoAm 94*
Bulich, Vera Sergeevna 1898-1954 *BlmGWL*
Bulifant, Joyce 1938- *WhoHol 92*
Bulin, Rene Henri 1920- *IntWW 93*
Bulitt, Patricia Ann 1949- *WhoWest 94*
Bulkeley, Richard Thomas W. *Who 94*
Bulkeley, William M. 1950- *WrDr 94*
Bulkin, Bernard Joseph 1942- *WhoScEn 94*
Bulkin, Michael Herbert 1938- *WhoFI 94*
Bulkley, Jonathan William 1938- *WhoMW 93*
Bull, A. Vivien 1921- *WhoAm 94*
Bull, Angela (Mary) 1936- *WrDr 94*
Bull, Anthony 1908- *Who 94*
Bull, Bergen Ira 1940- *WhoAm 94*
Bull, Brian Stanley 1937- *WhoAm 94, WhoFI 94*
Bull, Charles Edward d1971 *WhoHol 92*
Bull, David 1934- *WhoAm 94*
Bull, Emma 1954- *EncSF 93*
Bull, Fran 1938- *WhoAmA 93*
Bull, George Albert 1927- *WhoAm 94*
Bull, George Anthony 1929- *Who 94*
Bull, Hank *WhoAmA 93*
Bull, Henrik Helkand 1929- *WhoAm 94*
Bull, John 1740-1802 *WhAmRev*
Bull, John Michael 1934- *Who 94*
Bull, John Prince 1917- *Who 94*
Bull, Kenneth Winson 1930- *WhoAmP 93*
Bull, Louis Antal 1961- *WhoMW 93*
Bull, Megan Patricia 1922- *Who 94*
Bull, Odd 1907- *IntWW 93*
Bull, Peter d1984 *WhoHol 92*
Bull, Richard *WhoHol 92*
Bull, (Oliver) Richard (Silvester) 1930- *Who 94*
Bull, Roger John 1940- *Who 94*
Bull, Simeon (George) 1934- *Who 94*
Bull, Tony Raymond 1934- *Who 94*
Bull, Vivian Ann 1934- *WhoWest 94*
Bull, Walter (Edward Avenon) 1902- *Who 94*
Bull, William, II 1710-1791 *WhAmRev*
Bulla, Ben F. 1920- *WhoFI 94*
Bulla, Clyde Robert 1914- *WhoAm 94, WrDr 94*
Bullant, Antoine c. 1750-1821 *NewGrDO*
Bullard, Bill 1948- *WhoAmP 93*
Bullard, Claude Earl 1920- *WhoAm 94*
Bullard, David K. 1942- *WhoIns 94*
Bullard, Denys Gradwell 1912- *Who 94*
Bullard, Edgar John, III 1942- *WhoAm 94, WhoAmA 93*
Bullard, Edward A., Jr. 1947- *WhoBlA 94*
Bullard, Giles Lionel d1992 *Who 94N*
Bullard, Helen 1902- *WhoAm 94, WrDr 94*
Bullard, John Kilburn 1947- *WhoAm 94, WhoAmP 93*
Bullard, Julian (Leonard) 1928- *IntWW 93, Who 94*
Bullard, Keith *WhoBlA 94*
Bullard, Larcenia J. 1947- *WhoAmP 93*
Bullard, Marcia Lynn 1952- *WhoAm 94*
Bullard, Matt *WhoBlA 94*
Bullard, Perry 1942- *WhoAmP 93*
Bullard, Ray Elva, Jr. 1927- *WhoAm 94*
Bullard, Richard Forrest 1937- *WhoWest 94*
Bullard, Robert Oliver, Jr. 1943- *WhoAm 94*
Bullard, Roger Dale 1942- *WhoScEn 94*
Bullard, Terry Lynn *WhoFI 94*
Bullard, Thais Jeanne *WhoWest 94*
Bullard, Todd Hupp 1931- *WhoAm 94*
Bullard, Willis Clare, Jr. 1943- *WhoAm 94, WhoAmP 93, WhoMW 93*
Bullard, Willis Gale 1940- *WhoWest 94*
Bullaro, Joseph d1986 *WhoHol 92*
Bulleid, Oliver Vaughan Snell 1882-1970 *DcNaB MP*
Bulleit, Donald Victor 1936- *WhoAmL 94*
Bullen, Adelaide Kendall 1908- *WhAm 10*
Bullen, Daniel Bernard 1956- *WhoScEn 94*
Bullen, Frank Thomas 1857-1915 *DcNaB MP*
Bullen, Frederick Hamilton 1915- *WhoAmL 94*
Bullen, Reginald 1920- *Who 94*
Bullen, Richard Hatch 1919- *WhoAm 94*
Bullen, Sarah 1950- *WhoHol 92*
Bullen, Voy M. *WhoAm 94*
Bullen, William Alexander d1992 *Who 94N*
Buller *Who 94*
Buller, Arthur John 1923- *IntWW 93, Who 94*
Buller, Dennis Wilson 1944- *WhoWest 94*
Buller, Herman 1927- *WrDr 94*
Buller, James Harlan 1944- *WhoMW 93*
Buller, John 1927- *NewGrDO*
Bullerjahn, Eduard Henri 1920- *WhoAm 94*
Bullerman, Ivan Arthur 1950- *WhoFI 94*
Bullers, Ronald Alfred 1931- *Who 94*
Bullett, Audrey Kathryn 1937- *WhoAmP 93, WhoBlA 94*
Bullett, David B. 1938- *WhoIns 94*
Bulley, Allan Edgar, Jr. 1933- *WhoFI 94*
Bulliet, C. J. 1883-1952 *WhoAmA 93N*
Bulliet, Richard Williams 1940- *WhoAm 94*
Bullimore, John Wallace MacGregor 1945- *Who 94*
Bullin, Christine Neva 1948- *WhoAm 94, WhoWest 94*
Bullington, James R. 1940- *WhoAm 94*
Bullington, James Richard 1940- *WhoAmP 93*
Bullins, Ed 1935- *AfrAmAl 6 [port], BlkWr 2, ConDr 93, IntDcT 2, WhoAm 94, WhoBlA 94, WrDr 94*
Bullis, William Murray 1930- *WhoScEn 94*
Bull Lodge c. 1802-1886 *EncNAR*
Bullmore, (John) Jeremy David 1929- *Who 94*
Bulloch, Archibald 1730-1777 *AmRev, WhAmRev*
Bulloch, John 1928- *WrDr 94*
Bulloch, John Frederick Devon 1933- *WhoAm 94*
Bulloch, Joseph *WhoHol 92*
Bullock, Baron 1914- *Who 94*
Bullock, Lord 1914- *WrDr 94*
Bullock, Alan (Louis Charles) 1914- *ConAu 41NR*
Bullock, Alan Louis Charles 1914- *IntWW 93*
Bullock, Anna Mae 1939- *WhoAm 94*
Bullock, Bob 1929- *WhoAmP 93*
Bullock, Boris d1979 *WhoHol 92*
Bullock, Bruce Lewis 1947- *WhoWest 94*
Bullock, Bruce Stanley 1933- *WhoAmL 94*
Bullock, Byron Swanson 1955- *WhoBlA 94*
Bullock, Charles Spencer, III 1942- *WhoAm 94*
Bullock, Clifton Vernice 1928-1991 *WhoBlA 94N*
Bullock, Daniel Hugh 1952- *WhoScEn 94*
Bullock, Dick d1971 *WhoHol 92*

Bullock, Donald Wayne 1947- *WhoWest 94*
Bullock, Edward Anthony Watson 1926- *Who 94*
Bullock, Elbert L. 1934- *WhoBlA 94*
Bullock, Ellis Way, Jr. 1928- *WhoAm 94*
Bullock, Francis Jeremiah 1937- *WhoAm 94*
Bullock, Frank William, Jr. 1938- *WhoAm 94, WhoAmL 94*
Bullock, Gayle Nelson 1952- *WhoAm 94*
Bullock, George 1782?-1818 *DcNaB MP*
Bullock, George Daniel 1942- *WhoAmP 93*
Bullock, H. Ridgely 1934- *WhoAm 94*
Bullock, Hugh 1898- *Who 94, WhoAm 94*
Bullock, J. Jerome 1948- *WhoBlA 94*
Bullock, James 1926- *WhoBlA 94*
Bullock, James Benbow 1929- *WhoAmA 93*
Bullock, James Robert 1916- *WhoAmL 94, WhoWest 94*
Bullock, John 1933- *Who 94*
Bullock, John McDonell 1932- *WhoAm 94*
Bullock, Kathleen (Mary) 1946- *SmATA 77 [port]*
Bullock, Maurice Randolph 1913- *WhoAm 94*
Bullock, Michael (Hale) 1918- *WrDr 94*
Bullock, Norma Kathryn Rice 1945- *WhoAm 94*
Bullock, Peter Bradley 1934- *WhoFI 94*
Bullock, Richard Henry Watson 1920- *Who 94*
Bullock, Robert D. 1929- *WhoAm 94*
Bullock, Samuel Carey 1921- *WhoBlA 94*
Bullock, Stephen 1735-1816 *WhAmRev*
Bullock, Stephen G. 1950- *WhoAmL 94*
Bullock, Stephen Michael 1953- *Who 94*
Bullock, Theodore 1928- *WhoBlA 94*
Bullock, Theodore Holmes 1915- *IntWW 93, WhoAm 94, WhoScEn 94*
Bullock, Thomas Abbott 1922- *WhoAm 94*
Bullock, Thurman Ruthe 1947- *WhoBlA 94*
Bullock, William H. 1927- *WhoAm 94, WhoMW 93*
Bullock, William Horace 1919- *WhoBlA 94*
Bullock, Wynn 1902-1975 *WhoAmA 93N*
Bulloff, Jack John 1914- *WhoAm 94*
Bullough, Bonnie 1927- *WhoAm 94*
Bullough, Donald Auberon 1928- *Who 94*
Bullough, John Frank 1928- *WhoAm 94*
Bullough, Robert V., Jr. 1949- *WrDr 94*
Bullough, Ronald 1931- *Who 94*
Bullough, Vern L. 1928- *WrDr 94*
Bullough, William Sydney 1914- *Who 94*
Bullowa, Arthur M. d1993 *NewYTBS 93*
Bullrich, Silvina 1915-1989 *BlmGWL*
Bullus, Eric (Edward) 1906- *Who 94*
Bullus, Eric E(dward), Sir 1906- *WrDr 94*
Bulmahn, Edelgard 1951- *WhoWomW 91*
Bulman, Aaron E. *DrAPF 93*
Bulman, W. John A. 1929- *WhoMW 93*
Bulman, William Patrick 1925- *WhoFI 94, WhoScEn 94*
Bulman Page, Philip Charles 1955- *WhoScEn 94*
Bulmer, Esmond *Who 94*
Bulmer, (James) Esmond 1935- *Who 94*
Bulmer, Gerald 1920- *Who 94*
Bulmer, H.K. *EncSF 93*
Bulmer, Kenneth 1921- *EncSF 93*
Bulmer, (Henry) Kenneth 1914- *WrDr 94*
Bulmer-Thomas, Ivor *IntWW 93*
Bulmer-Thomas, Ivor 1905- *Who 94, WrDr 94*
Bulmer-Thomas, Victor Gerald 1948- *Who 94*
Buloff, Joseph d1985 *WhoHol 92*
Buloff, Joseph 1899-1985 *ConAu 141*
Bulow, Frieda Freiin von 1858-1909 *BlmGWL*
Bulow, Hans (Guido), Freiherr von 1830-1894 *NewGrDO*
Bulow, Margarethe Freiin von 1860-1884 *BlmGWL*
Bulpitt, Cecil Arthur Charles 1919- *Who 94*
Bulsara, Ardeshir Ratan 1951- *WhoAsA 94*
Bult, John A. *WhoAm 94*
Bulteel, Christopher Harris 1921- *Who 94*
Bulthuis, Douglas Allen 1948- *WhoWest 94*
Bultman, Fritz 1919-1985 *WhoAmA 93N*
Bultmann, William Arnold 1922- *WhoWest 94*
Bultsma, Peter Allan 1954- *WhoMW 93*
Bululu, Lunda *IntWW 93*
Bulusu, Suryanarayana 1927- *WhoAsA 94*
Bulwer, Edward *EncSF 93*
Bulwer, John 17th cent.- *EncDeaf*
Bulwer-Lytton, Edward *EncSF 93*
Bulwer-Lytton, Edward (George Earle) 1803-1873 *IntDcT 2*
Bulwer-Lytton, Edward (George Earle Lytton) 1803-1873 *NewGrDO*
Bulychev, Kir(ill) 1934- *EncSF 93*
Bulyk, John-Conrad 1949- *WhoFI 94*
Bulzacchelli, John G. 1939- *WhoAm 94*
Bumas, Jonathan Mark 1957- *WhoAmA 93*
Bumbeck, David A. 1940- *WhoAmA 93*
Bumbery, Joseph Lawrence 1929- *WhoAm 94*
Bumbova, Stanislava 1948- *WhoWomW 91*
Bumbry, George Nordlinger 1922- *WhoBlA 94*
Bumbry, Grace 1937- *ConBlB 5 [port], IntWW 93, Who 94, WhoAm 94*
Bumbry, Grace (Melzia Ann) 1937- *NewGrDO*
Bumbry, Grace Ann 1937- *AfrAmAl 6, WhoBlA 94*
Bumgardner, David Webster, Jr. 1921- *WhoAmP 93*
Bumgardner, James Arliss 1935- *WhoAmA 93*
Bumgardner, Larry G. 1957- *WhoWest 94*
Bumgarner, Gary Dale 1938- *WhoAmP 93*
Bumgarner, James McNabb 1919- *WhoAmL 94, WhoMW 93*
Bumgarner, James Scott 1928- *WhoAm 94*
Bump, Larry J. 1939- *WhoFI 94*
Bump, Mark William 1956- *WhoAmL 94*
Bump, Suzanne 1956- *WhoAmP 93*
Bump, Wilbur Neil 1929- *WhoAm 94*
Bumpas, Bob d1959 *WhoHol 92*
Bumpas, Scott Jackson 1944- *WhoFI 94*
Bumpas, Stuart Maryman 1944- *WhoAm 94*
Bumpass, Ronald Eugene 1948- *WhoAmL 94*
Bumpass, T. Merritt, Jr. 1943- *WhoAm 94, WhoAmL 94*
Bumpers, Dale 1925- *CngDr 93*
Bumpers, Dale L. 1925- *WhoAm 94, WhoAmP 93*
Bumpers, Dale Leon 1925- *IntWW 93*
Bumphus, Walter Gayle 1948- *WhoBlA 94*
Bumpus, F. Merlin d1993 *NewYTBS 93 [port]*
Bumpus, Frederick J. 1929- *WhoIns 94*
Bumpus, Frederick Joseph 1929- *WhoAm 94*
Bumpus, Ivy Renee 1961- *WhoMW 93*
Bumpus, Jerry *DrAPF 93*
Bumpus, John 1929- *WhoAmP 93*
Bumpus, Terry Keith 1958- *WhoMW 93*
Bumstead, Henry *IntDcF 2-4*
Bumsted, J(ohn) M(ichael) 1938- *WrDr 94*
Bumsted, Robert Milton 1944- *WhoAm 94*
Bunaes, Bard E. 1935- *WhoIns 94*
Bunag, Ruben David 1931- *WhoMW 93*
Bunbury *Who 94*
Bunbury, Bishop of 1932- *Who 94*
Bunbury, Michael *Who 94*
Bunbury, (Richard David) Michael (Richardson-) 1927- *Who 94*
Bunbury, Michael (William) 1946- *Who 94*
Bunce, Alan d1965 *WhoHol 92*
Bunce, Louis DeMott 1914-1983 *WhoAmA 93N*
Bunce, Michael John 1935- *Who 94*
Bunce, Michael John 1949- *Who 94*
Bunce, Stanley Chalmers 1917- *WhoAm 94*
Bunch, Austin (Wyeth) 1918- *Who 94*
Bunch, Barbara J. 1952- *WhoAmP 93*
Bunch, Chris *EncSF 93*
Bunch, David R(oosevelt) *EncSF 93*
Bunch, Franklin Swope 1913- *WhoAm 94*
Bunch, Fred R. 1952- *WhoAmP 93*
Bunch, James Terrance 1942- *WhoAmL 94*
Bunch, Jeffrey Omer 1958- *WhoScEn 94*
Bunch, Jennings Bryan, Jr. 1929- *WhoAm 94*
Bunch, John Blake 1940- *WhoAm 94*
Bunch, Kenneth Alan 1961- *WhoMW 93*
Bunch, Michael Brannen 1949- *WhoScEn 94*
Bunche, Ralph J. 1904-1971 *AfrAmAl 6, ConBlB 5 [port]*
Bunche, Ralph J(ohnson) 1904-1971 *BlkWr 2*
Bunche, Ralph Johnson 1904-1971 *AmSocL [port], HisWorL [port]*
Buncher, Charles Ralph 1938- *WhoScEn 94*
Buncher, James Edward 1936- *WhoAm 94*
Bunchman, Herbert Harry, II 1942- *WhoScEn 94, WhoWest 94*
Bund, Karlheinz 1925- *IntWW 93*
Bunda, Robert 1947- *WhoAmP 93*
Bundalo, Milan Richard 1951- *WhoMW 93*
Bunde, Con 1938- *WhoAmP 93, WhoWest 94*
Bunderson, Harold *WhoAmP 93*
Bunderson, William Eric 1956- *WhoMW 93*
Bundesen, Faye Stimers 1932- *WhoWest 94*
Bundgaard, Nils 1952- *WhoScEn 94*
Bundick, William Ross 1917- *WhoAm 94*
Bundles, A'Lelia Perry 1952- *SmATA 76 [port], WhoBlA 94*
Bundren, Bob D. 1952- *WhoFI 94*
Bundschuh, George A. W. 1933- *WhoIns 94*
Bundschuh, George August William 1933- *WhoAm 94, WhoFI 94*
Bundu, Abass 1948- *IntWW 93*
Bundy, Blakely Fetridge 1944- *WhoMW 93*
Bundy, Brooke 1944- *WhoHol 92*
Bundy, Charles Alan 1930- *WhoAm 94*
Bundy, Charlett Ann 1947- *WhoAmL 94*
Bundy, Dorothy 1916- *BuCMET*
Bundy, Harvey Hollister 1916- *WhoAm 94*
Bundy, James Lomax 1920- *WhoBlA 94*
Bundy, Kirk Jon 1947- *WhoScEn 94*
Bundy, M. John 1942- *WhoAmL 94*
Bundy, May Sutton 1886-1975 *BuCMET*
Bundy, McGeorge 1919- *IntWW 93, Who 94, WhoAm 94*
Bundy, William P. 1917- *WhoAmP 93*
Bundza, Maira 1955- *WhoMW 93*
Bunge, Charles Albert 1936- *WhoAm 94*
Bunge, David Bruce 1955- *WhoFI 94*
Bunge, Jonathan Gunn 1936- *WhoAm 94*
Bunge, Marcia JoAnn 1954- *WhoMW 93*
Bunge, Richard Paul 1932- *WhoScEn 94*
Bunge, William Ronald 1934- *WhoAmP 93*
Bunge de Galvez, Delfina 1881-1952 *BlmGWL*
Bunger, Rolf 1941- *WhoScEn 94*
Bungert, (Friedrich) August 1845-1915 *NewGrDO*
Bungert, D. Edward 1957- *ConAu 140*
Bungey, John Henry 1944- *WrDr 94*
Bungey, Michael 1940- *IntWW 93, Who 94*
Bungo, Michael William 1950- *WhoAm 94*
Bunich, Pavel Grigorevich 1925- *LoBiDrD*
Bunich, Pavel Grigoryevich 1929- *IntWW 93*
Bunim, Amos 1929- *WrDr 94*
Bunim, Mary-Ellis 1946- *WhoAm 94*
Bunin, Louis 1904- *WhoAmA 93*
Bunina, Anna Pertovna 1774-1829 *BlmGWL*
Buniva, Brian Lawrence 1950- *WhoAmL 94*
Bunke, Tamara 1937-1967 *HisWorL*
Bunker, Albert Rowland 1913- *Who 94*
Bunker, Anthony Louis 1933- *WhoAm 94*
Bunker, Debra J. 1955- *WhoMW 93*
Bunker, Edward *WhoHol 92*
Bunker, George 1923-1991 *WhoAmA 93N*
Bunker, John Birkbeck 1926- *WhoAm 94*
Bunker, Michael 1937- *Who 94*
Bunker, Norene Rae 1931- *WhoAmP 93*
Bunker, Ralph d1966 *WhoHol 92*
Bunker, William B. 1951- *WhoAmL 94*
Bunkers, Douglas Frederick 1958- *WhoMW 93*
Bunkley, Lonnie R. 1932- *WhoBlA 94*
Bunlet, Marcelle 1900-1991 *NewGrDO*
Bunn, Alfred c. 1797-1860 *NewGrDO*
Bunn, Anna Maria 1808-1899 *BlmGWL*
Bunn, Barbara Jean *WhoAmP 93*
Bunn, Charles Nixon 1926- *WhoFI 94, WhoWest 94*
Bunn, David 1950- *WhoAmA 93*
Bunn, Dorothy Irons 1948- *WhoAmL 94, WhoWest 94*
Bunn, Douglas Henry David 1928- *Who 94*
Bunn, George 1925- *WhoAm 94, WhoAmP 93*
Bunn, Jacqueline Faye 1962- *WhoAmL 94*
Bunn, James 1956- *WhoAmP 93*
Bunn, James Lee 1956- *WhoWest 94*
Bunn, Joe Millard 1932- *WhoScEn 94*
Bunn, Robert Burgess 1933- *WhoAmL 94*
Bunn, Ronald Freeze 1929- *WhoAm 94*
Bunn, Stan 1946- *WhoAmP 93*
Bunn, Timothy David 1946- *WhoAm 94*
Bunn, Warren J. 1914-1986 *WhoBlA 94N*
Bunn, William Bernice, III 1952- *WhoAm 94*
Bunnag, Marut 1925- *IntWW 93*
Bunnage, Avis d1990 *WhoHol 92*
Bunnell, David J., Jr. 1929- *WhoWest 94*
Bunnell, Jane 1952- *NewGrDO*
Bunnell, Lloyd d1981 *WhoHol 92*
Bunnell, Peter Curtis 1937- *WhoAm 94, WhoAmA 93*
Bunnell, Sandra Jean 1945- *WhoMW 93*
Bunnelle, Robert Ellsworth 1903-1988 *WhAm 10*
Bunnen, Lucinda Weil 1930- *WhoAmA 93*
Bunner, Patricia Andrea 1953- *WhoAmL 94*
Bunner, William Keck 1949- *WhoAmL 94*
Bunnett, Joseph Frederick 1921- *WhoAm 94, WhoScEn 94*
Bunney, Benjamin Stephenson 1938- *WhoScEn 94*
Bunney, William E. 1902-1992 *WhAm 10*
Bunni, Nael Georges 1939- *WhoScEn 94*
Bunning, James P. 1931- *WhoAmP 93*
Bunning, Jim 1931- *CngDr 93, WhoAm 94*
Bunny, George d1952 *WhoHol 92*
Bunny, John d1915 *WhoHol 92*
Bunny, John 1863-1915 *See* Bunny and Finch *WhoCom*
Bunny and Finch *WhoCom*
Bunsen, Robert 1811-1899 *WorInv*
Bunsen, Robert Wilhelm Eberhard 1811-1899 *WorScD*
Bunshaft, Gordon 1909-1990 *AmCulL, WhAm 10*
Bunsow, Henry C. 1948- *WhoAmL 94*
Bunster, Don Alvaro 1920- *Who 94*
Bunston, Herbert d1935 *WhoHol 92*
Bunt, James Richard 1941- *WhoAm 94, WhoFI 94*
Bunt, Randolph Cedric 1958- *WhoScEn 94*
Bunt, Raymond, Jr. 1944- *WhoAmP 93*
Bunte, Doris 1933- *WhoAmP 93, WhoBlA 94*
Bunten, William Daniel 1931- *WhoAm 94*
Bunten, William Wallace 1930- *WhoAmP 93*
Bunteska, Vera 1943- *WhoWomW 91*
Bunting, Arthur Hugh 1917- *IntWW 93, Who 94*
Bunting, Bainbridge 1913-1981 *WhoAmA 93N*
Bunting, Basil 1900-1985 *BlmGEL*
Bunting, Charles I. 1942- *WhoAm 94*
Bunting, David Cuyp 1940- *WhoWest 94*
Bunting, (Anne) Eve(lyn) 1928- *TwCYAW*
Bunting, (Anne) Eve(lyn Bolton) 1928- *WrDr 94*
Bunting, Gary Glenn 1947- *WhoScEn 94*
Bunting, George H., Jr. 1944- *WhoAmP 93*
Bunting, (Edward) John 1918- *Who 94*
Bunting, John Pearce 1929- *WhoFI 94*
Bunting, John Reginald 1916- *Who 94*
Bunting, Martin Brian 1934- *Who 94*
Bunton, Clifford Allen 1920- *WhoWest 94*
Bunton, George Louis 1920- *Who 94*
Bunton, Henry Clay 1903- *WhoBlA 94*
Bunton, Lucius Desha, III 1924- *WhoAm 94, WhoAmL 94*
Buntrock, Bobby d1974 *WhoHol 92*
Buntrock, Dean Lewis 1931- *WhoAm 94, WhoFI 94*
Buntrock, Gerhard Friedrich Richard 1954- *WhoScEn 94*
Bunts, Frank 1932- *WhoAmA 93*
Bunts, Frank Emory 1932- *WhoAm 94*
Bunty, Jacqueline Marie 1959- *WhoAmL 94*
Bunuel, Jean-Louis *WhoHol 92*
Bunuel, Luis d1983 *WhoHol 92*
Bunuel, Luis 1900-1983 *ConLC 80 [port], HispLC [port]*
Bunyan, John 1628-1688 *BlmGEL [port]*
Bunyan, Peter John 1936- *Who 94*
Bunyard, Alan Donald 1931- *WhoScEn 94*
Bunyard, Robert (Sidney) 1930- *Who 94*
Bunyon, Ronald S. 1935- *WhoBlA 94*
Bunzel, John Harvey 1924- *WhoAm 94, WhoWest 94*
Bunzl, Rudolph Hans 1922- *WhoAm 94*
Buoch, William Thomas 1923- *WhoFI 94*
Buonagurio, Edgar R. 1946- *WhoAmA 93*
Buonagurio, Toby Lee 1947- *WhoAmA 93*
Buonanni, Brian Francis 1945- *WhoAm 94, WhoFI 94, WhoScEn 94*
Buonanno, Christopher Paul 1952- *WhoAmP 93*
Buono, Victor d1982 *WhoHol 92*
Buonocore, Dominic A. 1930- *WhoAmP 93*
Buonocore, Michelina *DrAPF 93*
Buonocore, Thomas Anthony 1958- *WhoAmL 94*
Buontalenti, Bernardo 1531-1608 *NewGrDO*
Bupp, Sonny 1928- *WhoHol 92*
Bupp, Tommy 1927- *WhoHol 92*
Bupp, Walter *EncSF 93*
Bur, Charles Francis 1950- *WhoFI 94*
Burack, Elmer H(oward) 1927- *WrDr 94*
Burack, Elmer Howard 1927- *WhoAm 94*
Burack, Michael Leonard 1942- *WhoAm 94, WhoAmL 94*
Burack, Sylvia E. Kamerman 1916- *WhoAm 94*
Buraczynski, Anthony C. 1908- *WhoAmP 93*
Burak, Howard Paul 1934- *WhoAm 94, WhoAmL 94*

Burakoff, Steven James 1942- *WhoAm 94*
Burandt, Gary Edward 1943- *WhoFI 94*
Buranelli, Vincent 1919- *ConAu 43NR, WrDr 94*
Buranello, Il *NewGrDO*
Burani, Michelette d1957 *WhoHol 92*
Buras, Nathan 1921- *WhoWest 94*
Buras-Elsen, Brenda Allynn 1954- *WhoFI 94*
Buratti, Dennis P. 1949- *WhoAm 94, WhoAmL 94*
Burawa, Christopher Mark 1959- *WhoWest 94*
Burba, Edwin Hess, Jr. 1936- *WhoAm 94*
Burback, Steven Brent 1954- *WhoAm 94*
Burbage, Eleanor Claire 1951- *WhoAmP 93*
Burbage, James d1597 *BlmGEL*
Burbage, Richard 1567?-1619 *BlmGEL*
Burbank, John Thorn 1939- *WhoMW 93*
Burbank, Luther *WorInv*
Burbank, Luther 1849-1926 *AmSocL, WorScD*
Burbank, Michael Eddy 1947- *WhoFI 94*
Burbank, Nelson Stone 1920- *WhoAm 94*
Burbank, Robinson Derry 1921- *WhoScEn 94*
Burbea, Jacob N. 1942- *WhoAm 94, WhoScEn 94*
Burbeck, Frank d1930 *WhoHol 92*
Burbidge, Eleanor Margaret Peachey *WhoAm 94*
Burbidge, Geoffrey 1925- *IntWW 93, Who 94, WhoScEn 94*
Burbidge, Herbert (Dudley) 1904- *Who 94*
Burbidge, Keith A. 1920- *WhoAmP 93*
Burbidge, Margaret *Who 94*
Burbidge, (Eleanor) Margaret *Who 94*
Burbidge, (Eleanor) Margaret Peachey *IntWW 93*
Burbridge, Charles d1922 *WhoHol 92*
Burbridge, Elizabeth *WhoHol 92*
Burbridge, (John) Paul 1932- *Who 94*
Burbridge, Stephen Nigel 1934- *Who 94*
Burbulis, Gennady Eduardovich 1945- *IntWW 93, LoBiDrD*
Burbury, Stanley Charles 1909- *Who 94*
Burby, Kary Elizabeth 1969- *WhoMW 93*
Burcat, Joel Robin 1954- *WhoAmL 94*
Burch, Claire *DrAPF 93*
Burch, Claire 1925- *WhoWest 94*
Burch, Claire R. 1935- *WhoAmA 93*
Burch, Craig Alan 1954- *WhoFI 94*
Burch, Dean 1927-1991 *WhAm 10*
Burch, Donald Victor 1944- *WhoAmL 94*
Burch, Earl Allen, Jr. 1947- *WhoWest 94*
Burch, Elizabeth *WhoAmP 93*
Burch, Elmer Earl 1943- *WhoAm 94*
Burch, Francis Boucher, Jr. 1948- *WhoAm 94, WhoAmL 94*
Burch, Hamlin Doughty, III 1939- *WhoWest 94*
Burch, Harold Dee 1928- *WhoMW 93*
Burch, Harold Eugene 1941- *AfrAmG [port]*
Burch, James Leo 1942- *WhoAm 94*
Burch, Jerry W. 1945- *WhoAmP 93*
Burch, Joann J(ohansen) *ConAu 142, SmATA 75*
Burch, John d1969 *WhoHol 92*
Burch, John Christopher, Jr. 1940- *WhoFI 94*
Burch, John Thomas, Jr. 1942- *WhoAm 94, WhoAmL 94*
Burch, John Walter 1925- *WhoFI 94, WhoScEn 94*
Burch, Keith 1931- *Who 94*
Burch, Lucius Edward, Jr. 1912- *WhoAm 94*
Burch, Mary Lou 1930- *WhoWest 94*
Burch, Mary Seelye Quinn 1925- *WhoAmL 94*
Burch, Melvin Earl 1949- *WhoAm 94, WhoFI 94*
Burch, Michael Ira 1941- *WhoAm 94*
Burch, Paul Michael 1954- *WhoAmP 93*
Burch, Philip J. 1937- *WhoFI 94*
Burch, Reynold Edward 1910- *WhoBlA 94*
Burch, Robert 1925- *WrDr 94*
Burch, Robert Dale 1928- *WhoAm 94, WhoAmL 94*
Burch, Robert J(oseph) 1925- *SmATA 74 [port], TwCYAW*
Burch, Robert Joseph 1925- *WhoAm 94*
Burch, Robert L. *WhoAmP 93*
Burch, Shelly 1959- *WhoHol 92*
Burch, Stephen Kenneth 1945- *WhoMW 93*
Burch, Susan Ann 1946- *WhoMW 93*
Burch, Thaddeus Joseph, Jr. 1930- *WhoAm 94*
Burch, Thomas J. 1931- *WhoAmP 93*
Burch, Voris Reagan 1930- *WhoAm 94*
Burch, William Alva 1925- *WhoAmP 93*
Burch, William Gerald 1911- *Who 94*
Burcham, Barbara June 1952- *WhoFI 94*
Burcham, Eva Helen 1941- *WhoMW 93*
Burcham, Jeffrey Anthony 1964- *WhoScEn 94*
Burcham, Randall Parks 1917- *WhoAmL 94*
Burcham, Thomas H. 1936- *WhoIns 94*
Burcham, William Ernest 1913- *IntWW 93, Who 94, WrDr 94*
Burchard, John Kenneth 1936- *WhoAm 94*
Burchard, Peter Duncan 1921- *SmATA 74 [port], WhoAmA 93*
Burchard, Thomas Kirk 1948- *WhoWest 94*
Burchardt, Bill 1917- *WrDr 94*
Burchardt, Clara Chavez 1932- *WhoAm 94*
Burche, John *WhoMW 93*
Burchell, Charles R. 1946- *WhoBlA 94*
Burchell, Howard Bertram 1907- *WhoAm 94*
Burchell, Isabella *NewGrDO*
Burchell, Mary Cecilia *WhoAm 94*
Burchell, R(obert) A(rthur) 1941- *WrDr 94*
Burchell, Vicki Jo 1961- *WhoFI 94, WhoMW 93*
Burchell, William John c. 1782-1863 *WhWE*
Burcher, Robert Douglas, Jr. 1946- *WhoFI 94*
Burchess, Arnold 1912- *WhoAmA 93*
Burchett, Alan Edward 1943- *WhoAmL 94*
Burchett, Betty Martela 1934- *WhoAm 94*
Burchett, Debra 1955- *WhoAmA 93*
Burchett, Dewey Eldridge, Jr. 1939- *WhoAmP 93*
Burchett, Glenn R. 1952- *WhoMW 93*
Burchett, Kenneth Eugene 1942- *WhoAmA 93*
Burchett, Paul Preston 1948- *WhoAmP 93*
Burchette, Marissa Jeanette, Sr. 1967- *WhoWest 94*
Burchfiel, Burrell Clark 1934- *WhoAm 94, WhoScEn 94*
Burchfield, Bobby Roy 1954- *WhoAmL 94*
Burchfield, Charles 1893-1967 *WhoAmA 93N*
Burchfield, James R. 1924- *WhoIns 94*
Burchfield, Jerry Lee 1947- *WhoAmA 93*
Burchfield, Robert William 1923- *IntWW 93, Who 94, WrDr 94*
Burchfield, William H. 1935- *WhoFI 94*
Burchill, Julie 1960- *WrDr 94*
Burchinal, Frederick 1948- *NewGrDO*
Burchman, Leonard 1925- *WhoAm 94*
Burchmore, Eric 1920- *Who 94*
Burchuladze, Paata 1951- *NewGrDO*
Burciaga, Cecilia Preciado de 1945- *WhoHisp 94*
Burciaga, Jose Antonio *DrAPF 93*
Burciaga, José Antonio 1940- *WhoHisp 94*
Burciaga, Juan G. 1929- *WhoHisp 94*
Burciaga, Juan Guerrero 1929- *WhoAm 94, WhoAmL 94, WhoWest 94*
Burciaga, Juan Ramon 1953- *WhoHisp 94, WhoScEn 94*
Burck, Arthur Albert 1913- *WhoAm 94*
Burck, Jacob 1904-1982 *WhoAmA 93N*
Burckhardt, Johann Ludwig 1784-1817 *WhWE*
Burckhardt, Rudy 1914- *WhoAm 94, WhoAmA 93*
Burckhardt, Yvonne Helene *WhoAmA 93*
Burcroff, Richard Tomkinson, II 1939- *WhoFI 94*
Burczyk, Mary Elizabeth 1953- *WhoWest 94*
Burd, Francis John 1940- *WhoMW 93*
Burd, James M. 1931- *WhoAmP 93*
Burd, John Stephen 1939- *WhoAm 94*
Burd, Robert Meyer 1937- *WhoScEn 94*
Burda, Hubert 1940- *IntWW 93*
Burde, Ronald Marshall 1938- *WhoAm 94*
Burde, Samuel Gottlieb 1753-1831 *NewGrDO*
Burdekin, Frederick Michael 1938- *Who 94*
Burdekin, Katharine P(enelope) 1896-1963 *EncSF 93*
Burdelik, Thomas Louis 1959- *WhoAm 94, WhoAmL 94, WhoMW 93*
Burden, Baron 1916- *Who 94*
Burden, Carter 1941- *WhoAmA 93*
Burden, Chris 1946- *WhoAmA 93*
Burden, David Leslie 1943- *Who 94*
Burden, Derrick Frank 1918- *Who 94*
Burden, Hugh d1985 *WhoHol 92*
Burden, James Ewers 1939- *WhoAmL 94, WhoFI 94*
Burden, Jean *DrAPF 93*
Burden, Jean 1914- *WrDr 94*
Burden, Jean Prussing *WhoAm 94*
Burden, Ordway Partridge 1944- *WhoAm 94*
Burden, Pennie L. 1910- *WhoBlA 94*
Burden, Richard Haines 1954- *Who 94*
Burden, S. Carter 1941- *WhoAm 94*
Burden, Suzanne *WhoHol 92*
Burden, Willie James 1951- *WhoBlA 94*
Burde-Ney, Jenny *NewGrDO*
Burdetsky, Ben 1928- *WhoAm 94*
Burdett, Barbra Elaine 1947- *WhoMW 93, WhoScEn 94*
Burdett, George Craig 1943- *WhoFI 94, WhoMW 93*
Burdett, Howard William 1939- *WhoAm 94*
Burdett, James Richard 1934- *WhoFI 94, WhoMW 93*
Burdett, Peter Perez c. 1734-1793 *DcNaB MP*
Burdett, Savile (Aylmer) 1931- *Who 94*
Burdett, Winston d1993 *NewYTBS 93 [port]*
Burdett, Winston M. 1913-1993 *CurBio 93N*
Burdette, Keith 1955- *WhoAmP 93*
Burdette, LaVere Elaine *WhoBlA 94*
Burdette, Robert Soelberg 1955- *WhoFI 94, WhoWest 94*
Burdette, Walter James 1915- *WhoAm 94*
Burdette, William James 1962- *WhoFI 94*
Burdge, Rabel James 1937- *WhoAm 94*
Burdge, Richard James, Jr. 1949- *WhoAmL 94*
Burdi, Alphonse Rocco 1935- *WhoAm 94*
Burdick, Allan Bernard 1920- *WhoAm 94*
Burdick, Carol (Ruth) 1928- *WrDr 94*
Burdick, Charles Lalor 1892-1989 *WhAm 10*
Burdick, David Maaloe 1954- *WhoScEn 94*
Burdick, Dorothy Jeannette 1935- *WhoWest 94*
Burdick, Eugene Allan 1912- *WhoAm 94*
Burdick, Eugene L(eonard) 1918-1965 *EncSF 93*
Burdick, Glenn Arthur 1932- *WhoAm 94*
Burdick, Hal d1978 *WhoHol 92*
Burdick, Jocelyn *WhoAmP 93*
Burdick, Lou Brum 1943- *WhoAm 94*
Burdick, Neil *WhoHol 92*
Burdick, Quentin N. 1908-1992 *AnObit 1992*
Burdick, Quentin Northrop d1992 *IntWW 93N*
Burdick, Quentin Northrop 1908-1992 *WhAm 10*
Burdick, Rick L. 1951- *WhoAmL 94*
Burdick, Robert William 1943- *WhoFI 94*
Burdick, William MacDonald 1952- *WhoScEn 94*
Burdine, Glenn D. 1930- *WhoAmP 93*
Burdine, John A. 1936- *WhoAm 94*
Burdis, Ray 1958- *WhoHol 92*
Burditt, George Miller, Jr. 1922- *WhoAm 94, WhoAmL 94*
Burdock, Harriet 1944- *WhoAmA 93*
Burdsall, Dean Leroy 1935- *WhoWest 94*
Burdsall, Mark David 1962- *WhoMW 93*
Burdus, (Julia) Ann 1933- *Who 94*
Bure, Pavel 1971- *WhoAm 94, WhoWest 94*
Bureau, Michel Andre 1943- *WhoAm 94*
Burel, Leonce-Henry 1892-1977 *IntDcF 2-4*
Burelli Rivas, Miguel Angel 1922- *IntWW 93*
Burenga, Kenneth L. 1944- *IntWW 93, WhoAm 94, WhoFI 94*
Buresch, Charles Edward 1947- *WhoFI 94, WhoMW 93*
Buresh, C. John 1945- *WhoAm 94*
Buresh, James Francis 1942- *WhoAmL 94*
Buresh, Thomas Gordon 1951- *WhoFI 94*
Buresova, Dagmar 1929- *WhoWomW 91*
Burfield, Eva 1925- *WrDr 94*
Burfield, Joan *WhoHol 92*
Burford, Earl of 1965- *Who 94*
Burford, Alexander Mitchell, Jr. 1929- *WhoScEn 94*
Burford, Anne McGill 1942- *WhoAm 94*
Burford, Barbara c. 1946- *BlmGWL*
Burford, Byron Leslie 1920- *WhoAmA 93*
Burford, Dorothy Wright 1903- *WhoAmP 93*
Burford, Edna d1929 *WhoHol 92*
Burford, Effie Lois 1927- *WhoBlA 94*
Burford, Eleanor *ConAu 140, SmATA 74*
Burford, Eleanor 1906-1993 *WrDr 94N*
Burford, Jeremy Michael Joseph 1942- *Who 94*
Burford, Lolah 1931- *WrDr 94*
Burford, Robert F. 1923- *WhoAmP 93*
Burford, Robert Fitzpatrick 1923- *WhoAm 94*
Burford, William *DrAPF 93*
Burford, William (Skelly) 1927- *WrDr 94*
Burford, William E. 1936- *WhoAmA 93*
Burg, Anton Behme 1904- *WhoWest 94*
Burg, Barry Richard 1938- *WhoWest 94*
Burg, Eugen d1944 *WhoHol 92*
Burg, Fredric David 1940- *WhoAm 94*
Burg, Gary G. 1956- *WhoWest 94*
Burg, George Roscoe 1916- *WhoAm 94*
Burg, Gerald William 1923- *WhoWest 94*
Burg, Gisela Elisabeth 1939- *Who 94*
Burg, James Allen 1941- *WhoAmP 93*
Burg, Jerome Stuart 1935- *WhoWest 94*
Burg, John Parker 1931- *WhoAm 94*
Burg, Josef 1909- *IntWW 93*
Burg, Maurice Benjamin 1931- *WhoAm 94, WhoScEn 94*
Burg, Michael S. 1950- *WhoAmL 94*
Burg, Mitchell Marc 1954- *WhoAm 94*
Burg, Patricia Jean 1934- *WhoAmA 93*
Burg, Robert 1890-1946 *NewGrDO*
Burg, Ruth Cooper 1926- *WhoAm 94, WhoAmL 94*
Burgamy, Michael Barnet 1945- *WhoWest 94*
Burgan, Jeffrey Brandon 1955- *WhoFI 94*
Burgan, Mary Alice 1935- *WhoAm 94*
Burgan, Salih Khalil 1918- *IntWW 93*
Burgard, Horst 1929- *IntWW 93*
Burgarella, John Paul 1928- *WhoScEn 94*
Burgarino, Anthony Emanuel 1948- *WhoScEn 94, WhoWest 94*
Burgdoerfer, Jerry 1958- *WhoAmL 94*
Burgdoerfer, Jerry J. 1935- *WhoAm 94*
Burgdorf, Barry Daniels 1964- *WhoAmL 94*
Burge, Christopher *WhoAm 94*
Burge, David Russell 1930- *WhoAm 94*
Burge, Henry Charles 1911- *WhoAm 94*
Burge, James C. d1985 *WhoHol 92*
Burge, James Darrell 1934- *WhoAm 94*
Burge, John Wesley, Jr. 1932- *WhoAm 94*
Burge, Ronald Edgar 1932- *Who 94*
Burge, Stuart 1918- *Who 94, WhoHol 92*
Burge, Willard, Jr. 1938- *WhoWest 94*
Burge, William Lee 1918- *WhoAm 94*
Burgee, John Henry 1933- *WhoAm 94*
Burgen, Arnold (Stanley Vincent) 1922- *IntWW 93, Who 94*
Burgener, Clair W. 1921- *WhoAmP 93*
Burgener, Francis Andre 1942- *WhoAm 94*
Burgeon, Colette 1957- *WhoWomW 91*
Burgeon, G.A.L. *EncSF 93*
Burger, Alewyn Petrus 1927- *IntWW 93*
Burger, Ambrose William 1923- *WhoAm 94*
Burger, Charles N. 1940- *WhoAmL 94*
Burger, Chester 1921- *WhoAm 94*
Burger, Dionys 1923- *EncSF 93*
Burger, Edmund Ganes 1930- *WhoAm 94*
Burger, Gary C. 1943- *WhoAmA 93*
Burger, George Vanderkarr 1927- *WhoMW 93, WhoScEn 94*
Burger, Henry G. 1923- *WhoAm 94, WhoMW 93, WhoScEn 94*
Burger, Herbert Francis 1930- *WhoAm 94*
Burger, Janette Marie 1958- *WhoMW 93*
Burger, Joanna 1941- *WrDr 94*
Burger, John Barclay 1936- *WhoWest 94*
Burger, Leslie Morton 1940- *WhoAm 94*
Burger, Mary Louise *WhoAm 94*
Burger, Mary Williams *WhoBlA 94*
Burger, Michael Donald 1958- *WhoFI 94*
Burger, Micheline Zacharias 1947- *WhoAmL 94*
Burger, Philip Michael 1944- *WhoMW 93*
Burger, Robert (Eugene) 1931- *WrDr 94*
Burger, Robert Eugene 1931- *WhoAm 94*
Burger, Robert Mercer 1927- *WhoAm 94*
Burger, W. Carl 1925- *WhoAmA 93*
Burger, Warren E. 1907- *CngDr 93, WhoAmP 93*
Burger, Warren E(arl) 1907- *IntWW 93*
Burger, Warren Earl 1907- *Who 94, WhoAm 94, WhoAmL 94*
Burgert, Eran Omer, Jr. 1924- *WhoMW 93*
Burges, Alan *Who 94*
Burges, (Norman) Alan 1911- *Who 94*
Burges, (Margaret) Betty (Pierpoint) *Who 94*
Burges, Dempsey 1751-1800 *WhAmRev*
Burges, Melvin E. 1951- *WhoBlA 94*
Burges, Norman Alan 1911- *WrDr 94*
Burges, Rodney Lyon Travers 1914- *Who 94*
Burgess, Anthony *DrAPF 93*
Burgess, Anthony 1917- *BlmGEL, EncSF 93, IntWW 93, NewGrDO, TwCYAW, Who 94, WhoAm 94, WrDr 94*
Burgess, Anthony 1917-1993 *ConLC 81 [port], NewYTBS 93, News 94-2*
Burgess, Anthony Reginald Frank 1932- *Who 94*
Burgess, Averil 1938- *Who 94*
Burgess, Brio *DrAPF 93*
Burgess, Charles 1932- *WrDr 94*
Burgess, Charles Orville 1932- *WhoAm 94*
Burgess, Clara Woodward 1918- *WhoWest 94*
Burgess, Claude Bramall 1910- *Who 94*
Burgess, Cyril Duncan 1929- *Who 94*

Burgess, David 1948- *WhoAm 94, WhoAmL 94, WhoFI 94*
Burgess, David John 1939- *Who 94*
Burgess, David Lowry 1940- *WhoAm 94, WhoAmA 93*
Burgess, Dennis Lane 1953- *WhoMW 93*
Burgess, Dilys Averil *Who 94*
Burgess, Dorothy d1961 *WhoHol 92*
Burgess, Dwight A. 1927- *WhoBlA 94*
Burgess, Earl d1920 *WhoHol 92*
Burgess, Edward (Arthur) 1927- *Who 94*
Burgess, Edward Anderson 1956- *WhoFI 94*
Burgess, Edward S. *WhoAmP 93*
Burgess, Eric 1920- *ConAu 42NR*
Burgess, Eric (Alexander) 1912- *EncSF 93*
Burgess, Geoffrey Harold Orchard 1926- *Who 94*
Burgess, Geoffrey Kelsen 1935- *Who 94*
Burgess, Gladys d1933 *WhoHol 92*
Burgess, Greg *WhoAm 94*
Burgess, Guy Francis de Moncy 1911-1963 *DcNaB MP*
Burgess, Harold Dempster 1894-1989 *WhAm 10*
Burgess, Harry d1936 *WhoHol 92*
Burgess, Hayden Fern 1946- *WhoAmL 94*
Burgess, Hazel d1973 *WhoHol 92*
Burgess, Helen d1937 *WhoHol 92*
Burgess, Henry Ernest 1929- *WhoWest 94*
Burgess, Hugh 1929- *WhoAmP 93*
Burgess, Ian Glencross 1931- *IntWW 93*
Burgess, Isabel Andrews *WhoAmP 93*
Burgess, J. Wesley 1952- *WhoWest 94*
Burgess, James Edward 1936- *WhoAm 94, WhoMW 93*
Burgess, James Harland 1929- *WhoAm 94*
Burgess, James R., Jr. 1915- *WhoBlA 94*
Burgess, Jane K. 1928- *ConAu 42NR*
Burgess, Janet Helen 1933- *WhoAm 94, WhoFI 94*
Burgess, Jeffrey L. 1953- *WhoMW 93*
Burgess, John 1929- *Who 94*
Burgess, John Allen 1951- *WhoAm 94*
Burgess, John Edward 1930- *Who 94*
Burgess, John Frank 1917- *WhoAm 94*
Burgess, John Herbert 1933- *WhoAm 94*
Burgess, John Melville 1909- *WhoBlA 94*
Burgess, John Stuart 1920- *WhoAmP 93*
Burgess, Joseph E. 1891-1961 *WhoAmA 93N*
Burgess, Joseph Edward 1935- *WhoBlA 94*
Burgess, Joseph James, Jr. 1924- *WhoAmA 93, WhoWest 94*
Burgess, Kathryn Hoy *WhoScEn 94*
Burgess, Larry Lee 1942- *WhoScEn 94, WhoWest 94*
Burgess, Lee E. 1949- *WhoAm 94*
Burgess, Leonard Randolph 1919- *WhoAm 94*
Burgess, Linda Suzanne 1954- *WhoAmA 93*
Burgess, Lloyd Albert 1917- *WhoAm 94*
Burgess, Lord 1924- *WhoBlA 94*
Burgess, M. R. *ConAu 42NR*
Burgess, M. R. 1948- *WrDr 94*
Burgess, Magnus Mallory 1896-1953 *WhAm 10*
Burgess, Mary Alice 1938- *WhoAm 94, WhoWest 94*
Burgess, Mary Wickizer *EncSF 93*
Burgess, Melvin 1938- *WhoAm 94*
Burgess, Melvin Thomas, Sr. 1938- *WhoBlA 94*
Burgess, Michael *EncSF 93*
Burgess, Michael 1948- *WhoAm 94, WhoWest 94, WrDr 94*
Burgess, Michael (Roy) 1948- *ConAu 42NR*
Burgess, Mike *ConAu 42NR*
Burgess, Myrtle Marie 1921- *WhoAmL 94*
Burgess, Peter Malcolm 1950- *WhoAm 94*
Burgess, Philip Robert 1960- *WhoAm 94*
Burgess, R. William, Jr. 1959- *WhoAm 94*
Burgess, Richard Ball 1943- *WhoAm 94*
Burgess, Richard Henry 1934- *WhoFI 94*
Burgess, Richard Ray 1942- *WhoAm 94*
Burgess, Robert E., Sr. 1937- *WhoBlA 94*
Burgess, Robert John 1961- *WhoWest 94*
Burgess, Robert K. 1944- *WhoAm 94, WhoFI 94*
Burgess, Robert Kyle 1948- *WhoAm 94*
Burgess, Robert Lewis 1931- *WhoAm 94, WhoScEn 94*
Burgess, Roger 1927- *WhoAm 94*
Burgess, Sally 1953- *NewGrDO, Who 94*
Burgess, Scott *WhoHol 92*
Burgess, Stuart *Who 94*
Burgess, (Joseph) Stuart 1929- *Who 94*
Burgess, Thornton Waldo 1874-1965 *ConAu 41NR*
Burgess, Tony *Who 94*
Burgess, Warren E 1932- *WrDr 94*
Burgess, William d1948 *WhoHol 92*
Burgess, William Henry 1917- *WhoWest 94*
Burgess, William J. *WhoAmP 93*
Burgess, William Vander 1934- *WhoWest 94*
Burgess, Yvonne 1936- *BlmGWL*
Burgess-Kohn, Jane *ConAu 42NR*
Burgest, David Raymond 1943- *WhoBlA 94*
Burges Watson, Richard Eagleson Gordon *Who 94*
Burget, Franz Anthony, III 1939- *WhoWest 94*
Burget, Mark Edward 1954- *WhoAmL 94*
Burgett, Dolores Mary 1935- *WhoMW 93*
Burgett, George L. 1944- *WhoAm 94, WhoAmL 94*
Burgett, Paul Joseph *WhoBlA 94*
Burgett, William Brian 1951- *WhoAm 94*
Burgette, James M. 1937- *WhoBlA 94*
Burggraf, Frank Bernard, Jr. 1932- *WhoAm 94*
Burggraf, Ray Lowell 1938- *WhoAmA 93*
Burgh, Baron 1935- *Who 94*
Burgh, John (Charles) 1925- *Who 94*
Burgh, John Charles 1925- *IntWW 93*
Burgh, Ulick John de 1802-1874 *DcNaB MP*
Burgham, Edwin O. 1889-1969 *EncABHB 9 [port]*
Burghardt, Kurt Josef 1935- *WhoAm 94*
Burghardt, Raymond Francis, Jr. 1945- *WhoAm 94*
Burghardt, Walter J. 1914- *IntWW 93*
Burghardt, Walter J(ohn) 1914- *ConAu 41NR*
Burghart, Gary Robert 1953- *WhoAmL 94*
Burghart, James Henry 1938- *WhoAm 94*
Burghauser, Jarmil 1921- *NewGrDO*
Burghduff, John Brian 1958- *WhoScEn 94*
Burgheim, Richard Allan 1933- *WhoAm 94*
Burgher, Fairfax d1965 *WhoHol 92*
Burghersh, Lord 1784-1859 *NewGrDO*
Burghley, Lord 1970- *Who 94*
Burghley, Rose *WrDr 94*
Burghoff, Gary 1943- *IntMPA 94, WhoHol 92*
Burgie, Irving Louis 1924- *WhoBlA 94*
Burgin, Bruce L. 1947- *WhoBlA 94*
Burgin, Charles E. 1938- *WhoAmL 94*
Burgin, Deborah Morrison 1954- *WhoAmL 94*
Burgin, George Hans 1930- *WhoAm 94*
Burgin, Richard *DrAPF 93*
Burgin, Ruth L. W. *WhoBlA 94*
Burgin, Victor 1941- *IntWW 93*
Burgin, William Garner, Jr. 1924- *WhoAmP 93*
Burgio, Jane *WhoAmP 93*
Burgis, Grover Cornelius 1933- *WhoAm 94*
Burgland, Jane Harvey 1931- *WhoAmP 93*
Burgman, Dierdre Ann 1948- *WhoAmL 94, WhoFI 94*
Burgner, Thomas Ulric 1932- *Who 94*
Burgoa, John Francis 1948- *WhoHisp 94*
Burgon, Geoffrey 1941- *IntWW 93, Who 94*
Burgon, M. Kent 1936- *WhoWest 94*
Burgos, Fernando 1927- *WhoHisp 94*
Burgos, Hector Hugo 1954- *WhoFI 94*
Burgos, Joseph 1966- *WhoHisp 94*
Burgos, Joseph Agner, Jr. 1945- *WhoHisp 94*
Burgos, Julia de 1914-1953 *BlmGWL*
Burgos, Luis Noel 1963- *WhoHisp 94*
Burgos-Aguilar, Benjamin 1941- *WhoHisp 94*
Burgos-Sasscer, Ruth 1931- *WhoHisp 94*
Burgos Segui, Carmen de c. 1870-1932 *BlmGWL*
Burgoyne, Bruce E. 1924- *WrDr 94*
Burgoyne, Edward Eynon 1918- *WhoAm 94*
Burgoyne, J. Albert 1914- *WhoIns 94*
Burgoyne, John 1711-1792 *WhAmRev [port]*
Burgoyne, John 1722-1794 *AmRev*
Burgoyne, John 1723-1792 *NewGrDO*
Burgoyne, Robert Michael 1927- *Who 94*
Burgstahler, Sheryl Elaine 1948- *WhoWest 94*
Burgstaller, Alois 1871-1945 *NewGrDO*
Burgues, Irving Carl 1906- *WhoAmA 93*
Burguieres, John Berchman, Jr. 1945- *WhoAmL 94*
Burguieres, Philip 1943- *WhoAm 94*
Burgum, Katherine K. 1915- *WhoAmP 93*
Burgweger, Francis Joseph Dewes, Jr. 1942- *WhoAm 94, WhoAmL 94*
Burhans, Frank Malcolm 1920- *WhoScEn 94, WhoWest 94*
Burhenne, Hans Joachim 1925- *WhoAm 94, WhoScEn 94, WhoWest 94*
Burhoe, Brian W. 1941- *WhoAm 94*
Burhoe, Ralph Wendell 1911- *WhoAm 94*
Burhop, Kenneth Eugene 1953- *WhoMW 93*
Buri, Charles Edward 1950- *WhoAmL 94*
Buria, Silvia 1940- *WhoHisp 94*
Burian, Jarka M. 1927- *WrDr 94*
Burian, Robert J 1937- *WhoAm 94*
Burick, John Earle 1962- *WhoWest 94*
Burick, Lawrence T. 1943- *WhoAm 94*
Burilovich, Linda Jean 1949- *WhoFI 94*
Burin, Michael Thomas 1949- *WhoMW 93*
Burinbuhe, Ba 1928- *WhoPRCh 91 [port]*
Burin Des Roziers, Etienne 1913- *IntWW 93*
Burini, Sonia Montes de Oca 1935- *WhoAm 94*
Burk, A. Darlene 1929- *WhoAmA 93*
Burk, Carl John 1935- *WhoAm 94*
Burk, Francis Lewis, Jr. 1943- *WhoAm 94*
Burk, Gary Maurice 1943- *WhoFI 94, WhoWest 94*
Burk, James Mack 1931- *WhoMW 93*
Burk, Kathleen 1946- *WrDr 94*
Burk, Norman 1937- *WhoAm 94, WhoMW 93*
Burk, Robert David 1951- *WhoScEn 94*
Burk, Robert F(redrick) 1955- *WrDr 94*
Burk, Robert S. 1937- *WhoAm 94*
Burk, Robert W., Jr. 1939- *WhoAmP 93*
Burk, Sylvia Joan 1928- *WhoAm 94*
Burka, Maria Karpati 1948- *WhoScEn 94*
Burka, Mark B. 1950- *WhoIns 94*
Burka, Robert Alan 1944- *WhoAm 94*
Burkard, Michael *DrAPF 93*
Burkard, Michael 1947- *WrDr 94*
Burkard, Otto Michael 1908- *IntWW 93*
Burkart, Burke 1933- *WhoAm 94*
Burkart, Erika 1922- *BlmGWL*
Burkart, Jordan V. 1935- *WhoWest 94*
Burkart, Walter Mark 1921- *WhoAm 94*
Burkat, Leonard 1919-1992 *WhAm 10*
Burke, Alfred 1918- *IntMPA 94, WhoHol 92*
Burke, Annie d1952 *WhoHol 92*
Burke, Arleigh A. 1901- *HisDcKW*
Burke, Arleigh Albert 1901- *Who 94*
Burke, Arthur Thomas 1919- *WhoWest 94*
Burke, Austin-Emile *Who 94*
Burke, Bernard Flood 1928- *IntWW 93, WhoAm 94, WhoScEn 94*
Burke, Beryl D. 1958- *WhoAmP 93*
Burke, Bill *WhoAmA 93*
Burke, Billie d1970 *WhoHol 92*
Burke, Billy Brown 1928- *WhoAmP 93*
Burke, Brian *WhoAm 94*
Burke, Brian B. 1958- *WhoAmP 93, WhoMW 93*
Burke, Brian K. 1948- *WhoAmL 94*
Burke, Brian Thomas 1947- *IntWW 93, Who 94*
Burke, Cameron d1978 *WhoHol 92*
Burke, Caroline d1964 *WhoHol 92*
Burke, Cheryl C. 1947- *WhoAmL 94*
Burke, Chris 1965- *WhoAm 94*
Burke, Christine F. 1956- *WhoAmP 93*
Burke, Crescent Frederick 1961- *WhoMW 93*
Burke, Daniel 1951- *WhoAmP 93*
Burke, Daniel Barnett 1929- *WhoAm 94, WhoFI 94*
Burke, Daniel V. 1942- *WhoAmA 93*
Burke, Daniel William 1926- *WhoAm 94*
Burke, Delta 1956- *IntMPA 94*
Burke, Denis Patrick 1951- *WhoAm 94*
Burke, Dennis Andrew 1956- *WhoWest 94*
Burke, Denzer 1933- *WhoBlA 94*
Burke, Derek Clissold 1930- *Who 94*
Burke, E. Ainslie 1922- *WhoAm 94*
Burke, E. Ainslie 1922-1991 *WhoAmA 93N*
Burke, Edmond W. 1935- *WhoAmP 93*
Burke, Edmond Wayne 1935- *WhoAm 94, WhoAmL 94, WhoWest 94*
Burke, Edmund 1727-1797 *HisWorL [port]*
Burke, Edmund 1729-1797 *AmRev, BlmGEL, EncEth, WhAmRev [port]*
Burke, Edmund, Jr. d1993 *NewYTBS 93*
Burke, Edmund (Arbrickle) 1876-1970 *NewGrDO*
Burke, Edmund Charles 1921- *WhoAm 94*
Burke, Edmund William 1948- *WhoAm 94*
Burke, Edward Kenneth 1937- *WhoAmP 93*
Burke, Edward L. 1943- *WhoAmP 93*
Burke, Edward M. 1943- *WhoAmP 93*
Burke, Edward Newell 1916- *WhoAm 94*
Burke, Emmett C. 1920- *WhoBlA 94*
Burke, Emmett Charles 1920- *WhoMW 93*
Burke, France *DrAPF 93*
Burke, Frank Gerard 1927- *WhoAm 94*
Burke, Frank Welsh 1920- *WhoAmP 93*
Burke, Gary Lamont 1955- *WhoBlA 94*
Burke, Geoffrey 1913- *Who 94*
Burke, Georgia d1985 *WhoHol 92*
Burke, Gerard Patrick 1930- *WhoAmP 93*
Burke, Gordon B. 1941- *WhoAmP 93*
Burke, J. Frank d1918 *WhoHol 92*
Burke, Jack L. 1949- *WhoIns 94*
Burke, Jacqueline Yvonne 1949- *WhoAm 94, WhoFI 94*
Burke, James d1968 *WhoHol 92*
Burke, James 1936- *WrDr 94*
Burke, James 1941- *WhoFI 94*
Burke, James 1948- *WhoAmP 93*
Burke, James (Stanley Gilbert) 1956- *Who 94*
Burke, James Donald 1939- *WhoAm 94, WhoAmA 93, WhoMW 93*
Burke, James Edward 1925- *WhoAm 94*
Burke, James Joseph 1928- *WhoAm 94*
Burke, James Joseph, Jr. 1951- *WhoAm 94, WhoFI 94*
Burke, James Lee 1936- *ConAu 19AS [port], -41NR, WrDr 94*
Burke, Jan 1953- *ConAu 142*
Burke, Jeffrey Peter 1941- *Who 94*
Burke, Jerome A. 1937- *WhoAmP 93*
Burke, Jerry Alan 1937- *WhoScEn 94*
Burke, Joe *WhAm 10*
Burke, John 1947- *WhoAm 94*
Burke, John (Frederick) 1922- *WrDr 94*
Burke, John Charles 1946- *WhoWest 94*
Burke, John Francis 1922- *WhoScEn 94*
Burke, John Francis, Jr. 1937- *WhoMW 93*
Burke, John Garrett 1917-1989 *WhAm 10*
Burke, John James 1928- *WhoAm 94*
Burke, John Joseph 1875-1936 *DcAmReB 2*
Burke, John Kenneth 1939- *Who 94*
Burke, John Kirkland, Jr. 1952- *WhoAm 94, WhoAmL 94*
Burke, John L., Jr. 1945- *WhoAmL 94*
Burke, John Michael 1941- *WhoAmL 94*
Burke, John Michael 1946- *WhoScEn 94*
Burke, John Miles 1938-1990 *WhAm 10*
Burke, John Philip 1954- *WhoAm 94*
Burke, Johnny d1964 *WhoHol 92*
Burke, Jonathan 1922- *EncSF 93, WrDr 94*
Burke, Joseph d1942 *WhoHol 92*
Burke, Joseph C. 1932- *WhoAm 94*
Burke, Kathleen d1980 *WhoHol 92*
Burke, Kathleen B. 1948- *WhoAm 94, WhoAmL 94*
Burke, Kathleen Glen 1961- *WhoAmL 94*
Burke, Kathleen Mary 1950- *WhoAmL 94*
Burke, Kelly Howard 1929- *WhoAm 94*
Burke, Kenneth d1993 *NewYTBS 93 [port]*
Burke, Kenneth 1897- *IntWW 93*
Burke, Kenneth Andrew 1941- *WhoAm 94*
Burke, Kenneth John 1939- *WhoAm 94, WhoAmL 94*
Burke, Kerry *Who 94*
Burke, (Thomas) Kerry 1942- *Who 94*
Burke, Kevin d1969 *WhoHol 92*
Burke, Kevin Charles Antony 1929- *WhoAm 94*
Burke, Kevin Michael 1946- *WhoAmP 93*
Burke, Kim Kenneth 1955- *WhoAmL 94*
Burke, Kirkland R. 1948- *WhoBlA 94*
Burke, Laurence Declan 1939- *WhoScEn 94*
Burke, Lillian W. 1917- *WhoBlA 94*
Burke, Lillian Walker 1917- *WhoAm 94, WhoMW 93*
Burke, Logan 1933- *WhoAmP 93*
Burke, Lynda Billa *WhoAmP 93*
Burke, M. Virginia 1945- *WhoAmP 93*
Burke, Margaret Ann 1961- *WhoFI 94, WhoScEn 94*
Burke, Marie d1988 *WhoHol 92*
Burke, Marjorie 1932- *WhoAmP 93*
Burke, Martin B. 1940- *WhoAmP 93*
Burke, Martin Nicholas 1936- *WhoAm 94*
Burke, Mary *WhoAm 94*
Burke, Mary Catherine 1929- *WhoAmP 93*
Burke, Mary Thomas 1930- *WhoAm 94*
Burke, Maureen Helen 1950- *WhoAmL 94*
Burke, Michael Donald 1944- *WhoAm 94*
Burke, Michael Francis 1939- *WhoWest 94*
Burke, Michael Henry 1952- *WhoAmL 94*
Burke, Michael J. 1943- *WhoAmL 94*
Burke, Michele Christine *WhoAm 94*
Burke, Olga Pickering 1946- *WhoBlA 94*
Burke, Orrin d1946 *WhoHol 92*
Burke, Owen 1922- *WrDr 94*
Burke, Patricia 1917- *WhoHol 92*
Burke, Patricia H. 1941- *WhoAm 94*
Burke, Patrick Walton 1922- *WhoAmP 93*
Burke, Paul 1926- *IntMPA 94, WhoHol 92*
Burke, Paul E., Jr. 1934- *WhoAm 94, WhoAmP 93, WhoMW 93*
Burke, Paul Joseph 1952- *WhoMW 93*
Burke, Paul Norman 1955- *WhoFI 94, WhoMW 93*
Burke, Pauline d1978 *WhoHol 92*
Burke, Peter Arthur 1948- *WhoAm 94*
Burke, Philip George 1932- *IntWW 93, Who 94*
Burke, Ralph *EncSF 93*

Burke, Ralph 1960- WhoAmP 93
Burke, Ray 1943- IntWW 93
Burke, Raymond F. WhoAmL 94, WhoFI 94
Burke, Redmond A. 1914- WhoAm 94
Burke, Richard 1932- IntWW 93, Who 94
Burke, Richard Edward 1946- WhoAmL 94
Burke, Richard J., Jr. 1940- WhoAmP 93
Burke, Richard James 1917- WhoScEn 94
Burke, Richard Kitchens 1922- WhoAm 94
Burke, Richard William 1933- WhoAm 94
Burke, Robert 1961- WhoHol 92
Burke, Robert Bertram 1942- WhoAmL 94
Burke, Robert Easton WhoHol 92
Burke, Robert Harry 1945- WhoMW 93, WhoScEn 94
Burke, Robert James 1934- WhoAmP 93
Burke, Robert O'Hara 1820-1861 WhWE
Burke, Robert Thomas 1943- WhoAm 94, WhoAmL 94
Burke, Rosann Margaret 1927- WhoFI 94, WhoMW 93
Burke, Selma 1900- AfrAmAl 6
Burke, Selma Hortense 1900- WhoBlA 94
Burke, Shawn Edmund 1959- WhoScEn 94
Burke, Shawn Patrick 1958- WhoFI 94
Burke, Simon WhoHol 92
Burke, Stephen 1970- WhoAmP 93
Burke, Stephen S. 1945- WhoIns 94
Burke, Steven Francis 1952- WhoAm 94
Burke, Theresa Counts 1965- WhoAmL 94
Burke, Thomas c. 1747-1783 WhAmRev
Burke, Thomas (Aspinall) 1890-1969 NewGrDO
Burke, Thomas C. 1941- WhoIns 94
Burke, Thomas Edmund 1932- WhoAm 94
Burke, Thomas Francis 1929-1989 WhAm 10
Burke, Thomas John 1947- WhoMW 93
Burke, Thomas Joseph 1927- WhoMW 93, WhoScEn 94
Burke, Thomas Joseph 1949- WhoIns 94
Burke, Thomas Joseph, Jr. 1941- WhoAm 94, WhoAmL 94
Burke, Thomas Kerry 1942- IntWW 93
Burke, Thomas Michael 1956- WhoAmL 94
Burke, Timothy Francis, Jr. WhoAmL 94
Burke, Timothy J. 1948- WhoAmP 93
Burke, Timothy John 1946- WhoAm 94, WhoAmL 94
Burke, Tom d1969 WhoHol 92
Burke, Tom 1947- Who 94
Burke, Ulick Peter 1937- IntWW 93
Burke, Vivian H. WhoAmP 93, WhoBlA 94
Burke, Walter d1984 WhoHol 92
Burke, Waymon Eugene 1951- WhoAmP 93
Burke, William Arthur 1939- WhoBlA 94
Burke, William James 1912- WhoAm 94
Burke, William L. 1941- WhoAmL 94
Burke, William Lozier Munro 1906-1961 WhoAmA 93N
Burke, William M. 1942- WhoAm 94, WhoAmL 94
Burke, William R., Jr. 1943- WhoAmL 94
Burke, William Temple, Jr. 1935- WhoAm 94, WhoAmL 94
Burke, Yvonne Braithwaite 1932- AfrAmAl 6 [port]
Burke, Yvonne Watson Brathwaite 1932- WhoAm 94, WhoBlA 94, WhoWest 94
Burkee, Irvin 1918- WhoWest 94
Burkeen, Ernest Wisdom, Jr. 1948- WhoBlA 94
Burke-Gaffney, John Campion 1932- Who 94
Burke-Gaffney, Michael Anthony Bowes 1928- Who 94
Burken, Ruth Marie 1956- WhoFI 94, WhoMW 93
Burkert, Rebecca Jean 1961- WhoMW 93
Burkert, Robert Randall 1930- WhoAm 94, WhoAmA 93
Burkes, Leisa Jeanotta 1961- WhoFI 94
Burkes, Wayne O. 1929- WhoAmP 93
Burket, Gail Brook 1905- WhoMW 93
Burket, George Edward, Jr. 1912- WhoAm 94
Burket, Harriet WhoAm 94
Burkett, Eugene Herbert 1948- WhoWest 94
Burkett, Eugene John 1937- WhoScEn 94
Burkett, John David 1964- WhoAm 94, WhoWest 94
Burkett, Larry 1939- ConAu 140
Burkett, Laura WhoHol 92
Burkett, Marjorie Theresa 1931- WhoScEn 94
Burkett, Mary Elizabeth Who 94
Burkett, Mike 1948- WhoAmP 93
Burkett, William Andrew 1913- WhoAm 94
Burkett, William R(ay), Jr. 1943- EncSF 93
Burkett, William Ray, Jr. 1943- WhoWest 94
Burkette, Tyrone WhoBlA 94
Burkey, Jacob Brent 1946- WhoAm 94
Burkey, Lee Melville 1914- WhoAm 94, WhoAmL 94, WhoMW 93
Burkey, Michael Robert 1948- WhoAmL 94
Burkhalter, Mark 1960- WhoAmP 93
Burkhard, Willy 1900-1955 NewGrDO
Burkhardt, Charles Henry 1915- WhoFI 94
Burkhardt, David Gerard 1966- WhoMW 93
Burkhardt, Douglas A. 1947- WhoAm 94
Burkhardt, Francois 1936- IntWW 93
Burkhardt, Hans Gustav 1904- WhoAm 94, WhoAmA 93
Burkhardt, Harry d1943 WhoHol 92
Burkhardt, J. Bland, Jr. 1940- WhoAm 94
Burkhardt, James Kevin 1954- WhoMW 93
Burkhardt, Ronald Robert 1948- WhoAm 94
Burkhart, Betty M. 1931- WhoAmP 93
Burkhart, Bruce Wells 1939- WhoWest 94
Burkhart, Catherine Ray 1939- WhoWest 94
Burkhart, Charles Barclay 1914- WhoAm 94
Burkhart, David A. 1950- WhoMW 93
Burkhart, Elizabeth Flores 1935- WhoHisp 94
Burkhart, Glenn Randall 1947- WhoFI 94
Burkhart, Jennifer Ellen 1955- WhoFI 94
Burkhart, John Henry 1920- WhoAm 94
Burkhart, Kathe DrAPF 93
Burkhart, Kathe K. 1958- WhoAmA 93
Burkhart, Lona Jane Tankersley 1930- WhoWest 94
Burkhart, Monte d1976 WhoHol 92
Burkhart, Robert Edward 1937- WhoAm 94
Burkhart, Stephen 1931- WhoAmP 93
Burkhart, William Henry 1931- WhoAm 94
Burkhauser, Teresa Elaine 1955- WhoWest 94
Burkholder, Donald Lyman 1927- WhoAm 94, WhoScEn 94
Burkholder, Evan A. 1946- WhoAmL 94
Burkholder, James Peter 1954- WhoMW 93
Burkholder, Joyce Lynn 1951- WhoWest 94
Burkholder, Mabel 1881-1973 BlmGWL
Burkholder, Wendell Eugene 1928- WhoAm 94, WhoScEn 94
Burkholz, Herbert DrAPF 93, EncSF 93
Burkholz, Herbert 1932- ConAu 41NR
Burkholz, Spencer Alan 1963- WhoAmL 94
Burkholz, Yvonne 1934- WhoAmP 93
Burki, Fred Albert 1926- WhoAm 94
Burkill, John Charles d1993 Who 94N
Burkitt, Denis (Parsons) 1911-1993 ConAu 141
Burkitt, Denis P. 1911-1993 NewYTBS 93 [port]
Burkitt, Denis Parsons d1993 IntWW 93N, Who 94N
Burkitt, Denis Parsons 1911- IntWW 93
Burkley, Dennis WhoHol 92
Burkley, George Gregory 1902-1991 WhAm 10
Burkley, Paul Edwin 1919- WhoAmP 93
Burkman, Allan Maurice 1932- WhoMW 93
Burkman, George Kenderdine 1928- WhoMW 93
Burkman, Mary Ellen 1959- WhoMW 93
Burko, Diane 1945- WhoAmA 93
Burkov, Valery Anatolevich 1957- LoBiDrD
Burks, Arthur J. 1898-1974 EncSF 93
Burks, Darrell 1956- WhoBlA 94
Burks, Ellis Rena 1964- WhoBlA 94
Burks, Frederick Eugene 1947- WhoAmP 93
Burks, James William, Jr. 1938- WhoBlA 94
Burks, Juanita Pauline 1920- WhoBlA 94
Burks, Larry W. 1943- WhoAmL 94
Burks, Myrna R. 1943- WhoAmA 93
Burks, Rick d1989 WhoHol 92
Burks, Robert 1910-1968 IntDcF 2-4
Burks, Tommy 1940- WhoAmP 93
Burks, Verner Irwin 1923- WhoAm 94
Burkush, Peter 1921- WhoAmP 93
Burl, Jeffrey Brian 1956- WhoScEn 94
Burlamachi, Philip d1644 DcNaB MP
Burland, Brian DrAPF 93
Burland, Brian Berkeley 1931- WhoAm 94, WhoWest 94
Burland, Harris EncSF 93
Burland, James S. 1955- WhoAmL 94
Burland, John Boscawen 1936- Who 94
Burlando, Joseph d1951 WhoHol 92
Burlant, William Jack 1928- WhoAm 94, WhoScEn 94
Burlatsky, Fedor Mikhailovich 1927- IntWW 93
Burleigh, Anne Husted 1941- WhoMW 93
Burleigh, Bruce Daniel, Jr. 1942- WhoMW 93
Burleigh, Charles L., Jr. 1941- WhoAmL 94
Burleigh, Henry Thacker 1866-1949 AfrAmAl 6
Burleigh, Kimberly 1955- WhoAmA 93
Burleigh, Lewis Albert 1940- WhoAm 94, WhoAmL 94
Burleigh, Michael 1955- WrDr 94
Burleigh, Rita Jean 1943- WhoWest 94
Burleigh, Thomas Haydon 1911- Who 94
Burleigh, William Robert 1935- WhoAm 94
Burleski, Joseph Anthony, Jr. 1960- WhoFI 94, WhoScEn 94, WhoWest 94
Burleson, Charles Trentman 1952- WhoAmA 93
Burleson, George Robert 1933- WhoWest 94
Burleson, Helen L. 1929- WhoBlA 94
Burleson, Jack Lance 1952- WhoMW 93
Burleson, Jane Geneva 1928- WhoBlA 94
Burleson, Karen Tripp 1955- WhoAmL 94, WhoFI 94
Burleson, Lynn Pierce 1948- WhoAmL 94
Burleson, Omar 1906-1991 WhAm 10
Burleson, Robert Odell WhoAmP 93
Burlew, Ann Kathleen 1948- WhoBlA 94
Burlew, John Swalm 1910- WhoAm 94
Burley, Dale S. 1961- WhoBlA 94
Burley, Jeffery 1936- Who 94
Burley, John David 1958- WhoFI 94
Burley, Lina 1922- WhoAmA 93
Burley, Victor (George) 1914- Who 94
Burley, W(illiam) J(ohn) 1914- WrDr 94
Burlin, Paul 1886-1969 WhoAmA 93N
Burlin, Terence Eric 1931- Who 94
Burling, Daniel James 1947- WhoFI 94
Burling, Peter 1945- WhoAmP 93
Burling, Philip 1942- WhoAmL 94
Burling, Robbins 1926- WhoAm 94
Burlingame, Alma Lyman 1937- WhoScEn 94, WhoWest 94
Burlingame, Barbara C. 1947- WhoAmP 93
Burlingame, Daniel Wessels 1930- WhoAmL 94
Burlingame, David Hartley 1955- WhoFI 94
Burlingame, Edward Livermore 1935- WhoAm 94
Burlingame, James Montgomery, III 1926- WhoAm 94, WhoAmL 94
Burlingame, John Francis 1922- WhoAm 94
Burlingame, John Hunter 1933- WhoAm 94, WhoAmL 94
Burlingame, Jonathan Donald 1953- WhoWest 94
Burlingame, Judy Louise 1960- WhoWest 94
Burlingame, Leroy James 1929- WhoAm 94
Burlingame, Lloyd Lamson 1934- WhoAm 94
Burlingame, Stephen Lee 1950- WhoAmL 94
Burlingham, Rebecca Ann 1954- WhoAmL 94
Burlington, Earl of 1969- Who 94
Burlinson, Tom WhoHol 92
Burlison, Tom 1936- Who 94
Burluik, David 1882-1967 WhoAmA 93N
Burman, (John) Charles 1908- Who 94
Burman, David John 1952- WhoAm 94
Burman, Diane Berger 1936- WhoMW 93
Burman, Edward 1947- WrDr 94
Burman, Jose Lionel 1917- WrDr 94
Burman, Marsha Linkwald 1949- WhoFI 94
Burman, S. D. 1906-1977 IntDcF 2-4
Burman, Stephen France d1992 Who 94N
Burmaster, Augusta d1934 WhoHol 92
Burmaster, M. R. 1934- WhoAm 94
Burmaster, Mark Joseph 1961- WhoScEn 94
Burmeister, Annelies 1930-1988 NewGrDO
Burmeister, Edward D. 1944- WhoAmL 94
Burmeister, Edwin 1939- WhoAm 94
Burmeister, John Luther 1938- WhoAm 94
Burmeister, Paul Frederick 1938- WhoMW 93
Burmeister, Vladimir 1904-1971 IntDcB
Burmester, Leo WhoHol 92
Burn, Adrian Who 94
Burn, (Bryan) Adrian (Falconer) 1945- Who 94
Burn, Andrew Robert 1902-1991 WrDr 94N
Burn, Angus Maitland P. Who 94
Burn, Ian 1939-1993 NewYTBS 93
Burn, Michael Clive 1912- Who 94
Burn, Richard Hardy 1938- Who 94
Burn, Richard Hunt 1945- WhoFI 94
Burnaby, Davy d1949 WhoHol 92
Burnacini, Giovanni c. 1605-1655 NewGrDO
Burnacini, Ludovico Ottavio 1636-1707 NewGrDO
Burnam, Paul Wayne 1913- WhoAm 94
Burnand, F(rancis) C(owley) 1836-1917 NewGrDO
Burnash, Robert John Charles 1931- WhoWest 94
Burne, Arthur d1945 WhoHol 92
Burne, Nancy d1954 WhoHol 92
Burne, Rosamond d1975 WhoHol 92
Burnell, Bates Cavanaugh 1923- WhoAm 94
Burnell, James McIndoe 1921- WhoAm 94
Burnell, (Susan) Jocelyn B. Who 94
Burnell, Peter d1987 WhoHol 92
Burneo, Francisco Felipe, Jr. 1942- WhoHisp 94
Burner, Alpheus Wilson, Jr. 1947- WhoScEn 94
Burnes, Alexander 1805-1841 WhWE
Burnes, Carol DrAPF 93
Burnes, Kennett Farrar 1943- WhoAm 94
Burness, Pete 1910- IntDcF 2-4
Burnet, Alastair IntWW 93
Burnet, Alastair 1928- WrDr 94
Burnet, Frank MacFarlane 1899-1985 WorScD
Burnet, George, Jr. 1924- WhoAm 94
Burnet, George Wardlaw 1927- Who 94
Burnet, James William Alexander 1928- Who 94
Burnet, James William Alexander (Alastair) 1928- IntWW 93
Burnet, Jean R. 1920- WrDr 94
Burnet, John Elliot 1947- Who 94
Burnet, Roger Hasted 1929- WhoAm 94, WhoFI 94
Burnet, William 1730-1791 WhAmRev
Burnett, Alfred David 1937- ConAu 41NR, WrDr 94
Burnett, Andrew Michael 1952- Who 94
Burnett, Arthur Louis, Sr. 1935- WhoAm 94, WhoAmL 94, WhoBlA 94
Burnett, Barbara Ann 1927- WhoAmA 93
Burnett, Barbara Lorraine 1947- WhoAmL 94
Burnett, Bescye P. 1950- WhoBlA 94
Burnett, Bill Bendyshe 1917- IntWW 93, Who 94
Burnett, Bob J. 1933- WhoAmP 93
Burnett, Brian (Kenyon) 1913- Who 94
Burnett, Brian Laurience 1955- WhoMW 93
Burnett, Calvin 1921- WhoAmA 93
Burnett, Calvin W. 1932- WhoBlA 94
Burnett, Carol 1933- IntMPA 94, WhoAm 94, WhoCom, WhoHol 92
Burnett, Charles John 1940- Who 94
Burnett, Collie, Jr. 1950- WhoBlA 94
Burnett, David Grant 1940- WhoAmA 93
Burnett, David Humphery 1918- Who 94
Burnett, David Lawrence 1956- WhoBlA 94
Burnett, Don WhoHol 92
Burnett, Dorsey d1979 WhoHol 92
Burnett, Eric Stephen 1924- WhoWest 94
Burnett, Eugene Allen 1951- WhoMW 93
Burnett, Frances Eliza Hodgson 1849-1924 BlmGWL, DcNaB MP
Burnett, Frances Hodgson 1849-1924 DcLB 141 [port]
Burnett, Gary Boyd 1954- WhoAmL 94
Burnett, Glenda Morris 1953- WhoMW 93
Burnett, Hamilton S(ands) 1895- WhAm 10
Burnett, Harry d1993 NewYTBS 93
Burnett, Henry 1927- WhoAm 94
Burnett, Howard Jerome 1929- WhoAm 94
Burnett, James H. 1917- WhoAmP 93
Burnett, James Ray 1933- WhoScEn 94
Burnett, James Rufus 1949- WhoAm 94
Burnett, Jean Bullard 1924- WhoMW 93
Burnett, Jim 1947- WhoAmP 93
Burnett, Jody K. 1953- WhoAmL 94
Burnett, John 1925- WrDr 94
Burnett, John (Harrison) 1922- Who 94
Burnett, John F. ConTFT 11
Burnett, John Laurence 1932- WhoWest 94
Burnett, John Nicholas 1939- WhoAm 94
Burnett, Lonnie Sheldon 1927- WhoAm 94
Burnett, Lou Gehrig 1941- WhoAmP 93

Burnett, Lowell Jay 1941- *WhoAm 94*
Burnett, Luther C. 1925- *WhoBlA 94*
Burnett, Lynn Barkley 1948- *WhoWest 94*
Burnett, Mary Coghill 1907-1987 *WhoBlA 94N*
Burnett, Patricia Hill *WhoAmA 93, WhoAmP 93*
Burnett, Philip Whitworth 1908- *Who 94*
Burnett, Richard James 1922- *WhoAmP 93*
Burnett, Rita Marline 1954- *WhoMW 93*
Burnett, Robert A. 1927- *WhoAm 94*
Burnett, Robert Adair 1934- *WhoAm 94*
Burnett, Robert Clayton 1928- *WhoAm 94*
Burnett, Sam Thomas 1942- *WhoAmP 93*
Burnett, Sidney Obed 1924- *WhoBlA 94*
Burnett, W. R. 1899-1982 *IntDcF 2-4*
Burnett, Walter (John) 1921- *Who 94*
Burnett, Whit 1899-1973 *DcLB 137 [port]*
Burnett, Woodrow Wilson 1913- *WhoAmP 93*
Burnette, Ada Puryear *WhoBlA 94*
Burnette, Guy Ellington, Jr. 1952- *WhoAmL 94*
Burnette, Harry Forbes 1947- *WhoAmL 94*
Burnette, James Thomas 1959- *WhoAmL 94*
Burnette, Johnny d1964 *WhoHol 92*
Burnette, Lester *WhoHol 92*
Burnette, Mary Malissa 1950- *WhoAmL 94*
Burnette, Nancy Everitt 1932-1983 *WhAm 10*
Burnette, Olivia *WhoHol 92*
Burnette, Ollen Lawrence, Jr. 1927- *WhoAm 94*
Burnette, Ralph Edwin, Jr. 1953- *WhoAmL 94*
Burnette, Robert Vance 1955- *WhoWest 94*
Burnette, Smiley d1967 *WhoHol 92*
Burnette, Susan Lynn 1955- *WhoAmL 94*
Burnette, Ward Watkins 1941- *WhoAmP 93*
Burnett-Stuart, Joseph 1930- *Who 94*
Burney, Cecil (Denniston) 1923- *Who 94*
Burney, Charles 1726-1814 *BlmGEL, NewGrDO*
Burney, Derek H. 1939- *WhoAm 94, WhoFI 94*
Burney, Fanny 1752-1840 *BlmGEL*
Burney, Fanny 1752-1850 *BlmGWL*
Burney, Hal d1933 *WhoHol 92*
Burney, Harry L., Jr. 1913- *WhoBlA 94*
Burney, James 1750-1821 *WhWE*
Burney, Minna 1891-1958 *WhoAmA 93N*
Burney, Sarah Harriet 1772-1844 *BlmGWL*
Burney, Sayed Muzaffir Hussain 1923- *IntWW 93*
Burney, Thomas Edward 1948- *WhoFI 94*
Burney, Victoria Kalgaard 1943- *WhoWest 94*
Burney, William D., Jr. 1951- *WhoBlA 94*
Burnfield, Daniel Lee 1952- *WhoScEn 94*
Burnford, Sheila 1918-1984 *BlmGWL*
Burnham, Baron d1993 *Who 94N*
Burnham, Baron 1931- *Who 94*
Burnham, Anthony Gerald 1936- *Who 94*
Burnham, Bryson Paine 1917- *WhoAm 94*
Burnham, Charles Wilson 1933- *WhoAm 94*
Burnham, Christopher B. 1956- *WhoAmP 93*
Burnham, Daniel Hudson 1846-1912 *AmCulL*
Burnham, Daniel M. 1929- *WhoAmP 93*
Burnham, Daniel Patrick 1946- *WhoAm 94*
Burnham, David Bright 1933- *WhoAm 94*
Burnham, Dawn Addison 1954- *WhoAmP 93*
Burnham, Deborah *DrAPF 93*
Burnham, Donald Clemens 1915- *WhoAm 94*
Burnham, Duane Lee 1942- *WhoAm 94, WhoFI 94, WhoMW 93, WhoScEn 94*
Burnham, Edward *WhoHol 92*
Burnham, Gregory *DrAPF 93*
Burnham, Harold Arthur 1929- *WhoAm 94*
Burnham, Henry Clifton 1967- *WhoAmP 93*
Burnham, J. V. 1923- *WhoFI 94*
Burnham, Jack Wesley 1931- *WhoAmA 93*
Burnham, James B. 1939- *IntWW 93*
Burnham, Jeremy *WhoHol 92*
Burnham, John Chynoweth 1929- *WhoAm 94*
Burnham, Margaret Ann 1944- *WhoBlA 94*
Burnham, Nicholas d1925 *WhoHol 92*
Burnham, Philip Smith, II 1964- *WhoAmL 94*
Burnham, Robert Bailey 1947- *WhoAm 94*
Burnham, Robert Danner 1944- *WhoAm 94*
Burnham, Robert Roy 1956- *WhoMW 93*
Burnham, Sophy 1936- *WhoAm 94*
Burnham, Tom 1946- *WhoAm 94*
Burnham, Viola *WhoWomW 91*
Burnham, Virginia Schroeder 1908- *WhoScEn 94*
Burnham, Walter Dean 1930- *WhoAm 94*
Burnheimer, Richard James 1959- *WhoFI 94*
Burniece, Thomas Francis, III 1941- *WhoWest 94*
Burnier, Andreas 1931- *BlmGWL*
Burnim, Kalman Aaron 1928- *WhoAm 94*
Burnim, Mellonee Victoria 1950- *WhoBlA 94*
Burnim, Mickey L. 1949- *WhoBlA 94*
Burningham, Haven Ralph 1918- *WhoAmP 93*
Burningham, John (Mackintosh) 1936- *WrDr 94*
Burningham, John Mackintosh 1936- *Who 94*
Burningham, Kim Richard 1936- *WhoAmP 93*
Burnison, Boyd Edward 1934- *WhoAm 94, WhoAmL 94, WhoFI 94, WhoWest 94*
Burniston, Karen Sue 1939- *WhoMW 93*
Burnley, Bishop Suffragan of 1944- *Who 94*
Burnley, Christopher John 1936- *Who 94*
Burnley, James H., IV 1948- *IntWW 93*
Burnley, James Horace, IV 1948- *WhoAmP 93*
Burnley, Kenneth S. *WhoWest 94*
Burno, John Gordon, Jr. 1963- *WhoScEn 94*
Burns, A. Leslie 1948- *WhoAmP 93*
Burns, Alan *DrAPF 93*
Burns, Alan 1929- *EncSF 93, WrDr 94*
Burns, Alberta Otterbach 1952- *WhoAmP 93*
Burns, Alexandra Darrow 1946- *WhoWest 94*
Burns, Andrew *Who 94*
Burns, (Robert) Andrew 1943- *Who 94*
Burns, Ann *WhoBlA 94*
Burns, Anne 1915- *Who 94*
Burns, Anne M. 1921- *WhoAmP 93*
Burns, Annette Trainor 1959- *WhoAmL 94*
Burns, Arnold Irwin 1930- *WhoAm 94*
Burns, Arthur Frank 1904-1987 *AmSocL*
Burns, Arthur Lee 1924- *WhoAm 94*
Burns, Avon Lorraine 1952- *WhoMW 93*
Burns, B(enedict) Delisle 1915- *Who 94*
Burns, Barbara Belton 1944- *WhoFI 94*
Burns, Bart *WhoHol 92*
Burns, Benedict DeLisle 1915- *IntWW 93*
Burns, Beverly Hall 1945- *WhoAmL 94*
Burns, Bob d1956 *WhoHol 92*
Burns, Bob d1957 *WhoHol 92*
Burns, Bob 1893-1956 *WhoCom*
Burns, Brenda 1950- *WhoAmP 93*
Burns, Brendan *WhoHol 92*
Burns, Brent Emil 1952- *WhoWest 94*
Burns, Brian Douglas 1939- *WhoAmP 93*
Burns, Brian Patrick 1936- *WhoAm 94*
Burns, Brian Patrick 1962- *WhoFI 94, WhoScEn 94*
Burns, Calvin Louis 1952- *WhoBlA 94*
Burns, Carol *WhoHol 92*
Burns, Carol 1934- *WrDr 94*
Burns, Carol J. 1954- *WhoAm 94*
Burns, Carolyn *BlmGWL*
Burns, Carroll D. 1932- *WhoIns 94*
Burns, Carroll Dean 1932- *WhoAm 94*
Burns, Catherine 1943- *WhoHol 92*
Burns, Catherine Elizabeth 1953- *WhoAm 94*
Burns, Charles 1955- *EncSF 93*
Burns, Charles Patrick 1937- *WhoAm 94*
Burns, Chester Ray 1937- *WhoAm 94*
Burns, Clarence 1918- *WhoAmP 93*
Burns, Clarence Du 1918- *WhoBlA 94*
Burns, Clyde d1964 *WhoHol 92*
Burns, Conrad 1935- *CngDr 93*
Burns, Conrad R. 1935- *WhoAmP 93*
Burns, Conrad Ray 1935- *WhoAm 94, WhoWest 94*
Burns, Dan W. 1925- *WhoAm 94, WhoFI 94, WhoWest 94*
Burns, Daniel Hobart 1928- *WhoAm 94, WhoFI 94, WhoWest 94*
Burns, Daniel Michael 1927- *WhoWest 94*
Burns, Dargan J. 1925- *WhoBlA 94*
Burns, David d1971 *WhoHol 92*
Burns, David Alan 1945- *WhoAmL 94*
Burns, David Allan 1937- *Who 94*
Burns, David Mitchell 1928- *WhoAm 94*
Burns, Debra Linn 1956- *WhoAmL 94*
Burns, Denise *WhoBlA 94*
Burns, Denise Ruth 1943- *WhoWest 94*
Burns, Diane L. 1950- *WrDr 94*
Burns, Donald A. 1946- *WhoAmL 94*
Burns, Donald Carlton 1929- *WhoIns 94*
Burns, Donald Howard 1928- *WhoAmP 93*
Burns, Donald Raymond 1961- *WhoScEn 94*
Burns, Donald Snow 1925- *WhoWest 94*
Burns, Duncan Thorburn 1934- *IntWW 93*
Burns, Edmund 1892- *WhoHol 92*
Burns, Edward Bradford 1932- *WhoAm 94*
Burns, Edward Charles 1942- *WhoFI 94*
Burns, Edward Francis, Jr. 1931- *WhoAmP 93*
Burns, Edward Morton, II 1947- *WhoAmP 93*
Burns, Elizabeth Mary 1927- *WhoAm 94*
Burns, Ellen Bree 1923- *WhoAm 94, WhoAmL 94*
Burns, Emmett C. *WhoBlA 94*
Burns, Eugene Warren 1946- *WhoAmP 93*
Burns, Felton 1936- *WhoBlA 94*
Burns, Fred d1955 *WhoHol 92*
Burns, G. Joan 1918- *WhoAmA 93*
Burns, George *Who 94*
Burns, George 1896- *IntMPA 94, IntWW 93, WhoAm 94, WhoCom [port], WhoHol 92, WrDr 94*
Burns, (Walter Arthur) George 1911- *Who 94*
Burns, George Washington 1913- *WhoAm 94*
Burns, Gerald Edward 1936- *WhoMW 93*
Burns, Gerald Phillip 1918- *WhoAm 94*
Burns, Geraldine Hamilton *WhoBlA 94*
Burns, Glenn Richard 1951- *WhoMW 93*
Burns, Grover Preston 1918- *WhoFI 94*
Burns, Guy M. 1948- *WhoAmL 94*
Burns, H. Michael 1937- *WhoAm 94*
Burns, Harold W. 1926- *WhoAm 94*
Burns, Harold Wilbur 1926- *WhoAmP 93*
Burns, Harrison D. 1946-1991 *WhoAmA 93N*
Burns, Harry d1939 *WhoHol 92*
Burns, Harry d1948 *WhoHol 92*
Burns, Ian Morgan 1939- *Who 94*
Burns, Irving d1968 *WhoHol 92*
Burns, Ivan Alfred 1935- *WhoAm 94*
Burns, Jacob d1993 *NewYTBS 93 [port]*
Burns, James d1975 *WhoHol 92*
Burns, James 1902- *Who 94*
Burns, James 1931- *Who 94*
Burns, James Alvin 1935- *WhoWest 94*
Burns, James E., Jr. 1946- *WhoAmL 94*
Burns, James Edward 1950- *WhoAmP 93*
Burns, James Francis 1922-1988 *WhAm 10*
Burns, James Henderson 1921- *Who 94*
Burns, James Kent Jasper 1952- *WhoScEn 94*
Burns, James M. 1924- *WhoAm 94, WhoAmL 94, WhoWest 94*
Burns, James MacGregor 1918- *ConAu 43NR, WrDr 94*
Burns, James Marcus 1939- *WhoAmP 93*
Burns, James William 1929- *WhoAm 94, WhoFI 94*
Burns, Jeff, Jr. 1950- *WhoBlA 94*
Burns, Jere 1956- *WhoHol 92*
Burns, Jerome 1919- *WhoAmA 93*
Burns, Jim 1936- *WrDr 94*
Burns, Jim 1948- *EncSF 93*
Burns, Jimmy 1953- *WrDr 94*
Burns, Joan Simpson 1927- *WrDr 94*
Burns, John 1920- *IntWW 93*
Burns, John Dudley 1933- *WhoAm 94, WhoFI 94*
Burns, John E. *WhoAmP 93*
Burns, John F. 1945- *WhoAm 94*
Burns, John Francis 1933- *See* Burns and Schreiber *WhoCom*
Burns, John Francis 1945- *WhoAm 94*
Burns, John Joseph 1920- *WhoAm 94*
Burns, John Joseph 1924- *WhoAm 94*
Burns, John Joseph, Jr. 1931- *WhoAm 94, WhoFI 94*
Burns, John Lawrence 1908- *WhAm 10*
Burns, John Scott 1947- *WhoAm 94*
Burns, John Tolman 1922- *WhoAm 94*
Burns, John William 1945- *WhoAm 94*
Burns, Joseph d1946 *WhoHol 92*
Burns, Joseph Arthur 1941- *WhoAm 94*
Burns, Joseph M. 1938- *WhoFI 94*
Burns, Joseph William 1908- *WhoAm 94*
Burns, Josephine 1917- *WhoAmA 93*
Burns, Ken 1953- *ConTFT 11*
Burns, Ken(neth Lauren) 1953- *ConAu 141*
Burns, Kenneth 1920-1989 *See* Homer and Jethro *WhoCom*
Burns, Kenneth Dean 1930- *WhoAm 94*
Burns, Kenneth Jones, Jr. 1926- *WhoAm 94, WhoAmL 94*
Burns, Kenneth Lauren 1953- *WhoAm 94*
Burns, Kevin Francis Xavier 1930- *Who 94*
Burns, Lawrence Aloysius, Jr. 1949- *WhoFI 94, WhoMW 93*
Burns, Leonard L. 1922- *WhoBlA 94*
Burns, M. Susan 1954- *WhoAmL 94*
Burns, Marcelline *WhoScEn 94*
Burns, Marian Law 1954- *WhoAmL 94*
Burns, Marilyn *WhoHol 92*
Burns, Marion 1909- *WhoHol 92*
Burns, Mark 1937- *WhoHol 92*
Burns, Mark A. 1950- *WhoAmA 93*
Burns, Marsha 1945- *WhoAmA 93*
Burns, Marshall 1954- *WhoScEn 94*
Burns, Marshall Shelby, Jr. 1931- *WhoAmL 94*
Burns, Marvin Gerald 1930- *WhoAm 94, WhoAmL 94, WhoWest 94*
Burns, Mary Ferris 1952- *WhoWest 94*
Burns, Michael 1917- *Who 94*
Burns, Michael 1947- *WhoHol 92*
Burns, Michael 1958- *WhoAmP 93*
Burns, Michael Joseph 1943- *WhoAm 94*
Burns, Millie 1950- *WhoAmA 93*
Burns, Milton Jerome 1965- *WhoFI 94*
Burns, Mitchel Anthony 1942- *WhoAm 94, WhoFI 94*
Burns, Nancy Kay 1942- *WhoMW 93*
Burns, Nat d1962 *WhoHol 92*
Burns, Neal d1962 *WhoHol 92*
Burns, Neal Murray 1933- *WhoAm 94*
Burns, Ned Hamilton 1932- *WhoAm 94, WhoScEn 94*
Burns, Olive Ann 1924-1990 *ConAu 41NR, TwCYAW*
Burns, Ollie Hamilton 1911- *WhoBlA 94*
Burns, Padraic 1929- *WhoAm 94, WhoScEn 94*
Burns, Pat 1952- *WhoAm 94*
Burns, Pat Ackerman Gonia 1938- *WhoFI 94, WhoScEn 94*
Burns, Patout, Jr. 1939- *WhoAm 94*
Burns, Patricia Henrietta 1934- *WhoWest 94*
Burns, Paul E. d1967 *WhoHol 92*
Burns, Paul Edward 1959- *WhoAmL 94*
Burns, Peter David 1952- *WhoScEn 94*
Burns, Ralph *DrAPF 93*
Burns, Ralph 1922- *IntMPA 94*
Burns, Regina Lynn 1961- *WhoBlA 94*
Burns, Rex 1935- *WrDr 94*
Burns, Ric 1955?- *ConAu 141*
Burns, Richard 1958-1992 *AnObit 1992*
Burns, Richard Dean 1929- *WhoAm 94*
Burns, Richard Francis 1931- *WhoFI 94*
Burns, Richard Gordon 1925- *ConAu 142*
Burns, Richard James 1951- *WhoFI 94*
Burns, Richard Michael 1937- *WhoAm 94*
Burns, Richard Owen 1942- *WhoAmL 94*
Burns, Richard Ramsey 1946- *WhoAmL 94, WhoFI 94, WhoMW 93*
Burns, Robert *WhoAmP 93*
Burns, Robert 1759-1796 *BlmGEL*
Burns, Robert 1925- *WhoAmP 93*
Burns, Robert, Jr. 1936- *WhoScEn 94*
Burns, Robert A. *DrAPF 93*
Burns, Robert A. 1944- *WhoAm 94, WhoAmL 94*
Burns, Robert Andrew 1943- *IntWW 93*
Burns, Robert Charles 1961- *WhoWest 94*
Burns, Robert Edward 1919- *WhoAm 94, WhoMW 93*
Burns, Robert Edward 1953- *WhoAmL 94*
Burns, Robert F. *WhoAmP 93*
Burns, Robert Grant *DrAPF 93*
Burns, Robert Harrison 1941- *WhoIns 94*
Burns, Robert Henry 1929- *WhoAm 94*
Burns, Robert Ignatius 1921- *WhoAm 94*
Burns, Robert Obed 1910- *WhoWest 94*
Burns, Robert P. d1966 *WhoHol 92*
Burns, Robert Paschal 1933- *WhoAm 94*
Burns, Robert Patrick 1947- *WhoAmL 94*
Burns, Robert Wayne 1953- *WhoScEn 94*
Burns, Robin *WhoAm 94, WhoFI 94*
Burns, Roger George 1937- *WhoAm 94, WhoScEn 94*
Burns, Ronald Melvin 1942- *WhoBlA 94*
Burns, Ronald S. *WhoAm 94, WhoFI 94*
Burns, Ronnie 1935- *WhoHol 92*
Burns, Sally Ann 1959- *WhoScEn 94*
Burns, Sandra Pauline 1938- *Who 94*
Burns, Sarah Ann 1938- *WhoBlA 94*
Burns, Scott 1940- *WhoAm 94*
Burns, Sheila *WhoAmA 93*
Burns, Sid 1916-1979 *WhoAmA 93N*
Burns, Simon Hugh McGuigan 1952- *Who 94*
Burns, Stan *WhoAmA 93*
Burns, Stephan W. d1990 *WhoHol 92*
Burns, Stephen Gilbert 1953- *WhoAm 94*
Burns, Stephen James 1939- *WhoAm 94*
Burns, Steven Dwight 1948- *WhoAmL 94, WhoMW 93*
Burns, Terence 1944- *IntWW 93, Who 94*
Burns, Terrence Michael 1954- *WhoAmL 94*
Burns, Terry Dee 1956- *WhoMW 93*
Burns, Thagrus Asher 1917- *WhoAm 94*
Burns, Thomas C. 1928- *WhoAm 94, WhoFI 94*
Burns, Thomas David 1921- *WhoAm 94, WhoAmL 94*
Burns, Thomas Donald 1956- *WhoWest 94*
Burns, Thomas Ferrier 1906- *Who 94*

Burns, Thomas Gordon 1940- *WhoWest 94*
Burns, Thomas Raymond 1941- *WhoAmP 93*
Burns, Thomas Samuel 1945- *WhoAm 94*
Burns, Tom 1913- *IntWW 93, Who 94*
Burns, Tommie, Jr. 1933- *WhoBlA 94*
Burns, Vernon D. 1953- *WhoAmP 93*
Burns, Virginia Law 1925- *WhoMW 93*
Burns, W. Haywood 1940- *WhoBlA 94*
Burns, Ward 1928- *WhoAm 94*
Burns, Wendy Walther 1962- *WhoFI 94*
Burns, Willard Rainey 1963- *WhoAmL 94*
Burns, William *DrAPF 93*
Burns, William 1909- *Who 94*
Burns, William A. 1909- *WhoAm 94*
Burns, William Edgar 1924- *WhoScEn 94*
Burns, William Goodykoontz 1935- *WhoFI 94*
Burns, William J. d1932 *WhoHol 92*
Burns, William Robert 1922- *WhoIns 94*
Burns, Willie Miles *WhoBlA 94*
Burns and Allen *WhoCom*
Burns and Schreiber *WhoCom*
Burns-Bisogno, Louisa 1936- *WrDr 94*
Burns-Haindel, Jeanne Ellen 1957- *WhoAmL 94*
Burnshaw, Stanley *DrAPF 93*
Burnshaw, Stanley 1906- *WhoAm 94, WrDr 94*
Burnshide, Katherine Talbott *WhoAmA 93N*
Burnside, Cameron 1887-1952 *WhoAmA 93N*
Burnside, Donald Phillip 1949- *WhoMW 93*
Burnside, Edith *Who 94*
Burnside, Edward Blair 1937- *WhoScEn 94*
Burnside, John Wayne 1941- *WhoAm 94*
Burnside, Madeleine Hilding 1948- *WhoAmA 93*
Burnside, Mary Beth 1943- *WhoAm 94*
Burnside, Orvin Charles 1932- *WhoAm 94, WhoMW 93*
Burnside, Otis Halbert 1943- *WhoScEn 94*
Burnside, Roger Edward 1952- *WhoWest 94*
Burnside, William d1976 *WhoHol 92*
Burnsky, Paul John 1921- *WhoAm 94*
Burnson, George *NewGrDO*
Burnstein, Daniel 1946- *WhoAmL 94*
Burnstein, Frances 1935- *WhoAm 94*
Burnstock, Geoffrey 1929- *IntWW 93, Who 94*
Burnton, Stanley Jeffrey 1942- *Who 94*
Burnweit, Richard Chris 1950- *WhoWest 94*
Burnyeat, Myles Fredric 1939- *IntWW 93, Who 94*
Burokyavichus, Mikolas 1927- *IntWW 93*
Buron, Martine 1944- *WhoWomW 91*
Buros, Luella *WhoAmA 93*
Burose, Renee 1962- *WhoBlA 94*
Burpee, Charles Edward 1952- *WhoAmL 94*
Burpee, James Stanley 1938- *WhoAmA 93*
Burr, Aaron 1756-1836 *AmRev, WhAmRev*
Burr, Anne Christian 1947- *WhoAmL 94*
Burr, Anne Marie 1953- *WhoAmL 94*
Burr, Brooks Milo 1949- *WhoAm 94, WhoMW 93, WhoScEn 94*
Burr, Clive
See Iron Maiden *ConMus 10*
Burr, David D. 1963- *WhoFI 94*
Burr, Donald d1979 *WhoHol 92*
Burr, Donald David 1923-1990 *WhAm 10*
Burr, Edmund d1975 *WhoHol 92*
Burr, Edward B. 1923- *WhoIns 94*
Burr, Edward Benjamin 1923- *WhoAm 94*
Burr, Esther Edwards 1732-1758 *BlmGWL*
Burr, Eugene d1940 *WhoHol 92*
Burr, Francis Hardon 1914- *WhoAm 94*
Burr, Fritzi *WhoHol 92*
Burr, Gray *DrAPF 93*
Burr, Hiram Hale, Jr. 1943- *WhoAm 94*
Burr, Horace 1912- *WhoAmA 93*
Burr, John Roy 1933- *WhoAm 94*
Burr, Karen Lynne 1964- *WhoWest 94*
Burr, Lanny John 1960- *WhoFI 94*
Burr, Lawrence C. 1913-1990 *WhoBlA 94N*
Burr, Lee Reynolds 1936- *WhoAmA 93*
Burr, Michael Rodney 1941- *Who 94*
Burr, Ramiro 1956- *WhoHisp 94*
Burr, Raymond d1993 *IntMPA 94N, NewYTBS 93 [port]*
Burr, Raymond 1917- *IntMPA 94, WhoAm 94, WhoHol 92*
Burr, Raymond 1917-1993 *CurBio 93N, News 94-1*
Burr, Robert 1922- *WhoHol 92*
Burr, Robert Lyndon 1944- *WhoAm 94*
Burr, Ruth Basler 1932- *WhoAmA 93*
Burr, Sandra Lynn 1959- *WhoAmL 94*
Burr, Timothy John 1950- *Who 94*
Burr, Wesley R 1936- *WrDr 94*
Burrage, Jeanette Ruth 1952- *WhoAmP 93*
Burrall, Frederic H. 1935- *WhoAmP 93*
Burrell, Allen Lamar 1951- *WhoAmL 94*
Burrell, Barbara 1941- *WhoBlA 94*
Burrell, Carolyn C. 1946- *WhoAmL 94*
Burrell, Craig Donald 1926- *WhoAm 94*
Burrell, David Bakewell 1933- *WhoAm 94*
Burrell, Derek William 1925- *Who 94*
Burrell, Donald Eugene, Jr. 1960- *WhoAmL 94*
Burrell, Emma P. *WhoBlA 94*
Burrell, Garland E., Jr. 1947- *WhoAmL 94, WhoWest 94*
Burrell, George d1933 *WhoHol 92*
Burrell, George Reed, Jr. 1948- *WhoBlA 94*
Burrell, Jan *WhoHol 92*
Burrell, Joel Brion 1959- *WhoMW 93*
Burrell, Kenneth Earl 1931- *WhoAm 94, WhoBlA 94*
Burrell, Kenny 1931- *ConMus 11 [port]*
Burrell, Leroy *IntWW 93, WhoBlA 94*
Burrell, Maryedith *WhoHol 92*
Burrell, Morris 1908- *WhoBlA 94*
Burrell, Peter 1905- *Who 94*
Burrell, Raymond *Who 94*
Burrell, (John) Raymond 1934- *Who 94*
Burrell, Sam *WhoAmP 93*
Burrell, Sheila 1922- *WhoHol 92*
Burrell, Sidney Alexander 1917- *WhoAm 94*
Burrell, Stanley Kirk 1962- *WhoAm 94*
Burrell, Suzanne Elizabeth 1964- *WhoFI 94*
Burrell, Thomas J. *WhoAm 94, WhoMW 93*
Burrell, Thomas J. 1939- *WhoBlA 94*
Burrell, Thomas William 1923- *WrDr 94*
Burrell, Victor Gregory, Jr. 1925- *WhoAm 94, WhoScEn 94*
Burrenchobay, Dayendranath 1919- *IntWW 93, Who 94*
Burress, William d1948 *WhoHol 92*
Burrett, (Frederick) Gordon 1921- *Who 94*
Burri, Betty Jane 1955- *WhoWest 94*
Burri, Peter Hermann 1938- *WhoScEn 94*
Burrian, Carl 1870-1924 *NewGrDO*
Burridge, Alan 1921- *Who 94*
Burridge, Geoffrey d1987 *WhoHol 92*
Burridge, Michael John 1942- *WhoScEn 94*
Burrier, Gail Warren 1927- *WhoMW 93, WhoScEn 94*
Burright, Richard George 1934- *WhoScEn 94*
Burrill, Kathleen R. F. 1924- *WhoAm 94*
Burrill, Melinda Jane 1947- *WhoAm 94*
Burrill, Timothy 1931- *IntMPA 94, Who 94*
Burrington, David Edson 1931- *WhoAm 94*
Burrington, Ernest 1926- *IntWW 93, Who 94*
Burrington, James David 1951- *WhoMW 93*
Burris, Bertram Ray 1950- *WhoBlA 94*
Burris, Bill Buchanan, Jr. 1957- *WhoFI 94, WhoWest 94*
Burris, Bruce C. 1955- *WhoAmA 93*
Burris, Duane 1956- *WhoWest 94*
Burris, Harrison Robert 1945- *WhoScEn 94*
Burris, Hazel Lorene 1921- *WhoAmP 93*
Burris, James d1923 *WhoHol 92*
Burris, James Frederick 1947- *WhoAm 94, WhoScEn 94*
Burris, John Edward 1949- *WhoAm 94, WhoScEn 94*
Burris, John L. 1945- *WhoBlA 94*
Burris, John M. 1946- *WhoAmP 93*
Burris, Joseph Stephen 1942- *WhoAm 94*
Burris, Kathryn Ann 1957- *WhoFI 94*
Burris, Robert Harza 1914- *IntWW 93, WhoAm 94, WhoMW 93*
Burris, Roland W. 1937- *WhoBlA 94*
Burris, Roland Wallace 1937- *WhoAm 94, WhoAmL 94, WhoAmP 93, WhoMW 93*
Burris, Steven Michael 1952- *WhoAmL 94*
Burris, Troy 1921- *WhoAmP 93*
Burriss, John Hay, Sr. 1946- *WhoAmP 93*
Burriss, Milford D. 1937- *WhoAmP 93*
Burriss, R. (Riley) Hal 1892-1991 *WhoAmA 93N*
Burriss, Thomas Moffatt 1919- *WhoAmP 93*
Burrough, Alan 1917- *Who 94*
Burrough, Bryan 1961- *ConAu 140*
Burrough, John Outhit Harold 1916- *Who 94*
Burrough, John Paul 1916- *Who 94*
Burrough, Tom d1929 *WhoHol 92*
Burroughs, Baldwin Wesley 1915- *WhoBlA 94*
Burroughs, Charles Edward 1939- *WhoAm 94*
Burroughs, Clark d1937 *WhoHol 92*
Burroughs, Edgar Rice 1875-1950 *AmCulL, Au&Arts 11 [port], EncSF 93, TwCYAW*
Burroughs, Eric d1960 *WhoHol 92*
Burroughs, Franklin Troy 1936- *WhoAm 94*
Burroughs, Hugh Charles 1940- *WhoBlA 94*
Burroughs, Jack Eugene 1926- *WhoAm 94*
Burroughs, Jackie *WhoHol 92*
Burroughs, John 1827-1921 *EnvEnc [port]*
Burroughs, John A., Jr. 1936- *WhoAmP 93*
Burroughs, John Andrew, Jr. 1936- *WhoBlA 94*
Burroughs, John Coleman 1913-1979 *EncSF 93*
Burroughs, Kate 1953- *WhoWest 94*
Burroughs, Leonard 1921- *WhoBlA 94*
Burroughs, Margaret T. G. 1917- *WhoAmA 93*
Burroughs, Margaret Taylor 1917- *WhoBlA 94*
Burroughs, Nannie Helen 1878?-1961 *DcAmReB 2*
Burroughs, Nannie Helen 1879-1961 *AfrAmAl 6*
Burroughs, Nannie Helen 1883-1961 *AfrAmAl 6*
Burroughs, Pamela Gayle 1957- *WhoMW 93*
Burroughs, Robert A. 1948- *WhoBlA 94*
Burroughs, Roland Arthur 1935- *WhoAmP 93*
Burroughs, Sarah G. 1943- *WhoBlA 94*
Burroughs, Tim *WhoBlA 94*
Burroughs, Todd Steven 1968- *WhoBlA 94*
Burroughs, Walter Laughlin 1901-1990 *WhAm 10*
Burroughs, William S. *DrAPF 93*
Burroughs, William S. 1914- *News 94-2 [port], WhoHol 92*
Burroughs, William S(eward) 1914- *EncSF 93, GayLL, WrDr 94*
Burroughs, William Seward 1855-1898 *WorInv*
Burroughs, William Seward 1914- *IntWW 93, WhoAm 94*
Burrow, Charles C., III 1945- *WhoAmP 93*
Burrow, Gerard Noel 1933- *WhoAm 94*
Burrow, J(ohn) A(nthony) 1932- *WrDr 94*
Burrow, John Anthony 1932- *Who 94*
Burrow, John Halcrow 1935- *Who 94*
Burrow, John Wyon 1935- *IntWW 93, Who 94*
Burrow, Marie Brabham 1915- *WhoBlA 94*
Burrow, William Fite, Sr. 1907-1991 *WhAm 10*
Burroway, Janet *DrAPF 93*
Burroway, Janet (Gay) 1936 *WrDr 94*
Burroway, Janet G. 1936- *WhoAm 94*
Burrowes, Edmund Stanley Spencer 1906- *Who 94*
Burrowes, Mike 1937- *WrDr 94*
Burrowes, Norma 1944- *NewGrDO*
Burrowes, Norma Elizabeth *IntWW 93, Who 94*
Burrows, Abe 1910-1985 *ConDr 93*
Burrows, Adam Seth 1953- *WhoScEn 94*
Burrows, Barbara Ann 1947- *WhoScEn 94*
Burrows, Benjamin 1927- *WhoAm 94, WhoScEn 94*
Burrows, Bernard (Alexander Brocas) 1910- *Who 94*
Burrows, Brenda Lee 1960- *WhoFI 94*
Burrows, Brian William 1939- *WhoAm 94, WhoScEn 94*
Burrows, Cecil J. 1922- *WhoAmL 94, WhoMW 93*
Burrows, Cecil J. 1938- *WhoFI 94*
Burrows, Clare 1938- *WhoBlA 94*
Burrows, Donald Albert 1937- *WhoAm 94*
Burrows, E. G. *DrAPF 93*
Burrows, Edward William 1928- *WhoHisp 94*
Burrows, Elizabeth MacDonald 1930- *WhoAm 94*
Burrows, Eva 1929- *IntWW 93, Who 94*
Burrows, Fred 1925- *Who 94*
Burrows, Gates Wilson 1899- *WhoAm 94*
Burrows, George Bill 1930- *WhoAmP 93*
Burrows, Gordon W. *WhoAmP 93*
Burrows, James d1926 *WhoHol 92*
Burrows, James 1940- *IntMPA 94, WhoAm 94*
Burrows, James H. *WhoScEn 94*
Burrows, Janice H. 1944- *WhoBlA 94*
Burrows, John 1945- *ConDr 93*
Burrows, John Edward 1950- *WhoFI 94*
Burrows, Jon Hanes 1946- *WhoAmL 94*
Burrows, Kenneth David 1941- *WhoAmL 94*
Burrows, Lionel John 1912- *Who 94*
Burrows, Malcolm 1943- *Who 94*
Burrows, Mary McCauley 1932- *WhoAmP 93*
Burrows, Michael Donald 1944- *WhoAm 94, WhoAmL 94*
Burrows, Pearl 1903-1960 *WhoAmA 93N*
Burrows, Reginald Arthur 1918- *Who 94*
Burrows, Richard *Who 94*
Burrows, (George) Richard (William) 1946- *Who 94*
Burrows, Richard Steven 1966- *WhoScEn 94*
Burrows, Robert Nelson 1923- *WhoMW 93*
Burrows, Roberta *IntMPA 94*
Burrows, Ronald Montagu 1867-1920 *DcNaB MP*
Burrows, Ronna May 1956- *WhoWest 94*
Burrows, Selig S. 1913- *WhoAmA 93*
Burrows, Selig Saul 1913- *WhoAm 94*
Burrows, Simon Hedley 1928- *Who 94*
Burrows, Stephen 1943- *AfrAmAl 6*
Burrows, (James) Stuart *IntWW 93*
Burrows, (James) Stuart 1933- *NewGrDO*
Burrows, Virginia Moore 1956- *WhoAmL 94*
Burrows, William Claude 1925- *WhoAm 94*
Burrud, Billy d1990 *WhoHol 92*
Burrud, William James 1925-1990 *WhAm 10*
Burrus, Charles Andrew, Jr. 1927- *WhoAm 94*
Burrus, Charles Sidney 1934- *WhoAm 94*
Burrus, Clark 1928- *WhoBlA 94*
Burrus, Daniel Allen 1947- *WhoFI 94, WhoMW 93*
Burrus, Harry *DrAPF 93*
Burrus, John H. 1944- *WhoAmL 94*
Burrus, John Newell 1920- *WhoAm 94*
Burrus, Robert Lewis, Jr. 1934- *WhoAm 94, WhoAmL 94*
Burrus, William Henry 1936- *WhoBlA 94*
Burruss, George Wilson 1939- *WhoMW 93*
Burruss, Lloyd Earl, Jr. 1957- *WhoBlA 94*
Burry, Kenneth Arnold 1942- *WhoWest 94*
Bursal, Faruk Halil 1963- *WhoScEn 94*
Burse, Delores Tate 1940- *WhoAmP 93*
Burse, Luther 1937- *WhoBlA 94*
Burse, Raymond Malcolm 1951- *WhoAm 94, WhoBlA 94*
Bursell, David Hingston 1942- *Who 94*
Bursey, Joan Tesarek 1943- *WhoAm 94*
Bursey, Maurice M. 1939- *WhoAm 94*
Burshtan, Alvin 1935- *WhoFI 94*
Bursiek, Ralph David 1937- *WhoAm 94, WhoScEn 94*
Bursik, David James 1952- *WhoScEn 94*
Bursill, Tina *WhoHol 92*
Bursinger, JoEllen 1958- *WhoMW 93*
Bursk, Christopher *DrAPF 93*
Bursk, Edward Collins 1907-1990 *WhAm 10*
Bursky, Herman Aaron 1938- *WhoAm 94*
Bursley, Gilbert E. 1913- *WhoAmP 93*
Bursley, Kathleen A. 1954- *WhoAmL 94*
Bursma, Albert, Jr. 1937- *WhoAm 94*
Burson, Betsy Lee 1942- *WhoAm 94*
Burson, Charles W. *WhoAm 94, WhoAmL 94*
Burson, Charles W. 1944- *WhoAmP 93*
Burson, Harold 1921- *IntWW 93, WhoAm 94, WhoFI 94*
Burson, Nancy 1948- *WhoAmA 93*
Burstall, Clare 1931- *Who 94*
Burstein, Alan Stuart 1940- *WhoAmL 94*
Burstein, Albert 1922- *WhoAmP 93*
Burstein, Beatrice S. 1915- *WhoAmL 94*
Burstein, David 1947- *WhoWest 94*
Burstein, Elias 1917- *WhoAm 94*
Burstein, Karen 1942- *WhoAmP 93*
Burstein, Richard Joel 1945- *WhoAm 94, WhoAmL 94*
Burstein, Rose *Who 94*
Burstein, Sharon Ann Palma 1952- *WhoFI 94*
Burstein, Sol 1922- *WhoAm 94*
Burstein, Stephen David 1934- *WhoScEn 94*
Burstermann, Juliette Phifer 1905- *WhoBlA 94*
Burston, Richard Mervin 1924- *WhoFI 94*
Burston, Samuel (Gerald Wood) 1915- *Who 94*
Burstyn, Ellen 1932- *IntMPA 94, IntWW 93, WhoAm 94, WhoHol 92*
Burstyn, Mike *WhoHol 92*
Burstyn, Neil *WhoHol 92*
Burt, Alice Louise 1925- *WhoIns 94*
Burt, Alistair James Hendrie 1955- *Who 94*
Burt, Alvin Miller, III 1935- *WhoAm 94*
Burt, Alvin Victor, Jr. 1927- *WhoAm 94*
Burt, Benny d1980 *WhoHol 92*
Burt, Christopher Murray 1933- *WhoAm 94*

Burt, Clarissa *WhoHol 92*
Burt, Clyde Edwin d1981 *WhoAmA 93N*
Burt, Cyril O. 1923- *WhoAmP 93*
Burt, Dan 1930- *WhoAmA 93*
Burt, David Arlin 1949- *WhoIns 94*
Burt, David Sill 1917- *WhoAmA 93*
Burt, Francis 1926- *NewGrDO*
Burt, Francis (Theodore Page) 1918- *Who 94*
Burt, Frederick d1943 *WhoHol 92*
Burt, Gerald Raymond 1926- *Who 94*
Burt, James Roy 1935- *WhoMW 93*
Burt, Jeffrey Amsterdam 1944- *WhoAm 94, WhoAmL 94*
Burt, John Alan 1943- *WhoAm 94, WhoFI 94*
Burt, John Harris 1918- *WhoAm 94*
Burt, Laura d1952 *WhoHol 92*
Burt, Laurie 1949- *WhoAmL 94*
Burt, Marvin Roger 1937- *WhoFI 94*
Burt, Maurice Edward 1921- *Who 94*
Burt, Nathaniel 1913- *WrDr 94*
Burt, Nellie d1986 *WhoHol 92*
Burt, Peter Alexander 1944- *Who 94*
Burt, Richard 1947- *IntWW 93*
Burt, Richard R. 1947- *WhoAmP 93*
Burt, Robert Amsterdam 1939- *IntWW 93, WhoAm 94*
Burt, Robert Eugene 1926- *WhoMW 93*
Burt, Robert Norcross 1937- *WhoAm 94, WhoFI 94, WhoScEn 94*
Burt, Steven Richard 1954- *WhoFI 94*
Burt, Thomas William 1955- *WhoAmL 94*
Burt, Wallace Joseph, Jr. 1924- *WhoFI 94, WhoIns 94*
Burt, Wallace Lockwood 1948- *WhoIns 94*
Burt, Wayne Vincent 1917-1991 *WhAm 10*
Burt, William Austin 1792-1858 *WorInv*
Burt, William P. d1955 *WhoHol 92*
Burt-Andrews, Charles Beresford Eaton 1913- *Who 94*
Burtch, John Hamrick 1948- *WhoAm 94, WhoAmL 94*
Burtchaell, James Tunstead 1934- *IntWW 93, WrDr 94*
Burten, Barry Lee 1948- *WhoAm 94*
Burtenshaw, Claude Junior 1918- *WhoAmP 93*
Burti, Christopher Louis 1950- *WhoAmL 94*
Burtin, Carlos *WhoHisp 94*
Burtin, Margaret Irene 1939- *WhoAm 94*
Burtis, Carl A., Jr. 1937- *WhoScEn 94*
Burtis, James d1939 *WhoHol 92*
Burtis, Theodore Alfred 1922- *WhoAm 94*
Burtle, Debra Ann 1953- *WhoMW 93*
Burtle, James Lindley 1919- *WhoFI 94, WhoScEn 94*
Burtle, Paul Walter 1950- *WhoMW 93*
Burtnett, Earl d1935 *WhoHol 92*
Burtnett, Steven Charles 1942- *WhoAmL 94*
Burtoft, John Nelson, Jr. 1944- *WhoScEn 94*
Burton, Baron 1924- *Who 94*
Burton, Al *WhoAm 94, WhoWest 94*
Burton, Alan Harvey 1952- *WhoMW 93*
Burton, Alice Jean 1934- *WhoAm 94*
Burton, Anthony 1934- *WrDr 94*
Burton, Anthony George Graham 1934- *Who 94*
Burton, Arthur Henry, Jr. 1934- *WhoAm 94*
Burton, Barbara Ann 1941- *WhoBlA 94*
Burton, Benjamin Theodore 1919- *WhoAm 94*
Burton, Bertha Edwina 1949- *WhoWest 94*
Burton, Blanche d1934 *WhoHol 92*
Burton, Bruce Edgar 1948- *WhoMW 93*
Burton, Calvin E. *WhoBlA 94*
Burton, Carlisle (Archibald) 1921- *Who 94*
Burton, Charles Henning 1915- *WhoAm 94*
Burton, Charles Howard, Jr. 1945- *WhoBlA 94*
Burton, Charles Victor 1935- *WhoAm 94*
Burton, Charles Wesley 1897- *WhAm 10*
Burton, Charles Wesley 1934- *WhoMW 93*
Burton, Charlotte d1942 *WhoHol 92*
Burton, Clarence d1933 *WhoHol 92*
Burton, Dan 1938- *CngDr 93*
Burton, Dan L. 1938- *WhoAmP 93*
Burton, Daniel Frederick 1915- *WhoAmP 93*
Burton, Daniel G. 1935- *WhoFI 94, WhoIns 94*
Burton, Danny Lee 1938- *WhoAm 94, WhoMW 93*
Burton, Darrell Irvin 1926- *WhoAm 94, WhoMW 93*
Burton, David *Who 94*
Burton, David d1963 *WhoHol 92*
Burton, (Anthony) David 1937- *Who 94*
Burton, David Harold 1947- *Who 94*
Burton, David Lee 1966- *WhoMW 93*
Burton, David Lloyd 1956- *WhoBlA 94*
Burton, David R. 1959- *WhoAmL 94*
Burton, Dennis E. 1947- *WhoMW 93*
Burton, Diane Aurelia 1947- *WhoAmP 93*
Burton, Donald 1934- *ConTFT 11*
Burton, Donald C. 1938- *WhoBlA 94*
Burton, Donald Joseph 1934- *WhoAm 94*
Burton, Douglas Andrew *WhoMW 93*
Burton, Edward Lewis 1935- *WhoFI 94, WhoScEn 94, WhoWest 94*
Burton, Eugene *DrAPF 93*
Burton, Frederick d1957 *WhoHol 92*
Burton, Frederick Glenn 1939- *WhoWest 94*
Burton, Gabrielle *DrAPF 93*
Burton, Gary 1943- *ConMus 10 [port]*
Burton, Gary L. 1945- *WhoAmP 93*
Burton, George d1955 *WhoHol 92*
Burton, George (Vernon Kennedy) 1916- *Who 94*
Burton, George Aubrey, Jr. 1926- *WhoAmP 93*
Burton, Glenn Willard 1910- *IntWW 93*
Burton, Graham Stuart 1941- *Who 94*
Burton, Harry 1919- *Who 94*
Burton, Hester 1913- *WrDr 94*
Burton, Hester (Wood-Hill) 1913- *SmATA 74 [port], TwCYAW*
Burton, Humphrey McGuire 1931- *Who 94*
Burton, Ian 1935- *IntWW 93, WhoAm 94*
Burton, Iola Brantley *WhoBlA 94*
Burton, Iris Grace *Who 94*
Burton, Ivor (Flower) 1923- *WrDr 94*
Burton, Jay d1993 *NewYTBS 93*
Burton, Jeff d1988 *WhoHol 92*
Burton, Joan E. 1945- *WhoBlA 94*
Burton, Joe 1923- *WhoAmP 93*
Burton, John 1932- *WhoAmP 93*
Burton, John (Wear) 1915- *WrDr 94*
Burton, John Andrew 1944- *WrDr 94*
Burton, John Campbell 1932- *WhoAm 94, WhoFI 94*
Burton, John Charles 1920- *WhoAmP 93*
Burton, John Clyde 1957- *WhoFI 94*
Burton, John H. 1910- *WhoBlA 94*
Burton, John Harold Stanley d1993 *Who 94N*
Burton, John Lee 1927- *WhoFI 94*
Burton, John Paul 1943- *WhoAmL 94, WhoWest 94*
Burton, John Routh 1917- *WhoAm 94*
Burton, John W. d1920 *WhoHol 92*
Burton, Juanita Sharon 1946- *WhoBlA 94*
Burton, Karen 1946- *WhoMW 93*
Burton, Kate 1957- *IntMPA 94*
Burton, Kate 1958- *WhoHol 92*
Burton, Kay Fox 1938- *WhoMW 93*
Burton, Kenneth 1926- *IntWW 93, Who 94*
Burton, Kenneth Raymond 1944- *WhoWest 94*
Burton, Lana Doreen 1953- *WhoBlA 94*
Burton, Langhorne d1949 *WhoHol 92*
Burton, Lawrence DeVere 1943- *WhoScEn 94*
Burton, Leroy Melvin, Jr. 1940- *WhoBlA 94*
Burton, Levar 1957- *IntMPA 94, WhoBlA 94, WhoHol 92*
Burton, Levardis Robert Martyn *WhoAm 94*
Burton, Loren G. 1939- *WhoWest 94*
Burton, Margaret d1984 *WhoHol 92*
Burton, Martin d1976 *WhoHol 92*
Burton, Maurice 1898- *WrDr 94*
Burton, Melvin Matthew, Jr. 1929- *WhoAmP 93*
Burton, Michael (St. Edmund) 1937- *Who 94*
Burton, Michael Angelo 1956- *WhoBlA 94*
Burton, Michael John 1946- *Who 94*
Burton, Michael Ladd 1942- *WhoAm 94*
Burton, Mike 1941- *WhoAmP 93*
Burton, Miriam d1991 *WhoHol 92*
Burton, Nanci L. 1942- *WhoAm 94*
Burton, Ned d1922 *WhoHol 92*
Burton, Netta M. d1960 *WhoAmA 93N*
Burton, Niul Adam 1960- *WhoFI 94*
Burton, Norman *WhoHol 92*
Burton, Paul Floyd 1939- *WhoWest 94*
Burton, Peter *WhoHol 92*
Burton, Philip L. 1915- *WhoBlA 94*
Burton, Philip Ward 1910- *WhoAm 94*
Burton, R. Dal 1954- *WhoAmL 94*
Burton, R. Keith 1947- *WhoAm 94*
Burton, Ralph Joseph 1911- *WhoAm 94*
Burton, Randall James 1950- *WhoAmL 94, WhoWest 94*
Burton, Raymond Charles, Jr. 1938- *WhoAm 94, WhoFI 94*
Burton, Richard d1984 *WhoHol 92*
Burton, Richard 1821-1890 *NinCLC 42 [port]*
Burton, Richard Francis 1821-1890 *BlmGEL, WhWE [port]*
Burton, Richard Greene 1936- *WhoFI 94*
Burton, Richard Hilary 1923- *Who 94*
Burton, Richard Irving 1936- *WhoAm 94*
Burton, Richard Roghaar 1941- *WhoWest 94*
Burton, Robert d1962 *WhoHol 92*
Burton, Robert 1577-1640 *BlmGEL*
Burton, Robert 1747-1825 *WhAmRev*
Burton, Robert Gene 1938- *WhoAm 94, WhoFI 94*
Burton, Robert William 1927- *WhoAm 94*
Burton, Rodney Lane 1940- *WhoScEn 94*
Burton, Roger 1946- *Who 94*
Burton, Roger Vernon 1928- *WhoAm 94*
Burton, Ronald Allan 1939- *WhoWest 94*
Burton, Ronald E. 1936- *WhoBlA 94*
Burton, Ronald J. 1947- *WhoBlA 94*
Burton, Russell Rohan 1932- *WhoAm 94*
Burton, Sam A. d1946 *WhoHol 92*
Burton, Sandra *WrDr 94*
Burton, Scott 1939-1989 *WhAm 10, WhoAmA 93N*
Burton, Stephen Douglas 1943- *NewGrDO*
Burton, Sydney Harold 1916- *Who 94*
Burton, Terry C. *WhoAmP 93*
Burton, Theodore Allen 1935- *WhoMW 93*
Burton, Thomas 1907- *WrDr 94*
Burton, Thomas Lawson 1922- *WhoAmP 93*
Burton, Thomas M. 1941- *WhoMW 93*
Burton, Tim *IntWW 93*
Burton, Tim 1958- *IntMPA 94*
Burton, Tim 1960- *WhoAm 94*
Burton, Tom d1943 *WhoHol 92*
Burton, Tom d1955 *WhoHol 92*
Burton, Tony *WhoHol 92*
Burton, Verona Devine 1922- *WhoAmP 93*
Burton, Victoria Geraldine *Who 94*
Burton, Walter Brandon 1946- *WhoAmP 93*
Burton, Walter Ervin 1903- *WhoMW 93*
Burton, Warren *WhoHol 92*
Burton, Wayne M. 1944- *WhoAmP 93*
Burton, Wendell 1947- *WhoHol 92*
Burton, William *WorInv*
Burton, William H. d1926 *WhoHol 92*
Burton, William Joseph 1931- *WhoFI 94, WhoScEn 94*
Burton, Willie Ricardo 1968- *WhoBlA 94*
Burton, Woody 1945- *WhoAmP 93*
Burton-Bradley, Burton (Gyrth) 1914- *Who 94*
Burton-Chadwick, Joshua (Kenneth) 1954- *Who 94*
Burton-Junior, Eva Westbrook 1944- *WhoBlA 94*
Burton-Lyles, Blanche 1933- *WhoBlA 94*
Burton of Coventry, Baroness 1904- *WhoWomW 91*
Burton-Shannon, Clarinda 1959- *WhoBlA 94*
Burts, Ezunial *WhoBlA 94*
Burtschi, Mary Pauline 1911- *WrDr 94*
Burtt, Ben 1948- *IntDcF 2-4, WhoAm 94*
Burtt, Benjamin Pickering 1921- *WhoAm 94*
Burtt, Edward Howland, Jr. 1948- *WhoScEn 94*
Burtt, Everett Johnson 1914-1989 *WhAm 10*
Burtwell, Frederick d1948 *WhoHol 92*
Burwash, Peter Francis 1945- *WhoWest 94*
Burwell, Bill Loren 1952- *WhoWest 94*
Burwell, Bryan Ellis 1955- *WhoBlA 94*
Burwell, Dudley Sale 1931- *WhoAm 94*
Burwell, Lewis Carter, Jr. 1908-1988 *WhAm 10*
Burwell, Martin *DrAPF 93*
Burwell, Rex *DrAPF 93*
Burwell, Robert L., Jr. 1912- *IntWW 93*
Burwell, Robert Lemmon, Jr. 1912- *WhoAm 94, WhoMW 93*
Burwell, William David, Jr. 1942- *WhoBlA 94*
Burwitz, Nils 1940- *IntWW 93*
Bury, Bernard de 1720-1795 *NewGrDO*
Bury, Frank 1911- *WrDr 94*
Bury, John 1925- *NewGrDO, Who 94, WhoAm 94*
Bury, Lindsay Claude Neils 1939- *Who 94*
Bury, Michael Oswell 1922- *Who 94*
Bury, Pol 1922- *IntWW 93*
Bury, Shirley Joan 1925- *Who 94*
Bury, Thomas Malcolm Grahame 1918- *Who 94*
Buryak, Leonid Iosifovich 1953- *LoBiDrD*
Bury St Edmunds, Hugo of fl. 1130- *DcNaB MP*
Burzio, Eugenia 1872-1922 *NewGrDO*
Burzynski, J. Bradley 1955- *WhoAmP 93*
Burzynski, Norman Stephen 1928- *WhoAm 94*
Burzynski, Susan Marie 1953- *WhoAm 94*
Busa, Peter 1914-1983 *WhoAmA 93N*
Busa, Stephen K. *WhoMW 93*
Busack, Gary Lee 1952- *WhoMW 93*
Busbee, George D. 1927- *WhoAmP 93*
Busbee, Juliana Royster 1877-1962 *WhoAmA 93N*
Busbee, Kline Daniel, Jr. 1933- *WhoAm 94, WhoAmL 94*
Busbee, Maury Judson 1947- *WhoAmP 93*
Busbee, Shirlee 1941- *WrDr 94*
Busbey, Douglas Earle 1948- *WhoAm 94, WhoAmL 94*
Busbin, O. Mell, Jr. 1937- *WhoAm 94*
Busboom, Larry D. 1942- *WhoFI 94*
Busboom, Patricia Gail 1936- *WhoAmP 93*
Busby, David 1926- *WhoAm 94*
Busby, Edward Oliver 1926- *WhoAm 94*
Busby, Everett C. *WhoBlA 94*
Busby, F(rancis) M(arion) 1921- *EncSF 93, WrDr 94*
Busby, Jheryl *WhoBlA 94*
Busby, Jheryl 1949- *WhoAm 94*
Busby, John Arthur, Jr. 1933- *WhoAm 94*
Busby, Kenneth Owen 1950- *WhoScEn 94*
Busby, Marjorie Jean 1931- *WhoAm 94*
Busby, Matt(hew) 1909- *IntWW 93*
Busby, Matthew 1909- *Who 94*
Busby, Morris D. *WhoAm 94, WhoAmP 93*
Busby, Roger (Charles) 1941- *WrDr 94*
Busby, Ron D. 1958- *WhoWest 94*
Busby, Thomas 1755-1838 *NewGrDO*
Busby, V. Eugene 1937- *WhoBlA 94*
Busby, Zane *WhoHol 92*
Busca, Lodovico fl. 1670-1688 *NewGrDO*
Buscaglia, Adolfo Edgardo 1930- *WhoScEn 94*
Buscaglia, Leo F(elice) 1924- *WrDr 94*
Buscaglia, Leonardo 1924- *WhoAm 94*
Buscaglia, Marta Carmen 1953- *WhoHisp 94*
Buscemi, Peter 1950- *WhoAm 94, WhoAmL 94*
Buscemi, Steve *WhoHol 92*
Buscemi, Steve 1958- *IntMPA 94*
Busch, Arthur Allen 1954- *WhoAmL 94*
Busch, Arthur Winston 1926- *WhoAm 94*
Busch, August A., Jr. 1899-1989 *WhAm 10*
Busch, August Adolphus, III 1937- *WhoAm 94, WhoFI 94, WhoMW 93*
Busch, Briton Cooper 1936- *WhoAm 94, WrDr 94*
Busch, Charles (Louis) 1954- *ConDr 93*
Busch, Charles Gardner 1939- *WhoFI 94*
Busch, Constantinus Albertus Maria 1937- *Who 94*
Busch, Corey *WhoWest 94*
Busch, Ernst d1980 *WhoHol 92*
Busch, Frederick *DrAPF 93*
Busch, Frederick 1941- *WrDr 94*
Busch, Frederick Matthew 1941- *WhoAm 94*
Busch, Fritz 1890-1951 *NewGrDO*
Busch, H. Donald 1935- *IntMPA 94*
Busch, Harris 1923- *WhoAm 94*
Busch, J. Michael 1946- *WhoAmP 93*
Busch, John Arthur 1951- *WhoAm 94, WhoAmL 94*
Busch, Joyce Ida 1934- *WhoFI 94, WhoWest 94*
Busch, Lawrence Michael 1945- *WhoMW 93*
Busch, Mae d1946 *WhoHol 92*
Busch, Marc Allen 1953- *WhoWest 94*
Busch, Michael 1947- *WhoAmP 93*
Busch, Niven 1903-1991 *WhAm 10, WrDr 94N*
Busch, Noel Henry 1940- *WhoFI 94*
Busch, Richard 1941- *WhoAm 94*
Busch, Rita Mary 1926- *WhoAmA 93*
Busch, Rolf Trygue 1920- *IntWW 93*
Busch, Rolf Trygve 1920- *Who 94*
Busch, Steven Jeffrey 1954- *WhoMW 93*
Busch, Thomas Anthony 1947- *WhoWest 94*
Busch, William R., Jr. 1951- *WhoAmL 94*
Buschbach, Thomas Charles 1923- *WhoAm 94*
Busche, Robert Marion 1926- *WhoScEn 94*
Buschke, Herman 1932- *WhoAm 94*
Buschmann, James R. 1945- *WhoAmL 94*
Buschmann, Siegfried 1937- *WhoAm 94*
Busdicker, Gordon G. 1933- *WhoAm 94*
Buse, Don 1950- *BasBi*
Buseck, Peter Robert *WhoAm 94*
Busek, Erhard 1941- *IntWW 93*
Buselmeier, Bernard Joseph 1956- *WhoAm 94*
Buselt, Clara Irene 1921- *WhoMW 93*
Busemann, Herbert 1905- *WhoAm 94*
Busenberg, Stavros Nicholas 1941- *WhoWest 94*
Busenello, Giovanni Francesco 1598-1659 *NewGrDO*
Buser, Paul Joseph 1947- *WhoAmP 93*
Buser, Walter Emil 1926- *IntWW 93*
Busey, Gary 1944- *IntMPA 94, WhoAm 94, WhoHol 92*
Busey, James B. *WhoAmP 93*

Busey, Roxane C. 1949- *WhoAm 94, WhoAmL 94*
Busfield, Roger Melvil, Jr. 1926- *WhoFI 94*
Busfield, Timothy 1957- *IntMPA 94, WhoAm 94, WhoHol 92*
Bush, Alan 1900- *IntWW 93, Who 94*
Bush, Alan (Dudley) 1900- *NewGrDO*
Bush, Alvin C. 1924- *WhoAmP 93*
Bush, Anita d1974 *WhoHol 92*
Bush, Anita 1883-1974 *AfrAmAl 6*
Bush, Ann 1939- *WhoBlA 94*
Bush, Ann Kathleen 1960- *WhoFI 94*
Bush, Barbara 1963- *WhoHol 92*
Bush, Barbara (Pierce) 1925- *ConAu 141*
Bush, Barbara Pierce 1925- *IntWW 93, WhoAm 94, WhoWomW 91*
Bush, Barney *DrAPF 93*
Bush, Barry (Michael) 1938- *WrDr 94*
Bush, Beverly d1969 *WhoAmA 93N*
Bush, Beverly d1990 *WhAm 10*
Bush, Billie Voss 1914- *WhoAmP 93*
Bush, Billy Green *WhoHol 92*
Bush, Bryan 1936- *Who 94*
Bush, Charles Martin Peter 1952- *Who 94*
Bush, Charles R. 1940- *WhoAmL 94*
Bush, Charles Robert *WhoAmA 93*
Bush, Charles Vernon 1939- *WhoAm 94, WhoBlA 94*
Bush, David Frederic 1942- *WhoScEn 94*
Bush, Don E. 1923- *WhoAmP 93*
Bush, Donald John *WhoAmA 93*
Bush, Dorothy Vredenburgh *IntWW 93N*
Bush, Dorothy Walker 1901-1992 *AnObit 1992*
Bush, (John Nash) Douglas 1896-1983 *ConAu 41NR*
Bush, Ella Shepart 1863- *WhoAmA 93N*
Bush, Eugene Nyle 1952- *WhoMW 93, WhoScEn 94*
Bush, Evelyn 1953- *WhoBlA 94*
Bush, F. Brad 1951- *WhoAmL 94*
Bush, F. M., III 1945- *WhoAmL 94*
Bush, Frances Cleveland d1967 *WhoHol 92*
Bush, Fred Marshall, Jr. 1917- *WhoAm 94, WhoAmL 94*
Bush, Frederic Andrew 1904-1989 *WhAm 10*
Bush, Frederick Morris 1949- *WhoAm 94, WhoAmP 93*
Bush, Gary Graham 1950- *WhoWest 94*
Bush, Geoffrey 1920- *IntWW 93, NewGrDO*
Bush, Geoffrey Hubert 1942- *Who 94*
Bush, George d1937 *WhoHol 92*
Bush, George 1924- *NewYTBS 93 [port]*
Bush, George Herbert Walker 1924- *IntWW 93, Who 94, WhoAm 94, WhoAmP 93*
Bush, George Ray 1938- *WhoIns 94*
Bush, Graeme Webster 1950- *WhoAmL 94*
Bush, Guy Louis 1929- *WhoAm 94*
Bush, Jack 1909-1977 *WhoAmA 93N*
Bush, James *WhoHol 92*
Bush, James, III 1955- *WhoAmP 93*
Bush, James Michael 1955- *WhoWest 94*
Bush, James William, Jr. 1931- *WhoFI 94*
Bush, Jill Lobdill 1942- *WhoAmA 93*
Bush, John
See Anthrax *ConMus 11*
Bush, John (Fitzroy Duyland) 1914- *Who 94*
Bush, John Arthur Henry *WhoAm 94*
Bush, John Burchard, Jr. 1933- *WhoScEn 94*
Bush, John Michael 1954- *WhoFI 94*
Bush, John William 1909- *WhoAm 94, WhoScEn 94*
Bush, Judy Lynn 1938- *WhoMW 93*
Bush, June Lee 1942- *WhoFI 94, WhoWest 94*
Bush, Kate *IntWW 93*
Bush, Kate 1958- *WhoAm 94*
Bush, Kirk Bowen 1955- *WhoScEn 94*
Bush, Lenoris 1949- *WhoBlA 94*
Bush, M(ichael) L(accohee) 1938- *WrDr 94*
Bush, Mark Bennett 1958- *WhoScEn 94*
Bush, Martin H. 1930- *WhoAmA 93, WrDr 94*
Bush, Mary *DrAPF 93*
Bush, Mary K. 1948- *WhoBlA 94*
Bush, Nathaniel 1949- *WhoBlA 94*
Bush, Norman 1929- *WhoAm 94, WhoScEn 94*
Bush, Paul Stanley 1936- *WhoAm 94*
Bush, Pauline d1969 *WhoHol 92*
Bush, Peter John 1924- *Who 94*
Bush, Philip L. 1949- *WhoAmL 94*
Bush, Rebecca A. 1952- *WhoAmL 94*
Bush, Rex Curtis 1953- *WhoAmL 94*
Bush, Richard James 1921- *WhoAm 94*
Bush, Robert Donald 1939- *WhoAm 94*
Bush, Robert Finlay d1929 *WhoHol 92*
Bush, Robert G., III 1936- *WhoAmL 94, WhoAmP 93*
Bush, Ronald 1946- *WrDr 94*
Bush, Ronald Edward 1959- *WhoAmL 94*
Bush, Ronald L. 1946- *WhoAm 94, WhoWest 94*
Bush, Roy *DrAPF 93*
Bush, Sarah Lillian 1920- *WhoWest 94*
Bush, Solomon *WhAmRev*
Bush, Solomon 1753-1795 *AmRev*
Bush, Spencer Harrison 1920- *WhoAm 94*
Bush, Stanley Giltner 1928- *WhoWest 94*
Bush, Stephanie R. 1953- *WhoAmP 93*
Bush, Steven Alan 1955- *WhoMW 93*
Bush, T. W. *WhoBlA 94*
Bush, Thomas Norman 1947- *WhoAm 94, WhoAmL 94, WhoFI 94*
Bush, Tom 1948- *WhoAmP 93*
Bush, Vannevar 1890-1974 *WorInv*
Bush, Virginia A. 1952- *WhoAmL 94*
Bush, William Broughton 1911- *WhoAmA 93N*
Bush, William E. *WhoAmP 93*
Bush, William Read 1950- *WhoWest 94*
Busha, Gary C. *DrAPF 93*
Bush-Brown, Albert 1926- *WhoAm 94, WhoAmA 93*
Bushby, Frederick Henry 1924- *Who 94*
Bushe, Frederick Joseph William 1939- *Who 94*
Bushee, Andrea Margot 1955- *WhoFI 94*
Bushee, James Michael 1954- *WhoAmL 94*
Bushehri, Ali 1957- *WhoWest 94*
Bushell, Agnes 1949- *WrDr 94*
Bushell, Anthony 1904- *WhoHol 92*
Bushell, John Christopher Wyndowe 1919- *IntWW 93, Who 94*
Bushell, Raymond 1910- *WrDr 94*
Bushey, A. Scott 1930- *WhoIns 94*
Bushey, Alan Scott 1930- *WhoAm 94*
Bushey, Gerald Blair 1950- *WhoIns 94*
Bushey, Leonel H. 1922- *WhoAmP 93*
Bushey, Richard Kenneth 1940- *WhoAm 94*
Bushing, Jan *WhoAmP 93*
Bushinsky, Jay 1932- *WhoAm 94*
Bushkin, Joe 1916- *WhoHol 92*
Bushmaker, Sandra Jean 1947- *WhoAmL 94*
Bushman, David Franklin 1945- *WhoAmA 93*
Bushman, David Mark 1962- *WhoScEn 94*
Bushman, Edwin Francis Arthur 1919- *WhoWest 94*
Bushman, Francis X. d1966 *WhoHol 92*
Bushman, Francis X., Jr. d1978 *WhoHol 92*
Bushman, Naomi *DrAPF 93*
Bushman, Richard Lyman 1931- *WrDr 94*
Bushmann, Eugene G. *WhoAmP 93*
Bushmiller, Ernie Paul 1905- *WhoAmA 93N*
Bushnell, Alexander Lynn 1911- *Who 94*
Bushnell, Asa Smith 1925- *WhoWest 94*
Bushnell, Bill 1937- *WhoWest 94*
Bushnell, Blake Wayne 1959- *WhoAmL 94*
Bushnell, Clarence William 1916- *WhoAm 94*
Bushnell, David 1740-1824 *AmRev*
Bushnell, David 1742-1824 *WhAmRev, WorInv*
Bushnell, Dennis Meyer 1941- *WhoScEn 94*
Bushnell, Gene Raymond 1938- *WhoAmL 94*
Bushnell, George Edward, Jr. 1924- *WhoAmL 94*
Bushnell, George Edward, III 1952- *WhoAmL 94*
Bushnell, Horace 1802-1876 *DcAmReB 2*
Bushnell, John Alden 1933- *WhoAm 94, WhoAmP 93*
Bushnell, Kenneth Wayne *WhoAmA 93*
Bushnell, Mary B. 1932- *WhoAmP 93*
Bushnell, Roderick Paul 1944- *WhoAmL 94, WhoWest 94*
Bushnell, William Rodgers 1931- *WhoMW 93*
Bushouse, Daniel Bruce 1951- *WhoMW 93*
Bushre, Peter Alvin 1943- *WhoFI 94, WhoWest 94*
Bushuk, Walter 1929- *WhoScEn 94*
Bushway, Rodney John 1949- *WhoScEn 94*
Bushwick Bill
See Geto Boys, The *ConMus 11*
Bushy, Karen Marie 1940- *WhoMW 93*
Bushyeager, Peter *DrAPF 93*
Bushyhead, Jesse d1844 *EncNAR*
Busi, Aldo 1948- *GayLL*
Busia, Akosua *WhoHol 92*
Busia, Kofi Abrefa 1913?-1978 *BlkWr 2*
Busick, Charles Philip 1928- *WhoWest 94*
Busick, Denzel Rex 1945- *WhoAmL 94, WhoMW 93*
Busick, Robert James 1950- *WhoFI 94, WhoMW 93, WhoScEn 94*
Busig, Rick Harold 1952- *WhoWest 94*
Busigo, George Charles 1933- *WhoHisp 94*
Businger, John Arnold 1945- *WhoAmP 93*
Businger, Joost Alois 1924- *WhoAm 94*
Busino, Orlando Francis 1926- *WhoAmA 93*
Busk, Leslie Francis Harry 1937- *Who 94*
Busker, Leroy Henry 1929- *WhoAm 94*
Buskey, James E. *WhoAmP 93, WhoBlA 94*
Buskey, John *WhoBlA 94*
Buskirk, Elsworth Robert 1925- *WhoAm 94, WhoScEn 94*
Buskirk, Phyllis Richardson 1930- *WhoFI 94, WhoMW 93*
Buskirk, Richard Hobart 1927- *WhoAm 94*
Buskuhl, Carl Thomas 1952- *WhoWest 94*
Busky, Henry LeRoy 1938- *WhoFI 94*
Buslaev, Yuri Aleksandrovich 1929- *IntWW 93*
Busley, Jessie d1950 *WhoHol 92*
Busmann, Thomas Gary 1958- *WhoScEn 94*
Busner, Philip H. 1927- *WhoAm 94, WhoAmL 94*
Buso, Eduardo L. 1951- *WhoAmL 94*
Busoni, Ferruccio (Dante Michelangelo Benvenuto) 1866-1924 *NewGrDO*
Busonik, Stephen William 1952- *WhoMW 93*
Busquin, Philippe 1941- *IntWW 93*
Buss, Barbara Ann 1932- *Who 94*
Buss, Claude Albert 1903- *WhoAm 94*
Buss, Daniel Frank 1943- *WhoAm 94*
Buss, Dietrich G. 1939- *WhoWest 94*
Buss, Edward George 1921- *WhoScEn 94*
Buss, Frances Mary 1827-1894 *DcNaB MP*
Buss, Helen N. 1941- *WrDr 94*
Buss, Jerry 1933- *BasBi*
Buss, Jerry Hatten *WhoAm 94, WhoWest 94*
Buss, Leo William 1953- *WhoAm 94, WhoScEn 94*
Buss, Robin (Caron) 1939- *ConAu 141*
Buss, Samuel Rudolph 1957- *WhoWest 94*
Buss, Teresa Thacker 1957- *WhoWest 94*
Buss, Walter Richard 1905- *WhoAm 94*
Buss, William Charles 1938- *WhoAm 94*
Bussabarger, Robert Franklin 1922- *WhoAmA 93*
Bussani, Dorothea 1763-1810? *NewGrDO*
Bussani, Giacomo Francesco fl. 1673-1680 *NewGrDO*
Bussard, David Andrew 1955- *WhoAm 94*
Bussard, Richard Earl 1934- *WhoAm 94*
Bussard, Robert William 1928- *WhoAm 94*
Bussart, Ford Thomas 1945- *WhoAmP 93*
Bussart, Walter Woods 1942- *WhoAmP 93*
Bussche, Wolf Von Dem *WhoAmA 93*
Busse, Barry (Lee) 1946- *NewGrDO*
Busse, Bill E. 1919- *WhoAmP 93*
Busse, Ewald William 1917- *WhoAm 94*
Busse, Felix 1940- *IntWW 93*
Busse, Leonard Wayne 1938- *WhoAm 94, WhoWest 94*
Busse, Lu Ann 1956- *WhoAm 94*
Busse, Michael Clifford 1942- *WhoWest 94*
Bussell, Darcey 1969- *IntDcB [port]*
Bussell, Darcey Andrea 1969- *IntWW 93, Who 94*
Bussell, Mark Stephen 1953- *WhoAm 94*
Busselle, Rebecca *DrAPF 93*
Busselle, Rebecca 1941- *WrDr 94*
Busser, (Paul-)Henri 1872-1973 *NewGrDO*
Bussey, C. H. d1971 *WhoHol 92*
Bussey, Charles D. 1933- *AfrAmG [port]*
Bussey, Charles David 1933- *WhoBlA 94*
Bussey, George Davis 1949- *WhoWest 94*
Bussey, John W., III 1943- *WhoAmL 94*
Bussey, Patricia Jean 1923- *WhoWest 94*
Bussey, Reuben T. 1943- *WhoBlA 94*
Bussgang, Julian Jakob 1925- *WhoAm 94*
Bussian, John A., III 1954- *WhoAmL 94*
Bussie, John Norris 1957- *WhoFI 94*
Bussie, Victor 1919- *WhoAmP 93*
Bussieres, Raymond d1982 *WhoHol 92*
Bussieres, Yvan 1945- *WhoAm 94, WhoFI 94, WhoWest 94*
Bussing, Mary Agnes 1938- *WhoAmP 93*
Bussinger, Robert E. 1932- *WhoWest 94*
Bussman, Donald Herbert 1925- *WhoAmL 94, WhoMW 93*
Bussman, John Wood 1924- *WhoAm 94*
Bussoleni, Giovanni *NewGrDO*
Bussone, David Eben 1947- *WhoAm 94, WhoFI 94, WhoScEn 94*
Bussone, Frank Joseph *WhoMW 93*
Bussone, Karen Marie 1950- *WhoMW 93*
Bussotti, Sylvano 1931- *NewGrDO*
Bussy, Roger de Rabutin, comte de 1618-1693 *GuFrLit 2*
Busta, Christine 1915-1987 *BlmGWL*
Bustabad, Juan *WhoHisp 94*
Bustad, Leo Kenneth 1920- *WhoAm 94*
Bustamante, Albert G. 1935- *WhoAmP 93, WhoHisp 94*
Bustamante, Arturo 1944- *WhoHisp 94*
Bustamante, Cody Antonio 1955- *WhoHisp 94*
Bustamante, Cruz M. *WhoHisp 94*
Bustamante, David Anthony 1954- *WhoHisp 94*
Bustamante, J. W. Andre 1961- *WhoBlA 94*
Bustamante, Leonard Eliecer 1938- *WhoHisp 94*
Bustamante, Ricardo 1962- *WhoHisp 94*
Bustamante, Richard *WhoAm 94*
Bustamante, Roberto J. 1946- *WhoHisp 94*
Bustamante, Valentin M., Sr. 1931- *WhoHisp 94*
Bustamante, Z. Sonali 1958- *WhoBlA 94*
Bustamente, Cecilia *WhoHisp 94*
Bustard, Thomas Stratton 1934- *WhoScEn 94*
Busteed, Robert Charles 1907-1988 *WhAm 10*
Bustelli, Giuseppe d1781? *NewGrDO*
Bustelo Y Garcia Del Real, Carlos 1936- *IntWW 93*
Buster, Budd d1965 *WhoHol 92*
Buster, Carolyn 1942- *WhoMW 93*
Buster, Edmond Bate 1918- *WhoAm 94, WhoWest 94*
Buster, J. Kevin 1953- *WhoAmL 94*
Buster, Jim *WhoAmP 93*
Buster, John Edmond 1941- *WhoScEn 94*
Bustillo, Eloy 1951- *WhoHisp 94*
Bustillo, Oscar, Jr. *WhoHisp 94*
Bustillos, Herbert P., Jr. 1937- *WhoHisp 94*
Bustin, Beverly Miner 1936- *WhoAmP 93*
Bustin, Edouard Jean 1933- *WhoAm 94*
Bustin, George Leo 1948- *WhoAm 94, WhoAmL 94*
Busto, Ana Marie *WhoAmA 93*
Busto, Rafael Pedro 1939- *WhoHisp 94*
Bustos, Aida *WhoHisp 94*
Bustos Domecq, H. *ConWorW 93 RfGShF*
Bustos Domecq, H(onorio) *ConAu 43NR*
Busu, Fatima 1948- *BlmGWL*
Busvine, James Ronald 1912- *Who 94, WrDr 94*
Buszko, Irene J. 1947- *WhoAmA 93*
Butala, Sharon 1940- *BlmGWL*
Butch, James Nicholas 1951- *WhoScEn 94*
Butch, William Louis 1932- *WhoIns 94*
Butcher, Amanda Kay 1936- *WhoMW 93*
Butcher, Anthony John 1934- *Who 94*
Butcher, Bobby Gene 1936- *WhoAm 94*
Butcher, Brian Ronald 1947- *WhoScEn 94*
Butcher, Bruce Cameron 1947- *WhoAmL 94*
Butcher, Connie Joan 1960- *WhoAmL 94*
Butcher, David John 1948- *IntWW 93*
Butcher, Devereux 1906-1991 *WhAm 10*
Butcher, Donald Franklin 1937- *WhoAm 94*
Butcher, Duane Clemens 1939- *WhoFI 94*
Butcher, Ernest d1965 *WhoHol 92*
Butcher, Fred R. 1943- *WhoAm 94, WhoScEn 94*
Butcher, Goler Teal 1925- *WhoBlA 94*
Butcher, Grace *DrAPF 93*
Butcher, Harold 1893- *WhAm 10*
Butcher, Howard, III 1902-1991 *WhAm 10*
Butcher, Jack Robert 1941- *WhoFI 94, WhoWest 94*
Butcher, James R. *WhoAmP 93*
Butcher, James Walter 1917- *WhoAm 94*
Butcher, John Charles 1933- *IntWW 93*
Butcher, John Patrick *Who 94*
Butcher, Philip 1918- *WhoAm 94, WhoBlA 94*
Butcher, Richard James 1926- *Who 94*
Butcher, Richard Kent 1949- *WhoWest 94*
Butcher, Susan Howlet 1954- *WhoAm 94*
Butcher, Thomas Kennedy 1914- *WrDr 94*
Butcher, Willard Carlisle 1926- *IntWW 93, Who 94, WhoAm 94*
Butcher, (Charles) William 1951- *WrDr 94*
Butchkes, Sydney 1922- *WhoAm 94, WhoAmA 93*
Butchman, Alan A. 1938- *WhoAmP 93*
Butchvarov, Panayot Krustev 1933- *WhoAm 94*
Bute, Marquess of d1993 *Who 94N*
Bute, Marquess of 1793-1848 *DcNaB MP*
Bute, Marquess of 1958- *Who 94*
Bute, John Stuart, Earl of 1713-1792 *WhAmRev*

Bu-te-ge-qi *WhoPRCh 91*
Butenandt, Adolf 1903- *Who 94*
Butenandt, Adolf Friedrich 1903- *WorScD*
Butenandt, Adolf Friedrich Johann 1903- *IntWW 93, WhoScEn 94*
Butenhoff, Laura Lea 1960- *WhoFI 94*
Butenko, Constantine 1918- *WhoAmP 93*
Butera, Constance Diane 1936- *WhoAmL 94*
Butera, Paul 1942- *WhoFI 94*
Butera, Robert J. *WhoAm 94*
Butera, Robert James 1935- *WhoAmP 93*
Butera, Virginia Fabbri 1951- *WhoAmA 93*
Buth, Martin D. 1917- *WhoAmP 93*
Buthelezi, Manas 1935- *IntWW 93*
Buthelezi, Mangosuthu Gatsha 1928- *IntWW 93*
Buti, Francesco 1604-1682 *NewGrDO*
Butki, Arnold 1935- *WhoFI 94*
Butkovitz, Alan L. 1952- *WhoAmP 93*
Butkus, Dick *ProFbHF [port]*
Butkus, Dick 1942- *WhoAm 94*
Butkus, Dick 1943- *WhoHol 92*
Butland, Gilbert J(ames) 1910- *WrDr 94*
Butland, Jeffrey H. *WhoAmP 93*
Butler *Who 94*
Butler, Abbey J. *WhoAm 94, WhoFI 94*
Butler, Adam (Courtauld) 1931- *Who 94*
Butler, Aimee Mott d1993 *NewYTBS 93*
Butler, Alan 1940- *IntWW 93*
Butler, Aldis Perrin 1913- *WhoWest 94*
Butler, Alison 1954- *WhoScEn 94*
Butler, Allan Geoffrey Roy 1933- *Who 94*
Butler, Anna Land *BlkWr 2*
Butler, Anna M(abel Land) 1901- *BlkWr 2*
Butler, Annette Garner 1944- *WhoBlA 94*
Butler, Anthony John 1945- *Who 94*
Butler, Archie d1977 *WhoHol 92*
Butler, Arthur Maurice 1947- *WhoWest 94*
Butler, Arthur William 1929- *Who 94*
Butler, Audrey Maude Beman 1936- *Who 94*
Butler, B. Janelle 1949- *WhoBlA 94*
Butler, Barbara Kay 1961- *WhoMW 93*
Butler, Basil Richard Ryland 1930- *IntWW 93, Who 94*
Butler, Benjamin Willard 1933- *WhoBlA 94*
Butler, Bernard Francis 1937- *WhoMW 93*
Butler, Bill 1927- *WrDr 94*
Butler, Bill 1931- *ConTFT 11*
Butler, Broadus Nathaniel 1920- *WhoAm 94, WhoBlA 94*
Butler, Bruce W. 1939- *WhoIns 94*
Butler, Byron C. 1918- *WhoAmA 93*
Butler, Byron Clinton 1918- *WhoScEn 94, WhoWest 94*
Butler, Cass C. 1956- *WhoAmL 94*
Butler, Charles d1920 *WhoHol 92*
Butler, Charles David 1936- *WhoAm 94*
Butler, Charles H. 1925- *WhoBlA 94*
Butler, Charles R., Jr. 1940- *WhoAm 94*
Butler, Charles Randolph, Jr. 1940- *WhoAmL 94*
Butler, Charles Thomas 1951- *WhoAm 94, WhoAmA 93*
Butler, Charles W. 1922- *WhoBlA 94*
Butler, Charlotte c. 1660-1692? *NewGrDO*
Butler, Christine Ann 1951- *WhoAmL 94*
Butler, Christopher John 1950- *Who 94*
Butler, Clark Michael 1946- *WhoScEn 94*
Butler, Clary Kent 1948- *WhoBlA 94*
Butler, Clifford (Charles) 1922- *Who 94*
Butler, Clifford Charles 1922- *IntWW 93*
Butler, Colin G(asking) 1913- *WrDr 94*
Butler, Colin Gasking 1913- *IntWW 93, Who 94*
Butler, Dan M. 1947- *WhoMW 93*
Butler, Darraugh Clay 1955- *WhoBlA 94*
Butler, David *Who 94*
Butler, David d1979 *WhoHol 92*
Butler, David 1930- *WhoAm 94*
Butler, David 1936- *Who 94*
Butler, David 1941- *EncSF 93*
Butler, (Christopher) David 1942- *Who 94*
Butler, David (Edgeworth) 1924- *WrDr 94*
Butler, David Edgeworth 1924- *IntWW 93, Who 94*
Butler, David J. 1950- *WhoAmL 94*
Butler, Dean 1957- *WhoHol 92*
Butler, Deborah Ann 1949- *WhoMW 93*
Butler, Denis J. *WhoAmP 93*
Butler, Denis William Langford 1926- *Who 94*
Butler, Denver 1938- *WhoAmP 93*
Butler, Donald Earnest 1927- *WhoAm 94*
Butler, Donald K. 1944- *WhoAmL 94*
Butler, Donald Philip 1957- *WhoScEn 94*
Butler, Dorothy 1925- *WrDr 94*
Butler, Douglas 1948- *WhoAmL 94*
Butler, Douthard Roosevelt 1934- *WhoBlA 94*
Butler, Drew Mark 1960- *WhoFI 94*
Butler, Eddie d1944 *WhoHol 92*
Butler, Edward 1763-1803 *WhAmRev*
Butler, Edward Clive Barber 1904- *Who 94*
Butler, Edward Eugene 1919- *WhoAm 94*
Butler, Edward Franklyn 1937- *WhoAmL 94*
Butler, Edward Lee 1945- *WhoAm 94*
Butler, Edwin John 1874-1943 *DcNaB MP*
Butler, Eleanor *BlmGWL*
Butler, Elizur 1794- *EncNAR*
Butler, Eric Scott 1907- *Who 94*
Butler, Ernest Daniel 1913- *WhoBlA 94*
Butler, Eugene L. 1941- *WhoAm 94*
Butler, Eugene Thaddeus, Jr. 1922- *WhoBlA 94*
Butler, Eula M. 1927- *WhoBlA 94*
Butler, Francelia McWilliams 1913- *WhoAm 94*
Butler, Frank d1967 *WhoHol 92*
Butler, Frank Anthony 1942- *WhoAm 94*
Butler, Frank B. 1945- *WhoAmL 94*
Butler, Fred J. d1929 *WhoHol 92*
Butler, Fred Jay, Jr. 1929- *WhoAm 94*
Butler, Frederick Douglas 1942- *WhoBlA 94*
Butler, Frederick George 1919- *WhoAm 94*
Butler, Frederick Guy 1918- *IntWW 93*
Butler, Gary Lee 1934- *WhoAmP 93*
Butler, Geoffrey Scott 1958- *WhoScEn 94*
Butler, George 1904- *Who 94*
Butler, George Harrison 1917- *WhoAm 94*
Butler, George L. *WhoAm 94*
Butler, George Prentiss, IV 1956- *WhoAmL 94*
Butler, George Washington, Jr. 1944- *WhoAmL 94*
Butler, George William P. *Who 94*
Butler, Gerald Norman 1930- *Who 94*
Butler, Gertrude I. 1922- *WhoAmP 93*
Butler, Granger Hal 1960- *WhoMW 93*
Butler, (Frederick) Guy 1918- *ConAu 41NR, WrDr 94*
Butler, Gwendoline (Williams) 1922- *WrDr 94*
Butler, Hew Dacres George 1922- *Who 94*
Butler, Hiram 1951- *WhoAmA 93*
Butler, Homer L. 1934- *WhoBlA 94*
Butler, Hugh Alan 1952- *WhoAmP 93*
Butler, Ian Geoffrey 1925- *Who 94*
Butler, Iris Mary 1905- *WrDr 94*
Butler, Ivan 1909- *WrDr 94*
Butler, Ivan Scott 1962- *WhoFI 94*
Butler, J. Bradway 1941- *WhoAmL 94*
Butler, J. Murfree 1942- *WhoAm 94, WhoFI 94*
Butler, J. Ray 1923- *WhoBlA 94*
Butler, Jack 1944- *EncSF 93, WrDr 94*
Butler, Jack Fairchild 1933- *WhoAmA 93*
Butler, James *Who 94*
Butler, James d1781 *WhAmRev*
Butler, (Percy) James 1929- *Who 94*
Butler, James D. 1945- *WhoAmA 93*
Butler, James D. 1950- *WhoAm 94, WhoAmL 94*
Butler, James Hall 1948- *WhoScEn 94, WhoWest 94*
Butler, James Lawrence 1943- *WhoFI 94*
Butler, James Lee 1927- *WhoScEn 94*
Butler, James Martin 1948- *WhoMW 93*
Butler, James Newton 1934- *WhoAm 94*
Butler, James Patrick 1957- *WhoWest 94*
Butler, James Robert 1930- *WhoAm 94*
Butler, James Robertson, Jr. 1946- *WhoAmL 94, WhoFI 94*
Butler, James Walter 1931- *Who 94*
Butler, James Walter, III 1958- *WhoAmL 94*
Butler, Jeremy Edward 1930- *WhoAm 94*
Butler, Jerome M. 1944- *WhoBlA 94*
Butler, Jerry 1939- *WhoBlA 94*
Butler, Jerry O'Dell 1957- *WhoBlA 94*
Butler, Jesse Lee 1953- *WhoFI 94*
Butler, Jim *IntWW 93*
Butler, Jimmie d1945 *WhoHol 92*
Butler, Joan *EncSF 93*
Butler, John d1967 *WhoHol 92*
Butler, John d1993 *NewYTBS 93*
Butler, John 1728-1796 *AmRev, WhAmRev*
Butler, John 1920- *IntDcB*
Butler, John 1920-1993 *CurBio 93N*
Butler, John Alden 1930- *WhoAm 94*
Butler, John Ben, III 1948- *WhoScEn 94*
Butler, John Benson 1938- *WhoFI 94*
Butler, John Donald 1910- *WhoBlA 94*
Butler, John Gordon 1942- *WhoBlA 94*
Butler, John L., Jr. 1931- *WhoMW 93*
Butler, John Linton 1943- *WhoAmP 93*
Butler, John Manton 1909- *Who 94*
Butler, John Michael 1959- *WhoAmL 94*
Butler, John Michael, II 1969- *WhoFI 94, WhoWest 94*
Butler, John Musgrave 1928- *WhoAm 94*
Butler, John Nathaniel 1932- *WhoBlA 94*
Butler, John O. 1926- *WhoBlA 94*
Butler, John Paul 1935- *WhoFI 94*
Butler, John Sibley 1947- *WhoBlA 94*
Butler, Johnnella E. 1947- *WhoBlA 94*
Butler, Jon 1940- *WrDr 94*
Butler, Jon Terry 1943- *WhoAm 94*
Butler, Jonathan Putnam 1940- *WhoAm 94*
Butler, Joseph 1692-1752 *EncEth*
Butler, Joseph (Green) 1901-1981 *WhoAmA 93N*
Butler, Joseph Green, Jr. 1840-1927 *EncABHB 9*
Butler, Joseph T(homas) 1932- *WrDr 94*
Butler, Joseph Thomas 1932- *WhoAmA 93*
Butler, Joyce M. 1941- *WhoBlA 94*
Butler, Karla 1933- *WhoAm 94*
Butler, Katharine Gorrell 1925- *WhoAm 94*
Butler, Keith A. 1955- *WhoAmP 93*
Butler, Keith Andre 1955- *WhoBlA 94*
Butler, Keith Stephenson 1917- *Who 94*
Butler, Kent Alan 1958- *WhoWest 94*
Butler, Kevin Cornell 1963- *WhoScEn 94*
Butler, Kevin Gregory 1962- *WhoAm 94, WhoMW 93*
Butler, Larry Gene 1933- *WhoAm 94, WhoMW 93*
Butler, Leslie Ann 1945- *WhoAm 94, WhoWest 94*
Butler, Lillian Catherine 1919- *WhoWest 94*
Butler, Lorenza Phillips, Jr. 1960- *WhoBlA 94*
Butler, Loretta M. *WhoBlA 94*
Butler, Manley Caldwell 1925- *WhoAm 94, WhoAmL 94, WhoAmP 93*
Butler, Margaret (Gwendoline) *WrDr 94*
Butler, Margaret Kampschaefer 1924- *WhoAm 94, WhoMW 93*
Butler, Marigene H. 1931- *WhoAmA 93*
Butler, Marilyn (Speers) 1937- *WrDr 94*
Butler, Marilyn Speers 1937- *IntWW 93, Who 94*
Butler, Marjorie Johnson 1911- *WhoBlA 94*
Butler, Martin J. 1924- *WhoAmP 93*
Butler, Marty *WhoMW 93*
Butler, Martyn Don 1939- *WhoAmP 93*
Butler, Max R. 1912- *WhoBlA 94*
Butler, Melvin Lynn 1938- *WhoWest 94*
Butler, Merrill *WhoFI 94*
Butler, Michael *Who 94*
Butler, Michael (Dacres) 1927- *Who 94*
Butler, (Reginald) Michael (Thomas) 1928- *Who 94*
Butler, Michael Dacres 1927- *IntWW 93*
Butler, Michael Eugene 1950- *WhoBlA 94*
Butler, Michael Francis 1935- *WhoAm 94*
Butler, Michael Howard 1936- *Who 94*
Butler, Nathan *EncSF 93*
Butler, Nathan 1913- *WrDr 94*
Butler, Neil A. 1927-1992 *WhoBlA 94N*
Butler, Neville Roy 1920- *Who 94*
Butler, Newman N. 1914- *WhoAmP 93*
Butler, (John) Nicholas 1942- *Who 94*
Butler, Nicholas Murray 1862-1947 *AmSocL [port]*
Butler, Nick *Who 94*
Butler, Norman John Terence 1946- *Who 94*
Butler, Octavia 1947- *BlmGWL*
Butler, Octavia E. 1947- *AfrAmAl 6, WhoBlA 94, WrDr 94*
Butler, Octavia E(stelle) 1947- *BlkWr 2, EncSF 93, TwCYAW*
Butler, Oliver Richard 1941- *WhoBlA 94*
Butler, Owen Bradford 1923- *WhoAm 94*
Butler, Patricia 1958- *WhoMW 93*
Butler, Patrick 1917- *WrDr 94*
Butler, Patrick David 1952- *WhoWest 94*
Butler, Patrick Hampton 1933- *WhoBlA 94*
Butler, Paul *WhoHol 92*
Butler, Paul Bascomb, Jr. 1947- *WhoAmL 94*
Butler, Paul Clyde 1950- *WhoScEn 94*
Butler, Paul Thurman 1928- *WhoMW 93*
Butler, Paul William 1961- *WhoAmL 94*
Butler, Pearl d1987 *WhoHol 92*
Butler, Percival 1760-1821 *WhAmRev*
Butler, Peter 1951- *Who 94*
Butler, Pierce 1744-1822 *WhAmRev*
Butler, Pinkney L. 1948- *WhoBlA 94*
Butler, Raymond Leonard 1956- *WhoBlA 94*
Butler, Rebecca Batts *WhoBlA 94*
Butler, Rex Lamont 1951- *WhoAmL 94*
Butler, Richard 1743-1791 *AmRev, WhAmRev*
Butler, Richard (Clive) 1929- *Who 94*
Butler, Richard C., Jr. 1937- *WhoAmP 93*
Butler, Richard Colburn 1910- *WhoAm 94*
Butler, Richard Dean 1930- *WhoAm 94*
Butler, Richard Edmund 1926- *IntWW 93, Who 94*
Butler, Richard Noel 1942- *IntWW 93*
Butler, Robert Allan 1923- *WhoAm 94*
Butler, Robert Allen 1944- *WhoWest 94*
Butler, Robert Calvin 1959- *WhoBlA 94*
Butler, Robert Clifton 1930- *WhoAm 94, WhoFI 94*
Butler, Robert Leonard 1931- *WhoAm 94*
Butler, Robert Neil 1927- *WhoAm 94*
Butler, Robert Olen *DrAPF 93*
Butler, Robert Olen 1945- *ConLC 81 [port], WhoAm 94*
Butler, Robert P. 1924- *WhoFI 94*
Butler, Robert Russell 1954- *WhoScEn 94*
Butler, Robert Thomas 1925- *WhoAm 94*
Butler, Robin *IntWW 93, Who 94*
Butler, (Frederick Edward) Robin 1938- *IntWW 93, Who 94*
Butler, Rohan D'Olier 1917- *Who 94*
Butler, Ronnie 1931- *WrDr 94*
Butler, Rosemary Jane 1946- *Who 94*
Butler, Roy d1973 *WhoHol 92*
Butler, Roy 1949- *WhoBlA 94*
Butler, Roy Francis 1914- *WhAm 10*
Butler, Samuel 1612-1680 *BlmGEL*
Butler, Samuel 1835-1902 *BlmGEL, EncSF 93*
Butler, Samuel Coles 1930- *WhoAm 94*
Butler, Shirley Elaine 1949- *WhoMW 93*
Butler, Stephen J. 1952- *WhoAmL 94*
Butler, Susan Lowell 1944- *WhoAm 94*
Butler, Sydney J. *WhoAm 94*
Butler, Thelma Jean 1933- *WhoAmP 93*
Butler, Thomas 1754-1805 *WhAmRev*
Butler, Thomas Frederick *Who 94*
Butler, Thomas Joseph, Jr. 1965- *WhoAmL 94*
Butler, Thomas Pierce 1910- *Who 94*
Butler, Thomas Wayne 1944- *WhoAmP 93*
Butler, Thorne Gordon 1948- *WhoMW 93*
Butler, Timothy Harold 1945- *WhoAm 94, WhoAmL 94*
Butler, Toni Jean 1963- *WhoMW 93*
Butler, Velma Sydney 1902- *WhoBlA 94*
Butler, Vincent Frederick 1933- *Who 94*
Butler, Vincent Paul, Jr. 1929- *WhoAm 94*
Butler, (Christina) Violet 1884-1982 *DcNaB MP*
Butler, Vivian 1927- *WrDr 94*
Butler, Walter 1752-1781 *AmRev, WhAmRev*
Butler, Washington Roosevelt, Jr. 1933- *WhoBlA 94*
Butler, Wendell Harding 1924- *WhoBlA 94*
Butler, Wilford Arthur 1937- *WhoAm 94*
Butler, William d1789 *WhAmRev*
Butler, William fl. 1640-1660 *DcNaB MP*
Butler, William 1759-1821 *WhAmRev*
Butler, William 1929- *EncSF 93*
Butler, William A. 1951- *WhoAm 94*
Butler, William Allington 1940- *WhoAmL 94*
Butler, William Arthur Vivian 1927- *WrDr 94*
Butler, William E. 1931- *WhoAm 94, WhoFI 94*
Butler, William Elliott 1939- *Who 94*
Butler, William J. d1927 *WhoHol 92*
Butler, William Joseph 1924- *WhoAm 94*
Butler, William Joseph 1934- *IntWW 93*
Butler, William Oliver 1949- *WhoMW 93*
Butler, William Thomas 1932- *WhoAm 94*
Butler, Zebulon 1730-1795 *AmRev*
Butler, Zebulon 1731-1795 *WhAmRev*
Butler-Hamilton, Melba 1954- *WhoBlA 94*
Butler-Sloss, (Ann) Elizabeth (Oldfield) 1933- *IntWW 93, Who 94*
Butler-Sloss, Joseph William Alexander 1926- *Who 94*
Butlin, Martin (Richard Fletcher) 1929- *WrDr 94*
Butlin, Martin Richard Fletcher 1929- *IntWW 93, Who 94*
Butlin, Robin Alan 1938- *Who 94*
Butlin, Ron 1949- *WrDr 94*
Butman, John 1951- *ConAu 142*
Butner, Fred Washington, Jr. 1927- *WhoAm 94*
Butner, Richard Edward 1950- *WhoAmL 94*
Butor, Michel 1926- *EncSF 93, IntWW 93*
Butor, Michel (Marie Francois) 1926- *ConWorW 93*
Butow, Robert J. C. 1924- *WrDr 94*
Butow, Robert Joseph Charles 1924- *WhoAm 94, WhoWest 94*
Butowick, George Vincent 1945- *WhoWest 94*
Butowsky, David Martin 1936- *WhoAm 94*
Butragueno, Emilio 1963- *WorESoc*
Butrick, Daniel Sabin 1789-1851 *EncNAR*
Butrick, Merritt d1989 *WhoHol 92*
Butrimovitz, Gerald Paul *WhoWest 94*
Butros, Albert Jamil 1934- *IntWW 93, Who 94*
Butry, Paul John 1946- *WhoScEn 94*
Butsch, Don *WhoAmP 93*
Butsch, Richard (J.) 1943- *WrDr 94*
Butscher, Edward *DrAPF 93*

Butsko, Yury Markovich 1938- *NewGrDO*
Butson, Alton Thomas 1926- *WhoAm 94*
Butt, Bob d1958 *WhoHol 92*
Butt, Clara (Ellen) 1872-1936 *NewGrDO*
Butt, Edward Thomas, Jr. 1947- *WhoAm 94, WhoAmL 94*
Butt, Geoffrey Frank 1943- *Who 94*
Butt, Harlan W. 1950- *WhoAmA 93*
Butt, Howard Edward 1895-1991 *WhAm 10*
Butt, Howard Edward, Jr. 1927- *WhoAm 94*
Butt, Hugh Roland 1910- *WhoAm 94*
Butt, Jimmy Lee 1921- *WhoAm 94, WhoScEn 94*
Butt, John Baecher 1935- *WhoAm 94*
Butt, Johnny d1930 *WhoHol 92*
Butt, Kenneth *Who 94*
Butt, (Alfred) Kenneth (Dudley) 1908- *Who 94*
Butt, Lawson d1956 *WhoHol 92*
Butt, Michael Acton 1942- *IntWW 93, Who 94*
Butt, Richard Bevan 1943- *Who 94*
Butta, Deena Celeste 1950- *WhoMW 93*
Butta, J. Henry 1928- *WhoAm 94, WhoFI 94*
Buttaci, Sal St. John *DrAPF 93*
Buttaci, Salvatore Michael 1941- *WhoAmL 94*
Buttchen, Terry Gerard 1958- *WhoFI 94, WhoWest 94*
Butte, Anthony Jeffrey 1951- *WhoFI 94*
Buttenheim, Edgar Marion 1922- *WhoAm 94*
Buttenwieser, Benjamin Joseph 1900-1991 *WhAm 10*
Buttenwieser, Lawrence Benjamin 1932- *WhoAm 94*
Butter, David (Henry) 1920- *Who 94*
Butter, John Henry 1916- *Who 94*
Butter, Neil (McLaren) 1933- *Who 94*
Butter, Peter Herbert 1921- *Who 94, WrDr 94*
Butter, Peter Joseph Michael 1932- *Who 94*
Butter, Tom 1952- *WhoAmA 93*
Butterbaugh, Robert Clyde 1931- *WhoAmA 93*
Butterbrodt, John Ervin 1929- *WhoAm 94*
Butterfield, Baron 1920- *Who 94*
Butterfield, Alexander P. 1926- *IntWW 93*
Butterfield, Anthony Swindt 1931- *WhoWest 94*
Butterfield, Bruce Scott 1949- *WhoAm 94*
Butterfield, C. Robert 1943- *WhoAmL 94*
Butterfield, Charles Harris 1911- *Who 94*
Butterfield, D. Allan 1946- *WhoScEn 94*
Butterfield, Deborah Kay 1949- *WhoAmA 93*
Butterfield, Don 1923- *WhoBlA 94*
Butterfield, Everett d1925 *WhoHol 92*
Butterfield, Herb d1957 *WhoHol 92*
Butterfield, Jack Arlington 1919- *WhoAm 94*
Butterfield, Jim 1955- *WhoMW 93*
Butterfield, (William) John (Hughes) 1920- *IntWW 93, WrDr 94*
Butterfield, John Michael 1926- *Who 94*
Butterfield, Lander W(estgate) 1897- *WhAm 10*
Butterfield, Paul d1987 *WhoHol 92*
Butterfield, R. Keith 1941- *WhoAm 94*
Butterfield, Samuel Hale 1924- *WhoAm 94*
Butterfield, Walton d1966 *WhoHol 92*
Butterfield, William H(enry) 1910- *WrDr 94*
Butterfill, John Valentine 1941- *Who 94*
Butterick, Brian *DrAPF 93*
Butterick, Ebenezer *WorInv*
Butterick, Ellen *WorInv*
Butterly, Sean C. *WhoAmP 93*
Butters, Christopher *DrAPF 93*
Butters, Dorothy Gilman 1923- *WrDr 94*
Butters, John Patrick 1933- *WhoFI 94*
Butterss, Robert Leopold 1931- *Who 94*
Butterweck, Hans Juergen 1932- *WhoScEn 94*
Butterworth, Baron 1918- *Who 94*
Butterworth, Charles d1946 *WhoHol 92*
Butterworth, Charles E. 1938- *WhoAm 94*
Butterworth, Donna 1956- *WhoHol 92*
Butterworth, Edward Livingston 1914- *WhoAm 94, WhoFI 94, WhoWest 94*
Butterworth, Francis Macomber 1935- *WhoMW 93*
Butterworth, Frank Willoughby, III 1937-1988 *WhAm 10*
Butterworth, George William, III 1939- *WhoAm 94*
Butterworth, Henry 1926- *Who 94*
Butterworth, Ian 1930- *IntWW 93, Who 94*
Butterworth, Jane Rogers Fitch 1937- *WhoAm 94, WhoMW 93*
Butterworth, Kenneth W. 1925- *WhoAm 94, WhoFI 94*
Butterworth, Michael 1942- *WhoScEn 94*
Butterworth, Michael 1947- *EncSF 93*
Butterworth, Neville *Who 94*
Butterworth, (George) Neville 1911- *IntWW 93, Who 94*
Butterworth, Oliver 1915-1990 *WhAm 10, WrDr 94N*
Butterworth, Peter d1979 *WhoHol 92*
Butterworth, Robert A. 1942- *WhoAm 94, WhoAmL 94, WhoAmP 93*
Butterworth, Robert Roman 1946- *WhoWest 94*
Butterworth, Tyler *WhoHol 92*
Butterworth, Walter d1962 *WhoHol 92*
Butterworth, William Todd 1959- *WhoMW 93*
Buttfield, Nancy (Eileen) 1912- *Who 94*
Butti, Linda (Benincasa) 1951- *WhoAmA 93*
Buttiglier, Joseph P. 1950- *WhoAmL 94*
Buttinger, Catharine Sarina Caroline 1951- *WhoAm 94*
Buttinger, Joseph 1906-1992 *AnObit 1992*
Buttitta, Tony 1907- *WrDr 94*
Buttke, Thomas Frederick 1956- *WhoScEn 94*
Buttlar, Rudolph Otto 1934- *WhoAm 94*
Buttle, Edgar Allyn 1903-1990 *WhAm 10*
Buttle, Eileen 1937- *Who 94*
Buttner, Jean Bernhard 1934- *WhoAm 94, WhoFI 94*
Button, Daniel Evan 1917- *WhoAm 94*
Button, Dick 1929- *WhoHol 92*
Button, Henry George 1913- *Who 94*
Button, John 1932- *IntWW 93*
Button, Kenneth J(ohn) 1948- *WrDr 94*
Button, Kenneth John 1922- *WhoAm 94*
Button, Kenneth Rodman 1946- *WhoAm 94*
Button, Larry Irvin 1946- *WhoWest 94*
Button, Marian Lucille 1930- *WhoAmP 93*
Button, Rena Pritsker 1925- *WhoAm 94*
Button, Richard Totten 1929- *WhoAm 94*
Button, Thomas fl. 160-?- *WhWE*
Buttons, Red 1919- *IntMPA 94, WhoCom, WhoHol 92*
Buttram, James David 1941- *WhoMW 93*
Buttram, Pat *WhoHol 92*
Buttress, Donald Reeve 1932- *Who 94*
Buttrey, Donald Wayne 1935- *WhoAm 94*
Buttrey, Douglas Norton *WrDr 94*
Buttrey, Greg 1959- *WhoMW 93*
Buttrey, Theodore Vern 1929- *Who 94*
Buttrick, David Gardner 1927- *WhoAm 94*
Buttrick, John 1715-1791 *WhAmRev*
Buttrick, John Arthur 1919- *WhoAm 94*
Buttry, Daniel Alan 1955- *WhoAm 94*
Butts, Alfred M. d1993 *NewYTBS 93 [port]*
Butts, Alfred M(osher) 1899-1993 *CurBio 93N*
Butts, Arthur Edward 1947- *WhoFI 94*
Butts, Barbara Rosalyn 1955- *WhoAm 94*
Butts, Carlyle A. 1935- *WhoBlA 94*
Butts, Charles Dana 1921- *WhoAmL 94*
Butts, Charles Lewis 1942- *WhoAmP 93*
Butts, Craig E. 1958- *WhoBlA 94*
Butts, Cyril William, Jr. 1954- *WhoAmL 94*
Butts, David Phillip 1932- *WhoScEn 94*
Butts, David Wayne 1955- *WhoMW 93*
Butts, Edna Ramon *WhoIns 94*
Butts, Edward Eugene *WhoIns 94*
Butts, Edward P. 1958- *WhoScEn 94*
Butts, George B. 1945- *WhoAmL 94*
Butts, George Francis 1923- *WhoAm 94*
Butts, H. Daniel, III 1939- *WhoAmA 93*
Butts, Herbert Clell 1924- *WhoAm 94*
Butts, Hugh F. 1926- *WhoBlA 94*
Butts, Janie Pressley 1936- *WhoBlA 94*
Butts, Marion Stevenson, Jr. *WhoAm 94*
Butts, Marion Stevenson, Jr. 1966- *WhoBlA 94*
Butts, Mary 1890-1937 *BlmGWL*
Butts, Michael C. 1948- *WhoAm 94*
Butts, Virginia *WhoAm 94*
Butts, William Randolph 1966- *WhoScEn 94*
Butts, Wilson Henry 1932- *WhoBlA 94*
Buttz, Charles William 1932- *WhoFI 94*
Butwin, Richard William 1955- *WhoFI 94*
Butynski, William 1944- *WhoAm 94*
Butz, Andrew 1931- *WhoMW 93*
Butz, Earl 1909- *IntWW 93*
Butz, Earl Lauer 1909- *WhoAmP 93*
Butz, Geneva Mae 1944- *WhoAm 94*
Butz, Michael Ray 1962- *WhoScEn 94*
Butz, Otto William 1923- *WhoAm 94*
Butzer, Karl W. 1934- *WhoScEn 94, WrDr 94*
Butzin, Peter Alfred 1944- *WhoFI 94*
Butzner, John Decker, Jr. 1917- *WhoAm 94, WhoAmL 94*
Buuck, Roland John 1935- *WhoAm 94*
Bux, William John 1946- *WhoAm 94*
Buxbaum, David Charles 1933- *WhoAmL 94*
Buxbaum, Edward d1951 *WhoHol 92*
Buxbaum, James Monroe 1928- *WhoWest 94*
Buxbaum, Martin 1912- *WrDr 94*
Buxbaum, Richard M. 1930- *WhoAm 94, WhoAmL 94, WhoWest 94*
Buxbaum, Robert 1939- *WhoAmA 93*
Buxbaum, Wiebke L. 1936- *WhoAmL 94*
Buxie, Kathy Marie 1950- *WhoMW 93*
Buxman, Karyn Lynn 1956- *WhoMW 93*
Buxton *Who 94*
Buxton, Adrian Clarence 1925- *Who 94*
Buxton, Andrew Robert Fowell 1939- *IntWW 93, Who 94*
Buxton, Anne Marie 1968- *WhoMW 93*
Buxton, Charles Ingraham, II 1924- *WhoIns 94*
Buxton, Charles Michael 1946- *WhoAmL 94*
Buxton, Cindy 1950- *WrDr 94*
Buxton, David Roden 1910- *WrDr 94*
Buxton, Georgia B. 1929- *WhoAmP 93*
Buxton, Glenn 1953- *WhoWest 94*
Buxton, John Noel 1933- *Who 94*
Buxton, Jorge Norman 1921- *WhoAm 94*
Buxton, Kenneth Arthur 1944- *WhoWest 94*
Buxton, Neil Keith 1940- *Who 94*
Buxton, Patrick Richard 1955- *WhoFI 94*
Buxton, Paul William Jex 1925- *Who 94*
Buxton, Raymond Naylor 1915- *Who 94*
Buxton, Richard Joseph 1938- *Who 94*
Buxton, Richard Millard 1948- *WhoWest 94*
Buxton, Ron *WhoAmP 93*
Buxton, Ronald Carlile 1923- *Who 94*
Buxton, Susan Elizabeth 1963- *WhoAmL 94*
Buxton, Thomas Fowell Victor 1925- *Who 94*
Buxton, Winslow H. *WhoFI 94*
Buxton, Winslow Hurlbert *WhoAm 94*
Buxton Of Alsa, Baron 1918- *Who 94*
Buydens, Robert G. 1943- *WhoAmL 94*
Buydos, Geary Stephan 1950- *WhoWest 94*
Buyer, Linda Susan 1956- *WhoScEn 94*
Buyer, Steve 1958- *CngDr 93, WhoAmP 93*
Buyer, Steve 1959- *WhoAm 94*
Buyer, Steve E. 1959- *WhoMW 93*
Buyers, John William Amerman 1928- *WhoAm 94*
Buyers, Thomas Bartlett 1926- *Who 94*
Buyers, William James Leslie 1937- *WhoAm 94*
Buyoya, Pierre 1949- *IntWW 93*
Buys, Clifford Richards 1923- *WhoFI 94*
Buys Ballot, Christoph 1817-1890 *WorScD*
Buyse, Emile Jules 1927- *WhoAm 94*
Buyse, Leone Karena 1947- *WhoAm 94*
Buyske, Donald Albert 1927-1990 *WhAm 10*
Buzacott, John Alan 1937- *WhoAm 94*
Buzak, Edward Joseph 1948- *WhoAmL 94*
Buzanis, Alexandra Christine *WhoAmL 94*
Buzard, James 1959- *ConAu 141*
Buzard, James Albert 1927- *WhoAm 94*
Buzard, Kurt Andre 1953- *WhoScEn 94, WhoWest 94*
Buzatu, Gheorghe 1939- *IntWW 93*
Buzbee, Kenneth V. 1937- *WhoAmP 93*
Buzbee, Richard Edgar 1931- *WhoAm 94*
Buzgalin, Aleksandr Valdimirovich 1954- *LoBiDrD*
Buziak, Frank T. 1947- *WhoIns 94*
Buzick, William Alonson, Jr. 1920- *WhoAm 94*
Buznego, Angel *WhoHisp 94*
Buzo, Alexander 1944- *WrDr 94*
Buzo, Alexander (John) 1944- *ConDr 93, IntDcT 2*
Buzoianu, Catalina 1938- *IntWW 93*
Buzulencia, Michael Douglas 1958- *WhoAmL 94*
Buzunis, Constantine Dino 1958- *WhoAmL 94, WhoWest 94*
Buzydlowski, Frank P. 1954- *WhoAmP 93*
Buzzanca, Lando *WhoHol 92*
Buzzard, Anthony (Farquhar) 1935- *Who 94*
Buzzard, Steven Ray 1946- *WhoAmL 94*
Buzzati, Dino 1906-1972 *EncSF 93*
Buzzell, Donald Warren 1920- *WhoAmP 93*
Buzzell, Eddie d1985 *WhoHol 92*
Buzzell, Robert Dow 1933- *WhoAm 94*
Buzzelli, Elizabeth Kane *DrAPF 93*
Buzzelli, Joseph Anthony 1907- *WhoAmA 93N*
Buzzelli, Laurence Francis 1943- *WhoMW 93*
Buzzi, Paul F. 1941- *WhoAmL 94*
Buzzi, Ruth 1936- *WhoCom, WhoHol 92*
Buzzi, Ruth 1939- *IntMPA 94*
Buzzoleni, Giovanni fl. 1682-1722 *NewGrDO*
Buzzolla, Antonio 1815-1871 *NewGrDO*
By, Andre Bernard 1955- *WhoFI 94, WhoScEn 94*
Byam, Milton S. 1922- *WhoBlA 94*
Byam, Milton Sylvester 1922-1991 *WhAm 10*
Byam, Seward Groves, Jr. 1928- *WhoFI 94*
Byambasuren, Dashiin 1942- *IntWW 93*
Byam Shaw, Nicholas Glencairn 1934- *IntWW 93, Who 94*
Byard, Carole Marie 1941- *WhoAmA 93*
Byard, John Arthur, Jr. 1922- *WhoBlA 94*
Byars, Betsy 1928- *TwCYAW*
Byars, Betsy (Cromer) 1928- *WrDr 94*
Byars, Betsy Cromer 1928- *WhoAm 94*
Byars, Dennis M. *WhoAmP 93*
Byars, Donna *WhoAmA 93*
Byars, Keith 1963- *WhoAm 94, WhoBlA 94*
Byars, Samuel D. 1954- *WhoAmL 94*
Byars, Walter Ryland, Jr. 1928- *WhoAm 94*
Byas, Thomas Haywood 1922- *WhoBlA 94*
Byas, Ulysses 1924- *WhoBlA 94*
Byas, William Herbert 1932- *WhoBlA 94*
Byatt, A. S. 1936- *BlmGEL, BlmGWL*
Byatt, A(ntonia) S(usan) 1936- *WrDr 94*
Byatt, Antonia Susan 1936- *IntWW 93, Who 94*
Byatt, Hugh Campbell 1927- *IntWW 93, Who 94*
Byatt, Ian Charles Rayner 1932- *IntWW 93, Who 94*
Byatt, Ronald Archer Campbell 1930- *Who 94*
Byatt, Ronald (Robin) Archer Campbell 1930- *IntWW 93*
Bybee, Edward Joseph 1944- *WhoAmP 93*
Bybee, Jay Scott 1953- *WhoAm 94*
Bybee, Rodger Wayne 1942- *WhoAm 94*
Bybee, Shannon Larmer, Jr. 1938- *WhoAm 94, WhoAmL 94*
Bychkov, Aleksey Mikhailovich 1928- *IntWW 93*
Bychkov, Semyon 1952- *IntWW 93*
Byck, Robert Samuel 1933- *WhoAm 94*
Byczkowski, Janusz Zbigniew 1947- *WhoMW 93, WhoScEn 94*
Bydalek, David Allen 1943- *WhoWest 94*
Bydzovsky, Viktor 1944- *WhoScEn 94*
Bye, Arthur Edwin, Jr. 1919- *WhoAm 94*
Bye, Beryl (Joyce Rayment) 1926- *WrDr 94*
Bye, James Edward 1930- *WhoAm 94*
Bye, Ranulph 1916- *WhoAmA 93*
Bye, Ranulph DeBayeux 1916- *WhoAm 94*
Bye, Raymond Erwin, Jr. 1944- *WhoAm 94*
Bye, Reed *DrAPF 93*
Byer, Adam Mikael 1963- *WhoWest 94*
Byer, Hazel Mae S. 1948- *WhoMW 93*
Byer, Kathryn Stripling *DrAPF 93*
Byer, Kathryn Stripling 1944- *ConAu 142*
Byer, Robert Louis 1942- *WhoAm 94*
Byerly, Bruce Lloyd 1945- *WhoAmL 94*
Byerly, Greg (W.) 1949- *WrDr 94*
Byerly, LeRoy James 1931- *WhoAm 94*
Byerly, Radford, Jr. 1936- *WhoAm 94, WhoScEn 94*
Byerly, Rex R. *WhoAmP 93*
Byerly, Theodore Carroll 1902-1990 *WhAm 10*
Byerrum, Richard Uglow 1920- *WhoAm 94*
Byers, A. M. 1837-1900 *EncABHB 9*
Byers, Brent Eugene 1950- *WhoAm 94*
Byers, Dallas Canon *EncABHB 9*
Byers, Eben McBurney *EncABHB 9*
Byers, Fleur *WhoAmA 93*
Byers, Francis Robert 1920- *WhoAmP 93*
Byers, George William 1923- *WhoAm 94*
Byers, Horace (Robert) 1906- *WrDr 94*
Byers, Horace Robert 1906- *IntWW 93, WhoAm 94*
Byers, Jim Don 1954- *WhoScEn 94*
Byers, Jo Ann 1947- *WhoMW 93*
Byers, John Frederic *EncABHB 9*
Byers, John Kaye 1930- *WhoAmL 94*
Byers, John R. 1955- *WhoAmL 94*
Byers, Kenneth Vernon 1940- *WhoFI 94*
Byers, L. Eugene *WhoAmP 93*
Byers, Marianne 1941- *WhoBlA 94*
Byers, Maurice (Hearne) 1917- *Who 94*
Byers, Maurice Hearne 1917- *IntWW 93*
Byers, Nancy d1980 *WhoHol 92*
Byers, Nina 1930- *WhoAm 94, WhoScEn 94*
Byers, Pamela McLucas 1947- *WhoWest 94*
Byers, Paul Duncan 1922- *Who 94*
Byers, Raymond Lester, Jr. 1943- *WhoMW 93*
Byers, Robin Wayne 1954- *WhoMW 93*
Byers, Stephen John 1953- *Who 94*
Byers, Walter 1922- *WhoAm 94*

Byers Brown, (Dorothy) Betty 1927- *WrDr 94*
Byers-Jones, Charmian 1913- *WhoWest 94*
Byers-Pevitts, Beverley 1939- *WhoMW 93*
Byford, Lawrence 1925- *Who 94*
Byford, Roy d1939 *WhoHol 92*
Bygraves, Max 1922- *WhoHol 92*
Bygraves, Max Walter 1922- *Who 94*
Bygraves, May 1922- *IntMPA 94*
Byhan, Gottlieb fl. 1800- *EncNAR*
Byington, Cyrus 1793-1868 *EncNAR*
Byington, George David 1952- *WhoFI 94*
Byington, Homer Morrison, III 1934- *WhoAm 94*
Byington, Mary 1918- *WhoAmP 93*
Byington, S. John *WhoAm 94, WhoAmL 94*
Byington, Spring d1971 *WhoHol 92*
Bykat, Alexander 1940- *WhoAm 94*
Byker, Gary 1920- *WhoAmP 93*
Byker, Harlan Jay 1954- *WhoMW 93*
Bykhovsky, Arkadi Gregory 1943- *WhoAm 94*
Bykofsky, Seth Darryl 1956- *WhoAmL 94*
Bykov, Rolan *WhoHol 92*
Bykov, Vasily Viadimirovich 1924- *IntWW 93*
Byland, Peter *WhoAm 94, WhoFI 94*
Byler, Gary Clarence 1957- *WhoAmP 93*
Byles, Bobby d1969 *WhoHol 92*
Byles, Joan Montgomery *DrAPF 93*
Byles, Mather c. 1706-1788 *WhAmRev*
Byles, Robert Valmore 1937- *WhoAmP 93*
Bylinsky, Gene (Michael) 1930- *WrDr 94*
Bylinsky, Gene Michael 1930- *WhoAm 94*
Bylot, Robert fl. 160-?- *WhWE*
Bylsma, Frederick Wilburn 1957- *WhoScEn 94*
Bylund, David Bruce 1946- *WhoMW 93*
Bylund, David John 1954- *WhoWest 94*
Byman, Robert Leslie 1945- *WhoAm 94, WhoAmL 94*
Bynam, Sawyer Lee, III 1933- *WhoBlA 94*
Byner, Earnest Alexander 1962- *WhoAm 94, WhoBlA 94*
Byner, John *WhoHol 92*
Byner, John 1937- *WhoCom*
Bynes, Frank Howard, Jr. 1950- *WhoBlA 94, WhoScEn 94*
Byng *Who 94*
Byng, Douglas d1987 *WhoHol 92*
Byng, John 1743-1813 *DcNaB MP*
Bynoe, Hilda Louisa 1921- *Who 94*
Bynoe, John Garvey 1926- *WhoBlA 94*
Bynoe, Peter C. B. 1951- *WhoBlA 94*
Bynoe, Peter Charles Bernard 1951- *WhoAm 94, WhoWest 94*
Bynum, Barbara Stewart 1936- *WhoScEn 94*
Bynum, E. Anderson 1922- *WhoAmA 93*
Bynum, George T., III 1951- *WhoAm 94, WhoFI 94*
Bynum, Horace Charles, Sr. 1916- *WhoBlA 94*
Bynum, Jack Edward, Jr. 1929- *WhoAm 94*
Bynum, Raleigh Wesley 1936- *WhoBlA 94*
Bynum, Valerie Callymore 1942- *WhoBlA 94*
Byowitz, Michael Harvey 1952- *WhoAmL 94*
Byram, James Asberry, Jr. 1954- *WhoAmL 94*
Byram, Ronald d1919 *WhoHol 92*
Byram, Stanley Harold 1906- *WhoAmP 93*
Byrant, Sophie 1850-1922 *DcNaB MP*
Byrd, Albert Alexander 1927- *WhoBlA 94*
Byrd, Alma *WhoAmP 93*
Byrd, Andrew Wayne 1954- *WhoAmL 94*
Byrd, Anthony d1925 *WhoHol 92*
Byrd, Arthur W. 1943- *WhoBlA 94*
Byrd, Benjamin Franklin, Jr. 1918- *WhoAm 94*
Byrd, Bette Jean 1928- *WhoAm 94*
Byrd, Bobby *DrAPF 93*
Byrd, C. Don 1940- *WhoIns 94*
Byrd, Camolia Alcorn *WhoBlA 94*
Byrd, Caruth C. 1941- *IntMPA 94*
Byrd, Chris *WhoAm 94*
Byrd, Christine Waterman Swent 1951- *WhoAm 94, WhoAmL 94*
Byrd, Corine Williams 1946- *WhoBlA 94*
Byrd, D. Gibson 1923- *WhoAmA 93*
Byrd, Dan R. 1944- *WhoAmP 93*
Byrd, David *WhoHol 92*
Byrd, David Lamar 1922- *WhoAm 94*
Byrd, Don *DrAPF 93*
Byrd, Edward Travis 1946- *WhoAmP 93*
Byrd, Edwin R. 1920- *WhoBlA 94*
Byrd, Enola 1927- *WhoAmP 93*
Byrd, Estell Glynn 1933- *WhoFI 94*
Byrd, Frederick E. 1918- *WhoBlA 94*
Byrd, George Edward 1941- *WhoBlA 94*
Byrd, Gill Arnette 1961- *WhoAm 94, WhoBlA 94, WhoWest 94*
Byrd, Gwendolyn Pauline 1943- *WhoAm 94*
Byrd, Harold W. *WhoAmP 93*
Byrd, Harriett Elizabeth 1926- *WhoAmP 93, WhoBlA 94*
Byrd, Harry Flood, Jr. 1914- *IntWW 93, WhoAm 94, WhoAmP 93*
Byrd, Helen P. 1943- *WhoBlA 94*
Byrd, Herbert Lawrence, Jr. 1943- *WhoBlA 94*
Byrd, Isaac, Jr. 1952- *WhoBlA 94*
Byrd, Isaac Burlin 1925- *WhoAm 94*
Byrd, James W. 1925- *WhoBlA 94*
Byrd, Jan G. 1942- *WhoAmP 93*
Byrd, Jerry 1947- *WhoAmA 93*
Byrd, Jerry Stewart 1935- *WhoBlA 94*
Byrd, Joan Eda 1942- *WhoBlA 94*
Byrd, Joann Kathleen 1943- *WhoAm 94*
Byrd, Jonathan Eugene 1952- *WhoFI 94*
Byrd, Joseph Keys 1953- *WhoBlA 94*
Byrd, Katie W. *WhoBlA 94*
Byrd, Kevin B. 1951- *WhoAmL 94*
Byrd, Larry Donald 1936- *WhoAm 94*
Byrd, Linward Tonnett 1921- *WhoAm 94, WhoAmL 94*
Byrd, Lloyd Garland 1923- *WhoAm 94*
Byrd, Lorenda Sue 1941- *WhoMW 93*
Byrd, Lumus, Jr. 1942- *WhoBlA 94*
Byrd, Manford, Jr. 1928- *WhoBlA 94*
Byrd, Marc Robert 1954- *WhoWest 94*
Byrd, Mary Laager 1935- *WhoAm 94, WhoScEn 94*
Byrd, Mary Willing 1740-1814 *BlmGWL*
Byrd, Max 1942- *WrDr 94*
Byrd, Max (W.) 1942- *ConAu 142*
Byrd, Melvin L. 1935- *WhoBlA 94*
Byrd, Melvin Leon 1935- *AfrAmG [port]*
Byrd, Michael 1948- *WhoAmL 94*
Byrd, Michael Kenneth 1955- *WhoMW 93*
Byrd, Michaele Abner 1949- *WhoFI 94*
Byrd, Milton Bruce 1922- *WhoAm 94*
Byrd, Nellie J. 1924- *WhoBlA 94*
Byrd, Percy L. 1937- *WhoBlA 94*
Byrd, R. Wayne 1947- *WhoAmL 94*
Byrd, Ralph d1952 *WhoHol 92*
Byrd, Richard E. d1957 *WhoHol 92*
Byrd, Richard Edward 1931- *WhoAm 94, WhoMW 93*
Byrd, Richard Evelyn 1888-1957 *WhWE [port]*
Byrd, Richard Hays 1939- *WhoAm 94, WhoFI 94*
Byrd, Robert C. 1917- *CngDr 93, IntWW 93, WhoAmP 93*
Byrd, Robert Carlyle 1917- *WhoAm 94*
Byrd, Robert John 1942- *WhoAmA 93*
Byrd, Robert Lee 1949- *WhoAmP 93*
Byrd, Roger C. 1954- *WhoAmP 93*
Byrd, Ronald Dallas 1934- *WhoWest 94*
Byrd, Sherman Clifton 1928- *WhoBlA 94*
Byrd, Stephen Fred 1928- *WhoAm 94*
Byrd, Stephen Timothy 1957- *WhoAmL 94*
Byrd, Taylor 1940- *WhoBlA 94*
Byrd, Warren Edgar, II 1950- *WhoAm 94, WhoAmL 94*
Byrd, William, II 1674-1744 *DcLB 140 [port]*
Byrd, William, III 1728-1777 *WhAmRev*
Byrd, William Floyd 1943- *WhoAmP 93*
Byrd, William Garlen 1947- *WhoMW 93, WhoScEn 94*
Byrding, Holger 1891-1980 *NewGrDO*
Byrd-Lawler, Barbara Ann 1952- *WhoAm 94*
Byrd-Nethery, Miriam *WhoHol 92*
Byrdsong, Ricky *WhoBlA 94*
Byrd-Tillman, Jacqueline Pearl 1946- *WhoAmL 94*
Byrens, Myer d1933 *WhoHol 92*
Byrn, Stephen R. 1944- *WhoAm 94*
Byrne, Anne 1943- *WhoHol 92*
Byrne, Arthur Dillard 1918- *WhoAmL 94*
Byrne, Brendan Thomas 1924- *WhoAmP 93*
Byrne, Carol Susan 1943- *WhoAm 94*
Byrne, Catherine *WhoAm 94*
Byrne, Cecily d1975 *WhoHol 92*
Byrne, Charles Joseph 1943- *WhoAmA 93*
Byrne, Clarence (Askew) 1903- *Who 94*
Byrne, Cynthia Mary 1957- *WhoAmL 94*
Byrne, Daniel William 1958- *WhoScEn 94*
Byrne, David 1952- *IntMPA 94, IntWW 93, WhoAm 94, WhoHol 92*
Byrne, Dennis Michael 1947- *WhoMW 93*
Byrne, Donn E. 1931- *WrDr 94*
Byrne, Donn Erwin 1931- *WhoAm 94*
Byrne, Douglas Norman 1924- *Who 94*
Byrne, Eddie d1981 *WhoHol 92*
Byrne, Edward *DrAPF 93*
Byrne, Edward Blake 1935- *WhoAm 94*
Byrne, Francis d1923 *WhoHol 92*
Byrne, Frank Loyola 1928- *WhoAm 94, WhoMW 93*
Byrne, Gabriel 1950- *IntMPA 94, IntWW 93, WhoHol 92*
Byrne, Gary Cecil 1942- *WhoAm 94*
Byrne, George Melvin 1933- *WhoScEn 94, WhoWest 94*
Byrne, Gerard Anthony 1944- *WhoAm 94*
Byrne, Granville Bland, III 1952- *WhoAmL 94*
Byrne, James A. d1927 *WhoHol 92*
Byrne, James Frederick 1931- *WhoAm 94*
Byrne, James M. 1940- *WhoWest 94*
Byrne, James Peter 1956- *WhoWest 94*
Byrne, James Thomas, Jr. 1939- *WhoAm 94*
Byrne, Jane 1934- *WhoAmP 93*
Byrne, Jerome Camillus 1925- *WhoAm 94*
Byrne, John d1924 *WhoHol 92*
Byrne, John 1940- *ConDr 93, WrDr 94*
Byrne, John Anthony 1945- *Who 94*
Byrne, John Edward 1925- *WhoAm 94*
Byrne, John Joseph, Jr. 1932- *WhoAm 94, WhoFI 94*
Byrne, John Keyes *Who 94*
Byrne, John Keyes 1926- *WhoAm 94*
Byrne, John N. 1925- *WhoFI 94*
Byrne, John P. 1936- *WhoIns 94*
Byrne, John V. 1928- *IntWW 93*
Byrne, John Vincent 1928- *WhoAm 94, WhoScEn 94, WhoWest 94*
Byrne, Joseph 1923- *WhoAm 94*
Byrne, Kathleen A. 1936- *WhoAmP 93*
Byrne, Kevin Francis 1952- *WhoFI 94*
Byrne, Kevin O. *DrAPF 93*
Byrne, Kevin Thomas 1939- *WhoAmL 94*
Byrne, Leslie L. 1946- *CngDr 93*
Byrne, Leslie Larkin 1946- *WhoAm 94, WhoAmP 93*
Byrne, Michael *WhoHol 92*
Byrne, Michael Joseph 1928- *WhoFI 94, WhoMW 93*
Byrne, Niall 1973- *WhoHol 92*
Byrne, Noel Thomas 1943- *WhoFI 94, WhoWest 94*
Byrne, Olivia Sherrill 1957- *WhoAmL 94*
Byrne, Patrick Edward, II 1952- *WhoAmP 93*
Byrne, Patrick Eugene 1965- *WhoFI 94*
Byrne, Patrick James 1949- *WhoFI 94*
Byrne, Patrick Michael 1952- *WhoAm 94*
Byrne, Patsy 1933- *WhoHol 92*
Byrne, Paul Laurence 1932- *Who 94*
Byrne, Peggy 1949- *WhoAmP 93*
Byrne, Peter 1928- *WhoHol 92*
Byrne, Richard Hill 1915- *WhoAm 94*
Byrne, Robert 1930- *WrDr 94*
Byrne, Robert J. 1943- *WhoIns 94*
Byrne, Robert James 1953- *WhoFI 94*
Byrne, Robert Leo 1930- *WhoWest 94*
Byrne, Robert William 1958- *WhoAmL 94*
Byrne, Stuart J(ames) 1913- *EncSF 93*
Byrne, Terence Niall 1942- *Who 94*
Byrne, Thomas Ray 1958- *WhoFI 94*
Byrne, William Matthew, Jr. 1930- *WhoAm 94, WhoAmL 94, WhoWest 94*
Byrne, William Patrick 1959- *WhoMW 93*
Byrnes, Arthur Francis 1917- *WhoAm 94*
Byrnes, Burke *WhoHol 92*
Byrnes, Christopher Ian 1949- *WhoAm 94, WhoScEn 94*
Byrnes, Edd 1933- *IntMPA 94, WhoHol 92*
Byrnes, Frederick, Jr. *DrAPF 93*
Byrnes, James Bernard 1917- *WhoAm 94, WhoAmA 93*
Byrnes, James Lawrence 1952- *WhoAmP 93*
Byrnes, John Carroll 1939- *WhoAmP 93*
Byrnes, John Joseph 1942- *WhoScEn 94*
Byrnes, Michael Francis 1957- *WhoScEn 94*
Byrnes, R. John 1948- *WhoMW 93*
Byrnes, Robert Charles, Jr. 1958- *WhoFI 94*
Byrnes, Robert Francis 1917- *WhoAm 94, WrDr 94*
Byrnes, Thomas H., Jr. *WhoAmP 93*
Byrnes, Victor Allen 1906- *WhoAm 94*
Byrnes, William G. *WhoFI 94*
Byrnes, William George 1959- *WhoAmL 94*
Byrnes, William Joseph 1940- *WhoAmL 94*
Byrnn, Edward Paul 1942- *WhoAmP 93*
Byrnside, Oscar Jehu, Jr. 1935- *WhoAm 94*
Byrom, Fletcher Lauman 1918- *WhoAm 94*
Byrom, John 1692-1763 *BlmGEL*
Byrom, Peter Craig 1927- *Who 94*
Byron, Baron 1950- *Who 94*
Byron, Lord 1788-1824 *NewGrDO*
Byron, A. S. d1943 *WhoHol 92*
Byron, (Augusta) Ada, Countess of Lovelace 1815-1852 *DcNaB MP*
Byron, Allan d1945 *WhoHol 92*
Byron, Arthur d1943 *WhoHol 92*
Byron, Beverly B. 1932- *WhoAmP 93, WhoWomW 91*
Byron, Beverly Butcher 1932- *WhoAm 94*
Byron, Charles Anthony 1919- *WhoAmA 93*
Byron, Cheryl *DrAPF 93*
Byron, Frederick William, Jr. 1938- *WhoAm 94*
Byron, George Gordon, Lord 1788-1824 *BlmGEL [port]*
Byron, Gilbert *DrAPF 93*
Byron, H(enry) J(ames) 1835-1884 *IntDcT 2*
Byron, Jean *WhoHol 92*
Byron, Jeffrey 1955- *WhoHol 92*
Byron, John 1723-1786 *AmRev, WhAmRev, WhWE*
Byron, Joseph Winston 1930- *WhoScEn 94*
Byron, Kathleen 1922- *WhoHol 92*
Byron, Marion d1985 *WhoHol 92*
Byron, Michael 1954- *WhoAmA 93*
Byron, Paul d1959 *WhoHol 92*
Byron, Richard J. 1938- *WhoIns 94*
Byron, Rita Ellen Cooney *WhoMW 93*
Byron, Royal d1943 *WhoHol 92*
Byron, Walter d1972 *WhoHol 92*
Byron, William James 1927- *WhoAm 94*
Byrt, Edwin Andrew 1932- *WrDr 94*
Byrt, (Henry) John 1929- *Who 94*
Byrum, Charles L. 1944- *WhoAmL 94*
Byrum, Dianne 1954- *WhoAmP 93*
Byrum, Donald Roy 1942- *WhoAmA 93*
Byrum, John 1947- *IntMPA 94*
Byrum, Judith Miriam 1943- *WhoMW 93*
Byrum, Mark White, Jr. 1955- *WhoAmL 94*
Byrum, Marni Elaine 1955- *WhoAmL 94*
Byrum, McAuley Carnavious, Jr. 1938- *WhoFI 94*
Byrum, Ruthven Holmes 1896- *WhoAmA 93N*
Bysiewicz, Susan *WhoAmP 93*
Bystedt, (Petrus) Gosta 1929- *IntWW 93*
Bystryn, Jean-Claude 1938- *WhoAm 94*
Bywater, David Llewellyn 1937- *Who 94*
Bywater, Hector Charles 1884-1940 *EncSF 93*
Bywater, William Harold 1920- *WhoAm 94, WhoFI 94*
Bywaters, David R. 1932- *WhoAm 94*
Bywaters, Eric George Lapthorne 1910- *Who 94*
Bywaters, Jerry 1906- *WhAm 10*
Byyny, Richard Lee 1939- *WhoAm 94*
Byzantine, Julian Sarkis 1945- *IntWW 93*
Byzewski, Mark T. 1960- *WhoWest 94*
Bzik, David John 1955- *WhoScEn 94*
Bzoskie, James Steven 1949- *WhoAm 94*

C

Caan, James 1939- *IntWW 93, WhoHol 92*
Caan, James 1940- *WhoAm 94*
Cabai, Kevin Arthur 1958- *WhoMW 93*
Caballe, Montserrat *IntWW 93*
Caballe, Montserrat 1933- *NewGrDO, Who 94*
Caballero, Alfredo A. *WhoHisp 94*
Caballero, Anna Marie 1954- *WhoHisp 94*
Caballero, Bertha *WhoHisp 94*
Caballero, Eddie 1942- *WhoHisp 94*
Caballero, Eduardo *WhoHisp 94*
Caballero, Fernan *BlmGWL*
Caballero, Katia *WhoHol 92*
Caballero, Manuel Fernandez 1835-1906 *NewGrDO*
Caballero, Mario Gustavo 1959- *WhoFI 94*
Caballero, Raymond C. 1942- *WhoHisp 94*
Caballero, Roberto 1958- *WhoHisp 94*
Caballero, Santiago 1936- *WhoHisp 94*
Caballero, Servando 1942- *WhoHisp 94*
Caballero Calderon, Eduardo d1993 *IntWW 93N*
Caballero Calderon, Eduardo 1910- *IntWW 93*
Caballes, Romeo Lopez 1925- *WhoScEn 94*
Caballone, Michele 1692-1740 *NewGrDO*
Cabalquinto, Luis *DrAPF 93*
Caban, Beatriz L. 1962- *WhoHisp 94*
Cabán, Delia 1957- *WhoHisp 94*
Cabán, Juan Pedro, Jr. 1931- *WhoHisp 94*
Cabán, Luis A. 1939- *WhoHisp 94*
Cabán, Luis C., Jr. 1947- *WhoHisp 94*
Cabana, Veneracion Garganta 1942- *WhoAsA 94*
Cabanas, Humberto 1951- *WhoHisp 94*
Cabañas, Lázaro V. 1956- *WhoHisp 94*
Cabanero, Eladio 1930- *DcLB 134 [port]*
Cabanis, Jose 1922- *IntWW 93*
Cabaniss, Charles Davis 1927- *WhoAmL 94*
Cabaniss, Gerry Henderson 1935- *WhoScEn 94*
Cabaniss, Thomas Edward 1949- *WhoAm 94*
Cabaniss, W. J., Jr. 1938- *WhoAmP 93*
Cabanne, Christy d1950 *WhoHol 92*
Cabanting, George Paul 1953- *WhoAsA 94*
Cabanya, Mary Louise 1947- *WhoWest 94*
Cabaret, Joseph Ronald 1934- *WhoAm 94, WhoScEn 94*
Cabasso, Israel 1942- *WhoScEn 94*
Cabat, Erni 1914- *SmATA 74 [port]*
Cabaup, Joseph John 1940- *WhoScEn 94*
Cabbage, William Austin 1934- *WhoScEn 94*
Cabbell, Edward Joseph 1946- *WhoBlA 94*
Cabe, Gloria Burford 1941- *WhoAmP 93*
Cabe, Jerry Lynn 1953- *WhoScEn 94*
Cabeceiras, James 1930- *WrDr 94*
Cabel, Marie(-Josephe) 1827-1885 *NewGrDO*
Cabell, Elizabeth Arlisse 1947- *WhoAm 94*
Cabell, Fredrick, Jr. 1961- *WhoAmL 94*
Cabell, James Branch 1879-1958 *EncSF 93*
Cabell, William 1730-1798 *WhAmRev*
Cabello, Aida *WhoHisp 94*
Cabello, Marco V. 1960- *WhoHisp 94*
Cabello, Robert 1950- *WhoHisp 94*

Cabello-Argandoña, Roberto 1939- *WhoHisp 94*
Cabello de Carbonera, Mercedes 1845-1907 *BlmGWL*
Cabete, Adelaide 1867-1935 *BlmGWL*
Cabey, Alfred Arthur, Jr. 1935- *WhoFI 94*
Cabeza de Baca, Fernando E. 1937- *WhoHisp 94*
Cabeza De Vaca, Alvar Nunez c. 1490-c. 1564 *WhWE*
Cabeza de Vaca, James Hugo 1948- *WhoHisp 94*
Cabezas, Heriberto, Jr. 1952- *WhoHisp 94*
Cabezas, Rafael 1937- *WhoHisp 94*
Cabezut, Alejandro 1962- *WhoHisp 94*
Cabezut-Ortiz, Delores J. 1948- *WhoHisp 94*
Cabibbo, Nicola 1935- *IntWW 93*
Cabieles, Lucy 1924- *WhoHisp 94*
Cable, Charles Allen 1932- *WhoAm 94, WhoScEn 94*
Cable, Donald Aubrey 1927- *WhoAm 94, WhoAmL 94*
Cable, George Washington 1844-1925 *AmSocL*
Cable, Howard Reid 1920- *WhoAm 94*
Cable, James (Eric) 1920- *Who 94*
Cable, John Franklin 1941- *WhoAm 94, WhoAmL 94*
Cable, Maxine Roth *WhoAmA 93*
Cable, Paul Andrew 1939- *WhoAm 94, WhoAmL 94*
Cable, Richard Albert 1950- *WhoWest 94*
Cable-Alexander, Patrick (Desmond William) 1936- *Who 94*
Cabo, Federico *WhoHisp 94*
Caborn, Richard George 1943- *Who 94*
Cabot, Bruce d1972 *WhoHol 92*
Cabot, Ceil *WhoHol 92*
Cabot, Charles Codman, Jr. 1930- *WhoAm 94, WhoAmL 94*
Cabot, Elliott d1938 *WhoHol 92*
Cabot, Harold 1929- *WhoAm 94*
Cabot, Howard Ross 1947- *WhoAmL 94*
Cabot, Hugh 1930- *WhoAmA 93*
Cabot, Hugh, III 1930- *WhoWest 94*
Cabot, John c. 1450-c. 1498 *WhWE*
Cabot, John G. L. 1934- *WhoAm 94, WhoFI 94*
Cabot, John York *EncSF 93*
Cabot, Lewis Pickering 1937- *WhoFI 94*
Cabot, Louis Wellington 1921- *WhoAm 94*
Cabot, Paul Codman 1898- *IntWW 93*
Cabot, Sebastian d1977 *WhoHol 92*
Cabot, Sebastian c. 1476-1557 *WhWE [port]*
Cabot, Susan d1986 *WhoHol 92*
Cabot, Thomas Dudley 1897- *WhoAm 94*
Cabral, Alfredo Lopes 1946- *IntWW 93*
Cabral, Allen Manuel 1944- *WhoHisp 94*
Cabral, Antonio F. *WhoAmP 93*
Cabral, Bernardo Joseph 1944- *WhoAmL 94*
Cabral, Darien 1949- *WhoWest 94*
Cabral, Goncalo Velho fl. 143-?- *WhWE*
Cabral, Joao 1599-1669 *WhWE*
Cabral, Judith Ann 1951- *WhoAm 94, WhoFI 94*
Cabral, Luis de Almeida 1931- *IntWW 93*
Cabral, Olga *DrAPF 93*
Cabral, Othon 1942- *WhoFI 94*

Cabral, Pedro Alvares c. 1467-c. 1520 *WhWE [port]*
Cabral, Ramon 1956- *WhoHisp 94*
Cabral De Melo Neto, Joao *ConWorW 93*
Cabral de Melo Neto, Joao 1920- *ConLC 76 [port]*
Cabranes, José A. 1940- *WhoHisp 94*
Cabranes, Jose Alberto 1940- *WhoAm 94, WhoAmL 94*
Cabre, Mario d1990 *WhoHol 92*
Cabrera, Alejandro Leopoldo 1950- *WhoScEn 94*
Cabrera, Angelina *WhoAmP 93, WhoHisp 94*
Cabrera, Cesar Trinidad 1935- *WhoAsA 94*
Cabrera, Charles R. 1944- *WhoHisp 94*
Cabrera, Eloise J. 1932- *WhoBlA 94*
Cabrera, Emma Agramonte 1938- *WhoHisp 94*
Cabrera, Francisco 1966- *WhoHisp 94*
Cabrera, George Albert 1946- *WhoHisp 94*
Cabrera, Gilda 1949- *WhoHisp 94*
Cabrera, James S. *WhoHisp 94*
Cabrera, Lydia 1899- *BlmGWL*
Cabrera, Manuel Vasquez 1931- *WhoHisp 94*
Cabrera, Nestor L. 1957- *WhoHisp 94*
Cabrera, Richard Anthony 1941- *WhoHisp 94*
Cabrera, Rosa Maria 1918- *WhoHisp 94*
Cabrera-Baukus, María B. 1954- *WhoHisp 94*
Cabrera Infante, G(uillermo) 1929- *ConWorW 93*
Cabrera Infante, Guillermo 1929- *HispLC [port], IntWW 93*
Cabrillo, Juan Rodriguez c. 1500-1543 *WhWE*
Cabrini, Frances Xavier 1850-1917 *AmSocL, HisWorL [port]*
Cabrini, Frances Xavier 1850-1918 *DcAmReB 2*
Caccamo, Nicholas James 1944- *WhoAm 94*
Caccamo, Pedro 1936- *WhoHisp 94*
Cacchione, Patrick Joseph 1959- *WhoMW 93*
Caccia, Harold Anthony 1905-1990 *WhAm 10*
Cacciatore, Ronald Keith 1937- *WhoFI 94*
Cacciatore, S. Sammy, Jr. 1942- *WhoAm 94*
Cacciatore, Vera 1911- *WrDr 94*
Cacciavillan, Agostino 1926- *WhoAm 94*
Caccini, Francesca 1587-1637 *NewGrDO*
Caccini, Giulio 1551-1618 *NewGrDO*
Caccini, Settimia 1591-c. 1660 *NewGrDO*
Caccini Family *NewGrDO*
Cacciolfi, William Peter, Jr. 1960- *WhoMW 93*
Cacella, Estevao 1585-1630 *WhWE*
Caceres, Alfredo *WhoHisp 94*
Caceres, Esther de 1903-1971 *BlmGWL*
Caceres, John 1909- *WhoHisp 94*
Caceres, Virginia *WhoHisp 94*
Caceres Contreras, Carlos 1940- *IntWW 93*
Cachapero, Emilya *DrAPF 93*
Cacharel, Jean 1932- *IntWW 93*
Cachelin, Francy 1923- *Who 94*

Cacheris, James C. 1933- *WhoAm 94, WhoAmL 94*
Cacheris, Plato 1929- *WhoAmL 94*
Cacheux, Denise Jeanne Henriette 1932- *WhoWomW 91*
Cachia, Pierre (Jacques Elie) 1921- *WrDr 94*
Cachia, Pierre Jacques 1921- *WhoAm 94*
Cacho, Patrick Thomas 1950- *WhoWest 94*
Cachola, Romy Munoz 1938- *WhoAmP 93*
Cacicedo, Alberto Jesus 1952- *WhoHisp 94*
Cacicedo, Paul 1927- *WhoHisp 94*
Cacioppo, John Terrance 1951- *WhoAm 94*
Cacioppo, Paul Phillip 1939- *WhoAmL 94*
Cacioppo, Peter Thomas 1947- *WhoWest 94*
Cacouris, Elias Michael 1929- *WhoScEn 94*
Cacoyannis, Michael 1922- *ConTFT 11, IntMPA 94, IntWW 93, Who 94*
Cadahia, Aurelio *WhoHisp 94*
Cadamosto, Alvise Da 1432-1488 *WhWE*
Cadarette, John Robert, Jr. 1958- *WhoAmL 94*
Cadaval, Olivia 1943- *WhoHisp 94*
Cadbury, Adrian *Who 94*
Cadbury, (George) Adrian (Hayhurst) 1929- *IntWW 93, Who 94*
Cadbury, Dominic *Who 94*
Cadbury, (Nicholas) Dominic 1940- *IntWW 93, Who 94*
Cadbury, George Woodall 1907- *Who 94*
Cadbury, Henry Joel 1883-1974 *DcAmReB 2*
Cadbury, John 1801-1889 *DcNaB MP*
Cadbury, Peter (Egbert) 1918- *Who 94*
Cadbury-Brown, Henry Thomas 1913- *IntWW 93, Who 94*
Cadd, Gary Genoris 1953- *WhoWest 94*
Caddell, Foster 1921- *WhoAmA 93*
Caddell, John A. 1910- *WhoAm 94*
Cadden, Joan *WhoAmP 93*
Cadden, Thomas Scott 1923- *WrDr 94*
Caddoe, Sean *DrAPF 93*
Caddy, (Michael) Douglas 1938- *WrDr 94*
Caddy, Edmund Harrington Homer, Jr. 1928- *WhoAm 94*
Caddy, Ian (Graham) 1947- *NewGrDO*
Caddy, John *DrAPF 93*
Caddy, Michael Douglas 1938- *WhoAmL 94*
Cade, Alfred Jackal 1931- *AfrAmG [port], WhoBlA 94*
Cade, Harold Edward 1929- *WhoBlA 94*
Cade, Jack d1450 *BlmGEL*
Cade, John A. 1929- *WhoAmP 93*
Cade, Lillian Ferrara *WhoAmP 93*
Cade, Robin 1930- *WrDr 94*
Cade, Tommories 1961- *WhoBlA 94*
Cade, Toni 1939- *WhoBlA 94*
Cade, Toni *BlkWr 2*
Cade, Valarie Swain 1952- *WhoBlA 94*
Cade, Walter, III *WhoAm 94, WhoBlA 94*
Cade, Walter, III 1936- *WhoAmA 93*
Cade, William fl. 1150- *DcNaB MP*
Cadell, Colin Simson 1905- *Who 94*
Cadell, Jean d1967 *WhoHol 92*
Cadell, John (Frederick) 1929- *Who 94*
Cadell, Patrick Moubray 1941- *Who 94*

Cadell, Selina WhoHol 92
Cadell, Simon John 1950- Who 94
Cadena, Carlos C. WhoHisp 94
Cadena, Emilio E., II 1964- WhoHisp 94
Cadena, Guadalupe, Jr. 1966- WhoHisp 94
Cadena, Michael Manuel 1962- WhoHisp 94
Cadena, Val, Sr. 1929- WhoHisp 94
Cadenas, Ricardo A. 1953- WhoHisp 94
Cadenhead, Alfred Paul 1926- WhoAm 94
Cades, Julius Russell 1904- WhoAm 94, WhoAmL 94, WhoWest 94
Cades, Stewart Russell 1942- WhoAm 94
Cadge, William Fleming 1924- WhoAm 94
Cadieux, Leo 1908- Who 94
Cadieux, Michael Eugene 1940- WhoAmA 93
Cadieux, Pierre H. 1948- IntWW 93, WhoAm 94
Cadieux, Robert D. 1937- WhoAm 94, WhoFI 94
Cadieux, Roger Joseph 1945- WhoAm 94
Cadigan, Pat 1953- EncSF 93
Cadigan, Patrick Joseph 1936- WhoAm 94
Cadigan, Richard Foster 1930- WhoAmL 94
Cadilla, Manuel Alberto 1912- WhoHisp 94
Cadillac, Louise Roman WhoAmA 93
Cadle, Dean DrAPF 93
Cadle, Farris W(illiam) 1952- WrDr 94
Cadle, Ray Kenneth 1906- WhoAmA 93
Cadman, Baron 1938- Who 94
Cadman, Charles Wakefield 1881-1946 NewGrDO
Cadman, (D) (Albert) Edward 1918- Who 94
Cadman, Joshua WhoHol 92
Cadman, Theodore Wesley 1940- WhoAm 94
Cadman, Wilson Kennedy 1927- WhoAm 94
Cadmus, Paul 1904- WhoAm 94, WhoAmA 93
Cadmus, Robert Randall, Jr. 1946- WhoMW 93
Cadmus, William Albert 1945- WhoFI 94
Cadnum, Michael DrAPF 93
Cadogan, Earl 1914- Who 94
Cadogan, Edward John Patrick 1939- WhoWest 94
Cadogan, John (Ivan George) 1930- Who 94
Cadogan, John Ivan George 1930- IntWW 93
Cadogan, Marjorie A. 1960- WhoBlA 94
Cadogan, Mary (Rose) 1928- WrDr 94
Cadogan, Peter William 1921- Who 94
Cadogan, William J. 1948- WhoAm 94, WhoFI 94
Cadorette, Mary WhoHol 92
Cadoria, Sherian Grace 1940- AfrAmG [port], WhoBlA 94
Cadorin, Ettor 1876-1952 WhoAmA 93N
Cadou, Peter Brosius 1931- WhoMW 93
Cadugan, Richard Grant 1957- WhoFI 94
Caduto, Ralph 1927- WhoScEn 94
Cadwalader, John 1742-1786 AmRev, WhAmRev
Cadwalader, Lambert 1743-1823 WhAmRev
Cadwalder, Hugh Maurice 1924- WhoScEn 94
Cadwallader, Fay Margaret 1964- WhoWest 94
Cadwallader, Floyd Blair 1939- WhoMW 93
Cadwallader, Howard George 1919- Who 94
Cadwallader, James Kerrick 1927- WhoAmP 93
Cadwallader, John d1991 Who 94N
Cadwallader, John I. 1952- WhoAmL 94
Cadwell, David Robert 1934- WhoAmL 94
Cadwell, Franchellie Margaret 1937- WhoAm 94
Cady, Dennis Vern 1944- WhoAmA 93
Cady, Edwin H(arrison) 1917- WrDr 94
Cady, Edwin Harrison 1917- WhoAm 94
Cady, Elwyn Loomis, Jr. 1926- WhoMW 93, WhoScEn 94
Cady, Frank DrAPF 93, WhoHol 92
Cady, Gary 1960- WhoHol 92
Cady, Howard Stevenson 1914-1990 WhAm 10
Cady, Jack DrAPF 93
Cady, Jack 1932- EncSF 93
Cady, Joseph Howard 1959- WhoWest 94
Cady, Mary Margaret 1947- WhoMW 93
Cady, Samuel Lincoln 1943- WhoAmA 93
Cady Stanton, Elizabeth 1815-1902 WomPubS
Cadzow, James Archie 1936- WhoAm 94
Caedmon fl. 650-670 BlmGEL
Caen, Herb NewYTBS 93 [port]
Caen, Herb 1916- WhoAm 94
Caesar, Adolph d1986 WhoHol 92
Caesar, Anthony Douglass 1924- Who 94
Caesar, Augustus 63BC-14AD BlmGEL
Caesar, Berel 1927- WhoAmL 94
Caesar, Carol Ann 1945- WhoWest 94
Caesar, Gaius Julius 102BC-44BC BlmGEL
Caesar, Gaius Julius 100BC-44BC WhWE
Caesar, Harry WhoHol 92
Caesar, Harry 1928- WhoBlA 94
Caesar, Henry A., II 1914- WhoAm 94
Caesar, Irving 1895- IntMPA 94, Who 94
Caesar, Julius NewGrDO
Caesar, Julius 102BC-44BC HisWorL [port]
Caesar, Lois 1922- WhoBlA 94
Caesar, Mary 1677-1741 BlmGWL
Caesar, Shirley WhoBlA 94
Caesar, Sid 1922- IntMPA 94, WhoAm 94, WhoCom [port], WhoHol 92
Caesar, Vance Roy 1944- WhoAm 94
Cafaro, Pasquale 1716-1787 NewGrDO
Cafero, Lawrence F., Jr. WhoAmP 93
Caffarella, Edward Philip 1946- WhoAm 94
Caffarelli 1710-1783 NewGrDO
Caffarelli, Luis Angel 1948- WhoAm 94, WhoScEn 94
Caffee, Lorren Dale 1947- WhoAmL 94
Caffee, Marcus Pat 1948- WhoFI 94, WhoScEn 94
Cafferata, Patricia Dillon 1940- WhoAmP 93
Cafferky, Michael Edwin 1950- WhoFI 94, WhoWest 94
Cafferty, Michael Angelo 1927- Who 94
Cafferty, Pastora San Juan 1940- WhoHisp 94
Cafferty, Patrick J. 1951- WhoAmL 94
Caffery, Lisa Kaye 1960- WhoMW 93
Caffery, Taylor Liddell 1947- WhoAmL 94
Caffey, Benjamin Franklin 1927- WhoScEn 94
Caffey, Horace Rouse 1929- WhoAm 94
Caffey, James Enoch 1934- WhoScEn 94
Caffey, John 1895- WhAm 10
Caffin, A(rthur) Crawford 1910- Who 94
Caffin, Roger Neil 1945- WhoScEn 94
Caffrey, Andrew A. d1993 NewYTBS 93
Caffrey, Andrew Augustine 1920- WhoAm 94, WhoAmL 94
Caffrey, Augustine Joseph 1948- WhoWest 94
Caffrey, Francis David 1927- WhoAm 94
Caffrey, Margaret M. 1947- WrDr 94
Caffrey, Robert Daniel 1939- WhoFI 94
Caffrey, Stephen 1961- WhoHol 92
Cafiero, Eugene Anthony 1926- WhoAm 94
Cafiero, James S. 1928- WhoAmP 93
Cafiero, Renee Vera 1943- WhoAmP 93
Caflisch, Russel Edward 1954- WhoWest 94
Cafritz, Peggy Cooper 1947- WhoAm 94, WhoBlA 94
Cafritz, Robert Conrad 1953- WhoAmA 93
Cagan, Jonathan 1961- WhoScEn 94
Cagan, Martin B. 1941- WhoAm 94
Cagan, Phillip 1927- WrDr 94
Cagan, Robert H. 1938- WhoAm 94
Cagatay, Mustafa 1937- IntWW 93
Cage, John DrAPF 93
Cage, John d1992 IntWW 93N
Cage, John 1912- WrDr 94
Cage, John 1912-1992 AnObit 1992, WhAm 10, WhoAmA 93N
Cage, John (Milton, Jr.) 1912-1992 NewGrDO
Cage, John Milton, Jr. 1912-1992 AmCulL
Cage, Michael Jerome 1962- WhoBlA 94
Cage, Nicholas 1964- WhoAm 94
Cage, Nicolas 1964- IntMPA 94, IntWW 93, WhoHol 92
Cage, Patrick B. 1958- WhoBlA 94
Cagel, Nate WhoHisp 94
Caggiano, Joseph 1925- WhoAm 94
Caggine, Carolyn Cassandra 1932- WhoAm 94
Caggins, Ruth Porter 1945- WhoBlA 94
Cagiati, Andrea 1922- IntWW 93, Who 94
Cagin, Tahir 1956- WhoScEn 94
Caginalp, Aydin S. 1950- WhoAmL 94
Caglayangil, Ihsan Sabri 1908- IntWW 93
Cagle, Johnny WhoAmP 93
Cagle, Thomas Marquis 1927- WhoScEn 94
Cagle, William Rea 1933- WhoAm 94
Cagli, Augusto fl. 1865-1885 NewGrDO
Cagli, Bruno 1942- NewGrDO
Cagliero, Giorgio 1952- WhoWest 94
Caglioti, Vincenzo 1902- IntWW 93
Cagney, James d1986 WhoHol 92
Cagney, Jeanne d1984 WhoHol 92
Cagney, William d1988 WhoHol 92
Cagnoni, Antonio 1828-1896 NewGrDO
Caguiat, Carlos J. 1937- WhoHisp 94
Cahal, Mac Fullerton 1907- WhoAm 94
Cahalan, (John) Donald 1912-1992 WhAm 10
Cahalen, Shirley Leanore 1933- WhoMW 93
Cahan, James N. 1951- WhoAm 94
Cahan, Samuel G. d1974 WhoAmA 93N
Cahan, William George 1914- WhoAm 94
Cahana, Alice Lok 1929- WhoAmA 93
Cahay, Marc Michel 1959- WhoMW 93, WhoScEn 94
Cahen, Albert 1846-1903 NewGrDO
Cahen, Alfred 1929- IntWW 93
Cahen, David 1947- WhoScEn 94
Cahier, Charles, Mme. 1870-1951 NewGrDO
Cahill, Arthur Ripley 1907- WhoMW 93
Cahill, Barry WhoHol 92
Cahill, Charles L. 1933- WhoAm 94
Cahill, Clyde S. 1923- WhoAm 94, WhoMW 93
Cahill, Clyde S., Jr. 1923- WhoBlA 94
Cahill, Cornelius 1937- WhoFI 94
Cahill, Donald R. WhoIns 94
Cahill, Edward Eugene 1931- WhoAm 94
Cahill, George Francis, Jr. 1927- WhoAm 94
Cahill, Harry Amory 1930- WhoAm 94
Cahill, Holger 1893-1960 WhoAmA 93N
Cahill, James David 1924- WhoAmL 94
Cahill, James Francis 1926- WhoAm 94, WhoAmA 93
Cahill, John C. WhoAm 94, WhoFI 94
Cahill, John Conway 1930- IntWW 93, Who 94
Cahill, John Denis 1926- WrDr 94
Cahill, Kenneth Vern 1954- WhoMW 93
Cahill, Kevin A. WhoAmP 93
Cahill, Laurence James, Jr. 1924- WhoAm 94
Cahill, Lawrence Bernard 1947- WhoScEn 94
Cahill, Lawrence R. 1947- WhoAmL 94
Cahill, Lily d1955 WhoHol 92
Cahill, Mabel 1863- BuCMET
Cahill, Marie d1933 WhoHol 92
Cahill, Marvin Edward 1947- WhoMW 93
Cahill, Mary Frances 1965- WhoAmP 93
Cahill, Michael Leo 1928- Who 94
Cahill, Michael P. WhoAmP 93
Cahill, Pamela L. 1953- WhoAmP 93
Cahill, Paul Augustine 1959- WhoScEn 94
Cahill, Richard Frederick 1953- WhoAmL 94, WhoFI 94, WhoWest 94
Cahill, Teresa 1944- NewGrDO
Cahill, Teresa Mary 1944- IntWW 93, Who 94
Cahill, Thomas Andrew 1937- WhoAm 94, WhoScEn 94
Cahill, Thomas J. 1935- WhoIns 94
Cahill, William d1926 WhoHol 92
Cahill, William Joseph, Jr. 1923- WhoAm 94
Cahill, William Peter 1953- WhoAmP 93
Cahill, William Randall 1944- WhoAm 94
Cahill, William T. 1947- WhoAmL 94
Cahill, William Walsh, Jr. 1927- WhoAm 94
Cahillane, Sean Francis 1951- WhoAmP 93
Cahir, John Joseph 1933- WhoAm 94
Cahir, Thomas S. 1952- WhoAmP 93
Cahn, Albert Jonas 1924- Who 94
Cahn, Dana d1973 WhoHol 92
Cahn, David Stephen 1940- WhoAm 94
Cahn, Edgar Stuart 1935- WhoAm 94
Cahn, Edward N. 1933- WhoAm 94, WhoAmL 94
Cahn, Glenn Evan 1953- WhoScEn 94
Cahn, Jeffrey Barton 1943- WhoAm 94, WhoAmL 94
Cahn, John Werner 1928- WhoAm 94, WhoScEn 94
Cahn, Joseph M. 1931- WhoAmL 94
Cahn, Joshua Binion 1915- WhoAm 94
Cahn, Julius N. d1993 NewYTBS 93 [port]
Cahn, Matthew Alan 1961- WhoWest 94
Cahn, Peter H. 1932- WhoMW 93
Cahn, Richard Caleb 1932- WhoAmL 94
Cahn, Robert Nathan 1944- WhoScEn 94, WhoWest 94
Cahn, Robert Wolfgang 1924- Who 94
Cahn, Sammy d1993 IntMPA 94N, NewYTBS 93 [port], Who 94N
Cahn, Sammy 1913- IntMPA 94
Cahn, Sammy 1913-1993 ConAu 140, ConMus 11 [port], CurBio 93N, IntDcF 2-4
Cahn, Steven M. 1942- WhoAm 94
Cahn, Susan Leitz 1939- WhoMW 93
Cahoon, Howard C., Jr. WhoAmP 93
Cahoon, Susan Alice 1948- WhoAm 94, WhoAmL 94
Cahouet, Frank Vondell 1932- WhoAm 94, WhoFI 94
Cahusac, Louis de 1706-1759 IntDcB
Cahusac, (Jean-)Louis de 1706-1759 NewGrDO
Cai, Jin-Yi 1961- WhoAsA 94
Cai, Shelton Xuanqing 1954- WhoAsA 94
Cai, Zhengwei 1946- WhoScEn 94
Caicedo, Claudia 1955- WhoHisp 94
Caicedo, Eduardo 1945- WhoHisp 94
Caicedo, Harry 1928- WhoHisp 94
Cai Cehai 1954- WhoPRCh 91 [port]
Cai Chang 1900- WhoPRCh 91 [port]
Cai Cheng 1927- IntWW 93
Cai Cheng 1928- WhoPRCh 91 [port]
Cai-dan Zhuo-ma WhoPRCh 91
Caidin, Martin 1927- EncSF 93, WrDr 94
Cai Dizhi 1918- WhoPRCh 91 [port]
Caiel 1860-1929 BlmGWL
Cai Fangbo WhoPRCh 91
Cail, Carol 1937- ConAu 140
Cailiou, Alan 1914- WrDr 94
Caillard, (Hugh) Anthony 1927- Who 94
Caillat, Claude 1918- Who 94
Caille, Andre 1943- WhoAm 94
Cailletet, Louis Paul WorScD
Caillie, Rene-Auguste 1799-1838 WhWE
Caillier, James Allen 1940- WhoBlA 94
Cailliet, Marcel Emile 1914- WhoWest 94
Caillou, Alan WhoHol 92
Caillouet, Charles Wax, Jr. 1937- WhoScEn 94
Caillouette, James Clyde 1927- WhoAm 94
Cain Who 94
Cain, Albert Clifford 1933- WhoAm 94
Cain, B. Frank 1946- WhoAmL 94
Cain, Becky C. WhoAm 94
Cain, Bernest 1949- WhoAmP 93
Cain, Bruce Edward 1948- WhoAm 94
Cain, Burton Edward 1942- WhoScEn 94
Cain, C. Joseph 1949- WhoAmL 94
Cain, Charles Alan 1943- WhoAm 94
Cain, Charlotte WhoAmA 93
Cain, Christopher 1927- WrDr 94
Cain, Cyric William, Jr. WhoAmP 93
Cain, Dan M. 1940- WhoAmL 94
Cain, David H. 1947- WhoAmP 93
Cain, David Lee 1941- WhoFI 94
Cain, David Paul 1928- WhoAmA 93
Cain, Donald Ezell 1921- WhoAm 94
Cain, Douglas Mylchreest 1938- WhoAm 94, WhoAmL 94
Cain, Edmund Joseph 1918- WhoAm 94
Cain, Edney Who 94
Cain, (Henry) Edney (Conrad) 1924- IntWW 93, Who 94
Cain, Edward (Thomas) 1916- Who 94
Cain, Frank 1930- WhoBlA 94
Cain, Frank Edward, Jr. 1924- WhoBlA 94
Cain, Gary M. 1943- WhoIns 94
Cain, George (M.) 1943- BlkWr 2, ConAu 142
Cain, George Douglas 1940- WhoMW 93
Cain, George Harvey 1920- WhoAm 94, WhoAmL 94
Cain, George Robert T. Who 94
Cain, Gerry Ronald 1961- WhoBlA 94
Cain, Gordon A. 1913- WhoAm 94, WhoFI 94
Cain, Guy A., Jr. WhoAmP 93
Cain, Henri 1859-1937 NewGrDO
Cain, Herbert R., Jr. 1916- WhoBlA 94
Cain, Herman 1945- WhoBlA 94
Cain, James Clarence 1913-1992 WhAm 10
Cain, James Crookall 1927- Who 94
Cain, James David 1938- WhoAmP 93
Cain, James Marshall 1933- WhoAm 94, WhoFI 94
Cain, James Nelson 1930- WhoAm 94
Cain, John 1931- IntWW 93, Who 94
Cain, John Clifford 1924- Who 94
Cain, Johnnie M. 1940- WhoBlA 94
Cain, Joseph Alexander 1920- WhoAmA 93
Cain, Leo Francis 1909- WhoAm 94
Cain, Lester James, Jr. 1937- WhoBlA 94
Cain, Louie Stephen 1949- WhoMW 93
Cain, Madeline Ann 1949- WhoAmP 93, WhoMW 93
Cain, Margaret 1946- WhoIns 94
Cain, Michael Dean 1946- WhoScEn 94
Cain, Michael Peter 1941- WhoAmA 93
Cain, Michael Scott DrAPF 93
Cain, Michael Stephen 1952- WhoFI 94
Cain, Morrison Griffin 1946- WhoAmL 94
Cain, Nathaniel Z., Jr. 1946- WhoBlA 94
Cain, Patricia Jean 1931- WhoFI 94, WhoWest 94
Cain, Raymond Frederick 1937- WhoAm 94
Cain, Richard Duane 1941- WhoMW 93
Cain, Richard Harvey 1825-1887 DcAmReB 2
Cain, Robert d1954 WhoHol 92
Cain, Ruth WhoAm 94
Cain, Ruth Rodney 1935- WhoAmP 93
Cain, Simon Lawrence 1927- WhoBlA 94
Cain, Steven Lyle 1960- WhoScEn 94

Cain, Thomas G. 1938- *WhoAmP 93*
Cain, Thomas William 1935- *Who 94*
Cain, Victor Ralph 1934- *WhoAm 94*
Cain, Virginia Hartigan 1922- *WhoAmP 93, WhoWest 94*
Cain, Waldo 1921- *WhoBlA 94*
Cain, Walker O. d1993 *NewYTBS 93*
Cain, William 1931- *WhoHol 92*
Caine, Carol Whitacre 1925- *WhoWest 94*
Caine, Daniel M. 1942- *WhoAmL 94*
Caine, Derwent Hall d1971 *WhoHol 92*
Caine, Emma Harriet *Who 94*
Caine, Georgia d1964 *WhoHol 92*
Caine, (Thomas Henry) Hall 1853-1931 *EncSF 93*
Caine, Henry d1962 *WhoHol 92*
Caine, Howard 1928- *WhoHol 92*
Caine, Joan-Ellen d1983 *WhoHol 92*
Caine, Marco 1923- *IntWW 93*
Caine, Michael 1933- *IntMPA 94, IntWW 93, Who 94, WhoAm 94, WhoHol 92*
Caine, Michael (Harris) 1927- *Who 94*
Caine, Michael Harris 1927- *IntWW 93*
Caine, Nelson 1939- *WhoAm 94*
Caine, Raymond William, Jr. 1932- *WhoAm 94*
Caine, Richard *WhoHol 92*
Caine, Shulamith Wechter *DrAPF 93*
Caine, Stanley 1937- *WhoHol 92*
Caine, Stanley Paul 1940- *WhoAm 94*
Caine, Stephen Howard 1941- *WhoFI 94, WhoScEn 94, WhoWest 94*
Caines, Eleanor d1913 *WhoHol 92*
Caines, Eric 1936- *Who 94*
Caines, Gary Lee 1949- *WhoFI 94*
Caines, Jeannette (Franklin) 1938- *BlkWr 2*
Caines, John 1933- *Who 94*
Caines, Ken 1926- *WhoBlA 94*
Caines, Kenneth L.D. *WhoWest 94*
Cai Ninglin 1934- *IntWW 93, WhoPRCh 91 [port]*
Cai Qigong *WhoPRCh 91 [port]*
Cai Qijiao 1918- *IntWW 93, WhoPRCh 91 [port]*
Caird, Donald Arthur Richard *Who 94*
Caird, Donald Arthur Richard 1925- *IntWW 93*
Caird, Janet (Hinshaw Kirkwood) 1913- *WrDr 94*
Caird, John Newport 1948- *Who 94*
Caird, Mona 1858-1932 *BlmGWL*
Caird, William Douglas Sime 1917- *Who 94*
Caire, Reda d1963 *WhoHol 92*
Caire, William 1946- *WhoAm 94*
Cai Rengui *WhoPRCh 91*
Cairncross, Alexander (Kirkland), Sir 1911- *WrDr 94*
Cairncross, Alexander Kirkland 1911- *IntWW 93, Who 94, WhoAm 94*
Cairncross, Frances Anne 1944- *Who 94*
Cairncross, James 1915- *WhoHol 92*
Cairncross, Neil Francis 1920- *Who 94*
Cairnes, Joseph Francis 1907- *WhoAm 94*
Cairney, John 1930- *WhoHol 92*
Cairns, Earl 1939- *Who 94*
Cairns, Angus d1975 *WhoHol 92*
Cairns, David 1904-1992 *ConAu 140*
Cairns, David (Adam) 1926- *NewGrDO*
Cairns, David Adam 1926- *IntWW 93*
Cairns, Diane Patricia 1957- *WhoWest 94*
Cairns, Donald Fredrick 1924- *WhoAm 94*
Cairns, Earle E(dwin) 1910- *WrDr 94*
Cairns, Elizabeth 1685-1714 *BlmGWL*
Cairns, Elton James 1932- *WhoAm 94*
Cairns, Geoffrey Crerar 1926- *Who 94*
Cairns, H. Alan C. 1930- *IntWW 93, WhoAm 94*
Cairns, Helen Smith 1938- *WhoAm 94*
Cairns, Hugh John Forster 1922- *IntWW 93, Who 94*
Cairns, James Donald 1931- *WhoAm 94*
Cairns, James Ford 1914- *IntWW 93, Who 94*
Cairns, James George Hamilton Dickson 1920- *Who 94*
Cairns, James Robert 1930- *WhoAm 94*
Cairns, Janice 1954- *NewGrDO*
Cairns, John, Jr. 1923- *WhoAm 94, WhoScEn 94*
Cairns, John B. 1941- *WhoAmL 94*
Cairns, John Joseph 1927- *WhoAm 94*
Cairns, Marion G. 1928- *WhoAmP 93*
Cairns, Raymond Eldon, Jr. 1932- *WhoAm 94*
Cairns, Sally d1965 *WhoHol 92*
Cairns, Scott *DrAPF 93*
Cairns, Shirley Ann 1937- *WhoWest 94*
Cairns, Simon Dallas Cairns 1939- *IntWW 93*
Cairns, Theodore Lesueur 1914- *IntWW 93, WhoAm 94, WhoScEn 94*
Cairo, Jimmy Michael 1952- *WhoScEn 94*
Cai Ruohong *WhoPRCh 91*
Cai Ruo-Hong 1910- *IntWW 93*
Caiserman-Roth, Ghitta 1923- *WhoAmA 93*
Caisley, William T. 1939- *WhoMW 93*
Caison, Thelma Jann 1950- *WhoBlA 94*
Caisse, Albert Leo 1950- *WhoAmP 93*
Caisse, Susan Ann *WhoAmP 93*
Caisson, Joel Thomas 1934- *WhoAmP 93*
Caithamer, Claire S. 1955- *WhoIns 94*
Caithness, Earl of 1948- *Who 94*
Cai Tiyuan 1920- *WhoPRCh 91*
Caits, Joe d1957 *WhoHol 92*
Cai Wenhao 1913- *WhoPRCh 91 [port]*
Cai Wenji *BlmGWL*
Cai Xiaoyu 1930- *WhoPRCh 91 [port]*
Cai Yansong *WhoPRCh 91*
Cai Yen 177- *BlmGWL*
Cai Yuanpei 1868-1940 *HisWorL*
Cai Zaidu *WhoPRCh 91*
Cai Zimin 1920- *WhoPRCh 91 [port]*
Cajal, Rosa Maria 1920- *BlmGWL*
Cajero, Carmen *WhoAmP 93, WhoHisp 94*
Cajigal, Joseph A. 1953- *WhoFI 94*
Cajole, Benat le 1925-1992 *WrDr 94N*
Cajori, Charles F. 1921- *WhoAmA 93*
Cajori, Charles Florian 1921- *WhoAm 94*
Cajthaml, Michael Joseph 1955- *WhoFI 94*
Caju *BlmGWL*
Cakebread, Steven Robert 1946- *WhoWest 94*
Cakmak, Ahmet Sefik 1934- *WhoAm 94*
Cal, Luis Jesus 1943- *WhoHisp 94*
Cala, Jerry *WhoHol 92*
Cala, John Joseph 1960- *WhoWest 94*
Calabi, Eugenio 1923- *WhoScEn 94*
Calabia, Dawn Tennant 1941- *WhoAmP 93*
Calabrese, Arnold Joseph 1960- *WhoAmL 94*
Calabrese, Diane Marie 1949- *WhoAm 94*
Calabrese, Dominic 1963- *WhoMW 93*
Calabrese, Judith Marie 1943- *WhoFI 94*
Calabrese, Leonard M. 1946- *WhoMW 93*
Calabrese, Marta Pérez 1950- *WhoHisp 94*
Calabrese, Rosalie Sue 1938- *WhoAm 94*
Calabrese, Sylvia M. 1934- *WhoAmP 93*
Calabresi, Guido 1932- *WhoAm 94, WhoAmL 94*
Calabretta, Marti 1940- *WhoAmP 93*
Calabro, Joseph John, III 1955- *WhoScEn 94*
Calabro, Julie 1964- *WhoFI 94*
Calabro, Richard Paul 1937- *WhoAmA 93*
Calafati, Peter Gabe 1957- *WhoFI 94*
Calahan, Donald Albert 1935- *WhoAm 94*
Calamai, Clara 1915- *WhoHol 92*
Calamar, Gloria 1921- *WhoAm 94, WhoAmA 93*
Calamari, Andrew M. 1918- *WhoAmL 94*
Calamari, John Daniel 1921- *WhoAm 94*
Calamari, John Edward 1950- *WhoMW 93*
Calamaro, Raymond Stuart 1944- *WhoAm 94*
Calame, Alexandre Emile 1913- *WhoAm 94*
Calan, Pierre 1911- *IntWW 93*
Calandra, Michael A. 1945- *WhoAmL 94*
Calandra, Nicola fl. 1747-1759 *NewGrDO*
Calandrini, Cesar 1595-1665 *DcNaB MP*
Calapai, Letterio *WhoAm 94*
Calapai, Letterio 1902- *WhoAmA 93*
Calapristi, Santo d1987 *WhoHol 92*
Calarco, Antonino Pietro Romeo 1929- *WhoWest 94*
Calarco, Michael David 1953- *WhoAmL 94*
Calarco, N. Joseph 1938- *WhoMW 93*
Calarco, Patricia Gillam *WhoAm 94*
Calarco, Vincent Anthony 1942- *WhoAm 94, WhoFI 94*
Calardo, Stephen Paul 1955- *WhoAmL 94*
Calas, Nicholas d1989 *WhoAmA 93N*
Calasso, Roberto 1941- *ConLC 81 [port]*
Calatchi, Ralph Franklin 1944- *WhoAm 94*
Calati, Charles Paul, Jr. 1946- *WhoMW 93*
Calawa, Leon, Jr. 1929- *WhoAmP 93*
Calaway, Dennis Louis 1960- *WhoFI 94*
Calazans De Magalhaes, Camillo 1928- *IntWW 93*
Calbert, Roosevelt 1931- *WhoBlA 94*
Calbert, William Edward 1918- *WhoBlA 94*
Calbick, Ian MacKinnon 1938- *WhoAm 94*
Calbom, Cherie Marie 1947- *WhoWest 94*
Calcagnie, Kevin Frank 1955- *WhoAmL 94*
Calcagno, Anne *DrAPF 93*
Calcagno, Lawrence d1993 *NewYTBS 93*
Calcagno, Lawrence 1913- *WhoAmA 93*
Calcamuggio, Larry Glenn 1951- *WhoAmL 94, WhoMW 93*
Calcaterra, Edward Lee 1930- *WhoAm 94, WhoFI 94*
Calcaterra, Lynette Grala 1948- *WhoHisp 94*
Calcevecchia, Mark *WhoAm 94*
Calcott, Peter Howard 1948- *WhoWest 94*
Calcutt, David (Charles) 1930- *Who 94*
Calcutt, David Charles 1930- *IntWW 93*
Calcutta, Archbishop of 1926- *Who 94*
Calcutta, Bishop of 1934- *Who 94*
Calda, Pavel 1932- *WhoAm 94*
Caldabaugh, Karl 1946- *WhoFI 94*
Caldara, Antonio c. 1670-1736 *NewGrDO*
Caldara, Orme d1925 *WhoHol 92*
Caldarelli, David Donald 1941- *WhoAm 94*
Caldecote, Viscount 1917- *IntWW 93, Who 94*
Calden, Gertrude Beckwith 1909- *WhoAmP 93, WhoWest 94*
Calder, Alexander d1976 *WhoHol 92*
Calder, Alexander 1898-1976 *WhoAmA 93N*
Calder, Alexander Stirling 1898-1976 *AmCulL [port]*
Calder, Angus 1942- *WrDr 94*
Calder, Bruce 1925- *WhoAmP 93*
Calder, Bruce J. 1940- *WrDr 94*
Calder, Clarence Andrew 1937- *WhoWest 94*
Calder, Daniel Gillmore 1939- *WhoAm 94*
Calder, Elisabeth Nicole 1938- *Who 94*
Calder, Iain Wilson 1939- *WhoAm 94*
Calder, John (Mackenzie) 1927- *WrDr 94*
Calder, John Mackenzie 1927- *IntWW 93, Who 94*
Calder, Julian Richard 1941- *Who 94*
Calder, Kenneth Thomas 1918- *WhoAm 94*
Calder, Kent Eyring 1948- *WhoFI 94*
Calder, King d1964 *WhoHol 92*
Calder, Michael Eugene 1946- *WhoFI 94*
Calder, Nigel (David Ritchie) 1931- *WrDr 94*
Calder, Nigel David Ritchie 1931- *Who 94*
Calder, Robert Mac 1932- *WhoWest 94*
Calder, William Musgrave, III 1932- *WhoMW 93*
Caldera, Edward 1956- *WhoHisp 94*
Caldera, Louis 1956- *WhoAmP 93*
Caldera, Louis Edward 1956- *WhoWest 94*
Calderara, Giacinto 1730-1757? *NewGrDO*
Calderaro, Leonard Joseph 1935- *WhoAm 94*
Caldera Rodriguez, Rafael 1916- *IntWW 93*
Calderazzo, Joseph N., Jr. 1960- *WhoHisp 94*
Calderhead, William Dickson 1919- *WhoAm 94*
Calderin, Carolina *WhoHisp 94*
Calderin, Roberto Antonio 1952- *WhoHisp 94*
Calder-Marshall, Anna 1947- *WhoHol 92*
Calder-Marshall, Arthur 1908- *WrDr 94*
Caldero, Carmen P. *WhoHisp 94*
Calderon (De La Barca), Pedro 1600-1681 *IntDcT 2 [port]*
Calderon, Alberto P. 1920- *WhoAm 94, WhoScEn 94*
Calderon, Alberto Pedro 1920- *IntWW 93, WhoHisp 94*
Calderon, Alejandro A. 1963- *WhoHisp 94*
Calderón, Arnulfo Subia 1922- *WhoHisp 94*
Calderón, Calixto P. 1939- *WhoHisp 94*
Calderon, Cesar A., Jr. 1944- *WhoHisp 94*
Calderón, Charles 1950- *WhoHisp 94*
Calderon, Charles M. 1950- *WhoAmP 93*
Calderón, Edith M. 1962- *WhoHisp 94*
Calderon, Eduardo 1953- *WhoScEn 94*
Calderon, Ernesto 1928- *WhoHisp 94*
Calderon, Eulalio, Jr. 1932- *WhoHisp 94*
Calderon, Ivan 1962- *WhoBlA 94, WhoHisp 94*
Calderon, Jack 1929- *WhoHisp 94*
Calderón, Joseph A. 1944- *WhoHisp 94*
Calderon, Juan A. 1938- *WhoHisp 94*
Calderón, Larry A. 1950- *WhoHisp 94*
Calderon, Linda Mary 1950- *WhoWest 94*
Calderón, Margarita Espino *WhoHisp 94*
Calderón, Mark 1970- *WhoHisp 94*
Calderon, Nissim 1933- *WhoScEn 94*
Calderon, Peter J. 1943- *WhoAmL 94*
Calderon, Raul Morales 1954- *WhoAmL 94*
Calderón, Rosa Margarita 1952- *WhoHisp 94*
Calderón, Rossie 1951- *WhoHisp 94*
Calderón, Sandra Socorro 1963- *WhoHisp 94*
Calderon-Bartolomei, Jose Manuel 1952- *WhoHisp 94*
Calderon-Burris, Enna 1951- *WhoHisp 94*
Calderon de la Barca, Pedro 1600-1681 *LitC 23 [port], NewGrDO*
Calderone, Marlene Elizabeth 1940- *WhoScEn 94*
Calderone, Mary Steichen 1904- *AmSocL*
Calderon Fournier, Rafael Angel 1949- *IntWW 93*
Calderon Rodriguez, Elsie *WhoHisp 94*
Calderon-Van Stane, Zulma Cecilia 1943- *WhoWest 94*
Calderón Woodruff, Irma E. 1951- *WhoHisp 94*
Calderwood, Betty Louise 1937- *WhoMW 93*
Calderwood, James Albert 1941- *WhoAmL 94*
Calderwood, James Lee 1930- *WhoAm 94, WrDr 94*
Calderwood, Neil Moody 1910- *WhoWest 94*
Calderwood, Robert 1932- *Who 94*
Calderwood, Stanford Matson 1920- *WhoAm 94*
Calderwood, William Arthur 1941- *WhoScEn 94, WhoWest 94*
Caldesi, Vincenzo *NewGrDO*
Caldicot, Richard 1908- *WhoHol 92*
Caldicott, Fiona 1941- *Who 94*
Caldicott, Helen 1938- *EnvEnc [port]*
Caldito, Gloria Cruz 1944- *WhoAsA 94*
Caldow, William James 1919- *Who 94*
Caldwell, Adrian Bernard 1966- *WhoBlA 94*
Caldwell, Alethea Otti 1941- *WhoAm 94*
Caldwell, Allan Blair 1929- *WhoFI 94, WhoScEn 94, WhoWest 94*
Caldwell, Andrew Brian 1958- *WhoScEn 94*
Caldwell, Benjamin 1937- *WhoBlA 94*
Caldwell, Benjamin Hubbard, Jr. 1935- *WhoAmA 93*
Caldwell, Billy Ray 1932- *WhoScEn 94*
Caldwell, Brian Yancy 1961- *WhoWest 94*
Caldwell, Carl Howard 1944- *WhoMW 93*
Caldwell, Carlyle G. 1914- *WhoAm 94*
Caldwell, Charles Francis 1935- *WhoMW 93*
Caldwell, Claud Reid 1909- *WhoAmL 94*
Caldwell, Courtney Lynn 1948- *WhoAmL 94, WhoFI 94, WhoWest 94*
Caldwell, Curtis Irvin 1947- *WhoScEn 94*
Caldwell, Dale Gilbert 1960- *WhoFI 94*
Caldwell, Dan Edward 1948- *WhoWest 94*
Caldwell, Daniel Ralston 1936- *WhoAm 94*
Caldwell, David H(epburn) 1951- *WrDr 94*
Caldwell, David Orville 1925- *WhoWest 94*
Caldwell, Delois Whitaker *WhoMW 93*
Caldwell, Dennis Dana 1942- *WhoWest 94*
Caldwell, Dick *Who 94*
Caldwell, (Eric) Dick 1909- *Who 94*
Caldwell, Don d1986 *WhoHol 92*
Caldwell, Douglas Ray 1936- *WhoScEn 94, WhoWest 94*
Caldwell, Edward George 1941- *Who 94*
Caldwell, Edwin L., Jr. 1935- *WhoBlA 94*
Caldwell, Eleanor 1927- *WhoAmA 93*
Caldwell, Elvin R. 1919- *WhoBlA 94*
Caldwell, Elwood Fleming 1923- *WhoAm 94, WhoScEn 94*
Caldwell, Erskine (Preston) 1903-1987 *RfGShF*
Caldwell, Erskine Preston 1903-1987 *AmCulL*
Caldwell, Esly Samuel, II 1938- *WhoBlA 94*
Caldwell, Ethel Louise Lynch 1938- *WhoMW 93*
Caldwell, Frank Griffiths 1921- *Who 94*
Caldwell, Gail 1951- *WhoAm 94*
Caldwell, Garnett Ernest 1934- *WhoAm 94*
Caldwell, Gary Wayne 1953- *WhoScEn 94*
Caldwell, George Bruce 1930- *WhoAm 94*
Caldwell, George Theron, Sr. 1939- *WhoBlA 94*
Caldwell, Gilbert Raymond, III 1952- *WhoAmL 94*
Caldwell, H. Allan 1944- *WhoAmL 94*
Caldwell, Hayes 1949- *WhoAm 94*
Caldwell, Howard Bryant 1944- *WhoWest 94*
Caldwell, J. Edward 1927- *WhoAmP 93*
Caldwell, James 1734-1781 *WhAmRev*
Caldwell, James E. 1930- *WhoBlA 94*
Caldwell, James L. 1955- *WhoBlA 94*
Caldwell, James Richard, Jr. 1943- *WhoAmL 94*
Caldwell, James Russell 1896- *WhAm 10*
Caldwell, James Wiley 1923- *WhoAm 94, WhoAmL 94*
Caldwell, Jean Leonora 1928- *WhoMW 93*
Caldwell, Joe 1941- *BasBi*
Caldwell, John 1941- *WhoAmA 93*
Caldwell, John 1941-1993 *NewYTBS 93 [port]*

Caldwell, John Bernard 1926- *IntWW 93, Who 94*
Caldwell, John Edward 1937- *WhoBlA 94*
Caldwell, John Gilmore 1931- *WhoAm 94*
Caldwell, John L. 1940- *WhoAm 94*
Caldwell, John Rankin 1918- *WhoMW 93*
Caldwell, John Thomas, Jr. 1932- *WhoAm 94*
Caldwell, John Tyler 1911- *WhoAm 94*
Caldwell, Johnnie L. 1922- *WhoAmP 93*
Caldwell, Joni 1948- *WhoFI 94, WhoWest 94*
Caldwell, Judy Carol 1946- *WhoFI 94*
Caldwell, Justin *DrAPF 93*
Caldwell, Karen K. *WhoAmL 94*
Caldwell, Keesha Maria 1948- *WhoBlA 94*
Caldwell, Kenneth Carson 1949- *WhoMW 93*
Caldwell, L. Scott *WhoAm 94*
Caldwell, Lewis A. H. 1905- *WhoBlA 94*
Caldwell, Lisa Jeffries 1961- *WhoBlA 94*
Caldwell, Lynton Keith 1913- *EnvEnc [port], WhoAm 94, WhoMW 93, WhoScEn 94*
Caldwell, M. Milford 1928- *WhoBlA 94*
Caldwell, Marion Milford, Jr. 1952- *WhoBlA 94*
Caldwell, Mark R. 1953- *WhoWest 94*
Caldwell, Martha Belle 1931- *WhoAmA 93*
Caldwell, Mary Peri 1935- *WhoAm 94*
Caldwell, Michael DeFoix 1943- *WhoAm 94, WhoScEn 94*
Caldwell, Minna d1969 *WhoHol 92*
Caldwell, Oliver Johnson 1904- *WhAm 10*
Caldwell, Orville d1967 *WhoHol 92*
Caldwell, Patty Jean Grosskopf 1937- *WhoAm 94*
Caldwell, Paul Willis, Jr. 1930- *WhoWest 94*
Caldwell, Peter Derek 1940- *WhoScEn 94, WhoWest 94*
Caldwell, Philip 1920- *IntWW 93, Who 94, WhoAm 94*
Caldwell, Price *DrAPF 93*
Caldwell, Ravin, Jr. 1963- *WhoBlA 94*
Caldwell, Richard Lloyd 1939- *WhoFI 94*
Caldwell, Robert John 1949- *WhoWest 94*
Caldwell, Robert L. 1933- *WhoIns 94*
Caldwell, Rodney K. 1937- *WhoAmL 94*
Caldwell, Rossie Juanita Brower 1917- *WhoBlA 94*
Caldwell, Sandra Ishmael 1948- *WhoBlA 94*
Caldwell, Sarah 1924- *NewGrDO, WhoAm 94*
Caldwell, Stratton F. *DrAPF 93*
Caldwell, Stratton F(ranklin) 1926- *WrDr 94*
Caldwell, Stratton Franklin 1926- *WhoAm 94, WhoWest 94*
Caldwell, Susan Hanes 1938- *WhoAm 94*
Caldwell, Susan Havens 1938- *WhoAmA 93*
Caldwell, Taylor 1900- *BlmGWL*
Caldwell, (Janet Miriam) Taylor (Holland) 1900-1985 *EncSF 93*
Caldwell, Thomas Howell, Jr. 1934- *WhoFI 94*
Caldwell, Thomas Michael 1946- *WhoWest 94*
Caldwell, Toy Talmadge, Jr. d1993 *NewYTBS 93*
Caldwell, Walter Edward 1941- *WhoWest 94*
Caldwell, Warren A. 1958- *WhoAmP 93*
Caldwell, Warren Frederick 1928- *WhoAm 94*
Caldwell, Wesley Stuart, III 1946- *WhoAm 94, WhoAmL 94*
Caldwell, Will M. 1925- *WhoAm 94*
Caldwell, William Mackay, III 1922- *WhoAm 94, WhoFI 94, WhoWest 94*
Caldwell, William McNeilly 1953- *WhoFI 94*
Caldwell, William Wilson 1925- *WhoAm 94, WhoAmL 94*
Caldwell, Zoe 1933- *WhoAm 94, WhoHol 92*
Caldwell-Colbert, A. Toy 1951- *WhoMW 93*
Caldwell-Lee, Laurie Neilson 1947- *WhoAmL 94, WhoWest 94*
Caldwell-Moore, Patrick *Who 94*
Caldwell Swisher, Rozella Kathrine 1908- *WhoBlA 94*
Cale, Charles Griffin 1940- *WhoAm 94*
Cale, William Graham, Jr. 1947- *WhoScEn 94*
Caledon, Earl of 1955- *Who 94*
Caledonia, Bishop of 1937- *Who 94*
Calef, George (Waller) 1944- *WrDr 94*
Calegari, Antonio 1757-1828 *NewGrDO*
Calegari, Giuseppe c. 1750-1812 *NewGrDO*
Calegari, Luigi Antonio c. 1780-1849 *NewGrDO*
Calegari, Maria 1957- *IntDcB [port], WhoAm 94*
Calegari Family *NewGrDO*
Calendar, Lauren *WhoAmP 93*
Calenoff, Leonid 1923- *WhoAm 94*
Calentine, Mary Edith 1952- *WhoMW 93*
Calero, Ramôn *WhoHisp 94*
Calfa, Don *WhoHol 92*
Calfa, Marian 1946- *IntWW 93*
Calfan, Nicole 1947- *WhoHol 92*
Calfee, David Walker 1921- *WhoAmL 94, WhoWest 94*
Calfee, John Beverly, Sr. 1913- *WhoAm 94, WhoFI 94*
Calfee, Robert Chilton 1933- *WhoAm 94*
Calfee, William Howard 1909- *WhoAm 94, WhoAmA 93*
Calfee, William Lewis 1917- *WhoAm 94, WhoAmL 94*
Calfee, William Rushton 1947- *WhoFI 94*
Calfo, Cathryn Cathy 1957- *WhoAmP 93*
Calgaard, Ronald Keith 1937- *WhoAm 94*
Calgary, Bishop of 1933- *Who 94*
Calhern, Louis d1956 *WhoHol 92*
Calhoon, Ed Latta 1922- *WhoAmP 93*
Calhoon, John Charles 1957- *WhoWest 94*
Calhoun, Alice d1966 *WhoHol 92*
Calhoun, Calvin Lee 1927- *WhoBlA 94*
Calhoun, Calvin Lee, Sr. 1927- *WhoAm 94*
Calhoun, Cecelia C. 1922- *WhoBlA 94*
Calhoun, Charles d1984 *WhoHol 92*
Calhoun, Clayne Marsh 1950- *WhoAmL 94*
Calhoun, Craig (Jackson) 1952- *WrDr 94*
Calhoun, Credell 1945- *WhoAmP 93*
Calhoun, Don *NewYTBS 93 [port]*
Calhoun, Donald Eugene, Jr. 1926- *WhoAm 94, WhoAmL 94, WhoMW 93*
Calhoun, Dorothy Eunice 1936- *WhoBlA 94*
Calhoun, Ellsworth L. 1928- *WhoIns 94*
Calhoun, Eric A. 1950- *WhoBlA 94*
Calhoun, Evelyn Williams 1921- *WhoAm 94*
Calhoun, Frank Wayne 1933- *WhoAm 94*
Calhoun, Fred Steverson 1947- *WhoBlA 94*
Calhoun, Gordon James 1953- *WhoAm 94, WhoWest 94*
Calhoun, Gregory Bernard 1952- *WhoBlA 94*
Calhoun, Harold 1906- *WhoAm 94*
Calhoun, Jack Johnson, Jr. 1938- *WhoBlA 94*
Calhoun, James Clay 1962- *WhoWest 94*
Calhoun, Jerry L. 1943- *WhoAmP 93*
Calhoun, Jesse, Jr. 1958- *WhoScEn 94*
Calhoun, John 1937- *WhoBlA 94*
Calhoun, John Alfred 1939- *WhoAm 94*
Calhoun, John C. 1782-1850 *HisWorL [port]*
Calhoun, John C., Jr. 1917- *WhoAm 94*
Calhoun, John Cozart 1937- *WhoAm 94, WhoFI 94*
Calhoun, Joshua Wesley 1956- *WhoBlA 94*
Calhoun, Larry Darryl 1937- *WhoAmA 93*
Calhoun, Lee A. 1947- *WhoBlA 94*
Calhoun, Lillian Scott *WhoBlA 94*
Calhoun, Lyla Lea 1934- *WhoMW 93*
Calhoun, Mark Alan 1946- *WhoAmL 94*
Calhoun, Martin Lewis 1961- *WhoAm 94*
Calhoun, Milburn 1930- *WhoAm 94*
Calhoun, Nancy 1944- *WhoAmP 93*
Calhoun, Noah Robert 1921- *WhoAm 94, WhoBlA 94*
Calhoun, Richard d1977 *WhoHol 92*
Calhoun, Richard J(ames) 1926- *WrDr 94*
Calhoun, Richard James 1926- *WhoAm 94*
Calhoun, Robert L. 1937- *WhoAmP 93*
Calhoun, Robert Lathan 1937- *WhoAm 94*
Calhoun, Robert Lowry 1896- *WhAm 10*
Calhoun, Rory 1922- *IntMPA 94, WhoHol 92*
Calhoun, Shirley Meacham 1927- *WhoAmP 93*
Calhoun, Thomas 1932- *WhoBlA 94*
Calhoun, V. O., Jr. 1951- *WhoAmP 93*
Calhoun, Wes 1943- *WrDr 94*
Calhoun, William *See* Living Colour *News 93-3*
Calhoun-Senghor, Keith 1955- *WhoAmL 94*
Cali, Giulio d1967 *WhoHol 92*
Cali, Joseph *WhoHol 92*
Cali, Joseph John 1928- *WhoAm 94*
Calia, Vincent Frank 1926- *WhoAm 94*
Calian, Carnegie Samuel 1933- *WrDr 94*
Calie, Patrick Joseph 1953- *WhoScEn 94*
Caliendo, G. D. 1941- *WhoFI 94*
Calif, Ruth 1922- *WrDr 94*
Califano, Joseph A., Jr. 1931- *WhoAmP 93, WrDr 94*
Califano, Joseph Anthony, Jr. 1931- *IntWW 93, WhoAm 94, WhoAmL 94*
Califf, Marilyn Iskiwitz 1932- *WhoAmA 93*
Califia, Pat *DrAPF 93*
Califia, Pat 1954- *GayLL, WrDr 94*
Califice, Alfred 1916- *IntWW 93*
Caligari, Peter Douglas Savaria 1949- *Who 94*
Caligiuri, Joseph Frank 1928- *WhoAm 94*
Caligula 12-41 *HisWorL [port]*
Caligula, Gaius Caesar d41 *BlmGEL*
Calinescu, Adriana Gabriela 1941- *WhoAm 94*
Calinescu, Matei (Alexe) 1934- *WrDr 94*
Calingaert, Michael 1933- *WhoAm 94*
Calinger, Ronald Steve 1942- *WhoAm 94*
Calinoiu, Nicolae d1992 *IntWW 93N*
Calio, Anthony John 1929- *WhoAm 94, WhoAmP 93*
Caliri, David J. 1929- *WhoAmP 93*
Caliri, David Joseph 1929- *WhoAmL 94*
Caliri, Jon 1960- *WhoHol 92*
Calise, Anthony John 1943- *WhoScEn 94*
Calise, Nicholas James 1941- *WhoAm 94, WhoAmL 94*
Calise, Ronald Jan 1948- *WhoAm 94*
Calise, William Joseph, Jr. 1938- *WhoAm 94*
Calisher, Hortense *DrAPF 93*
Calisher, Hortense 1911- *EncSF 93, IntWW 93, RfGShF, WhoAm 94, WrDr 94*
Calistro, Paddy *ConAu 41NR*
Calistro McAuley, Patricia Ann 1948- *ConAu 41NR*
Calitri, Charles *DrAPF 93*
Calkin, Joy Durfee 1938- *WhoAm 94*
Calkins, Dick 1895-1962 *EncSF 93*
Calkins, Emily Virginia 1918- *WhoMW 93*
Calkins, Evan 1920- *WhoAm 94, WhoScEn 94*
Calkins, Gary Nathan 1911- *WhoAm 94*
Calkins, Hugh 1924- *WhoAm 94*
Calkins, Jean *DrAPF 93*
Calkins, Jerry Milan 1942- *WhoAm 94, WhoWest 94*
Calkins, John Thiers 1925- *WhoAmP 93*
Calkins, Judith Moritz 1942- *WhoFI 94*
Calkins, Kingsley Mark 1917- *WhoAmA 93*
Calkins, Loring Gary 1887-1960 *WhoAmA 93N*
Calkins, Ralph Nelson 1926- *WhoMW 93*
Calkins, Richard W. 1939- *WhoAm 94, WhoMW 93*
Calkins, Robert Bruce 1942- *WhoScEn 94, WhoWest 94*
Calkins, Robert G. 1932- *WhoAmA 93, WrDr 94*
Calkins, Susannah Eby 1924- *WhoAm 94*
Call, Anthony *WhoHol 92*
Call, Brandon 1976- *WhoHol 92*
Call, Craig M. 1948- *WhoAmP 93*
Call, David Lincoln 1932- *WhoAm 94*
Call, Gene 1944- *WhoAmP 93*
Call, John d1973 *WhoHol 92*
Call, John E. *WhoAmP 93*
Call, Joseph Rudd 1950- *WhoWest 94*
Call, Katherine Mary 1956- *WhoScEn 94*
Call, Merlin Wendell 1931- *WhoAmL 94, WhoWest 94*
Call, Neil Judson 1933- *WhoAm 94*
Call, Osborne Jay 1941- *WhoFI 94, WhoWest 94*
Call, R. D. *WhoHol 92*
Call, Richard William 1924- *WhoWest 94*
Calladine, Christopher Reuben 1935- *IntWW 93, Who 94*
Callaghan *Who 94*
Callaghan, Allan (Robert) 1903- *Who 94*
Callaghan, Barry 1937- *WrDr 94*
Callaghan, Bede (Bertrand) 1912- *Who 94*
Callaghan, Brendan Alphonsus 1948- *Who 94*
Callaghan, Catherine A. *DrAPF 93*
Callaghan, Desmond Noble 1915- *Who 94*
Callaghan, Donald E. 1946- *WhoFI 94*
Callaghan, Frank D. 1924- *WhoAmP 93*
Callaghan, J. Clair 1933- *WhoAm 94*
Callaghan, James 1927- *Who 94*
Callaghan, Lawrence A. 1942- *WhoAmL 94*
Callaghan, Mary Rose 1944- *BlmGWL, ConAu 43NR*
Callaghan, Morley (Edward) 1903-1990 *RfGShF*
Callaghan, Morley Edward 1903-1990 *WhAm 10*
Callaghan, William McCombe 1897-1991 *WhAm 10*
Callaghan, William Stuart 1945- *WhoAmP 93*
Callaghan Of Cardiff, Baron 1912- *IntWW 93, Who 94*
Callagy, John M. 1944- *WhoAmL 94*
Callaham, Betty Elgin 1929- *WhoAm 94*
Callaham, Thomas Hunter 1915- *WhoAm 94*
Callahan, Adelina Pena 1935- *WhoHisp 94*
Callahan, Aileen *WhoAmA 93*
Callahan, Bill d1981 *WhoHol 92*
Callahan, Bobby d1938 *WhoHol 92*
Callahan, Carroll Bernard 1908- *WhoAm 94*
Callahan, Charles Edward, III *WhoAm 94*
Callahan, Christine H. 1944- *WhoAmP 93*
Callahan, Chuck d1964 *WhoHol 92*
Callahan, Cleta 1935- *WhoMW 93*
Callahan, Daniel (J.) 1930- *WrDr 94*
Callahan, Daniel J. *WhoAmP 93*
Callahan, Daniel John 1930- *WhoAm 94*
Callahan, David 1965?- *ConAu 140*
Callahan, Dennis M. 1942- *WhoAmP 93*
Callahan, Dorothy Mott 1942- *WhoMW 93*
Callahan, Edward William 1930- *WhoAm 94*
Callahan, Elias Richard, Jr. 1938- *WhoAm 94*
Callahan, Era Eugene 1933- *WhoAmP 93*
Callahan, Francis Joseph 1923- *WhoAm 94*
Callahan, Geoffrey Louis 1949- *WhoFI 94*
Callahan, Gerald William 1936- *WhoAm 94, WhoAmL 94*
Callahan, H. L. 1932- *WhoAm 94, WhoAmP 93*
Callahan, H. Patrick 1947- *WhoAmL 94*
Callahan, Harry 1912- *WhoAmA 93*
Callahan, Harry Leslie 1923- *WhoAm 94*
Callahan, Harry M. 1912- *IntWW 93*
Callahan, Harry Morey 1912- *WhoAm 94*
Callahan, James 1930- *WhoHol 92*
Callahan, James Calvin 1942- *WhoWest 94*
Callahan, James P. 1939- *WhoAmP 93*
Callahan, John F. 1912- *WrDr 94*
Callahan, John William 1947- *WhoAmL 94*
Callahan, Joseph Murray *WhoAm 94*
Callahan, Joseph Patrick 1945- *WhoAm 94, WhoAmL 94*
Callahan, Kenneth 1905-1986 *WhoAmA 93N*
Callahan, Marilyn Joy 1934- *WhoWest 94*
Callahan, Michael Charles 1949- *WhoWest 94*
Callahan, Michael J. 1939- *WhoAm 94, WhoFI 94*
Callahan, Michael Thomas 1948- *WhoAmL 94*
Callahan, Mushy d1986 *WhoHol 92*
Callahan, Nelson J. 1927- *WrDr 94*
Callahan, North 1908- *WhoAm 94, WrDr 94*
Callahan, Patrick Henry 1865-1940 *DcAmReB 2*
Callahan, Patrick Michael 1947- *WhoAmL 94*
Callahan, Richard J. 1941- *WhoAm 94*
Callahan, Richard James 1928- *WhoFI 94*
Callahan, Rickey Don 1956- *WhoFI 94*
Callahan, Robert F., Jr. *WhoAm 94*
Callahan, Robert J. *WhoAmP 93*
Callahan, Robert J. 1926- *WhoAmP 93*
Callahan, Robert J. 1930- *WhoAm 94, WhoAmL 94*
Callahan, Ronald E. 1926- *WhoFI 94*
Callahan, Samuel P. 1924- *WhoBlA 94*
Callahan, Sonny 1932- *CngDr 93*
Callahan, Thomas Dennis 1952- *WhoIns 94*
Callahan, Tom *WhoHol 92*
Callahan, Vincent Francis, Jr. 1931- *WhoAmP 93*
Callahan, William *EncSF 93*
Callahan, William 1911- *WrDr 94*
Callahan Graham, Pia Laaster 1955- *WhoAm 94, WhoScEn 94*
Callan, Clair Marie 1940- *WhoMW 93*
Callan, Harold Garnet 1917- *IntWW 93, Who 94*
Callan, Herbert Quentin 1922- *WhoAmP 93*
Callan, Ivan Roy 1942- *Who 94*
Callan, Jamie *DrAPF 93*
Callan, Josi irene 1946- *WhoWest 94*
Callan, K. *WhoHol 92*
Callan, Michael 1925- *Who 94*
Callan, Michael 1935- *IntMPA 94, WhoHol 92*
Callan, Terrence A. 1939- *WhoAm 94*
Callanan, Kathleen Joan 1940- *WhoMW 93*
Calland, Diana Baker 1935- *WhoAm 94*
Callander, Bruce Douglas 1923- *WhoAm 94*
Callander, Kay Eileen Paisley 1938- *WhoMW 93*
Callard, Carole Crawford 1941- *WhoMW 93*
Callard, David Jacobus 1938- *WhoAm 94*
Callard, Eric John 1913- *Who 94*
Callard, Jack (Eric John) 1913- *IntWW 93*
Callard, Kay *WhoHol 92*
Callard, Maurice (Frederic Thomas) 1912- *WrDr 94*

Callari Galli, Matilde 1934- *WhoWomW 91*
Callas, Charlie 1924- *WhoHol 92*
Callas, Maria d1977 *WhoHol 92*
Callas, Maria 1923-1977 *AmCulL, ConMus 11 [port]*
Callas, (Cecilia Sophia Anna) Maria 1923-1977 *NewGrDO*
Callas, Michael G. 1921- *WhoAmP 93*
Callas, Peter G. *WhoAmP 93*
Callas, Theo 1928- *WrDr 94*
Callaway, Ben Anderson 1927- *WhoAm 94*
Callaway, Betty *Who 94*
Callaway, Clifford Wayne 1941- *WhoAm 94*
Callaway, David Henry, Jr. 1912- *WhoAm 94*
Callaway, Dwight W. 1932- *WhoBlA 94*
Callaway, Frank (Adams) 1919- *Who 94*
Callaway, Fuller Earle, Jr. 1907- *WhAm 10*
Callaway, Henry Abbott, III 1958- *WhoAmL 94*
Callaway, Howard H. 1927- *IntWW 93*
Callaway, Howard Hollis 1927- *WhoAm 94, WhoAmP 93, WhoWest 94*
Callaway, Joseph 1931- *WhoScEn 94*
Callaway, Karen Alice 1946- *WhoAm 94*
Callaway, Kathy *DrAPF 93*
Callaway, Louis Marshall, Jr. 1939- *WhoBlA 94*
Callaway, Richard Earl 1951- *WhoMW 93*
Callaway-Fittall, Betty Daphne 1928- *Who 94*
Callbeck, Catherine 1939- *WhoAm 94*
Calle, Craig R.L. 1959- *WhoAm 94*
Calle, Luz Marina 1947- *WhoHisp 94*
Calle, Paul 1928- *WhoAmA 93*
Calleia, Joseph d1975 *WhoHol 92*
Calleja, Rafael (Gomez) 1874-1938 *NewGrDO*
Callejas, Manuel Mancia, Jr. 1933- *WhoHisp 94*
Callejas, Marlene Therese 1957- *WhoHisp 94*
Callejas, Rafael *IntWW 93*
Callejo, Carlos 1951- *WhoHisp 94*
Callejo, Gerald Rodriguez 1963- *WhoScEn 94*
Callen, Hubert B. 1919-1993 *NewYTBS 93*
Callen, James Donald 1941- *WhoAm 94*
Callen, Jeffrey Phillip 1947- *WhoAm 94*
Callen, Jerry, Jr. *WhoAmP 93*
Callen, John Holmes, Jr. 1932- *WhoAm 94*
Callen, Lon Edward 1929- *WhoWest 94*
Callen, Michael d1993 *NewYTBS 93 [port]*
Callenbach, Ernest 1929- *EncSF 93, WhoAm 94, WrDr 94*
Callendar, Malcolm *WhoAmP 93*
Callender, Carl O. 1936- *WhoBlA 94*
Callender, Clive Orville 1936- *WhoAm 94, WhoBlA 94, WhoScEn 94*
Callender, Hannah 1737-1801 *BlmGWL*
Callender, John d1797 *AmRev*
Callender, John Francis 1944- *WhoAmL 94*
Callender, John Hancock 1908- *WhoAm 94*
Callender, Leroy R. 1932- *WhoBlA 94*
Callender, Lucinda R. 1957- *WhoBlA 94*
Callender, Maurice Henry 1916- *Who 94*
Callender, Norma Anne 1933- *WhoFI 94*
Callender, Ralph A. 1932- *WhoBlA 94*
Callender, Red 1916- *WrDr 94*
Callender, Red 1916-1992 *AnObit 1992*
Callender, Robert Howard 1942- *WhoScEn 94*
Callender, Valerie Dawn 1960- *WhoBlA 94*
Callender, Wilfred A. 1929- *WhoBlA 94*
Callender, William Lacey 1933- *WhoAm 94, WhoFI 94, WhoWest 94*
Caller, Maxwell Marshall 1951- *Who 94*
Callerame, Joseph 1950- *WhoScEn 94*
Calleros, Charles R. 1953- *WhoHisp 94*
Callery, Mary 1903-1977 *WhoAmA 93N*
Calles, Guillermo d1958 *WhoHol 92*
Calles, Rosa Maria 1949- *WhoHisp 94*
Callesen-Gyorgak, Jan Elaine 1959- *WhoMW 93*
Calles-Escandon, Jorge 1951- *WhoHisp 94*
Calleton, Theodore Edward 1934- *WhoAm 94*
Callewaert, Denis Marc 1947- *WhoAm 94*
Calley, Henry (Algernon) 1914- *Who 94*
Calley, Robert d1977 *WhoHol 92*
Callicott, Burton Harry 1907- *WhoAmA 93*
Callicott, Clint 1948- *WhoAmP 93*
Callicott, J(ohn) Baird 1941- *WrDr 94*
Callicott, John Baird 1941- *EnvEnc*
Callies, David Lee 1943- *WhoAm 94, WhoAmL 94*
Calliga, George d1976 *WhoHol 92*
Calligan, William Dennis 1925- *WhoAm 94*
Callighan, Phillip Edward 1951- *WhoMW 93*
Callihan, C. Michael 1947- *WhoAm 94, WhoAmP 93, WhoWest 94*
Callihan, Harriet K. 1930- *WhAm 10*
Callil, Carmen Therese 1938- *IntWW 93, Who 94*
Callinan, Bernard (James) 1913- *Who 94*
Callinan, Bernard J(ames) 1913- *WrDr 94*
Callinan, Dick *WhoHol 92*
Callis, Bruce *WhoIns 94*
Callis, Bruce 1939- *WhoAm 94, WhoAmP 93*
Callis, Clayton Fowler 1923- *WhoAm 94*
Callis, Daniel Leon 1958- *WhoWest 94*
Callis, David d1934 *WhoHol 92*
Callis, Jerry Jackson 1926- *WhoAm 94*
Callis, Jo Ann *WhoAmA 93*
Callisen, Sterling A. 1899-1988 *WhoAmA 93N*
Callison, Brian (Richard) 1934- *WrDr 94*
Callison, Charles H. d1993 *NewYTBS 93 [port]*
Callison, James W. 1928- *WhoAm 94, WhoAmL 94*
Callison, John Patrick 1950- *WhoMW 93*
Callison, Nancy Fowler 1931- *WhoWest 94*
Callison, Russell James 1954- *WhoAmL 94*
Callison, Scott Dale 1961- *WhoMW 93*
Callison, William Andrew, III 1945- *WhoAmL 94*
Calliss, Frank William 1962- *WhoWest 94*
Callister, John Richard 1961- *WhoScEn 94*
Callister, Louis Henry, Jr. 1935- *WhoAmL 94, WhoWest 94*
Callister, Marion Jones 1921- *WhoAm 94, WhoAmL 94, WhoWest 94*
Callister, Matthew Q. 1955- *WhoAmP 93*
Callman, Clive Vernon 1927- *Who 94*
Callmer, James Peter 1919- *WhoAm 94*
Callner, Bruce Warren 1948- *WhoAmL 94*
Callner, Richard 1927- *WhoAmA 93*
Callo, Joseph Francis 1929- *WhoAm 94*
Callos, Phyllis Marie 1923- *WhoWest 94*
Callow, Allan Dana 1916- *WhoAm 94*
Callow, Honour Henry William 1926- *Who 94*
Callow, James Arthur 1945- *Who 94*
Callow, Keith McLean 1925- *WhoAm 94, WhoAmL 94, WhoAmP 93, WhoWest 94*
Callow, Philip 1924- *WrDr 94*
Callow, Simon 1949- *IntMPA 94, WhoHol 92*
Callow, Simon Philip Hugh 1949- *IntWW 93*
Callow, Simon Phillip Hugh 1949- *Who 94*
Callow, William Grant 1921- *WhoAm 94, WhoAmL 94, WhoAmP 93, WhoMW 93*
Calloway, Al *WhoAmP 93*
Calloway, Cab 1907- *WhoHol 92*
Calloway, Cab, III 1907- *WhoBlA 94*
Calloway, Colin G(ordon) 1953- *WrDr 94*
Calloway, Curtis A. 1939- *WhoBlA 94*
Calloway, D. Wayne 1935- *WhoAm 94, WhoFI 94*
Calloway, Deverne Lee 1916- *WhoAmP 93, WhoBlA 94*
Calloway, Doris Howes 1923- *WhoAm 94*
Calloway, Jean Mitchener 1923- *WhoAm 94*
Calloway, Kirk *WhoHol 92*
Calloway, Rick *WhoBlA 94*
Calloway, Vanessa Bell *WhoBlA 94*
Callsen, Christian E. 1938- *WhoAm 94*
Callum, Agnes Kane 1925- *WhoBlA 94*
Callum, Myles 1934- *WhoAm 94*
Callwood, June *BlmGWL*
Callwood, June 1924- *IntWW 93, WrDr 94*
Calman, Kenneth Charles 1941- *IntWW 93, Who 94*
Calman, Mel 1931- *Who 94*
Calman, Robert Frederick 1932- *WhoAm 94*
Calman, W(endy L.) 1947- *WhoAmA 93*
Calmann, Arnold B. 1947- *WhoAmL 94*
Calmer, Charles Edward 1951- *WhoMW 93*
Calmes, Christian 1913- *IntWW 93*
Calmes, John Wintle 1942- *WhoScEn 94*
Calmettes, Andre d1942 *WhoHol 92*
Calmon De Sa, Angelo *IntWW 93*
Calnan, Charles Dermod 1917- *Who 94*
Calnan, James Stanislaus 1916- *Who 94*
Calne, Roy 1930- *WorInv*
Calne, Roy (Yorke) 1930- *Who 94*
Calne, Roy Yorke 1930- *IntWW 93*
Calne And Calstone, Viscount 1970- *Who 94*
Calo, Joseph Manuel 1944- *WhoAm 94*
Calof, Lawrence 1944- *WhoAmL 94*
Calogero, Pascal Frank, Jr. 1931- *WhoAm 94, WhoAmL 94, WhoAmP 93*
Calogero, Stefano 1954- *WhoAmL 94*
Calomee, Annie E. 1910- *WhoBlA 94*
Calori, Angiola 1732-c. 1790 *NewGrDO*
Calotta, Charles Joseph 1926- *WhoFI 94*
Calouri, Theodore Lawrence 1941- *WhoAmP 93*
Calovski, Mitko 1930- *IntWW 93, Who 94*
Caloz, Byron Victor 1959- *WhoMW 93*
Calpin, Martin J. 1934- *WhoIns 94*
Calprenede *GuFrLit 2*
Calrow, Robert F. 1916- *WhoAmA 93*
Caltagirone, Thomas Richard 1942- *WhoAmP 93*
Calthorpe *Who 94*
Calthorpe, Baron 1927- *Who 94*
Calthrop, Donald d1940 *WhoHol 92*
Calton, Gary Jim 1943- *WhoAm 94*
Calton, Lynn Barker 1942- *WhoMW 93*
Caltrider, Paul Gene 1935- *WhoMW 93*
Calvaer, Andre J. 1921- *WhoScEn 94*
Calvanese, Flora 1954- *WhoWomW 91*
Calvani, Terry 1947- *WhoAm 94, WhoAmP 93*
Calvanico, Thomas Paul 1955- *WhoAmL 94*
Calvaruso, Joseph Anthony 1949- *WhoAmL 94*
Calve (de Roquer), (Rosa-Noemie) Emma 1858-1942 *NewGrDO [port]*
Calve, Olga d1982 *WhoHol 92*
Calverley, Baron 1946- *Who 94*
Calverley, John Robert 1932- *WhoAm 94*
Calvert, Ann 1935- *WhoAmP 93*
Calvert, Barbara Adamson 1926- *Who 94*
Calvert, Catherine d1971 *WhoHol 92*
Calvert, Cecil 1606-1675 *DcNaB MP*
Calvert, Cecilius 1606-1675 *DcAmReB 2*
Calvert, Charles, Mrs. d1921 *WhoHol 92*
Calvert, David Victor 1934- *WhoScEn 94*
Calvert, Delbert William 1927- *WhoAm 94*
Calvert, Denis *Who 94*
Calvert, (Louis Victor) Denis 1924- *Who 94*
Calvert, E. H. d1941 *WhoHol 92*
Calvert, Eddie d1978 *WhoHol 92*
Calvert, Florence Irene 1912- *Who 94*
Calvert, George David 1964- *WhoScEn 94*
Calvert, Gordon Lee 1921- *WhoAm 94*
Calvert, Jack George 1923- *WhoAm 94*
Calvert, James Francis 1920- *WhoAm 94*
Calvert, James Henry 1898- *WhAm 10*
Calvert, Jay H., Jr. 1945- *WhoAm 94, WhoAmL 94*
Calvert, Jennie C. 1878- *WhoAmA 93N*
Calvert, John *WhoHol 92*
Calvert, John H. 1940- *WhoAmL 94*
Calvert, John Raymond 1937- *Who 94*
Calvert, Jon Channing 1941- *WhoAm 94*
Calvert, Ken 1953- *CngDr 93, WhoAm 94, WhoWest 94*
Calvert, Kenneth Elsworth 1928- *WhoAmP 93*
Calvert, Laura *DrAPF 93*
Calvert, Louis d1923 *WhoHol 92*
Calvert, Marilyn Rose Stewart 1959- *WhoMW 93*
Calvert, Mary 1941- *WrDr 94*
Calvert, Nancy Ann 1939- *WhoMW 93*
Calvert, Norman Hilton 1925- *Who 94*
Calvert, Patricia 1931- *SmATA 17AS [port], TwCYAW*
Calvert, Peter (Anthony Richard) 1936- *WrDr 94*
Calvert, Phyllis 1915- *Who 94, WhoHol 92*
Calvert, Sam J., Jr. 1928- *WhoAm 94*
Calvert, Thomas *EncSF 93*
Calvert, William Preston 1934- *WhoAm 94, WhoScEn 94*
Calvert, Wilma Jean 1958- *WhoBlA 94*
Calvert-Smith, David 1945- *Who 94*
Calvesi, Vincenzo fl. 1780-1794 *NewGrDO*
Calvet, Cesar E. *WhoHisp 94*
Calvet, Corinne 1925- *IntMPA 94, WhoHol 92*
Calvet, Jacques 1931- *IntWW 93, Who 94*
Calvey, Brian J. 1949- *WhoAm 94, WhoAmL 94*
Calviello, Joseph Anthony 1933- *WhoAm 94*
Calvillo, David Neal 1960- *WhoHisp 94*
Calvillo, Evelyn Ruiz 1943- *WhoHisp 94*
Calvillo, Ricardo C. *WhoAm 94*
Calvin, Allen David 1928- *WhoAm 94, WhoScEn 94*
Calvin, Charles D. 1948- *WhoAmL 94*
Calvin, Donald Lee 1931- *WhoFI 94*
Calvin, Dorothy Ver Strate 1929- *WhoAm 94, WhoFI 94, WhoWest 94*
Calvin, Earl David 1934- *WhoBlA 94*
Calvin, Henry d1975 *WhoHol 92*
Calvin, Henry 1922- *WrDr 94*
Calvin, Jean 1509-1564 *GuFrLit 2*
Calvin, John *WhoHol 92*
Calvin, John 1509-1564 *EncEth, HisWorL [port]*
Calvin, John 1509-1604 *BlmGEL*
Calvin, Lester d1978 *WhoHol 92*
Calvin, Mack 1949- *BasBi*
Calvin, Melvin 1911- *IntWW 93, Who 94, WhoAm 94, WhoScEn 94, WhoWest 94, WorScD, WrDr 94*
Calvin, Michael Byron *WhoBlA 94*
Calvin, Stafford Richard 1931- *WhoMW 93*
Calvin, Virginia Brown 1945- *WhoBlA 94*
Calvin, William H(oward) 1939- *WrDr 94*
Calvin, William Howard 1939- *WhoScEn 94*
Calvin, Willie J. 1913-1992 *WhoBlA 94N*
Calvino, Italo 1923-1985 *EncSF 93, RfGShF*
Calvino, Philippe Andre Marie 1939- *WhoScEn 94*
Calvo, Alberto 1957- *WhoHisp 94*
Calvo, Edward M. *WhoAmP 93*
Calvo, Francisco Omar 1948- *WhoHisp 94*
Calvo, Horace Lawrence 1927- *WhoAmL 94*
Calvo, J. Manuel 1949- *WhoHisp 94*
Calvo, Juan d1962 *WhoHol 92*
Calvo, Kevin Edward 1957- *WhoWest 94*
Calvo, Manuel Frank 1922- *WhoHisp 94*
Calvo, Paul McDonald *WhoAmP 93*
Calvo, Roberto Q. *Who 94*
Calvocoressi, Michel-Dimitri 1877-1944 *NewGrDO*
Calvocoressi, Peter 1912- *IntWW 93*
Calvocoressi, Peter (John Ambrose) 1912- *Who 94, WrDr 94*
Calvocoressi, Richard Edward Ion 1951- *Who 94*
Calvo de Aguilar, Isabel 1916- *BlmGWL*
Calvo-Roth, Fortuna 1934- *WhoHisp 94*
Calvo-Sotelo, Joaquin d1993 *IntWW 93N*
Calvo-Sotelo, Joaquin 1905- *IntWW 93*
Calvo-Sotelo Bustelo, Leopoldo 1926- *IntWW 93*
Cal Yilei 1969- *WhoPRCh 91 [port]*
Calzabigi, Ranieri (Simone Francesco Maria) de' 1714-1795 *NewGrDO*
Calzada, Edelmira C. 1930- *WhoHisp 94*
Calzada, Humberto 1944- *WhoHisp 94*
Calzolano, John Joseph 1940- *WhoFI 94*
Calzolari, Elaine 1950- *WhoAmA 93*
Cam, Diego *WhWE*
Cam, Theodore Victor 1928- *WhoBlA 94*
Camacci, Michael A. 1951- *WhoMW 93*
Camacho, Antonio Muna *WhoAmP 93*
Camacho, Eduardo Garcia 1928- *WhoFI 94*
Camacho, Ernest M. 1944- *WhoHisp 94*
Camacho, Felix 1957- *WhoAmP 93*
Camacho, Francisco 1941- *WhoAmP 93*
Camacho, Héctor 1967- *WhoHisp 94*
Camacho, Henry Francis 1930- *WhoFI 94*
Camacho, Henry Stephen, III 1947- *WhoHisp 94*
Camacho, James, Jr. 1956- *WhoHisp 94*
Camacho, Marco Antonio 1960- *WhoHisp 94*
Camacho, P. Bruce *WhoIns 94*
Camacho, Ralph Alberto 1954- *WhoHisp 94*
Camacho, Robert Gregory 1953- *WhoHisp 94*
Camacho, Salvador 1942- *WhoHisp 94*
Camacho-Gingerich, Alina Luisa 1947- *WhoHisp 94*
Camacho Solis, Manuel 1946- *WhoAm 94*
Camadona, Juan 1952- *WhoHisp 94*
Camalier, Charles A. 1951- *WhoAmL 94*
Camara, Assan Musa 1923- *IntWW 93*
Camara, Helder Pessoa 1909- *IntWW 93*
Camarata, Martin L. 1934- *WhoAmA 93*
Camarata, Martin Louis 1934- *WhoAm 94*
Camaren, James L. 1954- *WhoMW 93*
Camarena, Edward 1938- *WhoHisp 94*
Camarena Badia, Vicente 1941- *IntWW 93*
Camargo, Francis Javier 1929- *WhoHisp 94*
Camargo, Marie-Anne 1710-1770 *IntDcB [port]*
Camargo, Marie-Anne de Cupis de 1710-1770 *NewGrDO*
Camargo, Martin Joseph 1950- *WhoHisp 94, WhoMW 93*
Camargo, Sergio de 1930- *IntWW 93*
Camarillo, Albert (M.) 1948- *WrDr 94*
Camarillo, Albert Michael 1948- *WhoHisp 94*
Camarillo, Richard Jon 1959- *WhoAm 94, WhoWest 94*
Camarillo, Teresa 1943- *WhoHisp 94*
Camarra, Joseph A. 1946- *WhoAmL 94*
Camastro-Pritchett, Rose 1942- *WhoAmA 93*
Camata, Rita de Cassia Paste 1961- *WhoWomW 91*

Cambalouris, Michael Dimitrios 1959-
WhoScEn 94
Cambeiro, Arturo B. 1932- WhoHisp 94
Cambel, Ali Bulent 1923- WhoAm 94,
WhoScEn 94
Cambell, Dennis Royle Farquharson
1907- Who 94
Camber, Andrew ConAu 42NR
Camber, Diane Woolfe WhoAmA 93
Cambern, Donn ConTFT 11
Cambert, Robert c. 1628-1677 NewGrDO
Cambiaggio, Carlo 1798-1880 NewGrDO
Cambie, Richard Conrad 1931- IntWW 93
Cambier, Penelope Howland 1935-
WhoMW 93
Cambini, Giuseppe Maria (Gioacchino)
1746-1825 NewGrDO
Cambio, Bambilyn Breece 1956-
WhoAmP 93
Cambio, Frank Caesar 1895- WhAm 10
Cambitoglou, Alexander IntWW 93
Camblos, James L., III 1945- WhoAmL 94
Cambon, Charles-Antoine 1802-1875
NewGrDO
Camboni, Silvana Maria WhoScEn 94
Cambosos, Bruce Michael 1941-
WhoBlA 94
Cambray-Dignay, Louis Antoine Jean
Baptiste 1751-1822 AmRev
Cambray-Digny, Louis Antoine
Jean-Baptiste, Chevalier de 1751-1822
WhAmRev
Cambreling, Sylvain 1948- IntWW 93,
NewGrDO
Cambria, Paul J. 1947- WhoAmL 94
Cambrice, Robert Louis 1947-
WhoAmL 94
Cambridge, Ada 1844-1926 BlmGWL
Cambridge, Alan John 1925- Who 94
Cambridge, Dexter WhoBlA 94
Cambridge, Edward Jonathan 1922-
WhoAmL 94
Cambridge, Godfrey d1976 WhoHol 92
Cambridge, Godfrey 1933-1976
AfrAmAl 6 [port], WhoCom
Cambridge, Sydney John Guy 1928-
Who 94
Cambridge, William G. 1931- WhoAm 94,
WhoAmL 94, WhoMW 93
Camden, Marquess 1930- Who 94
Camden, Dorothea d1980 WhoHol 92
Camden, John 1925- IntWW 93, Who 94
Camdessus, Jean-Michel 1933- IntWW 93
Camdessus, Michel WhoAmP 93
Camdessus, Michel 1933- Who 94
Camdessus, Michel Jean 1933-
WhoAm 94, WhoFI 94
Camelia, Muriel d1925 WhoHol 92
Camelins, L. T. 1912- WrDr 94
Camenga, David LeRoy 1938-
WhoMW 93
Camenzind, Mark J. 1956- WhoWest 94
Camera, Michael J. 1954- WhoAmP 93
Camerano, Franklin 1936- WhoAm 94
Camerius, James Walter 1939- WhoFI 94,
WhoMW 93
Cameron Who 94
Cameron, Hon. Lord 1900- Who 94
Cameron, Alan Douglas Edward 1938-
Who 94
Cameron, Alastair Duncan 1920-
WhoAm 94
Cameron, Alastair Graham Walter 1925-
WhoAm 94
Cameron, Albert Neill 1946- WhoAm 94
Cameron, Alexander d1781 AmRev
Cameron, Alexander 1926- WrDr 94
Cameron, Allan John 1917- Who 94
Cameron, Allan Williams 1938-
WhoAmP 93
Cameron, Andrew Bruce Who 94
Cameron, Ann d1979 WhoHol 92
Cameron, Ann 1925- Who 94
Cameron, Anne 1938- BlmGWL
Cameron, (Barbara) Anne 1938- WrDr 94
Cameron, Averil Millicent 1940-
IntWW 93, Who 94
Cameron, Berl EncSF 93
Cameron, Brooke Bulovsky WhoAmA 93
Cameron, Bruce d1959 WhoHol 92
Cameron, Bruce Francis 1934- WhoAm 94
Cameron, Candace 1976- WhoHol 92
Cameron, Carey 1952- WrDr 94
Cameron, Carey Marbut 1935-
WhoAmL 94
Cameron, Charles 1743?-1812 DcNaB MP
Cameron, Charles Bruce 1954-
WhoScEn 94
Cameron, Charles Henry 1947-
WhoWest 94
Cameron, Charles Metz, Jr. 1923-
WhoAm 94
Cameron, Clive Bremner 1921- Who 94
Cameron, Clyde Robert 1913- IntWW 93
Cameron, Colin Campbell 1927-
WhAm 10
Cameron, Colleen Irene 1952- WhoAm 94,
WhoMW 93

Cameron, D.B. 1932- WhoMW 93
Cameron, David Brian 1953- WhoAm 94
Cameron, Dean WhoHol 92
Cameron, Dean L. 1961- WhoAmP 93
Cameron, Don R. 1937- WhoAm 94
Cameron, Donald d1955 WhoHol 92
Cameron, Donald d1987 WhoHol 92
Cameron, Donald 1901-1967 EncSPD
Cameron, Donald William 1946- Who 94
Cameron, Donna M. 1946- WhoAmL 94
Cameron, Douglas Maclean Who 94
Cameron, Duncan F. 1930- WhoAmA 93
Cameron, Duncan Ferguson 1930-
WhoWest 94
Cameron, Duncan Hume 1934-
WhoAm 94
Cameron, Earl 1925- WhoHol 92
Cameron, Edward Madison, III 1933-
WhoIns 94
Cameron, Eleanor 1912- BlmGWL
Cameron, Eleanor (Butler) 1912-
EncSF 93, WrDr 94
Cameron, Eleanor (Frances) 1912-
TwCYAW
Cameron, Eleanor Frances 1912-
WhoAm 94
Cameron, Ellen Who 94
Cameron, Elsa S. 1939- WhoAmA 93
Cameron, Elsa Sue 1939- WhoWest 94
Cameron, Eric 1935- WhoAmA 93
Cameron, Eugene Foster 1945- WhoAm 94
Cameron, Ewen Donald 1926- Who 94
Cameron, Francis (Ernest) 1927- Who 94
Cameron, Gene d1928 WhoHol 92
Cameron, George Edmund 1911- Who 94
Cameron, Goldie d1976 WhoHol 92
Cameron, Gordon Stewart 1916- Who 94
Cameron, Guy E. 1958- WhoAmP 93
Cameron, Howard K., Jr. 1930-1991
WhoBlA 94N
Cameron, Hugh d1941 WhoHol 92
Cameron, Iain Thomas 1956- Who 94
Cameron, Ian 1924- EncSF 93, WrDr 94
Cameron, Ian Alexander 1938- Who 94
Cameron, Ian Rennell 1936- Who 94
Cameron, J.D. EncSF 93
Cameron, J. Elliot 1923- WhoAm 94
Cameron, J(ames) Malcolm 1930- Who 94
Cameron, Jack Lyndon 1961- WhoBlA 94
Cameron, James 1954- IntMPA 94
Cameron, James 1956- EncSF 93
Cameron, James Duke 1925- WhoAm 94,
WhoAmL 94, WhoAmP 93, WhoWest 94
Cameron, James Munro 1910- Who 94,
WrDr 94
Cameron, James R. 1942- WhoAmL 94
Cameron, JoAnna WhoAm 94
Cameron, Joanna 1950- WhoHol 92
Cameron, Joanna 1951- IntMPA 94
Cameron, John Who 94
Cameron, John 1927- EncSF 93
Cameron, (Eustace) John 1913- Who 94
Cameron, John (Watson) 1901- Who 94
Cameron, John Alastair Who 94
Cameron, John Bell 1939- Who 94
Cameron, John Charles Finlay 1928-
Who 94
Cameron, John Clifford 1946- WhoAm 94,
WhoAmL 94
Cameron, John E. 1932- WhoBlA 94
Cameron, John Gray, Jr. 1949-
WhoAmL 94
Cameron, John Lansing 1916- WhoAm 94
Cameron, John Robinson 1936- Who 94
Cameron, John Taylor Who 94
Cameron, Joseph A. 1942- WhoBlA 94
Cameron, Joy 1912- WrDr 94
Cameron, Judith Elaine Moellering 1943-
WhoWest 94
Cameron, Judith Lynne 1945- WhoAm 94,
WhoWest 94
Cameron, Julie EncSF 93
Cameron, Kate ConAu 43NR
Cameron, Kenneth 1922- IntWW 93,
Who 94
Cameron, Kenneth Allan 1953-
WhoWest 94
Cameron, Kirk 1970- IntMPA 94,
WhoHol 92
Cameron, Krystol 1967- WhoBlA 94
Cameron, Lewis 1935- Who 94
Cameron, Liana L. 1954- WhoMW 93
Cameron, Lorna WrDr 94
Cameron, Lou 1924- EncSF 93, WrDr 94
Cameron, Lucille Wilson 1932-
WhoAm 94
Cameron, Mary Evelyn 1944- WhoBlA 94
Cameron, Maryellen 1943- WhoScEn 94
Cameron, Matthew d1988 WhoHol 92
Cameron, Mindy WhoAm 94
Cameron, Nicholas Allen 1939-
WhoAm 94
Cameron, Paul Scott 1940- WhoMW 93
Cameron, Peter Alfred Gordon 1930-
WhoAm 94
Cameron, Peter Duncanson 1952-
IntWW 93

Cameron, Prudence Lanegran 1934-
WhoAmP 93
Cameron, Randolph W. WhoBlA 94
Cameron, Richard Douglas 1937-
WhoAm 94
Cameron, Richard Irwin 1941- WhoFI 94,
WhoWest 94
Cameron, Richfield J. 1921- WhoIns 94
Cameron, Rita Giovannetti WhoAm 94
Cameron, Robert A. WhoAmP 93
Cameron, Robert H. 1953- WhoScEn 94
Cameron, Rod d1983 WhoHol 92
Cameron, Rondo 1925- WhoAm 94,
WrDr 94
Cameron, Roy James 1923- Who 94
Cameron, Rudolph d1958 WhoHol 92
Cameron, Sheila Morag Clark 1934-
Who 94
Cameron, Silver Donald 1937- WrDr 94
Cameron, Stuart Gordon 1924- Who 94
Cameron, Susan Kay 1960- WhoMW 93
Cameron, Thomas Anthony 1947- Who 94
Cameron, Thomas K. 1934- WhoIns 94
Cameron, Thomas William Lane 1927-
WhoAm 94
Cameron, Tom WhoAmP 93
Cameron, Ulysses 1930- WhoBlA 94
Cameron, Verney Lovett 1844-1894
WhWE
Cameron, Wilburn Macio, Jr. WhoBlA 94
Cameron, William Duncan 1925-
WhoFI 94, WhoScEn 94
Cameron Of Lochbroom, Baron 1931-
IntWW 93, Who 94
Cameron Of Lochiel, Donald (Hamish)
1910- Who 94
Cameron-Ramsay-Fairfax-Lucy Who 94
Cameron Watt, Donald 1928- IntWW 93,
Who 94, WrDr 94
Camfferman, Peter Marienus 1890-1957
WhoAmA 93N
Camfield, William Arnett 1934-
WhoAm 94, WhoAmA 93
Camhi, Morrie 1928- WhoAmA 93
Cami, Foto 1925- IntWW 93
Camic, David Edward 1954- WhoAmL 94
Camiener, Gerald W. 1932- WhoMW 93
Camilion, Oscar Hector 1930- IntWW 93
Camilleri, Charles 1931- IntWW 93
Camilleri, Joseph A. 1944- ConAu 41NR
Camilleri, Michael 1953- WhoAmL 94
Camilleri, Victor 1942- IntWW 93,
Who 94
Camilletti, Rob 1965- WhoHol 92
Camilo, Michel 1954- WhoHisp 94
Camin, Carlos WhoHisp 94
Caminiti, Donald Angelo WhoAmL 94
Camino, Mario d1981 WhoHol 92
Caminos-Medina, María A. 1941-
WhoHisp 94
Camins, Jacques Joseph 1904-1988
WhoAmA 93N
Camisa, George Lincoln 1929- WhoAm 94
Camisi, Domenick J. 1947- WhoFI 94
Camlin, James A. 1918-1982
WhoAmA 93N
Camm, A(lan) John 1947- Who 94
Camm, John 1718-1778 WhAmRev
Camma, Philip 1923- WhoFI 94,
WhoMW 93
Cammack, Charles Lee, Jr. 1954-
WhoBlA 94
Cammack, Trank Emerson 1919-
WhoAm 94
Cammaker, Sheldon Ira 1939- WhoAm 94,
WhoFI 94
Cammalleri, Joseph Anthony 1935-
WhoWest 94
Cammann, Helmuth Carl IntWW 93
Cammans, Stephen Charles 1954-
WhoWest 94
Cammarano, Salvadore 1801-1852
NewGrDO
Cammarata, Angelo 1936- WhoScEn 94
Cammarata, Bernard 1940- WhoFI 94
Cammarata, Richard John 1950-
WhoFI 94
Cammell, John Ernest 1932- Who 94
Cammock, Earl E. 1926- WhoAm 94
Camner, Howard DrAPF 93
Camoretti-Mercado, Blanca Del Socorro
1957- WhoMW 93
Camoys, Baron 1940- IntWW 93, Who 94
Camp, Alida Diane 1955- WhoWest 94
Camp, Anthony John 1937- Who 94
Camp, Billy Joe 1938- WhoAm 94,
WhoAmP 93
Camp, Candace (Pauline) 1949-
ConAu 42NR
Camp, Cassandra Ann 1950- WhoFI 94
Camp, Clifton Durrett, Jr. 1927-
WhoAm 94
Camp, Colleen 1953- IntMPA 94,
WhoHol 92
Camp, Dave 1953- CngDr 93, WhoAm 94,
WhoAmP 93, WhoMW 93
Camp, Donald A. WhoAm 94
Camp, Duane d1987 WhoHol 92

Camp, Frances Spencer 1924-
WhoScEn 94
Camp, George 1926- WhoAmP 93
Camp, Hamilton 1934- WhoHol 92
Camp, Hazel Lee Burt 1922- WhoAm 94
Camp, Herbert Latimer 1939- WhoAm 94,
WhoAmL 94
Camp, Herbert V., Jr. 1935- WhoAmP 93
Camp, Jack Tarpley, Jr. 1943- WhoAm 94,
WhoAmL 94
Camp, James DrAPF 93
Camp, Jeffery Bruce 1923- IntWW 93,
Who 94
Camp, Joe 1939- IntMPA 94
Camp, John 1939- WhoAmP 93
Camp, John W. 1949- WhoAmL 94
Camp, Joseph Shelton, Jr. 1939-
WhoAm 94
Camp, Kimberly Noreen 1956-
WhoBlA 94
Camp, Laurie Smith 1953- WhoAmL 94
Camp, Linda Joyce WhoAm 94
Camp, Maria Theresa de NewGrDO
Camp, Martin L. 1954- WhoAmL 94
Camp, Marva Jo 1961- WhoBlA 94
Camp, Roderic (Ai) 1945- ConAu 41NR
Camp, Shep d1929 WhoHol 92
Camp, Susan K. 1959- WhoMW 93
Camp, Thomas Harley 1929-
WhoScEn 94
Camp, William C. WhoAmP 93
Camp, William Curtis WhoWest 94
Camp, William Newton Alexander 1926-
Who 94
Camp, Wilson d1988 WhoHol 92
Campa, Gustavo E(milio) 1863-1934
NewGrDO
Campagna, Larry A. 1952- WhoAmL 94
Campagna, Richard Vincent 1952-
WhoAmL 94
Campagne, Thomas Elmer 1950-
WhoAmL 94
Campagnolo, Francesco 1584-1630
NewGrDO
Campaign, H. John WhoAmL 94
Campaigne, Ernest Edwin 1914-
WhoAm 94
Campan, Jeanne-Louise-Henriette Genest
1752-1822 BlmGWL
Campana, Ana Isabel 1934- WhoFI 94
Campana, Fabio 1819-1882 NewGrDO
Campana, Michael Emerson 1948-
WhoWest 94
Campana, Nina d1950 WhoHol 92
Campana, Richard John 1918- WhoAm 94
Campanari, Giuseppe 1855-1927
NewGrDO
Campanella, Americo 1922- WhoAmP 93
Campanella, Anton J. 1932- WhoAm 94,
WhoFI 94
Campanella, Frank WhoHol 92
Campanella, Joseph 1927- WhoHol 92
Campanella, Migdalia Cavazos 1961
WhoHisp 94
Campanella, Roy 1921-1993
AfrAmAl 6 [port], CurBio 93N,
NewYTBS 93 [port], News 94-1
Campanella, Roy, Sr. 1921-1993
WhoBlA 94N
Campanella, Tom 1944- IntMPA 94
Campanella, Tommaso 1568-1639
EncSF 93
Campanelli, Dan 1949- WhoAmA 93
Campanelli, John A. 1918- WhoAmP 93
Campanelli, Pauline Eble WhoAmA 93
Campanelli, Pauline Eble 1943-
WhoAm 94
Campaneris, Bert 1942- WhoHisp 94
Campanini, Barbara IntDcB
Campanini, Carlo d1984 WhoHol 92
Campanini, Cleofonte 1860-1919
NewGrDO
Campanini, Italo 1845-1896 NewGrDO
Campanius, Johan 1601-1683
DcAmReB 2, EncNAR
Company, Andrew Daniel 1956-
WhoWest 94
Campaspe, La NewGrDO
Campbell Who 94
Campbell, A. Stuart 1953- WhoAmL 94
Campbell, Alan 1957- ConTFT 11,
WhoHol 92
Campbell, Alan (Hugh) 1919- Who 94
Campbell, Alan Hugh 1919- IntWW 93
Campbell, Alan Keith 1923- Who 94
Campbell, Alexander d1970 WhoHol 92
Campbell, Alexander 1788-1866
DcAmReB 2
Campbell, Alexander Bradshaw 1933-
IntWW 93, Who 94
Campbell, Alexander Buchanan 1914-
Who 94
Campbell, Alexander Elmslie 1929-
Who 94
Campbell, Alice del Campillo 1928-
WhoWest 94
Campbell, Alice Shaw 1918- WhoMW 93

Campbell, Alistair (Te Ariki) 1925-
WrDr 94
Campbell, Allan McCulloch 1929-
IntWW 93, WhoAm 94
Campbell, Allen F. 1948- *WhoAmL 94*
Campbell, Alvis E. 1944- *WhoAmL 94*
Campbell, Andrew Garrett 1960-
WhoWest 94
Campbell, Andrew Robert 1954-
WhoWest 94
Campbell, Anita Joyce 1953- *WhoMW 93*
Campbell, Anne 1940- *Who 94*
Campbell, Anthony *Who 94*
Campbell, (William) Anthony 1936-
Who 94
Campbell, Archibald 1739-1791 *AmRev,
WhAmRev*
Campbell, Archibald 1914- *Who 94*
Campbell, Archie d1987 *WhoHol 92*
Campbell, Argyle d1940 *WhoHol 92*
Campbell, Arthur A(ndrews) 1924-
ConAu 43NR
Campbell, Arthur Andrews 1924-
WhoAm 94
Campbell, Arthur McLure 1932- *Who 94*
Campbell, Arthur Ree 1943- *WhoBlA 94*
Campbell, Arthur Russell 1898- *WhAm 10*
Campbell, Arthur Waldron 1944-
WhoWest 94
Campbell, Ashley Sawyer 1918-
WhoScEn 94
Campbell, Avril Kim 1947- *WhoAm 94*
Campbell, Barbara J. *WhoAmP 93*
Campbell, Barbara Seim 1932-
WhoAmP 93
Campbell, Barry Keith 1947- *WhoAmP 93*
Campbell, Beatrice d1980 *WhoHol 92*
Campbell, Beatrice Murphy 1908-
WhoBlA 94
Campbell, Bebe Moore *WhoBlA 94*
Campbell, Bebe Moore 1950- *BlkWr 2,
ConBlB 6 [port]*
Campbell, Ben D. 1947- *WhoAmP 93*
Campbell, Ben Nighthorse 1933-
*CngDr 93, IntWW 93, WhoAm 94,
WhoAmP 93, WhoWest 94*
Campbell, Bert Louis 1939- *WhoAmL 94*
Campbell, Bertrand Charles 1941-
WhoAmP 93
Campbell, Beverly *WhoHol 92*
Campbell, Blanch 1941- *WhoBlA 94*
Campbell, Bobby Lamar 1949-
WhoBlA 94
Campbell, Bonnie 1948- *WhoAmP 93,
WhoWomW 91*
Campbell, Bonnie Jean 1948- *WhoAm 94,
WhoAmL 94, WhoMW 93*
Campbell, Bonnie Jo 1962- *WhoMW 93*
Campbell, Brian C. d1993 *NewYTBS 93*
Campbell, Brian Edward 1962-
WhoAmP 93
Campbell, Bruce *WhoHol 92*
Campbell, Bruce d1993 *NewYTBS 93*
Campbell, Bruce 1954- *WhoAmL 94*
Campbell, Bruce Alan 1944- *WhoAm 94*
Campbell, Bruce Crichton 1947-
WhoAm 94
Campbell, Bruce D. 1953- *WhoAmL 94*
Campbell, Bruce Irving 1947-
WhoAmL 94
Campbell, Bud 1938- *WhoAmP 93*
Campbell, Byron *WhoAmP 93*
Campbell, Byron Chesser 1934-
WhoAm 94
Campbell, Calvin C. 1924- *WhoBlA 94*
Campbell, Carl Lester 1943- *WhoAm 94*
Campbell, Carlos, Sr. 1946- *WhoBlA 94*
Campbell, Carlos C. 1937- *WhoAmP 93*
Campbell, Carlos Cardozo 1937-
WhoBlA 94
Campbell, Carol Norton 1944-
WhoMW 93
Campbell, Carolyn Milburn 1961-
WhoAmL 94
Campbell, Carrol Nunn 1952- *WhoBlA 94*
Campbell, Carroll Ashmore 1940-
IntWW 93
Campbell, Carroll Ashmore, Jr. 1940-
WhoAm 94, WhoAmP 93
Campbell, Catherine Mary 1941-
WhoMW 93
Campbell, Charles *WhoScEn 94*
Campbell, Charles Alton 1944- *WhoFI 94*
Campbell, Charles Everett 1933-
WhoBlA 94
Campbell, Charles H. 1931- *WhoFI 94*
Campbell, Charles J. 1915- *WhoAm 94*
Campbell, Charles K. 1949- *WhoAm 94*
Campbell, Charles Lee 1953- *WhoScEn 94*
Campbell, Charles Malcolm 1908-1985
WhoAmA 93N
Campbell, Charles Philip, Jr. 1948-
WhoAmL 94
Campbell, Charlotte Catherine d1993
NewYTBS 93
Campbell, Cheryl 1950- *WhoHol 92*

Campbell, Cheryl (Anne) 1949- *Who 94*
Campbell, Cheryl Nichols 1948-
WhoMW 93
Campbell, Christian Larsen 1950-
WhoAmL 94
Campbell, Christopher James 1936-
Who 94
Campbell, Christopher Lundy 1954-
WhoBlA 94
Campbell, Clair Gilliland 1961-
WhoAmL 94
Campbell, Clifford V. 1921- *WhoAmP 93*
Campbell, Clyde Crane *EncSF 93*
Campbell, Clyde Del 1930- *WhoAm 94*
Campbell, Colin *Who 94*
Campbell, Colin d1966 *WhoHol 92*
Campbell, Colin 1927- *WhoAm 94*
Campbell, Colin 1937- *WhoHol 92*
Campbell, Colin, Lady *ConAu 140*
Campbell, (Alexander) Colin (Patton)
1908- *Who 94*
Campbell, Colin Dearborn 1917-
WhoAm 94
Campbell, Colin Goetze 1935- *WhoAm 94*
Campbell, Colin Herald 1911-
WhoWest 94
Campbell, Colin Kydd 1927- *IntWW 93,
WhoAm 94*
Campbell, Colin Malcolm 1953- *Who 94*
Campbell, Colin McLeod 1945-
WhoAm 94
Campbell, Colin Moffat 1925- *Who 94*
Campbell, Colin Murray 1944-
IntWW 93, Who 94
Campbell, Courtney Lee 1957-
WhoAmL 94
Campbell, Craig Bartlett 1938-
WhoAmP 93
Campbell, Daniel Lee 1956- *WhoMW 93*
Campbell, David *EncSF 93*
Campbell, David Alan 1954- *WhoWest 94*
Campbell, David Brian 1957-
WhoAmP 93
Campbell, David Bruce 1953-
WhoScEn 94
Campbell, David Douglas 1929-
WhoFI 94
Campbell, David G. 1952- *WhoAmL 94*
Campbell, David George 1949-
WhoScEn 94
Campbell, David Gwynne 1930-
WhoAm 94, WhoFI 94
Campbell, David James 1953-
WhoMW 93
Campbell, David John G. *Who 94*
Campbell, David Martin 1961- *WhoFI 94*
Campbell, David Ned 1929- *WhoAm 94*
Campbell, David Paul 1936- *WhoAmA 93*
Campbell, David Randall 1928-
WhoWest 94
Campbell, David Scott 1954- *WhoWest 94*
Campbell, David Stetson 1943-
WhoAm 94
Campbell, David White 1945- *WhoAm 94*
Campbell, Debra Lynn 1954- *WhoFI 94*
Campbell, Demarest Lindsay *WhoWest 94*
Campbell, Dennis George 1949-
WhoAm 94
Campbell, Dennis Marion 1945-
WhoAm 94
Campbell, Dennis Michael 1954-
WhoAmL 94
Campbell, Diana Butt 1943- *WhoAmL 94*
Campbell, Dianne Lynne 1958-
WhoMW 93
Campbell, Dick C. 1903- *WhoBlA 94*
Campbell, Doak Sheridan 1945-
WhoAmP 93
Campbell, Donald 1930- *Who 94*
Campbell, Donald 1940- *WrDr 94*
Campbell, Donald A. 1922- *WhoAmP 93*
Campbell, Donald Acheson 1919-
WhoScEn 94
Campbell, Donald Graham 1925-
WhoAm 94
Campbell, Donald K. 1926- *WhoAm 94*
Campbell, Donald le Strange 1919-
Who 94
Campbell, Donald Malcolm 1921-1967
DcNaB MP
Campbell, Donald Thomas 1916-
WhoAm 94
Campbell, Donovan, Jr. 1950-
WhoAmL 94
Campbell, Doris Klein *WhoScEn 94*
Campbell, Dorothy Bostwick 1899-
WhoAmA 93
Campbell, Douglas 1922- *WhoHol 92*
Campbell, Douglas Argyle 1929-
WhoAm 94, WhoFI 94
Campbell, Douglas G. *DrAPF 93*
Campbell, Douglas Michael 1943-
WhoWest 94
Campbell, Douglas Norman 1955-
WhoWest 94
Campbell, Douglass 1919- *WhoAm 94,
WhoFI 94*
Campbell, Duncan 1935- *Who 94*

Campbell, E. Alexander 1927- *WhoBlA 94*
Campbell, Earl *ProFbHF*
Campbell, Earl Christian 1955-
WhoBlA 94
Campbell, Edmund Douglas 1899-
WhoAm 94
Campbell, Edmund S. 1884-1950
WhoAmA 93N
Campbell, Edward Adolph 1936-
WhoAmL 94
Campbell, Edward Clinton 1929-
WhoFI 94
Campbell, Edward Fay, Jr. 1932-
WhoAm 94
Campbell, Edward Joseph 1928-
WhoAm 94
Campbell, Edwin Denton 1927-
WhoAm 94
Campbell, Elden 1968- *WhoBlA 94*
Campbell, Emmett Earle 1927-
WhoBlA 94
Campbell, Emory Shaw 1941- *WhoBlA 94*
Campbell, Eric d1917 *WhoHol 92*
Campbell, Eric Eldon 1929- *WhoAm 94*
Campbell, Eunice M. 1920- *WhoAmP 93*
Campbell, Everett O. 1934- *WhoBlA 94*
Campbell, Ewing *DrAPF 93*
Campbell, Fenton Gregory 1939-
WhoAm 94
Campbell, Fergus William d1993
Who 94N
Campbell, Fergus William 1924-
IntWW 93
Campbell, Finley Alexander 1927-
IntWW 93, WhoAm 94
Campbell, Flora d1978 *WhoHol 92*
Campbell, Foster L., Jr. 1947-
WhoAmP 93
Campbell, Francis James 1924-
WhoAm 94
Campbell, Francis Stuart 1909- *WrDr 94*
Campbell, Frank d1934 *WhoHol 92*
Campbell, Frank C. d1993 *NewYTBS 93*
Campbell, Frank Carter 1916- *WhoAm 94*
Campbell, Franklin Carter 1958-
WhoMW 93
Campbell, Franklyn D. 1947- *WhoBlA 94*
Campbell, Freda K. *Who 94*
Campbell, Frederick Hollister 1923-
WhoAmL 94, WhoWest 94
Campbell, G(aylon) S(anford) 1940-
WrDr 94
Campbell, Gary J. 1944- *WhoFI 94*
Campbell, Gary Lloyd 1951- *WhoBlA 94*
Campbell, Gavin Elliott 1960-
WhoMW 93
Campbell, Gaylon Sanford 1940-
WhoWest 94
Campbell, Gene *WhoAmP 93*
Campbell, George, Jr. 1945- *WhoBlA 94*
Campbell, George Anthony 1952-
WhoAmP 93
Campbell, George Emerson 1932-
WhoAm 94, WhoAmL 94, WhoFI 94
Campbell, George W. 1922- *WhoAmP 93*
Campbell, Georgia Arianna Ziadie 1949-
ConAu 140
Campbell, Gertrude M. 1923- *WhoBlA 94*
Campbell, Gilbert Godfrey 1920-
WhoBlA 94
Campbell, Gilbert R., Jr. 1932-
WhoAmL 94
Campbell, Gilbert Sadler 1924-
WhoAm 94
Campbell, Glen 1936- *IntMPA 94,
WhoAm 94, WhoHol 92*
Campbell, Gordon Muir 1948-
WhoAm 94, WhoFI 94
Campbell, Grace MacLennan 1895-1963
BlmGWL
Campbell, Graham F. 1939- *WhoBlA 94*
Campbell, Graham Gordon 1924- *Who 94*
Campbell, Gregory Ray 1955-
WhoWest 94
Campbell, Grover R. 1954- *WhoAmP 93*
Campbell, Guy Theophilus Halswell
d1993 *Who 94N*
Campbell, H(erbert) J. 1925- *EncSF 93*
Campbell, H. R. 1929- *WhoAmP 93*
Campbell, Hamish Manus d1993
Who 94N
Campbell, Harold Edward 1915- *Who 94*
Campbell, Harry Francis d1983
WhoHol 92
Campbell, Harry L. 1966- *WhoScEn 94*
Campbell, Harry Woodson 1946-
WhoWest 94
Campbell, Henry Cummings 1919-
WhoAm 94
Campbell, Henry J., Jr. 1922-
WhoScEn 94
Campbell, Herbert d1904 *WhoHol 92*
Campbell, Howard Ernest 1925-
WhoWest 94
Campbell, Hugh 1916- *Who 94*
Campbell, Hugh Hall 1944- *Who 94*
Campbell, Iain Leslie 1955- *WhoScEn 94*
Campbell, Ian 1926- *Who 94*

Campbell, Ian 1942- *WrDr 94*
Campbell, Ian (Tofts) 1923- *Who 94*
Campbell, Ian Barclay 1916- *WrDr 94*
Campbell, Ian Burns 1938- *Who 94*
Campbell, Ian David 1945- *NewGrDO,
WhoAm 94, WhoWest 94*
Campbell, Ian Dugald 1916- *Who 94*
Campbell, Ian James 1923- *Who 94*
Campbell, Ian Macdonald 1922- *Who 94*
Campbell, Ian Robert 1920- *Who 94*
Campbell, Ian Ross 1900- *Who 94*
Campbell, J. Cameron 1943- *WhoFI 94*
Campbell, J. Kenneth *WhoHol 92*
Campbell, J. Kermit 1939- *WhoAm 94,
WhoFI 94*
Campbell, Jack James Ramsay 1918-
WhoAm 94
Campbell, Jack L. 1945- *WhoAmL 94*
Campbell, Jackson Justice 1920-
WhoAm 94
Campbell, James 1935- *Who 94*
Campbell, James Albert Barton 1940-
WhoFI 94
Campbell, James Anson 1854-1933
EncABHB 9 [port]
Campbell, James Arthur 1916-1989
WhAm 10
Campbell, James Arthur 1924-
WhoAm 94, WhoMW 93
Campbell, James Edward 1943-
WhoScEn 94, WhoWest 94
Campbell, James Howard, Jr. 1958-
WhoFI 94
Campbell, James Hugh 1926- *Who 94*
Campbell, James Marshall 1895-
WhAm 10
Campbell, James Marshall 1942-
WhoAmP 93
Campbell, James Robert 1942-
WhoAm 94
Campbell, James Sargent 1938-
WhoAm 94
Campbell, James W. *WhoAmP 93*
Campbell, James W. 1945- *WhoBlA 94*
Campbell, Jane Louise 1953-
*WhoAmP 93, WhoMW 93,
WhoWomW 91*
Campbell, Jean 1925- *WhoFI 94*
Campbell, Jeanne Begien 1913-
WhoAmA 93
Campbell, Jerry Dean 1945- *WhoAm 94*
Campbell, Jewett 1912- *WhoAmA 93*
Campbell, Jim d1980 *WhoHol 92*
Campbell, Jimmy d1967 *WhoHol 92*
Campbell, Jo-Ann 1938- *WhoHol 92*
Campbell, Joan d1981 *WhoHol 92*
Campbell, Joan Brown *WhoAm 94*
Campbell, Joe Bill 1943- *WhoAmL 94*
Campbell, John d1806 *WhAmRev*
Campbell, John d1993 *NewYTBS 93*
Campbell, John 1753-1784 *WhAmRev*
Campbell, John 1766-c. 1840 *WhWE*
Campbell, John 1934- *WhoAmP 93*
Campbell, John 1936- *IntWW 93*
Campbell, John 1938- *WhoScEn 94*
Campbell, John Coert 1911- *WhoAm 94*
Campbell, John Davies 1921- *Who 94*
Campbell, John Douglas 1943-
WhoAm 94
Campbell, John Frank 1947- *WhoWest 94*
Campbell, John Jette 1947- *WhoFI 94*
Campbell, John Kelly 1929- *WhoAm 94*
Campbell, John L. 1906- *Who 94*
Campbell, John Morgan 1922- *WhoAm 94*
Campbell, John Palmer 1923-
WhoAmL 94, WhoAmP 93
Campbell, John Richard 1932- *WhoAm 94*
Campbell, John Roy 1933- *WhoAm 94,
WhoScEn 94*
Campbell, John Tucker 1912-1991
WhAm 10
Campbell, John W(ood), Jr. 1910-1971
EncSF 93
Campbell, Johnnie Jay 1946- *WhoFI 94*
Campbell, Jonathan Wesley 1950-
WhoScEn 94
Campbell, Joseph Leonard 1938-
WhoAm 94
Campbell, Joyce Marie 1936- *WhoMW 93*
Campbell, Judith 1914- *WrDr 94*
Campbell, Judith Lowe 1946- *WhoAm 94,
WhoMW 93, WhoScEn 94*
Campbell, Judith May 1938- *WhoAm 94*
Campbell, Judy 1916- *WhoHol 92*
Campbell, Julia *WhoHol 92*
Campbell, Juliet Jeanne D'Auvergne
1935- *IntWW 93, Who 94*
Campbell, Karen 1919- *WrDr 94*
Campbell, Karlyn Kohrs 1937-
WhoAm 94
Campbell, Katherine Ann 1949-
WhoWest 94
Campbell, Kathleen Charlotte Murphey
1952- *WhoScEn 94*
Campbell, Katie 1957- *WrDr 94*
Campbell, Kay d1985 *WhoHol 92*
Campbell, Kenneth Archibald 1936-
Who 94

Campbell, Kenneth Eugene, Jr. 1943-
WhoAm 94
Campbell, Kenneth Floyd 1925-
WhoAmA 93
Campbell, Kim *NewYTBS 93,*
WhoWomW 91
Campbell, Kim 1947- *IntWW 93,*
News 93 [port], Who 94
Campbell, Lachlan (Philip Kemeys) 1958-
Who 94
Campbell, Larry E. 1941- *WhoAm 94*
Campbell, Larry L. 1931- *WhoAmP 93*
Campbell, Larry Norton 1946-
WhoMW 93
Campbell, Laughlin Andrew 1942-
WhoWest 94
Campbell, Laurence Jamieson 1927-
Who 94
Campbell, (James) Lawrence 1914-
WhoAmA 93
Campbell, Lawrence G. 1939-
WhoAmL 94
Campbell, Leila 1911- *Who 94*
Campbell, Leonard Martin 1918-
WhoAm 94
Campbell, Levin H. *WhoAmP 93*
Campbell, Levin Hicks 1927- *WhoAm 94,*
WhoAmL 94
Campbell, Linzy Leon 1927- *WhoAm 94,*
WhoScEn 94
Campbell, Louis Lorne 1928- *WhoAm 94*
Campbell, Louise 1915- *WhoHol 92*
Campbell, Lucinda Solomon 1925-
WhoAmP 93
Campbell, Luther c. 1961-
ConMus 10 [port]
Campbell, Lyle Richard 1942- *WhoAm 94*
Campbell, M. Douglas, Jr. 1962-
WhoAmL 94
Campbell, Margaret d1939 *WhoHol 92*
Campbell, Margaret Amelia 1923-1992
WhAm 10
Campbell, Margaret M. 1928- *WhoAm 94*
Campbell, Margie 1954- *WhoBlA 94*
Campbell, Mari Elizabeth 1944-
WhoFI 94
Campbell, Maria 1940- *BlmGWL*
Campbell, Maria Bouchelle 1944-
WhoAmL 94
Campbell, María Dolores Delgado 1943-
WhoHisp 94
Campbell, Marilyn R. 1932- *WhoAmP 93*
Campbell, Marion 1948- *BlmGWL*
Campbell, Martin James 1965-
WhoWest 94
Campbell, Marty *DrAPF 93*
Campbell, Mary Allison 1937- *WhoBlA 94*
Campbell, Mary B(aine) 1954- *WrDr 94*
Campbell, Mary Belle *DrAPF 93*
Campbell, Mary Delois 1940- *WhoBlA 94*
Campbell, Mary Kathryn 1939-
WhoAm 94
Campbell, Mary Schmidt 1947-
WhoAm 94, WhoBlA 94
Campbell, Marybelle Schmitt 1923-
WhoAmP 93
Campbell, Matthew 1907- *Who 94*
Campbell, May d1951 *WhoHol 92*
Campbell, Meg 1937- *BlmGWL*
Campbell, Menzies *Who 94*
Campbell, (Walter) Menzies 1941-
Who 94
Campbell, Michael Edward 1947-
WhoAm 94
Campbell, Michael Lee 1958-
WhoWest 94
Campbell, Milton Gray 1933- *WhoBlA 94*
Campbell, Milton Hugh 1928- *WhoAm 94*
Campbell, Muriel d1986 *WhoHol 92*
Campbell, Nancy B. 1952- *WhoAmA 93*
Campbell, Nancy Edinger 1957-
WhoAm 94
Campbell, Nancy L. 1939- *WhoAm 94*
Campbell, Naomi 1970- *IntWW 93*
Campbell, Naomi Flowers 1960-
WhoScEn 94
Campbell, Nell *WhoHol 92*
Campbell, Neva Tipley 1933- *WhoAm 94,*
WhoAmL 94
Campbell, Newton Allen 1928-
WhoAm 94
Campbell, Niall (Alexander Hamilton)
1925- *Who 94*
Campbell, Niall Gordon 1941- *Who 94*
Campbell, Nicholas *WhoHol 92*
Campbell, Oliver 1871-1953 *BuCMET*
Campbell, Orland 1890-1972
WhoAmA 93N
Campbell, Orland, Jr. 1942- *WhoAmP 93*
Campbell, Otis, Jr. 1953- *WhoBlA 94*
Campbell, Otis Levy 1935- *WhoBlA 94*
Campbell, Patrick *WhoHol 92*
Campbell, Patrick, Mrs. d1940
WhoHol 92
Campbell, Patton 1926- *WhoAm 94*
Campbell, Paul 1929- *WhoHol 92*
Campbell, Paul, Jr. 1915- *WhoAmL 94*
Campbell, Paul, III 1946- *WhoAmL 94*

Campbell, Paul Barton 1930- *WhoAm 94*
Campbell, Paul N(ewell) 1923- *WrDr 94*
Campbell, Paula Marie 1943-
WhoAmP 93
Campbell, Paulina Yager 1927-
WhoAmP 93
Campbell, Peter *Who 94*
Campbell, (Charles) Peter 1926- *Who 94*
Campbell, Peter (Walter) 1926- *Who 94,*
WrDr 94
Campbell, Peter DeGray 1966-
WhoMW 93
Campbell, Peter Nelson 1921- *Who 94*
Campbell, Phil
See Motorhead ConMus 10
Campbell, Philip Laroche 1950-
WhoWest 94
Campbell, Phoebe Harriet d1978
WhoHol 92
Campbell, Phyllis J. Takisaki *WhoAsA 93*
Campbell, Pollyann S. 1949- *WhoAmL 94*
Campbell, Quentin *Who 94*
Campbell, (John) Quentin 1939- *Who 94*
Campbell, R. Wright 1927- *WrDr 94*
Campbell, Ralph, Jr. 1946- *WhoAmP 93*
Campbell, Ramsey 1946- *WrDr 94*
Campbell, Randy Linn 1953- *WhoAmP 93*
Campbell, Ray *WhoAmP 93*
Campbell, Raymond McKinly 1942-
WhoFI 94
Campbell, Reginald Lawrence 1943-
WhoWest 94
Campbell, Renoda Gisele 1963- *WhoFI 94*
Campbell, Richard *WhoAmP 93*
Campbell, Richard Alden 1926-
WhoAm 94, WhoWest 94
Campbell, Richard Arthur 1930-1985
WhAm 10
Campbell, Richard Bruce 1947-
WhoAm 94, WhoAmL 94
Campbell, Richard H., Jr. 1920-
WhoAmP 93
Campbell, Richard Horton 1921-
WhoAmA 93
Campbell, Richard P. 1947- *WhoAm 94,*
WhoAmL 94
Campbell, Richard Rice 1923- *WhoAm 94*
Campbell, Richard Watson 1927-
WhoAmL 94
Campbell, Robert 1804-1879 *WhWE*
Campbell, Robert 1808-1894 *WhWE*
Campbell, Robert 1926- *WrDr 94*
Campbell, Robert 1929- *Who 94*
Campbell, Robert 1937- *WhoAm 94*
Campbell, Robert (Wright) 1927- *WrDr 94*
Campbell, Robert Ayerst 1940-
WhoAm 94
Campbell, Robert Charles 1924-
WhoAm 94
Campbell, Robert Dale 1914- *WhoAm 94*
Campbell, Robert E. 1933- *WhoAm 94,*
WhoFI 94
Campbell, Robert H. 1937- *WhoAm 94,*
WhoFI 94
Campbell, Robert Hedgcock 1948-
WhoAm 94, WhoAmL 94, WhoFI 94,
WhoWest 94
Campbell, Robert J. d1987 *WhoHol 92*
Campbell, Robert J. 1937- *WhoAmP 93*
Campbell, Robert Kenneth 1930-1990
WhAm 10
Campbell, Robert Lewis 1941- *WhoFI 94*
Campbell, Robert M. *WhoAmP 93*
Campbell, Robert P. *WhoScEn 94*
Campbell, Robin Auchinbreck 1922-
Who 94
Campbell, Roderick Samuel Fisher 1924-
IntWW 93
Campbell, Roger D. 1946- *WhoFI 94*
Campbell, Rogers Edward, III 1951-
WhoBlA 94
Campbell, Ronald 1943- *Who 94*
Campbell, Ronald Bruce 1946-
WhoMW 93
Campbell, Ronald Francis Boyd 1912-
Who 94
Campbell, Ronald Hugh 1924- *IntWW 93*
Campbell, Ronald Kent 1934-
WhoAmP 93
Campbell, Ronald Neil 1926- *WhoAm 94*
Campbell, Ross 1916- *Who 94*
Campbell, Ross 1918- *Who 94*
Campbell, Roy 1902-1957 *BlmGEL*
Campbell, Sandra J. *WhoAmP 93*
Campbell, Sara Moores 1943-
WhoWest 94
Campbell, Sara Wendell 1886-1960
WhoAmA 93N
Campbell, Sarah Anne 1959- *WhoFI 94*
Campbell, Scott 1956- *WhoAm 94*
Campbell, Scott G. 1950- *WhoAm 94,*
WhoAmL 94
Campbell, Scott Lenn 1952- *WhoAm 94,*
WhoAmL 94
Campbell, Scott Robert 1946- *WhoAm 94,*
WhoWest 94
Campbell, Sean P. 1952- *WhoAmP 93*

Campbell, Selaura Joy 1944- *WhoAmL 94,*
WhoFI 94
Campbell, Sharon Lynn 1955-
WhoScEn 94
Campbell, Shirley Ann *WhoAmP 93*
Campbell, Sid Ellis 1944- *WhoWest 94*
Campbell, Stanley Richard 1949-
WhoAm 94
Campbell, Stanley Wallace 1926-
WhoAm 94
Campbell, Steven MacMillan 1953-
IntWW 93
Campbell, Stewart Fred 1931- *WhoAm 94,*
WhoFI 94
Campbell, Stewart J. 1961- *WhoFI 94*
Campbell, Susan L. 1956- *WhoIns 94*
Campbell, Sylvan Lloyd 1931- *WhoBlA 94*
Campbell, Talmage Alexander 1939-
WhoAm 94
Campbell, Tevin *WhoBlA 94*
Campbell, Thomas 1763-1854
DcAmReB 2
Campbell, Thomas 1777-1844 *BlmGEL*
Campbell, Thomas 1943- *WhoAm 94,*
WhoAmL 94
Campbell, Thomas C. *Who 94*
Campbell, Thomas Colin 1934-
WhoAm 94
Campbell, Thomas Corwith, Jr. 1920-
WhoAm 94
Campbell, Thomas Douglas 1951-
WhoAmL 94
Campbell, Thomas Gordy 1932-
WhoWest 94
Campbell, Thomas Humphreys, III 1932-
WhoAmP 93
Campbell, Thomas J. 1952- *WhoWest 94*
Campbell, Thomas M(oody) 1936-1993
ConAu 142
Campbell, Thomas Moody d1993
NewYTBS 93
Campbell, Thomas R., Jr. 1940-
WhoAmP 93
Campbell, Thomas W. 1957- *WhoBlA 94*
Campbell, Tisha *WhoBlA 94, WhoHol 92*
Campbell, Tom 1952- *WhoAmP 93*
Campbell, Tom 1954- *WhoWest 94*
Campbell, Tony 1962- *WhoBlA 94*
Campbell, Truman F. 1928- *WhoAmP 93*
Campbell, Van C. 1938- *WhoFI 94*
Campbell, Violet d1970 *WhoHol 92*
Campbell, Vivian 1919-1986
WhoAmA 93N
Campbell, Wallace J. 1910- *WrDr 94*
Campbell, Wallace Justin 1910-
WhoAm 94
Campbell, Walter (Benjamin) 1921-
Who 94
Campbell, Walter Gordon 1948-
WhoAmL 94
Campbell, Webster d1972 *WhoHol 92*
Campbell, Wendell J. 1927- *WhoBlA 94*
Campbell, Wendell Jerome 1927-
WhoAm 94
Campbell, Wesley Glenn 1924-
WhoAm 94, WhoWest 94
Campbell, Wilbur Harold 1945-
WhoScEn 94
Campbell, William d1778 *WhAmRev*
Campbell, William 1745-1781 *AmRev,*
WhAmRev
Campbell, William 1926- *IntMPA 94,*
WhoHol 92
Campbell, William 1935- *WhoAmP 93*
Campbell, William 1960- *WhoHol 92*
Campbell, William Buford, Jr. 1935-
WhoScEn 94
Campbell, William Cecil 1930-
WhoAm 94
Campbell, William Earl 1965- *WhoBlA 94*
Campbell, William Edward 1927-
WhoAm 94, WhoMW 93
Campbell, William Foley 1951-
WhoAm 94, WhoFI 94
Campbell, William Henry 1915-
WhoAmA 93
Campbell, William I. 1944- *WhoAm 94,*
WhoFI 94
Campbell, William J., Jr. 1948-
WhoAmL 94
Campbell, William Jackson 1929-
WhoWest 94
Campbell, William P. 1913- *WhoAmP 93*
Campbell, William Patrick 1914-1976
WhoAmA 93N
Campbell, William Steen 1919-
WhoAm 94, WhoFI 94, WhoWest 94
Campbell, William Tait 1912- *Who 94*
Campbell, Willis L. 1898- *WhAm 10*
Campbell, Willis Preston 1945-
WhoWest 94
Campbell, Woodrow Wilson, Jr. 1944-
WhoAm 94, WhoAmL 94
Campbell, Zerrie D. 1951- *WhoBlA 94*
Campbell-Gray *Who 94*
Campbell-Johnson, Alan 1913- *Who 94*

Campbell-Johnston, Michael Alexander
Ninian 1931- *Who 94*
Campbell of Alloway, Baron 1917-
Who 94
Campbell Of Croy, Baron 1921-
IntWW 93, Who 94
Campbell Of Eskan, Baron 1912-
IntWW 93, Who 94
Campbell of Succoth, Ilay (Mark) 1927-
Who 94
Campbell-Orde, John A. *Who 94*
Campbell-Preston, Frances (Olivia) 1918-
Who 94
Campbell-Preston of Ardchattan, Robert
Modan Thorne 1909- *Who 94*
Campbell-Savours, Dale Norman 1943-
Who 94
Campbell-White, Annette Jane 1947-
WhoAm 94, WhoFI 94
Campbell-White, Martin Andrew 1943-
Who 94
Campden, Viscount 1950- *Who 94*
Campdon, Alfred Ellis 1923- *WhoFI 94*
Campeau, Frank d1943 *WhoHol 92*
Campeau, George *WhoHol 92*
Campen, Philippus Canisius Maria van
1911- *IntWW 93*
Camper, Diane G. 1948- *WhoBlA 94*
Camper, Jeffrey Douglas 1960-
WhoScEn 94
Camper, John Jacob 1943- *WhoAm 94*
Camper, John Saxton 1929- *WhoWest 94*
Campfield, Regis William 1942-
WhoAm 94
Camphausen, Fred Howard 1933-
WhoWest 94
Camphor, Michael Gerard *WhoBlA 94*
Campigotto, Corrado Marco 1962-
WhoScEn 94
Campillo, Fred Grover 1956- *WhoMW 93*
Campioli fl. 1703-1738 *NewGrDO*
Campion, Alan 1951- *WhoAm 94*
Campion, Carol-Mae Sack 1950-
WhoAm 94
Campion, Cris *WhoHol 92*
Campion, Daniel *DrAPF 93*
Campion, Edmund 1540-1581 *BlmGEL*
Campion, Frank Davis 1921-1989
WhAm 10
Campion, Gerald *WhoHol 92*
Campion, Harry 1905- *Who 94*
Campion, Jane *NewYTBS 93 [port]*
Campion, Nicholas 1953- *AstEnc*
Campion, Peter James 1926- *Who 94*
Campion, Robert Thomas 1921-
WhoAm 94
Campion, Sarah 1906- *BlmGWL*
Campion, Thomas 1567-1620 *BlmGEL*
Campion, Thomas Francis 1935-
WhoAm 94
Campistron, Jean Galbert de 1656-1723
NewGrDO
Campling, Christopher Russell 1925-
Who 94, WrDr 94
Campling, Elizabeth 1948- *WrDr 94*
Campman, Marie Katherine 1917-
WhoAmP 93
Campo (y Zabaleta), Conrado del
1878-1953 *NewGrDO*
Campo, J. M. 1943- *WhoScEn 94*
Campo, Pupi *WhoHol 92*
Campo, Terry Thomas 1957- *WhoAmP 93*
Campoamar, Diana *WhoHisp 94*
Campobasso, Eleanor M. 1922-
WhoAmP 93
Campobasso d'Alessandro, Vincenzo
1760-1788? *NewGrDO*
Campolettano, Thomas Alfred 1946-
WhoFI 94
Campoli, Cosmo 1922- *WhoAmA 93*
Campoli, Douglas Martin 1964- *WhoFI 94*
Campoli, Ella Frances 1906- *WhoFI 94*
Campopiano, Remo *WhoAmA 93*
Campora, Giuseppe 1923- *NewGrDO*
Campora, Mario 1930- *IntWW 93,*
Who 94
Campos, Agustin De 1669-1737 *EncNAR*
Campos, Angel P. *WhoHisp 94*
Campos, Carlos de 1866-1927 *NewGrDO*
Campos, Christophe Lucien 1938- *Who 94*
Campos, Crisanto E. 1936- *WhoHisp 94*
Campos, Eduardo Javier, Sr. 1949-
WhoHisp 94
Campos, Elizabeth Marie 1955-
WhoHisp 94
Campos, Gloria 1954- *WhoHisp 94*
Campos, Javier F. 1947- *WhoHisp 94*
Campos, Joaquin Paul, III 1962-
WhoScEn 94, WhoHisp 94
Campos, Leonard Peter 1932-
WhoWest 94
Campos, Luis Manuel Braga da Costa
1950- *WhoScEn 94*
Campos, Maria Aparecida 1942-
WhoWomW 91
Campos, Natividad, Jr. 1947- *WhoHisp 94*
Campos, Paul F. 1959- *WhoHisp 94*

Campos, Pete 1953- *WhoAmP 93, WhoHisp 94*
Campos, Porfirio, Jr. 1941- *WhoHisp 94*
Campos, R. Yvonne 1948- *WhoHisp 94*
Campos, Rafael d1985 *WhoHol 92*
Campos, Rafael 1935- *WhoHisp 94*
Campos, Robert 1938- *WhoHisp 94*
Campos, Roberto A. 1958- *WhoHisp 94*
Campos, Roberto de Oliveria 1917- *Who 94*
Campos, Roberto de Oliviera *IntWW 93*
Campos, Rodolfo Estuardo 1967- *WhoHisp 94*
Campos, Santiago E. 1926- *WhoAm 94, WhoAmL 94, WhoHisp 94, WhoWest 94*
Campos, Victor *WhoHol 92*
Campos, Victor Manuel 1942- *WhoHisp 94*
Campos-Parsi, Hector M. 1922- *WhoHisp 94*
Campoy, Sylvia *WhoHisp 94*
Campra, Andre 1660-1744 *NewGrDO*
Campra, Frances L. 1940- *WhoWest 94*
Camps, Jeffrey Lowell 1954- *WhoFI 94*
Camps, William Anthony 1910- *Who 94*
Campton, David 1924- *ConDr 93, WrDr 94*
Campus, Peter 1937- *WhoAm 94, WhoAmA 93*
Campusano, Silvestre 1966- *WhoHisp 94*
Camras, Carl Bruce 1953- *WhoMW 93*
Camras, Marvin 1916- *WhoAm 94, WhoScEn 94, WorInv*
Camron, Rocky d1967 *WhoHol 92*
Camron, Roxanne *WhoAm 94*
Camrose, Viscount 1909- *Who 94*
Camu, Pierre 1923- *IntWW 93*
Camurati, Mireya B. 1934- *WhoHisp 94*
Camus, Albert 1913-1960 *EncEth, IntDcT 2, RfGShF*
Camus, Edward Poland 1932- *WhoAmL 94*
Canaan, Don 1938- *WhoMW 93*
Canada, Metropolitan of *Who 94*
Canada, Primate of *Who 94*
Canada, Primate of All *Who 94*
Canada, Andrew Joseph, Jr. 1939- *WhoAmP 93*
Canada, Benjamin Oleander 1944- *WhoBlA 94*
Canada, Bud 1925- *WhoAmP 93*
Canada, Mary Whitfield 1919- *WhoAm 94*
Canada, W. Ralph, Jr. 1955- *WhoAmL 94*
Canaday, Doris Charlene 1932- *WhoFI 94*
Canaday, Harry Edsel 1925- *WhoAmL 94*
Canaday, John Edwin 1907-1985 *WhoAmA 93N*
Canaday, Richard A. 1947- *WhoAmL 94*
Canade, Terrence Patrick 1962- *WhoAmL 94*
Canadeo, Tony *ProFbHF*
Canady, Alexa I. 1950- *WhoBlA 94*
Canady, Blanton Thandreus 1948- *WhoBlA 94*
Canady, Charles T. 1954- *CngDr 93, WhoAm 94, WhoAmP 93*
Canady, Herman G., Jr. *WhoBlA 94*
Canady, Hortense Golden 1927- *WhoBlA 94*
Canady, Mark Howard 1961- *WhoAmL 94*
Canady, Nathaniel Byron 1962- *WhoMW 93*
Canady-Davis, Alexa 1950- *WhoBlA 94*
Canaka, Togo William 1916- *WhoAm 94, WhoFI 94, WhoWest 94*
Canalas, Robert Anthony 1940- *WhoScEn 94*
Canale, Dee James 1932- *WhoAm 94*
Canale, Gianna Maria 1927- *WhoHol 92*
Canale-Parola, Ercole 1929- *WhoAm 94*
Canales, Adolph *WhoHisp 94*
Canales, Carmen L. 1944- *WhoHisp 94*
Canales, Charles John 1944- *WhoWest 94*
Canales, H. Paul *WhoHisp 94*
Canales, Herbert Glenn 1954- *WhoAm 94*
Canales, Judith Ann 1962- *WhoHisp 94*
Canales, Manuel *WhoHisp 94*
Canales, Maria Cristina 1949- *WhoHisp 94*
Canales, Martin A., Jr. *WhoHisp 94*
Canales, Oscar Mario 1939- *WhoHisp 94*
Canales, Ramiro R. 1950- *WhoHisp 94*
Canales, Terry A. *WhoHisp 94*
Canales De Mendieta, Sonia *WhoWomW 91*
Canan, Janine *DrAPF 93*
Canan, Michael J. 1941- *WhoAm 94*
Canan, Penelope 1946- *WhoWest 94*
Canapary, Herbert C. 1932- *WhoIns 94*
Canapary, Herbert Carton 1932- *WhoAm 94*
Canardo, Hernando Vicente 1957- *WhoFI 94*
Canary, David 1938- *WhoHol 92*
Canary, John Joseph 1925- *WhoAm 94*
Canary, Nancy Halliday 1941- *WhoAm 94*
Cañas, Alberto J. 1953- *WhoHisp 94*
Cañas, Angel 1939- *WhoHisp 94*
Cañas, Richard León 1941- *WhoHisp 94*
Canatsey, Sandy 1940- *WhoAmP 93*
Canavan, Bernard 1936- *WhoFI 94*
Canavan, Christine Estelle 1950- *WhoAmP 93*
Canavan, Dennis Andrew 1942- *Who 94*
Canavan, Ellen M. 1941- *WhoAmP 93*
Canavan, John James, Jr. 1933- *WhoFI 94*
Canavan, Vincent Joseph 1946- *Who 94*
Canberra And Goulburn, Archbishop of 1930- *Who 94*
Canberra And Goulburn, Bishop of 1942- *Who 94*
Canby, Craig Allen 1959- *WhoScEn 94*
Canby, Jeanny Vorys 1929- *WhoAmA 93*
Canby, Vincent 1924- *IntMPA 94, WhoAm 94*
Canby, William C., Jr. *WhoAmP 93*
Canby, William Cameron, Jr. 1931- *WhoAm 94, WhoAmL 94, WhoWest 94*
Cancel, Adrian R. 1946- *WhoHisp 94*
Cancel, Luis R. 1952- *WhoAmA 93, WhoHisp 94*
Cancela, José 1957- *WhoHisp 94*
Canchiani, Celia 1949- *WhoHisp 94*
Canchola, Acencion 1934- *WhoHisp 94*
Canchola, Joe Paul 1935- *WhoHisp 94*
Canchola, Jose L. 1931- *WhoHisp 94*
Canchola, Joseph Paul, Jr. 1954- *WhoHisp 94*
Canchola, Samuel Victor 1944- *WhoHisp 94*
Cancienne, Kenneth Michael 1963- *WhoFI 94*
Cancio, Norma Gloria 1961- *WhoHisp 94*
Cancro, Robert 1932- *WhoAm 94, WhoScEn 94*
Candage, Howard Everett 1952- *WhoFI 94*
Candal, Francisco Javier 1952- *WhoHisp 94*
Candales de López, María D. 1930- *WhoHisp 94*
Candau, Eugenie 1938- *WhoAmA 93, WhoWest 94*
Candea, Virgil 1927- *IntWW 93*
Candeille, (Amelie-) Julie 1767-1834 *NewGrDO*
Candeille, Pierre Joseph 1744-1827 *NewGrDO*
Candela (Outerino), Felix 1910- *IntWW 93*
Candela, Hilario Francisco 1934- *WhoHisp 94*
Candela Outerino, Felix 1910- *Who 94*
Candelaria, Cordelia Chávez 1943- *WhoHisp 94*
Candelaria, John 1953- *WhoHisp 94*
Candelaria, Michael Richard 1955- *WhoHisp 94*
Candelaria, Nash *DrAPF 93*
Candelaria, Nash 1928- *WhoHisp 94*
Candelario, Eva Nydia 1954- *WhoHisp 94*
Candelario, John S. 1916-1993 *WhoHisp 94N*
Candelario, Nilda 1947- *WhoHisp 94*
Candell, Victor 1903-1977 *WhoAmA 93N*
Cander, Leon 1926- *WhoAm 94*
Candi, Giovanni Pietro fl. 1703- *NewGrDO*
Candia, Oscar A. 1935- *WhoAm 94, WhoHisp 94, WhoScEn 94*
Candia, Rubén Araiza 1938- *WhoHisp 94*
Candib, Murray A. 1915- *WhoAm 94*
Candido, Raquel 1951- *WhoWomW 91*
Candilis, Georges 1913- *IntWW 93*
Candilis, Wray O. 1927- *WrDr 94*
Candioti, Beatriz A. *WhoAmA 93*
Candland, Douglas Keith 1934- *WhoAm 94, WrDr 94*
Candler, Ann (More) 1740-1814 *BlmGWL*
Candler, James Nall, Jr. 1943- *WhoAm 94, WhoAmL 94*
Candler, John Slaughter, II 1908- *WhoAm 94, WhoAmL 94*
Candlin, Christopher Noel 1940- *Who 94*
Candlin, Frances Ann 1945- *WhoWest 94*
Candlish, Thomas Tait 1926- *Who 94*
Candoli, Pete 1923- *WhoHol 92*
Candon, John C. *WhoAmP 93*
Candon, Mary Eva 1950- *WhoAmP 93*
Candon, Patrick James 1908- *WhoAmP 93*
Candon, Thomas Henry *WhoAmP 93*
Candrick, Thomas R., Jr. 1947- *WhoAmL 94*
Candris, Laura A. 1955- *WhoAm 94, WhoAmL 94*
Candy, Edward 1925- *WrDr 94*
Candy, Elizabeth Mary 1942- *Who 94*
Candy, John 1950- *IntMPA 94, WhoCom [port]*
Candy, John 1951- *WhoHol 92*
Candy, John Franklin 1950- *WhoAm 94*
Candy, Philip C(arne) 1950- *ConAu 140*
Cane, Charles d1973 *WhoHol 92*
Cane, Guy 1929- *WhoScEn 94*
Cane, Louis Paul Joseph 1943- *IntWW 93*
Cane, Marilyn Blumberg 1949- *WhoAmL 94*
Cane, Mark Alan 1944- *WhoAm 94, WhoScEn 94*
Cane, Paula P. 1945- *WhoAm 94*
Cane, Violet Rosina 1916- *Who 94*
Caneba, Gerard Tablada 1958- *WhoScEn 94*
Canel, Fausto 1939- *WhoHisp 94*
Canelas, Dale Brunelle 1938- *WhoAm 94*
Canella, Guido 1931- *IntWW 93*
Cañellas, Dionisio J., IV 1935- *WhoHisp 94*
Canellos, George P. 1934- *WhoAm 94*
Canellos, Peter Constantine 1944- *WhoAmL 94*
Canepa, Adolfo John 1940- *IntWW 93*
Canepa, John Charles 1930- *WhoAm 94, WhoFI 94*
Cánepa, Mario Alfredo 1932- *WhoHisp 94*
Canepa, Richard Thomas 1946- *WhoFI 94*
Canepa, Robert Frank 1947- *WhoFI 94*
Caner, George Colket, Jr. 1925- *WhoAm 94*
Caner, Marc 1936- *WhoScEn 94*
Canes, Carmen Dahlia 1952- *WhoAmL 94*
Canes, Michael Edwin 1941- *WhoAm 94*
Canes, Moira *AstEnc*
Canestrari, Ronald J. *WhoAmP 93*
Canestri, Giovanni 1918- *IntWW 93*
Canet, Lawrence George 1910- *Who 94*
Canete, Alfredo 1942- *IntWW 93*
Canetti, Elias 1905- *ConWorW 93, IntWW 93, Who 94*
Canevari, Charles Daniel 1920- *WhoAm 94*
Canfield, Andrew Trotter 1953- *WhoAm 94*
Canfield, Brian A. 1938- *WhoWest 94*
Canfield, Earle Lloyd 1918- *WhoAm 94*
Canfield, Edward Francis 1922- *WhoAm 94*
Canfield, Francis Xavier 1920- *WhoAm 94*
Canfield, Glenn, Jr. 1935- *WhoScEn 94*
Canfield, Grant Wellington, Jr. 1923- *WhoAm 94, WhoFI 94, WhoWest 94*
Canfield, Gregory Wayne 1956- *WhoAmL 94*
Canfield, Jane (White) 1897-1984 *WhoAmA 93N*
Canfield, Jimmie Gilliam *DrAPF 93*
Canfield, Judy Ohlbaum 1947- *WhoScEn 94*
Canfield, Mary Grace 1924- *WhoHol 92*
Canfield, Muriel Jean Nixon 1928- *WhoAm 94, WhoMW 93*
Canfield, Peter Crane 1954- *WhoAmL 94*
Canfield, Philip Charles 1956- *WhoScEn 94*
Canfield, William d1925 *WhoHol 92*
Canfield, William Newton 1920- *WhoAm 94*
Cangalovic, Miroslav 1921- *NewGrDO*
Cangelosi, Vincent Emanuel 1928-1988 *WhAm 10*
Cangemi, Joseph P. 1936- *IntWW 93*
Cangemi, Joseph Peter 1936- *WhoAm 94*
Cangemi, Michael Paul 1948- *WhoAm 94*
Cangiamila, Brion M. 1962- *WhoAmP 93*
Canham, Bryan Frederick 1920- *Who 94*
Canham, Paul George 1933- *Who 94*
Canham, Peter *Who 94*
Caniff, Milton Arthur 1907-1988 *WhoAmA 93N*
Caniglia, Maria 1905-1979 *NewGrDO*
Canike, Anthony Christopher 1946- *WhoFI 94*
Canin, Ethan *DrAPF 93*
Canin, Ethan 1960- *WrDr 94*
Canin, Stuart Victor 1926- *WhoAm 94*
Canine, Jonathan Albert 1951- *WhoMW 93*
Canino, Glorisa J. 1946- *WhoHisp 94*
Canino, Ian *WhoHisp 94*
Canino, Roberto A. *WhoHisp 94*
Canino, Victor Manuel, Jr. 1940- *WhoHisp 94*
Caniparoli, Val William 1951- *WhoAm 94*
Canizales, Lila Lisa 1960- *WhoHisp 94*
Canizales, Orlando *WhoHisp 94*
Canizalez, Thomas Manuel 1957- *WhoHisp 94*
Canizares, Claude Roger 1945- *WhoAm 94, WhoScEn 94*
Canizarro, Vincent, Jr. *DrAPF 93*
Canjar, Patricia McWade 1932- *WhoMW 93*
Cann, Alexander d1977 *WhoHol 92*
Cann, Charles Richard 1937- *Who 94*
Cann, Howard 1895- *BasBi*
Cann, James 1940- *IntMPA 94*
Cann, James Charles 1946- *Who 94*
Cann, John Rusweiler 1920- *WhoWest 94*
Cann, Johnson Robin 1937- *Who 94*
Cann, William Francis 1922- *WhoAm 94*
Cann, William Hopson 1916- *WhoAm 94, WhoWest 94*
Cannabich, (Johann) Christian (Innocenz Bonaventura) 1731-1798 *NewGrDO*
Cannadine, David 1950- *WrDr 94*
Cannady, Alonzo James 1947- *WhoBlA 94*
Cannady, Edward Wyatt, Jr. 1906- *WhoScEn 94, WhoWest 94*
Cannaliato, Vincent, Jr. 1941- *WhoAm 94, WhoFI 94*
Cannan, Denis 1919- *ConDr 93, Who 94, WhoHol 92, WrDr 94*
Cannell, Charles Frederick 1913- *WhoAm 94*
Cannell, John Redferne 1937- *WhoAm 94*
Cannell, Robert Quirk 1937- *Who 94*
Cannell, Stephen J. 1942- *IntMPA 94*
Cannell, Stephen Joseph 1941- *WhoAm 94*
Cannella, John Matthew 1908- *WhoAm 94, WhoAmL 94*
Cannella, Nicholas M. 1951- *WhoAmL 94*
Cannella, Sal *WhoAmP 93*
Canne-Meijer, Cora 1929- *NewGrDO*
Cannetti, Linda 1878-1960 *NewGrDO*
Canney, Carroll E. 1945- *WhoAmP 93*
Canney, Donald James 1930- *WhoAmP 93*
Canniff, Bryan Gregory 1948- *WhoAmA 93*
Canniff, Paul Joseph, Jr. *WhoWest 94*
Canning *Who 94*
Canning, Jessie Marie *WhoAm 94*
Canning, John Beckman 1943- *WhoFI 94*
Canning, John J. 1941- *WhoAm 94, WhoFI 94*
Canning, John Rafton 1927- *WhoAm 94*
Canning, Victor 1911-1986 *EncSF 93*
Cannistraci, John C. 1965- *WhoAmL 94*
Cannistraro, Nicholas, Jr. 1939- *WhoAm 94*
Cannistraro, Philip V(incent) 1942- *ConAu 141*
Cannizzaro, Stanislao 1826-1910 *WorScD*
Cannon, Albert Earl, Jr. 1951- *WhoScEn 94*
Cannon, Aleta 1942- *WhoBlA 94*
Cannon, Annie Jump 1863-1941 *WorScD*
Cannon, Anthon S., Jr. 1938- *WhoAmL 94*
Cannon, Barbara E. M. 1936- *WhoBlA 94*
Cannon, Bradford 1907- *WhoAm 94*
Cannon, Calvin Curtis 1952- *WhoBlA 94*
Cannon, Chapman Roosevelt, Jr. 1934- *WhoBlA 94*
Cannon, Charles C. 1928- *WhoAm 94*
Cannon, Charles Earl 1946- *WhoBlA 94, WhoMW 93*
Cannon, Chris J. 1954- *WhoAmL 94, WhoWest 94*
Cannon, Dale Joseph 1950- *WhoMW 93*
Cannon, Daniel Willard 1920- *WhoAm 94, WhoAmL 94, WhoFI 94*
Cannon, David Joseph 1933- *WhoAm 94*
Cannon, David Wadsworth, Jr. 1911?-1938 *BlkWr 2*
Cannon, Davita Louise 1949- *WhoBlA 94*
Cannon, Donnie E. 1929- *WhoBlA 94*
Cannon, Douglas Robert 1954- *WhoFI 94*
Cannon, Dyan 1936- *WhoHol 92*
Cannon, Dyan 1937- *IntMPA 94, WhoAm 94*
Cannon, Edith H. 1940- *WhoBlA 94*
Cannon, Elton Molock 1920- *WhoBlA 94*
Cannon, Esme d1973 *WhoHol 92*
Cannon, Eugene Nathaniel 1944- *WhoBlA 94*
Cannon, Francis V., Jr. 1935- *WhoAm 94*
Cannon, Frank *ConAu 42NR*
Cannon, Frank 1930- *WrDr 94*
Cannon, Freddy *WhoHol 92*
Cannon, Garland 1924- *WhoAm 94, WrDr 94*
Cannon, Grace Bert 1937- *WhoScEn 94*
Cannon, Grant G., Mrs. *WhAm 10*
Cannon, Gus 1883- *WhoHol 92*
Cannon, H. LeRoy 1916- *WhoBlA 94*
Cannon, Helen Leighton 1911- *WhoAm 94*
Cannon, Helen Virginia Graham 1913- *WhoFI 94*
Cannon, Herbert Seth 1931- *WhoAm 94*
Cannon, Howard Walter *WhoAmP 93*
Cannon, Howard Walter 1912- *WhoAm 94*
Cannon, Hugh 1931- *WhoAm 94, WhoAmL 94, WhoAmP 93, WhoFI 94*
Cannon, Ilvi Joe 1937- *WhoAmP 93*
Cannon, Isabella Walton 1904- *WhoAm 94*
Cannon, J. D. 1922- *WhoHol 92*
Cannon, James, Jr. 1864-1944 *DcAmReB 2*
Cannon, James Anthony 1938- *WhoAm 94, WhoFI 94*
Cannon, James Dean 1964- *WhoWest 94*
Cannon, James W. 1927- *WhoFI 94*
Cannon, Janet *DrAPF 93*
Cannon, Joan L. *DrAPF 93*

Capelja, Jad *WhoHol 92*
Capell *Who 94*
Capell, Peter d1986 *WhoHol 92*
Capellan, Angel 1942- *WhoHisp 94*
Capellani, Paul d1914 *WhoHol 92*
Capelle, Madelene Carole 1950- *WhoWest 94*
Capelle, Russell B(eckett) 1917- *WrDr 94*
Capelli, David August von *NewGrDO*
Capelli, Giovanni Maria 1648-1726 *NewGrDO*
Capelli, John Placido 1936- *WhoAm 94*
Capello, Phyllis *DrAPF 93*
Capellos, Chris Spiridon 1934- *WhoScEn 94*
Capellupo, John P. *WhoAm 94, WhoFI 94*
Capen, Charles Chabert 1936- *WhoAm 94, WhoScEn 94*
Capen, Richard Goodwin, Jr. 1934- *WhoAm 94*
Capener, Regner Alvin 1942- *WhoWest 94*
Capers, Charlotte 1913- *WhoAm 94*
Capers, Eliza Virginia 1925- *WhoBlA 94*
Capers, John D., Jr. 1953- *WhoAmL 94*
Capers, Virginia 1925- *WhoHol 92*
Caperton, Albert Franklin 1936- *WhoAm 94, WhoMW 93*
Caperton, Dee Kessel *WhoAm 94*
Caperton, Gaston 1940- *WhoAmP 93*
Caperton, Kent Allen 1949- *WhoAmP 93*
Caperton, Richard Walton 1948- *WhoFI 94*
Caperton, W. Gaston 1940- *WhoAm 94*
Capes, Richard Edward 1942- *WhoAmA 93*
Cape Town, Archbishop of 1931- *Who 94*
Cape Town, Bishop Suffragan of *Who 94*
Capey, Montague Martin *Who 94*
Capezza, Joseph C. 1955- *WhoIns 94*
Capgras, Jean Marie Joseph 1873-1950 *EncSPD*
Capice, Philip Charles 1931- *WhoAm 94*
Capineri, Joseph A. 1929- *WhoAmP 93*
Capistran, Eleno Pete, III 1958- *WhoHisp 94*
Capitan, William H(arry) 1933- *WrDr 94*
Capitan, William Harry 1933- *WhoAm 94*
Capitano, Francesco *WhoHol 92*
Capizzi, John A. 1954- *WhoIns 94*
Capizzi, Michael Robert 1939- *WhoAmL 94, WhoWest 94*
Capizzi, Robert Lawrence 1938- *WhoAm 94*
Caplan, Hon. Lord 1929- *Who 94*
Caplan, Albert Joseph 1908- *WhoAm 94*
Caplan, Arnold I. 1942- *WhoAm 94, WhoScEn 94*
Caplan, Arthur L. 1950- *WhoMW 93*
Caplan, Arthur L(eonard) 1950- *WrDr 94*
Caplan, Daniel 1915- *Who 94*
Caplan, David d1993 *NewYTBS 93*
Caplan, David Norman 1947- *WhoScEn 94*
Caplan, Edwin Harvey 1926- *WhoAm 94, WhoWest 94*
Caplan, Frank 1919- *WhoWest 94*
Caplan, Harry 1896- *WhAm 10*
Caplan, Jerry L. 1922- *WhoAmA 93*
Caplan, John Alan 1945- *WhoWest 94*
Caplan, John David 1926- *WhoAm 94*
Caplan, Jonathan Michael 1951- *Who 94*
Caplan, Joyce F. 1933- *WhoAmP 93*
Caplan, Lazarus David 1940- *WhoAm 94*
Caplan, Leonard 1909- *Who 94*
Caplan, Lester 1924- *WhoAm 94*
Caplan, Louis Robert 1936- *WhoAm 94*
Caplan, Milton Irving 1933- *WhoAmP 93*
Caplan, Philip Isaac *Who 94*
Caplan, Richard V. 1937- *WhoAm 94, WhoAmL 94*
Caplan, William J. 1953- *WhoAmL 94*
Caplan, Yale Howard 1941- *WhoScEn 94*
Caplan Ciarrochi, Sandra *WhoAmA 93*
Caplat, Moran Victor Hingston 1916- *Who 94*
Caples, Barbara Barrett 1914- *WhoAmA 93*
Caples, John 1900-1990 *WhAm 10*
Caples, Richard James 1949- *WhoAm 94*
Caples, William Goff 1909-1989 *WhAm 10*
Caplin, Donald *WhoFI 94*
Caplin, Jerrold Leon 1930- *WhoScEn 94*
Caplin, Mortimer M. 1916- *IntWW 93*
Caplin, Mortimer Maxwell 1916- *WhoAm 94*
Caplin, Ty 1935- *WhoWest 94*
Caplis, Kevin J. 1948- *WhoAm 94, WhoAmL 94*
Caplis, Stephen Bennett 1947- *WhoAm 94, WhoAmL 94*
Caplitz, Gregg D. 1959- *WhoFI 94*
Caplovitz, Coleman David 1925- *WhoAm 94*
Caplow, Steven Phillip 1961- *WhoAmL 94*
Caplow, Theodore 1920- *WhoAm 94*
Capmany Farnes, Maria Aurelia 1918- *BlmGWL*
Capo, Manuel *WhoHisp 94*
Capobianco, Domenick 1928- *WhoAmA 93*
Capobianco, Michael 1950- *EncSF 93*
Capobianco, Philip Daniel 1949- *WhoFI 94*
Capobianco, Tito 1931- *NewGrDO, WhoAm 94*
Capo-Chichi, Gratien Tonakpon 1938- *IntWW 93*
Capon, Edmund (George) 1940- *WrDr 94*
Capon, (Harry) Paul 1911-1969 *EncSF 93*
Capon, Robert Farrar 1925- *WrDr 94*
Capone, Alphonse William 1919- *WhoAm 94*
Capone, Antonio 1926- *WhoScEn 94*
Capone, Bert J. 1944- *WhoAmL 94*
Capone, Lucien, Jr. *WhoAm 94*
Capone, Nadia *WhoHol 92*
Caponegro, Ernest Mark 1957- *WhoFI 94*
Caponegro, Mary 1956- *WhoAm 94*
Caponi, Anthony 1921- *WhoAmA 93*
Caponigri, A(loysius) Robert 1915-1983 *ConAu 43NR*
Caponigro, Paul 1932- *WhoAmA 93*
Capoor, Asha 1941- *WhoAsA 94*
Caporael, Suzanne 1949- *WhoAmA 93*
Caporale, Charles Michael 1950- *WhoIns 94*
Caporale, D. Nick 1928- *WhoAm 94, WhoAmL 94, WhoAmP 93, WhoMW 93*
Caporali, Renso L. 1933- *WhoAm 94, WhoFI 94, WhoScEn 94*
Caporaso, Fredric 1947- *WhoWest 94*
Caporaso, Karen Denise 1953- *WhoWest 94*
Caporaso, Pat Marie *WhoAmA 93*
Capos, Claudia Ruth 1951- *WhoMW 93*
Capote, Luciano Caridad 1926- *WhoHisp 94*
Capote, María Romero 1935- *WhoHisp 94*
Capote, Truman d1984 *WhoHol 92*
Capote, Truman 1924-1984 *AmCulL, GayLL, RfGShF*
Capotorti, Luigi 1767-1842 *NewGrDO*
Capouano, Albert D. 1945- *WhoAmL 94*
Capouch, Edward Arthur 1942- *WhoMW 93*
Capoul, (Joseph) Victor (Amadee) 1839-1924 *NewGrDO*
Capozzi, Alberto d1945 *WhoHol 92*
Capozzi, Anthony Patrick 1945- *WhoAmP 93*
Capozzi, Kevin Leo 1957- *WhoWest 94*
Capozzi, Louis Joseph, Jr. 1961- *WhoAmL 94*
Capozzoli, Jeanne Johnson 1940- *WhoAmP 93*
Capp, Al d1979 *WhoHol 92*
Capp, Al 1909-1979 *WhoAmA 93N*
Capp, Bernard (Stuart) 1943- *WrDr 94*
Capp, David A. *WhoAmL 94*
Capp, Michael Paul 1930- *WhoAm 94*
Cappa, Donald 1930- *WhoWest 94*
Cappabianca, Italo S. 1936- *WhoAmP 93*
Capparelli, R. Cary 1953- *WhoMW 93*
Capparelli, Ralph C. 1924- *WhoAmP 93*
Cappas, Alberto O., Jr. 1946- *WhoHisp 94*
Cappas, Alberto Oscar *DrAPF 93*
Cappel, Carolyn M. 1952- *WhoAmL 94*
Cappel, Constance 1936- *WhoWest 94*
Cappelen, Andreas Zeier 1915- *IntWW 93*
Cappell, Joe Frederick 1927- *WhoAmP 93*
Cappellano, Francesca d1988 *WhoHol 92*
Cappelletti, Grace 1939- *WhoAm 94*
Cappelletti, Mauro 1927- *WhoAm 94*
Cappelletti, Norma Leone *WhoAmP 93*
Cappelli, Giovanni Maria *NewGrDO*
Cappelli, Louis Joseph 1931- *WhoAm 94*
Cappello, A. Barry 1942- *WhoAmL 94*
Cappello, Carmelo 1912- *IntWW 93*
Cappello, Juan C. *WhoHisp 94*
Cappello, Juan C. 1938- *WhoFI 94*
Cappello, Rosemary *DrAPF 93*
Capper, Edmund Michael Hubert 1908- *Who 94*
Capper, John Edward 1942- *WhoMW 93*
Capper, Roger Lee 1965- *WhoMW 93*
Cappiello, Agata Alma 1948- *WhoWomW 91*
Cappiello, Angela 1954- *WhoFI 94*
Cappiello, Frank Anthony, Jr. 1926- *WhoAm 94*
Cappiello, Rosa 1942- *BlmGWL*
Cappitella, Mauro John 1934- *WhoFI 94, WhoScEn 94*
Cappo, Joseph C. 1936- *WhoAm 94, WhoMW 93*
Cappolella, Lisa Jane 1966- *WhoAmL 94*
Cappon, Alexander Patterson 1900- *WhoAm 94*
Cappon, Andre Alfred 1948- *WhoAm 94, WhoFI 94*
Cappon, Daniel 1931- *WrDr 94*
Cappon, Rene Jacques 1924- *WhoAm 94*
Capps, Ben(jamin F.) 1922- *WrDr 94*
Capps, Charles Wilson, Jr. 1925- *WhoAmP 93*
Capps, Duane O. 1932- *WhoFI 94*
Capps, Ethan LeRoy 1924- *WhoAm 94*
Capps, Gilmer N. 1932- *WhoAmP 93*
Capps, James Leigh, II 1956- *WhoAmL 94, WhoWest 94*
Capps, John Paul 1934- *WhoAmP 93*
Capps, Kenneth P. 1939- *WhoAmA 93*
Capps, Richard Huntley 1928- *WhoAm 94*
Capps, Thomas Edward 1935- *WhoAm 94, WhoFI 94*
Cappuccilli, Piero 1929- *IntWW 93, NewGrDO*
Cappuyns, Hendrik Frans Ferdinand d1992 *IntWW 93N*
Cappy, Ralph J. 1943- *WhoAmP 93*
Cappy, Ralph Joseph 1943- *WhoAmL 94*
Cappy, Ted d1979 *WhoHol 92*
Capra, Carlo 1938- *IntWW 93*
Capra, Frank 1897-1991 *AmCulL [port], WhAm 10*
Capra, Frank, Jr. *IntMPA 94*
Capranica, Matteo 1708-1776? *NewGrDO*
Capranica Family *NewGrDO*
Capri, Ahna *WhoHol 92*
Capria, Nicola 1932- *IntWW 93*
Capriano, Michael Patrick 1928- *WhoAmL 94*
Capriati, Jennifer 1976- *BuCMET, IntWW 93*
Capriati, Jennifer Maria 1976- *WhoAm 94*
Capriccioso, Richard Paul 1956- *WhoFI 94*
Caprice, June d1936 *WhoHol 92*
Capricornus, Samuel Friedrich 1628-1665 *NewGrDO*
Caprio, Anthony S. 1945- *WhoAm 94*
Caprio, Frank Thomas 1966- *WhoAmP 93*
Caprio, Giuseppe 1914- *IntWW 93*
Caprioglio, Nino d1993 *NewYTBS 93*
Caprioli, Richard Michael 1943- *WhoScEn 94*
Caprioli, Vittorio d1989 *WhoHol 92*
Capriotti, John M., Jr. 1953- *WhoMW 93*
Caproli, Carlo 1615?-1692? *NewGrDO*
Capron, Alexander Morgan 1944- *IntWW 93, WhoAm 94*
Capron, (George) Christopher 1935- *Who 94*
Capron, John M. 1942- *WhoAmL 94*
Capshaw, Kate 1953- *IntMPA 94, WhoHol 92*
Capshaw, Tommie Dean 1936- *WhoAm 94, WhoAmL 94, WhoMW 93*
Capshew, James H. 1954- *WhoMW 93*
Capsir, Mercedes c. 1895-1969 *NewGrDO*
Capstick, Brian Eric 1927- *Who 94*
Capstick, Charles William 1934- *Who 94*
Captain Beefheart 1941- *ConMus 10 [port]*
Capua, Marcello da *NewGrDO*
Capuana, Franco 1894-1969 *NewGrDO*
Capuana, Maria 1891-1955 *NewGrDO*
Capucine d1990 *WhoHol 92*
Capute, Charles Thomas 1950- *WhoAm 94, WhoAmL 94*
Caputi, Anthony 1924- *WhoAm 94, WrDr 94*
Caputi, William James, Jr. 1936- *WhoAm 94*
Caputo, Bruce 1943- *WhoAmP 93*
Caputo, Dante 1943- *IntWW 93*
Caputo, David Armand 1943- *WhoAm 94*
Caputo, Joseph Anthony 1940- *WhoAm 94*
Caputo, Kathryn Mary 1948- *WhoAmL 94*
Caputo, Lucio 1935- *WhoFI 94*
Caputo, Philip 1941- *TwCYAW*
Caputo, Philip Joseph 1941- *WhoAm 94*
Caputo, Wayne James 1956- *WhoScEn 94*
Capuzzi, Giuseppe Antonio 1755-1818 *NewGrDO*
Cara, Irene 1957- *WhoHol 92*
Cara, Irene 1959- *IntMPA 94*
Caraballo, José Noel 1955- *WhoHisp 94*
Caraballo, Luis Benito 1954- *WhoHisp 94*
Caraballo, Manuel De J. 1936- *WhoHisp 94*
Caraballo, Wilfredo 1947- *WhoHisp 94*
Caraballo-Oramas, Jose A. 1961- *WhoHisp 94*
Carabe Lopez, Julio 1959- *WhoScEn 94*
Carabillo, Joseph Anthony 1946- *WhoIns 94*
Carabillo, Virginia A. 1926- *WhoAm 94*
Caracciola, Joseph John 1915- *WhoAmP 93*
Caractacus fl. 1st cent.BC- *BlmGEL*
Caradoc fl. 1st cent.BC- *BlmGEL*
Caradori-Allan, Maria (Caterina Rosalbina) 1800-1865 *NewGrDO*
Carafa (de Colobrano), Michele (Enrico-Francesco-Vincenzo-Aloisio-Paolo 1787-1872 *NewGrDO*
Carafotes, Paul *WhoHol 92*
Caragiale, Ion Luca 1852-1912 *IntDcT 2*
Caraher, Michael Edward 1953- *WhoScEn 94*
Caraker, Mary *EncSF 93*
Caraker, Mary 1929- *SmATA 74 [port]*
Caraley, Demetrios 1932- *WhoAm 94*
Caram, Dorothy Farrington 1933- *WhoHisp 94*
Caram, Eve La Salle *DrAPF 93*
Carameros, George Demitrius, Jr. 1924- *WhoAm 94*
Caramitru, Ion 1942- *IntWW 93*
Caranci, Anthony Benjamin, Jr. 1930- *WhoAmP 93*
Caranci, John Anthony, Jr. 1952- *WhoWest 94*
Caranci, Paul Francis 1955- *WhoAmP 93*
Carano, Boyd Gilardi 1959- *WhoAmL 94*
Caras, Joseph Sheldon 1924- *WhoAm 94*
Caras, Roger A(ndrew) 1928- *WrDr 94*
Caras, Roger Andrew 1928- *WhoAm 94*
Carasso, Alfred Sam 1939- *WhoScEn 94*
Carattini-Cooke, Valerie 1958- *WhoFI 94*
Caravatt, Paul Joseph, Jr. 1922- *WhoAm 94*
Caravia, Manuel A. *WhoHisp 94*
Caraway, Yolanda H. 1950- *WhoAmP 93, WhoBlA 94*
Caray, Harry Christopher 1919- *WhoAm 94*
Carazo Odio, Rodrigo 1926- *IntWW 93*
Carb, Stephen Ames 1930- *WhoAm 94*
Carbajal, Michael 1968- *WhoHisp 94*
Carbajal G., Enrique *WhoAmA 93*
Carballeira, David A. 1958- *WhoHisp 94*
Carballido (Fentanes), Emilio 1925- *ConWorW 93*
Carballido, Emilio 1925- *IntDcT 2*
Carballo, Julio R. 1946- *WhoHisp 94*
Carballo, Richard d1980 *WhoHol 92*
Carbaugh, John Edward, Jr. 1945- *WhoAmL 94, WhoFI 94*
Carberry, Charles M. 1950- *WhoAm 94*
Carberry, Charles Michael 1950- *WhoAmL 94*
Carberry, Deirdre *WhoAm 94*
Carberry, Edward Andrew 1941- *WhoScEn 94*
Carberry, Glenn Thomas 1955- *WhoAmP 93*
Carberry, James John 1925- *WhoScEn 94*
Carberry, Joe *WhoHol 92*
Carberry, Michael Glen 1941- *WhoAm 94*
Carbery, Baron 1920- *Who 94*
Carbery, Ethna 1866-1911 *BlmGWL*
Carbery, Muriel R. d1993 *NewYTBS 93*
Carbery, Thomas Francis 1925- *Who 94*
Carbet, Marie-Magdeleine *BlmGWL*
Carbine, James Edmond 1945- *WhoAm 94, WhoAmL 94*
Carbine, Sharon 1950- *WhoAmL 94*
Carbo, Michael D. 1956- *WhoAmL 94*
Carbo, Ramon 1940- *WhoScEn 94*
Carbo-Fite, Rafael 1942- *WhoScEn 94*
Carbon, Max William 1922- *WhoScEn 94*
Carbon, Susan Berkson 1953- *WhoAmL 94*
Carbonara, Robert Stephen 1937- *WhoMW 93*
Carbone, Antony *WhoHol 92*
Carbone, David 1950- *WhoAmA 93*
Carbone, James Joseph 1961- *WhoFI 94*
Carbone, John Vito 1922- *WhAm 10*
Carbone, Joyce *DrAPF 93*
Carbone, Leslie Ann 1964- *WhoHisp 94*
Carbone, Leslie Anne 1964- *WhoWest 94*
Carbone, Lewis Peter 1949- *WhoAm 94*
Carbone, Nicholas R. 1936- *WhoAmP 93*
Carbone, Paul Peter 1931- *WhoAm 94, WhoScEn 94*
Carbone, William John 1947- *WhoMW 93*
Carbonell, Carlos E. 1957- *WhoHisp 94*
Carbonell, Joseph Fernando 1936- *WhoHisp 94*
Carbonell, Néstor *WhoHisp 94*
Carbonell, Ramiro M. 1962- *WhoAmL 94*
Carbonell, Ruben Guillermo 1947- *WhoHisp 94, WhoScEn 94*
Carbonell, William Leycester Rouse 1912- *Who 94*
Carboni, Richard *DrAPF 93*
Carbonneau, Come 1923- *WhoScEn 94*
Carbonneau, Guy 1960- *WhoAm 94*
Carby, Fanny *WhoHol 92*
Carby, Hazel V. 1948- *BlmGWL, WhoBlA 94*
Carcani, Adil 1922- *IntWW 93*
Carcani, Giuseppe 1703-1778 *NewGrDO*
Carcaterra, Lorenzo 1954- *ConAu 140*
Carcieri, Anthony J. *WhoAmP 93*
Card, Andrew Hill, Jr. 1947- *WhoAmP 93*
Card, June 1942- *NewGrDO*
Card, Kathryn d1964 *WhoHol 92*
Card, Larry J. 1950- *WhoIns 94*
Card, Orson Scott 1951- *Au&Arts 11 [port], EncSF 93, TwCYAW, WhoAm 94, WrDr 94*
Card, Royden 1952- *WhoAmA 93*
Cardalena, Peter Paul, Jr. 1943- *WhoAmL 94*
Cardamone, Richard J. 1925- *WhoAm 94, WhoAmL 94, WhoAmP 93*
Cardano, Girolamo 1501-1576 *WorScD*

Cardarelli, Joseph DrAPF 93
Carde, Ring Richard Tomlinson 1943- WhoScEn 94
Cardella, Thomas J. 1954- WhoMW 93
Carden, Charles Buford 1944- WhoAm 94
Carden, Christopher Robert 1946- Who 94
Carden, David L. 1951- WhoAmL 94
Carden, Derrick Charles 1921- Who 94
Carden, Henry Christopher d1993 Who 94N
Carden, Joan 1937- NewGrDO
Carden, Joan Maralyn IntWW 93
Carden, John d1783 WhAmRev
Carden, John Craven 1926- Who 94
Carden, Joy Cabbage 1932- WhoWest 94
Carden, Richard John Derek 1943- Who 94
Carden, Thomas Ray WhoWest 94
Cardenal, Ernesto 1925- ConWorW 93, HispLC [port]
Cárdenas, Alberto Patricio 1937- WhoHisp 94
Cárdenas, Anthony J. 1946- WhoHisp 94
Cardenas, Deborah Ileana 1962- WhoHisp 94
Cardenas, Diana Delia 1947- WhoScEn 94
Cardenas, Elsa WhoHol 92
Cardenas, Gabriel Ricardo 1967- WhoFI 94
Cardenas, Garcia Lopez De fl. 154-?- WhWE
Cardenas, Gerardo Felipe 1962- WhoHisp 94
Cardenas, Gilberto 1947- WhoHisp 94
Cardenas, Henry WhoHisp 94
Cardenas, Henry Steven 1964- WhoWest 94
Cardenas, John I. 1924- WhoScEn 94
Cardenas, John R. WhoHisp 94
Cárdenas, Jose A. 1930- WhoHisp 94
Cardenas, Judith Frances 1961- WhoHisp 94
Cardenas, Lazaro 1895-1970 HisWorL [port]
Cardenas, Leo Elias 1935- WhoHisp 94
Cardenas, Lucy R. 1945- WhoHisp 94
Cardenas, Luis WhoHisp 94
Cárdenas, Maria de la Luz Rodriguez 1945- WhoHisp 94
Cárdenas, María Elena 1939- WhoHisp 94
Cardenas, Mario J. 1925- WhoHisp 94
Cardenas, Mike 1955- WhoHisp 94
Cardenas, Nick 1940- WhoHisp 94
Cardenas, Norma Yvette 1944- WhoHisp 94
Cardenas, Patricia Lorain Hicks 1939- WhoMW 93
Cardenas, Rafael 1949- WhoHisp 94
Cárdenas, Raúl 1937- WhoHisp 94
Cárdenas, Raúl R., Jr. 1929- WhoHisp 94
Cardenas, Raymond WhoHisp 94
Cardenas, Renato E. WhoHisp 94
Cardenas, Rene F. 1933- WhoHisp 94
Cardenas, Robert Isaac 1936- WhoHisp 94
Cárdenas, Robert Léon 1920- WhoHisp 94
Cardenas, Ruben Raul 1931- WhoHisp 94
Cardenas, Rudolfo Robert, Jr. 1949- WhoAmP 93
Cardenas-Escovar, Alberto 1917- WhoHisp 94
Cardenas-Garcia, Jaime Fernando 1950- WhoHisp 94
Cardenas-Jaffe, Veronica 1947- WhoHisp 94
Cardenes, Andres Jorge 1957- WhoAm 94
Cardente, Alfred W. 1925- WhoAmP 93
Carder, James Lewis 1944- WhoFI 94
Carder, John Arthur 1955- WhoWest 94
Carder, Larry William 1958- WhoFI 94, WhoWest 94
Carder, Paul Charles 1941- WhoAm 94
Cardew, William Joseph WhoAm 94
Cardi, Pat 1952- WhoHol 92
Cardiff, Archbishop of 1929- Who 94
Cardiff, Gladys H. DrAPF 93
Cardiff, Jack 1914- IntDcF 2-4, IntMPA 94, IntWW 93, Who 94
Cardigan, Earl of 1952- Who 94
Cardillo, Joe DrAPF 93
Cardillo, John Pollara 1942- WhoAmL 94
Cardillo, Joseph Bernard 1949- WhoFI 94
Cardillo, Rimer Angel 1944- WhoAmA 93
Cardin, Benjamin L. 1943- CngDr 93
Cardin, Benjamin Louis 1943- WhoAm 94, WhoAmP 93
Cardin, Meyer M. 1907- WhoFI 94
Cardin, Pierre 1922- IntWW 93, Who 94
Cardin, Shoshana Shoubin 1926- WhoAm 94
Cardin, Suzette 1950- WhoWest 94
Cardin, Tommie Sullivan 1961- WhoAmP 93
Cardinal, Claus 1943- WhoIns 94
Cardinal, Douglas Joseph 1934- IntWW 93
Cardinal, Marcelin 1920- WhoAm 94, WhoAmA 93
Cardinal, Marie 1929- BlmGWL, ConWorW 93
Cardinal, Robert Jean 1935- WhoFI 94
Cardinal, Roger 1940- WrDr 94
Cardinal, Roger Joseph 1950- WhoFI 94
Cardinal, Shirley Mae 1944- WhoMW 93
Cardinale, Claudia 1938- IntWW 93
Cardinale, Claudia 1939- IntMPA 94, WhoHol 92
Cardinale, Gerald 1934- WhoAmP 93
Cardinale, Kathleen Carmel 1933- WhoAm 94
Cardinali, Albert John 1934- WhoAm 94
Cardine, G. Joseph WhoAmP 93
Cardine, Godfrey Joseph 1924- WhoAm 94, WhoAmL 94, WhoWest 94
Cardis, Thomas Michael 1945- WhoScEn 94
Cardle, Janet Campbell 1934- WhoMW 93
Cardle, Maria Joan Pastuszek 1959- WhoWest 94
Cardman, Cecilia d1989 WhAm 10
Cardman, Lawrence S. 1944- WhoAm 94
Cardner, David Victor 1935- WhoScEn 94
Cardona, Alice 1930- WhoHisp 94
Cardona, Carlos J., Jr. 1940- WhoHisp 94
Cardona, Ed 1944- WhoMW 93
Cardona, Fernando 1935- WhoHisp 94
Cardona, Gilbert Tommy WhoHisp 94
Cardona, Manuel 1934- IntWW 93
Cardona, Rodolfo 1924- WhoAm 94
Cardona, Steven Carl 1956- WhoWest 94
Cardona-Hine, Alvaro DrAPF 93
Cardone, Bonnie Jean 1942- WhoAm 94
Cardoni, Horace Robert 1916- WhoAm 94
Cardonne, Jean-Baptiste 1730-1792? NewGrDO
Cardoso, Anthony 1930- WhoAmA 93
Cardoso, Dinora C. 1959- WhoHisp 94
Cardoso de Mello, Zelia 1954- WhoWomW 91
Cardoso E Cunha, Antonio Jose 1933- IntWW 93
Cardoso E Cunha, Antonio Jose Baptista 1934- Who 94
Cardoso Pires, Jose (Augusto Neves) 1925- ConWorW 93
Cardoza, Anne de Sola 1941- WhoAm 94, WhoWest 94
Cardoza, James Ernest 1944- WhoScEn 94
Cardoza, Jose Alfredo 1953- WhoHisp 94
Cardoza, Marvin Edmund 1913- WhoWest 94
Cardoza, Raul John 1944- WhoHisp 94
Cardoza, Robert J. WhoHisp 94
Cardozier, Virgus R. 1923- WhoAm 94
Cardozo, Benjamin Mordecai 1915- WhoAm 94
Cardozo, Michael A 1941- WhoAm 94
Cardozo, Michael Hart 1910- WhoAm 94
Cardozo, Michael Hart, V 1940- WhoAmP 93
Cardozo, Miguel Angel 1932- WhoScEn 94
Cardozo, Richard Nunez 1936- WhoAm 94
Cardross, Lord 1960- Who 94
Carducci, Vincent A. 1953- WhoAmA 93
Cardullo, Joseph P. 1945- WhoAmP 93
Cardus, David 1922- WhoAm 94
Cardwell, David Earl 1951- WhoAm 94
Cardwell, Donald Stephen Lowell 1919- IntWW 93
Cardwell, Horace Milton 1919- WhoAm 94
Cardwell, J. Thomas 1943- WhoAmL 94
Cardwell, James d1954 WhoHol 92
Cardwell, James William 1948- WhoAm 94
Cardwell, John James 1931- IntWW 93
Cardwell, John Nelson 1944- WhoMW 93
Cardwell, Kenneth Harvey 1920- WhoAm 94
Cardwell, Michael Dexter 1950- WhoWest 94
Cardwell, Nancy Lee 1947- WhoAm 94
Cardwell, Robert A. 1942- WhoAmL 94
Cardy, Andrew Gordon WhoAm 94
Cardy, John Lawrence 1947- Who 94
Cardy, Robert Willard 1936- WhoAm 94, WhoFI 94
Care, Norman Sydney 1937- WhoMW 93
Careaga, Richard WhoAmL 94
Careaga, Rogelio Antonio 1942- WhoWest 94
Carek, Donald John 1931- WhoAm 94
Carek, Gerald Allen 1960- WhoScEn 94
Carel, Roger WhoHol 92
Carell, Annette d1967 WhoHol 92
Carelli, Emma 1877-1928 NewGrDO
Carelli, Gabor Paul 1915- WhoAm 94
Caren, Robert Poston 1932- WhoAm 94
Carena, Maria 1891-1966 NewGrDO
Carere, Christine 1930- WhoHol 92
Carestini, Giovanni c. 1704-c. 1760 NewGrDO
Caret, Robert Laurent 1947- WhoAm 94
Carette d1966 WhoHol 92
Carette, Bruno d1989 WhoHol 92
Caretti, Richard Louis 1953- WhoAmL 94
Caretto, Albert Alexander 1928- WhoAm 94
Carew, Baron 1905- Who 94
Carew, Arthur Edmund d1937 WhoHol 92
Carew, Benjamin WhAmRev
Carew, Colin A. 1943- WhoBlA 94
Carew, James d1938 WhoHol 92
Carew, Jan (Rynveld) 1925- BlkWr 2, WrDr 94
Carew, Ora d1955 WhoHol 92
Carew, Rivers (Verain) 1935- Who 94
Carew, Rivers (Verain), Sir 1935- WrDr 94
Carew, Rodney Cline 1945- WhoAm 94, WhoBlA 94
Carew, Thomas 1594-1640 BlmGEL
Carew, Topper 1943- WhoBlA 94
Carewe, Edwin d1940 WhoHol 92
Carewe, Rita d1955 WhoHol 92
Carewe, Sylvia WhoAmA 93N
Carew Pole, John Gawen d1993 Who 94N
Carew Pole, (John) Richard (Walter Reginald) 1938- Who 94
Carey, Addison, Jr. 1933- WhoBlA 94
Carey, Alban M. 1906- Who 94
Carey, Anthony Morris 1935- WhoAm 94
Carey, Arthur Bernard, Jr. 1950- WhoAm 94
Carey, Audrey L. 1937- WhoBlA 94
Carey, Austin, Jr. 1943- WhoAmL 94
Carey, Barbara I. 1946- WhoIns 94
Carey, Bruce Douglas 1923- WhoAm 94
Carey, Carnice 1945- WhoBlA 94
Carey, Charles John 1933- Who 94
Carey, Claire Lamar 1943- WhoBlA 94
Carey, (Francis) Clive (Savill) 1883-1968 NewGrDO
Carey, Conan Jerome 1936- Who 94
Carey, D(avid) M(acbeth) M(oir) 1917- Who 94
Carey, de Vic Graham 1940- Who 94
Carey, Dean Lavere 1925- WhoAm 94
Carey, Denis d1986 WhoHol 92
Carey, Dennis Clarke 1949- WhoAm 94
Carey, Diane (L.) 1954- EncSF 93
Carey, Edward F. d1979 WhoHol 92
Carey, Edward John 1944- WhoAm 94
Carey, Edward Marshel, Jr. 1942- WhoAm 94, WhoFI 94, WhoMW 93
Carey, Ellen 1952- WhoAmA 93
Carey, Ernestine Gilbreth WrDr 94
Carey, Ernestine Gilbreth 1908- WhoAm 94
Carey, Francis James 1926- WhoAm 94, WhoFI 94
Carey, George Leonard Who 94
Carey, George Leonard 1935- IntWW 93
Carey, Gerald E. 1937- WhoIns 94
Carey, Gerald John, Jr. 1930- WhoAm 94, WhoScEn 94
Carey, Gerard V. 1926- WhoAm 94
Carey, Godfrey Mohun Cecil 1941- Who 94
Carey, Gregory Brian 1942- WhoAm 94
Carey, H. Bissell, III 1944- WhoAmL 94
Carey, Harmon Roderick 1936- WhoBlA 94
Carey, Harry d1947 WhoHol 92
Carey, Harry, Jr. 1921- IntMPA 94, WhoHol 92
Carey, Henry 1687-1743 NewGrDO
Carey, Howard H. 1937- WhoBlA 94
Carey, Hugh L. WhoAm 94, WhoAmL 94, WhoFI 94
Carey, Hugh L. 1919- WhoAmP 93
Carey, Hugh Leo 1919- Who 94
Carey, J. Edwin 1923- WhoAm 94
Carey, James Henry 1932- WhoAm 94
Carey, James Joseph 1939- WhoAmP 93
Carey, James William 1934- WhoAm 94
Carey, James William 1945- WhoBlA 94
Carey, Jana Howard 1945- WhoAm 94, WhoAmL 94
Carey, Jane Quellmalz 1952- WhoFI 94
Carey, Jean Lebeis 1943- WhoFI 94
Carey, Jennifer Davis 1956- WhoBlA 94
Carey, John 1924- WhoAm 94
Carey, John 1934- IntWW 93, Who 94, WhoAm 94, WrDr 94
Carey, John Allen 1959- WhoMW 93
Carey, John Andrew 1949- WhoFI 94
Carey, John J. 1928- WhoIns 94
Carey, John J. 1931- WhoFI 94
Carey, John Jesse 1931- WhoAm 94
Carey, John Leo 1920- WhoAm 94, WhoAmL 94
Carey, John M. 1933- WhoFI 94
Carey, John Thomas 1917-1990 WhoAmA 93N
Carey, John W. 1937- WhoAmL 94
Carey, Joseph Kuhn 1957- WrDr 94
Carey, Joyce d1993 NewYTBS 93 [port]
Carey, Joyce 1898- WhoHol 92
Carey, Katherine Burns 1963- WhoMW 93
Carey, Kathryn Ann 1949- WhoAm 94, WhoFI 94, WhoWest 94
Carey, Larry Campbell 1933- WhoAm 94
Carey, Leonard d1977 WhoHol 92
Carey, Macdonald 1913- IntMPA 94, WhoHol 92
Carey, Malcom Timothy 1944- WhoFI 94
Carey, Mariah WhoBlA 94, WhoHisp 94
Carey, Mariah 1969- WhoAm 94
Carey, Marsha Clifton 1951- WhoAmL 94
Carey, Martin Conrad 1939- WhoScEn 94
Carey, Mary 1609?-c. 1680 BlmGWL
Carey, Mary Jane d1990 WhoHol 92
Carey, Michael James 1957- WhoMW 93
Carey, Michael Richard 1953- WhoAmL 94
Carey, Michele WhoHol 92
Carey, Milburn Ernest 1912- WhoAm 94
Carey, Milton Gales 1926- WhoBlA 94
Carey, Nancy Sue 1942- WhoAmP 93
Carey, Olive d1988 WhoHol 92
Carey, Omer Ligon 1929- WhoWest 94
Carey, Patricia Elaine Stedman 1944- WhoAm 94
Carey, Patricia M. WhoBlA 94
Carey, Paul Richard 1945- WhoAm 94, WhoScEn 94
Carey, Pearl M. WhoBlA 94
Carey, Peter 1943- BlmGEL, EncSF 93, IntWW 93, WrDr 94
Carey, Peter (Philip) 1943- RfGShF
Carey, Peter (Willoughby) 1923- Who 94
Carey, Peter Kevin 1940- WhoAm 94
Carey, Peter Philip 1943- Who 94
Carey, Peter Willoughby 1923- IntWW 93
Carey, Phil 1925- IntMPA 94
Carey, Philip 1925- WhoHol 92
Carey, Phillip 1942- WhoBlA 94
Carey, Richard Edward 1957- WhoWest 94
Carey, Richard J. WhoAmP 93
Carey, Robert Munson 1940- WhoAm 94, WhoScEn 94
Carey, Robert Williams 1918- WhoAm 94
Carey, Ron 1935- WhoHol 92
Carey, Ron 1936- News 93-3 [port]
Carey, Ronald WhoAm 94, WhoFI 94
Carey, Rosa Nouchette 1840-1909 BlmGWL
Carey, Sarah Collins 1938- WhoAm 94
Carey, Stan 1955- WhoWest 94
Carey, Steve DrAPF 93
Carey, Terrence Michael 1949- WhoMW 93
Carey, Thomas Devore 1931- WhoAm 94
Carey, Thomas Hilton 1944- WhoAm 94
Carey, Timothy 1925- WhoHol 92
Carey, V. George 1928- WhoAmP 93
Carey, Wayne E. 1945- WhoBlA 94
Carey, Willard Keith 1929- WhoAm 94
Carey, William Arthur 1920- WhoAmP 93
Carey, William Bacon 1926- WhoAm 94
Carey, William Barker 1954- WhoAmL 94
Carey, William Craig 1942- WhoAmL 94
Carey, William Joseph 1922- WhoAm 94
Carey, William Polk 1930- WhoAm 94, WhoFI 94
Carey Evans, David Lloyd 1925- Who 94
Carey-Foster, George Arthur 1907- Who 94
Carey Jones, Norman Stewart 1911- Who 94
Carfagna, Peter A. 1953- WhoAmL 94
Carfax, Catherine 1928- WrDr 94
Carfora, John Michael 1950- WhoScEn 94
Cargas, Martin dePorres 1958- WhoAmL 94
Cargerman, Alan William 1945- WhoAmL 94
Cargile, Ann Peldo 1960- WhoAmL 94
Cargile, C. B., Jr. 1926- WhoBlA 94
Cargile, James Thomas 1938- WhoAm 94
Cargile, Michael Edward 1942- WhoMW 93
Cargile, William, III WhoBlA 94
Cargill, Mrs. NewGrDO
Cargill, Gilbert Allen 1916- WhoBlA 94
Cargill, Linda DrAPF 93
Cargill, Otto Arthur, Jr. 1914- WhAm 10
Cargill, Patrick 1918- WhoHol 92
Cargill, Robert Mason 1948- WhoAmL 94
Cargill, Sandra Morris 1953- WhoBlA 94
Cargiulo, Ralph J. 1935- WhoIns 94
Cargo, David Francis 1929- WhoAm 94
Cargo, Gerald Thomas 1930- WhoAm 94
Cargo, William Ira 1917- WhoAm 94
Carhart, Vera Margaret 1928- WhoAmP 93
Caridad, Jose Maria 1949- WhoScEn 94
Caridas, Evangeline Chris 1950- WhoFI 94
Cariddi, Alan Francis 1949- WhoAm 94
Carideo, Eddie d1985 WhoHol 92

Carides, Gia WhoHol 92
Caridi, Carmine WhoHol 92
Carignan, Claude 1950- WhoScEn 94
Carignan, Marc Alfred 1963- WhoWest 94
Carignon, Alain 1949- IntWW 93
Carigouan dc. 1634 EncNAR
Carillo, Mary 1957- BuCMET
Carillo, Michael A. 1951- WhoHisp 94
Carim, Altaf Hyder 1961- WhoScEn 94
Carim, Enver 1938- WrDr 94
Carin, Michael 1951- WrDr 94
Carine, James 1934- Who 94
Carington Who 94
Cariola, Robert J. 1927- WhoAmA 93
Cariola, Robert Joseph 1927- WhoAm 94
Carioti, Bruno Mario 1929- WhoScEn 94
Cariou, Len 1939- IntMPA 94, WhoHol 92
Cariou, Len Joseph 1939- WhoAm 94
Carisch, George 1935- IntMPA 94
Carisella, P(asquale) J. 1922- WrDr 94
Caris-McManus, Jeannemarie 1953- WhoMW 93
Carithers, Hugh Alfred 1913- WhoAm 94
Carithers, Jeanine Rutherford 1933- WhoAm 94
Carius, Jeffrey Rapp 1949- WhoMW 93
Carius, Robert Wilhelm 1929- WhoAm 94
Carkeet, David DrAPF 93
Carkeet, David 1946- SmATA 75, WrDr 94
Carl, Angela Reeves 1949- WhoMW 93
Carl, Douglas 1951- WhoAmP 93
Carl, Earl Lawrence 1919- WhoBlA 94
Carl, Janet A. 1948- WhoAmP 93
Carl, Joan 1926- WhoAmA 93
Carl, John L. 1948- WhoFI 94
Carl, Lillian Stewart 1949- ConAu 42NR
Carl, Renee d1954 WhoHol 92
Carl, Robert E. 1927- WhoFI 94
Carlander, John Robert 1943- WhoWest 94
Carlani, Carlo fl. 1743-1765 NewGrDO
Carlberg, Norman Kenneth 1928- WhoAmA 93
Carlberg, Ralph Norman 1943- WhoWest 94
Carle, Eric 1929- WrDr 94
Carle, Frankie 1903- WhoHol 92
Carle, Harry Lloyd 1927- WhoWest 94
Carle, Lawrence Jerry 1946- WhoMW 93
Carle, Lucky d1983 WhoHol 92
Carle, Richard d1941 WhoHol 92
Carle, William Daniel, III 1929- WhoAmL 94
Carlen, Claudia 1906- WhoAm 94
Carlen, Raymond Nils 1919-1989 WhAm 10
Carlen, Richard Donald 1932- WhoMW 93
Carleon, A. 1922- WrDr 94
Carleone, Joseph 1946- WhoWest 94
Carles, Arthur B. 1882-1952 WhoAmA 93N
Carles, Emilie 1900-1979 ConAu 141
Carles, Romeo d1971 WhoHol 92
Carleson, Robert Bazil 1931- WhoAm 94
Carless, Hugh Michael 1925- Who 94
Carless, John Edward 1922- Who 94
Carleton, Bruce Alan 1947- WhoMW 93
Carleton, Bukk Griffith 1909- WhoFI 94
Carleton, Christopher d1787 WhAmRev
Carleton, Claire d1979 WhoHol 92
Carleton, Don Edward 1947- WhoAm 94
Carleton, George d1950 WhoHol 92
Carleton, George 1529-1590 DcNaB MP
Carleton, Guy 1724-1808 AmRev, WhAmRev [port]
Carleton, Harry Guy d1922 WhoHol 92
Carleton, Janet (Buchanan) Who 94
Carleton, John Lowndes 1925- WhoWest 94
Carleton, Joseph G., Jr. 1945- WhoAmP 93
Carleton, Lloyd B. d1933 WhoHol 92
Carleton, Mark Thomas 1935- WrDr 94
Carleton, Mary 1633?-1673 BlmGWL
Carleton, Richard Allyn 1931- WhoAm 94
Carleton, Robert L. 1940- WhoFI 94
Carleton, Thomas 1735-1817 WhAmRev
Carleton, Willard Tracy 1934- WhoAm 94
Carleton, William P. d1947 WhoHol 92
Carleton, William T. d1922 WhoHol 92
Carleton-Smith, Michael Edward 1931- Who 94
Carl Eugen 1728-1793 NewGrDO
Carley, Charles Team, Jr. 1932- WhoAm 94
Carley, George H. 1938- WhoAmL 94, WhoAmP 93
Carley, James French 1923- WhoAm 94
Carley, John Blythe 1934- WhoFI 94, WhoWest 94
Carley, John Halliday 1941- WhoAm 94, WhoAmL 94, WhoAmP 93
Carley, L. David 1928- WhoAm 94
Carley, Lionel (Kenneth) 1936- WrDr 94
Carley, Robert Hillis, Jr. 1950- WhoFI 94
Carl Gustaf, XVI 1946- IntWW 93
Carlhian, Jean Paul 1919- WhoAm 94
Carli, Antonio Francesco fl. 1698-1723 NewGrDO
Carli, Guido d1993 IntWW 93N, NewYTBS 93 [port]
Carli, Guido 1914- IntWW 93
Carlie, Edward d1938 WhoHol 92
Carlier, Anthony Neil 1937- Who 94
Carlier, Jean Joachim 1926- WhoScEn 94
Carlile, Alexander Charles 1948- Who 94
Carlile, Edward Wilson 1915- Who 94
Carlile, Henry DrAPF 93
Carlile, Janet (Hildebrand) 1942- WhoAmA 93
Carlile, Janet Louise 1942- WhoAm 94
Carlile, Lynne 1947- WhoScEn 94
Carlile, Richard F. 1941- WhoAmL 94
Carlile, Robert Leslie 1924- WhoAm 94
Carlile, Thomas 1924- Who 94
Carlill, John Hildred 1925- Who 94
Carlill, Stephen Hope 1902- Who 94
Carlin, Benedict 1911- WhoFI 94
Carlin, Clair Myron 1947- WhoAmL 94, WhoMW 93
Carlin, David H. 1943- WhoAmL 94
Carlin, David Robert, Jr. 1938- WhoAmP 93
Carlin, Dennis J. 1941- WhoAm 94, WhoAmL 94, WhoMW 93
Carlin, Donald Walter 1934- WhoAm 94
Carlin, Edward Robert 1940- WhoAm 94
Carlin, Electra Marshall WhoAmA 93
Carlin, Gabriel S. 1921- WhoAm 94
Carlin, George 1937- IntMPA 94, WhoCom [port], WhoHol 92
Carlin, George Denis 1937- WhoAm 94
Carlin, Gloria WhoHol 92
Carlin, Herbert J. 1917- WhoAm 94, WhoScEn 94
Carlin, James 1910- WhoAmA 93
Carlin, James Boyce 1932- WhoAm 94
Carlin, Jeffrey John 1964- WhoAmL 94
Carlin, John William 1940- IntWW 93, WhoAm 94, WhoAmP 93
Carlin, Kevin Francis Christopher 1952- WhoAmL 94
Carlin, Lynn 1938- WhoHol 92
Carlin, Melissa Joann 1949- WhoHisp 94
Carlin, Paul Victor 1945- WhoAm 94, WhoAmL 94
Carlin, Sean Michael 1958- WhoAmL 94
Carlin, Thomas A. d1991 WhoHol 92
Carlin, Vivian F. 1919- WrDr 94
Carline, William Ralph 1910- WhoBlA 94
Carliner, David 1918- WhoAm 94
Carliner, Michael Simon 1945- WhoAm 94
Carling, Francis 1945- WhoAm 94, WhoAmL 94
Carling, Richard Junius 1937- WhoAmP 93
Carling, William David Charles 1965- IntWW 93, Who 94
Carlini, James 1954- WhoFI 94
Carlini, Lawrence J. 1949- WhoAmL 94
Carlini, Paolo d1979 WhoHol 92
Carlino, Guy Thomas 1928- WhoFI 94
Carlino, James Charles 1960- WhoAmL 94
Carlino, Lewis John 1932- ConDr 93, IntMPA 94, WrDr 94
Carlino di Ratta, Il NewGrDO
Carlisi, Olimpia WhoHol 92
Carlisle Who 94
Carlisle, Archdeacon of Who 94
Carlisle, Bishop of 1932- Who 94
Carlisle, Dean of Who 94
Carlisle, Earl of 1923- Who 94
Carlisle, Alan 1929- WhoAmL 94
Carlisle, Alan Robert WhoScEn 94
Carlisle, Alexandra d1936 WhoHol 92
Carlisle, Anne WhoHol 92
Carlisle, Brian Apcar 1919- Who 94
Carlisle, Carris 1943- WrDr 94
Carlisle, Charles Roger 1929- WhoAm 94
Carlisle, Dwight L., Jr. 1935- WhoAm 94
Carlisle, Ervin Frederick 1935- WhoAm 94
Carlisle, Frederick Howard, Earl of 1748-1825 WhAmRev
Carlisle, Henry DrAPF 93
Carlisle, Hugh Bernard Harwood 1937- Who 94
Carlisle, James Edward, Jr. 1944- WhoBlA 94
Carlisle, John Charles 1938- WhoMW 93
Carlisle, John Reid 1942- WhoAmP 93
Carlisle, John Russell 1942- Who 94
Carlisle, Kenneth Melville 1941- Who 94
Carlisle, Kitty 1915- WhoHol 92
Carlisle, Lilburn Wayne 1936- WhoAmP 93
Carlisle, Lilian Matarose Baker 1912- WhoAm 94
Carlisle, Margo Duer Black WhoAm 94, WhoAmP 93
Carlisle, Mark Ross 1966- WhoScEn 94
Carlisle, Mary 1912- WhoHol 92
Carlisle, Michael Who 94
Carlisle, (John) Michael 1929- Who 94
Carlisle, Patricia Kinley 1949- WhoFI 94
Carlisle, Rita d1949 WhoHol 92
Carlisle, Robert d1986 WhoHol 92
Carlisle, Ronald Dwight 1940- WhoAmP 93
Carlisle, Steve WhoHol 92
Carlisle, Thomas John DrAPF 93
Carlisle, Vervene WhoAmP 93
Carlisle, William Aiken 1918- WhoAm 94
Carlisle, William Todd 1966- WhoAmL 94
Carlisle Of Bucklow, Baron 1929- IntWW 93, Who 94
Carlman, Susan Frick 1957- WhoMW 93
Carlo, Dorothy 1943- WhoAmL 94
Carlo, George Louis 1953- WhoScEn 94
Carlo, Nelson WhoBlA 94
Carlo, Nelson 1938- WhoHisp 94
Carlock, Mahlon Waldo 1926- WhoMW 93
Carlomagno, Giovanni Maria 1940- WhoScEn 94
Carlon, Ancel R. 1940- WhoAmP 93
Carlon, Fran d1993 NewYTBS 93 [port]
Carlos, Andrea Jean 1965- WhoHisp 94
Carlos, (James) Edward 1937- WhoAmA 93
Carlos, Laurie DrAPF 93
Carlos, Marcelino Jose IntWW 93
Carlos, Michael C. 1927- WhoAm 94
Carlotta 1840-1927
See Maximilian 1832-1867 HisWorL
Carlotti, Ronald John 1942- WhoMW 93
Carlotti, Stephen Jon 1942- WhoAm 94, WhoAmL 94, WhoFI 94
Carlotto, Mark Joseph 1954- WhoScEn 94
Carlough, Edward J. WhoAm 94
Carlow, Viscount 1965- Who 94
Carlow, John Sydney 1943- WhoScEn 94
Carlozzi, Carlo, Jr. 1958- WhoFI 94
Carlquist, Sherwin 1930- WhoAm 94
Carlsen, Chris EncSF 93
Carlsen, Chris 1948- WrDr 94
Carlsen, Christopher Robert 1942- WhoAmL 94
Carlsen, Clifford Norman, Jr. 1927- WhoAm 94, WhoAmL 94
Carlsen, G(eorge) Robert 1917- WrDr 94
Carlsen, Ioanna DrAPF 93
Carlsen, James Caldwell 1927- WhoAm 94
Carlsen, Mary Baird 1928- WhoAm 94
Carlsen, Traute d1968 WhoHol 92
Carlsmith, James Merrill 1936- WhoAm 94
Carlsmith, Roger Snedden 1925- WhoScEn 94
Carlson, Al 1948- WhoAmP 93
Carlson, Alan G. 1945- WhoAmL 94
Carlson, Anders Johan 1894- WhAm 10
Carlson, Andrew R. 1934- WrDr 94
Carlson, Andrew Raymond 1934- WhoMW 93
Carlson, Arne H. 1934- WhoAmP 93
Carlson, Arne Helge 1934- WhoAm 94, WhoMW 93
Carlson, Arthur Eugene 1923- WhoMW 93
Carlson, Bernice Wells 1910- WrDr 94
Carlson, Bradley Dee 1951- WhoWest 94
Carlson, Brian Jay 1956- WhoMW 93
Carlson, Bruce Arnold 1949- WhoFI 94
Carlson, C. Craig 1942- WhoAmL 94
Carlson, C. Kent 1942- WhoAmL 94
Carlson, Carl Edward 1922- WhoWest 94
Carlson, Carl G. 1924- WhoWest 94
Carlson, Carolin McCormick Furst 1934- WhoFI 94
Carlson, Charles David 1954- WhoAmL 94
Carlson, Charles Evans 1941- WhoMW 93
Carlson, Charles Long 1917- WhoWest 94
Carlson, Charlotte Booth 1920- WhoAm 94
Carlson, Chester Floyd 1906-1968 WorInv [port]
Carlson, Christopher Eugene 1969- WhoMW 93
Carlson, Clarke 1956- WhoAmP 93
Carlson, Curtis Eugene 1942- WhoScEn 94, WhoWest 94
Carlson, Curtis LeRoy 1914- WhoAm 94, WhoFI 94, WhoMW 93
Carlson, Cynthia J. 1942- WhoAmA 93
Carlson, Cynthia Joanne WhoAm 94
Carlson, Dale Arvid 1925- WhoAm 94
Carlson, Dale Bick 1935- WhoAm 94
Carlson, Dale Lynn 1946- WhoAmL 94, WhoFI 94
Carlson, Daniel Erik 1954- WhoMW 93
Carlson, David Bret 1918- WhoAm 94
Carlson, David Emil 1942- WhoAm 94
Carlson, David Leroy 1942- WhoAm 94
Carlson, David Martin 1940- WhoAm 94
Carlson, David Wayne 1953- WhoMW 93
Carlson, Dennis Nobel 1946- WhoWest 94
Carlson, Devon McElvin 1917- WhoAm 94
Carlson, Doc 1894-1964 BasBi
Carlson, Don WhoAmP 93
Carlson, Don 1929- WhoAmP 93
Carlson, Don D. 1945- WhoAm 94, WhoAmL 94
Carlson, Don Marvin 1931- WhoAm 94
Carlson, Donald Robert 1961- WhoAmL 94
Carlson, Donna Jean 1938- WhoAmP 93
Carlson, Douglas DrAPF 93
Carlson, Douglas R. 1945- WhoAmL 94
Carlson, Douglas W. 1939- WhoAmP 93
Carlson, Dudley Louis 1932- WhoAm 94
Carlson, Edgar A. 1929- WhoAmP 93
Carlson, Edgar Magnus 1908-1992 WhAm 10
Carlson, Edward C. 1942- WhoAm 94
Carlson, Edward Elmer 1911-1990 WhAm 10
Carlson, Edwin Theodore 1946- WhoFI 94
Carlson, Elof Axel 1931- WhoAm 94, WhoScEn 94
Carlson, Elvin Palmer 1950- WhoAm 94
Carlson, Eric Dungan 1929- WhoMW 93
Carlson, Ernest d1940 WhoHol 92
Carlson, Frederick Paul 1938- WhoAm 94
Carlson, Gary Lee 1954- WhoWest 94
Carlson, George Arthur 1940- WhoAm 94, WhoAmA 93
Carlson, Gerhard Frederick 1937- WhoMW 93
Carlson, Guy Raymond 1918- WhoAm 94, WhoMW 93
Carlson, Harry WhoFI 94
Carlson, Harry 1919- WhoAm 94
Carlson, Herb WhoAmP 93
Carlson, Jack Wilson 1933-1992 WhAm 10
Carlson, James Ellsworth 1934- WhoAm 94
Carlson, James R. 1947- WhoAm 94, WhoAmL 94
Carlson, Jane C. 1928- WhoAmA 93
Carlson, Jay L. 1943- WhoAmL 94
Carlson, Jeannie Ann 1955- WhoAm 94
Carlson, Jeffery John 1947- WhoAmL 94
Carlson, Jerry Alan 1936- WhoAm 94
Carlson, Joan WhoAmP 93
Carlson, Joan 1928- WrDr 94
Carlson, John Earl 1952- WhoAm 94
Carlson, John H. 1945- WhoAm 94
Carlson, John Paul 1942- WhoMW 93
Carlson, Jon Gordon 1943- WhoAmL 94, WhoMW 93
Carlson, June 1924- WhoHol 92
Carlson, Karen WhoHol 92
Carlson, Katherine DrAPF 93
Carlson, Kathleen Bussart 1956- WhoAmL 94
Carlson, Kenneth George 1949- WhoMW 93
Carlson, Kit DrAPF 93
Carlson, Kristi Mork 1955- WhoMW 93
Carlson, Lance R. 1950- WhoAmA 93
Carlson, Larry D. 1953- WhoAmL 94
Carlson, Larry Vernon 1943- WhoMW 93
Carlson, Laurie 1952- ConAu 140
Carlson, Lawrence Evan 1944- WhoScEn 94
Carlson, Lenus 1945- NewGrDO
Carlson, Les WhoHol 92
Carlson, Lisa Marie 1956- WhoFI 94
Carlson, Loraine 1923- WrDr 94
Carlson, Loren Merle 1923- WhoAm 94
Carlson, Lyndon Richard 1940- WhoAmP 93, WhoMW 93
Carlson, Lynn Douglas 1934- WhoMW 93
Carlson, Margaret Ellen 1955- WhoWest 94
Carlson, Marian Bille 1952- WhoAm 94
Carlson, Marilyn A. 1938- WhoMW 93
Carlson, Marvin 1937- WhoScEn 94
Carlson, Marvin Albert 1935- WhoAm 94
Carlson, Mary 1939- WhoAmP 93
Carlson, Mary 1951- WhoAmA 93
Carlson, Mary Ann 1944- WhoAmP 93
Carlson, Mary Isabel 1931- WhoMW 93
Carlson, Merle Thomas 1932- WhoAmP 93
Carlson, Michael Paul 1952- WhoMW 93
Carlson, Mitchell Lans 1951- WhoAm 94, WhoWest 94
Carlson, Myron Frank 1910- WhoMW 93
Carlson, Nancy Lee 1950- WhoWest 94
Carlson, Natalie Savage 1906- WhoAm 94, WrDr 94
Carlson, Natalie Traylor 1938- WhoWest 94
Carlson, Norman A. 1933- WhoAm 94, WhoAmP 93
Carlson, Orville James 1944- WhoFI 94
Carlson, Oscar Norman 1920- WhoAm 94
Carlson, Paul Edwin 1944- WhoWest 94

Carlson, Per J. 1938- *WhoScEn 94*
Carlson, Ralph Jennings 1929- *WhoWest 94*
Carlson, Ralph Lawrence 1944- *WhoAm 94*
Carlson, Ralph William, Jr. 1936- *WhoWest 94*
Carlson, Randy Eugene 1948- *WhoMW 93*
Carlson, Raymond Louis 1955- *WhoAmL 94*
Carlson, Reynold Erland d1993 *NewYTBS 93*
Carlson, Richard d1977 *WhoHol 92*
Carlson, Richard Gregory 1949- *WhoMW 93*
Carlson, Richard Merrill 1925- *WhoScEn 94, WhoWest 94*
Carlson, Richard Raymond 1923- *WhoMW 93*
Carlson, Richard Raymond 1957- *WhoScEn 94*
Carlson, Richard Warner 1941- *WhoAm 94, WhoAmP 93, WhoFI 94*
Carlson, Robert Codner 1939- *WhoAm 94, WhoWest 94*
Carlson, Robert E. 1930- *WhoAm 94, WhoAmL 94*
Carlson, Robert E. 1936- *WhoIns 94*
Carlson, Robert Ernest 1924- *WhoWest 94*
Carlson, Robert Gideon 1938- *WhoAm 94*
Carlson, Robert J. 1929- *IntWW 93*
Carlson, Robert James 1944- *WhoAm 94*
Carlson, Robert John 1929- *WhoAm 94*
Carlson, Robert Lee 1924- *WhoAm 94*
Carlson, Robert Michael 1952- *WhoAmA 93*
Carlson, Roger Allan 1932- *WhoFI 94, WhoMW 93*
Carlson, Roger Charles 1937- *WhoIns 94*
Carlson, Roger David 1946- *WhoWest 94*
Carlson, Rolf Stanley 1943- *WhoScEn 94*
Carlson, Ron *DrAPF 93*
Carlson, Ron 1934- *WrDr 94*
Carlson, Ron 1947- *WrDr 94*
Carlson, Ronald Frank 1947- *WhoWest 94*
Carlson, Ronald Lee 1934- *WhoAm 94*
Carlson, Sarah *WhoAmP 93*
Carlson, Sarah Jane Price 1961- *WhoMW 93*
Carlson, Shawn Eric 1960- *WhoWest 94*
Carlson, Stanley Andrew 1939- *WhoAm 94, WhoAmL 94*
Carlson, Stephen Curtis 1951- *WhoAm 94*
Carlson, Stephen Thomas 1945- *WhoAmP 93*
Carlson, Steve *WhoHol 92*
Carlson, Steven Neil 1958- *WhoAmP 93*
Carlson, Suzanne Olive 1939- *WhoAm 94*
Carlson, Terrance L. 1953- *WhoAm 94*
Carlson, Theodore Joshua 1919- *WhoAm 94, WhoAmL 94*
Carlson, Thomas David 1944- *WhoAm 94, WhoAmL 94*
Carlson, Thomas J. 1953- *WhoAmP 93*
Carlson, Thomas Joseph 1953- *WhoAm 94, WhoAmL 94, WhoMW 93*
Carlson, Veronica 1944- *WhoHol 92*
Carlson, Walter Carl 1953- *WhoAm 94*
Carlson, Wayne Harold 1944- *WhoMW 93*
Carlson, William Clifford 1937- *WhoAm 94*
Carlson, William D. 1950- *WhoAmA 93*
Carlson, William Donald 1914-1988 *WhAm 10*
Carlson, William Dwight 1928- *WhoAm 94*
Carlson, William Hugh 1898- *WhAm 10*
Carlson, William K. *EncSF 93*
Carlson, William Scott 1963- *WhoScEn 94*
Carlsson, Anders Einar 1953- *WhoScEn 94*
Carlsson, Bo A. V. 1942- *WhoAm 94*
Carlsson, Gunnar Erik 1952- *WhoAm 94*
Carlsson, Ingvar Gosta 1934- *IntWW 93*
Carlsson, Roine 1937- *IntWW 93*
Carlston, Richard Charles 1929- *WhoFI 94*
Carlstrom, Lucinda 1950- *WhoAmA 93*
Carlstrom, R. William 1944- *WhoWest 94*
Carl Theodor 1724-1799 *NewGrDO*
Carlton, Viscount 1980- *Who 94*
Carlton, Alfred Pershing, Jr. 1947- *WhoAm 94, WhoAmL 94*
Carlton, Blaine L. 1946- *WhoAmL 94*
Carlton, Charles Merritt 1928- *ConAu 43NR, WhoAm 94*
Carlton, David 1938- *WrDr 94*
Carlton, Dean 1928- *WhoAm 94*
Carlton, Dennis William 1951- *WhoAm 94*
Carlton, Donald Morrill 1937- *WhoAm 94*
Carlton, Eric L. 1948- *WhoAmL 94*
Carlton, Fran 1936- *WhoAmP 93*
Carlton, George R., Jr. 1942- *WhoAmL 94*
Carlton, Hope Marie *WhoHol 92*
Carlton, James 1952- *WrDr 94*
Carlton, James D. 1948- *WhoFI 94*
Carlton, Jay 1952- *WrDr 94*
Carlton, Pamela Gean 1954- *WhoBlA 94*
Carlton, Patrick William 1937- *WhoAm 94*
Carlton, Paul Kendall 1921- *WhoAm 94*
Carlton, Richard 1919- *IntMPA 94*
Carlton, Richard Anthony 1951- *WhoFI 94, WhoWest 94*
Carlton, Richard E. 1939- *WhoAmL 94*
Carlton, Robert L. 1918- *WhoMW 93, WhoScEn 94*
Carlton, Roger *EncSF 93*
Carlton, Sara Boehlke 1937- *WhoAm 94*
Carlton, Stephen Edward 1952- *WhoFI 94*
Carlton, Steven Norman 1944- *WhoAm 94*
Carlton, Terry Scott 1939- *WhoAm 94*
Carlton, Timothy *WhoHol 92*
Carlton-Adams, Georgia M. *WhoWest 94*
Carlucci, Frank Charles 1930- *IntWW 93*
Carlucci, Frank Charles, III 1930- *WhoAm 94*
Carlucci, Joseph P. 1942- *WhoAmL 94*
Carluccio, Charles Goldhammer 1926- *WhoAm 94*
Carlyle, David d1987 *WhoHol 92*
Carlyle, Francis d1916 *WhoHol 92*
Carlyle, Helen d1933 *WhoHol 92*
Carlyle, Jane 1801-1866 *BlmGEL*
Carlyle, Jane Welsh 1801-1866 *BlmGWL*
Carlyle, Joan 1931- *NewGrDO*
Carlyle, Joan Hildred 1931- *IntWW 93, Who 94*
Carlyle, Richard *WhoHol 92*
Carlyle, Richard d1942 *WhoHol 92*
Carlyle, Thomas 1795-1881 *BlmGEL*
Carlyon, Candace Cay 1961- *WhoAmL 94*
Carlyon, Don J. 1924- *WhoMW 93*
Carlyss, Earl Winston 1939- *WhoAm 94*
Carlzon, Jan 1941- *IntWW 93*
Carmack, Comer Aston, Jr. 1932- *WhoFI 94*
Carmack, David Earl 1946- *WhoWest 94*
Carmack, Donald Gene 1932- *WhoAmP 93*
Carmack, Mildred Jean 1938- *WhoAm 94, WhoAmL 94*
Carmack, Paul R. 1895-1977 *WhoAmA 93N*
Carman, Charles Hallack 1949- *WhoAmL 94*
Carman, Charles Jerry 1938- *WhoFI 94, WhoMW 93, WhoScEn 94*
Carman, Edwin G. 1951- *WhoBlA 94*
Carman, Gary Michael 1949- *WhoAm 94*
Carman, George Alfred 1929- *Who 94*
Carman, George Henry 1928- *WhoAm 94*
Carman, Gregory W. 1937- *CngDr 93, WhoAmP 93*
Carman, Gregory Wright 1937- *WhoAm 94, WhoAmL 94*
Carman, Hoy Fred 1938- *WhoAm 94*
Carman, John Elwin 1946- *WhoAm 94*
Carman, Kenneth Philip 1953- *WhoAmL 94*
Carman, Michael Dennis 1938- *WhoAm 94, WhoWest 94*
Carman, Robert Eugene 1940- *WhoMW 93*
Carman, Robert Lincoln, Jr. 1941- *WhoScEn 94*
Carman, Steven F. 1959- *WhoAmL 94*
Carman, William Young 1909- *WrDr 94*
Carme, Pamela 1902- *WhoHol 92*
Carmean, E. A., Jr. 1945- *WhoAmA 93*
Carmean, Irl Russell 1949- *WhoAmL 94*
Carmean, Jerry Richard 1938- *WhoMW 93*
Carmel, Eddie d1972 *WhoHol 92*
Carmel, Roger C. d1986 *WhoHol 92*
Carmel, Simon Jacob 1938- *WhoAm 94*
Carmen, Gerald P. 1930- *WhoAmP 93*
Carmen, Ira Harris 1934- *WhoAm 94, WhoMW 93*
Carmen, Jean *WhoHol 92*
Carmen, Julie 1954- *WhoHol 92*
Carmen, Julie 1960- *WhoHisp 94*
Carmen, Loene 1970- *WhoHol 92*
Carmen, Marilyn *DrAPF 93*
Carmen, Sybil d1929 *WhoHol 92*
Carmet, Jean *WhoHol 92*
Carmi, Maria d1957 *WhoHol 92*
Carmi, Shlomo 1937- *WhoAm 94*
Carmi, T. 1925- *ConWorW 93*
Carmi, Vera d1969 *WhoHol 92*
Carmichael *Who 94*
Carmichael, Alexander Douglas 1929- *WhoAm 94*
Carmichael, Benjamin G. 1938- *WhoBlA 94*
Carmichael, Bill 1933- *WhoAmP 93*
Carmichael, Carole A. 1950- *WhoBlA 94*
Carmichael, Catherine McIntosh 1925- *Who 94*
Carmichael, Charles Elmore, Jr. 1923- *WhoAmP 93*
Carmichael, Charles Wesley 1919- *WhoFI 94, WhoMW 93, WhoScEn 94*
Carmichael, David Burton 1923- *WhoAm 94*
Carmichael, David Richard 1942- *WhoIns 94*
Carmichael, David William G. C. *Who 94*
Carmichael, Donald Ray 1922- *WhoAmA 93*
Carmichael, Donald Scott 1912- *WhoAm 94*
Carmichael, Dorothy S. 1925- *WhoAmP 93*
Carmichael, Eric Devon 1964- *WhoFI 94*
Carmichael, Gary Alan 1964- *WhoWest 94*
Carmichael, Gilbert E. *WhoAm 94, WhoFI 94*
Carmichael, Gilbert Ellzey 1927- *WhoAmP 93*
Carmichael, Hoagy d1981 *WhoHol 92*
Carmichael, Hoagy 1899-1981 *IntDcF 2-4*
Carmichael, Hugh 1906- *WhoAm 94*
Carmichael, Ian 1920- *IntMPA 94, WhoHol 92*
Carmichael, Ian (Gillett) 1920- *Who 94*
Carmichael, Ian Stuart Edward 1930- *WhoAm 94, WhoScEn 94*
Carmichael, Jae 1925- *WhoAmA 93*
Carmichael, Joel 1915- *WrDr 94*
Carmichael, John 1910- *Who 94*
Carmichael, Judy Lea 1952- *WhoFI 94*
Carmichael, Kay *Who 94*
Carmichael, Keith Stanley 1929- *Who 94*
Carmichael, Lawrence Ray 1958- *WhoAmP 93*
Carmichael, Lee Harold 1949- *WhoBlA 94*
Carmichael, Malcolm N. 1947- *WhoAmL 94*
Carmichael, Marc 1950- *WhoAmP 93*
Carmichael, Mary Mulloy 1916- *WhoAm 94*
Carmichael, Myra d1974 *WhoHol 92*
Carmichael, Nelson *WhoAm 94*
Carmichael, Peter 1933- *Who 94*
Carmichael, Stephen Webb 1945- *WhoScEn 94*
Carmichael, Stokely 1941- *AfrAmAl 6 [port], AmSocL, ConBlB 5 [port], HisWorL, WhoBlA 94*
Carmichael, Virgil Wesly 1919- *WhoAm 94, WhoMW 93, WhoScEn 94*
Carmichael, William d1795 *WhAmRev*
Carmichael, William Daniel 1929- *WhoAm 94*
Carmichael, William Jerome 1920- *WhoAm 94*
Carmichael Of Kelvingrove, Baron 1921- *Who 94*
Carmiciano, Mario 1946- *WhoScEn 94*
Carmin, Robert Leighton 1918- *WhoAm 94*
Carminati, Tullio d1971 *WhoHol 92*
Carmine, Michael d1989 *WhoHol 92*
Carmirelli, Pina d1993 *NewYTBS 93*
Carmody, Arthur Roderick, Jr. 1928- *WhoAm 94*
Carmody, George Edward 1931- *WhoAmL 94, WhoFI 94*
Carmody, Gerard Timothy 1949- *WhoAm 94, WhoAmL 94*
Carmody, Isobelle 1958- *EncSF 93*
Carmody, James Albert 1945- *WhoAm 94, WhoAmL 94*
Carmody, James Peter 1951- *WhoAmL 94*
Carmody, Richard Patrick 1942- *WhoAmL 94*
Carmody, Robert Edward 1942- *WhoFI 94*
Carmody, Thomas Roswell 1933- *WhoFI 94*
Carmody, Tim 1946- *WhoAmP 93*
Carmody, Timothy James 1946- *WhoAmL 94, WhoMW 93*
Carmody, Victor Wallace, Jr. 1945- *WhoAmL 94*
Carmon, Amalia Kahana *ConWorW 93*
Carmona, José Antonio 1960- *WhoHisp 94*
Carmona, Richard Henry 1949- *WhoHisp 94*
Carmona, Roel Guerra 1935- *WhoHisp 94*
Carmony, Donald Duane 1935- *WhoAm 94, WhoMW 93*
Carmony, Kevin Brackett 1959- *WhoWest 94*
Carmony, Marvin Dale 1923- *WhoAm 94*
Carmoy, Guy de 1907- *IntWW 93*
Carn, Andrew James 1950- *WhoAmP 93*
Carnabuci, Piero d1957 *WhoHol 92*
Carnac *Who 94*
Carnac, Levin *EncSF 93*
Carnahan, Brice 1933- *WhoScEn 94*
Carnahan, Clarence Earl 1935- *WhoIns 94*
Carnahan, Frances Morris 1937- *WhoAm 94*
Carnahan, John Anderson 1930- *WhoAm 94, WhoAmL 94*
Carnahan, John Hillis 1929- *WhoAmP 93*
Carnahan, John Russell 1958- *WhoAmP 93*
Carnahan, Karlyn Tasto 1958- *WhoWest 94*
Carnahan, Mel 1934- *WhoAm 94, WhoAmP 93, WhoMW 93*
Carnahan, Mel Eugene 1934- *IntWW 93*
Carnahan, Michael William 1946- *WhoAmL 94*
Carnahan, Orville D. 1929- *WhoAmP 93*
Carnahan, Orville Darrell 1929- *WhoAm 94, WhoWest 94*
Carnahan, Patrick William 1963- *WhoFI 94*
Carnahan, Robert Narvell 1928- *WhoAmL 94*
Carnahan, Suzanne d1952 *WhoHol 92*
Carnahan, Wanda Edwina 1929- *WhoAmP 93*
Carnall, Geoffrey Douglas 1927- *WrDr 94*
Carnarvon, Earl of 1924- *Who 94*
Carnase, Thomas Paul 1939- *WhoAm 94*
Carnathan, Gilbert William 1951- *WhoWest 94*
Carne, John E. 1946- *WhoAmL 94*
Carne, Judy 1939- *WhoHol 92*
Carne, Marcel 1906- *IntWW 93*
Carne, Stuart John 1926- *Who 94*
Carneal, George Upshur 1935- *WhoAm 94*
Carneal, James William 1918- *WhoAm 94*
Carneal, John T. 1950- *WhoAmL 94*
Carnecchia, Baldo M., Jr. 1947- *WhoAm 94, WhoAmL 94*
Carnegie *Who 94*
Carnegie, Lord 1989- *Who 94*
Carnegie, Andrew 1835-1919 *AmSocL [port]*
Carnegie, Dale 1888-1955 *AmSocL, TwCLC 53 [port]*
Carnegie, James Gordon 1934- *WhoAm 94*
Carnegie, Randolph David 1952- *WhoBlA 94*
Carnegie, Robin (Macdonald) 1926- *Who 94*
Carnegie, Roderick (Howard) 1932- *Who 94*
Carnegie, Roderick Howard 1932- *IntWW 93*
Carnegie, Sacha 1920- *WrDr 94*
Carnegy Of Lour, Baroness 1925- *Who 94, WhoWomW 91*
Carneiro, Andre *EncSF 93*
Carnell, Geoffrey Gordon 1918- *Who 94*
Carnell, (Edward) John 1912-1972 *EncSF 93*
Carnell, Lougenia Littlejohn 1947- *WhoBlA 94*
Carnell, Marion P. 1928- *WhoAmP 93*
Carnell, Paul Herbert 1917- *WhoAm 94*
Carnella, Frank Thomas 1934- *WhoFI 94*
Carnelley, Desmond 1929- *Who 94*
Carner, Gary 1955- *ConAu 140*
Carner, George 1945- *WhoAm 94*
Carner, Mosco 1904-1985 *NewGrDO*
Carner, William John 1948- *WhoFI 94*
Carnera, Primo d1967 *WhoHol 92*
Carnes, Edward E. *WhoAmP 93*
Carnes, Edward E. 1950- *WhoAmL 94*
Carnes, James Edward 1939- *WhoAm 94*
Carnes, James Robert 1909-1992 *WhAm 10*
Carnes, Julie E. 1950- *WhoAm 94, WhoAmL 94*
Carnes, Millard James 1945- *WhoMW 93*
Carnes, Robert Mann 1942- *WhoScEn 94*
Carnesale, Albert 1936- *ConAu 142*
Carneseca, Lou 1926- *BasBi [port]*
Carnesecca, Lou 1925- *WhoAm 94*
Carnesoltas, Ana-Maria 1948- *WhoAmL 94*
Carnevale, Anthony, Jr. *WhoAmP 93*
Carnevale, Anthony P(atrick) 1946- *WrDr 94*
Carnevale, Ben 1915- *BasBi*
Carnevale, Ronald A. 1942- *WhoFI 94*
Carney, Alan d1973 *WhoHol 92*
Carney, Alan 1911-1973 *See* Brown and Carney *WhoCom*
Carney, Alfonso Linwood, Jr. 1949- *WhoBlA 94*
Carney, Art 1918- *IntMPA 94, WhoCom, WhoHol 92*
Carney, Arthur William Matthew 1918- *WhoAm 94*
Carney, Bradford George Yost 1950- *WhoAm 94*
Carney, Callie I. 1934- *WhoBlA 94*
Carney, David 1925- *IntWW 93*
Carney, David Mitchel 1959- *WhoAm 94*
Carney, Deborah Leah Turner 1952- *WhoAmL 94, WhoWest 94*
Carney, Dennis Joseph 1921- *EncABHB 9, WhoAm 94*

Carney, Dennis Ray 1947- *WhoIns 94*
Carney, Don d1954 *WhoHol 92*
Carney, Edmund M. 1943- *WhoAmL 94*
Carney, Eliza Macaulay 1937- *WhoAmP 93*
Carney, Fred 1914- *IntMPA 94*
Carney, G. Daniel 1937- *WhoAmL 94*
Carney, George d1948 *WhoHol 92*
Carney, Harry d1974 *WhoHol 92*
Carney, Heath Joseph 1955- *WhoWest 94*
Carney, James d1955 *WhoHol 92*
Carney, James F. 1915-1990 *WhAm 10*
Carney, James Michael 1944- *WhoMW 93*
Carney, Jean Kathryn 1948- *WhoAm 94, WhoMW 93, WhoScEn 94*
Carney, John Francis 1939- *WhoAmL 94*
Carney, Joseph Buckingham 1928- *WhoAm 94, WhoAmL 94*
Carney, Joseph D. 1952- *WhoAmL 94*
Carney, Kim 1925- *WhoAm 94*
Carney, Larry Brady 1948- *WhoMW 93*
Carney, Mary d1984 *WhoHol 92*
Carney, Michael 1937- *Who 94*
Carney, Pat 1928- *WhoAmP 93*
Carney, Pat 1935- *WhoWomW 91*
Carney, Patricia 1935- *IntWW 93*
Carney, Phillita Toyia 1952- *WhoFl 94*
Carney, Richard Edgar 1923- *WhoWest 94*
Carney, Robert Alfred 1916- *WhoAm 94*
Carney, Robert Arthur 1937- *WhoFl 94*
Carney, Robert Bostwick 1895-1990 *WhAm 10*
Carney, Robert Matthew 1928- *WhoBlA 94*
Carney, Robert Thomas 1947- *WhoAm 94*
Carney, Ronald Eugene 1943- *WhoMW 93, WhoScEn 94*
Carney, Ryndee Skillman 1954- *WhoMW 93*
Carney, Thomas 1953- *WhoAmP 93*
Carney, Thomas Daly 1947- *WhoAm 94*
Carney, Thomas E. *WhoAmP 93*
Carney, Thomas Joseph 1934- *WhoAmP 93*
Carney, Thomas Mellis 1942- *WhoAm 94*
Carney, William H. 1840-1908 *AfrAmAl 6*
Carney, William Ray 1940- *WhoAmL 94*
Carney Stalnaker, Lisa Ann 1953- *WhoMW 93*
Carnicer (y Batlle), Ramon 1789-1855 *NewGrDO*
Carnicero, Jorge E. 1921- *WhoHisp 94*
Carnicero, Jorge Emilio 1921- *WhoAm 94*
Carnicom, Gene E. 1944- *WhoWest 94*
Carniglia, Stephen Davis 1950- *WhoAm 94*
Carnine, Douglas Wayne 1947- *WhoWest 94*
Carnley, Peter Frederick *Who 94*
Carnley, Peter Frederick 1937- *IntWW 93, WrDr 94*
Carnley, Samuel Fleetwood 1918- *WhoAmL 94*
Carnochan, John Low, Jr. 1918- *WhoFl 94*
Carnochan, W. B. 1930- *WrDr 94*
Carnochan, Walter Bliss 1930- *WhoAm 94*
Carnock, Baron 1920- *Who 94*
Carnogursky, Jan 1944- *IntWW 93*
Carnot, Nicolas-Leonard Sadi 1796-1832 *WorScD*
Carnovsky, Morris 1897- *WhAm 10, WhoHol 92*
Carnovsky, Morris 1897-1992 *AnObit 1992*
Carnow, Bertram Warren 1922- *WhoAm 94*
Carnoy, Martin 1938- *WhoAm 94*
Carns, Jim 1940- *WhoAmP 93*
Carns, Michael Patrick Chamberlain 1937- *WhoAm 94*
Carnwath, Andrew Hunter 1909- *Who 94*
Carnwath, Robert John Anderson 1945- *Who 94*
Carnwath, Squeak 1947- *WhoAmA 93*
Caro, Anthony 1924- *IntWW 93*
Caro, Anthony (Alfred) 1924- *Who 94*
Caro, Cesar M. 1954- *WhoHisp 94*
Caro, Charles Crawford 1946- *WhoFl 94*
Caro, David Edmund 1922- *IntWW 93, Who 94*
Caro, Dennis R. 1944- *EncSF 93*
Caro, Doris A. 1946- *WhoHisp 94*
Caro, Eugenio, Sr. *WhoHisp 94*
Caro, Francis 1938- *WhoAmA 93*
Caro, Heinrich 1834-1910 *WorInv*
Caro, Ivor 1946- *WhoAm 94*
Caro, Jacobina d1993 *NewYTBS 93*
Caro, Marcos Esteban 1961- *WhoHisp 94*
Caro, Mike 1944- *WhoWest 94*
Caro, Pauline 1835-1901 *BlmGWL*
Caro, Rafael 1952- *WhoHisp 94*
Caro, Robert A. *WrDr 94*
Caro, Robert A. 1936- *WhoHisp 94*
Caro, Robert Allan *WhoAm 94*
Caro, Warren 1907- *WhoAm 94*
Caro, William Allan 1934- *WhoAm 94*
Caroe, Martin Bragg 1933- *Who 94*

Caroff, Phyllis M. 1924- *WhoAm 94*
Carol, Sister *Who 94*
Carol, Bill J. 1927- *WrDr 94*
Carol, Cindy 1945- *WhoHol 92*
Carol, John d1968 *WhoHol 92*
Carol, Martine d1967 *WhoHol 92*
Carol, Sue d1982 *WhoHol 92*
Carolan, Donald Bartley Abraham, Jr. 1960- *WhoScEn 94*
Carolan, Douglas *WhoFl 94*
Caroli, Angelo Antonio 1701-1778 *NewGrDO*
Caroli, Betty Boyd 1938- *ConAu 43NR*
Carolin, Peter Burns 1936- *Who 94*
Caroline, J. C. 1933- *WhoBlA 94*
Caroline, Leona Ruth 1912- *WhoScEn 94*
Caroll, Robert 1916- *WrDr 94*
Carollo, James Paul 1946- *WhoIns 94*
Carolus, Cheryl *WhoWomW 91*
Caro Maillen de Soto, Ana c. 1590-1650 *BlmGWL*
Carome, Edward Francis 1927- *WhoMW 93*
Carome, Patrick Joseph 1957- *WhoAmL 94*
Caron, Edward L. *WhoAmP 93*
Caron, Elise *WhoHol 92*
Caron, Leslie 1931- *IntMPA 94, WhoHol 92*
Caron, Leslie (Claire Margaret) 1931- *Who 94*
Caron, Leslie Clair Margaret 1931- *IntWW 93*
Caron, Maurice Lawrence, Jr. 1945- *WhoAmP 93*
Caron, Michael 1960- *WhoAmP 93*
Caron, Michelle Denise 1968- *WhoMW 93*
Caron, Paul Eugene 1955- *WhoAmP 93*
Caron, Ronald Jacques *WhoAm 94, WhoMW 93*
Caron, Rose 1857-1930 *NewGrDO [port]*
Caron, Sandra *WhoHol 92*
Caron, Wilfred Rene 1931- *WhoAmL 94*
Carona, John 1955- *WhoAmP 93*
Caron de Beaumarchais, Pierre-Augustin *IntDcT 2*
Carone, Frank 1927- *WhoAm 94*
Carone, Patricia 1943- *WhoAmP 93*
Caronis, George John 1933- *WhoFl 94*
Caroselli, William R. 1941- *WhoAmL 94*
Carosio, Margherita 1908- *NewGrDO*
Caroso, Fabritio c. 1526-c. 1605 *IntDcB [port]*
Carosso, Vincent Philip d1993 *NewYTBS 93*
Carosso, Vincent Phillip 1922- *WhoAm 94*
Carosso, Vincent Phillip 1922-1993 *ConAu 141*
Carotenuto, Mario 1915- *WhoHol 92*
Carotenuto, Memmo 1908- *WhoHol 92*
Carothers, Charles Omsted 1923- *WhoAm 94*
Carothers, Donna June 1954- *WhoMW 93*
Carothers, Josiah S. Robins, Jr. 1938- *WhoAmP 93*
Carothers, Neil, III 1919- *WhoAmP 93*
Carothers, Richard Alton 1935- *WhoAm 94*
Carothers, Robert L. *DrAPF 93*
Carothers, Robert Lee 1942- *WhoAm 94*
Carothers, Steven Michael 1954- *WhoAm 94*
Carothers, Wallace Hume 1896-1937 *WorInv*
Carovano, John Martin 1935- *WhoAm 94*
Carozza, Davy Angelo 1926- *WhoAm 94*
Carozza, Gerald Nicholas, Jr. 1960- *WhoAmL 94*
Carp, Richard Lawrence 1926- *WhoAm 94*
Carp, Richard Merchant 1949- *WhoMW 93*
Carpani, Giuseppe 1752-1825 *NewGrDO*
Carpelan, Bo *EncSF 93*
Carpelan, Bo (Gustaf Bertellsson) 1926- *ConWorW 93*
Carpelan, Harry Campbell 1957- *WhoAmL 94*
Carpenetti, Ben Wallace 1960- *WhoFl 94*
Carpeni, Marcia E. 1944- *WhoAmL 94*
Carpenito, Eleanor Frances 1934- *WhoAmP 93*
Carpenito, James William 1956- *WhoAmP 93*
Carpentaria, Bishop of 1940- *Who 94*
Carpenter *GayLL, Who 94*
Carpenter (y Valmont), Alejo 1904-1980 *RfGShF*
Carpenter, Adelaide Trowbridge Clark 1944- *WhoAm 94*
Carpenter, Adelbert Wall 1943- *WhoWest 94*
Carpenter, Allan 1917- *WhoAm 94, WrDr 94*

Carpenter, (John) Allan 1917- *ConAu 42NR*
Carpenter, Allan Lee 1931- *WhoScEn 94*
Carpenter, Ann M. 1934- *WhoBlA 94*
Carpenter, Arthur Espenet *WhoAmA 93*
Carpenter, Arthur James 1931- *WhoAmP 93*
Carpenter, Bill *WhoAmP 93*
Carpenter, Bogdana 1941- *WrDr 94*
Carpenter, Brent 1959- *WhoAmL 94*
Carpenter, Bruce H. 1932- *WhoAm 94, WhoWest 94*
Carpenter, Carl, Jr. 1935- *WhoAmP 93*
Carpenter, Carl Anthony 1944- *WhoBlA 94*
Carpenter, Carleton 1926- *IntMPA 94, WhoHol 92*
Carpenter, Charles d1990 *WhoHol 92*
Carpenter, Charles Bernard 1933- *WhoAm 94*
Carpenter, Charles Colcock Jones 1931- *WhoAm 94*
Carpenter, Charles Congden 1921- *WhoAm 94*
Carpenter, Charles Elford, Jr. 1944- *WhoAmL 94*
Carpenter, Charles Francis 1957- *WhoAmL 94*
Carpenter, Charles Loren, Jr. 1947- *WhoAmL 94*
Carpenter, Christopher *EncSF 93*
Carpenter, Clarence E., Jr. 1941- *WhoBlA 94*
Carpenter, Clayton Duffey 1940- *WhoFl 94*
Carpenter, Constance d1992 *NewYTBS 93 [port]*
Carpenter, Constance 1906- *WhoHol 92*
Carpenter, D(avid) A(rscott) 1946- *WrDr 94*
Carpenter, Danny R. 1946- *WhoAmL 94*
Carpenter, Dante K. *WhoAmP 93*
Carpenter, Darwin R., Jr. 1947- *WhoFl 94*
Carpenter, David *WhoHol 92*
Carpenter, David Allan 1951- *WhoAmL 94*
Carpenter, David Bailey 1915-1988 *WhAm 10*
Carpenter, David Erwin 1939- *WhoMW 93*
Carpenter, David L. *WhoAmP 93*
Carpenter, David Lyle 1942- *WhoAmL 94*
Carpenter, David R. 1939- *WhoIns 94*
Carpenter, David Roland 1939- *WhoAm 94, WhoFl 94, WhoWest 94*
Carpenter, David William 1950- *WhoAm 94*
Carpenter, Deborah Joan 1958- *WhoAmL 94*
Carpenter, Delbert Stanley 1950- *WhoAm 94*
Carpenter, Dennis Wilkinson 1947- *WhoAmA 93*
Carpenter, Derr Alvin 1931- *WhoAm 94*
Carpenter, Don *DrAPF 93*
Carpenter, Donald Blodgett 1916- *WhoWest 94*
Carpenter, Dorothy F. 1933- *WhoAmP 93, WhoWomW 91*
Carpenter, Dorothy Fulton 1933- *WhoMW 93*
Carpenter, Earl L. 1931- *WhoAmA 93*
Carpenter, Ed *WhoAmP 93*
Carpenter, Edmund Mogford 1941- *WhoAm 94, WhoFl 94*
Carpenter, Edward 1844-1929 *GayLL*
Carpenter, Edward Frederick 1910- *Who 94*
Carpenter, Edwin Charles 1942- *WhoAmL 94*
Carpenter, Elizabeth Eileen 1953- *WhoMW 93*
Carpenter, Elizabeth Sutherland 1920- *WhoAm 94*
Carpenter, Elmer J. *EncSF 93*
Carpenter, F. Lynn 1944- *WhoScEn 94*
Carpenter, Francis J. *WhoAmP 93*
Carpenter, Frank Charles, Jr. 1917- *WhoScEn 94, WhoWest 94*
Carpenter, Frank Morton 1902- *WhoAm 94*
Carpenter, Frank Wilkinson 1931- *WhoAm 94*
Carpenter, Fred d1984 *WhoHol 92*
Carpenter, Frederic I(ves) 1903- *WrDr 94*
Carpenter, Frederick Charles 1920- *Who 94*
Carpenter, Gene Blakely 1922- *WhoAm 94*
Carpenter, Gilbert Frederick 1920- *WhoAmA 93*
Carpenter, Harry James d1993 *Who 94N*
Carpenter, Harry Leonard 1925- *Who 94*
Carpenter, Horace B. d1945 *WhoHol 92*
Carpenter, Howard Grant, Jr. 1939- *WhoAm 94*
Carpenter, Humphrey (William Bouverie) 1946- *WrDr 94*

Carpenter, Humphrey William Bouverie 1946- *Who 94*
Carpenter, Jack Duane 1951- *WhoWest 94*
Carpenter, James Morton 1914-1992 *WhAm 10, WhoAmA 93N*
Carpenter, James Russell 1927- *WhoAmP 93*
Carpenter, James Willard 1935- *WhoAmL 94*
Carpenter, JoAnn Finney 1954- *WhoMW 93*
Carpenter, John *DrAPF 93, Who 94*
Carpenter, John 1948- *EncSF 93, HorFD [port], IntMPA 94*
Carpenter, John (Howard) 1948- *WrDr 94*
Carpenter, (Victor Harry) John 1921- *Who 94*
Carpenter, John C. 1930- *WhoAmP 93*
Carpenter, John Everett 1923- *WhoWest 94*
Carpenter, John Howard 1948- *IntWW 93, WhoAm 94*
Carpenter, John Lindemann 1958- *WhoAmL 94*
Carpenter, John Marland 1935- *WhoAm 94*
Carpenter, John Wilson, III 1916- *WhoAm 94*
Carpenter, Joseph, II 1937- *WhoBlA 94*
Carpenter, Jot David 1938- *WhoAm 94*
Carpenter, Ken d1984 *WhoHol 92*
Carpenter, Kenneth E. 1936- *WhoAm 94*
Carpenter, Kenneth John 1923- *WhoAm 94*
Carpenter, Kenneth Russell 1955- *WhoFl 94, WhoMW 93, WhoScEn 94*
Carpenter, Kirk Duane 1950- *WhoAmP 93*
Carpenter, Leslie Arthur 1927- *IntWW 93, Who 94*
Carpenter, Lewis 1928- *WhoBlA 94*
Carpenter, Linda Buck 1952- *WhoAmA 93*
Carpenter, Lorayne d1979 *WhoHol 92*
Carpenter, Louise *Who 94*
Carpenter, Lucas *DrAPF 93*
Carpenter, Malcolm Breckenridge 1921- *WhoAm 94*
Carpenter, Malcolm Scott 1925- *WhoAm 94, WhoScEn 94*
Carpenter, Marj Collier 1926- *WhoAm 94*
Carpenter, Mary-Chapin *NewYTBS 93 [port]*
Carpenter, Mary-Chapin c. 1958- *News 94-1 [port]*
Carpenter, Mary-Chapin 1959- *WhoAm 94*
Carpenter, Mary Grace d1993 *NewYTBS 93*
Carpenter, Mary Laure 1953- *WhoMW 93*
Carpenter, Michael Alan 1947- *WhoAm 94, WhoFl 94*
Carpenter, Michael E. 1947- *WhoAm 94, WhoAmL 94*
Carpenter, Michael Eugene 1947- *WhoAmP 93*
Carpenter, Michael H. 1953- *WhoAm 94*
Carpenter, Myron Arthur 1938- *WhoAm 94*
Carpenter, Nan Cooke 1912- *WrDr 94*
Carpenter, Noble Olds 1929- *WhoAm 94*
Carpenter, Norman Roblee 1932- *WhoAm 94, WhoAmL 94*
Carpenter, Patricia 1923- *WhoAm 94*
Carpenter, Paul d1964 *WhoHol 92*
Carpenter, Paul Charles 1940- *WhoMW 93*
Carpenter, Paul Leonard 1920- *WhoAm 94*
Carpenter, Peter Rockefeller 1939- *WhoWest 94*
Carpenter, Philip Brian 1956- *WhoWest 94*
Carpenter, Philip David 1943- *WhoAm 94*
Carpenter, Randle Burt 1939- *WhoAmL 94*
Carpenter, Ray Warren 1934- *WhoAm 94, WhoScEn 94, WhoWest 94*
Carpenter, Raymond Leonard 1926- *WhoAm 94*
Carpenter, Richard Amon 1926- *WhoAm 94*
Carpenter, Richard M. 1927- *WhoAm 94, WhoFl 94*
Carpenter, Richard Norris 1937- *WhoAmL 94*
Carpenter, Robert C. 1924- *WhoAmP 93*
Carpenter, Robert L. 1927- *IntMPA 94*
Carpenter, Robert Van, Jr. 1965- *WhoScEn 94*
Carpenter, Russell H., Jr. 1941- *WhoAmL 94*
Carpenter, Sheila Jane 1950- *WhoAm 94, WhoAmL 94*
Carpenter, Susan Karen 1951- *WhoAm 94, WhoAmL 94*
Carpenter, Ted Galen 1947- *WhoAm 94*

Carpenter, Thomas Milton 1952- *WhoAmL 94*
Carpenter, Timothy W. 1960- *WhoAmP 93*
Carpenter, Torrey C. 1922- *WhoAmP 93*
Carpenter, Vivian L. 1952- *WhoBlA 94*
Carpenter, Will Dockery 1930- *WhoAm 94*
Carpenter, William *DrAPF 93*
Carpenter, William A. 1944- *WhoAmL 94*
Carpenter, William Arthur, II 1965- *WhoBlA 94*
Carpenter, William Levy 1926- *WhoAm 94*
Carpentier, Alejo 1904-1980 *HispLC [port]*
Carpentier, Georges d1975 *WhoHol 92*
Carpentier, Jean Claude Gabriel 1926- *IntWW 93*
Carper, Gertrude Esther 1921- *WhoFI 94*
Carper, Gloria G. 1930- *WhoBlA 94*
Carper, James David 1956- *WhoMW 93*
Carper, Kenneth Lynn 1948- *WhoScEn 94*
Carper, Stephen William 1958- *WhoScEn 94*
Carper, Thomas R. 1947- *WhoAmP 93*
Carper, Thomas Richard 1947- *IntWW 93, WhoAm 94*
Carper, William Grady, Jr. 1946- *WhoAmP 93*
Carper, William Robert 1935- *WhoMW 93*
Carpini, Giovanni Da Pian Del 1182-1252 *WhWE*
Carpino, Francesco 1905- *IntWW 93*
Carpino, Louis A. 1927- *WhoAm 94*
Carpinteri, Laura *BlmGWL*
Carpio, Julio Fernando 1947- *WhoHisp 94*
Carpio, Virginia Ann 1939- *WhoHisp 94*
Carr *Who 94*
Carr, Albert Anthony 1930- *WhoScEn 94*
Carr, Alexander d1946 *WhoHol 92*
Carr, Allan *WhoAm 94*
Carr, Allan 1939- *IntMPA 94*
Carr, Allen Wesley 1942- *WhoFI 94*
Carr, Antoine Labotte 1961- *WhoBlA 94*
Carr, Arthur Charles 1918- *WhoAm 94*
Carr, Arthur Japheth 1914-1991 *WhAm 10*
Carr, Arthur Wesley 1941- *Who 94*
Carr, Audri Joan 1936- *WhoFI 94*
Carr, Austin 1948- *BasBi*
Carr, Benjamin 1768-1831 *NewGrDO*
Carr, Bernard Francis 1919- *WhoAm 94*
Carr, Billie J. 1928- *WhoAmP 93*
Carr, Bob 1943- *CngDr 93*
Carr, Bonnie Jean 1947- *WhoMW 93*
Carr, Cameron 1876- *WhoHol 92*
Carr, Carolyn K. 1939- *WhoAmA 93*
Carr, Carolyn Kehlor 1948- *WhoMW 93*
Carr, Charles *EncSF 93*
Carr, Charles Jelleff 1910- *WhoAm 94*
Carr, Charles William 1917- *WhoAm 94, WhoMW 93*
Carr, Charmian 1947- *WhoHol 92*
Carr, Christopher 1944- *Who 94*
Carr, Christopher C. 1950- *WhoAmL 94*
Carr, Clara B. 1948- *WhoBlA 94*
Carr, Cynda Annette 1948- *WhoMW 93*
Carr, Cynthia 1953- *WhoAmL 94*
Carr, Dan *DrAPF 93*
Carr, Daniel Barry 1948- *WhoScEn 94*
Carr, Daniel Floyd 1959- *WhoAmP 93*
Carr, Darlene 1950- *WhoHol 92*
Carr, David Robert 1950- *WhoWest 94*
Carr, David Turner 1914- *WhoAm 94*
Carr, Davis Haden 1940- *WhoAmL 94*
Carr, Denis John 1915- *Who 94*
Carr, Doleen Pellett 1950- *WhoMW 93, WhoScEn 94*
Carr, Donald Bryce 1926- *Who 94*
Carr, Edward Albert, Jr. 1922- *WhoAm 94*
Carr, Edward Arthur John 1938- *Who 94*
Carr, Emily 1871-1945 *BlmGWL*
Carr, Eric Francis 1919- *Who 94*
Carr, Ernest James 1896- *WhAm 10*
Carr, Floyd Eugene 1955- *WhoMW 93, WhoScEn 94*
Carr, Francis E. *WhoAmP 93*
Carr, Frankie d1986 *WhoHol 92*
Carr, Gary Thomas 1946- *WhoAm 94, WhoAmL 94*
Carr, Gayle Charlene 1961- *WhoAmL 94*
Carr, George d1962 *WhoHol 92*
Carr, George Francis, Jr. 1939- *WhoAm 94*
Carr, George Leroy 1927- *WhoAm 94*
Carr, Georgia d1971 *WhoHol 92*
Carr, Gerald Paul 1932- *IntWW 93, WhoAm 94, WhoScEn 94*
Carr, Geraldine d1954 *WhoHol 92*
Carr, Gertrude d1969 *WhoHol 92*
Carr, Gilbert Randle 1928- *WhoAm 94*
Carr, Ginna d1972 *WhoHol 92*
Carr, Gladys d1940 *WhoHol 92*
Carr, Gladys Justin *WhoAm 94*
Carr, Glenna Dodson 1927- *WhoAm 94*
Carr, Glyn *Who 94*
Carr, Glyn 1908- *WrDr 94*
Carr, H. D. *GayLL*
Carr, Harold John 1895- *WhAm 10*
Carr, Harold Noflet 1921- *WhoAm 94, WhoFI 94*
Carr, Hobart Cecil 1912-1990 *WhAm 10*
Carr, Howard Earl 1915- *WhoAm 94*
Carr, Howard Ernest 1908- *WhoAm 94, WhoFI 94*
Carr, J(ames Joseph) L(loyd) 1912- *WrDr 94*
Carr, Jack d1967 *WhoHol 92*
Carr, Jack 1948- *IntWW 93*
Carr, Jack Richard 1937- *WhoAm 94*
Carr, Jacquelyn B. 1923- *WhoScEn 94*
Carr, Jacquelyn Carney 1956- *WhoWest 94*
Carr, James Drew 1935- *WhoAmP 93*
Carr, James Francis 1946- *WhoAmL 94*
Carr, James Lloyd 1912- *Who 94*
Carr, James Michael 1950- *WhoAm 94, WhoAmL 94*
Carr, James Patrick 1950- *WhoAmL 94*
Carr, James T. 1937- *WhoIns 94*
Carr, Jane d1957 *WhoHol 92*
Carr, Jane 1954- *WhoHol 92*
Carr, Jay Phillip 1936- *WhoAm 94*
Carr, Jayge 1940- *WrDr 94*
Carr, Jayge 1941- *EncSF 93*
Carr, Jeanette Irene 1955- *WhoWest 94*
Carr, Jess 1930- *WrDr 94*
Carr, Jesse Metteau, III 1952- *WhoAmL 94, WhoFI 94*
Carr, Joe d1939 *ProFbHF*
Carr, John Darcy B. *Who 94*
Carr, John Dickson 1906-1977 *EncSF 93*
Carr, John F(rancis) 1944- *EncSF 93*
Carr, John H. c. 1812- *EncNAR*
Carr, John Lyle, Jr. 1946- *WhoAm 94, WhoAmL 94*
Carr, John P. 1945- *WhoIns 94*
Carr, John Roger 1927- *Who 94*
Carr, Julian Lanier, Jr. 1946- *WhoFI 94*
Carr, Karen L. 1960- *ConAu 142*
Carr, Katherine Ann Camacho 1949- *WhoWest 94*
Carr, Katherine McIntosh 1963- *WhoFI 94*
Carr, Kenneth Lloyd 1932- *WhoAm 94*
Carr, Kenneth Monroe 1925- *WhoAm 94, WhoAmP 93*
Carr, Kenny 1955- *WhoBlA 94*
Carr, Kipley DeAne 1967- *WhoBlA 94*
Carr, Larry d1987 *WhoHol 92*
Carr, Lawrence d1969 *WhoHol 92*
Carr, Lawrence Edward, Jr. 1923- *WhoAm 94, WhoAmL 94*
Carr, Lawrence George d1990 *Who 94N*
Carr, Lenford 1938- *WhoBlA 94*
Carr, Leonard G. 1902- *WhoBlA 94*
Carr, Les 1935- *WhoAm 94*
Carr, Louella d1937 *WhoHol 92*
Carr, M. Robert 1943- *WhoAm 94, WhoAmP 93, WhoMW 93*
Carr, Margaret 1935- *WrDr 94*
Carr, Margaret Jo 1956- *WhoMW 93*
Carr, Marie Pinak 1954- *WhoFI 94*
Carr, Martin 1932- *IntMPA 94*
Carr, Mary d1973 *WhoHol 92*
Carr, Maurice Chapman 1937- *Who 94*
Carr, Michael 1946- *Who 94*
Carr, Michael 1951- *WhoScEn 94*
Carr, Michael Harold 1935- *WhoScEn 94*
Carr, Mildred Dolly d1949 *WhoHol 92*
Carr, Nat d1944 *WhoHol 92*
Carr, Noly Cruz 1940- *WhoWest 94*
Carr, Oscar Clark, III 1951- *WhoAmL 94*
Carr, Pat *DrAPF 93*
Carr, Patrick d1802 *AmRev*
Carr, Patrick E. 1922- *WhoAm 94*
Carr, Patrick Martin 1958- *WhoMW 93*
Carr, Paul *WhoHol 92*
Carr, Paul Henry 1935- *WhoAm 94*
Carr, Percy d1926 *WhoHol 92*
Carr, Percy L. 1941- *WhoBlA 94*
Carr, Peter Derek 1930- *Who 94*
Carr, Philip d1969 *WhoHol 92*
Carr, Philippa *ConAu 140, SmATA 74*
Carr, Philippa 1906-1993 *WrDr 94N*
Carr, Phyllis Anne 1935- *WhoAmP 93*
Carr, Pressley Rodney 1930- *WhoBlA 94*
Carr, Raymond *Who 94*
Carr, Raymond, Sir 1919- *WrDr 94*
Carr, (Albert) Raymond (Maillard) 1919- *IntWW 93, Who 94*
Carr, Robert Allen 1917- *WhoAm 94*
Carr, Robert B. *WhoAmP 93*
Carr, Robert Clifford 1940- *WhoAm 94*
Carr, Robert M. 1937- *WhoAmP 93*
Carr, Robert Spencer 1909- *EncSF 93*
Carr, Robert Stuart 1946- *WhoAm 94, WhoAmL 94*
Carr, Robert Wilson, Jr. 1934- *WhoAm 94, WhoMW 93*
Carr, Roberta 1925- *WrDr 94*
Carr, Robyn 1951- *WrDr 94*
Carr, Roderich Marion 1956- *WhoBlA 94*
Carr, Ronald Edward 1932- *WhoAm 94*
Carr, Ronald Gene 1946- *WhoAm 94, WhoAmL 94*
Carr, Roy Arthur 1929- *WhoAm 94*
Carr, Sade d1940 *WhoHol 92*
Carr, Sally Swan *WhoAmA 93*
Carr, Sandra Jean Irons 1940- *WhoBlA 94*
Carr, Sara Adnee 1963- *WhoAmL 94*
Carr, Stephen Howard 1942- *WhoAm 94*
Carr, Stephen W. 1943- *WhoAmL 94*
Carr, Steven Addison 1950- *WhoAm 94*
Carr, Terry (Gene) 1937-1987 *EncSF 93*
Carr, Thomas d1946 *WhoHol 92*
Carr, Thomas Eldridge 1953- *WhoAmL 94*
Carr, Thomas Ernest Ashdown 1915- *Who 94*
Carr, Thomas Jefferson, Jr. 1942- *WhoFI 94*
Carr, Thomas Michael 1953- *WhoMW 93, WhoScEn 94*
Carr, Victoria 1956- *WhoWest 94*
Carr, Vikki 1940- *WhoHisp 94*
Carr, Virgil H. *WhoBlA 94*
Carr, Walter James, Jr. 1918- *WhoAm 94*
Carr, Wiley Nelson 1940- *WhoAm 94*
Carr, Willard Zeller, Jr. 1927- *IntWW 93, WhoAm 94*
Carr, William d1937 *WhoHol 92*
Carr, William Anthony 1938- *WhoAm 94*
Carr, William Compton 1918- *Who 94*
Carr, William E. 1946- *WhoAmL 94*
Carr, William George 1901- *WrDr 94*
Carr, William Henry A. 1924- *WhoFI 94, WhoMW 93*
Carr, William Pitts 1947- *WhoAmP 93*
Carra, Andrew Joseph 1943- *WhoAm 94*
Carrad, David Clayton 1944- *WhoAmL 94*
Carradine, David 1936- *ConTFT 11, IntMPA 94, WhoAm 94, WhoHol 92*
Carradine, John d1988 *WhoHol 92*
Carradine, Keith 1949- *IntMPA 94, WhoHol 92*
Carradine, Keith Ian 1949- *WhoAm 94*
Carradine, Robert 1954- *IntMPA 94, WhoHol 92*
Carradini, Lawrence 1953- *WhoScEn 94*
Carragher, Audrey A. *WhoAmP 93*
Carragher, Frank Anthony 1932- *WhoFI 94*
Carragher, Mary A. 1960- *WhoAmL 94*
Carraher, Charles E., Jr. 1941- *WrDr 94*
Carraher, Charles Eugene, Jr. 1941- *WhoAm 94*
Carraher, Charles Jacob, Jr. 1922- *WhoMW 93*
Carraher, Daniel Peter 1953- *WhoFI 94*
Carraher, John Bernard 1934- *WhoAmL 94*
Carranca, Roberto 1952- *WhoFI 94*
Carranza, Fermin Albert 1926- *WhoWest 94*
Carranza, Norma *WhoAmP 93*
Carranza, Roque Guillermo 1919- *IntWW 93*
Carranza, Ruth 1949- *WhoHisp 94*
Carrara, Agata fl. 1772-1788 *NewGrDO*
Carrara, Arthur Alfonso 1914- *WhoAm 94*
Carraro, Franco 1939- *IntWW 93*
Carraro, Joseph J. *WhoAmP 93*
Carraro, Joseph John 1944- *WhoWest 94*
Carrasco, Alejandro 1962- *WhoHisp 94*
Carrasco, Carlos 1948- *WhoHisp 94*
Carrasco, Cecilia Carmiña 1966- *WhoHisp 94*
Carrasco, Connie M. *WhoHisp 94*
Carrasco, David 1944- *WhoHisp 94*
Carrasco, Emma J. *WhoHisp 94*
Carrasco, Hector R. 1948- *WhoHisp 94*
Carrasco, Lourdes 1947- *WhoHisp 94*
Carrasco, Margarita *BlmGWL*
Carrasco, Mario 1945- *WhoHisp 94*
Carrasco, Michael M. 1951- *WhoAmP 93*
Carrasco, Reynaldo Raul *WhoHisp 94*
Carrasco, Robert Anthony 1966- *WhoHisp 94*
Carrasco, Virginia 1958- *WhoHisp 94*
Carrasquillo, Angela L. 1941- *WhoHisp 94*
Carrasquillo, Frank *WhoHisp 94*
Carrasquillo, M. M. 1952- *WhoHisp 94*
Carrasquillo, Ramon Luis 1953- *WhoHisp 94, WhoScEn 94*
Carrasquillo-Molina, Edwin 1955- *WhoHisp 94*
Carre, Albert 1852-1938 *NewGrDO*
Carre, Bartlett d1971 *WhoHol 92*
Carre, Ben 1883-1978 *IntDcF 2-4*
Carre, Marguerite 1880-1947 *NewGrDO*
Carre, Marie *WhoHol 92*
Carre, Michel(-Florentin) 1822-1872 *NewGrDO*
Carreathers, Kevin R. 1957- *WhoBlA 94*
Carreker, Alphonso 1962- *WhoBlA 94*
Carreker, James D. *WhoAm 94, WhoFI 94*
Carreker, John Russell 1908- *WhoScEn 94*
Carreker, William, Jr. 1936- *WhoBlA 94*
Carrel, Alexis 1873-1944 *WorInv*
Carrel, Dany 1935- *WhoHol 92*
Carrel, Frederic 1869- *EncSF 93*
Carrel, James Elliott 1944- *WhoScEn 94*
Carrel, Mark *EncSF 93*
Carrel, Philip 1915- *Who 94*
Carrell, Bobby 1938- *WhoAmP 93*
Carrell, Daniel Allan 1941- *WhoAm 94, WhoAmL 94*
Carrell, Richard N. 1943- *WhoAmL 94*
Carrell, Robin Wayne 1936- *IntWW 93, Who 94*
Carrell, Terry Eugene 1938- *WhoFI 94*
Carrell, Thomas Tyrone *WhoAmP 93*
Carr-Ellison, Ralph (Harry) 1925- *Who 94*
Carren, Jeffrey P. 1946- *WhoAm 94*
Carreño, Eufronio Román 1941- *WhoHisp 94*
Carreño, José R. 1930- *WhoHisp 94*
Carreno, Kevin Andrew 1960- *WhoAmL 94*
Carreno, Mark *WhoHisp 94*
Carreño, Richard D. J. 1946- *WhoHisp 94*
Carreon, Jesus V. 1945- *WhoHisp 94*
Carreon, Mark Steven 1963- *WhoHisp 94*
Carreon, Martha E. 1944- *WhoHisp 94*
Carreon, Zulema 1939- *WhoHisp 94*
Carrer, Pavlos 1829-1896 *NewGrDO*
Carrera, Barbara 1947- *WhoHol 92*
Carrera, Barbara 1951- *IntMPA 94, WhoHisp 94*
Carrera, Eladio Santana 1953- *WhoHisp 94*
Carrera, José Luis 1932- *WhoHisp 94*
Carrera, Maria-Cecilia 1954- *WhoHisp 94*
Carrera, Martin Enrique 1960- *WhoScEn 94*
Carrera, Rodolfo 1953- *WhoScEn 94*
Carrera, Victor Manuel 1954- *WhoAmL 94*
Carreras, Francisco Jose 1932- *WhoAm 94*
Carreras, James 1909-1990 *IntDcF 2-4*
Carreras, Jose 1946- *ConAu 141, NewGrDO*
Carreras, Jose 1947- *IntWW 93, WhoAm 94*
Carreras, Leonardo Alfredo 1920- *WhoHisp 94*
Carrere, Charles Scott 1937- *WhoAmL 94*
Carrere, Tia 1966- *WhoHol 92*
Carrere, Tia 1967?- *ConTFT 11*
Carrere D'Encausse, Helene 1929- *IntWW 93*
Carrero, Jaime 1931- *WhoAmA 93, WhoHisp 94*
Carret, Philip Lord 1896- *WhoAm 94, WhoFI 94*
Carretta, Albert Aloysius 1907- *WhoAm 94, WhoAmL 94*
Carretta, Richard Louis 1939- *WhoAm 94*
Carretta, Vincent (Albert) 1945- *WrDr 94*
Carrey, Bernard S. 1940- *WhoAmL 94*
Carrey, Jim *WhoHol 92*
Carrey, Neil 1942- *WhoAmL 94, WhoWest 94*
Carr-Gomm, Richard Culling 1922- *Who 94*
Carr-Harris, Ian Redford 1941- *WhoAmA 93*
Carr-Hill, Roy A. 1943- *ConAu 141*
Carricart, Robert *WhoHol 92*
Carrick, Earl of d1992 *Who 94N*
Carrick, Earl of 1953- *Who 94*
Carrick, B. Cramton 1913- *WhoIns 94*
Carrick, Bruce Robert 1937- *WhoAm 94*
Carrick, Carol 1935- *SmATA 18AS [port]*
Carrick, David Stanley 1914- *WhoWest 94*
Carrick, Donald F. 1929- *WhoAmA 93N*
Carrick, Edward *Who 94*
Carrick, Edward 1905- *WrDr 94*
Carrick, John (Leslie) 1918- *Who 94*
Carrick, John Leslie 1918- *IntWW 93*
Carrick, Kathleen Michele 1950- *WhoAmL 94*
Carrick, Malcolm 1945- *WrDr 94*
Carrick, Paula Strecker 1944- *WhoAmL 94*
Carrick, Roger John 1937- *Who 94*
Carrick, Thomas Welsh 1914- *Who 94*
Carrico, Donald Jefferson 1944- *WhoWest 94*
Carrico, Fred Allen 1943- *WhoAm 94*
Carrico, Harry L. 1916- *WhoAmP 93*
Carrico, Harry Lee 1916- *WhoAm 94, WhoAmL 94*
Carrico, John Paul 1938- *WhoScEn 94*
Carrico, Michael Dicharry 1951- *WhoAmL 94*
Carriedo, Ruben Anthony 1943- *WhoHisp 94*
Carrier, Albert *WhoHol 92*
Carrier, Bernard 1929- *WhoAmP 93*
Carrier, Clara L. DeGay 1939- *WhoBlA 94*
Carrier, Constance 1908- *WrDr 94*
Carrier, Darel 1940- *BasBi*
Carrier, Estelle Stacy 1913- *WhoAm 94, WhoAmP 93*

Carrier, George Francis 1918- *IntWW 93, WhoAm 94, WhoScEn 94*
Carrier, Glass Bowling, Jr. 1931- *WhoAm 94*
Carrier, Herve 1921- *IntWW 93*
Carrier, John Mark 1965- *WhoBlA 94*
Carrier, Linda Susan 1954- *WhoFI 94*
Carrier, Mark Anthony 1968- *WhoAm 94, WhoBlA 94, WhoMW 93*
Carrier, Roch 1937- *ConLC 78 [port], WrDr 94*
Carrier, Ronald Edwin 1932- *WhoAm 94*
Carrier, Samuel Crowe, III 1945- *WhoAm 94*
Carrier, Warren *DrAPF 93*
Carrier, Warren 1918- *WrDr 94*
Carrier, Warren Pendleton 1918- *WhoAm 94*
Carrier, William David, III 1943- *WhoAm 94*
Carrier, Willis *WorInv*
Carriere, Jean-Claude 1931- *ConAu 140, IntDcF 2-4*
Carriere, Jean Paul Jacques 1932- *IntWW 93*
Carriere, Mathieu 1950- *WhoHol 92*
Carriere, Serge 1934- *WhoScEn 94*
Carrigan, Andrew G. *DrAPF 93*
Carrigan, Daniel James 1960- *WhoFI 94*
Carrigan, Daniel Joseph 1949- *WhoAm 94*
Carrigan, David Owen 1933- *WhoAm 94*
Carrigan, Jim Richard 1929- *WhoAm 94, WhoAmL 94, WhoWest 94*
Carrigan, John Richard 1948- *WhoAmL 94*
Carrigan, Martha Loretto 1961- *WhoMW 93*
Carrigan, Martin Dennis 1959- *WhoAmL 94*
Carrigan, Nancy 1933- *EncSF 93*
Carrigan, Richard 1932- *EncSF 93*
Carrigan, Sheila Patricia 1957- *WhoAmL 94*
Carrigan, Thomas J. d1941 *WhoHol 92*
Carrigg, James A. 1933- *WhoAm 94, WhoFI 94*
Carriker, Gordon Louis 1959- *WhoMW 93*
Carriker, Robert Charles 1940- *WhoWest 94*
Carriker, Steve Alan 1950- *WhoAmP 93*
Carril, Peter J. 1931- *WhoHisp 94*
Carril, Peter James 1958- *WhoAm 94*
Carrillo(-Trujillo), Julian (Antonio) 1875-1965 *NewGrDO*
Carrillo, Arsenio *WhoHisp 94*
Carrillo, Barbara *WhoHisp 94*
Carrillo, Carlos Gilberto *WhoHisp 94*
Carrillo, Carmen 1943- *WhoHisp 94*
Carrillo, Carmen 1960- *WhoHisp 94*
Carrillo, Charles Michael 1956- *WhoHisp 94*
Carrillo, Eduardo L. 1937- *WhoHisp 94*
Carrillo, Efraín de la Cerda 1953- *WhoHisp 94*
Carrillo, Elpidia *WhoHol 92*
Carrillo, Federico Martínez 1937- *WhoHisp 94*
Carrillo, Frank Quintero 1928- *WhoHisp 94*
Carrillo, Fred Anthony 1946- *WhoHisp 94*
Carrillo, George *WhoHisp 94*
Carrillo, Germán David *WhoHisp 94*
Carrillo, Gilberto 1926- *WhoWest 94*
Carrillo, Joe M., Jr. 1927- *WhoHisp 94*
Carrillo, Jose Arturo 1944- *WhoHisp 94*
Carrillo, Juan Carlos *WhoHisp 94*
Carrillo, Ken 1958- *WhoHisp 94*
Carrillo, Lawrence W. 1920- *WrDr 94*
Carrillo, Leo d1961 *WhoHol 92*
Carrillo, Lilia 1929-1974 *WhoAmA 93N*
Carrillo, Michael Anthony 1960- *WhoHisp 94*
Carrillo, Miguel Angel 1964- *WhoHisp 94*
Carrillo, Peter Joseph 1949- *WhoHisp 94*
Carrillo, Ray 1951- *WhoHisp 94*
Carrillo, Richard M. *WhoHisp 94*
Carrillo, Robert S. 1932- *WhoHisp 94*
Carrillo, Santiago 1915- *IntWW 93*
Carrillo-Beron, Carmen 1943- *WhoHisp 94*
Carrington, Baron 1919- *Who 94*
Carrington, Alan 1934- *IntWW 93, Who 94*
Carrington, Christine H. 1941- *WhoBlA 94*
Carrington, Colin Edward George 1936- *Who 94*
Carrington, Dora de Houghton 1893-1932 *DcNaB MP*
Carrington, Edward 1749-1810 *WhAmRev*
Carrington, Evelyn Carter d1942 *WhoHol 92*
Carrington, Frank d1975 *WhoHol 92*
Carrington, Glenda *DrAPF 93*
Carrington, Grant *DrAPF 93*
Carrington, Grant 1938- *EncSF 93*
Carrington, Helen d1963 *WhoHol 92*
Carrington, James 1904- *WhoBlA 94*
Carrington, Joy Harrell *WhoAmA 93*
Carrington, Laura Stock 1946- *WhoAmP 93*
Carrington, Marsha Solomon 1954- *WhoAmP 93*
Carrington, Matthew Hadrian Marshall 1947- *Who 94*
Carrington, Michael Davis 1938- *WhoMW 93*
Carrington, Murray d1941 *WhoHol 92*
Carrington, Omar Raymond 1904-1991 *WhoAmA 93N*
Carrington, Paul 1733-1818 *WhAmRev*
Carrington, Paul DeWitt 1931- *WhoAmL 94, WrDr 94*
Carrington, Peter Alexander Rupert 1919- *IntWW 93*
Carrington, Samuel Macon, Jr. 1939- *WhoAm 94*
Carrington, Terri Lyne 1965- *WhoBlA 94*
Carrino, David 1959- *WhoAmA 93*
Carrino, Michael *DrAPF 93*
Carrion, Daniel Edward 1958- *WhoHisp 94*
Carrion, Richard 1952- *WhoAm 94, WhoFI 94*
Carrion, Richard L. *WhoHisp 94*
Carrion, Teresita Milagros 1964- *WhoHisp 94*
Carrithers, David Wayne 1955- *WhoAmL 94*
Carriveau, Michael Jon 1956- *WhoMW 93*
Carrizal, Ernesto, Jr. 1933- *WhoHisp 94*
Carrizosa, Fernando 1943- *WhoHisp 94*
Carr Linford, Alan 1926- *Who 94*
Carr-Locke, David Leslie 1948- *WhoScEn 94*
Carro, John 1927- *WhoHisp 94*
Carro, John Placid 1920- *WhoHisp 94*
Carro, Jorge L. 1924- *WhoHisp 94*
Carro, Jorge Luis 1924- *WhoAm 94, WhoAmL 94*
Carr Of Hadley, Baron 1916- *IntWW 93, Who 94*
Carro-Figueroa, Eric Francisco 1949- *WhoHisp 94*
Carrol, Charles Gordon 1935- *Who 94*
Carrol, Robert Kelton 1952- *WhoAm 94*
Carroli, Silvano 1939- *NewGrDO*
Carroll, Albert d1956 *WhoHol 92*
Carroll, Albert 1914- *WhoAm 94*
Carroll, Annie Haywood 1904- *WhoBlA 94*
Carroll, Barry Joseph 1944- *WhoAm 94*
Carroll, Beeson *WhoHol 92*
Carroll, Bernard James 1940- *WhoAm 94*
Carroll, Beverly A. 1946- *WhoBlA 94*
Carroll, Billy Price 1920- *WhoAm 94*
Carroll, Brendan Thomas More 1960- *WhoMW 93*
Carroll, C. Edward 1923- *WrDr 94*
Carroll, Carmal Edward 1923- *WhoAm 94*
Carroll, Carol Ann 1945- *WhoMW 93*
Carroll, Cathleen Ann 1964- *WhoFI 94*
Carroll, Charlene O. 1950- *WhoBlA 94*
Carroll, Charles 1723-1783 *WhAmRev*
Carroll, Charles (of Carrollton) 1737-1832 *WhAmRev*
Carroll, Charles H. 1910- *WhoBlA 94*
Carroll, Charles Lemuel, Jr. 1916- *WhoScEn 94*
Carroll, Charles Michael 1921- *WhoAm 94*
Carroll, Charles William Desmond 1919- *Who 94*
Carroll, Christopher Steven 1952- *WhoAmL 94*
Carroll, Constance Marie 1945- *WhoBlA 94*
Carroll, Dana 1943- *WhoWest 94*
Carroll, Danford Frederic 1948- *WhoAmL 94*
Carroll, Daniel 1730-1796 *WhAmRev*
Carroll, David-James 1950-1992 *ConTFT 11*
Carroll, David Todd 1959- *WhoScEn 94, WhoWest 94*
Carroll, Dee d1980 *WhoHol 92*
Carroll, Dennis D. 1947- *WhoAmL 94*
Carroll, Derek Raymond 1919- *Who 94*
Carroll, Diahann 1935- *AfrAmAl 6, IntMPA 94, WhoBlA 94, WhoHol 92*
Carroll, Diane Camille 1960- *WhoAmL 94*
Carroll, Donal Shemus Allingham 1927- *IntWW 93*
Carroll, Donnell Philip 1950- *WhoAmP 93*
Carroll, Douglas Edward 1954- *WhoFI 94*
Carroll, Earl d1948 *WhoHol 92*
Carroll, Earl Hamblin 1925- *WhoAm 94, WhoAmL 94, WhoWest 94*
Carroll, Edith B. 1930- *WhoAmP 93*
Carroll, Edward Gonzalez 1910- *WhoBlA 94*
Carroll, Edward Major 1916- *WhoBlA 94*
Carroll, Edward William 1942- *WhoScEn 94*
Carroll, Edwin Winford 1912- *WhoAm 94*
Carroll, Elizabeth 1944- *WrDr 94*
Carroll, Elizabeth 1945- *WrDr 94*
Carroll, Ellen A. 1947- *WhoAmL 94*
Carroll, Eunice Saunders d1993 *NewYTBS 93*
Carroll, Francis Patrick *Who 94*
Carroll, Frank J. 1947- *WhoAmL 94*
Carroll, Frank Richard 1947- *WhoWest 94*
Carroll, George Arthur 1919- *WhoAmP 93*
Carroll, George D. 1923- *WhoBlA 94*
Carroll, George Joseph 1917- *WhoAm 94*
Carroll, Georgia 1919- *WhoHol 92*
Carroll, Gerald J. d1993 *NewYTBS 93*
Carroll, Ginny 1948- *WrDr 94*
Carroll, Gladys Hasty 1904- *WhoAm 94, WrDr 94*
Carroll, Gordon 1928- *IntMPA 94*
Carroll, Helena 1920- *WhoHol 92*
Carroll, Holbert Nicholson 1921- *WhoAm 94*
Carroll, Howard William 1942- *WhoAmP 93, WhoMW 93*
Carroll, J. Raymond 1922- *WhoScEn 94*
Carroll, J(efferson) Roy, Jr. 1904-1990 *WhAm 10*
Carroll, J. Speed 1936- *WhoAm 94*
Carroll, Jack Adien 1950- *WhoAm 94, WhoMW 93*
Carroll, James 1943- *WhoAm 94, WrDr 94*
Carroll, James Edward 1952- *WhoAmL 94*
Carroll, James F. L. 1934- *WhoAmA 93*
Carroll, James J. 1948- *WhoAm 94*
Carroll, James J., III 1946- *WhoAmL 94*
Carroll, James Kevin 1945- *WhoAmL 94*
Carroll, James L. 1945- *WhoAmL 94*
Carroll, James Robert 1940- *WhoWest 94*
Carroll, James S. 1945- *WhoBlA 94*
Carroll, James Vincent, III 1940- *WhoAm 94*
Carroll, Janice *WhoHol 92*
Carroll, Jean d1972 *WhoHol 92*
Carroll, Jeanne 1929- *WhoAm 94, WhoMW 93*
Carroll, Jill *WhoHol 92*
Carroll, Jim 1951- *ConAu 42NR*
Carroll, Joan 1932- *WhoHol 92*
Carroll, Joanne H. 1931- *WhoAmP 93*
Carroll, Joe Barry 1958- *BasBi, WhoBlA 94*
Carroll, Joel 1924- *WhoWest 94*
Carroll, John d1979 *WhoHol 92*
Carroll, John 1735-1815 *DcAmReB 2, WhAmRev*
Carroll, John 1892-1959 *WhoAmA 93N*
Carroll, John 1943- *WhoAmP 93*
Carroll, John Bissell 1916- *IntWW 93, WhoAm 94*
Carroll, John Douglas 1939- *WhoAm 94*
Carroll, John Edward 1934- *Who 94*
Carroll, John F. d1993 *NewYTBS 93*
Carroll, John H. *WhoAmP 93*
Carroll, John Howard 1927- *WhoFI 94, WhoMW 93*
Carroll, John J. 1947- *WhoMW 93*
Carroll, John M. 1941- *WhoAm 94*
Carroll, John Moore 1911- *WhoScEn 94*
Carroll, John S. 1929- *WhoAmP 93*
Carroll, John Sawyer 1942- *WhoAm 94*
Carroll, Joseph Francis 1910-1991 *WhAm 10*
Carroll, Joseph John 1936- *WhoAm 94*
Carroll, Julian Morton 1931- *IntWW 93, WhoAm 94, WhoAmP 93*
Carroll, June *WhoHol 92*
Carroll, Kenneth Kitchener 1923- *IntWW 93, WhoAm 94*
Carroll, Kenneth William 1947- *WhoMW 93*
Carroll, Kent Jean 1926- *WhoAm 94*
Carroll, Kim Marie 1958- *WhoMW 93*
Carroll, Larry Lester 1935- *WhoWest 94*
Carroll, Lawrence W. 1923- *WhoBlA 94*
Carroll, Lawrence William, III 1950- *WhoBlA 94*
Carroll, Leo G. d1972 *WhoHol 92*
Carroll, Lesley Gitzendanner 1965- *WhoAmL 94*
Carroll, Lewis *WorScD*
Carroll, Lewis 1832-1898 *BlmGEL, EncSF 93*
Carroll, Madeleine d1987 *WhoHol 92*
Carroll, Margaret Ann 1929- *WhoAm 94*
Carroll, Mark Bennett 1964- *WhoAmL 94*
Carroll, Mark Thomas 1956- *WhoAmL 94*
Carroll, Marshall Elliott 1923- *WhoAm 94*
Carroll, Martin 1935- *WrDr 94*
Carroll, Mary *WhoHol 92*
Carroll, Mary 1929- *WrDr 94*
Carroll, Mary Colvert 1940- *WhoAm 94*
Carroll, Maura *WhoAmP 93*
Carroll, Megan Elizabeth 1967- *WhoAmL 94*
Carroll, Michael L. 1950- *WhoMW 93*
Carroll, Michael M. 1936- *WhoAm 94*
Carroll, Nancy d1965 *WhoHol 92*
Carroll, Norman d1967 *WhoHol 92*
Carroll, Oscar Franklin 1950- *WhoFI 94*
Carroll, Pat 1927- *IntMPA 94, WhoAm 94, WhoHol 92, WhoWest 94*
Carroll, Patricia Whitehead 1954- *WhoFI 94*
Carroll, Patrick D. 1941- *WhoAmP 93*
Carroll, Patrick Joseph 1946- *WhoMW 93*
Carroll, Paul *DrAPF 93*
Carroll, Paul 1927- *WrDr 94*
Carroll, Paul Vincent 1900-1968 *IntDcT 2*
Carroll, Paula Marie 1933- *WhoFI 94, WhoWest 94*
Carroll, Peggy d1981 *WhoHol 92*
Carroll, Peter *WhoHol 92*
Carroll, Philip 1946- *Who 94*
Carroll, Philip Joseph 1937- *WhoAm 94*
Carroll, Raoul Lord 1950- *WhoAm 94, WhoAmL 94, WhoAmP 93, WhoBlA 94*
Carroll, Rhoda *DrAPF 93*
Carroll, Richard F. d1925 *WhoHol 92*
Carroll, Robert Alan 1935- *WhoWest 94*
Carroll, Robert Charles 1944- *WhoMW 93*
Carroll, Robert Eugene 1957- *WhoAm 94*
Carroll, Robert F. 1931- *WhoBlA 94*
Carroll, Robert Henry 1932- *WhoAm 94*
Carroll, Robert Lynn 1938- *WhoAm 94*
Carroll, Robert P(eter) 1941- *ConAu 43NR*
Carroll, Robert W. 1923- *WhoAm 94*
Carroll, Robert Wayne 1930- *WhoAm 94*
Carroll, Roger Clinton 1947- *WhoScEn 94*
Carroll, Sally G. *WhoBlA 94*
Carroll, Shirley deVaux Strong 1930- *WhoMW 93*
Carroll, Stephen Douglas 1943- *WhoScEn 94*
Carroll, Stephen John, Jr. 1930- *WhoAm 94*
Carroll, Stephen K. 1949- *WhoAmL 94*
Carroll, Steven R. 1956- *WhoAmP 93*
Carroll, Terence Patrick 1948- *Who 94*
Carroll, Thomas Andrew 1954- *WhoFI 94*
Carroll, Thomas Colas 1943- *WhoAmL 94*
Carroll, Thomas E. 1948- *WhoAmL 94*
Carroll, Thomas John 1929- *WhoAm 94*
Carroll, Thomas Joseph 1941- *WhoAm 94, WhoFI 94*
Carroll, Thomas Sylvester 1919- *WhoAm 94*
Carroll, Timothy Keenan 1938- *WhoAm 94*
Carroll, Vinnette 1922- *WhoHol 92*
Carroll, Vinnette Justine *WhoBlA 94*
Carroll, W. Donald, Jr. 1945- *WhoAmL 94*
Carroll, Wallace Edward 1907-1990 *WhAm 10*
Carroll, Wayne Jackson 1933- *WhoAmL 94*
Carroll, William 1936- *WhoBlA 94*
Carroll, William A. d1928 *WhoHol 92*
Carroll, William Jerome 1923- *WhoAm 94*
Carroll, William Joseph 1943- *WhoAmP 93*
Carroll, William Kenneth 1927- *WhoAm 94, WhoAmL 94*
Carroll, William Marion 1932- *WhoFI 94*
Carron, Arthur 1900-1967 *NewGrDO*
Carron, Maudee Lilyan *WhoAmA 93*
Carron, Reid 1947- *WhoAmL 94*
Carrothers, Alfred William Rooke 1924- *WhoAm 94*
Carrothers, Gerald Arthur Patrick 1925- *WhoAm 94*
Carrott, Jasper *WhoHol 92*
Carrott, John Arden 1947- *WhoFI 94, WhoWest 94*
Carrow, Leon Albert 1924- *WhoAm 94*
Carrow, Milton Michael 1912- *WhoAm 94*
Carr-Smith, Stephen Robert 1941- *Who 94*
Carruth, Carl B. 1947- *WhoAmL 94*
Carruth, David Barrow 1926- *WhoAm 94*
Carruth, Hayden *DrAPF 93*
Carruth, Hayden 1921- *WhoAm 94, WrDr 94*
Carruth, Joseph D. 1942- *WhoAmL 94*
Carruth, Paul H. 1892-1961 *WhoAmA 93N*
Carruthers, Alwyn Guy 1925- *Who 94*
Carruthers, Ben d1983 *WhoHol 92*
Carruthers, Bruce d1977 *WhoHol 92*
Carruthers, Claudelle Ann 1961- *WhoMW 93*
Carruthers, Colin Malcolm 1931- *Who 94*
Carruthers, Garrey E. 1939- *WhoAmP 93*
Carruthers, Garrey Edward 1939- *IntWW 93*
Carruthers, George d1992 *Who 94N*
Carruthers, George E. 1940- *AfrAmAl 6*
Carruthers, George Robert 1939- *WhoBlA 94*
Carruthers, James Edwin 1928- *Who 94*

Carruthers, John Robert 1935- *WhoAm 94*
Carruthers, Norman Harry 1935- *Who 94, WhoAm 94*
Carruthers, Peter Ambler 1935- *WhoAm 94, WhoScEn 94, WhoWest 94*
Carruthers, Philip C. 1953- *WhoAmP 93*
Carruthers, Robert d1992 *IntWW 93N*
Carruthers, S. George 1945- *WhoAm 94*
Carruthers, Thomas Neely, Jr. 1928- *WhoAm 94*
Carruthers, Walter Edward Royden 1938- *WhoAm 94*
Carruthers, William Buttrick 1929- *Who 94*
Carry, Helen Ward *WhoBlA 94*
Carry, Julius J., III 1952- *WhoBlA 94*
Carsberg, Bryan (Victor) 1939- *IntWW 93, Who 94*
Carse, Henry H. 1918- *WhoAmP 93*
Carsey, Lamberth S. 1924- *WhoAm 94*
Carsey, Marcia Lee Peterson 1944- *WhoAm 94*
Carsey, Mary d1973 *WhoHol 92*
Carson, Ada Lou 1932- *WhoMW 93*
Carson, Allan Grant 1897- *WhAm 10*
Carson, Anne (Regina) 1950- *WrDr 94*
Carson, Benjamin Solomon, Sr. 1951- *WhoBlA 94*
Carson, Carol S. 1939- *WhoAm 94, WhoFI 94*
Carson, Charles d1977 *WhoHol 92*
Carson, Charles William 1897- *WhAm 10*
Carson, Chris d1978 *WhoHol 92*
Carson, Christopher d1868 *HisWorL*
Carson, Christopher Houston 1809-1868 *WhWE [port]*
Carson, Ciaran 1948- *WrDr 94*
Carson, Clarence B. 1925- *WrDr 94*
Carson, Curtis C., Jr. 1920- *WhoBlA 94*
Carson, D(onald) A(rthur) 1946- *ConAu 142*
Carson, Dave *WhoAm 94, WhoAmP 93*
Carson, David Ellis Adams 1934- *WhoAm 94, WhoFI 94*
Carson, David Richard 1946- *WhoAmL 94*
Carson, Dwight Keith 1951- *WhoBlA 94*
Carson, Edward Mansfield 1929- *IntWW 93, WhoAm 94, WhoFI 94, WhoWest 94*
Carson, Eldridge Franklin d1978 *WhoHol 92*
Carson, Elizabeth Lorraine Neal 1958- *WhoWest 94*
Carson, Frances 1895- *WhoHol 92*
Carson, G. B. 1950- *WhoAmA 93*
Carson, Gerald Glen 1961- *WhoMW 93*
Carson, Gerald Hewes 1899-1989 *WhAm 10*
Carson, Gordon Bloom 1911- *WhoAm 94, WhoMW 93, WhoScEn 94*
Carson, Gregory L. 1958- *WhoAmP 93*
Carson, Hampton L(awrence) 1914- *IntWW 93*
Carson, Harry Albert 1913- *WhoAm 94*
Carson, Harry Donald 1953- *WhoBlA 94*
Carson, Herbert L. 1929- *WrDr 94*
Carson, Hunter 1976- *WhoHol 92*
Carson, Irma 1935- *WhoBlA 94*
Carson, Jack d1963 *WhoHol 92*
Carson, Jack 1910-1963 *WhoCom*
Carson, James d1958 *WhoHol 92*
Carson, James Donald 1929- *WhoAm 94*
Carson, James Elijah 1923- *WhoAm 94*
Carson, James Matthew 1944- *WhoWest 94*
Carson, James Patrick 1955- *WhoMW 93*
Carson, Jeannie 1928- *IntMPA 94, WhoHol 92*
Carson, Jeffrey Ellis 1956- *WhoMW 93*
Carson, John 1927- *WhoHol 92*
Carson, John 1934- *Who 94*
Carson, John Congleton 1927- *WhoAm 94*
Carson, John David 1951- *WhoHol 92*
Carson, John Little 1945- *WhoAm 94*
Carson, Johnnie 1943- *WhoAm 94, WhoAmP 93*
Carson, Johnny 1925- *IntMPA 94, IntWW 93, WhoAm 94, WhoCom [port], WhoHol 92*
Carson, Josephine *DrAPF 93*
Carson, Julia M. *WhoAmP 93*
Carson, Julia M. 1938- *WhoBlA 94*
Carson, Kit d1979 *WhoHol 92*
Carson, L. M. Kit *WhoHol 92*
Carson, Leonard Allen 1940- *WhoAm 94, WhoAmL 94*
Carson, Lillian Gershenson 1933- *WhoWest 94*
Carson, Linda Frances 1952- *WhoMW 93*
Carson, Lois Montgomery 1931- *WhoBlA 94*
Carson, Marvin Wayne 1955- *WhoWest 94*
Carson, Michael (Charles) 1946- *WrDr 94*
Carson, Nolan Wendell 1924- *WhoAm 94*
Carson, Rachel 1907-1964 *AmSocL, EnvEnc [port], WorScD*
Carson, Rachelle *WhoHol 92*
Carson, Regina Edwards *WhoFI 94, WhoScEn 94*
Carson, Regina M. Edwards *WhoBlA 94*
Carson, Richard McKee 1912- *WhoMW 93, WhoScEn 94*
Carson, Robert d1979 *WhoHol 92*
Carson, Robert Andrew Glendinning 1918- *Who 94*
Carson, Robin D. 1955- *WhoAm 94*
Carson, Samuel Goodman 1913- *WhoAm 94*
Carson, Stanley 1937- *WhoWest 94*
Carson, Steven Douglas 1951- *WhoMW 93*
Carson, Sunset d1990 *WhoHol 92*
Carson, Timothy Joseph 1949- *WhoAm 94, WhoAmL 94, WhoAmP 93*
Carson, Violet d1983 *WhoHol 92*
Carson, Virginia Gottschall *WhoWest 94*
Carson, Wallace P., Jr. 1934- *WhoAmP 93*
Carson, Wallace Preston, Jr. 1934- *WhoAm 94, WhoAmL 94, WhoWest 94*
Carson, Warren Jason, Jr. 1953- *WhoBlA 94*
Carson, Wayne d1982 *WhoHol 92*
Carson, Wayne Gilbert 1931- *WhoWest 94*
Carson, William Charles 1924- *WhoFI 94*
Carson, William Dean 1963- *WhoMW 93*
Carson, William Hunter 1942- *IntWW 93*
Carson, William Hunter Fisher 1942- *Who 94*
Carsrud, Alan Lee 1946- *WhoWest 94*
Carssow, Tim 1944- *WhoAmL 94*
Carstairs, Charles Young d1993 *Who 94N*
Carstairs, Sharon 1942- *WhoMW 93*
Carsten, Arlene Desmet 1937- *WhoAm 94*
Carsten, Francis Ludwig 1911- *Who 94, WrDr 94*
Carsten, Peter 1929- *WhoHol 92*
Carstens, Harold Henry 1925- *WhoAm 94*
Carstens, Jane Ellen 1922- *WhoAm 94*
Carstens, John Christopher 1937- *WhoMW 93*
Carstens, Karl d1992 *IntWW 93N*
Carstens, Karl 1914-1992 *AnObit 1992*
Carstens, Karl Walter 1914-1992 *WhAm 10*
Carstens, Lina d1978 *WhoHol 92*
Carstensen, Edwin Lorenz 1919- *WhoAm 94*
Carstensen, Jens Thuroe 1926- *WhoMW 93*
Carstensen, Marilyn Joyce 1938- *WhoAmP 93*
Carstensen, Roger (Norwood) 1920- *WrDr 94*
Carstenson, Cecil C. 1906-1991 *WhoAmA 93N*
Carswell, Allan Ian 1933- *WhoAm 94*
Carswell, Bruce 1930- *WhoAm 94, WhoFI 94*
Carswell, Gloria Nadine Sherman 1951- *WhoBlA 94*
Carswell, Jane Triplett 1932- *WhoAm 94*
Carswell, John 1931- *WhoAmA 93*
Carswell, John Patrick 1918- *Who 94, WrDr 94*
Carswell, Lois Malakoff 1932- *WhoAm 94*
Carswell, Robert 1928- *WhoAm 94, WhoAmP 93*
Carswell, Robert (Douglas) 1934- *Who 94*
Carswell, Rodney 1946- *WhoAmA 93*
Cart, Doran Lansing 1952- *WhoAm 94*
Carta, Franklin Oliver 1930- *WhoScEn 94*
Carta, Giorgio 1957- *WhoScEn 94*
Cartagena, Luis A. 1946- *WhoHisp 94*
Cartagena, Roberto A. 1947- *WhoHisp 94*
Cartagena, Ruben 1939- *WhoHisp 94*
Cartagena, Teresa de c. 1420-1470 *BlmGWL*
Cartan, Henri Paul 1904- *IntWW 93*
Cartan-Hansen, Joan Kathleen 1961- *WhoAmP 93*
Carte, Elliott Cook, Jr. 1908- *AmCulL*
Carte, George Wayne 1940- *WhoWest 94*
Carte, Richard D'Oyly 1844-1901 *NewGrDO*
Cartee, Thomas Edward, Jr. 1960- *WhoFI 94*
Cartel, Louis 1907- *WrDr 94*
Cartelli, Mary Anne *DrAPF 93*
Cartellieri, Ulrich 1937- *IntWW 93*
Carten, Francis Noel 1935- *WhoAmL 94*
Carter *Who 94*
Carter, Baron 1932- *Who 94*
Carter, Alan 1920- *IntDcB*
Carter, Alden R. *DrAPF 93*
Carter, Alden R. 1947- *SmATA 18AS [port]*
Carter, Alden R(ichardson) 1947- *TwCYAW, WrDr 94*
Carter, Allen D. 1947- *WhoBlA 94*
Carter, Alphonse H. 1928- *WhoBlA 94*
Carter, Andrew 1943- *Who 94*
Carter, Angela 1940- *BlmGEL [port]*
Carter, Angela 1940-1992 *AnObit 1992, BlmGWL [port], ConLC 76 [port], RfGShF, ShSCr 13 [port]*
Carter, Angela (Olive Stalker) 1940-1992 *EncSF 93, WrDr 94N*
Carter, Ann 1936- *WhoHol 92*
Carter, Ann Keeling 1949- *WhoAm 94*
Carter, Anne Cohen 1919- *WhoAm 94*
Carter, Annette Wheeler 1941- *WhoAmP 93*
Carter, Anthony 1960- *WhoAm 94, WhoBlA 94, WhoMW 93*
Carter, Anthony Jerome 1956- *WhoBlA 94*
Carter, Arlington W., Jr. 1933- *WhoBlA 94*
Carter, Arthur 1916- *WhoAmP 93*
Carter, Arthur Michael 1940- *WhoBlA 94*
Carter, Augustus D. 1895-1957 *WhoAmA 93N*
Carter, Barbara Lillian 1942- *WhoBlA 94*
Carter, Barry Edward 1942- *WhoAm 94, WhoAmL 94*
Carter, Ben d1947 *WhoHol 92*
Carter, Bennett Lester 1907- *WhoAm 94*
Carter, Benny 1907- *AfrAmAl 6, WhoHol 92*
Carter, Bernard Thomas 1920- *Who 94*
Carter, Bertha Mae 1945- *WhoMW 93*
Carter, Betty 1929- *WhoAm 94*
Carter, Betty 1930- *WhoBlA 94*
Carter, Bill G. 1928- *WhoAmP 93*
Carter, Billy L. *WhoBlA 94*
Carter, Brandon 1942- *IntWW 93, Who 94*
Carter, Bruce *Who 94*
Carter, Bruce 1922- *EncSF 93, WrDr 94*
Carter, (Charles) Bruce 1930- *WhoAmA 93*
Carter, Bruce D. *WhoAmP 93*
Carter, Calvert d1932 *WhoHol 92*
Carter, Calvin W. 1934- *WhoIns 94*
Carter, Carl Anthony 1964- *WhoBlA 94*
Carter, Carla Cifelli 1949- *WhoFI 94*
Carter, Carmen 1954- *EncSF 93*
Carter, Carol A. 1955- *WhoAmA 93*
Carter, Carolyn McCraw 1932- *WhoBlA 94*
Carter, Cary Warren 1947- *WhoAm 94, WhoFI 94*
Carter, Cecil Neal 1939- *WhoScEn 94*
Carter, Charleata A. 1960- *WhoScEn 94*
Carter, Charles (Frederick) 1919- *Who 94*
Carter, Charles (Frederick), Sir 1919- *WrDr 94*
Carter, Charles E. O. 1887-1968 *AstEnc*
Carter, Charles Edward 1925- *WhoBlA 94*
Carter, Charles Frederick 1919- *IntWW 93*
Carter, Charles Michael 1943- *WhoBlA 94*
Carter, Charlotte *DrAPF 93*
Carter, Cheryl A. 1960- *WhoMW 93*
Carter, Chester C. 1921- *WhoBlA 94*
Carter, Christopher Anthony 1963- *WhoBlA 94*
Carter, Clarence Holbrook 1904- *WhoAm 94, WhoAmA 93*
Carter, Claude Daniel 1932- *WhoAmP 93*
Carter, Craig Nash 1949- *WhoScEn 94*
Carter, Curtis Harold 1915-1992 *WhAm 10*
Carter, Curtis L. 1935- *WhoAmA 93*
Carter, Curtis Lloyd 1935- *WhoAm 94*
Carter, Curtis William 1927- *WhoAmP 93*
Carter, Cynthia Elaine Kinser 1964- *WhoAmL 94*
Carter, D. Martin d1993 *NewYTBS 93*
Carter, Daisy 1931- *WhoBlA 94*
Carter, Dale William 1949- *WhoScEn 94*
Carter, Dan T. 1940- *WhoAm 94*
Carter, Dan T. 1954- *WhoAmL 94*
Carter, Daniel Paul 1948- *WhoAmL 94*
Carter, Darline Louretha 1933- *WhoBlA 94*
Carter, David *Who 94*
Carter, (Ronald) David 1927- *Who 94*
Carter, David Clifford 1929- *WhAm 10*
Carter, David Craig 1940- *Who 94*
Carter, David Furrow 1946- *WhoFI 94*
Carter, David G., Sr. 1942- *WhoBlA 94*
Carter, David Giles 1921- *WhoAmA 93*
Carter, David J. 1934- *WhoWest 94*
Carter, David LaVere 1933- *WhoScEn 94, WhoWest 94*
Carter, David Martin 1936- *WhoAm 94, WhoScEn 94*
Carter, David S. 1946- *WhoWest 94*
Carter, Dean 1922- *WhoAm 94, WhoAmA 93*
Carter, Dee *EncSF 93*
Carter, Derrick (Hunton) 1906- *Who 94*
Carter, Dexter Anthony 1967- *WhoBlA 94*
Carter, Dixie *WhoAm 94*
Carter, Dixie 1939- *IntMPA 94, WhoHol 92*
Carter, Don 1928- *WhoAmP 93*
Carter, Don Earl 1917- *WhoAm 94*
Carter, Donald *WhoAm 94*
Carter, Donald Patton 1927- *WhoAm 94*
Carter, Donald Webster 1929- *WhoMW 93*
Carter, Dorothy Ethel Fleming 1928- *Who 94*
Carter, Dorval Ronald 1935- *WhoBlA 94*
Carter, Douglas 1911- *Who 94*
Carter, Duane d1993 *NewYTBS 93*
Carter, Dudley Christopher 1891- *WhAm 10*
Carter, Dudley Christopher 1891-1992 *WhoAmA 93N*
Carter, E(dward) Graydon 1949- *Who 94*
Carter, Edward Earl 1939- *WhoBlA 94*
Carter, Edward Fenton, III 1948- *WhoScEn 94*
Carter, Edward William 1911- *WhoWest 94*
Carter, Eleanor Elizabeth 1954- *WhoMW 93*
Carter, Elizabeth 1717-1806 *BlmGWL*
Carter, Ellin *DrAPF 93*
Carter, Elliott (Cook) 1908- *Who 94*
Carter, Elliott Cook, Jr. 1908- *IntWW 93, WhoAm 94*
Carter, Enrique Delano 1945- *WhoBlA 94*
Carter, Eric Bairstow 1912- *Who 94*
Carter, Eric Stephen 1923- *Who 94*
Carter, Ernest Trow 1866-1953 *NewGrDO*
Carter, Esther Young 1930- *WhoBlA 94*
Carter, Eva Meador 1921- *WhoAmP 93*
Carter, Everett 1919- *WrDr 94*
Carter, Felicity (Winifred) 1906- *WrDr 94*
Carter, Fran(ces) Tunnell *WrDr 94*
Carter, Frances Monet 1923- *WrDr 94*
Carter, Frances Tunnell *WhoAm 94*
Carter, Francis Jackson 1899- *Who 94*
Carter, Frank d1920 *WhoHol 92*
Carter, Frank Ernest Lovell 1909- *Who 94*
Carter, Fred 1945- *BasBi, WhoBlA 94*
Carter, Frederick Brian 1933- *Who 94*
Carter, Frederick James 1945- *WhoAm 94*
Carter, Frederick Timmins 1925- *WhoAmA 93*
Carter, G(erald) Emmett 1912- *Who 94*
Carter, Gary 1939- *WhoAmA 93*
Carter, Gary Lee 1939- *WhoWest 94*
Carter, Gene 1935- *WhoAm 94, WhoAmL 94*
Carter, Gene Raymond 1939- *WhoBlA 94*
Carter, Geoffrey Norton 1944- *WhoBlA 94*
Carter, George Carson 1957- *WhoAmL 94*
Carter, George E. 1925- *WhoBlA 94*
Carter, George Kent 1935- *WhoAm 94, WhoFI 94*
Carter, Gerald Emmett 1912- *IntWW 93, WhoAm 94*
Carter, Gilbert Lino 1945- *WhoBlA 94*
Carter, Glenn Douglas 1940- *WhoMW 93*
Carter, Glenn Thomas 1934- *WhoAmL 94*
Carter, Godfrey James 1919- *Who 94*
Carter, Granville Wellington 1920-1992 *WhAm 10*
Carter, Graydon *Who 94*
Carter, Gwendolen Margaret 1906-1991 *WhAm 10*
Carter, Gwendolyn Burns 1932- *WhoBlA 94*
Carter, Hanson 1932- *WhoAmP 93*
Carter, Harold 1925- *WrDr 94*
Carter, Harold Lloyd *WhoMW 93*
Carter, Harold M., Jr. 1952- *WhoAmL 94*
Carter, Harold O. 1932- *WhoAm 94*
Carter, Harriet LaShun 1963- *WhoBlA 94*
Carter, Harriet (Estelle) Manore 1929- *WhoAmA 93*
Carter, Harry L. 1946- *WhoAmL 94*
Carter, Harvey 1938- *WhoAmP 93*
Carter, Hazo William, Jr. *WhoBlA 94*
Carter, Helena 1923- *WhoHol 92*
Carter, Helene 1887-1960 *WhoAmA 93N*
Carter, Henry Lee 1935- *WhoAmP 93*
Carter, Henry Moore, Jr. 1932- *WhoAm 94*
Carter, Herbert E. 1919- *WhoBlA 94*
Carter, Herbert Edmund 1910- *IntWW 93, WhoAm 94*
Carter, Herbert Jacque 1953- *WhoScEn 94*
Carter, Hodding, III 1935- *WhoAm 94*
Carter, Howard Payne 1921- *WhoBlA 94*
Carter, Hubert d1934 *WhoHol 92*
Carter, Hugh Clendenin 1925- *WhoAm 94*
Carter, J. B., Jr. 1937- *WhoBlA 94*
Carter, Jack d1967 *WhoHol 92*
Carter, Jack 1923- *ConTFT 11, IntDcB [port], IntMPA 94, WhoCom, WhoHol 92*
Carter, Jaine Marie 1946- *WhoAm 94*
Carter, James 1944- *WhoBlA 94*
Carter, James Able 1926- *WhoFI 94*
Carter, James Clarence 1927- *WhoAm 94*
Carter, James Earl, Jr. 1924- *Who 94, WhoAm 94*
Carter, James Earl, Jr. 1943- *WhoBlA 94*
Carter, James Edward 1935- *WhoAmL 94*

Carter, James Edward, Jr. 1906- *WhoBlA 94*
Carter, James Edward, III 1938- *WhoBlA 94*
Carter, James H. 1935- *WhoAmL 94, WhoAmP 93, WhoMW 93*
Carter, James Hal, Jr. 1943- *WhoAm 94*
Carter, James Harvey 1934- *WhoBlA 94*
Carter, James L. 1933- *WhoBlA 94*
Carter, James McCord 1952- *WhoAm 94*
Carter, James Norman *Who 94*
Carter, James P. *WhoBlA 94*
Carter, James Rose, Jr. 1933- *WhoAm 94*
Carter, James Sumter 1948- *WhoScEn 94*
Carter, Jandra D. 1948- *WhoBlA 94*
Carter, Jane *Who 94*
Carter, Jane Foster 1927- *WhoAmP 93, WhoFI 94, WhoWest 94*
Carter, Janice Joene 1948- *WhoFI 94, WhoWest 94*
Carter, Janis 1917- *WhoHol 92*
Carter, Jared *DrAPF 93*
Carter, Jefferson *DrAPF 93*
Carter, Jenny L. 1959- *WhoAmL 94*
Carter, Jerry Williams 1941- *WhoAmA 93*
Carter, Jesse Lee, Sr. 1926- *WhoBlA 94*
Carter, Jim *WhoHol 92*
Carter, Jimmy *NewYTBS 93 [port]*
Carter, Jimmy 1924- *IntWW 93, WhoAm 94, WhoAmP 93, WrDr 94*
Carter, Joan Elizabeth 1937- *WhoBlA 94*
Carter, JoAnne Williams 1935- *WhoBlA 94*
Carter, Joe 1960- *News 94-2 [port]*
Carter, John *DrAPF 93, WhoAmP 93*
Carter, John 1737-1781 *WhAmRev*
Carter, John 1745-1814 *WhAmRev*
Carter, John 1919- *IntWW 93, Who 94*
Carter, John (Alexander) 1921- *Who 94*
Carter, John Angus 1935- *WhoScEn 94*
Carter, John Avery 1924- *WhoAm 94*
Carter, John Bernard *IntWW 93N*
Carter, John Bernard 1934-1991 *WhAm 10*
Carter, John Charleton 1924- *WhoAm 94*
Carter, John Coles 1920- *WhoAm 94*
Carter, John Dale 1944- *WhoAm 94, WhoMW 93*
Carter, John Douglas 1946- *WhoAm 94, WhoAmL 94*
Carter, John E. 1950- *ConAu 141*
Carter, John Francis, II 1939- *WhoAmL 94*
Carter, John H. 1948- *WhoBlA 94*
Carter, John Loyd 1948- *WhoAmL 94*
Carter, John Mack 1928- *WhoAm 94*
Carter, John Phillip 1950- *WhoScEn 94*
Carter, John R. 1941- *WhoBlA 94*
Carter, John Swain 1950- *WhoAm 94*
Carter, John T(homas) 1921- *WrDr 94*
Carter, John Thomas 1921- *WhoAm 94*
Carter, Joseph 1918- *WhoAmP 93*
Carter, Joseph 1960- *WhoBlA 94*
Carter, Joseph, Jr. 1927- *WhoBlA 94*
Carter, Joseph C., III 1951- *WhoAmL 94*
Carter, Joseph Carlyle, Jr. 1927- *WhoAm 94*
Carter, Joseph Chris 1960- *WhoAm 94*
Carter, Joseph Edwin 1915- *WhoAm 94*
Carter, Joy Eaton 1923- *WhoWest 94*
Carter, Judy L. 1942- *WhoBlA 94*
Carter, Judy Langford 1950- *WhoMW 93*
Carter, Judy Sharon 1951- *WhoBlA 94*
Carter, June 1929- *WhoHol 92*
Carter, Katharine Tipton 1950- *WhoAmA 93*
Carter, Kathy Ellen 1955- *WhoMW 93*
Carter, Kelly Elizabeth 1962- *WhoBlA 94*
Carter, Kenneth 1933- *WhoAmP 93*
Carter, Kenneth Gregory 1959- *WhoBlA 94*
Carter, Kenneth Wayne 1954- *WhoBlA 94*
Carter, L. Philip 1939- *WhoScEn 94, WhoWest 94*
Carter, Lamore Joseph 1925- *WhoBlA 94*
Carter, Lark P. 1930- *WhoAm 94*
Carter, Larry Alexander 1940- *WhoFI 94, WhoWest 94*
Carter, Lawrence 1942- *WhoBlA 94*
Carter, Lawrence E., Sr. 1941- *WhoBlA 94*
Carter, Lawrence Robert 1936- *WhoBlA 94*
Carter, Leigh 1925- *IntWW 93*
Carter, Lemorie, Jr. 1944- *WhoBlA 94*
Carter, Lenora 1941- *WhoBlA 94*
Carter, Leslie d1921 *WhoHol 92*
Carter, Leslie, Mrs. d1937 *WhoHol 92*
Carter, Lewis Aaron, Jr. 1941- *WhoAm 94*
Carter, Lewis Winston 1920- *WhoBlA 94*
Carter, Lila Mae *WhoMW 93*
Carter, Lillian d1956 *WhoHol 92*
Carter, Lin 1930-1988 *EncSF 93*
Carter, Lonnie 1942- *ConDr 93*
Carter, Louise d1957 *WhoHol 92*
Carter, Lynda *IntMPA 94*
Carter, Lynda 1951- *WhoHol 92*
Carter, Lynda Cordoba *WhoHisp 94*
Carter, Lynne d1985 *WhoHol 92*
Carter, Margaret L. 1935- *WhoWest 94*
Carter, Margaret Louise 1935- *WhoAmP 93, WhoBlA 94*
Carter, Marian Elizabeth 1935- *WhoAmP 93*
Carter, Marilyn 1912- *WrDr 94*
Carter, Marion Elizabeth *WhoBlA 94*
Carter, Marshall Nichols 1940- *WhoAm 94, WhoFI 94*
Carter, Marshall S. d1993 *NewYTBS 93 [port]*
Carter, Marshall Sylvester d1993 *IntWW 93N*
Carter, Marshall Sylvester 1909- *IntWW 93*
Carter, Martin (Wylde) 1927- *BlkWr 2, ConAu 42NR, WrDr 94*
Carter, Martin Joseph 1930- *WhoBlA 94*
Carter, Mary *DrAPF 93, WhoAmA 93*
Carter, Mary 1947- *WhoMW 93*
Carter, Mary Eddie 1925- *WhoAm 94*
Carter, Mary Elizabeth Arkley *WhoWest 94*
Carter, Mary Louise 1937- *WhoBlA 94*
Carter, Mason Carlton 1933- *WhoAm 94*
Carter, Melvin Whitsett 1941- *WhoWest 94*
Carter, Michael 1960- *WhoBlA 94*
Carter, Michael Allen 1947- *WhoAm 94*
Carter, Michael Ray 1953- *WhoWest 94*
Carter, Michelle Adair 1944- *WhoAm 94*
Carter, Milton O., Sr. 1912- *WhoBlA 94*
Carter, Monte d1950 *WhoHol 92*
Carter, Mother Maybelle d1978 *WhoHol 92*
Carter, Nanette Carolyn 1954- *WhoAm 94, WhoAmA 93, WhoBlA 94*
Carter, Nell 1948- *IntMPA 94, WhoBlA 94, WhoHol 92*
Carter, Nellie Bell d1981 *WhoHol 92*
Carter, Neville Louis 1934- *WhoAm 94*
Carter, Nick *ConAu 43NR, EncSF 93, WrDr 94*
Carter, Nick 1924- *WrDr 94*
Carter, Nick 1941- *WrDr 94*
Carter, Nick 1942- *WrDr 94*
Carter, Nick 1951- *WrDr 94*
Carter, Olice Cleveland, Jr. 1955- *WhoScEn 94*
Carter, Ora Williams 1925- *WhoBlA 94*
Carter, Orwin L. 1942- *WhoAm 94*
Carter, Oscar Earl, Jr. 1922- *WhoBlA 94*
Carter, Pam *WhoAmP 93*
Carter, Pamela Lynn 1949- *WhoAm 94, WhoAmL 94, WhoBlA 94, WhoMW 93*
Carter, Patrick Henry, Jr. 1939- *WhoBlA 94*
Carter, Paul A(llen) 1926- *EncSF 93*
Carter, Paul R. 1940- *WhoAm 94, WhoFI 94*
Carter, Paul R. 1955- *WhoScEn 94*
Carter, Paul Richard 1922- *WhoAm 94*
Carter, Paul Thomas 1922- *WhoAmP 93*
Carter, Paula J. *WhoAmP 93*
Carter, Peers Lee 1916- *Who 94*
Carter, Percy A., Jr. 1929- *WhoBlA 94*
Carter, Perry W. 1960- *WhoBlA 94*
Carter, Peter 1929- *WrDr 94*
Carter, Peter Basil 1921- *Who 94*
Carter, Philip (David) 1927- *Who 94*
Carter, Philip W., Jr. 1941- *WhoBlA 94*
Carter, Phyllis Harden 1948- *WhoBlA 94*
Carter, Powell Frederick 1931- *WhoAm 94*
Carter, R.M.H. *EncSF 93*
Carter, Ray Morgan 1941- *WhoAmP 93*
Carter, Raymond Gene, Sr. 1936- *WhoBlA 94*
Carter, Raymond John 1935- *Who 94*
Carter, Rebecca Davilene 1932- *WhoAm 94, WhoScEn 94*
Carter, Regina Roberts 1962- *WhoScEn 94*
Carter, Reinald Willis 1932- *WhoFI 94*
Carter, Rex Lyle 1925- *WhoAmP 93*
Carter, Rhonda Lee 1958- *WhoMW 93*
Carter, Richard 1918- *WhoAm 94*
Carter, Richard (Henry Alwyn) 1935- *Who 94*
Carter, Richard Bert 1916- *WhoWest 94*
Carter, Richard Dennis 1949- *WhoAmL 94*
Carter, Richard Duane *WhoAm 94*
Carter, Richard Gerald, Jr. 1947- *WhoAmP 93*
Carter, Robert Alfred Copsey 1910- *Who 94*
Carter, Robert Cornelius 1917- *WhoAmP 93*
Carter, Robert Henry, III 1941- *WhoBlA 94*
Carter, Robert Lee 1917- *WhoAm 94, WhoAmL 94, WhoBlA 94*
Carter, Robert Lee 1954- *WhoFI 94, WhoMW 93*
Carter, Robert LeRoy 1918- *WhoMW 93*
Carter, Robert Louis, Jr. 1937- *WhoBlA 94*
Carter, Robert Philip, Sr. 1946- *WhoAmL 94*
Carter, Robert S. 1925- *WhoAmP 93*
Carter, Robert Spencer 1915- *WhoWest 94*
Carter, Robert T. 1938- *WhoBlA 94*
Carter, Robert Thompson 1937- *WhoBlA 94*
Carter, Robert Warren 1941-1989 *WhAm 10*
Carter, Robert William Bernard 1913- *Who 94*
Carter, Roberta Eccleston *WhoWest 94*
Carter, Robyn Janine 1961- *WhoMW 93*
Carter, Rodney Carl 1964- *WhoBlA 94*
Carter, Roger 1939- *ConAu 43NR*
Carter, Roger James 1942- *WhoMW 93*
Carter, Roger Richard 1962- *WhoAmL 94*
Carter, Roland 1924- *Who 94*
Carter, Romelia Mae 1934- *WhoBlA 94*
Carter, Ronald 1937- *WhoAm 94*
Carter, Ronald Louis 1926- *Who 94*
Carter, Ronald Martin, Sr. 1925- *WhoAm 94*
Carter, Rosalynn (Smith) 1927- *WrDr 94*
Carter, Rosalynn Smith 1927- *WhoAm 94*
Carter, Roscoe Owen, III 1946- *WhoScEn 94*
Carter, Roy Ernst, Jr. 1922- *WhoAm 94*
Carter, Rubin 1952- *WhoBlA 94*
Carter, Ruth Durley 1922- *WhoBlA 94*
Carter, Sally Jo Hamrick 1929- *WhoAmP 93*
Carter, Sam John 1943- *WhoAmA 93*
Carter, Sandra Lee 1943- *WhoMW 93*
Carter, Saralee Lessman 1951- *WhoAm 94*
Carter, Shari Elaine *DrAPF 93*
Carter, Shelby Henry, Jr. 1931- *WhoFI 94*
Carter, Stephaney Dawn 1962- *WhoMW 93*
Carter, Stephen Edward 1954- *WhoAmL 94*
Carter, Steven R(ay) 1942- *ConAu 141*
Carter, Susan D. 1949- *WhoAmP 93*
Carter, Susanne 1950- *ConAu 141*
Carter, T. K. 1956- *WhoHol 92*
Carter, Terry 1929- *WhoHol 92*
Carter, Theodore Ulysses 1931- *WhoBlA 94*
Carter, Thomas 1953- *WhoHol 92*
Carter, Thomas Allen 1935- *WhoBlA 94, WhoFI 94, WhoScEn 94*
Carter, Thomas Barton 1949- *WhoAmL 94*
Carter, Thomas Floyd, Jr. 1927- *WhoBlA 94*
Carter, Thomas Heyward, Jr. 1946- *WhoAmL 94*
Carter, Thomas Smith, Jr. 1921- *WhoAm 94, WhoFI 94, WhoWest 94*
Carter, Timothy *Who 94*
Carter, (John) Timothy 1944- *Who 94*
Carter, Tom 1947- *WrDr 94*
Carter, Tommy 1934- *WhoAmP 93*
Carter, Troy A. 1963- *WhoAmP 93, WhoBlA 94*
Carter, Warrick L. 1942- *WhoBlA 94*
Carter, Wendell Patrick 1966- *WhoBlA 94*
Carter, Weptanomah Washington 1937- *WhoBlA 94*
Carter, Wesley Byrd 1942- *WhoBlA 94*
Carter, Wilbur Lee, Jr. 1922- *WhoAm 94*
Carter, Wilford 1947- *WhoAmP 93*
Carter, Wilfred 1912- *Who 94*
Carter, Wilfred Wilson 1923- *WhoAm 94*
Carter, Will J. *WhoBlA 94*
Carter, William (Oscar) 1905- *Who 94*
Carter, William Beverly, III 1947- *WhoBlA 94*
Carter, William Caswell 1917- *WhoAm 94*
Carter, William George, III 1944- *WhoAm 94, WhoWest 94*
Carter, William Hodding, Jr. 1907-1972 *AmSocL*
Carter, William Hodding, III 1935- *WhoAmP 93*
Carter, William Joseph 1949- *WhoAmL 94*
Carter, William Lacy 1925- *WhoAmP 93*
Carter, William Lynn 1936-1988 *WhAm 10*
Carter, William Nicholas 1912- *Who 94*
Carter, William Thomas, Jr. 1944- *WhoBlA 94*
Carter, William Walton 1921- *WhoAm 94*
Carter, Willie A. 1909- *WhoBlA 94*
Carter, Wilmoth Annette *WhoBlA 94*
Carter, Winstol Dean, Jr. 1954- *WhoAmL 94*
Carter, Yvonne P. 1939- *WhoBlA 94*
Carter, Yvonne Pickering 1939- *WhoAmA 93*
Carter, Zachary W. *WhoAmL 94*
Carteret, Anna 1942- *WhoHol 92*
Carteret, Philip 1733-1796 *WhWE*
Carter-Harrison, Paul *BlkWr 2*
Carter-Jones, Lewis 1920- *Who 94*
Carter-Ruck, Peter Frederick 1914- *IntWW 93, Who 94*
Cartey, Wilfred 1931-1992 *AnObit 1992*
Cartey, Wilfred (George Onslow) 1931-1992 *BlkWr 2*
Cartey, Wilfred G. O. 1931-1992 *WhoBlA 94N*
Cartey, Wilfred George Onslow 1931-1992 *WhAm 10*
Carthan, Eddie James 1949- *WhoBlA 94*
Carthaus, James Arthur 1940- *WhoAm 94*
Carthen, Billy Burton 1950- *WhoFI 94*
Carthen, Carlos J. 1957- *WhoMW 93*
Carthen, John, Jr. *WhoBlA 94*
Carthon, Maurice 1961- *WhoBlA 94*
Carthy, Margaret 1911-1992 *WhAm 10*
Cartier, Brian Evans 1950- *WhoAm 94, WhoFI 94*
Cartier, Carol Jean McMaster 1954- *WhoWest 94*
Cartier, Celine Paule 1930- *WhoAm 94*
Cartier, Edd 1914- *EncSF 93*
Cartier, Jacques 1491-1557 *WhWE [port]*
Cartier, Marie *DrAPF 93*
Cartier, Rudolph 1904- *Who 94*
Cartier, Thomas Nicholas 1950- *WhoMW 93*
Cartier, Xam Wilson 1949?- *BlkWr 2*
Cartier-Bresson, Henri 1908- *IntWW 93, Who 94*
Cartland, Barbara 1901- *WhoAm 94*
Cartland, Barbara 1904- *BlmGWL*
Cartland, Barbara (Hamilton) 1901- *IntWW 93, Who 94, WrDr 94*
Cartland, George (Barrington) 1912- *Who 94*
Cartledge, Bryan (George) 1931- *Who 94*
Cartledge, Bryan George 1931- *IntWW 93*
Cartledge, Raymond Eugene 1929- *WhoAm 94, WhoFI 94*
Cartlidge, Arthur J. 1942- *WhoBlA 94*
Cartlidge, William 1942- *IntMPA 94*
Cartmell, Helen 1923- *WhoAmA 93*
Cartmell, James V. 1938- *WhoScEn 94*
Cartmell, Nathaniel Madison, III 1951- *WhoAm 94*
Cartmell, Vinton Aikins 1925- *WhoAm 94*
Cartmill, Cleve 1908-1964 *EncSF 93*
Cartmill, George Edwin, Jr. 1918- *WhoAm 94*
Cartmill, Matt 1943- *WhoAm 94*
Cartner, Theodore Valentine 1949- *WhoMW 93*
Carto, Willis Allison 1926- *WhoFI 94*
Carton, Laurence Alfred 1918- *WhoAm 94*
Carton, Pauline d1974 *WhoHol 92*
Cartoun, Myer Fred 1898- *WhAm 10*
Cartright, Peter *WhoHol 92*
Carttiss, Michael Reginald Harry 1938- *Who 94*
Cartun, Lois B. 1933- *WhoMW 93*
Cartwright, Alton Stuart 1922- *WhoAm 94*
Cartwright, Angela 1952- *WhoHol 92*
Cartwright, Bill 1957- *WhoBlA 94*
Cartwright, Brian Grant 1947- *WhoFI 94*
Cartwright, Carol Ann 1941- *WhoMW 93*
Cartwright, Carole B. 1940- *WhoBlA 94*
Cartwright, Carroll L. *See* Cartwright, Constance B. & Cartwright, Carroll L. *WhoAmA 93*
Cartwright, Carroll L. *WhoAmA 93*
Cartwright, Charles Nelson 1933- *WhoAm 94*
Cartwright, Constance B. & Cartwright, Carroll L. *WhoAmA 93*
Cartwright, (Edward) David 1920- *Who 94*
Cartwright, David Edgar 1926- *Who 94*
Cartwright, Edmund 1743-1823 *WorInv*
Cartwright, Frederick *Who 94*
Cartwright, (William) Frederick 1906- *Who 94*
Cartwright, Harry 1919- *Who 94*
Cartwright, Howard Eugene 1924- *WhoAm 94*
Cartwright, James Elgin 1943- *WhoBlA 94*
Cartwright, Jim 1958- *ConDr 93*
Cartwright, John Cameron 1933- *Who 94*
Cartwright, Jon Kyle 1960- *WhoFI 94*
Cartwright, Judith Ellen 1941- *WhoMW 93*
Cartwright, Keros 1934- *WhoMW 93, WhoScEn 94*
Cartwright, Lynn *WhoHol 92*
Cartwright, Marguerite Dorsey *WhoBlA 94*
Cartwright, Mary Lou 1923- *WhoAm 94*
Cartwright, Mary Lucy 1900- *IntWW 93, Who 94*
Cartwright, Peter 1785-1872 *DcAmReB 2*
Cartwright, Richard Fox 1913- *Who 94*
Cartwright, Robert William 1945- *WhoMW 93*
Cartwright, Roscoe Conklin 1919- *AfrAmG [port]*
Cartwright, Roy R. *WhoAmA 93*
Cartwright, Silvia (Rose) 1943- *Who 94*
Cartwright, Veronica 1949- *IntMPA 94*

Casey, Barbara Ann Perea 1951- WhoHisp 94
Casey, Bernard J. 1942- WhoAm 94, WhoAmL 94
Casey, Bernard Terry 1939- BlkWr 2
Casey, Bernie BlkWr 2
Casey, Bernie 1939- IntMPA 94
Casey, Bernie 1940- WhoHol 92
Casey, Beverly Dionne 1953- WhoFI 94
Casey, Carey Walden, Sr. 1955- WhoBlA 94
Casey, Charles Francis 1927- WhoAm 94, WhoFI 94
Casey, Charles Philip 1942- WhoAm 94, WhoMW 93
Casey, Clifton G. 1924- WhoBlA 94
Casey, Coleman Hampton 1947- WhoAmL 94
Casey, Dan 1938- WhoAmP 93
Casey, Deb DrAPF 93
Casey, Denette C. 1954- WhoWest 94
Casey, Dolores d1945 WhoHol 92
Casey, Eamonn 1927- IntWW 93, Who 94
Casey, Edmund C. WhoBlA 94
Casey, Edward Dennis 1931- WhoAm 94
Casey, Edward Paul 1930- WhoAm 94
Casey, Elizabeth Temple 1901-1990 WhoAmA 93N
Casey, Ethel Laughlin 1926- WhoAm 94
Casey, Frank Leslie 1935- WhoBlA 94
Casey, G. Nicholas, Jr. 1953- WhoAmL 94
Casey, George Edward, Jr. 1946- WhoFI 94
Casey, Gerard William 1942- WhoAm 94
Casey, Gladys GayLL
Casey, Horace Craig, Jr. 1934- WhoAm 94
Casey, Jack d1956 WhoHol 92
Casey, Jacqueline Shepard 1927- WhoAmA 93
Casey, James G., Sr. 1917- WhoAmP 93
Casey, James M. 1949- WhoAmP 93
Casey, Jeanne Sullivan 1959- WhoAmL 94
Casey, John DrAPF 93
Casey, John (Dudley) 1939- WrDr 94
Casey, John Alexander 1945- WhoAm 94, WhoAmL 94
Casey, John Dudley 1939- WhoAm 94
Casey, John Joseph 1918- WhoAm 94
Casey, John K. 1933- WhoAm 94, WhoFI 94
Casey, John P. 1920- WhoAm 94
Casey, John Patrick 1928- WhoAm 94
Casey, John Thayer 1931- WhoAmA 93, WhoWest 94
Casey, John Thomas 1945- WhoAm 94
Casey, Joseph Edward 1913- WhoAmP 93
Casey, Joseph F. 1914- WhoBlA 94
Casey, Joseph T. 1931- WhoAm 94, WhoFI 94, WhoWest 94
Casey, Karen Anne 1955- WhoFI 94
Casey, Keith Allen 1961- WhoFI 94
Casey, Kenneth d1965 WhoHol 92
Casey, Kenneth Lyman 1935- WhoAm 94
Casey, Kevin 1940- WrDr 94
Casey, Kevin Robert 1957- WhoAmL 94
Casey, Lawrence 1941- WhoHol 92
Casey, Lawrence W. 1949- WhoAmP 93
Casey, Leslie d1942 WhoHol 92
Casey, Lew J. d1942 WhoHol 92
Casey, Linda M. WrDr 94
Casey, Lloyd Aloysius 1926- WhoAmP 93
Casey, Maria Terese 1963- WhoAmL 94
Casey, Mark Evan 1954- WhoWest 94
Casey, Mary Ann 1949- WhoAm 94, WhoAmP 93
Casey, Maureen Therese 1953- WhoAmL 94
Casey, Maurice (Eugene) 1923- Who 94
Casey, Michael DrAPF 93
Casey, Michael 1947- WrDr 94
Casey, Michael Bernard 1928- IntWW 93, Who 94
Casey, Michael Kirkland 1940- WhoAm 94
Casey, Michael P. 1943- WhoAmL 94
Casey, Michael Vince 1927- Who 94
Casey, Murray Joseph 1936- WhoFI 94, WhoMW 93, WhoScEn 94
Casey, Patricia Carolyn 1936- WhoWest 94
Casey, Patrick Anthony 1944- WhoAmL 94, WhoWest 94
Casey, Patrick Joseph 1913- Who 94
Casey, Patrick Joseph 1947- WhoAmL 94
Casey, Paul C. 1961- WhoAmP 93
Casey, Paul Foley 1942- WhoMW 93
Casey, Paula Jean 1951- WhoAmL 94
Casey, Phillip Earl 1942- WhoAm 94
Casey, Raymond 1917- Who 94
Casey, Raymond Richard 1935- WhoAm 94
Casey, Richard EncSF 93
Casey, Robert H. 1946- WhoMW 93
Casey, Robert J. 1923- WhoAm 94
Casey, Robert K. 1931- WhoAmP 93
Casey, Robert P. 1932- IntWW 93, WhoAm 94, WhoAmP 93
Casey, Robert Reisch 1946- WhoAm 94
Casey, Ronald Bruce 1951- WhoAm 94
Casey, Stella (Katherine) 1924- Who 94
Casey, Steven C. 1952- WhoAmP 93
Casey, Steven Michael 1952- WhoScEn 94
Casey, Stuart d1948 WhoHol 92
Casey, Sue WhoHol 92
Casey, Thomas A. 1931- WhoAmP 93
Casey, Thomas Clark 1929- WhoWest 94
Casey, Thomas J. 1952- WhoAm 94
Casey, Tim 1947- WhoAmA 93
Casey, Timothy John 1951- WhoAmP 93
Casey, Warren Peter 1935-1988 WhAm 10
Casey, William R., Jr. 1944- WhoAmP 93
Casey, William Robert, Jr. 1944- WhoAm 94
Casgar, Timothy R. 1941- WhoAmL 94
Cash, Alan Sherwin 1938- WhoMW 93
Cash, Anthony 1933- WrDr 94
Cash, Arlene Marie 1955- WhoBlA 94
Cash, Bettye Joyce 1936- WhoBlA 94
Cash, Carol Vivian 1929- WhoAm 94
Cash, Catherine 1939- ConAu 141
Cash, Claud V. 1935- WhoAmP 93
Cash, Francis Winford 1942- WhoAm 94
Cash, Frank Errette, Jr. 1921- WhoAm 94
Cash, Gerald (Christopher) 1917- Who 94
Cash, Gerald Christopher 1917- IntWW 93
Cash, J. R. 1932- IntWW 93
Cash, James Ireland, Jr. 1947- WhoBlA 94
Cash, John David 1936- Who 94
Cash, John R. ConAu 142
Cash, Johnny 1932- ConAu 142, WhoAm 94, WhoHol 92
Cash, Joseph L. WhoIns 94
Cash, June Carter 1929- WhoAm 94
Cash, LaVerne 1956- WhoScEn 94
Cash, Pamela J. 1948- WhoBlA 94
Cash, Pat 1965- IntWW 93
Cash, R. D. 1942- WhoWest 94
Cash, Robert Joseph 1955- WhoAmL 94
Cash, Rosalind 1938- IntMPA 94, WhoHol 92
Cash, Rosanne 1955- WhoAm 94
Cash, Roy Don 1942- WhoAm 94, WhoFI 94
Cash, William F. d1963 WhoHol 92
Cash, William L., Jr. 1915- WhoBlA 94
Cash, William McKinley 1930- WhoAm 94
Cash, William Nigel Paul 1940- Who 94
Cashatt, Charles Alvin 1929- WhoWest 94
Cashdan, Linda 1942- WrDr 94
Cashel, Thomas William 1930- WhoAm 94
Cashel And Emly, Archbishop of 1939- Who 94
Cashel And Ossory, Bishop of 1926- Who 94
Cashen, Henry Christopher, II 1939- WhoAm 94
Cashen, J. Frank WhoAm 94
Cashen, Joseph Larry 1942- WhoAmL 94
Cashier, Isidore d1948 WhoHol 92
Cashill, Thomas J. 1931- WhoAmP 93
Cashin, Edward Joseph 1927- WhoAm 94
Cashin, Francis Joseph 1924- WhoFI 94
Cashin, Richard Marshall 1924- WhoAm 94
Cashion, Bonnie Bingham 1926- WhoFI 94
Cashion, Marvin J. 1945- WhoIns 94
Cashion, Robert Nesbit 1947- WhoAm 94
Cashion, Shelley Jean 1955- WhoAmL 94
Cashman, David DrAPF 93
Cashman, David J. WhoAmP 93
Cashman, Edmund Joseph, Jr. 1936- WhoAm 94, WhoFI 94
Cashman, Gideon 1929- WhoAmL 94
Cashman, Harry d1912 WhoHol 92
Cashman, John Anthony 1950- WhoAmP 93
Cashman, John Prescott 1930- Who 94
Cashman, John W. 1923- WhoAm 94
Cashman, Michael Richard 1926- WhoWest 94
Cashman, Michael W., Sr. 1949- WhoIns 94
Cashman, Robert J. 1906-1988 WhAm 10
Cashman, William Elliott 1952- WhoFI 94
Cashman, William James, Jr. 1937- WhoAm 94
Cashmore, Patsy Joy 1943- WhoAm 94
Cashmore, Roger John 1944- Who 94
Cashorali, Peter DrAPF 93
Cash-Rhodes, Winifred E. WhoBlA 94
Casiano, Americo DrAPF 93
Casiano, Americo, Jr. 1951- WhoHisp 94
Casiano, Luz Nereida 1950- WhoHisp 94
Casiano, Manuel A., Jr. 1931- WhoHisp 94
Casida, John Edward 1929- WhoAm 94
Casida, Kati 1931- WhoAmA 93
Casiello, Nicholas, Jr. 1953- WhoAmL 94
Casilio, Joan Erica 1962- WhoAmL 94
Casilla, Robert 1959- SmATA 75 [port]
Casillas, Lucius 1926- WhoHisp 94
Casillas, Mark 1953- WhoAm 94, WhoAmL 94, WhoWest 94
Casillas, Robert Patrick 1962- WhoScEn 94
Casimir, Golda d1976 WhoHol 92
Casimir, Hendrik Brugt Gerhard 1909- IntWW 93
Casimiro, Jorge L. 1953- WhoHisp 94
Casimiro, Luis WhoHisp 94
Casinelli, Joseph L. 1937- WhoAmP 93
Casino, Joanne 1951- WhoAm 94
Casken, John (Arthur) 1949- NewGrDO
Caskey, Bethany Anne 1950- WhoMW 93
Caskey, Harold Leroy 1938- WhoAmP 93
Caskey, J. Thomas 1944- WhoAmL 94
Caskey, Priscilla C. 1946- WhoAmL 94
Caskey, William Joslin 1949- WhoAm 94
Caskie, William Wirt 1945- WhoFI 94, WhoWest 94
Caslavska, Vera 1942- IntWW 93
Caslin, Jean WhoAmA 93
Caslow, Patricia Norine 1934- WhoMW 93
Casner, Andrew James 1907-1990 WhAm 10
Casner, Bruce Morgan 1949- WhoAmP 93
Casner, Truman Snell 1933- WhoAm 94
Casnoff, Phillip WhoHol 92
Caso, Gasper 1933- WhoAm 94
Caso, Ralph George 1917- WhoAmP 93
Caso, Ronald George 1936- WhoAm 94
Cason, Barbara d1990 WhoHol 92
Cason, David, Jr. 1923- WhoAmP 93, WhoBlA 94
Cason, Gary Carlton 1943- WhoAmP 93
Cason, John L. d1961 WhoHol 92
Cason, Joseph L. 1939- WhoBlA 94
Cason, Marilynn Jean 1943- WhoBlA 94
Cason, Neal Martin 1938- WhoAm 94
Cason, Udell, Jr. 1940- WhoBlA 94
Casona, Alejandro 1903-1965 IntDcT 2, NewGrDO
Casorati, Francesco 1934- IntWW 93
Casoria, Giuseppe 1908- IntWW 93
Casorri, Ferdinando c. 1730-1792? NewGrDO
Caspar, Donald Louis Dvorak 1927- WhoAm 94, WhoScEn 94
Caspar, Horst d1952 WhoHol 92
Caspe, Naomi 1954- WhoWest 94
Casper, Anthony Albert 1958- WhoMW 93
Casper, Banjo 1937- WhoBlA 94
Casper, Barry Michael 1939- WhoAm 94
Casper, Charles B. 1952- WhoAm 94
Casper, Eric Michael 1959- WhoAmL 94
Casper, Gary Steven 1958- WhoMW 93
Casper, Gerhard NewYTBS 93 [port]
Casper, Gerhard 1937- WhoAm 94, WhoAmL 94, WhoWest 94
Casper, Lawrence A. 1962- WhoAmL 94
Casper, Leonard (Ralph) 1923- WrDr 94
Casper, Leonard Ralph 1923- WhoAm 94
Casper, Linda Ty BlmGWL
Casper, Patricia A. 1959- WhoScEn 94
Casper, Paul Alexander 1947- WhoAm 94
Casper, Richard Henry 1950- WhoAm 94
Casper, Robert J. 1943- WhoIns 94
Casper, Stewart Michael 1953- WhoAmL 94
Casper, Susan 1947- EncSF 93
Casper, William Earl 1931- IntWW 93
Caspersen, Finn Michael Westby 1941- WhoAm 94, WhoFI 94
Caspersen, O(laus) W(estby) 1896- WhAm 10
Caspersen, Ralph Frederick 1942- WhoAmL 94
Caspersen, Sven Lars 1935- IntWW 93
Caspy, Barbara Jane 1945- WhoWest 94
Cass, Bertrand M. 1944- WhoAmL 94
Cass, Bill 1954- WhoAmA 93
Cass, David WhoHol 92
Cass, David 1937- WhoAm 94, WhoFI 94
Cass, Edward Geoffrey 1916- Who 94
Cass, Francis d1927 WhoHol 92
Cass, Geoffrey (Arthur) 1932- Who 94
Cass, Geoffrey Arthur 1932- IntWW 93
Cass, George Frank 1939- WhoAm 94, WhoIns 94
Cass, George L. 1940- WhoAm 94
Cass, Guy d1959 WhoHol 92
Cass, James (Michael) 1915-1992 ConAu 140
Cass, Joan E(velyn) WrDr 94
Cass, John 1925- Who 94
Cass, John (Patrick) 1909- Who 94
Cass, Leslie d1987 WhoHol 92
Cass, Lou d1942 WhoHol 92
Cass, Maurice d1954 WhoHol 92
Cass, Millard 1916- WhoAm 94
Cass, Neil Earl 1952- WhoAm 94
Cass, Peggy 1924- IntMPA 94
Cass, Peggy 1925- WhoHol 92
Cass, Ray WhoHol 92
Cass, Richard W. 1946- WhoAmL 94
Cass, Robert Michael 1945- WhoAmL 94, WhoFI 94
Cass, Ronald Andrew 1949- WhoAm 94, WhoAmL 94
Cass, William F. WhoAmP 93
Cass, Zoe 1916- WrDr 94
Cassab, Judy 1920- IntWW 93
Cassady, Ann R. 1927- WhoAmP 93
Cassady, Carolyn (Elizabeth Robinson) 1923- WrDr 94
Cassady, James d1928 WhoHol 92
Cassady, Joseph Rudolph, III 1959- WhoAm 94
Cassady, Kenneth Edward 1948- WhoMW 93
Cassady, Marsh DrAPF 93
Cassady, Neal 1926-1968 ConAu 141
Cassady, Neely WhoAmP 93
Cassady, Philip Earl 1940- WhoScEn 94
Cassady, Sed Onstott d1980 WhoHol 92
Cassagne, Gilbert Michael 1956- WhoFI 94
Cassanego, Michael John 1950- WhoIns 94
Cassani, Giuseppe fl. 1700-1728 NewGrDO
Cassani, Vincenzo 1677?- NewGrDO
Cassanmagnago-Cerretti, Maria-Luisa 1940- WhoWomW 91
Cassar, Francis Felix Anthony 1934- Who 94
Cassar, Joseph 1918- IntWW 93
Cassara, Frank WhoAmA 93
Cassara, Frank 1913- WhoAm 94
Cassat, David Berryhill 1894- WhAm 10
Cassatt, Mary Stevenson 1844-1926 AmCulL
Cassavetes, John d1989 WhoHol 92
Cassavetes, Katherine d1983 WhoHol 92
Cassavetes, Nick 1959- WhoHol 92
Casseday, John Herbert 1934- WhoScEn 94
Cassedy, Edward Spencer, Jr. 1927- WhoScEn 94
Cassedy, James H(iggins) 1919- WrDr 94
Cassedy, Sylvia 1930-1989 SmATA 77 [port], TwCYAW
Cassel Who 94
Cassel, Alvin I. IntMPA 94
Cassel, Christine Karen 1945- WhoAm 94, WhoScEn 94
Cassel, Harold (Felix) 1916- Who 94
Cassel, Herbert William 1931- WhoAm 94
Cassel, Jean-Pierre 1932- IntMPA 94, IntWW 93, WhoHol 92
Cassel, John Elden 1934- WhoFI 94
Cassel, John Harmon WhoAmA 93N
Cassel, Marwin Shepard 1925- WhoAmL 94
Cassel, Russell N 1911- WrDr 94
Cassel, Seymour 1935- WhoHol 92
Cassel, Seymour 1937- IntMPA 94
Cassel, Sid d1960 WhoHol 92
Cassel, Timothy Felix Harold 1942- Who 94
Cassel, (John) Walter 1910- NewGrDO
Cassell, Alan WhoHol 92
Cassell, Beverly 1936- WhoAmA 93
Cassell, Eric Jonathan 1928- WhoAm 94
Cassell, Frank 1930- Who 94
Cassell, Frank Hyde 1916- WhoAm 94
Cassell, Joan 1929- WrDr 94
Cassell, Kay Ann 1941- WhoAm 94
Cassell, Michael Robert 1946- Who 94
Cassell, Wally WhoHol 92
Cassell, Wanda A. 1937- WhoAmP 93
Cassell, William Comyn 1934- WhoAm 94
Cassell, William Walter 1917- WhoAm 94
Cassella, William Nathan, Jr. 1920- WhoAm 94
Casselli, Henry C., Jr. 1946- WhoAmA 93
Casselli, Henry Calvin, Jr. 1946- WhoAm 94
Cassells, Cyrus DrAPF 93
Casselman, Barry DrAPF 93
Casselman, William E., II 1941- WhoAm 94, WhoAmL 94
Cassels, Alan 1929- WrDr 94
Cassels, Archibald James H. 1907- HisDcKW
Cassels, J(ohn) W(illiam) S(cott) 1922- ConAu 142
Cassels, (Archibald) James (Halkett) 1907- IntWW 93, Who 94
Cassels, James Macdonald 1924- IntWW 93, Who 94
Cassels, John (Seton) 1928- Who 94
Cassels, John William Scott 1922- IntWW 93, Who 94
Cassels, Peter 1949- IntWW 93
Cassels, Simon (Alastair Cassillis) 1928- Who 94
Cassen, Robert Harvey 1935- Who 94
Cassens, Nicholas, Jr. 1948- WhoWest 94
Cassens, Robert Gene 1937- WhoAm 94, WhoMW 93
Casserly, Charley 1949- WhoAm 94

Casserly, James Lund 1951- *WhoAm 94*
Casserly, Sandra Racine 1932- *WhoMW 93*
Cassesse, Andrew 1972- *WhoHol 92*
Cassetta, Sebastian Ernest 1948- *WhoScEn 94*
Cassetta, William M. 1949- *WhoAmL 94*
Cassette, Robert Louis, Sr. 1928- *WhoAmP 93*
Casseus, Frantz 1915-1993 *NewYTBS 93*
Cassian, Nina 1924- *BlmGWL, ConWorW 93*
Cassibry, Fred James 1918- *WhoAm 94*
Cassiday, Karen Lynn 1960- *WhoMW 93*
Cassidi, (Arthur) Desmond 1925- *Who 94*
Cassidy, Adrian Clyde 1916- *WhoFI 94*
Cassidy, Bill d1943 *WhoHol 92*
Cassidy, Bryan Michael Deece 1934- *Who 94*
Cassidy, Carl Eugene 1924- *WhoAm 94*
Cassidy, Charles Michael Ardagh 1936- *IntWW 93*
Cassidy, Charles Philip 1937- *WhoWest 94*
Cassidy, Christine *DrAPF 93*
Cassidy, David 1950- *IntMPA 94, WhoHol 92*
Cassidy, David C(harles) 1945- *ConAu 140*
Cassidy, David Michael 1954- *WhoAmL 94*
Cassidy, DeVallo Francis 1937- *WhoWest 94*
Cassidy, Donald Lawrence 1933- *WhoWest 94*
Cassidy, Ed d1968 *WhoHol 92*
Cassidy, Edward *Who 94*
Cassidy, (Idris) Edward 1924- *Who 94*
Cassidy, Eugene Patrick 1940- *WhoMW 93*
Cassidy, Francis E. 1928- *WhoFI 94*
Cassidy, Frank d1978 *WhoHol 92*
Cassidy, Frederic Gomes 1907- *WhoMW 93, WrDr 94*
Cassidy, George Henry 1942- *Who 94*
Cassidy, George Thomas 1939- *WhoFI 94*
Cassidy, Herbert 1935- *Who 94*
Cassidy, J. Peter, Jr. 1942- *WhoAmL 94*
Cassidy, Jack d1976 *WhoHol 92*
Cassidy, James Edward 1928- *WhoScEn 94*
Cassidy, James Edward 1945- *WhoAm 94*
Cassidy, James Joseph 1916- *WhoAm 94, WhoFI 94*
Cassidy, James Mark 1942- *WhoFI 94, WhoMW 93*
Cassidy, Joanna 1944- *IntMPA 94, WhoHol 92*
Cassidy, John Francis, Jr. 1943- *WhoScEn 94*
Cassidy, John Harold 1925- *WhoAm 94, WhoAmL 94*
Cassidy, John Lemont 1934- *WhoFI 94, WhoMW 93*
Cassidy, Joseph *Who 94*
Cassidy, Lee M. 1933- *WhoAmP 93*
Cassidy, Margaret Carol *WhoAmA 93*
Cassidy, Michael 1936- *WrDr 94*
Cassidy, Michael Edward 1955- *WhoAmP 93*
Cassidy, Patrick 1961- *IntMPA 94*
Cassidy, Patrick 1962- *WhoHol 92*
Cassidy, Patrick Edward 1937- *WhoAm 94*
Cassidy, Richard Arthur 1944- *WhoWest 94*
Cassidy, Richard Thomas 1916- *WhoAm 94*
Cassidy, Robert Charles, Jr. 1946- *WhoAm 94*
Cassidy, Robert Joseph 1930- *WhoAm 94, WhoFI 94*
Cassidy, Robert Valentine 1930- *WhoAmP 93*
Cassidy, Samuel H. *WhoWest 94*
Cassidy, Samuel H. 1950- *WhoAmP 93*
Cassidy, Shaun 1958- *IntMPA 94, WhoHol 92*
Cassidy, Sheila Anne 1937- *IntWW 93, Who 94*
Cassidy, Ted d1979 *WhoHol 92*
Cassidy, Victor Monod 1940- *WhoMW 93*
Cassidy, William Arthur 1928- *WhoAm 94*
Cassidy, William Dunnigan, III 1941- *WhoFI 94*
Cassidy, William J., Jr. 1946- *WhoAmL 94*
Cassiers, Juan 1931- *IntWW 93, WhoAm 94*
Cassil, Dorothy d1983 *WhoHol 92*
Cassill, Herbert Carroll 1928- *WhoAm 94, WhoAmA 93*
Cassill, Kay *DrAPF 93*
Cassill, R. V. *DrAPF 93*
Cassill, R(onald) V(erlin) 1919- *WrDr 94*
Cassill, Ronald Verlin 1919- *WhoAm 94*
Cassillis, Earl of 1956- *Who 94*
Cassilly, Richard 1927- *IntWW 93, NewGrDO, Who 94, WhoAm 94*
Cassimatis, Emanuel Andrew 1926- *WhoAmL 94*
Cassimatis, Peter John 1928- *WhoAm 94*
Cassin, James Richard 1933- *WhoMW 93*
Cassin, Maxine *DrAPF 93*
Cassin, William Bourke 1931- *WhAm 10*
Cassinelli, Claudio d1985 *WhoHol 92*
Cassinelli, Dolores d1984 *WhoHol 92*
Cassinelli, Joseph Patrick 1940- *WhoAm 94, WhoMW 93*
Cassini, Giovanni Domenico 1625-1712 *WorScD*
Cassini, Oleg Lolewski 1913- *WhoAm 94*
Cassirer, Aurora 1951- *WhoAmL 94*
Cassirer, Claude 1921- *WhoAmP 93*
Cassirer, Fritz 1871-1926 *NewGrDO*
Cassirer, Henry R. 1911- *IntWW 93*
Cassirer, Nadine *Who 94*
Cassis, Glenn Albert 1951- *WhoBlA 94*
Cassity, Turner *DrAPF 93*
Cassity, (Allen) Turner 1929- *WrDr 94*
Cassling, Donald Roger 1950- *WhoAm 94, WhoAmL 94*
Cassman, Frederick Stanley 1925- *WhoAmL 94*
Cassman, Marvin 1936- *WhoAm 94*
Casson, Andrew J. *WhoScEn 94*
Casson, Ann d1990 *WhoHol 92*
Casson, Francois Dollier De *WhWE*
Casson, Hugh (Maxwell) 1910- *Who 94*
Casson, Hugh (Maxwell), Sir 1910- *WrDr 94*
Casson, Hugh Maxwell 1910- *IntWW 93*
Casson, Joseph Edward 1943- *WhoAm 94*
Casson, Lewis d1969 *WhoHol 92*
Casson, Louis d1950 *WhoHol 92*
Casson, Margaret MacDonald 1913- *Who 94*
Casson, Mark Christopher 1945- *Who 94*
Casson, Michael *Who 94*
Casson, (Frederick) Michael 1925- *Who 94*
Casson, Richard Frederick 1939- *WhoAmL 94, WhoFI 94*
Cassoni, Vittorio d1992 *IntWW 93N*
Casstevens, Bill 1928- *WhoAmP 93*
Casstevens, Kay *WhoAmP 93*
Casstevens, Thomas William 1937- *WrDr 94*
Cassutt, Michael 1954- *EncSF 93*
Cassyd, Syd 1908- *WhoAmA 93*
Cast, Anita Hursh 1939- *WhoMW 93*
Castagna, Bruna 1905-1983 *NewGrDO*
Castagna, Joe d1970 *WhoHol 92*
Castagna, William John 1924- *WhoAm 94, WhoAmL 94*
Castagnede, Bernard Roger 1956- *WhoScEn 94*
Castagnetta, Grace Sharp 1912- *WhoAm 94*
Castagnetto, Perry Michael 1959- *WhoFI 94, WhoWest 94*
Castain, Ralph Henri 1954- *WhoScEn 94, WhoWest 94*
Castaing, Raimond Bernard Rene 1921- *IntWW 93*
Castaldi, David Lawrence 1940- *WhoAm 94*
Castan, Fran *DrAPF 93*
Castaneda, Aldo Ricardo 1930- *WhoHisp 94*
Castaneda, Antonia I. *WhoHisp 94*
Castañeda, Blas 1949- *WhoHisp 94*
Castaneda, Carlos 1925- *WhoHisp 94*
Castaneda, Carlos 1931- *WhoAm 94, WrDr 94*
Castaneda, Hector-Neri 1924-1991 *WhAm 10*
Castañeda, James Agustín 1933- *WhoHisp 94*
Castaneda, Jorge 1921- *IntWW 93*
Castaneda, Manuel R. 1948- *WhoHisp 94*
Castaneda, Mario 1954- *WhoScEn 94*
Castañeda, Martha *WhoHisp 94*
Castañeda, Octavio Emilio, Jr. 1960- *WhoHisp 94*
Castaneda, Omar S. *DrAPF 93*
Castaneda, Omar S. 1954- *WrDr 94*
Castaneda, Omar Sigfrido 1954- *WhoWest 94*
Castaneda, Oswaldo 1944- *WhoHisp 94*
Castaneda-Cornejo, Ricardo Guillermo 1938- *IntWW 93*
Castaneira Colon, Rafael 1936- *WhoAmP 93, WhoHisp 94*
Castanes, James Christopher 1951- *WhoScEn 94*
Castang, Veronica d1988 *WhoHol 92*
Castanis, Muriel (Julia Brunner) 1926- *WhoAmA 93*
Castano, Elvira 1929- *WhoAmA 93*
Castano, Giovanni 1896- *WhoAmA 93N*
Castano, Gregory Joseph 1929- *WhoAmL 94*
Castañón-Williams, Maria Isela 1949- *WhoHisp 94*
Castanuela, Elio *WhoHisp 94*
Castañuela, Mary Helen 1950- *WhoHisp 94*
Castberg, Eileen Sue 1946- *WhoWest 94*
Castedo, Elena *DrAPF 93*
Castedo, Elena 1937- *WhoHisp 94*
Casteel, Charles L. 1948- *WhoAmL 94*
Casteel, Cheryl Theodora 1955- *WhoWest 94*
Casteel, Mark Allen 1960- *WhoScEn 94*
Casteen, John T., III 1943- *IntWW 93, WhoAm 94*
Casteix, Michael John 1952- *WhoAm 94*
Castel, Albert Edward 1928- *WhoAm 94*
Castel, Gerard Joseph 1934- *WhoScEn 94*
Castel, Jean Gabriel 1928- *WhoAm 94*
Castel, John Christopher 1954- *WhoFI 94*
Castel, Jose fl. 1761-1781 *NewGrDO*
Castel, Lou *WhoHol 92*
Castel, Nico 1935- *WhoAm 94*
Castel, P. Kevin 1950- *WhoAm 94, WhoAmL 94*
Castelaz, Patrick Frank 1952- *WhoScEn 94*
Castele, Theodore John 1928- *WhoAm 94, WhoMW 93*
Casteleyn, Mary (Teresa) 1941- *WrDr 94*
Castell, Megan 1930- *WrDr 94*
Castell, William Martin 1947- *Who 94*
Castella, Xavier 1958- *WhoScEn 94*
Castellan, Gilbert William 1924- *WhoAm 94*
Castellan, Jeanne Anais 1819-1858? *NewGrDO*
Castellan, Norman John, Jr. 1939- *WhoAm 94*
Castellani, Maria 1898- *WhAm 10*
Castellani, Victor 1947- *WhoWest 94*
Castellano, Francesco fl. 1898-1918 *NewGrDO*
Castellano, Joe Cruz, Jr. 1944- *WhoHisp 94*
Castellano, Joseph Anthony 1937- *WhoWest 94*
Castellano, Michael Angelo 1956- *WhoWest 94*
Castellano, Richard d1988 *WhoHol 92*
Castellano-Hoyt, Julia 1941- *WhoHisp 94*
Castellanos, Diego Antonio 1933- *WhoHisp 94*
Castellanos, Jesus Antonio 1942- *WhoHisp 94*
Castellanos, Julio Jesus 1910- *WhoFI 94*
Castellanos, Laura 1965- *WhoHisp 94*
Castellanos, Ricardo C. 1945- *WhoHisp 94*
Castellanos, Richard Henry 1965- *WhoAmL 94*
Castellanos, Robert J. 1940- *WhoHisp 94*
Castellanos, Rosario 1925-1974 *HispLC [port], RfGShF*
Castellanos, Rosario 1925-1978 *BlmGWL*
Castellanos, Theodora 1940- *WhoHisp 94*
Castellett, Marisa *WhoAmA 93*
Castelli, Alexander Gerard 1929- *WhoAm 94*
Castelli, Leo 1907- *IntWW 93, WhoAm 94, WhoAmA 93*
Castelli, Ottaviano 1602?-1642 *NewGrDO*
Castelli, William 1931- *WhoAm 94, WhoScEn 94*
Castellina, Luciana 1929- *WhoWomW 91*
Castellini, William McGregor 1928- *WhoAmP 93*
Castellino, Francis Joseph 1943- *WhoAm 94*
Castellino, Ronald Augustus Dietrich 1938- *WhoAm 94*
Castellito, Sergio *WhoHol 92*
Castello, Hugo Martinez 1914- *WhoHisp 94*
Castello, Joe, Jr. 1943- *WhoAmL 94*
Castello, William d1953 *WhoHol 92*
Castelloe, Paul E. 1944- *WhoAmL 94*
Castellon, Christine New 1957- *WhoScEn 94*
Castellotti, Pete *NewYTBS 93 [port]*
Castellotti, Peter *WhoHol 92*
Castelloza, Na fl. 13th cent.- *BlmGWL*
Castelmary, Armand 1834-1897 *NewGrDO*
Castelnau, Francois De La Porte, Comte De 1812-1880 *WhWE*
Castelnuovo, Nino 1937- *WhoHol 92*
Castelnuovo-Tedesco, Mario 1895-1968 *NewGrDO*
Castelo, Henry L. *WhoIns 94*
Castelo, Joseph 1945- *WhoAmP 93*
Castelo, Julieta 1914- *WhoHol 92*
Castenada, Movita *WhoHol 92*
Castenell, Louis Anthony, Jr. 1947- *WhoBlA 94*
Castenschiold, Rene 1923- *WhoAm 94, WhoScEn 94*
Castenson, Roger R. 1943- *WhoMW 93, WhoScEn 94*
Caster, Bernard Harry 1921- *WhoAmA 93*
Caster, Caroleigh Tuitt 1947- *WhoBlA 94*
Caster, Sean Cauthers 1970- *WhoWest 94*
Casteras, Susan Paulette *WhoAmA 93*
Casteret, Norbert 1897- *EncSF 93*
Casterline, Cecil W. 1938- *WhoAm 94*
Casterline, James Larkin, Jr. 1931- *WhoScEn 94*
Casterlow, Carolyn B. 1948- *WhoBlA 94*
Castetter, Gregory Keeler 1935- *WhoMW 93*
Casti, Giovanni Battista 1724-1803 *NewGrDO*
Casti, J. *ConAu 141*
Casti, J. L. *ConAu 141*
Casti, John *ConAu 141*
Casti, John L(ouis) 1943- *ConAu 141*
Castiglione, Baldassare 1478-1529 *BlmGEL*
Castiglioni, Iphigenia d1963 *WhoHol 92*
Castiglioni, Niccolo 1932- *NewGrDO*
Castignetti, Domenic 1951- *WhoScEn 94*
Castil-Blaze 1784-1857 *NewGrDO*
Castile, Anthony Wayne 1961- *WhoFI 94*
Castile, Lynn d1975 *WhoHol 92*
Castile, Rand 1938- *WhoAmA 93*
Castilla, Rene *WhoHisp 94*
Castilla, Vinny 1967- *WhoHisp 94*
Castille, Armand 1943- *WhoAmP 93*
Castillo, Alba N. 1945- *WhoHisp 94*
Castillo, Allan Paul 1939- *WhoMW 93*
Castillo, Alvaro 1960- *WhoHisp 94*
Castillo, Amelia *WhoHisp 94*
Castillo, Ana *BlmGWL, DrAPF 93*
Castillo, Ana 1953- *WhoHisp 94*
Castillo, Angel, Jr. 1946- *WhoAmL 94*
Castillo, Beatriz V. 1954- *WhoHisp 94*
Castillo, Bernal Diaz Del c. 1492-1581 *WhWE*
Castillo, Brenda Victoria 1962- *WhoHisp 94*
Castillo, C. Thomas *WhoHisp 94*
Castillo, Carmen 1958- *WhoHisp 94*
Castillo, Craig Michael 1967- *WhoHisp 94*
Castillo, Debra A(nn Garsow) 1953- *WrDr 94*
Castillo, Diane M. González 1952- *WhoHisp 94*
Castillo, Eduardo A. *WhoHisp 94*
Castillo, Estela 1965- *WhoHisp 94*
Castillo, Evelyn C. 1958- *WhoHisp 94*
Castillo, Frank 1969- *WhoHisp 94*
Castillo, Franklin H. 1943- *WhoHisp 94*
Castillo, Gabriel Alejandro 1962- *WhoHisp 94*
Castillo, Gabriel Bermudez *EncSF 93*
Castillo, Gloria J. 1954- *WhoHisp 94*
Castillo, Guadalupe Trevino 1957- *WhoMW 93*
Castillo, Helen M. 1936- *WhoHisp 94*
Castillo, Horacio 1953- *WhoAmP 93*
Castillo, Jacob 1932- *WhoHisp 94*
Castillo, Javier M. 1967- *WhoHisp 94*
Castillo, John G. 1951- *WhoHisp 94*
Castillo, John Roy 1948- *WhoHisp 94, WhoMW 93*
Castillo, Jose G. *WhoHisp 94*
Castillo, Jose Ramon 1934- *WhoHisp 94*
Castillo, Joseph A. 1933- *WhoAmP 93, WhoHisp 94*
Castillo, Lazaro Jose, Sr. 1961- *WhoMW 93*
Castillo, Leonel Jabier 1939- *WhoAm 94*
Castillo, Leonel Javier 1939- *WhoAmP 93, WhoHisp 94*
Castillo, Lucy Narvaez 1943- *WhoFI 94*
Castillo, Manuel H. 1949- *WhoHisp 94*
Castillo, Mario Enrique *WhoAmA 93*
Castillo, Mario Enrique 1945- *WhoHisp 94, WhoMW 93*
Castillo, Mary 1947- *WhoHisp 94*
Castillo, Mary Helen M. *WhoHisp 94*
Castillo, Max *WhoAm 94*
Castillo, Max 1944- *WhoHisp 94*
Castillo, Michael Jay 1949- *WhoHisp 94*
Castillo, Michel Xavier Janicot del 1933- *IntWW 93*
Castillo, Miguel A. 1954- *WhoHisp 94*
Castillo, Mona 1928- *WhoHisp 94*
Castillo, Nilda 1956- *WhoHisp 94*
Castillo, Norman 1946- *WhoHisp 94*
Castillo, Osvaldo J. *WhoHisp 94*
Castillo, Pedro Antonio 1926- *WhoHisp 94*
Castillo, Rafael C. 1950- *WhoHisp 94*
Castillo, Ralph Amado 1961- *WhoFI 94*
Castillo, Ramona 1928- *WhoHisp 94*
Castillo, Ricardo Orlando 1948- *WhoHisp 94*
Castillo, Richard Cesar 1949- *WhoHisp 94*
Castillo, Robert Charles 1952- *WhoHisp 94*
Castillo, Rudolph Innocent 1927- *Who 94*
Castillo, Santos 1942- *WhoHisp 94*
Castillo, Steven David 1944- *WhoHisp 94*
Castillo, Tony 1963- *WhoHisp 94*

Castillo, Victor Rodriguez 1945- *WhoHisp 94*
Castillo Arriola, Eduardo 1914 *IntWW 93*
Castillo Lara, Rosalio Jose 1922- *IntWW 93*
Castillo Morales, Carlos Manuel 1928- *IntWW 93*
Castillon, Francisco L. 1954- *WhoHisp 94*
Castillo-Quiñones, Isabel 1953- *WhoHisp 94*
Castillo-Speed, Lillian 1949- *WhoHisp 94*
Castillo-Tovar, Maria-Lourdes 1950- *WhoHisp 94*
Castillo y Guevara, Maria Francisca Josefa del 1671-1742 *BlmGWL*
Castle *Who 94*
Castle, Alfred 1948- *WhoWest 94*
Castle, Alfred L., Mrs. 1886-1970 *WhoAmA 93N*
Castle, Carl Alan 1961- *WhoMW 93*
Castle, Christian Lancelot *WhoWest 94*
Castle, Damon *EncSF 93*
Castle, Don d1966 *WhoHol 92*
Castle, Emery Neal 1923- *WhoAm 94, WhoWest 94*
Castle, Enid 1936- *Who 94*
Castle, Frederick Ted *DrAPF 93*
Castle, Irene d1969 *WhoHol 92*
Castle, J(effery) Lloyd 1898- *EncSF 93*
Castle, James Cameron 1936- *WhoAm 94*
Castle, Jayne 1948- *WrDr 94*
Castle, Jeffrey Russell 1960- *WhoFI 94*
Castle, Joan 1914- *WhoHol 92*
Castle, John 1940- *WhoHol 92*
Castle, John Krob 1940- *WhoAm 94*
Castle, John Raymond, Jr. 1943- *WhoFI 94*
Castle, Keith L. *WhoBlA 94*
Castle, Lee d1990 *WhoHol 92*
Castle, Lillian d1959 *WhoHol 92*
Castle, Mary 1931- *WhoHol 92*
Castle, Michael N. 1939- *CngDr 93, IntWW 93, WhoAm 94*
Castle, Michael Newbold 1939- *WhoAmP 93*
Castle, Nick d1968 *WhoHol 92*
Castle, Nick 1947- *IntMPA 94*
Castle, Peggie d1973 *WhoHol 92*
Castle, Raymond Nielson 1916- *WhoAm 94, WhoScEn 94*
Castle, Robert *EncSF 93*
Castle, Robert Woods 1925- *WhoAm 94*
Castle, Roy 1932- *WhoHol 92*
Castle, Stephen Neil 1952- *WhoFI 94*
Castle, Terry 1953- *BlmGWL*
Castle, Vernon d1918 *WhoHol 92*
Castle, Vernon Charles 1931- *WhoFI 94*
Castle, Wendell Keith 1932- *WhoAm 94, WhoAmA 93*
Castle, William d1977 *WhoHol 92*
Castle, William 1914-1977 *HorFD [port]*
Castle, William Bosworth 1897-1990 *WhAm 10*
Castle, William Eugene 1929- *WhoAm 94, WhoScEn 94*
Castleberry, Arline Alrick 1919- *WhoWest 94*
Castleberry, Donald Grant 1929- *WhoAmP 93*
Castleberry, Edward J. 1928- *AfrAmAl 6, WhoBlA 94*
Castleberry, Kelly L. 1926- *WhoAmP 93*
Castleberry, May Lewis 1954- *WhoAm 94*
Castleberry, Rhebena Taylor 1917- *WhoBlA 94*
Castle-Kanerova, Mita 1948- *ConAu 142*
Castlemaine, Baron 1943- *Who 94*
Castleman, Albert Welford, Jr. 1936- *WhoAm 94*
Castleman, Christopher Norman Anthony 1941- *IntWW 93, Who 94*
Castleman, Elise Marie 1925- *WhoBlA 94*
Castleman, Louis Samuel 1918- *WhoAm 94*
Castleman, Riva 1930- *WhoAm 94, WhoAmA 93*
Castle Of Blackburn, Baroness 1910- *IntWW 93, Who 94*
Castlereagh, Viscount 1769-1822 *BlmGEL*
Castlereagh, Viscount 1972- *Who 94*
Castles, Amy 1880-1951 *NewGrDO*
Castles, John William 1947- *WhoFI 94*
Castles, William Albert, II 1949- *WhoMW 93*
Castle Stewart, Earl 1928- *Who 94*
Castleton, Barbara d1978 *WhoHol 92*
Castleton, David J. 1954- *WhoAmL 94*
Castner, Hamilton Young 1858-1899 *DcNaB MP*
Casto, Keith Michael 1947- *WhoAm 94*
Casto, Robert Clayton *DrAPF 93*
Caston, Geoffrey 1926- *IntWW 93*
Caston, Geoffrey Kemp 1926- *Who 94*
Caston, Jesse Douglas 1932- *WhoAm 94*
Castonguay, Claude 1929- *WhoAm 94*
Castor, Betty 1941- *WhoAmP 93*
Castor, C. William, Jr. 1925- *WhoAm 94*
Castor, Christina Pelayo *WhoMW 93*
Castor, Conrado Pelayo 1945- *WhoMW 93*
Castor, Jon Stuart 1951- *WhoWest 94*
Castor, Richard Gilbert 1927- *WhoIns 94*
Castor, Wilbur Wright 1932- *WhoWest 94*
Castor, William Stuart, Jr. 1926- *WhoAm 94*
Castori, Castore Antonio c. 1700-1740? *NewGrDO*
Castorino, Sue 1953- *WhoMW 93*
Castoro, Rosemarie 1939- *WhoAmA 93*
Castracane, James 1954- *WhoScEn 94*
Castrataro, Barbara Ann 1958- *WhoAmL 94*
Castrillón, José P. A. 1926- *WhoHisp 94*
Castris, Francesco de *NewGrDO*
Castro, Albert 1933-1988 *WhAm 10*
Castro, Alfonso 1950- *WhoHisp 94*
Castro, Alfonso H. Peter, III 1955- *WhoHisp 94*
Castro, Alfred A. 1932- *WhoHisp 94*
Castro, Amado Alejandro 1924- *IntWW 93*
Castro, Antonio Ramon 1933- *WhoHisp 94*
Castro, Bill 1931- *WhoHisp 94*
Castro, C. Elizabeth 1950- *WhoHisp 94*
Castro, Carlos Arturo, Sr. 1954- *WhoHisp 94*
Castro, Celia 1949- *WhoHisp 94*
Castro, Daniel Ray 1960- *WhoAmL 94*
Castro, David 1947- *WhoHisp 94*
Castro, David Alexander 1950- *WhoWest 94*
Castro, Emilio Enrique 1927- *Who 94*
Castro, Ernesto 1967- *WhoHisp 94*
Castro, Estrellita d1983 *WhoHol 92*
Castro, Federico *WhoHisp 94*
Castro, Fernanda de 1900- *BlmGWL*
Castro, Fernando A. 1952- *WhoHisp 94*
Castro, Fidel *IntWW 93*
Castro, Fidel 1926- *WhoHol 92*
Castro, Fidel 1927- *HispLC [port]*
Castro, George 1939- *WhoHisp 94*
Castro, George A. 1936- *WhoAmP 93, WhoBlA 94*
Castro, Giovanni 1946- *WhoAmA 93*
Castro, Gonzalo 1961- *WhoScEn 94*
Castro, Irma *WhoHisp 94*
Castro, Jaime 1943- *WhoHisp 94*
Castro, Jan Garden *DrAPF 93*
Castro, Jan Garden 1945- *WhoAm 94*
Castro, John M. 1951- *WhoHisp 94*
Castro, Jose Alfredo 1930- *WhoHisp 94*
Castro, José Ramón 1931- *WhoHisp 94*
Castro, Joseph Armand 1927- *WhoWest 94*
Castro, Joseph Ronald 1934- *WhoAm 94, WhoScEn 94*
Castro, Juan Jose 1895-1968 *NewGrDO*
Castro, Juana *BlmGWL*
Castro, Justiniano 1961- *WhoHisp 94*
Castro, Leonard Edward 1934- *WhoAm 94, WhoAmL 94, WhoWest 94*
Castro, Lillian 1954- *WhoHisp 94*
Castro, Manuel Francisco 1946- *WhoHisp 94*
Castro, Maria del Rosario 1947- *WhoHisp 94*
Castro, Mario Humberto 1934- *WhoHisp 94*
Castro, Marissa Barbers 1959- *WhoAsA 94*
Castro, Max Jose 1951- *WhoHisp 94*
Castro, Michael *DrAPF 93*
Castro, Michael 1945- *WhoHisp 94, WrDr 94*
Castro, Mike *WhoHisp 94*
Castro, Peter 1943- *WhoHisp 94*
Castro, Publia Hortensia de 1548-1595 *BlmGWL*
Castro, Rafaela Gonzales 1943- *WhoHisp 94*
Castro, Raul *IntWW 93*
Castro, Raul 1961- *WhoHisp 94*
Castro, Raul H. 1916- *WhoHisp 94*
Castro, Raul Hector 1916- *WhoAmP 93*
Castro, Rick R. 1938- *WhoHisp 94*
Castro, Rodolfo H. 1942-1991 *WhoHisp 94N*
Castro, Rosalia de 1837-1885 *BlmGWL*
Castro, Thomas *WhoHisp 94*
Castro, Victoria M. 1945- *WhoHisp 94*
Castro Alberty, Margarita 1947- *NewGrDO*
Castro-Blanco, David *WhoHisp 94*
Castro-Blanco, David Raphael 1958- *WhoScEn 94*
Castrodad, Felix A. *WhoAm 94*
Castro de DeLaRosa, Maria Guadalupe 1944- *WhoHisp 94*
Castrogiovanni, Anthony G. 1965- *WhoScEn 94*
Castro-Gomez, Margaret 1959- *WhoHisp 94*
Castro Herrera, Ricardo 1864-1907 *NewGrDO*
Castro Jijon, Ramon 1915- *IntWW 93*
Castro-Klarén, Sara 1942- *WhoHisp 94*
Castroleal, Alicia 1945- *WhoHisp 94*
Castronovo, David 1945- *WhoAm 94*
Castronovo, Michael Louis 1963- *WhoFI 94*
Castronovo, Thomas Paul 1932- *WhoMW 93*
Castro Ruz, Fidel 1927- *IntWW 93*
Castro Ruz, Raul 1931- *IntWW 93*
Castroviejo, Concha 1915- *BlmGWL*
Castrovillari, Daniele da fl. 1660-1662 *NewGrDO*
Castruita, Rudy *WhoWest 94*
Castruita, Rudy M. 1944- *WhoHisp 94*
Casty, Alan Howard 1929- *WrDr 94*
Casullo, Joanne M. *DrAPF 93*
Casuso, Jose A. 1932- *WhoHisp 94*
Caswall Devey, Emily Jane 1954- *WhoMW 93*
Caswell, Adam Gerard 1958- *WhoAmL 94*
Caswell, Albert, Jr. 1931- *WhoAmP 93*
Caswell, Catheryne Willis 1917- *WhoBlA 94*
Caswell, Donald *DrAPF 93*
Caswell, Dorothy Ann Cottrell 1938- *WhoAm 94*
Caswell, Hal 1949- *WhoScEn 94*
Caswell, Helen Rayburn 1923- *WhoAmA 93*
Caswell, Herbert Hall, Jr. 1923- *WhoAm 94*
Caswell, Jeffry Claxton 1959- *WhoFI 94*
Caswell, Jim 1948- *WhoAmA 93*
Caswell, Richard 1729-1789 *AmRev, WhAmRev*
Caswell, Robert Douglas 1946- *WhoScEn 94*
Catabelle, Jean-Marie Henri 1941- *WhoFI 94*
Catacalos, Rosemary 1944- *WhoHisp 94*
Catacosinos, Paul Anthony 1933- *WhoMW 93*
Catacosinos, William James 1930- *WhoAm 94, WhoFI 94*
Catala, Henry Leon 1951- *WhoWest 94*
Catala, Mario E., II 1942- *WhoHisp 94*
Catala, Muriel 1952- *WhoHol 92*
Catala, Nicole 1936- *WhoWomW 91*
Catala, Rafael *DrAPF 93*
Catalá, Rafael Enrique 1942- *WhoHisp 94*
Catala, Victor *BlmGWL*
Catalan, David 1941- *WhoHisp 94*
Catalan, Edgardo Omar *WhoAmA 93*
Catalani, Alfredo 1854-1893 *NewGrDO*
Catalani, Angelica 1780-1849 *NewGrDO [port]*
Catalano, Carlos Enrique 1954- *WhoHisp 94*
Catalano, Dennis Michael 1956- *WhoWest 94*
Catalano, Dominic 1956- *SmATA 76 [port]*
Catalano, Eduardo Fernando 1917- *WhoAm 94*
Catalano, Gene *WhoHisp 94*
Catalano, Gerald 1949- *WhoFI 94, WhoMW 93*
Catalano, Grace (A.) 1961- *ConAu 141*
Catalano, John Denis 1939- *WhoHisp 94*
Catalano, John George 1950- *WhoWest 94*
Catalano, Louis William, Jr. 1942- *WhoScEn 94*
Catalano, Michael Alfred 1947- *WhoWest 94*
Catalano, Robert Anthony 1956- *WhoFI 94, WhoScEn 94*
Catalano, Stephen 1952- *WrDr 94*
Cataldo, John William 1924- *WhoAmA 93*
Cataldo, Joseph M. 1837-1928 *EncNAR [port]*
Cataldo, Joseph Michael 1934- *WhoAm 94*
Cataldo, Michael *WhoAmP 93*
Catalfamo, Janice Stella 1936- *WhoAm 94*
Catalfo, Alfred, Jr. 1920- *WhoAm 94, WhoAmL 94*
Catalfo, Betty Marie 1942- *WhoFI 94, WhoScEn 94*
Catalfomo, Philip 1931- *WhoAm 94*
Catalifo, Patrick *WhoHol 92*
Catalina, Frank A. 1957- *WhoAmL 94*
Catalino, Kenneth James 1950- *WhoWest 94*
Catallo, Clarence Guerrino, Jr. 1940- *WhoAm 94, WhoFI 94*
Catalon, Virginia Keel 1925- *WhoAmP 93*
Catanach, J. N. *DrAPF 93*
Catanese, Anthony James 1942- *WhoAm 94*
Catania, Anthony Charles 1936- *WhoAm 94*
Catania, Frank 1941- *WhoAmP 93*
Catania, Fred d1978 *WhoHol 92*
Catania, Lorraine Laura 1942- *WhoAm 94*
Catania, Susan Kmetty 1941- *WhoAmP 93*
Catanzano, Dennis A. 1951- *WhoIns 94*
Catanzano, Frank Alexander 1947- *WhoFI 94*
Catanzarite, Catherine Marie 1925- *WhoAmP 93*
Catanzaro, James Lee, Jr. 1963- *WhoAmL 94*
Catanzaro, Marci-lee 1941- *WhoWest 94*
Catanzaro, Tony *WhoAm 94*
Catapano, Joseph John 1935- *WhoAm 94, WhoFI 94*
Catapano, Thomas F. 1949- *WhoAmP 93, WhoHisp 94*
Catarino, Cecilia Pita 1949- *WhoWomW 91*
Catasta, Anna 1952- *WhoWomW 91*
Catches, Peter c. 1915- *EncNAR*
Catcheside, David Guthrie 1907- *IntWW 93, Who 94*
Catchi 1920- *WhoAmA 93*
Catchings, Howard Douglas 1939- *WhoBlA 94*
Catchings, Walter J. 1933- *WhoBlA 94*
Catchings, Yvonne Parks *WhoBlA 94*
Catchpole, Margaret 1762-1819 *BlmGWL*
Catchpole, Nancy Mona 1929- *Who 94*
Catchpool, (Egerton) St John (Pettifor) 1890-1971 *DcNaB MP*
Cate, Alison Mather 1959- *WhoFI 94*
Cate, Barbara Kaufman *WhoAmA 93*
Cate, Benjamin Wilson Upton 1931- *WhoAm 94*
Cate, Byron Lee 1942- *WhoAmP 93*
Cate, Curtis (Wilson) 1924- *WrDr 94*
Cate, Donald James 1933- *WhoFI 94*
Cate, Floyd Mills 1917- *WhoWest 94*
Cate, Milton A. *WhoAmP 93*
Cate, Phillip Dennis 1944- *WhoAm 94, WhoAmA 93*
Cate, Rodney Michael 1942- *WhoScEn 94*
Cate, Tom 1956- *WhoAmP 93*
Cate, Wirt Armistead 1900-1991 *WhAm 10*
Catel, Charles-Simon 1773-1830 *NewGrDO*
Catelani, Angelo 1811-1866 *NewGrDO*
Catell, Grace Louise 1929- *WhoAm 94*
Cateora, Philip Rene 1932- *WhoAm 94*
Cater, Antony John E. *Who 94*
Cater, Douglass 1923- *IntWW 93, Who 94, WhoAm 94*
Cater, (Silas) Douglass, (Jr.) 1923- *WrDr 94*
Cater, Jack 1922- *IntWW 93, Who 94*
Cater, James Thomas 1948- *WhoAm 94, WhoFI 94*
Cater, John 1932- *WhoHol 92*
Cater, John Robert 1919- *Who 94*
Caterina da Siena, Santa 1347-1380 *BlmGWL*
Cates, Charles Bradley 1950- *WhoAmP 93*
Cates, Dalton Reede 1933- *WhoFI 94*
Cates, David Clay 1959- *WhoAmL 94*
Cates, Don Tate 1933- *WhoAm 94*
Cates, Ed *DrAPF 93*
Cates, Gilbert 1934- *IntMPA 94, WhoAm 94*
Cates, Harold Thomas 1941- *WhoScEn 94*
Cates, James William 1944- *WhoAmP 93*
Cates, Jo A. 1958- *WrDr 94*
Cates, Joseph 1924- *IntMPA 94*
Cates, Madelyn *WhoHol 92*
Cates, Phoebe 1963- *IntMPA 94*
Cates, Phoebe 1964- *WhoAm 94, WhoHol 92*
Cates, Sidney Hayward, III 1931- *WhoBlA 94*
Catesby, Mark c. 1679-1749 *WhWE*
Cateura, Linda Brandi 1924- *WrDr 94*
Catey, Laurie Lynn 1962- *WhoScEn 94*
Catford, (John) Robin 1923- *Who 94*
Cath, Stanley Howard 1921- *WhoAm 94, WhoScEn 94*
Cathala, Thierry Gerard 1925- *IntWW 93*
Cathcart, Earl 1919- *Who 94*
Cathcart, Allen 1938- *NewGrDO*
Cathcart, David Arthur 1940- *WhoAm 94, WhoAmL 94*
Cathcart, Dick d1993 *NewYTBS 93*
Cathcart, George LeBlanc 1947- *WhoWest 94*
Cathcart, Harold Robert 1924- *WhoAm 94*
Cathcart, Helen 1909- *WrDr 94*
Cathcart, James B. 1917- *WhoWest 94*
Cathcart, Kevin James 1939- *IntWW 93*
Cathcart, Linda 1947- *WhoAm 94*
Cathcart, Linda Louise *WhoAmA 93*
Cathcart, Mary R. *WhoAmP 93*
Cathcart, Patrick Alan 1945- *WhoAmL 94*
Cathcart, Rich 1946- *WhoAmP 93*
Cathcart, Richard C. 1944- *WhoAmP 93*
Cathcart, Robert Stephen 1923- *WhoAm 94*
Cathcart, William Schaw 1755-1843 *AmRev, WhAmRev [port]*
Cather, Donald Warren 1926- *WhoAm 94*

Cather, James Newton 1931- *WhoAm 94*
Cather, Willa 1873-1947 *BlmGWL [port]*
Cather, Willa (Sibert) 1873-1947 *GayLL, RfGShF*
Cather, Willa Sibert 1873-1947 *AmCulL [port]*
Catherall, Arthur 1906-1980 *SmATA 74*
Catherine, II 1729-1796 *BlmGWL [port], NewGrDO*
Catherine (The Great), II 1729-1796 *WhAmRev*
Catherine de Medici 1519-1589 *BlmGWL*
Catherine of Aragon 1485-1536 *BlmGWL*
Catherine the Great 1729-1796 *AmRev*
Catherine the Great, II 1729-1796 *HisWorL [port]*
Cathers, James O. 1934-1982 *WhoAmA 93N*
Catherwood, Cummins 1910-1990 *WhAm 10*
Catherwood, (Henry) Frederick (Ross) 1925- *IntWW 93, Who 94*
Catherwood, (Henry) Frederick (Ross), Sir 1925- *WrDr 94*
Catherwood, Herbert Sidney Elliott 1929- *Who 94*
Catherwood, Hugh Robert 1911- *WhoWest 94*
Catherwood, Mary Hartwell 1847-1902 *BlmGWL*
Cathey, Dean Edward 1946- *WhoWest 94*
Cathey, Sharon Sue Rinn 1940- *WhoWest 94*
Cathey, Wade Thomas 1937- *WhoScEn 94*
Cathey, William L. 1947- *WhoAmL 94*
Cathou, Renata Egone 1935- *WhoAm 94, WhoScEn 94*
Catic, Igor Julio 1936- *WhoScEn 94*
Catjakis, Athan 1931- *WhoAmP 93*
Catledge, Terry Dewayne 1963- *WhoBlA 94*
Catlett, Charles E. 1960- *WhoMW 93*
Catlett, Donna Snell 1959- *WhoMW 93*
Catlett, Elizabeth *AfrAmAl 6*
Catlett, Elizabeth 1919- *WhoAm 94, WhoAmA 93, WhoBlA 94*
Catlett, George Roudebush 1917- *WhoAm 94*
Catlett, Mary Jo *WhoHol 92*
Catlett, Meredith P. 1952- *WhoAmL 94*
Catlett, Richard H., Jr. 1921- *WhoAm 94*
Catlett, Walter d1960 *WhoHol 92*
Catley, Anne 1745-1789 *NewGrDO*
Catley-Carlson, Margaret 1942- *WhoAm 94*
Catlin, A. B. *WhoAmP 93*
Catlin, Alan *DrAPF 93*
Catlin, Avery 1924- *WhoAm 94*
Catlin, B. Wesley 1917- *WhoAm 94*
Catlin, Catherine M. 1961- *WhoAmL 94*
Catlin, Donald Edward 1936- *WhoAm 94*
Catlin, Francis Irving 1925- *WhoAm 94*
Catlin, George 1796-1872 *WhWE [port]*
Catlin, James C. 1947- *WhoAm 94*
Catlin, John Anthony 1947- *Who 94*
Catlin, Robert A. 1940- *WhoBlA 94*
Catlin, Robin John Oakley 1927- *WhoAm 94*
Catlin, Stanton Loomis 1915- *WhoAmA 93*
Catlin, William Arthur 1941- *WhoMW 93*
Catling, Hector William 1924- *Who 94*
Catling, Richard (Charles) 1912- *Who 94*
Catlow, Charles Richard Arthur 1947- *IntWW 93, Who 94*
Cato, Mr. d1978 *WhoHol 92*
Cato, Arnott Samuel 1912- *Who 94*
Cato, Brian Hudson 1928- *Who 94*
Cato, Harry F. 1958- *WhoAmP 93*
Cato, Marcus Porcius 95BC-46BC *BlmGEL*
Cato, (Robert) Milton 1915- *Who 94*
Cato, Nancy 1917- *BlmGWL, WrDr 94*
Cato, Robert Milton 1915- *IntWW 93*
Catoe, Bette Lorrina 1926- *WhoAm 94, WhoScEn 94*
Catok, Lottie Meyer *WhoAmA 93*
Catoline, Pauline Dessie 1937- *WhoMW 93*
Caton, Betty Ann 1917- *WhoAm 94*
Caton, Charles Allen 1937- *WhoWest 94*
Caton, David 1955- *WhoAmA 93*
Caton, Michael *WhoHol 92*
Catoni, Pedro Miguel 1957- *WhoHisp 94*
Caton-Jones, Michael 1958- *IntMPA 94, IntWW 93*
Cato the Censor 234BC-149BC *BlmGEL*
Catovsky, Julia Margaret *Who 94*
Catrambone, Eugene Dominic 1926- *WhoWest 94*
Catran, Jack 1918- *WhoScEn 94*
Catravas, George Nicholas 1919- *WhoAm 94*
Catrett, John Thomas, III 1947- *WhoWest 94*
Catrillo, Charles J. *WhoAmP 93*
Catron, Gary Wayne 1944- *WhoAmL 94*
Catron, Stephen Barnard 1949- *WhoAmL 94*
Catron, William G. 1945- *WhoFI 94*
Catronio, Ronald Joseph 1951- *WhoFI 94*
Catrufo, Gioseffo 1771-1851 *NewGrDO*
Catselli, Rina 1938- *WhoWomW 91*
Catsimatidis, John Andreas 1948- *WhoAm 94, WhoFI 94*
Catt, Carrie Lane Chapman 1859-1947 *AmSocL*
Cattan, Henry 1906-1992 *WrDr 94N*
Cattanach, Bruce MacIntosh 1932- *IntWW 93, Who 94*
Cattanach, Helen 1920- *Who 94*
Cattanach, Richard L. 1942- *WhoWest 94*
Cattanach, Robert Edward, Jr. 1949- *WhoAm 94, WhoAmL 94*
Cattaneo, Jacquelyn Annette Kammerer 1944- *WhoWest 94*
Cattaneo, John Leo 1944- *WhoWest 94*
Cattaneo, (Jacquelyn A.) Kammerer 1944- *WhoAmA 93*
Cattaneo, Michael S. 1948- *WhoMW 93*
Cattani, Lorenzo d1713 *NewGrDO*
Cattani, Luis Carlos 1962- *WhoFI 94*
Cattani, Maryellen B. 1943- *WhoAm 94*
Cattani, Richard John 1936- *WhoAm 94*
Cattarulla, Elliot Reynold 1931- *WhoFI 94*
Cattelino, Craig Alan 1958- *WhoFI 94*
Cattelino, Ronald E. 1948- *WhoMW 93*
Cattell, George Harold Bernard 1920- *Who 94*
Cattell, Heather Birkett 1936- *WhoScEn 94*
Cattell, Ray 1921- *WhoAmA 93*
Cattell, Raymond Bernard 1905- *WrDr 94*
Cattell, Roderic Geoffrey Galton 1953- *WhoWest 94*
Catterall, John Ashley 1928- *Who 94*
Catterall, John Edward 1940- *WhoAmA 93*
Catterall, John Stewart 1939- *Who 94*
Catterall, Lee 1944- *ConAu 141*
Catterall, Peter 1961- *WrDr 94*
Cattermole, Joan Eileen *Who 94*
Cattermole, Paul S. 1946- *WhoFI 94*
Catterton, Marianne Rose 1922- *WhoWest 94*
Catto, Baron 1923- *Who 94*
Catto, Henry E. 1930- *WhoAmP 93*
Catto, Henry Edward 1930- *IntWW 93, Who 94, WhoAm 94*
Catto, Max 1909-1992 *AnObit 1992*
Catto, Stephen Gordon 1923- *IntWW 93*
Cattoi, Robert Louis 1926- *WhoAm 94*
Catton, Ivan 1934- *WhoAm 94*
Catton, William Robert, Jr. 1926- *WhoAm 94*
Catto of Cairncatto, Stephen Gordon 1923- *WhoAm 94*
Cattrall, Kim 1956- *IntMPA 94, WhoHol 92*
Catty, Charles *GayLL*
Catudal, Honorae (Marc), Jr. 1944- *WrDr 94*
Catullus, Gaius Valerius 84?BC-54BC *BlmGEL*
Caturla, Alejandro Garcia 1906-1940 *NewGrDO*
Catusco, Louis *WhoAmA 93*
Catuzzi, J. P., Jr. 1938- *WhoAm 94*
Caty, J. Charles 1940- *WhoAm 94, WhoFI 94*
Catz, Boris 1923- *WhoWest 94*
Cau, Jean d1993 *NewYTBS 93*
Cau, Jean 1925- *IntWW 93*
Cauas, Jorge *IntWW 93*
Cauble, Sarah Jane *WhoMW 93*
Cauchy, Augustin-Louis 1789-1857 *WorScD*
Caudell, James A. 1929- *WhoAmP 93*
Caudella, Eduard 1842-1924 *NewGrDO*
Caudill, Charlotte 1953- *WhoMW 93*
Caudill, David L. 1937- *WhoAm 94*
Caudill, Franklin Terrell 1945- *WhoAm 94, WhoAmL 94*
Caudill, Harry Monroe 1922-1990 *WhAm 10*
Caudill, James Mason 1950- *WhoWest 94*
Caudill, Rebecca 1899-1985 *TwCYAW*
Caudill, Samuel Jefferson 1922- *WhoAm 94*
Caudill, Terry Lee 1947- *WhoWest 94*
Caudill, Tom Holden 1945- *WhoMW 93*
Caudill, William Howard 1951- *WhoAm 94, WhoAmL 94*
Caudle, Neil 1952- *WrDr 94*
Caudle, William Brandon, II 1942- *WhoAmP 93*
Caudron, John Armand 1944- *WhoWest 94*
Cauduro, Rafael 1950- *WhoAmA 93*
Caudwell, Sarah *WrDr 94*
Cauffiel, Lowell 1951- *WrDr 94*
Caughey, George Herbert 1953- *WhoWest 94*
Caughey, Thomas Harcourt Clarke 1911- *Who 94*
Caughlan, Georgeanne Robertson 1916- *WhoAm 94, WhoWest 94*
Caughlin, Donald Joseph, Jr. 1946- *WhoScEn 94*
Caughlin, Stephenie Jane 1948- *WhoFI 94, WhoWest 94*
Caulcott, Thomas Holt 1927- *Who 94*
Caulder, Jerry Dale 1942- *WhoScEn 94*
Cauldwell, Frank 1923- *WrDr 94*
Cauley, Colleen Ann 1963- *WhoMW 93*
Caulfeild *Who 94*
Caulfield, Barbara Ann 1947- *WhoAm 94, WhoAmL 94, WhoWest 94*
Caulfield, Bernard 1914- *Who 94*
Caulfield, Henry John *WhoAm 94, WhoScEn 94*
Caulfield, Ian George 1942- *Who 94*
Caulfield, James Benjamin 1927- *WhoAm 94*
Caulfield, Joan 1922-1991 *WhAm 10, WhoHol 92*
Caulfield, Joan 1943- *WhoMW 93*
Caulfield, Maxwell 1959- *IntMPA 94, WhoHol 92*
Caulfield, Patrick 1936- *IntWW 93, Who 94*
Caulfield, Sharon Elizabeth 1956- *WhoAmL 94*
Caulk, G. Wallace, Jr. 1941- *WhoAmP 93*
Caulkins, Charles S. 1949- *WhoAmL 94*
Caulo, Ralph Daniel 1935- *IntWW 93*
Caumont de la Force *BlmGWL*
Cauna, Nikolajs 1914- *WhoAm 94, WhoScEn 94*
Caunitz, William J. 1933- *WrDr 94*
Caunter, Tony 1937- *WhoHol 92*
Causey, Earl Wayne 1945- *WhoMW 93*
Causey, Gilbert 1907- *Who 94, WrDr 94*
Causey, Gill Terry 1950- *WhoWest 94*
Causey, John Michael 1959- *WhoAmL 94*
Causey, John Paul, Jr. 1943- *WhoAm 94, WhoAmL 94*
Causey, Paul Raymond 1938- *WhoAmL 94*
Causey, Robert Louis 1941- *WhoAm 94*
Causing, Amy Lynn 1962- *WhoFI 94*
Causley, Charles 1917- *BlmGEL, ChlLR 30 [port]*
Causley, Charles (Stanley) 1917- *WrDr 94*
Causley, Charles Stanley 1917- *IntWW 93, Who 94*
Causse, Jean-Pierre 1926- *IntWW 93*
Caussimon, Jean-Roger d1985 *WhoHol 92*
Causwell, Duane 1968- *WhoBlA 94*
Caute, David 1936- *BlmGEL*
Caute, (John) David 1936- *ConDr 93, IntWW 93, Who 94, WrDr 94*
Cauthen, Charles Edward, Jr. 1931- *WhoAm 94, WhoFI 94*
Cauthen, Cheryl G. 1957- *WhoBlA 94*
Cauthen, E. Larry 1930- *WhoIns 94*
Cauthen, Irby Bruce, Jr. 1919- *WhoAm 94, WrDr 94*
Cauthen, (W.) Kenneth 1930- *WrDr 94*
Cauthen, Richard L. 1944- *WhoBlA 94*
Cauthen, Richard Lee 1944- *WhoMW 93*
Cauthen, Stephen Mark 1960- *Who 94*
Cauthen, Steve 1960- *WhoAm 94*
Cauthorn, James Daniel 1955- *WhoAsA 94*
Cauthorn, Tom 1947- *WhoAmP 93*
Cauthron, Robin J. 1950- *WhoAm 94, WhoAmL 94*
Cava, Michael Patrick 1926- *WhoAm 94*
Cava, Paul 1949- *WhoAmA 93*
Cavaco Silva, Anibal 1939- *IntWW 93*
Cavafy, C(onstantine) P(eter) 1863-1933 *GayLL*
Cavaglieri, Giorgio 1911- *WhoAm 94*
Cavagnaro, Edmund Walter 1952- *WhoWest 94*
Cavalcanti, Edward L. 1963- *WhoHisp 94*
Cavalcanti, Giacomo 1952- *IntWW 93*
Cavalcanti, Sandra Martins 1925- *WhoWomW 91*
Cavalet, James Roger 1942- *WhoScEn 94*
Cavalier, Michael Antonio, Jr. 1954- *WhoMW 93*
Cavaliere, Barbara *WhoAmA 93*
Cavalieri, Caterina 1760-1801 *NewGrDO*
Cavalieri, Emilio de' c. 1550-1602 *NewGrDO*
Cavalieri, Gianni d1955 *WhoHol 92*
Cavalieri, Grace *DrAPF 93*
Cavalieri, Lina d1944 *WhoHol 92*
Cavalieri, Lina 1874-1944 *NewGrDO*
Cavalieri, Nick V. 1947- *WhoAmL 94*
Cavalieri, Vivian L. 1956- *WhoAmL 94*
Cavaliero, Roderick 1928- *Who 94*
Cavallada, Carlos *WhoHisp 94*
Cavallaro, Angelo L. *WhoHisp 94*
Cavallaro, Carmen d1989 *WhoHol 92*
Cavallaro, Joseph John 1932- *WhoScEn 94*
Cavallera, Charles 1909- *Who 94*
Cavallera, Felice Teresa Bloom 1939- *WhoFI 94*
Cavallero, Hazel Helen 1913- *WhoWest 94*
Cavalletti, Giulio Maria c. 1668-1755 *NewGrDO*
Cavalli, Dick 1923- *WhoAmA 93*
Cavalli, (Pietro) Francesco 1602-1676 *NewGrDO*
Cavalli-Sforza, Luigi Luca 1922- *WhoAm 94*
Cavallito, Albino 1905-1966 *WhoAmA 93N*
Cavallo, Diana *DrAPF 93*
Cavallo, Diana 1931- *WrDr 94*
Cavallo, Domingo Felipe 1946- *IntWW 93*
Cavallon, Betty Gabler 1918- *WhoAm 94*
Cavallon, Giorgio *WhoAmA 93N*
Cavallon, Giorgio 1904-1989 *WhAm 10*
Cavan, Earl of 1944- *Who 94*
Cavana, Giovanni Battista fl. 1684-1732 *NewGrDO*
Cavanagh, Carroll John 1943- *WhoAmL 94, WhoFI 94*
Cavanagh, Denis *WhoAm 94*
Cavanagh, Harrison Dwight 1940- *WhoAm 94*
Cavanagh, John Bryan 1914- *Who 94*
Cavanagh, John Charles 1932- *WhoAm 94, WhoWest 94*
Cavanagh, John Edward 1918- *WhoAm 94*
Cavanagh, John Henry 1955- *WhoAm 94*
Cavanagh, John Joseph, Jr. 1942- *WhoAmP 93*
Cavanagh, Michael F. *WhoAmP 93*
Cavanagh, Michael Francis 1940- *WhoAm 94, WhoAmL 94, WhoMW 93*
Cavanagh, Paul d1964 *WhoHol 92*
Cavanagh, Richard Edward 1946- *WhoAm 94, WhoFI 94*
Cavanaugh, Andrew *IntMPA 94*
Cavanaugh, Evelyn Beatrice 1940- *WhoAmL 94*
Cavanaugh, Francis Xavier 1928- *WhoAmP 93*
Cavanaugh, Gordon 1928- *WhoAm 94, WhoAmL 94*
Cavanaugh, Hobart d1950 *WhoHol 92*
Cavanaugh, James d1981 *WhoHol 92*
Cavanaugh, James David 1965- *WhoMW 93*
Cavanaugh, James Francis 1917- *WhoMW 93*
Cavanaugh, James Henry 1937- *WhoAm 94*
Cavanaugh, James Michael 1949- *WhoAm 94*
Cavanaugh, John G. 1936- *WhoIns 94*
Cavanaugh, John J., III 1945- *WhoAmP 93*
Cavanaugh, John W. 1921- *WhoAmA 93N*
Cavanaugh, Kenneth Clinton 1916- *WhoAm 94*
Cavanaugh, Kevin Stuart 1944- *WhoAmL 94*
Cavanaugh, Michael *WhoHol 92*
Cavanaugh, Michael Everett 1946- *WhoAm 94, WhoAmL 94*
Cavanaugh, Patricia L. 1954- *WhoMW 93*
Cavanaugh, Tom Richard 1923- *WhoAm 94*
Cavanaugh, William, III 1939- *WhoFI 94*
Cavaney, Red 1943- *WhoAm 94*
Cavani, Liliana 1937- *IntMPA 94*
Cavanna, Betty 1909- *TwCYAW, WrDr 94*
Cavanna, Elise d1963 *WhoHol 92*
Cavasso, Cam 1950- *WhoAmP 93*
Cavat, Irma *WhoAmA 93*
Cavazos, Ben 1950- *WhoHisp 94*
Cavazos, Eddie 1942- *WhoAmP 93, WhoHisp 94*
Cavazos, Henry J. *WhoHisp 94*
Cavazos, Irma Estella 1964- *WhoHisp 94*
Cavazos, Joel *WhoHisp 94*
Cavazos, Lauro F. 1927- *WhoHisp 94*
Cavazos, Lauro Fred 1927- *IntWW 93, WhoAm 94, WhoAmP 93*
Cavazos, Miguel A., Jr. 1943- *WhoHisp 94*
Cavazos, Norma Louise 1952- *WhoHisp 94*
Cavazos, Rosa I. 1954- *WhoHisp 94*
Cavazos, Ruben 1923- *WhoHisp 94*
Cavazza, Fabio Luca 1927- *WhoFI 94*
Cave (Winscom), Jane c. 1754-1813 *BlmGWL*
Cave, Alexander James Edward 1900- *Who 94*
Cave, Alfred Earl 1940- *WhoBlA 94*
Cave, Alison Ann 1960- *WhoAmL 94*
Cave, Charles (Edward Coleridge) 1927- *Who 94*
Cave, Claude Bertrand 1910- *WhoBlA 94*
Cave, David Ralph 1946- *WhoScEn 94*
Cave, Emma *WrDr 94*
Cave, Herbert G. 1922- *WhoBlA 94*
Cave, Joe d1912 *WhoHol 92*
Cave, John Arthur 1915- *Who 94*
Cave, Kathryn 1948- *SmATA 76*

Cave, Leonard Edward 1944- WhoAmA 93
Cave, Mac Donald 1939- WhoAm 94
Cave, Nick 1957- ConMus 10 [port]
Cave, Perstein Ronald 1947- WhoBlA 94
Cave, (Charles) Philip H. Who 94
Cave, Shannon Daily 1949- WhoAmP 93
Cave, Stanton L. 1963- WhoAmP 93
Cave, Terence (Christopher) 1938- ConAu 142
Cave, Terence Christopher 1938- Who 94
Cave, Thomas GayLL
Cave, Vernal G. WhoBlA 94
Cave-Browne-Cave, Robert 1929- Who 94
Cavedo, Bradley Brent 1955- WhoAmP 93
Cavell, John Kingsmill 1916- Who 94
Cavell, Marc WhoHol 92
Cavell, Stanley 1926- WhoAm 94
Caven, Allan d1941 WhoHol 92
Caven, Ingrid WhoHol 92
Cavenagh, Desmond Waring, Jr. 1937- WhoWest 94
Cavenagh, Winifred (Elizabeth) WrDr 94
Cavenagh, Winifred Elizabeth Who 94
Cavenagh-Mainwaring, Maurice Kildare 1908- Who 94
Cavender, Glen d1962 WhoHol 92
Cavendish Who 94
Cavendish, David d1960 WhoHol 92
Cavendish, Elizabeth 1626-1663 BlmGWL
Cavendish, Elizabeth (Georgiana Alice) 1926- Who 94
Cavendish, Henry 1731-1810 WorScD [port]
Cavendish, Jane 1621-1669 BlmGWL
Cavendish, Margaret 1623-1673 BlmGWL [port]
Cavendish, Margaret 1624?-1674 BlmGEL
Cavendish, Margaret Lucas, Duchess of Newcastle 1623-1673 DcLB 131 [port]
Cavendish, Michael c. 1565-1628 DcNaB MP
Cavendish, Peter Boucher 1925- Who 94
Cavendish, Richard 1930- WrDr 94
Cavendish Of Furness, Baron 1941- Who 94
Caveney, William John 1944- WhoAmL 94, WhoFI 94
Cavens, Fred d1962 WhoHol 92
Cavens, Sharon Sue 1942- WhoBlA 94
Caver, Carmen C. Murphy 1915- WhoBlA 94
Caver, Michael David 1942- WhoMW 93
Caver, William Ralph 1932- WhoAmA 93
Caverly, Gardner A. 1910- WhoAm 94
Caverly, Robert H. 1954- WhoScEn 94
Cavert, Henry Mead 1922- WhoAm 94
Caves, Richard E(arl) 1931- ConAu 41NR
Caves, Richard Earl 1931- WrDr 94
Cavett, Dick 1936- WhoAm 94, WhoCom, WhoHol 92
Cavett, Dick 1937- IntMPA 94
Cavey, Jay Von 1963- WhoFI 94
Cavezza, Carmen James 1937- WhoAm 94, WhoWest 94
Cavicchi, Leslie Scott 1954- WhoFI 94, WhoScEn 94
Cavicchio, Daniel Joseph, Jr. 1944- WhoFI 94
Cavigli, Henry James 1914- WhoScEn 94
Cavigliasso, Paola 1942- WhoWomW 91
Cavill, Ronald William 1944- WhoFI 94
Cavin, Alonzo C. 1939- WhoBlA 94
Cavin, Jess d1967 WhoHol 92
Cavin, William Brooks 1914- WhoAm 94
Cavin, William Pinckney 1925- WhoAm 94
Caviness, E. Theophilus 1928- WhoBlA 94
Caviness, Lorraine F. 1914- WhoBlA 94
Caviness, Madeline Harrison 1938- WhoAm 94
Cavior, Warren Joseph 1929- WhoAm 94
Cavis, Ella DrAPF 93
Cavitt, Bruce Edward 1945- WhoAmL 94
Cavnar, Samuel Melmon 1925- WhoAmP 93, WhoWest 94
Cavness, Marc Cleburne 1945- WhoAmL 94
Cavos, Catterino Al'bertovich 1775-1840 NewGrDO
Cavoukian, Raffi 1948- WhoAm 94
Cavour, Camillo di 1810-1861 HisWorL [port]
Cawarden, Thomas c. 1514-1559 DcNaB MP
Cawdor, Earl d1993 Who 94N
Cawdor, Earl 1962- Who 94
Cawdrey, Nancy Townsend 1948- WhoWest 94
Cawdron, George Edward 1943- Who 94
Cawdron, Robert WhoHol 92
Cawein, Kathrin 1895- WhoAmA 93
Cawley, Baron 1913- Who 94
Cawley, Charles (Mills) 1907- Who 94
Cawley, Charles M. WhoAm 94
Cawley, Charles Nash 1937- WhoScEn 94
Cawley, Edward Philip 1912- WhoAm 94
Cawley, Evonne Fay 1951- IntWW 93
Cawley, Gaynor 1941- WhoAmP 93
Cawley, James Hughes 1945- WhoAm 94, WhoAmL 94
Cawley, Joan Mae WhoAmA 93
Cawley, Rhya Noel 1947- WhoWest 94
Cawley, Robert Hugh 1924- Who 94
Cawley, Robert Lucian 1934- WhoAmP 93
Cawley, Thomas J. 1943- WhoAmL 94
Cawley, Winifred 1915- WrDr 94
Cawns, Albert Edward 1937- WhoScEn 94
Cawood, Elizabeth Jean 1947- WhoFI 94
Cawood, Gary Kenneth 1947- WhoAmA 93
Cawood, Hobart Guy 1935- WhoAm 94
Cawood, Merton Campbell 1947- WhoFI 94
Cawood, Stephen Carl 1943- WhoAmP 93
Caws, Genevra Fiona Penelope Victoria 1949- Who 94
Caws, Mary Ann 1933- WhoAm 94, WrDr 94
Caws, Peter (James) 1931- WrDr 94
Caws, Peter James 1931- WhoAm 94
Caws, Richard Byron 1927- Who 94
Cawson, Roderick Anthony 1921- Who 94
Cawthon, Frank H. 1930- WhoFI 94
Cawthon, William Connell 1922- WhoAm 94
Cawthorn, James 1929- EncSF 93
Cawthorn, Joseph d1949 WhoHol 92
Cawthorn, Robert Elston 1935- WhoAm 94, WhoFI 94
Cawthorne, Dennis Otto 1940- WhoAmP 93
Cawthorne, Kenneth Clifford 1936- WhoAm 94, WhoFI 94
Cawthorne, Nigel 1951- WrDr 94
Cawthra, Arthur James 1911- Who 94
Cawthra, David Wilkinson 1943- Who 94
Caxton EncSF 93
Caxton, William 1422?-1491 BlmGEL
Cayce, Edgar 1877-1945 DcAmReB 2
Cayce, W. H. WhoAm 94
Cayea, Donald Joseph 1948- WhoAmL 94
Cayer, D. M. GayLL
Cayer, D. M. 1933- WrDr 94
Cayetano, Benjamin J. 1939- WhoAsA 94
Cayetano, Benjamin Jerome 1939- WhoAm 94, WhoAmP 93, WhoWest 94
Cayford, Florence Evelyn 1897- Who 94
Caygill, David Francis 1948- IntWW 93, Who 94
Cayle DrAPF 93
Cayley, Arthur 1821-1895 WorScD
Cayley, Digby (William David) 1944- Who 94
Cayley, George 1773-1857 DcNaB MP, WorInv
Cayley, Michael Forde 1950- Who 94
Caylor, Dee Jerlyn 1942- WhoFI 94
Caylus, Madame de 1673- BlmGWL
Cayne, Bernard Stanley 1924- WhoAm 94
Cayne, James E. 1934- WhoAm 94, WhoFI 94
Cayou, Nontsizi Kirton 1937- WhoBlA 94
Cayrol, Jean 1910- IntWW 93
Cayrol, Roland 1941- IntWW 93
Caytas, Ivo George 1958- WhoAmL 94
Caywood, James Alexander, III 1923- WhoScEn 94
Caywood, Thomas Elias 1919- WhoWest 94
Cayz, Barbara WhoWomW 91
Cayzer Who 94
Cayzer, Baron 1910- Who 94
Cayzer, James Arthur 1931- Who 94
Cayzer, (William) Nicholas 1910- IntWW 93
Cazabon, Gilles 1933- WhoMW 93
Cazalas, Mary Rebecca Williams 1927- WhoAmL 94
Cazale, John d1978 WhoHol 92
Cazalet, Hon. Lady 1937- Who 94
Cazalet, Edward (Stephen) 1936- Who 94
Cazalet, Peter (Grenville) 1929- IntWW 93, Who 94
Cazares, Carlos A. WhoHisp 94
Cazares, Hector Robert 1945- WhoHisp 94
Cázares, Roger 1941- WhoHisp 94
Cazares, Roy B. WhoHisp 94
Cazayoux, Lawrence Marius 1897- WhAm 10
Cazden, Courtney Borden 1925- WhoAm 94
Cazeaux, Isabelle Anne Marie 1926- WhoAm 94
Cazel, Hugh Allen 1923- WhoFI 94
Cazenave, Noel Anthony 1948- WhoBlA 94
Cazeneuve, Jean 1915- IntWW 93
Cazeneuve, Paul d1925 WhoHol 92
Cazenove, Christopher 1945- IntMPA 94, WhoHol 92
Cazenove, Christopher de Lerisson 1945- IntWW 93
Cazes, Jack 1934- WhoScEn 94
Cazet, Denys 1938- WrDr 94
Cazette, Louis 1887-1922 NewGrDO
Cazier, Barry James 1943- WhoWest 94
Cazzati, Maurizio c. 1620-1677 NewGrDO
C de Baca, Celeste M. 1957- WhoHisp 94
C de Baca, Richard 1939- WhoHisp 94
Cea, Robert 1963- WhoHol 92
Cearlock, Dennis Bill 1941- WhoAm 94
Ceasar, Mitchell 1954- WhoAmL 94
Ceasar, Sherita Therese 1959- WhoBlA 94
Ceasar, Shirley 1938- AfrAmAl 6
Cease, Jane Hardy 1936- WhoAmP 93
Cease, Ron 1931- WhoAmP 93
Ceasor, Augusta Casey 1943- WhoScEn 94
Ceausescu, Nicolae 1918-1989 HisWorL [port]
Ceballos, Cedric Z. 1969- WhoBlA 94
Ceballos, Gerardo 1958- WhoScEn 94
Ceballos, Roderick Oscar 1952- WhoHisp 94
Ceballos Ordonez, Luz Priscila IntWW 93
Cebollero, Carlos 1927- WhoIns 94
Cebotari, Maria 1910-1949 NewGrDO
Cebrián, Teresa del Carmen 1960- WhoHisp 94
Cebrian Echarri, Juan Luis 1944- IntWW 93
Cebuc, Alexandru 1932- IntWW 93
Cebula, James E. 1942- WhoMW 93
Cebulash, Mel 1937- WrDr 94
Cecala, Ted Thomas, Jr. 1949- WhoAm 94
Ceccaldik, Daniel WhoHol 92
Ceccarelli, Francesco 1752-1814 NewGrDO
Ceccarelli, Odoardo d1668 NewGrDO
Ceccatelli, Anna Gabriella 1927- WhoWomW 91
Ceccato, Aldo 1934- IntWW 93, NewGrDO
Ceccherelli, Chiara NewGrDO
Cecchetti, Enrico 1850-1928 IntDcB [port]
Cecchetti, Giovanni 1922- WhoAm 94
Cecchi, Anna Maria Torri NewGrDO
Cecchi, Domenico c. 1650-1717? NewGrDO
Cecchi, Giuseppe 1930- WhoAm 94
Cecchi d'Amico, Suso 1914- IntDcF 2-4 [port]
Cecchi Gori, Mario d1993 NewYTBS 93
Cecchina, La NewGrDO
Cecchini, Angelo fl. 1619-1639 NewGrDO
Cecere, Carlo 1706-1761 NewGrDO
Cecere, Gaetano 1894- WhAm 10
Cecere, Gaetano 1894-1985 WhoAmA 93N
Cech, John Edward 1962- WhoWest 94
Cech, Joseph Harold 1951- WhoMW 93
Cech, Svatopluk EncSF 93
Cech, Svatopluk 1846-1908 NewGrDO
Cech, Thomas R. 1947- NobelP 91 [port]
Cech, Thomas Robert 1947- IntWW 93, WhoAm 94, WhoScEn 94, WhoWest 94
Cechova, Heda 1928- WhoWomW 91
Ceci, Jesse Arthur 1924- WhoAm 94, WhoWest 94
Ceci, Louis J. 1927- WhoAm 94, WhoAmL 94, WhoAmP 93
Ceci Bonifazi, Adriana 1942- WhoWomW 91
Cecich, Donald Edward 1950- WhoAm 94
Cecil Who 94
Cecil, Baron Who 94
Cecil, Charles Harkless 1945- WhoAm 94, WhoAmA 93
Cecil, David Rolf 1935- WhoAm 94
Cecil, Donald 1927- WhoFI 94
Cecil, Dorcas Ann 1945- WhoMW 93
Cecil, Edward d1940 WhoHol 92
Cecil, Elmer James 1922- WhoAmP 93
Cecil, Frances 1945- WhoMW 93
Cecil, Henry Richard Amherst 1943- Who 94
Cecil, Jane WhoHol 92
Cecil, John Lamont 1909- WhoAm 94
Cecil, Jonathan 1939- WhoHol 92
Cecil, Mary d1940 WhoHol 92
Cecil, Mildred Cooke 1526-1589 BlmGWL
Cecil, (Oswald) Nigel Amherst 1925- Who 94
Cecil, Nora 1879- WhoHol 92
Cecil, Richard DrAPF 93
Cecil, Robert 1913- Who 94
Cecil, William, Viscount Cranborne and Earl of Salisbury 1591-1668 DcNaB MP
Cecil, William A. V., Sr. WhoAm 94
Cecil, Winifred 1907-1985 NewGrDO
Cecilia 1915- WhoAmA 93
Cecilia, St. d230? BlmGEL
Cedain Zhoma 1937- IntWW 93, WhoPRCh 91 [port]
Cedar, Jon WhoHol 92
Cedar, Larry WhoHol 92
Cedar, Paul Arnold 1938- WhoAm 94, WhoMW 93
Cedarbaum, Jesse Michael 1951- WhoScEn 94
Cedarbaum, Miriam Goldman 1929- WhoAm 94, WhoAmL 94
Ceddia, Anthony Francis 1944- WhoAm 94
Cedeno, Andujar 1969- WhoHisp 94
Cedeno, Cesar 1951- WhoHisp 94
Cedeno, Cesar 1957- WhoBlA 94
Ceder, Elayne 1946- ConTFT 11
Cederbaum, Eugene E. 1942- WhoAm 94
Cederberg, John Edwin 1943- WhoAm 94, WhoFI 94
Cederberg, Jon C. 1952- WhoAmL 94
Cedering, Siv DrAPF 93
Cederna, Camilla 1921- BlmGWL
Cederquist, John 1946- WhoAm 94, WhoAmA 93
Cederschiold, Charlotte 1944- WhoWomW 91
Cederstrom, John Andrew 1929- WhoAmA 93
Cediel, Germán 1941- WhoHisp 94
Cedillo, Arnulfo 1951- WhoHisp 94
Cedillo, Rebecca Quintanilla 1954- WhoHisp 94
Cedoline, Anthony John 1942- WhoWest 94
Cedraschi, Tullio 1938- WhoAm 94, WhoFI 94
Cedric, Lyle Russell 1918- WhoAm 94
Cedrone, Louis Robert, Jr. 1923- WhoAm 94
Ceeley, Leonard d1977 WhoHol 92
Cefalo, Michael Joseph 1940- WhoAmP 93
Cefis, Eugenio 1921- IntWW 93
Cefkin, J. Leo 1916- WhoAmP 93
Cegani, Elisa 1911- WhoHol 92
Cegielka, Francis (Anthony) 1908- WrDr 94
Ceguerra, Lourdes Obieta 1963- WhoWest 94
Cehanovsky, George 1892-1986 NewGrDO
Ceibal, Alfredo 1952- WhoHisp 94
Ceisler, Robert Lester 1919- WhoAmL 94
Cejas, Paul L. 1943- WhoHisp 94
Cejka, Susan Ann 1950- WhoFI 94
Cela (y Trulock), Camilo Jose 1916- ConWorW 93
Cela, Camilo Jose 1916- HispLC [port], IntWW 93, NobelP 91 [port], Who 94
Celac, Sergiu 1939- Who 94
Celarie, Clementine WhoHol 92
Celati, Gianni 1937- ConWorW 93
Celaya, Carlos S. 1946- WhoHisp 94
Celaya, Frank WhoAmP 93, WhoHisp 94
Celaya, Mary Susan 1962- WhoHisp 94
Celaya, Oscar WhoHisp 94
Celebrezze, Anthony WhoAmL 94
Celebrezze, Anthony J., Jr. 1941- WhoAm 94, WhoAmL 94, WhoAmP 93, WhoMW 93
Celebrezze, Frank D. 1928- WhoAmP 93
Celebrezze, James P. 1938- WhoAmP 93
Celender, Don 1931- WhoAmA 93
Celentano, Adriano WhoHol 92
Celentano, Francis Michael 1928- WhoAm 94, WhoAmA 93, WhoWest 94
Celentino, Luciano 1940- IntMPA 94
Celesia, Gastone Guglielmo 1933- WhoAm 94
Celeste, Lino Joseph 1937- WhoAm 94
Celeste, Richard F. 1937- IntWW 93, WhoAmP 93
Celeste, Theodore Samuel 1945- WhoAmP 93
Celestin, Toussaint A. 1930- WhoBlA 94
Celi, Adolfo d1986 WhoHol 92
Celibidache, Sergiu 1912- IntWW 93, Who 94
Celier, Pierre 1917- IntWW 93
Celio, Nello 1914- IntWW 93
Celis, Claudia d1958 WhoHol 92
Celis, Manuel 1944- WhoWest 94
Celisova, Kvetoslava 1946- WhoWomW 91
Celizic, Mike 1948- WrDr 94
Cell, Edward Charles 1928- WrDr 94
Cella, Carl Edward 1941- WhoAmP 93
Cella, Francis Raymond 1909- WhoAm 94
Cella, Frank J. 1939- WhoIns 94
Cella, John Anthony 1926- WhoWest 94
Cella, John J. 1940- WhoAm 94, WhoFI 94
Cellan-Jones, James 1931- IntMPA 94
Cellan-Jones, James Gwynne 1931- WhoAm 94
Celletti, Rodolfo 1917- NewGrDO
Celli, Frank H. 1842-1904 NewGrDO
Celli, Kenneth Dana 1956- WhoWest 94
Celli, Paul 1935- WhoAmA 93
Cellier, Alfred 1844-1891 NewGrDO
Cellier, Antoinette 1909- WhoHol 92
Cellier, Caroline WhoHol 92
Cellier, Elizabeth BlmGWL
Cellier, Frank d1948 WhoHol 92
Cellier, Peter WhoHol 92
Celliers, Peter Joubert 1920- WhoFI 94
Cellini, Joseph 1924- WhoAmA 93

Cellucci, Argeo Paul 1948- *WhoAm 94, WhoAmP 93*
Cellura, Angele Raymond 1932- *WhoScEn 94*
Celniker, Susan Elizabeth 1954- *WhoScEn 94*
Celona, John Anthony 1953- *WhoAmP 93*
Celoniati, Ignazio c. 1731-1784 *NewGrDO*
Celoron de Blainville, Paul Louis 1753- *WhAmRev*
Celotti, Janice L. 1953- *WhoAmL 94*
Celsi, Dick 1933- *WhoAmP 93*
Celsius, Anders 1701-1744 *WorInv*
Celsor, Billy Frank 1924- *WhoAmP 93*
Cely, Margery fl. 15th cent.- *BlmGWL*
Cemal Pasha 1872-1920 *HisWorL*
Cember, Herman 1924- *WhoAm 94*
Cena fl. 8th cent.- *BlmGWL*
Cenac, Winston Francis 1925- *IntWW 93*
Cenarrusa, Pete T. 1917- *WhoAm 94, WhoHisp 94, WhoWest 94*
Cenarrusa, Peter Thomas 1917- *WhoAmP 93*
Cenci, Silvana 1926- *WhoAmA 93*
Cenerini, Frank Joseph 1944- *WhoAmP 93*
Cengle 1930- *WhoAmA 93*
Ceniceros, Joseph F. *WhoHisp 94*
Ceniceros, Kay *WhoHisp 94*
Cenkner, William 1930- *WhoAm 94*
Cennerazzo, Armando d1962 *WhoHol 92*
Cenotto, Lawrence Arthur 1931- *WhoWest 94*
Censits, Richard John 1937- *WhoAm 94, WhoFI 94*
Censor, Therese *WhoAmA 93*
Centeno, Herbert Elliott 1948- *WhoHisp 94*
Centeno, Martha Aixchel 1960- *WhoHisp 94*
Centeno, Miguel Angel 1957- *WhoHisp 94*
Centeno, Yvette Kace 1940- *BlmGWL*
Center, Charles R. 1958- *WhoAmL 94*
Center, Robert A. 1948- *WhoAm 94, WhoFI 94*
Centlivre, Susanna (Carroll) 1666-1723 *BlmGWL*
Centlivre, Susanna(h) c. 1669-1723 *IntDcT 2*
Centlivre, Susannah d1723 *BlmGEL*
Centner, Charles William 1915- *WhoAmL 94, WhoMW 93*
Centofanti, Joseph 1965- *WhoFI 94*
Centola, Lawrence Joseph 1946- *WhoAmL 94*
Centolella, Thomas Carmen 1952- *ConAu 140*
Centonze, Robert John 1959- *WhoFI 94*
Central Africa, Archbishop of 1935- *Who 94*
Cenwulf fl. 796-821 *DcNaB MP*
Ceo, Maria do 1658- *BlmGWL*
Ceo, Raymond Anthony 1956- *WhoWest 94*
Cepaitis, Elizabeth A. 1943- *WhoAmP 93*
Cepeda, Claudio 1942- *WhoHisp 94*
Cepeda, Joseph C. 1948- *WhoHisp 94*
Cepeda, Orlando Manuel Pennes 1937- *WhoHisp 94*
Cepeda Garcia, Samuel *WhoHisp 94*
Cepluch, Robert J. *WhoScEn 94*
Ceppos, Jerome Merle 1946- *WhoAm 94, WhoWest 94*
Cera, Jack *WhoAmP 93*
Cera, Lee Marie 1950- *WhoAm 94*
Cerami, Anthony 1940- *WhoAm 94, WhoScEn 94*
Ceraso, Chuck Martin 1951- *WhoWest 94*
Cerasoli, Robert Angelo 1947- *WhoAmP 93*
Cerato, Karen Lee 1963- *WhoWest 94*
Ceraul, David James 1955- *WhoAmL 94*
Cerbone, Robert 1960- *WhoWest 94*
Cerda, Clarissa 1964- *WhoHisp 94*
Cerda, David 1927- *WhoHisp 94*
Cerda, Ernestine Castro *WhoHisp 94*
Cerda, James John 1930- *WhoHisp 94*
Cerda, Martin G. 1964- *WhoHisp 94*
Cerdan, Marcel, Jr. *WhoHol 92*
Cere, Ronald Carl 1947- *WhoMW 93*
Cereghino, Warren Wood 1937- *WhoWest 94*
Cereijo, Manuel Ramon 1938- *WhoHisp 94*
Ceresney, Ian 1938- *WhoAm 94, WhoAmL 94*
Cerezo, Carmen Consuelo 1940- *WhoAm 94, WhoAmL 94, WhoHisp 94*
Cerezo Arevalo, Mario Vinicio 1942- *IntWW 93*
Cerf, Kurt d1979 *WhoHol 92*
Cerf, Vinton Gray 1943- *WhoAm 94*
Cerha, Friedrich 1926- *NewGrDO*
Cerilli, Francesco *NewGrDO*
Cerino, Angela Marie 1950- *WhoAmL 94*
Cerkas, Michael William 1956- *WhoMW 93*
Cerletti, Ugo 1877-1963 *EncSPD*
Cerlone, Francesco 1722-c. 1812 *NewGrDO*
Cermak, Jack Edward 1922- *WhoAm 94*
Cerna, Enrique Santiago 1953- *WhoHisp 94*
Cernak, Keith Patrick 1954- *WhoWest 94*
Cernan, Eugene A. 1934- *WhoAm 94*
Cerna-Plata, Angela 1941- *WhoHisp 94*
Cernay, Germaine 1900-1943 *NewGrDO*
Cernera, Anthony Joseph 1950- *WhoAm 94*
Cernik, Oldrich 1921- *IntWW 93*
Cerninova z Harasova, Zuzana 1601-1654 *BlmGWL*
Cernova, Darina 1924- *WhoWomW 91*
Cernuda, Luis 1902-1963 *DcLB 134 [port], GayLL*
Cernuda, Paloma 1948- *WhoAmA 93*
Cernuda, Ramon *WhoHisp 94*
Cernuda y Bidon, Luis *GayLL*
Cernugel, William John 1942- *WhoAm 94*
Cernuschi, Alberto C. *WhoAmA 93*
Cernuschi-Frias, Bruno 1952- *WhoScEn 94*
Cerny, Douglas Martin 1958- *WhoAmL 94*
Cerny, Edward Charles, III 1943- *WhoAmL 94*
Cerny, Howard J. d1993 *NewYTBS 93*
Cerny, Joseph, III 1936- *WhoAm 94, WhoWest 94*
Cerny, Joseph Charles 1930- *WhoAm 94, WhoMW 93, WhoScEn 94*
Cerny, Louis Thomas 1942- *WhoAm 94*
Cerny, William F., Jr. *WhoAmP 93*
Cerofolini, Gianfranco 1946- *WhoScEn 94*
Ceroke, Clarence John 1921- *WhoMW 93*
Cerone, David *WhoMW 93*
Cerquetti, Anita 1931- *NewGrDO*
Cerra, Joseph Michael 1962- *WhoAmL 94*
Cerra, Ramona Gail 1940- *WhoAmP 93*
Ceratto, Fernando 1939- *WhoHisp 94*
Cerri, Alberto 1948- *WhoWest 94*
Cerria, Philip Michael 1934- *WhoAmP 93*
Cerrito, Fanny 1817-1909 *IntDcB [port]*
Cerrito, Oratio Alfonso 1911- *WhoFI 94, WhoWest 94*
Cerro, Jose Antonio 1941- *WhoAm 94*
Cerrolaza, Miguel Enrique 1957- *WhoScEn 94*
Cerrone, Jean Baptiste 1912-1991 *WhAm 10*
Certan, Sergiu 1952- *LoBiDrD*
Cerullo, Alfred C., III 1961- *WhoAmP 93*
Cerutti, James Joseph 1942- *WhoMW 93*
Cerval, Claude d1972 *WhoHol 92*
Cervantes (Saavedra), Miguel de 1547-1616 *NewGrDO*
Cervantes, Alfonso 1937- *WhoHisp 94*
Cervantes, David Michael 1955- *WhoHisp 94*
Cervantes, Donald E. *WhoHisp 94*
Cervantes, Evelio 1937- *WhoHisp 94*
Cervantes, James V. *DrAPF 93*
Cervantes, Jorge Alberto 1961- *WhoHisp 94*
Cervantes, Joseph M. 1950- *WhoHisp 94*
Cervantes, Lorna Dee *DrAPF 93*
Cervantes, Lorna Dee 1954- *BlmGWL, WhoHisp 94*
Cervantes, Magdalena *WhoHisp 94*
Cervantes, Miguel de 1547-1616 *LitC 23 [port], ShSCr 12 [port]*
Cervantes, (Saveedra) Miguel de 1547-1616 *IntDcT 2 [port]*
Cervantes, Miguel R. 1938- *WhoHisp 94*
Cervantes, Olivia *WhoHisp 94*
Cervantes, Richard E. *WhoHisp 94*
Cervantes, Robert W. 1947- *WhoHisp 94*
Cervantes, Salvador A. 1948- *WhoHisp 94*
Cervantes Sahagún, Miguel 1959- *WhoHisp 94*
Cervántez, Pedro 1915- *WhoHisp 94*
Cervellione, Maurizio 1952- *WhoMW 93*
Cervena, Sona 1925- *NewGrDO*
Cervene, Richard *WhoAmA 93*
Cervenka, Barbara 1939- *WhoAmA 93*
Cervenka, Exene 1956- *See X ConMus 11*
Cervenka, Jaroslav 1933- *WhoMW 93*
Cervenka, William Joseph 1931- *WhoAmP 93*
Cerveny, Frank Stanley 1933- *WhoAm 94*
Cerveny, Libor 1942- *WhoScEn 94*
Cervera, Richard *WhoHisp 94*
Cervero, Jose Maria 1946- *WhoScEn 94*
Cervetti, Raymond Dean 1951- *WhoMW 93*
Cervi, Al 1917- *BasBi*
Cervi, Gino d1974 *WhoHol 92*
Cervieri, John Anthony, Jr. 1931- *WhoAm 94, WhoFI 94*
Cervilla, Constance Marlene 1951- *WhoFI 94, WhoMW 93*
Cervinkova-Riegrova, Marie 1854-1895 *NewGrDO*
Cervone, Anthony Louis 1962- *WhoAmL 94*
Cervoni, Robert Angelo 1953- *WhoFI 94*
Cesaire, Aime (Fernand) 1913- *BlkWr 2, ConAu 43NR, ConWorW 93, IntDcT 2*
Cesaire, Aime Fernand 1913- *IntWW 93*
Cesaire, Ina *BlmGWL*
Cesana, Renzo d1970 *WhoHol 92*
Cesar, Ana Cristina 1952-1983 *BlmGWL*
Cesar, M. d1921 *WhoHol 92*
Cesarani, Sal 1941- *WhoAm 94*
Cesarano, Gregory Morgen 1946- *WhoAm 94*
Cesarano, Michael Chapman 1944- *WhoAmL 94*
Cesari, Lamberto 1910-1990 *WhAm 10*
Cesarini, Carlo Francesco 1666-1741? *NewGrDO*
Cesario, Robert Charles 1941- *WhoMW 93*
Cesena, Alma *WhoHisp 94*
Cesinger, Joan 1936- *WhoAm 94*
Ceska, Miroslav 1932- *WhoScEn 94*
Cesnik, James Michael 1935- *WhoAm 94*
Cespedes, Rogelio Miguel 1943- *WhoHisp 94*
Cess, Robert Donald 1933- *WhoAm 94*
Cessar, Richard J. 1928- *WhoAmP 93*
Cessna, Jay Bertram 1950- *WhoAmP 93*
Cestari, Constance G. 1931- *WhoAmP 93*
Cestero, Herman J., Jr. 1941- *WhoHisp 94*
Cesti, Antonio 1623-1669 *NewGrDO*
Cesti, Remigio c. 1635-1710? *NewGrDO*
Cetegen, Baki M. 1956- *WhoScEn 94*
Ceterski, Dorothy 1950- *WhoAm 94*
Cetin, Anton 1936- *WhoAmA 93*
Cetin, Hikmet 1937- *IntWW 93*
Cetron, Marvin Jerome 1930- *WhoAm 94*
Cetrulo, Lawrence G. 1949- *WhoAmL 94*
Cetrulo, Robert Camillus 1935- *WhoAmL 94*
Cettei, Donna Lee 1951- *WhoAmL 94*
Ceu, Maria do 1658-1753 *BlmGWL*
Ceu, Violante do 1601-1693 *BlmGWL*
Cevallos, Carlos 1950- *WhoHisp 94*
Cevallos, Francisco Javier 1956- *WhoHisp 94*
Cevallos, Ramón Yuri 1963- *WhoHisp 94*
Cevallos, Victor Hugo 1949- *WhoHisp 94*
Cevasco, G(eorge) A(nthony) 1924- *WrDr 94*
Cevenini, Roberto Mauro 1957- *WhoFI 94, WhoScEn 94*
Ceverha, Bill 1936- *WhoAmP 93*
Cevetillo, Louis d1985 *WhoHol 92*
Cewang Jigmei 1945- *IntWW 93, WhoPRCh 91 [port]*
Ceyrac, Francois 1912- *IntWW 93*
Cha, Chang-Yul 1939- *WhoAsA 94*
Cha, Chuan-sin 1925- *WhoScEn 94*
Cha, Dae Yang 1936- *WhoMW 93*
Cha, Dong Se 1943- *WhoScEn 94*
Cha, Liang-Chien 1905- *IntWW 93*
Cha, Philip Dao 1962- *WhoScEn 94*
Cha, Soyoung Stephen 1944- *WhoAsA 94*
Cha, Sungman 1928- *WhoAsA 94*
Chaar, Alfonso Lopez 1938- *WhoAmP 93*
Chaban-Delmas, Jacques Michel Pierre 1915- *IntWW 93*
Chaban-Delmas, Jacques Pierre Michel 1915- *Who 94*
Chabanon, Michel-Paul-Guy de 1729?-1792 *NewGrDO*
Chabaud, Andre 1921- *IntWW 93*
Chaben, Steven Ross 1958- *WhoMW 93*
Chaber, M.E. *EncSF 93*
Chaberek, Ed *DrAPF 93*
Chabert, Jos 1933- *IntWW 93*
Chablais, Jean-Daniel 1961- *WhoAmL 94*
Chabon, Michael 1965- *WrDr 94*
Chabot, Aurore (Martha) 1949- *WhoAmA 93*
Chabot, Christopher Cleaves 1961- *WhoScEn 94*
Chabot, Elliot Charles 1955- *WhoAmL 94*
Chabot, Herbert L. 1931- *CngDr 93, WhoAm 94, WhoAmL 94*
Chabot, Philip Louis, Jr. 1951- *WhoAm 94, WhoAmL 94, WhoFI 94*
Chabot, Robert F. 1924- *WhoAmP 93*
Chabot-Fence, Dene 1932- *WhoWest 94*
Chabraja, Nicholas D. 1942- *WhoAm 94, WhoAmL 94*
Chabran, Richard 1950- *WhoHisp 94*
Chabre, Virgil *DrAPF 93*
Chabrier, (Alexis-)Emmanuel 1841-1894 *NewGrDO*
Chabrol, Claude 1930- *IntMPA 94, IntWW 93, WhoHol 92*
Chabrow, Penn Benjamin 1939- *WhoAmL 94*
Chabukiani, Vakhtang 1910-1992 *IntDcB [port]*
Chabukiani, Vakhtang Mikhailovich 1910-1992 *AnObit 1992*
Chace, Isobel 1934- *WrDr 94*
Chace, Malcolm 1875-1955 *BuCMET*
Chace, William Murdough 1938- *WhoAm 94*
Chacel (Arimon), Rosa 1898- *ConWorW 93*
Chacel, Rosa 1898- *BlmGWL, DcLB 134 [port]*
Chacholiades, Miltiades 1937- *WhoFI 94, WhoScEn 94*
Chackel, Charles Victor 1947- *WhoWest 94*
Chackes, Kenneth Michael 1949- *WhoAmL 94*
Chacko, George Kuttickal 1930- *WhoAm 94, WhoAsA 94, WhoFI 94, WhoScEn 94*
Chacko, Harsha E. 1952- *WhoAsA 94*
Chacko, Kurian 1949- *WhoAsA 94*
Chacko, Mariam Renate 1950- *WhoAsA 94*
Chacko, Ranjit C. 1948- *WhoAsA 94*
Chacko, Samuel 1942- *WhoMW 93*
Chacko, Varkki P. 1956- *WhoAsA 94*
Chacksfield, Bernard 1913- *Who 94*
Chacon, Alicia *WhoHisp 94*
Chacon, Carlos R. 1959- *WhoHisp 94*
Chacon, Claude Vincent 1952- *WhoHisp 94*
Chacón, Elia Margarita 1951- *WhoHisp 94*
Chacon, George 1953- *WhoHisp 94*
Chacon, Michael Ernest 1954- *WhoWest 94*
Chacón, Peter R. 1925- *WhoHisp 94*
Chacon, Raul 1956- *WhoHisp 94*
Chacon, Vince 1952- *WhoHisp 94*
Chacon Nardi, Rafaela 1926- *BlmGWL*
Chacron, Joseph 1936- *WhoScEn 94*
Chada, Sharon Lynne Wachtel 1960- *WhoWest 94*
Chadbon, Tom 1946- *WhoHol 92*
Chadbourn, Alfred Cheney 1921- *WhoAmA 93*
Chadbourne, Mary McConville 1947- *WhoMW 93*
Chadd, Charles M. 1941- *WhoAmL 94*
Chaddlesone, Sherman 1947- *WhoAmA 93*
Chaddock, Jack Bartley 1924- *WhoAm 94*
Chadeayne, Robert Osborne 1897- *WhoAmA 93*
Chadha, Indrajit Singh 1933- *IntWW 93*
Chadha, Kailash Chandra 1943- *WhoAsA 94*
Chadha, Navneet 1955- *WhoScEn 94*
Chadick, Gary Robert 1961- *WhoAmL 94*
Chadima, Sarah Anne 1956- *WhoScEn 94*
Chadirji, Rifat Kamil 1926- *IntWW 93*
Chadli, Bendjedid 1929- *IntWW 93*
Chadonic, John d1993 *NewYTBS 93*
Chadsey, Phillip Duke 1936- *WhoAm 94*
Chadsey, William Lloyd, III 1942- *WhoAm 94*
Chadwell, James Russell, Jr. 1948- *WhoFI 94*
Chadwell, Susie 1940- *WhoFI 94*
Chadwick, Alex *ConAu 142*
Chadwick, Charles McKenzie 1932- *Who 94*
Chadwick, Curtiss Floyd 1946- *WhoFI 94*
Chadwick, Derek James 1948- *Who 94*
Chadwick, Fiona 1960- *IntDcB [port]*
Chadwick, George W(hitefield) 1854-1931 *NewGrDO*
Chadwick, Gerald William St. John 1915- *Who 94*
Chadwick, Graham Charles 1923- *Who 94*
Chadwick, H. Beatty 1936- *WhoAm 94*
Chadwick, Helene d1940 *WhoHol 92*
Chadwick, Henry 1920- *IntWW 93, Who 94, WrDr 94*
Chadwick, Ina B. *DrAPF 93*
Chadwick, J. Scott 1953- *WhoAmP 93*
Chadwick, James 1891-1974 *WorScD*
Chadwick, John *Who 94*
Chadwick, John 1920- *IntWW 93, Who 94, WrDr 94*
Chadwick, (Gerald William St.) John 1915- *WrDr 94*
Chadwick, John (Murray) 1941- *Who 94*
Chadwick, John Edwin 1957- *WhoMW 93*
Chadwick, Joshua Kenneth B. *Who 94*
Chadwick, June *WhoHol 92*
Chadwick, Lynn Russell 1914- *IntWW 93, Who 94*
Chadwick, Owen *Who 94*
Chadwick, Owen 1916- *IntWW 93*
Chadwick, Owen, Sir 1916- *WrDr 94*
Chadwick, (William) Owen 1916- *ConAu 41NR, Who 94*
Chadwick, P(hilip) G(eorge) 1893-1955 *EncSF 93*
Chadwick, Peter 1931- *IntWW 93, Who 94*
Chadwick, Raymond G. 1947- *WhoAmL 94*
Chadwick, Robert 1924- *WhoAmL 94*
Chadwick, Robert Edwin, II 1947- *WhoMW 93*
Chadwick, Robert Everard 1916- *Who 94*
Chadwick, Robert William 1930- *WhoScEn 94*

Chamberlin, Paul Davis 1937-
WhoScEn 94
Chamberlin, Riley d1917 *WhoHol 92*
Chamberlin, Robert Joseph 1929-
WhoFI 94, WhoWest 94
Chamberlin, Robert Porter 1965-
WhoAmL 94
Chamberlin, Scott 1948- *WhoAmA 93*
Chamberlin, Terry McBride *WhoAm 94*
Chambers, Agnes Mae 1934- *WhoMW 93*
Chambers, Aidan 1934- *TwCYAW,
WrDr 94*
Chambers, Albert A. d1993
NewYTBS 93 [port]
Chambers, Alex A. 1934- *WhoBlA 94*
Chambers, Andrew David 1943- *Who 94*
Chambers, Andrew P. 1931-
AfrAmG [port]
Chambers, Anne Cox *WhoAm 94*
Chambers, Bruce William 1941-
WhoAmA 93
Chambers, Carolyn Silva 1931-
WhoWest 94
Chambers, Catherine E. *WrDr 94*
Chambers, Charles MacKay 1941-
WhoAm 94
Chambers, Charlotte d1821 *BlmGWL*
Chambers, Clarice Lorraine 1938-
WhoBlA 94
Chambers, Clytia Montllor 1922-
WhoFI 94, WhoWest 94
Chambers, Colin 1950 *WrDr 94*
Chambers, Curtis Allen 1924- *WhoAm 94*
Chambers, David Smith 1917-1989
WhAm 10
Chambers, Donald Arthur 1936-
WhoAm 94, WhoScEn 94
Chambers, Donald C. 1936- *WhoBlA 94*
Chambers, Donald Everard 1929-
WhoMW 93
Chambers, Dorothea 1878-1960
BuCMET [port]
Chambers, Dorothy Rose 1941-
WhoWest 94
Chambers, Douglas L. 1957- *WhoAmL 94*
Chambers, Douglas Robert 1929- *Who 94*
Chambers, Edmund 1866-1954 *BlmGEL*
Chambers, Edward Allen 1933-
WhoScEn 94
Chambers, Ernest *WhoAmP 93*
Chambers, Everett 1926- *IntMPA 94*
Chambers, Fred 1912- *WhoAm 94*
Chambers, Fredrick 1928- *WhoBlA 94*
Chambers, Gary Lee 1953- *WhoAmL 94,
WhoWest 94*
Chambers, George *DrAPF 93*
Chambers, George Michael 1928-
IntWW 93
Chambers, George Michael 1956- *Who 94*
Chambers, Guy Wayne 1956-
WhoAmL 94
Chambers, Harry, Jr. 1956- *WhoBlA 94*
Chambers, Harry Heyworth 1926-
Who 94
Chambers, Henry George 1956-
WhoScEn 94
Chambers, James 1948- *WhoAm 94*
Chambers, James Patrick 1968-
WhoScEn 94
Chambers, (Carolyn) Jane 1937-1983
GayLL
Chambers, Jerry Ray 1947- *WhoMW 93*
Chambers, Jessie *GayLL*
Chambers, Joan Louise 1937- *WhoAm 94*
Chambers, John 1931-1978
WhoAmA 93N
Chambers, John Paul 1958- *WhoMW 93*
Chambers, Jonathan Goetz 1955-
WhoWest 94
Chambers, Julius LeVonne 1936-
WhoAm 94, WhoAmL 94, WhoBlA 94
Chambers, Karen 1948- *WhoAmA 93*
Chambers, Kate *WrDr 94*
Chambers, Kenneth Carter 1956-
WhoScEn 94, WhoWest 94
Chambers, Kenton Lee 1929- *WhoAm 94,
WhoScEn 94*
Chambers, LaRoyce Francis 1944-
WhoMW 94
Chambers, Lawrence Cleveland 1929-
AfrAmG [port]
Chambers, Leigh Ross 1932- *IntWW 93,
WhoAm 94*
Chambers, Leland H. 1928- *ConAu 140*
Chambers, Linda *WhoAmP 93*
Chambers, Lois Irene 1935- *WhoFI 94,
WhoWest 94*
Chambers, Lyster d1947 *WhoHol 92*
Chambers, Madrith Bennett 1935-
WhoBlA 94
Chambers, Margaret d1965 *WhoHol 92*
Chambers, Margaret Warner 1959-
WhoAmL 94
Chambers, Marie d1933 *WhoHol 92*
Chambers, Marilyn 1952- *WhoHol 92*
Chambers, Marjorie Bell 1923-
WhoWest 94

Chambers, Mary Peyton 1931-
WhoAmP 93
Chambers, Maurice Ripley 1916-1990
WhAm 10
Chambers, Milton Warren 1928-
WhoFI 94, WhoWest 94
Chambers, Nicholas Mordaunt 1944-
Who 94
Chambers, Olivia Marie 1942-
WhoBlA 94
Chambers, Pamela S. 1961- *WhoBlA 94*
Chambers, Park A., Jr. 1942- *WhoAmA 93*
Chambers, Penny 1944- *WrDr 94*
Chambers, Peter 1924- *WrDr 94*
Chambers, Peter R. 1953- *WhoWest 94*
Chambers, Ralph d1968 *WhoHol 92*
Chambers, Ray Benjamin 1940-
WhoAmP 93
Chambers, Richard H. 1906- *WhoAm 94,
WhoAmL 94, WhoWest 94*
Chambers, Richard Lee 1947- *WhoAm 94*
Chambers, Robert Alexander H. *Who 94*
Chambers, Robert C. 1952- *WhoAmP 93*
Chambers, Robert Eugene 1910-
WhoAmP 93
Chambers, Robert Guy 1924- *Who 94*
Chambers, Robert Hunter, III 1939-
WhoAm 94
Chambers, Robert Jeffferson 1930-
WhoAm 94
Chambers, Robert William 1943-
WhoFI 94
Chambers, Ronald D. 1943- *WhoAm 94*
Chambers, Ruth-Marie Frances
WhoBlA 94
Chambers, Shirley *WhoHol 92*
Chambers, Stephen L.E. 1956-
WhoWest 94
Chambers, Steven Ralph 1961-
WhoWest 94
Chambers, Terry
See XTC *ConMus 10*
Chambers, Thomas Doane 1959-
WhoAm 94, WhoBlA 94
Chambers, Timothy Lachlan 1946-
Who 94
Chambers, Tom 1959- *BasBi*
Chambers, Virginia Ellen 1927-
WhoWest 94
Chambers, Wheaton d1958 *WhoHol 92*
Chambers, William Everett 1931-
WhoFI 94, WhoMW 93
Chambers, William McWille 1951-
WhoAmA 93
Chambers, YJean S. 1921- *WhoBlA 94*
Chambi, Martin 1891-1973 *WhoAmA 93N*
Chamblee, Carl 1933- *WhoAmP 93*
Chamblee, Cebron Daniel 1928-
WhoAmP 93
Chambless, Thomas Sidney 1943-
WhoAmP 93
Chambliss, Chris 1948- *WhoBlA 94*
Chambliss, Ida Belle 1935- *WhoBlA 94*
Chambliss, William Joseph 1933-
WhoAm 94
Chambliss, Woodrow d1981 *WhoHol 92*
Chamblit, Rebekah d1733 *BlmGWL*
Chambolle, Thierry Jean-Francois 1939-
WhoScEn 94
Chambon, Charles William 1954-
WhoWest 94
Chambon, Pierre 1931- *IntWW 93*
Chambre, Paul L. 1918- *WhoAm 94*
Chambrot, Joseph Abrahan 1952-
WhoAmL 94
Chameides, Steven B. 1946- *WhoAm 94,
WhoAmL 94*
Chameli, David Paul 1962- *WhoAmL 94*
Chamfort, Sebastien-Roch Nicolas de
1740-1794 *GuFrLit 2*
Chamier, Anthony Edward Deschamps
1935- *Who 94*
Chamis, Christos Constantinos 1930-
WhoMW 93, WhoScEn 94
Chamisso De Boncourt,
Louis-Charles-Adelaide 1781-1836
WhWE
Chamkha, Ali Jawad 1964- *WhoScEn 94*
Chamlee, Mario 1892-1966 *NewGrDO*
Chammah, Walid A. 1954- *WhoAm 94,
WhoFI 94*
Chamorro, H.E. Violeta Barrios de 1929-
WhoWomW 91
Chamorro, Violeta Barrios de *IntWW 93*
Chamoux, Francois 1915- *IntWW 93*
Champ, Frank Percival 1896- *WhAm 10*
Champ, Norman Barnard, Jr. 1928-
WhoAmP 93
Champ, Raymond Lester 1941-
WhoAm 94
Champ, Stanley Gordon 1919-
WhoScEn 94, WhoWest 94
Champa, Jo *WhoHol 92*
Champagne, Andree 1939- *WhoAm 94*
Champagne, Anthony Martin 1949-
WhoAmL 94

Champagne, Jennifer A. 1970-
WhoAmP 93
Champagne, Jocelyne D. 1942-
WhoAmP 93
Champagne, John *DrAPF 93*
Champagne, John F., Jr. 1952- *WhoAm 94*
Champagne, Martin Raymond 1964-
WhoFI 94
Champagne, Norman E. 1941-
WhoAmP 93
Champagne, Pierre d1929? *WhoHol 92*
Champagne, Richard L. 1926-
WhoAmP 93
Champagne, Ronald Oscar 1942-
WhoAm 94
Champane, James 1926- *WhoMW 93*
Champe, John c. 1752-c. 1798 *WhAmRev*
Champe, John c. 1758-1818 *AmRev*
Champein, Stanislas 1753-1830 *NewGrDO*
Champernowne, David (Gawen) 1912-
WrDr 94
Champernowne, David Gawen 1912-
Who 94
Champine, Dennis *WhoAmP 93*
Champion, Epaphroditus 1756-1834
WhAmRev
Champion, Gower d1980 *WhoHol 92*
Champion, Hale 1922- *WhoAm 94,
WhoAmP 93*
Champion, J(ustin) A. I. 1960- *ConAu 141*
Champion, James A. 1947- *WhoBlA 94*
Champion, Jean *WhoHol 92*
Champion, Jerrye G. 1940- *WhoBlA 94*
Champion, Jesse 1927- *WhoBlA 94*
Champion, John C. 1923- *IntMPA 94*
Champion, John Stuart 1921- *Who 94*
Champion, Larry S. 1932- *WrDr 94*
Champion, Marge 1919- *WhoHol 92*
Champion, Marge 1923- *IntMPA 94,
WhoAm 94, WhoWest 94*
Champion, Michael *WhoHol 92*
Champion, Norma Jean 1933-
WhoAmP 93, WhoMW 93
Champion, Richard Gordon 1931-
WhoAm 94
Champion, Tempii Bridgene 1961-
WhoBlA 94
Champkin, Peter 1918- *WrDr 94*
Champlain, Edward James 1948-
WhoAm 94
Champlain, Samuel De 1567-1635 *WhWE*
Champlain, Samuel de c. 1570-1635
HisWorL [port]
Champlin, Charles Davenport 1926-
WhoAm 94
Champlin, Irene d1990 *WhoHol 92*
Champlin, Joseph M(asson) 1930-
WrDr 94
Champlin, Malcolm McGregor 1911-
WhoAm 94
Champlin, Marjorie Weeden 1921-
WhoAm 94
Champlin, Richard H. 1935- *WhoAm 94*
Champlin, Steven K. 1944- *WhoAm 94,
WhoAmL 94*
Champlin, Tim 1937- *WrDr 94*
Champlin, William Glen 1923-
WhoScEn 94
Champney, Richard Edward Jr. 1952-
WhoFI 94
Champoux, Michael Francis 1962-
WhoAmP 93
Champseix, Leodile *BlmGWL*
Chamson, Sandra Potkorony 1933-
WhoAm 94
Chan, Adrian 1941- *WhoAsA 94*
Chan, Agnes Isabel 1917- *WhoAmP 93*
Chan, Ah Wing Edith 1963- *WhoScEn 94*
Chan, Albert 1949- *WhoScEn 94*
Chan, Allen Fong 1957- *WhoWest 94*
Chan, Andrew Mancheong 1957-
WhoScEn 94
Chan, Angela 1968- *WhoAsA 94*
Chan, Anson 1940- *WhoWomW 91*
Chan, Anthony Bernard 1944-
WhoAsA 94
Chan, Anthony Kit-Cheung 1960-
WhoAsA 94
Chan, Arthur H. 1950?- *WhoAsA 94*
Chan, Arthur Wing Kay 1941- *WhoAsA 94*
Chan, Bill 1951- *WhoAsA 94*
Chan, Carl Chiang 1950- *WhoAsA 94*
Chan, Carlyle Hung-lun 1949-
WhoAsA 94, WhoMW 93
Chan, Caroline Elaine 1965- *WhoAmL 94*
Chan, Cheung M. 1917- *WhoAsA 94*
Chan, Chiu Shui 1950- *WhoAsA 94*
Chan, Chiu Yeung 1941- *WhoAsA 94*
Chan, Cho-chak John 1943- *Who 94*
Chan, Cho Lik 1955- *WhoAsA 94*
Chan, Chong B. 1951- *WhoAsA 94*
Chan, Chun Kin 1953- *WhoAsA 94*
Chan, Clara Suet-Phang 1949-
WhoScEn 94
Chan, Daniel Chung-Yin 1948-
WhoAmP 94
Chan, David Chuk 1962- *WhoScEn 94*
Chan, David S. 1940- *WhoAsA 94*

Chan, David So Keung 1951- *WhoAsA 94*
Chan, Donald P. K. 1937- *WhoAsA 94*
Chan, Donald Pin-Kwan 1937-
WhoScEn 94
Chan, Edwin Y. 1960- *WhoAsA 94*
Chan, Eric Ping-Pang 1952- *WhoScEn 94*
Chan, Gary M. 1947- *WhoAsA 94*
Chan, George d1957 *WhoHol 92*
Chan, Glenn 1934- *WhoAsA 94*
Chan, Harvey Thomas, Jr. 1940-
WhoAsA 94
Chan, Heng Chee 1942- *IntWW 93*
Chan, Henry Y. S. 1947- *WhoAsA 94*
Chan, Jack-Kang 1950- *WhoAsA 94,
WhoScEn 94*
Chan, Jackie 1954- *WhoHol 92*
Chan, James C. 1937- *WhoAsA 94*
Chan, James C. M. 1937- *WhoAsA 94*
Chan, Jeffery Paul *DrAPF 93*
Chan, Jerry Kum Nam 1960-
WhoWest 94
Chan, John 1964- *WhoAsA 94*
Chan, John Doddson 1962- *WhoScEn 94*
Chan, John G. 1938- *WhoAsA 94*
Chan, Julius 1939- *IntWW 93, Who 94*
Chan, Kai Chiu 1934- *WhoAsA 94*
Chan, Kam Chuen 1959- *WhoAsA 94*
Chan, Kawei 1934- *WhoAsA 94*
Chan, Kenyon S. 1948- *WhoAsA 94*
Chan, Kwai Shing 1955- *WhoScEn 94*
Chan, Kwan M. 1935- *WhoAsA 94*
Chan, Kwok Hung 1954- *WhoAsA 94*
Chan, Lai Kow *WhoAm 94*
Chan, Laurence Kwong-Fai 1947-
WhoAsA 94
Chan, Lee-Nien Lillian 1941- *WhoAsA 94*
Chan, Lo-Yi C. Y. 1932- *WhoAsA 94*
Chan, Lo-Yi Cheung Yuen 1932-
WhoAm 94
Chan, Lois Mai 1934- *WhoAsA 94*
Chan, Loren Briggs 1943- *WhoWest 94*
Chan, Lung S. 1955- *WhoAsA 94*
Chan, Marsha J. 1952- *WhoAsA 94*
Chan, Mason C. 1937- *WhoAsA 94*
Chan, Mei-Mei 1959- *WhoAsA 94*
Chan, Michael Chiu-Hon 1961-
WhoScEn 94, WhoWest 94
Chan, Michele *WhoHol 92*
Chan, Nai Keong 1931- *Who 94*
Chan, Nelson Hao 1959- *WhoAmL 94*
Chan, Oie d1967 *WhoHol 92*
Chan, Paul T. 1956- *WhoFI 94*
Chan, Peng S. 1957- *WhoAsA 94*
Chan, Peter Wing Kwong 1949-
WhoWest 94
Chan, Phillip Paang 1946- *WhoAsA 94*
Chan, Po Chuen 1935- *WhoAsA 94*
Chan, Pui Kwong 1946- *WhoAsA 94*
Chan, Ray Chi-Moon 1957- *WhoWest 94*
Chan, Raymond Honfu 1958-
WhoScEn 94
Chan, Raymond Sun-Man 1955-
WhoFI 94
Chan, Richard Y. D. 1954- *WhoFI 94*
Chan, Rix Siu-Wong 1962- *WhoWest 94*
Chan, Robert T. P. 1943- *WhoAsA 94*
Chan, Samuel H. P. 1941- *WhoAsA 94*
Chan, Sham-Yuen 1949- *WhoAsA 94*
Chan, Shih Hung 1943- *WhoAm 94,
WhoAsA 94*
Chan, Shu-Park 1929- *WhoAm 94*
Chan, Shu Yan 1954- *WhoMW 93*
Chan, Spencer d1988 *WhoHol 92*
Chan, Stephen W. 1942- *WhoAsA 94*
Chan, Steven D. 1951- *WhoAsA 94*
Chan, Steven S. 1949- *WhoWest 94*
Chan, Su Han 1956- *WhoAsA 94*
Chan, Sucheng 1941- *WhoAsA 94*
Chan, Suitak Steve 1949- *WhoAsA 94*
Chan, Sunney Ignatius 1936- *WhoAm 94*
Chan, Tak-Biu 1961- *WhoWest 94*
Chan, Tak Hang 1941- *WhoAm 94,
WhoScEn 94*
Chan, Tat-Hing 1951- *WhoAsA 94*
Chan, Ted W. 1960- *WhoAsA 94*
Chan, Thomas d1942 *WhoHol 92*
Chan, Thomas O. 1954- *WhoAsA 94*
Chan, Thomas Tak-Wah 1950-
WhoAmL 94
Chan, Timothy T. 1945- *WhoAsA 94*
Chan, Ting Y. 1932- *WhoAsA 94*
Chan, Tsze Hau 1954- *WhoAsA 94*
Chan, Vivien Wai-Fan 1967- *WhoWest 94*
Chan, W. Y. 1932- *WhoAm 94*
Chan, Wai-Yee *WhoAsA 94*
Chan, Wai-Yee 1950- *WhoScEn 94*
Chan, Wan Choon 1937- *WhoScEn 94*
Chan, Wing-Chung 1947- *WhoScEn 94*
Chan, Yeung Yu 1962- *WhoAsA 94*
Chan, Yim Hung 1959- *WhoWest 94*
Chan, Yupo 1945- *WhoScEn 94*
Chanan, Michael 1946- *WrDr 94*
Chance, Alexander Macomb 1844-1917
DcNaB MP
Chance, Anna d1943 *WhoHol 92*
Chance, Britton 1913- *IntWW 93,
WhoAm 94, WhoScEn 94*
Chance, Charles 1936- *WhoIns 94*

Chance, Dudley Raymond 1916- *Who 94*
Chance, George A., Jr. 1918- *WhoAmP 93*
Chance, Henry Martyn, II 1912- *WhAm 94*
Chance, Hugh Nicholas 1940- *WhoScEn 94*
Chance, Jane *DrAPF 93*
Chance, Jean Carver 1938- *WhoAmP 93*
Chance, (George) Jeremy (ffolliott) 1926- *Who 94*
Chance, John Newton *EncSF 93*
Chance, John T. 1948- *WrDr 94*
Chance, Jonathan *EncSF 93*
Chance, Kathy Lynn 1957- *WhoWest 94*
Chance, Kenneth Bernard 1953- *WhoBlA 94*
Chance, Kenneth Donald 1948- *WhoWest 94*
Chance, Michael 1955- *NewGrDO*
Chance, Michael Edward Ferguson 1955- *Who 94*
Chance, Michael Spencer 1938- *Who 94*
Chance, Naomi 1930- *WhoHol 92*
Chance, Stephen 1925- *WrDr 94*
Chancel, Francois-Joseph de *NewGrDO*
Chancellor, Alexander Surtees 1940- *IntWW 93, Who 94*
Chancellor, Carl Eugene 1929- *WhoBlA 94*
Chancellor, Christopher 1904-1989 *WhAm 10*
Chancellor, John 1927- *IntMPA 94, IntWW 93, WrDr 94*
Chancellor, John William 1927- *WhoAm 94*
Chancellor, Richard d1556 *WhWE*
Chancellor, Rose Ann 1955- *WhoMW 93*
Chancellor, William Joseph 1931- *WhoAm 94, WhoScEn 94*
Chancey, C. Ray 1914- *WhoAmP 93*
Chancey, Malcolm B., Jr. *WhoAm 94, WhoFI 94*
Chancey, Velton Ray 1943- *WhoWest 94*
Chanco, Amado Garcia 1936- *WhoScEn 94*
Chan Costa, Vivian Rhoda *WhoAsA 94*
Chand, Meira (Angela) 1942- *BlmGWL*
Chand, Naresh 1951- *WhoAsA 94*
Chandan, Ramesh Chandra 1934- *WhoAsA 94*
Chandavimol, Abhai 1908- *IntWW 93*
Chandel, Thomas Phillip 1957- *WhoFI 94*
Chandernagor, Andre 1921- *IntWW 93*
Chandersekaran, Achamma C. *WhoAsA 94*
Chandler, A(rthur) Bertram 1912-1984 *EncSF 93*
Chandler, A. Lee 1922- *WhoAm 94, WhoAmL 94, WhoAmP 93*
Chandler, Adele Rico 1923- *WhoHisp 94*
Chandler, Albert Benjamin 1898-1991 *WhAm 10*
Chandler, Alfred D(upont), Jr. 1918- *WrDr 94*
Chandler, Alfred Dupont, Jr. 1918- *WhoAm 94*
Chandler, Allen E. 1935- *AfrAmG [port]*
Chandler, Allen Eugene 1935- *WhoBlA 94*
Chandler, Alton H. 1942- *WhoBlA 94*
Chandler, Anna d1957 *WhoHol 92*
Chandler, Arthur Bleakley 1926- *WhoAm 94*
Chandler, Bruce Frederick 1926- *WhoScEn 94, WhoWest 94*
Chandler, Brue Stanhope, III 1949- *WhoAm 94*
Chandler, Burton 1934- *WhoAmL 94*
Chandler, Caleb J. 1943- *WhoAmP 93*
Chandler, Carmen Ramos 1963- *WhoHisp 94*
Chandler, Chick d1988 *WhoHol 92*
Chandler, Chris 1951- *WhoAmP 93*
Chandler, Colby H. 1925- *IntWW 93*
Chandler, Colin (Michael) 1939- *IntWW 93, Who 94*
Chandler, Dana 1941- *AfrAmArt 6*
Chandler, Dana C., Jr. 1941- *WhoBlA 94*
Chandler, David 1944- *WhoAm 94*
Chandler, David (Geoffrey) 1934- *WrDr 94*
Chandler, David Benjamin 1953- *WhoWest 94*
Chandler, Dennis 1947- *WhoAmP 93*
Chandler, Douglas Edwin 1945- *WhoWest 94*
Chandler, Douglas R. 1946- *WhoAmL 94*
Chandler, Drake E. 1948- *WhoAmL 94*
Chandler, Earle W. 1913- *WhoAmP 93*
Chandler, Eddy d1948 *WhoHol 92*
Chandler, Edward William 1953- *WhoMW 93*
Chandler, Edwin Russell 1932- *WhoAm 94*
Chandler, Effie L. 1927- *WhoBlA 94*
Chandler, Elisabeth Gordon 1913- *WhoAm 94, WhoAmA 93*
Chandler, Elizabeth Margaret 1807-1834 *BlmGWL*
Chandler, Estee *WhoHol 92*

Chandler, Everett A. 1926- *WhoBlA 94*
Chandler, Floyd Copeland 1920- *WhoWest 94*
Chandler, Frank 1936- *WrDr 94*
Chandler, Gary *WhoAmP 93*
Chandler, Gene Giles 1947- *WhoAmP 93*
Chandler, Geoffrey 1922- *Who 94*
Chandler, George d1985 *WhoHol 92*
Chandler, George d1992 *IntWW 93N, Who 94N*
Chandler, George 1915-1992 *WrDr 94N*
Chandler, George Francis, III 1940- *WhoAmL 94*
Chandler, Gregory 1957- *WhoWest 94*
Chandler, Harold R. 1941- *WhoBlA 94*
Chandler, Harry Edgar 1920- *WhoAm 94*
Chandler, Harry S. 1938- *WhoAmL 94*
Chandler, Helen d1965 *WhoHol 92*
Chandler, Henry William 1961- *WhoScEn 94*
Chandler, Hubert Thomas 1933- *WhoAm 94*
Chandler, James d1988 *WhoHol 92*
Chandler, James A. 1931- *WhoAmP 93*
Chandler, James Barton 1922- *WhoMW 93*
Chandler, James John 1932- *WhoAm 94*
Chandler, James Kenneth 1948- *WhoAm 94*
Chandler, James P. 1938- *WhoBlA 94*
Chandler, James Williams 1904- *WhoAm 94*
Chandler, Janet Carncross *DrAPF 93*
Chandler, Jeff d1961 *WhoHol 92*
Chandler, Jill d1979 *WhoHol 92*
Chandler, Joan d1979 *WhoHol 92*
Chandler, John 1762-1841 *WhAmRev*
Chandler, John, Jr. 1920- *WhoAm 94*
Chandler, John A. 1944- *WhoAmL 94*
Chandler, John C. 1946- *WhoWest 94*
Chandler, John Davis 1937- *WhoHol 92*
Chandler, John Herrick 1928- *WhoAm 94*
Chandler, John P. H., Jr. 1911- *WhoAmP 93*
Chandler, John W. 1940- *WhoScEn 94*
Chandler, John Wesley 1923- *WhoAm 94*
Chandler, John William 1910- *WhoAm 93*
Chandler, Joyce A. *DrAPF 93*
Chandler, Kathleen Leone 1932- *WhoMW 93*
Chandler, Kenneth A. 1947- *WhoAm 94*
Chandler, Kent, Jr. 1920- *WhoAm 94, WhoAmL 94*
Chandler, Kevin M. 1960- *WhoAmP 93*
Chandler, Kimberley Ann 1952- *WhoAmL 94*
Chandler, Kris 1948- *WhoWest 94*
Chandler, Kyle *WhoHol 92*
Chandler, Lane d1972 *WhoHol 92*
Chandler, Lawrence Bradford, Jr. 1942- *WhoAmL 94*
Chandler, Louis 1911- *WhoAmL 94*
Chandler, Margaret Kueffner 1922-1991 *WhAm 10*
Chandler, Marguerite Nella 1943- *WhoAm 94*
Chandler, Marilyn R(uth) 1949- *ConAu 140*
Chandler, Mark 1931-1992 *WrDr 94N*
Chandler, Mark Joseph 1956- *WhoWest 94*
Chandler, Martha Marsh d1993 *NewYTBS 93*
Chandler, Michael Robert 1950- *WhoAmA 93*
Chandler, Michael Stephen 1959- *WhoWest 94*
Chandler, Mimi *WhoHol 92*
Chandler, Mittie Olion 1949- *WhoBlA 94*
Chandler, Nancy Ann 1933- *WhoAmP 93*
Chandler, Otis 1927- *IntWW 93, WhoAm 94*
Chandler, Paul Anderson 1933- *WhoScEn 94*
Chandler, Raymond 1888-1959 *BlmGEL, IntDcF 2-4*
Chandler, Reuben Carl 1917-1989 *WhAm 10*
Chandler, Rex W. 1937- *WhoAmP 93*
Chandler, Richard Gates 1952- *WhoMW 93*
Chandler, Robert d1950 *WhoHol 92*
Chandler, Robert Charles 1945- *WhoAm 94*
Chandler, Robert Flint, Jr. 1907- *WhoAm 94*
Chandler, Robert Leslie 1948- *WhoAm 94, WhoFI 94*
Chandler, Rod Dennis 1942- *WhoAmP 93*
Chandler, Rory Wayne 1959- *WhoBlA 94*
Chandler, S(tanley) Bernard 1921- *WrDr 94*
Chandler, Sharon Kay 1942- *WhoMW 93*
Chandler, Stephen S. 1899-1989 *WhAm 10*
Chandler, Tertius 1915- *WhoWest 94, WrDr 94*

Chandler, Theodore Alan 1949- *WhoBlA 94*
Chandler, Thomas Bradbury 1726-1790 *DcAmReB 2, WhAmRev*
Chandler, Thomas Eugene 1958- *WhoScEn 94*
Chandler, Thomas Franklin 1947- *WhoWest 94*
Chandler, Tom *DrAPF 93*
Chandler, Tony John 1928- *Who 94*
Chandler, William Everett 1943- *WhoAm 94, WhoFI 94*
Chandler, William Knox 1933- *WhoAm 94*
Chandley, Ann Chester 1936- *WhoScEn 94*
Chandley, Katherine Ragsdale 1937- *WhoAmP 93*
Chandley, Peter Warren 1934- *Who 94*
Chandonnet, Ann Fox *DrAPF 93*
Chandonnet, Ann Fox 1943- *WhoWest 94*
Chandor, Douglas 1897-1953 *WhoAmA 93N*
Chandor, Stebbins Bryant 1933- *WhoAm 94, WhoWest 94*
Chandos, Viscount 1953- *Who 94*
Chandos, John d1987 *WhoHol 92*
Chandos-Pole, John 1909- *Who 94*
Chandos-Pole, John Walkelyne 1913- *Who 94*
Chandra, Abhijit 1957- *WhoAsA 94, WhoWest 94*
Chandra, Ajey 1964- *WhoScEn 94*
Chandra, Avinash 1931- *IntWW 93*
Chandra, Kavitha 1961- *WhoScEn 94*
Chandra, Pramod 1930- *WhoAm 94*
Chandra, Purna 1929- *WhoMW 93*
Chandra, Ramesh 1925- *IntWW 93*
Chandra, Ramesh 1942- *WhoScEn 94*
Chandra, Sanjay 1965- *WhoFI 94*
Chandrachud, Yeshwant Vishnu 1920- *IntWW 93, Who 94*
Chandragupta, Bansi 1924-1981 *IntDcF 2-4*
Chandragupta Maurya c. 360BC-298BC *HisWorL*
Chandramouli, Ramamurti 1947- *WhoWest 94*
Chandramouli, S. *WhoAsA 94*
Chandran, Krishnan Bala 1944- *WhoAsA 94*
Chandran, Ravi 1954- *WhoAsA 94*
Chandran, Satish Raman 1938- *WhoAsA 94*
Chandrasekaran, Balakrishnan 1942- *WhoAm 94, WhoAsA 94*
Chandrasekaran, Perinkolam Raman 1949- *WhoAm 94*
Chandrasekaran, Rengaswami 1939- *WhoScEn 94*
Chandrasekhar, Bellur Sivaramiah 1928- *WhoAm 94*
Chandrasekhar, Bhagwat Subrahmanya 1945- *IntWW 93*
Chandra Sekhar, Hosakere K. 1932- *WhoAsA 94*
Chandrasekhar, Maragatham 1917- *WhoWomW 91*
Chandrasekhar, Sivaramakrishna 1930- *IntWW 93, Who 94*
Chandrasekhar, Sripati 1918- *IntWW 93*
Chandrasekhar, Subrahmanyan 1910- *IntWW 93, Who 94, WhoAm 94, WhoAsA 94, WhoMW 93, WhoScEn 94, WrDr 94*
Chandrasekhar, Subramanyan 1910- *WorScD [port]*
Chandrasekharam, Komaravolu 1920- *IntWW 93*
Chandra Sekharan, Pakkirisamy 1934- *WhoScEn 94*
Chandrashekar, Ramaswamy 1957- *WhoMW 93*
Chandrashekar, Varadaraj 1942- *WhoMW 93, WhoScEn 94*
Chandrawati 1928- *WhoWomW 91*
Chandross, Edwin A. 1934- *WhoScEn 94*
Chandy, Kanianthra Mani 1944- *WhoAm 94*
Chandy, Varughese Kuzhiyath 1946- *WhoAsA 94*
Chane, George Warren 1910- *WhoAm 94*
Chanel, Tally *WhoHol 92*
Chanen, Franklin Allen 1933- *WhoAm 94*
Chanen, Steven Robert 1953- *WhoAmL 94*
Chanenchuk, Claire Ann 1965- *WhoScEn 94*
Chaney, Alphonse 1944- *WhoBlA 94*
Chaney, Chubby d1936 *WhoHol 92*
Chaney, Don 1946- *WhoAm 94, WhoBlA 94, WhoHol 92*
Chaney, Edward (Paul de Gruyter) 1951- *WrDr 94*
Chaney, Frances d1967 *WhoHol 92*
Chaney, Frederick (Charles) 1914- *Who 94*

Chaney, Frederick Michael 1941- *IntWW 93*
Chaney, Jill 1932- *WrDr 94*
Chaney, John *WhoBlA 94*
Chaney, John Richard 1947- *WhoMW 93*
Chaney, Lon d1930 *WhoHol 92*
Chaney, Lon, Jr. d1973 *WhoHol 92*
Chaney, Mary Kathleen 1961- *WhoMW 93*
Chaney, Mike *WhoAmP 93*
Chaney, Ronald Claire 1944- *WhoScEn 94*
Chaney, Stephen Robert 1943- *WhoAmL 94*
Chaney, Verne Edward, Jr. 1923- *WhoAm 94*
Chaney, W. H. 1821-1903 *AstEnc*
Chaney, William Albert 1922- *WhoMW 93*
Chaney, William R. 1932- *WhoAm 94, WhoFI 94*
Chan Fang, Anson Maria Elizabeth 1940- *Who 94*
Chang, Albert 1941- *WhoAsA 94*
Chang, Alice Ching 1914- *WhoAsA 94*
Chang, Amy Lee 1952- *WhoAsA 94*
Chang, Andrew C. 1940- *WhoAsA 94, WhoScEn 94*
Chang, Ann Han-Chih 1963- *WhoAsA 94*
Chang, Anthony K. U. 1944- *WhoAsA 94*
Chang, Anthony Kai Ung 1944- *WhoAmP 93, WhoWest 94*
Chang, Ben 1950- *WhoAsA 94*
Chang, Benjamin Tai-An 1949- *WhoAsA 94*
Chang, Briankle G. 1954- *WhoAsA 94*
Chang, Byung Jin 1941- *WhoAsA 94*
Chang, C. Yul 1934- *WhoFI 94*
Chang, Carl Kochao 1952- *WhoAsA 94*
Chang, Caroline J. 1940- *WhoAsA 94*
Chang, Charles Hung 1922- *WhoAsA 94*
Chang, Charles Shing 1940- *WhoScEn 94*
Chang, Chawnshang 1955- *WhoAsA 94*
Chang, Che-Gil 1932- *WhoAsA 94*
Chang, Chein-I 1950- *WhoAsA 94*
Chang, Cheng-Hui 1948- *WhoAsA 94*
Chang, Cheng-Hui Karen 1948- *WhoScEn 94*
Chang, Chia-Cheh 1938- *WhoAsA 94*
Chang, Chia-ning 1950- *WhoAsA 94*
Chang, Chia-Wun 1957- *WhoScEn 94*
Chang, Chih-Wei David 1955- *WhoWest 94*
Chang, Chin Hao 1926- *WhoAsA 94*
Chang, Ching-jer 1942- *WhoAsA 94*
Chang, Ching M. *WhoFI 94*
Chang, Chong Eun 1938- *WhoScEn 94*
Chang, Chuan Chung 1938- *WhoAsA 94, WhoScEn 94*
Chang, Chun-Hao 1956- *WhoAsA 94*
Chang, Chun-hsing 1927- *WhoScEn 94*
Chang, Chung-Ho 1937- *WhoMW 93*
Chang, Clarence Dayton 1933- *WhoAm 94*
Chang, Claudia 1952- *WhoAsA 94*
Chang, Clement C. 1935- *WhoAsA 94*
Chang, Clifford Wah Jun 1938- *WhoAsA 94*
Chang, Craig 1943- *WhoAsA 94*
Chang, Daniel Hsing-Nan 1967- *WhoScEn 94*
Chang, Darwin 1954- *WhoAsA 94*
Chang, David Hsiang 1929- *WhoAsA 94*
Chang, David Ping-Chung 1929- *WhoAm 94*
Chang, David W. 1951- *WhoAsA 94*
Chang, David Wen-Wei 1929- *WhoAsA 94, WrDr 94*
Chang, Deanna BauKung 1946- *WhoAsA 94*
Chang, Deborah 1960- *WhoAmL 94, WhoFI 94, WhoWest 94*
Chang, Deborah I-Ju 1962- *WhoAsA 94*
Chang, Diana *BlmGWL, DrAPF 93*
Chang, Donald Choy 1942- *WhoScEn 94*
Chang, Donald S. M. 1934- *WhoWest 94*
Chang, Douglas Howe 1962- *WhoAsA 94*
Chang, Edmund Z. 1935- *WhoAsA 94*
Chang, Edward C. 1936- *WhoAsA 94*
Chang, Edward Shih-Tou 1940- *WhoAsA 94*
Chang, Edward Taehan 1956- *WhoAsA 94*
Chang, Eileen *BlmGWL, ConWorW 93, RfGShF*
Chang, Elden T. 1965- *WhoAsA 94*
Chang, Eric Chieh 1951- *WhoAsA 94*
Chang, Ernest Sun-Mei 1950- *WhoAsA 94*
Chang, Farland H. 1963- *WhoAsA 94*
Chang, Francis 1945- *WhoScEn 94*
Chang, Franklin 1942- *WhoWest 94*
Chang, Gene Hsin 1952- *WhoAsA 94, WhoMW 93*
Chang, Gordon H. 1948- *WhoAsA 94*
Chang, Helen Kuang 1962- *WhoAsA 94*
Chang, Helen T. 1943- *WhoAsA 94*
Chang, Henry C. 1941- *WhoAsA 94*
Chang, Henry Chung-Lien 1941- *WhoAm 94*

Chang, Howard F. 1960- *WhoAsA 94*
Chang, Hsu Hsin 1934- *WhoAsA 94*
Chang, Hsuan Hung 1950- *WhoScEn 94*
Chang, Huai Ted 1955- *WhoMW 93, WhoScEn 94*
Chang, Hui-Ching 1962- *WhoAsA 94*
Chang, Hyong Koo 1957- *WhoAsA 94*
Chang, Jack Che-man 1941- *WhoAm 94, WhoAsA 94*
Chang, Jack H. T. 1942- *WhoAsA 94*
Chang, Jae Chan 1941- *WhoMW 93, WhoScEn 94*
Chang, James C. 1930- *WhoAsA 94, WhoMW 93*
Chang, James H. 1942- *WhoAmL 94*
Chang, James Wan Chie 1965- *WhoAsA 94*
Chang, Jane Yueh 1961- *WhoAsA 94*
Chang, Jeffrey Chit-Fu 1928- *WhoAsA 94*
Chang, Jennie C. C. 1951- *WhoAsA 94*
Chang, Jerjang 1940- *WhoScEn 94*
Chang, Jerry L. 1947- *WhoAmP 93*
Chang, Jerry Leslie 1947- *WhoAsA 94*
Chang, Jhy-Jiun 1944- *WhoAsA 94*
Chang, Jian Cherng 1939- *WhoMW 93, WhoScEn 94*
Chang, John M. 1899-1966 *HisDcKW*
Chang, Joseph J. C. 1936- *WhoAsA 94*
Chang, Juang-Chi 1936- *WhoAsA 94*
Chang, Jung 1952- *ConAu 142*
Chang, Kai 1948- *WhoAsA 94*
Chang, Kai-Hsiung 1958- *WhoAsA 94*
Chang, Kai Siung 1939- *WhoScEn 94*
Chang, Kang-Tsung 1943- *WhoAsA 94, WhoWest 94*
Chang, Keh-Chin 1952- *WhoScEn 94*
Chang, Kelvin Yau-Min 1944- *WhoAsA 94*
Chang, Ker-Chi 1950- *WhoScEn 94*
Chang, Kern K. N. 1918- *WhoAsA 94*
Chang, Kow-Ching 1952- *WhoAsA 94*
Chang, Kuo-Tsun 1922- *WhoWest 94*
Chang, Kwang-Chih 1931- *IntWW 93, WhoAm 94, WhoAsA 94*
Chang, Kwang-Poo 1942- *WhoAsA 94*
Chang, Lee-Hong 1954- *WhoWest 94*
Chang, Leh 1960- *WhoWest 94*
Chang, Leroy L. 1936- *WhoAm 94, WhoScEn 94*
Chang, Louis Wai-Wah 1944- *WhoAsA 94, WhoScEn 94*
Chang, Lucia Sun 1932- *WhoFI 94*
Chang, Mabel Li *WhoAsA 94*
Chang, Maria Hsia 1950- *WhoAsA 94*
Chang, Marian S. 1958- *WhoAsA 94*
Chang, Mervin Henry 1946- *WhoAsA 94*
Chang, Michael 1972- *BuCMET, WhoAm 94, WhoAsA 94*
Chang, Michael Moonki 1944- *WhoWest 94*
Chang, Michael S. 1957- *WhoAsA 94*
Chang, Min-Chueh *WorInv*
Chang, Min Chueh 1908-1991 *WhAm 10*
Chang, Ming 1952?- *WhoAsA 94*
Chang, Mingteh 1939- *WhoAsA 94*
Chang, Moon K. 1941- *WhoAsA 94*
Chang, Mou-Hsiung 1944- *WhoAsA 94*
Chang, Myron N. 1941- *WhoAsA 94*
Chang, Nancy Siu 1940- *WhoAsA 94*
Chang, Nelson 1923- *WhoAsA 94*
Chang, Ngee-Pong 1940- *WhoAsA 94*
Chang, Parris Hsu-cheng 1936- *WhoAm 94*
Chang, Patricia W. *WhoAsA 94*
Chang, Paul Keub 1913- *WhoAsA 94*
Chang, Paul Peng-Cheng 1931- *WhoAsA 94*
Chang, Paul Steven 1956- *WhoAsA 94*
Chang, Pei K. 1936- *WhoAsA 94*
Chang, Peter Asha, Jr. 1937- *WhoAmL 94, WhoAsA 94*
Chang, Peter C. 1955- *WhoAsA 94*
Chang, Peter Hon-You *WhoMW 93*
Chang, Peter Tsu-Yuan 1935- *WhoAm 94*
Chang, Ping 1960- *WhoAsA 94*
Chang, Ping-Tung 1935- *WhoWest 94*
Chang, Pohua Paul 1966- *WhoWest 94*
Chang, R. P. H. 1941- *WhoScEn 94*
Chang, Ren-Fang 1938- *WhoAsA 94*
Chang, Richard 1962- *WhoAsA 94*
Chang, Robert C. 1928- *WhoAsA 94*
Chang, Robert Huei 1932- *WhoAm 94, WhoAsA 94*
Chang, Robert Shihman 1922- *WhoAm 94, WhoWest 94*
Chang, Robert Timothy 1958- *WhoAm 94, WhoFI 94*
Chang, Robin 1951- *WhoAm 94*
Chang, Rodney Eiu Joon 1945- *WhoWest 94*
Chang, Ruey-Jang 1957- *WhoScEn 94*
Chang, Ryan Chih-Kang 1964- *WhoFI 94*
Chang, Sari *WhoHol 92*
Chang, Sen-dou 1928- *WhoAsA 94*
Chang, Shau-Jin 1937- *WhoMW 93*
Chang, Shau-Jin 1939- *WhoAsA 94*
Chang, Sheldon Shou Lien 1920- *WhoAm 94*
Chang, Shen Chie 1931- *WhoAsA 94*
Chang, Shi-Kuo 1944- *WhoScEn 94*
Chang, Shih-Ger 1941- *WhoAsA 94*
Chang, Shin-Jyh Frank 1956- *WhoAsA 94*
Chang, Shing I. 1961- *WhoAsA 94*
Chang, Shirley Lin 1937- *WhoAsA 94*
Chang, Simon *WhoAsA 94*
Chang, Sookyung 1957- *WhoAsA 94*
Chang, Stephen S. 1918- *WhoAm 94, WhoAsA 94, WhoScEn 94*
Chang, Steven Daniel 1968- *WhoWest 94*
Chang, Sukjeong J. 1949- *WhoAsA 94*
Chang, Sung-sheng Yvonne 1951- *WhoAsA 94*
Chang, Sung Sook 1937- *WhoAsA 94*
Chang, Sylvia Tan 1940- *WhoAsA 94, WhoScEn 94*
Chang, Taiping 1949- *WhoWest 94*
Chang, Te-Wen 1920- *WhoAsA 94*
Chang, Theodore Chien-Hsin 1926- *WhoMW 93*
Chang, Thomas Ming Swi 1933- *WhoAm 94, WhoScEn 94*
Chang, Tien-Chien 1954- *WhoAsA 94*
Chang, Tim P. 1965- *WhoAsA 94*
Chang, Timothy S. 1925- *WhoAsA 94*
Chang, Tisa 1941- *WhoHol 92*
Chang, Tony H. 1951- *WhoAsA 94*
Chang, Tsan-Kuo 1950- *WhoAsA 94*
Chang, Warren W. 1956- *WhoAsA 94*
Chang, Wayne Wei 1963- *WhoAsA 94*
Chang, Wei 1945- *WhoScEn 94*
Chang, Weilin P. 1947- *WhoAsA 94*
Chang, Weilin Parrish 1947- *WhoAm 94*
Chang, William 1931- *WhoAsA 94*
Chang, William Shen Chie 1931- *WhoAm 94*
Chang, William Wei-Lien 1933- *WhoAsA 94*
Chang, William Y. B. 1948- *WhoAsA 94*
Chang, Winston Wen-Tsuen 1939- *WhoAsA 94*
Chang, Won Ho 1937- *WhoAsA 94*
Chang, Won Soon 1949- *WhoScEn 94*
Chang, Y. Austin *WhoAm 94*
Chang, Yang-Shim 1943- *WhoAsA 94*
Chang, Yankee d1989 *WhoHol 92*
Chang, Yen Fook 1949- *WhoAsA 94*
Chang, Yi-Cheng 1943- *WhoFI 94*
Chang, Yi-Chieh 1957- *WhoAsA 94*
Chang, Yia-Chung 1952- *WhoAsA 94*
Chang, Ying Ying 1940- *WhoMW 93*
Chang, Yoon Il 1942- *WhoAsA 94, WhoMW 93*
Chang, Yu Lo Cyrus 1958- *WhoAsA 94*
Chang, Yuan-Feng 1928- *WhoAm 94, WhoScEn 94*
Chang, Yung-Feng 1935- *WhoAsA 94*
Chang, Zhao Hua 1963- *WhoScEn 94*
Changalovich, Miroslav *NewGrDO*
Chang Ch'ien d107BC *WhWE*
Chang Chongxuan 1931- *IntWW 93, WhoPRCh 91 [port]*
Chang-Diaz, Franklin Ramon 1950- *WhoAsA 94, WhoHisp 94*
Chang Do Yung, General 1923- *IntWW 93*
Changeux, Jean-Pierre 1936- *IntWW 93*
Chang Han-Fu 1905-1972 *HisDcKW*
Chang-Hasnain, Constance Jui-Hua 1960- *WhoScEn 94*
Chang-Him, French Kitchener *Who 94*
Chang-Him, French Kitchener 1938- *IntWW 93*
Changho, Casto Ong 1939- *WhoScEn 94*
Chang Hsin-Hsin *ConWorW 93*
Chang Jie 1929- *WhoPRCh 91 [port]*
Chang Kang Jae d1993 *NewYTBS 93*
Chang King-Yuh 1937- *IntWW 93*
Chang Lifu *WhoPRCh 91*
Chang Lifu 1912- *IntWW 93*
Chang-Mota, Roberto 1935- *WhoScEn 94*
Chango, Clovr *DrAPF 93*
Chang-Rodriguez, Eugenio 1926- *WhoHisp 94*
Chang Shana 1931- *IntWW 93*
Chang Sha'no 1930- *WhoPRCh 91 [port]*
Chang Shouyi *WhoPRCh 91*
Chang Shuhong 1904- *IntWW 93*
Chang Shuhong 1905- *WhoPRCh 91 [port]*
Chang T'aek-Sang 1899-1969 *HisDcKW*
Chang Xiangyu 1921- *IntWW 93, WhoPRCh 91 [port]*
Chang Yanqing *WhoPRCh 91*
Chang Yao 1936- *WhoPRCh 91 [port]*
Chang Yu 1928- *WhoPRCh 91 [port]*
Chanick, Richard Alan 1953- *WhoWest 94*
Chanin, Abraham L. *WhoAmA 93N*
Chanin, Leah Farb 1929- *WhoAmL 94*
Chanin, Michael Henry 1943- *WhoAm 94*
Channel, A. R. *SmATA 74*
Channel, Elinor fl. 1654- *BlmGWL*
Channell, Eula L. 1928- *WhoBlA 94*
Channell, R. M. 1942- *WhoAmP 93*
Channick, Herbert S. 1929- *WhoAm 94*
Channing, Alan Harold 1945- *WhoAm 94*
Channing, Carol 1921- *IntMPA 94, IntWW 93, WhoHol 92*
Channing, Carol 1923- *WhoAm 94*
Channing, Rhoda Kramer 1941- *WhoAm 94*
Channing, Steven A. 1940- *WrDr 94*
Channing, Stockard *IntWW 93, WhoAm 94*
Channing, Stockard 1944- *IntMPA 94, WhoHol 92*
Channing, Susan Rose 1943- *WhoAmA 93*
Channing, William Ellery 1780-1842 *AmSocL, DcAmReB 2*
Channon, Derek French 1939- *Who 94*
Channon, (Henry) Paul (Guinness) 1935- *Who 94*
Channon, (Henry) Paul Guinness 1935- *IntWW 93*
Chant, (Elizabeth) Ann 1945- *Who 94*
Chant, Dixon S. *WhoAm 94*
Chant, Sperrin Noah Fulton 1896- *WhAm 10*
Chantal, Jeanne de 1572-1641 *BlmGWL*
Chantal, Marcelle d1960 *WhoHol 92*
Chantikian, Kosrof *DrAPF 93*
Chantrell, Robert Dennis 1793-1872 *DcNaB MP*
Chantry, George William 1933- *Who 94*
Chanturia, Georgi (Gia) 1960- *IntWW 93*
Chanussot, Guy 1943- *WhoScEn 94*
Chany, Charles 1920- *WhoScEn 94*
Chao, Allen Y. 1945- *WhoAsA 94*
Chao, Bei Tse 1918- *WhoAm 94, WhoAsA 94, WhoScEn 94*
Chao, Bruce *WhoAmA 93*
Chao, Cedric C. 1950- *WhoAm 94, WhoAmL 94*
Chao, Chiang-nan 1949- *WhoAsA 94*
Chao, Chih Hsu 1939- *WhoWest 94*
Chao, Ching Yuan 1921- *WhoAsA 94*
Chao, Chong-Yun 1930- *WhoAm 94*
Chao, Conrad Russell 1957- *WhoScEn 94*
Chao, Daniel Kung-Hua 1951- *WhoWest 94*
Chao, Edward C. T. 1919- *WhoAsA 94*
Chao, Elaine L. *WhoAm 94, WhoAmP 93, WhoFI 94*
Chao, Elaine Lan *WhoAsA 94*
Chao, Georgia Tze-Ying *WhoAsA 94*
Chao, James Lee 1954- *WhoScEn 94*
Chao, James Min-Tzu 1940- *WhoFI 94, WhoScEn 94, WhoWest 94*
Chao, Jowett 1915- *WhoAsA 94*
Chao, Koung-An 1940- *WhoScEn 94*
Chao, Kwang-Chu 1925- *WhoAsA 94, WhoScEn 94*
Chao, Lin 1950- *WhoAsA 94*
Chao, Marshall S. 1924- *WhoAm 94*
Chao, Paul W. F. 1950- *WhoAsA 94*
Chao, Rosalind *WhoAsA 94, WhoHol 92*
Chao, Stanley K. *WhoAsA 94*
Chao, Tim 1925- *WhoAsA 94*
Chao, Xiuli 1964- *WhoAsA 94*
Chao, Yei-chin 1955- *WhoAm 94, WhoScEn 94*
Chao, Yuh J. 1953- *WhoAsA 94*
Chao Qing 1928- *WhoPRCh 91 [port]*
Chao Yao-Tung 1915- *IntWW 93*
Chapa, Alfonso 1930- *WhoHisp 94*
Chapa, Amancio Jose, Jr. 1946- *WhoHisp 94*
Chapa, Armando 1944- *WhoHisp 94*
Chapa, Arthur *WhoHisp 94*
Chapa, Carmen 1947- *WhoHisp 94*
Chapa, David Clemente 1940- *WhoHisp 94*
Chapa, Elia Kay 1960- *WhoHisp 94*
Chapa, Joseph S. 1948- *WhoHisp 94*
Chapa, Judy J. 1957- *WhoHisp 94*
Chapa, Ramon, Jr. 1958- *WhoHisp 94*
Chapa, Raul Roberto 1948- *WhoHisp 94*
Chapa, Rodolfo Chino 1958- *WhoHisp 94*
Chapa-Guzmán, Hugo Gerardo 1953- *WhoHisp 94*
Chapanis, Alphonse 1917- *WhoAm 94, WhoScEn 94*
Chaparro, Carmen 1947- *WhoHisp 94*
Chaparro, José L. 1955- *WhoHisp 94*
Chaparro, Linda L. 1949- *WhoHisp 94*
Chaparro, Luis *WhoHisp 94*
Chaparro, Luis F. 1947- *WhoHisp 94*
Chapatwala, Kirit D. 1948- *WhoAsA 94*
Chapdelaine, Perry A(nthony) 1925- *EncSF 93*
Chapdelaine, Roland Joseph 1946- *WhoAm 94*
Chapel, Theron Theodore 1918- *WhoScEn 94*
Chapelain, Jean 1595-1674 *GuFrLit 2*
Chapelle, Pierre-David-Augustin 1756-1821 *NewGrDO*
Chapelli, Armando C., Jr. *WhoHisp 94*
Chapellier, George 1890-1978 *WhoAmA 93N*
Chapellier, Robert d1974 *WhoAmA 93N*
Chapellin, Helena *WhoAmA 93*
Chapgier, Pierre Andre 1941- *WhoWest 94*
Chapi (y Lorente), Ruperto 1851-1909 *NewGrDO*
Chapian, Grieg Hovsep 1913- *WhoAmA 93, WhoWest 94*
Chapin, Alice d1934 *WhoHol 92*
Chapin, Allan M. 1941- *WhoAmL 94*
Chapin, Benjamin d1918 *WhoHol 92*
Chapin, Billy 1943- *WhoHol 92*
Chapin, Charlotte d1977 *WhoHol 92*
Chapin, Diana Derby 1942- *WhoAmP 93*
Chapin, Doug *IntMPA 94*
Chapin, Dwight Allan 1938- *WhoAm 94*
Chapin, Edward William 1908- *WhoAm 94*
Chapin, Elizabeth Steinway d1993 *NewYTBS 93 [port]*
Chapin, Elliott Lowell 1917- *WhoAm 94*
Chapin, F. Stuart, Jr. 1916- *WrDr 94*
Chapin, Francis 1899-1965 *WhoAmA 93N*
Chapin, Frederic Lincoln 1929-1989 *WhAm 10*
Chapin, Harold d1915 *WhoHol 92*
Chapin, Howard B. *WhoAmP 93*
Chapin, Hugh A. 1925- *WhoAm 94*
Chapin, James Chris 1940- *WhoAm 94*
Chapin, John Carsten 1920- *WhoAmP 93*
Chapin, John Nettleton, Jr. 1933- *WhoFI 94*
Chapin, Melodee Ann 1951- *WhoMW 93*
Chapin, Melville 1918- *WhoAm 94, WhoAmL 94*
Chapin, Michael 1937- *WhoHol 92*
Chapin, Miles 1954- *WhoHol 92*
Chapin, Myron Butman 1887-1958 *WhoAmA 93N*
Chapin, Paul *EncSF 93*
Chapin, Richard 1923- *WhoAm 94*
Chapin, Richard Earl 1925- *WhoAm 94*
Chapin, Roy Dikeman, Jr. 1915- *WhoAm 94*
Chapin, Schuyler G(arrison) 1923- *NewGrDO*
Chapin, Schuyler Garrison 1923- *IntWW 93, WhoAm 94*
Chapin, Suzanne Phillips 1930- *WhoAm 94*
Chapin, Tom 1945- *ConMus 11 [port]*
Chaplais, Pierre Theophile Victorien Marie 1920- *Who 94*
Chapleau, Mark William 1955- *WhoMW 93*
Chaplin, Ansel Burt 1931- *WhoAm 94, WhoAmL 94*
Chaplin, Arthur Hugh 1905- *IntWW 93, Who 94*
Chaplin, Charles d1977 *WhoHol 92*
Chaplin, Charles 1889-1977 *WhoCom [port]*
Chaplin, Charles, Jr. d1968 *WhoHol 92*
Chaplin, Charles S. 1911- *IntMPA 94*
Chaplin, Charles Spencer 1889-1977 *AmCulL [port]*
Chaplin, Christopher 1963- *WhoHol 92*
Chaplin, Elizabeth 1947- *WrDr 94*
Chaplin, George 1914- *WhoAm 94, WhoWest 94*
Chaplin, George Edwin 1931- *WhoAmA 93*
Chaplin, Geraldine 1944- *IntMPA 94, IntWW 93, WhoAm 94, WhoHol 92*
Chaplin, Hugh, Jr. 1923- *WhoAm 94*
Chaplin, James Crossan, IV 1933- *WhoAm 94*
Chaplin, James Patrick 1919- *WrDr 94*
Chaplin, Jim 1944- *WhoAmP 93*
Chaplin, John Cyril 1926- *Who 94*
Chaplin, Josephine 1950- *WhoHol 92*
Chaplin, (Sybil) Judith d1993 *Who 94N*
Chaplin, Malcolm Hilbery *Who 94*
Chaplin, Michael 1947- *WhoHol 92*
Chaplin, Oona 1925- *WhoHol 92*
Chaplin, Peggy Fannon 1940- *WhoAm 94, WhoAmL 94*
Chaplin, Saul 1912- *IntMPA 94*
Chaplin, Stephan 1961- *WhoHol 92*
Chaplin, Sydney d1965 *WhoHol 92*
Chaplin, Sydney 1926- *WhoHol 92*
Chapline, Claudia Beechum 1930- *WhoAmA 93*
Chapline, George Frederick, Jr. 1942- *WhoScEn 94*
Chapman *Who 94*
Chapman, Alan Jesse 1925- *WhoAm 94*
Chapman, Albert Lee 1933- *WhoMW 93*
Chapman, Alger Baldwin 1931- *WhoAm 94, WhoFI 94, WhoMW 93*
Chapman, Alice Mariah 1947- *WhoBlA 94*
Chapman, Allen Floyd 1930- *WhoFI 94*
Chapman, Alvah Herman, Jr. 1921- *WhoAm 94, WhoFI 94*
Chapman, Amy R. 1962- *WhoAmP 93*
Chapman, Angela Mary 1940- *Who 94*
Chapman, (M.) Anne 1930-1986 *WhoAmA 93N*
Chapman, Audrey Bridgeforth 1941- *WhoBlA 94*
Chapman, Barbara Della 1952- *WhoMW 93*

Charkin, Richard Denis Paul 1949- *Who 94*
Charkoudian, Arppie 1925- *WhoAmP 93*
Charla, Leonard Francis 1940- *WhoAm 94, WhoAmL 94*
Charlemagne 742-814 *BlmGEL, HisWorL [port]*
Charlemont, Viscount 1934- *Who 94*
Charles, Duc d'Orleans 1394-1465 *BlmGEL*
Charles, I fl. 1625-1649 *BlmGEL*
Charles, II 1630-1685 *HisWorL [port]*
Charles, II fl. 1660-1685 *BlmGEL*
Charles, III 1716-1788 *AmRev, HisWorL [port], WhAmRev*
Charles, V 1500-1558 *HisWorL [port]*
Charles, VI 1685-1740 *NewGrDO*
Charles, VII 1402-1461 *HisWorL [port]*
Charles, Adrian Owen 1926- *Who 94*
Charles, Allan Frederick 1946- *WhoAm 94*
Charles, Allan G. 1928- *WhoAm 94*
Charles, Anita *WrDr 94*
Charles, Anne 1941- *WhoAmP 93*
Charles, Anthony d1987 *WhoHol 92*
Charles, Arthur William Hessin 1948- *Who 94*
Charles, Bernard L. 1927- *WhoBlA 94*
Charles, Bernard Leopold 1929- *Who 94*
Charles, Bertram 1918- *WhoAm 94*
Charles, Carol Morgan 1931- *WhoAm 94*
Charles, Caroline 1942- *IntWW 93, Who 94*
Charles, Clayton (Henry) 1913-1976 *WhoAmA 93N*
Charles, Daedra *WhoBlA 94*
Charles, Doreen Alicia 1960- *WhoBlA 94*
Charles, Durant *WhoAmA 93*
Charles, Eugenia *Who 94*
Charles, (Mary) Eugenia 1919- *IntWW 93, Who 94, WhoWomW 91*
Charles, Glen *WhoAm 94*
Charles, Hampton *Who 94*
Charles, Hampton 1931- *WrDr 94*
Charles, Henry 1925- *WrDr 94*
Charles, Isabel 1926- *WhoAm 94*
Charles, Jack 1923- *Who 94*
Charles, Jacques-Alexandre-Cesar 1746-1823 *WorScD [port]*
Charles, James Anthony 1926- *Who 94*
Charles, Jimmy 1960- *WhoAmP 93*
Charles, Joel 1914- *WhoScEn 94*
Charles, John d1921 *WhoHol 92*
Charles, John A. 1951- *WhoHisp 94*
Charles, Joseph, Jr. 1944- *WhoAmP 93*
Charles, Joseph (Quentin) 1908- *Who 94*
Charles, Joseph C. 1941- *WhoBlA 94*
Charles, Josh 1971- *WhoHol 92*
Charles, Josh 1972?- *ConTFT 11*
Charles, Judith Korey 1925- *WhoFI 94*
Charles, Kate 1950- *ConAu 141*
Charles, Kathleen J. 1950- *WhoAm 94*
Charles, Leon d1981 *WhoHol 92*
Charles, Les *WhoAm 94*
Charles, Leslie Stanley Francis 1917- *Who 94*
Charles, Lewis d1979 *WhoHol 92*
Charles, Lewis 1945- *WhoBlA 94*
Charles, Lyn Ellen 1951- *WhoFI 94*
Charles, M. Arthur 1941- *WhoScEn 94*
Charles, Maria 1929- *IntMPA 94, WhoHol 92*
Charles, Mark *ConAu 42NR*
Charles, Mary Louise 1922- *WhoWest 94*
Charles, Michael d1967 *WhoHol 92*
Charles, Michael Geoffrey A. *Who 94*
Charles, Michael Harrison 1952- *WhoFI 94*
Charles, Neil *EncSF 93*
Charles, Nicholas 1932- *WrDr 94*
Charles, Nicholas J. *ConAu 41NR*
Charles, Pearnel 1936- *IntWW 93*
Charles, Ray 1930- *IntWW 93, WhoAm 94, WhoBlA 94, WhoHol 92*
Charles, Ray 1932- *AfrAmAl 6*
Charles, Richard Frank *WhoFI 94*
Charles, Robert *EncSF 93*
Charles, Robert Bruce 1960- *WhoAmL 94*
Charles, Roderick Edward 1927- *WhoBlA 94*
Charles, Sara C(onnor) 1934- *WrDr 94*
Charles, Steven *EncSF 93*
Charles, Una *WhoWomW 91*
Charles, William John 1931- *WorESoc*
Charles of Sweden, XII 1687-1718 *HisWorL [port]*
Charleson, Ian d1990 *WhoHol 92*
Charleson, Ian 1949-1990 *ConTFT 11*
Charleson, Leslie 1945- *WhoHol 92*
Charleson, Mary d1961 *WhoHol 92*
Charleson, Ray *WhoHol 92*
Charles-Roux, Edmonde 1920- *IntWW 93*
Charleston, Gomez, Jr. 1950- *WhoBlA 94*
Charleston, Helen d1978 *WhoHol 92*
Charleston, Robert Jesse 1916- *Who 94, WrDr 94*
Charleston, Steve *WhoWest 94*
Charlesworth, Arthur Leonard 1927- *Who 94*
Charlesworth, Brian 1945- *Who 94, WhoAm 94*
Charlesworth, Ernest Neal 1945- *WhoScEn 94*
Charlesworth, James H(amilton) 1940- *WrDr 94*
Charlesworth, James Hamilton 1940- *WhoAm 94*
Charlesworth, John d1960 *WhoHol 92*
Charlesworth, Peter James 1944- *Who 94*
Charlesworth, Sarah E. 1947- *WhoAm 94, WhoAmA 93*
Charlesworth, Stanley d1992 *Who 94N*
Charlevoix, Pierre-Francois-Xavier De 1682-1761 *WhWE [port]*
Charley, Philip James 1921- *WhoAm 94, WhoFI 94, WhoScEn 94, WhoWest 94*
Charley, Ray Thomas 1951- *WhoFI 94*
Charlier, Roger Henri 1921- *WhoAm 94, WrDr 94*
Charlip, Remy 1929- *WrDr 94*
Charlish, Dennis Norman 1918- *Who 94*
Charlita *WhoHol 92*
Charlot, Andre d1956 *WhoHol 92*
Charlot, Gaston 1904- *IntWW 93*
Charlot, Jean 1898-1979 *WhoAmA 93N*
Charlot, Jean 1932- *IntWW 93*
Charlot, Martin Day 1944- *WhoAmA 93*
Charlson, David Harvey 1947- *WhoAm 94, WhoMW 93*
Charlson, Michael Lloyd 1958- *WhoAmL 94*
Charlton, Alethea d1976 *WhoHol 92*
Charlton, Betty Jo 1923- *WhoAmP 93, WhoMW 93*
Charlton, Bobby *Who 94*
Charlton, Bobby 1937- *WorESoc [port], WrDr 94*
Charlton, Charles Hayes 1940- *WhoBlA 94*
Charlton, Clifford Tyrone 1965- *WhoBlA 94*
Charlton, Clivel George *WhoScEn 94*
Charlton, David 1946- *NewGrDO*
Charlton, (Foster) Ferrier (Harvey) 1923- *Who 94*
Charlton, Gordon Randolph 1937- *WhoScEn 94*
Charlton, Gordon Taliaferro, Jr. 1923- *WhoAm 94*
Charlton, Graham *Who 94*
Charlton, Graham 1928- *Who 94*
Charlton, (Thomas Alfred) Graham 1913- *Who 94*
Charlton, Hal d1954 *WhoHol 92*
Charlton, Jack Fields 1928- *WhoBlA 94*
Charlton, Jesse Melvin, Jr. 1916- *WhoAm 94*
Charlton, John 1932- *WrDr 94*
Charlton, John 1935- *Who 94*
Charlton, John Kipp 1937- *WhoAm 94, WhoScEn 94, WhoWest 94*
Charlton, Kenneth 1925- *Who 94*
Charlton, Kevin Michael 1966- *WhoScEn 94*
Charlton, (Frederick) Noel 1906- *Who 94*
Charlton, Philip 1930- *Who 94*
Charlton, Robert 1937- *IntWW 93, Who 94*
Charlton, Robert William 1929- *IntWW 93*
Charlton, Samuel 1760-1843 *WhAmRev*
Charlton, Shannon Bruce 1957- *WhoWest 94*
Charlton, Thomàs Jackson 1960- *WhoAmL 94*
Charlton, Thomas Malcolm 1923- *Who 94, WrDr 94*
Charlwood, D(onald) E(rnest Cameron) 1915- *WrDr 94*
Charman, Janet 1954- *BlmGWL*
Charmatz, Bill 1925- *WhoAmA 93*
Charmichael, Stokely 1941- *AfrAmAl 6*
Charmot, Guy 1914- *IntWW 93*
Charnas, Michael 1947- *WhoAm 94*
Charnas, Suzy McKee *DrAPF 93*
Charnas, Suzy McKee 1939- *EncSF 93, WrDr 94*
Charnay, John Bruce 1949- *WhoWest 94*
Charneco, Jerry Charles 1947- *WhoHisp 94*
Charness, Michael Edward 1950- *WhoScEn 94*
Charney, Evan 1933- *WhoAm 94*
Charney, Jack G. 1946- *WhoAmL 94*
Charney, Jordan *WhoHol 92*
Charney, Lena London *DrAPF 93*
Charney, Mark J. 1956- *ConAu 141*
Charney, Melvin 1935- *WhoAm 94, WhoAmA 93*
Charney, Michael Jeffrey 1959- *WhoWest 94*
Charney, Philip 1939- *WhoScEn 94*
Charney, Scott Jason 1954- *WhoAmL 94*
Charniak, Eugene 1946- *WhoAm 94*
Charnin, Martin 1934- *WhoAm 94*
Charnley, Donn 1928- *WhoAmP 93*
Charnley, Douglas Glenn 1957- *WhoFI 94*
Charnley, John 1911-1982 *WorInv*
Charnley, (William) John 1922- *Who 94*
Charnley, Mitchell Vaughn 1898-1991 *WhAm 10*
Charnock, Henry 1920- *IntWW 93, Who 94*
Charnoff, Deborah Bernstein 1953- *WhoAm 94*
Charny, Carmi *ConWorW 93*
Charny, Israel 1931- *WrDr 94*
Charo 1951- *WhoHol 92*
Charobee, Danny David 1950- *WhoWest 94*
Charon, Jacques d1975 *WhoHol 92*
Charon, Lourdes 1956- *WhoHisp 94*
Charone, Irwin *WhoHol 92*
Charpak, Georges 1924- *IntWW 93, Who 94, WhoScEn 94*
Charpentier, Arthur Aldrich 1919-1989 *WhAm 10*
Charpentier, Gabriel 1925- *NewGrDO*
Charpentier, Gustave 1860-1956 *NewGrDO*
Charpentier, Marc-Antoine 1643-1704 *NewGrDO*
Charpin, Fernand d1944 *WhoHol 92*
Charrat, Janine 1924- *IntDcB [port]*
Charren, Peggy 1928- *WhoAm 94*
Charrier, Jacques 1936- *WhoHol 92*
Charrier, Michael Edward 1945- *WhoAm 94, WhoFI 94*
Charriere, Isabelle-Agnes-Elisabeth van Tuyll van 1740-1805 *BlmGWL*
Charron, Andre Joseph Charles Pierre 1936- *WhoAm 94*
Charron, Paul Richard 1942- *WhoAm 94*
Charron, Pierre 1541-1603 *GuFrLit 2*
Charron, Robert R. *WhoAmP 93*
Charry, Jonathan M. 1948- *WhoScEn 94*
Charry, Michael Ronald 1933- *WhoAm 94*
Charskaia, Lidiia Alekseevna 1875-1937 *BlmGWL*
Charsky, Boris d1956 *WhoHol 92*
Chartchaiganan, Suwit 1954- *WhoWest 94*
Charteris *Who 94*
Charteris, Leslie d1993 *IntWW 93N, NewYTBS 93, Who 94N*
Charteris, Leslie 1907- *EncSF 93, IntWW 93*
Charteris, Leslie 1907-1993 *ConAu 141, WrDr 94N*
Charteris Of Amisfield, Baron 1913- *Who 94*
Charters, Alexander Nathaniel 1916- *WhoAm 94*
Charters, Ann 1936- *WhoAm 94, WrDr 94*
Charters, Cynthia Grace 1949- *WhoWest 94*
Charters, Jimmy d1975 *WhoHol 92*
Charters, Samuel 1929- *WrDr 94*
Charters, Spencer d1943 *WhoHol 92*
Chartier, Charles Adrian 1955- *WhoMW 93*
Chartier, Janellen Olsen 1951- *WhoAm 94*
Chartier, Roger 1945- *IntWW 93*
Chartier, Vernon Lee 1939- *WhoAm 94, WhoWest 94*
Chartoff, Melanie *WhoHol 92*
Chartoff, Robert 1933- *IntMPA 94*
Chartoff, Robert Irwin *WhoAm 94*
Charton, George N., Jr. 1923- *WhoBlA 94*
Charton, Marvin 1931- *WhoAm 94*
Charton-Demeur, Anne 1824-1892 *NewGrDO*
Chartrain 1740-1793 *NewGrDO*
Chartrand, Bernard Francis 1925- *WhoAmP 93*
Chartrand, J. Claude *WhoIns 94*
Chartrand, Mark Ray 1943- *WhoAm 94*
Chartrand, Robert Lee 1928- *WhoAm 94*
Chartres, Richard John Carew *Who 94*
Chartroule, Marie-Amelie 1850- *BlmGWL*
Charusathira, Prapas 1912- *IntWW 93*
Charvet, Denis *WhoHol 92*
Charvet, Richard Christopher Larkins 1936- *Who 94*
Charwat, Andrew Franciszek 1925- *WhoAm 94*
Chary, Karudapuram Eachambadi Ranga 1936- *WhoFI 94*
Charyk, Joseph Vincent 1920- *IntWW 93, WhoAm 94, WhoScEn 94*
Charyk, William R. 1948- *WhoAmL 94*
Charyn, Jerome *DrAPF 93*
Charyn, Jerome 1937- *EncSF 93, WrDr 94*
Chasanow, Howard Stuart 1937- *WhoAm 94, WhoAmL 94, WhoAmP 93*
Chase, Adam *EncSF 93*
Chase, Alice *SmATA 77*
Chase, Alice Elizabeth 1906- *WhoAmA 93*
Chase, Alison *WhoAm 94*
Chase, Allan (Seamans) *WhoAmA 93*
Chase, Alston Hurd 1906- *WrDr 94*
Chase, Annazette *WhoHol 92*
Chase, Arline d1926 *WhoHol 92*
Chase, Arnett C. 1940- *WhoBlA 94*
Chase, Arthur E. *WhoAmP 93*
Chase, Aurin Moody, Jr. 1904- *WhoAm 94*
Chase, Barrie 1934- *WhoHol 92*
Chase, Borden 1900-1971 *IntDcF 2-4*
Chase, Brandon *IntMPA 94*
Chase, Charley d1940 *WhoHol 92*
Chase, Charley 1893-1940 *WhoCom*
Chase, Chaz d1983 *WhoHol 92*
Chase, Chevy 1943- *IntMPA 94, IntWW 93, WhoAm 94, WhoCom [port], WhoHol 92*
Chase, Chris *WhoHol 92*
Chase, Clarence d1964 *WhoHol 92*
Chase, Clinton Irvin 1927- *WhoAm 94*
Chase, Cochrane 1932- *WhoAm 94*
Chase, Colin d1937 *WhoHol 92*
Chase, Cyril Charles 1917- *WhoAmP 93*
Chase, David Marion 1930- *WhoAm 94*
Chase, David N. 1940- *WhoMW 93*
Chase, Doris (Totten) 1923- *WhoAmA 93*
Chase, Duane 1951- *WhoHol 92*
Chase, Edward 1884-1965 *WhoAmA 93N*
Chase, Elaine Raco *DrAPF 93*
Chase, Elaine Raco 1949- *WrDr 94*
Chase, Emily 1926- *WrDr 94*
Chase, Emily 1947- *WrDr 94*
Chase, Eric Lewis 1946- *WhoAmL 94*
Chase, Frank Swift 1886-1958 *WhoAmA 93N*
Chase, Gail M. *WhoAmP 93*
Chase, George H. 1874-1952 *WhoAmA 93N*
Chase, George Washington d1918 *WhoHol 92*
Chase, Gilbert 1906-1992 *WhAm 10*
Chase, Helen Louise 1943- *WhoFI 94*
Chase, Howard Marion 1938- *WhoAm 94*
Chase, Ilka d1978 *WhoHol 92*
Chase, J. Vincent 1949- *WhoAmP 93*
Chase, Jack S(paulding) 1941- *WhoAmA 93*
Chase, James d1987 *WhoBlA 94N*
Chase, James Keller 1927- *WhoAm 94*
Chase, James Richard 1930- *WhoAm 94*
Chase, James Staton 1932- *WhoAmP 93*
Chase, Jeanne Norman 1929- *WhoAmA 93*
Chase, Jeffrey A. 1946- *WhoAmL 94*
Chase, Jeremiah Townley 1748-1828 *WhAmRev*
Chase, Joan *WrDr 94*
Chase, John David 1920- *WhoAm 94*
Chase, John S. 1925- *WhoBlA 94*
Chase, Joseph Cummings 1878-1965 *WhoAmA 93N*
Chase, Judith Helfer 1939- *WhoWest 94*
Chase, Karen *DrAPF 93*
Chase, Kenneth Edward 1952- *WhoAmL 94*
Chase, Larry I 1945- *WhoWest 94*
Chase, Laurence F. 1915- *WhoAmP 93*
Chase, Lawrence Arthur, Jr. 1948- *WhoAmP 93*
Chase, Linda Kay 1957- *WhoMW 93*
Chase, Loriene Eck 1934- *WhoWest 94*
Chase, Lorraine 1951- *WhoHol 92*
Chase, Louisa L. 1951- *WhoAmA 93*
Chase, Lucia 1907-1986 *IntDcB [port]*
Chase, Lucius Peter 1902- *WhoAm 94*
Chase, Lyndon 1916- *WrDr 94*
Chase, Maria Elaine Garoufalis 1957- *WhoAm 94, WhoMW 93*
Chase, Mary (Coyle) 1907-1981 *ConDr 93*
Chase, Mary Jane 1938- *WhoAmP 93*
Chase, Merrill Wallace 1905- *WhoAm 94, WhoScEn 94*
Chase, Morris 1918- *WhoAm 94, WhoFI 94*
Chase, Naomi Feigelson *DrAPF 93*
Chase, Nicholas 1946- *WrDr 94*
Chase, Nicholas Joseph 1913- *WhoAm 94*
Chase, Norman Bradford 1924- *WhoAmP 93*
Chase, Oscar Gottfried *WhoAm 94, WhoAmL 94*
Chase, Paul Kenneth, Jr. 1945- *WhoAmP 93*
Chase, Pauline d1962 *WhoHol 92*
Chase, Philander 1775-1852 *DcAmReB 2*
Chase, Philip Noyes 1954- *WhoScEn 94*
Chase, Ramon L. 1933- *WhoScEn 94*
Chase, Richard Barth 1939- *WhoWest 94*
Chase, Richard Lionel St. Lucian 1933- *WhoAm 94, WhoScEn 94, WhoWest 94*
Chase, Robert Arthur 1923- *IntWW 93, WhoAm 94*
Chase, Robert John 1943- *Who 94*
Chase, Robert M. 1940- *WhoAmA 93*
Chase, Robert M. 1944- *WhoAmP 93*
Chase, Robert R(eynolds) 1948- *EncSF 93*
Chase, Robert William 1950- *WhoScEn 94*
Chase, Roger Robert 1928- *Who 94*

Chase, Samuel 1741-1811 *HisWorL, WhAmRev*
Chase, Samuel Brown 1932- *WhoFI 94*
Chase, Seymour M. 1924- *WhoAm 94*
Chase, Sharon Sue 1945- *WhoMW 93*
Chase, Sidney M. 1877-1957 *WhoAmA 93N*
Chase, Stanley *IntMPA 94*
Chase, Stephen d1982 *WhoHol 92*
Chase, Sylvia B. 1938- *WhoAm 94*
Chase, Theodore, Jr. 1938- *WhoAmP 93*
Chase, Thomas Newell 1932- *WhoAm 94*
Chase, Truddi 1937?- *ConAu 142*
Chase, W(illiam) Thomas 1940- *WhoAmA 93*
Chase, William Douglas 1959- *WhoFI 94*
Chase, William E. 1931- *WhoAmL 94*
Chase, William Howard 1910- *WhoAm 94*
Chase, William Rowell 1904- *WhoAm 94*
Chase, William Thomas, III 1940- *WhoAm 94*
Chaseman, Joel 1926- *WhoAm 94*
Chasen, Dave d1973 *WhoHol 92*
Chasen, Heather 1927- *WhoHol 92*
Chasen, Nancy H. 1945- *WrDr 94*
Chasen, Robert E. 1916- *WhoAm 94*
Chasen, Sylvan Herbert 1926- *WhoAm 94*
Chase-Riboud, Barbara 1939- *WhoAmA 93*
Chase-Riboud, Barbara (Dewayne Tosi) 1939- *BlkWr 2*
Chase-Riboud, Barbara Dewayne 1939- *WhoAm 94, WhoBlA 94*
Chasey-Czernekova, Jacqueline *WhoAmL 94*
Chasin, Helen *DrAPF 93*
Chasin, Judith Tripp 1948- *WhoWest 94*
Chasin, Marshall Lewis 1954- *WhoScEn 94*
Chasin, Martin 1938- *WhoAmA 93*
Chasin, Werner David 1932-1992 *WhAm 10*
Chasins, Edward A. 1920- *WhoAm 94*
Chaskelson, Marsha Ina 1950- *WhoAm 94*
Chaski, Hilda Cecelia 1951- *WhoMW 93*
Chasles, Robert de *GuFrLit 2*
Chasman, Daniel Benzion 1949- *WhoScEn 94*
Chasman, David 1925- *IntMPA 94*
Chasnis, John Alex 1948- *WhoAmL 94*
Chasnoff, Barry A. 1949- *WhoAmL 94*
Chasnoff, Ira Jay 1947- *WhoMW 93*
Chasnoff, Joel 1936- *WhoAmP 93*
Chasnoff, Michael Jay 1959- *WhoFI 94*
Chason, Jacob 1915- *WhoAm 94*
Chason, James R. 1950- *WhoAmL 94*
Chassay, Roger Paul, Jr. 1938- *WhoScEn 94*
Chasse (de Chinais), Claude Louis Dominique 1699-1786 *NewGrDO*
Chasse, Richard D. 1924- *WhoAmP 93*
Chassin, Mark Russell 1947- *WhoAm 94*
Chassman, Leonard Fredric 1935- *WhoAm 94*
Chastain, Denise Jean 1961- *WhoScEn 94*
Chastain, Don *WhoHol 92*
Chastain, Elijah Denton, Jr. 1925-1989 *WhAm 10*
Chastain, Larry Kent 1943- *WhoAm 94*
Chastain, Randall Meads 1945- *WhoAmL 94*
Chastain, Robert 1923- *WhoAmP 93*
Chastain, Roger W. 1941- *WhoFI 94*
Chastain, Sarah Frances 1949- *WhoFI 94*
Chastain, Thomas *WrDr 94*
Chastain, Vicki *WhoAmP 93*
Chastel, Andre Adrien 1912-1990 *WhAm 10*
Chastellux, Chevalier de (Francois-Jean de Beauvoir) 1734-1788 *AmRev*
Chastellux, Francois-Jean, Marquis de 1734-1788 *NewGrDO*
Chastellux, Francois-Jean de Beauvoir, Chevalier de 1734-1788 *WhAmRev [port]*
Chastenay de Lenty, Louise-Marie Victorine de 1770-1838? *BlmGWL*
Chatain, Robert *DrAPF 93*
Chataway, Christopher John 1931- *IntWW 93, Who 94*
Chateau, Francois Michel 1956- *WhoAmL 94*
Chateau, John Peter David 1942- *WhoAm 94*
Chatel, Peter *WhoHol 92*
Chatelet-Lomont, Gabrielle-Emilie Le Tonnelier de Berteuil, Marquise du 1706-1749 *BlmGWL*
Chatelier, Paul Richard 1938- *WhoScEn 94*
Chater, Anthony Philip John *Who 94*
Chater, Geoffrey 1921- *WhoHol 92*
Chater, Nancy 1915- *Who 94*
Chater, Shirley Sears 1932- *WhoAm 94*
Chatfield, Baron 1917- *Who 94*
Chatfield, Cheryl Ann 1946- *WhoAm 94, WhoFI 94, WhoWest 94*
Chatfield, E. Charles 1934- *WrDr 94*
Chatfield, Gail L. 1933- *WhoAmP 93*
Chatfield, Hale *DrAPF 93*
Chatfield, Joan 1932- *WhoWest 94*
Chatfield, John (Freeman) 1929- *Who 94*
Chatfield, Mary Van Abshoven *WhoAm 94*
Chatfield-Taylor, Richard Farwell 1958- *WhoAmL 94*
Chatham, Earl of *AmRev, WhAmRev*
Chatham, James Ray 1931- *WhoAm 94*
Chatham, Larry *ConAu 42NR*
Chatham, Sherri Irene 1958- *WhoWest 94*
Chatillon, Henri 1816-1875 *WhWE*
Chatilovicz, Peter 1946- *WhoAmL 94*
Chatinover, Marvin A. *WhoHol 92*
Chatlos, William Edward 1927- *WhoAm 94*
Chatlosh, Diane Lynn 1955- *WhoWest 94*
Chatman, Abraham David 1896- *WhAm 10*
Chatman, Alex 1943- *WhoBlA 94*
Chatman, Anna Lee 1919- *WhoBlA 94*
Chatman, Donald Leveritt 1934- *WhoBlA 94*
Chatman, Jacob L. 1938- *WhoBlA 94*
Chatman, James I. *WhoBlA 94*
Chatman, Melvin E. 1933- *WhoBlA 94*
Chatman, Paul Herbert 1944- *WhoAmP 93*
Chatman, Peter *WhAm 10*
Chatman, Peter 1915- *WhoHol 92*
Chatman, Rosie A. *WhoAm 94*
Chatman, Seymour 1928- *WrDr 94*
Chatmas, John T. *WhoAmA 93*
Chatmon, Linda Carol 1951- *WhoBlA 94*
Chato, John Clark 1929- *WhoAm 94, WhoScEn 94*
Chatoff, Michael Alan 1946- *WhoAm 94, WhoAmL 94*
Chatot-Travis, Judee Jules 1948- *WhoFI 94*
Chatrian, Alexandre *NewGrDO*
Chatrier, Philippe 1926- *BuCMET*
Chatroo, Arthur Jay 1946- *WhoAmL 94, WhoFI 94, WhoWest 94*
Chatry, Frederic Metzinger 1923- *WhoScEn 94*
Chatt, Allen Barrett 1949- *WhoScEn 94*
Chatt, Joseph 1914- *IntWW 93, Who 94*
Chatten, Harold Raymond Percy *Who 94*
Chatterjee, Amit 1943- *WhoScEn 94*
Chatterjee, Amitava 1956- *WhoScEn 94*
Chatterjee, Anil Kumar 1923- *WhoWest 94*
Chatterjee, Asima 1917- *WhoWomW 91*
Chatterjee, Bijoy Gopal 1937- *WhoWest 94*
Chatterjee, Hem Chandra 1940- *WhoScEn 94*
Chatterjee, Jay 1936- *WhoAmA 93*
Chatterjee, Lata Roy 1938- *WhoAsA 94*
Chatterjee, Lois Jordan 1940- *WhoBlA 94*
Chatterjee, Monish Ranjan 1959- *WhoAsA 94, WhoScEn 94*
Chatterjee, Pranab 1936- *WhoAm 94, WhoAsA 94*
Chatterjee, Pronoy Kumar 1936- *WhoAsA 94*
Chatterjee, Sankar 1943- *WhoAsA 94*
Chatterjee, Satya N. 1934- *WhoAsA 94*
Chatterjee, Satya Saran 1922- *Who 94*
Chatterjee, Sayan 1951- *WhoAsA 94*
Chatterjee, Siddhartha 1963- *WhoWest 94*
Chatterjee, Soumitra *WhoHol 92*
Chatterjee, Tapan Kumar 1952- *WhoScEn 94*
Chatterji, Debajyoti 1944- *WhoAm 94*
Chatterton, Clarence Kerr 1880-1973 *WhoAmA 93N*
Chatterton, N. Jerry 1939- *WhoAm 94*
Chatterton, Robert Treat, Jr. 1935- *WhoAm 94, WhoMW 93*
Chatterton, Ruth d1961 *WhoHol 92*
Chatterton, Thomas d1952 *WhoHol 92*
Chatterton, Thomas 1752-1770 *BlmGEL*
Chatterton, Vivienne d1974 *WhoHol 92*
Chatterton, William Alonzo 1926- *WhoAmL 94*
Chattin, Gilbert Marshall 1914- *WhoFI 94*
Chattman, Sanders M. 1947- *WhoAmL 94*
Chatto, Beth 1923- *Who 94*
Chatto, Daniel 1958- *WhoHol 92*
Chatto, Tom d1982 *WhoHol 92*
Chatton, Sydney d1966 *WhoHol 92*
Chattopadhyay, Aditi 1958- *WhoScEn 94*
Chattopadhyay, Kallol *WhoAsA 94*
Chattoraj, Sati Charan 1934- *WhoAm 94*
Chattoraj, Shib Charan 1924- *WhoMW 93*
Chattree, Mayank 1957- *WhoScEn 94*
Chaturvedi, Arvind Kumar 1947- *WhoAsA 94*
Chaturvedi, Ram Prakash 1931- *WhoAsA 94*
Chaturvedi, Rama Kant 1933- *WhoAsA 94*
Chaturvedi, Shive Kumar 1947- *WhoMW 93*
Chatwani, Jaswanti 1933- *Who 94*
Chatwin, (John) Malcolm 1945- *Who 94*
Chatzidakis, Manos 1925- *IntWW 93*
Chatzinoff, Howard 1952- *WhoAmL 94*
Chau, Henry Chun-Nam 1961- *WhoAsA 94*
Chau, Lai-Kwan 1956- *WhoScEn 94*
Chau, Peter 1950- *WhoAsA 94*
Chaucer, Daniel *EncSF 93*
Chaucer, Geoffrey c. 1340-1400 *BlmGEL [port]*
Chauchoin, Lily 1903- *WhoAm 94*
Chaudhari, Anshumali 1947- *WhoAsA 94*
Chaudhari, Praveen 1937- *WhoAsA 94*
Chaudhari, Shobhana Ashok 1950- *WhoAsA 94*
Chaudhary, Shaukat Ali 1931- *WhoScEn 94*
Chaudhary, Ved P. 1942- *WhoAsA 94*
Chaudhri, Amin Qamar 1942- *IntMPA 94*
Chaudhri, Rajiv Jahangir 1957- *WhoAsA 94*
Chaudhry, G. Rasul 1948- *WhoAsA 94, WhoScEn 94*
Chaudhry, Ghulam Miran 1951- *WhoMW 93*
Chaudhuri, Dilip Kumar 1938- *WhoAm 94*
Chaudhuri, Jharna 1947- *WhoMW 93*
Chaudhuri, Kirti Narayan 1934- *Who 94*
Chaudhuri, Naranarain (Sankho) 1916- *IntWW 93*
Chaudhuri, Nirad Chandra 1897- *Who 94*
Chaudhuri, Probal 1963- *WhoMW 93*
Chaudhuri, Tapan K. 1944- *WhoAsA 94*
Chauffard, Jacques-Rene d1972 *WhoHol 92*
Chaufournier, Roger 1924- *IntWW 93*
Chauhan, Ved Pal Singh 1953- *WhoScEn 94*
Chaulet, Emmanuelle 1961- *WhoHol 92*
Chaumel, Adele *NewGrDO*
Chaumonot, Pierre-Joseph-Marie 1611-1693 *EncNAR*
Chauncey, Beatrice Arlene *WhoAm 94*
Chauncey, Minion Kenneth 1946- *WhoBlA 94*
Chauncey, Tom 1913- *WhoWest 94*
Chauncey, Tom Webster, II 1947- *WhoAmL 94, WhoWest 94*
Chauncy, Charles 1705-1787 *DcAmReB 2*
Chauncy, Nan 1900-1970 *BlmGWL*
Chaunu, Pierre 1923- *IntWW 93*
Chaussard, Bessie Rose 1936- *WhoMW 93*
Chausson, (Amedee-)Ernest 1855-1899 *NewGrDO*
Chautard, Emile d1934 *WhoHol 92*
Chauveau, Zoe *WhoHol 92*
Chauveaux, Billie 1925- *WhoAmP 93*
Chauvel, Jean M. H. 1897-1979 *HisDcKW*
Chauvet, Guy 1933- *NewGrDO*
Chauvet, Marie 1916-1973 *BlmGWL*
Chauvette, Claude R. 1939- *WhoAm 94*
Chauvin, Leonard Stanley, Jr. 1935- *WhoAmL 94*
Chauvin, Lilyan *WhoHol 92*
Chauvire, Yvette *WhoHol 92*
Chauvire, Yvette 1917- *IntDcB [port], IntWW 93, Who 94*
Chavan, Sangita D. 1965- *WhoAsA 94*
Chavan, Shankarrao Bhaorao 1920- *IntWW 93*
Chavarria, Adam, Jr. 1949- *WhoHisp 94*
Chavarria, Dolores Esparza 1952- *WhoFI 94*
Chavarria, Doroteo *WhoHisp 94*
Chavarria, Ernest M., Jr. 1955- *WhoHisp 94*
Chavarria, Ernest Montes, Jr. 1955- *WhoAm 94, WhoFI 94*
Chavarria, Fernando 1952- *WhoHisp 94*
Chavarria, Hector Manuel 1934- *WhoHisp 94*
Chavarria, Jesus *WhoHisp 94*
Chavarria, Oscar 1947- *WhoHisp 94*
Chavarria, Phil 1929- *WhoHisp 94*
Chavarria Chairez, Rebecca 1956- *WhoHisp 94*
Chavas, John Joseph, Jr. 1939- *WhoMW 93*
Chavasse, Christopher Patrick Grant 1928- *Who 94*
Chave, Keith Ernest 1928- *WhoWest 94*
Chavel, Francois M. 1946- *WhoIns 94*
Chaves, Christi Cahill 1955- *WhoMW 93*
Chaves, Jose A. 1941- *WhoIns 94*
Chaves, Jose Maria 1922- *WhoAm 94*
Chaves, Lloyd Zamora, Jr. 1948- *WhoHisp 94*
Chaves, Manuel 1945- *IntWW 93*
Chaves, Maria Isabel 1956- *WhoHisp 94*
Chaves, Mark Alan 1960- *WhoMW 93*
Chaves, Melvin *WhoHisp 94*
Chaves-Carballo, Enrique 1936- *WhoHisp 94*
Chaves De Mendonca, Antonio Aureliano 1929- *IntWW 93*
Chavez (y Ramirez), Carlos (Antonio de Padua) 1899-1978 *NewGrDO*
Chavez, Abel Max 1951- *WhoHisp 94*
Chávez, Abraham 1927- *WhoHisp 94*
Chavez, Albert Blas 1952- *WhoFI 94, WhoWest 94*
Chavez, Alice Diaz 1956- *WhoHisp 94*
Chavez, Andrew 1939- *WhoHisp 94*
Chavez, Angelico, Fray 1910- *WhoHisp 94*
Chavez, Anita *WhoHisp 94*
Chavez, Arthur L. *WhoHisp 94*
Chavez, Benjamin Anthony *WhoHisp 94*
Chavez, Bernadette Louise 1947- *WhoHisp 94*
Chavez, Bernadette Marie 1955- *WhoHisp 94*
Chavez, Carmela B. 1950- *WhoHisp 94*
Chávez, Carmen L. 1955- *WhoHisp 94*
Chavez, Cesar 1927-1993 *NewYTBS 93 [port], News 93*
Chavez, Cesar (Estrada) 1927-1993 *CurBio 93N*
Chavez, Cesar Estrada 1927-1993 *AmSocL [port], WhoHisp 94N*
Chavez, Cesar Tizoc 1952- *WhoHisp 94*
Chavez, Cynthia 1967- *WhoHisp 94*
Chávez, Darlene 1950- *WhoHisp 94*
Chavez, David Mario 1955- *WhoWest 94*
Chavez, Denise 1948- *BlmGWL, HispLC [port]*
Chávez, Denise Elia 1948- *WhoHisp 94*
Chavez, Dennis C. *WhoAmP 93, WhoHisp 94*
Chavez, Dennis M. 1954- *WhoHisp 94*
Chavez, Don Antonio 1950- *WhoHisp 94*
Chavez, Eduardo Arcenio 1917- *WhoAmA 93, WhoHisp 94*
Chavez, Edward John 1943- *WhoHisp 94*
Chavez, Edward L. 1963- *WhoHisp 94, WhoWest 94*
Chavez, Elaine Juanita 1964- *WhoHisp 94*
Chavez, Elida *WhoHisp 94*
Chávez, Eliverio 1940- *WhoHisp 94*
Chavez, Ernest L. 1949- *WhoHisp 94*
Chavez, Fabian 1924- *WhoHisp 94*
Chavez, Felix P. 1933- *WhoHisp 94*
Chavez, Frank 1929- *WhoHisp 94*
Chavez, Gabriel Anthony 1955- *WhoHisp 94*
Chavez, Gilbert Espinoza 1932- *WhoWest 94*
Chavez, Helen Pappas 1925- *WhoAmP 93*
Chavez, Ida Lillian 1944- *WhoHisp 94*
Chavez, Ingrid 1964- *WhoHol 92*
Chavez, Isidro Ontiveros 1948- *WhoHisp 94*
Chavez, J. Anthony 1955- *WhoAmL 94*
Chavez, Joe Robert 1958- *WhoHisp 94*
Chavez, John *WhoHisp 94*
Chavez, John G. *WhoHisp 94*
Chavez, John I. E. 1949- *WhoHisp 94*
Chavez, John J. 1935- *WhoHisp 94*
Chavez, John Montoya 1952- *WhoHisp 94*
Chavez, John S. *WhoHisp 94*
Chavez, Joseph Arnold 1939- *WhoAmA 93, WhoHisp 94*
Chavez, Julio Cesar *NewYTBS 93 [port], WhoHisp 94*
Chavez, Larry Sterling 1948- *WhoHisp 94*
Chavez, Leo E. 1947- *WhoHisp 94*
Chavez, Linda *WhoHisp 94*
Chavez, Linda 1947- *WhoFI 94, WhoHisp 94*
Chavez, Lloyd G. 1929- *WhoHisp 94*
Chavez, Luis 1953- *WhoHisp 94*
Chavez, Manuel C. 1914- *WhoHisp 94*
Chavez, Manuel Camacho, Sr. 1930- *WhoHisp 94*
Chavez, Marcelo d1970 *WhoHol 92*
Chávez, Maria D. 1939- *WhoHisp 94*
Chavez, Mariano, Jr. *WhoHisp 94*
Chavez, Martin J. 1952- *WhoAmP 93*
Chavez, Martin Joseph 1952- *WhoHisp 94, WhoWest 94*
Chavez, Mary 1952- *WhoHisp 94*
Chavez, Mary B. 1925- *WhoHisp 94*
Chavez, Mauro 1947- *WhoHisp 94*
Chavez, Melchor 1934- *WhoAmP 93*
Chavez, Melesio Romo 1935- *WhoHisp 94*
Chavez, Michael Mendez 1959- *WhoHisp 94*
Chávez, Nora W. 1952- *WhoHisp 94*
Chavez, Octavio Vega 1939- *WhoHisp 94*
Chavez, Pablo R. 1935- *WhoHisp 94*
Chavez, Patricia L. 1954- *WhoHisp 94*
Chavez, Ramiro Rosales 1945- *WhoHisp 94*
Chavez, Ray 1950- *WhoHisp 94*
Chavez, Raymond M. 1947- *WhoHisp 94*
Chavez, Richard G. *WhoHisp 94*
Chavez, Richard J. 1946- *WhoHisp 94*
Chavez, Rodolfo Lucas 1950- *WhoHisp 94*
Chavez, Sam J. *WhoHisp 94*
Chavez, Sonny *WhoHisp 94*
Chavez, Tibo J. *WhoHisp 94*
Chavez, Tim A. 1958- *WhoHisp 94*
Chavez, Tito David 1947- *WhoAmP 93, WhoHisp 94*
Chavez, Tony, Jr. 1939- *WhoHisp 94*

Chavez, Tony A. 1931- *WhoHisp 94*
Chavez, Trinidad Jose, Jr. 1937- *WhoHisp 94*
Chavez, Victor B. 1945- *WhoHisp 94*
Chavez, Victor Edwin 1930- *WhoAm 94*
Chavez, Victoria Marie 1933- *WhoHisp 94*
Chávez, William Xavier, Jr. 1955- *WhoHisp 94*
Chavez Ahner, Yolanda 1937- *WhoHisp 94*
Chavez-Andonegui, Carlos E. 1946- *WhoHisp 94*
Chavez-Cornish, Patricia Marie 1951- *WhoHisp 94*
Chávez Kelley, Christina L. G. 1953- *WhoHisp 94*
Chávez-Méndez, Ricardo 1953- *WhoHisp 94*
Chávez Ortiz, Genovevo Teodoro 1945- *WhoHisp 94*
Chávez-Thompson, Linda *WhoHisp 94*
Chavez-Vasquez, Gloria *WhoHisp 94*
Chaviano, Daina *EncSF 93*
Chaviano, Hugo 1952- *WhoHisp 94*
Chavin, Walter 1925- *WhoAm 94*
Chavis, Benjamin 1948- *ConBlB 6 [port], News 93 [port]*
Chavis, Benjamin F. 1948- *WhoAmP 93*
Chavis, Benjamin Franklin, Jr. 1948- *AfrAmAl 6 [port], NewYTBS 93 [port], WhoAm 94, WhoBlA 94*
Chavis, Theodore R. 1922- *WhoBlA 94*
Chavolla Ramos, Francisco Javier 1946- *WhoAm 94*
Chavooshian, Marge 1925- *WhoAm 94, WhoAmA 93*
Chavous, Barney Lewis 1951- *WhoBlA 94*
Chavous, Kevin P. *WhoAmP 93*
Chavous, Mildred L. *WhoBlA 94*
Chavunduka, Gordon Lloyd 1931- *IntWW 93*
Chawaf, Chantal *BlmGWL*
Chawla, Amrik Singh 1941- *WhoScEn 94*
Chawla, Krishan Kumar 1942- *WhoAm 94*
Chawla, Lal Muhammad 1917- *WhoScEn 94*
Chawla, Manmohan Singh 1940- *WhoScEn 94*
Chawla, Sudhir Kumar 1951- *WhoFI 94*
Chayanne 1969- *WhoHisp 94*
Chayasirisobhon, Sirichai 1944- *WhoWest 94*
Chayefsky, Paddy 1923-1981 *ConDr 93, EncSF 93, IntDcF 2-4, IntDcT 2*
Chayes, Abram 1922- *IntWW 93, WhoAm 94, WhoAmL 94*
Chaykin, Howard V(ictor) 1950- *EncSF 93*
Chaykin, Maury *WhoHol 92*
Chaykin, Robert Leroy 1944- *WhoFI 94, WhoWest 94*
Chaykovsky, Alexander Vladimirovich 1946- *NewGrDO*
Chaykovsky, Modest Il'ich *NewGrDO*
Chaykovsky, Pyotr Il'ich *NewGrDO*
Chaytor, George Reginald 1912- *Who 94*
Chazel, Marie-Anne *WhoHol 92*
Chazell, Russell Earl 1964- *WhoScEn 94*
Chazen, Hartley James 1932- *WhoAm 94*
Chazen, Jerome A. 1927- *WhoAm 94, WhoFI 94*
Chazen, Melvin Leonard 1933- *WhoScEn 94, WhoWest 94*
Chazot, Jacques d1993 *NewYTBS 93*
Chazov, Yevgeny Ivanovich 1929- *IntWW 93*
Chbosky, Fred G. 1944- *WhoAm 94, WhoFI 94*
Che, Chico d1989 *WhoHol 92*
Che, Chuang 1934- *WhoAmA 93*
Che, Chun-Tao 1953- *WhoScEn 94*
Cheadle, Walter Butler 1835-1919 *WhWE*
Cheaney, Calbert *WhoBlA 94*
Cheatham, Adolphus A. 1905- *WhoBlA 94*
Cheatham, Betty L. 1940- *WhoBlA 94*
Cheatham, Charlotte *DrAPF 93*
Cheatham, Daniel Lee 1950- *WhoMW 93*
Cheatham, David G. 1951- *WhoAmP 93*
Cheatham, Frank Reagan 1936- *WhoAmA 93*
Cheatham, Glenn Wallace 1934- *WhoAm 94*
Cheatham, Henry Boles 1943- *WhoBlA 94*
Cheatham, Jack d1971 *WhoHol 92*
Cheatham, John Bryan 1896- *WhoAmP 93*
Cheatham, Karyn Follis *DrAPF 93*
Cheatham, Linda Moye 1948- *WhoBlA 94*
Cheatham, Marie *WhoHol 92*
Cheatham, Mary Ann 1944- *WhoMW 93*
Cheatham, Richard Reed 1943- *WhoAm 94, WhoAmL 94*
Cheatham, Robert William 1938- *WhoAm 94*
Cheatham, Roy E. 1941- *WhoBlA 94*
Cheatham, Thomas Edward, Jr. 1929- *WhoScEn 94*
Cheatley, Susan Rae 1947- *WhoMW 93*
Cheatwood, Earl 1928- *WhoAmP 93*
Cheatwood, Roy Clifton 1946- *WhoAm 94, WhoAmL 94*
Cheavens, Frank 1905- *WrDr 94*
Cheavens, Joseph D. 1940- *WhoAm 94*
Chebrikov, Viktor Mikhailovich 1923- *IntWW 93*
Checa, Eduardo 1959- *WhoFI 94*
Checchi, Alfred A. 1948- *WhoAm 94, WhoFI 94*
Checchi, Robert J. d1993 *NewYTBS 93*
Checchi, Vincent Victor 1918- *WhoAm 94*
Checci, Andrea d1974 *WhoHol 92*
Checco, Al 1925- *WhoHol 92*
Checco, Jessie d1983 *WhoHol 92*
Check, Melvin Anthony 1951- *WhoMW 93*
Checker, Chubby 1941- *WhoBlA 94, WhoHol 92*
Checketts, David (John) 1930- *Who 94*
Checketts, David Wayne 1955- *WhoAm 94*
Checketts, Guy Tresham 1927- *Who 94*
Checketts, Keith Thomas 1935- *WhoWest 94*
Checkland, Michael 1936- *IntWW 93, Who 94*
Checkley, Stuart Arthur 1945- *Who 94*
Checkman, Neil Bruce 1947- *WhoAmL 94*
Checole, Kassahun 1947- *WhoBlA 94*
Checota, Joseph W. 1939- *WhoAmP 93*
Checota, Joseph Woodrow 1939- *WhoAm 94*
Checote, Samuel c. 1819-1884 *EncNAR*
Cheddar, Donville Glen 1946- *WhoScEn 94, WhoWest 94*
Chediak, Natalio 1909- *WhoHisp 94*
Chedid, Andree 1920- *IntWW 93*
Chedid, Andree 1921- *BlmGWL*
Chedid, John G. 1923- *WhoWest 94*
Chedister, America d1975 *WhoHol 92*
Chedlow, Barry William 1921- *Who 94*
Chee, Cheng-Khee 1934- *WhoAm 94, WhoAmA 93, WhoAsA 94*
Chee, Percival Hon Yin 1936- *WhoAm 94, WhoWest 94*
Cheech 1946- *WhoAm 94*
Cheech and Chong *WhoCom, WhoHol 92*
Cheek, Donald Kato 1930- *WhoBlA 94*
Cheek, Donna Marie 1963- *WhoBlA 94*
Cheek, James Edward 1932- *IntWW 93, WhoAm 94, WhoBlA 94*
Cheek, James Howe, III 1942- *WhoAm 94, WhoAmL 94*
Cheek, James Richard 1936- *WhoAm 94, WhoAmP 93*
Cheek, John Henry 1929- *WhoAm 94*
Cheek, King Virgil, Jr. 1937- *WhoAm 94, WhoBlA 94*
Cheek, Mary Louise 1942- *WhoMW 93*
Cheek, Robert Benjamin, III 1931- *WhoBlA 94*
Cheek, Ronald Edward 1942- *WhoAmA 93*
Cheek, Timothy Newton 1958- *WhoAmL 94*
Cheek, Will T. 1943- *WhoAmP 93*
Cheek, Will Tompkins 1943- *WhoFI 94*
Cheeks, Carl L. 1937- *WhoBlA 94*
Cheeks, Darryl Lamont 1968- *WhoBlA 94*
Cheeks, Donald E. 1931- *WhoAmP 93*
Cheeks, Maurice 1956- *BasBi [port]*
Cheeks, Maurice Edward 1956- *WhoBlA 94*
Cheeley, Robert David 1957- *WhoAmL 94*
Cheely, Daniel Joseph 1949- *WhoAm 94, WhoAmL 94*
Cheese, Pauline Staten *WhoBlA 94*
Cheeseman, Clara 1852-1943 *BlmGWL*
Cheeseman, Douglas Taylor, Jr. 1937- *WhoAm 94, WhoWest 94*
Cheeseman, Ian Clifford 1926- *Who 94*
Cheeseman, Martin d1924 *WhoHol 92*
Cheeseman, William John 1943- *WhoAm 94, WhoAmL 94*
Cheesman, John Michael 1943- *WhoMW 93*
Cheesman, Steven Miles 1958- *WhoMW 93*
Cheetham, Ann 1944- *WrDr 94*
Cheetham, Anthony John Valerian 1943- *IntWW 93, Who 94*
Cheetham, Anthony Kevin 1946- *Who 94*
Cheetham, Francis William 1928- *Who 94*
Cheetham, John Frederick Thomas 1919- *Who 94*
Cheetham, Juliet 1939- *Who 94*
Cheetham, Nicolas (John Alexander) 1910- *Who 94*
Cheever, Abigail A. 1944- *WhoAmL 94*
Cheever, Allen Williams 1932- *WhoScEn 94*
Cheever, Dan J. 1955- *WhoWest 94*
Cheever, Daniel Sargent 1916- *WhoAm 94*
Cheever, George Martin 1947- *WhoAm 94*
Cheever, Herbert Edward, Jr. 1938- *WhoAmP 93*
Cheever, John (William) 1912-1982 *RfGShF*
Cheever, Raymond Craig 1926- *WhoMW 93*
Cheever, Susan 1943- *WrDr 94*
Cheevers, Sarah *BlmGWL*
Cheevers, William Harold 1918- *Who 94*
Chefe, Jack d1975 *WhoHol 92*
Cheffer, Scott Gerard 1964- *WhoAm 94*
Cheffetz, Asa 1897-1965 *WhoAmA 93N*
Cheffy, Edward Kefgen 1953- *WhoAmL 94*
Chefitz, Harold Neal 1935- *WhoAm 94*
Chefitz, Joel Gerald 1951- *WhoAm 94, WhoAmL 94*
Chegini, Nasser 1949- *WhoScEn 94*
Cheh, Huk Yuk 1939- *WhoAm 94, WhoFI 94*
Chehak, Susan Taylor 1951- *WrDr 94*
Cheifetz, Lorna Gale 1953- *WhoAm 94, WhoWest 94*
Cheiffou, Amadou *IntWW 93*
Cheirel, Micheline *WhoHol 92*
Cheit, Earl Frank 1926- *WhoAm 94*
Chejonska, Irena *WhoWomW 91*
Chekanauskas, Vitautas 1930- *IntWW 93*
Cheke, Dudley John d1993 *Who 94N*
Cheke, John 1514-1557 *DcLB 132 [port]*
Chekhov, Anton (Pavlovich) 1860-1904 *IntDcT 2 [port], RfGShF*
Chekhov, Anton Pavlovich 1860-1904 *BlmGEL, NewGrDO*
Chekhov, Michael d1955 *WhoHol 92*
Chekova, Olga d1980 *WhoHol 92*
Chelard, Hippolyte-Andre(-Jean)-Baptiste 1789-1861 *NewGrDO*
Chelberg, Bruce Stanley 1934- *WhoAm 94, WhoFI 94*
Chelberg, Robert Douglas 1938- *WhoAm 94*
Chelette, Kathryn Fontenot 1966- *WhoFI 94*
Chelf, Carl P. 1937- *WrDr 94*
Cheli, Giovanni 1918- *IntWW 93*
Cheli, Ronald Peter 1952- *WhoAmL 94*
Chelidze, Otar Silovanovich 1925- *IntWW 93*
Chelikowsky, James Robert 1948- *WhoMW 93*
Chelios, Christos K 1962- *WhoAm 94*
Chelios, Nicole 1960- *WhoMW 93*
Chelius, James Robert 1943- *WhoAm 94*
Chell, Beverly C. 1942- *WhoAm 94, WhoAmL 94*
Chellappa, Rama 1953- *WhoAsA 94*
Chellas, Brian Farrell 1941- *WhoAm 94*
Chelleri, Fortunato 1686?-1757 *NewGrDO*
Chellgren, Paul Wilbur 1943- *WhoAm 94*
Chellis, Sharon Lee Hayes 1943- *WhoAmP 93*
Chelmer, Baron 1914- *Who 94*
Chelminiak, Charles Thomas 1953- *WhoFI 94, WhoMW 93*
Chelmsford, Bishop of 1930- *Who 94*
Chelmsford, Provost of *Who 94*
Chelmsford, Viscount 1931- *Who 94*
Chelsea, Viscount 1937- *Who 94*
Chelsom, Peter *WhoHol 92*
Chelsom, Peter 1956- *ConTFT 11*
Chelstrom, Marilyn Ann *WhoMW 93*
Cheltenham, Archdeacon of *Who 94*
Chelton, John 1921- *WrDr 94*
Chelton, Lewis William Leonard 1934- *Who 94*
Chelton, Tsilla 1918- *WhoHol 92*
Chelyuskin, Simeon fl. 174-?- *WhWE*
Chema, Thomas V. 1946- *WhoAm 94, WhoAmL 94, WhoMW 93*
Chemeche, George 1934- *WhoAmA 93*
Chementi, Margherita *NewGrDO*
Chemerow, David Irving 1951- *WhoAm 94*
Chemers, Robert Marc 1951- *WhoAmL 94*
Chemetov, Paul 1928- *IntWW 93*
Chemin-Petit, Hans (Helmuth) 1902-1981 *NewGrDO*
Chemsak, J. A. 1932- *WhoAm 94*
Chen, Alan Keith 1960- *WhoAsA 94*
Chen, Alice Wu 1937- *WhoAsA 94*
Chen, Amy L. 1957- *WhoAsA 94*
Chen, Andrew Houng-Yhi 1937- *WhoAsA 94*
Chen, Angela Tzu-Yau 1958- *WhoAsA 94*
Chen, Anne Chi 1962- *WhoAsA 94*
Chen, Audrey Huey-Wen 1964- *WhoAsA 94*
Chen, Augustine Cheng-Hsin 1927- *WhoAsA 94*
Chen, Bang-Yen 1943- *WhoAsA 94*
Chen, Basilio 1953- *WhoWest 94*
Chen, Benjamin Yun-Hai 1951- *WhoAsA 94*
Chen, Bernard Shao-Wen 1960- *WhoAsA 94*
Chen, Bessie B. 1958- *WhoAsA 94*
Chen, Bill Shun-Zer 1941- *WhoAm 94*
Chen, Bintong 1964- *WhoAsA 94*
Chen, C. L. Philip 1959- *WhoAsA 94*
Chen, Carl Wan-Cheng 1936- *WhoAsA 94*
Chen, Catherine W. 1938- *WhoAsA 94*
Chen, Chao 1953- *WhoAsA 94*
Chen, Chao Ling 1937- *WhoAsA 94*
Chen, Chaozong 1935- *WhoScEn 94*
Chen, Char-Nie 1938- *IntWW 93*
Chen, Charles T. M. 1934- *WhoAsA 94*
Chen, Chaur-Fong 1956- *WhoScEn 94*
Chen, Chen-Tung Arthur 1949- *WhoScEn 94*
Chen, Cheyenne 1963- *WhoAsA 94*
Chen, Chi 1912- *WhoAm 94*
Chen, Chi Hau 1937- *WhoAsA 94*
Chen, Chi-Tsong 1936- *WhoAm 94*
Chen, Chi-yun 1933- *WhoAsA 94*
Chen, Chih-Ying 1951- *WhoScEn 94*
Chen, Chin 1927- *WhoAsA 94*
Chen, Chin-Lin 1937- *WhoAsA 94*
Chen, Ching-chih 1937- *WhoAsA 94*
Chen, Ching-Hong 1935- *WhoScEn 94*
Chen, Chong-Maw *WhoAsA 94, WhoMW 93*
Chen, Chong-Tong 1935- *WhoAsA 94*
Chen, Chu-Chin 1954- *WhoScEn 94*
Chen, Chuan Fang 1932- *WhoAm 94*
Chen, Chuan Ju 1947- *WhoAsA 94*
Chen, Chun-fan 1937- *WhoScEn 94*
Chen, Chung 1953- *WhoAsA 94*
Chen, Chung-Hsuan 1948- *WhoAsA 94, WhoScEn 94*
Chen, Chung Long 1958- *WhoScEn 94*
Chen, Concordia Chao *WhoScEn 94*
Chen, David Ta-Fu 1935- *WhoAsA 94*
Chen, David Ting-Kai 1935- *WhoAsA 94*
Chen, David W. 1939- *WhoAsA 94*
Chen, Derrick A. 1966- *WhoAsA 94*
Chen, Di 1929- *WhoAm 94, WhoAsA 94*
Chen, Ding-Bond 1947- *WhoAsA 94*
Chen, Donald S. 1940- *WhoAsA 94*
Chen, Edward C. H. 1954- *WhoAsA 94*
Chen, Er-Ping 1944- *WhoAsA 94*
Chen, Fang Chu *WhoScEn 94*
Chen, Francis F. 1929- *WhoAm 94, WhoAsA 94, WhoScEn 94, WhoWest 94*
Chen, Franklin Ming-kai 1946- *WhoMW 93*
Chen, George Chi-Ming 1923- *WhoAsA 94*
Chen, Gong 1953- *WhoAsA 94*
Chen, Gong Ning 1939- *WhoScEn 94*
Chen, Guanrong 1948- *WhoAsA 94, WhoScEn 94*
Chen, Gui-Qiang 1962- *WhoMW 93, WhoScEn 94*
Chen, Gwo-Liang 1948- *WhoScEn 94*
Chen, Hai-chin 1924- *WhoScEn 94*
Chen, Haiyang 1955- *WhoAsA 94*
Chen, Han-Ping 1949- *WhoWest 94*
Chen, Harry W. 1937- *WhoAsA 94*
Chen, Helen T. W. *WhoAsA 94*
Chen, Henry 1941- *WhoAsA 94*
Chen, Henry 1959- *WhoAsA 94, WhoScEn 94*
Chen, Henry J. 1960- *WhoAsA 94*
Chen, Hilo 1942- *WhoAmA 93*
Chen, Hilo C. H. 1942- *WhoAsA 94*
Chen, Ho-Hong H. H. 1933- *WhoAm 94, WhoScEn 94*
Chen, Hollis Ching 1935- *WhoAsA 94*
Chen, Hong Chyi 1954- *WhoAsA 94*
Chen, Hongda 1957- *WhoAsA 94*
Chen, Houn-Gee 1956- *WhoAsA 94*
Chen, Hsin-Piao Patrick 1950- *WhoAsA 94*
Chen, Hung-Liang 1959- *WhoAsA 94*
Chen, Irvin Shao Yu 1955- *WhoScEn 94*
Chen, Ivan Mao-Chang 1956- *WhoAsA 94*
Chen, Jackson W. 1941- *WhoAsA 94*
Chen, James *WhoAsA 94*
Chen, James Jen-Chuan 1964- *WhoScEn 94*
Chen, James Pai-fun 1929- *WhoAsA 94, WhoScEn 94*
Chen, Jay 1950- *WhoAsA 94*
Chen, Jei-Po 1936- *WhoWest 94*
Chen, Jian Ning 1959- *WhoScEn 94*
Chen, Jianhua 1954- *WhoAsA 94*
Chen, Jie 1955- *WhoAsA 94*
Chen, Jin 1967- *WhoFI 94*
Chen, Jinya 1952- *WhoAmL 94*
Chen, Jizeng 1950- *WhoAsA 94*
Chen, Joan 1961- *WhoAsA 94, WhoHol 92*
Chen, John Calvin 1949- *WhoWest 94*
Chen, John L. 1934- *WhoAsA 94*
Chen, John Shaoming 1935- *WhoAsA 94*
Chen, Joseph T. 1925- *WrDr 94*
Chen, Joseph Tao 1925- *WhoAm 94*
Chen, Juh Wah 1928- *WhoAsA 94*
Chen, Jyh-Hong Eric 1951- *WhoAsA 94*
Chen, Kangping 1961- *WhoAsA 94*
Chen, Kao 1919- *WhoAm 94, WhoAsA 94*
Chen, Karl A. 1935- *WhoAsA 94*
Chen, Kenny T. 1961- *WhoAsA 94*
Chen, Ker-Sang 1946- *WhoMW 93*
Chen, King C. d1993 *NewYTBS 93*
Chen, Kok-Choo 1947- *WhoAmL 94*

Chen, Kuang Chung 1954- WhoAsA 94
Chen, Kuang Yu 1946- WhoAsA 94
Chen, Kun-Mu 1933- WhoAm 94, WhoAsA 94
Chen, Le Chun 1956- WhoAsA 94
Chen, Lea D. 1952- WhoMW 93
Chen, Lea Der 1952- WhoAsA 94
Ch'en, Lena B. 1949- WhoAsA 94
Chen, Li-Fu 1944- WhoAsA 94
Ch'en, Li-li 1934- WhoAm 94, WhoAsA 94
Chen, Lih-Juann 1946- WhoScEn 94
Chen, Lihtorng Robert 1952- WhoAmL 94
Chen, Lincoln Chin-ho 1942- WhoAm 94
Chen, Linda 1957- WhoAsA 94
Chen, Linda Li-yueh 1937- WhoAsA 94
Chen, Lung-chu 1935- WhoAm 94
Chen, Meanshang 1953- WhoAsA 94
Chen, Michael Chia-Chao 1947- WhoAsA 94
Chen, Michael M. 1932- WhoAsA 94
Chen, Michael Ming 1933- WhoAm 94, WhoScEn 94
Chen, Michael Y. M. 1941- WhoAsA 94
Chen, Min-Chu 1949- WhoScEn 94
Chen, Ming 1955- WhoAsA 94
Chen, Ming Chih 1920- WhoAsA 94
Chen, Moon Shao-Chuang, Jr. 1947- WhoAsA 94
Chen, Mu-Tsai 1945- WhoFI 94
Chen, Nai-Fu 1950- WhoWest 94
Chen, Nai-Ni WhoAsA 94
Chen, Nai Y. 1926- WhoAsA 94
Chen, Naixing 1933- WhoScEn 94
Chen, Pamela Ki Mai 1961- WhoAsA 94
Chen, Paul Kuan Yao 1924- WhoAsA 94
Chen, Pengyuan 1961- WhoMW 93
Chen, Peter WhoScEn 94
Chen, Peter Pin-Shan 1947- WhoAm 94, WhoScEn 94
Chen, Peter Wei-Teh 1942- WhoWest 94
Chen, Philip S., Jr. 1932- WhoAm 94
Chen, Ping-fan 1917- WhoAm 94, WhoAsA 94
Chen, Robert Chia-Hua 1946- WhoAsA 94
Chen, Roger Ko-chung 1951- WhoMW 93, WhoScEn 94
Chen, Rong 1955- WhoMW 93
Chen, Rong Yaw 1933- WhoAsA 94
Chen, S. Steve 1950- WhoAsA 94
Chen, Sam W. 1945- WhoAsA 94
Chen, Shi-Han 1936- WhoAsA 94
Chen, Shih-Hsiung 1955- WhoScEn 94
Chen, Shilu 1920- WhoScEn 94
Chen, Shoei-Sheng 1940- WhoAm 94, WhoAsA 94
Chen, Simon Ying 1948- WhoAsA 94
Chen, Siu Loong 1970- WhoAsA 94
Chen, Sow-Hsin 1935- WhoAm 94
Chen, Stanford 1947- WhoAsA 94
Chen, Stephen C. 1941- WhoAsA 94
Chen, Stephen Shau-tsi 1934- WhoWest 94
Chen, Steve S. 1944- WhoAsA 94
Chen, Stuart S. 1957- WhoAsA 94
Chen, Su-chiung 1937- WhoAsA 94
Chen, Ta-Shen 1932- WhoAsA 94
Chen, Tai 1951- WhoAsA 94
Chen, Terry 1951- WhoAsA 94
Chen, Terry Li-Tseng 1949- WhoAsA 94
Chen, Theodore Tien Yiu 1946- WhoWest 94
Chen, Thomas K. S. WhoAsA 94
Chen, Thomas Shih-Nien 1936- WhoAsA 94
Chen, Tian-Jie 1939- WhoScEn 94
Chen, Tina WhoHol 92
Chen, Tony Young 1929- WhoAsA 94
Chen, Tseh An 1928- WhoAsA 94
Chen, Tsong-Ming 1934- WhoAsA 94
Chen, Tuan Wu 1925- WhoAsA 94
Chen, Tung-Shan 1939- WhoAsA 94
Chen, Victor John 1952- WhoAsA 94
Chen, Victoria Liu 1945- WhoAsA 94
Chen, Virginia L. 1959- WhoAsA 94
Chen, Wai Fah 1936- WhoAsA 94, WhoMW 93
Chen, Wai Jun 1942- WhoAsA 94
Chen, Wai-Kai 1936- WhoAm 94, WhoAsA 94, WhoMW 93
Chen, Walter Yi-Chen 1956- WhoScEn 94
Chen, Wayne G. 1950- WhoAsA 94
Chen, Wayne H. 1922- WhoScEn 94
Chen, Wayne Y. 1942- WhoAsA 94
Chen, Wei R. 1958- WhoScEn 94
Chen, Wei-Yin 1950- WhoAsA 94
Chen, Weihang 1940- WhoAsA 94
Chen, Wen Fu 1942- WhoMW 93, WhoScEn 94
Chen, Wen H. 1938- WhoScEn 94
Chen, Wen L. 1934- WhoAsA 94
Chen, Wen-Yih 1958- WhoScEn 94
Chen, Wenxiong 1952- WhoAsA 94, WhoMW 93
Chen, Wesley 1954- WhoAmL 94
Chen, William Hok-Nin 1950- WhoAsA 94
Chen, William Lin-Tang 1938- WhoMW 93
Chen, William Shao-Chang 1939- WhoAm 94
Chen, Winston H. 1941?- WhoAsA 94
Chen, Wun-ee Chelsea 1964- WhoAsA 94
Chen, Xiangming 1955- WhoAsA 94
Chen, Xiangning 1963- WhoAsA 94
Chen, Xinfu 1964- WhoAsA 94
Chen, Yang-Fang 1953- WhoScEn 94
Chen, Ye-Hwa 1956- WhoAsA 94
Chen, Ye-Sho 1954- WhoAsA 94
Chen, Yea-Mow 1953- WhoAsA 94
Chen, Yen-Hsu 1952- WhoAsA 94
Chen, Yi-Chao 1952- WhoAsA 94
Chen, Yi-Leng 1950- WhoAsA 94
Chen, Yi-Shon 1939- WhoAsA 94
Chen, Yih-Wen David 1948- WhoAsA 94
Chen, Yohchia 1956- WhoAsA 94
Chen, Yu 1921- WhoAsA 94
Chen, Yu-Charn 1954- WhoAsA 94
Chen, Yuan James 1949- WhoScEn 94
Chen, Yubao 1958- WhoAsA 94
Chen, Yuki Y. Kuo 1930- WhoAm 94
Chen, Yung 1937- WhoAsA 94
Chen, Yung-Lin 1952- WhoWest 94
Chen, Zhan 1945- WhoScEn 94
Chen, Zhen 1958- WhoScEn 94
Chen, Zhengxin 1947- WhoMW 93
Chen, Zhong-Ying 1943- WhoAsA 94
Chen, Zuohuang 1947- WhoAm 94
Chen Ailian 1939- IntWW 93, WhoPRCh 91 [port]
Chen Anyu 1922- WhoPRCh 91 [port]
Chenault, James Stouffer 1923- WhoAmL 94
Chenault, Kenneth 1952- WhoBlA 94
Chenault, Kenneth Irvine 1951- WhoAm 94, WhoFI 94
Chenault, Lawrence Royce 1897-1990 WhAm 10
Chenault, Myron Maurice 1949- WhoBlA 94
Chenault, William J. 1928- WhoBlA 94
Chenaux, Henry Eliot 1947- WhoHisp 94
Chen Baichen 1908- IntWW 93, WhoPRCh 91 [port]
Chen Baigao 1931- WhoPRCh 91 [port]
Chen Bangzhu 1934- IntWW 93, WhoPRCh 91 [port]
Chen Baoshun WhoPRCh 91
Chen Benting WhoPRCh 91 [port]
Chen Bin 1921- WhoPRCh 91 [port]
Chen Binfan 1933- WhoPRCh 91 [port]
Chen Bingquan 1931- WhoPRCh 91 [port]
Chen Bingxin WhoPRCh 91
Chen Bo WhoPRCh 91
Chen Chao WhoPRCh 91
Chen Chi 1912- WhoAm 94
Chen Chi-Lu 1923- IntWW 93
Chen Chunxian WhoPRCh 91 [port]
Chen Cuiting 1971- WhoPRCh 91 [port]
Chenda, Alfonso NewGrDO
Chen Daisun 1900- WhoPRCh 91 [port]
Chen Danqing 1953- WhoPRCh 91 [port]
Chen Dayu 1912- WhoPRCh 91 [port]
Chen Dazhi WhoPRCh 91
Chen Dehe WhoPRCh 91
Chen Dehong 1936- WhoPRCh 91
Chen Dengke 1918- WhoPRCh 91 [port]
Chen Dexi 1936- WhoPRCh 91
Chen Dingmao WhoPRCh 91 [port]
Chen Dongsheng WhoPRCh 91
Chen Duansheng fl. c. 18th cent.- BlmGWL
Chen Dun WhoPRCh 91
Chen Duxiu 1879-1942 HisWorL
Chene, Ethel d1972 WhoHol 92
Cheneler, John B. 1953- WhoFI 94
Chenery, Hollis (Burnley) 1918- WrDr 94
Chenery, Hollis Burnley 1918- IntWW 93
Chenery, Peter James 1946- Who 94
Chenery, Robin 1945- WhoAm 94, WhoFI 94
Chenevert, Edward Valmore, Jr. 1923- WhoAm 94
Chenevert, Phillip Joseph 1948- WhoBlA 94
Cheney, Daniel Lavern 1928- WhoAm 94
Cheney, Darwin Leroy 1940- WhoAm 94
Cheney, Dick 1941- WhoAm 94, WhoWest 94
Cheney, Elizabeth Joan 1924- WhoWest 94
Cheney, Glenn Alan 1951- WhoFI 94
Cheney, James Addison 1927- WhoAm 94
Cheney, Liana De Girolami 1942- WhoAmA 93
Cheney, Lynn V. 1941- WhoAmP 93
Cheney, Lynne V. 1941- WhoAm 94
Cheney, Nathaniel Boynton 1944- WhoFI 94
Cheney, Peter A. 1942- WhoIns 94
Cheney, Richard B. 1941- IntWW 93
Cheney, Richard Bruce 1941- Who 94, WhoAmP 93
Cheney, Richard Eugene 1921- WhoAm 94, WhoFI 94
Cheney, Richard Eugene 1922- WhoAmL 94
Cheney, Richard P. 1937- WhoAmP 93
Cheney, Sheldon 1886-1980 WhoAmA 93N
Cheney, Stuart F. 1942- WhoAmL 94
Cheney, Thomas Ward 1914- WhoAm 94
Chen Fangyun WhoPRCh 91
Chen Fawen 1930- WhoPRCh 91 [port]
Chen Fuli 1916- WhoPRCh 91 [port]
Cheng, Alexander H-D. 1952- WhoAsA 94
Cheng, Alexander Lihdar 1956- WhoFI 94, WhoScEn 94
Cheng, Amy I. 1956- WhoAsA 94
Cheng, Andrew F. 1951- WhoAsA 94
Cheng, Ansheng 1938- WhoScEn 94
Cheng, Benjamin Shujung 1937- WhoAsA 94
Cheng, Brian Kai-Ming 1958- WhoAsA 94
Cheng, Carl F. K. 1942- WhoAmA 93
Cheng, Carlos 1946- WhoAsA 94
Cheng, Carol Wai Yee 1964- WhoMW 93
Cheng, Charles Ching-an 1948- WhoAsA 94
Cheng, Charmian S. 1942- WhoAsA 94
Cheng, Cheng-Yin 1930- WhoAsA 94
Cheng, Chu-yuan 1927- ConAu 42NR, WhoAsA 94, WhoMW 93
Cheng, Chuen Yan 1954- WhoScEn 94
Cheng, Chung-Kuan WhoAsA 94
Cheng, Chung P. 1954- WhoScEn 94
Cheng, David Hong 1920- WhoAm 94, WhoAsA 94
Cheng, David Keun 1918- WhoAsA 94, WhoScEn 94
Cheng, Emily 1953- WhoAmA 93
Cheng, Eugene Y. 1954- WhoAsA 94
Cheng, Franklin Yih 1936- WhoAm 94, WhoAsA 94
Cheng, Fu-Ding 1943- WhoAmA 93, WhoAsA 94
Cheng, H. H. 1932- WhoAsA 94
Cheng, Heng-Da 1944- WhoWest 94
Cheng, Herbert S. 1929- WhoAsA 94
Cheng, Herbert Su-Yuen 1929- WhoAm 94, WhoScEn 94
Cheng, Hsiang-tai 1952- WhoAsA 94
Cheng, Hsien K. 1923- WhoAsA 94
Cheng, Hsien Kei 1923- WhoAm 94
Cheng, Hsueh-Jen 1937- WhoAsA 94
Cheng, Hwei Hsien 1932- WhoAm 94, WhoMW 93, WhoScEn 94
Cheng, J(ames) Chester 1926- WrDr 94
Cheng, J. S. 1914- WhoScEn 94
Cheng, Jane WhoAsA 94
Cheng, Jill Tsui 1945- WhoAsA 94
Cheng, Joe Zen 1958- WhoAsA 94
Cheng, Joseph Kwang-Chao 1934- WhoAsA 94
Cheng, Josephine 1958- WhoAsA 94
Cheng, Kuang Lu 1919- WhoAsA 94
Cheng, Kwong Man 1952- WhoScEn 94
Cheng, Lanna 1941- WhoAsA 94
Cheng, Lawrence Kai-Leung 1954- WhoAsA 94
Cheng, Li 1963- WhoScEn 94
Cheng, Louis Tsz-Wan 1961- WhoAsA 94
Cheng, Mei-Fang 1938- WhoAm 94
Cheng, Mei-Fang Hsieh 1938- WhoAsA 94
Cheng, Minquan 1965- WhoScEn 94
Cheng, Nancy C. 1931- WhoAsA 94
Cheng, Nelly Ching-yun 1933- WhoAsA 94
Cheng, Norman Alan 1957- WhoAsA 94
Cheng, Paifong Robert d1993 NewYTBS 93
Cheng, Paul Hung-Chiao 1930- WhoFI 94
Cheng, Ping WhoAsA 94
Cheng, Richard Tien-Ren 1934- WhoAsA 94
Cheng, Samson 1934- WhoFI 94
Cheng, Sheng-San 1952- WhoScEn 94
Cheng, Sheue-yann WhoAsA 94
Cheng, Sin I. 1921- WhoAsA 94
Cheng, Songlin 1949- WhoAsA 94
Cheng, Stephen Z. D. 1949- WhoAsA 94
Cheng, Stephen Zheng Di 1949- WhoScEn 94
Cheng, Ta-Pei 1941- WhoAsA 94
Cheng, Thomas Clement 1930- WhoAm 94, WhoScEn 94
Cheng, Tsen-Chung 1944- WhoAm 94
Cheng, Tsung O. 1925- WhoAm 94
Cheng, Tu-chen 1938- WhoAsA 94
Cheng, Tung Chao 1931- WhoAsA 94
Cheng, Wan-Lee 1945- WhoAm 94, WhoWest 94
Cheng, Wing-Tai Savio 1955- WhoScEn 94
Cheng, Ying-wan WhoAsA 94
Cheng, Yung-Sung 1947- WhoAsA 94
Cheng Andong WhoPRCh 91
Chen Gang 1935- IntWW 93
Chen Gaohua WhoPRCh 91
Cheng Chunshu WhoPRCh 91
Chengery, Albert Edward 1940- WhoFI 94
Cheng Faguang 1942- WhoPRCh 91 [port]
Cheng-Guajardo, Miguel A. 1943- WhoHisp 94
Cheng Ho 1371-1433 HisWorL [port]
Cheng Ho 1371-c. 1434 WhWE
Cheng Jinfa WhoPRCh 91
Cheng Jinxiang 1928- WhoPRCh 91 [port]
Cheng Kaijia WhoPRCh 91
Cheng Kejie 1933- IntWW 93, WhoPRCh 91 [port]
Cheng Li 1924- WhoPRCh 91 [port]
Cheng Lianchang 1931- IntWW 93, WhoPRCh 91 [port]
Cheng Mian 1933- IntWW 93, WhoPRCh 91
Cheng Naishan 1946- WhoPRCh 91 [port]
Cheng Ruisheng WhoPRCh 91
Cheng Shengsan 1912- WhoPRCh 91 [port]
Cheng Shicai 1912- WhoPRCh 91 [port]
Cheng Shicai, Lieut.-Gen. IntWW 93
Cheng Shifa 1921- IntWW 93, WhoPRCh 91 [port]
Chen Guangjian 1928- WhoPRCh 91 [port]
Chen Guangyi 1933- IntWW 93, WhoPRCh 91 [port]
Chen Guangzhong WhoPRCh 91
Chen Guizun 1931- WhoPRCh 91 [port]
Chen Guoda 1912- WhoPRCh 91 [port]
Chen Guodong 1911- WhoPRCh 91 [port]
Chen Guokai 1938- WhoPRCh 91 [port]
Cheng Wanzhu WhoPRCh 91
Cheng Weigao 1933- IntWW 93, WhoPRCh 91 [port]
Cheng Wendong WhoPRCh 91
Cheng Xiaowu WhoPRCh 91
Cheng Xihe WhoPRCh 91
Cheng Xu 1919- WhoPRCh 91 [port]
Cheng Yanan 1936- IntWW 93
Cheng Yuqi 1912- WhoPRCh 91 [port]
Cheng Zemin WhoPRCh 91
Cheng Zhenhua WhoPRCh 91
Cheng Zhiping 1926- WhoPRCh 91 [port]
Cheng Zihua 1905- WhoPRCh 91 [port]
Chenhall, Robert Gene 1923- WhoAm 94
Chen Hanseng 1897- IntWW 93
Chen Hansheng 1897- WhoPRCh 91 [port]
Chen Hanyuan WhoPRCh 91
Chen Haosu 1942- WhoPRCh 91 [port]
Chen Haozhu 1924- WhoPRCh 91 [port]
Chen Heng WhoPRCh 91
Chen Hengping WhoPRCh 91
Chen Heqiao WhoPRCh 91
Chen Hong WhoPRCh 91
Chen Hongchang WhoPRCh 91 [port]
Chen Hongyou 1942- WhoPRCh 91
Chen Huailong WhoPRCh 91
Chen Huakui 1914- IntWW 93
Chen Huangmei 1913- IntWW 93, WhoPRCh 91 [port]
Chen Huanyou 1934- IntWW 93, WhoPRCh 91 [port]
Chen Huiguang 1938- WhoPRCh 91 [port]
Chen Huiguang 1939- IntWW 93
Cheniae, George Maurice 1928- WhoAm 94
Chenier, Andre-Marie 1762-1794 GuFrLit 2
Chenier, Phil 1950- BasBi
Chen Jiaer WhoPRCh 91
Chen Jialiang WhoPRCh 91 [port]
Chen Jialing 1937- WhoPRCh 91
Chen Jiangong 1949- WhoPRCh 91 [port]
Chen Jianning WhoPRCh 91
Chen Jie 1957- WhoPRCh 91 [port]
Ch'en Jing WhoPRCh 91 [port]
Chen Jingkai WhoPRCh 91 [port]
Chen Jingrong 1917- BlmGWL [port]
Chen Jingrun 1933- IntWW 93, WhoPRCh 91 [port]
Chen Jinhua WhoPRCh 91
Chen Jiuchang WhoPRCh 91
Chen Jiyuan WhoPRCh 91
Chen Jo Hsi BlmGWL, ConWorW 93
Chen Junsheng 1927- IntWW 93, WhoPRCh 91 [port]
Chen Junyong WhoPRCh 91
Chen Kaige 1954- IntWW 93
Chen Lantong WhoPRCh 91
Chen Lei 1917- IntWW 93, WhoPRCh 91
Chen Lemin 1930- WhoPRCh 91
Chen Li WhoPRCh 91
Chen Li-An 1937- IntWW 93
Chen Lin 1970- WhoPRCh 91 [port]
Chen Liquan WhoPRCh 91 [port]
Chen Liying 1934- WhoPRCh 91 [port]
Chen Liying, Miss 1934- IntWW 93
Chen Liyou WhoPRCh 91
Chen Longcan WhoPRCh 91 [port]
Chen Luzhi WhoPRCh 91
Chen Miaolan WhoPRCh 91
Chen Ming 1919- WhoPRCh 91 [port]
Chen Mingshan 1916- WhoPRCh 91 [port]
Chen Mingshan 1931- WhoPRCh 91 [port]
Chen Mingshao 1914- WhoPRCh 91 [port]
Chen Mingtong 1926- IntWW 93
Chen Mingyi 1940- WhoPRCh 91 [port]

Chen Mingyuan 1941- *IntWW 93, WhoPRCh 91 [port]*
Chen Minzhang 1931- *IntWW 93, WhoPRCh 91 [port]*
Chen Muhua 1920- *WhoPRCh 91 [port]*
Chen Muhua 1921- *IntWW 93, WhoWomW 91*
Chen Musen 1920- *WhoPRCh 91 [port]*
Chen Naishan 1946- *BlmGWL*
Chen Nanxian 1937- *WhoPRCh 91 [port]*
Chennault, Anna Chan 1925- *WhoAmP 93*
Chennault, Madelyn 1934- *WhoBlA 94*
Chen Nengkuan *WhoPRCh 91*
Chenok, Philip Barry 1935- *WhoAm 94, WhoFI 94*
Chenot, Bernard 1909- *IntWW 93*
Chenoweth, Carol Kathryn 1928- *WhoAmP 93*
Chenoweth, Christopher Evan 1957- *WhoAmL 94*
Chenoweth, Joe Elling 1936- *WhoFI 94*
Chenoweth, Walter A. 1930- *WhoWest 94*
Chenoweth, William Lyman 1928- *WhoWest 94*
Chen Peimin 1927- *WhoPRCh 91 [port]*
Chen Peiqiu 1922- *WhoPRCh 91 [port]*
Chen Pixian 1916- *IntWW 93, WhoPRCh 91 [port]*
Chen Puru 1918- *WhoPRCh 91 [port]*
Chen Qiaoyi 1932- *WhoPRCh 91*
Chen Qimao *WhoPRCh 91 [port]*
Chen Qingzi 1935?- *WhoPRCh 91 [port]*
Chen Qiqi 1941- *IntWW 93, WhoPRCh 91 [port]*
Chen Qiucao 1906- *WhoPRCh 91 [port]*
Chen Qizhi 1925- *WhoPRCh 91 [port]*
Chen Ren 1929- *WhoPRCh 91 [port]*
Chen Rong 1936- *WhoPRCh 91 [port]*
Chen Rongti *WhoPRCh 91*
Chen Rongti 1919- *IntWW 93*
Chen Ruiqing 1932- *BlmGWL*
Chen Ruoxi 1938- *BlmGWL, ConWorW 93*
Chen Ruyu 1920- *IntWW 93*
Chen Shaowu *WhoPRCh 91*
Chen Shengwu *WhoPRCh 91*
Chen Shijun *WhoPRCh 91*
Chen Shineng 1938- *WhoPRCh 91 [port]*
Chen Shiqiu *WhoPRCh 91*
Chen Shixu 1947- *WhoPRCh 91 [port]*
Chen Shize *WhoPRCh 91*
Chen Shunli *WhoPRCh 91 [port]*
Chen Shunli 1917- *IntWW 93*
Chen Shupeng 1920- *IntWW 93, WhoPRCh 91*
Chen Songlu *WhoPRCh 91*
Chen Suhou *WhoPRCh 91*
Chen Suiheng 1915- *WhoPRCh 91 [port]*
Chen Suzhi 1931- *IntWW 93, WhoPRCh 91 [port], WhoWomW 91*
Chen Tianren 1914- *WhoPRCh 91 [port]*
Chen Ticdi 1936- *WhoPRCh 91 [port]*
Chen Tingyuan 1925- *WhoPRCh 91 [port]*
Chen-Tsai, Charlotte Hsiao-yu 1955- *WhoAsA 94*
Chen Weiming *WhoPRCh 91*
Chen Weiqiang 1958- *WhoPRCh 91*
Chen Weiren *WhoPRCh 91*
Chen Xian 1919- *WhoPRCh 91 [port]*
Chen Xianglin 1944- *WhoPRCh 91 [port]*
Chen Xiaojin *WhoPRCh 91*
Chen Xiaoqun *WhoPRCh 91 [port]*
Chen Xieyang 1939- *IntWW 93, WhoPRCh 91 [port]*
Chen Xifu 1924- *WhoPRCh 91 [port]*
Chen Xilian 1913- *WhoPRCh 91 [port]*
Chen Xin 1930- *WhoPRCh 91 [port]*
Chen Xingyin *WhoPRCh 91*
Chen Xinmin 1912- *WhoPRCh 91 [port]*
Chen Xinren 1915- *IntWW 93, WhoPRCh 91*
Chen Xitong 1930- *IntWW 93, WhoPRCh 91 [port]*
Chen Xizhong 1904- *WhoPRCh 91*
Chen Xuejun 1919- *WhoPRCh 91 [port]*
Chen Xueshi *WhoPRCh 91*
Chen Yanfa 1930- *WhoPRCh 91 [port]*
Chen Yanxi *WhoPRCh 91*
Chen Yaobang 1935- *WhoPRCh 91 [port]*
Chen Ye *WhoPRCh 91*
Chen Yeping *WhoPRCh 91*
Chen Yi *WhoPRCh 91*
Ch'en Yi 1901-1972 *HisDcKW*
Chen Yicun *WhoPRCh 91*
Chen Yifei *WhoPRCh 91*
Chen Ying 1919- *WhoPRCh 91 [port]*
Chen Yisong 1907- *WhoPRCh 91 [port]*
Chen Yizi *WhoPRCh 91*
Chen Yong 1919- *WhoPRCh 91 [port]*
Chen Yong 1952- *WhoPRCh 91*
Chen Yongcai *WhoPRCh 91*
Chen Yongling *WhoPRCh 91*
Chen Yu 1916- *WhoPRCh 91 [port]*
Chen Yu 1965- *WhoPRCh 91*
Chen Yuan 1918- *WhoPRCh 91 [port]*
Chen Yuan 1945- *WhoPRCh 91 [port]*
Chen Yuanmu *WhoPRCh 91*
Chen Yujie 1942- *WhoPRCh 91 [port], WhoWomW 91*
Chen Yun 1905- *IntWW 93, WhoPRCh 91 [port]*
Chen Yunlin 1941- *WhoPRCh 91 [port]*
Chen Yuntai *WhoPRCh 91*
Chen Yuntian 1908- *WhoPRCh 91 [port]*
Chen Yuqing 1947- *WhoPRCh 91 [port]*
Chen Yuying *WhoPRCh 91, WhoWomW 91*
Chen Zhaobo *WhoPRCh 91*
Chen Zhaoyuan 1918- *Who 94*
Chen Zhenkang 1932- *WhoPRCh 91 [port]*
Chen Zhili 1943- *WhoPRCh 91 [port], WhoWomW 91*
Chen Zhongbiao *WhoPRCh 91*
Chen Zhongjing 1915- *WhoPRCh 91 [port]*
Chen Zhongwei 1928- *WhoPRCh 91 [port]*
Chen Zhongwei 1929- *IntWW 93*
Chen Zhongyi 1923- *WhoPRCh 91*
Chen Zhuo *WhoPRCh 91*
Chen Zonggao 1931- *WhoPRCh 91 [port]*
Chen Zongji 1922- *WhoPRCh 91 [port]*
Chen Zude 1944- *WhoPRCh 91 [port]*
Chen Zufen 1943- *BlmGWL, WhoPRCh 91 [port]*
Chen Zuohuang 1947- *IntWW 93, WhoPRCh 91*
Chen Zuolin 1923- *IntWW 93, WhoPRCh 91 [port]*
Chen Zupei 1916- *WhoPRCh 91 [port]*
Chen Zutao *WhoPRCh 91*
Cheo, Li-hsiang S. 1932- *WhoAsA 94*
Cheo, Peter K. 1930- *WhoAsA 94*
Cheo, Peter Kiong-Liang 1930- *WhoAm 94*
Cheong, Fiona 1961- *WhoAsA 94*
Che Peiqin *WhoPRCh 91*
Chepiga, Michael Joseph 1948- *WhoAmL 94*
Chepiga, Pamela Rogers 1949- *WhoAm 94, WhoAmL 94*
Chepik, Sergei 1953- *IntWW 93*
Chepp, Mark *WhoAmA 93*
Chepurnyi, Anatolii Grygorovych 1941- *LoBiDrD*
Cher *IntWW 93*
Cher 1946- *IntMPA 94, WhoAm 94, WhoHol 92*
Cher, Beatrice *WhoAmA 93*
Cherbas, Peter Thomas 1946- *WhoMW 93*
Cherberg, John Andrew 1910- *WhAm 10*
Cherches, Peter *DrAPF 93*
Cherchiglia, Dean Kenneth 1956- *WhoAmL 94*
Chercover, Murray 1929- *WhoAm 94, WhoFI 94*
Chereau, Patrice 1944- *IntWW 93, NewGrDO*
Cherem, Barbara Frances 1946- *WhoAm 94*
Cheremisinoff, Paul Nicholas 1929- *WhoScEn 94*
Cherenkov, Pavel Alexeyevich 1904- *WhoScEn 94*
Cherenzia, Bradley James 1931- *WhoMW 93*
Cherepakhov, Galina 1936- *WhoScEn 94*
Cherepanov, Genady Petrovich 1937- *WhoScEn 94*
Cherepnin, Alexander *NewGrDO*
Cherepnin, Nikolay *NewGrDO*
Chereskin, Alvin 1928- *WhoAm 94*
Cherewka, Michael 1955- *WhoAmL 94*
Cherian, Joy 1942- *WhoAm 94, WhoAmP 93, WhoAsA 94*
Cherici, Pier Raoul 1948- *WhoFI 94*
Cherici, Sebastiano 1647-1703 *NewGrDO*
Cherins, Robert Howard 1940- *WhoAm 94*
Cheris, Elaine Gayle Ingram 1946- *WhoWest 94*
Cheris, Samuel David 1945- *WhoAmL 94*
Cherkas, Constantine 1919- *WhoAmA 93*
Cherkasky, Martin 1911- *WhoAm 94*
Cherkassky, Shura 1911- *IntWW 93, Who 94*
Cherkassov, Nikolai d1966 *WhoHol 92*
Cherken, Harry Sarkis, Jr. 1949- *WhoAm 94, WhoAmL 94*
Cherkesov, Georgy Mashtaevich 1938- *LoBiDrD*
Cherkin, Adina 1921- *WhoWest 94*
Cherkis, Laurence D. 1942- *WhoAmL 94*
Chermak, Cy 1929- *IntMPA 94*
Chermayeff, Ivan 1932- *WhoAm 94, WhoAmA 93*
Chermayeff, Peter 1936- *IntWW 93*
Chermayeff, Serge 1900- *IntWW 93, Who 94*
Chern, Jeng-Shing 1947- *WhoScEn 94*
Chern, Jenn-Chuan 1954- *WhoScEn 94*
Chern, Ji-Wang 1953- *WhoScEn 94*
Chern, Jiun-Der 1962- *WhoScEn 94*
Chern, Shiing-Shen 1911- *IntWW 93, WhoAm 94, WhoScEn 94, WhoWest 94*
Chernaik, Judith *DrAPF 93*
Chernak, John Andrew 1929- *WhoMW 93*
Chernak, Ronald V. 1949- *WhoAmL 94*
Chernavin, Vladimir Nikolaevich 1928- *LoBiDrD*
Chernenko, John G. 1924- *WhoAmP 93*
Chernenko, Konstantin 1911-1985 *HisWorL [port]*
Cherner, Anne *DrAPF 93*
Cherner, Paul Jordan 1943- *WhoAmL 94*
Chernesky, Richard John 1939- *WhoAm 94, WhoAmL 94*
Chernev, Melvin 1928- *WhoAm 94*
Cherney, Emanuel S. 1951- *WhoAmL 94*
Cherney, James Alan 1948- *WhoAm 94, WhoAmL 94*
Cherney, Marvin d1966 *WhoAmA 93N*
Cherney, Michael Gerard 1957- *WhoMW 93*
Cherniack, Helen Wessel 1911- *WhoMW 93*
Cherniack, Nathan 1897- *WhAm 10*
Cherniack, Neil Stanley 1931- *WhoAm 94*
Cherniack, Saul Mark 1917- *WhoAm 94*
Cherniak, Volodymyr Kurylovych 1941- *LoBiDrD*
Cherniavsky, John Charles 1947- *WhoScEn 94*
Cherniawski, Anthony Michael 1950- *WhoFI 94, WhoMW 93*
Chernichaw, Mark 1946- *WhoAm 94*
Chernichenko, Yury Dmitrievich 1929- *LoBiDrD*
Chernick, Cedric L. 1931- *WhoMW 93, WhoScEn 94*
Chernick, Myrel *WhoAmA 93*
Chernick, Richard 1945- *WhoAm 94, WhoAmL 94*
Chernik, Barbara Eisenlohr 1938- *WhoMW 93*
Chernin, Fredric David 1939- *WhoAm 94*
Chernin, Peter *WhoAm 94, WhoFI 94, WhoWest 94*
Chernish, Stanley Michael 1924- *WhoAm 94, WhoMW 93, WhoScEn 94*
Cherniss, David Alan 1954- *WhoAmL 94*
Cherniss, Michael David 1940- *WhoAm 94*
Cherno, Melvin 1929- *WhoAm 94*
Chernof, David 1935- *WhoAm 94*
Chernof, Stephen L. 1944- *WhoAmL 94*
Chernoff, Amoz Immanuel 1923- *WhoAm 94*
Chernoff, Daniel Paregol 1935- *WhoAm 94*
Chernoff, Herman 1923- *IntWW 93, WhoAm 94*
Chernoff, Maxine *DrAPF 93*
Chernoff, Maxine 1952- *WrDr 94*
Chernoff, Robert 1922- *WhoAm 94*
Chernoff, Sanford *DrAPF 93*
Chernoff Pate, Diana 1942- *WhoWest 94*
Chernomyrdin, Viktor Stepanovich 1938- *IntWW 93, LoBiDrD*
Chernow, Ann 1936- *WhoAmA 93*
Chernow, Burt 1933- *WhoAmA 93*
Chernow, David A. 1922- *WhoAm 94*
Chernow, Jeffrey Scott 1951- *WhoAmL 94*
Chernow, Ron 1949- *ConAu 142, WhoAm 94*
Cherny, David Edward 1957- *WhoAmL 94*
Cherny, Gorimir Gorimirovich 1923- *IntWW 93*
Cherny, Robert W(allace) 1943- *WrDr 94*
Cherny, Robert Wallace 1943- *WhoAm 94*
Chernyak, Boris Victor 1954- *WhoScEn 94*
Chernyayev, Anatoly Sergeyevich 1921- *IntWW 93*
Cheron, Andre d1952 *WhoHol 92*
Cheron, Elisabeth-Sophie 1648-1711 *BlmGWL*
Cheron, James Clinton 1943- *WhoScEn 94*
Cherone, Gary c. 1961- *See* Extreme *ConMus 10*
Cherot, Nicholas Maurice 1947- *WhoBlA 94*
Cheroutes, Michael Louis 1940- *WhoAm 94*
Cherovsky, Erwin Louis 1933- *WhoAm 94*
Cherrelle *WhoBlA 94*
Cherrill, Christine d1989 *WhoHol 92*
Cherrill, Virginia 1908- *WhoHol 92*
Cherry, Andrew Jackson 1927- *WhoBlA 94*
Cherry, Andrew L., Jr. 1943- *WhoScEn 94*
Cherry, Bridget Katherine 1941- *Who 94*
Cherry, Byron *WhoHol 92*
Cherry, Carolyn Janice 1942- *TwCYAW*
Cherry, Cassandra Brabble 1947- *WhoBlA 94*
Cherry, Charles d1931 *WhoHol 92*
Cherry, Charles Conrad 1937- *WrDr 94*
Cherry, Charles William 1928- *WhoBlA 94*
Cherry, Colin 1931- *Who 94*
Cherry, David A. 1949- *EncSF 93*
Cherry, David Earl 1944- *WhoAmL 94*
Cherry, Deborah Lee 1954- *WhoMW 93*
Cherry, Don 1934- *News 93 [port]*
Cherry, Don 1936- *ConMus 10 [port]*
Cherry, Edward Earl 1926- *WhoAm 94*
Cherry, Edward Earl, Sr. 1926- *WhoBlA 94*
Cherry, Frances 1937- *BlmGWL*
Cherry, Gordon Emanuel 1931- *Who 94*
Cherry, Harold 1931- *WhoAm 94*
Cherry, Helen 1915- *WhoHol 92*
Cherry, Herman 1909-1992 *WhAm 10, WhoAmA 93N*
Cherry, James Donald 1930- *WhoAm 94*
Cherry, Jeffrey L. 1960- *WhoFI 94*
Cherry, John 1942- *Who 94*
Cherry, John D., Jr. 1951- *WhoAmP 93*
Cherry, John Mitchell 1937- *Who 94*
Cherry, Kelly *DrAPF 93, WrDr 94*
Cherry, Lee Otis 1944- *WhoBlA 94, WhoWest 94*
Cherry, Linda Lea 1956- *WhoMW 93*
Cherry, Linda Z. 1951- *WhoAmP 93*
Cherry, Malcolm d1925 *WhoHol 92*
Cherry, Paul Stephen 1943- *WhoAmL 94*
Cherry, Peter Ballard 1947- *WhoAm 94*
Cherry, Robert Earl Patrick 1924- *WhoAm 94*
Cherry, Robert Lee 1941- *WhoBlA 94*
Cherry, Robert Steven, III 1951- *WhoMW 93*
Cherry, Rona Beatrice 1948- *WhoAm 94*
Cherry, Ronald Lee 1934- *WhoAm 94, WhoAmL 94*
Cherry, Sandra Wilson 1941- *WhoAmL 94*
Cherry, Theodore W. 1932- *WhoBlA 94*
Cherry, Walter Lorain 1917- *WhoAm 94*
Cherry, Wendell d1991 *WhAm 10*
Cherry, William Ashley 1924- *WhoAm 94*
Cherryh, C. J. 1942- *BlmGWL, EncSF 93, WhoAm 94, WrDr 94*
Cherryh, Carolyn Janice 1942- *TwCYAW*
Cherryholmes, James Gilbert 1917- *WhoAm 94*
Cherryman, John Richard 1932- *Who 94*
Cherryman, Rex d1928 *WhoHol 92*
Chertack, Melvin M. 1923- *WhoAm 94*
Chertoff, Michael *WhoAmL 94*
Chertok, Jack 1906- *IntMPA 94*
Chertow, Mark 1946- *WhoMW 93*
Cherubini, Lillian M. Williams 1916- *WhoAmP 93*
Cherubini, (Maria) Luigi (Carlo Zanobi Salvadore) 1760-1842 *NewGrDO*
Cherundolo, John Charles 1948- *WhoAmL 94*
Chervinskaia, Lidiia Davydovna 1907-1988 *BlmGWL*
Chervokas, John Vincent 1936- *WhoAm 94*
Cherwin, Joel Ira 1942- *WhoAmL 94*
Cheryan, Munir 1946- *WhoAsA 94*
Chesbro, George C(lark) 1940- *WrDr 94*
Chesbro, Ray T. 1925- *WhoAmP 93*
Chesbro, Vern 1925- *WhoAmP 93*
Chesbrough, Geoffrey Lynn 1940- *WhoAm 94*
Chesebro', Caroline 1825-1873 *BlmGWL*
Chesebro, George d1959 *WhoHol 92*
Chesen, Eli S. 1944- *WrDr 94*
Chesham, Baron 1941- *Who 94*
Chesham, Henry *ConAu 42NR*
Chesham, Sallie *WrDr 94*
Cheshier, Stephen Robert 1940- *WhoAm 94*
Cheshire, Baron d1992 *IntWW 93N*
Cheshire, Craig Gifford 1936- *WhoAmA 93*
Cheshire, Geoffrey Leonard 1917-1992 *AnObit 1992*
Cheshire, Harry d1968 *WhoHol 92*
Cheshire, John Anthony 1942- *Who 94*
Cheshire, William Polk 1931- *WhoAm 94, WhoWest 94*
Cheski, Richard Michael 1935- *WhoAm 94*
Chesky, Evelyn G. *WhoAmP 93*
Chesler, Carol Ann 1938- *WhoMW 93*
Chesler, Ellen 1947- *ConAu 140*
Chesler, Evan Robert 1949- *WhoAm 94, WhoAmL 94*
Chesler, Stanley Richard 1947- *WhoAm 94, WhoAmL 94*
Chesley, Larry J. 1938- *WhoAmP 93*
Chesley, Paul Alexander 1946- *WhoAmA 93*
Chesley, Robert c. 1943-1990 *GayLL*
Chesley, Roger T., Sr. 1959- *WhoBlA 94*
Chesley, Stanley Morris 1936- *WhoAm 94, WhoAmL 94, WhoMW 93*
Chesley-Lahm, Diane 1942- *WhoAmL 94*
Chesman, Andrea 1952- *WrDr 94*
Chesnais, Patrick *WhoHol 92*

Chesnard De La Giraudais, Francois fl. 176-?- WhWE
Chesner, Robert W. 1942- WhoIns 94
Chesney, Ann 1930- WrDr 94
Chesney, Arthur d1949 WhoHol 92
Chesney, Charles Frederic 1942- WhoMW 93
Chesney, Diana WhoHol 92
Chesney, George T(omkyns) 1830-1895 EncSF 93
Chesney, John 1949- WhoAmL 94
Chesney, Lee R., Jr. 1920- WhoAmA 93
Chesney, Lee Roy, Jr. 1920- WhoAm 94
Chesney, Lee Roy, III 1945- WhoAmA 93
Chesney, Marion 1936- WrDr 94
Chesney, Russell Wallace 1941- WhoAm 94
Chesney, Weatherby EncSF 93
Chesnick, Joyce Bailes 1925- WhoAm 94
Chesnik, Earl 1934- WhoAmP 93
Chesnin, Leon 1919- WhoMW 93
Chesnin, Sidney 1942- WhoAmL 94
Chesnut, Carol Fitting 1937- WhoAm 94, WhoWest 94
Chesnut, Donald Blair 1932- WhoAm 94
Chesnut, Franklin Gilmore 1919- WhoAm 94
Chesnut, Mary Boykin Miller 1823-1886 BlmGWL
Chesnutt, Charles Waddell 1858-1932 AfrAmAl 6, RfGShF
Chess, Faye Rosalind 1962- WhoAmL 94
Chess, Sammie, Jr. 1934- WhoBlA 94
Chessells, Arthur David 1941- Who 94
Chesser, Al H. 1914- WhoAm 94
Chesser, Kerry Royce 1956- WhoFI 94
Chessex, Jacques 1934- ConWorW 93
Chessey, Joseph J., Jr. 1948- WhoAmP 93
Chesshyre, (David) Hubert (Boothby) 1940- Who 94
Chessman, John Michael 1943- WhoAmP 93
Chesson, Eugene, Jr. 1928- WhoAm 94
Chestang, Leon Wilbert 1937- WhoBlA 94
Chesteen, Richard Dallas 1939- WhoAmP 93
Chester, Archdeacon of Who 94
Chester, Bishop of 1930- Who 94
Chester, Dean of Who 94
Chester, Alexander Campbell, III 1947- WhoAm 94
Chester, Alfred d1978 WhoHol 92
Chester, Alfred 1928-1971 DcLB 130 [port]
Chester, Alma d1953 WhoHol 92
Chester, Arthur Noble 1940- WhoAm 94, WhoScEn 94
Chester, Betty d1943 WhoHol 92
Chester, Charles Frederick 1954- WhoAmL 94
Chester, Charlotte Wanetta WhoAmA 93
Chester, Colby WhoHol 92
Chester, Deborah 1957- ConAu 41NR
Chester, Eric Stanton 1960- WhoAmL 94
Chester, Francis 1936- WhoAmL 94
Chester, Geoffrey 1951- WhoAm 94
Chester, George Randolph 1869-1924 EncSF 93
Chester, Giraud 1922- WhoAm 94
Chester, Hally 1921- WhoHol 92
Chester, James Johnson 1962- WhoAmL 94
Chester, John Ervin 1932- WhoAm 94, WhoFI 94
Chester, John Geoffrey 1951- WhoAmL 94
Chester, John Jonas 1920- WhoAm 94
Chester, Joseph A., Sr. 1914- WhoBlA 94
Chester, Laura DrAPF 93
Chester, Malcolm Paul 1948- WhoMW 93
Chester, Marvin 1930- WhoWest 94
Chester, Peter 1924- WrDr 94
Chester, Peter Francis 1929- Who 94
Chester, Robert Simon George 1949- WhoAmL 94
Chester, Roberta DrAPF 93
Chester, Russell Gilbert, Jr. 1947- WhoMW 93
Chester, Sharon Rose 1942- WhoWest 94
Chester, Sherman E., Sr. 1921- WhoAmP 93
Chester, Stephanie Ann 1951- WhoAmL 94, WhoMW 93
Chester, Tessa Rose 1950- WrDr 94
Chester, Timothy J. WhoAm 94, WhoMW 93
Chester, Virginia d1927 WhoHol 92
Chester, William L. 1907- EncSF 93
Chesterfield, Archdeacon of Who 94
Chesterfield, Rhydonia Ruth Epperson 1919- WhoFI 94, WhoWest 94
Chester Jones, Ian 1916- Who 94
Chesterman, Ross 1909- Who 94
Chesters, Alan David Who 94
Chesters, Charles Geddes Coull d1993 Who 94N
Chesters, Graham 1944- WrDr 94
Chesters, John Hugh 1906- Who 94
Chesterton, Cecil Edward 1879-1918 DcNaB MP
Chesterton, David 1930- WhoAmA 93N
Chesterton, David 1939- Who 94
Chesterton, Elizabeth (Ursula) 1915- Who 94
Chesterton, G. K. 1874-1936 BlmGEL
Chesterton, G(ilbert) K(eith) 1874-1936 EncSF 93, RfGShF
Chesterton, Oliver (Sidney) 1913- Who 94
Chestnut, Cynthia Moore 1949- WhoAmP 93
Chestnut, David Hill 1952- WhoMW 93
Chestnut, Dennis Earl 1947- WhoBlA 94
Chestnut, Edwin, Sr. 1924- WhoBlA 94
Chestnut, Harold 1917- WhoAm 94, WhoScEn 94
Chestnut, Kathi Lynne 1959- WhoAmL 94
Chestnut, Morris WhoBlA 94
Cheston, George Morris 1917- WhoAm 94
Cheston, Theodore C. 1922- WhoAm 94
Cheston, Warren Bruce 1926- WhoAm 94
Chesworth, George Arthur 1930- Who 94
Cheszek, Linda Ann 1951- WhoMW 93
Chetelat, Roger Topping 1957- WhoScEn 94
Chetham, Charles WhoAmA 93
Chethlahe 1926-1984 WhoAmA 93N
Chetkovich, Michael N. 1916- WhoAm 94
Chettle, Henry 1560-1607 BlmGEL, DcLB 136
Chetwin, Grace TwCYAW, WrDr 94
Chetwode, Baron 1937- Who 94
Chetwode, R.D. EncSF 93
Chetwood, Clifford (Jack) 1928- Who 94
Chetwyn, Robert 1933- Who 94
Chetwynd, Viscount 1935- Who 94
Chetwynd, Arthur (Ralph Talbot) 1913- Who 94
Chetwynd, Bridget 1910- EncSF 93
Chetwynd, Lionel WhoWest 94
Chetwynd, Lionel 1940- IntMPA 94
Chetwynd-Talbot Who 94
Cheung, Cindy Siu-Whei 1970- WhoAsA 94
Cheung, David F. 1965- WhoAsA 94
Cheung, Fernando C. H. 1957- WhoAsA 94
Cheung, Herbert Chiu-Ching 1933- WhoAsA 94
Cheung, John Yan-Poon 1950- WhoAsA 94
Cheung, Joseph Y. 1950- WhoAsA 94
Cheung, Julian F. Y. 1956- WhoAsA 94
Cheung, Kwok-wai 1956- WhoScEn 94
Cheung, Lim H. 1953- WhoAsA 94
Cheung, Lim Hung 1953- WhoScEn 94
Cheung, Luke P. WhoAsA 94
Cheung, Oswald (Victor) 1922- Who 94
Cheung, Philip 1958- WhoAsA 94
Cheung, Shun Yan 1958- WhoAsA 94
Cheung, Wai Yiu 1933- WhoAsA 94
Cheung, Wesley Hoi Pang 1956- WhoWest 94
Cheung, Wilkin Wai-Kuen 1941- WhoScEn 94
Cheung, Wilson D. 1966- WhoScEn 94
Cheung Man-Yee 1946- WhoWomW 91
Cheuse, Alan 1940- WrDr 94
Chevalier, Mlle 1722-1789? NewGrDO
Chevalier, Albert d1923 WhoHol 92
Chevalier, Albert d1959 WhoHol 92
Chevalier, Gus d1947 WhoHol 92
Chevalier, Haakon (Maurice) 1902-1985 EncSF 93
Chevalier, Jean 1936- WhoScEn 94
Chevalier, Louis 1911- IntWW 93
Chevalier, Maurice d1972 WhoHol 92
Chevalier, Paul Edward 1939- WhoAm 94
Chevalier, Roger 1922- IntWW 93
Chevalier, Roger Alan 1949- WhoAm 94, WhoScEn 94
Chevalier, Samuel Fletcher 1934- WhoAm 94, WhoFI 94
Chevalier of St. George BlmGEL
Chevallaz, Georges-Andre 1915- IntWW 93
Chevat, Edith DrAPF 93
Cheveallier, Jesse David 1950- WhoFI 94
Cheveldae, Tim 1968- WhoAm 94, WhoMW 93
Chevenement, Jean-Pierre 1939- IntWW 93
Cheverton, Richard E. WhoAm 94
Cheverton, William Kearns 1944- WhoWest 94
Cheverus, Jean Louis Lefebre de 1768-1836 DcAmReB 2
Chevigne EncSPD
Cheville, Norman Frederick 1934- WhoAm 94
Chevins, Anthony Charles 1921- WhoAm 94
Chevins, Christopher M. 1951- WhoAmA 93
Chevis, Cheryl Ann 1947- WhoAmL 94
Chevray, Rene 1937- WhoAm 94
Chevret, Lita 1908- WhoHol 92
Chevreuille, Raymond 1901-1976 NewGrDO
Chevreul, Michel Eugene 1786-1889 WorScD
Chevrier, Jean Marc 1916- WhoAm 94
Chevrillon, Olivier 1929- IntWW 93
Chew, Ada Nield 1870-1945 DcLB 135 [port]
Chew, Allen F. 1924- WrDr 94
Chew, Benjamin 1722-1810 WhAmRev
Chew, Bettye L. 1940- WhoBlA 94
Chew, Frances Sze-Ling WhoAsA 94
Chew, Geoffrey Foucar 1924- IntWW 93, WhoAm 94
Chew, Harry 1925- WhoAmA 93N
Chew, Ka-Wing 1957- WhoWest 94
Chew, Keith Elvin 1957- WhoMW 93
Chew, (Victor) Kenneth 1915- Who 94
Chew, Kenneth Sze-Ying 1953- WhoAsA 94
Chew, Linda Lee 1941- WhoWest 94
Chew, Mary Catherine WhoFI 94
Chew, Pamela Christine 1953- WhoAsA 94
Chew, Paul Albert 1925- WhoAmA 93
Chew, Richard ConTFT 11
Chew, Richard Franklin 1940- WhoAsA 94
Chew, Ronald A. 1953- WhoAsA 94
Chew, Sam, Jr. WhoHol 92
Chew, Virgilia d1987 WhoHol 92
Chew, Wellington Lum 1922- WhoAsA 94
Chew, Weng Cho 1953- WhoAsA 94, WhoMW 93
Chewning, Emily Blair DrAPF 93
Chewning, John Andrew 1949- WhoMW 93
Chewning, Richard Carter 1933- WhoAm 94
Chewton, Viscount 1940- Who 94
Chey, William Yoon 1930- WhoAm 94
Cheyfitz, Eric DrAPF 93
Cheyne, Joseph (Lister Watson) 1914- Who 94
Cheyney, Edward 1803-1884 DcNaB MP
Cheyney-Coker, Syl 1945- WrDr 94
Cheysson, Claude 1920- IntWW 93, Who 94
Chezem, Curtis Gordon 1924- WhoAm 94
Chezy, Helmina von 1783-1856 BlmGWL
Chezy, Helmina (Christiane) von 1783-1856 NewGrDO
Chhabildas, Lalit Chandra 1945- WhoWest 94
Chhatwal, Surbir Jit Singh 1931- IntWW 93
Chhim, Him S. 1941- WhoAsA 94
Chi, Bo Kyung 1956- WhoAsA 94
Chi, Chang Hwi 1934- WhoWest 94
Chi, Chen 1912- WhoAmA 93
Chi, Cheng-Ching 1939- WhoAsA 94
Chi, David Bokyung 1956- WhoAsA 94
Chi, David Shyh-Wei 1943- WhoAsA 94
Chi, Donna Sherman 1954- WhoWest 94
Chi, Hsin 1949- WhoScEn 94
Chi, Jacob 1952- WhoAsA 94
Chi, Lotta C. J. Li 1930- WhoAsA 94
Chi, Myung Sun 1940- WhoAsA 94
Chi, Vernon L. 1940- WhoScEn 94
Chi, Yinliang 1934- WhoAsA 94
Chia, David 1959- WhoAsA 94
Chia, Fu-Shiang 1931- WhoWest 94
Chia, Kai 1925- WhoAsA 94
Chia, Ning 1955- WhoAsA 94
Chia, Pei-Yuan 1939- WhoFI 94
Chia, Rosina Chih-Hung 1939- WhoAsA 94
Chia, Sandro 1946- WhoAmA 93
Chia, Swee Lim 1962- WhoAsA 94
Chiabrera, Gabriello 1552-1638 NewGrDO
Chialvo, Ariel Augusto 1955- WhoScEn 94
Chiang, Albert Chin-Liang 1937- WhoWest 94
Chiang, Albert Chinfa 1946- WhoScEn 94
Chiang, Asuntha Maria Ming-Yee 1970- WhoAsA 94
Chiang, Berttram 1945- WhoAsA 94
Chiang, Chao-Kuo 1936- WhoAsA 94
Chiang, Cheng-Wen 1943- WhoScEn 94
Chiang, Chin Long 1916- WhoAsA 94
Chiang, Chwan K. 1943- WhoAsA 94
Chiang, Erick 1950- WhoAsA 94
Chiang, Fay DrAPF 93
Chiang, Huai C. WhoAsA 94
Chiang, Huai Chang 1915- WhoAm 94, WhoMW 93
Chiang, Joseph F. 1938- WhoAsA 94
Chiang, Kin Seng 1957- WhoScEn 94
Chiang, Oscar C. K. 1932- WhoAsA 94
Chiang, Ping-Wang WhoAsA 94
Chiang, Richard Yi-Ning 1953- WhoScEn 94
Chiang, Samuel Edward 1959- WhoAm 94
Chiang, Shiao-Hung 1929- WhoAm 94, WhoAsA 94
Chiang, Sie Ling 1938- WhoAsA 94
Chiang, Soong T. 1937- WhoAsA 94
Chiang, Tai-Chang 1949- WhoScEn 94
Chiang, Ted EncSF 93
Chiang, Theresa Yi-Chin Tung 1947- WhoAsA 94
Chiang, Thomas Minghung 1940- WhoAsA 94
Chiang, Tom Chuan-Hsien 1944- WhoScEn 94
Chiang, Tsung Ting 1936- WhoAsA 94
Chiang, Yaojen Peter 1964- WhoWest 94
Chiang, Yi-ling F. 1934- WhoAsA 94
Chiang, Yuen-Sheng 1936- WhoAsA 94
Chiang, Yung Frank 1936- WhoAsA 94
Chiang Kai-Shek 1887-1975 HisWorL [port], HisDcKW
Chiang Kai-Shek, Madame Who 94
Chiang Kai-Shek, Madame 1900- IntWW 93
Chiao, Jen Wei WhoAsA 94
Chiao, Leroy 1960- WhoAsA 94
Ch'iao, Sung 1915- WrDr 94
Chiao, Yu-Chih 1949- WhoAsA 94
Chiapella, Edward Emile 1889-1951 WhoAmA 93N
Chiappelli, John Arthur 1949- WhoFI 94
Chiara, Alan Robert 1936- WhoAmA 93
Chiara, Maria 1939- IntWW 93
Chiara, Maria(-Rita) 1939- NewGrDO
Chiarchiaro, Frank John 1945- WhoAm 94
Chiarella, Peter Ralph 1932- WhoAm 94
Chiarelli, Joseph 1946- WhoFI 94
Chiarelli, Luigi 1880-1947 IntDcT 2
Chiarello, Donald Frederick 1940- WhoAm 94, WhoAmL 94
Chiarenza, Carl 1935- WhoAm 94, WhoAmA 93
Chiarenza, Frank John 1926- WhoAm 94
Chiari, Pietro 1712-1785 NewGrDO
Chiari, Walter 1924- WhoHol 92
Chiarini, Pietro dc. 1765 NewGrDO
Chiarkas, Nicholas L. WhoAmL 94
Chiaro, A. William 1928- WhoFI 94
Chiarucci, Vincent A. 1929- WhoFI 94, WhoMW 93
Chiarugi, Vincenzo 1759-1820 EncSPD
Chiasson, Donat Who 94
Chiasson, Robert Breton 1925- WhoWest 94
Chiat, Jay 1931- WhoAm 94
Chiat, Marilyn Joyce 1932- WhoMW 93
Chiate, Kenneth Reed 1941- WhoAm 94, WhoAmL 94
Chiaverini, John Edward 1924- WhoAm 94, WhoFI 94
Chiazze, Leonard, Jr. 1934- WhoAm 94
Chiba, Kazuo 1925- IntWW 93, Who 94
Chiba, Keiko 1948- WhoWomW 91
Chiba, Kiyoshi 1946- WhoScEn 94
Chiba, Lee I. 1951- WhoAsA 94
Chiba, Sonny WhoHol 92
Chiba, Yoshihiko 1931- WhoScEn 94
Chibbaro, Anthony Joseph 1946- WhoScEn 94
Chibeau, Edmond DrAPF 93
Chi Biqing 1920- WhoPRCh 91 [port]
Chibnall, Marjorie McCallum 1915- Who 94, WrDr 94
Chiburdanidze, Maiya Grigorevna 1961- IntWW 93
Chicago, Judy 1939- WhoAm 94, WhoAmA 93
Chichester Who 94
Chichester, Archdeacon of Who 94
Chichester, Bishop of 1915- Who 94
Chichester, Dean of Who 94
Chichester, Earl of 1944- Who 94
Chichester, Viscount 1990- Who 94
Chichester, (Edward) John 1916- Who 94
Chichester, John H. 1937- WhoAmP 93
Chichester, Suzy M. C. 1949- WhoAmP 93
Chichester-Clark Who 94
Chichester Clark, Emma 1955- WrDr 94
Chichester-Clark, Robert 1928- Who 94
Chichetto, James William DrAPF 93
Chichura, Diane B. WhoAmA 93
Chick, John Stephen 1935- Who 94
Chick, Stacy Ayers 1962- WhoFI 94
Chickering, F. William 1953- WhoAm 94
Chickering, Howard Allen 1942- WhoAm 94
Chicks, Charles Hampton 1930- WhoWest 94
Chico, Gery J. 1956- WhoHisp 94
Chicoine, Roland A. 1922- WhoAmP 93
Chicoine, Roland Alvin 1922- WhoMW 93
Chicorel, Marietta Eva WhoAm 94, WhoWest 94
Chicot, Etienne WhoHol 92
Chicoye, Etzer 1926- WhoBlA 94
Chicz-DeMet, Aleksandra 1951- WhoScEn 94
Chiddix, James Alan 1945- WhoAm 94
Chidester, Alfred C. 1945- WhoAm 94
Chidester, Gene Roger 1948- WhoWest 94

Christ, Ronald 1936- *WrDr 94*
Christ, Ronald Lee 1935- *WhoWest 94*
Christ, Thomas Warren 1944- *WhoAm 94*
Christ, Vincent B. 1931- *WhoMW 93*
Christakos, Sylvia 1946- *WhoAm 94*
Christaldi, Brian 1940- *WhoAm 94*
Christaller, Helene 1872-1953 *BlmGWL*
Christchurch, Bishop of 1943- *Who 94*
Christ Church, Dublin, Dean of *Who 94*
Christ Church, Oxford, Dean of *Who 94*
Christen, Ada 1839-1901 *BlmGWL*
Christen, Brenda Jean 1962- *WhoMW 93*
Christen, Peter 1953- *WhoIns 94*
Christenberry, William 1936-
WhoAmA 93
Christenbury, Edward Samuel 1941-
WhoAm 94, WhoAmL 94
Christenbury, Jerry Dean 1935-
WhoIns 94
Christensen, Adele Marie 1951-
WhoMW 93
Christensen, Albert Kent 1927-
WhoAm 94
Christensen, Albert Sherman 1905-
WhoAm 94, WhoAmL 94, WhoWest 94
Christensen, Allen Clare 1935-
WhoWest 94
Christensen, Amy Jean 1968- *WhoMW 93*
Christensen, Arnold 1936- *WhoAm 94,*
WhoAmP 93
Christensen, Barbara Jean 1951-
WhoAmP 93
Christensen, Benjamin d1959 *WhoHol 92*
Christensen, Betty *WhoAmA 93*
Christensen, Boake 1939- *WhoAmL 94*
Christensen, Bruce LeRoy 1943-
WhoAm 94, WhoFI 94
Christensen, Burke Arthur 1945-
WhoAmL 94, WhoIns 94
Christensen, Carl Roland 1919-
WhoAm 94
Christensen, Caroline 1936- *WhoWest 94*
Christensen, Charles Lewis 1936-
WhoFI 94
Christensen, Chris Lauriths 1894-
WhAm 10
Christensen, Christian Lingo 1855-1940
EncNAR
Christensen, Clyde Martin 1905-
WhoMW 93, WhoScEn 94
Christensen, Craig A. 1947- *WhoAmL 94*
Christensen, Curtis Lee 1950- *WhoAm 94*
Christensen, Cyrus Robert 1926-
WhoFI 94
Christensen, Dan 1942- *WhoAmA 93*
Christensen, Dana Lane 1961-
WhoWest 94
Christensen, David Allen 1935-
WhoAm 94, WhoMW 93
Christensen, David Arthur 1960-
WhoMW 93
Christensen, David G. *WhoAmP 93*
Christensen, David William 1937-
WhoScEn 94
Christensen, Dieter 1932- *WhoAm 94*
Christensen, Don B. 1948- *WhoAmA 93*
Christensen, Don M. 1929- *WhoFI 94*
Christensen, Donn Wayne 1941-
WhoWest 94
Christensen, Emil Hass d1982 *WhoHol 92*
Christensen, Eric Herbert *Who 94N*
Christensen, Erik Regnar 1943-
WhoMW 93
Christensen, Erleen J. *DrAPF 93*
Christensen, Erma H. 1909- *WhoAmP 93*
Christensen, George B. 1905- *WhoAm 94*
Christensen, George Curtis 1924-
WhoAm 94
Christensen, George Manford 1920-
WhoAmP 93
Christensen, Gordon Johnson 1936-
WhoWest 94
Christensen, Gwen Joyner 1930-
WhoWest 94
Christensen, Hal 1935- *WhoAmP 93*
Christensen, Halvor Niels 1915-
WhoAm 94
Christensen, Henry, III 1944- *WhoAm 94,*
WhoAmL 94
Christensen, Inger 1935- *BlmGWL*
Christensen, J(ack) A(rden) 1927-
WrDr 94
Christensen, Jay D. 1946- *WhoAmL 94,*
Who 94
Christensen, Jens 1921- *IntWW 93,*
Who 94
Christensen, Joan K. *WhoAmP 93*
Christensen, John William 1914-
WhoAm 94
Christensen, Julien Martin 1918-
WhoAm 94, WhoScEn 94
Christensen, Kai 1916- *IntWW 93*
Christensen, Karen Kay 1947-
WhoAmL 94
Christensen, Karl Reed 1962-
WhoScEn 94
Christensen, Larry R. 1936- *WhoAmA 93*
Christensen, Lew 1908?-1984
IntDcB [port]

Christensen, Lydell Lee 1934- *WhoAm 94*
Christensen, Maren J. 1943- *WhoAmL 94*
Christensen, Margaret Anna 1938-
WhoFI 94
Christensen, Mari Alice 1934-
WhoMW 93
Christensen, Mark Dean 1956-
WhoMW 93
Christensen, Martha 1932- *WhoAm 94*
Christensen, Marvin Nelson 1927-
WhoFI 94, WhoMW 93
Christensen, Nadia *DrAPF 93*
Christensen, Neil C. 1947- *WhoAmA 93*
Christensen, Nikolas Ivan 1937-
WhoAm 94
Christensen, Ole 1944- *WhoScEn 94*
Christensen, Patricia Anne Watkins
1947- *WhoAmL 94*
Christensen, Paul *DrAPF 93*
Christensen, Paul 1943- *WrDr 94*
Christensen, Paul Walter, Jr. 1925-
WhoAm 94
Christensen, Ralph 1897-1961
WhoAmA 93N
Christensen, Ralph J. 1953- *WhoScEn 94*
Christensen, Ray Richards 1922-
WhoAm 94
Christensen, Raymond A. 1922-
WhoAmP 93
Christensen, Raymond Gordon 1944-
WhoMW 93
Christensen, Richard Monson 1932-
WhoScEn 94
Christensen, Robert A. 1940- *WhoAm 94*
Christensen, Robert Wayne, Jr. 1948-
WhoWest 94
Christensen, Ronald Robert 1943-
WhoAmL 94
Christensen, Sally H. 1935- *WhoAmP 93*
Christensen, Sharlene 1939- *WhoAmA 93*
Christensen, Soren Brogger 1947-
WhoScEn 94
Christensen, Steven Brent 1959-
WhoWest 94
Christensen, Susan L. 1959- *WhoMW 93*
Christensen, Ted 1911- *WhoAmA 93*
Christensen, Tom 1925- *WhoAm 94*
Christensen, Val Alan 1946- *WhoAmA 93*
Christensen, William 1902- *IntDcB [port]*
Christenson, Andrew Lewis 1950-
WhoWest 94
Christenson, Bernard Wyman 1938-
WhoAmP 93
Christenson, Charles Elroy 1942-
WhoWest 94
Christenson, Charles John 1930-
WhoAm 94
Christenson, Donald Robert 1937-
WhoMW 93
Christenson, Gordon A. 1932-
WhoAm 94, WhoAmL 94
Christenson, Hans-Jorgen Thorvald
1924-1983 *WhoAmA 93N*
Christenson, James M. 1946- *WhoAmL 94*
Christenson, Le Roy Howard 1948-
WhoAm 94, WhoFI 94
Christenson, LeRoy H. 1948- *WhoIns 94*
Christenson, Philip L. 1947- *WhoAmP 93*
Christenson, Steven Maurice 1951-
WhoMW 93
Christenson, Susan Elizabeth 1951-
WhoAm 94
Christenson, Vicki 1947- *WhoWest 94*
Christenson, William Newcome 1925-
WhoAm 94
Christesen, C(lement) B(yrne) 1911-
WrDr 94
Christesen, Clement Byrne 1911-
IntWW 93
Christesen, Russell J. 1923- *WhoFI 94*
Christgau, John *DrAPF 93*
Christgau, Victor 1894-1991 *WhAm 10*
Christhilf, David Michael 1959-
WhoScEn 94
Christi, Frank d1982 *WhoHol 92*
Christiaens, B. F. Chris 1940-
WhoAmP 93
Christiaens, Chris 1940- *WhoAm 94,*
WhoWest 94
Christian, IV 1577-1648 *HisWorL [port]*
Christian, Almeric L. 1919- *WhoBlA 94*
Christian, Ann Seger 1954- *WhoAmL 94,*
WhoWest 94
Christian, Barbara 1943- *BlmGWL*
Christian, Betty Jo 1936- *WhoAm 94,*
WhoAmP 93
Christian, Carl Franz 1929- *WhoScEn 94*
Christian, Carol Cathay 1923- *WrDr 94*
Christian, Charlie 1916-1942 *AfrAmAl 6,*
ConMus 11 [port]
Christian, Clarence Wendol 1927-
WhoAmP 93
Christian, Claudia *WhoHol 92*
Christian, Clifford Stuart 1907- *Who 94*
Christian, Cora LeEthel 1947- *WhoBlA 94*
Christian, Darrell L. 1948- *WhoAm 94*
Christian, David C. 1948- *WhoAmP 93*

Christian, David Ralph 1952-
WhoAmP 93
Christian, Dolly Lewis *WhoBlA 94*
Christian, Donald Jacobs 1951-
WhoFI 94, WhoWest 94
Christian, Douglas Lee 1949-
WhoAmL 94
Christian, Edith Ann 1950- *WhoAmL 94*
Christian, Edward Kieren 1944-
WhoAm 94
Christian, Eric Oliver, Jr. 1951-
WhoBlA 94
Christian, Ernest Silsbee, Jr. 1937-
WhoAm 94
Christian, Frederick Ade 1937-
WhoScEn 94
Christian, Frederick H. 1931- *WrDr 94*
Christian, Gary Dale 1937- *WhoAm 94*
Christian, Gary Irvin 1951- *WhoAm 94,*
WhoAmL 94
Christian, George Eastland 1927-
WhoAm 94
Christian, George Lloyd, Jr. 1927-
WhoAm 94
Christian, Geraldine Ashley McConnell
1929- *WhoBlA 94*
Christian, James M. 1948- *WhoAmP 93*
Christian, James Wayne 1934- *WhoAm 94*
Christian, Jerald Cronis 1933- *WhoBlA 94*
Christian, Joe Clark 1934- *WhoAm 94,*
WhoScEn 94
Christian, John *WhoHol 92*
Christian, John 1930- *WrDr 94*
Christian, John Catlett, Jr. 1929-
WhoAm 94, WhoAmL 94
Christian, John Edward 1917- *WhoAm 94*
Christian, John Kenton 1927- *WhoAm 94*
Christian, John L. 1940- *WhoBlA 94*
Christian, John M. 1948- *WhoAmL 94*
Christian, John Wyrill 1926- *IntWW 93,*
Who 94, WrDr 94
Christian, Joseph Ralph 1920- *WhoAm 94*
Christian, Linda 1923- *WhoHol 92*
Christian, Linda 1924- *IntMPA 94*
Christian, Lynda Gregorian 1938-
WhoAmL 94
Christian, Mae Armster 1934- *WhoBlA 94*
Christian, Mary Blount 1933- *WrDr 94*
Christian, Mary Taylor 1924-
WhoAmP 93
Christian, Michael 1943- *WhoHol 92*
Christian, Nelson Frederick 1949-
WhoAm 94
Christian, Paul 1917- *WhoHol 92*
Christian, Paulette Therese 1947-
WhoWest 94
Christian, Percy Willis 1907-1990
WhAm 10
Christian, Peter *ConAu 141*
Christian, Rebecca Anne 1952-
WhoMW 93
Christian, Reginald Frank 1924- *Who 94*
Christian, Richard Carlton 1924-
WhoAm 94, WhoMW 93
Christian, Robert d1983 *WhoHol 92*
Christian, Robert Henry 1922-
WhoAm 94
Christian, Roland Carl 1938- *WhoWest 94*
Christian, Roy Cloberry 1914- *WrDr 94*
Christian, Spencer 1947- *AfrAmAl 6 [port],*
WhoBlA 94
Christian, Suzanne Hall 1935- *WhoFI 94,*
WhoWest 94
Christian, Theresa *WhoBlA 94*
Christian, Thomas Franklin, Jr. 1946-
WhoScEn 94
Christian, William c. 1743-1786
WhAmRev
Christian, William Richardson 1950-
WhoWest 94
Christiana, Edward 1912- *WhoAmA 93*
Christian-Allgaier, Donna 1950-
WhoMW 93
Christian-Green, Donna-Marie 1945-
WhoBlA 94
Christiano, Paul P. 1942- *WhoAm 94*
Christians, Darnell Dean 1961-
WhoMW 93
Christians, F. Wilhelm 1922- *IntWW 93*
Christians, George d1921 *WhoHol 92*
Christians, Kimberly Kay 1960-
WhoMW 93
Christians, Mady d1951 *WhoHol 92*
Christians, Margarete *WhoHol 92*
Christians, Rudolph d1921 *WhoHol 92*
Christiansen, Andrew Perry 1953-
WhoAmP 93
Christiansen, Arthur d1963 *WhoHol 92*
Christiansen, Christian Carl, Jr. 1933-
WhoAm 94
Christiansen, David K. 1952- *WhoAm 94*
Christiansen, Dennis Lee 1948-
WhoScEn 94
Christiansen, Diane 1958- *WhoAmA 93*
Christiansen, Donald David 1927-
WhoAm 94
Christiansen, Eric Alan 1958-
WhoWest 94

Christiansen, Eric George 1931-
WhoMW 93
Christiansen, Ernest Bert 1910-1988
WhAm 10
Christiansen, H. J. 1930- *WhoAmP 93*
Christiansen, Jack d1986 *ProFbHF [port]*
Christiansen, James Edward 1930-
WhoAm 94
Christiansen, Jay David 1952-
WhoAm 94, WhoAmL 94
Christiansen, John Rees 1927- *WhoAm 94*
Christiansen, Jon Peter 1950- *WhoAm 94*
Christiansen, Kathleen Marie 1955-
WhoMW 93
Christiansen, Keith A. 1943- *WhoAm 94,*
WhoAmL 94
Christiansen, Kenneth Allen 1924-
WhoAm 94
Christiansen, Marjorie Miner 1922-
WhoWest 94
Christiansen, Mark D. 1955- *WhoAmL 94*
Christiansen, Mogens Erik d1993
NewYTBS 93
Christiansen, Norman Juhl 1923-
WhoAm 94
Christiansen, Patrick T. 1947-
WhoAmL 94
Christiansen, Paul Arthur 1932-
WhoMW 93
Christiansen, Raymond Stephan 1950-
WhoMW 93
Christiansen, Richard Dean 1931-
WhoAm 94
Christiansen, Richard Louis 1935-
WhoAm 94
Christiansen, Robert Lester 1927-1992
WhAm 10
Christiansen, Robert Lorenz 1935-
WhoWest 94
Christiansen, Robert W. *IntMPA 94*
Christiansen, Roy Hvidkaer 1932-
WhoAmL 94
Christiansen, Rupert 1954- *WrDr 94*
Christiansen, Russell 1935- *WhoAm 94,*
WhoFI 94
Christiansen, Steven John 1955-
WhoAmL 94
Christiansen, Susan Putnam 1938-
WhoWest 94
Christiansen, Tim Alan 1951-
WhoScEn 94
Christiansen, Walter Henry 1934-
WhoAm 94
Christianson, Alan 1909- *Who 94*
Christianson, Dana Paul 1957-
WhoWest 94
Christianson, Floyd Kenneth 1917-
WhoMW 93
Christianson, James Duane 1952-
WhoMW 93
Christianson, Kevin *DrAPF 93*
Christianson, Lloyd Fenton 1914-
WhoAm 94
Christianson, Roger Allen 1943-
WhoAmP 93
Christianson, Roger Gordon 1947-
WhoWest 94
Christianson, T. Loren *WhoAmP 93*
Christie, A(ndrew) B(arnett) 1909-
WrDr 94
Christie, Agatha 1890-1976 *BlmGEL,*
BlmGWL
Christie, Agatha (Mary Clarissa)
1890-1976 *ConDr 93, TwCYAW*
Christie, Andrew, Jr. 1943- *WhoAmP 93*
Christie, Andrew George 1936-
WhoAm 94
Christie, Ann Philippa *Who 94*
Christie, Audrey d1989 *WhoHol 92*
Christie, Campbell 1937- *Who 94*
Christie, Charles d1812 *WhWE*
Christie, Clarence J. 1930- *WhoAm 94*
Christie, David George 1930- *WhoFI 94*
Christie, Elizabeth Mary *Who 94*
Christie, Fred Atherton 1936-
WhoMW 93
Christie, George d1949 *WhoHol 92*
Christie, George (William Langham)
1934- *Who 94*
Christie, George Custis 1934- *WhoAm 94*
Christie, George Nicholas 1924-
WhoFI 94
Christie, George William Langham 1934-
IntWW 93
Christie, Hans Frederick 1933-
WhoAm 94, WhoWest 94
Christie, Herbert 1933- *Who 94*
Christie, Ian (Ralph) 1919- *WrDr 94*
Christie, Ian R(alph) 1919- *ConAu 42NR*
Christie, Ian Ralph 1919- *IntWW 93,*
Who 94
Christie, Ivan d1949 *WhoHol 92*
Christie, John 1882-1962 *NewGrDO*
Christie, John Arthur Kingsley 1915-
Who 94
Christie, John Belford Wilson 1914-
Who 94
Christie, John Rankin 1918- *Who 94*

Christie, John Reginald Halliday 1899-1953 *DcNaB MP*
Christie, Judith Marjorie 1940- *WhoFI 94*
Christie, Julie 1940- *WhoAm 94, WhoHol 92*
Christie, Julie 1941- *IntMPA 94*
Christie, Julie (Frances) 1940- *Who 94*
Christie, Julie Frances 1940- *IntWW 93*
Christie, Kim d1979 *WhoHol 92*
Christie, Laurence Glenn, Jr. 1930- *WhoAm 94, WhoScEn 94*
Christie, Linford 1960- *IntWW 93, Who 94*
Christie, Mary Anne 1934- *WhoAmP 93*
Christie, Nan (Stevenson) 1948- *NewGrDO*
Christie, Richard G. 1934- *WhoScEn 94*
Christie, Robert Brent 1952- *WhoAm 94*
Christie, Robert Duncan 1946- *WhoAmA 93*
Christie, Scott Graham 1953- *WhoFI 94*
Christie, Shannon *WhoHol 92*
Christie, Steven Lee 1960- *WhoScEn 94*
Christie, Thomas J. 1942- *WhoAmP 93*
Christie, Thomas Philip 1934- *WhoAm 94*
Christie, Vernon (Howard Colville) 1909- *Who 94*
Christie, Walter Scott 1922- *WhoFI 94, WhoMW 93*
Christie, William 1913- *Who 94*
Christie, William 1960- *ConAu 140*
Christie, William (Lincoln) 1944- *NewGrDO*
Christie, William James 1932- *Who 94*
Christie-Murray, David (Hugh Arthur) 1913- *WrDr 94*
Christina 1626-1689 *NewGrDO*
Christina, Martha *DrAPF 93*
Christina-Marie *DrAPF 93*
Christina of Markyate c. 1096- *DcNaB MP*
Christina of Sweden 1626-1689 *HisWorL [port]*
Christine, Henri 1867-1941 *NewGrDO*
Christine, Virginia 1917- *WhoHol 92*
Christine, Virginia 1920- *IntMPA 94*
Christine, Virginia Feld 1920- *WhoAm 94*
Christine de Pisan 1364?-1434? *BlmGWL [port]*
Christison, Kent F. 1946- *WhoAmL 94*
Christison, Muriel B. *WhoAmA 93*
Christison, Philip d1993 *NewYTBS 93 [port]*
Christison, (Alexander Frank) Philip 1893- *Who 94*
Christison, William Henry, III 1936- *WhoAm 94*
Christ-Janer, Albert William 1910-1973 *WhoAmA 93N*
Christ-Janer, Arland F. 1922- *WhoAmA 93*
Christ-Janer, Arland Frederick 1922- *WhoAm 94*
Christman, Arthur Castner, Jr. 1922- *WhoAm 94*
Christman, Bruce Lee 1955- *WhoAmL 94*
Christman, Edward Arthur 1943- *WhoScEn 94*
Christman, Elizabeth *DrAPF 93*
Christman, Helen Dorothy Nelson 1922- *WhoWest 94*
Christman, James A. 1948- *WhoAmL 94*
Christman, James Edward 1930- *WhoAm 94*
Christman, John Francis 1924- *WhoAm 94*
Christman, Luther Parmalee 1915- *IntWW 93, WhoAm 94, WhoScEn 94*
Christman, Paul J. 1952- *WrDr 94*
Christman, Quentin E. *WhoAmP 93*
Christman, Robert Alan 1955- *WhoAm 94*
Christmas, Arthur Napier 1913- *Who 94*
Christmas, Eric *WhoHol 92*
Christmas, Jason d1991 *WhoHol 92*
Christmas, Jeffrey L. d1993 *NewYTBS 93*
Christmas, Joyce 1939- *WrDr 94*
Christner, David Lee 1949- *WhoMW 93*
Christo 1935- *IntWW 93, WhoAm 94, WhoAmA 93*
Christodoulou, Anastasios 1932- *IntWW 93, Who 94*
Christodoulou, Aris Peter 1939- *WhoAm 94*
Christodoulou, Demetrios 1919- *WrDr 94*
Christodoulou, Demetrios 1951- *WhoScEn 94*
Christodoulou, Efthymios 1932- *IntWW 93*
Christofas, Kenneth (Cavendish) d1992 *IntWW 93N*
Christofas, Kenneth Cavendish d1992 *Who 94N*
Christofes, Fritz *NewGrDO*
Christoff, Boris d1993 *Who 94N*
Christoff, Boris 1914-1993 *NewYTBS 93 [port]*
Christoff, Boris 1919- *IntWW 93*
Christoff, Boris (Kirilov) 1914- *NewGrDO [port]*
Christoffel, Ivan 1921- *WhoFI 94*
Christoffel, James Francis 1954- *WhoAmL 94*
Christoffel, Kurt Matthew 1953- *WhoMW 93*
Christoffersen, Ralph Earl 1937- *WhoAm 94*
Christoffersson, John Goran 1945- *WhoAm 94*
Christofi, Andreas Charalambos 1949- *WhoAm 94*
Christoforidis, A. John 1924- *WhoAm 94, WhoScEn 94*
Christol, Carl Quimby 1913- *WhoAm 94*
Christon, Mark Allen 1958- *WhoScEn 94*
Christoph, James B. 1928- *WrDr 94*
Christoph, Siegfried Richard 1950- *WhoMW 93*
Christoph, Susan Catherine 1960- *WhoFI 94*
Christophe, Henri 1767-1820 *HisWorL [port], WhAmRev*
Christophe, Pascale *WhoHol 92*
Christopher, Alexander George 1941- *WhoFI 94, WhoMW 93*
Christopher, Ann 1947- *Who 94*
Christopher, Anthony Martin Grosvenor 1925- *Who 94*
Christopher, Colin Alfred 1932- *Who 94*
Christopher, Dennis 1955- *IntMPA 94, WhoHol 92*
Christopher, Diana 1930- *WrDr 94*
Christopher, Glenn A. *WhoAm 94, WhoFI 94, WhoMW 93*
Christopher, James Walker 1930- *WhoAm 94*
Christopher, Joe Randell 1935- *WhoAm 94*
Christopher, John 1922- *EncSF 93, TwCYAW, WrDr 94*
Christopher, John A. 1941- *WhoBlA 94*
Christopher, John Anthony 1924- *Who 94*
Christopher, John Anthony 1947- *WhoAmL 94*
Christopher, Jordan 1940- *WhoHol 92*
Christopher, Jordan 1941- *IntMPA 94*
Christopher, Lee Neil 1940- *WhoWest 94*
Christopher, M. Ronald 1941- *WhoAmL 94, WhoAmP 93*
Christopher, Matt(hew) F. 1917- *WrDr 94*
Christopher, Maurine Brooks *WhoAm 94*
Christopher, Nancy B. 1942- *WhoAmP 93*
Christopher, Nicholas *DrAPF 93*
Christopher, Nicholas 1951- *ConAu 43NR*
Christopher, Raymond Joseph 1945- *WhoFI 94*
Christopher, Richard d1982 *WhoHol 92*
Christopher, Richard Douglas 1953- *WhoAmP 93*
Christopher, Robert 1924-1992 *AnObit 1992*
Christopher, Roy *ConTFT 11*
Christopher, Russell Lewis 1930- *WhoAm 94*
Christopher, Sharon A. Brown 1944- *WhoAm 94, WhoMW 93*
Christopher, Stephen M. 1951- *WhoIns 94*
Christopher, Susan Roxanne 1952- *WhoWest 94*
Christopher, Thomas Weldon 1917- *WhoAm 94*
Christopher, Warren 1925- *IntWW 93, Who 94, WhoAm 94, WhoAmP 93*
Christopher, Wilford Scott 1916- *WhoAm 94*
Christopher, William *WhoAm 94, WhoHol 92*
Christopher, William Garth 1940- *WhoAm 94, WhoAmL 94*
Christopher, William R. 1924-1973 *WhoAmA 93N*
Christophersen, Dale Bjorn 1940- *WhoAmP 93*
Christophersen, Edward Rea 1940- *WhoMW 93*
Christophersen, Henning 1939- *IntWW 93, Who 94*
Christophersen, Paul (Hans) 1911- *WrDr 94*
Christopherson, Christine Young 1950- *WhoAmP 93*
Christopherson, Derman (Guy) 1915- *Who 94*
Christopherson, Derman Guy 1915- *IntWW 93*
Christopherson, Fred Carl 1896- *WhAm 10*
Christopherson, Harald Fairbairn 1920- *Who 94*
Christopherson, Myrvin Frederick 1939- *WhoMW 93*
Christopherson, Romola Carol Andrea 1939- *Who 94*
Christopherson, Weston Robert 1925- *WhoAm 94*
Christophides, Andreas Nicolaou 1937- *IntWW 93*
Christophides, Takis 1931- *IntWW 93*
Christou, Jani 1926-1970 *NewGrDO*
Christov, Dragan Spirov 1934- *WhoFI 94*
Christowe, Margaret Wooters *WhoAmP 93*
Christy, Ann d1987 *WhoHol 92*
Christy, Arthur Hill 1923- *WhoAm 94*
Christy, Bill d1946 *WhoHol 92*
Christy, C. Dana 1913- *WhoAmP 93*
Christy, Dorothy d1977 *WhoHol 92*
Christy, Floyd d1962 *WhoHol 92*
Christy, Gary Christopher 1948- *WhoAmL 94*
Christy, Howard Chandler 1872-1952 *WhoAmA 93N*
Christy, James Walter 1938- *WhoAm 94*
Christy, John Gilray 1932- *WhoAm 94, WhoFI 94*
Christy, June d1990 *WhoHol 92*
Christy, Ken d1962 *WhoHol 92*
Christy, Nicholas Pierson 1923- *WhoAm 94*
Christy, Perry T. 1941- *WhoAmP 93*
Christy, Perry Thomas 1941- *WhoAm 94*
Christy, Robert Allen 1956- *WhoFI 94*
Christy, Suzanne 1904- *WhoHol 92*
Christy, Ted d1976 *WhoHol 92*
Christy, Thomas Patrick 1943- *WhoFI 94, WhoWest 94*
Chritton, George A. 1933- *WhoWest 94*
Chrobak, Dennis Steven 1939- *WhoFI 94*
Chromizky, William Rudolph 1955- *WhoMW 93*
Chromow, Sheri P. 1946- *WhoAm 94, WhoAmL 94*
Chronic, Byron John 1921- *WhoAm 94*
Chronister, Gregory Michael 1953- *WhoAm 94*
Chronister, Harry B. 1922- *WhoAmP 93*
Chronister, Richard Davis 1943- *WhoScEn 94*
Chronister, Rochelle Beach 1939- *WhoAmP 93*
Chronley, James Andrew 1930- *WhoAm 94*
Chruszcz, Charles Francis 1950- *Who 94*
Chrysikopoulos, Constantinos Vassilios 1960- *WhoScEn 94*
Chrysis, International d1990 *WhoHol 92*
Chrysochoos, John 1934- *WhoScEn 94*
Chrysostom, John c. 344-407 *HisWorL [port]*
Chrysostomos of Oreoietna 1943- *WhoAm 94*
Chrysoulakis, Gennadios 1924- *WhoAm 94*
Chryss, George 1941- *WhoFI 94, WhoScEn 94*
Chryssa 1933- *IntWW 93, WhoAm 94, WhoAmA 93*
Chryssafopoulos, Nicholas 1919- *WhoAm 94*
Chryssanthou, Christodoulos 1935- *IntWW 93*
Chryssis, George Christopher 1947- *WhoAm 94, WhoFI 94*
Chryst, Gary 1949- *WhoAm 94*
Chrystall, Belle 1910- *WhoHol 92*
Chrystie, Thomas Ludlow 1933- *WhoFI 94*
Chrystos *DrAPF 93*
Chrzanowski, Wieslaw Marian 1923- *IntWW 93*
Chrzan-Seelig, Patricia Ann 1954- *WhoFI 94*
Chu, Adam 1965- *WhoAsA 94*
Chu, Alexander Hang-Torng 1955- *WhoMW 93, WhoScEn 94*
Chu, Allen Yum-Ching 1951- *WhoScEn 94, WhoWest 94*
Chu, Benjamin 1932- *WhoAsA 94*
Chu, Benjamin Thomas Peng-Nien 1932- *WhoAm 94, WhoScEn 94*
Chu, C. K. 1927- *WhoAm 94*
Chu, Chi-Ming 1917- *IntWW 93*
Chu, Ching-Wu 1941- *WhoAsA 94*
Chu, Christopher Kar Fai 1955- *WhoWest 94*
Chu, Chung Kwang 1941- *WhoAsA 94*
Chu, Chung-Yu Chester 1950- *WhoAsA 94*
Chu, Daniel Tim-Wo 1941- *WhoAsA 94, WhoMW 93*
Chu, David 1954- *WhoAsA 94*
Chu, David S. C. 1944- *WhoAm 94, WhoAmP 93, WhoAsA 94*
Chu, David Yuk 1945- *WhoScEn 94*
Chu, Deeing 1943- *WhoWest 94*
Chu, Elizabeth Chan 1955- *WhoAsA 94*
Chu, Felix T. 1949- *WhoAsA 94*
Chu, Foo 1921- *WhoAm 94*
Chu, Franklin Dean 1948- *WhoAm 94*
Chu, Franklin Janen 1955- *WhoAsA 94*
Chu, Gene 1936- *WhoAmA 93*
Chu, George Hao 1939- *WhoWest 94*
Chu, Hung Manh 1944- *WhoAsA 94*
Chu, James Chien-Hua 1948- *WhoScEn 94*
Chu, Jeffrey Chuan 1919- *WhoAm 94*
Chu, Johnson Chin Sheng 1918- *WhoAm 94, WhoMW 93, WhoScEn 94*
Chu, Jonathan Moseley 1945- *WhoAsA 94*
Chu, Judy M. 1953- *WhoAsA 94*
Chu, Judy May 1953- *WhoWest 94*
Chu, Julia Nee 1940- *WhoAmA 93*
Chu, Julia Nee 1941- *WhoAsA 94*
Chu, Kong 1926- *WhoAsA 94*
Chu, Kuang-Han 1919- *WhoAm 94, WhoAsA 94*
Chu, Lon-Chan 1963- *WhoMW 93*
Chu, Merri Theresa 1959- *WhoFI 94*
Chu, Mon-Li Hsiung 1948- *WhoScEn 94*
Chu, Morgan 1950- *WhoAm 94, WhoAmL 94*
Chu, Nhan V. 1951- *WhoAsA 94*
Chu, Nori Yaw-Chyuan 1939- *WhoAsA 94*
Chu, Patricia Pei-chang *WhoAsA 94*
Chu, Patrick 1955- *WhoHol 92*
Chu, Paul Ching-Wu 1941- *WhoAm 94, WhoAsA 94*
Chu, Peter Cheng 1944- *WhoAsA 94*
Chu, Regina Maria 1953- *WhoAmL 94*
Chu, Richard Chao-Fan 1933- *WhoAm 94*
Chu, Richard Shao-hung 1946- *WhoFI 94*
Chu, Roderick Gong-Wah 1949- *WhoAm 94, WhoFI 94*
Chu, Shirley S. 1929- *WhoAsA 94*
Chu, Shirley Shan-Chi 1929- *WhoScEn 94*
Chu, Steven 1948- *WhoAm 94, WhoScEn 94*
Chu, Sung Nee George 1947- *WhoAsA 94*
Chu, Terence 1959- *WhoAsA 94*
Chu, Tien Lu 1934- *WhoAsA 94*
Chu, Ting L. 1924- *WhoAsA 94*
Chu, Ting Li 1924- *WhoScEn 94*
Chu, Tsann Ming 1938- *WhoAm 94*
Chu, Tsuchin Philip 1952- *WhoAsA 94*
Chu, Victor Fu Hua 1918- *WhoAsA 94*
Chu, Vincent Hao-Kwong 1918- *WhoAsA 94*
Chu, Warren 1951- *WhoAsA 94*
Chu, Wayne Shu-Wing 1949- *WhoScEn 94*
Chu, Wei-Kan 1940- *WhoAsA 94*
Chu, Wen-djang 1914- *WhoAm 94*
Chu, Wesley Wei-Chin 1936- *WhoAm 94*
Chu, William Tongil 1934- *WhoAsA 94*
Chua, Amy Lynn 1962- *WhoAsA 94*
Chua, Conrad E. 1951- *WhoAsA 94*
Chua, Leon O. *WhoAsA 94*
Chua, Leon O. 1936- *WhoWest 94*
Chua, Nam-Hai 1944- *IntWW 93, Who 94, WhoAm 94*
Chua, Tommy Dy 1955- *WhoFI 94*
Chuan, Raymond Lu-Po 1924- *WhoWest 94*
Chu-Andrews, Jennifer 1948- *WhoAsA 94*
Chuang, De-Maw 1942- *WhoAsA 94*
Chuang, Frank Shiunn-Jea 1942- *WhoAm 94, WhoScEn 94*
Chuang, Harold Hwa-Ming 1941- *WhoFI 94*
Chuang, Henry Ning 1937- *WhoAsA 94*
Chuang, Jerry T. 1943- *WhoAsA 94*
Chuang, Strong C. 1939- *WhoAsA 94*
Chuang, Tze-jer 1943- *WhoAsA 94*
Chuang, Vincent P. 1940- *WhoAsA 94*
Chuang Tzu 4th cent.BC- *EncEth*
Chuan Leekpai 1938- *IntWW 93*
Chua Sian Chin 1934- *IntWW 93*
Chub, Vladimir Fedorovich 1948- *LoBiDrD*
Chubais, Anatoly Borisovich 1955- *IntWW 93, LoBiDrD*
Chubb *Who 94*
Chubb, Anthony Gerald Trelawny 1928- *Who 94*
Chubb, Frederick Basil 1921- *IntWW 93, Who 94*
Chubb, John Oliver 1920- *Who 94*
Chubb, Joseph 1940- *WhoAm 94*
Chubb, Louise B. 1927- *WhoBlA 94*
Chubb, Paul *WhoHol 92*
Chubb, Percy, III 1934- *WhoAm 94, WhoFI 94, WhoIns 94*
Chubb, Scott Robinson 1953- *WhoScEn 94*
Chubb, Stephen Darrow 1944- *WhoAm 94*
Chubb, Talbot Albert 1923- *WhoAm 94*
Chubukov, Andrey Vadim 1959- *WhoScEn 94*
Chuchel, Paul B. *WhoIns 94*
Chu Chuanheng *WhoPRCh 91*
Chuck, Leon 1955- *WhoScEn 94*
Chuck, Steven Lee 1958- *WhoWest 94*
Chuck, Walter Goonsun 1920- *WhoAm 94, WhoAmL 94, WhoFI 94, WhoWest 94*
Chucks, Jerry 1957- *WhoBlA 94*
Chudakov, Aleksandr Yevgeniyevich 1921- *IntWW 93*
Chudd, Reeve E. 1951- *WhoAmL 94*
Chudleigh, Mary 1656-1710 *BlmGWL*
Chudnovsky, Gregory Volfovich 1952- *WhoAm 94*

Chudobiak, Walter James 1942- *WhoFI 94*
Chudzik, Douglas Walter 1946- *WhoScEn 94*
Chudzinski, Mark Adam 1956- *WhoAmL 94, WhoMW 93*
Chue, Seck Hong 1942- *WhoScEn 94*
Chueca, Federico 1846-1908 *NewGrDO*
Chu Fu-Sung 1915- *IntWW 93*
Chugh, Ashok Kumar 1942- *WhoAsA 94*
Chugh, Yoginder Paul *WhoScEn 94*
Chughtai, Ismat 1915-1991 *BlmGWL*
Chughtai, Shahid H. 1958- *WhoAsA 94*
Chu Hsi 1130-1200 *EncEth*
Chu Huy Man, Gen. 1913- *IntWW 93*
Chui, Charles K. 1940- *WhoAsA 94*
Chukhadjian, Tigran *NewGrDO*
Chukhrai, Grigoriy Naumovich 1921- *IntWW 93*
Chukovskaia, Lidiia Korneevna 1910- *BlmGWL*
Chukovskaya, Lidia Korneyevna 1907- *IntWW 93*
Chukovsky, Kornei (Ivanovich) 1882-1969 *ConAu 42NR*
Chuks-Orji, Austin *WhoBlA 94*
Chukwueke, Gerald Ndudi 1957- *WhoBlA 94*
Chulack, Peter G., Sr. 1945- *WhoAmP 93*
Chulasapya, Dawee 1914- *IntWW 93*
Chum, Helena L. 1946- *WhoWest 94*
Chumakov, Mikhail Petrovich 1909- *IntWW 93*
Chumas, Henry John 1933- *Who 94*
Chumbley, Avery B. 1955- *WhoAmP 93*
Chumley, Donnie Ann 1942- *WhoFI 94*
Chumley, John Wesley 1928- *WhoAmA 93N*
Chummers, Paul *WhoWest 94*
Chumney, Carol *WhoAmP 93*
Chun, Alvin 1950- *WhoWest 94*
Chun, Aulani 1952- *WhoAsA 94*
Chun, Hon Ming 1960- *WhoAsA 94*
Chun, Jerrold Yeu-Quong 1948- *WhoAmP 93*
Chun, Joe Y. F. 1935- *WhoAsA 94*
Chun, Lowell Koon Wa 1944- *WhoAm 94, WhoFI 94, WhoScEn 94, WhoWest 94*
Chun, Raymond W. M. 1926- *WhoAsA 94*
Chun, Shinae 1943- *WhoAsA 94*
Chun, Sun Woong 1934- *WhoAsA 94*
Chun, Suzanne 1961- *WhoAmP 93*
Chun, Wei Foo 1916- *WhoAsA 94*
Chun, Wendy Sau Wan 1951- *WhoWest 94*
Chunder, Pratap Chandra 1919- *IntWW 93*
Chun Doo-Hwan, Gen. 1931- *IntWW 93*
Chunduri, Narendra R. *WhoWest 94*
Chung, Alison Li *WhoMW 93*
Chung, Anni Yuet-Kuen 1951- *WhoAsA 94*
Chung, (Raymond) Arthur 1918- *IntWW 93*
Chung, Byung Hwa 1966- *WhoWest 94*
Chung, Catherine L. 1951- *WhoAsA 94*
Chung, Chai-sik 1930- *WhoAsA 94*
Chung, Chen Hua 1951- *WhoAsA 94*
Chung, Chin Sik 1924- *WhoAsA 94*
Chung, Cho Man 1918- *WhoScEn 94*
Chung, Connie 1946- *IntMPA 94, WhoAsA 94*
Chung, Constance Yu-hwa 1946- *WhoAm 94*
Chung, David Yih 1936- *WhoAsA 94*
Chung, Dean I. 1958- *WhoMW 93*
Chung, Deborah Duen Ling 1952- *WhoAsA 94*
Chung, Douglas Chu 1951- *WhoScEn 94*
Chung, Douglas Kuei-Nan 1943- *WhoAsA 94*
Chung, Ed Baik 1928- *WhoAsA 94*
Chung, Edward K. 1931- *WhoAsA 94*
Chung, Edward Kooyoung 1931- *WhoAm 94*
Chung, Eugene 1969- *WhoAsA 94*
Chung, Fay *WhoWomW 91*
Chung, Frank Huan-Chen 1930- *WhoAsA 94*
Chung, Fung-Lung 1949- *WhoScEn 94*
Chung, H. Michael *WhoAsA 94*
Chung, Harold *WhoAsA 94*
Chung, Ho Young 1934- *WhoAsA 94*
Chung, Hwan Yung 1927- *WhoScEn 94*
Chung, Hyun S. 1928- *WhoAsA 94*
Chung, Jesse Y. W. 1942- *WhoAsA 94*
Chung, Jin Soo 1937- *WhoAsA 94*
Chung, Jong Rak Philip 1931- *WhoAsA 94*
Chung, Joseph Sang-hoon 1929- *WhoAm 94*
Chung, Kea Sung 1935- *WhoWest 94*
Chung, Kevin Kyu-Bong 1957- *WhoFI 94*
Chung, King-Thom 1943- *WhoAsA 94, WhoScEn 94*
Chung, Kwong T. 1938- *WhoAsA 94*
Chung, Kyung Cho 1921- *WhoAm 94*
Chung, Kyung-Wha 1948- *IntWW 93, Who 94*
Chung, Kyung Won 1938- *WhoAsA 94*
Chung, L. A. *WhoAsA 94*
Chung, Ling Jia 1941- *WhoAsA 94*
Chung, Lisa A. *WhoAsA 94*
Chung, Luke Tsun 1964- *WhoAsA 94*
Chung, Myung-Whun 1953- *IntWW 93*
Chung, Paul Myungha 1929- *WhoAm 94, WhoAsA 94, WhoFI 94, WhoMW 93, WhoScEn 94*
Chung, Robert 1949- *WhoAsA 94*
Chung, Ronald Aloysius 1936- *WhoAm 94, WhoAsA 94*
Chung, Simon Lam-Ying 1948- *WhoAsA 94*
Chung, Stewart 1956- *WhoWest 94*
Chung, Sue Fawn 1944- *WhoAsA 94, WhoWest 94*
Chung, Sung-Kee 1945- *WhoScEn 94*
Chung, Sze-Yuen 1917- *IntWW 93, Who 94*
Chung, T. S. *WhoAsA 94*
Chung, Tae-Soo 1937- *WhoAsA 94*
Chung, Tchang-Il 1932- *WhoFI 94*
Chung, Thomas D. 1956- *WhoAsA 94*
Chung, Thomas Yongbong 1927- *WhoAsA 94*
Chung, Tze-Chiang 1953- *WhoAsA 94*
Chung, Y. David 1959- *WhoAsA 94*
Chung, Yip-Wah 1950- *WhoAsA 94*
Chung, Young Chu 1956- *WhoScEn 94*
Chung, Young-Iob 1928- *WhoAsA 94*
Chung Il Kwon 1917- *HisDcKW*
Chung Il Kwon, Gen. 1917- *IntWW 93*
Chung Shih-Yi 1914- *IntWW 93*
Chung-Welch, Nancy Yuen Ming 1960- *WhoScEn 94*
Chung Won Shik *IntWW 93*
Chun-Hoon, Lowell Koon Ying 1949- *WhoAmL 94*
Chunko, Daniel Lucian 1950- *WhoAmL 94*
Chunn, Jay Carrington, II 1938- *WhoBlA 94*
Chunovich, Larry Walter 1942- *WhoAmP 93*
Chuong, Cheng-Ming 1952- *WhoAsA 94*
Chuong, Thach 1938- *WhoAsA 94*
Chupik, Eugene Jerry 1931- *WhoFI 94*
Chupka, William Andrew 1923- *WhoAm 94*
Chupp, Diana Lynn 1945- *WhoMW 93*
Chupp, Timothy E. 1954- *WhoScEn 94*
Chuquet, Nicolas c. 1445-c. 1500 *WorScD*
Chur, Daniel Eric 1956- *WhoAmL 94*
Chura, David *DrAPF 93*
Churanov, Vladimir Timofeevich 1945- *LoBiDrD*
Churbanov, Yuriy Mikhailovich 1930- *IntWW 93*
Church, Alonzo 1903- *WhoWest 94*
Church, Benjamin 1734-c. 1777 *WhAmRev*
Church, Benjamin 1734-1778 *AmRev*
Church, Billy d1942 *WhoHol 92*
Church, Brooks Davis 1918- *WhAm 10*
Church, C. Howard 1904- *WhoAm 94, WhoAmA 93*
Church, Dale Walker 1939- *WhoAm 94, WhoAmL 94*
Church, Elva Mae 1931- *WhoMW 93*
Church, Ernest Elliott 1897- *WhAm 10*
Church, Esme d1972 *WhoHol 92*
Church, Eugene Lent 1925- *WhoAm 94*
Church, F(rank) Forrester, (IV) 1948- *WrDr 94*
Church, Frank Forrester 1948- *WhoAm 94*
Church, Fred d1936 *WhoHol 92*
Church, Frederick E. 1826-1900 *WhoAmA 93N*
Church, Frederick Edwin 1826-1900 *AmCulL*
Church, G. Russell *WhoHisp 94*
Church, George Millord 1924- *WhoFI 94*
Church, Herbert Stephen, Jr. 1920- *WhoAm 94*
Church, Ian David 1941- *Who 94*
Church, Irene Zaboly 1947- *WhoAm 94, WhoMW 93*
Church, James Anthony *Who 94*
Church, Jay Kay 1927- *WhoMW 93*
Church, John Carver 1929- *Who 94*
Church, John Franklin, Jr. 1936- *WhoAm 94*
Church, John H. 1892-1953 *HisDcKW*
Church, John I. *DrAPF 93*
Church, John Trammell 1917- *WhoAm 94, WhoAmP 93*
Church, Kern Everidge 1926- *WhoScEn 94*
Church, Lorene Kemmerer 1929- *WhoWest 94*
Church, Martha Eleanor 1930- *WhoAm 94*
Church, Maude 1949- *WhoAmA 93*
Church, Philip Throop 1931- *WhoAm 94*
Church, Randolph Warner, Jr. 1934- *WhoAm 94, WhoAmL 94*
Church, Richard Dwight 1936- *WhoScEn 94*
Church, Robert Max, Jr. 1949- *WhoScEn 94*
Church, Robert T., Sr. 1909- *WhoBlA 94*
Church, Ronald James H. *Who 94*
Church, Russell Miller 1930- *WhoAm 94*
Church, Ruth Joan 1927- *WhoAmP 93*
Church, Sandra 1938- *WhoHol 92*
Church, Thomas Trowbridge 1919- *WhoAm 94*
Church, Tony 1930- *Who 94, WhoHol 92*
Church, Walter, Sr. *WhoAmP 93*
Churcher, John Bryan 1905- *Who 94*
Churchhouse, Robert Francis 1927- *Who 94*
Churchill *Who 94*
Churchill, Viscount 1934- *Who 94*
Churchill, Allen Delos 1921- *WhoAmL 94*
Churchill, Berton d1940 *WhoHol 92*
Churchill, Bonnie Jeane 1937- *WhoWest 94*
Churchill, Caryl 1938- *BlmGEL, BlmGWL, ConDr 93, IntDcT 2 [port], IntWW 93, Who 94, WrDr 94*
Churchill, Charles 1731-1764 *BlmGEL*
Churchill, Daniel Wayne 1947- *WhoFI 94*
Churchill, David James 1945- *WhoAmP 93*
Churchill, Diana 1913- *WhoHol 92*
Churchill, Diana (Josephine) 1913- *Who 94*
Churchill, Diane 1941- *WhoAmA 93*
Churchill, Donald 1930- *WhoHol 92*
Churchill, E. Richard 1937- *WrDr 94*
Churchill, Elizabeth 1922- *WrDr 94*
Churchill, James Allen 1935- *WhoAm 94*
Churchill, James Paul 1924- *WhoAm 94, WhoAmL 94, WhoMW 93*
Churchill, Jeanette 1854-1921 *DcNaB MP*
Churchill, John 1650-1722 *HisWorL [port]*
Churchill, Joseph Lacy 1944- *WhoAmL 94*
Churchill, Joyce *EncSF 93*
Churchill, Justina Anne 1963- *WhoMW 93*
Churchill, Larry Raymond 1945- *WhoAm 94*
Churchill, Marguerite 1909- *WhoHol 92*
Churchill, Mary Carey *WhoAm 94*
Churchill, Michael 1939- *WhoAmL 94*
Churchill, Neil Center 1927- *WhoAm 94*
Churchill, Odette Maria Celine *IntWW 93*
Churchill, R(eginald) C(harles) 1916- *EncSF 93*
Churchill, Ralph John 1944- *WhoScEn 94*
Churchill, Randolph Frederick Edward Spencer- 1911-1968 *DcNaB MP*
Churchill, Robert Wilson 1947- *WhoMW 93*
Churchill, Robert Winston 1947- *WhoAmP 93*
Churchill, Sarah d1982 *WhoHol 92*
Churchill, Sharon Anne-Kernicky 1957- *WhoScEn 94*
Churchill, Steven W. 1963- *WhoAmP 93*
Churchill, Steven Wayne 1963- *WhoMW 93*
Churchill, Stuart Winston 1920- *WhoAm 94*
Churchill, Thomas *DrAPF 93*
Churchill, Thomas John 1961- *WhoMW 93*
Churchill, Ward 1947- *WrDr 94*
Churchill, William DeLee 1919- *WhoWest 94*
Churchill, William Lloyd 1929- *WhoAmP 93*
Churchill, Winston d1965 *WhoHol 92*
Churchill, Winston 1874-1965 *HisWorL [port], HisDcKW*
Churchill, Winston John 1940- *WhoAm 94*
Churchill, Winston S(pencer) 1940- *WrDr 94*
Churchill, Winston Spencer 1940- *Who 94*
Churchill-Lentz, Carla K. 1959- *WhoMW 93*
Churchland, Paul M. 1942- *WrDr 94*
Churchman, David Alan 1938- *WhoWest 94*
Churchward, George Jackson 1857-1933 *DcNaB MP*
Churchward, L(loyd) G(ordon) 1919- *WrDr 94*
Churchwell, Caesar Alfred 1932- *WhoBlA 94*
Churchwell, Charles Darrett 1926- *WhoAm 94, WhoBlA 94*
Churchwell, Edward Bruce 1940- *WhoAm 94, WhoScEn 94*
Churchyard, Thomas 1520?-1604 *DcLB 132*
Churg, Jacob 1910- *WhoAm 94, WhoScEn 94*
Churikova, Inna Mikhailovna 1945- *IntWW 93*
Churkin, Vitaly Ivanovich 1952- *IntWW 93, LoBiDrD*
Churston, Baron 1934- *Who 94*
Churuti, Susan Hamilton 1954- *WhoAmL 94*
Chusid, Martin 1925- *NewGrDO*
Chusid, Michael Joseph 1944- *WhoMW 93*
Chusid, Michael Thomas 1952- *WhoScEn 94*
Chustz, J. Steve 1948- *WhoAmL 94*
Chute, Carolyn 1947- *WrDr 94*
Chute, Harold LeRoy 1921- *WhoFI 94*
Chute, John 1701-1776 *DcNaB MP*
Chute, Marchette 1909- *Who 94, WhoAm 94, WrDr 94*
Chute, Marchette (Gaylord) 1909- *TwCYAW*
Chute, Phillip Bruce 1938- *WhoWest 94*
Chute, Robert Maurice 1926- *IntWW 93, WhoAm 94*
Chu Thompson, Jane 1957- *WhoMW 93*
Chutich, Margaret Helen 1958- *WhoAmL 94*
Chutjian, Seta Leonie *WhoAmA 93*
Chutkow, Jerry Grant 1933- *WhoAm 94*
Chu Tunan 1899- *IntWW 93, WhoPRCh 91 [port]*
Chuyman, Howard d1978 *WhoHol 92*
Chu Zhuang 1928- *WhoPRCh 91 [port]*
Chvala, Charles Joseph 1954- *WhoAmP 93*
Chwalek, Adele Ruth 1939- *WhoAm 94*
Chwast, Seymour 1931- *WhoAm 94, WhoAmA 93*
Chwat, John 1950- *WhoAmP 93*
Chyba, Christopher F. 1959- *WhoWest 94*
Chylinski-Polubinski, Roger 1945- *WhoAm 94*
Chyngyshev, Tursunbek 1942- *LoBiDrD*
Chynoweth, Alan Gerald 1927- *IntWW 93, WhoAm 94, WhoScEn 94*
Chynoweth, David Boyd 1940- *Who 94*
Chynoweth, Neville James 1922- *Who 94*
Chytil, Frank 1924- *WhoAm 94*
Chyu, Jih-Jiang 1935- *WhoScEn 94*
Chyung, Chi Han 1933- *WhoFI 94*
Chyung, Dong Hak 1937- *WhoAsA 94*
Cia, Manuel Lopez 1937- *WhoHisp 94*
Ciabattari, Jane *DrAPF 93*
Ciaccio, Leonard Louis 1924- *WhoScEn 94*
Cialente, Fausta Terni 1898- *BlmGWL*
Cialente, Renato d1943 *WhoHol 92*
Cialli, Rinaldo fl. 1684-1698 *NewGrDO*
Cialone, Joseph A., II 1944- *WhoAmL 94*
Ciampa, Dan 1946- *WhoAm 94*
Ciampa, Vincent Paul *WhoAmP 93*
Ciampaglia, Carlo 1891-1975 *WhoAmA 93N*
Ciampi, Carlo Azeglio 1920- *IntWW 93*
Ciampi, Francesco c. 1690-1764? *NewGrDO*
Ciampi, Maria Louise 1959- *WhoAmL 94*
Ciampi, Vincenzo (Legrenzio) 1719?-1762 *NewGrDO*
Cianchette, Alton E. *WhoAmP 93*
Cianci, Vincent Albert 1941- *WhoAmP 93*
Cianci, Vincent Albert, Jr. 1941- *WhoAm 94*
Ciancio, June (Kirkpatrick) 1920- *WhoAmA 93*
Ciancio, Sebastian Gene 1937- *WhoAm 94*
Cianciolo, Patricia Jean 1929- *WhoMW 93*
Cianfoni, Emilio 1946- *WhoAmA 93*
Ciani, Alfred Joseph 1946- *WhoMW 93*
Ciannella, Giuliano 1943- *NewGrDO*
Ciannelli, Alma d1968 *WhoHol 92*
Ciannelli, Eduardo d1969 *WhoHol 92*
Ciano, Mario C. 1942- *WhoAmL 94*
Ciappenelli, Donald John 1943- *WhoScEn 94*
Ciappi, Mario Luigi 1909- *IntWW 93*
Ciaramitaro, Nick 1951- *WhoAmP 93*
Ciardiello, Joseph G. 1953- *WhoAmA 93*
Ciarlillo, Marjorie Ann 1940- *WhoMW 93*
Ciarlone, Anthony Michael 1929- *WhoAmP 93*
Ciarrochi, Ray *WhoAmA 93*
Ciatteo, Carmen Thomas 1921- *WhoMW 93*
Ciavarro, Massimo *WhoHol 92*
Cibber, Colley 1671-1757 *BlmGEL, IntDcT 2 [port]*
Cibber, Katherine c. 1669-1734 *BlmGEL*
Cibber, Susanna Maria 1714-1766 *BlmGEL, NewGrDO*
Cibber, Theophilus 1703-1758 *BlmGEL*
Cibes, William Joseph, Jr. 1943- *WhoAmP 93*
Cibilis Viana, Marcia Maria d'Avila 1949- *WhoWomW 91*
Cibischino, Ray 1954- *WhoFI 94*
Cicansky, Victor 1935- *WhoAmA 93*
Cicarella, Thomas A. 1949- *WhoAmL 94*
Ciccarelli, Salvatore 1941- *WhoAmP 93*
Ciccarone, Richard Anthony 1952- *WhoAm 94*
Ciccerelli, Chiara fl. 1796-1808 *NewGrDO*

Cicchetti, Mark Anthony 1956- *WhoFI 94*
Cicciarelli, James Carl 1947- *WhoAm 94, WhoWest 94*
Ciccimarra, Giuseppe 1790-1836 *NewGrDO*
Ciccolino *NewGrDO*
Ciccone, Amy Navratil 1950- *WhoAmA 93*
Ciccone, Anne Panepinto 1943- *WhoAm 94*
Ciccone, Francis Anthony 1949- *WhoFI 94*
Ciccone, J. Richard 1943- *WhoAm 94*
Ciccone, Madonna Louise Veronica 1958- *WhoAm 94*
Ciccone, Peter M. 1942- *WhoFI 94*
Ciccone, Richard 1940- *WhoMW 93*
Cicconi, James William 1952- *WhoAm 94, WhoAmL 94, WhoAmP 93*
Ciccotelli, Patricia Ann 1942- *WhoMW 93*
Cicellis, Kay 1926- *EncSF 93, WrDr 94*
Ciceri, Pierre-Luc-Charles 1782-1868 *NewGrDO*
Cicero 106BC-43BC *HisWorL [port]*
Cicero, Carmen L. *WhoAmA 93*
Cicero, Frank, Jr. 1935- *WhoAm 94, WhoAmL 94*
Cicero, Marcus Tullius 106BC-43BC *BlmGEL, EncEth*
Cicet, Donald James 1940- *WhoAmL 94, WhoFI 94*
Cichoke, Anthony Joseph, Jr. 1931- *WhoWest 94*
Cichon, Joanne M. 1959- *WhoIns 94*
Cichy, Martin d1962 *WhoHol 92*
Cicilline, J. Clement 1940- *WhoAmP 93*
Cicilline, Stephen E. 1942- *WhoAmP 93*
Cicilline, Stephen Edward 1942- *WhoAmL 94*
Cicirelli, Victor George 1926- *WhoAm 94*
Cicognini, Giacinto Andrea 1606-c. 1650 *NewGrDO*
Cid, A. Louis 1923- *WhoHisp 94*
Cidoncha, Carlos Saiz *EncSF 93*
Cidoni, Jomar *WhoHol 92*
Cid Perez, José 1906- *WhoHisp 94*
Cidre, Cynthia 1957- *WhoHisp 94*
Ciechanover, Joseph 1933- *WhoAm 94*
Ciee, Grace 1961- *BlkWr 2, ConAu 140*
Cielo, William Clyde, Jr. 1955- *WhoFI 94*
Ciemniewski, Jerzy 1939- *IntWW 93*
Cienciala, Anna Maria 1929- *WhoMW 93*
Ciereszko, Leon Stanley 1917- *WhoAm 94, WhoScEn 94*
Cierkes, Vincent d1979 *WhoHol 92*
Ciernia, James Richard 1933- *WhoWest 94*
Ciesielski, Thomas Gregory 1949- *WhoMW 93*
Ciesinski, Katherine 1950- *NewGrDO*
Ciesinski, Kristine (Frances) 1952- *NewGrDO*
Ciesla, Andrew R. 1953- *WhoAmP 93*
Cieslak, Arthur Kazimer 1915- *WhoAm 94*
Cieslinski, L. John *DrAPF 93*
Cifariello, Antonio d1968 *WhoHol 92*
Cifelli, John Louis 1923- *WhoAm 94*
Cifolelli, Alberta 1931- *WhoAmA 93*
Cifuentes, Arturo Ovalle 1953- *WhoScEn 94*
Cifuentes, Luis Arturo 1956- *WhoHisp 94*
Cigna, Gina 1900- *NewGrDO*
Cigna-Santi, Vittorio Amedeo c. 1730-1795? *NewGrDO*
Cigoli 1559-1613 *NewGrDO*
Cigoli, Emilio d1980 *WhoHol 92*
Cihlarz, Wolfgang 1954- *IntWW 93*
Cikker, Jan 1911-1989 *NewGrDO*
Cikovsky, Nicolai 1894-1984 *WhoAmA 93N*
Cikovsky, Nicolai, Jr. 1933- *WhoAm 94, WhoAmA 93*
Cilea, Francesco 1866-1950 *NewGrDO*
Cilek, James Edwin 1952- *WhoScEn 94*
Cilella, Salvatore G., Jr. 1941- *WhoAmA 93*
Cilella, Salvatore George, Jr. 1941- *WhoAm 94*
Cilento, Diane 1933- *WhoHol 92*
Cilento, Diane 1934- *IntMPA 94*
Cillario, Carlo Felice 1915- *NewGrDO*
Cilley, Joseph 1735-1799 *WhAmRev*
Cillie, Petrus Johannes 1917- *IntWW 93*
Cilliers, Jana *WhoHol 92*
Cillo, Paul A. 1953- *WhoAmP 93*
Cilz, Douglas Arthur 1949- *WhoAmL 94*
Cima, Daniel F. 1951- *WhoHisp 94*
Cima, Laura 1942- *WhoWomW 91*
Cimador, Giambattista 1761-1805 *NewGrDO*
Cimara, Luigi d1962 *WhoHol 92*
Cimarosa, Domenico 1749-1801 *NewGrDO*
Cimatti, Giovanni Ermanno 1945- *WhoScEn 94*
Cimbala, Stephen J. 1943- *ConAu 142*
Cimbalo, Robert W. *WhoAmA 93*
Cimbleris, Borisas 1923- *WhoScEn 94*
Ciment, Jill *DrAPF 93*
Ciminello, Emanuel, Jr. *WhoHisp 94*
Cimini, Anthony J. 1922- *WhoAmP 93*
Cimini, Joseph Fedele 1948- *WhoAm 94, WhoAmL 94*
Cimino, Anthony John 1947- *WhoAmP 93*
Cimino, James Ernest 1928- *WhoAm 94*
Cimino, Joseph Anthony 1934- *WhoAm 94*
Cimino, Leonardo *WhoHol 92*
Cimino, Michael 1943- *IntMPA 94, IntWW 93, WrDr 94*
Cimino, Michael 1948- *WhoAm 94*
Cimino, Richard Dennis 1947- *WhoAmL 94*
Cimino, Salvatore P. 1933- *WhoAmP 93*
Cimino, Thomas 1935- *WhoIns 94*
Cimochowicz, Diane Marie 1955- *WhoWest 94*
Cimonetti, William J. 1931- *WhoAmP 93*
Cimpl, Dennis Richard 1950- *WhoAmL 94*
Cimrmancic, Mary Ann 1956- *WhoMW 93*
Cinader, Bernhard 1919- *IntWW 93, WhoAm 94*
Cinciotta, Linda Ann 1943- *WhoAmL 94*
Cinelli, Ferdinando Oreste Federico 1916- *WhoMW 93*
Cinelli, Giovanna M. 1959- *WhoAmL 94*
Cing, David M. *WhoAmP 93*
Cingolani, Judith 1938- *WhoMW 93*
Cink, James Henry 1959- *WhoScEn 94*
Cinlar, Erhan 1941- *WhoAm 94*
Cinotti, Alfonse Anthony 1923- *WhoAm 94*
Cinque c. 1814-c. 1879 *HisWorL [port]*
Cinquegrana, Americo Ralph 1942- *WhoAmL 94*
Cinquemani, Joseph Robert 1952- *WhoFI 94*
Cinquevalli, Paul d1918 *WhoHol 92*
Cinti-Damoreau, Laure (Cinthie) 1801-1863 *NewGrDO [port]*
Cintrón, Benigno, Jr. 1955- *WhoHisp 94*
Cintron, Charles 1936- *WhoHisp 94*
Cintron, Emma V. 1926- *WhoHisp 94*
Cintron, Guillermo B. 1942- *WhoHisp 94*
Cintron, Joseph M. 1921- *WhoAmA 93*
Cintron, Martin 1948- *WhoHisp 94*
Cintron, Nitza Margarita *WhoHisp 94*
Cintron-Budet, Nancy *WhoHisp 94*
Cintron de Frias, Marlene 1951- *WhoHisp 94*
Cintrón-García, Angel *WhoHisp 94*
Cioccio, Ellen Lacey 1935- *WhoMW 93*
Ciochon, Russell Lynn 1948- *WhoMW 93*
Cioffi, Charles *WhoHol 92*
Cioffi, Michael Lawrence 1953- *WhoAmL 94*
Cioffi, Ronald Ernest 1955- *WhoFI 94*
Cioffi-Revilla, Claudio 1951- *WhoWest 94*
Ciolli, Augusta d1967 *WhoHol 92*
Cion, Judith Ann 1943- *WhoAm 94, WhoAmL 94, WhoFI 94*
Cion, Richard M. 1943- *WhoAm 94, WhoFI 94*
Ciosek, Nancy Carol 1942- *WhoMW 93*
Ciosek, Stanislaw 1939- *IntWW 93*
Ciotti, Eugene Barney 1928- *WhoFI 94*
Cipa, Walter Johannes 1928- *IntWW 93*
Cipale, Joseph Michael 1958- *WhoScEn 94*
Ciparick, Carmen Beauchamp *WhoHisp 94*
Cipes, Arianne Ulmer 1937- *IntMPA 94*
Cipes, Jay H. 1928- *IntMPA 94*
Ciplijauskaite, Birute 1929- *WhoAm 94*
Cipolla, Carlo M. 1922- *WrDr 94*
Cipollone, Anthony Dominic 1939- *WhoAmL 94*
Cipparone, Josephine Magnino 1931- *WhoMW 93*
Ciprandi, Ercole d1790? *NewGrDO*
Cipriani, Frank Anthony 1933- *WhoAm 94*
Cipriani, Harriet Emily *WhoAmP 93*
Cipriano, Irene P. 1942- *WhoHisp 94*
Cipriano, Michael R. 1942- *WhoAmA 93*
Cipriano, Patricia Ann 1946- *WhoWest 94*
Cirafesi, Robert J. 1942- *WhoAm 94*
Cirando, John Anthony 1942- *WhoAmL 94*
Ciraulo, Stephen Joseph 1960- *WhoScEn 94*
Circeo, Louis Joseph, Jr. 1934- *WhoAm 94*
Circle, Lilias Wagner 1928- *WhoMW 93*
Circo, Carl J. 1949- *WhoAmL 94*
Cire, Richard Camile 1933- *WhoWest 94*
Cirello, John 1943- *WhoFI 94*
Cirese, Robert Charles 1938- *WhoFI 94*
Ciresi, Anthony David 1907- *WhAm 10*
Ciresi, Michael Vincent 1946- *WhoAm 94, WhoAmL 94*
Ciriacks, Jean Lorraine 1925- *WhoAmP 93*
Ciriani, Henri 1936- *IntWW 93*
Cirici, Cristian 1941- *IntWW 93*
Cirillo, Francesco 1623-1667? *NewGrDO*
Cirillo, Michael d1968 *WhoHol 92*
Cirillo, Richard Allan 1951- *WhoAm 94, WhoAmL 94*
Cirillo, Vincent A. 1927- *WhoAmL 94*
Cirino, Leonard John *DrAPF 93*
Cirker, Hayward 1917- *IntWW 93, WhoAm 94*
Cirolia, Donna Mary 1958- *WhoMW 93*
Cirone, Anthony James 1941- *WhoAm 94*
Ciruelas, Dominador Benedicto 1940- *WhoAm 94*
Ciruli, Floyd 1946- *WhoAmP 93*
Ciruti, Joan Estelle 1930- *WhoAm 94*
Ciry, Michel 1919- *IntWW 93*
Cis, Mark Michael 1950- *WhoIns 94*
Cisko, George Joseph, Jr. 1958- *WhoScEn 94*
Cisky, Jon 1941- *WhoAmP 93*
Cisler, Dennis Keith 1949- *WhoIns 94*
Cisler, Theresa Ann 1951- *WhoAm 94*
Cisler, Walker Lee 1897- *WhAm 10*
Cislo, Donald Michael 1935- *WhoAmL 94*
Cisneros, Antonio 1942- *ConWorW 93*
Cisneros, Arnoldo 1951- *WhoHisp 94*
Cisneros, Carlos R. *WhoAmP 93, WhoHisp 94*
Cisneros, Connie P. *WhoHisp 94*
Cisneros, Eleonora de 1878-1934 *NewGrDO*
Cisneros, Evelyn 1955- *WhoAm 94, WhoHisp 94*
Cisneros, Florencio Garcia *WhoAmA 93*
Cisneros, Frank G. 1942- *WhoHisp 94*
Cisneros, Henry 1947- *IntWW 93*
Cisneros, Henry G. *NewYTBS 93 [port]*
Cisneros, Henry G. 1947- *CngDr 93, WhoAm 94*
Cisneros, Henry Gabriel 1947- *WhoAmP 93, WhoHisp 94*
Cisneros, James M. 1951- *WhoHisp 94*
Cisneros, Joe Alvarado 1935- *WhoHisp 94*
Cisneros, Marc Anthony 1939- *WhoAm 94*
Cisneros, Rafael 1934- *WhoHisp 94*
Cisneros, Sandra *DrAPF 93, NewYTBS 93 [port]*
Cisneros, Sandra 1954- *HispLC [port], TwCYAW, WhoHisp 94*
Cisneros, Sandra 1955- *BlmGWL*
Cisneros de Perez, Imelda 1946- *WhoWomW 91*
Cisney, Marcella d1989 *WhoHol 92*
Cissell, James Charles 1940- *WhoAm 94, WhoAmL 94*
Cissik, John Henry 1943- *WhoAm 94*
Cissoko, Alioune Badara 1952- *WhoBlA 94*
Cissoko, Filifing 1936- *IntWW 93*
Cist, Charles 1738-1805 *WhAmRev*
Ciszewski, Bohdan 1922- *IntWW 93*
Cita, Maria 1922- *WhoScEn 94*
Citardi, Mattio H. 1966- *WhoScEn 94*
Citarella, Victor Thomas 1951- *Who 94*
Citarelli, Michael Robert 1957- *WhoFI 94*
Citati, Pietro 1930- *ConAu 43NR*
Citino, David *DrAPF 93*
Citran, Roberto *WhoHol 92*
Citrin, Phillip Marshall 1931- *WhoAm 94*
Citrin, Willie 1947- *WhoWest 94*
Citrine, Baron 1914- *Who 94*
Citro, Angelo T. *WhoAmP 93*
Citroen, Charles Louis 1939- *WhoScEn 94*
Citron, Beatrice Sally 1929- *WhoAmL 94*
Citron, David Sanford 1920- *WhoAm 94*
Citron, Diane 1953- *WhoAm 94*
Citron, Harvey Lewis 1942- *WhoAmA 93*
Citron, M. Sloane 1956- *WhoWest 94*
Citron, Minna Wright 1896-1991 *WhoAmA 93N*
Citron, Richard Ira 1944- *WhoAm 94*
Cittafino, Ricardo *ConAu 42NR*
Citti, Christine *WhoHol 92*
Citti, Franco *WhoHol 92*
Ciuca, Gary Eugene 1950- *WhoFI 94*
Ciuha, Joze 1924- *IntWW 93*
Ciulei, Liviu 1923- *IntWW 93*
Ciullo, Rosemary *WhoMW 93*
Ciurczak, Alexis 1950- *WhoAm 94*
Civale, Biagio A. 1935- *WhoAmA 93*
Civello, Anthony Ned 1944- *WhoFI 94*
Civera, Mario J., Jr. 1946- *WhoAmP 93*
Civiletti, Benjamin R. 1935- *IntWW 93, WhoAm 94, WhoAmL 94*
Civins, Jeff 1946- *WhoAmL 94*
Civish, Gayle Ann 1948- *WhoScEn 94*
Civitello, John Patrick 1939- *WhoAmA 93*
Civitello, Robert Charles 1947- *WhoWest 94*
Civitico, Bruno 1942- *WhoAmA 93*
Ciwang Zunmei *WhoPRCh 91*
Cixi 1835-1908 *HisWorL [port]*
Cixous, Helene 1937- *ConWorW 93, IntWW 93*
Cixous, Helene 1938- *BlmGWL*
Ci Yungui *WhoPRCh 91*
Cizek, David John 1959- *WhoMW 93*
Cizek, John Gary 1948- *WhoScEn 94*
Cizewski, Jolie Antonia 1951- *WhoScEn 94*
Cizik, Robert 1931- *IntWW 93, WhoAm 94, WhoFI 94*
Cizza, John Anthony 1952- *WhoFI 94, WhoMW 93*
Claassen, Sherida Dill 1948- *WhoMW 93*
Claassen, Stephen Charles 1950- *WhoFI 94*
Claassen, Walter Marshall 1943- *WhoFI 94, WhoMW 93*
Clabaugh, Elmer Eugene, Jr. 1927- *WhoAmL 94, WhoFI 94, WhoWest 94*
Clabaugh, Henry Edward Doyle 1942- *WhoMW 93*
Clabby, William Robert 1931- *WhoAm 94*
Clabes, Judith Grisham 1945- *WhoAm 94*
Claborn, David Warren 1952- *WhoMW 93*
Clabots, Joseph Paul 1951- *WhoWest 94*
Clack, Charles Gilbert 1937- *WhoAmP 93*
Clack, Doris H. 1928- *WhoBlA 94*
Clack, Floyd 1940- *WhoAmP 93, WhoBlA 94*
Clack, Jerry 1926- *WhoAm 94*
Clack, Leigh Langston 1956- *WhoAmL 94*
Clack, R. C. 1938- *WhoBlA 94*
Clacy, Ellen *BlmGWL*
Claes, August Joseph 1943- *WhoFI 94*
Claes, Daniel John 1931- *WhoAm 94, WhoFI 94, WhoScEn 94, WhoWest 94*
Claes, Willy 1938- *IntWW 93*
Claeson, Robert W. 1943- *WhoAmL 94*
Claeson, Tord Claes 1938- *IntWW 93*
Claessens, Pierre 1939- *WhoScEn 94*
Claeys, Richard G. *WhoWest 94*
Claffey, Stephen Allen 1945- *WhoAm 94, WhoAmL 94*
Clafin, Lola White *DrAPF 93*
Claflin, Arthur Cary 1950- *WhoAm 94*
Claflin, (Alan) Avery 1898-1979 *NewGrDO*
Claflin, Douglas Morgan 1963- *WhoWest 94*
Claflin, Robert Malden 1921- *WhoAm 94*
Claflin, Tennessee Celeste 1845-1923 *AmSocL*
Claflin Woodhull, Victoria 1838-1927 *WomPubS*
Clagett, Arthur Frank, Jr. 1916- *WhoAm 94, WhoScEn 94*
Clagett, Brice McAdoo 1933- *WhoAm 94*
Clagett, Gordon Jell 1945- *WhoFI 94*
Clagett, John (Henry) 1916- *EncSF 93*
Clagett, Marshall 1916- *WhoAm 94*
Clagett, Oscar Theron 1908-1990 *WhAm 10*
Clagett, William H., IV 1938- *WhoAm 94*
Claghorn, George 1748-1824 *WhAmRev*
Clague, Christopher K. 1938- *ConAu 141*
Clague, Joan 1931- *Who 94*
Clague, John Rogers 1928- *WhoAmA 93*
Clague, William Donald 1920- *WhoWest 94*
Claiborn, Stephen Allan 1948- *WhoAm 94*
Claiborne, Craig 1920- *WhoAm 94, WrDr 94*
Claiborne, Earl Ramsey 1921- *WhoBlA 94*
Claiborne, Jarvis Jerome 1957- *WhoAmL 94*
Claiborne, Jimmy David 1961- *WhoScEn 94*
Claiborne, Liz 1929- *WhoAm 94*
Claiborne, Lloyd R. 1936- *WhoBlA 94*
Claiborne, Sybil *DrAPF 93*
Claiborne, Sybil 1923-1992 *ConAu 140*
Claiborne, Vernal 1946- *WhoBlA 94*
Clair, Areatha G. 1931- *WhoBlA 94*
Clair, Carolyn Green 1907- *WhoAm 94*
Clair, Denise d1970 *WhoHol 92*
Clair, Ethlyne 1908- *WhoHol 92*
Clair, Louis Serge 1940- *IntWW 93*
Clair, Rene d1981 *WhoHol 92*
Clair, Richard d1988 *WhoHol 92*
Clair, Theodore Nat 1929- *WhoWest 94*
Claire, Anne Marie Arancibia 1948- *WhoWest 94*
Claire, Bernice 1911- *WhoHol 92*
Claire, Cyrielle 1956- *WhoHol 92*
Claire, Evelyn *WrDr 94*
Claire, Fred *WhoWest 94*
Claire, Gertrude d1928 *WhoHol 92*
Claire, Helen d1974 *WhoHol 92*
Claire, Imogen *WhoHol 92*
Claire, Ina d1985 *WhoHol 92*
Claire, Ludi d1990 *WhoHol 92*
Claire, Marion *WhoHol 92*
Claire, Mavis 1916- *WhoHol 92*
Claire, Thomas Andrew 1951- *WhoAm 94, WhoFI 94*
Claire, William *DrAPF 93*
Clairville 1811-1879 *NewGrDO*
Claitor, Daniel Albert 1961- *WhoAmL 94*
Clama, Renee 1908- *WhoHol 92*
Clamageran, Alice Germaine Suzanne 1906- *Who 94*
Clamar, Aphrodite J. 1933- *WhoAm 94*

Clampett, Bob 1915?-1985 *IntDcF 2-4 [port]*
Clampitt, Amy *DrAPF 93*
Clampitt, Amy 1920- *WrDr 94*
Clampitt, Amy Kathleen 1920- *WhoAm 94*
Clampitt, Otis Clinton, Jr. 1947- *WhoScEn 94*
Clanagan, Mazzetta Price 1920- *WhoBlA 94*
Clancarty, Earl of 1911- *Who 94*
Clancey, Delores Ann 1930- *WhoIns 94*
Clanchy, Joan Lesley 1939- *Who 94*
Clancy, Donna L. 1943- *WhoIns 94*
Clancy, Edward Bede *Who 94*
Clancy, Edward Bede 1923- *IntWW 93*
Clancy, Edward J., Jr. *WhoAmP 93*
Clancy, Eric Robert 1961- *WhoFI 94*
Clancy, John d1981 *WhoAmA 93N*
Clancy, John Patrick 1942- *WhoFI 94*
Clancy, Joseph Howard 1939- *WhoAmL 94*
Clancy, Joseph Patrick 1931- *WhoAm 94*
Clancy, Laurie 1942- *WrDr 94*
Clancy, Louis John 1946- *WhoAm 94*
Clancy, Magalene Aldoshia 1938- *WhoBlA 94*
Clancy, Michael James 1946- *WhoAmL 94*
Clancy, Patrick 1941- *WhoAmA 93*
Clancy, Sam 1958- *WhoBlA 94*
Clancy, Terrence Patrick 1955- *WhoMW 93*
Clancy, Thomas Gerald 1934- *WhoAm 94*
Clancy, Thomas H. 1923- *WrDr 94*
Clancy, Thomas Joseph 1946- *WhoScEn 94*
Clancy, Thomas L. 1947- *WhoAm 94*
Clancy, Tom d1990 *WhoHol 92*
Clancy, Tom 1947- *IntWW 93, WrDr 94*
Clanfield, Viscount 1976- *Who 94*
Clanmorris, Baron 1937- *Who 94*
Clanon, Thomas Lawrence 1929- *WhoAm 94*
Clanricarde, Marquess of 1802-1874 *DcNaB MP*
Clanton, Albert Phil 1946- *WhoMW 93*
Clanton, David Albert 1944- *WhoAmP 93*
Clanton, Jimmy 1940- *WhoHol 92*
Clanton, Lemuel Jacque 1931- *WhoBlA 94*
Clanton, Ralph 1914- *WhoHol 92*
Clanvow, John c. 1341-1391 *DcNaB MP*
Clanvowe, John 1341-1391 *BlmGEL*
Clanwilliam, Earl of 1919- *Who 94*
Clapham, Brian Ralph 1913- *Who 94*
Clapham, Charlie d1959 *WhoHol 92*
Clapham, Christopher 1941- *WrDr 94*
Clapham, John 1908- *WrDr 94*
Clapham, Leonard d1963 *WhoHol 92*
Clapham, Michael 1943- *Who 94*
Clapham, Michael (John Sinclair) 1912- *Who 94*
Clapham, Michael John Sinclair 1912- *IntWW 93*
Clapham, Peter Brian 1940- *Who 94*
Clapham, Wentworth Beggs, Jr. 1942- *WhoMW 93*
Clapham, William Montgomery 1948- *WhoScEn 94*
Clapisson, (Antonin) Louis 1808-1866 *NewGrDO*
Claplanhoo, Edward E. 1928- *WhoAmP 93*
Clapman, Peter C. 1936- *WhoIns 94*
Clapman, Peter Carlyle 1936- *WhoAm 94, WhoAmL 94*
Clapp, Allen Linville 1943- *WhoFI 94*
Clapp, Beverly Booker 1954- *WhoScEn 94*
Clapp, Charles E., II 1923- *CngDr 93, WhoAm 94, WhoAmL 94*
Clapp, Charles Edward 1930- *WhoAm 94, WhoMW 93*
Clapp, Elinor 1925- *WhoWomW 91*
Clapp, Elinor J. 1925- *WhoAmP 93*
Clapp, Eugene Howard, II 1913- *WhoAm 94*
Clapp, Gayle Laurene *WhoMW 93*
Clapp, Gordan *WhoHol 92*
Clapp, James Brennan 1948- *WhoAmL 94*
Clapp, James Ford, Jr. 1908- *WhoAm 94*
Clapp, Joseph Mark 1936- *WhoAm 94, WhoFI 94*
Clapp, Laurel Rebecca 1944- *WhoAmL 94*
Clapp, Lloyd *WhoAmP 93*
Clapp, Marcus R. 1942- *WhoAmL 94*
Clapp, Maude Caroline Ede 1876-1960 *WhoAmA 93N*
Clapp, Michael Cecil 1932- *Who 94*
Clapp, Patricia 1912- *SmATA 74 [port], TwCYAW, WrDr 94*
Clapp, Roger Alvin 1909- *WhoAm 94*
Clapp, Roger Howland 1928- *WhoAm 94, WhoFI 94*
Clappe, Louise Amelia Knapp Smith 1819-1906 *BlmGWL*
Clapper, George Raymond 1931- *WhoFI 94*
Clapper, Lyle Nielsen 1941- *WhoAm 94*
Clapper, Marie Anne 1942- *WhoAm 94*
Clapper, Samuel David 1946- *WhoAmL 94*
Clapperton, Hugh 1788-1827 *WhWE [port]*
Clappison, (William) James 1956- *Who 94*
Clapprood, Marjorie A. O'Neill *WhoAmP 93*
Claps, Joseph Michael 1948- *WhoAmL 94*
Clapsaddle, Jerry 1941- *WhoAmA 93*
Clapton, Eric 1945- *ConMus 11 [port], IntWW 93, News 93-3 [port], WhoAm 94*
See Also Yardbirds, The *ConMus 10*
Claramunt, Javier Fernando 1960- *WhoWest 94*
Clardy, Thelma Sanders 1955- *WhoAmL 94*
Clardy, Virginia Mae 1923- *WhoAmP 93*
Clardy, William J. 1935- *WhoBlA 94*
Clare, Anthony Ward 1942- *Who 94*
Clare, David Ross 1925- *IntWW 93*
Clare, Ellen 1923- *WrDr 94*
Clare, George 1930- *WhoFI 94, WhoScEn 94*
Clare, George (Peter) 1920- *WrDr 94*
Clare, Helen 1921- *WrDr 94*
Clare, Herbert Mitchell N. *Who 94*
Clare, James Paley S. *Who 94*
Clare, John 1793-1864 *BlmGEL*
Clare, John Charles 1950- *Who 94*
Clare, Josephine *DrAPF 93*
Clare, Madelyn d1975 *WhoHol 92*
Clare, Mary d1970 *WhoHol 92*
Clare, Mildred *WhoHol 92*
Clare, Phyllis d1947 *WhoHol 92*
Clare, Samantha 1936- *WrDr 94*
Clare, Stewart 1913-1992 *WhoAmA 93N*
Claremon, Neil *DrAPF 93*
Claremont, Chris 1950- *EncSF 93*
Clarenbach, David E. 1953- *WhoAmP 93*
Clarence, O. B. d1955 *WhoHol 92*
Clarendon, Earl of 1933- *Who 94*
Clarendon, Edward Hyde, Earl of 1609-1674 *BlmGEL*
Clarendon, Jean d1952 *WhoHol 92*
Clarens, Angel *WhoHisp 94*
Clarens, Carlos d1987 *WhoHol 92*
Clarens, Elsie d1917 *WhoHol 92*
Clarens, John Gaston 1924- *WhoAm 94*
Clareson, Thomas D. d1993 *NewYTBS 93*
Clareson, Thomas D(ean) 1926- *EncSF 93*
Clareson, Thomas D(ean) 1926-1993 *ConAu 141*
Clarey, Cynthia 1949- *NewGrDO*
Clarey, Donald Alexander 1950- *WhoAm 94*
Clarey, John Robert 1942- *WhoAm 94, WhoFI 94, WhoMW 93*
Clarfelt, Jack Gerald 1914- *Who 94*
Clarges, Verner d1911 *WhoHol 92*
Clari, Giovanni Carlo Maria 1677-1754 *NewGrDO*
Claridge, Michael Frederick 1934- *Who 94*
Claridge, Norman d1985 *WhoHol 92*
Claridge, Richard Allen 1932- *WhoScEn 94*
Claringbull, Katharine Ruth 1949- *WhoWest 94*
Clariond, Aime d1960 *WhoHol 92*
Clarizio, Josephine Delores 1922- *WhoAm 94*
Clark *Who 94*
Clark, Abraham 1726-1794 *WhAmRev*
Clark, Alan (Kenneth McKenzie) 1928- *Who 94*
Clark, Alan Barthwell 1936- *WhoAm 94, WhoWest 94*
Clark, Alan Charles *Who 94*
Clark, Alan Fred 1936- *WhoAm 94*
Clark, Alan Hedgecock 1964- *WhoFI 94*
Clark, Alan Richard 1939- *Who 94*
Clark, Albert William 1922- *Who 94*
Clark, Alfred Joseph 1885-1941 *DcNaB MP*
Clark, Alice Thompson 1926- *WhoAm 94, WhoMW 93*
Clark, Alicia Garcia *WhoAm 94*
Clark, Alistair Campbell 1933- *Who 94*
Clark, Allan 1896-1950 *WhoAmA 93N*
Clark, Allen LeRoy 1938- *WhoWest 94*
Clark, Alson Skinner 1876-1949 *WhoAmA 93N*
Clark, Amanda *WrDr 94*
Clark, Ameera H. 1919- *WhoBlA 94*
Clark, Andrew J., III 1938- *WhoAmL 94*
Clark, Andy d1960 *WhoHol 92*
Clark, Ann Nolan 1898- *WhAm 10*
Clark, Anne Margaret Eberhardt 1961- *WhoWest 94*
Clark, Anthony Morris 1923-1976 *WhoAmA 93N*
Clark, Anthony Warner 1951- *WhoAmL 94*
Clark, Archie 1941- *BasBi*
Clark, Arthur Brodie 1935- *WhoFI 94*
Clark, Arthur Joseph, Jr. 1921- *WhoWest 94*
Clark, Arthur Watts 1922- *WhoAm 94*
Clark, Augusta Alexander 1932- *WhoAmP 93, WhoBlA 94*
Clark, Barbara *WhoAmP 93*
Clark, Barbara M. 1939- *WhoAmP 93*
Clark, Barbara Susan 1949- *WhoMW 93*
Clark, Barry Wayne 1941- *WhoMW 93*
Clark, Benjamin Cates, Jr. *WhoScEn 94*
Clark, Benjamin F. 1910- *WhoBlA 94*
Clark, Benjamin G. 1950- *WhoAmL 94*
Clark, Bernard F. 1921- *WhoAm 94, WhoFI 94*
Clark, Bertha Smith 1943- *WhoBlA 94*
Clark, Bettie I. 1927- *WhoBlA 94*
Clark, Betty Elizabeth 1928- *WhoAmP 93*
Clark, Betty Jean 1920- *WhoAmP 93*
Clark, Beverly A. *WhoAmP 93*
Clark, Bill 1944- *WhoAmP 93*
Clark, Bill 1946- *WhoAmP 93*
Clark, Billy Pat 1939- *WhoAm 94, WhoFI 94, WhoScEn 94*
Clark, Birge Malcolm 1893-1989 *WhAm 10*
Clark, Blake 1908- *WhoAm 94*
Clark, Bob 1941- *HorFD [port], IntMPA 94*
Clark, Bobby d1960 *WhoHol 92*
Clark, Bobby 1888-1960
See Clark and McCullough *WhoCom*
Clark, Brett *WhoHol 92*
Clark, Brian (Robert) 1932- *ConDr 93, WrDr 94*
Clark, Brian D. 1956- *WhoAmP 93*
Clark, Brian Robert 1932- *Who 94*
Clark, Brian Thomas 1951- *WhoScEn 94, WhoWest 94*
Clark, Bruce (Budge) 1918- *WrDr 94*
Clark, Bruce Budge 1918- *WhoAm 94*
Clark, Bruce E. 1946- *WhoAmL 94*
Clark, Bruce Quinton *Who 94*
Clark, Bruce Robert 1941- *WhoAm 94*
Clark, Buddy d1949 *WhoHol 92*
Clark, Burnill Fred 1941- *WhoWest 94*
Clark, Burton Robert 1921- *WhoAm 94*
Clark, C. A. *WhoAm 94*
Clark, C. Ray 1939- *WhoAmP 93*
Clark, C. Scott *IntWW 93*
Clark, Caesar A. W. 1914- *WhoBlA 94*
Clark, Caleb Morgan 1945- *WhoWest 94*
Clark, Cameron 1944- *WhoAm 94, WhoAmL 94*
Clark, Candy *IntMPA 94, WhoAm 94*
Clark, Candy 1947- *WhoHol 92*
Clark, Carl Arthur 1911- *WhoMW 93, WhoScEn 94*
Clark, Carleton Earl 1942- *WhoFI 94*
Clark, Carol 1947- *WhoAmA 93*
Clark, Carol C. 1949- *WhoAmL 94*
Clark, Carol Lois 1948- *WhoAm 94*
Clark, Carolyn Archer 1944- *WhoAm 94, WhoScEn 94*
Clark, Carolyn Cochran 1941- *WhoAm 94, WhoAmL 94*
Clark, Catherine Anthony 1892-1977 *BlmGWL*
Clark, Chapin DeWitt 1930- *WhoAm 94*
Clark, Charles 1925- *WhoAm 94, WhoAmP 93*
Clark, Charles Anthony 1940- *Who 94*
Clark, Charles Champ, Sr. 1926- *WhoAmP 93*
Clark, Charles D. 1917- *WhoAmA 93*
Clark, Charles David Lawson 1933- *Who 94*
Clark, Charles Dow d1959 *WhoHol 92*
Clark, Charles E. 1929- *WrDr 94*
Clark, Charles Edward 1921- *WhoAmL 94*
Clark, Charles Edward, Jr. 1923- *WhoFI 94*
Clark, Charles Joseph 1939- *Who 94, WhoAm 94*
Clark, Charles Sutter 1927- *WhoWest 94*
Clark, Charles Taliferro 1917- *WhoAm 94*
Clark, Charles Warfield 1917- *WhoBlA 94*
Clark, Chester d1987 *WhoHol 92*
Clark, Christine May 1957- *WhoAm 94*
Clark, Christopher Adam 1965- *WhoMW 93*
Clark, Christopher Harvey 1946- *Who 94*
Clark, Clarence 1859-1937 *BuCMET*
Clark, Clarence Bendenson, Jr. 1943- *WhoBlA 94*
Clark, Clarence C. 1894- *WhAm 10*
Clark, Claude 1915- *WhoAmA 93, WhoWest 94*
Clark, Claude Lockhart 1945- *WhoBlA 94*
Clark, Claudia J. 1949- *WhoAm 94*
Clark, Clayton 1912- *WhoAm 94*
Clark, Cliff d1953 *WhoHol 92*
Clark, Clifford Edward, Jr. 1941- *WhoAm 94*
Clark, Clifton Bob 1927- *WhoAm 94*
Clark, Colin (Douglas) 1918- *Who 94*
Clark, Colin Whitcomb 1931- *WhoAm 94*
Clark, Curt *EncSF 93*
Clark, Curt 1933- *WrDr 94*
Clark, Dane 1915- *IntMPA 94, WhoHol 92*
Clark, Daniel F. 1954- *WhoAmP 93*
Clark, Dave 1913- *WhoBlA 94*
Clark, Dave 1943- *WhoHol 92*
Clark, David 1933- *WrDr 94*
Clark, David 1941- *WhoAmL 94*
Clark, David, Sr. 1922- *WhoAmP 93*
Clark, David (George) 1939- *Who 94, WrDr 94*
Clark, David Beatson 1933- *Who 94*
Clark, David Delano 1924- *WhoAm 94*
Clark, David Gillis 1933- *WhoWest 94*
Clark, David John 1947- *Who 94*
Clark, David Keith 1952- *WhoMW 93*
Clark, David Leigh 1931- *WhoAm 94, WhoScEn 94*
Clark, David Neil 1953- *WhoWest 94*
Clark, David R. 1942- *WhoAm 94*
Clark, David Randolph 1943- *WhoAm 94*
Clark, David Ridgley 1920- *WrDr 94*
Clark, David Willard 1930- *WhoAm 94*
Clark, David Wright 1948- *WhoAmL 94*
Clark, Davison d1972 *WhoHol 92*
Clark, Dayle Meritt 1933- *WhoFI 94*
Clark, Denis 1943- *Who 94*
Clark, Dennis J. d1993 *NewYTBS 93 [port]*
Clark, Dennis J. 1927-1993 *ConAu 142*
Clark, Dennis J. 1948- *WhoAmL 94*
Clark, Derek John 1929- *Who 94*
Clark, Desmond *Who 94*
Clark, Dewey P. 1934- *WhoIns 94*
Clark, Diana Brewster d1993 *NewYTBS 93 [port]*
Clark, Diane Marie 1954- *WhoMW 93*
Clark, Dianna Lea 1956- *WhoFI 94, WhoMW 93*
Clark, Dick 1928- *IntWW 93, WhoAm 94*
Clark, Dick 1929- *IntMPA 94, WhoAm 94, WhoHol 92, WrDr 94*
Clark, Donald Cameron 1931- *WhoAm 94, WhoFI 94*
Clark, Donald Lewis 1935- *WhoBlA 94*
Clark, Donald M. 1923- *WhoAmP 93*
Clark, Donald Malin 1929- *WhoAm 94*
Clark, Donald Otis 1934- *WhoAm 94, WhoAmL 94*
Clark, Donald Robert 1924- *WhoAm 94*
Clark, Donald Rowlee 1925- *WhoWest 94*
Clark, Doran *WhoHol 92*
Clark, Dort d1989 *WhoHol 92*
Clark, Douglas (Malcolm Jackson) 1919- *WrDr 94*
Clark, Douglas Henderson d1991 *Who 94N*
Clark, Douglas Kenneth 1947- *WhoWest 94*
Clark, Douglas L. 1935- *WhoBlA 94*
Clark, Drew 1946- *WhoAmP 93, WhoWest 94*
Clark, Duncan C. 1952- *IntMPA 94*
Clark, E. Holman d1925 *WhoHol 92*
Clark, Earl d1978 *ProFbHF*
Clark, Earl Wesley 1901-1990 *WhAm 10*
Clark, Earnest Hubert, Jr. 1926- *WhoAm 94, WhoWest 94*
Clark, Ed d1954 *WhoHol 92*
Clark, Edgar Sanderford 1933- *WhoAm 94, WhoFI 94, WhoWest 94*
Clark, Edward 1926- *WhoAmA 93, WhoBlA 94*
Clark, Edward Alan 1947- *WhoWest 94*
Clark, Edward Depriest, Sr. 1930- *WhoBlA 94*
Clark, Edward E. 1930- *WhoAmP 93*
Clark, Edward Emerson 1930- *WhoAmL 94*
Clark, Edward Ferdnand 1921- *WhoAm 94*
Clark, Edythe Audrey 1929- *WhoWest 94*
Clark, Eleanor *DrAPF 93, WhoAm 94*
Clark, Eleanor 1913- *ConAu 41NR, WrDr 94*
Clark, Eliot Candee 1883-1980 *WhoAmA 93N*
Clark, Elmer J. 1919- *WhoAm 94*
Clark, Eloise Elizabeth 1931- *WhoAm 94, WhoMW 93*
Clark, Emery Ann 1950- *WhoAmA 93*
Clark, Emory Eugene 1931- *WhoFI 94*
Clark, Eric 1937- *WrDr 94*
Clark, Eric Charles 1951- *WhoAmP 93*
Clark, Ernest 1912- *WhoHol 92*
Clark, Ernest John 1905-1992 *WhAm 10*
Clark, Esther 1716-1794 *DcNaB MP*
Clark, Esther Frances 1929- *WhoAm 94*
Clark, Ethel d1964 *WhoHol 92*
Clark, Eugene Bradley 1873-1942 *EncABHB 9 [port]*
Clark, Eugene T. 1947- *WhoAmP 93*
Clark, Eugene Walter 1915- *WhoAmP 93*
Clark, Eugenie 1922- *WhoAm 94*
Clark, Ezekail Louis 1912- *WhoWest 94*
Clark, Findlay *Who 94*
Clark, (Samuel) Findlay 1909- *Who 94*
Clark, Forrester A., Jr. 1934- *WhoAmP 93*
Clark, Francis (Drake) 1924- *Who 94*
Clark, Francis Edward 1851-1927 *DcAmReB 2*

Clark, Frank d1945 *WhoHol 92*
Clark, Frank Rinker, Jr. 1912- *WhoAm 94*
Clark, Fred d1968 *WhoHol 92*
Clark, Fred 1930- *WhoFI 94*
Clark, Fred Allen 1929- *WhoBlA 94*
Clark, Frederic William 1939- *WhoAm 94, WhoAmL 94*
Clark, Frederick A. 1942- *WhoAmL 94*
Clark, Frederick R. 1916-1990 *WhAm 10*
Clark, G. Fletcher 1899-1982 *WhoAmA 93N*
Clark, Garth Reginald 1947- *WhoAmA 93*
Clark, Gary C. 1962- *WhoAm 94, WhoBlA 94, WhoWest 94*
Clark, Gary Carl 1947- *WhoAmL 94*
Clark, Gary Kenneth 1936- *WhoWest 94*
Clark, Gary M. 1935- *WhoAm 94, WhoFI 94*
Clark, Gary R. 1946- *WhoAm 94, WhoMW 93*
Clark, Geoffrey 1946- *WhoFI 94*
Clark, Geoffrey D. *DrAPF 93*
Clark, George d1976 *WhoHol 92*
Clark, George 1932- *WrDr 94*
Clark, George Bryan 1925- *WhoAm 94*
Clark, George L. 1941- *WhoAmP 93*
Clark, George M., Jr. 1947- *WhoIns 94*
Clark, George Roberts 1910- *WhoAm 94*
Clark, George Rogers 1752-1818 *AmRev, HisWorL [port], WhAmRev [port]*
Clark, George Whipple 1928- *IntWW 93*
Clark, Gerald 1933- *Who 94*
Clark, Gerald Edmondson 1935- *Who 94*
Clark, Gerald L. 1938- *WhoIns 94*
Clark, Gilbert Michael 1944- *WhoAm 94*
Clark, Glen Edward 1943- *WhoAm 94, WhoAmL 94, WhoWest 94*
Clark, Glenwood 1926- *WhoAm 94*
Clark, Gordon Hostetter, Jr. 1947- *WhoScEn 94*
Clark, Gordon Meredith 1934- *WhoMW 93*
Clark, Grady William 1897- *WhAm 10*
Clark, Graham 1941- *NewGrDO*
Clark, Grahame *Who 94*
Clark, (John) Grahame (Douglas) 1907- *Who 94*
Clark, (John) Grahame (Douglas), Sir 1907- *WrDr 94*
Clark, Granville E., Sr. 1927- *WhoBlA 94*
Clark, Gregor Munro 1946- *Who 94*
Clark, Gregory Alton 1947- *WhoScEn 94*
Clark, Greydon *WhoHol 92*
Clark, Greydon 1943- *IntMPA 94*
Clark, Harold Steve 1947- *WhoAm 94*
Clark, Harry d1956 *WhoHol 92*
Clark, Harry R. *WhoAmP 93*
Clark, Harry W. 1946- *WhoBlA 94*
Clark, Harvey d1938 *WhoHol 92*
Clark, Helen 1950- *IntWW 93*
Clark, Helen Elizabeth 1950- *Who 94, WhoWomW 91*
Clark, Henry Benjamin, Jr. 1913- *WhoAm 94, WhoWest 94*
Clark, Henry Maitland 1929- *Who 94*
Clark, Henry Ogden 1944- *WhoMW 93*
Clark, Herbert Edward 1945- *WhoAmP 93*
Clark, Herbert Forrester 1943- *WhoAm 94*
Clark, Herman 1942- *WhoAmL 94, WhoAmP 93*
Clark, Hilary J. 1976- *IntMPA 94*
Clark, Hilton Bancroft 1943- *WhoAmP 93*
Clark, Howard Charles 1929- *IntWW 93*
Clark, Howard Longstreth 1916- *IntWW 93, WhoAm 94*
Clark, Howard Longstreth, Jr. 1944- *WhoAm 94, WhoFI 94*
Clark, Hunter R. 1955- *ConAu 141*
Clark, I. E. 1919- *WhoAm 94*
Clark, Ian Douglas 1946- *WhoAm 94*
Clark, Ian Robertson 1939- *IntWW 93, Who 94*
Clark, Ira C. *WhoAm 94*
Clark, J(onathan) C(harles) D(ouglas) 1951- *WrDr 94*
Clark, J(ohn) Desmond 1916- *IntWW 93, Who 94, WrDr 94*
Clark, J. Thomas *WhoAm 94, WhoFI 94*
Clark, Jack 1932- *WhoAm 94, WhoFI 94*
Clark, Jack I. *WhoScEn 94*
Clark, James Allen 1948- *WhoAm 94*
Clark, James Benton 1914- *WhoAm 94*
Clark, James C., Jr. 1944- *WhoAmL 94*
Clark, James E. 1948- *WhoAm 94*
Clark, James Erle 1929- *WhoAmL 94*
Clark, James Eugene 1950- *WhoMW 93*
Clark, James H. 1944- *WhoAm 94, WhoFI 94, WhoWest 94*
Clark, James H. 1952- *WhoAmP 93*
Clark, James Henry 1931- *WhoAm 94, WhoWest 94*
Clark, James Irving, Jr. 1936- *WhoBlA 94*
Clark, James Kendall 1948- *WhoAmL 94*
Clark, James Leonard 1923- *Who 94*
Clark, James McAdam 1916- *Who 94*
Clark, James Milford 1930- *WhoAm 94*
Clark, James N. 1934- *WhoBlA 94*
Clark, James Norman 1932- *WhoAm 94, WhoIns 94*
Clark, James Orie, II 1950- *WhoWest 94*
Clark, James Richard 1946- *WhoAm 94*
Clark, James Robert 1950- *WhoMW 93*
Clark, James S. *WhoAm 94*
Clark, James S. 1921- *WhoAmP 93*
Clark, Jameson d1984 *WhoHol 92*
Clark, Jane Angela 1955- *WhoMW 93*
Clark, Janet d1987 *WhoHol 92*
Clark, Janet Eileen 1940- *WhoWest 94*
Clark, Jean *DrAPF 93*
Clark, Jeanenne Frances 1954- *WhoMW 93*
Clark, Jeff Ray 1947- *WhoFI 94, WhoScEn 94*
Clark, Jeffrey Alan 1959- *WhoScEn 94*
Clark, Jeffrey Raphiel 1953- *WhoFI 94, WhoWest 94*
Clark, Jeffrey Wade 1950- *WhoMW 93*
Clark, Jeffry Russell 1950- *WhoWest 94*
Clark, Jerald Dwayne 1963- *WhoBlA 94*
Clark, Jerry 1944- *WhoAmP 93*
Clark, Jesse B., III 1925- *WhoBlA 94*
Clark, Jessie L. 1960- *WhoBlA 94*
Clark, Jimmy d1972 *WhoHol 92*
Clark, Jimmy E. 1934-1985 *WhoBlA 94*
Clark, Joan 1905- *WrDr 94*
Clark, Joan 1934- *BlmGWL*
Clark, JoAnn 1953- *WhoWest 94*
Clark, Jocelyn Hamlar 1954- *WhoBlA 94*
Clark, Joe *Who 94*
Clark, Joe 1861-1956 *BuCMET*
Clark, Joe 1939- *AfrAmAl 6 [port], WhoAm 94*
Clark, Joe Louis 1939- *WhoBlA 94*
Clark, John 1797-1854 *EncNAR*
Clark, John (Allen) 1926- *Who 94*
Clark, John A. 1926- *IntWW 93*
Clark, John Albert 1933- *WhoMW 93*
Clark, John Alden 1923- *WhoAm 94*
Clark, John Arthur 1920- *WhoAm 94*
Clark, John Benjamin 1941- *Who 94*
Clark, John C., III 1943- *WhoAmL 94*
Clark, John Conrad 1913-1990 *WhAm 10*
Clark, John Desmond 1916- *WhoAm 94*
Clark, John Edward 1932- *Who 94*
Clark, John Elwood 1931- *WhoAmP 93*
Clark, John F. 1920- *WhoAm 94, WhoScEn 94*
Clark, John Graham, III 1950- *WhoAmL 94*
Clark, John Grahame Douglas 1907- *IntWW 93*
Clark, John H., Jr. 1928- *WhoAm 94*
Clark, John Hallett, III 1918- *WhoAm 94*
Clark, John Holley, III 1918- *WhoAmL 94*
Clark, John Howard 1946- *WhoAmP 93*
Clark, John Ives 1958- *WhoAmP 93*
Clark, John J. d1947 *WhoHol 92*
Clark, John Joseph 1954- *WhoBlA 94*
Clark, John Paul 1940- *WhoAmP 93*
Clark, John Pepper 1935- *ConDr 93, IntDcT 2, WrDr 94*
Clark, John Peter, III 1942- *WhoAm 94*
Clark, John Phelps 1932- *WhoAm 94*
Clark, John R(ichard) 1930- *WrDr 94*
Clark, John Robert 1943- *WhoFI 94*
Clark, John Robert 1955- *WhoAmP 93*
Clark, John Russell 1927- *WhoAm 94*
Clark, John S. *Who 94*
Clark, John Stewart 1957- *WhoFI 94*
Clark, John W., Jr. 1938- *WhoAmL 94*
Clark, John Walter, Jr. 1919- *WhoAm 94*
Clark, John Welwyn 1954- *WhoMW 93*
Clark, John Whitcomb 1918- *WhoAm 94*
Clark, Johnny d1967 *WhoHol 92*
Clark, Jon Frederic 1947- *WhoAmA 93*
Clark, Jonas 1731-1805 *WhAmRev*
Clark, Jonathan Charles Douglas 1951- *IntWW 93*
Clark, Jonathan Montgomery 1937- *WhoAm 94, WhoAmL 94*
Clark, Joseph *IntWW 93*
Clark, (Charles) Joseph 1939- *IntWW 93*
Clark, Joseph Daniel 1957- *WhoScEn 94*
Clark, Joseph S. 1901-1990 *WhAm 10*
Clark, June *Who 94*
Clark, (Margaret) June 1941- *Who 94*
Clark, Karen *WhoAmP 93*
Clark, Karen Heath 1944- *WhoAm 94*
Clark, Katherine Judkins d1993 *NewYTBS 93*
Clark, Keith 1944- *Who 94*
Clark, Kelly 1957- *WhoAmP 93*
Clark, Kelly James 1956- *WhoMW 93*
Clark, Ken *WhoHol 92*
Clark, Kendall d1983 *WhoHol 92*
Clark, Kenneth B. 1914- *ConBlB 5 [port]*
Clark, Kenneth Bancroft 1914- *AmSocL, IntWW 93, WhoAm 94, WhoBlA 94, WrDr 94*
Clark, Kenneth Courtright 1919- *WhoAm 94*
Clark, Kenneth Edwin 1914- *WhoAm 94*
Clark, Kenneth James 1922- *Who 94*
Clark, Kenneth R. 1947- *WhoAmP 93*
Clark, Kenneth William 1960- *WhoMW 93, WhoScEn 94*
Clark, L. D. *DrAPF 93*
Clark, La Verne Harrell 1929- *WrDr 94*
Clark, Laron Jefferson, Jr. 1937- *WhoBlA 94*
Clark, Larry 1943- *WhoAm 94*
Clark, Larry 1945- *WhoAmP 93*
Clark, Larry Kenneth 1945- *WhoWest 94*
Clark, Laurie Jane 1951- *WhoAmL 94*
Clark, LaVerne Harrell *DrAPF 93*
Clark, LaWanna Gibbs 1941- *WhoBlA 94*
Clark, Lawrence M., Sr. 1934- *WhoBlA 94*
Clark, Leif Michael 1947- *WhoAm 94, WhoAmL 94*
Clark, Leigh Mallet 1901- *WhAm 10*
Clark, Leo *Who 94*
Clark, (Francis) Leo 1920- *Who 94*
Clark, Leon Henry 1941- *WhoBlA 94*
Clark, Leon Stanley 1930- *WhoBlA 94*
Clark, Leonard J., Jr. 1934- *WhoFI 94*
Clark, Leonard Vernon 1938- *WhoAm 94*
Clark, Leonard Weslorn, Jr. 1942- *WhoBlA 94*
Clark, LeRoy D. 1917- *WhoBlA 94*
Clark, Les d1959 *WhoHol 92*
Clark, Letitia Z. 1945- *WhoAm 94, WhoAmL 94*
Clark, Liddy *WhoHol 92*
Clark, Ligia 1920- *IntWW 93*
Clark, Lisa R. 1967- *WhoWest 94*
Clark, Lloyd 1923- *WhoWest 94*
Clark, Lonnie Paul 1943- *WhoAmP 93*
Clark, Louie Max *WhoAmP 93*
Clark, Louis James 1940- *WhoBlA 94*
Clark, Loyal Frances 1958- *WhoFI 94, WhoWest 94*
Clark, Luther Johnson 1941- *Who 94*
Clark, Lynda K. 1969- *WhoAmA 93*
Clark, Lynda Margaret *Who 94*
Clark, Lynn C. 1947- *WhoIns 94*
Clark, Lynne Wilson 1947- *WhoScEn 94*
Clark, M. R. *SmATA 74*
Clark, M. Rita 1915- *WhoAmP 93*
Clark, Mabel Beatrice Smith d1957 *WhoAmA 93N*
Clark, Major 1917- *WhoBlA 94*
Clark, Malcolm 1931- *Who 94*
Clark, Malcolm Aiken 1905- *Who 94*
Clark, Malcolm Dowdles 1940- *WhoFI 94*
Clark, Mamo d1986 *WhoHol 92*
Clark, Margaret Goff 1913- *ConAu 43NR, WrDr 94*
Clark, Margaret Pruitt 1946- *WhoAmP 93*
Clark, Marguerite d1940 *WhoHol 92*
Clark, Marie *WhoAmA 93*
Clark, Marilyn 1929- *WhoHol 92*
Clark, Mario Sean 1954- *WhoBlA 94*
Clark, Mark A. 1931- *WhoAmA 93*
Clark, Mark W. 1896-1984 *HisDcKW*
Clark, Marlene *WhoHol 92*
Clark, Martha F. 1942- *WhoAmP 93*
Clark, Martin Fillmore, Jr. 1959- *WhoAmL 94*
Clark, Mary Diane 1953- *WhoScEn 94*
Clark, Mary E. d1993 *NewYTBS 93*
Clark, Mary Higgins 1929- *TwCYAW, WrDr 94*
Clark, Mary Higgins 1931- *WhoAm 94*
Clark, Mary Margaret 1925- *WhoAm 94*
Clark, Mary T. *WrDr 94*
Clark, Mary Twibill *WhoAm 94*
Clark, Matt *WhoHol 92*
Clark, Matt 1930- *WhoAm 94*
Clark, Matt 1936- *IntMPA 94*
Clark, Matthew Harvey 1937- *WhoAm 94*
Clark, Mavis Thorpe 1909- *SmATA 74 [port], WrDr 94*
Clark, Mavis Thorpe 1912- *ChlLR 30 [port]*
Clark, Maxine 1949- *WhoAm 94, WhoFI 94*
Clark, Mayree Carroll 1957- *WhoFI 94*
Clark, Melinda Lee 1962- *WhoMW 93*
Clark, Melville, Jr. 1921- *WhoAm 94*
Clark, Melvin Eugene 1916- *WhoAm 94*
Clark, Merle 1919- *WrDr 94*
Clark, Merlyn Wesley 1937- *WhoAmL 94*
Clark, Merrell Edward, Jr. 1922- *WhoAm 94*
Clark, Merrell Mays 1935- *WhoAm 94*
Clark, Michael *DrAPF 93*
Clark, Michael 1935- *Who 94*
Clark, Michael 1948- *WhoAm 94, WhoWest 94*
Clark, Michael A. 1954- *WhoAmL 94*
Clark, Michael Earl 1951- *WhoScEn 94*
Clark, Michael Emory 1956- *WhoAmL 94*
Clark, Michael Jay 1945- *WhoAmP 93*
Clark, Michael P. 1950- *WhoWest 94*
Clark, Michael Scott 1962- *WhoAmL 94*
Clark, Michael Vinson 1946- *WhoAmA 93*
Clark, Michael Wayne 1939- *WhoMW 93*
Clark, Michael William 1927- *Who 94*
Clark, Michal Charles 1945- *WhoWest 94*
Clark, Micheal Dale 1954- *WhoWest 94*
Clark, Mildred E. 1936- *WhoBlA 94*
Clark, Morris Shandell 1945- *WhoBlA 94*
Clark, Nancy Filstrup 1921- *WhoMW 93*
Clark, Nancy Kissel 1919- *WhoAmA 93*
Clark, Nancy Randall *WhoWomW 91*
Clark, Nancy Randall 1938- *WhoAmP 93*
Clark, Naomi *DrAPF 93*
Clark, Nathan Stewart, Jr. 1959- *WhoMW 93*
Clark, Nicholas L. 1944- *WhoAm 94*
Clark, Noreen Morrison 1943- *WhoAm 94, WhoMW 93*
Clark, Oliver *WhoHol 92*
Clark, Oswald William Hugh 1917- *Who 94*
Clark, Pamela Morris 1937- *WhoAmP 93*
Clark, Pat English 1940- *WhoAm 94*
Clark, Patricia *DrAPF 93*
Clark, Patricia 1928- *WhoScEn 94*
Clark, Patricia Ann 1936- *WhoAm 94, WhoAmL 94, WhoWest 94*
Clark, Patricia Ann 1951- *WhoBlA 94*
Clark, Patricia Frances 1951- *WhoMW 93*
Clark, Patricia Jean 1951- *WhoAmP 93*
Clark, Patti Lynn 1950- *WhoWest 94*
Clark, Paul d1960 *WhoHol 92*
Clark, Paul 1932- *WhoAmP 93*
Clark, Paul Derek 1939- *Who 94*
Clark, Paul Newton 1947- *WhoFI 94*
Clark, Paul Nicholas Rowntree 1940- *Who 94*
Clark, Paul Sleman 1942- *WhoAmP 93*
Clark, Paul Thomas 1954- *WhoAmL 94*
Clark, Peggy 1915- *WhoAm 94*
Clark, Pendleton Scott 1895- *WhAm 10*
Clark, Peter Bruce 1928- *WhoAm 94*
Clark, Petula 1932- *IntMPA 94, WhoHol 92*
Clark, Petula 1934- *IntWW 93, Who 94*
Clark, Philip Raymond 1930- *WhoAm 94, WhoScEn 94*
Clark, Phillip R. 1948- *WhoAmL 94*
Clark, Priscilla Alden 1940- *WhoAm 94*
Clark, R. Bradbury 1924- *WhoAm 94, WhoAmL 94, WhoFI 94, WhoWest 94*
Clark, R. Thomas 1951- *WhoAmL 94*
Clark, Ramsey 1927- *IntWW 93, Who 94, WhoAm 94, WhoAmP 93*
Clark, Randall Livingston 1943- *WhoAm 94*
Clark, Randolph A. 1939- *WhoBlA 94*
Clark, Raymond John 1951- *WhoMW 93, WhoScEn 94*
Clark, Raymond Oakes 1944- *WhoWest 94*
Clark, Raymond Robert 1938- *WhoFI 94*
Clark, Raymond Skinner 1913- *WhoAm 94*
Clark, Reginald J. 1953- *WhoAmL 94*
Clark, Reuben Grove, Jr. 1923- *WhoAm 94*
Clark, Richard 1939- *WhoAm 94*
Clark, Richard A. 1949- *WhoAm 94*
Clark, Richard Charles 1935- *WrDr 94*
Clark, Richard Clarence 1928- *WhoAmP 93*
Clark, Richard David 1934- *Who 94*
Clark, Richard K. 1944- *WhoAmL 94*
Clark, Richard Lee 1940- *WhoAm 94*
Clark, Richard McCourt 1937- *WhoAm 94, WhoAmL 94, WhoFI 94*
Clark, Richard R. 1943- *WhoAmP 93*
Clark, Richard Walter 1936- *WhoWest 94*
Clark, Richard Ward 1938- *WhoFI 94, WhoWest 94*
Clark, Rickie G. 1952- *WhoBlA 94*
Clark, Ricky Merle 1955- *WhoAmP 93*
Clark, Robert 1911- *WrDr 94*
Clark, Robert 1929- *HisWorL*
Clark, Robert (Anthony) 1924- *Who 94*
Clark, Robert Anthony 1924- *IntWW 93*
Clark, Robert Arthur 1923- *WhoAm 94*
Clark, Robert Bernard 1923- *Who 94*
Clark, Robert Brewster 1927- *WhoAmP 93*
Clark, Robert C. 1942- *WhoAmP 93*
Clark, Robert Charles 1920- *WhoAmA 93*
Clark, Robert Charles 1944- *WhoAmL 94*
Clark, Robert Frederick 1942- *WhoMW 93*
Clark, Robert G. 1929- *WhoBlA 94*
Clark, Robert George, Jr. 1929- *WhoAmP 93*
Clark, Robert Henry, Jr. 1941- *WhoAm 94, WhoFI 94*
Clark, Robert James Vodden 1907- *Who 94*
Clark, Robert King 1934- *WhoAm 94*
Clark, Robert Lloyd, Jr. 1945- *WhoAm 94*
Clark, Robert M., Jr. 1948- *WhoAmL 94, WhoAmP 93*
Clark, Robert Newhall 1925- *WhoAm 94*
Clark, Robert Phillips 1921- *WhoAm 94*
Clark, Robert Stokes 1954- *WhoAmL 94*
Clark, Robert W. *WhoAmP 93*
Clark, Robert William, III 1945- *WhoAm 94, WhoAmL 94*
Clark, Roberta Carter 1924- *WhoAmA 93*

Clark, Roberta Humphrey 1942- WhoAmL 94
Clark, Robin Jon Hawes 1935- IntWW 93, Who 94
Clark, Roger Arthur 1932- WhoAm 94, WhoAmL 94
Clark, Roger Gordon 1937- WhoAm 94
Clark, Roger Harrison 1939- WhoAm 94
Clark, Roger M. 1938- WhoAmL 94
Clark, Roland 1874-1957 WhoAmA 93N
Clark, Ron Dean 1947- WhoAm 94
Clark, Ronald Dean 1943- WhoAm 94, WhoMW 93
Clark, Ronald George 1928- Who 94
Clark, Ronald Harry 1904- WrDr 94
Clark, Ronald Hurley 1953- WhoAmL 94
Clark, Ronald W(illiam) 1916-1987 EncSF 93
Clark, Rosalind K. 1943- WhoBlA 94
Clark, Rose Francis d1962 WhoHol 92
Clark, Ross Bert, II 1932- WhoAm 94, WhoAmL 94
Clark, Roy 1933- WhoAm 94, WhoHol 92
Clark, Russell Gentry 1925- WhoAm 94, WhoAmL 94, WhoMW 93
Clark, Ruth 1942- WhoBlA 94
Clark, Sally Newbert 1934- WhoWest 94
Clark, Sam WhoAmP 93
Clark, Samuel Delbert 1910- WhoAm 94
Clark, Samuel H., Jr. 1949- WhoAmL 94
Clark, Samuel Smith 1932- WhoAm 94
Clark, Sandra Helen Becker 1938- WhoAm 94
Clark, Sandra Marie 1942- WhoFI 94
Clark, Sanza Barbara 1940- WhoBlA 94
Clark, Savanna M. Vaughn 1927- WhoBlA 94
Clark, Scott H. 1946- WhoAmL 94
Clark, Sharon Kay 1946- WhoAmP 93
Clark, Sheila Wheatley 1948- WhoBlA 94
Clark, Shirley 1946- WhoFI 94
Clark, Shirley Lorraine 1936- WhoBlA 94
Clark, Stanford E. 1917- WhoAm 94
Clark, Stanley Ralph 1945- WhoMW 93
Clark, Stephen P. 1923- WhoAm 94, WhoAmP 93
Clark, Stephen R. DrAPF 93
Clark, Stephen Russell 1949- WhoAmP 93
Clark, Steve d1954 WhoHol 92
Clark, Steven C. 1968- WhoAmP 93
Clark, Steven English 1950- WhoAmP 93
Clark, Steven Eugene 1953- WhoAmL 94
Clark, Steven Joseph 1957- WhoScEn 94
Clark, Stuart Alan 1962- WhoScEn 94
Clark, Susan 1940- IntMPA 94
Clark, Susan 1943- WhoHol 92
Clark, Susan 1944- WhoAm 94
Clark, Susan Matthews 1950- WhoAm 94, WhoMW 93, WhoScEn 94
Clark, Sydney Procter 1929- WhoScEn 94
Clark, Tama Myers WhoBlA 94
Clark, Terence (Joseph) 1934- Who 94
Clark, Teresa Watkins 1953- WhoScEn 94
Clark, Terrence Patrick 1960- WhoScEn 94
Clark, Terry N(ichols) 1940- WrDr 94
Clark, Terry Nichols 1940- WhoMW 93
Clark, Theodore Lee 1907- WhoBlA 94
Clark, Thomas 1926- WhoAmP 93
Clark, Thomas (Edwin) 1916- Who 94
Clark, Thomas A. 1920- WhoAmP 93
Clark, Thomas Alonzo 1920- WhoAm 94, WhoAmL 94
Clark, Thomas Bertram, Sr. 1943- WhoFI 94, WhoMW 93
Clark, Thomas Carlyle 1947- WhoAm 94
Clark, Thomas Francis WhoFI 94
Clark, Thomas Garis 1925- WhoAm 94
Clark, Thomas Joseph 1926- WhoWest 94
Clark, Thomas Lloyd 1939- WhoAm 94
Clark, Thomas P., Jr. 1943- WhoAmL 94
Clark, Thomas Ryan 1925- WhoWest 94
Clark, Thomas Sullivan 1947- WhoWest 94
Clark, Thomas Willard 1941- ConAu 43NR, WhoAm 94
Clark, Timothy John 1951- WhoAmA 93
Clark, Timothy John Hayes 1935- Who 94
Clark, Tom ConAu 43NR, DrAPF 93
Clark, Tom 1941- WrDr 94
Clark, Tony Who 94
Clark, Vernon E. 1911-1967 AstEnc
Clark, VeVe A. 1944- WhoBlA 94
Clark, Vicky A. WhoAmA 93
Clark, Vicky Jo 1937- WhoAmA 93
Clark, Vincent W. 1950- WhoBlA 94
Clark, Virginia Lee 1948- WhoMW 93
Clark, Vivian Rae 1940- WhoAmP 93
Clark, W. Murray WhoAmP 93
Clark, W. Richard 1939- WhoFI 94
Clark, W. T. d1925 WhoHol 92
Clark, Wallace Who 94
Clark, Wallace d1960 WhoHol 92
Clark, (Henry) Wallace (Stuart) 1926- Who 94
Clark, Wallace Thomas, III 1953- WhoWest 94
Clark, Wallis d1961 WhoHol 92
Clark, Wally d1920 WhoHol 92
Clark, Walter H. 1928- WhoBlA 94
Clark, Ward Christopher 1939- WhoAm 94
Clark, Warren, Jr. 1936- WhoAmP 93
Clark, Warren L. 1952- WhoAmL 94
Clark, Wendell Mark 1954- WhoAm 94
Clark, Wesley Clarke 1907-1990 WhAm 10
Clark, Will 1964- WhoAm 94, WhoWest 94
Clark, William 1770-1838 WhWE [port]
Clark, William 1937- WhoBlA 94
Clark, William, Jr. 1930- IntWW 93, WhoAm 94, WhoAmP 93
Clark, William A. 1937- WhoAmP 93
Clark, William A. 1958- WhoAmP 93
Clark, William Alfred 1928- WhoAm 94, WhoAmL 94
Clark, William Anthony 1961- WhoScEn 94
Clark, William B. WhoIns 94
Clark, William Burton, IV 1947- WhoScEn 94
Clark, William Cummin 1948- WhoAm 94
Clark, William David 1954- WhoAmP 93
Clark, William E. WhoAmP 93
Clark, William Franklin 1947- WhoAm 94, WhoAmL 94
Clark, William Frederick 1941- WhoAmL 94
Clark, William G. 1924- WhoAmP 93
Clark, William G. 1933- WhoIns 94
Clark, William Hartley 1930- WhoAm 94
Clark, William Howard, Jr. 1951- WhoAmL 94, WhoFI 94
Clark, William J. 1923- WhoAm 94, WhoFI 94, WhoIns 94
Clark, William James 1923- WhoAm 94
Clark, William Lee 1950- WhoAm 94
Clark, William Noble 1921- WhoAmP 93
Clark, William P. 1931- IntWW 93, Who 94
Clark, William Roger 1949- WhoAmA 93
Clark, William Stratton 1914- WhoAm 94
Clark, William W. 1940- WhoAmA 93
Clark, Winston Craig 1949- WhoAm 94
Clark, Worley H., Jr. 1932- WhoAm 94, WhoFI 94
Clark and McCullough WhoCom
Clarke, A(ubrey) V(incent) EncSF 93
Clarke, Aidan 1933- IntWW 93
Clarke, Alan Douglas Benson 1922- Who 94
Clarke, Alexander Ross 1828-1914 DcNaB MP
Clarke, Allan J. 1949- WhoAm 94
Clarke, Allen Who 94
Clarke, (Cyril Alfred) Allen 1910- Who 94
Clarke, Allen Bruce 1927- WhoAm 94
Clarke, Allen Richard 1957- WhoWest 94
Clarke, Alured c. 1745-1832 AmRev, WhAmRev
Clarke, Alyce Griffin WhoAmP 93, WhoWomW 91
Clarke, Alyce Griffin 1939- WhoBlA 94
Clarke, Andrew WhoHol 92
Clarke, Angela WhoHol 92
Clarke, Angela 1905- WhoHol 92
Clarke, Angela Webb 1932- WhoBlA 94
Clarke, Ann 1944- WhoAmA 93
Clarke, Anna 1919- WrDr 94
Clarke, Anthony (Peter) 1943- Who 94
Clarke, Arthur C(harles) 1917- EncSF 93, TwCYAW, WrDr 94
Clarke, Arthur Charles 1917- IntWW 93, Who 94, WhoAm 94
Clarke, Arthur Grenfell d1993 Who 94N
Clarke, Arthur S. 1923- Who 94
Clarke, Ashley Who 94
Clarke, (Henry) Ashley 1903- IntWW 93, Who 94
Clarke, Athalie R. d1993 NewYTBS 93 [port]
Clarke, Austin (Ardinel) C(hesterfield) 1934- WrDr 94
Clarke, Austin C(hesterfield) 1934- RfGShF
Clarke, Bart Lyman 1956- WhoMW 93
Clarke, Benjamin Louis 1944- WhoBlA 94
Clarke, Bernard Who 94
Clarke, (John) Bernard 1934- Who 94
Clarke, Betty Ross d1947 WhoHol 92
Clarke, Bobby 1949- WhoAm 94
Clarke, Boden ConAu 42NR, EncSF 93
Clarke, Brenda 1926- WrDr 94
Clarke, Brian 1953- IntWW 93
Clarke, Brian Patrick 1953- WhoHol 92
Clarke, Bryan Campbell 1932- IntWW 93, Who 94
Clarke, Bud 1941- WhoAmA 93
Clarke, C. J. WhoIns 94
Clarke, Caitlin WhoHol 92
Clarke, Charles Fenton 1916- WhoAm 94
Clarke, Charles G. 1899-1983 IntDcF 2-4
Clarke, Cheryl DrAPF 93
Clarke, Cheryl 1947- BlkWr 2
Clarke, Christopher Michael 1952- Who 94
Clarke, Christopher Simon Courtenay Stephenson 1947- Who 94
Clarke, Clifford Montreville 1925- WhoAm 94
Clarke, Cordelia Kay Knight Mazuy 1938- WhoAm 94
Clarke, Cynthia Therese 1952- WhoAm 94
Clarke, Cyril (Astley) 1907- Who 94
Clarke, Cyril (Astley), Sir 1907- WrDr 94
Clarke, Cyril Astley 1907- IntWW 93
Clarke, David 1908- WhoHol 92
Clarke, David A. 1943- WhoAmP 93
Clarke, David Clive 1942- Who 94
Clarke, David H. 1941- WhoAm 94, WhoFI 94
Clarke, David Marshall 1927- WhoAm 94, WhoWest 94
Clarke, David Stuart 1942- Who 94
Clarke, David William 1943- Who 94
Clarke, Denise Jo 1947- WhoMW 93
Clarke, Derrick Harry 1919- WrDr 94
Clarke, Donald Dudley 1930- WhoBlA 94
Clarke, Donald Roberts 1933- Who 94
Clarke, Dorothy Clotelle 1908- WrDr 94
Clarke, Douglas E. 1948- WhoAmL 94
Clarke, Downing d1930 WhoHol 92
Clarke, Edmund Arthur Stanley 1862-1931 EncABHB 9
Clarke, Edward 1649?-1710 DcNaB MP
Clarke, Edward Nielsen 1925- WhoAm 94
Clarke, Edward Owen, Jr. 1929- WhoAm 94, WhoAmL 94
Clarke, Edwin (Sisterson) 1919- Who 94
Clarke, Edwin Kent Who 94
Clarke, Eleanora Norwood 1927- WhoBlA 94
Clarke, Elijah 1733-1799 WhAmRev
Clarke, Elijah 1742-1799 AmRev
Clarke, Elizabeth Bleckly 1915- Who 94
Clarke, Ellis (Emmanuel Innocent) 1917- Who 94
Clarke, Ellis Emmanuel Innocent 1917- IntWW 93
Clarke, Eric Lionel 1933- Who 94
Clarke, Eugene H., Jr. 1920- WhoBlA 94
Clarke, Everee Jimerson 1926- WhoBlA 94
Clarke, "Fast" Eddie
See Motorhead ConMus 10
Clarke, Fletcher James 1942- WhoBlA 94
Clarke, Florence Myres 1927- WhoMW 93
Clarke, Frank d1948 WhoHol 92
Clarke, Franklyn Roselle 1926- WhoAm 94
Clarke, Frederic B., III 1942- WhoAm 94
Clarke, Frederick 1928- Who 94
Clarke, Gage d1964 WhoHol 92
Clarke, Garry Evans 1943- WhoAm 94
Clarke, Garry Kenneth Connal 1941- WhoAm 94
Clarke, Garvey Elliott 1935- WhoFI 94
Clarke, Gary 1936- WhoHol 92
Clarke, Gary Kendrick 1939- WhoAm 94
Clarke, Geoffrey 1924- IntWW 93, Who 94
Clarke, George d1946 WhoHol 92
Clarke, Gillian 1937- WrDr 94
Clarke, Gordon B. d1972 WhoHol 92
Clarke, Graeme Wilber 1934- IntWW 93
Clarke, Graham WhoHol 92
Clarke, Graham Neil 1956- Who 94
Clarke, Greta Fields WhoBlA 94
Clarke, Guy Hamilton 1910- Who 94
Clarke, H(enry) Harrison 1902- WrDr 94
Clarke, (James) Hamilton (Smee) 1840-1912 NewGrDO
Clarke, Hansen 1957- WhoAmP 93
Clarke, Harold G. 1927- WhoAmP 93
Clarke, Harold Gravely 1927- WhoAm 94, WhoAmL 94
Clarke, Helen 1939- Who 94
Clarke, Henry Benwell 1950- Who 94
Clarke, Henry Lee 1941- WhoAm 94
Clarke, Henry Leland 1907- NewGrDO
Clarke, Henry Louis 1908- WhoBlA 94
Clarke, Hilton Swift 1909- Who 94
Clarke, Hope WhoAm 94, WhoHol 92
Clarke, Hugh Vincent 1919- ConAu 41NR, WrDr 94
Clarke, I(gnatius) F(rederic) 1918- EncSF 93
Clarke, Irene Fortune Irwin 1903- IntWW 93
Clarke, J. SmATA 75
Clarke, J. Calvitt, Jr. 1920- WhoAm 94, WhoAmL 94
Clarke, J. D. WhoHol 92
Clarke, J(oseph) Henry 1930- WhAm 10
Clarke, Jack 1939- WhoAmL 94
Clarke, Jack Frederick 1936- WhoWest 94
Clarke, Jack Graeme 1927- WhoAm 94, WhoFI 94
Clarke, James Alexander 1924- WhoBlA 94
Clarke, James Freeman 1810-1888 DcAmReB 2
Clarke, James McClure 1917- WhoAmP 93
Clarke, James Samuel 1921- Who 94
Clarke, James T. d1993 NewYTBS 93
Clarke, James W(eston) 1937- ConAu 42NR
Clarke, James Weston 1937- WhoAm 94
Clarke, Joan L(orraine) 1920- WrDr 94
Clarke, John DrAPF 93, WhoHol 92
Clarke, John 1609-1676 DcAmReB 2
Clarke, John 1942- IntWW 93, Who 94, WhoAm 94
Clarke, John Clem 1937- WhoAm 94, WhoAmA 93
Clarke, John Frederick 1927- Who 94
Clarke, John Henrik 1915- BlkWr 2, ConAu 43NR, WhoBlA 94
Clarke, John Innes 1929- Who 94
Clarke, John Kevin Aloysius 1931- IntWW 93
Clarke, John L. 1905-1991 WhAm 10
Clarke, John Patrick 1930- WhoAm 94
Clarke, John R. 1945- ConAu 141, WhoAmA 93
Clarke, John Robert Who 94
Clarke, John W. 1937- WhoAmL 94
Clarke, Jonathan (Dennis) 1930- Who 94
Clarke, Joseph Lance 1941- WhoBlA 94
Clarke, Joy Adele 1937- WhoBlA 94
Clarke, Judith 1943- ConAu 142, SmATA 75 [port]
Clarke, Kenneth 1940- Who 94
Clarke, Kenneth Harry 1940- IntWW 93
Clarke, Kenneth Kingsley 1924- WhoAm 94
Clarke, Kenneth Stevens 1931- WhoAm 94
Clarke, Kenny 1914-1985 AfrAmAl 6
Clarke, Kenton 1951- WhoBlA 94
Clarke, Kevin Mattes 1959- WhoAmL 94
Clarke, Kit Hansen 1944- WhoScEn 94
Clarke, Lambuth McGeehee 1923- WhoAm 94
Clarke, Laurence R. 1944- WhoAmL 94
Clarke, Laurie 1934- IntMPA 94
Clarke, Leon Edison 1949- WhoBlA 94
Clarke, LeRoy P. 1938- WhoBlA 94
Clarke, Lewis Douglas 1936- WhoMW 93
Clarke, Lewis James 1927- WhoAm 94
Clarke, Linda Dumas 1944- WhoAmP 93
Clarke, (Victor) Lindsay 1939- WrDr 94
Clarke, Logan, Jr. 1927- WhoAm 94
Clarke, Lydia WhoHol 92
Clarke, Mae 1907- WhoHol 92
Clarke, Malcolm WhoAm 94
Clarke, Malcolm Roy 1930- Who 94
Clarke, Marcus (Andrew Hislop) 1846-1881 RfGShF
Clarke, Margaret 1941- WrDr 94
Clarke, Margi 1956- WhoHol 92
Clarke, Marshal Butler C. Who 94
Clarke, Martin Lowther 1909- Who 94, WrDr 94
Clarke, Mary 1923- Who 94, WrDr 94
Clarke, Mary Cowden 1809-1898 BlmGWL
Clarke, Mary Stetson 1911- WrDr 94
Clarke, Matthew Gerard Who 94
Clarke, Mercer Kaye 1944- WhoAm 94, WhoAmL 94
Clarke, Michael Gilbert 1944- Who 94
Clarke, Michael Hugo Friend 1936- Who 94
Clarke, Mike d1993 NewYTBS 93
Clarke, Milton Charles 1929- WhoAm 94, WhoAmL 94
Clarke, Neil Who 94
Clarke, Neil 1937- WhoAmP 93
Clarke, (John) Neil 1934- IntWW 93, Who 94
Clarke, Nicholas Charles 1948- WhoScEn 94
Clarke, Nigel d1976 WhoHol 92
Clarke, Norman 1916- Who 94
Clarke, Norman Eley d1993 Who 94N
Clarke, Oscar Withers 1919- WhoAm 94, WhoMW 93
Clarke, P. Joseph 1933- WhoAmP 93
Clarke, Patricia Hannah 1919- Who 94
Clarke, Pauline 1921- WrDr 94
Clarke, Peter 1922- Who 94
Clarke, Peter 1936- WhoAm 94, WhoWest 94
Clarke, Peter Anthony 1933- WhoWest 94
Clarke, Peter Cecil 1927- Who 94
Clarke, Peter Frederick 1942- Who 94, WrDr 94
Clarke, Peter James 1934- Who 94
Clarke, Philip Joseph 1956- WhoWest 94
Clarke, Philip Ream, Jr. 1914- WhoAm 94, WhoFI 94
Clarke, Priscilla 1960- WhoBlA 94
Clarke, Randall Lee 1958- WhoWest 94
Clarke, Raymond d1987 WhoHol 92

Clarke, Raymond 1950- *WhoBlA 94*
Clarke, Redfield d1928 *WhoHol 92*
Clarke, Richard *WhoHol 92*
Clarke, Richard 1711-1795 *WhAmRev*
Clarke, Richard A. *WhoAm 94*
Clarke, Richard Alan 1930- *WhoAm 94, WhoFI 94, WhoWest 94*
Clarke, Richard Lewis 1948- *WhoAm 94, WhoMW 93*
Clarke, Richard M. 1931- *WhoFI 94*
Clarke, Richard Stewart 1934- *WhoMW 93*
Clarke, Richard V. 1927- *WhoBlA 94*
Clarke, Robert *EncSF 93, WhoHol 92*
Clarke, Robert (Cyril) 1929- *Who 94*
Clarke, Robert Bradstreet 1928-1990 *WhAm 10*
Clarke, Robert C. 1929- *IntWW 93*
Clarke, Robert Earle 1949- *WhoAm 94*
Clarke, Robert F. *WhoFI 94*
Clarke, Robert Logan 1942- *WhoAm 94, WhoAmP 93*
Clarke, Robert Sydney 1935- *Who 94*
Clarke, Robert Warner 1896- *WhAm 10*
Clarke, Robin *WhoHol 92*
Clarke, Robin Mitchell 1917- *Who 94*
Clarke, Rockne Wayne 1949- *WhoAmP 93*
Clarke, Roger Eric 1939- *Who 94*
Clarke, Roger Howard 1943- *Who 94*
Clarke, Roy 1947- *WhoScEn 94*
Clarke, Rupert W.J. 1919- *IntWW 93*
Clarke, Rupert William John 1919- *Who 94*
Clarke, S. Bruce 1940- *WhoFI 94*
Clarke, Samuel 1675-1729 *EncEth*
Clarke, Samuel Harrison 1903- *Who 94*
Clarke, Samuel Laurence Harrison 1929- *Who 94*
Clarke, Shirley 1925- *WhoHol 92*
Clarke, Stanley 1951- *ConTFT 11*
Clarke, Stanley George 1914- *Who 94*
Clarke, Stanley Marvin 1951- *WhoBlA 94*
Clarke, Stella Rosemary 1932- *Who 94*
Clarke, T. E. B. 1907-1989 *IntDcF 2-4 [port]*
Clarke, Terence Michael 1937- *WhoAm 94, WhoFI 94*
Clarke, Theodore Henson 1923- *WhoBlA 94, WhoMW 93*
Clarke, Thomas 1941- *Who 94*
Clarke, Thomas Crawford 1932- *WhoAm 94, WhoFI 94*
Clarke, Thomas Edward 1942- *WhoScEn 94*
Clarke, Thomas Hal 1914- *WhoAm 94*
Clarke, Thomas Joseph 1949- *WhoAmL 94*
Clarke, Thomas P. 1917- *WhoBlA 94*
Clarke, Tobias *Who 94*
Clarke, (Charles Mansfield) Tobias 1939- *Who 94*
Clarke, Tom d1993 *Who 94N*
Clarke, Una *WhoAmP 93*
Clarke, Urana 1902- *WhoWest 94*
Clarke, Velma Greene 1930- *WhoBlA 94*
Clarke, Vince 1960- *See* Erasure *ConMus 11*
Clarke, W. Hall 1927- *WhoAm 94*
Clarke, Walter Sheldon 1934- *WhoAm 94*
Clarke, Warren *WhoHol 92*
Clarke, Westcott B. d1959 *WhoHol 92*
Clarke, Wilfred d1945 *WhoHol 92*
Clarke, William J. 1937- *WhoIns 94*
Clarke, William Malpas 1922- *Who 94*
Clarke, William Newton 1841-1912 *DcAmReB 2*
Clark-Eddington, Paul *Who 94*
Clarke Hall, Denis 1910- *Who 94*
Clarke-Smith, D. A. d1959 *WhoHol 92*
Clarkeson, John Anthony 1953- *WhoAmP 93*
Clark-Gates, Brenda *WhoBlA 94*
Clark Hutchison, George Ian *Who 94*
Clarkin, John Francis 1936- *WhoFI 94*
Clarkin, Peter Arthur 1958- *WhoAmL 94*
Clark-Langager, Sarah Ann 1943- *WhoAmA 93*
Clark Of Kempston, Baron 1917- *Who 94*
Clarkson, Alan Geoffrey 1934- *Who 94*
Clarkson, Andrew MacBeth 1937- *WhoAm 94, WhoFI 94*
Clarkson, Barbara Moore *DrAPF 93*
Clarkson, Brian Leonard 1930- *IntWW 93, Who 94*
Clarkson, C. Jack 1930- *WhoAmP 93*
Clarkson, Charles Andrew 1945- *WhoAm 94*
Clarkson, David M. 1927- *WhoAmP 93*
Clarkson, Derek Joshua 1929- *Who 94*
Clarkson, E. Margaret 1915- *WrDr 94*
Clarkson, Elizabeth Diane 1958- *WhoMW 93*
Clarkson, Ewan 1929- *WrDr 94*
Clarkson, Geoffrey Peniston Elliott 1934- *Who 94, WhoAm 94*
Clarkson, Gerald Dawson 1939- *Who 94*
Clarkson, Helen 1904- *EncSF 93, WrDr 94*
Clarkson, J. F. 1919- *WrDr 94*
Clarkson, Jocelyn Adrene 1952- *WhoAm 94, WhoScEn 94*
Clarkson, John J. 1941- *WhoScEn 94*
Clarkson, Julian Derieux 1929- *WhoAm 94*
Clarkson, Kenneth Wright 1942- *WhoAm 94, WhoFI 94, WhoScEn 94*
Clarkson, Lawrence William 1938- *WhoAm 94, WhoFI 94, WhoWest 94*
Clarkson, Matthew 1758-1825 *WhAmRev*
Clarkson, Max Boydell Elliott 1922- *WhoAm 94*
Clarkson, Patricia 1960- *WhoHol 92*
Clarkson, Patrick Robert James 1949- *Who 94*
Clarkson, Paul R. 1935- *WhoIns 94*
Clarkson, Paul Sumpter 1928- *WhoAmP 93*
Clarkson, Peter David 1945- *Who 94*
Clarkson, Thomas Boston 1931- *WhoScEn 94*
Clarkson, Thomas William 1932- *IntWW 93, WhoAm 94*
Clarkson, William Morris 1954- *WhoMW 93*
Clarkston, Ronne 1941- *WhoFI 94*
Clark-Taylor, Kristin 1959- *WhoBlA 94*
Clark-Thomas, Eleanor M. 1938- *WhoBlA 94*
Clarno, Beverly A. 1936- *WhoAmP 93*
Clarno, Beverly Ann 1936- *WhoWest 94*
Clarno, Robert John 1948- *WhoMW 93*
Claro, Jaime 1936- *WhoAm 94*
Clarren, Sterling Keith 1947- *WhoScEn 94, WhoWest 94*
Clarricoats, Peter John Bell 1932- *Who 94*
Clarson, Stephen John 1959- *WhoMW 93*
Clary, Alexia Barbara 1954- *WhoAm 94, WhoFI 94*
Clary, Ben 1940- *WhoAm 94, WhoMW 93*
Clary, Bradley Grayson 1950- *WhoAm 94, WhoAmL 94*
Clary, Charles d1931 *WhoHol 92*
Clary, Daniel K. 1958- *WhoAmL 94*
Clary, David Allen 1946- *WhoMW 93*
Clary, Everett Burton 1921- *WhoAm 94*
Clary, Glenn Warren 1955- *WhoAmP 93*
Clary, Keith Uhl 1921- *WhoMW 93*
Clary, Killarney *DrAPF 93*
Clary, Richard Wayland 1953- *WhoAm 94, WhoAmL 94*
Clary, Robert 1926- *WhoHol 92*
Clary, Ronald Gordon 1940- *WhoFI 94*
Clary, Rosalie Brandon Stanton 1928- *WhoAm 94, WhoFI 94, WhoMW 93*
Clary, Warren Powell 1936- *WhoWest 94*
Clasen, George Henry 1916- *WhoAmP 93*
Clasper, Michael 1953- *Who 94*
Claspill, James Louis 1946- *WhoFI 94, WhoMW 93*
Class, Loretta Mina 1913- *WhoAmP 93*
Class-Rivera, Ana Nydia 1951- *WhoHisp 94*
Clatterbaugh, Barbara Ann 1944- *WhoAmP 93*
Clatworthy, Robert 1928- *IntWW 93, Who 94*
Claud, Joseph Gillette 1927- *WhoAm 94*
Claude, Georges 1870-1960 *WorInv*
Claude, Inis Lothair, Jr. 1922- *WhoAm 94*
Claude, James L. 1942- *WhoFI 94*
Claude, Richard Pierre 1934- *WrDr 94*
Claude, Robert Woodward 1956- *WhoAmL 94*
Claudel, Paul (Louis Charles Marie) 1868-1955 *IntDcT 2*
Claudia, Susan 1949- *WrDr 94*
Claudio, Pete 1956- *WhoHisp 94*
Claudius 10BC-54AD *HisWorL [port]*
Claudius fl. 41-54 *BlmGEL*
Claudius, Dane d1946 *WhoHol 92*
Claudy, Carl H(arry) 1879-1957 *EncSF 93*
Claus, Christian Daniel 1727-1787 *AmRev*
Claus, Hugo (Maurice Julien) 1929- *ConWorW 93, IntDcT 2*
Clause, Calley E. 1963- *WhoFI 94*
Clausen, Alden Winship 1923- *Who 94*
Clausen, Alden Winship (Tom) 1923- *IntWW 93*
Clausen, Alf Heiberg 1941- *WhoWest 94*
Clausen, Andy *DrAPF 93*
Clausen, Betty Jane Hansen 1925- *WhoMW 93*
Clausen, Bret Mark 1958- *WhoWest 94*
Clausen, Christopher (John) 1942- *WrDr 94*
Clausen, Don H. 1923- *WhoAmP 93*
Clausen, Donald Neath 1898- *WhAm 10*
Clausen, Edgar Clemens 1951- *WhoAm 94*
Clausen, Edwin George 1946- *WhoWest 94*
Clausen, Hans Peter 1928- *IntWW 93*
Clausen, Hugh Joseph 1926- *WhoAm 94*
Clausen, Jan *DrAPF 93*
Clausen, Jerry Lee 1939- *WhoAm 94, WhoScEn 94*
Clausen, John Adam 1914- *WhoAm 94*
Clausen, Sally Ilene 1945- *WhoAm 94*
Clausen, Thomas G. *WhoAmP 93*
Clausen, Thomas Hans Wilhelm 1950- *WhoScEn 94*
Clausen, Wendell Vernon 1923- *WhoAm 94*
Clauser, Angela Frances 1955- *WhoMW 93*
Clauser, Donald Roberdeau 1941- *WhoAm 94*
Clauser, Francis H. 1913- *WhoAm 94*
Clausing, Alice 1944- *WhoAmP 93*
Clausing, Arthur M. 1936- *WhoAm 94*
Clausius, Rudolf Julius Emmanuel 1822-1888 *WorScD*
Clausman, Gilbert Joseph 1921- *WhoAm 94*
Clausner, Marlin David, Jr. 1941- *WhoWest 94*
Clausnitzer, Dale A. 1951- *WhoAmP 93*
Clauson, James Wilson 1913- *WhoAm 94*
Clauson, Peter A. 1955- *WhoIns 94*
Clauson, Sharyn Ferne 1946- *WhoFI 94*
Clauss, Alfred 1906- *WhoAm 94*
Clauss, Heinz 1935- *IntDcB [port]*
Clauss, Wayne Francis 1947- *WhoAmL 94*
Claussen, Bonnie Addison, II 1942- *WhoWest 94*
Claussen, Eileen Barbara 1945- *WhoAm 94*
Claussen, Julia 1879-1941 *NewGrDO*
Claussen, Karen *DrAPF 93*
Claussen, Kelli 1943- *WhoWest 94*
Claussen, Ron d1977 *WhoHol 92*
Claussen, Ronald Vernon 1938- *WhoWest 94*
Clave, Antoni 1913- *IntWW 93*
Clavel, Bernard 1923- *IntWW 93*
Clavell, James *Who 94*
Clavell, James 1924- *IntWW 93, WhoAm 94, WrDr 94*
Clavelli, Louis John 1939- *WhoScEn 94*
Clavenna, George Brian 1948- *WhoMW 93*
Claver, Robert Earl 1928- *WhoAm 94*
Claverie, Philip deVilliers 1941- *WhoAm 94*
Clavering, Eric *WhoHol 92*
Clavers, Mary, Mrs. *BlmGWL*
Clavier, Christian *WhoHol 92*
Clavijo, Ruy Gonzalez De d1412 *WhWE*
Clawater, Wayne 1954- *WhoAmL 94*
Clawges, Russell Maxwell, Jr. 1950- *WhoAmL 94*
Clawson, Charles Bernard 1957- *WhoMW 93*
Clawson, David Kay 1927- *WhoAm 94*
Clawson, Harry Quintard Moore 1924- *WhoFI 94*
Clawson, John Addison 1922- *WhoAm 94*
Clawson, John David 1934- *WhoFI 94*
Clawson, John Thomas 1945- *WhoAmP 93*
Clawson, Kim Roger 1953- *WhoMW 93*
Clawson, Michael Scott 1958- *WhoAmL 94*
Clawson, Raymond Walden 1906- *WhoFI 94*
Claxton, Bradford Wayne 1934- *WhoAm 94*
Claxton, Patrick Fisher 1915- *Who 94*
Clay, Alberta Z. *WhoAmP 93*
Clay, Ambrose Whitlock Winston 1941- *WhoAm 94, WhoScEn 94*
Clay, Andrew Dice 1957- *WhoHol 92*
Clay, Andrew Dice 1958- *ConTFT 11, WhoAm 94, WhoCom*
Clay, Bill, Jr. 1956- *WhoAmP 93*
Clay, Camille Alfreda 1946- *WhoBlA 94*
Clay, Cassius *WhoHol 92*
Clay, Cassius Marcellus 1810-1903 *AmSocL*
Clay, Cassius Marcellus 1942- *WhoAm 94, WhoBlA 94*
Clay, Charles Commander 1950- *WhoAmP 93*
Clay, Cliff *WhoBlA 94*
Clay, Don d1993 *NewYTBS 93*
Clay, Don Richard 1937- *WhoAm 94*
Clay, Eric Lee 1948- *WhoBlA 94*
Clay, Ernest H., III 1972- *WhoBlA 94*
Clay, Franklin Delano 1947- *WhoMW 93*
Clay, Frederic Emes 1838-1889 *NewGrDO*
Clay, George Harry 1911- *WhoAm 94*
Clay, George Henry 1941- *WhoAmP 93*
Clay, George R. *DrAPF 93*
Clay, Harold R. 1936- *WhoBlA 94*
Clay, Harris Aubrey 1911- *WhoAm 94, WhoFI 94, WhoScEn 94*
Clay, Henry 1777-1852 *HisWorL [port]*
Clay, Henry Carroll, Jr. 1928- *WhoBlA 94*
Clay, James Franklin 1911- *WhoAmL 94*
Clay, James Jordan, Jr. 1962- *WhoMW 93*
Clay, James Ray 1938- *WhoWest 94*
Clay, Jasper R. 1933- *WhoAm 94, WhoAmL 94*
Clay, Jesse fl. 1912-1920 *EncNAR*
Clay, John Ernest 1921- *WhoAm 94*
Clay, John Lionel 1918- *Who 94*
Clay, John Martin 1927- *IntWW 93, Who 94*
Clay, Joseph 1741-1804 *WhAmRev*
Clay, Kelli Suzanne 1964- *WhoScEn 94*
Clay, Laura 1849-1941 *WomPubS*
Clay, Margaret Leone 1923- *WhoMW 93*
Clay, Marie (Mildred) 1926- *Who 94*
Clay, Nathaniel, Jr. 1943- *WhoBlA 94*
Clay, Nicholas 1947- *WhoHol 92*
Clay, Orson C. 1930- *WhoAm 94, WhoFI 94, WhoIns 94*
Clay, Philip G. 1952- *WhoIns 94*
Clay, Reuben Anderson, Jr. 1938- *WhoBlA 94*
Clay, Richard (Henry) 1940- *Who 94*
Clay, Rickter Samuel 1946- *WhoMW 93*
Clay, Robert Alan 1946- *Who 94*
Clay, Robert N. 1946- *WhoAm 94*
Clay, Ross Collins 1908- *WhoBlA 94*
Clay, Rudolph 1935- *WhoBlA 94*
Clay, Stanley Bennett 1950- *WhoBlA 94*
Clay, Stanton Tower 1932- *WhoScEn 94*
Clay, Theodore Roosevelt, Jr. 1931- *WhoBlA 94*
Clay, Timothy Byron 1955- *WhoBlA 94*
Clay, Trevor 1936- *Who 94*
Clay, William 1931- *AfrAmAl 6 [port], CngDr 93*
Clay, William L. 1931- *WhoBlA 94*
Clay, William Lacy 1931- *WhoAm 94, WhoAmP 93, WhoMW 93*
Clay, William Lacy, Jr. 1956- *WhoBlA 94, WhoMW 93*
Clay, William Roger 1919- *WhoBlA 94*
Clay, Willie B. 1929- *WhoBlA 94*
Claybaker, Beth 1930- *WhoAmP 93*
Clayberger, Samuel Robert 1926- *WhoAmA 93*
Clayborn, Ray Dewayne 1955- *WhoBlA 94*
Clayborn, Wilma W. *WhoBlA 94*
Clayborne, Oneal 1940- *WhoAmP 93, WhoBlA 94*
Claybourne, Doug 1947- *IntMPA 94*
Claybourne, Edward P. 1927- *WhoBlA 94*
Clayburgh, Bennie James 1924- *WhoAmP 93*
Clayburgh, Jill 1944- *IntMPA 94, IntWW 93, WhoAm 94, WhoHol 92*
Clayburgh, Richard Scott *WhoAmP 93*
Claycamp, Henry Gregg 1952- *WhoScEn 94*
Claycomb, Cecil Keith 1920- *WhoAm 94*
Claycomb, Hugh Murray 1931- *WhoAmL 94*
Claydon, Geoffrey Bernard 1930- *Who 94*
Claye, Charlene Marette 1945- *WhoBlA 94*
Clayman, David 1934- *Who 94*
Clayman, Ralph Victor 1947- *WhoMW 93*
Claypole, Eugene 1938- *WhoAmP 93*
Claypool, David L. 1946- *WhoAm 94, WhoAmL 94*
Claypool, Les c. 1964- *See* Primus *ConMus 11*
Claypool, William, III *WhoFI 94*
Claypoole, Robert Edwin 1936- *WhoAm 94*
Clayre, Berenice d1978 *WhoHol 92*
Clayson, Christopher William 1903- *Who 94*
Clayson, (S.) Hollis 1946- *ConAu 140*
Clayson, S. Hollis *WhoAmA 93*
Clayson, Susan Hollis *WhoMW 93*
Clayton, Barbara (Evelyn) 1922- *Who 94*
Clayton, Bernard Miles, Jr. 1953- *WhoFI 94*
Clayton, Billy Wayne 1928- *WhoAmP 93*
Clayton, Bob d1979 *WhoHol 92*
Clayton, Bruce David 1947- *WhoMW 93*
Clayton, Buck (Wilbur) d1991 *WhoBlA 94N*
Clayton, C. Guy 1936- *WrDr 94*
Clayton, Charles Andrew 1957- *WhoWest 94*
Clayton, Charles M. 1889-1992 *WhoBlA 94N*
Clayton, Claude F., Jr. 1948- *WhoAmL 94*
Clayton, Claude Feemster, Jr. 1948- *WhoAmP 93*
Clayton, Constance *WhoAm 94*
Clayton, Constance Elaine *WhoBlA 94*
Clayton, Daniel Louis 1963- *WhoAmL 94*
Clayton, David (Robert) 1936- *Who 94*
Clayton, Dick *WhoHol 92*
Clayton, Donald d1964 *WhoHol 92*
Clayton, Donald Delbert 1935- *WhoAm 94, WhoScEn 94*
Clayton, Donald W. 1936- *WhoWest 94*
Clayton, Dwight Alan 1958- *WhoScEn 94*
Clayton, Ethel d1966 *WhoHol 92*
Clayton, Eva *WhoAm 94, WhoAmP 93*
Clayton, Eva 1934- *CngDr 93*

Clayton, Eva 1938- *WhoBlA 94*
Clayton, Evelyn Williams 1951- *WhoFI 94*
Clayton, Frances Elizabeth 1922- *WhoAm 94*
Clayton, Frederic d1925 *WhoHol 92*
Clayton, Frederick William 1913- *Who 94*
Clayton, George 1922- *Who 94*
Clayton, Gilbert d1950 *WhoHol 92*
Clayton, Hazel *WhoHol 92*
Clayton, Ina Smiley 1924- *WhoBlA 94*
Clayton, Jack 1921- *HorFD [port], IntMPA 94, IntWW 93, Who 94*
Clayton, James Edwin 1929- *WhoAm 94*
Clayton, James Henry 1944- *WhoBlA 94*
Clayton, Jan d1983 *WhoHol 92*
Clayton, Janet Theresa 1955- *WhoBlA 94*
Clayton, Jay *DrAPF 93*
Clayton, Jeffrey Alan 1955- *WhoWest 94*
Clayton, (Patricia) Jo 1939- *EncSF 93*
Clayton, Joe Don 1934- *WhoAm 94*
Clayton, Joe Todd 1924- *WhoAm 94*
Clayton, John *WhoHol 92*
Clayton, John 1930- *WhoScEn 94*
Clayton, John Charles 1924- *WhoAm 94*
Clayton, John J. *DrAPF 93*
Clayton, John Pilkington 1921- *Who 94*
Clayton, Joshua 1744-1798 *WhAmRev*
Clayton, Kathleen R. 1952- *WhoBlA 94*
Clayton, Keith Martin 1928- *Who 94*
Clayton, Laura Ancelina 1960- *WhoBlA 94*
Clayton, Lawrence (Otto, Jr.) 1945- *ConAu 142, SmATA 75 [port]*
Clayton, Lawrence Dean 1957- *WhoWest 94*
Clayton, Lawrence Ray 1938- *WhoAm 94*
Clayton, Lloyd E. 1921- *WhoBlA 94*
Clayton, Lou d1950 *WhoHol 92*
Clayton, Lucie *Who 94*
Clayton, Lucille d1923 *WhoHol 92*
Clayton, Margaret Ann 1941- *Who 94*
Clayton, Marguerite d1968 *WhoHol 92*
Clayton, Mark Gregory 1961- *WhoAm 94, WhoMW 93*
Clayton, Marvin Courtland 1938- *WhoFI 94*
Clayton, Mary 1954- *WrDr 94*
Clayton, Mary Jo *WhoAm 94*
Clayton, Matthew D. 1941- *WhoBlA 94*
Clayton, Mayme Agnew 1923- *WhoBlA 94, WhoWest 94*
Clayton, Michael Aylwin 1934- *Who 94*
Clayton, Michael Thomas Emilius 1917- *Who 94*
Clayton, Minnie H. *WhoBlA 94*
Clayton, Paula Jean 1934- *WhoScEn 94*
Clayton, Peter A(rthur) 1937- *WrDr 94*
Clayton, Preston Copeland 1903- *WhoAm 94*
Clayton, Randy Joe 1954- *WhoFI 94*
Clayton, Richard Henry Michael 1907- *Who 94*
Clayton, Richard Reese 1938- *WhoAm 94, WhoFI 94*
Clayton, Robert (James) 1915- *Who 94*
Clayton, Robert Beville 1948- *WhoFI 94*
Clayton, Robert James 1915- *IntWW 93*
Clayton, Robert L. 1938- *WhoBlA 94*
Clayton, Robert Louis 1934- *WhoBlA 94*
Clayton, Robert Norman 1930- *IntWW 93, Who 94, WhoAm 94*
Clayton, Ronald A. 1947- *WhoAmL 94*
Clayton, Sheryl Anne Howard 1929- *WhoMW 93*
Clayton, Stanley James 1919- *Who 94*
Clayton, Theaoseus T. 1930- *WhoBlA 94*
Clayton, Thomas 1673-1725 *NewGrDO*
Clayton, Verna L. *WhoAmP 93*
Clayton, Verna Lewis 1937- *WhoMW 93*
Clayton, William Alexander, Jr. 1946- *WhoWest 94*
Clayton, William E. 1938- *WhoAm 94*
Clayton, William Francis 1923- *WhoAmL 94, WhoMW 93*
Clayton, William Howard 1927- *WhoAm 94*
Clayton, William L. 1929- *WhoAm 94*
Clayton, William Lewis 1930- *WhoAm 94*
Clayton, Willie Burke, Jr. 1922- *WhoBlA 94*
Clayton, Xernona 1930- *WhoBlA 94*
Clayton, Xerona 1930- *AfrAmAl 6 [port]*
Clayton-Hill, Kelli 1965- *WhoWest 94*
Claytor, Arthur Adams 1893- *WhAm 10*
Claytor, Charles E. 1936- *WhoBlA 94*
Claytor, Richard Anderson 1927- *WhoAm 94*
Claytor, Robert Buckner d1993 *NewYTBS 93*
Claytor, W. Graham, Jr. 1912- *WhoAmP 93*
Claytor, William Graham, Jr. 1912- *WhoAm 94*
Clayworth, June *WhoHol 92*
Clayworth, June d1993 *NewYTBS 93*
Cleage, Albert B., Jr. 1911- *WhoBlA 94*
Cleage, Pearl (Michelle) 1948- *BlkWr 2*
Cleall, Charles 1927- *Who 94, WrDr 94*
Clear, Albert F., Jr. 1920- *WhoAm 94*
Clear, Charles V. *WhoAmA 93N*
Clear, John Michael 1948- *WhoAm 94, WhoAmL 94*
Clear, Robert Douglas 1947- *WhoWest 94*
Cleare, John S. 1936- *WrDr 94*
Clearfield, Abraham 1927- *WhoAm 94*
Clearfield, Harris Reynold 1933- *WhoAm 94*
Cleary, Audrey *WhoAmP 93*
Cleary, Audrey 1930- *WhoMW 93*
Cleary, B. J. B. *WhoAmA 93*
Cleary, Barbara Ann 1940- *WhoMW 93*
Cleary, Barbara B. 1935- *WhoAmA 93*
Cleary, Beverly 1916- *WrDr 94*
Cleary, Beverly Atlee 1916- *WhoAm 94*
Cleary, David Laurence 1941- *WhoAmL 94*
Cleary, Denis Mackrow 1907- *Who 94*
Cleary, Dennis H. *WhoAmP 93*
Cleary, Edward L. 1929- *ConAu 140*
Cleary, Edward William 1919- *WhoAm 94*
Cleary, Fritz 1914- *WhoAmA 93*
Cleary, Gary Wynn 1942- *WhoWest 94*
Cleary, James Roy 1926- *WhoAm 94*
Cleary, James W. 1927- *WhoScEn 94*
Cleary, James William 1926- *WhoMW 93*
Cleary, John Elliott 1943- *WhoMW 93*
Cleary, John Joseph 1946- *WhoAm 94, WhoAmL 94*
Cleary, John Vincent 1901- *WhAm 10*
Cleary, John Washington 1911- *WhoAm 94*
Cleary, Jon (Stephen) 1917- *WrDr 94*
Cleary, Jon Stephen 1917- *IntWW 93, Who 94*
Cleary, Joseph Jackson d1993 *Who 94N*
Cleary, Leo d1955 *WhoHol 92*
Cleary, Lynda Woods 1950- *WhoFI 94*
Cleary, Manon Catherine 1942- *WhoAmA 93*
Cleary, Martin Joseph 1935- *WhoAm 94*
Cleary, Michael *WhoScEn 94*
Cleary, Pamela Ann 1947- *WhoMW 93*
Cleary, Patrick James 1929- *WhoAmP 93*
Cleary, Paul Joseph 1950- *WhoAmL 94*
Cleary, Peggy d1972 *WhoHol 92*
Cleary, Philip Edward 1947- *WhoAmL 94*
Cleary, Polly Chase *DrAPF 93*
Cleary, Richard Edward 1963- *WhoFI 94*
Cleary, Richard Simon 1956- *WhoAmL 94*
Cleary, Robert Emmet 1937- *WhoScEn 94*
Cleary, Russell George 1933- *WhoAm 94*
Cleary, Shirley 1942- *WhoAmA 93*
Cleary, Shirley Jean 1942- *WhoWest 94*
Cleary, Sue Allene Shorney 1935- *WhoMW 93*
Cleary, Suzanne *DrAPF 93*
Cleary, Theresa Anne 1935-1992 *WhAm 10*
Cleary, Timothy Finbar 1925- *WhoAmP 93*
Cleary, William Joseph, Jr. 1942- *WhoFI 94, WhoWest 94*
Cleary, William Richard 1933- *WhoAm 94*
Cleasby, John LeRoy 1928- *WhoAm 94*
Cleasby, Thomas Wood Ingram 1920- *Who 94*
Cleave, James H. *WhoAm 94, WhoFI 94*
Cleave, Mary L. 1947- *WhoScEn 94*
Cleaveland, Moses 1754-1806 *WhAmRev*
Cleaveland, Samuel c. 1727-1794 *AmRev*
Cleavelin, Leonard Robert 1957- *WhoAmL 94*
Cleaver, Alan Richard 1952- *IntWW 93*
Cleaver, Anthony (Brian) 1938- *Who 94*
Cleaver, Anthony Brian 1938- *IntWW 93*
Cleaver, Bill 1920-1981 *TwCYAW*
Cleaver, Dale Gordon 1928- *WhoAmA 93*
Cleaver, Eldridge 1935- *ConBlB 5 [port], HisWorL, WhoBlA 94, WrDr 94*
Cleaver, (Leroy) Eldridge 1935- *TwCYAW*
Cleaver, Emanuel, II 1944- *WhoAm 94, WhoBlA 94, WhoMW 93*
Cleaver, James Edward 1938- *WhoWest 94*
Cleaver, Leonard Harry 1909- *Who 94*
Cleaver, Leroy Eldridge, Jr. 1935- *AmSocL [port]*
Cleaver, Peter (Charles) 1919- *Who 94*
Cleaver, Vera 1919-1992 *SmATA 76 [port], TwCYAW, WrDr 94N*
Cleaver, Vera 1919-1993 *Au&Arts 12 [port]*
Cleaver, William Benjamin 1921- *Who 94*
Cleaver, William Lehn 1949- *WhoAmL 94*
Cleaver, William Pennington 1914- *WhoAm 94*
Cleaves, Mark Andrew 1960- *WhoAmL 94*
Cleaves, Muriel Mattock d1947 *WhoAmA 93N*
Clecak, Dvera Vivian Bozman 1944- *WhoWest 94*
Clecak, Peter 1938- *WrDr 94*
Cleckley, Betty J. *WhoBlA 94*
Clediere, Bernard fl. 1673-1680 *NewGrDO*
Cledwyn Of Penrhos, Baron 1916- *IntWW 93, Who 94*
Cleere, Adrienne J. *WhoAm 94*
Cleere, Henry Forester 1926- *Who 94*
Cleese, John 1939- *IntMPA 94, WhoCom, WhoHol 92*
Cleese, John (Marwood) 1939- *WrDr 94*
Cleese, John Marwood 1939- *IntWW 93, Who 94, WhoAm 94*
Cleeve, Brian (Talbot) 1921- *WrDr 94*
Cleeves, Ann (Richardson) 1954- *WrDr 94*
Clegg, Brian George Herbert 1921- *Who 94*
Clegg, Edward John 1925- *Who 94*
Clegg, Hugh Armstrong 1920- *Who 94*
Clegg, John 1909- *WrDr 94*
Clegg, John Cardwell 1927- *WhoWest 94*
Clegg, Legrand H., II 1944- *WhoBlA 94*
Clegg, Michael Tran 1941- *WhoAm 94*
Clegg, Philip Charles 1942- *Who 94*
Clegg, Richard Ninian Barwick 1938- *Who 94*
Clegg, Roger Burton 1955- *WhoAm 94*
Clegg, Ronald Anthony 1937- *IntWW 93, Who 94*
Clegg, Valce d1947 *WhoHol 92*
Clegg, Walter 1920- *Who 94*
Clegg, William 1949- *Who 94*
Clegg-Hill *Who 94*
Cleghorn, Bruce Elliot 1946- *Who 94*
Cleghorn, John E. 1941- *IntWW 93*
Cleghorn, John Edward 1941- *WhoAm 94, WhoFI 94*
Cleghorn, Reese 1930- *WhoAm 94*
Clein, A. Michael 1937- *WhoAmL 94*
Cleitagora fl. c. 6th cent.BC- *BlmGWL*
Cleland, Charles Carr 1924- *WhoAm 94*
Cleland, Edward Gordon 1949- *WhoAmL 94*
Cleland, John 1709-1789 *BlmGEL*
Cleland, Joseph Maxwell 1942- *WhoAm 94, WhoAmP 93*
Cleland, Ned Murray 1951- *WhoScEn 94*
Cleland, Rachel 1906- *Who 94*
Cleland, Robert Erksine 1932- *WhoAm 94*
Cleland, Robert Hardy 1947- *WhoAm 94, WhoAmL 94, WhoMW 93*
Cleland, Sherrill 1924- *WhoAm 94*
Cleland, Thomas Maitland 1880-1964 *WhoAmA 93N*
Cleland, William Paton 1912- *Who 94*
Cleland, William Wallace 1930- *WhoAm 94, WhoScEn 94*
Clelland, David Gordon 1943- *Who 94*
Clelland, Michael Darr 1947- *WhoScEn 94*
Clelland, Richard Cook 1921- *WhoAm 94*
Clelland, Robert Theodore 1943- *WhoAmL 94*
Clem, Alan L(eland) 1929- *WrDr 94*
Clem, Alan Leland 1929- *WhoAm 94*
Clem, Chester 1937- *WhoAmP 93*
Clem, David Bruce 1946- *WhoMW 93*
Clem, Elizabeth Ann Stumpf 1945- *WhoMW 93*
Clem, John Richard 1938- *WhoAm 94, WhoScEn 94*
Clem, Lane William 1944- *WhoWest 94*
Clem, Richard Paul 1961- *WhoAmL 94*
Clemeau, Carol *DrAPF 93*
Clemen, John Douglas 1944- *WhoAm 94*
Clemenceau, Georges 1841-1929 *HisWorL [port]*
Clemenceau, Paul B. 1940- *WhoAm 94*
Clemence of Barking fl. 12th cent.- *BlmGWL*
Clemencia, Marina *BlmGWL*
Clemendor, Anthony Arnold 1933- *WhoBlA 94, WhoScEn 94*
Clemenhagen, Carol Jane 1954- *WhoAm 94*
Clemens, Alvin Honey 1937- *WhoAm 94, WhoFI 94*
Clemens, Brian *EncSF 93*
Clemens, Brian 1931- *IntMPA 94*
Clemens, Charles 1944- *WhoFI 94*
Clemens, Charles D. d1947 *WhoHol 92*
Clemens, Clive Carruthers 1924- *Who 94*
Clemens, David Allen 1946- *WhoAm 94, WhoAmL 94*
Clemens, Donald Faull 1929- *WhoAm 94*
Clemens, Frank Joseph 1940- *WhoAmL 94*
Clemens, Paul *WhoHol 92*
Clemens, Peter John, III 1943- *WhoFI 94*
Clemens, Richard Glenn 1940- *WhoAm 94*
Clemens, Roger 1962- *WhoAm 94*
Clemens, Roger Allyn 1946- *WhoScEn 94*
Clemens, Samuel L. *EncSF 93*
Clemens, T. Pat 1944- *WhoFI 94, WhoMW 93*
Clemens, Walter C., Jr. 1933- *WrDr 94*
Clemens, William Alvin 1932- *WhoWest 94*
Clemensen, Mariel Christi 1952- *WhoFI 94*
Clement, IX, Pope *NewGrDO*
Clement, Alain Gerard *WhoAmA 93*
Clement, Allan M., III 1955- *WhoIns 94*
Clement, Alvis Macon 1912- *WhoAm 94*
Clement, Andree d1954 *WhoHol 92*
Clement, Arthur *WhoAmP 93*
Clement, Arthur John Howard, III 1934- *WhoAmP 93*
Clement, Aurore *WhoHol 92*
Clement, Betty Waidlich 1937- *WhoWest 94*
Clement, Bob 1943- *CngDr 93, WhoAm 94, WhoAmP 93*
Clement, Catherine *BlmGWL*
Clement, Clay d1956 *WhoHol 92*
Clement, Clayton Emerson 1943- *WhoAmL 94*
Clement, D. B. *WhoAmP 93*
Clement, Daniel Roy, III 1943- *WhoAm 94, WhoFI 94, WhoMW 93*
Clement, David James 1930- *Who 94*
Clement, David Morris 1911- *Who 94*
Clement, Donald d1970 *WhoHol 92*
Clement, Douglas Bruce 1933- *WhoScEn 94*
Clement, Edith Brown 1948- *WhoAm 94, WhoAmL 94*
Clement, Edmond 1867-1928 *NewGrDO*
Clement, Hal 1922- *EncSF 93, WrDr 94*
Clement, Henry Joseph, Jr. 1942- *WhoAm 94*
Clement, Hope Elizabeth Anna 1930- *WhoAm 94*
Clement, Howard Wheeler 1917- *WhoAm 94*
Clement, Janice Faye 1946- *WhoMW 93*
Clement, John 1932- *IntWW 93, Who 94, WhoAm 94*
Clement, John Handel 1920- *Who 94*
Clement, Joseph 1779-1844 *DcNaB MP*
Clement, Joseph Dale 1928- *WhoAm 94*
Clement, Josephine Dobbs 1918- *WhoBlA 94*
Clement, Kathleen (Ruth) 1928- *WhoAmA 93*
Clement, Marc Ray d1990 *WhoHol 92*
Clement, Margaret Bush d1993 *NewYTBS 93*
Clement, Meredith Owen 1926- *WhoAm 94*
Clement, Paul Platts, Jr. 1935- *WhoMW 93*
Clement, Rene 1913- *IntWW 93, Who 94*
Clement, Richard 1937- *Who 94*
Clement, Richard Francis 1906- *WhoAm 94, WhoMW 93*
Clement, Robert Lebby, Jr. 1928- *WhoAmL 94*
Clement, Robert William 1927- *WhoAm 94*
Clement, Ronald E. 1948- *WhoWest 94*
Clement, Shirley 1922- *WhoAmA 93*
Clement, Stephen Le Roy 1944- *WhoWest 94*
Clement, Thomas Earl 1932- *WhoAm 94*
Clement, Walter Hough 1931- *WhoWest 94*
Clement, Whittington Whiteside 1947- *WhoAmP 93*
Clement, William A. 1912- *WhoBlA 94*
Clement, William A., Jr. 1943- *WhoBlA 94*
Clement, William Alexander 1912- *WhoAm 94*
Clement, Zack A. 1949- *WhoAmL 94*
Clemente, Carmine Domenic 1928- *IntWW 93, WhoAm 94, WhoScEn 94*
Clemente, Celestino 1922- *WhoAm 94*
Clemente, Constantine Louis 1937- *WhoAm 94, WhoAmL 94, WhoFI 94*
Clemente, Francesco 1952- *WhoAmA 93*
Clemente, Holly Anne *WhoFI 94*
Clemente, Patrocinio Ablola 1941- *WhoWest 94*
Clemente, Robert Stephen 1956- *WhoAmL 94*
Clemente, Steve d1950 *WhoHol 92*
Clemente, Vince *DrAPF 93*
Clementi, Aldo 1925- *NewGrDO*
Clementi, Mark Anthony 1955- *WhoWest 94*
Clementi, Muzio 1752-1832 *DcNaB MP*
Clementi, Pierre 1942- *WhoHol 92*
Clementin c. 1655-1714? *NewGrDO*
Clements, Alan William 1928- *Who 94*
Clements, Andrew Joseph 1950- *Who 94*
Clements, Arthur L. *DrAPF 93*
Clements, Arthur L. 1932- *WrDr 94*
Clements, Bernadette Stone 1943- *WhoAm 94*
Clements, Brian Matthew 1946- *WhoAm 94, WhoFI 94, WhoScEn 94*
Clements, Bruce 1931- *TwCYAW, WhoAm 94, WrDr 94*
Clements, Bruce W. 1942- *WhoIns 94*
Clements, David *EncSF 93*
Clements, Dudley d1947 *WhoHol 92*

Clinard, Joseph Hiram, Jr. 1938- *WhoFI 94*
Clinard, Marshall Barron 1911- *WhoAm 94*
Clinard, Robert Noel 1946- *WhoAm 94, WhoAmL 94*
Clinch, David John 1937- *Who 94*
Clinch, Harry Anselm 1908- *WhoWest 94*
Clinch, John Edmund 1940- *WhoFI 94*
Clinch, Nicholas Bayard, III 1930- *WhoWest 94*
Cline, Andrew Haley 1951- *WhoAm 94, WhoAmL 94*
Cline, Athol Louis 1936- *WhoWest 94*
Cline, Beth Ellen 1957- *WhoFI 94*
Cline, Bobby James 1932- *WhoAm 94*
Cline, Bryan M. 1959- *WhoWest 94*
Cline, C(harles) Terry, Jr. 1935- *EncSF 93*
Cline, Carolyn Joan 1941- *WhoScEn 94, WhoWest 94*
Cline, Cathie B. 1943- *WhoAm 94, WhoMW 93*
Cline, Charles *DrAPF 93*
Cline, Charles William 1937- *WhoAm 94*
Cline, Clarence Lee 1905- *WhoAm 94*
Cline, Clinton C. 1934- *WhoAmA 93*
Cline, David Bruce 1933- *WhoScEn 94, WhoWest 94*
Cline, David Christopher 1955- *WhoScEn 94*
Cline, Douglas 1934- *WhoScEn 94*
Cline, Eddie d1961 *WhoHol 92*
Cline, Eileen Tate 1935- *WhoBlA 94*
Cline, Fred Albert, Jr. 1929- *WhoWest 94*
Cline, Glen Edwin 1920- *WhoAm 94*
Cline, James Michael 1960- *WhoScEn 94*
Cline, Jane Lynn 1956- *WhoAmP 93*
Cline, John L. 1942- *WhoAmL 94*
Cline, Judy Butler 1952- *WhoFI 94*
Cline, Judy Elizabeth 1944- *WhoAmP 93*
Cline, Kenneth Scott 1958- *WhoAmL 94*
Cline, Lee Williamson 1944- *WhoAmL 94*
Cline, Linda Blair 1950- *WhoMW 93*
Cline, Lowell Eugene 1935- *WhoAmP 93*
Cline, Martin Jay 1934- *WhoAm 94*
Cline, Michael Robert 1949- *WhoAmL 94*
Cline, Mischelle Rae 1960- *WhoMW 93*
Cline, Nancy M. 1946- *WhoAm 94*
Cline, Ned Aubrey 1938- *WhoAm 94*
Cline, Paul Charles 1933- *WhoAm 94, WhoAmP 93*
Cline, Philip Lee 1945- *WhoFI 94*
Cline, Platt Herrick 1911- *WhoWest 94*
Cline, Ray S(teiner) 1918- *WrDr 94*
Cline, Ray Steiner 1918- *WhoAm 94*
Cline, Richard Allen 1955- *WhoAmL 94*
Cline, Richard Gordon 1935- *WhoAm 94, WhoFI 94*
Cline, Robert *DrAPF 93*
Cline, Robert Corde 1933- *WhoAmP 93*
Cline, Robert Stanley 1937- *WhoAm 94, WhoFI 94, WhoWest 94*
Cline, Robert Thomas 1925- *WhoFI 94*
Cline, Russell Brian 1959- *WhoWest 94*
Cline, Thomas Warren 1946- *WhoScEn 94*
Cline, Thomas William 1932- *WhoAm 94*
Cline, William Chambers 1949- *WhoMW 93*
Cline, William Richard 1941- *WhoAm 94*
Cline, Wilson Ettason 1914- *WhoAm 94, WhoAmL 94, WhoFI 94, WhoWest 94*
Clinebell, Howard J., Jr. 1922- *WrDr 94*
Clineburg, William A. 1943- *WhoAmL 94*
Clinedinst, Katherine Parsons 1903- *WhoAmA 93*
Clinedinst, May Spear 1887- *WhoAmA 93N*
Clinefelter, Ruth Elizabeth Wright 1930- *WhoMW 93*
Clingan, Lee 1921- *WhoAmP 93*
Clingan, Wanda Jacqueline 1928- *WhoMW 93*
Clingan, William d1790 *WhAmRev*
Clinger, William F., Jr. 1929- *CngDr 93*
Clinger, William Floyd, Jr. 1929- *WhoAm 94, WhoAmP 93*
Clingerman, Edgar Allen, Sr. 1934- *WhoFI 94*
Clingerman, John R. 1931- *WhoAmP 93*
Clingerman, John Rufus 1931- *WhoFI 94*
Clingerman, Mildred (McElroy) 1918- *EncSF 93*
Clingerman, Roger Brian 1961- *WhoFI 94*
Clingerman, Stanley Lee 1952- *WhoMW 93*
Clingham, Leonard F., Jr. 1938- *WhoAmP 93*
Clingman, Kevin Loren 1961- *WhoBlA 94*
Clingman, William Edward, Jr. 1953- *WhoAmL 94*
Clingman, William Herbert, Jr. 1929- *WhoFI 94*
Clinkscales, Jerry A. 1933- *WhoBlA 94*
Clinkscales, John William, Jr. 1925- *WhoBlA 94*
Clinkscales, William Abner, Jr. 1928- *WhoAm 94*
Clinque, Joseph 1811-1852 *AfrAmAl 6 [port]*
Clinton *Who 94*
Clinton, Baron 1934- *Who 94*
Clinton, Alan *Who 94*
Clinton, (Robert) Alan 1931- *Who 94*
Clinton, Bill *NewYTBS 93 [port], Who 94*
Clinton, Bill 1946- *WhoAm 94, WhoAmP 93*
Clinton, Bill Jefferson 1946- *IntWW 93*
Clinton, Catherine 1952- *WrDr 94*
Clinton, Charles A. *WhoIns 94*
Clinton, Charles A. 1943- *WhoFI 94*
Clinton, DeWitt *DrAPF 93*
Clinton, Dirk *EncSF 93*
Clinton, Edward Xavier 1930- *WhoAmL 94*
Clinton, F. G. 1927- *WrDr 94*
Clinton, George 1739-1812 *WhAmRev [port]*
Clinton, George 1941?- *CurBio 93 [port]*
Clinton, Gordon Stanley 1920- *WhoAm 94*
Clinton, Henry 1730-1795 *AmRev, WhAmRev [port]*
Clinton, Hillary Rodham 1947- *CurBio 93 [port], IntWW 93, NewYTBS 93 [port], WhoAm 94, WhoAmL 94, WhoAmP 93*
Clinton, James 1733-1812 *AmRev, WhAmRev [port]*
Clinton, James Harmon 1946- *WhoAm 94*
Clinton, Jeff *EncSF 93*
Clinton, Jeff 1930- *WrDr 94*
Clinton, John Philip Martin 1935- *WhoFI 94*
Clinton, Joseph Edward 1948- *WhoAm 94*
Clinton, Judith Mary Myers 1945- *WhoMW 93*
Clinton, Larry d1985 *WhoHol 92*
Clinton, Lawrence Paul 1945- *WhoScEn 94*
Clinton, Mariann Hancock 1933- *WhoAm 94*
Clinton, Michael *WhoAm 94*
Clinton, Paul Arthur 1942- *WhoAmA 93*
Clinton, Richard M. 1941- *WhoAm 94*
Clinton, Sam Houston 1923- *WhoAmL 94*
Clinton, Stephen William 1950- *WhoMW 93*
Clinton, Tracy Peter, Sr. 1948- *WhoFI 94*
Clinton, William Jefferson 1946- *Who 94, WhoAm 94*
Clinton-Davis, Baron 1928- *IntWW 93, Who 94*
Clipper, Lawrence Jon 1930- *WhoMW 93*
Clipper, Milton Clifton, Jr. 1948- *WhoBlA 94*
Clipper, Scott Alan 1963- *WhoMW 93*
Clippert, Charles Frederick 1931- *WhoAm 94, WhoAmL 94*
Clipsham, Robert Charles 1955- *WhoWest 94*
Clisby, Roger David 1939- *WhoAmA 93*
Clithero, Donley James 1941- *WhoWest 94*
Clithero, Monte Paul 1953- *WhoAmL 94*
Clithero, Paul Harvey 1952- *WhoAm 94*
Clitheroe, Baron 1929- *Who 94*
Clitheroe, Jimmy d1973 *WhoHol 92*
Clive, Viscount 1979- *Who 94*
Clive, Catherine 1711-1785 *BlmGEL*
Clive, Colin d1937 *WhoHol 92*
Clive, Dennis *EncSF 93*
Clive, E. E. d1940 *WhoHol 92*
Clive, Eric McCredie 1938- *Who 94*
Clive, Henry d1960 *WhoHol 92*
Clive, John *ConAu 43NR*
Clive, John 1938- *WhoHol 92*
Clive, John (Leonard) 1924- *WrDr 94*
Clive, John Leonard 1924-1990 *ConAu 43NR, WhAm 10*
Clive, Kitty 1711-1785 *NewGrDO*
Clive, Nigel David 1917- *Who 94*
Clive, Richard R. 1912- *WhoAmA 93*
Clive, Robert 1725-1774 *HisWorL [port]*
Clive, Teagan *WhoHol 92*
Clive, Vincent d1943 *WhoHol 92*
Cliver, Al *WhoHol 92*
Cliver, Dean Otis 1935- *WhoAm 94*
Cliver, Kendra-Jean *WhoAmA 93*
Clizbe, John Anthony 1942- *WhoAm 94*
Cloake, John (Cecil) 1924- *WrDr 94*
Cloake, John Cecil 1924- *Who 94*
Cloar, Carroll 1913- *WhoAmA 93*
Cloar, Carroll 1913-1993 *NewYTBS 93 [port]*
Clock, Herbert 1890-1979 *EncSF 93*
Clocksin, Donald E. 1944- *WhoAmP 93*
Clod, Bente 1946- *BlmGWL*
Clode, (Emma) Frances (Heather) 1903- *Who 94*
Clodfelter, Daniel Gray 1950- *WhoAm 94, WhoAmL 94*
Clodfelter, David Shibley 1953- *WhoFI 94*
Clodius, Albert Howard 1911- *WhoAm 94, WhoWest 94*
Clodius, Robert LeRoy 1921- *WhoAm 94*
Cloer, Carl Thomas, Jr. 1945- *WhoAm 94*
Cloes, Roger Arthur Josef 1956- *WhoScEn 94*
Clogan, Paul Maurice 1934- *WhoAm 94*
Clogg, Clifford Collier 1949- *WhoScEn 94*
Clogher, Bishop of 1934- *Who 94*
Clogher, Bishop of 1936- *Who 94*
Clohesy, William Warren 1946- *WhoMW 93*
Cloke, Kenneth 1941- *WhoAmL 94*
Cloke, Kristen *WhoHol 92*
Cloke, Richard *DrAPF 93*
Cløkey, Frank R. 1939- *WhoAm 94*
Clokie, Hilary Ann *Who 94*
Clompus, Bradley *DrAPF 93*
Clonch, L. Dale 1944- *WhoAmP 93*
Clonch, Leslie Allen, Jr. 1961- *WhoFI 94*
Clonebaugh, G. Butler d1943 *WhoHol 92*
Cloninger, Claude Robert 1944- *WhoAm 94, WhoMW 93*
Cloninger, Franklin Dale 1938- *WhoMW 93*
Cloninger, Kriss, III 1947- *WhoAm 94*
Cloninger, Ralph d1962 *WhoHol 92*
Cloonan, Clifford B. 1928- *WhoAm 94, WhoWest 94*
Cloonan, James Brian 1931- *WhoAm 94*
Clooney, George 1961- *WhoHol 92*
Clooney, Rosemary 1928- *WhoAm 94, WhoHol 92*
Cloos, Ernst 1898- *WhAm 10*
Clopet, Julian *WhoAm 94, WhoFI 94*
Clopine, Gordon Alan 1936- *WhoWest 94*
Cloquet, Ghislain 1924-1981 *IntDcF 2-4*
Cloran, John James 1958- *WhoAmL 94*
Clore, Duncan L. 1948- *WhoAmL 94*
Clore, Lawrence H. 1944- *WhoAm 94, WhoAmL 94*
Clore, Leon 1918-1992 *AnObit 1992*
Clos, Charles 1919- *WrDr 94*
Close, Charles Thomas 1940- *WhoAm 94*
Close, Chuck 1940- *WhoAmA 93*
Close, Daryl Lyndon 1947- *WhoMW 93*
Close, David Palmer 1915- *WhoAm 94, WhoAmL 94*
Close, Dean Purdy 1905- *WhoAmA 93*
Close, Del *WhoHol 92*
Close, Del 1934- *WhoCom*
Close, Donald Pembroke 1920- *WhoFI 94*
Close, Edward Roy 1936- *WhoScEn 94*
Close, Elizabeth Scheu 1912- *WhoAm 94*
Close, Elmer Harry 1937- *WhoAmP 93*
Close, Frank 1947- *WhoAmA 93*
Close, Glenn 1947- *IntMPA 94, IntWW 93, WhoAm 94, WhoHol 92*
Close, Ivy d1968 *WhoHol 92*
Close, Jay Charles 1961- *WhoWest 94*
Close, John d1964 *WhoHol 92*
Close, Marjorie (Perry) 1899-1978 *WhoAmA 93N*
Close, Melvin Dilkes, Jr. 1934- *WhoAmP 93*
Close, Michael John 1943- *WhoAm 94, WhoAmL 94*
Close, Reginald Arthur 1909- *WrDr 94*
Close, Richard Charles 1949- *Who 94*
Close, Roy Edwin 1920- *Who 94*
Close, Winston Arthur 1906- *WhoAm 94*
Closen, Ludwig von (Closen-Haydenburg) c. 1752-1830 *WhAmRev*
Closen, Michael Lee 1949- *WhoAm 94*
Closen-Haydenburg, Hans Christoph Friedrich Ignatz Ludwig c. 1754-1830 *AmRev*
Closets, Francois de 1933- *IntWW 93*
Closs, Gerhard Ludwig 1928-1992 *WhAm 10*
Closset, Gerard Paul 1943- *WhoAm 94*
Closson, Kay L. *DrAPF 93*
Closson, Nanci Blair 1943- *WhoAmA 93*
Closure, Vanilla Threats 1946- *WhoBlA 94*
Clotet, Lluis 1941- *IntWW 93*
Clotfelter, Beryl E. 1926- *WrDr 94*
Clotfelter, Charles T. 1947- *WrDr 94*
Clothier, Bill 1891-1962 *BuCMET*
Clothier, Cecil (Montacute) 1919- *Who 94*
Clothier, Peter *DrAPF 93*
Clothier, Peter Dean 1936- *WhoAmA 93*
Clothier, Richard John 1945- *Who 94*
Clothier, William H. 1903- *IntDcF 2-4*
Clotworthy, John Harris 1924- *WhoAm 94*
Cloud, Albert Hadden, Jr. 1926- *WhoFI 94*
Cloud, Bruce Benjamin, Sr. 1920- *WhoAm 94, WhoFI 94*
Cloud, Darrah 1955- *ConDr 93*
Cloud, Gary Lee 1937- *WhoMW 93*
Cloud, Henry Roe 1886-1950 *AmSocL*
Cloud, Jack L. 1925- *WhoAmA 93*
Cloud, Jack Leslie 1925- *WhoFI 94, WhoMW 93*
Cloud, Jack Leslie 1951- *WhoMW 93*
Cloud, James Merle 1947- *WhoWest 94*
Cloud, Mabel d1921 *WhoHol 92*
Cloud, Preston 1912-1991 *WhAm 10*
Cloud, Sanford, Jr. 1944- *WhoBlA 94*
Cloud, Stanley Wills 1936- *WhoAm 94*
Cloud, Stephen R. 1949- *WhoAmP 93*
Cloud, W. Eric 1946- *WhoBlA 94*
Clouden, LaVerne C. 1933- *WhoBlA 94*
Cloudman, Francis Harold, III 1944- *WhoAm 94*
Cloudman, Ruth Howard 1948- *WhoAmA 93*
Cloudsley, Donald Hugh 1925- *WhoAm 94*
Cloudsley-Thompson, John (Leonard) 1921- *WrDr 94*
Cloudsley-Thompson, John Leonard 1921- *IntWW 93, Who 94*
Cloues, Edward Blanchard, II 1947- *WhoAm 94, WhoAmL 94*
Clough, Alan *Who 94*
Clough, (John) Alan 1924- *Who 94*
Clough, Anson W. 1936- *WhoIns 94*
Clough, Arthur Hugh 1819-1861 *BlmGEL*
Clough, Charles Elmer 1930- *WhoAm 94*
Clough, Charles Marvin 1928- *WhoFI 94*
Clough, Charles Sidney 1951- *WhoAmA 93*
Clough, Charles Thomas 1852-1916 *DcNaB MP*
Clough, David Alan 1955- *WhoAmL 94*
Clough, Eleanor 1953- *WhoAmA 93*
Clough, (Arthur) Gordon 1934- *Who 94*
Clough, John Scott *WhoHol 92*
Clough, Nadine Doerr 1942- *WhoAm 94*
Clough, Philip Gerard 1924- *Who 94*
Clough, Prunella 1919- *Who 94*
Clough, Ray William, Jr. 1920- *IntWW 93, WhoAm 94, WhoScEn 94*
Clough, Shepard Bancroft 1901-1990 *WhAm 10*
Clough, Wilson Ober 1894-1990 *WhAm 10*
Clougherty, Dennis Paul *WhoWest 94*
Clous, James M. 1959- *WhoFI 94, WhoMW 93*
Clouse, Bill 1952- *WhoAmP 93*
Clouse, John Daniel 1925- *WhoAmL 94, WhoFI 94, WhoMW 93*
Clouse, Jon Monroe 1954- *WhoMW 93*
Clouse, Robert Gordon 1931- *WrDr 94*
Clouse, Robert Wilburn 1937- *WhoAm 94*
Clouser, Christopher E. 1953- *WhoAm 94*
Clouser, E. Randall 1957- *WhoFI 94, WhoMW 93*
Clouser, Michael Allen 1963- *WhoWest 94*
Clouston, J(oseph) Storer 1870-1944 *EncSF 93*
Clouston, Ross Neal 1922- *WhoAm 94*
Clout, Colin *BlmGEL*
Cloutier, Charles Edgar 1941- *WhoAmL 94*
Cloutier, Gilles G. 1928- *IntWW 93*
Cloutier, Gilles Georges 1928- *WhoAm 94*
Cloutier, John R. 1957- *WhoAmP 93*
Cloutier, Peter *WhoAmP 93*
Cloutier, Raymond Arthur 1938- *WhoAmL 94*
Cloutier, Stephen Edward 1949- *WhoScEn 94*
Cloutier, Suzanne 1927- *WhoHol 92*
Cloutier, Sylvain 1929- *IntWW 93*
Cloutier, Terry Wayne 1955- *WhoMW 93*
Cloutman, Geoffrey William 1920- *Who 94*
Clouzot, Vera d1960 *WhoHol 92*
Clovelly, Cecil d1965 *WhoHol 92*
Clover, Marian *DrAPF 93*
Clover, Philip Thornton 1935- *WhoFI 94*
Clover, Robert Gordon d1993 *Who 94N*
Clover, Timothy Dale 1963- *WhoMW 93*
Clovis, I 466-511 *HisWorL [port]*
Clovis, Albert L. 1935- *WhoAm 94*
Clovis, Donna L. *DrAPF 93*
Clow, Barbara Hand 1943- *WrDr 94*
Clow, Gordon Henry 1942- *WhoFI 94*
Clow, Lee *WhoAm 94*
Clow, William Hammond 1939- *WhoWest 94*
Cloward, Richard Andrew 1926- *WhoAm 94*
Clowe, Curtis James 1959- *WhoMW 93*
Clower, Robert Wayne 1926- *WhoAm 94*
Clower, William Dewey 1935- *WhoAm 94*
Clowers, Myles Leonard 1944- *WhoWest 94*
Clowes, A. W. 1931- *Who 94*
Clowes, Alexander Whitehill 1946- *WhoWest 94*
Clowes, Allen Whitehill 1917- *WhoAmA 93*
Clowes, Edith W. 1951- *WhoMW 93*
Clowes, Garth Anthony 1926- *WhoFI 94, WhoScEn 94, WhoWest 94*
Clowes, Henry Nelson d1993 *Who 94N*
Clowney, Audrey E. 1961- *WhoBlA 94*
Clowney, Frank Sherman, III 1952- *WhoAmL 94*
Cloyd, George Thomas 1944- *WhoMW 93*
Clubb, Bruce Edwin 1931- *WhoAm 94, WhoAmL 94*
Clubb, O. Edmund 1901-1989 *HisDcKW*

Coelho, Raymond C. 1933- *WhoAmP 93*
Coelho, Rui 1892-1986 *NewGrDO*
Coelho, Susie *WhoHol 92*
Coelho, Tony 1942- *WhoAm 94, WhoAmP 93, WhoWest 94*
Coello, Elena Coromoto 1952- *WhoAm 94*
Coeme, Guy 1946- *IntWW 93*
Coen, Daniel Kennedy, Jr. 1932- *WhoAm 94*
Coen, Edward Darby 1961- *WhoMW 93*
Coen, Ethan 1958- *IntMPA 94, WhoAm 94*
Coen, Guido *IntMPA 94*
Coen, Jeffrey V. 1951- *WhoAmL 94*
Coen, Joel 1954- *IntMPA 94*
Coen, Joel 1955- *WhoAm 94*
Coen, Massimo (Aldo) 1918- *Who 94*
Coen, Rena Neumann 1925- *WrDr 94*
Coen, Robert Joseph 1923- *WhoAm 94*
Coerne, Louis (Adolphe) 1870-1922 *NewGrDO*
Coerper, Milo George 1925- *WhoAm 94*
Coerr, Eleanor Beatrice 1922- *WrDr 94*
Coertse, Mimi (Maria Sophia) 1932- *NewGrDO*
Coerver, Elizabeth Ann 1941- *WhoMW 93*
Coes, Betsy A. 1952- *WhoAmP 93*
Coes, Kent Day 1910- *WhoAm 94, WhoAmA 93*
Coetsee, Hendrik Jacobus 1931- *IntWW 93*
Coetzee, J(ohn) M(ichael) 1940- *ConAu 41NR, WrDr 94*
Coetzee, John M. 1940- *IntWW 93, Who 94*
Coeur-Brulant, Vicomtesse de *BlmGWL*
Coey, John Michael David 1945- *IntWW 93*
Cofer, Berdette Henry *WhoFI 94, WhoWest 94*
Cofer, Charles Norval 1916- *WhoAm 94*
Cofer, James Henry 1925- *WhoBlA 94*
Cofer, Judith Ortiz *DrAPF 93*
Cofer, Judith Ortiz 1952- *WhoHisp 94, WrDr 94*
Cofer, Michael Lynn 1960- *WhoBlA 94*
Cofer, Suzanne Marie 1948- *WhoWest 94*
Coffee, Gary 1956- *WhoAmP 93*
Coffee, James Frederick 1918-1989 *WhAm 10*
Coffee, Joseph Denis, Jr. 1918- *WhoAm 94*
Coffee, Lawrence Winston 1929- *WhoBlA 94*
Coffee, Lenore d1984 *WhoHol 92*
Coffee, Lenore J. c. 1896-1983 *IntDcF 2-4*
Coffee, Richard J. *WhoAmP 93*
Coffee, Virginia Claire 1920- *WhoMW 93*
Coffelt, Gina Crews 1959- *WhoMW 93*
Coffer, David Edwin 1913- *Who 94*
Coffer, Jack d1967 *WhoHol 92*
Coffey, Aeneas c. 1780-1852 *DcNaB MP*
Coffey, Ann *Who 94*
Coffey, (Margaret) Ann 1946- *Who 94*
Coffey, Barbara J. 1931- *WhoBlA 94*
Coffey, Bert *WhoAmP 93*
Coffey, Brian *EncSF 93, TwCYAW*
Coffey, Brian 1945- *WrDr 94*
Coffey, C. Shelby, III *WhoAm 94, WhoFI 94*
Coffey, Charles d1745 *NewGrDO*
Coffey, Daniel 1950- *WrDr 94*
Coffey, Daniel William 1962- *WhoAmL 94*
Coffey, David L. 1932- *WhoAmP 93*
Coffey, David Roy 1941- *IntWW 93, Who 94*
Coffey, Denise 1936- *WhoHol 92*
Coffey, Dennis James 1940- *WhoFI 94, WhoMW 93*
Coffey, Douglas Robert 1937- *WhoAmA 93*
Coffey, Frank *WrDr 94*
Coffey, Gilbert Haven, Jr. 1926- *WhoBlA 94*
Coffey, Harold F. 1898- *WhAm 10*
Coffey, Howard Thomas 1934- *WhoScEn 94*
Coffey, John J. *WhoAmP 93*
Coffey, John Joseph 1936- *WhoAmL 94*
Coffey, John L. 1922- *WhoAmP 93*
Coffey, John Louis 1922- *WhoAm 94, WhoAmL 94*
Coffey, John William, II 1954- *WhoAmA 93*
Coffey, Joseph Daniel 1938- *WhoAm 94*
Coffey, Joseph Irving 1916- *WhoAm 94*
Coffey, Kathryn Robinson *WhoWest 94*
Coffey, Kendall Brindley 1952- *WhoAmL 94*
Coffey, Kevin Robert 1954- *WhoScEn 94*
Coffey, Larry Bruce 1940- *WhoAmL 94*
Coffey, Lee d1993 *NewYTBS 93*
Coffey, Mabel 1874-1949 *WhoAmA 93N*
Coffey, Marilyn *DrAPF 93*
Coffey, Marvin Dale 1930- *WhoAm 94*
Coffey, Matthew B. 1941- *WhoAm 94*
Coffey, Michael Desmond 1928- *WhoAmP 93*
Coffey, Paul 1961- *WhoAm 94*
Coffey, Raymond Richard 1929- *WhoAm 94*
Coffey, Richard *WhoBlA 94*
Coffey, Scott 1967- *WhoHol 92*
Coffey, Sean O. 1950- *WhoAmP 93*
Coffey, Sean Owen 1950- *WhoAm 94*
Coffey, Shelby, III *IntWW 93, WhoAm 94, WhoWest 94*
Coffey, Thomas *IntWW 93*
Coffey, Thomas Francis, Jr. 1923- *WhoAm 94*
Coffey, Thomas William 1959- *WhoAmL 94*
Coffey, Timothy 1941- *WhoAm 94, WhoScEn 94*
Coffey, Virginia Mae 1929- *WhoAmP 93*
Coffey, William David, III 1950- *WhoAmL 94*
Coffey, William Edward 1948- *WhoMW 93*
Coffield, Conrad Eugene 1930- *WhoAmL 94*
Coffield, Peter d1983 *WhoHol 92*
Coffield, Ronald Dale 1943- *WhoScEn 94*
Coffield, Shirley A. 1945- *WhoAm 94*
Coffill, Charles Frederick, Jr. 1946- *WhoScEn 94*
Coffill, Marjorie Louise 1917- *WhoWest 94*
Coffill, William Charles 1908-1989 *WhAm 10*
Coffin, Adeline Hayden 186-?- *WhoHol 92*
Coffin, Audress Marie 1949- *WhoFI 94*
Coffin, Bertha Louise 1919- *WhoFI 94, WhoMW 93*
Coffin, C. Hayden d1935 *WhoHol 92*
Coffin, Cyril Edwin 1919- *Who 94*
Coffin, David Linwood 1925- *WhoAm 94, WhoFI 94*
Coffin, David R. 1918- *WrDr 94*
Coffin, David R. 1954- *WhoWest 94*
Coffin, David Robbins 1918- *WhoAm 94*
Coffin, Debra Peters 1958- *WhoScEn 94*
Coffin, Dwight Clay 1938- *WhoFI 94*
Coffin, Frank Morey 1919- *IntWW 93, WhoAm 94, WhoAmL 94*
Coffin, Frederick 1943- *WhoHol 92*
Coffin, Hank d1966 *WhoHol 92*
Coffin, Harold Walter 1908- *WhoWest 94*
Coffin, Helen Kingsbury 1907- *WhoMW 93*
Coffin, Henry Sloane 1877-1954 *DcAmReB 2*
Coffin, Isaac 1759-1839 *WhAmRev*
Coffin, James Robert 1942- *WhoAmP 93, WhoHisp 94*
Coffin, John 1756-1838 *WhAmRev*
Coffin, Judy Sue 1953- *WhoAm 94*
Coffin, Laurence Edmondston, Jr. 1928- *WhoAm 94*
Coffin, Levi 1789-1877 *DcAmReB 2*
Coffin, Louis Fussell, Jr. 1917- *WhoAm 94*
Coffin, Lyn *DrAPF 93*
Coffin, Richard Keith 1940- *WhoAm 94, WhoAmL 94*
Coffin, Robert Parker 1917- *WhoMW 93*
Coffin, Thomas Ashton 1754-1810 *WhAmRev*
Coffin, Thomas M. 1945- *WhoAm 94, WhoAmL 94, WhoWest 94*
Coffin, Tris d1990 *WhoHol 92*
Coffin, Tristram 1912- *WhoAm 94, WrDr 94*
Coffin, Tristram Potter 1922- *WrDr 94*
Coffin, Violet 1920- *WhoWomW 91*
Coffin, Violet B. 1920- *WhoAmP 93*
Coffin, William Sloane, Jr. 1924- *AmSocL*
Coffin, Winifred d1986 *WhoHol 92*
Coffindaffer, Bernard d1993 *NewYTBS 93*
Coffing, Janet S. 1951- *WhoMW 93*
Coffinger, Maralin Katharyne 1935- *WhoWest 94*
Coffin Mott, Lucretia 1793-1880 *WomPubS*
Coffman, Barbara Frances 1907-1992 *WrDr 94N*
Coffman, Dallas Whitney 1957- *WhoFI 94*
Coffman, Edward M. 1929- *WrDr 94*
Coffman, Edward McKenzie 1929- *WhoAm 94*
Coffman, Franklin Edward 1942- *WhoAm 94*
Coffman, Hal 1883-1958 *WhoAmA 93N*
Coffman, Harry Thomas 1910- *WhoAmL 94*
Coffman, Hugh Marshall 1948- *WhoAmP 93*
Coffman, James Richard 1938- *WhoAm 94*
Coffman, Jay Denton 1928- *WhoAm 94*
Coffman, Mike 1955- *WhoAmP 93*
Coffman, Orene Burton 1938- *WhoFI 94*
Coffman, Phillip Hudson 1936- *WhoAm 94*
Coffman, Ralph I. 1950- *WhoAmP 93*
Coffman, Ramon Peyton 1896- *WhAm 10*
Coffman, Roy Walter, III 1943- *WhoAm 94*
Coffman, Samuel Leroy 1951- *WhoMW 93*
Coffman, Sandra Jeanne 1945- *WhoAm 94*
Coffman, Stanley Knight, Jr. 1916- *WhoAm 94*
Coffman, Steven *DrAPF 93*
Coffman, Terrence J. *WhoMW 93*
Coffman, Virginia (Edith) 1914- *WrDr 94*
Coffman, William Eugene 1913- *WhoAm 94*
Coffman, William Thomas 1940- *WhoAmL 94*
Coffrin, Albert Wheeler 1919- *WhoAm 94*
Cofield, Elizabeth Bias 1920- *WhoBlA 94*
Cofield, Howard John 1926- *WhoAm 94, WhoAmL 94*
Cofield, James E., Jr. 1945- *WhoBlA 94*
Cofield, Philip Thomas 1951- *WhoWest 94*
Cofoid, Paul Brian 1945- *WhoMW 93*
Cofran, George Lee 1945- *WhoAm 94*
Cofrancesco, Donald George 1953- *WhoFI 94, WhoScEn 94*
Cogan, Alma d1966 *WhoHol 92*
Cogan, David G. d1993 *NewYTBS 93*
Cogan, David Glendenning 1908- *WhoAm 94*
Cogan, Fanny Hay d1929 *WhoHol 92*
Cogan, J. Kevin 1951- *WhoAm 94*
Cogan, James Richard 1928- *WhoAm 94*
Cogan, John Francis, Jr. 1926- *WhoAm 94*
Cogan, Kenneth George 1960- *WhoScEn 94*
Cogan, Marshall S. 1937- *WhoAm 94, WhoFI 94*
Cogan, Philip 1748-1833 *NewGrDO*
Cogan, Robert David 1930- *WhoAm 94*
Cogbill, John V., III 1948- *WhoAmL 94*
Cogburn, Max Oliver 1927- *WhoAmL 94*
Cogcave, Serge O. 1924- *WrDr 94*
Cogdell, D. Parthenia 1938- *WhoAmP 93, WhoBlA 94*
Cogdell, Joe Bennett, Jr. 1953- *WhoAm 94*
Cogdell, Josephine d1969 *WhoHol 92*
Cogen, Tess 1904-1993 *NewYTBS 93*
Coger, Rick 1940- *WhoMW 93*
Coggan, Baron 1909- *Who 94*
Coggan, Lord 1909- *WrDr 94*
Coggan, (Frederick) Donald 1909- *IntWW 93*
Coggeshall, Bruce Amsden 1941- *WhoAmL 94*
Coggeshall, Janice Reddig 1935- *WhoAmP 93*
Coggeshall, Norman David 1916- *WhoFI 94, WhoScEn 94*
Coggeshall, Rosanne *DrAPF 93*
Coggin, Betty Ferguson 1943- *WhoAmL 94*
Coggin, Charlotte Joan 1928- *WhoAm 94, WhoWest 94*
Coggin, David Anthony 1950- *WhoAmL 94*
Coggin, Frank E. *WhoAmP 93*
Coggin, Michael Wright 1955- *WhoFI 94*
Coggin, Philip A(nnett) 1917- *WrDr 94*
Coggins, Dana Chandler 1931- *WhoAm 94*
Coggins, Douglas Edward 1955- *WhoWest 94*
Coggins, Frank Edward 1946- *WhoWest 94*
Coggins, Freeman Wescoat, Jr. 1942- *WhoFI 94*
Coggins, George Miller, Jr. 1939- *WhoFI 94*
Coggins, Homer Dale 1922- *WhoAm 94*
Coggins, Jack B. 1914- *WrDr 94*
Coggins, Jack Banham 1914- *WhoAmA 93*
Coggins, John Richard 1944- *Who 94*
Coggins, Paul Edward, Jr. 1951- *WhoAmL 94*
Coggins, Wilmer Jesse 1925- *WhoAm 94*
Coggio, Roger *WhoHol 92*
Coggs, G. Spencer 1949- *WhoAmP 93*
Coggs, Granville Coleridge 1925- *WhoBlA 94*
Coggs, Marcia P. 1928- *WhoAmP 93*
Coggshall, Gene *DrAPF 93*
Coggs-Jones, Elizabeth Monette 1956- *WhoAmP 93*
Coghill, Egerton James Nevill Tobias 1930- *Who 94*
Coghill, John B. 1925- *WhoAmP 93*
Coghill, John Bruce 1925- *WhoAm 94, WhoWest 94*
Coghill, Joy *WhoHol 92*
Coghill, Marvin W. 1933- *WhoFI 94*
Coghill, Nikki *WhoHol 92*
Coghill, William Thomas, Jr. 1927- *WhoAm 94, WhoAmL 94*
Coghlan, Charles d1972 *WhoHol 92*
Coghlan, Gertrude d1952 *WhoHol 92*
Coghlan, James Thomas 1955- *WhoWest 94*
Coghlan, Junior 1916- *WhoHol 92*
Coghlan, Katherine d1965 *WhoHol 92*
Coghlan, Kelly Jack 1952- *WhoAm 94, WhoAmL 94*
Coghlan, Rose d1932 *WhoHol 92*
Coghlan, Terence Augustine 1945- *Who 94*
Cogley, Allen C. *WhoScEn 94*
Cogley, Nick d1936 *WhoHol 92*
Coglitore, Frank Joseph 1942- *WhoFI 94*
Cogman, Frederick Walter 1913- *Who 94*
Cognata, Joseph Anthony 1946- *WhoWest 94*
Cograve, John Edwin 1929- *WhoAm 94*
Cogsville, Donald J. 1937- *WhoBlA 94*
Cogswell, Alice 1805-1830 *EncDeaf*
Cogswell, Dorothy McIntosh 1909- *WhoAmA 93*
Cogswell, Fred(erick William) 1917- *ConAu 43NR, WrDr 94*
Cogswell, Frederick William 1917- *WhoAm 94*
Cogswell, Glenn Dale 1922- *WhoAm 94*
Cogswell, John Heyland 1933- *WhoAm 94*
Cogswell, Kenneth Mark 1957- *WhoMW 93*
Cogswell, Margaret Price 1925- *WhoAmA 93*
Cogswell, Mason Fitch 1761-1830 *EncDeaf*
Cogswell, Richard L. 1948- *WhoAmP 93*
Cogswell, Theodore R(ose) 1918-1987 *EncSF 93*
Cogut, Theodore Louis 1928- *WhoScEn 94*
Cohalan, Peter Fox 1938- *WhoAmP 93*
Cohan, Agnes Merrill d1972 *WhoHol 92*
Cohan, Anthony Robert 1939- *WhoWest 94*
Cohan, George M. d1942 *WhoHol 92*
Cohan, George M(ichael) 1878-1942 *NewGrDO*
Cohan, George Sheldon 1924- *WhoAm 94*
Cohan, Helen *WhoHol 92*
Cohan, John Robert 1931- *WhoAm 94, WhoAmL 94*
Cohan, Leon Sumner 1929- *WhoAm 94, WhoAmL 94, WhoFI 94*
Cohan, Philip L. 1939- *WhoAmL 94*
Cohan, Robert Paul 1925- *IntWW 93, Who 94*
Cohan, Tony *DrAPF 93*
Cohan, Zara R. 1928- *WhoAmA 93*
Coheleach, Guy Joseph *WhoAm 94, WhoAmA 93*
Cohen *Who 94*
Cohen, Aaron 1931- *WhoScEn 94*
Cohen, Abraham Ezekiel *WhoFI 94*
Cohen, Abraham J. 1932- *WhoAm 94*
Cohen, Adam Lloyd 1958- *WhoWest 94*
Cohen, Adele *WhoAmA 93*
Cohen, Alain *WhoHol 92*
Cohen, Alan 1932- *WhoScEn 94*
Cohen, Alan Barry 1943- *WhoAmA 93*
Cohen, Alan Jay 1956- *WhoWest 94*
Cohen, Alan Norman 1930- *WhoAm 94*
Cohen, Alan Seymour 1926- *WhoAm 94, WhoScEn 94*
Cohen, Albert 1929- *WhoAm 94*
Cohen, Albert Diamond 1914- *WhoAm 94, WhoFI 94*
Cohen, Alberto 1932- *WhoMW 93, WhoScEn 94*
Cohen, Alex 1927- *WhoAm 94*
Cohen, Alexander H. 1920- *IntWW 93, WhoAm 94*
Cohen, Alexander Perlin 1964- *WhoMW 93*
Cohen, Alfred Martin 1941- *WhoAm 94*
Cohen, Alice Eve *DrAPF 93*
Cohen, Allan Richard 1923-1989 *WhAm 10*
Cohen, Allan Richard 1947- *WhoAm 94, WhoMW 93*
Cohen, Allan Yale 1939- *WhoAm 94*
Cohen, Allen Barry 1939- *WhoScEn 94*
Cohen, Amaziah VanBuren 1916- *WhoBlA 94*
Cohen, Amy 1942- *WhoAm 94*
Cohen, Andrea Robin 1966- *WhoFI 94*
Cohen, Andrew (Z.) 1955- *WrDr 94*
Cohen, Andrew Stuart 1930- *WhoAm 94*
Cohen, Anne Constant 1935- *WhoWest 94*
Cohen, Anthea 1913- *WrDr 94*
Cohen, Arie 1948- *WhoMW 93*
Cohen, Arnold A. 1914- *WhoAm 94*
Cohen, Arnold Norman 1949- *WhoWest 94*
Cohen, Arthur *Who 94*
Cohen, (Nathaniel) Arthur (Jim) 1898- *Who 94*
Cohen, Arthur A(llen) 1928-1986 *ConAu 42NR*
Cohen, Arthur Abram 1917- *WhoAmL 94*
Cohen, Arthur Morris 1928- *WhoAm 94, WhoAmA 93*
Cohen, Arthur Nathan 1947- *WhoMW 93*
Cohen, B. Stanley 1923- *WhoAm 94*

Cohen, Barbara 1932-1992 *AnObit 1992, ConAu 140, SmATA 74, -77 [port]*
Cohen, Barbara (Kauder) 1932-1992 *WrDr 94N*
Cohen, Barney *EncSF 93*
Cohen, Barry Jay 1949- *WhoMW 93*
Cohen, Benjamin Harry 1951- *WhoMW 93*
Cohen, Benjamin Jack 1948- *WhoAm 94, WhoAmL 94*
Cohen, Benjamin R. 1942- *WhoAmP 93*
Cohen, Bennett Jay 1925-1990 *WhAm 10*
Cohen, Bernard (Cecil) 1926- *WrDr 94*
Cohen, Bernard Barrie 1944- *WhoAmL 94*
Cohen, Bernard Cecil 1926- *WhoAm 94*
Cohen, Bernard Lande 1902- *WrDr 94*
Cohen, Bernard Leonard 1924- *WhoAm 94*
Cohen, Bernard S. 1934- *WhoAmL 94, WhoAmP 93*
Cohen, Bernard Woolf 1933- *IntWW 93, Who 94*
Cohen, Bertram David 1923- *WhoAm 94*
Cohen, Betty *Who 94*
Cohen, Bonnie R. 1942- *WhoAm 94, WhoAmL 94*
Cohen, Bruce Joel 1953- *WhoAmA 93*
Cohen, Bruce Michael 1947- *WhoAm 94*
Cohen, Bruce Preston 1940- *WhoAmL 94*
Cohen, Bryant Benjamin 1960- *WhoFI 94*
Cohen, Burton 1950- *WhoAmP 93*
Cohen, Burton David 1940- *WhoAm 94*
Cohen, Burton Jerome 1933- *WhoAm 94*
Cohen, Carl Mordecai 1954- *WhoFI 94*
Cohen, Carole Knipp *DrAPF 93*
Cohen, Charles E. 1942- *WhoAmA 93*
Cohen, Charles F. 1945- *WhoAm 94*
Cohen, Charles I. 1945- *WhoAmL 94*
Cohen, Cheryl Diane Durda 1947- *WhoFI 94, WhoMW 93*
Cohen, Christopher B. 1942- *WhoAm 94, WhoAmL 94*
Cohen, Clarence Budd 1925- *WhoAm 94, WhoWest 94*
Cohen, Cora 1943- *WhoAm 94, WhoAmA 93*
Cohen, Cynthia Marylyn 1945- *WhoAm 94, WhoAmL 94*
Cohen, Daniel Booth 1955- *WhoFI 94*
Cohen, Daniel Edward 1936- *WhoAm 94*
Cohen, Daniel Morris 1930- *WhoAm 94*
Cohen, Darcy M. d1993 *NewYTBS 93*
Cohen, Darryl Brandt 1944- *WhoAmL 94*
Cohen, David *WhoAmP 93*
Cohen, David Alan 1963- *WhoAmL 94*
Cohen, David B. 1947- *WhoAmP 93*
Cohen, David Harris 1938- *WhoAm 94, WhoMW 93*
Cohen, David Michael 1942- *WhoAm 94, WhoAmL 94*
Cohen, David R. 1959- *WhoAmL 94*
Cohen, David Richard 1949- *WhoAm 94*
Cohen, David Saul 1945- *WhoAmL 94*
Cohen, David Walter 1926- *WhoAm 94*
Cohen, Deborah Fuchs 1950- *WhoAm 94, WhoAmL 94*
Cohen, Donald Jay 1940- *WhoAm 94, WhoScEn 94*
Cohen, Donald S. 1946- *WhoAmL 94*
Cohen, Donald W. 1934- *WhoAmL 94*
Cohen, Donna Eden 1956- *WhoAmL 94*
Cohen, Dorothy 1918- *WhoAm 94*
Cohen, Earl Harding 1948- *WhoAmL 94*
Cohen, Edmund Stephen 1946- *WhoAm 94, WhoAmL 94*
Cohen, Edward 1912- *Who 94*
Cohen, Edward 1921- *WhoAm 94, WhoFI 94, WhoScEn 94*
Cohen, Edward 1930- *WhoScEn 94*
Cohen, Edward Arthur 1936- *WhoAmL 94*
Cohen, Edward Barth 1949- *WhoAm 94*
Cohen, Edward Herschel 1938- *WhoAm 94*
Cohen, Edward Philip 1932- *WhoAm 94*
Cohen, Edwin Robert 1939- *WhoFI 94*
Cohen, Edwin Samuel 1914- *WhoAm 94*
Cohen, Elaine Lustig 1927- *WhoAmA 93*
Cohen, Eli Edward 1912- *WhoAm 94*
Cohen, Eliot Kenneth 1928- *WhoAmL 94*
Cohen, Elizabeth G. 1931- *WhoAm 94*
Cohen, Elliot Gene 1945- *WhoAm 94*
Cohen, Ellis A. 1945- *IntMPA 94*
Cohen, Eric Martin 1955- *WhoAmL 94*
Cohen, Esther *DrAPF 93*
Cohen, Eugene Erwin 1917- *WhoAm 94*
Cohen, Ezechiel Godert David 1923- *WhoAm 94*
Cohen, Ezra Harry 1942- *WhoAm 94, WhoAmL 94*
Cohen, Felissa L. 1941- *WhoMW 93*
Cohen, Felix Asher 1943- *WhoAm 94, WhoAmL 94*
Cohen, Florence Emery 1944- *WhoFI 94*
Cohen, Frank Burton 1927- *WhoFI 94*
Cohen, Fred Howard 1948- *WhoAm 94, WhoAmL 94*
Cohen, Frederick 1935- *WhoAm 94, WhoAmL 94*
Cohen, Gabriel Murrel 1908- *WhoAm 94, WhoMW 93*
Cohen, Gary Dale 1951- *WhoAmL 94*
Cohen, Gary J. 1946- *WhoAm 94*
Cohen, George Cormack 1909- *Who 94*
Cohen, George Leon 1930- *WhoAm 94*
Cohen, George Michael 1958- *WhoAmA 93*
Cohen, Gerald *DrAPF 93*
Cohen, Gerald Allan 1941- *IntWW 93, Who 94*
Cohen, Gerson David 1924-1991 *WhAm 10*
Cohen, Geula 1927- *WhoWomW 91*
Cohen, Gloria Ernestine 1942- *WhoFI 94*
Cohen, Gordon S. 1937- *WhoFI 94*
Cohen, H. George 1913-1980 *WhoAmA 93N*
Cohen, Harlan P. 1948- *WhoAmL 94*
Cohen, Harley 1933- *WhoAm 94, WhoScEn 94*
Cohen, Harold 1928- *WhoAmA 93*
Cohen, Harold Larry 1925- *WhoAmA 93*
Cohen, Harry 1949- *Who 94*
Cohen, Harry Bruce 1938- *WhoWest 94*
Cohen, Harvey Jay 1940- *WhoAm 94, WhoScEn 94*
Cohen, Hennig 1919- *WhoAm 94*
Cohen, Henry 1933- *WrDr 94*
Cohen, Henry C. 1945- *WhoAmL 94*
Cohen, Henry Rodgin 1944- *WhoAm 94, WhoAmL 94*
Cohen, Herbert Jesse 1935- *WhoAm 94*
Cohen, Herman 1894-1990 *WhAm 10*
Cohen, Herman 1932- *WhoAmP 93*
Cohen, Herman Jay 1932- *WhoAm 94*
Cohen, Herman Nathan 1949- *WhoAm 94*
Cohen, Hirsh Joel 1942- *WhoAm 94*
Cohen, Hollace T. 1948- *WhoAm 94, WhoAmL 94*
Cohen, Howard 1942- *WhoAm 94*
Cohen, Howard M. 1944- *WhoAmL 94*
Cohen, Howard William 1918- *WhoAm 94*
Cohen, Hy 1901- *WhoAmA 93*
Cohen, Ida Bogin *WhoFI 94*
Cohen, Ira *DrAPF 93*
Cohen, Ira D. 1951- *WhoFI 94*
Cohen, Ira Myron 1937- *WhoAm 94, WhoScEn 94*
Cohen, Irving David 1945- *WhoAm 94*
Cohen, Irving Elias 1946- *WhoAm 94*
Cohen, Irving I. 1950- *WhoAm 94, WhoFI 94*
Cohen, Irving P. 1941- *WhoAmL 94*
Cohen, Irwin 1936- *WhoAm 94, WhoFI 94, WhoScEn 94*
Cohen, Irwin 1941- *WhoAmL 94*
Cohen, Irwin R. 1924- *IntMPA 94*
Cohen, Isaac Louis 1948- *WhoFI 94, WhoScEn 94*
Cohen, Isidore Leonard 1922- *WhoAm 94*
Cohen, Israel 1912- *WhoAm 94, WhoFI 94*
Cohen, Ivor (Harold) 1931- *Who 94*
Cohen, Jack S(idney) 1938- *WrDr 94*
Cohen, James Robert *WhoWest 94*
Cohen, Jane R(abb) 1938- *WrDr 94*
Cohen, Jay Loring 1953- *WhoAmL 94*
Cohen, Jean 1927- *WhoAmA 93*
Cohen, Jean R. 1935- *WhoAmA 93*
Cohen, Jeff *WhoAm 94*
Cohen, Jeffrey A. 1952- *ConAu 141*
Cohen, Jeffrey Elliott 1951- *WhoMW 93*
Cohen, Jeffrey M. 1940- *WhoAm 94*
Cohen, Jeffrey Michael 1940- *WhoAmL 94*
Cohen, Jene Barr 1900-1985 *ConAu 42NR*
Cohen, Jeremy 1953- *WrDr 94*
Cohen, Jeremy Patrick 1960- *WhoAmL 94, WhoWest 94*
Cohen, Jerome 1925- *WhoAm 94*
Cohen, Jerome Bernard 1932- *WhoAm 94, WhoScEn 94*
Cohen, Jerry d1993 *NewYTBS 93*
Cohen, Joan Lebold 1932- *WhoAmA 93*
Cohen, Joel Ephraim 1944- *WhoAm 94*
Cohen, Joel J. 1938- *WhoAm 94*
Cohen, Joel Mark 1946- *WhoAmL 94*
Cohen, Jon Stephan 1943- *WhoAm 94, WhoAmL 94*
Cohen, Jonathan *DrAPF 93*
Cohen, Jonathan 1915- *WhoScEn 94*
Cohen, Jonathan Brewer 1944- *WhoAm 94*
Cohen, Jonathan Jacob 1955- *WhoAmA 93*
Cohen, Jonathan Little 1939- *WhoAm 94*
Cohen, Jose, Sr. 1938- *WhoHisp 94*
Cohen, Joseph 1926- *WhoAm 94*
Cohen, Joseph D. 1948- *WhoAmL 94*
Cohen, Joyce E. 1937- *WhoAmP 93*
Cohen, Jozef 1921- *WhoAm 94*
Cohen, Judith Beth *DrAPF 93*
Cohen, Judith Lynne 1951- *WhoFI 94*
Cohen, Jules 1931- *WhoAm 94*
Cohen, Jules Simon 1937- *WhoAm 94*
Cohen, Julius George 1921- *WhoAm 94*
Cohen, Karl Paley 1913- *WhoAm 94*
Cohen, Keith *DrAPF 93*
Cohen, Kenneth A. 1945- *WhoAmL 94*
Cohen, Kenneth Allan 1953- *WhoScEn 94*
Cohen, Kenneth Bruce 1950- *WhoAm 94*
Cohen, Kenneth Bruce 1953- *WhoMW 93*
Cohen, Larry 1936- *IntMPA 94*
Cohen, Larry 1938- *EncSF 93*
Cohen, Larry 1941- *HorFD [port]*
Cohen, Larry 1945- *ConAu 142*
Cohen, Laurence Joel 1932- *WhoAmL 94*
Cohen, Laurence Jonathan 1923- *IntWW 93, Who 94, WrDr 94*
Cohen, Lawrence 1926- *WhoAm 94, WhoMW 93*
Cohen, Lawrence Alan 1953- *WhoAm 94, WhoFI 94*
Cohen, Lawrence David 1933- *WhoAmP 93*
Cohen, Lawrence Edward 1945- *WhoAm 94*
Cohen, Lawrence N. 1932- *WhoAm 94*
Cohen, Lawrence Sorel 1933- *WhoAm 94*
Cohen, Leon Warren 1903-1992 *WhAm 10*
Cohen, Leonard 1925- *WhoAm 94, WhoFI 94, WhoWest 94*
Cohen, Leonard 1934- *WhoAm 94, WrDr 94*
Cohen, Leonard Harold Lionel 1922- *Who 94*
Cohen, Lester *WhoFI 94*
Cohen, Lewis Cobrain 1947- *WhoAm 94*
Cohen, Lewis Isaac 1932- *WhoAm 94*
Cohen, Lita Indzel *WhoAmP 93*
Cohen, Lois Ruth Kushner 1938- *WhoScEn 94*
Cohen, Louis 1925- *Who 94*
Cohen, Louis Richard 1940- *WhoAm 94, WhoAmL 94*
Cohen, Lynne G. 1944- *WhoAmA 93*
Cohen, Malcolm Martin 1937- *WhoAm 94, WhoScEn 94*
Cohen, Marc *DrAPF 93*
Cohen, Marc Kami *WhoAm 94*
Cohen, Marc M. 1952- *WhoWest 94*
Cohen, Marc S. 1950- *WhoAmL 94*
Cohen, Marion D. *DrAPF 93*
Cohen, Mark B. 1949- *WhoAmP 93*
Cohen, Mark Daniel 1951- *WhoFI 94*
Cohen, Mark David 1960- *WhoFI 94*
Cohen, Mark Herbert 1932- *WhoAm 94*
Cohen, Mark N. 1947- *WhoAm 94, WhoFI 94*
Cohen, Mark Nathan 1943- *WrDr 94*
Cohen, Marlene Lois 1945- *WhoAm 94*
Cohen, Marlene Zichi 1951- *WhoWest 94*
Cohen, Marsha A. 1952- *WhoIns 94*
Cohen, Marsha Nan 1947- *WhoAmL 94*
Cohen, Marshall *WhoAm 94*
Cohen, Marshall Harris 1926- *WhoAm 94*
Cohen, Martin 1932- *WhoAm 94*
Cohen, Martin Gilbert 1938- *WhoAm 94, WhoScEn 94*
Cohen, Marty *DrAPF 93*
Cohen, Marvin *DrAPF 93*
Cohen, Marvin Lou 1935- *IntWW 93, WhoAm 94*
Cohen, Marvin S. 1931- *WhoAmP 93*
Cohen, Mary Ann 1943- *CngDr 93, WhoAm 94, WhoAmL 94*
Cohen, Matt 1942- *ConAu 18AS [port], EncSF 93, WrDr 94*
Cohen, Max Harry 1940- *WhoAm 94*
Cohen, Max Mark 1939- *WhoWest 94*
Cohen, Maxwell 1910- *WrDr 94*
Cohen, Maynard Manuel 1920- *WhoAm 94*
Cohen, Melanie Rovner 1944- *WhoAm 94, WhoAmL 94*
Cohen, Melvin Arthur 1943- *WhoFI 94*
Cohen, Melvin Irwin 1936- *WhoAm 94*
Cohen, Melvin Joseph 1928- *WhoAm 94*
Cohen, Melvin R. 1911- *WhoAm 94, WhoScEn 94*
Cohen, Melvin Samuel 1918- *WhoAm 94*
Cohen, Melvin Stephen 1919- *WhoAm 94*
Cohen, Melvyn Douglas 1943- *WhoFI 94*
Cohen, Michael 1930- *WhoAm 94*
Cohen, Michael Antony 1940- *Who 94*
Cohen, Michael I. 1935- *WhoAm 94*
Cohen, Michael L. 1943- *WhoAmL 94*
Cohen, Michael Lee 1953- *WhoScEn 94*
Cohen, Michael Paul Austern 1965- *WhoAmL 94*
Cohen, Michael S. 1936- *WhoAmA 93*
Cohen, Mildred Thaler 1921- *WhoAm 94, WhoAmA 93*
Cohen, Miles Jon 1941- *WhoMW 93*
Cohen, Miriam 1926- *WhoAm 94*
Cohen, Mitchell Harry 1904-1991 *WhAm 10*
Cohen, Montague 1925- *WhoScEn 94*
Cohen, Mordaunt 1916- *Who 94*
Cohen, Morley Mitchell 1917- *WhoAm 94*
Cohen, Morrel Herman 1927- *WhoAm 94*
Cohen, Morris 1911- *IntWW 93, WhoAm 94*
Cohen, Morris Leo 1927- *WhoAm 94, WhoAmL 94*
Cohen, Morton N(orton) 1921- *WrDr 94*
Cohen, Moses Elias 1937- *WhoAm 94*
Cohen, Myer 1907- *WhoAm 94*
Cohen, Myrella 1927- *Who 94*
Cohen, Myron 1902-1986 *WhoCom*
Cohen, Myron 1927- *WhoAmL 94*
Cohen, Myron Leslie 1934- *WhoAm 94*
Cohen, N. Jerold 1935- *WhoAm 94*
Cohen, Naomi Kurnitsky 1941- *WhoAmP 93, WhoWomW 91*
Cohen, Natalie Shulman 1938- *WhoWest 94*
Cohen, Nathan Leslie 1908- *Who 94*
Cohen, Neil M. *WhoAmP 93*
Cohen, Nelson Craig 1947- *WhoAmL 94*
Cohen, Nicholas 1938- *WhoAm 94*
Cohen, Noel Lee 1930- *WhoAm 94, WhoScEn 94*
Cohen, Nora *SmATA 75 [port]*
Cohen, Norm 1936- *WhoAm 94*
Cohen, Norman 1934- *WhoAm 94*
Cohen, Norton Jacob 1935- *WhoAmL 94*
Cohen, Patricia Ann 1944- *WhoScEn 94*
Cohen, Paul Edward 1957- *WhoAmL 94*
Cohen, Paul Frederick 1944- *WhoWest 94*
Cohen, Peter Zachary 1931- *WrDr 94*
Cohen, Philip 1931- *WhoAm 94, WhoScEn 94*
Cohen, Philip 1945- *Who 94*
Cohen, Philip Francis 1911- *WhoAm 94*
Cohen, Philip G(ary) 1954- *WrDr 94*
Cohen, Philip M. 1947- *WhoAmL 94*
Cohen, Philip Pacy d1993 *NewYTBS 93*
Cohen, Philip Pacy 1908- *WhoAm 94*
Cohen, Phyllis Joanne 1935- *WhoMW 93*
Cohen, R. Scott 1954- *WhoAmL 94*
Cohen, Rachelle Sharon 1946- *WhoAm 94*
Cohen, Randy Wade 1954- *WhoScEn 94*
Cohen, Raquel E. 1922- *WhoHisp 94*
Cohen, Raymond 1923- *WhoAm 94, WhoScEn 94*
Cohen, Raymond James 1948- *WhoScEn 94*
Cohen, Reina Joyce 1931- *WhoAmA 93*
Cohen, Richard 1952- *ConAu 140, WhoAm 94, WhoFI 94*
Cohen, Richard 1955- *WhoAmL 94*
Cohen, Richard Gerard 1931- *WhoAm 94*
Cohen, Richard Henry Lionel 1907- *Who 94*
Cohen, Richard J. 1949- *WhoAmP 93*
Cohen, Richard Lawrence 1937- *WhoScEn 94*
Cohen, Richard Martin 1941- *WhoAm 94*
Cohen, Richard Norman 1923- *WhoAm 94*
Cohen, Richard Paul 1945- *WhoAmL 94*
Cohen, Richard S. 1947- *WhoAmL 94*
Cohen, Richard Schley 1945- *WhoWest 94*
Cohen, Richard Steven 1942- *WhoAm 94, WhoFI 94*
Cohen, Richard Stockman 1937- *WhoAm 94*
Cohen, Rob 1949- *IntMPA 94*
Cohen, Robert 1957- *WhoAmL 94, WhoFI 94, WrDr 94*
Cohen, Robert 1959- *IntWW 93*
Cohen, Robert A. 1946- *WhoAmL 94*
Cohen, Robert Abraham 1909- *WhoAm 94*
Cohen, Robert Alan 1953- *WhoMW 93*
Cohen, Robert Avram 1929- *WhoAmL 94*
Cohen, Robert B. *IntMPA 94*
Cohen, Robert Donald 1933- *Who 94*
Cohen, Robert Edward 1947- *WhoAm 94*
Cohen, Robert F. 1951- *WhoWest 94*
Cohen, Robert Fadian 1969- *WhoScEn 94*
Cohen, Robert Garrett 1963- *WhoAmL 94*
Cohen, Robert Sonne 1923- *WhoAm 94, WhoScEn 94*
Cohen, Robert Stephen 1938- *WhoAm 94, WhoWest 94*
Cohen, Robin 1944- *WrDr 94*
Cohen, Roger L. 1935- *WhoAm 94, WhoFI 94*
Cohen, Ronald Eli 1937- *WhoAm 94*
Cohen, Ronald J. 1950- *WhoAmL 94*
Cohen, Ronald Jay 1948- *WhoAmL 94*
Cohen, Ronald S. 1937- *WhoFI 94*
Cohen, Ronny 1950- *WhoAmA 93*
Cohen, Roy Alan 1954- *WhoAmL 94*
Cohen, Sammy d1979 *WhoHol 92*
Cohen, Samuel Israel 1933- *WhoFI 94*
Cohen, Sanford Irwin 1928- *WhoAm 94*
Cohen, Sanford Ned 1935- *WhoAm 94*
Cohen, Saul (Bernard) 1925- *WrDr 94*
Cohen, Saul Bernard 1925- *WhoAm 94*
Cohen, Saul G. 1916- *WhoAm 94*
Cohen, Saul Mark 1924- *WhoScEn 94*
Cohen, Saul Zelman 1926-1992 *WhAm 10*
Cohen, Selma Jeanne 1920- *WhoAm 94, WrDr 94*
Cohen, Seymour 1917- *WhoAm 94, WhoAmL 94*
Cohen, Seymour I. 1931- *WhoWest 94*

Cohen, Seymour Stanley 1917- *WhoAm 94*
Cohen, Sharleen Cooper *ConAu 41NR*
Cohen, Sharon Ann *WhoMW 93*
Cohen, Shayne Del 1946- *WhoWest 94*
Cohen, Sheldon Gilbert 1918- *WhoAm 94*
Cohen, Sheldon Hersh 1934- *WhoAm 94*
Cohen, Sheldon Irwin 1937- *WhoAmL 94*
Cohen, Sheldon Stanley 1927- *WhoAm 94*
Cohen, Sorel *WhoAmA 93*
Cohen, Stanley 1922- *IntWW 93, Who 94, WhoAm 94, WhoScEn 94, WorScD*
Cohen, Stanley 1927- *Who 94*
Cohen, Stanley 1935- *IntWW 93*
Cohen, Stanley 1937- *IntWW 93, WhoAm 94*
Cohen, Stanley 1942- *Who 94*
Cohen, Stanley I. *DrAPF 93*
Cohen, Stanley I. 1928- *WrDr 94*
Cohen, Stanley Norman 1935- *WhoAm 94, WhoWest 94, WorScD*
Cohen, Stephen Bruce 1939- *WhoAmL 94*
Cohen, Stephen Douglas 1944- *WhoScEn 94*
Cohen, Stephen F(rand) 1938- *WrDr 94*
Cohen, Stephen Frand 1938- *WhoAm 94*
Cohen, Stephen Ira 1949- *WhoAmP 93*
Cohen, Stephen Mark 1952- *WhoFI 94*
Cohen, Stephen Marshall 1929- *WhoAm 94, WhoWest 94*
Cohen, Stephen Martin 1957- *WhoAmL 94*
Cohen, Stephen Philip 1936- *WhoAm 94*
Cohen, Steven (A.) 1953- *ConAu 142*
Cohen, Stuart I. 1942- *WhoAmL 94*
Cohen, Susan Gloria 1952- *WhoWest 94*
Cohen, Susan Lois 1938- *WhoAm 94*
Cohen, Sydney 1921- *IntWW 93, Who 94*
Cohen, Sylvan M. 1914- *WhoAm 94*
Cohen, Ted 1939- *WhoAm 94*
Cohen, Vincent H. 1936- *WhoBlA 94*
Cohen, Vincent Hamilton 1936- *WhoAm 94*
Cohen, Wallace M. d1993 *NewYTBS 93*
Cohen, Wallace M. 1908- *WhoAm 94, WhoAmL 94*
Cohen, Walter Stanley 1936- *WhoAm 94*
Cohen, Warren I. 1934- *WhoAm 94*
Cohen, William A(lan) 1937- *ConAu 42NR*
Cohen, William Alan 1937- *WhoAm 94*
Cohen, William B. *WhoWest 94*
Cohen, William Benjamin 1941- *WhoAm 94, WrDr 94*
Cohen, William Jay 1950- *WhoAmL 94*
Cohen, William Nathan 1935- *WhoAm 94*
Cohen, William S. 1940- *CngDr 93, IntWW 93, WhoAmP 93*
Cohen, William Sebastian 1940- *WhoAm 94*
Cohen-Albrecht, Patricia Rebeca 1957- *WhoHisp 94*
Cohen-Tannoudji, Claude Nessim 1933- *WhoScEn 94*
Cohick, James Allen, Jr. 1959- *WhoFI 94*
Cohill, Maurice Blanchard, Jr. 1929- *WhoAm 94, WhoAmL 94*
Cohl, Emile 1857-1938 *IntDcF 2-4*
Cohler, Bertram Joseph 1938- *WhoAm 94*
Cohlon, William 1941- *WhoAmA 93*
Cohn, Andrew Howard 1945- *WhoAm 94, WhoAmL 94*
Cohn, Avern Levin 1924- *WhAm 10, WhoAm 94, WhoAmL 94*
Cohn, Barbara *WhoAmA 93*
Cohn, Bertram Josiah 1925- *WhoAm 94*
Cohn, Cindy A. 1963- *WhoAmL 94*
Cohn, Daniel Howard 1955- *WhoWest 94*
Cohn, David Herc 1923- *WhoAm 94*
Cohn, David Stephen 1945- *WhoAm 94*
Cohn, David Valor 1926- *WhoAm 94*
Cohn, Elchanan 1941- *WhoAm 94*
Cohn, Eric Alan 1964- *WhoAmL 94*
Cohn, Frederick Donald 1931- *WhoAmA 93*
Cohn, George Herschel 1947- *WhoFI 94, WhoMW 93*
Cohn, Gerald Bernard 1939- *WhoAmL 94*
Cohn, H. Miles 1955- *WhoAmL 94*
Cohn, Haim 1911- *IntWW 93*
Cohn, Harry 1891-1958 *IntDcF 2-4*
Cohn, Harvey 1923- *WhoAm 94*
Cohn, Henry S. 1945- *ConAu 141*
Cohn, Herbert B. 1912- *WhoAm 94*
Cohn, Howard 1922- *WhoAm 94*
Cohn, Howard T. 1929- *WhoIns 94*
Cohn, Isidore, Jr. 1921- *WhoAm 94*
Cohn, Jess Victor 1908- *WhoAm 94*
Cohn, Jim *DrAPF 93*
Cohn, John J. 1941- *WhoHisp 94*
Cohn, John Robert 1963- *WhoAmL 94*
Cohn, Jonathan Daniel 1959- *WhoMW 93*
Cohn, Joseph Theodore 1958- *WhoWest 94*
Cohn, Judith 1950- *WhoMW 93*
Cohn, Judith R. 1943- *WhAm 10*
Cohn, Julia d1975 *WhoHol 92*
Cohn, Lawrence Steven 1945- *WhoWest 94*
Cohn, Leonard Allan 1929- *WhoAm 94*
Cohn, Marcus E. 1942- *WhoAmL 94*
Cohn, Marjorie B. 1939- *WhoAmA 93*
Cohn, Marjorie Benedict 1939- *WhoAm 94*
Cohn, Martin 1945- *WhoAm 94*
Cohn, Marvin 1928- *WhoAm 94*
Cohn, Max Arthur 1903- *WhoAmA 93*
Cohn, Mildred 1913- *IntWW 93, WhoAm 94, WhoScEn 94*
Cohn, Mindy 1966- *WhoHol 92*
Cohn, Nathan 1907-1989 *WhAm 10*
Cohn, Nathan 1918- *WhoAmL 94, WhoWest 94*
Cohn, Norman d1993 *NewYTBS 93*
Cohn, Norman 1915- *IntWW 93, Who 94, WrDr 94*
Cohn, Norman Stanley 1930- *WhoAm 94*
Cohn, Paul Moritz 1924- *IntWW 93, Who 94*
Cohn, Richard A. 1924- *WhoAmA 93*
Cohn, Richard J. 1943- *WhoAmL 94*
Cohn, Robert 1920- *IntMPA 94*
Cohn, Robert E. 1945- *WhoAmL 94*
Cohn, Robert Greer 1921- *WhoWest 94*
Cohn, Ronald Dennis 1942- *WhoAm 94*
Cohn, Ronald Elliot 1933- *WhoAm 94*
Cohn, Ronald Ira 1936- *WhoAm 94*
Cohn, Sam 1929- *WhoAm 94*
Cohn, Samuel Maurice 1915- *WhoAm 94*
Cohn, Scott Howard 1960- *WhoMW 93*
Cohn, Sherman Louis 1932- *WhoAm 94*
Cohn, Sidney Elliott 1908-1991 *WhAm 10*
Cohn, Stuart Harris 1950- *WhoFI 94*
Cohn, Theodore 1923- *WhoAm 94*
Cohn, Theodore Roy 1938- *WhoFI 94*
Cohn, Victor Edward 1919- *WhoAm 94*
Cohn, Zanvil Alexander d1993 *NewYTBS 93 [port]*
Cohn, Zanvil Alexander 1926- *WhoAm 94*
Cohodes, Barry Joel 1948- *WhoMW 93*
Cohodes, Donald R. 1949- *WhoFI 94*
Cohodes, Eli Aaron 1927- *WhoAm 94*
Cohoe, Grey 1944- *WhoAmA 93N*
Cohon, Peter 1942- *WhoAm 94*
Co Hongming *WhoPRCh 91*
Cohoon, Dennis M. 1953- *WhoAmP 93*
Cohu, Henry Wallace 1897- *WhAm 10*
Coia, Arthur A. *WhoAm 94, WhoFI 94*
Coia, Arthur E. d1993 *NewYTBS 93*
Coia, Theodore N. 1947- *WhoIns 94*
Coicy, Madame de fl. 18th cent.- *BlmGWL*
Coignard, Gabrielle de d1594 *BlmGWL*
Coignet, Horace 1735-1821 *NewGrDO*
Coil, Henry Wilson, Jr. 1932- *WhoAmP 93*
Coil, James H., III 1945- *WhoAmL 94*
Coiley, John Arthur 1932- *Who 94*
Coin, Sheila Regan 1942- *WhoMW 93*
Coiner, Charles T. 1897-1989 *WhoAmA 93N*
Coing, Helmut 1912- *IntWW 93*
Cointat, Michel 1921- *IntWW 93*
Coiro, Domenico Pietro 1960- *WhoScEn 94*
Coit, M. B. *WhoAmA 93*
Coit, Margaret Louise 1919- *WhoAm 94*
Coit, Mehetabel Chandler 1673-1758 *BlmGWL*
Coit, R. Ken 1943- *WhoWest 94*
Coit, Sam d1933 *WhoHol 92*
Coiter, Volcher 1534-1600 *EncDeaf*
Cojuangco, Eduardo *IntWW 93*
Cokayne *Who 94*
Coke *Who 94*
Coke, Viscount 1986- *Who 94*
Coke, Chauncey Eugene *WhoAm 94, WhoFI 94*
Coke, F. Van Deren 1921- *WhoAmA 93*
Coke, Frank Van Deren 1921- *WhoAm 94, WhoWest 94*
Coke, Richard d1955 *WhoHol 92*
Coke, Thomas 1747-1814 *DcAmReB 2*
Cokelet, Giles Roy 1932- *WhoAm 94*
Cokendolpher, Eunice Loraine 1931- *WhoAmA 93*
Coker, Carl David 1928- *WhoAmA 93*
Coker, Charles Westfield 1933- *WhoAm 94, WhoFI 94*
Coker, Charlotte Noel 1930- *WhoAmP 93*
Coker, Donna Sue 1957- *WhoFI 94*
Coker, Elizabeth Boatwright 1909-1993 *ConAu 142, CurBio 93N, NewYTBS 93*
Coker, Harold L. 1929- *WhoAmP 93*
Coker, Lynda 1946- *WhoAmP 93*
Coker, Pamela Lee 1948- *WhoWest 94*
Coker, Paul 1938- *Who 94*
Coker, Peter Godfrey 1926- *IntWW 93, Who 94*
Coker, Robert Hilton 1947- *WhoAm 94, WhoFI 94*
Colabella, Richard d1993 *NewYTBS 93*
Colaco, Branca de Gonta 1880-1944 *BlmGWL*
Colacurcio, Daniel V. 1948- *WhoIns 94*
Coladarci, Peter Paul 1927-1991 *WhAm 10*
Colafella, Nick A. 1939- *WhoAmP 93*
Colagiovanni, Joseph Alfred, Jr. 1956- *WhoAmL 94*
Colaianni, Deborah 1953- *WhoBlA 94*
Colaianni, Joseph Vincent 1935- *WhoAm 94*
Colaizzi, John Louis 1938- *WhoAm 94*
Colaizzo, Anthony L. 1930- *WhoAmP 93*
Colakovic, Bozidar 1931- *IntWW 93*
Colamarino, Katrin Belenky 1951- *WhoAmL 94*
Colan, Bruce Jay 1941- *WhoAmL 94*
Colander, David Charles 1947- *WhoAm 94*
Colander, Valerie Nieman *DrAPF 93*
Colandrea, Thomas Richard 1938- *WhoWest 94*
Colangelo, Jerry John 1939- *WhoAm 94, WhoWest 94*
Colangelo, Rocco, Jr. 1964- *WhoFI 94*
Colantuono, Anthony 1958- *WhoAmA 93*
Colantuono, Joseph R. 1951- *WhoAmL 94*
Colantuono, Thomas 1951- *WhoAmP 93*
Colao, Anthony F. *WhoIns 94*
Colao, Rudolph 1927- *WhoAmA 93*
Colapietro, Thomas A., Jr. *WhoAmP 93*
Colardyn, Francis Achille 1944- *WhoScEn 94*
Colarelli, Nick John 1960- *WhoMW 93*
Colarelli, Stephen Michael 1951- *WhoScEn 94*
Colarossi, Steven A. 1964- *WhoAmL 94*
Colarusso, Corrine Camille 1952- *WhoAmA 93*
Colas, Antonio Espada 1928- *WhoAm 94, WhoHisp 94*
Colas, Emile Jules 1923- *WhoAm 94*
Colasanti, Brenda Karen 1945- *WhoAm 94*
Colasanto, Nick d1985 *WhoHol 92*
Colasse, Pascal *NewGrDO*
Colasuonno, Louis Christopher 1948- *WhoAm 94*
Colasurd, Richard Michael 1928- *WhoAm 94*
Colautti, Arturo 1851-1914 *NewGrDO*
Colavita, Anthony Joseph 1935- *WhoAmP 93*
Colavito, James Samuel 1945- *WhoAmL 94*
Colbaugh, Richard Donald 1958- *WhoScEn 94*
Colbeck, J. Richard 1939- *WhoAmL 94*
Colbeck, Maurice 1925- *WrDr 94*
Colbeck, William 1871-1930 *DcNaB MP*
Colbeck-Welch, Edward Lawrence 1914- *Who 94*
Colberg, Marshall Rudolph 1913- *WhoAm 94*
Colberg, Thomas Pearsall 1948- *WhoAm 94, WhoFI 94*
Colberg-Poley, Anamaris Martha 1954- *WhoScEn 94*
Colbert, Alison *DrAPF 93*
Colbert, Annette Darcia 1959- *WhoFI 94*
Colbert, Benjamin James 1942- *WhoBlA 94*
Colbert, Charles Ralph 1921- *WhoAm 94*
Colbert, Claudette 1903- *IntWW 93, Who 94, WhoAm 94, WhoCom, WhoHol 92*
Colbert, Claudette 1905- *IntMPA 94*
Colbert, Edward Bruce 1957- *WhoWest 94*
Colbert, Edward Tuck 1947- *WhoAmL 94*
Colbert, Edwin Harris 1905- *IntWW 93, WhoAm 94, WhoScEn 94, WrDr 94*
Colbert, Ernest, Sr. 1916- *WhoBlA 94*
Colbert, George Clifford 1949- *WhoBlA 94*
Colbert, James W., III 1945- *WhoAmL 94*
Colbert, Jean-Baptiste 1619-1683 *HisWorL [port]*
Colbert, John W. 1950- *WhoAmL 94*
Colbert, Joseph d1978 *WhoHol 92*
Colbert, Lester Lum 1905- *WhoAm 94*
Colbert, Lester Lum, Jr. 1934- *WhoAm 94*
Colbert, Marvin Jay 1923- *WhoAm 94*
Colbert, Olga 1959- *WhoWest 94*
Colbert, Paul 1949- *WhoAmP 93*
Colbert, Robert *WhoHol 92*
Colbert, Robert B., Jr. 1921- *WhoAm 94*
Colbert, Robert Floyd 1960- *WhoScEn 94*
Colbert, Robert Reed, Jr. 1949- *WhoFI 94*
Colbert, Thelma Quince 1949- *WhoBlA 94*
Colbert, Thomas Burnell 1947- *WhoMW 93*
Colbert, Virgis W. 1939- *WhoBlA 94*
Colbert, Virgis William 1939- *WhoFI 94*
Colbin, Rod 1923- *WhoHol 92*
Colborn, Gene Louis 1935- *WhoAm 94, WhoScEn 94*
Colborn, Harry Walter 1921- *WhoAm 94*
Colborn, Jane Taylor 1913-1983 *WhoAmA 93N*
Colbourne, Edwin Denis 1941- *WhoFI 94*
Colbourne, Maurice d1965 *WhoHol 92*
Colbran, Isabella (Angela) 1785-1845 *NewGrDO [port]*
Colburn, C. William 1939- *WhoAmP 93*
Colburn, Carrie d1932 *WhoHol 92*
Colburn, David Dunton 1958- *WhoFI 94*
Colburn, Donald D. 1948- *WhoAm 94, WhoAmL 94*
Colburn, Francis Peabody 1909-1984 *WhoAmA 93N*
Colburn, Gene Lewis 1932- *WhoFI 94, WhoWest 94*
Colburn, Harold L., Jr. 1925- *WhoAmP 93*
Colburn, James Allan 1942- *WhoAmL 94*
Colburn, Kathleen Ann 1950- *WhoMW 93*
Colburn, Kenneth Hersey 1952- *WhoAm 94, WhoFI 94*
Colburn, Larry B. 1944- *WhoIns 94*
Colburn, Mickey 1929- *WhoAmP 93*
Colburn, Paul Leroy 1948- *WhoWest 94*
Colburn, Ralph Jonathan 1916- *WhoWest 94*
Colburn, Richard Dunton 1911- *WhoAm 94*
Colburn, Richard F. 1950- *WhoAmP 93*
Colburn, Wayne Alan 1947- *WhoWest 94*
Colby, Anita 1914- *WhoHol 92*
Colby, Anne 1946- *WhoAm 94*
Colby, Barbara d1975 *WhoHol 92*
Colby, Barbara Diane 1932- *WhoAm 94, WhoWest 94*
Colby, Bill 1927- *WhoAmA 93*
Colby, George Vincent, Jr. 1931- *WhoScEn 94*
Colby, Herbert d1912 *WhoHol 92*
Colby, Homer Wayland 1874-1950 *WhoAmA 93N*
Colby, Jean Poindexter 1907- *WrDr 94*
Colby, Jeff 1956- *WhoAmA 93*
Colby, Joan *DrAPF 93*
Colby, Joy Hakanson *WhoAm 94, WhoAmA 93*
Colby, Kenneth P., Sr. 1908- *WhoIns 94*
Colby, Kenneth Poole 1908- *WhoAm 94*
Colby, Marion d1987 *WhoHol 92*
Colby, Marvelle Seitman 1932- *WhoAm 94*
Colby, Patricia Farley 1958- *WhoAm 94, WhoMW 93*
Colby, Ralph Hayes 1958- *WhoScEn 94*
Colby, Robert Alan 1920- *WhoAm 94*
Colby, Robert Lester 1941- *WhoWest 94*
Colby, Ronald *IntMPA 94*
Colby, Stanley Brent 1964- *WhoScEn 94*
Colby, Tamara 1960- *WhoWest 94*
Colby, Victor E. 1917- *WhoAmA 93*
Colby, William Egan 1920- *IntWW 93, WhoAm 94, WhoAmP 93*
Colby, William Michael 1942- *WhoAmL 94*
Colby-Hall, Alice Mary 1932- *WhoAm 94*
Colchado, José D., Jr. 1946- *WhoHisp 94*
Colchester, Archdeacon of *Who 94*
Colchester, Area Bishop of 1929- *Who 94*
Colchester, Halsey Sparrowe 1918- *Who 94*
Colchester, Nicholas Benedick Sparrowe 1946- *Who 94*
Colchester, Trevor Charles 1909- *Who 94*
Colclaser, H. Alberta 1911- *WhoAm 94*
Colclough, Michael John 1944- *Who 94*
Colclough, Oswald S. 1898- *WhAm 10*
Colcord, Herbert Nathaniel, III 1951- *WhoFI 94*
Colcord, Mabel d1952 *WhoHol 92*
Colcord, Ray, III 1949- *WhoAm 94*
Cold, Ulrik (Thestrup) 1939- *NewGrDO*
Colden, Cadwallader 1688-1776 *AmRev, WhAmRev [port]*
Coldewey, John Christopher 1944- *WhoAm 94*
Coldoney, Nathan Jay 1963- *WhoFI 94*
Coldren, Diane 1945- *WhoMW 93*
Coldren, John 1944- *WhoAmP 93*
Coldren, Lee O. 1943- *WhoAm 94*
Coldrick, Albert Percival 1913- *Who 94*
Coldsmith, Don(ald C.) 1926- *WrDr 94*
Coldstream, George (Phillips) 1907- *Who 94*
Coldstream, John Nicolas 1927- *Who 94*
Coldstream, John Richard Francis 1947- *Who 94*
Coldwell, Philip Edward 1922- *WhoAm 94*
Coldwells, Alan Alfred 1930- *Who 94*
Cole *Who 94*
Cole, Adolph 1923- *WhoBlA 94*
Cole, Adrian (Christopher Synnot) 1949- *EncSF 93*
Cole, Albert, Jr. 1894-1989 *WhAm 10*
Cole, Alexander, Jr. 1965- *WhoBlA 94*
Cole, Allan 1943- *EncSF 93*
Cole, Alonzo Deen d1971 *WhoHol 92*
Cole, Arthur 1942- *WhoBlA 94*
Cole, Aubrey Louis 1923- *WhoAm 94*
Cole, Babette *WrDr 94*
Cole, Barbara Ruth 1941- *WhoAm 94*
Cole, Barry 1936- *WrDr 94*
Cole, Benjamin Richason 1916- *WhoAm 94*

Cole, Benjamin Theodore 1921- WhoAm 94
Cole, Boris Norman 1924- Who 94
Cole, Bradley C. 1955- WhoMW 93
Cole, Brady Marshall 1936- WhoAm 94
Cole, Brock 1938- TwCYAW, WrDr 94
Cole, Bruce 1938- WhoAmA 93, WrDr 94
Cole, Bruce Milan 1938- WhoAm 94
Cole, Buddy d1964 WhoHol 92
Cole, Burt 1930- EncSF 93
Cole, Carolyn Jo 1943- WhoAm 94, WhoFI 94
Cole, Charles Chester, Jr. 1922- WhoAm 94
Cole, Charles Dewey, Jr. 1952- WhoAmL 94
Cole, Charles E. 1927- WhoAmP 93
Cole, Charles Edward 1927- WhoAm 94, WhoAmL 94, WhoWest 94
Cole, Charles Glaston 1952- WhoAm 94, WhoAmL 94
Cole, Charles R. 1942- WhoScEn 94
Cole, Charles W., Jr. 1935- WhoAm 94, WhoFI 94
Cole, Charles Zhivaga 1957- WhoBlA 94
Cole, Clarence Russell 1918- WhoAm 94
Cole, Clark H. 1955- WhoAmL 94
Cole, Clifford Adair 1915- WhoAm 94
Cole, Clyde Curtis, Jr. 1932- WhoAm 94
Cole, Colin Who 94
Cole, (Alexander) Colin 1922- IntWW 93, Who 94
Cole, Corinne WhoHol 92
Cole, Curtis Allen 1946- WhoAm 94, WhoAmL 94
Cole, Cyrus EncSF 93
Cole, Daniel J., Jr. 1944- WhoAmL 94
Cole, David Who 94
Cole, (Claude Neville) David 1928- Who 94
Cole, David (Lee) 1920- Who 94
Cole, David Andrew 1942- WhoAm 94
Cole, David lee 1947- WhoIns 94
Cole, David Rodney 1931- WhoWest 94
Cole, David Winslow 1947- WhoFI 94, WhoWest 94
Cole, Dean Allen 1952- WhoScEn 94
Cole, Dennis 1943- WhoHol 92
Cole, Donald 1930- WhoAmA 93
Cole, Donald Charles 1937- WhoAmP 93
Cole, Dorthy Gattin 1933- WhoAmP 93
Cole, Douglas 1934- WhoAm 94
Cole, Douglas Leon 1947- WhoWest 94
Cole, E. R. DrAPF 93
Cole, E(ugene) R(oger) 1930- WrDr 94
Cole, Edmund Keith 1919- WrDr 94
Cole, Edward L. 1944- WhoAmP 93
Cole, Edward Nelson WhoAmP 93
Cole, Edyth Bryant WhoBlA 94
Cole, Eileen Marie Lucy 1924- Who 94
Cole, Elma Phillipson 1909- WhoAm 94
Cole, Eric Stuart d1992 Who 94N
Cole, Everett B. 1910- EncSF 93
Cole, Florence M. 1917- WhoAmP 93
Cole, Frances Elaine 1937-1983 AfrAmAl 6
Cole, Frank Who 94
Cole, Franklin Alan 1926- WhoAm 94
Cole, Fred d1964 WhoHol 92
Cole, Gary IntMPA 94
Cole, Geoffrey Alexander 1963- WhoIns 94
Cole, George 1925- IntMPA 94, Who 94, WhoHol 92
Cole, George David 1925- WhoAm 94
Cole, George Francis 1918- Who 94
Cole, George Thomas 1946- WhoAm 94
Cole, George Watson 1850-1939 DcLB 140 [port]
Cole, Gerald Ainsworth 1917- WhoWest 94
Cole, Grace WhoAmP 93
Cole, Grace V. WhoAmA 93
Cole, Gretchen Bornor 1927- WhoMW 93
Cole, Hannah 1954- SmATA 74
Cole, Harold David 1940- WhoAmA 93
Cole, Harry A. WhoAmP 93
Cole, Harry A. 1921- WhoBlA 94
Cole, Heather E. 1942- WhoAm 94
Cole, Helen 1922- WhoAmP 93
Cole, Herbert Milton 1935- WhoAmA 93
Cole, Hugo 1917- NewGrDO
Cole, Humphrey John Douglas 1928- Who 94
Cole, J. Chase 1954- WhoAmL 94
Cole, J. P. ConAu 41NR
Cole, J. Weldon 1936- WhoAm 94
Cole, Jack d1974 WhoHol 92
Cole, Jack 1914-1974 IntDcF 2-4
Cole, Jack Howard 1934- WhoScEn 94
Cole, James M. WhoAmP 93
Cole, James Mariner, Jr. 1915- WhoFI 94
Cole, James O. 1941- WhoBlA 94
Cole, James Ray 1944- WhoAmL 94
Cole, Janet 1922- WhoAm 94
Cole, Jeanette 1952- WhoAmA 93
Cole, Jeffrey Clark 1966- WhoMW 93
Cole, Jerome Foster 1940- WhoAm 94
Cole, Joanne W. 1958- WhoMW 93
Cole, Joe Clinton 1938- WhoWest 94
Cole, John Adam 1951- WhoFI 94
Cole, John Donald 1949- WhoAm 94
Cole, John L., Jr. 1928- WhoBlA 94
Cole, John Morrison 1927- Who 94
Cole, John P(eter) 1928- ConAu 41NR
Cole, John Peter 1928- Who 94
Cole, John Pope, Jr. 1930- WhoAm 94
Cole, John Y(oung), Jr. 1940- ConAu 41NR
Cole, Johnetta 1936- AfrAmAl 6 [port]
Cole, Johnnetta B. 1936- ConBlB 5 [port]
Cole, Johnnetta Betsch 1936- WhoAm 94, WhoBlA 94
Cole, Jojo WhoHol 92
Cole, Jonathan 1942- WrDr 94
Cole, Jonathan Edward 1945- WhoAm 94, WhoAmL 94
Cole, Jonathan Jay 1953- WhoScEn 94
Cole, Jonathan Otis 1925- WhoAm 94
Cole, Jonathan Richard 1942- WhoAm 94
Cole, Joseph Derham 1952- WhoAmP 93
Cole, Joseph Edmund 1915- WhoMW 93
Cole, Joseph H. 1913- WhoBlA 94
Cole, Joyce WhoAmA 93
Cole, Julian D. 1925- WhoScEn 94
Cole, Julian Wayne 1937- WhoAm 94, WhoScEn 94, WhoWest 94
Cole, Julie Kramer 1942- WhoAmA 93
Cole, June Marie 1957- WhoMW 93
Cole, June Robertson 1931- WhoAm 94
Cole, Kathleen Ann 1946- WhoMW 93
Cole, Kay 1948- WrDr 94
Cole, Keith David 1929- IntWW 93
Cole, Kenneth A. 1938- WhoAmP 93
Cole, Kenneth Bridges, Jr. 1959- WhoAmL 94
Cole, Kenneth Duane 1932- WhoAm 94
Cole, Kenneth J. 1936- WhoAmP 93
Cole, Kenneth M., III 1946- WhoAmL 94
Cole, Kenneth Merle, III 1946- WhoAmP 93
Cole, Larry Don 1937- WhoWest 94
Cole, Leonard Aaron 1933- WhoAm 94
Cole, Lester d1962 WhoHol 92
Cole, Lewis George 1931- WhoAm 94
Cole, Lois Lorraine 1932- WhoMW 93
Cole, Luther Francis 1925- WhoAm 94, WhoAmP 93
Cole, Maceola Louise 1934- WhoBlA 94
Cole, Malvin 1933- WhoScEn 94, WhoWest 94
Cole, Marie Keith d1975 WhoHol 92
Cole, Mark Allen 1961- WhoMW 93
Cole, Mark Julian 1955- WhoFI 94
Cole, Max 1937- WhoAm 94, WhoAmA 93
Cole, Michael 1945- WhoHol 92
Cole, Michael Allen 1943- WhoMW 93
Cole, Monica M. 1922- Who 94
Cole, Monroe 1933- WhoAm 94
Cole, Murray Lee 1922- WhoAmL 94
Cole, Nancy Stooksberry 1942- WhoAm 94
Cole, Nat 1919-1965 AfrAmAl 6 [port]
Cole, Nat King d1965 WhoHol 92
Cole, Natalie 1950- AfrAmAl 6, WhoBlA 94
Cole, Natalie Maria 1950- WhoAm 94
Cole, Olivia 1942- WhoHol 92
Cole, Patricia A. 1940- WhoBlA 94
Cole, Peter DrAPF 93
Cole, Peter Geoffrey 1945- Who 94
Cole, Peter Wayne 1939- WhoMW 93
Cole, Phillip Allen 1940- WhoAmL 94
Cole, Phyllis M. 1945- WhoAmP 93
Cole, Priscilla Marina 1926- WhoMW 93
Cole, Ralph WhoAmP 93
Cole, Ralph A. 1915- WhoAmP 93
Cole, Ransey Guy, Jr. 1951- WhoAm 94, WhoAmL 94, WhoBlA 94
Cole, Richard DrAPF 93
Cole, Richard 1928- WrDr 94
Cole, Richard A. 1951- WhoAm 94
Cole, Richard Cargill 1926- WhoAm 94
Cole, Richard Charles 1950- WhoAm 94
Cole, Richard George 1948- WhoWest 94
Cole, Richard Henry 1926- WhoFI 94
Cole, Richard John 1926- WhoAm 94
Cole, Richard Louis 1946- WhoAm 94
Cole, Richard P. 1948- WhoAmL 94
Cole, Richard Ray 1942- WhoAm 94
Cole, Richard Raymond Buxton 1937- Who 94
Cole, Rick 1953- WhoAm 94
Cole, Rickey Lloyd 1954- WhoFI 94
Cole, Robert Bates 1911- WhoAm 94
Cole, Robert Dennis 1949- WhoMW 93
Cole, Robert Hugh 1914-1991 WhAm 10
Cole, Robert Lane 1941- WhoAmL 94
Cole, Robert Taylor 1905-1991 WhAm 10
Cole, Robert Templeman 1918- Who 94
Cole, Robert W(illiam) EncSF 93
Cole, Roger David 1924- WhoAm 94
Cole, Roland Jay 1948- WhoAmL 94
Cole, Ronald Berkeley 1913- Who 94
Cole, Ronnie M. WhoAmP 93
Cole, Ruby Marie 1929- WhoMW 93
Cole, (Hugh) Sam(uel) (David) 1943- WrDr 94
Cole, Samuel Joseph 1950- WhoScEn 94
Cole, Samuel Thornton 1932- WhoIns 94
Cole, Sarah 1963- WhoAmL 94, WhoMW 93
Cole, Sheila R. 1939- WrDr 94
Cole, Sherwood Orison 1930- WhoAm 94
Cole, Stacey W. 1921- WhoAmP 93
Cole, Stephen Salisbury 1950- WhoFI 94
Cole, Sylvan 1918- WhoAmA 93
Cole, Sylvan, Jr. 1918- WhoAm 94
Cole, Terrence (Michael) 1953- WrDr 94
Cole, Terri Lynn 1951- WhoAm 94, WhoWest 94
Cole, Theodore John 1953- WhoMW 93, WhoScEn 94
Cole, Thomas 1801-1848 AmCulL
Cole, Thomas Alan 1936- WhoMW 93
Cole, Thomas Amor 1948- WhoAm 94, WhoAmL 94, WhoMW 93
Cole, Thomas E. 1933- WhoAmP 93
Cole, Thomas R(ichard) 1949- ConAu 141
Cole, Thomas Winston, Sr. 1915- WhoBlA 94
Cole, Thomas Winston, Jr. 1941- WhoBlA 94
Cole, Timothy David 1955- WhoScEn 94
Cole, Tina 1943- WhoHol 92
Cole, Todd G. 1921- WhoFI 94
Cole, Tom ConAu 141
Cole, Tom 1949- WhoAmP 93
Cole, Tom C. 1937- WhoAmP 93
Cole, Vinson WhoAm 94
Cole, Vinson 1950- NewGrDO
Cole, W(illiam) Owen 1931- ConAu 43NR
Cole, W. Storrs 1902-1989 WhAm 10
Cole, Walter R(andall) 1933- EncSF 93
Cole, Warren 1948- WhoAmL 94
Cole, Warren Henry 1898-1990 WhAm 10
Cole, Wayne S. 1922- WrDr 94
Cole, Wayne Stanley 1922- WhoAm 94
Cole, Wendell Gordon 1914- WhoAm 94
Cole, William DrAPF 93, Who 94
Cole, William 1919- WrDr 94
Cole, (Robert) William 1926- Who 94
Cole, William Charles 1909- Who 94
Cole, William Edward 1931- WhoAm 94
Cole, William Graham 1917- WhoMW 93
Cole, William James 1948- WhoAmP 93
Cole, William Kaufman 1914- WhoAm 94
Cole, William L. 1952- WhoAmL 94
Cole, William Manning 1930- WhoAm 94
Cole, William Scott d1992 Who 94N
Colebrook, George, Jr. 1942- WhoBlA 94
Colebrook, Philip Victor Charles 1924- Who 94
Colebrooke, George 1729-1809 DcNaB MP
Coleburt, James Russell 1920- WrDr 94
Coleby, Anthony Laurie 1935- Who 94
Coleby, Robert WhoHol 92
Coleclough, Peter Cecil 1917- Who 94
Colee, Forest R. d1962 WhoHol 92
Colef, Michael 1956- WhoScEn 94
Colegate, Isabel 1931- WrDr 94
Colegate, Isabel Diana 1931- Who 94
Colegate, Raymond 1927- Who 94
Cole-Hamilton, David John 1948- IntWW 93
Cole-Hamilton, (Arthur) Richard 1935- Who 94
Colelli, Marc Vincent 1959- WhoWest 94
Colello, Daniel R. 1948- WhoIns 94
Coleman, A(llan) D(ouglass) 1943- WhoAmA 93, WrDr 94
Coleman, Alan Brouse 1929- WhoWest 94
Coleman, Albert John 1918- WhoAm 94
Coleman, Alice Mary 1923- Who 94
Coleman, Almand Rouse 1905- WhoAm 94
Coleman, Alyce Marie 1911- WhoAmP 93
Coleman, Andrew Lee 1960- WhoBlA 94
Coleman, Arlene Florence 1926- WhoWest 94
Coleman, Arthur DrAPF 93
Coleman, Arthur H. 1920- WhoBlA 94
Coleman, Arthur Percy 1922- Who 94
Coleman, Arthur Robert 1916- WhoFI 94
Coleman, Audrey Rachelle 1934- WhoBlA 94
Coleman, Avant Patrick 1936- WhoBlA 94
Coleman, Barbara Lee 1948- WhoWest 94
Coleman, Barbara Sims 1932- WhoBlA 94
Coleman, Beatrice 1916-1990 WhAm 10
Coleman, Bernard 1928- Who 94
Coleman, Bernell 1929- WhoAm 94
Coleman, Brian Fitzgerald 1960- WhoScEn 94
Coleman, Brittin Turner 1942- WhoAm 94
Coleman, Brooks P., Jr. 1939- WhoAmP 93
Coleman, Bryan WhoHol 92
Coleman, Bryan Douglas 1948- WhoAmL 94, WhoFI 94
Coleman, C. Norman 1945- WhoAm 94
Coleman, Caesar David 1919- WhoBlA 94
Coleman, Carolyn S. 1952- WhoAmP 93
Coleman, Catherine d1669? NewGrDO
Coleman, Cecil R. 1934- WhoBlA 94
Coleman, Charles d1664 NewGrDO
Coleman, Charles d1951 WhoHol 92
Coleman, Charles Clyde 1937- WhoAm 94
Coleman, Charles Payson, Jr. 1950- WhoAmL 94
Coleman, Charles W. 1932- WhoAmP 93
Coleman, Chrisena Anne 1963- WhoBlA 94
Coleman, Clare EncSF 93
Coleman, Clarence J. 1897- WhAm 10
Coleman, Clarence William 1909-1992 WhoFI 94
Coleman, Claude M. 1940- WhoBlA 94
Coleman, Claudia d1938 WhoHol 92
Coleman, Collie WhoBlA 94
Coleman, Columbus E., Jr. 1948- WhoBlA 94
Coleman, Constance Depler 1926- WhoAmA 93
Coleman, Corinne d1981 WhoHol 92
Coleman, Cy WhoAm 94
Coleman, Cy 1929- ConTFT 11, NewGrDO
Coleman, D. Jackson 1934- WhoAm 94
Coleman, Dabney 1932- IntMPA 94, WhoCom, WhoHol 92
Coleman, Dabney W. 1932- WhoAm 94
Coleman, Dale Lynn 1958- WhoScEn 94, WhoWest 94
Coleman, David Cecil 1937- WhoFI 94
Coleman, David Manley 1948- WhoAm 94
Coleman, Denis Patrick, Jr. 1946- WhoAm 94, WhoFI 94
Coleman, Dennis 1951- WhoBlA 94
Coleman, Derrick 1967- WhoBlA 94
Coleman, Don d1985 WhoHol 92
Coleman, Don Edwin 1928- WhoBlA 94
Coleman, Donald Alvin 1952- WhoBlA 94
Coleman, Donald Cuthbert 1920- IntWW 93, Who 94
Coleman, Donald Lee 1936- WhoWest 94
Coleman, Donna 1949- WhoAmP 93
Coleman, E. Thomas 1943- WhoAmP 93
Coleman, Earl d1983 WhoHol 92
Coleman, Earl Maxwell 1916- WhoAm 94
Coleman, Edmund Benedict 1926- WhoAm 94
Coleman, Edward d1977 WhoHol 92
Coleman, Edward H. 1928- WhoAmA 93
Coleman, Edward M. WhoAmP 93
Coleman, Edwin DeWitt, III 1954- WhoScEn 94
Coleman, Edwin Leon, II 1932- WhoBlA 94
Coleman, Elijah 1924- WhoAmP 93
Coleman, Elizabeth 1937- WhoAm 94
Coleman, Elizabeth Sheppard WhoBlA 94
Coleman, Emil d1965 WhoHol 92
Coleman, Emily R. 1947- WrDr 94
Coleman, Emmett BlkWr 2
Coleman, Emmett 1938- WhoBlA 94
Coleman, Eric Dean 1951- WhoAmP 93, WhoBlA 94
Coleman, Ernest Albert 1929- WhoAm 94
Coleman, Everod A. 1920- WhoBlA 94
Coleman, F. Woodrow 1944- WhoAmL 94
Coleman, Finnos Weinford 1951- WhoMW 93
Coleman, Floyd Willis 1939- WhoAmA 93
Coleman, Francis J., Jr. 1945- WhoAmL 94
Coleman, Frank d1970 WhoHol 92
Coleman, Frank Thomas 1950- WhoMW 93
Coleman, Frankie Lynn 1950- WhoBlA 94
Coleman, Garnet F. 1961- WhoAmP 93
Coleman, Garry Dale 1961- WhoFI 94
Coleman, Gary 1968- IntMPA 94, WhoBlA 94, WhoHol 92
Coleman, Gary William 1945- WhoMW 93
Coleman, Gayle 1954- WhoAmA 93
Coleman, George Edward 1935- WhoAm 94, WhoBlA 94
Coleman, George Joseph, III 1958- WhoAmL 94
Coleman, George Michael 1953- WhoMW 93
Coleman, George Willard 1912- WhoFI 94
Coleman, Gerald Christopher 1939- WhoAm 94, WhoFI 94
Coleman, Gilbert Irving 1940- WhoBlA 94
Coleman, Gloria Jean 1952- WhoMW 93
Coleman, Greg Jerome 1954- WhoBlA 94
Coleman, Harry Theodore 1943- WhoBlA 94
Coleman, Herman Oscar 1923- WhoFI 94
Coleman, Herman W. 1939- WhoBlA 94
Coleman, Horace DrAPF 93
Coleman, Howard S. 1917- WhoAm 94, WhoScEn 94
Coleman, Hume Field 1938- WhoAm 94
Coleman, Hurley J., Jr. 1953- WhoBlA 94
Coleman, Isobel Mary Who 94
Coleman, J. Grant 1950- WhoAmL 94

Coleman, J. Tom, Jr. 1928- *WhoAmP 93*
Coleman, Jack 1924- *BasBi*
Coleman, Jack L., Jr. 1953- *WhoAmP 93*
Coleman, James *DrAPF 93*
Coleman, James (Samuel) 1926- *WrDr 94*
Coleman, James A. 1921- *WrDr 94*
Coleman, James D. 1949- *WhoAmL 94*
Coleman, James Howard, Jr. 1909- *WhoAmL 94*
Coleman, James Julian, Jr. 1941- *WhoAmL 94, WhoFI 94*
Coleman, James Malcolm 1935- *WhoAm 94*
Coleman, James Nelson *EncSF 93*
Coleman, James Plemon 1914-1991 *WhAm 10*
Coleman, James Regis 1946- *WhoMW 93*
Coleman, James Samuel 1926- *IntWW 93, WhoAm 94*
Coleman, James William 1935- *WhoBlA 94*
Coleman, Jane Candia *DrAPF 93*
Coleman, Jane Candia 1939- *WrDr 94*
Coleman, Jean Ellen *WhoBlA 94*
Coleman, Jean Stapleton 1925- *WhoAmP 93*
Coleman, Jeffrey Peters 1959- *WhoAmL 94*
Coleman, Jerry Todd 1957- *WhoScEn 94*
Coleman, Joel Clifford 1930- *WhoAm 94, WhoAmL 94*
Coleman, Joel Gregory 1957- *WhoFI 94*
Coleman, John B. 1929- *WhoBlA 94*
Coleman, John Ennis 1930- *Who 94*
Coleman, John H. 1928- *WhoBlA 94*
Coleman, John Hewson 1912- *WhoAm 94*
Coleman, John Howard 1925- *WhoScEn 94*
Coleman, John James 1926- *WhoAm 94*
Coleman, John James, III 1956- *WhoAmL 94*
Coleman, John Joseph 1937- *WhoAm 94*
Coleman, John Michael 1949- *WhoAm 94, WhoAmL 94*
Coleman, John Morley 1948- *WhoScEn 94*
Coleman, John Royston 1921- *WhoAm 94*
Coleman, John Winston 1898- *WhAm 10*
Coleman, Joseph E. *WhoAmP 93*
Coleman, Joseph E. 1922- *WhoBlA 94*
Coleman, Joseph Michael 1945- *WhoAm 94*
Coleman, Judy 1944- *WhoAmA 93*
Coleman, Karen Jones 1961- *WhoMW 93*
Coleman, Kenneth L. 1942- *WhoBlA 94*
Coleman, Kenneth William 1930- *WhoFI 94*
Coleman, Kit 1856-1915 *BlmGWL*
Coleman, Lamar William 1934- *WhoAm 94*
Coleman, Leighton Hammond d1993 *NewYTBS 93 [port]*
Coleman, Lemon, Jr. 1935- *WhoBlA 94*
Coleman, Leonard *WhoBlA 94*
Coleman, Lester Earl 1930- *WhoAm 94, WhoFI 94*
Coleman, Lester Laudy 1911- *WhoAm 94, WhoScEn 94*
Coleman, Lewis Waldo 1942- *WhoAm 94, WhoFI 94, WhoWest 94*
Coleman, Linda *WhoAmP 93*
Coleman, Loren (Elwood), Jr. 1947- *WrDr 94*
Coleman, M. L. 1941- *WhoAmA 93*
Coleman, Malina 1954- *WhoAmL 94*
Coleman, Marian M. 1948- *WhoBlA 94*
Coleman, Marion Leslie 1925- *WhoFI 94*
Coleman, Mark David 1960- *WhoScEn 94*
Coleman, Martin Stone 1913- *WhoAm 94*
Coleman, Mary Ann *DrAPF 93*
Coleman, Mary Louise 1949- *WhoMW 93*
Coleman, Mary Stallings *WhoAm 94*
Coleman, Melvin D. 1948- *WhoBlA 94*
Coleman, Michael 1946- *WhoAmA 93*
Coleman, Michael B. 1946- *WhoWest 94*
Coleman, Michael Bennett *WhoBlA 94*
Coleman, Michael C(hristopher) 1946- *ConAu 43NR*
Coleman, Michael Dortch 1944- *WhoScEn 94*
Coleman, Michael Murray 1938- *WhoAm 94*
Coleman, Michael Victor 1953- *WhoBlA 94*
Coleman, Monte 1957- *WhoBlA 94*
Coleman, Morton 1939- *WhoAm 94*
Coleman, Nancy 1914- *WhoHol 92*
Coleman, Nancy 1917- *IntMPA 94*
Coleman, Nancy Pees 1955- *WhoAm 94*
Coleman, Norman Arthur 1923- *WhoFI 94*
Coleman, Ornette 1930- *AfrAmAl 6, AmCulL, WhoAm 94, WhoBlA 94*
Coleman, Paul David 1927- *WhoAm 94*
Coleman, Paul Jerome, Jr. 1932- *WhoFI 94, WhoScEn 94*
Coleman, Peter Everard *Who 94*
Coleman, Peter Tali 1919- *WhoAm 94, WhoAmP 93*
Coleman, Ralph Edward 1943- *WhoAm 94*
Coleman, Ralph P. 1892-1968 *WhoAmA 93N*
Coleman, Raymond Cato 1918- *WhoBlA 94*
Coleman, Renee *WhoHol 92*
Coleman, Richard *DrAPF 93*
Coleman, Richard Walter 1922- *WhoMW 93, WhoScEn 94*
Coleman, Richard William 1935- *WhoAmL 94*
Coleman, Rita Denise 1959- *WhoAmL 94*
Coleman, Robert A. 1932- *WhoBlA 94*
Coleman, Robert Earl, Jr. 1961- *WhoBlA 94*
Coleman, Robert George Gilbert 1929- *Who 94*
Coleman, Robert Griffin 1923- *WhoAm 94, WhoScEn 94*
Coleman, Robert J. 1937- *WhoAmL 94*
Coleman, Robert John 1943- *Who 94*
Coleman, Robert Lee 1929- *WhoAm 94, WhoAmL 94, WhoMW 93*
Coleman, Robert Marshall 1925- *WhoAm 94*
Coleman, Robert Samuel 1959- *WhoScEn 94*
Coleman, Robert Trent 1936- *WhoWest 94*
Coleman, Robert Winston 1942- *WhoAm 94, WhoAmL 94*
Coleman, Roderick Flynn 1958- *WhoAmL 94*
Coleman, Rodney Albert 1938- *WhoBlA 94*
Coleman, Roger Dixon 1915- *WhoWest 94*
Coleman, Roger Haven 1930- *WhoMW 93*
Coleman, Roger William 1929- *WhoAm 94, WhoWest 94*
Coleman, Rolf d1976 *WhoHol 92*
Coleman, Ronald D. 1941- *CngDr 93, WhoAm 94, WhoAmP 93*
Coleman, Ronald Frederick 1931- *Who 94*
Coleman, Ronald Gerald 1944- *WhoBlA 94*
Coleman, Ronald K. 1934- *WhoBlA 94*
Coleman, Ronny Jack 1940- *WhoWest 94*
Coleman, Roy Melvin 1930- *WhoAm 94*
Coleman, Rudolph W. 1929- *WhoBlA 94*
Coleman, Rudy B. 1947- *WhoAmL 94*
Coleman, Ruth M. 1917-1990 *WhoBlA 94N*
Coleman, Samuel Ebow 1945- *WhoScEn 94*
Coleman, Samuel Melville 1961- *WhoAmL 94*
Coleman, Shirley 1955- *WhoAmP 93*
Coleman, Sidney 1937- *IntWW 93*
Coleman, Sidney Richard 1937- *WhoAm 94, WhoScEn 94*
Coleman, Sinclair B. 1946- *WhoBlA 94*
Coleman, Steven Laurence 1940- *WhoAm 94*
Coleman, Tamara Ann 1958- *WhoMW 93*
Coleman, Ted 1953- *WhoWest 94*
Coleman, Terry 1931- *IntWW 93, Who 94, WrDr 94*
Coleman, Terry L. 1943- *WhoAmP 93*
Coleman, Thomas Britt 1952- *WhoAmL 94*
Coleman, Thomas D. *WhoAmP 93*
Coleman, Thomas J. 1950- *IntMPA 94*
Coleman, Thomas Loyd 1947- *WhoAmP 93*
Coleman, Thomas Young 1949- *WhoAm 94*
Coleman, Timothy Stewart 1950- *WhoMW 93*
Coleman, Tommy Lee 1952- *WhoScEn 94*
Coleman, Valerie Dickerson 1946- *WhoBlA 94*
Coleman, Verna (Scott) *WrDr 94*
Coleman, Veronica Freeman *WhoAmL 94*
Coleman, Vincent Maurice 1961- *WhoBlA 94*
Coleman, Virginia Flood 1945- *WhoAm 94, WhoAmL 94*
Coleman, Wade Hampton, III 1932- *WhoAm 94*
Coleman, Wanda *DrAPF 93, WhoBlA 94*
Coleman, Wanda 1946- *BlkWr 2, ConAu 43NR, DcLB 130 [port]*
Coleman, Warren d1968 *WhoHol 92*
Coleman, Warren B. 1932- *WhoBlA 94*
Coleman, Wendell Lawrence 1946- *WhoAmP 93*
Coleman, William Carleton, Jr. 1925- *WhoAmP 93*
Coleman, William Eliah 1921- *WhoScEn 94*
Coleman, William Gilbert 1951- *WhoWest 94*
Coleman, William Matthew 1922- *WhoAmP 93*
Coleman, William Robert 1916- *WhoWest 94*
Coleman, William Robert 1917- *Who 94*
Coleman, William T., Jr. 1920- *WhoBlA 94*
Coleman, William Thaddeus, Jr. 1920- *WhoAm 94, WhoAmL 94*
Coleman, William Thomas 1938- *WhoAmL 94*
Coleman, William V. 1943- *WhoAmL 94*
Coleman, Wilson 1875- *WhoHol 92*
Coleman, Winson 1905- *WhoBlA 94*
Coleman, Wisdom F. 1944- *WhoBlA 94*
Coleman-Burns, Patricia Wendolyn 1947- *WhoBlA 94*
Coleman Family *NewGrDO*
Colemon, Johnnie *WhoBlA 94*
Colen, B. D. 1946- *WhoAm 94*
Colen, Donald Jerome 1917- *WhoAm 94*
Colen, Frederick Haas 1947- *WhoAm 94, WhoAmL 94*
Colenso, William 1811-1899 *WhWE*
Coler, Joel H. 1931- *IntMPA 94*
Coler, Myron Abraham 1913- *WhoAm 94*
Coleraine, Baron 1931- *Who 94*
Coleridge, Baron 1937- *Who 94*
Coleridge, David Ean 1932- *IntWW 93, Who 94*
Coleridge, Ethel d1976 *WhoHol 92*
Coleridge, (Marguerite) Georgina 1916- *Who 94*
Coleridge, Geraldine Margaret 1948- *Who 94*
Coleridge, John *EncSF 93*
Coleridge, Mary 1861-1907 *BlmGWL*
Coleridge, Nicholas David 1957- *Who 94*
Coleridge, Paul James Duke 1949- *Who 94*
Coleridge, Samuel Taylor 1772-1834 *BlmGEL [port]*
Coleridge, Sara 1802-1852 *BlmGWL*
Coleridge, Sylvia d1986 *WhoHol 92*
Coleridge-Taylor, Samuel 1875-1912 *AfrAmAl 6 [port], NewGrDO*
Colerio, Maire Louise *WhoWomW 91*
Coles, Adrian Michael 1954- *Who 94*
Coles, Anna Bailey 1925- *WhoBlA 94*
Coles, Anna L. Bailey 1925- *IntWW 93*
Coles, Anna Louise Bailey 1925- *WhoAm 94*
Coles, Bimbo 1968- *WhoBlA 94*
Coles, Bruce *Who 94*
Coles, (Norman) Bruce (Cameron) 1937- *Who 94*
Coles, Bryan Randell 1926- *IntWW 93, Who 94*
Coles, Charles (Honi) d1992 *WhoBlA 94N*
Coles, Charles Honi c. 1911-1992 *AnObit 1992*
Coles, Darnell 1962- *WhoBlA 94*
Coles, David John *Who 94*
Coles, Don 1928- *WrDr 94*
Coles, Donald Earl 1924- *WhoAm 94*
Coles, Dwight Ross 1952- *WhoWest 94*
Coles, Edwin Lee 1952- *WhoMW 93*
Coles, Gerald James Kay 1933- *Who 94*
Coles, Graham 1948- *WhoMW 93*
Coles, Honi 1911- *WhoHol 92*
Coles, James Reed *WhoAmP 93*
Coles, Janis 1936- *WrDr 94*
Coles, Joan M(yers) 1947- *WrDr 94*
Coles, John *Who 94*
Coles, (Arthur) John 1937- *IntWW 93, Who 94*
Coles, John Edward 1951- *WhoBlA 94*
Coles, John Morton 1930- *IntWW 93, Who 94, WrDr 94*
Coles, Joseph C. 1902- *WhoBlA 94*
Coles, Joseph Carlyle, Jr. 1926-1981 *WhoBlA 94N*
Coles, Kenneth George 1926- *Who 94*
Coles, Lorraine McClellan 1929- *WhoMW 93*
Coles, Mabel Irene *Who 94*
Coles, Michael *WhoHol 92*
Coles, Norman 1914- *Who 94*
Coles, Richard Scott 1957- *WhoMW 93*
Coles, Richard Warren 1939- *WhoScEn 94*
Coles, Robert 1929- *WhoAm 94, WrDr 94*
Coles, Robert Martin 1929- *IntWW 93*
Coles, Robert Traynham 1929- *WhoAm 94, WhoBlA 94*
Coles, Thelma 1952- *WhoAmA 93*
Coles, William Henry *WhoAm 94*
Colescott, Robert 1925- *AfrAmAl 6*
Colescott, Robert H. 1925- *WhoAmA 93*
Colescott, Robert Hutton 1925- *WhoAm 94*
Colescott, Warrington W. 1921- *WhoAmA 93*
Colescott, Warrington Wickham 1921- *WhoAm 94*
Colet, John 1467-1519 *DcLB 132 [port]*
Colet, Louise 1810-1876 *BlmGWL*
Coletta, Ralph John 1921- *WhoAmL 94*
Colette 1873-1954 *NewGrDO*
Colette 1952- *WhoAmA 93*
Colette, (Sidonie-Gabrielle) 1873-1954 *GayLL, RfGShF*
Colette, Sidonie Gabrielle 1873-1954 *BlmGWL [port]*
Coletti, Agostino Bonaventura c. 1680-1752 *NewGrDO*
Coletti, Filippo 1811-1894 *NewGrDO*
Coletti, John Anthony 1952- *WhoAmL 94*
Coletti, Joseph Arthur 1898-1973 *WhoAmA 93N*
Coley, Betty 1933- *WhoAm 94*
Coley, Donald Lee 1953- *WhoBlA 94*
Coley, Gerald Sydney 1914- *WhoBlA 94*
Coley, H. Turner, Jr. 1942- *WhoIns 94*
Coley, John Ford *WhoHol 92*
Coley, Randolph C. 1947- *WhoAmL 94*
Coley, Robert *EncSF 93*
Coley, Robert Bernard 1951- *WhoFI 94*
Coley, Thomas d1989 *WhoHol 92*
Colfax, David (John) 1936- *ConAu 140*
Colfax, J. David *ConAu 140*
Colfin, Bruce Elliott 1951- *WhoAmL 94*
Colford, Francis Xavier 1952- *WhoAm 94*
Colfox, (William) John 1924- *Who 94*
Colgan, Charles Joseph 1926- *WhoAmP 93*
Colgan, Evan George 1960- *WhoScEn 94*
Colgan, Michael Anthony 1950- *IntWW 93*
Colgan, Michael Byrley 1948- *WhoAmL 94*
Colgan, Samuel Hezlett 1945- *Who 94*
Colgate, Doris Eleanor 1941- *WhoFI 94*
Colgate, Samuel Oran 1933- *WhoScEn 94*
Colgate, Stirling Auchincloss 1925- *WhoAm 94, WhoScEn 94*
Colglazier, Michael D. 1948- *WhoAmL 94*
Colglazier, Patrick V. 1950- *WhoAmP 93*
Colgrain, Baron 1920- *Who 94*
Colgrass, Michael (Charles) 1932- *NewGrDO*
Colgrass, Michael Charles 1932- *WhoAm 94*
Colgren, Richard Dean 1961- *WhoWest 94*
Colgrove, Thomas Michael 1930- *WhoMW 93*
Colhapp, Barbara Jones 1935- *WhoAmP 93*
Colhoun, Howard Post 1935- *WhoAm 94*
Colhoun, John 1913- *Who 94*
Coli, Guido John 1921- *WhoAm 94*
Colice, Gene Leslie 1950- *WhoScEn 94*
Colice-Cadwell, Michele Irene 1953- *WhoMW 93*
Colicos, John 1928- *WhoHol 92*
Coligny, Louise de 1555-1620 *BlmGWL*
Colihan, Patrice 1965- *WhoHol 92*
Colin, George H. *WhoBlA 94*
Colin, Georges d1979 *WhoHol 92*
Colin, Georgia T. *WhoAmA 93*
Colin, Georgia Talmey *WhoAm 94*
Colin, Gerald Fitzmaurice 1913- *Who 94*
Colin, Jean d1989 *WhoHol 92*
Colin, Julia d1975 *WhoHol 92*
Colin, Lawrence 1931- *WhoAm 94*
Colin, Margaret 1957- *WhoHol 92*
Colin, Margaret 1958- *IntMPA 94*
Colin, Ralph Frederick 1900- *WhoAmA 93N*
Colina, Armando G. 1935- *WhoAmA 93*
Colinas, Antonio 1946- *DcLB 134 [port]*
Colin Clout *BlmGEL*
Colingo, Joe Ross 1939- *WhoAmL 94*
Colini, Filippo 1811-1863 *NewGrDO*
Colino, Richard Ralph 1936- *WhoFI 94*
Colish, Marcia Lillian 1937- *WhoAm 94, WrDr 94*
Colista, Feliciano Philip, Jr. 1933- *WhoAmL 94*
Colitti, Michael Joseph, Jr. 1965- *WhoFI 94*
Colitti, Rik *WhoHol 92*
Colker, Edward 1927- *WhoAm 94, WhoAmA 93*
Colker, Marvin Leonard 1927- *WhoAm 94*
Coll, Blasini Nestor 1931- *Who 94*
Coll, Colleen *WhoAmP 93*
Coll, Edward Girard, Jr. 1934- *WhoAm 94*
Coll, Elizabeth Anne Loosemore E. *Who 94*
Coll, Helen F. 1921- *WhoAm 94*
Coll, Ivonne *WhoHisp 94*
Coll, John Peter, Jr. 1943- *WhoAm 94, WhoAmL 94*
Coll, Max 1932- *WhoAmP 93*
Coll, Stephen Wilson 1958- *WhoAm 94*
Colla, Giuseppe 1731-1806 *NewGrDO*
Colla, Marcel 1943- *IntWW 93*
Colla, Virginia Covert 1937- *WhoWest 94*
Colladay, Robert S. 1940- *WhoAm 94*
Collado, Emilio Gabriel 1910- *WhoAm 94*
Collado, Francisco 1951- *WhoHisp 94*
Collado, Lisa 1944- *WhoAmA 93, WhoHisp 94*
Collamore, Jerome d1987 *WhoHol 92*

Collamore, Thomas Jones 1959- *WhoAm 94, WhoAmP 93*
Collan, Yrjo Urho 1941- *WhoScEn 94*
Collantes, Augurio L. 1928- *WhoAsA 94*
Collantes, Lourdes Yapchiongco *WhoAsA 94*
Collar, Leo Linford 1930- *WhoFI 94*
Collard, Cyril 1957-1993 *NewYTBS 93*
Collard, Douglas Reginald 1916- *Who 94*
Collard, Jean Philippe 1948- *IntWW 93*
Collard, Lorraine Fullmer 1957- *WhoWest 94*
Collard, Randle Scott 1951- *WhoScEn 94*
Collaro, Andrew *WhoAmP 93*
Collas, Juan Garduno, Jr. 1932- *WhoAm 94, WhoAmL 94*
Collasse, Pascal 1649-1709 *NewGrDO*
Collazo, Carlos Erick 1956-1990 *WhoAmA 93N*
Collazo, Ernest J. *WhoHisp 94*
Collazo, Francisco Jose 1931- *WhoHisp 94*
Collazo, Frank, Jr. 1931- *WhoAmP 93, WhoHisp 94*
Collazo, Joe Manuel 1945- *WhoHisp 94*
Collazo, Jose Antonio 1943- *WhoHisp 94*
Collazo, Miguel *EncSF 93*
Collazo, Salvador 1948- *WhoHisp 94*
Collazos Gonzalez, Julio 1955- *WhoScEn 94*
Collbohm, Franklin Rudolf 1907-1990 *WhAm 10*
Colleano, Bonar, Jr. d1958 *WhoHol 92*
Colleano, Mark 1956- *WhoHol 92*
Colledge, Malcolm (Andrew Richard) 1939- *WrDr 94*
Collee, John Gerald 1929- *Who 94*
Collen, Henri d1924 *WhoHol 92*
Collen, John 1954- *WhoAmL 94*
Collen, Morris Frank 1913- *WhoAm 94, WhoScEn 94, WhoWest 94*
Collen, Sheldon Orrin 1922- *WhoAm 94*
Collender, Andrew Robert 1946- *Who 94*
Collens, Lewis Morton 1938- *WhoAm 94, WhoMW 93*
Collens, William S. 1897- *WhAm 10*
Coller, Donna Jean 1938- *WhoMW 93*
Colleran, Bill 1922- *IntMPA 94*
Colleran, Kevin 1941- *WhoAmL 94*
Collery, Arnold 1927-1989 *WhAm 10*
Collery, Paula 1954- *WhoAmA 93*
Colles, Gertrude 1869-1957 *WhoAmA 93N*
Collet, Bernt Johan 1941- *IntWW 93*
Collet, Camilla 1813-1895 *BlmGWL*
Collet, Christopher 1968- *WhoHol 92*
Collett, Christopher 1931- *Who 94*
Collett, Farrell Reuben 1907- *WhoAmA 93*
Collett, Ian (Seymour) 1953- *Who 94*
Collett, Joan *WhAm 10*
Collett, Lorraine d1983 *WhoHol 92*
Collett, Merrill Judson 1914- *WhoWest 94*
Collett, Robert Lee 1940- *WhoAm 94*
Collett, Wayne Neville 1941- *WhoAm 94*
Collette, Charles T. 1944- *WhoAmL 94*
Collette, Christine 1947- *WrDr 94*
Colleville, Anne-Hyacinthe de Saint Leger de 1761-1824 *BlmGWL*
Colley, Barbara Marie 1958- *WhoWest 94*
Colley, (David) Bryan (Hall) 1934- *Who 94*
Colley, Denise *WhoHol 92*
Colley, Don Pedro *WhoHol 92*
Colley, Ian Harris 1922- *Who 94*
Colley, John Leonard, Jr. 1930- *WhoAm 94*
Colley, Kenneth 1937- *WhoHol 92*
Colley, Linda 1949- *WrDr 94*
Colley, Michael F. 1936- *WhoAmP 93*
Colley, Nathaniel S., Jr. 1956- *WhoBlA 94*
Colley, Peter Michael 1949- *WhoWest 94*
Colley, Roger J. 1938- *WhoScEn 94*
Colley, Susan Jane 1959- *WhoMW 93*
Colley, Thomas Elbert, Jr. 1928- *WhoScEn 94*
Colley, William, Jr. 1910-1984 *WhoAmA 93N*
Colli, Bart Joseph 1948- *WhoAm 94*
Colliander, Alan Clare 1948- *WhoFI 94*
Colliander, Douglas C. 1943- *WhoIns 94*
Collias, Elsie Cole 1920- *WhoAm 94*
Collias, Nicholas E(lias) 1914- *WrDr 94*
Collie, Alexander Conn 1913- *Who 94*
Collie, John, Jr. 1934- *WhoFI 94, WhoMW 93*
Collie, Kelsey E. 1935- *WhoBlA 94*
Collie, Marvin Key 1918-1989 *WhAm 10*
Collier *Who 94*
Collier, Alan Caswell 1911-1990 *WhAm 10, WhoAmA 93N*
Collier, Albert 1921- *WhoAmP 93*
Collier, Albert, III 1926- *WhoBlA 94*
Collier, Alberta 1911-1987 *WhoAmA 93N*
Collier, Andrew James 1923- *Who 94*
Collier, Andrew John 1939- *Who 94*
Collier, Beverly Joanne 1936- *WhoMW 93*
Collier, Calvin Joseph 1942- *WhoAmP 93*
Collier, Charles Arthur, Jr. 1930- *WhoAm 94*
Collier, Christopher 1930- *TwCYAW*
Collier, Clarence Marie *WhoBlA 94*
Collier, Clarence Robert 1919- *WhoAm 94*
Collier, Clifford Warthen, Jr. 1927- *WhoAm 94*
Collier, Constance d1955 *WhoHol 92*
Collier, David Alan 1947- *WhoAm 94*
Collier, David English 1960- *WhoMW 93*
Collier, Don *WhoHol 92*
Collier, Duaine Alden 1950- *WhoFI 94*
Collier, Eugenia W. 1928- *WhoBlA 94*
Collier, Eugenia W(illiams) 1928- *BlkWr 2*
Collier, Everett Dolton 1914-1992 *WhAm 10*
Collier, Felton Moreland 1924- *WhoAm 94*
Collier, Gaylan Jane 1924- *WhoAm 94*
Collier, George 1738-1795 *AmRev, WhAmRev*
Collier, Graham 1937- *WrDr 94*
Collier, H. M., Jr. 1916- *WhoBlA 94*
Collier, Herman Edward, Jr. 1927- *WhoAm 94*
Collier, Irene Dea 1948- *WhoAsA 94*
Collier, James Bruce 1920- *WhoAmL 94*
Collier, James Burton, Jr. 1953- *WhoMW 93*
Collier, James Lincoln 1928- *TwCYAW, WrDr 94*
Collier, James Warren 1940- *WhoAm 94*
Collier, Jane *ConAu 43NR*
Collier, Jane 1710-1754? *BlmGWL, DcNaB MP*
Collier, Jean 1926- *WrDr 94*
Collier, John (Henry Noyes) 1901-1980 *EncSF 93*
Collier, John Gordon 1935- *Who 94, WhoScEn 94*
Collier, Kenneth (Gerald) 1910- *WrDr 94*
Collier, Kenneth Gerald 1938- *Who 94*
Collier, Lacey Alexander 1935- *WhoAm 94, WhoAmL 94*
Collier, Leo Nathan 1884-1901 *WhoAmA 93N*
Collier, Lesley 1947- *IntDcB [port]*
Collier, Lesley Faye 1947- *IntWW 93, Who 94*
Collier, Leslie Harold 1921- *Who 94*
Collier, Lois 1919- *WhoHol 92*
Collier, Louis Malcolm 1919- *WhoBlA 94*
Collier, Lucille Ann *WhoAm 94*
Collier, Marian *WhoHol 92*
Collier, Marie 1927-1971 *NewGrDO*
Collier, Marsha Ann 1950- *WhoWest 94*
Collier, Mary 1679-c. 1762 *BlmGWL*
Collier, Mary 1688-c. 1762 *DcNaB MP*
Collier, Matthew S. 1957- *WhoAmP 93*
Collier, Michael *DrAPF 93*
Collier, Nathan Morris 1924- *WhoMW 93*
Collier, Oscar 1924- *WhoAm 94*
Collier, Patience d1987 *WhoHol 92*
Collier, Paul 1949- *Who 94*
Collier, Peter (Anthony) 1939- *WrDr 94*
Collier, Peter Neville 1948- *Who 94*
Collier, Richard 1924- *WrDr 94*
Collier, Richard Bangs 1918- *WhoWest 94*
Collier, Sherlee d1972 *WhoHol 92*
Collier, Shirley Lucille 1933- *WhoAmP 93*
Collier, Steven Edward 1952- *WhoFI 94, WhoScEn 94*
Collier, Torrence Junis 1932- *WhoBlA 94*
Collier, Troy 1941- *WhoBlA 94*
Collier, William, Sr. d1944 *WhoHol 92*
Collier, William, Jr. d1987 *WhoHol 92*
Collier, William H. 1926- *WhoAmP 93*
Collier, Willye 1922- *WhoBlA 94*
Collier, Zena *DrAPF 93*
Collier, Zena 1926- *ConAu 43NR, WrDr 94*
Collier-Evans, Demetra Frances 1937- *WhoAm 94*
Collier-Griffith, Julia Marie 1949- *WhoBlA 94*
Collier-Thomas, Bettye *WhoBlA 94*
Collier-Wright, John Hurrell 1915- *Who 94*
Colligan, Elsa *DrAPF 93*
Colligan, John Clifford 1906- *Who 94*
Collignon, Stefan Colin 1951- *IntWW 93*
Collin, Arthur Edwin 1929- *WhoAm 94*
Collin, Dwight R. 1940- *WhoAmL 94*
Collin, Geoffrey de Egglesfield 1921- *Who 94*
Collin, Jack 1945- *Who 94*
Collin, Jean 1924- *IntWW 93*
Collin, John 1931- *WhoHol 92*
Collin, Marion (Cripps) 1928- *WrDr 94*
Collin, Robert Emanuel 1928- *WhoAm 94*
Collin, Thomas James 1949- *WhoAm 94, WhoAmL 94*
Collin de Blamont, Francois 1690-1760 *NewGrDO*
Collinet, Georges Andre 1940- *WhoBlA 94*
Colling, Cecilia Gail 1949- *WhoAmP 93*
Colling, David Allen 1935- *WhoScEn 94*
Colling, Dennis Robert 1947- *WhoAmP 93*
Colling, James Oliver 1930- *Who 94*
Colling, Kenneth Frank 1945- *WhoAm 94*
Collinge, Jared Edward 1932- *WhoAmL 94*
Collinge, Patricia d1974 *WhoHol 92*
Collingridge, Jean Mary 1923- *Who 94*
Collings, Betty 1934- *WhoAmA 93*
Collings, Blanche d1968 *WhoHol 92*
Collings, Celeste Louise 1948- *WhoWest 94*
Collings, Charles LeRoy 1925- *WhoAm 94, WhoWest 94*
Collings, David 1940- *WhoHol 92*
Collings, I. J. *WrDr 94*
Collings, Juliet Jeanne d'Auvergne *Who 94*
Collings, Michael (Robert) 1947- *WrDr 94*
Collings, Michael R. *DrAPF 93*
Collings, Michael R(obert) 1947- *EncSF 93*
Collings, Robert Biddlecombe 1942- *WhoAm 94, WhoAmL 94*
Collings, Robert L. 1950- *WhoAm 94*
Collingsworth, Ann Taylor 1933- *WhoAmP 93*
Collingwood, Harry 1851-1922 *EncSF 93*
Collingwood, John Gildas 1917- *Who 94*
Collingwood, Lawrance (Arthur) 1887-1982 *NewGrDO*
Collingwood, Peter *WhoHol 92*
Collins, Adrian Anthony 1937- *WhoAm 94*
Collins, Alan *WhoHol 92*
Collins, Alan 1928- *WrDr 94*
Collins, Alana *WhoHol 92*
Collins, Albert 1932-1993 *NewYTBS 93 [port], News 94-2*
Collins, Allan Wayne 1934- *WhoWest 94*
Collins, An *BlmGWL*
Collins, An fl. c. 1653- *DcLB 131*
Collins, Andre 1968- *WhoBlA 94*
Collins, Andrew David 1942- *Who 94*
Collins, Andy Ray 1966- *WhoMW 93*
Collins, Angelo 1944- *WhoScEn 94*
Collins, Anita Marguerite 1947- *WhoAm 94, WhoScEn 94*
Collins, Anne 1943- *NewGrDO*
Collins, Arthur (James Robert) 1911- *Who 94*
Collins, Arthur John 1931- *Who 94*
Collins, Arthur Worth, Jr. 1929- *WrDr 94*
Collins, Barbara Ballin 1955- *WhoMW 93*
Collins, Barbara-Rose 1939- *CngDr 93, WhoAm 94, WhoAmP 93, WhoBlA 94, WhoMW 93, WhoWomW 91*
Collins, Barry 1941- *ConDr 93, WrDr 94*
Collins, Basil Eugene Sinclair 1923- *IntWW 93, Who 94*
Collins, Bernice Elaine 1957- *WhoBlA 94*
Collins, Bert 1934- *WhoBlA 94, WhoIns 94*
Collins, Billy *DrAPF 93*
Collins, Bob *IntWW 93*
Collins, Bobby L. *WhoBlA 94*
Collins, Brien T. d1993 *NewYTBS 93*
Collins, Bruce W. 1953- *WhoAmL 94*
Collins, Bud *WhoAm 94*
Collins, Byron Griggs 1939- *WhoAm 94*
Collins, C. E. d1951 *WhoHol 92*
Collins, C. W. Tom, Jr. 1950- *WhoAmP 93*
Collins, Cardiss 1924- *WhoWomW 91*
Collins, Cardiss 1931- *AfrAmAl 6 [port], CngDr 93, WhoAm 94, WhoAmP 93, WhoBlA 94, WhoMW 93*
Collins, Carl Russell, Jr. 1926- *WhoAm 94*
Collins, Carter Compton 1925- *WhoAm 94*
Collins, Carter H. 1928- *WhoBlA 94*
Collins, Carvel 1912-1990 *WhAm 10*
Collins, Charles Curtis 1954- *WhoScEn 94*
Collins, Charles Miller 1947- *WhoBlA 94*
Collins, Charles Patrick 1947- *WhoMW 93*
Collins, Charles Roland 1931- *WhoAm 94*
Collins, Chick d1981 *WhoHol 92*
Collins, Christiane C. *WhoAmA 93*
Collins, Christopher Carl 1950- *WhoAm 94, WhoFI 94*
Collins, Clark *EncSF 93*
Collins, Clifford Jacob, III 1947- *WhoBlA 94*
Collins, Constance Renee Wilson 1932- *WhoBlA 94*
Collins, Copp 1914- *WhoAm 94*
Collins, Cora Sue 1927- *WhoHol 92*
Collins, Corene 1948- *WhoBlA 94*
Collins, Curtis Allan 1940- *WhoAm 94, WhoWest 94*
Collins, Daisy G. 1937- *WhoBlA 94*
Collins, Dan 1954- *WhoAmA 93*
Collins, Dana Jon 1956- *WhoMW 93*
Collins, Dane H. 1961- *WhoWest 94*
Collins, Daniel A. 1916- *WhoBlA 94*
Collins, Daniel Francis 1942- *WhoAm 94, WhoAmL 94*
Collins, Daniel W. 1946- *WhoAm 94*
Collins, David Browning 1922- *WhoAm 94*
Collins, David Edmond 1934- *WhoFI 94*
Collins, David R. 1940- *WrDr 94*
Collins, Denis 1956- *WhoMW 93*
Collins, Dennis Arthur 1940- *WhoAm 94*
Collins, Dennis G. 1942- *WhoAmL 94*
Collins, Dennis Glenn 1944- *WhoMW 93, WhoScEn 94*
Collins, Diana Josephine 1944- *WhoAm 94*
Collins, Donald F. *WhoAmP 93*
Collins, Dorothy Lee 1932- *WhoBlA 94*
Collins, Doug 1951- *BasBi*
Collins, Earlean *WhoAmP 93*
Collins, Eddie d1940 *WhoHol 92*
Collins, Eddy d1916 *WhoHol 92*
Collins, Eileen Louise 1942- *WhoAm 94*
Collins, Eileen Marie 1956- *WhoScEn 94*
Collins, Elizabeth Louise 1954- *WhoMW 93*
Collins, Elliott 1943- *WhoBlA 94*
Collins, Elsie *WhoBlA 94*
Collins, Emmanuel Gye 1959- *WhoScEn 94*
Collins, Erik 1938- *WhoScEn 94*
Collins, Eugene Boyd 1917- *WhoScEn 94*
Collins, Evan R. d1993 *NewYTBS 93 [port]*
Collins, Fern Sharon 1945- *WhoWest 94*
Collins, Francis James 1933- *WhoAmP 93*
Collins, Francis S. *WhoAm 94, WhoScEn 94*
Collins, Frank Charles, Jr. 1927- *WhoAm 94, WhoFI 94*
Collins, G. Bryan 1960- *WhoAmL 94*
Collins, G. Pat d1959 *WhoHol 92*
Collins, Gary 1938- *IntMPA 94, WhoHol 92*
Collins, Gene *WhoAmP 93*
Collins, George Bradford 1964- *WhoFI 94*
Collins, George Briggs 1906- *WhoScEn 94*
Collins, George Joseph *WhoAm 94*
Collins, George Joseph 1948- *WhoScEn 94*
Collins, George R. d1993 *NewYTBS 93*
Collins, George R. 1917- *WhoAmA 93*
Collins, George R(oseborough) 1917-1993 *ConAu 140*
Collins, George Timothy 1943- *WhoWest 94*
Collins, Gerard *Who 94*
Collins, (James) Gerard 1938- *Who 94*
Collins, Gerry 1938- *IntWW 93*
Collins, Gilbert 1900- *EncSF 93*
Collins, Gordon Geoffrey 1958- *WhoBlA 94*
Collins, Harker 1924- *WhoAm 94*
Collins, Harold R(eeves) 1915- *WrDr 94*
Collins, Harry David 1931- *WhoFI 94, WhoScEn 94*
Collins, Harvey Arnold 1927- *WhoAmA 93*
Collins, Heather Lynne 1951- *WhoScEn 94*
Collins, Helen (Francis) *ConAu 141*
Collins, Henry Edward 1903- *Who 94*
Collins, Henry James, III 1927- *WhoAm 94*
Collins, Herbert Francis 1930- *WhoAm 94, WhoFI 94*
Collins, Herschel Douglas 1928- *WhoAm 94*
Collins, Howard F. 1922- *WhoAmA 93*
Collins, Hubert 1936- *WhoAmP 93*
Collins, Hunt *EncSF 93*
Collins, Hunt 1926- *WrDr 94*
Collins, J. Barclay, II 1944- *WhoAm 94, WhoAmL 94, WhoFI 94*
Collins, J. Lawton 1896-1987 *HisDcKW*
Collins, J. Michael 1935- *WhoAm 94*
Collins, Jack *WhoHol 92*
Collins, Jack 1943- *WhoAmP 93*
Collins, Jackie *IntWW 93, WhoAm 94, WrDr 94*
Collins, Jackie 1937- *BlmGWL*
Collins, Jackie 1940- *WhoHol 92*
Collins, James B. 1944- *WhoAmL 94*
Collins, James Douglas 1931- *WhoBlA 94*
Collins, James Foster 1922- *WhoAm 94*
Collins, James Francis 1942- *WhoWest 94*
Collins, James Francis 1943- *WhoAm 94, WhoAmL 94, WhoFI 94, WhoMW 93*
Collins, James H. 1946- *WhoBlA 94*
Collins, James Lawton, Jr. 1917- *WhoAm 94*
Collins, James Linton 1950- *WhoMW 93*
Collins, James Mitchell 1916-1989 *WhAm 10*
Collins, James Slade, II 1937- *WhoAmL 94*
Collins, James Thomas 1946- *WhoFI 94*
Collins, James William 1942- *WhoAmL 94*
Collins, James X. d1993 *NewYTBS 93*
Collins, Jan 1943- *WhoAmP 93*
Collins, Jay Wilson 1917- *WhoMW 93*

Colombi, la Marchesa 1846-1920 BlmGWL
Colombine BlmGWL
Colombini, Leda 1929- WhoWomW 91
Colombini, Susan Murphy WhoAmA 93
Colombo, Metropolitan Archbishop of 1932- Who 94
Colombo, Antonio 1950- WhoScEn 94
Colombo, Charles 1927- WhoAmA 93
Colombo, Christopher Joseph 1965- WhoFI 94
Colombo, Emilio 1920- IntWW 93, Who 94
Colombo, Frank V. 1956- WhoAm 94
Colombo, Furio Marco 1931- WhoAm 94
Colombo, Gino R. 1939- WhoAmP 93
Colombo, Giovanni d1992 IntWW 93N
Colombo, John Robert 1936- EncSF 93, IntWW 93, WhoAm 94, WrDr 94
Colombo, Louis A. 1947- WhoAm 94, WhoAmL 94
Colombo, Louis Robert 1925- WhoAmP 93
Colombo, Michael Patrick 1966- WhoScEn 94
Colombo, Umberto 1927- IntWW 93
Colombo, Umberto Paolo 1927- WhoScEn 94
Colombo, Vittorino 1925- IntWW 93
Colomby, Scott 1952- WhoHol 92
Colomer Viadel, Vicente 1946- IntWW 93
Colon, Alex WhoHol 92
Colón, Alicia V. 1944- WhoHisp 94
Colon, Anthony Ezequiel 1955- WhoHisp 94
Colón, Diego L. 1943- WhoHisp 94
Colon, Doris E. 1930-1988 WhAm 10
Colon, Eduardo Anibal 1953- WhoMW 93
Colon, Edwin 1960- WhoMW 93
Colón, Gilberto 1963- WhoHisp 94
Colón, Gustavo Alberto 1938- WhoHisp 94
Colón, Israel 1940- WhoHisp 94
Colon, Joseph Q. 1930- WhoHisp 94
Colón, Linda M. WhoHisp 94
Colon, Marta I. 1955- WhoHisp 94
Colón, Matilde Cristina 1942- WhoHisp 94
Colón, Miriam 1945- WhoHisp 94, WhoHol 92
Colon, Myrna 1948- WhoHisp 94
Colon, Nelson 1960- WhoHisp 94
Colón, Nicholas, Jr. 1909- WhoHisp 94
Colón, Oscar A. 1937- WhoHisp 94
Colón, Ramiro Luis, Jr. 1936- WhoHisp 94
Colon, Richard J. WhoHisp 94
Colon, Robert Raymond 1946- WhoHisp 94
Colón, Samuel Alberto 1950- WhoHisp 94
Colón, Vicente Franklin 1937- WhoHisp 94
Colón, Vilma Estrella 1945- WhoHisp 94
Colon, William Ralph 1930- WhoHisp 94
Colón, Willie 1950- WhoHisp 94, WhoHol 92
Colon Alvarado, Carlos WhoHisp 94
Colon Alvarado, Charlie WhoAmP 93
Colón-Arroyo, David 1950- WhoHisp 94
Colon-Carlo, Ileana M. 1949- WhoAmP 93
Colonel, Sheri Lynn 1955- WhoAm 94
Colonello, Attilio 1930- NewGrDO
Coloney, Wayne Herndon 1925- WhoAm 94, WhoFI 94, WhoScEn 94
Colonia, Regina Celia 1940- BlmGWL
Colonna, Giovanni Paola 1637-1695 NewGrDO
Colonna, Jerry d1986 WhoHol 92
Colonna, Jerry 1904-1986 WhoCom
Colonna, Rocco J. WhoAmP 93
Colonna, Vittoria 1490-1547 BlmGWL
Colonna, William Mark 1956- WhoMW 93
Colonnier, Marc Leopold 1930- WhoAm 94
Colon-Otero, Gerardo 1956- WhoScEn 94
Colon-Pacheco, Rico Butch 1927- WhoHisp 94
Colorado, Antonio J. 1939- WhoAmP 93, WhoHisp 94
Colorado, Antonio Jose 1939- WhoFI 94
Colorado, Hortensia WhoHol 92
Colosimo, Mary Lynn Sukurs 1950- WhoMW 93
Colosimo, Vince WhoHol 92
Coloske, Steven Robert 1960- WhoScEn 94
Colotka, Peter 1925- IntWW 93
Colp, Norman B. 1944- WhoAmA 93
Colpacci, Viorica WhoAmA 93
Colpi, Henri 1921- IntDcF 2-4 [port]
Colpitt, Frances 1952- WhoAmA 93
Colpron, Merlyn Dallas 1933- WhoFI 94
Colquhoun, Andrew John 1949- Who 94
Colquhoun, Cyril (Harry) 1903- Who 94
Colquhoun, David 1936- Who 94
Colquhoun, Frank 1909- Who 94
Colquhoun, Ian Charles 1959- WhoMW 93
Colquhoun, Keith 1937- WrDr 94
Colquhoun, Maureen Morfydd 1928- Who 94
Colquhoun Of Luss, Ivar 1916- Who 94
Colson, Charles W(endell) 1931- WrDr 94
Colson, Charles Wendell 1931- WhoAm 94
Colson, Chester E. 1917-1985 WhoAmA 93N
Colson, Earl M. 1930- WhoAm 94
Colson, Elizabeth 1917- WrDr 94
Colson, Elizabeth Florence 1917- IntWW 93, WhoAm 94
Colson, Joseph S., Jr. 1947- WhoBlA 94
Colson, Kate d1944 WhoHol 92
Colson, Kenneth Merritt 1939- WhoWest 94
Colson, Lewis Arnold 1947- WhoBlA 94
Colson, Steven Douglas 1941- WhoAm 94
Colston, Colin Charles 1937- Who 94
Colston, Freddie C. 1936- WhoBlA 94
Colston, Karen WhoHol 92
Colston, Michael 1932- Who 94
Colston, Monroe James 1933- WhoBlA 94
Colston Barge, Gayle S. 1951- WhoBlA 94
Colt, Clem 1907- WrDr 94
Colt, Edward (William Dutton) 1936- Who 94
Colt, Henri Gaston 1956- WhoWest 94
Colt, James D. 1932- WhoAmP 93
Colt, John Drew d1975 WhoHol 92
Colt, John Nicholson 1925- WhoAmA 93
Colt, Marshall IntMPA 94, WhoHol 92
Colt, Samuel 1814-1862 WorInv [port]
Colt, Samuel Barrymore d1986 WhoHol 92
Colt, Zandra WrDr 94
Coltart, Simon Stewart 1946- Who 94
Coltellini, Celeste 1760-1829 NewGrDO
Coltellini, Marco 1719-1777 NewGrDO
Colten, Harvey Radin 1939- WhoAm 94
Colter, Cyrus 1910- WhoAm 94, WrDr 94
Colter, Cyrus J. 1910- WhoBlA 94
Colter, Dale 1946- WrDr 94
Colter, John c. 1775-1813 WhWE
Colter, Steve 1962- WhoBlA 94
Colter-Thielemann, Theresa 1965- WhoMW 93
Coltharp, Lurline H(ughes) 1913- WrDr 94
Colthurst, Richard La Touche 1928- Who 94
Coltman, John Wesley 1915- WhoAm 94
Coltman, (Arthur) Leycester (Scott) 1938- Who 94
Coltman, Will ConAu 42NR
Coltoff, Beth Jamie 1955- WhoAm 94
Colton, Arlan Miller 1955- WhoWest 94
Colton, Clarence Eugene 1914- WrDr 94
Colton, Clark Kenneth 1941- WhoAm 94, WhoScEn 94
Colton, David Lem 1943- WhoAm 94
Colton, Frank Benjamin 1923- WhoAm 94, WhoScEn 94
Colton, Frank G. 1939- WhoAmP 93
Colton, Jacque Lynn WhoHol 92
Colton, James GayLL
Colton, James 1923- WrDr 94
Colton, Joel 1918- WhoAm 94, WrDr 94
Colton, John Patrick, Jr. 1938- WhoAmP 93
Colton, Judith 1943- WhoAmA 93
Colton, Kent W. 1943- WhoFI 94
Colton, Marie W. WhoAmP 93
Colton, Milo WhoAmP 93
Colton, Nelson Burton 1930- WhoAm 94
Colton, Robert Craig 1943- WhoAm 94, WhoAmL 94
Colton, Roy Charles 1941- WhoFI 94, WhoWest 94
Colton, Sterling Don 1929- WhoAm 94, WhoAmL 94
Colton, Victor Robert 1930- WhoFI 94, WhoMW 93
Coltrane, Alice Turiya 1937- WhoBlA 94
Coltrane, John 1926-1967 AfrAmAl 6 [port]
Coltrane, John William 1926-1967 AmCulL [port]
Coltrane, Robbie 1950- IntMPA 94, WhoHol 92
Colucci, Marius WhoHol 92
Colucci, Robert Dominick 1961- WhoScEn 94
Coluccio, Lynne M. 1956- WhoScEn 94
Coluche d1986 WhoHol 92
Colum, Padraic 1881-1972 IntDcT 2
Columba, St. 521-597 BlmGEL
Columbo, Russ d1934 WhoHol 92
Columbus, Chris 1959- IntMPA 94
Columbus, Christopher 1451-1506 HisWorL [port], WhWE [port]
Columbus, R. Timothy 1949- WhoAmL 94
Columbus, Robert Howard 1952- WhoFI 94
Columna, Francisca de la c. 1600-1660 BlmGWL
Colussy, Dan Alfred 1931- WhoAm 94
Coluzzi, Niccolo fl. 173-?- NewGrDO
Colvard, Dean Wallace 1913- WhoAm 94
Colvard, Landon, Sr. 1921- WhoAmP 93
Colver, C. Phillip 1935- WhoWest 94
Colver, Hugh Bernard 1945- Who 94
Colvig, Vance d1967 WhoHol 92
Colvig, Vance d1991 WhoHol 92
Colville Who 94
Colville, Master of 1959- Who 94
Colville, Alexander 1920- WhoAmA 93
Colville, David 1813-1898 DcNaB MP
Colville, David Alexander 1920- WhoAm 94
Colville, Elizabeth Melville fl. 1599-1603 BlmGWL
Colville, Margaret 1918- Who 94
Colville, Robert E. 1935- WhoAmL 94
Colville, Sam L. 1942- WhoAmL 94
Colville, William Warner 1934- WhoAmL 94, WhoFI 94
Colville Of Culross, Viscount 1933- Who 94
Colvin, Alonza James 1931- WhoBlA 94
Colvin, Andrew James 1947- Who 94
Colvin, Burton Houston 1916- WhoAm 94
Colvin, David 1931- Who 94
Colvin, David Hugh 1941- Who 94
Colvin, Donald Andrew 1915- WhoWest 94
Colvin, Edwin A. 1927- WhoAmP 93
Colvin, Ernest J. 1935- WhoBlA 94
Colvin, Gary Robert 1956- WhoWest 94
Colvin, H(oward) M(ontagu) 1919- WrDr 94
Colvin, Harry Walter, Jr. 1921- WhoAm 94
Colvin, Herbert, Jr. 1923- WhoAm 94
Colvin, Howard Montagu 1919- IntWW 93, Who 94
Colvin, Ian 1912-1975 EncSF 93
Colvin, James EncSF 93
Colvin, James 1939- WrDr 94
Colvin, John WhoHol 92
Colvin, John Horace Ragnar 1922- Who 94
Colvin, John O. 1946- CngDr 93, WhoAm 94, WhoAmL 94
Colvin, John Trevor 1957- WhoScEn 94
Colvin, Lance Elliott 1944- WhoWest 94
Colvin, Lloyd Dayton 1915- WhoWest 94
Colvin, Michael Keith Beale 1932- Who 94
Colvin, Robert Alan 1953- WhoMW 93
Colvin, Shawn 1956- ConMus 11 [port]
Colvin, Thomas Stuart 1947- WhoMW 93, WhoScEn 94
Colvin, Warwick, Jr. EncSF 93
Colvin, William d1930 WhoHol 92
Colvin, William E. 1930- WhoBlA 94
Colvin, William H. 1897-1972 EncABHB 9 [port]
Colvis, John Paris 1946- WhoScEn 94, WhoWest 94
Colway, James R. 1920- WhoAmA 93
Colwell, Carlton H. 1926- WhoAmP 93
Colwell, Howard Otis 1929- WhoAm 94
Colwell, James Lee 1926- WhoWest 94
Colwell, John Amory 1928- WhoAm 94
Colwell, John Edwin 1930- WhoMW 93
Colwell, Judith Kogod 1949- WhoAmA 93
Colwell, Kent Leigh 1931- WhoAm 94
Colwell, Rita Rossi WhoAm 94
Colwell, Rita Rossi 1934- IntWW 93
Colwell, Rita Rossi 1956- WhoScEn 94
Colwell, Robbie Elena 1956- WhoAmP 93
Colwill, Jack Marshall 1932- WhoAm 94
Colwin, Arthur Lentz 1911- WhoAm 94
Colwin, Laurie c. 1944-1992 AnObit 1992, WrDr 94N
Colwyn, Baron 1942- Who 94
Colyar, Ardell Benton 1914- WhoAm 94
Colyer, Dale Keith 1931- WhoAm 94
Colyer, Henry D. 1920- WhoAmP 93
Colyer, John Stuart 1935- Who 94
Colyer, Kirk Klein 1956- WhoAmP 93
Colyer, Richard Moore ConAu 141
Colyer, Sheryl Lynn 1959- WhoAm 94, WhoBlA 94
Colyer-Fergusson, James Herbert Hamilton 1917- Who 94
Colyton, Baron 1902- Who 94
Colzani, Anselmo 1918- NewGrDO
Coma-Canella, Isabel 1948- WhoScEn 94
Coman, Morgan d1947 WhoHol 92
Coman, William LeRoy 1948- WhoAmL 94
Comaneci, Nadia 1961- IntWW 93, WhoAm 94
Comanor, William S. 1937- WhoAm 94
Comans, Raymond 1930- WhoAmP 93
Comas Bacardi, Adolfo T. 1944- WhoHisp 94
Comaschino, Il NewGrDO
Comay, Sholom David 1937-1991 WhAm 10
Combe, David Alfred 1942- WhoAm 94, WhoAmL 94
Combe, Gordon Desmond 1917- WrDr 94
Combe, Ivan DeBlois 1911- WhoAm 94, WhoFI 94
Combe, John Clifford, Jr. 1939- WhoAm 94
Combee, Byron R. 1947- WhoAmP 93
Comber, Anthony James 1927- Who 94
Comber, Bobbie d1942 WhoHol 92
Comber, Neil M. 1951- WhoHisp 94
Comberg, Hans-Ulrich 1948- WhoScEn 94
Combermere, Viscount 1929- Who 94
Combest, Larry 1945- CngDr 93, WhoAmP 93
Combest, Larry Ed 1945- WhoAm 94
Combi, Giampiero 1902-1956 WorESoc
Combie, Joan Diane 1946- WhoWest 94
Combie, Robert Graham 1956- WhoWest 94
Combs, Bert Thomas 1911-1991 WhAm 10
Combs, Dan Jack 1924- WhoAm 94, WhoAmL 94, WhoAmP 93
Combs, Delia 1941- WhoAmP 93
Combs, Don E. 1934- WhoIns 94
Combs, Gene Donald 1926- WhoAmP 93
Combs, J. Andrew 1950- WhoWest 94
Combs, Jack B. 1942- WhoAmL 94
Combs, Janet Louise 1959- WhoFI 94
Combs, Jeffrey WhoHol 92
Combs, Jo Karen Kobeck 1944- WhoAm 94
Combs, John Francis 1950- WhoFI 94
Combs, Julius V. 1931- WhoBlA 94
Combs, Kathryn Louise 1957- WhoWest 94
Combs, Linda Jones 1948- WhoFI 94, WhoScEn 94
Combs, Maxine DrAPF 93
Combs, Melvin, Jr. 1941- WhoAmL 94
Combs, Mike 1947- WhoAmP 93
Combs, Susan 1945- WhoAmP 93
Combs, Sylvester Lawrence 1919- WhoBlA 94
Combs, Thomas Neal 1942- IntWW 93, WhoAmL 94
Combs, Timothy Lee 1947- WhoAmP 93
Combs, Tram DrAPF 93
Combs, Willa R. 1925- WhoBlA 94
Combs, William Henry, III 1949- WhoAmL 94, WhoWest 94
Combs, Willis (Ide) 1916- Who 94
Comchoc, Rudolph A. WhoFI 94
Comden, Betty 1919- IntDcF 2-4, IntMPA 94, WhoAm 94, WhoHol 92
Comeau, Anne Bradley 1934- WhoMW 93
Comeau, Lorene Anita Emerson 1952- WhoFI 94
Comeau, Michael Gerard 1956- WhoAmL 94
Comeau, Paul R. 1948- WhoAmL 94
Comeau, Reginald Alfred 1934- WhoAm 94
Comegys, Daphne D. 1932- WhoBlA 94
Comegys, Kathleen 1895- WhoHol 92
Comegys, Walker Brockton 1929- WhoAm 94, WhoAmL 94
Comelli-Rubini, Adelaide c. 1796-1874 NewGrDO
Comen, Steven Joel 1941- WhoAm 94
Comer, Anjanette 1942- WhoHol 92
Comer, Braxton Bragg, II 1951- WhoFI 94
Comer, Clarence C. 1948- WhoFI 94
Comer, Dawn WhoHol 92
Comer, Donald, III 1938- WhoAm 94
Comer, Evan Philip 1927- WhoAm 94
Comer, Gary C. 1927- WhoFI 94
Comer, James P. 1934- ConBlB 6 [port]
Comer, James P(ierpont) 1934- BlkWr 2, ConAu 43NR
Comer, James Pierpont 1934- WhoAm 94, WhoBlA 94, WhoScEn 94
Comer, Jonathan 1921- WhoBlA 94
Comer, Marian Wilson 1938- WhoBlA 94
Comer, Nathan Lawrence 1923- WhoAm 94, WhoScEn 94
Comer, Norman David 1935- WhoBlA 94
Comer, Russell Wayne 1959- WhoFI 94
Comer, William Joseph 1935- WhoAmP 93
Comer, Zeke 1938- WhoBlA 94
Comerford, George Emory 1928- WhoAmP 93
Comes, Marcella WhoAmA 93
Comes, Pietro fl. 1739-1755 NewGrDO
Comes, Robert George 1931- WhoWest 94
Comet, Catherine WhoAm 94, WhoMW 93
Cometto-Muniz, Jorge Enrique 1954- WhoScEn 94
Comey, Dale Raymond 1941- WhoAm 94, WhoFI 94
Comey, J. Martin 1934- WhoAm 94, WhoFI 94
Comey, James H. DrAPF 93
Comfort, Alex(ander) 1920- EncSF 93, WrDr 94

Comfort, Alexander 1920- *IntWW 93, Who 94, WhoAm 94*
Comfort, Anthony Francis 1920- *Who 94*
Comfort, Charles Fraser 1900- *Who 94*
Comfort, Jane d1979 *WhoHol 92*
Comfort, Nemo Robert 1932-1991 *WhoBlA 94N*
Comfort, Patrick Connell 1930- *WhoWest 94*
Comfort, Robert Dennis 1950- *WhoAm 94, WhoAmL 94*
Comfort, William Twyman, Jr. 1937- *WhoAm 94*
Comfort, William Wistar 1933- *WhoAm 94*
Comfrey, Kathleen Marie 1951- *WhoAm 94, WhoAmL 94*
Comi, Paul *WhoHol 92*
Comienski, James Sigmon 1948- *WhoMW 93*
Comingore, Dorothy d1971 *WhoHol 92*
Comings, David Edward 1935- *WhoAm 94*
Comings, William Daniel, Jr. 1938- *WhoAm 94*
Comini, Alessandra 1934- *WhoAm 94, WhoAmA 93, WrDr 94*
Cominos, Achilles Zachariah 1911- *WhoFI 94*
Comins, Frederic Marshall, Jr. 1948- *WhoAm 94*
Comis, Robert Leo 1945- *WhoScEn 94*
Comisar, Chris Farah-Lynn 1952- *WhoMW 93*
Comiskey, Brendan 1935- *IntWW 93*
Comiskey, Edward Alan 1942- *WhoAm 94*
Comiskey, Michael Peter 1948- *WhoAm 94*
Comisky, Hope A. 1953- *WhoAm 94*
Comisky, Ian Michael 1950- *WhoAmL 94*
Comisky, Marvin 1918- *WhoAm 94, WhoAmL 94*
Comiso, Josefino Cacas 1940- *WhoScEn 94*
Comissiona, Sergiu 1928- *NewGrDO, WhoAm 94, WhoWest 94*
Comitas, Lambros 1927- *WhoAm 94*
Comito, Richard Le 1939- *WhoAmP 93*
Comizio, V. Gerard 1955- *WhoAmL 94*
Commager, Henry Steele 1902- *IntWW 93, Who 94, WrDr 94*
Commander, Eugene R. 1953- *WhoAmL 94*
Commerford, Kathleen Anne 1951- *WhoAm 94*
Commerford, Thomas d1920 *WhoHol 92*
Commers, Tim *WhoAmP 93*
Commerson, Joseph-Philibert 1727-1773 *WhWE*
Commes, Thomas A. 1942- *WhoAm 94, WhoFI 94*
Commire, Anne *WhoAm 94*
Commito, Richard William 1951- *WhoMW 93, WhoScEn 94*
Common, John 1778-1868 *DcNaB MP*
Commoner, Barry 1917- *EnvEnc [port], IntWW 93, WhoAm 94, WhoScEn 94, WrDr 94*
Commons, Giselle *GayLL*
Commons, John Rogers 1862-1945 *AmSocL*
Como, Francis W. 1931- *WhoScEn 94*
Como, Perry 1912- *IntMPA 94, WhoHol 92*
Como, Perry 1913- *WhoAm 94*
Como, Rossella d1986 *WhoHol 92*
Comoglio, Paolo Maria 1945- *WhoScEn 94*
Comola, James Paul 1931- *WhoAm 94, WhoAmL 94*
Comont, Mathilde d1938 *WhoHol 92*
Comp, Philip Cinnamon 1945- *WhoAm 94*
Compadre, Cesar Manuel 1953- *WhoScEn 94*
Compagna, Robert A. 1918- *WhoAmP 93*
Compagnet, Alex *WhoHisp 94*
Compagni, Frederick George, Sr. 1923- *WhoAmP 93*
Compagnon, Antoine Marcel Thomas 1950- *IntWW 93*
Compaore, Blaise *IntWW 93*
Comparin, Robert Anton 1928- *WhoAm 94*
Compas, Lolita Burgos 1946- *WhoAsA 94*
Comper, Francis Anthony 1945- *IntWW 93*
Compere, Clinton Lee 1911-1991 *WhAm 10*
Compere, Lee 1790-1871 *EncNAR*
Compernolle, Paul J. 1952- *WhoAm 94*
Compert, Cindy Ellen 1961- *WhoWest 94*
Comfort, Marjorie Lenore *DrAPF 93*
Compitello, Malcolm Alan 1946- *WrDr 94*
Compiuta Donzella, la fl. 13th cent.- *BlmGWL*
Compo, Lawrence Judd 1955- *WhoFI 94*
Compo, Susan 1955- *WrDr 94*

Comporese, Violante 1785-1839 *NewGrDO*
Composto, Russell John 1960- *WhoScEn 94*
Compratt, Robert Arthur 1942- *WhoAmMW 93*
Compretta, Joseph Patrick 1945- *WhoAmP 93*
Compson, Betty d1974 *WhoHol 92*
Compson, John d1913 *WhoHol 92*
Compston, Alastair *Who 94*
Compston, (David) Alastair (Standish) 1948- *Who 94*
Compston, Christopher Dean 1940- *Who 94*
Compston, Peter (Maxwell) 1915- *Who 94*
Compston, William 1931- *Who 94*
Compton *Who 94*
Compton, Earl 1973- *Who 94*
Compton, A. Christian 1929- *WhoAmP 93*
Compton, Allen T. 1938- *WhoAmL 94, WhoAmP 93, WhoWest 94*
Compton, Angela 1961- *WhoMW 93*
Compton, Ann Woodruff 1947- *WhoAm 94*
Compton, Arthur Holly 1892-1962 *WorScD*
Compton, Asbury Christian 1929- *WhoAm 94, WhoAmL 94*
Compton, Betty d1944 *WhoHol 92*
Compton, Charles Daniel 1915- *WhoAm 94*
Compton, D(avid) G(uy) 1930- *EncSF 93, WrDr 94*
Compton, Dale Leonard 1935- *WhoAm 94, WhoScEn 94*
Compton, David Bruce 1952- *WhoMW 93*
Compton, Denis (Charles Scott) 1918- *WrDr 94*
Compton, Denis Charles Scott 1918- *IntWW 93, Who 94*
Compton, Duane W. 1918- *WhoAmP 93*
Compton, Edmund (Gerald) 1906- *Who 94*
Compton, Erlinda Rae 1947- *WhoHisp 94*
Compton, Fay d1978 *WhoHol 92*
Compton, Forrest *WhoHol 92*
Compton, Francis d1964 *WhoHol 92*
Compton, George Wade 1946- *WhoAmP 93*
Compton, Guy 1930- *WrDr 94*
Compton, H. C. 1924- *WhoMW 93*
Compton, James Allan 1951- *WhoScEn 94*
Compton, James V(incent) 1928- *WrDr 94*
Compton, James W. 1939- *WhoBlA 94*
Compton, John Carroll 1941- *WhoFI 94*
Compton, John George Melvin 1926- *IntWW 93, Who 94*
Compton, John Robinson 1923- *WhoAm 94*
Compton, Joyce 1907- *IntMPA 94, WhoHol 92*
Compton, Juleen 1933- *WhoHol 92*
Compton, Linn *WhoWest 94*
Compton, Madge d1970 *WhoHol 92*
Compton, Mark Melville 1953- *WhoScEn 94*
Compton, Mary Pearl 1930- *WhoAmP 93*
Compton, Merlin David 1924- *WhoWest 94*
Compton, Michael Graeme 1927- *Who 94*
Compton, Norma Haynes 1924- *WhoAm 94*
Compton, Olin Randall 1925- *WhoAm 94*
Compton, Patricia A. 1936- *ConAu 142, SmATA 75 [port]*
Compton, R. Tom 1953- *WhoMW 93*
Compton, Ralph Theodore, Jr. 1935- *WhoAm 94*
Compton, Richard Wesley 1925- *WhoAmP 93*
Compton, Robert David 1949- *WhoMW 93*
Compton, Robert Edward John 1922- *Who 94*
Compton, Robert H. *WhoFI 94*
Compton, Ronald E. 1933- *WhoAm 94, WhoFI 94*
Compton, Ronald Edward 1933- *WhoIns 94*
Compton, Russell Frederick 1921- *WhoWest 94*
Compton, Shannon Leigh 1953- *WhoAm 94*
Compton, Susan LaNell 1917- *WhoAm 94*
Compton, Viola d1971 *WhoHol 92*
Compton, W. Dale 1929- *WhoAm 94, WhoScEn 94*
Compton, William Avera 1927- *WhoMW 93*
Compton-Burnett, I(vy) 1884-1969 *GayLL*
Compton-Burnett, Ivy 1884-1969 *BlmGEL, BlmGWL*
Compton Miller, John Francis d1992 *Who 94N*
Compton-Rickett, Joseph *EncSF 93*
Comras, Rema 1936- *WhoAm 94*

Comrie, Bernard Sterling 1947- *WhoWest 94*
Comrie, (Alexander) Peter 1924- *Who 94*
Comrie, Sandra Melton 1940- *WhoAm 94*
Comstock, Anthony 1844-1915 *AmSocL [port]*
Comstock, Clark d1934 *WhoHol 92*
Comstock, Dale Robert 1934- *WhoAm 94, WhoWest 94*
Comstock, Glen David 1945- *WhoAm 94*
Comstock, Mary Joan 1946- *WhoScEn 94*
Comstock, Rebecca Ann 1950- *WhoAm 94, WhoAmL 94*
Comstock, Robert Francis 1936- *WhoAm 94*
Comstock, Robert Ray 1927- *WhoAm 94*
Comstock-Jones, Janis Lou 1956- *WhoMW 93*
Comte, Auguste 1798-1857 *BlmGEL*
Comte, P. D. Q. *ConAu 142*
Comtois, Mary Elizabeth *WhoWest 94*
Comus, Louis F., Jr. 1942- *WhoAmL 94*
Comvalius, Nadia Hortense 1926- *WhoBlA 94*
Comyn, James 1921- *Who 94*
Comyns, Barbara 1909-1992 *EncSF 93*
Comyns, Jacqueline Roberta 1943- *Who 94*
Conable, Barber B. 1922- *IntWW 93*
Conable, Gordon M. 1947- *WhoMW 93*
Conaboy, Richard Paul 1925- *WhoAm 94, WhoAmP 93*
Conacher, Desmond John 1918- *IntWW 93, WhoAm 94*
Conafay, Stephen Rogers 1943- *WhoAm 94*
Conahan, Cormac C. 1947- *WhoAmL 94*
Conahan, Walter Charles 1927- *WhoAmP 93*
Conal, Robbie 1941- *WhoAmA 93*
Conan, Laure 1845-1924 *BlmGWL*
Conan, Robert James, Jr. 1924- *WhoAm 94*
Conan Doyle, Jean (Lena Annette) 1912- *Who 94*
Conant, Allah B., Jr. 1939- *WhoAm 94*
Conant, Colleen Christner 1947- *WhoAm 94*
Conant, David Arthur 1945- *WhoScEn 94, WhoWest 94*
Conant, Howard Rosset 1924- *WhoAm 94*
Conant, Howard Somers 1921- *WhoAm 94, WhoWest 94*
Conant, James Bryant 1893-1978 *AmSocL*
Conant, Jan Royce 1930- *WhoAmA 93*
Conant, Joan Anderson 1943- *WhoAmP 93*
Conant, John (Ernest Michael) 1923- *Who 94*
Conant, Kenneth John 1894- *WhAm 10*
Conant, Miriam Bernheim 1931- *WhoAm 94*
Conant, Oliver 1955- *WhoHol 92*
Conant, Ralph W. 1926- *WrDr 94*
Conant, Robert Scott 1928- *WhoAm 94*
Conant, Steven George 1949- *WhoMW 93*
Conant, William *WhAmRev*
Conard, Brad *DrAPF 93*
Conard, Frederick Underwood, Jr. 1918- *WhoAm 94*
Conard, John Joseph 1921- *WhoAm 94*
Conard, Richard D. 1948- *WhoAmL 94*
Conarroe, Joel Osborne 1934- *WhoAm 94*
Conary, David Arlan 1937- *WhoAm 94, WhoFI 94*
Conason, Rick Steven 1954- *WhoAmL 94*
Conaslo, Robert 1932- *WhoAmL 94*
Conaton, Michael Joseph 1933- *WhoAm 94*
Conaway, Christine Yerges 1901-1989 *WhAm 10*
Conaway, Gerald 1933- *WhoAmA 93*
Conaway, J. Michal 1948- *WhoAm 94*
Conaway, James D. 1932- *WhoAmA 93*
Conaway, Jane Ellen 1941- *WhoMW 93*
Conaway, Jeff 1950- *IntMPA 94, WhoHol 92*
Conaway, John Bolyn 1934- *WhoAm 94*
Conaway, Mary Ward Pindle 1943- *WhoBlA 94*
Conaway, Orrin Bryte 1918- *WhoAm 94*
Conaway Williams, Ellen 1956- *WhoWomW 91*
Conboy, James C., Jr. 1947- *WhoAmL 94*
Conboy, Kenneth 1938- *WhoAm 94, WhoAmL 94*
Conboy, Kevin 1952- *WhoAmL 94*
Conboy, Patrick M. 1944- *WhoAmP 93*
Concannon, Ann Worth 1946- *WhoAmA 93*
Concannon, Donald O. 1927- *WhoAmP 93*
Concannon, George Robert *WhoAmA 93*
Concannon, John Dennis 1930- *Who 94*
Concannon, Kevin William 1940- *WhoWest 94*
Concannon, Richard James 1933- *WhoAm 94, WhoAmL 94*
Concannon, Terry *WhoAmP 93*

Concato, Augusta 1895-1964 *NewGrDO*
Conceicao, Josie 1961- *WhoScEn 94*
Concello, Antoinette d1984 *WhoHol 92*
Concepcion, Dave 1948- *WhoHisp 94*
Concepcion, David Alden 1935- *WhoWest 94*
Concepcion, David Ismael 1948- *WhoBlA 94*
Concepcion Baez, Arcadio *WhoHisp 94*
Concevitch, Bill Byron 1958- *WhoFI 94*
Concha, Jerry 1935- *WhoAmA 93*
Concha, Joseph L. *DrAPF 93*
Concha, Luis A. 1937- *WhoHisp 94*
Conchita d1940 *WhoHol 92*
Concholar, Dan Robert 1939- *WhoAm 94*
Conchon, Georges 1925-1990 *WhAm 10*
Concon, Eileen Mary 1962- *WhoAmL 94*
Concone, (Paolo) Giuseppe (Gioacchino) 1801-1861 *NewGrDO*
Concordia, Charles 1908- *WhoAm 94*
Concus, Paul 1933- *WhoAm 94*
Condamine, Charles-Marie De La *WhWE*
Condayan, John 1933- *WhoAm 94*
Conde (Abellan), Carmen 1907- *ConWorW 93*
Conde, Alice 1946- *WhoAm 94, WhoHisp 94*
Conde, Anselmo 1944- *WhoHisp 94*
Conde, Carlos D. 1936- *WhoHisp 94*
Conde, David 1943- *WhoHisp 94*
Conde, Emilia *WhoHisp 94*
Conde, Maryse 1934- *ConWorW 93*
Conde, Maryse 1937- *BlkWr 2, BlmGWL*
Conde, Rita *IntMPA 94*
Conde, Rita d1989 *WhoHol 92*
Conde, Rosa *WhoWomW 91*
Conde Abellan, Carmen 1907- *BlmGWL*
Conde Conde, Mario 1948- *IntWW 93*
Condeff, David W. 1942- *WhoAmL 94*
Condell, Henry d1627 *BlmGEL*
Condeni, Joseph Anthony 1956- *WhoAmL 94*
Conder, George Anthony 1950- *WhoMW 93, WhoScEn 94*
Conder, James Richard *WhoAmP 93*
Condeso, Orlando 1947- *WhoAmA 93*
Condict, Edgar Rhodes 1940- *WhoAm 94, WhoFI 94*
Condict, Jemima 1754-1779 *BlmGWL*
Condict, Silas 1738-1801 *WhAmRev*
Condie, Carol Joy 1931- *WhoAm 94, WhoWest 94*
Condie, Michael Wilfred 1939- *WhoWest 94*
Condit, Carl W(ilbur) 1914- *WrDr 94*
Condit, Carl Wilbur 1914- *WhoAm 94*
Condit, Doris Elizabeth *WhoAm 94*
Condit, Gary A. 1948- *CngDr 93, WhoAm 94, WhoWest 94*
Condit, Gary Adrian 1948- *WhoAmP 93*
Condit, Jeffrey John 1958- *WhoMW 93*
Condit, Linda Faulkner 1947- *WhoAm 94, WhoFI 94*
Condit, Michael Francis 1960- *WhoAmL 94*
Condit, Philip Murray 1941- *WhoAm 94, WhoFI 94, WhoWest 94*
Condit, Ralph Howell 1929- *WhoWest 94*
Condo, James Robert 1952- *WhoAmL 94*
Condodemetraky, George 1936- *WhoAmP 93*
Condon, Breen O'Malley 1944- *WhoFI 94*
Condon, Chris J. 1922- *IntMPA 94*
Condon, David *WhoHol 92*
Condon, David Patrick 1963- *WhoAmL 94*
Condon, Deborah Rene 1955- *WhoMW 93*
Condon, Denis David 1910- *Who 94*
Condon, Donald Stephen 1930- *WhoFI 94*
Condon, Edward John, Jr. 1940- *WhoAm 94, WhoMW 93*
Condon, Francis Edward 1919- *WhoAm 94*
Condon, George Edward 1916- *WhoAm 94*
Condon, Irvin G. 1959- *WhoAmL 94*
Condon, Jackie d1977 *WhoHol 92*
Condon, John 1918- *BasBi*
Condon, Lester P. 1922- *WhoAmP 93*
Condon, Margaret Jean *DrAPF 93*
Condon, Paul 1947- *IntWW 93*
Condon, Paul Leslie *WhoWest 94*
Condon, Richard (Thomas) 1915- *EncSF 93, WrDr 94*
Condon, Richard Thomas 1915- *IntWW 93, WhoAm 94*
Condon, Rita Veronica Knaga 1947- *WhoMW 93*
Condon, Robert Edward 1929- *WhoAm 94*
Condon, Stanley Charles 1931- *WhoWest 94*
Condon, Thomas Brian 1942- *WhoFI 94, WhoScEn 94*
Condon, Thomas J. 1930- *WhoAm 94*
Condon, Verner Holmes, Jr. 1926- *WhoAm 94*
Condor, Robert *WhoAm 94*

Condorcet, Marie-Jean-Antoine-Nicolas Caritat, Marquis de 1743-1794 *GuFrLit 2*
Condos, Nick d1988 *WhoHol 92*
Condos, Steve d1990 *WhoHol 92*
Condra, Allen Lee 1950- *WhoAmL 94*
Condray, Bruno G. 1921- *EncSF 93*
Condrell, William Kenneth 1926- *WhoAmL 94*
Condrey, William V. 1947- *WhoAmL 94*
Condrill, Jo Ellaresa 1935- *WhoAm 94*
Condron, Barbara O'Guinn 1953- *WhoMW 93*
Condry, Dorothea *DrAPF 93*
Condry, John C. d1993 *NewYTBS 93*
Condry, Robert Stewart 1941- *WhoAm 94, WhoMW 93*
Condry, William (Moreton) 1918- *WrDr 94*
Condy, Henry Bollmann 1826-1907 *DcNaB MP*
Condy, Sylvia Robbins 1931- *WhoScEn 94*
Cone, Anne DiMaria 1949- *WhoAmL 94*
Cone, Carl B. 1916- *WrDr 94*
Cone, Carl Bruce 1916- *WhoAm 94*
Cone, Cecil Wayne 1937- *WhoBlA 94*
Cone, Cynthia Abbott 1934- *WhoMW 93*
Cone, David Brian 1963- *WhoAm 94*
Cone, Edward Toner 1917- *WhoAm 94*
Cone, Edwin Earl 1916- *WhoWest 94*
Cone, Frances McFadden 1938- *WhoFI 94*
Cone, Gerrit Craig 1947- *WhoAmA 93*
Cone, Helen Bess 1906- *WhoMW 93*
Cone, James 1938- *AfrAmAl 6*
Cone, James H. 1938- *WhoBlA 94*
Cone, James Hal 1938- *WhoAm 94*
Cone, Joseph Jay 1955- *WhoAm 94*
Cone, Juanita Fletcher 1947- *WhoBlA 94*
Cone, June Elizabeth 1918- *WhoWest 94*
Cone, Lawrence Arthur 1928- *WhoWest 94*
Cone, Marvin 1891-1964 *WhoAmA 93N*
Cone, Mike d1969 *WhoHol 92*
Cone, Richard Allen 1936- *WhoScEn 94*
Cone, Spencer Burtis 1910- *WhoAm 94*
Cone, Sydney M., III 1930- *WhoAm 94*
Conejo, Mary Lynn 1951- *WhoHisp 94*
Conerly, Richard Pugh 1924- *WhoAm 94*
Conerton, Stella M. 1916- *WhoAmP 93*
Cones, Van Buren 1918- *WhoScEn 94*
Conesa, Miguel A. 1952- *WhoAmA 93*
Cone-Skelton, Annette 1942- *WhoAmA 93*
Coney, Aims C., Jr. 1929- *WhoAm 94*
Coney, Hydia Lutrice 1963- *WhoBlA 94*
Coney, Loraine Chapell 1935- *WhoBlA 94*
Coney, Michael G(reatrex) 1932- *EncSF 93, WrDr 94*
Coneyrs, Sue Ann 1942- *WhoFI 94*
Confer, Anthony W. 1947- *WhoAm 94*
Conford, Ellen 1942- *TwCYAW, WrDr 94*
Conforte, Renee *WhoAmA 93*
Conforti, Gino *WhoHol 92*
Conforti, Joanne 1944- *WhoAm 94*
Conforti, Michael Peter 1945- *WhoAm 94, WhoAmA 93*
Conforti, Oria *WhoHol 92*
Conforti, Ronald Anthony, Jr. 1960- *WhoScEn 94*
Conforto, Nicola 1718-1788? *NewGrDO*
Confucius 6th cent.BC- *EncEth*
Confucius c. 551BC-479BC *HisWorL [port]*
Congalton, Christopher William 1946- *WhoAmL 94*
Congalton, Susan Tichenor 1946- *WhoAm 94, WhoFI 94*
Congar, (Georges) Yves (Marie) 1904- *IntWW 93*
Congdon, Constance S. 1944- *ConDr 93*
Congdon, David Leonard 1949- *Who 94*
Congdon, James *WhoHol 92*
Congdon, John Rhodes 1933- *WhoAm 94*
Congdon, Kirby *DrAPF 93*
Congdon, Lee (Walter) 1939- *WrDr 94*
Congdon, Marsha B. 1947- *WhoAm 94, WhoFI 94*
Congdon, Richard Allen 1949- *WhoAmP 93*
Congdon, Rita Isabel 1948- *WhoHisp 94*
Congdon, Roger Douglass 1918- *WhoWest 94*
Congdon, Sarah-Braeme 1952- *WhoFI 94*
Congdon, Thomas B., Jr. 1931- *WhoAm 94*
Congdon, Timothy George 1951- *Who 94*
Congdon, William (Grosvenor) 1912- *WhoAmA 93*
Congel, Frank Joseph 1943- *WhoAm 94*
Congeni, Donna M. 1951- *WhoAmL 94*
Conger, Bob Vernon 1938- *WhoAm 94*
Conger, Cary Alan 1940- *WhoMW 93*
Conger, Clement E. 1912- *WhoAmA 93*
Conger, Clement Ellis 1912- *WhoAm 94*
Conger, Dwight G. 1949- *WhoAmL 94*
Conger, Franklin Barker 1929- *WhoAm 94*
Conger, Harry Calvin 1931- *WhoWest 94*
Conger, Harry Milton 1930- *WhoAm 94, WhoFI 94, WhoWest 94*
Conger, Jay A. 1952- *WrDr 94*
Conger, Jeffrey Scott 1961- *WhoScEn 94*
Conger, John (Janeway) 1921- *WrDr 94*
Conger, John Janeway 1921- *WhoAm 94*
Conger, Kyril B. 1913- *WhoAm 94*
Conger, Stephen Halsey 1927- *WhoAm 94*
Conger, William 1937- *WhoAmA 93*
Conger, William Frame 1937- *WhoAm 94*
Cong Fukui 1942- *WhoPRCh 91 [port]*
Congleton, Baron 1930- *Who 94*
Congleton, Joseph Patrick 1947- *WhoAmL 94*
Congleton, William C. 1935- *WhoBlA 94*
Congo, Sonia *Who 94*
Congreve, Ambrose 1907- *Who 94*
Congreve, Mario Ricardo 1957- *WhoWest 94*
Congreve, William 1670-1729 *BlmGEL, IntDcT 2 [port], NewGrDO*
Congreve, William 1743-1814 *AmRev*
Cong Weixi 1933- *WhoPRCh 91 [port]*
Cong Yuzhen 1963- *WhoPRCh 91 [port]*
Coni, Peter d1993 *NewYTBS 93*
Coni, Peter Richard Carstairs d1993 *Who 94N*
Conibear, Elizabeth Jenkins d1965 *WhoHol 92*
Conibear, Shirley Ann 1946- *WhoAm 94*
Conidi, Daniel Joseph 1957- *WhoAm 94, WhoMW 93*
Conine, Ernest 1925- *WhoAm 94*
Coningsby, Thomas Arthur Charles 1933- *Who 94*
Conino, Joseph Aloysius 1920- *WhoAmL 94*
Coniston, Ed *ConAu 42NR*
Conkel, Robert Dale 1936- *WhoAmL 94*
Conkin, Paul Keith 1929- *WhoAm 94*
Conkle, D. Steven *DrAPF 93*
Conklin, Andrew Sterrett 1961- *WhoAmA 93*
Conklin, Anna Immaculata G. 1951- *WhoAm 94*
Conklin, Charles D. 1938- *WhoFI 94, WhoIns 94*
Conklin, Chester d1971 *WhoHol 92*
Conklin, Chester 1886-1971 *WhoCom*
Conklin, Daral G. 1926- *WhoAm 94, WhoAmL 94*
Conklin, Donald David 1944- *WhoAm 94, WhoFI 94*
Conklin, Donald Ransford 1936- *WhoAm 94*
Conklin, Frances d1935 *WhoHol 92*
Conklin, Frank d1945 *WhoHol 92*
Conklin, Frederick Meade d1929 *WhoHol 92*
Conklin, Gayle Underwood 1948- *WhoAmP 93*
Conklin, George Melville 1921- *WhoAm 94*
Conklin, George William 1908- *WhoAmP 93*
Conklin, Gerald Thomas 1935- *WhoIns 94*
Conklin, Gloria Zamko 1925- *WhoAmA 93*
Conklin, Gordon Leroy 1927- *WhoAm 94*
Conklin, (Edward) Groff 1904-1968 *EncSF 93*
Conklin, Hal 1945- *WhoWest 94*
Conklin, Harold Colyer 1926- *WhoAm 94, WhoScEn 94*
Conklin, Heinie d1959 *WhoHol 92*
Conklin, Hugh Randolph 1911- *WhoAm 94*
Conklin, John 1937- *NewGrDO*
Conklin, John E. 1943- *WrDr 94*
Conklin, John Evan 1943- *WhoAm 94*
Conklin, John Roger 1933- *WhoFI 94, WhoScEn 94*
Conklin, Kenneth Edward 1939- *WhoAm 94*
Conklin, Peggy 1912- *WhoHol 92*
Conklin, Richard Allan 1939- *WhoFI 94*
Conklin, Richard James 1930- *WhoAmP 93*
Conklin, Robert B. 1943- *WhoAmL 94*
Conklin, Robert Eugene 1925- *WhoScEn 94*
Conklin, Steven John 1956- *WhoFI 94*
Conklin, Susan Joan 1950- *WhoAm 94*
Conklin, Thomas J. 1946- *WhoAm 94*
Conklin, Thomas William 1938- *WhoAm 94*
Conklin, William d1935 *WhoHol 92*
Conkling, Roger Linton 1917- *WhoAm 94*
Conlan, Bernard 1923- *Who 94*
Conlan, Frank d1955 *WhoHol 92*
Conlan, John B., Jr. 1930- *WhoAmP 93*
Conlan, Michael J. 1946- *WhoAmL 94*
Conland, Stephen 1916- *WhoAm 94*
Conlee, Jaelyn *WrDr 94*
Conley, Blair J. 1954- *WhoAmP 93*
Conley, Bruce H. 1950- *WhoMW 93*
Conley, Carroll Lockard 1915- *WhoAm 94*
Conley, Charles S. 1921- *WhoBlA 94*
Conley, Clare Dean 1929- *WhoAm 94*
Conley, Darlene *WhoHol 92*
Conley, Diana Mae 1942- *WhoMW 93*
Conley, Edward F. d1993 *NewYTBS 93*
Conley, Edward Vincent, Jr. 1940- *WhoScEn 94*
Conley, Elizabeth-Lucy Carter 1919- *WhoBlA 94*
Conley, Elizabeth Simona 1942- *WhoWest 94*
Conley, Emmitt Jerome 1922- *WhoBlA 94*
Conley, Eugene Allen 1925- *WhoAm 94*
Conley, Gerard P., Jr. 1930- *WhoAmP 93*
Conley, H. Dean 1946- *WhoAmP 93*
Conley, Harry J. d1975 *WhoHol 92*
Conley, Harry V. 1927- *WhoAmP 93*
Conley, Herbert A. 1942- *WhoBlA 94*
Conley, James Daniel 1928- *WhoAm 94*
Conley, James E. d1993 *NewYTBS 93*
Conley, James Monroe 1915- *WhoBlA 94*
Conley, James Sylvester, Jr. 1942- *WhoBlA 94*
Conley, Joe *WhoHol 92*
Conley, John A. 1928- *WhoBlA 94*
Conley, John Joseph 1912- *WhoScEn 94*
Conley, Karyne 1953- *WhoAmP 93*
Conley, Lige d1937 *WhoHol 92*
Conley, Linda Susan 1953- *WhoMW 93*
Conley, Mariita Arosemena 1951- *WhoHisp 94*
Conley, Martha Richards 1947- *WhoBlA 94*
Conley, Mary Therese 1955- *WhoMW 93*
Conley, Mike *WhoAm 94*
Conley, Mike 1962- *WhoBlA 94*
Conley, Ned Leroy 1925- *WhoAm 94*
Conley, Norman Eddy 1943- *WhoMW 93*
Conley, Paul A. d1993 *NewYTBS 93 [port]*
Conley, Philip James, Jr. 1927- *WhoAm 94, WhoWest 94*
Conley, Raymond K., Jr. *WhoAmP 93*
Conley, Robert Eugene 1936- *WhoAmP 93*
Conley, Robert J. *DrAPF 93*
Conley, Robert J. 1929- *WhoAmP 93*
Conley, Robert J(ackson) 1940- *WrDr 94*
Conley, Sarah Ann 1942- *WhoMW 93*
Conley, Tom Clark 1943- *WhoAm 94*
Conley, Toni *DrAPF 93*
Conley, William d1962 *WhoHol 92*
Conley, William Edward 1962- *WhoMW 93*
Conley, Zeb Bristol, Jr. 1936- *WhoAmA 93, WhoWest 94*
Conlin, Alfred Thomas 1921- *WhoAm 94*
Conlin, Jimmy d1962 *WhoHol 92*
Conlin, Roxanne Barton 1944- *WhoAm 94, WhoAmL 94, WhoAmP 93, WhoMW 93*
Conlin, Thomas Byrd 1944- *WhoAm 94*
Conlin, Veronica 1951- *WhoMW 93*
Conlin, William Patrick 1933- *WhoFI 94*
Conlin, William Richard, II 1913- *WhoWest 94*
Conliss, Edward B. d1981 *WhoHol 92*
Conlon, Brian Thomas 1958- *WhoFI 94*
Conlon, Donald Robert 1931- *WhoAmP 93*
Conlon, Evelyn 1952- *BlmGWL [port]*
Conlon, Faith Eleanor 1955- *WhoWest 94*
Conlon, Harry B., Jr. 1935- *WhoAm 94*
Conlon, James 1950- *IntWW 93*
Conlon, James (Joseph) 1950- *NewGrDO*
Conlon, James Charles *WhoAmP 93*
Conlon, James Edward 1935- *WhoAmA 93*
Conlon, James Joseph 1950- *WhoAm 94*
Conlon, Joseph R. *WhoIns 94*
Conlon, Jud d1966 *WhoHol 92*
Conlon, Kathleen (Annie) 1943- *WrDr 94*
Conlon, Kathryn Ann 1958- *WhoMW 93*
Conlon, Michael William 1946- *WhoAm 94, WhoAmL 94*
Conlon, Patrick C. 1962- *WhoMW 93*
Conlon, Peter John, Jr. 1951- *WhoFI 94*
Conlon, Raymond Joseph 1962- *WhoAmL 94*
Conlon, Suzanne B. 1939- *WhoAm 94, WhoAmL 94*
Conlon, Thomas James 1935- *WhoAm 94*
Conlon, Thomas Julius 1960- *WhoMW 93*
Conlon, Walter 1947- *WhoAmP 93*
Conlon, William F. 1945- *WhoAm 94, WhoAmL 94*
Conly, Jane Leslie *EncSF 93, TwCYAW*
Conly, John Franklin 1933- *WhoAm 94*
Conly, Michael Frederick 1945- *WhoMW 93*
Conmy, Patrick A. 1934- *WhoAm 94, WhoAmL 94, WhoMW 93*
Conn, Anita Ruth 1927- *WhoAmP 93*
Conn, Billy d1993 *NewYTBS 93 [port]*
Conn, Billy 1917-1993 *CurBio 93N*
Conn, David Edward 1941- *WhoAmA 93*
Conn, Didi 1951- *WhoHol 92*
Conn, Edward 1918- *Who 94*
Conn, Eric Edward 1923- *WhoAm 94*
Conn, Gordon Brainard, Jr. 1944- *WhoAm 94, WhoAmL 94*
Conn, Hadley Lewis, Jr. 1921- *WhoAm 94*
Conn, Harold O. 1925- *WhoAm 94*
Conn, Jerome W. 1907- *IntWW 93, WhoAm 94*
Conn, John Farquhar Christie d1993 *Who 94N*
Conn, Laurence 1945- *WhoAmA 93*
Conn, Rex Boland, Jr. 1927- *WhoAm 94, WhoScEn 94*
Conn, Richard George 1928- *WhoAmA 93*
Conn, Robert A. 1926- *IntMPA 94*
Conn, Robert Henry 1925- *WhoAmP 93*
Conn, Robert William 1942- *WhoAm 94, WhoScEn 94*
Conn, Ross Edward 1913- *WhoAmP 93*
Conn, Stewart 1936- *ConDr 93, WrDr 94*
Conn, Walter Jennings 1922- *WhoAmP 93*
Connable, Alfred Barnes 1904- *WhoAm 94*
Connah, Douglas D., Jr. 1934- *WhoAmL 94*
Connair, Pierce F. 1926- *WhoAmP 93*
Connally, C. Ellen 1945- *WhoBlA 94*
Connally, Ernest Allen 1921- *WhoAm 94*
Connally, John 1917-1993 *News 94-1*
Connally, John B. 1917-1993 *NewYTBS 93 [port]*
Connally, John B(owden, Jr.) 1917-1993 *CurBio 93N*
Connally, John Bowden d1993 *Who 94N*
Connally, John Bowden, Jr. 1917- *IntWW 93*
Connally, Julia A. 1938- *WhoAmP 93*
Connally, Merrill *WhoHol 92*
Connally, Sandra Jane Oppy 1941- *WhoMW 93*
Connally, Tom 1877-1963 *HisDcKW*
Connally, Tom 1940- *WhoAm 94*
Connar, Richard Grigsby 1920-1990 *WhAm 10*
Connare, William Graham 1911- *WhoAm 94*
Connarty, Michael 1947- *Who 94*
Connatser, Larry Stuart 1938- *WhoAmA 93*
Connavino, Nicholas Anthony 1946- *WhoFI 94*
Connaway, Jay Hall 1893- *WhAm 10*
Connaway, Jay Hall 1893-1970 *WhoAmA 93N*
Conneally, P. Michael *WhoScEn 94*
Connealy, Patricia Sue 1947- *WhoMW 93*
Conneen, Jane W. 1921- *WhoAmA 93*
Conneen, Mari M. 1946- *WhoAmA 93*
Connell, Alastair McCrae 1929- *WhoAm 94*
Connell, Brian Lindsay 1947- *WhoWest 94*
Connell, Brian Reginald 1916- *WrDr 94*
Connell, Cameron 1944- *WhoBlA 94*
Connell, Charles Percy 1902- *Who 94*
Connell, David R. 1950- *WhoAmP 93*
Connell, Desley William 1938- *WhoScEn 94*
Connell, Desmond *Who 94*
Connell, Elizabeth *IntWW 93*
Connell, Elizabeth 1946- *NewGrDO*
Connell, Elizabeth Jane 1951- *WhoMW 93*
Connell, Eugene C. 1954- *WhoFI 94, WhoIns 94*
Connell, Evan S(helby), Jr. 1924- *WrDr 94*
Connell, Evan Shelby, Jr. 1924- *WhoAm 94, WhoWest 94*
Connell, Francis Joseph, III 1946- *WhoAm 94, WhoAmL 94*
Connell, George B(oyce, II) 1957- *ConAu 141*
Connell, George Edward 1930- *IntWW 93, Who 94, WhoAm 94*
Connell, Gerald A. 1934- *WhoAm 94, WhoAmL 94*
Connell, Gordon 1923- *WhoHol 92*
Connell, Grover 1918- *WhoAm 94*
Connell, Hugh P. 1931- *WhoAm 94*
Connell, Jack 1919- *WhoAmP 93*
Connell, James Joseph, Jr. 1928- *WhoWest 94*
Connell, James Roger 1929- *WhoScEn 94*
Connell, Jan *ConAu 140*
Connell, Jane 1925- *WhoHol 92*
Connell, Janice T. *WhoAmL 94*
Connell, Janice T(imchak) 1939- *ConAu 140*
Connell, Jerome F., Sr. *WhoAmP 93*
Connell, John Gibbs, Jr. 1914- *WhoAm 94*
Connell, John J. 1947- *WhoAmL 94*
Connell, John Jeffrey 1927- *Who 94*
Connell, John MacFarlane 1924- *Who 94*
Connell, John Morris 1911- *Who 94*
Connell, Joseph Edward 1930- *WhoAm 94*
Connell, Kathleen 1937- *WhoAmP 93, WhoWomW 91*
Connell, Lawrence 1936- *WhoAm 94, WhoFI 94*
Connell, Michael (Bryan) 1939- *Who 94*
Connell, Ninette *Who 94*
Connell, Philip Francis 1924- *WhoAm 94*

Connell, Philip Henry 1921- *IntWW 93, Who 94*
Connell, Polly d1986 *WhoHol 92*
Connell, Robert Ivey 1955- *WhoWest 94*
Connell, Steven John 1951- *WhoMW 93*
Connell, Ted 1946- *WhoFI 94*
Connell, William (Fraser) 1916- *WrDr 94*
Connell, William D. 1955- *WhoAm 94, WhoAmL 94, WhoWest 94*
Connell, William Francis 1938- *WhoAm 94, WhoFI 94*
Connellan, D. Michael 1947- *WhoFI 94*
Connellan, Leo *DrAPF 93*
Connellee-Clay, Barbara 1929- *WhoScEn 94, WhoWest 94*
Connell-Smith, Gordon Edward 1917- *Who 94*
Connell-Tatum, Elizabeth Bishop 1925- *WhoAm 94*
Connelly, Alan B. *WhoScEn 94*
Connelly, Albert R. 1908- *WhoAm 94*
Connelly, Anne 1950- *WhoAmL 94*
Connelly, Arch 1950-1993 *NewYTBS 93*
Connelly, Bobby d1922 *WhoHol 92*
Connelly, Brian Robert 1935- *WhoAmP 93*
Connelly, Charles Michael 1938- *WhoAmL 94*
Connelly, Christopher d1988 *WhoHol 92*
Connelly, Chuck 1955- *WhoAmA 93*
Connelly, Colin Charles 1956- *WhoAmL 94*
Connelly, Donald Preston 1939- *WhoAm 94*
Connelly, Edward d1928 *WhoHol 92*
Connelly, Elizabeth Ann *WhoAmP 93*
Connelly, Erwin d1931 *WhoHol 92*
Connelly, James P. 1947- *WhoAmL 94*
Connelly, Jane d1925 *WhoHol 92*
Connelly, Jennifer 1970- *WhoHol 92*
Connelly, Joe Turner 1926- *WhoAmP 93*
Connelly, John Dooley 1946- *WhoMW 93*
Connelly, John Francis *IntWW 93N*
Connelly, John Francis 1905-1990 *WhAm 10*
Connelly, John James 1935- *WhoMW 93*
Connelly, John Matthew 1942- *WhoAm 94*
Connelly, John P. *WhoAmL 94*
Connelly, Lewis Branch Sutton 1950- *WhoAmL 94*
Connelly, Lloyd G. 1945- *WhoAmP 93*
Connelly, Marc d1980 *WhoHol 92*
Connelly, Marc(us Cook) 1890-1980 *ConDr 93, IntDcT 2*
Connelly, Mary Ellen *WhoAmP 93*
Connelly, Michael Robert 1947- *WhoAmL 94, WhoAmP 93*
Connelly, Michele *DrAPF 93*
Connelly, Paul V. 1923- *IntMPA 94*
Connelly, R. Terry 1946- *WhoAmP 93*
Connelly, Rebecca Buehler 1963- *WhoAmL 94*
Connelly, Sharon Rudolph 1940- *WhoAm 94*
Connelly, Theodore Sample 1925- *WhoWest 94*
Connelly, Thomas 1949- *WhoFI 94*
Connelly, Thomas John d1991 *Who 94N*
Connelly, Thomas Joseph 1940- *WhoAmL 94*
Connelly, Vincent J. 1950- *WhoAm 94, WhoAmL 94*
Connelly, Warren E. 1946- *WhoAmL 94*
Connelly, William Howard 1920- *WhoAm 94*
Connelly, William Joseph 1931- *WhoFI 94*
Connelly-Beckman, Eileen Marie 1963- *WhoMW 93*
Conner, Ann 1948- *WhoAmA 93*
Conner, Bruce 1933- *WhoAm 94, WhoAmA 93*
Conner, Daryl R(iles) 1946- *ConAu 142*
Conner, David Allen 1939- *WhoAm 94*
Conner, David John 1947- *Who 94*
Conner, Dennis 1943- *WhoAm 94*
Conner, Doyle E. 1928- *WhoAmP 93*
Conner, Ernest Lee, Jr. 1955- *WhoAmL 94*
Conner, Finis F. 1943- *WhoAm 94, WhoFI 94, WhoWest 94*
Conner, Fred L. 1909- *WhoAmL 94*
Conner, Gail Patricia 1948- *WhoBlA 94*
Conner, Jeffrey T. 1966- *WhoAmP 93*
Conner, John Ramsey 1869-1952 *WhoAmA 93N*
Conner, Laban Calvin 1936- *WhoBlA 94*
Conner, Laurie Catherine 1954- *WhoWest 94*
Conner, Leland Lavon 1930- *WhoMW 93*
Conner, Lester Allen 1959- *WhoBlA 94*
Conner, Lindsay Andrew 1956- *WhoWest 94*
Conner, Lois 1951- *WhoAmA 93*
Conner, Lucy Shull 1938- *WhoBlA 94*
Conner, Marcia Lynne 1958- *WhoBlA 94*
Conner, Michael R. 1951- *WhoAmL 94*
Conner, Mike 1951- *EncSF 93*
Conner, Nadine 1913- *NewGrDO, WhoHol 92*
Conner, Pat *WhoAmP 93*
Conner, Patrick (Roy Mountifort) 1947- *WrDr 94*
Conner, Patrick John 1965- *WhoWest 94*
Conner, Paul H. 1925- *WhoAmP 93*
Conner, Prudence Ophelia 1963- *WhoAmL 94*
Conner, Rearden 1907- *WrDr 94*
Conner, Richard D. 1945- *WhoAmL 94*
Conner, Stewart Edmund 1941- *WhoAm 94*
Conner, Terry W. 1951- *WhoAmL 94*
Conner, Timothy Mark 1961- *WhoFI 94*
Conner, Troy Blaine, Jr. 1926- *WhoAm 94*
Conner, Virginia S. 1950- *WhoHisp 94*
Conner, Warren Wesley 1932- *WhoAmL 94*
Conner, William Curtis 1920- *WhoAm 94*
Conner, William Herbert 1940- *WhoAmL 94*
Conners, Barry d1933 *WhoHol 92*
Conners, John B. 1945- *WhoIns 94*
Conners, John Brendan 1945- *WhoAm 94, WhoFI 94*
Conners, Kenneth Wray 1909- *WrDr 94*
Conners, Maynard Gilbert 1918- *WhoAmP 93*
Conners, Michael Dennis 1962- *WhoMW 93*
Conners, Richard J. 1910- *WhoAmP 93*
Connery, Brian Arthur 1951- *WhoMW 93*
Connery, Jason 1962- *WhoHol 92*
Connery, Neil 1938- *WhoHol 92*
Connery, Robert Howe 1907- *WhoAm 94*
Connery, Sean 1930- *CurBio 93 [port], IntMPA 94, IntWW 93, Who 94, WhoAm 94, WhoHol 92*
Connery, Steven Charles 1950- *WhoScEn 94*
Conness, Robert d1941 *WhoHol 92*
Connett, Dee M. 1935- *WhoAmA 93*
Conney, Allan Howard 1930- *WhoAm 94*
Connick, C(harles) Milo *WrDr 94*
Connick, Charles Milo 1917- *WhoAm 94*
Connick, Harry, Jr. 1967- *ConTFT 11, IntMPA 94*
Connick, Harry, Jr. 1968- *WhoAm 94, WhoHol 92*
Connick, Robert Elwell 1917- *IntWW 93, WhoAm 94, WhoScEn 94*
Conniff, Gregory 1944- *WhoAmA 93*
Conniff, Ray 1916- *WhoAm 94*
Connington, J.J. 1880-1947 *EncSF 93*
Connley, Virginia Ann d1977 *WhoHol 92*
Connolly, Andrew *WhoHol 92*
Connolly, Arthur Guild 1905- *WhoAm 94*
Connolly, Billy 1943- *ConTFT 11, WhoHol 92*
Connolly, Connie Christine 1947- *WhoScEn 94*
Connolly, David I. 1934- *WhoFI 94*
Connolly, Edward G. *WhoAmP 93*
Connolly, Edward Joseph 1936- *WhoAmP 93*
Connolly, Edward Thomas 1935- *Who 94*
Connolly, Elizabeth Anne 1957- *WhoAm 94*
Connolly, Elma Troutman 1931- *WhoFI 94*
Connolly, Eugene B., Jr. 1932- *WhoAm 94, WhoFI 94*
Connolly, Gerald Edward 1943- *WhoAm 94, WhoAmL 94*
Connolly, Geraldine *DrAPF 93*
Connolly, Grace *WhoAmP 93*
Connolly, James 1868-1916 *DcNaB MP*
Connolly, James Louis 1894- *WhAm 10*
Connolly, Janet Claire Whitty 1936- *WhoAmP 93*
Connolly, Jerome Patrick 1931- *WhoAmA 93*
Connolly, John 1750- *AmRev, WhAmRev*
Connolly, John Earle 1923- *WhoAm 94, WhoScEn 94, WhoWest 94*
Connolly, John Joseph 1940- *WhoAm 94*
Connolly, John Stephen 1936- *WhoAm 94*
Connolly, Joseph 1950- *WrDr 94*
Connolly, Joseph M. *WhoAmP 93*
Connolly, K. Thomas 1940- *WhoAmL 94*
Connolly, L. William 1923- *WhoAm 94, WhoAmL 94*
Connolly, Laurence E., Jr. *WhoAmP 93*
Connolly, Mark Victor 1957- *WhoAmL 94*
Connolly, Matthew B., Jr. 1941- *WhoAm 94*
Connolly, Maureen 1934-1969 *BuCMET [port]*
Connolly, Michael J. 1949- *WhoAmL 94*
Connolly, Michael Joseph 1947- *WhoAm 94, WhoAmP 93*
Connolly, Michael W. 1945- *WhoAmP 93*
Connolly, Norma *WhoHol 92*
Connolly, Pat 1943- *SmATA 74 [port]*
Connolly, Patricia Ann Stacy 1939- *WhoScEn 94*
Connolly, Paul 1926- *WrDr 94*
Connolly, Paul K., Jr. 1944- *WhoAm 94, WhoAmL 94*
Connolly, Peggy 1951- *WhoAmL 94, WhoMW 93*
Connolly, Peter 1935- *WrDr 94*
Connolly, Phyllis Fern 1929- *WhoAmP 93*
Connolly, Ray 1940- *WrDr 94*
Connolly, Robert Michael 1955- *WhoAmL 94*
Connolly, Roberta Sue 1947- *WhoMW 93*
Connolly, Ronald Cavanagh 1932- *WhoAm 94, WhoFI 94*
Connolly, Roy *EncSF 93*
Connolly, Terrence J. 1954- *WhoAmL 94*
Connolly, Thomas Arthur 1899-1991 *WhAm 10*
Connolly, Thomas B. 1963- *WhoAmP 93*
Connolly, Thomas Edward 1942- *WhoAmL 94, WhoFI 94*
Connolly, Thomas Joseph 1922- *WhoAm 94, WhoWest 94*
Connolly, Tom *WhoAmP 93*
Connolly, Walter d1940 *WhoHol 92*
Connolly, William Gerard 1937- *WhoAm 94*
Connolly, William Michael 1952- *WhoScEn 94*
Connolly-O'Neill, Barrie Jane 1943- *WhoWest 94*
Connor, Bishop of 1926- *Who 94*
Connor, Charles William 1935- *WhoScEn 94*
Connor, David John 1953- *WhoWest 94*
Connor, David Thomas 1939- *WhoMW 93*
Connor, Dolores L. 1950- *WhoHisp 94*
Connor, Dolores Lillie 1950- *WhoBlA 94*
Connor, Edmond M. 1950- *WhoAmL 94*
Connor, Edric d1968 *WhoHol 92*
Connor, Edward d1932 *WhoHol 92*
Connor, Edward Francis 1952- *WhoAm 94*
Connor, Gary Edward 1948- *WhoWest 94*
Connor, Geoffrey Michael 1946- *WhoAm 94*
Connor, George *ProFbHF [port]*
Connor, George C., Jr. 1921- *WhoBlA 94*
Connor, Gerald Raymond 1946- *WhoFI 94*
Connor, Herman P. 1932- *WhoBlA 94*
Connor, J. Robert 1927- *WhoAm 94*
Connor, James A. 1936- *WhoAmP 93*
Connor, James Edward, Jr. 1924- *WhoAm 94*
Connor, James Michael 1951- *Who 94*
Connor, James Richard 1928- *WhoAm 94*
Connor, James Russell 1940- *WhoBlA 94*
Connor, Jeremy George 1938- *Who 94*
Connor, John Arthur 1940- *WhoAm 94, WhoScEn 94*
Connor, John Bernard 1946- *WhoAm 94*
Connor, John Murray 1943- *WhoFI 94, WhoScEn 94*
Connor, John Robert 1916- *WhoFI 94*
Connor, John Thomas 1914- *WhoAm 94*
Connor, John Thomas, Jr. 1941- *WhoAm 94, WhoFI 94*
Connor, John William 1930- *WhoWest 94*
Connor, Joseph Andrew 1952- *WhoFI 94*
Connor, Joseph E. 1931- *IntWW 93, WhoAm 94*
Connor, Joseph Patrick, III 1953- *WhoAmL 94*
Connor, Kenneth 1918- *WhoHol 92*
Connor, Kenneth 1937- *IntMPA 94*
Connor, Kevin 1940- *HorFD*
Connor, Laurence Davis 1938- *WhoAm 94*
Connor, Linda Stevens 1944- *WhoAmA 93*
Connor, Martin 1945- *WhoAmP 93*
Connor, Martin Edward 1945- *WhoAm 94*
Connor, Richard L. 1947- *WhoAm 94*
Connor, Robert Joseph 1927- *WhoAmP 93*
Connor, Robert Patrick 1948- *WhoAm 94*
Connor, Robert T. 1919- *WhoAm 94*
Connor, Robert Thomas 1938- *WhoAmP 93*
Connor, Roger David 1939- *Who 94*
Connor, Seymour Vaughan 1923- *WhoAm 94*
Connor, Steven 1955- *ConAu 141*
Connor, Terence Gregory 1942- *WhoAm 94*
Connor, Thelma d1981 *WhoHol 92*
Connor, Thomas Byrne 1921- *WhoAm 94*
Connor, Thomas Maxwell, Sr. 1924- *WhoAmP 93*
Connor, Tony *DrAPF 93*
Connor, Tony 1930- *WrDr 94*
Connor, Ulysses J., Jr. 1948- *WhoBlA 94*
Connor, Velma d1987 *WhoHol 92*
Connor, Virginia M. d1987 *WhoHol 92*
Connor, Walter Robert 1934- *WhoAm 94*
Connor, Walter Thomas 1877-1952 *DcAmReB 2*
Connor, Whitfield d1988 *WhoHol 92*
Connor, Wilda 1947- *WhoAm 94*
Connor, William Elliott 1921- *WhoAm 94*
Connor, Zack d1939 *WhoHol 92*
Connor-Bey, Brenda *DrAPF 93*
Connors, Andree *DrAPF 93*
Connors, Bruton 1931- *WrDr 94*
Connors, Carol Ekern 1953- *WhoAmP 93*
Connors, Christopher J. 1956- *WhoAmP 93*
Connors, Chuck 1921- *WhoHol 92*
Connors, Chuck 1921-1992 *AnObit 1992, ConTFT 11*
Connors, Chuck Kevin Joseph 1921-1992 *WhAm 10*
Connors, Dennis Michael 1943- *WhoFI 94*
Connors, Donald Louis 1936- *WhoAm 94, WhoAmL 94*
Connors, Dorsey *WhoAm 94*
Connors, Edward Joseph 1929- *WhoAm 94*
Connors, Eugene Kenneth 1946- *WhoAm 94, WhoAmL 94*
Connors, Frank Joseph 1944- *WhoAmL 94*
Connors, Henry Joseph 1931- *WhoAmP 93*
Connors, Hollis Gay 1912- *WhoAmP 93*
Connors, James Patrick 1952- *WhoAmL 94*
Connors, James Scott 1952- *IntWW 93*
Connors, Jimmy 1952- *BuCMET [port], WhoAm 94*
Connors, John H. *WhoAmP 93*
Connors, John Henry 1929- *WhoAmP 93*
Connors, John Michael, Jr. 1942- *WhoAm 94*
Connors, Joseph Aloysius, III 1946- *WhoAmL 94*
Connors, Joseph Conlin 1948- *WhoAmL 94*
Connors, Kenneth Antonio 1932- *WhoAm 94*
Connors, Kevin Gerard 1961- *WhoWest 94*
Connors, Leo Gerard 1927- *WhoAm 94*
Connors, Leonard T., Jr. 1929- *WhoAmP 93*
Connors, Mary Eileen 1953- *WhoAm 94, WhoMW 93*
Connors, Maureen Stotler 1955- *WhoFI 94*
Connors, Michele Perrott 1952- *WhoFI 94*
Connors, Mike 1925- *IntMPA 94, WhoAm 94, WhoHol 92*
Connors, Robert Leo 1940- *WhoFI 94*
Connors, Stephen Wilfred 1918-1991 *WhAm 10*
Connors, Thomas P., Sr. *WhoAmP 93*
Connors, W. Bruce 1943- *WhoFI 94*
Connorton, John V. 1943- *WhoAmL 94*
Conoby, Joseph Francis 1930- *WhoFI 94, WhoScEn 94*
Conole, Clement Vincent 1908- *WhoAm 94, WhoFI 94*
Conole, Richard Clement 1936- *WhoAm 94, WhoFI 94*
Conoley, Gillian *DrAPF 93*
Conolly, John 1794-1866 *EncSPD*
Conolly, Yvonne Cecile 1939- *Who 94*
Conolly-Carew *Who 94*
Conom, Tom Peter 1949- *WhoAmL 94*
Conombo, Joseph Issoufou 1917- *IntWW 93*
Conomikes, George Spero 1925- *WhoWest 94*
Conomy, John Paul 1938- *WhoAm 94*
Conoscenti, Thomas C. 1945- *WhoAm 94*
Conot, Robert E. 1929- *WrDr 94*
Conour, William Frederick 1947- *WhoAmL 94*
Conover, Clarence Millard 1939- *WhoWest 94*
Conover, Claude 1907- *WhoAmA 93*
Conover, Frederic King 1933- *WhoAm 94*
Conover, Harvey 1925- *WhoAm 94*
Conover, Lloyd Hillyard 1923- *WhoScEn 94*
Conover, Max *WhoAmP 93*
Conover, Nellie Coburn 1921- *WhoMW 93*
Conover, Robert A. *WhoIns 94*
Conover, Robert Fremont 1920- *WhoAm 94, WhoAmA 93*
Conover, Robert Warren 1937- *WhoWest 94*
Conover, Roger L. *DrAPF 93*
Conover, Roger L(loyd) 1950- *WrDr 94*
Conover, William Jay 1936- *WhoAm 94*
Conquest, Arthur d1945 *WhoHol 92*
Conquest, Joan 1883?-1941 *EncSF 93*
Conquest, Loveday Loyce 1948- *WhoWest 94*
Conquest, Ned 1931- *WrDr 94*
Conquest, (George) Robert (Acworth) 1917- *EncSF 93, Who 94, WrDr 94*
Conquest, Robert Acworth 1917- *WhoAm 94*
Conquest, (George) Robert Acworth 1917- *IntWW 93*
Conrad, Albert H., Jr. 1951- *WhoAmL 94*
Conrad, Allen Lawrence 1940- *WhoAmP 93*

Conrad, Bruce R. *WhoScEn 94*
Conrad, Christina 1942- *BlmGWL*
Conrad, Con d1938 *WhoHol 92*
Conrad, Conrad A. 1946- *WhoFI 94*
Conrad, David K. 1956- *WhoAmL 94*
Conrad, David Paul 1946- *WhoFI 94*
Conrad, Deborah I. 1950- *WhoAmL 94*
Conrad, Donald Glover 1930- *IntWW 93, WhoAm 94*
Conrad, Donald Lewis 1927- *WhoMW 93*
Conrad, Earl 1912-1986 *EncSF 93*
Conrad, Eddie d1941 *WhoHol 92*
Conrad, Emmett J. 1923- *WhoBlA 94*
Conrad, George 1916- *WhoAmA 93*
Conrad, Gregg *EncSF 93*
Conrad, Harold Theodore 1934- *WhoScEn 94*
Conrad, Jan *WhoHol 92*
Conrad, Jeffrey Philip 1950- *WhoScEn 94*
Conrad, Jess 1940- *WhoHol 92*
Conrad, John Regis 1955- *WhoAmL 94*
Conrad, John W. 1935- *WhoAmA 93*
Conrad, John Wilfred 1935- *WhoWest 94*
Conrad, Joseph 1857-1924 *BlmGEL [port], EncSF 93, RfGShF*
Conrad, Joseph Henry 1950- *WhoMW 93*
Conrad, Joseph M., Jr. 1936- *WhoBlA 94*
Conrad, Judy Lynn 1952- *WhoFI 94*
Conrad, Kelley Allen 1941- *WhoAm 94*
Conrad, Kent 1948- *CngDr 93, IntWW 93, WhoAm 94, WhoAmP 93, WhoMW 93*
Conrad, Larry A. *WhoAmP 93*
Conrad, Larry Allyn 1935-1990 *WhAm 10*
Conrad, Loretta Jane 1934- *WhoMW 93*
Conrad, Lori Lynn 1963- *WhoMW 93*
Conrad, M.G. *EncSF 93*
Conrad, Marcel Edward 1928- *WhoAm 94*
Conrad, Margit 1952- *WhoWomW 91*
Conrad, Marian Rideout *WhoAmP 93*
Conrad, Marian Sue 1946- *WhoMW 93*
Conrad, Michael d1983 *WhoHol 92*
Conrad, Michael Earl 1941- *WhoMW 93*
Conrad, Nancy Lu 1927- *WhoMW 93*
Conrad, Nancy R. 1940- *WhoAmA 93*
Conrad, Osmond 1936- *WhoAm 94*
Conrad, Pam 1947- *TwCYAW, WhoAm 94, WrDr 94*
Conrad, Paul 1924- *EncSF 93*
Conrad, Paul Edward 1956- *WhoAm 94*
Conrad, Paul Ernest 1927- *WhoAm 94*
Conrad, Paul Francis 1924- *WhoAm 94, WhoAmA 93, WhoWest 94*
Conrad, Peter 1948- *WrDr 94*
Conrad, Robert 1935- *IntMPA 94, WhoAm 94, WhoHol 92*
Conrad, Sally 1941- *WhoAmP 93*
Conrad, Stuart W. 1947- *WhoAmL 94*
Conrad, William 1920- *IntMPA 94, WhoHol 92*
Conrad, William Merrill 1926- *WhoAm 94, WhoMW 93*
Conrad, Winthrop Brown, Jr. 1945- *WhoAm 94, WhoAmL 94*
Conradi, Madame c. 1680-1719? *NewGrDO*
Conradi, August 1821-1873 *NewGrDO*
Conradi, Johann Georg d1699 *NewGrDO*
Conradi, Mark Stephen 1952- *WhoScEn 94*
Conradi, Peter J(ohn) 1945- *WrDr 94*
Conrado, George Francis 1955- *WhoHisp 94*
Conrady, James Louis 1933- *WhoWest 94*
Conran, Anthony 1931- *WrDr 94*
Conran, Elizabeth Margaret 1939- *Who 94*
Conran, James Michael 1952- *WhoWest 94*
Conran, Jasper Alexander Thirlby 1959- *IntWW 93, Who 94*
Conran, Joseph Palmer 1945- *WhoAm 94, WhoAmL 94*
Conran, Shirley (Ida) 1932- *WrDr 94*
Conran, Shirley Ida 1932- *IntWW 93, Who 94*
Conran, Terence (Orby) 1931- *Who 94*
Conran, Terence Orby 1931- *IntWW 93*
Conrat, Richard Fraenkel *WhoAm 94*
Conray, Mickey *WhoAmP 93*
Conried, Hans d1982 *WhoHol 92*
Conroe, Mark Gustav 1958- *WhoWest 94*
Conron, John Phelan 1921- *WhoAm 94, WhoScEn 94, WhoWest 94*
Conrow, Wilford Seymour 1880- *WhoAmA 93N*
Conroy, David James 1918- *WhoAm 94*
Conroy, Douglas C. 1942- *WhoAmL 94*
Conroy, Frances *WhoHol 92*
Conroy, Frank d1964 *WhoHol 92*
Conroy, Harry 1943- *Who 94*
Conroy, Jack 1898-1990 *WhAm 10*
Conroy, James R. 1947- *WhoFI 94*
Conroy, Janet M. 1931- *WhoAmP 93*
Conroy, Joe *WhoAmP 93*
Conroy, John 1951- *WrDr 94*
Conroy, John Alexander 1951- *WhoMW 93*
Conroy, John Ponsonby 1786-1854 *DcNaB MP*
Conroy, Mary A. *WhoAmP 93*
Conroy, Nora Elizabeth 1962- *WhoAmL 94*
Conroy, Pat 1945- *WhoAm 94*
Conroy, (Donald) Pat(rick) 1945- *WrDr 94*
Conroy, Robert John 1953- *WhoAmL 94*
Conroy, Robert Warren 1938- *WhoAm 94*
Conroy, Sarah Booth 1927- *WhoAm 94*
Conroy, Sue d1968 *WhoHol 92*
Conroy, Tamara Boks *WhoFI 94*
Conroy, Thom d1971 *WhoHol 92*
Conroy, Thomas Francis 1935- *WhoFI 94*
Conroy, Thomas Francis 1938- *WhoAm 94*
Conroy, Thomas Hyde 1922- *WhoAmL 94, WhoMW 93*
Conroy, Thomas R. 1934- *WhoAmP 93*
Conroy, Williams Eugene 1933- *WhoIns 94*
Conry, Thomas Francis 1942- *WhoAm 94*
Cons, Derek 1928- *Who 94*
Cons, Emma 1838-1912 *DcNaB MP*
Cons, Richard *WhoHisp 94*
Consagra, Pier 1954- *WhoAmA 93*
Consagra, Pietro 1920- *IntWW 93*
Consagra, Sophie Chandler 1927- *WhoAm 94*
Consalvi, Simon Alberto 1929- *IntWW 93*
Consejo, Eduardo 1957- *WhoScEn 94*
Consey, Kevin E. 1952- *WhoAmA 93*
Consey, Kevin Edward 1952- *WhoAm 94, WhoMW 93*
Considine, David D. 1939- *WhoAmP 93*
Considine, Frank William 1921- *IntWW 93, WhoAm 94, WhoMW 93*
Considine, John *WhoHol 92*
Considine, John Joseph 1941- *WhoAm 94*
Considine, Terry 1947- *WhoAmP 93*
Considine, Tim 1940- *WhoHol 92*
Considine, William Howard 1947- *WhoAm 94*
Consiglio, Helen 1962- *WhoMW 93*
Consilio, Barbara Ann 1938- *WhoAmL 94*
Consola, Mary Frances 1946- *WhoMW 93*
Console, Frank Milton 1924- *WhoAm 94*
Consoli, John F. *WhoAmP 93*
Consoli, Marc-Antonio 1941- *WhoAm 94*
Constable, Elinor Greer 1934- *WhoAm 94*
Constable, Henry 1562-1613 *DcLB 136*
Constable, (Charles) John 1936- *Who 94*
Constable, Robert Frederick S. *Who 94*
Constable, Robert Lee 1942- *WhoAm 94*
Constable, Rosalind *WhoAmA 93*
Constable, William 1783-1861 *DcNaB MP*
Constable, William George 1887-1976 *WhoAmA 93N*
Constance, Eugene Roy 1937- *WhoHisp 94*
Constance, Joseph William, Jr. 1952- *WhoAm 94*
Constance, Mervyn 1950- *WhoScEn 94*
Constance, Thomas Ernest 1936- *WhoAm 94*
Constancio, Vitor 1943- *IntWW 93*
Constanduros, Mabel d1957 *WhoHol 92*
Constandy, John Peter 1924- *WhoAm 94*
Constans, Henry Philip, Jr. 1928- *WhoAm 94*
Constant, Anita Aurelia 1945- *WhoAm 94, WhoFI 94*
Constant, Antony 1916- *Who 94*
Constant, Clinton 1912- *WhoAm 94, WhoFI 94, WhoScEn 94, WhoWest 94*
Constant, George 1892-1978 *WhoAmA 93N*
Constant, Jan 1936- *WrDr 94*
Constant, Max d1943 *WhoHol 92*
Constant, Paule 1944- *IntWW 93*
Constant, Stephen 1931- *WrDr 94*
Constant, William David 1954- *WhoScEn 94*
Constant, Yvonne 1935- *WhoHol 92*
Constantaras, Lambros d1985 *WhoHol 92*
Constantelos, Demetrios J. 1927- *WrDr 94*
Constantikes, Penelope Louise 1956- *WhoWest 94*
Constantin, Michel *WhoHol 92*
Constantine *Who 94*
Constantine, I 285-337 *HisWorL [port]*
Constantine, II 1940- *IntWW 93*
Constantine, D. Lee 1952- *WhoAmP 93*
Constantine, David (John) 1944- *ConAu 142, WrDr 94*
Constantine, Eddie 1915- *WhoHol 92*
Constantine, Eddie 1917-1993 *NewYTBS 93 [port]*
Constantine, Greg John 1938- *WhoAmA 93*
Constantine, Jan Friedman 1948- *WhoAm 94*
Constantine, K. C. *WrDr 94*
Constantine, Kathy Smith 1954- *WhoFI 94*
Constantine, Michael 1927- *WhoHol 92*
Constantine, Mildred 1913- *WhoAmA 93*
Constantine, Murray *EncSF 93*
Constantine, Storm 1956- *EncSF 93*
Constantine, Virginia *WhoAmP 93*
Constantineau, Constance Juliette 1937- *WhoWest 94*
Constantine Of Stanmore, Baron *Who 94*
Constantinescu, Dan 1953- *IntWW 93*
Constantinescu, Gheorghe M. 1932- *WhoMW 93*
Constantinescu, Paul 1909-1963 *NewGrDO*
Constantini, JoAnn M. 1948- *WhoFI 94*
Constantini, Louis Orlando 1948- *WhoFI 94*
Constantinides, Dinos Demetrios 1929- *WhoAm 94*
Constantino, Florencio 1869-1919 *NewGrDO*
Constantino, James Peter 1953- *WhoAmL 94*
Constantino, Renato 1919- *ConAu 42NR*
Constantino, William, Jr. *WhoAmP 93*
Constantino-Bana, Rose Eva 1940- *WhoScEn 94*
Constantinou, Clay 1951- *WhoAmL 94*
Constine, Karen Robin 1960- *WhoWest 94*
Conston, Henry Siegismund 1928- *WhoAm 94*
Conta, Bart Joseph 1914- *WhoAm 94*
Conta, Lewis Dalcin 1912- *WhAm 10*
Contag, Christopher Heinz 1959- *WhoScEn 94*
Contag, Pamela Reilly 1957- *WhoScEn 94*
Contamine, Claude Maurice 1929- *IntWW 93*
Contamine, Philippe 1932- *IntWW 93*
Contarini, Marco 1632-1689 *NewGrDO*
Conte, Arthur 1920- *IntWW 93*
Conte, Gregory Michael 1947- *WhoAmP 93*
Conte, James D. 1959- *WhoAmP 93*
Conte, Jean Jacques 1938- *WhoScEn 94*
Conte, Jeanne Larner 1928- *WhoAmA 93*
Conte, John 1915- *IntMPA 94, WhoHol 92*
Conte, Joseph John, II 1932- *WhoAm 94*
Conte, Lansana *IntWW 93*
Conte, Lou 1942- *WhoMW 93*
Conte, Nicholas *WhoHol 92*
Conte, Rafael 1925- *WhoHisp 94*
Conte, Richard d1975 *WhoHol 92*
Conte, Richard Nicholas 1918- *WhoAm 94*
Conte, Richard R. 1947- *WhoAm 94, WhoFI 94*
Conte, Samuel Daniel 1917- *WhoAm 94*
Conte, Silvio Otto 1921-1991 *WhAm 10*
Conte, Steve *WhoHol 92*
Contee, Benjamin 1755-1815 *WhAmRev*
Contee, Carolyn Ann 1945- *WhoBlA 94*
Conteh, Abdulai Osman 1945- *IntWW 93*
Conteh, Barbara Allison 1951- *WhoMW 93*
Contento, William G(uy) 1947- *EncSF 93*
Conterato, Bruno Paul 1920- *WhoAm 94*
Conti, Albert d1967 *WhoHol 92*
Conti, Ann Patricia 1933- *WhoAmP 93*
Conti, Bill 1942- *IntMPA 94, WhoAm 94*
Conti, Carlo 1796-1868 *NewGrDO*
Conti, Daniel Joseph 1949- *WhoWest 94*
Conti, David John 1951- *WhoAm 94*
Conti, David Victor 1939- *WhoAmP 93*
Conti, Edmund *DrAPF 93*
Conti, Francesco Bartolomeo 1681-1732 *NewGrDO*
Conti, Gioacchino 1714-1761 *NewGrDO*
Conti, Ignazio Maria 1699?-1759 *NewGrDO*
Conti, Isabella 1942- *WhoAm 94, WhoWest 94*
Conti, James Joseph 1930- *WhoAm 94*
Conti, Joy Flowers 1948- *WhoAm 94, WhoAmL 94*
Conti, Laura 1921- *WhoWomW 91*
Conti, Lee Ann *WhoAm 94*
Conti, Louis Thomas Moore 1949- *WhoAm 94, WhoAmL 94*
Conti, Mario Giuseppe 1934- *IntWW 93*
Conti, Mario Joseph *Who 94*
Conti, Niccolo Dei c. 1395-1469 *WhWE*
Conti, Nicola fl. 1733-1754 *NewGrDO*
Conti, Patricia d1929 *WhoHol 92*
Conti, Paul Louis 1945- *WhoAm 94, WhoMW 93*
Conti, Peter Selby 1934- *WhoAm 94*
Conti, Samuel 1922- *WhoAm 94, WhoAmL 94*
Conti, Tom *IntWW 93*
Conti, Tom 1941- *IntMPA 94, WhoAm 94, WhoHol 92*
Conti, Tom 1942- *Who 94*
Conti, William J. 1953- *WhoAm 94*
Conticchio, Linda Anne *WhoFI 94*
Contie, Leroy John, Jr. 1920- *WhoAm 94, WhoAmL 94, WhoMW 93*
Contillo, Paul J. 1929- *WhoAmP 93*
Contini, Anita 1944- *WhoAmA 93*
Contini, Domenico Filippo fl. 1669-1687 *NewGrDO*
Contini, Francesco Bartolomeo *NewGrDO*
Contini, Gianfranco 1912-1990 *WhAm 10*
Contino, Dick *WhoHol 92*
Continos, Anna *WhoAmA 93*
Contney, John Joseph 1932- *WhoAm 94*
Conto, Aristides 1931- *WhoWest 94*
Contogeorgis, George 1912- *Who 94*
Contois, David Francis 1963- *WhoScEn 94*
Contos, Larry D 1940- *WhoAm 94*
Contos, Paul Anthony 1926- *WhoWest 94*
Contoski, Victor *DrAPF 93*
Contouri, Chantal *WhoHol 92*
Contrada, Charles Vincent 1951- *WhoAmL 94*
Contrada, Joseph Guy 1950- *WhoAm 94*
Contrada, Richard Jude 1954- *WhoScEn 94*
Contreni, John Joseph, Jr. 1944- *WhoAm 94*
Contreras, Abraham 1965- *WhoHisp 94*
Contreras, Adela Marie 1960- *WhoHisp 94*
Contreras, Benigno, Jr. 1941- *WhoHisp 94*
Contreras, Carl Toby 1957- *WhoHisp 94*
Contreras, Carlos 1942- *WhoHisp 94*
Contreras, Carlos Arturo 1922- *WhoHisp 94*
Contreras, Don L. 1962- *WhoHisp 94*
Contreras, Esther Cajahuaringa 1962- *WhoHisp 94*
Contreras, Fernando, Jr. 1950- *WhoHisp 94*
Contreras, Francis 1950- *WhoHisp 94*
Contreras, Frank R. 1942- *WhoHisp 94*
Contreras, Hiram *WhoHisp 94*
Contreras, James *WhoHisp 94*
Contreras, Joe W. *WhoHisp 94*
Contreras, Jose Antonio 1953- *WhoHisp 94*
Contreras, Joseph Louis 1957- *WhoHisp 94*
Contreras, Luis A. 1952- *WhoHisp 94*
Contreras, Mariano d1979 *WhoHol 92*
Contreras, Mark Gerard 1961- *WhoMW 93*
Contreras, Matias Ricardo 1946- *WhoHisp 94*
Contreras, Miguel d1956 *WhoHol 92*
Contreras, Raoul Lowery 1941- *WhoHisp 94*
Contreras, Thomas José 1945- *WhoHisp 94*
Contreras, Vincent John 1943- *WhoHisp 94*
Contreras-Sweet, Maria *WhoHisp 94*
Contreras-Velásquez, Simón Rafael 1956- *WhoHisp 94*
Contrivo, Frank Joseph 1957- *WhoAmL 94*
Conversano, Guy John 1924- *WhoScEn 94*
Converse, Elizabeth 1946- *WhoAmA 93*
Converse, Frank 1938- *IntMPA 94, WhoHol 92*
Converse, Frederick Shepherd 1871-1940 *NewGrDO*
Converse, James Clarence 1942- *WhoAm 94*
Converse, Kenneth E. 1930- *WhoAmP 93*
Converse, Kristin Ashley 1965- *WhoFI 94*
Converse, Peggy *WhoHol 92*
Converse, Philip E. 1928- *IntWW 93, WrDr 94*
Converse, Philip Ernest 1928- *WhoAm 94*
Converse, Rob Roy McGregor 1917- *WhoAmP 93*
Converse, Robert E., Jr. 1945- *WhoAm 94, WhoAmL 94*
Converse, William Rawson Mackenzie 1937- *WhoAm 94*
Converse-Roberts, William *WhoHol 92*
Converti, Vincenzo 1925- *WhoAm 94*
Convertino, Victor Anthony 1949- *WhoAm 94*
Convery, Patrick George 1953- *WhoMW 93*
Convery, Robert 1954- *NewGrDO*
Convery, Samuel V. *WhoAmP 93*
Conviser, Richard 1944- *WhoWest 94*
Conviser, Richard James 1938- *WhoAm 94, WhoAmL 94, WhoMW 93*
Convisser, Martin 1932- *WhoAmP 93*
Convy, Bert 1933-1991 *WhAm 10*
Convy, Bert 1934-1991 *WhoHol 92*
Conway, Alan 1920- *WrDr 94*
Conway, Alvin James 1925- *WhoAm 94*
Conway, Anne 1631-1679 *BlmGWL*
Conway, Anne Callaghan 1950- *WhoAm 94, WhoAmL 94*
Conway, Barbara Elaine 1955- *WhoFI 94*
Conway, Casey Anthony 1953- *WhoFI 94*
Conway, Celine *WrDr 94*
Conway, Charles D. 1947- *WhoAmL 94*
Conway, Curt d1974 *WhoHol 92*
Conway, Cyril *WhoHol 92*
Conway, Daniel Edward 1941- *WhoMW 93*
Conway, David 1939- *WrDr 94*

Conway, David Antony 1941- WhoAm 94
Conway, Derek Leslie 1953- Who 94
Conway, Dominic J. Who 94
Conway, Dwight Colbur 1930- WhoAm 94
Conway, E. Virgil 1929- WhoAm 94
Conway, Earl Cranston 1931- WhoMW 93
Conway, Frank Harrison 1913- WhoAmP 93
Conway, French Hoge 1918- WhoAmL 94
Conway, Gary 1936- IntMPA 94, WhoHol 92
Conway, Gerald A. 1947- WhoAmP 93
Conway, Gerard F. 1952- EncSF 93
Conway, Gordon Richard 1938- Who 94
Conway, Hobart McKinley, Jr. 1920- WhoAm 94
Conway, Jack d1951 WhoHol 92
Conway, Jack d1952 WhoHol 92
Conway, James Francis 1932- WhoAmP 93
Conway, James Stephen 1930- WhoAmP 93
Conway, James Valentine Patrick 1917- WhoAm 94
Conway, Jeff 1948- WhoAmP 93
Conway, Jill Kathryn Ker 1934- WhoAm 94
Conway, John E. 1934- WhoAm 94, WhoAmL 94, WhoWest 94
Conway, John Horton IntWW 93, Who 94
Conway, John K. WhoAmL 94
Conway, John S. 1929- WhoAm 94
Conway, John Thomas 1924- WhoAm 94
Conway, John Thomas 1956- WhoScEn 94
Conway, Kathleen M. 1940- WhoAmL 94
Conway, Kenneth Edwin 1934- WhoMW 93
Conway, Kevin 1942- IntMPA 94, WhoAm 94, WhoHol 92
Conway, Kevin John 1951- WhoAmL 94
Conway, Lizzie d1916 WhoHol 92
Conway, Lynn Ann 1938- WhoAm 94, WhoScEn 94
Conway, Maria Joanne 1962- WhoFI 94
Conway, Mark Allyn 1957- WhoAmL 94
Conway, Martin Who 94
Conway, (David) Martin 1935- Who 94
Conway, Michael A. 1947- WhoIns 94
Conway, Michael Anthony 1947- WhoAm 94
Conway, Michael J. 1945- WhoAm 94, WhoFI 94, WhoWest 94
Conway, Michael Maurice 1946- WhoAm 94, WhoAmL 94
Conway, Michael Thomas WhoAmL 94
Conway, Morgan d1981 WhoHol 92
Conway, Morna Helen 1945- WhoFI 94
Conway, Nancy Ann 1941- WhoAm 94
Conway, Neil James, III 1950- WhoAmL 94, WhoFI 94, WhoMW 93
Conway, Norman H. 1942- WhoAmP 93
Conway, Pat 1936 WhoHol 92
Conway, Patrick d1981 WhoHol 92
Conway, Peter P. 1936- WhoIns 94
Conway, Richard 1936- WhoWest 94
Conway, Richard Ashley 1931- WhoAm 94
Conway, Richard Francis 1954- WhoFI 94
Conway, Richard Walter 1931- WhoAm 94
Conway, Robert WhoAmP 93
Conway, Robert Alfred 1927- WhoAm 94
Conway, Robert George, Jr. 1951- WhoAmL 94
Conway, Robert P. 1946- WhoAm 94
Conway, Robert Patrick 1914- WhoWest 94
Conway, Ronald Anthony 1958- WhoAmL 94
Conway, Russ 1913- WhoHol 92
Conway, Sari Elizabeth 1951- Who 94
Conway, Shirl 1916- WhoHol 92
Conway, Steve Edward 1944- WhoAmP 93
Conway, Thomas 1735-c. 1800 WhAmRev
Conway, Thomas F. WhoAmP 93
Conway, Thomas James 1913- WhoAm 94
Conway, Thomas William 1931- WhoMW 93
Conway, Tim 1933- IntMPA 94, WhoAm 94, WhoCom, WhoHol 92
Conway, Tim, Jr. 1963- WhoHol 92
Conway, Tina Marie DrAPF 93
Conway, Tom d1967 WhoHol 92
Conway, Troy EncSF 93
Conway, Troy 1924- WrDr 94
Conway, Tyrrell 1957- WhoMW 93
Conway, Wallace Xavier, Sr. 1920- WhoBlA 94
Conway, William d1924 WhoHol 92
Conway, William Frederick, Sr. 1928- WhoMW 93
Conway, William Gaylord 1929- WhoAm 94
Conway Carey, Allison Brandes 1957- WhoFI 94
Conway Morris, Simon 1951- Who 94
Conwell, Carolyn WhoHol 92
Conwell, Esther Marly 1922- WhoAm 94
Conwell, Russell Herman 1843-1925 AmSocL, DcAmReB 2
Conwill, Allan Franklin 1921-1989 WhAm 10
Conwill, Giles 1944- WhoBlA 94
Conwill, Houston 1947- AfrAmAl 6
Conwill, Houston E. 1947- WhoAmA 93
Conwill, William Louis 1946- WhoBlA 94
Conybeare, Charles Augustus ConAu 41NR
Conyers, Abda Johnson, III 1944- WhoAm 94
Conyers, Charles L. 1927- WhoBlA 94
Conyers, Darcy d1973 WhoHol 92
Conyers, James E. 1932- WhoBlA 94
Conyers, Jean Louise 1932- WhoMW 93
Conyers, John 1929- AfrAmAl 6 [port]
Conyers, John, Jr. 1929- CngDr 93, WhoAm 94, WhoAmP 93, WhoBlA 94, WhoMW 93
Conyers, Joseph d1920 WhoHol 92
Conyers, Nathan WhoBlA 94
Conyers, Nathan G. 1932- WhoBlA 94
Conyers, Richard Lee 1958- WhoFI 94
Conyers, Selma Harris 1935- WhoAmP 93
Conyngham, Marquess 1924- Who 94
Conyngham, Barry 1944- NewGrDO
Conyngham, Fred 1909- WhoHol 92
Conyngham, Gustavus c. 1744-1819 WhAmRev
Conyngham, Gustavus 1747-1819 AmRev
Conza, Anthony P. 1940- WhoFI 94
Conzelman, James Ken 1953- WhoAmP 93
Conzelman, Jimmy d1970 ProFbHF
Coobar, Abdulmegid 1909- IntWW 93
Cooch, Edward Webb, Jr. 1920- WhoAmL 94
Cooder, Ry 1947- WhoAm 94
Coodley, Alfred Edgar 1922- WhoAm 94
Cooey, William Randolph 1942- WhoAm 94, WhoFI 94, WhoScEn 94
Coogan, Gene d1972 WhoHol 92
Coogan, Jack d1935 WhoHol 92
Coogan, Jackie d1984 WhoHol 92
Coogan, Jackie 1914-1984 WhoCom
Coogan, Keith 1969- WhoHol 92
Coogan, Keith 1970- IntMPA 94
Coogan, Philip Shields 1938- WhoAm 94
Coogan, Robert d1978 WhoHol 92
Coogan, Robert Arthur William 1929- Who 94
Coogan, Thomas Phillips 1898- WhAm 10
Coogle, Joseph Moore, Jr. 1933- WhoAm 94
Coohill, Thomas Patrick 1941- WhoScEn 94
Cook fl. 1701-1718 NewGrDO
Cook, Addison Gilbert 1933- WhoAm 94, WhoScEn 94
Cook, Alan (Hugh) 1922- Who 94
Cook, Alan (Hugh), Sir 1922- WrDr 94
Cook, Alan Hugh 1922- IntWW 93
Cook, Albert DrAPF 93
Cook, Albert 1925- WrDr 94
Cook, Albert Spaulding 1925- WhoAm 94
Cook, Albert Thomas Thornton, Jr. 1940- WhoFI 94, WhoWest 94
Cook, Alexander Burns 1924- WhoAm 94, WhoFI 94, WhoMW 93
Cook, Alfred Alden 1930- WhoScEn 94
Cook, Anda Suna 1935- WhoMW 93
Cook, Andrew Robert 1965- WhoScEn 94
Cook, Ann Who 94
Cook, Ann Jennalie 1934- WhoAm 94
Cook, Anthony Lacquise 1967- WhoBlA 94
Cook, Anthony Malcolm 1936- WhoScEn 94
Cook, Arthur Thompson 1923- Who 94
Cook, August Charles 1897- WhoAmA 93
Cook, August Joseph 1926- WhoAmL 94
Cook, B. Thomas 1946- WhoAm 94, WhoAmL 94
Cook, Bart R. 1950- WhoAm 94
Cook, Beryl 1926- IntWW 93
Cook, Beryl Frances 1926- Who 94
Cook, Beth Marie 1933- WhoAm 94
Cook, Bette Walker Philpott 1941- WhoFI 94
Cook, Betty 1929- WhoAmP 93
Cook, Billy d1981 WhoHol 92
Cook, Blanche Wiesen 1941- WhoAm 94
Cook, Bob 1961- WrDr 94
Cook, Brian Francis 1933- Who 94
Cook, Brian Hartley K. Who 94
Cook, Brian (Robert) Rayner 1945- IntWW 93
Cook, Bruce, Sr. WhoAmP 93
Cook, Bruce Alan 1929- WhoFI 94
Cook, Bruce Martin 1954- WhoWest 94
Cook, Bryson Leitch 1948- WhoAm 94, WhoAmL 94
Cook, Camille Wright WhoAm 94
Cook, Carole WhoHol 92
Cook, Cathy Welles WhoAmP 93
Cook, Charles A. 1946- WhoBlA 94
Cook, Charles Alfred George 1913- Who 94
Cook, Charles Beckwith, Jr. 1929- WhoAm 94, WhoFI 94
Cook, Charles Conway 1917-1991 WhoBlA 94N
Cook, Charles Davenport 1919- WhoAm 94
Cook, Charles David 1924- WhoAm 94
Cook, Charles David 1935- WhoAmP 93
Cook, Charles Emerson 1926- WhoAm 94
Cook, Charles Francis 1941- WhoAm 94, WhoFI 94
Cook, Charles Smith d1892 EncNAR
Cook, Charles Terrence 1949- WhoMW 93
Cook, Charles Wilkerson, Jr. 1934- WhoAm 94
Cook, Charles William 1927- WhoAm 94
Cook, Chauncey William Wallace 1909- WhoAm 94
Cook, Chris(topher) 1945- WrDr 94
Cook, Christopher Capen 1932- WhoAm 94, WhoAmA 93
Cook, Christopher Wymondham Rayner Herbert 1938- Who 94
Cook, Clarence Edgar 1936- WhoAm 94
Cook, Clarence Sharp 1918- WhoAm 94
Cook, Clayton Henry 1912- WhoAm 94, WhoAmP 93
Cook, Clyde d1984 WhoHol 92
Cook, Curtis Dale 1961- WhoMW 93
Cook, David 1940- WrDr 94
Cook, David Alastair 1942- WhoAm 94
Cook, David Bruce 1957- WhoWest 94
Cook, David Charles, III 1912-1990 WhAm 10
Cook, David George 1937- WhoFI 94
Cook, David Lee 1952- WhoAmL 94
Cook, David S. 1921- WhAm 10
Cook, David Somerville 1944- Who 94
Cook, Deborah 1938- NewGrDO
Cook, Delores Woodrum 1933- WhoAmP 93
Cook, Derek Edward 1931- Who 94
Cook, Dick d1986 WhoHol 92
Cook, Dierdre Ruth Goorman 1956- WhoWest 94
Cook, Don 1920- WhoAm 94, WrDr 94
Cook, Donald d1961 WhoHol 92
Cook, Donald E. 1928- WhoAm 94, WhoWest 94
Cook, Donald Jean 1920- WhoAm 94
Cook, Donald Lloyd 1948- WhoWest 94
Cook, Doris Jean 1934- WhoAmP 93
Cook, Doris Marie 1924- WhoAm 94, WhoFI 94
Cook, Douglas Neilson 1929- WhoAm 94, WhoWest 94
Cook, Douglas Ray 1962- WhoMW 93
Cook, Edward Joseph 1925- WhoAm 94
Cook, Edward Marks, Jr. 1944- WhoMW 93
Cook, Edward Willingham 1922- WhoAm 94, WhoFI 94
Cook, Elisha, Jr. 1903- IntMPA 94
Cook, Elisha, Jr. 1906- WhoHol 92
Cook, Eliza 1818-1889 BlmGWL
Cook, Elizabeth G. 1960- WhoBlA 94
Cook, Eric L. 1963- WhoAm 94
Cook, Ethyle d1949 WhoHol 92
Cook, Eugene A. 1938- WhoAmP 93
Cook, Eugene Augustus 1938- WhoAm 94, WhoAmL 94
Cook, F. A. d1940 WhoHol 92
Cook, Fielder WhoAm 94
Cook, Fielder 1923- IntMPA 94
Cook, Frances D. 1945- WhoAm 94, WhoAmP 93
Cook, Francis 1935- Who 94
Cook, Francis John Granville 1913- Who 94
Cook, Frank Patrick 1920- Who 94
Cook, Frank Robert, Jr. 1923- WhoBlA 94
Cook, Fred Harrison, III 1952- WhoBlA 94
Cook, Fred James 1911- WhoAm 94
Cook, Freda Maxine 1928- WhoWest 94
Cook, Frederick Albert 1865-1940 WhWE [port]
Cook, G(eorge) Bradford 1937- IntWW 93
Cook, Gail Fairman 1937- WhoAm 94
Cook, Garry Aron WhoHol 92
Cook, Gary Dean 1947- WhoAmP 93
Cook, Gary Dennis 1951- WhoWest 94
Cook, Gary L. WhoAmP 93
Cook, Gary Raymond 1950- WhoAm 94
Cook, Geoffrey DrAPF 93
Cook, George David 1925- Who 94
Cook, George Edward 1938- WhoAm 94
Cook, George Henry, Jr. 1951- WhoAm 94
Cook, George Steveni L. Who 94
Cook, George Valentine 1927- WhoAm 94
Cook, George Wallace Foster 1919- WhoAm 94
Cook, Georgia Mae 1929- WhoAmP 93
Cook, Gerald 1937- WhoAm 94
Cook, Gerald S. 1942- WhoAmL 94
Cook, Gladys Emerson 1899- WhoAmA 93N
Cook, Glen (Charles) 1944- EncSF 93, WrDr 94
Cook, Gordon Charles 1932- IntWW 93, Who 94
Cook, Gregory D. 1948- WhoWest 94
Cook, Gregory John 1951- WhoAmL 94
Cook, Haney Judaea 1926- WhoBlA 94
Cook, Harold Dale 1924- WhoAm 94, WhoAmL 94
Cook, Harold J. 1946- WhoBlA 94
Cook, Harold James 1926- Who 94
Cook, Harold Rodney 1944- WhoFI 94, WhoScEn 94
Cook, Harry Clayton, Jr. 1935- WhoAm 94
Cook, Heidemarie Gertrude 1958- WhoFI 94
Cook, Henry George 1906- Who 94
Cook, Henry Home 1918- Who 94
Cook, Henry Lee, Sr. 1939- WhoBlA 94
Cook, Howard Norton 1901-1980 WhoAmA 93N
Cook, Hugh (Murray William) 1957- EncSF 93
Cook, Hugh (Walter Gilbert) 1956- WrDr 94
Cook, J. Rowland 1942- WhoAm 94
Cook, Jack McPherson 1945- WhoAm 94, WhoMW 93
Cook, James 1728-1779 HisWorL [port], WhWE [port]
Cook, James 1926- WhoAm 94
Cook, James Curtis 1896- WhAm 10
Cook, James E. 1925- WhoBlA 94
Cook, James Ivan 1925- WhoAm 94
Cook, James L(ister) 1932- ConAu 142
Cook, James Lee 1955- WhoAmP 93
Cook, James William Dunbar 1921- Who 94
Cook, Jan 1939- WhoAm 94
Cook, Jan 1955- WhoAmP 93
Cook, Jay F. 1948- WhoAm 94, WhoAmL 94
Cook, Jay Michael 1942- WhoAm 94, WhoFI 94
Cook, Jeannine Harriss 1929- WhoMW 93
Cook, Jeffrey 1934- WrDr 94
Cook, Jeffrey L. 1952- WhoAmP 93
Cook, Jeffrey Ross 1934- WhoAm 94
Cook, Jeffrey Sherard 1947- WhoAmL 94
Cook, Joe d1959 WhoHol 92
Cook, Joe 1890-1959 WhoCom
Cook, John WhoAm 94
Cook, John 1926- Who 94
Cook, John 1944- WhoAmP 93
Cook, John (Alfred) 1930- WhoAmA 93
Cook, John Alfred 1930- WhoAm 94
Cook, John Alvin 1952- WhoFI 94
Cook, John Barry 1940- Who 94
Cook, John Bell 1933- WhoScEn 94
Cook, John C. 1941- WhoAmL 94
Cook, John Manuel 1910- Who 94
Cook, John R. 1943- WhoIns 94
Cook, Joseph 1838-1901 DcAmReB 2
Cook, Joseph 1917- Who 94
Cook, Joseph Daniel 1951- WhoFI 94
Cook, Joseph S. 1936- WhoAmA 93
Cook, Joseph T. 1941- WhoAmL 94
Cook, Joyce Mitchell 1933- WhoBlA 94
Cook, Judith (Anne) 1933- WrDr 94
Cook, Julia Lea 1958- WhoScEn 94
Cook, Julian Abele, Jr. 1930- WhoAm 94, WhoAmL 94, WhoBlA 94, WhoMW 93
Cook, Karen Gullberg 1951- WhoAmL 94
Cook, Kathleen L. 1949- WhoAmA 93
Cook, Kenneth (Bernard) 1929- WrDr 94
Cook, Kenneth L. 1934- WhoIns 94
Cook, Kevin Joe 1960- WhoFI 94
Cook, Ladda Banks 1935- WhoBlA 94
Cook, LeAnn Cecilia 1950- WhoAmL 94
Cook, Leeland d1981 WhoHol 92
Cook, Leland G. 1942- WhoAmL 94
Cook, Leonard Clarence 1936- WhoAm 94
Cook, Lester d1953 WhoHol 92
Cook, Lia 1942- WhoAmA 93
Cook, Lillian d1918 WhoHol 92
Cook, Lisle M. 1936- WhoAmP 93
Cook, Liz DrAPF 93
Cook, Lloyd E., Sr. 1928- WhoAmP 93
Cook, Lodwrick M. 1928- IntWW 93
Cook, Lodwrick Monroe 1928- WhoAm 94, WhoFI 94, WhoWest 94
Cook, Lois Anna 1924- WhoMW 93
Cook, Louisa Fay 1925- WhoWest 94
Cook, Lucius d1952 WhoHol 92
Cook, Lyle Edwards 1918- WhoAm 94, WhoWest 94
Cook, Lyn 1918- WrDr 94
Cook, Lynette Rene 1961- WhoWest 94
Cook, Marian Alice 1928- WhoAm 94
Cook, Marianne WhoHol 92
Cook, Marjorie Ellen 1942- WhoMW 93
Cook, Mark d1987 WhoHol 92
Cook, Mark 1942- WrDr 94
Cook, Marvin Eugene 1966- WhoAm 94
Cook, Mary Louise 1933- WhoAmP 93

Coomaraswamy, Ananda K. 1877-1947 *WhoAmA 93N*
Coombe, Carol d1966 *WhoHol 92*
Coombe, George William, Jr. 1925- *IntWW 93, WhoAm 94*
Coombe, Gerald Hugh 1925- *Who 94*
Coombe, Michael Rew 1930- *Who 94*
Coombe, Richard Irwin 1942- *WhoAmP 93*
Coombe, V. Anderson 1926- *WhoAm 94*
Coomber, James Elwood 1942- *WhoMW 93*
Coombes, Keva Christopher 1949- *Who 94*
Coombes, Terri Lee 1954- *WhoAmP 93*
Coombs, Allen Kelso 1932- *WhoFI 94*
Coombs, Ann *WrDr 94*
Coombs, Anthony Michael Vincent 1952- *Who 94*
Coombs, Bertha I. 1961- *WhoHisp 94*
Coombs, Camilla H. 1944- *WhoAmP 93*
Coombs, C'Ceal Phelps *WhoWest 94*
Coombs, D. A. L. *WhoAm 94, WhoFI 94*
Coombs, Derek Michael 1937- *Who 94*
Coombs, Douglas Saxon 1924- *IntWW 93*
Coombs, Douglas Stafford 1924- *Who 94*
Coombs, Eugene G. 1911- *WhoAmL 94*
Coombs, Fletcher 1924- *WhoBlA 94*
Coombs, Harry James 1935- *WhoBlA 94*
Coombs, Herbert Cole 1906- *IntWW 93, Who 94*
Coombs, Jerry Donald 1955- *WhoFI 94*
Coombs, Jim Le 1964- *WhoWest 94*
Coombs, John Wendell 1905- *WhoAm 94*
Coombs, Michael John 1946- *WhoWest 94*
Coombs, Nina *WrDr 94*
Coombs, Orde *WhoBlA 94*
Coombs, Pat 1930- *WhoHol 92*
Coombs, Patricia 1926- *WrDr 94*
Coombs, Peter Bertram 1928- *Who 94*
Coombs, Peter Richard 1951- *WhoAmP 93*
Coombs, Philip (Hall) 1915- *WrDr 94*
Coombs, Philip H. 1915- *IntWW 93*
Coombs, Robert Eugene 1936- *WhoWest 94*
Coombs, Robert H(olman) 1934- *ConAu 41NR*
Coombs, Robert Holman 1934- *WhoAm 94*
Coombs, Robert Royston Amos 1921- *IntWW 93, Who 94*
Coombs, Simon Christopher 1947- *Who 94*
Coombs, Walter Paul 1920- *WhoAm 94*
Coombs, William Elmer 1911- *WhoAmL 94, WhoAmP 93, WhoFI 94, WhoWest 94*
Coomer, Joe *DrAPF 93*
Coomer, Joe 1958- *WrDr 94*
Coon, Carleton S., Sr. 1927- *WhoAmP 93*
Coon, Charles Edward 1933- *WhoAm 94*
Coon, Duane Edward 1936- *WhoMW 93*
Coon, Fred Albert, III 1949- *WhoScEn 94*
Coon, Gary M. 1964- *WhoAmP 93*
Coon, Hilary Huntington 1961- *WhoScEn 94*
Coon, Horace 1897-1961 *EncSF 93*
Coon, J. Frederick 1951- *WhoIns 94*
Coon, Jane A. 1929- *WhoAmP 93*
Coon, Julian Barham 1939- *WhoAm 94*
Coon, Ken *WhoAmP 93*
Coon, Minor Jesser 1921- *IntWW 93*
Coon, Saundra Kay 1943- *WhoMW 93*
Coon, Susan *EncSF 93*
Coonan, Dorothy *WhoHol 92*
Coonan, Sheila d1989 *WhoHol 92*
Cooney, Barbara 1917- *WhoAm 94*
Cooney, Blanche 1917- *ConAu 142*
Cooney, C. Hayes 1937- *WhoAmL 94*
Cooney, Charles Leland 1944- *WhoAm 94*
Cooney, Daniel Ellard 1949- *WhoWest 94*
Cooney, David Francis 1954- *WhoAmL 94*
Cooney, David Martin 1930- *WhoAm 94*
Cooney, Ellen *DrAPF 93*
Cooney, Frank James 1941- *WhoFI 94*
Cooney, J. Michael 1950- *WhoAmL 94*
Cooney, James Patrick d1993 *NewYTBS 93*
Cooney, James Patrick 1944- *WhoAmL 94*
Cooney, Joan Ganz 1929- *IntMPA 94, WhoAm 94*
Cooney, John Fontana 1949- *WhoAm 94, WhoAmL 94*
Cooney, John Gordon 1930- *WhoAm 94, WhoAmL 94*
Cooney, John Gordon, Jr. 1959- *WhoAmL 94*
Cooney, John Patrick, Jr. 1944- *WhoAm 94, WhoAmL 94*
Cooney, John Richardson 1942- *WhoWest 94*
Cooney, John Thomas 1927- *WhoAm 94*
Cooney, Kevin Patrick 1955- *WhoWest 94*
Cooney, Leighton H., Jr. 1944- *WhoAmP 93*
Cooney, Lynn Futch 1961- *WhoAmL 94*
Cooney, Michael Rodman 1954- *WhoAmP 93*
Cooney, Mike 1954- *WhoWest 94*
Cooney, Miriam P. 1925- *WhoMW 93*
Cooney, Ned Lyhne 1955- *WhoScEn 94*
Cooney, Patricia Noel 1950- *WhoWest 94*
Cooney, Patrick 1931- *IntWW 93*
Cooney, Patrick Ronald 1934- *WhoAm 94, WhoMW 93*
Cooney, Ray(mond George Alfred) 1932- *ConDr 93, WrDr 94*
Cooney, Raymond George Alfred 1932- *Who 94*
Cooney, Robert John 1924- *WhoAmL 94*
Cooney, Thomas Michael 1926- *WhoAm 94*
Cooney, Thomas O. 1944- *WhoAmL 94*
Cooney, Timothy J., Jr. *WhoAmP 93*
Cooney, William J. 1929- *WhoAmL 94*
Cooney, Wilson Charles 1934- *WhoIns 94*
Coonrod, Richard Allen 1931- *WhoAm 94*
Coons, Clifford Vernon 1911-1990 *WhAm 10*
Coons, Eldo Jess, Jr. 1924- *WhoFI 94, WhoWest 94*
Coons, Harold Meredith 1911- *WhoAmP 93*
Coons, Marion McDowell 1915- *WhoFI 94*
Coons, Ronald Edward 1936- *WhoAm 94*
Coonts, Stephen (Paul) 1946- *WrDr 94*
Coontz, Bill d1978 *WhoHol 92*
Coontz, Morris Stephen 1946- *WhoAmL 94*
Coontz, Stephanie 1944- *WrDr 94*
Coony, Thomas M. *WhoAmP 93*
Coop, Eddie Paul 1946- *WhoAmP 93*
Coop, Franco d1962 *WhoHol 92*
Coop, Frederick Robert 1914- *WhoAm 94*
Coop, Louise C. 1913- *WhoAmP 93*
Coop, Maurice (Fletcher) 1907- *Who 94*
Cooper *Who 94*
Cooper, Adrian 1968- *WhoAm 94*
Cooper, Alan *Who 94*
Cooper, (William Hugh) Alan 1909- *Who 94*
Cooper, Alan Samuel 1942- *WhoAm 94*
Cooper, Albert, Sr. 1934- *WhoBlA 94*
Cooper, Albert Samuel 1905- *Who 94*
Cooper, Alcie Lee, Jr. 1939- *WhoFI 94*
Cooper, Alice 1948- *WhoAm 94, WhoHol 92*
Cooper, Allan B. 1949- *WhoAmL 94*
Cooper, Allen David 1942- *WhoAm 94, WhoScEn 94*
Cooper, Almeta E. 1950- *WhoBlA 94*
Cooper, Alva C. d1993 *NewYTBS 93*
Cooper, Andrew Charles 1952- *WhoFI 94*
Cooper, Andrew Ramsden 1902- *Who 94*
Cooper, Anna Julia Haywood 1858-1964 *BlmGWL*
Cooper, Anne 1935- *WhoAmP 93*
Cooper, Anthony J. 1907-1992 *WhoAmA 93N*
Cooper, Anthony Kemble 1908- *WhoHol 92*
Cooper, April Helen 1951- *WhoAm 94*
Cooper, Arnold Michael 1923- *WhoAm 94*
Cooper, Arthur Irving 1922- *WhoAm 94*
Cooper, Arthur Martin 1937- *WhoAm 94*
Cooper, Arthur Wells 1931- *WhoAm 94*
Cooper, Ashley d1952 *WhoHol 92*
Cooper, Ashley 1936- *BuCMET*
Cooper, Augusta Mosley 1903- *WhoBlA 94*
Cooper, Austin Morris 1959- *WhoWest 94*
Cooper, B.J. 1935- *WhoAmL 94*
Cooper, B. Jay 1950- *WhoAm 94*
Cooper, Barbara Jean *WhoBlA 94*
Cooper, Ben 1930- *WhoHol 92*
Cooper, Ben 1933- *IntMPA 94*
Cooper, Benita Ann 1944- *WhoAm 94, WhoScEn 94*
Cooper, Bernard *DrAPF 93*
Cooper, Bernard 1951- *WrDr 94*
Cooper, Beryl Phyllis 1927- *Who 94*
Cooper, Bill *WhoAmP 93*
Cooper, Bobby G. 1938- *WhoBlA 94*
Cooper, Bonnie Sue 1934- *WhoAmP 93*
Cooper, Brian (Newman) 1919- *WrDr 94*
Cooper, Bryan 1932- *WrDr 94*
Cooper, C. Everett *ConAu 42NR, EncSF 93*
Cooper, C. Everett 1948- *WrDr 94*
Cooper, Camille 1969- *WhoHol 92*
Cooper, Camille Sutro 1946- *WhoIns 94*
Cooper, Candace D. 1948- *WhoBlA 94*
Cooper, Candace Lucretia 1961- *WhoBlA 94*
Cooper, Carl Wade 1957- *WhoAmL 94*
Cooper, Carol Diane 1953- *WhoAm 94, WhoFI 94*
Cooper, Caroline Ann 1943- *WhoFI 94*
Cooper, Carolyn Kraemer *DrAPF 93*
Cooper, Cary Lynn 1940- *Who 94*
Cooper, Cary Wayne 1939- *WhoAm 94*
Cooper, Cecil 1949- *WhoBlA 94*
Cooper, Charles Donald 1932- *WhoAm 94*
Cooper, Charles Gerson 1932- *WhoAm 94*
Cooper, Charles Gilbert 1928- *WhoAm 94, WhoFI 94*
Cooper, Charles Gordon 1927- *WhoAm 94*
Cooper, Charles Grafton 1927- *WhoAm 94*
Cooper, Charles Howard 1923- *WhoAm 94*
Cooper, Charles Justin 1952- *WhoAm 94*
Cooper, Charles Neilson 1935- *WhoAmL 94*
Cooper, Charles W. 1929- *WhoBlA 94*
Cooper, Chester Lawrence 1917- *WhoScEn 94*
Cooper, Chris 1951- *WhoHol 92*
Cooper, Christopher (Donald Huntington) 1942- *WrDr 94*
Cooper, Chuck 1928- *BasBi*
Cooper, Clancy d1975 *WhoHol 92*
Cooper, (Brenda) Clare 1935- *ConAu 41NR*
Cooper, Clare Dunlap 1938- *WhoAm 94*
Cooper, Clarence 1942- *WhoBlA 94*
Cooper, Clarence L(avaugn), Jr. 1942- *BlkWr 2*
Cooper, Claude d1932 *WhoHol 92*
Cooper, Clement Theodore 1930- *WhoBlA 94*
Cooper, Clyde James, Jr. 1931- *WhoAmL 94*
Cooper, Colin (Symons) 1926- *EncSF 93*
Cooper, Colin Symons 1926- *WrDr 94*
Cooper, Constance Deloris Carter d1992 *WhoBlA 94N*
Cooper, Constance Marie 1952- *WhoBlA 94*
Cooper, Corinne 1952- *WhoAmL 94*
Cooper, Curtis V. *WhoBlA 94*
Cooper, Daneen Ravenell 1958- *WhoBlA 94*
Cooper, Daniel 1931- *WhoAm 94*
Cooper, Daniel T. 1961- *WhoAmP 93*
Cooper, Darren Scott 1961- *WhoMW 93*
Cooper, David *WhoAmP 93*
Cooper, David Antony 1945- *Who 94*
Cooper, David Booth, Jr. 1956- *WhoAm 94, WhoFI 94*
Cooper, David Edward 1942- *Who 94*
Cooper, David Robert 1956- *WhoScEn 94*
Cooper, Dee 1920- *WhoHol 92*
Cooper, Delmar Clair 1896- *WhAm 10*
Cooper, Dennis 1953- *GayLL*
Cooper, Derek (Macdonald) 1925- *WrDr 94*
Cooper, Derek Macdonald 1925- *Who 94*
Cooper, Dolores G. 1922- *WhoAmP 93*
Cooper, Dominic (Xavier) 1944- *WrDr 94*
Cooper, Donald Arthur 1930- *Who 94*
Cooper, Donald Lee 1928- *WhoAm 94*
Cooper, Doug d1977 *WhoHol 92*
Cooper, Douglas E. 1912- *WhoWest 94*
Cooper, Douglas Kenneth 1947- *WhoAmL 94*
Cooper, Douglas Winslow 1942- *WhoScEn 94*
Cooper, Drucilla Hawkins 1950- *WhoBlA 94*
Cooper, Duane *WhoBlA 94*
Cooper, Dulcie d1981 *WhoHol 92*
Cooper, E. Camron 1939- *WhoAm 94, WhoFI 94*
Cooper, Earl, II 1944- *WhoBlA 94*
Cooper, Edith *BlmGWL*
Cooper, Edmund 1926-1982 *EncSF 93*
Cooper, Edna Mae d1986 *WhoHol 92*
Cooper, Edward d1945 *WhoHol 92*
Cooper, Edward d1956 *WhoHol 92*
Cooper, Edward Hayes 1941- *WhoAm 94*
Cooper, Edward S. 1926- *ConBlB 6 [port]*
Cooper, Edward Sawyer 1926- *WhoBlA 94*
Cooper, Edwin d1961 *WhoHol 92*
Cooper, Edwin d1984 *WhoHol 92*
Cooper, Edwin Lowell 1936- *WhoAm 94*
Cooper, Elaine Janice 1937- *WhoMW 93*
Cooper, Emil (Albertovich) 1877-1960 *NewGrDO*
Cooper, Emmett E., Jr. 1921- *WhoBlA 94*
Cooper, Ernest, Jr. 1941- *WhoBlA 94*
Cooper, Ethel Thomas 1919- *WhoBlA 94*
Cooper, Ethna Bennert 1955- *WhoAmL 94*
Cooper, Eugene Bruce 1933- *WhoAm 94, WhoScEn 94*
Cooper, Evelyn Kaye 1941- *WhoBlA 94*
Cooper, Florence d1993 *NewYTBS 93*
Cooper, Francis Loren 1919- *WhoAm 94*
Cooper, Frank d1918 *WhoHol 92*
Cooper, Frank 1922- *Who 94*
Cooper, Franklin Seaney 1908- *WhoAm 94*
Cooper, Fred G. 1883-1962 *WhoAmA 93N*
Cooper, Frederick d1945 *WhoHol 92*
Cooper, Frederick Eansor 1942- *WhoAm 94, WhoAmP 93*
Cooper, Gary d1961 *WhoHol 92*
Cooper, Gary 1901-1961 *AmCulL*
Cooper, Gary Allan 1947- *WhoAmL 94*
Cooper, Gary T. 1948- *WhoBlA 94*
Cooper, Geoffrey 1907- *Who 94*
Cooper, George d1943 *WhoHol 92*
Cooper, George (Leslie Conroy) 1925- *Who 94*
Cooper, George A. 1915- *Who 94*
Cooper, George A. 1916- *WhoHol 92*
Cooper, George Brinton 1916- *WhoAm 94*
Cooper, George Edward 1915- *Who 94*
Cooper, George Emery 1916- *WhoAm 94*
Cooper, George Kile 1920- *WhoMW 93*
Cooper, George Robert 1921- *WhoAm 94*
Cooper, George Ryan 1954- *WhoWest 94*
Cooper, Georgie d1968 *WhoHol 92*
Cooper, Gerald Rice 1914- *WhoScEn 94*
Cooper, Ginnie 1945- *WhoAm 94, WhoWest 94*
Cooper, Gladys d1971 *WhoHol 92*
Cooper, Gloria 1931- *WhoAm 94*
Cooper, Gordon Mayo 1925- *WhoAm 94*
Cooper, Gordon R., II 1941- *WhoBlA 94*
Cooper, Grant Burr 1903-1990 *WhAm 10*
Cooper, Grey d1801 *WhAmRev*
Cooper, Guy 1948- *WhoAm 94*
Cooper, Hal 1923- *IntMPA 94, WhoAm 94*
Cooper, Hal Dean 1934- *WhoAm 94*
Cooper, Hannah *ConAu 43NR*
Cooper, Hannah 1923- *WrDr 94*
Cooper, Helen *DrAPF 93*
Cooper, Henry 1924- *WrDr 94*
Cooper, Henry 1934- *Who 94*
Cooper, Henry Noble 1896- *WhAm 10*
Cooper, Herman E. d1993 *NewYTBS 93*
Cooper, Homer Chassell 1923- *WhoAmP 93*
Cooper, Ilene Linda 1948- *WhoAm 94*
Cooper, Imogen 1949- *IntWW 93, Who 94*
Cooper, Iris N. 1942- *WhoBlA 94*
Cooper, Irmgard M. 1946- *WhoBlA 94*
Cooper, Irving Ben 1902- *WhoAm 94, WhoAmL 94*
Cooper, Isabel Rosario d1960 *WhoHol 92*
Cooper, J. California *Au&Arts 12 [port], WhoBlA 94*
Cooper, Jack d1970 *WhoHol 92*
Cooper, Jack Ross 1924- *WhoAm 94*
Cooper, Jackie 1921- *WhoHol 92*
Cooper, Jackie 1922- *IntMPA 94, WhoAm 94, WrDr 94*
Cooper, James Albert, Jr. 1946- *WhoAm 94, WhoMW 93*
Cooper, James Fenimore 1789-1851 *AmCulL, EncSF 93*
Cooper, James Ford 1935- *IntWW 93*
Cooper, James H. 1929- *WhoFI 94*
Cooper, James Hayes Shofner 1954- *WhoAm 94, WhoAmP 93*
Cooper, James J. 1924- *WhoAmP 93*
Cooper, James M., Jr. 1941- *WhoIns 94*
Cooper, James Michael 1939- *WhoAm 94*
Cooper, James Randall 1960- *WhoWest 94*
Cooper, James Ray, Jr. 1949- *WhoWest 94*
Cooper, James Wayne 1904-1989 *WhAm 10*
Cooper, Jane *DrAPF 93*
Cooper, Jane (Marvel) 1924- *WrDr 94*
Cooper, Jane Todd 1943- *WhoAm 94*
Cooper, Janelle Lunette 1955- *WhoMW 93, WhoScEn 94*
Cooper, Jay Leslie 1929- *WhoAm 94*
Cooper, Jean Saralee 1946- *WhoAm 94, WhoAmP 93*
Cooper, Jeanne 1928- *WhoHol 92*
Cooper, Jeff *WhoHol 92*
Cooper, Jeremy 1946- *WrDr 94*
Cooper, Jerome A. 1913- *WhoAm 94*
Cooper, Jerome Gary 1936- *AfrAmG [port], WhoAmP 93, WhoBlA 94*
Cooper, Jerome Maurice 1930- *WhoAm 94*
Cooper, Jerrold Stephen 1942- *WhoAm 94*
Cooper, Jerry W. 1948- *WhoAmP 93*
Cooper, Jerry William 1937- *WhoFI 94*
Cooper, Jilly 1937- *Who 94*
Cooper, Jilly (Sallitt) 1937- *WrDr 94*
Cooper, Jim 1954- *CngDr 93*
Cooper, Joan d1989 *WhoHol 92*
Cooper, Joan Davies 1914- *Who 94*
Cooper, JoAnn Sobkowiak 1945- *WhoMW 93*
Cooper, John 1729-1785 *WhAmRev*
Cooper, John Allen Dicks 1918- *IntWW 93, WhoAm 94*
Cooper, John Arnold 1917- *WhoAm 94, WhoFI 94, WhoMW 93*
Cooper, John C., III 1942- *WhoAmL 94*
Cooper, John Charles *DrAPF 93*
Cooper, John Edgar, Sr. 1947- *WhoScEn 94*
Cooper, John Edwin 1948- *WhoScEn 94*
Cooper, John G. 1945- *WhoAmL 94*
Cooper, John Joseph 1924- *WhoAm 94*
Cooper, John Leslie 1933- *Who 94*
Cooper, John Milton, (Jr.) 1940- *WrDr 94*
Cooper, John Milton, Jr. 1940- *WhoAm 94*
Cooper, John Philip 1923- *IntWW 93, Who 94*

Cooper, John Sherman 1901-1991 WhAm 10
Cooper, John Spencer 1933- Who 94
Cooper, John Wesley 1946- WhoMW 93
Cooper, Jon Hugh 1940- WhoAm 94, WhoWest 94
Cooper, Joseph WhoBlA 94
Cooper, Joseph 1912- IntWW 93, Who 94
Cooper, Joseph 1933- WhoAm 94
Cooper, Joseph Girard 1956- WhoMW 93
Cooper, Josephine H. 1936- WhoBlA 94
Cooper, Josephine Smith 1945- WhoAm 94
Cooper, Joyce Beatrice 1941- WhoMW 93
Cooper, Judith DrAPF 93
Cooper, Judson Merri 1931- WhoAmP 93
Cooper, Julian M. 1945- WrDr 94
Cooper, Julius, Jr. 1944- WhoBlA 94
Cooper, Karin Ruth 1962- WhoMW 93
Cooper, Kathleen Bell 1945- WhoAm 94
Cooper, Keith Harvey 1936- WhoAm 94
Cooper, Ken Errol 1939- WhoAm 94
Cooper, Kenneth Banks 1923- WhoAm 94
Cooper, Kenneth Ernest d1993 Who 94N
Cooper, Kenneth H(ardy) 1931- WrDr 94
Cooper, Kenneth Joseph 1955- WhoBlA 94
Cooper, Kenneth Reginald 1931- IntWW 93, Who 94
Cooper, Kent DrAPF 93
Cooper, Khershed Pessie 1952- WhoScEn 94
Cooper, LaMoyne Mason 1931- WhoBlA 94
Cooper, Larry B. 1946- WhoBlA 94
Cooper, Larry S. 1957- WhoWest 94
Cooper, Lawrence 1937- WhoFI 94
Cooper, Lawrence Allen 1948- WhoAmL 94
Cooper, Lawrence John 1959- WhoFI 94
Cooper, Lee Pelham 1926- WrDr 94
Cooper, Leon Melvin 1924- WhoAm 94
Cooper, Leon N. 1930- IntWW 93, Who 94, WhoAm 94, WhoScEn 94, WorScD
Cooper, Leonard Jay 1938- WhoAm 94
Cooper, Leroy Gordon, Jr. 1927- WhoAm 94, WhoScEn 94
Cooper, Lettice 1897- WrDr 94
Cooper, Lillian Kemble d1977 WhoHol 92
Cooper, Linda G. 1954- WhoBlA 94
Cooper, Lois Louise 1931- WhoBlA 94
Cooper, Louis Jacques B. Who 94
Cooper, Louisa Sinclair 1931- WhoWest 94
Cooper, Louise Field 1905-1992 CurBio 93N, WhAm 10
Cooper, M. E. 1936- WrDr 94
Cooper, M. Scott 1950- WhoAmL 94
Cooper, M. Truman DrAPF 93
Cooper, Margaret Jean Drummond 1922- Who 94
Cooper, Marian WhoHol 92
Cooper, Marianne 1938- WhoAm 94
Cooper, Marilyn WhoAm 94
Cooper, Mario 1905- WhoAm 94, WhoAmA 93
Cooper, Marsh Alexander 1912- WhoAm 94
Cooper, Martin 1928- WhoAm 94
Cooper, Martin (Du Pre) 1910-1986 NewGrDO
Cooper, Marve H. 1939- WhoAmA 93N
Cooper, Mary Campbell 1940- WhoScEn 94
Cooper, Mary Wright 1714-1778 BlmGWL
Cooper, Matthew N. 1914- WhoBlA 94
Cooper, Maudine R. 1941- WhoBlA 94
Cooper, Max Dale 1933- WhoAm 94, WhoScEn 94
Cooper, Melrose SmATA 76
Cooper, Melville d1973 WhoHol 92
Cooper, Merian C. 1893-1973 IntDcF 2-4
Cooper, Merri-Ann 1946- WhoAm 94
Cooper, Merrill Pittman 1921- WhoBlA 94
Cooper, Michael 1956- BasBi
Cooper, Michael Anthony 1936- WhoAm 94
Cooper, (Frederick Howard) Michael C. Who 94
Cooper, Michael Gary 1954- WhoBlA 94
Cooper, Michael Jerome 1956- WhoBlA 94
Cooper, Michael John 1937- Who 94
Cooper, Miki Jean 1943- WhoAmP 93
Cooper, Milford J. 1920- WhoAmP 93
Cooper, Milton 1929- WhoAm 94, WhoFI 94
Cooper, Miriam d1976 WhoHol 92
Cooper, Myles 1735-1785 WhAmRev
Cooper, Nigel Cookson 1929- Who 94
Cooper, Norman Streich 1920- WhoAm 94
Cooper, Norton J. 1931- WhoAm 94
Cooper, Olin Cecil, Jr. 1925- WhoAm 94
Cooper, Olive d1950 WhoHol 92
Cooper, Olive d1987 WhoHol 92
Cooper, Pat 1929- WhoCom
Cooper, Patrick Graham Astley 1918- Who 94
Cooper, Paul 1926- WhoAm 94
Cooper, Paul Douglas 1941- WhoAm 94
Cooper, Paul Roy 1950- WhoAmL 94
Cooper, Paula 1938- WhoAm 94, WhoAmA 93
Cooper, Paulette Marcia 1942- WhoAm 94
Cooper, Peter 1791-1883 AmSocL [port], WorInv
Cooper, Peter James 1947- Who 94
Cooper, Peter Semler 1949- WhoScEn 94
Cooper, Philip John 1929- Who 94
Cooper, R. John, III 1942- WhoAm 94, WhoAmL 94, WhoFI 94
Cooper, Ralph WhoHol 92
Cooper, Ralph d1992 WhoBlA 94N
Cooper, Raymond Louis 1961- WhoMW 93
Cooper, Reginald Rudyard 1932- WhoAm 94, WhoMW 93, WhoScEn 94
Cooper, Rhonda H. 1950- WhoAmA 93
Cooper, Richard d1947 WhoHol 92
Cooper, Richard 1945-1979 WhoAmA 93N
Cooper, Richard (Powell) 1934- Who 94
Cooper, Richard Alan 1936- WhoAm 94
Cooper, Richard Alan 1953- WhoAmL 94, WhoMW 93
Cooper, Richard Arthur 1936- WhoScEn 94
Cooper, Richard Casey 1942- WhoAmL 94
Cooper, Richard Conrad 1903-1982 EncABHB 9 [port]
Cooper, Richard Craig 1941- WhoAm 94
Cooper, Richard Harris 1940- WhoFI 94
Cooper, Richard Kent 1937- WhoWest 94
Cooper, Richard Lee 1946- WhoAm 94
Cooper, Richard Melvin 1942- WhoAm 94, WhoAmL 94
Cooper, Richard Newell 1934- WhoAm 94, WhoAmP 93, WrDr 94
Cooper, Robert Arthur, Jr. 1932-1992 WhAm 10
Cooper, Robert Elbert 1920- WhoAm 94, WhoAmL 94, WhoAmP 93
Cooper, Robert Francis 1947- Who 94
Cooper, Robert George 1936- Who 94
Cooper, Robert H. 1925- WhoAm 94, WhoFI 94
Cooper, Robert James 1929- WhoMW 93
Cooper, Robert L. 1956- WhoAmL 94
Cooper, Robert Michael 1948- WhoScEn 94
Cooper, Robert Shanklin 1932- WhoAm 94
Cooper, Roger Frank 1944- WhoAm 94
Cooper, Roger Harvey 1941- WhoFI 94
Cooper, Roger M. 1944- WhoAmP 93
Cooper, Roger Merlin 1943- WhoAm 94
Cooper, Ron 1943- WhoAmA 93
Cooper, Ron 1948- WhoWest 94
Cooper, Ronald Cecil Macleod 1931- Who 94
Cooper, Ronald Louis 1961- WhoBlA 94
Cooper, Ronald Stephen 1945- WhoAm 94, WhoAmL 94
Cooper, Roy Asberry, III 1957- WhoAmP 93
Cooper, Ruffin 1942- WhoAmA 93
Cooper, Russell Who 94
Cooper, (Theo) Russell 1941- Who 94
Cooper, Sally WhoHol 92
Cooper, Samuel H., Jr. 1955- WhoBlA 94
Cooper, Scott Francis 1953- WhoAmL 94
Cooper, Scott Kendrick 1967- WhoAm 94
Cooper, Sharon Marsha 1944- WhoFI 94
Cooper, Sheldon IntMPA 94, WhoMW 93
Cooper, Shirley Fields 1943- WhoAmP 93
Cooper, Sidney G. Who 94
Cooper, Sidney Pool 1919- Who 94
Cooper, Simon (Christie) 1936- Who 94
Cooper, Stephanie R. 1944- WhoAmL 94
Cooper, Stephen C. 1944- WhoAmP 93
Cooper, Stephen Herbert 1939- WhoAm 94, WhoAmL 94
Cooper, Stephen Randolph 1950- WhoScEn 94
Cooper, Steven Jon 1941- WhoWest 94
Cooper, Stuart Leonard 1941- WhoAm 94, WhoScEn 94
Cooper, Susan 1947- WhoAmA 93
Cooper, Susan (Mary) 1935- EncSF 93, TwCYAW, WrDr 94
Cooper, Susan Fenimore 1813-1894 BlmGWL
Cooper, Susan Rogers 1947- WrDr 94
Cooper, Susie 1902- Who 94
Cooper, Syretha C. 1930- WhoBlA 94
Cooper, Tarzan 1926- BasBi
Cooper, Terrence WhoHol 92
Cooper, Terry L. 1938- ConAu 142
Cooper, Tex d1951 WhoHol 92
Cooper, Theodore d1993 IntWW 93N, NewYTBS 93 [port]
Cooper, Theodore 1928- IntWW 93, WhoFI 94
Cooper, Theodore A. 1943- WhoAmA 93
Cooper, Thomas Astley 1936- WhoAm 94
Cooper, Thomas Louis 1938- WhoAm 94
Cooper, Thomas Luther 1917- WhoAm 94
Cooper, Thomas M. 1939- WhoAmL 94
Cooper, Thomas McNeil 1951- WhoWest 94
Cooper, Thomas Thornville 1839-1878 WhWE
Cooper, Valerie Antionette 1961- WhoBlA 94
Cooper, Vern Edward 1957- WhoMW 93
Cooper, Violet Kemble d1961 WhoHol 92
Cooper, Wallace J. 1926- WhoAm 94
Cooper, Walter 1928- WhoBlA 94
Cooper, Warren Ernest 1933- IntWW 93, Who 94
Cooper, Warren Stanley 1922- WhoFI 94
Cooper, Wayne 1942- WhoAmA 93
Cooper, Wayne 1956- WhoBlA 94
Cooper, Wendy 1919- WrDr 94
Cooper, Wendy E. 1950- WhoIns 94
Cooper, Wendy Fein 1946- WhoAmL 94
Cooper, Whina 1895- Who 94
Cooper, William 1910- BlmGEL, ConAu 42NR, Who 94, WrDr 94
Cooper, William (Daniel Charles) 1955- Who 94
Cooper, William Allen 1943- WhoAm 94, WhoFI 94
Cooper, William Allen, Jr. 1932- WhoScEn 94
Cooper, William B. 1956- WhoBlA 94
Cooper, William Clark 1912- WhoWest 94
Cooper, William Eugene 1924- WhoAm 94, WhoScEn 94
Cooper, William Ewing, Jr. 1929- WhoAm 94
Cooper, William Frank 1921- Who 94
Cooper, William Hurlbert 1924- WhoAmP 93
Cooper, William James 1945- WhoScEn 94
Cooper, William James, Jr. 1940- WhoAm 94
Cooper, William Luther, III 1956- WhoAmL 94
Cooper, William Marion 1919- WhoAm 94
Cooper, William Russell 1936- WhoAm 94
Cooper, William Secord 1935- WhoAm 94, WhoWest 94
Cooper, William Thomas 1934- WhoScEn 94
Cooper, Winston Lawrence 1946- WhoBlA 94
Cooper, Wyatt d1978 WhoHol 92
Cooper, Wylola 1926- WhoMW 93
Cooper-Fratrik, Julie DrAPF 93
Cooper-Lewter, Marcia Jean 1959- WhoFI 94, WhoMW 93
Cooper-Lewter, Nicholas Charles 1948- WhoBlA 94
Cooperman, Alvin IntMPA 94
Cooperman, Barry S. 1941- WhoAm 94
Cooperman, Hasye WrDr 94
Cooperman, Robert DrAPF 93
Cooperman, Saul 1934- WhoAm 94
Cooperrider, David Loy 1954- WhoMW 93
Cooperrider, Ruth Hung 1952- WhoAmL 94
Cooperrider, Tom Smith 1927- WhoAm 94, WhoMW 93, WhoScEn 94
Cooper-Servaites, Pamela Sue 1941- WhoMW 93
Coopersmith, Bernard Ira 1914- WhoMW 93, WhoScEn 94
Coopersmith, Esther Lipsen WhoAmP 93
Coopersmith, Fran M. 1956- WhoAm 94, WhoFI 94
Coopersmith, Fredric S. WhoFI 94, WhoWest 94
Coopersmith, Georgia A. 1950- WhoAmA 93
Cooperstein, Claire DrAPF 93
Cooperstein, Paul Andrew 1953- WhoAmL 94
Cooperstein, Sherwin Jerome 1923- WhoAm 94
Coor, Lattie Finch 1936- IntWW 93, WhoAm 94, WhoWest 94
Cooray, (Bulathsinhalage) Anura (Siri) 1936- Who 94
Coordsen, George WhoAmP 93
Coore, David Hilton 1925- IntWW 93
Coorens, Claudette 1940- WhoWomW 91
Coorey, Chandana Aelian 1921- IntWW 93
Coors, Jeffrey H. 1945- WhoAm 94, WhoWest 94
Coors, Joseph 1917- WhoWest 94
Coors, Peter Hanson 1946- WhoWest 94
Coors, William K. 1916- WhoAm 94, WhoFI 94, WhoScEn 94, WhoWest 94
Coorts, Gerald Duane 1932- WhoAm 94
Coote, Bert d1938 WhoHol 92
Coote, Christopher (John) 1928- Who 94
Coote, Colin Reith 1893- WhAm 10
Coote, John Haven 1937- Who 94
Coote, John Oldham d1993 Who 94N
Coote, Robert d1982 WhoHol 92
Coote, Roderic Norman 1915- Who 94
Cooter, Dale A. 1948- WhoAmL 94
Cootes, Frank Graham 1879-1960 WhoAmA 93N
Coovelis, Mark DrAPF 93
Coover, Harry Wesley 1919- WhoAm 94
Coover, James Burrell 1925- WhoAm 94
Coover, Robert DrAPF 93
Coover, Robert 1932- WrDr 94
Coover, Robert (Lowell) 1932- EncSF 93, RfGShF
Coover-Clark, Carol 1955- WhoAm 94
Coox, Alvin D. 1924- WrDr 94
Coox, Alvin David 1924- WhoAm 94
Copage, Marc Diego 1962- WhoBlA 94
Copani, Anthony Frank 1957- WhoAmL 94
Copans, Kenneth Gary 1946- WhoFI 94
Copas, Lloyd d1963 WhoHol 92
Copas, Virgil 1915- Who 94
Cope, Alfred Haines 1912- WhoFI 94
Cope, Anthony Leon 1911- WhoMW 93
Cope, Charles Dudley 1943- WhoAmP 93
Cope, David DrAPF 93
Cope, David 1948- WrDr 94
Cope, David Robert 1944- Who 94
Cope, David Robert 1946- Who 94
Cope, Donald Lloyd 1936- WhoBlA 94
Cope, F(rederick) Wolverson 1909- Who 94
Cope, Harold Cary 1918- WhoAm 94
Cope, Jack 1913- WrDr 94
Cope, Jackson I. 1925- WrDr 94
Cope, James Dudley 1932- WhoAm 94
Cope, James Francis 1907- Who 94
Cope, Jeannette Naylor 1956- WhoAm 94
Cope, Joe L. 1953- WhoAmL 94
Cope, John (Ambrose) 1937- Who 94
Cope, John Robert 1942- WhoAm 94, WhoAmL 94
Cope, Joseph Adams 1945- WhoAmL 94
Cope, Kenneth 1931- WhoHol 92
Cope, Kenneth Wayne 1924- WhoAm 94
Cope, Larry Morgan 1946- WhoAm 94
Cope, Laurence Brian 1951- WhoFI 94
Cope, Lewis 1934- WhoAm 94
Cope, Louise Todd 1930- WhoAmA 93
Cope, Nancy Elizabeth 1952- WhoWest 94
Cope, Randolph Howard, Jr. 1927- WhoAm 94
Cope, Robert Gary 1936- WhoMW 93
Cope, Thom K. 1948- WhoAmL 94
Cope, Thomas Field 1948- WhoAm 94, WhoAmL 94
Cope, Wendy 1945- ConAu 140, WrDr 94
Cope, Wendy Mary 1945- Who 94
Cope, William Robert 1942- WhoAmL 94
Copeau, Jacques d1949 WhoHol 92
Copek, Peter Joseph 1945- WhoWest 94
Copeland, Adrian Dennis 1928- WhoAm 94
Copeland, Alvin Charles 1944- WhoFI 94
Copeland, Ann BlmGWL, ConAu 41NR, DrAPF 93
Copeland, Ann 1932- WrDr 94
Copeland, Anne Pitcairn 1951- WhoAm 94
Copeland, Barry Bernard 1957- WhoBlA 94
Copeland, Betty Marable 1946- WhoBlA 94
Copeland, Danny Ray 1960- WhoBlA 94
Copeland, David Y., III 1931- WhoAmP 93
Copeland, Donald Eugene 1912- WhoAm 94
Copeland, Douglas Allen 1956- WhoAmL 94
Copeland, Douglas Wallace, Jr. 1952- WhoAmP 93
Copeland, Edward Jerome 1933- WhoAm 94
Copeland, Edward Meadors, III 1937- WhoAm 94
Copeland, Edwin (Luther) 1916- WrDr 94
Copeland, Elaine Johnson 1943- WhoBlA 94
Copeland, Emily America 1918- WhoBlA 94
Copeland, Floyd Dean 1939- WhoAm 94, WhoAmL 94
Copeland, Fred E. 1932- WhoAmP 93
Copeland, Helen M. DrAPF 93
Copeland, Henry Jefferson, Jr. 1936- WhoAm 94, WhoMW 93
Copeland, Howard Edgar 1944- WhoAmP 93
Copeland, Hunter Armstrong 1918- WhoAm 94
Copeland, James 1923- WhoHol 92
Copeland, Joan WhoHol 92
Copeland, Joan Miller WhoAm 94

Corcoran, Michael E. 1951- *WhoFI 94*
Corcoran, Michael John 1960- *WhoScEn 94*
Corcoran, Neil (Cornelius) 1948- *WrDr 94*
Corcoran, Noreen 1943- *WhoHol 92*
Corcoran, Paul John 1934- *WhoAm 94*
Corcoran, Robert J. *WhoAmP 93*
Corcoran, Robert J. 1934- *WhoAmL 94*
Corcoran, Robert Joseph 1929- *WhoFI 94*
Corcoran, Robert Lee, Jr. 1944- *WhoAm 94*
Corcoran, Susan 1950- *WhoMW 93*
Corcoran, Thomas Joseph 1920- *WhoAm 94*
Corcoran, Thomas Joseph 1922- *WhoAmP 93*
Corcoran, Timothy R. 1950- *WhoAmP 93*
Corcoran, Tom 1939- *WhoAmP 93*
Corcoran, Victoria 1951- *WhoAm 94, WhoAmL 94*
Corcos, Lucille 1908-1973 *WhoAmA 93N*
Corcuera Cuesta, Jose Luis 1945- *IntWW 93*
Cord, Alex 1931- *WhoHol 92*
Cord, Alex 1933- *IntMPA 94*
Corda, Maria d1965? *WhoHol 92*
Cordain, Loren 1950- *WhoScEn 94*
Cordans, Bartolomeo c. 1700-1757 *NewGrDO*
Cordaro, Matthew Charles 1943- *WhoAm 94*
Cordasco, Francesco 1920- *WhoAm 94*
Cordati, Rosaia Luigia 1926- *WhoWomW 91*
Corday, Barbara 1944- *IntMPA 94*
Corday, Ben d1938 *WhoHol 92*
Corday, Mara 1932- *WhoHol 92*
Corday, Marcelle *WhoHol 92*
Corday, Paula 1924- *WhoHol 92*
Corddry, Paul Imlay 1936- *WhoAm 94, WhoFI 94*
Cordeiro, Joseph *Who 94*
Cordeiro, Joseph 1918- *IntWW 93*
Cordeiro da Silva, Joao *NewGrDO*
Cordel, Virginia Ann 1927- *WhoAmP 93*
Cordelier, Jeanne *BlmGWL*
Cordell, Alexander 1914- *WrDr 94*
Cordell, Cathleen 1917- *WhoHol 92*
Cordell, Francis Merritt 1932- *WhoScEn 94*
Cordell, Frank d1977 *WhoHol 92*
Cordell, Joe B. 1927- *WhAm 10*
Cordell, La Doris Hazzard 1949- *WhoBlA 94*
Cordell, Michael Bragg 1946- *WhoFI 94*
Cordell, Robert James 1917- *WhoAm 94*
Cordell, Steven Mark 1955- *WhoMW 93*
Cordella, Giacomo 1786-1846? *NewGrDO*
Corden, Henry *WhoHol 92*
Corden, Warner Max 1927- *IntWW 93, WhoAm 94, WrDr 94*
Corder, Frederick 1852-1932 *NewGrDO*
Corder, Loren David 1949- *WhoScEn 94*
Corder, Loren David Zeke 1949- *WhoWest 94*
Corder, Michael Paul 1940- *WhoAm 94*
Corder, Rodney Joe 1962- *WhoWest 94*
Corderi, Victoria Marta 1957- *WhoHisp 94*
Corderman, Douglas George 1931- *WhoMW 93*
Corderman, John Printz 1942- *WhoAm 94, WhoAmL 94, WhoAmP 93*
Cordero, Angel T., Jr. 1942- *WhoAm 94*
Cordero, Angel Tomas, Jr. 1942- *WhoHisp 94*
Cordero, Brenda Sue 1967- *WhoHisp 94*
Cordero, Carlos *WhoHisp 94*
Cordero, Fausto 1954- *WhoHisp 94*
Cordero, Joseph A. 1953- *WhoHisp 94*
Cordero, Manuel A., III 1955- *WhoHisp 94*
Cordero, Rafael *WhoAmP 93*
Cordero, Ronald Anthony 1940- *WhoHisp 94*
Cordero, Roque 1917- *AfrAmAl 6, WhoHisp 94*
Cordero, Sylvia D. 1959- *WhoHisp 94*
Cordero, Wilfredo 1971- *WhoHisp 94*
Cordero de Noriega, Diane C. 1943- *WhoHisp 94*
Cordero Jimenez, Carlos O. 1948- *WhoHisp 94*
Cordero-Santiago, Rafael 1942- *WhoHisp 94*
Cordero-Spampinato, Sylvia D. 1959- *WhoHisp 94*
Corderoy, Graham Thomas 1931- *Who 94*
Cordery, Sara Brown 1920- *WhoBlA 94*
Cordes, Alexander Charles 1925- *WhoAm 94*
Cordes, Brent Ray 1969- *WhoMW 93*
Cordes, Clifford Frederick, III 1946- *WhoAmL 94*
Cordes, Donald Wesley 1917- *WhoAm 94*
Cordes, Eugene Harold 1936- *WhoAm 94, WhoScEn 94*
Cordes, Fauno Lancaster 1927- *WhoWest 94*
Cordes, James F. 1940- *WhoFI 94*
Cordes, Loverne Christian 1927- *WhoAm 94*
Cordes, William H. 1945- *WhoAmL 94*
Cordiano, Dean Martin 1952- *WhoAm 94*
Cordier, Andrew W. 1901-1975 *HisDcKW*
Cordiner, William Lawson 1935- *Who 94*
Cording, Edward James 1937- *WhoFI 94*
Cording, Harry d1954 *WhoHol 92*
Cordingley, James John 1960- *WhoScEn 94*
Cordingley, John Edward 1916- *Who 94*
Cordingley, Mary Bowles 1918- *WhoAmA 93*
Cordingley, Mary Jeanette Bowles 1918- *WhoAm 94*
Cordingley, Patrick Anthony John 1944- *Who 94*
Cordingly, David 1938- *WrDr 94*
Cordingly, David Michael Bradley 1938- *Who 94*
Cordis, Maria 1929- *WhoAm 94*
Cordle, John Howard 1912- *Who 94*
Cordner, Blaine d1971 *WhoHol 92*
Cordoba, Becky Abbate 1956- *WhoHisp 94*
Cordoba, Francisco Fernandez De d1518 *WhWE*
Cordoba, Francisco Fernandez De c. 1475-c. 1526 *WhWE*
Cordoba, Jose *IntWW 93*
Córdoba, Mariano 1924- *WhoHisp 94*
Cordobés, Roland Esteban 1938- *WhoHisp 94*
Cordon, Glenda Sue 1943- *WhoMW 93*
Cordon, Norman d1964 *WhoHol 92*
Cordoni, Barbara Keene 1933- *WhoMW 93*
Cordova, Alexander M. 1943- *WhoWest 94*
Cordova, Carlos A. 1947- *WhoHisp 94*
Córdova, Carlos D. 1954- *WhoHisp 94*
Cordova, Donald E. 1938- *WhoWest 94*
Cordova, Fabian D. 1931- *WhoHisp 94*
Cordova, France Anne-Dominic 1947- *WhoAm 94, WhoHisp 94, WhoScEn 94*
Cordova, Francisco Ray 1963- *WhoHisp 94*
Cordova, J. Gustavo 1949- *WhoHisp 94*
Cordova, John Lawrence 1948- *WhoHisp 94*
Córdova, Johnny Amezquita 1946- *WhoHisp 94*
Córdova, José Hernán *WhoHisp 94*
Cordova, Kandy 1936- *WhoHisp 94*
Córdova, Kathryn M. 1947- *WhoHisp 94*
Cordova, Linda L. 1957- *WhoHisp 94*
Cordova, Manuel 1949- *WhoHisp 94*
Cordova, Mark Allan 1956- *WhoHisp 94*
Cordova, Moses E. *WhoHisp 94*
Cordova, Ralph Aguirre 1933- *WhoHisp 94*
Cordova, Randy 1955- *WhoHisp 94*
Cordova, Sam 1932- *WhoHisp 94*
Cordova, Terry Mark 1961- *WhoMW 93*
Cordova, Victor *WhoHisp 94*
Cordova, William 1930- *WhoHisp 94*
Cordover, Mitchell Burton 1947- *WhoMW 93*
Cordover, Ronald Harvey 1943- *WhoAm 94*
Cordoves, Margarita 1947- *WhoHisp 94*
Cordovez Zegers, Diego 1935- *IntWW 93*
Cordray, Richard Adams 1959- *WhoAmP 93*
Cordray, Richard Lynn 1952- *WhoWest 94*
Cordrey, Richard Stephen 1933- *WhoAm 94, WhoAmP 93*
Cordurer, Alan *WhoHol 92*
Cordy, Annie 1928- *WhoHol 92*
Cordy, Henry d1965 *WhoHol 92*
Cordy, Raymond d1956 *WhoHol 92*
Cordy, Timothy Soames 1949- *Who 94*
Cordy-Collins, Alana (Kathleen) 1944- *WhoAmA 93*
Cordy-Simpson, Roderick Alexander 1944- *Who 94*
Core, Edward K. *WhoAmP 93*
Core, Mary Carolyn W. Parsons 1949- *WhoAm 94*
Core, Orville Ben 1924- *WhoAmL 94*
Corea, Chick 1941- *WhoAm 94*
Corea, Gamani 1925- *IntWW 93*
Coreen, Marcelle d1977 *WhoHol 92*
Corell, Robert Walden 1934- *WhoAm 94, WhoScEn 94*
Corella, John C. *WhoHisp 94*
Corelli, Franco *IntWW 93*
Corelli, Franco 1921- *NewGrDO*
Corelli, Franco 1923- *WhoHol 92*
Corelli, John Charles 1930- *WhoAm 94*
Corelli, Marie 1855-1924 *BlmGEL, BlmGWL, EncSF 93, TwCLC 51 [port]*
Coren, Alan 1938- *IntWW 93, Who 94, WrDr 94*
Coren, Victoria 1972- *WrDr 94*
Corena, Fernando 1916-1984 *NewGrDO*
Coreth, Joseph Herman 1937- *WhoAm 94*
Corette, John E. 1908- *WhoAm 94*
Corey, Amalia 1931- *WhoAmP 93*
Corey, Arthur d1950 *WhoHol 92*
Corey, Charles William 1952- *WhoFI 94*
Corey, David Thomas 1960- *WhoMW 93*
Corey, Dorian d1993 *NewYTBS 93*
Corey, Elias James 1928- *IntWW 93, NobelP 91 [port], Who 94, WhoAm 94, WhoScEn 94*
Corey, Glenn Michael 1950- *WhoMW 93*
Corey, Gordon Richard 1914- *WhoAm 94*
Corey, Irwin 1912- *WhoCom*
Corey, Jeff 1914- *IntMPA 94, WhoAm 94, WhoHol 92*
Corey, Jill 1935- *WhoHol 92*
Corey, Joseph d1972 *WhoHol 92*
Corey, Katherine 1635?- *BlmGEL*
Corey, Kenneth Edward 1938- *WhoAm 94*
Corey, Leroy Dale 1942- *WhoAmP 93*
Corey, Mary Lou *WhoAmP 93*
Corey, Milton R., Sr. d1951 *WhoHol 92*
Corey, Orlin Russell 1926- *WhoAm 94*
Corey, Paul 1903- *WrDr 94*
Corey, Paul (Frederick) 1903- *EncSF 93*
Corey, "Professor" Irwin 1912- *WhoHol 92*
Corey, Ronald 1938- *WhoAm 94*
Corey, Stephen *DrAPF 93*
Corey, Virgil E. *WhoAmP 93*
Corey, Wendell d1968 *WhoHol 92*
Corey, William Ellis 1866-1934 *EncABHB 9*
Corfield, Frederick (Vernon) 1915- *Who 94*
Corfield, Frederick Vernon 1915- *IntWW 93*
Corfield, Kenneth (George) 1924- *Who 94*
Corfield, Kenneth George 1924- *IntWW 93*
Corfield, Robin Bell 1952- *SmATA 74 [port]*
Corfu, Haim 1921- *IntWW 93*
Corghi, Azio 1937- *NewGrDO*
Cori, Angelo Maria d1741? *NewGrDO*
Cori, Carl F. 1896-1984 *WorScD [port]*
Cori, Carl Tom 1937- *WhoAm 94, WhoFI 94*
Cori, Gerty Theresa Radnitz 1896-1957 *WorScD [port]*
Coriell, Bruce Richard 1956- *WhoWest 94*
Coriell, Lewis Lemon 1911- *WhoAm 94*
Corigliano, John (Paul, Jr.) 1938- *NewGrDO*
Corigliano, John Paul 1938- *WhoAm 94*
Corinaldi, Austin 1921- *WhoAm 94, WhoBlA 94*
Corinna fl. c. 5th cent.BC- *BlmGWL*
Corinne, Tee (A.) 1943- *GayLL*
Corinthios, Michael Jean George 1941- *WhoAm 94, WhoScEn 94*
Corio, Ann 1914- *WhoHol 92*
Coriolanus *WrDr 94*
Corish, Joseph Ryan 1909-1988 *WhoAmA 93N*
Corish, Patrick Joseph 1921- *IntWW 93*
Cork, Donald Burl 1949- *WhoMW 93*
Cork, Edwin Kendall *WhoAm 94*
Cork, Holly A. 1966- *WhoAmP 93*
Cork, Linda Katherine 1936- *WhoAm 94*
Cork, Randall Charles 1948- *WhoScEn 94, WhoWest 94*
Cork, Richard (Graham) 1947- *WrDr 94*
Cork, Richard Graham 1947- *Who 94*
Cork, Roger William 1947- *Who 94*
Cork, William Herbert 1959- *WhoMW 93*
Cork And Orrery, Earl of 1910- *Who 94*
Cork, Cloyne, and Ross, Bishop of 1930- *Who 94*
Corker, Bruce D. 1945- *WhoAmL 94*
Corker, Charles Edward 1917- *WhoAm 94*
Corkery, Christopher Jane *DrAPF 93*
Corkery, James Caldwell 1925- *WhoAm 94*
Corkery, Michael 1926- *Who 94*
Corkery, Neil A. 1940- *WhoAmP 93*
Corkery, Tim 1931- *WhoAmA 93*
Corkill, Daniel Bryan *WhoHol 92*
Corkle, Joseph Patrick 1951- *WhoAmP 93*
Corl, William Edward 1964- *WhoScEn 94*
Corlan, Anthony 1947- *WhoHol 92*
Corless, Dorothy Alice 1943- *WhoWest 94*
Corlett, Clive William 1938- *Who 94*
Corlett, Ewan Christian Brew 1923- *Who 94*
Corlett, Gerald Lingham 1925- *Who 94*
Corlett, William 1938- *EncSF 93, WrDr 94*
Corlette, Edith 1942- *WhoBlA 94*
Corlew, John Gordon 1943- *WhoAmL 94*
Corley, Al 1956- *WhoHol 92*
Corley, Daniel Martin 1940- *WhoScEn 94*
Corley, Eddie B. *WhoBlA 94*
Corley, Edwin 1931-1981 *EncSF 93*
Corley, Elizabeth A. 1955- *WhoMW 93*
Corley, Ernest 1914- *WrDr 94*
Corley, James 1947- *EncSF 93*
Corley, Jean Arnette Leister 1944- *WhoScEn 94*
Corley, Kenneth (Sholl Ferrand) 1908- *Who 94*
Corley, Leslie M. 1946- *WhoAm 94*
Corley, Michael Early Ferrand 1909- *Who 94*
Corley, O. Wayne 1938- *WhoAmL 94*
Corley, Pat *WhoHol 92*
Corley, Pat 1930- *WhoAm 94*
Corley, Peter Maurice Sinclair 1933- *Who 94*
Corley, Ralph Randall 1941- *WhoFI 94*
Corley, Roger David 1933- *Who 94*
Corley, Thomas Anthony Buchanan 1923- *WrDr 94*
Corley, William Angus d1993 *NewYTBS 93*
Corley, William Edward 1942- *WhoMW 93*
Corley, William Gene 1935- *WhoAm 94, WhoFI 94, WhoScEn 94*
Corley-Saunders, Angela Rose 1947- *WhoBlA 94*
Corley Smith, Gerard Thomas 1909- *Who 94*
Corliss, Edward d1981 *WhoHol 92*
Corliss, George Henry 1817-1888 *WorInv*
Corliss, John Ozro 1922- *WhoAm 94*
Corliss, Richard Nelson 1944- *WhoAm 94*
Corma, Avelino 1951- *WhoScEn 94*
Cormack, Alan *WorInv*
Cormack, Allan MacLeod 1924- *IntWW 93, Who 94, WhoAm 94, WhoScEn 94*
Cormack, Douglas 1939- *Who 94*
Cormack, G. J. *WhoAm 94, WhoFI 94*
Cormack, John 1922- *Who 94*
Cormack, Magnus (Cameron) 1906- *Who 94*
Cormack, Malcolm 1935- *WhoAmA 93*
Cormack, Patrick (Thomas) 1939- *WrDr 94*
Cormack, Patrick Thomas 1939- *Who 94*
Cormack, Richard Lowell 1948- *WhoWest 94*
Cormack, Robert George Hall 1904- *WhoAm 94*
Cormack, Robert Linklater Burke 1935- *Who 94*
Cormack, William MacIntosh 1941- *WhoWest 94*
Corman, Avery 1935- *WhoAm 94*
Corman, Cid 1924- *WhoAm 94, WrDr 94*
Corman, Eugene Harold 1927- *WhoAm 94*
Corman, Gene 1927- *IntMPA 94*
Corman, Jacob Doyle, Jr. 1932- *WhoAmP 93*
Corman, Larry 1958- *WhoAmL 94*
Corman, Maddie 1969- *WhoHol 92*
Corman, Randy 1960- *WhoAmP 93*
Corman, Rebecca Davis 1935- *WhoAmP 93*
Corman, Roger 1926- *EncSF 93, HorFD [port]*
Corman, Roger William 1926- *IntMPA 94, IntWW 93, WhoAm 94*
Cormanick, Rosa-Maria 1946- *WhoMW 93*
Cormany, Michael 1951- *WrDr 94*
Cormia, Frank Howard 1936- *WhoScEn 94*
Cormie, Donald Mercer 1922- *WhoAm 94, WhoWest 94*
Cormier, Jean G. 1941- *WhoAm 94*
Cormier, Lawrence J. 1927- *WhoBlA 94*
Cormier, Mark Stephen 1960- *WhoWest 94*
Cormier, Robert 1925- *WrDr 94*
Cormier, Robert (Edmund) 1925- *TwCYAW*
Cormier, Robert Edmund 1925- *WhoAm 94*
Cormier, Robert John 1932- *WhoAmA 93*
Cormier, Rufus, Jr. 1948- *WhoBlA 94*
Cormon, Eugene 1810-1903 *NewGrDO*
Corn, Alfred *DrAPF 93*
Corn, Alfred 1943- *WrDr 94*
Corn, Alfred DeWitt 1943- *WhoAm 94*
Corn, Barry Francis 1938- *WhoAmL 94*
Corn, Bennett Julian 1944- *WhoFI 94*
Corn, Jack W. 1929- *WhoAm 94, WhoFI 94*
Corn, Joseph Edward, Jr. 1932- *WhoAm 94*
Corn, Milton 1928- *WhoAm 94*
Corn, Morton 1933- *WhoAm 94*
Corn, Robert Bowden 1952- *WhoAmP 93*
Corn, Wanda M. 1940- *WhoAmA 93*
Corna, Mark Steven 1949- *WhoFI 94*
Cornaby, Kay Sterling 1936- *WhoAmL 94, WhoAmP 93, WhoWest 94*
Cornacchio, Joseph Vincent 1934- *WhoAm 94*
Cornacchioli, Giacinto c. 1598?-1673? *NewGrDO*

Courtheoux, Richard James 1949-
  WhoFI 94, WhoMW 93
Courthion, Pierre-Barthelemy 1902-
  IntWW 93
Courths-Mahler, Hedwig 1867-1950
  BlmGWL
Courtice, Rody Kenny d1973
  WhoAmA 93N
Courtice, Thomas Barr 1943- WhoAm 94
Courtier, S(idney) H(obson) EncSF 93
Courtiss, Eugene Howard 1930-
  WhoAm 94
Courtland, Jerome 1926- IntMPA 94,
  WhoHol 92
Courtleigh, Stephen d1968 WhoHol 92
Courtleigh, William, Jr. d1930
  WhoHol 92
Courtneidge, Charles d1935 WhoHol 92
Courtneidge, Cicely d1980 WhoHol 92
Courtney, Alex WhoHol 92
Courtney, Alex d1985 WhoHol 92
Courtney, Barbara Wood 1929-
  WhoAmA 93
Courtney, Brian Christopher 1962-
  WhoAmL 94
Courtney, Caroline 1920- WrDr 94
Courtney, Cassandra Hill 1949-
  WhoBlA 94
Courtney, Charles Edward 1936-
  WhoAm 94
Courtney, Charles Tyrone 1952-
  WhoAmP 93
Courtney, Christopher Andrew 1966-
  WhoMW 93
Courtney, Constance E. 1960-
  WhoAmL 94
Courtney, Dan d1982 WhoHol 92
Courtney, David Michael 1941-
  WhoAmP 93
Courtney, Dayle 1944- WrDr 94
Courtney, Edward 1932- Who 94,
  WhoAm 94
Courtney, Eugene Whitmal 1936-
  WhoAm 94, WhoMW 93
Courtney, Gladys Atkins 1930-
  WhoAm 94
Courtney, Gwendoline WrDr 94
Courtney, Henry Thomas 1941-
  WhoAmL 94
Courtney, Howard Perry 1911-
  WhoAm 94
Courtney, Inez d1975 WhoHol 92
Courtney, James Edmond 1931-
  WhoAm 94
Courtney, James McNiven 1940-
  WhoScEn 94
Courtney, James Patrick, Jr. 1952-
  WhoAm 94
Courtney, James Robert 1936-
  WhoAmP 93
Courtney, Joseph D. 1953- WhoAmP 93
Courtney, Kathleen D'Olier 1878-1974
  DcNaB MP
Courtney, Keith Townsend 1949-
  WhoAmA 93
Courtney, Oscar W. d1962 WhoHol 92
Courtney, Peter 1943- WhoAmP 93
Courtney, Richard Augustus 1953-
  WhoAmL 94
Courtney, Richard Howard 1938-
  WhoWest 94
Courtney, Robert 1926- WrDr 94
Courtney, Roger Graham 1946- Who 94
Courtney, Stephen Alexander 1957-
  WhoBlA 94
Courtney, Suzan 1947- WhoAmA 93
Courtney, Victoria Black 1943-
  WhoWest 94
Courtney, Wayne C. 1909- WhoAmP 93
Courtney, William Francis 1914-
  WhoAm 94
Courtney, William H. 1944- WhoAmP 93
Courtney, William Harrison 1944-
  WhoAm 94
Courtney, William Reid 1927- Who 94
Courtois, B. A. WhoAm 94, WhoFI 94
Courtois, Edmond Jacques 1920-
  WhoAm 94
Courtois, Yves 1940- WhoScEn 94
Courtot, Marguerite d1986 WhoHol 92
Courtot, Martha DrAPF 93
Courtown, Earl of 1954- Who 94
Courtright, Clyde d1967 WhoHol 92
Courtright, Lee Flippen 1937- WhoFI 94
Courtright, Morris, Jr. 1930- WhoAmP 93
Courtright, Robert 1926- WhoAmA 93
Courtsal, Donald Preston 1929-
  WhoAm 94
Courtwright, William d1933 WhoHol 92
Coury, Edmund Anthony, Jr. 1961-
  WhoMW 93
Coury, John, Jr. 1921- WhoAm 94
Coury, Louis Albert, Jr. 1960-
  WhoScEn 94
Couse, Philip Edward 1936- Who 94
Couser, William Griffith 1939-
  WhoAm 94
Cousin, Philip R. 1933- WhoBlA 94

Cousin Jacques NewGrDO
"Cousin Jody" d1975 WhoHol 92
Cousins, Althea L. 1932- WhoBlA 94
Cousins, Brian Harry 1933- Who 94
Cousins, David 1942- Who 94
Cousins, Frank G., Jr. WhoAmP 93
Cousins, James Mackay 1944- Who 94
Cousins, James R., Jr. 1906- WhoBlA 94
Cousins, John Peter 1931- Who 94
Cousins, Linda DrAPF 93
Cousins, Margaret 1905- DcLB 137 [port],
  WhoAm 94, WrDr 94
Cousins, Morison Stuart 1934- WhoAm 94
Cousins, Norman 1915-1990
  DcLB 137 [port], WhAm 10
Cousins, Peter Edward 1928- WrDr 94
Cousins, Philip 1923- Who 94
Cousins, Richard Francis 1955-
  WhoFI 94, WhoWest 94
Cousins, Robert John 1941- WhoAm 94
Cousins, William, Jr. 1927- WhoAmL 94,
  WhoBlA 94
Cousins, William Joseph 1917-
  WhoAmL 94
Cousser, Jean Sigismond NewGrDO
Cousteau, Jacques 1910- WorInv [port]
Cousteau, Jacques-Yves 1910-
  EnvEnc [port], IntMPA 94, IntWW 93,
  Who 94, WhoAm 94, WhoHol 92,
  WhoScEn 94
Cousteau, Philipe d1979 WhoHol 92
Cousy, Bob 1928- BasBi
Cousy, Bob Joseph 1928- WhoAm 94
Coutard, Raoul 1924- IntDcF 2-4 [port],
  IntMPA 94, IntWW 93
Coutinho, Albino EncSF 93
Coutinho, Antonio Alba Rosa 1926-
  IntWW 93
Coutinho, Sonia 1939- BlmGWL
Couto, Nancy (Vieira) 1942- WrDr 94
Couto, Nancy Vieira DrAPF 93
Coutsoheras, Yannis 1904- IntWW 93
Coutts Who 94
Coutts, Francis Burdett Money NewGrDO
Coutts, Gordon Who 94
Coutts, Herbert 1944- Who 94
Coutts, Ian Dewar 1927- Who 94
Coutts, John Archibald 1909- Who 94
Coutts, John Wallace 1923- WhoAm 94
Coutts, Linda Dale 1947- WhoMW 93
Coutts, Robert Francis 1941- WhoWest 94
Coutts, Ronald Thomson 1931-
  IntWW 93
Coutts, T(homas) Gordon 1933- Who 94
Coutu, Jean 1927- WhoFI 94
Couture, Armand WhoAm 94, WhoFI 94
Couture, Barbara WhoMW 93
Couture, Daniel Archie 1945-
  WhoAmP 93
Couture, Jean Desire 1913- IntWW 93
Couture, Jean G. 1924- WhoAm 94
Couture, Jean Guy 1929- WhoAm 94
Couture, Marvin Dean 1945- WhoAmL 94
Couture, Mary Michelle 1967-
  WhoMW 93
Couture, Maurice Who 94
Couture, Maurice 1926- WhoAm 94
Couture, Ronald David 1944- WhoAm 94
Couturier, Marion B. WhoAmA 93
Couve De Murville, Maurice 1907-
  Who 94
Couve De Murville, (Jacques) Maurice
  1907- IntWW 93
Couve De Murville, Maurice Noel Leon
  Who 94
Couve De Murville, Maurice Noel Leon
  1929- IntWW 93
Couvillion, David Irvin 1934-
  WhoAmL 94
Couvreur, Jessie 1848-1897 BlmGWL
Couzens, Kenneth (Edward) 1925-
  IntWW 93, Who 94
Couzinou, Robert 1888-1958 NewGrDO
Couzyn, Jeni 1942- BlmGEL, BlmGWL,
  WrDr 94
Covacevich, (Anthony) Thomas 1915-
  Who 94
Coval-Apel, Naomi Miller 1914-
  WhoAm 94
Covalt, Robert Byron 1931- WhoAm 94
Covalt, Roger Calvin 1959- WhoWest 94
Covan, DeForest W. 1917- WhoBlA 94
Covan, Willie d1989 WhoHol 92
Covarrubias, Edgar Angel 1942-
  WhoHisp 94
Covarrubias, Gonzalo A. 1950-
  WhoHisp 94
Covarrubias, Leopoldo Humberto 1942-
  WhoHisp 94
Covarrubias, Manuel fl. 1838-1844
  NewGrDO
Covarrubias, Patricia Olivia 1951-
  WhoWest 94
Covarrubias-Lugo, Irma Yolanda 1959-
  WhoHisp 94
Covatta, Anthony Gallo, Jr. 1944-
  WhoAmL 94

Covault, Lloyd R., Jr. 1928- WhoAm 94,
  WhoMW 93, WhoScEn 94
Cove, Rosemary 1936- WhoAmA 93
Cove, Ruth d1981 WhoHol 92
Covell, Alan Carter 1952- WhoAmA 93
Covell, Roger David 1931- IntWW 93
Covello, Aldo 1935- WhoScEn 94
Covello, Alfred B. WhoAmP 93
Covello, Alfred Vincent 1933- WhoAm 94,
  WhoAmL 94
Coven, Berdeen 1941- WhoAm 94
Coven, Edwina Olwyn 1921- Who 94
Coven, Frank 1910- Who 94
Coveney, James 1920- IntWW 93, Who 94
Coveney, Michael William 1948- Who 94
Coveney, Peter (Vivian) 1958- ConAu 140
Coventry, Archdeacon of Who 94
Coventry, Bishop of 1930- Who 94
Coventry, Earl of 1934- Who 94
Coventry, Provost of Who 94
Coventry, Florence d1939 WhoHol 92
Coventry, John Seton 1915- IntWW 93,
  Who 94
Cover, Arthur Byron 1950- EncSF 93,
  WrDr 94
Cover, Eva Nast Timrud 1946- WhoFI 94
Cover, Franklin 1928- WhoAm 94
Cover, Franklin Edward 1928- WhoAm 94
Cover, Margaret Peery 1927- WhoAmP 93
Cover, Norman Bernard 1935- WhoFI 94
Coverdale, Gabriela 1963- WhoHisp 94
Coverdale, Herbert Linwood 1940-
  WhoBlA 94
Coverdale, Miles 1488-1568 BlmGEL
Coverdell, Paul 1939- CngDr 93
Coverdell, Paul D. WhoAm 94
Coverdell, Paul D. 1939- WhoAmP 93
Coverston, Harry Scott 1953- WhoAmL 94
Covert, Earl d1975 WhoHol 92
Covert, Eugene Edzards 1926- WhoAm 94,
  WhoScEn 94
Covert, John 1882-1960 WhoAmA 93N
Covert, Michael Henri 1949- WhoAm 94
Covey, Arthur 1878-1960 WhoAmA 93N
Covey, Charles William 1918- WhoAm 94
Covey, Cyclone 1922- WhoAm 94
Covey, F. Don 1934- WhoAm 94,
  WhoFI 94
Covey, Frank Michael, Jr. 1932-
  WhoAm 94, WhoFI 94
Covey, Harold D. 1930- WhoIns 94
Covey, Harold Dean 1930- WhoAm 94,
  WhoFI 94
Covey, Stephen Merrill Richards 1962-
  WhoWest 94
Covey, Stephen R. 1932- ConAu 41NR
Covey, Victor Charles B. 1928-1989
  WhoAmA 93N
Covi, Dario A. 1920- WhoAmA 93
Coviello, Robert Frank 1941- WhoFI 94
Covilha, Pedro Da c. 1460-c. 1540 WhWE
Coville, Bruce 1950- EncSF 93,
  SmATA 77 [port]
Coville, Christopher Charles Cotton
  1945- Who 94
Covin, David L. 1940- WhoBlA 94
Covin, David L(eroy) 1940- BlkWr 2
Covina, Gina DrAPF 93
Covington, Ann K. WhoAmP 93
Covington, Ann K. 1942- WhoAm 94,
  WhoAmL 94, WhoMW 93
Covington, Dean 1916- WhoAmP 93
Covington, George Morse 1942-
  WhoAm 94, WhoAmL 94
Covington, H. Douglas 1935- WhoBlA 94
Covington, Harrison Wall 1924-
  WhoAmA 93
Covington, James Arthur 1927-
  WhoBlA 94
Covington, James W. 1917- WrDr 94
Covington, John Ryland 1936- WhoBlA 94
Covington, Julie WhoHol 92
Covington, Kim Ann 1964- WhoBlA 94
Covington, M. Stanley 1937- WhoBlA 94
Covington, Marlow Stanley 1937-
  WhoAmL 94
Covington, Nicholas 1929- Who 94
Covington, Pamela Jean 1956- WhoAm 94
Covington, Patricia Ann 1946-
  WhoAm 94, WhoMW 93
Covington, Robert Geoffry 1949-
  WhoMW 93
Covington, Robert Newman 1936-
  WhoAm 94
Covington, Stephanie Stewart 1942-
  WhoScEn 94
Covington, Suzanne 1949- WhoAmL 94
Covington, Vicki 1952- WrDr 94
Covington, Willa Alma Greene 1902-
  WhoBlA 94
Covington, William Clyde, Jr. 1932-
  WhoAm 94
Covington, William Slaughter 1897-
  WhAm 10
Covington, Z. Wall d1941 WhoHol 92
Covington-Kent, Dawna Marie 1948-
  WhoMW 93

Covino, Benjamin Gene 1930-1991
  WhAm 10
Covino, Charles Peter 1923- WhoAm 94
Covino, Joseph, Jr. 1954- WhoWest 94
Covino, Michael DrAPF 93
Covino, Michael 1950- WrDr 94
Covino, Michael Angelo, Jr. 1953-
  WhoFI 94
Covitz, Carl D. 1939- WhoAm 94
Covone, James Michael 1948- WhoAm 94
Cowal, Sally G. 1944- WhoAmP 93
Cowal, Sally Grooms 1944- WhoAm 94
Cowan, Aileen Hooper 1926- WhoAmA 93
Cowan, Alan Who 94
Cowan, (James) Alan (Comrie) 1923-
  Who 94
Cowan, Andrew Glenn 1951- WhoAm 94
Cowan, Barton Zalman 1934- WhoAm 94
Cowan, Charles Donald 1923- Who 94
Cowan, Charles Gibbs 1928- WhoAm 94
Cowan, Colin Hunter 1920- Who 94
Cowan, Edward 1933- WhoAm 94
Cowan, Edward (James) 1944- WrDr 94
Cowan, Fairman Chaffee 1913-
  WhoAm 94
Cowan, Finis Ewing 1929- WhoAm 94
Cowan, Frank 1844-1905 EncSF 93
Cowan, Frederic J. 1945- WhoAmP 93
Cowan, Frederic Joseph 1945- WhoAm 94,
  WhoAmL 94
Cowan, George Arthur 1920- WhoAm 94,
  WhoFI 94, WhoScEn 94, WhoWest 94
Cowan, George Llewellyn 1931-
  WhoWest 94
Cowan, George T. 1951- WhoAmL 94
Cowan, Gordon 1933- WrDr 94
Cowan, Henry (Jacob) 1919- WrDr 94
Cowan, Henry Jacob 1919- WhoScEn 94
Cowan, Homer H., Jr. 1923- WhoIns 94
Cowan, Irving 1932- WhoAm 94
Cowan, J Milton 1907- WhoAm 94
Cowan, James 1870-1943 EncSF 93
Cowan, James C. 1927- WrDr 94
Cowan, James Donald, Jr. 1943-
  WhoAmL 94
Cowan, James Edington 1930-
  WhoWest 94
Cowan, James R. 1919- WhoBlA 94
Cowan, James Robertson 1919- Who 94
Cowan, James Spencer 1952- WhoAm 94
Cowan, Jeremy Who 94
Cowan, Jerome d1972 WhoHol 92
Cowan, Jerry Louis 1927- WhoAm 94
Cowan, Joel Harvey 1936- WhoAmP 93
Cowan, John Joseph 1932- WhoAmL 94
Cowan, John Stephen 1937- WhoMW 93
Cowan, John Willard 1935- WhoMW 93
Cowan, Larine Yvonne 1949- WhoBlA 94
Cowan, Lionel David 1929- Who 94
Cowan, Lynn P. d1973 WhoHol 92
Cowan, Mark Douglas 1949- WhoAm 94
Cowan, Martin B. 1935- WhoAm 94
Cowan, Mary Elizabeth 1907
  WhoScEn 94
Cowan, Michael John 1953- WhoScEn 94
Cowan, Nelson 1951- WhoScEn 94
Cowan, Patricia d1978 WhoHol 92
Cowan, Paul Earl 1946- WhoAmP 93
Cowan, Penelope Sims 1966- WhoScEn 94
Cowan, Penney Lee 1948- WhoWest 94
Cowan, Peter 1914- WrDr 94
Cowan, Peter (Walkinshaw) 1914-
  RfGShF
Cowan, Ralph Wolfe 1931- WhoAmA 93
Cowan, Richard 1957- NewGrDO,
  WhoAm 94
Cowan, Robert d1993 Who 94N
Cowan, Robert Jenkins 1937- WhoAm 94
Cowan, Rosalie 1912- WhoAmP 93
Cowan, Ruth Baldwin 1901-1993
  NewYTBS 93 [port]
Cowan, Stephen A. 1943- WhoAm 94,
  WhoAmL 94
Cowan, Stuart DuBois 1917- WhoAm 94
Cowan, Stuart Marshall 1932-
  WhoWest 94
Cowan, Susan Alison 1959- WhoWest 94
Cowan, Suzanne Trocinski 1951-
  WhoFI 94
Cowan, Ted M. 1940- WhoAmP 93
Cowan, Thaddeus McKelvey 1934-
  WhoMW 93
Cowan, Thomas F., Sr. 1927- WhoAmP 93
Cowan, Tom Keith 1916- WrDr 94
Cowan, Wallace Edgar 1924- WhoAm 94,
  WhoAmL 94
Cowan, Warren J. IntMPA 94
Cowan, William James 1919- Who 94
Cowan, William Maxwell 1931-
  IntWW 93, Who 94, WhoAm 94,
  WhoScEn 94
Cowan, William Walker 1963- WhoFI 94
Cowan, Woodson Messick 1886-1977
  WhoAmA 93N
Cowans, Alvin Jeffrey 1955- WhoBlA 94
Cowap, Charles Richardson 1931-1989
  WhAm 10
Coward, Barry 1941- WrDr 94

Coward, Curtis M. 1946- WhoAmL 94
Coward, David John 1917- Who 94
Coward, Denise 1958- WhoHol 92
Coward, Jasper Earl 1932- WhoBlA 94
Coward, John (Francis) 1937- Who 94
Coward, John Stephen 1937- Who 94
Coward, Noel d1973 WhoHol 92
Coward, Noel 1899-1973 BlmGEL, IntDcF 2-4 [port]
Coward, Noel (Pierce) 1899-1973 ConDr 93, IntDcT 2 [port], NewGrDO
Coward, Onida Lavoneia 1964- WhoBlA 94
Coward, Richard Edgar 1927- Who 94
Coward, Rosalind BlmGWL
Cowardin, Richard Murrel 1930- WhoWest 94
Cowart, Bill Frank 1932- WhoWest 94
Cowart, Elgin Courtland, Jr. 1923- WhoAm 94
Cowart, Jack 1945- WhoAm 94, WrDr 94
Cowart, Jim Cash 1951- WhoWest 94
Cowart, R. Greg 1956- WhoWest 94
Cowart, Thomas David 1953- WhoAm 94, WhoAmL 94
Cowasjee, Saros 1931- ConAu 43NR, WrDr 94
Cowburn, Norman 1920- Who 94
Cowden, James N. 1949- WhoAmL 94
Cowden, Jere Lee 1947- WhoAm 94, WhoFI 94
Cowden, Louis Fredrick 1929- WhoWest 94
Cowden, Michael E. 1951- WhoBlA 94
Cowden, Robert Laughlin 1933- WhoAm 94
Cowden, Ronald Reed 1931- WhoScEn 94
Cowderoy, Brenda 1925- Who 94
Cowdery, Robert Douglas 1926- WhoMW 93
Cowdray, Viscount 1910- IntWW 93, Who 94
Cowdrey, Colin Who 94
Cowdrey, (Michael) Colin 1932- IntWW 93, Who 94
Cowdrey, (Michael) Colin, Sir 1932- WrDr 94
Cowdrey, Herbert Edward John 1926- Who 94
Cowdrey, Mary Bartlett 1910-1974 WhoAmA 93N
Cowdry, Rex William 1947- WhoAm 94, WhoScEn 94
Cowe, (Robert George) Collin 1917- Who 94
Cowee, John Widmer 1918- WhoAm 94
Cowee, John Widmer, Jr. 1949- WhoWest 94
Cowell, Catherine 1921- WhoBlA 94
Cowell, Ernest Saul 1927- WhoWest 94
Cowell, Frank A WrDr 94
Cowell, Henry (Dixon) 1897-1965 NewGrDO
Cowell, John Richard 1933- Who 94
Cowell, Marion Aubrey, Jr. 1934- WhoAmL 94
Cowell, Raymond 1937- Who 94
Cowell, Ronald Raymond 1946- WhoAmP 93
Cowell, Stephanie Amy DrAPF 93
Cowen, Brian 1960- IntWW 93
Cowen, Bruce David 1953- WhoFI 94, WhoScEn 94
Cowen, Donald Eugene 1918- WhoScEn 94, WhoWest 94
Cowen, Edward S. 1936- WhoAm 94, WhoAmL 94
Cowen, Emory L. 1926- WhoAm 94
Cowen, Eugene Sherman 1925- WhoAm 94
Cowen, Frances 1915- WrDr 94
Cowen, Frederick Hymen 1852-1935 NewGrDO
Cowen, Joseph Eugene 1946- WhoScEn 94
Cowen, Robert E. 1930- WhoAm 94, WhoAmL 94, WhoAmP 93
Cowen, Robert Henry 1915- WhoAm 94
Cowen, Robert Nathan 1948- WhoAm 94
Cowen, Ron(ald) 1944- ConDr 93, WrDr 94
Cowen, Roy Chadwell, Jr. 1930- WhoAm 94
Cowen, Sonia Sue 1952- WhoWest 94
Cowen, Stanton Jonathan 1954- WhoScEn 94
Cowen, Wilson 1905- CngDr 93, WhoAm 94, WhoAmL 94
Cowen, Wilson Walker 1934-1987 WhAm 10
Cowen, Zelman 1919- IntWW 93, Who 94, WrDr 94
Cowenhoven, Garret Peter 1941- WhoAmP 93
Cowens, Alfred Edward, Jr. 1951- WhoBlA 94
Cowens, Dave 1948- BasBi
Cowens, David William 1948- WhoAm 94
Cowern, Nicholas Edward Benedict 1953- WhoScEn 94
Cowey, Alan 1935- Who 94
Cowey, Bernard Turing Vionnee 1911- Who 94
Cowgill, Bryan 1927- Who 94
Cowgill, Frank Brooks 1932- WhoAm 94
Cowgill, Jeffery William 1962- WhoMW 93
Cowgill, Nancy L. 1951- WhoAmL 94
Cowgill, Robert Lee, III 1947- WhoFI 94
Cowgill, Ursula Moser 1927- WhoAm 94, WhoScEn 94
Cowher, Bill 1957- WhoAm 94
Cowherd, Edwin Russell 1921- WhoAm 94
Cowhey, Peter Francis 1948- WhoWest 94
Cowhill, William Joseph 1928- WhoAm 94
Cowie, Hon. Lord 1926- Who 94
Cowie, Bruce Edgar 1938- WhoAm 94
Cowie, Catherine Christine 1953- WhoAm 94
Cowie, Donald (John) 1911- EncSF 93
Cowie, Edward 1943- NewGrDO
Cowie, Hamilton Russell 1931- WrDr 94
Cowie, Laura d1969 WhoHol 92
Cowie, Lennox Lauchlan 1950- WhoAm 94
Cowie, Leonard Wallace 1919- WrDr 94
Cowie, Mervyn 1909- WrDr 94
Cowie, Mervyn Hugh 1909- Who 94
Cowie, Thomas 1922- Who 94
Cowie, William Lorn Kerr Who 94
Cowin, Eileen 1947- WhoAmA 93
Cowin, Stephen Corteen 1934- WhoAm 94, WhoScEn 94
Cowing, Paul D. 1950- WhoAmL 94
Cowing, Sheila DrAPF 93
Cowing, Thomas William 1951- WhoScEn 94
Cowings, Everett Alvin 1963- WhoWest 94
Cowings, John Sherman 1943- AfrAmG [port]
Cowl, Darry 1925- WhoHol 92
Cowl, George d1942 WhoHol 92
Cowl, Jane d1950 WhoHol 92
Cowles, Charles 1941- WhoAm 94, WhoAmA 93
Cowles, Chauncey D. 1911- WhoIns 94
Cowles, David William 1954- WhoWest 94
Cowles, Donald Thurston 1947- WhoAmL 94
Cowles, Fleur WhoAm 94, WhoAmA 93, WrDr 94
Cowles, Frederick Oliver 1937- WhoAm 94
Cowles, Gardner, Jr. 1903-1985 DcLB 137 [port]
Cowles, Joe Richard 1941- WhoAm 94
Cowles, John, Jr. 1929- WhoAm 94
Cowles, Jules d1943 WhoHol 92
Cowles, Julia 1785-1803 BlmGWL
Cowles, Matthew WhoHol 92
Cowles, Michael David 1965- WhoMW 93
Cowles, Milly 1932- WhoAm 94
Cowles, Robert L., III 1950- WhoAmP 93
Cowles, Roger William 1945- WhoAm 94
Cowles, Ronald Eugene 1941- WhoMW 93
Cowles, Russell 1887-1979 WhoAmA 93N
Cowles, William Hutchinson, III 1932-1992 WhAm 10
Cowles, William Stacey 1960- WhoFI 94
Cowley, Earl 1934- Who 94
Cowley, Abraham 1618-1667 BlmGEL, DcLB 131 [port]
Cowley, Abraham 1816-1887 EncNAR
Cowley, Alan H. IntWW 93
Cowley, Alan Herbert 1934- Who 94
Cowley, Benjamin Dollar 1956- WhoMW 93
Cowley, Cassia Joy 1936- BlmGWL
Cowley, Colin Patrick d1993 Who 94N
Cowley, Edward P. 1925- WhoAmA 93
Cowley, Eric d1948 WhoHol 92
Cowley, Gerald Dean 1931- WhoFI 94
Cowley, Hannah 1743-1809 BlmGEL
Cowley, Hannah (Parkhouse) 1743-1809 BlmGWL
Cowley, John WhoHol 92
Cowley, John Cain 1918- Who 94
Cowley, John Guise d1993 Who 94N
Cowley, John Maxwell 1923- IntWW 93, Who 94, WhoAm 94, WhoScEn 94
Cowley, Joseph DrAPF 93
Cowley, Kenneth Martin 1912- Who 94
Cowley, Malcolm 1898-1989 WhAm 10
Cowley, R. Adams 1917-1991 WhAm 10
Cowley, Roger A. 1939- IntWW 93
Cowley, Roger Arthur 1939- Who 94
Cowley, Scott West 1945- WhoScEn 94
Cowley, William Eugene 1909- WhoAm 94
Cowling, Bruce d1986 WhoHol 92
Cowling, David Edward 1951- WhoAm 94, WhoAmL 94
Cowling, Gareth Who 94
Cowling, (Thomas) Gareth 1944- Who 94
Cowling, James Roy 1940- Who 94
Cowling, Maurice John 1926- Who 94
Cowlishaw, Mary Lou 1932- WhoAmP 93, WhoMW 93
Cowman, Roz 1942- BlmGWL
Cowman, William Henry 1910- WhoAmP 93
Cownie, John Bowler 1940- WhAm 10
Cowper, Edward Alfred 1819-1893 DcNaB MP
Cowper, Gerry 1958- WhoHol 92
Cowper, Nicola WhoHol 92
Cowper, Richard 1926- EncSF 93, WrDr 94
Cowper, Stephen Cambreleng 1938- WhoAmP 93
Cowper, Steve Cambreleng 1938- IntWW 93
Cowper, William 1731-1800 BlmGEL [port]
Cowper, William C. d1918 WhoHol 92
Cowperthwaite, David Jarvis 1921- Who 94
Cowperthwaite, John James 1915- Who 94
Cowser, Danny Lee 1948- WhoAmL 94
Cowser, Robert DrAPF 93
Cowsik, Ramanath 1940- WhoScEn 94
Cowtan, Frank Willoughby John 1920- Who 94
Cox Who 94
Cox, Baroness 1937- Who 94, WhoWomW 91
Cox, Adrian EncSF 93
Cox, Alan 1970- WhoHol 92
Cox, Alan George 1936- Who 94
Cox, Alan Seaforth 1915- Who 94
Cox, Albert Harrington, Jr. 1932- WhoAm 94
Cox, Albert Reginald 1928- WhoAm 94
Cox, Alex 1954- IntMPA 94
Cox, Alfred Bertram 1902- WrDr 94
Cox, Alister Stransom 1934- Who 94
Cox, Allan James 1937- WhoAm 94
Cox, Allyn 1896-1982 WhoAmA 93N
Cox, Alvin Earl 1918- WhoAm 94
Cox, Alvin Joseph, Jr. 1907-1990 WhAm 10
Cox, Andrew Hood 1917- WhoAmL 94
Cox, Andrew Paul, Jr. 1937- WhoFI 94
Cox, Ann Bruger WhoAm 94
Cox, Anthony Who 94
Cox, (James) Anthony 1924- Who 94
Cox, Anthony Robert 1938- Who 94
Cox, Anthony Wakefield d1993 Who 94N
Cox, Archibald 1912- IntWW 93, Who 94, WhoAm 94, WhoAmP 93, WrDr 94
Cox, Archibald, Jr. 1940- Who 94, WhoAm 94, WhoFI 94
Cox, Arthur Dean 1961- WhoBlA 94
Cox, Arthur George Ernest S. Who 94
Cox, Arthur James, Sr. 1943- WhoBlA 94
Cox, Arthur Nelson 1927- WhoWest 94
Cox, Barbara Roose 1951- WhoAm 94
Cox, Beau WhoHol 92
Cox, Beverly E. WhoMW 93
Cox, Bobby 1941- WhoAm 94
Cox, Brian Who 94
Cox, Brian 1946- WhoHol 92
Cox, (Charles) Brian 1928- Who 94
Cox, Brian Dennis 1946- Who 94
Cox, Brian (Robert) Escott 1932- Who 94
Cox, Carol DrAPF 93
Cox, Cathy 1958- WhoAmP 93
Cox, Chad William 1949- WhoScEn 94
Cox, Chapman Beecher 1940- WhoAm 94, WhoAmP 93
Cox, Charles Anthony 1957- WhoMW 93
Cox, Charles Brian 1928- WrDr 94
Cox, Charles C. 1945- WhoAm 94, WhoMW 93
Cox, Charles Raymond 1891-1962 EncABHB 9 [port]
Cox, Charles Shipley 1922- WhoAm 94, WhoScEn 94, WhoWest 94
Cox, Charles Wesley 1918-1992 WhAm 10
Cox, Christopher 1952- CngDr 93, WhoAm 94, WhoAmP 93, WhoWest 94
Cox, Christopher Barry 1931- Who 94, WrDr 94
Cox, Clair Edward, II 1933- WhoAm 94
Cox, Clifford Ernest 1942- WhoFI 94, WhoMW 93
Cox, Clifford Laird 1935- WhoAm 94
Cox, Clinton SmATA 74
Cox, Corine 1944- WhoBlA 94
Cox, Courteney 1964- IntMPA 94, WhoHol 92
Cox, Cynthia Lee 1960- WhoAmL 94
Cox, Dallas Wendell, Jr. 1943- WhoAmL 94
Cox, Daniel Dean 1968- WhoMW 93
Cox, Daniel Thomas 1946- WhoIns 94
Cox, David (Roxbee) 1924- IntWW 93, Who 94
Cox, David Brummal 1940- WhoAm 94
Cox, David Carson 1937- WhoAm 94, WhoMW 93
Cox, David G. 1958- WhoAmL 94
Cox, David H. 1952- WhoAm 94
Cox, David Jackson 1934- WhoAm 94
Cox, David Leon 1952- WhoScEn 94
Cox, David S. 1942- WhoIns 94
Cox, David W. 1951- WhoAmP 93
Cox, David Willis Frank 1923- WhoMW 93
Cox, Dennis George 1914- Who 94
Cox, Dennis Joseph 1951- WhoScEn 94
Cox, Dianne Fitzgerald 1951- WhoBlA 94
Cox, Donald Clyde 1937- WhoAm 94, WhoScEn 94
Cox, Douglas Charles 1944- WhoWest 94
Cox, Douglas Lynn 1945- WhoAm 94, WhoFI 94
Cox, Duane L. 1940- WhoWest 94
Cox, DuBois V. 1950- WhoBlA 94
Cox, E. Morris 1903- WhoAmA 93
Cox, Ebbie Lee 1927- WhoAm 94
Cox, Ed DrAPF 93
Cox, Edward Charles 1937- WhoAm 94
Cox, Elbert Frank 1895-1969 AfrAmAl 6
Cox, Elizabeth 1942- WrDr 94
Cox, Elizabeth 1953- WrDr 94
Cox, Emmett R. WhoAmP 93
Cox, Emmett Ripley 1935- WhoAm 94, WhoAmL 94
Cox, Erle 1873-1950 EncSF 93
Cox, Ernest Lee 1937- WhoAmA 93
Cox, Euola Wilson WhoBlA 94
Cox, Exum Morris 1903- WhoAm 94
Cox, Frank D. 1932- WhoScEn 94
Cox, Frederick Moreland 1928- WhoAm 94
Cox, Gary Evans 1937- WhoWest 94
Cox, Geoffrey (Sandford) 1910- Who 94
Cox, Geoffrey (Sandford), Sir 1910- WrDr 94
Cox, George Wyatt 1935- WhoWest 94
Cox, Georgetta Manning 1947- WhoBlA 94
Cox, Geraldine Vang 1944- WhoAm 94
Cox, Gilbert Edwin 1917- WhoAm 94
Cox, Gladys M. 1911- WhoAmP 93
Cox, Glenda Evonne 1937- WhoAmL 94
Cox, Glenn A. 1929- IntWW 93
Cox, Glenn Andrew, Jr. 1929- WhoAm 94
Cox, Gordon Who 94
Cox, (Ernest) Gordon 1906- IntWW 93, Who 94
Cox, Graham Campbell 1932- IntWW 93
Cox, Gregory Richardson 1948- WhoAmP 93
Cox, Hannibal Maceo, Jr. 1923- WhoBlA 94
Cox, Hardin Charles 1928- WhoAmP 93
Cox, Harry Seymour 1923- WhoAm 94
Cox, Harvey 1929- WrDr 94
Cox, Harvey Gallagher, Jr. 1929- AmSocL
Cox, Headley Morris, Jr. 1916- WhoAm 94
Cox, Henry 1935- WhoAm 94
Cox, Henry Reid 1956- WhoAmL 94
Cox, Herbert Bartle 1944- WhoAm 94
Cox, Hollace Lawton 1935- WhoScEn 94
Cox, Hollis Utah 1944- WhoAm 94
Cox, Horace B. T. Who 94
Cox, Howard Ellis, Jr. 1944- WhoAm 94
Cox, J. Halley 1910- WhoAmA 93N
Cox, J. William 1928- WhoAm 94
Cox, James 1753-1810 WhAmRev
Cox, James Carl, Jr. 1919- WhoFI 94, WhoScEn 94
Cox, James Clarence 1929- WhoAm 94
Cox, James Darrell 1950- WhoAmL 94
Cox, James David 1945- WhoAm 94
Cox, James Grady 1949- WhoScEn 94
Cox, James L. 1922- WhoBlA 94
Cox, James Oliver, III 1946- WhoAm 94
Cox, James Steven 1958- WhoAmP 93
Cox, James Talley 1921- WhoAm 94
Cox, James William 1937- WhoAm 94
Cox, Jean 1922- NewGrDO
Cox, Jeffery WhoAmP 93
Cox, Jennie Palmero 1940- WhoAmP 93
Cox, Jeralynn Lee 1944- WhoAmL 94
Cox, Jerome Rockhold, Jr. 1925- WhoAm 94
Cox, Jesse L. 1946- WhoBlA 94
Cox, Jim 1934- WhoAmP 93
Cox, Joan (Irene) 1942- EncSF 93
Cox, John WhoAmP 93, WhoHol 92
Cox, John 1935- NewGrDO, Who 94
Cox, John (Michael Holland) 1928- Who 94
Cox, John C. 1950- WhoAmL 94
Cox, John Colin Leslie 1933- Who 94
Cox, John D. 1945- WhoMW 93
Cox, John David 1964- WhoAmP 93
Cox, John F. WhoAmP 93
Cox, John Francis 1929- WhoAm 94
Cox, John Frederick 1955- WhoWest 94
Cox, John Jeffrey 1954- WhoAmP 93
Cox, John Robert 1945- WhoWest 94
Cox, John Thomas, Jr. 1943- WhoAmL 94

Cox, John Wesley 1929- WhoBlA 94
Cox, Joseph King 1950- WhoAmL 94
Cox, Joseph Lawrence 1932- WhoAmL 94
Cox, Joseph Mason Andrew 1930- WhoBlA 94
Cox, Joseph William 1937- WhoAm 94, WhoWest 94
Cox, Kathryn Cullen 1943- WhoWest 94
Cox, Keith Gordon 1933- Who 94
Cox, Kenneth Allen 1916- WhoAm 94
Cox, Kenneth Roger 1928- WhoAmP 93
Cox, Kevin C. 1949- WhoBlA 94
Cox, Kevin Creuzot 1949- WhoAmP 93
Cox, Kevin Robert 1939- WrDr 94
Cox, Kim Carroll 1955- WhoAmP 93
Cox, Lester Lee 1922- WhoAm 94
Cox, Lewis Calvin 1924- WhoAmL 94
Cox, Loren Charles 1938- WhoAmP 93
Cox, M. Maurice 1951- WhoBlA 94
Cox, Marilyn Butler 1946- WhoWest 94
Cox, Marion Averal WhoAmA 93
Cox, Marjorie Herrmann 1918- WhoAmP 93
Cox, Mark DrAPF 93
Cox, Mark 1943- BuCMET
Cox, Mark Edward 1959- WhoMW 93
Cox, Mark Lewis 1957- WhoMW 93
Cox, Marshall 1932- WhoAm 94
Cox, Marvin Kirkland 1957- WhoAmP 93
Cox, Marvin Melvin, Jr. 1953- WhoFI 94
Cox, Mary E. 1937- WhoMW 93
Cox, Mary Linda 1946- WhoMW 93
Cox, Mencea Ethereal 1906- Who 94
Cox, Meridith Brittan 1941- WhoWest 94
Cox, Merrill Anthony 1952- WhoAmP 93
Cox, Michael Graham 1938- WhoHol 92
Cox, Michael Matthew 1952- WhoMW 93
Cox, Mitchel Neal 1956- WhoAm 94
Cox, Murray Glenn WhoFI 94
Cox, Myron Keith 1926- WhoMW 93
Cox, Norman Ernest 1921- Who 94
Cox, Norman Roy 1949- WhoScEn 94
Cox, Oliver Jasper 1920- Who 94
Cox, Otha P. WhoBlA 94
Cox, Otis Edward 1941- WhoAmP 93
Cox, Otis Graham, Jr. 1941- WhoBlA 94
Cox, Owen Devol 1910- WhAm 10
Cox, Patricia Ann 1931- Who 94
Cox, Patricia Anne Who 94
Cox, Paul 1940- ConTFT 11, IntWW 93
Cox, Paul William 1957- Who 94
Cox, Peter Arthur 1922- Who 94
Cox, Peter Denzil John H. Who 94
Cox, Peter Frederick 1945- Who 94
Cox, Peter Richmond 1914- Who 94
Cox, Philip (Joseph) 1922- Who 94
Cox, Philip Sutton 1939- IntWW 93
Cox, Randy J. 1953- WhoAmL 94
Cox, Ray L. WhoAmP 93
Cox, Raymond Whitten, III 1949- WhoWest 94
Cox, Richard c. 1776-1845 DcNaB MP
Cox, Richard 1949- WhoHol 92
Cox, Richard (Hubert Francis) 1931 WrDr 94
Cox, Richard Charles 1920- Who 94
Cox, Richard D. 1951- WhoAmL 94
Cox, Richard Horton 1920- WhoAm 94
Cox, Richard Joseph 1929- WhoAm 94
Cox, Richard William 1942- WhoAmA 93
Cox, Robert d1974 WhoHol 92
Cox, Robert De Lafayette 1934- WhoHisp 94
Cox, Robert Gene 1929- WhoAm 94
Cox, Robert Hames 1923- WhoScEn 94
Cox, Robert Harold 1937- WhoScEn 94
Cox, Robert L. 1933- WhoBlA 94
Cox, Robert M., Jr. 1945- WhoFI 94
Cox, Robert O. 1917- WhoAmP 93
Cox, Robert Osborne 1917- WhoAm 94
Cox, Robert Sayre, Jr. 1925- WhoAm 94
Cox, Robert Winfred 1937- WhoAmL 94
Cox, Rody Powell 1926- WhoAm 94
Cox, Roger (Kenneth) 1936- WrDr 94
Cox, Roger Charles 1941- Who 94
Cox, Roger Frazier 1939- WhoAm 94, WhoAmL 94
Cox, Roger L. 1931- WrDr 94
Cox, Ronald Baker 1943- WhoAm 94
Cox, Ronald E. 1945- WhoAmL 94
Cox, Ronnie 1952- WhoBlA 94
Cox, Ronny 1938- IntMPA 94, WhoHol 92
Cox, Roy Arthur 1925- Who 94
Cox, Sammie Tyree 1943- WhoAm 94
Cox, Sandra Hicks 1939- WhoBlA 94
Cox, Sanford Curtis, Jr. 1929- WhoAmL 94
Cox, Shenikwa Nowlin NewYTBS 93 [port]
Cox, Shirley Ann 1950- WhoAmL 94
Cox, Stanley Brian 1949- WhoAmP 93, WhoMW 93
Cox, Stephen (LeRoy) 1966- WrDr 94
Cox, Stephen James 1946- Who 94
Cox, Stephen Joseph 1946- IntWW 93
Cox, Steven Mark 1949- WhoMW 93
Cox, Sue Green 1940- WhoAmP 93
Cox, Susie 1949- AstEnc, WhoWest 94
Cox, Taylor H., Sr. 1926- WhoBlA 94
Cox, Terrence Guy 1956- WhoFI 94, WhoScEn 94
Cox, Terry Allen 1939- WhoAm 94
Cox, Thomas A. 1951- WhoAmL 94
Cox, Thomas J., Jr. 1935- WhoAmP 93
Cox, Thomas Michael 1930- Who 94
Cox, Thomas Patrick 1946- WhoScEn 94
Cox, Timothy Martin 1948- Who 94
Cox, Trenchard 1905- IntWW 93, Who 94
Cox, (George) Trenchard Who 94
Cox, Velma Jean 1933- WhoAmP 93
Cox, Verne Caperton 1938- WhoScEn 94
Cox, Wally d1973 WhoHol 92
Cox, Wally 1924-1973 WhoCom
Cox, Walter Thompson, III 1942- CngDr 93, WhoAm 94, WhoAmL 94
Cox, Warren E. 1936- WhoBlA 94
Cox, Warren Jacob 1935- IntWW 93, WhoAm 94
Cox, Wendell 1914- WhoBlA 94
Cox, Wendell 1944- WhoMW 93
Cox, Whitson William 1921- WhoAm 94
Cox, Wilford Donald 1925- WhoAm 94
Cox, William Andrew 1925- WhoAm 94, WhoScEn 94
Cox, William Donald, Jr. 1957- WhoAmL 94
Cox, William Harvey, Jr. 1942- WhoAmP 93
Cox, William Jackson 1921- WhoAm 94
Cox, William Martin 1922- WhoAmL 94
Cox, William Stanley, III 1962- WhoAmL 94
Cox, William Trevor Who 94
Cox, William V. 1936- WhoAmL 94
Cox, William Walter 1947- WhoScEn 94
Cox, Winston H. 1941- WhoFI 94
Cox, Zainab Nagin 1965- WhoWest 94
Coxe, Daniel 1640-1730 DcNaB MP
Coxe, Daniel 1741-1826 WhAmRev
Coxe, G. Caliman 1908- WhoBlA 94
Coxe, Louis DrAPF 93
Coxe, Louis (Osborne) 1918- WrDr 94
Coxe, Louis O. d1993 NewYTBS 93 [port]
Coxe, Tench 1755-1824 WhAmRev
Coxe, Tench Charles 1925- WhoAm 94, WhoAmL 94
Coxe, Thomas C., III 1930- WhoFI 94
Coxe, Weld 1929- WhoAm 94
Coxe, William Haddon 1920- WhoBlA 94
Coxen, Ed d1954 WhoHol 92
Coxen, Gervis 1937- WhoFI 94
Coxeter, Harold Scott MacDonald 1907- IntWW 93, Who 94, WhoAm 94, WrDr 94
Coxey, Jacob Sechler 1854-1951 AmSocL [port]
Coxhead, George Leavell 1920- WhoAmP 93
Cox-Johnson, Ann 1930- WrDr 94
Cox-Murphy, Sarah Joann 1933- WhoAmP 93
Coxon, Michele 1950- SmATA 76 [port]
Cox-Pursley, Carol Sue 1951- WhoFI 94
Cox-Rawles, Rani 1927- WhoBlA 94
Coxwell-Rogers, Richard Annesley 1932- Who 94
Coy, Charles Russell 1926- WhoAmP 93
Coy, David DrAPF 93
Coy, George Somerville 1943- WhoAmP 93
Coy, Jeffrey Wayne 1951- WhoAmP 93
Coy, John T. 1939- WhoBlA 94
Coy, Johnny d1973 WhoHol 92
Coy, Patricia Ann 1952- WhoMW 93
Coy, Robert Earl 1931- WhoAmL 94
Coy, Walter d1974 WhoHol 92
Coy, William Raymond 1923- WhoScEn 94
Coye, Dena E. WhoBlA 94
Coyer, Max R. 1954-1988 WhoAmA 93N
Coykendall, Alan Littlefield 1937- WhoScEn 94
Coyle, Beverly (Jones) 1946- WrDr 94
Coyle, Dennis Patrick 1938- WhoAmL 94, WhoFI 94
Coyle, Eurfron Gwynne Who 94
Coyle, Harold (W.) 1952- ConAu 140
Coyle, Harold William 1952- WhoAm 94
Coyle, John d1964 WhoHol 92
Coyle, Joseph William d1993 NewYTBS 93
Coyle, Marie Bridget 1935- WhoAm 94
Coyle, Marion J. d1981 WhoHol 92
Coyle, Martin Adolphus, Jr. 1941- WhoAm 94, WhoAmL 94, WhoFI 94, WhoMW 93
Coyle, Mary Dee 1916- WhoBlA 94
Coyle, Michael Lee 1944- WhoAmL 94
Coyle, Michele C. 1951- WhoAmL 94
Coyle, Robert Everett 1930- WhoAm 94, WhoAmL 94, WhoWest 94
Coyle, Terence 1925- WhoAmA 93
Coyle, William 1917- WhoAm 94
Coyne, Bill WhoHol 92
Coyne, Brian D. 1959- WhoAmP 93
Coyne, Charles Cole 1948- WhoAmL 94
Coyne, Frank J. 1948- WhoAm 94
Coyne, James Elliott 1910- Who 94
Coyne, James K. 1946- WhoAmP 93
Coyne, James K(itchenman) 1946- ConAu 141
Coyne, James Oliver 1928- WhoFI 94
Coyne, Jeanne d1973 WhoHol 92
Coyne, John Martin 1916- WhoAmP 93
Coyne, John Michael 1950- WhoAmA 93
Coyne, Lolafaye F. 1926- WhoMW 93
Coyne, M. Jeanne 1926- WhoAmL 94, WhoAmP 93, WhoMW 93
Coyne, Mary Downey 1938- WhoAm 94
Coyne, Michael Patrick 1952- WhoAmL 94
Coyne, Nancy Carol 1949- WhoAm 94
Coyne, Patrick Ivan 1944- WhoAm 94, WhoScEn 94
Coyne, Petah E. 1953- WhoAmA 93
Coyne, Robert Patrick 1961- WhoAmL 94
Coyne, Thomas Joseph 1933- WhoAm 94
Coyne, William J. 1936- CngDr 93
Coyne, William Joseph 1934- WhoAmL 94
Coyne, William Joseph 1936- WhoAm 94, WhoAmP 93
Coyote, Peter 1941- WhoHol 92
Coyote, Peter 1942- IntMPA 94, WhoAm 94
Coyro, William Frederick, Jr. 1943- WhoHisp 94
Coz, Mary Kathleen 1952- WhoMW 93
Cozad, James W. 1927- WhoAm 94
Cozad, James William 1927- IntWW 93
Cozad, John Condon 1944- WhoAmL 94
Cozan, Lee WhoAm 94
Cozart, Bert C. 1965- WhoWest 94
Cozart, John 1928- WhoBlA 94
Coze-Dabija, Paul 1903-1975 WhoAmA 93N
Cozen, Lewis 1911- WhoAm 94, WhoWest 94
Cozen, Stephen Allen 1939- WhoAm 94, WhoAmL 94
Cozens, (Florence) Barbara 1906- Who 94
Cozens, Henry Iliffe 1904- Who 94
Cozens, Peter d1968 WhoHol 92
Cozens, Richard 1952- WhoWest 94
Cozens, Robert William 1927- Who 94
Cozens, Thomas Joseph 1958- WhoFI 94
Cozine, Ann 1941- WhoAmP 93
Cozmo-Th'-Mystik DrAPF 93
Cozort, Amber Lynne 1963- WhoMW 93
Cozort, H. Wayne 1931- WhoAmP 93
Cozzarelli, Nicholas R. 1938- WhoScEn 94
Cozzens, Peter 1957- ConAu 140
Cozzi, Hugo Louis 1934- WhoAm 94
Cozzi, Joanne WhoAm 94
Cozzi, Ronald Lee 1943- WhoFI 94
Craane, Janine Lee 1961- WhoHisp 94
Crabb, Allan Edward 1933- WhoMW 93
Crabb, Barbara Brandriff 1939- WhoAm 94, WhoAmL 94, WhoMW 93
Crabb, Carol Ann 1944- WhoWest 94
Crabb, Delbert Elmo 1916- WhoAmP 93
Crabb, Frederick Hugh Wright 1915- Who 94
Crabb, Henry Stuart Malcolm 1922- WrDr 94
Crabb, Jeremiah 1760-1800 WhAmRev
Crabb, Joe 1939- WhoAmP 93
Crabb, Kenneth Wayne 1950- WhoMW 93
Crabb, Patrick Shia 1947- WhoWest 94
Crabb, Robert James 1949- WhoWest 94
Crabb, Tony William 1933- Who 94
Crabbe, Armand (Charles) 1883-1947 NewGrDO
Crabbe, George 1754-1832 BlmGEL, NewGrDO
Crabbe, John Crozier 1914- WhoAm 94
Crabbe, John Roth 1906- WhAm 10
Crabbe, Katharyn W. 1945- WrDr 94
Crabbe, Kenneth Herbert Martineau 1916- Who 94
Crabbe, Larry d1983 WhoHol 92
Crabbe, Pauline 1914- Who 94
Crabbe, Reginald James Williams 1909- Who 94
Crabbe, Samuel Azu 1918- IntWW 93
Crabbie, Christopher Donald 1946- Who 94
Crabbie, (Margaret) Veronica 1910- Who 94
Crabbs, Roger Alan 1928- WhoAm 94, WhoWest 94
Crable, Dallas Eugene 1927- WhoBlA 94
Crable, Deborah J. 1957- WhoBlA 94
Crable, James Harbour 1939- WhoAmA 93
Crabs, Donald Benjamin 1926- WhoWest 94
Crabtree, Aubrey 1898- WhAm 10
Crabtree, Beverly June 1937- WhoAm 94
Crabtree, Bruce Isbester, Jr. 1923- WhoAm 94
Crabtree, Bruce Isbester, III 1951- WhoAmL 94
Crabtree, Burnie R. WhoAmP 93
Crabtree, Derek Thomas 1930- Who 94
Crabtree, Garvin Dudley 1929- WhoWest 94
Crabtree, Jack Turner 1936- WhoAm 94
Crabtree, James L. 1947- WhoFI 94
Crabtree, John David 1947- WhoFI 94, WhoMW 93
Crabtree, John Henry, Jr. 1925- WhoAm 94
Crabtree, Jonathan 1934- Who 94
Crabtree, Judith 1928- ConAu 42NR
Crabtree, Lewis Frederick 1924- Who 94, WhoScEn 94
Crabtree, Paul d1979 WhoHol 92
Crabtree, Ray S. 1935- WhoIns 94
Crabtree, Robert H. 1948- IntWW 93
Crabtree, Robert Howard 1948- WhoScEn 94
Crabtree, Simon Who 94
Crabtree, Vivian Sucher 1923- WhoWest 94
Cracco, Roger Quinlan 1934- WhoAm 94
Crace, Jim 1946- WrDr 94
Cracium, John Odie 1944- WhoMW 93
Crackanthorpe, Hubert 1870-1896 DcLB 135 [port]
Crackel, Theodore Joseph 1938- WhoAm 94
Cracken, Jael EncSF 93
Cracknell, Basil Edward 1925- WrDr 94
Cracknell, Malcolm Thomas 1943- Who 94
Cracknell, (William) Martin 1929- Who 94
Cracknell, Ruth 1925- WhoHol 92
Cracroft, Peter Dicken 1907- Who 94
Craddick, Donald Lee 1932- WhoAmP 93
Craddick, Thomas Russell 1943- WhoAmP 93
Craddock, (William) Aleck 1924- Who 94
Craddock, Campbell 1930- WhoAm 94, WhoMW 93
Craddock, Charles Egbert BlmGWL
Craddock, Claudia d1945 WhoHol 92
Craddock, Fred B(renning) 1928- WrDr 94
Craddock, Mariam Narcissa 1897- WhAm 10
Craddock, Robert Glen 1931- WhoAmP 93
Craddock, Shirley Anne 1934- WhoAmP 93
Craddock, Thomas Wofford 1946- WhoAmL 94
Cradock, John Anthony 1921- Who 94
Cradock, Percy 1923- IntWW 93, Who 94
Cradock-Hartopp, J. E. Who 94
Crady, George 1931- WhoAmP 93
Craft, Benjamin Cole, III 1955- WhoScEn 94
Craft, David Ralph 1945- WhoAmA 93
Craft, David Walton 1957- WhoScEn 94
Craft, Donald Bruce 1935- WhoAm 94
Craft, Douglas D. 1924- WhoAmA 93
Craft, Douglas Durwood 1924- WhoAm 94
Craft, E. Carrie 1928- WhoBlA 94
Craft, Edmund Coleman 1939- WhoAm 94
Craft, Guy Calvin 1929- WhoBlA 94
Craft, Harold Dumont, Jr. 1938- WhoAm 94
Craft, Ian Logan 1937- Who 94
Craft, John Charles 1938- WhoAmL 94
Craft, John Edward 1943- WhoWest 94
Craft, John Richard 1909- WhoAmA 93
Craft, Joseph W., III WhoFI 94
Craft, Maurice 1932- Who 94
Craft, Randal Robert, Jr. 1941- WhoAm 94, WhoAmL 94
Craft, Robbie Wright 1951- WhoWest 94
Craft, Robert 1923- WrDr 94
Craft, Robert Homan 1906- WhoAm 94
Craft, Robert Homan, Jr. 1939- WhoAm 94, WhoAmL 94
Craft, Rolf V. 1937- WhoAmP 93
Craft, Ruth 1935- WrDr 94
Craft, Sally-Ann Roberts 1953- WhoBlA 94
Craft, Thomas J., Sr. 1924- WhoBlA 94
Craft, Timothy George 1960- WhoScEn 94
Crafton, Richard Douglas 1932- WhoAm 94
Crafts, Alden Springer 1897-1990 WhAm 10
Crafts, Griffin d1973 WhoHol 92
Crafts, Nicholas Francis Robert 1949- Who 94
Cragg, Anthony Douglas 1949- IntWW 93, Who 94
Cragg, Anthony John 1943- Who 94
Cragg, Ernest Elliott 1927- WhoAm 94
Cragg, Gordon Mitchell 1936- WhoScEn 94
Cragg, James Birkett 1910- Who 94
Cragg, Kenneth Who 94

Crampton, Howard d1922 *WhoHol 92*
Crampton, Mary *BlmGWL*
Crampton, Peter Duncan 1932- *Who 94*
Crampton, Rollin 1886-1970 *WhoAmA 93N*
Crampton, Scott Paul 1913- *WhoAm 94*
Crampton, (Arthur Edward) Sean 1918- *Who 94*
Crampton, Stuart Jessup Bigelow 1936- *WhoAm 94*
Crampton, Tom *BlmGWL*
Crampton, William DeVer 1920- *WhoAm 94*
Crampton Smith, Alex *Who 94*
Cramton, Roger Conant 1929- *WhoAm 94*
Cran, James Douglas 1944- *Who 94*
Cran, Mark Dyson Gordon 1948- *Who 94*
Cranborne, Viscount 1591-1668 *DcNaB MP*
Cranborne, Viscount 1946- *Who 94*
Cranbrook, Earl of 1933- *Who 94*
Cranch, Elizabeth 1743-1811 *BlmGWL*
Crandall, Brian Douglas 1965- *WhoMW 93*
Crandall, Christian Stuart 1959- *WhoScEn 94*
Crandall, David Hugh 1942- *WhoScEn 94*
Crandall, Edward d1968 *WhoHol 92*
Crandall, Edward David 1938- *WhoAm 94*
Crandall, Ira Carlton 1931- *WhoAm 94*
Crandall, Jerry C. 1935- *WhoAmA 93*
Crandall, John Lynn 1927- *WhoFI 94*
Crandall, Judith Ann 1948- *WhoAmA 93*
Crandall, Kathleen M. 1943- *WhoWest 94*
Crandall, Lee Walter 1913- *WhoAm 94*
Crandall, Loree Yoko Yamada 1964- *WhoWest 94*
Crandall, Nancy 1940- *WhoAmP 93*
Crandall, Nancy Lee 1940- *WhoAm 94*
Crandall, Nelson David, III 1954- *WhoAmL 94*
Crandall, Norma (Rand) *WrDr 94*
Crandall, Richard Eugene 1947- *WhoAm 94*
Crandall, Robert *NewYTBS 93 [port]*
Crandall, Robert Earl 1917- *WhoWest 94*
Crandall, Robert Lloyd 1935- *IntWW 93, WhoAm 94, WhoFI 94*
Crandall, Stephen Harry 1920- *WhoAm 94, WhoScEn 94*
Crandall, Theodore David 1955- *WhoFI 94*
Crandell, Bradshaw d1966 *WhoAmA 93N*
Crandell, Dwight Samuel 1943- *WhoMW 93*
Crandell, Jodie Leigh 1959- *WhoMW 93*
Crandell, Judith Speizer *DrAPF 93*
Crandell, Kenneth James 1957- *WhoAm 94, WhoFI 94*
Crandell, William Dean 1950- *WhoWest 94*
Crandles, George Marshal 1917- *WhoAm 94*
Crandon, John Howland 1912- *WhoAm 94*
Crane, A. Stoddard 1947- *WhoMW 93*
Crane, Andrew B. 1946- *WhoAm 94*
Crane, Barbara Bachmann 1928- *WhoAm 94, WhoAmA 93*
Crane, Barbara Joyce 1934- *WhoAm 94*
Crane, Benjamin Field 1929- *WhoAm 94*
Crane, Bob d1978 *WhoHol 92*
Crane, Bonnie L. 1930- *WhoAmA 93*
Crane, Bruce 1909- *WhoAmP 93*
Crane, Burton *DrAPF 93*
Crane, Carl 1939- *WhoAmP 93*
Crane, Caroline 1930- *ConAu 41NR, WrDr 94*
Crane, Charles Arthur 1938- *WhoAm 94*
Crane, Darlene Barrientos 1948- *WhoWest 94*
Crane, David Franklin 1953- *WhoAmA 93*
Crane, Dwight Burdick 1937- *WhoAm 94*
Crane, Edward Harrison, III 1944- *WhoAm 94*
Crane, Ernest F. 1921- *WhoAmP 93*
Crane, Eva 1912- *CurBio 93 [port]*
Crane, Faye 1947- *WhoMW 93*
Crane, Frank H. d1948 *WhoHol 92*
Crane, Fred 1918- *WhoHol 92*
Crane, Frederick Loring 1925- *WhoMW 93*
Crane, Gardner, Mrs. d1963 *WhoHol 92*
Crane, Geoffrey David 1934- *Who 94*
Crane, Harold Hart 1899-1932 *AmCulL*
Crane, (Harold) Hart 1899-1932 *GayLL*
Crane, Henrietta Page *WhoAmP 93*
Crane, Hewitt David 1927- *WhoAm 94*
Crane, Horace Richard 1907- *WhoAm 94, WhoScEn 94*
Crane, Irving Donald 1913- *WhoAm 94*
Crane, Jack Wilbur 1932- *WhoFI 94, WhoScEn 94*
Crane, James d1968 *WhoHol 92*
Crane, James (William Donald) 1921- *Who 94*
Crane, Jameson 1926- *WhoAm 94*
Crane, Jean 1933- *WhoAmA 93*
Crane, Jim (James G) 1927- *WhoAmA 93*
Crane, John 1744-1805 *WhAmRev*
Crane, John 1774-1805 *AmRev*
Crane, Julia Gorham 1925- *WhoAm 94*
Crane, Julian Coburn 1918- *WhoAm 94*
Crane, Laura Jane 1941- *WhoAm 94*
Crane, Leo Stanley 1915- *WhoAm 94, WhoFI 94*
Crane, Lloyd *WhoHol 92*
Crane, Louis Arthur 1922- *WhoAm 94*
Crane, Mae d1969 *WhoHol 92*
Crane, Margaret Ann 1940- *WhoFI 94, WhoMW 93*
Crane, Mark 1930- *WhoAm 94*
Crane, Michael Patrick 1948- *WhoAm 94, WhoAmA 93*
Crane, Mitchell Gregory 1947- *WhoAmL 94*
Crane, Neal Dahlberg 1916- *WhoAm 94*
Crane, Norma d1973 *WhoHol 92*
Crane, Ogden d1940 *WhoHol 92*
Crane, Peter Francis 1940- *Who 94*
Crane, Philip M. 1930- *CngDr 93*
Crane, Philip Miller 1930- *WhoAm 94, WhoAmP 93, WhoMW 93*
Crane, Phyllis *WhoHol 92*
Crane, Richard d1969 *WhoHol 92*
Crane, Richard (Arthur) 1944- *ConDr 93, WrDr 94*
Crane, Richard Clement 1925- *WhoAm 94*
Crane, Richard Turner 1951- *WhoScEn 94*
Crane, Robert 1908-1990 *EncSF 93*
Crane, Robert Kendall 1935- *WhoAm 94*
Crane, Robert Q. 1926- *WhoAmP 93*
Crane, Roger *Who 94*
Crane, (Francis) Roger 1910- *Who 94*
Crane, Roger Alan 1942- *WhoScEn 94*
Crane, Ron 1948- *WhoAmP 93*
Crane, Roy (Campbell) 1901-1977 *WhoAmA 93N*
Crane, Samuel *WhoAm 94*
Crane, Stephen 1709-1780 *WhAmRev*
Crane, Stephen 1871-1900 *RfGShF*
Crane, Stephen (Townley) 1871-1900 *ConAu 140*
Crane, Stephen A. 1949- *WhoAmL 94*
Crane, Stephen Andrew 1945- *WhoAm 94*
Crane, Stephen Townley 1871-1900 *AmCulL [port]*
Crane, Stephen Wallace 1944- *WhoMW 93*
Crane, Steve d1985 *WhoHol 92*
Crane, Steven 1959- *WhoFI 94, WhoWest 94*
Crane, Ward d1928 *WhoHol 92*
Crane, William H. d1928 *WhoHol 92*
Cranefield, Paul F. 1925- *ConAu 141*
Cranefield, Paul Frederic 1925- *WhoAm 94, WhoScEn 94*
Craney, Terrance Lee 1950- *WhoMW 93*
Cranfield, Charles Ernest Burland 1915- *IntWW 93, Who 94, WrDr 94*
Cranfield, Ingrid 1945- *ConAu 141, SmATA 74 [port]*
Cranford, J. Wayne 1933- *WhoAm 94*
Cranford, James Blease 1950- *WhoFI 94*
Cranford, James Michael 1946- *WhoAmL 94*
Cranford, Page Deronde 1935- *WhoAm 94*
Cranford, Sharon Hill 1946- *WhoBlA 94*
Crang, Richard Francis Earl 1936- *WhoAm 94*
Crangle, Joseph F. 1932- *WhoAmP 93*
Cranham, Kenneth 1944- *ConTFT 11, WhoHol 92*
Cranin, Marilyn Sunners 1932- *WhoAm 94*
Cranko, John 1927-1973 *IntDcB [port]*
Crankshaw, John Hamilton 1914- *WhoFI 94, WhoScEn 94*
Cranley, Viscount 1967- *Who 94*
Cranmer, Arthur (Henry) 1885-1954 *NewGrDO*
Cranmer, Philip 1918- *Who 94*
Cranmer, Thomas 1489-1556 *BlmGEL, DcLB 132 [port]*
Cranmer, Thomas William 1951- *WhoAmL 94*
Crannell, Hall Leinster 1936- *WhoScEn 94*
Cranney, Marilyn Kanrek 1949- *WhoAmL 94, WhoFI 94*
Cranor, John 1946- *WhoAm 94, WhoFI 94*
Cranshaw, Janet Louise 1961- *WhoMW 93*
Cranshaw, Patrick 1919- *WhoHol 92*
Cranston, Alan 1914- *IntWW 93, WhoAm 94, WhoWest 94*
Cranston, Alan MacGregor 1914- *WhoAmP 93*
Cranston, Howard Stephen 1937- *WhoFI 94, WhoWest 94*
Cranston, Mary B. 1947- *WhoAm 94, WhoAmL 94*
Cranston, Maurice d1993 *NewYTBS 93*
Cranston, Maurice (William) 1920- *IntWW 93, Who 94, WrDr 94*
Cranston, Mildred Welch 1898- *WhAm 10*
Cranston, Monroe G. 1915- *WhoBlA 94*
Cranston, Wilber Charles 1933- *WhoScEn 94*
Cranston, William Ian 1928- *Who 94*
Cranwell, Charles Richard 1942- *WhoAmP 93*
Cranworth, Baron 1940- *Who 94*
Crapo, John Jennings 1937- *WhoAmP 93*
Crapo, Michael D. 1951- *CngDr 93*
Crapo, Michael Dean 1951- *WhoAm 94, WhoAmP 93, WhoWest 94*
Crapo, Richley H. 1943- *WhoWest 94*
Crapo, Sheila Anne 1951- *WhoWest 94*
Crapo, Terry LaVelle 1939- *WhoAmP 93*
Crapsey, Algernon Sidney 1847-1927 *DcAmReB 2*
Crapster, Gary Clark 1949- *WhoAmL 94*
Crary, Jonathan Knight *WhoAmA 93*
Crary, Miner Dunham, Jr. 1920- *WhoAm 94, WhoAmL 94*
Crary, Selden Bronson 1949- *WhoMW 93*
Crary, William Frederick, II 1954- *WhoAmL 94*
Cras, Jean (Emile Paul) 1879-1932 *NewGrDO*
Crase, Douglas *DrAPF 93*
Crase, Douglas 1944- *WhoAm 94*
Crasemann, Bernd 1922- *WhoAm 94*
Crash 1961- *WhoAmA 93*
Crashaw, Richard 1612?-1649 *BlmGEL*
Crashaw, Richard 1613?-1649 *LitC 24*
Crashing Thunder *See* Blowsnake, Sam 1875- *EncNAR*
Craske, Leonard d1950 *WhoAmA 93N*
Craske, Margaret 1892-1990 *IntDcB*
Crass, Franz 1928- *NewGrDO*
Craston, (Richard) Colin 1922- *Who 94*
Craswell, Ellen 1932- *WhoAmP 93*
Craswell, Ellen 1953- *WhoWomW 91*
Crater, Timothy Andrews 1966- *WhoMW 93*
Crathorne, Baron 1939- *Who 94*
Cratty, Bryant J. 1929- *WrDr 94*
Cratz, Benjimin Arthur 1888- *WhoAmA 93N*
Crauchet, Paul *WhoHol 92*
Craufurd, Robert (James) 1937- *Who 94*
Craugh, Joseph Patrick, Jr. 1934- *WhoAm 94*
Cravat, Nick 1911- *WhoHol 92*
Cravat, Noel d1960 *WhoHol 92*
Cravath, Glenn d1964 *WhoAmA 93N*
Craven, Earl of 1989- *Who 94*
Craven, Charles Warren 1947- *WhoAmL 94*
Craven, Daniel Hartman d1993 *IntWW 93N*
Craven, David James 1946- *WhoAmA 93*
Craven, Donald B. 1941- *WhoAmL 94*
Craven, Frank d1945 *WhoHol 92*
Craven, Gemma 1950- *IntMPA 94, WhoHol 92*
Craven, George W. 1951- *WhoAm 94*
Craven, Homer Henry, Jr. 1925- *WhoFI 94*
Craven, James J., Jr. *WhoAmP 93*
Craven, James M. *WhoAmP 93*
Craven, James Michael 1946- *WhoWest 94*
Craven, John Anthony 1940- *IntWW 93, Who 94*
Craven, John Pinna 1924- *WhoAm 94, WhoAmL 94*
Craven, Judith *WhoBlA 94*
Craven, Matt *WhoHol 92*
Craven, Pauline 1808-1891 *BlmGWL*
Craven, Robert Edward 1916- *Who 94*
Craven, Robin d1978 *WhoHol 92*
Craven, Roy Curtis, Jr. 1924- *WhoAm 94, WhoAmA 93*
Craven, Stanley E. 1946- *WhoAmL 94*
Craven, Stephen M. 1944- *WhoMW 93*
Craven, Walter d1918 *WhoHol 92*
Craven, Wayne 1930- *WhoAmA 93*
Craven, Wes 1939- *IntMPA 94*
Craven, Wes 1949- *HorFD [port]*
Craven, William A. 1921- *WhoAmP 93*
Cravens, Gerald McAdoo 1918- *WhoScEn 94*
Cravens, Gwyneth *DrAPF 93*
Cravens, Hartley Dodge 1935- *WhoIns 94*
Cravens, Malcolm 1907- *WhoIns 94*
Cravens, Raymond Lewis 1930- *WhoAm 94*
Craver, James Bernard 1943- *WhoAm 94, WhoAmL 94*
Cravez, Glenn Edward 1957- *WhoAmL 94*
Cravins, Donald R. 1948- *WhoAmP 93*
Craw, Freeman *WhoAm 94*
Craw, Nicholas Wesson 1936- *WhoWest 94*
Crawfis, Robert P. 1950- *WhoAmL 94, WhoWest 94*
Crawford, Earl of 1927- *Who 94*
Crawford, Alan 1943- *WrDr 94*
Crawford, Andrea Steen 1963- *WhoMW 93*
Crawford, Andrew 1917- *WhoHol 92*
Crawford, Andrew Charles 1949- *Who 94*
Crawford, Anne d1956 *WhoHol 92*
Crawford, Barbara Hopkins *WhoBlA 94*
Crawford, Betty Marilyn 1948- *WhoBlA 94*
Crawford, Bill 1941- *WhoAmA 93*
Crawford, Bo *WhoAmP 93*
Crawford, Bob 1948- *WhoAmP 93*
Crawford, Brian Louis 1956- *WhoWest 94*
Crawford, Broderick d1986 *WhoHol 92*
Crawford, Bruce Edgar 1929- *WhoAm 94, WhoFI 94*
Crawford, Bryce, Jr. 1914- *IntWW 93*
Crawford, Bryce Low, Jr. 1914- *WhoAm 94*
Crawford, Burnett Hayden 1922- *WhoAmL 94*
Crawford, Carl Benson 1923- *WhoAm 94*
Crawford, Carl M. 1932- *WhoBlA 94*
Crawford, Carol Forsyth 1911- *WhoAmP 93*
Crawford, Catherine Betty 1910- *WhoAmA 93*
Crawford, Charles L. 1929- *WhoBlA 94*
Crawford, Charles McNeil 1918- *WhoAm 94*
Crawford, Charles Merle 1924- *WhoAm 94*
Crawford, Charles Renville 1837-1920 *EncNAR*
Crawford, Christina 1939- *WhoHol 92, WrDr 94*
Crawford, Cindy 1966- *CurBio 93 [port], IntWW 93, News 93-3 [port], WhoAm 94*
Crawford, Claude Cecil, III 1943- *WhoScEn 94*
Crawford, Clifton d1920 *WhoHol 92*
Crawford, Cranford L., Jr. 1940- *WhoBlA 94*
Crawford, Curtis Scott 1960- *WhoMW 93*
Crawford, Daniel J. 1942- *WrDr 94*
Crawford, Daniel Mollenhoff 1941- *WhoAmL 94*
Crawford, David 1941- *WhoBlA 94*
Crawford, David 1951- *WrDr 94*
Crawford, David Coleman 1930- *WhoAm 94*
Crawford, Dean *DrAPF 93*
Crawford, Deborah Collins 1947- *WhoBlA 94*
Crawford, Desiree White 1953- *WhoAmP 93*
Crawford, Dewey Byers 1941- *WhoAm 94, WhoAmL 94*
Crawford, Dewitt Charles, Sr. 1923- *WhoAmP 93*
Crawford, Dick *WhoAmP 93*
Crawford, Don Lee 1947- *WhoAm 94*
Crawford, Donald Wayne 1929- *WhoMW 93*
Crawford, Donald Wesley 1938- *WhoAm 94*
Crawford, Douglas *Who 94*
Crawford, (George) Douglas 1939- *Who 94*
Crawford, Earl 1890-1960 *WhoAmA 93N*
Crawford, Ed c. 1964- *See* fIREHOSE *ConMus 11*
Crawford, Edward Hamon 1925- *WhoAm 94, WhoFI 94, WhoIns 94*
Crawford, Edwin Ben 1944- *WhoScEn 94*
Crawford, Edwin L. d1993 *NewYTBS 93*
Crawford, Edwin Mack 1949- *WhoAm 94, WhoFI 94*
Crawford, Ella Mae 1932- *WhoBlA 94*
Crawford, Evelyn Carlene 1931- *WhoAmP 93*
Crawford, Frederick (William) 1931- *Who 94*
Crawford, Frederick William 1931- *IntWW 93*
Crawford, George (Hunter) 1911- *Who 94*
Crawford, George David 1930- *WhoMW 93*
Crawford, George Gordon 1869-1936 *EncABHB 9 [port]*
Crawford, George Oswald 1902- *Who 94*
Crawford, George Truett 1936- *WhoFI 94, WhoWest 94*
Crawford, Gerald Marcus 1940- *WhoAmL 94*
Crawford, Gerald Wayne 1949- *WhoAmP 93*
Crawford, H. R. 1939- *WhoAmP 93*
Crawford, Hank 1950- *WrDr 94*
Crawford, Harold Bernard 1934- *WhoAm 94*
Crawford, Hazle R. 1939- *WhoBlA 94*
Crawford, Homer 1916- *WhoFI 94*
Crawford, Howard Allen 1917- *WhoAm 94*
Crawford, Howard Marion d1969 *WhoHol 92*
Crawford, Howard T. 1947- *WhoAmP 93*
Crawford, Hunt Dorn, Jr. 1948- *WhoFI 94*

Crawford, Iain 1938- *Who 94*
Crawford, Ian Drummond 1945- *WhoScEn 94*
Crawford, Isabella Valancy 1850-1887 *BlmGWL*
Crawford, Isaiah 1960- *WhoScEn 94*
Crawford, J. Douglas 1948- *WhoWest 94*
Crawford, Jack 1908-1991 *BuCMET [port]*
Crawford, Jack, Jr. *DrAPF 93*
Crawford, Jacob Wendell 1942- *WhoBlA 94*
Crawford, James *WhoAmP 93*
Crawford, James Douglas 1932- *WhoAm 94*
Crawford, James Maurice 1946- *WhoBlA 94*
Crawford, James Richard 1948- *Who 94*
Crawford, James W., Jr. 1937- *WhoAmP 93*
Crawford, James Weldon 1927- *WhoAm 94*
Crawford, James Wesley 1942- *WhoBlA 94*
Crawford, Jayne Suzanne 1958- *WhoBlA 94*
Crawford, Jean Andre 1941- *WhoMW 93*
Crawford, Jeffrey Allen 1963- *WhoAmL 94*
Crawford, Jerry LeRoy 1934- *WhoWest 94*
Crawford, Jesse d1962 *WhoHol 92*
Crawford, Jimmy d1980 *WhoHol 92*
Crawford, Joan d1977 *WhoHol 92*
Crawford, Joanna *WhoHol 92*
Crawford, John *NewYTBS 93 [port], WhoHol 92*
Crawford, John Andrew 1956- *WhoAmL 94*
Crawford, John Edward 1924- *WhoAm 94*
Crawford, John Emerson 1943- *WhoWest 94*
Crawford, John Gilliand 1946- *WhoAmP 93*
Crawford, John Michael 1938- *Who 94*
Crawford, John Richard 1932- *WrDr 94*
Crawford, John T. *WhoIns 94*
Crawford, Johnny 1946- *WhoHol 92*
Crawford, Joyce Catherine Holmes 1918- *WhoWest 94*
Crawford, Judith Ann 1952- *WhoFI 94*
Crawford, Katherine 1945- *WhoHol 92*
Crawford, Kathryn d1980 *WhoHol 92*
Crawford, Kenneth Charles 1918- *WhoAm 94*
Crawford, Kevan Charles 1956- *WhoScEn 94, WhoWest 94*
Crawford, Lawrence Douglas 1949- *WhoAmP 93, WhoBlA 94*
Crawford, Lester d1962 *WhoHol 92*
Crawford, Lester Mills, Jr. 1938- *WhoAm 94, WhoFI 94, WhoScEn 94*
Crawford, Lewis Cleaver 1925- *WhoAm 94*
Crawford, Linda *DrAPF 93*
Crawford, Linda Sibery 1947- *WhoAmL 94*
Crawford, Lionel Vivian 1932- *Who 94*
Crawford, Lucy A. 1947- *WhoIns 94*
Crawford, Marc *DrAPF 93*
Crawford, Margaret Ward 1937- *WhoBlA 94*
Crawford, Maria Luisa 1939- *WhoAm 94*
Crawford, Maria Luisa Buse 1939- *WhoScEn 94*
Crawford, Mark Harwood 1950- *WhoScEn 94*
Crawford, Mary B. 1949- *WhoMW 93*
Crawford, Mary Catherine 1947- *WhoWomW 91*
Crawford, Mary Greer *WhoBlA 94*
Crawford, Meredith Pullen 1910- *WhoAm 94*
Crawford, Michael 1942- *ConTFT 11, IntMPA 94, IntWW 93, News 94-2 [port], Who 94, WhoHol 92*
Crawford, Michael Anthony 1955- *WhoFI 94*
Crawford, Michael Hewson 1939- *IntWW 93, Who 94*
Crawford, Michael Howard 1943- *WhoWest 94*
Crawford, Michael Howard 1958- *WhoFI 94*
Crawford, Mildred Wynters d1978 *WhoHol 92*
Crawford, Muriel C. *WhoBlA 94*
Crawford, Muriel Laura *WhoAm 94, WhoAmL 94, WhoWest 94*
Crawford, Myron Lloyd 1938- *WhoAm 94, WhoWest 94*
Crawford, Nan d1975 *WhoHol 92*
Crawford, Narvel J., Jr. 1929- *WhoAmP 93*
Crawford, Natalie Wilson 1939- *WhoWest 94*
Crawford, Nathaniel, Jr. 1951- *WhoBlA 94*
Crawford, Ned *EncSF 93*
Crawford, (Robert) Norman 1923- *Who 94*

Crawford, Norman Crane, Jr. 1930- *WhoAm 94*
Crawford, Odel 1952- *WhoBlA 94*
Crawford, Patricia A. 1928- *WhoAmP 93*
Crawford, Patrick *Who 94*
Crawford, (Ian) Patrick 1933- *Who 94*
Crawford, Peter John 1930- *Who 94*
Crawford, Peter S. 1945- *WhoAm 94*
Crawford, Philip Stanley 1944- *WhoAm 94, WhoFI 94, WhoWest 94*
Crawford, Purdy *WhoAm 94, WhoFI 94*
Crawford, Ralston 1906-1977 *WhoAmA 93N*
Crawford, Raymon Edward 1939- *WhoBlA 94*
Crawford, Raymond Maxwell, Jr. 1933- *WhoAm 94*
Crawford, Richard 1935- *WhoAm 94*
Crawford, Richard Bradway 1933- *WhoAm 94*
Crawford, Richard Eben, Jr. 1930- *WhoWest 94*
Crawford, Richard L. 1951- *WhoAmP 93*
Crawford, Richard M. *WhoScEn 94*
Crawford, Robert 1935- *WrDr 94*
Crawford, Robert Gammie 1924- *Who 94*
Crawford, Robert John 1942- *WhoFI 94*
Crawford, Robert M. 1954- *WhoAmP 93*
Crawford, Robert Platt 1893- *WhAm 10*
Crawford, Robert Webb 1924- *WhoFI 94*
Crawford, Robert William Kenneth 1945- *Who 94*
Crawford, Ronald Lyle 1947- *WhoWest 94*
Crawford, Roy Edgington, III 1938- *WhoAm 94*
Crawford, Russell 1939- *WhoAmP 93*
Crawford, Samuel D. 1936- *WhoBlA 94*
Crawford, Scott Lee 1955- *WhoFI 94*
Crawford, Stanley *DrAPF 93*
Crawford, (Robert) Stewart 1913- *Who 94*
Crawford, Stewart Montgomery 1936- *WhoFI 94*
Crawford, Susan J. 1947- *CngDr 93*
Crawford, Susan Jean 1947- *WhoAm 94, WhoAmL 94*
Crawford, Tad *DrAPF 93*
Crawford, Tad 1946- *WrDr 94*
Crawford, Theodore d1993 *Who 94N*
Crawford, Thom Cooney 1944- *WhoAmA 93*
Crawford, Thomas James *WhoAmP 93*
Crawford, Thomas Mark 1954- *WhoScEn 94*
Crawford, Timothy d1978 *WhoHol 92*
Crawford, Tom *DrAPF 93*
Crawford, Vanella Alise 1947- *WhoBlA 94*
Crawford, Vanessa Reese 1952- *WhoBlA 94*
Crawford, Vernon (E.) 1946- *WrDr 94*
Crawford, Wayne *WhoHol 92*
Crawford, William 1732-1782 *AmRev, WhAmRev*
Crawford, William (Godfrey) 1907- *Who 94*
Crawford, William A. 1936- *WhoAmP 93, WhoBlA 94*
Crawford, William Avery 1915- *IntWW 93*
Crawford, William Basil, Jr. 1941- *WhoAm 94*
Crawford, William David 1945- *WhoFI 94*
Crawford, William F. 1911- *WhoAm 94*
Crawford, William H. 1913- *WhoAmA 93N*
Crawford, William Hamilton Raymund 1936- *Who 94*
Crawford, William Henry, II 1957- *WhoAmL 94*
Crawford, William L(evi) 1911-1984 *EncSF 93*
Crawford, William Rex 1928- *WhoAmP 93*
Crawford, William Rex, Jr. 1928- *WhoAm 94*
Crawford, William Richard 1936- *WhoAm 94*
Crawford, William S. *WhoAmP 93*
Crawford, William Walsh 1927- *WhoAm 94, WhoAmL 94*
Crawford-Mason, Clare Wootten 1936- *WhoAm 94*
Crawley, A. Bruce 1946- *WhoBlA 94*
Crawley, Aidan (Merivale) 1908- *WrDr 94*
Crawley, Aidan Merivale 1908- *Who 94*
Crawley, Alexander Radford 1947- *WhoAm 94*
Crawley, Bettye Jean 1955- *WhoBlA 94*
Crawley, Charles William d1992 *Who 94N*
Crawley, Christine Mary 1950- *Who 94, WhoWomW 91*
Crawley, Clifford 1929- *NewGrDO*
Crawley, Constance d1919 *WhoHol 92*
Crawley, Dan d1912 *WhoHol 92*
Crawley, Darline 1941- *WhoBlA 94*
Crawley, David *Who 94*

Crawley, Desmond John Chetwode d1993 *Who 94N*
Crawley, Frederick William 1926- *IntWW 93, Who 94*
Crawley, George Claudius 1934- *WhoBlA 94*
Crawley, Harriet 1948- *WrDr 94*
Crawley, Jacqueline Nina 1950- *WhoAm 94*
Crawley, John *WhoAmP 93*
Crawley, John Boevey 1946- *WhoAm 94*
Crawley, John Cecil 1909- *Who 94*
Crawley, John Maurice 1933- *Who 94*
Crawley, Oscar Lewis 1942- *WhoBlA 94*
Crawley, Robert d1987 *WhoHol 92*
Crawley, Sayre d1948 *WhoHol 92*
Crawley, Stephen David 1960- *WhoAmL 94*
Crawley, Thomas Michael 1963- *WhoAm 94*
Crawley, Timothy Dale 1959- *WhoAmL 94*
Crawley, Vernon Obadiah 1936- *WhoMW 93*
Crawley-Boevey, Thomas (Michael Blake) 1928- *Who 94*
Crawshaw, Baron 1933- *Who 94*
Crawshaw, Ralph 1921- *WhoAm 94, WhoWest 94*
Crawshay, Elisabeth Mary Boyd 1927- *Who 94*
Crawshay, William (Robert) 1920- *Who 94*
Craxi, Bettino 1934- *IntWW 93*
Craxton, Antony 1918- *Who 94*
Cray, Charles Francis 1961- *WhoMW 93*
Cray, Cloud Lanor, Jr. 1922- *WhoAm 94*
Cray, Edward 1933- *WrDr 94*
Cray, Graham Alan 1947- *Who 94*
Cray, Robert 1953- *WhoAm 94, WhoBlA 94*
Cray, Seymour *WorInv*
Cray, Seymour R. 1925- *WhoAm 94*
Craycraft, Allie V., Jr. *WhoAmP 93*
Crayder, Teresa *TwCYAW, WrDr 94*
Crayne, Dani 1934- *WhoHol 92*
Craypo, Charles 1936- *WhoAm 94*
Craythorne, Norman William Brian 1931- *WhoAm 94*
Crayton, Billy Gene 1931- *WhoMW 93*
Crayton, James Edward 1943- *WhoBlA 94*
Crayton, Samuel S. 1916- *WhoBlA 94*
Crazy Horse 1841-1877 *HisWorL [port]*
Crazy Mule dc. 1889 *EncNAR*
Creach, David Cleo 1918- *WhoWest 94*
Creagan, Robert Joseph 1919- *WhoAm 94*
Creager, Clara 1930- *WrDr 94*
Creager, Clifford Raymond 1937- *WhoWest 94*
Creager, Joe Scott 1929- *WhoAm 94, WhoScEn 94*
Creagh, George d1962 *WhoHol 92*
Creagh, Kilner Rupert B. *Who 94*
Creal, David Bruce 1959- *WhoFI 94*
Creamer, Brian 1926- *Who 94*
Creamer, Bruce Cunningham 1941- *WhoMW 93*
Creamer, James Edward, Jr. 1958- *WhoAmP 93*
Creamer, Robert Allan 1941- *WhoAm 94, WhoAmL 94*
Creamer, Robert W. 1922- *WrDr 94*
Creamer, William Henry, III 1927- *WhoAm 94*
Crean, Frank 1916- *IntWW 93, Who 94*
Crean, Gerald Philip, Jr. 1936- *WhoAmP 93*
Crean, John C. 1925- *WhoAm 94, WhoFI 94, WhoMW 93*
Crean, John Gale 1910- *WhoAm 94*
Crean, Simon 1949- *IntWW 93*
Creany, Cathleen Annette 1950- *WhoAm 94*
Creary, Ludlow Barrington 1930- *WhoBlA 94*
Creasey, John 1908-1973 *EncSF 93*
Creasia, Donald Anthony 1937- *WhoScEn 94*
Creasman, William Paul 1952- *WhoAmL 94*
Creasman, William Thomas 1934- *WhoAm 94*
Creason, Karen Kay 1943- *WhoAm 94, WhoAmL 94*
Creason, Norwood A. 1918- *WhoAmP 93*
Creasy, Leonard Richard 1912- *Who 94*
Creasy, William Russel 1958- *WhoScEn 94*
Creath, Katherine 1958- *WhoWest 94*
Creato, Anthony Edmund 1945- *WhoAmL 94*
Creaven, Patrick Joseph 1933- *WhoAm 94*
Crebbin, Anthony Micek 1952- *WhoAmL 94*
Crebillon, Claude-Prosper Jolyot de 1707-1777 *GuFrLit 2*
Crebillon, Prosper Jolyot, sieur de 1674-1762 *GuFrLit 2*

Crebillon, Prosper Jolyot de 1674-1762 *NewGrDO*
Crebo, Alan Richard 1940- *WhoMW 93*
Crebs, Paul Terence 1938- *WhoAmL 94, WhoMW 93*
Crecco, Marion *WhoAmP 93*
Crecine, John Patrick 1939- *WhoAm 94*
Crecy, Jeanne 1930- *WrDr 94*
Crede, Robert Henry 1915- *WhoAm 94, WhoWest 94*
Crediton, Bishop Suffragan of 1928- *Who 94*
Creditt, Thelma Cobb 1902- *WhoBlA 94*
Cree, Albert Alexander 1898- *WhAm 10*
Cree, Gerald Hilary 1905- *Who 94*
Creech, Billy James 1943- *WhoAmP 93*
Creech, Franklin Underwood 1941- *WhoAmA 93*
Creech, Fulton Hunter 1929- *WhoAm 94*
Creech, Hugh John 1910- *WhoAm 94*
Creech, John Lewis 1920- *WhoAm 94*
Creech, Philip 1950- *AfrAmAl 6*
Creech, Wilbur Lyman 1927- *WhoAm 94, WhoWest 94*
Creech, William Ayden 1925- *WhoAmP 93*
Creech-Eakman, Michelle Jeanne 1967- *WhoScEn 94*
Creecy, Charles Melvin 1920- *WhoAmP 93*
Creecy, Herbert Lee 1939- *WhoAmA 93*
Creecy, Jimmy Glen 1947- *WhoAmL 94*
Creed, Barbara B. 1944- *WhoAmL 94*
Creed, Catherine d1978 *WhoHol 92*
Creed, John Henry 1940- *WhoWest 94*
Creed, Robert Payson, Sr. 1925- *WhoAm 94*
Creed, Thomas G. 1933- *WhoFI 94*
Creedon, John J. 1924- *WhoAm 94*
Creedon, Michael C. 1946- *WhoAmP 93*
Creegan, Robert Francis 1915- *WhoAm 94*
Creeggan, Jack Burnett 1902- *Who 94*
Creek, Malcolm Lars 1931- *Who 94*
Creekmore, David Dickason 1942- *WhoAmL 94*
Creekmore, Frederick Hillary 1937- *WhoAmP 93*
Creekmore, Marion V., Jr. *WhoAmP 93*
Creel, Austin Bowman 1929- *WhoAm 94*
Creel, Luther Edward, III 1937- *WhoAm 94*
Creel, Ronald Joseph 1938- *WhoAmP 93*
Creel, Thomas Leonard 1937- *WhoAm 94*
Creeley, Bobbie *DrAPF 93*
Creeley, Robert *DrAPF 93*
Creeley, Robert 1926- *ConLC 78 [port]*
Creeley, Robert (White) 1926- *ConAu 43NR, WrDr 94*
Creeley, Robert White 1926- *IntWW 93, WhoAm 94*
Creelman, Marjorie Broer 1908- *WhoMW 93, WhoScEn 94*
Creenan, Katherine Heras 1945- *WhoAmL 94*
Creer, James Read 1942- *WhoWest 94*
Creer, Philip Douglas 1903- *WhoAm 94*
Creese, Nigel Arthur Holloway 1927- *Who 94*
Creese, Walter Littlefield 1919- *WhoAmA 93*
Creese, Wesley William 1959- *WhoFI 94*
Creevey, Thomas 1768-1838 *DcNaB MP*
Creevy, Bill 1942- *WhoAmA 93*
Creevy, Donald Charles 1936- *WhoAm 94*
Creevy, Patrick Joseph 1947- *ConAu 141*
Cregan, David (Appleton Quartus) 1931- *ConDr 93, WrDr 94*
Cregan, John B. 1930- *WhoIns 94*
Cregan, N. R. d1939 *WhoHol 92*
Cregar, Laird d1944 *WhoHol 92*
Cregeen, Archibald 1774-1841 *DcNaB MP*
Cregg, Hugh Anthony, III 1951- *WhoAm 94*
Cregor, John Marshall, Jr. 1945- *WhoWest 94*
Crehan, Joseph d1966 *WhoHol 92*
Crehan, Joseph Edward 1938- *WhoAm 94, WhoAmL 94*
Crehore, Charles Aaron 1946- *WhoAmL 94*
Creider, Jane Tapsubei *BlmGWL*
Creigh, Thomas, Jr. 1912- *WhoAm 94, WhoMW 93*
Creightmore, Peter Beauchamp 1928- *Who 94*
Creighton, Alan Joseph 1936- *Who 94*
Creighton, Dale Edward 1934- *WhoAm 94*
Creighton, Don 1914- *WrDr 94*
Creighton, Douglas George 1923- *WhoWest 94*
Creighton, Harold Digby Fitzgerald 1927- *Who 94*
Creighton, John Douglas 1928- *WhoAm 94*
Creighton, John W., Jr. 1932- *WhoAm 94, WhoFI 94, WhoWest 94*
Creighton, Neal 1930- *WhoAm 94*
Creighton, Tom 1927- *WhoAmP 93*

Cronin, Thomas E(dward) 1940- *ConAu 42NR*
Cronin, Thomas Francis, Jr. 1939- *WhoFI 94*
Cronin, Tim d1919 *WhoHol 92*
Cronin, Timothy Cornelius, III 1927- *WhoAm 94*
Cronin, Tony d1979 *WhoAmA 93N*
Cronin, Vincent Archibald Patrick 1924- *Who 94*
Cronin, Vincent Sean 1957- *WhoScEn 94*
Cronin, William F. 1948- *WhoAmL 94*
Cronin Seligson, Karen 1956- *WhoAmL 94*
Cronjager, Edward 1904-1960 *IntDcF 2-4*
Cronk, Daniel Thompson 1953- *WhoAmL 94*
Cronk, Duane Anthony 1952- *WhoAmP 93*
Cronk, George 1938- *WhoAmL 94*
Cronk, Mildred Schiefelbein 1909- *WhoWest 94*
Cronkhite, Leonard Wolsey, Jr. 1919- *WhoAm 94*
Cronkite, Eugene Pitcher 1914- *IntWW 93, WhoAm 94*
Cronkite, Kathy 1950- *WhoHol 92*
Cronkite, Walter *NewYTBS 93 [port]*
Cronkite, Walter 1916- *IntMPA 94, WhoAm 94*
Cronkite, Walter (Leland, Jr.) 1916- *WrDr 94*
Cronkite, Walter Leland, Jr. 1916- *IntWW 93*
Cronkleton, Thomas Eugene 1928- *WhoScEn 94, WhoWest 94*
Cronon, Edmund David, Jr. 1924- *WhoAm 94*
Cronon, William 1954- *WhoAm 94, WrDr 94*
Cronquist, Arthur John 1919-1992 *WhAm 10*
Cronson, Harry Marvin 1937- *WhoAm 94*
Cronson, Robert Granville 1924- *WhoAm 94*
Cronyn, Hume 1911- *IntMPA 94, IntWW 93, WhoAm 94, WhoHol 92*
Cronyn, Marshall William 1919- *WhoAm 94*
Cronyn, Tandy 1945- *WhoHol 92*
Crook, Baron 1926- *Who 94*
Crook, Arthur Charles William 1912- *Who 94*
Crook, Charles Samuel, III 1944- *WhoAmL 94*
Crook, Colin 1942- *Who 94*
Crook, Compton N. *EncSF 93*
Crook, Donald Martin 1947- *WhoAmL 94*
Crook, Frances Rachel 1952- *Who 94*
Crook, Gaines Morton 1923- *WhoWest 94*
Crook, Jacquelyn Elaine Terry 1943- *WhoMW 93*
Crook, James Cooper 1923- *Who 94*
Crook, John Anthony 1921- *Who 94*
Crook, John Robert 1947- *WhoAmL 94*
Crook, Joseph Mordaunt 1937- *Who 94, WrDr 94*
Crook, K. Eric 1953- *WhoFI 94*
Crook, Kenneth Roy 1920- *Who 94*
Crook, Paul 1948- *WhoMW 93*
Crook, Paul Edwin 1915- *Who 94*
Crook, Robert Lacey 1929- *WhoAmP 93*
Crook, Robert Wayne 1936- *WhoAm 94*
Crook, Sean Paul 1953- *WhoWest 94*
Crook, Stephen Richard 1963- *WhoMW 93*
Crook, Theo Helsel 1898- *WhAm 10*
Crook, Troy Norman 1928- *WhoScEn 94*
Crooke, Edward A. 1938- *WhoAm 94, WhoFI 94*
Crooke, James Augustine 1955- *WhoMW 93*
Crooke, Stanley Thomas 1945- *WhoAm 94, WhoFI 94, WhoWest 94*
Crookenden, George Wayet Derek 1920- *Who 94*
Crookenden, Napier 1915- *Who 94*
Crooker, Barbara *DrAPF 93*
Crooker, John H., Jr. 1914- *WhoAm 94*
Crookes, William 1832-1919 *WorInv, WorScD [port]*
Crooks, Archibald Muir 1935- *WhoFI 94*
Crooks, Barbara Lyn *WhoFI 94*
Crooks, Bruce Philip 1944- *WhoAm 94*
Crooks, David Lloyd 1963- *WhoMW 93*
Crooks, David Manson 1931- *Who 94*
Crooks, Edwin William 1919- *WhoAm 94*
Crooks, John A. 1936- *WhoWest 94*
Crooks, John Robert Megaw 1914- *Who 94*
Crooks, Joseph William 1942- *WhoAmL 94*
Crooks, Richard (Alexander) 1900-1972 *NewGrDO*
Crooks, Thomas Jackson 1953- *WhoAm 94*
Crooks, W. Spencer 1917- *WhoAm 94, WhoAmA 93*
Crookshanks, Betty Dorsey 1944- *WhoAmP 93*
Crookston, Robert Kent 1943- *WhoAm 94, WhoMW 93*
Croom, Frederick Hailey 1941- *WhoAm 94*
Croom, Henrietta Brown 1940- *WhoAm 94*
Croom, John Henry, III 1932- *WhoAm 94, WhoFI 94*
Croom, Wanda Joyce 1944- *WhoMW 93*
Croome, (John) Lewis 1907- *Who 94*
Croom-Johnson, David Powell 1914- *Who 94*
Croom-Johnson, Henry Powell 1910- *Who 94*
Croon, Gregory Steven 1960- *WhoMW 93, WhoScEn 94*
Cropp, Dwight Sheffery 1939- *WhoBlA 94*
Cropp, J. Wayne 1952- *WhoAmL 94*
Cropp, Linda W. *WhoAmP 93*
Cropper, Andre Dominic 1961- *WhoScEn 94*
Cropper, Anna 1938- *WhoHol 92*
Cropper, James Anthony 1938- *Who 94*
Cropper, M. Elizabeth 1944- *WhoAmA 93*
Cropper, Peter John 1927- *Who 94*
Cropper, Rebecca Lynn 1957- *WhoMW 93*
Cropper, Susan Peggy 1941- *WhoAm 94*
Cropsey, Alan L. 1952- *WhoAmP 93*
Cropsey, Alan Lee 1952- *WhoMW 93*
Cropsey, Harmon 1917- *WhoAmP 93*
Cropsey, Joseph 1919- *WhoAm 94*
Crory, Elizabeth Lupien *WhoAmP 93*
Crosa, Jorge Homero 1941- *WhoWest 94*
Crosa, Michael L. 1942- *WhoHisp 94*
Crosato, Giambattista 1685?-1758 *NewGrDO*
Crosbie, Alfred Linden 1942- *WhoAm 94, WhoScEn 94*
Crosbie, Annette 1934- *WhoHol 92*
Crosbie, Helen Blair *WhoAmA 93*
Crosbie, John Carnell 1931- *IntWW 93, Who 94*
Crosbie, Martin *WhoHol 92*
Crosbie, Stanley Blandford 1906-1989 *WhAm 10*
Crosbie, William 1915- *Who 94*
Crosby, Alfred W., Jr. 1931- *WrDr 94*
Crosby, Alfred Worcester 1931- *WhoAm 94*
Crosby, Archie R. 1924- *WhoAmP 93*
Crosby, Bing d1977 *WhoHol 92*
Crosby, Bing 1903-1977 *WhoCom*
Crosby, Bob d1993 *IntMPA 94N, NewYTBS 93 [port]*
Crosby, Bob 1913- *IntMPA 94, WhoHol 92*
Crosby, Cathy *WhoHol 92*
Crosby, Cathy Lee *IntMPA 94*
Crosby, Cathy Lee 1944- *WhoHol 92*
Crosby, Denise 1957- *WhoHol 92*
Crosby, Dennis d1991 *WhoHol 92*
Crosby, Don d1985 *WhoHol 92*
Crosby, Donald Allen 1932- *WhoWest 94*
Crosby, Edward Warren 1932- *WhoBlA 94*
Crosby, Enoch 1750-1835 *WhAmRev [port]*
Crosby, Faye Jacqueline 1947- *WhoAm 94*
Crosby, Floyd 1899-1985 *IntDcF 2-4 [port]*
Crosby, Frances Jane 1820-1915 *DcAmReB 2*
Crosby, Fred McClellan 1928- *WhoAm 94*
Crosby, Fred McClellen 1928- *WhoBlA 94*
Crosby, Gary 1933- *WhoHol 92*
Crosby, George M. 1916- *WhoAmP 93*
Crosby, Glenn Arthur 1928- *WhoAm 94, WhoWest 94*
Crosby, Gordon E., Jr. 1920- *WhoIns 94*
Crosby, Harry 1958- *WhoHol 92*
Crosby, Harry C. *EncSF 93*
Crosby, Jacqueline Garton 1961- *WhoAm 94*
Crosby, James Philip 1953- *WhoMW 93*
Crosby, Jane A. 1920- *WhoAmP 93*
Crosby, Joan Carew 1934- *WhoAm 94*
Crosby, John (Campbell) 1912-1991 *WrDr 94N*
Crosby, John Campbell 1912-1991 *WhAm 10*
Crosby, John O('Hea) 1926- *NewGrDO*
Crosby, John O'Hea 1926- *WhoAm 94, WhoWest 94*
Crosby, Juliette d1969 *WhoHol 92*
Crosby, Kathryn 1933- *IntMPA 94*
Crosby, La Rhonda Smith 1960- *WhoWest 94*
Crosby, Lavon K. 1924- *WhoAmP 93*
Crosby, LaVon Kehoe Stuart 1924- *WhoMW 93*
Crosby, Lindsay d1989 *WhoHol 92*
Crosby, Lou d1984 *WhoHol 92*
Crosby, Lucinda *WhoHol 92*
Crosby, Margaree Seawright 1941- *WhoBlA 94*
Crosby, Marshall d1954 *WhoHol 92*
Crosby, Marshall Robert 1943- *WhoScEn 94*
Crosby, Mary 1959- *IntMPA 94, WhoHol 92*
Crosby, Norm 1927- *WhoCom*
Crosby, Norman Lawrence 1927- *WhoAm 94*
Crosby, Peter Alan 1945- *WhoAm 94*
Crosby, Philip 1922- *WhoAmL 94*
Crosby, Phillip 1934- *WhoHol 92*
Crosby, Ranice W. 1915- *WhoAmA 93*
Crosby, Robert d1984 *WhoHol 92*
Crosby, Robert Berkey 1911- *WhoAmL 94, WhoAmP 93*
Crosby, Robert Lewis 1932- *WhoAmL 94*
Crosby, Sumner McKnight 1909-1982 *WhoAmA 93N*
Crosby, Susan 1945- *WhoMW 93*
Crosby, Susan R. 1945- *WhoAmP 93*
Crosby, Theo 1925- *Who 94, WrDr 94*
Crosby, Thomas 1840-1914 *EncNAR*
Crosby, Thomas Manville, Jr. 1938- *WhoAm 94*
Crosby, Tom, Jr. 1928- *WhoAmP 93*
Crosby, Wade d1975 *WhoHol 92*
Crosby, William Duncan, Jr. 1943- *WhoAmL 94, WhoAmP 93*
Crosby, Willis Herman, Jr. 1941- *WhoBlA 94*
Crosby-Langley, Loretta 1957- *WhoBlA 94*
Croser, Mary Doreen 1944- *WhoAm 94*
Croset, Michel Roger 1943- *WhoScEn 94*
Croset, Paula *WhoHol 92*
Crosfield, John 1832-1901 *DcNaB MP*
Crosfield, (George) Philip (Chorley) 1924- *Who 94*
Croshal, Kathleen Klotz 1947- *WhoAmL 94*
Croshaw, Glenn Randall 1950- *WhoAmP 93*
Crosier, Helen Rose 1955- *WhoMW 93*
Crosier, John David 1937- *WhoAm 94*
Croslan, John Arthur 1939- *WhoBlA 94*
Crosland, Alan d1936 *WhoHol 92*
Crosland, John, Jr. 1928- *WhoAm 94*
Crosland, Margaret *WrDr 94*
Crosland, Maurice P. 1931- *WrDr 94*
Crosland, Philip Crawford 1943- *WhoAm 94*
Crosland, Susan Barnes *Who 94*
Crosman, Christopher Byron 1946- *WhoAmA 93*
Crosman, Henrietta d1944 *WhoHol 92*
Cross, Viscount 1920- *Who 94*
Cross, Alexander Dennis 1932- *WhoAm 94*
Cross, Alexander Galbraith 1908- *Who 94*
Cross, Alexander Urquhart 1906- *Who 94*
Cross, Alfred d1938 *WhoHol 92*
Cross, Alistair Robert Sinclair B. *Who 94*
Cross, Amanda *BlmGWL*
Cross, Amanda 1926- *WrDr 94*
Cross, Anthony Glenn 1936- *Who 94, WrDr 94*
Cross, Aureal Theophilus 1916- *WhoAm 94*
Cross, Austin Devon 1928- *WhoBlA 94*
Cross, Barry (Albert) 1925- *IntWW 93, Who 94*
Cross, Ben 1947- *IntMPA 94, WhoHol 92*
Cross, Betty Jean 1946- *WhoBlA 94*
Cross, Beverley 1931- *Who 94*
Cross, (Alan) Beverley 1931- *ConDr 93, WrDr 94*
Cross, Brenda 1919- *WrDr 94*
Cross, Bruce Michael 1942- *WhoAmL 94*
Cross, Carla Jean 1941- *WhoWest 94*
Cross, Charles Frederick 1855-1935 *WorInv*
Cross, Chester Joseph 1931- *WhoAmL 94*
Cross, Christopher 1951- *WhoAm 94*
Cross, Christopher Charles 1952- *WhoAmL 94, WhoWest 94*
Cross, Christopher T. 1940- *WhoAm 94*
Cross, (Margaret) Claire 1932- *WrDr 94*
Cross, Clifford Thomas 1920- *Who 94*
Cross, Clyde Cleveland 1918- *WhoAm 94*
Cross, David 1940- *WrDr 94*
Cross, Dennis Gerald 1945- *WhoAmL 94*
Cross, Dennis Ward 1943- *WhoFI 94*
Cross, Dewain Kingsley 1937- *WhoFI 94*
Cross, Dolores E. 1938- *WhoBlA 94*
Cross, Dolores Evelyn 1938- *Who 94, WhoAm 94, WhoMW 93*
Cross, Donald Melvin 1935- *WhoAmP 93*
Cross, Elmo Garnett, Jr. 1942- *WhoAmP 93*
Cross, Frank Bradley 1897- *WhAm 10*
Cross, Frank Moore, Jr. 1921- *WhoAm 94*
Cross, G(eorge) L(ynn) 1905- *IntWW 93*
Cross, George Alan Martin 1942- *IntWW 93, Who 94, WhoAm 94, WhoScEn 94*
Cross, George Lynn 1905- *WhoAm 94*
Cross, George R. 1923- *WhoAm 94*
Cross, Gerald *WhoHol 92*
Cross, Gillian (Clare) 1945- *TwCYAW, WrDr 94*
Cross, Gillian Clare 1945- *Who 94*
Cross, Glenn Laban 1941- *WhoFI 94, WhoScEn 94, WhoWest 94*
Cross, Haman, Jr. 1949- *WhoBlA 94*
Cross, Hannah Margaret 1908- *Who 94*
Cross, Harley *WhoHol 92*
Cross, Harold Zane 1941- *WhoMW 93, WhoScEn 94*
Cross, Harry Maybury 1913- *WhoAm 94*
Cross, Herbert James 1934- *WhoWest 94*
Cross, Irvie Keil 1917- *WhoAm 94*
Cross, J. Bruce 1949- *WhoAm 94, WhoAmL 94*
Cross, Jack 1926- *WhoBlA 94*
Cross, James *DrAPF 93*
Cross, James d1981 *WhoHol 92*
Cross, James 1916- *WhoAm 94, WrDr 94*
Cross, James Richard 1921- *Who 94*
Cross, Jayne Roberta 1953- *WhoFI 94*
Cross, Jeffery M. 1946- *WhoAmL 94*
Cross, Jeremy Ladd 1939- *WhoFI 94*
Cross, Jerry 1941- *WhoAmP 93*
Cross, Jimmy d1981 *WhoHol 92*
Cross, Joan 1900- *NewGrDO, Who 94*
Cross, John Keir 1914-1967 *EncSF 93*
Cross, Judith Anne 1945- *WhoMW 93*
Cross, June Victoria 1954- *WhoAm 94, WhoBlA 94*
Cross, K. Patricia 1926- *WrDr 94*
Cross, Kathryn Patricia 1926- *WhoWest 94*
Cross, Kenneth (Brian Boyd) 1911- *Who 94*
Cross, Larry d1976 *WhoHol 92*
Cross, Leland Briggs, Jr. 1930- *WhoAm 94*
Cross, Letitia c. 1681-1737 *NewGrDO*
Cross, Margaret Natalie *Who 94*
Cross, Michael Aduron 1944- *WhoAmP 93*
Cross, Oliver d1971 *WhoHol 92*
Cross, Paul Edward 1948- *WhoWest 94*
Cross, Peter 1951- *ConAu 141*
Cross, Peter A. 1947- *WhoAm 94, WhoAmL 94*
Cross, Polton *EncSF 93*
Cross, Ralph Emerson 1910- *WhoAm 94*
Cross, Richard Eugene 1910- *WhoAm 94*
Cross, Richard John 1929- *WhoAm 94*
Cross, Richard K. 1940- *WrDr 94*
Cross, Robert Clark 1939- *WhoAm 94*
Cross, Robert Craigie 1911- *Who 94*
Cross, Robert Louis 1937- *WhoWest 94*
Cross, Robert R. 1945- *WhoAmL 94*
Cross, Robert Roy 1935- *WhoIns 94*
Cross, Robert William 1937- *WhoFI 94*
Cross, Roger David 1947- *WhoAmP 93*
Cross, Ronald Anthony 1937- *EncSF 93*
Cross, Ruel P. 1926- *WhoAmP 93*
Cross, Samuel S. 1919- *WhoAm 94, WhoAmL 94*
Cross, Steven Jasper 1954- *WhoFI 94*
Cross, Terry I. 1951- *WhoAmL 94*
Cross, Theodore Lamont 1924- *WhoAm 94*
Cross, Thomas B. 1949- *WrDr 94*
Cross, Thomas Gary 1947- *WhoFI 94*
Cross, Thomas H., III 1958- *WhoAmP 93*
Cross, Thomas Michael 1961- *WhoFI 94*
Cross, Thomas Robert 1942- *WhoAmL 94*
Cross, Travis 1927- *WhoWest 94*
Cross, Trevor Arthur 1960- *WhoScEn 94*
Cross, Verda 1914- *ConAu 142, SmATA 75 [port]*
Cross, Victor 1914- *WrDr 94*
Cross, Victoria 1868-1952 *DcLB 135 [port], EncSF 93*
Cross, W. Thomas 1949- *WhoFI 94*
Cross, Watson, Jr. 1918- *WhoAmA 93*
Cross, Wayne A. 1945- *WhoAmL 94*
Cross, Wilbur (Lucius, III) 1918- *WrDr 94*
Cross, William 1936- *WhoAmP 93*
Cross, William Dennis 1940- *WhoAm 94, WhoAmL 94*
Cross, William Howard 1946- *WhoBlA 94*
Cross, William Lee 1936- *WhoIns 94*
Cross, William Redmond 1959- *WhoFI 94*
Cross, William Redmond, Jr. 1917- *WhoAm 94*
Cross, Yvonne *WhoAmA 93*
Cross, Zora 1890-1964 *BlmGWL*
Crossan, G(regory) D(ixon) 1950- *WrDr 94*
Crossan, John Robert 1947- *WhoAm 94, WhoAmL 94, WhoMW 93*
Crosse, Gordon 1937- *NewGrDO, Who 94*
Crosse, Robert c. 1547-1611 *DcNaB MP*
Crosse, Rupert d1973 *WhoHol 92*
Crosse, Rupert 1928-1973 *AfrAmAl 6*
Crosse, St. George Idris Bryon 1939- *WhoBlA 94*
Crossen, Forest *DrAPF 93*
Crossen, Gary Charles 1951- *WhoAmL 94*
Crossen, John Jacob 1932- *WhoAm 94*
Crossen, Kendell Foster 1910-1981 *EncSF 93*

Crossett, Robert Nelson 1938- *Who 94*
Crossfield, Albert Scott 1921- *WhoAm 94*
Crossgrove, Roger Lynn 1921- *WhoAmA 93*
Crossland, Anthony 1931- *Who 94*
Crossland, Bernard 1923- *IntWW 93, Who 94*
Crossland, Harriet Kent 1902- *WhoAm 94*
Crossland, Ivan, Sr. *WhoHisp 94*
Crossland, Leonard 1914- *Who 94*
Crossland, Marjorie d1954 *WhoHol 92*
Crossland, Pete Nelson 1937- *WhoAmP 93*
Crossland, Ronald Arthur 1920- *Who 94*
Crossler, Johnnie Charles 1954- *WhoWest 94*
Crossley *Who 94*
Crossley, Charles R., II 1938- *WhoBlA 94*
Crossley, Francis Rendel Erskine 1915- *WhoScEn 94*
Crossley, Frank Alphonso 1925- *WhoAm 94, WhoBlA 94*
Crossley, Geoffrey Allan 1920- *Who 94*
Crossley, Gertrude Comilla 1925- *WhoAmP 93*
Crossley, Harry 1918- *Who 94*
Crossley, Kent Bertram 1942- *WhoMW 93*
Crossley, Linda Susan 1950- *WhoMW 93*
Crossley, Nicholas John 1962- *Who 94*
Crossley, Paul Christopher Richard 1944- *Who 94*
Crossley, Ralph John 1933- *Who 94*
Crossley, Randolph Allin 1904- *WhoAm 94*
Crossley, Sid d1960 *WhoHol 92*
Crossley-Holland, Kevin (John William) 1941- *SmATA 74 [port], TwCYAW, WrDr 94*
Crossley-Holland, Kevin John William 1941- *Who 94*
Crosslin, Anna Eriko 1950- *WhoMW 93*
Crosslin, Evelyn Stocking 1919- *WhoBlA 94*
Crosslin, Justin Dell 1943- *WhoFI 94*
Crossman, Harold G., Jr. 1922- *WhoAmP 93*
Crossman, John Sherman 1943- *WhoWest 94*
Crossman, Richard (Howard Stafford) 1907-1974 *ConAu 43NR*
Crossman, Stafford Mac Arthur 1953- *WhoScEn 94*
Crossman, William Whittard 1927- *WhoAm 94*
Crosson, Albert J. 1934- *WhoFI 94, WhoWest 94*
Crosson, Frederick James 1926- *WhoAm 94*
Crosson, John Albert 1961- *WhoWest 94*
Crosson, Joseph Patrick 1950- *WhoScEn 94*
Crosson, Matthew Thomas 1949- *WhoAmL 94*
Crosson, Robert *DrAPF 93*
Crosswhite, Bob H. 1929- *WhoFI 94*
Crosthwait, David N., Jr. 1898-1976 *WorInv*
Crosthwait, Timothy Leland 1915- *Who 94*
Crosthwaite, Ivy d1962 *WhoHol 92*
Croston, Arthur Michael 1942- *WhoScEn 94*
Croteau, Denis 1932- *WhoWest 94*
Crothers, Donald Morris 1937- *WhoAm 94, WhoScEn 94*
Crothers, Rachel 1878-1958 *BlmGWL, IntDcT 2*
Crothers, Scatman d1986 *WhoHol 92*
Crotti, Joseph Robert 1923- *WhoWest 94*
Crotto, Paul 1922- *WhoAmA 93*
Crotts, Mike D. 1947- *WhoAmP 93*
Crotty, Edward John 1923- *WhoAmP 93*
Crotty, Leo William 1927- *WhoFI 94*
Crotty, Paul A. 1941- *WhoAmL 94*
Crotty, Richard Thomas 1948- *WhoAmP 93*
Crotty, Robert Bell 1951- *WhoAmL 94*
Crotty, Robert E. 1944- *WhoAmL 94*
Crotty, William 1936- *WhoAm 94*
Crotty, William Henry 1947- *WhoMW 93*
Crouch, Andrae 1942- *AfrAmAl 6, WhoBlA 94*
Crouch, Anna Maria 1763-1805 *NewGrDO*
Crouch, Colin John 1944- *Who 94*
Crouch, David (Lance) 1919- *Who 94*
Crouch, George Sanford 1896- *WhAm 10*
Crouch, Jay Thomas 1960- *WhoMW 93*
Crouch, Joyce Knowles 1935- *WhoAmP 93*
Crouch, Judith Ann 1953- *WhoMW 93*
Crouch, Marcus S. 1913- *WrDr 94*
Crouch, Ned Philbrick 1948- *WhoAmA 93*
Crouch, Robert Allen 1955- *WhoBlA 94*
Crouch, Robert P., Jr. 1948- *WhoAmL 94, WhoAmP 93*
Crouch, Stanley *DrAPF 93*
Crouch, Stanley 1945- *ConAu 141*
Crouch, Steven L. 1943- *WhoScEn 94*
Crouch, Thomas Gene 1933- *WhoAmL 94, WhoAmP 93*
Crouch, Walter H. 1943- *WhoAmL 94*
Crouchett, Lawrence Paul 1922- *WhoBlA 94*
Crouch-Robinson, Myra 1960- *WhoMW 93*
Crough, Daniel Francis 1936- *WhoAm 94, WhoAmL 94, WhoIns 94*
Croughton, Amy H. 1880-1951 *WhoAmA 93N*
Crouse, Farrell R. 1963- *WhoAmL 94*
Crouse, Farrell Rondall 1932- *WhoAm 94*
Crouse, Lindsay 1948- *IntMPA 94, WhoAm 94, WhoHol 92*
Crouse, Lloyd Roseville 1918- *WhoAm 94*
Crouse, Michael Glenn 1949- *WhoAmA 93*
Crouse, Ted *WhoFI 94*
Croushoré, Bruce Joseph 1947- *WhoAmL 94*
Crout, Daniel Wesley 1937- *WhoAmL 94*
Crout, John J. 1937- *WhoIns 94*
Crout, John Richard 1929- *WhoAm 94*
Crouter, Richard Earl 1937- *WhoAm 94*
Crouther, Betty Jean 1950- *WhoBlA 94*
Crouther, Betty M. 1931- *WhoBlA 94*
Crouther, Melvin S., Jr. 1926- *WhoBlA 94*
Croutier, Alev Lytle 1944- *ConAu 142*
Crouton, Francois (Lafortune) 1921- *WhoAmA 93*
Crouzet, Francois Marie-Joseph 1922- *ConAu 42NR, IntWW 93*
Crouzet, Roger *WhoHol 92*
Crovitz, Charles K. 1953- *WhoAm 94, WhoFI 94*
Crow, Allan Brian 1953- *WhoAmP 93*
Crow, Bill 1927- *ConAu 140*
Crow, Bobby C. 1932- *WhoAmP 93*
Crow, Carl A., Jr. 1951- *WhoAmP 93*
Crow, Carol (Wilson) 1915- *WhoAmA 93*
Crow, Charles Delmar 1945- *WhoFI 94*
Crow, Dolores J. *WhoAmP 93*
Crow, Edwin Louis 1916- *WhoAm 94, WhoWest 94*
Crow, Elizabeth Smith *WhoAm 94*
Crow, Emilia 1957- *WhoHol 92*
Crow, F. Trammell *WhoAm 94, WhoFI 94*
Crow, Harold Eugene 1933- *WhoAm 94*
Crow, Hershal Hilliar, Jr. 1935- *WhoAmP 93*
Crow, Hiawatha Moore 1907- *WhoBlA 94*
Crow, James F(ranklin) 1916- *IntWW 93*
Crow, James Franklin 1916- *WhoAm 94*
Crow, James Sylvester 1915- *WhoAm 94*
Crow, John Armstrong 1906- *WhoAm 94*
Crow, John Michael *WhoFI 94*
Crow, John W. 1937- *IntWW 93*
Crow, John William 1937- *WhoAm 94*
Crow, Judson Lewis 1936- *WhoMW 93*
Crow, Kenneth Arthur 1938- *WhoWest 94*
Crow, Levi *EncSF 93*
Crow, Lynne Campbell Smith 1942- *WhoFI 94*
Crow, Martha Ellen 1944- *WhoMW 93*
Crow, Mary *DrAPF 93*
Crow, Nancy Rebecca 1948- *WhoAmL 94, WhoWest 94*
Crow, Neil Byrne 1927- *WhoScEn 94*
Crow, Neil Edward 1926- *WhoAm 94*
Crow, Paul Abernathy, Jr. 1931- *WhoAm 94*
Crow, Richard Thomas 1939- *WhoAm 94*
Crow, Sam Alfred 1926- *WhoAm 94, WhoAmL 94, WhoMW 93*
Crow, (Hilary) Stephen 1934- *Who 94*
Crow, T. J. *EncSPD*
Crow, Terry Tom 1931- *WhoAm 94*
Crow, Timothy Alan 1962- *WhoWest 94*
Crow, Timothy John 1938- *Who 94*
Crow, Trammell *NewYTBS 93 [port]*
Crow, William Beryl 1931- *WhoAm 94, WhoAmL 94*
Crow, William Cecil 1904- *WhoAm 94*
Crowcroft, Peter d1982 *WhoHol 92*
Crowcroft, (William) Peter 1925- *EncSF 93*
Crowden, Graham 1922- *WhoHol 92*
Crowden, James Gee Pascoe 1927- *Who 94*
Crowder, Barbara Lynn 1956- *WhoAmL 94, WhoMW 93*
Crowder, Charles Harper, Jr. 1927- *WhoAmP 93*
Crowder, David Lester 1941- *WhoWest 94*
Crowder, Diane Griffin 1948- *WhoMW 93*
Crowder, F(rederick) Petre 1919- *Who 94*
Crowder, Norman Harry 1926- *Who 94*
Crowder, Robert McKnight 1944- *WhoAmP 93*
Crowder, William Harvey 1945- *WhoAmL 94*
Crowdus, Gary Alan 1945- *WhoAm 94*
Crowdy, Joseph Porter 1923- *Who 94*
Crowe, Brian Lee 1938- *Who 94*
Crowe, Cameron 1957- *IntMPA 94*
Crowe, Cameron Macmillan 1931- *WhoAm 94*
Crowe, Catherine 1800?-1872 *BlmGWL*
Crowe, Cecily Bentley (Teague) *WrDr 94*
Crowe, Christopher Everett 1954- *WhoWest 94*
Crowe, Dale Jody 1946- *WhoMW 93*
Crowe, Danny C. 1949- *WhoAmL 94*
Crowe, Devon George 1948- *WhoScEn 94*
Crowe, Dewey E., II 1947- *WhoAmP 93*
Crowe, Eileen d1978 *WhoHol 92*
Crowe, Eugene Bertrand 1916- *WhoAm 94*
Crowe, F. J. *GayLL*
Crowe, Gerald Patrick 1930- *Who 94*
Crowe, Hal Scott 1953- *WhoScEn 94*
Crowe, James Joseph 1935- *WhoAm 94, WhoAmL 94*
Crowe, Jeffrey C. 1946- *WhoAm 94, WhoFI 94*
Crowe, John 1924- *WrDr 94*
Crowe, John Carl 1937- *WhoAm 94*
Crowe, John T. 1938- *WhoAmL 94, WhoFI 94, WhoWest 94*
Crowe, Martin David 1962- *IntWW 93*
Crowe, Michael John 1936- *WhoMW 93*
Crowe, Michael John 1937- *Who 94*
Crowe, Norma Jean 1938- *WhoAmP 93*
Crowe, Patrick J. 1944- *WhoIns 94*
Crowe, Philip Anthony 1936- *Who 94*
Crowe, Richard Allan 1952- *WhoWest 94*
Crowe, Robert William 1924- *WhoAm 94*
Crowe, Russell *WhoHol 92*
Crowe, Sackville 1600-1683 *DcNaB MP*
Crowe, Sylvia 1901- *Who 94*
Crowe, Thomas Hunter 1935- *WhoMW 93*
Crowe, Thomas Leonard 1944- *WhoAm 94, WhoAmL 94*
Crowe, Vincil Penny 1897- *WhAm 10*
Crowe, William J., Jr. 1925- *ConAu 142, WhoAmP 93*
Crowe, William James, Jr. 1925- *IntWW 93, WhoAm 94*
Crowe, William Joseph 1947- *WhoAm 94*
Crowell, Bernard G. 1930- *WhoBlA 94*
Crowell, Dean W. 1949- *WhoAmL 94*
Crowell, Donald Rex 1943- *WhoAmP 93*
Crowell, Edward Prince 1926- *WhoAm 94*
Crowell, Eldon Hubbard 1924- *WhoAm 94*
Crowell, Elizabeth A. Chase 1939- *WhoAmP 93*
Crowell, Gentry 1932-1989 *WhAm 10*
Crowell, John B., Jr. 1930- *WhoAm 94, WhoAmP 93*
Crowell, John Chambers 1917- *WhoAm 94*
Crowell, John Durand, III 1957- *WhoAmL 94*
Crowell, Josephine d1932 *WhoHol 92*
Crowell, Lucius 1911-1988 *WhoAmA 93N*
Crowell, Michael Earl 1949- *WhoWest 94*
Crowell, Nancy Melzer 1948- *WhoFI 94*
Crowell, Prince Sears, Jr. 1909- *WhoMW 93*
Crowell, Richard Henry 1928- *WhoAm 94*
Crowell, Richard Lane 1930- *WhoAm 94*
Crowell, Robert Lamson 1945- *WhoAmL 94, WhoAmP 93*
Crowell, Rodney J. 1950- *WhoAm 94*
Crowell, Wayne Franklin 1937- *WhoFI 94*
Crowell-Moustafa, Julia J. 1923- *WhoBlA 94*
Crowfoot, Anthony Bernard 1936- *Who 94*
Crowhurst, Viscount 1983- *Who 94*
Crowl, John Allen 1935- *WhoAm 94*
Crowl, Philip Axtell 1914-1991 *WhAm 10*
Crowl, Samuel 1940- *ConAu 142*
Crowl, Samuel Renninger 1940- *WhoAm 94*
Crowley, Aleister 1875-1947 *AstEnc, DcNaB MP, GayLL*
Crowley, Allen L., Sr. 1932- *WhoFI 94*
Crowley, Ambrose 1658-1713 *DcNaB MP*
Crowley, Beryl Ponton 1949- *WhoAmL 94*
Crowley, Cassandra Ann 1949- *WhoMW 93*
Crowley, Christina 1945- *WhoWest 94*
Crowley, Daniel John 1921- *WhoAm 94, WhoWest 94*
Crowley, Don W. *WhoAmP 93*
Crowley, Ed *WhoHol 92*
Crowley, Edward Alexander *GayLL*
Crowley, Edward Alexander 1875-1947 *DcNaB MP*
Crowley, Eileen Lopez 1949- *WhoHisp 94*
Crowley, Elizabeth Marlene 1940- *WhoMW 93*
Crowley, Ellen 1916- *WhoAmP 93*
Crowley, Frank 1948- *WhoAmL 94*
Crowley, Frederic Charles 1944- *WhoAmP 93*
Crowley, George Clement 1916- *Who 94*
Crowley, Hank 1918- *WhoAmP 93*
Crowley, James M. 1942- *WhoIns 94*
Crowley, James T. 1943- *WhoAmL 94*
Crowley, James Worthington 1930- *WhoAm 94, WhoAmL 94*
Crowley, Jane d1970 *WhoHol 92*
Crowley, Janeen Lou 1954- *WhoMW 93*
Crowley, Jerome Joseph, Jr. 1939- *WhoAm 94*
Crowley, Joanne Katherine 1932- *WhoMW 93*
Crowley, John *Who 94*
Crowley, John 1942- *ConAu 43NR, EncSF 93, WrDr 94*
Crowley, John Crane 1919- *WhoWest 94*
Crowley, John Desmond 1938- *Who 94*
Crowley, John J., Jr. 1928- *WhoAmP 93*
Crowley, John Joseph, Jr. 1928- *WhoAm 94*
Crowley, John P. 1936- *WhoAmP 93*
Crowley, John William 1945- *WhoAm 94*
Crowley, Joseph 1962- *WhoAmP 93*
Crowley, Joseph Michael 1940- *WhoAm 94, WhoScEn 94*
Crowley, Joseph Neil 1933- *WhoAm 94, WhoWest 94*
Crowley, Kathleen 1931- *WhoHol 92*
Crowley, Kevin Xavier 1949- *WhoAmL 94*
Crowley, L. C. 1949- *WhoFI 94*
Crowley, Leo T. 1955- *WhoAmL 94*
Crowley, Maria Elena Pérez *WhoHisp 94*
Crowley, Marilyn 1935- *WhoMW 93*
Crowley, Mart 1935- *GayLL, WrDr 94*
Crowley, Mart 1935-1991 *ConDr 93*
Crowley, Matt *WhoHol 92*
Crowley, Michael Joseph 1962- *WhoScEn 94*
Crowley, Michael Summers 1928- *WhoScEn 94*
Crowley, Nathaniel J., Sr. *WhoAmP 93*
Crowley, Niall 1926- *Who 94*
Crowley, Patricia 1929- *WhoHol 92*
Crowley, Paul William 1949- *WhoAmP 93*
Crowley, Rosemary Anne 1938- *WhoWomW 91*
Crowley, Suzan *WhoHol 92*
Crowley, Thomas B. 1914- *WhoAm 94, WhoWest 94*
Crowley, Thomas M. 1935- *WhoAmP 93*
Crowley, William Francis, Jr. 1943- *WhoAm 94, WhoScEn 94*
Crowley-Milling, Denis 1919- *Who 94*
Crowley-Milling, Michael Crowley 1917- *Who 94*
Crowling, Patrick McGuire, Jr. 1942- *WhoAmL 94*
Crown, Alan D(avid) 1932- *ConAu 141*
Crown, David Allan 1928- *WhoAm 94, WrDr 94*
Crown, Henry 1896-1990 *WhAm 10*
Crown, Keith Allen 1918- *WhoAmA 93*
Crown, Lester 1925- *WhoAm 94, WhoFI 94*
Crown, Roberta Lila *WhoAmA 93*
Crowne, John 1640?-1703? *BlmGEL*
Crowninshield, Edward Augustus 1817-1859 *DcLB 140*
Crowser, Linda Ann 1969- *WhoWest 94*
Crowsey, Cheryl Ann 1959- *WhoFI 94*
Crowson, Dan Michael 1953- *WhoWest 94*
Crowson, James Lawrence 1938- *WhoAm 94, WhoAmL 94*
Crowson, P(aul) S(piller) 1913- *WrDr 94*
Crowson, Richard Borman 1929- *Who 94*
Crowston, Wallace Bruce Stewart 1934- *WhoAm 94, WhoFI 94*
Crowther, Bryan 1765-1814 *EncSPD*
Crowther, Derek *Who 94*
Crowther, Eric (John Ronald) 1924- *Who 94*
Crowther, H. David 1930- *WhoAm 94*
Crowther, Harold Francis 1920- *WrDr 94*
Crowther, James Earl 1930- *WhoAm 94*
Crowther, Leslie 1933- *IntMPA 94*
Crowther, Richard Anthony 1942- *Who 94*
Crowther, Richard Layton 1910- *WhoAm 94, WhoScEn 94*
Crowther, (Joseph) Stanley 1925- *Who 94*
Crowther, Thomas Rowland 1937- *Who 94*
Crowther, William Ronald Hilton 1941- *Who 94*
Croxford, Ian Lionel 1953- *Who 94*
Croxford, Lynne Louise 1947- *WhoFI 94*
Croxon, Raymond Patrick Austen 1928- *Who 94*
Croxton, C(live) A(nthony) 1945- *WrDr 94*
Croxton, Frederick Emory 1899-1991 *WhAm 10*
Croxton, Frederick Emory, Jr. 1923- *WhoAm 94*
Croxton, Gayle Tennison 1964- *WhoAmL 94*
Croxton-Smith, Claude 1901- *Who 94*
Croydon, Area Bishop of 1936- *Who 94*
Croydon, Joan *WhoHol 92*
Croydon, John Edward Kenneth 1929- *Who 94*
Croydon, Michael Benet 1931- *WhoAmA 93*

Crozer, Robert P. 1947- *WhoFI 94*
Crozier, Andrew 1943- *WrDr 94*
Crozier, Brian 1918- *WrDr 94*
Crozier, Brian Rossiter 1918- *IntWW 93, Who 94*
Crozier, Caroline Sanchez *WhoHisp 94*
Crozier, David Wayne 1958- *WhoScEn 94*
Crozier, Eric 1914- *NewGrDO*
Crozier, Eric John 1914- *Who 94*
Crozier, Francis Rawdon Moira 1796-1848 *WhWE*
Crozier, Lorna 1948- *BlmGWL, WrDr 94*
Crozier, Nancy Joyce 1933- *WhoMW 93*
Crozier, Richard Lewis 1944- *WhoAmA 93*
Crozier, Scott A. 1950- *WhoAmL 94*
Crozier, William K., Jr. 1926- *WhoAmA 93*
Crozier, William Marshall, Jr. 1932- *WhoAm 94, WhoFI 94*
Cruanes Molina, Asuncion 1925- *WhoWomW 91*
Cruce, Doug 1947- *WhoAmP 93*
Cruddas, Thomas Rennison 1921- *Who 94*
Cruden, John *AmRev*
Cruden, John Charles 1946- *WhoAmL 94*
Crudup, Gwendolyn M. 1961- *WhoBlA 94*
Crudup, Warren George, Sr. 1923- *WhoAm 94*
Crue, Benjamin Lane, Jr. 1925- *WhoWest 94*
Cruea, Dudley 1956- *WhoAmP 93*
Cruea, Edmond D. *IntMPA 94*
Cruess, Richard Leigh 1929- *WhoAm 94, WhoScEn 94*
Cruft, John Herbert 1914- *Who 94*
Cruger, John Harris 1738-1807 *WhAmRev*
Cruickshank, Alistair Ronald 1944- *Who 94*
Cruickshank, Andrew d1988 *WhoHol 92*
Cruickshank, Donald Gordon 1942- *Who 94*
Cruickshank, Duncan Redford 1965- *WhoWest 94*
Cruickshank, Durward William John 1924- *IntWW 93, Who 94*
Cruickshank, Eric Kennedy 1914- *Who 94*
Cruickshank, Herbert James 1912- *Who 94*
Cruickshank, James David 1936- *WhoWest 94*
Cruickshank, John 1924- *Who 94, WrDr 94*
Cruickshank, John Alexander 1920- *Who 94*
Cruickshank, Laura *WhoHol 92*
Cruickshank, Su *WhoHol 92*
Cruickshank, William Mellon 1915-1992 *WhAm 10*
Cruickshanks, Reid *WhoHol 92*
Cruikshank, David C. 1946- *WhoIns 94*
Cruikshank, George 1792-1878 *BlmGEL*
Cruikshank, John W., III 1933- *WhoAm 94*
Cruikshank, Margaret 1940- *GayLL*
Cruikshank, Robert Lane 1936- *WhoAm 94*
Cruikshank, Thomas Henry 1931- *WhoAm 94, WhoFI 94*
Cruikshank, Warren Lott 1916- *WhoAm 94*
Cruise, R. David 1956- *WhoAmP 93*
Cruise, Tom 1962- *IntMPA 94, IntWW 93, WhoAm 94, WhoHol 92*
Cruise, Warren Michael 1939- *WhoBlA 94*
Cruls, Gastao *EncSF 93*
Crum, Albert B. 1931- *WhoBlA 94*
Crum, Albert Byrd 1931- *WhoAm 94, WhoFI 94, WhoScEn 94*
Crum, Colleen Ruth 1957- *WhoMW 93*
Crum, David 1938- *WhoAmA 93*
Crum, Denny 1943- *BasBi*
Crum, Denny Edwin 1937- *WhoAm 94*
Crum, James Francis 1934- *WhoAm 94, WhoMW 93*
Crum, John Kistler 1936- *WhoAm 94, WhoFI 94, WhoScEn 94*
Crum, Katherine B. 1941- *WhoAmA 93*
Crum, Katherine Rosemary 1963- *WhoMW 93*
Crum, Lawrence Lee 1933- *WhoAm 94*
Crum, M. Elizabeth 1948- *WhoAmL 94*
Crum, William H., Jr. 1948- *WhoAmP 93*
Crumb, George 1929- *IntWW 93*
Crumb, George Henry 1929- *AmCulL, WhoAm 94*
Crumb, Owen Joseph 1925- *WhoAm 94*
Crumbaker, Don E. *WhoAmP 93*
Crumbaugh, David Gordon 1951- *WhoAm 94*
Crumbaugh, Lee Forrest 1947- *WhoAm 94*
Crumbley, Alex *WhoAmP 93*
Crumbley, Donald Larry 1941- *WhoAm 94*
Crumbley, John David 1951- *WhoWest 94*
Crumbley, R. Alex 1942- *WhoAmL 94*
Crumbliss, Alvin Lee 1942- *WhoAm 94*
Crumer, Jane *WhAmRev*
Crumes, William Edward 1914- *WhoAm 94*
Crumit, Frank d1943 *WhoHol 92*
Crumley, James *DrAPF 93*
Crumley, James 1939- *WrDr 94*
Crumley, James Robert, Jr. 1925- *WhoAm 94*
Crumley, John Walter 1944- *WhoAmL 94*
Crummell, Alexander 1819-1898 *AfrAmAl 6, DcAmReB 2*
Crummett, Warren Berlin 1922- *WhoMW 93*
Crummey, Robert Owen 1936- *WhoAm 94*
Crump, Arthel Eugene 1947- *WhoBlA 94*
Crump, Barry (John) 1935- *WrDr 94*
Crump, C(harles) G(eorge) 1862-1935 *EncSF 93*
Crump, Charles H. *DrAPF 93*
Crump, Constance Louise 1948- *WhoMW 93*
Crump, Dewey G. 1946- *WhoAmP 93*
Crump, Diana Lynne 1950- *WhoMW 93*
Crump, Francis Jefferson, III 1942- *WhoAmL 94*
Crump, Fred H., Jr. 1931- *ConAu 41NR, SmATA 76 [port]*
Crump, Galbraith Miller 1929- *WhoAm 94*
Crump, Gerald Franklin 1935- *WhoAmL 94, WhoWest 94*
Crump, Gwyn Norman, Sr. 1932- *WhoMW 93*
Crump, Irving 1887-1979 *EncSF 93*
Crump, James G., Jr. *WhoFI 94*
Crump, Janice Renae 1947- *WhoBlA 94*
Crump, John *WhoAmL 94*
Crump, Julianne Juanita 1950- *WhoWest 94*
Crump, Kathleen (Wheeler) 1884-1977 *WhoAmA 93N*
Crump, Lisa M. 1963- *WhoMW 93*
Crump, Maurice 1908- *Who 94*
Crump, Nathaniel L., Sr. 1920- *WhoBlA 94*
Crump, Paul (Orville) 1930?- *BlkWr 2*
Crump, Ronald Cordell 1951- *WhoAmL 94*
Crump, Spencer *WhoAm 94, WhoWest 94*
Crump, W. Leslie 1894-1962 *WhoAmA 93N*
Crump, Walter Moore, Jr. 1941- *WhoAmA 93*
Crump, Wayne F. 1950- *WhoAmP 93*
Crump, Wilbert S. *WhoBlA 94*
Crump, William Henry Howes 1903- *Who 94*
Crump, William L. 1920- *WhoBlA 94*
Crump, William Maurice Esplen *Who 94*
Crumpecker, C. W., Jr. 1945- *WhoAmL 94*
Crumpton, Evelyn 1924- *WhoScEn 94, WhoWest 94*
Crumpton, Michael Joseph 1929- *IntWW 93, Who 94*
Crupi, Karen Michele 1963- *WhoAmL 94*
Crupper, Clay 1935- *WhoAmP 93*
Crusa, Michael Charles 1947- *WhoWest 94*
Crusat, Paulina 1900- *BlmGWL*
Cruse, Allan Baird 1941- *WhoWest 94*
Cruse, Clyde Lansford, III 1956- *WhoWest 94*
Cruse, David C. *DrAPF 93*
Cruse, Denton W. 1944- *WhoWest 94*
Cruse, Harold Wright 1916- *WhoBlA 94*
Cruse, Peggy *WhoAmP 93*
Cruse, Rex Beach, Jr. 1941- *WhoFI 94*
Crusell, Bernhard Henrik 1775-1838 *NewGrDO*
Crush, Jonathan 1953- *ConAu 141*
Crusius, Christian August c. 1715-1775 *EncEth*
Crusoe, Edwin *DrAPF 93*
Crust, Arnold *ConTFT 11*
Cruster, Aud d1938 *WhoHol 92*
Crusto, Mitchell Ferdinand 1953- *WhoAm 94, WhoAmL 94, WhoBlA 94*
Crutcher, Betty Neal 1949- *WhoBlA 94*
Crutcher, Chris(topher C.) 1946- *TwCYAW*
Crutcher, Edward Torrence 1920- *WhoBlA 94*
Crutcher, Harold Trabue, Jr. 1938- *WhoAm 94, WhoMW 93*
Crutcher, Harry, III 1938- *WhoAmP 93*
Crutcher, J. Thomas 1947- *WhoAmL 94*
Crutcher, John William 1916- *WhoAm 94, WhoAmP 93*
Crutcher, Michael Bayard 1944- *WhoAm 94, WhoAmL 94, WhoFI 94*
Crutcher, Ronald Andrew 1947- *WhoBlA 94*
Crutcher, Ronald James 1954- *WhoAmP 93*
Crutchfield, Alexander 1958- *WhoFI 94, WhoWest 94*
Crutchfield, Edward Elliott, Jr. 1941- *WhoAm 94, WhoFI 94*
Crutchfield, Inez *WhoAmP 93*
Crutchfield, James N. 1947- *WhoBlA 94*
Crutchfield, James Patrick 1955- *WhoWest 94*
Crutchfield, Jimmie d1993 *NewYTBS 93*
Crutchfield, Sabrina Dames 1957- *WhoBlA 94*
Crutchfield, Sam Shaw, Jr. 1934- *WhoAm 94*
Crutchfield, Susan Ellis 1940- *WhoBlA 94*
Crutchfield, William Richard 1932- *WhoAm 94, WhoAmA 93*
Crutchfield, William Ward 1928- *WhoAmP 93*
Crutchfield-Baker, Verdenia 1958- *WhoBlA 94*
Crutchley, Brooke 1907- *Who 94*
Crutchley, Donald Osborne 1927- *WhoAmP 93*
Crutchley, Rosalie 1921- *WhoHol 92*
Crutchlow, John Adrian 1946- *Who 94*
Crute, Beverly Jean *WhoMW 93*
Crute, Sally d1971 *WhoHol 92*
Cruthers, James (Winter) 1924- *Who 94*
Cruthird, J. Robert Lee 1944- *WhoBlA 94*
Crutsinger, Robert Keane 1930- *WhoAm 94, WhoFI 94*
Cruttwell, Geraldine *Who 94*
Cruttwell, Hugh (Percival) 1918- *Who 94*
Crutzen, Yves Robert 1950- *WhoScEn 94*
Cruvelli, (Jeanne) Sophie (Charlotte) 1826-1907 *NewGrDO*
Cruyff, John 1947- *WorESoc [port]*
Cruz, Abraham 1949- *WhoHisp 94*
Cruz, Adolph F. *WhoHisp 94*
Cruz, Agata *BlmGWL*
Cruz, Albert Raymond 1933- *WhoHisp 94*
Cruz, Amada Lourdes 1961- *WhoHisp 94*
Cruz, Amado Luis 1956- *WhoAmL 94*
Cruz, Antonio L. *WhoHisp 94*
Cruz, Aurelio R. 1934- *WhoHisp 94*
Cruz, B. Roberto 1941- *WhoHisp 94*
Cruz, Bárbara Caridad 1961- *WhoHisp 94*
Cruz, Ben Ruben 1918- *WhoHisp 94*
Cruz, Benjamin J. *WhoAmP 93*
Cruz, Benjamin Joseph Franquez 1951- *WhoAm 94, WhoAmL 94*
Cruz, Bobby *WhoAm 94*
Cruz, Brandon 1962- *WhoHol 92*
Cruz, Camilo Fernando 1960- *WhoHisp 94*
Cruz, Carlos 1940- *WhoHisp 94*
Cruz, Celia *WhoHisp 94*
Cruz, Celia c. 1929- *ConMus 10 [port]*
Cruz, Cosme 1942- *WhoHisp 94*
Cruz, Daniel 1941- *WhoHisp 94*
Cruz, Daniel Louis 1951- *WhoHisp 94*
Cruz, Doris *WhoHisp 94*
Cruz, Edwin O. *WhoHisp 94*
Cruz, Emilio *WhoAmA 93*
Cruz, Emilio 1938- *AfrAmAl 6, WhoBlA 94*
Cruz, Erasmo, Sr. 1940- *WhoHisp 94*
Cruz, Félix Miguel 1958- *WhoHisp 94*
Cruz, Gilbert R. 1929- *WhoHisp 94*
Cruz, Gregory A. *WhoHisp 94*
Cruz, Iluminado Angeles 1936- *WhoBlA 94*
Cruz, John F. *WhoAmP 93*
Cruz, John Frank 1936- *WhoHisp 94*
Cruz, Jose Bejar, Jr. 1932- *WhoAm 94, WhoAsA 94, WhoScEn 94*
Cruz, Jose Manuel 1968- *WhoHisp 94*
Cruz, Joseph *WhoHisp 94*
Cruz, Juan Sanjurjo 1924- *WhoHisp 94*
Cruz, Juana Ines de la *BlmGWL*
Cruz, Julia Margarita 1948- *WhoHisp 94*
Cruz, Julio 1942- *WhoHisp 94*
Cruz, Lucy *WhoAmP 93*
Cruz, Manuel Franklin 1937- *WhoAm 94*
Cruz, Maximo Leonardo 1939- *WhoHisp 94*
Cruz, Michael J. 1952- *WhoHisp 94*
Cruz, Migdalia 1958- *WhoHisp 94*
Cruz, Miriam I. *WhoHisp 94*
Cruz, Norma Irene 1952- *WhoHisp 94*
Cruz, Phillip 1955- *WhoHisp 94*
Cruz, Pura *WhoAmA 93*
Cruz, Pura Isabel 1947- *WhoHisp 94*
Cruz, Raymond 1953- *WhoHisp 94*
Cruz, Renier 1952- *WhoAmL 94*
Cruz, Ricardo Cortez 1964- *BlkWr 2*
Cruz, Ruben 1956- *WhoHisp 94*
Cruz, Secundino 1938- *WhoHisp 94*
Cruz, Silvia 1959- *WhoHisp 94*
Cruz, Tim R. 1959- *WhoHisp 94*
Cruz, Victor Hernandez 1949- *BlkWr 2, HispLC [port], WhoHisp 94, WrDr 94*
Cruz, Virgil 1929- *WhoBlA 94*
Cruz, Wilfredo *WhoHisp 94*
Cruz, Willie *WhoHisp 94*
Cruzada, Rodolfo Omega 1930- *WhoAsA 94*
Cruzado, George *WhoHisp 94*
Cruz Aponte, Ramon Aristides 1927- *WhoAm 94, WhoHisp 94*
Cruzat, Edward Pedro 1926- *WhoBlA 94*
Cruzat, Gwendolyn S. *WhoBlA 94*
Cruzat, Liza *WhoHol 92*
Cruz-Diez, Carlos 1923- *IntWW 93*
Cruz Domenech, Antonio 1951- *WhoHisp 94*
Cruze, Alvin M. 1939- *WhoAm 94, WhoScEn 94*
Cruze, Deborah Kaye 1957- *WhoAmL 94, WhoWest 94*
Cruze, James d1942 *WhoHol 92*
Cruze, John Joseph 1943- *WhoAm 94, WhoAmL 94*
Cruze, Julie Jane d1946 *WhoHol 92*
Cruze, Kathryn 1954- *WhoAmL 94*
Cruze, Mae d1965 *WhoHol 92*
Cruz-Emeric, Jorge A. 1951- *WhoHisp 94*
Cruzen, Matt Earl 1962- *WhoScEn 94*
Cruzen, Patrick Richard 1947- *WhoFI 94*
Cruzerio, Maria-Manuela da Silva Nunes Ribeiro 1934- *IntWW 93*
Cruzkatz, Ida Maria *DrAPF 93*
Cruz Martinez, Alejandro d1987 *SmATA 74*
Cruzon, Virginia *WhoHol 92*
Cruz-Pinto, Jose Joaquim C. 1948- *WhoScEn 94*
Cruz-Rodriguez, Elba Teresa 1953- *WhoMW 93*
Cruz-Rodriguez, Escolastico 1931- *WhoHisp 94*
Cruz Rodriguez, Roberto *WhoAmP 93*
Cruz-Romeo, Gilda 1940- *NewGrDO*
Cruz-Romo, Gilda *WhoAm 94, WhoHisp 94*
Cruz Santiago, Gladys M. 1956- *WhoHisp 94*
Cruz-Uribe, Eugene David 1952- *WhoWest 94*
Cruz-Velez, David F. 1951- *WhoAmP 93*
Cruz-Velez, David Francisco 1951- *WhoHisp 94*
Crvenkovski, Krste 1921- *IntWW 93*
Crwys-Williams, David Owen 1940- *Who 94*
Cryden, David William 1955- *WhoWest 94*
Cryder, Cathy M. 1953- *WhoScEn 94*
Cryer, Clifford Loper 1948- *WhoWest 94*
Cryer, David 1936- *WhoHol 92*
Cryer, Dennis Robert 1944- *WhoScEn 94*
Cryer, Eugene Edward 1935- *WhoAm 94*
Cryer, Gretchen *WhoHol 92*
Cryer, Gretchen 1935- *WhoAm 94*
Cryer, Jon 1965- *IntMPA 94, WhoHol 92*
Cryer, Linkston T. 1933- *WhoBlA 94*
Cryer, Philip Eugene 1940- *WhoMW 93*
Cryer, (George) Robert 1934- *Who 94*
Cryer, Rodger Earl 1940- *WhoWest 94*
Cryer, Theodore Hudson 1946- *WhoScEn 94*
Crymble, John Frederick 1916- *WhoScEn 94*
Crymes, Ronald Jack 1935- *WhoScEn 94*
Crystal, Billy 1947- *IntMPA 94, IntWW 93, WhoAm 94, WhoCom [port], WhoHol 92*
Crystal, Boris 1931- *WhoAm 94, WhoAmA 93*
Crystal, David 1941- *Who 94, WrDr 94*
Crystal, James William 1937- *WhoAm 94, WhoFI 94*
Crystal, Jonathan Andrew 1943- *WhoFI 94*
Crystal, Joseph 1940- *WhoAmL 94*
Crystal, Jules I. 1946- *WhoAmL 94*
Crystal, Lester Martin 1934- *WhoAm 94*
Crystal, Michael 1948- *Who 94*
Crystal, Michael R. 1951- *WhoFI 94*
Crystal, Richard 1967- *WhoAmL 94*
Crystal, Vearl Charles 1919- *WhoAmP 93*
Crystall, Joseph N. 1922- *WhoWest 94*
Csaky, Susan Dischka 1926- *WhoAmL 94*
Csanady, Gabriel Tibor 1925- *WhoAm 94, WhoScEn 94*
Csango, Peter Andras 1942- *WhoScEn 94*
Csanyi-Salcedo, Zoltan F. 1964- *WhoHisp 94*
Csar, Michael F. 1950- *WhoAmL 94*
Csaszar, Akos 1924- *IntWW 93, WhoScEn 94*
Csaszar, Gyorgy 1813-1850 *NewGrDO*
Csavinszky, Peter John 1931- *WhoAm 94*
Csehak, Judit *WhoWomW 91*
Csendes, Ernest 1926- *WhoAm 94, WhoFI 94, WhoScEn 94, WhoWest 94*
Csermely, Thomas John 1931- *WhoScEn 94*
Cserna, Jozsef *EncSF 93*
Csernai, Zoltan *EncSF 93*
Csernak, Stephen Francis 1952- *WhoScEn 94*
Csernus, Tibor 1927- *WhoAmA 93*
Cserr, Robert 1936- *WhoAm 94*
C'Shiva, Oya *WhoBlA 94*
Csia, Susan Rebecca 1945- *WhoAm 94*
Csikos-Nagy, Bela 1915- *IntWW 93*
Csikszentmiha'lyi, Miha'ly 1934- *IntWW 93, WhoAm 94*
Csiky, Boldizsar 1937- *NewGrDO*

Cslza, Charles Karoly 1937- *WhoScEn 94*
Csoka, Stephen d1989 *WhoAmA 93N*
Csoka, Stephen 1897-1989 *WhAm 10*
Csonka, Larry *ProFbHF [port], WhoHol 92*
Csoori, Sandor 1930- *ConWorW 93, IntWW 93*
Csorgo, Miklos 1932- *WhoAm 94*
Ctesias Of Cnidus fl. 40-?BC- *WhWE*
Cua, Antonio S. 1932- *WhoAm 94, WhoAsA 94, WrDr 94*
Cuadra, Carlos Albert 1925- *WhoAm 94*
Cuadra, Dorothy Elizabeth 1932- *WhoAmL 94*
Cuadra, Julio C. 1946- *WhoHisp 94*
Cuadrado, John J. *WhoHisp 94*
Cuadros, Alvaro Julio 1926- *WhoHisp 94*
Cuajao, Tracy Lee 1953- *WhoAsA 94*
Cuarenta, Jayne Stephanie 1959- *WhoHisp 94*
Cuarón, Alicia Valladolid 1939- *WhoHisp 94*
Cuarón, Marco A. 1944- *WhoHisp 94*
Cuartas, Francisco Ignacio 1939- *WhoHisp 94*
Cuatrecasas, Pedro 1936- *WhoHisp 94*
Cuatrecasas, Pedro Martin 1936- *IntWW 93, WhoAm 94*
Cuba, Robert Gregory 1959- *WhoMW 93*
Cubas, Jorge L. 1951- *WhoAm 94*
Cubas, Jose M. *WhoHisp 94*
Cubbison, Christopher Allen 1948- *WhoAm 94*
Cubbon, Brian (Crossland) 1928- *Who 94*
Cubbon, John Hamilton 1911- *Who 94*
Cubeiro, Emilio *DrAPF 93*
Cubell, Howard Alan 1948- *WhoAm 94*
Cubena 1941- *WhoHisp 94*
Cuberli, Lella 1945- *NewGrDO*
Cubero, Linda Garcia 1958- *WhoHisp 94*
Cubeta, Michael John, Jr. 1951- *WhoAmP 93*
Cubeta, Paul (Marsden) 1925- *WrDr 94*
Cubides, Carlos 1931- *WhoHisp 94*
Cubie, George 1943- *Who 94*
Cubillas, Teofilo 1949- *WhoHisp 94, WorESoc*
Cubillos, Ignacio 1947- *WhoFI 94*
Cubillos Sallato, Hernan 1936- *IntWW 93*
Cubin, Barbara L. 1946- *WhoAmP 93*
Cubin, Barbara Lynn *WhoWest 94*
Cubita, Peter Naylor 1957- *WhoAmL 94*
Cubitt *Who 94*
Cubitt, Hugh (Guy) 1928- *IntWW 93, Who 94*
Cubitto, Robert J. 1950- *WhoAm 94, WhoAmL 94*
Cucci, Anthony *WhoAmP 93*
Cucci, Cesare Eleuterio 1925- *WhoAm 94*
Cucci, Edward Arnold 1944- *WhoAm 94*
Cuccia, Mae Ruth d1952 *WhoHol 92*
Cucciolla, Ricardo 1932- *WhoHol 92*
Cucco, Ulisse P. 1929- *WhoAm 94*
Cucina, Vincent Robert 1936- *WhoWest 94*
Cuckney, John (Graham) 1925- *Who 94*
Cuckney, John Graham 1925- *IntWW 93*
Cuclin, Dimitrie 1885-1978 *NewGrDO*
Cucu, Vasile 1927- *IntWW 93*
Cudaback, Jim D. 1938- *WhoAmP 93*
Cudahy, Gregory Christian 1963- *WhoFI 94*
Cudahy, Richard D. 1926- *WhoAm 94, WhoAmL 94, WhoAmP 93, WhoMW 93*
Cudd, Robert A. N. 1946- *WhoAmL 94*
Cuddigan, Timothy John 1949- *WhoAmL 94*
Cuddon, J(ohn) A(nthony) 1928- *WrDr 94*
Cuddy, Charles D. *WhoAmP 93*
Cuddy, Daniel Hon 1921- *WhoAm 94*
Cuddy, David Warren 1952- *WhoAmP 93*
Cude, Reginald Hodgin 1936- *WhoAm 94*
Cudjoe, Selwyn Reginald 1943- *WhoBlA 94*
Cudlip, Charles Thomas 1940- *WhoAm 94*
Cudlipp, Baron 1913- *Who 94*
Cudlipp, Hugh 1913- *IntWW 93*
Cudlipp, Michael John 1934- *Who 94*
Cudlipp, Reginald 1910- *Who 94*
Cudmore, Byron Glen 1952- *WhoAmL 94*
Cudmore, Dana (D.) 1954- *WrDr 94*
Cudmore, Wynn Watson 1955- *WhoWest 94*
Cudworth, Ralph 1617-1688 *EncEth*
Cuebas-Incle, Esteban Luis 1955- *WhoHisp 94*
Cuelho, Art, Jr. *DrAPF 93*
Cuellar, Alfredo 1946- *WhoHisp 94*
Cuellar, Benjamin 1942- *WhoHisp 94*
Cuellar, Enrique Roberto 1955- *WhoHisp 94*
Cuellar, Evelio *WhoHisp 94*
Cuellar, Fernando Daniel 1941- *WhoHisp 94*
Cuellar, Gilbert, Jr. *WhoHisp 94*
Cuellar, Henry R. 1955- *WhoAmP 93*
Cuellar, Jose B. 1941- *WhoHisp 94*
Cuellar, Michael J. 1956- *WhoHisp 94*
Cuellar, Mike 1937- *WhoHisp 94*
Cuellar, Orlando 1934- *WhoHisp 94*
Cuellar, Renato 1927- *WhoAmP 93, WhoHisp 94*
Cuellar, Robert 1949- *WhoHisp 94*
Cuellar, Salvador M., Jr. 1949- *WhoHisp 94*
Cuello, Augusto Claudio Guillermo 1939- *WhoAm 94, WhoScEn 94*
Cuello, Jose 1945- *WhoHisp 94*
Cuenca, Carlos Fernandez d1977 *WhoHol 92*
Cuenca, Peter Nicolas 1943- *WhoHisp 94*
Cuenca I Valero, Maria Eugenia 1948- *WhoWomW 91*
Cuenod, Hugues 1902- *Who 94*
Cuenod, Hugues (Adhemar) 1902- *NewGrDO*
Cuervo, Leon Andres 1929- *WhoHisp 94*
Cuesta, Emerita de las Mercedes 1956- *WhoHisp 94*
Cuesta, Yolanda *WhoHisp 94*
Cuestas, David *WhoHisp 94*
Cueto, Alex *WhoAsA 94*
Cueto, Jose Manuel 1924- *WhoHisp 94*
Cueto, Luis M. 1931- *WhoHisp 94*
Cuevas, Betty 1953- *WhoHisp 94*
Cuevas, Carlos 1941- *WhoHisp 94*
Cuevas, Carlos M. 1951- *WhoHisp 94*
Cuevas, David 1947- *WhoHisp 94, WhoScEn 94*
Cuevas, Gabino S. 1924- *WhoHisp 94*
Cuevas, Helen 1952- *WhoHisp 94*
Cuevas, Hipolito 1966- *WhoHisp 94*
Cuevas, Jose, Jr. *WhoHisp 94*
Cuevas, Jose Luis 1934- *IntWW 93, WhoAm 94, WhoAmA 93*
Cuevas, Joseph B. 1942- *WhoHisp 94*
Cuevas, Marcial 1943- *WhoHisp 94*
Cuevas, Milton Joseph 1934- *WhoAm 94*
Cuevas Cancino, Francisco 1921- *IntWW 93, Who 94*
Cueya y Silva, Leonor de la c. 1600-1660 *BlmGWL*
Cuff, Brian C. 1948- *WhoAmL 94*
Cuff, George Wayne 1923- *WhoBlA 94*
Cuffe, Paul 1759-1817 *AfrAmAl 6*
Cuffe, Stafford Sigesmund 1949- *WhoMW 93*
Cuffey, Roger J. 1939- *WhoScEn 94*
Cuffney, Robert Howard 1959- *WhoScEn 94*
Cugat, Carmen d1967 *WhoHol 92*
Cugat, Xavier d1990 *WhoHol 92*
Cugat, Xavier 1900-1990 *WhAm 10*
Cuggino, Michael Joseph 1963- *WhoFI 94*
Cugnot, Nicholas-Joseph 1725-1804 *WorInv*
Cui, Cesar Antonovich 1835-1918 *NewGrDO*
Cui Daoyi *WhoPRCh 91*
Cuiffo, Frank Wayne 1943- *WhoAmL 94*
Cui Jianmin 1932- *WhoPRCh 91 [port]*
Cui Jie *WhoPRCh 91*
Cui Lin 1927- *WhoPRCh 91 [port]*
Cui Naifu 1928- *IntWW 93, WhoPRCh 91 [port]*
Cui Ronghan 1922- *WhoPRCh 91 [port]*
Cuiscard, Henri *EncSF 93*
Cui Shifang *WhoPRCh 91*
Cuisia, Jose L. 1944- *IntWW 93*
Cuisia, Jose L., Jr. 1944- *WhoIns 94*
Cui Weiyue *WhoPRCh 91*
Cui Yanxu *WhoPRCh 91*
Cui Yi 1930- *WhoPRCh 91 [port]*
Cui Yueli 1920- *WhoPRCh 91 [port]*
Cui Yueli, Gen. 1920- *IntWW 93*
Cui Yuling *WhoPRCh 91*
Cui Zifan 1915- *WhoPRCh 91 [port]*
Cuk, Slobodan *WhoScEn 94*
Cuka, Frances 1936- *WhoHol 92*
Cukierski, Matthew John 1958- *WhoWest 94*
Cukor, Peter 1936- *WhoAm 94*
Cukras, Roger 1943- *WhoAmL 94*
Culberg, Paul S. 1942- *IntMPA 94*
Culberson, Gary Michael 1955- *WhoMW 93*
Culberson, John 1956- *WhoAmP 93*
Culberson, William Louis 1929- *WhoAm 94, WhoScEn 94*
Culbert, Patrick 1948- *WhoAmP 93*
Culbert, Read Shephard 1966- *WhoWest 94*
Culbertson, Andrea Caroline 1961- *WhoMW 93*
Culbertson, Ely d1955 *WhoHol 92*
Culbertson, Frances Mitchell 1921- *WhoAm 94*
Culbertson, James Clifford 1953- *WhoScEn 94*
Culbertson, James Thomas 1911- *WhoWest 94*
Culbertson, Janet Lynn 1932- *WhoAm 94, WhoAmA 93*
Culbertson, John Harrison 1905-1988 *WhAm 10*
Culbertson, John Mathew 1921- *WhoAm 94*
Culbertson, Katheryn Campbell 1920- *WhoAm 94*
Culbertson, Philip Edgar 1925- *WhoAm 94*
Culbertson, R. Scott 1945- *WhoFI 94*
Culbreath, Myrna *EncSF 93*
Culbreath-Manly, Tongila M. 1959- *WhoBlA 94*
Culbreth, Carl R. 1952- *WhoAmA 93*
Culbreth, Martha Elizabeth 1942- *WhoAmL 94*
Culbreth, Ronnie 1954- *WhoAmP 93*
Culham, Michael John 1933- *Who 94*
Culhane, John Leonard *Who 94*
Culhane, John Leonard 1937- *IntWW 93*
Culhane, John William 1934- *WhoAm 94*
Culhane, Rosalind *Who 94*
Culhane, Shamus 1908- *WhoAm 94*
Culhane, Shamus H. 1908- *WhoAmA 93*
Culick, Fred Ellsworth Clow 1933- *WhoAm 94, WhoScEn 94*
Culik, Karel 1934- *WhoAm 94*
Culikova, Vera 1951- *WhoWomW 91*
Culkar, D. J. 1963- *WhoMW 93*
Culkin, Gerald P. d1993 *NewYTBS 93 [port]*
Culkin, John M. d1993 *NewYTBS 93 [port]*
Culkin, John Michael 1928- *WhoAmA 93*
Culkin, Macaulay 1980- *IntMPA 94, WhoAm 94, WhoHol 92*
Cull, Chris Alan 1947- *WhoWest 94*
Cull, Robert Robinette 1912- *WhoAm 94*
Cullan, David James 1940- *WhoAmP 93*
Cullari, Salvatore Santino 1952- *WhoScEn 94*
Cullberg, Birgit 1908- *IntDcB*
Cullberg, Brigit Ragnhild 1908- *IntWW 93*
Cullen, Hon. Lord 1935- *Who 94*
Cullen, Alexander Lamb 1920- *IntWW 93, Who 94*
Cullen, Barry John 1964- *WhoAm 94*
Cullen, Bill 1920-1990 *WhAm 10*
Cullen, Brett *WhoHol 92*
Cullen, Charles Thomas 1940- *WhoAm 94*
Cullen, Claudia P. 1956- *WhoHisp 94*
Cullen, Countee 1903-1946 *AfrAmAl 6 [port]*
Cullen, David A. 1960- *WhoAmP 93*
Cullen, Douglas *Who 94*
Cullen, E. J. *DrAPF 93*
Cullen, Edward d1964 *WhoHol 92*
Cullen, Ernest Andre 1926- *WhoScEn 94*
Cullen, Gordon *Who 94*
Cullen, (Thomas) Gordon 1914- *Who 94*
Cullen, Jack J. 1951- *WhoAmL 94*
Cullen, Jack Sydney George Bud 1927- *WhoAm 94*
Cullen, James D. 1925- *WhoAmL 94*
Cullen, James Douglas 1945- *WhoAm 94*
Cullen, James G. 1942- *WhoAm 94, WhoFI 94*
Cullen, James Patrick 1944- *WhoAm 94, WhoFI 94*
Cullen, James Reynolds 1900- *Who 94*
Cullen, James Thaddeus, Jr. 1935- *WhoAm 94*
Cullen, John *Who 94*
Cullen, (Edward) John 1926- *Who 94*
Cullen, John B. 1911- *WhoFI 94*
Cullen, John Knox, Jr. 1936- *WhoScEn 94*
Cullen, Jonna Lynne 1941- *WhoAmP 93*
Cullen, Linda Jo Krozser 1955- *WhoMW 93*
Cullen, Marion Permilla 1931- *WhoScEn 94*
Cullen, Mark 1956- *ConAu 141*
Cullen, Max *WhoHol 92*
Cullen, Michael John 1945- *IntWW 93*
Cullen, Mike 1927- *WhoAmP 93*
Cullen, Patrick Colborn 1940- *WhoAm 94*
Cullen, Paul 1803-1878 *HisWorL [port]*
Cullen, Paula Bramsen *DrAPF 93*
Cullen, Philip Michael 1947- *WhoAmL 94*
Cullen, Raymond 1913- *Who 94*
Cullen, Raymond T. 1937- *WhoAmL 94*
Cullen, Robert (B.) 1949- *WrDr 94*
Cullen, Robert John 1949- *WhoFI 94, WhoWest 94*
Cullen, Terence Lindsay Graham 1930- *Who 94*
Cullen, Thomas Francis, Jr. 1949- *WhoAm 94, WhoAmL 94*
Cullen, Timothy F. 1944- *WhoAmP 93*
Cullen, William 1710-1790 *EncSPD*
Cullen, William, Jr. *DrAPF 93*
Cullen, William P. 1954- *WhoIns 94*
Cullen-Benson, Scott Paul 1952- *WhoMW 93*
Cullenbine, Clair Stephens 1905- *WhoAm 94*
Cullen Of Ashbourne, Baron 1912- *Who 94*
Cullens, Joseph Roy 1947- *WhoAmL 94*
Cullens, William Scott 1930- *WhoFI 94*
Culler, Arthur Dwight 1917- *WhoAm 94*
Culler, David Ethan 1959- *WhoWest 94*
Culler, Eugene R. 1938- *WhoFI 94*
Culler, Floyd LeRoy, Jr. 1923- *WhoScEn 94*
Culler, Jonathan 1944- *BlmGEL*
Culler, Jonathan Dwight 1944- *WhoAm 94, WrDr 94*
Cullerne Bown, Matthew 1956- *WrDr 94*
Cullers, Samuel James *WhoBlA 94*
Cullers, Vincent T. *WhoBlA 94*
Cullerton, John James 1948- *WhoAmP 93, WhoMW 93*
Culleton, Beatrice *BlmGWL*
Culley, Frank d1966 *WhoHol 92*
Culley, Frederick d1942 *WhoHol 92*
Culley, J. Kent 1940- *WhoAmL 94*
Culley, Peter William 1943- *WhoAmL 94*
Culliford, Pierre 1928-1992 *AnObit 1992, ConAu 140, SmATA 74*
Culligan, John William 1916- *WhoAm 94*
Cullimore, Charles Augustine Kaye 1933- *Who 94*
Cullimore, Colin Stuart 1931- *Who 94*
Cullina, William Michael 1921- *WhoAm 94, WhoAmL 94*
Cullinan, Brendan Peter 1927- *IntWW 93*
Cullinan, Edward Horder 1931- *IntWW 93, Who 94*
Cullinan, Elizabeth *DrAPF 93*
Culling, Richard Edward 1951- *WhoAmA 93*
Cullingford, Eric Coome Maynard 1910- *Who 94*
Cullingford, Guy 1907- *WrDr 94*
Cullington, Margaret d1925 *WhoHol 92*
Cullingworth, (John) Barry 1929- *Who 94*
Cullingworth, J(ohn) Barry 1929- *WrDr 94*
Cullingworth, Larry Ross 1939- *WhoFI 94*
Cullingworth, N(icholas) J(ohn) *EncSF 93*
Cullins, James Thomas 1930- *WhoAmP 93*
Cullis, Charles 1838-1892 *DcAmReB 2*
Cullis, Charles Fowler 1922- *Who 94*
Cullis, Christopher Ashley 1945- *WhoAm 94*
Cullis, Michael Fowler 1914- *Who 94*
Cullis, Rita 1952- *NewGrDO*
Cullison, Alexander C. 1951- *WhoAm 94*
Cullison, Robert Virl 1936- *WhoAmP 93*
Culliton, Edward Milton 1906-1991 *WhAm 10*
Culliton, James Joseph 1937- *WhoFI 94*
Cullman, Edgar M., Jr. 1946- *WhoFI 94*
Cullman, Edgar Meyer 1918- *WhoAm 94, WhoFI 94*
Cullman, Hugh 1923- *WhoAm 94*
Cullman, Joe 1912- *BuCMET*
Cullman, Joseph Frederick, III 1912- *IntWW 93*
Cullmann, Oscar 1902- *IntWW 93*
Cullom, Hale Ellicott 1935- *WhoAm 94, WhoFI 94*
Cullom, William Otis 1932- *WhoAm 94, WhoFI 94*
Cullum, Colin Munro 1959- *WhoScEn 94*
Cullum, John 1930- *IntMPA 94, WhoAm 94, WhoHol 92*
Cullum, John David *WhoHol 92*
Cullum, Robert B., Jr. 1948- *WhoFI 94*
Cully, Zara d1978 *WhoHol 92*
Culmann, Herbert Ernst 1921- *IntWW 93*
Culmer, Marjorie Mehne 1912- *WhoAm 94*
Culme-Seymour, Michael *Who 94*
Culotta, Rodi William 1952- *WhoAmL 94*
Culp, Arlie Franklin, Jr. 1926- *WhoAmP 93*
Culp, Benjamin B., Jr. 1948- *WhoAmL 94*
Culp, Bethany Kelly 1951- *WhoAmL 94*
Culp, Bobbie A. 1947- *WhoAmP 93*
Culp, Carl Lester 1922- *WhoAmP 93*
Culp, Charles Allen 1930- *WhoAm 94*
Culp, Donald Allen 1938- *WhoAm 94*
Culp, Even Asher 1952- *WhoAm 94*
Culp, Gary 1940- *WhoWest 94*
Culp, George Hart 1938- *WhoAm 94*
Culp, Gordon Louis 1939- *WhoAm 94*
Culp, Joe Carl 1933- *WhoAm 94, WhoFI 94*
Culp, John H(ewett, Jr.) 1907- *WrDr 94*
Culp, Joseph *WhoHol 92*
Culp, Kenneth, Jr. 1936- *WhoAmP 93*
Culp, Mae Ng 1935- *WhoAsA 94*
Culp, Margaret Geralyn 1954- *WhoFI 94*
Culp, Michael 1952- *WhoAm 94*
Culp, Mildred Louise 1949- *WhoAm 94, WhoWest 94*
Culp, Robert 1930- *IntMPA 94, WhoAm 94, WhoHol 92*
Culp, Sandra Kay 1938- *WhoAmP 93*
Culp, Stephanie (Anne) 1947- *WrDr 94*
Culp, William Newton 1923- *WhoAm 94*
Culpeper, Edmund c. 1670-1738 *DcNaB MP*
Culpepper, Betty M. 1941- *WhoBlA 94*
Culpepper, Bobby L. 1941- *WhoAmP 93*

Culpepper, David Charles 1946-
WhoAm 94, WhoAmL 94
Culpepper, David M. 1952- *WhoAmL 94*
Culpepper, Dellie L. 1941- *WhoBlA 94*
Culpepper, George Bryant 1947-
WhoAmP 93
Culpepper, Lucy Nell 1951- *WhoBlA 94*
Culpepper, Nicolas 1616-1654 *AstEnc*
Culpepper, Robert Sammon 1927-
WhoWest 94
Culshaw, John 1924-1980 *NewGrDO*
Culshaw, John Douglas 1927- *Who 94*
Culshaw, Robert Nicholas 1952- *Who 94*
Culter, John Dougherty 1937-
WhoMW 93, WhoScEn 94
Culton, Paul Melvin 1932- *WhoWest 94*
Culton, Ruth Ann 1937- *WhoAmP 93*
Culton, Sarah Alexander 1927-
WhoScEn 94
Cultra, John William, Jr. 1945- *WhoFI 94*
Culvahouse, Arthur Boggess, Jr. 1948-
WhoAm 94, WhoAmL 94
Culver, Barbara Green 1926- *WhoAmP 93*
Culver, Bob Ed 1934- *WhoAmP 93*
Culver, Bruce Vernon 1958- *WhoFI 94*
Culver, Charles George 1937- *WhoAm 94,
WhoFI 94*
Culver, David Alan 1945- *WhoMW 93,
WhoScEn 94*
Culver, David M. 1924- *IntWW 93*
Culver, Edward Holland 1918- *WhoAm 94*
Culver, Florence Morrow 1915-
WhoMW 93
Culver, Howard d1984 *WhoHol 92*
Culver, James 1939- *WhoFI 94*
Culver, John Eskridge 1932- *WhoAm 94*
Culver, John Howard 1947- *Who 94*
Culver, Kathleen Bartzen 1966-
WhoMW 93
Culver, Marjorie *DrAPF 93*
Culver, Michael 1938- *WhoHol 92*
Culver, Michael L. 1947- *WhoAmA 93*
Culver, Rhonda 1960- *WhoBlA 94*
Culver, Robert Elroy 1926- *WhoAm 94,
WhoMW 93*
Culver, Roland d1984 *WhoHol 92*
Culver, Timothy J. *EncSF 93*
Culver, Timothy J. 1933- *WrDr 94*
Culver, Walter Julius 1937- *WhoAm 94*
Culverhouse, Hugh Franklin 1919-
WhoAm 94
Culvern, Julian Brewer 1919-
WhoScEn 94
Culverwell, Albert Henry 1913-
WhoAm 94
Culverwell, Rosemary Jean 1934-
WhoMW 93
Culwell, Charles Louis 1927- *WhoAm 94*
Culwell, Warren Dale 1925- *WhoFI 94*
Culyer, A(nthony) J(ohn) 1942- *WrDr 94*
Culyer, Anthony John 1942- *Who 94*
Cumani, Luca Matteo 1949- *Who 94*
Cumber, Victoria Lillian 1920-
WhoBlA 94
Cumberland, Duke of 1819-1878
DcNaB MP
Cumberland, John 1880- *WhoHol 92*
Cumberland, Richard 1632-1718 *EncEth*
Cumberland, Richard 1732-1811
BlmGEL, IntDcT 2, WhAmRev
Cumberland, William Edwin 1938-
WhoAmL 94
Cumberlege, Baroness 1943- *Who 94*
Cumberlege, Marcus (Crossley) 1938-
WrDr 94
Cumbey, Constance Elizabeth 1944-
WhoAmL 94
Cumbrae, Provost of *Who 94*
Cumbuka, Ji-Tu 1941- *WhoHol 92*
Cumby, George Edward 1956- *WhoBlA 94*
Cumerford, William Richard 1916-
WhoAm 94
Cuming, Beatrice 1903-1975
WhoAmA 93N
Cuming, Frederick George Rees 1930-
IntWW 93, Who 94
Cuming, George Scott 1915- *WhoAm 94*
Cumings, Anne Flower 1942-
WhoAmL 94
Cumings, Edwin Harlan 1933-
WhoAm 94, WhoScEn 94
Cumley, Robert Dale 1943- *WhoMW 93*
Cummens, Linda Talaba *WhoAmA 93*
Cummer, William Jackson 1922-
WhoAm 94
Cummin, Alfred Samuel 1924- *WhoFI 94,
WhoMW 93*
Cumming *Who 94*
Cumming, (John) Alan 1932- *Who 94*
Cumming, David Robert, Jr. 1927-
WhoAm 94
Cumming, Dorothy d1983 *WhoHol 92*
Cumming, George Anderson, Jr. 1942-
WhoAm 94, WhoAmL 94
Cumming, Glen Edward 1936-
WhoAm 94, WhoAmA 93
Cumming, Ian M. 1940- *WhoAm 94,
WhoFI 94*

Cumming, Janice Dorothy 1953-
WhoScEn 94
Cumming, Joseph Bryan 1893- *WhAm 10*
Cumming, Mansfield George Smith
1859-1923 *DcNaB MP*
Cumming, Patricia *DrAPF 93*
Cumming, Primrose (Amy) 1915-
WrDr 94
Cumming, Robert *DrAPF 93*
Cumming, Robert Emil 1933- *WhoAm 94*
Cumming, Robert H. 1943- *WhoAmA 93*
Cumming, Robert Hugh 1943- *WhoAm 94*
Cumming, Ruth d1967 *WhoHol 92*
Cumming, Thomas Alexander 1937-
WhoAm 94
Cumming, Valerie Lynn 1946- *Who 94*
Cumming, Virgil H. 1945- *WhoIns 94*
Cumming, William *WhAmRev*
Cumming, William Patterson 1900-1989
WhAm 10
Cumming-Bruce, (James) Roualeyn
Hovell-Thurlow- 1912- *Who 94*
Cummingham, Billy 1943- *BasBi [port]*
Cummings, Albert R. 1940- *WhoBlA 94*
Cummings, Ann 1933- *WhoAmP 93*
Cummings, Barton 1946- *WhoAm 94*
Cummings, Belinda 1963- *WhoScEn 94*
Cummings, Bill 1929- *WhoAmP 93*
Cummings, Bob 1910-1990 *WhAm 10*
Cummings, Brian Thomas 1945-
WhoAm 94
Cummings, Cary, III 1949- *WhoBlA 94*
Cummings, Charles Edward 1931-
WhoBlA 94
Cummings, Charles Rogers 1930-
WhoAm 94, WhoAmL 94
Cummings, Charles William 1935-
WhoAm 94
Cummings, Conrad 1948- *NewGrDO*
Cummings, Constance *Who 94,
WhoAm 94*
Cummings, Constance 1910- *IntMPA 94,
IntWW 93, WhoHol 92*
Cummings, Daniel O'Donnell 1954-
WhoWest 94
Cummings, Danny d1984 *WhoHol 92*
Cummings, Darold Bernard 1944-
WhoWest 94
Cummings, David 1932- *WhoWest 94*
Cummings, David K. 1941- *WhoIns 94*
Cummings, David William 1937-
WhoAm 94, WhoAmA 93
Cummings, Donald Wayne 1935-
WhoWest 94
Cummings, Donn Paul 1949- *WhoMW 93*
Cummings, Donna Louise 1944-
WhoBlA 94
Cummings, E. Emerson 1917- *WhoBlA 94*
Cummings, Edward Estlin 1894-1962
AmCulL [port]
Cummings, Elijah E. 1951- *WhoAmP 93*
Cummings, Erwin Karl 1954- *WhoMW 93*
Cummings, Frances McArthur 1941-
WhoAmP 93, WhoBlA 94
Cummings, Frank 1929- *WhoAm 94,
WhoAmL 94*
Cummings, Frederick James 1933-1990
WhoAmA 93N
Cummings, George d1946 *WhoHol 92*
Cummings, Gregg Alex 1963-
WhoWest 94
Cummings, Irving d1959 *WhoHol 92*
Cummings, J. Greer, Jr. 1948-
WhoAmL 94
Cummings, Jack *ConAu 41NR*
Cummings, Jack 1925- *WrDr 94*
Cummings, James C., Jr. 1929-
WhoBlA 94
Cummings, James Edward d1991
WhoBlA 94N
Cummings, Jill Ann 1958- *WhoMW 93*
Cummings, Joan E. *WhoMW 93*
Cummings, John Chester, Jr. 1947-
WhoScEn 94
Cummings, John Scott 1943- *Who 94*
Cummings, John W(illiam), Jr. 1940-
ConAu 41NR
Cummings, Josephine Anna 1949-
WhoAm 94
Cummings, Katherine d1950 *WhoHol 92*
Cummings, Katina 1956- *WhoAmP 93*
Cummings, Larry Lee 1937- *WhoAm 94*
Cummings, M(onette) A. 1914- *EncSF 93*
Cummings, Martha Clark *DrAPF 93*
Cummings, Martin Marc 1920-
WhoAm 94
Cummings, Mary Dappert 1922-
WhoFI 94
Cummings, Mary T. 1951- *WhoAmA 93*
Cummings, Milton C(urtis), Jr. 1933-
WrDr 94
Cummings, Nancy Boucot 1927-
WhoAm 94
Cummings, Nicholas Andrew 1924-
WhoAm 94, WhoScEn 94, WhoWest 94
Cummings, Pat 1950- *WhoBlA 94*
Cummings, Pat (Marie) 1950- *BlkWr 2*

Cummings, Patrick Henry 1941-
WhoFI 94
Cummings, Paul *WhoAmA 93*
Cummings, Quinn 1965- *WhoHol 92*
Cummings, Ralph W. 1911- *IntWW 93*
Cummings, Ralph Waldo 1911-
WhoAm 94
Cummings, Ray 1887-1957 *EncSF 93*
Cummings, Richard d1938 *WhoHol 92*
Cummings, Richard J. 1932- *WhoMW 93*
Cummings, Richard LeRoy 1933-
WhoMW 93
Cummings, Robert d1949 *WhoHol 92*
Cummings, Robert d1990 *WhoHol 92*
Cummings, Roberta Spikes 1944-
WhoBlA 94
Cummings, Roger David 1944-
WhoWest 94
Cummings, Roger Holt 1949- *WhoAm 94*
Cummings, Roy d1940 *WhoHol 92*
Cummings, Russell Mark 1955-
WhoWest 94
Cummings, Sam R. 1944- *WhoAm 94,
WhoAmL 94*
Cummings, Sandy *WhoHol 92*
Cummings, Spangler 1936- *WhoWest 94*
Cummings, Terry 1961- *BasBi,
WhoBlA 94*
Cummings, Theresa Faith *WhoBlA 94*
Cummings, Thomas 1945- *WhoAmL 94*
Cummings, Thomas Gerald 1944-
WhoAm 94
Cummings, Vicki d1969 *WhoHol 92*
Cummings, Walter J. 1916- *WhoAm 94,
WhoAmL 94, WhoAmP 93*
Cummings, William Robert, Jr. 1937-
WhoMW 93
Cummins, Alfred Byron 1905-1991
WhAm 10
Cummins, Bruce Wynn 1947- *WhoMW 93*
Cummins, Charles Fitch, Jr. 1939-
WhoAmL 94, WhoWest 94
Cummins, Delmer Duane 1935-
WhoAm 94
Cummins, Evelyn Freeman 1904-
WhoFI 94
Cummins, Frank 1924- *Who 94*
Cummins, George David 1822-1876
DcAmReB 2
Cummins, Gus 1943- *Who 94*
Cummins, Harle Owen *EncSF 93*
Cummins, Herman Zachary 1933-
WhoAm 94
Cummins, James *DrAPF 93*
Cummins, John David 1946- *WhoAm 94*
Cummins, John Stephen 1928-
WhoAm 94, WhoWest 94
Cummins, Karen Gasco 1945-
WhoAmA 93
Cummins, Kenneth Burdette 1911-
WhoAm 94
Cummins, Light Townsend 1946-
ConAu 141
Cummins, Maria Susanna 1827-1866
BlmGWL
Cummins, Nancyellen Heckeroth 1948-
WhoScEn 94, WhoWest 94
Cummins, Paul Zach, II 1936- *WhoFI 94*
Cummins, Peggy 1925- *IntMPA 94,
WhoHol 92*
Cummins, Peter *WhoHol 92*
Cummins, Shirley Jean 1948- *WhoAm 94*
Cummins, Walter *DrAPF 93*
Cummis, Clive Sanford 1928- *WhoAm 94,
WhoAmL 94*
Cummiskey, Chris *WhoAmP 93*
Cummiskey, J. Kenneth 1928- *WhoAm 94*
Cummiskey, John William 1917-
WhoAmL 94
Cumpian, Carlos *DrAPF 93, WhoHisp 94*
Cumpson, John R. d1913 *WhoHol 92*
Cunard, Grace d1967 *WhoHol 92*
Cunard, Mina d1978 *WhoHol 92*
Cunard, Nancy 1896-1965 *BlmGWL*
Cunconan-Lahr, Robin Lynn 1960-
WhoAmL 94
Cundall, Donald R. 1925- *WhoAmP 93*
Cundall, Kathleen Foy 1948- *WhoWest 94*
Cundey, Dean *ConTFT 11*
Cundiff, Carl Copeland 1941-
WhoAmP 93
Cundiff, Edward William 1919-
WhoAm 94
Cundiff, John Howard *WhoBlA 94*
Cundiff, Paul Arthur 1909- *WhoAm 94*
Cundy, Ian Patrick Martyn *Who 94*
Cundy, Vic Arnold 1950- *WhoAm 94*
Cunefare, Kenneth Arthur 1961-
WhoScEn 94
Cuneo, Dennis Clifford 1950- *WhoFI 94,
WhoWest 94*
Cuneo, Donald Lane 1944- *WhoAm 94,
WhoWest 94*
Cuneo, Ernest L. *WhAm 10*
Cuneo, Jack Alfred 1947- *WhoFI 94*
Cuneo, Lester d1925 *WhoHol 92*
Cuneo, Terence Tenison 1907- *Who 94*
Cung, Tien Thuc 1938- *WhoAsA 94*

Cungu, Bukurije *WhoWomW 91*
Cunha, Fausto *EncSF 93*
Cunha, John Henry, Jr. 1950-
WhoAmL 94
Cunha, Mark Geoffrey 1955- *WhoAmL 94*
Cunha, Richard E. *HorFD*
Cunhal, Alvaro 1913- *IntWW 93*
Cunha-Vaz, Jose Guilherme Fernandes
1938- *WhoScEn 94*
Cunill, Buenaventura Cesar 1935-
WhoHisp 94
Cuningham, Elizabeth Bayard
WhoAmA 94
Cuningham, Philip d1928 *WhoHol 92*
Cuninghame, John Christopher Foggo M.
Who 94
Cuninghame, William Henry F. *Who 94*
Cunitz, Maria 1610-1664 *BlmGWL*
Cunitz, Maud 1911-1987 *NewGrDO*
Cunkelman, Brian Lee 1969- *WhoScEn 94*
Cunliffe, Baron 1932- *Who 94*
Cunliffe, Barrington Windsor 1939-
Who 94
Cunliffe, Barry 1939- *WrDr 94*
Cunliffe, Christopher Joseph 1916-
Who 94
Cunliffe, David Ellis 1957- *Who 94*
Cunliffe, John (Arthur) 1933- *WrDr 94*
Cunliffe, Lawrence Francis 1929- *Who 94*
Cunliffe, Peter Whalley 1926- *Who 94*
Cunliffe, Stella Vivian 1917- *Who 94*
Cunliffe, Thomas Alfred d1993 *Who 94N*
Cunliffe, Walter 1855-1920 *DcNaB MP*
Cunliffe-Lister *Who 94*
Cunliffe-Owen, Hugo Dudley 1966-
Who 94
Cunnane, James Joseph 1938- *WhoAm 94,
WhoFI 94*
Cunnane, Joseph 1913- *Who 94*
Cunnane, Patricia S. 1946- *WhoWest 94*
Cunnick, Gloria Helen *WhoAmA 93*
Cunniff, Patrick Francis 1933- *WhoAm 94*
Cunningham, Alexander Alan 1926-
Who 94
Cunningham, Alfred Joe 1928-
WhoAmP 93
Cunningham, Allan 1791-1839 *WhWE*
Cunningham, Andrea Lee 1956-
WhoAm 94, WhoFI 94
Cunningham, Ann Marie 1947-
WhoAm 94
Cunningham, Arthur 1928- *NewGrDO*
Cunningham, Arthur Francis 1922-
WhoAm 94
Cunningham, Arthur H. 1928- *WhoBlA 94*
Cunningham, Atlee Marion, Jr. 1938-
WhoAm 94, WhoScEn 94
Cunningham, Benjamin Frazier
1904-1975 *WhoAmA 93N*
Cunningham, Beryl *WhoHol 92*
Cunningham, Billy 1943- *WhoAm 94*
Cunningham, Blenna A. 1946- *WhoBlA 94*
Cunningham, Bob *WhoHol 92*
Cunningham, Brian C. 1943- *WhoAm 94*
Cunningham, (Charles) Bruce 1943-
WhoAmA 93
Cunningham, Bruce Arthur 1940-
WhoAm 94
Cunningham, Bruce Edward 1955-
WhoMW 93
Cunningham, Cathy 1928- *WrDr 94*
Cunningham, Cecil d1959 *WhoHol 92*
Cunningham, Charles (Craik) 1906-
Who 94
Cunningham, Charles Baker, III 1941-
WhoAm 94
Cunningham, Charles Crehore 1910-1979
WhoAmA 93N
Cunningham, Charles Duane 1956-
WhoMW 93
Cunningham, Charles Joseph 1948-
WhoAmL 94
Cunningham, Chet 1928- *WrDr 94*
Cunningham, Clark Edward 1934-
WhoAm 94
Cunningham, Courtney 1962- *WhoBlA 94*
Cunningham, Dale Everett 1927-
WhoFI 94
Cunningham, David 1924- *Who 94*
Cunningham, David S., Jr. 1935-
WhoBlA 94
Cunningham, Dennis Dean 1939-
WhoAm 94
Cunningham, Donna *AstEnc*
Cunningham, Dorothy Jane 1927-
WhoAm 94, WhoMW 93
Cunningham, E. Brice 1931- *WhoBlA 94*
Cunningham, E. C. 1956- *WhoAmA 93*
Cunningham, E.V. *EncSF 93*
Cunningham, E. V. 1914- *WrDr 94*
Cunningham, Edward 1862-1920 *EncNAR*
Cunningham, Edward Patrick 1934-
IntWW 93
Cunningham, Edward Preston, Jr. 1945-
WhoFI 94
Cunningham, Elizabeth Ann 1953-
WhoMW 93

Cunningham, Emmett Thomas, Jr. 1960-
WhoAm 94
Cunningham, Ernest 1936- *WhoAmP 93*
Cunningham, Erskine 1955- *WhoBlA 94*
Cunningham, Evelyn 1936- *WhoAmP 93*
Cunningham, F. Malcolm 1927-
WhoBlA 94
Cunningham, Francis 1931- *WhoAmA 93*
Cunningham, George *WhoAmP 93*
Cunningham, George d1962 *WhoHol 92*
Cunningham, George 1931- *Who 94*
Cunningham, George D. 1948-
WhoAmL 94
Cunningham, George John 1906- *Who 94*
Cunningham, George Woody 1930-
WhoAm 94
Cunningham, Glenn C. 1912-
WhoAmP 93
Cunningham, Glenn Clarence 1912-
WhoAm 94
Cunningham, Glenn Dale 1943-
WhoAmP 93, WhoBlA 94
Cunningham, Gordon Ross 1944-
WhoAm 94, WhoFI 94
Cunningham, Gregg Lee 1947-
WhoAmP 93
Cunningham, Harry 1907-1992
AnObit 1992
Cunningham, Harry Blair d1992
IntWW 93N
Cunningham, Hugh (Patrick) 1921-
Who 94
Cunningham, Imogen 1883-1976
WhoAmA 93N
Cunningham, Isabella Clara Mantovani
1942- *WhoAm 94*
Cunningham, J. 1940- *WhoAmA 93*
Cunningham, Jack d1967 *WhoHol 92*
Cunningham, James Carroll, Jr. 1955-
WhoFI 94
Cunningham, James Dolan 1941- *Who 94*
Cunningham, James Everett 1923-
WhoAm 94
Cunningham, James Gerald, Jr. 1930-
WhoAm 94
Cunningham, James J. 1938- *WhoBlA 94*
Cunningham, James Joseph 1949-
WhoAmL 94
Cunningham, James Melvin 1946-
WhoFI 94
Cunningham, James Steven 1957-
WhoFI 94
Cunningham, James V. 1923- *WrDr 94*
Cunningham, Janis Ann 1952-
WhoAm 94, WhoAmL 94
Cunningham, Jean Wooden 1946-
WhoAmP 93
Cunningham, Jeffrey Milton 1952-
WhoFI 94
Cunningham, Jerry Glenn 1941-
WhoAmP 93
Cunningham, Joe d1943 *WhoHol 92*
Cunningham, Joel Dean 1948-
WhoAmL 94
Cunningham, John *WhoHol 92*
Cunningham, John 1917- *Who 94*
Cunningham, John A. 1939- *IntWW 93, Who 94*
Cunningham, John F. 1941- *WhoBlA 94*
Cunningham, John Fabian 1928-
WhoAm 94
Cunningham, John J., III 1942-
WhoAmL 94
Cunningham, John Michael 1950-
WhoFI 94
Cunningham, John Randolph 1954-
WhoScEn 94
Cunningham, Joseph F. 1924-
WhoAmP 93
Cunningham, Joseph Francis, Jr. 1924-
WhoAm 94, WhoAmL 94
Cunningham, Judy Marie 1944-
WhoAmL 94
Cunningham, Julia W(oolfolk) 1916-
WrDr 94
Cunningham, Julia Woolfolk 1916-
WhoAm 94
Cunningham, Keith Allen, II 1948-
WhoFI 94, WhoScEn 94
Cunningham, Kenneth Carl 1954-
WhoAmL 94
Cunningham, Kirk B. 1943- *WhoIns 94*
Cunningham, Larry J. 1944- *WhoAm 94*
Cunningham, LeMoine Julius 1934-
WhoScEn 94
Cunningham, Leon William 1927-
WhoAm 94
Cunningham, Letitia fl. 1783- *BlmGWL*
Cunningham, Louis Ernest 1951-
WhoBlA 94
Cunningham, Malena Ann 1958-
WhoBlA 94
Cunningham, Margaret 1915- *WhoBlA 94*
Cunningham, Marion 1911-
WhoAmA 93N
Cunningham, Marion (Elizabeth) 1922-
WrDr 94

Cunningham, Mark Eric 1962-
WhoMW 93
Cunningham, Mary Elizabeth 1931-
WhoAm 94
Cunningham, Merce *WhoAm 94*
Cunningham, Merce 1919- *AmCulL [port],
IntDcB [port], IntWW 93, Who 94*
Cunningham, Michael 1952- *WrDr 94*
Cunningham, Milamari Antoinella 1949-
WhoMW 93
Cunningham, Murray Hunt, Jr. 1942-
WhoAm 94
Cunningham, Neil Lewis 1924-
WhoAm 94
Cunningham, Noble E., Jr. 1926-
WhoMW 93
Cunningham, Patrick c. 1743-1790 *AmRev*
Cunningham, Patrick Joseph 1943-
WhoAm 94, WhoFI 94
Cunningham, Patrick Joseph, III 1950-
WhoMW 93
Cunningham, Paul A. 1946- *WhoAmL 94*
Cunningham, Paul Bernard 1943-
WhoWest 94
Cunningham, Paul Johnston 1928-
WhoAmP 93
Cunningham, Paul Raymond Goldwyn
1949- *WhoBlA 94*
Cunningham, Pierce Edward 1934-
WhoAmL 94
Cunningham, R. John 1926- *WhoAm 94*
Cunningham, R. Walter 1932- *WhoAm 94,
WhoScEn 94*
Cunningham, Ralph Eugene, Jr. 1927-
WhoAmL 94
Cunningham, Randall 1963- *WhoAm 94,
WhoBlA 94*
Cunningham, Randy 1941- *CngD 93,
WhoAm 94, WhoAmP 93, WhoWest 94*
Cunningham, Raymond Leo 1934-
WhoMW 93, WhoScEn 94
Cunningham, Richard H. G. 1944-
WhoAmP 93
Cunningham, Richard O. 1942-
WhoAmL 94
Cunningham, Richard T. 1918-
WhoBlA 94
Cunningham, Robert c. 1739-1813
WhAmRev
Cunningham, Robert 1741-1813 *AmRev*
Cunningham, Robert Cyril 1914-
WhoAm 94
Cunningham, Robert D. *WhoAmL 94*
Cunningham, Robert James 1942-
WhoAm 94, WhoAmL 94
Cunningham, Robert Kerr 1923- *Who 94*
Cunningham, Robert Kuhlman, Sr. 1922-
WhoAmP 93
Cunningham, Robert Morton 1907-
WhoAm 94
Cunningham, Robert Shannon, Jr. 1958-
WhoBlA 94
Cunningham, Robert Stephen 1942-
WhoWest 94
Cunningham, Roger Alan 1951-
WhoWest 94
Cunningham, Rosemary Thomas 1957-
WhoFI 94
Cunningham, Samuel Lewis, Jr. 1950-
WhoBlA 94
Cunningham, Samuel S. 1958-
WhoAmL 94
Cunningham, Sarah d1986 *WhoHol 92*
Cunningham, Sean S. 1941- *HorFD [port],
IntMPA 94*
Cunningham, Stanley Lloyd 1938-
WhoAmL 94
Cunningham, Sue 1932- *WhoAmA 93*
Cunningham, Sue Carol 1940-
WhoMW 93
Cunningham, T. J. 1930- *WhoBlA 94*
Cunningham, Terence Thomas, III 1943-
WhoAm 94
Cunningham, Thomas B. 1946-
WhoScEn 94
Cunningham, Tom Alan 1946-
WhoAm 94, WhoAmL 94
Cunningham, Verenessa Smalls-Brantley
1949- *WhoBlA 94*
Cunningham, W. Pete 1929- *WhoAmP 93*
Cunningham, Walter Jack 1917-
WhoAm 94
Cunningham, William d1787 *WhAmRev*
Cunningham, William c. 1717-1791
WhAmRev
Cunningham, William 1756-1787 *AmRev*
Cunningham, William 1929- *WhoBlA 94*
Cunningham, William Dean 1937-
WhoBlA 94
Cunningham, William E. 1920-
WhoBlA 94
Cunningham, William Francis 1945-
WhoAmL 94
Cunningham, William Francis, Jr. 1931-
WhoAm 94
Cunningham, William Henry 1930-
WhoAm 94

Cunningham, William Hughes 1944-
WhoAm 94
Cunningham, William J., III 1951-
WhoAmL 94
Cunningham, William L. 1939-
WhoBlA 94
Cunningham, William Patrick 1947-
WhoFI 94
Cunningham, Zamah d1967 *WhoHol 92*
Cunningham-Jardine, Ronald Charles
1931- *Who 94*
Cunnyngham, Jon 1935- *WhoAm 94*
Cunqueiro, Alvaro 1911-1981
DcLB 134 [port]
Cuntz, Manfred Adolf 1958- *WhoScEn 94,
WhoWest 94*
Cuny, Alain 1908- *WhoHol 92*
Cuny, John Dana 1956- *WhoMW 93*
Cunynghame, Andrew (David Francis)
1942- *Who 94*
Cuoco, Daniel Anthony 1937- *WhoFI 94*
Cuomo, George *DrAPF 93*
Cuomo, George (Michael) 1929- *WrDr 94*
Cuomo, Jerome John 1936- *WhoAm 94,
WhoScEn 94*
Cuomo, Kerry Kennedy
NewYTBS 93 [port]
Cuomo, Mario (Matthew) 1932- *WrDr 94*
Cuomo, Mario Matthew 1932- *IntWW 93,
Who 94, WhoAm 94, WhoAmP 93*
Cuozzo, Steven David 1950- *WhoAm 94*
Cupeda, Donato c. 1661-1704 *NewGrDO*
Cupery, Robert Rink 1944- *WhoWest 94*
Cupit, Danny E. *WhoAmP 93*
Cupitt, Don 1934- *IntWW 93, Who 94*
Cupka, Jeffrey Albert 1955- *WhoMW 93*
Cupp, David Foster 1938- *WhoAm 94*
Cupp, Jon Michael 1955- *WhoMW 93,
WhoScEn 94*
Cupp, Robert R. 1950- *WhoAmP 93*
Cupp, Robert Richard 1950- *WhoMW 93*
Cupp, Samuel B. 1945- *WhoIns 94*
Cuppage, Francis Edward 1932-
WhoMW 93, WhoScEn 94
Cuppaidge, Virginia 1943- *WhoAmA 93*
Cupples, Stephen Elliot 1955-
WhoAmL 94
Cuprak, Peter V. *WhoAmP 93*
Cuprien, Frank W. 1871-1948
WhoAmA 93N
Curatolo, Alphonse Frank 1936-
WhoAm 94
Curb, Michael *WhoAmP 93*
Curbelo, Silvia Maria 1955- *WhoHisp 94*
Curbow, Deryl Crawford 1922-
WhoAmP 93
Curboy, Robert Edward 1928- *WhoFI 94*
Curchack, Walter H. 1951- *WhoAmL 94*
Curchoe, Carl A. 1944- *WhoFI 94*
Curci, Gennaro d1955 *WhoHol 92*
Curci, Giuseppe 1808-1877 *NewGrDO*
Curci-Gonzalez, Lucy 1955- *WhoAmL 94*
Curcio, Christopher Frank 1950-
WhoFI 94, WhoWest 94
Curcio, Giuseppe Maria fl. 1780-1809
NewGrDO
Curcio, John Baptist 1934- *WhoAm 94*
Curcio, Paul V. 1952- *WhoAmL 94*
Curcuru, Felix 1947- *WhoIns 94*
Curd, Freed 1933- *WhoAmP 93*
Curd, John Gary 1945- *WhoWest 94*
Curds, Colin Robert 1937- *Who 94*
Cure, Carol Campbell 1944- *WhoAmL 94*
Cure, Harding B. 1942- *WhoAmL 94*
Cure, Kenneth Graham 1924- *Who 94*
Cure, (George) Nigel C. *Who 94*
Cure-Awl, Dr. *EncSPD*
Cureton, Benjamin, Jr. 1947- *WhoWest 94*
Cureton, Bryant Lewis 1938- *WhoAm 94*
Cureton, Claudette Hazel Chapman 1932-
WhoScEn 94
Cureton, John Porter 1936- *WhoBlA 94*
Cureton, Michael 1955- *WhoBlA 94*
Cureton, Stewart Cleveland 1930-
WhoBlA 94
Curet-Ramos, Jose Antonio 1957-
WhoScEn 94
Curfiss, Robert C. 1946- *WhoAm 94*
Curfman, David Ralph 1942- *WhoAm 94,
WhoScEn 94*
Curfman, Floyd Edwin 1929-
WhoMW 93, WhoScEn 94
Curfman, Lawrence Everett 1909-
WhoAm 94, WhoAmL 94, WhoMW 93
Curiale, Salvatore R. 1945- *WhoIns 94*
Curie, Eve 1904- *Who 94*
Curie, Leonardo Rodolfo 1950-
WhoHisp 94
Curie, Marie 1867-1934 *WorScD [port]*
Curie, Pierre 1859-1906 *WorScD [port]*
Curiel, Frederico d1985 *WhoHol 92*
Curiel, Gonzalo d1958 *WhoHol 92*
Curiel, Herman F., II 1934- *WhoHisp 94*
Curiel, Imma Jacinta 1960- *WhoHisp 94*
Curiel, Tony 1953- *WhoHisp 94*
Curiel, Tyler Jay 1956- *WhoHisp 94*
Curien, Gilles 1922- *IntWW 93*

Curien, Hubert 1924- *IntWW 93,
WhoScEn 94*
Curioli, Paul D. 1948- *WhoIns 94*
Curioni, Alberico c. 1785-1875 *NewGrDO*
Curioni, Rosa fl. 1753-1762 *NewGrDO*
Curkendall, Brenda Irene 1954- *WhoFI 94*
Curl, Eileen Deges 1954- *WhoMW 93*
Curl, James Stevens 1937- *WrDr 94*
Curl, Paul Thomas 1958- *WhoScEn 94*
Curl, Rane Locke 1929- *WhoScEn 94*
Curl, Robert Floyd, Jr. 1933- *WhoAm 94,
WhoScEn 94*
Curl, Samuel Everett 1937- *WhoAm 94,
WhoScEn 94*
Curle, James Leonard 1925- *Who 94*
Curle, John (Noel Ormiston) 1915-
Who 94
Curle, Robin Lea 1950- *WhoScEn 94*
Curlee, Lane 1955- *WhoAmP 93*
Curlee, Richard Frederick 1935-
WhoAm 94
Curler, Howard J. 1925- *WhoAm 94,
WhoFI 94*
Curless, Larry Dean 1931- *WhoAm 94,
WhoFI 94*
Curley, Arthur 1938- *WhoAm 94*
Curley, Donald Houston 1940-
WhoAmA 93
Curley, Edwin Munson 1937- *WhoAm 94*
Curley, Jack R. 1928- *WhoWest 94*
Curley, John Francis, Jr. 1939-
WhoAm 94, WhoFI 94
Curley, John J. 1938- *WhoAm 94,
WhoFI 94*
Curley, Jonathan Edward 1953-
WhoWest 94
Curley, Kevin J. 1943- *WhoAmL 94*
Curley, Leo d1960 *WhoHol 92*
Curley, Michael Edward 1946-
WhoAmL 94
Curley, Michael Edward 1947- *WhoAm 94*
Curley, Pauline *WhoHol 92*
Curley, Robert Ambrose, Jr. 1949-
WhoAmL 94
Curley, Robert E. 1935- *WhoAm 94*
Curley, Sarah Sharer *WhoAm 94,
WhoAmL 94*
Curley, Thomas *DrAPF 93*
Curley, Thomas 1948- *WhoAm 94*
Curley, Walter J. P. *WhoAmP 93*
Curley, Walter Joseph Patrick, Jr. 1922-
IntWW 93, WhoAm 94
Curlis, David Alan 1950- *WhoScEn 94*
Curlook, Walter 1929- *WhoAm 94,
WhoFI 94*
Curls, Phillip B. 1942- *WhoAmP 93,
WhoBlA 94*
Curly-Headed Doctor d1890 *EncNAR*
Curman, Johan 1919- *IntWW 93*
Curmano, Billy *WhoAmA 93*
Curneal, Rick Owen 1951- *WhoMW 93*
Curnes, Terry Wayne 1959- *WhoFI 94*
Curnin, Thomas Francis 1933-
WhoAmL 94
Curnow, Allen 1911- *ConDr 93, WrDr 94*
Curnow, (Elizabeth) Ann (Marguerite)
1935- *Who 94*
Curnow, Frank 1927-1991 *WrDr 94N*
Curnutte, John Tolliver, III 1951-
WhoWest 94
Curnutte, Mark William 1954- *WhoAm 94*
Curotto, Ricky Joseph 1931- *WhoAm 94,
WhoAmL 94, WhoFI 94, WhoWest 94*
Curphey, Margaret 1938- *NewGrDO*
Currall, Alexander 1917- *Who 94*
Curran, Armil O. 1935- *WhoAmP 93*
Curran, Barbara A. 1940- *WhoAmP 93*
Curran, Barbara Adell 1928- *WhoAm 94,
WhoAmL 94*
Curran, Charles E. 1934- *IntWW 93,
WrDr 94*
Curran, Charles John 1921-1980
DcNaB MP
Curran, Daniel Richard 1961-
WhoWest 94
Curran, Darryl Joseph 1935- *WhoAm 94,
WhoAmA 93*
Curran, Dian Beard 1956- *WhoScEn 94*
Curran, Donald Charles 1933- *WhoAm 94*
Curran, Douglas Edward 1952-
WhoAmA 93
Curran, Francis X. 1914-1993 *WrDr 94N*
Curran, Geoffrey Michael 1949-
WhoAm 94, WhoAmL 94
Curran, Gerald Joseph 1939- *WhoAmP 93*
Curran, Henry M. d1993 *NewYTBS 93*
Curran, J. Joseph, Jr. 1931- *WhoAm 94,
WhoAmL 94, WhoAmP 93*
Curran, J. P. d1919 *WhoHol 92*
Curran, John J. 1931- *WhoAmL 94*
Curran, John Roger 1934- *WhoWest 94*
Curran, Joseph Patrick 1951- *WhoAm 94*
Curran, Leo Gabriel Columbanus 1930-
Who 94
Curran, Lynette *WhoHol 92*
Curran, M. Scot 1952- *WhoAmL 94*
Curran, Marcella Joyce 1953-
WhoWest 94

Curran, Mark Albert 1954- *WhoFI 94, WhoWest 94*
Curran, Mary 1947- *WhoAmL 94*
Curran, Maurice Francis 1931- *WhoAmL 94*
Curran, Michael D. 1945- *WhoAmP 93*
Curran, Michael Walter 1935- *WhoAm 94, WhoMW 93*
Curran, Paul d1986 *WhoHol 92*
Curran, Philip E. *WhoAmP 93*
Curran, R. T. 1931- *WhoAm 94*
Curran, Robert Bruce 1948- *WhoAm 94, WhoAmL 94*
Curran, Robert Crowe 1921- *Who 94*
Curran, Samuel (Crowe) 1912- *Who 94*
Curran, Samuel Crowe 1912- *IntWW 93*
Curran, Thomas d1941 *WhoHol 92*
Curran, Thomas 1956- *WhoScEn 94*
Curran, Thomas J. 1924- *WhoAm 94, WhoAmL 94, WhoMW 93*
Curran, Ward Schenk 1935- *WhoAm 94*
Curran, William Edward 1948- *WhoAm 94*
Curran, William James, III 1940- *WhoAmL 94*
Curran, William Stephen 1935- *WhoAm 94*
Currás, Margarita C. 1960- *WhoHisp 94*
Currell, William Dennis 1951- *WhoAmL 94*
Currelley, Lorraine Rainie *DrAPF 93*
Current, Gloster Bryant 1913- *WhoBlA 94*
Current, Richard Nelson 1912- *WhoAm 94*
Currer, Barney *DrAPF 93*
Curreri, John Robert 1922- *WhoScEn 94*
Curreri, Lee 1961- *WhoHol 92*
Curreri, Peter Angelo 1952- *WhoScEn 94*
Currey, Dave 1953- *ConAu 140*
Currey, Edmund Neville Vincent 1906- *Who 94*
Currey, Harry Lloyd Fairbridge 1925- *Who 94*
Currey, L(oyd) W(esley) 1942- *EncSF 93*
Currey, Melody A. *WhoAmP 93*
Currey, Patricia Lou 1954- *WhoFI 94*
Currey, R(alph) N(ixon) 1907- *WrDr 94*
Currey, Richard *DrAPF 93*
Currey, Richard 1949- *WrDr 94*
Currey-Wilson, Robert Thomas 1958- *WhoAmL 94*
Currid, Cheryl Clarke 1950- *WhoFI 94*
Currie, Alastair (Robert) 1921- *Who 94*
Currie, Austin *Who 94*
Currie, (Joseph) Austin 1939- *Who 94*
Currie, Barbara Flynn 1940- *WhoAmP 93, WhoMW 93*
Currie, Bruce 1911- *WhoAm 94, WhoAmA 93*
Currie, Bruce LaMonte 1945- *WhoScEn 94*
Currie, Cherie *WhoHol 92*
Currie, Christopher Clyde 1966- *WhoWest 94*
Currie, Clifford William Herbert 1918- *WhoAm 94*
Currie, Clive d1935 *WhoHol 92*
Currie, Constance Mershon 1950- *WhoMW 93*
Currie, David Anthony 1946- *IntWW 93, Who 94*
Currie, David P(ark) 1936- *WrDr 94*
Currie, Donald Scott 1930- *Who 94*
Currie, Earl James 1939- *WhoAm 94*
Currie, Eddie L. 1927- *WhoBlA 94*
Currie, Edward Jones, Jr. 1951- *WhoAmL 94*
Currie, Edwina 1946- *IntWW 93, Who 94, WhoWomW 91*
Currie, Finlay d1968 *WhoHol 92*
Currie, Frances H. Light 1923- *WhoAmP 93*
Currie, Francis Sparre 1950- *WhoAm 94*
Currie, Glenn Kenneth 1943- *WhoAm 94*
Currie, Heriot Whitson 1952- *Who 94*
Currie, Jackie L. 1932- *WhoBlA 94*
Currie, James McGill 1941- *Who 94*
Currie, James Morton 1933- *WhoFI 94*
Currie, John Thornton 1928- *WhoAm 94, WhoFI 94*
Currie, John W. 1946- *WhoAmL 94*
Currie, Katy *ConAu 141*
Currie, Lauchlin d1993 *NewYTBS 93*
Currie, Lauchlin MacLaurin 1898- *WhAm 10*
Currie, Leah Rae 1942- *WhoMW 93*
Currie, Leonard James 1913- *WhoAm 94*
Currie, Louise *WhoHol 92*
Currie, Madeline Ashburn 1922- *WhoWest 94*
Currie, Malcolm Roderick 1927- *WhoAm 94, WhoFI 94, WhoWest 94*
Currie, Michael *WhoHol 92*
Currie, Michael Robert 1952- *WhoAmL 94*
Currie, Neil (Smith) 1926- *Who 94*
Currie, Neil William 1946- *WhoFI 94*
Currie, Piers William Edward 1913- *Who 94*
Currie, Richard James 1937- *WhoFI 94*
Currie, Robert 1948-1993 *NewYTBS 93 [port]*
Currie, Robert Alexander 1905- *Who 94*
Currie, Robert Emil 1937- *WhoAm 94, WhoAmL 94*
Currie, Ronald Ian 1928- *Who 94*
Currie, Ross Stewart 1959- *WhoMW 93*
Currie, Russell 1954- *NewGrDO*
Currie, Sandee *WhoHol 92*
Currie, Sondra *WhoHol 92*
Currie, Steve
See T. Rex *ConMus 11*
Currie, Steve 1954- *WhoAmA 93*
Currie, Ulysses 1937- *WhoAmP 93*
Currier, Barry Arthur 1946- *WhoAmL 94*
Currier, Benjamin Atkinson 1933- *WhoIns 94*
Currier, Cyrus Bates 1868- *WhoAmA 93N*
Currier, David P. 1944- *WhoAmP 93*
Currier, Frank d1928 *WhoHol 92*
Currier, Frederick Plumer 1923- *WhoAm 94*
Currier, Gene Mark 1943- *WhoAmL 94, WhoMW 93*
Currier, Jeffrey L. 1940- *WhoFI 94*
Currier, Paul Jon 1952- *WhoMW 93*
Currier, Robert David 1925- *WhoAm 94, WhoScEn 94*
Currier, Ruth 1926- *WhoAm 94*
Curris, Constantine William 1940- *WhoAm 94, WhoMW 93*
Currivan, John Daniel 1947- *WhoAm 94, WhoAmL 94, WhoFI 94*
Currlin, William Egon 1945- *WhoAmP 93*
Curry, Alan C. 1933- *WhoIns 94*
Curry, Alan Chester 1933- *WhoAm 94*
Curry, Alan Stewart 1925- *Who 94*
Curry, Alton Frank 1933- *WhoAm 94*
Curry, Anne *WhoHol 92*
Curry, Beatrice Chesrown 1932- *WhoAm 94*
Curry, Bernard Francis 1918- *WhoAm 94*
Curry, Bill Perry 1937- *WhoMW 93*
Curry, Charles E. 1934- *WhoBlA 94*
Curry, Charles H. *WhoBlA 94*
Curry, Clarence F., Jr. 1943- *WhoBlA 94*
Curry, Clifton Conrad, Jr. 1957- *WhoAmL 94*
Curry, Daniel Arthur 1937- *WhoAmL 94*
Curry, Daniel Francis Myles 1946- *WhoWest 94*
Curry, David *DrAPF 93*
Curry, David Lee 1942- *WhoMW 93*
Curry, David Maurice 1944- *Who 94*
Curry, David Park 1946- *WhoAmA 93*
Curry, Dell 1964- *WhoBlA 94*
Curry, Denise 1959- *BasBi*
Curry, Donald Robert 1943- *WhoAmL 94*
Curry, Donald Scott 1958- *WhoAmL 94*
Curry, Francis John 1911- *WhoAm 94*
Curry, G(len) David 1948- *WrDr 94*
Curry, George E. 1947- *WhoBlA 94*
Curry, George Edward 1947- *WhoAm 94*
Curry, Gladys J. 1931- *WhoBlA 94*
Curry, Gordon Barrett 1954- *Who 94*
Curry, Jack *WhoAm 94*
Curry, James Trueman, Jr. 1936- *WhoAm 94, WhoWest 94*
Curry, Jane (Louise) 1932- *WrDr 94*
Curry, Jane Anne 1945- *WhoMW 93*
Curry, Jane Louise 1932- *ChlLR 31 [port], WhoAm 94*
Curry, Jerry Ralph *WhoAmP 93*
Curry, Jerry Ralph 1932- *AfrAmG [port], WhoBlA 94*
Curry, John Anthony 1949- *Who 94*
Curry, John Anthony, Jr. 1934- *WhoAm 94*
Curry, John Arthur Hugh 1938- *Who 94*
Curry, John Joseph 1936- *WhoAm 94*
Curry, John Michael 1942- *WhoAm 94*
Curry, John Patrick 1934- *WhoMW 93*
Curry, Johnny Lynville 1956- *WhoAmP 93*
Curry, Julian 1937- *ConTFT 11, WhoHol 92*
Curry, Kathleen Bridget 1931- *WhoMW 93*
Curry, Kelly Edwin 1955- *WhoAm 94*
Curry, Kevin Lee 1957- *WhoAmA 93*
Curry, Lawrence H. 1935- *WhoAmP 93*
Curry, Levy Henry 1949- *WhoBlA 94*
Curry, Mark *WhoBlA 94*
Curry, Mason d1980 *WhoHol 92*
Curry, Michael Bruce 1938- *WhoWest 94*
Curry, Michael Bruce 1953- *WhoBlA 94*
Curry, Michael Joseph 1953- *WhoMW 93*
Curry, Mitchell L. 1935- *WhoBlA 94*
Curry, Nancy Ellen 1931- *WhoAm 94*
Curry, Nathan d1964 *WhoHol 92*
Curry, Norval Herbert 1914- *WhoAm 94, WhoScEn 94*
Curry, Norvelle 1930- *WhoBlA 94*
Curry, (Thomas) Peter (Ellison) *Who 94*
Curry, Peter Harwood 1945- *WhoAmL 94*
Curry, Phyllis Joan 1929- *WhoBlA 94*
Curry, Raymond Howard 1956- *WhoMW 93*
Curry, Richard Charles 1937- *WhoAmP 93*
Curry, Richard O(rr) 1931- *WrDr 94*
Curry, Richard Orr 1931- *WhoAm 94*
Curry, Robert Emmet, Jr. 1946- *WhoAm 94, WhoAmL 94*
Curry, Robert Lee 1923- *WhoAm 94*
Curry, Robert Lee, III 1931- *WhoAmL 94*
Curry, Robert M. 1953- *WhoAmL 94*
Curry, Robert Michael 1947- *WhoScEn 94*
Curry, Roger D. 1953- *WhoAmL 94*
Curry, Sadye Beatryce *WhoBlA 94*
Curry, Thomas Fortson 1926- *WhoAm 94*
Curry, Tim 1946- *IntMPA 94, WhoAm 94, WhoHol 92*
Curry, Victor Tyrone 1960- *WhoBlA 94*
Curry, William E., Jr. 1951- *WhoAmP 93*
Curry, William Sims 1938- *WhoWest 94*
Curry, William Thomas 1943- *WhoBlA 94*
Curry-Swann, Lynne Marie 1951- *WhoFI 94*
Curschmann, Michael Johann Hendrik 1936- *WhoAm 94*
Curson, Theodore 1935- *WhoAm 94, WhoBlA 94*
Curteis, Ian (Bayley) 1935- *WrDr 94*
Curteis, Ian Bayley 1935- *IntWW 93, Who 94*
Curteis, Joanna *Who 94*
Curthoys, Ann 1942- *WhoHol 92*
Curthoys, Norman P. 1944- *WhoAm 94*
Curti, Merle 1897- *IntWW 93*
Curti, Merle Eugene 1897- *WhoAm 94*
Curties, Henry 1860- *EncSF 93*
Curtin, Brian Joseph 1921- *WhoAm 94*
Curtin, Christopher James 1951- *WhoAmL 94*
Curtin, Cynthia Kay 1961- *WhoAmL 94*
Curtin, Daniel Joseph, Jr. 1933- *WhoAm 94*
Curtin, David Stephen 1955- *WhoAm 94*
Curtin, David Yarrow 1920- *IntWW 93, WhoAm 94, WhoScEn 94*
Curtin, Gary Lee 1943- *WhoAm 94*
Curtin, Jane 1947- *IntMPA 94, WhoCom, WhoHol 92*
Curtin, Jane Therese 1947- *WhoAm 94*
Curtin, John Dorian, Jr. 1932- *WhoFI 94*
Curtin, John Joseph, Jr. 1933- *WhoAm 94*
Curtin, John Joseph, Jr. 1941- *WhoFI 94*
Curtin, John T. 1921- *WhoAm 94, WhoAmL 94, WhoBlA 94*
Curtin, John William 1922- *WhoAm 94*
Curtin, Lawrence *WhoHol 92*
Curtin, Lawrence N. 1950- *WhoAmL 94*
Curtin, Leah Louise 1942- *WhoAm 94, WhoMW 93*
Curtin, Margaret Mary 1934- *WhoAmP 93*
Curtin, Michael Daniel 1938- *WhoWest 94*
Curtin, Michael Edward 1939- *IntWW 93*
Curtin, Neal J. 1944- *WhoAmL 94*
Curtin, Phyllis *WhoAm 94*
Curtin, Phyllis 1922- *NewGrDO*
Curtin, Richard Daniel 1915- *WhoAm 94*
Curtin, Richard N. 1944- *WhoAmL 94*
Curtin, Richard T. 1941- *WhoAmL 94*
Curtin, Susan Connaughton 1943- *WhoAm 94*
Curtin, Thomas Lee 1932- *WhoWest 94*
Curtin, Thomas R. 1943- *WhoAmL 94*
Curtin, Timothy John 1942- *WhoAm 94, WhoAmL 94*
Curtin, Valerie *WhoHol 92, WrDr 94*
Curtin, William Joseph 1931- *WhoAm 94*
Curtis, Alan d1953 *WhoHol 92*
Curtis, Alan 1934- *NewGrDO*
Curtis, Albert Bradley, II 1957- *WhoFI 94*
Curtis, Allegra 1966- *WhoHol 92*
Curtis, Allen d1961 *WhoHol 92*
Curtis, Alva Marsh 1911- *WhoAm 94*
Curtis, Anthony 1926- *WrDr 94*
Curtis, Arnold Bennett 1940- *WhoAm 94*
Curtis, Barry (John) 1939- *Who 94*
Curtis, Beatrice d1963 *WhoHol 92*
Curtis, Bill 1948- *WhoScEn 94*
Curtis, Billy d1988 *WhoHol 92*
Curtis, Blake *WhoAmP 93*
Curtis, Brian Albert 1936- *WhoMW 93*
Curtis, C(hristopher) Michael 1934- *WrDr 94*
Curtis, Candace A. *WhoAmP 93*
Curtis, Carl T. 1905- *WhoAmP 93*
Curtis, Carl Thomas 1905- *WhoAm 94*
Curtis, Charles David 1939- *Who 94*
Curtis, Charles Edward 1931- *WhoAm 94*
Curtis, Chester Harris 1913- *WhoAm 94*
Curtis, Christopher Michael 1934- *WhoAm 94*
Curtis, Clark Britten 1951- *WhoFI 94, WhoMW 93, WhoScEn 94*
Curtis, Colin Hinton Thomson 1920- *Who 94*
Curtis, Constance d1959 *WhoAmA 93N*
Curtis, Dale Jay 1942- *WhoAmL 94*
Curtis, Dan 1928- *HorFD, IntMPA 94*
Curtis, David *DrAPF 93*
Curtis, David 1949- *WhoAmA 93*
Curtis, David Roderick 1927- *IntWW 93, Who 94*
Curtis, Dick d1952 *WhoHol 92*
Curtis, Dolly Powers 1942- *WhoAmA 93*
Curtis, Donald *WhoHol 92*
Curtis, Douglas Homer 1934- *WhoAm 94*
Curtis, Edward Joseph, Jr. 1942- *WhoFI 94, WhoScEn 94*
Curtis, Ernest Edwin 1906- *Who 94*
Curtis, Floyd d1988 *WhoHol 92*
Curtis, Frank *Who 94*
Curtis, (Robert) Frank 1926- *Who 94*
Curtis, (Wilfred) Frank 1923- *Who 94*
Curtis, Frank R. 1946- *WhoAm 94*
Curtis, Genevra Fiona Penelope Victoria *Who 94*
Curtis, George Bartlett 1947- *WhoAm 94, WhoAmL 94*
Curtis, George Clifton 1926- *WhoAm 94*
Curtis, George Darwin 1928- *WhoWest 94*
Curtis, George Martin, III 1935- *WhoMW 93*
Curtis, George Warren 1936- *WhoAmL 94*
Curtis, Glen Russell 1947- *WhoAmP 93, WhoWest 94*
Curtis, Grant Bradley 1948- *WhoFI 94*
Curtis, Grant E. d1993 *NewYTBS 93*
Curtis, Gregory Dyer 1947- *WhoAm 94*
Curtis, Harry S. 1934- *WhoBlA 94*
Curtis, Israel B. 1932- *WhoAmP 93*
Curtis, J(ulie) A. E. 1955- *ConAu 141*
Curtis, J. Vaughan 1951- *WhoAmL 94*
Curtis, Jack *DrAPF 93*
Curtis, Jack d1956 *WhoHol 92*
Curtis, Jackie *ConAu 42NR*
Curtis, Jackie d1985 *WhoHol 92*
Curtis, Jackie 1947-1985 *ConDr 93*
Curtis, James Austin 1927- *WhoAm 94*
Curtis, James L. 1922- *WhoAm 94, WhoBlA 94*
Curtis, James Theodore 1923- *WhoAmL 94*
Curtis, James William Ockford 1946- *Who 94*
Curtis, Jamie Lee 1958- *IntMPA 94, IntWW 93, WhoAm 94, WhoHol 92*
Curtis, Jean-Louis 1917- *EncSF 93, IntWW 93*
Curtis, Jean Trawick *WhoAm 94, WhoBlA 94, WhoMW 93*
Curtis, Jeff Bain 1953- *WhoAmL 94*
Curtis, Jesse William, Jr. 1905- *WhoAm 94, WhoWest 94*
Curtis, Jim 1945- *WhoAmL 94*
Curtis, John Barry *Who 94*
Curtis, John E., Jr. 1945- *WhoAm 94, WhoAmL 94*
Curtis, John Edward 1946- *Who 94*
Curtis, John Henry 1920- *Who 94*
Curtis, John Joseph 1942- *WhoAm 94*
Curtis, John W. d1925 *WhoHol 92*
Curtis, Joseph F., Sr. 1916- *WhoBlA 94*
Curtis, Joseph W. 1930- *WhoAmP 93*
Curtis, Juanita Gwendolyn 1920- *WhoBlA 94*
Curtis, Keene 1923- *WhoHol 92*
Curtis, Kelly 1956- *WhoHol 92*
Curtis, Ken d1991 *WhoHol 92*
Curtis, Kenneth M. 1931- *WhoAmL 94*
Curtis, Kenneth Merwin 1931- *WhoAmP 93*
Curtis, Kenneth Stewart 1925- *WhoAm 94*
Curtis, King d1971 *WhoHol 92*
Curtis, Lance *WhoHol 92*
Curtis, Laurence 1893-1989 *WhAm 10*
Curtis, Lawrence Andrew 1942- *WhoScEn 94*
Curtis, LeGrand R., Jr. 1952- *WhoAmL 94*
Curtis, Leo *Who 94*
Curtis, (Edward) Leo 1907- *Who 94*
Curtis, Liane *WhoHol 92*
Curtis, Linda Jenarie 1941- *WhoWest 94*
Curtis, Linda Lee *DrAPF 93*
Curtis, Loretta O'Ellen 1937- *WhoMW 93*
Curtis, Lynne Katherine 1950- *WhoWest 94*
Curtis, Marcia 1931- *WhoAm 94*
Curtis, Marie Therese Dodge 1935- *WhoWest 94*
Curtis, Mark Hubert 1920- *WhoAm 94*
Curtis, Marvin Vernell 1951- *WhoBlA 94*
Curtis, Mary C. 1953- *WhoBlA 94*
Curtis, Mary Cranfill 1925- *WhoAmA 93*
Curtis, Mary Ellen 1946- *WhoAm 94*
Curtis, Mary Hronik 1941- *WhoMW 93*
Curtis, Michael Howard 1920- *Who 94*
Curtis, Nancy Jane 1935- *WhoMW 93*
Curtis, Nevius Minot 1929- *WhoFI 94*
Curtis, Norma Lynn 1947- *WhoMW 93*
Curtis, Orlie Lindsey, Jr. 1934- *WhoAm 94*
Curtis, Paul James 1927- *WhoAm 94*
Curtis, Paul Nelson 1944- *WhoWest 94*
Curtis, Philip 1908- *Who 94*

Curtis, Philip C. 1907- *WhoAm 94*
Curtis, Philip Campbell 1907- *WhoAmA 93*
Curtis, Philip Hamilton 1953- *WhoMW 93*
Curtis, Philip James 1918- *WhoAm 94*
Curtis, Philip Kerry 1945- *WhoAmL 94*
Curtis, Richard A(lan) 1937- *EncSF 93*
Curtis, Richard Earl 1930- *WhoAm 94*
Curtis, Richard Herbert *Who 94*
Curtis, Richard Kenneth 1924- *WhoMW 93*
Curtis, Robert D. 1948- *WhoAmA 93*
Curtis, Robert Joseph 1945- *WhoAm 94*
Curtis, Robert Kern 1940- *WhoAmL 94*
Curtis, Roger William 1910- *WhoAm 94, WhoAmA 93*
Curtis, Sharon 1951- *WrDr 94*
Curtis, Sheldon 1932- *WhoAm 94*
Curtis, Spencer M. d1921 *WhoHol 92*
Curtis, Staton Russell 1921- *WhoAm 94*
Curtis, Stephen P. 1949- *WhoAmP 93*
Curtis, Stephen Russell 1948- *Who 94*
Curtis, Susan 1956- *WhoMW 93*
Curtis, Susan Grace 1950- *WhoAm 94*
Curtis, Terry Wayne 1951- *WhoAmA 93*
Curtis, Thomas Alan 1957- *WhoAmL 94*
Curtis, Thomas B. d1993 *NewYTBS 93 [port]*
Curtis, Thomas B(radford) 1911-1993 *CurBio 93N*
Curtis, Thomas Bradford 1911-1993 *ConAu 140*
Curtis, Thomas Dale 1952- *WrDr 94*
Curtis, Tom 1951- *WrDr 94*
Curtis, Tom 1952- *WrDr 94*
Curtis, Tony 1924- *WhoHol 92*
Curtis, Tony 1925- *IntMPA 94, IntWW 93, WhoAm 94*
Curtis, Tony 1946- *WrDr 94*
Curtis, Verna P. *WhoAmA 93*
Curtis, Wade *EncSF 93*
Curtis, Wade 1933- *WrDr 94*
Curtis, Walt *DrAPF 93*
Curtis, Wardon Allan 1867-1940 *EncSF 93*
Curtis, Warren Edward 1914- *WhoAmP 93*
Curtis, Will 1908- *WrDr 94*
Curtis, Willa Pearl d1970 *WhoHol 92*
Curtis, William (Peter) 1935- *Who 94*
Curtis, William Edgar 1914- *WhoAm 94*
Curtis, William Hall 1915-1991 *WhAm 10*
Curtis, William J. R. 1948- *WrDr 94*
Curtis, William Patrick, Jr. 1961- *WhoFI 94*
Curtis, William Shepley 1915- *WhoWest 94*
Curtis-Raleigh, Jean Margaret Macdonald 1933- *Who 94*
Curtiss, Aubyn A. *WhoAmP 93*
Curtiss, Charles Francis 1921- *WhoAm 94*
Curtiss, Elden F. 1932- *WhoAm 94, WhoWest 94*
Curtiss, Howard Crosby, Jr. 1930- *WhoAm 94*
Curtiss, Jack Daniel 1942- *WhoAmL 94*
Curtiss, Jeffrey Eugene 1948- *WhoFI 94*
Curtiss, John (Bagot) 1924- *Who 94*
Curtiss, Joseph August 1938- *WhoScEn 94*
Curtiss, Robert Louis 1932- *WhoMW 93*
Curtiss, Robert Roy 1948- *WhoMW 93*
Curtiss, Roy, III 1934- *WhoAm 94*
Curtiss, Sidney Q. *WhoAmP 93*
Curtiss, Thomas, Jr. 1941- *WhoAm 94, WhoAmL 94*
Curtiss, Trumbull Cary 1940- *WhoAm 94, WhoFI 94*
Curtner, Gregory L. 1945- *WhoAmL 94*
Curtner, Mary Elizabeth 1957- *WhoScEn 94*
Curtoni, Vittorio *EncSF 93*
Curtright, Jorja d1985 *WhoHol 92*
Curval, Philippe 1929- *EncSF 93*
Curvey, Troy, Jr. 1957- *WhoHol 92*
Curvin, Robert 1934- *WhoBlA 94*
Curwen, Christopher (Keith) 1929- *Who 94*
Curwen, John Christian 1756-1828 *DcNaB MP*
Curwen, Patric d1949 *WhoHol 92*
Curwen, Randall William 1946- *WhoAm 94*
Curwen, Samuel 1715-1802 *WhAmRev*
Curwin, Norma Pauline 1937- *WhoWest 94*
Curwin, Ronald 1930- *WhoFI 94*
Curwood, Stephen Thomas 1947- *WhoBlA 94*
Curzi, Pierre *WhoHol 92*
Curzio, Francis Xavier 1944- *WhoAm 94, WhoFI 94*
Curzon *Who 94*
Curzon, Clare 1922- *WrDr 94*
Curzon, Daniel *DrAPF 93*
Curzon, Daniel 1938- *GayLL*
Curzon, David *DrAPF 93*
Curzon, George d1976 *WhoHol 92*
Curzon, Leonard Henry 1912- *Who 94*
Curzon, Lucia *WrDr 94*
Curzon, Nathaniel 1726-1804 *DcNaB MP*
Curzon, Sarah Anne 1833-1898 *BlmGWL*
Cusack, Anne E. *DrAPF 93*
Cusack, Cyril 1910- *IntMPA 94, WhoHol 92*
Cusack, Cyril 1910-1993 *NewYTBS 93 [port]*
Cusack, Cyril James 1910- *IntWW 93*
Cusack, Dick *WhoHol 92*
Cusack, Dymphna 1902-1981 *BlmGWL [port]*
Cusack, Henry Vernon 1895- *Who 94*
Cusack, Joan 1962- *IntMPA 94, WhoHol 92*
Cusack, John 1966- *IntMPA 94, WhoAm 94*
Cusack, John 1967- *WhoHol 92*
Cusack, John Francis 1937- *WhoAmP 93*
Cusack, Margaret Weaver 1945- *WhoAmA 93*
Cusack, Sinead 1948- *WhoHol 92*
Cusack, Thomas Joseph 1938- *WhoAm 94*
Cusak, Joan 1962- *WhoAm 94*
Cusano, Cristino 1941- *WhoAm 94, WhoScEn 94*
Cusanovich, Michael Anthony 1942- *WhoWest 94*
Cusatis, John Anthony 1951- *WhoScEn 94*
Cuscaden, Sarah d1954 *WhoHol 92*
Cuscaden, William H. d1955 *WhoHol 92*
Cusdin, Sidney Edward Thomas 1908- *Who 94*
Cusens, Anthony Ralph 1927- *Who 94*
Cush, Geoffrey 1956- *EncSF 93*
Cushing, David Henry 1920- *Who 94*
Cushing, David Walker 1961- *WhoFI 94*
Cushing, Frederic Sanford 1920- *WhoAm 94*
Cushing, George Littleton 1943- *WhoAmL 94*
Cushing, Harry Cooke, IV *WhoAm 94*
Cushing, Harvey Williams 1869-1939 *WorScD*
Cushing, Peter 1913- *IntMPA 94, IntWW 93, WhoHol 92*
Cushing, Ralph Harvey 1922- *WhoMW 93*
Cushing, Richard James 1895-1970 *DcAmReB 2*
Cushing, Robert Charles 1952- *WhoFI 94*
Cushing, Robert Hunter 1953- *WhoAm 94*
Cushing, Robert Reynolds, Jr. 1952- *WhoAmP 93*
Cushing, Steven 1948- *WhoAm 94, WhoFI 94, WhoScEn 94*
Cushing, Thomas 1725-1788 *WhAmRev*
Cushingberry, George, Jr. 1953- *WhoAmP 93, WhoBlA 94*
Cushman, Aaron D. 1924- *WhoAm 94, WhoFI 94*
Cushman, Anne Caroline 1951- *WhoAmP 93*
Cushman, Dan 1909- *WrDr 94*
Cushman, David Wayne 1939- *WhoAm 94*
Cushman, Edward L. 1914-1992 *WhAm 10*
Cushman, Eugene Crocker 1944- *WhoAmP 93*
Cushman, Helen Merle Baker *WhoAm 94*
Cushman, James Butler 1936- *WhoAm 94*
Cushman, John Palmer 1932- *WhoWest 94*
Cushman, Kenneth Dean 1945- *WhoMW 93*
Cushman, Nancy d1979 *WhoHol 92*
Cushman, Oris Mildred 1931- *WhoMW 93*
Cushman, Paul 1930- *WhoAm 94*
Cushman, Robert Earl 1913- *WhoAm 94*
Cushman, Robert Fairchild 1918- *WhoAm 94*
Cushman, Vera F. 1944- *WhoBlA 94*
Cushwa, William Wallace 1937- *WhoAm 94*
Cusick, Albert 1846- *EncNAR*
Cusick, Jerry G. 1954- *WhoMW 93*
Cusick, Joseph David 1929- *WhoScEn 94*
Cusick, Mark A. 1948- *WhoAmL 94*
Cusick, Michael F. 1944- *WhoAmL 94*
Cusick, Nancy Taylor *WhoAmA 93*
Cusick, Ralph A., Jr. 1934- *WhoAm 94*
Cusick, Richie Tankersley 1952- *TwCYAW, WrDr 94*
Cusick, Robert I. 1944- *WhoAmL 94*
Cusimano, Adeline Mary 1939- *WhoAm 94*
Cusimano, Charles Vincent, II 1953- *WhoAmP 93*
Cusinelli, Peter d1945 *WhoHol 92*
Cuskaden, Everett *WhoAmL 94*
Cussler, Clive *WhoHol 92*
Cussler, Clive (Eric) 1931- *EncSF 93, IntWW 93, WrDr 94*
Cussler, Clive Eric 1931- *WhoAm 94*
Cusson, Theodore J., Sr. 1936- *WhoAmP 93*
Cussons, Sheila 1922- *BlmGWL*
Cust *Who 94*
Custalow, Otha Thomas fl. 20th cent.- *EncNAR*
Custance, Michael Magnus Vere 1916- *Who 94*
Custer, Benjamin Scott, Jr. 1937- *WhoAm 94*
Custer, Betty J. 1948- *WhoFI 94*
Custer, Bob d1974 *WhoHol 92*
Custer, Charles Francis 1928- *WhoAm 94*
Custer, Edith 1923- *AstEnc*
Custer, George Armstrong 1839-1876 *HisWorL [port]*
Custer, John Charles 1934- *WhoAm 94*
Custer, Mary Louise 1936- *WhoAmP 93*
Custer, Samuel George 1958- *WhoMW 93*
Custer-Chen, Johnnie M. 1948- *WhoBlA 94*
Custis, Clarence A. *WhoBlA 94*
Custis, Patrick James 1921- *Who 94*
Custis, Ronald Alfred 1931- *Who 94*
Cusumano, James Anthony 1942- *WhoAm 94, WhoScEn 94, WhoWest 94*
Cusumano, Michele *DrAPF 93*
Cusumano, Robert Francis 1956- *WhoAmL 94*
Cusumano, Stefano 1912-1975 *WhoAmA 93N*
Cutchall, Michael Alan 1949- *WhoMW 93*
Cutcher, Alan David 1939- *WhoAmP 93*
Cutchins, Clifford Armstrong, III 1923- *WhoAm 94, WhoFI 94*
Cutchins, Clifford Armstrong, IV 1948- *WhoAm 94, WhoAmL 94*
Cutforth, Roger 1944- *WhoAmA 93*
Cuthbert, Lady 1904- *Who 94*
Cuthbert, Alan William 1932- *IntWW 93, Who 94*
Cuthbert, Ian Holm *Who 94*
Cuthbert, Robert Allen *WhoAm 94*
Cuthbert, Robert Lowell 1939- *WhoScEn 94*
Cuthbert, Robert P. 1947- *WhoIns 94*
Cuthbert, Versie 1960- *WhoScEn 94*
Cuthbert, Virginia 1908- *WhoAmA 93*
Cuthbertson, Allan d1988 *WhoHol 92*
Cuthbertson, Betsy Alice 1952- *WhoAmL 94*
Cuthbertson, Harold (Alexander) 1911- *Who 94*
Cuthbertson, Iain 1930- *WhoHol 92*
Cuthbertson, John 1743-1821 *DcNaB MP*
Cuthill, Robert T. *WhoMW 93*
Cuthrell, Carl Edward 1934- *WhoAm 94*
Cutillo, Louis Sabino 1934- *WhoAmP 93*
Cutino, Bert Paul 1939- *WhoWest 94*
Cutkomp, Laurence Kremer 1916- *WhoMW 93*
Cutkosky, Richard Edwin 1928- *WhoAm 94, WhoScEn 94*
Cutler, Alan Jay 1949- *WhoMW 93*
Cutler, Alexander MacDonald 1951- *WhoAm 94*
Cutler, Arnold Lloyd 1938- *WhoMW 93*
Cutler, Arnold Robert 1908- *WhoAm 94, WhoAmL 94, WhoFI 94*
Cutler, Benjamin M., II 1944- *WhoIns 94*
Cutler, Bernard Joseph 1924- *WhoAm 94*
Cutler, Bess 1949- *WhoAmA 93*
Cutler, Brian *WhoHol 92*
Cutler, Bruce *DrAPF 93, NewYTBS 93 [port]*
Cutler, Bruce 1930- *ConAu 41NR, WhoMW 93*
Cutler, Bruce 1943- *WhoMW 93*
Cutler, Cassius Chapin 1914- *WhoAm 94, WhoScEn 94*
Cutler, Charles (Benjamin) 1918- *Who 94*
Cutler, Charles Russell 1924- *WhoAm 94, WhoAmL 94*
Cutler, Donald 1943- *WhoBlA 94*
Cutler, Douglas, Jr. *WhoAmP 93*
Cutler, Edward I. 1913- *WhoAm 94*
Cutler, Ethel Rose *WhoAmA 93*
Cutler, Everette Wayne 1938- *WhoAm 94*
Cutler, Frank Charles 1949- *WhoFI 94*
Cutler, Goldie *WhoAmP 93*
Cutler, Grayce E. *WhoAmA 93*
Cutler, Horace (Walter) 1912- *Who 94*
Cutler, Horace Walter 1912- *IntWW 93*
Cutler, Howard Armstrong 1918- *WhoAm 94, WhoWest 94*
Cutler, Irwin Herbert 1943- *WhoAmL 94*
Cutler, Ivor 1923- *Who 94, WrDr 94*
Cutler, Jane *DrAPF 93*
Cutler, Jane 1936- *ConAu 142, SmATA 75 [port]*
Cutler, Jay B. 1930- *WhoAmL 94, WhoAmP 93*
Cutler, John *WhoHol 92*
Cutler, John Charles 1915- *WhoAm 94*
Cutler, Kate d1955 *WhoHol 92*
Cutler, Kenneth Burnett 1932- *WhoAm 94*
Cutler, Kenneth Lance 1947- *WhoAm 94, WhoAmL 94*
Cutler, Kenneth Ross 1920- *WhoWest 94*
Cutler, Laurence Stephan 1940- *WhoAm 94*
Cutler, Leonard Samuel 1928- *WhoAm 94, WhoScEn 94*
Cutler, Linda Lefstein 1947- *WhoMW 93*
Cutler, Lloyd Norton 1917- *WhoAm 94*
Cutler, Lorraine Masters 1943- *WhoWest 94*
Cutler, Lynn Germain 1938- *WhoAmP 93*
Cutler, Manasseh 1742-1823 *WhAmRev*
Cutler, Max 1912-1988 *WhAm 10*
Cutler, Miriam 1953- *WhoAmL 94*
Cutler, Morene Parten 1911- *WhoAm 94*
Cutler, Neal Evan *WhoAm 94, WhoScEn 94*
Cutler, Norman Barry 1942- *WhoFI 94, WhoMW 93*
Cutler, Phyllis L. 1928- *WhoAm 94*
Cutler, Rhoda *WhoAm 94*
Cutler, Richard Bruce 1931- *WhoWest 94*
Cutler, Richard Schuyler 1898- *WhAm 10*
Cutler, Richard Woolsey 1917- *WhoAm 94*
Cutler, Robert 1895-1974 *HisDcKW*
Cutler, Robert Porter 1917- *WhoAm 94*
Cutler, Robert W. d1993 *NewYTBS 93*
Cutler, Robert Ward 1905- *WhoAm 94*
Cutler, Robin *Who 94*
Cutler, Roden *IntWW 93, Who 94*
Cutler, (Arthur) Roden 1916- *IntWW 93, Who 94*
Cutler, Roland *DrAPF 93*
Cutler, Ronnie *WhoAmA 93*
Cutler, Stephen Joel 1943- *WhoAm 94*
Cutler, Steve Keith 1948- *WhoAmP 93*
Cutler, Theodore John 1941- *WhoAm 94*
Cutler, Timothy 1684-1765 *DcAmReB 2*
Cutler, Timothy Robert 1934- *Who 94*
Cutler, Tom 1951- *WrDr 94*
Cutler, Victor *WhoHol 92*
Cutler, Walter Leon 1931- *IntWW 93, WhoAm 94*
Cutler-Shaw, Joyce *WhoAmA 93*
Cutliff, John Wilson 1923- *WhoBlA 94*
Cutlip, Randall Brower 1916- *WhoAm 94, WhoScEn 94*
Cutlip, Scott Munson 1915- *WhoAm 94*
Cutrate, Joe 1948- *ConLC 76*
Cutrell, Benjamin Elwood 1923- *WhoAm 94*
Cutrie, Sherri Ann 1948- *WhoFI 94*
Cutright, Bonnie Joann 1956- *WhoMW 93*
Cutright, Frances Larson 1935- *WhoWest 94*
Cutright, James Marr 1927- *WhoAmL 94*
Cutrona, Salvatore Michael 1951- *WhoFI 94*
Cutrone, Ronnie Blaise 1948- *WhoAmA 93*
Cutrow, Allan B. 1946- *WhoAmL 94*
Cutshall, Ronny L. 1946- *WhoAmL 94*
Cutshaw, James Michael 1950- *WhoAmL 94*
Cutshaw, Kenneth Andrew 1953- *WhoAm 94, WhoAmL 94*
Cutt, Samuel Robert 1925- *Who 94*
Cutter, Ammi 1735-1819 *WhAmRev*
Cutter, Charles Richard, III 1924- *WhoAm 94*
Cutter, David Lee 1929- *WhoAm 94*
Cutter, Edward Ahern 1939- *WhoAmL 94*
Cutter, Elizabeth Graham 1929- *Who 94*
Cutter, Gary Lee 1948- *WhoMW 93*
Cutter, Glenn Terry 1939- *WhoMW 93*
Cutter, John Michael 1952- *WhoMW 93*
Cutter, Lise *WhoHol 92*
Cutter, Reginald 1951- *WhoWest 94*
Cutting, Harold D. 1929- *WhoAmP 93*
Cutting, Heyward 1921- *WhoAm 94*
Cutting, Mable Goodhue 1910- *WhoAmP 93*
Cutting, Richard d1972 *WhoHol 92*
Cutting, Robert Thomas 1929- *WhoAm 94*
Cuttle, Tracy Donald 1908- *WhoAm 94*
Cuttler, Charles David 1913- *WhoAmA 93*
Cutts, Charles Eugene 1914- *WhoAm 94*
Cutts, Patricia d1974 *WhoHol 92*
Cutts, Richard Stanley 1919- *Who 94*
Cutts, Simon 1944- *IntWW 93*
Cuvier, Georges Leopold Chretien Frederic Dagobert, Baron 1769-1832 *WorScD*
Cuyas y Bores, Vicenc 1816-1839 *NewGrDO*
Cuyjet, Aloysius Baxter 1947- *WhoBlA 94*
Cuyjet, Cynthia K. 1948- *WhoBlA 94*
Cuyler, Milton 1968- *WhoBlA 94*
Cuza Malé, Belkis 1942- *WhoHisp 94*
Cuzzetto, Charles Edward 1954- *WhoFI 94*
Cuzzoni, Francesca 1696-1778 *NewGrDO*
Cvar, Duane Emil 1944- *WhoWest 94*
Cvejic, Biserka 1923- *NewGrDO*

Cvengros, Joseph Michael 1931-
  WhoMW 93
Cvengros, William D. 1948- WhoIns 94
Cvensros, Katherine Anne 1961-
  WhoAmL 94
Cvetanovich, Danny L. 1952- WhoAm 94
Cvijanovic, Vince Vojislav 1960-
  WhoMW 93
Cwejdzinska, Gabriela WhoWomW 91
Cwik, Wayne S. 1947- WhoIns 94
Cybulski, Joanne Karen 1950- WhoAm 94
Cybulski, Zbigniew d1967 WhoHol 92
Cyccone, Louis Anthony 1956-
  WhoMW 93
Cycmanick, Carol George 1944-
  WhoAmP 93, WhoWomW 91
Cycyota, Thomas A. 1958- WhoMW 93
Cyert, Richard Michael 1921- WhoAm 94
Cylke, Frank Kurt 1932- WhoAm 94
Cymbala, Robert Joseph 1937-
  WhoAm 94
Cymbalista, Debbie DrAPF 93
Cymbler, Murray Joel 1948- WhoFI 94
Cymrot, Mark Alan 1947- WhoAm 94,
  WhoAmL 94
Cynader, Max Sigmund 1947- WhoAm 94
Cynamon, David J. 1949- WhoAmL 94
Cynar, Sandra Jean 1941- WhoAm 94,
  WhoScEn 94
Cynewulf fl. 800- BlmGEL
Cyniburg fl. 8th cent.- BlmGWL
Cynthia ConAu 41NR
Cypert, Charles Leroy 1950- WhoFI 94
Cypert, James Dean 1934- WhoAmP 93
Cypert, Jimmy Dean 1934- WhoAm 94
Cypher, Jon WhoHol 92
Cyphers, Charles WhoHol 92
Cyphers, Daniel Clarence 1964-
  WhoScEn 94
Cyphers, Peggy K. 1954- WhoAmA 93
Cyphert, Frederick Ralph 1928-
  WhoAm 94
Cyphert, Michael A. 1948- WhoAmL 94
Cypress Hill ConMus 11 [port]
Cyprus And The Gulf, Bishop in 1930-
  Who 94
Cypser, Darlene Ann 1958- WhoAmL 94
Cyr, Arthur 1945- WhoAm 94,
  WhoMW 93
Cyr, Conrad K. 1931- WhoAmP 93
Cyr, Conrad Keefe 1931- WhoAm 94,
  WhoAmL 94
Cyr, J. V. Raymond 1934- WhoAm 94,
  WhoFI 94
Cyrano de Bergerac 1619-1655 EncSF 93
Cyrano de Bergerac, Savinien de
  1619-1655 GuFrLit 2
Cyrus, Bernard E. J., Jr. 1953-
  WhoAmP 93
Cyrus, Billy Ray WhoAm 94
Cyrus, Billy Ray 1961- ConMus 11 [port]
Cyrus, Kenneth M. WhoAm 94,
  WhoAmL 94, WhoFI 94
Cyrus, Ronald R. 1935- WhoAmP 93
Cyrus the Great, II c. 590-529BC
  HisWorL [port]
Cys, Richard L. 1944- WhoAmL 94
Cytowic, Richard Edmund 1952-
  WhoAm 94
Cytraus, Aldona Ona 1947- WhoFI 94
Cywinska, Izabella 1935- IntWW 93
Czach, Marie WhoAmA 93
Czachura, Kimberly Ann Napua 1963-
  WhoScEn 94
Czajka, James Vincent 1950- WhoFI 94
Czajkowski, Carl Joseph 1948-
  WhoScEn 94
Czajkowski, Eva Anna 1961- WhoFI 94,
  WhoScEn 94
Czajkowski, Frank Henry 1936-
  WhoAmL 94
Czajkowski, Ned J. 1949- WhoAmL 94
Czajkowski-Barrett, Karen Angela 1957-
  WhoFI 94
Czaplewski, Lynn Marie 1950-
  WhoMW 93
Czaplewski, Mark Monty 1953-
  WhoMW 93
Czaplewski, Raymond Lawrence 1949-
  WhoWest 94
Czapor, Edward P. WhoFI 94
Czarcinski, Donald Paul 1947-
  WhoAmP 93
Czarnecki, Caroline MaryAnne 1929-
  WhoAm 94, WhoMW 93
Czarnecki, Gerald Milton 1940-
  WhoAm 94, WhoWest 94
Czarnecki, Gregory James 1959-
  WhoScEn 94
Czarnecki, Richard Edward 1931-
  WhoAm 94
Czarnezki, Joseph John 1954-
  WhoAmP 93
Czarnezki, Mary Elaine 1952-
  WhoMW 93
Czarniecki, M. J., III 1948- WhoAmA 93
Czarniecki, Myron James, III 1948-
  WhoAm 94, WhoMW 93

Czarnik, Marvin Ray 1932- WhoAm 94
Czarnik-Sojka, Teresa WhoWomW 91
Czarnopys, Thomas J. 1957- WhoAmA 93
Czarra, Edgar F., Jr. 1928- WhoAm 94,
  WhoAmL 94
Czartolomny, Piotr Antoni 1946-
  WhoWest 94
Czech, Grover E. 1942- WhoIns 94
Czechowski, Mary Ann 1942- WhoMW 93
Czekanowska, Anna 1929- ConAu 140
Czenezek, Maria WhoWomW 91
Czepa, Friedl d1973 WhoHol 92
Czernilofsky, Armin Peter 1945-
  WhoScEn 94
Czerwenka, Oskar 1924- NewGrDO
Czerwinski, Barbara Lynn 1954-
  WhoAmP 93
Czerwinski, Edward Joseph 1929-
  WhoAm 94
Czerwinski, Henry Richard 1933-
  WhoAm 94
Czerwonka, Kevin Mark 1965-
  WhoAmL 94
Czestochowski, Joseph Stephen 1950-
  WhoAmA 93
Czeswik, Frederick Randall 1946-
  WhoMW 93
Czibere, Tibor 1930- IntWW 93
Czibulka, Alphons 1842-1894 NewGrDO
Cziffra Who 94
Cziffra, Georges 1921- IntWW 93
Czigany, Lorant (Gyorgy) 1935- WrDr 94
Czimbalmos, Magdolna Paal WhoAmA 93
Czimbalmos, Szabo Kalman 1914-
  WhoAmA 93
Czipott, Peter Victor 1954- WhoWest 94
Czirbik, Rudolf Joseph 1953-
  WhoScEn 94
Czrtoryska, Izabela 1746-1835 BlmGWL
Czufin, Rudolf 1901-1979 WhoAmA 93N
Czulowski, Edward Joseph 1914-
  WhoAmP 93
Czuma, Stanislaw J. 1935- WhoAmA 93
Czupala-Hologa, Stefania WhoWomW 91
Czuprynski, Charles Joseph 1953-
  WhoMW 93
Czury, Craig DrAPF 93
Czuszak, Janis Marie 1956- WhoFI 94
Czysz, David Eugene 1948- WhoMW 93
Czyz, Henryk 1923- NewGrDO

D

Daab-Krzykowski, Andre 1949- *WhoFI 94*
Daane, James Dewey 1918- *IntWW 93,*
  WhoAm 94
Daay, Badie Peter 1940- *WhoScEn 94*
Dabadie, Henri-Bernard 1797-1853
  NewGrDO
Dabadie, Louise 1804-1877 *NewGrDO*
Dabah, Haim 1951- *WhoAm 94,*
  WhoFI 94
Dabah, Isaac 1958- *WhoFI 94*
Dabah, Morris 1925- *WhoAm 94,*
  WhoFI 94
Dabareiner, Thomas John 1956-
  WhoMW 93
Dabb, Wayne C., Jr. 1946- *WhoAmL 94*
Dabbieri, Susan Lynn 1964- *WhoMW 93*
Dabbs, Henry Erven 1932- *WhoAm 94,*
  WhoBlA 94
Dabbs, Roy Andrew 1950- *WhoAmP 93*
Dabby, Sabah Salman 1946- *WhoAm 94*
Daberko, David A. 1945- *WhoAm 94,*
  WhoFI 94
Dabich, Danica 1930- *WhoMW 93*
Dabich, Eli, Jr. 1939- *WhoAm 94*
Dabill, Phillip Alvin 1942- *WhoAm 94,*
  WhoFI 94
Dabkowski, John 1933- *WhoMW 93,*
  WhoScEn 94
Dablow, Dean Clint 1946- *WhoAmA 93*
Dabney, Augusta 1920- *WhoHol 92*
Dabney, David Hodges 1927- *WhoBlA 94*
Dabney, Fred E., II 1937- *WhoIns 94*
Dabney, H. Slayton, Jr. 1949- *WhoAm 94,*
  WhoAmL 94
Dabney, Hovey Slayton 1923- *WhoAm 94*
Dabney, Joseph Earl 1929- *WrDr 94*
Dabney, Robert Lewis 1820-1898
  DcAmReB 2
Dabney, Seth Mason, III 1918-
  WhoAm 94
Dabney, Virginia *WhoHol 92*
Dabney, Virginius 1901- *WhoAm 94,*
  WrDr 94
Dabney, Watson Barr 1923- *WhoAm 94,*
  WhoFI 94
d'Abo, Jennifer Mary Victoria 1945-
  Who 94
Dabo, Leon 1868-1960 *WhoAmA 93N*
d'Abo, Maryam 1961- *WhoHol 92*
d'Abo, Olivia 1969- *WhoHol 92*
Daboll, Nathan 1750-1818 *WhAmRev*
D'Aboville, Francois Marie *WhAmRev*
Dabravolski, Aliaksandr Alhiertavic 1958-
  LoBiDrD
d'Abreu, Francis Arthur 1904- *Who 94*
Dabrowska, Maria 1889-1965 *BlmGWL*
Dabrowski, Adam Miroslaw 1953-
  WhoScEn 94
Dabrowski, Doris Jane 1950- *WhoAmL 94*
Dabrowski, Edward John 1957-
  WhoMW 93
Dabrowski, Konrad Ryszard 1949-
  WhoMW 93
Dabydeen, Cyril 1945- *WrDr 94*
Dabydeen, David 1956- *WrDr 94*
Dacca *Who 94*
D'Accone, Frank Anthony 1931-
  WhoAm 94
Dace, Tish 1941- *WhoAm 94, WrDr 94*
Dacek, Raymond Francis 1930-
  WhoAm 94
Dacey, Eileen M. 1948- *WhoAm 94,*
  WhoAmL 94

Dacey, Florence Chard *DrAPF 93*
Dacey, George Clement 1921- *WhoAm 94*
Dacey, Kathleen Ryan *WhoAm 94*
Dacey, Michael F. *WhoAm 94, WhoFI 94*
Dacey, Philip *DrAPF 93*
Dacey, Philip 1939- *WrDr 94*
Dacey, Richard Norman 1959- *WhoFI 94*
Dacey, Robert Frank 1954- *WhoFI 94*
Dache, Lilly d1990 *WhAm 10*
Dacheville, Colette 1932- *IntWW 93*
Dachowski, Peter Richard 1948-
  WhoAm 94
Dacie, John (Vivian) 1912- *IntWW 93,*
  Who 94
Dacier, Anne Le Ferre 1651-1720
  BlmGWL
Dack, Christopher Edward Hughes 1942-
  WhoAm 94
Dack, Simon 1908- *WhoAm 94*
Dackawich, S. John 1926- *WhoAm 94*
Dacko, David 1930- *IntWW 93*
Dackow, Orest Taras 1936- *WhoAm 94*
Dacla, Corinne *WhoHol 92*
Dacombe, William John Armstrong 1934-
  Who 94
Dacosta, Claude Antoine *IntWW 93*
DaCosta, Edward Hoban 1918-
  WhoAm 94
da Costa, Harvey Lloyd 1914- *Who 94*
da Costa, Margaret Anne 1941-
  WhoMW 93
da Costa, Newton Carneiro Affonso 1929-
  WhoScEn 94
da Costa, Sergio Correa 1919- *Who 94*
Da Costa Salema Roseta, Maria Helena do
  Rego 1947- *WhoWomW 91*
Dacquino, Vincent T. *DrAPF 93*
Dacre, Baroness 1929- *Who 94*
Dacre, Paul Michael 1948- *IntWW 93,*
  Who 94
Dacre Of Glanton, Baron 1914-
  IntWW 93, Who 94
Da Cruz, Daniel 1921-1991 *EncSF 93*
da Cunha, John Wilfrid 1922- *Who 94*
Da Cunha, Julio 1929- *WhoAmA 93*
Dacus, Claudette Jill 1953- *WhoMW 93*
Dadabhai, Naoroji 1825-1917 *DcNaB MP*
Dadakis, John D. 1951- *WhoAm 94,*
  WhoAmL 94
D'Adamo, Michael Anthony 1953-
  WhoFI 94
Dadd, Richard 1817-1886 *DcNaB MP*
Daddah, Moktar Ould 1924- *IntWW 93*
D'Addario, Alice Marie 1942- *WhoAm 94*
Daddario, Emilio Quincy 1918-
  WhoAm 94, WhoAmP 93
Daddi, Francesco 1864-1945 *NewGrDO*
Daddona, Joseph S. 1933- *WhoAmP 93*
Dadds, Susan Margaret 1957- *WhoMW 93*
Daddy Mack c. 1979-
  See Kris Kross *ConMus 11*
Dade, Frances d1968 *WhoHol 92*
Dade, Malcolm G., Jr. 1931- *WhoBlA 94*
Dadez, Christine D. 1958- *WhoMW 93*
Dadie, Bernard (Binlin) 1916-
  ConWorW 93
Dadie, Bernard Binlin 1916- *IntDcT 2*
Dadisman, Joseph Carrol 1934-
  WhoAm 94
Dadisman, Lynn Ellen 1946- *WhoWest 94*
Dadley, Arlene Jeanne 1941- *WhoAm 94*
Dadlez, Christopher M. 1953- *WhoAm 94*
Dado, Arnold Emmett 1938- *WhoWest 94*

Dadrian, Vahakn Norair 1926-
  WhoAm 94
Dady, J. Michael 1949- *WhoAm 94,*
  WhoAmL 94
Dady, Robert Edward 1936- *WhoAm 94*
Dadyburjor, Dady B. 1949- *WhoAm 94*
Dadzie, Kenneth 1930- *IntWW 93*
Dae, Frank d1959 *WhoHol 92*
Daeger, Phillip James 1942- *WhoAmP 93*
Daehn, Glenn Steven 1961- *WhoAm 94,*
  WhoScEn 94
Daemen, Jaak Joseph K. *WhoWest 94*
Daemer, Will 1920- *WrDr 94*
Daems, Marie *WhoHol 92*
Daenzer, Bernard J(ohn) 1916- *WrDr 94*
Daenzer, Bernard John 1916- *WhoAm 94,*
  WhoIns 94
Daepp-Heiniger, Susanna 1938-
  WhoWomW 91
Daerr, Richard Leo, Jr. 1944- *WhoFI 94*
Daeschner, Charles William, Jr. 1920-
  WhoAm 94
Daeschner, Richard Wilbur 1917-
  WhoAm 94
D'Aeth, Richard 1912- *Who 94*
Dafallah, Gizouli 1935- *IntWW 93*
Dafermos, Constantine Michael 1941-
  WhoAm 94, WhoScEn 94
Daffern, Paul George 1953- *Who 94*
Daffron, MaryEllen 1946- *WhoAm 94*
Dafis, Cynog Glyndwr 1938- *Who 94*
Da Foe, Allan d1943 *WhoHol 92*
Dafoe, Christopher Randy 1962-
  WhoFI 94
Dafoe, Willem 1955- *IntMPA 94,*
  IntWW 93, WhoAm 94, WhoHol 92
da Fonseca, Eduardo Giannetti 1957-
  ConAu 141
da Fonseca, Manuel d1993 *NewYTBS 93*
Daft, Jack Robert 1929- *WhoAm 94*
Daft, William Stanley 1957- *WhoMW 93*
Daftari, Inder Krishen 1947- *WhoScEn 94*
Daftary, Farhad 1938- *WrDr 94*
Daga, Raman Lall 1944- *WhoAsA 94*
Da Gagliano, Marco *NewGrDO*
Da Gama, Vasco *WhWE*
Dagenais, Camille A. 1920- *IntWW 93*
Dagenais, Don Frederick 1951-
  WhoAmL 94
Dagenais, Marcel Gilles 1935- *IntWW 93,*
  WhoAm 94
Dagenhart, Larry Jones 1932- *WhoAm 94*
Dager, Fernando E. 1961- *WhoHisp 94*
Dager, Robert Arnold *WhoMW 93*
Dagerman, Stig (Halvard) 1923-1954
  IntDcT 2
Daget, Robert T. d1975 *WhoHol 92*
Daggett, Albert H. 1898- *WhAm 10*
Daggett, Beverly C. *WhoAmP 93*
Daggett, Horace 1931- *WhoAmP 93*
Daggett, Jimason Jackson 1915-
  WhoAmL 94
Daggett, John P. *WhoAmP 93*
Daggett, Naphtali 1727-1780 *WhAmRev*
Daggett, Robert Sherman 1930-
  WhoAm 94, WhoAmL 94, WhoFI 94,
  WhoWest 94
Daggett, Wesley John 1963- *WhoScEn 94*
Daggs, Leon, Jr. 1941- *WhoBlA 94*
Daggs, LeRoy W. 1924- *WhoBlA 94*
Daghofer, Fritz d1936 *WhoHol 92*
Dagit, Charles Edward, Jr. 1943-
  WhoAm 94

Daglarca, Fazil Husnu 1914-
  ConWorW 93
Dagley, Larry Jack 1948- *WhoFI 94*
Dagli, Cihan Hayreddin 1949-
  WhoMW 93
Dagmar *EncSF 93*
Dagmar, Peter *EncSF 93*
D'Agnese, Helen Jean 1922- *WhoAm 94*
Dagnol, Jules N. *EncSF 93*
Dagnon, James Bernard 1940-
  WhoAm 94, WhoFI 94
D'Agostino, Albert S. 1893-1970
  IntDcF 2-4
D'Agostino, Angelo Rocco 1943-
  WhoAmP 93
D'Agostino, Anthony Carmen 1939-
  WhoAm 94
D'Agostino, Harry J. 1931- *WhoAmP 93*
D'Agostino, James Samuel, Jr. 1946-
  WhoAm 94, WhoIns 94
D'Agostino, Paul Anthony 1963-
  WhoScEn 94
D'Agostino, Peler 1945- *WhoAmA 93*
D'Agostino, Ralph Benedict 1940-
  WhoAm 94, WhoScEn 94
D'Agostino, Stephen I. 1933- *WhoAm 94*
D'Agostino, Thomas C. 1940-
  WhoAmL 94
d'Agoult, Marie *BlmGWL*
Dagover, Lil 1887?-1980 *WhoHol 92*
Dagri Diabate, Henriette Rose
  WhoWomW 91
Daguerre, Louis Jacque Mande
  1789-1851 *WorInv [port]*
Daguerre, Louis-Jacques-Mande
  1787-1851 *NewGrDO*
D'Aguiar, Fred 1960- *WrDr 94*
Dagum, Camilo 1925- *WhoScEn 94*
D'Agusto, Karen Rose 1952- *WhoAmL 94*
Dagworthy Prew, Wendy Ann 1950-
  IntWW 93
Dagys, Jacob 1905-1989 *WhoAmA 93N*
Dahab, Abdul-Rahman Swar al- 1934-
  IntWW 93
Dahanayake, Wijeyananda 1902-
  IntWW 93
Daheim, Mary Rene 1937- *WhoWest 94*
Dahill, Thomas Henry, Jr. 1925-
  WhoAmA 93
Dahiya, Jai Bhagwan 1956- *WhoMW 93,*
  WhoScEn 94
Dahiya, Jai Narain 1946- *WhoMW 93,*
  WhoScEn 94
Dahiya, Rajbir Singh 1940- *WhoScEn 94*
Dahl, Alan Richard 1944- *WhoWest 94*
Dahl, Andrew Wilbur 1943- *WhoScEn 94*
Dahl, Arlene 1928- *IntMPA 94,*
  WhoAm 94, WhoHol 92
Dahl, Arlene (Carol) 1928- *ConAu 140*
Dahl, Arthur Ernest 1916- *WhoAm 94*
Dahl, Bernhoff Allen 1938- *WhoFI 94*
Dahl, Birgitta 1937- *IntWW 93,*
  WhoWomW 91
Dahl, Bonnie Lou 1956- *WhoMW 93*
Dahl, Bren Bennington 1954- *WhoAm 94*
Dahl, Bruce Eric 1963- *WhoAmL 94*
Dahl, Christopher T. 1943- *WhoAm 94*
Dahl, Curtis 1920- *WhoAm 94,*
  WhoAmP 93, WrDr 94
Dahl, Donald Douglas 1920- *WhoWest 94*
Dahl, Francis W. 1907-1973
  WhoAmA 93N

Dahl, Gardar Godfrey, Jr. 1946- *WhoWest 94*
Dahl, George Leighton 1894- *WhAm 10*
Dahl, Gerald LuVern 1938- *WhoMW 93, WhoScEn 94*
Dahl, Gregory L. *WhoAmP 93*
Dahl, Harry Waldemar 1927- *WhoAm 94, WhoAmL 94, WhoFI 94, WhoMW 93*
Dahl, Henry Lawrence, Jr. 1933- *WhoFI 94*
Dahl, Hilbert Douglas 1942- *WhoAm 94, WhoScEn 94*
Dahl, Jeffrey Alan 1953- *WhoAmL 94*
Dahl, John Anton 1922- *WhoAm 94*
Dahl, John L. 1920- *WhoAmP 93*
Dahl, Joyle Cochran 1935- *WhoAm 94*
Dahl, Lance Christopher 1951- *WhoAm 94*
Dahl, Laurel Jean *WhoMW 93*
Dahl, Lawrence Frederick 1929- *WhoAm 94, WhoMW 93, WhoScEn 94*
Dahl, Loren Silvester 1921- *WhoAm 94, WhoAmL 94, WhoWest 94*
Dahl, Martin Astor 1933- *WhoIns 94*
Dahl, Mildred *Who 94*
Dahl, Reynold Paul 1924- *WhoAm 94*
Dahl, Roald 1916-1990 *ConLC 79 [port], DcLB 139 [port], EncSF 93, RfGShF, TwCYAW, WhAm 10*
Dahl, Robert (Alan) 1915- *WrDr 94*
Dahl, Robert Alan 1915- *IntWW 93, WhoAm 94*
Dahl, Robert Henry 1910- *Who 94*
Dahl, Stephen M. *WhoAmA 93*
Dahl, Terrence Curtis 1954- *WhoWest 94*
Dahl, Tessa 1957- *WhoHol 92*
Dahl, Tyrus Vance, Jr. 1949- *WhoAmL 94*
Dahlbeck, Eva 1920- *IntWW 93, WhoHol 92*
Dahlberg, Albert A. d1993 *NewYTBS 93*
Dahlberg, Albert Edward 1938- *WhoAm 94*
Dahlberg, Alfred William 1940- *WhoAm 94, WhoFI 94*
Dahlberg, Burton Francis 1932- *WhoAm 94, WhoFI 94*
Dahlberg, Carl Fredrick, Jr. 1936- *WhoFI 94*
Dahlberg, Edwin Lennart 1901-1984 *WhoAmA 93N*
Dahlberg, Richard Craig 1929- *WhoWest 94*
Dahlberg, Thomas Robert 1961- *WhoAmL 94, WhoWest 94*
Dahleen, Lynn Sue 1962- *WhoMW 93*
Dahlen, Beverly *DrAPF 93, WrDr 94*
Dahlen, Laurel June 1949- *WhoWest 94*
Dahlenburg, Lyle Marion 1935- *WhoAm 94*
Dahler, John Spillers 1930- *WhoAm 94*
Dahler, Warren 1897-1961 *WhoAmA 93N*
Dahlerup, Troels 1925- *IntWW 93*
Dahlfors, John Ragnar 1934- *IntWW 93*
Dahlgren, Carl Herman Per 1929- *WhoAm 94*
Dahlgren, John Onsgard 1913-1989 *WhAm 10*
Dahlgren, Paul Andrew 1959- *WhoFI 94*
Dahlhaus, Carl 1928-1989 *NewGrDO*
Dahlheimer, Donald Joseph 1931- *WhoWest 94*
Dahlie, Hallvard 1925- *WrDr 94*
Dahlin, Dennis John 1947- *WhoWest 94*
Dahlin, Donald Clifford 1941- *WhoAm 94*
Dahlin, Robert Steven 1953- *WhoScEn 94*
Dahling, E. Gunter 1931- *WhoIns 94*
Dahling, Gerald Vernon 1947- *WhoAmL 94*
Dahlke, Walter Emil 1910- *WhoAm 94*
Dahlke, Wayne Theodore 1941- *WhoAm 94, WhoFI 94*
Dahllof, Urban Sigurd 1928- *IntWW 93*
Dahlman, Martha Clarke 1960- *WhoMW 93*
Dahlquist, Gregory Edward 1957- *WhoWest 94*
Dahlquist, James Lewis 1950- *WhoAmL 94*
Dahlquist, Lasse d1979 *WhoHol 92*
Dahlstedt, Kate *DrAPF 93*
Dahlsten, Donald L 1933- *WrDr 94*
Dahlsten, Donald Lee 1933- *WhoWest 94*
Dahlsten, Gunnar 1927- *IntWW 93*
Dahlsten, Shirley Annette 1940- *WhoWest 94*
Dahlstrom, Donald Albert 1920- *WhoAm 94*
Dahlstrom, Grant Russell 1954- *WhoFI 94, WhoWest 94*
Dahlstrom, Nancy Gail 1948- *WhoAmA 93*
Dahlstrom, Norman Herbert 1931- *WhoFI 94, WhoScEn 94*
Dahlstrom, William Grant 1922- *WhoAm 94*
Dahm, Alfons George 1942- *WhoFI 94*
Dahm, Arnold Jay 1932- *WhoScEn 94*
Dahm, Marion 1918- *WhoAmP 93*
Dahmer, Michael D. 1950- *WhoAmP 93*
Dahmer, Wayne d1980 *WhoHol 92*
Dahms, Arthur Robert, III 1944- *WhoFI 94*
Dahms, William Lauritz 1959- *WhoMW 93*
Dahn, Carl James 1936- *WhoMW 93*
Dahn, Felix 1834-1912 *DcLB 129 [port]*
Dahn, Michael Steven 1949- *WhoMW 93*
Dahod, Aarif Mansur 1952- *WhoFI 94*
Dahotre, Narendra Bapurao 1956- *WhoScEn 94*
Dahrendorf, Baron 1929- *Who 94*
Dahrendorf, Ralf, Sir 1929- *WrDr 94*
Dahrendorf, Ralf (Gustav) 1929- *IntWW 93*
Dai, Charles Mun-Hong 1953- *WhoScEn 94*
Dai, Hai-Lung 1954- *WhoAsA 94, WhoScEn 94*
Dai, Lin d1964 *WhoHol 92*
Dai, Liyi 1961- *WhoAsA 94*
Dai, Peter Kuang-Hsun 1934- *WhoScEn 94*
Dai Ailian 1916- *IntWW 93, WhoPRCh 91 [port]*
Dai Bang 1917- *WhoPRCh 91*
Daiber, Albert *EncSF 93*
Daiber, Hans Joachim 1942- *IntWW 93*
Dai Bingguo *WhoPRCh 91*
Daiches, David 1912- *IntWW 93, Who 94, WrDr 94*
Daiches, Lionel Henry 1911- *Who 94*
Dai Chuanzeng *WhoPRCh 91*
Daidone, Lewis Eugene 1957- *WhoFI 94*
Dai Dunbang 1938- *WhoPRCh 91*
Daie, Jaleh 1948- *WhoScEn 94*
Daigh, Robin Demarest 1957- *WhoFI 94*
Daigle, Paul Nelson 1938- *WhoAm 94, WhoAmL 94*
Daigle, Robert A. 1921- *WhoAmP 93*
Daigle, Ronald Elvin 1944- *WhoScEn 94, WhoWest 94*
Daignault, David William 1939- *WhoWest 94*
Daigneault, Gilles 1943- *WhoAmA 93*
Daigon, Ruth *DrAPF 93*
Dai Houying 1938- *BlmGWL, WhoPRCh 91 [port]*
Daija, Tish 1926- *NewGrDO*
Dai Jie 1928- *IntWW 93, WhoPRCh 91 [port]*
Daiker, Donald Arthur 1938- *WhoAmP 93*
Dail, C(harles) C(urtis) 1851-1902 *EncSF 93*
Dail, Gerry Joseph 1956- *WhoFI 94*
Dail, Hilda Lee 1920- *WhoAm 94*
Dail, Joseph Garner, Jr. 1932- *WhoAm 94, WhoAmL 94*
Daileda, David Allen 1949- *WhoAm 94*
Dailey, Anna Marie 1954- *WhoAmL 94*
Dailey, Benjamin Peter 1919- *WhoAm 94*
Dailey, Chuck 1935- *WhoAmA 93*
Dailey, Coleen Hall 1955- *WhoAmL 94*
Dailey, Dan d1978 *WhoHol 92*
Dailey, Dan 1947- *WhoAmA 93*
Dailey, Daniel Owen 1947- *WhoAm 94*
Dailey, Donald Earl 1914- *WhoAm 94*
Dailey, Franklyn Edward, Jr. 1921- *WhoFI 94, WhoScEn 94*
Dailey, Fred William 1908- *WhoWest 94*
Dailey, Frederick M. 1945- *WhoAmP 93*
Dailey, Garrett Clark 1947- *WhoAmL 94*
Dailey, Irene 1920- *WhoAm 94, WhoHol 92*
Dailey, James Roberts 1919- *WhoAmP 93*
Dailey, Janet 1944- *WhoAm 94, WrDr 94*
Dailey, Joel *DrAPF 93*
Dailey, John Revell 1934- *WhoAm 94*
Dailey, John William 1943- *WhoMW 93*
Dailey, Joseph d1940 *WhoHol 92*
Dailey, Joseph Charles *WhoAmA 93*
Dailey, Kathleen Cecilia 1950- *WhoMW 93*
Dailey, Mark W. *WhoAmP 93*
Dailey, Michael Dennis 1938- *WhoAmA 93*
Dailey, Mitch R. 1953- *WhoAmP 93*
Dailey, Pauline F. 1930- *WhoAmP 93*
Dailey, Peter H. 1930- *WhoAmP 93*
Dailey, Peter Heath 1930- *WhoAm 94*
Dailey, Quintin 1961- *WhoBlA 94*
Dailey, Thelma *WhoBlA 94*
Dailey, Tom E., Jr. 1964- *WhoFI 94*
Dailey, Truman fl. 1940-1970 *EncNAR*
Dailey, Ulysses Grant 1885-1961 *AfrAmAl 6*
Dailey, Victoria Ann 1945- *WhoFI 94, WhoScEn 94*
Dailey, Victoria Keilus 1948- *WhoAmA 93*
Daily, Augustus Dee, Jr. 1920- *WhoScEn 94*
Daily, Bill 1930- *WhoHol 92*
Daily, Eileen M. *WhoAmP 93*
Daily, Elizabeth 1962- *WhoHol 92*
Daily, Evelynne Mess 1903- *WhoAmA 93*
Daily, Frank Jerome 1942- *WhoAm 94, WhoAmL 94*
Daily, Fred 1945- *WhoAmP 93*
Daily, Frederick William 1942- *WhoAmL 94*
Daily, James L., Jr. 1929- *WhoAm 94*
Daily, James Wallace 1913- *WhAm 10*
Daily, Louis 1919- *WhoScEn 94*
Daily, Lynn Y. 1955- *WhoHisp 94*
Daily, Pete d1986 *WhoHol 92*
Daily, Richard W. 1945- *WhoWest 94*
Daily, Sherrill Idus 1936- *WhoFI 94*
Daily, Susan *DrAPF 93*
Daily, Thomas V. 1927- *WhoAm 94*
Daily, William Allen 1912- *WhoMW 93, WhoScEn 94*
Daimler, Gottlieb 1834-1900 *WorInv*
Dai Moan *WhoPRCh 91 [port]*
Dai Mu 1925- *WhoPRCh 91*
Dain, Alex *EncSF 93*
Dain, Arthur John 1912- *Who 94*
Dain, David John Michael 1940- *Who 94*
Daines, Darrel 1922- *WhoAmP 93*
Daingerfield, Marjorie Jay d1977 *WhoAmA 93N*
Daintith, Terence Charles 1942- *IntWW 93, Who 94*
Dainton, Baron 1914- *Who 94*
Dainton, Frederick 1914- *WrDr 94*
Dainton, Frederick Sydney 1914- *IntWW 93*
Dainton, Patricia 1930- *WhoHol 92*
Dainty, (John) Christopher 1947- *Who 94*
Dai Ping 1932- *IntWW 93*
Dai Qianding 1925- *IntWW 93*
Dai Qing 1941- *BlmGWL*
Daire, Alberto 1967- *WhoHisp 94*
Dais, Larry 1945- *WhoBlA 94*
Dai Shihe 1948- *WhoPRCh 91*
Dai Shiqi *WhoPRCh 91*
Dai Shuhe 1923- *WhoPRCh 91 [port]*
Dai Shunzhi *WhoPRCh 91*
Daisley, Richard John 1930- *WhoAmP 93*
Daisley, William Prescott 1935- *WhoAm 94*
Dai Suli 1919- *WhoPRCh 91 [port]*
Daitch, Susan *DrAPF 93*
Daitz, Ronald Frederick 1940- *WhoAm 94*
Dai Wei 1943- *WhoPRCh 91 [port]*
Dai Xianglong *WhoPRCh 91*
Dai Xuejiang *WhoPRCh 91*
Dai Yi *WhoPRCh 91*
Dai Yuanben 1928- *WhoPRCh 91*
Dai Yuhua *WhoPRCh 91*
Dajani, Esam Zapher 1940- *WhoMW 93, WhoScEn 94*
Dajani, M(unther) S(uleiman) 1951- *WrDr 94*
Dajani, Virginia 1936- *WhoAm 94*
Dakay, Alan R. 1952- *WhoIns 94*
Dake, Charles Romyn *EncSF 93*
Dake, Karl Manning 1954- *WhoScEn 94*
Dake, Marcia Allene 1923- *WhoAm 94*
Daken, Richard Joseph, Jr. 1947- *WhoScEn 94*
Daker, David *WhoHol 92*
Dakers, Lionel Frederick 1924- *Who 94*
Dakin, Carol F. 1943- *WhoAm 94, WhoAmL 94*
Dakin, Christine Whitney 1949- *WhoAm 94*
Dakin, Dorothy Danvers 1919- *Who 94*
Dakin, Karl Jonathan 1954- *WhoWest 94*
Dakin, Mary Meier 1956- *WhoMW 93*
Dakin, Robert Edwin 1949- *WhoScEn 94*
Dakofsky, Andrew Eric 1960- *WhoWest 94*
Dakos, Minas James 1937- *WhoAmP 93*
Dakov, Mako 1920- *IntWW 93*
Dal, Erik 1922- *IntWW 93, WhoScEn 94*
Dalager, Jon Karl 1956- *WhoMW 93*
Dalai Lama *Who 94*
Dalai Lama 1935- *NewYTBS 93 [port], NobelP 91 [port]*
Dalai Lama, The 1935- *IntWW 93*
Dalai Lama, XIV *ConAu 141*
Dalais, (Adrien) Pierre 1929- *Who 94*
Dalal, Fram R. 1935- *WhoAsA 94*
Dalal, Maneck Ardeshir Sohrab 1918- *Who 94*
Dalal, Mayur Thakorbhai 1958- *WhoFI 94*
Dalal, Siddhartha Ramanlal 1948- *WhoAsA 94*
Dalambakis, Christopher A. 1960- *WhoMW 93*
Dalayrac, Nicolas-Marie 1753-1809 *NewGrDO*
Dal Barba, Daniel (Pius) 1715-1801 *NewGrDO*
Dalbeck, Richard Bruce 1929- *WhoAm 94*
Dalberg, Frederick 1908-1988 *NewGrDO*
Dalbert, Suzanne d1971 *WhoHol 92*
Dalberto, Michel 1955- *IntWW 93*
D'Albie, Julian d1978 *WhoHol 92*
Dalborg, Hans Folkeson 1941- *IntWW 93*
D'Albray, Muse *WhoHol 92*
D'Albrook, Sidney d1948 *WhoHol 92*
Dalby, Alan James 1937- *WhoAm 94*
Dalby, Amy d1969 *WhoHol 92*
Dalby, (Terry) David (Pereira) 1933- *Who 94*
Dalby, John Mark Meredith 1938- *Who 94*
DalCanton, James Angelo 1956- *WhoFI 94*
Dalcourt, Gerard Joseph 1927- *WrDr 94*
D'Alcy, Jeanne d1956 *WhoHol 92*
Dalderup, Louise Maria 1925- *WhoScEn 94*
Daldry, Stephen *IntWW 93*
Dale, Adam *EncSF 93*
Dale, Antony 1912- *WrDr 94*
Dale, Barry Gordon 1938- *Who 94*
Dale, Benjamin Moran 1889-1951 *WhoAmA 93N*
Dale, Beverly Ann 1942- *WhoWest 94*
Dale, Charlene Boothe 1942- *WhoScEn 94*
Dale, Charles d1971 *WhoHol 92*
Dale, Charles 1929- *WhoAm 94*
Dale, Charles Jeffrey 1944- *WhoScEn 94*
Dale, Charlie 1881-1971 *See* Smith and Dale *WhoCom*
Dale, Clamma Churita 1953- *WhoBlA 94*
Dale, Colin *WhoHol 92*
Dale, Cynthia *WhoHol 92*
Dale, Dana d1977 *WhoHol 92*
Dale, David C. 1940- *WhoAm 94*
Dale, David Kenneth Hay 1927- *Who 94*
Dale, Denver Thomas, III 1931- *WhoWest 94*
Dale, Dick *WhoHol 92*
Dale, Dorothy d1937 *WhoHol 92*
Dale, Dorothy d1957 *WhoHol 92*
Dale, Edwin L., Jr. 1923- *WhoAmP 93*
Dale, Ellis *WhoHol 92*
Dale, Erwin Randolph 1915- *WhoAm 94*
Dale, Esther d1961 *WhoHol 92*
Dale, Floyd D. *EncSF 93*
Dale, Francis L. d1993 *NewYTBS 93 [port]*
Dale, Francis Lykins 1921- *WhoAm 94, WhoWest 94*
Dale, George 1940- *WhoAmP 93*
Dale, George E. *SmATA 74*
Dale, George E. 1920-1992 *ConLC 76 [port]*
Dale, Grover 1936- *WhoHol 92*
Dale, Harvey Philip 1937- *WhoAm 94, WhoAmL 94*
Dale, Henry Hallett *WorScD*
Dale, James d1985 *WhoHol 92*
Dale, Jean d1981 *WhoHol 92*
Dale, Jennifer *WhoHol 92*
Dale, Jim 1935- *IntMPA 94, Who 94, WhoAm 94, WhoHol 92*
Dale, John Denny 1916- *WhoAm 94*
Dale, John Sorensen 1945- *WhoFI 94*
Dale, Joseph 1923- *WhoAmP 93*
Dale, K. Diane 1946- *WhoMW 93*
Dale, Kenneth Ray 1948- *WhoMW 93*
Dale, Larry Huston 1946- *WhoAm 94, WhoFI 94*
Dale, Laurence 1957- *NewGrDO*
Dale, Leon Andrew 1921- *WhoAm 94, WhoFI 94, WhoWest 94*
Dale, Lisa Lynne 1967- *WhoAmP 93*
Dale, Louis 1935- *WhoBlA 94*
Dale, Madeline Houston McWhinney 1922- *WhoAm 94*
Dale, Margaret d1972 *WhoHol 92*
Dale, Martha Ericson 1914- *WhoScEn 94*
Dale, Martin Albert 1932- *WhoAm 94, WhoFI 94*
Dale, Nicholas Daniel 1948- *WhoAmL 94*
Dale, Peggy d1967 *WhoHol 92*
Dale, Peter 1938- *WrDr 94*
Dale, Philip Scott 1943- *WhoScEn 94*
Dale, Richard 1756-1826 *WhAmRev [port]*
Dale, Richard 1932- *WrDr 94*
Dale, Richard Ray 1958- *WhoAm 94*
Dale, Richard Scott 1950- *WhoFI 94*
Dale, Robert Alan 1938- *Who 94*
Dale, Robert Gordon 1920- *WhoAm 94*
Dale, Robert J. 1943- *WhoBlA 94*
Dale, Ron G. 1949- *WhoAmA 93*
Dale, Ron Lewis 1950- *WhoMW 93*
Dale, Sam *WhoHol 92*
Dale, Sharon R. 1955- *WhoWest 94*
Dale, Suzanne *DrAPF 93*
Dale, Virginia 1918- *WhoHol 92*
Dale, Virginia Marie 1925- *WhoBlA 94*
Dale, Walter R. 1944- *WhoBlA 94*
Dale, Wesley John 1921- *WhoAm 94*
Dale, William 1905- *WrDr 94*
Dale, William (Leonard) 1906- *Who 94*
Dale, William Scott Abell 1921- *WhoAmA 93*
Daleke, David Leo 1957- *WhoMW 93*
D'Alembert, Jean Le Rond *WorScD*
D'Alemberte, Talbot 1933- *WhoAm 94, WhoAmL 94*
Dalen, James Eugene 1932- *WhoAm 94*
Dalen, Nils 1869-1937 *WorInv*
Dales, Catharina Isabella (Ien) 1931- *IntWW 93*

Dales, Ien 1931- *WhoWomW 91*
Dales, Richard Clark 1926- *WhoAm 94*
Dales, Richard Nigel 1942- *Who 94*
Dales, Samuel 1927- *WhoAm 94*
Dalesio, Wesley Charles 1930- *WhoWest 94*
Daleski, H. M. 1926- *WrDr 94*
D'Alessandro, Angelo Michael 1930- *WhoAm 94*
D'Alessandro, Daniel Anthony 1949- *WhoAmL 94*
D'Alessandro, David Francis 1951- *WhoAm 94*
D'Alessandro, Mary Patricia 1924- *WhoWest 94*
Dalessio, Anthony Thomas 1952- *WhoScEn 94*
Dalessio, Donald John 1931- *WhoAm 94*
d'Alessio, Gregory d1993 *NewYTBS 93*
D'Alessio, Gregory 1904- *WhoAmA 93*
D'Alessio, Hilda Terry *WhoAmA 93*
D'Alessio, Natalie Marino *WhoAmA 93*
D'Alexander, William Joseph 1927- *WhoAm 94*
Daley, Arthur James 1916- *WhoAm 94*
Daley, Arthur Stuart 1908- *WhoAm 94, WhoWest 94*
Daley, Brian C. 1947- *EncSF 93, WrDr 94*
Daley, Cass d1975 *WhoHol 92*
Daley, David Walter 1967- *WhoMW 93*
Daley, George Quentin 1960- *WhoScEn 94*
Daley, Guilbert Alfred 1923- *WhoBlA 94*
Daley, Henry Owen, Jr. 1936- *WhoScEn 94*
Daley, Jack d1967 *WhoHol 92*
Daley, James E. 1941- *WhoAm 94, WhoFI 94*
Daley, James P. 1948- *WhoAm 94, WhoAmL 94*
Daley, John 1923- *WhoAmP 93*
Daley, John P. 1946- *WhoAmP 93*
Daley, John Patrick 1958- *WhoScEn 94*
Daley, Mabel d1942 *WhoHol 92*
Daley, Michael Edward 1952- *WhoFI 94*
Daley, Paul Patrick 1941- *WhoAm 94, WhoAmL 94*
Daley, Peter Edmund 1943- *WhoFI 94*
Daley, Peter John, II 1950- *WhoAmP 93*
Daley, Richard Halbert 1948- *WhoWest 94*
Daley, Richard M. 1942- *WhoAmP 93*
Daley, Richard Michael 1942- *WhoAm 94, WhoMW 93*
Daley, Robert *IntMPA 94*
Daley, Robert (Blake) 1930- *WrDr 94*
Daley, Robert Edward 1939- *WhoAm 94*
Daley, Robert Emmett 1933- *WhoAm 94, WhoMW 93*
Daley, Royston Tuttle 1929- *WhoAm 94*
Daley, Susan Jean 1959- *WhoAmL 94*
Daley, Thelma Thomas *WhoBlA 94*
Daley, Victor Neil 1943- *WhoIns 94*
Daley, Vincent Raymond, Jr. 1940- *WhoMW 93*
Daley, William P. 1925- *WhoAmA 93*
Daley-Kauffman, Sandra 1933- *WhoAmP 93*
Dalferes, Edward R., Jr. 1931- *WhoBlA 94*
Dalferes, Edward Roosevelt, Jr. 1931- *WhoScEn 94*
D'Alfonso, Mario Joseph 1951- *WhoAmL 94*
Dalgaard, Niels 1956- *EncSF 93*
Dalgarno, Alexander 1928- *IntWW 93, Who 94, WhoAm 94*
Dalgarno, George 1626?-1687 *EncDeaf*
Dalgety, Ramsay Robertson 1945- *Who 94*
Dalgleish, James 1936- *WrDr 94*
Dalglish, Edward Russell 1913- *WrDr 94*
Dalglish, James Stephen 1913- *Who 94*
Dalglish, Jamie 1947- *WhoAmA 93*
Dalglish, Meredith Rennels 1941- *WhoAmA 93*
D'Algy, Helena *WhoHol 92*
D'Algy, Tony d1977 *WhoHol 92*
Dalhouse, Warner Norris 1934- *WhoAm 94*
Dalhousie, Earl of 1914- *Who 94*
Dalhousie, Simon Ramsay, Earl of 1914- *IntWW 93*
Da Li *WhoPRCh 91*
Dali, Salvador 1904-1989 *WhoAmA 93N*
Dalibard, Francoise-Therese Aumerle de Saint Phalier d1757 *BlmGWL*
D'Alibert, Giacomo *NewGrDO*
Dalida d1987 *WhoHol 92*
Daligand, Daniel 1942- *WhoScEn 94*
Dalinka, Murray Kenneth 1938- *WhoAm 94*
Dalio, Marcel d1983 *WhoHol 92*
Dalis, Irene 1925- *NewGrDO, WhoAm 94, WhoWest 94*
Dalitz, Richard Henry 1925- *IntWW 93, Who 94, WrDr 94*
Dalke, Robert Lynn 1945- *WhoAm 94*
Dalkeith, Earl of 1954- *Who 94*
Dall, Arthur G. 1929- *WhoMW 93*
Dall, Bobby
See Poison *ConMus 11*
Dall, Caroline Wells Healey 1822-1912 *BlmGWL*
Dall, John d1971 *WhoHol 92*
dalla Chiesa, Romeo 1924- *IntWW 93*
Dallapiccola, Luigi 1904-1975 *NewGrDO*
Dallapozza, Adolf 1940- *NewGrDO*
Dallara, Charles H. 1948- *IntWW 93*
Dall'Argine, Costantino 1842-1877 *NewGrDO*
Dalla Rizza, Gilda 1892-1975 *NewGrDO*
Dallas, Charlene *WhoHol 92*
Dallas, Daniel George 1932- *WhoMW 93*
Dallas, Dorothy B. *WhoAmA 93*
Dallas, Ruth 1919- *BlmGWL, WrDr 94*
Dallas, Thomas Abraham 1923- *WhoAm 94*
Dallas, William Moffit, Jr. 1949- *WhoAm 94, WhoAmL 94*
Dalla-Vicenza, Mario Joseph 1938- *WhoAm 94*
Dalle, Beatrice 1965- *WhoHol 92*
Dalle, Francois Leon Marie-Joseph 1918- *IntWW 93*
Dallek, Robert 1934- *WhoAm 94, WrDr 94*
Daller, Walter E., Jr. 1939- *WhoAm 94*
Dallesandro, Joe 1948- *WhoHol 92*
Dalleu, Gilbert d1931 *WhoHol 92*
Dalley, Christopher Mervyn 1913- *IntWW 93, Who 94*
Dalley, George Albert 1941- *WhoAm 94, WhoAmP 93, WhoBlA 94*
Dalley, Ted d1952 *WhoHol 92*
Dallimore, Maurice d1973 *WhoHol 92*
Dallin, Alexander 1924- *WhoAm 94*
Dalling, John d1798 *WhAmRev*
Dalling, John c. 1731-1798 *AmRev*
Dallis, Nicholas Peter 1911-1991 *WhAm 10*
Dallman, Elaine *DrAPF 93*
Dallman, Paul Jerald 1939- *WhoAm 94*
Dallman, Robert E. 1947- *WhoAmL 94*
Dallmann, Daniel F. 1942- *WhoAm 94*
Dallmann, Daniel Forbes 1942- *WhoAmA 93*
Dallmann-Schaper, Mary Louise 1951- *WhoMW 93*
Dallmar, Howie 1922- *BasBi*
Dallmayr, Winfried Reinhard 1928- *WhoAm 94*
Dallmeier, Francisco 1953- *WhoHisp 94*
Dallos, Peter John 1934- *WhoAm 94*
Dallosto, Raymond Michael 1952- *WhoAmL 94*
Dallura, Sal Anthony 1960- *WhoMW 93*
Dally, Ann 1926- *WrDr 94*
Dally, James William 1929- *WhoAm 94*
Dalman, Gisli Conrad 1917- *WhoAm 94*
Dalman, Jessie Fiesselmann 1933- *WhoAmP 93*
Dalmas, John *SmATA 76*
Dalmas, John 1926- *EncSF 93*
Dalmau, Edward Martinez 1893-1987 *WhAm 10*
Dalmbert, Robert Lorts 1930- *WhoAmL 94*
D'Almeida, George 1934- *WhoAmA 93*
Dalmeny, Lord 1967- *Who 94*
Dalmia, Mriduhari 1941- *IntWW 93*
Dalmia, Vishnu Hari 1924- *IntWW 93*
Dalmores, Charles 1871-1939 *NewGrDO*
D'Aloia, Giambattista Peter 1945- *WhoAmL 94*
Dal Pane, Domenico c. 1630-1694 *NewGrDO*
Dalpiaz, Julius Anthony 1931- *WhoAmP 93*
Dal Prato, Vincenzo 1756-1828 *NewGrDO*
D'Alpuget, Blanche 1944- *BlmGWL*
Dal Re, Vincenzo *NewGrDO*
Dalroy, Rube d1954 *WhoHol 92*
Dalrymple *Who 94*
Dalrymple, Viscount 1961- *Who 94*
Dalrymple, Elizabeth Barkley 1945- *WhoAmP 93*
Dalrymple, Frederick *NewGrDO*
Dalrymple, Frederick Rawdon 1930- *IntWW 93*
Dalrymple, Gary Brent 1937- *WhoAm 94, WhoScEn 94, WhoWest 94*
Dalrymple, Glenn Vogt 1955- *WhoScEn 94*
Dalrymple, Gordon Bennett 1924- *WhoAm 94*
Dalrymple, Hew (Fleetwood) Hamilton- 1926- *Who 94*
Dalrymple, Ian 1903-1989 *IntDcF 2-4*
Dalrymple, Jack *WhoAmP 93*
Dalrymple, Jean 1902- *WrDr 94*
Dalrymple, Jean Van Kirk 1902- *WhoAm 94*
Dalrymple, John 1749-1821 *WhAmRev*
Dalrymple, Margaret Fisher *WhoAm 94*
Dalrymple, Martha d1993 *NewYTBS 93*
Dalrymple, Richard William 1943- *WhoAm 94*
Dalrymple, Thomas Lawrence 1921- *WhoAm 94*
Dalrymple, William d1807 *WhAmRev*
Dalrymple-Hamilton of Bargany, North Edward Frederick 1922- *Who 94*
Dalrymple-Hay, James Brian 1928- *Who 94*
Dalrymple-White, Henry Arthur Dalrymple 1917- *Who 94*
Dalsace, Lucien d1980 *WhoHol 92*
Dalsager, Poul 1929- *Who 94*
Dalsager, Poul Christian 1929- *IntWW 93*
Dal Santo, Diane 1949- *WhoAmL 94*
Dalsimer, Susan *IntMPA 94*
Daltas, Arthur John 1945- *WhoAm 94*
Dalthorp, George Carrol 1929- *WhoAmL 94*
Dalto, Michael 1956- *WhoScEn 94*
Dalton, Abby 1935- *WhoHol 92*
Dalton, Alan (Nugent Goring) 1923- *Who 94*
Dalton, Alfred Hyam 1922- *Who 94*
Dalton, Andrew 1950- *NewGrDO*
Dalton, Audrey 1934- *WhoHol 92*
Dalton, Cathy Ratcliff 1957- *WhoFI 94*
Dalton, Charles d1942 *WhoHol 92*
Dalton, Clair Eugene 1939- *WhoWest 94*
Dalton, D. Paul 1950- *WhoAmL 94*
Dalton, Daniel J. 1949- *WhoAm 94, WhoAmP 93*
Dalton, Dennis Gilmore 1938- *WhoAm 94*
Dalton, Dick Newton 1937- *WhoFI 94*
Dalton, Dolores Ann 1955- *WhoAmL 94*
Dalton, Dorothy *DrAPF 93*
Dalton, Dorothy d1972 *WhoHol 92*
Dalton, Frank H., Jr. 1956- *WhoMW 93*
Dalton, G(raham) E(yre) 1942- *WrDr 94*
Dalton, Geoffrey (Thomas James Oliver) 1931- *Who 94*
Dalton, Harry 1928- *WhoAm 94*
Dalton, Harry Lee 1895- *WhAm 10*
Dalton, Henry Robert S(amuel) 1835- *EncSF 93*
Dalton, Howard 1944- *Who 94*
Dalton, Howard Edward 1937- *WhoAm 94*
Dalton, Irene d1934 *WhoHol 92*
Dalton, Irwin 1932- *Who 94*
Dalton, James Edward 1930- *WhoAm 94*
Dalton, Jane Leslie 1944- *WhoAmL 94*
Dalton, Jessy Kid 1942- *WrDr 94*
Dalton, John 1766-1844 *WorScD*
Dalton, John Charles 1931- *WhoAm 94*
Dalton, John George 1961- *WhoAmL 94*
Dalton, John Howard 1941- *WhoAm 94*
Dalton, John J. 1943- *WhoAm 94, WhoAmL 94*
Dalton, John Jay T. 1951- *WhoAmL 94*
Dalton, Judy 1937- *BuCMET*
Dalton, Kenneth M. 1954- *WhoAmL 94*
Dalton, Larry R. 1942- *WhoAmL 94*
Dalton, Larry Raymond 1945- *WhoAm 94*
Dalton, Margaret Anne 1951- *WhoAmL 94*
Dalton, Matthew William 1828-1918 *EncNAR*
Dalton, Maurice Leonard 1944- *Who 94*
Dalton, Oren Navarro 1929- *WhoScEn 94*
Dalton, Pamela Yvonne Werton 1943- *WhoWest 94*
Dalton, Patrick Daly, Jr. 1922- *WhoAm 94*
Dalton, Peter Gerald Fox 1914- *Who 94*
Dalton, Peter John 1944- *WhoFI 94, WhoScEn 94*
Dalton, Phyllis Irene 1909- *WhoWest 94*
Dalton, Priscilla 1924- *WrDr 94*
Dalton, Raymond Andrew 1942- *WhoBlA 94*
Dalton, Robert Edgar 1938- *WhoScEn 94*
Dalton, Robert Lowry, Jr. 1931- *WhoScEn 94*
Dalton, Ruth Margaret 1926- *WhoMW 93*
Dalton, Sammy Dale 1951- *WhoAmP 93*
Dalton, Sean *ConAu 41NR, EncSF 93*
Dalton, Ted 1901-1989 *WhAm 10*
Dalton, Thomas George 1940- *WhoWest 94*
Dalton, Timothy 1944- *IntMPA 94*
Dalton, Timothy 1945- *WhoHol 92*
Dalton, Timothy 1946- *IntWW 93*
Dalton, William Matthews 1922- *WhoAm 94*
Daltrey, Roger 1944- *IntMPA 94, WhoAm 94, WhoHol 92*
D'Alvarez, Marguerite d1953 *WhoHol 92*
D'Alvarez, Marguerite 1886-1953 *NewGrDO*
Dalven, Rae 1904-1992 *AnObit 1992*
Dalvesco, Rebecca 1962- *WhoWest 94*
Dalvi, Ramesh R. 1938- *WhoAsA 94*
Daly, Arnold d1927 *WhoHol 92*
Daly, (John) Augustin 1838-1899 *IntDcT 2*
Daly, Brenda O. 1941- *ConAu 142*
Daly, Brendan 1940- *IntWW 93*
Daly, Cahal Brendan *Who 94*
Daly, Cahal Brendan 1917- *IntWW 93*
Daly, Cahal Brendan, Cardinal 1917- *WrDr 94*
Daly, Charles Arthur 1945- *WhoAm 94*
Daly, Charles Patrick 1930- *WhoAm 94*
Daly, Charles Ulick 1927- *WhoAm 94*
Daly, Charles Wason 1916- *WhoAmL 94*
Daly, Chuck 1933- *WhoAm 94*
Daly, Clinton Riggs 1956- *WhoAm 94, WhoFI 94*
Daly, Denis Jon 1940- *WhoAm 94*
Daly, Donald Francis 1928- *WhoFI 94*
Daly, Edward Kevin 1933- *IntWW 93*
Daly, Francis Lenton 1938- *Who 94*
Daly, Frederica Y. 1925- *WhoBlA 94*
Daly, Gabriel Conor 1927- *IntWW 93*
Daly, Gay 1951- *WrDr 94*
Daly, Gene B. 1918- *WhoAmP 93*
Daly, George Garman 1940- *WhoAm 94, WhoFI 94*
Daly, Gerald 1948- *WhoAm 94*
Daly, Hamlin *EncSF 93*
Daly, Ita 1945- *WrDr 94*
Daly, Ita 1955- *BlmGWL*
Daly, Jack d1968 *WhoHol 92*
Daly, James d1933 *WhoHol 92*
Daly, James d1978 *WhoHol 92*
Daly, James F. 1949- *WhoAmL 94*
Daly, James Joseph 1921- *WhoAm 94*
Daly, James William 1931- *WhoAm 94*
Daly, Jane *WhoHol 92*
Daly, Jim 1938- *IntMPA 94*
Daly, Jim Roy 1940- *WhoWest 94*
Daly, Joe Ann Godown 1924- *WhoAm 94*
Daly, John 1928- *WhoFI 94*
Daly, John 1937- *ConTFT 11, IntMPA 94*
Daly, John 1966- *WhoAm 94*
Daly, John Augustin 1838-1899 *AmCulL*
Daly, John B. *WhoAmP 93*
Daly, John Charles, Jr. 1914-1991 *WhAm 10*
Daly, John Charles Sydney d1993 *Who 94N*
Daly, John Dennis 1936- *WhoFI 94*
Daly, John Francis 1922- *WhoAm 94*
Daly, John Lawrence 1953- *WhoFI 94*
Daly, John Neal 1937- *WhoAm 94*
Daly, John Paul 1939- *WhoAm 94, WhoAmL 94*
Daly, John W. 1931- *WhoAmP 93*
Daly, Jonathan *WhoHol 92*
Daly, Joseph Leo 1942- *WhoAm 94, WhoAmL 94, WhoMW 93*
Daly, Joseph Patrick 1957- *WhoAmL 94*
Daly, Judith Marie 1950- *WhoFI 94*
Daly, Kathleen 1898- *WhoAmA 93*
Daly, Lawrence 1924- *Who 94*
Daly, Leo (Arthur) 1920- *WrDr 94*
Daly, Lloyd William 1910-1989 *WhAm 10*
Daly, Lowrie J. 1914- *WrDr 94*
Daly, Lowrie John 1914- *WhoMW 93*
Daly, Margaret Elizabeth 1938- *Who 94, WhoWomW 91*
Daly, Maria Vega 1950- *WhoHisp 94*
Daly, Marie Maynard 1921- *WhoBlA 94*
Daly, Mark d1957 *WhoHol 92*
Daly, Mary 1928- *GayLL, WrDr 94*
Daly, Maureen 1921- *TwCYAW, WrDr 94*
Daly, Michael de Burgh 1922- *Who 94*
Daly, Michael Francis 1931- *Who 94*
Daly, Nicholas 1946- *SmATA 76 [port]*
Daly, Niki *SmATA 76*
Daly, Norman 1911- *WhoAmA 93*
Daly, Pat d1947 *WhoHol 92*
Daly, Paul Sylvester 1934- *WhoWest 94*
Daly, Robert A. 1936- *IntMPA 94*
Daly, Robert Anthony 1936- *IntWW 93, WhoAm 94*
Daly, Robert J. 1933- *WhoAm 94*
Daly, Robert J., Jr. 1928- *WhoAmP 93*
Daly, Robert W. 1932- *WhoAm 94*
Daly, Ronald Edwin 1947- *WhoBlA 94*
Daly, Saralyn R. *DrAPF 93*
Daly, Simeon Philip John 1922- *WhoAm 94*
Daly, Stephen Jeffrey 1942- *WhoAmA 93*
Daly, Thomas (Joseph) 1913- *Who 94*
Daly, Thomas Francis 1902-1990 *WhAm 10*
Daly, Thomas Francis Gilroy 1931- *WhoAm 94, WhoAmL 94*
Daly, Timothy 1956- *IntMPA 94, WhoAm 94, WhoHol 92*
Daly, Timothy Patrick 1959- *WhoAmL 94, WhoWest 94*
Daly, Tom *WhoAmP 93*
Daly, Tyne 1946- *IntMPA 94, WhoHol 92*
Daly, Tyne 1947- *WhoAm 94*
Daly, Walter Joseph 1930- *WhoAm 94, WhoMW 93*
Daly, Warren B., Jr. 1944- *WhoAm 94, WhoAmL 94*
Daly, William d1940 *WhoHol 92*
Daly, William Gerald 1924- *WhoAm 94*
Daly, William James 1917- *WhoAm 94*
Daly, William Joseph 1928- *WhoAm 94, WhoAmL 94*
Dalya, Jacqueline *WhoHol 92*

Dalyell, Kathleen Mary Agnes 1937- *Who 94*
Dalyell, Tam 1932- *ConAu 142, Who 94*
Dalzell, Fred Briggs 1922- *WhoAm 94*
Dalzell, Robert Fenton, Jr. 1937- *WhoAm 94*
Dalzell, Stewart 1843- *WhoAm 94*
Dalzell, Stewart 1943- *WhoAmL 94*
Dalzell Payne, Henry Salusbury Legh 1929- *Who 94*
Dalziel, Charles Meredith, Jr. 1956- *WhoAmL 94*
Dalziel, Geoffrey Albert 1912- *Who 94*
Dalziel, Ian Martin 1947- *Who 94*
Dalziel, Keith 1921- *Who 94*
Dalziel, Lianne 1960- *WhoWomW 91*
Dalziel, Malcolm Stuart 1936- *Who 94*
Dalziel, Robert David 1934- *WhoAm 94*
Dam, A. Scott 1946- *WhoScEn 94*
Dam, Carl Peter Henrik *WorScD*
Dam, Dwight E. 1917- *WhoAmP 93*
Dam, Jose Van *NewGrDO*
Dam, Kenneth W. 1932- *IntWW 93, WhoAm 94, WhoAmL 94, WhoFI 94*
Dam, Quy T. T. 1942- *WhoAsA 94*
Damadian, Raymond *WorInv*
Daman, Ernest Ludwig 1923- *WhoAm 94*
Damanaki, Maria 1952- *WhoWomW 91*
Damas, David (John) 1926- *WrDr 94*
Damase, Jean-Michel 1928- *NewGrDO*
Damashek, Philip Michael 1940- *WhoAmL 94*
Damasio, Antonio R. 1944- *WhoAm 94*
Damaska, Mirjan Radovan 1931- *WhoAm 94*
Damast, Elba Cecilia 1944- *WhoAmA 93*
D'Amato, Alfonse M. 1937- *CngDr 93, IntWW 93, WhoAm 94, WhoAmP 93*
D'Amato, Anthony 1937- *WhoAm 94, WrDr 94*
D'Amato, Anthony Roger 1931- *WhoAm 94*
D'Amato, Anthony S. 1930- *WhoAm 94, WhoFI 94*
D'Amato, Anthony Salvatore 1930- *WhoScEn 94*
D'Amato, Armand P. 1944- *WhoAmP 93*
D'Amato, Brian *ConAu 141*
Damato, David Joseph 1953- *WhoScEn 94*
D'Amato, Domenico Donald 1911- *WhoAm 94*
D'Amato, Janet Potter *WhoAmA 93*
D'Amato, Joe 1936- *HorFD*
DaMatta, Roberto Augusto 1936- *WhoAm 94*
Damaz, Paul F. 1917- *WhoAm 94, WhoAmA 93, WrDr 94*
Dambenzet, Jeanne *WhoWomW 91*
Dambis, Pauls 1936- *NewGrDO*
Dambman, Mary Elizabeth 1935- *WhoAmP 93*
D'Amboise, *WhAmRev*
D'Amboise, Charlotte 1964- *WhoHol 92*
D'Amboise, Charlotte 1965?- *ConTFT 11*
d'Amboise, Christopher 1960- *WhoAm 94*
D'Amboise, Jacques 1934- *IntDcB [port], WhoHol 92*
D'Amboise, Jacques Joseph 1934- *WhoAm 94*
D'Ambra, Michael V. 1947- *WhoAmP 93*
D'Ambricourt, Adrienne d1957 *WhoHol 92*
D'Ambrosia, Robert Dominick 1938- *WhoAm 94*
D'Ambrosio, Charles Anthony, Sr. 1932- *WhoAm 94*
d'Ambrosio, Madeleine B. 1950- *WhoAm 94*
D'Ambrosio, Vinni Marie *DrAPF 93*
Dambruch, Edward L. *WhoAmP 93*
Dame, Enid *DrAPF 93*
Dame, Rose A. 1941- *WhoAmP 93*
Dame, Thomas Michael 1954- *WhoScEn 94*
Dame, William Page, III 1940- *WhoAm 94, WhoFI 94*
Damer *Who 94*
Damer, Linda K. 1938- *WhoMW 93*
Damerel, Donna d1941 *WhoHol 92*
Damerell, Derek Vivian 1921- *Who 94*
Dameron, Chip *DrAPF 93*
Dameron, Del Stiltner 1953- *WhoAm 94*
Dameron, Kenneth Oliver 1938- *WhoFI 94*
Dameron, Larry Wright 1949- *WhoFI 94*
Dameron, Thomas Barker, Jr. 1924- *WhoAm 94*
Dameron, William *WhoAm 94, WhoAmP 93*
Damery, David Thomas 1958- *WhoFI 94*
Dames, George P. 1937- *WhoAmP 93*
Dames, Joan Foster 1934- *WhoAm 94*
Dames, Rob(ert L.) 1944- *WrDr 94*
Dames, Sandra A. 1957- *WhoBlA 94*
Dameshek, Harold Lee 1937- *WhoAm 94*
Dame Shirley *BlmGWL*

Damewood, Rachel Wang 1952- *WhoWest 94*
Damgard, John Michael 1939- *WhoAm 94*
Damia d1978 *WhoHol 92*
Damia, Carol G. 1939- *WhoMW 93*
Damiani, Victor 1897-1962 *NewGrDO*
Damiano, Anthony D. 1962- *WhoAmL 94*
Damianos, Sylvester 1933- *WhoAm 94*
Damiao Vieira, Elisa Maria Ramos 1946- *WhoWomW 91*
Damich, Edward John 1948- *WhoAmL 94*
D'Amico, Andrew John 1942- *WhoAm 94*
D'Amico, Dawn Marie 1966- *WhoMW 93*
D'Amico, Fedele 1912-1990 *NewGrDO*
Damico, James Anthony 1932- *WhoAm 94*
D'Amico, John C. 1936- *WhoAmP 93*
D'Amico, Joseph Allen 1962- *WhoAmL 94, WhoFI 94*
D'Amico, Michael 1936- *WhoWest 94*
Damico, Nicholas Peter 1937- *WhoAmP 93*
Damico, Nuncio Joseph 1938- *WhoAmP 93*
D'Amico, Salvatore J. 1924- *WhoAmP 93*
D'Amico, Thomas F. 1948- *WhoAm 94, WhoFI 94*
D'Amico, William Peter, Jr. 1944- *WhoScEn 94*
D'Amico, William S. 1938- *WhoAmL 94*
Damicone-McCullough, Mary Susan 1946- *WhoMW 93*
Damin, David E. 1947- *WhoFI 94, WhoMW 93*
Damisch, Mark William 1956- *WhoAmP 93*
Damita, Lili 1904- *WhoHol 92*
Damji, Karim Sadrudin 1959- *WhoScEn 94*
Damken, John August 1950- *WhoScEn 94*
Damlos, Jack d1993 *NewYTBS 93*
Dammann, David Patrick 1965- *WhoScEn 94*
Dammann, Richard Weil 1911-1988 *WhAm 10*
Dammerman, Dennis Dean 1945- *WhoFI 94*
Dammers, Alfred Hounsell 1921- *Who 94*
Dammers, Steven Willem 1942- *WhoAm 94, WhoFI 94*
Dammeyer, Rodney Foster 1940- *WhoAm 94, WhoFI 94*
Dammin, Gustave John 1911-1991 *WhAm 10*
Damon, Cathryn d1987 *WhoHol 92*
Damon, Christopher Andrew 1951- *WhoMW 93*
Damon, Edmund Holcombe 1929- *WhoAm 94*
Damon, Gabriel *WhoHol 92*
Damon, Gene *GayLL*
Damon, Henry Eugene 1926- *WhoAmP 93*
Damon, James Christian 1951- *WhoWest 94*
Damon, Les d1962 *WhoHol 92*
Damon, Mark 1933- *IntMPA 94, WhoHol 92*
Damon, Michael 1962- *WhoWest 94*
Damon, Miracyl Jane 1927- *WhoAmP 93*
Damon, Richard Winslow 1923- *WhAm 10*
Damon, Stuart 1937- *WhoHol 92*
Damon, William Van Buren 1944- *WhoAm 94*
Damon, William Winchell 1943- *WhoAm 94*
Damone, Vic 1928- *IntMPA 94, WhoHol 92*
Damonte, James C. 1949- *WhoIns 94*
Damonte, Magali *NewGrDO*
Damoose, Carol Sweeney 1942- *WhoFI 94*
Damoose, George Lynn 1938- *WhoAm 94*
Damora, Robert Matthew *WhoAm 94*
D'Amore, Thomas J., Jr. 1941- *WhoAmP 93*
Damory, Roger d1322 *DcNaB MP*
DaMotta, Lorraine 1957- *WhoFI 94*
D'Amour, Claire Marie 1956- *WhoAm 94*
Damour, Frederick Windle 1940- *WhoAmL 94*
D'Amours, Norman Edward 1937- *WhoAmP 93*
Dampeer, John Lyell 1916- *WhoAm 94, WhoAmL 94*
Damper, Ronald Eugene 1946- *WhoBlA 94*
Damphousse, Vincent 1967- *WhoAm 94, WhoWest 94*
Dampier, Claude d1955 *WhoHol 92*
Dampier, Harold Dean, Jr. 1962- *WhoAmL 94*
Dampier, Louie 1944- *BasBi*
Dampier, William c. 1652-1715 *WhWE [port]*
Damrell, Liz 1956- *SmATA 77*
Damria, Mulkh Raj 1942- *WhoAsA 94*

Damron, Charles Franklin 1948- *WhoWest 94*
Damron, Charles Hoadley 1944- *WhoAmP 93*
Damron, Hillel *EncSF 93*
Damron, Jeffrey Dale 1962- *WhoAmL 94*
Damron, Robert R. 1954- *WhoAmP 93*
Damrosch, Leopold 1832-1885 *NewGrDO*
Damrosch, Walter d1950 *WhoHol 92*
Damrosch, Walter (Johannes) 1862-1950 *NewGrDO*
Damroth, George d1939 *WhoHol 92*
Damrow, Kathleen A. 1953- *WhoMW 93*
Damsbo, Ann Marie 1931- *WhoAm 94, WhoScEn 94, WhoWest 94*
Damschroder, Gene 1922- *WhoAmP 93*
Damschroder, Louis George 1953- *WhoMW 93*
Damse, Jozef 1789-1852 *NewGrDO*
Damsel, Charles H., Jr. 1929- *WhoAmL 94*
Damsey, Joan 1931- *WhoAm 94, WhoFI 94*
Damsgaard, Kell Marsh 1949- *WhoAm 94, WhoAmL 94*
Damski, Mel 1946- *ConTFT 11, IntMPA 94*
Damsky, Robert Philip 1921- *WhoWest 94*
Damson, Barrie Morton 1936- *WhoAm 94*
Damstra, Wanda Lou 1936- *WhoAmP 93*
Damtoft, Walter Atkinson 1922- *WhoAm 94*
Damusis, Adolfas 1908- *WhoAm 94*
Damuth, John Erwin 1942- *WhoScEn 94*
Dan, Ikuma 1924- *NewGrDO*
Dan, Lars 1960- *WhoAmA 93*
Dan, Phan Quang 1918- *WhoAsA 94*
Dan, Zhao d1980 *WhoHol 92*
Dana 1951- *WhoHol 92*
Dana, Barbara *WhoHol 92*
Dana, Bill 1924- *IntMPA 94, WhoCom [port], WhoHol 92*
Dana, Charles Anderson 1819-1897 *AmSocL*
Dana, Charles H. *WhoFI 94*
Dana, Charles Harold, Jr. 1950- *WhoWest 94*
Dana, Clara d1956 *WhoHol 92*
Dana, Deane, Jr. 1926- *WhoAmP 93*
Dana, Dick d1976 *WhoHol 92*
Dana, Edward Runkle 1919- *WhoAm 94*
Dana, Francis 1743-1811 *WhAmRev*
Dana, Frank Mitchell 1942- *WhoAm 94*
Dana, Howard H. Jr. *WhoAmL 94*
Dana, Hugh Richard 1950- *WhoWest 94*
Dana, Jacqueline *BlmGWL*
Dana, James Dwight 1813-1895 *WhWE*
Dana, Jerilyn Denise 1949- *WhoAm 94*
Dana, Lauren Elizabeth 1950- *WhoAmL 94*
Dana, Leora d1983 *WhoHol 92*
Dana, Mark 1920- *WhoHol 92*
Dana, Randall M. 1945- *WhoAmL 94*
Dana, Richard Henry, Jr. 1815-1882 *AmSocL*
Dana, Robert *DrAPF 93*
Dana, Robert (Patrick) 1929- *WrDr 94*
Dana, Viola d1987 *WhoHol 92*
Dana, William Milam, Jr. 1950- *WhoMW 93*
Dana-Davidson, Laoma Cook 1925- *WhoWest 94*
Danaher, Frank Erwin 1936- *WhoScEn 94*
Danaher, James William 1929- *WhoAm 94*
Danaher, John Anthony 1899-1990 *WhAm 10*
Danaher, Kevin 1913- *WrDr 94*
Danahy, James Patrick 1944- *WhoAm 94, WhoFI 94*
Danak, Shehnaaz Siddharth 1958- *WhoMW 93*
Dan-ba Jian-zuo *WhoPRCh 91*
Danbom, David Byers 1947- *WhoMW 93*
Danburg, Debra 1951- *WhoAmP 93*
Danburg, Jerome Samuel 1940- *WhoScEn 94*
Danby, James Charles 1940- *WhoAmP 93*
Danby, Ken 1940- *WhoAmA 93*
Danby, Kenneth Edison 1940- *WhoAm 94*
Danby, Mary 1941- *WrDr 94*
Dance, Brian David 1929- *Who 94*
Dance, Charles 1946- *ConTFT 11, IntMPA 94, IntWW 93, WhoHol 92*
Dance, Daryl Cumber 1938- *BlkWr 2, WhoBlA 94, WhoWest 94*
Dance, Francis Esburn Xavier 1929- *WhoAm 94, WhoWest 94*
Dance, Gloria Fenderson 1932- *WhoAm 94*
Dance, Helen Oakley 1913- *ConAu 140*
Dance, Maurice Eugene 1923- *WhoAm 94*
Dance, Robert Bartlett 1934- *WhoAmA 93*
Dance, Stanley 1910- *WrDr 94*
Dance, William Elijah 1930- *WhoScEn 94*
Dancer, J. B. 1938- *WrDr 94*

Dancer, John Benjamin 1812-1887 *DcNaB MP*
Dancewicz, John Edward 1949- *WhoAm 94, WhoFI 94*
Dancey, Charles Lohman 1916- *WhoAm 94*
Dancey, Roger William 1945- *Who 94*
Dancey, William Sherwood 1941- *WhoMW 93*
Danchet, Antoine 1671-1748 *NewGrDO*
Danco, Leon Antoine 1923- *WhoAm 94*
Danco, Suzanne 1911- *NewGrDO*
D'Ancona, Hedy 1937- *IntWW 93, WhoWomW 91*
d'Ancona, John Edward William 1935- *Who 94*
Dancourt, Florent Carton 1661-1725 *GuFrLit 2*
Dancy, John Albert 1936- *WhoAm 94*
Dancy, John Christopher 1920- *Who 94*
Dancy, Shenia Marie 1962- *WhoAmL 94*
Dancy, William F. 1924- *WhoBlA 94*
Dandashi, Fayad Alexander 1959- *WhoScEn 94*
Dandavate, Madhu 1924- *IntWW 93*
Dandeneau, Marcel 1931- *WhoAmP 93*
Dando, A. Jeffrey 1938- *WhoAm 94*
Dando, Howard C. 1943- *WhoWest 94*
Dando, Neal Richard 1957- *WhoScEn 94*
Dandona, Paresh 1943- *WhoScEn 94*
Dandoy, Maxima Antonio *WhoAm 94*
Dandoy, Suzanne Eggleston 1935- *WhoAm 94*
D'Andrade, Francisco 1859-1921 *NewGrDO*
D'Andrade, Hugh Alfred 1938- *WhoAm 94*
D'Andrea, Albert Philip 1897- *WhAm 10*
D'Andrea, Albert Philip 1897-1983 *WhoAmA 93N*
D'Andrea, Jeanne 1925- *WhoAmA 93*
D'Andrea, Mark 1960- *WhoScEn 94*
D'Andrea, Robert Anthony 1933- *WhoAmP 93*
D'Andrea, Tom 1909- *WhoHol 92*
Dandridge, Bob 1947- *BasBi, WhoBlA 94*
Dandridge, Cheryl 1947- *WhoAmP 93*
Dandridge, Dorothy d1965 *WhoHol 92*
Dandridge, Dorothy 1922-1965 *AfrAmaL 6 [port]*
Dandridge, Raymond Emmett 1913- *WhoBlA 94*
Dandridge, Rita B(ernice) 1940- *BlkWr 2, ConAu 141*
Dandridge, Rita Bernice *WhoAm 94*
Dandridge, Rita Bernice 1940- *WhoBlA 94*
Dandridge, Ruby d1987 *WhoHol 92*
Dandridge, William Shelton 1914- *WhoScEn 94*
D'Andrie, Sonia d1990 *WhoHol 92*
Dandrow, Ann P. *WhoAmP 93*
Dandy, Clarence L. 1939- *WhoBlA 94*
Dandy, Jess d1923 *WhoHol 92*
Dandy, Ned d1948 *WhoHol 92*
Dandy, Roscoe Greer 1946- *WhoBlA 94*
Dandzin 1946- *WhoPRCh 91 [port]*
Dane, Alexandra *WhoHol 92*
Dane, Bill 1938- *WhoAmA 93*
Dane, Carl d1981 *WhoHol 92*
Dane, Clemence 1887-1965 *BlmGWL*
Dane, Clemence 1888-1965 *EncSF 93*
Dane, Eva *WrDr 94*
Dane, Karl d1934 *WhoHol 92*
Dane, Lawrence *WhoHol 92*
Dane, Leila Finlay 1936- *WhoAm 94*
Dane, Mark 1924- *WrDr 94*
Dane, Maxwell 1906- *WhoAm 94*
Dane, Nathan 1752-1835 *WhAmRev*
Dane, Patricia *WhoHol 92*
Dane, Peter *WrDr 94*
Dane, Stephen Mark 1956- *WhoAmL 94*
Dane, William Jerald 1925- *WhoAmA 93*
Dane, Wilmer Ray 1953- *WhoMW 93*
Daneault, Gabriel 1924- *WhoAmP 93*
Daneel, Sylvia 1931- *WhoHol 92*
Danegger, Theodor d1959 *WhoHol 92*
Daneholt, Per Bertil Edvard 1940- *WhoScEn 94*
Danehy, James Philip 1912- *WhoMW 93*
Danehy, Thomas William 1929- *WhoAmP 93*
Danek, Vladimir 1940- *WhoScEn 94*
Danelius, Hans Carl Yngve 1934- *IntWW 93*
Danelo, Peter Anthony 1950- *WhoAm 94, WhoAmL 94*
Danelski, David Joseph 1930- *WhoAm 94*
Daneman, Paul 1925- *WhoHol 92*
Daner, Paul 1919- *WrDr 94*
Danese, Shera *WhoHol 92*
Danesh, Abol Hassan 1952- *ConAu 140*
Danesh, Hossain Banadake 1938- *WhoAm 94*
Daneshvar, Simin 1921- *ConWorW 93*
Danford, Ardath Anne 1930- *WhoAm 94*
Danforth, Arthur Edwards 1925- *WhoAm 94, WhoFI 94*

Danforth, David Newton 1912-1990 WhAm 10
Danforth, David Newton, Jr. 1942- WhoScEn 94
Danforth, Elizabeth Turner 1953- WhoWest 94
Danforth, Elliot, Jr. 1933- WhoAm 94
Danforth, George Lewis, Jr. 1879- EncABHB 9
Danforth, Jack Timothy 1946- WhoWest 94
Danforth, John C. 1936- CngDr 93
Danforth, John Claggett 1936- IntWW 93, WhoAm 94, WhoAmP 93, WhoMW 93
Danforth, Louis Fremont 1913- WhoAm 94
Danforth, Paul M. 1921- WrDr 94
Danforth, Robert L. 1945- WhoBlA 94
Danforth, William d1941 WhoHol 92
Danforth, William Henry 1926- WhoAm 94, WhoMW 93
Dang, Harish C. 1947- WhoAsA 94
Dang, Marvin S.C. 1954- WhoAmL 94, WhoAmP 93, WhoWest 94
Dang, Phu Ngoc 1954- WhoAsA 94
Dang, Tim WhoAsA 94
Dangan, Viscount 1965- Who 94
Dangarembga, Tsitsi c. 1958- BlmGWL
Dangcil, Linda 1942- WhoHol 92
D'Angelo, Alfred John, Jr. 1948- WhoAm 94, WhoAmL 94
D'Angelo, Andrew William 1924- WhoScEn 94
D'Angelo, Beverly 1953- WhoHol 92
D'Angelo, Beverly 1954- IntMPA 94, WhoAm 94
D'Angelo, Carlo d1973 WhoHol 92
D'Angelo, Carmen 1949- WhoIns 94
Dangelo, Charles H. 1950- WhoIns 94
D'Angelo, Christopher Scott 1953- WhoAm 94, WhoAmL 94
D'Angelo, Greg See Anthrax ConMus 11
D'Angelo, Joseph Francis 1930- WhoAm 94
Dangelo, Kathleen Birkel 1965- WhoAmL 94
D'Angelo, Patricia Jones 1945- WhoAmL 94
D'Angelo, Robert William 1932- WhoAm 94
Dangerfield, Clyde Moultrie 1915- WhoAmP 93
Dangerfield, Rodney 1921- IntMPA 94, WhoCom [port], WhoHol 92
Dangerfield, Rodney 1922- WhoAm 94
D'Angeri, Anna 1853-1907 NewGrDO
Dang-Hoang 1938- WhoAsA 94
D'Angio, Giulio John 1922- WhoAm 94
Dangler, Anita WhoHol 92
Dangler, Richard Reiss 1940- WhoAm 94
D'Angona, Teresita 1937- WhoHisp 94
Dangoor, David Ezra Ramsi 1949- WhoAm 94, WhoFI 94
D'Angri, Elena NewGrDO
Danhausen, Eldon WhoAmA 93
Daniel, Alan 1939- SmATA 76 [port]
Daniel, Alan 1942- WhoMW 93
Daniel, Alfred Irwin 1934- WhoBlA 94
Daniel, Antoine 1601-1648 EncNAR
Daniel, Aubrey Marshall, III 1941- WhoAm 94
Daniel, Beth 1956- WhoAm 94
Daniel, Charles Dwelle, Jr. 1925- WhoAm 94
Daniel, Charles Timothy 1958- WhoScEn 94
Daniel, Clarence Huber 1917- WhoMW 93
Daniel, (Elbert) Clifton, (Jr.) 1912- ConAu 142
Daniel, Colin ConAu 42NR, TwCYAW
Daniel, Colin 1938- WrDr 94
Daniel, David James 1938- WhoFI 94
Daniel, David L. 1906- WhoBlA 94
Daniel, David Logan 1906- WhoAm 94, WhoMW 93
Daniel, David Ronald 1930- WhoAm 94
Daniel, Donald Clifton 1942- WhoScEn 94
Daniel, E. C., Jr. ConAu 142
Daniel, Eddy Wayne 1960- WhoScEn 94
Daniel, Elaine Marie 1963- WhoMW 93
Daniel, Elbert Clifton 1912- WhoAm 94
Daniel, Eleanor Sauer 1917- WhoFI 94
Daniel, Gabriel 1649-1728 EncSF 93
Daniel, Gary Wayne 1948- WhoWest 94
Daniel, George Berkley 1951- WhoAmP 93
Daniel, Gerald Ernest 1919- Who 94
Daniel, Gerard Lucian 1927- WhoAm 94
Daniel, Goronwy Hopkin 1914- Who 94
Daniel, Griselda 1938- WhoBlA 94
Daniel, Gruffydd Huw Morgan 1939- Who 94
Daniel, Idus Jerome 1960- WhoAmL 94
Daniel, J. Reese 1924- WhoAmL 94
Daniel, Jack Who 94
Daniel, (Reginald) Jack 1920- Who 94
Daniel, Jack L. 1942- WhoBlA 94
Daniel, James 1916- WhoAm 94
Daniel, James Edward 1935- WhoAmP 93
Daniel, James L. 1945- WhoBlA 94
Daniel, James Richard 1940- WhoFI 94
Daniel, James Richard 1947- WhoAm 94
Daniel, Jaquelin James 1916-1990 WhAm 10
Daniel, Jean 1920- IntWW 93
Daniel, Jennifer 1939- WhoHol 92
Daniel, Jessica Henderson 1944- WhoBlA 94
Daniel, John 1932- Who 94
Daniel, John Mahendra Kumar 1964- WhoScEn 94
Daniel, John Sagar 1942- IntWW 93, Who 94, WhoAm 94
Daniel, John T. DrAPF 93
Daniel, Kenneth Rule 1913- WhoAm 94, WhoFI 94
Daniel, (Donna) Lea 1944- SmATA 76 [port]
Daniel, Leon 1931- WhoAm 94
Daniel, Levi Garland 1918- WhoBlA 94
Daniel, Lewis C. 1901-1952 WhoAmA 93N
Daniel, Mark 1954- WrDr 94
Daniel, Mark D. 1950- WhoFI 94
Daniel, Mark Paul 1962- WhoScEn 94
Daniel, Mary Reed WhoBlA 94
Daniel, Melvin Randolph 1942- WhoAmL 94
Daniel, Michael Edwin 1948- WhoMW 93
Daniel, Michael R. 1940- WhoAmP 93
Daniel, Pete 1938- WrDr 94
Daniel, Peter Maxwell 1910- Who 94
Daniel, Phillip T. K. 1947- WhoBlA 94
Daniel, Ramon, Jr. 1936- WhoScEn 94
Daniel, Richard C. 1966- WhoHisp 94
Daniel, Richard Nicholas 1935- WhoAm 94, WhoFI 94
Daniel, Robert Edwin 1906-1992 WhAm 10
Daniel, Robert Michael 1947- WhoAm 94, WhoAmL 94
Daniel, Robert Williams, Jr. 1936- WhoAm 94, WhoAmP 93
Daniel, Royal Thomas, III 1956- WhoAmL 94, WhoFI 94
Daniel, Samuel 1562-1619 BlmGEL, LitC 24 [port]
Daniel, Samuel Phillips 1932- WhoAmL 94
Daniel, Sean 1951- IntMPA 94
Daniel, Simmie Childrey 1934- WhoBlA 94
Daniel, Suzanne 1936- WhoMW 93
Daniel, Tony 1963- ConAu 141
Daniel, Walter C. 1922- WhoBlA 94
Daniel, Walter Randy 1950- WhoAmP 93
Daniel, Wayne W. 1929- WrDr 94
Daniel, Wiley Y. 1946- WhoAm 94, WhoAmL 94
Daniel, Wiley Young 1946- WhoBlA 94
Daniel, William W. 1922- WhoBlA 94
Daniel, William Wentworth 1938- Who 94
Daniel, Yuli 1925-1988 EncSF 93
Daniel, Yvette Felice 1959- WhoAm 94
Daniel-Alston, Tracey Ann 1961- WhoBlA 94
Daniele, Graciela 1939- WhoHisp 94
Daniele, Joan O'Donnell 1958- WhoScEn 94
Danielescu, George 1949- IntWW 93
Danielewski, Tad d1993 IntMPA 94N
Danielewski, Tad 1921-1993 NewYTBS 93 [port]
Danieli, Isa WhoHol 92
Danielian, Leon 1920- IntDcB
Daniell, Averell John 1903- Who 94
Daniell, Henry d1963 WhoHol 92
Daniell, Herman Burch 1929- WhoAm 94
Daniell, Jere Rogers, II 1932- WhoAm 94
Daniell, John Frederic 1790-1845 WorInv
Daniell, Laura Christine 1957- WhoScEn 94
Daniell, Peter (Averell) 1909- Who 94
Daniell, Ralph Allen 1915- Who 94
Daniell, Robert F. IntWW 93
Daniell, Robert F. 1933- WhoAm 94, WhoFI 94
Daniell, Rosemary DrAPF 93
Danielle, Suzanne WhoHol 92
Daniel-Lesur 1908- NewGrDO
Daniel-Lesur, J. Y. 1908- IntWW 93
Daniels, A. Raiford 1944- WhoBlA 94
Daniels, Alex 1956- WhoHol 92
Daniels, Alfred Claude Wynder 1934- WhoBlA 94
Daniels, Alfred Harvey 1912- WhoAm 94
Daniels, Alrie McNiff 1962- WhoFI 94
Daniels, Anthea Rena WhoAmL 94
Daniels, Anthony 1946- WhoHol 92
Daniels, Anthony Hawthorne 1950- WhoBlA 94
Daniels, Arlene Kaplan 1930- WhoAm 94
Daniels, Astar 1920- WhoAmA 93
Daniels, Barbara 1946- NewGrDO
Daniels, Baverly Andria 1956- WhoMW 93
Daniels, Bebe d1971 WhoHol 92
Daniels, Billy d1962 WhoHol 92
Daniels, Billy d1988 WhoHol 92
Daniels, Carlos Ruben 1928- WhoHisp 94
Daniels, Carolyn Elizabeth 1946- WhoAm 94, WhoAmL 94
Daniels, Cary 1912- WhoAmP 93
Daniels, Casandra 1957- WhoBlA 94
Daniels, Cecil Tyrone 1941- WhoBlA 94
Daniels, Charles Joseph, III 1941- WhoScEn 94
Daniels, Charles William 1945- WhoWest 94
Daniels, Charlie 1936- WhoAm 94, WhoHol 92
Daniels, Charlie 1939- WhoAmP 93
Daniels, Cindy Lou 1959- WhoFI 94, WhoScEn 94
Daniels, Curtis A. 1941- WhoBlA 94
Daniels, Danny 1924- WhoHol 92
Daniels, David Herbert, Jr. 1941- WhoBlA 94
Daniels, David M. 1927- WhoAmA 93
Daniels, David Wilder 1933- WhoMW 93
Daniels, Dean Wilson 1952- WhoMW 93
Daniels, Deborah Jean WhoAm 94
Daniels, Diana M. WhoAm 94, WhoAmL 94
Daniels, Doral Lee 1925- WhoMW 93
Daniels, Doria Lynn 1951- WhoFI 94, WhoMW 93
Daniels, Doris Groshen 1931- WrDr 94
Daniels, Dorothy (Smith) 1915- WrDr 94
Daniels, Drew 1958- WhoAmP 93
Daniels, Earl Hodges 1963- WhoBlA 94
Daniels, Elizabeth Adams 1920- WhoAm 94, WrDr 94
Daniels, Faith 1958- News 93-3 [port], WhoAm 94
Daniels, Fletcher 1919- WhoAmP 93
Daniels, Frank d1935 WhoHol 92
Daniels, Frank Arthur, Jr. 1931- WhoAm 94
Daniels, Frank Arthur, III 1956- WhoAm 94
Daniels, Frederick Thomas 1947- WhoScEn 94
Daniels, Gary L. 1954- WhoAmP 93
Daniels, George 1926- Who 94
Daniels, George Benjamin 1953- WhoAmL 94, WhoBlA 94
Daniels, Geraldine L. WhoBlA 94
Daniels, Geraldine L. 1933- WhoAmP 93
Daniels, Gill D. 1948- WhoBlA 94
Daniels, Hank, Jr. d1973 WhoHol 92
Daniels, Harold IntMPA 94
Daniels, Harold d1971 WhoHol 92
Daniels, Harold Albert 1915- Who 94
Daniels, Henry Ellis 1912- IntWW 93, Who 94
Daniels, Hugh Allan 1952- WhoWest 94
Daniels, Jack 1921- WhoAmP 93
Daniels, James Arthur 1937- WhoWest 94
Daniels, James Douglas 1935- WhoAm 94
Daniels, James Eliot 1941- WhoAmL 94
Daniels, James Maurice 1924- WhoAm 94
Daniels, James Walter 1945- WhoAm 94, WhoAmL 94
Daniels, Jean E. WhoBlA 94
Daniels, Jeff 1955- ConTFT 11, IntMPA 94, WhoAm 94, WhoHol 92
Daniels, Jerry Franklin 1915- WhoBlA 94
Daniels, Jesse 1935- WhoBlA 94
Daniels, Jim DrAPF 93
Daniels, John WhoHol 92
Daniels, John 1936- WhoBlA 94
Daniels, John C. WhoBlA 94
Daniels, John Clifford 1936- WhoAmP 93
Daniels, John Draper 1939- WhoAmL 94
Daniels, John Hancock 1921- WhoAm 94
Daniels, John Peter 1937- WhoAm 94
Daniels, John W., Jr. 1948- WhoAmL 94
Daniels, Jordan, Jr. 1923- WhoBlA 94
Daniels, Joseph 1931- WhoBlA 94, WhoMW 93
Daniels, Joseph Jerard 1953- WhoAm 94
Daniels, Kathryn DrAPF 93
Daniels, Keith Allen DrAPF 93
Daniels, Kurt R. 1954- WhoMW 93
Daniels, Laurence John 1916- Who 94
Daniels, Lee A. 1942- WhoAmP 93
Daniels, Legree S. 1917- WhoAmP 93
Daniels, LeGree Sylvia 1920- WhoBlA 94
Daniels, Lemuel Lee 1945- WhoBlA 94
Daniels, Lincoln, Sr. 1932- WhoBlA 94
Daniels, Linda 1954- WhoAmA 93
Daniels, Lisa WhoHol 92
Daniels, Lloyd 1967- WhoBlA 94
Daniels, Lori S. WhoAmP 93
Daniels, Lori S. 1955- WhoWest 94
Daniels, Lorna Theresa WhoAmP 93
Daniels, Louis G. EncSF 93
Daniels, Lydia M. 1932- WhoWest 94
Daniels, M. K. WhoAmP 93
Daniels, Mark 1916- WhoHol 92
Daniels, Mary 1937- WrDr 94
Daniels, Max 1927- EncSF 93, WrDr 94
Daniels, Mel 1944- BasBi
Daniels, Melvin J. 1944- WhoBlA 94
Daniels, Melvin R., Jr. 1925- WhoAmP 93
Daniels, Michael Alan 1946- WhoAmL 94, WhoFI 94
Daniels, Michael Paul 1930- WhoAm 94
Daniels, Mickey d1970 WhoHol 92
Daniels, Mitchell Elias, Jr. 1949- WhoAmP 93
Daniels, Molly Ann 1932- WhoMW 93
Daniels, Myra Janco WhoAm 94
Daniels, Ned Eugene 1949- WhoAmP 93
Daniels, Norma L. WhoAmP 93
Daniels, Norman A 1905- WrDr 94
Daniels, Olga 1923- WrDr 94
Daniels, Patricia Ann 1940- WhoBlA 94
Daniels, Paul 1938- IntMPA 94
Daniels, Peter F. 1928- WhoBlA 94
Daniels, Phil 1958- WhoHol 92
Daniels, Philip 1924- WrDr 94
Daniels, Philip Bliss 1928- WhoWest 94
Daniels, Phyllis WhoHol 92
Daniels, Rahul Ebenezer 1966- WhoMW 93
Daniels, Rebecca Haywood 1943- WhoBlA 94
Daniels, Reginald Shiffon 1963- WhoBlA 94
Daniels, Richard Bernard 1944- WhoBlA 94
Daniels, Richard D. 1931- WhoBlA 94
Daniels, Richard Martin 1942- WhoWest 94
Daniels, Robert (Vincent) 1926- WrDr 94
Daniels, Robert Alan 1944- WhoAm 94
Daniels, Robert George Reginald d1993 Who 94N
Daniels, Robert Sanford 1927- WhoAm 94
Daniels, Robert Vincent 1926- WhoAm 94, WhoAmP 93
Daniels, Roger 1927- WhoMW 93
Daniels, Ron D. WhoBlA 94
Daniels, Ruben 1917- WhoBlA 94
Daniels, Sarah 1956- WrDr 94
Daniels, Sarah 1957- ConDr 93
Daniels, Shouri DrAPF 93
Daniels, Sidney 1923- WhoBlA 94
Daniels, Stephen Bushnell 1950- WhoScEn 94
Daniels, Stephen Hall 1953- WhoAm 94, WhoAmL 94
Daniels, Stephen M. 1947- WhoAm 94
Daniels, Terry L. 1951- WhoBlA 94
Daniels, Thomas Kirk 1953- WhoFI 94
Daniels, Thomas Tyler 1960- WhoFI 94
Daniels, Timothy Holm 1949- WhoMW 93
Daniels, Walter d1928 WhoHol 92
Daniels, Wilbur d1993 NewYTBS 93
Daniels, Wilbur 1923- WhoAm 94
Daniels, William 1927- IntMPA 94, WhoHol 92
Daniels, William B. 1930- IntWW 93
Daniels, William Burton 1930- WhoAm 94, WhoScEn 94
Daniels, William Carlton, Jr. 1920- WhoAm 94
Daniels, William H. 1895-1970 IntDcF 2-4
Daniels, William James 1940- WhoBlA 94
Daniels, William Orlan 1944- WhoBlA 94
Danielsen, Karen Christine 1958- WhoWest 94
Danielski, Frederick d1993 NewYTBS 93
Daniels-Lee, Elizabeth 1938- WhoBlA 94
Daniels-McGhee, Susan 1958- WhoMW 93
Danielson, Craig WhoFI 94
Danielson, Gary R. 1953- WhoAmL 94
Danielson, George Elmore WhoAmP 93
Danielson, Gordon Douglas 1942- WhoWest 94
Danielson, Gordon Kenneth, Jr. 1931- WhoAm 94
Danielson, James Leonard 1938- WhoMW 93
Danielson, Judith 1951- WhoAmP 93
Danielson, Lynn WhoHol 92
Danielson, Neil David 1950- WhoScEn 94
Danielson, Phyllis I. WhoAmA 93
Danielson, Robert E. 1958- WhoAmL 94
Danielson, Wayne Allen 1929- WhoAm 94
Daniels-Race, Theda Marcelle WhoScEn 94
Danielsson, Bengt Emmerik 1921- IntWW 93
Danielsson, Tage d1985 WhoHol 92
Daniely, Lisa 1930- WhoHol 92
Danies Rincones, Enrique E. IntWW 93
Daniher, John M. 1926- WhoWest 94
Danilek, Donald J. 1937- WhoAm 94
Daniloff, Stephen 1954- WhoMW 93
Danilov, Victor Joseph 1924- WhoAm 94
Danilova, Alexandra WhoAm 94
Danilova, Alexandra 1903?- IntDcB [port]

Danilova, Alexandra 1906- Who 94, WhoHol 92
Danilov-Danilyan, Viktor Ivanovich 1938- LoBiDrD
Danilowicz, Delores Ann 1935- WhoAm 94
Danin, Mary Ann 1928- WhoAm 94
Daninos, Pierre 1913- IntWW 93, Who 94
Danis, Gary Fred WhoAmL 94
Danis, Marcel 1943- IntWW 93, WhoAm 94, WhoFI 94
Danis, Peter G., Jr. 1932- WhoAm 94, WhoWest 94
Danish, Barbara DrAPF 93
Danish, Roy Bertram 1919- WhoAm 94
Danishefsky, Isidore 1923- WhoAm 94
Danisman, Tarhan Ahmet 1937- WhoFI 94
Danitz, Marilynn Patricia WhoAm 94
Dank, Leonard D. 1929- WhoAmA 93
Dank, Leonard Dewey 1929- WhoAm 94
Dankanyin, Robert John 1934- WhoAm 94, WhoFI 94, WhoWest 94
Dankert, Pieter 1934- IntWW 93, Who 94
Dan'kevych, Kostyantyn Fedorovych 1905-1984 NewGrDO
Dankner, Donald K. 1947- WhoAm 94
Dankner, Jay Warren 1949- WhoAmL 94
Dankner, Laura ConAu 142
Danko, Edward Thomas 1952- WhoScEn 94
Danko, Joseph Christopher 1927- WhoAm 94, WhoScEn 94
Dankowska, Adela WhoWomW 91
Danks, Alan (John) 1914- Who 94
Danks, Anthony Cyril 1945- WhoScEn 94
Danks, Dale A., Jr. WhoAmP 93
Dankworth, C. D. Who 94
Dankworth, Charles Henry 1950- WhoFI 94
Dankworth, Clementina Dinah 1927- WhoAm 94
Dankworth, John Philip William 1927- IntWW 93, Who 94
Dankworth, Margaret Anne 1920- WhoMW 93
Danley, William Shurtleff 1948- WhoAmP 93
Danly, Donald Robert 1923- WhoAm 94
Danly, Susan 1948- WhoAmA 93
Dann, Colin (Michael) 1943- WrDr 94
Dann, Jack DrAPF 93
Dann, Jack 1945- WrDr 94
Dann, Jack (Mayo) 1945- EncSF 93
Dann, Jill 1929- Who 94
Dann, Robert William 1914- Who 94
Danna, Jo J. WhoAm 94
Dannatt, (James) Trevor 1920- Who 94
Dannay, Frederic 1905-1982 DcLB 137 [port]
Danneels, Godfried 1933- IntWW 93
Dannehy, Joseph F. WhoAmP 93
Danneker, Henry Louis 1919- WhoAmP 93
Dannelly, William D. 1951- WhoAm 94, WhoAmL 94
Danneman, Edward Carl 1959- WhoFI 94, WhoWest 94
Dannemeyer, William Edwin 1929- WhoAmP 93, WhoWest 94
Dannemiller, Edward Paul 1934- WhoWest 94
Dannemiller, John C. 1938- WhoFI 94
Dannemiller, Nicholas Stephen 1961- WhoFI 94
Dannen, Avrum H. 1935- WhoAmL 94
Dannen, Fredric 1955- ConAu 140
Dannenberg, Arthur Milton, Jr. 1923- WhoAm 94
Dannenberg, Konrad K. 1912- WhoScEn 94
Dannenberg, Martin Ernest 1915- WhoAm 94
Dannenhauer, Kenneth S. d1993 NewYTBS 93
Danner, Blythe 1943- IntMPA 94, WhoHol 92
Danner, Blythe Katharine 1944- WhoAm 94
Danner, George Wilson 1919- WhoMW 93
Danner, Margaret DrAPF 93
Danner, Margaret Essie 1915- WhoBlA 94
Danner, Pat 1934- CngDr 93, WhoAmP 93
Danner, Patsy Ann 1934- WhoAm 94, WhoMW 93
Danner, Paul Kruger, III 1957- WhoFI 94, WhoWest 94
Danner, Richard Allen 1947- WhoAm 94, WhoAmL 94
Danner, Sharon Kay 1946- WhoMW 93
Danner, Steve WhoAmP 93
Dannewitz, Stephen Richard 1948- WhoScEn 94
Dannhauser, Stephen J. 1950- WhoAm 94
Dannheim, Lawrence C. 1934- WhoAmP 93
Danni, F. Robert 1939- WhoFI 94
D'Anniballe, Priscilla Lucille 1950- WhoFI 94
Danning, Sybil WhoHol 92
D'Annunzio, Eleonora 1932- WhoWest 94
D'Annunzio, Gabriele 1863-1938 IntDcT 2, NewGrDO
D'Annunzio, Lola d1956 WhoHol 92
Dano, Garth Louis 1953- WhoWest 94
Dano, Royal 1922- IntMPA 94, WhoHol 92
Dano, Sven 1922- IntWW 93
da Nobrega, Mailson Ferreira IntWW 93
Danochowska, Maria WhoWomW 91
Danoff, Dudley Seth 1937- WhoWest 94
Danoff, Eric Michael 1949- WhoAm 94, WhoAmL 94
Danoff, I. Michael 1940- WhoAm 94, WhoAmA 93, WhoMW 93
Danoff-Kraus, Pamela Sue 1946- WhoFI 94
Danon, Giuliana Maria 1957- WhoAmL 94
Danon, Oskar 1913- NewGrDO
Danon, Ruth DrAPF 93
Danos, Robert McClure 1929- WhoAm 94, WhoWest 94
Danova, Cesare 1926- WhoHol 92
Dansby, Harry Bishop 1945- WhoAmL 94
Dansby, Jesse L., Jr. 1942- WhoBlA 94
Dansby, John Walter 1944- WhoAm 94, WhoFI 94
Danse, Ilene Homnick Raisfeld 1940- WhoScEn 94
Danser, Bonita Kay 1949- WhoAmL 94
Dansereau, Pierre 1911- IntWW 93, WhoAm 94
Dansey, Claude Edward Marjoribanks 1876-1947 DcNaB MP
Dansey, Herbert d1917 WhoHol 92
Dansford, Robert Granville d1924 WhoHol 92
Danski, Jon Frank 1952- WhoFI 94
Danson, Barnett Jerome Who 94
Danson, Barnett Jerome 1921- IntWW 93
Danson, Linda d1975 WhoHol 92
Danson, Stephen Michael 1943- WhoAm 94
Danson, Ted 1947- ConTFT 11, IntMPA 94, IntWW 93, WhoAm 94, WhoHol 92
Dant, Alan Hale 1935- WhoAm 94
Dante, Harris Loy 1912- WhoAm 94
Dante, Joe IntMPA 94
Dante, Joe 1947- EncSF 93
Dante, Joe, Jr. 1946- HorFD [port]
Dante, Lionel d1974 WhoHol 92
Dante, Michael 1935- WhoHol 92
Dante, Nicholas 1941-1991 ConTFT 11
Dante, Robert DrAPF 93
Dante, Ronald 1920- WhoFI 94
Dante Aligheri 1265-1321 BlmGEL
Dante Alighieri 1265-1321 EncSF 93, NewGrDO
Dante The Magician d1955 WhoHol 92
Dantin, Maurice 1929- WhoAmL 94
Dantine, Helmut d1982 WhoHol 92
Dantine, Nikki WhoHol 92
Dantley, Adrian 1956- BasBi
Dantley, Adrian Delano 1956- WhoBlA 94
Danto, Arthur C(oleman) 1924- WrDr 94
Danto, Arthur Coleman 1924- WhoAm 94
Danton, Georges-Jacques 1759-1794 HisWorL [port]
Danton, J. Periam 1908- IntWW 93
Danton, Joseph Periam 1908- WhoAm 94
Danton, Peter W. WhoAmP 93
Danton, Ray 1931- HorFD, WhoHol 92
Danton, Ray 1931-1992 ConTFT 11
Dantone, Joseph John, Jr. 1942- WhoAm 94
D'Antoni, Hector Luis 1943- WhoWest 94
D'Antoni, Philip 1929- IntMPA 94
D'Antonio, Carmen d1986 WhoHol 92
D'Antonio, Gregory Douglas 1951- WhoAmL 94
D'Antonio, James Joseph 1959- WhoAmL 94
D'Antonio, Michael 1955- ConAu 140
Dantuono, Louise Mildred 1916- WhoScEn 94
Dantus, Marcos 1962- WhoMW 93
Dantzic, Cynthia Maris 1933- WhoAmA 93
Dantzic, Roy Matthew 1944- Who 94
Dantzig, George Bernard 1914- IntWW 93, WhoAm 94, WhoScEn 94, WhoWest 94
Dantzig, Jonathan A. 1951- WhoScEn 94
Dantzig, Rudi van IntDcB
Dantzig, Rudi Van 1933- IntWW 93
Dantzker, Steven R. 1947- WhoAmL 94
Dantzler, Deryl Daugherty 1944- WhoAmL 94
Dantzler, Herman 1937- WhoBlA 94
Dantzler, Rick 1956- WhoAmP 93
Dantzman, Gregory Peter 1965- WhoMW 93
Danuatmodjo, Cheryl Lynn 1962- WhoMW 93
Danuser, Menga 1951- WhoWomW 91
Danusis, George 1948- WhoFI 94
Danvers, Jack 1909- EncSF 93
Danyluk, George Edward, III 1960- WhoFI 94
Danysh, Richard C. 1948- WhoAmL 94
Danz, Fredric A. 1918- IntMPA 94
Danza, Tony 1951- IntMPA 94, WhoAm 94, WhoHol 92
Danzansky, Stephen Ira 1939- WhoAmP 93
Danzberger, Alexander Harris 1932- WhoAm 94
Danzeisen, John R. WhoAm 94, WhoFI 94
Danzeisen, Rhonda Leigh 1967- WhoWest 94
Danzell, George EncSF 93
Dan Zeng WhoPRCh 91
Danzi, Franz (Ignaz) 1763-1826 NewGrDO
Danzi, (Maria) Margarethe 1768-1800 NewGrDO
Danzi Family NewGrDO
Danzig, Aaron Leon 1913- WhoAm 94
Danzig, Allison 1898-1987 BuCMET
Danzig, Douglas J. 1949- WhoAmL 94
Danzig, Frederick Paul 1925- WhoAm 94
Danzig, Jerome Alan 1913- WhoAm 94
Danzig, Richard Jeffrey 1944- WhoAm 94, WhoAmL 94
Danzig, Robert James 1932- WhoWest 94
Danzig, Sarah H. Palfrey 1912- WhoAm 94
Danzig, Sheila Ring 1948- WhoFI 94
Danzig, William Harold 1947- WhoFI 94
Danziger, Avery C. 1953- WhoAmA 93
Danziger, Fred Frank 1946- WhoAmA 93
Danziger, Frederick Michael 1940- WhoAm 94
Danziger, Glenn Norman 1930- WhoAm 94
Danziger, James Norris 1945- WhoAm 94
Danziger, Jeff 1943- WhoAm 94
Danziger, Jerry 1924- WhoAm 94, WhoWest 94
Danziger, Joan 1934- WhoAm 94, WhoAmA 93
Danziger, Louis 1923- WhoAm 94
Danziger, Maia WhoHol 92
Danziger, Martin Breitel 1931- WhoAm 94
Danziger, Paula 1944- TwCYAW, WrDr 94
Danziger, Robert Falzer 1928- WhoAmL 94
Danziger, Sheldon H. 1948- ConAu 43NR
Danzin, Charles Marie 1944- WhoScEn 94
Danzis, Rose Marie WhoAm 94
Danzl, Daniel Frank 1950- WhoScEn 94
Danzy, LeRoy Henry 1929- WhoBlA 94
Dao, Anh Huu 1933- WhoAsA 94
Dao, Larry 1960- WhoScEn 94
Dao, Minh Quang 1955- WhoAsA 94
Dao, Tuan Anh 1966- WhoAsA 94
Dao Anju WhoPRCh 91
Dao Guodong 1913- WhoPRCh 91 [port]
Daong Khin Khin Lay 1913- BlmGWL
Dao Shuren WhoPRCh 91
Daoud, George Jamil 1948- WhoFI 94
Daoud, Mohamed 1947- WhoFI 94, WhoScEn 94
Daoudi, Mohammed Suleiman Dajani 1946- WrDr 94
Daoust, Donald Roger 1935- WhoAm 94
Da Parma, Claire Elizabeth 1945- WhoMW 93
Daphnis, Nassos 1914- WhoAm 94, WhoAmA 93
Dapice, Ronald R. 1937- WhoAm 94
Da Ponte, Lorenzo 1749-1838 NewGrDO
Dapper, G. Steven 1946- WhoAm 94
Dapples, Edward Charles 1906- WhoAm 94, WhoScEn 94, WhoWest 94
Dapporto, Carlo d1989 WhoHol 92
DaPrato, Frank J. 1916- WhoAmP 93
DaPrato, Robert H. 1945- WhoMW 93
Dapremont, Delmont, Jr. WhoBlA 94
Dapron, Elmer Joseph, Jr. 1925- WhoAm 94, WhoFI 94
Da Pron, Louis d1987 WhoHol 92
D'Aquila, James Anthony 1960- WhoWest 94
D'Aquino, Albert John 1960- WhoAmL 94
d'Aquino, Thomas 1940- WhoAm 94
Dar, Dina 1939- WhoAmA 93
Dar, Mohammad Saeed 1937- WhoScEn 94
Dara, Enzo 1938- NewGrDO
Darack, Arthur J. 1918- WhoAm 94
Daragan, Thomas William 1946- WhoFI 94
Daramola, Olubunmi 1954- WhoMW 93
Darany, George Thomas 1956- WhoMW 93
Darany, Michael Anthony 1946- WhoFI 94
Darawalla, Keki N(asserwanji) 1937- WrDr 94
Darazsdi, James Joseph 1949- WhoAm 94
Darbaker, James Mateer 1898- WhAm 10
D'Arbanville, Patti 1951- IntMPA 94, WhoHol 92
Darbaud, Monique d1971 WhoHol 92
d'Arbeloff, Nicholas Coe 1961- WhoFI 94
D'Arblay, Madame BlmGEL
Darbo, Bakary Bunja 1946- IntWW 93
Dar Boggia, Henry d1976 WhoHol 92
Darboven, Hanne 1941- IntWW 93, WhoAmA 93
Darby, Abraham 1678?-1717 WorInv
Darby, Ann K. DrAPF 93
Darby, Castilla A., Jr. 1946- WhoBlA 94
Darby, Catherine 1935- WrDr 94
Darby, Edwin Wheeler 1922- WhoAm 94
Darby, Francis John 1920- Who 94
Darby, G. Harrison 1942- WhoAm 94
Darby, Harold Richard 1919- Who 94
Darby, Henry Clifford, Sir 1909- WrDr 94
Darby, Howard Darrel 1928- WhoAmP 93
Darby, John 1940- WrDr 94
Darby, John J. d1946 WhoHol 92
Darby, John Oliver Robertson 1930- Who 94
Darby, John William 1953- WhoWest 94
Darby, Joseph Branch, Jr. 1925- WhoAm 94
Darby, Karen Sue 1947- WhoAmL 94
Darby, Ken 1909- WhoHol 92
Darby, Ken 1909-1992 ConTFT 11
Darby, Kim 1948- IntMPA 94, WhoHol 92
Darby, Lawrence A., III 1947- WhoAmL 94
Darby, Michael Douglas 1944- Who 94
Darby, Michael Rucker 1945- WhoAm 94
Darby, Peter (Howard) 1924- Who 94
Darby, Robert E. 1947- WhoAmL 94
Darby, Suzanna Victoria 1948- WhoMW 93
D'Arby, Terence Trent 1962- WhoBlA 94
Darby, Wesley Andrew 1928- WhoWest 94
Darby, William D(uane) 1942- ConAu 141
Darby, William Elliott 1928- WhoAmP 93
Darby, Willie Samuel 1952- WhoAmP 93
Darbyshire, Robyn Willey 1958- WhoWest 94
Darc, Mireille 1938- WhoHol 92
D'Arcais, Francesco 1830-1890 NewGrDO
D'Arcangelo, Allan M. 1930- WhoAmA 93
D'Arcangelo, Allan Matthew 1930- WhoAm 94
D'Arcangelo, Maria Terese 1963- WhoWest 94
Darcel, Denise 1925- WhoHol 92
Darchun, Lino Auksutis 1942- WhoFI 94
Darcis, Francois-Joseph 1759?-c. 1783 NewGrDO
Darclee, Hariclea 1860-1939 NewGrDO
D'Arcy, Alex 1908- WhoHol 92
D'Arcy, Camille d1916 WhoHol 92
Darcy, Clare WrDr 94
D'Arcy, Ella 1857-1937 DcLB 135 [port]
D'Arcy, Eric Who 94
D'Arcy, Gene d1984 WhoHol 92
Darcy, George Robert 1920- WhoAm 94
Darcy, Georgine WhoHol 92
D'Arcy, Gerald Paul 1933- WhoAm 94
D'Arcy, Hugh d1925 WhoHol 92
Darcy, John Joseph 1928- WhoAmL 94
D'Arcy, John Michael 1932- WhoAm 94, WhoMW 93
D'Arcy, Margaretta IntWW 93, WrDr 94
D'Arcy, Pamela 1930- WrDr 94
Darcy, Robert WhoHol 92
D'Arcy, Roy d1969 WhoHol 92
Darcy, Sheila WhoHol 92
Darcy, Thomas Francis, Jr. 1895- WhAm 10
D'Arcy, William Knox 1849-1917 DcNaB MP
Darcy De Knayth, Baroness 1938- Who 94, WhoWomW 91
D'Arcy Hart, Philip Montagu Who 94
Darden, Anne d1977 WhoHol 92
Darden, Charles R. 1911- WhoBlA 94
Darden, Christine Mann 1942- WhoBlA 94
Darden, David Putnam 1958- WhoAmL 94
Darden, Edwin Speight, Sr. 1920- WhoAm 94
Darden, George 1943- CngDr 93
Darden, George H., Jr. 1930- WhoAmP 93
Darden, George Harry 1934- WhoAmL 94, WhoBlA 94
Darden, George W. 1943- WhoAmP 93
Darden, George Washington, III 1943- WhoAm 94
Darden, John F. 1946- WhoIns 94
Darden, Joseph S., Jr. 1925- WhoBlA 94
Darden, Margaret Furr 1937- WhoAmP 93
Darden, Marshall Taylor 1952- WhoAmL 94

Darden, Orlando William 1930- *WhoBlA 94*
Darden, Severn 1929- *WhoHol 92*
Darden, Thomas Vincent 1950- *WhoBlA 94*
Darden, William Boone 1925- *WhoBlA 94*
Darden, William Horace 1923- *CngDr 93*
Darden, William Howard, Jr. 1937- *WhoAm 94, WhoScEn 94*
Dardenne, John L., Jr. *WhoAmP 93*
Dardick, Kenneth Regen 1946- *WhoAm 94*
Dardis, Thomas (Anthony) 1926- *WrDr 94*
Dare, Alan *EncSF 93*
Dare, Charles Ernest 1938- *WhoScEn 94*
Dare, Dorris d1927 *WhoHol 92*
Dare, Eva d1931 *WhoHol 92*
Dare, Helena d1972 *WhoHol 92*
Dare, Phyllis d1975 *WhoHol 92*
Dare, Richard d1964 *WhoHol 92*
Dare, Virginia d1962 *WhoHol 92*
Dare, Zena d1975 *WhoHol 92*
Dareff, Hal 1920- *WhoAm 94*
Darehshori, Nader Farhang 1936- *WhoAm 94, WhoFI 94*
Darell, Jeffrey (Lionel) 1919- *Who 94*
Daresbury, Baron 1928- *Who 94*
Darewski, Herman d1947 *WhoHol 92*
Dargan, Stephen *WhoAmP 93*
D'Argenteuil, Paul *EncSF 93*
Darget, Chantal d1988 *WhoHol 92*
Dargie, William Alexander 1912- *IntWW 93, Who 94*
Dargin, Errol Ramone 1945- *WhoAmP 93*
Dargomizhsky, Alexander Sergeyevich 1813-1869 *NewGrDO*
d'Argyre, Gilles *EncSF 93*
Darias, Alicia 1949- *WhoAmL 94*
Darida, Clelio 1927- *IntWW 93*
Daridan, Jean-Henri 1906- *IntWW 93*
Darien, Frank d1955 *WhoHol 92*
Darien, Steven Martin 1942- *WhoAm 94*
D'Arienzo, Marco 1811-1877 *NewGrDO*
D'Arienzo, Nicola 1842-1915 *NewGrDO*
Darin, Bobby d1973 *WhoHol 92*
Darin, Frank Victor John 1930- *WhoAm 94, WhoFI 94, WhoMW 93*
Darino, Eduardo 1944- *WhoHisp 94*
Dario, Ronald A. 1937- *WhoAmP 93*
Dario, Ruben 1867-1916 *HispLC [port]*
Darion, Ellen *DrAPF 93*
Darion, Joe 1917- *WhoAm 94*
Darios, Bobbi Alice 1949- *WhoFI 94*
Dariotis, Terrence Theodore 1946- *WhoAmL 94*
Daris, Phillip Isaac 1949- *WhoAmL 94*
Darity, Evangeline Royall 1927- *WhoBlA 94*
Darity, William A. 1924- *WhoBlA 94*
Dariu, Al. N. *EncSF 93*
Darius, Denyll 1942-1976 *WhoAmA 93N*
Darius the Great, I c. 550BC-486BC *HisWorL*
Darji, Bhuleshwar S. 1939- *WhoAsA 94*
Dark, Alice Elliott *DrAPF 93*
Dark, Alvin Ralph 1922- *WhoAm 94*
Dark, Anthony Michael B. *Who 94*
Dark, Christopher d1971 *WhoHol 92*
Dark, Eleanor 1901-1985 *BlmGWL*
Dark, John *IntMPA 94*
Dark, Larry 1959- *WrDr 94*
Dark, Lawrence Jerome 1953- *WhoBlA 94*
Dark, Okianer Christian 1954- *WhoAmL 94, WhoBlA 94*
Dark, Philip John Crosskey 1918- *WhoAm 94*
Dark, T. R. 1934- *WhoMW 93*
Dark Cloud, Beulah d1946 *WhoHol 92*
Darke, Charles B. 1937- *WhoBlA 94*
Darke, Geoffrey James 1929- *Who 94*
Darke, James *EncSF 93*
Darke, Marjorie (Sheila) 1929- *WrDr 94*
Darke, Marjorie Sheila 1929- *Who 94*
Darke, Nick 1948- *ConDr 93, WrDr 94*
Darke, Roy R. 1946- *WhoAmL 94*
Darke, William 1736-1801 *WhAmRev*
Darkes, Leroy William 1924- *WhoBlA 94*
Darkey, Kermit Louis 1930- *WhoWest 94*
Darkins, Duane Adrian 1934- *WhoBlA 94*
Darko, Paula A. 1952- *WhoAmP 93*
D'Arkor, Andre 1901-1971 *NewGrDO*
Darkovich, Sharon Marie 1949- *WhoMW 93*
Darley, Brian d1924 *WhoHol 92*
Darley, Dick *IntMPA 94*
Darley, Gillian Mary 1947- *Who 94*
Darley, John Gordon 1910-1990 *WhAm 10*
Darley, John McConnon 1938- *WhoAm 94*
Darling *Who 94*
Darling, Baron 1919- *Who 94*
Darling, Alberta 1944- *WhoAmP 93*
Darling, Alistair Maclean 1953- *Who 94*
Darling, Anne 1915- *WhoHol 92*
Darling, Candy d1974 *WhoHol 92*
Darling, Charles M., IV 1948- *WhoAmL 94*
Darling, Cheryl MacLeod 1949- *WhoMW 93, WhoScEn 94*
Darling, Clifford 1922- *Who 94*
Darling, Diana 1947- *ConAu 142*
Darling, Earl Douglas 1948- *WhoFI 94*
Darling, Edward Flewett *Who 94*
Darling, Elaine Elizabeth *WhoWomW 91*
Darling, Frank Clayton 1925- *WhoAm 94*
Darling, Gary Lyle 1941- *WhoFI 94*
Darling, George Bapst, Jr. 1905- *WhoAm 94*
Darling, Gerald Ralph Auchinleck 1921- *Who 94*
Darling, Gladys d1983 *WhoHol 92*
Darling, Henry Shillington 1914- *Who 94*
Darling, Herbert A. *WhoAmP 93*
Darling, Ida d1936 *WhoHol 92*
Darling, James Ralph 1899- *IntWW 93, Who 94*
Darling, Jay Norwood (Ding) 1876-1962 *WhoAmA 93N*
Darling, Jean 1922- *WhoHol 92*
Darling, Joan 1935- *WhoHol 92*
Darling, John Rothburn, Jr. 1937- *WhoAm 94*
Darling, Kenneth (Thomas) 1909- *Who 94*
Darling, Lawrence Dean 1936- *WhoMW 93*
Darling, Mary Albert 1956- *WhoMW 93*
Darling, Michael Lashawne 1965- *WhoMW 93*
Darling, Richard Reid 1940- *WhoMW 93*
Darling, Robert Edward 1937- *WhoAm 94*
Darling, Robert Howard 1947- *WhoAmL 94*
Darling, Ron 1960- *WhoAsA 94*
Darling, Ruth d1918 *WhoHol 92*
Darling, Sandra L. Woodward 1941- *WhoAm 94*
Darling, Scott Edward 1949- *WhoAmL 94, WhoWest 94*
Darling, Sharon Sandling 1943- *WhoAmA 93*
Darling, Stephen Edward 1949- *WhoAmL 94*
Darling, Stephen Foster 1901-1990 *WhAm 10*
Darling, Susan 1942- *Who 94*
Darling, T.H. *BlkWr 2, ConAu 141*
Darling, Terry William 1956- *WhoMW 93*
Darling, Thomas, Jr. 1903- *WhoAm 94*
Darling, William Martindale 1934- *Who 94*
Darlington, Charles (Roy) 1910- *Who 94*
Darlington, David William 1945- *WhoFI 94*
Darlington, Henry, Jr. 1925- *WhoAm 94, WhoFI 94*
Darlington, Joyce *Who 94*
Darlington, Julian Trueheart 1918- *WhoScEn 94*
Darlington, Oscar Gilpin 1909- *WhoAm 94*
Darlington, Richard Benjamin 1937- *WhoAm 94, WhoScEn 94*
Darlington, Ronald Lawrence 1936- *WhoWest 94*
Darlington, Stephen Mark 1952- *Who 94*
Darlow, Julia Donovan 1941- *WhoAm 94, WhoAmL 94*
Darlton, Clark 1920- *EncSF 93*
Darman, Richard Gordon 1943- *IntWW 93, WhoAm 94, WhoAmP 93*
Darmody, Stephen Jerome 1957- *WhoAmL 94*
Darmojuwono, Justine 1914- *IntWW 93*
Darmon, Gerard *WhoHol 92*
Darmon, Marco 1930- *IntWW 93*
Darmond, Grace d1963 *WhoHol 92*
D'Arms, John Haughton 1934- *WhoAm 94*
Darmstaetter, Jay Eugene 1937- *WhoWest 94*
Darmstandler, Harry Max 1922- *WhoAm 94*
Darnall, Robert J. *WhoAm 94, WhoFI 94*
Darnall, Roberta Morrow 1949- *WhoWest 94*
Darnas, Clara 1956- *WhoHisp 94*
Darnay, Arsen *WrDr 94*
Darnay, Arsen (Julius) 1936- *EncSF 93*
Darnay, Toni d1938 *WhoHol 92*
Darnell, Alan Mark 1946- *WhoAm 94*
Darnell, Alfred Jerome 1924- *WhoScEn 94*
Darnell, Catherine Margaret 1957- *WhoWest 94*
Darnell, Diane Marie 1962- *WhoFI 94*
Darnell, Edward Buddy 1930- *WhoBlA 94*
Darnell, Emma Ione 1937- *WhoBlA 94*
Darnell, Gerald Thomas 1942- *WhoMW 93*
Darnell, James Edwin, Jr. 1930- *WhoScEn 94*
Darnell, James Oral 1955- *WhoAmL 94*
Darnell, Jean d1961 *WhoHol 92*
Darnell, Larry d1983 *WhoHol 92*
Darnell, Linda d1965 *WhoHol 92*
Darnell, Lonnie Lee 1928- *WhoScEn 94*
Darnell, Mark Lawrence 1958- *WhoMW 93*
Darnell, Randall Howard 1944- *WhoFI 94*
Darnell, Regna (Diebold) *WrDr 94*
Darnell, Riley Carlisle 1940- *WhoAm 94, WhoAmP 93*
Darnell, Robert Carter 1927- *WhoWest 94*
Darner, L. Karen 1945- *WhoAmP 93*
Darney, Philip Dempsey 1943- *WhoAm 94*
Darnley, Earl of 1941- *Who 94*
Darnley, Herbert d1947 *WhoHol 92*
Darnley-Thomas, John, Mrs. *Who 94*
D'Arno, Albert d1977 *WhoHol 92*
Darnton, Robert 1939- *WrDr 94*
Darnton, Robert Choate 1939- *IntWW 93*
Daro, Gino d1977 *WhoHol 92*
Daroff, Robert Barry 1936- *WhoAm 94*
Daron, Harlow H. 1930- *WhoScEn 94*
da Roza, Victoria Cecilia 1945- *WhoWest 94*
D'Arpino, Tony *DrAPF 93*
D'Arquier, Joseph *NewGrDO*
Darr, Alan Phipps 1948- *WhoAm 94, WhoAmA 93*
Darr, Ann *DrAPF 93*
Darr, Ann Catherine 1958- *WhoFI 94*
Darr, Carol C. 1951- *WhoAmL 94*
Darr, James Earl, Jr. 1943- *WhoAmL 94, WhoFI 94*
Darr, John 1951- *WhoFI 94*
Darr, Milton Freeman, Jr. 1921- *WhoAm 94*
Darr, Walter Robert 1956- *WhoFI 94*
Darragh, Alexander James 1955- *WhoMW 93*
Darragh, Daniel Meyer 1946- *WhoAm 94, WhoAmL 94*
Darragh, John K. 1929- *WhoAm 94, WhoFI 94*
Darragh, Lydia Barrington 1729-1789 *WhAmRev*
Darrah, James Gore 1928- *WhoScEn 94*
Darrah, Joan *WhoAm 94, WhoAmP 93, WhoWest 94*
Darrah, Larry Lynn 1943- *WhoAm 94*
Darran, Douglas Charles 1941- *WhoFI 94*
Darrell, Betty Louise 1934- *WhoBlA 94*
Darrell, Elizabeth *WrDr 94*
Darrell, George Albert 1931- *WhoAm 94*
Darrell, Joseph A. 1945- *WhoAmL 94*
Darrell, Lewis E. 1932- *WhoBlA 94*
Darrell, Norris, Jr. 1929- *WhoAm 94*
Darrell, Peter 1929-1987 *IntDcB*
Darrell, Steve d1970 *WhoHol 92*
Darren, James 1936- *IntMPA 94, WhoHol 92*
Darriau, Jean-Paul 1929- *WhoAmA 93*
Darrid, Bill 1923- *WhoHol 92*
Darrieux, Danielle 1917- *IntMPA 94, IntWW 93, WhoHol 92*
D'Arrigo, Stephen, Jr. 1922- *WhoFI 94*
Darrin, David Kevin 1956- *WhoWest 94*
Darrin, Diana *WhoHol 92*
Darrington, Denton C. 1940- *WhoAmP 93*
Darrington, Hugh 1940- *EncSF 93*
Darro, Frankie d1976 *WhoHol 92*
Darrone, Donald William 1916- *WhoAm 94*
Darrow, Barbara 1933- *WhoHol 92*
Darrow, Christopher 1945- *WhoAmL 94*
Darrow, Clarence Allison 1940- *WhoAmP 93*
Darrow, Clarence Seward 1857-1938 *AmSocL [port]*
Darrow, Duncan Noble 1948- *WhoAm 94*
Darrow, George F. 1924- *WhoScEn 94, WhoWest 94*
Darrow, Henry *WhoHisp 94*
Darrow, Henry 1933- *WhoHol 92*
Darrow, Jill Ellen 1954- *WhoAm 94, WhoAmL 94*
Darrow, John d1980 *WhoHol 92*
Darrow, Paul Gardner *WhoAmA 93*
Darrow, Peter H. 1942- *WhoAmL 94*
Darrow, Peter P. 1919- *WhoAmP 93*
Darrow, Peter V. 1950- *WhoAmL 94*
Darrow, Philip Hokanson 1959- *WhoAmL 94*
Darrow, Steve 1949- *WhoAmP 93*
Darrow, Tony *WhoHol 92*
Darrow, Whitney, Jr. 1909- *WhoAmA 93*
Darrow, William Richard 1939- *WhoAm 94, WhoFI 94*
Darsey, Jerome Anthony 1946- *WhoScEn 94*
Darsonval, Lycette 1912- *IntDcB*
Darst, Bette-Jean *DrAPF 93*
Darst, David Martin 1947- *WhoAm 94*
Darst, Richard L. 1944- *WhoAmL 94*
Dart, Charles Edward 1915- *WhoAm 94*
Dart, John Seward 1936- *WhoAm 94, WhoWest 94*
Dart, Judith Candelor Lalka 1947- *WhoAm 94, WhoAmL 94*
Dart, Justin, Jr. 1930- *WhoAm 94, WhoFI 94*
Dart, Stephen Howard 1953- *WhoMW 93*
Dart, Stephen Plauche 1924- *WhoAmP 93*
Dart, Thomas J. *WhoAmP 93*
Dartez, Charles Bennett 1951- *WhoScEn 94*
Dartez, Franklin 1934- *WhoAm 94*
Darting, Edith Anne 1945- *WhoMW 93*
Dartmouth, Earl of 1731-1801 *AmRev*
Dartmouth, Earl of 1924- *Who 94*
Dartmouth, William Legge, Earl of 1731-1801 *WhAmRev [port]*
Dartnall, Gary 1937- *IntMPA 94*
Darton, Christopher 1945- *WhoAmA 93*
Darton, Edythe M. 1921- *WhoBlA 94*
Darton, Eric *DrAPF 93*
Darvall, Roger *Who 94*
Darvall, (Charles) Roger 1906- *Who 94*
Darvarova, Elmira *WhoAm 94*
Darvas, Charles d1930 *WhoHol 92*
Darvas, Endre Peter 1946- *WhoWest 94*
Darvas, Lili d1974 *WhoHol 92*
Darvennes, Corinne Marcelle 1961- *WhoScEn 94*
Darvi, Bella d1971 *WhoHol 92*
Darvill, Alan G. 1952- *WhoScEn 94*
D'Arville, Camille d1932 *WhoHol 92*
Darwall Smith, Simon Crompton 1946- *Who 94*
Darwall Smith, Susan Patricia 1946- *Who 94*
Darwell, Jane d1967 *WhoHol 92*
Darwen, Baron 1938- *Who 94*
Darwent, Frederick Charles 1927- *Who 94*
Darwin, Charles 1809-1882 *WorScD [port]*
Darwin, Charles Robert 1809-1882 *BlmGEL [port], EnvEnc [port], WhWE*
Darwin, Christopher John 1944- *WhoScEn 94*
Darwin, Erasmus 1731-1802 *BlmGEL, EncSF 93*
Darwin, Kenneth 1921- *Who 94*
Darwish, Adel 1945- *WrDr 94*
Darwish, Mahmud 1942- *ConWorW 93*
Darwish, Sayed 1892-1923 *NewGrDO*
Dary, David Archie 1934- *WhoAm 94, WrDr 94*
Daryanani, Michael *WhoAsA 94*
Daryngton, Baron 1908- *Who 94*
Daryush, Elizabeth 1887-1977 *BlmGEL, BlmGWL*
Das, Anath 1953- *WhoMW 93*
Das, D(eb) K(umar) 1935- *WrDr 94*
Das, Dilip Kumar 1941- *WhoScEn 94*
Das, Ishwar 1952- *WhoScEn 94*
Das, Kalyan 1956- *WhoAmL 94*
Das, Kamala 1934- *BlmGWL, WrDr 94*
Das, Kamalendu 1944- *WhoAsA 94, WhoScEn 94*
Das, Kumudeswar 1932- *WhoScEn 94*
Das, Mahadai *BlmGWL*
Das, Man Singh 1932- *WhoAsA 94*
Das, Mohan N. 1947- *WhoAsA 94*
Das, Phanindramohan 1926- *WhoAsA 94*
Das, Purna Chandra 1954- *WhoScEn 94*
Das, Rathin C. 1948- *WhoAm 94*
Das, Sajal Kumar 1960- *WhoScEn 94*
Das, Salil Kumar 1940- *WhoAsA 94, WhoScEn 94*
Das, Shovan 1954- *WhoAsA 94*
Das, Shyam 1944- *WhoAsA 94*
Das, Sujit 1958- *WhoScEn 94*
Das, Suman Kumar 1944- *WhoScEn 94*
Das, T. K. 1938- *WhoFI 94*
Das, Utpal 1955- *WhoScEn 94*
D'Asaro, Lucian Arthur 1927- *WhoScEn 94*
Dasburg, Andrew Michael 1887-1979 *WhoAmA 93N*
Dasburg, John Harold 1944- *WhoAm 94, WhoFI 94, WhoMW 93*
Dascal, Marcelo 1940- *ConAu 140*
Dascalescu, Constantin 1923- *IntWW 93*
Dascalos, Danielle Merrie 1960- *WhoWest 94*
Daschbach, Charles Clark 1948- *WhoWest 94*
Daschbach, Richard Joseph 1936- *WhoAmP 93*
Dascher, Paul Edward 1942- *WhoAm 94*
Daschle, Thomas A. 1947- *CngDr 93*
Daschle, Thomas Andrew 1947- *IntWW 93, WhoAm 94, WhoAmP 93, WhoMW 93*
d'Ascoli, Bernard Jacques-Henri Marc 1958- *IntWW 93*
Das Dasgupta, Shamita *WhoAsA 94*
Dasenbrock, Doris (Nancy) Voss 1939- *WhoAmA 93*
Dasgupta, Dipankar 1952- *WhoWest 94*
Dasgupta, Partha Sarathi 1942- *IntWW 93, Who 94*
Dasgupta, Purnendu Kumar 1949- *WhoScEn 94*
Dasgupta, Ranjit Kumar *WhoMW 93, WhoScEn 94*
Dash 1804-1872 *BlmGWL*

Davenport, Pamela Beaver 1948- WhoFI 94
Davenport, Paul WhoAm 94
Davenport, Paul 1946- WrDr 94
Davenport, Paul Theodore 1946- IntWW 93
Davenport, Ray 1926- WhoAmA 93
Davenport, Rebecca Read 1943- WhoAmA 93
Davenport, Roger (Hamilton) 1946- WrDr 94
Davenport, Roger Lee 1955- WhoWest 94
Davenport, Ronald R. 1936- WhoBlA 94
Davenport, Thomas 1802-1851 WorInv
Davenport, Thomas Herbert 1933- WhoMW 93
Davenport, W. Bennett 1931- WhoIns 94
Davenport, Walter Arthur B. Who 94
Davenport, Wilbur Bayley, Jr. 1920- WhoAm 94
Davenport, William d1941 WhoHol 92
Davenport, William H(enry) 1908- WrDr 94
Davenport, William Harold 1935- WhoWest 94
Davenport, William Wallace 1948- WhoAmL 94
Davenport, Willie D. WhoBlA 94
Davenport-Handley, David (John) 1919- Who 94
Davenport-Hines, Richard (Peter Treadwell) 1953- WrDr 94
Daventry, Viscount 1921- Who 94
Daventry, Leonard (John) 1915- EncSF 93
Daves, Delmer d1977 WhoHol 92
Daves, Glenn Doyle 1915- WhoAmP 93
Daves, Glenn Doyle, Jr. 1936- WhoAm 94
Davey, Bruce James 1927- WhoAm 94, WhoFI 94
Davey, Charles Bingham 1928- WhoAm 94, WhoScEn 94
Davey, Cheryl Davis 1961- WhoAmL 94
Davey, Clark William 1928- WhoAm 94
Davey, Cyril J(ames) 1911- ConAu 41NR
Davey, David Garnet 1912- Who 94
Davey, David Herbert P. Who 94
Davey, Francis 1932- Who 94
Davey, Frank(land Wilmot) 1940- WrDr 94
Davey, Geoffrey Wallace 1924- Who 94
Davey, Idris Wyn 1917- Who 94
Davey, James Joseph 1945- WhoScEn 94
Davey, Jocelyn Who 94
Davey, Jocelyn 1908- WrDr 94
Davey, John WhoHol 92
Davey, John Michael 1937- WhoAm 94
Davey, John Trevor 1923- Who 94
Davey, Jon Colin 1938- Who 94
Davey, Keith Alfred Thomas 1920- Who 94
Davey, Kenneth George 1932- IntWW 93, WhoAm 94
Davey, Lycurgus Michael 1918- WhoAm 94
Davey, (Henry) Norman 1888- EncSF 93
Davey, Nuna d1977 WhoHol 92
Davey, Pete Bruce-Wood 1964- WhoMW 93
Davey, Peter (John) 1940- WrDr 94
Davey, Peter Gordon 1935- Who 94
Davey, Peter John 1940- Who 94
Davey, Randall 1887-1964 WhoAmA 93N
Davey, Ronald A. WhoAmA 93
Davey, Ronald William 1943- Who 94
Davey, Roy Charles 1915- Who 94
Davey, William DrAPF 93
Davey, William 1917- Who 94
Davi, Robert 1953- WhoHol 92
Daviau, Allen 1942- IntMPA 94, WhoAm 94
Davico, Vincenzo 1889-1969 NewGrDO
David, Baroness 1913- Who 94, WhoWomW 91
David, King fl. 1010BC-970BC HisWorL [port]
David, Alexandra Mascolo 1962- WhoMW 93
David, Alfred 1929- WhoMW 93
David, Allen N. 1952- WhoAmL 94
David, Almitra DrAPF 93
David, Arthur LaCurtiss 1938- WhoBlA 94
David, Barbara Marie 1935- WhoMW 93
David, Brad WhoHol 92
David, Catherine Anne 1963- WhoMW 93
David, Clifford 1933- WhoHol 92
David, Clive 1934- WhoAm 94
David, Cyril Frank 1920- WhoAmA 93
David, Daniel Allen 1958- WhoAmL 94
David, Domenico d1698 NewGrDO
David, Don Raymond 1906- WhoAmA 93
David, Donald Kirk 1896- WhAm 10
David, Ebenezer c. 1751-1778 WhAmRev
David, Edward Emil, Jr. 1925- IntWW 93, WhoAm 94
David, Edward Joseph 1942- WhoAmL 94
David, Eleanor 1956- WhoHol 92
David, Elizabeth d1992 IntWW 93N, WrDr 94N
David, Elizabeth 1913-1992 AnObit 1992
David, Felicien(-Cesar) 1810-1876 NewGrDO
David, Florence Nightingale d1993 NewYTBS 93
David, Frank WhoHol 92
David, George 1940- WhoAm 94, WhoScEn 94, WhoWest 94
David, George Alfred Lawrence 1942- WhoFI 94
David, George F., III 1923- WhoBlA 94
David, Geraldine R. 1938- WhoBlA 94
David, Hal WhoAm 94
David, Herbert Aron 1925- WhoAm 94, WhoMW 93
David, Ibolya WhoWomW 91
David, Jacques Henri 1943- IntWW 93
David, James R. 1950- WhoFI 94
David, Joanna 1947- WhoHol 92
David, Johnny d1979 WhoHol 92
David, Karl Heinrich 1884-1951 NewGrDO
David, Keith 1954- IntMPA 94
David, Keith 1956- WhoBlA 94, WhoHol 92
David, Larry WhoHol 92
David, Lawrence T. 1930- WhoBlA 94
David, Leon 1867-1962 NewGrDO
David, Leon Thomas 1901- WhoAmL 94, WhoWest 94
David, Lourdes Tenmatay 1944- WhoScEn 94
David, Lynn Allen 1948- WhoFI 94
David, (Jean) Marc 1925- Who 94
David, Michael Paul 1951- WhoAmP 93
David, Michel Louis 1945- WhoAm 94
David, Miles 1926- WhoAm 94
David, Miriam Lang 1945- WhoAm 94
David, Nat DrAPF 93
David, Paul Theodore 1906- WhoAm 94
David, Percival Victor David Ezekiel 1892-1964 DcNaB MP
David, Peter 1954- EncSF 93
David, Pierre 1944- IntMPA 94
David, Ray 1925- WhoAmP 93
David, Richard Francis 1938- WhoAm 94
David, Richard William d1993 Who 94N
David, Robert Allan 1937- Who 94
David, Robert Jefferson 1943- WhoAmL 94
David, Robert Porter 1956- WhoWest 94
David, Robin (Robert) Daniel George 1922- Who 94
David, Ronald Sigmund 1940- WhoWest 94
David, Saul 1921- IntMPA 94
David, Thayer d1978 WhoHol 92
David, Thomas Meredith 1941- WhoAm 94
David, Timothy James 1947- Who 94
David, Tudor 1921- Who 94
David, Wayne 1957- Who 94
David, William d1965 WhoHol 92
Davide, Giacomo 1750-1830 NewGrDO
Davide, Giovanni 1790-1864 NewGrDO
Davidek, Stefan 1924- WhoAmA 93
Davidenko, Alexander Alexandrovich 1899-1934 NewGrDO
David-Neel, Alexandra 1868-1969 WhWE
Davidoff, Alexander 1872-1944 NewGrDO
Davidoff, Frances Mack d1967 WhoHol 92
Davidoff, Richard Sayles 1932- WhoAmL 94
Davidov, Stepan Ivanovich 1777-1825 NewGrDO
Davidovich, Bella 1928- IntWW 93, WhoAm 94
Davidovich, Jaime 1936- WhoAm 94, WhoAmA 93
Davidovich, Lolita 1961- IntMPA 94
Davidovich, Lolita 1962- WhoHol 92
Davidovsky, Mario 1934- WhoAm 94
Davidow, Jeffrey 1944- WhoAm 94, WhoAmP 93
Davidow, Joel 1938- WhoAm 94
Davidow, Robert 1947- WhoAm 94
Davids, Cary Nathan 1940- WhoMW 93
Davids, Greg 1958- WhoAmP 93
Davids, Kenneth Hawley 1937- WhoWest 94
Davids, Norman 1918- WhoAm 94
Davids, Robert Norman 1938- WhoScEn 94
Davidsen, Donald R. WhoAmP 93
Davidsmeyer, Kay L. 1953- WhoAmP 93
Davidson, Hon. Lord 1929- Who 94
Davidson, Viscount 1928- Who 94
Davidson, A. N. 1930- WhoIns 94
Davidson, Abraham A. 1935- WhoAm 94, WhoAmA 93
Davidson, Alan Charles 1937- WhoFI 94
Davidson, Alan Eaton 1924- Who 94, WrDr 94
Davidson, Alexander T. 1925- WhoAm 94
Davidson, Alfred E. 1911- IntWW 93
Davidson, Alfred Edward 1911- Who 94, WhoAm 94
Davidson, Allan Albert 1913-1988 WhoAmA 93N
Davidson, Alphonzo Lowell 1941- WhoBlA 94
Davidson, Andrew John 1957- WhoFI 94
Davidson, Anne Stowell 1949- WhoAmL 94
Davidson, Arthur 1928- Who 94
Davidson, Arthur B. 1929- WhoBlA 94
Davidson, Arthur Turner 1923- WhoBlA 94
Davidson, Avram 1923- WrDr 94
Davidson, Avram (James) 1923- EncSF 93
Davidson, Basil 1914- IntWW 93, WrDr 94
Davidson, Basil Risbridger 1914- Who 94
Davidson, Bill 1918- WhoWest 94
Davidson, Bonnie Jean 1941- WhoMW 93
Davidson, Brian 1909- Who 94
Davidson, Brian Y. 1933- WhoFI 94
Davidson, Bruce C. 1943- WhoAmL 94
Davidson, C. Girard 1910- WhoAmP 93
Davidson, Carl B. 1933- WhoAm 94
Davidson, Cathy Notari 1949- WhoAm 94
Davidson, Charles Kemp Who 94
Davidson, Charles Odell 1935- WhoBlA 94
Davidson, Charles Peter Morton 1938- Who 94
Davidson, Charles Robert 1922- WhoBlA 94
Davidson, Charles Sprecher 1910- WhoAm 94
Davidson, Charles Tompkins 1940- WhoFI 94
Davidson, Clayton Leslie 1930- WhoMW 93
Davidson, Cliff 1941- WhoAmP 93
Davidson, Colin Henry 1928- WhoAm 94
Davidson, Crow Girard 1910- WhoAm 94
Davidson, Dalwyn Robert 1918- WhoAm 94
Davidson, Daniel M. 1950- WhoAm 94
Davidson, David Neal 1956- WhoFI 94
Davidson, David Scott 1925- WhoAm 94
Davidson, Debra Ann 1956- WhoMW 93
Davidson, Dennis Michael 1939- WhoWest 94
Davidson, Donald 1917- IntWW 93
Davidson, Donald (Herbert) 1917- WrDr 94
Davidson, Donald Herbert 1917- WhoAm 94
Davidson, Donald Lee 1937- WhoAmP 93
Davidson, Donald Rae 1943- WhoBlA 94
Davidson, Donald William 1938- WhoAm 94
Davidson, Donetta Lea 1943- WhoAmP 93
Davidson, Dore d1930 WhoHol 92
Davidson, Doug WhoHol 92
Davidson, Earnest Jefferson 1946- WhoBlA 94
Davidson, Edwin Dow, Jr. 1953- WhoWest 94
Davidson, Eileen WhoHol 92
Davidson, Elizabeth H. Donnally 1948- WhoAmA 93
Davidson, Ellen WhoHol 92
Davidson, Elvyn Verone 1923- WhoBlA 94
Davidson, Emily DrAPF 93
Davidson, Eric Harris 1937- WhoAm 94, WhoWest 94
Davidson, Ernest Roy 1936- WhoScEn 94
Davidson, Eugene 1902- WrDr 94
Davidson, Eugene Abraham 1930- WhoAm 94
Davidson, Eugene Arthur 1902- WhoAm 94
Davidson, Eugene Erbert 1947- WhoAmP 93
Davidson, Ezra C., Jr. 1933- WhoAm 94, WhoBlA 94
Davidson, Fletcher Vernon, Jr. 1947- WhoBlA 94
Davidson, Francis 1905- Who 94
Davidson, Frank Geoffrey 1920- WrDr 94
Davidson, Frank Paul 1918- WhoAmL 94, WhoFI 94, WhoScEn 94
Davidson, Frederic McShan 1941- WhoAm 94
Davidson, Garrison H(olt) 1904-1992 CurBio 93N
Davidson, George WhAmRev
Davidson, George A., Jr. 1938- WhoAm 94, WhoFI 94
Davidson, George Allan 1942- WhoAm 94, WhoAmL 94
Davidson, Gerard H., Jr. 1943- WhoAmL 94
Davidson, Glen Harris 1941- WhoAm 94, WhoAmL 94
Davidson, Gordon 1933- WhoAm 94
Davidson, Gordon Byron 1926- WhoAm 94
Davidson, Gordon K. 1948- WhoAmL 94
Davidson, Harold French, Jr. 1920- WhoMW 93
Davidson, Herbert Alan 1932- WhoAm 94
Davidson, Herbert Laurence 1930- WhoAmA 93
Davidson, Herbert M. Tippen, Jr. 1925- WhoAm 94
Davidson, Howard William 1911- Who 94
Davidson, Hugh EncSF 93
Davidson, Ian Douglas 1901- WhAm 10
Davidson, Ian Graham 1950- Who 94
Davidson, Ian J. 1925- WhoAmA 93
Davidson, Ian Thomas Rollo 1925- Who 94
Davidson, Inger IntWW 93
Davidson, Inger Margareta 1944- WhoWomW 91
Davidson, Ivor Macaulay 1924- Who 94
Davidson, Jack Leroy 1927- WhoAm 94
Davidson, James Alfred 1922- Who 94
Davidson, James Duncan Gordon 1927- Who 94
Davidson, James F. 1952- WhoFI 94
Davidson, James Joseph, Jr. 1904-1990 WhAm 10
Davidson, James Joseph, III 1940- WhoAmL 94
Davidson, James Madison, III 1930- WhoFI 94, WhoScEn 94, WhoWest 94
Davidson, James Michael 1962- WhoWest 94
Davidson, James Patton 1928- Who 94
Davidson, James W. 1939- WhoFI 94
Davidson, James Wilson 1950- WhoMW 93
Davidson, Janet Marjorie 1941- IntWW 93
Davidson, Janet Toll 1939- WhoAm 94
Davidson, Jaye 1967?- ConBlB 5 [port]
Davidson, Jean WhoAmA 93
Davidson, Jeff 1951- WrDr 94
Davidson, Jeffrey P(hilip) 1951- ConAu 41NR
Davidson, Jo 1883-1952 WhoAmA 93N
Davidson, Jo Ann WhoAmP 93, WhoWomW 91
Davidson, Joan Gather 1934- WhoScEn 94
Davidson, John WhoAmP 93
Davidson, John d1968 WhoHol 92
Davidson, John 1857-1909 BlmGEL, EncSF 93
Davidson, John 1916- WhoAm 94
Davidson, John 1941- IntMPA 94, WhoHol 92
Davidson, John A. 1924- WhoAmP 93
Davidson, John Frank 1926- IntWW 93, Who 94
Davidson, John Hunter 1914- WhoScEn 94
Davidson, John Kenneth, Sr. 1939- WhoAm 94, WhoMW 93
Davidson, John Macdonald 1926- IntWW 93
Davidson, John Pirnie 1924- WhoAm 94
Davidson, John Robert 1947- WhoMW 93
Davidson, John Robert Jay 1950- WhoWest 94
Davidson, John Roderick 1937- Who 94
Davidson, Joseph d1981 WhoHol 92
Davidson, Joseph Q., Jr. 1941- WhoAmL 94
Davidson, Joy Elaine 1940- WhoAm 94
Davidson, Juli 1960- WhoFI 94, WhoWest 94
Davidson, Karen Sue 1950- WhoFI 94, WhoScEn 94
Davidson, Keith Who 94
Davidson, (William) Keith 1926- Who 94
Davidson, Keith Dewayne 1955- WhoScEn 94
Davidson, Kenneth Darrell 1967- WhoBlA 94
Davidson, Kenneth Lawrence 1945- WhoAmL 94
Davidson, Kerry 1935- WhoBlA 94
Davidson, Lacinda Susan 1958- WhoAm 94
Davidson, Lawrence Ira 1949- WhoAm 94, WhoAmL 94
Davidson, Lenny WhoHol 92
Davidson, Leroy 1920- WhAm 10
Davidson, Lionel 1922- ConAu 43NR, EncSF 93, WrDr 94
Davidson, Lisa Trnoska 1963- WhoMW 93
Davidson, Lurlean G. 1931- WhoBlA 94
Davidson, Mark 1938- WhoWest 94
Davidson, Mark Edward 1952- WhoAm 94, WhoAmL 94
Davidson, Mark S. 1950- WhoAmL 94
Davidson, Marshall B(owman) 1907-1989 ConAu 42NR
Davidson, Marshall Bowman 1907-1990 WhAm 10
Davidson, Martin 1939- IntMPA 94
Davidson, Mary Theresa 1952- WhoMW 93

Davidson, Max d1950 *WhoHol 92*
Davidson, Maxwell, III 1939- *WhoAmA 93*
Davidson, Mayer B. 1935- *WhoAm 94*
Davidson, Michael *DrAPF 93, EncSF 93*
Davidson, Michael 1944- *WrDr 94*
Davidson, Michael 1949- *WhoScEn 94*
Davidson, Michael Martin 1943- *WhoAmL 94*
Davidson, Michael Walker 1947- *WhoAm 94*
Davidson, Morris 1898-1979 *WhoAmA 93N*
Davidson, Nancy *WhoAmA 93*
Davidson, Nancy Brachman 1943- *WhoAm 94*
Davidson, Nicholas Ranking 1951- *Who 94*
Davidson, Norman Ralph 1916- *IntWW 93, WhoAm 94*
Davidson, Osha Gray 1954- *WhoMW 93*
Davidson, Owen 1943- *BuCMET*
Davidson, Pamela 1954- *WrDr 94*
Davidson, Peggy Eileen 1947- *WhoMW 93*
Davidson, Phebe *DrAPF 93*
Davidson, Phillip B. 1915- *WrDr 94*
Davidson, Ralph Kirby 1921- *WhoAm 94*
Davidson, Ralph P. 1927- *IntWW 93*
Davidson, Richard *DrAPF 93*
Davidson, Richard Alan 1946- *WhoMW 93, WhoScEn 94*
Davidson, Richard K. 1942- *WhoAm 94*
Davidson, Rick Bernard 1951- *WhoBlA 94*
Davidson, Robert 1927- *Who 94*
Davidson, Robert (James) 1928- *Who 94*
Davidson, Robert Bruce 1945- *WhoAm 94, WhoAmL 94*
Davidson, Robert C., Jr. 1945- *WhoBlA 94*
Davidson, Robert Laurenson Dashiell 1909- *WhoAm 94*
Davidson, Robert Miller d1993 *NewYTBS 93*
Davidson, Robert William 1949- *WhoAm 94, WhoWest 94*
Davidson, Robyn 1950- *ConAu 142*
Davidson, Roger H(arry) 1936- *WrDr 94*
Davidson, Roger Harry 1936- *WhoAm 94*
Davidson, Ronald d1965 *WhoHol 92*
Davidson, Ronald Crosby 1941- *WhoAm 94, WhoScEn 94*
Davidson, Ross J. 1949- *WhoIns 94*
Davidson, Rudolph Douglas 1941- *WhoBlA 94*
Davidson, Shelby 1868-1931 *WorInv*
Davidson, Sheldon Jerome 1939- *WhoAm 94*
Davidson, Shepard 1964- *WhoAmL 94*
Davidson, Sinclair Melville 1922- *Who 94*
Davidson, Sol M. 1924- *WrDr 94*
Davidson, Stanley J. 1946- *WhoAm 94, WhoAmL 94*
Davidson, Stephen J. 1948- *WhoAmL 94*
Davidson, Suzette Morton 1911- *WhoAmA 93*
Davidson, Sven 1928- *BuCMET*
Davidson, Sylvia Audrey 1922- *WhoAmP 93*
Davidson, Teresa D. *WhoWest 94*
Davidson, Terry Lee 1951- *WhoScEn 94*
Davidson, Thomas Ferguson 1930- *WhoScEn 94, WhoWest 94*
Davidson, Thomas Maxwell 1937- *WhoAm 94*
Davidson, Thomas Noel 1939- *WhoAm 94*
Davidson, Thyra 1926- *WhoAmA 93*
Davidson, Tom William 1952- *WhoAm 94*
Davidson, Tommy *WhoBlA 94*
Davidson, U. S., Jr. 1954- *WhoBlA 94*
Davidson, Van Michael, Jr. 1945- *WhoAmL 94*
Davidson, Wayne A. 1931- *WhoFI 94*
Davidson, Wayne Douglas 1947- *WhoAmL 94*
Davidson, William B. d1947 *WhoHol 92*
Davidson, William C. 1941- *WhoAmL 94*
Davidson, William George, III 1938- *WhoFI 94*
Davidson, William Lee c. 1746-1781 *AmRev, WhAmRev*
Davidson, William M. 1921- *WhoMW 93*
Davidson-Arnott, Frances E. 1946- *WhoAm 94*
Davidson-Harger, Joan Carole 1946- *WhoBlA 94*
Davidson-Houston, Aubrey Claud 1906- *Who 94*
Davidson-Moore, Kathy Louise 1949- *WhoScEn 94*
David-Weill, Michel 1932- *IntWW 93*
David-Weill, Michel Alexandre 1932- *Who 94, WhoAm 94, WhoFI 94*
Davie, Alan 1920- *IntWW 93, Who 94*
Davie, Antony Francis F. *Who 94*
Davie, Donald 1922- *BlmGEL*
Davie, Donald (Alfred) 1922- *WrDr 94*
Davie, Donald Alfred 1922- *IntWW 93, Who 94*
Davie, Helen K(ay) 1952- *SmATA 77*
Davie, Ian 1924- *WrDr 94*
Davie, Joseph Myrten 1939- *WhoAm 94*
Davie, Rex *Who 94*
Davie, (Stephen) Rex 1933- *Who 94*
Davie, Ronald 1929- *Who 94*
Davie, William Richardson 1756-1820 *AmRev, WhAmRev [port]*
Daviee, Jerry Michael 1947- *WhoAmA 93*
Davies *Who 94*
Davies, Baron 1940- *Who 94*
Davies, A. Michael 1934- *IntWW 93*
Davies, Alan (Cyril) 1924- *Who 94*
Davies, Albert John 1919- *Who 94*
Davies, Alfred Robert 1933- *WhoAm 94*
Davies, Alun Radcliffe 1923- *Who 94*
Davies, Alun Talfan 1913- *Who 94*
Davies, Alwyn George 1926- *Who 94*
Davies, Andrew (Wynford) 1936- *WrDr 94*
Davies, Andrew Owen Evan 1936- *Who 94*
Davies, Andrew Wynford 1936- *Who 94*
Davies, Anna Elbina 1937- *Who 94*
Davies, Anthony 1912- *Who 94*
Davies, Arthur 1906- *Who 94*
Davies, Arthur 1941- *NewGrDO*
Davies, Arthur Gordon 1917- *Who 94*
Davies, Betty Ann d1955 *WhoHol 92*
Davies, Bob 1920- *BasBi*
Davies, Brian 1938- *WhoHol 92*
Davies, Brian Meredith *Who 94*
Davies, (James) Brian Meredith 1920- *Who 94*
Davies, Brigid Catherine Brennan 1941- *Who 94*
Davies, Bryan 1939- *Who 94*
Davies, Bryn 1932- *Who 94*
Davies, Caleb, IV 1954- *WhoAmL 94*
Davies, Caleb William 1916- *Who 94*
Davies, Cecilia c. 1757-1836 *NewGrDO*
Davies, Christie 1941- *WrDr 94*
Davies, Christopher Evelyn K. *Who 94*
Davies, Colin 1948- *Who 94*
Davies, Colin Godfrey 1934- *Who 94*
Davies, Cynog Glyndwr *Who 94*
Davies, Cyril James 1923- *Who 94*
Davies, Daniel R. 1911- *WhoAm 94*
Davies, Darren Allen 1961- *WhoWest 94*
Davies, David 1818-1890 *DcNaB MP*
Davies, David 1939- *Who 94*
Davies, David (Henry) 1909- *Who 94*
Davies, David Brian 1950- *WhoIns 94*
Davies, David Brian Arthur Llewellyn 1932- *Who 94*
Davies, David Cyril 1925- *Who 94*
Davies, David E. N. 1935- *IntWW 93*
Davies, David Evan Naunton 1935- *Who 94*
Davies, David George 1928- *WhoAm 94*
Davies, David Glyn 1961- *WhoFI 94*
Davies, David John 1940- *Who 94*
Davies, David Keith 1940- *WhoAm 94*
Davies, David Levric 1925- *Who 94*
Davies, David Margerison 1923- *WrDr 94*
Davies, David Reginald 1927- *IntWW 93*
Davies, David Ronald 1910- *Who 94*
Davies, David Roy 1932- *Who 94*
Davies, David Stephen 1954- *WhoFI 94*
Davies, David Theodore Alban 1940- *Who 94*
Davies, Debra Lynn 1956- *WhoFI 94*
Davies, Deddie 1938- *WhoHol 92*
Davies, Dennis Russell 1944- *CurBio 93 [port], NewGrDO, WhoAm 94*
Davies, Denzil *Who 94*
Davies, (David John) Denzil 1938- *Who 94*
Davies, Dickie *Who 94*
Davies, Donald 1924- *Who 94*
Davies, Donald Watts 1924- *Who 94*
Davies, Douglas *Who 94*
Davies, (Percy) Douglas 1921- *Who 94*
Davies, (Gwilym) E(dnyfed) Hudson *Who 94*
Davies, E(benezer) T(homas) 1903-1992 *WrDr 94N*
Davies, Edna 1905- *WhoHol 92*
Davies, Ednyfed Hudson 1929- *Who 94*
Davies, Elidir (Leslie Wish) 1907- *Who 94*
Davies, Elmer David 1926- *WhoAmL 94*
Davies, Emlyn Glyndwr 1916- *Who 94*
Davies, Emrys 1934- *IntWW 93*
Davies, Emrys Thomas 1934- *Who 94*
Davies, Ernest Arthur 1926- *Who 94*
Davies, Eurfil Rhys 1929- *Who 94*
Davies, Fredric *EncSF 93*
Davies, Gareth 1930- *Who 94*
Davies, Gareth John 1944- *WhoAm 94*
Davies, Gareth Lewis 1936- *Who 94*
Davies, Garfield *Who 94*
Davies, (David) Garfield 1935- *Who 94*
Davies, Gavyn 1950- *Who 94*
Davies, Geoffrey 1941- *WhoHol 92*
Davies, George N. 1960- *WhoAmL 94*
Davies, George Raymond 1916- *Who 94*
Davies, George William 1941- *Who 94*
Davies, Geraint Talfan 1943- *Who 94*
Davies, Glyn *Who 94*
Davies, (Thomas) Glyn 1905- *Who 94*
Davies, Glyn Arthur Owen 1933- *Who 94*
Davies, Graeme John 1937- *IntWW 93, Who 94*
Davies, Grant William 1937- *WhoWest 94*
Davies, Gwynne Henton 1906- *Who 94*
Davies, Handel *Who 94*
Davies, Harry 1915- *Who 94*
Davies, Harry Clayton 1940- *WhoAmA 93*
Davies, Haydn Llewellyn 1921- *WhoAmA 93*
Davies, Horton (Marlais) 1916- *WrDr 94*
Davies, Horton Marlais 1916- *WhoAm 94*
Davies, Howard d1947 *WhoHol 92*
Davies, Howard John 1951- *IntWW 93, Who 94*
Davies, Howell 1717?-1770 *DcNaB MP*
Davies, Howell Haydn 1927- *Who 94*
Davies, Hugh Llewelyn 1941- *Who 94*
Davies, Hugh Marlais 1948- *WhoAmA 93, WhoWest 94*
Davies, Hugh Sykes 1909-1984 *EncSF 93*
Davies, Humphrey *Who 94*
Davies, (Morgan Wynn) Humphrey 1911- *Who 94*
Davies, Hunter *Who 94*
Davies, Hunter 1936- *WrDr 94*
Davies, (Edward) Hunter 1936- *Who 94*
Davies, Huw Humphreys 1940- *Who 94*
Davies, Hywel *Who 94*
Davies, (David) Hywel 1929- *Who 94*
Davies, Hywel William 1945- *Who 94*
Davies, Ian Hewitt 1931- *Who 94*
Davies, Ian Leonard 1924- *Who 94*
Davies, J(ohn) R(obert) Lloyd 1913- *Who 94*
Davies, Jack Gale Wilmot d1992 *Who 94N*
Davies, Jack Lloyd 1923- *WhoWest 94*
Davies, Jacob Arthur Christian 1925- *Who 94*
Davies, Jane Badger 1913- *WhoAm 94*
Davies, Janet d1986 *WhoHol 92*
Davies, Janet Mary H. *Who 94*
Davies, Jean *Who 94*
Davies, John *Who 94*
Davies, John 1569-1626 *BlmGEL*
Davies, John 1945- *WhoAmP 93*
Davies, (Lewis) John 1921- *Who 94*
Davies, John Alun Emlyn 1909- *Who 94*
Davies, John Arthur 1927- *IntWW 93, WhoAm 94*
Davies, John Brian 1932- *Who 94*
Davies, John Dudley *Who 94*
Davies, John Duncan 1929- *Who 94*
Davies, John Edward 1936- *WhoAm 94*
Davies, John G. *NewYTBS 93 [port]*
Davies, John G. 1929- *WhoAm 94, WhoAmL 94, WhoWest 94*
Davies, John Gordon 1919-1990 *WrDr 94N*
Davies, John Henry Vaughan 1921- *Who 94*
Davies, John Howard 1929- *Who 94*
Davies, John Howard 1939- *IntMPA 94, WhoHol 92*
Davies, John Howard Gay 1923- *Who 94*
Davies, John Irfon 1930- *Who 94*
Davies, John J. 1947- *WhoAmP 93*
Davies, John Kenyon 1937- *Who 94*
Davies, John McRoy 1958- *WhoAmP 93*
Davies, John Michael 1940- *Who 94*
Davies, John, of Hereford 1565?-1618 *BlmGEL*
Davies, John Paton 1908- *HisDcKW*
Davies, John Rhys 1942- *WhoHol 92*
Davies, John S. 1926- *WhoAmP 93*
Davies, John Sherrard 1917-1990 *WhAm 10*
Davies, John Thomas 1933- *IntWW 93, Who 94*
Davies, John Tudor 1937- *WhoWest 94*
Davies, Joseph Marie 1916- *Who 94*
Davies, Keith Laurence M. *Who 94*
Davies, Kelvin James Anthony 1951- *WhoScEn 94*
Davies, Kenneth 1928- *WhoWest 94*
Davies, Kenneth Southworth 1925- *WhoAmA 93*
Davies, L(eslie) P(urnell) 1914- *EncSF 93*
Davies, Lancelot Richard B. *Who 94*
Davies, Lane *WhoHol 92*
Davies, Lawrence A. 1930- *WhoBlA 94*
Davies, Lewis Mervyn 1922- *Who 94*
Davies, Lillian d1932 *WhoHol 92*
Davies, Linda 1963- *WhoWest 94*
Davies, Linda Hillary 1945- *Who 94*
Davies, Lindy *WhoHol 92*
Davies, Lloyd *Who 94*
Davies, Lorys Martin 1936- *Who 94*
Davies, Lucy Myfanwy 1913- *Who 94*
Davies, Marcus John A. *Who 94*
Davies, Margaret (Constance) 1923- *WrDr 94*
Davies, Margaret Caroline Llewelyn 1861-1944 *DcNaB MP*
Davies, Marion d1961 *WhoHol 92*
Davies, Martin (Brett) 1936- *WrDr 94*
Davies, Marvin 1934- *WhoBlA 94*
Davies, Meredith *Who 94*
Davies, (Albert) Meredith 1922- *NewGrDO, Who 94*
Davies, Merton Edward 1917- *WhoWest 94*
Davies, Mervyn *Who 94*
Davies, (David Herbert) Mervyn 1918- *Who 94*
Davies, Michael *Who 94*
Davies, (Alfred William) Michael 1921- *Who 94*
Davies, (Angie) Michael 1934- *Who 94*
Davies, Michael Norman Arden 1932- *WhoAm 94*
Davies, Michael Scott 1955- *WhoFI 94*
Davies, Neil *Who 94*
Davies, (William Michael) Neil 1931- *Who 94*
Davies, Nick 1953- *WrDr 94*
Davies, Nicola Velfor 1953- *Who 94*
Davies, Nicolas *Who 94*
Davies, (Frederic) Nicolas (John) 1939- *Who 94*
Davies, Nigel *Who 94*
Davies, Nigel 1920- *WrDr 94*
Davies, (Claude) Nigel (Byam) 1920- *Who 94*
Davies, Noel Anthony 1942- *Who 94*
Davies, Norman 1939- *WrDr 94*
Davies, Norman Thomas 1933- *Who 94*
Davies, Olwen *Who 94*
Davies, (Norah) Olwen 1926- *Who 94*
Davies, Oswald 1920- *Who 94*
Davies, P(aul) C(harles) W(illiam) 1946- *WrDr 94*
Davies, Patrick Taylor 1927- *Who 94*
Davies, Paul (Charles Williams) 1946- *EncSF 93*
Davies, Paul Lewis, Jr. 1930- *WhoAm 94, WhoAmL 94, WhoFI 94, WhoWest 94*
Davies, Paul R. 1939- *WhoIns 94*
Davies, Pete 1959- *EncSF 93*
Davies, Peter *Who 94*
Davies, (Roger) Peter (Havard) 1919- *Who 94*
Davies, Peter Douglas Royston 1936- *Who 94*
Davies, Peter George 1927- *Who 94*
Davies, Peter Howell 1950- *WhoFI 94*
Davies, Peter J. 1937- *WrDr 94*
Davies, Peter John 1940- *WhoAm 94, WhoScEn 94*
Davies, Peter Julian 1963- *WhoMW 93*
Davies, Peter Maxwell 1934- *IntWW 93, NewGrDO, Who 94*
Davies, Peter Ronald 1938- *Who 94*
Davies, Philip Bertram 1933- *Who 94*
Davies, Philip Middleton 1932- *Who 94*
Davies, Piers Anthony David 1941- *WrDr 94*
Davies, Quentin *Who 94*
Davies, (John) Quentin 1944- *Who 94*
Davies, R(obert) R(ees) 1938- *WrDr 94*
Davies, R. Scott 1944- *WhoAm 94, WhoAmL 94*
Davies, Ralph Kenneth 1897- *WhAm 10*
Davies, Ray *WhoHol 92*
Davies, Raymond Douglas 1944- *WhoAm 94*
Davies, Rees *Who 94*
Davies, (Robert) Rees 1938- *Who 94*
Davies, Reine d1938 *WhoHol 92*
Davies, Rhys 1901-1978 *DcLB 139 [port]*
Davies, Rhys Everson 1941- *Who 94*
Davies, Richard Harries 1916- *Who 94*
Davies, Richard Thomas 1946- *WhoMW 93*
Davies, Robert, Mrs. 1923- *WhoMW 93*
Davies, Robert Abel, III 1935- *WhoAm 94, WhoFI 94*
Davies, Robert David 1927- *Who 94*
Davies, Robert Edward 1913- *Who 94*
Davies, Robert Ernest d1993 *IntWW 93N, Who 94N*
Davies, Robert Henry 1921- *Who 94*
Davies, Robert Wallace 1959- *WhoFI 94*
Davies, Robert William 1925- *WrDr 94*
Davies, Robertson 1913- *IntWW 93, WhoAm 94, WrDr 94*
Davies, (William) Robertson 1913- *ConAu 42NR, ConDr 93*
Davies, Robin 1954- *WhoHol 92*
Davies, Rodney Deane 1930- *Who 94*
Davies, Roger *Who 94*
Davies, Roger 1948- *WhoScEn 94*
Davies, (Anthony) Roger 1940- *Who 94*
Davies, Roger Oliver 1945- *Who 94*
Davies, Ronald 1946- *Who 94*
Davies, Ronald Norwood 1904- *WhoAm 94, WhoAmL 94, WhoMW 93*
Davies, Ronald Wynn 1941- *WhoAm 94*
Davies, Rosemary d1963 *WhoHol 92*
Davies, Roy Thomas *Who 94*
Davies, Rudi *WhoHol 92*
Davies, Rupert d1976 *WhoHol 92*
Davies, Rupert E(ric) 1909- *WrDr 94*
Davies, Rupert Eric 1909- *Who 94*

Davies, Ryland 1943- IntWW 93, NewGrDO, Who 94
Davies, Sam Who 94
Davies, Samuel 1723-1761 DcAmReB 2
Davies, Siobhan Who 94
Davies, Siobhan 1950- ConTFT 11
Davies, Sonja M.L. 1923- WhoWomW 91
Davies, Stanley Mason 1919- Who 94
Davies, Stephen WhoHol 92
Davies, Stephen Graham 1950- IntWW 93
Davies, Steven A. 1949- WhoAmP 93
Davies, Stuart Duncan 1906- Who 94
Davies, Susan 1950- Who 94
Davies, Susan Elizabeth 1933- Who 94
Davies, Theodore Peter 1928- WhoAmA 93
Davies, Thomas Mockett, Jr. 1940- WhoAm 94
Davies, Trevor Arthur L. Who 94
Davies, Tudor 1892-1958 NewGrDO
Davies, Vivian Who 94
Davies, (William) Vivian 1947- Who 94
Davies, W.X. EncSF 93
Davies, Walter 1920- Who 94
Davies, Walter C. EncSF 93
Davies, Walter Merlin 1910- WrDr 94
Davies, Wendy Elizabeth 1942- Who 94
Davies, William D., Jr. 1928- WhoAm 94
Davies, William Llewellyn M. Who 94
Davies, William Ralph 1955- WhoFI 94, WhoWest 94
Davies, William Rhys 1932- Who 94
Davies, William Robert 1942- WhoFI 94
Davies, William S. 1942- WhoAmL 94
Davies, Windsor 1930- WhoHol 92
Davies, Zelma Ince 1930- Who 94
Daviess, John Howard 1923- WhoFI 94
Davies-Scourfield, Edward Grismond Beaumont 1918- Who 94
Davignon, Etienne 1932- IntWW 93, Who 94
Davila, Alberto 1955- WhoHisp 94
Davila, Diana 1966- WhoAmP 93
Davila, Edwin 1954- WhoAmL 94
Dávila, Elisa 1944- WhoHisp 94
Dávila, Hernando 1935- WhoHisp 94
Davila, Jaime WhoHisp 94
Dávila, José Rámon 1934- WhoHisp 94
Davila, Manuel 1955- WhoHisp 94
Davila, Maritza 1952- WhoAmA 93, WhoHisp 94
Davila, Pedrarias WhWE
Davila, Robert Refugio 1932- WhoHisp 94
Davila, Ruben Allen 1956- WhoHisp 94
Davila, Sonia J. 1942- WhoHisp 94
Davila, William A., Jr. 1952- WhoHisp 94
Davila, William Joseph 1950- WhoHisp 94
Davila, William S. 1931- WhoHisp 94
Dávila-Colón, Luis R. 1952- WhoHisp 94
Davila Ostolaza, Iván E. 1946- WhoHisp 94
Dávila Poupart, Pedro Juan 1940- WhoHisp 94
Davin, Dan(iel Marcus) 1913-1990 RfGShF, WrDr 94N
Davin, James Martin 1958- WhoAmL 94
Davin, Jana McCullough 1951- WhoWest 94
Davin, Thomas A., Jr. WhoAmP 93
da Vinci, Leonardo WorInv
Da Vinci, Mona DrAPF 93
Davino, Carmencita Fernandez 1948- WhoAsA 94
Davino, Donald J. 1941- WhoAmP 93
Davinson, Donald (Edward) 1932- WrDr 94
Davion, Albert d1726 WhWE
Davion, Alexander 1929- WhoHol 92
Daviot, Gordon BlmGWL
Daviot, Gordon 1896-1952 DcNaB MP
Davis Who 94
Davis, A. Arthur 1928- WhoAm 94, WhoAmP 93
Davis, A. Dano 1945- WhoAm 94, WhoFI 94
Davis, Abraham, Jr. 1923- WhoBlA 94
Davis, Ada Romaine ConAu 142
Davis, Adrianne 1945- WhoBlA 94
Davis, Alan DrAPF 93
Davis, Alan d1943 WhoHol 92
Davis, Alan Jay 1937- WhoAm 94
Davis, Alan Robert 1947- WhoScEn 94
Davis, Alan Roger M. Who 94
Davis, Aldrich B. 1946- WhoAmL 94
Davis, Alexander Jackson 1803-1892 AmCulL
Davis, Alfred, IV 1945- WhoAmP 93
Davis, Alfred Austin 1940- WhoWest 94
Davis, Alfred C., Sr. 1938- WhoBlA 94
Davis, Alfred Lewis 1941- WhoAm 94, WhoFI 94
Davis, Algenita Scott 1950- WhoBlA 94
Davis, Alice R. 1904- WhoBlA 94
Davis, Allan Who 94
Davis, (William) Allan 1921- IntWW 93, Who 94
Davis, Allen 1929- WhoAm 94, WhoWest 94
Davis, Allen F. 1931- WrDr 94
Davis, Allen Freeman 1931- WhoAm 94
Davis, Allen Kent 1962- WhoAmL 94
Davis, Alonzo J. 1942- WhoBlA 94
Davis, Alonzo Joseph 1942- WhoAmA 93
Davis, Alton Thomas 1947- WhoAmP 93
Davis, Altovise WhoHol 92
Davis, Alvin Glenn 1960- WhoBlA 94
Davis, Alvin Robert, Jr. 1954- WhoScEn 94
Davis, Ames 1945- WhoAmL 94
Davis, Amos 1932- WhoBlA 94
Davis, Amy Fogel 1943- WhoAmL 94
Davis, Andre Maurice 1949- WhoBlA 94
Davis, Andrew IntMPA 94
Davis, Andrew 1944- IntWW 93
Davis, Andrew (Frank) 1944- NewGrDO
Davis, Andrew Frank 1944- Who 94, WhoAm 94
Davis, Andrew Jackson 1826-1910 DcAmReB 2
Davis, Angela 1944- AfrAmAl 6 [port], ConBlB 5 [port], ConLC 77 [port], HisWorL
Davis, Angela (Yvonne) 1944- BlkWr 2
Davis, Angela Y(vonne) 1944- WrDr 94
Davis, Angela Yvonne 1944- WhoBlA 94
Davis, Anita Louise 1936- WhoBlA 94
Davis, Ann d1961 WhoHol 92
Davis, Ann B. 1926- WhoHol 92
Davis, Anna d1945 WhoHol 92
Davis, Anthony 1951- NewGrDO
Davis, Anthony Michael John 1939- WhoAm 94
Davis, Anthony Ronald William James 1931- Who 94
Davis, Arnor S. 1919- WhoBlA 94
Davis, Arrie W. 1940- WhoBlA 94
Davis, Art d1987 WhoHol 92
Davis, Arthur, Jr. 1933- WhoBlA 94
Davis, Arthur, III 1942- WhoBlA 94
Davis, Arthur D. WhoBlA 94
Davis, Arthur David WhoAm 94, WhoWest 94
Davis, Arthur H. 1917- IntWW 93
Davis, Arthur John 1924- IntWW 93
Davis, Arthur P(aul) 1904- BlkWr 2
Davis, Arthur Paul 1904- WhoBlA 94
Davis, B. Lynch ConAu 43NR, ConWorW 93
Davis, Barbara D. WhoBlA 94
Davis, Barbara L. 1957- WhoFI 94
Davis, Barry Robert 1952- WhoScEn 94
Davis, Bart McKay 1955- WhoAmL 94
Davis, Belva 1933- WhoBlA 94
Davis, Ben 1947- WhoAmA 93
Davis, Benjamin F., Jr. 1946- WhoAmL 94
Davis, Benjamin O., Sr. 1877-1970 AfrAmAl 6 [port]
Davis, Benjamin O., Jr. 1912- AfrAmG [port], AfrAmAl 6 [port], WhoBlA 94
Davis, Benjamin O(liver), Jr. 1912- BlkWr 2, WrDr 94
Davis, Benjamin Oliver, Sr. 1877-1970 AfrAmG [port]
Davis, Benjamin Oliver, Jr. 1912- WhoAmP 93
Davis, Bennie L. 1927- WhoBlA 94
Davis, Bennie Luke 1928- WhoAm 94
Davis, Bernard D(avid) 1916- IntWW 93
Davis, Bernard David 1916- WhoAm 94
Davis, Bertha G. 1918- WhoAmA 93
Davis, Bertram George 1919- WhoAm 94
Davis, Bertram Hylton 1918- WhoAm 94
Davis, Bette d1989 WhoHol 92
Davis, Bette 1908-1989 AmCulL [port]
Davis, Bette Ruth Elizabeth 1908-1989 WhAm 10
Davis, Betty Jean Bourbonia 1931- WhoWest 94
Davis, Bettye J. 1938- WhoBlA 94
Davis, Bettye Jean 1938- WhoAmP 93, WhoWest 94
Davis, Billy, Jr. 1938- WhoBlA 94
Davis, Bob WhoBlA 94
Davis, Boyce Ray 1938- WhoAmL 94
Davis, Boyd d1963 WhoHol 92
Davis, Brad 1942- WhoAmA 93
Davis, Brad 1949- WhoHol 92
Davis, Brad 1949-1991 WhAm 10
Davis, Bradley B. DrAPF 93
Davis, Brenda Lightsey-Hendricks 1943- WhoBlA 94
Davis, Brian Michael 1937- Who 94
Davis, Brian Newton Who 94
Davis, Brian Newton 1934- IntWW 93
Davis, Brian Richard 1934- WhoScEn 94
Davis, Brian William 1930- Who 94
Davis, Britt 1913- WhoAmP 93
Davis, Britton Anthony 1936- WhoAm 94
Davis, Brownie W. 1933- WhoBlA 94
Davis, Bruce Livingston, Jr. 1929- WhoAm 94
Davis, Bryce Scott 1949- WhoAmP 93
Davis, Burke 1913 WrDr 94
Davis, Burl Edward 1930- WhoAm 94
Davis, Byron Preston 1944- WhoAmL 94
Davis, C. Morris 1942- WhoAmL 94
Davis, C. Ray 1946- WhoAmP 93
Davis, C. VanLeer, III 1942- WhoAmL 94
Davis, Cabell Seal, Jr. 1926- WhoAm 94
Davis, Calvin De Armond 1927- WhoAm 94
Davis, Carl 1936- IntMPA 94, IntWW 93, Who 94
Davis, Carl George 1937- WhoAm 94
Davis, Carol Ann 1955- WhoFI 94
Davis, Carol Pinney 1926- WhoAmP 93
Davis, Carole 1962- WhoHol 92
Davis, Carole Joan 1942- WhoAm 94
Davis, Carolyn Ann McBride 1952- WhoBlA 94
Davis, Carolyn Kahle 1932- WhoAm 94
Davis, Carolyn Leigh 1936- WhoWest 94
Davis, Carrie L. Filer 1924- WhoBlA 94
Davis, Chandler 1926- WhoAm 94
Davis, Charles WhoHol 92
Davis, Charles 1944- WhoBlA 94
Davis, Charles (Sigmund) 1909- Who 94
Davis, Charles A. 1922- WhoBlA 94
Davis, Charles Alexander 1936- WhoBlA 94, WhoScEn 94
Davis, Charles Arthur 1921- WhoWest 94
Davis, Charles Burdis, III 1945- WhoAmA 93
Davis, Charles Carroll 1911- WhoAm 94
Davis, Charles Edward 1958- WhoBlA 94
Davis, Charles Francis, Jr. 1908- WhoAm 94
Davis, Charles Franklin 1964- WhoBlA 94
Davis, Charles Gregory WhoAmP 93
Davis, Charles Hargis 1938- WhoAm 94
Davis, Charles Joseph 1949- WhoAmL 94
Davis, Charles R. 1945- WhoAmP 93
Davis, Charlotte L. Poole 1947- WhoAmP 93
Davis, Cheri WhoAmP 93
Davis, Cheryl Eileen 1946- WhoMW 93
Davis, Chester R., Jr. 1930- WhoAm 94, WhoAmL 94
Davis, Chili 1960- WhoBlA 94
Davis, Chip WhoAm 94
Davis, Chloe Marion 1909- Who 94
Davis, Chris Mark 1954- WhoWest 94
Davis, Christine Eurich 1937- WhoMW 93
Davis, Christine R. WhoBlA 94
Davis, Christopher DrAPF 93
Davis, Christopher 1928- WrDr 94
Davis, Christopher Lee 1950- WhoAmL 94
Davis, Clarence 1939- WhoBlA 94
Davis, Clarence 1942- WhoAmP 93, WhoBlA 94
Davis, Clarence, Jr. 1926- WhoAmP 93
Davis, Clarence A. 1941- WhoBlA 94
Davis, Clarence Ephraim 1941- WhoAm 94
Davis, Clarice McDonald 1941- WhoAm 94, WhoAmL 94
Davis, Clark Sackett 1953- WhoMW 93
Davis, Claude-Leonard 1944- WhoAmL 94, WhoFI 94
Davis, Clay 1944- WhoAmP 93
Davis, Clayton Arthur Larsh 1955- WhoAmL 94
Davis, Clifton 1945- WhoHol 92
Davis, Clifton D. 1945- WhoBlA 94
Davis, Clive Jay 1934- WhoAm 94
Davis, Coleen Cockerill 1930- WhoWest 94
Davis, Colin IntMPA 94
Davis, Colin (Rex) 1927- NewGrDO, Who 94
Davis, Colin Rex 1927- IntWW 93
Davis, Conrad d1969 WhoHol 92
Davis, Constance A. 1949- WhoAmP 93
Davis, Corneal A. 1900- WhoAmP 93
Davis, Corneal Aaron 1900- WhoBlA 94
Davis, Cortney DrAPF 93
Davis, Courtland Harwell, Jr. 1921- WhoAm 94
Davis, Craig Alphin 1940- WhoAm 94
Davis, Craig Carlton 1919- WhoFI 94
Davis, Curtis Carroll 1916- WhoAm 94
Davis, Cyprian 1930- WhoBlA 94
Davis, D. Frank 1946- WhoAmL 94
Davis, D. Jack 1938- WhoAmA 93
Davis, Dale 1969- WhoBlA 94
Davis, Daniel WhoHol 92
Davis, Danny 1925- WhoAm 94
Davis, Danny K. 1941- WhoAmP 93, WhoBlA 94
Davis, Darlene Rose 1959- WhoBlA 94
Davis, Darrell L. 1939- WhoAm 94, WhoFI 94, WhoWest 94
Davis, Darwin N. 1932- WhoBlA 94
Davis, David Who 94
Davis, David (Howard) 1941- WrDr 94
Davis, David Aaron 1959- WhoAm 94
Davis, David Brion 1927- WhoAm 94, WrDr 94
Davis, David Ensos 1920- WhoAmA 93
Davis, David George 1945- WhoAm 94
Davis, David Michael 1948- Who 94
Davis, David Murrel 1947- WhoAmL 94
Davis, David Oliver 1933- WhoAm 94
Davis, Dean Earl 1952- WhoScEn 94
Davis, Deane Chandler 1900-1990 WhAm 10
Davis, Debbie Ann d1976 WhoHol 92
Davis, Debbie McCune 1951- WhoAmP 93
Davis, Deborah Cecilia 1952- WhoMW 93
Davis, Deborah Lynn 1948- WhoAmL 94
Davis, Delmont Alvin, Jr. 1935- WhoAm 94
Davis, Denice Faye 1953- WhoBlA 94
Davis, Denise Whitlock 1959- WhoFI 94
Davis, Dennis Albert 1934- WhoWest 94
Davis, Dennis M. 1951- WhoAmP 93
Davis, Denyvetta 1949- WhoBlA 94
Davis, Deralyn Riles 1935- WhoAmP 93
Davis, Derek Alan 1929- Who 94
Davis, Derek Richard 1945- Who 94
Davis, Derek Russell d1993 Who 94N
Davis, Diane Lynn 1954- WhoBlA 94
Davis, Dick 1945- WrDr 94
Davis, Dolores 1925- WhoAmP 93
Davis, Don Clarence 1943- WhoAmP 93
Davis, Don Paul 1950- WhoAmP 93
Davis, Donald WhoBlA 94
Davis, Donald 1928- WhoHol 92
Davis, Donald Alan 1939- WhoAm 94
Davis, Donald Fred 1935- WhoBlA 94
Davis, Donald Gordon, Jr. 1939- WhoAm 94
Davis, Donald Ray 1934- WhoAm 94
Davis, Donald Robert 1909-1990 WhoAmA 93N
Davis, Donald Russell 1932- WhoWest 94
Davis, Donald W. 1934- WhoBlA 94
Davis, Donald W. 1943- WhoMW 93
Davis, Doreen S. 1954- WhoAmL 94
Davis, Dorinne Sue Taylor Lovas 1949- WhoAm 94
Davis, Doris Ann WhoBlA 94
Davis, Doris Ann 1939- WhoAmP 93
Davis, Dorothy Patrick WhoHol 92
Davis, Dorothy Salisbury 1916- WhoAm 94, WrDr 94
Davis, Douglas (Matthew) 1933- WrDr 94
Davis, Douglas Matthew 1933- WhoAm 94, WhoAmA 93
Davis, Douglas Russell 1963- WhoAmL 94
Davis, Douglas Whitfield 1945- WhoAmL 94
Davis, Douglas Witfield 1945- WhoAm 94
Davis, Drexell WhoAmP 93
Davis, Dupree Daniel 1908- WhoBlA 94
Davis, Dwight 1879-1945 BuCMET
Davis, Dwight 1948- WhoAm 94, WhoScEn 94
Davis, Dwight E. 1944- WhoIns 94
Davis, E. Lawrence, III 1937- WhoAmP 93
Davis, E. Marcus 1951- WhoAmL 94
Davis, Earl James 1934- WhoAm 94
Davis, Earl S. WhoBlA 94
Davis, Earnestine Bady 1943- WhoBlA 94
Davis, Eddie d1987 WhoHol 92
Davis, Edgar Glenn 1931- WhoAm 94, WhoFI 94, WhoScEn 94
Davis, Edith Pancoast 1911- WhoAmP 93
Davis, Edmond Ray 1928- WhoAm 94
Davis, Edward 1914- WhoBlA 94
Davis, Edward 1935- WhoAmP 93, WhoBlA 94
Davis, Edward Bertrand 1933- WhoAm 94, WhoAmL 94
Davis, Edward D. 1904- WhoBlA 94
Davis, Edward L. 1943- WhoBlA 94
Davis, Edward Michael 1916- WhoAmP 93
Davis, Edward Mott 1918- WhoAm 94
Davis, Edward P., Jr. 1948- WhoAmL 94
Davis, Edward Shippen 1932- WhoAm 94
Davis, Edward Wilson 1935- WhoAm 94
Davis, Edwards d1936 WhoHol 92
Davis, Edwin Dyer 1925- WhoAm 94
Davis, Egbert Lawrence, III 1937- WhoAm 94
Davis, Elaine Carsley 1921- WhoBlA 94
Davis, Elberta Coleman 1946- WhoBlA 94
Davis, Eleanor Kay 1935- WhoAm 94
Davis, Elisa Elaine 1963- WhoWest 94
Davis, Elizabeth Emily Louise Thorpe 1948- WhoScEn 94
Davis, Ellen N. 1937- WhoAmA 93
Davis, Ellis James EncSF 93
Davis, Elmer d1958 WhoHol 92
Davis, Elnathan 1922- WhoAmP 93
Davis, Emery Stephen 1940- WhoAm 94, WhoFI 94
Davis, Emily 1944- WhoIns 94
Davis, Emma-Jo Levey 1932- WhoAm 94
Davis, Erellon Ben 1912- WhoBlA 94
Davis, Eric Keith 1962- WhoAm 94, WhoBlA 94, WhoWest 94
Davis, Erroll B., Jr. WhoBlA 94

Davis, Erroll Brown, Jr. 1944- *WhoAm 94, WhoFI 94*
Davis, Ervin 1926- *WhoAmP 93*
Davis, Esther Gregg 1934- *WhoBlA 94*
Davis, Esther M. 1893-1974 *WhoAmA 93N*
Davis, Etheldra S. 1931- *WhoBlA 94*
Davis, Eugenia Asimakopoulos 1938- *WhoMW 93*
Davis, Evan Anderson 1944- *WhoAm 94, WhoAmL 94*
Davis, Evelyn d1982 *WhoHol 92*
Davis, Evelyn K. 1921- *WhoBlA 94*
Davis, Evelyn Marguerite Bailey *WhoMW 93*
Davis, Evelyn Yvonne *WhoAm 94*
Davis, Ferd Leary, Jr. 1941- *WhoAm 94, WhoAmL 94*
Davis, Finis E. 1911- *WhoAm 94*
Davis, France Albert 1946- *WhoBlA 94*
Davis, Frances Kay 1952- *WhoAmL 94*
Davis, Francis 1946- *WrDr 94*
Davis, Francis A. 1893- *WhAm 10*
Davis, Francis D. 1923- *WhoBlA 94*
Davis, Francis Keith 1928- *WhoAm 94, WhoMW 93*
Davis, Frank 1947- *WhoBlA 94*
Davis, Frank Allen 1960- *WhoBlA 94*
Davis, Frank B. 1928- *WhoAm 94*
Davis, Frank Derocher 1934- *WhoBlA 94*
Davis, Frank I. 1919- *IntMPA 94*
Davis, Frank Marshall 1905-1987 *BlkWr 2, ConAu 42NR*
Davis, Frank Tradewell, Jr. 1938- *WhoAm 94*
Davis, Frank W. 1936- *WhoAmP 93*
Davis, Frank Wayne 1936- *WhoAmL 94*
Davis, Fred 1934- *WhoBlA 94*
Davis, Frederick Athie 1938- *WhoMW 93*
Davis, Frederick Benjamin 1926- *WhoAmL 94*
Davis, Frederick C(lyde) 1902-1977 *EncSF 93*
Davis, Frederick D. 1935- *WhoBlA 94*
Davis, Frederick Townsend 1945- *WhoAm 94, WhoAmL 94, WhoFI 94*
Davis, Freeman d1974 *WhoHol 92*
Davis, G. Cullom 1935- *WhoMW 93*
Davis, G. Reuben 1943- *WhoAmL 94*
Davis, Gail 1925- *WhoHol 92*
Davis, Garry Wayne 1957- *WhoMW 93*
Davis, Gary 1945- *WhoAmP 93*
Davis, Geena *IntWW 93*
Davis, Geena 1957- *IntMPA 94, WhoAm 94*
Davis, Geena 1958- *WhoHol 92*
Davis, Gene *WhoHol 92*
Davis, Gene 1945- *WhoAmP 93, WhoWest 94*
Davis, Gene A. 1939- *WhoBlA 94*
Davis, Gene B. 1920-1985 *WhoAmA 93N*
Davis, George *DrAPF 93, WhoIns 94*
Davis, George d1965 *WhoHol 92*
Davis, George Alfred 1928- *WhoAm 94, WhoFI 94*
Davis, George B. 1939- *WhoBlA 94*
Davis, George Donald 1942- *WhoAm 94*
Davis, George Edward 1850-1952 *DcNaB MP*
Davis, George Edward 1928- *WhoAm 94, WhoFI 94*
Davis, George Kelso 1910- *IntWW 93, WhoAm 94*
Davis, George Linn 1934- *WhoAm 94*
Davis, George Lynn 1940- *WhoAm 94*
Davis, George Nelson, Jr. 1936- *WhoBlA 94*
Davis, George W. 1914- *IntMPA 94*
Davis, George Wilmot 1933- *WhoAm 94, WhoFI 94*
Davis, Georgia d1976 *WhoHol 92*
Davis, Gerald U. *WhoAmP 93*
Davis, Gerry *WrDr 94*
Davis, Gerry 1930-1991 *EncSF 93*
Davis, Gilbert d1983 *WhoHol 92*
Davis, Gita 1925- *WrDr 94*
Davis, Glendell Kirk *WhoBlA 94*
Davis, Glenn *WhoHol 92*
Davis, Glenn Gallery 1955- *WhoMW 93*
Davis, Glenn Mark-Alan 1951- *WhoAmP 93*
Davis, Gloria 1938- *WhoAmP 93, WhoWomW 91*
Davis, Gloria Ann 1933- *EncNAR*
Davis, Gloria-Jeanne 1945- *WhoBlA 94*
Davis, Godfrey Rupert Carless 1917- *Who 94*
Davis, Gordon 1918- *WrDr 94*
Davis, Gordon B. 1930- *WhoMW 93*
Davis, Gordon Dale, II 1956- *WhoScEn 94*
Davis, Gordon J. 1941- *WhoAmL 94*
Davis, Gordon Richard Fuerst 1925- *WhoAm 94*
Davis, Grace Montañez 1926- *WhoHisp 94*
Davis, Grace W. *WhoAmP 93*
Davis, Grady D., Sr. *WhoBlA 94*
Davis, Grania *EncSF 93*
Davis, Grant Douglas 1954- *WhoMW 93*
Davis, Gray 1942- *WhoAmP 93*
Davis, Gregory A. 1948- *WhoBlA 94*
Davis, Gregory John 1959- *WhoScEn 94*
Davis, Gregory Thomas 1952- *WhoMW 93*
Davis, Guy Gaylon 1941- *WhoAmP 93*
Davis, H. Bernard 1945- *WhoBlA 94*
Davis, H. Ray 1927- *WhoAm 94, WhoFI 94*
Davis, Hal d1960 *WhoHol 92*
Davis, Hamilton E. 1937- *WhoAmP 93*
Davis, Harley *ConAu 41NR*
Davis, Harley Cleo 1941- *WhoAm 94*
Davis, Harold 1950- *WhoAm 94*
Davis, Harold Matthew 1946- *WhoBlA 94*
Davis, Harold R. 1926- *WhoBlA 94*
Davis, Harold Truscott 1895- *WhAm 10*
Davis, Harry d1929 *WhoHol 92*
Davis, Harry 1909- *WhAm 10*
Davis, Harry Allen 1914- *WhoAmA 93*
Davis, Harry Rex 1921- *WhoAm 94*
Davis, Harry Scott, Jr. 1943- *WhoAm 94*
Davis, Helen Elizabeth *Who 94*
Davis, Helen Gordon *WhoAmP 93, WhoWomW 91*
Davis, Helene *DrAPF 93*
Davis, Henry Barnard, Jr. 1923- *WhoAmL 94, WhoFI 94, WhoMW 93*
Davis, Henry Jefferson, Jr. 1929- *WhoAm 94*
Davis, Herbert Lowell 1933- *WhoAm 94*
Davis, Herbert Owen 1935- *WhoAm 94*
Davis, Herman E. 1935- *WhoBlA 94*
Davis, Heywood Hodder 1931- *WhoAmL 94*
Davis, Hiram Logan 1943- *WhoBlA 94*
Davis, Hope Hale *DrAPF 93, WrDr 94*
Davis, Horace Bancroft 1898- *WrDr 94*
Davis, Horance Gibbs, Jr. 1924- *WhoAm 94*
Davis, Howard *Who 94*
Davis, (Ernest) Howard 1918- *Who 94*
Davis, Howard C. 1928- *WhoBlA 94*
Davis, Howard Ted 1937- *WhoAm 94, WhoMW 93*
Davis, Howard Walter 1945- *WhoAm 94*
Davis, Hubert *NewYTBS 93 [port]*
Davis, Hubert Ira, Jr. 1970- *WhoBlA 94*
Davis, Humphrey d1987 *WhoHol 92*
Davis, Humphrey Denny 1927- *WhoAmP 93, WhoFI 94, WhoMW 93*
Davis, Isaac 1745-1775 *WhAmRev [port]*
Davis, Ivor John Guest 1925- *Who 94*
Davis, J. Alan 1961- *WhoWest 94*
Davis, J. Gunnis d1937 *WhoHol 92*
Davis, J. Mac 1952- *WhoAmP 93*
Davis, J. Madison *DrAPF 93*
Davis, J(ames) Madison, (Jr.) 1951- *WrDr 94*
Davis, J. Mason, Jr. 1935- *WhoAmP 93, WhoBlA 94*
Davis, J. Max 1938- *WhoAmP 93*
Davis, J. Morton 1929- *WhoFI 94*
Davis, J. Steve 1945- *WhoAm 94, WhoFI 94*
Davis, Jack *WhoHol 92*
Davis, Jack d1968 *WhoHol 92*
Davis, Jack 1917- *BlmGEL*
Davis, Jack (Leonard) 1917- *ConDr 93, WrDr 94*
Davis, Jack D. 1935- *WhoAmP 93*
Davis, Jack R. *WhoAmA 93*
Davis, Jack Wayne, Jr. 1947- *WhoAm 94*
Davis, Jackson Beauregard 1918- *WhoAmP 93*
Davis, Jacob E., II 1934- *WhoAm 94*
Davis, Jacqueline Marie Vincent d1989 *WhAm 10*
Davis, Jacquelyn Kay 1950- *WhoAm 94*
Davis, James *WhoBlA 94*
Davis, James 1901-1974 *WhoAmA 93N*
Davis, James A. 1924- *WhoBlA 94*
Davis, James Allan 1953- *WhoAm 94*
Davis, James B. *WhoAm 94*
Davis, James D. *WhoAmP 93*
Davis, James Evans 1918- *WhoAm 94, WhoScEn 94*
Davis, James F. 1943- *WhoBlA 94*
Davis, James Granberry 1931- *WhoAmA 93*
Davis, James Gresham 1928- *Who 94*
Davis, James H. 1941- *WhoBlA 94*
Davis, James Harold 1932- *WhoBlA 94*
Davis, James Harold 1939- *WhoBlA 94*
Davis, James Henry 1932- *WhoAm 94*
Davis, James Holmes 1930- *WhoAmL 94*
Davis, James Hornor, III 1928- *WhoAm 94*
Davis, James Ivey 1937- *WhoWest 94*
Davis, James Keet 1940- *WhoBlA 94*
Davis, James Lee 1940- *WhoAmL 94*
Davis, James Lee 1953- *WhoMW 93*
Davis, James Lloyd 1928- *WhoAmP 93*
Davis, James Luther 1924- *WhoAm 94, WhoWest 94*
Davis, James McCoy 1914- *WhoFI 94*
Davis, James Minor, Jr. 1936- *WhoAm 94, WhoFI 94*
Davis, James Morris 1927- *WhoFI 94*
Davis, James Norman 1939- *WhoAm 94*
Davis, James O., III 1957- *WhoAmP 93*
Davis, James Othello 1916- *IntWW 93, WhoAm 94*
Davis, James Parker 1921- *WhoBlA 94*
Davis, James Richard 1939- *WhoAm 94*
Davis, James Robert 1945- *ConAu 41NR, WhoAm 94, WhoAmA 93*
Davis, James S. 1945- *WhoAmL 94*
Davis, James Verlin 1935- *WhoAm 94*
Davis, James W. 1926- *WhoBlA 94*
Davis, James Wesley 1940- *WhoAmA 93*
Davis, James Z. 1943- *WhoAmL 94*
Davis, Jana Valerie 1951- *WhoFI 94*
Davis, Jane Strauss 1944- *WhoMW 93*
Davis, Janet 1959- *WhoFI 94*
Davis, Jay Barry 1959- *WhoAmL 94*
Davis, Jean E. *WhoBlA 94*
Davis, Jean M. 1932- *WhoBlA 94*
Davis, Jefferson 1808-1889 *HisWorL [port]*
Davis, Jefferson B. *WhoAmP 93*
Davis, Jeffrey J. 1947- *WhoAm 94, WhoAmL 94*
Davis, Jeffrey Stuart 1942- *WhoWest 94*
Davis, Jenny 1953- *SmATA 74 [port], TwCYAW*
Davis, Jeremy Matthew 1953- *WhoWest 94*
Davis, Jerome 1950- *WhoBlA 94*
Davis, Jerrold 1926- *WhoAmA 93*
Davis, Jerry, Jr. 1925- *WhoBlA 94*
Davis, Jerry Arnold 1946- *WhoAm 94*
Davis, Jerry Ray 1938- *WhoAm 94*
Davis, Jesse F. 1908- *WhoAmP 93*
Davis, Jim *ConAu 41NR*
Davis, Jim d1981 *WhoHol 92*
Davis, Jimmie 1902- *WhoHol 92*
Davis, Jimmie Dan 1940- *WhoAm 94*
Davis, Jimmy Frank 1945- *WhoAmL 94*
Davis, Jimmy Kyle 1954- *WhoAmP 93*
Davis, Joan d1961 *WhoHol 92*
Davis, Joan 1907-1961 *WhoCom*
Davis, JoAn 1947- *WhoFI 94*
Davis, Joe W. *WhoAmP 93*
Davis, Joel 1934- *WhoAm 94*
Davis, Joel Allen 1956- *WhoWest 94*
Davis, John *Who 94*
Davis, John dc. 1840 *EncNAR*
Davis, John c. 1550-1605 *WhWE*
Davis, John 1773-1839 *NewGrDO*
Davis, (Arthur) John 1924- *Who 94*
Davis, John (Gilbert) 1936- *Who 94*
Davis, John Aaron, Jr. 1928- *WhoWest 94*
Davis, John Adams, Jr. 1944- *WhoFI 94, WhoScEn 94*
Davis, John Albert 1935- *WhoBlA 94*
Davis, John Albert 1940- *WhoAmL 94*
Davis, John Alexander 1960- *WhoBlA 94*
Davis, John Allen 1923- *Who 94*
Davis, John Allen, Jr. 1952- *WhoFI 94*
Davis, John Aubrey 1912- *WhoBlA 94*
Davis, John Byron 1922- *WhoAm 94*
Davis, John Charles 1943- *WhoAm 94, WhoAmL 94*
Davis, John Christopher 1944- *WhoAm 94*
Davis, John Clements 1938- *WhoAm 94*
Davis, John Darelan R. *Who 94*
Davis, John David 1937- *WrDr 94*
Davis, John Edward *WhoFI 94*
Davis, John Edward 1913- *WhoAmP 93*
Davis, John Edward 1913-1990 *WhAm 10*
Davis, John Edward 1942- *WhoAm 94, WhoFI 94*
Davis, John Gilbert *WrDr 94*
Davis, John Henry 1906- *IntWW 93*
Davis, John Henry Harris d1993 *Who 94N*
Davis, John Herschel 1924- *WhoAm 94*
Davis, John Horsley Russell 1938- *Who 94*
Davis, John Howard 1920- *WhoAm 94*
Davis, John I. 1939- *WhoAmL 94*
Davis, John James 1936- *WhoAm 94*
Davis, John Kennerly, Jr. 1945- *WhoFI 94*
Davis, John Kerr 1956- *WhoAmL 94*
Davis, John MacDougall 1914- *WhoAm 94*
Davis, John Mason 1935- *WhoAm 94*
Davis, John Michael N. *Who 94*
Davis, John Phillips, Jr. 1925- *WhoAm 94*
Davis, John R., Jr. 1927- *WhoAmP 93*
Davis, John Robert 1951- *WhoAmP 93*
Davis, John Roger, Jr. 1927- *WhoAm 94*
Davis, John Rowland 1927- *WhoAm 94*
Davis, John Sherwood 1942- *WhoAmA 93N*
Davis, John Sidney 1942- *WhoFI 94*
Davis, John Staige, IV 1931- *WhoAm 94, WhoScEn 94*
Davis, John Stewart 1952- *WhoScEn 94*
Davis, John W., III 1942- *WhoAm 94, WhoFI 94*
Davis, John W., III 1958- *WhoBlA 94*
Davis, John Wesley, Sr. 1934- *WhoBlA 94*
Davis, John Westley 1933- *WhoBlA 94*
Davis, Johnetta Garner 1939- *WhoBlA 94*
Davis, Johnny d1983 *WhoHol 92*
Davis, Johnny Reginald 1955- *WhoBlA 94*
Davis, Jolene Bryant 1942- *WhoFI 94*
Davis, Jon Francis 1936- *WhoMW 93*
Davis, Jonathan Farr 1893- *WhAm 10*
Davis, Jordan Ray 1921- *WhoAmP 93*
Davis, Joseph 1942- *WhoBlA 94*
Davis, Joseph Barton 1942- *WhoAmP 93*
Davis, Joseph Edward 1926- *WhoAm 94, WhoWest 94*
Davis, Joseph La Roy 1932- *WhoWest 94*
Davis, Joseph Lloyd 1927- *WhoAm 94, WhoMW 93*
Davis, Joseph M. 1937-1992 *WhoBlA 94N*
Davis, Joseph Samuel 1930- *WhoAm 94, WhoWest 94*
Davis, Joseph Solomon 1938- *WhoBlA 94*
Davis, Josephine D. *WhoBlA 94*
Davis, Joy Lee 1931- *WhoMW 93*
Davis, Judy 1955?- *CurBio 93 [port], IntWW 93*
Davis, Judy 1956- *IntMPA 94, WhoHol 92*
Davis, Judy Ann 1942- *WhoMW 93*
Davis, Julia 1900?-1993 *ConAu 140, SmATA 75*
Davis, Julia McBroom 1930- *WhoAm 94*
Davis, Julian Mason, Jr. 1935- *WhoAm 94*
Davis, June Leah 1922- *WhoMW 93, WhoScEn 94*
Davis, K. Paul 1940- *WhoAmL 94*
Davis, Karen 1952- *WhoIns 94*
Davis, Karen Elaine 1957- *WhoMW 93*
Davis, Karen Lee 1954- *WhoFI 94*
Davis, Karen Padgett 1942- *WhoAm 94*
Davis, Karl d1977 *WhoHol 92*
Davis, Karla Jean Barrett 1963- *WhoFI 94*
Davis, Kathryn Ward 1949- *WhoMW 93*
Davis, Kathryn Wasserman 1907- *WhoAm 94*
Davis, Kathy 1957- *WhoMW 93*
Davis, Katie Campbell 1936- *WhoBlA 94*
Davis, Keith 1918- *WrDr 94*
Davis, Keith Eugene 1936- *WhoAm 94*
Davis, Keith Frederic 1952- *WhoAmA 93*
Davis, Keith Robert 1957- *WhoScEn 94*
Davis, Kenn 1932- *WrDr 94*
Davis, Kenneth Dudley 1958- *WhoAmL 94*
Davis, Kenneth Earl, Sr. 1937- *WhoScEn 94*
Davis, Kenneth Leon 1949- *WhoScEn 94*
Davis, Kenneth Sidney 1912- *WhoAm 94*
Davis, Kent Andrew 1960- *WhoMW 93*
Davis, Kevin Jon 1963- *WhoScEn 94*
Davis, Kimberly Brooke 1953- *WhoAmA 93*
Davis, Kingsley 1908- *WhoAm 94*
Davis, Kristin Woodford 1944- *WhoFI 94*
Davis, Kurt R. 1962- *WhoAmP 93*
Davis, L. Clarice *WhoAmA 93*
Davis, L. Clifford 1925- *WhoBlA 94*
Davis, L. J. *DrAPF 93*
Davis, Lambert d1993 *NewYTBS 93*
Davis, LaNay Flint 1933- *WhoMW 93*
Davis, Lance Alan 1939- *WhoAm 94*
Davis, Lance Edwin 1928- *WhoAm 94, WhoWest 94*
Davis, Lance Roosevelt 1962- *WhoBlA 94*
Davis, Lanny J. 1945- *WhoAmL 94*
Davis, Lanny Jesse 1945- *WhoAmP 93*
Davis, Lant B. 1954- *WhoAmL 94*
Davis, Larry Albert 1939- *WhoMW 93*
Davis, Larry Allen 1950- *WhoAmL 94*
Davis, Larry Earl 1946- *WhoBlA 94*
Davis, Larry Jon 1961- *WhoMW 93*
Davis, Larry Michael 1947- *WhoMW 93*
Davis, Laura Alice 1943- *WhoAmP 93*
Davis, Laura Ann 1959- *WhoFI 94*
Davis, Laura Arlene 1935- *WhoAm 94*
Davis, Laurel Elizabeth 1956- *WhoAmL 94*
Davis, Laurence Laird 1915- *WhoAm 94, WhoMW 93*
Davis, Laurence Richard 1934- *WhoWest 94*
Davis, Lavene 1918- *WhoAmP 93*
Davis, Lawrence Arnette, Jr. 1937- *WhoBlA 94*
Davis, Lawrence C. 1935- *WhoIns 94*
Davis, Lawrence Clark 1945- *WhoMW 93*
Davis, Lawrence Hale 1943- *WhoFI 94*
Davis, Lawrence William 1935- *WhoScEn 94*
Davis, Lee Anna 1936- *WhoAmP 93*
Davis, Lee Jarrell *WhoAmP 93*
Davis, Leita R. 1916- *WhoAmP 93*
Davis, Leland Cunningham, Jr. 1922- *WhoAmP 93*
Davis, Lelia Kasenia 1941- *WhoBlA 94*
Davis, Leodis 1933- *WhoBlA 94*
Davis, Leon 1933- *WhoBlA 94*
Davis, Leonard 1919- *WhoAm 94*
Davis, Leonard Harry 1927- *WhoBlA 94*
Davis, Leonard McCutchan 1919- *WhoAm 94*

Davis, Walter d1981 WhoHol 92
Davis, Walter d1991 WhoAmA 93N
Davis, Walter 1954- BasBi
Davis, Walter, Mrs. d1991 WhoAmA 93N
Davis, Walter Barry 1942- WhoScEn 94
Davis, Walter Jackson, Jr. 1936- AfrAmG [port], WhoBlA 94
Davis, Walter Lee 1954- WhoAmL 94
Davis, Walter Lewis 1937- WhoAmA 93
Davis, Walter Lowry, Jr. 1946- WhoAmP 93
Davis, Walter Paul 1954- WhoBlA 94
Davis, Walter Richard 1935- WhoAm 94
Davis, Walter Stewart 1924- WhoAm 94, WhoMW 93
Davis, Wanda M. 1952- WhoBlA 94
Davis, Wanda Rose 1937- WhoAmL 94, WhoWest 94
Davis, Warren B. 1947- WhoBlA 94
Davis, Warren Judson 1937- WhoAmL 94
Davis, Warwick 1969- WhoHol 92
Davis, Watson 1896- WhAm 10
Davis, Wayne Alton 1931- WhoAm 94
Davis, Wayne Lambert 1904-1988 WhoAmA 93N
Davis, Wendell, Jr. 1933- WhoAm 94
Davis, Wendell Tyrone 1966- WhoBlA 94
Davis, Wiley M. 1927- WhoBlA 94
Davis, Will David 1929- WhoAmP 93
Davis, William 1933- Who 94, WrDr 94
Davis, William A. 1948- WhoAmL 94
Davis, William Albert 1946- WhoAm 94
Davis, William Allison, II 1942- WhoAm 94
Davis, William Arthur 1932- WhoAm 94
Davis, William C., Jr. 1948- WhoMW 93
Davis, William Charles 1933- WhoScEn 94
Davis, William Columbus 1910- WhoAm 94
Davis, William D. 1936- WhoAmA 93
Davis, William E. WhoAm 94, WhoFI 94
Davis, William E., Sr. 1930- WhoBlA 94
Davis, William Emrys 1942- WhoAm 94
Davis, William Eric 1908- Who 94
Davis, William Eugene 1929- WhoAm 94
Davis, William Eugene 1936- WhoAm 94, WhoAmL 94
Davis, William F. 1948- WhoAmP 93
Davis, William Grenville 1929- Who 94, WhoAm 94, WhoFI 94
Davis, William Hayes, Sr. 1947- WhoBlA 94
Davis, William Herbert 1919- Who 94
Davis, William Howard 1922-1991 WhAm 10
Davis, William Howard 1951- WhoAmL 94
Davis, William L. 1933- WhoBlA 94
Davis, William Maxie, Jr. 1932- WhoAmL 94
Davis, William Michael 1951- WhoAmP 93
Davis, William O. 1948- WhoAmL 94
Davis, William R. 1921- WhoBlA 94
Davis, William R. 1934- WhoBlA 94
Davis, William R. 1945- WhoAmP 93
Davis, William Robert 1929- WhoAm 94
Davis, William Ross, Jr. 1953- WhoWest 94
Davis, William Selassie, Jr. 1918- WhoBlA 94
Davis, William Steeple 1884-1961 WhoAmA 93N
Davis, William Virgil DrAPF 93
Davis, Willie ProFbHF
Davis, Willie A. 1948- WhoBlA 94
Davis, Willie D. 1934- WhoBlA 94
Davis, Willie J. 1935- WhoBlA 94
Davis, Willie James 1940- WhoBlA 94
Davis, Willis H. 1937- WhoBlA 94
Davis, Wylie Herman 1919- WhoAm 94
Davis, Yvonne 1955- WhoAmP 93
Davis Anthony, Vernice 1945- WhoBlA 94
Davis-Banks, Phyllis Eileen 1918- WhoWest 94
Davis-Bruno, Karen L. 1961- WhoScEn 94
Davis-Cartey, Catherine B. 1954- WhoBlA 94
Davis-Cartey, Catherine Bernice 1954- WhoMW 93
Davis-Friedmann, Deborah 1945- ConAu 41NR
Davis-Gardner, Angela DrAPF 93
Davis-Goff, Annabel DrAPF 93
Davis-Goff, Robert William Who 94
Davis-Kimball, Jeannine 1929- WhoWest 94
Davis-McFarland, E. Elise 1946- WhoBlA 94
Davison Who 94
Davison, Alan Nelson 1925- Who 94
Davison, Arthur Lee 1936- WhoAm 94, WhoScEn 94, WhoWest 94
Davison, Beaumont 1929- WhoAm 94
Davison, Bill 1941- WhoAmA 93
Davison, Bruce 1946- IntMPA 94, WhoAm 94, WhoHol 92
Davison, Bruce C. 1950- WhoAmL 94
Davison, Burns Harris, II 1931- WhoAmL 94
Davison, Calvin 1932- WhoAm 94
Davison, Charles 1858-1940 DcNaB MP
Davison, Charles Hamilton 1926- WhoAm 94
Davison, Dale 1955- IntMPA 94
Davison, Daniel Pomeroy 1925- WhoAm 94
Davison, Davey WhoHol 92
Davison, Dennis 1923- WrDr 94
Davison, Edward Joseph 1938- IntWW 93, WhoAm 94
Davison, Edward L. 1943- WhoBlA 94
Davison, Emily Wilding 1872-1913 DcNaB MP
Davison, Endicott Peabody 1923- WhoAm 94
Davison, Frederic E. 1917- WhoBlA 94
Davison, Frederic Ellis 1917- AfrAmG [port]
Davison, Frederick Corbet 1929- WhoAm 94
Davison, Geoffrey 1927- WrDr 94
Davison, George Frederick, Jr. 1950- WhoAmL 94
Davison, Glenn Alan 1963- WhoScEn 94
Davison, Helen Irene 1926- WhoWest 94
Davison, Ian Frederic Hay 1931- IntWW 93, Who 94
Davison, Irwin Stuart 1942- WhoAmL 94
Davison, Jeffrey Blair 1956- WhoAmL 94
Davison, John Herbert 1930- WhoAm 94
Davison, Jon 1949- IntMPA 94
Davison, Kenneth Edwin 1924- WhoAm 94
Davison, Lawrence H. GayLL
Davison, Luella May 1922- WhoMW 93
Davison, Nancy Reynolds 1944- WhoAm 94
Davison, Paul Sioussa 1955- WhoAmL 94
Davison, Peter DrAPF 93
Davison, Peter (Hubert) 1928- ConAu 43NR, WrDr 94
Davison, Peter Fitzgerald 1927- WhoAm 94
Davison, Peter Hubert 1928- WhoAm 94
Davison, Richard 1937- WhoAm 94
Davison, Roderic Hollett 1916- WhoAm 94
Davison, Ronald (Keith) 1920- Who 94
Davison, Ronald Keith 1920- IntWW 93
Davison, Sid I., Jr. 1936- WhoMW 93
Davison, Stanley Who 94
Davison, (John) Stanley 1922- Who 94
Davison, Tito d1985 WhoHol 92
Davison, Warren Malcolm 1933- WhoAm 94
Davis-Rice, Peter 1930- Who 94
Davisson, Clinton Joseph 1881-1958 WorScD
Davisson, Homer G. 1866- WhoAmA 93N
Davisson, Lee David 1936- WhoAm 94
Davisson, Muriel Trask 1941- WhoScEn 94
Davisson, Ross Olen, Sr. 1940- WhoAmP 93
Davis-Voss, Sammi 1964- IntMPA 94
Davis Wagnon, Joan 1940- WhoWomW 91
Davis-Williams, Phyllis A. 1947- WhoBlA 94
Davit, Frank Torino 1961- WhoFI 94
Davitz, J(oel) R(obert) 1926- WrDr 94
Davlin, Michael C. 1955- WhoIns 94
Davon, Ofira d1993 NewYTBS 93
Davoodi, Hamid 1959- WhoScEn 94
D'Avril, Yola 1907- WhoHol 92
Davson, Geoffrey Leo Simon Who 94
Davtian, Vaagn Armenakovich 1922- IntWW 93
Davy, Gloria 1931- NewGrDO
Davy, Gloria 1937- WhoBlA 94
Davy, Humphry 1778-1829 WorInv [port], WorScD
Davy, John 1763-1824 NewGrDO
Davy, Michael Francis 1946- WhoMW 93, WhoScEn 94
Davy, Sarah (Roane) c. 1636-1670 BlmGWL
Davy, Woods 1949- WhoAmA 93, WhoWest 94
Davydov, Aleksandr Sergeivich 1912-1993 NewYTBS 93
Davydov, Gavriil Ivanovich 1784-1809 WhWE
Davydov, Yuri Vladimirovich 1924- IntWW 93
Davys, Mary 1674-1732 BlmGWL
Daw, Evelyn d1970 WhoHol 92
Daw, Harold John 1926- WhoAm 94
Daw, Marjorie d1979 WhoHol 92
Daw, Paul Curtis 1947- WhoAmL 94
Dawahare, Sandra Mendez 1950- WhoAmL 94
Dawalt, Kenneth Francis 1911- WhoAm 94
Dawbarn, Simon (Yelverton) 1923- Who 94
Dawber, Pam WhoAm 94
Dawber, Pam 1951- WhoHol 92
Dawber, Pam 1954- IntMPA 94
Dawda, Edward C. 1952- WhoAmL 94
Dawdy, David Russell 1926- WhoScEn 94
Dawdy, Doris Ostrander WhoAmA 93, WhoWest 94
Dawe, (Donald) Bruce 1930- WrDr 94
Dawe, Donovan Arthur 1915- Who 94
Dawe, Roger James 1941- Who 94
Dawes, Carol J. 1931- WhoAm 94
Dawes, Dennis William 1945- WhoAm 94
Dawes, Dominique Margaux 1976- WhoBlA 94
Dawes, Douglas Charles 1952- WhoWest 94
Dawes, Edna WrDr 94
Dawes, Edward Naasson 1914- WrDr 94
Dawes, Edwin Alfred 1925- Who 94
Dawes, Geoffrey Sharman 1918- IntWW 93, Who 94, WhoAm 94
Dawes, Michael Francis 1942- WhoAm 94, WhoAmL 94
Dawes, Paul H. 1945- WhoAm 94, WhoAmL 94
Dawes, Peter Spencer Who 94
Dawes, Robyn Mason 1936- WhoAm 94
Dawes, William 1745-1799 WhAmRev
Dawick, Viscount 1961- Who 94
Dawicki, Doloretta Diane 1956- WhoScEn 94
Dawid, Annie 1960- ConAu 141
Dawid, Igor Bert 1935- WhoAm 94, WhoScEn 94
Dawida, Michael Mathew 1949- WhoAmP 93
Dawidowicz, Lucy S 1915- WrDr 94
Dawidowicz, Lucy Schildkret 1915-1990 WhAm 10
Dawis, Rene V. 1928- WhoAm 94
Daw Khin Myo Chit 1915- BlmGWL
Dawkins, Andrew John 1950- WhoMW 93
Dawkins, Andy 1950- WhoAmP 93
Dawkins, Cecil DrAPF 93
Dawkins, Darryl 1957- BasBi, WhoBlA 94
Dawkins, David Michael 1948- WhoFI 94
Dawkins, Donald M. WhoAmP 93
Dawkins, Douglas Alfred 1927- Who 94
Dawkins, Harrill L. 1946- WhoAmP 93
Dawkins, Irma d1972 WhoHol 92
Dawkins, John Sydney 1947- IntWW 93, Who 94
Dawkins, Marva Phyllis 1948- WhoAm 94, WhoMW 93
Dawkins, Maurice Anderson 1921- WhoAm 94, WhoAmP 93
Dawkins, Michael James 1953- WhoBlA 94
Dawkins, Miller J. 1925- WhoAmP 93, WhoBlA 94
Dawkins, Paul d1979 WhoHol 92
Dawkins, Richard Who 94
Dawkins, Richard 1941- IntWW 93
Dawkins, (Clinton) Richard 1941- Who 94
Dawkins, Simon John Robert 1945- Who 94
Dawkins, Stan Barrington Bancroft 1933- WhoBlA 94
Dawkins, Stephen A. 1960- WhoBlA 94
Dawkins, Wayne J. 1955- WhoBlA 94
Dawkins, William Chester, Jr. 1933- WhoAmP 93
Dawkins, William Lee, Jr. 1960- WhoAmL 94
Dawlatabadi, Mahmud 1940- ConWorW 93
Dawley, Alan 1943- ConAu 140
Dawley, Donald Lee 1936- WhoFI 94, WhoMW 93
Dawley, Joseph William 1936- WhoAmA 93
Dawley, Melvin Emerson 1905-1989 WhAm 10
Daw Mi Mi Khaing 1916-1990 BlmGWL
Dawn, Clarence Ernest 1918- WhoAm 94
Dawn, Deborah WhoAm 94
Dawn, Dolly 1921- WhoHol 92
Dawn, Frederic Samuel 1916- WhoAm 94, WhoScEn 94
Dawn, Gloria d1978 WhoHol 92
Dawn, Hazel d1988 WhoHol 92
Dawn, Hazel, Jr. WhoHol 92
Dawn, Marpessa WhoHol 92
Dawnay Who 94
Dawood, Mohamed Yusoff 1943- WhoScEn 94
Dawood, Nessim Joseph 1927- Who 94
Daws, Joyce (Margaretta) 1925- Who 94
Daws, Russell Winston 1962- WhoFI 94
Daw San San BlmGWL
Dawson, Amos Council, III 1948- WhoAmL 94
Dawson, Andre Fernando 1954- WhoAm 94
Dawson, Andre Nolan 1954- WhoBlA 94
Dawson, Anthony 1916- WhoHol 92
Dawson, Anthony (Michael) 1928- Who 94
Dawson, Armetta K. 1938- WhoMW 93
Dawson, B. W. WhoBlA 94
Dawson, Bess Phipps WhoAmA 93
Dawson, Billy WhoHol 92
Dawson, Bobby H. WhoBlA 94
Dawson, Brian Robert 1947- WhoMW 93, WhoScEn 94
Dawson, Bruce Arnold 1959- WhoFI 94
Dawson, Carol 1945- WhoAmP 93
Dawson, Carol 1951- ConAu 141
Dawson, Carol Gene 1937- WhoAm 94, WhoAmP 93
Dawson, Chandler R. 1930- WhoScEn 94
Dawson, Charles 1864-1916 DcNaB MP
Dawson, (Henry) Christopher 1889-1970 DcNaB MP
Dawson, Craig NewYTBS 93 [port]
Dawson, Craig William 1956- WhoMW 93
Dawson, Curt d1985 WhoHol 92
Dawson, Daryl (Michael) 1933- Who 94
Dawson, David Eugene 1949- WhoMW 93
Dawson, Dennis Ray 1948- WhoAm 94, WhoAmL 94
Dawson, Donald Andrew 1937- WhoAm 94
Dawson, Donald H., Jr. 1949- WhoAmL 94
Dawson, Doris d1986 WhoHol 92
Dawson, Doug 1944- WhoAmA 93, WhoWest 94
Dawson, Earl Bliss 1930- WhoScEn 94
Dawson, Edward Joseph 1944- WhoFI 94
Dawson, Elizabeth 1930- WrDr 94
Dawson, Elizabeth Abbott 1924- WhoAmP 93
Dawson, Eric Emmanuel 1937- WhoAmP 93, WhoBlA 94
Dawson, Ernest 1882-1947 DcLB 140 [port]
Dawson, Eve WhoAmA 93N
Dawson, Fielding DrAPF 93
Dawson, Fielding 1930- DcLB 130 [port]
Dawson, Frances Emily 1952- WhoWest 94
Dawson, Frank d1953 WhoHol 92
Dawson, George Glenn 1925- WhoAm 94, WrDr 94
Dawson, Gerald Lee 1933- WhoScEn 94
Dawson, Geraldine 1951- WhoScEn 94
Dawson, Gilbert Edward, II 1945- WhoWest 94
Dawson, Glenn V. 1944- WhoAmP 93
Dawson, Hal K. d1987 WhoHol 92
Dawson, Hazel d1948 WhoHol 92
Dawson, Horace 1897- WhAm 10
Dawson, Horace Greeley, Jr. 1926- WhoAm 94, WhoBlA 94
Dawson, Howard A., Jr. 1922- CngDr 93
Dawson, Howard Athalone, Jr. 1922- WhoAm 94, WhoAmL 94
Dawson, Ian David 1934- Who 94
Dawson, Ivo d1934 WhoHol 92
Dawson, J. Steve 1949- WhoAmL 94
Dawson, James Ambrose 1937- WhoAm 94
Dawson, James Gordon 1916- Who 94
Dawson, James Linwood 1959- WhoBlA 94
Dawson, James Richard 1936- WhoMW 93
Dawson, Janis 1936- WrDr 94
Dawson, Jeffrey Robert 1941- WhoScEn 94
Dawson, Jennifer WrDr 94
Dawson, John Who 94
Dawson, John 1762-1814 WhAmRev
Dawson, (Edward) John 1935- Who 94
Dawson, John Alan 1944- Who 94
Dawson, John Alan 1946- WhoWest 94
Dawson, John Allan 1946- WhoAmA 93
Dawson, John Anthony Lawrence 1950- Who 94
Dawson, John Frederick 1930- WhoAm 94
Dawson, John H. 1921- WhoAmP 93
Dawson, John Hallam 1936- WhoFI 94
Dawson, John Howel 1944- WhoMW 93
Dawson, John Joseph 1947- WhoAm 94, WhoAmL 94
Dawson, John Leonard 1932- Who 94
Dawson, John Myrick 1930- WhoAm 94, WhoScEn 94
Dawson, John R. 1941- WhoAmL 94
Dawson, John William, Jr. 1920- WhoMW 93
Dawson, Keith Who 94
Dawson, (Archibald) Keith 1937- Who 94
Dawson, Larry Ross 1946- WhoMW 93
Dawson, Lawrence 1953- WhoWest 94
Dawson, Lawrence E. WhoBlA 94
Dawson, Leland Bradley 1950- WhoWest 94
Dawson, Len ProFbHF

Dawson, Leonard Ervin 1934- *WhoBlA 94*
Dawson, Les *WhoHol 92*
Dawson, Lin 1959- *WhoBlA 94*
Dawson, Linda 1949- *WrDr 94*
Dawson, Lumell Herbert 1934- *WhoBlA 94*
Dawson, Lynne 1956- *NewGrDO*
Dawson, Marion d1975 *WhoHol 92*
Dawson, Mark 1920- *WhoHol 92*
Dawson, Mark H. *WhoWest 94*
Dawson, Martha E. 1922- *WhoBlA 94*
Dawson, Martha Morgan 1908- *WhoWest 94*
Dawson, Mary Ruth 1931- *WhoAm 94*
Dawson, Matel, Jr. 1921- *WhoBlA 94*
Dawson, Maxine Virginia 1909- *WhoAmP 93*
Dawson, Melissa Jane 1963- *WhoWest 94*
Dawson, Michael *Who 94*
Dawson, (Hugh) Michael (Trevor) 1957- *Who 94*
Dawson, Mimi 1944- *WhoAm 94*
Dawson, Muriel 1956- *WhoAmP 93*
Dawson, Peter *Who 94*
Dawson, Peter 1929- *Who 94*
Dawson, Peter 1933- *Who 94*
Dawson, (Joseph) Peter 1940- *Who 94*
Dawson, Peter Edward 1931- *WhoBlA 94*
Dawson, Philip M. 1945- *WhoAmL 94*
Dawson, Ray Fields 1911- *WhoAm 94*
Dawson, Reginald Thomas 1930- *Who 94*
Dawson, Rex Malcolm Chaplin 1924- *Who 94*
Dawson, Rhett 1943- *WhoAmL 94*
Dawson, Richard 1932- *WhoHol 92*
Dawson, Richard Thomas 1945- *WhoAm 94*
Dawson, Robert Earle 1923- *WhoAm 94*
Dawson, Robert Edward 1918- *WhoBlA 94*
Dawson, Robert Kent 1946- *WhoAm 94, WhoAmP 93*
Dawson, Robert M. 1954- *WhoAmL 94*
Dawson, Robert Oscar 1939- *WhoAm 94*
Dawson, Roger 1940- *ConAu 142*
Dawson, Ronald d1984 *WhoHol 92*
Dawson, Samuel Cooper, Jr. 1909- *WhoAm 94*
Dawson, Sea-Flower White Cloud *DrAPF 93*
Dawson, Sidney L., Jr. 1920- *WhoBlA 94*
Dawson, Stephen Everette 1946- *WhoAm 94, WhoAmL 94*
Dawson, Stuart Owen 1935- *WhoAm 94*
Dawson, Suzanne Stockus 1941- *WhoAm 94*
Dawson, Theresa Marie 1959- *WhoWest 94*
Dawson, Thomas C. 1948- *WhoAmP 93*
Dawson, Thomas C., II 1948- *IntWW 93*
Dawson, Thomas Cleland, II 1948- *WhoAm 94*
Dawson, Thomas Cordner 1948- *Who 94*
Dawson, Thomas Thiel 1935- *WhoMW 93*
Dawson, Tom Henry 1937- *WhoAmP 93*
Dawson, Vicki *WhoHol 92*
Dawson, Wallace Douglas, Jr. 1931- *WhoAm 94, WhoScEn 94*
Dawson, Walter Lloyd 1902- *Who 94*
Dawson, Warren Hope 1939- *WhoBlA 94*
Dawson, Wilfred Thomas 1928- *WhoAm 94*
Dawson, William B. 1949- *WhoAmL 94*
Dawson, William John Richard Geoffrey Patrick 1926- *Who 94*
Dawson, William Ryan 1927- *WhoAm 94, WhoScEn 94*
Dawson, William Thomas, III 1943- *WhoAmP 93*
Dawson Boyd, Candy 1946- *WhoBlA 94*
Dawson-Damer *Who 94*
Dawson-Moray, Edward Bruce 1909- *Who 94*
Dawtry, Alan 1915- *Who 94*
Dax, Scott Louis 1959- *WhoScEn 94*
Daxon, Thomas Edward 1947- *WhoAmP 93*
Day, Agnes Adeline 1952- *WhoScEn 94*
Day, Aidan 1952- *WrDr 94*
Day, Alan Charles Lynn 1924- *Who 94*
Day, Alexandra *WrDr 94*
Day, Alexandra 1941- *WhoAm 94*
Day, Alice 1905- *WhoHol 92*
Day, Ann *WhoAmP 93, WhoWest 94*
Day, Anne W. 1926- *WhoMW 93*
Day, Anthony 1933- *WhoAm 94*
Day, Arthur Grove 1904- *WhoAm 94, WhoWest 94*
Day, Barry Leonard 1934- *WhoAm 94*
Day, Barton D. 1956- *WhoAmL 94*
Day, Bernard Maurice 1928- *Who 94*
Day, Bill 1955- *WhoAmP 93*
Day, Bradford M(arshall) 1916- *EncSF 93*
Day, Burnis Calvin 1940- *WhoAmA 93, WhoBlA 94*
Day, Castle Nason 1933- *WhoAm 94*
Day, Catherine-Ann 1942- *WhoAmP 93*
Day, Cecil LeRoy 1922- *WhoAm 94, WhoScEn 94*
Day, Charles Roger, Jr. 1947- *WhoAm 94*
Day, Chon 1907- *WhoAm 94, WhoAmA 93*
Day, Clint M. 1959- *WhoAmP 93*
Day, Colin Leslie 1944- *WhoAm 94*
Day, Connie J. 1949- *WhoAmP 93*
Day, Daniel Edgar 1913- *WhoAm 94, WhoBlA 94*
Day, David John 1932- *WhoWest 94*
Day, David Vivian 1936- *Who 94*
Day, (Stephen) Deforest 1941- *WrDr 94*
Day, Delbert Edwin 1936- *WhoAm 94, WhoScEn 94*
Day, Dennis d1988 *WhoHol 92*
Day, Dennis Gene 1936- *WhoAm 94, WhoWest 94*
Day, Dennis M. 1943- *WhoAmL 94*
Day, Derek (Malcolm) 1927- *IntWW 93, Who 94*
Day, Donald B(yrne) 1909-1978 *EncSF 93*
Day, Donald Joseph 1929- *WhoFI 94*
Day, Donald K. 1936- *WhoBlA 94*
Day, Donald Sheldon 1924- *WhoAm 94, WhoAmL 94*
Day, Doris 1924- *IntMPA 94, IntWW 93, WhoAm 94, WhoCom, WhoHol 92*
Day, Dorothy 1897-1980 *AmSocL, DcAmReB 2, HisWorL [port]*
Day, Douglas Henry 1943- *Who 94*
Day, Dulce d1954 *WhoHol 92*
Day, Edith d1971 *WhoHol 92*
Day, Edward C. 1932- *WrDr 94*
Day, Edward Francis, Jr. 1946- *WhoAm 94, WhoAmL 94*
Day, Emerson 1913- *WhoAm 94*
Day, Eric Therander 1952- *WhoBlA 94*
Day, Eugene Davis, Sr. 1925- *WhoAm 94*
Day, Frances 1908- *WhoHol 92*
Day, Fred L. 1937- *WhoAmP 93*
Day, Gary *WhoHol 92*
Day, Gary Lewis 1950- *WhoAmA 93*
Day, George Richard 1950- *WhoAm 94*
Day, Gerald W. *WhoFI 94*
Day, Graham *Who 94*
Day, (Judson) Graham 1933- *IntWW 93, Who 94*
Day, Helen Nevitt 1913- *WhoAmP 93*
Day, Holliday T. 1936- *WhoAmA 93*
Day, Horace Talmage 1909- *WhoAmA 93N*
Day, Howard Wilman 1942- *WhoAm 94*
Day, J. Edward 1914- *WhoAmP 93*
Day, James Edward 1914- *WhoAm 94, WhoAmL 94*
Day, James McAdam, Jr. 1948- *WhoAmL 94*
Day, James Milton 1931- *WhoAm 94*
Day, Janice Eldredge 1919- *WhoWest 94*
Day, Jennie D. 1921- *WhoAmP 93*
Day, Jerome Michael 1955- *WhoAmL 94*
Day, Jill d1990 *WhoHol 92*
Day, John *WhoHol 92*
Day, John 1574-1640 *BlmGEL*
Day, John 1932-1984 *WhoAmA 93N*
Day, John Arthur 1956- *WhoAmL 94*
Day, John Denton 1942- *WhoFI 94, WhoWest 94*
Day, John Francis 1920- *WhoAm 94*
Day, John Franklin 1928- *WhoAm 94*
Day, John Frederick 1938- *WhoAmL 94*
Day, John G. *WhoAmL 94*
Day, John H. 1952- *WhoAm 94, WhoScEn 94*
Day, John J. 1937- *WhoAmP 93*
Day, John King 1909- *Who 94*
Day, John Sidney 1917- *WhoAm 94*
Day, John W. 1933- *WhoAm 94*
Day, Joseph Dennis 1942- *WhoAm 94, WhoWest 94*
Day, Josette d1978 *WhoHol 92*
Day, Julian Charles 1952- *WhoWest 94*
Day, Juliette d1957 *WhoHol 92*
Day, Kathleen Patricia 1947- *WhoFI 94*
Day, Kevin Ross 1960- *WhoWest 94*
Day, L. B. 1944- *WhoWest 94*
Day, Lance Reginald 1927- *Who 94*
Day, (Gerald William) Langston 1894- *EncSF 93*
Day, Laraine 1917- *WhoHol 92*
Day, Laraine 1920- *IntMPA 94*
Day, Larry 1921- *WhoAmA 93*
Day, Leora Gregg 1937- *WhoAmP 93*
Day, LeRoy Edward 1925- *WhoAm 94*
Day, Lionel *EncSF 93*
Day, Lucienne 1917- *Who 94*
Day, Lucille *DrAPF 93*
Day, Lucille Elizabeth 1947- *WhoScEn 94, WhoWest 94*
Day, Lyn Tibbits 1935- *WhoMW 93*
Day, Lynda *WhoHol 92*
Day, Mabel K. 1884- *WhoAmA 93N*
Day, Marceline 1907- *WhoHol 92*
Day, Marie L. d1939 *WhoHol 92*
Day, Marilyn Lee 1949- *WhoWest 94*
Day, Mary *WhoAm 94*
Day, Mary Jane Thomas 1927- *WhoAm 94, WhoScEn 94*
Day, Maurice Jerome 1913- *WhoAm 94*
Day, Melvin Sherman 1923- *WhoAm 94, WhoFI 94, WhoScEn 94*
Day, Michael (John) 1933- *Who 94*
Day, Michael Herbert 1927- *WrDr 94*
Day, Morris 1957- *WhoBlA 94, WhoHol 92*
Day, Neil (Atherton) 1945- *ConAu 140*
Day, Neil McPherson 1935- *WhoFI 94*
Day, Nicholas Edward 1939- *Who 94*
Day, Paul Richard 1922- *WhoAm 94*
Day, Peter 1938- *IntWW 93, Who 94*
Day, Peter Rodney 1928- *IntWW 93, Who 94, WhoScEn 94*
Day, Phyllis Arlene 1961- *WhoMW 93*
Day, Pietrina Ann 1943- *WhoWest 94*
Day, Richard d1973 *WhoHol 92*
Day, Richard 1896-1972 *IntDcF 2-4*
Day, Richard Cortez *DrAPF 93*
Day, Richard Earl 1929- *WhoAmL 94*
Day, Richard Edward 1960- *WhoWest 94*
Day, Richard Erwin 1933- *WhoAmL 94*
Day, Richard H. 1937- *WhoAmP 93*
Day, Richard Lawrence 1905-1989 *WhAm 10*
Day, Richard Putnam 1930- *WhoAm 94*
Day, Richard Somers 1928- *WhoWest 94*
Day, Robert *DrAPF 93*
Day, Robert 1922- *ConTFT 11, IntMPA 94*
Day, Robert Androus 1924- *WhoAm 94*
Day, Robert Dwain, Jr. 1950- *WhoAm 94*
Day, Robert Edgar 1919- *WhoAm 94*
Day, Robert Hugh 1952- *WhoWest 94*
Day, Robert Michael 1950- *WhoScEn 94*
Day, Robert P 1941- *WrDr 94*
Day, Robert Winsor 1930- *WhoAm 94, WhoScEn 94, WhoWest 94*
Day, Robin 1915- *Who 94*
Day, Robin 1923- *IntWW 93, Who 94*
Day, Robin, Sir 1923- *WrDr 94*
Day, Roger F. 1929- *WhoAm 94*
Day, Roland B. 1919- *WhoAmP 93*
Day, Roland Bernard 1919- *WhoAm 94, WhoAmL 94*
Day, Ronald Elwin 1933- *WhoFI 94*
Day, Ronald Richard 1934- *WhoFI 94*
Day, Russell Clover 1943- *WhoFI 94*
Day, Russell R. *WhoAmP 93*
Day, Shannon d1977 *WhoHol 92*
Day, Simon James 1935- *Who 94*
Day, Stacey B. 1927- *WrDr 94*
Day, Stacey Biswas 1927- *WhoAm 94, WhoScEn 94*
Day, Stephen Martin 1931- *WhoAm 94*
Day, Stephen Nicholas 1947- *Who 94*
Day, Stephen Peter 1938- *Who 94*
Day, Stephen Richard 1948- *Who 94*
Day, Steven M. 1960- *WhoFI 94*
Day, Stuart Reid 1959- *WhoAmL 94*
Day, Thomas Brennock 1932- *WhoAm 94, WhoWest 94*
Day, Todd F. 1970- *WhoBlA 94*
Day, Vera 1939- *WhoHol 92*
Day, Walter M., Sr. 1917- *WhoAmP 93*
Day, Weston S. 1945- *WhoIns 94*
Day, William Charles, Jr. 1937- *WhoBlA 94*
Day, William Hudson 1937- *WhoAm 94*
Day, Worden 1916-1986 *WhoAmA 93N*
Dayal, Rajeshwar 1909- *WrDr 94*
Dayal, Sandeep 1960- *WhoScEn 94*
Dayal, Vijay Shanker 1936- *WhoMW 93*
Dayal, Vinay 1950- *WhoScEn 94*
Dayala, Haji Farooq 1948- *WhoWest 94*
Dayan, Assaf 1945- *WhoHol 92*
Dayan, Moshe 1915-1981 *HisWorL [port]*
Dayan, Rodney S. 1933- *WhoAm 94, WhoAmL 94*
Dayananda, Mysore Ananthamurthy 1934- *WhoAm 94*
Dayanim, Farangis *WhoScEn 94*
Dayao, Firmo Salvador 1949- *WhoAsA 94*
Dayday, Henry *WhoWest 94*
Dayde, Liane 1932- *IntDcB [port]*
Daye, Charles Edward 1944- *WhoAmL 94, WhoBlA 94*
Daye, Darren 1960- *WhoBlA 94*
Daye, Walter O. 1918- *WhoBlA 94*
Day-Gowder, Patricia Joan 1936- *WhoWest 94*
Daykarhanova, Tamara d1980 *WhoHol 92*
Daykin, Christopher David 1948- *Who 94*
Day Lewis, Cecil 1904-1972 *BlmGEL*
Day-Lewis, Daniel *IntWW 93*
Day-Lewis, Daniel 1957- *IntMPA 94, WhoAm 94, WhoHol 92*
Day-Lewis, Sean 1931- *Who 94*
Day-Lewis, Sean (Francis) 1931- *WrDr 94*
Day-Lyon, Karen 1951- *WhoWest 94*
Daynard, Richard Alan 1943- *WhoAmL 94*
Daynes, Raymond Austin *WhoScEn 94*
Days, Drew S., III 1941- *WhoAm 94, WhoAmL 94*
Days, Drew Saunders, III 1941- *WhoAmP 93, WhoBlA 94*
Days, Michael Irvin 1953- *WhoBlA 94*
Days, Rosetta Hill *WhoBlA 94*
Days, Virginia Mae *WhoHisp 94*
Dayson, Rodney Andrew 1964- *WhoScEn 94*
Dayton, Bruce McLean 1934- *WhoIns 94*
Dayton, Danny *WhoHol 92*
Dayton, David *DrAPF 93*
Dayton, Deane Kraybill 1949- *WhoScEn 94*
Dayton, Douglas Emory 1951- *WhoWest 94*
Dayton, Elias 1737-1807 *AmRev, WhAmRev*
Dayton, Frank d1924 *WhoHol 92*
Dayton, Irene *DrAPF 93*
Dayton, John Thomas, Jr. 1955- *WhoScEn 94*
Dayton, Jonathan 1760-1824 *WhAmRev*
Dayton, June *WhoHol 92*
Dayton, Lyman D. 1941- *IntMPA 94*
Dayton, Mark *WhoAmP 93*
Dayton, Richard Lee 1934- *WhoAm 94*
Dayton, Robert D. 1944- *WhoAmL 94*
Dayton, Samuel Grey, Jr. 1921- *WhoAm 94*
Daza, Pedro 1925- *IntWW 93*
Dazai Osamu 1909-1948 *RfGShF*
Daze, Mercedes d1945 *WhoHol 92*
Dazey, William Boyd 1915- *WhoAm 94*
Dazie, Mlle. d1952 *WhoHol 92*
D'Azzo, John Joachim 1919- *WhoAm 94*
DCamp, Kathryn Acker 1956- *WhoFI 94, WhoMW 93*
D'Costa, Jean 1937- *BlmGWL*
D'Cruz, Jonathan 1963- *WhoScEn 94*
D. D. R. O. 1922- *WrDr 94*
De, Sukla *WhoWest 94*
De, Suranjan 1954- *WhoAsA 94*
Dea, David Young Fong 1924- *WhoFI 94*
Deacon, Brian 1949- *WhoHol 92*
Deacon, David Emmerson 1949- *WhoAm 94*
Deacon, Eric *WhoHol 92*
Deacon, Henry 1822-1876 *DcNaB MP*
Deacon, John C. 1920- *WhoAmL 94*
Deacon, Keith Vivian 1935- *Who 94*
Deacon, Paul Septimus 1922- *WhoAm 94*
Deacon, Richard d1984 *WhoHol 92*
Deacon, Richard 1911- *WrDr 94*
Deacon, Robert Thomas 1944- *WhoWest 94*
Deacon Elliott, Robert 1914- *Who 94*
de Acosta, Alejandro Daniel 1941- *WhoAm 94*
Deacy, Thomas Edward, Jr. 1918- *WhoAm 94, WhoAmL 94*
Deaderick, Joseph 1930- *WhoAmA 93*
Deadman, Leonard John 1932- *WhoAm 94*
Deadrich, Paul Eddy 1925- *WhoAmL 94, WhoWest 94*
Deagle, Edwin Augustus, Jr. 1937- *WhoAm 94*
Deagon, Ann *DrAPF 93*
De Aguiar, Ricardo Jorge Frutuoso 1963- *WhoScEn 94*
De Ahna(-Strauss), Pauline 1863-1950 *NewGrDO*
Deak, Charles Karol 1928- *WhoMW 93, WhoScEn 94*
Deak, Istvan 1926- *WhoAm 94, WrDr 94*
Deak, Michael S. *WhoHol 92*
Deak, Peter 1952- *WhoScEn 94*
Deak, Tibor 1935- *WhoScEn 94*
Deakin, Edward B. 1943- *WhoAm 94*
Deakin, Michael 1939- *Who 94*
Deakin, Nicholas Dampier 1936- *Who 94*
Deakin, William 1913- *Who 94*
Deakin, (Frederick) William, Sir 1913- *WrDr 94*
Deakin, (Frederick) William (Dampier) *Who 94*
Deakins, Eric Petro 1932- *Who 94*
Deakins, Lucy 1971- *WhoHol 92*
Deakins, Roger 1949- *IntMPA 94*
Deaktor, Darryl Barnett 1942- *WhoAm 94*
Deal, Borden 1922-1985 *BlkWr 2, ConAu 43NR*
Deal, Bruce Elmer 1927- *WhoAm 94*
Deal, Ernest Linwood, Jr. 1929- *WhoAm 94*
Deal, George Edgar 1920- *WhoAm 94, WhoFI 94*
Deal, Gregory R. 1941- *WhoAmL 94*
Deal, J. Nathan 1942- *WhoAmP 93*
Deal, Jo Anne McCoy 1953- *WhoScEn 94*
Deal, Joe 1947- *WhoAmA 93*
Deal, Joseph Maurice 1947- *WhoAm 94*
Deal, Lynn Eaton Hoffmann 1953- *WhoWest 94*
Deal, Nathan 1942- *CngDr 93, WhoAm 94*
Deal, Pamela Ellis 1950- *WhoAmL 94*
Deal, Susan Strayer *DrAPF 93*
Deal, Terrance E. 1939- *WrDr 94*
Deal, Terry Dean 1948- *WhoWest 94*

Deal, Timothy 1940- WhoAm 94
Deal, W. P. d1955 WhoHol 92
Deal, W. W. 1936- WhoAmP 93
Deal, William Thomas 1949- WhoMW 93
Dealaman, Doris W. 1919- WhoAmP 93
De Alba, Marlys Ann 1956- WhoHisp 94
De Alba-Avila, Abraham 1955- WhoScEn 94
DeAlessandro, Joseph Paul 1930- WhoAm 94, WhoFI 94
de Almeida, Acacio 1938- IntDcF 2-4
De Almeida, Antonio IntWW 93
De Almeida, Antonio Castro Mendes 1934- WhoScEn 94
De Almeida, Joaquim 1957- WhoHol 92
Dealtry, (Thomas) Richard 1936- Who 94
Dealy, Catherine Ann 1949- WhoMW 93
Dealy, John Francis 1939- WhoAm 94
Dealy, John Michael 1937- WhoAm 94
Deam, Connie M. 1952- WhoMW 93
Deamer, Bartley C. 1945- WhoAmL 94
Deamer, Dulcie 1890-1972 BlmGWL
Deamer, (Mary Elizabeth Kathleen) Dulcie 1890-1972 EncSF 93
De Amicis, Anna Lucia c. 1733-1816 NewGrDO
Dean Who 94
Dean, Alan Loren 1918- WhoAm 94
Dean, Alberta LaVaun 1925- WhoMW 93
Dean, Allison WhoHol 92
Dean, Anabel 1915- WrDr 94
Dean, Anne Who 94
Dean, Antony Musgrave 1921- IntWW 93
Dean, Arthur 1898-1987 HisDcKW
Dean, Arthur Truman 1946- AfrAmG
Dean, Barney d1954 WhoHol 92
Dean, Basil d1978 WhoHol 92
Dean, Basil 1888-1978 IntDcF 2-4
Dean, Beale 1922- WhoAm 94, WhoAmL 94
Dean, Beryl 1911- WrDr 94
Dean, Bill Verlin, Jr. 1957- WhoAmL 94
Dean, Billy 1967- WhoAm 94
Dean, Bradley P. 1954- ConAu 141
Dean, Britten 1935- WhoWest 94
Dean, Burton Victor 1924- WhoAm 94
Dean, Carol Carlson 1944- WhoAmP 93
Dean, Carolynn Leslie 1952- WhoWest 94
Dean, Charles Henry, Jr. 1925- WhoAm 94
Dean, Charles R., Jr. 1949- WhoAmL 94
Dean, Charles Thomas 1918- WhoAm 94
Dean, Clara Russell 1927- WhoBlA 94
Dean, Cleon Eugene 1957- WhoScEn 94
Dean, Dallas, Jr. 1947- WhoAmP 93
Dean, Daniel R. 1941- WhoBlA 94
Dean, David Allen 1948- WhoAm 94, WhoAmL 94
Dean, David Edis 1922- Who 94
Dean, Dearest 1911- WhoAm 94
Dean, Denis Allen 1942- WhoAmL 94
Dean, Diane D. 1949- WhoBlA 94
Dean, Dinky WhoHol 92
Dean, Donald W. WhoAmP 93
Dean, Douglas C. WhoAmP 93
Dean, Dwight Gantz 1918- WhAm 10
Dean, E. Joseph 1949- WhoAm 94, WhoAmL 94
Dean, Eddie 1907- IntMPA 94, WhoHol 92
Dean, Elinor ConAu 142, SmATA 75
Dean, Eric Walter d1993 Who 94N
Dean, Ernest H. 1914- WhoAmP 93
Dean, Ernest Wilfrid WhoAmA 93N
Dean, Fabian d1971 WhoHol 92
Dean, Felicity WhoHol 92
Dean, Francis Hill 1922- WhoAm 94
Dean, Frank Warren, Jr. 1954- WhoScEn 94
Dean, Gary Edward 1950- WhoMW 93
Dean, Gary Neal 1953- WhoScEn 94
Dean, Geoffrey 1940- WhoAm 94
Dean, George Alden 1929- WhoAm 94
Dean, George R. 1933- WhoAmP 93
Dean, George W., Jr. d1993 NewYTBS 93
Dean, Hannah WhoHol 92
Dean, (Frederick) Harold 1908- Who 94
Dean, Harvey Ray 1943- WhoFI 94
Dean, Helen d1930 WhoHol 92
Dean, Henry Lamar 1938- WhoAmP 93
Dean, Howard 1948- WhoAm 94
Dean, Howard B. 1948- WhoAmP 93
Dean, Howard M., Jr. 1937- WhoAm 94, WhoFI 94
Dean, Isabel 1918- WhoHol 92
Dean, Ivor d1964 WhoHol 92
Dean, J. Thomas 1933- WhoAmL 94, WhoAmP 93
Dean, Jack d1950 WhoHol 92
Dean, Jack Pearce 1931- WhoAm 94
Dean, James d1955 WhoHol 92
Dean, James 1931- WhoAmA 93
Dean, James B. 1941- WhoAm 94
Dean, James Edward 1944- WhoBlA 94
Dean, Jean WhoHol 92
Dean, Jeffrey David 1960- WhoFI 94
Dean, Jimmy 1928- IntMPA 94, WhoAm 94, WhoHol 92
Dean, John Aurie 1921- WhoAm 94, WhoScEn 94
Dean, John Francis 1946- WhoScEn 94
Dean, John Francis 1950- WhoMW 93
Dean, John Gunther 1926- IntWW 93, WhoAm 94, WhoAmP 93
Dean, John Wilson, Jr. 1918- WhoAm 94
Dean, Joseph (Jolyon) 1921- Who 94
Dean, Julia d1952 WhoHol 92
Dean, Katharine Mary Hope Who 94
Dean, Laura 1963- WhoHol 92
Dean, Laura Ann 1958- WhoMW 93
Dean, Leslie Alan 1940- WhoAm 94
Dean, Loren 1967- WhoHol 92
Dean, Loren 1969- ConTFT 11
Dean, Louis d1933 WhoHol 92
Dean, Lydia Margaret Carter 1919- WhoAm 94
Dean, Mal 1941-1974 EncSF 93
Dean, Man Mountain d1953 WhoHol 92
Dean, Margia WhoHol 92
Dean, Margo 1927- WhoAm 94
Dean, Martyn EncSF 93
Dean, May d1937 WhoHol 92
Dean, Michael 1938- Who 94
Dean, Michael Anthony 1942- WhoWest 94
Dean, Michael M. 1933- WhoAm 94
Dean, Morris Jonathan 1931- WhoAm 94
Dean, Morton 1935- IntMPA 94
Dean, Nancy Ann 1959- WhoFI 94
Dean, Nat(alie Carol) 1956- WhoAmA 93
Dean, Nathan 1934- WhoAmP 93
Dean, Nelson d1923 WhoHol 92
Dean, Nicholas Brice 1933- WhoAmA 93
Dean, Norman Emerson 1943- WhoFI 94
Dean, Patrick (Henry) 1909- Who 94
Dean, Patrick Henry 1909- IntWW 93
Dean, Paul 1933- Who 94
Dean, Paul John 1941- WhoAm 94
Dean, Paul Regis 1918- WhoAm 94
Dean, Peter 1934-1993 NewYTBS 93
Dean, Peter 1939- WhoAmA 93
Dean, Peter Henry 1939- Who 94
Dean, Phillip Hayes ConDr 93, WrDr 94
Dean, Priscilla d1987 WhoHol 92
Dean, Raymond Who 94
Dean, (Charles) Raymond 1923- Who 94
Dean, Richard Albert 1924- WhoWest 94
Dean, Richard Anthony 1935- WhoScEn 94
Dean, Robert Bruce 1949- WhoScEn 94
Dean, Robert Charles 1903- WhoAm 94
Dean, Robert Charles, Jr. 1928- WhoAm 94
Dean, Roger 1944- EncSF 93
Dean, Roger Alan 1947- WhoAmP 93
Dean, Ron WhoHol 92
Dean, Ronald Glenn 1944- WhoAmL 94
Dean, Roy Who 94
Dean, (Cecil) Roy 1927- Who 94
Dean, S. F. X. WrDr 94
Dean, Shelley 1907- WrDr 94
Dean, Sidney Walter, Jr. 1905- WhoAm 94
Dean, Stafford (Roderick) 1937- NewGrDO
Dean, Stafford Roderick 1937- IntWW 93
Dean, Stanley Rochelle 1908- WhoAm 94
Dean, Stephen Odell 1936- WhoAm 94
Dean, Thomas Scott 1924- WhoAm 94
Dean, Vicky Charlene 1949- WhoMW 93
Dean, Vyvyan Coleman 1945- WhoBlA 94
Dean, Wally WhoHol 92
Dean, Walter Clark 1898- WhAm 10
Dean, Walter R., Jr. 1934- WhoBlA 94
Dean, Walter Raleigh, Jr. 1934- WhoAmP 93
Dean, Wanda Luther 1948- WhoAmP 93
Dean, William 1907- WorESoc [port]
Dean, William Denard 1937- WrDr 94
Dean, William Evans 1930- WhoAm 94
Dean, William F. 1899-1981 HisDcKW
Dean, William George 1921- WhoAm 94
Dean, Willie B. 1951- WhoBlA 94
Dean, Winton (Basil) 1916- NewGrDO, Who 94
Dean, Winton Basil 1916- IntWW 93
De Anda, Arnold 1946- WhoHisp 94
DeAnda, James 1925- WhoAm 94, WhoAmL 94, WhoHisp 94
De Anda, Mike d1988 WhoHol 92
DeAnda, Peter 1938- WhoBlA 94
De Anda, Raul WhoHisp 94
De Andino, Jean-Pierre M. 1946- WhoAmA 93
De Andrade, Fernando Freyre d1946 WhoHol 92
De Andrade, Francisco NewGrDO
DeAndrea, William L(ouis) 1952- WrDr 94
Deane Who 94
Deane, Basil 1928- Who 94
Deane, Debbe 1950- WhoWest 94
Deane, Doris d1974 WhoHol 92
Deane, Grant Biden 1961- WhoScEn 94
Deane, Herbert Andrew 1921-1991 WhAm 10
Deane, Horace Albert, Jr. 1940- WhoMW 93
Deane, James Garner 1923- WhoAm 94
Deane, James Richard 1935- WhoAm 94
Deane, John Herbert 1952- WhoScEn 94
Deane, Lyttleton Nicholas 1954- WhoAmL 94
Deane, Morgan R. 1922- WhoBlA 94
Deane, Palmer d1990 WhoHol 92
Deane, Phyllis Mary 1918- IntWW 93, Who 94
Deane, Ralph d1955 WhoHol 92
Deane, Richard d1977 WhoHol 92
Deane, Richard fl. 1647-1696 DcNaB MP
Deane, Robert Armistead 1919- WhoBlA 94
Deane, Robert Donald 1936- WhoAmP 93
Deane, Seamus (Francis) 1940- ConAu 42NR
Deane, Seamus Francis 1940- IntWW 93
Deane, Shirley d1983 WhoHol 92
Deane, Silas 1737-1789 AmRev, WhAmRev [port]
Deane, Thomas Andersen 1921- WhoAm 94
Deane, William (Patrick) Who 94
Deane-Drummond, Anthony (John) 1917- WrDr 94
Deane-Drummond, Anthony John 1917- Who 94
Deaner, R. Milton 1924- WhoAm 94
Deangelis, Aldo A. 1931- WhoAmP 93, WhoMW 93
de Angelis, Angela 1952- WrDr 94
DeAngelis, Catherine D. 1940- WhoScEn 94
De Angelis, Gina WhoHol 92
deAngelis, Jacqueline DrAPF 93
De Angelis, Jefferson d1933 WhoHol 92
DeAngelis, John Louis, Jr. 1951- WhoAmL 94
DeAngelis, Joseph 1946- WhoAmP 93
DeAngelis, Joseph Rocco 1938- WhoAmA 93
DeAngelis, Lisa Marie 1955- WhoScEn 94
De Angelis, Nazzareno 1881-1962 NewGrDO
DeAngelis, Thomas P. 1951- WhoScEn 94
DeAngelis, William Martin 1929- WhoAmP 93
DeAngelo, Anthony James 1956- WhoMW 93
De Angelo, George Washington, Jr. 1945- WhoFI 94
DeAngelo, Robert Carmen 1951- WhoMW 93
DeAngelus, Ronald Patrick 1935- WhoAmL 94
Deano, Edward J., Jr. 1952- WhoAmP 93
Dean Of Beswick, Baron 1922- Who 94
Dean Of Harptree, Baron 1924- Who 94
Dean Of Thornton-Le-Fylde, Baroness 1943 Who 94
Deanovich, Connie DrAPF 93
Deans, David Henry 1954- WhoWest 94
Deans, Herbert d1967 WhoHol 92
Deans, Rodger William 1917- Who 94
De Antoni, Edward Paul 1941- WhoAm 94
Dean-Zubritsky, Cynthia Marian 1950- WhoAm 94
De Aparicio, Vibiana Chamberlin DrAPF 93
Dear, Geoffrey James 1937- Who 94
Dear, Homer 1930- WhoAmP 93
Dear, Nick 1955- ConDr 93
Dear, Noach 1953- WhoAmP 93
de Aragón, Ray John 1946- WhoHisp 94
De Araugo, Tess (S.) 1930- WrDr 94
De Araugo-O'Mullane, Tess 1930- WrDr 94
De Araujo, Joao Gomes NewGrDO
Dearbaugh, Wesley N. 1952- WhoFI 94
Dearborn, Bruce Burritt 1949- WhoMW 93
Dearborn, Henry 1751-1829 AmRev, WhAmRev
Dearborn, Keith W. 1944- WhoAmL 94
Dearborn, Mary V. 1955- ConAu 142
Dearborn, Robert D. 1949- WhoAmL 94
Dearborn, Robert Wesley 1911- WhoAmP 93
de Arce, Carmen 1952- WhoHisp 94
Dearden, James 1949- IntMPA 94, WrDr 94
Dearden, James Shackley 1931- WrDr 94
Deardorf, David A. 1937- WhoWest 94
Deardorff, John Milton, Jr. 1935- WhoMW 93
Deardorff, Michael Kent 1949- WhoIns 94
Deardourff, John D. 1933- WhoAm 94
Deare, Jennifer Laurie 1952- WhoAm 94
de Arechaga, Eduardo Jimenez IntWW 93
Dearhammer, William Gregory 1934- WhoMW 93
Dearholt, Ashton d1942 WhoHol 92
Dearie, John C. 1940- WhoAmP 93
Dearie, Raymond J. 1944- WhoAm 94, WhoAmL 94
Dearin, Ray Dean 1941- WhoAmP 93
Dearing, Dorothy d1965 WhoHol 92
Dearing, Edgar d1974 WhoHol 92
Dearing, Robert M. 1935- WhoAmP 93
Dearing, Ronald (Ernest) 1930- Who 94
Dearing, Ronald Ernest 1930- IntWW 93
Dearing, Thomas Clyde 1946- WhoAmL 94
Dearing, Vinton Adams 1920- WhoAm 94
Dearing, William Ray 1963- WhoAmL 94
Dearington, Michael 1942- WhoAmL 94
Dearli, Bruno d1950 WhoHol 92
Dearly, Max d1943 WhoHol 92
Dearman, Henry Hursell 1934- WhoAm 94
Dearman, John Edward 1931- WhoBlA 94
de Armas, Frederick A. 1945- WhoHisp 94
De Armas, Frederick Alfred 1945- WhoAm 94
De Armas, Jorge Benito 1931- WhoHisp 94
de Armas, Luis A. 1952- WhoAmL 94, WhoHisp 94
Dearmer, Geoffrey 1893- EncSF 93
Dearmin, Vauda Lewis 1947- WhoAmP 93
DeArmitt, Walter Henry 1946- WhoMW 93
DeArmon, Shari Kathryn 1961- WhoAmL 94
Dearmon, Thomas Alfred 1937- WhoFI 94
De Armond, Dale B. WhoAmA 93
DeArmond, M. Keith 1935- WhoWest 94
Dearmore, Thomas Lee 1927- WhoAm 94
Dearnaley, Geoffrey 1930- Who 94
Dearnley, Christopher Hugh 1930- IntWW 93, Who 94
Dearth, Jeffrey L. 1950- WhoAm 94
Deas, Larry 1945- WhoBlA 94
Dease, Bobby d1958 WhoHol 92
Dease, John d1979 WhoHol 92
Deason, Edward Joseph 1955- WhoAmL 94
Deason, Herold McClure 1942- WhoAmL 94
Deason, Jonathan P. 1948- WhoScEn 94
De Assis, Auricelia Freitas 1958- WhoWomW 91
Deasy, Austin 1936- IntWW 93
Deasy, Cornelius Michael 1918- WhoAm 94
Deasy, Donald Wayne 1938- WhoWest 94
Deasy, John Berchmans 1911- WhoWest 94
Deasy, Kevin 1953- WhoAmL 94
Deasy, Theresa 1958- WhoFI 94, WhoMW 93
Deasy, William John 1937- WhoAm 94
Deatherage, Junior Lee 1940- WhoAmP 93
Deatherage, Philip Roy 1948- WhoWest 94
Deatherage, Scott Dean 1961- WhoAmL 94
Deatherage, William Vernon 1927- WhoAmL 94
Deathridge, John (William) 1944- NewGrDO, WrDr 94
DeAtley, James Harry WhoAmL 94
Deaton, Angus Stewart 1945- WhoAm 94
Deaton, Charles M. 1931- WhoAmP 93
Deaton, Dianne Lynne 1967- WhoMW 93
Deaton, John Earl 1949- WhoScEn 94
Deaton, Lewis Edward 1949- WhoScEn 94
Deaton, Robert Lester 1936- WhoWest 94
Deaton, Timothy Lee 1951- WhoScEn 94
Deaton, William Weldon, Jr. 1930- WhoAmL 94
Deatrick, David Ross, Jr. 1958- WhoAmL 94
Deats, James Lawton 1948- WhoFI 94
Deats, Margaret 1942- WhoAmA 93
Deats, Paul Kindred, Jr. 1918- WhoAm 94
Deats, Richard L 1932- WrDr 94
D'Eau, Jean 1944- WrDr 94
D'eaubonne, Jean 1903-1970 IntDcF 2-4
De Aubry, Diane d1969 WhoHol 92
Deaux, George DrAPF 93
Deave, John James 1928- Who 94
Deaver, Darwin Holloway 1914- WhoAm 94
Deaver, E. Allen 1935- WhoAm 94, WhoFI 94
Deaver, Julie Reece 1953- TwCYAW
Deaver, Michael Keith 1938- WhoAm 94
Deaver, Phillip Lester 1952- WhoAmL 94, WhoFI 94, WhoWest 94
Deavers, Karl Alan 1934- WhoAm 94
Deaves, Ada d1920 WhoHol 92
De Azevedo, Lorenco 1958- WhoHisp 94
Deb, Arun Kumar 1936- WhoAsA 94
Deb, Satyen K. 1932- WhoWest 94
DeBacco, R. DrAPF 93
De Baer, Jean WhoHol 92
De Baets, Marc Hubert 1950- WhoScEn 94
DeBaker, Brian Glenn 1961- WhoScEn 94

DeBakey, Ernest George 1912- *WhoAm 94*
DeBakey, Lois *WhoAm 94*
DeBakey, Michael Ellis 1908- *IntWW 93, Who 94, WhoAm 94, WhoScEn 94, WrDr 94*
DeBakey, Selma *WhoAm 94*
De Bankole, Isaach 1956- *WhoHol 92*
De Banzie, Brenda d1981 *WhoHol 92*
de Banzie, Lois *WhoHol 92*
deBarbadillo, John Joseph 1942- *WhoAm 94*
DeBard, Roger 1941- *WhoFI 94, WhoWest 94*
De Bardeleben, Arthur 1918- *WhoAm 94*
DeBardeleben, Henry Fairchild 1840-1910 *EncABHB 9 [port]*
DeBardeleben, John Thomas, Jr. 1926- *WhoAm 94*
DeBari, Vincent Anthony 1946- *WhoScEn 94*
DeBarr, John R. 1920- *WhoAmL 94*
De Barras, Louis *WhAmRev*
deBarros, Leonard G. *WhoHisp 94*
DeBartolo, Edward J., Sr. 1919- *WhoAm 94, WhoFI 94, WhoMW 93*
DeBartolo, Edward John, Jr. 1946- *WhoAm 94, WhoMW 93, WhoWest 94*
DeBartolo, Jack, Jr. 1938- *WhoAm 94*
de Bary, Paul Ambrose 1946- *WhoAmL 94*
de Bary, William Theodore 1919- *WhoAm 94*
Debas, Haile T. 1937- *WhoAm 94, WhoBlA 94, WhoScEn 94, WhoWest 94*
De Basil, Wassily 1888-1951 *IntDcB*
De Bassini, Achille 1819-1881 *NewGrDO*
de Basto, Gerald Arthur 1924- *Who 94*
DeBat, Donald Joseph 1944- *WhoAm 94*
DeBaun, Burt 1922- *WhoAmP 93*
De Bayser, Clotilde *WhoHol 92*
Debbasch, Charles 1937- *IntWW 93*
deBear, Richard Stephen 1933- *WhoFI 94, WhoMW 93*
DeBeary, Herberth H., Sr. *WhoAmP 93*
De Beaumont, Etienne 1883-1956 *IntDcB*
de Beauregard, Georges 1920-1984 *IntDcF 2-4*
Debeaussaert, Kenneth Joseph 1954- *WhoAmP 93*
de Beauvior, Simone (Lucie Ernestine Marie Bertrand) 1908-1986 *EncEth*
De Beauvoir, Simone 1908-1986 *BlmGEL, BlmGWL*
De Beauvolers, Maj. J. J. d1960 *WhoHol 92*
Debeche, Jamila *BlmGWL*
De Beck, Billy d1942 *WhoHol 92*
De Becker, Harold d1947 *WhoHol 92*
De Becker, Marie d1946 *WhoHol 92*
de Beer, Sam 1944- *IntWW 93*
De Beer, Zacharias Johannes 1928- *IntWW 93*
De Begnis, Giuseppe *NewGrDO*
Debele, Gary Alan 1962- *WhoAmL 94*
De Bell, Kristine *WhoHol 92*
DeBella Bodley, Sandra Anne 1943- *WhoAm 94*
de Bellaigue, Eric 1931- *WhoAm 94*
de Bellaigue, Geoffrey 1931- *Who 94*
De Belleville, Frederic d1923 *WhoHol 92*
DeBello, Marguerite Catherine 1964- *WhoMW 93*
de Belloy, Geoffrey L. 1936- *WhoFI 94*
De Benedetti, Carlo 1934- *IntWW 93, Who 94*
Debenedetti, Pablo Gaston 1953- *WhoScEn 94*
De Benedictis, Dario 1918- *WhoAm 94*
Debenham, Gilbert Ridley 1906- *Who 94*
Debenham, Ray Gene 1935- *WhoFI 94, WhoWest 94*
Debenham Taylor, John 1920- *Who 94*
De Benko, Eugene 1917- *WhoAm 94*
De Benning, Burr *WhoHol 92*
de Bergerac, Cyrano *EncSF 93*
DeBernardo, Pasquale Frank 1940- *WhoAmP 93*
de Bernieres, Louis 1954- *WrDr 94*
de Berniere-Smart, Reginald Piers Alexander 1924- *Who 94*
DeBerry, Arthur St. Clair 1929- *WhoFI 94*
DeBerry, Dennis Charles 1932- *WhoAmL 94*
Deberry, Lois *WhoWomW 91*
DeBerry, Lois M. 1945- *WhoAmP 93*
DeBerry, Lois Marie 1945- *WhoBlA 94*
Debevec, Paul Timothy 1946- *WhoMW 93*
DeBevoise, Charles Henry 1958- *WhoAmL 94*
Debevoise, Dickinson Richards 1924- *WhoAm 94, WhoAmL 94*
Debevoise, Eli Whitney 1899-1990 *WhAm 10*
Debevoise, Thomas McElrath 1929- *WhoAm 94*
Debeyre, Guy Edouard Pierre Albert 1911- *IntWW 93*
Debeyssey, Mark Sammer 1966- *WhoScEn 94*
de Bhaldraithe, Tomas 1916- *IntWW 93*
de Biasi, Ronaldo Sergio 1943- *WhoScEn 94*
De Blanck, Hubert 1856-1932 *NewGrDO*
de Blank, Justin Robert 1927- *Who 94*
De Blas, Angel Luis 1950- *WhoMW 93, WhoScEn 94*
DeBlase, Anthony Frank 1942- *WhoWest 94*
DeBlasi, Robert Vincent 1936- *WhoScEn 94*
De Blasi, Tony 1933- *WhoAm 94, WhoAmA 93*
DeBlasio, Chris d1993 *NewYTBS 93*
De Blasio, Michael Peter 1937- *WhoAm 94, WhoFI 94*
DeBlasio, Peter Edward 1929- *WhoAmL 94*
DeBlasis, Celeste N(inette) 1946- *WrDr 94*
de Blasis, James Michael 1931- *WhoAm 94, WhoMW 93*
Deblieck, Norman R. 1926- *WhoAmP 93*
DeBlieu, Ivan Knowlton 1919- *WhoScEn 94*
De Blieux, Joseph Davis 1912- *WhoAmP 93*
de Blij, Harm J(an) 1935- *WrDr 94*
de Blij, Harm Jan 1935- *WhoAm 94*
Debnam, Chadwick Basil 1950- *WhoBlA 94*
Debnath, Lokenath 1935- *WhoScEn 94*
Debo, Vincent Joseph 1940- *WhoAm 94*
DeBock, Florent Alphonse 1924- *WhoAm 94, WhoFI 94*
de Bode, Oleg 1956- *WhoWest 94*
DeBoe, Patricia Ann 1967- *WhoFI 94*
de Boer, Anthony Peter 1918- *Who 94*
De Boer, Darrell Wayne 1940- *WhoMW 93*
DeBoer, Jay Wayne 1953- *WhoAmP 93*
De Boer, Pieter Cornelis Tobias 1930- *WhoAm 94, WhoScEn 94*
de Boer, Thymen Jan 1924- *IntWW 93*
DeBois, James Adolphus 1929- *WhoAm 94*
de Boissière, Ralph (Anthony Charles) 1907- *WrDr 94*
De Bokx, Pieter Klaas 1955- *WhoScEn 94*
de Bold, Adolfo J. 1942- *WhoAm 94, WhoScEn 94*
DeBold, C. Rowan 1948- *WhoMW 93*
De Bolt, Donald Walter 1952- *WhoWest 94*
DeBolt, Edward S. 1938- *WhoAmP 93*
DeBolt, Virginia Faye 1941- *WhoWest 94*
DeBon, George A. *WhoFI 94*
DeBonis, Anthony, Jr. 1950- *WhoAmP 93*
De Bonis, Donato 1930- *IntWW 93*
DeBonis, Michael A. 1912- *WhoAmP 93*
de Bono, Edward 1933- *ConAu 43NR*
deBono, Edward (Francis Charles) 1933- *WrDr 94*
de Bono, Edward Francis Charles Publius 1933- *IntWW 93, Who 94*
Debono, Giovanna *WhoWomW 91*
DeBono, Kenneth George 1958- *WhoScEn 94*
Debono, Manuel 1936- *WhoMW 93*
De Bont, Jan *ConTFT 11*
Deboo, Behram Savakshaw 1931- *WhoScEn 94*
de Boor, Carl 1937- *WhoAm 94, WhoMW 93, WhoScEn 94*
De Borba, Dorothy 1925- *WhoHol 92*
de Borbon, Juan 1913-1993 *NewYTBS 93 [port]*
de Borchgrave, Arnaud 1926- *WhoAm 94*
DeBord, Jerry L. 1943- *WhoAmP 93*
De Bord, Sharon 1939- *WhoHol 92*
De Borhegyi, Stephen 1921-1969 *WhoAmA 93N*
De Boschnek, Chris (Christian Charles) 1947- *WhoAmA 93*
De Bosset, Vera d1982 *WhoHol 92*
de Botton, Gilbert 1935- *Who 94*
De Botton, Jean Philippe d1978 *WhoAmA 93N*
De Bow, James Dunwoody Brownson 1820-1867 *AmSocL*
DeBow, Jay Howard Camden 1932- *WhoAm 94, WhoFI 94*
De Bozoky, Barbara d1937 *WhoHol 92*
DeBra, Daniel B. 1930- *WhoAm 94*
DeBracy, Warren 1942- *WhoBlA 94*
de Braga, Marcia D. 1937- *WhoAmP 93*
de Branges de Bourcia, Louis 1932- *WhoAm 94, WhoMW 93*
De Bray, Henri d1965 *WhoHol 92*
Debray, Regis 1940- *IntWW 93*
Debray, (Jules) Regis 1940- *ConAu 43NR*
De Bray, Yvonne d1954 *WhoHol 92*
Debre, Michel 1912- *IntWW 93*
Debre, Michel Jean-Pierre 1912- *Who 94*
Debreczeny, Paul 1932- *WhoAm 94, WrDr 94*
DeBree, Susan Kidder 1943- *WhoWest 94*
De Bremaecker, Jean-Claude 1923- *WhoAm 94*
De Bremont, Anna 1864-1922 *BlmGWL*
De Breteuil, Gilberte d1972 *WhoHol 92*
de Bretteville, Sheila Levrant 1940- *WhoAm 94, WhoAmA 93*
Debreu, Gerard 1921- *IntWW 93, Who 94, WhoAm 94, WhoFI 94, WhoWest 94, WrDr 94*
De Briac, Jean d1970 *WhoHol 92*
De Brier, Donald Paul 1940- *WhoAm 94*
DeBrincat, Susan Jeanne 1943- *WhoMW 93*
Debro, Jesse, III 1935- *WhoAmP 93*
Debro, Joseph Rollins 1928- *WhoBlA 94*
Debro, Julius 1931- *WhoAm 94, WhoBlA 94*
De Broca, Philippe 1933- *IntMPA 94*
DeBroeck, Dennis Alan 1957- *WhoScEn 94, WhoWest 94*
DeBroeck, Dennis R. 1951- *WhoAmL 94*
DeBroff, Scott H. 1963- *WhoAmL 94*
de Broglie, Gabriel Marie Joseph Anselme 1931- *IntWW 93*
De Broglie, Louis Victor *WorScD*
de Broke *Who 94*
Debrosky, Christine A. 1951- *WhoAmA 93*
De Brosses, Charles 1709-1777 *WhWE*
De Brouwer, Nathalie 1962- *WhoScEn 94*
De Broux, Lee *WhoHol 92*
Debrovner, Steven H. *WhoIns 94*
Debroy, Chitrita 1946- *WhoAsA 94*
De Bruhl, Arthur Marshall 1935- *WhoAm 94*
DeBrule, William J. 1930- *WhoAm 94, WhoFI 94*
DeBruler, Roger O. 1934- *WhoAm 94, WhoAmL 94, WhoAmP 93, WhoMW 93*
De Brulier, Nigel d1948 *WhoHol 92*
DeBrunner, Gerald Joseph 1937- *WhoAm 94, WhoMW 93*
Debrunner, Peter George 1931- *WhoAm 94*
DeBruycker, Dirk H. A. 1955- *WhoAmA 93*
Debruycker, Jane 1936- *WhoAmP 93*
Debruycker, Roger 1936- *WhoAmP 93*
De Bruyn, Peter Paul Henry 1910- *WhoAm 94*
DeBruyn, Robert L. 1934- *WhoMW 93*
de Bruyne, Dirk 1920- *IntWW 93, Who 94*
de Bruyne, Norman Adrian 1904- *Who 94*
Debs, Barbara Knowles 1931- *WhoAm 94*
Debs, Eugene V. 1855-1926 *HisWorL [port]*
Debs, Eugene Victor 1855-1926 *AmSocL*
Debs, Richard A. 1930- *WhoAm 94, WhoFI 94*
Debu-Bridel, Jacques 1902- *IntWW 93*
Debucourt, Jean d1958 *WhoHol 92*
DeBunda, Salvatore Michael 1943- *WhoAm 94, WhoAmL 94*
DeBuono, Barbara Ann 1955- *WhoAm 94*
De Burgh, Celia *WhoHol 92*
de Burlo, Comegys Russell, Jr. *WhoAm 94*
Debus, Allen George 1926- *WhoAm 94, WrDr 94*
Debus, Eleanor Viola 1920- *WhoWest 94*
Debusk, Edith M. 1912- *WhAm 10*
DeBusk, George Henry, Jr. 1966- *WhoScEn 94*
DeBusk, Manuel Conrad 1914- *WhoAm 94*
DeBusschere, Dave 1940- *BasBi*
DeBusschere, David Albert 1949- *WhoAm 94*
Debussy, Claude 1862-1918 *IntDcB*
Debussy, (Achille-)Claude 1862-1918 *NewGrDO*
De Butts, Frederick Manus 1916- *Who 94*
deButts, Harry Ashby 1895- *WhAm 10*
deButts, Robert Edward Lee 1927- *WhoFI 94*
DeBuys, John F., Jr. 1942- *WhoAmL 94*
deBuys, William (Eno), Jr. 1949- *WrDr 94*
Deby, Idriss *IntWW 93*
Deby, John Bedford 1931- *Who 94*
Debyasuvan, Boonlua Kunjara *BlmGWL*
Decae, Henri 1915-1987 *IntDcF 2-4 [port]*
DeCair, Thomas Palmer 1945- *WhoAmP 93*
Decaminada, Joseph P. 1935- *WhoIns 94*
Decaminada, Joseph Pio 1935- *WhoAm 94*
De Camp, Catherine A. Crook *EncSF 93*
de Camp, Catherine Crook 1907- *WrDr 94*
De Camp, Gayle S. d1977 *WhoHol 92*
DeCamp, Graydon 1934- *WhoAm 94*
Decamp, John William 1941- *WhoAmP 93*
De Camp, L(yon) Sprague 1907- *EncSF 93, WrDr 94*
De Camp, Maria Theresa 1775-1838 *NewGrDO*
De Camp, Rosemary 1910- *WhoHol 92*
De Camp, Rosemary 1913- *IntMPA 94*
DeCamp, Rosemary Shirley 1910- *WhoAm 94*
DeCandia, Donald Alan 1964- *WhoAmL 94*
de Cani, John Stapley 1924- *WhoAm 94*
De Capitani, Grace *WhoHol 92*
De Caprio, Al *IntMPA 94*
DeCaprio, Alice 1919- *WhoAmA 93*
DeCarava, Roy 1919- *AfrAmAl 6 [port]*
DeCarava, Roy R. 1919- *WhoAm 94*
DeCarava, Roy Rudolph 1919- *WhoAmA 93, WhoBlA 94*
De Carbonnel, Francois Eric 1946- *WhoAm 94*
De Cárdenas, Gilbert Lorenzo 1941- *WhoHisp 94*
de Cardi, Beatrice Eileen 1914- *Who 94*
De Cardo, Walton d1953 *WhoHol 92*
DeCaria, Michael Dee 1946- *WhoWest 94*
DeCarlo, Donald Thomas *WhoAmL 94*
DeCarlo, Guy Richard 1939- *WhoFI 94*
De Carlo, Vinnie d1989 *WhoHol 92*
DeCarlo, William S. 1950- *WhoAm 94*
De Carlo, Yvonne 1922- *IntMPA 94, WhoHol 92*
de Carmoy, Herve Pierre 1937- *Who 94*
de Caro, Frank Anthony 1943- *WhoAm 94*
Decas, Charles N. 1937- *WhoAmP 93*
Decas, George Charles 1937- *WhoAmP 93*
De Casabianca, Camille *WhoHol 92*
De Casalis, Jeanne d1966 *WhoHol 92*
de Castella, (Francois) Robert 1957- *IntWW 93*
De Castris, Francesco c. 1650-1724 *NewGrDO*
DeCastris, Valeri Dawn 1956- *WhoMW 93*
De Castro, German *WhoHisp 94*
de Castro, Godfrey R. 1922- *WhoAmP 93*
de Castro, Hugo Daniel 1935- *WhoAm 94*
De Castro, John Manuel 1947- *WhoHisp 94*
de Castro, Julian Edmund 1930- *WhoAmL 94*
De Castro, Julio O. 1959- *WhoHisp 94*
De Castro, L. Felippe C. *WhoHisp 94*
De Castro, Lorraine 1946- *WhoAmA 93*
De Castro Font, Jorge *WhoAmP 93*
Decatur, Stephen 1752-1808 *WhAmRev*
De Caunes, Antoine *WhoHol 92*
Decaux, Alain 1925- *IntWW 93*
Deccio, Alex A. 1927- *WhoAmP 93*
de Cecco, Marcello 1939- *IntWW 93*
De Celles, Charles Edouard 1942- *WhoAm 94*
DeCesare, James Charles 1931- *WhoFI 94*
De Cespedes, Alba 1911- *BlmGWL*
de Cespedes, Carlos M. *WhoHisp 94*
De Ceuster, Luc Frans 1959- *WhoScEn 94*
DeChaine, Dean Dennis 1936- *WhoAm 94, WhoAmL 94*
de Chair, Somerset 1911- *Who 94*
De Chair, Somerset (Struben) 1911- *EncSF 93, WrDr 94*
de Chambrun, Comtesse 1929- *Who 94*
De Champlain, Vera Chopak *WhoAmA 93*
de Champlain, Vera Chopak 1928- *WhoAm 94*
Dechamps, Charles d1958 *WhoHol 92*
DeChancie, John 1946- *ConAu 41NR, EncSF 93*
Dechant, Virgil C. 1930- *WhoAm 94*
Dechar, Peter 1942- *WhoAmA 93*
Dechar, Peter Henry 1942- *WhoAm 94*
Dechario, Tony Houston 1940- *WhoWest 94*
de Chassiron, Charles Richard Lucien 1948- *Who 94*
de Chastelain, Alfred John Gardyne Drumm 1937- *WhoAm 94*
de Chazal, Claire Denise 1955- *WhoAmL 94*
DeChellis, Michael Anthony 1940- *WhoWest 94*
Dechene, James Charles 1953- *WhoAm 94*
Decher, Rudolf 1927- *WhoAm 94, WhoScEn 94*
Decherd, Robert William 1951- *WhoAm 94*
De Cherney, Alan Hersh 1942- *WhoAm 94, WhoScEn 94*
DeCherney, George Stephen 1952- *WhoScEn 94*
Dechert, Michael Salvatore Alfred 1958- *WhoFI 94*
Dechert, Peter 1924- *WhoWest 94*
De Chino, Karen Linnia 1955- *WhoScEn 94*
Dechmann, Manfred 1942- *WhoScEn 94*
Dechter, Warren *WhoAm 94*
Deci, Edward Lewis 1942- *WhoAm 94*
DeCicco, Anne Lommel 1950- *WhoFI 94*
DeCicco, Peter Dominick 1955- *WhoMW 93*
DeCicco, Yvonne Angela 1960- *WhoMW 93*

Decies, Baron d1992 *Who 94N*
Decies, Baron 1948- *Who 94*
De Cinque, William C. 1941- *WhoIns 94*
Decio, Arthur Julius 1930- *WhoAm 94, WhoMW 93*
deCiutiis, Alfred Charles Maria 1945- *WhoAm 94, WhoWest 94*
Deck, Allan Figueroa 1945- *WhoHisp 94*
Deck, Armida Amparo 1941- *WhoHisp 94*
Deck, Joseph Francis 1907- *WhoAm 94*
Deck, Paul Wayne, Jr. 1946- *WhoAm 94, WhoAmL 94*
Deck, Robert A. 1931- *WhoFI 94*
Deckard, Homer Edward 1955- *WhoFI 94*
Deckard, Ivan Lowell 1928- *WhoWest 94*
Deckard, Jerry 1942- *WhoAmP 93*
Deckelbaum, Nelson 1928- *WhoAm 94*
Decker, Anne Rebecca 1941- *WhoMW 93*
Decker, Arthur John 1941- *WhoScEn 94*
Decker, Bernard Martin d1993 *NewYTBS 93 [port]*
Decker, Bob 1922- *WhoAmP 93*
Decker, Charles David 1945- *WhoAm 94*
Decker, Charles L. *WhoAm 94*
Decker, Charles Richard 1937- *WhoAm 94*
Decker, Christian Lucien 1940- *WhoScEn 94*
Decker, David Garrison 1917-1990 *WhAm 10*
Decker, David R. 1942- *WhoAmL 94*
Decker, Diana 1926- *WhoHol 92*
Decker, Donna *DrAPF 93*
Decker, Francis Keil, Jr. 1936- *WhoAm 94*
Decker, George John 1955- *WhoWest 94*
Decker, Gilbert Felton 1937- *WhoAm 94*
Decker, Gloria Ann 1932- *WhoAmP 93*
Decker, Hannah Shulman 1937- *WhoAm 94*
Decker, Hans Wilhelm 1929- *WhoAm 94, WhoFI 94*
Decker, Jack Neal 1944- *WhoFI 94*
Decker, James Harrison, Jr. 1948- *WhoAmL 94*
Decker, James Ludlow 1923- *WhoFI 94*
Decker, John 1895- *WhoAmA 93N*
Decker, John Alvin, Jr. 1935- *WhoWest 94*
Decker, John Laws 1921- *WhoAm 94*
Decker, John Robert 1952- *WhoAmL 94*
Decker, John William 1948- *WhoMW 93*
Decker, Kathryn Browne d1919 *WhoHol 92*
Decker, Kurt Hans 1946- *WhoAmL 94, WhoFI 94*
Decker, Leon Theodore 1946- *WhoMW 93*
Decker, Malcolm Doyle 1946- *WhoFI 94*
Decker, Mary Ellen Lafferty 1949- *WhoMW 93*
Decker, Mary Katherine 1951- *WhoMW 93*
Decker, Melissa *WhoHol 92*
Decker, Michael Lynn 1953- *WhoAmL 94*
Decker, Michael P. 1944- *WhoAmP 93*
Decker, Peter William 1919- *WhoMW 93*
Decker, Purley John 1947- *WhoWest 94*
Decker, Raymond Frank 1930- *WhoAm 94*
Decker, Richard Henry 1934- *WhoMW 93*
Decker, Richard Jeffrey 1959- *WhoWest 94*
Decker, Richard Kelsey 1927- *WhoWest 94*
Decker, Richard Knore 1913- *WhoAm 94*
Decker, Russell S. 1953- *WhoAmP 93*
Decker, Suelyn 1948- *WhoWest 94*
Decker, Veronica Blaha 1952- *WhoMW 93*
Decker, Wayne H. d1993 *NewYTBS 93*
Decker, Wayne Leroy 1922- *WhoAm 94, WhoMW 93*
Decker, William *DrAPF 93*
Decker, William 1926- *WrDr 94*
Deckers, Eugene d1977 *WhoHol 92*
Decker Slaney, Mary Teresa 1958- *WhoAm 94, WhoWest 94*
Deckert, Curtis Kenneth 1939- *WhoWest 94*
Deckert, Gordon Harmon 1930- *WhoAm 94*
Deckert, Harlan Kennedy, Jr. 1923- *WhoWest 94*
Deckler, Daniel Carl 1963- *WhoMW 93*
Decko, Kenneth Owen 1944- *WhoAm 94*
Deckrosh, Hazen Douglas 1936- *WhoMW 93*
Deckter, Louis Larry 1941- *WhoAmL 94*
DeClerck, Timothy Edward 1956- *WhoAmL 94*
De Clercq, Willy 1927- *Who 94*
De Cleyre, Voltairine 1866-1912 *WomPubS*
de Clifford, Baron 1928- *Who 94*
DeClue, Anita *WhoBlA 94*
de Clue, David Marshall-Rutledge 1957- *WhoAmL 94*
De Coma, Eddie d1938 *WhoHol 92*
Decomble, Guy d1964 *WhoHol 92*
DeConcini, Dennis 1937- *CngDr 93, IntWW 93, WhoAm 94, WhoAmP 93, WhoWest 94*
DeConcini, John Cyrus 1918- *WhoFI 94*
De Conde, Syn *WhoHol 92*
De Cordoba, Pedro d1950 *WhoHol 92*
De Cordova, Arturo d1973 *WhoHol 92*
De Cordova, Frederick 1910- *IntMPA 94*
de Cordova, Frederick Timmins 1910- *WhoAm 94*
De Cordova, Leander d1969 *WhoHol 92*
De Cordova, Rudolph d1941 *WhoHol 92*
deCormier-Shekerjian, Regina *DrAPF 93*
De Corsia, Ted d1973 *WhoHol 92*
DeCorte, Robert Vincent 1941- *WhoMW 93*
De Costa, Edwin J. 1906- *WhoAm 94*
DeCosta, Herbert Alexander, Jr. 1923- *WhoBlA 94*
De Costa, James 1963- *WhoFI 94*
DeCosta, Peter F. *WhoScEn 94*
DeCosta, William Joseph 1960- *WhoScEn 94*
DeCosta-Willis, Miriam 1934- *BlkWr 2, ConAu 142, WhoBlA 94*
De Coster, Cyrus Cole 1914- *WhoAm 94*
de Cotret, Robert Rene 1944- *IntWW 93*
de Cou, Emil *WhoAm 94*
de Courcy *Who 94*
de Courcy, Kenneth Hugh 1909- *Who 94*
deCourcy, Lynne Hugo *DrAPF 93*
de Courcy-Ireland, Patrick Gault 1933- *Who 94*
de Courcy Ling, John 1933- *Who 94*
DeCoursey, Elizabeth Jean 1958- *WhoMW 93*
Decoursey, William Leslie 1931- *WhoScEn 94*
DeCourten, Frank L. 1950- *WhoWest 94*
Decourtray, Albert 1923- *IntWW 93*
De Coux, Janet *WhoAmA 93*
Decowski, Piotr 1940- *WhoScEn 94*
De Craene, Jacques Maria 1929- *WhoFI 94*
Decramer, Gary M. 1944- *WhoAmP 93*
DeCrane, Alfred C., Jr. 1931- *IntWW 93*
DeCrane, Alfred Charles, Jr. 1931- *Who 94, WhoAm 94, WhoFI 94*
DeCrane, Vincent Francis 1927- *WhoMW 93*
DeCredico, Mary A. 1959- *WrDr 94*
De Creeft, Jose 1884-1982 *WhoAmA 93N*
De Creeft, Lorrie J. *WhoAmA 93*
de Crespigny, (Richard) Rafe (Champion) 1936- *WrDr 94*
DeCristoforo, Romeo John 1917- *WrDr 94*
Decroce, Alex 1936- *WhoAmP 93*
DeCrosta, Edward Francis, Jr. 1926- *WhoScEn 94*
Decroux, Etienne d1991 *WhoHol 92*
DeCrow, Karen 1937- *WhoAm 94, WrDr 94*
Decter, Betty Eva 1927- *WhoAmA 93*
Decter, Midge 1927- *WhoAm 94*
Decter, Midge (Rosenthal) 1927- *WrDr 94*
De Cuevas, George 1885-1961 *IntDcB [port]*
DeCuir, John F., Jr. 1941- *IntMPA 94*
Decuir, Joseph Charles 1950- *WhoWest 94*
Decuir, Oswald A. 1940- *WhoAmP 93*
De Cunto, John Giovanni *WhoAmA 93*
De Cusatis, Casimer Maurice 1964- *WhoScEn 94*
Decyk, Viktor Konstantyn 1948- *WhoScEn 94*
Dedalus *ConWorW 93*
DeDanaan, Llyn Patterson 1942- *WhoWest 94*
De Datta, Surajit Kumar 1936- *WhoScEn 94*
Deddeh, Wadie Peter 1920- *WhoAmP 93*
Dedeaux, Paul J. 1937- *WhoWest 94*
Dedekind, (Julius Wilhelm) Richard *WorScD*
De Dell, Gary Jerome *WhoFI 94*
Dedema *WhoPRCh 91 [port]*
de Deney, Geoffrey Ivor 1931- *Who 94*
De Deo, Joseph E. 1936- *IntWW 93*
De Deo, Joseph E. 1937- *WhoAm 94, WhoFI 94*
Dederer, James W. 1946- *WhoAmL 94*
Dederer, John Morgan 1951- *WrDr 94*
Dederer, Michael Eugene 1932- *WhoAm 94, WhoFI 94*
Dederer, William Bowne 1945- *WhoAm 94*
Dederich-Pejovich, Susan Russell 1951- *WhoAm 94*
Dederick, Robert Gogan 1929- *WhoAm 94*
Dederick, Ronald Osburn 1935- *WhoAm 94*
Dedert, Joanne Lucille 1950- *WhoFI 94*
Dedert, Steven Ray 1953- *WhoMW 93*
Dedeurwaerder, Jose Joseph 1932- *IntWW 93*
Dedeyan, Charles 1910- *IntWW 93*
Dedeyn, Carey P. 1941- *WhoAmL 94*
Dedhia, Navin Shamji 1940- *WhoAsA 94, WhoWest 94*
Dedic, Michael Robert 1965- *WhoMW 93*
De Diego, Julio d1979 *WhoHol 92*
De Diego, Julio 1900-1979 *WhoAmA 93N*
Dedijer, Vladimir 1914-1990 *WhAm 10*
Dedini, Eldon Lawrence 1921- *WhoAm 94, WhoAmA 93, WhoWest 94*
De Dios Muniz, Juan d1951 *WhoHol 92*
Dedman, Bertram Cottingham 1914- *WhoAm 94*
Dedman, Bill 1960- *WhoAm 94*
Dedman, James Monroe, III 1944- *WhoAmL 94*
Dedo, Dorothy Junell Turner 1920- *WhoMW 93*
DeDona, Francis Alfred 1924- *WhoFI 94, WhoWest 94*
DeDonato, Donald Michael 1952- *WhoMW 93*
De Donato, Louis 1934- *WhoAmA 93*
Dedrick, James R. *WhoAmL 94*
Dedrick, Kent Gentry 1923- *WhoScEn 94, WhoWest 94*
Dedrick, Robert Lyle 1933- *WhoScEn 94*
de Duve, Christian Rene 1917- *IntWW 93, WhoAm 94, WhoScEn 94*
de Duve, Christian Rene Marie Joseph 1917- *Who 94*
Dee, Blanche d1987 *WhoHol 92*
Dee, David Scott 1952- *WhoAmL 94*
Dee, Elaine Evans 1924- *WhoAmA 93*
Dee, Frances 1907- *WhoHol 92*
Dee, Francis X. 1944- *WhoAmL 94*
Dee, Freddie d1958 *WhoHol 92*
Dee, George d1974 *WhoHol 92*
Dee, Ivan Richard 1935- *WhoMW 93*
Dee, Joey 1940- *WhoHol 92*
Dee, John 1527-1609 *DcLB 136 [port]*
Dee, Leo Joseph 1931- *WhoAmA 93*
Dee, Merri 1936- *WhoBlA 94*
Dee, Michael 1964- *WhoWest 94*
Dee, Mikkey
See Motorhead *ConMus 10*
Dee, Roger 1914- *EncSF 93*
Dee, Ruby *WhoAm 94, WhoBlA 94*
Dee, Ruby 1923- *AfrAmAl 6 [port], SmATA 77*
Dee, Ruby 1924- *IntMPA 94, WhoHol 92*
Dee, Sandra 1942- *IntMPA 94, WhoHol 92*
Deeb, George Phillip 1922- *WhoAmL 94*
Deebel, George Franklin 1911- *WhoAmP 93*
Deech, Ruth Lynn 1943- *Who 94*
Deecken, George Christian 1922- *WhoAm 94*
Deed, Andre d1931 *WhoHol 92*
Deedes, Baron 1913- *Who 94*
Deedes, Charles Julius 1913- *Who 94*
Deedes, William Francis 1913- *IntWW 93*
Deeds, Robert Creigh 1958- *WhoAmL 94, WhoAmP 93*
Deeds, William Edward 1920- *WhoScEn 94*
Deedy, John Gerard, Jr. 1923- *WhoAm 94*
Deeg, Emil Wolfgang 1926- *WhoFI 94*
Deegan, Derek James 1940- *WhoAm 94*
Deegan, John, Jr. 1944- *WhoAm 94*
Deegan, Jon J. *EncSF 93*
Deegan, Rose Mary Groetken 1917- *WhoAmP 93*
Deegear, James Otis, III 1948- *WhoAmL 94*
Deegen, Uwe Frederick 1948- *WhoScEn 94*
Deeik, Khalil George 1937- *WhoFI 94, WhoScEn 94*
Deeken, Michael George 1952- *WhoMW 93*
Deeks, William George 1933- *WhoFI 94*
Deel, Frances Quinn 1939- *WhoAm 94*
Deel, Sandra *WhoHol 92*
Deeley, Ben d1924 *WhoHol 92*
Deeley, C. Carey, Jr. 1951- *WhoAmL 94*
Deeley, Edward Joseph 1956- *WhoFI 94*
Deeley, Michael 1932- *IntMPA 94, Who 94*
Deem, George 1932- *WhoAm 94, WhoAmA 93*
Deem, J. Frank 1928- *WhoAmP 93*
Deem, James L. 1951- *WhoAmL 94*
Deem, James M(organ) 1950- *ConAu 142, SmATA 75 [port]*
Deem, Patrick D. 1944- *WhoAmL 94*
Deemer, Bill *DrAPF 93*
Deems, Andrew William 1946- *WhoAm 94, WhoWest 94*
Deems, Mickey 1925- *WhoHol 92*
Deems, Nyal David 1948- *WhoAm 94*
Deems, Richard Emmet 1913- *WhoAm 94*
Deen, David Lewis, III 1944- *WhoAmP 93*
Deen, Jesse C. 1922- *WhoAmP 93*
Deen, Nedra d1975 *WhoHol 92*
Deen, Thomas Blackburn 1928- *WhoAm 94*
Deene, Lally d1988 *WhoHol 92*
Deeny, Raymond M. 1951- *WhoAmL 94*
Deeny, Robert Joseph 1941- *WhoAm 94, WhoAmL 94*
Deep, Ira Washington 1927- *WhoAm 94, WhoMW 93*
Deepak, Adarsh 1936- *WhoScEn 94*
Deep Chin 1944- *WrDr 94*
Deeping, (George) Warwick 1877-1950 *EncSF 93*
Deep Purple *ConMus 11 [port]*
Deer, Ada Elizabeth 1935- *WhoAmP 93*
Deer, Darrell Duane 1966- *WhoMW 93*
Deer, (Arthur) Frederick 1910- *Who 94*
Deer, James William 1922- *WhoScEn 94*
Deer, James Willis 1917- *WhoAmL 94, WhoFI 94*
Deer, John J. d1940 *WhoHol 92*
Deer, M.J. *EncSF 93*
Deer, M. J. 1922- *WrDr 94*
Deer, Richard Elliott 1932- *WhoAm 94*
Deer, William Alexander 1910- *IntWW 93, Who 94*
De Erdely, Francis 1904-1959 *WhoAmA 93N*
Deere, Cyril Thomas 1924- *WhoAm 94*
Deere, John 1804-1886 *WorInv*
Deere, Phillip c. 1920-1985 *EncNAR*
Deerhurst, Viscount 1957- *Who 94*
Deering, Allan Brooks 1934- *WhoAm 94*
Deering, Anthony Wayne Marion 1945- *WhoFI 94*
Deering, Fred A. 1928- *WhoIns 94*
Deering, Fred Arthur 1928- *WhoAm 94, WhoFI 94, WhoWest 94*
Deering, Frederick Henry 1923- *WhoAmP 93*
Deering, John d1955 *WhoHol 92*
Deering, Joseph William 1940- *WhoFI 94*
Deering, Marda d1961 *WhoHol 92*
Deering, Mark Stephen 1966- *WhoWest 94*
Deering, Olive d1986 *WhoHol 92*
Deering, Patricia 1916- *WhoHol 92*
Deering, Terry W. 1958- *WhoAmP 93*
Deering, Terry William 1958- *WhoMW 93*
Deering, Thomas Phillips 1929- *WhoAm 94*
Deery, Jack d1965 *WhoHol 92*
Deery, Sandy *DrAPF 93*
Dees, Anse 1920- *WhoAmP 93*
Dees, Bowen Causey 1917- *IntWW 93*
Dees, C. Stanley 1938- *WhoAm 94*
Dees, Julian Worth 1933- *WhoAm 94*
Dees, Lynne 1954- *WhoAm 94*
Dees, Mary 1911- *WhoHol 92*
Dees, Michael Kenneth 1952- *WhoAmP 93*
Dees, Morris Seligman, Jr. 1936- *WhoAmL 94*
Dees, Richard Houston 1960- *WhoMW 93*
Dees, Sandra Kay Martin 1944- *WhoAm 94*
Dees, Stephen Phillip 1943- *WhoAmL 94*
Dees, Tom Moore 1931- *WhoScEn 94*
Dees, Tony *WhoAm 94*
Deese, James Earle 1921- *WhoAm 94*
Deese, James LaMotte 1944- *WhoAm 94*
Deese, Manuel 1941- *WhoBlA 94*
Deese, Pamela McCarthy 1958- *WhoAmL 94*
Deeter, Allen C. 1931- *WhoMW 93*
Deeths, Lenore Clair 1940- *WhoMW 93*
Deetman, Willem Joost 1945- *IntWW 93*
Deets, Dwain Aaron 1939- *WhoAm 94, WhoScEn 94*
Deets, Horace 1938- *WhoAm 94, WhoFI 94*
Deevey, Edward Smith, Jr. 1914-1988 *WhAm 10*
Deevi, Seetharama C. 1955- *WhoScEn 94*
Deezen, Eddie *WhoHol 92*
DeFabees, Richard d1993 *NewYTBS 93*
De Fabo, Edward Charles 1937- *WhoScEn 94*
De Fabritiis, Oliviero (Carlo) 1902-1982 *NewGrDO*
DeFalaise, Louis Gaylord 1945- *WhoAmP 93*
DeFalco, Frank Damian 1934- *WhoAm 94*
DeFanti, Michael Peter 1942- *WhoAmL 94*
de Faria, Antonio Leite 1904- *Who 94*
de Farrell, Pauline 1932- *WhoHisp 94*
De Fazio, John 1959- *WhoAmA 93*
DeFazio, Lynette Stevens 1930- *WhoWest 94*
De Fazio, Marjorie *DrAPF 93*
DeFazio, Peter A. 1947- *CngDr 93, WhoAm 94, WhoAmP 93, WhoWest 94*
DeFazio, Teresa Galligan 1941- *WhoAmA 93*
Defebaugh, James Elliott 1926- *WhoAmP 93*

Defechereux, Philippe Henry 1945-
WhoAm 94
DeFelice, Eugene Anthony 1927-
WhoAm 94
DeFelice, Jim 1956- *ConAu 142*
DeFelice, Jonathan Peter 1947-
WhoAm 94
DeFelice, Ronald J. 1943- *WhoAmL 94*
De Felitta, Frank Paul *WhoAm 94*
Defenbaugh, Richard Eugene 1946-
WhoAm 94
DeFeo, John Eugene 1946- *WhoWest 94*
DeFeo, Stephen Joseph 1960-
WhoAmL 94
DeFeo, Thomas Anthony 1936-
WhoAm 94
De Feraudy, Maurice d1932 *WhoHol 92*
De Feria, Antenor Armando 1960-
WhoHisp 94
de Ferranti, Sebastian Basil Joseph Ziani
1927- *Who 94*
de Ferranti, Sebastian Ziani 1927-
IntWW 93
De Ferrari, Gabriella 1941- *WhoAm 94*
De Ferrari, Serafino (Amedeo) 1824-1885
NewGrDO
De Ferreire, Mary Elizabeth 1949-
WhoHisp 94
Deffand, Marie de Vichy-Chamrond,
Marquise du 1697-1780 *BlmGWL*
Deffenbaugh, Kent Bradley 1943-
WhoMW 93
Deffenbaugh, Ralston H., Jr. 1952-
WhoAm 94
Deffes, Pierre-Louis 1819-1900 *NewGrDO*
Deffeyes, Robert Joseph 1935-
WhoMW 93
Deffner, Barbara Dunning *DrAPF 93*
DeFilippes, Mary Wolpert 1939-
WhoScEn 94
DeFilippi, Walter Arthur 1926-
WhoAmP 93
DeFilippis, Carl William 1931-
WhoScEn 94
De Filippis, Daisy Cocco 1949-
WhoHisp 94
De Filippo, Eduardo d1984 *WhoHol 92*
De Filippo, Eduardo 1900-1984 *IntDcT 2*
DeFilippo, Paul R. 1953- *WhoAmL 94*
Di Filippo, Peppino d1980 *WhoHol 92*
De Filippo, Titina d1963 *WhoHol 92*
De Fina, Barbara *IntMPA 94*
DeFino, Anthony Michael 1936-
WhoAmP 93
Deflassieux, Jean Sebastien 1925-
IntWW 93
Defleur, Lois B. 1936- *WhoAm 94*
DeFleur, Melvin Lawrence 1923-
WhoAm 94
Defliese, Philip Leroy 1915- *WhoAm 94*
Deflo, Gilbert 1944- *NewGrDO*
DeFlorio, Mary Lucy *WhoScEn 94*
DeFlyer, Joseph Eugene 1943-
WhoWest 94
De Foe, Annette d1960 *WhoHol 92*
Defoe, Daniel 1660-1731 *BlmGEL [port],
EncSF 93*
Defoe, Daniel 1661-1736 *EncSPD*
DeFoe, Mark *DrAPF 93*
de Fonblanque, John Robert 1943-
Who 94
Defontenay, C(harlemagne) I(schir)
1814-1856 *EncSF 93*
de Fontenay, Patrick B. 1934- *IntWW 93*
de Fonville, Paul Bliss 1923- *WhoWest 94*
DeFoor, James Allison, II 1953-
WhoAmL 94
Defoor, Nathan Dwight 1952- *WhoAm 94*
Deford, Frank 1938- *WhoAm 94, WrDr 94*
DeFord, Harry Alonzo, II 1941-
WhoAmL 94
deFord, Miriam Allen 1888-1975
EncSF 93
DeFore, Don d1993 *NewYTBS 93 [port]*
De Fore, Don 1917- *WhoHol 92*
Defore, Jimmy d1987 *WhoHol 92*
De Forest, Calvert 1921- *WhoHol 92*
De Forest, Edgar Lester *WhoWest 94*
De Forest, Hal d1938 *WhoHol 92*
De Forest, Lee 1873-1961 *WorInv [port]*
DeForest, Orrin L. 1923- *WrDr 94*
De Forest, Roy Dean 1930- *WhoAmA 93*
De Forest, Sherwood Searle 1921-
WhoAm 94, WhoScEn 94
DeForest, Walter Pattison, III 1944-
WhoAm 94, WhoAmL 94
DeForge, William J. 1940- *WhoIns 94*
Deforges, Regine *BlmGWL*
De Fossett, William K. 1920- *WhoBlA 94*
Defossez, Rene 1905-1998 *NewGrDO*
DeFrain, Donna Raye 1943- *WhoMW 93*
Defranceschi, Carlo Prospero fl.
1798-1800 *NewGrDO*
Defrancesco, Italo I. 1901-1967
WhoAmA 93N
De Francesco, John Blaze, Jr. 1936-
WhoAm 94
de Francia, Peter Laurent 1921- *Who 94*

De Francisci, Anthony 1887-1964
WhoAmA 93N
DeFrancisco, John A. 1946- *WhoAmP 93*
De Frank, Vincent 1915- *WhoAm 94*
DeFrantz, Anita L. 1952- *WhoBlA 94*
De Freece, Lauri d1921 *WhoHol 92*
De Frees, Madeline *DrAPF 93*
DeFrees, Madeline 1919- *WrDr 94*
DeFreese, Vernon Lee, Jr. 1962-
WhoWest 94
De Freitas, Frederico (Guedes) *NewGrDO*
De Freitas, Rosilda 1949- *WhoWomM 91*
De Freyne, Baron 1927- *Who 94*
De Fries, John Clarence 1934-
WhoAm 94, WhoScEn 94
De Frietas, Cecil d1925 *WhoHol 92*
De Frumerie, (Per) Gunnar (Fredrik)
NewGrDO
De Fuentes, Eduardo Sanchez *NewGrDO*
De Funes, Louis d1983 *WhoHol 92*
Dega, Igor d1976 *WhoHol 92*
Dega, Wiktor 1896- *IntWW 93*
de Gabriak, Cherubina 1887-1928
BlmGWL
Degady, Marc 1957- *WhoScEn 94*
De Gaetani, Jan 1933-1989 *WhAm 10*
Degal, Aldion *EncSF 93*
De Gali, Ernesto 1939- *WhoWest 94*
De Gamerra, Giovanni 1743-1803
NewGrDO
Deganawida fl. 1500- *EncNAR*
de Garcia, Lucia 1941- *WhoWest 94*
De Garcia, Orlando Frank 1947-
WhoHisp 94
De Gaster, Zachary 1926- *WhoAm 94*
deGavre, Chester B. d1993 *NewYTBS 93*
deGavre, Robert Thompson 1940-
WhoFI 94
Degazon, Frederick *IntWW 93*
De Geer, Carl 1923- *IntWW 93*
Degeilh, Robert 1927- *WhoScEn 94*
Degen, Bernard John, II 1937-
WhoAm 94, WhoAmP 93
Degen, Jessica d1978 *WhoHol 92*
Degen-Cohen, Helen *DrAPF 93*
DeGeneste, Henry Irving 1940-
WhoBlA 94
Degenevieve, Barbara 1947- *WhoAmA 93*
Degenfisz, Helen *DrAPF 93*
Degenford, James Edward 1938-
WhoAm 94
Degenhardt, Harold F. 1946- *WhoAmL 94*
Degenhardt, Henry W 1910- *WrDr 94*
Degenhardt, Johannes Joachim 1926-
IntWW 93
Degenhardt, Robert Allan 1943-
WhoAm 94
Degenhart, Bernhard 1907- *IntWW 93*
Degenkolb, Henry John 1913-1989
WhAm 10
De Gennaro, Richard 1926- *WhoAm 94*
De Gennes, Pierre-Gilles 1932-
*IntWW 93, NobelP 91 [port], Who 94,
WhoScEn 94*
DeGeorge, Francis Donald 1929-
WhoAm 94
DeGeorge, Gail 1950- *WhoWest 94*
De George, Lawrence Joseph 1916-
WhoAm 94
DeGeorge, Richard T(homas) 1933-
WrDr 94
De George, Richard Thomas 1933-
WhoAm 94
de Gerenday, Laci Anthony 1911-
WhoAm 94
Degermark, Pia 1949- *WhoHol 92*
Degerstrom, James Marvin 1933-
WhoMW 93
Degette, Diana L. 1957- *WhoAmP 93*
De Gette, Diana Louise 1957-
WhoWest 94
DeGeus, Wendell Ray 1948- *WhoMW 93*
DeGhetto, Kenneth Anselm 1924-
WhoAm 94
Deghy, Guy 1912- *WhoHol 92*
Degiardino, Felice *NewGrDO*
De Giorgi, Ennio 1928- *WhoScEn 94*
De Giosa, Nicola 1819-1885 *NewGrDO*
DeGiovanni-Donnelly, Rosalie Frances
1926- *WhoAm 94*
De Girondo, Norah Langue *BlmGWL*
DeGiusti, Dominic Lawrence 1911-
WhoAm 94
De Givenchy, Hubert James Marcel Taffin
1927- *WhoAm 94*
Deglane, Bobby d1983 *WhoHol 92*
Degler, Carl Neumann 1921- *WhoAm 94*
Deglise, Elisabeth 1931- *WhoWomW 91*
Degnan, Herbert Raymond 1921-
WhoAm 94
Degnan, John James, III 1945-
WhoScEn 94
Degnan, John Michael 1948- *WhoAmL 94*
Degnan, Joseph 1955- *WhoAm 94*
Degnan, Martin J. *WhoAmL 94*
Degnan, Michael John 1955- *WhoMW 93*
Degnan, Peter M. 1946- *WhoAmL 94*

Degnan, Thomas Leonard 1909-
WhoAm 94
De Goff, Victoria Joan 1945-
WhoAmL 94, WhoWest 94
DeGood, Douglas Kent 1947-
WhoAmP 93
DeGooyer, John G. 1942- *WhoAmL 94*
De Gooyer, Rijk 1925- *WhoHol 92*
De Graaf, Regnier *WorScD*
DeGraaff, Robert M(ark) 1942-
ConAu 141
de Graaff-Nauta, Dieuwke 1930-
WhoWomW 91
Degrada, Francesco 1940- *NewGrDO*
De Graeff, Allen 1921- *EncSF 93*
De Graff, Jacques Andre 1949
WhoBlA 94
De Graff, Johannes *WhAmRev*
de Graffenreid, Adrian L. 1940-
WhoAm 94
DeGraffenreidt, Andrew 1928-
WhoBlA 94
De Graffenried, Micheal *WhoMW 93*
de Graffenried, Velda Mae Camp
WhoMW 93
Degraffenried, William Ryan, Jr. 1950-
WhoAmP 93
de Graft, J. C. *ConAu 43NR*
deGraft, J(oseph) C(oleman) 1924-1978
BlkWr 2
deGraft, Joe *BlkWr 2*
Degraft, Joe 1932-1978 *ConDr 93*
de Graft, Joe (Coleman) 1924-1978
ConAu 43NR
de Graft-Hanson, J(ohn) O(rleans) 1932-
WrDr 94
DeGrandi, Joseph Anthony 1927-
WhoAm 94, WhoAmL 94
DeGrandis, Donald James 1948-
WhoAm 94
De Grandis, Francesco fl. 1685-1729
NewGrDO
De Grandis, Renato 1927- *NewGrDO*
DeGrandpre, Charles Allyson 1936-
WhoAmL 94
De Grandy, Miguel A. 1958- *WhoAmP 93,
WhoHisp 94*
De Grasse, Comte *WhAmRev*
De Grasse, Joseph d1940 *WhoHol 92*
De Grasse, Sam d1953 *WhoHol 92*
DeGrassi, Leonard Rene 1928-
WhoWest 94
Degrave, Alex G. 1957- *WhoScEn 94*
DeGrave, Kathleen Rose 1950-
WhoMW 93
de Gravelles, William Decatur, Jr. 1928-
WhoAm 94
DeGraw, Richard G. 1946- *WhoAmP 93*
DeGraw, Stephen Todd 1956-
WhoWest 94
DeGray, Thomas Alan 1939- *WhoAm 94*
DeGrazia, Emilio *DrAPF 93*
DeGrazia, Emilio 1941- *ConAu 140*
De Grazia, Ettore Ted 1909-1982
WhoAmA 93N
De Grazia, Julio d1989 *WhoHol 92*
de Grazia, Sebastian 1917- *ConAu 43NR,
WhoAm 94, WrDr 94*
De Grecis, Nicola 1773-1826? *NewGrDO*
Degreeff, Betty A. 1936- *WhoAmP 93*
DeGreif, Larry Lee 1941- *WhoWest 94*
de Grey *Who 94*
De Grey, (Constance) Gladys 1859-1917
NewGrDO
De Grey, Roger 1918- *IntWW 93, Who 94*
De Grey, Sydney d1941 *WhoHol 92*
De Groat, Diane 1947- *WhoAmA 93*
De Groat, George Hugh 1917-
WhoAmA 93
deGroat, William Chesney 1938-
WhoAm 94, WhoScEn 94
De Groen, Alma 1941- *ConDr 93,
IntDcT 2*
DeGroff, Ralph Lynn, Jr. 1936-
WhoAm 94, WhoFI 94
De Groot, Albert 1945- *IntWW 93*
De Groot, John 1941- *WhoAm 94*
de Groot, John Weert, Jr. 1927-
WhoAmP 93
de Groot, Katherine Hynes d1993
NewYTBS 93 [port]
Degroot, Leslie Jacob 1928- *WhoAm 94*
DeGroot, Loren Edward 1935-
WhoMW 93
De Groot, Morris Herman 1931-1989
WhAm 10
De Groot, Myra *WhoHol 92*
de Groote, Jacques 1927- *IntWW 93*
DeGroote, Judith *DrAPF 93*
DeGross, Pierce Edward, III 1964-
WhoFI 94
de Grouchy, Robert Travis, Jr. 1953-
WhoWest 94
Degrow, Dan L. 1953- *WhoAmP 93*
de Gruchy, John W(esley) 1939- *WrDr 94*
de Gruchy, Nigel Ronald Anthony 1943-
Who 94

de Grunwald, Anatole 1910-1967
IntDcF 2-4
DeGruson, Eugene Henry 1932-
WhoAm 94
De Gruttla, Germaine Edna 1931-
WhoAmP 93
De Guatemala, Joyce 1938- *WhoAmA 93*
De Guingand, Pierre d1964 *WhoHol 92*
DeGuire, Mark Robert 1958-
WhoScEn 94
de Guise, Elizabeth Mary Teresa 1934-
WrDr 94
Deguy, Michel 1930- *ConWorW 93*
De Guzman, Evelyn Lopez 1947-
WhoAmA 93
de Guzman, Roman de Lara 1941-
WhoScEn 94
De Haan, Hendrik 1941- *IntWW 93*
DeHaan, Norman Richard 1927-1990
WhAm 10
De Haan-Puls, Joyce Elaine 1941-
WhoMW 93
DeHaas, John Neff, Jr. 1926- *WhoAm 94*
De Haas, Louis H. 1941- *WhoAmL 94*
Dehaene, Jean-Luc 1940- *IntWW 93,
Who 94*
de Hamel, Christopher Francis Rivers
1950- *Who 94*
de Hamel, Joan (Littledale) 1924-
WrDr 94
DeHarde, William M. 1933- *WhoAm 94*
DeHart, Dan William 1951- *WhoAmP 93*
DeHart, Henry R. 1931- *WhoBlA 94*
DeHart, Panzy H. 1934- *WhoBlA 94*
de Hartog, Jan 1914- *WhoAm 94*
De Hass, John Philip 1735-1786
WhAmRev
De Hauteclocque, Nicole 1913-
WhoWomW 91
De Haven, Carter d1977 *WhoHol 92*
De Haven, Carter, Mrs. d1950 *WhoHol 92*
De Haven, Carter, Jr. d1979 *WhoHol 92*
De Haven, Edwin Jesse 1816-1865 *WhWE*
DeHaven, Ernest Thomas 1928-
WhoMW 93
De Haven, Gloria 1925- *WhoHol 92*
DeHaven, Kenneth Le Moyne 1913-
WhoScEn 94, WhoWest 94
DeHaven, Michael Allen 1950-
WhoAm 94, WhoAmL 94
De Haven, Richard 1958- *WhoHol 92*
De Haven, Tom *DrAPF 93*
De Haven, Tom 1949- *EncSF 93,
WrDr 94*
De Havilland, Olivia 1916- *IntMPA 94,
WhoHol 92*
de Havilland, Olivia Mary 1916-
IntWW 93, Who 94, WhoAm 94
DeHay, Jerry Marvin 1939- *WhoAm 94*
DeHayes, Daniel Wesley 1941-
WhoAm 94
Dehejia, Vidya 1942- *WrDr 94*
Dehelly, Jean d1964 *WhoHol 92*
Dehem, Roger Jules 1921- *IntWW 93*
Dehennin, Herman 1929- *IntWW 93,
Who 94*
Dehennin, Herman Baron 1929-
WhoAm 94
Deherrera, Guillermo A. 1950-
WhoAmP 93
DeHerrera, Guillermo Alejandro 1950-
WhoHisp 94
DeHerrera, Helen L. *WhoHisp 94*
de Herrera, Nancy Cooke *ConAu 142*
De Herrera, Rick *WhoHisp 94*
De Hertogh, August Albert 1935-
WhoScEn 94
De Heusch, Lucio 1946- *WhoAmA 93*
Dehghan, Elizabeth Irene 1951-
WhoWest 94
De Hirsch, Storm *DrAPF 93*
De Hita, Antonio Rodriguez *NewGrDO*
Dehler, Steve 1950- *WhoAmP 93*
Dehlinger, Peter 1917- *WhoAm 94*
Dehmelt, Hans G. 1922- *NobelP 91 [port]*
Dehmelt, Hans Georg 1922- *IntWW 93,
Who 94, WhoAm 94, WhoScEn 94,
WhoWest 94*
Dehmlow, Louis Henry Theodore, III
1927- *WhoAm 94*
Dehmlow, Nancy Jean 1952- *WhoMW 93*
Dehn, Adolf 1895-1968 *WhoAmA 93N*
Dehn, Conrad Francis 1926- *Who 94*
Dehn, Joseph William, Jr. 1928-
WhoAm 94
Dehn, Letha Arlene 1916- *WhoMW 93*
Dehn, Olive 1914- *WrDr 94*
Dehn, Paul 1912-1976 *IntDcF 2-4*
Dehn, Paul (Edward) 1912-1976
NewGrDO
Dehner, Dorothy 1901-
NewYTBS 93 [port], WhoAmA 93
Dehner, John 1915- *WhoHol 92*
Dehner, Joseph Julnes 1948- *WhoAm 94,
WhoAmL 94, WhoMW 93*
De Hoek, William Richard 1955-
WhoAmL 94
DeHoff, George W. 1913- *WhoAmP 93*

De Hoff, John Burling 1913- *WhoScEn 94*
De Hoffmann, Frederic 1924-1989 *WhAm 10*
de Hoghton, (Richard) Bernard (Cuthbert) 1945- *Who 94*
DeHoogh, Noreen Beth 1943- *WhoMW 93*
De Hoop, Adrianus Teunis 1927- *IntWW 93*
DeHope, Edward Kim 1952- *WhoAm 94*
DeHoratius, Raphael Joseph 1942- *WhoScEn 94*
DeHority, Edward Havens, Jr. 1930- *WhoAm 94*
De Hory, Elmyr d1976 *WhoHol 92*
Dehousse, Jean-Maurice 1936- *WhoScEn 94*
de Hoyos, Angela *DrAPF 93*
de Hoyos, Angela 1940- *BlmGWL, WhoHisp 94*
de Hoyos, David Treviño 1945- *WhoHisp 94*
de Hoyos, Debora 1953- *WhoHisp 94*
de Hoyos, Debora M. 1953- *WhoAm 94*
De Hoyos, Librado R., Jr. 1933- *WhoHisp 94*
DeHoyos, Orlando Flores 1959- *WhoHisp 94*
Dehqani-Tafti, Hassan Barnaba 1920- *Who 94*
Deibel, Jill 1961- *WhoMW 93*
Deiber *NewGrDO*
Deiber, Julio Alcides 1945- *WhoScEn 94*
Deibler, William Edwin 1932- *WhoAm 94*
Deichman, Shane Daniel 1967- *WhoWest 94*
Deichmann, Bernhard Ernst 1935- *WhoFI 94*
Deieso, Donald Allan 1949- *WhoAm 94*
Deighton, Len 1929- *EncSF 93, IntWW 93, WhoAm 94, WrDr 94*
Deighton, Marga Ann d1971 *WhoHol 92*
Deignan, Robert E. 1938- *WhoAm 94*
Deihl, Charles L. 1937- *WhoAm 94*
Deihl, Michael Allen 1952- *WhoAm 94*
Deihl, Richard Harry 1928- *WhoAm 94, WhoFI 94, WhoWest 94*
Deike, James M. 1943- *WhoIns 94*
Deikel, Theodore *WhoFI 94*
Deikman, Eugene Lawrence 1927- *WhoAmL 94*
Deinekin, Petr Stepanovich 1937- *LoBiDrD*
Deinekin, Piotr Stepanovich 1937- *IntWW 93*
Deiner, John B. 1940- *WhoIns 94*
Deines, E. Hubert 1894-1967 *WhoAmA 93N*
Deines, Harry J. 1909- *WhoFI 94, WhoWest 94*
Deines, Vernon Phillip 1929- *WhoMW 93*
Deininger, David G. 1947- *WhoAmP 93*
Deininger, David George 1947- *WhoMW 93*
Deinzer, George William 1934- *WhoAm 94*
Deinzer, George William 1934-1993 *WhoMW 93*
Deiotte, Charles Edward 1946- *WhoWest 94*
de Irala, Mikel *WhoHisp 94*
Deisenhofer, Johann 1943- *NobelP 91 [port], Who 94, WhoAm 94, WhoScEn 94*
Deisenroth, Clinton Wilbur 1941- *WhoAm 94, WhoWest 94*
Deisler, Paul Frederick, Jr. 1926- *WhoAm 94*
Deiss, Joseph Jay 1915- *WrDr 94*
Deissler, Mary A. 1955- *WhoAm 94*
Deissler, Robert George 1921- *WhoAm 94*
Deisz, Shawn Lynette 1959- *WhoFI 94*
Deitch, Arline Douglis 1922- *WhoAm 94*
Deitch, Irene 1930- *WhoAm 94*
Deitch, Jeffrey 1952- *WhoAmA 93*
Deitcher, Herbert 1933- *WhoAm 94*
Deitchman, Bnzeion Buzz 1949- *WhoAmL 94*
Deiter, Newton Elliott 1931- *WhoAm 94, WhoScEn 94, WhoWest 94*
Deiters, Joan Adele 1934- *WhoAm 94*
Deitrich, Lawrence Walter 1938- *WhoMW 93*
Deitrich, Richard Adam 1931- *WhoWest 94*
Deitrick, William Edgar 1944- *WhoAm 94, WhoAmL 94*
Deitsch, Jeremy Stafford *ConAu 141*
Deitz, Melvin Eugene 1940- *WhoFI 94*
Deitz, Paula 1938- *WhoAm 94*
Deitz, Robert L. 1946- *WhoAmL 94*
Deitzler, Harry G. 1951- *WhoAmL 94*
Deivanayagam, Subramaniam 1941- *WhoAsA 94*
Deiz, Mercedes F. 1917- *WhoBlA 94, WhoHisp 94*
Dejaegher, M. Bob *WhoAmP 93*
De Jager, Cornelis 1921- *IntWW 93*
De-Ja-Gou *Who 94*
Dejanovic, Draga 1843-1870 *BlmGWL*
DeJarmon, Elva Pegues 1921- *WhoBlA 94*
Dejarnette, Edmund, Jr. 1938- *WhoAmP 93*
DeJean, Joan (Elizabeth) 1948- *WrDr 94*
Dejean De La Batie, Bernard 1927- *IntWW 93*
De Jesús, Confesor 1944- *WhoHisp 94*
De Jesus, Gary 1962- *WhoHisp 94*
DeJesus, Hiram Raymon 1957- *WhoHisp 94*
De Jesús, Isaías 1942- *WhoHisp 94*
De Jesús, Ivette 1960- *WhoHisp 94*
de Jesus, Jose *WhoHisp 94*
DeJesus, Jose 1965- *WhoHisp 94*
De Jesus, Nydia Rosa 1930- *WhoAm 94, WhoScEn 94*
De Jesús, Sara *WhoHisp 94*
De Jesus-Burgos, Sylvia Teresa 1941- *WhoHisp 94*
De Jesús-Torres, Migdalia 1944- *WhoHisp 94*
de Jeude, Erland van Lidth 1954- *WhoHol 92*
Dejid, Bugyn 1927- *IntWW 93*
Dejmek, Kazimierz 1924- *IntWW 93*
De Johnette, Jack 1942- *WhoAm 94*
Dejoie, C. C., Jr. 1914- *WhoBlA 94*
Dejoie, Carolyn Barnes Milanes *WhoBlA 94*
Dejoie, Michael C. 1947- *WhoBlA 94*
De Jong, Arthur Jay 1934- *WhoAm 94*
DeJong, Bruce Allen 1946- *WhoWest 94*
DeJong, Caspar Karel 1946- *WhoMW 93*
Dejong, Constance *DrAPF 93*
De Jong, David Samuel 1951- *WhoAmL 94, WhoFI 94*
de Jong, Eveline D(orothea) 1948- *WrDr 94*
De Jong, Gary Joel 1947- *WhoScEn 94*
DeJong, Gerben 1946- *WhoAm 94*
De Jong, Gerrit, Jr. 1892-1979 *WhoAmA 93N*
DeJong, James Gerald 1951- *WhoAmL 94*
De Jong, Jan Willem 1921- *IntWW 93*
De Jong, Lloyd Lambert 1944- *WhoMW 93*
de Jong, Mechtild 1939- *WhoWomW 91*
De Jong, Meindert 1906-1991 *WrDr 94N*
DeJong, Patricia Ellen 1949- *WhoMW 93*
De Jong, Russell Nelson 1907-1990 *WhAm 10*
de Jonge, Alex 1938- *ConAu 42NR, WrDr 94*
DeJonge, Christopher John 1958- *WhoScEn 94*
de Jongh, Eduard 1931- *IntWW 93*
De Jongh, James *DrAPF 93*
de Jongh, James Laurence 1942- *WhoBlA 94*
de Jongh, Nicholas Raymond 1946- *Who 94*
De Josselin De Jong, Patrick Edward 1922- *IntWW 93*
Dejouany, Guy Georges Andre 1920- *Who 94*
de Jouvenel, Hugues Alain 1946- *WrDr 94*
DeJulio, Ellen Louise 1946- *WhoMW 93*
Dekany, Imre Lajos 1946- *WhoScEn 94*
Dekat, Joseph Carroll Francis 1952- *WhoFI 94*
Deken, Aagje 1741-1804 *BlmGWL*
De Kerekjarto, Duci d1962 *WhoHol 92*
De Kergommeaux, Duncan 1927- *WhoAmA 93*
De Keyser, David *WhoHol 92*
De Keyzer, Patrick Maurice 1954- *WhoFI 94*
Dekich, Sherlie Eugene 1929- *WhoFI 94*
deKieffer, Donald Eulette 1945- *WhoAm 94, WhoAmL 94*
Dekker, Albert d1968 *WhoHol 92*
Dekker, Carl 1924- *WrDr 94*
Dekker, Eugene Earl 1927- *WhoAm 94*
Dekker, Fred 1959- *HorFD*
Dekker, George 1934- *WrDr 94*
Dekker, George Gilbert 1934- *WhoAm 94, WhoWest 94*
Dekker, Marcel 1931- *WhoAm 94*
Dekker, Maurits 1899- *WhoAm 94*
Dekker, Thomas 1570?-1632 *BlmGEL*
Dekker, Thomas c. 1572-1632 *IntDcT 2, LitC 22 [port]*
Dekker, W. 1924- *IntWW 93*
de Klerk, Albert 1917- *IntWW 93*
de Klerk, F. W. *NewYTBS 93 [port]*
de Klerk, Frederik Willem 1936- *IntWW 93, Who 94*
Dekmejian, Richard Hrair 1933- *WhoAm 94*
Deknatel, Frederick Brockway 1905-1973 *WhoAmA 93N*
De Knight, Avel 1933- *WhoAmA 93, WhoBlA 94*
DeKock, William Henry 1938- *WhoMW 93*
De Kok, Ingrid 1951- *BlmGWL*
Dekom, Peter James 1946- *WhoAm 94, WhoAmL 94*
De Konink, Servaas *NewGrDO*
De Kooning, Elaine Marie Catherine 1920-1989 *WhoAmA 93N*
de Kooning, Willem 1904- *AmCulL, IntWW 93, WhoAm 94*
De Kooning, William 1904-1988 *WhoAmA 93N*
Dekorsi, Ann Elizabeth 1947- *WhoMW 93*
De Korte, Rudolf Willem 1936- *IntWW 93*
De Koster, Lucas James 1918- *WhoAmP 93*
De Kova, Frank d1981 *WhoHol 92*
DeKoven, Reginald, III 1948- *WhoAm 94*
De Koven, (Henry Louis) Reginald 1859-1920 *NewGrDO*
Dekoven, Roger d1988 *WhoHol 92*
De Kowa, Viktor d1973 *WhoHol 92*
de Krasinski, Joseph Stanislas 1914- *WhoScEn 94*
DeKrey, Duane L. 1956- *WhoAmP 93*
DeKrey, Duane Lee 1956- *WhoFI 94*
de Kruif, Jack H. 1921- *WhoAm 94, WhoWest 94*
De Kruyf, Ton *NewGrDO*
Dekster, Boris Veniamin 1938- *WhoScEn 94*
de la Barre de Nanteuil, Luc 1925- *IntWW 93, Who 94*
DelaBarre Powers, Nancy May 1941- *WhoFI 94*
Delabbio, Daryl Joseph 1953- *WhoMW 93*
De la Bere, Cameron 1933- *Who 94*
de la Billiere, Peter (Edgar de la Cour) 1934- *IntWW 93, Who 94*
De La Brosse, Simon *WhoHol 92*
De La Cadena, Raul Alvarez 1959- *WhoScEn 94*
De La Cancela, Victor 1952- *WhoHisp 94*
Delacato, Carl Henry 1923- *WhoAm 94*
Delacey, Deborah Hartwell 1952- *WhoFI 94*
De Lacey, John d1924 *WhoHol 92*
De Lacey, Philippe 1917- *WhoHol 92*
de la Colina, Rafael 1898- *WhoAm 94*
Delacorte, George Thomas, Jr. 1894-1991 *WhAm 10*
Delacote, Jacques *IntWW 93*
Delacour, Jean-Paul 1930- *Who 94*
Delacour, Yves Jean Claude Marie 1943- *WhoFI 94, WhoScEn 94*
Delacourt-Smith Of Alteryn, Baroness 1916- *Who 94*
DeLaCroix, Alice 1940- *ConAu 142, SmATA 75 [port]*
de la Cruz, Carlos Manuel, Sr. 1941- *WhoHisp 94*
De La Cruz, Daniel F. 1941- *WhoHisp 94*
De la Cruz, Dimitri 1957- *WhoHisp 94*
De La Cruz, Jerry John 1948- *WhoHisp 94*
De La Cruz, Joe *WhoHisp 94*
Dela Cruz, Jose Santos 1948- *WhoAm 94, WhoAmL 94, WhoWest 94*
De La Cruz, Joseph d1961 *WhoHol 92*
De La Cruz, Juan d1953 *WhoHol 92*
De La Cruz, Pedro 1950- *WhoHisp 94*
De La Cruz-Cartagena, Luis T. 1950- *WhoHisp 94*
de la Cruz Meléndez, Francisco 1955- *WhoHisp 94*
de la Cuadra, Bruce *WhoHisp 94*
de la Cuesta, Leonel A. 1937- *WhoHisp 94*
De La Cueva, Julio Jose Iglesias 1943- *WhoAm 94*
DeLacy, James Peter 1937- *WhoFI 94*
De Lacy, Leigh d1966 *WhoHol 92*
de la Fe, Frank Arthur 1940- *WhoHisp 94*
Delafield, E. M. 1890-1943 *BlmGWL [port]*
Delafield, Joseph Livingston, III 1940- *WhoAmL 94*
Delafons, John 1930- *Who 94*
De La Fuente, Arnoldo Romeo 1959- *WhoHisp 94*
de la Fuente, Javier Ramirez 1947- *WhoHisp 94*
de la Fuente, Roque *WhoHisp 94*
De La Garza, Charles H. 1948- *WhoAmL 94*
De La Garza, E. 1927- *CngDr 93, WhoAmP 93*
De la Garza, Eddie 1952- *WhoHisp 94*
de la Garza, Eligio 1927- *WhoAm 94, WhoHisp 94*
de la Garza, Kika 1927- *WhoHisp 94*
de la Garza, Leonardo 1937- *WhoHisp 94*
de la Garza, Luis Adolfo 1943- *WhoHisp 94*
De La Garza, Pete 1945- *WhoHisp 94*
de la Garza, Ray 1958- *WhoWest 94*
De La Garza, Rene E. 1961- *WhoHisp 94*
de la Garza, Rodolfo O. 1942- *WhoHisp 94*
Delage, Marie M. 1936- *WhoAmP 93*
de la Guardia, Mario Francisco 1936- *WhoAm 94*
de la Gueronniere, Raphael *WhoAm 94, WhoFI 94*
del Aguila, Juan Manuel 1950- *WhoHisp 94*
de Laguna, Frederica 1906- *WhoAm 94*
Delahanty, Edward Lawrence 1942- *WhoFI 94*
Delahanty, Thomas Edward, II 1945- *WhoAmP 93*
Delahay, Paul 1921- *WhoScEn 94*
De La Haye, Ina d1972 *WhoHol 92*
Delahaye, Michael (John) 1946- *WrDr 94*
Delahoussaye, Eddie *NewYTBS 93 [port]*
De La Hoya, Oscar *WhoAm 94*
De La Hoya, Oscar 1973- *WhoHisp 94*
Delahunty, Joseph L. 1935- *WhoAmP 93*
De La Iglesia, Felix Alberto 1939- *WhoAm 94*
D'Elaine 1932- *WhoAmA 93*
Delair, Suzy 1916- *WhoHol 92*
Delaire, Jean *EncSF 93*
De Laittre, Eleanor 1911- *WhoAmA 93*
Delakas, Daniel Liudviko 1921- *WhoAm 94*
Delalande, Michel-Richard *NewGrDO*
de la Lanne-Mirrlees, Robin Ian Evelyn Stuart *Who 94*
DeLalio, George M. d1993 *NewYTBS 93*
Delaloye, Bernard 1928- *WhoAm 94, WhoScEn 94*
Delaloye, John Francis 1945- *WhoIns 94*
De La Luz, Nilsa 1946- *WhoHisp 94*
de Lama, George 1957- *WhoHisp 94*
de la Madrid Hurtado, Miguel 1934- *Who 94*
De La Madrid Hurtado, Miguel 1935- *IntWW 93*
de la Mare, Albinia Catherine 1932- *Who 94*
de la Mare, Arthur 1914- *IntWW 93*
de la Mare, Arthur (James) 1914- *Who 94*
Delamare, Lise *WhoHol 92*
De la Mare, Walter 1873-1956 *BlmGEL, RfGShF, ShSCr 14 [port], TwCLC 53 [port]*
Delamarter, Thelda Jean Harvey 1924- *WhoMW 93*
de la Martinez, Odaline 1949- *Who 94*
DeLamater, James Newton 1912- *WhoAm 94*
Delamere, Baron 1934- *Who 94*
Delamere, Monita (Eru) 1921- *Who 94*
De Lamerie, Paul Jacques 1688-1751 *DcNaB MP*
DeLamonica, Roberto 1933- *WhoAmA 93*
de la Mora, Juan Fernandez 1952- *WhoHisp 94*
de la Morena, Felipe 1927- *IntWW 93, Who 94*
De La Motte, Marguerite d1950 *WhoHol 92*
Delamotte, Philip Henry 1821-1889 *DcNaB MP*
Delamuraz, Jean-Pascal 1936- *IntWW 93*
De Lancey, James 1746-1802 *AmRev*
De Lancey, James (the Elder) 1732-1800 *WhAmRev*
De Lancey, James (the Younger) 1746-1804 *WhAmRev*
De Lancey, Oliver 1718-1785 *AmRev*
De Lancey, Oliver, Jr. 1749-1822 *AmRev*
De Lancey, Oliver (the Elder) 1718-1785 *WhAmRev*
De Lancey, Oliver (the Younger) 1749-1822 *WhAmRev*
DeLancey, Scott Cameron 1949- *WhoWest 94*
De Lancey, William J. 1916- *EncABHB 9*
De Lancie, John *WhoHol 92*
Deland, Margaret Wade Campbell 1857-1945 *BlmGWL*
Deland, Michael Reeves 1941- *WhoAm 94*
De Landa, Juan d1968 *WhoHol 92*
Delandro, Donald J. 1935- *AfrAmG [port]*
de Lanerolle, Nimal Gerard 1945- *WhoScEn 94*
Delaney, Andrew 1920- *WhoFI 94*
Delaney, Andrew John 1962- *WhoAmL 94*
DeLaney, Ann M. 1946- *WhoAmP 93*
Delaney, Beauford 1902-1979 *WhoAmA 93N*
Delaney, Beauford 1910-1979 *AfrAmAl 6*
Delaney, Cassandra *WhoHol 92*
Delaney, Charles d1959 *WhoHol 92*
Delaney, Cornelius Francis 1938- *WhoAm 94, WhoMW 93*
Delaney, Daniel Peter 1949- *WhoAm 94*
Delaney, Denis 1924- *WrDr 94*
Delaney, Edward Norman 1927- *WhoAmL 94, WhoFI 94*
DeLaney, Edward O'Donnell 1943- *WhoAm 94, WhoAmL 94*
Delaney, Francis James Joseph 1942- *Who 94*
Delaney, Gayle (M. V.) 1949- *ConAu 142*
Delaney, Harold 1919- *WhoBlA 94*

Del Prato, Vincenzo *NewGrDO*
Del Prete, John F. 1927- *WhoAmP 93*
Del Propost, John Joseph 1962- *WhoAmL 94*
Del Puente, Giuseppe 1841-1900 *NewGrDO*
Delpy, Julie 1969- *WhoHol 92*
Del Raso, Joseph Vincent 1952- *WhoAmL 94*
DelRaso, Nicholas John 1957- *WhoMW 93*
Delray, Chester *EncSF 93*
Del Razo, Erick Silva 1967- *WhoWest 94*
Del Re, Vincenzo *NewGrDO*
del Regato, Juan Angel 1909- *WhoAm 94, WhoScEn 94*
Del Regno, Ugo d1981 *WhoHol 92*
Del Rey, Alfred J. 1946- *WhoAmL 94*
del Rey, Judy-Lynn 1943-1986 *EncSF 93*
del Rey, Lester d1993 *NewYTBS 93*
del Rey, Lester 1915- *EncSF 93, WrDr 94*
del Rey, Lester 1915-1993 *ConAu 141, SmATA 76*
Del Rey, Pilar *WhoHol 92*
Del Rio, Carlos H. 1949- *WhoHisp 94*
del Rio, Carmen Maria 1947- *WhoHisp 94*
Del Rio, Dolores d1983 *WhoHol 92*
Del Rio, Fernando Rene 1932- *WhoHisp 94*
del Rio, Graciela 1955- *WhoHisp 94*
del Rio, Israel H. 1948- *WhoHisp 94*
Del Rio, Jack d1978 *WhoHol 92*
Del Rio, Joaquín 1941- *WhoHisp 94*
Del Rio, Luis Raul 1939- *WhoHisp 94*
Del Rio-Diaz, Estyne 1945- *WhoAm 94*
Del Rosario, Franco R. *WhoHisp 94*
Del Rosario, Mirza 1957- *WhoHisp 94*
del Rosario Sintes Ulloa, Maria *WhoWomW 91*
Del Rossi, Paul R. 1942- *IntMPA 94*
Delroy, Irene *WhoHol 92*
Delruelle-Ghobert, Janine 1931- *WhoWomW 91*
del Russo, Alessandra Luini 1916- *WhoAmL 94*
Del Ruth, Thomas Anthony 1943- *WhoAm 94*
Del Santo, Lawrence A. 1934- *WhoAm 94, WhoFI 94, WhoWest 94*
Del Sol, Laura *WhoHol 92*
del Solar, Daniel 1940- *WhoWest 94*
Delson, Elizabeth 1932- *WhoAm 94, WhoAmA 93*
Delson, Robert 1905- *WhoAm 94*
Delson, Sidney Leon 1932- *WhoAm 94*
Delta, Penelope 1871-1941 *BlmGWL*
Deltgen, Rene d1979 *WhoHol 92*
Del Tito, Benjamin John, Jr. 1955- *WhoScEn 94*
Delton, Judy 1931- *SmATA 77 [port]*
Del Toro, Ana I. 1950- *WhoHisp 94*
Del Toro, Angelo 1947- *WhoAmP 93, WhoHisp 94*
Del Toro, Margaret 1949- *WhoHisp 94*
del Toro, Raul *WhoHisp 94*
Del Tredici, David 1937- *WhoAm 94*
Deltry, William d1924 *WhoHol 92*
Del Tufo, Robert J. 1933- *WhoAm 94, WhoAmL 94, WhoAmP 93*
delTufo, Theresa Lallana Izon 1943- *WhoAm 94*
De Lubac, Henri Sonier 1896-1991 *WhAm 10*
Deluc, Xavier *WhoHol 92*
DeLuca, Anthony *WhoAmP 93*
Deluca, Anthony M. 1937- *WhoAmP 93*
DeLuca, August Frank, Jr. 1943- *WhoFI 94*
De Luca, Carlo John 1943- *WhoAm 94*
DeLuca, Diana Macintyre 1943- *WhoWest 94*
DeLuca, Donald Paul 1940- *WhoAm 94, WhoFI 94*
De Luca, Giuseppe d1950 *WhoHol 92*
De Luca, Giuseppe 1876-1950 *NewGrDO [port]*
DeLuca, John 1956- *WhoScEn 94*
De Luca, Joseph Victor 1935- *WhoAmA 93*
Deluca, Louis C. *WhoAmP 93*
DeLuca, Marc David 1963- *WhoMW 93*
DeLuca, Mary 1960- *WhoScEn 94*
DeLuca, Patrick Phillip 1935- *WhoAm 94, WhoScEn 94*
DeLuca, Ronald 1924- *WhoAm 94*
De Luca, Rudy *WhoHol 92*
De Luca, Severo fl. 1685-1720 *NewGrDO*
De Luca, Thomas George 1950- *WhoAmL 94*
DeLuca, Thomas Henry 1962- *WhoMW 93*
DeLucca, Gregory James 1937- *WhoWest 94*
DeLucca, Leopoldo Eloy 1952- *WhoMW 93*
Delucchi, George Paul 1938- *WhoWest 94*
De Lucchi, Michele 1951- *IntWW 93*
DeLuce, Richard David 1928- *WhoAm 94*
de Luce, Virginia 1921- *WhoAm 94, WhoHol 92*
De Lucia, Fernando 1860-1925 *NewGrDO*
De Lucia, Frank Charles 1943- *WhoAm 94*
DeLucia, Richard L. 1948- *WhoAmL 94*
De Lucia-Weinberg, Diane Marie 1964- *WhoScEn 94*
Delugach, Albert Lawrence 1925- *WhoAm 94*
De Lugo, Ron 1930- *CngDr 93, WhoAm 94, WhoHisp 94*
de Lugo, Ronald 1930- *WhoAmP 93*
Deluhery, Patrick John 1942- *WhoAmP 93, WhoMW 93*
Deluigi, Janice Cecilia Weil Lefton *WhoAmA 93*
De Luise, Dom 1933- *IntMPA 94, WhoAm 94, WhoCom, WhoHol 92*
De Luise, Peter *WhoHol 92*
De Lullo, Giorgio d1981 *WhoHol 92*
de Lumen, Benito O. 1940- *WhoWest 94*
De Luna, Evangelina S. 1939- *WhoHisp 94*
De Luna, Rosalinda 1953- *WhoMW 93*
Delunas, Linda 1955- *WhoMW 93*
De Lung, Jane Solberger 1944- *WhoFI 94*
De Lungo, Tony 1892- *WhoHol 92*
Delurey, Michael William 1962- *WhoScEn 94*
De Lurgio, Stephen Anthony 1945- *WhoMW 93*
DeLury, Bernard E. 1938- *WhoAm 94, WhoFI 94*
De Lussan, Zelie 1861-1949 *NewGrDO*
DeLustro, Frank Anthony 1948- *WhoAm 94*
DeLustro, Frank Joseph 1947- *WhoFI 94*
De Lutis, Donald Conse 1934- *WhoAm 94*
DeLuze, James Robert 1948- *WhoWest 94*
Deluzio, Vincent C. 1947- *WhoAmL 94*
Del Val, Jean d1975 *WhoHol 92*
Delvalie, Eduardo *WhoAmA 93*
del Valle, Antonio M. 1954- *WhoHisp 94*
Del Valle, Carlos Sergio 1951- *WhoHisp 94*
Del Valle, Cezar Jose 1945- *WhoAmA 93*
Del Valle, David d1934 *WhoHol 92*
del Valle, Eduardo N. 1961- *WhoHisp 94*
Delvalle, Eric Arturo 1937- *IntWW 93*
Del Valle, Hector L. 1963- *WhoHisp 94*
Del Valle, Irma *DrAPF 93*
del Valle, John 1904- *IntMPA 94*
Del Valle, Jose M. *WhoAmP 93, WhoHisp 94*
Del Valle, Joseph Bourke 1919- *WhoAmA 93*
Del Valle, M. 1931- *WhoHisp 94*
del Valle, Manuel Luis 1924- *WhoFI 94*
Del Valle, Miguel 1951- *WhoAmP 93, WhoHisp 94*
Del Valle, Tony 1955- *WhoHisp 94*
Del Valle Alliende, Jaime 1931- *IntWW 93*
Del Valle-Iovino, Jean Marie 1961-1993 *WhoHisp 94N*
del Valle-Sepúlveda, Edwin Alberto 1962- *WhoHisp 94*
Del Vando, Amapola d1988 *WhoHol 92*
Delvaux, Paul 1897- *IntWW 93*
Delvaux-Stehres, Mady 1950- *WhoWomW 91*
Delve, Frederick (William) 1902- *Who 94*
Delventhal, Robert W. 1944- *WhoAmL 94*
Del Villar, Laura 1958- *WhoHisp 94*
Delvin, Lord *Who 94*
Delvin, David George 1939- *Who 94*
Delvincourt, Claude 1888-1954 *NewGrDO*
Del Violone, Giovanni *NewGrDO*
Delvoye, Jacques Victor 1947- *WhoFI 94, WhoWest 94*
Delwiche, Lyle Dean 1934- *WhoMW 93*
Delwiche, Patricia Ellen 1952- *WhoMW 93*
Dely, Steven 1943- *WhoAm 94*
Delyannis, Leonidas T. 1926- *WhoAmP 93*
DeLynn, Jane *DrAPF 93*
De Lyrot, Alain Herve 1926- *WhoAm 94*
Delysia, Alice d1979 *WhoHol 92*
Delz, William Ronald 1932- *WhoAm 94*
Delza-Munson, Elizabeth *WhoAm 94*
Delzeit, Linda Doris 1954- *WhoWest 94*
Delzell, Charles F 1920- *WrDr 94*
Delzer, Jeff W. *WhoAmP 93*
deMaar, Natalie Shana 1950- *WhoWest 94*
de MaCarty, Peter Charles Ridgway 1952- *WhoWest 94*
De Macchi, Maria *NewGrDO*
de Macedo, Carlyle Guerra 1937- *WhoAm 94*
de Madariaga (Y Rojo), Salvador *EncSF 93*
de Madariaga, Isabel 1919- *IntWW 93*
de Madeiros, Maria 1965- *WhoHol 92*
Demain, Arnold Lester 1927- *WhoScEn 94*
De Main, Gordon d1967 *WhoHol 92*
DeMain, John 1944- *NewGrDO, WhoAm 94*
Demain, Paul 1955- *WhoAmP 93*
De Maio, Victoria Antoinette 1947- *WhoWest 94*
de Maiziere, Lothar 1940- *IntWW 93*
de Maiziere, Ulrich 1912- *IntWW 93*
De Majo, Gian Francesco *NewGrDO*
De Majo, Giuseppe *NewGrDO*
de Majo, William Maks 1917- *Who 94*
De Man, Paul 1919-1983 *BlmGEL*
De Mance, Henri 1871-1948 *WhoAmA 93N*
Demanche, Michel S. 1953- *WhoAmA 93*
Demangone, Dominic Donald 1949- *WhoAmP 93*
DeMann, Jack Frank 1933- *WhoAmP 93*
De Mar, Carrie d1963 *WhoHol 92*
Demar, Claire 1800-1833 *BlmGWL*
de Mar, Leoda Miller 1929- *WhoAm 94*
Demara, F. W. d1982 *WhoHol 92*
De Maranville, Nancy Joan 1932- *WhoWest 94*
Demaray, Donald E(ugene) 1926- *WrDr 94*
Demaray, Mark Marston 1953- *WhoAmL 94*
De Marchi, Emilio 1861-1917 *NewGrDO*
Demarchi, Ernest Nicholas 1939- *WhoAm 94, WhoScEn 94, WhoWest 94*
DeMarchis, Linda Weatherby 1946- *WhoMW 93*
De Marco, Guido 1931- *IntWW 93*
De Marco, Jean Antoine 1898-1990 *WhoAmA 93N*
DeMarco, Kenneth F. 1948- *WhoAmL 94*
DeMarco, Michael 1936- *WhoAmP 93*
DeMarco, Peter Vincent 1955- *WhoScEn 94*
DeMarco, Ralph John 1924- *WhoFI 94, WhoWest 94*
Demarco, Richard 1930- *Who 94*
DeMarco, Robert Thomas 1950- *WhoAm 94*
DeMarco, Roland R. 1910- *WhoAm 94, WhoFI 94*
De Marco, Sally *WhoHol 92*
De Marco, Thomas Joseph 1942- *WhoAm 94*
De Marco, Tony d1965 *WhoHol 92*
Demarco, Tony d1985 *WhoHol 92*
DeMarco, Vincent 1957- *WhoAmP 93*
De Marco Sisters, The *WhoHol 92*
De Marcus, Jamima Powell *WhoAmP 93*
de Mare, Eric 1910- *Who 94*
De Mare, Rolf 1888-1964 *IntDcB [port]*
DeMaree, Betty 1918- *WhoAmA 93*
Demaree, David Harry 1939- *WhoMW 93*
Demaree, Duane David 1925- *WhoFI 94*
Demaree, Robert Glenn 1920- *WhoScEn 94*
Demarest, Daniel Anthony 1924- *WhoAm 94*
Demarest, David Franklin, Jr. 1951- *WhoAm 94*
Demarest, David N. *NewYTBS 93 [port]*
Demarest, Drew d1949 *WhoHol 92*
Demarest, Harold H., Jr. 1946- *WhoAmP 93*
Demarest, Rube d1962 *WhoHol 92*
Demarest, Sylvia M. 1944- *WhoAm 94*
Demarest, William d1983 *WhoHol 92*
Demarest, William 1882-1983 *WhoCom*
Demarest, William F. 1947- *WhoAmL 94*
de Margerie, Jean-M. 1927- *WhoAm 94*
de Margitay, Gedeon 1924- *WhoFI 94*
De Maria, Anthony John 1931- *WhoAm 94*
DeMaria, Anthony Nicholas 1943- *WhoAm 94*
DeMaria, Joseph Carminus 1947- *WhoAmL 94*
DeMaria, Peter James 1934- *WhoAm 94*
Demaria, Robert *DrAPF 93*
Demaria, Walter 1935- *WhoAm 94, WhoAmA 93*
Demarinis, Nancy A. *WhoAmP 93*
DeMarinis, Rick 1934- *EncSF 93, WrDr 94*
De Marino, Donald Nicholson 1945- *WhoAm 94, WhoFI 94*
DeMaris, Daphne Lynn 1965- *WhoMW 93*
Demaris, Ovid 1919- *WrDr 94*
Demaris, Ovis 1919- *WhoAm 94*
De Maris, Ron *DrAPF 93*
DeMark, Richard Reid 1925- *WhoAm 94*
de Marneffe, Francis 1924- *WhoAm 94*
De Marney, Derrick d1978 *WhoHol 92*
De Marney, Terence d1971 *WhoHol 92*
De Marr, Mary Jean 1932- *WhoAm 94, WhoMW 93*
DeMars, Bruce *WhoAm 94, WhoScEn 94*
DeMars, Dan Richard 1943- *WhoAm 94*
DeMars, Gene 1937- *WhoAmP 93*
DeMars, Robert A. 1930- *WhoAmP 93*
De Martelly, John Stockton 1903-1980 *WhoAmA 93N*
DeMartin, Charles Peter 1952- *WhoAmL 94*
DeMartini, Edward John 1932- *WhoAmL 94*
De Martini, Joseph 1896- *WhoAmA 93N*
DeMartini, Richard Michael 1952- *WhoAm 94, WhoFI 94*
Demartini, Robert John 1919- *WhoAm 94*
DeMartino, Anthony Gabriel 1931- *WhoAm 94*
De Martino, Ciro 1903- *IntWW 93*
De Martino, Francesco 1907- *IntWW 93*
Demartis, James J. 1926- *WhoAmA 93*
Demas, William Gilbert 1929- *IntWW 93*
DeMascio, Robert Edward 1923- *WhoAm 94, WhoAmL 94, WhoMW 93*
Demaso, Harry A. 1921- *WhoAmP 93*
DeMaso, Jeffrey Anthony 1964- *WhoAmL 94*
De Massa, Jessie G. *WhoWest 94*
De' Massimi, Francesco *NewGrDO*
De Matos Proenca, Joao Uva *IntWW 93*
deMatties, Nicholas Frank 1939- *WhoAm 94*
DeMatties, Nick 1939- *WhoAmA 93*
de Mauley, Baron 1921- *Who 94*
de Mauret, Kevin John 1957- *WhoScEn 94*
deMause, Lloyd 1931- *WhoAm 94*
De Mave, Jack *WhoHol 92*
De Max, Edouard Alexandre d1924 *WhoHol 92*
De May, Robert Lee 1946- *WhoAmL 94*
de Mayo, Paul 1924- *IntWW 93, Who 94*
Dembeck, Mary Grace 1931- *WhoAm 94*
Dembek, Zygmunt Francis 1950- *WhoScEn 94*
Dember, Jean Wilkins 1930- *WhoBlA 94*
Dember, William Norton 1928- *WhoAm 94*
Dembinski, David Thomas 1965- *WhoMW 93*
Dembling, Paul Gerald 1920- *WhoAm 94, WhoAmP 93*
Dembner, S. Arthur 1920-1990 *WhAm 10*
Dembo, Joseph T. *WhoAm 94*
Dembo, Lawrence Sanford 1929- *WhoAm 94*
Dembo, Tamara d1993 *NewYTBS 93*
Dembowski, Peter Florian 1925- *WhoAm 94*
Dembroski, George Steven 1934- *WhoAm 94*
Dembrow, Dana Lee 1953- *WhoAmP 93*
Dembs, Marcy Robinson 1958- *WhoAmL 94*
Dembski, Stephen Michael 1949- *WhoAm 94*
Demby, Emanuel H. 1919- *IntMPA 94*
Demby, James E. 1936- *WhoBlA 94*
Demby, William E., Jr. 1922- *WhoBlA 94*
Demcoe, Lloyd Robert 1930- *WhoMW 93*
de Medici, Lorenza 1926- *ConAu 141*
De Meester-Demeyer, Wivina 1943- *WhoWomW 91*
De Mel, Ronnie 1925- *IntWW 93*
Demell, Harry A. 1951- *WhoAmL 94*
De Mello, Alberto *WhoHol 92*
DeMello, Austin Eastwood 1939- *WhoWest 94*
De Melo, Eurico 1925- *IntWW 93*
De Menezes, Etevalda Grassi 1948- *WhoWomW 91*
de Menezes, Ruth *DrAPF 93*
DeMenil, Dominique 1908- *WhoAm 94*
De Menil, John 1904-1973 *WhoAmA 93N*
Dement, Franklin Leroy, Jr. 1966- *WhoScEn 94*
De Ment, Ira 1931- *WhoAm 94, WhoAmL 94*
De Ment, Jack Andrew 1920- *WhoWest 94*
De Ment, James Alderson 1920- *WhoScEn 94*
DeMent, James Alderson, Jr. 1947- *WhoAm 94, WhoAmL 94*
Dement, William Charles 1928- *WhoAm 94*
Dementis, Katharine Hopkins 1922- *WhoScEn 94*
DeMeo, Edgar Anthony 1942- *WhoWest 94*
Demerath, Jeffrey Titus 1948- *WhoAmL 94*
Demerath, Nicholas Jay, III 1936- *WhoAm 94*
Demerdash, Nabeel Aly Omar 1943- *WhoAm 94*
DeMere, McCarthy 1925- *WhoAmL 94*
Demeree, Gloria 1931- *WhoWest 94*
De Meric, Josephine 1801-1877 *NewGrDO*
Demeritte, Edwin T. 1935- *WhoBlA 94*
Demeritte, Richard C. 1939- *IntWW 93*
Demeritte, Richard Clifford 1939- *Who 94*
Demerjian, Kenneth L. 1945- *WhoScEn 94*
DeMers, Gerald Louis 1956- *WhoMW 93*

Demers, Jacques 1944- *WhoAm 94*
Demers, Judy L. 1944- *WhoAmP 93*
DeMers, Judy Lee 1944- *WhoMW 93*
Demers, Laurence Maurice 1938- *WhoScEn 94*
DeMers, Patricia A. *WhoAmP 93*
Demers, Sharon Washington 1951- *WhoAmP 93*
De Mesquita, Henrique Alves *NewGrDO*
Demeter, Nancy Ford 1957- *WhoMW 93*
DeMeter, Robert F. 1948- *WhoAmL 94*
Demeter, Stephen Louis 1949- *WhoMW 93*
Demetillo, Ricaredo 1920- *WrDr 94*
Demetracopoulos, Anthony 1953- *WhoAmP 93*
Demetree, Frances Mary 1943- *WhoFI 94*
Demetrescu, Mihai Constantin 1929- *WhoScEn 94, WhoWest 94*
Demetri, Patricia *DrAPF 93*
Demetrio, Anna d1959 *WhoHol 92*
Demetrio, Thomas A. 1947- *WhoAmL 94*
Demetrion, James Thomas 1930- *WhoAm 94, WhoAmA 93*
Demetrios, George 1896-1974 *WhoAmA 93N*
Demetriou, Ioannes Constantine 1956- *WhoScEn 94*
Demetrious, Mary 1950- *WhoAmP 93*
De Meules, James Head 1945- *WhoAm 94, WhoAmL 94*
Demeure de Lespaul, Edouard Henri 1928- *Who 94*
De Meuse, Donald Howard 1936- *WhoAm 94, WhoFI 94, WhoMW 93*
De Mey, Guy 1955- *NewGrDO*
De Meyere, Robert Emmet 1951- *WhoScEn 94*
DeMezzo, Pietro c. 1730-1794? *NewGrDO*
Demian, Wilhelm 1910- *NewGrDO*
Demianoff, Renee Lockhart 1910-1962 *WhoAmA 93N*
De Michele, O. Mark 1934- *WhoAm 94, WhoFI 94, WhoWest 94*
De Michelis, Gianni 1940- *IntWW 93*
Demick, Irina 1937- *WhoHol 92*
De Micoli, Salvatore 1939- *WhoAm 94*
Demidova, Alla Sergeyevna 1936- *IntWW 93*
DeMieri, Joseph L. 1940- *WhoAm 94*
Demijohn, Thom *EncSF 93*
Demijohn, Thom 1937- *WrDr 94*
Demijohn, Thom 1940- *WrDr 94*
DeMik, Anita Lorraine 1945- *WhoMW 93*
D'Emilio, John 1948- *GayLL, WrDr 94*
D'Emilio, Sandra *WhoHisp 94*
de Mille, Agnes *ConAu 142, IntWW 93, WhoAm 94*
De Mille, Agnes 1905?- *IntDcB [port]*
de Mille, Agnes 1905-1993 *NewYTBS 93 [port], News 94-2*
de Mille, Agnes George *Who 94*
de Mille, Agnes George 1909- *AmCulL*
DeMille, Cecil B. d1959 *WhoHol 92*
DeMille, Cecil Blount 1881-1959 *AmCulL [port]*
De Mille, Cecilia d1984 *WhoHol 92*
DeMille, Darcy *WhoBlA 94*
De Mille, James 1833-1880 *EncSF 93*
De Mille, Katherine 1911- *WhoHol 92*
De Mille, Leslie Benjamin 1927- *WhoAmA 93*
Demille, Nelson (Richard) 1943- *WrDr 94*
de Mille, Peter Noel 1944- *Who 94*
De Mille, Richard *DrAPF 93*
de Mille, Richard 1922- *WrDr 94*
DeMille, Thomas W. 1938- *WhoAmL 94*
deMille, Valerie Cecilia 1949- *WhoBlA 94*
De Mille, William C. d1955 *WhoHol 92*
DeMillo, Richard A. 1947- *WhoAm 94*
Deming, Alison Hawthorne *DrAPF 93*
Deming, David Lawson 1943- *WhoAm 94, WhoAmA 93*
Deming, Donald Livingston 1924- *WhoAm 94*
Deming, Frank Stout 1927- *WhoAm 94*
Deming, Frederick Lewis 1912- *WhoAm 94*
Deming, John *DrAPF 93*
Deming, Laura *DrAPF 93*
Deming, N. Karen 1953- *WhoAmL 94*
Deming, Thomas Edward 1954- *WhoFI 94*
Deming, W. Edwards 1900- *CurBio 93 [port]*
Deming, W. Edwards 1900-1993 *NewYTBS 93 [port], News 94-2*
Deming, Wendy Anne 1968- *WhoScEn 94*
Deming, William Edwards *WhoAm 94, WhoScEn 94*
Deming, Willis Riley 1914- *WhoAm 94*
Demiray, Tanel 1946- *WhoFI 94*
Demirbilek, Zeki 1949- *WhoScEn 94*
Demirel, Suleyman 1924- *IntWW 93*
Demirgian, Jack Charles 1947- *WhoScEn 94*
Demiris, Okan 1940- *NewGrDO*
DeMirjian, Arto, Jr. *DrAPF 93*
Demiroz, Marco Y. 1957- *WhoFI 94*
Demise, Phil *DrAPF 93*
De Miskey, Julian d1986 *WhoAmA 93N*
De Mist, Augusta 1783-1832 *BlmGWL*
De Mita, Luigi Ciriaco 1928- *IntWW 93*
DeMitchell, Terri Ann 1953- *WhoAmL 94*
Demitz, Heinz-Jurgen 1946-1989 *NewGrDO*
Demkovitz, Russell Bernard 1949- *WhoAmP 93*
Demling, John William 1951- *WhoAmL 94*
Demlong, William Maurice 1960- *WhoAmL 94*
Demma, James J. 1939- *WhoAmL 94*
Demme, Jonathan 1944- *IntMPA 94, IntWW 93, WhoAm 94*
Demmer, William Roy 1933- *WhoAm 94*
Demmerle, Daniel H. 1948- *WhoAmL 94*
Demmler, John Henry 1932- *WhoAm 94*
Demmler, Ralph Henry 1904- *WhoAm 94*
Demo, Janine Louise Gracy 1962- *WhoMW 93*
Democritus c. 460BC-c. 370BC *EncEth, WorScD*
Demoff, Marvin Alan 1942- *WhoAmL 94, WhoWest 94*
Demoff, Samuel Louis 1909- *WhoAm 94*
De Moivre, Abraham *WorScD*
Demokan, Muhtesem Suleyman 1948- *WhoScEn 94*
De Moleyns *Who 94*
De Molina, Raul 1959- *WhoHisp 94*
De Molli, Anna Lugo 1950- *WhoHisp 94*
Demonbreun, Thelma M. 1928- *WhoBlA 94*
de Monchaux, Wendy Lynne 1959- *WhoFI 94*
Demond, Joan *WhoAm 94*
Demond, Walter Eugene 1947- *WhoAmL 94*
DeMone, Robert Stephen 1932- *WhoAm 94*
Demongeot, Mylene 1935- *WhoHol 92*
Demons, Leona Marie 1928- *WhoBlA 94*
deMonsabert, Winston Russel 1915- *WhoScEn 94*
Demont, William *WhAmRev*
De Monte, Claudia 1947- *WhoAmA 93*
DeMonte, Claudia Ann 1947- *WhoAm 94*
de Montebello, (Guy) Philippe (Lannes) 1936- *Who 94*
de Montebello, Philippe Lannes 1936- *WhoAm 94, WhoAmA 93*
de Monte-Campbell, Alpha *WhoWest 94*
DeMontier, Paulette LaPointe 1948- *WhoAm 94*
deMontmollin, Nina Snead 1920- *WhoAmP 93*
de Montmorency, Arnold (Geoffroy) 1908- *Who 94*
Demopulos, Chris 1924- *WhoAm 94*
DeMordaunt, Walter J(ulius) 1925- *WrDr 94*
Demorest, Allan Frederick 1931- *WhoMW 93*
DeMorest, Jon D. 1954- *WhoAmL 94*
De Morgan, John 1848-c. 1920 *EncSF 93*
De Mori, Renato 1941- *WhoAm 94*
De Mornay, Rebecca 1961- *WhoAm 94*
De Mornay, Rebecca 1962- *ConTFT 11, IntMPA 94, WhoHol 92*
Demos, John Putnam 1937- *WhoAm 94*
DeMoss, Harold R., Jr. *WhoAmP 93*
DeMoss, Harold R., Jr. 1930- *WhoAm 94, WhoAmL 94*
DeMoss, Jon W. 1947- *WhoAm 94, WhoAmL 94*
Demosthenes 384BC-322BC *HisWorL [port]*
Demosthenes fl. 4th cent.- *BlmGEL*
Demotes, Michael *ConAu 42NR*
Demott, Benjamin *DrAPF 93*
Demott, Benjamin (Hailer) 1924- *WrDr 94*
Demott, Deborah Ann 1948- *WhoAm 94*
De Mott, John A. d1975 *WhoHol 92*
DeMott, Robert (James) 1943- *ConAu 141*
Demougeot, Marcelle 1876-1931 *NewGrDO*
DeMoulas, Telemachus A. 1923- *WhoFI 94*
De Moura Sobral, Luis 1943- *WhoAmA 93*
Demouth, Robin Madison 1939- *WhoAm 94*
Dempsey, Andrew *Who 94*
Dempsey, (James) Andrew 1942- *Who 94*
Dempsey, Barbara Matthea 1943- *WhoWest 94*
Dempsey, Bernard Hayden, Jr. 1942- *WhoAmL 94*
Dempsey, Brian S. *WhoAmP 93*
Dempsey, Bruce Harvey 1941- *WhoAmA 93*
Dempsey, Clifford d1938 *WhoHol 92*
Dempsey, David (Knapp) 1914- *WrDr 94*
Dempsey, David B. 1949- *WhoAm 94, WhoAmL 94*
Dempsey, Edward A. 1939- *WhoFI 94*
Dempsey, Edward Joseph 1943- *WhoAmL 94*
Dempsey, Francis Burke 1962- *WhoFI 94*
Dempsey, Gerard Robert 1942- *WhoMW 93*
Dempsey, Gregory 1931- *NewGrDO*
Dempsey, Hank *EncSF 93*
Dempsey, Howard Stanley 1939- *WhoAm 94*
Dempsey, Ivy *DrAPF 93*
Dempsey, Jack d1983 *WhoHol 92*
Dempsey, James Harold 1953- *WhoWest 94*
Dempsey, James Howard, Jr. 1916- *WhoAm 94, WhoAmL 94*
Dempsey, James Randall 1954- *WhoMW 93*
Dempsey, James Raymon 1921- *WhoAm 94*
Dempsey, Jerome *WhoHol 92*
Dempsey, Jerry *WhoAmP 93*
Dempsey, Jerry Edward 1932- *WhoAm 94, WhoFI 94*
Dempsey, John Cornelius 1914- *WhoAm 94, WhoFI 94*
Dempsey, Joseph P. 1930- *WhoBlA 94*
Dempsey, Louis Francis, III 1926- *WhoAm 94*
Dempsey, Margaret A. 1950- *WhoWest 94*
Dempsey, Martin *WhoHol 92*
Dempsey, Neal, III 1941- *WhoFI 94*
Dempsey, Patrick 1966- *IntMPA 94, WhoHol 92*
Dempsey, Paul Stephen 1950- *WhoWest 94*
Dempsey, Pauline d1923 *WhoHol 92*
Dempsey, Raymond Leo, Jr. 1949- *WhoScEn 94*
Dempsey, Richard W. 1909- *WhoAmA 93N*
Dempsey, Robert Armstrong 1935- *WhoAmP 93*
Dempsey, Terry M. 1932- *WhoAmP 93*
Dempsey, Thomas d1947 *WhoHol 92*
Dempsey, Thomas W. 1931- *WhoAmP 93*
Dempsey, Timothy Michael 1939- *WhoAm 94*
Dempsey, Tracy 1950- *WhoAmP 93*
Dempsey, William Lawrence 1894- *WhAm 10*
Dempster, Carol d1991 *WhoHol 92*
Dempster, George 1887-1964 *WorInv*
Dempster, Hugh d1987 *WhoHol 92*
Dempster, John William Scott 1938- *Who 94*
Dempster, Lauramay Tinsley 1905- *WhoAm 94*
Dempster, Nigel Richard Patton 1941- *Who 94*
Dempster, Richard Vreeland 1928- *WhoAm 94*
Dempster, Stuart Ross 1936- *WhoWest 94*
Dempwolf, Gertrud 1936- *WhoWomW 91*
Demsetz, Harold 1930- *WhoAm 94*
Demske, James Michael 1922- *WhoAm 94*
Demski, Thomas J. 1944- *WhoAmL 94*
Demszky, Gabor 1952- *IntWW 93*
De Munn, Jeffrey 1947- *IntMPA 94, WhoHol 92*
De Muro, Bernardo 1881-1955 *NewGrDO*
DeMuro, Paul Robert 1954- *WhoAmL 94*
Demus, Jorg 1928- *IntWW 93*
Demus, Leslie Margot 1950- *WhoAmL 94*
DeMuse, Toni Ann 1947- *WhoAmP 93*
DeMuth, Alan Cornelius 1935- *WhoAmL 94, WhoFI 94, WhoWest 94*
DeMuth, Christopher Clay 1946- *WhoAm 94, WhoAmP 93, WhoFI 94*
Demuth, Joseph E. 1946- *WhoScEn 94*
DeMuth, Laurence Wheeler, Jr. *WhoAmL 94, WhoFI 94*
Demuth, Leopold 1861-1910 *NewGrDO*
Demuth, Richard H. 1910- *IntWW 93*
Demuzio, Vince 1941- *WhoAmP 93*
Demy, Jacques d1990 *WhoHol 92*
Demy, Mathieu *WhoHol 92*
Denaburg, Charles Robert 1935- *WhoAm 94, WhoScEn 94*
DeNafio, Teresa Louise 1957- *WhoAmP 93*
De Nagy, Eva *WhoAmA 93*
de Nagy, Tibor 1908-1993 *NewYTBS 93 [port]*
De Nagy, Tibor 1910- *WhoAmA 93*
de Nagy, Tibor Julius 1910- *WhoAm 94*
de Naray, Andrew Thomas 1942- *WhoWest 94*
Denard, Bob *NewYTBS 93 [port]*
Denard, Michael 1944- *IntDcB [port]*
DeNardis, Lawrence Joseph 1938- *WhoAmP 93*
DeNardis, Richard R. 1949- *WhoAmL 94*
DeNardo, James P. 1942- *WhoAmL 94*
Denaro, Gregory 1954- *WhoAm 94, WhoAmL 94*
Denaro, John Michael 1950- *WhoFI 94*
De Natale, Andrew Peter 1950- *WhoAm 94, WhoAmL 94*
De Natale, Francine 1939- *WrDr 94*
De Navarro, Mary d1940 *WhoHol 92*
de Navarro, Michael Antony 1944- *Who 94*
De Navrotzki, Igor *WhoHol 92*
Denbigh, Earl of 1943- *Who 94*
Denbigh, Kenneth George 1911- *IntWW 93, Who 94, WrDr 94*
Denbo, Jack *WhoHol 92*
Denbo, Jerry L. 1950- *WhoAmP 93*
DenBoer, James Drew 1937- *WhoWest 94*
den Breejen, Jan-Dirk 1963- *WhoScEn 94*
Denburg, Howard S. 1945- *WhoAmL 94*
Denby, James Orr 1896- *WhAm 10*
Denby, Patrick Morris Coventry 1920- *Who 94*
Dence, Edward William, Jr. 1938- *WhoAm 94*
Dence, Michael Robert 1931- *WhoAm 94, WhoScEn 94*
Dench, Judi 1934- *ConTFT 11, IntMPA 94, WhoHol 92*
Dench, Judith Olivia 1934- *IntWW 93, Who 94*
Dencklau, John Emery 1956- *WhoFI 94*
Dencoff, John Edgar 1968- *WhoScEn 94*
Dende, Henry John 1918- *WhoAmP 93*
Dendle, Brian J(ohn) 1936- *ConAu 42NR*
Den Dooven, Leslie *WhoHol 92*
Dendrinos, Dimitrios Spyros 1944- *WhoFI 94, WhoMW 93*
Dendurent, Harold Oscar 1941- *WhoMW 93*
Dendurent, Sharon Drwall 1945- *WhoMW 93*
Dendy, Gail Carter 1945- *WhoAmP 93*
Dendy, H. Benson, III 1956- *WhoAmP 93*
Dendy, Roger Paul 1964- *WhoScEn 94*
Dendy, Tometta Moore 1932- *WhoBlA 94*
Dene, Jozsef 1938- *NewGrDO*
Deneau, Sidney G. *IntMPA 94*
Deneberg, Jeffrey N. 1943- *WhoScEn 94*
de Necochea, Fernando *WhoHisp 94*
de Necochea, Gladys *WhoHisp 94*
De Neef, Diny d1978 *WhoHol 92*
Denegall, John Palmer, Jr. 1959- *WhoFI 94*
Denegre, George 1923- *WhoAm 94*
Denehy, Robert Corneilius 1931- *WhoFI 94*
Denell, Robin Ernest 1942- *WhoMW 93*
Denenberg, Herbert 1929- *WrDr 94*
Denenberg, Herbert Sidney 1929- *IntWW 93, WhoAm 94, WhoIns 94*
Denenberg, Victor Hugo 1925- *WhoAm 94*
DeNero, Henry T. *WhoAm 94, WhoFI 94*
DeNero, Nancy Sturdy 1946- *WhoFI 94*
Denes, Agnes *WhoAmA 93*
Denes, Agnes C. 1931- *WhoAm 94*
Denes, Michel Janet 1950- *WhoMW 93*
de Neufville, Richard 1939- *WrDr 94*
de Neufville, Richard Lawrence 1939- *WhoAm 94*
Deneuve, Catherine 1943- *IntMPA 94, IntWW 93, Who 94, WhoAm 94, WhoHol 92*
Denevan, William Maxfield 1931- *WhoAm 94*
de Nevers, Roy Olaf 1922- *WhoFI 94, WhoMW 93, WhoScEn 94*
DeNevi, Mary Kathryn 1954- *WhoAmL 94*
Deng, Ming-Dao 1954- *WhoAsA 94*
Deng, Rosaline Zhuang 1933- *WhoMW 93*
Dengel, Jake *WhoHol 92*
Dengel, Mary Cedella, Sister 1908- *WhoMW 93*
Denger, Michaël L. 1945- *WhoAm 94, WhoAmL 94*
Deng Gang 1917- *WhoPRCh 91*
Deng Gang 1945- *WhoPRCh 91 [port]*
Deng Hainan 1955- *WhoPRCh 91*
Deng Hongxun *WhoPRCh 91*
Deng Jiatai 1914- *WhoPRCh 91 [port]*
Dengler, Madison Luther 1935- *WhoScEn 94*
Dengler, Renee Aird 1946- *WhoMW 93*
Dengler, Robert Anthony 1947- *WhoMW 93*
Deng Li *WhoPRCh 91*
Deng Lin 1941- *WhoPRCh 91*
Deng Liqun 1914- *WhoPRCh 91 [port]*
Deng Pufang 1943- *IntWW 93, WhoPRCh 91 [port]*
Deng Weizhi 1938- *WhoPRCh 91 [port]*
Deng Xiaoping 1904- *HisWorL [port], IntWW 93, WhoPRCh 91 [port]*
Deng Ximing *WhoPRCh 91*
Deng Xingqi *WhoPRCh 91*
Deng Yiming *WhoPRCh 91*
Deng Yingchao d1992 *IntWW 93N*
Deng Yingchao 1904- *WhoPRCh 91 [port]*
Deng Youmei 1931- *IntWW 93, WhoPRCh 91*

Deng Yuzhi 1900- *WhoPRCh 91*
Deng Zhaoxiang 1902- *WhoPRCh 91 [port]*
Deng Zili 1920- *WhoPRCh 91 [port]*
Denham, Baron 1927- *Who 94*
Denham, Alice *DrAPF 93*
Denham, Dixon 1786-1828 *WhWE*
Denham, Ernest William 1922- *Who 94*
Denham, Frederick Ronald 1929- *WhoAm 94*
Denham, H(enry) M(angles) 1897-1993 *ConAu 142*
Denham, Henry Mangles d1993 *Who 94N*
Denham, John 1615-1669 *BlmGEL*
Denham, John Yorke 1953- *Who 94*
Denham, Mark Edward 1951- *WhoMW 93*
Denham, Maurice 1909- *IntMPA 94, Who 94, WhoHol 92*
Denham, Robert Edwin 1945- *WhoAm 94, WhoFI 94*
Denham, Seymour Vivian G. *Who 94*
Denham, Vera d1981 *WhoHol 92*
Denham, Vernon Robert, Jr. 1948- *WhoAmL 94*
Denhardt, David Tilton 1939- *IntWW 93, WhoAm 94, WhoScEn 94*
Den Hartog, Jacob Pieter 1901-1989 *WhAm 10*
Den Hertog, Johanna Agatha 1952- *WhoWomW 91*
Denhof, Miki *WhoAm 94*
Denholm, Allan *Who 94*
Denholm, (James) Allan 1936- *Who 94*
Denholm, David 1924- *WrDr 94*
Denholm, Elliott 1922-1992 *AnObit 1992*
Denholm, Ian *Who 94*
Denholm, Ian (John Ferguson) 1927- *IntWW 93*
Denholm, John Ferguson 1927- *Who 94*
Denholm, Thom W. 1966- *WhoWest 94*
Denholtz, Elaine *DrAPF 93*
Deniau, Jean Francois 1928- *IntWW 93*
Deniaud, Yves d1959 *WhoHol 92*
De Nicola, Peter Francis 1954- *WhoFI 94*
Denier, Robert E. 1921- *WhoAmP 93*
De Nike, Michael Nicholas 1923- *WhoAmA 93*
Denikin, Anton 1872-1947 *HisWorL [port]*
De Nil, Luc Frans 1957- *WhoScEn 94*
Denington, Baroness 1907- *Who 94, WhoWomW 91*
deNiord, Chard *DrAPF 93*
Denious, Robert Wilbur 1936- *WhoAm 94*
De Niro, Robert *NewYTBS 93 [port]*
De Niro, Robert 1922-1993 *NewYTBS 93*
De Niro, Robert 1943- *CurBio 93 [port], IntMPA 94, IntWW 93, WhoAm 94, WhoHol 92*
Denis, Armand *WhoHol 92*
Denis, Howard A. 1939- *WhoAmP 93*
Denis, Jean Baptiste 1643-1704 *EncSPD*
Denis, Michaela *WhoHol 92*
Denis, Paul-Yves 1932- *WhoAm 94, WhoScEn 94*
Denis, Prince d1984 *WhoHol 92*
Denise, Robert Phillips 1936- *WhoAm 94*
Denise, Theodore Cullom 1919- *WhoAm 94*
Denisoff, R. Serge 1939- *WhoAm 94, WrDr 94*
Denison *Who 94*
Denison, Ann *Who 94*
Denison, Anthony 1950- *WhoHol 92*
Denison, Dulcie Winifred Catherine 1920- *Who 94*
Denison, Edward F(ulton) 1915-1992 *ConAu 140, WrDr 94N*
Denison, Edward Fulton 1915- *IntWW 93*
Denison, Edward Fulton 1915-1992 *WhAm 10*
Denison, Edwin d1928 *WhoHol 92*
Denison, Floyd G. 1943- *WhoIns 94*
Denison, Floyd Gene 1943- *WhoAm 94*
Denison, John Law 1911- *Who 94*
Denison, Mary Boney 1956- *WhoAmL 94*
Denison, Michael *Who 94*
Denison, Michael 1915- *IntMPA 94, WhoHol 92*
Denison, (John) Michael 1915- *WrDr 94*
Denison, (John) Michael (Terence Wellesley) 1915- *Who 94*
Denison, Nathan 1740-1809 *WhAmRev*
Denison, Spencer T. 1944- *WhoAmL 94*
Denison, William Clark 1928- *WhoWest 94*
Denison, William Mason 1929- *WhoAmP 93*
Denison, William Neil 1929- *Who 94*
Denison-Pender *Who 94*
Denison-Smith, Anthony Arthur 1942- *Who 94*
Denisov, Edison (Vasil'yevich 1929- *NewGrDO*
Denisov, Edison Vasilyevich 1929- *IntWW 93*
Denisse, Jean-Francois 1915- *IntWW 93*

Denius, Franklin Wofford 1925- *WhoAmL 94, WhoFI 94*
Denize, Nadine 1943- *NewGrDO*
De Nizio, John Albert 1951- *WhoFI 94*
Denke, Paul Herman 1916- *WhoWest 94*
Denkenberger, John David 1963- *WhoWest 94*
Denker, Henry 1912- *WhoAm 94, WrDr 94*
Denker, John Stewart 1954- *WhoScEn 94*
Denker, Robert Wayne 1950- *WhoMW 93*
Denker, Susan A. 1948- *WhoAmA 93*
Denko, Joanne D. 1927- *WhoMW 93, WhoScEn 94*
Denkowicz, Stephanie 1952- *WhoAmL 94*
Denktas, Rauf R. 1924- *IntWW 93*
Denlea, Leo Edward, Jr. 1932- *WhoAm 94, WhoFI 94*
Denlinger, Edgar Jacob 1939- *WhoAm 94*
Denlinger, John Kenneth 1942- *WhoAm 94*
Denman, Baron 1916- *Who 94*
Denman, Don Curry 1946- *WhoAmP 93*
Denman, Donald Robert 1911- *Who 94, WrDr 94*
Denman, George Roy *Who 94*
Denman, Joe Carter, Jr. 1923- *WhoAm 94*
Denman, John Willard 1957- *WhoFI 94*
Denman, Patricia Price 1932- *WhoAmA 93*
Denman, Roy 1924- *IntWW 93, Who 94*
Denman, Sylvia Elaine *Who 94*
Denman, William Foster 1929- *WhoAm 94*
Denmark, Bernhardt 1917- *WhoAm 94*
Denmark, Harrison *EncSF 93*
Denmark, Robert Richard 1930- *WhoBlA 94*
Denn, Cyril Joseph 1948- *WhoFI 94, WhoMW 93*
Denn, Morton Mace 1939- *WhoAm 94, WhoScEn 94*
Dennard, Brazeal Wayne 1929- *WhoBlA 94*
Dennard, Cleveland L. d1992 *WhoBlA 94N*
Dennard, Cleveland Leon 1929-1992 *WhAm 10*
Dennard, Darryl W. 1957- *WhoBlA 94*
Dennard, H. Lane, Jr. 1943- *WhoAmL 94*
Dennard, Robert Heath 1932- *WhoAm 94, WhoScEn 94*
Dennard, Turner Harrison 1913- *WhoBlA 94*
Dennay, Charles William 1935- *Who 94*
Denne, Christopher James Alured 1945- *Who 94*
Denneen, John Paul 1940- *WhoAm 94, WhoAmL 94*
Denne-Hinnov, Gerd Boel 1954- *WhoScEn 94*
Dennehy, Brian 1938- *ConTFT 11, WhoHol 92*
Dennehy, Brian 1939- *IntMPA 94, WhoAm 94*
Dennehy, Brian 1940- *IntWW 93*
Dennen, David Warren 1932-1990 *WhAm 10*
Dennen, Keith Cameron 1962- *WhoAmL 94*
Denneny, James Clinton, Jr. 1924- *WhoAm 94*
Denner, Charles 1926- *WhoHol 92*
Denner, Melvin Walter 1933- *WhoAm 94*
Denner, William Howard Butler 1944- *Who 94*
Dennert, Dutch 1898- *BasBi*
Dennert, H. Paul *WhoAmP 93*
Dennery, Moise Waldhorn 1915- *WhoAm 94*
Dennett, Daniel Clement 1942- *IntWW 93, WhoAm 94*
Dennett, Lissy W. 1926- *WhoAmA 93*
Dennett, Nolan Alma 1950- *WhoWest 94*
Denney, Arthur Hugh 1916- *WhoAm 94*
Denney, Dick d1981 *WhoHol 92*
Denney, Doris Elaine 1940- *WhoWest 94*
Denney, George Covert, Jr. 1921- *WhoAm 94*
Denney, Jim 1953- *WhoHol 92*
Denney, Lawerence E. *WhoAmP 93*
Denney, Lucinda Ann 1938- *WhoMW 93*
Denney, Nancy Wadsworth 1944- *WhoMW 93*
Denney, Robert (Eugene) 1929- *ConAu 140*
Denney, Ruell *DrAPF 93*
Dennie, Abigail Colman 1715-1745 *BlmGWL*
Dennin, Joseph Francis 1943- *WhoAm 94, WhoAmL 94*
Dennin, Robert Aloysius, Jr. 1951- *WhoScEn 94*
Denning, Baron 1899- *Who 94*
Denning, Lord 1899- *WrDr 94*
Denning, Alfred Thompson 1899- *IntWW 93*

Denning, Bernadine Newsom 1930- *WhoBlA 94*
Denning, Eileen Bonar 1944- *WhoFI 94*
Denning, Joe William 1945- *WhoBlA 94*
Denning, Joseph P. 1907-1990 *WhAm 10*
Denning, Keith Meyer 1955- *WhoMW 93*
Denning, Michael Marion 1943- *WhoFI 94, WhoScEn 94, WhoWest 94*
Denning, Peter James 1942- *WhoAm 94*
Denning, Richard 1914- *WhoHol 92*
Denningmann, Elroy 1937- *WhoFI 94*
Dennington, Dudley 1927- *Who 94*
Dennis, Alastair Wesley 1931- *Who 94*
Dennis, Andre L. 1943- *WhoBlA 94*
Dennis, Anthony James 1963- *WhoAmL 94*
Dennis, Barbara Rodgers 1946- *WhoBlA 94*
Dennis, Bengt 1930- *IntWW 93*
Dennis, Benjamin Franklin, III 1942- *WhoAmL 94*
Dennis, Bert R. 1932- *WhoWest 94*
Dennis, Bruce *EncSF 93*
Dennis, Burt Morgan 1892-1960 *WhoAmA 93N*
Dennis, Carl *DrAPF 93*
Dennis, Charles Erwin, Jr. 1925- *WhoFI 94*
Dennis, Charles Houston 1921- *WhoAmA 93*
Dennis, Clarence 1909- *WhoAm 94*
Dennis, Conrad Vance 1953- *WhoMW 93*
Dennis, Crystal d1973 *WhoHol 92*
Dennis, Danny *WhoHol 92*
Dennis, David W. 1912- *WhoAmP 93*
Dennis, Dennis Michael 1949- *WhoWest 94*
Dennis, Don W. 1923- *WhoAmA 93*
Dennis, Donald Daly 1928- *WhoAm 94*
Dennis, Donna Frances 1942- *IntWW 93, WhoAm 94, WhoAmA 93*
Dennis, Doris Lavelle 1928- *WhoAmP 93*
Dennis, Edward S. G., Jr. 1945- *WhoBlA 94*
Dennis, Edward Spencer Gale, Jr. 1945- *WhoAm 94, WhoAmL 94*
Dennis, Everette Eugene, Jr. 1942- *WhoAm 94*
Dennis, Evie *WhoWest 94*
Dennis, Evie Garrett 1924- *WhoBlA 94*
Dennis, Frank George, Jr. 1932- *WhoAm 94*
Dennis, Geoffrey (Pomeroy) 1892-1963 *EncSF 93*
Dennis, Gerald C. 1947- *WhoAmP 93*
Dennis, Gertrude Weyhe *WhoAmA 93*
Dennis, Gertrude Zelma Ford 1927- *WhoBlA 94*
Dennis, Howard Willis 1927- *WhoWest 94*
Dennis, Hugo, Jr. 1936- *WhoAmP 93, WhoBlA 94*
Dennis, Jack Bonnell 1931- *WhoAm 94*
Dennis, James Carlos 1947- *WhoBlA 94*
Dennis, James L. 1936- *WhoAmP 93*
Dennis, James Leon 1936- *WhoAm 94, WhoAmL 94*
Dennis, James M. *WhoWest 94*
Dennis, John *Who 94, WhoHol 92*
Dennis, John 1657-1734 *BlmGEL*
Dennis, John 1917- *WhoAmP 93*
Dennis, John Emory, Jr. 1939- *WhoAm 94, WhoScEn 94*
Dennis, Larry Walter 1939- *WhoWest 94*
Dennis, Lawrence Edward 1920-1990 *WhAm 10*
Dennis, Lyle B. 1953- *WhoAmP 93*
Dennis, Mark Allen 1961- *WhoFI 94*
Dennis, Maxwell Lewis 1909- *Who 94*
Dennis, Michael Mark 1942- *IntWW 93*
Dennis, Nadine d1979 *WhoHol 92*
Dennis, Nick d1980 *WhoHol 92*
Dennis, Nigel 1912-1989 *BlmGEL*
Dennis, Nigel (Forbes) 1912-1989 *ConDr 93, EncSF 93*
Dennis, Patricia Diaz 1946- *WhoAmP 93, WhoHisp 94*
Dennis, Peggy d1993 *NewYTBS 93*
Dennis, Peter Ray 1938- *WhoMW 93*
Dennis, Philip H. 1925- *WhoBlA 94*
Dennis, Robert 1933- *WhoAm 94*
Dennis, Robert D. 1943- *WhoAmL 94*
Dennis, Rodney Howard 1936- *WhoBlA 94*
Dennis, Roger Wilson 1902- *WhoAmA 93*
Dennis, Ronald Marvin 1950- *WhoScEn 94*
Dennis, Russell d1964 *WhoHol 92*
Dennis, Rutledge M. 1939- *WhoBlA 94*
Dennis, Samuel Elliott 1929- *WhoAm 94*
Dennis, Samuel Sibley, III 1910- *WhoAm 94*
Dennis, Sandy 1937- *WhoHol 92*
Dennis, Sandy 1937-1992 *AnObit 1992, WhAm 10*
Dennis, Shirley M. 1938- *WhoAmP 93, WhoBlA 94*
Dennis, Sonya Renee 1965- *WhoWest 94*

Dennis, Stephen Neal 1943- *WhoAmI. 94*
Dennis, Steven Pellowe 1960- *WhoAm 94*
Dennis, Walter Decoster 1932- *WhoAm 94, WhoBlA 94*
Dennis, Ward Brainerd 1922- *WhoAm 94*
Dennis, Ward Haldan 1938-1992 *WhAm 10*
Dennis, Wayne Allen 1941- *WhoMW 93*
Dennis, William Littleton 1950- *WhoAmL 94*
Dennis, Willye E. 1926- *WhoAmP 93*
Dennis, Winston Robert, Jr. 1941- *WhoWest 94*
Dennish, George William, III 1945- *WhoAm 94, WhoWest 94*
Dennis-Jones, Harold 1915- *WrDr 94*
Dennison, Anna Nasvik *WhoWest 94*
Dennison, Byron Lee 1930- *WhoAm 94*
Dennison, Charles Stuart 1918- *WhoAm 94*
Dennison, Daniel B. 1947- *WhoScEn 94*
Dennison, David Short, Jr. 1918- *WhoAm 94, WhoAmP 93*
Dennison, George Marshel 1935- *WhoAm 94, WhoWest 94*
Dennison, Jack Lee 1951- *WhoWest 94*
Dennison, Jo-Carroll 1925- *WhoHol 92*
Dennison, John Manley 1934- *WhoAm 94*
Dennison, Karen D. 1946- *WhoAmL 94*
Dennison, Keith Elkins 1939- *WhoAmA 93*
Dennison, Malcolm Gray 1924- *Who 94*
Dennison, Mervyn William d1993 *Who 94N*
Dennison, Robert Abel, III 1951- *WhoScEn 94*
Dennison, Ronald Walton 1944- *WhoWest 94*
Dennison, Stanley Raymond d1992 *Who 94N*
Dennison, Stanley Richard 1930- *Who 94*
Dennison, Stanley Scott 1920- *WhoAm 94*
Denniss, Gordon Kenneth 1915- *Who 94*
Denniston, Brackett Badger, III 1947- *WhoAm 94, WhoAmL 94*
Denniston, Dorothy L. 1944- *WhoBlA 94*
Denniston, Douglas 1921- *WhoAmA 93*
Denniston, John Baker 1936- *WhoAm 94*
Denniston, Martha Kent 1920- *WhoWest 94*
Denniston, Pamela Boggs 1948-, *WhoMW 93*
Denniston, Reynolds d1943 *WhoHol 92*
Denniston, Robin Alastair 1926- *IntWW 93, Who 94*
Denny, Alistair (Maurice Archibald) 1922- *Who 94*
Denny, Alma *DrAPF 93*
Denny, Anthony Coningham de Waltham 1925- *Who 94*
Denny, Barry Lyttelton 1928- *Who 94*
Denny, Bob *WhoAmP 93*
Denny, Brewster Castberg 1924- *WhoAm 94*
Denny, Charles M., Jr. 1931- *WhoAm 94, WhoFI 94*
Denny, Collins, III 1933- *WhoAm 94, WhoAmL 94*
Denny, Ebenezer 1761-1822 *WhAmRev*
Denny, Floyd Wolfe, Jr. 1923- *IntWW 93, WhAm 94*
Denny, Ike *WhoHol 92*
Denny, James Clifton 1922- *WhoWest 94*
Denny, James McCahill 1932- *WhoAm 94, WhoFI 94*
Denny, Margaret Bertha Alice 1907- *Who 94*
Denny, Norwyn Ephraim 1924- *Who 94*
Denny, Otway B., Jr. 1949- *WhoAm 94, WhoAmL 94*
Denny, Patricia G. 1963- *WhoAmL 94*
Denny, Raymond A., III 1961- *WhoAmP 93*
Denny, Reginald d1967 *WhoHol 92*
Denny, Richard Alden, Jr. 1931- *WhoAm 94*
Denny, Robert 1920- *WrDr 94*
Denny, Robert Richard 1939- *WhoMW 93*
Denny, Robert William, Jr. 1953- *WhoScEn 94*
Denny, Robyn (Edward M. F.) 1930- *IntWW 93*
Denny, Ronald Maurice 1927- *Who 94*
Denny, Thomas Albert 1933- *WhoScEn 94*
Denny, William 1847-1887 *DcNaB MP*
Denny, William C., Jr. 1930- *WhoAmP 93*
Denny, William Eric 1927- *Who 94*
Denny, William Murdoch, Jr. 1934- *WhoFI 94*
Dennys, Nicholas Charles Jonathan 1951- *Who 94*
Dennys, Rodney Onslow d1993 *NewYTBS 93, Who 94N*
Dennys, Rodney Onslow 1911-1993 *ConAu 142*
De Nobili, Lila 1916- *NewGrDO*

Denomme, Robert Thomas 1930- *WhoAm 94*
Denoon, Clarence England, Jr. 1915- *WhoAm 94*
Denoon, David Baugh Holden 1945- *WhoAm 94*
De Normand, George d1976 *WhoHol 92*
Den Otter, Cornelis Johannes 1935- *WhoScEn 94*
Den Ouden, Gaylin L. R. 1945- *WhoAmP 93*
Denov, Sam 1923- *WhoAm 94*
De Novara, Medea *WhoHol 92*
DeNovio, Susan Williams 1948- *WhoFI 94*
DeNovo, John August 1916- *WhoAm 94*
Denoyer, Arsene J. 1904- *WhoMW 93*
DeNoyer, Georgia Ann 1948- *WhoMW 93*
Densen, Paul Maximillian 1913- *WhoAm 94*
Densen-Gerber, Judianne 1934- *WhoAm 94, WrDr 94*
Denslow, Dorothea Henrietta 1900-1971 *WhoAmA 93N*
Denslow, Sharon Phillips 1947- *WrDr 94*
Denslow, Victor Allen 1922- *WhoFI 94*
Densmore, Douglas Warren 1948- *WhoAmL 94*
Densmore, Edward D. 1940- *WhoAmP 93*
Densmore, James *WorInv*
Densmore, John 1944- *WrDr 94*
Densmore, William Phillips 1924- *WhoAm 94*
Denson, Alexander Bunn 1936- *WhoAm 94, WhoAmL 94*
Denson, Fred L. 1937- *WhoBlA 94*
Denson, G. Roger 1956- *WhoAmA 93*
Denson, John Boyd d1992 *IntWW 93N*
Denson, Nancy Rae 1951- *WhoWest 94*
Denson, William Frank, III 1943- *WhoAm 94*
Dent, Anthony L. 1943- *WhoBlA 94*
Dent, Arthur L., III 1947- *WhoAmL 94*
Dent, Carl Ashley 1914- *WhoBlA 94*
Dent, Catherine Gale 1953- *WhoMW 93*
Dent, Cedric Carl 1962- *WhoBlA 94*
Dent, Charles W. 1960- *WhoAmP 93*
Dent, Doris A. 1945- *WhoIns 94*
Dent, Edward Dwain 1950- *WhoAmL 94*
Dent, Edward J(oseph) 1876-1957 *NewGrDO*
Dent, Ernest DuBose, Jr. 1927- *WhoAm 94, WhoFI 94, WhoScEn 94, WhoWest 94*
Dent, Frederick Baily 1922- *WhoAm 94, WhoAmP 93*
Dent, Gary Kever 1950- *WhoBlA 94*
Dent, George 1756-1813 *WhAmRev*
Dent, Guy *EncSF 93*
Dent, Harold Collett 1894- *Who 94*
Dent, Harry Shuler 1930- *WhoAmP 93*
Dent, John 1923- *IntWW 93, Who 94*
Dent, Jonathan Hugh Baillie 1930- *Who 94*
Dent, Josephine d1978 *WhoHol 92*
Dent, Lester 1905-1959 *EncSF 93*
Dent, Preston L. 1939- *WhoBlA 94*
Dent, Richard Lamar 1960- *WhoAm 94, WhoBlA 94, WhoMW 93*
Dent, Robin (John) 1929- *Who 94*
Dent, Roger Eugene 1937- *WhoMW 93*
Dent, Ronald Henry 1913- *Who 94*
Dent, Thomas Covington 1932- *WhoBlA 94*
Dent, Thomas G. 1942- *WhoAmL 94*
Dent, Tom *DrAPF 93*
Dent, V. Edward 1918- *WhoAm 94*
Dent, Vernon d1963 *WhoHol 92*
Dentel, Steven Keith 1951- *WhoScEn 94*
Dentine, Margaret Raab 1947- *WhoScEn 94*
Dentinger, Ronald Lee 1941- *WhoFI 94*
Dentinger, Stephen *EncSF 93*
Dentiste, Paul George 1930- *WhoAm 94*
Dentler, Marion d1988 *WhoHol 92*
Dentler, Robert Arnold 1928- *WhoAm 94*
Denton *Who 94*
Denton, Arnold Eugene 1925- *WhoFI 94*
Denton, Betty F. 1945- *WhoAmP 93*
Denton, Bobby Eugene 1938- *WhoAmP 93*
Denton, Bradley (Clayton) 1958- *EncSF 93*
Denton, Catherine Margaret Mary *Who 94*
Denton, Charles 1937- *IntWW 93, Who 94*
Denton, Charles Mandaville 1924- *WhoAm 94*
Denton, Charles William 1951- *WhoAmL 94*
Denton, Crahan d1966 *WhoHol 92*
Denton, D. Keith 1948- *WhoAm 94*
Denton, David Edward 1935- *WhoAm 94*
Denton, David Harrison 1945- *WhoFI 94, WhoMW 93*
Denton, David Lee 1952- *WhoScEn 94*
Denton, Derek Ashworth 1924- *IntWW 93*
Denton, Donald A. 1939- *WhoAmL 94*
Denton, Dorothea Mary 1938- *WhoScEn 94*
Denton, Elwood Valentine 1912- *WhoFI 94*
Denton, Eric (James) 1923- *Who 94*
Denton, Eric James 1923- *IntWW 93*
Denton, Frank d1945 *WhoHol 92*
Denton, Frank M. 1945- *WhoAm 94, WhoMW 93*
Denton, Frank Marion 1935- *WhoFI 94*
Denton, Frank Trevor 1930- *IntWW 93*
Denton, George d1918 *WhoHol 92*
Denton, Harold Ray 1936- *WhoAm 94*
Denton, Jack d1986 *WhoHol 92*
Denton, Jeremiah A. 1924- *WhoAmP 93*
Denton, Joan Cameron *WhoMW 93*
Denton, John Douglas 1939- *Who 94*
Denton, John Grant 1929- *Who 94*
Denton, John Joseph 1915- *WhoAm 94*
Denton, Kady MacDonald *WrDr 94*
Denton, Kirk Alexander 1955- *WhoMW 93*
Denton, Laurie R. 1951- *WhoAm 94*
Denton, M. Bonner 1944- *WhoScEn 94*
Denton, Margaret *Who 94*
Denton, Patry 1943- *WhoAmA 93*
Denton, Ray Douglas 1937- *WhoFI 94, WhoMW 93*
Denton, Robert William 1944- *WhoFI 94*
Denton, Timothy Lynn 1951- *WhoAmL 94*
Denton, Victoria Villena- 1959- *WhoAsA 94*
Denton, William Lewis 1932- *WhoWest 94*
Denton Of Wakefield, Baroness 1935- *Who 94*
Denton-Thompson, Aubrey Gordon 1920- *Who 94*
D'Entrecasteaux, Antoine-Raymond-Joseph De Bruni, Chevalier *WhWE*
Dentzel, Carl Schaefer 1913-1980 *WhoAmA 93N*
Denu, Marie E. 1931- *WhoAmP 93*
DeNucci, A. Joseph 1939- *WhoAmP 93*
DeNunzio, Michael Joseph 1968- *WhoMW 93*
DeNunzio, Ralph Dwight 1931- *WhoAm 94*
Den Uyl, Simon Danker 1896- *WhAm 10*
DeNuzzo, Rinaldo Vincent 1922- *WhoAm 94, WhoScEn 94*
Denver, Andrew Malcolm 1947- *WhoFI 94*
Denver, Bob 1935- *IntMPA 94, WhoCom, WhoHol 92*
Denver, Drake C. 1907- *WrDr 94*
Denver, Eileen Ann 1942- *WhoAm 94*
Denver, John 1943- *IntMPA 94, IntWW 93, WhoAm 94, WhoHol 92*
Denver, Maryesther d1980 *WhoHol 92*
Denver, Thomas H. R. 1944- *WhoAmL 94*
Denvir, James Peter, III 1950- *WhoAm 94, WhoAmL 94*
Denvir, Robert F. 1945- *WhoAm 94, WhoAmL 94*
Denworth, Raymond K. 1932- *WhoAm 94*
DeNye, Blaine A. 1933- *WhoBlA 94*
Denyer, Nicholas (Charles) 1955- *WrDr 94*
Denyer, Roderick Lawrence 1948- *Who 94*
Denys, Edward Paul 1927- *WhoMW 93*
Denys, Marie-Jose 1950- *WhoWomW 91*
Denysyk, Bohdan 1947- *WhoAm 94*
Denza, Eileen 1937- *Who 94*
Denza, Luigi 1846-1922 *NewGrDO*
Denzel, Justin F(rancis) 1917- *ConAu 42NR*
Denzel, Ken John 1940- *WhoAmL 94*
Denzio, Antonio c. 1690-1763? *NewGrDO*
Denzler, Robert 1892-1972 *NewGrDO*
Deo, Marjoree Nee 1907- *WhoAmA 93*
Deo, Narsingh 1936- *WhoAm 94*
de Oddone, Barbara S. 1943- *WhoAmL 94*
Deol, Harjyot 1957- *WhoAsA 94*
Deol, Malkiat Singh 1928- *Who 94*
de Olloqui, Jose Juan 1931- *Who 94*
Deom, Carol Pearce 1959- *WhoMW 93*
Deon, Michel 1919- *IntWW 93*
Deones, Jack E. 1931- *WhoAm 94*
De Orchis, M. E. 1923- *WhoAmL 94*
DeOrchis, Vincent Moore 1949- *WhoAmL 94*
De Orduna, Juan d1974 *WhoHol 92*
Deori, Omem Moyong 1943- *WhoWomW 91*
Deorio, Anthony Joseph 1945- *WhoMW 93, WhoScEn 94*
de Oriol Y Urquijo, Antonio Maria 1913- *IntWW 93*
de Ossorio, Amando 1925- *HorFD*
Deoul, Neal 1931- *WhoAm 94, WhoFI 94, WhoScEn 94*
De Pablo, Luis *NewGrDO*
DePace, Nicholas Louis 1953- *WhoAm 94*
de Padilla, Maria Luisa Beltranena *WhoWomW 91*
De Palma, Brett 1949- *WhoAmA 93*
De Palma, Brian 1940- *HorFD [port], IntMPA 94, IntWW 93*
De Palma, Brian Russell 1940- *WhoAm 94*
DePalma, Ralph George 1931- *WhoAm 94, WhoScEn 94*
DePalma, Stephanie Marie 1960- *WhoFI 94*
De Panafieu, Francoise Marie-Therese 1948- *WhoWomW 91*
DePaola, Dominick Philip 1942- *WhoAm 94*
De Paola, Tomie 1934- *WhoAmA 93, WrDr 94*
DePaoli, Geri Mary 1941- *WhoAm 94*
De Paolis, Alessio 1893-1964 *NewGrDO*
DePaolis, Peter Candito 1949- *WhoAmL 94*
dePaolis, Potito Umberto 1925- *WhoAm 94, WhoFI 94, WhoWest 94*
DePaolo, Donald James 1951- *WhoAm 94, WhoScEn 94, WhoWest 94*
dePaolo, Ronald Francis 1938- *WhoAm 94*
de Papp, Elise Wachenfeld 1933- *WhoAm 94*
Depardieu, Elisabeth *WhoHol 92*
Depardieu, Gerard 1948- *IntMPA 94, IntWW 93, WhoAm 94, WhoHol 92*
Depardon, Raymond 1942- *IntWW 93*
deParrie, Paul 1949- *SmATA 74 [port]*
DePasco, Ronnie Nick 1943- *WhoAmP 93*
DePasquale, Daniel A. d1993 *NewYTBS 93*
Depasquale, Ed *DrAPF 93*
Depasquale, Francesco 1954- *WhoScEn 94*
De Pasquale, John Anthony 1942- *WhoAm 94*
De Pasquali, Bernice *NewGrDO*
DePass, William Brunson, Jr. 1947- *WhoAmP 93*
De Passe, Derrel Blauvelt 1950- *WhoWest 94*
de Passe, Suzanne *WhoAm 94, WhoFI 94, WhoWest 94*
de Passe, Suzanne 1948- *WhoBlA 94*
de Pater, Imke 1952- *WhoWest 94*
DePatie, David Hudson 1930- *WhoAm 94*
DePaul, John Phil 1963- *WhoMW 93*
de Paula, (Frederic) Clive 1916- *Who 94*
De Paula, Francisco d1985 *WhoHol 92*
De Pauli, Frank Edward 1927- *WhoAmL 94*
DePaulis, Palmer 1945- *WhoAmP 93*
DePaur, Leonard *WhoBlA 94*
De Pauw, Gommar Albert 1918- *WhoAm 94*
De Pauw, Linda Grant 1940- *WhoAm 94*
Depazzo, Louis L. 1932- *WhoAmP 93*
Depecol, Benjamin J. 1951- *WhoAmP 93*
De Pedery-Hunt, Dora 1913- *WhoAmA 93*
de Pedrolo, Manuel *EncSF 93*
De Pena, Hector, Jr. *WhoHisp 94*
Depestre, Rene 1926- *ConWorW 93*
DePetrillo, Paolo Bartolomeo 1956- *WhoScEn 94*
DePew, Alfred (Mansfield) 1952- *ConAu 141*
Depew, Charles Gardner 1930- *WhoAm 94*
Depew, Joseph d1988 *WhoHol 92*
DePew, Marie Kathryn 1928- *WhoWest 94*
Depew, Richard H. 1925- *IntMPA 94*
Depew, Wally *DrAPF 93*
DePew, William Earl 1948- *WhoWest 94*
de Peyer, David Charles 1934- *Who 94*
De Peyer, Gervase 1926- *IntWW 93, Who 94*
De Peyster, Abraham 1753-c. 1799 *WhAmRev*
DePeyster, Arent Schuyler 1736-1822 *AmRev*
De Peyster, Arent Schuyler 1736-1832 *WhAmRev*
dePeyster, Frederic Augustus 1914- *WhoAm 94*
De Peyster, Frederick *WhAmRev*
De Peyster, James d1793 *WhAmRev*
De Pfyffer, Andre 1928- *WhoAm 94, WhoAmL 94, WhoFI 94*
Dephillips, Paul S. 1939- *WhoIns 94*
Depiante, Eduardo Victor 1959- *WhoMW 93, WhoScEn 94*
DePiero, Joseph Anthony 1953- *WhoMW 93*
DePillars, Murry N. 1938- *WhoAmA 93*
DePillars, Murry Norman 1938- *WhoBlA 94*
de Piñeres, Oscar G. 1932- *WhoHisp 94*
de Pinies, Jaime 1918- *IntWW 93*
DePinna, Vivian 1883-1978 *WhoAmA 93N*
Depino, Chris *WhoAmP 93*
DePinto, Joseph Anthony 1951- *WhoWest 94*
DePinto, Ronald Duncan 1932- *WhoWest 94*
de Piro, Alan C. H. *Who 94*
De Pirro, Nicola 1898-1979 *NewGrDO*
Depke, Nancy Elizabeth 1932- *WhoMW 93*
Depkovich, Francis John 1924- *WhoAm 94*
de Planque, E. Gail 1945- *WhoAm 94*
Depner, Steven John 1955- *WhoFI 94*
De Pol, John 1913- *WhoAm 94, WhoAmA 93*
De Polnay, Peter 1906-1984 *EncSF 93*
De Pomes, Felix d1969 *WhoHol 92*
de Posada, Robert G. 1966- *WhoHisp 94*
de Posadas, Luis Maria 1927- *Who 94*
Depp, Harry d1957 *WhoHol 92*
Depp, Johnny 1963- *IntMPA 94, IntWW 93, WhoAm 94, WhoHol 92*
Depp, Richard, III 1938- *WhoAm 94*
Deppe, Henry A. 1920- *WhoAm 94, WhoFI 94*
Deppe, Theodore *DrAPF 93*
Depperschmidt, Thomas Orlando 1935- *WhoAm 94*
De Pré, Jean-Anne 1924- *WrDr 94*
De Pree, Max O. 1924- *WhoFI 94*
De Pree, Willard Ames 1928- *WhoAmP 93*
DePreist, James Anderson 1936- *AfrAmAl 6 [port], WhoAm 94, WhoBlA 94, WhoWest 94*
De Premonville, Myrene Sophie Marie 1949- *IntWW 93*
De Prey, Juan d1962 *WhoAmA 93N*
Deprez, Deborah Ann 1952- *WhoMW 93*
Deprez, Luisa Stormer *WhoAmP 93*
DePriest, C. E. *WhoAmP 93*
DePriest, Darryl Lawrence 1954- *WhoBlA 94*
DePriest, James Bradley 1956- *WhoMW 93*
De Priest, James E. *WhoHol 92*
DePriest, Oscar Stanton 1871-1951 *AfrAmAl 6*
DePriest, Oscar Stanton, III 1928- *WhoBlA 94*
De Prima, Charles Raymond 1918- *WhAm 10*
DePristo, Andrew E. 1951- *WhoScEn 94*
Deprit, Andre Albert 1926- *WhoAm 94*
Depta, Victor M. *DrAPF 93*
Depte, Larry D. 1950- *WhoBlA 94*
Deptula, George Stanley 1942- *WhoAmL 94*
DePue, Bobbie Lee 1938- *WhoFI 94*
DePue, Josephine Helen 1948- *WhoMW 93*
Depukat, Thaddeus Stanley 1936- *WhoMW 93*
De Puma, Richard Daniel 1942- *WhoAmA 93, WhoMW 93*
De Putti, Lya d1931 *WhoHol 92*
DePuy, Charles Herbert 1927- *WhoAm 94, WhoWest 94*
DePuy, R. David 1945- *WhoAmL 94*
Dequae, Andre 1915- *IntWW 93*
Dequasie, Andrew Eugene 1929- *WhoScEn 94*
DeQuattro, Vincent Louis 1933- *WhoAm 94*
de Queiroz, Kevin 1956- *WhoScEn 94*
De Queiroz, Rachel *ConWorW 93*
De Quick, Alfo d1978 *WhoHol 92*
De Quincey, Thomas 1785-1859 *BlmGEL*
De Quiros, Beltran *DrAPF 93*
Der, Henry 1947?- *WhoAsA 94*
DeRaad, Brent Eugene 1966- *WhoWest 94*
de Rachewiltz, Igor 1929- *IntWW 93*
Derain, Andre 1880-1954 *IntDcB*
Deraismes, Maria 1828-1894 *BlmGWL*
Deram, Sharon Frances 1958- *WhoMW 93*
D'Eramo, David 1942- *WhoAm 94*
Deramore, Baron 1911- *Who 94*
De Ramsey, Baron d1993 *Who 94N*
De Ramsey, Baron 1942- *Who 94*
DeRamus, Betty Jean 1941- *WhoAm 94*
DeRamus, Judson Davie, Jr. 1945- *WhoAmP 93*
Deramus, William Neal, III 1915-1989 *WhAm 10*
DeRan, David 1946- *SmATA 76 [port]*
DeRango, Mary Laura Keul *WhoMW 93*
De Ranter, Camiel Joseph 1937- *WhoScEn 94*
Deratany, Tim 1939- *WhoAmP 93*
de Rath, Suzanne Marie 1963- *WhoAmL 94, WhoMW 93*
De Ravenne, Caroline Marie d1962 *WhoHol 92*
Derba, Mimi d1953 *WhoHol 92*
Derbes, Albert Joseph, III 1940- *WhoAmL 94*
Derbes, Daniel William 1930- *WhoAm 94, WhoFI 94*
Derbes, Max Joseph, Jr. 1923- *WhoFI 94*
Derbigny, Rhoda L. 1960- *WhoBlA 94*
Der Boggia, Henry d1976 *WhoHol 92*
Derby, Archdeacon of *Who 94*

Derby, Bishop of 1928 Who 94
Derby, Earl of 1918- Who 94
Derby, Provost of Who 94
Derby, Christopher William 1963- WhoScEn 94
Derby, Ernest Stephen 1938- WhoAm 94, WhoAmL 94
Derby, Jill T. 1940- WhoWest 94
Derby, Loyd P. 1939- WhoAmL 94
Derby, Mark 1960- WhoAmA 93
Derby, Mark Garald 1965- WhoWest 94
Derby, Ted d1976 WhoHol 92
Derbyshire, Andrew (George) 1923- Who 94
Derbyshire, Andrew George 1923- IntWW 93
Derchin, Michael Wayne 1942- WhoAm 94, WhoFI 94
D'Ercole, S. Frank 1939- WhoAmL 94
Derdarian, Christine Anne 1948- WhoAmL 94
Derdenger, Patrick 1946- WhoAm 94, WhoAmL 94, WhoFI 94, WhoWest 94
Dere, Willard Honglen 1954- WhoScEn 94
Derechin, Moises 1924- WhoScEn 94
de Regnier, Kevin Vincent 1957- WhoMW 93
de Regniers, Beatrice Schenk 1914- WrDr 94
Dereham, Elias of d1245 DcNaB MP
Derek, Bo 1956- IntMPA 94
Derek, Bo 1958- WhoHol 92
Derek, John 1926- IntMPA 94, WhoHol 92
Derelanko, Michael Joseph 1951- WhoScEn 94
DeRemee, Richard Arthur 1933- WhoAm 94
De Remer, Edgar Dale 1935- WhoScEn 94
De Remer, Rubye d1984 WhoHol 92
Deren, Donald David 1949- WhoAmL 94
DeRensis, Paul Ronald 1944- WhoAmL 94
Deresiewicz, Herbert 1925- WhoAm 94, WhoScEn 94
Deresiewicz, Robert Leslie 1958- WhoScEn 94
de Reszke, Edouard 1853-1917 NewGrDO [port]
de Reszke, Jean 1850-1925 NewGrDO [port]
de Reszke, Josephine 1855-1891 NewGrDO
De Reszke Family NewGrDO
Deretich, George 1933- WhoAmL 94
DeReus, Harry Bruce 1964- WhoScEn 94
Derevan, Richard A. 1949- WhoAmL 94
De Reyna, Jorge EncSF 93
Derfler, Eugene L. 1924- WhoWest 94
Derfler, Gene 1924- WhoAmP 93
Derfler, (Arnold) Leslie 1933- WrDr 94
Derfler, Steven L. 1951- WhoMW 93
Dergalis, George 1928- WhoAmA 93
Dergarabedian, Paul 1922- WhoAm 94
Derge, David Richard 1928- WhoAm 94, WhoAmP 93
Derham, Arthur Morgan 1915- WrDr 94
de Rham, Casimir, Jr. 1924- WhoAm 94
Derham, John P(ickens) 1896- WhAm 10
Derham, Peter (John) 1925- Who 94
Derham, Richard Andrew 1940- WhoAm 94, WhoAmP 93
Der Harootian, Khoren 1909- WhoAm 94
Der-Houssikian, Haig 1938- WhoAm 94
Der Hovanessian, Diana DrAPF 93
Der'i, Arye 1959- IntWW 93
Deriabin, Peter 1921- WrDr 94
Deriabin, Peter 1921-1992 AnObit 1992
Derian, Patricia Murphy WhoAmP 93
Deric, Arthur J. 1926- WhoIns 94
Deric, Arthur Joseph 1926- WhoAmL 94, WhoFI 94
De Ricco, Hank 1946- WhoAmA 93
DeRicco, Lawrence Albert 1923- WhoAm 94
Derickson, Jeffrey Cline 1950- WhoWest 94
DeRienzo, Harold 1953- WhoAmL 94
DeRight, Robert E., Jr. 1938- WhoAmL 94
Dering, Edward 1625-1684 DcNaB MP
Deringer, Arved 1913- IntWW 93
Derise, Nellie Louise 1937- WhoAm 94
De Riso, Camillo d1924 WhoHol 92
DeRita, Curly Joe d1993 NewYTBS 93 [port]
De Rita, Joe WhoHol 92
DeRita, Joe d1993 IntMPA 94N
DeRita, Joe 1909- See Three Stooges, The WhoCom
de Rivas, Carmela Foderaro 1920- WhoAm 94
De Rivera, Jose 1904-1985 WhoAmA 93N
Derivis, Henri-Etienne 1780-1856 NewGrDO
Derivis, Maria c. 1845-1877? NewGrDO
Derivis, (Nicholas) Prosper 1808-1880 NewGrDO
Derivis Family NewGrDO
de Rivoyre, Christine Berthe Claude Denis 1921- IntWW 93
Derkach, Ihor Stepanovych 1963- LoBiDrD
Derks, Frederick Julius 1945- WhoMW 93
Derlacki, Eugene Lubin 1913- WhoAm 94
Derleth, August W(illiam) 1909-1971 EncSF 93
Derman, Cyrus 1925- WhoAm 94
Derman, Donald A. 1933- WhoAmP 93
Derman, Harriet 1943- WhoAmP 93
Derman, Herbert 1921- WhoMW 93
Derman, Martha (Winn) 20th cent.- SmATA 74
Dermer, Stephen N. 1945- WhoAmL 94
Dermo, Pierre d1976 WhoHol 92
Dermody, Frank d1978 WhoHol 92
Dermody, Frank 1951- WhoAmP 93
Dermota, Anton d1989 WhoHol 92
Dermota, Anton 1910-1989 NewGrDO
Dermott, Jon Alan 1938- WhoAmL 94
Dermott, William 1924- Who 94
Dermout, Maria 1888-1962 BlmGWL
Dermoz, Germaine d1966 WhoHol 92
Dern, Bruce 1936- IntMPA 94, WhoHol 92
Dern, Bruce MacLeish 1936- WhoAm 94
Dern, F. Carl 1936- WhoAmA 93
Dern, Laura 1966- IntWW 93
Dern, Laura 1967- IntMPA 94, WhoHol 92
Dern, Laura Elizabeth 1967- WhoAm 94
Dernesch, Helga 1939- IntWW 93, NewGrDO
Dernovich, Donald Frederick 1942- WhoAmA 93
De Robertis, Eduardo Diego Patricio 1913- IntWW 93
DeRoburt, Hammer d1992 IntWW 93N
De Roburt, Hammer 1923-1992 WhAm 10
De Rocco, Andrew Gabriel 1929- WhoAm 94
De Roche, Charles d1952 WhoHol 92
de Rochemont, Louis 1899-1978 IntDcF 2-4 [port]
de Roe Devon 1934- WhoScEn 94, WhoWest 94
de Roe Devon, The Marchioness 1934- WhoFI 94
De Roes, Nanda Yvonne 1945- WhoFI 94
De Rogatis, Francesco Saverio 1745-1827 NewGrDO
De Rogatis, Pascual NewGrDO
DeRoma, Leonard James 1953- WhoAm 94
Derome, Jacques Florian 1941- WhoAm 94
De Romilly, Jacqueline 1913- IntWW 93
Deron, Edward Michael 1945- WhoAmL 94
DeRonde, John Allen, Jr. 1947- WhoAmL 94
de Roo, Anne (Louise) 1931- WrDr 94
De Roo, Edward DrAPF 93
De Roo, Remi Joseph 1924- WhoAm 94, WhoWest 94
de Ros, Baron 1958- Who 94
DeRosa, Francis Dominic 1936- WhoFI 94, WhoWest 94
DeRosa, Michael Louis 1965- WhoAmA 93
DeRosa, Patti Jean 1946- WhoMW 93
De Rosa Amorim, Maria Luisa Rodrigues Garcia 1946- WhoWomW 91
De Rosas, Enrique d1948 WhoHol 92
Derose, Candace Margaret 1949- WhoAmP 93
De Rose, Louis John 1952- WhoFI 94
De Rose, Sandra Michele WhoAm 94, WhoScEn 94
DeRosier, Arthur Henry, Jr. 1931- WhoAm 94
Derosier, David John 1939- WhoAm 94
DeRoss, Evelyn Jones 1927- WhoAmP 93
DeRoss, Thomas Charles 1946- WhoMW 93
de Rosso, Diana 1921- WrDr 94
de Rothschild Who 94
DeRouchey, Beverly Jean 1958- WhoFI 94
De Rouen, Reed R(andolph) 1917- EncSF 93
Derouin, James G. 1944- WhoAmL 94
De Roulet, Yvonn d1950 WhoHol 92
Derounian, Steven B. 1918- WhoAmP 93
Derounian, Steven Boghos 1918- WhoAm 94
DeRousie, Charles Stuart 1947- WhoAm 94, WhoAmL 94, WhoMW 93
DeRoux, Daniel Edward 1951- WhoAmA 93
De Roux, Tomas E. 1961- WhoScEn 94
Derow, Peter Alfred 1940- WhoAm 94
Derr, Gilbert S. 1917- WhoBlA 94
Derr, John Sebring 1941- WhoWest 94
Derr, John W. 1941- WhoAmP 93
Derr, Kenneth T. IntWW 93
Derr, Kenneth T. 1936- WhoAm 94, WhoFI 94, WhoWest 94
Derr, Lee E. 1948- WhoMW 93
Derr, Mark (Burgess) 1950- WrDr 94
Derr, Mary Louise 1917- WhoWest 94
Derr, Richard 1917- WhoHol 92
Derr, Thomas Burchard 1929- WhoFI 94
Derr, Thomas Sieger 1931- WhoAm 94
Derr, Vernon Ellsworth 1921- WhoAm 94
Derrett, (John) Duncan (Martin) 1922- Who 94, WrDr 94
Derrick, Butler C., Jr. 1936- CngDr 93
Derrick, Butler Carson, Jr. 1936- WhoAm 94, WhoAmP 93
Derrick, Charles Warren, Jr. 1935- WhoAm 94
Derrick, Gary Wayne 1953- WhoAmL 94
Derrick, Homer 1906- WhoFI 94
Derrick, James V., Jr. 1945- WhoAmL 94
Derrick, John Martin, Jr. 1940- WhoAm 94, WhoFI 94
Derrick, Laura Jean 1962- WhoMW 93
Derrick, Malcolm 1933- WhoAm 94
Derrick, Patricia Who 94
Derrick, Paul Wayne 1947- WhoAmP 93
Derrick, William Dennis 1946- WhoWest 94
Derricks, Cleavant 1953- WhoHol 92
Derrickson, James Harrison 1944- WhoScEn 94
Derrickson, Steve Bruce 1952- WhoAmA 93
Derrickson, William Borden 1940- WhoAm 94, WhoFI 94, WhoScEn 94
Derrick-White, Elizabeth 1940- WhoAm 94
Derricotte, C. Bruce 1928- WhoBlA 94
Derricotte, Eugene Andrew 1926- WhoBlA 94
Derricotte, Toi DrAPF 93
Derricotte, Toi 1941- BlkWr 2
Derrida, Jacques BlmGWL
Derrida, Jacques 1930- BlmGEL, CurBio 93 [port], IntWW 93
Derrough, Neil E. 1936- WhoAm 94, WhoWest 94
Derry, John (Wesley) 1933- WrDr 94
Derry, Thomas Kingston 1905- Who 94, WrDr 94
Derry, William R., Jr. 1946- WhoAmL 94
Derry And Raphoe, Bishop of 1931- Who 94
Derryberry, Larry Dale 1939- WhoAmP 93
Derryberry, Thomas Kelly 1959- WhoAmP 93
Derryck, Vivian Lowery 1945- WhoAm 94
Dersh, Rhoda E. 1934- WhoAm 94, WhoFI 94
Dershem, Larry Douglas 1948- WhoAmL 94
Dershem, Stephen Michael 1954- WhoWest 94
Dershimer, Harold H. 1961- WhoWest 94
Dershowitz, Alan M. 1938- WrDr 94
Dershowitz, Alan Morton 1938- IntWW 93, WhoAm 94, WhoAmL 94
Derstadt, Ronald Theodore 1950- WhoAm 94, WhoMW 93, WhoScEn 94
Derstine, Mark Stephen 1961- WhoScEn 94
Dertadian, Richard Norman 1938- WhoAm 94
Derthick, L(awrence) G(ridley) 1905-1992 CurBio 93N
Derthick, Martha Ann 1933- WhoAm 94
Dertien, James LeRoy 1942- WhoAm 94, WhoMW 93
Dertouzos, Michael Leonidas 1936- WhoAm 94
Deru, Terry M. 1954- WhoFI 94
DeRubertis, Patricia Sandra 1950- WhoWest 94
Derucher, Kenneth Noel 1949- WhoFI 94
De Rue, Carmen d1986 WhoHol 92
De Rue, Eugene d1985 WhoHol 92
DeRugeris, C. K. DrAPF 93
de Ruiter, Hendrikus 1934- IntWW 93
de Ruiter, Jacob 1930- IntWW 93
Derujinsky, Gleb W. 1888-1975 WhoAmA 93N
De Ruth, Jan 1922-1991 WhoAmA 93N
DeRuyter, Steven D. 1946- WhoAmL 94
Dervaird, Hon. Lord 1935- Who 94
Dervan, Peter Brendan 1945- WhoAm 94, WhoScEn 94, WhoWest 94
Dervin, Brenda Louise 1938- WhoAm 94
Dervis, Suat 1905-1972 BlmGWL
Derwent, Baron 1930- Who 94
Derwent, Clarence d1959 WhoHol 92
Derwent, Henry Clifford Sydney 1951- Who 94
Derwin, Jordan 1931- WhoAmL 94, WhoFI 94
Derwinski, Dennis Anthony 1941- WhoMW 93
Derwinski, Edward J. 1926- WhoAmP 93
Derwinski, Edward Joseph 1926- IntWW 93
Derx, Donald John 1928- Who 94
Dery (Schenbach-Szeppataky), Roza 1793-1872 NewGrDO
Dery, Mark DrAPF 93
Deryagin, Aleksandr Vasilevich 1941- LoBiDrD
Derzai, Amy Ruth 1904- WhoAmP 93
Derzaw, Richard Lawrence 1954- WhoAmL 94
D'erzell, Catalina 1897- BlmGWL
Derzhinskaya, Kseniya Georgiyevna 1889-1951 NewGrDO
Derzon, Gordon M. 1934- WhoAm 94, WhoMW 93
Derzon, Robert Alan 1930- WhoAm 94
De Sabata, Victor 1892-1967 NewGrDO
De Sade, Ana WhoHol 92
De Saeger, Jozef 1911- IntWW 93
Desai, Baron 1940- IntWW 93, Who 94
Desai, Anita 1937- BlmGEL, BlmGWL [port], IntWW 93, Who 94, WrDr 94
Desai, Ashok Govindji 1949- WhoAsA 94
Desai, Boman 1950- WrDr 94
Desai, Cawas Jal 1938- WhoAm 94
Desai, Chandra 1936- WhoAsA 94
Desai, Chandrakant S. 1936- WhoAsA 94, WhoWest 94
Desai, Hiren Sharad 1969- WhoAsA 94
Desai, Hitendra Kanaiyalal 1915- IntWW 93
Desai, Kantilal Panachand 1929- WhoAsA 94
Desai, Mahendrabhai Nanubhai 1931- IntWW 93
Desai, Mahesh Kumar 1964- WhoFI 94
Desai, Manisha 1958- WhoAsA 94
Desai, Manubhai Haribhai 1933- WhoScEn 94
Desai, Morarji Ranchhodji 1896- IntWW 93
Desai, Mukund Ramanlal 1946- WhoMW 93, WhoScEn 94
Desai, Sharad P. 1946- WhoAsA 94
Desai, Shri Morarji Ranchhodji 1896- Who 94
Desai, Smita 1959- WhoFI 94
Desai, Sudhir G. 1937- WhoAsA 94
Desai, Suresh A. 1933- WhoAsA 94
Desai, Suresh A. 1942- WhoAsA 94
Desai, Uday 1943- WhoAsA 94
Desai, Vijay 1953- WhoAsA 94
Desai, Vikram J. 1945- WhoAsA 94
Desai, Vimal H. 1951- WhoAsA 94
Desai, Vishakha N. 1949- WhoAm 94
Desaides, Nicholas NewGrDO
Desaigoudar, Chan 1937- WhoAsA 94
Desailly, Jean 1920- IntWW 93, WhoHol 92
de Ste. Croix, Geoffrey Ernest Maurice 1910- Who 94
de Saint-Erne, Nicholas John 1958- WhoWest 94
de St. Jorre, Danielle WhoWomW 91
De St. Jorre, Danielle Marie-Madeleine 1941- IntWW 93
De St. Jorre, Danielle Marie-Madeleine J. Who 94
de St. Jorre, John 1936- WrDr 94
de St. Paer, Virginia Beth 1918- WhoAmP 93
de Saint Phalle, Francois 1946- WhoAm 94, WhoFI 94
de Saint Phalle, Pierre Claude 1948- WhoAm 94
de Saint Phalle, Thibaut 1918- WhoAm 94
De Sales, Francis d1988 WhoHol 92
De Salva, Salvatore Joseph 1924- WhoAm 94, WhoScEn 94
DeSalve, Dennis Wayne 1946- WhoMW 93
De Salvo, Anne 1950- WhoHol 92
De Sanctis, Roman William 1930- IntWW 93, WhoAm 94
De Sanctis, Sante 1862-1935 EncSPD
DeSandies, Kenneth Andre 1948- WhoBlA 94
Desani, G(ovindas) V(ishnoodas) 1909- WrDr 94
De Santi, Anna c. 1772-1802 NewGrDO
de Santiago, Jose Eduardo, Sr. 1944- WhoHisp 94
DeSantiago, Michael Francis 1956- WhoScEn 94
De Santis, Anthony 1914- WhoAm 94
DeSantis, Donald Anthony 1950- WhoAm 94
De Santis, Gregory Joseph 1947- IntMPA 94
De Santis, Inma d1989 WhoHol 92
De Santis, James Joseph 1958- WhoScEn 94
De Santis, Joe d1989 WhoHol 92
De Santis, Luigi fl. 179-?- NewGrDO
De Santis, Tony WhoHol 92

Devlin, Lord 1905-1992 *WrDr 94N*
Devlin, Alan *WhoHol 92*
Devlin, Alexander 1927- *Who 94*
Devlin, Anne 1951- *BlmGWL, WrDr 94*
Devlin, (Josephine) Bernadette *Who 94*
Devlin, Cathy Stegman 1964- *WhoFI 94*
Devlin, Gerald M. 1930- *WhoIns 94*
Devlin, Gerard Francis 1933- *WhoAmP 93*
Devlin, Gerry 1931- *WhoAmP 93*
Devlin, Harry 1918- *SmATA 74 [port], WhoAmA 93*
Devlin, J. G. *WhoHol 92*
Devlin, James Richard 1950- *WhoAm 94, WhoAmL 94*
Devlin, Joe d1973 *WhoHol 92*
Devlin, Keith 1947- *ConAu 141*
Devlin, Keith Michael 1933- *Who 94*
Devlin, Michael (Coles) 1942- *NewGrDO*
Devlin, Michael Coles 1942- *WhoAm 94*
Devlin, Michael Gerard 1947- *WhoAmL 94, WhoFI 94*
Devlin, Patricia 1945- *WhoAmL 94*
Devlin, Patrick 1905-1992 *AnObit 1992*
Devlin, Paul 1903-1989 *WhAm 10*
Devlin, Polly 1944- *BlmGWL*
Devlin, Robert G. 1949- *WhoAmL 94*
Devlin, Robert Manning 1941- *WhoAm 94*
Devlin, Roy P. *EncSF 93*
Devlin, Stuart Leslie 1931- *IntWW 93, Who 94*
Devlin, Thomas McKeown 1929- *WhoAm 94*
Devlin, Tim 1944- *Who 94*
Devlin, Timothy Robert 1959- *Who 94*
Devlin, Wende 1918- *WhoAmA 93*
Devlin, (Dorothy) Wende 1918- *SmATA 74 [port]*
Devlin, William d1987 *WhoHol 92*
Devney, John Leo 1938- *WhoAm 94*
DeVoe, Barbara Maines 1945- *WhoAmP 93*
Devoe, Bert d1930 *WhoHol 92*
DeVoe, Kenneth Nickolas 1944- *WhoWest 94*
Devoe, Lawrence Daniel 1944- *WhoScEn 94*
DeVoe, Robert Carl 1933- *WhoWest 94*
DeVoe, Robert Donald 1934- *WhoMW 93*
DeVoe, Ronnie *WhoBlA 94*
De Vogt, Carl d1970 *WhoHol 92*
DeVogt, John Frederick 1930- *WhoAm 94*
De Vol, Frank 1911- *WhoHol 92*
Devol, Kenneth Stowe 1929- *WhoAm 94*
DeVol, Luana 1942- *NewGrDO*
DeVoll, Ray d1993 *NewYTBS 93*
DeVolpi, Alexander 1931- *WhoMW 93*
Devon, Earl of 1916- *Who 94*
DeVon, Albert J., Jr. 1947- *WhoIns 94*
Devon, Laura 1940- *WhoHol 92*
Devon, Richard 1931- *WhoHol 92*
Devon, Warren 1947- *WhoAm 94*
Devon, Wesley Scott 1939- *WhoMW 93*
Devonport, Viscount 1944- *Who 94*
Devons, Samuel 1914- *IntWW 93, Who 94, WhoAm 94*
Devonshire, Duke of 1920- *Who 94*
Devonshire, Michael Norman 1930- *Who 94*
Devontine, Julie Elizabeth Jacqueline 1934- *WhoFI 94, WhoScEn 94, WhoWest 94*
DeVor, Richard Earl 1944- *WhoScEn 94*
DeVore, Ann G. 1936- *WhoAmP 93*
DeVore, Carl Brent 1940- *WhoAm 94*
DeVore, Charles Stuart 1962- *WhoWest 94*
DeVore, Daun Aline 1955- *WhoAmL 94*
Devore, Dorothy d1976 *WhoHol 92*
DeVore, Galvin Fray 1949- *WhoAmL 94*
DeVore, Jonathan Kip 1955- *WhoMW 93*
Devore, Kimberly K. 1947- *WhoFI 94*
DeVore, Ophelia *WhoBlA 94*
DeVore, Paul Cameron 1932- *WhoAm 94*
De Vore, Paul Warren 1926- *WhoAm 94*
De Vore, Richard E. 1933- *WhoAmA 93*
De Vorsey, Louis, Jr. 1929- *WrDr 94*
De Vos, Alois J. 1947- *WhoScEn 94*
Devos, Elisabeth 1958- *WhoAmP 93*
de Vos, Peter Jon 1938- *WhoAm 94, WhoAmP 93*
DeVos, Richard Marvin 1926- *WhoAm 94*
DeVos, Richard Marvin, Jr. 1955- *WhoAm 94, WhoFI 94*
DeVoss, David Arlen 1947- *WhoWest 94*
DeVoss, James Thomas 1916- *WhoAm 94*
Devoti, William *DrAPF 93*
Devoto, John fl. 1708-1752 *NewGrDO*
De Voto, Terence Alan 1946- *WhoWest 94*
Devoy, Kimball John 1941- *WhoAmL 94*
Devree, Howard 1890-1966 *WhoAmA 93N*
DeVriendt, David Mark 1962- *WhoMW 93*
Devrient, Eduard 1801-1877 *NewGrDO*
De Vries, Bert 1938- *IntWW 93*
DeVries, Beverly Mae 1935- *WhoMW 93*
Devries, David 1881-1934 *NewGrDO*
Devries, Fides 1851-1941 *NewGrDO*
DeVries, Frederick William 1930- *WhoScEn 94*
De Vries, Gary Alan 1955- *WhoMW 93*
DeVries, Geert Jan 1954- *WhoScEn 94*
De Vries, Henri 1863- *WhoHol 92*
Devries, Hermann 1858-1949 *NewGrDO*
De Vries, Hugo *WorScD*
DeVries, Jack *WhoFI 94*
de Vries, Jacobus E. 1934- *WhoAm 94*
DeVries, James Howard 1932- *WhoAmL 94*
Devries, Jeanne 1850-1924 *NewGrDO*
DeVries, Judith Leigh 1945- *WhoAmP 93*
De Vries, Kenneth Lawrence 1933- *WhoAm 94, WhoScEn 94, WhoWest 94*
de Vries, Margaret Garritsen 1922- *WhoAm 94*
DeVries, Marvin Frank 1937- *WhoAm 94, WhoScEn 94*
Devries, Maurice 1854-1919 *NewGrDO*
De Vries, Michiel Josias 1933- *IntWW 93*
De Vries, Peter *DrAPF 93*
De Vries, Peter d1993 *NewYTBS 93 [port]*
De Vries, Peter 1910- *ConAu 41NR, IntWW 93, Who 94, WhoAm 94, WrDr 94*
De Vries, Peter 1910-1993 *ConAu 142*
De Vries, Rachel (Guido) 1947- *WrDr 94*
deVries, Rachel Guido *DrAPF 93*
de Vries, Rimmer 1929- *WhoAm 94*
DeVries, Robert Allen 1936- *WhoAm 94*
De Vries, Robert John 1932- *WhoFI 94, WhoMW 93*
DeVries, Robert K. 1932- *WhoAm 94*
Devries, William Castle 1943- *IntWW 93, WhoAm 94*
Devries Family *NewGrDO*
de Vries-van Os, Rosa 1828-1889 *NewGrDO*
deVroede, Peter John 1960- *WhoWest 94*
Devrouax, Paul S., Jr. 1942- *WhoBlA 94*
Devroy, Craig Allen 1960- *WhoMW 93*
Devry, Elaine 1935- *WhoHol 92*
DeVylder, Edgar Paul, Jr. 1945- *WhoAmL 94*
DeVylder, Emil Raymond 1930- *WhoWest 94*
Dew, Charles Burgess 1937- *WhoAm 94*
Dew, Eddie d1972 *WhoHol 92*
Dew, Hartwell Coleman 1953- *WhoIns 94*
Dew, Jess Edward 1920- *WhoAm 94*
Dew, John 1944- *NewGrDO*
Dew, Leslie Robert 1914- *Who 94*
Dew, Robb Forman *DrAPF 93*
Dew, Ronald Beresford 1916- *Who 94*
Dew, Thomas Roderick 1940- *WhoWest 94*
Dew, William Waldo, Jr. 1935- *WhoAm 94, WhoWest 94*
de Waal, Constant Hendrik 1931- *Who 94*
de Waal, Hugo Ferdinand *Who 94*
DeWaal, Ian C. Smith 1950- *WhoAmL 94*
De Waal, Marius Theodorus 1925- *IntWW 93*
De Waal, Ronald Burt 1932- *WhoAmA 93, WrDr 94*
de Waal, Victor Alexander 1929- *Who 94*
de Waart, Edo 1941- *IntWW 93, NewGrDO, WhoAm 94, WhoMW 93*
Dewaere, Patrick d1982 *WhoHol 92*
Dewald, Bruce Wayne 1955- *WhoAmL 94*
DeWald, John Edward 1946- *WhoAmL 94*
Dewald, Paul A 1920- *WrDr 94*
Dewald, Paul Adolph 1920- *WhoAm 94*
DeWall, Karen Marie 1943- *WhoWest 94*
DeWall, Richard Allison 1926- *WhoAm 94*
Dewan, Karan d1979 *WhoHol 92*
De Wan-Carlson, Anna 1949- *WhoAmA 93*
De Wandeleer, Patrick Jules 1949- *WhoScEn 94*
Dewanjee, Mrinal Kanti 1941- *WhoScEn 94*
Dewar *Who 94*
Dewar, David Alexander 1934- *Who 94*
Dewar, Donald Campbell 1937- *IntWW 93, Who 94*
Dewar, George Duncan Hamilton 1916- *Who 94*
Dewar, Graeme Alexander 1951- *WhoMW 93*
Dewar, Ian Stewart 1929- *Who 94*
Dewar, James 1842-1923 *WorInv, WorScD*
Dewar, James McEwen 1943- *WhoAm 94, WhoFI 94, WhoScEn 94*
Dewar, Margaret Elizabeth 1948- *WhoMW 93*
Dewar, Michael J(ames Steuart) 1918- *WrDr 94*
Dewar, Michael James Steuart 1918- *IntWW 93, Who 94, WhoAm 94, WhoScEn 94*
Dewar, Norman Ellison 1930- *WhoAm 94*
Dewar, Robert James 1923- *Who 94*
Dewar, Robert Scott 1949- *Who 94*
Dewar, Thomas 1909- *Who 94*
de Wardener, Hugh Edward 1915- *Who 94*
Deware, Mable Margaret 1926- *WhoWomW 91*
De Warfaz, George d1959 *WhoHol 92*
Dewart, Gilbert 1932- *WrDr 94*
Dewart, Katherine *DrAPF 93*
Dewart, Leslie 1922- *WrDr 94*
DeWaters, Clarke 1931- *WhoIns 94*
Dewayne, Jessie *WhoHol 92*
Dewberry, Betty Bauman 1930- *WhoAmL 94*
Dewberry, David Albert 1941- *Who 94*
Dewberry, Thomas E. *WhoAmP 93*
Dewberry-Williams, Madelina Denise 1958- *WhoBlA 94*
Dewbre, J. W. 1933- *WhoIns 94*
Dewbre, Ross James 1963- *WhoAmL 94*
Dewdney, A(lexander) K(eewatin) 1941- *ConAu 142*
Dewdney, Christopher 1951- *WrDr 94*
Dewdney, Duncan Alexander Cox 1911- *Who 94*
Dewdney, John Christopher 1928- *WrDr 94*
Dewe, Roderick Gorrie 1935- *Who 94*
de Weck, Philippe 1919- *IntWW 93*
De Weerdt, Mark Murray 1928- *IntWW 93, WhoWest 94*
DeWees, Bill Irvin, Jr. 1959- *WhoMW 93*
Dewees, Donald Charles 1931- *WhoAm 94*
DeWees, James H. 1933- *WhoFI 94*
Dewees, Mary Coburn fl. 1787-1788 *BlmGWL*
De Wees, Samuel 1760- *WhAmRev*
De Weese, Bob M. 1934- *WhoAmP 93*
DeWeese, David Downs 1913- *WhAm 10*
De Weese, Frank d1928 *WhoHol 92*
DeWeese, Gene 1934- *EncSF 93, WrDr 94*
Deweese, Glen S. 1932- *WhoAmP 93*
Deweese, H. William 1950- *WhoAmP 93*
DeWeese, James Arville 1925- *WhoAm 94*
DeWeese, Jean *EncSF 93*
DeWeese, Jean 1934- *WrDr 94*
Deweese, Malcolm Leslie, Jr. 1935- *WhoWest 94*
DeWeese, Marion Spencer 1915- *WhoAm 94*
Dewell, Julian C. 1930- *WhoAmL 94*
Dewell, Michael 1931- *WhoAm 94, WhoWest 94*
Dewe Mathews, Marina Sarah *Who 94*
DeWerth, Gordon Henry 1939- *WhoAm 94*
De Wet, Carel 1924- *IntWW 93, Who 94*
De Wet, Reza 1953- *BlmGWL*
de Wetter, Herman Peter 1920- *WhoAm 94, WhoFI 94*
Dewey, A. A. *DrAPF 93*
Dewey, Alan H. 1957- *WhoScEn 94*
Dewey, Anna d1967 *WhoHol 92*
Dewey, Anthony Hugh 1921- *Who 94*
Dewey, Bradley, III 1943- *WhoAm 94*
Dewey, Cameron Boss 1961- *WhoScEn 94*
Dewey, Craig Douglas 1950- *WhoMW 93, WhoScEn 94*
Dewey, Donald O(dell) 1930- *WrDr 94*
Dewey, Donald Odell 1930- *WhoAm 94, WhoWest 94*
Dewey, Donald William 1933- *WhoAm 94, WhoFI 94, WhoWest 94*
Dewey, Earl Frederick, II 1953- *WhoAmL 94*
Dewey, Earl S. d1950 *WhoHol 92*
Dewey, Edward Allen 1932- *WhoAm 94*
Dewey, Elmer d1954 *WhoHol 92*
Dewey, Gene Lawrence 1938- *WhoAm 94*
Dewey, Henry Bowen 1924- *WhoAmL 94*
Dewey, Joel Allen 1956- *WhoAmL 94*
Dewey, John 1859-1952 *AmSocL, EncEth*
Dewey, John Edwin 1939- *WhoAmP 93*
Dewey, John F. 1937- *WhoScEn 94*
Dewey, John Frederick 1937- *IntWW 93, Who 94*
Dewey, Michael Lee 1944- *WhoWest 94*
Dewey, Pat Parker 1923- *WhoFI 94*
Dewey, Phelps 1928- *WhoAm 94*
Dewey, Robert Manson, Jr. 1931- *WhoFI 94*
Dewey, Robert V., Jr. 1944- *WhoAmL 94*
Dewey, Roger William 1928- *WhoWest 94*
Dewhirst, Glenn Eric 1966- *WhoAmP 93*
Dewhirst, Ian 1936- *WrDr 94*
Dewhirst, John Ward 1937- *WhoAmL 94*
Dewhurst, Charles Kurt 1948- *WhoAm 94, WhoScEn 94*
Dewhurst, Colleen 1924-1991 *ConTFT 11*
Dewhurst, Colleen 1926- *WhoHol 92*
Dewhurst, Colleen 1926-1991 *WhAm 10*
Dewhurst, Eileen (Mary) 1929- *WrDr 94*
Dewhurst, (Christopher) John 1920- *Who 94*
Dewhurst, Keith 1931- *ConDr 93, WrDr 94*
Dewhurst, Peter 1944- *WhoScEn 94*
Dewhurst, Stephen B. 1942- *WhoAm 94*
Dewhurst, Timothy Littleton 1920- *Who 94*
Dewhurst, William d1937 *WhoHol 92*
Dewhurst, William George 1926- *WhoAm 94, WhoScEn 94, WhoWest 94*
Dewhurst, William Harvey 1929- *WhoWest 94*
De Wied, David 1925- *IntWW 93*
De Wilde, Brandon d1972 *WhoHol 92*
deWilde, David Michael 1940- *WhoAm 94, WhoFI 94*
de Wilde, (Alan) Robin 1945- *Who 94*
de Windt, Edward Mandell 1921- *WhoAm 94, WhoFI 94*
DeWine, Michael 1947- *WhoAmP 93*
DeWine, Paul Robert 1957- *WhoWest 94*
DeWine, R. Michael 1947- *WhoAm 94, WhoMW 93*
Dewing, Henry Woods 1962- *WhoFI 94*
Dewing, Merlin Eugene 1934- *WhoAm 94*
de Winter, Carl 1934- *Who 94*
De Winter, Jo *WhoHol 92*
de Winton, Michael Geoffrey 1916- *Who 94*
DeWire, John W. 1916-1990 *WhAm 10*
De Wit, Cornelis T. 1924- *IntWW 93*
de Wit, Jacqueline 1916- *WhoHol 92*
De Witt, Alan d1976 *WhoHol 92*
De Witt, Bryce S. 1923- *IntWW 93*
De Witt, Bryce Seligman 1923- *WhoAm 94*
DeWitt, Calvin B. 1935- *WrDr 94*
De Witt, Charles 1727-1787 *WhAmRev*
DeWitt, Charles Barbour 1950- *WhoAm 94*
DeWitt, Charles Benjamin, III 1952- *WhoAmL 94*
DeWitt, Charles C., Jr. 1951- *WhoAmL 94*
Dewitt, Charles W. 1947- *WhoAmP 93*
De Witt, Eugene A. 1943- *WhoAm 94*
De Witt, Fay 1935- *WhoHol 92*
DeWitt, Frances Marie De Jong 1939- *WhoAmP 93*
DeWitt, Frank John 1929- *WhoFI 94*
DeWitt, Franklin Roosevelt 1936- *WhoAmL 94, WhoAmP 93, WhoBlA 94*
De Witt, George d1979 *WhoHol 92*
DeWitt, Gerry 1952- *WhoWest 94*
Dewitt, Harry Morton 1920- *WhoFI 94*
DeWitt, James Howard 1952- *WhoScEn 94*
Dewitt, John *DrAPF 93*
DeWitt, John 1929- *WhoAmP 93*
Dewitt, John Belton 1937- *WhoWest 94*
DeWitt, John Hibbett, Jr. 1906- *WhoAm 94*
DeWitt, Jon F. 1938- *WhoAm 94*
De Witt, Joyce 1949- *IntMPA 94*
De Witt, Lew d1990 *WhoHol 92*
DeWitt, Lew C. 1938- *See* Statler Brothers, The *WhoHol 92*
De Witt, Lew Calvin 1938-1990 *WhAm 10*
DeWitt, Michelle Lynn 1962- *WhoMW 93*
DeWitt, Nicholas 1950- *WhoAmL 94*
De Witt, Paul d1978 *WhoHol 92*
DeWitt, Rufus B. 1915- *WhoBlA 94*
DeWitt, Sheila Hobbs 1960- *WhoMW 93, WhoScEn 94*
DeWitt, Simeon 1756-1834 *AmRev, WhAmRev*
De Witt, William Gerald 1937- *WhoAm 94*
De Witt-Morette, Cecile 1922- *WhoAm 94*
DeWitt-Rogers, Johari Marilyn 1950- *WhoWest 94*
DeWitz, Loren *WhoAmP 93*
Dewlen, Al 1921- *WrDr 94*
de Wolf, David Alter 1934- *WhoAm 94*
De Wolf, Harry George 1903- *Who 94*
De Wolfe, Billy d1974 *WhoHol 92*
De Wolfe, Elsie d1950 *WhoHol 92*
DeWolfe, Fred Stanley 1928- *WhoWest 94*
DeWolfe, Gregory S. *WhoAmL 94*
DeWolfe, James Pernette 1895- *WhAm 10*
DeWolfe, John Chauncey, Jr. 1913- *WhoAm 94*
De Wolff, Francis 1913- *WhoHol 92*
de Wolff, Frederik Albert 1944- *WhoScEn 94*
DeWolff, Maurice Konrad 1941- *WhoAm 94*
de Woody, Charles 1914- *WhoWest 94*
Deworme, Elie 1932- *IntWW 93*
DeWoskin, Alan Ellis 1940- *WhoAmL 94, WhoMW 93*
De Wreder, Paul *EncSF 93*
De Wright, Yvonne *WhoHisp 94*
Dews, Peter 1929- *Who 94*
Dews, Peter Booth 1922- *IntWW 93, WhoAm 94*
Dewsbury, Donald Allen 1939- *WhoAm 94*
de Wys, Egbert Christiaan 1924- *WhoScEn 94, WhoWest 94*
Dexheimer, Karl D. 1942- *WhoAmL 94*
Dexheimer, Larry William 1941- *WhoAm 94*
Dexter, Alan d1983 *WhoHol 92*
Dexter, Anthony 1919- *WhoHol 92*
Dexter, Aubrey d1958 *WhoHol 92*

Diaz, Lope Max WhoAmA 93
Diaz, Lucy Alice 1950- WhoHisp 94
Diaz, Luis A. WhoHisp 94
Diaz, Luis F. 1946- WhoHisp 94
Diaz, Magna M. 1951- WhoHisp 94
Diaz, Manuel G. 1921- WhoHisp 94
Diaz, Maria Cristina 1955- WhoHisp 94
Diaz, Maria M. 1960- WhoHisp 94
Diaz, Maria V. 1949- WhoHisp 94
Diaz, Mario WhoHisp 94
Diaz, Maximo, Jr. 1944- WhoHisp 94
Diaz, Melchior d1540 WhWE
Diaz, Mercedes 1938- WhoHisp 94
Diaz, Michael A. 1944- WhoHisp 94
Diaz, Michael Anthony 1956- WhoHisp 94
Diaz, Nelson A. 1947- WhoHisp 94
Diaz, Nils J. 1938- WhoHisp 94
Diaz, Nils Juan 1938- WhoScEn 94
Diaz, Octavio 1951- WhoHisp 94
Diaz, Olga WhoHisp 94
Diaz, Oliver E., Jr. 1959- WhoAmP 93, WhoHisp 94
Diaz, Oscar J. 1947- WhoHisp 94
Diaz, Pedro 1949- WhoHisp 94
Diaz, Pedro J. 1937- WhoIns 94
Diaz, Porfirio 1830-1915 HisWorL [port]
Diaz, Rafael, Jr. 1939- WhoHisp 94
Diaz, Ramon V. WhoAmP 93
Diaz, Ramon Valero 1918- WhoAm 94, WhoAmL 94, WhoWest 94
Diaz, Raul J. 1947- WhoHisp 94
Diaz, Raul Zaragoza 1953- WhoHisp 94
Diaz, Raymond Franco 1952- WhoHisp 94
Diaz, Raymond Julio 1945- WhoAmL 94
Diaz, René Michel 1961- WhoHisp 94
Diaz, Rey N. WhoHisp 94
Diaz, Ricardo d1979 WhoHol 92
Diaz, Ricardo 1951- WhoHisp 94
Diaz, Ricardo L. 1956- WhoHisp 94
Diaz, Rita M. 1941- WhoHisp 94
Diaz, Robert 1960- WhoHisp 94
Diaz, Robert James 1946- WhoHisp 94
Diaz, Romulo, Jr. WhoHisp 94
Diaz, Rosita d1986 WhoHol 92
Diaz, Ruben 1943- WhoHisp 94
Diaz, Rudolph A. 1942- WhoHisp 94
Diaz, Rudy WhoHol 92
Diaz, Samuel, Jr. 1943- WhoHisp 94
Diaz, Steven A. 1948- WhoHisp 94
Diaz, Teo 1955- WhoHisp 94
Diaz, Tony d1988 WhoHol 92
Diaz, Vic WhoHol 92
Diaz, Victor Manuel, Jr. 1960- WhoAmL 94
Diaz, William Adams 1945- WhoHisp 94
Diaz, William Emilio 1957- WhoHisp 94
Diaz-Alemany, Daisy 1948- WhoHisp 94
Diaz-Arias, Alberto A. 1958- WhoHisp 94
Diaz-Arrastia, George Ravelo 1959- WhoAmL 94
Diaz-Balart, Jose A. 1960- WhoHisp 94
Diaz-Balart, Lincoln 1954- CngDr 93, WhoAm 94, WhoAmP 93, WhoHisp 94
Diaz-Balart, Mario 1961- WhoAmP 93, WhoHisp 94
Diaz-Blanco, Eduardo J. 1944- WhoHisp 94
Diaz Bosch, Mario 1944- WhoHisp 94
Diaz-Cancela, Frank J. 1949- WhoHisp 94
Diaz-Coller, Carlos 1916- WhoAm 94
Diaz-Cruz, Jorge Hatuey 1914- WhoHisp 94
Diaz Cruz, Luis Ramon 1951- WhoHisp 94
Diaz de Aldrey, Iván 1925- WhoHisp 94
Diaz Del Castillo, Bernal WhWE
Diaz De Solis, Juan WhWE
Diaz de Vivar, Rodrigo c. 1043-1099 HisWorL [port]
Diaz-Duque, Ozzie Francis 1955- WhoHisp 94
Diaz-Franco, Carlos Hernan 1956- WhoMW 93
Diaz-Gilbert, Miriam M. 1959- WhoHisp 94
Diaz Gomez, Ramon L. WhoHisp 94
Diaz-Hernández, Jaime Miguel 1950- WhoHisp 94
Diaz-Herrera, Jorge Luis 1950- WhoHisp 94
Diaz-Jimeno, Felipe WhoHisp 94
Diaz Lane, Enriqueta WhoHisp 94
Diaz Lozano, Argentina 1912- BlmGWL
Diaz-Oliver, Remedios 1938- WhoHisp 94
Diaz Perez, Clemente 1949- WhoHisp 94
Diaz-Peterson, Rosendo 1935- WhoHisp 94
Diaz-Rousselot, Guillermo WhoHisp 94
Diaz-Saldana, Manuel WhoAmP 93
Diaz Tirado, Miguel WhoHisp 94
Diaz Vargas, Alejandro WhoHisp 94
Diaz Vela, Luis Humberto 1953- WhoFI 94, WhoScEn 94
Diaz-Vélez, Félix 1942- WhoHisp 94
Diaz-Verson, Salvador, Jr. 1951- WhoFI 94, WhoHisp 94
Diaz y Perez, Elias 1933- WhoHisp 94
Diaz-Zubieta, Agustin 1936- WhoWest 94
Diba, Farah IntWW 93
Dibak, Igor 1947- NewGrDO
Diballa de Lopez, Susan 1958- WhoWest 94
DiBartolomeo, Albert 1952- ConAu 141
DiBartolomeo, Dennis 1949- WhoWest 94
Dibb, David Walter 1943- WhoAm 94, WhoScEn 94
Dibben, Michael Alan Charles 1943- Who 94
Dibble, Cameron Shawn 1951- WhoMW 93
Dibble, George 1904- WhoAmA 93
Dibble, George Smith, Jr. 1933- WhoAm 94
Dibble, Gordon Lynch 1928- WhoAm 94
Dibble, J(ames) Birney 1925- WrDr 94
Dibble, John C. 1946- WhoAmL 94
Dibble, Jonathan A. 1946- WhoAmL 94
Dibdin, Charles 1745-1814 NewGrDO [port]
Dibdin, Michael 1947- WrDr 94
Dibela, Kingsford 1932- IntWW 93, Who 94
Di Belgiojoso, Lodovico Barbiano 1909- IntWW 93
Dibella, William A. 1944- WhoAmP 93
DiBenedetto, Anthony Thomas 1933- WhoAm 94, WhoScEn 94
DiBenedetto, Joseph A. 1946- WhoAm 94
Dibenedetto, Mary Rowan 1963- WhoIns 94
Di Benedetto, Tony WhoHol 92
DiBerardinis, Louis Joseph 1947- WhoScEn 94
DiBerardino, Marie Antoinette 1926- WhoAm 94
Dibert, Nicholas J. 1947- WhoAmL 94
Dibert, Rita Jean 1946- WhoAmA 93
Dibiaggio, John A. 1932- IntWW 93, WhoAm 94
Dibianca, Joseph Philip 1954- WhoAm 94
DiBlasi, Gandolfo Vincent 1953- WhoAmL 94
Dible, Dennis D. 1946- WhoAm 94
Dible, Rose Harpe McFee 1927- WhoWest 94
Dibner, Bern 1897- WhAm 10
Dibner, David Robert 1926- WhoAm 94
Dibner, Mark Douglas 1951- WhoScEn 94
DiBoise, James A. 1952- WhoAmL 94
Dibona, Anthony 1896- WhoAmA 93N
DiBona, Charles Joseph 1932- WhoAm 94, WhoFI 94, WhoScEn 94
Dibos, Dennis Robert 1942- WhoFI 94
Dibrell, Louis Nelson, III 1945- WhoAm 94, WhoFI 94
Dibrienza, Stephen 1954- WhoAmP 93
diBuono, Anthony Joseph 1930- WhoAm 94, WhoAmL 94, WhoFI 94
DiCamillo, Gary Thomas 1950- WhoAm 94, WhoFI 94
DiCamillo, Peter John 1953- WhoScEn 94
DiCara, Lawrence S. 1949- WhoAmL 94, WhoAmP 93
DiCarlo, David Jon 1965- WhoAmL 94
DiCarlo, Dominick L. 1928- CngDr 93, WhoAm 94, WhoAmL 94
DiCarlo, Dominick L. 1938- WhoAmP 93
Dice, Brian Charles 1936- Who 94
Dice, Bruce Burton 1926- WhoFI 94, WhoScEn 94
Dice, Elizabeth Jane 1919- WhoAmA 93
Dicello, John Francis, Jr. 1938- WhoAm 94
Dicenta, Manuel d1974 WhoHol 92
diCenzo, Colin Domenic 1923- IntWW 93
Di Cenzo, George WhoHol 92
Di Cerbo, Michael 1947- WhoAmA 93
Di Certo, J(oseph) J(ohn) 1933- ConAu 42NR, WrDr 94
Di Cesare, Mario A 1928- WrDr 94
Dicharry, Richard N. 1951- WhoAmL 94
Di Chiara, Gerald J. 1951- WhoAmL 94
DiChiera, David 1935- NewGrDO
Di Chiera, David 1937- WhoAm 94, WhoMW 93
Dichter, Barry Joel 1950- WhoAm 94, WhoAmL 94, WhoFI 94
Dichter, Ernest 1907-1991 WhAm 10, WrDr 94N
Dichter, Mark S. 1943- WhoAm 94, WhoAmL 94
Dichter, Misha 1945- IntWW 93, WhoAm 94
Di Cicco, Bobby 1955- WhoHol 92
Di Cicco, Joseph Nicholas, Jr. 1917- WhoFI 94
Di Cicco, Pat d1978 WhoHol 92
Di Cicco, Pier Giorgio 1949- WrDr 94
Dick, Alan David 1924- Who 94
Dick, Albert Blake, III 1918-1989 WhAm 10
Dick, Barclay L. 1948- WhoWest 94
Dick, Bernard 1935- WrDr 94
Dick, Bertram Gale, Jr. 1926- WhoAm 94, WhoWest 94
Dick, Brett R. 1945- WhoAmL 94
Dick, Charles H., Jr. 1942- WhoAmL 94
Dick, Douglas 1920- WhoHol 92
Dick, Douglas Patrick 1953- WhoAm 94
Dick, Edward Francis 1924- WhoFI 94
Dick, Ellen A. WhoScEn 94
Dick, Gary Lowell 1954- WhoScEn 94
Dick, Gavin Colquhoun 1928- Who 94
Dick, George (Williamson Auchinvole) 1914- Who 94
Dick, George Albert 1940- WhoBlA 94
Dick, Harold L. 1943- WhoAm 94
Dick, Henry Henry 1922- WhoAm 94
Dick, Iain Charles M. Who 94
Dick, James Brownlee 1919- Who 94
Dick, John (Alexander) 1920- Who 94
Dick, John Kenneth 1913- IntWW 93, Who 94
Dick, Kay 1915- EncSF 93, Who 94, WrDr 94
Dick, Kent Edward 1963- WhoFI 94
Dick, Mike fl. 1930- EncNAR
Dick, Nancy E. 1930- WhoAmP 93
Dick, Neil Alan 1941- WhoFI 94
Dick, Patricia A. 1929- WhoMW 93
Dick, Paul Douglas 1956- WhoWest 94
Dick, Paul Wyatt 1940- IntWW 93, WhoAm 94
Dick, Philip K(indred) 1928-1982 EncSF 93
Dick, Randall G. 1945- WhoAmL 94
Dick, Raymond Dale 1930- WhoAm 94
Dick, Richard Irwin 1935- WhoAm 94
Dick, Robert C(hristopher) 1938- WrDr 94
Dick, Rollin Merle 1931- WhoFI 94
Dick, Ronald 1931- Who 94
Dick, Samuel 1740-1812 WhAmRev
Dick, William A. WhAm 10
Dickamore, Henry James 1933- WhoAmP 93
Dickason, Glen E. 1953- WhoAmP 93
Dickason, John Hamilton 1931- WhoAm 94
Dickason, Olive Patricia 1920- WrDr 94
Dick B. ConAu 142
Dicke, Arnold A. 1942- WhoIns 94
Dicke, Candice Edwards 1949- WhoAm 94
Dicke, James Frederick, II 1945- WhoAm 94
Dicke, Robert H 1916- WrDr 94
Dicke, Robert H(enry) 1916- IntWW 93
Dicke, Robert Henry 1916- WhoAm 94, WhoScEn 94
Dickel, Friedrich 1913- IntWW 93
Dickel, HeLene Ramseyer 1938- WhoMW 93
Dickelman, James Howard 1947- WhoFI 94
Dicken, Michael John Charles Worwood 1935- Who 94
Dicken-Garcia, Hazel Faye 1939- WhoMW 93
Dickens, Arthur Geoffrey 1910- IntWW 93, Who 94, WrDr 94
Dickens, Bernard Morris 1937- WhoAm 94
Dickens, Charles 1812-1870 BlmGEL [port], NewGrDO
Dickens, Charles (John Huffam) 1812-1870 RfGShF
Dickens, Charles (John Huffham) 1812-1870 EncSF 93
Dickens, Charles Stafford d1967 WhoHol 92
Dickens, Doris Lee WhoAm 94, WhoBlA 94, WhoScEn 94
Dickens, Edwin Larry 1938- WhoAmP 93
Dickens, Geoffrey Kenneth 1931- Who 94
Dickens, Helen Octavia WhoBlA 94
Dickens, Jacoby 1931- WhoBlA 94
Dickens, James McCulloch York 1931- Who 94
Dickens, James Ralph 1942- WhoAmL 94
Dickens, Monica 1915- BlmGWL
Dickens, Monica 1915-1992 AnObit 1992
Dickens, Monica (Enid) 1915- WrDr 94
Dickens, Monica (Enid) 1915-1992 ConAu 140, SmATA 74
Dickens, Monica Enid d1992 IntWW 93N, Who 94N
Dickens, Patricia A. 1941- WhoAmP 93
Dickens, Robert Allen 1941- WhoMW 93
Dickens, Samuel 1926- WhoBlA 94
Dickens, Thomas Allen 1959- WhoScEn 94
Dickens, William Theodore 1953- WhoWest 94
Dickenson, Aubrey Fiennes T. Who 94
Dickenson, Charles Royal 1907- Who 94
Dickenson, George-Therese DrAPF 93
Dickenson, Joseph Frank 1924- Who 94
Dickenson, Nancy Combs 1960- WhoAmP 93
Dicker, Herbert 1921- WhoAm 94
Dicker, Marvin 1933- WhoAm 94
Dicker, Richard d1993 NewYTBS 93
Dickerman, Dorothea Wilhelmina 1958- WhoAmL 94
Dickerman, Herbert William 1928-1991 WhAm 10
Dickerman, John Melvin 1914- WhoAmL 94
Dickerson, Adolphus Sumner 1914- WhoBlA 94
Dickerson, Allen Bruce 1938- WhoMW 93
Dickerson, Angela Darby 1963- WhoAmL 94
Dickerson, Arthur Neal 1930- WhoIns 94
Dickerson, Barbara Ann Ransom 1952- WhoWest 94
Dickerson, Beach 1935- WhoHol 92
Dickerson, Bette Jeanne 1951- WhoBlA 94
Dickerson, Brian 1956- WhoAm 94
Dickerson, Brian S. 1951- WhoAmA 93
Dickerson, Claire Moore 1950- WhoAmL 94
Dickerson, Colleen Bernice Patton 1922- WhoWest 94
Dickerson, Cynthia Rowe 1956- WhoFI 94, WhoWest 94
Dickerson, Daniel Jay 1922- WhoAmA 93
Dickerson, Dennis Clark 1949- WhoBlA 94
Dickerson, Dudley d1968 WhoHol 92
Dickerson, Edward Ted 1932- WhoAmA 93
Dickerson, Ellis L., Jr. 1934- WhoBlA 94
Dickerson, Eric Demetric 1960- WhoAm 94, WhoBlA 94, WhoWest 94
Dickerson, Ernest 1952?- ConBlB 6 [port], IntMPA 94
Dickerson, Ernest 1954?- ConTFT 11
Dickerson, Frank Secor, III 1939- WhoFI 94
Dickerson, Frederick Reed 1909-1991 WhAm 10
Dickerson, George WhoHol 92
Dickerson, Glenda J. 1945- WhoBlA 94
Dickerson, Gordon Edwin 1912- WhoMW 93
Dickerson, Harvey G., Jr. 1926- WhoBlA 94
Dickerson, Jaffe Dean 1950- WhoAm 94
Dickerson, Janet Smith 1944- WhoBlA 94
Dickerson, Jennie d1943 WhoHol 92
Dickerson, Jill Louise 1965- WhoMW 93
Dickerson, Lawrence Loton, Jr. 1956- WhoAmP 93
Dickerson, Lowell Dwight 1944- WhoBlA 94
Dickerson, Matthew Ennis 1961- WhoFI 94
Dickerson, Michael Joe 1967- WhoScEn 94
Dickerson, Monar Stephen 1947- WhoFI 94
Dickerson, Nancy Whitehead WhoAm 94
Dickerson, Pamela Ann 1953- WhoBlA 94
Dickerson, Ron 1948- WhoBlA 94
Dickerson, Thomas Arthur 1944- WhoAmL 94
Dickerson, Thomas L., Jr. 1949- WhoBlA 94
Dickerson, Thomas Milton 1898- WhAm 10
Dickerson, Thomas Patrick 1955- WhoAmL 94
Dickerson, Tim Edward 1948- WhoFI 94
Dickerson, Tommy WhoAmP 93
Dickerson, Vera Mason 1946- WhoAmA 93
Dickerson, Warner Lee 1937- WhoBlA 94
Dickerson, William J. 1943- WhoAmA 93
Dickerson, William Judson 1904- WhoAmA 93N
Dickerson, William Roy 1928- WhoAmL 94, WhoWest 94
Dickes, Bruce E. 1950- WhoIns 94
Dickes, Robert 1912- WhoAm 94
Dickeson, Ludmila Weir 1941- WhoMW 93
Dickeson, Robert Celmer 1940- WhoAm 94
Dickey, Bette Ellyn 1936- WhoFI 94
Dickey, Bill 1907-1993 NewYTBS 93 [port]
Dickey, Christopher 1951- WrDr 94
Dickey, Curtis Raymond 1956- WhoBlA 94
Dickey, David G. 1969- WhoScEn 94
Dickey, David Herschel 1951- WhoAm 94, WhoAmL 94
Dickey, David Jerry 1939- WhoAmP 93
Dickey, Don Allen 1945- WhoAmL 94
Dickey, Donald Floyd 1927- WhoAmP 93
Dickey, Duval Frederick 1916- WhoAm 94
Dickey, Erma Cook 1929- WhoBlA 94
Dickey, Gary Alan 1946- WhoWest 94
Dickey, Glenn Ernest, Jr. 1936- WhoAm 94, WhoWest 94
Dickey, James DrAPF 93, WhoHol 92

Dickey, James 1923- *IntWW 93, WhoAm 94*
Dickey, James (Lafayette) 1923- *WrDr 94*
Dickey, Jay 1939- *CngDr 93, WhoAmP 93*
Dickey, Jay W., Jr. 1940- *WhoAm 94*
Dickey, John Horace 1914- *WhoAm 94*
Dickey, John Miller 1911-1990 *WhAm 10*
Dickey, John Miller 1954- *WhoAm 94*
Dickey, John Sloan 1907-1991 *WhAm 10*
Dickey, Joseph Waldo 1939- *WhoScEn 94*
Dickey, Julia Edwards 1940- *WhoMW 93*
Dickey, Lloyd V. *WhoBlA 94*
Dickey, Lucinda *WhoHol 92*
Dickey, Lynn 1949- *WhoAmP 93*
Dickey, M. Jane 1948- *WhoAmL 94*
Dickey, Paul d1933 *WhoHol 92*
Dickey, R. P. *DrAPF 93*
Dickey, Robert Marvin 1950- *WhoWest 94*
Dickey, Robert Preston 1936- *WhoAm 94, WhoWest 94*
Dickey, Ronald Wayne 1938- *WhoMW 93*
Dickey, Samuel Stephens 1921- *WhoAmL 94*
Dickey, Wilhelmina Kuehn 1937- *WhoAmP 93*
Dickey, William *DrAPF 93*
Dickey, William 1928- *WhoAm 94, WhoWest 94, WrDr 94*
Dickey, William K., Jr. 1920- *WhoAmP 93*
Dickie, Brian 1941- *NewGrDO, WhoAm 94*
Dickie, Brian James 1941- *Who 94*
Dickie, Dean A. 1944- *WhoAmL 94*
Dickie, Helen Aird 1913-1988 *WhAm 10*
Dickie, Lloyd M. 1926- *IntWW 93*
Dickie, Lloyd Merlin 1926- *WhoAm 94*
Dickie, Margaret McKenzie 1935- *WhoAm 94*
Dickie, Murray 1924- *NewGrDO*
Dickins, Barry 1949- *ConDr 93*
Dickins, Basil Gordon 1908- *Who 94*
Dickins, Mark Frederick Hakon S. *Who 94*
Dickinson, Baron 1926- *Who 94*
Dickinson, Alfred James 1916- *WhoAm 94*
Dickinson, Angie 1931- *IntMPA 94, WhoAm 94*
Dickinson, Angie 1932- *WhoHol 92*
Dickinson, Ann 1961- *WhoWest 94*
Dickinson, Anna E. 1842-1932 *WomPubS*
Dickinson, Anne *Who 94*
Dickinson, (Vivienne) Anne 1931- *Who 94*
Dickinson, Basil Philip Harriman 1916- *Who 94*
Dickinson, Ben *Who 94*
Dickinson, Bradley William 1948- *WhoAm 94*
Dickinson, Brian Henry Baron 1940- *Who 94*
Dickinson, Calhoun 1931- *WhoAm 94*
Dickinson, Catherine Schatz 1927- *WhoAm 94*
Dickinson, Christopher John 1927- *IntWW 93, Who 94*
Dickinson, Daniel Oliver 1950- *WhoMW 93*
Dickinson, David Budd, Jr. 1936- *WhoAm 94*
Dickinson, David Charles 1940- *WhoAmA 93*
Dickinson, David Walter 1946- *WhoAm 94*
Dickinson, Donald Charles 1927- *WhoAm 94, WhoWest 94*
Dickinson, Ed Frank 1948- *WhoAm 94*
Dickinson, Edwin W. 1891-1979 *WhoAmA 93N*
Dickinson, Eleanor Creekmore 1931- *WhoAm 94, WhoAmA 93*
Dickinson, Emily 1830-1886 *BlmGWL*
Dickinson, Emily Elizabeth 1830-1886 *AmCulL*
Dickinson, Gloria Harper 1947- *WhoBlA 94*
Dickinson, Hal d1970 *WhoHol 92*
Dickinson, Harold (Herbert) 1917- *Who 94*
Dickinson, Harry Thomas 1939- *Who 94, WrDr 94*
Dickinson, Homer d1959 *WhoHol 92*
Dickinson, Howard C., Jr. 1936- *WhoAmP 93*
Dickinson, Hugh Geoffrey 1929- *Who 94*
Dickinson, Hugh Gordon 1944- *Who 94*
Dickinson, Jacob John Louis 1957- *WhoWest 94*
Dickinson, James Gordon 1940- *WhoAm 94, WhoFI 94, WhoWest 94*
Dickinson, Janet Mae Webster 1929- *WhoFI 94, WhoWest 94*
Dickinson, Jerold Thomas 1941- *WhoWest 94*
Dickinson, John 1732-1808 *WhAmRev [port]*
Dickinson, John D. 1937- *WhoAmP 93*
Dickinson, John Hubert d1993 *Who 94N*
Dickinson, John Lawrence 1913- *Who 94*
Dickinson, Jonathan 1688-1747 *DcAmReB 2*
Dickinson, Joshua Clifton, Jr. 1916- *WhoAm 94*
Dickinson, Katherine Diana 1954- *WhoScEn 94*
Dickinson, Lee George 1935- *WhoWest 94*
Dickinson, Lloyd J. 1947- *WhoAmL 94*
Dickinson, Loren Eric 1943- *WhoAmP 93*
Dickinson, Mae 1933- *WhoAmP 93*
Dickinson, Margaret 1942- *WrDr 94*
Dickinson, Norman 1921- *WhoAmA 93*
Dickinson, Patric (Thomas) 1914- *Who 94, WrDr 94*
Dickinson, Patric Laurence 1950- *Who 94*
Dickinson, Patric Thomas 1914- *ConAu 43NR*
Dickinson, Paul Bruce 1958- *See* Iron Maiden *ConMus 10*
Dickinson, Paul R. 1947- *WhoHisp 94*
Dickinson, Peter 1927- *WrDr 94*
Dickinson, Peter 1934- *Who 94, WhoAm 94*
Dickinson, Peter (Malcolm de Brissac) 1927- *EncSF 93, TwCYAW*
Dickinson, Peter Malcolm de Brissac 1927- *Who 94*
Dickinson, Philemon 1739-1809 *AmRev, WhAmRev*
Dickinson, Randolph Paul 1945- *WhoWest 94*
Dickinson, Richard Donald Nye 1929- *WhoAm 94*
Dickinson, Richard Henry 1944- *WhoFI 94*
Dickinson, Richard Raymond 1931- *WhoAm 94, WhoFI 94*
Dickinson, Rick 1953- *WhoAmP 93*
Dickinson, Rita Harkins 1949- *WhoWest 94*
Dickinson, Robert Earl 1940- *WhoAm 94, WhoWest 94*
Dickinson, Roger Allyn 1929- *WhoAm 94*
Dickinson, Samuel Benson 1912- *Who 94*
Dickinson, Spencer 1943- *WhoAmP 93*
Dickinson, Temple 1956- *WhoAmL 94*
Dickinson, Vivian Earl 1924- *WhoAmP 93*
Dickinson, Wade 1926- *WhoAm 94*
Dickinson, William Boyd, Jr. 1931- *WhoAm 94*
Dickinson, William Louis 1925- *WhoAmP 93*
Dickinson, William Michael 1930- *Who 94*
Dickinson, William Richard 1931- *WhoAm 94, WhoScEn 94, WhoWest 94*
Dickinson, William Streit, Jr. 1918- *WhoAmP 93*
Dickinson, William Trevor 1939- *WhoAm 94*
Dickinson-Brown, Roger *DrAPF 93*
Dick-Lauder, George (Andrew) 1917-1981 *EncSF 93*
Dick-Lauder, Piers Robert *Who 94*
Dickler, Howard Byron 1942- *WhoScEn 94*
Dicklich, Ronald Robert 1951- *WhoAmP 93*
Dickman, Craig Steven 1960- *WhoMW 93*
Dickman, Dean Anthony 1961- *WhoScEn 94*
Dickman, Donna McCord 1942- *WhoFI 94*
Dickman, Francois M. 1924- *WhoAmP 93*
Dickman, Francois Moussiegt 1924- *WhoAm 94*
Dickman, James Bruce 1949- *WhoAm 94*
Dickman, James Earl 1963- *WhoFI 94*
Dickman, James Joseph d1993 *NewYTBS 93 [port]*
Dickman, Murray G. 1947- *WhoAmP 93*
Dickman, Robert Laurence 1947- *WhoScEn 94*
Dickman, Steven Gary 1962- *WhoScEn 94*
Dickmann, Fritz 1948- *WhoMW 93*
Dickons, Maria (Francis) Caroline 1776-1833 *NewGrDO*
Dickow, James Fred 1943- *WhoFI 94, WhoMW 93*
Dicks, John G., III 1951- *WhoAm 94*
Dicks, John Gaudry, III 1951- *WhoAmP 93*
Dicks, Norman D. 1940- *CngDr 93*
Dicks, Norman De Valois 1940- *WhoAm 94, WhoWest 94*
Dicks, Norman DeValois 1940- *WhoAmP 93*
Dicks, Randall James 1950- *WhoAmL 94*
Dicks, Robert J. 1941- *WhoIns 94*
Dicks, Terence Patrick 1937- *Who 94*
Dickson, Alan T. 1931- *WhoFI 94*
Dickson, Alex Dockery 1926- *WhoAm 94*
Dickson, Alexander Graeme 1914- *Who 94*
Dickson, Arthur Richard Franklin 1913- *Who 94*
Dickson, Brent E. 1941- *WhoAmL 94, WhoAmP 93, WhoMW 93*
Dickson, Brian 1916- *Who 94, WhoAm 94*
Dickson, Brian 1950- *WhoScEn 94*
Dickson, Carter *EncSF 93*
Dickson, Cecil B. 1935- *WhAm 10*
Dickson, Charles d1927 *WhoHol 92*
Dickson, Charlie Jones *WhoBlA 94*
Dickson, Constance Pierce *WhoAmL 94*
Dickson, David John Scott 1947- *Who 94*
Dickson, David W. D. 1919- *WhoBlA 94*
Dickson, David Watson Daly 1919- *WhoAm 94*
Dickson, Donald d1972 *WhoHol 92*
Dickson, Dorothy 1900- *WhoHol 92*
Dickson, Eileen Wadham *Who 94*
Dickson, Ella Irene 1914- *WhoAmP 93*
Dickson, Frank Wilson 1922- *WhoWest 94*
Dickson, Frederic Howard 1946- *WhoFI 94*
Dickson, George 1931- *Who 94*
Dickson, Gloria d1945 *WhoHol 92*
Dickson, Gordon (Rupert) 1923- *WrDr 94*
Dickson, Gordon R(upert) 1923- *EncSF 93, SmATA 77*
Dickson, Gordon Ross 1932- *Who 94*
Dickson, James Edwin, II 1943- *WhoScEn 94*
Dickson, James Francis, III 1924- *WhoAm 94*
Dickson, James Lothar 1949- *WhoAm 94*
Dickson, Jane Leone 1952- *WhoAmA 93*
Dickson, Jennifer 1936- *IntWW 93*
Dickson, Jennifer (Joan) 1936- *Who 94*
Dickson, Jennifer Joan 1936- *WhoAmA 93*
Dickson, John *DrAPF 93*
Dickson, John Abernethy 1915- *Who 94*
Dickson, John H. 1935- *WhoAmP 93*
Dickson, John H. 1943- *WhoFI 94*
Dickson, John R. 1930- *WhoAm 94, WhoFI 94*
Dickson, John V. d1941 *WhoHol 92*
Dickson, Joseph 1745-1825 *WhAmRev*
Dickson, Joseph Craig, Jr. 1935- *WhoAmL 94*
Dickson, Kwesi A(botsia) 1929- *WrDr 94*
Dickson, Lamont d1944 *WhoHol 92*
Dickson, Leonard Elliot 1915- *Who 94*
Dickson, Lydia d1928 *WhoHol 92*
Dickson, Mark Amos 1946- *WhoAmA 93*
Dickson, Markham Allen 1922- *WhoFI 94*
Dickson, Marnell 1952- *WhoMW 93*
Dickson, Mora Agnes 1918- *WrDr 94*
Dickson, Murray Graeme 1911- *Who 94*
Dickson, Neil *WhoHol 92*
Dickson, Onias D., Jr. 1958- *WhoBlA 94*
Dickson, Patrick *WhoHol 92*
Dickson, Paul 1939- *WrDr 94*
Dickson, Paul Wesley, Jr. 1931- *WhoAm 94, WhoScEn 94*
Dickson, Peter George Muir 1929- *IntWW 93, Who 94*
Dickson, Ray Clark *DrAPF 93*
Dickson, Reecy L. *WhoAmP 93*
Dickson, Reginald D. 1946- *WhoBlA 94*
Dickson, Richard Eugene 1932- *WhoMW 93*
Dickson, Robert Andrew 1943- *Who 94*
Dickson, Robert Frank 1933- *WhoMW 93*
Dickson, Robert George Brian *Who 94*
Dickson, Robert George Brian 1916- *IntWW 93*
Dickson, Robert Hamish 1945- *Who 94*
Dickson, Robert Lee 1932- *WhoAm 94, WhoWest 94*
Dickson, Rush Stuart 1929- *WhoAm 94, WhoFI 94*
Dickson, Sally Isabelle *WhoAm 94*
Dickson, Stewart Price 1956- *WhoWest 94*
Dickson, Temple 1934- *WhoAmP 93*
Dickson, W. W. *WhoAmP 93*
Dickson, William Brown 1865-1942 *EncABHB 9 [port]*
Dickson Mabon, Jesse *Who 94*
Dickstein, Harold David 1929- *WhoWest 94*
Dickstein, Harvey Leonard 1936- *WhoFI 94*
Dickstein, Sidney 1925- *WhoAm 94*
Dickstein, Zena Manes 1957- *WhoAmL 94*
DiClerico, Joseph Anthony, Jr. 1941- *WhoAmL 94*
DiColo, Robert Louis 1958- *WhoFI 94*
Di Conza, Peter James, Jr. 1948- *WhoAmL 94*
Di Cosimo, Joanne Violet 1953- *WhoAm 94*
Di Cosola, Lois 1935- *WhoAmA 93*
Dicterow, Glenn Eugene 1948- *WhoAm 94*
Dictor, Cary L. 1949- *WhoAmL 94*
Dicus, Brian George 1961- *WhoAmL 94*
Dicus, John Carmack 1933- *WhoAm 94*
Dicus, Stephen Howard 1948- *WhoAmL 94*
Di Cyan, Erwin 1918- *WrDr 94*
Diddle, Ed 1895- *BasBi*
Diddley, Bo 1928- *WhoBlA 94, WhoHol 92*
Didelot, Charles-Louis 1767-1837 *IntDcB*
Didelot, Charles-Louis (Frederic) 1767-1837 *NewGrDO*
Diderot, Denis 1713-1784 *GuFrLit 2, NewGrDO [port]*
Didi 1928- *WorESoc [port]*
Didich, Jan 1952- *WhoMW 93*
Didieo, James 1949- *WhoFI 94*
Didier, Gordon 1948- *WhoAmL 94*
DiDio, Anthony Michael 1951- *WhoFI 94*
DiDio, Liberato John Alphonse 1920- *WhoAm 94*
Didion, Joan *DrAPF 93*
Didion, Joan 1934- *BlmGWL, IntWW 93, WhoAm 94, WrDr 94*
Didion, Maureen Anne 1938- *WhoAmP 93*
Didlake, Ralph Hunter, Jr. 1953- *WhoScEn 94*
Didlick, Wells S. 1925- *WhoBlA 94*
Di Domenica, Robert Anthony 1927- *WhoAm 94*
Di Domenico, Gianpaolo *NewGrDO*
DiDomenico, Mauro, Jr. 1937- *WhoAm 94*
DiDomenico, Nikki 1948- *WhoAmA 93*
DiDomenico, Paul B. 1968- *WhoScEn 94*
DiDonato, Greg L. 1961- *WhoAmP 93*
di Donato, Pietro 1911-1992 *AnObit 1992*
DiDonna, Richard A. *WhoFI 94*
Didrickson, Loleta Anderson 1941- *WhoAmP 93*
Didsbury, Howard Francis 1924- *WhoScEn 94*
Didur, Adam 1874-1946 *NewGrDO*
Die, Beatrice, Comtesse de fl. 12th cent.- *BlmGWL*
Dieball, Scott Alan 1961- *WhoAmL 94*
Diebel, Nelson *WhoAm 94*
Diebenkorn, Richard 1922- *WhoAmA 93*
Diebenkorn, Richard 1922-1993 *NewYTBS 93 [port], News 93*
Diebenkorn, Richard (Clifford, Jr.) 1922-1993 *CurBio 93N*
Diebenkorn, Richard Clifford d1993 *IntWW 93N*
Diebenkorn, Richard Clifford 1922- *IntWW 93*
Diebenkorn, Richard Clifford, Jr. 1922-1993 *AmCulL*
Diebold, Charles Harbou 1909- *WhoScEn 94*
Diebold, Foster Frank 1932- *WhoAm 94*
Diebold, John 1926- *IntWW 93, WhoAm 94, WrDr 94*
Diebolt, Judy 1948- *WhoAm 94*
Dieck, William Wallace Sandford 1924- *WhoScEn 94*
Diecke, Friedrich Paul Julius 1927- *WhoAm 94*
Diederich, Anne Marie 1943- *WhoMW 93*
Diederich, Evelyn Tomlinson 1915- *WhoAmP 93*
Diederich, John William 1929- *WhoAm 94, WhoFI 94, WhoWest 94*
Diederichs, John Kuensting 1921- *WhoAm 94*
Diedrich, Jayne F. 1956- *WhoHisp 94*
Diedrich, Michael G. *WhoAmP 93*
Diedrich, William Lawler 1923-1992 *WhAm 10*
Diedrick, Geraldine Rose 1928- *WhoWest 94*
Diedtrich, Elmer *WhoAmP 93*
Diefenbach, Dale Alan 1933- *WhoAmL 94*
Diefenbach, Viron Leroy 1922- *WhoAm 94*
Diefenderfer, William Martin, III 1945- *WhoAm 94*
Diefendorf, David *DrAPF 93*
Diegel, Roger Louis 1934- *WhoFI 94*
Diegelmann, Wilhelm d1934 *WhoHol 92*
Diego, Gerardo 1896-1987 *DcLB 134 [port]*
Dieguez, Clemente 1935- *WhoHisp 94*
Dieguez, Richard P. 1960- *WhoHisp 94*
Diehl, Beth M. *WhoHisp 94*
Diehl, Carol Lou 1929- *WhoMW 93*
Diehl, Cynthia Barre 1933- *WhoAmP 93*
Diehl, Deborah Hilda 1951- *WhoAm 94*
Diehl, Digby Robert 1940- *WhoAm 94, WhoWest 94*
Diehl, Gerald George 1916- *WhoAm 94*
Diehl, Guy Louis 1949- *WhoAmA 93*
Diehl, Hans-Jurgen 1940- *WhoAmA 93*
Diehl, John *WhoHol 92*
Diehl, John Bertram Stuart 1944- *Who 94*
Diehl, John E. 1941- *WhoAmL 94*
Diehl, Joseph Burnett 1949- *WhoAm 94*
Diehl, Lesley Ann 1943- *WhoAm 94*
Diehl, Mary Grace 1952- *WhoAmL 94*
Diehl, Michael 1949- *WhoAmL 94*
Diehl, Myron Herbert, Jr. 1951- *WhoScEn 94*
Diehl, Paul W. 1933- *WhoAmP 93*
Diehl, Randy Lee 1949- *WhoScEn 94*
Diehl, Richard Crocker 1949- *WhoMW 93*

Diehl, Richard Kurth 1935- *WhoAm 94*
Diehl, Sevilla S. *WhoAmA 93*
Diehl, Sharon Fay 1951- *WhoWest 94*
Diehl, Stephen Anthony 1942- *WhoAm 94*
Diehl, Walter Francis 1907-1991 *WhAm 10*
Diehl, William *WhoHol 92*
Diehm, James Warren 1944- *WhoAm 94*
Diekema, Anthony J. 1933- *WhoAm 94*
Diekmann, Gilmore Frederick, Jr. 1946- *WhoAm 94, WhoAmL 94*
Diel, Rolf 1922- *IntWW 93*
Dieleman, William W. 1931- *WhoAmP 93*
Dieleman, William Wilbur 1931- *WhoMW 93*
Diemand, Kim Eugene 1953- *WhoMW 93*
Diemar, Robert Emery, Jr. 1942- *WhoAm 94*
Diemecke, Enrique 1952- *WhoHisp 94*
Diemecke, Enrique Arturo 1952- *WhoAm 94, WhoMW 93*
Diemer, Arthur William 1925- *WhoFI 94*
Diemer, Emma Lou 1927- *WhoAm 94, WhoWest 94*
Diemer, Marvin E. 1924- *WhoAmP 93*
Dienelt, John F. 1943- *WhoAmL 94*
Diener, Bert 1915- *WhoAm 94*
Diener, Betty Jane 1940- *WhoAm 94*
Diener, Erwin 1932- *WhoAm 94*
Diener, Royce 1918- *WhoAm 94, WhoFI 94, WhoWest 94*
Diener, Theodor Otto 1921- *IntWW 93, WhoAm 94*
Diener, William Paul 1941- *WhoAm 94*
Dienes, Sari 1898-1992 *WhoAmA 93N*
Dienstbier, Jiri 1937- *IntWW 93*
Diepgen, Eberhard 1941- *IntWW 93*
Diepholz, Daniel Ray 1964- *WhoFI 94, WhoWest 94*
Dieppa, Margaret *WhoHisp 94*
Dierauf, Leslie Ann 1948- *WhoAm 94*
Diercks, Chester William, Jr. 1926- *WhoAm 94*
Diercks, Eileen Kay 1944- *WhoMW 93*
Diercks, Frederick Otto 1912- *WhoAm 94, WhoScEn 94*
Diercks, Ross 1957- *WhoAmP 93*
Diercks, Walter Elmer 1945- *WhoAm 94*
Dierdorf, Daniel Lee 1949- *WhoAm 94*
Dierdorff, John Ainsworth 1928- *WhoAm 94*
Dierenfield, Richard Bruce 1922- *WrDr 94*
Dierickx, Mary Fahy 1941- *WhoWest 94*
Dierkers, Joseph Andrew 1930- *WhoFI 94*
Dierkes, John d1975 *WhoHol 92*
Dierking, Herminia D. *WhoAmP 93*
Dierkop, Charles 1936- *WhoHol 92*
Dierks, Henry Alfred 1894- *WhAm 10*
Dierks, Merton L. 1932- *WhoAmP 93*
Dierks, Merton Lyle 1932- *WhoMW 93*
Dierks, Richard Ernest 1934- *WhoAm 94*
Dierner-Aeppli, Verena 1949 *WhoWomW 91*
Diers, Carol Jean 1933- *WhoAm 94*
Diers, Hank H. 1931- *WhoAm 94*
Diersen, David John 1948- *WhoMW 93*
Diersing, Robert Joseph 1949- *WhoScEn 94*
Dies, Douglas Hilton 1913- *WhoAm 94*
Dies, Martin, Jr. 1921- *WhoAmP 93*
Diesch, Stanley La Verne 1925- *WhoAm 94*
Diesel, John Phillip 1926- *IntWW 93*
Diesel, Rudolf Christian Karl 1858-1913 *WorInv*
Diesem, Charles David 1921- *WhoAm 94*
Diesem, John Lawrence 1941- *WhoAm 94, WhoFI 94, WhoMW 93, WhoScEn 94*
Diesi, Sal L. 1930- *WhoAmP 93*
Diesing, Daryl L. 1953- *WhoAmL 94*
Dieskau, Dietrich F. *Who 94*
Diessl, Gustav d1948 *WhoHol 92*
Diessner, A. W. 1923- *WhoAmP 93*
Diessner, Charles F. 1944- *WhoAmL 94*
Diessner, Daniel Joseph 1963- *WhoScEn 94*
Dieste St. Martin, Eladio 1917- *IntWW 93*
Dietch, Henry Xerxes 1913- *WhoAm 94*
Dietel, James Edwin 1941- *WhoAmL 94*
Dietel, William Moore 1927- *WhoAm 94*
Dieter, Christian Ludwig 1757-1822 *NewGrDO*
Dieter, George E., Jr. 1928- *WhoAm 94, WhoScEn 94*
Dieter, Raymond Andrew, Jr. 1934- *WhoAm 94*
Dieter, Werner H. 1929- *IntWW 93*
Dieterich, Douglas Thomas 1951- *WhoScEn 94*
Dieterich, Janet E. 1943- *WhoAmP 93*
Dieterich, Neil *WhoAmP 93*
Dieterich, Russell Burks 1943- *WhoMW 93*
Dieterle, Donald Lyle 1908- *WhoAm 94*
Dieterle, Robert *WhoScEn 94*
Dieterle, William d1972 *WhoHol 92*
Diethelm, Arnold Gillespie 1932- *WhoAm 94*
Diethrich, Edward Bronson 1935- *WhoAm 94, WhoWest 94*
Dietl, Frank d1923 *WhoHol 92*
Dietmeyer, Donald Leo 1932- *WhoAm 94, WhoMW 93*
Dietrich, Bruce Leinbach 1937- *WhoAm 94, WhoAmA 93*
Dietrich, Dena *WhoHol 92*
Dietrich, James Robert 1944- *WhoAmP 93*
Dietrich, Joseph Jacob 1932- *WhoAm 94*
Dietrich, Laura Jordan 1952- *WhoAm 94*
Dietrich, Marlene 1901- *WhoHol 92*
Dietrich, Marlene 1901-1992 *AmCulL, AnObit 1992*
Dietrich, Marlene 1924-1992 *WhAm 10*
Dietrich, Martha Jane 1916- *WhoAm 94*
Dietrich, Paul George 1949- *WhoAm 94*
Dietrich, Richard Thomas 1939- *WhoFI 94*
Dietrich, Richard Vincent 1924- *WhoAm 94*
Dietrich, Robert Anthony 1933- *WhoAm 94*
Dietrich, Suzanne Claire 1937- *WhoMW 93*
Dietrich, Thomas W. 1952- *WhoAmL 94*
Dietrich, William Alan 1951- *WhoAm 94, WhoWest 94*
Dietrich, William Gale 1925- *WhoAm 94*
Dietrick, Harry Joseph 1922- *WhoMW 93*
Dietrict, Robert 1918- *WrDr 94*
Dietsch, Alfred John 1931- *WhoAm 94*
Dietsch, C. Percival 1881-1961 *WhoAmA 93N*
Dietsch, (Pierre-)Louis(-Philippe) 1808-1865 *NewGrDO*
Dietterich, Thomas Glen 1954- *WhoWest 94*
Dietterick, Scott 1941- *WhoAmP 93*
Dietz, Albert George Henry 1908- *WhoAm 94, WhoScEn 94*
Dietz, Alma 1922- *WhoScEn 94*
Dietz, Charles LeMoyne 1910- *WhoAmA 93*
Dietz, Charlton Henry 1931- *WhoAm 94, WhoAmL 94, WhoFI 94*
Dietz, David 1946- *WhoWest 94*
Dietz, David F. 1949- *WhoAmL 94*
Dietz, Dayle 1928- *WhoAmP 93*
Dietz, Deborah Dorothy 1949- *WhoAmP 93*
Dietz, Deborah Jean 1958- *WhoAmL 94*
Dietz, Donald Elmore, III 1946- *WhoAm 94*
Dietz, Earl Daniel 1928- *WhoAm 94*
Dietz, Gerald Paul 1933- *WhoFI 94*
Dietz, James d1987 *WhoHol 92*
Dietz, James G. 1942- *WhoAmP 93*
Dietz, James Lowell 1947- *WhoWest 94*
Dietz, James Michael 1960- *WhoAmL 94*
Dietz, John Raphael 1912- *WhoAm 94*
Dietz, Kathryn Ann 1961- *WhoMW 93*
Dietz, Margaret Jane 1924- *WhoMW 93*
Dietz, Milton S. 1931- *WhoAm 94*
Dietz, Patricia Ann 1958- *WhoWest 94*
Dietz, Pattye d1981 *WhoHol 92*
Dietz, Peter (John) 1924- *WrDr 94*
Dietz, Robert Barron 1942- *WhoAmL 94*
Dietz, Robert Eldon 1931- *WhoWest 94*
Dietz, Robert Sheldon 1950- *WhoAmL 94*
Dietz, Robert Sinclair 1914- *WhoAm 94, WhoWest 94*
Dietz, Russell Scott 1963- *WhoFI 94, WhoWest 94*
Dietz, Stephen I. 1934- *WhoIns 94*
Dietz, Steven 1958- *ConDr 93*
Dietz, Thomas Gordon 1955- *WhoScEn 94*
Dietz, Thomas Michael 1949- *WhoScEn 94*
Dietz, Vida Lee 1952- *WhoWest 94*
Dietz, William C(orey) 1945- *EncSF 93*
Dietz, William Ronald 1942- *WhoAm 94*
Dietze, Gerald Roger 1959- *WhoScEn 94*
Dietze, Gottfried 1922- *WhoAm 94*
Dietzman, Leslie *WhoFI 94*
Dieudonne, Albert d1976 *WhoHol 92*
Dieudonne, Florence (Lucinda) Carpenter 1850- *EncSF 93*
Dieudonne, Helene d1980 *WhoHol 92*
Dieulafoy, Jane 1851-1916 *BlmGWL*
Dieulangard, Marie-Madeleine Jeanne Colette 1936- *WhoWomW 91*
Diez, Charles F. *WhoHisp 94*
Diez, Gerald F. *WhoHisp 94*
Diez, John C. 1944- *WhoAmP 93, WhoHisp 94*
Diez, Jose Alberto 1956- *WhoScEn 94*
Diez, Sherry Mae 1968- *WhoHisp 94*
DiezCanseco, Carmen Rosa 1950- *WhoHisp 94*
Diez De Rivera Icaza, Carmen 1942- *WhoWomW 91*
Diez de Velasco, Manuel 1926- *IntWW 93*
Diez-Pinto, Migdonia Maria 1964- *WhoHisp 94*
Di Fabio, Michael D. 1963- *WhoAmL 94*
DiFalco, John Patrick 1943- *WhoWest 94*
Di Falco, Laura 1910- *BlmGWL*
Di Fate, Vincent 1945- *EncSF 93, WhoAmA 93*
Diffenbaugh, Craig Alan 1951- *WhoFI 94*
Diffendaffer, Gary Lee 1946- *WhoFI 94*
Diffendal, Anne P. 1943- *WhoAm 94*
Diffie, Joe 1958- *ConMus 10 [port]*
Diffie, Joe 1960- *WhoAm 94*
Diffrient, Niels 1928- *WhoAm 94*
Diffring, Anton d1989 *WhoHol 92*
DiFilippo, Fernando, Jr. 1948- *WhoAm 94*
DiFillippo, Anthony Francis 1927- *WhoAm 94*
DiFino, Santo Michael 1948- *WhoScEn 94*
Difiore, Juliann Marie 1962- *WhoScEn 94*
DiForio, James P., Jr. 1951- *WhoIns 94*
Diforio, Robert G. 1940- *IntWW 93, WhoAm 94*
DiFrancesco, Donald Thomas 1944- *WhoAmP 93*
DiFranco, Anthony *DrAPF 93*
Di Franco, Loretta Elizabeth 1942- *WhoAm 94*
DiFranza, Americo M. 1919- *WhoAmA 93*
DiGaetano, Paul 1953- *WhoAmP 93*
DiGangi, Frank Edward 1917- *WhoAm 94*
Di Gatano, Adam d1966 *WhoHol 92*
Di Gatti, Theobaldo *NewGrDO*
Digby, Baron 1924- *Who 94*
Digby, Lady 1934- *Who 94*
Digby, Adrian 1909- *Who 94*
Digby, James Foster 1921- *WhoWest 94*
Digby, James Keith 1950- *WhoAmP 93*
Digby, Richard Shuttleworth W. *Who 94*
Digby, Robert 1732-1814 *AmRev, WhAmRev*
Digby, Simon Wingfield 1910- *Who 94*
Digby, Stephen Basil W. *Who 94*
diGenova, Joseph E. 1945- *WhoAm 94, WhoAmL 94*
diGenova, Joseph Egidio 1945- *WhoAmP 93*
di Gesu, Antony d1993 *NewYTBS 93*
Digges, Dudley d1947 *WhoHol 92*
Digges, Dudley Perkins 1918- *WhoAm 94*
Digges, Edward Simms, Jr. 1946- *WhoAmL 94*
Digges, Sam Cook 1916-1990 *WhAm 10*
Digges, Thomas c. 1546-1595 *DcLB 136*
Diggins, Eddie d1927 *WhoHol 92*
Diggins, Peggy 1921- *WhoHol 92*
Diggins, Peter Sheehan 1938- *WhoAm 94*
Diggle, James 1944- *Who 94*
Diggle, Judith Margaret *Who 94*
Diggory, Colin 1954- *Who 94*
Diggs, Bradley C. 1948- *WhoAmL 94*
Diggs, Charles Coles, Jr. 1922- *WhoAmP 93*
Diggs, David Michael 1958- *WhoMW 93*
Diggs, Estella B. 1916- *WhoBlA 94*
Diggs, Irene 1906- *WhoBlA 94*
Diggs, Jesse Frank 1917- *WhoAm 94*
Diggs, Lawrence Edward 1947- *WhoAmP 93*
Diggs, Matthew O'Brien, Jr. 1933- *WhoAm 94*
Diggs, Robert Maclary 1912- *WhoAmL 94*
Diggs, Roy Dalton, Jr. 1929- *WhoBlA 94*
Diggs, Walter Edward, Jr. 1936- *WhoAm 94*
Diggs, Walter Whitley 1932- *WhoAm 94*
Diggs, William P. 1926- *WhoBlA 94*
Dighe, Krishna S. 1959- *WhoAmL 94*
Dighe, Shrikant Vishwanath 1933- *WhoAsA 94*
Dighton, Robert Duane 1934- *WhoScEn 94*
Di Giacinto, Sharon 1960- *WhoAmA 93, WhoWest 94*
DiGiacomo, Robert James 1950- *WhoMW 93*
DiGiacomo, Ruth Ann 1966- *WhoScEn 94*
Di Giacomo, Salvatore 1860-1934 *NewGrDO*
Di Giacomo, Thomas Anthony 1941- *WhoAm 94, WhoFI 94*
DiGiamarino, Marian Eleanor 1947- *WhoFI 94*
Digiorgio, Joseph J. 1931- *WhoAmA 93*
Di Giorgio, Robert 1911-1991 *WhAm 10*
DiGiorno, Vincent John 1963- *WhoMW 93*
Di Giovanni, Anthony 1919- *WhoAm 94*
Di Giovanni, Edoardo *NewGrDO*
DiGiovanni, Eleanor Elma 1944- *WhoFI 94*
Digirolamo, Edward Leonard 1944- *WhoFI 94*
DiGirolamo, Rudolph Gerard 1934- *WhoWest 94*
Digiusto, Gerald N. 1929-1987 *WhoAmA 93N*
Digman, Lester Aloysius 1938- *WhoAm 94, WhoFI 94, WhoMW 93*
Dignac, Geny 1932- *WhoAm 94, WhoAmA 93*
Dignam, Arthur *WhoHol 92*
Dignam, Basil d1979 *WhoHol 92*
Dignam, Mark d1989 *WhoHol 92*
Dignam, Robert Joseph 1925- *WhoAm 94*
Dignam, William Joseph 1920- *WhoAm 94*
Dignan, Albert Patrick 1920- *Who 94*
Dignan, Jim *WhoAmP 93*
Dignan, Ruth Swensen *DrAPF 93*
Dignan, Thomas Galvin 1934- *WhoAm 94*
Dignan, Thomas Gregory, Jr. 1940- *WhoAm 94, WhoAmL 94*
Dignani Grimaldi, Vanda 1930- *WhoWomW 91*
Digney, James Brian 1946- *WhoIns 94*
Dignt, Ken d1978 *WhoHol 92*
Dignum, Charles c. 1765-1827 *NewGrDO*
Dignum, Kim 1954- *WhoFI 94*
DiGregorio, Ernie 1952- *BasBi*
Di Gregorio, Mario A(urelio Umberto) 1950- *WrDr 94*
Dihle, Albrecht Gottfried Ferdinand 1923- *WhoScEn 94*
Dijeau, Edward Francis 1946- *WhoWest 94*
di Jeso, Fernando 1931- *WhoScEn 94*
Diji, Augustine Ebun 1932- *WhoBlA 94*
Dijkstra, Edsger Wybe 1930- *WhoAm 94, WhoScEn 94*
Dijkstra, Minne 1937- *IntWW 93*
Dijoud, Paul Charles Louis 1938- *IntWW 93*
DiJulio, Peter Stephen 1951- *WhoAm 94*
Dike, Fatima 1948- *BlmGWL*
Dike, Kenneth Onwuka 1917- *WhoBlA 94*
Dike, Phil 1906-1990 *WhAm 10*
Dikeman, May *DrAPF 93*
Dikie, Alexei d1955 *WhoHol 92*
Dikranjan, Dikran Nishan 1950- *WhoScEn 94*
Dikshit, Uma Shankar 1901- *IntWW 93*
Diktas, Christos James 1955- *WhoAmL 94*
Dikty, T(haddeus Maxim) E(ugene) 1920-1991 *EncSF 93*
DiLalla, Lisabeth Anne 1959- *WhoScEn 94*
DiLaurenti, Marco Italo 1933- *WhoAmA 93*
DiLauro, Stephen 1950- *ConTFT 11*
Dilbeck, Charles Stevens, Jr. 1944- *WhoFI 94, WhoWest 94*
Dilcher, David Leonard 1936- *WhoAm 94*
Dilday, Judith Nelson 1943- *WhoBlA 94*
Dilday, William Horace, Jr. 1937- *WhoBlA 94*
Dildy, Catherine Greene 1940- *WhoBlA 94*
Dileepan, Kottarappat Narayanan 1947- *WhoScEn 94*
Di Lelio, Umberto 1894-1946 *NewGrDO*
Di Lella, Alexander Anthony 1929- *WhoAm 94, WrDr 94*
Dilenschneider, Robert 1943- *IntWW 93*
Dilenschneider, Robert Louis 1943- *WhoAm 94, WhoFI 94*
DiLeo, Anthony M. 1946- *WhoAmL 94*
DiLeo, Jeffrey Richard 1963- *WhoMW 93*
Di Leo, Joseph H 1902- *WrDr 94*
Dileski, Patricia Parra *WhoHisp 94*
Dilg, Joseph Carl 1951- *WhoAmL 94*
Dilger, Margaret Anne 1952- *WhoFI 94*
Dilhorne, Viscount 1932- *Who 94*
Dilibaier Younusi 1958- *WhoPRCh 91 [port]*
Diliberto, Helen Bratney 1920- *WhoWest 94*
Diliberto, Pamela Allen 1956- *WhoScEn 94*
DiLiberto, Richard A., Jr. 1961- *WhoAmP 93*
Di Liello, Salvatore 1958- *WhoMW 93*
DiLieto, Biagio *WhoAmP 93*
Diligensky, German Germanovich 1930- *IntWW 93*
DiLillo, Leonard Michael 1935- *WhoAm 94*
Dilitkanich, Kenneth Rodger 1954- *WhoWest 94*
Dilke *Who 94*
Dilke, Annabel Mary 1942- *WrDr 94*
Dilke, John Fisher Wentworth 1906- *Who 94*
Dilke, O(swald) A(shton) W(entworth) 1915-1993 *ConAu 142*
Dilke, Oswald Ashton Wentworth 1915- *WrDr 94*
Dilks, David Neville 1938- *IntWW 93, Who 94*
Dilks, John Morris Whitworth 1950- *Who 94*
Dilks, Park Bankert, Jr. 1928- *WhoAm 94*
Dill, (Nicholas) Bayard d1993 *Who 94N*
Dill, Charles Anthony 1939- *WhoAm 94, WhoFI 94*
Dill, Ellen Renee 1949- *WhoMW 93*

Dill, Ellis Harold 1932- WhoAm 94, WhoScEn 94
Dill, Frederick Hayes 1932- WhoAm 94
Dill, Guy 1946- WhoAm 94
Dill, Guy Girard 1946- WhoAmA 93
Dill, John Francis 1934- WhoAm 94
Dill, John Junior 1939- WhoAm 94
Dill, Kenneth Austin 1947- WhoScEn 94
Dill, Laddie John 1943- WhoAm 94, WhoAmA 93, WhoWest 94
Dill, Lesley 1950- WhoAmA 93
Dill, Max d1949 WhoHol 92
Dill, Melville Reese, Jr. 1937- WhoAm 94
Dill, Michael Nickolas 1957- WhoFI 94
Dill, Virginia S. 1938 WhoAm 94
Dill, William Allen 1918- WhoAmL 94
Dill, William Joseph 1935- WhoAm 94, WhoMW 93
Dill, William Rankin 1930- WhoAm 94
Dillabaugh, Roy Grant 1940- WhoFI 94
Dillaber, Philip Arthur 1922- WhoAm 94
Dillahunty, Wilbur Harris 1928- WhoAmL 94
Dillamore, Ian Leslie 1938- Who 94
Dillard, Annie BlmGWL, DrAPF 93
Dillard, Annie 1945- ConAu 43NR, IntWW 93, WhoAm 94, WrDr 94
Dillard, Art d1960 WhoHol 92
Dillard, Bert d1960 WhoHol 92
Dillard, Cecil R. 1906- WhoBlA 94
Dillard, David Brownrigg 1935- WhoAm 94
Dillard, David Hugh 1923- WhoAm 94
Dillard, Dean Innes 1947- WhoMW 93
Dillard, Dennis Wayne 1953- WhoMW 93
Dillard, Dudley 1913- WhoAm 94
Dillard, Dudley 1913-1991 WhAm 10
Dillard, Emil L. DrAPF 93
Dillard, Ernest WhoAmP 93
Dillard, Faye Graham 1933- WhoAmP 93
Dillard, George Douglas 1942- WhoAmP 93
Dillard, Howard Lee 1946- WhoBlA 94
Dillard, J(eanne) M. 1954- EncSF 93
Dillard, Jackie Smith 1948- WhoBlA 94
Dillard, James Hardy, II 1933- WhoAmP 93
Dillard, Joan Helen 1951- WhoAm 94, WhoFI 94
Dillard, Joey L. 1924- WhoBlA 94
Dillard, John Martin 1945- WhoAmL 94, WhoWest 94
Dillard, June White 1937- WhoBlA 94
Dillard, Marilyn Dianne 1940- WhoFI 94, WhoWest 94
Dillard, Martin Gregory 1935- WhoBlA 94
Dillard, Melvin Rubin 1941- WhoBlA 94
Dillard, Oliver Williams 1926- AfrAmG
Dillard, R.H.W. DrAPF 93
Dillard, R(ichard) H(enry) W(ilde) 1937- WrDr 94
Dillard, Richard Henry Wilde 1937- WhoAm 94
Dillard, Robert Lionel, Jr. 1913- WhoAm 94
Dillard, Rodney Jefferson 1939- WhoAm 94, WhoFI 94
Dillard, Samuel Dewell 1913- WhoBlA 94
Dillard, Stephen C. 1946- WhoAmL 94
Dillard, Thelma Deloris 1946- WhoBlA 94
Dillard, Thelma Deloris Bivins 1946- WhoAmP 93
Dillard, W. Thomas 1941- WhoAm 94
Dillard, William, II 1945- WhoAm 94, WhoFI 94
Dillard, William Elbert 1898- WhAm 10
Dillard, William T. 1914- WhoAm 94, WhoFI 94
Dillaway, Donald d1982 WhoHol 92
Dillaway, Robert Beacham 1924- WhoAm 94
Dille, Earl Kaye 1927- WhoAm 94, WhoFI 94
Dille, John Flint, Jr. 1913- WhoAm 94, WhoMW 93
Dille, John Robert 1931- WhoAm 94, WhoScEn 94
Dille, Roland Paul 1924- WhoAm 94, WhoMW 93
Dille, Stephen E. 1945- WhoAmP 93
Dillehay, Ronald Clifford 1935- WhoWest 94
Dillemans, Roger Henri 1932- IntWW 93
Dillenback, Robert G. 1921- WhoAmP 93
Dillenberger, John 1918- WhoAm 94, WrDr 94
Diller, Barry 1942- IntMPA 94, IntWW 93, WhoAm 94, WhoFI 94
Diller, Burgoyne 1906-1965 WhoAmA 93N
Diller, Edward Dietrich 1947- WhoAm 94, WhoAmL 94
Diller, Janelle Marie 1955- WhoAmL 94
Diller, Phyllis 1917- IntMPA 94, WhoAm 94, WhoCom [port], WhoHol 92
Dillery, Carl Edward 1930- WhoAmP 93
Dillett, Gregory Craft 1943- WhoAm 94
Dilley, David Ross 1934- WhoScEn 94
Dilley, Leslie ConTFT 11
Dilley, Richard A. 1936- WhoMW 93
Dilley, William Gregory 1922- WhoWest 94
Dillihay, Tanya Clarkson 1958- WhoBlA 94
Dillin, John Woodward, Jr. 1936- WhoAm 94
Dillin, S. Hugh 1914- WhoAm 94, WhoAmL 94, WhoMW 93
Dilling, Kirkpatrick Wallwick 1920- WhoAm 94, WhoAmL 94, WhoFI 94, WhoMW 93
Dilling, Mildred d1982 WhoHol 92
Dillingham, Catherine Knight 1930- WhoScEn 94
Dillingham, Frederick 1948- WhoAmP 93
Dillingham, John Allen 1939- WhoAm 94, WhoMW 93
Dillingham, Rick, II 1952- WhoAmA 93
Dillingham, Robert Bulger 1932- WhoAm 94
Dillingham, William B 1930- WrDr 94
Dillingham, William Byron 1930- WhoAm 94
Dillingham-Evans, Donna Faye 1948- WhoWest 94
Dillingofski, Mary Sue 1944- WhoMW 93
Dillion, Arthur 1750-1794 AmRev
Dillion, Gregory Lee 1954- WhoAmL 94
Dillistone, Frederick William 1903- Who 94
Dillman, Alan D. 1946- WhoAmP 93
Dillman, Bradford 1930- IntMPA 94, WhoAm 94, WhoHol 92
Dillman, Charles Norman 1938- WhoAm 94
Dillman, Grant 1918- WhoAm 94
Dillman, Joseph Francis 1924- WhoFI 94
Dillman, Joseph John Thomas 1941- WhoFI 94
Dillman, Lowell Thomas 1931- WhoMW 93
Dillman, Norman Gregg 1938- WhoMW 93
Dillman, Richard Howard 1942- WhoMW 93
Dillman, Rodney J. 1952- WhoAm 94
Dilloff, Neil Joel 1948- WhoAm 94, WhoAmL 94
Dillon, Viscount 1973- Who 94
Dillon, Aubrey 1938- WhoBlA 94
Dillon, Brendan 1924- IntWW 93
Dillon, Brendan Thomas WhoHol 92
Dillon, Brian Who 94
Dillon, (George) Brian (Hugh) 1925- Who 94
Dillon, C. Douglas 1909- IntWW 93, WhoAmA 93
Dillon, C(larence) Douglas 1909- Who 94
Dillon, Carmen 1908- IntDcF 2-4 [port]
Dillon, Clarence Douglas 1909- WhoAm 94
Dillon, Clifford Brien 1921- WhoAm 94
Dillon, David 1957- WhoAm 94
Dillon, David Anthony 1947- WhoAm 94
Dillon, David Brian 1951- WhoAm 94
Dillon, Dick d1961 WhoHol 92
Dillon, Donald Ward 1936- WhoAm 94
Dillon, Douglas J. 1953- WhoAmL 94
Dillon, Edouard 1750-1839 AmRev
Dillon, Edward d1933 WhoHol 92
Dillon, Eilis 1920- SmATA 74 [port], WrDr 94
Dillon, Ellis 1920- TwCYAW
Dillon, Enoch DrAPF 93
Dillon, Francis Patrick 1937- WhoFI 94, WhoWest 94
Dillon, Francis Richard 1939- WhoAm 94
Dillon, Francois Theobald 1764-1837 AmRev
Dillon, George d1965 WhoHol 92
Dillon, George Chaffee 1922- WhoWest 94
Dillon, Gloria Ann 1955- WhoBlA 94
Dillon, Gregory Russell 1922- WhoAm 94, WhoFI 94, WhoWest 94
Dillon, Herman George 1926- WhoAmP 93
Dillon, Howard Burton 1935- WhoMW 93, WhoScEn 94
Dillon, J. C., Jr. WhoAmP 93
Dillon, Jack d1934 WhoHol 92
Dillon, James Joseph 1948- WhoAm 94, WhoAmL 94
Dillon, James Lee 1928- WhoAm 94
Dillon, James M. 1933- WhoAm 94
Dillon, John d1937 WhoHol 92
Dillon, John (Vincent) 1908- Who 94
Dillon, John Robert, III 1941- WhoAm 94
Dillon, John T. 1938- WhoFI 94
Dillon, John Webb d1949 WhoHol 92
Dillon, Joseph Francis, Jr. 1924- WhoScEn 94
Dillon, Josephine d1971 WhoHol 92
Dillon, Kathleen Gereaux 1957- WhoScEn 94
Dillon, Kevin 1965- IntMPA 94
Dillon, Kevin 1966- WhoHol 92
Dillon, Leo 1933- EncSF 93
Dillon, Linda Jean 1941- WhoMW 93
Dillon, M(artin) C. 1938- ConAu 140
Dillon, Matt 1964- IntMPA 94, IntWW 93, WhoAm 94, WhoHol 92
Dillon, Max 1913- Who 94
Dillon, Melinda 1939- IntMPA 94, WhoHol 92
Dillon, Merton Lynn 1924- WhoAm 94
Dillon, Mia WhoHol 92
Dillon, Michael Earl 1946- WhoFI 94, WhoScEn 94
Dillon, Mildred (Murphy) 1907- WhoAmA 93
Dillon, Millicent G. DrAPF 93
Dillon, Neal Winfield 1925- WhoAm 94
Dillon, Owen C. 1934- WhoBlA 94
Dillon, Patricia Anne 1948- WhoAmP 93
Dillon, Paul Andrew 1945- WhoMW 93
Dillon, Paul Michael, Jr. 1963- WhoMW 93
Dillon, Paul Sanford 1943- WhoAm 94, WhoAmA 93
Dillon, Phillip Michael 1944- WhoFI 94, WhoMW 93
Dillon, Ray William 1954- WhoFI 94, WhoScEn 94, WhoWest 94
Dillon, Richard Hugh 1924- WhoAm 94
Dillon, Robert Guillaume 1754-1837 AmRev
Dillon, Robert Morton 1923- WhoAm 94, WhoFI 94
Dillon, Rodney Lee 1938- WhoAmL 94
Dillon, Theobald Hyacinthe 1745-1792 AmRev
Dillon, Thomas Michael 1927- Who 94
Dillon, Thomas Ray 1948- WhoMW 93
Dillon, Tom d1962 WhoHol 92
Dillon, Tom d1965 WhoHol 92
Dillon, Vermon Lemar 1958- WhoBlA 94
Dillon, W. Martin 1910-1989 WhAm 10
Dillon, Wentworth 1633?-1685 BlmGEL
Dillon, Wilton Sterling 1923- WhoAm 94, WrDr 94
Dillow, Jean Carmen IntMPA 94
Dillow, Jean Carmen d1993 IntMPA 94N
Dillow, John David 1946- WhoAm 94, WhoAmL 94
Dillow, Nancy E. 1928- WhoAmA 93
Dillree, Marda 1945- WhoAmP 93
Dills, James Arlof 1930- WhoAm 94
Dills, James Carl 1954- WhoFI 94
Dills, Ralph C. 1910- WhoAmP 93
Dillson, Clyde d1957 WhoHol 92
Dillwyn, (Elizabeth) Amy 1845-1935 DcNaB MP
Dillwyn-Venables-Llewelyn, John Michael Who 94
Dilly, Ronald Lee 1956- WhoScEn 94
Dilnot, Mary 1921- Who 94
DiLonardo, Joseph A. 1928- WhoAmP 93
Di Lorenzo, John Florio, Jr. 1940- WhoAm 94, WhoMW 93
DiLorenzo, Joseph L. WhoFI 94
DiLorenzo, Louis Patrick 1952- WhoAm 94, WhoAmL 94
Di Loreto, Andrew P. 1958- WhoIns 94
Dilov, Ljuben EncSF 93
Dilsaver, Steven Charles 1953- WhoScEn 94
Dilson, John d1944 WhoHol 92
Dilthey, Wilhelm 1833-1911 DcLB 129 [port]
Dilts, David Alan 1947- WhoScEn 94
Dilts, David Michael 1950- WhoAm 94
Dilts, Mervin Robert 1938- WhoAm 94
Dilts, Michael Curtis 1956- WhoFI 94
Diltz, Daniel H. 1950- WhoMW 93
DiLuglio, Thomas Ross 1931- WhoAmP 93
Di Lullo, Charles S. 1938- WhoIns 94
Dilworth, Charles Dewees 1956- WhoWest 94
Dilworth, Cindy Parker 1958- WhoMW 93
Dilworth, David A. 1934- WrDr 94
Dilworth, Edwin Earle 1914- WhoAm 94
Dilworth, Joseph Richardson 1916- WhoAm 94
Dilworth, Mary Elizabeth 1950- WhoBlA 94
Dilworth, Robert Holden 1942- WhoAm 94
Dilworth, Robert Lexow 1936- WhoAm 94
Dilworth, Sharon 1958- WrDr 94
Dilworth, Stephen James 1959- WhoScEn 94
Dimaggio, Dennis WhoIns 94
DiMaggio, Frank Louis 1929- WhoAm 94
DiMaggio, Joe 1914- WhoHol 92
Di Maggio, Joseph Paul 1914- WhoAm 94
Di Maio, Vincent Joseph Martin 1941- WhoScEn 94
DiMaio, Virginia Sue 1921- WhoFI 94, WhoWest 94
Diman, Homer 1914-1974 WhoAmA 93N
DiMarco, Anthony F. 1948- WhoMW 93
Di Marco, Gabriel Robert 1927- WhoFI 94
DiMarco, Mario Anthony 1931- WhoAmP 93
Di Maria, Charles Walter 1927- WhoScEn 94
Di Maria, Valerie Theresa 1957- WhoFI 94
DiMario, Judith L. WhoAmP 93
Di Martino, Rita 1937- WhoAmP 93, WhoHisp 94
DiMartino, Santo John 1946- WhoWest 94
Dimarzio, Dennis A. 1943- WhoIns 94
Dimas, Armando NewYTBS 93 [port]
Dimas, Trent WhoAm 94
Di Mascio, John Philip 1944- WhoAmL 94
DiMasi, Salvatore Francis 1945- WhoAmP 93
DiMatteo, Anthony J. 1925- WhoAmP 93
DiMauro, Anthony F. d1993 NewYTBS 93
Dimauro, Theodore E. 1933- WhoAmP 93
Dimbleby, Bel Who 94
Dimbleby, David 1938- IntWW 93, Who 94
Dimbleby, Jonathan 1944- IntWW 93, Who 94, WrDr 94
Dimbleby, Josceline Rose 1943- Who 94
Dimbleby, Richard d1965 WhoHol 92
Dime, James d1981 WhoHol 92
Dimechkie, Nadim 1919- IntWW 93, Who 94
Dimen, Muriel Vera 1942- WhoAm 94
Dimeny, Imre 1922- IntWW 93
Di Meo, Dominick 1927- WhoAm 94, WhoAmA 93
Dimeo, Lucien A. WhoAmP 93
Dimeo, Steven DrAPF 93
DiMercurio, Michael 1958- ConAu 140
di Michele, Mary 1949- BlmGWL
DiMichele, Rosalie L. 1919- WhoFI 94
Di Mino, Andre Anthony 1955- WhoFI 94
Dimino, Joseph T. 1923- WhoAm 94
Dimitrescu, Constantin 1847-1928 NewGrDO
Dimitrescu, Giovanni 1860-1913 NewGrDO
Di Mitri, Piero 1933- WhoAm 94
Dimitri, Richard WhoHol 92
Dimitriadis, Andre C. 1940- WhoAm 94
Dimitric, Ivko Milan 1957- WhoScEn 94
Dimitrios, I, Ecumenical Patriarch WhAm 10
Dimitrios, Don Fedon 1928- WhoScEn 94
Dimitriou, Michael Anthony 1951- WhoScEn 94
Dimitrov, Filip IntWW 93
Dimitrova, Blaga 1922- BlmGWL, ConWorW 93
Dimitrova, Ghena 1941- IntWW 93, NewGrDO
Dimitry, John Randolph 1929- WhoAm 94
Dimitry, Theodore George 1937- WhoAm 94
Dimitt, Sharon Marie 1943- WhoMW 93
Dimkoff, Graydon Woodard 1947- WhoAmP 93
Dimler, Charles Henry 1943- WhoAmP 93
Dimling, John Arthur 1938- WhoAm 94
Dimma, William Andrew 1928- WhoAm 94
Dimmerling, Harold J. 1914-1987 WhAm 10
Dimmers, Albert Worthington 1904- WhoAmL 94
Dimmick, Carolyn Reaber 1929- WhoAm 94, WhoAmL 94, WhoWest 94
Dimmick, Charles William 1940- WhoAm 94
Dimmick, Kris Douglas 1963- WhoScEn 94
Dimmig, Bruce David 1956- WhoScEn 94
Dimmitt, Lawrence Andrew 1941- WhoAmL 94
Dimmler, Franz Anton 1753-1827 NewGrDO
Dimmock, John Oliver 1936- WhoAm 94
Dimmock, Peter Who 94
Dimmock, Peter 1920- IntMPA 94
Dimmock, Roger Charles 1935- Who 94
Dimock, Florence Irene d1962 WhoHol 92
Dimock, George E(dward) 1917- WrDr 94
Dimock, Maitland Stuart 1940- WhoFI 94
Dimock, Marshall Edward 1903-1991 WhAm 10, WrDr 94N
Dimon, James 1956- WhoAm 94, WhoFI 94
Dimon, John Edward 1916- WhoAmP 93
Dimond, Alan Theodore 1943- WhoAm 94, WhoAmL 94
Dimond, Edmunds Grey 1918- WhoAm 94
Dimond, Paul Stephen 1944- Who 94
Dimond, Robert Edward 1936- WhoAm 94

Dimond, Roberta Ralston 1940- WhoScEn 94
Dimond, Thomas 1916- WhoFI 94
Dimondstein, Morton 1920- WhoAmA 93
Dimont, Penelope 1918- WrDr 94
Dimora, Jimmy Carl 1955- WhoAmP 93
Dimos, Jimmy N. 1938- WhoAmP 93
Dimson, Gladys Felicia Who 94
Dimson, Theo Aeneas 1930- WhoAmA 93
Di Muccio, Mary Jo 1930- WhoAm 94
Di Muccio, Robet A. 1957- WhoIns 94
Di Murska, Ilma 1836-1889 NewGrDO
Din, Ayub Khan WhoHol 92
Din, Gilbert C. 1932- WhoWest 94
Dinaburg, Mary Ellen 1954- WhoAm 94
Dinan, Donald Robert 1949- WhoAmL 94
Dinan, James Gerard 1959- WhoFI 94
DiNapoli, Thomas John 1943- WhoFI 94
DiNapoli, Thomas P. WhoAmP 93
DiNatale, Joseph Nicholas 1942- WhoAmL 94
Dinberg, Michael David 1944- WhoScEn 94
Dinbergs, Anatol d1993 NewYTBS 93
Dinbergs, Kornelius 1925- WhoMW 93
Dinc, Alev Necile WhoAmA 93
Dincerler, M. Vehbi 1940- IntWW 93
Dinculeanu, Nicolae 1925- WhoAm 94
Dindoffer, Fredrick John 1950- WhoAmL 94
Dine, Carol DrAPF 93
Dine, James 1935- IntWW 93, WhoAmA 93
Dine, Jim 1935- WhoAm 94
Dineen, Bill 1932- WhoAm 94
Dineen, John K. 1928- WhoAm 94, WhoAmL 94
Dineen, Robert Joseph 1929- WhoFI 94, WhoMW 93
Dinehart, Alan d1944 WhoHol 92
Dinel, Richard Henry 1942- WhoAmL 94, WhoFI 94, WhoWest 94
DiNello, Gilbert John 1935- WhoAmP 93
Dinello, Mark S. 1955- WhoMW 93
Diner, Wilma Canada 1926- WhoAm 94
Dinerman, Beatrice 1933- WrDr 94
D'Ines, Denis d1968 WhoHol 92
Dines, George B. 1931- WhoBlA 94
Dines, Peter Munn 1929- Who 94
Dinesen, Isak BlmGWL
Dinesen, Isak 1885-1962 RfGShF
Dinev, Patricia WhoHol 92
Dinevor Who 94
Ding, Aihao 1945- WhoScEn 94
Ding, Chen 1919- WhoFI 94
Ding, Hai 1969- WhoScEn 94
Ding, Jonathan Zhong 1952- WhoWest 94
Ding, Kung-Hau 1956- WhoWest 94
Ding, Mae Lon 1954- WhoWest 94
Ding, Mingzhou 1960- WhoScEn 94
Ding, Ni 1957- WhoScEn 94
Ding Cong 1916- WhoPRCh 91 [port]
Dingeldine, Janet Sue 1952- WhoMW 93
Dingell, Christopher Dennis 1957- WhoAmP 93
Dingell, James Victor 1931- WhoAm 94
Dingell, John D. 1926- CngDr 93, WhoAmP 93
Dingell, John David, Jr. 1926- WhoAm 94, WhoMW 93
Dingelstedt, Franz von 1814-1881 DcLB 133 [port]
Dingeman, Thomas Edward 1950- WhoScEn 94
Dingemans, Peter George Valentin 1935- Who 94
Dinger, Henry C. 1952- WhoAmL 94
Dinger, John Russell 1952- WhoAmP 93
Dinger, Marvin L. 1921- WhoAmP 93
Dinges, Richard Allen 1945- WhoFI 94, WhoWest 94
Ding Fengying 1943- IntWW 93, WhoPRCh 91 [port]
Ding Guangen 1929- IntWW 93, WhoPRCh 91 [port]
Ding Guangxun 1915- IntWW 93, WhoPRCh 91 [port]
Ding Guoyu WhoPRCh 91
Ding Henggao 1931- WhoPRCh 91 [port]
Ding Henggao, Lieut.-Gen. 1931- IntWW 93
Dingilian, Robert d1993 NewYTBS 93
Ding Jieyin 1926- IntWW 93
Dingle, Charles d1956 WhoHol 92
Dingle, Charles H. 1924- WhoAmP 93
Dingle, Graeme 1945- WrDr 94
Dingle, John Thomas 1927- Who 94
Dingle, Robert Balson 1926- Who 94
Dingler, Maurice Eugene 1952- WhoScEn 94
Dingley, Mark A. 1953- WhoAmL 94
Dingley, Robert 1710-1781 DcNaB MP
Ding Ling 1905-1986 BlmGWL [port]
Dingman, Douglas Wayne 1953- WhoScEn 94
Dingman, James E. d1993 NewYTBS 93 [port]
Dingman, Michael David 1931- WhoAm 94, WhoFI 94
Dingman, Norman Ray 1936- WhoScEn 94
Dingman, Richard B. 1935- WhoAmP 93
Dingman, Robert Walter 1926- WhoAm 94
Ding Ning 1924- BlmGWL
Ding Ruopeng WhoPRCh 91
Dings, Fred DrAPF 93
Ding Shande WhoPRCh 91 [port]
Ding Shisun 1927- IntWW 93, WhoPRCh 91 [port]
Ding Tingmo 1936- IntWW 93, WhoPRCh 91 [port]
Dingus, Phillip Rick 1951- WhoAmA 93
Dingwall, Baron Who 94
Dingwall, Craig David 1956- WhoAmL 94
Dingwall, John James 1907- Who 94
Dingwall-Smith, Ronald Alfred 1917- Who 94
Ding Weizhi 1931- WhoPRCh 91 [port]
Dingwell, Everett W. 1931- WhoFI 94
Dingwell, Joyce 1912- WrDr 94
Dingwell, Kelly WhoHol 92
Ding Wenchang 1933- WhoPRCh 91 [port]
Ding Wenchang, Maj.-Gen. 1933- IntWW 93
Ding Xiaqi WhoPRCh 91
Ding Xiling 1918- WhoPRCh 91 [port]
Ding Ximan WhoPRCh 91
Ding Xiu WhoPRCh 91
Ding Xuesong WhoPRCh 91 [port]
Ding Yangyan WhoPRCh 91
Ding Yinnan 1938- WhoPRCh 91 [port]
Ding Yuanhong WhoPRCh 91
Ding Zhaomin WhoPRCh 91
Ding Zhenyu 1913- WhoPRCh 91 [port]
Dinh, Nicholas Nguyen 1941- WhoAsA 94
Dinh, Steven M. 1955- WhoAsA 94
Dinh, Thuy Tu Bich 1962- WhoAsA 94
Dinh, Tung Van 1930- WhoAsA 94
Dinh, Yuk-Ching Tse 1956- WhoAsA 94
Dinhofer, Alfred D 1930- WrDr 94
Dinhofer, Shelly Mehlman 1927- WhoAmA 93
Dinhut, Patrice WhoAm 94
Dini, Joseph Edward, Jr. 1929- WhoAm 94, WhoAmP 93, WhoWest 94
Dini, Joseph J. 1941- WhoFI 94
Dini Ahmed, Ahmed 1932- IntWW 93
Dininni, Rudolph 1926- WhoAmP 93
Dinitz, Simcha 1929- IntWW 93
Dinkel, Allen Joseph 1956- WhoMW 93
Dinkel, John George 1944- WhoAm 94
Dinkel, Shiela Darlene 1964- WhoMW 93
Dinkelspiel, Martin J(errold) 1898- WhAm 10
Dinkelspiel, Paul Gaines 1935- WhoAm 94, WhoFI 94, WhoWest 94
Dinkevich, Solomon 1934- WhoScEn 94
Dinkey, Alva C. 1866-1931 EncABHB 9 [port]
Dinkin, Anthony David 1944- Who 94
Dinkins, Carol Eggert 1945- WhoAm 94, WhoAmL 94
Dinkins, David NewYTBS 93 [port]
Dinkins, David 1927- AfrAmAl 6 [port], IntWW 93
Dinkins, David N. 1927- WhoAm 94, WhoAmP 93, WhoBlA 94
Dinkins, Thomas Allen, III 1946- WhoMW 93
Dinkla, Dwight WhoAmP 93
Dinman, Bertram David 1925- WhoAm 94
Dinneen, Gerald Paul 1924- WhoAm 94
Dinneen, James Francis 1915- WhoAm 94
Dinner, Marie Bernice 1947- WhoWest 94
Dinnerstein, Harvey 1928- WhoAm 94, WhoAmA 93
Dinnerstein, Leonard 1934- WhoAm 94, WrDr 94
Dinnerstein, Lois 1932- WhoAmA 93
Dinnerstein, Michael 1960- WhoAmL 94
Dinnerstein, Simon A. 1943- WhoAmA 93
Dinnerstein, Simon Abraham 1943- WhoAm 94
Dinniman, Andrew Eric 1944- WhoAmP 93, WhoFI 94
Dinning, Ginger See Dinning Sisters, The WhoHol 92
Dinning, James Smith 1922- WhAm 10
Dinning, Jean See Dinning Sisters, The WhoHol 92
Dinning, Lou See Dinning Sisters, The WhoHol 92
Dinning, Woodford Wyndham, Jr. 1954- WhoAmL 94
Dinning Sisters, The WhoHol 92
D'Innocenzo, Nick 1934- WhoAmA 93
Di Nola, Raffaello IntWW 93N
Dinome, Jerry WhoHol 92
Dinos, Nicholas 1934- WhoAm 94
Dinosaur Jr. ConMus 10 [port]
Dinoso, Vicente Pescador, Jr. 1936- WhoAm 94
Dinov, Todor 1919- IntDcF 2-4
Dinsdale, Grace Katherine 1957- WhoWest 94
Dinsdale, Reece WhoHol 92
Dinsdale, Richard Lewis 1907- Who 94
Dinse, John Merrell 1925- WhoAm 94, WhoAmL 94
Dinsmoor, James Arthur 1921- WhoAm 94
Dinsmore, Charles E(arle) 1947- ConAu 142
Dinsmore, Charles Earle 1947- WhoMW 93
Dinsmore, Gordon Griffith 1917- WhoAm 94
Dinsmore, Philip Wade 1942- WhoAm 94, WhoWest 94
Dinsmore, Stephen Pul 1952- WhoAmA 93
Dinsmore, Wiley 1934- WhoAm 94
Dinstber, George Charles 1966- WhoScEn 94
Dinstel, Edward R. 1954- WhoIns 94
Dintenfass, Mark DrAPF 93
Dintenfass, Mark 1941- WrDr 94
Dintenfass, Terry WhoAm 94
Dintenfass, Terry 1920- WhoAmA 93
Dintiman, George B(lough) 1936- ConAu 42NR
Dinwiddie, Stephen Hunt 1955- WhoMW 93
Dinwiddy, Bruce Harry 1946- Who 94
Diocletian 240-312 HisWorL [port]
Dioda, Adolph T. 1915-1991 WhoAmA 93N
Diodati, Giuseppe Maria (Rossi) fl. 18th cent.- NewGrDO
Diogenes fl. 4-?-5-? WhWE
Diogenes, Marvin DrAPF 93
Diogenes the Cynic BlmGEL
DioGuardi, Joseph J. 1940- ConAu 140
DioGuardi, Joseph John 1940- WhoAmP 93
Dioguardi, Mark David 1956- WhoAmP 93
Diokno, Ananias Cornejo 1942- WhoAsA 94
Diomede, John K. EncSF 93
Diomede, Matthew DrAPF 93
Dion, Gerard 1912-1990 WhAm 10
Dion, Jerrold Mark 1936- WhoAm 94
Dion, Nancy Logan 1941- WhoAm 94
Dione, Rose d1936 WhoHol 92
Diong, Billy Ming 1962- WhoMW 93
Dionigi, Christopher Paul 1957- WhoScEn 94
Dionisio, Silvia WhoHol 92
Dionisio, William Pasquale 1933- WhoWest 94
Dionisopoulos, George Allan 1954- WhoAmL 94
Dionisopoulos, P(anagiotes) Allan 1921-1993 ConAu 141
Dionisotti-Casalone, Carlo 1908- Who 94
Dionne, Albert J. 1946- WhoAmP 93
Dionne, Annette 1934- WhoHol 92
Dionne, Cecile 1934- WhoHol 92
Dionne, E(ugene) J., Jr. 1952- ConAu 140
Dionne, Emilie 1934-1954 WhoHol 92
Dionne, Gary S. 1953- WhoAmP 93
Dionne, Gerald Francis 1935- WhoScEn 94
Dionne, Gregory Vincent 1958- WhoMW 93
Dionne, Joseph Lewis 1933- IntWW 93, WhoAm 94, WhoFI 94
Dionne, Marcel Elphege 1951- WhoAm 94
Dionne, Marie 1934-1970 WhoHol 92
Dionne, Ovila Joseph 1947- WhoScEn 94
Dionne, Paul R. 1951- WhoAmP 93
Dionne, Yvonne 1934- WhoHol 92
Dionyse de Munchensy fl. 13th cent.- BlmGWL
Dionysia fl. c. 1200- BlmGWL
Diop, Birago (Ismael) 1906-1989 BlkWr 2
Diop, Cheikh Anta 1923-1986 BlkWr 2
Diop, David Mandessi 1927-1960 BlkWr 2
Diop, Majhemout 1922- IntWW 93
Diophantus of Alexandria c. 210-c. 290 WorScD
Dioramananda DrAPF 93
D'Iorio, Antoine 1925- IntWW 93
Diorio, Margaret DrAPF 93
Dioscorides, Dr. EncSF 93
Diosdado, Ana 1938- BlmGWL
Diotte, Alfred Peter 1925- WhoAm 94
Diouf, Abdou 1935- IntWW 93
Diouf, Jacques 1938- IntWW 93
DiPalma, Daniel 1958- WhoWest 94
Di Palma, Joseph Alphonse 1931- WhoAm 94, WhoFI 94, WhoWest 94
DiPalma, Joseph Rupert 1916- WhoAm 94
DiPalma, Ray DrAPF 93
Di Palma, Vera June 1931- Who 94
Dipaola, James WhoAmP 93
Di Paola, Robert Arnold 1933- WhoAm 94
Di Paolo, Joseph Amadeo 1924- WhoScEn 94
Di Paolo, Nicholas P. 1941- WhoFI 94
DiPasquale, Benn S. 1944- WhoAmL 94
DiPasquale, Dominic Theodore 1932- WhoAmA 93
Di Pasquale, Emanuel DrAPF 93
DiPentima, Renato Anthony 1941- WhoAm 94
DiPerna, Frank Paul 1947- WhoAm 94, WhoAmA 93
DiPiazza, Michael Charles 1953- WhoFI 94
Di Pietra, Rosemary IntMPA 94
DiPietro, Angela Lee 1967- WhoWest 94
Dipietro, Anthony M., Jr. 1935- WhoAmP 93
DiPietro, Carmela M. 1925- WhoAmP 93
DiPietro, Dominic 1905- WhoAmP 93
Di Pietro, Frank Anthony 1926- WhoMW 93
DiPietro, Mark Joseph 1947- WhoAmL 94
DiPietro, Melanie 1944- WhoAm 94
DiPietro, Ralph Anthony 1942- WhoAm 94, WhoFI 94
Di Pietro, Robert Joseph 1932-1991 WhAm 10, WrDr 94N
Dipietro, Santo WhoAmP 93
Dipinto, Joseph G. 1932- WhoAmP 93
Diplock, Anthony Tytherleigh 1935- Who 94
Dipoko, Mbella Sonne 1936- BlkWr 2
Dippel, Andreas 1866-1932 NewGrDO
Dipprey, Duane Floyd 1929- WhoWest 94
Diprete, Edward D. 1934- IntWW 93
DiPrete, Edward Daniel 1934- WhoAmP 93
Di Prima, Diane DrAPF 93
Di Prima, Diane 1934- BlmGWL, WrDr 94
DiPrima, Lawrence 1910- WhoAmP 93
Di Prima, Stephanie Marie 1952- WhoMW 93
Di Primo, Marie Ann 1952- WhoAmL 94
Di Prisco, Elisabetta 1950- WhoWomW 91
Diprizio, Rosario Peter 1940- WhoMW 93, WhoScEn 94
DiPrizio, Victor Anthony 1947- WhoMW 93
Dirac, Paul Adrien Maurice 1902-1984 WorScD
Diracles, John Michael, Jr. 1944- WhoAm 94, WhoFI 94
Dirck, Edwin L. 1928- WhoAmP 93
Dirda, Michael 1949- WhoAm 94
Director, Stephen William 1943- WhoAm 94, WhoScEn 94
DiRenzo, Gordon James 1934- WhoAm 94
Dirheimer, Guy 1931- WhoScEn 94
Dirichlet, Peter Gustav Lejeune 1805-1859 WorScD
Di Rienzo, Frederick J. 1948- WhoIns 94
Dirige, Ofelia Villa 1940- WhoAsA 94
Dirk, Nathaniel 1896-1961 WhoAmA 93N
Dirkes, George R. 1943- WhoAmL 94
Dirks, A. Stephen 1943- WhoAmP 93
Dirks, David McCormick 1941- WhoWest 94
Dirks, John 1917- WhoAmA 93
Dirks, Kenneth Ray 1925- WhoAm 94
Dirks, Laura McClure 1946- WhoWest 94
Dirks, Lee Edward 1935- WhoAm 94
Dirks, Leslie Chant 1936- WhoAm 94
Dirks, Rudolph d1968 WhoAmA 93N
Dirks, Vickie Ellen 1953- WhoMW 93
Dirkse, Ronald John 1945- WhoMW 93
Dirksen, Gebhard 1929- IntWW 93
Dirksen, Jean 1949- WhoAm 94
Dirksen, Richard Wayne 1921- WhoAm 94
Dirlam, David Kirk 1942- WhoScEn 94
Diroll, David John 1951- WhoAmL 94, WhoMW 93
Dirube, Rolando Lopez 1928- WhoAmA 93
DiRuscio, Lawrence William 1941- WhoFI 94, WhoWest 94
Di Russo, Erasmo Victor 1955- WhoScEn 94
Dirvin, Gerald Vincent 1937- WhoAm 94
Dirvin, Joseph I. d1993 NewYTBS 93
Dirvin, Joseph I. 1917-1993 ConAu 141
Di Sabato, Louis Roman 1931- WhoAm 94
DiSabato, Mary Keating Croce WhoAmP 93
DiSaia, Philip John 1937- WhoScEn 94
Di Salvo, Arthur Francis 1932- WhoAm 94
DiSalvo, Beverly Jane 1952- WhoWest 94
Di Salvo, Francis Joseph 1944- WhoScEn 94
DiSalvo, Mark Sebastian 1954- WhoAmP 93
Di Salvo, Nicholas Armand 1920- WhoAm 94

DiSalvo, Thomas Joseph 1953- WhoAmL 94
DiSalvo, Vera June 1928- WhoMW 93
Disandro, Domenic A., III 1959- WhoAmP 93
DiSandro, Edmond A. 1932- WhoAmL 94
Di Sangro, Elena d1969 WhoHol 92
Di Santo, Grace Johanne DeMarco 1924- WhoAm 94
Disbrey, William Daniel 1912- Who 94
Disbrow, Lynn Marie 1961- WhoMW 93
Disbrow, Michael Ray 1959- WhoFI 94, WhoMW 93
Disbrow, Richard Edwin 1930- IntWW 93, WhoAm 94, WhoFI 94
Disbrow, Sidney Arden, Jr. 1946- WhoMW 93
Disch, Thomas M. DrAPF 93
Disch, Thomas M(ichael) 1940- EncSF 93, WrDr 94
Disch, Thomas Michael 1940- WhoAm 94
Disch, Wayne Harlow 1935- WhoMW 93
Dischinger, Hugh Charles 1924- WhoScEn 94
Dischinger, Terry 1940- BasBi
Discipolo, Enrique Santos d1951 WhoHol 92
Disend, Michael DrAPF 93
Disharoon, Leslie Benjamin 1932- WhoAm 94
Disher, David Alan 1944- WhoAmL 94
Disher, John Howard 1921-1988 WhAm 10
Disher, Spencer C., III 1957- WhoBlA 94
Disheroon, Fred Russell 1931- WhoAmL 94
Dishman, Cris Edward 1965- WhoAm 94
Dishman, Leonard I. 1920- WhoAm 94
Dishmon, Samuel Quinton, Jr. 1956- WhoScEn 94
Dishy, Bob IntMPA 94, WhoAm 94, WhoHol 92
DiSilvestro, Roger L. 1949- EncSF 93
DiSimone, Rita Louise WhoAmP 93
Disinger, John Franklin 1930- WhoAm 94
Diska, (P) WhoAmA 93
Diskant, Gregory L. 1948- WhoAm 94, WhoAmL 94
Diski, Jenny 1947- BlmGWL
Diskin, Michael Edward 1946- WhoFI 94
Disko, Michael David, Jr. 1962- WhoFI 94
Disley, John Ivor 1928- Who 94
Dismuke, Leroy 1937- WhoBlA 94, WhoMW 93
Dismuke, Mary Eunice 1942- WhoBlA 94
Dismukes, Mary Ethel d1952 WhoAmA 93N
Dismukes, Valena Broussard 1938- WhoWest 94
Disnard, George F. 1923- WhoAmP 93
Disney, Anthea 1944- WhoAm 94
Disney, Harold Vernon 1907- Who 94
Disney, Michael George 1955- WhoFI 94, WhoWest 94
Disney, Roy E. 1930- IntMPA 94
Disney, Roy Edward 1930- WhoAm 94, WhoFI 94, WhoWest 94
Disney, Walt d1966 WhoHol 92
Disney, Walt 1901-1966 IntDcF 2-4 [port]
Disney, Walter Elias 1901-1966 AmCulL [port]
Dispeker, Thea WhoAm 94
Di Spigna, Tony 1943- WhoAm 94
Di Spigno, Guy Joseph 1948- WhoMW 93
DiSpirito, Robert George, Jr. 1959- WhoAmP 93
Disraeli, Benjamin 1804-1881 BlmGEL, EncSF 93, HisWorL [port]
Diss, Eileen 1931- Who 94
Dissanayake, Chandra WhoWest 94
Disse, Diane Marie 1943- WhoWest 94
Disser, Maria-Elena 1946- WhoHisp 94
Disston, Harry 1899- WhAm 10
DiStasio, James Shannon 1947- WhoAm 94
DiStefano, Ana Maria 1961- WhoHisp 94
Di Stefano, Anthony Ferdinand 1945- WhoAm 94
Di Stefano, Giuseppe 1921- NewGrDO
Distefano, Peter Andrew 1939- WhoFI 94, WhoWest 94
Di Stefano Lauthe, Alfredo 1926- WorESoc [port]
Distel, Sacha WhoHol 92
Distel, Sacha 1933- IntWW 93
Distelbrink, Jan Hendrik 1946- WhoScEn 94
Distelhorst, Craig Tipton 1941- WhoFI 94
Distelhorst, Garis Fred 1942- WhoAm 94
Distler, Jim T. 1934- WhoAmP 93
Distler, Theodore August 1898-1991 WhAm 10
Distler, William Francis 1917- WhoAm 94
D'Istria, Dora 1828-1882 BlmGWL
Di Suvero, Mark 1933- WhoAm 94, WhoAmA 93
Ditch, Michael Terry 1944- WhoFI 94
Ditchburn, Anne WhoHol 92
Ditchik, Robert Andrew 1958- WhoWest 94
Ditchoff, Pamela DrAPF 93
Ditelberg, Dennis Leonard 1932- WhoAmL 94
Ditka, Michael Keller 1939- WhoAm 94
Ditka, Mike ProFbHF [port]
Ditkowsky, Kenneth K. 1936- WhoAmL 94
Ditlevsen, Tove 1918-1976 BlmGWL
Ditlev-Simonsen, Per 1932- IntWW 93
Ditmanson, Dennis L. 1947- WhoWest 94
Ditmars, David Walter 1948- WhoMW 93
Ditmars, Donald Melick, Jr. 1934- WhoMW 93
DiTolla, Alfred W. 1926- IntMPA 94
Di Tomaso, Nick WhoAm 94, WhoFI 94
D'Itri, Frank Michael 1933- WhoAm 94
Ditrichstein, Leo d1928 WhoHol 92
Ditsky, John DrAPF 93
Ditt, Josephine d1939 WhoHol 92
Dittberner, Gerald John 1941- WhoScEn 94
Dittemore, David H. 1953- WhoScEn 94
Dittenber, LaVern Morrell 1935- WhoMW 93
Dittenhafer, Brian Douglas 1942- WhoAm 94
Ditter, John William, Jr. 1921- WhoAm 94, WhoAmL 94
Ditterich, (Eric) Keith 1913- WrDr 94
Dittersdorf, Carl Ditters von 1739-1799 NewGrDO
Dittert, J. Lee, Jr. 1931- WhoAm 94
Dittert, Lewis William 1934- WhoAm 94
Dittes, James Edward 1926- WhoAm 94
Dittman, Dean d1989 WhoHol 92
Dittman, Deborah Ruth 1932- WhoWest 94
Dittman, Duane Arthur 1924- WhoAm 94
Dittman, Mark Allen 1950- WhoMW 93
Dittman, Richard Henry 1937- WhoMW 93
Dittmann, Albert Stephen, Jr. 1941- WhoAm 94
Dittmann, Reidar 1922- WhoAm 94
Dittmar, Robert L. 1931- WhoAmP 93
Dittmer, Clarence Christian 1895- WhAm 10
Dittmer, Terry Keith 1948- WhoMW 93
Dittmer, Timothy Wilfred 1964- WhoMW 93
Ditto, John Kane, Jr. 1944- WhoAmP 93
Ditto, Kane 1944- WhoAm 94
Dittoe, John E. 1954- WhoAmL 94
Dittoe, Robert Bradley 1956- WhoMW 93
Ditton, Carl Rossini 1886-1962 AfrAmAl 6
Ditton, James 1919- WrDr 94
Dittrich, Denise Marie 1960- WhoMW 93
Dittrich, Herbert 1955- WhoScEn 94
Dittrich, Raymond Joseph 1932- WhoAm 94
Ditty, Marilyn Louise WhoScEn 94
Dityatin, Aleksandr 1957- IntWW 93
Ditzig, Michael Curtis 1956- WhoFI 94
Ditzion, Grace WhoAmA 93
Ditzler, James (R.) 1933- WrDr 94
Diu, Chin Kee 1952- WhoWest 94
Diuguid, Lewis Walter 1955- WhoBlA 94
Diuguid, Lincoln I. 1917- WhoBlA 94
DiUlio, Albert Joseph 1943- WhoAm 94
Divakaran, Subramaniam 1938- WhoScEn 94
Divakaruni, Chitra Banerjee 1956- WhoAsA 94
Divale, William T(ulio) 1942- WrDr 94
Divall, Richard 1945- NewGrDO
DiVelez, Gilbert Julian 1950- WhoWest 94
Di Venanzo, Gianni 1920-1966 IntDcF 2-4 [port]
Divendal, Joost 1955- WrDr 94
DiVenere, Anthony Joseph 1941- WhoAmL 94
Diver, Colin S. 1943- WhoAmL 94
Diver, Jeffrey Rouse 1942- WhoMW 93
Diver, Leslie Charles 1899- Who 94
Diver, William 1921- WhoAm 94
Diveris, Aristeidie Michael 1961- WhoMW 93
Diverres, Armel Hugh 1914- Who 94
Divich, Duane G. 1937- WhoIns 94
Divine d1988 WhoHol 92
Divine, Father 1877-1965 AfrAmAl 6 [port], DcAmReB 2
Divine, Father c. 1880-1965 HisWorL
Divine, Charles Hamman 1945- WhoWest 94
Divine, Father c. 1880-1965 AmSocL
Divine, James Robert 1939- WhoWest 94
Divine, Robert A(lexander) 1929- ConAu 42NR, WrDr 94
Divine, Robert Alexander 1929- WhoAm 94
Divine, Theodore Emry 1943- WhoWest 94
Divinsky, Nathan (Joseph) 1925- WrDr 94
Divinsky, Nathan Joseph 1925- WhoWest 94
Divirgilio, Albert V. WhoAmP 93
Divis, Rita W. WhoHisp 94
DiVita, Merle R. 1952- WhoFI 94
DiVito, Gary Francis 1946- WhoAmL 94
Divok, Mario DrAPF 93
Divola, John 1949- WhoWest 94
Divola, John Manford, Jr. 1949- WhoAmA 93
Diwan, Romesh Kumar 1933- WhoAm 94
Diwoky, Roy John 1910- WhoAm 94
Dix, Alan Michael 1922- Who 94
Dix, Bernard Hubert 1925- Who 94
Dix, Billy d1973 WhoHol 92
Dix, David Arthur 1932- WhoAmP 93
Dix, Dorothea 1802-1887 HisWorL [port]
Dix, Dorothea Lynde 1802-1887 AmSocL [port], BlmGWL, EncSPD
Dix, Dorothy d1970 WhoHol 92
Dix, Fred Andrew, Jr. 1931- WhoAm 94, WhoScEn 94
Dix, Geoffrey Herbert 1922- Who 94
Dix, Gerald Bennett 1926- Who 94
Dix, Lillian d1922 WhoHol 92
Dix, Richard d1949 WhoHol 92
Dix, Robert WhoHol 92
Dix, Rollin Cumming 1936- WhoAm 94
Dix, Rollo d1973 WhoHol 92
Dix, Scott 1957- WhoAmP 93
Dix, Tommy 1924- WhoHol 92
Dix, William 1956- WhoHol 92
Dixey, Henry E. d1943 WhoHol 92
Dixey, John 1926- Who 94
Dixey, Paul (Arthur Groser) 1915- Who 94
Dixey, Paul Arthur Groser 1915- IntWW 93
Dixey, Phyllis d1964 WhoHol 92
Dixie, Florence (Caroline) 1855-1905 EncSF 93
Dixit, Ajit S. 1950- WhoAsA 94
Dixit, Avinash Kamalakar 1944- Who 94
Dixit, Balwant N. 1933- WhoAsA 94
Dixit, Balwant Narayan 1933- WhoAm 94
Dixit, Jyotindranath 1936- IntWW 93
Dixit, Padmakar Kashinath 1921- WhoAsA 94
Dixit, Sudhakar Gajanan 1939- WhoAsA 94
Dixit, Sudhir Sharan 1951- WhoAsA 94
Dixon Who 94
Dixon (Robertson), Lucille 1923- AfrAmAl 6
Dixon, Alan 1927- WhoBlA 94
Dixon, Alan John 1927- IntWW 93, WhoAmP 93
Dixon, Amzi Clarence 1854-1925 DcAmReB 2
Dixon, Andrew Derart 1925- WhoAm 94
Dixon, Andrew Lee, Jr. 1942- WhoAm 94
Dixon, Ann R. 1954- SmATA 77 [port]
Dixon, Anthony 1947- WhoAmL 94
Dixon, Anthony Philip G. Who 94
Dixon, Ardena S. 1927- WhoBlA 94
Dixon, Arrington Liggins 1942- WhoAmP 93, WhoBlA 94
Dixon, Barbara IntMPA 94
Dixon, Benjamin 1939- WhoBlA 94
Dixon, Benjamin Rollin 1930- WhoAmP 93
Dixon, Bernard 1938- Who 94, WrDr 94
Dixon, Bernard Tunbridge 1928- Who 94
Dixon, Billy Gene 1935- WhoAm 94
Dixon, Blanche V. WhoBlA 94
Dixon, Brenda Joyce 1954- WhoBlA 94
Dixon, Brian Gilbert 1951- WhoScEn 94
Dixon, Carl Franklin 1948- WhoAmL 94
Dixon, Charles 1858-1926 EncSF 93
Dixon, Clay WhoAmP 93
Dixon, Conway d1943 WhoHol 92
Dixon, Dean 1915-1976 AfrAmAl 6 [port]
Dixon, Denver d1972 WhoHol 92
Dixon, Diane L. 1964- WhoBlA 94
Dixon, Donald 1929- Who 94
Dixon, Donna 1957- IntMPA 94, WhoHol 92
Dixon, Dougal 1947- EncSF 93, WrDr 94
Dixon, Emmett d1969 WhoHol 92
Dixon, Ernest H. 1952- WhoWest 94
Dixon, Ernest Thomas, Jr. 1922- WhoAm 94, WhoBlA 94
Dixon, Eustace A(ugustus) 1934- WrDr 94
Dixon, Fitz Eugene, Jr. 1923- WhoAm 94
Dixon, Floyd Eugene 1964- WhoBlA 94
Dixon, Francis S. 1879-1967 WhoAmA 93N
Dixon, Frank James 1920- IntWW 93, WhoAm 94
Dixon, Franklin W. EncSF 93
Dixon, Franklin W. 1949- WrDr 94
Dixon, Gale Harllee 1944- WhoAm 94
Dixon, Gemma Barbara 1951- WhoHisp 94
Dixon, George ConAu 140, ConTFT 11
Dixon, George David 1936- WhoMW 93
Dixon, George Francis, Jr. 1918- WhoAm 94
Dixon, George Lane, Jr. 1928- WhoAm 94
Dixon, Glenn WhoHol 92
Dixon, Gordon Henry 1930- IntWW 93, Who 94, WhoAm 94, WhoScEn 94
Dixon, Guy Holford d1993 Who 94N
Dixon, Hanford 1958- WhoBlA 94
Dixon, Harland d1969 WhoHol 92
Dixon, Harry Dale, Jr. 1942- WhoAmP 93
Dixon, Harry Donival 1925- WhoAmP 93
Dixon, Hortense 1926- WhoBlA 94
Dixon, Irma Muse 1952- WhoAm 94, WhoAmP 93, WhoBlA 94
Dixon, Isaiah, Jr. 1922- WhoAmP 93, WhoBlA 94
Dixon, Ivan 1931- WhoHol 92
Dixon, Ivan N. 1931- WhoBlA 94
Dixon, J. A. 1952- WhoAmP 93
Dixon, Jack Shawcross 1918- Who 94
Dixon, James WhoHol 92
Dixon, James Andrew, Jr. 1951- WhoAm 94
Dixon, James Anthony 1967- WhoBlA 94
Dixon, Jean d1981 WhoHol 92
Dixon, Jean T. 1949- WhoAmP 93
Dixon, Jeane 1918- WhoAm 94
Dixon, Jenny (Jane Hodley) 1950- WhoAmA 93
Dixon, Jeremiah 1733-1779 DcNaB MP
Dixon, Jeremy Who 94
Dixon, (David) Jeremy 1939- IntWW 93, Who 94
Dixon, Jerome Wayne 1955- WhoAmL 94
Dixon, Jerry B. WhoAm 94
Dixon, Jerry B. 1937- WhoAmP 93
Dixon, Jim d1974 WhoHol 92
Dixon, Jimmy 1943- WhoBlA 94
Dixon, Jo-Ann Conte 1942- WhoFI 94
Dixon, Joan DeVee 1963- ConAu 142
Dixon, Joe Boris 1930- WhoAm 94
Dixon, John Aldous 1923-1992 WhAm 10
Dixon, John Allen, Jr. 1920- WhoAmP 93
Dixon, John Frederick 1949- WhoBlA 94
Dixon, John Fulton 1946- WhoMW 93
Dixon, John Kenneth 1915- WhoAmP 93
Dixon, John M. 1938- WhoBlA 94
Dixon, John Morris 1933- WhoAm 94
Dixon, John Morris, Jr. 1940- WhoAm 94, WhoAmL 94
Dixon, John Spencer 1957- WhoFI 94
Dixon, John Wayne 1944- WhoFI 94, WhoMW 93
Dixon, John Wesley, Jr. 1919- WhoAm 94
Dixon, Jon Edmund 1928- Who 94
Dixon, Jonathan (Mark) 1949- Who 94
Dixon, Juanita Clark 1936- WhoAmP 93
Dixon, Julian C. 1934- AfrAmAl 6 [port], CngDr 93, WhoAmP 93, WhoBlA 94
Dixon, Julian Carey 1934- WhoAm 94, WhoWest 94
Dixon, Katie Loosle 1925- WhoAmP 93
Dixon, Ken 1943- WhoAmA 93
Dixon, Kenneth Herbert Morley 1929- IntWW 93, Who 94
Dixon, Kent H. DrAPF 93
Dixon, Larry Dean 1942- WhoAmP 93
Dixon, Lawrence Paul 1938- WhoAm 94, WhoFI 94
Dixon, Lee d1953 WhoHol 92
Dixon, Leon Martin 1927- WhoBlA 94
Dixon, Lorraine WhoAmP 93
Dixon, Louis Frederick 1928- WhoAm 94
Dixon, Louis Tennyson 1941- WhoBlA 94
Dixon, Lynn Diane 1947- WhoWest 94
Dixon, Macintyre WhoHol 92
Dixon, Marcia WhoHol 92
Dixon, Margaret Rumer Haynes Who 94
Dixon, Melvin DrAPF 93
Dixon, Melvin 1950-1992 GayLL
Dixon, Melvin (Winfred) 1950- WrDr 94
Dixon, Melvin (Winfred) 1950-1992 BlkWr 2
Dixon, Melvin W. 1950- WhoBlA 94
Dixon, Michael Wayne 1942- WhoWest 94
Dixon, Norman (Frank) 1922- WrDr 94
Dixon, Norman Rex 1932- WhoAm 94
Dixon, Paige DrAPF 93, SmATA 77
Dixon, Paige 1911- WrDr 94
Dixon, Patricia Sue 1960- WhoScEn 94
Dixon, Paul Edward 1944- WhoAmL 94, WhoFI 94
Dixon, Peter Vibart 1932- Who 94
Dixon, Piers 1928- Who 94
Dixon, Rachel 1952- SmATA 74 [port]
Dixon, Randall Carl 1953- WhoAmL 94
Dixon, Richard B 1937- WhoWest 94
Dixon, Richard Clay WhoBlA 94
Dixon, Richard Cressie 1929- WhoAm 94
Dixon, Richard N. 1938- WhoAmP 93
Dixon, Richard Nathaniel 1938- WhoBlA 94
Dixon, Richard Newland 1930- IntWW 93, Who 94
Dixon, Richard Wayne 1936- WhoAm 94
Dixon, Robert Gene 1934- WhoScEn 94
Dixon, Robert J. 1936- WhoMW 93
Dixon, Robert James 1920- WhoAm 94
Dixon, Robert Keith 1955- WhoScEn 94

Dixon, Roger 1930- *EncSF 93, WrDr 94*
Dixon, Roscoe 1949- *WhoBlA 94*
Dixon, Roscoe, Jr. 1949- *WhoAmP 93*
Dixon, Rosie *ConAu 43NR*
Dixon, Rosina Berry 1942- *WhoFI 94*
Dixon, Roy Laurence Cayley 1924- *Who 94*
Dixon, Ruth F. 1931- *WhoBlA 94*
Dixon, Sally Foy *WhoAmA 93*
Dixon, Sandra Wise 1964- *WhoScEn 94*
Dixon, Sarah 1672-1765 *DcNaB MP*
Dixon, Sharon Pratt 1944- *AfrAmAl 6 [port], WhoWomW 91*
Dixon, Shirley Juanita 1935- *WhoFI 94*
Dixon, Stanley 1900- *Who 94*
Dixon, Stephen *DrAPF 93*
Dixon, Stephen 1936- *DcLB 130 [port], WrDr 94*
Dixon, Stephen Bruce 1936- *WhoAm 94*
Dixon, Stewart Strawn 1930- *WhoAm 94*
Dixon, Thomas 1864-1946 *EncSF 93*
Dixon, Thomas F. 1916- *IntWW 93*
Dixon, Thomas Francis 1916- *WhoAm 94*
Dixon, Tom L. 1932- *WhoBlA 94*
Dixon, Valena Alice 1953- *WhoBlA 94*
Dixon, Victor Lee 1966- *WhoScEn 94*
Dixon, Wheeler Winston 1950- *IntMPA 94*
Dixon, Wilfrid Joseph *WhoAm 94*
Dixon, Willard 1942- *WhoAmA 93*
Dixon, Willard Michael 1942- *WhoWest 94*
Dixon, William Cornelius 1904- *WhoAm 94, WhoAmL 94*
Dixon, William Gordon, Jr. 1931- *WhoMW 93*
Dixon, William Michael 1920- *Who 94*
Dixon, William R. 1925- *WhoBlA 94*
Dixon, William Robert 1917- *WhoAm 94*
Dixon, William Robert 1925- *WhoAm 94*
Dixon, William S. 1943- *WhoAmL 94*
Dixon, Willie d1992 *WhoBlA 94N*
Dixon, Willie 1915-1992 *ConMus 10 [port]*
Dixon, Willie B. 1915-1992 *AnObit 1992*
Dixon, Willie James 1915-1992 *AmCulL, WhAm 10*
Dixon, Wright Tracy, Jr. 1921- *WhoAmL 94*
Dixon-Balsiger, Nancy Marie 1958- *WhoWest 94*
Dixon-Brown, Totlee *WhoBlA 94*
Dixon-Smith, Baron 1934- *Who 94*
Dixon-Ward, Frank 1922- *Who 94*
Dixson, Maurice Christopher Scott 1941- *Who 94*
Dixson, Wendy Fay 1931- *WhoAmA 93*
Diz, Adolfo Cesar 1931- *IntWW 93*
Dizard, Wilson Paul, Jr. 1922- *WhoAm 94*
Dizdarevic, Raif 1926- *IntWW 93*
Dizenzo, Charles (John) 1938- *ConDr 93, WrDr 94*
di Zerega, Thomas William 1927- *WhoAm 94*
Dizhur, Bella Abramovna 1906- *BlmGWL*
Dizmang, Gloria Ann 1943- *WhoAmP 93*
Dizney, Robert Edward 1937- *WhoMW 93*
Dizon, Jesse 1950- *WhoHol 92*
Dizon, Jose Solomon 1960- *WhoScEn 94*
Djang, Edward B. 1937- *WhoAmL 94*
Djanikian, Gregory *DrAPF 93*
Djanogly, Harry Ari Simon 1938- *Who 94*
Djao, Angela Wei *WhoAsA 94*
Djaout, Tahar d1993 *NewYTBS 93*
Djavid, Ismail Faridoon 1908- *WhoScEn 94, WhoWest 94*
Djawad, Said Tayeb 1958- *WhoWest 94*
DJ Domination
See Geto Boys, The *ConMus 11*
Djebar, Assia 1936- *BlmGWL*
Djeddah, Richard Nissim *WhoFI 94*
Djeghaba, Mohamed 1935- *IntWW 93*
Djerassi, Carl *DrAPF 93*
Djerassi, Carl 1923- *IntWW 93, WhoAm 94, WhoScEn 94, WhoWest 94, WrDr 94*
Djerassi, Isaac 1925- *WhoAm 94*
Djerejian, Edward Peter 1939- *WhoAm 94, WhoAmP 93*
Djilas, Milovan 1911- *IntWW 93*
D.J. Minutemix 197-?-
See P. M. Dawn *ConMus 11*
Djohar, Said Ahmed *IntWW 93*
Djokic, Georgije 1949- *WhoAm 94*
Djola, Badja *WhoHol 92*
Djoleto, (Solomon Alexander) Amu 1929- *BlkWr 2, ConAu 141*
Djordjevic, Borislav Boro 1951- *WhoScEn 94*
Djordjevic, Cirila 1926- *WhoAm 94*
Djordjevic, Dimitrije 1922- *WhoAm 94*
Djordjevich, Michael 1936- *WhoAm 94*
DJ Ready Red
See Geto Boys, The *ConMus 11*
Djukanovic, Milo 1962- *IntWW 93*
Djuranovic, Veselin 1925- *IntWW 93*
Djurdjevic, Robert Slobodan 1945- *WhoWest 94*
Djwa, Sandra (Ann) 1939- *WrDr 94*
Dlab, Vlastimil 1932- *WhoAm 94, WhoScEn 94*
Dlabach, Gregory Wayne 1964- *WhoScEn 94*
Dlamini, Bhekimpi Alpheus *IntWW 93*
Dlamini, Obed Mfanyana 1937- *IntWW 93*
Dlamini, Sotsha *IntWW 93*
Dlamini, Timothy Lutfo Lucky 1952- *IntWW 93*
Dla'upac fl. 1800- *EncNAR*
Dlesk, George 1914- *WhoAm 94*
Dlott, Susan Judy 1949- *WhoAmL 94*
Dlouhy, Phillip Edward 1941- *WhoAm 94*
Dlouhy, Vladimir 1953- *IntWW 93*
D'Lower, Del 1912- *WhoFI 94*
Dlugoff, Marc Alan 1955- *WhoAmL 94*
Dlugoszewski, Lucia 1934- *NewGrDO*
D'Luhy, John James 1933- *WhoFI 94*
Dluski, Erazm 1857-1923 *NewGrDO*
Dmitrich, Mike 1936- *WhoAmP 93*
Dmitrieva, Elizaveta Ivanovna *BlmGWL*
Dmitrieva, Valentina Ionovna 1859-1948 *BlmGWL*
Dmytruk, Ihor R. 1938- *WhoAmA 93*
Dmytruk, Maksym, Jr. 1958- *WhoScEn 94*
Dmytryk, Edward 1908- *IntMPA 94*
Dmytryshyn, Basil 1925- *WhoAm 94, WhoWest 94*
Dneprov, Eduard Dmitrievich 1936- *LoBiDrD*
Do, Kim V. 1954- *WhoAmA 93*
Do, Tai Huu 1942- *WhoScEn 94, WhoWest 94*
Do, Toa Quang 1950- *WhoAsA 94*
Doa, Vincent, Sr. *WhoHisp 94*
Doak, Wade (Thomas) 1940- *WrDr 94*
Do Amaral, Diogo Freitas 1941- *IntWW 93*
Do Amaral, Luiz Henrique De Filippis De 1952- *WhoWest 94*
Doan, Charles Austin 1896-1990 *WhAm 10*
Doan, Eleanor Lloyd 1914- *WrDr 94*
Doan, Herbert Dow 1922- *WhoScEn 94*
Doan, James O. 1909- *WhoAmP 93*
Doan, Michael Frederick 1942- *WhoAm 94*
Doan, Phung Lien 1940- *WhoAsA 94*
Doan, Xuyen Van 1949- *WhoAmL 94*
Doane, Doris Chase 1913- *AstEnc*
Doane, Gilbert H(arry) 1897- *WhAm 10*
Doane, Helen Mitzi 1952- *WhoMW 93*
Doane, (R.) Michael 1952- *WrDr 94*
Doane, Paul Vincent 1943- *WhoAmP 93*
Doane, Thomas Roy 1947- *WhoScEn 94*
Doane, William McKee 1930- *WhoMW 93*
Doane, Woolson Whitney 1939- *WhoScEn 94*
Doanes-Bergin, Sharyn F. *WhoBlA 94*
Doar, William Walter, Jr. 1935- *WhoAmP 93*
Dobard, Raymond Gerard 1947- *WhoAmA 93*
Dobay, Donald G. 1924- *WhoScEn 94*
Dobb, Barbara J. *WhoAmP 93*
Dobb, Barbara Jeane 1949- *WhoMW 93*
Dobb, Erlam Stanley 1910- *Who 94*
Dobbel, Rodger Francis 1934- *WhoScEn 94, WhoWest 94*
Dobberstein, Shawn Albert 1963- *WhoMW 93*
Dobbie, Dorothy *WhoWomW 91*
Dobbie, George Herbert 1918- *WhoAm 94*
Dobbie, Robert Charles 1942- *Who 94*
Dobbie, William George Shedden 1879-1964 *DcNaB MP*
Dobbin, Edmund J. 1935- *WhoAm 94*
Dobbin, Ronald Denny 1944- *WhoScEn 94*
Dobbing, John 1922- *Who 94*
Dobbins, Albert Greene, III 1949- *WhoBlA 94*
Dobbins, Alphondus Milton 1924- *WhoBlA 94*
Dobbins, Ben d1930 *WhoHol 92*
Dobbins, Benjamin Knox 1951- *WhoAmL 94*
Dobbins, Bennie d1988 *WhoHol 92*
Dobbins, David Foster 1928- *WhoAm 94*
Dobbins, Deborah Wood 1958- *WhoAmL 94*
Dobbins, E. Fred *WhoAmP 93*
Dobbins, Earl d1949 *WhoHol 92*
Dobbins, James Francis, Jr. 1942- *WhoAm 94*
Dobbins, James Joseph 1924- *WhoAm 94*
Dobbins, James Talmage, Jr. 1926- *WhoScEn 94*
Dobbins, John Steve 1948- *WhoBlA 94*
Dobbins, Lucille R. *WhoBlA 94*
Dobbs, Bernard *Who 94*
Dobbs, (William) Bernard (Joseph) 1925- *Who 94*
Dobbs, Betty Jo (Teeter) 1930- *WrDr 94*
Dobbs, C. Edward 1949- *WhoAmL 94*
Dobbs, Charles Luther 1952- *WhoScEn 94*
Dobbs, Charles M. 1950- *WhoWest 94*
Dobbs, Dan Byron 1932- *WhoAm 94*
Dobbs, Denny Michael 1945- *WhoAmP 93*
Dobbs, Dorothy 1945- *WhoIns 94*
Dobbs, Ella Victoria 1866-1952 *WhoAmA 93N*
Dobbs, Frank Wilbur 1932- *WhoAm 94*
Dobbs, Gregory Allan 1946- *WhoAm 94*
Dobbs, James Frederick 1945- *WhoFI 94*
Dobbs, Jeannine *DrAPF 93*
Dobbs, John Barnes 1931- *WhoAm 94, WhoAmA 93*
Dobbs, John Wesley 1931- *WhoBlA 94*
Dobbs, Joseph Alfred 1914- *Who 94*
Dobbs, Mattiwilda *IntWW 93, Who 94, WhoBlA 94*
Dobbs, Mattiwilda 1925- *AfrAmAl 6, NewGrDO*
Dobbs, Michael John 1948- *Who 94*
Dobbs, Michael Sean 1950- *WhoAm 94*
Dobbs, Richard (Arthur Frederick) 1919- *Who 94*
Dobbs, Roland *Who 94*
Dobbs, (Edwin) Roland 1924- *Who 94*
Dobelbower, Peter Martin 1959- *WhoAmL 94*
Dobelis, George 1940- *WhoWest 94*
Dobell, Byron Maxwell 1927- *WhoAm 94*
Dobell, Sydney Thompson 1824-1874 *NinCLC 43 [port]*
Dobereiner, Johann Wolfgang 1780-1849 *WorScD*
Dobereiner, Johanna 1924- *WhoScEn 94*
Dobereiner, Peter Arthur Bertram 1925- *Who 94*
Doberenz, Alexander R. 1936- *WhoAm 94*
Doberneck, Raymond C. 1932- *WhoAm 94*
Doberstein, Audrey K. 1932- *WhoAm 94*
Dobes, Ivan Rastislav 1937- *WhoFI 94*
Dobes, William Lamar, Jr. 1943- *WhoScEn 94*
Dobesch, Gerhard 1939- *IntWW 93*
Dobesh, Ernest Leonard 1921- *WhoMW 93*
Dobey, James Kenneth 1919- *WhoAm 94*
D'Obici, Valeria *WhoHol 92*
Dobie, Alan 1932- *WhoHol 92*
Dobie, Colleen Langeland 1947- *WhoMW 93*
Dobie, Jeanne *WhoAmA 93*
Dobie, Shirley Imogene 1930- *WhoMW 93*
Dobielinska-Eliszewska, Teresa Katarzyna 1941- *WhoWomW 91*
Dobies, Eugene Stephen 1961- *WhoFI 94*
Dobis, Chester F. 1942- *WhoAmP 93*
Dobis, Lori Jean 1963- *WhoMW 93*
Dobkin, Alexander 1908-1975 *WhoAmA 93N*
Dobkin, Irving Bern 1918- *WhoAm 94, WhoMW 93, WhoScEn 94*
Dobkin, James Allen 1940- *WhoAm 94*
Dobkin, John Howard 1942- *WhoAm 94, WhoAmA 93*
Dobkin, Lawrence *WhoHol 92*
Doblado, Carlos Manuel 1950- *WhoHisp 94*
Doble, Denis Henry 1936- *Who 94*
Doble, Frances d1969 *WhoHol 92*
Doble, John Frederick 1941- *Who 94*
Dobler, Donald William 1927- *WhoAm 94*
Dobler, Norma Mae 1917- *WhoAmP 93*
Dobler, Patricia *DrAPF 93*
Doblin, Alfred *ConAu 141, EncSF 93*
Doblin, Hugo d1960 *WhoHol 92*
Doblin, Jay 1920-1989 *WhAm 10*
Dobmeyer, Douglas Charles 1949- *WhoMW 93*
Dobos, Barbara M. *WhoAmP 93*
Dobraczynski, Jan 1910- *IntWW 93*
Dobranski, Bernard 1939- *WhoAm 94*
Dobree, John Hatherley 1914- *Who 94*
Dobriansky, Lev Eugene 1918- *WhoAm 94, WhoAmP 93*
Dobriansky, Paula Jon 1955- *WhoAm 94*
Dobrick, Roger Harvey 1950- *WhoMW 93*
Dobrin, Arthur *DrAPF 93*
Dobrin, Bernard Robert 1937- *WhoAm 94*
Dobrin, Lyn 1942- *WrDr 94*
Dobrin, Raymond Allen 1942- *WhoScEn 94*
Dobrin, Sheldon L. 1945- *WhoMW 93*
Dobrin, Tamara Maria *WhoWomW 91*
Dobrinski, Everett *WhoAmP 93*
Dobrinski, Gail Margaret 1946- *WhoMW 93*
Dobrish, Robert Zachary 1940- *WhoAmL 94*
Dobronic, Antun 1878-1955 *NewGrDO*
Dobronski, Agnes M. 1925- *WhoAmP 93*
Dobronski, Agnes Marie 1925- *WhoMW 93*
Dobrosielski, Marian 1923- *Who 94*
Dobroski, H. Edward 1942- *WhoAmL 94*
Dobroven, Issay Alexandrovich 1891-1953 *NewGrDO*
Dobrovolny, Jerry Stanley 1922- *WhoAm 94*
Dobrovolny, John Henry 1933- *WhoMW 93*
Dobrovolny, Kenneth Ray 1947- *WhoWest 94*
Dobrowolska, Gosia *WhoHol 92*
Dobrowolski, Francis Joseph 1936- *WhoScEn 94*
Dobrowolski, Kathleen 1954- *WhoScEn 94*
Dobrski, Julian 1811?-1886 *NewGrDO*
Dobry, George Leon Severyn 1918- *Who 94*
Dobrynin, Anatoliy Fedorovich 1919- *IntWW 93*
Dobrynin, Anatoly Fedorovich 1919- *Who 94*
Dobrzynski, Ignacy Feliks 1807-1867 *NewGrDO*
Dobschensky, Carolyn Sue 1943- *WhoMW 93*
Dobson, Alan 1928- *WhoAm 94*
Dobson, Allen 1943- *WhoAm 94*
Dobson, Andrew (Nicholas Howard) 1957- *WrDr 94*
Dobson, Bridget McColl Hursley 1938- *WhoAm 94, WhoFI 94, WhoWest 94*
Dobson, Byron Eugene 1957- *WhoBlA 94*
Dobson, Christopher Selby Austin 1916- *Who 94*
Dobson, David (Stuart) 1938- *Who 94*
Dobson, David Irving 1883-1957 *WhoAmA 93N*
Dobson, Denis (William) 1908- *Who 94*
Dobson, Donald Alfred 1928- *WhoAm 94*
Dobson, Dorothy Ann 1934- *WhoBlA 94*
Dobson, Dorothy Grace 1928- *WhoWest 94*
Dobson, F. Stephen 1949- *WhoScEn 94*
Dobson, Frank Gordon 1940- *IntWW 93, Who 94*
Dobson, Helen Sutton 1926- *WhoBlA 94*
Dobson, James d1987 *WhoHol 92*
Dobson, James C. 1936- *WrDr 94*
Dobson, Jesse C. d1993 *NewYTBS 93*
Dobson, John 1930- *NewGrDO*
Dobson, John McCullough 1940- *WhoAm 94*
Dobson, Judith Elise 1934- *WhoAm 94*
Dobson, Julia 1941- *WrDr 94*
Dobson, Keith *Who 94*
Dobson, (William) Keith 1945- *Who 94*
Dobson, Kevin 1943- *IntMPA 94, WhoAm 94, WhoHol 92*
Dobson, Michael 1960- *ConAu 142*
Dobson, Michael William Romsey 1952- *Who 94*
Dobson, Patrick John H. *Who 94*
Dobson, Peter 1964- *WhoHol 92*
Dobson, R(ichard) Barrie 1931- *WrDr 94*
Dobson, Regina Louise 1965- *WhoBlA 94*
Dobson, Richard (Portway) 1914- *Who 94*
Dobson, Richard Barrie 1931- *Who 94*
Dobson, Richard Lawrence 1928- *WhoAm 94*
Dobson, Robert Albertus, III 1938- *WhoAmL 94*
Dobson, Robert Albertus, IV 1957- *WhoFI 94*
Dobson, Roger Swinburne 1936- *Who 94*
Dobson, Rosemary 1920- *BlmGWL, WrDr 94*
Dobson, Sue 1946- *Who 94*
Dobson, Tamara 1947- *WhoHol 92*
Dobson, Terrance James 1940- *WhoWest 94*
Dobson, Thomas W. 1942- *WhoAmL 94*
Dobtcheff, Vernon *WhoHol 92*
Doby, Allen E. 1934- *WhoBlA 94*
Doby, Kathryn *WhoHol 92*
Doby, Lawrence Eugene 1924- *WhoBlA 94*
Dobynes, Elizabeth 1930- *WhoBlA 94*
Dobyns, James Robert 1926- *WhoAmP 93*
Dobyns, John 1944- *WhoAmP 93*
Dobyns, Lloyd Allen 1936- *WhoAm 94*
Dobyns, Stephen *DrAPF 93*
Dobyns, Stephen 1941- *WrDr 94*
Dobyns, Zipporah 1921- *AstEnc*
Dobzhansky, Theodosius Grigorievich 1900-1975 *WorScD*
Doche, Joseph-Denis 1766-1825 *NewGrDO*
Docherty, Daniel Joseph 1924- *Who 94*
Docherty, James A. 1932- *WhoAmP 93*
Docherty, John Joseph 1941- *WhoMW 93*
Docherty, Robert Kelliehan, III 1959- *WhoScEn 94*
Dochez, Alphonse Raymond 1882-1964 *WorScD*
Dochniak, James M. *DrAPF 93*
Dochtermann, Trudi *WhoHol 92*
Dockendorf, Denise D. 1953- *WhoIns 94*
Docker, Ivor Colin 1925- *Who 94*

Dockerty, John Malcolm 1945- *WhoMW 93*
Dockery, Harva Ruth 1950- *WhoAmL 94*
Dockery, Herbert Donald 1954- *WhoFI 94*
Dockery, J. Lee 1932- *WhoAm 94*
Dockery, Martin J. 1938- *WhoAmL 94*
Dockery, Richard L. *WhoBlA 94*
Dockery, Robert W. 1954- *WhoAmL 94*
Dockery, Robert Wyatt 1909- *WhoBlA 94*
Dockett, Alfred B. 1935- *WhoBlA 94*
Dockham, Jerry C. *WhoAmP 93*
Dockhorn, Robert John 1934- *WhoAm 94, WhoMW 93, WhoScEn 94*
Docking, Thomas Robert 1954- *WhoAm 94, WhoAmP 93*
Dockser, William Barnet 1937- *WhoAm 94*
Dockson, Evllyn d1952 *WhoHol 92*
Dockson, Robert Ray 1917- *WhoAm 94, WhoWest 94*
Dockstader, Emmett Stanley 1923- *WhoFI 94*
Dockstader, Frederick J. 1919- *WhoAmA 93*
Dockstader, George d1987 *WhoHol 92*
Dockstader, Jack Lee 1936- *WhoWest 94*
Dockstader, Lew d1924 *WhoHol 92*
Dockterman, Michael 1954- *WhoAm 94, WhoAmL 94, WhoMW 93*
Docktor, William Jay 1951- *WhoWest 94*
Docktor-Smith, Mary Ann 1957- *WhoMW 93*
Dockweiler, Joseph H. *EncSF 93*
Docobo, Richard Douglas 1956- *WhoHisp 94*
Docter, Charles Alfred 1931- *WhoAm 94, WhoAmP 93*
Doctor, Henry, Jr. 1932- *AfrAmG [port]*
Doctor, Kenneth Jay 1950- *WhoAm 94, WhoMW 93*
Doctor Charley fl. 1880- *EncNAR*
Doctor George dc. 1930 *EncNAR*
Doctorian, David 1934- *WhoAmP 93*
Doctorian, Sam Emmanuel, Jr. 1962- *WhoWest 94*
Doctoroff, Martin Myles 1933- *WhoAm 94*
Doctorow, E. L. *DrAPF 93*
Doctorow, E(dgar) L(aurence) 1931- *EncSF 93, WrDr 94*
Doctorow, Edgar Lawrence 1931- *IntWW 93, Who 94, WhoAm 94*
Doctors, Samuel I. 1936- *WhoAmL 94, WhoWest 94*
Dod, Charlotte 1871-1960 *DcNaB MP*
Dod, Lottie 1871-1960 *BuCMET*
Dodak, Lewis 1946- *WhoMW 93*
Dodak, Lewis N. 1946- *WhoAmP 93*
Dodani, Mahesh Hassomal 1958- *WhoMW 93*
Dodaro, Joseph John 1954- *WhoMW 93*
Dodd, Anna Bowman 1855-1929 *EncSF 93*
Dodd, Arthur Edward 1913- *WrDr 94*
Dodd, Charles Gardner 1915- *WhoAm 94*
Dodd, Chester Curtin, Jr. 1928- *WhoAmP 93*
Dodd, Christopher J. 1944- *CngDr 93, IntWW 93, WhoAm 94, WhoAmP 93*
Dodd, Claire d1973 *WhoHol 92*
Dodd, Debbie Lynn 1959- *WhoWest 94*
Dodd, Ed(ward Benton) 1902-1991 *WhAm 10*
Dodd, Edward William 1936- *WhoAmP 93*
Dodd, Edwin Dillon 1919- *IntWW 93*
Dodd, Elizabeth d1928 *WhoHol 92*
Dodd, Ellen d1935 *WhoHol 92*
Dodd, Eric M. *WhoAmA 93*
Dodd, Frank Leslie d1993 *Who 94N*
Dodd, Gerald Dewey, Jr. 1922- *WhoAm 94*
Dodd, Jack Gordon, Jr. 1926- *WhoAm 94*
Dodd, James C. 1923- *WhoBlA 94*
Dodd, James Robert 1934- *WhoAm 94*
Dodd, Jeanne Dolores 1957- *WhoAmL 94*
Dodd, Jerry Lee 1953- *WhoMW 93*
Dodd, Jimmy d1964 *WhoHol 92*
Dodd, Joe David 1920- *WhoFI 94, WhoWest 94*
Dodd, John Newton 1922- *IntWW 93, WhoScEn 94*
Dodd, Kenneth Arthur 1931- *Who 94*
Dodd, Lamar 1909- *WhoAmA 93*
Dodd, Lawrence Roe 1944- *WhoAmL 94*
Dodd, Lester Paul 1895- *WhAm 10*
Dodd, Lionel G. 1940- *WhoAm 94*
Dodd, Lois 1927- *WhoAm 94, WhoAmA 93*
Dodd, Lynley Stuart 1941- *BlmGWL*
Dodd, Lynley Stuart (Weeks) 1941- *WrDr 94*
Dodd, M(ary) Irene 1941- *WhoAmA 93*
Dodd, Michael F. 1938- *WhoIns 94*
Dodd, Molly d1981 *WhoHol 92*
Dodd, Neal d1966 *WhoHol 92*
Dodd, Philip Kevin 1938- *Who 94*
Dodd, Richard B. 1944- *WhoAmL 94*
Dodd, Robert 1938- *WhoAmP 93*
Dodd, Robert Bruce 1921- *WhoAm 94*
Dodd, Roger James 1951- *WhoAmL 94, WhoFI 94*
Dodd, Stephen M. 1946- *WhoAmL 94*
Dodd, Steven Louis 1953- *WhoScEn 94*
Dodd, Susan M. *DrAPF 93*
Dodd, Susan M 1946- *WrDr 94*
Dodd, Thomas *WhoAm 94*
Dodd, Valerie A. 1944- *WrDr 94*
Dodd, Virginia Marilyn 1950- *WhoAm 94*
Dodd, Walta Sue 1944- *WhoAmP 93*
Dodd, Wayne *DrAPF 93*
Dodd, Wayne D. 1930- *WrDr 94*
Dodd, William Atherton 1923- *Who 94*
Dodd, William Luther, Jr. 1921- *WhoAmP 93*
Doddapaneni, Narayan 1942- *WhoAsA 94*
Dodderidge, Esme 1916- *EncSF 93*
Dodderidge, Morris 1915- *Who 94*
Dodderidge, Richard William 1926- *WhoAm 94*
Dodds, Brenda Kay 1961- *WhoMW 93*
Dodds, Claudette La Vonn 1947- *WhoAm 94, WhoMW 93*
Dodds, Dale Irvin 1915- *WhoScEn 94, WhoWest 94*
Dodds, Dayle Ann 1952- *ConAu 142, SmATA 75 [port]*
Dodds, Denis George 1913- *Who 94*
Dodds, Douglas Allen 1950- *WhoAm 94*
Dodds, George Christopher Buchanan 1916- *Who 94*
Dodds, J. Allan 1947- *WhoWest 94*
Dodds, James Pickering 1913- *Who 94*
Dodds, John Wendell 1902-1989 *WhAm 10*
Dodds, Michael Bruce 1952- *WhoAmL 94*
Dodds, Nigel Alexander 1958- *Who 94*
Dodds, R. Harcourt 1938- *WhoBlA 94*
Dodds, Ralph (Jordan) 1928- *Who 94*
Dodds, Robert J., III 1943- *WhoAmA 93*
Dodds, Robert James, Jr. 1916- *WhoAm 94*
Dodds, Robert James, III 1943- *WhoAm 94*
Dodds-Parker, (Arthur) Douglas 1909- *Who 94*
Doddy, Reginald Nathaniel 1952- *WhoBlA 94*
Dodenhoff, Helen Jean 1938- *WhoMW 93*
Doderer, Minnette Frerichs 1923- *WhoAmP 93, WhoMW 93*
Dodes, Irving Allen d1993 *NewYTBS 93*
Dodge, Alwyn Conrad 1929- *WhoMW 93*
Dodge, Anna d1945 *WhoHol 92*
Dodge, Arthur G., Jr. 1929- *WhoAmP 93*
Dodge, Bertha Sanford 1902- *WrDr 94*
Dodge, Calvert Renaul 1921- *WhoFI 94*
Dodge, Charles Malcolm 1942- *WhoAm 94*
Dodge, Cleveland Earl, Jr. 1922- *WhoAm 94*
Dodge, Clifford F. 1939- *WhoAmP 93*
Dodge, David A. 1943- *WhoAm 94*
Dodge, Douglas Stuart 1951- *WhoWest 94*
Dodge, Earl Farwell 1932- *WhoAm 94, WhoAmP 93*
Dodge, Emma M. 1930- *WhoAmP 93*
Dodge, Gloria Evelyn *WhoFI 94*
Dodge, Hazel 1903-1957 *WhoAmA 93N*
Dodge, Henry 1782-1867 *WhWE*
Dodge, Jim 1945- *ConAu 141*
Dodge, Joseph Jeffers 1917- *WhoAmA 93*
Dodge, Lawrence Burnham 1942- *WhoAmP 93*
Dodge, Mary Abigail 1833-1896 *BlmGWL*
Dodge, Mary Elizabeth Mapes 1831-1905 *BlmGWL*
Dodge, Paul Cecil 1943- *WhoAm 94*
Dodge, Peter 1926- *WrDr 94*
Dodge, Peter Hampton 1929- *WhoAm 94*
Dodge, Philip Rogers 1923- *WhoAm 94*
Dodge, Richard Allan 1930- *WhoAmP 93*
Dodge, Robert G. 1939- *WhoAmA 93*
Dodge, William Douglas 1937- *WhoAm 94*
Dodgen, Andrew Clay 1961- *WhoAmL 94*
Dodgen, Harold Warren 1921- *WhoAm 94*
Dodgen, James 1921- *WhoWest 94*
Dodgshon, Robert A(ndrew) 1941- *WrDr 94*
Dodgson, Charles Lutwidge 1832-1898 *WorScD*
Dodimead, David 1919- *WhoHol 92*
Dodin, Lev Abramovich 1944- *IntWW 93*
Dodington, Sven H. M. 1912-1992 *WhAm 10*
Dodrill, Donald Lawrence 1922- *WhoAmA 93, WhoMW 93*
Dodrill, Robert Lee, Sr. 1933- *WhoAmP 93*
Dods, Robert Douglas 1942- *WhoAmP 93*
Dods, Walter Arthur, Jr. 1941- *WhoAm 94, WhoFI 94, WhoWest 94*
Dodson *Who 94*
Dodson, Angela Pearl 1951- *WhoBlA 94*
Dodson, Bruce J. 1937- *WhoFI 94, WhoMW 93*
Dodson, Catherine E. Brown 1948- *WhoAmL 94*
Dodson, Christopher Thomas 1964- *WhoWest 94*
Dodson, D. Keith 1943- *WhoAm 94*
Dodson, Daniel B 1918- *WrDr 94*
Dodson, Daniel Boone 1918-1991 *WhAm 10*
Dodson, Daryl Theodore 1934- *WhoAm 94*
Dodson, David Philip 1939- *WhoWest 94*
Dodson, Derek (Sherborne Lindsell) 1920- *Who 94*
Dodson, Derek Sherborne Lindsell 1920- *IntWW 93*
Dodson, Don Charles 1944- *WhoWest 94*
Dodson, Donald Mills 1937- *WhoAm 94*
Dodson, Fitzhugh d1993 *NewYTBS 93*
Dodson, Fitzhugh (James) 1923-1993 *ConAu 141*
Dodson, George W. 1937- *WhoScEn 94*
Dodson, Howard, Jr. 1939- *WhoBlA 94*
Dodson, Jack 1932- *WhoHol 92*
Dodson, James Noland 1963- *WhoScEn 94*
Dodson, Joanna 1945- *Who 94*
Dodson, John Paul 1938- *WhoWest 94*
Dodson, Jon d1964 *WhoHol 92*
Dodson, Jualynne E. 1942- *WhoBlA 94*
Dodson, Kenneth (MacKenzie) 1907- *WrDr 94*
Dodson, Oscar Henry 1905- *WhoMW 93*
Dodson, Owen 1914-1983 *ConLC 79 [port]*
Dodson, Robert North *Who 94*
Dodson, Ronald Franklin 1942- *WhoScEn 94*
Dodson, Samuel Robinette, III 1943- *WhoAm 94*
Dodson, Selma L. 1955- *WhoBlA 94*
Dodson, Vernon Nathan 1923- *WhoAm 94*
Dodson, Vivian M. 1934- *WhoBlA 94*
Dodson, William Alfred, Jr. 1950- *WhoBlA 94*
Dodson, William Patrick 1948- *WhoAmP 93*
Dodsworth, Geoffrey Hugh 1928- *Who 94*
Dodsworth, John d1964 *WhoHol 92*
Dodsworth, John Christopher S. *Who 94*
Dodsworth, Martin *Who 94*
Dodsworth, (James) Martin 1935- *Who 94*
Dodunekova, Penka Mihaylova (Ivanova) 1930- *WhoWomW 91*
Dodwell, Charles Reginald 1922- *IntWW 93, Who 94*
Dodworth, Allen Stevens 1938- *WhoAmA 93, WhoWest 94*
Dodworth, Peter 1940- *Who 94*
Doe, Bruce Roger 1931- *WhoAm 94*
Doe, John 1954- *See X ConMus 11*
Doe, Richard Philip 1926- *WhoAm 94, WhoScEn 94, WhoWest 94*
Doebele, Robert Garrick 1965- *WhoMW 93*
Doebler, James Carl 1939- *WhoAm 94*
Doebler, Paul Dickerson 1930- *WhoAm 94*
Doeblin, Alfred 1878-1957 *ConAu 141*
Doede, John Henry 1937- *WhoAm 94*
Doederlein, Deloris *WhoAmP 93*
Doeg, Johnny 1908-1978 *BuCMET*
Doege, Theodore Charles 1928- *WhoMW 93*
Doehne, Dorothy P. *WhoAmP 93*
Doehr, Ruth Nadine 1932- *WhoMW 93*
Doehr-Blanck, Denise Louise 1963- *WhoMW 93*
Doehrin, James *WhoAm 94*
Doel, Kenneth John 1948- *WhoAm 94*
Doelling, Hellmut Hans 1930- *WhoWest 94*
Doelling, Ralph Peter 1936- *WhoFI 94*
Doellman, John L. 1952- *WhoIns 94*
Doellman, Michael Anthony 1945- *WhoMW 93*
Doelman-Pel, Ali 1932- *WhoWomW 91*
D'Oench, Ellen Gates 1930- *WhoAmA 93*
D'Oench, Russell Grace, Jr. 1927- *WhoAm 94, WhoFI 94*
Doenecke, Carol Anne 1942- *WhoAm 94*
Doenecke, Justus Drew 1938- *ConAu 43NR*
Doenges, Byron Frederick 1922- *WhoAm 94*
Doenges, Norman Arthur 1926- *WhoAm 94*
Doenges, Rudolph Conrad 1930- *WhoAm 94*
Doenim, Susan *EncSF 93*
Doepke, Katherine Louise Guldberg 1921- *WhoMW 93*
Doepkens, Frederick Henry 1958- *WhoScEn 94*
Doepker, John Frederick, Jr. 1949- *WhoMW 93*
Doeppner, Thomas Walter 1920- *WhoAm 94, WhoScEn 94*
Doeres, Jurgen *WhoHol 92*
Doerfel, Ken Sue 1944- *WhoAmP 93*
Doerfler, Leo G. 1919- *WhoAm 94*
Doerfler, Ronald John 1941- *WhoAm 94*
Doerfling, Hank 1936- *WhoWest 94*
Doerflinger, Marlys Irene 1943- *WhoMW 93*
Doerge, Everett 1935- *WhoAmP 93*
Doerhoff, Dale Charles 1946- *WhoAmL 94*
Doering, Roger William 1951- *WhoFI 94*
Doering, William von Eggers 1917- *IntWW 93, WhoAm 94, WhoScEn 94*
Doermann, Humphrey 1930- *WhoAm 94*
Doermann, Paul Edmund 1926- *WhoAm 94*
Doerner, Martin David 1960- *WhoWest 94*
Doerper, John Erwin 1943- *WhoWest 94*
Doerr, Harriet *DrAPF 93*
Doerr, Harriet 1910- *WhoAm 94*
Doerr, Howard P. 1929- *WhoAm 94*
Doerr, Jana Rae 1948- *WhoAmP 93*
Doerr, John F. 1945- *WhoAmP 93*
Doerr, Mary Ann 1954- *WhoMW 93*
Doerr, Ray E. 1926- *WhoAmP 93*
Doerr, Ronald H. 1940- *WhoFI 94*
Doerr, Stephen Eugene 1959- *WhoScEn 94*
Doerr, York J. 1941- *WhoMW 93*
Doerries, Reinhard Rene 1934- *WhoAm 94*
Doerry, Norbert Henry 1962- *WhoScEn 94*
Doersch, Todd Dayton *WhoFI 94*
Doese, Helena 1946- *NewGrDO*
Doetsch, Paul William 1954- *WhoScEn 94*
Doetschman, David Charles 1942- *WhoScEn 94*
Doffou, Ako Dagobert 1955- *WhoFI 94*
Dogali, Jo Marie 1949- *WhoAmL 94*
Dogan, Husnu 1944- *IntWW 93*
Doganata, Yurdaer Nezihi 1959- *WhoScEn 94*
Dogancay, Burhan C. 1929- *WhoAm 94*
Dogancay, Burhan Cahit 1929- *WhoAmA 93*
Doggart, George Hubert Graham 1925- *Who 94*
Doggett, Aubrey Clayton, Jr. 1928- *WhoAm 94*
Doggett, Douglass M., Sr. *WhoBlA 94*
Doggett, John Nelson, Jr. 1918- *WhoBlA 94, WhoMW 93*
Doggett, Lloyd 1946- *WhoAm 94, WhoAmL 94*
Doggett, Lloyd Alton, II 1946- *WhoAmP 93*
Doggett, Mary Lousie Wallis 1928- *WhoAmP 93*
Doggrell, Henry Patton 1948- *WhoAmL 94*
Doglione, Arthur George 1938- *WhoWest 94*
Dogole, Saul Harrison 1922- *WhoAmP 93*
Dogoloff, Lee Israel 1939- *WhoAmP 93*
Dogoloff, Lee Israel 1962- *WhoAm 94*
Dogramaci, Ihsan 1915- *IntWW 93*
Doguzhiev, Vitaliy Khusseynovich 1935- *IntWW 93*
Doha, Aminur Rahman S. *Who 94*
Doha, Aminur Rahman S. 1929- *IntWW 93*
Dohanian, Diran Kavork 1931- *WhoAm 94*
Dohanos, Stevan 1907- *WhoAmA 93*
Doheny, Carrie Estelle 1875-1958 *DcLB 140 [port]*
Doheny, Donald Aloysius 1924- *WhoAm 94, WhoAmL 94, WhoFI 94, WhoMW 93*
Doheny, James Jerome 1906- *WhoMW 93*
Doheny, John T. 1948- *WhoAm 94, WhoAmL 94*
Doherty, Adrian Walter, Jr. 1952- *WhoAm 94*
Doherty, Alfred Edward 1929- *WhoWest 94*
Doherty, Barbara 1931- *WhoAm 94*
Doherty, Berlie 1943- *TwCYAW, WrDr 94*
Doherty, Brian Gerard 1957- *WhoAmP 93*
Doherty, Charla d1988 *WhoHol 92*
Doherty, Charles Vincent 1933- *WhoAm 94, WhoFI 94*
Doherty, Cornelius Gregory 1962- *WhoWest 94*
Doherty, Daniel Edward 1952- *WhoAmL 94*
Doherty, Evelyn Marie 1941- *WhoFI 94*
Doherty, George William 1941- *WhoWest 94*
Doherty, Gerald Paul, IV 1946- *WhoAmP 93*
Doherty, Henry Joseph 1933- *WhoAm 94*

Dombrowski, Edmund Theodore 1930-
WhoAmP 93
Dombrowski, Frank Paul, Jr. 1943-
WhoScEn 94
Dombrowski, Gerard *DrAPF 93*
Dombrowski, John Micheal 1959-
WhoScEn 94
Dombrowski, Joseph Patrick 1943-
WhoMW 93
Dombrowski, Raymond Edward, Jr.
1954- *WhoAmL 94*
Dombu, Sivert Rolf 1938- *WhoWest 94*
Domcq, H. Bustos *ConWorW 93,*
EncSF 93
Domecq, H(onorio) Bustos *ConAu 43NR*
Domeier, David John 1953- *WhoAm 94*
Domeij, Asa Elisabeth 1962-
WhoWomW 91
Domeischel, Jack R. *WhoMW 93*
Domenech i Escate de Canellas, Maria
1877-1952 *BlmGWL*
Domenici, Pete 1932- *WhoAm 94,*
WhoWest 94
Domenici, Pete V. 1932- *CngDr 93,*
IntWW 93, WhoAmP 93
Domenico d1963 *EncNAR*
Domenico, Gianpaolo di fl. 1706-1741
NewGrDO
Domenico de Piacenza c. 1425-c. 1465
IntDcB
Domeny, Rose Marie 1941- *WhoMW 93*
Domer, Floyd Ray 1931- *WhoAm 94*
Domeracki, Henry Stefan 1956-
WhoAmP 93
Domergue, Faith 1925- *WhoHol 92*
Domett, Douglas Brian 1932- *Who 94*
Domgraf-Fassbander, Willi 1897-1978
NewGrDO
Domgraf-Fassbender, Willi d1978
WhoHol 92
Domin, Hilde 1912- *BlmGWL, IntWW 93*
Domingo, Anni *WhoHol 92*
Domingo, Cynthia Garciano 1953-
WhoAsA 94, WhoWest 94
Domingo, Francisco *WhoHisp 94*
Domingo, Placido 1941- *IntWW 93,*
NewGrDO, Who 94, WhoAm 94,
WhoHol 92
Domingue, Emery 1926- *WhoAm 94*
Domingue, Gerald James 1937-
WhoAm 94
Domingue, Raymond Pierre 1959-
WhoScEn 94
Dominguez, A. M., Jr. 1943- *WhoHisp 94*
Dominguez, Abraham A. 1927-
WhoHisp 94
Dominguez, Al Manuel, Jr. 1943-
WhoAmL 94
Dominguez, Alfredo, Jr. 1935-
WhoHisp 94
Dominguez, Alvaro Jose 1954-
WhoHisp 94
Dominguez, Angel 1953- *SmATA 76 [port]*
Dominguez, Angel De Jesus 1950-
WhoHisp 94
Dominguez, Antonio 1951- *WhoHisp 94*
Dominguez, Beatrice d1921 *WhoHol 92*
Dominguez, Cari M. 1949- *WhoHisp 94*
Dominguez, Eddie 1957- *WhoAmA 93*
Dominguez, Eduardo Ramiro 1953-
WhoHisp 94
Dominguez, Edward Anthony 1960-
WhoHisp 94
Dominguez, Francisco Atanasio c.
1740-1805 *WhWE*
Dominguez, Hernan 1930- *WhoHisp 94*
Dominguez, Janie C. 1939- *WhoHisp 94*
Dominguez, Jesus Ygnacio 1940-
WhoHisp 94
Dominguez, Joe d1970 *WhoHol 92*
Dominguez, Jorge Ignacio 1945-
WhoAm 94, WhoHisp 94
Dominguez, Jose Raul 1970- *WhoHisp 94*
Dominguez, Joseph R. 1938- *WhoHisp 94*
Dominguez, Julio P. *WhoHisp 94*
Dominguez, Lorenzo 1953- *WhoHisp 94*
Dominguez, Maria Alicia 1908- *BlmGWL*
Dominguez, Marine 1952- *IntMPA 94*
Dominguez, Miguel A. 1961- *WhoHisp 94*
Dominguez, Oralia 1928- *NewGrDO*
Dominguez, Peter Joseph 1956-
WhoHisp 94
Dominguez, Rachel 1936- *WhoHisp 94*
Dominguez, Ralph, Jr. 1952- *WhoHisp 94*
Dominguez, Richard M. *WhoHisp 94*
Dominguez, Roberto 1955- *WhoHisp 94*
Dominguez, Ronald *WhoHisp 94*
Dominguez, Russell Guadalupe 1960-
WhoHisp 94
Dominguez, Steven 1953- *WhoHisp 94*
Dominguez-Mayoral, Rodrigo 1947-
WhoHisp 94
Dominguez Ortega, Luis 1941-
WhoScEn 94
Dominguin, Luis Miguel 1925-
WhoHol 92
Dominh, Thap 1938- *WhoAsA 94*
Domini, Irene C. 1933- *WhoAmP 93*

Domini, John A. *DrAPF 93*
Domini, Rey *GayLL*
Dominiak, Geraldine Florence 1934-
WhoAm 94
Dominian, Jack 1929- *WrDr 94*
Dominian, Jacobus 1929- *IntWW 93,*
Who 94
Dominianni, Emilio Anthony 1931-
WhoAm 94
Dominic, Irwing 1930- *WhoBlA 94*
Dominic, R. B. *WrDr 94*
Dominic, Zoe Denise 1920- *Who 94*
Dominiceti, Cesare 1821-1888 *NewGrDO*
Dominici, Mario d1942 *WhoHol 92*
Dominick, Alan R. 1944- *WhoAm 94,*
WhoAmL 94
Dominick, Betty Garrett 1938-
WhoAmP 93
Dominick, Charles Alva 1943-
WhoMW 93
Dominick, David DeWitt 1937-
WhoAm 94
Dominick, Paul Allen 1954- *WhoAmL 94*
Dominick, Paul Scott 1962- *WhoScEn 94*
Dominico, Michael d1977 *WhoHol 92*
Dominik, Hans *EncSF 93*
Dominik, Jack Edward 1924- *WhoAm 94,*
WhoAmL 94
Dominioni, Angelo Maria Francesco
1932- *WhoFI 94*
Dominique, Daniel Roy 1918- *WhoIns 94*
Dominique, Ivan d1973 *WhoHol 92*
Dominique, John August 1893-
WhoAmA 93
Dominique, Meg 1929- *WrDr 94*
Domino, Edward Felix 1924- *WhoAm 94*
Domino, Fats 1928- *WhoAm 94*
Domino, Fats 1928- *AfrAmAl 6,*
WhoAm 94, WhoBlA 94
Dominoski, Ronald Alan 1948-
WhoWest 94
Dominy, Eric Norman 1918- *WrDr 94*
Dominy, Sam 1945- *WhoAmP 93*
Dominy, Wendell Richard 1942-
WhoMW 93
Domir, Subhash Chandra 1944-
WhoMW 93
Domit, Moussa M. 1932- *WhoAmA 93*
Domitian 51-96 *HisWorL [port]*
Domitien, Elisabeth *IntWW 93*
Domjan, Joseph 1907- *WhoAm 94*
Domjan, Joseph (Spiri) 1907- *WhoAmA 93*
Domjan, Laszlo Karoly 1947- *WhoAm 94,*
WhoMW 93
Domke, Gary Edward *WhoMW 93*
Domm, Alice 1954- *WhoAm 94,*
WhoAmL 94
Domm, Lincoln Valentine 1896-1989
WhAm 10
Dommartin, Solveig 1961- *WhoHol 92*
Dommel, Darlene Hurst 1940-
WhoMW 93
Dommen, Arthur John 1934- *WhoAm 94*
Dommer, Allison Elizabeth 1967-
WhoWest 94
Dommer, Earl Michael 1952- *WhoMW 93*
Dommermuth, William P. *WhoAm 94,*
WhoMW 93, WrDr 94
Dommisse, Ebbe 1940- *IntWW 93*
Domna, H. fl. c. 1220-1240 *BlmGWL*
Domnie, Scott Harold 1954- *WhoWest 94*
Domokos, Gabor 1933- *WhoAm 94*
Domokos, Matyas 1930- *Who 94*
Domondon, Oscar 1924- *WhoAsA 94,*
WhoWest 94
Domoto, Akiko 1932- *WhoWomW 91*
Domoto, Douglass T. 1943- *WhoAsA 94*
Domoto, Hisao 1928- *IntWW 93*
Dompke, Norbert Frank 1920-
WhoMW 93
Domroe, Barbara 1939- *WhoAmA 93*
Doms, Keith 1920- *WhoAm 94*
Domsky, Ira Michael 1951- *WhoWest 94*
Do Muoi 1917- *IntWW 93*
Don, Carl *WhoHol 92*
Don, David d1949 *WhoHol 92*
Don, James E. 1932- *WhoAsA 94*
Don, Rasa c. 1969-
See Arrested Development *News 94-2*
Donabedian, Avedis 1919- *IntWW 93,*
WhoAm 94
Donadio, Giulio d1951 *WhoHol 92*
Donagan, Alan Harry 1925-1991
WhAm 10
Donaggio, Pino 1941- *IntDcF 2-4*
Donaghy, Henry James 1930- *WhoAm 94*
Donaghy, Michael 1954- *ConAu 140,*
WrDr 94
Donaghy, Patrick Christopher 1933-
WhoAm 94
Donaghy Craig, Sandra Noel 1954-
WhoAmL 94
Donahey, Beverly Ellinger 1948-
WhoMW 93
Donahey, Gertrude Walton 1908-
WhoAmP 93
Donahey, James Harrison 1875-1949
WhoAmA 93N

Donahey, Rex Craig 1955- *WhoScEn 94*
Donahoe, David Lawrence 1949-
WhoAm 94
Donahoe, Jim *DrAPF 93*
Donahoo, Melvin Lawrence 1930-
WhoScEn 94
Donahoo, Stanley Ellsworth 1933-
WhoWest 94
Donahue, Al d1983 *WhoHol 92*
Donahue, Barbara Lynn Sean 1956-
WhoAm 94
Donahue, Benedict, Sr. *WhoAmA 93N*
Donahue, Charlotte Mary 1954-
WhoAmL 94
Donahue, Daniel William 1942-
WhoAm 94
Donahue, Dennis Donald 1940-
WhoWest 94
Donahue, Donald Jordan 1924-
WhoAm 94, WhoFI 94, WhoWest 94
Donahue, Douglas Aidan, Jr. 1951-
WhoAm 94
Donahue, Elinor 1937- *IntMPA 94,*
WhoAm 94, WhoHol 92
Donahue, Hayden Hackney 1912-
WhoAm 94
Donahue, Jack *DrAPF 93*
Donahue, James J., Jr. 1919- *WhoWest 94*
Donahue, James Richard 1930-
WhoMW 93
Donahue, John Edward 1950-
WhoAmL 94
Donahue, John F. 1936- *WhoIns 94*
Donahue, John Lawrence, Jr. 1939-
WhoMW 93
Donahue, John McFall 1924- *WhoAm 94*
Donahue, John Michael 1952-
WhoAmL 94
Donahue, John Richard 1964- *WhoFI 94*
Donahue, Karin Victoria 1945-
WhoAmL 94
Donahue, Kevin Edward 1963-
WhoMW 93
Donahue, Laura Kent 1949- *WhoAmP 93,*
WhoMW 93
Donahue, Lauri Michele 1961-
WhoWest 94
Donahue, Leigh Richmond *WrDr 94*
Donahue, Mary Rosenberg 1932-
WhoScEn 94
Donahue, Patricia *WhoHol 92*
Donahue, Phil 1935- *IntMPA 94,*
IntWW 93, WhoAm 94
Donahue, Philip Richard 1943-
WhoAmA 93
Donahue, Richard King 1927-
WhoWest 94
Donahue, Robert Edward 1954-
WhoScEn 94
Donahue, Roberta Lucille 1950-
WhoMW 93
Donahue, Shirley Ohnstad 1937-
WhoMW 93
Donahue, Terry Lee 1946- *WhoAmP 93*
Donahue, Thomas Michael 1921-
IntWW 93, WhoAm 94, WhoMW 93,
WhoScEn 94
Donahue, Thomas Reilly 1928-
WhoAm 94, WhoFI 94
Donahue, Timothy James 1949-
WhoFI 94
Donahue, Timothy Patrick 1955-
WhoAmL 94
Donahue, Troy 1937- *IntMPA 94,*
WhoHol 92
Donahue, Vincent d1976 *WhoHol 92*
Donahue, William Francis d1981
WhoHol 92
Donahue, William T. 1943- *WhoBlA 94*
Donahue, Wilma Thompson d1993
NewYTBS 93
Donahugh, Robert Hayden 1930-
WhoAm 94
Donais, Gary Warren 1952- *WhoAm 94*
Donald, III c. 1039- *DcNaB MP*
Donald, Aida DiPace 1930- *WhoAm 94*
Donald, Alan (Ewen) 1931- *IntWW 93,*
Who 94
Donald, Alastair Geoffrey 1926- *Who 94*
Donald, Alexander Grant 1928-
WhoAm 94
Donald, Arnold Wayne 1954- *WhoBlA 94*
Donald, Bernice Bouie 1951- *WhoBlA 94*
Donald, Craig Reid Cantlie 1914- *Who 94*
Donald, David Herbert 1920- *WhoAm 94*
Donald, Edward Milton, Jr. 1947-
WhoMW 93
Donald, Eric Paul 1930- *WhoAm 94*
Donald, George Malcolm 1943- *Who 94*
Donald, Harvey C. *WhoAmP 93*
Donald, Ian *WhoAm 94, WhoFI 94,*
WhoWest 94
Donald, Jack C. 1934- *WhoAm 94*
Donald, James d1993 *NewYTBS 93 [port]*
Donald, James 1917- *WhoHol 92*
Donald, James L. 1931- *WhoAm 94,*
WhoFI 94
Donald, James Robert 1933- *WhoAm 94*

Donald, John (George) 1927- *Who 94*
Donald, Juliana 1964- *WhoHol 92*
Donald, Kenneth William 1911- *Who 94*
Donald, Larry Watson 1945- *WhoAm 94*
Donald, Norman Henderson, III 1937-
WhoAm 94, WhoAmL 94
Donald, Paul Aubrey 1929- *WhoAm 94*
Donald, Robert Graham 1943- *WhoAm 94*
Donald, William (Spooner) 1910-
WrDr 94
Donald, William Waldie 1950-
WhoMW 93
Donalda, Pauline 1882-1970 *NewGrDO*
Donalds, Gordon 1914- *WrDr 94*
Donaldson *Who 94*
Donaldson, Alexander Ivan 1942- *Who 94*
Donaldson, Alexander MacFarland 1953-
WhoAmL 94
Donaldson, Arthur d1955 *WhoHol 92*
Donaldson, Brian Eric 1969- *WhoMW 93*
Donaldson, Charles Ian Edward 1935-
IntWW 93
Donaldson, Charles Russell 1919-
WhAm 10
Donaldson, Coleman duPont 1922-
WhoAm 94
Donaldson, David Abercrombie 1916-
Who 94
Donaldson, David Howard, Jr. 1951-
WhoAmL 94
Donaldson, David Marbury 1938-
WhoAm 94
Donaldson, David Torrance 1943-
Who 94
Donaldson, Deirdre Hunter 1953-
WhoWest 94
Donaldson, Dennis C. 1938- *WhoAmP 93*
Donaldson, Edward Mossop 1939-
WhoAm 94
Donaldson, Frances 1907- *WrDr 94*
Donaldson, Frances Annesley 1907-
Who 94
Donaldson, Frank Arthur, Jr. 1919-1991
WhAm 10
Donaldson, George Burney 1945-
WhoWest 94
Donaldson, Gordon d1993 *Who 94N*
Donaldson, Gordon 1913- *WrDr 94*
Donaldson, Gordon 1913-1993
ConAu 141, SmATA 76
Donaldson, Hamish 1936- *Who 94*
Donaldson, Howard Meyer 1952-
WhoAm 94
Donaldson, Ian *Who 94*
Donaldson, (Charles) Ian (Edward) 1935-
Who 94
Donaldson, Islay (Eila) Murray 1921-
WrDr 94
Donaldson, Jack d1975 *WhoHol 92*
Donaldson, James 1957- *BasBi*
Donaldson, James Adrian 1930-
WhoAm 94
Donaldson, James Lee, III 1957-
WhoBlA 94
Donaldson, James Oswell, III 1942-
WhoScEn 94
Donaldson, Jeff R. 1932- *WhoAmA 93*
Donaldson, Jeff Richardson 1932-
WhoAm 94, WhoBlA 94
Donaldson, John 1928- *WhoAm 94*
Donaldson, John Anthony 1938-
WhoAm 94
Donaldson, John Cecil, Jr. 1933-
WhoAm 94, WhoFI 94
Donaldson, John Laurence 1950-
WhoMW 93
Donaldson, John Riley 1925- *WhoWest 94*
Donaldson, John Weber 1926-
WhoAmP 93
Donaldson, John William 1941-
WhoAmP 93
Donaldson, Laura Elizabeth 1947-
WhoMW 93
Donaldson, Lauren R. 1903- *WhoAm 94*
Donaldson, Leigh *DrAPF 93*
Donaldson, Leon Matthew 1933-
WhoBlA 94
Donaldson, Leslie Allan 1958-
WhoWest 94
Donaldson, Leslie Anne 1955-
WhoWest 94
Donaldson, Linda Margaret 1941-
WhoAmP 93
Donaldson, Loraine *ConAu 140*
Donaldson, Mary *Who 94*
Donaldson, (Dorothy) Mary 1921-
IntWW 93, Who 94
Donaldson, Mary Kendrick 1937-
WhoWest 94
Donaldson, Merle Richard 1920-
WhoAm 94
Donaldson, Michael Cleaves 1939-
WhoAmL 94, WhoAmP 93
Donaldson, Michael Phillips 1943-
Who 94
Donaldson, Michael Porter 1962-
WhoAmL 94

Donofrio, Richard Michael 1938- WhoFI 94
D'Onofrio, Steven John 1956-
D'Onofrio, Vincent Phillip 1960- IntMPA 94, WhoHol 92
Donoghue, Denis 1928- IntWW 93, Who 94, WrDr 94
Donoghue, John F. 1928- WhoAm 94
Donoghue, John P. 1957- WhoAmP 93
Donoghue, Mildred R(ansdorf) 1929- WrDr 94
Donoghue, Mildred Ransdorf WhoAm 94
Donoghue, Norman E., II 1944- WhoAm 94, WhoAmL 94
Donoghue, Richard S. 1943- WhoAmL 94
Donoho, Carolyn Staples 1949- WhoFI 94
Donoho, Laurel Roberta 1952- WhoScEn 94
Donohoe, Tim Mark 1955- WhoFI 94
Donohoe, Amanda WhoHol 92
Donohoe, Amanda 1963?- ConTFT 11
Donohoe, Brian Harold 1948- Who 94
Donohoe, Jerome Francis 1939- WhoAm 94, WhoAmL 94
Donohoe, Peter 1953- IntWW 93
Donohoe, Peter Howard 1953- Who 94
Donohoe, Robert James 1956- WhoScEn 94
Donohoe, Victoria WhoAmA 93
Donohue, Brian E. 1951- WhoAmL 94
Donohue, Carroll John 1917- WhoAm 94, WhoAmL 94, WhoFI 94, WhoMW 93
Donohue, Gail ConAu 140
Donohue, George L. 1944- WhoAm 94, WhoWest 94
Donohue, Gerald Joseph, Jr. 1959- WhoMW 93
Donohue, Hubert Francis 1921- WhoAmP 93
Donohue, Jack d1984 WhoHol 92
Donohue, James J. 1947- WhoAm 94
Donohue, James Patrick 1950- WhoAm 94, WhoAmL 94
Donohue, Jill 1940- WhoHol 92
Donohue, John Joseph 1923- WhoAmP 93
Donohue, Marc David 1951- WhoAm 94, WhoScEn 94
Donohue, Michael Joseph WhoAmL 94
Donohue, P. Daniel 1949- WhoAmL 94
Donohue, Patricia Jean 1947- WhoWest 94
Donohue, Thomas Joseph 1938- WhoAm 94, WhoFI 94
Donohugh, Donald Lee 1924- WhoScEn 94, WhoWest 94
Donop, Carl Emil Kurt von 1740-1777 WhAmRev
Donop, Karl Armilius Kurt von 1740-1777 AmRev
Donoso (Yanez), Jose 1924- ConWorW 93, RfGShF
Donoso, Alvaro 1951- IntWW 93
Donoso, Jose 1924- HispLC [port], IntWW 93
Donoughmore, Earl of 1927- Who 94
Donoughue, Baron 1934- Who 94
Donoughue, Bernard 1934- WrDr 94
Donovan 1946- WhoHol 92
Donovan, Alan Barton 1937- WhoAm 94
Donovan, Allen Francis 1914- WhoAm 94
Donovan, Ann 1955?- BasBi
Donovan, Arlene IntMPA 94
Donovan, Art ProFbHF
Donovan, Arthur WhoHol 92
Donovan, Bernard Timothy 1940- WhoAmP 93
Donovan, Brian Joseph 1953- WhoFI 94, WhoScEn 94
Donovan, Bruce Elliot 1937- WhoAm 94
Donovan, C. Steven 1951- WhoAmL 94
Donovan, Carol A. WhoAmP 93
Donovan, Charles Edward 1934- Who 94
Donovan, Charles J. 1938- WhoAmP 93
Donovan, Charles Stephen 1951- WhoAmL 94, WhoWest 94
Donovan, Christopher G. WhoAmP 93
Donovan, Daniel J. 1958- WhoIns 94
Donovan, Desmond Thomas 1921- Who 94
Donovan, Diane C. DrAPF 93
Donovan, Dick EncSF 93
Donovan, Donna Mae 1952- WhoAm 94
Donovan, Eddie 1921- BasBi
Donovan, Francis X. 1912- WhoAmP 93
Donovan, George Joseph 1935- WhoAm 94
Donovan, Gerald Alton 1925- WhoAm 94
Donovan, Hedley Williams 1914-1990 WhAm 10
Donovan, Henry B. IntMPA 94
Donovan, Herbert Alcorn, Jr. 1931- WhoAm 94
Donovan, Ian Edward 1940- Who 94
Donovan, James Patrick 1945- WhoAmL 94
Donovan, James Robert 1932- WhoAm 94

Donovan, Jane Fagan 1929- WhoAmL 94
Donovan, Jason WhoHol 92
Donovan, John 1928-1992 TwCYAW, WrDr 94N
Donovan, John Arthur 1942- WhoAm 94, WhoAmL 94, WhoWest 94
Donovan, John Edward 1949- WhoScEn 94
Donovan, John Joseph, Jr. 1916- WhoFI 94, WhoWest 94
Donovan, Kathleen 1952- WhoAmP 93
Donovan, King d1987 WhoHol 92
Donovan, Kreag 1933- WhoAm 94
Donovan, Laurie B. 1932- WhoAmP 93
Donovan, Lawrence 1952- WhoScEn 94
Donovan, Leslie, Sr. WhoAmP 93
Donovan, Margaret 1950- WhoMW 93
Donovan, Margaret Mary 1911- WhoAmP 93
Donovan, Marjorie Elizabeth 1946- WhoMW 93
Donovan, Mary Marcia 1936- WhoMW 93
Donovan, Maurice John 1954- WhoAmL 94
Donovan, Michael Joseph 1948- WhoAmL 94
Donovan, Michael Patrick WhoHol 92
Donovan, Michael Richard 1952- WhoWest 94
Donovan, Patricia Hasselhorn 1927- WhoMW 93
Donovan, Paul 1947- WhoAm 94, WhoFI 94
Donovan, Paul Joseph 1951- WhoAmL 94
Donovan, Paul V. 1924- WhoAm 94, WhoMW 93
Donovan, R. Michael 1943- WhoAm 94
Donovan, Raymond J. 1930- IntWW 93, WhoAmP 93
Donovan, Richard Edward 1952- WhoAmL 94
Donovan, Robert Alan 1921- WhoAm 94
Donovan, Robert H. 1957- WhoFI 94
Donovan, Robert J(ohn) 1912- ConAu 41NR
Donovan, Robert John 1912- WhoAm 94
Donovan, Stephan Michael 1950- WhoMW 93
Donovan, Stephen James 1951- WhoScEn 94
Donovan, Stephen Patrick, Jr. 1941- WhoFI 94
Donovan, Steven Robert 1941- WhoWest 94
Donovan, Tate WhoHol 92
Donovan, Tate 1964- IntMPA 94
Donovan, Terence WhoHol 92
Donovan, Terence Daniel 1936- Who 94
Donovan, Thomas B. 1942- WhoAm 94, WhoAmL 94
Donovan, Thomas Roy 1937- WhoAm 94, WhoFI 94
Donovan, Timothy Matthew 1952- WhoAmL 94
Donovan, Timothy Paul 1927-1990 WhAm 10
Donovan, Vergene 1924- WhoAmP 93
Donovan, Walt 1926- WhoAmP 93
Donovan, Walter Edgar 1926- WhoAm 94, WhoWest 94
Donovan, Warde d1988 WhoHol 92
Donovon, Patricia J. 1947- WhoAmP 93
Donsbach, Frank Joseph 1943- WhoFI 94
Donskoi, Mark d1981 WhoHol 92
Donskoy, Dimitri Michailovitch 1955- WhoScEn 94
Donson, Cyril EncSF 93
Donson, G. Jack, Jr. 1946- WhoAmL 94
DonTigny, Richard Louis 1931- WhoWest 94
Don-Wauchope, Roger Hamilton Who 94
Donze, Jerry Lynn 1943- WhoWest 94
Donzella, Niccolo DrAPF 93
Donzelli, Domenico 1790-1873 NewGrDO
Doo, Jack P., Jr. 1953- WhoAsA 94
Doo, Leigh-Wai 1946- WhoAmP 93, WhoAsA 94
Doo, Yi-Chung 1954- WhoScEn 94
Doob, Joseph Leo 1910- IntWW 93, WhoAm 94, WhoMW 93
Doob, Leonard W. 1909- IntWW 93, WrDr 94
Doob, Leonard William 1909- WhoAm 94
Doo Da Post, III 1949- WhoAmA 93
Doody, Agnes G. WhoFI 94
Doody, Alison 1965- WhoHol 92
Doody, Alton Frederick 1934- WhoFI 94, WhoMW 93
Doody, Daniel Patrick 1952- WhoScEn 94
Doody, Margaret Anne 1939- IntWW 93, WhoAm 94
Dooge, James Clement Ignatius 1922- IntWW 93, Who 94
Doohan, James 1920- IntMPA 94, WhoHol 92
Doo Kingue, Michel 1934- IntWW 93
Dookun, Dewoonarain 1929- Who 94
Doolan, Toby d1946 WhoHol 92

Dooley, Ann Elizabeth 1952- WhoAm 94
Dooley, Arch Richard 1925- WhoAm 94
Dooley, Billy d1938 WhoHol 92
Dooley, Calvin 1954- WhoAmP 93
Dooley, Calvin M. 1954- CngDr 93
Dooley, Calvin Millard 1954- WhoAm 94, WhoWest 94
Dooley, Dan 1948- WhoIns 94
Dooley, Deborah Ann 1962- WhoFI 94
Dooley, Delmer John 1920- WhoAm 94
Dooley, Dennis James 1955- WhoFI 94
Dooley, Donald John 1921- WhoAm 94
Dooley, George Elijah 1918- WhoAm 94
Dooley, Gordon d1930 WhoHol 92
Dooley, Helen Bertha 1907- WhoAmA 93
Dooley, J. Gordon 1935- WhoFI 94, WhoMW 93
Dooley, Jed d1973 WhoHol 92
Dooley, Jo Ann Catherine 1930- WhoMW 93
Dooley, John A. 1944- WhoAmP 93
Dooley, John Augustine, III 1944- WhoAmL 94
Dooley, Johnny d1928 WhoHol 92
Dooley, Joseph T. 1944- WhoIns 94
Dooley, Kevin C. 1952- WhoAmL 94
Dooley, Norah 1953- SmATA 74 [port]
Dooley, Patrick Kiaran 1942- WhoAm 94
Dooley, Paul 1928- IntMPA 94, WhoHol 92, WrDr 94
Dooley, Ray d1984 WhoHol 92
Dooley, Richard M. 1943- WhoAmL 94
Dooley, Sue Ann WhoFI 94
Dooley, Vincent Joseph 1932- WhoAm 94
Dooley, Wallace Troy 1917- WhoBlA 94
Dooley, William 1932- NewGrDO
Doolin, James Lawrence 1932- WhoAmA 93
Doolin, John B. 1918- WhoAm 94
Dooling, John E., Jr. 1952- WhoAmL 94
Dooling, Lucinda WhoHol 92
Doolittle, Amos 1754-1832 WhAmRev
Doolittle, Arthur K(ing) 1896- WhAm 10
Doolittle, Hilda d1961 WhoHol 92
Doolittle, Hilda 1886-1961 BlmGEL, GayLL
Doolittle, James H. WhoFI 94
Doolittle, James H. d1993 Who 94N
Doolittle, James H. 1896- IntWW 93, Who 94
Doolittle, James H. 1896-1993 NewYTBS 93 [port]
Doolittle, Jesse William, Jr. 1929- WhoAm 94
Doolittle, John 1950- WhoAmP 93
Doolittle, John T. 1950- CngDr 93
Doolittle, John Taylor 1950- WhoAm 94, WhoWest 94
Doolittle, Michael Jim 1956- WhoAmL 94
Doolittle, Quenten 1925- NewGrDO
Doolittle, Robert Frederick 1902- WhoAm 94
Doolittle, Russell Francis 1931- WhoAm 94, WhoWest 94
Doolittle, Sidney Newing 1934- WhoAm 94
Doolittle, Timothy Norris 1961- WhoMW 93
Doolittle, William Hotchkiss 1929- WhoAm 94
Doolittle, William Lawrence 1959- WhoWest 94
Dooly, John d1780 AmRev
Doomes, Earl 1943- WhoBlA 94
Doon, Roger Hugh 1938- WhoIns 94
Doonan, George d1973 WhoHol 92
Doonan, Patric d1958 WhoHol 92
Dooner, John Joseph, Jr. 1948- WhoAm 94, WhoFI 94
Dooner, Pierton W. 1844-1907? EncSF 93
Doonkeen, William 1933- WhoHisp 94
Doordan, Dennis Paul 1951- WhoMW 93
Doorenbos, Clinger d1978 WhoHol 92
Doorish, John Francis 1957- WhoScEn 94
Doorley, Thomas Lawrence, III 1944- WhoAm 94
Doory, Ann Marie 1954- WhoAmP 93
Doory, Robert Leonard, Jr. 1948- WhoAm 94, WhoMW 93
Dooskin, Herbert P. 1941- WhoAm 94
Doot, Carl Lee 1950- WhoFI 94
Doot, Timothy Allan 1957- WhoWest 94
Dopf, Glenn William 1953- WhoAmL 94
Dopheide, Fred J. 1924- WhoIns 94
Doppelt, Earl H. WhoFI 94
Dopper, Cornelis 1870-1939 NewGrDO
Doppler, Christian Johann 1803-1853 WorScD
Doppler, (Albert) Franz 1821-1883 NewGrDO

Doran, Ann 1911- WhoHol 92
Doran, Carrie d1977 WhoHol 92
Doran, Charles d1964 WhoHol 92
Doran, Charles Edward 1928- WhoAm 94, WhoFI 94
Doran, Christopher Miller 1946- WhoWest 94
Doran, Frank 1949- Who 94
Doran, George C., Sr. WhoFI 94
Doran, James Marion, Jr. 1943- WhoAmL 94
Doran, James Martin 1933- WhoAm 94
Doran, John Frederick 1916- Who 94
Doran, Johnny WhoHol 92
Doran, Lindsay IntMPA 94
Doran, Mark Richard 1954- WhoFI 94
Doran, Maureen O'Keefe 1947- WhoAm 94
Doran, Michael 1958- WhoAmL 94
Doran, Robert Stuart 1937- WhoAm 94, WhoScEn 94
Doran, Stephen William 1956- WhoAmP 93
Doran, Thomas E. 1944- WhoAm 94, WhoAmL 94
Doran, Vincent James 1917- WhoWest 94
Doran, William Michael 1940- WhoAm 94, WhoAmL 94
Dorantes, Ruth E. 1955- WhoHisp 94
Dorati, Antal 1906-1988 NewGrDO
Dorato, Peter 1932- WhoAm 94
Doray, Andrea Wesley 1956- WhoWest 94
Doray, Audrey Capel 1931- WhoAmA 93
Dorazio 1927- IntWW 93
D'Orbigny, Alcide-Charles-Victor Dessalines WhWE
Dorbin, Janet B. 1939- WhoAmP 93
Dorcas, William Gary 1949- WhoFI 94
Dorcey, Mary 1950- BlmGWL
Dorchester, Area Bishop of 1943- Who 94
Dorchester, Lord WhAmRev
Dordal, Erl 1927- WhoAm 94
Dordal, Peter Lars 1957- WhoMW 93
Dordelman, William Forsyth 1940- WhoAm 94
D'Ordonez, Carlo NewGrDO
Dore, Adrienne 1910- WhoHol 92
Dore, Alexander 1923- WhoHol 92
Dore, Bonny Ellen 1947- WhoAm 94
Dore, Edna WhoHol 92
Dore, Fred H. 1925- WhoAmP 93
Dore, Fred Hudson 1925- WhoAm 94, WhoAmL 94, WhoWest 94
Dore, James Francis 1946- WhoAm 94
Dore, Jean WhoAm 94
Dore, Michael 1950- WhoAm 94, WhoAmL 94
Dore, Roland 1938- WhoScEn 94
Dore, Ronald Philip 1925- IntWW 93, Who 94
Dore, Russell Lee 1937- WhoMW 93
Dore, Stephen Edward, Jr. 1918- WhoAm 94
Dore, Susan E. WhoAmP 93
Dorelli, Johnny WhoHol 92
Doremus, Ogden 1921- WhoAm 94, WhoAmL 94
Doremus, Robert Heward 1928- WhoAm 94, WhoScEn 94
Doren, A(rnold T.) 1935- WhoAmA 93
Doren, Henry J. T. 1929- WhoAmA 93
Dorenfest, Sheldon I. 1935- WhoFI 94, WhoMW 93
Dorer, Frances (Catherine) EncSF 93
Dorer, Fred Harold 1936- WhoAm 94, WhoWest 94
Dorer, Nancy (Jane) EncSF 93
Doreski, William DrAPF 93
Doret, David Maris 1946- WhoAmL 94
Doret, Gustave 1866-1943 NewGrDO
Doret, Michel R. DrAPF 93
Dorethy, Rex E. 1938- WhoAmA 93
Dorey, Graham Martyn 1932- Who 94
Dorf, Carol DrAPF 93
Dorf, Jerome 1936- WhoFI 94
Dorf, Michael C. 1964- WrDr 94
Dorf, Philip d1993 NewYTBS 93
Dorf, Richard Carl 1933- WhoAm 94
Dorf, Robert L. 1949- WhoAm 94
Dorfer, Ingemar (Nils Hans) 1939- WrDr 94
Dorff, Eugene Joseph 1930- WhoAmP 93
Dorff, Gerald J. 1938- WhoScEn 94
Dorff, Stephen WhoHol 92
Dorff, Steven Douglas 1955- WhoMW 93
Dorffi, William Edward 1932- WhoFI 94
Dorfi, Klaus G. 1942- WhoIns 94
Dorfman, Allen Bernard 1930- WhoAm 94
Dorfman, Ariel WhoHol 92
Dorfman, Ariel 1942- ConLC 77 [port], ConWorW 93, HispLC [port], WrDr 94
Dorfman, Bruce 1936- WhoAmA 93
Dorfman, Donald E. 1947- WhoAmL 94
Dorfman, Elsa 1937- WhoAmA 93
Dorfman, Fred 1946- WhoAmA 93
Dorfman, Henry S. 1922- WhoAm 94, WhoFI 94

Dorfman, Joel Marvin 1951- *WhoAm 94*
Dorfman, John Charles 1925- *WhoAm 94, WhoAmL 94*
Dorfman, Joseph 1904-1991 *WhAm 10*
Dorfman, Martin Stanley 1945- *WhoAmL 94*
Dorfman, Robert 1916- *WhoAm 94*
Dorfman, Steven David 1935- *WhoAm 94, WhoWest 94*
Dorfzaun, Richard S. 1943- *WhoAmL 94*
Dorgan, Byron L. 1942- *CngDr 93, WhoAmP 93*
Dorgan, Byron Leslie 1942- *IntWW 93, WhoAm 94, WhoMW 93*
Dorgay, Charles Kenneth 1956- *WhoScEn 94*
D'Orgaz, Elena d1947 *WhoHol 92*
Doria, Anthony Notarnicola 1927- *WhoAm 94, WhoAmL 94*
Doria, Charles *DrAPF 93*
Doria, Faye Kathryn 1953- *WhoFI 94*
Doria, Joseph V., Jr. 1946- *WhoAmP 93*
Dorian, Angela *WhoHol 92*
Dorian, Charles d1942 *WhoHol 92*
Dorian, Ernest d1969 *WhoHol 92*
Dorian, Harry Aram 1928- *WhoAm 94*
Dorian, Nancy Currier 1936- *WhoAm 94*
Dorian, Nancy Marilyn 1933- *WhoMW 93*
Doriani, Beth Maclay 1961- *WhoMW 93*
Doriani, Daniel Muldoon 1953- *WhoMW 93*
Dorin, Bernard J. 1929- *IntWW 93*
Dorin, Bernard Jean Robert 1929- *Who 94*
Dorin, Francoise Andree Renee 1928- *IntWW 93*
Dorio, Martin Matthew 1945- *WhoFI 94, WhoMW 93*
Dorion, Marie 1786-c. 1853 *WhWE*
Dorion, Pierre, Sr. c. 1750-c. 1820 *WhWE*
Dorion, Pierre, Jr. d1814 *WhWE*
Dorion, Robert Charles 1926- *WhoFI 94*
Doris, Alan Sanford 1947- *WhoAm 94, WhoAmL 94*
Doris, Francis D. *WhoAmP 93*
Doris, Peter A. 1956- *WhoScEn 94*
Doris Ann 1917- *WhoAm 94*
Dorius, Earl Fredric 1947- *WhoWest 94*
Dorius, Kermit Parrish 1926- *WhoAm 94*
Dorival, Bernard 1914- *IntWW 93*
Dorkey, Charles Edward, III 1948- *WhoFI 94*
Dorkin, Frederic Eugene 1932- *WhoAm 94*
Dorking, Archdeacon of *Who 94*
Dorking, Suffragan Bishop of 1930- *Who 94*
Dorko, Ernest Alexander 1936- *WhoScEn 94*
Dorland, Dodge Oatwell 1948- *WhoAm 94, WhoFI 94*
Dorland, Frank Norton 1914- *WhoWest 94*
Dorleac, Catherine 1943- *WhoAm 94*
Dorleac, Francoise d1967 *WhoHol 92*
Dorleac, Jean-Pierre *ConTFT 11*
Dorler, Ronald *WhoAmP 93*
Dorlhac De Borne, Helene 1935- *WhoWomW 91*
Dorman, Mrs. *NewGrDO*
Dorman, Albert A. 1926- *WhoAm 94, WhoWest 94*
Dorman, Arthur 1926- *WhoAmP 93*
Dorman, Charles (Geoffrey) 1920- *Who 94*
Dorman, Craig Emery 1940- *WhoAm 94, WhoScEn 94*
Dorman, Harry Gaylord, III 1943- *WhoAm 94*
Dorman, Hattie L. 1932- *WhoBlA 94*
Dorman, Henry 1916- *WhoAmP 93*
Dorman, J. Michael 1950- *WhoAmL 94*
Dorman, Jeffrey Lawrence 1949- *WhoAm 94*
Dorman, John Frederick 1928- *WhoAm 94*
Dorman, Linneaus C. 1935- *WhoBlA 94*
Dorman, Linneaus Cuthbert 1935- *WhoAm 94*
Dorman, Luke *ConAu 42NR*
Dorman, Maurice Henry 1912- *IntWW 93, Who 94*
Dorman, Michael L 1932- *WrDr 94*
Dorman, Rex Lee 1934- *WhoFI 94*
Dorman, Richard Bostock 1925- *Who 94*
Dorman, Richard Frederick, Jr. 1944- *WhoAm 94*
Dorman, Richard W. 1948- *WhoIns 94*
Dorman, Sonya (Hess) 1924- *EncSF 93, WrDr 94*
Dorman, Thomas Patrick 1950- *WhoWest 94*
Dormand *Who 94*
Dormand Of Easington, Baron 1919- *Who 94*
Dormandy, John Adam 1937- *IntWW 93*
Dormanen, Tammy Lynn 1966- *WhoMW 93*
Dormann, Henry O. 1932- *WhoAm 94, WhoFI 94*
Dormann, Rosemarie 1947- *WhoWomW 91*
Dormer, Baron 1914- *Who 94*
Dormer, James Thomas 1934- *WhoWest 94*
D'Ormeville, Carlo 1840-1924 *NewGrDO*
Dorminey, Elizabeth Kline 1956- *WhoAmL 94*
Dormire, Corwin Brooke 1942- *WhoAm 94, WhoAmL 94*
Dormitzer, Henry, II 1935- *WhoAm 94*
Dorn, Alfred *DrAPF 93*
Dorn, Charles Meeker 1927- *WhoAm 94*
Dorn, Dieter 1935- *IntWW 93*
Dorn, Dolores *WhoAm 94*
Dorn, Dolores 1934- *WhoHol 92*
Dorn, Ed(ward Merton) 1929- *WrDr 94*
Dorn, Edward *DrAPF 93*
Dorn, Edward (Merton) 1929- *ConAu 42NR*
Dorn, Edward Harvey 1952- *WhoMW 93*
Dorn, Edward Merton 1929- *WhoAm 94, WhoWest 94*
Dorn, Frank *EncSF 93*
Dorn, Heinrich Ludwig Egmont 1804-1892 *NewGrDO*
Dorn, James Andrew 1945- *WhoAm 94*
Dorn, Jennifer Lynn 1950- *WhoAm 94*
Dorn, John W. 1943- *WhoAmP 93*
Dorn, Joseph W. 1948- *WhoAmL 94*
Dorn, Marian Margaret 1931- *WhoWest 94*
Dorn, Peter Klaus 1932- *WhoAmA 93*
Dorn, Philip d1975 *WhoHol 92*
Dorn, Randy *WhoAmP 93*
Dorn, Robert Murray 1921- *WhoAm 94*
Dorn, Roosevelt F. 1935- *WhoAmL 94, WhoBlA 94*
Dorn, Ruth (Dornbush) 1925- *WhoAmA 93*
Dorn, Wanda Faye 1945- *WhoAm 94*
Dorn, William Jennings Bryan 1916- *WhoAmP 93*
Dornacker, Jane d1986 *WhoHol 92*
Dornan, James Jeffrey 1961- *WhoFI 94*
Dornan, Robert *WhoHol 92*
Dornan, Robert K. 1933- *CngDr 93, WhoAmP 93*
Dornan, Robert Kenneth 1933- *WhoAm 94, WhoWest 94*
Dornan, Wayne Allen 1953- *WhoMW 93*
Dornberg, John 1931- *WrDr 94*
Dornburg, Ralph Christoph 1952- *WhoScEn 94*
Dornburgh, William Walter 1931- *WhoAm 94*
Dornbusch, Arthur A., II 1943- *WhoAm 94, WhoAmL 94*
Dornbusch, Rudiger 1942- *IntWW 93, WhoAm 94*
Dornbusch, Sanford Maurice 1926 *WhoAm 94, WhoWest 94*
Dornbush, Vicky Jean 1951- *WhoWest 94*
Dorne, David J. 1946- *WhoAmL 94*
Dorne, Sandra 1925- *WhoHol 92*
Dorneman, Robert Wayne 1949- *WhoFI 94, WhoWest 94*
Dorner, Alexander 1893- *WhoAmA 93N*
Dorner, Douglas Bloom 1941- *WhoMW 93*
Dorner, Marjorie 1942- *WrDr 94*
Dorner, Peter Paul 1925- *WhoAm 94*
Dorner, Robert W. 1924- *WhoMW 93*
Dornette, Ralph Meredith 1927- *WhoWest 94*
Dornette, William Stuart 1951- *WhoAm 94, WhoAmL 94*
Dornfeld, David A. 1949- *WhoScEn 94*
Dornfeld, James Lee 1954- *WhoIns 94*
Dornfeld, Sharon Wicks 1952- *WhoAmL 94*
Dornhelm, Marilyn Celia 1945- *WhoWest 94*
Dornhorst, Antony Clifford 1915- *Who 94*
Dornin, Christopher *DrAPF 93*
Dorning, John Joseph 1938- *WhoAm 94, WhoScEn 94*
Dorning, Robert d1989 *WhoHol 92*
Dorning, Stacy 1958- *WhoHol 92*
Doro, Marie d1956 *WhoHol 92*
Doro, Marion Elizabeth 1928- *WhoAm 94*
Dorocke, Lawrence Francis 1946- *WhoAmL 94*
Dorodnitsyin, Anatoliy Alekseyevich 1910- *IntWW 93*
Dorokhin, Nikolai d1953 *WhoHol 92*
Doron, Harvey Haldiman 1926- *WhoFI 94*
Doron, Mary Ellen 1946- *WhoMW 93*
Doron, Sarah 1925- *WhoWomW 91*
Doronina, Tatyana Vasiliyevna 1933- *IntWW 93*
Doronzo, John Fred 1958- *WhoMW 93*
Dorosh, Daria 1943- *WhoAmA 93*
Doroshkin, Milton 1914- *WrDr 94*
Doroszkiewicz, Bazyli 1914- *IntWW 93*
Dorothy, Vogel, Mrs. 1935- *See* Vogel, Herbert, Mr. 1922- & Dorothy, Vogel, Mrs. 1935- *WhoAmA 93*
Dorough, H. Wyman 1936- *WhoAm 94*
Dorpat, Theodore Lorenz 1925- *WhoAm 94*
Dorr, Donald W. 1939- *WhoAmP 93*
Dorr, James P. 1944- *WhoAmL 94*
Dorr, Janet Kay 1943- *WhoAmP 93*
Dorr, John d1993 *NewYTBS 93*
Dorr, Lester d1980 *WhoHol 92*
Dorr, (Virginia) Nell 1893- *WhoAmA 93N*
Dorr, Noel 1933- *IntWW 93, Who 94*
Dorr, Ralze Wheeler 1929- *WhoAm 94*
Dorr, Robert Charles 1946- *WhoAmL 94*
Dorr, Robert Thomas 1951- *WhoWest 94*
Dorr, Sandra *DrAPF 93*
Dorr, Williams Peter 1944- *WhoAm 94, WhoAmL 94*
Dorra, Henri 1924- *WhoAmA 93*
Dorrance, John Thompson, Jr. 1919-1989 *WhAm 10*
Dorrance, Richard Christopher 1948- *Who 94*
Dorree, Bobbie d1974 *WhoHol 92*
Dorrell, Ernest John 1915- *Who 94*
Dorrell, Stephen James 1952- *Who 94*
Dorrell, Vernon Andrew 1932- *WhoScEn 94*
Dorrenbacher, Carl James 1928- *WhoAm 94, WhoFI 94*
Dorrian, John *WhoAmP 93*
Dorrien, Carlos Guillermo 1948- *WhoAmA 93*
Dorrien, Gary J. 1952- *WrDr 94*
Dorrier, Lindsay Gordon, Jr. 1943- *WhoAmL 94, WhoAmP 93*
Dorrill, William Franklin 1931- *WhoAm 94*
Dorrington, Albert 1871- *EncSF 93*
Dorris, Michael (Anthony) 1945- *SmATA 75 [port], WrDr 94*
Dorris, Michael A. *SmATA 75*
Dorris, Michael Anthony 1945- *TwCYAW, WhoAm 94*
Dorris, Sheila Robin 1956- *WhoMW 93*
Dorris, William E. 1955- *WhoAmL 94*
Dorris, Wilton Howard 1930- *WhoAmP 93*
Dorritie, John Francis 1934-1991 *WhAm 10*
Dorros, Irwin 1929- *WhoAm 94, WhoScEn 94*
Dorrycott, Joyce Whigham 1930- *WhoAmP 93*
Dors, Diana d1984 *WhoHol 92*
Dorsay, Edmund d1959 *WhoHol 92*
D'Orsay, Fifi d1983 *WhoHol 92*
D'Orsay, Lawrence d1931 *WhoHol 92*
Dorse, Bernice Perry 1931- *WhoBlA 94*
Dorsen, David Milton 1935- *WhoAmL 94*
Dorsen, Norman 1930- *WhoAm 94, WrDr 94*
Dorset, Archdeacon of *Who 94*
Dorset, Earl of 1638-1706 *BlmGEL*
Dorset, Lord *BlmGEL*
Dorset, Phyllis (Flanders) 1924- *WrDr 94*
Dorset and Middlesex, Earl of 1643-1706 *DcLB 131 [port]*
Dorsett, Burt 1930- *WhoFI 94*
Dorsett, Charles Barclay, Sr. 1927- *WhoWest 94*
Dorsett, Charles Irvin 1945- *WhoScEn 94*
Dorsett, Danielle 1915- *WrDr 94*
Dorsett, Katie G. 1932- *WhoAmP 93*
Dorsett, Katie Grays 1932- *WhoBlA 94*
Dorsett, Thomas A. *DrAPF 93*
Dorsett, Tony Drew 1954- *WhoBlA 94*
Dorsey, Arnold George 1936- *WhoAm 94*
Dorsey, Candas Jane 1952- *EncSF 93*
Dorsey, Carolyn Ann *WhoBlA 94*
Dorsey, Charles Henry, Jr. 1930- *WhoBlA 94*
Dorsey, Clinton George 1931- *WhoBlA 94*
Dorsey, Deborah Worthington *WhoAmA 93*
Dorsey, Denise 1953- *WhoBlA 94*
Dorsey, Dolores Florence 1928- *WhoAm 94*
Dorsey, Edmund d1959 *WhoHol 92*
Dorsey, Elbert 1941- *WhoBlA 94*
Dorsey, Eric Hall 1964- *WhoBlA 94*
Dorsey, Eugene Carroll 1927- *WhoAm 94, WhoFI 94*
Dorsey, Francis Edward 1931- *WhoAmL 94*
Dorsey, Frank James 1930- *WhoAm 94*
Dorsey, Gray Lankford 1918- *WhoAm 94, WhoMW 93*
Dorsey, Harold Aaron 1933- *WhoBlA 94*
Dorsey, Helen Danner 1928- *WhoAm 94*
Dorsey, Herman Sherwood, Jr. 1945- *WhoBlA 94*
Dorsey, Ivory Jean 1947- *WhoBlA 94*
Dorsey, James Baker 1927- *WhoAmL 94, WhoScEn 94*
Dorsey, James E. 1940- *WhoAmL 94*
Dorsey, James Francis, Jr. 1934- *WhoAm 94*
Dorsey, James Owen 1848-1895 *EncNAR*
Dorsey, James R. 1944- *WhoAmL 94*
Dorsey, Jeremiah Edmund 1944- *WhoFI 94*
Dorsey, Jimmy d1957 *WhoHol 92*
Dorsey, John H. 1937- *WhoAmP 93*
Dorsey, John L. 1935- *WhoBlA 94*
Dorsey, John Russell 1938- *WhoAm 94*
Dorsey, John Wesley, Jr. 1936- *WhoAm 94*
Dorsey, Joseph *WhoHol 92*
Dorsey, Joseph A. 1932- *WhoBlA 94*
Dorsey, Julie Ann 1961- *WhoWest 94*
Dorsey, L. C. 1938- *WhoBlA 94*
Dorsey, Laurens 1925- *WhoAm 94*
Dorsey, Leon D., Sr. 1909- *WhoBlA 94*
Dorsey, Lucia Iannone 1959- *WhoAmA 93*
Dorsey, Marc G. 1959- *WhoAmL 94*
Dorsey, Michael A. 1949- *WhoAmA 93*
Dorsey, Michael Dean 1959- *WhoMW 93*
Dorsey, Norbert M. 1929- *WhoAm 94*
Dorsey, Peter 1922- *WhoAm 94*
Dorsey, Peter Collins 1931- *WhoAm 94, WhoAmL 94*
Dorsey, Rhoda Mary 1927- *WhoAm 94*
Dorsey, Richard P., III 1959- *WhoAmP 93*
Dorsey, Robert Burgess 1932- *WhoFI 94*
Dorsey, Thomas A. d1993 *NewYTBS 93 [port]*
Dorsey, Thomas A. 1899-1993 *ConMus 11 [port], News 93-3, WhoBlA 94N*
Dorsey, Tommy d1956 *WhoHol 92*
Dorsey, Valerie Lynn 1961- *WhoBlA 94*
Dorsey, William Oscar Parks, III 1948- *WhoMW 93*
Dorsey, William Walter 1934- *WhoScEn 94*
Dorsey-Wong, Kathleen M. 1954- *WhoMW 93*
Dorsi, Stephen Nathan 1947- *WhoAmL 94*
D'Orsi, Umberto d1976 *WhoHol 92*
Dorsky, Alvin H. 1928- *WhoAm 94*
Dorsky, Morris 1918- *WhoAmA 93*
Dorsky, Samuel 1914- *WhoAmA 93*
Dorso, John M. 1943- *WhoAmP 93*
Dorst, Claire V. 1922- *WhoAmA 93*
Dorst, Howard Earl 1904- *WhoScEn 94, WhoWest 94*
Dorst, Jean P(ierre) 1924- *IntWW 93*
Dorst, John Phillips 1926- *WhoAm 94*
Dorst, Mary Crowe *WhoAmA 93*
Dorst, Neal Martin 1955- *WhoScEn 94*
Dorst, Stanley Elwood 1897- *WhAm 10*
Dorst, Tankred 1925- *IntDcT 2, IntWW 93*
Dortch, Carl Raymond 1914- *WhoAm 94*
Dortch, Clarence, III 1962- *WhoAmL 94*
Dortch, H. Wayne 1931- *WhoIns 94*
Dortch, Heyward 1939- *WhoMW 93*
Dortch, Thomas Wesley, Jr. 1950- *WhoBlA 94*
Dorton, David R. 1953- *WhoAmL 94*
Dortort, David 1916- *IntMPA 94*
Dorus-Gras, Julie(-Aimee-Josephe) 1805-1896 *NewGrDO [port]*
Dorville d1941 *WhoHol 92*
D'Orville, Albert *WhWE*
Dorvillier, William J. d1993 *NewYTBS 93 [port]*
Dorward, Judith A. 1941- *WhoFI 94*
Dorward, William 1929- *Who 94*
Dorwart, Brian Curtis 1949- *WhoScEn 94*
Dorwart, Donald Bruce 1949- *WhoAm 94, WhoAmL 94*
Dorweiler, Vernon Paul 1931- *WhoAmL 94, WhoMW 93*
Dorwick, Keith 1957- *WhoMW 93*
Dorziat, Gabrielle d1979 *WhoHol 92*
Dosamantes, Susana *WhoHol 92*
Dosanjh, Darshan Singh 1921- *WhoAm 94*
Doscher, Doris d1970 *WhoHol 92*
Dose, Frederick Philip, Jr. 1946- *WhoMW 93*
Dosek, Edwin Francis 1920- *WhoAmP 93*
Dosher, John Rodney 1936- *WhoAm 94*
Doshi, Balkrishna Vithaldas 1927- *IntWW 93*
Doshi, Bipin N. 1939- *WhoAsA 94*
Doshi, Vinod 1932- *IntWW 93*
Doskocil, Larry 1932- *WhoFI 94*
Dos Passos, John Roderigo 1896-1970 *AmCulL*
Doss, Chriss Herschel 1935- *WhoAmP 93*
Doss, Evan, Jr. 1948- *WhoBlA 94*
Doss, Ezzat Danial 1945- *WhoMW 93, WhoScEn 94*
Doss, James Daniel 1939- *WhoWest 94*
Doss, Juanita King 1942- *WhoBlA 94*
Doss, LaRoy Samuel 1936- *WhoBlA 94*
Doss, Lawrence Paul 1927- *WhoAm 94, WhoBlA 94*
Doss, Margot P(atterson) 1920- *WrDr 94*
Doss, Theresa *WhoBlA 94*

Dos Santos, Alexander Jose Maria 1924- *IntWW 93*
dos Santos, Domitilia M. *WhoFI 94*
Dos Santos, Errol Lionel d1992 *Who 94N*
Dos Santos, Jose Eduardo 1942- *IntWW 93*
dos Santos, Joyce Audy 1949- *WrDr 94*
Dos Santos, Manuel 1944- *IntWW 93*
Dos Santos, Marcelino 1931- *IntWW 93*
Dos Santos, Maria Odete 1941- *WhoWomW 91*
Dosser, Douglas George Maurice 1927- *Who 94*
Dossetor, John Beamish 1925- *WhoAm 94*
Dossett, Chappell d1961 *WhoHol 92*
Dossett, Dorothy Nell Morris 1938- *WhoFI 94*
Dossett, John *WhoHol 92*
Dossett, Lawrence Sherman 1936- *WhoWest 94*
Dossey, Larry *NewYTBS 93 [port]*
Dossey, Richard L. 1937- *WhoAm 94*
Dost, Mohammad 1929- *IntWW 93*
Dostal, Cyril A. *DrAPF 93*
Dostal, Milan Mathias 1929- *WhoAmL 94*
Dostal, Raymond F. 1943- *WhoIns 94*
Dostart, Paul Joseph 1951- *WhoAmL 94, WhoWest 94*
Dostart, Steven Peter 1963- *WhoFI 94*
Doster, Gregory W. 1954- *WhoAmP 93*
Doster, Joseph C. 1928- *WhoAm 94*
Dostoevskii, Fedor (Mikhailovich) 1821-1881 *RfGShF*
Dostoevsky, Fyodor 1821-1881 *NinCLC 43 [port]*
Dostoyevsky, Fyodor Mikhaylovich 1821-1881 *NewGrDO*
Doswald, Herman Kenneth 1932- *WhoAm 94*
Doten, Arthur Louis 1941- *WhoAm 94, WhoAmL 94*
Dothager, Julie Ann 1965- *WhoAm 94*
Doto, Irene Louise 1922- *WhoWest 94*
Doto, Paul Jerome 1917- *WhoFI 94*
Dotrice, Karen 1955- *WhoHol 92*
Dotrice, Michele 1947- *WhoHol 92*
Dotrice, Roy 1923- *WhoHol 92*
Dotrice, Roy 1925- *IntWW 93, Who 94*
Dotsenko, Paul 1894-1988 *ConAu 140*
Dotson, Betty Lou 1930- *WhoBlA 94*
Dotson, Bob 1946- *WrDr 94*
Dotson, Bruce *WhoAmP 93*
Dotson, Daniel Boyd, Jr. 1940- *WhoAmP 93*
Dotson, Donald L. 1938- *WhoAm 94, WhoAmP 93*
Dotson, George Stephen 1940- *WhoAm 94*
Dotson, Gerald Richard 1937- *WhoAm 94, WhoScEn 94, WhoWest 94*
Dotson, John Louis, Jr. 1937- *WhoAm 94*
Dotson, Philip Randolph 1948- *WhoBlA 94*
Dotson, Robert Charles 1946- *WhoAm 94*
Dotson, Rosetta Delores 1936- *WhoAmP 93*
Dotson, William Francis 1915- *WhoAmP 93*
Dotson, William S. 1911- *WhoBlA 94*
Dotson-Williams, Henrietta 1940- *WhoBlA 94*
Dott, Robert Henry, Jr. 1929- *WhoAm 94, WhoScEn 94*
Dotten, Michael Chester 1952- *WhoAm 94, WhoAmL 94*
Dotti, Anna Vincenza fl. 1715-1727 *NewGrDO*
Dottin, Robert Philip 1943- *WhoBlA 94*
Dottin, Roger Allen 1945- *WhoBlA 94*
Dotts, Harold William 1904-1990 *WhAm 10*
Dotts, Maryann J 1933- *WrDr 94*
Doty, Carl K. 1931- *WhoAm 94, WhoFI 94*
Doty, Carolyn *DrAPF 93*
Doty, Dale Douglas 1962- *WhoWest 94*
Doty, David Singleton 1929- *WhoAm 94, WhoAmL 94, WhoMW 93*
Doty, Dawn 1964- *WhoMW 93*
Doty, Donald D. 1928- *WhoAm 94*
Doty, Gene *DrAPF 93*
Doty, George Richard 1928- *WhoAm 94*
Doty, Gordon Leroy 1931- *WhoAm 94*
Doty, Horace Jay, Jr. 1924- *WhoWest 94*
Doty, J.E. 1941- *WhoWest 94*
Doty, James Edward 1922- *WhoAm 94*
Doty, James Robert 1940- *WhoAm 94*
Doty, Karen M. *WhoAmP 93*
Doty, Mark *DrAPF 93*
Doty, Natalie Johnston 1939- *WhoMW 93*
Doty, Paul Mead 1920- *IntWW 93*
Doty, Philip Edward 1943- *WhoAm 94*
Doty, Richard Leroy 1944- *WhoScEn 94*
Doty, Robert Kenneth 1946- *WhoMW 93*
Doty, Robert McIntyre 1933- *WhoAmA 93*
Doty, Robert McIntyre 1933-1992 *WhAm 10*
Doty, Robert Walter 1942- *WhoAm 94*
Doty, Robert William 1920- *WhoAm 94*
Doty, Romeo A. 1938- *WhoBlA 94*
Doty, Shirley L. *WhoAmP 93*
Doty, Weston *WhoHol 92*
Doty, Winston *WhoHol 92*
Dotzenrod, James A. 1946- *WhoAmP 93*
Dotzenrod, Ralph Clarence 1909- *WhoAmP 93*
Doub, Jack Rowland 1943- *WhoMW 93*
Doub, James C. 1947- *WhoAmL 94*
Doub, Randy Davis 1955- *WhoAmP 93*
Doub, William Offutt 1931- *WhoAm 94, WhoAmL 94, WhoAmP 93*
Doubiago, Sharon *DrAPF 93*
Double, Barbara Turner 1926- *WhoAmP 93*
Doubleday, Frank *WhoHol 92*
Doubleday, John Vincent 1947- *Who 94*
Doubleday, Nelson *WhoAm 94*
Doubledee, Deanna Gail 1958- *WhoScEn 94*
Doubrava, Jaroslav 1909-1960 *NewGrDO*
Doubrovska, Felia 1896-1981 *IntDcB [port]*
Doubt, Keith Dennis 1954- *WhoMW 93*
Doubtfire, Dianne (Joan) 1918- *WrDr 94*
Douce, John Leonard 1932- *Who 94*
Douce, Patrice 1942- *WhoFI 94*
Doucet, Catherine d1958 *WhoHol 92*
Doucet, Clive 1946- *ConAu 42NR*
Doucet, Eddie A. 1924- *WhoAmP 93*
Doucet, Paul d1928 *WhoHol 92*
Doucette, Concetta Ciccozzi *DrAPF 93*
Doucette, David Robert 1946- *WhoFI 94*
Doucette, John *WhoHol 92*
Doucette, Mary-Alyce 1924- *WhoFI 94*
Doucette, Paul Stanislaus 1966- *WhoScEn 94*
Doucette, Richard F. 1918- *WhoAmP 93*
Douchkess, George 1911- *WhoAmL 94*
Doud, Kenneth Eugene, Jr. 1953- *WhoAm 94*
Doud, Wallace C. 1925- *WhoAm 94*
Doudart De Lagree, Ernest-Marc-Louis De Gonzague 1823-1868 *WhWE*
Doudera, Gerard 1932- *WhoAmA 93*
Doudna, Martin Kirk 1930- *WhoWest 94*
Doudrick, Robert Lawrence 1950- *WhoScEn 94*
Douds, H. James 1930- *WhoIns 94*
Douek, Ellis Elliot 1934- *Who 94*
Douenias, Natalie 1940- *WhoAmA 93*
Dougal, Arwin Adelbert 1926- *WhoAm 94*
Dougal, Jerold Lynn 1953- *WhoWest 94*
Dougal, Malcolm Gordon 1938- *Who 94*
Dougall, Christopher Richardson 1956- *WhoFI 94*
Dougall, Lily 1858-1923 *BlmGWL*
Dougan, David John 1936- *Who 94*
Dougan, Deborah Rae 1952- *WhoScEn 94*
Dougan, (Alexander) Derek 1938- *Who 94*
Dougan, Robert Ormes 1904- *WhoAm 94*
Dougan, Vikki *WhoHol 92*
Doughan, Thomas Bruce 1960- *WhoFI 94, WhoMW 93*
Dougher, Joseph P. 1948- *WhoAmL 94*
Dougherty, Alonzo D., Jr. 1926- *AfrAmG [port]*
Dougherty, Barbara Lee 1949- *WhoWest 94*
Dougherty, Betsey Olenick 1950- *WhoAm 94*
Dougherty, Celia Berniece 1935- *WhoWest 94*
Dougherty, Charles John 1949- *WhoAm 94*
Dougherty, Charles Joseph 1919- *WhoAm 94*
Dougherty, Charlotte Anne 1947- *WhoFI 94, WhoMW 93*
Dougherty, Douglas Alexander 1952- *WhoMW 93*
Dougherty, Douglas Wayne 1943- *WhoAm 94*
Dougherty, Elmer Lloyd, Jr. 1930- *WhoAm 94, WhoScEn 94*
Dougherty, Harry Melville, III 1959- *WhoScEn 94*
Dougherty, Ivan Noel 1907- *Who 94*
Dougherty, J. Patrick 1948- *WhoAmP 93*
Dougherty, James 1926- *WhoAm 94, WhoScEn 94*
Dougherty, James E(dward) 1923- *WrDr 94*
Dougherty, Jay *DrAPF 93*
Dougherty, Joe d1978 *WhoHol 92*
Dougherty, John Chrysostom, III 1915- *WhoAm 94, WhoAmL 94, WhoFI 94*
Dougherty, John E. 1922- *WhoAmP 93*
Dougherty, John Ernest 1924- *WhoAm 94, WhoAmL 94*
Dougherty, John James 1924- *WhoAm 94, WhoWest 94*
Dougherty, Jude Patrick 1930- *WhoAm 94*
Dougherty, Lucia A. 1949- *WhoAmL 94*
Dougherty, Marion *IntMPA 94*
Dougherty, Michael Joseph 1949- *WhoWest 94*
Dougherty, Nancy Marie 1954- *WhoMW 93*
Dougherty, Patrick T. *WhoAmA 93*
Dougherty, Percy H. 1943- *WhoScEn 94*
Dougherty, Raleigh Gordon 1928- *WhoWest 94*
Dougherty, Ray 1942- *WhoAmA 93*
Dougherty, Richard Martin 1935- *WhoAm 94, WhoScEn 94*
Dougherty, Robert Anthony 1928- *WhoAm 94*
Dougherty, Robert Charles 1929- *WhoWest 94*
Dougherty, Ronald Jary 1936- *WhoWest 94*
Dougherty, Russell Elliott 1920- *WhoAm 94*
Dougherty, Sharon Ann 1952- *WhoMW 93*
Dougherty, Sherilyne Earnest 1950- *WhoFI 94*
Dougherty, Thomas James 1948- *WhoAm 94*
Doughten, Mary Katherine 1923- *WhoMW 93*
Doughtie, Venton Levy 1897- *WhAm 10*
Doughty, Charles d1977 *WhoHol 92*
Doughty, Charles M(ontagu) 1843-1926 *EncSF 93*
Doughty, Charles Montagu 1843-1926 *WhWE [port]*
Doughty, Francis W(orcester) 1850-1917 *EncSF 93*
Doughty, George Franklin 1946- *WhoAm 94*
Doughty, George Henry 1911- *Who 94*
Doughty, John 1754-1826 *AmRev*
Doughty, John Robert 1936- *WhoWest 94*
Doughty, Leslie John Trevalyn 1922- *WhoFI 94*
Doughty, Michael Dean 1947- *WhoFI 94*
Doughty, Robert Allen 1945- *WhoAm 94*
Doughty, Robin W 1941- *WrDr 94*
Doughty, Warren Browe 1921- *WhoAmP 93*
Doughty, William (Roland) 1925- *Who 94*
Dougill, John Wilson 1934- *Who 94*
Douglas *Who 94*
Douglas, Aaron 1899-1988 *AfrAmAl 6*
Douglas, Aaron 1900-1979 *WhoAmA 93N*
Douglas, Alexander Stuart 1921- *Who 94*
Douglas, Andrew 1932- *WhoAm 94, WhoAmL 94*
Douglas, Andy 1932- *WhoAmP 93*
Douglas, Angela 1940- *WhoHol 92*
Douglas, Archibald fl. 14th cent.- *BlmGEL*
Douglas, Arthur 1926- *WrDr 94*
Douglas, Arthur E. 1933- *WhoBlA 94*
Douglas, Arthur John Alexander 1920- *Who 94*
Douglas, Aubry Carter 1943- *WhoBlA 94*
Douglas, Barbara *WrDr 94*
Douglas, Barry 1960- *IntWW 93, Who 94*
Douglas, Betty C. 1920- *WhoAmP 93*
Douglas, Black *BlmGEL*
Douglas, Bob W. 1934- *WhoAmP 93*
Douglas, Bobby Eddie 1942- *WhoBlA 94*
Douglas, Bruce Lee 1925- *WhoAm 94*
Douglas, Bryce 1924- *WhoAm 94*
Douglas, Buster 1960- *WhoBlA 94*
Douglas, Byron d1935 *WhoHol 92*
Douglas, Carlyle Colin d1992 *WhoBlA 94N*
Douglas, Carole Nelson 1944- *EncSF 93*
Douglas, Charles d1789 *AmRev*
Douglas, Charles Francis 1930- *WhoAm 94*
Douglas, Charles Gwynne, III 1942- *WhoAmP 93*
Douglas, Charles Primrose 1921- *IntWW 93, Who 94*
Douglas, Charles W. 1948- *WhoAm 94, WhoAmL 94*
Douglas, Charles Wesley 1933- *WhoWest 94*
Douglas, Clarence James, Jr. 1924- *WhoFI 94*
Douglas, Clive (Martin) 1903-1977 *NewGrDO*
Douglas, Colin 1912- *WhoHol 92*
Douglas, Dale Stuart 1957- *WhoFI 94*
Douglas, David William 1924- *WhoMW 93*
Douglas, Diana 1923- *WhoHol 92*
Douglas, Diane Miriam 1957- *WhoWest 94*
Douglas, Don d1945 *WhoHol 92*
Douglas, Donald Macleod d1993 *Who 94N*
Douglas, Donna 1939- *WhoHol 92*
Douglas, Doris d1970 *WhoHol 92*
Douglas, Dwight Oliver 1941- *WhoAm 94*
Douglas, Edna M. 1904- *WhoBlA 94*
Douglas, Edwin Perry 1935- *WhoAmA 93*
Douglas, Eileen 1946- *WhoAm 94*
Douglas, Eleanor Davies 1590-1652 *BlmGWL*
Douglas, Elizabeth Asche 1930- *WhoBlA 94*
Douglas, Ellen *ConAu 41NR, DrAPF 93*
Douglas, Eric 1962- *WhoHol 92*
Douglas, Florence M. 1933- *WhoBlA 94*
Douglas, Frank Fair 1945- *WhoAm 94*
Douglas, Fred Robert 1924- *WhoAm 94*
Douglas, Frederic Huntington 1897-1956 *WhoAmA 93N*
Douglas, Frederick d1929 *WhoHol 92*
Douglas, Frederick William 1913- *WhoBlA 94*
Douglas, Garry *EncSF 93*
Douglas, Garry 1941- *WrDr 94*
Douglas, Gary 1945- *WhoFI 94, WhoWest 94*
Douglas, Gavin 1475?-1522 *BlmGEL*
Douglas, Gavin 1476-1522 *DcLB 132*
Douglas, Gavin Stuart 1932- *Who 94*
Douglas, George Halsey 1934- *WhoMW 93*
Douglas, George Warren 1938- *WhoAmP 93*
Douglas, Gilbert d1959 *WhoHol 92*
Douglas, Gordon d1993 *NewYTBS 93*
Douglas, Gordon 1907- *IntMPA 94, WhoHol 92*
Douglas, Gordon Watkins 1921- *WhoAm 94*
Douglas, Gregory A. *DrAPF 93*
Douglas, H. Eugene 1940- *WhoAmP 93*
Douglas, Harry E., III 1938- *WhoBlA 94*
Douglas, Henry Russell 1925- *Who 94*
Douglas, Herbert P., Jr. 1922- *WhoBlA 94*
Douglas, Iain *EncSF 93*
Douglas, Jack 1908-1989 *WhoCom*
Douglas, Jack 1927- *WhoHol 92*
Douglas, James *WhoHol 92*
Douglas, James 1286?-1330 *BlmGEL*
Douglas, James 1803-1877 *DcNaB MP*
Douglas, James 1960- *WhoBlA 94*
Douglas, James Buster *WhoAm 94*
Douglas, James Buster 1960- *IntWW 93*
Douglas, James Dixon 1922- *WrDr 94*
Douglas, James Franklin 1963- *WhoWest 94*
Douglas, James Holley 1951- *WhoAm 94, WhoAmP 93*
Douglas, James Matthew 1944- *WhoAmL 94, WhoBlA 94*
Douglas, James Murray 1925- *Who 94*
Douglas, Janice Green 1944- *WhoBlA 94*
Douglas, Jeff *EncSF 93*
Douglas, Jocelyn Fielding 1927- *WhoAm 94*
Douglas, Joe, Jr. 1928- *WhoBlA 94*
Douglas, Joel Bruce 1948- *WhoAmL 94*
Douglas, John (Frederick James) 1929- *WrDr 94*
Douglas, John Breed, III 1953- *WhoAmL 94*
Douglas, John Daniel 1945- *WhoBlA 94*
Douglas, John Edwin 1939- *WhoAmP 93*
Douglas, John Hoffmann 1920- *WhoFI 94*
Douglas, John Lewis 1950- *WhoAm 94, WhoAmL 94*
Douglas, John W. 1944- *WhoIns 94*
Douglas, Joseph Francis 1926- *WhoBlA 94*
Douglas, Josephine *WhoHol 92*
Douglas, Judy Carol 1948- *WhoMW 93*
Douglas, Keith *WhoHol 92*
Douglas, Keith 1920-1944 *BlmGEL*
Douglas, Keith Castellain 1920-1944 *DcNaB MP*
Douglas, Kenneth d1923 *WhoHol 92*
Douglas, Kenneth 1920- *Who 94*
Douglas, Kenneth Jay 1922- *WhoAm 94, WhoMW 93*
Douglas, Kent d1966 *WhoHol 92*
Douglas, Kirk 1916- *IntWW 93, WhoHol 92*
Douglas, Kirk 1918- *IntMPA 94, WhoAm 94, WrDr 94*
Douglas, Kordice Majella 1955- *WhoAmL 94*
Douglas, L. J. 1948- *WhoAmA 93*
Douglas, Leslie 1914- *WhoAm 94*
Douglas, Lester 1894-1961 *WhoAmA 93N*
Douglas, Lewis Williams 1894- *WhAm 10*
Douglas, Mae Alice 1951- *WhoBlA 94*
Douglas, Mansfield, III 1930- *WhoBlA 94*
Douglas, Margaret Elizabeth 1934- *Who 94*
Douglas, Maria d1973 *WhoHol 92*
Douglas, Marian *WhoHol 92*
Douglas, Marion Joan 1940- *WhoFI 94, WhoWest 94*
Douglas, (Margaret) Mary 1921- *Who 94*
Douglas, Mary Tew 1921- *WhoAm 94*
Douglas, Melvyn d1981 *WhoHol 92*
Douglas, Michael *NewYTBS 93 [port], TwCYAW*
Douglas, Michael 1942- *WrDr 94*
Douglas, Michael 1944- *ConTFT 11, IntMPA 94, WhoHol 92*
Douglas, Michael Gilbert 1945- *WhoScEn 94*

Douglas, Michael Kirk 1944- *IntWW 93, WhoAm 94*
Douglas, Mike 1925- *IntMPA 94, WhoHol 92*
Douglas, Milton d1970 *WhoHol 92*
Douglas, Nigel 1929- *NewGrDO*
Douglas, (George) Norman 1868-1952 *EncSF 93*
Douglas, O. 1878-1948 *BlmGWL*
Douglas, Patricia Jeanne 1939- *WhoFI 94, WhoScEn 94*
Douglas, Paul d1959 *WhoHol 92*
Douglas, Peter Roderick 1950- *WhoAm 94, WhoAmL 94*
Douglas, Philip Le Breton 1950- *WhoAm 94*
Douglas, R. M. 1918- *WrDr 94*
Douglas, Richard Giles 1932- *Who 94*
Douglas, Robert 1909- *WhoHol 92*
Douglas, Robert (McCallum) 1899- *Who 94*
Douglas, Robert Andrew 1954- *WhoScEn 94*
Douglas, Robert Gordon, Jr. 1934- *WhoAm 94*
Douglas, Robert L. 1884- *BasBi*
Douglas, Robert Langton d1951 *WhoAmA 93N*
Douglas, Robert Lee 1936- *WhoMW 93*
Douglas, Roger (Owen) 1937- *Who 94*
Douglas, Roger Owen 1937- *IntWW 93*
Douglas, Ronald Albert Neale 1922- *Who 94*
Douglas, Ronald George 1938- *WhoAm 94*
Douglas, Ronald Lynn 1942- *WhoFI 94*
Douglas, Ronald Walter 1910- *Who 94*
Douglas, Royal d1924 *WhoHol 92*
Douglas, Sally Jeanne 1964- *WhoWest 94*
Douglas, Samuel Horace 1928- *WhoBlA 94*
Douglas, Sarah 1953- *WhoHol 92*
Douglas, Scott *WhoHol 92*
Douglas, Sharon *WhoHol 92*
Douglas, Sherman 1966- *WhoBlA 94*
Douglas, Shirley *WhoHol 92*
Douglas, Sholto *Who 94*
Douglas, (Edward) Sholto 1909- *Who 94*
Douglas, Stephen 1954- *WhoWest 94*
Douglas, Stephen A. 1813-1861 *HisWorL [port]*
Douglas, Steve d1993 *NewYTBS 93*
Douglas, Steven Craig 1952- *WhoAmL 94*
Douglas, Stewart 1918- *WhoWest 94*
Douglas, Susan 1926- *WhoHol 92*
Douglas, Susan 1946- *WhoFI 94*
Douglas, Suzzanne *WhoBlA 94*
Douglas, Suzzanne 1957- *WhoHol 92*
Douglas, Teresa Lynn 1956- *WhoMW 93*
Douglas, Thomas Alexander 1926- *Who 94*
Douglas, Tom d1978 *WhoHol 92*
Douglas, Tom Howard 1957- *WhoAmA 93*
Douglas, Valerie *IntMPA 94*
Douglas, Valerie d1969 *WhoHol 92*
Douglas, Vicki V. 1937- *WhoAmP 93*
Douglas, W.H. Russel 1952- *WhoFI 94*
Douglas, Wallace d1958 *WhoHol 92*
Douglas, Walter Edmond 1933- *WhoBlA 94*
Douglas, Warren 1913- *WhoHol 92*
Douglas, Willard H., Jr. 1932- *WhoBlA 94*
Douglas, William 1743-1777 *WhAmRev*
Douglas, William (Randolph) 1921- *Who 94*
Douglas, William Alan 1929- *WhoFI 94*
Douglas, William Ernest 1930- *WhoAm 94, WhoFI 94*
Douglas, William Wilton 1922- *IntWW 93, Who 94*
Douglas And Clydesdale, Marquess of 1978- *Who 94*
Douglas-Chilton, Cher *WhoHisp 94*
Douglas-Hamilton *Who 94*
Douglas-Hamilton, James Alexander 1942- *Who 94, WrDr 94*
Douglas-Home *Who 94*
Douglas-Home, David Alexander Cospatrick 1943- *Who 94*
Douglas-Home, William d1992 *IntWW 93N*
Douglas-Mann, Bruce Leslie Home 1927- *Who 94*
Douglas Miller, Robert Alexander Gavin 1937- *Who 94*
Douglas-Pennant *Who 94*
Douglass, Amy d1980 *WhoHol 92*
Douglass, Andrew Ian 1943- *WhoAm 94, WhoFI 94*
Douglass, Billie 1945- *WrDr 94*
Douglass, Brooks 1963- *WhoAmP 93*
Douglass, Bruce E. 1917- *WhoAm 94*
Douglass, Carl Dean 1925- *WhoAm 94*
Douglass, Clyde J. 1925- *WhoAmP 93*
Douglass, David Fulton, Jr. 1957- *WhoFI 94*
Douglass, Donald Robert 1934- *WhoWest 94*
Douglass, Ellsworth *EncSF 93*
Douglass, Enid Hart 1926- *WhoAm 94, WhoWest 94*
Douglass, Frank Russell 1933- *WhoAmL 94*
Douglass, Frederick c. 1817-1875 *AfrAmAl 6 [port]*
Douglass, Frederick c. 1817-1895 *AmSocL [port]*
Douglass, Frederick 1818-1895 *HisWorL [port]*
Douglass, Gus R. 1927- *WhoAmP 93*
Douglass, Harry Robert 1937- *WhoAm 94*
Douglass, Jane Dempsey 1933- *WhoAm 94*
Douglass, John H. 1933- *WhoBlA 94*
Douglass, John Jay 1922- *WhoAm 94, WhoAmL 94*
Douglass, John Michael 1939- *WhoAm 94, WhoWest 94*
Douglass, John W. 1942- *WhoBlA 94*
Douglass, John William 1942- *WhoAmP 93*
Douglass, Laura Lee 1964- *WhoMW 93*
Douglass, Lewis Lloyd 1930- *WhoBlA 94*
Douglass, Maureen *WhoHol 92*
Douglass, Melvin Isadore 1948- *WhoAm 94, WhoBlA 94*
Douglass, Mike Reese 1955- *WhoBlA 94*
Douglass, Robert Lee 1928- *WhoAmP 93, WhoBlA 94*
Douglass, Robert Royal 1931- *WhoAm 94, WhoFI 94*
Douglass, Robyn 1950- *WhoHol 92*
Douglass, Sarah Mapp 1806-1882 *AfrAmAl 6*
Douglass, Thomas E. 1944- *WhoAmL 94*
Douglass, William Birch, III 1943- *WhoAm 94, WhoAmL 94*
Douglas-Scott, Douglas Andrew Montagu *Who 94*
Douglas-Scott-Montagu *Who 94*
Douglas-Talley, Rita Faye 1957- *WhoAmL 94*
Douglas-Wilson, Ian 1912- *Who 94*
Douglas-Withers, John Keppel Ingold 1919- *Who 94*
Douglis, Avron 1918- *WhoAm 94*
Douillard, Paul Arthur 1927- *WhoScEn 94*
Dou Jianzhong *WhoPRCh 91*
Douka, Maro 1947- *BlmGWL*
Douke, Daniel W. 1943- *WhoAmA 93*
Doulis, Thomas *DrAPF 93*
Doulton, Alfred John Farre 1911- *Who 94*
Doulton, John Hubert Farre 1942- *Who 94*
Douma, Harry Hein 1933- *WhoMW 93*
Douma, Jacob Hendrick 1912- *WhoAm 94*
Doumakes, Donald James 1955- *WhoAmP 93*
Doumar, George R. A. 1961- *WhoAmL 94*
Doumar, Robert George 1930- *WhoAm 94, WhoAmL 94*
Doumas, Basil Thomas 1930- *WhoScEn 94*
Doumas, Gena Kathleen 1963- *WhoFI 94*
Doumato, Lamia 1947- *WhoAmA 93*
Doumenc, Philippe 1934- *IntWW 93*
Doumlele, Ruth Hailey 1925- *WhoFI 94*
Doune, Lord 1966- *Who 94*
Doupe, Robert N. 1941- *WhoWest 94*
Doupnik, Craig Allen 1962- *WhoScEn 94*
Dourian, Ohan 1922- *NewGrDO*
Dourif, Brad 1950- *IntMPA 94, WhoHol 92*
Dourlen, Victor-Charles-Paul 1780-1864 *NewGrDO*
Dourney, Martin W. 1944- *WhoIns 94*
Douro, Marquess of 1945- *Who 94*
Dours, Jean 1913- *IntWW 93*
Douskey, Franz *DrAPF 93*
Douskey, Theresa Kathryn 1938- *WhoScEn 94*
Dout, Anne Jacqueline 1955- *WhoAm 94, WhoMW 93, WhoScEn 94*
Douthat, James Evans 1946- *WhoAm 94*
Douthett, Jill A. 1951- *WhoAmL 94*
Douthit, William E. 1925- *WhoBlA 94*
Douthitt, Wilfried *NewGrDO*
Doutt, Geraldine Moffatt 1927- *WhoMW 93*
Doutt, Jeffrey Thomas 1947- *WhoWest 94*
Doutt, Richard Leroy 1916- *WhoAm 94*
Doutt, Sam Blair 1927- *WhoAmP 93*
Douty, Richard Thomas 1930- *WhoScEn 94*
Douvan, Elizabeth 1926- *WhoAm 94*
Douvan-Kulesha, Irina 1938- *WhoScEn 94*
Douvier, Guy d1993 *NewYTBS 93*
Douvier, Mary Ann 1932- *WhoAmP 93*
Douville, Arthur *WhoAmP 93*
Douy, Max 1914- *IntDcF 2-4*
DoVale, Antonio Joseph, Jr. 1954- *WhoFI 94*
DoVale, Fern Louise 1956- *WhoScEn 94*
Dovaleff, Theodore Philip 1943- *WhoFI 94*
Dovalina, Fernando, Jr. 1942- *WhoHisp 94*
Dove, Arthur Allan 1933- *Who 94*
Dove, Arthur Garfield 1880-1946 *WhoAmA 93N*
Dove, Billie 1901- *WhoHol 92*
Dove, Donald Augustine 1930- *WhoWest 94*
Dove, James Leroy 1960- *WhoWest 94*
Dove, Pearlie C. *WhoBlA 94*
Dove, Rita *DrAPF 93, NewYTBS 93 [port]*
Dove, Rita 1952- *AfrAmAl 6, ConAu 19AS [port], ConBlB 6 [port], ConLC 81 [port]*
Dove, Rita (Frances) 1952- *BlkWr 2, ConAu 42NR, WrDr 94*
Dove, Rita Frances 1952- *WhoAm 94, WhoBlA 94*
Dove, Toni 1946- *WhoAmA 93*
Dove, Ulysses 1947- *ConBlB 5 [port]*
Dover, Suffragan Bishop of 1938- *Who 94*
Dover, Den 1938- *Who 94*
Dover, James Burrell 1927- *WhoAm 94*
Dover, K(enneth) J(ames), Sir 1920- *WrDr 94*
Dover, Kenneth James 1920- *IntWW 93, Who 94*
Dover, William J. 1945- *WhoAmP 93*
Doverspike, Terry Richard 1951- *WhoAmL 94*
Dovey, Alice d1969 *WhoHol 92*
Dovey, Brian Hugh 1941- *WhoAm 94*
Dovey, Irma *DrAPF 93*
Dovhan, Serhii Vasylovych *LoBiDrD*
Doviak, Richard James 1933- *WhoAm 94*
Dovich, Robert Arthur 1951- *WhoMW 93*
Dovidio, John Francis 1951- *WhoScEn 94*
Dovima d1990 *WhoHol 92*
Dovlatian, Frunze Vaginakovich 1927- *IntWW 93*
Dovring, Folke 1916- *WhoFI 94, WhoScEn 94*
Dovring, Karin Elsa Ingeborg 1919- *WhoAm 94, WhoMW 93*
Dow, Andrew Richard George 1943- *Who 94*
Dow, Arthur 1928- *WhoAmP 93*
Dow, Charles G. *WhoAmP 93*
Dow, Christopher *Who 94*
Dow, (John) Christopher (Roderick) 1916- *IntWW 93, Who 94*
Dow, Daniel Gould 1930- *WhoAm 94*
Dow, David O. 1948- *WhoAmP 93*
Dow, Dennis R. 1953- *WhoAmL 94*
Dow, Dorothy 1920- *NewGrDO*
Dow, Douglas Morrison 1935- *Who 94*
Dow, Faye Lynn *WhoAsA 94*
Dow, Frederick Warren 1917- *WhoAm 94, WhoWest 94*
Dow, Geoffrey Graham *Who 94*
Dow, Harold Peter Bourner 1921- *Who 94*
Dow, Helen Jeannette 1926- *WhoAmA 93*
Dow, Herbert Henry 1866-1930 *WorInv*
Dow, Herbert Henry 1927- *WhoAm 94*
Dow, Jean Louise 1955- *WhoFI 94, WhoMW 93*
Dow, Jennings Bryan 1897- *WhAm 10*
Dow, Jim D. 1942- *WhoAmA 93*
Dow, Jody DeRoma 1935- *WhoAmP 93*
Dow, John Goodchild 1905- *WhoAmP 93*
Dow, Mary Alexis 1949- *WhoFI 94, WhoWest 94*
Dow, Melvin Abbe 1928- *WhoAmL 94*
Dow, Neal 1804-1897 *AmSocL*
Dow, Peggy 1928- *WhoHol 92*
Dow, Peter Anthony 1933- *WhoAm 94*
Dow, Philip *DrAPF 93*
Dow, Robert Stone 1908- *WhoWest 94*
Dow, Rodney H. 1948- *WhoAmL 94*
Dow, Tony 1945- *WhoHol 92*
Dow, Wilbur Egerton, Jr. 1906-1991 *WhAm 10*
Dow, William F. 1941- *WhoAmL 94*
Dow, William Gould 1895- *WhoAm 94, WhoScEn 94*
Dowben, Robert Morris 1927- *WhoAm 94, WhoScEn 94*
Dowd, Andrew Joseph 1929- *WhoAm 94, WhoAmL 94*
Dowd, David D., Jr. 1929- *WhoAm 94, WhoAmL 94*
Dowd, David Joseph 1924- *WhoAm 94*
Dowd, Donny c. 194-?- *EncNAR*
Dowd, Edwin L. *WhoAmL 94*
Dowd, Harrison 1897- *WhoHol 92*
Dowd, Jack 1938- *WhoAmA 93*
Dowd, James Patrick 1937- *WhoMW 93*
Dowd, James Patrick 1951- *Who 94*
Dowd, John Maguire 1941- *WhoAm 94, WhoAmL 94*
Dowd, Kaye *WhoHol 92*
Dowd, Kevin Thomas 1956- *WhoAmL 94*
Dowd, M'el *WhoHol 92*
Dowd, Morgan Daniel 1933- *WhoAm 94*
Dowd, Patrick Francis 1955- *WhoMW 93*
Dowd, Peter Jerome 1942- *WhoAm 94*
Dowd, Robert 1937- *WhoAmA 93*
Dowd, (Eric) Ronald 1914-1990 *NewGrDO*
Dowd, Sandra K. 1950- *WhoAmP 93*
Dowd, Thomas F. 1943- *WhoAm 94, WhoAmL 94*
Dowd, Travis 1940- *WhoAmP 93*
Dowd, Wayne 1941- *WhoAmP 93*
Dowd, William Francis 1943- *WhoAmP 93*
Dowd, William Timothy 1927- *WhoAmL 94*
Dowdall, John Michael 1944- *Who 94*
Dowdalls, Edward Joseph 1926- *Who 94*
Dowdell, Dennis, Jr. 1919- *WhoBlA 94*
Dowdell, Dennis, Jr. 1945- *WhoBlA 94*
Dowdell, Dorothy Florence 1910- *WhoAm 94*
Dowdell, Kevin Crawford 1961- *WhoBlA 94*
Dowdell, Marcus L. 1970- *WhoBlA 94*
Dowdell, Robert *WhoHol 92*
Dowden, Albert Ricker 1941- *WhoAm 94, WhoFI 94*
Dowden, Anne Ophelia 1907- *WhoWest 94*
Dowden, Anne Ophelia Todd 1907- *WhoAmA 93, WrDr 94*
Dowden, Carroll Vincent 1933- *WhoAm 94*
Dowden, Craig Phillips 1947- *WhoMW 93*
Dowden, George *DrAPF 93*
Dowden, Richard George 1949- *Who 94*
Dowdeswell, Wilfrid Hogarth 1914- *WrDr 94*
Dowdeswell, (John) Windsor 1920- *Who 94*
Dowding, Baron d1992 *Who 94N*
Dowding, Baron 1949- *Who 94*
Dowding, Henry Wallace 1888?-1967? *EncSF 93*
Dowding, Peter M'Callum 1943- *Who 94*
Dowdle, Patrick Dennis 1948- *WhoAmL 94, WhoWest 94*
Dowdle, Walter Reid 1930- *WhoAm 94, WhoScEn 94*
Dowds, John Joseph 1938- *WhoAm 94*
Dowdy, C. Wayne 1943- *WhoAmP 93*
Dowdy, James H. 1932- *WhoBlA 94*
Dowdy, John Vernard 1912- *WhoAmL 94*
Dowdy, John Wesley 1912- *WhoAm 94*
Dowdy, Lewis C. 1917- *WhoBlA 94*
Dowdy, Linda Katherine 1943- *WhoMW 93*
Dowdy, Regera 1925- *WrDr 94*
Dowdy, Ronald Raymond 1944- *WhoAm 94*
Dowell, Anthony 1943- *IntDcB [port], WhoHol 92*
Dowell, Anthony (James) 1943- *Who 94*
Dowell, Anthony James 1943- *IntWW 93, WhoAm 94*
Dowell, Coleman 1925-1985 *DcLB 130 [port]*
Dowell, Earl Hugh 1937- *WhoAm 94, WhoScEn 94*
Dowell, Ian Malcolm 1940- *Who 94*
Dowell, James Dale 1932- *WhoAmP 93*
Dowell, John Derek 1935- *IntWW 93, Who 94*
Dowell, John E., Jr. 1941- *WhoAmA 93*
Dowell, Michael Brendan 1942- *WhoAm 94*
Dowell, Ollie Willette 1957- *WhoBlA 94*
Dowell, Tim 1947- *WhoAmP 93*
Dowell, Timothy John 1947- *WhoWest 94*
Dowell-Cerasoli, Patricia R. 1957- *WhoBlA 94*
Dower, Michael Shillito Trevelyan 1933- *Who 94*
Dowery, Mary *WhoBlA 94*
Dowgiewicz, Michael John 1952- *WhoFI 94*
Dowiakowska-Klimowiczowa, Bronislawa (Apolonia Izabela) 1840-1910 *NewGrDO*
Dowie, Ian James 1938- *WhoAm 94*
Dowis, Lenore 1934- *WhoAmL 94, WhoFI 94*
Dowiyogo, Bernard 1946- *IntWW 93*
Dowkings, Wendy Lanell 1964- *WhoBlA 94*
Dowlan, William C. d1947 *WhoHol 92*
Dowlatabadi, Mahmud *ConWorW 93*
Dowler, David P. 1944- *WhoAmA 93*
Dowler, James R. 1925- *WrDr 94*
Dowley, Jennifer *WhoAmA 93*
Dowley, Joseph K. 1946- *WhoAm 94*
Dowlin, Charles Edwin 1933- *WhoWest 94*
Dowlin, Kenneth Everett 1941- *WhoAm 94, WhoWest 94*
Dowling, Ann Patricia 1952- *Who 94, WhoScEn 94*
Dowling, Basil (Cairns) 1910- *WrDr 94*
Dowling, Constance d1969 *WhoHol 92*
Dowling, Doris 1921- *WhoHol 92*
Dowling, Eddie d1976 *WhoHol 92*

Dowling, Edward Thomas 1938- *WhoAm 94*
Dowling, Elaine Michele 1964- *WhoAmL 94*
Dowling, Ellen Catherine 1948- *WhoWest 94*
Dowling, Eva d1956 *WhoHol 92*
Dowling, James G., Jr. 1952- *WhoAmL 94*
Dowling, James Hamilton 1931- *IntWW 93, WhoAm 94, WhoFI 94*
Dowling, Joan d1954 *WhoHol 92*
Dowling, John Elliott 1935- *IntWW 93, WhoAm 94*
Dowling, Joseph d1928 *WhoHol 92*
Dowling, Joseph Albert 1926- *WhoAm 94*
Dowling, Kathryn *WhoHol 92*
Dowling, Kenneth 1933- *Who 94*
Dowling, Monroe Davis, Jr. 1934- *WhoBlA 94*
Dowling, Owen Douglas 1934- *Who 94*
Dowling, Patricia A. 1942- *WhoAmP 93*
Dowling, Patrick Henry 1954- *WhoFI 94*
Dowling, Patrick Joseph 1939- *Who 94*
Dowling, Rachael *WhoHol 92*
Dowling, Richard O. d1993 *NewYTBS 93 [port]*
Dowling, Robert Murray 1932- *WhoAm 94*
Dowling, Robert W. 1895-1973 *WhoAmA 93N*
Dowling, Roderick Anthony 1940- *WhoAm 94*
Dowling, Terry 1947- *EncSF 93*
Dowling, Thomas Allan 1941- *WhoAm 94*
Dowling, Thomas J. 1940- *WhoAmL 94*
Dowling, Timothy Paul 1955- *WhoAmL 94*
Dowling, Vincent 1929- *ConTFT 11, IntWW 93*
Dowling, Vincent John 1927- *WhoAmL 94*
Dowling, William J. 1942- *WhoAmL 94*
Down, Alastair (Frederick) 1914- *Who 94*
Down, Alastair Frederick 1914- *IntWW 93*
Down, Angela 1943- *WhoHol 92*
Down, Antony Turnbull L. *Who 94*
Down, Barbara Langdon *Who 94*
Down, Dorita deLemos 1928- *WhoHisp 94*
Down, John Langdon Haydon Langdon- 1828-1896 *DcNaB MP*
Down, Larry Eugene d1980 *WhoHol 92*
Down, Lesley-Anne 1954- *IntMPA 94, WhoHol 92*
Down, Michael (Graham) 1951- *ConAu 42NR*
Down, William John Denbigh *Who 94*
Down And Connor, Bishop of 1931- *Who 94*
Down And Dromore, Bishop of 1934- *Who 94*
Downard, Daniel Patrick 1946- *WhoScEn 94*
Downe, Viscount 1935- *Who 94*
Downen, David Earl 1940- *WhoAm 94*
Downend, Paul Eugene 1907- *WhoAmP 93*
Downer, Alan Seymour 1949- *WhoWest 94*
Downer, Eliphalet 1744-1806 *WhAmRev*
Downer, Eugene Debs, Jr. 1939- *WhoAm 94*
Downer, Hunt Blair, Jr. 1946- *WhoAmP 93*
Downer, Jocelyn Anita *Who 94*
Downer, Lesley 1949- *WrDr 94*
Downer, Luther Henry 1913- *WhoBlA 94*
Downer, Martin Craig 1931- *Who 94*
Downer, Michael C. 1954- *WhoScEn 94*
Downer, Robert Nelson 1939- *WhoAmL 94, WhoMW 93*
Downer, Roger George H. 1942- *WhoScEn 94*
Downer, William John, Jr. 1932- *WhoAm 94*
Downes, Bryan 1939- *WrDr 94*
Downes, Bryan Trevor 1939- *WhoWest 94*
Downes, Cathy *WhoHol 92*
Downes, David A(nthony) 1927- *WrDr 94*
Downes, David Malcolm 1938- *Who 94*
Downes, Dwight 1944- *WhoBlA 94*
Downes, Edward 1924- *IntWW 93*
Downes, Edward (Thomas) 1924- *NewGrDO, Who 94*
Downes, Edward Olin Davenport 1911- *WhoAm 94*
Downes, Edward Ray d1968 *WhoHol 92*
Downes, George Robert 1911- *Who 94*
Downes, George Stretton 1914- *Who 94*
Downes, Gregory 1939- *WhoFI 94, WhoScEn 94*
Downes, John 1936- *WhoFI 94*
Downes, (John) Kerry 1930- *Who 94, WrDr 94*
Downes, M. P. *Who 94*
Downes, Quentin 1907- *WrDr 94*
Downes, Rackstraw 1939- *WhoAm 94, WhoAmA 93*
Downes, Ralph (William) 1904- *IntWW 93, Who 94*
Downes, Robin 1932- *WhoAm 94*
Downes, Theron Winship 1941- *WhoMW 93*
Downey, Anne Elisabeth 1936- *Who 94*
Downey, Arthur Harold, Jr. 1938- *WhoAm 94*
Downey, Arthur T., III 1937- *WhoAm 94*
Downey, Aurelia Richie 1917- *WhoBlA 94*
Downey, Bruce Joseph 1962- *WhoFI 94*
Downey, Christine 1949- *WhoAmP 93*
Downey, Deoborah Ann 1958- *WhoFI 94, WhoMW 93*
Downey, Ellen *WhoFI 94*
Downey, Fairfax Davis 1893-1990 *WhAm 10*
Downey, Gordon (Stanley) 1928- *IntWW 93, Who 94*
Downey, Heidi Suzanne 1965- *WhoAmL 94*
Downey, James 1939- *IntWW 93, WhoAm 94*
Downey, James Edgar 1950- *WhoWest 94*
Downey, John Alexander 1930- *WhoAm 94*
Downey, John Charles 1926- *WhoAm 94*
Downey, John Chegwyn Thomas 1920- *Who 94*
Downey, John Harold 1956- *WhoFI 94*
Downey, John Wilham 1927- *WhoAm 94, WhoMW 93*
Downey, Joseph L. *WhoFI 94*
Downey, Juan 1940- *WhoAmA 93*
Downey, Juan 1940-1993 *NewYTBS 93*
Downey, Michael J. *WhoAm 94*
Downey, Mortimer Leo, III 1936- *WhoAm 94, WhoAmP 93, WhoFI 94*
Downey, Morton d1985 *WhoHol 92*
Downey, Norma Jean 1935- *WhoMW 93*
Downey, Richard Morgan 1946- *WhoScEn 94*
Downey, Richard Ralph 1934- *WhoAm 94, WhoAmL 94, WhoFI 94*
Downey, Robert 1936- *WhoHol 92*
Downey, Robert, Jr. 1965- *IntMPA 94, WhoAm 94, WhoHol 92*
Downey, Robert Anthony 1953- *WhoFI 94*
Downey, Sarah Meredith *Who 94*
Downey, Thomas Joseph 1949- *WhoAmP 93*
Downey, William Conner 1952- *WhoFI 94*
Downey, William George 1912- *Who 94*
Downie, Freda (Christina) 1929- *WrDr 94*
Downie, John Francis 1934- *WhoAm 94*
Downie, Leonard, Jr. 1942- *IntWW 93, WhoAm 94, WrDr 94*
Downie, Mary Alice 1934- *BlmGWL, WrDr 94*
Downie, Pamela 1954- *WhoWest 94*
Downie, R(obert) S(ilcock) 1933- *WrDr 94*
Downie, Robert Silcock 1933- *IntWW 93, Who 94*
Downie, Romana Anzi 1925- *WhoAmA 93*
Downie, Winsome Angela 1948- *WhoBlA 94*
Downing, Alvin Joseph 1916- *WhoBlA 94*
Downing, Andrew Jackson 1815-1852 *AmCulL*
Downing, Anthony Leighton 1926- *Who 94*
Downing, Brian Thomas 1947- *WhoAm 94*
Downing, Carl Seldon 1935- *WhoAmL 94*
Downing, Cynthia Hurst 1942- *WhoMW 93*
Downing, David *WhoHol 92*
Downing, David Francis 1926- *Who 94*
Downing, Delbert F. 1931- *WhoAmP 93*
Downing, Douglas Allan 1957- *WhoWest 94*
Downing, Forrest W. *WhoIns 94*
Downing, Forrest William 1949- *WhoAm 94*
Downing, George 1934- *WhoAm 94*
Downing, Graham 1954- *WrDr 94*
Downing, Harry d1972 *WhoHol 92*
Downing, Henry Julian 1919- *Who 94*
Downing, James Christie 1924- *WhoAmL 94*
Downing, Jeffrey M. 1948- *WhoMW 93*
Downing, Joan Forman 1934- *WhoAm 94*
Downing, John Henry 1936- *WhoAm 94*
Downing, John William, Jr. 1936- *WhoBlA 94*
Downing, Joseph d1975 *WhoHol 92*
Downing, K.K. *See* Judas Priest *ConMus 10*
Downing, Kathleen Dimmick 1944- *WhoMW 93*
Downing, Lewis 1823-1872 *EncNAR*
Downing, Lucy Winthrop 1600?-1679 *BlmGWL*
Downing, Margaret Mary 1952- *WhoAm 94*
Downing, Michael William 1947- *WhoScEn 94*
Downing, Paula E. 1951- *EncSF 93, WrDr 94*
Downing, Robert d1975 *WhoHol 92*
Downing, Robert Allan 1929- *WhoAm 94*
Downing, Stephen 1950- *WhoBlA 94*
Downing, Vic *WhoAmP 93*
Downing, Walter d1937 *WhoHol 92*
Downman, Francis *EncSF 93*
Downpatrick, Lord 1988- *Who 94*
Downs, Anthony 1930- *WhoAm 94*
Downs, Bill d1978 *WhoHol 92*
Downs, Cathy d1976 *WhoHol 92*
Downs, Clark Evans 1946- *WhoAm 94, WhoAmL 94*
Downs, Crystal 1964- *WhoBlA 94*
Downs, David Douglas 1938- *WhoMW 93*
Downs, Diarmuid 1922- *IntWW 93, Who 94*
Downs, Donald Alexander, Jr. 1948- *WhoMW 93*
Downs, Douglas Walker 1945- *WhoAmA 93, WhoWest 94*
Downs, Floyd L. 1931- *WhoScEn 94*
Downs, George Wallingford, Mrs. *Who 94*
Downs, George Warthen 1933- *WhoAm 94, WhoAmL 94*
Downs, Harry 1932- *WhoAm 94*
Downs, Hartley H., III 1949- *WhoFI 94, WhoScEn 94*
Downs, Hugh 1921- *IntMPA 94, WhoHol 92*
Downs, Hugh Malcolm 1921- *WhoAm 94*
Downs, Jane *WhoHol 92*
Downs, Johnny 1913- *WhoHol 92*
Downs, Kathleen Joan 1950- *WhoWest 94*
Downs, Linda Anne 1945- *WhoAmA 93*
Downs, Michael Patrick 1940- *WhoAm 94*
Downs, Robert B(ingham) 1903- *WrDr 94*
Downs, Robert Bingham 1903-1991 *WhAm 10*
Downs, Robert C. S. *DrAPF 93*
Downs, Robert C. S. 1937- *WrDr 94*
Downs, Stuart Clifton 1950- *WhoAmA 93*
Downs, Thomas K. 1949- *WhoAmL 94*
Downs, Thomas Michael 1943- *WhoAm 94*
Downs, Watson d1969 *WhoHol 92*
Downs, Wilbur George 1913-1991 *WhAm 10*
Downs, William Fredrick 1942- *WhoWest 94*
Downshire, Marquess of 1929- *Who 94*
Downside, Abbot of *Who 94*
Downward, Peter Aldcroft 1924- *Who 94*
Downward, William (Atkinson) 1912- *Who 94*
Dowriche, Anne *BlmGWL*
Dows, David Alan 1928- *WhoAm 94*
Dowse, Robert Edward *WrDr 94*
Dowsett, Charles James Frank 1924- *IntWW 93, Who 94*
Dowsett, Robert Chipman 1929- *WhoIns 94*
Dowson, Duncan 1928- *IntWW 93, Who 94*
Dowson, Ernest 1867-1900 *DcLB 135 [port]*
Dowson, Ernest Christopher 1867-1900 *DcNaB MP*
Dowson, Graham Randall 1923- *IntWW 93, Who 94*
Dowson, Philip (Manning) 1924- *IntWW 93, Who 94*
Dowty, Alan K. 1940- *WrDr 94*
Doxey, Gordon Earl 1954- *WhoWest 94*
Doxey, Ralph Hindman 1950- *WhoAmP 93*
Doxie, Marvin Leon, Sr. 1943- *WhoBlA 94*
Doxsee, Lawrence Edward 1934- *WhoAm 94*
Doxtader, John *WhAmRev*
Doyel, David Elmond 1946- *WhoWest 94*
Doyen, Ross O. 1926- *WhoAmP 93*
Doyle, A. Patrick 1948- *WhoAmL 94*
Doyle, Anthony Ian 1925- *Who 94*
Doyle, Anthony Peter 1953- *WhoAmL 94*
Doyle, Arthur Conan d1930 *WhoHol 92*
Doyle, Arthur Conan 1859-1930 *BlmGEL, EncSF 93, RfGShF, ShSCr 12 [port], TwCYAW*
Doyle, Austin Joseph, Jr. 1941- *WhoAmL 94*
Doyle, Bernard *Who 94*
Doyle, (Frederick) Bernard 1940- *Who 94*
Doyle, Billy d1945 *WhoHol 92*
Doyle, Brian 1935- *TwCYAW, WrDr 94*
Doyle, Brian Andre 1911- *IntWW 93, Who 94*
Doyle, Buddy d1939 *WhoHol 92*
Doyle, Charles (Desmond) 1928- *WrDr 94*
Doyle, Charles Robert *WhoAmP 93*
Doyle, Constance Talcott Johnston 1945- *WhoMW 93*
Doyle, Daniel G. 1935- *WhoAmP 93*
Doyle, David *WhoAmP 93*
Doyle, David 1929- *WhoHol 92*
Doyle, David C. 1951- *WhoAmL 94*
Doyle, Donald Vincent 1925- *WhoAmP 93*
Doyle, Erie R. 1917- *WhoBlA 94*
Doyle, Eugenie Fleri 1921- *WhoAm 94*
Doyle, Francis Robert 1938- *WhoMW 93*
Doyle, Frank Lawrence 1926- *WhoAm 94*
Doyle, Frederick Bernard 1940- *IntWW 93*
Doyle, Frederick Joseph 1920- *WhoAm 94*
Doyle, Gerard Francis 1942- *WhoAm 94, WhoAmL 94*
Doyle, Harley Joseph 1942- *WhoWest 94*
Doyle, Harrison *WhoHol 92*
Doyle, Helen Elizabeth 1936- *WhoAmP 93*
Doyle, Henry Eman 1910- *WhoBlA 94*
Doyle, Jack David 1952- *WhoWest 94*
Doyle, James *DrAPF 93*
Doyle, James Aloysius 1921- *WhoAm 94*
Doyle, James E. 1945- *WhoAmP 93*
Doyle, James Edward 1945- *WhoAm 94, WhoAmL 94, WhoMW 93*
Doyle, James Edwin (Ned) 1902-1989 *WhAm 10*
Doyle, James M., Jr. 1944- *WhoAmL 94*
Doyle, James Thomas 1933- *WhoAm 94*
Doyle, Jane Frances 1950- *WhoAmP 93*
Doyle, Jean (Lena Annette) C. *Who 94*
Doyle, Joe 1941- *WhoAmA 93*
Doyle, John c. 1750-1834 *WhAmRev*
Doyle, John 1942- *WhoAmP 93*
Doyle, John C. 1953- *WhoAmL 94*
Doyle, John Laurence 1931- *WhoAm 94*
Doyle, John Lawrence 1939- *WhoAm 94, WhoAmA 93*
Doyle, John Paul 1942- *WhoAmP 93*
Doyle, John Peter 1942- *WhoIns 94*
Doyle, John Robert 1950- *WhoAm 94, WhoAmL 94*
Doyle, John Robert, Jr. 1910- *WhoAm 94*
Doyle, John T. d1935 *WhoHol 92*
Doyle, Johnny d1919 *WhoHol 92*
Doyle, Joseph Anthony 1920- *WhoAm 94*
Doyle, Joseph Theobald 1918- *WhoAm 94*
Doyle, Joyce Ann 1937- *WhoAm 94, WhoAmP 93*
Doyle, Judith Warner 1943- *WhoAm 94*
Doyle, Justin Emmett 1935- *WhoAm 94, WhoAmL 94*
Doyle, Justin P 1948- *WhoAm 94, WhoAmL 94*
Doyle, Katherine Lee Lee 1932- *WhoAm 94*
Doyle, Kenneth Joseph 1940- *WhAm 10*
Doyle, Kevin 1933- *IntMPA 94*
Doyle, Kevin John 1943- *WhoAm 94*
Doyle, L. F. Boker 1931- *WhoAm 94*
Doyle, Marion Wade 1894- *WhAm 10*
Doyle, Mary Ellen 1938- *WhoAmA 93*
Doyle, Mathias Francis 1933- *WhoAm 94*
Doyle, Maxine d1973 *WhoHol 92*
Doyle, Michael Anthony 1937- *WhoAm 94, WhoAmL 94*
Doyle, Michael James 1939- *WhoWest 94*
Doyle, Michael Matthew 1950- *WhoAmP 93*
Doyle, Michael Norbert 1948- *WhoWest 94*
Doyle, Michael Patrick 1949- *WhoScEn 94*
Doyle, Michael Phillip 1955- *WhoScEn 94*
Doyle, Mike 1928- *WrDr 94*
Doyle, Mimi d1979 *WhoHol 92*
Doyle, Morris McKnight 1909- *WhoAm 94*
Doyle, O'Brien John, Jr. 1950- *WhoMW 93*
Doyle, Patricia d1975 *WhoHol 92*
Doyle, Patricia Anne 1953- *WhoAm 94*
Doyle, Patrick Francis 1948- *WhoScEn 94*
Doyle, Patrick John 1926- *WhoAm 94*
Doyle, Patrick Lee 1929- *WhoAm 94*
Doyle, Paul A. 1925- *WrDr 94*
Doyle, Paul Francis 1946- *WhoAm 94, WhoAmL 94*
Doyle, Peter 1938- *Who 94*
Doyle, Peter Thomas 1928- *WhoWest 94*
Doyle, Ransom Grant 1956- *WhoFI 94*
Doyle, Ray d1954 *WhoHol 92*
Doyle, Regina d1931 *WhoHol 92*
Doyle, Reginald (Derek Henry) 1929- *Who 94*
Doyle, Richard 1948- *WrDr 94*
Doyle, Richard Henry, IV 1949- *WhoAmL 94, WhoMW 93*
Doyle, Richard James 1923- *WhoAm 94*
Doyle, Richard Nason 1941- *WhoAmL 94*
Doyle, Richard Robert 1937- *WhoMW 93*
Doyle, Robert H. 1942- *WhoAmP 93*
Doyle, Roddy 1958?- *ConLC 81 [port]*
Doyle, Ruth Narita *WhoAsA 94*
Doyle, Terence Nicholas 1936- *WhoAm 94*
Doyle, Tom 1928- *WhoAmA 93*
Doyle, Wilfred Emmett 1913- *WhoAm 94*
Doyle, William d1993 *NewYTBS 93*
Doyle, William 1932- *IntWW 93*
Doyle, William 1942- *Who 94, WrDr 94*

Doyle, William Edward 1951- *WhoWest 94*
Doyle, William Jay, II 1928- *WhoFI 94, WhoMW 93*
Doyle, William Joseph, Jr. 1954- *WhoAmL 94*
Doyle, William Patrick 1932- *Who 94, WhoFI 94*
Doyle, William Stowell 1944- *WhoAm 94, WhoFI 94*
Doyle, William Thomas 1925- *WhoAm 94*
Doyle, William Thompson 1926- *WhoAmP 93*
Doyle-Murray, Brian *IntMPA 94*
D'Oyly, Nigel Hadley Miller 1914- *Who 94*
D'Oyly Carte, Richard *NewGrDO*
Doyon, Bruno *WhoHol 92*
Doyon, Gerard Maurice 1923-1990 *WhoAmA 93N*
Doza, Lawrence O. 1938- *WhoAm 94, WhoFI 94*
Dozier, D. J. 1965- *WhoBlA 94*
Dozier, Daniel Preston 1944- *WhoAmP 93*
Dozier, David Charles, Jr. 1938- *WhoAm 94*
Dozier, Flora Grace 1937- *WhoWest 94*
Dozier, Glenn Joseph 1950- *WhoAm 94, WhoFI 94*
Dozier, James Lee 1931- *WhoAm 94*
Dozier, Morris, Sr. 1921- *WhoBlA 94*
Dozier, Ollin Kemp 1929- *WhoAm 94*
Dozier, Pat Kennedy 1921- *WhoAmP 93*
Dozier, Richard K. 1939- *WhoBlA 94*
Dozier, Rush Watkins, Jr. 1950- *WhoAmP 93*
Dozier, Weldon Grady 1938- *WhoFI 94*
Dozier, William 1908-1991 *WhAm 10*
Dozier, Zoe 1930- *WrDr 94*
Dozois, Gardner 1947- *EncSF 93, WrDr 94*
Dozono, Sho G. 1944- *WhoAsA 94*
Dr. A *SmATA 74*
Dr. A. 1920-1992 *ConLC 76 [port]*
Drabanski, Emily Ann 1952- *WhoAm 94*
Drabble, Bernard J. 1925- *IntWW 93*
Drabble, Bernard James 1925- *WhoAm 94*
Drabble, Jane 1947- *Who 94*
Drabble, Margaret 1939- *BlmGEL [port], BlmGWL, IntWW 93, Who 94, WhoAm 94, WrDr 94*
Drabek, Doug 1962- *WhoAm 94*
Drabek, Zdenek 1945- *WhoFI 94*
Drabik, Alexander A. d1993 *NewYTBS 93*
Drabik, Harry Francis 1944- *WhoMW 93*
Drabinowicz, A. Theresa 1923- *WhoAmP 93*
Drabkin, David 1942- *WhoAm 94*
Drabkin, Murray 1928- *WhoAm 94, WhoAmL 94*
Drabkin, Stella 1900-1976 *WhoAmA 93N*
Drace-Francis, Charles David Stephen 1943- *Who 94*
Drach, George Wisse 1935- *WhoAm 94*
Drach, Ivan Fedorovych 1936- *LoBiDrD*
Drach, Ivan Fyodorovich 1936- *IntWW 93*
Drach, John Charles 1939- *WhoAm 94*
Drache, Heinz *WhoHol 92*
Drachler, Norman 1912- *WhoAm 94*
Drachman, Daniel Bruce 1932- *WhoScEn 94*
Drachman, David Alexander 1932- *WhoAm 94*
Drachman, Frank Emanuel, Jr. 1930- *WhoAmL 94*
Drachnik, Catherine Meldyn 1924- *WhoWest 94*
Drack, Paul E. 1928- *WhoFI 94*
Drackett, Phil(ip Arthur) 1922- *WrDr 94*
Draco, F. *ConAu 140, SmATA 75*
Dracopoulou, Theony 1883-1968 *BlmGWL*
Dracup, Angela 1943- *ConAu 141, SmATA 74 [port]*
Draddy, Vincent De Paul 1907-1990 *WhAm 10*
Draeger, Wayne Harold 1946- *WhoAm 94*
Draegert, David Allison 1940- *WhoAmL 94*
Draeseke, Felix (August Bernhard) 1835-1913 *NewGrDO*
Drafke, Michael Walter 1954- *WhoMW 93*
Dragan, Joseph Constantin 1917- *IntWW 93*
Draganescu, Mihai 1929- *WhoScEn 94*
Drage, Thomas Brochmann, Jr. 1948- *WhoAmP 93*
Drager, Barbara Rissman 1952- *WhoMW 93*
Dragging Canoe c. 1730-1792 *AmRev*
Draggon, Rodney Winston 1956- *WhoWest 94*
Draghi, Antonio c. 1634-1700 *NewGrDO*
Drago, Billy *WhoHol 92*
Drago, Cathleen d1938 *WhoHol 92*
Drago, Charles Grady *WhoMW 93*
Drago, Eugene Joseph 1926- *WhoAmP 93*
Drago, Patricia Ann 1953- *WhoFI 94*
Drago, Robert John 1958- *WhoScEn 94*
Drago, Russell Stephen 1928- *WhoAm 94*
Dragoi, Danut 1952- *WhoScEn 94*
Dragoi, Sabin Vasile 1894-1968 *NewGrDO*
Dragon, Albert 1937- *WhoAmL 94*
Dragon, William, Jr. 1942- *WhoAm 94, WhoWest 94*
Dragone, Allan R. 1926- *WhoAm 94*
Dragonette, Jessica d1980 *WhoHol 92*
Dragonwagon, Crescent *DrAPF 93*
Dragonwagon, Crescent 1952- *SmATA 75 [port], WhoAm 94*
Dragoo, Donald Wayne 1925-1988 *WhAm 10*
Dragoti, Stan 1932- *IntMPA 94*
Dragoumis, Paul 1934- *WhoAm 94*
Dragovic, Ljubisa Jovan 1950- *WhoMW 93*
Dragt, Alexander James 1936- *WhoAm 94, WhoScEn 94*
Dragun, James 1949- *WhoMW 93, WhoScEn 94*
Dragutsky, Howard William 1941- *WhoWest 94*
Draheim, Jennifer Ellen 1961- *WhoAmL 94*
Drahmann, Theodore 1926- *WhoAm 94*
Drai, Victor 1947- *IntMPA 94*
Draime, Doug *DrAPF 93*
Drain, Albert Sterling 1925- *WhoAm 94*
Drain, Alton Paul 1947- *WhoAmP 93*
Drain, Charles Michael 1959- *WhoScEn 94*
Drain, Geoffrey Ayrton d1993 *Who 94N*
Drain, Gershwin A. *WhoBlA 94*
Drain, Lee 1925- *WhoAm 94*
Drain, Patricia Welch 1935- *WhoAmP 93*
Drainie, John d1966 *WhoHol 92*
Draisen, Marc D. 1956- *WhoAmP 93*
Drake, Albert *DrAPF 93*
Drake, Albert (Dee) 1935- *ConAu 43NR, WrDr 94*
Drake, Albert Estern 1927- *WhoAm 94*
Drake, Alfred 1914- *WhoHol 92*
Drake, Alfred 1914-1992 *AnObit 1992*
Drake, Barbara *DrAPF 93*
Drake, Betsy 1923- *WhoHol 92*
Drake, Bonnie 1945- *WrDr 94*
Drake, Bryan (Ernest Hare) 1925- *NewGrDO*
Drake, Charles 1914- *IntMPA 94, WhoHol 92*
Drake, Charles D 1924- *WrDr 94*
Drake, Charles Whitney 1926- *WhoAm 94*
Drake, Charlie 1925- *WhoHol 92*
Drake, Daniel D. 1931- *WhoBlA 94*
Drake, David A. 1945- *WrDr 94*
Drake, David A(llen) 1945- *EncSF 93*
Drake, David Anderson 1952- *WhoWest 94*
Drake, David Lee 1960- *WhoScEn 94*
Drake, Dona d1989 *WhoHol 92*
Drake, Donald Charles 1935- *WhoAm 94*
Drake, Dorothy *WhoHol 92*
Drake, Dwight J. 1948- *WhoAmL 94*
Drake, E Maylon 1920- *WhoAm 94, WhoWest 94*
Drake, Edwin *WorInv*
Drake, Elisabeth Mertz 1936- *WhoAm 94*
Drake, Elizabeth Mullikin 1958- *WhoAmL 94*
Drake, (Arthur) Eric (Courtney) 1910- *IntWW 93, Who 94*
Drake, Fabia d1990 *WhoHol 92*
Drake, Frances 1908- *WhoHol 92*
Drake, Francis c. 1538-1596 *HisWorL [port]*
Drake, Francis c. 1540-1596 *WhWE [port]*
Drake, Francis 1549?-1596 *BlmGEL*
Drake, Francis LeBaron 1944- *WhoAmL 94, WhoMW 93*
Drake, Frank Donald 1930- *IntWW 93, WhoAm 94, WhoScEn 94, WhoWest 94*
Drake, Gordon William Frederic 1943- *WhoAm 94*
Drake, Grace L. *WhoAmP 93*
Drake, Grace L. 1926- *WhoAm 94, WhoMW 93*
Drake, Harold Allen 1942- *WhoWest 94*
Drake, Herbert R. 1923- *WhoAmP 93*
Drake, Hudson Billings 1935- *WhoAm 94, WhoFI 94*
Drake, Jack *WhoAmP 93*
Drake, Jack Thomas Arthur H. *Who 94*
Drake, James 1946- *WhoAmA 93*
Drake, James A. 1944- *WrDr 94*
Drake, Jean Elizabeth R. *Who 94*
Drake, Jim d1976 *WhoHol 92*
Drake, Joan *WrDr 94*
Drake, John d1985 *WhoHol 92*
Drake, John Gair 1930- *Who 94*
Drake, John Walter 1932- *WhoAm 94, WhoScEn 94*
Drake, John Warren 1930- *WhoAm 94, WhoMW 93*
Drake, Josephine d1929 *WhoHol 92*
Drake, Judith fl. 1696- *BlmGWL, DcNaB MP*
Drake, Ken d1987 *WhoHol 92*
Drake, Larry 1949- *WhoHol 92*
Drake, Larry 1950?- *ConTFT 11*
Drake, Lucius Charles, Jr. 1946- *WhoWest 94*
Drake, Lynn Annette 1949- *WhoAm 94*
Drake, Maurice *Who 94*
Drake, (Frederick) Maurice 1923- *Who 94*
Drake, Miriam Anna 1936- *WhoAm 94*
Drake, Paul W(oodhull) 1897- *WhAm 10*
Drake, Pauline *WhoHol 92*
Drake, Pauline Lilie 1926- *WhoBlA 94*
Drake, Peter 1957- *WhoAmA 93*
Drake, Richard Francis 1927- *WhoAmP 93, WhoMW 93*
Drake, Richard Lee 1950- *WhoMW 93*
Drake, Richard Paul 1954- *WhoScEn 94*
Drake, Robert Arthur 1924- *WhoWest 94*
Drake, Rodman Leland 1943- *WhoAm 94, WhoFI 94*
Drake, Roger Allan 1943- *WhoScEn 94*
Drake, Sarah Frances Ashford 1943- *WhoFI 94*
Drake, Shannon *ConAu 141, WrDr 94*
Drake, Shirley Jean 1927- *WhoAmP 93*
Drake, Simon Robert 1961- *WhoScEn 94*
Drake, Stephen Douglas 1947- *WhoScEn 94*
Drake, Stillman 1910- *IntWW 93, WhoAm 94*
Drake, Sylvie 1930- *WhoAm 94*
Drake, Thomas E. *WhoAmP 93*
Drake, Tom d1982 *WhoHol 92*
Drake, Virgil d1946 *WhoHol 92*
Drake, W. Anders *ConAu 42NR*
Drake, W(alter) Raymond 1913- *WrDr 94*
Drake, William Earle 1903- *WrDr 94*
Drake, William Everett 1939- *WhoAm 94*
Drake, William Frank, Jr. 1932- *WhoAm 94*
Drake-Brockman, Henrietta 1902-1968 *BlmGWL*
Drake-Brockman, Thomas Charles d1992 *Who 94N*
Drakeford, Jack 1937- *WhoBlA 94*
Drakeman, Donald Lee 1953- *WhoAm 94*
Drakert, Douglas Fulton 1942- *WhoFI 94*
Drakes, Muriel B. 1935- *WhoBlA 94*
Draklich, Nick 1926- *IntMPA 94*
Drakos, Charles Peter 1945- *WhoAm 94*
Drakos, Irene Sasso 1932- *WhoAm 94*
Drakulic, Slavenka 1949- *BlmGWL [port]*
Drance, Stephen Michael 1925- *WhoScEn 94*
Drane, Gary d1989 *WhoHol 92*
Drane, Sam Dade d1916 *WhoHol 92*
Drane, Walter Harding 1915- *WhoAm 94*
Dranem d1935 *WhoHol 92*
Dranias, Dean Anthony 1936- *WhoAm 94*
Dranishnikov, Vladimir Alexandrovich 1893-1939 *NewGrDO*
Dranow, John (Theodore) 1948- *ConAu 140*
Dransfield, Robert D. 1951- *WhoAmL 94*
Drantz, Veronica Ellen 1943- *WhoMW 93*
Drapeau, Jean 1916- *IntWW 93*
Drapeau, Phillip David 1938- *WhoAm 94*
Drapeau, William Lawrence 1929- *WhoAmP 93*
Drapell, Joseph 1940- *WhoAmA 93*
Draper, Alan Gregory 1926- *Who 94*
Draper, Alfred Ernest 1924- *WrDr 94*
Draper, Charles Stark 1901-1987 *WorInv*
Draper, Daniel, Jr. 1945- *WhoAmL 94*
Draper, Daniel Clay 1920- *WhoAm 94*
Draper, David Eugene 1949- *WhoAm 94*
Draper, Don d1990 *WhoHol 92*
Draper, E. Linn, Jr. 1942- *WhoAm 94*
Draper, Edgar 1926- *WhoAm 94*
Draper, Edgar Daniel 1921- *WhoBlA 94*
Draper, Elisabeth 1900-1993 *NewYTBS 93 [port]*
Draper, Everett T., Jr. 1939- *WhoBlA 94*
Draper, Frances Murphy 1947- *WhoBlA 94*
Draper, Frederick Webster 1945- *WhoBlA 94*
Draper, Gerald Carter 1926- *Who 94*
Draper, Hastings 1926- *WrDr 94*
Draper, James David 1943- *WhoAm 94*
Draper, James F. 1931- *WhoFI 94*
Draper, James Wilson 1926- *WhoAm 94*
Draper, Jo 1949- *ConAu 43NR*
Draper, Joe d1978 *WhoHol 92*
Draper, John Clayton 1945- *WhoAm 94*
Draper, John William 1811-1882 *DcAmReB 2*
Draper, Josiah Everett 1915- *WhoAmA 93*
Draper, Line Bloom *WhoAm 94*
Draper, Margaret c. 1730-1807 *WhAmRev*
Draper, Mary *WhAmRev*
Draper, Michael William 1928- *Who 94*
Draper, Norman Richard 1931- *WhoAm 94, WhoMW 93*
Draper, Paul *Who 94*
Draper, Paul 1909- *WhoHol 92*
Draper, (John Haydn) Paul 1916- *Who 94*
Draper, Peter Sydney 1935- *Who 94*
Draper, Polly 1956- *WhoHol 92*
Draper, R(onald) P(hilip) 1928- *WrDr 94*
Draper, Robert S. 1942- *WhoAmL 94*
Draper, Ronald Philip 1928- *Who 94*
Draper, Ruth 1884-1956 *WhoCom*
Draper, Theodore 1912- *WhoAm 94, WrDr 94*
Draper, Verden Rolland 1916- *WhoAm 94*
Draper, William Franklin 1912- *WhoAm 94, WhoAmA 93*
Draper, William Henry, III 1928- *IntWW 93, WhoAm 94, WhoAmP 93*
Draper-Peroulas, Maria 1950- *WhoAmP 93*
Drapkin, Arnold Howard 1931- *WhoAm 94*
Drapkin, Steven G. 1950- *WhoAm 94, WhoAmL 94*
Drasco, Dennis J. 1948- *WhoAmL 94*
Draskovic, Vuk 1946- *IntWW 93*
Drasner, Fred *WhoAm 94*
Dratz, Stephen Louis 1955- *WhoFI 94*
Draughon, Scott Wilson 1952- *WhoAmL 94, WhoFI 94*
Dravins, Dainis 1949- *IntWW 93*
Drawe, Scott Patrick 1955- *WhoAmL 94*
Drawicz, Andrzej 1932- *IntWW 93*
Drawz, John Englund 1942- *WhoAm 94*
Dray, Dwight Leroy 1918- *WhoMW 93*
Dray, Mark S. 1943- *WhoAm 94, WhoAmL 94*
Dray, Tevian 1956- *WhoWest 94*
Dray, William Herbert 1921- *IntWW 93, WhoAm 94*
Dray, William Perry 1940- *WhoAmL 94*
Draycott, Douglas Patrick 1918- *Who 94*
Draycott, Gerald Arthur 1911- *Who 94*
Drayer, Cynthia *WhoAm 94*
Draylin, Paul d1970 *WhoHol 92*
Drayson, Robert Quested 1919- *Who 94*
Drayton, Alfred d1949 *WhoHol 92*
Drayton, Henry S(hipman) 1840-1923 *EncSF 93*
Drayton, Mary Ann 1941- *WhoAmP 93*
Drayton, Michael 1563-1631 *BlmGEL*
Drayton, Noel d1981 *WhoHol 92*
Drayton, William 1943- *WhoAm 94, WhoAmL 94*
Drayton, William Henry 1742-1779 *AmRev, WhAmRev*
Drazen, Lori *IntMPA 94*
Draznin, Anne L. 1945- *WhoAmL 94*
Draznin, Jules Nathan 1923- *WhoWest 94*
Dr Brute 1940- *WhoAmA 93*
Drea, Edward Joseph 1954- *WhoScEn 94, WhoWest 94*
Drebbel, Cornelius Van 1572-1633 *WorInv*
Dreben, Burton Spencer 1927- *WhoAm 94*
Dreben, Raya Spiegel 1927- *WhoAm 94*
Drebsky, Dennis Jay 1946- *WhoAm 94, WhoAmL 94*
Drebus, Richard William 1924- *WhoAm 94, WhoFI 94, WhoMW 93, WhoScEn 94*
Drechney, Michaelene *WhoMW 93*
Drechsel, Edwin Jared 1914- *WhoAm 94, WhoWest 94*
Drechsler, Joseph 1782-1852 *NewGrDO*
Drechsler, Randall Richard 1945- *WhoWest 94*
Drechsler-Parks, Deborah Marie 1952- *WhoWest 94*
Dreeben, Robert 1930- *WhoMW 93*
Drees, Barry D. 1943- *WhoAmL 94*
Drees, Willem 1922- *IntWW 93*
Dregne, Harold Ernest 1916- *WhoAm 94*
Dreher, Darrell L. 1944- *WhoAm 94, WhoAmL 94*
Dreher, Lawrence John 1955- *WhoScEn 94*
Dreher, Lucille G. 1910- *WhoBlA 94*
Dreher, Murphy Andrew, Jr. 1930- *WhoAmP 93*
Dreher, Nancy C. 1942- *WhoAm 94, WhoAmL 94*
Dreher, Nicholas C. 1948- *WhoAmL 94*
Dreiband, Laurence 1944- *WhoAmA 93*
Dreier, Alex *WhoHol 92*
Dreier, David 1952- *CngDr 93, WhoAmP 93*
Dreier, David Timothy 1952- *WhoAm 94, WhoWest 94*
Dreier, Douglas H. *WhoFI 94*
Dreier, Hans 1885-1966 *IntDcF 2-4*
Dreier, Katherine S. 1877-1952 *WhoAmA 93N*
Dreier, Marc S. 1950- *WhoAmL 94*
Dreier, Ralf 1931- *IntWW 93*
Dreier Robins, Margaret 1868-1945 *WomPubS*
Dreifke, Gerald Edmond 1918- *WhoAm 94*
Dreifuss, Arthur 1908- *IntMPA 94*
Dreifuss, Fritz Emanuel 1926- *WhoAm 94*

Dreikausen, Margret 1937- *WhoAmA 93*
Dreiling, David A. 1918-1991 *WhAm 10*
Dreiling, Howard James 1951- *WhoFI 94*
Dreiling, Larry Joseph 1958- *WhoMW 93*
Dreilinger, Charles Lewis 1945- *WhoAm 94*
Dreimanis, Aleksis 1914- *IntWW 93, WhoAm 94*
Dreisbach, Clarence Ira 1903- *WhoAmA 93*
Dreisbach, John Gustave 1939- *WhoFI 94, WhoWest 94*
Dreiser, Theodore 1871-1945 *DcLB 137 [port]*
Dreiser, Theodore Herman Albert 1871-1945 *AmCulL*
Dreiss, L. Jack 1948- *WhoAm 94*
Dreitzer, Albert J. 1902-1985 *WhoAmA 93N*
Dreizen, Alison M. 1952- *WhoAm 94*
Dreizen, Samuel 1918- *WhoScEn 94*
Dreja, Chris 1944-
See Yardbirds, The *ConMus 10*
Drelich, Iris M. 1951- *WhoAm 94*
Drell, Sidney David 1926- *IntWW 93, WhoAm 94, WhoScEn 94, WhoWest 94*
Drell, William 1922- *WhoAm 94*
Dreman, David Nasaniel 1936- *WhoAm 94*
Drengler, William Allan John 1949- *WhoAmL 94, WhoAmP 93, WhoMW 93*
Drennan, Charles N. 1946- *WhoAmL 94*
Drennan, Donna Jane 1944- *WhoAmL 94*
Drennan, Michael Eldon 1946- *WhoWest 94*
Drennen, Elizabeth Jo 1953- *WhoMW 93*
Drennen, Gordon 1947- *WhoBlA 94*
Drennen, William Miller 1914- *CngDr 93, WhoAm 94*
Drennen, William Miller, Jr. 1942- *WhoAm 94*
Drenning, John B. 1937- *WhoAm 94*
Drenth, Pieter Johan Diederik 1935- *IntWW 93*
Drenth, Pieter Johan Diederk 1935- *WhoScEn 94*
Drenz, Charles Francis 1930- *WhoAm 94*
Dresbach, David Philip 1947- *WhoMW 93*
Dresbach, Janice Joy 1964- *WhoMW 93*
Dresbach, Mary Louise 1950- *WhoMW 93*
Dresch, Stephen Paul 1943- *WhoAm 94, WhoAmP 93, WhoMW 93*
Drescher, Edwin Anthony 1956- *WhoScEn 94*
Drescher, Fran 1957- *WhoHol 92*
Drescher, Henrik 1955- *WrDr 94*
Drescher, James Henry 1957- *WhoAmL 94*
Drescher, Judith Altman 1946- *WhoAm 94*
Drescher, Seymour 1934- *WhoAm 94*
Dreschhoff, Gisela Auguste Marie 1938- *WhoAm 94*
Dreschler, Wouter Albert 1953- *WhoScEn 94*
Dresdel, Sonia d1976 *WhoHol 92*
Dresden, Sem 1881-1957 *NewGrDO*
Dresdnere, Simon 1920- *WhoAmA 93*
Drese, Claus Helmut 1922- *IntWW 93*
Dresen, Adolf 1935- *NewGrDO*
Dresher, James T. 1919- *WhoAm 94, WhoFI 94*
Dresher, Paul Joseph 1951- *WhoAm 94*
Dresher, William Henry 1930- *WhoAm 94*
Dreska, John Paul 1938- *WhoAm 94*
Dreskin, Jeanet Steckler 1921- *WhoAmA 93*
Dreskin, Stephen Charles 1949- *WhoWest 94*
Dresner, Bruce Michael 1948- *WhoFI 94*
Dresner, Byron 1927- *WhoAmL 94*
Dresnick, Ronald C. 1944- *WhoAmL 94*
Dressel, Barry 1947- *WhoAm 94*
Dressel, Diane Lisette 1955- *WhoAm 94*
Dressel, Erwin 1909-1972 *NewGrDO*
Dressel, Irene Emma Ringwald 1926- *WhoMW 93*
Dressel, Jon *DrAPF 93*
Dressel, Paul Leroy 1910-1989 *WhAm 10*
Dressel, Roy Robert 1923- *WhoAm 94*
Dresselhaus, Mildred Spiewak 1930- *WhoAm 94, WhoScEn 94*
Dresser, Christopher 1834-1904 *DcNaB MP*
Dresser, Jesse Dale 1906- *WhoAm 94, WhoWest 94*
Dresser, Louisa 1907-1988 *WhoAmA 93N*
Dresser, Louise d1965 *WhoHol 92*
Dresser, Marcia van 1877-1937 *NewGrDO*
Dresser, Miles Joel 1935- *WhoWest 94*
Dresser, Norine 1931- *WrDr 94*
Dresser, Paul Alton, Jr. 1942- *WhoFI 94*
Dresser, Phyllis Howe *WhoAmP 93*
Dressick, Walter J. 1955- *WhoScEn 94*
Dressler, Alan Michael 1948- *WhoAm 94, WhoWest 94*
Dressler, David Charles 1928- *WhoFI 94*
Dressler, Joshua 1947- *WhoMW 93*
Dressler, Lieux *WhoHol 92*
Dressler, Marie d1934 *WhoHol 92*
Dressler, Marie 1869-1934 *WhoCom*
Dressler, Robert A. 1945- *WhoAm 94*
Dressler, Robert Anthony 1945- *WhoAmP 93*
Dressler, Robert Eugene 1922-1990 *WhAm 10*
Dressler, Robert Eugene 1944- *WhoMW 93*
Dressler, Susan Alice 1946- *WhoMW 93*
Dressner, Howard Roy 1919- *WhoAm 94*
Dretske, Frederick Irwin 1932- *IntWW 93*
Dreumont, Antonio Alcides 1939- *WhoHisp 94*
Drever, Richard Alston, Jr. 1936- *WhoWest 94*
Drevets, Wayne Curtis 1957- *WhoMW 93*
Drevinsky, David Matthew 1957- *WhoScEn 94*
Drew, Ann d1974 *WhoHol 92*
Drew, Arthur (Charles Walter) 1912- *Who 94*
Drew, Bruce Arthur 1924- *WhoMW 93*
Drew, Charles Milton 1921- *WhoWest 94*
Drew, Charles Richard 1904-1950 *AfrAmAl 6, WorInv*
Drew, Clifford James 1943- *WhoAm 94*
Drew, Delphine d1979 *WhoHol 92*
Drew, Donald Allen 1945- *WhoAm 94*
Drew, Elizabeth 1935- *WhoAm 94*
Drew, Elizabeth Heineman 1940- *WhoAm 94*
Drew, Ellen 1915- *WhoHol 92*
Drew, Ernest Harold 1937- *WhoAm 94, WhoFI 94*
Drew, Fraser (Bragg Robert) 1913- *WrDr 94*
Drew, Fraser Bragg Robert 1913- *WhoAm 94*
Drew, G. John 1940- *WhoAmP 93*
Drew, Gayden, IV 1953- *WhoAmL 94*
Drew, Gene d1990 *WhoHol 92*
Drew, George *DrAPF 93*
Drew, George Charles 1911- *Who 94*
Drew, Gerald John 1939- *WhoIns 94*
Drew, Horace Rainsford, Jr. 1918- *WhoAm 94*
Drew, Jack Hunter 1925- *WhoAmP 93*
Drew, James Brown 1922- *WhoBlA 94*
Drew, Jane Beverly 1911- *IntWW 93, Who 94*
Drew, Joanna Marie 1929- *Who 94*
Drew, John 1954- *BasBi*
Drew, John Alexander 1907- *Who 94*
Drew, John Sydney Neville 1936- *IntWW 93, Who 94*
Drew, Judy Morine 1951- *WhoMW 93*
Drew, Katherine Fischer 1923- *WhoAm 94*
Drew, Kathleen Kurlinski 1960- *WhoAmP 93*
Drew, Kenny d1993 *NewYTBS 93*
Drew, Larry Donelle 1958- *WhoBlA 94*
Drew, Lillian d1924 *WhoHol 92*
Drew, Lowell d1942 *WhoHol 92*
Drew, Max d1987 *WhoHol 92*
Drew, Nicholas 1910- *WrDr 94*
Drew, Paul 1935- *WhoAm 94*
Drew, Peter Robert Lionel 1927- *Who 94*
Drew, Philip 1943- *WrDr 94*
Drew, Philip Garfield 1932- *WhoAm 94*
Drew, Philip Yale d1940 *WhoHol 92*
Drew, Philippa Catherine 1946- *Who 94*
Drew, Richard *WorInv*
Drew, Richard Allen 1941- *WhoScEn 94*
Drew, Robert J. *WhoHol 92*
Drew, Roland d1988 *WhoHol 92*
Drew, Russell Cooper 1931- *WhoAm 94*
Drew, S. Rankin d1918 *WhoHol 92*
Drew, Sharon Lee 1946- *WhoWest 94*
Drew, Sidney d1919 *WhoHol 92*
Drew, Sidney, Mrs. d1925 *WhoHol 92*
Drew, Stephen Richard 1949- *WhoAmL 94, WhoBlA 94*
Drew, Thelma Lucille *WhoBlA 94*
Drew, Walter Harlow 1935- *WhoAm 94*
Drew, Wayland 1932- *EncSF 93*
Drew, Weldon 1935- *WhoBlA 94*
Drewal, Henry John 1943- *WhoAmA 93*
Drewe, Robert 1943- *WrDr 94*
Drewek, Gerard Alan 1963- *WhoScEn 94*
Drewery, Ida Mae Moore 1927- *WhoAm 94*
Drewes, Werner 1899-1985 *WhoAmA 93N*
Drewitt, (Lionel) Frank 1932- *Who 94*
Drewitz, Ingeborg 1923-1986 *BlmGWL*
Drewlow, Bruce 1956- *WhoMW 93*
Drewlowe, Eve 1924-1988 *WhoAmA 93N*
Drew-Peeples, Brenda 1947- *WhoBlA 94*
Drewry, Anthony B. 1947- *WhoAmL 94*
Drewry, Cecelia Hodges *WhoBlA 94*
Drewry, David John 1947- *Who 94*
Drewry, Guy Carleton 1901-1991 *WhAm 10*
Drewry, Henry Nathaniel 1924- *WhoBlA 94*
Drews, Juergen 1933- *IntWW 93*
Drews, Jurgen 1933- *WhoScEn 94*
Drews, Robert Carrel 1930- *WhoAm 94*
Drewsen, Jette 1943- *BlmGWL*
Drexel, Jay B. *EncSF 93*
Drexel, Katharine 1858-1955 *DcAmReB 2*
Drexel, Katherine 1858-1955 *EncNAR*
Drexel, Nancy d1989 *WhoHol 92*
Drexler, Arthur Justin 1925-1987 *WhoAmA 93N*
Drexler, Clyde 1962- *BasBi, WhoAm 94, WhoBlA 94, WhoWest 94*
Drexler, Douglas E. 1949- *WhoFI 94*
Drexler, Fred 1915- *WhoAm 94*
Drexler, Joanne Lee 1944- *WhoFI 94*
Drexler, Kenneth 1941- *WhoAmL 94, WhoWest 94*
Drexler, Kim Eric 1955- *WhoWest 94*
Drexler, Lloyd 1918- *WhoFI 94*
Drexler, Lynne *WhoAmA 93*
Drexler, Mary Sanford 1954- *WhoFI 94, WhoMW 93*
Drexler, Michael David 1938- *WhoAm 94, WhoFI 94*
Drexler, Millard S. 1944- *CurBio 93 [port], WhoFI 94*
Drexler, Paul 1947- *WhoWest 94*
Drexler, Richard Allan 1947- *WhoAm 94, WhoMW 93*
Drexler, Rosalyn 1926- *ConDr 93, WrDr 94*
Drexler, Rudy Matthew, Jr. 1941- *WhoMW 93*
Dreyer, Clarice A. 1946- *WhoAmA 93*
Dreyer, David E. *WhoAm 94*
Dreyer, Desmond (Parry) 1910- *Who 94*
Dreyer, Gay 1915- *WhoAmA 93*
Dreyer, Johann Conrad 1672-1742 *NewGrDO*
Dreyer, Leo Philip 1944- *WhoAmL 94*
Dreyfus, Alfred Stanley 1921- *WhoAm 94*
Dreyfus, Brandon Balfred 1953- *WhoFI 94*
Dreyfus, George 1928- *IntWW 93, NewGrDO*
Dreyfus, George Joseph 1920- *WhoAm 94*
Dreyfus, Howard Marlow 1942- *WhoIns 94*
Dreyfus, James K. 1947- *WhoAmL 94*
Dreyfus, John Gustave 1918- *Who 94*
Dreyfus, Lee Sherman 1926- *IntWW 93, WhoAmP 93*
Dreyfus, Pierre 1907- *IntWW 93, Who 94*
Dreyfus, Rene d1993 *NewYTBS 93*
Dreyfuss, Joel P. 1945- *WhoBlA 94*
Dreyfuss, John Alan 1933- *WhoAm 94*
Dreyfuss, Lorin *WhoHol 92*
Dreyfuss, Max Peter 1932- *WhoMW 93*
Dreyfuss, Michael d1960 *WhoHol 92*
Dreyfuss, Patricia 1932- *WhoMW 93, WhoScEn 94*
Dreyfuss, Randy *WhoHol 92*
Dreyfuss, Richard 1947- *IntMPA 94, WhoHol 92*
Dreyfuss, Richard Stephan 1947- *IntWW 93, WhoAm 94*
Drezdzon, William Lawrence 1934- *WhoMW 93*
Dreze, Jean 1959- *WrDr 94*
Drezner, Stephen M. 1937- *WhoScEn 94*
Dribin, Leland George 1944- *WhoAmL 94*
Dribin, Michael A. 1951- *WhoAmL 94*
Drickamer, Harry George 1918- *IntWW 93, WhoAm 94, WhoMW 93, WhoScEn 94*
Driedger, Florence Gay 1933- *WhoAm 94*
Driedger, Paul Edwin 1948- *WhoScEn 94*
Driegert, Robert S. 1942- *WhoAmP 93*
Driehaus, Robert J. 1928- *WhoIns 94*
Driehuys, Leonardus Bastiaan 1932- *WhoAm 94*
Drielsma, Claude Dunbar H. *Who 94*
Drier, Moosie 1964- *WhoHol 92*
Dries, Kathleen Marie 1946- *WhoMW 93*
Driesbach, David Fraiser 1922- *WhoAmA 93*
Driesbach, Walter Clark, Jr. 1929- *WhoAmA 93*
Driesell, Lefty 1939- *BasBi*
Driessel, Kenneth Richard 1940- *WhoWest 94*
Driessen, Angela Kosta *WhoAmA 93*
Driessen, Anthony Hartman 1948- *WhoAmL 94*
Driessen, Dan 1951- *WhoBlA 94*
Driessen, Henry, Jr. 1927- *WhoBlA 94*
Driessen, Paul 1940- *IntDcF 2-4*
Driessler, Johannes 1921- *NewGrDO*
Drif, Zohra 1941- *BlmGWL*
Driggers, Don d1972 *WhoHol 92*
Driggers, Timothy Gerald 1947- *WhoAmP 93*
Driggriss, Daphne Bernice Sutherland *WhoBlA 94*
Driggs, Charles Mulford 1924- *WhoAm 94, WhoAmL 94*
Driggs, Don Wallace 1924- *WhoAmP 93*
Driggs, Elsie 1898-1992 *WhoAmA 93N*
Driker, Eugene 1937- *WhoAm 94, WhoAmL 94*
Drikow, Dawn Lynn 1965- *WhoMW 93*
Drill, Lisa Marie 1959- *WhoAmL 94*
Drillinger, Brian 1960- *WhoHol 92*
Drimmer, Melvin 1934-1992 *WhAm 10*
Drinan, Robert F. 1920- *IntWW 93*
Drinan, Robert Frederick 1920- *WhoAm 94, WhoAmL 94, WhoAmP 93*
Drinane, Suleika Cabrera 1943- *WhoHisp 94*
Dring, Richard Paddison 1913- *Who 94*
Drinkall, John Kenneth 1922- *Who 94*
Drinkard, William H. *WhoAmP 93*
Drinker, Elizabeth Sandwith 1734-1807 *BlmGWL*
Drinko, John Deaver 1921- *WhoAm 94, WhoAmL 94, WhoMW 93*
Drinkrow, John *ConAu 42NR, Who 94*
Drinkrow, John 1924- *WrDr 94*
Drinkwater, Carol 1948- *WhoHol 92*
Drinkwater, Herbert *WhoAmP 93*
Drinkwater, Herbert R. *WhoWest 94*
Drinkwater, John (Muir) 1925- *Who 94*
Drinkwater, Penny 1929- *WrDr 94*
Drinkwater, William Wayne 1949- *WhoAmL 94*
Drinkwine, Edward Allen 1946- *WhoMW 93*
Drinnan, Alan John 1932- *WhoAm 94*
Drinnon, Richard 1925- *WhoAm 94*
Drinnon, Robert Steve 1944- *WhoAmP 93*
Driscol, Jeffrey William 1961- *WhoScEn 94*
Driscoll, Abigail Julia Hannah 1958- *WhoAmA 93*
Driscoll, Bobby d1968 *WhoHol 92*
Driscoll, Charles F. 1950- *WhoScEn 94*
Driscoll, Charles Francis 1943- *WhoMW 93*
Driscoll, Dawn-Marie 1946- *WhoAmL 94*
Driscoll, Edgar Joseph, Jr. 1920- *WhoAmA 93*
Driscoll, Edward Carroll, Jr. 1952- *WhoWest 94*
Driscoll, Edward Maurice 1936- *WhoAmP 93*
Driscoll, Ellen *WhoAmA 93*
Driscoll, Frances *DrAPF 93*
Driscoll, Frederick Donaghue 1957- *WhoFI 94*
Driscoll, Geoffrey C. 1953- *WhoAmP 93*
Driscoll, Glen Robert 1920- *WhoAm 94*
Driscoll, Henry Keane 1953- *WhoScEn 94*
Driscoll, James 1925- *Who 94*
Driscoll, James Glynn 1948- *WhoAmL 94*
Driscoll, James Michael 1939- *WhoAm 94*
Driscoll, James Philip 1943- *Who 94*
Driscoll, Jerry A. 1946- *WhoMW 93*
Driscoll, Jerry L. 1944- *WhoAmP 93*
Driscoll, John d1968 *ProFbHF*
Driscoll, John Brian 1946- *WhoAmP 93*
Driscoll, John Gerald, Jr. 1897- *WhAm 10*
Driscoll, John Paul 1949- *WhoAmA 93*
Driscoll, John R. 1924- *WhoAmP 93*
Driscoll, Joseph Aloysius 1940- *WhoFI 94*
Driscoll, Joseph D. *WhoAmP 93*
Driscoll, Joseph L. d1993 *NewYTBS 93*
Driscoll, Judith Ann 1944- *WhoMW 93*
Driscoll, Lee Francis, Jr. 1926- *WhoAm 94*
Driscoll, Loren 1928- *NewGrDO*
Driscoll, Mary Harris *DrAPF 93*
Driscoll, Michael Hardee 1946- *WhoAmL 94*
Driscoll, Michael John 1947- *Who 94*
Driscoll, Michael P. 1939- *WhoWest 94*
Driscoll, Patricia 1927- *WhoHol 92*
Driscoll, Peter 1942- *WrDr 94*
Driscoll, Robert L. 1939- *WhoAm 94*
Driscoll, Robert Miller d1983 *WhoHol 92*
Driscoll, Sean *NewYTBS 93 [port]*
Driscoll, Terence Patrick 1948- *WhoScEn 94*
Driscoll, Tex d1979 *WhoHol 92*
Driscoll, William J. 1913- *WhoAmP 93*
Driscoll, William Michael 1929- *WhoAm 94*
Driskell, Claude Evans 1926- *WhoAm 94, WhoBlA 94, WhoMW 93, WhoScEn 94*
Driskell, David C. 1931- *WhoBlA 94*
Driskell, David Clyde 1931- *AfrAmAl 6, WhoAmA 93*
Driskill, Clarence 1945- *WhoAm 94*
Driskill, Frank A. 1912- *WrDr 94*
Driskill, John R. 1934- *WhoIns 94*
Driskill, John Ray 1934- *WhoAm 94*
Driskill, Joseph L. 1955- *WhoAmP 93*
Driskill, Kevin 1957- *WhoAmL 94*
Drisko, Barbara Lucille 1932- *WhoAmP 93*
Drisko, Elliot Hillman 1917- *WhoAm 94*
Driss, Rachid 1917- *IntWW 93*
Dritsas, George Vassilios 1940- *WhoScEn 94*
Drivas, Robert d1986 *WhoHol 92*
Driver, Antony (Victor) 1920- *Who 94*

Driver, Bryan 1932- *Who 94*
Driver, C(harles) J(onathan) 1939- *WrDr 94*
Driver, C. Stephen 1936- *WhoFI 94*
Driver, Charles Jonathan 1939- *Who 94*
Driver, Christopher (Prout) 1932- *WrDr 94*
Driver, Christopher Prout 1932- *Who 94*
Driver, Claudia Laraine 1956- *WhoAmL 94*
Driver, Elwood T. 1921-1992 *WhoBlA 94N*
Driver, Eric (William) 1911- *Who 94*
Driver, Joe 1946- *WhoAmP 93*
Driver, Joe L. 1946- *WhoFI 94*
Driver, Johnie M. 1933- *WhoBlA 94*
Driver, Lottie Elizabeth 1918- *WhoAm 94*
Driver, Louie M., Jr. 1924- *WhoBlA 94*
Driver, Olga Lindholm *Who 94*
Driver, Richard J. 1937- *WhoAmL 94*
Driver, Richard John 1937- *WhoAmP 93*
Driver, Richard Sonny, Jr. 1926- *WhoBlA 94*
Driver, Robert Baylor, Jr. 1942- *WhoAm 94*
Driver, Rodney D. 1932- *WhoAmP 93*
Driver, Rodney David 1932- *WhoAm 94, WhoScEn 94*
Driver, Rogers W. 1921- *WhoBlA 94*
Driver, Tom Faw 1925- *WhoAm 94*
Driver, Walter W., Jr. 1945- *WhoAmL 94*
Driver, William Raymond, Jr. 1907- *WhoAm 94, WhoFI 94*
Drizulis, Aleksandrs 1920- *IntWW 93*
Drnevich, Vincent Paul 1940- *WhoScEn 94*
Drobac, Nikola 1953- *WhoFI 94*
Drobile, James Albert 1927- *WhoAm 94*
Drobinski, Roger J. 1951- *WhoIns 94*
Drobis, David R. *WhoAm 94, WhoFI 94*
Drobny, Jaroslav 1921- *BuCMET*
Drobot, Eve 1951- *WrDr 94*
Droege, Anthony Joseph, II 1943- *WhoAmA 93*
Droege, Harrison David 1961- *WhoFI 94, WhoWest 94*
Droegemueller, William 1934- *WhoAm 94*
Droegmueller, Lee *WhoAm 94*
Droessler, Earl G. *WhoScEn 94*
Drogheda, Earl of 1910-1989 *NewGrDO*
Drogheda, Earl of 1937- *Who 94*
Droghierina, La *NewGrDO*
Drogkamp, Charles d1958 *WhoAmA 93N*
Drohan, Thomas H. 1936- *WhoAm 94*
Drohojowska, Hunter 1952- *WhoAmA 93*
Drohojowska-Philp, Hunter 1952- *WhoWest 94*
Droit, Michel 1923- *IntWW 93*
Drolet, Paul Joseph 1951- *WhoAmL 94*
Drolet, Paul L. 1928- *WhoAmP 93*
Droll, Marian Clarke 1931- *WhoAm 94*
Droll, Raymond John 1956- *WhoScEn 94*
Dromberg, Kaarina 1942- *WhoWomW 91*
Dromer, Jean 1929- *IntWW 93*
Dromgold, George d1948 *WhoHol 92*
Dromgoole, Ida Hilda Acuna 1948- *WhoHisp 94*
Dromgoole, Jolyon 1926- *Who 94*
Dromgoole, Patrick 1930- *IntMPA 94*
Dromgoole, Patrick Shirley Brookes Fleming 1930- *Who 94*
Dromi, Jose Roberto 1945- *IntWW 93*
Dromore, Bishop of 1924- *Who 94*
Droms, William George 1944- *WhoAm 94*
Dronenburg, Ernest Justin, Jr. 1943- *WhoAmP 93*
Droney, Christopher *WhoAmL 94*
Droney, John F., Jr. 1946- *WhoAmP 93*
Dronfield, Ronald 1924- *Who 94*
Dronke, (Ernst) Peter (Michael) 1934- *IntWW 93, Who 94*
Droogan, Cornelius James 1948- *WhoAmL 94*
Droogleever Fortuyn, Jan 1906- *IntWW 93*
Drooyan, Richard E. 1950- *WhoAmL 94*
Dropkin, Allen Hodes 1930- *WhoAmL 94, WhoMW 93*
Droppers, Carl H 1918- *WrDr 94*
Drossman, Jay Lewis 1932- *WhoScEn 94*
Drossoyiannis, Anthony 1922- *IntWW 93*
Drost, Cristina Llorente 1934- *WhoMW 93*
Drost, Cynthia Mae Van Veldhuizen 1961- *WhoAmP 93*
Drost, Marianne 1950- *WhoAm 94, WhoAmL 94*
Droste, Donald Casper *WhoFI 94*
Droste, Jean Rasmusen 1941- *WhoMW 93*
Droste-Hulshoff, Annette von 1797-1848 *BlmGWL, DcLB 133 [port], RfGShF*
Drotning, John Evan 1932- *WhoAm 94*
Drott, Martin Ardo 1948- *WhoMW 93*
Drouat, Jean-Claude *WhoHol 92*
Drouet, Robert d1914 *WhoHol 92*
Drouilhet, Paul Raymond, Jr. 1933- *WhoAm 94*
Drouillard, George c. 1770-1810 *WhWE*
Drouin, Richard *WhoFI 94*
Droukas, Ann Hantis 1923- *WhoFI 94*
Drovdal, David *WhoAmP 93*
Drower, G(eorge) M(atthew) F(rederick) 1954- *WrDr 94*
Drower, Margaret Stefana 1911- *WrDr 94*
Drower, Sara Ruth 1938- *WhoAmA 93*
Drown, Eugene Ardent 1915- *WhoWest 94*
Drown, Henry 1920- *WrDr 94*
Drown, Merle *DrAPF 93*
Drowota, Frank F., III 1938- *WhoAmL 94, WhoAmP 93*
Droz, Charles Clinton 1924- *WhoAmP 93*
Droz, Georges Andre Leopold 1931- *IntWW 93*
Droz, Henry 1926- *WhoAm 94*
Drozd, Joseph Duane 1957- *WhoScEn 94*
Drozd, Leon Frank, Jr. 1948- *WhoWest 94*
Drozd, Phyllis Ann 1932- *WhoMW 93*
Drozda, Helen Dorothy 1924- *WhAm 10*
Drozda, Joseph Michael 1943- *WhoFI 94, WhoMW 93*
Drozda, William 1948- *WhoAmP 93*
Drozdeck, Steven Richard 1951- *WhoFI 94*
Drozdova, Margarita Sergeyevna 1948- *IntWW 93*
Drozdziel, Marion John 1924- *WhoFI 94, WhoScEn 94*
Dr. Seuss *SmATA 75*
Dru, Joanne 1923- *IntMPA 94, WhoHol 92*
Drubin, Charles d1976 *WhoHol 92*
Druce, Hubert d1931 *WhoHol 92*
Druce, Tom *WhoAmP 93*
Druck, James Burton 1941- *WhoAm 94, WhoAmL 94*
Druck, Kalman Breschel 1914- *WhoAm 94*
Druck, Mark *WhoAm 94*
Drucker, A. Norman 1930- *WhoAmL 94*
Drucker, Alan Steven 1948- *WhoFI 94*
Drucker, Barry Jules 1940- *WhoMW 93*
Drucker, Daniel Charles 1918- *IntWW 93, WhoAm 94, WhoScEn 94, WrDr 94*
Drucker, H. M. 1942- *WrDr 94*
Drucker, Harvey 1941- *WhoScEn 94*
Drucker, Henry Matthew 1942- *Who 94*
Drucker, Jacquelin F. *WhoAmL 94*
Drucker, Jean Maurice 1941- *IntWW 93*
Drucker, Johanna *DrAPF 93*
Drucker, Melvin Bruce 1927- *WhoAm 94*
Drucker, Mort 1929- *WhoAm 94, WrDr 94*
Drucker, Norm 1929- *BasBi*
Drucker, Peter (Ferdinand) 1909- *Who 94, WrDr 94*
Drucker, Peter Ferdinand 1909- *IntWW 93, WhoAm 94, WhoWest 94*
Drucker, Sally Ann *DrAPF 93*
Drucker, William Richard 1922- *WhoAm 94*
Druckman, Jacob Raphael 1928- *WhoAm 94*
Druckman, Jeffrey J. 1954- *WhoAmL 94*
Druckman, William Frank 1939- *WhoScEn 94*
Druckrey, Gerald Richard 1933- *WhoMW 93*
Drudge, Junior Harold 1922- *WhoAm 94*
Drudi, John Louis 1935- *WhoFI 94, WhoMW 93*
Dru Drury, Martin *Who 94*
Drudy, Patrick 1943- *WhoAm 94*
Drue, Kerry Erica 1966- *WhoAmL 94*
Druehl, Louis Dix 1936- *WhoAm 94, WhoScEn 94*
Druen, William Sidney 1942- *WhoAm 94*
Druery, Charles Thomas 1843-1917 *EncSF 93*
Druett, Joan 1939- *ConAu 140*
Drufenbrock, Diane Joyce 1929- *WhoAmP 93*
Drugan, Cornelius Bernard 1946- *WhoMW 93*
Druhot, Theodore Joseph 1934- *WhoAm 94*
Druick, Douglas Wesley 1945- *WhoAm 94*
Druillet, Philippe 1944- *EncSF 93*
Druillettes, Gabriel 1610-1681 *EncNAR*
Druk, Mirchea 1941- *IntWW 93*
Druke, William Erwin 1938- *WhoAmL 94*
Druker, Henry Leo 1953- *WhoAm 94*
Druker, Isaac E. 1937- *WhoAm 94*
Druks, Herbert 1937- *WrDr 94*
Drum, James d1976 *WhoHol 92*
Drum, Sydney Maria 1952- *WhoAmA 93*
Drumheller, George Jesse 1933- *WhoWest 94*
Drumheller, Helen E. 1931- *WhoAmP 93*
Drumheller, Jerry Paul 1948- *WhoScEn 94*
Drumheller, John Earl 1931- *WhoWest 94*
Drumier, Jack d1929 *WhoHol 92*
Drumke, Ronald Alfred 1941- *WhoAmL 94*
Drumlanrig, Viscount 1967- *Who 94*
Drumm, Chris 1949- *EncSF 93*
Drumm, D.B. *EncSF 93*
Drumm, D. B. 1950- *WrDr 94*
Drumm, David Gary 1955- *WhoAmL 94*
Drumm, Don 1935- *WhoAmA 93*
Drumm, Kevin James 1967- *WhoMW 93*
Drumm, Mitchell Lewis 1960- *WhoMW 93*
Drumm, Walter Gregory 1940- *Who 94*
Drummer, Donald Raymond 1941- *WhoAm 94, WhoWest 94*
Drummer, William Richard 1925- *WhoAmA 93*
Drummey, Charles E. 1933- *WhoAmL 94*
Drummond *Who 94*
Drummond, Alice 1928- *WhoHol 92*
Drummond, Anthony John D. *Who 94*
Drummond, Arthur A. 1891- *WhoAmA 93N*
Drummond, David Classon 1928- *Who 94*
Drummond, David L., Sr. 1918- *WhoBlA 94*
Drummond, Dugald 1840-1912 *DcNaB MP*
Drummond, Edward Joseph 1906-1991 *WhAm 10*
Drummond, Emma *WrDr 94*
Drummond, Garry N. *WhoAm 94*
Drummond, Gerard Kasper 1937- *WhoAm 94, WhoFI 94, WhoWest 94*
Drummond, Ian M 1933- *WrDr 94*
Drummond, Ivor 1929- *WrDr 94*
Drummond, James Everman 1932- *WhoAm 94*
Drummond, John 1919- *WhoAmP 93*
Drummond, John Richard Gray 1934- *Who 94*
Drummond, June 1923- *WrDr 94*
Drummond, Kevin *Who 94*
Drummond, (Thomas Anthony) Kevin 1943- *Who 94*
Drummond, Malcolm McAllister 1937- *WhoFI 94*
Drummond, Maldwin Andrew Cyril 1932- *Who 94*
Drummond, Marshall Edward 1941- *WhoAm 94, WhoWest 94*
Drummond, Martha Mason 1958- *WhoWest 94*
Drummond, Norman Walker 1952- *Who 94*
Drummond, Peter 1850-1918 *DcNaB MP*
Drummond, Richard Henry 1916- *WhoAm 94*
Drummond, Robert Kendig 1939- *WhoAm 94*
Drummond, Roger Otto 1931- *WhoScEn 94*
Drummond, Sally Hazelet 1924- *WhoAm 94, WhoAmA 93*
Drummond, Thornton B., Jr. 1927- *WhoBlA 94*
Drummond, V(iolet) H(ilda) 1911- *WrDr 94*
Drummond, William Eckel 1927- *WhoScEn 94*
Drummond, William Joe 1944- *WhoBlA 94, WhoWest 94*
Drummond, William John 1949- *WhoMW 93*
Drummond, William Norman 1927- *Who 94*
Drummond, William, of Hawthornden 1585-1649 *BlmGEL*
Drummond, Winslow 1933- *WhoAm 94*
Drummond Young, James Edward 1950- *Who 94*
Drumright, Everett F. d1993 *NewYTBS 93 [port]*
Drumright, Everett F. 1907- *HisDcKW*
Druon, Maurice Samuel Roger Charles 1918- *IntWW 93, Who 94*
Drury, Allen (Stuart) 1918- *EncSF 93, WrDr 94*
Drury, Allen Stuart 1918- *IntWW 93, Who 94, WhoAm 94*
Drury, Charles Louis, Jr. 1955- *WhoAm 94, WhoFI 94*
Drury, Charles Mills 1912-1991 *WhAm 10*
Drury, Clifford Merrill 1897- *WhAm 10*
Drury, David J. 1944- *WhoIns 94*
Drury, David Michael 1951- *WhoMW 93*
Drury, George *DrAPF 93*
Drury, James 1934- *IntMPA 94, WhoHol 92*
Drury, John *DrAPF 93*
Drury, John 1936- *WrDr 94*
Drury, John Henry 1936- *Who 94*
Drury, Kenneth Clayton 1945- *WhoScEn 94*
Drury, Lance Richer 1953- *WhoMW 93*
Drury, Leonard Leroy 1928- *WhoAm 94*
Drury, Martin Dru 1938- *Who 94*
Drury, Maxine Cole 1914- *WrDr 94*
Drury, Michael *Who 94*
Drury, (Victor William) Michael 1926- *Who 94*
Drury, Susie B. 1927- *WhoAmP 93*
Drury, William H. 1888-1960 *WhoAmA 93N*
Druschitz, Alan Peter 1955- *WhoScEn 94*
Druss, David Lloyd 1953- *WhoScEn 94*
Druss, Richard George 1933- *WhoScEn 94*
Drutchas, Gerrick Gilbert 1953- *WhoFI 94, WhoWest 94*
Drutchas, Gregory G. 1949- *WhoAm 94, WhoAmL 94*
Druten, John van *IntDcT 2*
Drutt, Helen Williams 1930- *WhoAmA 93*
Drutz, David Jules 1938- *WhoFI 94*
Drutz, June 1920- *WhoAmA 93*
Druyan, Mary Ellen 1938- *WhoMW 93*
Drvota, Mojmir 1923- *WhoAm 94*
Dryasdust *EncSF 93*
Dryden, Charles Walter 1920- *WhoBlA 94*
Dryden, David Charles 1947- *WhoFI 94*
Dryden, John 1631-1700 *BlmGEL [port], DcLB 131 [port], IntDcT 2 [port], NewGrDO*
Dryden, John (Stephen Gyles) 1943- *Who 94*
Dryden, Leo d1939 *WhoHol 92*
Dryden, Martin Francis, Jr. 1915- *WhoAm 94*
Dryden, Pamela *WrDr 94*
Dryden, Phylis Campbell *DrAPF 93*
Dryden, Richie Sloan 1938- *WhoScEn 94*
Dryden, Robert Charles 1936- *WhoAm 94*
Dryden, Robert Eugene 1927- *WhoAm 94, WhoAmL 94, WhoWest 94*
Dryden, Wheeler d1957 *WhoHol 92*
Dryden-Quadros, Mary Elizabeth 1949- *WhoAmL 94*
Dryer, Clayton Christopher 1951- *WhoWest 94*
Dryer, Douglas Poole 1915- *IntWW 93, WhoAm 94*
Dryer, Fred 1946- *WhoHol 92*
Dryer, Glen J. 1958- *WhoAmL 94*
Dryer, Moira Jane 1957-1992 *WhoAmA 93N*
Dryer, Murray 1925- *WhoAm 94*
Dryer, Randy L. 1949- *WhoAmL 94*
Dryer, Robert *WhoHol 92*
Dryer, Shawn Peter 1946- *WhoMW 93*
Dryfoos, Michael G. 1959- *WhoWest 94*
Dryfoos, Nancy 1918-1991 *WhoAmA 93N*
Dryfoos, Nancy Proskauer d1991 *WhAm 10*
Dryfoos, Robert J. 1942- *WhoAmP 93*
Drygalski, Erich von 1865-1949 *WhWE [port]*
Dryhurst, Glenn 1939- *WhoAm 94*
Drylie, Christine Marie 1966- *WhoAmL 94, WhoMW 93*
Drymalski, Raymond Hibner 1936- *WhoAm 94*
Drynan, Jeanie *WhoHol 92*
Drysdale, Andrew 1935- *IntWW 93*
Drysdale, Cliff 1941- *BuCMET*
Drysdale, Don d1993 *NewYTBS 93 [port]*
Drysdale, Don 1936-1993 *CurBio 93N, News 94-1*
Drysdale, George Marsman 1954- *WhoAmL 94, WhoWest 94*
Drysdale, Learmont 1866-1909 *NewGrDO*
Drysdale, Lee *WhoHol 92*
Drysdale, Nancy McIntosh 1931- *WhoAmA 93*
Drysdale, Thomas Henry 1942- *Who 94*
Drysdale Wilson, John Veitch 1929- *Who 94*
Drzewiecki, David Samuel 1953- *WhoScEn 94*
Drzewiecki, Gary F. 1954- *WhoAmP 93*
Drzewiecki, Tadeusz Maria 1943- *WhoAm 94*
Drzewinski, Michael Anthony 1958- *WhoScEn 94*
D'Souza, Anthony Frank 1929- *WhoAm 94*
D'Souza, Austin 1950- *WhoMW 93*
D'Souza, Eugene 1917- *IntWW 93*
D'Souza, Harry J. 1955- *WhoAsA 94*
D'Souza, Henry Sebastian *Who 94*
D'Souza, Maximian Felix 1965- *WhoScEn 94*
D'Souza, Russell Raj 1962- *WhoFI 94*
Du, Ding-Zhu 1948- *WhoScEn 94*
Du, Gonghuan 1934- *WhoScEn 94*
Du, Julie Yi-Fang Tsai 1937- *WhoAm 94*
Dua, Octave 1882-1952 *NewGrDO*
Dual, J. Fred, Jr. 1942- *WhoBlA 94*
Dual, Peter Alfred 1946- *WhoBlA 94*
Duane, Diane *WrDr 94*
Duane, Diane 1952- *TwCYAW*
Duane, Diane E(lizabeth) 1952- *EncSF 93*
Duane, Jack d1960 *WhoHol 92*
Duane, James 1733-1797 *WhAmRev*
Duane, John F. 1953- *WhoAmP 93*
Duane, Tanya *WhoAmA 93N*
Duane, Thomas D. d1993 *NewYTBS 93 [port]*
Duane, Thomas K. *WhoAmP 93*
Duane, William Francis 1948- *WhoAm 94*

Duan Jin *WhoPRCh 91*
Duan Junyi 1910- *WhoPRCh 91 [port]*
Duanmu Hongliang 1912- *WhoPRCh 91 [port]*
Duanmu Hongliang 1921- *IntWW 93*
Duanmu Zheng 1920- *WhoPRCh 91 [port]*
Duan Ruiyu *WhoPRCh 91*
Duan Suquan 1916- *WhoPRCh 91 [port]*
Duan Wenjie *WhoPRCh 91 [port]*
Duany, Luis Alberto 1965- *WhoHisp 94*
Duan Yinming *WhoPRCh 91*
Duan Yuanpei *WhoPRCh 91*
Duan Yuhua *WhoPRCh 91*
Duan Zijun *WhoPRCh 91 [port]*
Duarte, Amalia Maria 1962- *WhoHisp 94*
Duarte, Cristobal G. 1929- *WhoScEn 94*
Duarte, David *WhoHisp 94*
Duarte, Elena M. *WhoAmP 93*
Duarte, Eva d1952 *WhoHol 92*
Duarte, Jose Napoleon 1925-1990 *WhAm 10*
Duarte, Leroy Wilson 1947- *WhoAmL 94*
Duarte, Patricia *WhoHisp 94*
Duarte, Patricia 1938- *WhoFI 94*
Duarte, Ramon Gonzalez 1948- *WhoScEn 94, WhoWest 94*
Duarte, Y. E. 1948- *WhoHisp 94*
Duarte-Valverde, Gloria A. 1950- *WhoHisp 94*
Duax, William Leo 1939- *WhoAm 94, WhoScEn 94*
Duayen, Cesar *BlmGWL*
Dub, Stanley M. 1950- *WhoAmL 94*
Duba, Darcie Ann 1965- *WhoWest 94*
Duback, Charles S. 1926- *WhoAmA 93*
Duback, Steven Rahr 1944- *WhoAm 94, WhoAmL 94*
Dubai, Ruler of *IntWW 93*
Du Bain, Myron 1923- *WhoAm 94*
Duband, Wayne 1947- *IntMPA 94*
Dubaniewicz, Peter Paul 1913- *WhoAmA 93*
Du Bar, Jules Ramon 1923- *WhoAm 94*
Du Barry, Denise *WhoHol 92*
Du Bartas, Guillaume de Saluste 1544-1590 *BlmGEL*
Dubasky, Valentina 1951- *WhoAmA 93*
Dubaz, Larry, Jr. *WhoAmP 93*
Dubbert, Patricia Marie 1947- *WhoAm 94*
Dubbins, Don 1929- *WhoHol 92*
Dubble, Curtis William 1922- *WhoAm 94*
Dubbs, John William, III 1951- *WhoAm 94*
Dubcek, Alexander d1992 *IntWW 93N*
Dubcek, Alexander 1921-1992 *AnObit 1992, CurBio 93N, HisWorL [port]*
Dube, Ellen C. 1947- *WhoAmP 93*
Dube, Ghyslain *WhoScEn 94*
Dube, Lawrence Edward, Jr. 1948- *WhoAmL 94*
Dube, Leroy S. 1908- *WhoAmP 93*
Dube, Marcel 1930- *IntDcT 2*
Dube, Richard Lawrence 1950- *WhoScEn 94*
Dube, Thomas M. T. 1938- *WhoBlA 94*
Dubellamy, Charles Clementine d1793 *NewGrDO*
Du Bellay, Joachim 1522-1560 *BlmGEL*
du Bellay, Joachim 1524-1560 *GuFrLit 2*
Dubenion, Elbert 1933- *WhoBlA 94*
Du Benjie 1927- *WhoPRCh 91 [port]*
Duberg, John Edward 1917- *WhoAm 94, WhoFI 94, WhoScEn 94*
Duberman, Martin 1930- *WrDr 94*
Duberman, Martin (Bauml) 1930- *ConDr 93*
Duberman, Martin Bauml 1930- *GayLL*
Duberstein, Conrad B. 1915- *WhoAm 94, WhoAmL 94*
Duberstein, Helen *DrAPF 93*
Duberstein, Helen (Laura) 1926- *WrDr 94*
Duberstein, Kenneth Marc 1944- *WhoAmP 93*
Duberstein, Larry 1944- *WrDr 94*
Duberstein, Maxine K. 1923- *WhoAmL 94*
Dubes, George Richard 1926- *WhoAm 94, WhoMW 93*
Dubes, Michael J. 1942- *WhoAm 94, WhoFI 94*
Dubes, Richard Charles 1934- *WhoAm 94*
Dubetz, Shirley Arlene 1927- *WhoAmL 94*
Dubey, Ram Janam 1941- *WhoScEn 94*
Dubey, Satya Deva 1930- *WhoAm 94, WhoAsA 94*
Dubey, Stephen Arthur 1947- *WhoMW 93*
Dubick, Julie P. 1949- *WhoAmL 94*
Dubicki, Robert John 1954- *WhoFI 94*
Dubie, Norman *DrAPF 93*
Dubie, Norman (Evans, Jr.) 1945- *WrDr 94*
Dubiel, Thomas Wieslaw 1929- *WhoScEn 94*
Dubin, Al d1945 *WhoHol 92*
Dubin, Alan S. 1951- *WhoAm 94, WhoAmL 94*
Dubin, Arthur Detmers 1923- *WhoAm 94*
Dubin, Barry A. 1946- *WhoAmL 94*
Dubin, Charles Leonard 1921- *WhoAm 94*
Dubin, Charles S. 1919- *ConTFT 11*
Dubin, David Meyer 1956- *WhoAmL 94*
Dubin, Gerald Paul 1929- *WhoFI 94*
Dubin, Howard Victor 1938- *WhoAm 94*
Dubin, James Michael 1946- *WhoAm 94, WhoAmL 94, WhoFI 94*
Dubin, Joseph William 1948- *WhoFI 94*
Dubin, Leonard 1934- *WhoAm 94*
Dubin, Mark William 1942- *WhoAm 94*
Dubin, Martin David 1927- *WhoAm 94*
Dubin, Michael 1943- *WhoAm 94, WhoFI 94*
Dubin, Morton Donald 1931- *WhoAm 94*
Dubin, Seth Harris 1933- *WhoAm 94*
Dubina, Joel Fredrick 1947- *WhoAm 94, WhoAmL 94, WhoAmP 93*
Dubinin, Nikolay Petrovich 1907- *IntWW 93*
Dubinin, Yuri Vladimirovich 1930- *IntWW 93*
Dubinskis, Anda 1952- *WhoAmA 93*
Dubinsky, David 1892-1982 *AmSocL*
Dubinsky, Rostislav (D.) 1923- *WrDr 94*
Dublac, Robert Revak 1938- *WhoAmA 93*
Duble, Harold G. 1938- *WhoIns 94*
Duble, Lu 1896-1970 *WhoAmA 93N*
Dublin, Archbishop of 1925- *Who 94*
Dublin, Archbishop of 1926- *Who 94*
Dublin, Auxiliary Bishop of *Who 94*
Dublin, (Christ Church), Dean of *Who 94*
Dublin, (St. Patrick's), Dean of *Who 94*
Dublin, Elvie Wilson 1937- *WhoMW 93*
Dublin, Jessica *WhoHol 92*
Dublin, Kirk A. 1948- *WhoAmL 94*
Dublin, Thomas David 1912- *WhoAm 94*
Dubner, Ronald 1934- *WhoAm 94*
Dubnick, Bernard 1928- *WhoAm 94*
DuBoff, Leonard David 1941- *WhoAmL 94, WhoWest 94*
Duboff, Robert Samuel 1948- *WhoAm 94*
DuBoff, Scott M. 1947- *WhoAm 94, WhoAmL 94*
DuBois, Alan Beekman 1935- *WhoAm 94, WhoAmA 93*
DuBois, Arthur Brooks 1923- *WhoAm 94, WhoScEn 94*
Du Bois, Cora 1903-1991 *WhAm 10*
DuBois, D'Anne 1950- *WhoMW 93*
Dubois, David Graham *DrAPF 93*
Du Bois, David Graham 1925- *WhoBlA 94*
DuBois, Douglas J. *WhoAmA 93*
Dubois, Duane R. 1934- *WhoIns 94*
DuBois, Ellen Carol 1947- *WrDr 94*
DuBois, Frank A., III 1947- *WhoWest 94*
DuBois, G. Macy 1929- *IntWW 93*
Du Bois, Guy Pene 1884-1958 *WhoAmA 93N*
Dubois, Jacques-Emile 1920- *IntWW 93*
DuBois, James Clemens 1936- *WhoAmP 93*
DuBois, Jan Ely 1931- *WhoAm 94, WhoAmL 94*
DuBois, Ja'Net 1943- *WhoHol 92*
Dubois, Janice Ann 1961- *WhoScEn 94*
DuBois, Jean Gabriel 1926- *WhoScEn 94*
DuBois, John 1921- *WhoAmP 93*
DuBois, Jonathan Delafield 1941- *WhoAm 94*
Du Bois, Louis-Alexis d1967 *WhoHol 92*
Dubois, Louise H. 1947- *WhoFI 94*
Dubois, M. 1925- *WrDr 94*
DuBois, Macy 1929- *WhoAmA 93*
Dubois, Marie 1937- *WhoHol 92*
DuBois, Mark Benjamin 1955- *WhoMW 93*
Du Bois, Marta *WhoHol 92*
DuBois, Melodee Ann 1948- *WhoAm 94*
Du Bois, Nelson S. D'Andrea, Jr. 1930- *WhoBlA 94*
Dubois, Normand Rene 1938- *WhoScEn 94*
Du Bois, Paul Zinkhan 1936- *WhoAm 94*
Du Bois, Philip Hunter 1903- *WhoAm 94, WhoMW 93, WhoScEn 94*
Dubois, Pierre Max 1930- *NewGrDO*
DuBois, Rachel Davis d1993 *NewYTBS 93*
DuBois, Suzanne Lutzen 1946- *WhoFI 94*
Du Bois, Theodora (McCormick) 1890-1986 *EncSF 93*
Dubois, (Francois Clement) Theodore 1837-1924 *NewGrDO*
Du Bois, W. E. B. 1868-1963 *HisWorL [port]*
DuBois, William Edward Burghardt 1868-1963 *AfrAmAl 6 [port], AmSocL [port]*
Du Bois, William Pene 1916- *EncSF 93*
du Bois, William Pène 1916-1993 *WrDr 94N*
du Bois, William (Sherman) Pene *ConAu 41NR*
du Bois, William (Sherman) Pene 1916-1993 *ConAu 140, SmATA 74*
Dubon, Charles F. 1945- *WhoHisp 94*
Dubos, Rene 1901-1982 *EnvEnc [port]*
Dubosc, Andre d1935 *WhoHol 92*
Dubose, Catherine 1959- *NewGrDO*
DuBose, Charles Wilson 1949- *WhoAm 94*
Dubose, Cullen Lanier 1935- *WhoBlA 94*
DuBose, Francis Marquis 1922- *WhoWest 94*
DuBose, Maria Deborah 1952- *WhoHisp 94*
DuBose, Otelia 1949- *WhoBlA 94*
Du Bose, Robert Earl, Jr. 1927- *WhoBlA 94*
Du Bose, William Porcher 1836-1918 *DcAmReB 2*
Dubost, Paulette *WhoHol 92*
du Boulay *Who 94*
Du Boulay, F(rancis) R(obin) H(oussemayne) 1920- *WrDr 94*
Du Boulay, Francis Robin Houssemayne 1920- *IntWW 93*
Du Boulay, (Francis) Robin (Houssemayne) 1920- *Who 94*
DuBourdieu, Daniel John 1956- *WhoScEn 94*
Dubourg, Louis Guillaume Valentin 1766-1833 *DcAmReB 2*
Dubourg, Olivier Jean 1952- *WhoScEn 94*
Dubov, Paul d1979 *WhoHol 92*
Dubovich, Debra Lynch 1955- *WhoMW 93*
Dubovik, G. J. *DrAPF 93*
Dubow, Arthur Myron 1933- *WhoAm 94*
Dubowitz, Victor 1931- *IntWW 93, Who 94*
Dubowsky, Steven 1942- *WhoAm 94*
Duboy, Antonio 1963- *WhoHisp 94*
Dubrawski, Peter Andrew 1950- *WhoAm 94, WhoAmL 94*
Dubreuil, Francis W. 1948- *WhoAmL 94*
Du Brey, Claire 1893- *WhoHol 92*
DuBridge, Lee A(lvin) 1901- *Who 94*
DuBridge, Lee Alvin 1901- *WhoAm 94, WhoScEn 94*
DuBrin, Andrew John 1935- *WhoAm 94*
DuBrin, Stanley 1928- *WhoWest 94*
Dubris, Maggie *DrAPF 93*
Dubro, Alec 1944- *WrDr 94*
Dubroff, Charles Mark 1948- *WhoAm 94, WhoAmL 94*
Dubroff, Jerome M. 1948- *WhoScEn 94*
Dubrovay, Jaeson 1955- *WhoWest 94*
Dubrow, Gary S. 1961- *WhoAmL 94*
Dubrow, John 1958- *WhoAm 94*
Dubrow, Marsha Ann 1948- *WhoFI 94*
DuBrul, Stephen McKenzie, Jr. 1929- *WhoFI 94*
Dubs, Alfred 1932- *Who 94*
Dubs, Arthur R. 1930- *IntMPA 94*
Dubs, Darryl Dean 1960- *WhoMW 93*
Dubs, Kathy *WhoAmP 93*
Dubs, Patrick Christian 1947- *WhoAm 94*
Dubsky, Countess *BlmGWL*
Dubuc, Carroll Edward 1933- *WhoAm 94, WhoAmL 94*
Dubuc, Deborah Jo 1957- *WhoMW 93*
Dubuc, Kenneth E 1939- *WhoAm 94*
Dubuc, Serge 1939- *WhoAm 94*
Dubuque, Gregory Lee 1948- *WhoScEn 94*
Dubuque, Julien 1762-1810 *WhWE*
Dubus, Andre *DrAPF 93*
Dubus, Andre 1936- *DcLB 130 [port], WrDr 94*
Dubus, Andre, III *DrAPF 93*
Dubus, Andre, III 1959- *WrDr 94*
Dubuysson, Charles Francois 1752-1786 *WhAmRev*
Duby, Georges Michel Claude 1919- *IntWW 93*
Duby, Jean Jacques 1940- *IntWW 93*
Dubynin, Viktor Petrovich 1943- *LoBiDrD*
Duca, Alfred Milton 1920- *WhoAm 94, WhoAmA 93*
Duca, James Francis 1958- *WhoAmL 94*
Du Cane, John Peter 1921- *Who 94*
Ducanis, Alex Julius 1931- *WhoAm 94*
du Cann, Edward (Dillon Lott) 1924- *Who 94*
du Cann, Edward Dillon Lott 1924- *IntWW 93*
Du Cann, Richard Dillon Lott 1929- *Who 94*
Ducat, Dawn *Who 94*
Ducat-Amos, Barbara Mary 1921- *Who 94*
Ducceschi, James Martin Michael 1936- *WhoFI 94*
Ducci, Roberto 1914- *IntWW 93, Who 94*
Duce, David W. 1959- *WhoAmL 94*
Du Cello, Countess d1921 *WhoHol 92*
Duceppe, Jean d1990 *WhoHol 92*
Ducet, Paul d1928 *WhoHol 92*
Ducey, Michael E. 1948- *WhoMW 93*
Duch, Thomas J. 1956- *WhoAmP 93*
Duchac, Kenneth Farnham 1923-1989 *WhAm 10*
Du Chaillu, Paul Belloni c. 1831-1903 *WhWE*
Duchamp, Henri-Robert-marcel 1887-1968 *AmCulL [port]*
Duchamp, Marcel d1968 *WhoHol 92*
Duchane, Stephen Michael 1956- *WhoMW 93*
Du Changjin *WhoPRCh 91*
Du Changqing *WhoPRCh 91*
DuCharme, Donald Walter 1937- *WhoMW 93*
Ducharme, Doris R. *WhoAmP 93*
Ducharme, Gerry 1939- *WhoMW 93*
duCharme, Gillian Drusilla Brown 1938- *Who 94*
Ducharme, Howard Maurice 1950- *WhoMW 93*
Du Charme, Lawrence M. 1933- *WhoMW 93*
Duchaussoy, Michel 1938- *WhoHol 92*
Duche, Jacob 1738-1789 *WhAmRev*
Duche de Vancy, Joseph-Francois 1668-1704 *NewGrDO*
Duchek, Michael Gerard 1966- *WhoFI 94, WhoMW 93*
Duchene, Louis-Francois 1927- *Who 94, WrDr 94*
Duchesne, (Peter) Robin 1936- *Who 94*
Duchesne, Rose Philippine 1769-1852 *DcAmReB 2, EncNAR*
Duchin, Eddy d1951 *WhoHol 92*
Duchin, Peter 1937- *WhoHol 92*
Duchin, Peter Oelrichs 1937- *WhoAm 94*
Duchnowski, Edward Martin 1942- *WhoWest 94*
Duchon, Roseann Marie 1950- *WhoMW 93*
Duchovny, David *WhoHol 92*
Duchow, Paul Gerhardt 1938- *WhoFI 94*
Duci, Frank Joseph 1922- *WhoAmP 93*
Ducie, Earl of 1951- *Who 94*
duCille, Ann *DrAPF 93*
Duck, Hywel Ivor 1933- *Who 94*
Duck, Steve Weatherill 1946- *WhoMW 93*
Duck, Vaughn Michael 1943- *WhoFI 94*
Ducken, Lynn Kathryn 1943- *WhoFI 94*
Duckenfield, Thomas Adams 1935-1992 *WhoBlA 94N*
Ducker, Bruce 1938- *WhoAm 94*
Ducker, Herbert Charles 1900- *Who 94*
Ducker, James H. 1950- *WrDr 94*
Ducker, James Howard 1950- *WhoWest 94*
Duckers, Sarah Ann 1961- *WhoAmL 94*
Duckert, Audrey Rosalind 1927- *WhoAm 94*
Duckett, Bernadine Johnal 1939- *WhoMW 93*
Duckett, Gregory Morris 1960- *WhoBlA 94*
Duckett, Joan 1934- *WhoAmL 94*
Duckett, Louis 1929- *AfrAmG [port]*
Duckett, Thomas Ross 1924- *WhoAmP 93*
Duckles, Sue Piper 1946- *WhoWest 94*
Duckmanton, Talbot (Sydney) 1921- *Who 94*
Duckmanton, Talbot Sydney 1921- *IntWW 93*
Ducksworth, Marilyn Jacoby *WhoBlA 94*
Duckwall, Ralph 1925- *WhoAmP 93*
Duckworth, Brian Roy 1934- *Who 94*
Duckworth, Carol Kay 1941- *WhoMW 93*
Duckworth, Christopher Sayre 1948- *WhoMW 93*
Duckworth, Colin *WhoHol 92*
Duckworth, Donald Reid 1945- *WhoMW 93, WhoScEn 94*
Duckworth, Dortha *WhoHol 92*
Duckworth, Eleanor 1935- *ConAu 142*
Duckworth, Eric *Who 94*
Duckworth, (Walter) Eric 1925- *Who 94*
Duckworth, Guy 1923- *WhoAm 94, WhoWest 94*
Duckworth, Jerrell James 1940- *WhoScEn 94*
Duckworth, John Clifford 1916- *Who 94*
Duckworth, Kevin Jerome 1964- *WhoBlA 94*
Duckworth, Kim Pelto 1956- *WhoFI 94, WhoWest 94*
Duckworth, Marilyn 1935- *BlmGWL*
Duckworth, Marvin E. 1942- *WhoAmL 94*
Duckworth, Richard Dyce 1918- *Who 94*
Duckworth, Robert Vincent 1938- *WhoIns 94*
Duckworth, Roy 1929- *Who 94*
Duckworth, Ruth 1919- *WhoAmA 93*
Duckworth, Sandra Lee 1936- *WhoAmP 93*
Duckworth, Walter Donald 1935- *WhoScEn 94, WhoWest 94*
Duckworth, Winston Howard 1918- *WhoAm 94*
Duclon, Warren Eugene 1924- *WhoMW 93*
Duclos, Charles Pinot- 1704-1772 *GuFrLit 2*
Duclos-Guyot, Pierre-Nicolas 1722-1794 *WhWE*
Ducoff, Howard S. 1923- *WhoScEn 94*
DuComb, Robert James, Jr. 1943- *WhoAmP 93*

Dufranne, Eva 1857-1905 NewGrDO
Dufranne, Hector 1871-1951 NewGrDO
Dufrenoy, Adelaide 1765-1825 BlmGWL
Dufresne, Armand Alphee, Jr. 1909- WhoAm 94
DuFresne, Armand Frederick 1917- WhoAm 94, WhoFI 94, WhoScEn 94, WhoWest 94
DuFresne, Elizabeth Jamison 1942- WhoAm 94
Dufresne, Guy Georges 1941- WhoAm 94
Dufresne, Isabelle Collin WhoAmA 93
Dufresne, John DrAPF 93
duFresne, Yvonne 1929- BlmGWL
Dufty, (Arthur) Richard 1911- Who 94
Dugal, Hardev S. 1937- WhoAsA 94
Dugal, Louis Paul 1911- WhoAm 94
Dugan, Alan DrAPF 93
Dugan, Alan 1923- WrDr 94
Dugan, Charles Francis, II 1939- WhoAm 94
Dugan, Dennis 1946- IntMPA 94
Dugan, Dennis 1947- WhoHol 92
Dugan, Edward Francis 1934- WhoAm 94
Dugan, Eileen C. 1945- WhoAmP 93
Dugan, Elsie d1934 WhoHol 92
Dugan, Gerald J. 1948- WhoAmL 94
Dugan, Gerard A. 1945- WhoIns 94
DuGan, Gordon Frank 1966- WhoAm 94
Dugan, Gregory Thomas 1957- WhoMW 93
Dugan, Jack R. 1940- WhoAmL 94
Dugan, John F. 1935- WhoAm 94, WhoAmL 94
Dugan, John Leslie, Jr. 1921- WhoAm 94
Dugan, John Patrick 1958- WhoScEn 94
Dugan, John Vincent, Jr. 1936- WhoScEn 94
Dugan, Karen Vernon WhoAmA 93
Dugan, Michael J. 1937- WhoAm 94
Dugan, Mike WhoAmP 93
Dugan, Patrick Raymond 1931- WhoAm 94, WhoScEn 94
Dugan, Robert Perry, Jr. 1932- WhoAm 94
Dugan, Robert Peter 1961- WhoFI 94
Dugan, Ruth Puglisi 1947- WhoAmP 93
Dugan, Tom WhoHol 92
Dugan, Tom d1955 WhoHol 92
Dugan, Walter James 1922- WhoWest 94
Dugan Gindhart, Andrea Claire 1961- WhoWest 94
Dugard, Arthur Claude 1904- Who 94
Du Garde, Barry d1980 WhoHol 92
Dugas, Henry C. 1917- WhoBlA 94
Dugas, Jeffrey Alan, Sr. 1953- WhoBlA 94
Dugas, Louis, Jr. 1928- WhoAm 94
Dugaw, John Edward, Jr. 1945- WhoWest 94
Dugazon, (Alexandre-Louis-)Gustave 1782?-1826? NewGrDO
Dugazon, Louise-Rosalie 1755-1821 NewGrDO [port]
Dugdale Who 94
Dugdale, John, Mrs. Who 94
Dugdale, John Robert Stratford 1923- Who 94
Dugdale, Kathryn Edith Helen 1923- Who 94
Dugdale, Norman 1921- Who 94, WrDr 94
Dugdale, Peter Robin 1928- Who 94
Dugdale, William (Stratford) 1922- Who 94
Dugersuren, Mangalyn 1922- IntWW 93
Duggal, Arun Sanjay 1962- WhoScEn 94
Duggan, Andrew d1988 WhoHol 92
Duggan, Bessie Lou 1931- WhoAmP 93
Duggan, Dennis Michael 1927- WhoAm 94
Duggan, Eileen May 1894-1972 BlmGWL
Duggan, Ervin S. WhoAmP 93
Duggan, Ervin S. 1939- WhoAm 94, WhoFI 94
Duggan, Gordon Aldridge 1937- Who 94
Duggan, James Edgar 1961- WhoAmL 94
Duggan, James H. 1935- WhoFI 94
Duggan, Jan d1977 WhoHol 92
Duggan, Jerome Timothy 1914-1990 WhAm 10
Duggan, John Coote 1918- Who 94
Duggan, John Peter 1946- WhoAm 94
Duggan, Joseph F. 1928- WhoAmP 93
Duggan, Joseph John 1938- WhoWest 94
Duggan, Kevin 1944- WhoFI 94
Duggan, Mae Mosher 1919- WhoMW 93
Duggan, Maurice (Noel) 1922-1974 RfGShF
Duggan, Patrick James 1933- WhoAm 94, WhoAmL 94, WhoMW 93
Duggan, Thomas Patrick 1946- WhoFI 94
Duggan, Tom d1969 WhoHol 92
Dugger, Clinton George 1929- WhoBlA 94
Dugger, Edward, III 1949- WhoBlA 94
Dugger, Edwin Ellsworth 1940- WhoAm 94
Dugger, John Scott 1948- IntWW 93
Dugger, Myron W. 1936- WhoAmP 93

Dugger, Ronnie E. 1930- WhoAm 94
Duggin, Lorraine DrAPF 93
Duggin, Richard DrAPF 93
Duggin, Thomas Joseph 1947- Who 94
Duggins, David C. 1953- WhoAmL 94
Duggins, Ralph Hereford, III 1952- WhoAmL 94
Dugin, Andrej 1955- SmATA 77 [port]
Dugina, Olga 1964- SmATA 77 [port]
Dugmore, Edward 1915- WhoAm 94, WhoAmA 93
Dugmore, Kent Clyde 1939- WhoWest 94
Dugoff, Howard 1936- WhoAmP 93
Du Gong WhoPRCh 91
Dugoni, Arthur A. 1925- WhoAm 94
Duguid, Andrew Alexander 1944- Who 94
Duguid, James Paris 1919- Who 94
Duguid, Sandra R. DrAPF 93
Dugundji, John 1925- WhoAm 94
Duhamel, Antoine 1925- NewGrDO
Duhamel, Denise DrAPF 93
Duhamel, Pierre Albert 1920- WhoAm 94
Duhan, Hans 1890-1971 NewGrDO
Du Haoran WhoPRCh 91
Duhart, Harold B. 1938- WhoBlA 94
Duhe, John M., Jr. 1933- WhoAmP 93
Duhe, John Malcolm, Jr. 1933- WhoAm 94, WhoAmL 94
Duhe, Theodore Louis 1946- WhoAmP 93
Duhl, Leonard 1926- WhoAm 94, WhoWest 94
Duhl, Leonard J 1926- WrDr 94
Duhl, Michael Foster 1944- WhoAm 94, WhoAmL 94
Duhme, H. Richard, Jr. 1914- WhoAmA 93
Duhme, Herman Richard, Jr. 1914- WhoAm 94
Duhmke, Eckhart 1942- WhoScEn 94
Duhnke, Robert Emmet, Jr. 1935- WhoWest 94
Du Hongben WhoPRCh 91
Duhs, William Andrew 1939- WhoFI 94
Duigan, John IntMPA 94
Duis, Rita WhoAmA 93
Duisenberg, Willem Frederik 1935- IntWW 93
Du Jardin, Gussie 1918- WhoAmA 93
Duka, Ivo 1913-c. 1988 EncSF 93
Dukakis, John 1968- WhoHol 92
Dukakis, Kitty 1937- WrDr 94
Dukakis, Michael Stanley 1933- IntWW 93, Who 94, WhoAm 94, WhoAmP 93
Dukakis, Olympia IntWW 93
Dukakis, Olympia 1931- IntMPA 94, WhoAm 94, WhoHol 92
Dukas, James WhoHol 92
Dukas, Paul (Abraham) 1865-1935 NewGrDO
Dukas, Peter 1919- WhoAm 94
Dukas, Philip Alexander 1954- WhoMW 93
Dukat, Alexander Joseph 1941- WhoMW 93
Duke Who 94
Duke, A. Don 1933- WhoAmP 93
Duke, Angier Biddle 1915- IntWW 93, WhoAm 94, WhoAmP 93
Duke, Anna Marie 1946- WrDr 94
Duke, Anthony Drexel 1918- WhoAm 94
Duke, Bernard 1927- WhoFI 94
Duke, Bill 1943- IntMPA 94, WhoHol 92
Duke, Cecil Howard Armitage 1912- Who 94
Duke, Charles 1942- WhoAmP 93
Duke, Charles Bryan 1938- WhoAm 94, WhoScEn 94
Duke, Claire Diane 1935- WhoAmP 93
Duke, Clifford Frank 1953- WhoFI 94
Duke, David 1950- WhoAmP 93
Duke, David Allen 1935- WhoAm 94
Duke, Donald 1929- WrDr 94
Duke, Donald Norman 1929- WhoAm 94, WhoWest 94
Duke, Doris 1912-1993 NewYTBS 93 [port], News 94-2
Duke, E. L. Tony d1982 WhoHol 92
Duke, Edward 1953- WhoHol 92
Duke, Emanuel 1916- WhoAm 94
Duke, Gary James 1947- WhoFI 94
Duke, Gary Philip 1957- WhoHol 92
Duke, George F. 1935- WhoAmL 94
Duke, George M. 1946- WhoBlA 94
Duke, Harold Benjamin, Jr. 1922- WhoAm 94, WhoFI 94
Duke, Ivy 1896- WhoHol 92
Duke, J(ames) A. 1929- WrDr 94
Duke, J. Dale 1938- WhoIns 94
Duke, James Alan 1929- WhoAm 94
Duke, Kathleen Anne 1961- WhoAmL 94
Duke, Lance Brittain 1958- WhoAm 94
Duke, Leilani Lattin 1943- WhoAmA 93
Duke, Leslie Dowling, Sr. 1924- WhoBlA 94
Duke, Madelaine (Elizabeth) 1925- EncSF 93, WrDr 94
Duke, Merlin 1941- WhoAmP 93

Duke, Michael d1947 WhoHol 92
Duke, Michael B. 1935- WhoScEn 94
Duke, Michael Charles 1956- WhoAmL 94
Duke, Michael Geoffrey H. Who 94
Duke, Michael S. 1940- WrDr 94
Duke, Neville Frederick 1922- Who 94
Duke, Pamela Ruth 1945- WhoWest 94
Duke, Patty 1946- IntMPA 94, WhoAm 94, WhoHol 92
Duke, Paul Robert 1929- WhoAm 94
Duke, Robert 1917- WhoHol 92
Duke, Robert Dominick 1928- WhoAm 94
Duke, Robin Chandler Tippett 1923- WhoFI 94
Duke, Ruth White 1927- WhoBlA 94
Duke, Stephen Oscar 1944- WhoScEn 94
Duke, Steven Barry 1934- WhoAm 94
Duke, Thomas Walter Daniel 1896- WhAm 10
Duke, Vernon 1903-1969 NewGrDO
Duke, Will 1910- WrDr 94
Duke, William Edward 1932- WhoWest 94
Duke, William Henry, Jr. 1943- WhoBlA 94
Dukek, Nancy Bowman 1916- WhoFI 94
Dukelan, George d1933 WhoHol 92
Duke Of Paducah, The WhoHol 92
Duker, Laura Thompson 1905- WhoWest 94
Dukerschein, Jeanne Therese 1951- WhoScEn 94
Dukert, Betty Cole 1927- WhoAm 94
Dukert, Joseph M(ichael) 1929- WrDr 94
Dukert, Joseph Michael 1929- WhoAmP 93
Dukes, Alan M. 1945- IntWW 93, Who 94
Dukes, Caroline WhoAmA 93
Dukes, Constance T. WhoBlA 94
Dukes, David 1945- IntMPA 94, WhoHol 92
Dukes, Gene W. 1943- WhoAmP 93
Dukes, Hazel Nell 1932- WhoAmP 93, WhoBlA 94
Dukes, Henry Hugh 1895- WhAm 10
Dukes, Jack Richard 1941- WhoMW 93
Dukes, James Otis 1946- WhoAmL 94
Dukes, Jerome Erwin 1938- WhoBlA 94
Dukes, Joan 1947- WhoAmP 93, WhoWest 94
Dukes, Joseph 1811-1861 EncNAR
Dukes, Justin Paul 1941- Who 94
Dukes, LaJenne Marie 1931- WhoWest 94
Dukes, Ofield 1932- WhoBlA 94
Dukes, Paul 1934- WrDr 94
Dukes, Philip ConAu 42NR
Dukes, Ronald 1942- WhoBlA 94
Dukes, Ronnie d1981 WhoHol 92
Dukes, Walter 1930- BasBi
Dukes, Walter L. 1933- WhoBlA 94
Dukler, Abraham Emanuel 1925- WhoAm 94, WhoScEn 94
Dukore, Bernard F 1931- WrDr 94
Dukore, Bernard Frank 1931- WhoAm 94
Dukore, Margaret Mitchell DrAPF 93
Dula, Brett M. 1942- WhoAm 94
Dulac, Arthur d1962 WhoHol 92
Dulai, Surjit Singh WhoAm 94
Dulaine, Pierre WhoAm 94
Dulan, Harold Andrew 1911- WhoAm 94
Dulanto, Juan Carlos 1958- WhoHisp 94
Dulany, Daniel 1722-1797 AmRev
Dulany, Daniel (the Younger) 1722-1797 WhAmRev
Dulany, Elizabeth Gjelsness 1931- WhoAm 94
Dulany, Harris DrAPF 93
Dulany, William Bevard 1927- WhoAm 94
Dulatt, Lorraine Edwina Simon 1949- WhoMW 93
DuLaux, Russell Frederick 1918- WhoAmL 94, WhoFI 94
Dulbecco, Renato 1914- IntWW 93, Who 94, WhoAm 94, WhoScEn 94, WhoWest 94
Dulberg, Michael Seth 1954- WhoAmL 94
Dulchinos, Peter 1935- WhoAmL 94, WhoFI 94
Dulcich, James Frank 1954- WhoAmL 94
Dulcich, Thomas Vincent 1953- WhoAmL 94
Duldulao, Julie R. 1947- WhoAmP 93
Duley, Charlotte Dudley 1920- WhoWest 94
Duley, Margaret 1894-1968 BlmGWL
Dulin, Davison Randolph 1958- WhoFI 94
Dulin, Robert O., Jr. 1941- WhoBlA 94
Dulin, Thomas N. 1949- WhoAmL 94
Dull, Charles W. 1930- WhoAmL 94
Dull, Orville O. d1978 WhoHol 92
Dull, Robert J. 1947- WhoAmP 93
Dull, Wilbur Robbins 1914- WhoAmL 94
Dull, William Martin 1924- WhoAm 94
Dullea, Charles W. WhoAm 94
Dullea, Keir 1936- IntMPA 94, WhoHol 92

Dullemen, Inez van 1925- BlmGWL
Dulles, Avery 1918- WhoAm 94, WrDr 94
Dulles, Eleanor Lansing 1895- WhoAm 94
Dulles, John Foster 1888-1959 HisWorL [port], HisDcKW
Dullin, Charles d1949 WhoHol 92
Dulloo, Madum Murlidas 1949- IntWW 93
Dullzell, Paul d1961 WhoHol 92
Dulmes, Steven Lee 1957- WhoMW 93, WhoScEn 94
Dulo, Jane WhoHol 92
Du Locle, Camille 1832-1903 NewGrDO
Dulski, Thomas R. 1942- WhoScEn 94
Dulsky, Beryl I. 1930- WhoAmL 94
Dulude, Donald Owen 1928- WhoAm 94
Dulude, Gary Joseph 1966- WhoWest 94
Dulude, Richard 1933- WhoAm 94
Duluth, Daniel Greysolon, Sieur 1636-1710 WhWE
Dulverton, Baron 1944- Who 94
Duly, Leslie C. d1993 NewYTBS 93
Duma, Richard Joseph 1933- WhoAm 94
Dumaine, F. C. 1902- WhoFI 94
DuMaine, R. Pierre 1931- WhoAm 94, WhoWest 94
Dumais-Berube, Yvette 1930- WhoAmA 93
Dumaresq, John Edward 1913- WhoAm 94
Dumarot, Dan Peter 1956- WhoScEn 94
Dumars, Joe, III 1963- WhoAm 94, WhoBlA 94, WhoMW 93
Dumas, Alexandre 1802-1870 NewGrDO
Dumas, Alexandre 1824-1895 NewGrDO
Dumas, Antoine 1932- WhoAmA 93
Dumas, Charles William Frederic 1721-1796 WhAmRev
Dumas, Claudine 1939- WrDr 94
Dumas, David W. 1943- WhoAmP 93
Dumas, Floyd E. 1926- WhoBlA 94
Dumas, Gerald DrAPF 93
Dumas, Jean-Louis Robert Frederic 1938- IntWW 93
Dumas, Jeffrey Mack 1945- WhoAmL 94, WhoScEn 94
Dumas, Karen Marie 1962- WhoBlA 94
Dumas, Louise Isabelle WhoWest 94
Dumas, Mathieu, Comte de 1753-1837 WhAmRev [port]
Dumas, Peter J. 1955- WhoIns 94
Dumas, Pierre 1924- IntWW 93
Dumas, Rhetaugh Etheldra Graves 1928- IntWW 93
Dumas, Rhetaugh Graves 1928- WhoBlA 94
Dumas, Richard WhoBlA 94
Dumas, Roger WhoHol 92
Dumas, Roland 1922- IntWW 93, Who 94
Dumas-Dubourg, Francoise Therese Bernadette Marie 1932- IntWW 93
Dumas fils, Alexandre 1824-1895 IntDcT 2
Dumas pere, Alexandre (Davy de la Pailleterie) 1802-1870 IntDcT 2 [port]
du Maurier, Daphne 1907-1989 BlmGWL [port], EncSF 93, RfGShF, WhAm 10
Du Maurier, George 1834-1896 BlmGEL
Du Maurier, George (Louis Palmella Busson) 1834-1896 EncSF 93
Du Maurier, Gerald d1934 WhoHol 92
Dumbacher, John Philip 1965- WhoScEn 94
Dumbauld, Edward 1905- WhoAm 94
Dumbell, Keith Rodney 1922- Who 94
Dumbrille, Douglass d1974 WhoHol 92
Dumbutshena, Enoch 1920- IntWW 93, Who 94
Dumcke, Ernst d1940 WhoHol 92
Dumeny, Marcel Jacque 1950- WhoAm 94, WhoAmL 94
Dumesnil d1702 NewGrDO
Dumfries, Earl of 1989- Who 94
Dumisai, Kwame 1939- WhoBlA 94
Dumit, Thomas A. 1942- WhoAmL 94
Dumitrescu, Domnita WhoWest 94
Dumitrescu, Gheorghe 1914- NewGrDO
Dumitrescu, Lucien Z. 1931- WhoScEn 94
Dumke, Glenn S. 1917-1989 WhAm 10
Dumke, Melvin Philip 1920- WhoMW 93
Dumke, Ralph d1964 WhoHol 92
Dumler, Franz Anton NewGrDO
Dumm, Demetrius Robert 1923- WhoAm 94
Dummer, David E. 1944- WhoMW 93
Dummett, (Agnes Margaret) Ann 1930- Who 94, WrDr 94
Dummett, Clifton Orrin 1919- WhoAm 94, WhoBlA 94
Dummett, George Anthony 1907- Who 94
Dummett, Jocelyn Angela 1956- WhoBlA 94
Dummett, M(ichael) A(nthony) E(ardley) 1925- WrDr 94
Dummett, Michael Anthony Eardley 1925- IntWW 93, Who 94
Dummont, Denise WhoHol 92

Dumon, Bernard Claude Jean-Pierre 1935- *IntWW 93*
DuMond, Charles David 1947- *WhoAmL 94*
Du Mond, Frank V. 1865-1951 *WhoAmA 93N*
Dumont, Allan Eliot 1924- *WhoAm 94*
DuMont, Bruce *WhoAm 94*
Dumont, Carlotta *BlmGWL*
Dumont, Gordon d1965 *WhoHol 92*
Dumont, Hyacinthe de Gaureault, Sieur de 1647?-1726 *NewGrDO*
Dumont, J. M. d1959 *WhoHol 92*
Dumont, Kala Scott 1965- *WhoAmL 94*
Dumont, Karen Mae 1944- *WhoFI 94*
Dumont, Margaret d1965 *WhoHol 92*
Dumont, Margaret 1889-1965 *WhoCom*
Dumont, Mark Eliot 1950- *WhoScEn 94*
Dumont, Michael Gerard 1961- *WhoScEn 94*
Du Mont, Nicolas 1954- *WhoHisp 94*
Dumont, Rene 1904- *IntWW 93*
Dumont, Robert E. 1922- *WhoAmP 93*
Du Mont, Rosemary Ruhig 1947- *WhoAm 94*
Dumont, Sandra Jean 1955- *WhoFI 94*
Dumont, W. Hunt 1941- *WhoAmL 94*
Dumont D'Urville, Jules-Sebastien-Cesar 1790-1842 *WhWE [port]*
Dumoulin, Charles Lucian 1956- *WhoScEn 94*
Dumoulin, Donald Dwain 1960- *WhoFI 94*
Dumovich, Loretta 1930- *WhoAm 94*
Dumper, Anthony Charles 1923- *Who 94*
Dumpson, James R. *WhoBlA 94*
Dumsha, David Allen 1957- *WhoFI 94, WhoScEn 94*
Dun, Mlle d1713 *NewGrDO*
Dun, Mlle d1756? *NewGrDO*
Dun, Dennis *WhoHol 92*
Dun, Jean d1735 *NewGrDO*
Dun, Jean d1772 *NewGrDO*
Duna, Steffi 1913- *WhoHol 92*
Dunagan, James Alan 1954- *WhoWest 94*
Dunagan, Walter Benton 1937- *WhoAmL 94*
Dunaif, Alexandra Louise 1957- *WhoFI 94*
Dunalley, Baron 1948- *Who 94*
Dunant, Jean Henri 1828-1910 *HisWorL [port]*
Dunant, Sarah 1950- *WrDr 94*
Dunaskiss, Mat J. 1951- *WhoAmP 93*
Dunathan, Harmon Craig 1932- *WhoAm 94*
Dunau, Andrew T. 1959- *WhoScEn 94*
Dunavant, Leonard Clyde 1919- *WhoAmP 93*
Dunavant, Richard Hannah 1952- *WhoAmP 93*
Dunavant, William Buchanan, Jr. 1932- *WhoAm 94*
Dunaway, David R. 1939- *WhoWest 94*
Dunaway, Dorothy Faye 1941- *IntWW 93*
Dunaway, Faye 1941- *IntMPA 94, WhoAm 94, WhoHol 92*
Dunaway, Frank Rosser, III 1953- *WhoMW 93*
Dunaway, Margaret Ann 1943- *WhoWest 94*
Dunaway, Robert Lee 1942- *WhoWest 94*
Dunaway, Victor Allan 1928- *WhoAm 94*
Dunaway, William Preston 1936- *WhoAm 94*
Dunayevsky, Isaak Iosifovich 1900-1955 *NewGrDO*
Dunbar, Alexander Arbuthnott 1929- *Who 94*
Dunbar, Andrea 1961- *WrDr 94*
Dunbar, Andrea 1961-1991 *ConDr 93*
Dunbar, Anne Cynthia 1938- *WhoBlA 94*
Dunbar, Anthony Paul 1949- *WhoAmL 94*
Dunbar, Blanche d1926 *WhoHol 92*
Dunbar, Bonnie J. 1949- *WhoScEn 94*
Dunbar, Charles 1907- *Who 94*
Dunbar, Charles Edward, III 1926- *WhoAmP 93*
Dunbar, Charles F. 1937- *WhoAmP 93*
Dunbar, Christine c. 14th cent.- *BlmGWL*
Dunbar, David d1953 *WhoHol 92*
Dunbar, David H. *Who 94*
Dunbar, David Wesley 1952- *WhoFI 94*
Dunbar, Dixie 1918- *WhoHol 92*
Dunbar, Dorothy *WhoHol 92*
Dunbar, Gary Leo 1949- *WhoScEn 94*
Dunbar, Harry B. 1925- *WhoBlA 94*
Dunbar, Helen d1933 *WhoHol 92*
Dunbar, Ian Duncan 1948- *Who 94*
Dunbar, Ian Malcolm 1934- *Who 94*
Dunbar, Jack d1961 *WhoHol 92*
Dunbar, James V., Jr. 1937- *WhoAm 94, WhoAmL 94*
Dunbar, Jill H. 1949- *WhoAmA 93*
Dunbar, John 1804-1857 *EncNAR*
Dunbar, John Burton 1929- *WhoAm 94*
Dunbar, John D. 1939- *WhoAmL 94*
Dunbar, John Greenwell 1930- *Who 94*
Dunbar, John Raine 1911- *WhoAm 94*
Dunbar, John Robert 1929- *WhoMW 93*
Dunbar, Joseph C. 1944- *WhoBlA 94*
Dunbar, Joyce 1944- *SmATA 76 [port]*
Dunbar, Lawrence Gregory, Sr. 1953- *WhoAmL 94*
Dunbar, Leslie W(allace) 1921- *WrDr 94*
Dunbar, Leslie Wallace 1921- *WhoAm 94*
Dunbar, Lou 1956- *BasBi*
Dunbar, Marjorie Henderson 1932- *WhoBlA 94*
Dunbar, Maurice Victor 1928- *WhoWest 94*
Dunbar, Maxwell John 1914- *IntWW 93, WhoAm 94, WhoScEn 94*
Dunbar, Michael Austin 1947- *WhoAmA 93*
Dunbar, Moses 1746-1777 *WhAmRev*
Dunbar, Patricia Lynn 1953- *WhoWest 94*
Dunbar, Paul Laurence 1872-1906 *AfrAmAl 6*
Dunbar, Prescott Nelson 1942- *WhoFI 94*
Dunbar, Richard Paul 1951- *WhoWest 94*
Dunbar, Robert d1943 *WhoHol 92*
Dunbar, Robert Copeland 1943- *WhoScEn 94*
Dunbar, Robert William 1942- *WhoFI 94*
Dunbar, Rudolph 1917-1988 *AfrAmAl 6*
Dunbar, Thomas Jerome 1959- *WhoBlA 94*
Dunbar, Wallace Huntington 1931- *WhoAm 94*
Dunbar, William 1460?-1513? *DcLB 132*
Dunbar, William 1460?-1520? *BlmGEL*
Dunbar, William 1749-1810 *WhWE*
Dunbar, William Charles 1942- *WhoAmP 93*
Dunbar, Wylene Wisby 1949- *WhoAmL 94*
Dunbar-Nasmith, David Arthur 1921- *Who 94*
Dunbar-Nasmith, James Duncan 1927- *Who 94*
Dunbar of Durn, Drummond Cospatrick Ninian 1917- *Who 94*
Dunbar of Hempriggs, Maureen Daisy Helen 1906- *Who 94*
Dunbar of Mochrum, Jean Ivor 1918- *Who 94*
Dunbar of Northfield, Archibald (Ranulph) 1927- *Who 94*
Dunbavin, Philip Richard 1953- *WhoScEn 94*
Dunboyne, Baron 1917- *Who 94*
Dunboyne, Lord 1917- *WrDr 94*
Duncalf, Deryck 1926- *WhoAm 94*
Duncan, A(rchibald) A(lexander) M(cBeth) 1926- *WrDr 94*
Duncan, A(lastair) R(obert) C(ampbell) 1915- *WrDr 94*
Duncan, Agnes Lawrie Addie 1947- *Who 94*
Duncan, Alan Eugene 1951- *WhoFI 94*
Duncan, Alan James Carter 1957- *Who 94*
Duncan, Alan William 1954- *WhoAmL 94*
Duncan, Alastair Robert Campbell 1915- *WhoAm 94*
Duncan, Alice Geneva 1917- *WhoBlA 94*
Duncan, Andrew *WhoHol 92*
Duncan, Andrew Malcolm 1960- *WhoWest 94*
Duncan, Angus *WhoHol 92*
Duncan, Anita F. 1931- *WhoAmP 93*
Duncan, Ann Q. *WhoAmP 93*
Duncan, Anna d1980 *WhoHol 92*
Duncan, Ansley McKinley 1932- *WhoFI 94, WhoWest 94*
Duncan, Anthony Douglas 1930- *WrDr 94*
Duncan, Archibald Alexander McBeth 1926- *IntWW 93, Who 94*
Duncan, Archibald Sutherland d1992 *Who 94N*
Duncan, Archie d1979 *WhoHol 92*
Duncan, Arletta d1938 *WhoHol 92*
Duncan, Bob d1967 *WhoHol 92*
Duncan, Brian Arthur Cullum 1908- *Who 94*
Duncan, Brooke, III 1952- *WhoAmL 94*
Duncan, Bruce *EncSF 93*
Duncan, Bud d1960 *WhoHol 92*
Duncan, Carmen *WhoHol 92*
Duncan, Charles d1942 *WhoHol 92*
Duncan, Charles Clifford 1907- *WhoAm 94*
Duncan, Charles Howard 1924- *WhoAm 94*
Duncan, Charles Lee 1939- *WhoAm 94, WhoScEn 94*
Duncan, Charles Tignor 1924- *WhoAm 94, WhoBlA 94*
Duncan, Charles Wesley 1951- *WhoMW 93*
Duncan, Charles William, Jr. 1926- *WhoAm 94*
Duncan, Clydell 1946- *WhoMW 93*
Duncan, Constance Catharine 1948- *WhoFI 94, WhoScEn 94*
Duncan, Dave 1933- *EncSF 93*
Duncan, David 1913- *EncSF 93, WrDr 94*
Duncan, David Douglas 1916- *WhoAm 94*
Duncan, David Edward 1926- *WhoBlA 94*
Duncan, David Francis 1923- *Who 94*
Duncan, Denis Macdonald 1920- *Who 94*
Duncan, Donald Pendleton 1916- *WhoAm 94*
Duncan, Donald William 1932- *WhoAm 94*
Duncan, Doris Gottschalk 1944- *WhoFI 94, WhoScEn 94, WhoWest 94*
Duncan, Douglas John Stewart 1945- *Who 94*
Duncan, Ed Eugene 1948- *WhoAm 94, WhoAmL 94*
Duncan, Edward Howard *GayLL*
Duncan, Edwin Williams 1945- *WhoAm 94, WhoAmL 94*
Duncan, Elizabeth 1925- *WrDr 94*
Duncan, Elizabeth Charlotte 1919- *WhoAm 94*
Duncan, Erika *DrAPF 93*
Duncan, Ernest Louis, Jr. *WhoAmL 94*
Duncan, Evelyn d1972 *WhoHol 92*
Duncan, Francis 1922- *WhoAm 94*
Duncan, Freeman B. 1946- *WhoAmP 93*
Duncan, Geneva 1935- *WhoBlA 94*
Duncan, Geoffrey Stuart 1938- *Who 94*
Duncan, George 1927- *WrDr 94*
Duncan, George 1933- *Who 94*
Duncan, George Alexander 1902- *Who 94*
Duncan, George Douglas *Who 94*
Duncan, George H. 1931- *WhoAm 94*
Duncan, George Ronald 1923- *WhoIns 94*
Duncan, Harry Alvin 1916- *WhoAmA 93*
Duncan, Hearst Randolph 1905- *WhoAm 94*
Duncan, Irma Wagner 1912- *WhoWest 94*
Duncan, Isadora 1878-1927 *AmCulL*
Duncan, J. Santford 1948- *WhoAmP 93*
Duncan, Jack G. 1939- *WhoAmL 94*
Duncan, James (Blair) 1927- *Who 94*
Duncan, James Anthony 1954- *WhoAmP 93*
Duncan, James Byron 1947- *WhoWest 94*
Duncan, James Herbert, Jr. 1947- *WhoMW 93*
Duncan, James Knox 1928- *WhoAmP 93*
Duncan, James Playford 1919- *Who 94*
Duncan, James Richard 1948- *WhoWest 94*
Duncan, James Wendell 1942- *WhoAmP 93*
Duncan, Janice Elaine *WhoFI 94*
Duncan, Joan A. 1939- *WhoBlA 94*
Duncan, John *WhoHol 92*
Duncan, John Alexander 1937- *WhoAmL 94*
Duncan, John Bonner 1910- *WhoAm 94*
Duncan, John C., Jr. 1942- *WhoBlA 94*
Duncan, John C., III 1939- *WhoAmL 94*
Duncan, John Dean, Jr. 1950- *WhoAm 94*
Duncan, John Finch 1933- *Who 94*
Duncan, John Frederick 1961- *WhoMW 93*
Duncan, John J., Jr. 1947- *CngDr 93, WhoAm 94, WhoAmP 93*
Duncan, John Patrick Cavanaugh 1949- *WhoAm 94, WhoAmL 94*
Duncan, John Spenser Ritchie 1921- *IntWW 93, Who 94*
Duncan, John Wiley 1947- *WhoScEn 94, WhoWest 94*
Duncan, Joseph Wayman 1936- *WhoAm 94, WhoFI 94*
Duncan, Joyce Louise 1946- *WhoAm 94, WhoMW 93*
Duncan, Julia K. 1905- *WrDr 94*
Duncan, Julia Nunnally *DrAPF 93*
Duncan, Kate Corbin 1942- *WhoWest 94*
Duncan, Kenne d1972 *WhoHol 92*
Duncan, Kenneth Playfair 1924- *Who 94*
Duncan, Larry *WhoAmP 93*
Duncan, Laura *Who 94*
Duncan, Lewis Mannan, III 1951- *WhoScEn 94*
Duncan, Lindsay *IntMPA 94, WhoHol 92*
Duncan, Lisa Sandra 1963- *WhoScEn 94*
Duncan, Lois 1934- *SmATA 75 [port], TwCYAW, WrDr 94*
Duncan, Louis Davidson, Jr. 1932- *WhoBlA 94*
Duncan, Lynda J. *WhoBlA 94*
Duncan, Malcolm McGregor 1922- *Who 94*
Duncan, Malcom d1942 *WhoHol 92*
Duncan, Margaret Caroline 1930- *WhoAm 94*
Duncan, Mariano 1963- *WhoHisp 94*
Duncan, Mark (Winchester) 1952- *WrDr 94*
Duncan, Marvin E. 1939- *WhoBlA 94*
Duncan, Marvin R. 1935- *WhoAmP 93*
Duncan, Mary 1905- *WhoHol 92*
Duncan, Myrl Leland 1948- *WhoMW 93*
Duncan, Parker W., Jr. 1942- *WhoAmL 94*
Duncan, Paul R. 1940- *WhoFI 94*
Duncan, Pearl PRD *DrAPF 93*
Duncan, Peter 1954- *WhoHol 92*
Duncan, Phillip Charles 1956- *WhoScEn 94*
Duncan, Pope Alexander 1920- *WhoAm 94*
Duncan, Randy *WhoAmP 93*
Duncan, Richard 1913- *WhoAm 94*
Duncan, Richard (Hurley) 1944- *WhoAmA 93*
Duncan, Richard G., Jr. 1938- *WhoAmL 94*
Duncan, Robert 1942-1988 *GayLL*
Duncan, Robert Bannerman 1942- *WhoAm 94*
Duncan, Robert Blackford 1920- *WhoAmP 93*
Duncan, Robert Clifton 1923- *WhoAm 94*
Duncan, Robert L. 1953- *WhoAmP 93*
Duncan, Robert L(ipscomb) 1927- *WrDr 94*
Duncan, Robert Lloyd 1953- *WhoAmL 94*
Duncan, Robert M. 1927- *WhoBlA 94*
Duncan, Robert Michael 1931-1991 *WhAm 10*
Duncan, Robert Michael 1951- *WhoAmP 93, WhoFI 94*
Duncan, Robert Todd 1903- *AfrAmAl 6, WhoBlA 94*
Duncan, Robin Barclay 1956- *WhoBlA 94*
Duncan, Ronald 1914-1982 *NewGrDO*
Duncan, Ronald (Frederick Henry) 1914-1982 *EncSF 93*
Duncan, Ronald (Fredrick Henry) 1914-1982 *ConDr 93*
Duncan, Ronny Rush 1946- *WhoAm 94*
Duncan, Rosetta d1959 *WhoHol 92*
Duncan, Rosetta 1900-1959
See Duncan Sisters, The *WhoCom*
Duncan, Royal Robert 1952- *WhoMW 93*
Duncan, Ruby 1932- *WhoBlA 94*
Duncan, Ruth 1908- *WhoAmA 93*
Duncan, Sandra Rhodes 1944- *WhoBlA 94*
Duncan, Sandy 1946- *IntMPA 94, WhoAm 94, WhoHol 92*
Duncan, Sandy Frances 1942- *BlmGWL*
Duncan, Sarah Jeannette 1861-1922 *BlmGWL*
Duncan, Sean Bruce 1942- *Who 94*
Duncan, Stanley Frederick St. Clare 1927- *Who 94*
Duncan, Starkey Davis, Jr. 1935- *WhoAm 94*
Duncan, Stephan W. 1924- *WhoBlA 94*
Duncan, Stephen Mack 1941- *WhoAm 94, WhoAmP 93*
Duncan, Steven Merle 1954- *WhoWest 94*
Duncan, Taylor d1957 *WhoHol 92*
Duncan, Terence 1928- *WrDr 94*
Duncan, Thomas Alton 1942- *WhoAm 94*
Duncan, Todd 1903- *WhoHol 92*
Duncan, (Robert) Todd 1903- *NewGrDO*
Duncan, Tommy d1967 *WhoHol 92*
Duncan, Verdell 1946- *WhoBlA 94*
Duncan, Verne Allen 1934- *WhoAmP 93, WhoWest 94*
Duncan, Virginia Bauer 1929-1991 *WhAm 10*
Duncan, Vivian d1986 *WhoHol 92*
Duncan, Vivian 1902-1986
See Duncan Sisters, The *WhoCom*
Duncan, William d1945 *WhoHol 92*
Duncan, William d1961 *WhoHol 92*
Duncan, William 1832-1918 *EncNAR*
Duncan, William (Robert) 1944- *WrDr 94*
Duncan, William Henry 1805-1863 *DcNaB MP*
Duncan, William Louis 1945- *WhoWest 94*
Duncan, William Millen 1939- *WhoAm 94, WhoFI 94*
Duncan, Willis Paschal, Jr. 1942- *WhoFI 94*
Duncan-Jones, Geri 1958- *WhoBlA 94*
Duncan-Jones, Richard Phare 1937- *Who 94*
Duncan Millar, Ian Alastair 1914- *Who 94*
Duncan Sisters, The *WhoCom*
Duncan Smith, (George) Iain 1954- *Who 94*
Duncanson, Donald George 1928- *WhoMW 93*
Duncanson, Robert 1817-1872 *AfrAmAl 6, WhoAmA 93N*
Duncker, Michael Charles 1950- *WhoWest 94*
Duncombe *Who 94*
Duncombe, C. Beth 1948- *WhoAmL 94, WhoBlA 94*
Duncombe, David Eliot 1961- *WhoFI 94*
Duncombe, John 1622-1687 *DcNaB MP*
Duncombe, Philip (Digby) Pauncefort- 1927- *Who 94*
Duncombe, Raynor Bailey 1942- *WhoAmL 94*
Duncombe, Raynor Lockwood 1917- *WhoAm 94, WhoScEn 94*
Duncombe, Roy 1925- *Who 94*
Duncombe, Susanna 1725-1812 *BlmGWL*

Duncumb, Peter 1931- *Who 94*
Dundas *Who 94*
Dundas, Hugh (Spencer Lisle) 1920- *Who 94*
Dundas, Jennie *WhoHol 92*
Dundas, Philip Blair, Jr. 1948- *WhoAm 94, WhoAmL 94*
Dundas, Thomas 1750-1794 *AmRev, WhAmRev*
Dundee, Earl of 1949- *Who 94*
Dundee (St. Paul's Cathedral), Provost of *Who 94*
Dundee, Jimmy d1953 *WhoHol 92*
Dundes, Alan 1934- *WhoAm 94*
Dundes, Jules 1913-1992 *WhAm 10*
Dundon, Brian R. 1946- *WhoFI 94*
Dundon, Margo Elaine 1950- *WhoAm 94*
Dundonald, Earl of 1961- *Who 94*
Dundonald, James 1918- *WrDr 94*
Dundy, Elaine 1927- *WrDr 94*
Dune, Steve Charles 1931- *WhoAm 94, WhoAmL 94*
Dune, T. L. *WhoAmP 93*
Dunea, George 1933- *WhoAm 94*
Dunedin, Bishop of 1942- *Who 94*
Dunegan, James H. 1940- *WhoAmP 93*
Dunetz, Lora *DrAPF 93*
Dun Family *NewGrDO*
Dunfee, Thomas Wylie 1941- *WhoAm 94, WhoAmL 94*
Dunfey, Robert John 1928- *WhoAmP 93*
Dunfield, David Mark 1952- *WhoMW 93*
Dunford, David J. *WhoAmP 93*
Dunford, Max Patterson 1930- *WhoWest 94*
Dunford, Robert A. 1931- *WhoAm 94, WhoFI 94*
Dunford, Robert Walter 1946- *WhoScEn 94*
Dung, Hou Chi 1936- *WhoAsA 94*
Dungan, Malcolm Thon 1922- *WhoAm 94, WhoAmL 94*
Dungan, William Joseph, Jr. 1956- *WhoFI 94*
Dungee, Margaret R. *WhoBlA 94*
Dungey, James Wynne 1923- *Who 94*
Dungie, Ruth Spigner *WhoBlA 94*
Dunglass, Lord *Who 94*
Dungworth, Donald L. 1931- *WhoAm 94, WhoWest 94*
Dungy, Claibourne I. 1938- *WhoBlA 94*
Dungy, Madgetta Thornton *WhoBlA 94*
Dunham, Aileen 1897- *WhAm 10*
Dunham, Archie W. *WhoFI 94*
Dunham, Benjamin Starr 1944- *WhoAm 94*
Dunham, Christine *WhoAm 94*
Dunham, Christopher Cooper 1937- *WhoAmP 93*
Dunham, Clarence E. 1934- *WhoBlA 94*
Dunham, Corydon Busnell 1927- *WhoAm 94*
Dunham, D. Ross 1928- *WhoAm 94*
Dunham, Dave 1941- *WhoAmP 93*
Dunham, Donald Carl 1908- *WhoAm 94*
Dunham, Frank G., Jr. 1930- *WhoIns 94*
Dunham, Frank L. 1940- *WhoAm 94*
Dunham, Glen Curtis 1956- *WhoWest 94*
Dunham, Gloria 1949- *WhoMW 93*
Dunham, Gregory Mark 1958- *WhoScEn 94*
Dunham, Jeffrey Solon 1953- *WhoScEn 94*
Dunham, Joanna 1936- *WhoHol 92*
Dunham, Katherine *IntWW 93*
Dunham, Katherine 1909- *WhoAm 94*
Dunham, Katherine 1910- *AfrAmAl 6, WhoBlA 94*
Dunham, Katherine 1912- *WhoHol 92*
Dunham, Kingsley (Charles) 1910- *Who 94*
Dunham, Kingsley (Charles), Sir 1910- *WrDr 94*
Dunham, Kingsley C. 1910- *IntWW 93*
Dunham, Phil d1972 *WhoHol 92*
Dunham, Philip Bigelow 1937- *WhoAm 94*
Dunham, Robert 1932- *WhoBlA 94*
Dunham, Rosemarie *WhoHol 92*
Dunham, Scott H. 1950- *WhoAmL 94*
Dunham, Stephen Sampson 1945- *WhoAm 94, WhoAmL 94*
Dunham, William 1947- *WrDr 94*
Dunham, Wolcott Balestier, Jr. 1943- *WhoAm 94, WhoAmL 94*
Dunham-Griggs, Margaret 1922- *WhoAmA 93*
Dunhill, Robert W. 1929- *WhoAm 94*
Dunhill, Thomas (Frederick) 1877-1946 *NewGrDO*
Duni, Antonio c. 1700-1766? *NewGrDO*
Duni, Egidio 1708-1775 *NewGrDO*
Duniecki, Stanislaw 1839-1870 *NewGrDO*
Dunifer, Stephen *NewYTBS 93*
Dunigan, Breon Nina 1961- *WhoAmA 93*
Dunigan, David Deeds 1951- *WhoScEn 94*
Dunigan, Dennis Wayne 1952- *WhoFI 94, WhoMW 93*
Dunigan, James Patrick 1952- *WhoFI 94*
Dunigan, Mayme O. 1921- *WhoBlA 94*
Dunigan, Paul Francis Xavier, Jr. 1948- *WhoWest 94*
Duning, George 1908- *IntDcF 2-4, IntMPA 94*
Dunipace, Ian Douglas 1939- *WhoAm 94, WhoAmL 94, WhoWest 94*
Dunitz, Jack David 1923- *IntWW 93, Who 94, WhoScEn 94*
Dunitz, Jay 1956- *WhoAmA 93*
Dunivent, John Thomas 1928- *WhoMW 93*
Duniway, John Mason 1942- *WhoAm 94*
Dunkel, Arthur 1932- *IntWW 93, Who 94*
Dunkel, Elizabeth 1951- *ConAu 142*
Dunkel, Florence Vaccarello 1942- *WhoAm 94*
Dunkel, Nancy Ann 1955- *WhoMW 93*
Dunkelberger, Harry Edward, Jr. 1930- *WhoAm 94*
Dunkeld, Bishop of 1941- *Who 94*
Dunkelman, Loretta 1937- *WhoAmA 93*
Dunkelman, Martha Levine 1947- *WhoAmA 93*
Dunker, Robert Ferdinand 1931- *WhoIns 94*
Dunkerley, George William 1919- *Who 94*
Dunkerley, James 1953- *WrDr 94*
Dunkerly, Inez Kathleen 1914- *WhoAmP 93*
Dunkerson, Dennis L. 1947- *WhoIns 94*
Dunkinson, Harry d1936 *WhoHol 92*
Dunklau, Rupert Louis 1927- *WhoAm 94*
Dunkle, Joan Osborn *WhoAmA 93*
Dunkle, Lisa Marie 1946- *WhoScEn 94*
Dunkle, Stephen T. 1951- *WhoAmP 93*
Dunkley, Carlyle Anthony 1939- *IntWW 93*
Dunkley, Christopher 1944- *Who 94*
Dunkley, James Lewis 1908- *Who 94*
Dunklin, Juni *DrAPF 93*
Dunklin, Mae Ola 1948- *WhoMW 93*
Dunkly, James Warren 1942- *WhoAm 94*
Dunlap, Al d1988 *WhoHol 92*
Dunlap, Burnie Harold 1943- *WhoWest 94*
Dunlap, Clarence Rupert 1908- *Who 94*
Dunlap, Connie 1924- *WhoAm 94*
Dunlap, Connie Sue Zimmerman 1952- *WhoMW 93*
Dunlap, Dale Richard 1960- *WhoScEn 94*
Dunlap, Daniel Girard 1948- *WhoFI 94*
Dunlap, David Graydon 1949- *WhoAmL 94*
Dunlap, David Houston 1947- *WhoAmL 94, WhoMW 93*
Dunlap, E. T. 1914- *WhoAm 94*
Dunlap, Ellen S. 1951- *WhoAm 94*
Dunlap, Estelle Cecilia Diggs 1912- *WhoBlA 94*
Dunlap, Ethel Margaret d1968 *WhoHol 92*
Dunlap, F. Thomas, Jr. 1951- *WhoAmL 94, WhoFI 94*
Dunlap, George Alan 1925- *WhoMW 93*
Dunlap, George Carter 1936- *WhoAm 94*
Dunlap, Jack Stuart 1930- *WhoWest 94*
Dunlap, James Cleveland 1941- *WhoFI 94*
Dunlap, James Lapham 1937- *WhoAm 94*
Dunlap, James Riley, Sr. 1925- *WhoWest 94*
Dunlap, James Robert 1961- *WhoAmP 93*
Dunlap, Jane fl. 1771- *BlmGWL*
Dunlap, John 1747-1812 *WhAmRev*
Dunlap, John Frederick 1943- *WhoAmL 94*
Dunlap, Lawrence Hallowell 1910- *WhoScEn 94*
Dunlap, Leslie W 1911- *WrDr 94*
Dunlap, Loren Edward 1932- *WhoAmA 93*
Dunlap, Michele Marie 1960- *WhoMW 93*
Dunlap, Patricia C. 1926- *WhoAmP 93*
Dunlap, Philip Stanley 1918- *WhoAm 94*
Dunlap, Richard D. 1923- *IntMPA 94*
Dunlap, Riley E. 1943- *WhoScEn 94*
Dunlap, Robert 1942- *ConTFT 11*
Dunlap, Scott d1970 *WhoHol 92*
Dunlap, Susan D. (Sullivan) 1943- *WrDr 94*
Dunlap, William 1766-1839 *IntDcT 2*
Dunlap, William Crawford 1918- *WhoAm 94*
Dunlap, William DeWayne, Jr. 1938- *WhoAm 94*
Dunlap, William Phillip 1942- *WhoAm 94*
Dunlap, William Wayne 1933- *WhoFI 94*
Dunlap King, Virgie M. 1940- *WhoBlA 94*
Dunleath, Baron d1993 *Who 94N*
Dunleath, Baron 1915- *Who 94*
Dunleavy, James Patrick 1939- *WhoAmP 93*
Dunleavy, Janet Frank Egleson 1928- *WhoAm 94*
Dunleavy, Michael Joseph 1954- *WhoAm 94, WhoMW 93*
Dunleavy, Patrick 1952- *WrDr 94*
Dunleavy, Philip 1915- *Who 94*
Dunleavy, Rosemary *WhoAm 94*
Dunleavy, Terence Martin 1957- *WhoMW 93*
Dunlevy, Kevin John 1955- *WhoAmL 94*
Dunlevy, William Sargent 1952- *WhoAmL 94*
Dunlop, Andrew Reed 1953- *WhoMW 93*
Dunlop, Colin Charles Harrison 1918- *Who 94*
Dunlop, David John 1941- *WhoAm 94*
Dunlop, Donald William 1939- *WhoMW 93*
Dunlop, Edward d1993 *NewYTBS 93*
Dunlop, (Ernest) Edward d1993 *Who 94N*
Dunlop, Eileen (Rhona) 1938- *SmATA 76 [port], TwCYAW, WrDr 94*
Dunlop, Eliza Hamilton 1796-1880 *BlmGWL*
Dunlop, Ernest Edward 1907- *IntWW 93*
Dunlop, Frank 1927- *IntWW 93, Who 94*
Dunlop, Fred Hurston 1946- *WhoAm 94, WhoAmL 94*
Dunlop, George Rodgers 1906- *WhoAm 94*
Dunlop, Gordon *Who 94*
Dunlop, (Norman) Gordon (Edward) 1928- *Who 94*
Dunlop, Ian (Geoffrey David) 1925- *WrDr 94*
Dunlop, Ian Geoffrey David 1925- *Who 94*
Dunlop, John 1910- *Who 94*
Dunlop, John Barrett 1942- *WhoAm 94*
Dunlop, John Boyd 1840-1921 *WorInv*
Dunlop, John T. 1914- *IntWW 93*
Dunlop, John T(homas) 1914- *WrDr 94*
Dunlop, John Thomas 1914- *WhoAm 94, WhoAmP 93*
Dunlop, Laurence James 1939- *WhoWest 94*
Dunlop, Lesley 1956- *WhoHol 92*
Dunlop, Mark Joseph 1960- *WhoFI 94*
Dunlop, Michael John 1962- *WhoFI 94*
Dunlop, Richard B. *Who 94*
Dunlop, Robert Galbraith 1909- *WhoAm 94*
Dunlop, Robert Hugh 1929- *WhoAm 94*
Dunlop, Thomas 1912- *Who 94*
Dunlop, William 1792-1848 *DcNaB MP*
Dunlop, William (Norman Gough) 1914- *Who 94*
Dunluce, Viscount *Who 94*
Dunman, Leonard Joe, III 1952- *WhoFI 94*
Dunmire, Ronald Warren 1937- *WhoAm 94, WhoMW 93*
Dunmire, William Werden 1930- *WhoAm 94*
Dunmore, Earl of 1913- *Who 94*
Dunmore, Lord *AmRev*
Dunmore, Charlotte J. 1926- *WhoBlA 94*
Dunmore, Gregory Charles 1958- *WhoBlA 94*
Dunmore, John 1923- *WrDr 94*
Dunmore, John Murray, Earl of 1732-1809 *WhAmRev*
Dunmore, Lawrence A., Jr. 1923- *WhoBlA 94*
Dunmore, Spencer S 1928- *WrDr 94*
Dunn, Baroness 1940- *Who 94*
Dunn, Alan (Cantwell) 1900-1974 *WhoAmA 93N*
Dunn, Alan Michael 1953- *WhoAmL 94*
Dunn, Andrea Lee 1951- *WhoScEn 94*
Dunn, Andrew Fletcher 1922- *WhoAm 94*
Dunn, Arnold Samuel 1929- *WhoAm 94*
Dunn, Bobby d1937 *WhoHol 92*
Dunn, Bonnie Brill 1953- *WhoAm 94*
Dunn, Bruce Eric 1959- *WhoBlA 94*
Dunn, Bruce Sidney 1948- *WhoAm 94, WhoScEn 94*
Dunn, Bryant Winfield Culberson 1927- *WhoAmP 93*
Dunn, Cal 1915- *WhoAmA 93*
Dunn, Charles DeWitt 1945- *WhoAm 94*
Dunn, Charles W(illiam) 1915- *WrDr 94*
Dunn, Charles William 1915- *WhoAm 94*
Dunn, Charles Wythe 1940- *WhoAmP 93*
Dunn, Charlie d1993 *NewYTBS 93*
Dunn, Christopher Allan 1951- *WhoAm 94*
Dunn, Clara d1986 *WhoHol 92*
Dunn, Clark Allan 1901- *WhoAm 94*
Dunn, Clive 1922- *WhoHol 92*
Dunn, David Cameron 1941- *WhoWest 94*
Dunn, David E. 1935- *WhoAm 94*
Dunn, David John 1943- *WhoMW 93*
Dunn, David Joseph 1930- *WhoAm 94, WhoWest 94*
Dunn, David Lewis 1952- *WhoMW 93*
Dunn, David N. 1940- *WhoIns 94*
Dunn, Delmer Delano 1941- *WhoAm 94*
Dunn, Donald Allen 1925- *WhoAm 94*
Dunn, Donald Dean 1955- *WhoMW 93*
Dunn, Donald Jack 1945- *WhoAmL 94*
Dunn, Douglas 1942- *BlmGEL*
Dunn, Douglas (Eaglesham) 1942- *WrDr 94*
Dunn, Douglas Eaglesham 1942- *IntWW 93, Who 94*
Dunn, Eddie d1951 *WhoHol 92*
Dunn, Edgar M., Jr. 1939- *WhoAmP 93*
Dunn, Edward S., Jr. 1943- *WhoFI 94*
Dunn, Edwin Rydell 1942- *WhoAmL 94*
Dunn, Elwood 1906- *WhoAm 94*
Dunn, Emma d1966 *WhoHol 92*
Dunn, Eric (Clive) 1927- *Who 94*
Dunn, Floyd 1924- *WhoAm 94, WhoMW 93*
Dunn, Fontaine *WhoAmA 93*
Dunn, Francis Michael 1955- *WhoMW 93*
Dunn, Frank 1933- *WhoFI 94, WhoMW 93*
Dunn, Geoffrey 1903- *WhoHol 92*
Dunn, Geoffrey (Thomas) 1903-1981 *NewGrDO*
Dunn, George d1982 *WhoHol 92*
Dunn, George William 1930- *WhoBlA 94*
Dunn, George Willoughby 1914- *Who 94*
Dunn, Gordon Harold 1932- *WhoScEn 94, WhoWest 94*
Dunn, Grace Veronica *WhoFI 94*
Dunn, Gregg d1964 *WhoHol 92*
Dunn, Guy Wesley 1960- *WhoWest 94*
Dunn, H. Glenn Tolson 1944- *WhoAmL 94*
Dunn, H. Stewart, Jr. 1929- *WhoAm 94*
Dunn, Harry Lippincott 1894-1988 *WhAm 10*
Dunn, Harvey B. d1968 *WhoHol 92*
Dunn, Harvey T. 1884-1952 *WhoAmA 93N*
Dunn, Henry Hampton 1916- *WhoAm 94*
Dunn, Herbert Stanley d1979 *WhoHol 92*
Dunn, Horton, Jr. 1929- *WhoAm 94, WhoFI 94, WhoMW 93, WhoScEn 94*
Dunn, Hugh Alexander 1923- *IntWW 93*
Dunn, Hugh Patrick 1916- *WrDr 94*
Dunn, J. Malcolm d1946 *WhoHol 92*
Dunn, Jack d1938 *WhoHol 92*
Dunn, Jack Hibbard 1944- *WhoWest 94*
Dunn, James d1967 *WhoHol 92*
Dunn, James B. *WhoAmP 93*
Dunn, James Bernard 1927- *WhoMW 93*
Dunn, James Earl 1955- *WhoAmP 93, WhoBlA 94*
Dunn, James Joseph 1920- *WhoAm 94*
Dunn, James R. *WhoAmP 93*
Dunn, James Robert 1921- *WhoAm 94*
Dunn, James T. 1946- *WhoAmL 94*
Dunn, James Taylor 1912- *ConAu 43NR*
Dunn, James Whitney 1943- *WhoAmP 93*
Dunn, Jan d1986 *WhoHol 92*
Dunn, Jeffrey William 1947- *WhoMW 93*
Dunn, Jennifer 1941- *CngDr 93*
Dunn, Jennifer Blackburn 1941- *WhoAm 94, WhoAmP 93, WhoWest 94, WhoWomW 91*
Dunn, John (Montfort) 1940- *WrDr 94*
Dunn, John Churchill 1934- *Who 94*
Dunn, John F. 1936- *WhoAmP 93*
Dunn, John Francis 1936- *WhoMW 93*
Dunn, John M. 1951- *WhoAmL 94*
Dunn, John Montfort 1940- *IntWW 93, Who 94*
Dunn, John P. 1949- *WhoAm 94, WhoAmL 94*
Dunn, Johnny d1938 *WhoHol 92*
Dunn, Jon Michael 1941- *WhoAm 94*
Dunn, Josephine d1983 *WhoHol 92*
Dunn, Karl Lindemann 1942- *WhoScEn 94*
Dunn, Katherine (Karen) 1945- *EncSF 93*
Dunn, Kaye 1910- *WhoBlA 94*
Dunn, Kenneth Ralph 1958- *WhoFI 94*
Dunn, Lawrence William 1942- *WhoAmP 93*
Dunn, Leo James 1931- *WhoAm 94*
Dunn, Leslie D. 1945- *WhoAm 94, WhoAmL 94*
Dunn, Liam d1976 *WhoHol 92*
Dunn, Linda Kay 1947- *WhoAm 94*
Dunn, Linwood 1904- *IntDcF 2-4*
Dunn, Loretta Lynn 1955- *WhoAm 94*
Dunn, Lydia 1940- *WhoWomW 91*
Dunn, Lydia Selina 1940- *IntWW 93*
Dunn, M. Catherine 1934- *WhoAm 94*
Dunn, Margaret Mary Coyne 1909- *WhoAm 94*
Dunn, Marilyn Paulette 1964- *WhoAmL 94*
Dunn, Mark Dalton 1958- *WhoAmL 94*
Dunn, Mark R. 1961- *WhoAmL 94*
Dunn, Martin 1955- *Who 94*
Dunn, Martin J. 1956- *WhoAmP 93*
Dunn, Martin Joseph 1935- *WhoAm 94*
Dunn, Marvin 1940- *WhoBlA 94*
Dunn, Marvin Irvin 1927- *WhoAm 94, WhoScEn 94*
Dunn, Mary Jarratt 1942- *WhoAm 94, WhoAmP 93*
Dunn, Mary Maples 1931- *WhoAm 94*
Dunn, Mary Price 1952- *WhoWest 94*
Dunn, Melvin B. 1936- *WhoIns 94*
Dunn, Melvin Bernard 1936- *WhoAm 94*
Dunn, Michael d1973 *WhoHol 92*

Dunn, Michael Joseph 1951- *WhoWest 94*
Dunn, Mignon *WhoAm 94*
Dunn, Mignon 1931- *NewGrDO*
Dunn, Miriam D. 1927- *WhoAmP 93*
Dunn, Morris Douglas 1944- *WhoAm 94, WhoAmL 94*
Dunn, Nell 1936- *BlmGWL [port], WrDr 94*
Dunn, Nell (Mary) 1936- *ConDr 93*
Dunn, Nora 1952- *ConTFT 11, WhoHol 92*
Dunn, Norman Samuel 1921- *WhoAm 94*
Dunn, Parker Southerland 1910- *WhoAm 94*
Dunn, Patricia d1990 *WhoHol 92*
Dunn, Patrick Hunter 1912- *Who 94*
Dunn, Patrick W. 1946- *WhoAmL 94*
Dunn, Peter d1990 *WhoHol 92*
Dunn, Peter 1946- *WhoIns 94*
Dunn, Peter Norman 1926- *WrDr 94*
Dunn, Philip M. *EncSF 93*
Dunn, Phillip Charles 1947- *WhoAmA 93*
Dunn, Ralph d1968 *WhoHol 92*
Dunn, Ralph 1914- *WhoAmP 93*
Dunn, Randy Edwin 1954- *WhoAmL 94*
Dunn, Randy J. 1958- *WhoMW 93*
Dunn, Rebecca Diane 1948- *WhoFI 94*
Dunn, Rebecca Jo *WhoAmP 93*
Dunn, Reginald Arthur *WhoBlA 94*
Dunn, Richard Johann 1943- *Who 94*
Dunn, Richard John 1938- *WhoAm 94*
Dunn, Richard Joseph 1924- *WhoFI 94*
Dunn, Richard Lee 1944- *WhoAmL 94*
Dunn, Richard Maxwell 1942- *WhoFI 94*
Dunn, Richard S(lator) 1928- *WrDr 94*
Dunn, Robert *DrAPF 93*
Dunn, Robert d1960 *WhoHol 92*
Dunn, Robert Alan 1941- *WhoWest 94*
Dunn, Robert G. 1923- *WhoAmP 93*
Dunn, Robert John 1946- *Who 94*
Dunn, Robert Lawrence 1938- *WhoAmL 94*
Dunn, Robert Leland 1946- *WhoScEn 94*
Dunn, Robert Sigler 1926- *WhoMW 93*
Dunn, Robin Horace Walford 1918- *Who 94*
Dunn, Roger Terry 1946- *WhoAmA 93*
Dunn, Ronald Holland 1937- *WhoFI 94, WhoScEn 94*
Dunn, Ronald Leslie 1954- *WhoAmL 94*
Dunn, Ronnie 1953- *WhoAm 94*
Dunn, Ross *WhoBlA 94*
Dunn, Roy J. 1946- *WhoAm 94*
Dunn, S(amuel) Watson 1918- *WrDr 94*
Dunn, Saul 1946- *EncSF 93*
Dunn, Stanley Martin 1956- *WhoScEn 94*
Dunn, Stephen *DrAPF 93*
Dunn, Stephen 1939- *WrDr 94*
Dunn, Steven Allen 1948- *WhoScEn 94, WhoWest 94*
Dunn, Stuart Thomas 1940- *WhoWest 94*
Dunn, Susan 1954- *NewGrDO, WhoAm 94*
Dunn, T. R. 1955- *WhoBlA 94*
Dunn, Theresa Rose 1962- *WhoFI 94*
Dunn, Thomas Aquinas 1942- *WhoAmP 93, WhoMW 93*
Dunn, Thomas G. *WhoAmP 93*
Dunn, Thomas Guy 1935- *WhoWest 94*
Dunn, Thomas Henry 1956- *WhoAmL 94*
Dunn, Violet *WhoHol 92*
Dunn, Vivian *Who 94*
Dunn, (Francis) Vivian 1908- *Who 94*
Dunn, W. Carleton 1932- *WhoIns 94*
Dunn, W. Paul 1938- *WhoBlA 94*
Dunn, Walter Scott, Jr. 1928- *WhoAm 94*
Dunn, Warren Howard 1934- *WhoAm 94, WhoFI 94*
Dunn, Wendell Earl, III 1945- *WhoAm 94, WhoFI 94*
Dunn, Wesley B. 1951- *WhoAmP 93*
Dunn, Wesley John 1924- *WhoAm 94*
Dunn, William Bradley 1939- *WhoAmL 94, WhoMW 93*
Dunn, William Francis N. *Who 94*
Dunn, William Hubert 1933- *Who 94*
Dunn, William L. 1919- *WhoBlA 94*
Dunnachie, James Francis 1930- *Who 94*
Dunnahoo, Terry 1927- *WhoAm 94*
Dunnam, Stephanie *WhoHol 92*
Dunn-Barker, Lillian Joyce 1938- *WhoBlA 94*
Dunne, Dana Philip C. 1963- *WhoFI 94*
Dunne, Diane C. *WhoFI 94*
Dunne, Dominick *IntMPA 94*
Dunne, Dominick 1925- *WhoAm 94, WrDr 94*
Dunne, Dominique d1982 *WhoHol 92*
Dunne, Eithne d1988 *WhoHol 92*
Dunne, Elizabeth d1954 *WhoHol 92*
Dunne, Griffin 1955- *IntMPA 94, WhoHol 92*
Dunne, Irene d1990 *WhoHol 92*
Dunne, Irene 1901-1990 *WhAm 10*
Dunne, Irene 1904-1990 *WhoCom*
Dunne, J(ohn) W(illiam) 1875-1949 *EncSF 93*
Dunne, James Michael 1942- *WhoWest 94*
Dunne, James Robert 1929- *WhoFI 94*
Dunne, John Gregory 1932- *WhoAm 94, WrDr 94*
Dunne, John Richard 1930- *WhoAm 94, WhoAmP 93*
Dunne, John S(cribner) 1929- *WrDr 94*
Dunne, John William 1875-1949 *DcNaB MP*
Dunne, Kevin J. 1941- *WhoAm 94*
Dunne, Kevin Joseph 1941- *WhoAmL 94*
Dunne, Mary Chavelita *BlmGWL*
Dunne, Matthew Bailey 1969- *WhoAmP 93*
Dunne, Michael *WhoHol 92*
Dunne, Murphy *WhoHol 92*
Dunne, Philip 1908- *IntDcF 2-4*
Dunne, Philip 1908-1992 *WhAm 10*
Dunne, Richard E., III 1950- *WhoAm 94, WhoAmL 94*
Dunne, Steve d1977 *WhoHol 92*
Dunne, Thomas 1943- *WhoAm 94, WhoWest 94*
Dunne, Thomas Gregory 1930- *WhoAm 94*
Dunne, Thomas Leo 1946- *WhoAm 94*
Dunne, Thomas Raymond 1933- *Who 94*
Dunnebacke-Dixon, Thelma Hudson 1925- *WhoWest 94*
Dunnell, Robert Chester 1942- *WhoAm 94*
Dunner, Donald Robert 1931- *WhoAm 94*
Dunner, Leslie B. 1956- *WhoBlA 94*
Dunnet, George Mackenzie 1928- *Who 94*
Dunnett, Alastair M(acTavish) 1908- *WrDr 94*
Dunnett, Alastair MacTavish 1908- *IntWW 93, Who 94*
Dunnett, Dennis George 1939- *WhoWest 94*
Dunnett, Denzil Inglis 1917- *Who 94*
Dunnett, Dorothy 1923- *ConAu 43NR*
Dunnett, Dorothy (Halliday) 1923- *WrDr 94*
Dunnett, Jack 1922- *Who 94*
Dunnett, (Ludovic) James 1914- *Who 94*
Dunnigan, Frank Joseph 1914-1990 *WhAm 10*
Dunnigan, Jerry 1941- *WhoBlA 94*
Dunnigan, Mary Ann 1915- *WhoWest 94*
Dunnigan, Mary Catherine 1922- *WhoAmA 93*
Dunnigan, T. Kevin 1938- *WhoAm 94, WhoFI 94*
Dunnihoo, Dale Russell 1928- *WhoAm 94*
Dunning, Alan Smith 1946- *WhoAm 94, WhoAmL 94*
Dunning, Ann Marie 1942- *WhoAm 94*
Dunning, George 1920-1979 *IntDcF 2-4*
Dunning, Herbert Neal 1923- *WhoAm 94*
Dunning, James Morse 1904-1991 *WhAm 10*
Dunning, Jessica d1990 *WhoHol 92*
Dunning, John H 1927- *WrDr 94*
Dunning, John Harry 1927- *Who 94*
Dunning, Joseph 1920- *Who 94*
Dunning, Kenneth Laverne 1914- *WhoWest 94*
Dunning, Lawrence *DrAPF 93*
Dunning, Robert L., Sr. *WhoAmP 93*
Dunning, Robert William 1938- *ConAu 42NR*
Dunning, Ruth d1983 *WhoHol 92*
Dunning, Sally 1945- *WhoMW 93*
Dunning, Simon (William Patrick) 1939- *Who 94*
Dunning, Stephen *DrAPF 93*
Dunning, Thomas E. 1944- *WhoAm 94, WhoMW 93*
Dunnings, Stuart, II 1952- *WhoBlA 94*
Dunnington, Walter Grey, Jr. 1927- *WhoAm 94*
Dunnington-Jefferson, Mervyn (Stewart) 1943- *Who 94*
Dunnock, Mildred 1900-1991 *WhoHol 92*
Dunnock, Mildred 1932-1991 *WhAm 10*
Dunn-Rankin, Peter 1929- *WhoWest 94*
Dunnuck, Samuel R., III 1947- *WhoAmP 93*
Dunow, Esti 1948- *WhoAmA 93*
du Noyer, Anne-Marguerite Petit 1663-1720 *BlmGWL*
Dunphie, Charles (Anderson Lane) 1902- *Who 94*
Dunphy, Edward James 1940- *WhoAm 94, WhoScEn 94*
Dunphy, Jack 1914-1992 *AnObit 1992*
Dunraven and Mount-Earl, Earl of 1939- *Who 94*
Dunrossil, Viscount 1926- *IntWW 93, Who 94*
Dunsany, Baron of 1906- *Who 94*
Dunsany, Lord 1878-1957 *EncSF 93, IntDcT 2*
Dunsford, Harold Atkinson 1941- *WhoScEn 94*
Dunshee, Hans *WhoAmP 93*
Dunsire, Peter Kenneth 1932- *WhoAm 94*
Dunski, Jonathan Frank 1969- *WhoScEn 94*
Dunsky, Menahem 1930- *WhoAm 94*
Dunsmore, Allison Rosina Tippman 1954- *WhoMW 93*
Dunsmore, George M. 1942- *WhoAmP 93*
Dunsmore, Lorri Anne 1962- *WhoAmL 94*
Dunson, Carrie Lee 1946- *WhoBlA 94*
Dunson, Daniel 1947- *WhoAmL 94*
Dunson, James Blake, Jr. 1939- *WhoFI 94*
Dunson, William Albert 1941- *WhoAm 94, WhoScEn 94*
Duns Scotus, John 1265?-1308? *BlmGEL*
Duns Scotus, John c. 1266-1308 *EncEth*
Dunst, Isabel Paula 1947- *WhoAm 94*
Dunst, Laurence David 1941- *WhoAm 94*
Dunstan, Andrew *EncSF 93*
Dunstan, (Andrew Harold) Bernard 1920- *IntWW 93, Who 94*
Dunstan, Cliff d1968 *WhoHol 92*
Dunstan, Donald (Beaumont) 1923- *Who 94*
Dunstan, Donald Allan 1926- *Who 94*
Dunstan, G(ordon) R(eginald) 1917- *WrDr 94*
Dunstan, Gordon Reginald 1917- *IntWW 93, Who 94*
Dunstan, Ivan 1930- *Who 94*
Dunstan, James Roscoe 1927- *WhoWest 94*
Dunstan, Larry Kenneth 1948- *WhoWest 94*
Dunstan, Robert Owen 1927- *WhoAmP 93*
Dunster, Henry 1609-1659 *DcAmReB 2*
Dunster, (Herbert) John 1922- *Who 94*
Dunston, Alfred G. 1915- *WhoBlA 94*
Dunston, Alfred Gilbert, Jr. 1915- *WhoAm 94*
Dunston, Leigh Everett 1944- *WhoAmL 94*
Dunston, Leonard G. 1940- *WhoBlA 94*
Dunston, Shawon Donnell 1963- *WhoBlA 94*
Dunston, Victor 1926- *WhoBlA 94*
Dunston, Walter T. 1935- *WhoBlA 94*
Dunteman, George Henry 1935- *WhoAm 94*
Dunton, Franklin Roy 1921- *WhoAmP 93*
Dunton, Susan Beth 1955- *WhoMW 93*
Duntze, Daniel (Evans) 1926- *Who 94*
Dunwich, Bishop Suffragan of 1940- *Who 94*
Dunwich, Viscount 1961- *Who 94*
Dunwich, Gerina 1959- *WhoAm 94, WhoWest 94*
Dunwiddie, Charlotte *WhoAmA 93*
Dunwiddie, Charlotte 1907- *WhoAm 94*
Dunwiddie, Peter William 1953- *WhoScEn 94*
Dunwody, Eugene Cox 1933- *WhoAm 94*
Dunwoody, Gwyneth (Patricia) 1930- *Who 94*
Dunwoody, Gwyneth Patricia 1930- *WhoWomW 91*
Dunwoody, John (Elliott Orr) 1929- *Who 94*
Dunwoody, Kenneth Reed 1953- *WhoAm 94*
Dunwoody, Sharon Lee 1947- *WhoMW 93*
Dunworth, John 1924- *WhoAm 94*
Dunworth, John Vernon 1917- *Who 94*
Duoba 1932- *WhoPRCh 91 [port]*
Duo-ji Cai-rang *WhoPRCh 91*
Duo-jie Cai-dan *WhoPRCh 91*
Duojizha Jiangbai Luosang *WhoPRCh 91*
Duong, Cambao De 1943- *WhoAsA 94*
Duong, Duc Hong 1939- *WhoAsA 94*
Duong, Minh Truc 1938- *WhoScEn 94*
Duong, Ngo Dinh 1962- *WhoAsA 94*
Duong, Taihung 1956- *WhoScEn 94*
Duong, Victor Viet Hong 1956- *WhoScEn 94*
Du Par, Richard Conway 1933- *WhoAmL 94*
Duparc, Elisabeth d1778? *NewGrDO*
Dupas, Mark Kirby 1959- *WhoBlA 94*
Dupasquier, Philippe 1955- *WrDr 94*
Dupea, Tatzumbia d1970 *WhoHol 92*
Du Pen, Everett George 1912- *WhoAm 94, WhoAmA 93, WhoWest 94*
Du Pengcheng 1921- *WhoPRCh 91 [port]*
Duper, Mark Super 1959- *WhoAm 94*
Duperey, Anny 1947- *WhoHol 92*
Duperrey, Louis-Isadore 1786-1865 *WhWE*
Dupetit-Thouars, Abel-Aubert 1793-1864 *WhWE*
Dupies, Donald Albert 1934- *WhoAm 94*
Dupin, Jacques 1927- *ConWorW 93*
Du Ping 1905- *WhoPRCh 91 [port]*
Duplantier, Adrian Guy 1929- *WhoAm 94, WhoAmL 94*
Duplat, Jean-Louis *IntWW 93*
Duplechan, Larry 1956- *BlkWr 2, ConAu 141*
Du Plessis, Barend Jacobus 1940- *IntWW 93, Who 94*
Du Plessis, Christian 1944- *IntWW 93*
Du Plessis, Christian Johannes 1944- *NewGrDO*
Du Plessis, Daniel Jacob 1918- *IntWW 93, Who 94*
Duplessis, Harry Y. 1915- *WhoBlA 94*
Du Plessis, Menan 1952- *BlmGWL*
du Plessis, Nancy *DrAPF 93*
DuPlessis, Rachel Blau *DrAPF 93*
Duplessis, Susan Dubay 1956- *WhoAmP 93*
Duplessis, Suzanne 1940- *WhoWomW 91*
Duplessis, Thomas *WhAmRev*
Duplissea, William Patrick 1950- *WhoAmP 93*
Duponchel, Charles (Edmond) 1794-1868 *NewGrDO*
Dupond, Patrick 1959- *IntDcB [port]*
Dupont, Miss d1973 *WhoHol 92*
Dupont, Alexis 1796-1874 *NewGrDO*
Dupont, Colyer Lee 1957- *WhoWest 94*
Dupont, Edward Charles, Jr. 1950- *WhoAm 94, WhoAmP 93*
Dupont, Gabriel Edouard Xavier 1878-1914 *NewGrDO*
Dupont, Henry F. 1880-1969 *WhoAmA 93N*
DuPont, Herbert Lancashire 1938- *WhoAm 94*
Dupont, Jacqueline 1934- *WhoAm 94*
DuPont, James Benjamen 1953- *WhoAmP 93*
duPont, Margaret Osborne 1918- *BuCMET [port]*
duPont, Marka Truesdale d1993 *NewYTBS 93*
du Pont, Pierre Samuel 1935- *WhoAmP 93*
du Pont, Pierre Samuel, IV 1935- *IntWW 93, WhoAm 94*
Dupont, Ralph Paul 1929- *WhoAm 94, WhoAmL 94*
Dupont, Richard G. 1943- *WhoAmP 93*
DuPont, Robert Louis 1936- *WhoAm 94, WhoAmP 93*
DuPont, Stephen Carter 1958- *WhoAm 94*
Dupont, Todd F. 1942- *WhoAm 94*
DuPont-Morales, Maria A. Toni 1948- *WhoHisp 94*
Duport, Louis-Antoine 1781-1853 *IntDcB*
Duportail, Louis Le Beque de Presle 1743-1802 *WhAmRev*
Duportail, Louis Lebeque de Presle 1743-1802 *AmRev*
Duppa-Miller, John Bryan Peter *Who 94*
Dupper, Frank Floyd 1933- *WhoAm 94*
Dupplin, Viscount 1962- *Who 94*
Duppong, Margie Ann Claus 1939- *WhoMW 93*
Duppstadt, Marlyn Henry 1947- *WhoAm 94*
Duprato, Jules Laurent (Anacharsis) 1827-1892 *NewGrDO*
Dupray, Claire *WhoHol 92*
Dupray, Gaston d1976 *WhoHol 92*
Dupre, Emilo Joseph 1945- *WhoAmP 93, WhoBlA 94*
Dupre, John Lionel 1953- *WhoBlA 94*
Dupre, Louis *WhoAm 94, WrDr 94*
Dupre, Louis c. 1697-1774 *IntDcB*
Dupre, Tumun 1923- *Who 94*
Dupree, Anderson Hunter 1921- *WhoAm 94*
Dupree, Champion Jack 1910-1992 *AnObit 1992*
DuPree, David 1946- *WhoBlA 94*
Dupree, David H. 1959- *WhoBlA 94*
DuPree, Don Keck *DrAPF 93*
Dupree, Edward A. 1943- *WhoBlA 94*
Dupree, Franklin Taylor, Jr. 1913- *WhoAm 94, WhoAmL 94*
Dupree, George d1951 *WhoHol 92*
Dupree, Louis Benjamin 1925-1989 *WhAm 10*
Dupree, Minnie d1947 *WhoHol 92*
Dupree, Peter 1924- *Who 94*
Dupree, Roland 1925- *WhoHol 92*
Dupree, Sandra Kay 1956- *WhoBlA 94*
DuPree, Sherry Sherrod 1946- *WhoBlA 94*
Dupree, Stanley M. 1946- *WhoAm 94, WhoAmL 94*
Dupree, Thomas Andrew 1950- *WhoScEn 94*
Duprey, Joann 1945- *WhoAmP 93*
Duprey, Richard Lawrence 1962- *WhoAmP 93*
Duprey, Stephen Michael 1953- *WhoAmP 93*
Duprey, Wilson Gilliland 1924- *WhoAm 94*
Duprez, Fred d1938 *WhoHol 92*
Duprez, Gilbert(-Louis) 1806-1896 *NewGrDO*
Duprez, June d1984 *WhoHol 92*
DuPriest, Douglas Millhollen 1951- *WhoAmL 94*
Dupuis, Adrian M(aurice) 1919- *WrDr 94*
Dupuis, Albert 1877-1967 *NewGrDO*
Dupuis, Art d1952 *WhoHol 92*
Dupuis, Claude Paul 1942- *WhoFI 94*
Du Puis, George Bonello 1928- *IntWW 93*
Dupuis, Jean 1829-1912 *WhWE*

Dupuis, Jose 1831-1900 *NewGrDO*
Dupuis, Josephine Mabel 1920- *WhoAmP 93*
Dupuis, Paul d1976 *WhoHol 92*
Dupuis, Rene 1898- *WhAm 10*
Dupuis, Robert 1926- *ConAu 141*
Dupuis, Robert Simeon 1941- *WhoFI 94*
Dupuis, Russell Dean 1947- *WhoAm 94*
Dupuis, Sylvio Louis 1934- *WhoAm 94, WhoAmP 93*
Dupuis, Victor Lionel 1934- *WhoAm 94*
Dupuy, Arnold C. 1962- *WrDr 94*
Du Puy, (Jean Baptiste) Edouard (Louis Camille) c. 1770-1822 *NewGrDO*
Dupuy, Eliza Ann 1814-1881 *BlmGWL*
DuPuy, F. Russell, III 1961- *WhoAmL 94*
Dupuy, Frank Russell, Jr. 1907- *WhoAm 94*
Dupuy, Martine 1952- *NewGrDO*
Dupuy, Robert W. 1946- *WhoAmL 94*
Dupuy, T(revor) N(evitt) 1916- *WrDr 94*
Dupuy, Trevor Nevitt 1916- *WhoAm 94*
Du Qinglin 1946- *WhoPRCh 91 [port]*
Duquesne, Jacques Henri Louis 1930- *IntWW 93*
Duquesnoy, Charles-Francois-Honore 1759-1822 *NewGrDO*
Duquette, Dan *WhoAm 94*
Duquette, Diane Rhea 1951- *WhoWest 94*
Duquette, Donald Norman 1947- *WhoAm 94*
Duquette, Jean-Pierre 1939- *WhoAm 94*
Dur, Philip Alphonse 1944- *WhoAm 94*
Dur, Philip Francis 1914- *WhoAm 94*
Durac, Jack 1934- *WrDr 94*
Durack, David Tulloch 1944- *WhoAm 94*
Durack, Mary 1913- *Who 94, WrDr 94*
Duraczynski, Donna Moore 1937- *WhoAmP 93*
Durafour, Michel Andre Francois 1920- *IntWW 93*
Durai-Swamy, Kandaswamy 1945- *WhoWest 94*
Durall, Dolis, Jr. 1943- *WhoBlA 94*
Duran, Alfredo G. 1936- *WhoHisp 94*
Duran, Alfredo R. 1961- *WhoHisp 94*
Duran, Antonio Valdez 1942- *WhoHisp 94*
Duran, Arthur Eligio 1937- *WhoHisp 94*
Duran, Benita Ann 1960- *WhoHisp 94*
Duran, Benjamin S. 1939- *WhoHisp 94*
Duran, Beverly 1948- *WhoHisp 94*
Duran, Cathy L. 1946- *WhoHisp 94*
Duran, David 1950- *WhoHisp 94*
Duran, Dianna J. *WhoAmP 93*
Duran, Dianna J. 1955- *WhoHisp 94*
Duran, Dick 1935- *WhoHisp 94*
Duran, Elena 1948- *WhoHisp 94*
Duran, Emilio 1963- *WhoScEn 94*
Duran, Frank *WhoHisp 94*
Duran, Frank Velasquez 1940- *WhoHisp 94*
Durán, Gonzalo *WhoHisp 94*
Duran, J. R. *WhoHisp 94*
Duran, Jess 1953- *WhoHisp 94*
Duran, Josep d1791? *NewGrDO*
Durán, Julio C. 1937- *WhoHisp 94*
Duran, June Clark 1919- *WhoAmP 93*
Duran, Karin Jeanine 1948- *WhoHisp 94*
Duran, Massimiliano *WhoHisp 94*
Duran, Michael Carl 1953- *WhoWest 94*
Duran, Michael S. 1958- *WhoHisp 94*
Duran, Philip 1936- *WhoHisp 94*
Duran, Richard Fierro *WhoHisp 94*
Duran, Roberto 1951- *IntWW 93, WhoHisp 94*
Duran, Tino *WhoHisp 94*
Duran, Val d1937 *WhoHol 92*
Duran, Victor Manuel *WhoHisp 94*
Duran Ballen, Sixto *IntWW 93*
Duran-Carvajal, Natalie 1955- *WhoHisp 94*
Durand, Bernice Black 1942- *WhoMW 93*
Durand, Catherine d1736 *BlmGWL*
Durand, (Henry Mortimer) Dickon (Marion St. George) d1992 *Who 94N*
Durand, Edouard d1926 *WhoHol 92*
Durand, Edward (Alan Christopher David Percy) 1974- *Who 94*
Durand, G. Forbes *ConAu 42NR*
Durand, Henry J., Jr. 1948- *WhoBlA 94*
Durand, Hugo G. 1930- *WhoAmP 93*
Durand, James Howard 1951- *WhoScEn 94*
Durand, Jean d1946 *WhoHol 92*
Durand, Kemper Bartlett 1939- *WhoAmL 94*
Durand, Robert A. *WhoAmP 93*
Durand, Sydnie Mae 1934- *WhoAmP 93*
Durand, Victor Albert Charles *Who 94*
Durand, Whitney *WhoAmP 93*
Durand, Winsley, Jr. 1941- *WhoBlA 94*
Durandi, Jacopo 1737-1817 *NewGrDO*
Durand-Rival, Pierre J. H. 1930- *IntWW 93*
Durang, Christopher 1949- *WhoHol 92, WrDr 94*
Durang, Christopher (Ferdinand) 1949- *ConDr 93, GayLL, IntDcT 2*
Duran Salguero, Carlos 1956- *WhoHisp 94*
Durant, Anita 1938- *WhoBlA 94*
Durant, Anthony *Who 94*
Durant, (Robert) Anthony (Bevis) 1928- *Who 94*
Durant, Celeste Millicent 1947- *WhoBlA 94*
Durant, Charles E. 1949- *WhoBlA 94*
Durant, Charles Edward, Jr. 1951- *WhoAm 94*
Durant, David Norton 1925- *WrDr 94*
Durant, Frederick Clark, III 1916- *WhoAm 94, WhoScEn 94*
Durant, Gerald Wayne 1936- *WhoScEn 94*
Durant, Graham John 1934- *WhoAm 94*
Durant, Jack d1984 *WhoHol 92*
Durant, John Ridgeway 1930- *WhoAm 94, WhoScEn 94*
Durant, John Robert 1950- *Who 94*
Durant, Marc 1947- *WhoAmL 94*
Durant, Naomi C. 1938- *WhoBlA 94*
Durant, Stanton Vincent 1942- *Who 94*
Durant, Thomas James, Jr. 1941- *WhoBlA 94*
Durant, Will d1981 *WhoHol 92*
Durante, Charles J. 1951- *WhoAmP 93*
Durante, Checco d1976 *WhoHol 92*
Durante, Jimmy d1980 *WhoHol 92*
Durante, Jimmy 1893-1980 *WhoCom [port]*
Durante, Larry Anthony 1960- *WhoBlA 94*
Durante, Salvatore 1946- *WhoWest 94*
Durante, Viviana 1967- *IntDcB [port], Who 94*
Durante, Viviana Paola 1967- *IntWW 93*
Duranti, Francesca 1935- *BlmGWL [port]*
Durant-Paige, Beverly *WhoBlA 94*
Duras, Claire de 1778-1828 *BlmGWL*
Duras, Marguerite *Who 94*
Duras, Marguerite 1914- *BlmGWL, ConWorW 93, IntDcT 2 [port], IntWW 93*
Durastanti, Margherita fl. 1700-1734 *NewGrDO*
Durate, Geneva M. 1949- *WhoHisp 94*
Durazo, Guillermo, Jr. 1952- *WhoWest 94*
Durazo, María Elena *WhoHisp 94*
Durazo, Raymond 1942- *WhoHisp 94*
Durazzo, Giacomo 1717-1794 *NewGrDO*
Durban, Pam *DrAPF 93*
Durband, Alan 1927- *WrDr 94*
Durbetaki, N. John 1955- *WhoWest 94*
Durbetaki, Pandeli 1928- *WhoAm 94*
Durbin, Alan C. 1942- *WhoAmL 94*
Durbin, David P. 1948- *WhoAmL 94*
Durbin, Deanna 1921- *WhoHol 92*
Durbin, Enoch Job 1922- *WhoAm 94*
Durbin, James 1923- *Who 94*
Durbin, James E. 1944- *WhoAmL 94*
Durbin, James Harold 1898- *WhAm 10*
Durbin, Leslie 1913- *Who 94*
Durbin, Richard J. 1944- *CngDr 93*
Durbin, Richard Joseph 1944- *WhoAm 94, WhoAmP 93, WhoMW 93*
Durbin, Richard Louis, Sr. 1928- *WhoAm 94*
Durbin, Richard Louis, Jr. 1955- *WhoAm 94, WhoAmL 94*
Durbin, Robert Cain 1931- *WhoAm 94*
Durbin, Rosamond 1952- *WhoFI 94, WhoMW 93*
Durbin, William P., Jr. 1956- *WhoAmL 94*
Durbridge, Francis (Henry) 1912- *Who 94, WrDr 94*
Durbrow, Brian Richard 1940- *WhoAm 94*
Durcan, Paul 1944- *WrDr 94*
Durchslag, Stephen P. 1940- *WhoAm 94*
Durda, Daniel Joseph 1948- *WhoMW 93*
Durdahl, Carol Lavaun 1933- *WhoMW 93*
Durdel, Sonna Merrilee 1949- *WhoFI 94*
Durden, Charles Dennis 1930- *WhoAm 94*
Durden, Christopher John 1940- *WhoAm 94*
Durden, Earnel 1937- *WhoBlA 94*
Durden, Robert F(ranklin) 1925- *WrDr 94*
Durden, Robert Franklin 1925- *WhoAm 94*
Durden-Smith, Neil 1933- *WhoHol 92*
Durden-Smith, Richard *WhoHol 92*
Durdy, James Dirk 1957- *WhoWest 94*
Durdynets, Vaysl Vasylovich 1937- *LoBiDrD*
Durek, Thomas Andrew 1929- *WhoFI 94, WhoScEn 94*
Durell, Ann 1930- *WrDr 94*
Duren, Emma Thompson 1925- *WhoBlA 94*
Duren, Peter Larkin 1935- *WhoAm 94*
Duren, Stephen D. 1948- *WhoAmA 93*
Durenberger, Dave 1934- *CngDr 93*
Durenberger, David F. 1934- *WhoAmP 93*
Durenberger, David Ferdinand 1934- *IntWW 93, WhoAm 94, WhoMW 93*
Duret, Cecile *NewGrDO*
Durey, Louis (Edmond) 1888-1979 *NewGrDO*
Du Rey, Peter d1943 *WhoHol 92*
Durey, Peter Burrell 1932- *IntWW 93*
Durfee, Edmund Howell 1959- *WhoMW 93*
Durfee, Harold Allen 1920- *WhoAm 94*
Durfee, Minta d1975 *WhoHol 92*
Durfee, Raymond M. 1922- *WhoAmP 93*
Durfey, Robert Walker 1925- *WhoAm 94*
Durflinger, Elizabeth Ward 1912- *WhoMW 93*
Durflinger, Jeffrey Duane 1961- *WhoWest 94*
Durgin, Diane 1946- *WhoAmL 94, WhoFI 94*
Durgnat, Raymond (Eric) 1932- *WrDr 94*
Durham, Archdeacon of *Who 94*
Durham, Baron 1961- *Who 94*
Durham, Bishop of 1925- *Who 94*
Durham, Dean of *Who 94*
Durham, Earl of *Who 94*
Durham, Archer L. 1932- *AfrAmG [port]*
Durham, Barbara 1942- *WhoAm 94, WhoAmL 94, WhoAmP 93, WhoWest 94*
Durham, Barbee William 1910- *WhoBlA 94*
Durham, Christine 1945- *WhoAmP 93*
Durham, Christine Meaders 1945- *WhoAm 94, WhoAmL 94, WhoWest 94*
Durham, Davis Godfrey 1914- *WhoAm 94*
Durham, Eddie L., Sr. 1946- *WhoBlA 94*
Durham, (Mary) Edith 1863-1944 *DcNaB MP*
Durham, Ernie d1992 *WhoBlA 94N*
Durham, G. Robert 1929- *WhoAm 94, WhoFI 94*
Durham, Harry Blaine, III 1946- *WhoAmL 94, WhoWest 94*
Durham, James Michael, Sr. 1937- *WhoAm 94, WhoFI 94, WhoMW 93*
Durham, James W. 1937- *WhoAm 94*
Durham, Jeanette R. 1945- *WhoAmA 93*
Durham, Joseph Thomas 1923- *WhoBlA 94*
Durham, Kathrynann 1951- *WhoAmP 93*
Durham, Kenneth 1924- *IntWW 93, Who 94*
Durham, Kenneth Joe 1953- *WhoMW 93*
Durham, Lawrence Bradley 1941- *WhoScEn 94*
Durham, Leon 1957- *WhoBlA 94*
Durham, Louis d1937 *WhoHol 92*
Durham, Marilyn *DrAPF 93*
Durham, Marilyn (Wall) 1930- *WrDr 94*
Durham, Mary Lynn 1948- *WhoAm 94, WhoAmL 94*
Durham, Michael Jonathan 1951- *WhoAm 94, WhoFI 94*
Durham, Norman Nevill 1927- *WhoAm 94*
Durham, Richard Monroe 1954- *WhoAmL 94*
Durham, Robert J., Jr. 1941- *WhoAmL 94*
Durham, Robert Lewis 1912- *WhoAm 94*
Durham, Sandra Kay 1953- *WhoAm 94*
Durham, Sidney Down 1943- *WhoAmL 94*
Durham, Steve *WhoHol 92*
Durham, Steven Jackson 1947- *WhoAmP 93*
Durham, Susan B. 1939- *WhoAmP 93*
Durham, Walter Albert, Jr. 1910- *WhoWest 94*
Durham, William 1937- *WhoAmA 93*
Durham, William Lloyd 1928- *WhoAm 94*
Durham, William R. 1945- *WhoBlA 94*
Durick, Mary Lynn 1960- *WhoMW 93*
Durie, Alexander (Charles) 1915- *Who 94*
Durie, David Robert Campbell 1944- *Who 94*
Durie, Jack Frederick, Jr. 1944- *WhoAmL 94*
Durie, Thomas Peter 1926- *Who 94*
Durieux, Tilla d1971 *WhoHol 92*
Durigon, Michel Louis 1942- *WhoScEn 94*
Duringer, Annemarie *WhoHol 92*
Duringer, Jacob Clyde 1956- *WhoWest 94*
Durisova, Irena 1918- *WhoWomW 91*
Durkan, Michael Joseph 1925- *WhoAm 94*
Durkee, Arthur Bowman 1928-1982 *WhAm 10*
Durkee, Jackson Leland 1922- *WhoAm 94*
Durkee, Joe Worthington, Jr. 1956- *WhoScEn 94*
Durkee, John 1728-1782 *WhAmRev*
Durkee, William Robert 1923- *WhoAm 94*
Durkheim, Emile 1858-1917 *EncEth*
Durkheimer, John H. 1953- *WhoAmL 94*
Durkin, Anthony Joseph 1963- *WhoScEn 94*
Durkin, Eleanor d1957 *WhoHol 92*
Durkin, Gertrude d1970 *WhoHol 92*
Durkin, Herbert 1922- *Who 94*
Durkin, James d1934 *WhoHol 92*
Durkin, John A. *WhoAmP 93*
Durkin, John Charles 1951- *WhoScEn 94*
Durkin, Junior d1935 *WhoHol 92*
Durkin, Lee Ann 1955- *WhoMW 93*
Durkin, Raymond Michael 1936- *WhoAmP 93*
Durkin, Trent *WhoHol 92*
Durko, Zsolt 1934- *IntWW 93, NewGrDO*
Durlabhji, Subhash 1947- *WhoAsA 94*
Durlach, Marcus Russell 1911-1991 *WhoAmA 93N*
Durlacher, Nicholas John 1946- *Who 94*
Durland, Jack Raymond 1916- *WhoAm 94*
Durland, Sven O. 1944- *WhoScEn 94*
Durley, Alexander 1912- *WhoBlA 94*
Durley, Richard Charles 1943- *WhoMW 93*
Durme, Jef van 1907-1965 *NewGrDO*
Durn, Raymond Joseph 1925- *WhoAm 94*
Durnbaugh, Donald F. 1927- *WrDr 94*
Durnbaugh, Donald Floyd 1927- *WhoAm 94*
Durnell, Noland Reed 1939- *WhoFI 94*
Durney, Michael Cavalier 1943- *WhoAm 94*
Durnil, Gordon K. 1936- *WhoAmP 93*
Durnil, Gordon Kay 1936- *WhoAmL 94, WhoMW 93*
Durnil, James B. 1942- *WhoAm 94*
Durning, Bernard J. d1923 *WhoHol 92*
Durning, Charles 1923- *WhoAm 94*
Durning, Charles 1933- *IntMPA 94, WhoHol 92*
Duro, Akin 1941- *WhoBlA 94*
Durocher, Cort Louis 1946- *WhoAm 94, WhoScEn 94*
Du Rocher, James Howard 1945- *WhoAmL 94*
DuRocher, Jeffrey L. 1945- *WhoAmL 94*
Durocher, Leo 1905-1991 *WhAm 10*
Durock, Dick *WhoHol 92*
Durojaiye, Prince 1931- *WhoBlA 94*
Duron, Armando 1954- *WhoHisp 94*
Duron, Sebastian 1660-1716 *NewGrDO*
Duron, Susan Budde 1947- *WhoWest 94*
Duron, Ysabel 1947- *WhoHisp 94*
Durón, Ziyad H. 1959- *WhoHisp 94*
Duroni, Charles Eugene 1933- *WhoAm 94, WhoAmL 94*
Duros, Sally Arlene 1955- *WhoMW 93*
DuRose, Richard Arthur 1937- *WhoAm 94, WhoAmL 94*
DuRose, Stanley Charles, Jr. 1923- *WhoAm 94*
Duroselle, Jean-Baptiste 1917- *IntWW 93*
Du Roullet, Marie Francois Louis Gand Leblanc *NewGrDO*
Duroure, David Alan 1954- *WhoFI 94*
Durova, Nadezhda Andreevna 1783-1866 *BlmGWL*
Duroy, Edwin *WhoHisp 94*
Durr, Frankie 1942- *BuCMET*
Durr, Heinz 1933- *IntWW 93*
Durr, Kent Skelton 1941- *IntWW 93, Who 94*
Durr, Pat *WhoAmA 93*
Durr, Robert Joseph 1932- *WhoAm 94*
Durr, William K 1924- *WrDr 94*
Durrands, Kenneth James 1929- *Who 94*
Durrani, Sajjad Haidar 1928- *WhoAm 94, WhoAsA 94*
Durrani, Shakirullah 1928- *IntWW 93*
Durrant, Anthony Harrisson 1931- *Who 94*
Durrant, Dan Martin 1933- *WhoAm 94, WhoAmL 94*
Durrant, Geoffrey Hugh 1913- *WhoAm 94*
Durrant, Jennifer Ann 1942- *IntWW 93*
Durrant, William Henry Estridge 1901- *Who 94*
Durrell, Gerald (Malcolm) 1925- *WrDr 94*
Durrell, Gerald Malcolm 1925- *IntWW 93, Who 94, WhoAm 94*
Durrell, Lawrence 1912-1990 *BlmGEL*
Durrell, Lawrence (George) 1912-1990 *EncSF 93*
Durrell, Lawrence (George) 1912-1991 *ConDr 93*
Durrell, Lawrence George 1912-1990 *WhAm 10*
Durrell, Michael 1943- *WhoHol 92*
Durren, John *WhoHol 92*
Durrenberger, William John 1917- *WhoAm 94*
Durrence, James Larry 1939- *WhoAm 94*
Durrenmatt, Friedrich 1921-1990 *IntDcT 2, WhAm 10*
Durrenmatt, Peter Ulrich 1904- *IntWW 93*
Durrer, Christopher Thomas 1949- *WhoAm 94*
Durrett, Andrew Manning 1924- *WhoScEn 94*
Durrett, George Mann 1917- *WhoFI 94*
Durrett, James Frazer, Jr. 1931- *WhoAm 94, WhoAmL 94*
Durrill, Wayne Keith 1953- *WhoMW 93*
Durschmied, Erik 1930- *ConAu 140*

Durso, John J. 1952- WhoAm 94
D'Urso, Joseph Paul 1943- WhoAm 94
Durst, Edward L. d1945 WhoHol 92
Durst, Eric WhoAm 94
Durst, Gary Michael 1945- WhoMW 93
Durst, Martha Lynn 1944- WhoMW 93
Durst, Paul 1921- WrDr 94
Durst, Robert Joseph, II 1943- WhoAmL 94
Durston, David E. 1925- IntMPA 94
Duru, Alfred 1829-1890 NewGrDO
Durum, Daryl Eugene 1940- WhoIns 94
Du Runsheng 1909- WhoPRCh 91 [port]
Du Runsheng 1913- IntWW 93
Durward, (Alan) Scott 1935- Who 94
Durwood, Edward D. 1950- WhoAm 94, WhoFI 94
Durwood, Richard M. 1929- IntMPA 94
Durwood, Stanley H. 1920- IntMPA 94, WhoFI 94
Dury, Raymonde 1947- WhoWomW 91
Duryea, Dan d1968 WhoHol 92
Duryea, George d1963 WhoHol 92
Duryea, Lee Vaughn 1932- WhoAmP 93
Duryea, Perry Belmont, Jr. 1921- WhoAm 94, WhoAmP 93
Duryea, Peter 1940- WhoHol 92
Duryee, David Anthony 1938- WhoFI 94, WhoWest 94
Duryee, Harold Taylor 1930- WhoAm 94, WhoMW 93
Dusansky, Richard 1942- WhoAm 94
Dusard, Jay 1937- WhoAmA 93
Du Sautoy, Carmen 1950- WhoHol 92
du Sautoy, Peter Francis 1912- Who 94
Dusay, Marj 1936- WhoHol 92
Duscha, Julius Carl 1924- WhoAm 94
Duscha, Lloyd Arthur 1925- WhoAm 94
Duschl, Wolfgang Josef 1958- WhoScEn 94
Duse, Carlo d1956 WhoHol 92
Duse, Eleonora d1924 WhoHol 92
Dusenberry, Ann WhoHol 92
Dusenberry, Philip Bernard 1936- WhoAm 94, WhoFI 94
Dusenbery, Walter 1939- WhoAmA 93
Dusenbery, Walter Condit 1939- WhoAm 94
Dusenbury, Ruth Cole 1929- WhoAmP 93
Du Shane, James William 1912- WhoAm 94
DuShane, Phyllis Miller 1924- WhoWest 94
DuShane, Richard Leo 1940- WhoMW 93
Du Shicheng WhoPRCh 91
DuSimitiere, Pierre Eugene 1726-1784 WhAmRev
Duskin, Ruthie ConAu 43NR
Dusl, Frank 1918- WhoAmP 93
Dusold, Laurence Richard 1944- WhoScEn 94
Dussault, Ann Mary 1946- WhoAmP 93
Dussault, Marilyn Black 1943- WhoAmL 94
Dussault, Nancy 1936- IntMPA 94, WhoHol 92
Dusseault, C. Dean 1938- WhoAm 94
Dussman, Judith Ann 1947- WhoMW 93
Dussolier, Andre 1946- WhoHol 92
Duster, Benjamin C. 1927- WhoBlA 94
Duster, Donald Leon 1932- WhoBlA 94
Duster, Troy 1936- WhoBlA 94
Dusthimer, Jerry C. 1934- WhoAmL 94
Dustmann-Meyer, (Marie) Louise 1831-1899 NewGrDO
Duston, Jennifer 1954- WhoWest 94
Duszynski, Donald Walter 1943- WhoAm 94
Dutcher, Flora Mae 1908- WhoMW 93
Dutcher, Janice Jean Phillips 1950- WhoScEn 94
Dutcher, Phillip Charles 1950- WhoMW 93
Dutfield, Ray 1924- IntMPA 94
Duthie, Herbert Livingston 1929- Who 94
Duthie, Robert Buchan 1925- Who 94
Duthie, Robert Grieve 1928- Who 94
Duthler, Charles Dirk 1956- WhoWest 94
Dutile, Fernand Neville 1940- WhoAm 94, WhoAmL 94
Dutilleux, Henri 1916- IntWW 93
Dutillieu, Irene Tomeoni NewGrDO
Dutillieu, Pierre 1754-1798 NewGrDO
Dutkowski, Michael Mieczyslaw 1946- WhoWest 94
Dutoit, Charles 1936- WhoAm 94
Dutoit, Charles E. 1936- IntWW 93
Dutremble, Dennis L. WhoAmP 93
Dutremble, Lucien A. WhoAmP 93
Dutro, John Thomas, Jr. 1923- WhoAm 94
Dutronc, Jacques WhoHol 92
Dutsch, Otto Johann Anton 1823-1863 NewGrDO
Dutson, Thayne R. 1942- WhoScEn 94
Dutt, David Alan 1962- WhoScEn 94
Dutt, Nikil D. 1958- WhoAsA 94
Dutt, Ray Horn 1913- WhoScEn 94
Dutt, Toru 1856-1877 BlmGWL
Dutt, Utpal 1929- IntWW 93
Dutta, Arunava 1958- WhoScEn 94
Dutta, Hirian Moyee WhoMW 93
Dutta, Kanak 1927- WhoAmP 93
Dutta, Mitra 1953- WhoAsA 94
Dutta, Prabhat Kumar 1940- WhoMW 93
Dutta, Pulak 1951- WhoAsA 94, WhoScEn 94
Dutta, Shib Prasad 1935- WhoAsA 94
Dutta, Subijoy 1950- WhoScEn 94
Duttera, Brian Cleve 1963- WhoMW 93
Duttman, Martina ConAu 142
Dutton, Allen A. 1922- WhoAmA 93
Dutton, Anne fl. 1743- BlmGWL
Dutton, Bryan Hawkins 1943- Who 94
Dutton, Carol Tyminski 1946- WhoFI 94
Dutton, Charles S. 1951- IntMPA 94, WhoBlA 94, WhoHol 92
Dutton, Clarence Benjamin 1917- WhoAm 94, WhoAmL 94
Dutton, Denise Kitashima 1965- WhoFI 94
Dutton, Diana Cheryl 1944- WhoAm 94, WhoAmL 94
Dutton, Geoffrey (Piers Henry) 1922- WrDr 94
Dutton, Geoffrey Piers Henry 1922- IntWW 93
Dutton, Guy G. S. WhoWest 94
Dutton, Harold Vermont, Jr. 1945- WhoAmP 93
Dutton, J. Craig 1951- WhoMW 93, WhoScEn 94
Dutton, James Macfarlane 1922- Who 94
Dutton, John Altnow 1936- WhoAm 94
Dutton, John Coatsworth 1918- WhoAm 94
Dutton, Judson Dunlap 1908- WhoAmP 93
Dutton, Leland Summers 1905-1991 WhAm 10
Dutton, Pauline Mae WhoWest 94
Dutton, Peter Leslie 1941- Who 94
Dutton, Reginald David Ley 1916- Who 94
Dutton, Robert Edward, Jr. 1924- WhoAm 94
Dutton, Stephen James 1942- WhoAmL 94
Dutton, Uriel Elvis 1930- WhoAm 94
Dutu, Alexandru 1928- IntWW 93
Duty, Michael W. 1951- WhoAm 94
Duty, Tony Edgar 1928-1990 WhAm 10
Duus, Gordon Cochran 1954- WhoAmL 94
Duus, Peter 1908- WhoScEn 94
Duus, Peter 1933- WhoAm 94
Duva, Donna Marie 1956- WhoFI 94
Duva, Philip 1945- WhoAm 94
du Vair, Guillaume 1556-1621 GuFrLit 2
Duval, Albert Frank 1920- WhoAm 94
Duval, Barry E. WhoAmP 93
Duval, Clive L., II 1912- WhoAmP 93
DuVal, Daniel H. 1953- WhoAmL 94
Duval, Daniel Webster 1936- WhoAm 94
Duval, Denise 1921- NewGrDO
Duval, Diane WhoHol 92
DuVal, Everett Carl 1917- WhoFI 94
Duval, Gaetan Who 94
Duval, (Charles) Gaetan 1930- IntWW 93, Who 94
Duval, Jeanne 1914- WrDr 94
Du Val, Joe d1966 WhoHol 92
Duval, Jose F. d1993 NewYTBS 93
Duval, Juan d1954 WhoHol 92
Duval, Katherine 1945- WrDr 94
Duval, Kathy J. WhoAmP 93
Duval, Leon-Etienne 1903- IntWW 93
Duval, Michael Raoul 1938- WhoAm 94, WhoFI 94
Duval, Robert 1937- WhoAmL 94
Duvaleix, Christian d1979 WhoHol 92
Duvalier, Francois 1907-1971 HisWorL [port]
Duvalier, Jean-Claude 1951- HisWorL, IntWW 93
Duvalier, Simone 1913- IntWW 93
Duvall, C. Dale 1933- WhoAmP 93
Duvall, David Garland 1949- WhoFI 94
Duvall, Donald Edward 1950- WhoMW 93
Duvall, Donald Knox 1925- WhoAmL 94
Duvall, Evelyn Millis 1906- WrDr 94
Duvall, Gabriel 1752-1844 WhAmRev
Duvall, Gary Carlson 1949- WhoAmL 94
Duvall, Henry F., Jr. 1949- WhoBlA 94
DuVall, Jack 1946- WhoFI 94
Duvall, John Edward 1947- WhoAmL 94
Duvall, Lawrence Del 1942- WhoIns 94
Duvall, Lawrence Delbert 1942- WhoFI 94
Duvall, Leslie 1924- WhoAmP 93
DuVall, Lorraine 1925- WhoFI 94
Duvall, Paul Hamilton 1947- WhoAmL 94
Duvall, Robert 1930- WhoHol 92
Duvall, Robert 1931- IntMPA 94, IntWW 93, WhoAm 94
Duvall, Robert F. WhoWest 94
Duvall, Shelley 1949- IntMPA 94, WhoAm 94, WhoHol 92
Duvall, Wallace Lee 1926- WhoAm 94
Duvalles d1971 WhoHol 92
Duvall-Itjen, Phyllis 1951- WhoFI 94
Duvar, Ivan Ernest Hunter 1939- WhoAm 94, WhoFI 94
Duvaul, Virginia C. 1914- WrDr 94
Duvdevani, Ilan 1938- WhoScEn 94
Duveen, Anneta 1924- WhoAmA 93
Duverger, Maurice 1917- IntWW 93
Duvergier de Hauranne, Jean GuFrLit 2
Duvernoy, Roger DrAPF 93
Duveyrier, Henri 1840-1892 WhWE
Duvick, Donald Nelson 1924- WhoAm 94, WhoMW 93
Du Vigneaud, Vincent 1901-1978 WorScD
Duvillard, Henri 1910- IntWW 93
Duvin, Robert Phillip 1937- WhoAm 94, WhoAmL 94
Duvivier, George d1985 WhoHol 92
Duvivier, Jean Fernand 1926- WhoScEn 94
DuVivier, Katharine Keyes 1953- WhoAmL 94
DuVivier, Kathryn Shelley 1952- WhoWest 94
Duvo, Mechelle Louise 1962- WhoFI 94
Duvoisin, Roger 1904-1980 WhoAmA 93N
Duvoisin, Roger C(lair) 1927- WrDr 94
Duvoisin, Roger Clair 1927- WhoScEn 94
Du Weiyou 1921- WhoPRCh 91 [port]
Dux, Claire 1885-1967 NewGrDO
Dux, Pierre d1990 WhoHol 92
Duxbury, Alyn Crandall 1932- WhoWest 94
Duxbury, (John) Barry 1934- Who 94
Duxbury, Elspeth d1967 WhoHol 92
Duxbury, Philip Thomas 1928- Who 94
Duxbury, Robert N. 1933- WhoAmP 93
Du Xianzhong 1932- WhoPRCh 91 [port]
Du Xingyuan 1914- WhoPRCh 91 [port]
Duyfhuizen, Bernard Boyd 1953- WhoMW 93
Du Yide 1912- WhoPRCh 91 [port]
Du Yijin 1936- WhoPRCh 91 [port]
Du Yuzhou 1942- IntWW 93, WhoPRCh 91 [port]
Duzan, Stephen Andrew 1941- WhoWest 94
Duzgunes, Nejat A. 1950- WhoScEn 94, WhoWest 94
Du Ziwei 1932- WhoPRCh 91 [port]
Duzy, Merrilyn Jeanne 1946- WhoAmA 93
Dverin, Anatoly 1935- WhoAmA 93
Dvoracek, Jiri 1928- NewGrDO
Dvorak, Allen Dale 1943- WhoAm 94
Dvorak, Ann d1979 WhoHol 92
Dvorak, Antonin (Leopold) 1841-1904 NewGrDO
Dvorak, Clarence Allen 1942- WhoMW 93, WhoScEn 94
Dvorak, George J. WhoScEn 94
Dvorak, Harold F. 1937- WhoAm 94
Dvorak, Jane Ann 1955- WhoMW 93
Dvorak, Michael A. 1948- WhoAmP 93
Dvorak, Ray P. 1931- WhoWest 94
Dvorak, Roger G. 1934- WhoAm 94
Dvorak, Thomas Paul 1962- WhoAmL 94
Dvorakova, Ludmila 1923- NewGrDO
Dvorchak, Thomas Edward 1933- WhoAm 94
Dvoretzky, Edward 1930- WrDr 94
Dvorkin, Daniel EncSF 93
Dvorkin, David 1943- EncSF 93
Dvorkin, Donald 1942- WhoFI 94
Dvorkin, Louis 1951- WhoMW 93
Dvorsky, Peter 1951- IntWW 93, NewGrDO
Dvorsky, Robert E. 1948- WhoAmP 93
Dvury, Norma d1978 WhoHol 92
Dwan, Dorothy d1970 WhoHol 92
Dwass, Meyer 1923- WhoAm 94
Dwek, Cyril S. 1936- WhoAm 94
Dwek, Raymond Allen 1941- IntWW 93, Who 94
Dwenger, Thomas Andrew 1945- WhoMW 93, WhoScEn 94
Dwiggens, Jay d1919 WhoHol 92
Dwiggins, Alvin WhoAmP 93
Dwiggins, Clare 1874-1958 WhoAmA 93N
Dwiggins, W(illiam) A(ddison) 1880-1956 EncSF 93
Dwiggins, William Addison 1880-1956 WhoAmA 93N
Dwight, Charles Bishop, IV 1955- WhoAmL 94
Dwight, Donald Rathbun 1931- WhoAm 94
Dwight, Donald Stearns 1921- WhoWest 94
Dwight, Edward Harold 1919-1981 WhoAmA 93N
Dwight, Harvey Alpheus 1928- WhoFI 94
Dwight, Herbert M., Jr. WhoScEn 94
Dwight, James 1852-1917 BuCMET
Dwight, James Scutt, Jr. 1934- WhoAm 94
Dwight, Olivia DrAPF 93
Dwight, Reginald Kenneth Who 94
Dwight, Reginald Kenneth 1947- WhoAm 94
Dwight, Timothy 1752-1817 DcAmReB 2, WhAmRev
Dwight, William, Jr. 1929- WhoAm 94
Dwinell, Lane 1906- WhoAmP 93
Dwire, Earl d1940 WhoHol 92
Dwivedi, Chandradhar 1948- WhoAsA 94
Dwivedy, Keshab K. 1943- WhoAsA 94
Dwivedy, Ramesh Chandra 1943- WhoAsA 94
Dwon, Larry 1913- WhoAm 94
Dworak, Donald N. 1934- WhoAmP 93
Dworakowski, Marian WhoHol 92
Dworetzky, Joseph Anthony 1951- WhoAm 94, WhoAmL 94
Dworetzky, Murray 1917- WhoAm 94
Dworkin, Andrea 1946- GayLL, IntWW 93, WrDr 94
Dworkin, Gerald 1933- Who 94
Dworkin, Gerald 1937- WhoAm 94
Dworkin, Howard Jerry 1932- WhoAm 94
Dworkin, Larry Udell 1936- WhoScEn 94
Dworkin, Martin 1927- WhoAm 94, WhoScEn 94
Dworkin, Martin S. DrAPF 93
Dworkin, Michael Leonard 1947- WhoAmL 94
Dworkin, Paul David 1937- Who 94
Dworkin, Ronald (Myles) 1931- WrDr 94
Dworkin, Ronald Myles 1931- Who 94, WhoAm 94
Dworkin, Samuel Franklin 1933- WhoAm 94
Dworkoski, Robert John 1946- WhoWest 94
Dworschak, Scott Justin 1960- WhoAmP 93
Dworsky, Clara Weiner 1918- WhoAmL 94
Dworsky, Daniel Leonard 1927- WhoAm 94
Dworsky, Leonard B. 1915- WhoAm 94
Dworsky, Marc Trapedo Graham 1961- WhoFI 94
Dworsky, Steven Gene 1944- WhoAmP 93
Dworzan, George R. 1924- WhoAmA 93
Dworzan, Helene DrAPF 93
Dworzanski, Jacek Pawel 1952- WhoScEn 94
Dwyer, Andrew T. 1948- WhoAm 94, WhoFI 94
Dwyer, Ann Elizabeth 1953- WhoAm 94
Dwyer, Augusta (Maria) 1956- WrDr 94
Dwyer, Bernard J. 1921- WhoAmP 93
Dwyer, Charles Breen 1952- WhoFI 94
Dwyer, Claire Buckley 1930- WhoAmP 93
Dwyer, Cornelius J., Jr. 1943- WhoAmL 94
Dwyer, Darrell James 1946- WhoFI 94
Dwyer, David Charles 1948- WhoMW 93
Dwyer, Deanna TwCYAW
Dwyer, Deanna 1945- WrDr 94
Dwyer, Deanne EncSF 93
Dwyer, Dennis D. 1943- WhoFI 94, WhoMW 93, WhoScEn 94
Dwyer, Ethel d1985 WhoHol 92
Dwyer, Eugene Joseph 1943- WhoAmA 93
Dwyer, Francis Gerard 1931- WhoAm 94, WhoScEn 94
Dwyer, Frank DrAPF 93
Dwyer, Gary Colburn 1943- WhoWest 94
Dwyer, Gerald Paul, Jr. 1947- WhoFI 94, WhoScEn 94
Dwyer, Hilary 1935- WhoHol 92
Dwyer, James 1921- WhoAmA 93
Dwyer, James Francis 1874-1952 EncSF 93
Dwyer, Jeffry R. 1946- WhoAm 94, WhoAmL 94
Dwyer, John d1936 WhoHol 92
Dwyer, John D. 1946- WhoAmL 94
Dwyer, John James 1928- WhoScEn 94
Dwyer, John M. 1937- WhoMW 93
Dwyer, Joseph Anthony 1939- Who 94
Dwyer, K.R. EncSF 93, TwCYAW
Dwyer, K. R. 1945- WrDr 94
Dwyer, Leslie d1986 WhoHol 92
Dwyer, Maureen Quinn 1947- WhoIns 94
Dwyer, Patricia R. 1962- WhoAmP 93
Dwyer, Ralph Daniel, Jr. 1924- WhoAmL 94
Dwyer, Richard A. 1934- WrDr 94
Dwyer, Robert James 1920- WhoMW 93
Dwyer, Robert Jeffrey 1947- WhoAm 94
Dwyer, Ruth d1978 WhoHol 92
Dwyer, William J. 1934- WhoAmP 93
Dwyer, William L. 1929- WhoAm 94, WhoAmL 94, WhoWest 94
Dwyer-Carpenter, Aleta 1948- WhoBlA 94
Dwyre, William Patrick 1944- WhoAm 94
Dy, Francisco Justiniano 1912- IntWW 93
Dyadkin, Lev Joseph 1955- WhoWest 94
Dyagilev, Sergey Pavlovich 1872-1929 NewGrDO
Dyak, Miriam DrAPF 93

Dyal, Desta Casey 1922- *WhoAmP 93*
Dyal, William M., Jr. 1928- *WhoAm 94*
Dyall, Franklin d1950 *WhoHol 92*
Dyall, Valentine d1985 *WhoHol 92*
Dyar, Kathryn Wilkin 1945- *WhoAm 94*
Dyas, Dave d1929 *WhoHol 92*
Dyas, Patricia Ann 1952- *WhoBlA 94*
Dyba, Karel 1940- *IntWW 93*
Dybeck, Alfred Charles 1928- *WhoAm 94*
Dybek, Stuart *DrAPF 93*
Dybek, Stuart 1942- *DcLB 130 [port]*
Dybel, Michael Wayne 1946- *WhoMW 93*
Dybkjaer, Lone 1940- *IntWW 93, WhoWomW 91*
Dybvig, Douglas Howard 1935- *WhoScEn 94*
Dyce, Barbara J. *WhoBlA 94*
Dyce, Hamilton d1972 *WhoHol 92*
Dyche, David Bennett 1902-1990 *WhAm 10*
Dyche, David Bennett, Jr. 1932- *WhoAm 94*
Dyck, Andrew Roy 1947- *WhoAm 94, WhoWest 94*
Dyck, Arthur James 1932- *WhoAm 94*
Dyck, Ernest Van *NewGrDO*
Dyck, George 1937- *WhoAm 94, WhoMW 93, WhoScEn 94*
Dyck, Harold Peter 1920- *WhoAmP 93*
Dyck, Paul 1917- *WhoAmA 93*
Dyck, Peter J. 1914- *ConAu 142, SmATA 75*
Dyck, Robert Gilkey 1930- *WhoAmP 93*
Dyck, Walter Peter 1935- *WhoAm 94*
Dyckman, Thomas Richard 1932- *WhoAm 94*
d'Yd, Jean d1964 *WhoHol 92*
Dye, Alan Louis *WhoAm 94, WhoAmL 94*
Dye, Betty Lee 1921- *WhoAmP 93*
Dye, Bradford Johnson, Jr. 1933- *WhoAm 94, WhoAmP 93*
Dye, Bru *DrAPF 93*
Dye, Cameron *WhoHol 92*
Dye, Charles 1927-1955 *EncSF 93*
Dye, Clinton Elworth, Jr. 1942- *WhoBlA 94*
Dye, Dale 1944- *WhoHol 92*
Dye, David Ray 1951- *WhoFI 94*
Dye, Glenn W. 1921- *WhoFI 94*
Dye, Jack Bertie 1919- *Who 94*
Dye, James Louis 1927- *WhoAm 94, WhoScEn 94*
Dye, John *WhoHol 92*
Dye, Luther V. 1933- *WhoBlA 94*
Dye, Marvin Reed 1895- *WhAm 10*
Dye, Myron L. *WhoIns 94*
Dye, Patrick Fain 1939- *WhoAm 94*
Dye, Robert Fulton 1920- *WhoScEn 94*
Dye, Robert Lloyd 1952- *WhoFI 94*
Dye, Sherman 1915- *WhoAm 94, WhoAmL 94*
Dye, Stuart S. 1939- *WhoAm 94, WhoAmL 94*
Dye, Thomas Roy 1935- *WhoAm 94*
Dye, William Ellsworth 1926- *WhoAmL 94, WhoMW 93*
Dyen, Isidore 1913- *WhoAm 94, WrDr 94*
Dyens, Georges Maurice 1932- *WhoAmA 93*
Dyer, Mrs. *NewGrDO*
Dyer, Albert Gill 1951- *WhoAmL 94*
Dyer, Alexander Patrick 1932- *WhoAm 94*
Dyer, Alfred *EncSF 93*
Dyer, Alice Mildred 1929- *WhoAm 94, WhoWest 94*
Dyer, Allen Ralph 1944- *WhoAm 94*
Dyer, Bernard Joel 1933- *WhoBlA 94*
Dyer, Carolyn Price 1931- *WhoAmA 93, WhoWest 94*
Dyer, Charles 1928- *Who 94, WhoHol 92*
Dyer, Charles (Raymond) 1928- *ConDr 93, WrDr 94*
Dyer, Charles Arnold 1940- *WhoAmL 94*
Dyer, Charles Austen 1936- *WhoBlA 94*
Dyer, Cynthia Myers 1955- *WhoMW 93*
Dyer, David William 1910- *WhoAm 94, WhoAmL 94*
Dyer, Dennis Avery 1953- *WhoFI 94*
Dyer, Donald R(ay) 1918- *ConAu 140*
Dyer, Edward 1543-1607 *DcLB 136*
Dyer, Edward James, Jr. 1937- *WhoAmP 93*
Dyer, Eliphalet 1721-1807 *AmRev, WhAmRev*
Dyer, Frederick C(harles) 1918- *WrDr 94*
Dyer, Frederick Charles 1918- *WhoAm 94*
Dyer, Frederick T. 1941- *WhoAmP 93*
Dyer, George Carroll 1898- *WhAm 10*
Dyer, Geraldine Ann 1921- *WhoAm 94*
Dyer, Gregory Clark 1947- *WhoAmL 94*
Dyer, Henry Peter Francis S. *Who 94*
Dyer, Ira 1925- *WhoAm 94*
Dyer, Ira Jack 1929- *WhoAmP 93*
Dyer, James (Frederick) 1934- *WrDr 94*
Dyer, Joe, Jr. 1934- *WhoBlA 94*
Dyer, John 1700?-1758 *BlmGEL*
Dyer, John H., Jr. 1958- *WhoAmP 93*
Dyer, John M(artin) 1920- *WrDr 94*

Dyer, John Martin 1920- *WhoAm 94, WhoAmL 94*
Dyer, Joseph P., Jr. 1940- *WhoAmL 94*
Dyer, Lois Edith 1925- *Who 94*
Dyer, M. Wayne 1950- *WhoAmA 93*
Dyer, Mark 1928- *Who 94*
Dyer, Mary d1660 *DcAmReB 2*
Dyer, Merton S. 1930- *WhoAmP 93*
Dyer, Michael Rodney 1949- *WhoWest 94*
Dyer, Michael W. 1947- *WhoAmL 94*
Dyer, Noel John 1913- *WhoAm 94*
Dyer, Philip E. *WhoAmP 93*
Dyer, Ralph Andrew 1938- *WhoAmL 94*
Dyer, Richard Dennis 1949- *WhoMW 93*
Dyer, Richard Hutchins 1931- *WhoFI 94*
Dyer, Robert Francis, Jr. 1926- *WhoAm 94*
Dyer, Robert Theodore 1945- *WhoMW 93*
Dyer, Simon 1939- *Who 94*
Dyer, T. A. *DrAPF 93*
Dyer, Thomas Michael 1945- *WhoAmL 94*
Dyer, Tim Alan 1958- *WhoWest 94*
Dyer, Timothy J. *WhoAm 94*
Dyer, Travis Neal 1939- *WhoAm 94*
Dyer, Wayne W(alter) 1940- *WrDr 94*
Dyer, Wayne Walter 1940- *WhoAm 94*
Dyer, William d1960 *WhoHol 92*
Dyer, William Allan, Jr. d1993 *NewYTBS 93*
Dyer, William Earl, Jr. 1927- *WhoAm 94, WhoMW 93*
Dyer-Bennet, Richard 1913-1991 *WhAm 10*
Dyer-Dawson, Diane Faye 1941- *WhoMW 93*
Dyer-Goode, Pamela Theresa 1950- *WhoBlA 94*
Dyer-Smith, John Edward 1918- *Who 94*
Dyess, Bobby Dale 1935- *WhoAm 94*
Dyess, Edwin Earl 1949- *WhoWest 94*
Dyess, John (Foster) 1939- *SmATA 76 [port]*
Dyess, William J. 1929- *WhoAmP 93*
Dygert, Harold Paul, Jr. 1919- *WhoWest 94*
Dyhouse, Henry Norval 1945- *WhoAm 94*
Dyk, Timothy Belcher 1937- *WhoAm 94*
Dyka, Zbigniew 1928- *IntWW 93*
Dykas, James Donald 1940- *WhoFI 94*
Dyke, Who 94*
Dyke, Charles William 1935- *WhoAm 94*
Dyke, Gregory 1947- *Who 94*
Dyke, Henry Van *DrAPF 93*
Dyke, James Trester 1937- *WhoAm 94*
Dyke-Acland, John 1747-1778 *AmRev*
Dykema, Henry L. 1939- *WhoAm 94*
Dykema, John Russel 1918- *WhoAm 94*
Dykeman, Wilma *WrDr 94*
Dyken, Dorothy Catherine 1935- *WhoMW 93*
Dyken, Mark Lewis 1928- *WhoAm 94*
Dykes, Archie Reece 1931- *WhoAm 94, WhoFI 94*
Dykes, David Wilmer 1933- *Who 94*
Dykes, DeWitt S., Jr. 1938- *WhoBlA 94*
Dykes, DeWitt Sanford, Sr. 1903- *WhoBlA 94*
Dykes, Fred William 1928- *WhoScEn 94, WhoWest 94*
Dykes, Hugh John 1939- *Who 94*
Dykes, James Edgar 1919- *WhoAm 94*
Dykes, Jefferson Chenowth 1900-1989 *WhAm 10*
Dykes, John Henry, Jr. 1934- *WhoAm 94, WhoFI 94*
Dykes, Kathryn A. 1951- *WhoMW 93*
Dykes, Marie Draper 1942- *WhoBlA 94*
Dykes, Michael H. M. 1931-1990 *WhAm 10*
Dykes, Osborne Jefferson, III 1944- *WhoAm 94, WhoAmL 94*
Dykes, Robert Gregory 1950- *WhoAmL 94*
Dykes, Roland A. *WhoBlA 94*
Dykes, Virginia Chandler 1930- *WhoAm 94*
Dykes Bower, S(tephen) E(rnest) 1903- *Who 94*
Dykhouse, David Jay 1936- *WhoAm 94, WhoAmL 94*
Dykhouse, David Wayne 1949- *WhoAm 94, WhoAmL 94*
Dykhuis, Randy 1956- *WhoMW 93*
Dykla, Edward George 1933- *WhoAm 94*
Dykman, Roscoe Arnold 1920- *WhoScEn 94*
Dykstra, Craig Richard 1947- *WhoAm 94*
Dykstra, Daniel James 1916- *WhoAm 94*
Dykstra, David Allen 1938- *WhoMW 93*
Dykstra, David Charles 1941- *WhoAm 94, WhoWest 94*
Dykstra, Lenny 1963- *News 93 [port]*
Dykstra, Leona 1928- *WhoAmP 93*
Dykstra, Mary Elizabeth 1939- *WhoAm 94*

Dykstra, Paul Hopkins 1943- *WhoAm 94, WhoAmL 94*
Dykstra, Philip Rouse 1929- *WhoWest 94*
Dykstra, Robert 1930- *WhoMW 93*
Dykstra, Roger Everett 1949- *WhoFI 94*
Dykstra, Ronald Gerrit Malcolm 1934- *Who 94*
Dykstra, Vergil Homer 1925- *WhoAm 94*
Dykstra, William Henry 1928- *WhoAm 94*
Dykstra-Erickson, Elizabeth Ann 1954- *WhoWest 94*
Dylan, Bob 1941- *AmCulL, ConLC 77 [port], IntWW 93, WhoAm 94, WhoHol 92, WrDr 94*
Dylan, Sara *WhoHol 92*
Dy Liacco, Tomas Enciso 1920- *WhoAm 94*
Dym, Clive Lionel 1942- *WhoAm 94, WhoWest 94*
Dym, Elaine Marjorie 1925- *WhoAmP 93*
Dymally, Lynn V. 1958- *WhoBlA 94*
Dymally, Mervyn M. 1926- *WhoAmP 93, WhoBlA 94*
Dymally, Mervyn Malcolm 1926- *WhoAm 94, WhoBlA 94*
Dyment, John Joseph 1933- *WhoAm 94*
Dyment, Paul George 1935- *WhoAm 94*
Dymicky, Michael 1929- *WhoScEn 94*
Dymoke, John Lindley Marmion 1926- *Who 94*
Dymoke, Juliet 1919- *WrDr 94*
Dymoke, Lionel Dorian 1921- *Who 94*
Dymond, Lewis Wandell 1920- *WhoAm 94*
Dymond, Michael John 1936- *Who 94*
Dymov, Ossip d1959 *WhoHol 92*
Dynda, Ernest Francis 1934- *WhoWest 94*
Dyne, Michael d1989 *WhoHol 92*
Dyneley, Peter d1978 *WhoHol 92*
Dynes, Wayne R. 1934- *GayLL*
Dynevor, Baron 1935- *Who 94*
Dynkin, Eugene B. 1924- *WhoScEn 94*
Dynowska, Anna *WhoWomW 91*
Dyott, Richard Burnaby 1924- *WhoAm 94, WhoMW 93*
Dypski, Cornell N. 1931- *WhoAmP 93*
Dyregrov, Michael 1931- *WhoAm 94, WhoMW 93, WhoScEn 94*
Dyremose, Henning 1945- *IntWW 93*
Dyrensforth, James d1973 *WhoHol 92*
Dyrness, William A. 1943- *WrDr 94*
Dyroff, David Ray, Jr. 1966- *WhoAmL 94*
Dyrstad, Joanell M. 1942- *WhoAm 94, WhoAmP 93, WhoMW 93*
Dyrud, Jarl Edvard 1921- *WhoAm 94*
Dysart, Countess of 1914- *Who 94*
Dysart, Benjamin Clay, III 1940- *WhoAm 94, WhoFI 94, WhoScEn 94*
Dysart, Richard 1929- *WhoHol 92*
Dysart, Richard A. 1929- *IntMPA 94, WhoAm 94*
Dysinger, Paul William 1927- *WhoAm 94*
Dyson, A(nthony) E(dward) 1928- *WrDr 94*
Dyson, Allan Judge 1942- *WhoAm 94*
Dyson, Anne *WhoHol 92*
Dyson, Anthony Oakley 1935- *Who 94*
Dyson, Brian 1944- *WhoAmA 93*
Dyson, Brian G. 1935- *WhoFI 94*
Dyson, Freeman (John) 1923- *WrDr 94*
Dyson, Freeman J(ohn) 1923- *EncSF 93*
Dyson, Freeman John 1923- *IntWW 93, Who 94, WhoAm 94, WhoScEn 94*
Dyson, Humfrey d1633 *DcNaB MP*
Dyson, John Anthony 1943- *Who 94*
Dyson, John Michael 1929- *Who 94*
Dyson, John Stuart 1943- *WhoAmP 93*
Dyson, Michael Eric 1958- *WhoBlA 94*
Dyson, Noel 1916- *WhoHol 92*
Dyson, Raymond Clegg 1902- *WhoAm 94*
Dyson, Robert Harris 1927- *WhoAm 94*
Dyson, Roger Franklin 1940- *Who 94*
Dyson, Roy 1948- *WhoAmP 93*
Dyson, William Riley 1940- *WhoAmP 93, WhoBlA 94*
Dystel, Jane Dee 1945- *WhoAm 94*
Dystel, Oscar 1912- *WhoAm 94*
Dytrych, Karl Paul 1949- *WhoFI 94*
Dyutsch, Otton Ivanovich *NewGrDO*
Dyvig, Peter 1934- *Who 94*
Dyvig, Peter P. 1934- *WhoAm 94*
Dywan, Jeffery Joseph 1949- *WhoAmL 94*
Dyyon, Frazier 1946- *WhoAm 94, WhoAmA 93*
Dzasokhov, Aleksandr Sergeyevich 1934- *IntWW 93*
Dzelzkalns, LeeAnn 1956- *WhoMW 93*
Dzerzhinsky, Ivan Ivanovich 1909-1978 *NewGrDO*
Dzhanibekov, Vladimir Aleksandrovich 1942- *IntWW 93*
Dzharimov, Aslan Alievich 1939- *LoBiDrD*
Dzhelepov, Venedikt Petrovich 1913- *IntWW 93*
Dzhemilev, Mustafa 1943- *IntWW 93*

Dzhigarkhanian, Armen Borisovich 1935- *IntWW 93*
Dziadyk, Bohdan 1948- *WhoMW 93*
Dzialo, Raymond John 1931- *WhoAmP 93*
Dziech, Billie Wright 1941- *ConAu 43NR*
Dzieciol, George 1960- *WhoWest 94*
Dzierski, Vincent Paul 1930- *WhoAmA 93*
Dziewanowska, Zofia Elizabeth 1939- *WhoScEn 94*
Dziewanowski, Kazimierz 1930- *IntWW 93*
Dziewanowski, Marian Kamil 1913- *WhoAm 94*
Dzigan, Shimen d1980 *WhoHol 92*
Dzigurski, Alex 1911- *WhoAmA 93*
Dziuba, Henry Frank 1918- *WhoAm 94*
Dziuba, Ivan 1931- *LoBiDrD*
Dziubek, Edmund Andrew 1951- *WhoFI 94*
Dziubla, Robert W. 1952- *WhoAm 94, WhoAmL 94*
Dziuk, Philip John 1926- *WhoMW 93*
Dzodin, Harvey Cary 1947- *WhoAm 94*
Dzubas, Friedel 1915- *WhoAmA 93*
Dzundza, George *WhoHol 92*
Dzundza, George 1945- *IntMPA 94*
Dzyuba, Ivan Mikhailovich 1931- *IntWW 93*

E

E, Sheila *WhoHisp 94*
E., Sheila 1958- *WhoHol 92*
Eaborn, Colin 1923- *IntWW 93, Who 94, WrDr 94*
Eachus, Alan Campbell 1939- *WhoMW 93*
Eachus, Joseph Jackson 1911- *WhoAm 94*
Eadburg (Bugga) fl. 8th cent.- *BlmGWL*
Eade, George James 1921- *WhoAm 94*
Eaden, Maurice Bryan d1993 *Who 94N*
Eades, James Beverly, Jr. 1923- *WhoAm 94*
Eades, Joan *DrAPF 93*
Eades, Luis Eric 1923- *WhoAmA 93*
Eades, Vincent W. 1956- *WhoBlA 94*
Eadie, Alexander 1920- *Who 94*
Eadie, Dennis d1928 *WhoHol 92*
Eadie, Douglas George Arnott 1931- *Who 94*
Eadie, Ellice (Aylmer) 1912- *Who 94*
Eadie, John William 1935- *WhoAm 94*
Eadie, Nicholas *WhoHol 92*
Eadie, Noel 1901-1950 *NewGrDO*
Eads, Billy Gene 1940- *WhoScEn 94*
Eads, George Curtis 1942- *WhoAm 94, WhoFI 94*
Eads, M. Adela *WhoAmP 93, WhoWomW 91*
Eads, Ora Wilbert *DrAPF 93*
Eads, Ora Wilbert 1914- *WhoAm 94*
Eads, Ronald Preston 1948- *WhoFI 94*
Eady *Who 94*
Eady, Carol Murphy 1918- *WhoAm 94*
Eady, Cornelius Robert *DrAPF 93*
Eady, David 1943- *Who 94*
Eady, Eric Thomas 1915-1966 *DcNaB MP*
Eady, Lydia Davis 1958- *WhoBlA 94, WhoMW 93*
Eady, Mary E. *WhoBlA 94*
Eagan, Andrea Boroff d1993 *NewYTBS 93 [port]*
Eagan, Andrea Boroff 1943-1993 *ConAu 140*
Eagan, Claire Veronica 1950- *WhoAmL 94*
Eagan, Emma Louise 1928- *WhoBlA 94*
Eagan, Francis Owen 1930- *WhoAm 94, WhoAmL 94*
Eagan, James Joseph 1926- *WhoAmP 93*
Eagan, Sherman G. 1942- *WhoAm 94*
Eagan, William Edward 1943- *WhoAmP 93*
Eagan, William Leon 1928- *WhoAmL 94*
Eagar, Thomas Waddy 1950- *WhoScEn 94*
Eagels, Jeanne d1929 *WhoHol 92*
Eagen, Christopher T. 1956- *WhoAmA 93*
Eager, George Sidney, Jr. 1915- *WhoAm 94*
Eager, Henry Ide 1895-1989 *WhAm 10*
Eager, Johnny d1963 *WhoHol 92*
Eager, Robert Donald 1950- *WhoScEn 94*
Eager, Robert W., Jr. 1944- *WhoIns 94*
Eager, William Earl 1946- *WhoAm 94*
Eagers, Derek *Who 94*
Eagerton, Robert Pierce 1940- *WhoAmA 93*
Eagland, Arthur Austin 1898- *Who 94*
Eagland, (Ralph) Martin 1942- *Who 94*
Eagle, Angela 1961- *Who 94*
Eagle, Arnold Elliott 1941- *WhoBlA 94*
Eagle, Charles Steven 1958- *WhoFI 94*
Eagle, Harry d1992 *IntWW 93N*

Eagle, Harry 1905-1992 *WhAm 10*
Eagle, Jack 1926- *WhoAm 94*
Eagle, James C. d1959 *WhoHol 92*
Eagle, Judith Graybeal 1944- *WhoAmL 94*
Eagle, Paul Martin 1952- *WhoAm 94*
Eagleburger, Lawrence Sidney 1930- *IntWW 93, WhoAmP 93*
Eagle Eye, William d1927 *WhoHol 92*
Eagleman, Joe Roe 1936- *WhoMW 93*
Eaglen, Jane 1960- *NewGrDO*
Eagles, David M. 1935- *WhoScEn 94*
Eagles, (Charles Edward) James 1918- *Who 94*
Eagles, Sidney Smith, Jr. 1939- *WhoAm 94, WhoAmL 94*
Eagles, Stuart Ernest 1929- *WhoAm 94*
Eaglesfield, Francis 1905-1992 *WrDr 94N*
Eagleson, Halson Vashon 1903-1992 *WhoBlA 94N*
Eagleson, Peter Sturges 1928- *WhoAm 94*
Eagleson, William Boal, Jr. 1925- *WhoAm 94*
Eagleson Wyatt, Theresa Anne 1968- *WhoMW 93*
Eaglet, Robert Danton 1934- *WhoAm 94*
Eagleton, Lee Chandler 1923-1990 *WhAm 10*
Eagleton, Robert Don 1937- *WhoAm 94, WhoScEn 94*
Eagleton, Robert Lee 1945- *WhoScEn 94*
Eagleton, Terence (Francis) 1943- *WrDr 94*
Eagleton, Terence Francis 1943- *IntWW 93, Who 94*
Eagleton, Terry 1943- *BlmGEL*
Eagleton, Thomas F. 1929- *WhoAmP 93*
Eagleton, Thomas Francis 1929- *IntWW 93, Who 94*
Eagleton, William Lester, Jr. 1926- *WhoAm 94*
Eaglin, Fulton B. 1941- *WhoBlA 94*
Eagling, Wayne 1950- *IntDcB [port]*
Eagling, Wayne John *IntWW 93, Who 94*
Eaglstein, William Howard 1940- *WhoAm 94*
Eagly, Alice Hendrickson 1938- *WhoAm 94*
Eakeley, Douglas Scott 1946- *WhoAm 94, WhoAmL 94*
Eaker, Ira 1922- *WhoAm 94*
Eaker, Ira C. 1896- *WhAm 10*
Eakes, Grady M. *WhoAmP 93*
Eakin, Charles Gillilan 1927- *WhoWest 94*
Eakin, Margaretta Morgan 1941- *WhoAmL 94, WhoWest 94*
Eakin, Paul John 1938- *WhoMW 93*
Eakin, Richard Ronald 1938- *WhoAm 94*
Eakin, Thomas Capper 1933- *WhoAm 94*
Eakins, Joel Kenneth 1930- *WhoWest 94*
Eakins, Patricia *DrAPF 93*
Eakins, Thomas 1844-1916 *AmCulL*
Eakle, Arlene H. 1936- *WhoAm 94*
Eaks, Duane L. 1940- *AstEnc*
Ealdred fl. 1046-1069 *DcNaB MP*
Eales, John Geoffrey 1937- *WhoAm 94*
Eales, Victor Henry James 1922- *Who 94*
Ealey, Adolphus 1941- *WhoBlA 94*
Ealey, Mark E. 1926- *WhoBlA 94*
Ealing, Abbot of *Who 94*
Ealy, Jonathan Bruce 1960- *WhoAmL 94*
Ealy, Lawrence Orr 1915- *WhoAm 94*

Ealy, Mary Newcomb 1948- *WhoBlA 94*
Eaman, Frank Dwight 1944- *WhoMW 93*
Eamer, Richard Keith 1928- *WhoAm 94, WhoFI 94, WhoWest 94*
Eames, Charles 1907-1978 *AmCulL*
Eames, Clare d1930 *WhoHol 92*
Eames, Edwin Jacob 1930- *WhoWest 94*
Eames, Emma 1865-1952 *NewGrDO [port]*
Eames, Eric James 1917- *Who 94*
Eames, John d1989 *WhoHol 92*
Eames, John Byron 1941- *WhoAmL 94*
Eames, John Heagan 1900- *WhoAm 94, WhoAmA 93*
Eames, Robert Henry Alexander *Who 94*
Eames, Robert Henry Alexander 1937- *IntWW 93*
Eames, Virginia d1971 *WhoHol 92*
Eames, Wilberforce 1855-1937 *DcLB 140 [port]*
Eames, Wilmer Ballou 1914- *WhoAm 94*
Eanes, Antonio dos Santos Ramalho 1935- *IntWW 93*
Eanes, James Jeffrey 1956- *WhoAmP 93*
Eanes, Joseph Cabel, Jr. 1935- *WhoAm 94, WhoIns 94*
Eannace, Ralph J., Jr. *WhoAmP 93*
Eannes, Gil fl. 143-?- *WhWE*
Eapen, Gill Roy 1963- *WhoFI 94*
Earbery, Matthias 1690-1740 *DcNaB MP*
Eardley, Cynthia 1946- *WhoAmA 93*
Eardley, Richard Roy 1928- *WhoAmP 93*
Eardley-Wilmot, John (Assheton) 1917- *Who 94*
Earhart, Donald Marion 1944- *WhoAm 94*
Earhart, Eileen Magie 1928- *WhoAm 94*
Earhart, H. Byron 1935- *WrDr 94*
Earl, Anthony S. 1936- *WhoAmP 93*
Earl, Anthony Scully 1936- *WhoAm 94*
Earl, Archie William, Sr. 1946- *WhoBlA 94*
Earl, Boyd L. 1944- *WhoAm 94*
Earl, Catherine d1946 *WhoHol 92*
Earl, Christopher Joseph 1925- *Who 94*
Earl, Clifford *WhoHol 92*
Earl, Elizabeth *WhoHol 92*
Earl, Eric Stafford 1928- *Who 94*
Earl, Jack Eugene 1934- *WhoAmA 93*
Earl, John Richard 1934- *WhoIns 94*
Earl, Kathleen d1954 *WhoHol 92*
Earl, Lewis Harold 1918- *WhoAm 94*
Earl, Max d1954 *WhoHol 92*
Earlcott, Gladys d1939 *WhoHol 92*
Earle, Arthur Frederick 1921- *IntWW 93, Who 94*
Earle, Arthur Percival 1922- *WhoAm 94*
Earle, Arthur Scott 1924- *WhoAm 94*
Earle, Blanche d1952 *WhoHol 92*
Earle, Clifford John, Jr. 1935- *WhoAm 94*
Earle, David Prince, Jr. 1910- *WhoAm 94*
Earle, Dorothy d1958 *WhoHol 92*
Earle, E(dward) E(rnest) Maples 1900- *Who 94*
Earle, Edward d1972 *WhoHol 92*
Earle, Edward W. 1951- *WhoAmA 93*
Earle, Ernest Joseph *WhoAmP 93*
Earle, George *Who 94*
Earle, (Hardman) George (Algernon) *Who 94*
Earle, George Hughes 1925- *Who 94*
Earle, Harry Woodward 1924- *WhoAm 94*
Earle, Ion 1916- *Who 94*

Earle, Jack d1952 *WhoHol 92*
Earle, James A. 1945- *WhoMW 93*
Earle, James A. 1945- *WhoMW 93*
Earle, Joel Vincent 1952- *Who 94*
Earle, John *BlmGEL*
Earle, John Nicholas Francis 1926- *Who 94*
Earle, Josephine d1929 *WhoHol 92*
Earle, Julius Richard, Jr. 1954- *WhoWest 94*
Earle, Kenneth Martin 1919- *WhoAm 94*
Earle, Lewis Samuel 1933- *WhoAmP 93*
Earle, Merie d1984 *WhoHol 92*
Earle, Pliny 1809-1892 *EncSPD*
Earle, Ralph 1751-1801 *WhAmRev*
Earle, Ralph, II 1928- *WhoAm 94, WhoAmP 93*
Earle, Richard Alan 1941- *WhoAm 94, WhoAmL 94*
Earle, Richard Edmund d1962 *WhoHol 92*
Earle, Roderick 1952 *NewGrDO*
Earle, Steve *WhoAm 94*
Earle, Sylvia Alice 1935- *WhoAm 94, WhoWest 94*
Earle, Victor Montagne, III 1933- *WhoAm 94*
Earle, Virginia d1937 *WhoHol 92*
Earle, William George 1940- *WhoAmL 94*
Earles, Daisy d1980 *WhoHol 92*
Earles, Harry d1985 *WhoHol 92*
Earles, Rene Martin 1940- *WhoBlA 94*
Earles, Stanley William Edward 1929- *Who 94*
Earles, William Eugene 1928-1989 *WhAm 10*
Earley, Anthony Francis, Jr. 1949- *WhoAm 94, WhoAmL 94, WhoFI 94*
Earley, Charity (Edna) Adams 1918- *WrDr 94*
Earley, Charity Edna 1918- *WhoBlA 94*
Earley, Charles Willard 1933- *WhoScEn 94*
Earley, Jacqui *DrAPF 93*
Earley, Keith H. 1952- *WhoBlA 94*
Earley, Laurence Elliott 1931- *WhoAm 94*
Earley, Mark Lawrence 1954- *WhoAmP 93*
Earley, Robert 1960- *WhoAmP 93*
Earley, Stanley Armstead, Jr. 1919- *WhoBlA 94*
Earley, Tom 1911- *WrDr 94*
Earll, Jerry Miller 1928- *WhoAm 94*
Earlougher, Robert Charles, Sr. 1914- *WhoAm 94, WhoScEn 94*
Earls, Donald Edward 1941- *WhoAmL 94*
Earls, Julian Manly 1942- *WhoBlA 94*
Earls, Paul 1934- *WhoAmA 93*
Earls-Solari, Bonnie 1951- *WhoAmA 93*
Early, Bert Hylton 1922- *WhoAm 94, WhoAmL 94, WhoFI 94*
Early, Deloreese Patricia 1931- *WhoAm 94*
Early, Edward M. 1935- *WhoAmP 93*
Early, Edward William 1934- *WhoAmP 93*
Early, Ezzard Dale 1953- *WhoBlA 94*
Early, Gerald 1952- *WhoBlA 94, WrDr 94*
Early, Glen Alan 1948- *WhoAm 94*
Early, Ida H. 1952- *WhoBlA 94*
Early, Jack *ConAu 41NR, GayLL*
Early, Jack Jones 1925- *WhoAm 94*
Early, James Counts 1947- *WhoBlA 94*

313

Eaton, Trevor (Michael William) 1934- *WrDr 94*
Eaton, Vernet Eller 1895- *WhAm 10*
Eaton, Wallas 1917- *WhoHol 92*
Eaton, William Charles 1927- *WhoAm 94*
Eaton, William Edward 1943- *WhoMW 93*
Eaton, William Lee 1947- *WhoAmL 94*
Eaton, William Mellon 1924-1992 *WhAm 10*
Eatough, Craig Norman 1958- *WhoScEn 94*
Eatwell, Baron 1945- *Who 94*
Eaubonne, Francoise d' 1920- *BlmGWL*
Eaves, A. Reginald 1935- *WhoBlA 94*
Eaves, Allen Charles Edward 1941- *WhoAm 94, WhoScEn 94*
Eaves, George Newton 1935- *WhoAm 94*
Eaves, Gerald R. 1939- *WhoAmP 93*
Eaves, Mary Marie 1939- *WhoAmP 93, WhoWest 94*
Eaves, Morris Emery 1944- *WhoAm 94*
Eaves, Ronald Weldon 1937- *WhoAm 94*
Eayrs, James George 1926- *WhoAm 94*
Eayrs, John Thomas 1913- *Who 94*
Ebacher, Roger 1936- *WhoAm 94*
Eban, Abba 1915- *IntWW 93, Who 94*
Ebara, Ryuichiro 1942- *WhoScEn 94*
Ebata, Duane 1950- *WhoAsA 94*
Ebaugh, Franklin Gessford, Jr. 1921-1990 *WhAm 10*
Ebaugh, Helen Rose 1942- *WhoAm 94*
Ebaugh, William Lee 1930- *WhoWest 94*
Ebb, Fred 1936- *WhoAm 94*
Ebb, Lawrence Forrest 1918- *WhoAmL 94*
Ebbe, Obi N. I. 1949- *WhoBlA 94*
Ebben, James Adrian *WhoAm 94*
Ebbers, Larry Harold 1941- *WhoAm 94, WhoMW 93*
Ebbert, Arthur, Jr. 1922- *WhoAm 94*
Ebbert, John Voorhees 1936- *WhoMW 93*
Ebbesen, Samuel Emanuel 1938- *AfrAmG [port]*
Ebbett, Eve 1925- *WrDr 94*
Ebbing, Darrell Delmar 1933- *WhoAm 94, WhoMW 93*
Ebbitt, Kenneth Cooper 1908- *WhoAm 94*
Ebbitt, Kenneth Cooper, Jr. 1941- *WhoAm 94*
Ebbitts, Mark Hobart 1949- *WhoFI 94, WhoMW 93*
Ebbs, George Heberling, Jr. 1942- *WhoAm 94, WhoFI 94*
Ebejer, Francis 1925- *ConDr 93*
Ebel, A. James 1913- *WhoMW 93*
Ebel, Alfred d1993 *NewYTBS 93*
Ebel, Alfred Richard 1942- *WhoWest 94*
Ebel, David M. *WhoAmP 93*
Ebel, David M. 1940- *WhoAm 94, WhoAmL 94, WhoWest 94*
Ebel, Jack Edward 1949- *WhoAmL 94*
Ebel, Lynne Carol 1950- *WhoMW 93*
Ebel, Marvin Emerson 1930- *WhoAm 94*
Ebel, Roland H. 1928- *ConAu 140*
Ebel, Suzanne 1916- *WrDr 94*
Ebel, Wilfred Louis 1930- *WhoAmP 93*
Ebele, Ed d1936 *WhoHol 92*
Ebeling-Koning, Derek Bram 1955- *WhoScEn 94*
Ebell, Heinrich Carl 1775-1824 *NewGrDO*
Eben, Al 1918- *WhoHol 92*
Eben, John Eugene 1958- *WhoMW 93*
Eben, Petr 1929- *IntWW 93*
Ebenhoeh, Patrick Edward 1936- *WhoMW 93*
Ebenstein, Alan Oliver 1959- *WhoFI 94*
Eber, Herbert Wolfgang 1928- *WhoAm 94*
Eber, Lorenz 1963- *WhoScEn 94*
Eber, Michel 1943- *WhoScEn 94*
Eberenz, Jon G. 1942- *WhoWest 94*
Eberg, Victor d1972 *WhoHol 92*
Eberhard, David *WhoAmP 93*
Eberhard, Giustina Maria fl. 1727-1745 *NewGrDO*
Eberhard, John Paul 1927- *WhoAm 94*
Eberhard, Marc Olivier 1962- *WhoScEn 94*
Eberhard, William Thomas 1952- *WhoMW 93*
Eberhardt, Allen Craig 1950- *WhoScEn 94*
Eberhardt, Clifford 1947- *WhoBlA 94*
Eberhardt, Daniel Hugo 1938- *WhoAmL 94*
Eberhardt, Gary A. 1940- *WhoAmL 94*
Eberhart, Howard Davis d1993 *NewYTBS 93*
Eberhart, Mary Ann Petesie 1940- *WhoAm 94*
Eberhart, Mignon G. 1899- *WrDr 94*
Eberhart, Richard *DrAPF 93*
Eberhart, Richard 1904- *IntWW 93, WhoAm 94*
Eberhart, Richard (Ghormley) 1904- *Who 94, WrDr 94*
Eberhart, Robert Clyde 1937- *WhoAm 94*
Eberhart, Steve A. 1931- *WhoAm 94, WhoScEn 94, WhoWest 94*
Eberl, Anton (Franz Josef) 1765-1807 *NewGrDO*
Eberl, James Joseph 1916- *WhoScEn 94*
Eberle, August William 1916-1990 *WhAm 10*
Eberle, Charles Edward 1928- *WhoAm 94, WhoFI 94*
Eberle, Don 1948- *WhoAmP 93*
Eberle, Edward Samuel 1944- *WhoAmA 93*
Eberle, James (Henry Fuller) 1927- *Who 94*
Eberle, James Henry Fuller 1927- *IntWW 93*
Eberle, Leo Thomas 1948- *WhoAmL 94*
Eberle, Mary U. 1949- *WhoAmP 93*
Eberle, Merab d1959 *WhoAmA 93N*
Eberle, Peter Richard 1941- *WhoWest 94*
Eberle, Ray d1979 *WhoHol 92*
Eberle, Robert William 1931- *WhoAm 94*
Eberle, Shirley 1929- *ConAu 142*
Eberle, Todd Bailey 1946- *WhoAm 94, WhoAmL 94*
Eberle, William Denman 1923- *IntWW 93, WhoAm 94*
Eberlein, Patricia James 1925- *WhoAm 94*
Eberley, Helen-Kay 1947- *WhoAm 94*
Eberlin, Johann Ernst 1702-1762 *NewGrDO*
Eberly, Bob d1981 *WhoHol 92*
Eberly, Donald Eugene 1953- *WhoAmP 93*
Eberly, Harry Landis 1924- *WhoAm 94*
Eberly, Kathryn *DrAPF 93*
Eberly, Raina Elaine 1952- *WhoScEn 94*
Eberly, Robert Edward 1918- *WhoAm 94*
Eberly, Vickie 1956- *WhoAmA 93*
Eberly, William Robert 1926- *WhoMW 93*
Eberman, Edwin 1905-1988 *WhoAmA 93N*
Ebers, Clara 1902- *NewGrDO*
Ebers, John c. 1785-c. 1830 *NewGrDO*
Ebersberg, Horst *WhoHol 92*
Ebersohn, Wessel (Schalk) 1940- *WrDr 94*
Ebersol, Dick *WhoAm 94*
Ebersole, Brian 1947- *WhoAmP 93*
Ebersole, Christine 1953- *WhoHol 92*
Ebersole, Frederick Levi, Sr. 1939- *WhoMW 93*
Ebersole, Gary Linn 1950- *WhoMW 93*
Ebersole, George David 1936- *WhoFI 94*
Ebersole, J. Glenn, Jr. 1947- *WhoFI 94*
Ebersole, Lucinda 1956- *ConAu 142*
Ebersole, Mark Chester 1921- *WhoAm 94*
Eberspacher, Charles H. 1947- *WhoAmP 93*
Eberstadt, Fernanda 1960- *WrDr 94*
Eberstein, Arthur 1928- *WhoAm 94*
Ebert, Alan 1935- *WrDr 94*
Ebert, Alfred H., Jr. 1929- *WhoAm 94*
Ebert, Carl d1980 *WhoHol 92*
Ebert, (Anton) Carl 1887-1980 *NewGrDO*
Ebert, James D(avid) 1921- *WrDr 94*
Ebert, James David 1921- *IntWW 93, WhoAm 94, WhoScEn 94*
Ebert, Paul Allen 1932- *WhoAm 94*
Ebert, Peter 1918- *IntWW 93, Who 94*
Ebert, Richard Vincent 1912- *WhoAm 94*
Ebert, Robert Alvin 1915- *WhoAm 94*
Ebert, Robert Higgins 1914- *IntWW 93, WhoAm 94*
Ebert, Roger (Joseph) 1942- *WrDr 94*
Ebert, Roger Joseph 1942- *WhoAm 94, WhoMW 93*
Ebertin, Reinhold 1901-1988 *AstEnc*
Eberts, David 1976- *WhoHol 92*
Eberts, John David 1941- *IntMPA 94, Who 94*
Eberty, Paula d1929 *WhoHol 92*
Eberwein, Barton Douglas 1951- *WhoWest 94*
Eberwein, (Franz) Carl (Adalbert) 1786-1868 *NewGrDO*
Eberwine, C. Donald 1937- *WhoMW 93*
Eberwine, James Allen 1933- *WhoAm 94*
Ebey, Carl Finley 1940- *WhoAm 94*
Ebie, Teresa Hayes 1957- *WhoWest 94*
Ebie, William D. 1942- *WhoAm 94, WhoWest 94*
Ebie, William Dennis 1942- *WhoAmA 93*
Ebi-Kryston, Kristie Lee 1950- *WhoWest 94*
Ebin, Robert Felix 1940- *WhoAm 94*
Ebiner, Robert Maurice 1927- *WhoAmL 94, WhoWest 94*
Ebitz, David MacKinnon 1947- *WhoWest 94*
Ebitz, Elizabeth Kelly 1950- *WhoAmL 94*
Eble, Diana 1956- *SmATA 74 [port]*
Eblen, George Thomas 1936- *WhoAm 94*
Ebling, Glenn Russell 1956- *WhoScEn 94*
Ebner, Christine 1277-c. 1355 *BlmGWL*
Ebner, Kurt Ewald 1931- *WhoAm 94*
Ebner, Margarethe c. 1291-1351 *BlmGWL*
Ebner-Eschenbach, Marie von 1830-1916 *BlmGWL*
Ebneter, Stewart Dwight 1933- *WhoScEn 94*
Ebo, Antona 1924- *WhoBlA 94*
Ebon, Martin 1917- *WrDr 94*
Ebong, Regina U. 1953- *WhoBlA 94*
Ebrahim, (Mahomed) Currimbhoy 1935- *Who 94*
Ebrahim, Omar 1956- *NewGrDO*
Ebrey, Patricia Buckley 1947- *WhoMW 93*
Ebright, Peggy Linden Short 1928- *WhoWest 94*
Ebron, Betty Liu 1956- *WhoAsA 94*
Ebsen, Alf K. 1908- *WhoAmA 93*
Ebsen, Buddy 1908- *IntMPA 94, WhoAm 94, WhoHol 92*
Ebsen, Vilma *WhoHol 92*
Ebsworth, Ann (Marian) 1937- *Who 94*
Ebsworth, Evelyn Algernon Valentine 1933- *Who 94*
Ebtehaj, Abol Hassan 1899- *IntWW 93*
Eburne, Maude d1960 *WhoHol 92*
Eburne, Sidney (Alfred William) 1918- *IntWW 93, Who 94*
Ebury, Baron 1934- *Who 94*
Eby, Al R. 1935- *WhoAmP 93*
Eby, Cecil D(eGrotte) 1927- *ConAu 43NR*
Eby, Cecil DeGrotte 1927- *WhoAm 94*
Eby, David W. 1962- *WhoScEn 94*
Eby, Earl d1973 *WhoHol 92*
Eby, Frank Shilling 1924- *WhoScEn 94, WhoWest 94*
Eby, George W. 1914- *IntMPA 94*
Eby, Lawrence Thornton 1916- *WhoMW 93*
Eby, Martin Keller, Jr. 1934- *WhoAm 94, WhoMW 93*
Eby, Michael John 1949- *WhoWest 94*
Eby-Rock, Helyn d1979 *WhoHol 92*
Ebzeev, Boris Safarovich 1950- *LoBiDrD*
Ecabert, Peter Leo 1948- *WhoAmL 94*
Eccard, Walter Thomas 1946- *WhoAmL 94*
Eccles *Who 94*
Eccles 1912- *WhoAm 94*
Eccles, Viscount 1904- *Who 94*
Eccles, Aimee 1949- *WhoHol 92*
Eccles, David McAdam 1904- *IntWW 93*
Eccles, Donald d1986 *WhoHol 92*
Eccles, Geoffrey 1925- *Who 94*
Eccles, Homer Gordon 1937- *WhoAmP 93*
Eccles, Jack Fleming 1922- *Who 94*
Eccles, Jane d1966 *WhoHol 92*
Eccles, John c. 1668-1735 *NewGrDO*
Eccles, John (Carew), Sir 1903- *WrDr 94*
Eccles, John Carew 1903- *IntWW 93, Who 94, WhoAm 94, WhoScEn 94*
Eccles, John Dawson 1931- *Who 94*
Eccles, Patrick *Who 94*
Eccles, (Hugh William) Patrick 1946- *Who 94*
Eccles, Peter Wilson 1936- *WhoBlA 94*
Eccles, Spencer Fox 1934- *WhoAm 94, WhoFI 94, WhoWest 94*
Eccles, Ted *WhoHol 92*
Eccles Of Moulton, Baroness 1933- *Who 94*
Eccleston, Harry Norman 1923- *Who 94*
Ecclestone, Jacob Andrew 1939- *Who 94*
Eccles-Williams, Hilary a'Beckett 1917- *Who 94*
Ecevit, Bulent 1925- *IntWW 93*
Ecgfrith c. 645-685 *DcNaB MP*
Echandi Jimenez, Mario 1915- *IntWW 93*
Echartea, Laura Alicia 1958- *WhoHisp 94*
Echave-Stock, Sylvia 1945- *WhoHisp 94*
Echegaray (Y Eizaguirre), Jose 1832-1916 *IntDcT 2 [port]*
Echegaray (y Eizaguirre), Miguel 1848-1927 *NewGrDO*
Echegoyen, Luis Dernelio 1938- *WhoHisp 94*
Echement, John R. 1935- *WhoAm 94*
Echenique, Marcial Hernan 1943- *Who 94*
Echenique, Miguel 1923- *WhoHisp 94*
Echenique, Pedro Miguel 1950- *WhoScEn 94*
Echeruo, Michael (Joseph Chukwudalu) 1937- *WrDr 94*
Echeruo, Michael J(oseph) C(hukwudalu) 1937- *BlkWr 2*
Echevarria, Abraham 1942- *WhoHisp 94*
Echevarria, Angel M. *WhoHisp 94*
Echevarria, David Philip 1941- *WhoHisp 94*
Echevarria, Efrain Franco, Jr. 1949- *WhoHisp 94*
Echevarria, Juan Carlos 1949- *WhoHisp 94*
Echevarria, Margarita 1951- *WhoHisp 94*
Echevarrieta, John 1959- *WhoHisp 94*
Echeverria, Dorothy Nalani 1966- *WhoFI 94*
Echeverria, Durand 1913- *WrDr 94*
Echeverria Alvarez, Luis 1922- *IntWW 93*
Echeverri-Carroll, Elsie Lucia 1959- *WhoHisp 94*
Echeveste, John Anthony 1949- *WhoHisp 94*
Echeveste, Samuel P. *WhoHisp 94*
Echikson, Richard 1929- *WhoAm 94*
Echikson, William 1959- *WrDr 94*
Echlin, Bernard Joseph 1918- *WhoAm 94*
Echlin, John Edward 1897- *WhAm 10*
Echlin, Norman David Fenton 1925- *Who 94*
Echohawk, Brummett 1922- *WhoAmA 93*
Echohawk, John Ernest 1945- *WhoAm 94*
EchoHawk, Larry 1948- *WhoAm 94, WhoAmL 94, WhoAmP 93, WhoWest 94*
Echols, Alvin E. 1930- *WhoBlA 94*
Echols, Clarence LeRoy, Jr. 1947- *WhoBlA 94*
Echols, David Lorimer 1937- *WhoBlA 94*
Echols, Earl, Jr. *WhoAmP 93*
Echols, Harrison d1993 *NewYTBS 93*
Echols, Horace Richard 1942- *WhoWest 94*
Echols, Ivor Tatum 1919- *WhoBlA 94*
Echols, J. Kermit d1978 *WhoHol 92*
Echols, James Albert 1950- *WhoBlA 94*
Echols, M. Eileen 1951- *WhoAmL 94*
Echols, Mary Ann 1950- *WhoBlA 94*
Echols, Mary Evelyn 1915- *WhoAm 94*
Echols, Richard Nathan 1943- *WhoMW 93*
Echols, Robert L. 1941- *WhoAm 94, WhoAmL 94*
Echtenkamp, Stephen Frederick 1951- *WhoScEn 94*
Eck, Bernard John 1928- *WhoMW 93*
Eck, Charles Peter 1944- *WhoWest 94*
Eck, Dennis K. 1942- *WhoAm 94, WhoFI 94, WhoWest 94*
Eck, Dorothy 1924- *WhoAmP 93*
Eck, Dorothy Fritz 1924- *WhoWest 94*
Eck, E. C. *WhoAmP 93*
Eck, Gail Ann 1948- *WhoMW 93*
Eck, George Gregory 1950- *WhoAm 94, WhoAmL 94*
Eck, Imre 1930- *IntDcB*
Eck, Johnny d1991 *WhoHol 92*
Eck, Kenneth Frank 1917- *WhoScEn 94*
Eck, Michael John 1956- *WhoWest 94*
Eck, Robert Edwin 1938- *WhoAm 94*
Eck, Ronald Warren 1949- *WhoScEn 94*
Eck, Theresa Ann 1941- *WhoMW 93*
Eckardt, A(rthur) Roy 1918- *ConAu 42NR, WrDr 94*
Eckardt, Alice L(yons) 1923- *ConAu 42NR*
Eckardt, Arthur Roy 1918- *WhoAm 94*
Eckardt, Carl R. 1931- *WhoFI 94*
Eckardt, Charles Lincoln 1930- *WhoWest 94*
Eckart, Christian 1959- *WhoAmA 93*
Eckart, Dennis Edward 1950- *WhoAm 94, WhoAmP 93*
Eckart, Gabriele 1954- *ConAu 142*
Eckart, Jean 1921-1993 *NewYTBS 93*
Eckaus, Richard Samuel 1926- *WhoAm 94*
Eckblad, Edith Berven 1923- *WrDr 94*
Eckbo, Garrett 1910- *WhoAm 94, WrDr 94*
Eckdahl, Donald Edward 1924- *WhoAm 94*
Ecke, Betty Tseng Yu-Ho *WhoAmA 93*
Ecke, Gustav d1971 *WhoAmA 93N*
Ecke, Robert Everett 1953- *WhoScEn 94*
Eckel, James Robert, Jr. 1927- *WhoFI 94*
Eckel, John M. 1942- *WhoAm 94*
Eckelberry, Don Richard 1921- *WhoAmA 93*
Eckelman, Richard Joel 1951- *WhoWest 94*
Eckelmann, Frank Donald 1929- *WhoAm 94*
Eckels, Jon *DrAPF 93*
Eckels, Robert Allen 1957- *WhoAmP 93*
Eckenfelder, William Wesley, Jr. 1926- *WhoAm 94*
Eckenhoff, Edward Alvin 1943- *WhoAm 94*
Eckenhoff, James Edward 1915- *WhoAm 94*
Eckenrode, Robert J. 1931- *WhoAm 94, WhoFI 94*
Ecker, Anthony Joseph 1937- *WhoWest 94*
Ecker, Bart Edward 1942- *WhoAmL 94*
Ecker, Carol Adele 1940- *WhoAm 94*
Ecker, Edwin Duain 1934- *WhoMW 93*
Ecker, G. T. Dunlop 1940- *WhoAm 94*
Ecker, Harry Allen 1935- *WhoAm 94*
Ecker, Peder Kaloides 1929- *WhoAm 94, WhoAmL 94, WhoAmP 93*
Ecker, Terry Lee 1963- *WhoMW 93*
Eckerberg, (Carl) Lennart 1928- *IntWW 93, Who 94*
Eckerlein, John E. d1926 *WhoHol 92*
Eckerman, Jerome 1925- *WhoAm 94*
Eckerman, Roy Emmanuel 1921- *WhoWest 94*

Eckermann, Gerald Carlton 1934- *WhoWest 94*
Eckers, Christine 1957- *WhoScEn 94*
Eckersley, Dennis Lee 1954- *WhoAm 94, WhoWest 94*
Eckersley, Donald (Payze) 1922- *Who 94*
Eckersley, John Alan 1945- *WhoFI 94*
Eckersley, Norman Chadwick 1924- *WhoAm 94, WhoWest 94*
Eckersley, Peter Pendleton 1892-1963 *DcNaB MP*
Eckersley, Thomas 1914- *Who 94*
Eckersley, Thomas Cyril 1941- *WhoAmA 93*
Eckersley-Maslin, David Michael 1929- *Who 94*
Eckert, Alfred Carl, III 1948- *WhoAm 94*
Eckert, Allan W. 1931- *WhoAm 94*
Eckert, Allan W(esley) 1931- *EncSF 93*
Eckert, Brian H. 1954- *WhoFI 94*
Eckert, Charles Alan 1938- *WhoAm 94*
Eckert, Ernst R. G. 1904- *WhoAm 94, WhoMW 93*
Eckert, Geraldine Gonzales 1948- *WhoWest 94*
Eckert, J(ohn) Presper, Jr. 1913- *WorInv*
Eckert, Jean Patricia 1935- *WhoAm 94*
Eckert, John Andrew 1941- *WhoScEn 94*
Eckert, John M. *IntMPA 94*
Eckert, Laura E. 1950- *WhoAmP 93*
Eckert, Lou 1928- *WhoAmA 93*
Eckert, Michael Joseph 1947- *WhoAm 94*
Eckert, Michael Louis 1950- *WhoAmL 94*
Eckert, Opal Effie 1905- *WhoMW 93*
Eckert, Ralph J. 1929- *WhoIns 94*
Eckert, Richard E. *WhoAmP 93*
Eckert, Roger Earl 1926- *WhoAm 94*
Eckert, William Dean 1927- *WhoAmA 93*
Eckert, Winfield Scott 1936- *WhoMW 93*
Eckes, Alfred Edward, Jr. 1942- *WhoAm 94, WhoAmP 93*
Eckhardt, August Gottlieb 1917- *WhoAm 94*
Eckhardt, Caroline Davis 1942- *WhoAm 94*
Eckhardt, Craig Jon 1940- *WhoAm 94*
Eckhardt, Donald Henry 1932- *WhoAm 94*
Eckhardt, Ferdinand 1902- *WhoAmA 93*
Eckhardt, Fritz d1970 *WhoHol 92*
Eckhardt, Oliver J. d1952 *WhoHol 92*
Eckhardt, Richard Dale 1918- *WhoAm 94*
Eckhardt, Roger Lee 1963- *WhoWest 94*
Eckhardt, Sandor 1927- *IntWW 93*
Eckhart, James F. 1923- *WhoAmP 93*
Eckhart, Myron, Jr. 1923- *WhoAm 94, WhoScEn 94*
Eckhart, Walter 1938- *WhoAm 94, WhoScEn 94*
Eckhaus, Jay Elliot 1944- *WhoAm 94*
Eckhoff, Carl D. 1933- *WhoAm 94*
Eckhoff, Norman Dean 1938- *WhoMW 93*
Eckhoff, Rosalee 1930- *WhoMW 93*
Eckholm, William Arthur 1951- *WhoMW 93*
Eckl, William Wray 1936- *WhoAmL 94*
Eckler, A. Ross 1901-1991 *WhAm 10*
Eckler, John Alfred 1913- *WhoAm 94*
Eckles, Lew d1950 *WhoHol 92*
Eckles, Robert d1975 *WhoHol 92*
Eckley, Stephen Ross 1957- *WhoAmL 94*
Eckley, Wilton Earl, Jr. 1929- *WhoAm 94*
Ecklin, M. Irenita 1908- *WhoAmA 93*
Ecklin, Robert Luther 1938- *WhoAm 94*
Ecklund, Carol Ann d1939 *WhoHol 92*
Ecklund, Robert Earl 1931- *WhoMW 93*
Ecklund, Sheila Wilcox 1950- *WhoMW 93*
Eckman, David Walter 1942- *WhoAm 94, WhoAmL 94*
Eckman, Fern Marja *WhoAm 94*
Eckman, Frederick *DrAPF 93*
Eckman, John W. 1919-1993 *NewYTBS 93 [port]*
Eckmiller, Rolf Eberhard 1942- *WhoScEn 94*
Eckroad, Steven Wallace 1942- *WhoScEn 94*
Eckroth, Tony *WhoAmP 93*
Eckstein, Harry 1924- *WhoAm 94*
Eckstein, Jerome 1925- *WhoAm 94*
Eckstein, John William 1923- *WhoAm 94, WhoScEn 94*
Eckstein, Marlene R. 1948- *WhoAm 94*
Eckstein, Michael Lehman 1954- *WhoAmL 94*
Eckstein, Paul Franklin 1940- *WhoAm 94*
Eckstein, Ruth 1916- *WhoAmA 93*
Eckstine, Billy 1914- *WhoHol 92*
Eckstine, Billy 1914-1993 *CurBio 93N, NewYTBS 93 [port], News 93, WhoBlA 94N*
Eckstine, Ed *WhoBlA 94*
Eckstrom, Daniel W. 1947- *WhoHisp 94*
Eckstrom, Marta d1952 *WhoHol 92*
Eckstut, Michael Kauder 1952- *WhoAm 94*
Ecleo, Glenda B. 1937- *WhoWomW 91*
Eco, Umberto 1932- *ConWorW 93, EncSF 93, IntWW 93, WhoAm 94*
Ecochard, Jeanine 1939- *WhoWomW 91*
Ecoffey, Jean-Philippe *WhoHol 92*
Economaki, Chris Constantine 1920- *WhoAm 94*
Economides, Floyd A. 1928- *WhoWest 94*
Economos, Chris 1937- *WhoMW 93*
Economos, Michael E. 1936- *WhoAmA 93*
Economou, Eleftherios Nickolas 1940- *WhoScEn 94*
Economou, George *DrAPF 93*
Economou, George 1934- *WrDr 94*
Economou, Steve George 1922- *WhoAm 94*
Economy, James 1929- *WhoAm 94*
E Costa, Oliveira *WhoWomW 91*
Ecroyd, Lawrence Gerald 1918- *WhoAm 94*
Ecton, Donna R. 1947- *WhoAm 94, WhoMW 93*
Ecton, Virgil E. 1940- *WhoBlA 94*
Ed, Carl 1890-1959 *WhoAmA 93N*
Eda-Pierre, Christiane 1932- *NewGrDO*
Eda-Young, Barbara 1945- *WhoHol 92*
Edberg, Stefan 1966- *BuCMET [port], IntWW 93, WhoAm 94*
Edberg, Stephen J. 1952- *WhoWest 94*
Edblom, Dale Clarence 1934- *WhoWest 94*
Edblom, Linda Jane 1956- *WhoAmP 93*
Edde, Howard Jasper 1937- *WhoAm 94*
Eddery, Patrick James John 1952- *Who 94*
Eddey, Howard Hadfield 1910- *Who 94*
Eddie, Russell J. 1938- *WhoAmP 93*
Eddinger, Wallace d1929 *WhoHol 92*
Eddings, Cynthia *WhoBlA 94*
Eddington, Arthur Stanley 1882-1944 *WorScD*
Eddington, Herbert Hoover 1929- *WhoBlA 94*
Eddington, Paul 1927- *IntMPA 94, IntWW 93, WhoHol 92*
Eddington, Paul Clark- 1927- *Who 94*
Eddins, Boyd L. 1933- *WhoAmP 93*
Eddins, Dwight 1939- *WrDr 94*
Eddison, E(ric) R(ucker) 1882-1945 *EncSF 93*
Eddison, Elizabeth Bole 1928- *WhoAm 94*
Eddison, Robert 1908- *WhoHol 92*
Eddleman, Clyde Davis 1902- *Who 94*
Eddleman, Dwight 1922- *BasBi*
Eddleman, Floyd Eugene 1930- *WhoAm 94*
Eddleman, Lew Eugene 1955- *WhoFI 94*
Eddleman, William Roseman 1913- *WhoAm 94*
Eddleman, William Thomas 1900-1973 *WhoBlA 94N*
Eddo, James Ekundayo 1936- *WhoScEn 94*
Eddy, Alfred Alan 1926- *Who 94*
Eddy, Augusta Rossner d1925 *WhoHol 92*
Eddy, Charles Alan 1948- *WhoMW 93, WhoScEn 94*
Eddy, Dana Franklin 1959- *WhoAmL 94*
Eddy, Darlene M. *DrAPF 93*
Eddy, Darlene Mathis 1937- *WhoAm 94*
Eddy, David Corbett 1953- *WhoAm 94*
Eddy, David Latimer 1936- *WhoAm 94*
Eddy, Don 1944- *WhoAm 94, WhoAmA 93*
Eddy, Donald Davis 1929- *WhoAm 94*
Eddy, Dorothy d1959 *WhoHol 92*
Eddy, Duane 1938- *WhoHol 92*
Eddy, Edward A. 1938- *WhoBlA 94*
Eddy, Edward Danforth 1921- *WhoAm 94*
Eddy, Elizabeth *DrAPF 93*
Eddy, Esther Dewitz 1926- *WhoAm 94*
Eddy, Helen Jerome d1990 *WhoHol 92*
Eddy, Howard N. *WhoWest 94*
Eddy, John Joseph 1933- *WhoAm 94*
Eddy, Jonathan 1726-1804 *AmRev*
Eddy, Leon d1978 *WhoHol 92*
Eddy, Lynne Jones 1944- *WhoWest 94*
Eddy, Mary Baker 1821-1910 *DcAmReB 2, HisWorL [port]*
Eddy, Mary Morse Baker 1821-1910 *AmSocL [port]*
Eddy, Nelson d1967 *WhoHol 92*
Eddy, Robert, Jr. 1959- *WhoFI 94*
Eddy, Robert Phillip 1919- *WhoWest 94*
Eddy, Shirley Kathryn 1922- *WhoAmP 93*
Eddy, William Crawford 1902-1989 *WhAm 10*
Ede, Dennis 1931- *Who 94*
Ede, George 1931- *WhoHol 92*
Ede, Jeffery Raymond 1918- *Who 94*
Ede, Joyce Kinlaw 1936- *WhoMW 93*
Edeiken, Louise 1956- *ConAu 140*
Edel, Abraham 1908- *WhoAm 94, WrDr 94*
Edel, Leon 1907- *WhoAm 94, WhoWest 94*
Edel, (Joseph) Leon 1907- *IntWW 93, Who 94, WrDr 94*
Edelbaum, Philip R. 1936- *WhoAmL 94*
Edelbrock, Andrew Jason 1962- *WhoMW 93*
Edelcup, Norman Scott 1935- *WhoAm 94*
Edelen, Mary Beaty 1944- *WhoAmP 93, WhoWomW 91*
Edelen, Roberta Marie 1960- *WhoMW 93*
Edelhauser, Henry F. 1937- *WhoScEn 94*
Edelheit, Abraham J. 1958- *WrDr 94*
Edelheit, Hershel 1926- *WrDr 94*
Edelheit, Martha *WhoAmA 93*
Edelhertz, Helaine Wolfson 1953- *WhoScEn 94*
Edelin, Kenneth C. 1939- *WhoBlA 94*
Edelin, Ramona Hoage 1945- *AfrAmAl 6*
Edell, Nancy 1942- *WhoAmA 93*
Edell, Robert Thomas 1932- *WhoMW 93*
Edell, Stephen Bristow 1932- *Who 94*
Edelman, Alan Irwin 1958- *WhoAmL 94*
Edelman, Alma Ann 1918- *WhoAmP 93*
Edelman, Alvin 1916- *WhoAm 94*
Edelman, Ann *WhoAmA 93*
Edelman, Daniel Joseph 1920- *WhoAm 94, WhoFI 94, WhoMW 93*
Edelman, Edmund Douglas 1930- *WhoAmP 93*
Edelman, Elaine *DrAPF 93*
Edelman, Fredric Mark 1958- *WhoFI 94*
Edelman, Gerald Maurice 1929- *IntWW 93, Who 94, WhoAm 94, WhoScEn 94, WhoWest 94*
Edelman, Gregg *WhoHol 92*
Edelman, Harold 1923- *WhoAm 94*
Edelman, Harry Rollings, III 1928- *WhoAm 94*
Edelman, Hendrik 1937- *WhoAm 94*
Edelman, Herb 1930- *IntMPA 94*
Edelman, Herb 1933- *WhoHol 92*
Edelman, Herbert Stephen 1938- *WhoAm 94*
Edelman, Isidore Samuel 1920- *WhoAm 94*
Edelman, Joel 1931- *WhoAm 94*
Edelman, Judith Hochberg 1923- *WhoAm 94*
Edelman, Keith Graeme 1950- *Who 94*
Edelman, Marian Wright 1939- *AfrAmAl 6, AmSocL [port], BlkWr 2, ConBlB 5 [port], WhoAm 94, WhoAmL 94, WhoBlA 94*
Edelman, Mark L. 1943- *WhoAmP 93*
Edelman, Murray J 1919- *WrDr 94*
Edelman, Murray R. 1939- *WhoAm 94, WhoFI 94*
Edelman, Norma Lou 1939- *WhoWest 94*
Edelman, Norman H. 1937- *WhoAm 94*
Edelman, Paul Sterling 1926- *WhoAm 94, WhoAmL 94*
Edelman, Peter B. *WhoAmP 93*
Edelman, Peter Benjamin 1938- *WhoAm 94*
Edelman, Raymond Howard 1956- *WhoAmL 94*
Edelman, Richard Winston 1954- *WhoAm 94, WhoFI 94*
Edelman, Rita 1930- *WhoAmA 93*
Edelman, Thomas Jeffery 1951- *WhoAm 94*
Edelmann, Chester Monroe, Jr. 1930- *WhoAm 94*
Edelmann, Jean-Frederic 1749-1794 *NewGrDO*
Edelmann, Otto *WhoHol 92*
Edelmann, Otto 1917- *NewGrDO*
Edelmann, Otto Karl 1917- *IntWW 93*
Edelsbrunner, Herbert 1958- *WhoScEn 94*
Edelson, Burton Irving 1926- *WhoAm 94*
Edelson, David 1919- *WhoMW 93*
Edelson, Gilbert S. 1928- *WhoAmA 93*
Edelson, Gilbert Seymour 1928- *WhoAm 94*
Edelson, Ira J. 1946- *WhoAm 94, WhoFI 94*
Edelson, Jonathan Victor 1952- *WhoScEn 94*
Edelson, Marshall 1928- *WhoAm 94*
Edelson, Martin Charles 1943- *WhoMW 93*
Edelson, Mary Beth *WhoAmA 93*
Edelstein, Alan Shane 1936- *WhoScEn 94*
Edelstein, Alex S. 1920- *WrDr 94*
Edelstein, Chaim Y. 1942- *WhoAm 94, WhoFI 94*
Edelstein, Dad d1927 *WhoHol 92*
Edelstein, David Northon 1910- *WhoAm 94, WhoAmL 94*
Edelstein, Haskell 1933- *WhoAm 94*
Edelstein, J. M. 1924- *WhoAmA 93*
Edelstein, Jerome Melvin 1924- *WhoAm 94, WhoWest 94*
Edelstein, Leonard 1938- *WhoFI 94*
Edelstein, Scott *DrAPF 93*
Edelstein, Scott Samuel 1954- *WhoMW 93*
Edelstein, Terese 1950- *WrDr 94*
Edelstein, Teri J. 1951- *WhoAm 94, WhoAmA 93, WhoMW 93*
Edelstein, Tilden G. 1931- *WhoAm 94*
Edelstein, Victor 1945- *IntWW 93*
Edelstein, Victor Arnold 1945- *Who 94*
Edem, Benjamin G. 1952- *WhoWest 94*
Edemeka, Udo Edemeka 1944- *WhoScEn 94*
Eden *Who 94*
Eden, Anthony 1897-1977 *HisWorL [port], HisDcKW*
Eden, Barbara 1934- *IntMPA 94, WhoHol 92*
Eden, Barbara Janiece 1951- *WhoAm 94*
Eden, Barbara Jean 1934- *WhoAm 94*
Eden, Bronson B. 1949- *WhoAmA 93*
Eden, Cathy *WhoAmP 93*
Eden, Charles Henry 1895- *WhAm 10*
Eden, Conrad W. *Who 94*
Eden, Elana 1940- *WhoHol 92*
Eden, Emily 1797-1869 *BlmGEL*
Eden, F(lorence) Brown 1916- *WhoAmA 93*
Eden, Glenn 1951- *WhoAmA 93*
Eden, James Gary 1950- *WhoAm 94, WhoScEn 94*
Eden, Lee Smythe 1937- *WhoAm 94*
Eden, Mark 1928- *WhoHol 92*
Eden, Melinda Sue 1948- *WhoAmL 94*
Eden, Murray 1920- *WhoAm 94*
Eden, Nathan E. 1944- *WhoAmL 94*
Eden, Richard John 1922- *Who 94*
Eden, Robert 1741-1784 *WhAmRev*
Eden, William 1744-1814 *WhAmRev*
Edenberg, Howard Joseph 1948- *WhoMW 93*
Edenfield, Berry Avant 1934- *WhoAm 94, WhoAmL 94*
Edenfield, Thomas Keen, Jr. 1943- *WhoWest 94*
Eden Of Winton, Baron 1925- *IntWW 93, Who 94*
Edens, Bob *WhoAmP 93*
Edens, Donald Keith 1928- *WhoAm 94*
Edens, Gary Denton 1942- *WhoAm 94, WhoWest 94*
Edens, Glenn Thomas 1952- *WhoWest 94*
Edens, Richard Woodward 1928- *WhoIns 94*
Edens, Roger 1905-1970 *IntDcF 2-4*
Eder, (Henry) Bernard 1952- *Who 94*
Eder, George Jackson 1900- *WhoAm 94*
Eder, Helmut 1916- *NewGrDO*
Eder, Howard Abram 1917- *WhoAm 94*
Eder, James Alvin 1942- *WhoAmA 93*
Eder, Richard Gray 1932- *WhoAm 94*
Ederer, Brigitte 1956- *WhoWomW 91*
Ederer, Ronald Frank 1943- *WhoAmP 93*
Ederle, Douglas Richard 1962- *WhoAmL 94*
Ederle, Gertrude *WhoHol 92*
Edes, Benjamin 1732-1803 *WhAmRev*
Edes, (John) Michael 1930- *Who 94*
Edes, Nik Bruce 1943- *WhoAm 94*
Edeson, Arthur 1891-1970 *IntDcF 2-4 [port]*
Edeson, Robert d1931 *WhoHol 92*
Edey, Harold Cecil 1913- *Who 94*
Edey, Maitland A. 1910-1992 *AnObit 1992*
Edey, Maitland A(rmstrong) 1910-1992 *WrDr 94N*
Edey, Maitland Armstrong 1910-1992 *WhAm 10*
Edgar, Alvis, Jr. 1929- *WhoAm 94*
Edgar, Archer L. 1938- *WhoIns 94*
Edgar, David 1948- *BlmGEL, ConDr 93, IntDcT 2, IntWW 93, WrDr 94*
Edgar, David Burman 1948- *Who 94*
Edgar, Gilbert Hammond, III 1947- *WhoFI 94*
Edgar, Harold Simmons Hull 1942- *WhoAm 94*
Edgar, Jacqueline L. 1948- *WhoBlA 94*
Edgar, James 1946- *IntWW 93*
Edgar, James Macmillan, Jr. 1936- *WhoAm 94, WhoWest 94*
Edgar, Jim 1946- *WhoAm 94, WhoAmP 93, WhoMW 93*
Edgar, John M. 1943- *WhoAm 94, WhoAmL 94*
Edgar, Josephine 1907-1991 *WrDr 94N*
Edgar, Marriott d1951 *WhoHol 92*
Edgar, Robert Allan 1940- *WhoAm 94, WhoAmL 94*
Edgar, Robert William 1943- *WhoAmP 93, WhoWest 94*
Edgar, Ronald Dale 1943- *WhoFI 94*
Edgar, Shirley Anne 1935- *WhoAm 94*
Edgar, Thomas Flynn 1945- *WhoAm 94, WhoScEn 94*
Edgar, Walter Bellingrath 1943- *WhoAm 94*
Edgar, William 1938- *Who 94*
Edgar, William John 1933- *WhoAm 94*
Edgard, Lewis d1917 *WhoHol 92*
Edgcumbe *Who 94*
Edgcumbe, Richard *NewGrDO*
Edge, Arthur B., IV 1955- *WhoAmP 93*
Edge, Charles Geoffrey 1920- *WhoAm 94*
Edge, Douglas Benjamin 1942- *WhoAmA 93*

Edge, Eldon 1926- *WhoAmP 93*
Edge, Findley Bartow 1916- *WhoAm 94*
Edge, Geoffrey 1943- *Who 94*
Edge, Harold Lee 1933- *WhoAm 94*
Edge, James Edward 1948- *WhoFI 94, WhoScEn 94*
Edge, Julian Dexter, Jr. 1942- *WhoAm 94, WhoAmL 94*
Edge, (Philip) Malcolm 1931- *Who 94*
Edge, Raymond Cyril Alexander 1912- *Who 94*
Edge, Ronald Dovaston 1929- *WhoAm 94, WhoScEn 94*
Edge, William *Who 94*
Edgecombe, Nydia R. 1951- *WhoHisp 94*
Edgell, Robert Louis 1922-1991 *WhAm 10*
Edgell, Zee *BlmGWL*
Edgerly, William Skelton 1927- *WhoAm 94*
Edgerton, Art Joseph 1928- *WhoBlA 94*
Edgerton, Brenda Evans 1949- *WhoAm 94, WhoBlA 94*
Edgerton, Clyde 1944- *WrDr 94*
Edgerton, Clyde (Carlyle) 1944- *TwCYAW*
Edgerton, H. Quincy, Jr. 1950- *WhoAmP 93*
Edgerton, Harold E. 1903-1990 *WorInv*
Edgerton, Harold Eugene 1903-1990 *WhAm 10*
Edgerton, John Palmer 1917- *WhoAmP 93*
Edgerton, Mills Fox, Jr. 1931- *WhoAm 94*
Edgerton, Milton Thomas, Jr. 1921- *WhoAm 94*
Edgerton, Rebecca Jane 1953- *WhoMW 93*
Edgerton, Richard 1911- *WhoFI 94*
Edgerton, Robert Frank 1935- *WhoScEn 94*
Edgerton, William B. 1914- *WhoAm 94*
Edgerton, Winfield Dow 1924- *WhoAm 94*
Edgett, Steven Dennis 1948- *WhoWest 94*
Edgett, William Maloy 1927- *WhoAm 94*
Edgeworth, Maria 1767-1849 *BlmGEL*
Edgeworth, Maria 1768-1849 *BlmGWL*
Edgeworth, Patrick *WhoHol 92*
Edgeworth, Robert Joseph 1947- *WhoAm 94*
Edgeworth Johnstone, Robert *Who 94*
Edghill, John W. 1921- *WhoBlA 94*
Edgington, Eugene Sinclair 1924- *WrDr 94*
Edgington, Mary Carter 1947- *WhoMW 93*
Edginton, John Arthur 1935- *WhoAm 94*
Edgley, Michael Christopher 1943- *IntWW 93*
Edgren, Gary Robert 1947- *WhoAmA 93*
Edib, (Adivar) Halide 1883-1964 *BlmGWL*
Edidin, Michael Aaron 1939- *WhoAm 94*
Edie, Thomas Ker 1916- *Who 94*
Ediger, Mark D. 1957- *WhoScEn 94*
Ediger, Marlow 1927- *WhoMW 93*
Ediger, Nicholas Martin 1928- *WhoAm 94, WhoFI 94*
Ediger, Robert Ike 1937- *WhoAm 94*
Edin, Charles Thomas 1955- *WhoAmL 94*
Edinburgh, Bishop of 1933- *Who 94*
Edinburgh, Dean of *Who 94*
Edinburgh, Provost of *Who 94*
Edinburgh, Philip, Duke of 1921- *IntWW 93*
Edinger, John Walter 1959- *WhoMW 93*
Edinger, Lewis Joachim 1922- *WhoAm 94*
Edinger, Lois Virginia 1925- *WhoAm 94*
Edington, Donald Malvin 1942- *WhoFI 94*
Edington, Patricia Ann 1941- *WhoMW 93*
Edington, Patricia Gentry 1938- *WhoAmP 93*
Edington, Robert Van 1935- *WhoAm 94*
Edis, Richard John Smale 1943- *Who 94*
Edison, Allen Ray 1926- *WhoAm 94*
Edison, Ann Osterhout d1993 *NewYTBS 93*
Edison, Bernard Alan 1928- *WhoAm 94*
Edison, Peter Cornelius 1944- *WhoAmL 94*
Edison, Thomas Alva 1847-1931 *AmSocL, WorInv [port]*
Ediss, Connie d1934 *WhoHol 92*
Edith d1075 *BlmGWL*
Edland, Robert William 1932- *WhoMW 93*
Edlen, Bengt 1906- *IntWW 93*
Edler, Charles d1942 *WhoHol 92*
Edler, Robert P. 1944- *WhoAmL 94*
Edler, Robert Weber 1936- *WhoAm 94*
Edles, Gary J. 1941- *WhoAmL 94*
Edleson, L. B. Chip 1955- *WhoAmL 94*
Edley, Bill 1948- *WhoAmP 93*
Edley, Christopher F., Sr. 1928- *WhoBlA 94*
Edley, Christopher F., Jr. 1953- *WhoBlA 94*
Edlich, Richard French 1939- *WhoAm 94, WhoScEn 94*
Edlin, Jamie Ann 1950- *WhoWest 94*
Edlin, Ted d1974 *WhoHol 92*
Edlow, Kenneth Lewis 1941- *WhoAm 94, WhoFI 94*
Edlund, Carl E. 1936- *WhoScEn 94*
Edlund, Milton Carl 1924- *WhoAm 94*
Edlund, Philip Arthur 1941- *WhoAm 94, WhoAmL 94*
Edlund, Richard *IntDcF 2-4*
Edlund, Richard J. 1924- *WhoAmP 93*
Edman, Robin 1956- *WhoMW 93*
Edmenson, Walter Alexander d1992 *Who 94N*
Edmisten, Patricia Taylor 1939- *WrDr 94*
Edmisten, Rufus Ligh 1941- *WhoAm 94, WhoAmP 93*
Edmiston, Joseph Tasker 1948- *WhoWest 94*
Edmiston, Mark Morton 1943- *WhoAm 94*
Edmiston, Sara Joanne 1935- *WhoAmA 93*
Edmond, Alfred Adam, Jr. 1960- *WhoBlA 94*
Edmond, John Marmion 1943- *IntWW 93, Who 94*
Edmond, Lauris (Dorothy) 1924- *WrDr 94*
Edmond, Lauris Dorothy 1924- *BlmGWL [port]*
Edmond, Murray (Donald) 1949- *WrDr 94*
Edmond, Paul Edward 1944- *WhoBlA 94*
Edmond, William Henry, Jr. 1969- *WhoMW 93*
Edmonds, Albert J. 1942- *AfrAmG [port], WhoAm 94*
Edmonds, Albert Joseph 1942- *WhoBlA 94*
Edmonds, Andrew Nicola 1955- *WhoScEn 94*
Edmonds, Anne Carey 1924- *WhoAm 94*
Edmonds, Campbell Ray 1930- *WhoBlA 94*
Edmonds, Carol R. 1947- *WhoAmP 93*
Edmonds, Charles Henry 1919- *WhoWest 94*
Edmonds, David Albert 1944- *Who 94*
Edmonds, Elizabeth *WhoHol 92*
Edmonds, Harry (Moreton Southey) 1891-1989 *EncSF 93*
Edmonds, Ivy Gordon 1917- *WhoWest 94*
Edmonds, John Christopher 1921- *Who 94*
Edmonds, John Christopher Paul 1936- *Who 94*
Edmonds, John Walter 1944- *Who 94*
Edmonds, Josephine E. 1921- *WhoBlA 94*
Edmonds, Kenneth *WhoBlA 94*
Edmonds, Louis *WhoHol 92*
Edmonds, Mary Patricia 1922- *WhoAm 94*
Edmonds, Norman Douglas 1938- *WhoBlA 94*
Edmonds, Paul *EncSF 93*
Edmonds, Richard Lee 1953- *WhoScEn 94*
Edmonds, Robert Humphrey Gordon 1920- *Who 94*
Edmonds, Robert Scott 1951- *WhoAm 94*
Edmonds, Ronald Allen 1946- *WhoAm 94*
Edmonds, Sheila May 1916- *Who 94*
Edmonds, Terry Dean 1945- *WhoMW 93*
Edmonds, Thomas Andrew 1938- *WhoAmL 94*
Edmonds, Thomas Leon 1932- *WhoAmL 94*
Edmonds, Thomas Nathaniel 1936- *WhoBlA 94*
Edmonds, Walter D(umaux) 1903- *WrDr 94*
Edmonds, Walter Dumaux 1903- *WhoAm 94*
Edmonds, William Fleming 1923- *WhoAm 94*
Edmonds, Winston Godward 1912- *Who 94*
Edmonds-Brown, (Cedric Wilfred) George 1939- *Who 94*
Edmondson *Who 94*
Edmondson, Adrian *WhoHol 92*
Edmondson, Anthony Arnold 1920- *Who 94*
Edmondson, Betty Lavern 1924- *WhoAmP 93*
Edmondson, Frank Kelley 1912- *WhoAm 94*
Edmondson, Frank Kelley, Jr. 1936- *WhoAmL 94*
Edmondson, G.C. 1922- *EncSF 93, WrDr 94*
Edmondson, J. L. *WhoAmP 93*
Edmondson, James *WhoCom*
Edmondson, James Howard 1931- *WhoAmP 93*
Edmondson, James Larry 1947- *WhoAm 94, WhoAmL 94*
Edmondson, James W. 1930- *WhoIns 94*
Edmondson, James William 1930- *WhoAm 94*
Edmondson, Jennifer Lee 1961- *WhoAmL 94*
Edmondson, John Richard 1927- *WhoAm 94, WhoFI 94*
Edmondson, Keith Henry 1924- *WhoAm 94*
Edmondson, Leonard 1916- *WhoAmA 93*
Edmondson, Leonard Firby 1912- *Who 94*
Edmondson, Mark 1954- *BuCMET*
Edmondson, Scott Thomas 1955- *WhoWest 94*
Edmondson, Wallace *EncSF 93*
Edmondson, Wallace Thomas 1916- *WhoAm 94, WhoScEn 94, WhoWest 94*
Edmondson, William Brockway 1927- *WhoAm 94*
Edmonson, Bernie L. 1918-1987 *WhoBlA 94N*
Edmonson, Karen Marie 1957- *WhoMW 93*
Edmonson, Munro S 1924- *WrDr 94*
Edmonson, Munro Sterling 1924- *WhoAm 94*
Edmonson, Randall W. 1947- *WhoAmA 93*
Edmonson, William d1979 *WhoHol 92*
Edmonson, William 1882-1951 *AfrAmAl 6*
Edmonston, Paul 1922- *WhoAmA 93*
Edmonston, William Edward, Jr. 1931- *WhoAm 94, WhoScEn 94*
Edmonstone, Archibald (Bruce Charles) 1934- *Who 94*
Edmonton, Archbishop of 1924- *Who 94*
Edmonton, Area Bishop of 1932- *Who 94*
Edmonton, Bishop of 1933- *Who 94*
Edmund, Lada, Jr. 1948- *WhoHol 92*
Edmund-Davies, Baron d1992 *IntWW 93N, Who 94N*
Edmunds, Allan Logan 1949- *WhoAmA 93*
Edmunds, David L., Jr. *WhoBlA 94*
Edmunds, Ferrell, Jr. 1965- *WhoBlA 94*
Edmunds, Jane Clara 1922- *WhoAm 94*
Edmunds, Joseph Edsel 1935- *IntWW 93*
Edmunds, Lowell 1938- *WhoAm 94*
Edmunds, Nancy Garlock 1947- *WhoAm 94, WhoAmL 94, WhoMW 93*
Edmunds, Niel Arthur 1931- *WhoMW 93*
Edmunds, Robert Thomas 1924- *WhoAm 94, WhoScEn 94*
Edmunds, Walter Richard 1928- *WhoBlA 94*
Edmunds, William d1981 *WhoHol 92*
Edmundsen, Al d1954 *WhoHol 92*
Edmundson, Charles Wayne 1942- *WhoMW 93*
Edmunson, James 1951- *WhoAmP 93*
Ednam, Viscount 1947- *Who 94*
Edney, Beatie *WhoHol 92*
Edney, Florence d1950 *WhoHol 92*
Edney, Leon A. *WhoAm 94*
Edney, Norris Allen, I 1936- *WhoBlA 94*
Edney, Steve 1917- *WhoBlA 94*
Edouard, Pierre 1959- *WhoAmA 93*
Edouart, Farciot 1895-1980 *IntDcF 2-4*
Edozien, Margaret Ekwutozia 1959- *WhoAmL 94*
Edquist, Erhart David 1898- *WhAm 10*
Edrich, Leslie Howard 1953- *WhoWest 94*
Edris, Charles Lawrence 1942- *WhoAm 94*
Edsall, Howard Linn *DrAPF 93*
Edsall, Howard Linn 1904- *WhoFI 94*
Edsall, John Tileston 1902- *IntWW 93, WhoAm 94*
Edsall, Mary D(eutsch) 1943- *ConAu 142*
Edsall, Thomas Byrne 1941- *WhoAm 94*
Edsberg, John Christian *Who 94*
Edson, Charles Louis 1934- *WhoAm 94, WhoAmL 94*
Edson, Edward Marshall 1947- *WhoAmL 94*
Edson, Gary F. 1937- *WhoAmA 93*
Edson, Herbert Robbins 1931- *WhoFI 94, WhoScEn 94*
Edson, J(ohn) T(homas) 1928- *WrDr 94*
Edson, Richard 1954- *WhoHol 92*
Edson, Russell *DrAPF 93*
Edson, Russell 1935- *WrDr 94*
Edson, Wayne E. 1947- *WhoMW 93*
Edson, William Alden 1912- *WhoAm 94, WhoWest 94*
Edstrom, Eric Wayne 1950- *WhoFI 94*
Edstrom, Jan-Erik 1931- *IntWW 93*
Edstrom, John Olof 1926- *WhoFI 94*
Edthofer, Anton d1971 *WhoHol 92*
Eduardo *IntDcT 2*
Educato, John Saverio 1961- *WhoAmL 94*
Edvi Illes, Emma *WhoAmA 93*
Edvina, (Marie) Louise (Lucienne Juliette) 1880-1948 *NewGrDO*
Edwall, Allan *WhoHol 92*
Edwall, Chris Wendell 1958- *WhoFI 94*
Edward, Prince 1964- *Who 94R*
Edward, I 1239-1307 *HisWorL [port]*
Edward, I 1272-1307 *BlmGEL*
Edward, II 1307-1327 *BlmGEL*
Edward, III 1312-1377 *HisWorL [port]*
Edward, III 1327-1377 *BlmGEL*
Edward, IV 1461-1483 *BlmGEL*
Edward, V 1483- *BlmGEL*
Edward, VI 1547-1553 *BlmGEL*
Edward, VII 1841-1910 *HisWorL [port]*
Edward, Coleman 1622-1669 *NewGrDO*
Edward, David Alexander Ogilvy 1934- *IntWW 93, Who 94*
Edward, John Thomas 1919- *WhoAm 94*
Edward, Marion *WhoHol 92*
Edward, William N. 1929- *WhoIns 94*
Edward Atheling d1057 *DcNaB MP*
Edwardes *Who 94*
Edwardes, Michael (Owen) 1930- *Who 94*
Edwardes, Michael Owen 1930- *IntWW 93*
Edward of Westminster d1265 *DcNaB MP*
Edwards *Who 94*
Edwards fl. 1737-1753 *NewGrDO*
Edwards, A. Wilson 1908- *WhoBlA 94*
Edwards, Al 1937- *WhoAmP 93*
Edwards, Al E. 1937- *WhoBlA 94*
Edwards, Alan d1954 *WhoHol 92*
Edwards, Albert Glen d1973 *ProFbHF*
Edwards, Alexander Comstock 1953- *WhoFI 94*
Edwards, Alfred L. 1920- *WhoBlA 94*
Edwards, Alfred Leroy 1920- *WhoAm 94*
Edwards, Alison Edith 1952- *WhoWest 94*
Edwards, Allen Jack 1926- *WrDr 94*
Edwards, Amelia 1831-1892 *BlmGWL*
Edwards, Amy L. 1953- *WhoAmL 94*
Edwards, Andrew John Cumming 1940- *Who 94*
Edwards, Anne 1927- *WrDr 94*
Edwards, Anthony 1962- *IntMPA 94, WhoHol 92*
Edwards, Ardis Lavonne Quam 1930- *WhoWest 94*
Edwards, Arthur Anderson 1926- *WhoAm 94*
Edwards, Arthur Frank George 1920- *Who 94*
Edwards, Arthur James 1902- *WhoBlA 94*
Edwards, Atticus Fitzgerald 1890- *WhoAmP 93*
Edwards, Audrey Marie 1947- *WhoBlA 94*
Edwards, Bert Tvedt 1937- *WhoAm 94, WhoFI 94*
Edwards, Bessie Regina 1942- *WhoBlA 94*
Edwards, Betty 1926- *WrDr 94*
Edwards, Bill 1918- *WhoHol 92*
Edwards, Bingham David 1943- *WhoAmP 93*
Edwards, Blake 1922- *IntMPA 94, IntWW 93, WhoAm 94, WhoHol 92*
Edwards, Blue 1965- *WhoBlA 94*
Edwards, Bob 1947- *WhoAm 94*
Edwards, Brian 1942- *Who 94*
Edwards, Bruce George 1942- *WhoWest 94*
Edwards, Carl Normand 1943- *WhoFI 94*
Edwards, Carl Ray, II 1947- *WhoBlA 94*
Edwards, Carleton Ephraim 1909- *WhoAmP 93*
Edwards, Cassandra *WhoHol 92*
Edwards, Cassie *DrAPF 93*
Edwards, Cecile Hoover 1926- *WhoBlA 94*
Edwards, Chancy Rudolph 1925- *WhoAmP 93*
Edwards, Charles d1978 *WhoHol 92*
Edwards, Charles 1925- *WhoAm 94*
Edwards, Charles Archibald 1945- *WhoAm 94, WhoAmL 94*
Edwards, Charles Arthur 1940- *WhoMW 93*
Edwards, Charles Berkley 1942- *WhoAmL 94*
Edwards, Charles C., Jr. 1947- *WhoAm 94, WhoMW 93*
Edwards, Charles Cornell 1923- *WhoAmP 93, WhoWest 94*
Edwards, Charles Harold 1913- *Who 94*
Edwards, Charles Lloyd 1940- *WhoAm 94*
Edwards, Charles M. 1931- *WhoAm 94, WhoMW 93*
Edwards, Charles Marvin 1925- *WhoAmP 93*
Edwards, Charles Mundy, III 1935- *WhoFI 94*
Edwards, Charles Richard 1931- *WhoWest 94*
Edwards, Charles Richard 1945- *WhoScEn 94*
Edwards, Chet 1951- *CngDr 93, WhoAm 94, WhoAmP 93*
Edwards, Christine Annette 1952- *WhoAm 94, WhoFI 94*
Edwards, Christopher (John Churchill) 1941- *Who 94*
Edwards, Christopher Richard Watkin 1942- *Who 94*
Edwards, Claybon Jerome 1929- *WhoBlA 94*
Edwards, Cliff d1971 *WhoHol 92*
Edwards, Clive *Who 94*
Edwards, (John) Clive (Leighton) 1916- *Who 94*
Edwards, D. M. 1953- *WhoFI 94*

Edwards, Daniel James 1928- *WhAm 10*
Edwards, Daniel Paul 1940- *WhoAmL 94*
Edwards, Daniel Walden 1950- *WhoAmL 94, WhoWest 94*
Edwards, Darrel 1943- *WhoScEn 94*
Edwards, Daryl *WhoHol 92*
Edwards, David *EncSF 93*
Edwards, David 1929- *Who 94*
Edwards, David C. 1948- *WhoBlA 94*
Edwards, David Charles 1937- *WhoAm 94*
Edwards, David H., Jr. 1922-1992 *WhoBlA 94N*
Edwards, David Lawrence 1929- *Who 94*
Edwards, David Michael 1940- *Who 94*
Edwards, David Northrop 1923- *WhoAm 94*
Edwards, David Olaf 1932- *Who 94*
Edwards, Dawn Ann 1956- *WhoFI 94*
Edwards, Debora Michele 1958- *WhoFI 94*
Edwards, Delores A. 1965- *WhoBlA 94*
Edwards, Dennis, Jr. 1922- *WhoBlA 94*
Edwards, Dennis L. 1941- *WhoBlA 94*
Edwards, Dennis S. *DrAPF 93*
Edwards, Derek d1993 *Who 94N*
Edwards, Don *CngDr 93*
Edwards, Don 1915- *WhoAm 94, WhoAmP 93, WhoWest 94*
Edwards, Donald 1904- *WrDr 94*
Edwards, Donald Kenneth 1932- *WhoScEn 94*
Edwards, Donald Mervin 1938- *WhoAm 94*
Edwards, Donald O. 1931- *WhoBlA 94*
Edwards, Donald Philip 1947- *WhoBlA 94*
Edwards, Doris d1981 *WhoHol 92*
Edwards, Doris Steck 1944- *WhoMW 93*
Edwards, Dorothy R. 1911- *WhoAmP 93*
Edwards, Dorothy Wright 1914- *WhoBlA 94*
Edwards, Douglas d1993 *NewYTBS 93*
Edwards, Douglas 1917-1990 *WhAm 10*
Edwards, Douglas John 1916- *Who 94*
Edwards, Ed, Jr. 1927- *WhoBlA 94*
Edwards, Eddie 1954- *WhoBlA 94*
Edwards, Edna Park d1967 *WhoHol 92*
Edwards, Edward George 1914- *Who 94*
Edwards, Edwin W. 1927- *WhoAmP 93*
Edwards, Edwin Washington 1927- *IntWW 93, WhoAm 94*
Edwards, Eleanor d1968 *WhoHol 92*
Edwards, Eleanor Cecile 1940- *WhoFI 94*
Edwards, Elgan *Who 94*
Edwards, (David) Elgan (Hugh) 1943- *Who 94*
Edwards, Elizabeth Alice 1937- *Who 94*
Edwards, Ella Raino *WhoHol 92*
Edwards, Ella Raino 1938- *WhoBlA 94*
Edwards, Ellender Morgan *WhoAmA 93*
Edwards, Ellis 1947- *WhoAmP 93*
Edwards, Elton 1923- *WhoAmP 93*
Edwards, Emmet 1907- *WhoAmA 93N*
Edwards, Ernest Gray 1927- *WhoWest 94*
Edwards, Ernest L., Jr. 1944- *WhoAmL 94*
Edwards, Ernest Preston 1919- *WhoAm 94*
Edwards, Erwyd *Who 94*
Edwards, (Thomas) Erwyd (Pryse) 1933- *Who 94*
Edwards, Esther Gordy *WhoBlA 94*
Edwards, Ethel *WhoAmA 93*
Edwards, Eunice L. *WhoBlA 94*
Edwards, F.E. *EncSF 93*
Edwards, F. E. 1928- *WrDr 94*
Edwards, Florida d1990 *WhoHol 92*
Edwards, Floyd Kenneth 1917- *WhoAm 94, WhoWest 94*
Edwards, Francis Henry 1897- *WhAm 10*
Edwards, Franklin R. 1937- *WhoAm 94*
Edwards, Frederick Edward 1931- *Who 94*
Edwards, Frederick Mason 1948- *WhoAmP 93*
Edwards, Gail *WhoHol 92*
Edwards, Gareth Owen 1940- *Who 94*
Edwards, Gareth Owen 1947- *Who 94*
Edwards, Gawain *EncSF 93*
Edwards, Geoff *WhoHol 92*
Edwards, Geoffrey Francis 1917- *Who 94*
Edwards, Geoffrey Hartley 1936- *WhoAm 94*
Edwards, George *NewGrDO*
Edwards, George (Robert) 1908- *Who 94*
Edwards, George Alva 1916- *WhoAm 94*
Edwards, George C. 1948- *WhoAmP 93*
Edwards, George Clifton, Jr. 1914- *WhoMW 93*
Edwards, George Eugene 1960- *WhoMW 93*
Edwards, George Henry 1932- *WhoScEn 94*
Edwards, George Kent 1939- *WhoAm 94*
Edwards, George R. 1938- *WhoBlA 94*
Edwards, George Robert 1908- *IntWW 93*
Edwards, George W., Jr. 1939- *WhoAm 94*
Edwards, George Wharton 1869-1950 *WhoAmA 93N*
Edwards, Gerald Douglas 1950- *WhoBlA 94*
Edwards, Gilbert Franklin 1915- *WhoAm 94, WhoBlA 94*
Edwards, Glenn Thomas 1931- *WhoAm 94*
Edwards, Gloria d1988 *WhoHol 92*
Edwards, Glynn 1931- *WhoHol 92*
Edwards, Griffith *Who 94*
Edwards, (James) Griffith 1928- *Who 94*
Edwards, Grover Lewis, Sr. 1944- *WhoBlA 94*
Edwards, Gus d1945 *WhoHol 92*
Edwards, Guy d1986 *WhoHol 92*
Edwards, Guy Arthur 1950- *WhoAmP 93*
Edwards, Hank 1946- *WrDr 94*
Edwards, Harold Hugh, Jr. 1926- *WhoScEn 94*
Edwards, Harold Mills 1930- *WhoAm 94*
Edwards, Harold Mortimer 1936- *WhoAm 94*
Edwards, Harry d1952 *WhoHol 92*
Edwards, Harry 1942- *WhoBlA 94*
Edwards, Harry LaFoy 1936- *WhoAmL 94, WhoFI 94*
Edwards, Harry T. 1940- *CngDr 93, WhoAm 94, WhoAmL 94, WhoAmP 93, WhoBlA 94*
Edwards, Harvey 1929- *WrDr 94*
Edwards, Henry d1952 *WhoHol 92*
Edwards, Henry Percival 1939- *WhoAm 94*
Edwards, Hilton d1982 *WhoHol 92*
Edwards, Horace Burton 1925- *WhoAm 94, WhoBlA 94*
Edwards, Howard Dawson 1923- *WhoAm 94*
Edwards, Howard Lee 1931- *WhoAm 94*
Edwards, Huw William Edmund 1953- *Who 94*
Edwards, Ian Keith 1926- *WhoAm 94, WhoMW 93*
Edwards, Iorwerth (Eiddon Stephen) 1909- *WrDr 94*
Edwards, Iorwerth Eiddon Stephen 1909- *IntWW 93, Who 94*
Edwards, J. Michele 1945- *WhoMW 93*
Edwards, Jack 1928- *WhoAm 94, WhoAmP 93*
Edwards, Jack A. 1948- *WhoWest 94*
Edwards, Jack Donald 1933- *WhoAm 94*
Edwards, Jack Elmer 1955- *WhoScEn 94*
Edwards, Jack Trevor 1920- *Who 94*
Edwards, James d1970 *WhoHol 92*
Edwards, James 1756-1816 *DcNaB MP*
Edwards, James 1955- *BasBi*
Edwards, James A. 1954- *WhoAmL 94*
Edwards, James Burrows 1927- *IntWW 93, WhoAm 94, WhoAmP 93*
Edwards, James Clifford 1930- *WhoAm 94*
Edwards, James Cook 1923- *WhoAm 94*
Edwards, James D. 1943- *WhoAm 94*
Edwards, James Dallas, III 1937- *WhoFI 94, WhoMW 93*
Edwards, James Edwin 1914- *WhoAmL 94, WhoFI 94*
Edwards, James F. 1948- *WhoAmA 93*
Edwards, James Franklin 1955- *WhoBlA 94*
Edwards, James H. 1927- *IntMPA 94*
Edwards, James H. 1947- *WhoFI 94*
Edwards, James Harrell 1926- *WhoAmP 93*
Edwards, James Kennedy 1943- *WhoAm 94*
Edwards, James Lynn 1952- *WhoAm 94*
Edwards, James Malone 1931- *WhoAm 94*
Edwards, James Owen 1943- *WhoAm 94*
Edwards, James Stewart 1936- *WhoAm 94*
Edwards, James Valentine 1925- *Who 94*
Edwards, Jason *WhoHol 92*
Edwards, Jean Curtis 1929- *WhoAmP 93, WhoBlA 94*
Edwards, Jean Marie 1952- *WhoFI 94*
Edwards, Jennifer 1959- *WhoHol 92*
Edwards, Jenny Ellen 1952- *WhoAmL 94*
Edwards, Jeremy John Cary 1937- *Who 94*
Edwards, Jerome 1912- *WhoAm 94*
Edwards, Jesse Efrem 1911- *WhoAm 94*
Edwards, Jimmie Garvin 1934- *WhoScEn 94*
Edwards, Jimmy d1988 *WhoHol 92*
Edwards, Joan d1981 *WhoHol 92*
Edwards, JoAnn Louise 1955- *WhoFI 94*
Edwards, Jody d1967 *WhoHol 92*
Edwards, John d1929 *WhoHol 92*
Edwards, John Basil 1909- *Who 94*
Edwards, John Charles 1925- *Who 94*
Edwards, John Coates 1934- *IntWW 93, Who 94*
Edwards, John David 1958- *WhoFI 94, WhoMW 93*
Edwards, John Frederick 1960- *WhoAmL 94*
Edwards, John Hamilton 1922- *WhoAm 94*
Edwards, John Henry 1930- *WhoWest 94*
Edwards, John Hilton 1928- *IntWW 93, Who 94*
Edwards, John L. 1930- *WhoBlA 94*
Edwards, John Lionel 1915- *Who 94*
Edwards, John Loyd, III 1948- *WhoBlA 94*
Edwards, John M., Jr. 1945- *WhoAmL 94*
Edwards, John Phillip 1927- *Who 94*
Edwards, John Ralph 1937- *WhoAm 94, WhoScEn 94*
Edwards, John Saul 1943- *WhoAmP 93*
Edwards, John Stuart 1931- *WhoAm 94, WhoWest 94*
Edwards, John W., Jr. 1933- *WhoBlA 94*
Edwards, John Wesley, Jr. 1933- *WhoScEn 94, WhoWest 94*
Edwards, John Wesley, II 1948- *WhoAm 94, WhoAmL 94*
Edwards, John White *WhoAm 94*
Edwards, John William 1955- *WhoScEn 94*
Edwards, John Wilson 1942- *WhoBlA 94*
Edwards, Jonathan 1703-1758 *AmSocL, DcAmReB 2, EncEth, EncNAR*
Edwards, Jonathan, Jr. 1745-1801 *DcAmReB 2*
Edwards, Joseph Castro 1909- *WhoAm 94*
Edwards, Joseph Clay 1963- *WhoAmL 94*
Edwards, Joseph Robert 1908- *Who 94*
Edwards, Juanelle Barbee 1923- *WhoAmP 93*
Edwards, Judith Elizabeth 1933- *WhoMW 93*
Edwards, Julia d1976 *WhoHol 92*
Edwards, Julia Spalding 1920- *WhoAm 94*
Edwards, Julie Andrews *Who 94*
Edwards, June 1919- *WrDr 94*
Edwards, Junius 1929- *BlkWr 2, ConAu 142*
Edwards, Karin Redekopp 1948- *WhoMW 93*
Edwards, Kenneth *Who 94*
Edwards, (Alfred) Kenneth 1926- *Who 94*
Edwards, Kenneth J. 1947- *WhoBlA 94*
Edwards, Kenneth John Richard 1934- *IntWW 93, Who 94*
Edwards, Kenneth Neil 1932- *WhoAm 94, WhoScEn 94, WhoWest 94*
Edwards, Kenneth Ward 1933- *WhoScEn 94*
Edwards, Kevin 1965- *WhoBlA 94*
Edwards, Kirk Lewis 1950- *WhoFI 94, WhoWest 94*
Edwards, Larry David 1937- *WhoAm 94*
Edwards, Lee d1978 *WhoHol 92*
Edwards, Leo Derek 1937- *WhoBlA 94*
Edwards, Leroy 1913- *BasBi*
Edwards, Leslie 1916- *IntDcB [port]*
Edwards, Leverett 1902-1989 *WhAm 10*
Edwards, Lewis 1953- *WhoBlA 94*
Edwards, Linda 1951- *WhoAmA 93*
Edwards, Lionel Antony 1944- *Who 94, WhoFI 94*
Edwards, Lisa Michele 1956- *WhoMW 93*
Edwards, Llewellyn (Roy) 1935- *Who 94*
Edwards, Lonnie *WhoBlA 94*
Edwards, Lori 1957- *WhoAmP 93*
Edwards, Louis Ward, Jr. 1936- *WhoAm 94*
Edwards, Lucy Hadinoto 1963- *WhoWest 94*
Edwards, Luke 1980- *WhoHol 92*
Edwards, Lum 1902-1980 *See* Lum and Abner *WhoCom*
Edwards, Luther Howard 1954- *WhoBlA 94*
Edwards, Lydia Justice 1937- *WhoAmP 93, WhoWest 94*
Edwards, Malcolm (John) 1949- *EncSF 93*
Edwards, Malcolm John 1934- *Who 94*
Edwards, Marcus *Who 94*
Edwards, (Charles) Marcus 1937- *Who 94*
Edwards, Margaret *DrAPF 93*
Edwards, Margaret Hart 1950- *WhoAmL 94*
Edwards, Margo H. 1961- *WhoScEn 94*
Edwards, Marie Babare *WhoWest 94*
Edwards, Mark A. 1959- *WhoMW 93*
Edwards, Mark Brownlow 1939- *WhoAmL 94*
Edwards, Mark Robert 1948- *WhoWest 94*
Edwards, Marvin E. 1943- *WhoBlA 94*
Edwards, Marvin Earle 1943- *WhoAm 94*
Edwards, Marvin H. 1937- *WhoAmP 93*
Edwards, Mary Kathleen 1938- *WhoMW 93*
Edwards, Mary Matthews 1919- *WhoAmP 93*
Edwards, Mattie d1944 *WhoHol 92*
Edwards, Mattie Smith 1931- *WhoBlA 94*
Edwards, Meredith 1917- *WhoHol 92*
Edwards, Michael *Who 94*
Edwards, Michael 1938- *WrDr 94*
Edwards, (John) Michael (McFadyean) 1925- *Who 94*
Edwards, Michael David 1955- *WhoWest 94*
Edwards, Miles Stanley 1951- *WhoBlA 94*
Edwards, Monica 1912- *WrDr 94*
Edwards, Monique Marie 1961- *WhoBlA 94*
Edwards, Nancy *DrAPF 93*
Edwards, Ned Carmack, Jr. 1942- *WhoScEn 94*
Edwards, Neely d1965 *WhoHol 92*
Edwards, (Roger) Nicholas *IntWW 93*
Edwards, Ninian Murry 1922- *WhoAmL 94*
Edwards, Norman *EncSF 93*
Edwards, Norman 1938- *WrDr 94*
Edwards, Norman L. *Who 94*
Edwards, Oscar Lee 1953- *WhoBlA 94*
Edwards, Otis Carl, Jr. 1928- *WhoAm 94*
Edwards, Ovie C. 1929- *WhoAmP 93*
Edwards, Owen 1933- *Who 94*
Edwards, Page *DrAPF 93*
Edwards, Page, Jr. 1941- *WrDr 94*
Edwards, Page Lawrence, Jr. 1941- *WhoAm 94*
Edwards, Patricia Anne 1944- *Who 94*
Edwards, Patricia Burr 1918- *WhoWest 94*
Edwards, Patrick Michael 1947- *WhoWest 94*
Edwards, Patrick Ross 1940- *WhoAm 94*
Edwards, Paul Beverly 1915- *WhoScEn 94*
Edwards, Paul Burgess *WhoAmA 93*
Edwards, Paul Burgess 1934- *WhoAmA 93*
Edwards, Paul Robert 1940- *WhoWest 94*
Edwards, Penny 1928- *WhoHol 92*
Edwards, Peter 1946- *EncSF 93*
Edwards, Peter Robert 1937- *Who 94*
Edwards, Philip (Walter) 1923- *WrDr 94*
Edwards, Philip Walter 1923- *IntWW 93, Who 94*
Edwards, Phyllis Mae 1921- *WhoFI 94, WhoWest 94*
Edwards, Pierpont 1750-1826 *WhAmRev*
Edwards, Prentice Dearing 1895- *WhAm 10*
Edwards, Preston Joseph 1943- *WhoBlA 94*
Edwards, Quentin Tytler 1925- *Who 94*
Edwards, Ralph 1913- *IntMPA 94, WhoHol 92*
Edwards, Ralph M. 1933- *WhoAm 94, WhoWest 94*
Edwards, Ray Conway 1913- *WhoAm 94, WhoFI 94*
Edwards, Raymond, Jr. *WhoBlA 94*
Edwards, Richard 1523-1566 *BlmGEL*
Edwards, Richard Alan 1938- *WhoAm 94, WhoAmL 94*
Edwards, Richard Alan 1957- *WhoMW 93*
Edwards, Richard Ambrose 1922-1992 *WhAm 10*
Edwards, Richard Augustus, III 1945- *WhoAmP 93*
Edwards, Richard Charles 1949- *WhoScEn 94*
Edwards, Richard Humphrey Tudor 1939- *Who 94*
Edwards, Richard LeRoy 1943- *WhoAm 94*
Edwards, Rick *WhoHol 92*
Edwards, Rob 1963- *ConTFT 11*
Edwards, Robert d1981 *WhoHol 92*
Edwards, Robert 1879-1948 *WhoAmA 93N*
Edwards, Robert 1939- *WhoBlA 94*
Edwards, Robert Geoffrey 1925- *IntWW 93, Who 94*
Edwards, Robert Hazard 1935- *WhoAm 94*
Edwards, Robert John 1925- *IntWW 93, Who 94*
Edwards, Robert Mitchell 1950- *WhoScEn 94*
Edwards, Robert P., Jr. 1953- *WhoAmL 94*
Edwards, Robert Roy 1947- *WhoAm 94*
Edwards, Robert Septimus Friar 1910- *Who 94*
Edwards, Robert Valentino 1940- *WhoBlA 94*
Edwards, Robin Anthony 1939- *Who 94*
Edwards, Robin Morse 1947- *WhoAm 94, WhoAmL 94*
Edwards, Roger Snowden 1904- *Who 94*
Edwards, Ronald Alfred 1939- *WhoBlA 94*
Edwards, Ronald Gary 1948- *WhoMW 93*
Edwards, Ronald George 1930- *WrDr 94*
Edwards, Ronald Walter 1930- *Who 94*
Edwards, Ronald Wayne 1958- *WhoBlA 94*
Edwards, Rondle E. 1934- *WhoBlA 94*
Edwards, Ronnie Claire 1940- *WhoHol 92*
Edwards, Rupert L. 1929- *WhoBlA 94*
Edwards, Russell 1909-1991 *WhAm 10*
Edwards, Ruth McCalla 1949- *WhoBlA 94*
Edwards, Ryan Hayes *WhoAm 94*
Edwards, Sam *WhoHol 92*
Edwards, Sam d1921 *WhoHol 92*
Edwards, Sam(uel Frederick) 1928- *IntWW 93*

Edwards, Samuel Frederick 1928- *Who 94*
Edwards, Sarah d1965 *WhoHol 92*
Edwards, Sarah Pierpont 1710-1758 *BlmGWL*
Edwards, Scott d1983 *WhoHol 92*
Edwards, Sebastian 1953- *WhoAm 94*
Edwards, Shirley Heard 1949- *WhoBlA 94*
Edwards, Sian *IntWW 93*
Edwards, Sian 1959- *NewGrDO, Who 94*
Edwards, Snitz d1937 *WhoHol 92*
Edwards, Solomon 1932- *WhoBlA 94*
Edwards, Stanley Dean 1941- *WhoAmA 93*
Edwards, Stephen Allen 1953- *WhoAm 94*
Edwards, Stephen Glenn 1964- *WhoScEn 94*
Edwards, Stephen William 1958- *WhoAmL 94*
Edwards, Steven Alan 1956- *WhoAmL 94*
Edwards, Steven L. 1947- *WhoAmL 94*
Edwards, Steven Lawrence 1946- *WhoMW 93*
Edwards, Steven Mark 1947- *WhoAmL 94*
Edwards, Stewart Leslie 1914- *Who 94*
Edwards, Susan Harris 1948- *WhoAmA 93*
Edwards, Sylvia 1947- *WhoBlA 94*
Edwards, Ted d1945 *WhoHol 92*
Edwards, Theodore 1965- *WhoBlA 94*
Edwards, Theodore Thomas 1917- *WhoBlA 94*
Edwards, Theodore Unaldo 1934- *WhoBlA 94*
Edwards, Thomas Ashton 1960- *WhoAmL 94, WhoFI 94*
Edwards, Thomas Henry, Jr. 1918- *WhoFI 94*
Edwards, Thomas Oliver 1943- *WhoBlA 94*
Edwards, Thomas R(obert) 1928- *WrDr 94*
Edwards, Thomas Robert, Jr. 1928- *WhoAm 94*
Edwards, Timothy Ernest 1942- *WhoWest 94*
Edwards, Tom W., Jr. 1929- *WhoAmP 93*
Edwards, Tony *Who 94*
Edwards, Tony M. 1950- *WhoAm 94*
Edwards, Verba L. 1950- *WhoBlA 94*
Edwards, Vero C. W. *Who 94*
Edwards, Victor Henry 1940- *WhoAm 94, WhoScEn 94*
Edwards, Vince 1926- *WhoHol 92*
Edwards, Vince 1928- *IntMPA 94*
Edwards, Virginia d1964 *WhoHol 92*
Edwards, Vivian J. 1915- *WhoBlA 94*
Edwards, W. Cary, Jr. 1944- *WhoAmP 93*
Edwards, Wallace Edward, Jr. 1954- *WhoAmP 93*
Edwards, Wallace Winfield 1922- *WhoAm 94*
Edwards, Walter Meayers 1908- *WhoAm 94, WhoWest 94*
Edwards, Ward Dennis 1927- *WhoAm 94, WhoScEn 94*
Edwards, Wayne Forrest 1934- *WhoAm 94*
Edwards, Wilbur Patterson, Jr. 1949- *WhoBlA 94*
Edwards, Wilbur Shields 1916- *WhoAm 94*
Edwards, William 1723-1808 *DcNaB MP*
Edwards, William (Henry) 1938- *Who 94*
Edwards, William Charles 1934- *WhoAmP 93*
Edwards, William Foster 1946- *WhoFI 94*
Edwards, William George 1935- *WhoMW 93*
Edwards, William James 1915- *WhoAm 94*
Edwards, William Martin 1951- *WhoWest 94*
Edwards, William Philip Neville 1904- *IntWW 93, Who 94*
Edwards, William Sterling, III 1920- *WhoAm 94*
Edwards, Zeno L., Jr. *WhoAmP 93*
Edwards-Aschoff, Patricia Joann 1940- *WhoBlA 94*
Edwardsen, Kenneth Robert 1934- *WhoWest 94*
Edwards-Hollaway, Sheri Ann 1963- *WhoScEn 94*
Edwards-Jones, Ian 1923- *Who 94*
Edwards-Moss, David John *Who 94*
Edwardson, John Albert, Jr. 1949- *WhoAm 94, WhoFI 94*
Edwardson, John Richard 1923- *WhoScEn 94*
Edwards-Stuart, Antony James Cobham 1946- *Who 94*
Edwards-Tucker, Yvonne 1941- *WhoAmA 93*
Edwards-Vidal, Dimas Francisco 1965- *WhoScEn 94*
Edward the Black Prince 1330-1376 *HisWorL [port]*
Edward the Confessor fl. 1042-1066 *BlmGEL*
Eeden, Jan van den 1842-1917 *NewGrDO*
Eek, Nathaniel Sisson 1927- *WhoAm 94*
Eekman, Thomas Adam 1923- *WhoAm 94*
Eelkema, Robert Cameron 1930- *WhoAm 94*
Eells, Cushing 1810-1893 *DcAmReB 2, EncNAR*
Eells, Myron 1843-1907 *EncNAR*
Eells, Richard 1917-1992 *WhAm 10*
Eells, Richard S(edric) F(ox) 1917- *WrDr 94*
Eells, William Hastings 1924- *WhoAm 94*
Eelsen, Pierre Henri Maurice 1933- *IntWW 93*
Eernisse, Errol Peter 1940- *WhoAm 94*
Eerola, Osmo Tapio 1956- *WhoScEn 94*
Efaw, Cary R. 1949- *WhoFI 94*
Effel, Laura 1945- *WhoAmL 94*
Efferson, Henry Manning 1897- *WhAm 10*
Effert, Sven 1922- *IntWW 93*
Effinger, Cecil 1914-1990 *WhAm 10*
Effinger, Charles Edward, Jr. 1954- *WhoScEn 94*
Effinger, Charles Harvey Williams, Jr. 1935- *WhoFI 94*
Effinger, George Alec 1947- *EncSF 93, WrDr 94*
Effingham, Earl of 1905- *Who 94*
Effland, Robert E. 1939- *WhoMW 93*
Efford, Michael Robert 1950- *WhoWest 94*
Effort, Edmund D. 1949- *WhoBlA 94*
Effrat, John d1965 *WhoHol 92*
Effros, Richard Matthew 1935- *WhoScEn 94*
Efholm, Mogens 1910- *IntWW 93*
Efi, Taisi Tupuola Tufuga 1938- *IntWW 93*
Efimov *IntWW 93*
Efimov, Vitaly 1938- *WhoWest 94*
Efimov, Vitaly Borisovich 1940- *LoBiDrD*
Efken, Joel C. 1963- *WhoMW 93*
Efland, Simpson Lindsay 1913- *WhoAm 94, WhoFI 94*
Eforo, John Francis 1930- *WhoAm 94*
Efrat, Yona d1993 *NewYTBS 93*
Efremov, Ivan Antonovich *EncSF 93*
Efron, Bradley 1938- *WhoAm 94, WhoScEn 94*
Efron, Marc Fred 1942- *WhoAm 94, WhoAmL 94*
Efron, Marshall *WhoHol 92*
Efron, Robert 1927- *WhoScEn 94*
Efron, Samuel 1915- *WhoAm 94, WhoAmL 94, WhoFI 94*
Efroni, Yehuda *WhoHol 92*
Efros, Ellen Ann 1950- *WhoAm 94, WhoAmL 94*
Efros, Susan *DrAPF 93*
Efroymson, Robert Abraham 1905-1988 *WhAm 10*
Efstathiou, George Petros 1955- *Who 94*
Efstratiades, Anastasius 1951- *WhoAmL 94*
Efthimides, Aris D. 1929- *WhoHisp 94*
Eftimoff, Anita Kendall 1927- *WhoMW 93*
Ega, Francoise 1920-1976 *BlmGWL*
Egal, Mohamed Ibrahim 1928- *IntWW 93*
Egan, Bruce A. *WhoScEn 94*
Egan, Charles Joseph, Jr. 1932- *WhoAm 94, WhoAmL 94*
Egan, Charles R. d1993 *NewYTBS 93*
Egan, Cheryl Cobb 1960- *WhoWest 94*
Egan, Daniel Francis 1915- *WhoAm 94*
Egan, Eddie 1930- *WhoHol 92*
Egan, Edward M. 1932- *WhoAm 94*
Egan, Ferol 1923- *WrDr 94*
Egan, Greg 1961- *EncSF 93*
Egan, James Timothy 1946- *WhoWest 94*
Egan, Jenny *WhoHol 92*
Egan, Jerome P. 1943- *WhoAmP 93*
Egan, John (Leopold) 1939- *Who 94*
Egan, John Francis 1944- *WhoAmL 94*
Egan, John Frederick 1935- *WhoAm 94*
Egan, John Leopold 1939- *IntWW 93*
Egan, John Thomas 1937- *WhoScEn 94*
Egan, John Tinnerman 1948- *WhoWest 94*
Egan, Kevin *EncSF 93*
Egan, Kevin James 1950- *WhoAm 94, WhoAmL 94*
Egan, M. Sylvia 1930- *WhoAm 94*
Egan, M. Sylvia, Sister 1930- *WhoMW 93*
Egan, Michael James 1923- *WhoAmP 93*
Egan, Michael Joseph 1926- *WhoAm 94*
Egan, Michael Joseph, Jr. 1926- *WhoAmP 93*
Egan, Mike F. 1962- *WhoAmL 94*
Egan, Mishka d1964 *WhoHol 92*
Egan, Patrick Valentine Martin 1930- *Who 94*
Egan, Peter 1945- *WhoHol 92*
Egan, Raymond C. *WhoFI 94*
Egan, Richard d1987 *WhoHol 92*
Egan, Richard, Jr. *WhoHol 92*
Egan, Richard Leo 1917- *WhoAm 94*
Egan, Robert Joseph 1931- *WhoAmP 93*
Egan, Roger Edward 1921- *WhoAm 94*
Egan, Rory Bernard 1942- *WhoAm 94*
Egan, Russell E. 1907- *WhoAmP 93*
Egan, Sallie 1963- *WhoAmL 94*
Egan, Seamus 1924- *Who 94*
Egan, Shirley Anne *WhoAm 94*
Egan, Sister M. Ellene 1946- *WhoWest 94*
Egan, Susan Chan 1946- *WhoFI 94, WhoWest 94*
Egan, Susan S. 1944- *WhoAmL 94*
Egan, Timothy 1954- *ConAu 141*
Egan, Vincent Joseph 1921- *WhoAm 94*
Egan, Wesley William, Jr. 1946- *WhoAm 94*
Egan, William Joseph 1956- *WhoAmL 94*
Egar, Joseph Michael 1930- *WhoMW 93*
Egar, Thomas Arthur 1958- *WhoMW 93*
Egar, William Thomas 1955- *WhoScEn 94*
Egas, Camilo 1897-1962 *WhoAmA 93N*
Egas Moniz, Antonio 1874-1955 *WorScD*
Egbert, Albert d1942 *WhoHol 92*
Egbert, Elizabeth Frances 1945- *WhoAmA 93*
Egbert, Emerson Charles 1924- *WhoAm 94*
Egbert, H.M. *EncSF 93*
Egbert, Richard Cook 1927- *WhoAm 94*
Egbert, Robert Iman 1950- *WhoAm 94, WhoScEn 94*
Egbogah, Emmanuel Onu 1942- *WhoScEn 94*
Egbuna, Obi (Benedict) 1938- *WrDr 94*
Egbuna, Obi B(enedict) 1938- *ConDr 93*
Egbuonu, Zephyrinus Chiedu 1965- *WhoScEn 94*
Egburg fl. 8th cent.- *BlmGWL*
Egdahl, Richard H. 1926- *IntWW 93*
Egdahl, Richard Harrison 1926- *WhoAm 94, WhoScEn 94*
Egdell, John Duncan 1938- *Who 94*
Ege, Hans Alsnes 1924- *WhoFI 94*
Ege, Julie 1948- *WhoHol 92*
Ege, Otto F. 1888-1951 *WhoAmA 93N*
Egede, Hans 1686-1758 *WhWE*
Egede, Hans Povelsen 1686-1758 *EncNAR*
Egede, Povl d1789 *EncNAR*
Egekvist, W. Soren 1918- *WhoAm 94*
Egel, Christoph 1962- *WhoScEn 94*
Egeland, Leif 1903- *IntWW 93, Who 94*
Egeli, Cedric Baldwin 1936- *WhoAmA 93*
Egeli, Peter Even 1934- *WhoAmA 93*
Egelston, Roberta Riethmiller 1946- *WhoAm 94*
Egelston, William E. 1959- *WhoMW 93*
Egenolf, Robert F. 1946- *WhoAmL 94*
Eger, Denise Leese 1960- *WhoAm 94*
Eger, Joseph 1925- *WhoAm 94*
Eger, Marilyn Rae 1953- *WhoWest 94*
Egeria fl. 5th cent.- *BlmGWL*
Egerton *Who 94*
Egerton, David Boswell 1914- *Who 94*
Egerton, Francis 1930- *NewGrDO*
Egerton, George 1859-1945 *BlmGWL, DcLB 135 [port]*
Egerton, John Alfred Roy 1918- *Who 94*
Egerton, Philip John Caledon G. *Who 94*
Egerton, Sarah Fyge 1670-1723 *DcNaB MP*
Egerton, Seymour (John Louis) 1915- *Who 94*
Egerton, Stephen (Loftus) 1932- *Who 94*
Egerton, Stephen Loftus 1932- *IntWW 93*
Eggan, Fred Russell 1906-1991 *WhAm 10*
Eggan, Hugh Melford 1930- *WhoFI 94*
Eggar, Samantha 1939- *IntMPA 94, WhoHol 92*
Eggar, Timothy John Crommelin 1951- *Who 94*
Eggellestion, Josephus, Jr. 1949- *WhoAmP 93*
Eggeman, James Lewis 1956- *WhoAmL 94*
Eggen, Eric Carl 1946- *WhoAmP 93*
Eggen, Olin Jeuck 1919- *WhoAm 94, WhoScEn 94*
Eggenschwiler, James E. *WhoAmL 94*
Eggenton, Joseph d1946 *WhoHol 92*
Egger, Josef d1966 *WhoHol 92*
Egger, Louis Magnus 1919- *WhoAmP 93*
Egger, Roscoe L., Jr. 1920- *WhoAm 94*
Eggers, Alfred John, Jr. 1922- *WhoAm 94*
Eggers, David Frank, Jr. 1922- *WhoAm 94*
Eggers, Ernest Russell 1931- *WhoAm 94*
Eggers, George William 1883-1958 *WhoAmA 93N*
Eggers, George William Nordholtz, Jr. 1929- *WhoAm 94*
Eggers, Idamarie Rasmussen 1925- *WhoAm 94*
Eggers, James Wesley 1925- *WhoFI 94, WhoMW 93*
Eggers, Paul Walter 1919- *WhoAmL 94, WhoFI 94*
Eggers, Richard F. 1918-1979 *WhoAmA 93N*
Eggers, Richard Howell 1938- *WhoWest 94*
Eggers, Richard Lewis 1942- *WhoMW 93*
Eggert, Gerald Gordon 1926- *WhoAm 94*
Eggert, Joachim Georg Nikolas 1779-1813 *NewGrDO*
Eggert, Karen McMahan 1959- *WhoWest 94*
Eggert, Nicole *WhoHol 92*
Eggert, Robert John, Sr. 1913- *WhoAm 94, WhoFI 94, WhoScEn 94, WhoWest 94*
Eggert, Russell Raymond 1948- *WhoAm 94, WhoAmL 94, WhoMW 93*
Eggerth, Marta 1912- *WhoHol 92*
Eggertsen, Claude Andrew 1909- *WhoAm 94*
Eggertsen, Frank Thomas 1913- *WhoWest 94*
Eggertsen, John Hale 1947- *WhoAm 94*
Eggertsen, Paul Fred 1925- *WhoAm 94*
Eggington, William Robert Owen 1932- *Who 94*
Egginton, Anthony Joseph 1930- *Who 94*
Egginton, Joyce *ConAu 142*
Eggleston, Anthony Francis 1928- *Who 94*
Eggleston, Carl Ulysses 1950- *WhoAmP 93*
Eggleston, Charles Haggett 1941- *WhoFI 94*
Eggleston, Claud Hunt, III 1954- *WhoFI 94*
Eggleston, Drake Stephen 1954- *WhoScEn 94*
Eggleston, Harold Gordon 1921- *Who 94*
Eggleston, James Frederick 1927- *Who 94*
Eggleston, Jessica Chernay 1947- *WhoAmL 94*
Eggleston, Kim 1960- *BlmGWL*
Eggleston, Neverett A., Jr. *WhoBlA 94*
Eggleston, Samuel John 1926- *Who 94*
Eggleston, Willie Alexander, Jr. 1960- *WhoFI 94*
Eggleton, Anthony 1932- *Who 94*
Eggleton, Arthur C. *WhoAm 94*
Eggleton, Charles Edward 1937- *WhoFI 94*
Eggman, Jack Ray 1954- *WhoWest 94*
Egharevba, Jacob U(wadiae) 1920?- *BlkWr 2*
Eghbal, Morad 1952- *WhoScEn 94*
Egiebor, Sharon E. 1959- *WhoBlA 94*
Egilsson, Olafur 1936- *IntWW 93, Who 94*
Eginoire, Steven Louis 1953- *WhoMW 93*
Eginton, Charles Theodore 1914- *WhoAm 94*
Eginton, Warren William 1924- *WhoAm 94, WhoAmL 94*
Egizziello *NewGrDO*
Egk, Werner 1901-1983 *NewGrDO*
Egle, Davis Max 1939- *WhoAm 94, WhoScEn 94*
Egle, Jack 1924- *WhoAm 94*
Egler, Frank E(dwin) 1911- *WrDr 94*
Egler, Frank Edwin 1911- *WhoScEn 94*
Egler, Steven Lenhart 1949- *WhoMW 93*
Egleson, Jim 1907- *WhoAmA 93N*
Egleston, Fred R. 1947- *WhoAmP 93*
Egleston, Joseph 1754-1811 *WhAmRev*
Egleston, Truman G. 1931- *WhoAmA 93*
Egleton, Clive 1927- *WrDr 94*
Egleton, Clive (Frederick) 1927- *EncSF 93*
Eglevsky, Andre d1977 *WhoHol 92*
Eglevsky, Andre 1917-1977 *IntDcB [port]*
Egley, Thomas Arthur 1945- *WhoWest 94*
Egli, Alphons 1924- *IntWW 93*
Eglin, Colin Wells 1925- *IntWW 93*
Eglington, Charles Richard John 1938- *Who 94*
Eglinski, Georgann Hansen 1941- *WhoAmL 94*
Eglinton, Geoffrey 1927- *IntWW 93, Who 94*
Eglinton, William Matthew *WhoFI 94*
Eglinton and Winton, Earl of 1939- *Who 94*
Eglitis, Laimons 1929- *WhoAmA 93*
Egloff, Fred Robert 1934- *WhoMW 93*
Egmont, Earl of 1914- *Who 94*
Egnoski, Tina *DrAPF 93*
Ego-Aguirre, Ernesto 1928- *WhoScEn 94*
Egoff, Sheila A. 1918- *WrDr 94*
Egolf, C. Allan 1938- *WhoAmP 93*
Egolf, Kenneth Lee 1938- *WhoScEn 94*
Egolf, Paul Donald 1966- *WhoFI 94*
Egon, Joel d1979 *WhoHol 92*
Egorov, Nikolai Dmitrievich 1951- *LoBiDrD*
Egorov, Vladimir Grigorevich 1938- *LoBiDrD*
Egorova, Lyubov 1880-1972 *IntDcB*
Egremont, Baron 1948- *Who 94*
Egremont, Michael *EncSF 93*
Egremont, Michael 1907- *WrDr 94*
Egressy, Beni 1814-1851 *NewGrDO*

Egri, Gladys 1930- *WhoHisp 94*
Egri, Ted 1913- *WhoAmA 93*
Egual, Maria 1698-1735 *BlmGWL*
Eguchi, Kazuyuki 1952- *WhoFI 94*
Eguchi, Teiji 1926- *IntWW 93*
Eguchi, Tomonaru 1920- *IntWW 93*
Eguchi, Yasu 1938- *WhoAm 94, WhoWest 94*
Egudu, R.N. *BlkWr 2*
Egudu, Romanus N(nagbo) 1940- *BlkWr 2*
Eguiagaray Ucelay, Juan Manuel 1945- *IntWW 93*
Ehfe, William d1940 *WhoHol 92*
Ehgotz, Timothy Jon 1953- *WhoFI 94*
Ehinger, Albert Louis, Jr. 1927- *WhoAm 94*
Ehle, John *DrAPF 93*
Ehle, John 1925- *WrDr 94*
Ehle, John Marsden, Jr. 1925- *WhoAm 94*
Ehle, Robert Cannon 1939- *WhoWest 94*
Ehler, Herbert 1958- *WhoScEn 94*
Ehler, Kenneth Walter 1946- *WhoWest 94*
Ehler, Lester Ervin 1946- *WhoWest 94*
Ehler, Richard Lee 1930- *WhoWest 94*
Ehlerman, Paul Michael 1938- *WhoAm 94*
Ehlermann, Claus-Dieter 1931- *IntWW 93*
Ehlers, Carol A. 1952- *WhoAmA 93*
Ehlers, Charles H. d1993 *NewYTBS 93*
Ehlers, Eleanor May Collier 1920- *WhoWest 94*
Ehlers, Jerome *WhoHol 92*
Ehlers, Kathryn Hawes 1931- *WhoAm 94*
Ehlers, Vernon James 1934- *WhoAmP 93*
Ehlers, William Albert 1942- *WhoWest 94*
Ehlert, John Ambrose 1945- *WhoAm 94*
Ehlert, Marilyn Ann 1947- *WhoMW 93*
Ehlert, Nancy Lynne 1954- *WhoMW 93*
Ehli, Gerald James 1947- *WhoAm 94*
Ehlinger, John Joseph, Jr. 1949- *WhoAmL 94*
Ehlmann, Steven E. 1950- *WhoAmP 93*
Ehmann, Anthony Valentine 1935- *WhoAmL 94*
Ehmann, Carl William 1942- *WhoAm 94, WhoScEn 94*
Ehmann, William Donald 1931- *WhoAm 94*
Ehmen, Betty Hersey 1927- *WhoAmP 93*
Ehmen, Eldred Eugene 1944- *WhoMW 93*
Ehmke, Dale William 1944- *WhoScEn 94*
Ehmling, Miles Allen 1955- *WhoAmL 94*
Ehn, Leonore d1978 *WhoHol 92*
Ehnamani, Artemas c. 1827-c. 1902 *EncNAR*
Ehni, Bruce Loyal 1948-1986 *WhAm 10*
Ehora, Peggy Ann 1961- *WhoMW 93*
Ehre, Ida d1989 *WhoHol 92*
Ehre, Victor Tyndall 1913- *WhoAm 94*
Ehren, Charles Alexander, Jr. 1932- *WhoAm 94*
Ehrenbard, Robert 1925- *WhoAm 94*
Ehrenberg, Edward 1930- *WhoAm 94*
Ehrenberg, Herbert 1926- *IntWW 93*
Ehrenberg, Vladimir Georgiyevich 1874?-1923 *NewGrDO*
Ehrenfeld, David William 1938- *WhoAm 94, WhoScEn 94*
Ehrenfeld, John Henry 1917- *WhoAm 94*
Ehrenhaft, Johann Leo 1915- *WhoAm 94, WhoMW 93*
Ehrenhaft, Peter David 1933- *WhoAm 94*
Ehrenkrantz, David 1952- *WhoScEn 94*
Ehrenkranz, Joel S. 1935- *WhoAm 94*
Ehrenkranz, Shirley Malakoff 1920- *WhoAm 94*
Ehrenpreis, Seymour 1927- *WhoAm 94*
Ehrenreich, Barbara 1941- *WhoAm 94*
Ehrenreich, Henry 1928- *WhoAm 94*
Ehrenreich, Ron 1950- *WhoAmP 93*
Ehrensberger, Ray 1904- *WhoAm 94*
Ehrenstein, Gerald 1931- *WhoScEn 94*
Ehrenwerth, David Harry 1947- *WhoAm 94, WhoAmL 94*
Ehresmann, Donald Louis 1937- *WhoAmA 93*
Ehret, Christopher 1941- *WrDr 94*
Ehret, Robert 1925- *IntWW 93*
Ehrhardt, Anton F. 1960- *WhoScEn 94*
Ehrhart, Carl Yarkers 1918- *WhoAm 94*
Ehrhart, Earl *WhoAmP 93*
Ehrhart, Steven E. *WhoAm 94, WhoWest 94*
Ehrhart, W. D. *DrAPF 93*
Ehrhorn, Jean Helen 1943- *WhoWest 94*
Ehrhorn, Richard William 1934- *WhoAm 94*
Ehrich, Fredric F. 1928- *WhoAm 94, WhoScEn 94*
Ehrich, Sandra K. 1947- *WhoAmP 93*
Ehrig, Hartmut 1944- *WhoScEn 94*
Ehringer, Ann Graham 1938- *WhoWest 94*
Ehringer, Martha Lucy Miller 1940- *WhoWest 94*
Ehringer, William Dennis 1964- *WhoScEn 94*
Ehrke, Galen Lawrence 1949- *WhoMW 93*
Ehrle, Roy W. 1928- *WhoAm 94*
Ehrler, Bremer *WhoAmP 93*
Ehrlich, Abel 1915- *NewGrDO*
Ehrlich, Amy 1942- *TwCYAW, WhoAm 94*
Ehrlich, Bernard Herbert 1927- *WhoAm 94*
Ehrlich, Clifford John 1938- *WhoAm 94, WhoFI 94*
Ehrlich, Daniel Jacob 1951- *WhoAm 94, WhoScEn 94*
Ehrlich, Danuta 1931- *WhoMW 93*
Ehrlich, Eugene 1922- *WrDr 94*
Ehrlich, Everett Michael 1950- *WhoAm 94*
Ehrlich, Frederick 1932- *WhoScEn 94*
Ehrlich, George 1925- *WhoAmA 93, WhoMW 93*
Ehrlich, George Edward 1928- *WhoAm 94*
Ehrlich, Gert 1926- *WhoAm 94, WhoMW 93*
Ehrlich, Gertrude 1923- *WhoAm 94*
Ehrlich, Grant Conklin 1916- *WhoAm 94, WhoWest 94*
Ehrlich, Gretel *DrAPF 93*
Ehrlich, Gretel 1946- *ConAu 140*
Ehrlich, Ira Robert 1926- *WhoAm 94*
Ehrlich, Jack 1930- *WrDr 94*
Ehrlich, Joel Julius 1949- *WhoAm 94*
Ehrlich, Joseph 1950- *WhoAmL 94*
Ehrlich, Ken *ConTFT 11*
Ehrlich, M. Gordon 1930- *WhoAm 94*
Ehrlich, Margaret Isabella Gorley 1950- *WhoScEn 94*
Ehrlich, Max (Simon) 1909-1983 *EncSF 93*
Ehrlich, Melvin 1944- *WhoFI 94*
Ehrlich, Morton 1934- *WhoAm 94*
Ehrlich, Nancy Mills 1938- *WhoMW 93*
Ehrlich, Paul 1854-1915 *WorScD*
Ehrlich, Paul 1923- *WhoAm 94*
Ehrlich, Paul 1932- *EnvEnc, WrDr 94*
Ehrlich, Paul Ralph 1932- *IntWW 93, WhoAm 94, WhoScEn 94*
Ehrlich, Raymond 1918- *WhoAm 94, WhoAmL 94, WhoAmP 93*
Ehrlich, Robert L., Jr. 1957- *WhoAmP 93*
Ehrlich, Roy Melven 1928- *WhoAmP 93*
Ehrlich, S. Paul, Jr. 1932- *IntWW 93*
Ehrlich, Saul Paul, Jr. 1932- *WhoAm 94*
Ehrlich, Stephen Richard 1949- *WhoAmL 94*
Ehrlich, Thomas 1934- *IntWW 93, WhoAm 94, WhoAmL 94, WhoMW 93*
Ehrlich, Vivian Fenster 1942- *WhoAm 94*
Ehrlichman, John *DrAPF 93*
Ehrlichman, John 1925- *WrDr 94*
Ehrlichman, John Daniel 1925- *IntWW 93, WhoAm 94*
Ehrlichman, Peter S. 1950- *WhoAmL 94*
Ehrling, Sixten 1918- *NewGrDO, WhoAm 94*
Ehrman, Frederick L. 1906-1973 *WhoAmA 93N*
Ehrman, Joachim Benedict 1929- *WhoAm 94*
Ehrman, John (Patrick William) 1920- *WrDr 94*
Ehrman, John Patrick William 1920- *IntWW 93, Who 94*
Ehrman, Joseph S. 1931- *WhoAm 94, WhoAmL 94*
Ehrman, Lee 1935- *WhoAm 94*
Ehrman, Sally *DrAPF 93*
Ehrman, William Geoffrey 1950- *Who 94*
Ehrmann, Marianne 1753-1795 *BlmGWL*
Ehrmann, Robert Lincoln 1922- *WhoScEn 94*
Ehrmann, Thomas William 1935- *WhoAm 94, WhoAmL 94*
Ehrnschwender, Arthur Robert 1922- *WhoAm 94*
Ehsan, Fazl 1958- *WhoMW 93*
Ehsani, Mehrdad 1950- *WhoScEn 94*
Ehteshami, Keyoumars 1938- *WhoFI 94*
Eibel, Andrew H. 1950- *WhoAmL 94*
Eiben, Robert Michael 1922- *WhoAm 94*
Eiberger, Carl Frederick 1931- *WhoAm 94*
Eibl-Eibesfeldt, Irenaus 1928- *IntWW 93*
Eich, John Martin 1954- *WhoMW 93*
Eich, Stephen B. *WhoMW 93*
Eichacker, Milton Julian 1961- *WhoAmL 94*
Eichbaum, Edgar G. 1926- *WhoMW 93*
Eichberger, Joseph Michael 1947- *WhoAmL 94*
Eichberger, LeRoy Carl 1927- *WhoScEn 94*
Eichel, Edward W. 1932- *WhoAmA 93*
Eichelbaum, Melvin N. 1942- *WhoAmL 94*
Eichelbaum, (Johann) Thomas 1931- *Who 94*
Eichelberger, Brenda 1939- *WhoBlA 94*
Eichelberger, Charles Bell 1934- *WhoAm 94*
Eichelberger, Ethyl d1990 *WhoHol 92*
Eichelberger, John Henry, Jr. 1958- *WhoAmP 93*
Eichelberger, Robert John 1921- *WhoAm 94*
Eichelberger, William L. 1922- *WhoBlA 94*
Eichelman, Burr Simmons, Jr. 1943- *WhoAm 94*
Eichen, Marc Alan 1949- *WhoScEn 94*
Eichenberg, Fritz 1901-1990 *WhAm 10, WhoAmA 93N*
Eichenwald, Heinz Felix 1926- *WhoAm 94*
Eicher, Benjamin James 1959- *WhoAmL 94*
Eicher, David John 1961- *WhoMW 93*
Eicher, George John 1916- *WhoAm 94*
Eicher, Lawrence D. 1938- *IntWW 93*
Eicher, Roma Jean 1942- *WhoFI 94*
Eichholz, Geoffrey Gunther 1920- *WhoAm 94, WhoScEn 94*
Eichhorn, Arthur David 1953- *WhoMW 93*
Eichhorn, Bradford Reese 1954- *WhoMW 93*
Eichhorn, Douglas *DrAPF 93*
Eichhorn, Frederick Foltz, Jr. 1930- *WhoAm 94*
Eichhorn, Gunther Louis 1927- *WhoAm 94*
Eichhorn, Heinrich Karl 1927- *WhoAm 94*
Eichhorn, Lisa 1952- *IntMPA 94, WhoHol 92*
Eichinger, Marilynne H. *WhoAm 94, WhoWest 94*
Eichler, Franklin Roosevelt 1933- *WhoAm 94*
Eichler, John Frederick 1946- *WhoAmL 94*
Eichler, Ned 1930- *WrDr 94*
Eichler, Peter M. 1936- *WhoAm 94*
Eichler, Thomas P. 1944- *WhoAm 94*
Eichling, Mary Tourond 1947- *WhoMW 93*
Eichman, Charles Melvin 1950- *WhoMW 93*
Eichmann, Adolf 1906-1962 *HisWorL*
Eichner, Adelheid (Maria) 1760?-1787 *NewGrDO*
Eichner, Gregory Thomas 1961- *WhoScEn 94*
Eichner, Hans 1921- *ConAu 41NR, WhoAm 94, WrDr 94*
Eichner, Kay Marie 1955- *WhoMW 93*
Eichner, Maura *DrAPF 93*
Eichold, Samuel 1916- *WhoAm 94*
Eichorn, John Frederick Gerard, Jr. 1924- *WhoAm 94*
Eichstadt, Hermann Werner 1948- *WhoScEn 94*
Eichstaedt, Gregory Owen 1949- *WhoMW 93*
Eichwald, F. Ken 1954- *WhoHisp 94*
Eick, James E. 1937- *WhoIns 94*
Eickelberg, W. Warren Barbour 1925- *WhoScEn 94*
Eickhoff, Dennis Raymond 1944- *WhoAm 94*
Eickhoff, Harold Walter 1928- *WhoAm 94*
Eickhoff, Theodore Carl 1931- *WhoAm 94*
Eickhorst, William Sigurd 1941- *WhoAmA 93*
Eickleberg, John Edwin 1944- *WhoAm 94*
Eickman, Jennifer Lynn 1946- *WhoMW 93*
Eid, Leroy Victor 1932- *WhoMW 93*
Eid, Ursula 1949- *WhoWomW 91*
Eide, John 1943- *WhoAmA 93*
Eide, Palmer 1906-1991 *WhoAmA 93N*
Eide, Stephen Ralph 1955- *WhoAmL 94*
Eide, Tracey J. *WhoAmP 93*
Eidel, Hermann Karl 1955- *WhoFI 94*
Eidelberg, Martin 1941- *WhoAmA 93*
Eidell, Ronald George 1944- *WhoAm 94, WhoFI 94*
Eidelman, Cliff 1964- *ConTFT 11*
Eidels, Leon 1942- *WhoScEn 94*
Eidem, Bjarne Mork 1936- *IntWW 93*
Eidemiller, Donald Roy 1943- *WhoScEn 94*
Eiden, Michael Josef 1949- *WhoScEn 94*
Eiding, Paul 1957- *WhoHol 92*
Eidlitz, Walther *EncSF 93*
Eidson, Frank M. 1961- *WhoAmL 94*
Eidson, Thomas E. 1944- *WhoAm 94, WhoFI 94*
Eidson, Wanda Carroll 1922- *WhoAmP 93*
Eidsvold, Robert Henry, Jr. 1938- *WhoMW 93*
Eidt, Clarence Martin, Jr. 1935- *WhoAm 94*
Eidus, Janice *DrAPF 93*
Eidy, Jean E. *WhoAmP 93*
Eifert, Donald A. 1929- *WhoIns 94*
Eifler, Carl Frederick 1906- *WhoScEn 94, WhoWest 94*
Eifman, Boris 1946- *IntDcB*
Eifrig, David Eric 1935- *WhoAm 94*
Eig, Norman 1941- *WhoAm 94*
Eige, (Elizabeth) Lillian 1915- *WrDr 94*
Eigel, Christopher John *WhoMW 93*
Eigel, Edwin George, Jr. 1932- *WhoAm 94*
Eigeman, Christopher 1964- *WhoHol 92*
Eigen, Howard 1942- *WhoAm 94, WhoScEn 94*
Eigen, Manfred 1927- *IntWW 93, Who 94, WhoAm 94, WhoScEn 94*
Eigenbrodt, Harold John 1928- *WhoMW 93*
Eiger, Norman Nathan 1903-1990 *WhAm 10*
Eiger, Richard William 1933- *WhoAm 94*
Eighmey, Douglas Joseph, Jr. 1946- *WhoAm 94*
Eigler, Donald Mark 1953- *WhoScEn 94, WhoWest 94*
Eigner, Larry 1927- *WrDr 94*
Eigner, Richard Martin 1929- *WhoAm 94*
Eigo, J. *DrAPF 93*
Eigsti, Roger Harry 1942- *WhoAm 94, WhoFI 94, WhoWest 94*
Eiguren, Roy Lewis 1952- *WhoAm 94*
Eihusen, Virgil R. 1930- *WhoAm 94*
Eijkman, Christiaan 1858-1930 *WorScD*
Eikenberry, Arthur Raymond 1920- *WhoWest 94*
Eikenberry, Jill 1947- *IntMPA 94, WhoAm 94, WhoHol 92*
Eikenberry, Kenneth Otto 1932- *WhoAmP 93, WhoWest 94*
Eikerenkoetter, Frederick J., II 1935- *WhoBlA 94*
Eikerman, Alma *WhoAmA 93*
Eikermann, Ruth Ann 1921- *WhoMW 93*
Eiland, Gary Wayne 1951- *WhoAmL 94*
Eiland, Ray Maurice 1932- *WhoBlA 94*
Eilbacher, Cynthia 1959- *WhoHol 92*
Eilbacher, Leonard Eugene 1934- *WhoAmL 94*
Eilbacher, Lisa *IntMPA 94*
Eilbacher, Lisa 1957- *WhoHol 92*
Eilber, Janet 1951- *WhoHol 92*
Eilberg, Joshua 1921- *WhoAmP 93*
Eilbott, Don A. 1950- *WhoAmP 93*
Eilbracht, Lee Paul 1924- *WhoAm 94*
Eilen, Howard Scott 1954- *WhoAmL 94*
Eilenberg, Lawrence Ira 1947- *WhoAm 94, WhoWest 94*
Eilenberg, Samuel 1913- *IntWW 93, WhoAm 94*
Eiler, G. Roger 1944- *WhoIns 94*
Eilerman, Betty Jean 1942- *WhoWest 94*
Eilers, Fred *WhoAmA 93*
Eilers, Hazel Kraft 1910- *WrDr 94*
Eilers, Sally d1978 *WhoHol 92*
Eilers, Theresa G. 1952- *WhoAmL 94*
Eilert, Ed *WhoAmP 93*
Eilledge, Elwyn Owen Morris 1935- *Who 94*
Eilon, Samuel 1923- *Who 94, WrDr 94*
Eilts, Hermann Frederick 1922- *IntWW 93, WhoAm 94, WhoAmP 93*
Eilts, Michael Dean 1959- *WhoScEn 94*
Eilts, Susanne Elizabeth 1955- *WhoScEn 94*
Eimer, Nathan Philip 1949- *WhoAm 94, WhoAmL 94*
Eimicke, Victor William 1925- *WhoAm 94*
Ein, Daniel 1938- *WhoScEn 94*
Ein, Melvin Bennett 1932- *WhoAm 94*
Einaga, Hisahiko 1936- *WhoScEn 94*
Einaga, Yoshiyuki 1945- *WhoScEn 94*
Einarson, Baldvin Oliver 1934- *WhoAmL 94*
Einaudi, Giulio 1912- *IntWW 93*
Einaudi, Luigi R. 1936- *WhoAmP 93*
Einav, Shmuel 1942- *WhoScEn 94*
Einbender, Alvin H. 1929- *WhoAm 94, WhoFI 94*
Einbond, Bernard Lionel *DrAPF 93*
Einbond, Bernard Lionel 1937- *WrDr 94*
Einem, Gottfried von 1918- *IntWW 93, NewGrDO*
Eineman, Thomas Ralph 1957- *WhoAmL 94*
Einfalt, Linda Mary 1950- *WhoMW 93*
Einhellig, Frank Arnold 1938- *WhoMW 93*
Einhorn, Bruce Jeffrey 1954- *WhoWest 94*
Einhorn, David 1809-1879 *DcAmReB 2*
Einhorn, David Allen 1961- *WhoAmL 94, WhoFI 94*
Einhorn, Edward Martin 1936- *WhoAm 94, WhoMW 93*
Einhorn, Harold 1929- *WhoAmL 94, WhoFI 94*
Einhorn, Lawrence Henry 1942- *WhoAm 94*
Einhorn, Stephen Edward 1943- *WhoFI 94, WhoMW 93*
Einhorn, Steven Gary 1948- *WhoAm 94*
Einhorn, Wendy *DrAPF 93*
Einiger, Carol Blum 1949- *WhoAm 94*

Einiger, Roger W. 1947- WhoAm 94, WhoFI 94
Eino 1940- WhoAmA 93
Einoder, Camille Elizabeth 1937- WhoMW 93
Einreinhofer, Nancy Anne 1943- WhoAmA 93
Eins, Stefan WhoAmA 93
Einsel, David William, Jr. 1928- WhoMW 93, WhoScEn 94
Einselen, Kenneth Lee 1954- WhoMW 93
Einspruch, Burton Cyril 1935- WhoAm 94
Einspruch, Norman Gerald 1932- WhoAm 94
Einstein, Albert 1879-1955 AmSocL [port], WorScD [port]
Einstein, Alfred 1880-1952 NewGrDO
Einstein, Bob 1940- WhoCom
Einstein, Charles 1926- EncSF 93
Einstein, Clifford Jay 1939- WhoAm 94
Einstein, Frederick William Boldt 1940- WhoScEn 94
Einstein, Gilbert W. 1942- WhoAmA 93
Einstein, Stephen Jan 1945- WhoWest 94
Einsweiler, Robert Charles 1929- WhoAm 94
Einthoven, Willem 1860-1927 WorInv
Einzig, Barbara DrAPF 93
Einzig, Stanley 1942- WhoScEn 94
Eipperle, Trude 1910- NewGrDO
Eiriksdottir, Karolina 1951- NewGrDO
Eirman, Thomas Fredrick 1947- WhoWest 94
Eis, Jacalyn DrAPF 93
Eisa, Mohamed Shawky 1940- WhoFI 94
Eisaman, Josiah Reamer, III 1924- WhoAm 94
Eisberg, John Frederic 1938- WhoAmL 94
Eisberg, Robert Martin 1928- WhoAm 94
Eisch, John Joseph 1930- WhoAm 94, WhoScEn 94
Eischen, James J., Jr. 1962- WhoAmL 94
Eischen, Michael Hugh 1931- WhoAm 94
Eisele, Carolyn 1902- WhoScEn 94
Eisele, Garnett Thomas 1923- WhoAm 94, WhoAmL 94
Eisele, Milton Douglas 1910- WhoWest 94
Eisele, William David 1927- WhoFI 94
Eiselein, Frederick Elvin 1945- WhoMW 93
Eiseman, A. Quillen 1938- WhoAmP 93
Eisemann, Kurt 1923- WhoWest 94
Eisen, Charles Lee 1942- WhoAm 94, WhoAmL 94
Eisen, David John 1949- WhoMW 93
Eisen, Eric Anshel 1950- WhoAmL 94
Eisen, Frederick 1930- WhoAm 94
Eisen, Glenn Philip 1940- WhoFI 94
Eisen, Henry 1921- WhoAm 94
Eisen, Herman N(athaniel) 1918- IntWW 93
Eisen, Herman Nathaniel 1918- WhoAm 94
Eisen, Leonard 1934- WhoAm 94
Eisen, Mark 1959- WhoAm 94
Eisen, Marlene Ruth 1931- WhoMW 93
Eisen, Sydney 1929- WrDr 94
Eisenach, Robert L. 1942- WhoAmP 93
Eisenacher, Craig E. 1947- WhoIns 94
Eisenbarth, Gary L. 1947- WhoIns 94
Eisenbeis, Robert A. 1941- WhoAm 94
Eisenberg, Adi 1935- WhoAm 94, WhoScEn 94
Eisenberg, Alan 1935- WhoAm 94
Eisenberg, Albert Charles 1946- WhoAmP 93
Eisenberg, Andrew Lewis 1949- WhoAmL 94
Eisenberg, Avner WhoHol 92
Eisenberg, Barbara Anne K. 1945- WhoAm 94
Eisenberg, Bertram William 1930- WhoAmL 94
Eisenberg, David Henry 1936- WhoFI 94
Eisenberg, David Samuel 1939- WhoAm 94
Eisenberg, Deborah DrAPF 93
Eisenberg, Dorothy 1929- WhoAm 94, WhoAmL 94
Eisenberg, Howard Bruce 1946- WhoAmL 94
Eisenberg, Howard Edward 1946- WhoScEn 94
Eisenberg, Jerome Martin 1930- WhoAmA 93
Eisenberg, John Meyer 1946- WhoAm 94
Eisenberg, Jonathan Lee 1955- WhoAmL 94
Eisenberg, Jonathan Neil 1952- WhoAm 94
Eisenberg, Larry 1919- EncSF 93, WrDr 94
Eisenberg, Lawrence D. 1943- WhoAm 94, WhoAmL 94
Eisenberg, Lee B. 1946- WhoAm 94
Eisenberg, Leon 1922- IntWW 93, WhoAm 94
Eisenberg, Marc S. 1948- WhoAmA 93
Eisenberg, Marvin WhoAmA 93
Eisenberg, Marvin 1922- WhoAm 94
Eisenberg, Melvin A. 1934- WhoAm 94
Eisenberg, Meyer 1931- WhoAm 94, WhoAmL 94
Eisenberg, Milton 1928- WhoAm 94
Eisenberg, Ned WhoHol 92
Eisenberg, Pablo Samuel 1932- WhoAm 94
Eisenberg, Paul David 1939- WhoMW 93
Eisenberg, R. Neal 1936- WhoFI 94
Eisenberg, Richard M. 1942- WhoAm 94
Eisenberg, Richard S. 1943- WhoAm 94
Eisenberg, Ronald Lee 1945- WhoWest 94
Eisenberg, Ruth F. DrAPF 93
Eisenberg, Sonja Miriam 1926- WhoAm 94, WhoAmA 93
Eisenberg, Steven 1945- WhoAm 94, WhoFI 94
Eisenberg, Susan DrAPF 93
Eisenberg, Theodore 1947- WhoAm 94
Eisenberg, Theodore M. 1949- WhoAmL 94
Eisenbies, Ray Fred 1897- WhAm 10
Eisenbraun, Eric Charles 1955- WhoAmL 94
Eisenbud, Merril 1915- WhoAm 94
Eisendrath, Charles Rice 1940- WhoMW 93
Eisendrath, Edwin 1958- WhoAmP 93
Eisenhardt, Auban Ann 1946- WhoAmL 94
Eisenhardt, Roy 1939- WhoAm 94, WhoWest 94
Eisenhart, Frank J., Jr. 1945- WhoAmL 94
Eisenhauer, Gregory John 1958- WhoFI 94
Eisenhauer, John Allen 1959- WhoWest 94
Eisenhauer, Scott Albert 1962- WhoWest 94
Eisenhauer, William Joseph, Jr. 1964- WhoScEn 94
Eisenhower, Dwight D. NewYTBS 93 [port]
Eisenhower, Dwight D. 1890-1969 HisWorL [port], HisDcKW
Eisenhower, John S(heldon) D(oud) 1922- WrDr 94
Eisenhower, John Sheldon Doud 1922- IntWW 93, WhoAm 94, WhoAmP 93
Eisenkramer, Charles Carl, Jr. 1937- WhoMW 93
Eisenloh R., Edward G. 1873-1961 WhoAmA 93N
Eisenman, Peter D 1932- WrDr 94
Eisenman, Peter David 1932- WhoAm 94
Eisenman, Stephen F. 1956- ConAu 140
Eisenman, Trudy Fox 1940- WhoAm 94, WhoMW 93
Eisenmann, Ike WhoHol 92
Eisenmenger, Linda Thate 1956- WhoMW 93
Eisenpreis, Alfred 1924- WhoAm 94
Eisenshtat, Sidney Herbert 1914- WhoAm 94
Eisenson, Jon 1907- WrDr 94
Eisenstadt, Abraham S. 1920- WhoAm 94
Eisenstadt, G. Michael 1928- WhoAm 94
Eisenstadt, Jill 1963- ConAu 140
Eisenstadt, Pauline Bauman 1938- WhoAmP 93
Eisenstadt, Robert 1960- WhoMW 93
Eisenstadt, Shmuel N. 1923- IntWW 93
Eisenstadt, Shmuel Noah 1923- WrDr 94
Eisenstaedt, Alfred 1898- IntWW 93, WhoAm 94
Eisenstark, Abraham 1919- WhoScEn 94
Eisenstat, Albert A. 1930- WhoAm 94, WhoFI 94
Eisenstat, Benjamin 1915- WhoAmA 93
Eisenstat, David H. 1951- WhoAm 94
Eisenstein, Alex 1945- EncSF 93
Eisenstein, Bruce Allan 1941- WhoAm 94, WhoScEn 94
Eisenstein, Elizabeth Lewisohn 1923- WhoAm 94
Eisenstein, Julian, Mrs. 1921- WhoAmA 93
Eisenstein, Laurence Jay 1960- WhoAmP 93
Eisenstein, Michael 1950- WhoAmL 94
Eisenstein, Paul Allan 1953- WhoMW 93
Eisenstein, Phyllis 1946- EncSF 93
Eisenstein, Phyllis (Kleinstein) 1946- WrDr 94
Eisenstein, Phyllis Leah 1946- WhoMW 93
Eisenstein, Reuben 1929- WhoMW 93
Eisenstein, Samuel A. DrAPF 93
Eisenstein, Toby K. 1942- WhoAm 94
Eisentein, Sergey (Mikhaylovich) 1898-1948 NewGrDO
Eisenthal, Kenneth B. 1933- WhoAm 94
Eisentrager, James A. 1929- WhoAmA 93
Eisentraut, Madame c. 1700-c. 1735? NewGrDO
Eisenzimmer, Betty Wenner 1939- WhoFI 94
Eiser, Barbara J.A. WhoFI 94
Eiserer, Leonard Albert Carl 1916- WhoAm 94
Eiserling, Frederick Allen 1938- WhoAm 94, WhoWest 94
Eisermann, Eckehard Hermann 1943- WhoMW 93
Eisert, Debra Claire 1952- WhoAm 94
Eisert, Edward Gaver 1948- WhoAm 94, WhoAmL 94
Eisfelder, Bart E. 1946- WhoAmL 94
Eisiminger, Sterling, (Jr.) 1941- ConAu 141
Eisinger, Erica Mendelson 1944- WhoAmL 94
Eisinger, Harry 1932- WhoAmA 93
Eisinger, Irene 1903- NewGrDO
Eisinger, Peter Kendall 1942- WhoAm 94
Eisland, June M. WhoAmP 93
Eisler, Benita 1937- WrDr 94
Eisler, Colin Tobias 1931- WhoAm 94
Eisler, David Lee 1951- WhoWest 94
Eisler, Hanns 1898-1962 IntDcF 2-4, NewGrDO
Eisler, Millard Marcus 1950- WhoMW 93
Eisler, Robert David 1952- WhoWest 94
Eisler, Steven EncSF 93
Eisler, Susan Krawetz 1946- WhoAm 94
Eisley, Anthony 1925- WhoHol 92
Eisner, Carole Swid 1937- WhoAmA 93
Eisner, Dorothy 1906- WhoAmA 93N
Eisner, Elisabeth 1943- WhoAmL 94
Eisner, Elliot Wayne 1933- WhoAmA 93
Eisner, Elliott Roy 1945- WhoAmL 94
Eisner, Gisela 1925- WrDr 94
Eisner, Harvey Brian 1958- WhoWest 94
Eisner, Henry Wolfgang 1920- WhoAm 94
Eisner, Howard 1935- WhoAm 94, WhoScEn 94
Eisner, Janet Margaret 1940- WhoAm 94
Eisner, Michael D. 1942- IntMPA 94
Eisner, Michael Dammann 1942- IntWW 93, WhoAm 94, WhoFI 94, WhoWest 94
Eisner, Neil Robert 1943- WhoAmL 94
Eisner, Peter Norman 1950- WhoAm 94
Eisner, Richard Alan 1934- WhoFI 94
Eisner, Robert 1922- WhoAm 94, WrDr 94
Eisner, Ronald Richard 1933- WhoWest 94
Eisner, Thomas 1929- CurBio 93 [port], IntWW 93, WhoAm 94, WhoScEn 94
Eisner, Will 1917- WhoAm 94
Eissfeldt, Theodore L. 1950- WhoAm 94
Eissmann, Robert Fred 1924- WhoFI 94
Eiswerth, Barry Neil 1942- WhoAm 94
Eiszner, James Richard 1927-1990 WhAm 10
Eitan, Raphael 1929- IntWW 93
Eitel, Cliffe Dean 1909- WhoAmA 93N
Eitelberg, Cathie G. 1949- WhoFI 94
Eiteljorg, Harrison 1904- WhoAmA 93
Eitner, Lorenz E. A. 1919- WhoAmA 93, WrDr 94
Eitner, Lorenz Edwin Alfred 1919- WhoAm 94, WhoWest 94
Eitrheim, Norman Duane 1929- WhoMW 93
Eittreim, Richard MacNutt 1945- WhoAm 94
Eitzen, D(avid) Stanley 1934- ConAu 41NR
Eitzen, David Stanley 1934- WhoAm 94
Eizenstat, Stuart E. 1943- WhoAm 94, WhoAmL 94
Eizenstat, Stuart Elliot 1943- WhoAmP 93
Ejeta, Gebisa 1949- WhoMW 93
Ejiogu, Lem Onyeaduzim 1939- WhoMW 93
Ejsmont, Krystyna Stefania 1934- WhoWomW 91
Ek, Alan Ryan 1942- WhoAm 94
Ek, Anders 1916- WhoHol 92
Ekandem, Dominic Ignatius 1917- IntWW 93
Ekangaki, Nzo 1934- IntWW 93
Ekberg, Anita 1931- IntMPA 94, WhoHol 92
Ekberg, Carl Edwin, Jr. 1920- WhoAm 94
Ekberg, Kent Francis 1947- WhoFI 94
Ekblad, Stina WhoHol 92
Ekblaw, George Elbert 1895- WhAm 10
Ekborg, Lars d1969 WhoHol 92
Ekdahl, Janis Kay 1946- WhoAmA 93
Ekdahl, Jon Nels 1942- WhoAm 94, WhoFI 94
Eke, Abudu Yesufu 1923- IntWW 93
Eke, Kenoye Kelvin 1956- WhoBlA 94
Ekechi, Felix K. 1934- WhoBlA 94
Ekedahl, David D. 1930- WhoAm 94, WhoFI 94
Ekeland, Arne Erling 1942- WhoScEn 94
Ekelberry, Emogene 1934- WhoAmP 93
Ekelman, Daniel Louis 1926- WhoAm 94
Ekelof, Tord Johan Carl 1945- WhoScEn 94
Eker, Bjarne Reidar 1903- IntWW 93
Ekern, George Patrick 1931- WhoAm 94, WhoAmL 94
Ekern, Halvor O. 1917- WhoAmP 93
Ekernas, Sven Anders 1945- WhoAm 94
Ekirch, Arthur A., Jr. 1915- WrDr 94
Ekis, Imants 1943- WhoFI 94, WhoScEn 94
Ekizian, Harry 1921- WhoScEn 94
Ekland, Britt 1942- IntMPA 94, WhoHol 92
Eklof, Svea Christine 1951- WhoAm 94
Eklund, Bengt WhoHol 92
Eklund, Carl Andrew 1943- WhoAm 94, WhoAmL 94
Eklund, Donald Arthur 1929- WhoAm 94
Eklund, Gordon 1945- EncSF 93, WrDr 94
Eklund, Greg R. 1969- WhoAmP 93
Eklund, (Arne) Sigvard 1911- IntWW 93, Who 94
Ekman, Gosta WhoHol 92
Ekman, Gosta d1938 WhoHol 92
Ekman, Hasse 1915- WhoHol 92
Ekman, John d1949 WhoHol 92
Ekman, Kerstin 1933- BlmGWL
Ekman, Richard 1945- WhoAm 94
Ekman, Vagn Walfrid 1874-1954 WorScD
Ekmanner, Agneta WhoHol 92
Ekong, Ruth J. WhoWest 94
Ekrom, Roy Herbert 1929- WhoAm 94
Eksteen, Jacobus Adriaan 1942- IntWW 93
Ekstract, Richard Evan 1931- WhoAm 94
Ekstrand, AnnaLee Jones 1966- WhoMW 93
Ekstrand, Bruce Rowland 1940- WhoAm 94
Ekstrom, Robert Carl 1917- WhoAm 94, WhoMW 93
Ekstrom, Ruth Burt 1931- WhoAm 94
Ekstrom, Walter F. 1927- WhoFI 94
Ekstrom, William Ferdinand 1912- WhoAm 94
Ekvall, Bernt 1915- WhoMW 93
Ekwensi, C.O.D. BlkWr 2, ConAu 42NR
Ekwensi, Cyprian 1921- IntWW 93, WrDr 94
Ekwensi, Cyprian (Odiatu Duaka) 1921- BlkWr 2, ConAu 42NR
Ekwueme, Alex Ifeanyichukwu 1932- IntWW 93
Ela, Patrick H. 1948- WhoAmA 93
Ela, Patrick Hobson 1948- WhoWest 94
El-Abiad, Ahmed Hanafy 1926-1987 WhAm 10
Elad, Avri d1993 NewYTBS 93
Elad, Emanuel 1935- WhoAm 94
Elagin, Vladimir Vasilevich 1955- LoBiDrD
El-Agraa, Ali M. 1941- WhoScEn 94
Elaine, Karen 1965- WhoWest 94
Elam, Andrew Gregory, II 1932- WhoFI 94
Elam, Caroline Mary 1945- Who 94
Elam, Dorothy R. 1904- WhoBlA 94
Elam, Fred Eldon 1937- WhoAm 94
Elam, Harper Johnston, III 1926- WhoAm 94
Elam, Harry Justin 1922- WhoBlA 94
Elam, Harry Penoy 1919- WhoBlA 94
Elam, Henry d1993 Who 94N
Elam, Jack 1916- IntMPA 94, WhoHol 92
Elam, John Carlton 1924- WhoAm 94, WhoAmL 94
Elam, Leslie Albert 1938- WhoAm 94
Elam, Lloyd C. 1928- WhoBlA 94
Elam, (John) Nicholas 1939- Who 94
Elam, Pamela Lynn 1950- WhoAmP 93
El-Amin, Sa'ad 1940- WhoBlA 94
Elan, Joan d1981 WhoHol 92
Eland, Michael John 1952- Who 94
El-Ansary, Adel Ibrahim 1941- WhoAm 94
Elaraby, Nabil 1935- IntWW 93
El-Ashry, Mohamed Taha 1940- WhoAmP 93
Elath, Eliahu 1903-1990 WhAm 10
Elbarbary, Ibrahim Abdel Tawab 1933- WhoScEn 94
Elbaum, Charles 1926- WhoAm 94, WhoScEn 94
Elbaum, Marek 1941- WhoScEn 94
El-Bayya, Majed Mohammed 1963- WhoScEn 94
El-Baz, Farouk 1938- WhoAm 94, WhoScEn 94
Elbaz, Sohair Wastawy 1954- WhoAm 94
Elben, Ulrich 1950- WhoScEn 94
Elberg, Darryl Gerald 1944- WhoAm 94
Elberg, Sanford Samuel 1913- WhoAm 94
Elberger, Ronald Edward 1945- WhoAmL 94
Elbert, Joanna WhoFI 94
Elbert, Joyce WrDr 94

Elbert, Samuel 1740-1788 *AmRev, WhAmRev*
Elbert, Sarah 1937- *WrDr 94*
Elble, Rodger Jacob 1948- *WhoMW 93*
Elbon, Julia Lockridge 1941- *WhoAmP 93*
Elcar, Dana 1927- *WhoHol 92*
Elchibey (Aliev), Abulfaz Gadirgulu Ogly 1938- *LoBiDrD*
Elchuk, Steve *WhoScEn 94*
Elcoat, George Alastair 1922- *Who 94*
Elcock, Claudius Adolphus Rufus 1923- *WhoBlA 94*
Elcock, Howard (James) 1942- *WrDr 94*
El-Dabh, Halim (Abdul Messieh) 1921- *NewGrDO*
Eldard, Ron *WhoHol 92*
El-Dars, Aly Mohammed Saad 1958- *WhoMW 93*
Eldem, M. Necat 1928- *IntWW 93*
Elden, Gary Michael 1944- *WhoAm 94, WhoAmL 94*
Elder, Alexander West 1962- *WhoMW 93*
Elder, Almora Kennedy 1920- *WhoBlA 94*
Elder, Anne 1918-1976 *BlmGWL*
Elder, Arthur John 1874- *WhoAmA 93N*
Elder, Bessie Ruth 1935- *WhoScEn 94*
Elder, Curtis Harold 1921- *WhoWest 94*
Elder, David A. 1942- *WhoAmP 93*
Elder, David Morton 1936- *WhoAmA 93*
Elder, David Renwick 1920- *Who 94*
Elder, Eldon 1921- *WhoAm 94*
Elder, Fred Kingsley, Jr. 1921- *WhoAm 94*
Elder, Gary *DrAPF 93*
Elder, Geraldine H. 1937- *WhoBlA 94*
Elder, Gregory Dean 1956- *WhoWest 94*
Elder, Irma B. *WhoHisp 94*
Elder, James Carl 1947- *WhoAmL 94*
Elder, Jean Katherine 1941- *WhoAm 94, WhoMW 93*
Elder, John 1947- *WrDr 94*
Elder, John (William) 1933- *WrDr 94*
Elder, Joseph Stephen 1956- *WhoAmL 94*
Elder, Joseph Walter 1930- *WhoAm 94*
Elder, Karl *DrAPF 93*
Elder, Lee 1934- *AfrAmAl 6 [port], ConBlB 6 [port], WhoBlA 94*
Elder, Lonne, III 1931- *ConDr 93, WhoBlA 94, WhoHol 92, WrDr 94*
Elder, Marjorie Jeanne 1921- *WhoMW 93*
Elder, Mark (Philip) 1947- *NewGrDO*
Elder, Mark Lee 1935- *WhoScEn 94*
Elder, Mark Philip 1947- *IntWW 93, Who 94, WhoAm 94*
Elder, Michael (Aiken) 1931- *EncSF 93*
Elder, Michael Aiken 1931- *WrDr 94*
Elder, Muldoon 1935- *WhoAmA 93*
Elder, Murdoch George 1938- *Who 94*
Elder, R. Bruce 1947- *WhoAmA 93*
Elder, Rex Alfred 1917- *WhoAm 94*
Elder, Robert Laurie 1938- *WhoAm 94*
Elder, Robert Lee 1934- *WhoAm 94*
Elder, Ruth d1977 *WhoHol 92*
Elder, Samuel Adams 1929- *WhoAm 94*
Elder, Shirley (A.) 1931- *WrDr 94*
Elder, Stewart Taylor 1917- *WhoAm 94*
Elder, William John 1929- *WhoIns 94*
Elderfield, John 1943- *Who 94, WhoAm 94, WhoAmA 93, WrDr 94*
Elderfield, Maurice 1926- *Who 94*
Eldering, Herman George 1930- *WhoScEn 94*
Elderkin, Charles Edwin 1930- *WhoAm 94*
Elderkin, Edwin Judge 1932- *WhoAm 94*
Elderkin, Philip Leroy 1926- *WhoWest 94*
Elders, Jocelyn 1933- *WhoAmP 93*
Elders, Joycelyn *NewYTBS 93 [port]*
Elders, Joycelyn 1933- *ConBlB 6 [port], News 94-1 [port]*
Elders, M. Joycelyn 1933- *WhoBlA 94*
Elders, Minnie Joycelyn 1933- *WhoAm 94*
Eldershaw, Flora 1897-1956 *BlmGWL*
Eldershaw, M. Barnard *BlmGWL, EncSF 93*
Eldin, Gerard 1927- *IntWW 93*
Eldin, Raymond 1938- *WrDr 94*
Eldlitz, Doroth Meigs 1891-1976 *WhoAmA 93N*
Eldon, Earl of 1937- *Who 94*
Eldon, Michael Hartley 1931- *IntWW 93*
Eldon, Thor *See* Sugarcubes, The *ConMus 10*
Eldred, David Marsh 1966- *WhoFI 94*
Eldred, Gerald Marcus 1934- *WhoAm 94*
Eldred, Kenneth McKechnie 1929- *WhoAm 94, WhoScEn 94*
Eldred, Nelson Richards 1921- *WhoScEn 94*
Eldredge, Bruce B. 1952- *WhoAmA 93*
Eldredge, Bruce Beard 1952- *WhoAm 94*
Eldredge, Charles Child, III 1944- *WhoAm 94, WhoAmA 93, WhoMW 93*
Eldredge, Clifford Murray 1943- *WhoAm 94*
Eldredge, George Badge 1950- *WhoAmL 94*
Eldredge, Hanford Wentworth 1909-1991 *WhAm 10*
Eldredge, Irene d1950 *WhoHol 92*
Eldredge, Jane MacDougal 1944- *WhoAmP 93*
Eldredge, John d1961 *WhoHol 92*
Eldredge, Mary Agnes 1942- *WhoAmA 93*
Eldredge, Niles 1943- *WhoAm 94*
Eldredge, Ruth d1939 *WhoHol 92*
Eldredge, Stuart Edson 1902-1992 *WhoAmA 93N*
Eldredge, Todd *WhoAm 94*
Eldredge, William Augustus, Jr. 1925- *WhoAm 94*
Eldredge-Thompson, Linda Gaile 1959- *WhoScEn 94*
Eldridge, Bruce Frederick 1933- *WhoWest 94*
Eldridge, Charles d1922 *WhoHol 92*
Eldridge, Colin Clifford 1942- *WrDr 94*
Eldridge, David Carlton 1949- *WhoAm 94*
Eldridge, Douglas Alan 1944- *WhoAmL 94*
Eldridge, Eugene John 1956- *WhoMW 93*
Eldridge, Florence d1988 *WhoHol 92*
Eldridge, George *WhoHol 92*
Eldridge, James F. 1946- *WhoIns 94*
Eldridge, James Francis 1946- *WhoAm 94*
Eldridge, John Barron *Who 94*
Eldridge, John C. 1933- *WhoAmP 93*
Eldridge, John Cole 1933- *WhoAm 94, WhoAmL 94*
Eldridge, John E. T. 1936- *WrDr 94*
Eldridge, Josiah Baker 1927-1989 *WhAm 10*
Eldridge, Larry 1932- *WhoAm 94*
Eldridge, Marian 1936- *WrDr 94*
Eldridge, Marian (Favel Clair) 1936- *ConAu 42NR*
Eldridge, Paul 1888-1982 *EncSF 93*
Eldridge, Peter John 1937- *WhoScEn 94*
Eldridge, Richard Mark 1951- *WhoAmL 94*
Eldridge, Robert Coulter 1917- *WhoFI 94*
Eldridge, Roger *EncSF 93*
Eldridge, Ronnie 1931- *WhoAmP 93*
Eldridge, Roy d1989 *WhoHol 92*
Eldridge, Roy 1911-1989 *AfrAmAl 6*
Eldridge, Truman Kermit, Jr. 1944- *WhoAm 94, WhoAmL 94*
El-Duweini, Aadel Khalaf 1945- *WhoScEn 94*
Eleando, Mona Lisa 1960- *WhoWest 94*
Eleanor of Aquitaine c. 1122-1204 *BlmGWL, HisWorL [port]*
Eleanor of Provence 1223-1291 *BlmGWL*
Eleazer, George Robert, Jr. 1956- *WhoBlA 94*
Eleccion, Marcelino 1936- *WhoWest 94*
Elefante, Tom *IntMPA 94*
Elegant, Robert (Sampson) 1928- *WrDr 94*
Elegant, Robert Sampson 1928- *WhoAm 94*
Elegante, James M. 1947- *WhoAmL 94*
Elejalde, Cesar Carlos 1960- *WhoScEn 94*
Elek, Istvan *EncSF 93*
Elen, Gus d1940 *WhoHol 92*
Eleonore von Osterreich 1433-1480 *BlmGWL*
Elephantis fl. c. 3rd cent.BC- *BlmGWL*
Elequin, Cleto, Jr. 1933- *WhoScEn 94*
Elers, Karl Emerson 1938- *WhoAm 94*
Eles, Sandor 1936- *WhoHol 92*
Elesh, David Bert 1940- *WhoScEn 94*
Eleveld, Robert Jay 1936- *WhoAmP 93*
Elevitch, M. D. *DrAPF 93*
Elewonibi, Mohammed Thomas David 1965- *WhoBlA 94*
Eley, Daniel Douglas 1914- *IntWW 93, Who 94*
Eley, John Duane 1951- *WhoMW 93*
Eley, John L. *Who 94*
Eley, Lynn W. 1925- *WhoAm 94*
Eley, Thomas Wendell 1953- *WhoAm 94*
Elfand, Martin 1937- *IntMPA 94*
El-Fayoumy, Joanne Patricia Quinn 1930- *WhoAm 94*
Elfelt, James Sidle 1929- *WhAm 10*
Elfer, David Francis 1941- *Who 94*
Elfers, William 1918- *WhoAm 94*
Elfin, Mel 1929- *WhoAm 94*
El-Fishawy, Saad Samuel 1924- *WhoAmL 94*
Elfman, Danny 1953- *IntMPA 94, WhoAm 94*
Elfman, Danny 1954- *IntWW 93*
Elfman, Eric Michael 1954- *WhoAmL 94*
Elfner, Albert Henry, III 1944- *WhoAm 94*
Elfred, Frank Stillman 1893- *WhAm 10*
Elfring, Robert Lowell 1921- *WhoIns 94*
Elfstrom, Gary Macdonald 1944- *WhoScEn 94*
Elfvin, John Thomas 1917- *WhoAm 94, WhoAmL 94*
Elg, Taina 1930- *IntMPA 94, WhoHol 92*
El-Gammal, Abdel-Aziz Mohamed 1946- *WhoScEn 94*
Elgar, Avril 1932- *WhoHol 92*
Elgar, Edward (William) 1857-1934 *NewGrDO*
Elgart, Larry Joseph 1922- *WhoAm 94*
Elgart, Mervyn L. 1933- *WhoAm 94*
Elgavish, Ada 1946- *WhoScEn 94*
Elgavish, Gabriel Andreas 1942- *WhoScEn 94*
Elgee, Neil Johnson 1926- *IntWW 93, WhoAm 94*
Elger, William Robert, Jr. 1950- *WhoFI 94, WhoMW 93*
Elgeti, Alexander d1977 *WhoHol 92*
El-Gewely, M. Raafat 1942- *WhoScEn 94*
Elghammer, Richard William 1951- *WhoMW 93, WhoScEn 94*
Elgin, Earl of 1924- *Who 94*
Elgin, Charles Robert 1956- *WhoScEn 94*
Elgin, Gita *WhoScEn 94, WhoWest 94*
Elgin, Ron Alan 1941- *WhoAm 94, WhoFI 94, WhoWest 94*
Elgin, Suzette Haden 1936- *EncSF 93*
Elgin, (Patricia Anne) Suzette Haden (Wilkins) 1936- *WrDr 94*
Elgison, Martin J. 1951- *WhoAmL 94*
El-Gizawy, Ahmed Sherif 1945- *WhoMW 93*
Elgort, Andrew Charles 1953- *WhoScEn 94*
El-Hage, Nabil Nazih 1958- *WhoFI 94*
El-Hamalaway, Mohamed-Younis Abd-El-Sami 1947- *WhoAm 94, WhoScEn 94*
El Hanani, Jacob 1947- *WhoAmA 93*
El Hassan, Sayed Abdullah *Who 94*
El-Hodiri, Mohamed A. 1937- *WhoMW 93*
El-Husban, Tayseer Khalaf 1955- *WhoScEn 94*
Elia, Michele 1945- *WhoScEn 94*
Eliade, Mircea *EncSF 93*
Eliades, Elias 1947- *IntWW 93*
Eliades, George C. 1969- *WhoAmP 93*
Elias, Alix *WhoHol 92*
Elias, Antonio L. *WhoScEn 94*
Eliás, Blas, Jr. 1936- *WhoHisp 94*
Elias, Donald Francis 1949- *WhoScEn 94*
Elias, Fred, Sr. d1993 *NewYTBS 93*
Elias, Gerard 1944- *Who 94*
Elias, Hal 1899- *IntMPA 94*
Elias, Harold John 1920- *WhoAm 94, WhoAmA 93*
Elias, Hector *WhoHol 92*
Elias, Houghton F. 1911- *WhoMW 93*
Elias, Jack Angel 1951- *WhoScEn 94*
Elias, Jeannie *WhoHol 92*
Elias, Karen *DrAPF 93*
Elias, Marisel 1956- *WhoHisp 94*
Elias, Patrick 1947- *Who 94*
Elias, Paul S. 1926- *WhoAm 94*
Elias, Peter 1923- *IntWW 93, WhoAm 94*
Elias, Rosalind 1929- *NewGrDO*
Elias, Rosalind 1931- *WhoAm 94*
Elias, Samy E. G. 1930- *WhoAm 94, WhoScEn 94*
Elias, Santiago 1948- *WhoHisp 94*
Elias, Sheila *WhoAmA 93, WhoWest 94*
Elias, Stephen Arthur 1960- *WhoMW 93*
Elias, Steven Ernest 1952- *WhoAmL 94*
Elias, Taslim Olawale 1914-1991 *WhAm 10*
Elias, Thomas Ittan 1947- *WhoScEn 94*
Elias, Thomas Sam 1942- *WhoAm 94, WhoScEn 94, WhoWest 94*
Elias, Victor 1937- *WhoFI 94*
Elias, Ziad Malek 1934- *WhoAm 94, WhoWest 94*
Elias Octenjak, Jack 1960- *WhoFI 94*
Elias of Dereham d1245 *DcNaB MP*
Eliason, Alan Lewis 1939- *WhoWest 94*
Eliason, Bonnie Mae 1947- *WhoMW 93*
Eliason, Edward Best 1940- *WhoIns 94*
Eliason, Jon Tate 1938- *WhoMW 93*
Eliason, Norman Ellsworth 1907-1991 *WhAm 10*
Eliason, Richard I. *WhoAmP 93*
Eliason, Russell Allen 1944- *WhoAm 94, WhoAmL 94*
Eliason, Shirley 1926-1988 *WhoAmA 93N*
Eliasoph, Paula 1895- *WhoAmA 93N*
Eliasoph, Philip *WhoAmA 93*
Eliassen, Jon Eric 1947- *WhoAm 94, WhoWest 94*
Eliassen, Kjell 1929- *IntWW 93, Who 94*
Eliassen, Rolf 1911- *WhoAm 94*
Eliasson, Jan 1940- *IntWW 93*
Eliasson, Kerstin Elisabeth 1945- *WhoScEn 94*
Eliasson, Sven Olof 1933- *NewGrDO*
Elibank, Lord 1923- *Who 94*
Elibank, Master of 1964- *Who 94*
Elic, Josip *WhoHol 92*
Elicker, Gordon Leonard 1940- *WhoAm 94*
Elicker, Paul Edgar 1894- *WhAm 10*
Elicker, Paul Hamilton 1923- *IntWW 93*
Elie, Jean Andre 1943- *WhoAm 94*
Elie, Mehrdad 1959- *WhoWest 94*
Elie de Beaumont, Anne-Louise Morin-Dumesnil 1730-1783 *BlmGWL*
Elieff, Lewis Steven 1929- *WhoFI 94*
Eliel, Ernest L. 1921- *IntWW 93*
Eliel, Ernest Ludwig 1921- *WhoAm 94, WhoScEn 94*
Elien, Mona Marie 1932- *WhoFI 94, WhoScEn 94, WhoWest 94*
Eliezer, Isaac 1934- *WhoMW 93, WhoScEn 94*
Eligon, Ann Marie Paula 1957- *WhoScEn 94*
Elikann, Lawrence S. 1923- *WhoAm 94*
Elikann, Peter Todd 1953- *WhoAmL 94*
Elin, Ronald John 1939- *WhoAm 94, WhoScEn 94*
Eline, Marie d1981 *WhoHol 92*
Eling, Allen Fredrick 1952- *WhoIns 94*
Elinger, Wayne John 1943- *WhoWest 94*
Elinski, Donald Anthony *WhoMW 93*
Elinson, Henry David 1935- *WhoWest 94*
Elinson, Jack 1917- *IntWW 93, WhoAm 94*
Elioff, Irma Mercado 1956- *WhoHisp 94*
Elion, Gertrude B. 1918- *NobelP 91 [port]*
Elion, Gertrude Belle 1918- *IntWW 93, Who 94, WhoAm 94, WhoScEn 94, WorScD [port]*
Elion, Herbert A. 1923- *WhoAm 94, WhoFI 94, WhoScEn 94, WhoWest 94*
Eliopulos, Alex James 1930- *WhoAmL 94*
Eliot *Who 94*
Eliot, Lord 1966- *Who 94*
Eliot, Alexander 1919- *WhoAm 94*
Eliot, Charles William 1834-1926 *AmSocL*
Eliot, Charles William, II d1993 *NewYTBS 93 [port]*
Eliot, Charles William John 1928- *IntWW 93, WhoAm 94*
Eliot, George *NinCLC 41*
Eliot, George 1819-1880 *BlmGEL [port], BlmGWL [port], RfGShF*
Eliot, George 1936- *WrDr 94*
Eliot, John 1604-1690 *DcAmReB 2, EncNAR*
Eliot, Lucy Carter *WhoAmA 93*
Eliot, Lucy Carter 1913- *WhoAm 94*
Eliot, Peter Charles 1910- *Who 94*
Eliot, Robert Salim 1929- *WhoAm 94*
Eliot, T(homas) S(tearns) 1888-1965 *ConAu 41NR, IntDcT 2 [port]*
Eliot, Theodore Lyman, Jr. 1928- *WhoAm 94*
Eliot, Thomas Hopkinson 1907-1991 *WhAm 10*
Eliot, Thomas Stearns 1888-1965 *AmCulL [port], BlmGEL*
Eliott, E.C. 1900- *EncSF 93*
Eliott Of Stobs, Charles (Joseph Alexander) 1937- *Who 94*
Elisa, Henriqueta d1885 *BlmGWL*
Elisabeth von Nassau-Saarbrucken 1397-1456 *BlmGWL*
Elisabeth von Schonau c. 1129-1164 *BlmGWL*
Elisburg, Donald E. 1938- *WhoAmP 93*
Elisburg, Donald Earl 1938- *WhoAmL 94*
Eliscu, Fernanda d1968 *WhoHol 92*
Eliscu, Frank 1912- *WhoAm 94, WhoAmA 93*
Elish, Dan 1960- *WrDr 94*
Elish, Herbert 1933- *WhoAm 94, WhoFI 94*
Elisha, Ron 1951- *ConDr 93*
Elisha, Walter Y. 1932- *WhoAm 94, WhoFI 94*
Elisheva 1888-1949 *BlmGWL*
Elisi, Filippo c. 1724-c. 1775 *NewGrDO*
Elisofon, Eliot 1911-1973 *WhoAmA 93N*
Elis-Thomas, Baron 1946- *Who 94*
Elivas, Knarf *EncSF 93*
Elizabeth, Queen Mother 1900- *Who 94R*
Elizabeth, I *BlmGWL*
Elizabeth, I 1533-1603 *DcLB 136 [port], HisWorL [port]*
Elizabeth, I 1558-1603 *BlmGEL*
Elizabeth, II 1926- *IntWW 93*
Elizabeth, II, Queen 1926- *Who 94R, WhoWomW 91*
Elizabeth, Martha *DrAPF 93*
Elizabeth Angela Marguerite 1900- *IntWW 93*
Elizabeth II 1926- *WhoAm 94*
Elizabeth Tudor 1533-1603 *BlmGWL [port]*
Elizalde, Angel, Jr. 1953- *WhoHisp 94*
Elizalde, Felix 1931- *WhoHisp 94*
Elizardo, Kelly Patricia 1963- *WhoScEn 94*
Elizey, Chris William 1947- *WhoBlA 94*
Elizondo, Arturo 1956- *WhoHisp 94*
Elizondo, Hector 1936- *IntMPA 94, WhoAm 94, WhoHisp 94, WhoHol 92*
Elizondo, Hector G. 1939- *WhoHisp 94*
Elizondo, Joaquin d1952 *WhoHol 92*
Elizondo, Patricia Irene 1955- *WhoHisp 94*
Elizondo, Paul *WhoHisp 94*
Elizondo, Paul 1935- *WhoAmP 93*

Elizondo, Rey Soto 1940- *WhoHisp 94*
Elizondo, Rita *WhoHisp 94*
Elizondo, Roy Jesse, Jr. 1950- *WhoHisp 94*
Elizondo, Sergio D. *DrAPF 93*
Elizondo, Sergio D. 1930- *WhoHisp 94*
Elizondo, Tonatiuh 1953- *WhoHisp 94*
Elizondo, Virgil P. *WhoHisp 94*
Elizur, Joel 1952- *WrDr 94*
Elizza, Elise 1870-1926 *NewGrDO*
Elkan, Walter 1923- *Who 94*
El-Kati, Mahhmoud 1936- *WhoBlA 94*
Elkes, Joel 1913- *IntWW 93, Who 94*
Elkes, Terrence Allen 1934- *WhoAm 94*
El Khadem, Hassan S. 1923- *WhoAm 94*
Elkhadem, Saad (Eldin Amin) 1932- *WrDr 94*
Elkhadem, Saad Eldin Amin 1932- *WhoAm 94*
Elk Hair c. 1859- *EncNAR*
El-Khatib, Shukri Muhammed 1931- *WhoScEn 94*
Elkies, Noam D. *WhoScEn 94*
Elkin, Alexander 1909- *IntWW 93, Who 94*
Elkin, Benjamin 1911- *WrDr 94*
Elkin, Beverly Dawn 1933- *WhoAmA 93*
Elkin, Irvin J. *WhoAm 94, WhoFI 94*
Elkin, Jeffrey H. 1946- *WhoAm 94*
Elkin, Judith Laikin 1928- *ConAu 41NR*
Elkin, Milton 1916- *WhoAm 94*
Elkin, Rowena Caldwell 1917- *WhoAmA 93*
Elkin, Sonia Irene Linda 1932- *Who 94*
Elkin, Stanley *DrAPF 93*
Elkin, Stanley 1930- *ShSCr 12 [port]*
Elkin, Stanley (Lawrence) 1930- *WrDr 94*
Elkin, Stanley Lawrence 1930- *IntWW 93, WhoAm 94*
Elkind, David 1931- *WhoAm 94*
Elkind, Jerome Isaac 1929- *WhoScEn 94*
Elkind, Mort William 1925- *WhoFI 94*
Elkind, Mortimer Murray 1922- *WhoAm 94, WhoScEn 94, WhoWest 94*
Elkind, Sue Saniel *DrAPF 93*
Elkind, Thomas I. 1951- *WhoAm 94, WhoAmL 94*
Elkington, (Reginald) Geoffrey d1993 *Who 94N*
Elkington, William C. *DrAPF 93*
Elkins, Aaron 1935- *ConAu 18AS [port]*
Elkins, Aaron J. 1935- *WrDr 94*
Elkins, Angela Moncrief 1933- *WhoAmP 93*
Elkins, Anita Louise 1965- *WhoMW 93*
Elkins, Bettye Swales 1941- *WhoAm 94*
Elkins, David G. 1942- *WhoAmL 94*
Elkins, David J. 1941- *WhoAm 94*
Elkins, David Michael 1956- *WhoAmL 94*
Elkins, Donald Marcum 1940- *WhoAm 94*
Elkins, Dov Peretz 1937- *WrDr 94*
Elkins, Eddie d1984 *WhoHol 92*
Elkins, Francis Clark 1923- *WhoAm 94*
Elkins, Glen Ray 1933- *WhoAm 94, WhoWest 94*
Elkins, Hillard 1929- *IntMPA 94, WhoAm 94*
Elkins, James Anderson, Jr. 1919- *WhoAm 94*
Elkins, James Anderson, III 1952- *WhoFI 94*
Elkins, James E. *WhoAmP 93*
Elkins, James Paul 1924- *WhoMW 93*
Elkins, Ken Joe 1937- *WhoAm 94, WhoMW 93*
Elkins, (E) Lane 1925- *WhoAmA 93*
Elkins, Lincoln Feltch 1918- *WhoAm 94*
Elkins, Lloyd Edwin, Sr. 1912- *WhoAm 94*
Elkins, Margreta 1932- *NewGrDO*
Elkins, Michael David 1966- *WhoBlA 94*
Elkins, Robert N. 1943- *WhoScEn 94*
Elkins, Roland Lucien 1945- *WhoWest 94*
Elkins, Saul 1907- *IntMPA 94*
Elkins, Stanley Maurice 1925- *WhoAm 94*
Elkins, Toni Marcus 1946- *WhoAmA 93*
Elkins, Virgil Lynn 1925- *WhoBlA 94*
Elkman, Steven Munro 1946- *WhoFI 94*
Elko, Nicholas Thomas 1909-1991 *WhAm 10*
El Kodsi, Baroukh 1923- *WhoScEn 94*
Elkomoss, Sabry Gobran 1925- *WhoScEn 94*
Elkon, Jon 1949- *WrDr 94*
Elkon, Robert 1928-1983 *WhoAmA 93N*
Elkouri, Frank 1921- *WhoAm 94*
Elkourie, Paul 1947- *WhoScEn 94*
Elkowitz, Allan Barry 1948- *WhoScEn 94*
Elkowitz, Lloyd Kent 1936- *WhoAm 94, WhoScEn 94*
Elks, William Chester, Jr. 1952- *WhoAm 94, WhoFI 94*
Elkus, Howard Felix 1938- *WhoAm 94*
Elkus, Jonathan (Britton) 1931- *NewGrDO*
Elkus, Richard J. 1910- *WhoAm 94*
Elkus, Richard J., Jr. 1935- *WhoAm 94*
Ellacombe, John Lawrence Wemyss 1920- *Who 94*
Ellam, Gunnar 1929- *WhoWest 94*
Ellaraino 1938- *WhoBlA 94*
Ellard, Henry 1961- *WhoBlA 94*
Ellard, Hugh *WhoAmP 93*
Ellebrecht, Mark Gerard 1954- *WhoAm 94*
Elledge, Charles Cowles d1986 *WhoHol 92*
Elledge, Jim *DrAPF 93*
Elledge, Scott Bowen 1914- *WhoAm 94*
Ellefson, Judy Fay 1958- *WhoMW 93*
Ellefson, Karen Ann 1943- *WhoFI 94*
Ellefson, Timothy Harold 1953- *WhoMW 93*
Ellegood, Donald Russell 1924- *WhoAm 94, WhoWest 94*
Elleman, Barbara 1934- *WhoAm 94*
Elleman, Lawrence Robert 1940- *WhoAm 94*
Ellemann-Jensen, Uffe 1941- *IntWW 93*
Ellen *DrAPF 93*
Ellen, Eric Frank 1930- *Who 94*
Ellen, Jaye *TwCYAW*
Ellen, Minetta d1965 *WhoHol 92*
Ellen, Patricia Mae Hayward *Who 94*
Ellenbaum, Charles Otto 1944- *WhoMW 93*
Ellenberger, Diane Marie 1946- *WhoMW 93*
Ellenberger, Jack Stuart 1930- *WhoAm 94*
Ellenbogen, George 1934- *WhoAm 94*
Ellenbogen, Joan 1954- *WhoAmL 94*
Ellenbogen, Leon 1927- *WhoAm 94*
Ellenbogen, Milton Joseph 1935- *WhoAm 94*
Ellenbogen, Tina Rochelle 1952- *WhoAm 94*
Ellenborough, Baron 1926- *Who 94*
Ellenshaw, Peter 1913- *IntDcF 2-4*
Ellenstein, Robert 1923- *WhoHol 92*
Ellenzweig, Allen Bruce 1950- *WhoAmA 93*
Eller, Andrew Joseph 1963- *WhoFI 94*
Eller, Carl 1942- *WhoAm 94*
Eller, Carl L. 1942- *WhoBlA 94*
Eller, Charles Howe 1904-1992 *WhAm 10*
Eller, Evelyn 1933- *WhoAmA 93*
Eller, Gregory William 1957- *WhoWest 94*
Eller, Joseph Burton, Jr. 1941- *WhoAm 94, WhoFI 94*
Eller, Thomas Julian 1937- *WhoScEn 94, WhoWest 94*
Eller, Vernard 1927- *WrDr 94*
Eller, William Kyle 1934- *WhoFI 94*
Elleray, Anthony John 1954- *Who 94*
Ellerbe, Harry c. 1905- *WhoHol 92*
Ellerbeck, Rosemary *WrDr 94*
Ellerbee, Linda 1944- *News 93-3, WhoAm 94, WhoHol 92*
Ellerbrook, Niel Cochran 1948- *WhoAm 94, WhoFI 94*
Ellerbusch, Fred 1951- *WhoScEn 94*
Ellerby, William Mitchell 1946- *WhoAmP 93*
Ellerby, William Mitchell, Sr. 1946- *WhoBlA 94*
Ellerd, Robert A. *WhoAmP 93*
Ellerhusen, Florence Cooney d1950 *WhoAmA 93N*
Ellerhusen, Ulric H. 1879-1957 *WhoAmA 93N*
Ellerman, Annie Winifred *BlmGWL, GayLL*
Ellerman, Beverly Vigil 1952- *WhoHisp 94*
Ellerman, Curtis Howell 1959- *WhoWest 94*
Ellerman, Gene *EncSF 93*
Ellern, William B. *EncSF 93*
Ellers, Joseph Clinton 1959- *WhoAmP 93*
Ellerton, Geoffrey (James) 1920- *Who 94*
Ellerton, John 1826-1893 *DcNaB MP*
Ellerton, John Lodge 1801-1873 *NewGrDO*
Ellertson, R. Lee 1936- *WhoAmP 93*
Ellery, Arthur d1945 *WhoHol 92*
Ellery, John Blaise 1920- *WhoAm 94, WhoMW 93*
Ellery, William 1727-1820 *WhAmRev*
Elles, Baroness 1921- *Who 94, WhoWomW 91*
Elles, James Edmund Moncrieff 1949- *Who 94*
Elles, Neil Patrick Moncrieff 1919- *Who 94*
Elletson, Harold Daniel Hope 1960- *Who 94*
Ellett, Alan Sidney 1930- *WhoAm 94, WhoFI 94, WhoMW 93*
Ellett, E. Tazewell 1952- *WhoAm 94, WhoAmL 94*
Ellett, John Spears, II 1923- *WhoAmL 94*
Elleviou, (Pierre-)Jean(-Baptiste-Francois) 1769-1842 *NewGrDO*
Ellfeldt, Howard James 1937- *WhoAm 94, WhoMW 93*
Ellias, Diane *DrAPF 93*
Ellickson, Robert Chester 1941- *WhoAm 94*
Ellicott, Harold Christiansen 1918- *WhoWest 94*
Ellicott, John LeMoyne 1929- *WhoAm 94, WhoAmL 94*
Ellicott, Robert James 1927- *IntWW 93*
Ellig, Bruce Robert 1936- *WhoAm 94, WhoFI 94*
Elligan, Irvin, Jr. 1915- *WhoBlA 94*
Elligott, Linda A. 1955- *WhoScEn 94*
Ellik, Ron(ald) 1938-1968 *EncSF 93*
Elliman, Donald *WhoAm 94*
Elliman, Yvonne 1953- *WhoHol 92*
Ellin, David d1986 *WhoHol 92*
Ellin, Marvin 1923- *WhoAm 94, WhoAmL 94, WhoFI 94*
Elling, David L. 1952- *WhoAmP 93*
Elling, Laddie Joe 1917- *WhoMW 93*
Ellinger, Carol Eloise 1931- *WhoAmP 93*
Ellinger, Ilona E. 1913- *WhoAmA 93*
Ellinger, John Henry 1919- *WrDr 94*
Ellinger, John Michael 1948- *WhoMW 93*
Ellingford, William d1936 *WhoHol 92*
Ellinghaus, William M. 1922- *IntWW 93, WhoAm 94*
Ellings, Richard James 1950- *WhoWest 94*
Ellingsen, Olav 1941- *WhoFI 94*
Ellingson, Bertrum Edwin 1921- *WhoAmP 93*
Ellingson, Carol A. 1948- *WhoAmL 94*
Ellingson, David P. 1944- *WhoIns 94*
Ellingson, Lynn Marie 1957- *WhoMW 93*
Ellingson, Mark d1993 *NewYTBS 93 [port]*
Ellingson, Mark 1904-1993 *CurBio 93N*
Ellingson, Reynold Wallace 1934- *WhoAmP 93*
Ellingson, Steve 1910-1990 *WhAm 10*
Ellingson, William John 1933- *WhoAmA 93*
Ellington, Brenda Andrea 1960- *WhoBlA 94*
Ellington, Charles Ronald 1941- *WhoAm 94*
Ellington, Duke d1974 *WhoHol 92*
Ellington, Duke 1899-1974 *ConBlB 5 [port]*
Ellington, Edward Kennedy 1899-1974 *AmCulL*
Ellington, Edward Kennedy 1899-1975 *AfrAmAl 6*
Ellington, Howard W. 1938- *WhoAmA 93*
Ellington, Howard Wesley 1938- *WhoMW 93*
Ellington, James Willard 1927- *WhoScEn 94, WhoWest 94*
Ellington, Jim 1943- *WhoAmP 93*
Ellington, Joel William 1936- *WhoAmP 93*
Ellington, Joseph Andrews, Jr. 1953- *WhoAmL 94*
Ellington, Mercedes *WhoBlA 94*
Ellington, Mercer Kennedy 1919- *WhoAm 94*
Ellington, Noble 1942- *WhoAmP 93*
Ellingwood, Bruce Russell 1944- *WhoAm 94*
Ellingwood, Elmer d1971 *WhoHol 92*
Ellingwood, Herbert E. 1931- *WhoAmP 93*
Ellingworth, Richard Henry 1926- *Who 94*
Ellins, Howard A. 1951- *WhoAmL 94*
Elliot *Who 94*
Elliot, Alistair 1932- *WrDr 94*
Elliot, Andrew d1830 *WhAmRev*
Elliot, Biff 1923- *WhoHol 92*
Elliot, Bob 1950- *WhoFI 94*
Elliot, Bruce *DrAPF 93*
Elliot, Cass d1974 *WhoHol 92*
Elliot, Catherine J. 1947- *WhoAmA 93*
Elliot, Cecil d1982 *WhoHol 92*
Elliot, David Clephan 1917- *WhoAm 94*
Elliot, David H. 1941- *WhoAm 94, WhoFI 94*
Elliot, David Hawksley 1936- *WhoAm 94*
Elliot, Del d1945 *WhoHol 92*
Elliot, Denholm d1992 *IntMPA 94N*
Elliot, Douglas Gene 1941- *WhoFI 94, WhoScEn 94*
Elliot, George 1814-1893 *DcNaB MP*
Elliot, Gerald (Henry) 1923- *Who 94*
Elliot, Harry 1920- *Who 94*
Elliot, Jane 1947- *WhoHol 92*
Elliot, Jared 1928- *WhoAm 94*
Elliot, Jeffrey M. 1947- *EncSF 93, WhoAm 94, WrDr 94*
Elliot, John d1808 *WhAmRev*
Elliot, John 1918- *EncSF 93*
Elliot, John T. *WhoAm 94*
Elliot, John Theodore 1929- *WhoAmA 93*
Elliot, Laura 1926- *WhoHol 92*
Elliot, Lee *EncSF 93*
Elliot, Ralph Gregory 1936- *WhoAm 94, WhoAmL 94*
Elliot, Robert 1933- *WhoFI 94*
Elliot, Sarah Barnwell 1848-1928 *BlmGWL*
Elliot, Sean Michael 1968- *WhoAm 94*
Elliot, Sheila 1946- *WhoAmA 93*
Elliot, Willard Somers 1926- *WhoAm 94*
Elliot-Murray-Kynynmound *Who 94*
Elliot Of Harwood, Baroness 1903- *Who 94, WhoWomW 91*
Elliot-Smith, Alan Guy 1904- *Who 94*
Elliott *Who 94*
Elliott, Hon. Lord 1922- *Who 94*
Elliott, A. Wright *WhoAm 94*
Elliott, Albert Randle 1914-1990 *WhAm 10*
Elliott, Anne 1944- *WhoAmA 93*
Elliott, Anthony Daniel, III 1948- *WhoBlA 94*
Elliott, Anthony Michael Manton 1947- *Who 94*
Elliott, Arthur James 1941- *WhoAm 94*
Elliott, Barbara Jean 1927- *WhoMW 93*
Elliott, Ben G. d1993 *NewYTBS 93*
Elliott, Benjamin Paul 1920- *WhoAm 94*
Elliott, Bert d1972 *WhoHol 92*
Elliott, Bette G. 1920- *WhoAmA 93*
Elliott, Bob 1923- *WhoHol 92, WrDr 94*
Elliott, Brady Gifford 1943- *WhoAmL 94*
Elliott, Brian Robinson d1991 *IntWW 93N*
Elliott, Brian Robinson 1910- *WrDr 94*
Elliott, Bruce (Walter Gardner Lively Stacy) 1914-1973 *EncSF 93*
Elliott, Bruce John d1993 *Who 94N*
Elliott, Byron Kauffman 1899- *WhoAm 94, WhoAmL 94, WhoFI 94*
Elliott, Carl Hartley 1922- *WhoAm 94*
Elliott, Carol Harris 1950- *WhoAm 94*
Elliott, Cathy 1956- *WhoBlA 94*
Elliott, Charles Kennedy d1992 *Who 94N*
Elliott, Charles Middleton 1939- *IntWW 93, Who 94*
Elliott, Charles Thomas 1939- *Who 94*
Elliott, Charles W. 1932- *WhoFI 94*
Elliott, Chris *WhoAm 94*
Elliott, Clive (Christopher Hugh) 1945- *Who 94*
Elliott, Craig 1947- *WhoAmP 93*
Elliott, Daniel Robert, Jr. 1939- *WhoFI 94*
Elliott, Daniel Whitacre 1922- *WhoAm 94*
Elliott, Darrell Kenneth 1952- *WhoAm 94, WhoWest 94*
Elliott, Darrell Stanley, Sr. 1953- *WhoBlA 94*
Elliott, David Duncan, III 1930- *WhoAm 94*
Elliott, David H. 1941- *WhoFI 94*
Elliott, David Joseph 1953- *WhoAm 94*
Elliott, David LeRoy 1932- *WhoAm 94*
Elliott, David Murray 1930- *Who 94*
Elliott, David Stuart 1949- *Who 94*
Elliott, Denholm 1922- *WhoHol 92*
Elliott, Denholm 1922-1992 *ConTFT 11*
Elliott, Denholm Mitchell d1992 *Who 94N*
Elliott, Denholm Mitchell 1922-1992 *WhAm 10*
Elliott, Dennis Dawson 1945- *WhoFI 94*
Elliott, Derek Wesley 1958- *WhoBlA 94*
Elliott, Dick d1961 *WhoHol 92*
Elliott, Dick 1937- *WhoAmP 93*
Elliott, Donald B. 1931- *WhoAmP 93*
Elliott, Donald Harrison 1932- *WhoAm 94*
Elliott, Dorothy Baden 1914- *WhoAmA 93*
Elliott, Dorothy Gale 1948- *WhoMW 93*
Elliott, Douglas Charles 1952- *WhoWest 94*
Elliott, Eddie Mayes 1938- *WhoAm 94, WhoMW 93*
Elliott, Edward 1915- *WhoAm 94*
Elliott, Edward Procter 1916- *WhoAm 94*
Elliott, Edwin Donald, Jr. 1948- *WhoAm 94*
Elliott, Eleanor Thomas 1926- *WhoAm 94*
Elliott, Elton P. *EncSF 93*
Elliott, Emerson John 1933- *WhoAm 94*
Elliott, Emory Bernard 1942- *WhoAm 94*
Elliott, Errol Thomas 1894- *WhAm 10*
Elliott, Ewell H., Jr. 1936- *WhoAmP 93*
Elliott, Forriss Dugas *WhoBlA 94*
Elliott, Frank 1880- *WhoHol 92*
Elliott, Frank Abercrombie 1910- *Who 94*
Elliott, Frank Alan 1937- *Who 94*
Elliott, Frank George 1913- *WhoBlA 94*
Elliott, Frank Nelson 1926- *WhoAm 94*
Elliott, Frank Wallace 1930- *WhoAm 94, WhoAmL 94*
Elliott, G. H. d1962 *WhoHol 92*
Elliott, George 1932- *Who 94*
Elliott, George Arthur 1945- *WhoAm 94*
Elliott, George Byron 1928- *WhoFI 94*
Elliott, George P(aul) 1918-1980 *EncSF 93*
Elliott, Gerald Roland 1937- *WhoMW 93*

Elliott, Gertrude d1950 WhoHol 92
Elliott, Gordon d1965 WhoHol 92
Elliott, Gordon Jefferson 1928- WhoWest 94
Elliott, Graham 1960- WhoAm 94
Elliott, H(arry) Chandler 1907- EncSF 93
Elliott, Harley DrAPF 93
Elliott, Harold Marshall 1943- WhoWest 94
Elliott, Heenan d1970 WhoHol 92
Elliott, Homer Lee 1938- WhoAm 94, WhoAmL 94
Elliott, Howard, Jr. 1933- WhoAm 94
Elliott, Hugh Percival 1911- Who 94
Elliott, Humphrey Taylor 1933- WhoAmP 93
Elliott, Irvin Wesley 1925- WhoBlA 94
Elliott, J. Russell WhoBlA 94
Elliott, James A. 1941- WhoAm 94
Elliott, James Alton 1904- WhoAmP 93
Elliott, James Earl, Jr. 1957- WhoAmL 94
Elliott, James Heyer 1924- WhoAm 94, WhoAmA 93, WhoWest 94
Elliott, James Philip 1929- IntWW 93, Who 94
Elliott, James Robert 1910- WhoAm 94, WhoAmL 94
Elliott, James Sewell 1922- WhoAmP 93
Elliott, James Ward 1954- WhoAmL 94
Elliott, James William, Jr. 1950- WhoFI 94
Elliott, Janice 1931- EncSF 93, WrDr 94
Elliott, Jarrell Richard, Jr. 1958- WhoScEn 94
Elliott, Jean Ann 1933- WhoAm 94
Elliott, Jeanne Marie Koreltz 1943- WhoAm 94, WhoWest 94
Elliott, Jim 1942- WhoAmP 93
Elliott, Joe WhoAmP 93
Elliott, John WhoBlA 94
Elliott, John d1956 WhoHol 92
Elliott, John, Jr. 1921- WhoAm 94
Elliott, John Dewey 1948- WhoAmL 94
Elliott, John Dorman 1941- Who 94
Elliott, John Earl 1946- WhoScEn 94
Elliott, John Gregory 1948- WhoWest 94
Elliott, John Huxtable 1930- IntWW 93, Who 94, WrDr 94
Elliott, John Michael 1941- WhoAm 94
Elliott, Joseph Gordon, Jr. 1914- WhoAm 94
Elliott, Joy WhoBlA 94
Elliott, Karen Crawford 1955- WhoMW 93
Elliott, Kathleen Adele 1956- WhoWest 94
Elliott, Lang 1949- IntMPA 94
Elliott, Larry Doc 1953- WhoBlA 94
Elliott, Larry Gene 1965- WhoAmP 93
Elliott, Larry Leroy 1955- WhoAmP 93
Elliott, Larry Paul 1931- WhoAm 94
Elliott, Lawrence 1924- WhoAm 94
Elliott, Lee Ann WhoAm 94
Elliott, Lee Ann 1923- WhoAm 94
Elliott, Lee Ann 1927- WhoAmP 93
Elliott, Leonard d1989 WhoHol 92
Elliott, Leroy 1944- WhoWest 94
Elliott, Lillian WhoAmA 93
Elliott, Lillian d1959 WhoHol 92
Elliott, Lisa Elaine 1965- WhoAmL 94
Elliott, Lois Lawrence 1931- WhoAm 94
Elliott, Lora Louise 1962- WhoMW 93
Elliott, Lori Karen 1959- WhoBlA 94
Elliott, Mabel Agnes 1898- WhAm 10
Elliott, Marc Eldon 1955- WhoMW 93, WhoScEn 94
Elliott, Marguerite d1951 WhoHol 92
Elliott, Marianne 1948- IntWW 93, WrDr 94
Elliott, Mark 1939- Who 94
Elliott, Mark Lee 1956- WhoAmL 94
Elliott, Marvin Moore 1934- WhoMW 93
Elliott, Mary WhoHol 92
Elliott, Mary Ellen 1956- WhoMW 93
Elliott, Matthew 1739-1814 AmRev
Elliott, Maxine d1940 WhoHol 92
Elliott, Michael 1924- IntWW 93, Who 94
Elliott, Michael Alwyn 1936- Who 94
Elliott, Michael Norman 1932- Who 94
Elliott, Mildred Ellen 1927- WhoAmP 93
Elliott, Mitchell Lee 1958- WhoFI 94
Elliott, Nathan EncSF 93
Elliott, Odette 1939- ConAu 142, SmATA 75 [port]
Elliott, Odus Vernon 1940- WhoWest 94
Elliott, Oliver Douglas 1925- Who 94
Elliott, Osborn 1924- IntWW 93, WhoAm 94
Elliott, Patricia 1942- WhoHol 92
Elliott, Peggy Gordon 1937- WhoAm 94, WhoMW 93
Elliott, Peter WhoHol 92
Elliott, Peter 1941- Who 94
Elliott, Peter R. 1926- WhoAm 94, WhoMW 93
Elliott, Philip Clarkson 1903-1985 WhoAmA 93N
Elliott, R. Keith 1942- WhoFI 94
Elliott, R. L. d1977 WhoHol 92
Elliott, R. Lance 1943- WhoAm 94
Elliott, Randal (Forbes) 1922- Who 94
Elliott, Richard EncSF 93
Elliott, Richard Gibbons, Jr. 1940- WhoAm 94, WhoAmL 94
Elliott, Richard Howard 1933- WhoAmL 94, WhoFI 94
Elliott, Richard Wayne 1942- WhoAm 94, WhoAmL 94
Elliott, Robbins Leonard 1920- WhoAm 94
Elliott, Robert d1951 WhoHol 92
Elliott, Robert d1963 WhoHol 92
Elliott, Robert Anthony K. Who 94
Elliott, Robert B. 1923- WhoAm 94
Elliott, Robert Betzel 1926- WhoMW 93, WhoScEn 94
Elliott, Robert D. Who 94
Elliott, Robert Irvin WhoHol 92
Elliott, Robert James 1940- WhoWest 94
Elliott, Robert John 1934- WhoAm 94
Elliott, Robert M. 1923- WhoAm 94
Elliott, Robert Marc 1948- WhoMW 93
Elliott, Roger (James) 1928- IntWW 93, Who 94
Elliott, Roger Harley 1931- WhoAmP 93
Elliott, Ronald (Stuart) 1918- Who 94
Elliott, Ross WhoHol 92
Elliott, Ross Cox 1948- WhoWest 94
Elliott, Roy Fraser 1921- WhoAm 94
Elliott, Sam 1944- ConTFT 11, IntMPA 94, WhoAm 94, WhoHol 92
Elliott, Scott Cameron 1941- WhoAmA 93
Elliott, Scott Oller 1957- WhoAmL 94
Elliott, Sean Michael 1968- WhoBlA 94
Elliott, Shawn WhoHol 92
Elliott, Sherman John 1954- WhoMW 93
Elliott, Stephan Charles 1948- WhoWest 94
Elliott, Stephen 1920- WhoHol 92
Elliott, Sumner Locke 1917-1991 EncSF 93, WrDr 94N
Elliott, Susan Spoehrer 1937- WhoMW 93
Elliott, T. Mark 1956- WhoAmP 93
Elliott, Thomas Joseph 1941- WhoWest 94
Elliott, Thomas Michael 1942- WhoAm 94
Elliott, Tim 1948- WhoAm 94
Elliott, Timothy Stanley 1950- Who 94
Elliott, Tyron Clifford 1942- WhoAmP 93
Elliott, Vicki Jean 1952- WhoFI 94
Elliott, W. Neil 1948- WhoWest 94
Elliott, Walter Archibald Who 94
Elliott, Ward Edward Yandell 1937- WhoWest 94
Elliott, Warren G. 1927- WhoAm 94
Elliott, Wayne Allen 1939- WhoAmP 93
Elliott, Wayne Thomas 1944- WhoAmL 94
Elliott, "Wild Bill" d1965 WhoHol 92
Elliott, William d1932 WhoHol 92
Elliott, William d1983 WhoHol 92
Elliott, William Crawford 1955- WhoScEn 94
Elliott, William David 1934- WhoBlA 94
Elliott, William Gibson 1934- WhoAmL 94
Elliott, William Hall 1932- WhoAm 94
Elliott, William Homer, Jr. 1918- WhoAm 94
Elliott, William I. DrAPF 93
Elliott, William Rowcliffe 1910- Who 94, WrDr 94
Elliott Of Morpeth, Baron 1920- Who 94
Elliott-Smith, Paul Henry 1919- WhoAm 94
Elliott-Watson, Doris Jean 1932- WhoAm 94, WhoMW 93, WhoScEn 94
Ellis Who 94
Ellis, Aaron Edmund 1954- WhoWest 94
Ellis, Adrian Foss 1944- Who 94
Ellis, Albert 1913- WhoAm 94, WrDr 94
Ellis, Albert C(harles) 1947- EncSF 93
Ellis, Alec (Charles Owen) 1932- WrDr 94
Ellis, Alfred Wright 1943- WhoAmL 94
Ellis, Alice Marie 1932- WhoMW 93
Ellis, Alice Thomas Who 94
Ellis, Alice Thomas 1932- WrDr 94
Ellis, Alice Thomas (Anna Haycraft) 1932- BlmGWL
Ellis, Allan D. 1951- WhoBlA 94
Ellis, Alvin A., Jr. 1936- WhoAmP 93
Ellis, Andra 1948- WhoAmA 93
Ellis, Andrew Jackson, Jr. 1930- WhoAm 94, WhoAmL 94
Ellis, Andrew Steven 1952- Who 94
Ellis, Anita 1926- WhoHol 92
Ellis, Anne Elizabeth 1945- WhoAm 94
Ellis, Arthur Baron 1951- WhoAm 94, WhoScEn 94
Ellis, Arthur John 1932- Who 94
Ellis, Arthur Robert Malcolm 1912- Who 94
Ellis, Audrey WrDr 94
Ellis, Barnes Humphreys 1940- WhoAm 94
Ellis, Benjamin F., Jr. 1939- WhoBlA 94
Ellis, Benjamin F., Jr. 1941- WhoBlA 94
Ellis, Bernice WhoFI 94
Ellis, Bernice Allred 1932- WhoAm 94
Ellis, Birk Wolfgang 1966- WhoWest 94
Ellis, Bobby James 1941- WhoAmP 93
Ellis, Brenda Lee 1965- WhoMW 93, WhoScEn 94
Ellis, Brent 1946- NewGrDO
Ellis, Bret Easton 1964- WhoAm 94, WrDr 94
Ellis, Brian Norman 1932- WhoAm 94, WhoScEn 94
Ellis, Bruce W. 1939- WhoScEn 94
Ellis, Bryan James 1934- Who 94
Ellis, Calvert N. 1904- WhoAm 94
Ellis, Calvin H., III 1941- WhoBlA 94
Ellis, Carl Eugene 1932-1977 WhoAmA 93N
Ellis, Carlton Case 1954- WhoFI 94, WhoWest 94
Ellis, Carol Jacqueline 1929- Who 94
Ellis, Carolyn Terry 1949- WhoAm 94, WhoAmL 94
Ellis, Charles Calvert 1919-1990 WhAm 10
Ellis, Charles Richard 1935- WhoAm 94
Ellis, Cheryl Bonini 1951- WhoAm 94
Ellis, Clifford Aubrey 1935- WhoScEn 94
Ellis, Courtenay 1946- WhoAm 94, WhoAmL 94
Ellis, Craig DrAPF 93, EncSF 93
Ellis, Cynthia Atkinson 1955- WhoAmL 94
Ellis, D.E. EncSF 93
Ellis, Dale 1960- BasBi, WhoBlA 94
Ellis, Danny L. 1955- WhoAmP 93
Ellis, David Dunham 1953- WhoMW 93
Ellis, David H. 1945- WhoScEn 94
Ellis, David Maldwyn 1914- WhoAm 94
Ellis, David R. 1935- WhoScEn 94
Ellis, David Wertz 1936- WhoAm 94
Ellis, Diane d1930 WhoHol 92
Ellis, Dick WhoHol 92
Ellis, Donald Lee 1950- WhoAmL 94
Ellis, Dorsey Daniel, Jr. 1938- WhoAm 94, WhoMW 93
Ellis, Douglas, Jr. 1947- WhoBlA 94
Ellis, Dwight Holmes, III 1947- WhoAmL 94
Ellis, Dwight W., III 1940- WhoAmL 94
Ellis, E. BlmGWL
Ellis, Edna Small d1917 WhoHol 92
Ellis, Edward d1952 WhoHol 92
Ellis, Edward Robb 1911- WrDr 94
Ellis, Edward S(ylvester) 1840-1916 EncSF 93
Ellis, Edward V. 1924- WhoBlA 94
Ellis, Edward William 1918- Who 94
Ellis, Edwin d1958 WhoHol 92
Ellis, Effie O'Neal 1913- WhoBlA 94
Ellis, Eileen Mary 1933- Who 94
Ellis, Eldon Eugene 1922- WhoWest 94
Ellis, Eleanor d1982 WhoHol 92
Ellis, Elizabeth G. WhoBlA 94
Ellis, Ella T(horp) 1928- WrDr 94
Ellis, Ella Thorp DrAPF 93
Ellis, Ellen 1829-1895 BlmGWL
Ellis, Ellen Wilkins 1962- WhoFI 94
Ellis, Elliot Frederic 1929- WhoAm 94
Ellis, Elmer IntWW 93N
Ellis, Elmer Gene 1941- WhoAm 94
Ellis, Elmo Israel 1918- WhoAm 94
Ellis, Elward Dwayne 1948- WhoBlA 94
Ellis, Emory Nelson, Jr. 1929- WhoAm 94
Ellis, Ernest W. 1940- WhoBlA 94
Ellis, Eugene Joseph 1919- WhoWest 94
Ellis, Eva Lillian 1920- WhoAm 94, WhoWest 94
Ellis, Evelyn d1958 WhoHol 92
Ellis, Francis M. d1993 NewYTBS 93
Ellis, Frank d1969 WhoHol 92
Ellis, Frank C. 1913- WhoAmP 93
Ellis, Frank Corley, Jr. 1940- WhoAmP 93
Ellis, Frank Hale 1916- WhoAm 94
Ellis, Franklin Henry, Jr. 1920- WhoAm 94
Ellis, Fred K. 1939- WhoIns 94
Ellis, Fred Wilson 1914- WhoAm 94
Ellis, Frederic L. 1915- WhoBlA 94
Ellis, Fremont 1897-1985 WhoAmA 93N
Ellis, Gene DrAPF 93
Ellis, George Edwin, Jr. 1921- WhoAm 94, WhoFI 94, WhoScEn 94, WhoWest 94
Ellis, George Fitzallen, Jr. 1923- WhoAm 94
Ellis, George Francis Rayner 1939- IntWW 93, WhoScEn 94
Ellis, George Hathaway 1920- WhoAm 94
Ellis, George Richard 1937- WhoAm 94, WhoAmA 93, WhoWest 94
Ellis, George Washington 1925- WhoBlA 94
Ellis, Gerry Lynn 1957- WhoBlA 94
Ellis, Glen Edward, Jr. 1960- WhoFI 94
Ellis, Gregory Mac 1958- WhoAmL 94
Ellis, Gwynn Pennant WrDr 94
Ellis, Harold 1926- Who 94, WrDr 94
Ellis, Harold Bernard 1917- WhoAm 94
Ellis, Harrell Victor 1923- WhoAmP 93
Ellis, Harry Bearse 1921- WrDr 94
Ellis, (Henry) Havelock 1859-1939 GayLL
Ellis, Henry Havelock 1859-1939 BlmGEL
Ellis, Herb WhoHol 92
Ellis, Herbert Who 94
Ellis, (William) Herbert (Baxter) 1921- Who 94
Ellis, Herbert Wayne 1948- WhoAmL 94
Ellis, Houston d1928 WhoHol 92
Ellis, Howard Sylvester 1898- WhAm 10
Ellis, Howard Woodrow 1914- WhoAm 94
Ellis, Humphry Francis 1907- Who 94, WrDr 94
Ellis, J. Delano, II 1944- WhoBlA 94
Ellis, J. Sam WhoAmP 93
Ellis, Jack WhoHol 92
Ellis, James Alvis, Jr. 1943- WhoAmL 94
Ellis, James D. 1943- WhoAmL 94
Ellis, James Leonard 1928- WhoAmP 93
Ellis, James Reed 1921- WhoAm 94, WhoAmL 94
Ellis, James Richard 1938- WhoMW 93
Ellis, James Watson 1927- WhoAm 94
Ellis, Janet Bagshaw 1940- WhoMW 93
Ellis, Janice Rider 1939- WhoWest 94
Ellis, Jeffrey Orville 1944- WhoAmL 94
Ellis, John WhoAmP 93
Ellis, John 1925- Who 94
Ellis, John 1929- WhoAm 94
Ellis, John 1930- Who 94
Ellis, John (Rogers) 1916- Who 94
Ellis, John Carroll, Jr. 1948- WhoFI 94
Ellis, John Hagood 1928- WhoAmP 93
Ellis, John Martin 1936- IntWW 93, WhoAm 94
Ellis, John Munn, III WhoFI 94
Ellis, John Norman 1939- Who 94
Ellis, John Romaine 1922- Who 94
Ellis, John Russell 1938- Who 94
Ellis, John Taylor 1920- WhoAm 94, WhoScEn 94
Ellis, John Tracy 1905-1992 AnObit 1992, CurBio 93N, WhAm 10
Ellis, John W. 1928- WhoAm 94, WhoFI 94, WhoWest 94
Ellis, Johnell A. 1945- WhoBlA 94
Ellis, Johnny 1960- WhoAmP 93
Ellis, Johnny Charles d1968 WhoHol 92
Ellis, Jonathan Richard 1946- IntWW 93, Who 94
Ellis, Joseph Bailey 1890- WhoAmA 93N
Ellis, Joseph Newlin 1928- WhoAm 94
Ellis, Joseph Stanley d1993 Who 94N
Ellis, Julie 1933- ConAu 142, WrDr 94
Ellis, June Who 94
Ellis, (Dorothy) June 1926- Who 94
Ellis, June C. WhoHol 92
Ellis, Kate Ferguson DrAPF 93
Ellis, Keith 1927- WrDr 94
Ellis, Kent 1921- WhoAm 94
Ellis, Kerwin Ray 1959- WhoBlA 94
Ellis, LaPhonso 1970- WhoBlA 94
Ellis, Larry Rudell 1946- AfrAmG
Ellis, Laurence Edward 1932- Who 94
Ellis, Leander Theodore, Jr. 1929- WhoBlA 94
Ellis, Lee 1924- WhoWest 94
Ellis, Lee T., Jr. 1945- WhoAm 94
Ellis, Leo H. 1925- WhoWest 94
Ellis, Leroy 1940- BasBi
Ellis, Lester Neal, Jr. 1948- WhoAm 94, WhoAmL 94
Ellis, Lillian d1951 WhoHol 92
Ellis, Loren Elizabeth 1953- WhoAmA 93
Ellis, Loretta Busby 1958- WhoWest 94
Ellis, Lynn Webster 1928- WhoAm 94
Ellis, Marilyn Pope 1938- WhoBlA 94
Ellis, Mark (Karl) 1945- WrDr 94
Ellis, Martin Arthur 1933- Who 94
Ellis, Marvin Earl 1934-1982 WhAm 10
Ellis, Mary 1899- WhoHol 92
Ellis, Mary 1900- NewGrDO, Who 94
Ellis, Mary Louise Helgeson 1943- WhoAm 94
Ellis, Maxwell (Philip) 1906- Who 94
Ellis, Michael 1917- WhoAm 94
Ellis, Michael David 1952- WhoScEn 94
Ellis, Michael Eugene 1946- WhoFI 94, WhoMW 93
Ellis, Michael G. 1941- WhoAmP 93
Ellis, Michael G. 1962- WhoBlA 94
Ellis, Michael Paul 1946- WhoAmP 93
Ellis, Michael Wayne 1954- WhoMW 93
Ellis, Mollie WhoHol 92
Ellis, Nanette C. 1943- WhoMW 93
Ellis, Neal DrAPF 93
Ellis, Norman David 1943- Who 94
Ellis, O. Herbert 1916- WhoBlA 94
Ellis, Osian Gwynn 1928- IntWW 93, Who 94
Ellis, P. J. 1911- WhoBlA 94
Ellis, Patricia d1970 WhoHol 92
Ellis, Patrick 1928- WhoAm 94

Ellis, Patrick D. 1930- *WhoAmP 93*
Ellis, Peter B. 1941- *WhoAmL 94*
Ellis, Peter Hudson 1944- *WhoAm 94*
Ellis, Phyllis Mary 1939- *WhoWomW 91*
Ellis, Randall Blake 1966- *WhoFI 94*
Ellis, Ray 1921- *WhoAmA 93*
Ellis, Raymond Clinton, Jr. 1921- *WhoFI 94*
Ellis, Raymond G. 1943- *WhoAmL 94*
Ellis, Raymond Joseph 1923- *Who 94*
Ellis, Reginald John 1935- *IntWW 93, Who 94*
Ellis, Richard 1938- *WhoAmA 93*
Ellis, Richard (J.) 1960- *WrDr 94*
Ellis, Richard Hastings 1919-1989 *WhAm 10*
Ellis, Richard Peter 1931- *Who 94*
Ellis, Richard Salisbury 1950- *Who 94*
Ellis, Richard W. 1942- *WhoAmL 94*
Ellis, Robert d1973 *WhoHol 92*
Ellis, Robert d1974 *WhoHol 92*
Ellis, Robert Carroll 1923-1979 *WhoAmA 93N*
Ellis, Robert Griswold 1908- *WhoAm 94, WhoFI 94, WhoMW 93*
Ellis, Robert Harry 1928- *WhoWest 94*
Ellis, Robert Jeffry 1935- *WhoScEn 94*
Ellis, Robert Lawson, Jr. 1922- *WhoAmP 93*
Ellis, Robert M. 1922- *WhoAmA 93*
Ellis, Robert Malcolm 1922- *WhoAm 94, WhoWest 94*
Ellis, Robert Paul 1944- *WhoWest 94*
Ellis, Robert William 1939- *WhoAm 94*
Ellis, Robin 1943- *WhoHol 92*
Ellis, Robin Gareth 1935- *Who 94*
Ellis, Rodney 1954- *WhoBlA 94*
Ellis, Rodney G. 1954- *WhoAmP 93*
Ellis, Roger Henry 1910- *Who 94*
Ellis, Roger Wykeham 1929- *Who 94*
Ellis, Ronald 1925- *IntWW 93, Who 94*
Ellis, Roswell P. 1934- *WhoIns 94*
Ellis, Royston 1941- *WrDr 94*
Ellis, Rudolph Lawrence 1911- *WhoAm 94*
Ellis, Sally Strand *WhoAmA 93*
Ellis, Sarah 1952- *TwCYAW*
Ellis, Sarah Stickney 1799-1872 *BlmGWL*
Ellis, Scott 1953- *WrDr 94*
Ellis, Stephen 1951- *WhoAmA 93*
Ellis, Stephen C. 1947- *WhoAmL 94*
Ellis, Stephen Roger 1947- *WhoScEn 94*
Ellis, Susan Renee 1965- *WhoMW 93*
Ellis, Sydney 1917- *WhoAm 94*
Ellis, T(homas) Mullett 1850-1919 *EncSF 93*
Ellis, Tellis B., III 1943- *WhoBlA 94*
Ellis, Terry *WhoAmP 93*
Ellis, Terry c. 1967- *See* En Vogue *ConMus 10*
Ellis, Terry c. 1967- *See* En Vogue *News 94-1*
Ellis, (Robert) Thomas 1924- *Who 94*
Ellis, Thomas Edward 1859-1899 *DcNaB MP*
Ellis, Thomas Selby, III 1940- *WhoAm 94, WhoAmL 94*
Ellis, Tom *Who 94*
Ellis, Tyrone 1946- *WhoAmP 93*
Ellis, Verlyn Alfred 1912- *WhoAmP 93*
Ellis, Verna Jeanne 1928- *WhoAmP 93*
Ellis, Victor Seigfried 1955- *WhoWest 94*
Ellis, Vivian *Who 94*
Ellis, Vivian Elizabeth *WhoWest 94*
Ellis, Ward d1985 *WhoHol 92*
Ellis, Wayne Enoch 1945- *WhoScEn 94*
Ellis, Welbore 1713-1802 *WhAmRev*
Ellis, William Ben 1940- *WhoAm 94, WhoFI 94*
Ellis, William Grenville 1940- *WhoMW 93*
Ellis, William Harold 1925- *WhoAm 94*
Ellis, William Leigh 1908-1990 *WhAm 10*
Ellis, William Ray 1952- *WhoMW 93*
Ellis, William Reuben 1917- *WhoBlA 94*
Ellis, Willis Hill 1927- *WhoAm 94*
Ellis, Winford Gerald 1941- *WhoAm 94*
Ellis, Zachary L. *WhoBlA 94*
Ellisen, Stanley A(rthur) 1922- *WrDr 94*
Ellison, Arthur James 1920- *Who 94*
Ellison, Carol Rinkleib 1938- *WhoScEn 94*
Ellison, Curtis William 1943- *WhoMW 93*
Ellison, Cyril Lee 1916- *WhoAm 94, WhoWest 94*
Ellison, Dale Leo 1963- *WhoMW 93*
Ellison, David Charles 1957- *WhoMW 93*
Ellison, David Lee 1955- *WhoBlA 94*
Ellison, Edith d1944 *WhoHol 92*
Ellison, Elaine 1926- *WhoMW 93*
Ellison, Eugene Curtis 1949- *WhoAm 94*
Ellison, Gerald Alexander d1992 *IntWW 93N, Who 94N*
Ellison, Greg H. 1946- *WhoIns 94*
Ellison, Harlan *DrAPF 93*
Ellison, Harlan 1934- *ShSCr 14 [port]*
Ellison, Harlan (Jay) 1934- *EncSF 93, WrDr 94*
Ellison, Harlan Jay 1934- *IntWW 93, WhoAm 94*
Ellison, Henry S. 1923- *WhoBlA 94*
Ellison, Herbert Jay 1929- *WhoAm 94*
Ellison, James 1910- *WhoHol 92*
Ellison, James Oliver 1929- *WhoAm 94, WhoAmL 94*
Ellison, Joan Audrey 1928- *WrDr 94*
Ellison, John Alexander *Who 94*
Ellison, John Harold 1916- *Who 94*
Ellison, Julian, Jr. 1942- *WhoFI 94*
Ellison, Kathleen R. 1951- *WhoAmL 94*
Ellison, Keith P. 1950- *WhoAmL 94*
Ellison, Lawrence J. 1944- *WhoFI 94*
Ellison, Lorin Bruce 1932- *WhoAm 94*
Ellison, Luther Frederick 1925- *WhoScEn 94*
Ellison, Nolen M. 1941- *WhoBlA 94*
Ellison, Orval S. 1921- *WhoAmP 93*
Ellison, Pauline Allen *WhoBlA 94*
Ellison, Pervis 1967- *WhoAm 94, WhoBlA 94*
Ellison, Peter Kemp 1942- *WhoAmP 93*
Ellison, Ralph *DrAPF 93*
Ellison, Ralph 1914- *AfrAmAl 6 [port], CurBio 93 [port]*
Ellison, Ralph (Waldo) 1914- *IntWW 93, RfGShF, TwCYAW, WrDr 94*
Ellison, Ralph Henry C. *Who 94*
Ellison, Ralph Waldo 1914- *AmCulL, WhoAm 94, WhoBlA 94*
Ellison, Robert A. 1915- *WhoBlA 94*
Ellison, Robert Gordon 1916- *WhoAm 94*
Ellison, Robert W. 1946- *WhoAmA 93*
Ellison, Samuel Porter, Jr. 1914- *WhoAm 94*
Ellison, Solon Arthur 1922- *WhoAm 94*
Ellison, Thorleif 1902- *WhoScEn 94*
Ellison, Virginia Howell 1910- *WrDr 94*
Ellis-Rees, Hugh Francis 1929- *Who 94*
Elliston, Grace d1950 *WhoHol 92*
Elliston, Larry Joe 1951- *WhoFI 94*
Elliston, Mark d1925 *WhoHol 92*
Ellis-Tracy, Jo *WhoAmA 93*
Ellis-Vant, Karen McGee 1950- *WhoWest 94*
Ellman, Louise Joyce 1945- *Who 94*
Ellman-Brown, Geoffrey 1910- *Who 94*
Ellmann, Douglas Stanley 1956- *WhoAmL 94*
Ellmann, Sheila Frenkel 1931- *WhoFI 94, WhoMW 93*
Ellmann, William Marshall 1921- *WhoAm 94, WhoAmL 94*
Ellner, Carolyn Lipton 1932- *WhoAm 94, WhoWest 94*
Ellner, Paul D. 1925- *WhoAm 94, WhoScEn 94*
Elloian, Carolyn Autry *WhoAmA 93*
Elloian, Peter 1936- *WhoAmA 93*
Ellois, Edward R., Jr. 1922- *WhoBlA 94*
Ellram, Lisa Marie 1960- *WhoWest 94*
Ellroy, James 1948- *WrDr 94*
Ellsaesser, Adrienne Sue 1956- *WhoWest 94*
Ellsaesser, Hugh Walter 1920- *WhoScEn 94, WhoWest 94*
Ellsberry, Elizabeth Prather 1923- *WhoAmP 93*
Ellsler, Effie d1942 *WhoHol 92*
Ellstrand, Norman Carl 1952- *WhoWest 94*
Ellstrom-Calder, Annette 1952- *WhoMW 93*
Ellsworth, Arthur Whitney 1936- *WhoAm 94*
Ellsworth, Bob 1948- *WhoAm 94*
Ellsworth, Clarence A. 1885-1961 *WhoAmA 93N*
Ellsworth, Cynthia Ann 1950- *WhoMW 93*
Ellsworth, David G. 1941- *WhoAm 94*
Ellsworth, Duncan Steuart, Jr. 1928- *WhoAm 94*
Ellsworth, Frank L. 1943- *WhoAm 94*
Ellsworth, Gary George 1948- *WhoAmL 94*
Ellsworth, Jack d1949 *WhoHol 92*
Ellsworth, Jack Cutler 1948- *WhoFI 94*
Ellsworth, Lincoln 1880-1951 *WhWE [port]*
Ellsworth, Lucius Fuller 1941- *WhoAm 94*
Ellsworth, Oliver 1745-1807 *WhAmRev*
Ellsworth, Peter Campbell 1960- *WhoScEn 94*
Ellsworth, Ralph E. 1907- *IntWW 93, WrDr 94*
Ellsworth, Richard German 1950- *WhoWest 94*
Ellsworth, Robert 1926- *Who 94*
Ellsworth, Robert Fred 1926- *WhoAm 94*
Ellsworth, Samuel George 1916- *WhoAm 94*
Ellsworth, Stephen R. d1985 *WhoHol 92*
Ellsworth, Warren 1951- *NewGrDO*
Ellsworth, Warren Aldrich, III d1993 *NewYTBS 93*
Ellsworth, William Wallace 1918- *WhoAmP 93*
Ellwanger, C. Scott 1947- *WhoIns 94*
Ellwanger, J. David 1937- *WhoAm 94*
Ellwanger, Mike 1925- *WhoAm 94*
Ellwanger, Thomas John 1949- *WhoAm 94, WhoAmL 94*
Ellwood, Aubrey Beauclerk d1992 *Who 94N*
Ellwood, Brooks Beresford 1942- *WhoScEn 94*
Ellwood, David T. 1953- *WhoAm 94*
Ellwood, Edith E. Muesing *DrAPF 93*
Ellwood, Paul Murdock, Jr. 1926- *WhoAm 94*
Ellwood, Peter Brian 1943- *IntWW 93, Who 94*
Ellwood, Scott 1936- *WhoAm 94*
Ellwood-Filkins, Lea Beatrice 1955- *WhoFI 94*
Elly, (Richard) Charles 1942- *Who 94*
Ellzey, G. Daniel 1947- *WhoAmL 94*
Ellzey, Joe S. *WhoAmP 93*
Ellzey, Randal Edmond 1958- *WhoFI 94*
Elmachat, Ridha 1941- *WhoFI 94*
Elmaghraby, Salah Eldin 1927- *WhoAm 94*
El-Mahdi, Anas Morsi 1935- *WhoAm 94*
Elmalan, Mireille C. 1949- *WhoWomW 91*
Elmaloglou, Rebekah *WhoHol 92*
Elman, Gerry Jay 1942- *WhoAm 94*
Elman, Howard Lawrence 1938- *WhoFI 94, WhoScEn 94*
Elman, Mischa d1967 *WhoHol 92*
Elman, Naomi Geist *WhoAm 94*
Elman, Philip 1918- *WhoAm 94*
Elman, Richard *DrAPF 93*
Elman, Ziggy d1968 *WhoHol 92*
Elmandjra, Mahdi 1933- *IntWW 93*
Elmasry, Mohamed Ibrahim 1943- *WhoAm 94*
Elmendorf, DuMont Frelinghuysen, Jr. d1993 *NewYTBS 93*
Elmendorf, William Welcome 1912- *WhoAm 94*
Elmendorff, Karl (Eduard Maria) 1891-1962 *NewGrDO*
Elmer, Billy d1945 *WhoHol 92*
Elmer, Brian Christian 1936- *WhoAm 94*
Elmer, Jonathan 1745-1817 *WhAmRev*
Elmer, Michael C. 1944- *WhoAmL 94*
Elmer, Thomas J. 1948- *WhoIns 94*
Elmer, W. Owen 1938- *WhoAmP 93*
Elmer, William Morris 1915- *WhoAm 94*
Elmes, David Gordon 1942- *WhoAm 94*
Elmes, Peter Cardwell 1921- *Who 94*
Elmets, Craig Allan 1949- *WhoMW 93*
Elmets, Douglas Gregory 1958- *WhoWest 94*
Elmets, Harry Barnard 1920- *WhoAm 94*
El Mligi, Mahmoud d1983 *WhoHol 92*
Elmo, Cloe 1910-1962 *NewGrDO*
Elmore, Bob 1953- *WhoHol 92*
Elmore, C. Lamar d1993 *NewYTBS 93*
Elmore, Edward Whitehead 1938- *WhoAm 94, WhoAmL 94*
Elmore, Ernest (Carpenter) 1901-1957 *EncSF 93*
Elmore, James Walter 1917- *WhoAm 94*
Elmore, Joyce A. 1937- *WhoBlA 94*
Elmore, Louie Franklin 1951- *WhoAmL 94*
Elmore, Patricia *DrAPF 93*
Elmore, Stancliff Churchill 1921- *WhoAm 94*
Elmore, Stanley McDowell 1933- *WhoScEn 94*
Elmore, Stephen A., Sr. 1952- *WhoBlA 94*
Elmore, Timothy Scott 1959- *WhoWest 94*
Elmore, Walter A. 1925- *WhoAm 94*
El-Moursi, Houssam Hafez 1944- *WhoScEn 94*
Elmquist, David W. 1952- *WhoAmL 94*
Elmquist, Donna Lois 1948- *WhoWest 94*
Elmquist, Ronald E. *WhoAm 94*
Elms, Lauris 1931- *NewGrDO*
Elmslie, Alexander Frederic Joseph 1905- *Who 94*
Elmslie, Kenward *DrAPF 93*
Elmslie, Kenward 1929- *WrDr 94*
Elmslie, Kenward Gray 1929- *WhoAm 94*
Elmstrom, George P. 1925- *WhoWest 94*
El Mudo *EncDeaf*
El Nahass, Mohammed Refat Ahmed 1938- *WhoScEn 94*
Elnomrossy, Mokhtar Malek 1946- *WhoScEn 94*
Elodie *WhoHol 92*
Elon, Amos 1926- *WrDr 94*
Elon, Florence *DrAPF 93*
Eloranta, Edwin Walter 1943- *WhoScEn 94*
el Oudaii, Hashmi 1952- *WrDr 94*
Eloul, Kosso 1920- *WhoAmA 93*
Elous, Marv *EncSF 93*
Elovic, Barbara *DrAPF 93*
Elowitch, Annette 1942- *WhoAmA 93*
Elowitch, Robert Jason 1943- *WhoAmA 93*
Elozua, Raymon 1947- *WhoAmA 93*
Elperin, Louis Solomon 1958- *WhoWest 94*
Elphick, Michael 1946- *WhoHol 92*
Elphin, Bishop of 1918- *Who 94*
Elphinstone, Lord 1953- *Who 94*
Elphinstone, Master of 1980- *Who 94*
Elphinstone, Douglas *Who 94*
Elphinstone, (Maurice) Douglas (Warburton) 1909- *Who 94*
Elphinstone, George Keith 1746-1823 *WhAmRev*
Elphinstone, Margaret 1948- *EncSF 93*
Elphinstone of Glack, John 1924- *Who 94*
El Ramey, Ralph 1926- *WhoAmP 93*
Elrick, R. Peter M. 1946-1993 *NewYTBS 93*
Elrington, Christopher Robin 1930- *Who 94*
Elrod, Ben Moody 1930- *WhoAm 94*
Elrod, Dale Kendall 1948- *WhoMW 93*
Elrod, David Wayne 1952- *WhoScEn 94*
Elrod, Eugene Richard 1949- *WhoAm 94, WhoAmL 94*
Elrod, Harold Glenn 1918- *WhoAm 94*
Elrod, James Lake, Jr. 1954- *WhoFI 94*
Elrod, Linda Diane Henry 1947- *WhoAmL 94*
Elrod, Michael C. 1952- *WhoAmL 94*
Elrod, Richard Bryan 1949- *WhoAmL 94*
Elrod, Robert Grant 1940- *WhoAm 94*
El-Ruby, Mohamed Hassan 1956- *WhoWest 94*
El-Saadawi, Nawal *ConWorW 93*
El-Saden, Dhiya 1952- *WhoAmL 94*
Elsaesser, Robert James 1926- *WhoAm 94*
El-Saiedi, Ali Fahmy 1936- *WhoScEn 94*
Elsas, Louis Jacob, II 1937- *WhoAm 94*
Elsass, Rex 1962- *WhoAmP 93*
Elsass, Tobias Harold 1954- *WhoAmL 94*
Elsasser, Hans Friedrich 1929- *IntWW 93*
Elsasser, Walter Maurice 1904-1991 *WhAm 10*
El Sawi, Amir 1921- *Who 94*
El-Sayed, Ahmed Fayez 1948- *WhoScEn 94*
El-Sayed, Karimat Mahmoud 1933- *WhoScEn 94*
El-Sayed, Mostafa Amr 1933- *WhoScEn 94*
Elsberg, John *DrAPF 93*
Elsberg, Stuart Michael 1939- *WhoAm 94*
Elsberry, Susan Davise 1953- *WhoWest 94*
Elsbree, John Francis 1912- *WhoAm 94*
Elsbree, Langdon 1929- *WhoWest 94*
Elsbree, Wayland Hoyt 1898- *WhAm 10*
Elsbury, Ernest Edward 1937- *WhoMW 93*
Elsden, Sidney Reuben 1915- *Who 94*
Else, Carolyn Joan 1934- *WhoAm 94, WhoWest 94*
Else, Donald Peter 1932- *WhoMW 93*
Else, John 1911- *Who 94*
Else, Robert John 1918- *WhoAmA 93*
Elsea, Gene *WhoAmP 93*
Elsen, Albert Edward 1927- *WhoAm 94, WhoAmA 93, WrDr 94*
Elsen, Sheldon Howard 1928- *WhoAm 94, WhoAmL 94*
Elsener, James Edward 1943- *WhoAm 94*
Elsenhans, John Williams 1952- *WhoFI 94*
Elser, Danny Ray 1953- *WhoWest 94*
Elser, John Robert 1912- *WhoFI 94*
Elsesser, James R. *WhoFI 94*
Elsey, David *DrAPF 93*
Elsey, George M., Jr. 1918- *HisDcKW*
Elsey, George McKee 1918- *WhoAm 94, WhoFI 94*
Elsey, John H. 1945- *WhoIns 94*
El-Shawan, Aziz 1916- *NewGrDO*
Elsherbeni, Atef Zakaria 1954- *WhoScEn 94*
El-Shishini, Ali Salem 1939- *WhoFI 94*
Elsholtz, Peter d1977 *WhoHol 92*
Elsie, Lily d1962 *WhoHol 92*
Elsila, David August 1939- *WhoAm 94*
Elslande, Renaat van 1916- *IntWW 93*
Elsman, James Leonard, Jr. 1936- *WhoAm 94, WhoAmL 94*
Elsmore, Lloyd 1913- *Who 94*
Elsner, Frederick Harvey 1963- *WhoScEn 94*
Elsner, Gisela 1937- *BlmGWL*
Elsner, Jozef (Antoni Franciszek) 1769-1854 *NewGrDO*
Elsner, Larry Edward 1930- *WhoAmA 93N*
Elsner, Sidney Edgar 1919- *WhoAm 94*
Elsner Furman, Susan 1957- *WhoFI 94*
Elsom, Cecil Harry 1912- *Who 94*
Elsom, Clint Gary 1946- *WhoWest 94*
Elsom, Isobel d1981 *WhoHol 92*

Emery, George Edward 1920- Who 94
Emery, Gilbert d1945 WhoHol 92
Emery, Herschell Gene 1923- WhoAm 94
Emery, Howard Ivan, Jr. 1932- WhoFI 94
Emery, James W. WhoAmP 93
Emery, Joan Dawson Who 94
Emery, John d1964 WhoHol 92
Emery, John C. 1930- WhoAm 94
Emery, Joyce Margaret Who 94
Emery, Katherine d1980 WhoHol 92
Emery, Kenneth (Orris) 1914- WrDr 94
Emery, Kenneth O. 1914- IntWW 93
Emery, Kenneth Orris 1914- WhoAm 94
Emery, Lin WhoAmA 93
Emery, Lina Who 94
Emery, Marcia Rose 1937- WhoAm 94
Emery, Mark Lewis 1957- WhoScEn 94
Emery, Mary d1988 WhoHol 92
Emery, Nancy Beth 1952- WhoAm 94
Emery, Paul Emile 1922- WhoAm 94, WhoScEn 94
Emery, Peter (Frank Hannibal) 1926- Who 94
Emery, Philip Anthony 1934- WhoWest 94
Emery, Pollie d1958 WhoHol 92
Emery, Ralph 1932?- ConAu 142
Emery, Robert Firestone 1927- WhoAm 94, WrDr 94
Emery, Sherman Raymond 1924- WhoAm 94
Emery, Stephenson Dow 1959- WhoAmL 94
Emery, Sue 1920- WhoAm 94
Emery, Thomas V. d1921 WhoHol 92
Emery, Virginia Olga Beattie 1938- WhoScEn 94
Emery-Wallis, Frederick Alfred John 1927- Who 94
Emes, William 1730-1803 DcNaB MP
Emets, Oleksandr Ivanovych 1959- LoBiDrD
Emge, Thomas Michael 1957- WhoScEn 94
Emhardt, Robert 1914- WhoHol 92
Emick, Dudley Joseph, Jr. WhoAmP 93
Emick, William John 1931- WhoFI 94
Emigh, Elizabeth Evelyn 1924- WhoWest 94
Emil, Allan D. 1898-1976 WhoAmA 93N
Emil, Arthur D. 1924- WhoAmA 93
Emil, Michael WhoHol 92
Emiliani, Cesare 1922- WhoAm 94
Emiliani, Vittorio 1935- IntWW 93
Emilio IntWW 93
Emilio, Frank Anthony 1935- WhoAmP 93
Emin Pasha, Mehmed 1840-1892 WhWE
Emiroglu, Metin 1943- IntWW 93
Emison, James W. 1930- WhoAm 94
Emisteseguo of Little Tallassee d1782 AmRev
Emken, Robert Allan 1929- WhoAm 94
Emlen, Robert P. 1946- WrDr 94
Emlen, Stephen Thompson 1940- WhoAm 94
Emlen, Warren Metz 1932- WhoFI 94
Emler, Jay Scott 1949- WhoMW 93
Emlet, Richard Bond 1955- WhoWest 94
Emley, Charles Lee 1927- WhoAmP 93
Emley, William Earl 1948- WhoAmP 93
Emling, William Harold 1957- WhoScEn 94
Emlyn Jones, John Hubert 1915- Who 94
Emma 1844-1929 BlmGWL
Emma, Charles Joseph, Jr. 1956- WhoAmL 94
Emmanouilides, George Christos 1926- WhoAm 94, WhoWest 94
Emmanuel, Jorge Agustin 1954- WhoScEn 94, WhoWest 94
Emmanuel, Lenny DrAPF 93
Emmanuel, (Marie Francois) Maurice 1862-1938 NewGrDO
Emmanuel, Rahm WhoAm 94
Emmanuel, Tsegai 1940- WhoBlA 94
Emma of Normandy d1052 BlmGWL
Emmel, Bruce Henry 1942- WhoMW 93, WhoScEn 94
Emmel, Robert Shafer 1954- WhoMW 93
Emmeluth, Bruce Palmer 1940- WhoAm 94, WhoFI 94, WhoWest 94
Emmen, Dennis R. 1933- WhoAm 94
Emmens, Clifford Walter 1913- IntWW 93
Emmerich, Adam Oliver 1960- WhoAmL 94
Emmerich, Andre 1924- WhoAm 94, WhoAmA 93, WrDr 94
Emmerich, Irene Hillebrand WhoAmA 93N
Emmerich, Karol Denise 1948- WhoAm 94, WhoFI 94
Emmerich, Robert D. d1988 WhoHol 92
Emmerich, Walter 1929- WhoAm 94
Emmerich, Werner Sigmund 1921-

Emmerman, Michael N 1945- WhoAm 94, WhoFI 94
Emmerson, Donald Kenneth 1940- WhoFI 94
Emmerson, Ralph 1913- Who 94
Emmert, Gilbert Arthur 1938- WhoAm 94
Emmert, Johann Joseph 1732-1809 NewGrDO
Emmert, Pauline Gore 1923- WhoAmA 93
Emmert, Richard Eugene 1929- WhoAm 94, WhoScEn 94
Emmerth, Barbara 1958- WhoMW 93
Emmerton, William James 1947- WhoFI 94
Emmet, Dorothy Mary 1904- IntWW 93, Who 94, WrDr 94
Emmet, Herman LeRoy 1943- ConAu 141
Emmet, Joseph d1936 WhoHol 92
Emmet, Katherine d1960 WhoHol 92
Emmet, Lydia Field 1886-1952 WhoAmA 93N
Emmett, Bryan David 1941- Who 94
Emmett, E. V. H. d1971 WhoHol 92
Emmett, Edward Martin 1949- WhoAmP 93
Emmett, Fern d1946 WhoHol 92
Emmett, Frederick Joseph, Jr. 1945- WhoAm 94
Emmett, James Robert 1940- WhoAmL 94
Emmett, Rita 1943- WhoMW 93
Emmett, Robert 1921- ConTFT 11
Emmett, Robert Addis, III 1943- WhoAm 94
Emmett, Robert Andrew 1922- WhoAmP 93
Emmett, Stephanie Rose 1966- WhoFI 94
Emmett, Walter Charles 1925- WhoFI 94
Emmons, Alice M. 1955- WhoAmP 93
Emmons, Arthur B., III 1910-1962 HisDcKW
Emmons, Cynthia Wagner DrAPF 93
Emmons, Dale Clifton 1952- WhoAmP 93
Emmons, Delia McQuade 1947- WhoFI 94
Emmons, Donald Ray 1965- WhoBlA 94
Emmons, Donn 1910- WhoAm 94
Emmons, George Foster 1811-1884 WhWE
Emmons, Howard Wilson 1912- IntWW 93, WhoAm 94
Emmons, Joanne 1934- WhoMW 93
Emmons, Joanne Clara 1934- WhoAmP 93
Emmons, Larry d1978 WhoHol 92
Emmons, Linda N. 1937- WhoAmP 93
Emmons, Louise d1935 WhoHol 92
Emmons, Nathaniel 1745-1840 DcAmReB 2
Emmons, Rayford E. 1948- WhoBlA 94
Emmons, Richard William 1931- WhoWest 94
Emmons, Robert Duncan 1932- WhoAm 94
Emmons, Robert John 1934- WhoFI 94
Emmons, William David 1924- WhoScEn 94
Emmons, William Monroe, III 1959- WhoFI 94
Emmott, Bill 1956- WrDr 94
Emmott, William John 1956- Who 94
Emms, David Acfield 1925- Who 94
Emms, Peter Fawcett 1935- Who 94
Emney, Fred d1980 WhoHol 92
Emond, Robert R. J. 1930- WhoAmP 93
Emont, George Daniel 1958- WhoScEn 94
Emont, Michael J. 1948- WhoAmL 94
Emorey, Howard Omer 1928- WhoAm 94
Emori, Richard Ichiro 1924- WhoScEn 94
Emory, Carl d1966 WhoHol 92
Emory, Emerson 1925- WhoBlA 94
Emory, Hugh Mercer 1945- WhoAm 94
Emory, Linda B. 1938- WhoIns 94
Emory, Meade 1931- WhoAm 94
Emory, Samuel Thomas 1933- WhoAmP 93
Emory, William Hemsley 1811-1887 WhWE [port]
Emovon, Emmanuel Uwumagbuhunmwun 1929- IntWW 93
Empedocles fl. 5th cent.- BlmGEL
Emperado, Mercedes Lopez 1941- WhoAm 94
Emperor, Gerald Alan 1957- WhoMW 93
Empey, Gene F. 1923- WhoWest 94
Empey, Guy d1963 WhoHol 92
Empey, Reginald Norman Morgan 1947- Who 94
Empey, Walton Newcombe Francis Who 94
Emplit, Raymond Henry 1948- WhoFI 94, WhoScEn 94
Empress, Marie d1919 WhoHol 92
Empson, Cheryl Diane 1962- WhoScEn 94
Empson, Cindy WhoAmP 93
Empson, Cynthia Sue 1947- WhoMW 93
Empson, (Leslie) Derek 1918- Who 94
Empson, William 1906-1984 BlmGEL

Emrich, Edmund Michael 1956- WhoAmL 94
Emrich, Grover Harry 1929- WhoFI 94
Emrick, Donald Day 1929- WhoMW 93, WhoScEn 94
Emrick, Tammy Sue 1963- WhoFI 94
Emrick, Terry Lamar 1935- WhoAm 94
Emroch, Walter H. WhoAmP 93
Emsh, Ed EncSF 93
Emshwiller, Carol DrAPF 93
Emshwiller, Carol (Fries) 1921- EncSF 93, WrDr 94
Emshwiller, Ed 1925-1990 EncSF 93, WhAm 10
Emsley, John 1938- ConAu 142
Emslie, Baron 1919- Who 94
Emslie, Derek Robert Alexander 1949- Who 94
Emslie, George Carlyle 1919- IntWW 93
Emslie, (George) Nigel (Hannington) 1947- Who 94
Emslie, Ronald Douglas 1915- Who 94
Emslie, William Arthur 1947- WhoScEn 94
Emson, Harry Edmund 1927- WhoAm 94
Emson, Reginald (Herbert Embleton) 1912- Who 94
Emtman, Steve WhoAm 94, WhoMW 93
Emtsev, Mikhail (Tikhonovich) 1930- EncSF 93
Emura, Cynthia Sanae 1944- WhoAsA 94
Enahoro, Anthony 1923- IntWW 93
Enarson, Harold L. 1919- WhoAm 94
Enberg, Dick WhoAm 94
Enberg, Dick 1935- WhoHol 92
Enberg, Henry Winfield 1940- WhoAmL 94, WhoFI 94
Enchi Fumiko 1905-1988 BlmGWL
Encinas, Lalo d1959 WhoHol 92
Encinas, Salvador, Jr. 1963- WhoHisp 94
Encinias, Art WhoHisp 94
Enciso, Jose Raul 1954- WhoHisp 94
Encombe, Viscount 1962- Who 94
End, Henry 1915- WhoAm 94
End, William Thomas 1947- WhoAm 94, WhoFI 94
Endahl, Lowell Jerome 1922- WhoScEn 94
Endara Galimany, Guillermo IntWW 93
Endean, Leslie Ann 1944- WhoAmL 94
Endean, Stephen R. d1993 NewYTBS 93
Ende-Andriessen, Pelagie NewGrDO
Endeley, E. M. L. 1916- IntWW 93
Endeman, Ronald Lee 1936- WhoAmL 94
Endemann, Carl T. DrAPF 93
Ender, Elma Teresa Salinas 1953- WhoHisp 94
Ender, Jon Terry 1942- WhoAm 94
Ender, Richard Louis 1945- WhoWest 94
Enderby, John Edwin 1931- IntWW 93, Who 94
Enderby, Kenneth Albert 1920- Who 94
Enderby, Keppel Earl 1926- IntWW 93
Enderby, Samuel 1907- Who 94
Enderlein, Erik (Emil) 1887-c. 1928 NewGrDO
Enders, Allen Coffin 1928- WhoAm 94, WhoScEn 94
Enders, Anthony Talcott 1937- WhoFI 94
Enders, Elizabeth McGuire 1939- WhoAmA 93, WhoFI 94
Enders, John F. 1897-1985 WorScD
Enders, Murvin S. 1942- WhoBlA 94
Enders, Pat M. DrAPF 93
Enders, Robert IntMPA 94
Enders, Thomas O. 1931- IntWW 93
Enders, Thomas Ostrom 1931- WhoAmP 93
Endersby, Clive 1944- WrDr 94
Enderud, Wilbur Donald, Jr. 1945- WhoWest 94
Endick, Marshal S. 1947- WhoAmL 94
Endicott, Frank Simpson 1904-1990 WhAm 10
Endicott, John 1946- WhoAmL 94
Endicott, John Fredrick 1932- WhoMW 93
Endicott, William F. 1935- WhoAm 94, WhoWest 94
Endler, Norman Solomon 1931- WhoAm 94
Endlich, Leatrice Ann 1928- WhoMW 93
Endo, Amy Arakawa 1961- WhoWest 94
Endo, Burton Yoshiaki 1926- WhoScEn 94
Endo, Frank 1923- WhoAsA 94
Endo, Hajime 1950- WhoScEn 94
Endo, Kaname 1915- IntWW 93
Endo, Paula Sayoko Tsukamoto 1938- WhoAsA 94
Endo, Shusaku Paul 1923- IntWW 93
Endoh, Ryohei 1954- WhoScEn 94
Endore, S(amuel) Guy 1901-1970 EncSF 93
Endorf, Verlane L. 1944- WhoAm 94, WhoAmL 94
Endo Shusaku 1923- ConWorW 93, RfGShF

Endraske, Marilyn Joann 1947- WhoAm 94
Endrenyi, Janos 1927- WhoAm 94
Endres, Debra Jo 1959- WhoMW 93
Endres, Kathleen Lillian 1949- WhoMW 93
Endres, Patricia Sue 1961- WhoFI 94
Endresse, Clara d1979 WhoHol 92
Endreze, Arthur 1893-1975 NewGrDO
Endrezze, Anita DrAPF 93
Endries, John Michael 1942- WhoAm 94, WhoFI 94
Endris, Glenn Edwin 1938- WhoAmP 93
Endriss, Marilyn Jean 1953- WhoAmL 94
Endsley, John Patrick 1928- WhoAm 94, WhoAmL 94
Endt, Alvin Claude 1933- WhoAmP 93
Endy, William R. 1936- WhoAmP 93
Endyke, Debra Joan 1955- WhoAm 94
Endyke, Mary Beth 1961- WhoAmL 94
Enegess, David Norman 1946- WhoScEn 94
Enei, Yevgeni 1890-1971 IntDcF 2-4
Enelow, Allen Jay 1922- WhoAm 94
Ener, Guner 1935- BlmGWL
Enersen, Burnham 1905- WhoAm 94, WhoAmL 94
Enescu, George 1881-1955 NewGrDO
Enfield, Viscount 1964- Who 94
Enfield, Donald Michael 1945- WhoFI 94, WhoWest 94
Enfield, Franklin D. 1933- WhoAm 94
Enfield, Harry 1906-1958 WhoAmA 93N
Enfield, Hugh d1949 WhoHol 92
Enflo, Anita Margarita 1943- WhoScEn 94
Eng, Ana Mar 1939- WhoAsA 94
Eng, Anne Chin 1950- WhoFI 94
Eng, Henry 1940- WhoAsA 94
Eng, Jamie Pearl 1951- WhoAsA 94
Eng, Kee Juen 1950- WhoAmL 94
Eng, Lawrence Fook 1931- WhoAm 94, WhoAsA 94, WhoWest 94
Eng, Mamie 1954- WhoAsA 94
Eng, Patricia WhoAsA 94
Eng, Phoebe NewYTBS 93 [port]
Eng, Richard Shen 1930- WhoScEn 94
Eng, Steve DrAPF 93
Eng, William 1950- WhoAsA 94
Engar, Richard Charles 1953- WhoWest 94
Engberg, (Johanna) Susan 1940- ConAu 41NR
Engdahl, Brian Edward 1952- WhoScEn 94
Engdahl, Richard Bott 1914- WhoAm 94
Engdahl, Sylvia L(ouise) 1933- WrDr 94
Engdahl, Sylvia Louise 1933- EncSF 93, TwCYAW
Engebrecht, P. A. DrAPF 93
Engebretsen, Alan C. DrAPF 93
Engebretson, Douglas Kenneth 1946- WhoAm 94
Engebretson, Milton Benjamin 1920- WhoAm 94
Engel, Alan 1941- WrDr 94
Engel, Albert Edward 1916- IntWW 93
Engel, Albert Joseph 1924- WhoAm 94, WhoAmL 94, WhoMW 93
Engel, Alexander d1968 WhoHol 92
Engel, Alfred Julius 1927- WhoAm 94
Engel, Andrew Carl 1946- WhoFI 94
Engel, Andrew George 1930- WhoAm 94, WhoScEn 94
Engel, Antonie Jacobus 1896- WhAm 10
Engel, Austin George, Jr. 1928- WhoAmP 93
Engel, Bernard F. 1921- WrDr 94
Engel, Bernard Theodore 1928- WhoAm 94
Engel, Brian K. 1956- WhoIns 94
Engel, Charles F. 1937- IntMPA 94
Engel, Charles Robert 1922- WhoAm 94, WhoScEn 94
Engel, David Anthony 1951- WhoAm 94
Engel, David Chapin 1931- WhoAmL 94
Engel, David Lewis 1947- WhoAm 94, WhoAmL 94
Engel, Eliot L. 1947- CngDr 93, WhoAmP 93
Engel, Elliot L. 1947- WhoAm 94
Engel, Erich d1955 WhoHol 92
Engel, George Larry 1947- WhoAm 94, WhoAmL 94
Engel, George Libman 1913- WhoAm 94
Engel, Georgia 1948- WhoHol 92
Engel, Harry 1901-1970 WhoAmA 93N
Engel, Herbert M. 1918- ConAu 43NR
Engel, Howard 1931- WrDr 94
Engel, James Harry 1946- WhoScEn 94
Engel, Jerome, Jr. 1938- WhoScEn 94, WhoWest 94
Engel, Joanne Netter 1955- WhoScEn 94
Engel, Joel Stanley 1936- WhoAm 94, WhoMW 93
Engel, Johannes 1927- IntWW 93
Engel, John 1943- WhoAm 94, WhoAmL 94
Engel, John Jacob 1936- WhoAm 94

Engel, Juergen Kurt 1945- *WhoScEn 94*
Engel, Lawrence Edward 1943- *WhoIns 94*
Engel, (A.) Lehman 1910-1982 *NewGrDO*
Engel, Leonard 1916-1964 *EncSF 93*
Engel, Leslie Carroll 1949- *WhoMW 93*
Engel, Linda Jeanne 1949- *WhoWest 94*
Engel, Lyle Kenyon 1915-1986 *EncSF 93*
Engel, Marian 1933-1985 *BlmGWL*
Engel, Marie d1971 *WhoHol 92*
Engel, Mark A. 1953- *WhoAmL 94*
Engel, Matthew Lewis 1951- *Who 94*
Engel, Michael M. 1896-1969 *WhoAmA 93N*
Engel, Michael Martin, II 1919- *WhoAmA 93*
Engel, Monroe 1921- *WrDr 94*
Engel, Paul Bernard 1926- *WhoAm 94*
Engel, Ralph 1934- *WhoAm 94*
Engel, Ralph Manuel 1944- *WhoAm 94, WhoAmL 94*
Engel, Regula 1761-1853 *BlmGWL*
Engel, Richard Gardner 1944- *WhoAmL 94*
Engel, Richard Lee 1936- *WhoAmL 94*
Engel, Robert Andrew 1963- *WhoFI 94*
Engel, Robert G. d1993 *NewYTBS 93*
Engel, Roy d1980 *WhoHol 92*
Engel, Stientje *NewGrDO*
Engel, Susan 1935- *WhoHol 92*
Engel, Thomas 1942- *WhoAm 94*
Engel, Thomas Gregory 1959- *WhoScEn 94*
Engel, Walter F. 1908- *WhoAmA 93*
Engel, William R. 1930- *WhoIns 94*
Engel-Arieli, Susan Lee 1954- *WhoMW 93*
Engelbach, David (Charles) 1946- *WrDr 94*
Engelbardt, Robert Miles 1931- *WhoAm 94*
Engelberg, Alan (D.) 1941- *WrDr 94*
Engelberg, Mort *IntMPA 94*
Engelberg, Stephen Paul 1958- *WhoAm 94*
Engelbert, Arthur Ferdinand 1903- *WhoAm 94*
Engelbrecht, Richard Stevens 1926- *WhoAm 94, WhoScEn 94*
Engelbrecht, Rudolf 1928- *WhoAm 94*
Engeler, William Ernest 1928- *WhoAm 94*
Engel'gardt, Sof'ia Vladimirovna 1828-1894 *BlmGWL*
Engelhard, Hans Arnold 1934- *IntWW 93*
Engelhard, Jack 1940- *WrDr 94*
Engelhard, Joseph A. 1898- *WhAm 10*
Engelhard, Magdalene Philippine 1756-1831 *BlmGWL*
Engelhard, Robert John 1927- *WhoAmP 93*
Engelhardt, Albert George 1935- *WhoAm 94, WhoWest 94*
Engelhardt, Dean Lee 1940- *WhoAm 94*
Engelhardt, Frederick *EncSF 93*
Engelhardt, Helen *DrAPF 93*
Engelhardt, Hugo Tristram, Jr. 1941- *WhoAm 94*
Engelhardt, Jerry M. 1942- *WhoWest 94*
Engelhardt, John Hugo 1946- *WhoAmL 94, WhoFI 94*
Engelhardt, Klaus 1932- *IntWW 93*
Engelhardt, LeRoy A. 1924- *WhoAm 94*
Engelhardt, M. Veronice 1912- *WrDr 94*
Engelhardt, Sara Lawrence 1943- *WhoAm 94*
Engelhardt, Thomas Alexander 1930- *WhoAm 94, WhoAmA 93*
Engelhardt, Tom 1930- *WrDr 94*
Engelhart, Michael Steven 1953- *WhoFI 94*
Engelke, Kent Eric 1963- *WhoFI 94*
Engelkes, Donald J. 1938- *WhoIns 94*
Engelkes, Donald John 1938- *WhoAm 94*
Engelking, Ellen Melinda 1942- *WhoFI 94*
Engelking, Paul Craig 1948- *WhoWest 94*
Engell, Hans 1948- *IntWW 93*
Engell, James 1951- *WrDr 94*
Engelman, Donald Max 1941- *WhoAm 94*
Engelman, Karl 1933- *WhoAm 94*
Engelman, Melvin Alkon 1921- *WhoAm 94, WhoScEn 94*
Engelman, Robert S. 1912- *WhoAm 94*
Engelmann, Bernt J. 1921- *IntWW 93*
Engelmann, Hans Ulrich 1921- *NewGrDO*
Engelmann, Hugo Otto 1917- *WhoMW 93*
Engelmann, Lothar Klaus 1926- *WhoAm 94*
Engelmann, Paul Victor 1958- *WhoScEn 94*
Engelmann, Rudolf Jacob 1930- *WhoAm 94*
Engelmann, Rudolph Herman 1929- *WhoScEn 94*
Engelmann, Thomas Charles 1957- *WhoMW 93*
Engelmeyer, Alice Catherine 1936- *WhoMW 93*
Engels, Frederick 1820-1895 *EncEth*
Engels, Friedrich 1820-1895 *DcLB 129 [port]*
Engels, John *DrAPF 93*
Engels, John (David) 1931- *WrDr 94*
Engels, Thomas Joseph 1958- *WhoMW 93*
Engels, Virginia d1956 *WhoHol 92*
Engelschman, Niek d1988 *WhoHol 92*
Engelson, Carol 1944- *WhoAmA 93*
Engelstad, Stephen Phillip 1957- *WhoScEn 94*
Engelthal, Christina von *BlmGWL*
Engeman, William Knowles 1939- *WhoAm 94*
Engen, Donald Davenport 1924- *WhoAmP 93*
Engen, Donald Travis 1944- *WhoAm 94, WhoFI 94*
Engen, Keith 1925- *NewGrDO*
Engen, Lee Emerson 1921- *WhoFI 94*
Engen, Rene Leopold Alexis 1918- *IntWW 93*
Enger, Kari Jo 1965- *WhoWest 94*
Enger, Kathleen May 1944- *WhoMW 93*
Enger, Walter Melvin 1914- *WhoAm 94*
Engeran, Whitney John, Jr. 1934- *WhoAmA 93*
Engerbretson, David Lance 1936- *WhoWest 94*
Engerman, Stanley Lewis 1936- *WhoAm 94*
Engerrand, Doris Dieskow 1925- *WhoFI 94*
Engerrand, Kenneth G. 1952- *WhoAmL 94*
Engeset, Jetmund 1938- *Who 94*
Enget, June Y. 1930- *WhoAmP 93*
Engfer, Susan Marvel 1943- *WhoAm 94, WhoWest 94*
Enggaard, Knud 1929- *IntWW 93*
Enggass, Robert 1921- *WhoAmA 93*
Engh, M(ary) J(ane) 1933- *EncSF 93*
Engh, N. Rolf 1953- *WhoAmL 94*
Engheta, Nader 1955- *WhoScEn 94*
Engholm, Bjorn 1939- *IntWW 93*
Engiles, Jim George 1947- *WhoWest 94*
Engl, Walter L. 1926- *IntWW 93*
Englade, Kenneth Francis 1938- *WhoWest 94*
England, Alphonse 1961- *WhoWest 94*
England, Anthony Wayne 1942- *WhoAm 94, WhoScEn 94*
England, Arthur Jay, Jr. 1932- *WhoAm 94*
England, Barry 1934- *ConDr 93, WrDr 94*
England, Daisy d1943 *WhoHol 92*
England, Don d1987 *WhoHol 92*
England, Frank Raymond Wilton 1911- *Who 94*
England, Gary Alan 1939- *WhoScEn 94*
England, George Allan 1877-1936 *EncSF 93*
England, George Leslie 1935- *Who 94*
England, Glyn 1921- *IntWW 93, Who 94*
England, James *EncSF 93*
England, Jimmy Leon 1952- *WhoFI 94*
England, John 1786-1842 *DcAmReB 2*
England, John Melvin 1932- *WhoAmL 94*
England, Joseph Walker 1940- *WhoAm 94*
England, Kathleen Jane 1953- *WhoAmL 94*
England, Lynne Lipton 1949- *WhoAmL 94*
England, Martin Nicholas 1954- *WhoScEn 94*
England, Norman 1914- *WrDr 94*
England, Paul d1968 *WhoHol 92*
England, Richard 1937- *IntWW 93*
England, Rodney Wayne 1932- *WhoBlA 94*
England, Rudy Alan 1959- *WhoAmL 94*
England, Sharon E. 1939- *WhoWest 94*
England, Sue *WhoHol 92*
England, Timothy John 1942- *Who 94*
England, Timothy Scott 1964- *WhoMW 93*
Englander, Gertrud 1904- *WhoAmA 93*
Englander, Morris K. 1934- *IntMPA 94*
Englander, Roger Leslie 1926- *WhoAm 94*
Englar, John David 1947- *WhoAmL 94*
Engle, Barbara L. 1945- *WhoAmP 93*
Engle, Billy d1966 *WhoHol 92*
Engle, Carole Ruth 1952- *WhoAm 94*
Engle, Chet 1918- *WhoAmA 93*
Engle, Daniel T. 1955- *WhoAmL 94*
Engle, Darleen d1985 *WhoHol 92*
Engle, Donald Edward 1927- *WhoAm 94, WhoAmL 94, WhoFI 94*
Engle, Ed, Jr. *DrAPF 93*
Engle, Eloise 1923- *WrDr 94*
Engle, George (Lawrence Jose) 1926- *Who 94*
Engle, Howard Eugene, Jr. 1935- *WhoWest 94*
Engle, James Bruce 1919- *WhoAm 94, WhoAmP 93*
Engle, James Wayne 1951- *WhoMW 93*
Engle, John D., Jr. *DrAPF 93*
Engle, Kenneth William 1937- *WhoWest 94*
Engle, Leslie Love 1940- *WhoAmL 94*
Engle, Margarita M. 1951- *WhoHisp 94*
Engle, Mary Allen English 1922- *WhoAm 94*
Engle, Morris d1986 *WhoHol 92*
Engle, Paul Hamilton 1908-1991 *WhAm 10*
Engle, Ralph Landis, Jr. 1920- *WhoAm 94*
Engle, Ray 1934- *WhoWest 94*
Engle, Richard Carlyle 1934- *WhoAm 94*
Engle, Robert H. 1895- *WhAm 10*
Engle, Robert Irwin 1945- *WhoWest 94*
Engle, Steve 1950- *WhoAmA 93*
Engle, Thelburn L 1901- *WrDr 94*
Engle, William Thomas, Jr. 1957- *WhoAmL 94*
Englebach, George 1941- *WhoAmP 93*
Englebienne, Patrick P. 1949- *WhoScEn 94*
Englebright, Steven C. *WhoAmP 93*
Engledow, Jack Lee 1931- *WhoAm 94*
Englefield, Dermot John Tryal 1927- *Who 94*
Englehart, Bob 1945- *WrDr 94*
Englehart, Edwin Thomas 1921- *WhoScEn 94*
Englehart, Robert Michael 1943- *Who 94*
Englehaupt, William Myles 1918- *WhoAm 94*
Engleman, David S. 1937- *WhoAm 94, WhoFI 94, WhoWest 94*
Engleman, Dennis Eugene 1948- *WhoScEn 94*
Engleman, Donald James 1947- *WhoAm 94, WhoAmL 94*
Engleman, Ephraim Philip 1911- *WhoAm 94, WhoScEn 94*
Engleman, Paul 1953- *WrDr 94*
Engler, Colleen House 1952- *WhoAmP 93*
Engler, George Nichols 1944- *WhoAm 94*
Engler, Henry Julius, Jr. 1916- *WhoAmP 93*
Engler, J. Curtis 1947- *WhoFI 94*
Engler, John 1948- *WhoAm 94, WhoMW 93*
Engler, John M. 1948- *WhoAmP 93*
Engler, Kathleen Girdler 1951- *WhoAmA 93*
Engler, Lori-Ann *WhoHol 92*
Engler, Mary B. *WhoWest 94*
Engler, Robert 1922- *WhoAm 94*
Engler, W. Joseph, Jr. 1940- *WhoAm 94, WhoAmL 94*
Englert, Roy Theodore 1922- *WhoAm 94*
Engles, David 1946- *WhoIns 94*
Englesbe, Andrew Joseph 1950- *WhoIns 94*
Englesmith, Tejas 1941- *WhoAm 94*
Engleson, David Charles 1928- *WhoMW 93*
Engling, Richard (David George Patrick) 1952- *EncSF 93*
Engling, Robert John 1945- *WhoAm 94, WhoFI 94*
Englisch, Lucie d1956 *WhoHol 92*
English, Albert J. 1967- *WhoBlA 94*
English, Alex *WhoHol 92*
English, Alex 1954- *BasBi, WhoBlA 94*
English, Barbara (Anne) 1933- *WrDr 94*
English, Bill *WhoAmP 93*
English, Bill 1930- *WhoAmP 93*
English, Brenda H. 1897-1991 *WrDr 94N*
English, Bruce Vaughan 1921- *WhoAm 94, WhoScEn 94*
English, Charles *EncSF 93*
English, Charles Brand 1924- *WhoAm 94*
English, Charles E. 1935- *WhoAmL 94*
English, Charles Royal 1938- *WhoAmL 94*
English, Clarence R. 1915- *WhoBlA 94*
English, Clifford, Jr. 1940- *WhoIns 94*
English, Cyril 1923- *Who 94*
English, Cyril (Rupert) 1913- *Who 94*
English, David 1931- *IntWW 93, Who 94*
English, David Floyd 1948- *WhoAmL 94*
English, Deborah *WhoBlA 94*
English, Diane 1948- *CurBio 93 [port], NewYTBS 93 [port], WhoAm 94*
English, Diane 1949?- *ConTFT 11*
English, Donald 1930- *Who 94*
English, Donald Marvin 1951- *WhoWest 94*
English, Elias d1977 *WhoHol 92*
English, Elsa Granger d1955 *WhoHol 92*
English, Floyd Leroy 1934- *WhoAm 94, WhoMW 93, WhoScEn 94*
English, Francis Peter 1932- *WhoScEn 94*
English, Gary Emery 1962- *WhoScEn 94*
English, Gerald 1925- *Who 94*
English, Gerald Marion 1931- *WhoWest 94*
English, Glenn 1940- *CngDr 93, WhoAm 94, WhoAmP 93*
English, H. Elwood 1945- *WhoAmL 94, WhoWest 94*
English, Hal 1910- *WhoAmA 93*
English, Helen Williams Drutt *WhoAmA 93*
English, Henry L. 1942- *WhoBlA 94*
English, Isobel 1925- *WrDr 94*
English, James Fairfield, Jr. 1927- *WhoAm 94*
English, Jerry Fitzgerald 1934- *WhoAmP 93*
English, John 1947- *WhoAmL 94*
English, John Arbogast 1913- *WhoAmA 93*
English, John Dwight 1949- *WhoAmL 94*
English, John Winfield 1933- *WhoAm 94*
English, Joseph Thomas 1933- *IntWW 93*
English, Karan 1939- *WhoAm 94, WhoWest 94*
English, Karan 1949- *CngDr 93, WhoAmP 93*
English, Kenneth 1947- *WhoBlA 94*
English, Lawrence P. 1940- *WhoAm 94, WhoFI 94*
English, Malcolm Darnell 1962- *WhoMW 93*
English, Marion S. 1912- *WhoBlA 94*
English, Marla 1935- *WhoHol 92*
English, Michael 1930- *Who 94*
English, Nicholas Conover 1912- *WhoAm 94*
English, O. Spurgeon d1993 *NewYTBS 93*
English, Perry T., Jr. 1933- *WhoBlA 94*
English, Philip Sheridan 1956- *WhoAmP 93*
English, Ray 1946- *WhoAm 94*
English, Richard A. 1936- *WhoBlA 94*
English, Richard Allyn 1936- *WhoAm 94*
English, Richard D. 1948- *WhoAm 94*
English, Robert 1878- *WhoHol 92*
English, Robert Eugene 1953- *WhoScEn 94*
English, Robert Jackson 1951- *WhoWest 94*
English, Robert Joseph 1932- *WhoAm 94*
English, Stephen F. 1948- *WhoAmL 94*
English, Stephen Raymond 1946- *WhoAm 94*
English, Terence (Alexander Hawthorne) 1932- *Who 94*
English, Terence Alexander Hawthorne 1932- *IntWW 93*
English, Terence Michael 1944- *Who 94*
English, Thomas James 1942- *WhoAm 94*
English, Whittie 1917- *WhoBlA 94*
English, William deShay 1924- *WhoAm 94*
English, William Hazen 1929- *WhoAm 94*
English, Woodruff Jones 1909- *WhoAm 94*
Englot, Joseph Michael 1950- *WhoScEn 94*
Englund, Gage Bush 1931- *WhoAm 94*
Englund, John Arthur 1926- *WhoAm 94, WhoScEn 94*
Englund, Ken d1993 *NewYTBS 93*
Englund, Kenneth d1993 *IntMPA 94N*
Englund, Patricia *WhoHol 92*
Englund, Paul Theodore 1938- *WhoAm 94*
Englund, Robert 1948- *WhoHol 92*
Englund, Robert 1949- *IntMPA 94*
Engman, John *DrAPF 93*
Engman, John Daniel 1950- *WhoMW 93*
Engman, Lewis August 1936- *IntWW 93, WhoAm 94, WhoAmL 94*
Engo, Paul Bamela 1931- *IntWW 93*
Engoren, Sampson Seymour 1929- *WhoAm 94*
Engoron, Edward David 1946- *WhoWest 94*
Engram, Beverly *WhoAmP 93*
Engs, Robert Francis 1943- *WhoBlA 94*
Engseth, William 1933- *IntWW 93*
Engstrand, Craig S. 1949- *WhoAmL 94*
Engstrom, Donald Wayne 1953- *WhoMW 93*
Engstrom, Elizabeth *DrAPF 93*
Engstrom, Eric Gustaf 1942- *WhoAm 94*
Engstrom, Frederick William 1948- *WhoMW 93*
Engstrom, John Eric 1943- *WhoAmL 94*
Engstrom, Kenneth Robert 1951- *WhoMW 93*
Engstrom, Lyle Eugene 1948- *WhoMW 93*
Engstrom, Odd 1941- *IntWW 93*
Engvild, Kjeld Christensen 1940- *WhoScEn 94*
Enhorning, Goran 1924- *WhoScEn 94*
Enis, Thomas Joseph 1937- *WhoAmL 94*
Enix, Agnes Lucille 1933- *WhoAm 94*
Enix-Ross, Deborah Delores 1956- *WhoAmL 94*
Enke, Alan A. 1943- *WhoAmL 94*
Enke, Dennis Keith 1962- *WhoMW 93*
Enkemann, John Edward, Jr. 1955- *WhoMW 93*
Enloe, Cortez Ferdinand, Jr. 1910- *WhoAm 94*
Enloe, Jeff H., Jr. 1914- *WhoAmP 93*
Enlow, Donald Hugh 1927- *WhoAm 94*
Enlow, Fred Clark 1940- *WhoAm 94*

Enman, Tom Kenneth 1928- *WhoAmA 93*
Enmegahbowh c. 1810-1902 *EncNAR*
Enna, August (Emil) 1859-1939 *NewGrDO*
Ennals, Baron 1922- *Who 94*
Ennals, David Hedley 1922- *IntWW 93*
Ennals, Kenneth Frederick John 1932- *Who 94*
Ennals, Martin Francis Antony 1927-1991 *WhAm 10*
Ennen, Edith 1907- *IntWW 93*
Ennest, John William 1942- *WhoAm 94*
Enney, James Crowe 1930- *WhoAm 94*
Ennico, Clifford Robert 1954- *WhoAmL 94*
Ennis, Bruce C. 1939- *WhoAmP 93*
Ennis, Bruce J. 1940- *WhoAm 94, WhoAmL 94*
Ennis, Charles Roe 1932- *WhoAmL 94*
Ennis, David H. 1940- *WhoAmP 93*
Ennis, Edgar William, Jr. 1945- *WhoAm 94, WhoAmL 94*
Ennis, Joel Brian 1959- *WhoScEn 94*
Ennis, Robert Washington 1951- *WhoAmL 94*
Ennis, Skinnay d1963 *WhoHol 92*
Ennis, Thomas Michael 1931- *WhoAm 94, WhoFI 94, WhoWest 94*
Ennis, William Lee 1949- *WhoWest 94*
Enniskillen, Earl of 1942- *Who 94*
Ennismore, Viscount 1964- *Who 94*
Enniss, Leonard Franklin 1955- *WhoWest 94*
Ennix, Coyness Loyal, Jr. 1942- *WhoBlA 94*
Enns, Harry John *WhoMW 93*
Enns, Kevin Scott 1959- *WhoMW 93, WhoScEn 94*
Enns, Mark Kynaston 1931- *WhoAm 94*
Ennulat, Egbert M. 1929- *ConAu 142*
Eno, Arthur L., Jr. 1924- *WhoAmL 94*
Eno, Brian 1948- *WhoAm 94*
Eno, James Lorne 1887-1952 *WhoAmA 93N*
Eno, Larry E. 1969- *WhoAmP 93*
Eno, Paul Frederick 1953- *WhoAm 94*
Enoch, Craig *WhoAmP 93*
Enoch, Craig Trively 1950- *WhoAmL 94*
Enoch, Hollace J. 1950- *WhoBlA 94*
Enoch, Jay Martin 1929- *WhoAm 94*
Enoch, John D. *WhoBlA 94*
Enoch, Mark Charles 1953- *WhoAmL 94*
Enoch, Russell *WhoHol 92*
Enochs, Richmond M., Jr. 1938- *WhoAmL 94*
Enoff, Louis D. 1942- *WhoAm 94*
Enoki, Donald Yukio 1937- *WhoWest 94*
Enoki, Elliot *WhoAmL 94*
Enomoto, Jiro 1926- *WhoAsA 94*
Enos, Paul 1934- *WhoAm 94, WhoScEn 94*
Enos, Paul R. 1931- *WhoIns 94*
Enos, Priscilla Beth 1952- *WhoAmL 94*
Enos, Randall 1936- *WhoAm 94*
Enos, Roger 1729-1808 *WhAmRev*
Enos, William 1955- *WhoAmP 93*
Enouch, Vernon d1981 *WhoHol 92*
Enouen, William Albert 1928- *WhoAm 94*
Enquist, David Wayne 1957- *WhoMW 93*
Enquist, Irving Fridtjof 1920- *WhoAm 94*
Enquist, Per Olov 1934- *ConWorW 93*
Enrici, Domenico 1909- *Who 94*
Enrick, Norbert Lloyd 1920- *ConAu 43NR*
Enrico, David Russell 1959- *WhoScEn 94*
Enrico, Roger *WhoFI 94*
Enright, Cynthia Lee 1950- *WhoWest 94*
Enright, D. J. 1920- *BlmGEL*
Enright, D(ennis) J(oseph) 1920- *ConAu 42NR, WrDr 94*
Enright, Dennis Joseph 1920- *IntWW 93, Who 94*
Enright, Derek Anthony 1935- *Who 94*
Enright, Florence d1961 *WhoHol 92*
Enright, Georgann McGee 1943- *WhoMW 93*
Enright, John Carl 1948- *WhoScEn 94*
Enright, Josephine d1976 *WhoHol 92*
Enright, Juanita 1911- *WhoHisp 94*
Enright, Michael Joseph 1955- *WhoScEn 94*
Enright, Nick 1950- *ConDr 93*
Enright, Stephanie Veselich 1929- *WhoFI 94, WhoWest 94*
Enright, Thomas Michael 1954- *WhoAmL 94*
Enright, William Benner 1925- *WhoAmL 94, WhoWest 94*
Enrile, Juan Ponce *IntWW 93*
Enriques, Terence Bill 1955- *WhoFI 94*
Enrique Y Tarancon, Vicente 1907- *IntWW 93*
Enriquez, Carola Rupert 1954- *WhoAm 94, WhoWest 94*
Enriquez, Francisco Javier 1955- *WhoScEn 94, WhoWest 94*
Enriquez, Gaspar 1942- *WhoAmA 93*
Enriquez, Jaime 1958- *WhoHisp 94*
Enriquez, Oscar 1963- *WhoHisp 94*
Enriquez, Rene d1990 *WhAm 10, WhoHol 92*
Enriquez de Guzman, Feliciana c. 1580-1640 *BlmGWL*
Enriquez-Dougherty, Suzanne Provencio 1959- *WhoHisp 94*
Enriquez Savignac, Antonio 1931- *IntWW 93*
Enroth, Tess *DrAPF 93*
Enroth-Cugell, Christina Alma Elisabeth 1919- *WhoAm 94*
Enroughty, Christopher James 1961- *WhoScEn 94*
Ens, William *WhoHol 92*
Enscoe, Jon 1949- *WhoAmL 94*
Ensenat, Donald Burnham 1946- *WhoAmL 94, WhoAmP 93*
Enser, George 1890-1961 *WhoAmA 93N*
Enserro, Michael d1981 *WhoHol 92*
Ensign, David James 1950- *WhoAmL 94*
Ensign, Michael 1944- *WhoHol 92*
Ensign, Richard Papworth 1919- *WhoAm 94, WhoWest 94*
Ensign, William Lloyd 1928- *WhoAm 94*
Ensing, Riemke 1939- *BlmGWL*
Enslein, Vincent David 1952- *WhoMW 93*
Enslen, Pamela Chapman 1953- *WhoAmL 94*
Enslen, Richard Alan 1931- *WhoAm 94, WhoAmL 94, WhoMW 93*
Ensley, Rodney Gene 1934- *WhoIns 94*
Enslin, Donald William 1933- *WhoFI 94*
Enslin, Jon S. 1938- *WhoMW 93*
Enslin, Theodore *DrAPF 93*
Enslin, Theodore (Vernon) 1925- *ConAu 41NR, WrDr 94*
Enslin, Theodore Vernon 1925- *WhoAm 94*
Enslow, Ridley Madison, Jr. 1926- *WhoAm 94*
Enslow, Sam 1946- *WrDr 94*
Ensminger, Aldie *WhoAmP 93*
Ensminger, Dale 1923- *WhoMW 93, WhoScEn 94*
Ensminger, John C. 1934- *WhoAmP 93*
Ensminger, Luther Glenn 1919- *WhoAm 94*
Ensminger, Marion Eugene 1908- *WhoAm 94, WhoScEn 94*
Ensminger, Mark Douglas 1955- *WhoWest 94*
Ensom, Donald 1926- *Who 94*
Ensor, David 1924- *Who 94*
Ensor, Donald Gene 1947- *WhoMW 93*
Ensor, George Anthony 1936- *Who 94*
Ensor, Michael de Normann 1919- *Who 94*
Ensor Walters, P. H. B. *Who 94*
Ensrud, Wayne 1934- *WhoAmA 93*
Ensslin, Robert Frank, Jr. 1928- *WhoAm 94*
Ensslin, Theodore Gustav 1927- *WhoWest 94*
Enstad, Gale Sinclair 1932- *WhoWest 94*
Enstedt, Howard d1928 *WhoHol 92*
Enstice, Wayne 1943- *WhoAmA 93*
Enstine, Raymond Wilton, Jr. 1946- *WhoFI 94*
Enstrom, Robert (William) 1946- *EncSF 93*
Ensworth, Marvin D. 1934- *WhoAmP 93*
Enteman, Willard Finley 1936- *WhoAm 94*
Entenman, John Alfred 1948- *WhoAm 94, WhoAmL 94*
Enterline, Sandra 1960- *WhoAmA 93*
Enters, Angna 1907-1989 *WhAm 10*
Entezam, Nasrollah 1900- *HisDcKW*
Entezari, Shirin Ozra *WhoAmL 94*
Enthoven, Alain *NewYTBS 93 [port]*
Enthoven, Dirk 1924- *WhoScEn 94*
Entian, Karl-Dieter 1952- *WhoScEn 94*
Entin, Jonathan Lowe 1947- *WhoMW 93*
Entmacher, Paul Sidney 1924- *WhoAm 94*
Entman, June Henrietta 1945- *WhoAmL 94*
Entman, Robert M. 1949- *WrDr 94*
Entman, Robert Mathew 1949- *WhoMW 93*
Enton, Harry *EncSF 93*
Entorf, Richard Carl 1929- *WhoAm 94*
Entov, Revold Mikhailovich 1931- *IntWW 93*
Entratter, Jack d1971 *WhoHol 92*
Entrecasteaux, Antoine-Raymond-Joseph De Bruni, Chevalier D' 1737-1793 *WhWE*
Entrekin, Charles *DrAPF 93*
Entremont, Philippe 1934- *IntWW 93, WhoAm 94*
Entriken, Robert Kersey 1913- *WhoWest 94*
Entriken, Robert Kersey, Jr. 1941- *WhoMW 93*
Entringer, Robert Rufus 1938- *WhoAmP 93*
Entwisle, Doris Roberts 1924- *WhoAm 94*
Entwisle, Eric Arthur 1900- *WrDr 94*
Entwistle, Andrew John 1959- *WhoFI 94*
Entwistle, Harold d1944 *WhoHol 92*
Entwistle, James Tobit 1944- *WhoIns 94*
Entwistle, Kenneth Mercer 1925- *Who 94*
Entwistle, (John Nuttall) Maxwell 1910- *Who 94*
Entwistle, Peg d1932 *WhoHol 92*
Entwistle, Robert d1922 *WhoHol 92*
Entz, Lewis H. 1931- *WhoAmP 93*
Entzminger, John Nelson, Jr. 1936- *WhoAm 94*
Envallsson, Carl 1756-1806 *NewGrDO*
Enver Pasha 1881-1922 *HisWorL [port]*
En Vogue *ConMus 10 [port], News 94-1 [port]*
Enwonu, Benedict Chuka 1921- *IntWW 93*
Enyeart, James L. 1943- *WhoAm 94, WrDr 94*
Enyeart, James Lyle 1943- *WhoAmA 93*
Enyedy, Gustav, Jr. 1924- *WhoAm 94*
Enzensberger, Hans Magnus 1929- *ConWorW 93, IntWW 93*
Enzi, Michael B. 1944- *WhoAmP 93*
Enzi, Michael Bradley 1944- *WhoWest 94*
Eoff, W. S. 1920- *WhoAmP 93*
Eoga, Michael Gerard 1966- *WhoScEn 94*
Eom, Kie-Bum 1954- *WhoScEn 94*
Eon de Beaumont, Chevalier d' 1728-1810 *BlmGWL*
Eorsi, Gyula d1992 *IntWW 93N*
Eotvos, Peter *Who 94*
Eotvos, Peter 1944- *IntWW 93*
Eoyang, Eugene Chen 1939- *ConAu 140, WhoMW 93*
Epailly, Jules d1967 *WhoHol 92*
Epcar, Richard Michael 1955- *WhoWest 94*
Epee, Charles Michel de l' 1712-1789 *EncDeaf*
Epel, David 1937- *WhoAm 94*
Epel, Lidia Marmurek 1941- *WhoScEn 94*
Eperon, Alastair David Peter 1949- *IntWW 93*
Epes, Travis Fredricks 1959- *WhoAmL 94*
Ephelia *BlmGWL*
Ephland, John Russell 1952- *WhoAm 94*
Ephraim, Charles 1924- *WhoAm 94*
Ephraim, Charlesworth W. *WhoBlA 94*
Ephraim, Donald Morley 1932- *WhoAm 94*
Ephraim, Max, Jr. 1918- *WhoAm 94*
Ephram, George 1934- *IntWW 93*
Ephraums, Roderick Jarvis 1927- *Who 94*
Ephremides, Anthony 1943- *WhoAm 94*
Ephron, Delia 1944- *WrDr 94*
Ephron, Henry 1912-1992 *AnObit 1992*
Ephron, Nora 1941- *IntMPA 94, IntWW 93, WhoAm 94*
Epictetus c. 55-c. 135 *EncEth*
Epicurus 342BC-270BC *BlmGEL*
Epicurus 341BC-270BC *EncEth*
Epinay, Louise-Florence-Petronille Tardieu d' 1726-1783 *BlmGWL*
Epler, Jerry L. *WhoIns 94*
Epler, Katherine Susan 1962- *WhoScEn 94*
Epley, Lewis Everett, Jr. 1936- *WhoAm 94*
Epley, Marion Jay 1907- *WhoAm 94, WhoScEn 94*
Eplin, Tom 1960- *WhoHol 92*
Epling, Richard Louis 1951- *WhoAm 94*
EPMD *ConMus 10 [port]*
Epner, Steven Arthur *WhoAm 94*
Epp, Arthur Jacob 1939- *WhoAm 94*
Epp, Eldon Jay 1930- *WhoAm 94, WrDr 94*
Epp, Jacob B. 1874- *EncNAR*
Epp, Jake 1939- *IntWW 93*
Epp, Leonard George *WhoMW 93*
Epp, Margaret Agnes 1913- *WrDr 94*
Epp, Mary Elizabeth 1941- *WhoFI 94, WhoMW 93*
Epp, Susanna Samuels 1943- *WhoMW 93*
Eppele, David Louis 1939- *WhoWest 94*
Eppelheimer, Linda Louise 1949- *WhoMW 93*
Eppen, Gary Dean 1936- *WhoAm 94*
Eppenberger, Susi 1931- *WhoWomW 91*
Eppenstein, Theodore G. 1946- *WhoAmL 94*
Epperson, Aurelia Anne 1963- *WhoFI 94*
Epperson, Bryan Keith 1957- *WhoWest 94*
Epperson, Craig E. 1945- *WhoAmL 94*
Epperson, David E. 1935- *WhoBlA 94*
Epperson, David Ernest 1935- *WhoAm 94*
Epperson, Dwight J.L. 1956- *WhoAmL 94*
Epperson, Eleanor Louise 1916- *WhoWest 94*
Epperson, Eric Robert 1949- *WhoFI 94, WhoWest 94*
Epperson, John Walker 1950- *WhoMW 93*
Epperson, Kraettli Quynton 1949- *WhoAmL 94*
Epperson, Vaughn Elmo 1917- *WhoFI 94, WhoScEn 94*
Eppig, Aileen 1951- *WhoFI 94*
Epping, Florence Luella d1986 *WhoHol 92*
Eppink, Andreas 1946- *WhoScEn 94*
Epple, Anne Orth 1927- *WrDr 94*
Epple, Bob *WhoAmP 93*
Epple, Dennis Norbert 1946- *WhoAm 94*
Eppler, Jerome Cannon 1924- *WhoAm 94*
Eppley, Roland Raymond, Jr. 1932- *WhoAm 94, WhoFI 94*
Eppner, Gerald Allen 1939- *WhoAm 94*
Epprecht, Russell *DrAPF 93*
Epps, A. Glenn 1929- *WhoBlA 94*
Epps, Anna Cherrie 1930- *WhoBlA 94*
Epps, Augustus Charles 1916- *WhoAm 94*
Epps, C. Roy 1941- *WhoBlA 94*
Epps, Carl B., III 1944- *WhoAmL 94*
Epps, Carl Von 1948- *WhoAmP 93*
Epps, Charles H., Jr. 1930- *WhoAm 94*
Epps, Charles Harry, Jr. 1930- *WhoBlA 94*
Epps, Constance Arnettres 1950- *WhoBlA 94*
Epps, Dolzie C. B. 1907- *WhoBlA 94*
Epps, Edgar G. 1929- *WhoBlA 94*
Epps, Garrett *DrAPF 93*
Epps, George Allen, Jr. 1940- *WhoBlA 94*
Epps, Jack, Jr. 1949- *WrDr 94*
Epps, James Haws, III 1936- *WhoAmL 94*
Epps, James Vernon 1928- *WhoIns 94*
Epps, Lawrence Edward 1957- *WhoAmP 93*
Epps, Mary Ellen 1934- *WhoAmP 93*
Epps, Naomi Newby 1909- *WhoBlA 94*
Epps, Phillip Earl 1958- *WhoBlA 94*
Epps, Roselyn Elizabeth Payne 1930- *WhoAm 94*
Epps, Roselyn Payne *WhoBlA 94*
Epright, Charles John 1932- *WhoScEn 94*
Epsen, Robert A. 1939- *WhoAmL 94*
Epstein, Alan 1954- *WhoAmL 94*
Epstein, Alan Bruce 1944- *WhoAmL 94*
Epstein, Alexander Maxim 1963- *WhoWest 94*
Epstein, Alvin 1925- *WhoAm 94*
Epstein, (Michael) Anthony 1921- *IntWW 93, Who 94*
Epstein, Anthony C. 1952- *WhoAm 94*
Epstein, Arthur Joseph 1945- *WhoAm 94*
Epstein, Arthur William 1923- *WhoAm 94*
Epstein, Barbara 1929- *WhoAm 94*
Epstein, Barry R. 1942- *WhoAm 94*
Epstein, Beryl 1910- *SmATA 17AS [port]*
Epstein, Betty O. 1920- *WhoAmA 93*
Epstein, Bruce Howard 1952- *WhoAmL 94*
Epstein, Charles Joseph 1933- *WhoAm 94*
Epstein, Charlotte 1921- *WrDr 94*
Epstein, Cynthia Fuchs *WhoAm 94*
Epstein, Cynthia Fuchs 1933- *WrDr 94*
Epstein, Daniel Mark *DrAPF 93*
Epstein, Daniel Mark 1948- *WhoAm 94*
Epstein, David A. 1943- *WhoAmL 94*
Epstein, David Aaron 1942- *WhoScEn 94*
Epstein, David Frederick 1954- *WhoMW 93*
Epstein, David Gustav 1943- *WhoAm 94*
Epstein, David Lee 1947- *WhoFI 94*
Epstein, David Mayer 1930- *WhoAm 94*
Epstein, David Robert *WhoFI 94*
Epstein, Donald Robert 1945- *WhoAmL 94*
Epstein, Edna Selan 1938- *WhoAmP 93*
Epstein, Edward Joseph 1920- *WhoFI 94*
Epstein, Edward Louis 1936- *WhoAm 94*
Epstein, Edward S. 1931- *WhoAm 94*
Epstein, Eileen M. L. 1953- *WhoAmL 94*
Epstein, Elaine *DrAPF 93*
Epstein, Eleni Sakes 1925- *WhAm 10*
Epstein, Elissa 1933- *WhoAmP 93*
Epstein, Emanuel 1916- *IntWW 93, WhoAm 94*
Epstein, Ervin Harold, Jr. 1941- *WhoWest 94*
Epstein, Ethel S. *WhoAmA 93N*
Epstein, Franklin Harold 1924- *WhoAm 94*
Epstein, Gabriel 1918- *IntWW 93*
Epstein, Gary Marvin 1946- *WhoAm 94, WhoAmL 94*
Epstein, George Allan 1953- *WhoAmL 94*
Epstein, Gerald Lewis 1956- *WhoScEn 94*
Epstein, Henrietta *WhoMW 93*
Epstein, Henry David 1927- *WhoAm 94*
Epstein, Irving Robert 1945- *WhoAm 94*
Epstein, Israel 1915- *WhoPRCh 91 [port]*
Epstein, Jason 1928- *WhoAm 94*
Epstein, Jaye Mark 1950- *WhoFI 94*
Epstein, Jeremiah Fain 1924- *WhoAm 94*
Epstein, Jeremy G. 1946- *WhoAm 94, WhoAmL 94*
Epstein, Joan Hirsch 1923- *WhoMW 93*
Epstein, John Howard 1926- *WhoAm 94*
Epstein, Jon David 1942- *WhoAmL 94*
Epstein, Jonathan Akiba 1963- *WhoWest 94*

Epstein, Jonathan Stone 1957- WhoScEn 94
Epstein, Joseph d1993 NewYTBS 93
Epstein, Joseph 1937- WhoAm 94, WrDr 94
Epstein, Joseph Allen 1917- WhoScEn 94
Epstein, Joseph Z. 1941- WhoAmL 94
Epstein, Judith Ann 1942- WhoAmL 94
Epstein, Judith Sue DrAPF 93
Epstein, Julius 1909- IntDcF 2-4
Epstein, Julius J. 1909- IntMPA 94, WhoAm 94
Epstein, Kalman Noel 1938- WhoAm 94
Epstein, Laura 1914- WhoAm 94
Epstein, Lawrence J(effrey) 1946- WrDr 94
Epstein, Leon David 1919- WhoMW 93
Epstein, Leon Joseph 1917- WhoAm 94
Epstein, Leslie DrAPF 93
Epstein, Leslie (Donald) 1938- WrDr 94
Epstein, Lionel Charles 1924- WhoAm 94
Epstein, Louis Ralph 1926- WhoAm 94
Epstein, Matthew IntWW 93
Epstein, Matthew 1947- NewGrDO
Epstein, Max 1925- WhoAm 94
Epstein, Mel 1910- IntMPA 94
Epstein, Melvin 1938- WhoAm 94
Epstein, Michael Alan 1954- WhoAm 94, WhoAmL 94
Epstein, Mitch 1952- WhoAmA 93
Epstein, Philip 1909-1952 IntDcF 2-4
Epstein, Pierre 1930- WhoHol 92
Epstein, Raymond 1918- WhoAm 94
Epstein, Richard A. 1943- WhoAm 94, WhoAmL 94
Epstein, Robert C. 1951- WhoAmL 94
Epstein, Robert Marvin 1928- WhoAm 94
Epstein, Roger Harris 1945- WhoAmL 94
Epstein, Samuel 1909- SmATA 17AS [port]
Epstein, Samuel 1919- WhoAm 94
Epstein, Samuel Seth 1948- WhoScEn 94
Epstein, Sandra Gail 1939- WhoScEn 94
Epstein, Scott Mitchell 1958- WhoScEn 94
Epstein, Selma 1927- WhoAm 94
Epstein, Seth Paul 1958- WhoScEn 94
Epstein, Seymour DrAPF 93
Epstein, Seymour 1917- WrDr 94
Epstein, Sidney 1920- WhoAm 94
Epstein, Sidney 1923- WhoAm 94, WhoFI 94
Epstein, Simon Jules 1934- WhoAm 94
Epstein, Stephen Roger 1947- WhoFI 94
Epstein, Steven B. 1943- WhoAmL 94
Epstein, William 1912- IntWW 93
Epstein, William 1931- WhoAm 94
Epstein, William Eric 1949- WhoAm 94
Epstein, William Louis 1925- WhoAm 94, WhoScEn 94
Epstein, William Stuart 1940- WhoAm 94
Epstein, Wolfgang 1931- WhoAm 94, WhoMW 93
Epstein, Yale 1934- WhoAmA 93
Epstien, Jay Alan 1951- WhoAm 94
Epting, C. Christopher WhoAm 94, WhoMW 93
Epting, Marion WhoBlA 94
Epting, Marion Austin 1940- WhoAmA 93
Eqin Jamsu 1925- WhoPRCh 91 [port]
Equi, Elaine DrAPF 93
Equi, Glenn C. 1937- WhoAmL 94
Equiluz, Kurt 1929- NewGrDO
Erasistratus c. 304BC-c. 250BC WorScD
Erasmus, Charles John 1921- WhoAm 94
Erasmus, Desiderius 1466?-1536 BlmGEL
Erasmus, Desiderius c. 1467-1536 DcLB 136 [port]
Erastoff, Edith d1945 WhoHol 92
Erasure ConMus 11 [port]
Erath, Edward Hyde 1929- WhoWest 94
Eraut, Michael Ruarc 1940- Who 94
Erazmus, Walter Thomas 1947- WhoFI 94
Erb, Christian Stehman, Jr. 1931- WhoAmL 94
Erb, Dick 1928- WhoAmP 93
Erb, Donald 1927- WhoAm 94
Erb, Doretta Louise Barker 1932- WhoScEn 94
Erb, James J. 1946- WhoAm 94
Erb, John Charles 1946- WhoAmL 94
Erb, Karl 1877-1958 NewGrDO
Erb, Karl Albert 1942- WhoScEn 94
Erb, Lillian Edgar 1922- WhoAmP 93
Erb, Paul 1894- WhAm 10
Erb, Richard David 1941- WhoAm 94
Erb, Richard Louis Lundin 1929- WhoAm 94
Erb, Robert Allan 1932- WhoAm 94
Erb, Thomas C. 1953- WhoAmL 94
Erba, Luciano 1922- ConWorW 93
Erbakan, Necmettin 1926- IntWW 93
Erbe, Gary Thomas 1944- WhoAmA 93
Erbe, Joan 1926- WhoAmA 93
Erbe, Johannes Petrus 1927- IntWW 93
Erbe, Pamela DrAPF 93
Erbel, Raimund 1948- WhoScEn 94
Erben, Heinrich Karl 1921- IntWW 93
Erber, Thomas 1930- WhoAm 94
Erbert, Virgil 1924- WhoFI 94
Erbes, John Fredric 1954- WhoAmL 94
Erbes, Roslyn Maria WhoAmA 93
Erbil, Ahmet 1955- WhoScEn 94
Erbil, Leyla 1931- BlmGWL
Erbse, Heimo 1924- NewGrDO
Erbsen, Claude Ernest 1938- WhoAm 94
Erbst, Lawrence Arnold 1930- WhoWest 94
Erbstein, Keith Sandy 1946- WhoAmL 94
Erburu, Robert F. 1930- WhoAm 94, WhoFI 94, WhoWest 94
Erby, Morris d1978 WhoHol 92
Erce, Ignacio, III 1964- WhoScEn 94
Erck, Robert Alan 1954- WhoMW 93
Ercklentz, Alexander Tonio 1936- WhoAm 94, WhoFI 94
Ercklentz, Enno Wilhelm, Jr. 1931- WhoAm 94
Erckmann-Chatrian 1822-1899 NewGrDO
Erckmann-Chatrian 1826-1890 NewGrDO
Ercole, Robert Michael 1954- WhoAmL 94
Ercolini, Elaine Evelyn 1959- WhoAmL 94
Erdahl, Lowell O. 1931- WhoMW 93
Erdal, Bruce Robert 1939- WhoWest 94
Erdberg, Mindel Ruth 1916- WhoScEn 94
Erdel, Bert Paul 1943- WhoAm 94
Erdelac, Joseph Mark WhoAmA 93
Erdeljac, Daniel Joseph 1932- WhoAm 94
Erdely, Stephen Lajos 1921- WhoAm 94
Erdelyi, Miklos 1928- IntWW 93, NewGrDO
Erdem, Kaya 1928- IntWW 93
Erdemir, Ali 1954- WhoScEn 94
Erden, Sybil Isolde 1950- WhoAm 94
Erdle, Rob 1949- WhoAmA 93
Erdman, Barbara 1936- WhoAm 94
Erdman, Carl L. N. 1915- WhoAm 94
Erdman, Edward Louis 1906- Who 94
Erdman, Howard Loyd 1935- WhoAm 94
Erdman, Joseph 1935- WhoAm 94
Erdman, Leon R. 1950- WhoFI 94
Erdman, Lowell Paul 1926- WhoAm 94
Erdman, Nikolai Robertovich 1902-1970 IntDcT 2
Erdman, Pamela Ann 1962- WhoMW 93
Erdman, Paul E. 1932- WrDr 94
Erdman, Paul E(mil) 1932- ConAu 43NR, EncSF 93
Erdman, Paul Emil 1932- WhoAm 94
Erdman, Richard 1925- IntMPA 94, WhoHol 92
Erdman, William James, II 1921-1989 WhAm 10
Erdmann, August WhoMW 93
Erdmann, Joachim Christian 1928- WhoWest 94
Erdmann, John Baird 1950- WhoScEn 94
Erdmann, Terrance Gene 1965- WhoMW 93
Erdner, Jon W. 1942- WhoFI 94
Erdos, Andre 1941- IntWW 93
Erdos, Ervin George 1922- WhoAm 94
Erdos, Paul 1913- IntWW 93
Erdreich, Ben 1938- WhoAmP 93
Erdreich, John 1943- WhoScEn 94
Erdrich, Karen Louise 1954- IntWW 93, WhoAm 94
Erdrich, Louise 1954- BlmGWL, ConAu 41NR, WhoAm 94, WrDr 94
Ereaut, (Herbert) Frank (Cobbold) 1919- Who 94
Erede, Alberto 1908- NewGrDO
Erediauwa, Omo N'Oba N'Edo Uku-Akpolokpolo 1923- IntWW 93
Eremin, Alvin Evstafevich 1932- LoBiDrD
Eremin, Oleg 1938- Who 94
Erenberg, Vladimir Georgiyevich NewGrDO
Erenburg, Steven Alan 1937- WhoFI 94
Erens, Jay Allan 1935- WhoAm 94
Erens, Patricia 1938- WrDr 94
Eres, Eugenia 1928- WhoAmA 93
Eret, Donald 1931- WhoAmP 93
Erevia, Angela, Sister 1934- WhoHisp 94
E-Rex ConAu 142
Erf, Stephen D. 1953- WhoAm 94, WhoAmL 94
Erfani, Shervin 1948- WhoScEn 94
Erfman, David John 1953- WhoAmP 93
Erford, Esther DrAPF 93
Ergas, Enrique 1938- WhoAm 94, WhoScEn 94
Ergas, Jean-Pierre Maurice 1939- WhoAm 94, WhoFI 94
Ergazos, John William 1924- WhoMW 93
Erhard, Michael Paul 1948- WhoAm 94
Erhard, Tom 1923- WrDr 94
Erhardt, Edward Richard 1957- WhoAm 94
Erhardt, Ron WhoAmP 93
Erhardt, Warren Richard 1924- WhoAm 94
Eri, (Vincent) Serei d1993 Who 94N
Eri, Vincent (Serei) 1936- WrDr 94
Eri, Vincent Serei d1993 NewYTBS 93
Eriacho, Belinda Pearl 1963- WhoWest 94
Eribes, Richard A. WhoHisp 94
Eric, Fred d1935 WhoHol 92
Ericksen, Jerald Laverne 1924- WhoAm 94, WhoScEn 94
Erickson, Alan WhoAmP 93
Erickson, Alan Eric 1928- WhoAm 94
Erickson, Andrew M. 1939- WhoIns 94
Erickson, Arthur Charles 1924- IntWW 93, WhoAm 94, WhoWest 94
Erickson, Bernard 1944- WhoAmP 93
Erickson, Bob d1941 WhoHol 92
Erickson, Brice Carl 1957- WhoScEn 94
Erickson, Calvin Howard 1946- WhoWest 94
Erickson, Carol Ann 1933- WhoWest 94
Erickson, Catherine DrAPF 93
Erickson, Charles Burton 1932- WhoAm 94
Erickson, Charles Edward 1947- WhoAm 94, WhoIns 94
Erickson, Charles Henry 1940- WhoMW 93
Erickson, Charles John 1931- WhoWest 94
Erickson, Charlotte J(oanne) 1923- WrDr 94
Erickson, Charlotte Joanne 1923- Who 94
Erickson, Christopher Andrew 1957- WhoWest 94
Erickson, Darlene Ellen 1941- WhoMW 93
Erickson, David Belnap 1951- WhoAmL 94
Erickson, David Martin 1953- WhoAmL 94
Erickson, Dennis WhoAm 94
Erickson, Dennis Alseth 1954- WhoAmP 93
Erickson, Dennis Duane 1938- WhoAm 94
Erickson, Diane WhoHol 92
Erickson, Don 1937- WhoAmP 93
Erickson, Donald Arthur 1925- WhoWest 94
Erickson, Donald Craig 1950- WhoAm 94, WhoAmL 94
Erickson, Edward Leonard 1946- WhoFI 94
Erickson, Eric Douglas 1955- WhoWest 94
Erickson, Frank William 1923- WhoAm 94
Erickson, Gerald Meyer 1927- WhoAm 94
Erickson, Gordon Karl 1960- WhoMW 93
Erickson, Gregory Kevin 1953- WhoIns 94
Erickson, Hal 1950- ConAu 142
Erickson, Homer Theodore 1925- WhoScEn 94
Erickson, James Gardner 1925- WhoWest 94
Erickson, James H. 1939- WhoWest 94
Erickson, James Paul 1929- WhoAm 94
Erickson, Jeffrey Lee 1960- WhoMW 93
Erickson, John 1929- Who 94
Erickson, John Duff 1933- WhoAm 94
Erickson, John Ronald 1934- WhoScEn 94
Erickson, Joy M. 1932- WhoAmA 93
Erickson, Judith Bowen 1934- WhoMW 93
Erickson, Kenneth W. 1947- WhoAm 94
Erickson, Kim L. 1951- WhoMW 93
Erickson, Knute d1946 WhoHol 92
Erickson, Larry Alvin 1950- WhoMW 93
Erickson, Larry Eugene 1938- WhoMW 93
Erickson, Lawrence Wilhelm 1915- WhoAm 94
Erickson, Leif d1986 WhoHol 92
Erickson, Leif B. 1942- WhoAm 94, WhoAmL 94, WhoWest 94
Erickson, Leroy WhoAmP 93
Erickson, Luther Eugene 1933- WhoAm 94
Erickson, Margaret Jane WhoAmA 93
Erickson, Margaret Kathryn 1954- WhoAmL 94, WhoMW 93
Erickson, Mark D. 1955- WhoAmA 93
Erickson, Mark Robert 1956- WhoMW 93
Erickson, Marsha A. 1945- WhoAmA 93
Erickson, Nancy Annette Polzin 1934- WhoAmL 94
Erickson, Nancy Salome 1945- WhoAmL 94
Erickson, Ralph D. 1922- WhoAm 94
Erickson, Ralph Ernest 1928- WhoAm 94, WhoAmL 94
Erickson, Ralph O. 1914- WhoAm 94
Erickson, Raymond Leroy 1925- WhoAm 94
Erickson, Richard Ames 1923- WhoAm 94
Erickson, Richard Beau 1952- WhoWest 94
Erickson, Richard J. 1946- WhoAm 94
Erickson, Richard John 1943- IntWW 93
Erickson, Richard L. 1942- WhoAm 94
Erickson, Richard Lee 1938- WhoFI 94
Erickson, Richard Theodore 1932- WhoAm 94
Erickson, Robert 1917- NewGrDO
Erickson, Robert Allen 1940- WhoWest 94
Erickson, Robert Anders 1962- WhoMW 93, WhoScEn 94
Erickson, Robert Daniel 1943- WhoAm 94
Erickson, Robert L. 1938- WhoWest 94
Erickson, Robert Stanley 1944- WhoAmL 94
Erickson, Rolf Herbert 1940-1992 WhAm 10
Erickson, Roy Frederick, Jr. 1928- WhoAm 94
Erickson, Roy Lydeen 1923- WhoAm 94, WhoAmL 94
Erickson, Russell John WhoWest 94
Erickson, Scott Timothy 1961- WhoAmL 94
Erickson, Staci Kennedy 1969- WhoWest 94
Erickson, Stephen Emory 1945- WhoFI 94
Erickson, Stephen Paul 1951- WhoAmP 93
Erickson, Steve 1950- EncSF 93, WrDr 94
Erickson, Tamara Jo 1954- WhoFI 94
Erickson, Theodore Henning 1935- WhoMW 93
Erickson, Thomas J. 1954- WhoIns 94
Erickson, Timothy Eric 1954- WhoWest 94
Erickson, Virginia Bemmels 1948- WhoWest 94
Erickson, Walter 1914- WrDr 94
Erickson, Walter Bruce 1938- WhoAm 94
Erickson, Waltor Bruce WhoMW 93
Erickson, Wendell O. 1925- WhoAmP 93
Erickson, William Hurt 1924- WhoAm 94, WhoAmL 94, WhoAmP 93, WhoWest 94
Erickstad, Ralph John 1922- WhoAm 94, WhoAmL 94, WhoAmP 93
Ericson, Barbro 1930- NewGrDO
Ericson, Beatrice WhoAmA 93
Ericson, Bruce Alan 1952- WhoAm 94
Ericson, David F. 1950- ConAu 142
Ericson, David Paul 1949- WhoWest 94
Ericson, Devon WhoHol 92
Ericson, Ernest d1981 WhoAmA 93N
Ericson, Fritsi Hancock 1938- WhoWest 94
Ericson, James Donald 1935- WhoAm 94, WhoAmL 94
Ericson, John 1926- IntMPA 94, WhoHol 92, WhoWest 94
Ericson, Jon Meyer 1928- WhoAm 94
Ericson, Jonathon Edward 1942- WhoWest 94
Ericson, Karen WhoHol 92
Ericson, Kate 1955- See Ziegler, Mel(vin) 1956- & Ericson, Kate 1955- WhoAmA 93
Ericson, Mark Frederick 1957- WhoWest 94
Ericson, Richard Charles 1933- WhoMW 93
Ericson, Robert W. 1948- WhoAm 94, WhoAmL 94
Ericson, Roger Delwin 1934- WhoAm 94, WhoAmL 94, WhoFI 94
Ericson, Ruth Ann WhoAm 94
Ericsson, Dianne K. 1950- WhoAmL 94
Ericsson, John 1803-1889 WorInv
Ericsson, Leif c. 970-c. 1020 WhWE
Ericsson, Ronald James 1935- WhoFI 94
Ericsson, Thorvald dc. 1007 WhWE
Eric The Red c. 950-1010 WhWE
Erie, Gretchen Ann 1945- WhoMW 93
Eriksen, Charles Walter 1923- WhoAm 94, WhoScEn 94
Eriksen, Clyde Hedman 1933- WhoScEn 94
Eriksen, Gary 1943- WhoAmA 93
Eriksen, Gerald Bruce 1951- WhoAmP 93
Eriksen, Inge EncSF 93
Eriksen, Otto Louis 1930- WhoAm 94
Eriksen, Peter Bendtsen 1918- WhoMW 93
Eriksen, Richard Eugene 1945- WhoAmL 94
Erikson, Erik H(omburger) 1902- WrDr 94
Erikson, Erik Homburger 1902- AmSocL, IntWW 93, WhoAm 94
Erikson, George Emil 1920- WhoAm 94, WhoScEn 94
Erikson, Gregory 1944- WhoMW 93
Erikson, J. Lance 1943- WhoAmL 94
Erikson, Kai 1931- WhoAm 94
Erikson, Kai T(heodor) 1931- ConAu 142
Erikson, Nancy Watson DrAPF 93

Erikson, Raymond Leo 1936- *WhoAm 94, WhoScEn 94*
Eriksson, Goran Olof 1929- *IntWW 93*
Eriksson, James Ernest 1943- *WhoMW 93*
Eriksson, Karl-Erik Lennart 1932- *WhoScEn 94*
Eriksson, Larry John 1945- *WhoAm 94*
Eriksson, Per-Olof 1938- *IntWW 93*
Erim, Kenan Tevfik 1929-1990 *WhAm 10*
Erin, Viktor Fedorovich 1944- *LoBiDrD*
Erinna fl. c. 4th cent.BC- *BlmGWL*
Erinni *BlmGWL*
Eriphanis *BlmGWL*
Erisman, Frank 1943- *WhoAm 94, WhoAmL 94*
Erisman, Fred Raymond 1937- *WhoAm 94*
Eristoff, Andrew 1963- *WhoAmP 93*
Eristoff, Nestor d1961 *WhoHol 92*
Erith, John 1904- *WrDr 94*
Erkel, Ferenc 1810-1893 *NewGrDO*
Erkfritz, Donald Spencer 1925- *WhoFI 94*
Erkkila, Betsy 1944- *ConAu 140*
Erkmen, Hayrettin 1915- *IntWW 93*
Erla, Karen 1942- *WhoAm 94, WhoAmA 93*
Erland, Cynthia *WhoHol 92*
Erlande-Brandenburg, Alain 1937- *IntWW 93*
Erlandson, David Alan 1936- *WhoAm 94*
Erlandson, Douglas Kent 1946- *WhoMW 93*
Erlanger, Bernard Ferdinand 1923- *WhoAm 94*
Erlanger, Camille 1863-1919 *NewGrDO*
Erlanger, Elizabeth N. 1901-1975 *WhoAmA 93N*
Erlanger, Frederic d' 1868-1943 *NewGrDO*
Erlanger, Philippe *IntWW 93N*
Erlanger, Steven Jay 1952- *WhoAm 94*
Erlanson, Deborah McFarlin 1943- *WhoMW 93*
Erle, Walter 1586-1665 *DcNaB MP*
Erlebach, Philipp Heinrich 1657-1714 *NewGrDO*
Erlebacher, Albert 1932- *WhoAm 94*
Erlebacher, Arlene Cernik 1946- *WhoAm 94, WhoAmL 94*
Erlebacher, Martha Mayer 1937- *WhoAmA 93*
Erleigh, Viscount 1986- *Who 94*
Erlenberger, Maria *BlmGWL*
Erlenborn, John Neal 1927- *WhoAm 94*
Erlenmeyer-Kimling, L. *WhoAm 94*
Erlewine, Richard Henry 1914- *WhoMW 93*
Erlich, Victor 1914- *WhoAm 94*
Erlicht, Lewis Howard 1939- *WhoAm 94*
Erlick, Everett Howard 1921- *WhoAm 94*
Erline, N. T. 1949- *WrDr 94*
Erling, Jacque J. 1925- *WhoAmP 93*
Erlo, Louis 1929- *NewGrDO*
Erlo, Louis Jean-Marie 1929- *IntWW 93*
Ermak *WhWE*
Erman, Bruce 1945- *WhoAmA 93*
Erman, Geraldine *WhoAmA 93*
Erman, Jacques DeForest *EncSF 93*
Erman, John 1935- *IntMPA 94, WhoAm 94*
Erman, William Francis 1931- *WhoMW 93*
Ermelli, Claudio d1964 *WhoHol 92*
Ermenc, Joseph John 1912- *WhoAm 94*
Ermer, James 1942- *WhoAm 94, WhoFI 94*
Ermey, Lee 1944- *WhoHol 92*
Ermolenko, Vitaly Petrovich 1942- *LoBiDrD*
Ermolenko-Yuzhina, Nataliya *NewGrDO*
Ernaut, Peter Gordon 1964- *WhoAmP 93*
Ernaux, Annie *BlmGWL*
Erne, Earl of 1937- *Who 94*
Ernemann, Andre 1923- *IntWW 93*
Ernesaks, Gustav Gustavovich 1908- *NewGrDO*
Ernest, Albert Devery, Jr. 1930- *WhoAm 94*
Ernest, George 1921- *WhoHol 92*
Ernest, J. Terry 1935- *WhoScEn 94*
Ernest, Jonathan Alexander 1961- *WhoAmL 94*
Ernest, Max Wesley 1930- *WhoMW 93*
Erni, Hans 1909- *IntWW 93*
Erno, Richard B(ruce) 1923- *WrDr 94*
Ernsberger, Fred Martin 1919- *WhoScEn 94*
Ernsberger, George *EncSF 93*
Ernsberger, Paul Roos 1956- *WhoScEn 94*
Ernst, II 1818-1893 *NewGrDO*
Ernst, Albert 1949- *WhoAm 94, WhoAmL 94*
Ernst, Calvin Bradley 1934- *WhoAm 94*
Ernst, Christopher Mark 1966- *WhoAmL 94*
Ernst, Cliff 1953- *WhoAmL 94*
Ernst, Daniel Pearson 1931- *WhoAmL 94, WhoMW 93*
Ernst, Edward Willis 1924- *WhoAm 94, WhoScEn 94*
Ernst, Eldon Gilbert 1939- *WhoWest 94*
Ernst, Gregory Alan 1960- *WhoScEn 94*
Ernst, Jimmy 1920- *WhoAmA 93N*
Ernst, John Louis 1932- *WhoAm 94*
Ernst, Joseph Richard 1934- *WhoMW 93*
Ernst, K. S. *DrAPF 93*
Ernst, Laura *WhoHol 92*
Ernst, Lois Geraci 1933- *WhoAm 94*
Ernst, Max 1891-1976 *WhoAmA 93N*
Ernst, Michael J. 1966- *WhoAmP 93*
Ernst, Norman Frank, Jr. 1942- *WhoIns 94*
Ernst, Paul (Frederick) 1899-1985 *EncSF 93*
Ernst, Reginald H. 1928- *WhoBlA 94*
Ernst, Richard R. 1933- *IntWW 93, NobelP 91 [port]*
Ernst, Richard Robert 1933- *Who 94, WhoScEn 94*
Ernst, Robert 1915- *WrDr 94*
Ernst, Roger 1924- *WhoAm 94, WhoFI 94*
Ernst, Roger Charles 1914- *WhoAm 94*
Ernst, Wallace Gary 1931- *WhoAm 94, WhoScEn 94*
Ernst de la Graete, Brigitte 1957- *WhoWomW 91*
Ernster, Deszo d1981 *WhoHol 92*
Ernster, Dezso 1898-1981 *NewGrDO*
Ernsting, John 1928- *Who 94*
Ernsting, Walter *EncSF 93*
Ernstrom, Adele Mansfield 1930- *WhoAmA 93*
Ernstthal, Henry L. 1940- *WhoAm 94*
Ernt, Bruce William 1942- *WhoFI 94*
Ernzen, Mary Anne *WhoMW 93*
Erofeev, Oleg Aleksandrovich 1949- *LoBiDrD*
Erofeyev, Victor 1947- *ConAu 140*
Erokan, Dennis William 1950- *WhoAm 94, WhoWest 94*
Eron, Leonard David 1920- *WhoAm 94*
Eron, Madeline Marcus 1919- *WhoMW 93*
Erosh, William Daniel 1956- *WhoAm 94, WhoFI 94*
Erpelding, Curtis Michael 1950- *WhoWest 94*
Erpelding, Kevin Luke 1968- *WhoMW 93*
Erquiaga, Elisa Piper Cafferata 1962- *WhoWest 94*
Err, Lydie Clementine Nicole 1949- *WhoWomW 91*
Erramilli, Shyamsunder 1957- *WhoAsA 94*
Errampalli, Deena 1958- *WhoScEn 94*
Errazuriz, (Talavera) Hernan 1941- *Who 94*
Erreca, Charles M. *WhoHisp 94*
Errecart, Joyce Hier 1950- *WhoAmL 94*
Errichelli, Pasquale 1730-1775? *NewGrDO*
Errickson, Krista *WhoHol 92*
Errington, Geoffrey (Frederick) 1926- *Who 94*
Errington, Lancelot 1917- *Who 94*
Errington, Richard Percy 1904- *Who 94*
Errington, Stuart Grant 1929- *IntWW 93, Who 94*
Erritt, (Michael) John (Mackey) 1931- *Who 94*
Errol, Leon d1951 *WhoHol 92*
Errol, Leon 1881-1951 *WhoCom*
Erroll, Earl of 1948- *Who 94*
Erroll Of Hale, Baron 1914- *IntWW 93, Who 94*
Ersboll, Niels 1926- *IntWW 93*
Ersek, Gregory Joseph Mark 1956- *WhoAmL 94, WhoFI 94*
Ersek, Robert Allen 1938- *WhoAm 94*
Ersgaard, Ole Kristian 1948- *WhoFI 94*
Ershad, Hossain Mohammad 1930- *IntWW 93*
Ershad, Hussain Muhammad 1930- *Who 94*
Ershler, William Baldwin 1949- *WhoAm 94*
Ershov, Ivan Vasil'yevich *NewGrDO*
Ersin, Nurettin 1918- *IntWW 93*
Erskin, John *WhoAmP 93*
Erskine *Who 94*
Erskine, Lord 1949- *Who 94*
Erskine, Albert 1911-1993 *DcLB Y93N [port]*
Erskine, Albert R., Jr. d1993 *NewYTBS 93 [port]*
Erskine, David *Who 94*
Erskine, (Thomas) David 1912- *Who 94*
Erskine, David John 1957- *WhoScEn 94*
Erskine, George *EncSF 93*
Erskine, Harold Perry 1879-1951 *WhoAmA 93N*
Erskine, Howard 1926- *WhoHol 92*
Erskine, James Lorenzo 1942- *WhoAm 94*
Erskine, John Morse 1920- *WhoAm 94, WhoWest 94*
Erskine, Kenneth F. *WhoBlA 94*
Erskine, Laurie York 1894- *WhAm 10*
Erskine, Margaret *WrDr 94*
Erskine, Marilyn 1924- *WhoHol 92*
Erskine, Matthew Forbes 1959- *WhoAmL 94*
Erskine, Ralph 1914- *IntWW 93, Who 94*
Erskine, Robert 1735-1780 *AmRev, WhAmRev*
Erskine, Robin Richardson 1963- *WhoWest 94*
Erskine, Rosalind 1929- *WrDr 94*
Erskine, Thomas 1788-1870 *EncSF 93*
Erskine, Thomas Ralph 1933- *Who 94*
Erskine, Wallace d1943 *WhoHol 92*
Erskine, William 1728-1795 *WhAmRev*
Erskine-Hill, (Henry) Howard 1936- *Who 94*
Erskine-Hill, Roger *Who 94*
Erskine-Hill, (Alexander) Roger 1949- *Who 94*
Erskine-Murray *Who 94*
Erskine Of Rerrick, Baron 1926- *Who 94*
Erslev, Allan Jacob 1919- *WhoAm 94*
Erslev, Eric Allan 1954- *WhoScEn 94*
Erstad, Leon Robert 1947- *WhoAmL 94, WhoMW 93*
Erte, Romain De Tirtoff 1892-1990 *WhAm 10*
Ertegun, Ahmet 1923- *ConMus 10 [port]*
Ertegun, Ahmet Munir 1923- *WhoAm 94*
Ertel, Allen Edward 1936- *WhoAm 94, WhoAmL 94, WhoAmP 93*
Ertel, Denise Marlene 1956- *WhoFI 94*
Ertel, Gary Arthur 1954- *WhoFI 94, WhoMW 93*
Ertem, Ozcan 1962- *WhoScEn 94*
Erteza, Ireena Ahmed 1965- *WhoScEn 94*
Ertl, Josef 1925- *IntWW 93*
Ertl, Joseph L. *WhoAmP 93*
Ertl, Peter 1959- *WhoScEn 94*
Ertl, Ronald Frank 1946- *WhoScEn 94*
Ertle, William Justin 1968- *WhoMW 93*
Ertman, Earl Leslie 1932- *WhoAmA 93*
Ertmann, Minny d1981 *WhoHol 92*
Ertz, Susan 1894-1985 *EncSF 93*
Ervin, Connie Yvonne 1954- *WhoMW 93*
Ervin, Deborah Green 1956- *WhoBlA 94*
Ervin, Hazel Arnett 1948- *WhoBlA 94*
Ervin, Howard Guy, III 1947- *WhoAm 94*
Ervin, John B. 1916-1992 *WhoBlA 94N*
Ervin, Kathey 1952- *WhoAmA 93*
Ervin, Naomi Estalee 1942- *WhoMW 93*
Ervin, Noca Celia 1953- *WhoMW 93*
Ervin, Patrick Franklin 1946- *WhoWest 94*
Ervin, Robert Crawford 1960- *WhoAmL 94*
Ervin, Robert Marvin 1917- *WhoAm 94*
Ervin, Sam J., III 1926- *WhoAmP 93*
Ervin, Samuel James, III 1926- *WhoAm 94, WhoAmL 94*
Ervin, Samuel James, IV 1955- *WhoAmP 93*
Ervin, Tom J. 1952- *WhoAmP 93*
Ervine-Andrews, Harold Marcus 1911- *Who 94*
Erving, Claude Moore, Jr. 1952- *WhoWest 94*
Erving, Julius 1950- *AfrAmAl 6, BasBi [port], WhoHol 92*
Erving, Julius Winfield 1950- *WhoAm 94, WhoBlA 94*
Erway, Ben d1981 *WhoHol 92*
Erwin, Barbara *WhoHol 92*
Erwin, Bill *WhoHol 92*
Erwin, Cheryl Janette 1956- *WhoFI 94*
Erwin, Claude F., Sr. 1906- *WhoBlA 94*
Erwin, Dennis Keith 1953- *WhoAmP 93*
Erwin, Diane Jean 1946- *WhoAmP 93*
Erwin, Donald Carroll 1920- *WhoAm 94, WhoWest 94*
Erwin, Douglas Homer 1954- *WhoFI 94*
Erwin, Edgar E. 1920- *WhoAmP 93*
Erwin, Elmer Louis 1926- *WhoAm 94*
Erwin, Fran *WhoAmA 93*
Erwin, Frank William 1931- *WhoAm 94*
Erwin, James C. 1927- *WhoWest 94*
Erwin, James Otis 1922- *WhoBlA 94*
Erwin, James Walter 1946- *WhoAm 94*
Erwin, John Preston 1939- *WhoAmP 93*
Erwin, Judith Ann 1939- *WhoAm 94*
Erwin, Judy *WhoAmP 93*
Erwin, June d1965 *WhoHol 92*
Erwin, Kenton Lane 1957- *WhoAmL 94*
Erwin, Madge d1967 *WhoHol 92*
Erwin, Martin Nesbitt 1938- *WhoAm 94, WhoAmL 94*
Erwin, Phyllis R. 1929- *WhoAmP 93*
Erwin, Randall Lee 1951- *WhoAmP 93*
Erwin, Richard C. 1923- *WhoBlA 94*
Erwin, Richard Cannon 1923- *WhoAm 94, WhoAmL 94*
Erwin, Robert Earl 1943- *WhoAmP 93*
Erwin, Robert Lester 1953- *WhoAm 94*
Erwin, Roy d1958 *WhoHol 92*
Erwin, Stuart d1967 *WhoHol 92*
Erwin, Sue Carlanne 1950- *WhoAmL 94*
Erwin, Timothy J. *WhoAmP 93*
Erwin, William Walter 1925- *WhoAmP 93*
Erwitt, Elliott Romano 1928- *WhoAm 94*
Erxleben, William Charles 1942- *WhoAm 94, WhoAmL 94*
Erysian, Bill Myron 1957- *WhoWest 94*
Eryurek, Evren 1963- *WhoScEn 94*
Erzinger, Kim L. 1952- *WhoAmP 93*
Erzurumlu, H. Chik M. 1934- *WhoWest 94*
Esahak, George Michael 1958- *WhoAmL 94*
Esaki, Leo 1925- *IntWW 93, Who 94, WhoAm 94, WhoScEn 94, WorScD*
Esaki, Masumi 1915- *IntWW 93*
Esaki, Toshiyuki 1947- *WhoScEn 94*
Esaki, Yasuhiro 1941- *WhoAmA 93*
Esau, Erika 1949- *WhoAmA 93*
Esau, Gilbert D. 1919- *WhoAmP 93*
Esau, John Nicholas 1944- *WhoWest 94*
Esbensen, Barbara Juster *DrAPF 93*
Esbensen, Barbara Juster 1925- *WrDr 94*
Esbin, Jerry 1931- *IntMPA 94*
Escajeda, Henry *WhoHisp 94*
Escajeda, Richard Martin 1930- *WhoHisp 94*
Escala, Veronica *WhoHisp 94*
Escalada, Tito d1986 *WhoHol 92*
Escaladas, Emilio, III 1948- *WhoHisp 94*
Escalais, Leon 1859-1941 *NewGrDO*
Escalante, Efraim 1947- *WhoHisp 94*
Escalante, Francisco Silvestre Velez De 1745-1780 *EncNAR, WhWE*
Escalante, Jaime 1930- *WhoHisp 94*
Escalante, Judson Robert 1930- *WhoFI 94*
Escalante, Lalo d1970 *WhoHol 92*
Escalante, Roel 1937- *WhoHisp 94*
Escalante Cooper, Barbara 1967- *WhoHisp 94*
Escalera, Albert D. 1943- *WhoHisp 94*
Escalera, Nitza Milagros 1951- *WhoAmL 94*
Escalet, Edwin Michael 1952- *WhoHisp 94*
Escalet, Frank Diaz 1930- *WhoAmA 93, WhoFI 94*
Escalet, Frank Diaz, Jr. 1930- *WhoHisp 94*
Escamilla, Belinda 1956- *WhoHisp 94*
Escamilla, Gerardo M. 1958- *WhoHisp 94*
Escamilla, James R. 1959- *WhoHisp 94*
Escamilla, Kathy *WhoHisp 94*
Escamilla, Linda Garcia 1952- *WhoHisp 94*
Escamilla, Manuel 1947- *WhoHisp 94*
Escande, Maurice d1973 *WhoHol 92*
Escandell, Noemi *DrAPF 93*
Escandon, Jose De 1700-1770 *WhWE*
Escandón, Ralph 1928- *WhoHisp 94*
Escarraz, Enrique, III 1944- *WhoAmL 94*
Esch, Gerald Wisler 1936- *WhoScEn 94*
Esch, Raymond Gates 1940- *WhoMW 93*
Esch, Tyler Sue 1966- *WhoMW 93*
Eschbach, Jesse Ernest 1920- *WhoAm 94, WhoAmL 94*
Eschbach, Joseph Wetherill 1933- *WhoAm 94*
Escheikh, Abdelhamid 1935- *IntWW 93*
Eschenbach, Arthur Edwin 1918- *WhoWest 94*
Eschenbach, Christoph 1940- *IntWW 93, Who 94, WhoAm 94*
Eschenbrenner, Gunther Paul 1925- *WhoAm 94*
Eschenmoser, Albert 1925- *IntWW 93*
Eschenroeder, Alan Quade 1933- *WhoAm 94*
Escherich, Rudolf Johann 1923- *IntWW 93*
Escherny, Francois-Louis 1733-1815 *NewGrDO*
Eschevarria, Brunilda Soto *WhoAmP 93*
Eschmann, Jean Charles 1896-1961 *WhoAmA 93N*
Eschmeyer, William Neil 1939- *WhoAm 94*
Eschscholtz, Johann Friedrich 1793-1831 *WhWE*
Eschstruth, Nataly von 1860-1939 *BlmGWL*
Esclamado, Alejandro A. 1929- *WhoAsA 94*
Esco, Fred, Jr. 1954- *WhoBlA 94*
Escobar, Anna Maria 1956- *WhoHisp 94*
Escobar, Javier I., Sr. 1943- *WhoHisp 94*
Escobar, Javier Ignacio 1943- *WhoAm 94*
Escobar, Jesus Ernesto 1948- *WhoHisp 94*
Escobar, Jose Fernando 1954- *WhoMW 93*
Escobar, Juan Manuel 1950- *WhoHisp 94*
Escobar, Luis d1991 *WhoHol 92*
Escobar, Luis A. *WhoHisp 94*
Escobar, Luis Fernando 1957- *WhoScEn 94*
Escobar, Maria Luisa 1909- *IntWW 93*
Escobar, Marisol *WhoAm 94, WhoAmA 93*
Escobar, Martha Alicia 1965- *WhoHisp 94*
Escobar, Roberto E. *WhoHisp 94*

Escobar, Sandra Lynn Hayduk 1946- WhoFI 94
Escobar, William Alfred 1955- WhoHisp 94
Escobar Cerda, Luis 1927- IntWW 93
Escobar-Haskins, Lillian WhoHisp 94
Escobedo, Edmundo, Sr. 1932- WhoHisp 94
Escobedo, Helen 1936- WhoAmA 93
Escobedo, Joana 1942- BlmGWL
Escobedo, John WhoHisp 94
Escobedo, Luis Gerardo 1951- WhoHisp 94
Escobedo, Lydia Martinez 1930- WhoHisp 94
Escobedo, Marilyn B. 1945- WhoHisp 94
Escobedo, Theresa WhoHisp 94
Escoffery, Gloria 1923- BlmGWL
Escoffier, Paul d1941 WhoHol 92
Escontrias, Manuel 1945- WhoHisp 94
Escorza, Monica Marie 1958- WhoHisp 94
Escott, Margaret 1908- BlmGWL
Escott, Shoolah Hope 1952- WhoScEn 94
Escott, Sundra Erma 1954- WhoBlA 94
Escott Cox, Brian Robert Who 94
Escott-Russell, Sundra Erma 1954- WhoAmP 93
Escovar, Fernando 1944- WhoHisp 94
Escovar Salom, Ramon 1926- IntWW 93
Escovedo, Pete M. 1935- WhoHisp 94
Escover, Matthew Manuel 1957- WhoAmP 93
Escover, Thomas Frank 1947- WhoWest 94
Escritt, Frederick Knowles d1993 Who 94N
Escudero, Ernesto 1953- WhoHisp 94
Escudero, Gilbert 1945- WhoHisp 94
Escudero, Robert WhoHisp 94
Escudero, Vincente d1980 WhoHol 92
Escutia, Martha WhoAmP 93, WhoHisp 94
Esdale, Charles d1937 WhoHol 92
Esdale, Patricia Joyce Who 94
Eseki, Bruno BlkWr 2
Esekle, Bruno 1919- WrDr 94
Esenwein, J(oseph) Berg EncSF 93
Eseoghene BlkWr 2
Eseonu, Maxwell Obioma 1955- WhoFI 94
Eser, Gunter Otto 1927- Who 94
Esfandiari-Fard, Omid David 1961- WhoScEn 94
Esfandiary, F. M. WrDr 94
Esfandiary, Mary S. 1929- WhoFI 94
Esgate, Thomas Wagner 1949- WhoAmP 93
Esgdaille, Elias 1953- WhoHisp 94
Esguerra, Arturo Sazon 1941- WhoAsA 94
Esham, Faith 1948- NewGrDO
Esham, Richard Henry 1942- WhoScEn 94
Eshbach, Lloyd Arthur 1910- ConAu 42NR, EncSF 93, WrDr 94
Eshbach, William Wallace 1917- WhoAm 94
Eshbaugh, William Hardy 1936- WhoAm 94, WhoScEn 94
Eshe, Aisha DrAPF 93
Eshe, Montsho c. 1974- See Arrested Development News 94-2
Eshelman, David Richard 1949- WhoAmL 94
Eshelman, Enos Grant, Jr. 1943- WhoWest 94
Eshelman, John D. WhoWest 94
Eshelman, John Leo, Jr. 1927- WhoAmP 93
Eshelman, William Robert 1921- WhoAm 94
Esher, Viscount 1913- Who 94
Esher, Brian Richard 1948- WhoAm 94, WhoFI 94
Esherick, Joseph 1914- WhoAm 94
Esherick, W. Harton 1887-1970 WhoAmA 93N
Eshleman, Clayton DrAPF 93
Eshleman, Clayton 1935- WrDr 94
Eshleman, Silas Kendrick, III 1928- WhoAm 94
Eshleman, Von Russel 1924- WhoScEn 94
Eshley, Norman 1945- WhoHol 92
Eshoo, Anna Georges 1942- WhoAm 94, WhoAmP 93, WhoWest 94
Eshoo, Robert 1926- WhoAmA 93
Esiason, Boomer 1961- WhoAm 94
Esin, Joseph Okon 1953- WhoScEn 94
Esiri, Margaret Miriam 1941- Who 94
Eskandarian, Edward 1936- WhoAm 94
Eskdaill, Lord 1984- Who 94
Eskenazi, Gerard Andre 1931- IntWW 93
Eskenazi, Giuseppe 1939- Who 94
Eskesen, Ruth E. 1939- WhoAmP 93
Eskew, Cathleen Cheek 1953- WhoWest 94
Eskew, Rhea Taliaferro 1923- WhoAm 94
Eski, John Robert 1932- WhoMW 93
Eskin, Barry Sanford 1943- WhoAmL 94
Eskin, Frada 1936- WrDr 94
Eskind, Jane Greenebaum 1933- WhoAmP 93
Eskoff, Richard Joseph WhoAm 94, WhoFI 94, WhoWest 94
Eskola, Antti Aarre 1934- IntWW 93
Eskow, John DrAPF 93
Eskridge, James Arthur 1942- WhoFI 94
Eskridge, John Clarence 1943- WhoBlA 94
Eskuri, Neil WhoAm 94
Eslami, Hossein Hojatol 1927- WhoAm 94
Eslami, Mohammad Reza 1945- WhoScEn 94
Eslava (y Elizondo), (Miguel) Hilarion 1807-1878 NewGrDO
Esler, Anthony DrAPF 93
Esler, Anthony James 1934- WhoAm 94, WrDr 94
Esler, John Kenneth 1933- WhoAm 94, WhoAmA 93, WhoWest 94
Esler, Tika Amelia 1949- WhoWest 94
Eslick, Donald Farrell 1934- WhoAmP 93
Esman, Aaron H. 1924- WhoAm 94
Esman, Rosa 1927- WhoAmA 93
Esmelton, Fred d1933 WhoHol 92
Esmenard, Francis 1936- IntWW 93
Esmeria, Virgilio Reyes 1946- WhoWest 94
Esmond, Annie d1945 WhoHol 92
Esmond, Carl 1906- IntMPA 94, WhoHol 92
Esmond, H. V. d1922 WhoHol 92
Esmond, Harriet 1922- WrDr 94
Esmond, Jill d1990 WhoHol 92
Esmonde, Thomas (Francis Grattan) 1960- Who 94
Esogbue, Augustine O. 1940- WhoBlA 94
Espada, Martin DrAPF 93, WhoHisp 94
Espada, Pedro, Jr. 1953- WhoAmP 93, WhoHisp 94
Espaillat, Edwin R. 1934- WhoHisp 94
Espaillat, Rhina P. DrAPF 93
Espaldon, Ernesto Mercader 1926- WhoAmP 93, WhoWest 94
Espana, Caroline Sophie 1965- WhoWest 94
Espana, Jean Philippe 1961- WhoWest 94
Espanca, Florbela 1894-1930 BlmGWL
Espander, William Robert 1947- WhoWest 94
Espantaleon, Juan d1966 WhoHol 92
Esparza, Edward Duran 1942- WhoScEn 94
Esparza, Henry WhoHisp 94
Esparza, Hugo R. 1955- WhoHisp 94
Esparza, Jesus 1932- WhoHisp 94
Esparza, Leonardo Rodriguez 1949- WhoHisp 94
Esparza, Lili V. 1937- WhoHisp 94
Esparza, Manuel, Jr. 1946- WhoHisp 94
Esparza, Moctesuma Diaz 1949- WhoAmP 93, WhoHisp 94
Esparza, Phillip W. 1949- WhoHisp 94
Esparza, Ralph Robert 1947- WhoHisp 94
Esparza, Thomas, Jr. 1952- WhoHisp 94
Espat, Roberto E. WhoHisp 94
Espejo, Antonio De fl. 158-?- WhWE
Espeland, Pamela (Lee) 1951- WrDr 94
Espenet 1920- WhoAmA 93
Espenoza, Cecelia M. 1958- WhoAmL 94, WhoHisp 94
Espenschied, Clyde WhoAmA 93
Espenshade, Edward Bowman, Jr. 1910- WhoAm 94
Esperian, Kallen Rose 1961- WhoAm 94
Espert, Nuria 1935- NewGrDO
Espert Romero, Nuria 1935- IntWW 93
Espey, John DrAPF 93
Espey, John (Jenkins) 1913- WrDr 94
Espich, Jeffrey K. WhoAmP 93
Espie, Frank (Fletcher) 1917- Who 94
Espin, Mario Andre 1950- WhoFI 94
Espín, Oliva María 1938- WhoHisp 94
Espin, Orlando Oscar 1947- WhoHisp 94
Espina, Concha 1869-1955 BlmGWL
Espinasse, Jacques Paul 1943- IntWW 93
Espinassy, Louise-Florence-Petronille Tardieu d'Esclavelle, Marquise d' d1777 BlmGWL
Espinda, David d1976 WhoHol 92
Espinet, Rambabai 1948- BlmGWL
Espino, David Ramirez 1963- WhoWest 94
Espino, David Virgil 1956- WhoHisp 94
Espino, Federico (Liesi, Jr.) 1939- WrDr 94
Espino, Fern R. WhoHisp 94
Espinola, Aida 1920- WhoScEn 94
Espino Ramírez, Rosa María 1964- WhoHisp 94
Espinosa, Alma Olga 1942- WhoHisp 94
Espinosa, Augusto d1989 Who 94N
Espinosa, Aurelio Macedonio, Jr. 1907- WhoHisp 94
Espinosa, Dula Joanne 1958- WhoHisp 94
Espinosa, Edmundo 1927-1992 WhoHisp 94N
Espinosa, Edouard d1950 WhoHol 92
Espinosa, Fernando WhoHisp 94
Espinosa, Francisco C. 1936- WhoHisp 94
Espinosa, Genevieve 1950- WhoHisp 94
Espinosa, Gustavo Adolfo 1943- WhoHisp 94
Espinosa, Hector WhoHisp 94
Espinosa, James 1938- WhoHisp 94
Espinosa, Jose Manuel, Jr. 1942- WhoHisp 94
Espinosa, Judith M. WhoWest 94
Espinosa, Luisito WhoHisp 94
Espinosa, Paul 1950- WhoHisp 94
Espinosa, Paula Maria 1939- WhoWest 94
Espinosa, Reynaldo, Jr. 1945- WhoHisp 94
Espinosa, Ruben William WhoHisp 94
Espinosa, Rudy DrAPF 93
Espinosa, Segundo Jorge 1959- WhoHisp 94
Espinosa y Almodóvar, Juan 1941- WhoHisp 94
Espinoza, Alvaro 1962- WhoHisp 94
Espinoza, Elena Emilia 1960- WhoHisp 94
Espinoza, Eloisa 1960- WhoHisp 94
Espinoza, Gerardo 1955- WhoHisp 94
Espinoza, Isidro 1958- WhoHisp 94
Espinoza, Jesus I. 1937- WhoHisp 94
Espinoza, Laurie Edith 1943- WhoHisp 94
Espinoza, Luis R. 1943- WhoHisp 94
Espinoza, Manuel R. 1942- WhoHisp 94
Espinoza, Michael Dan WhoHisp 94
Espinoza, Narcisa Margarita Monreal 1923- WhoHisp 94
Espinoza, Noe 1954- WhoHisp 94
Espinoza, Orlando P. 1953- WhoHisp 94
Espinoza, Pete E., Jr. 1948- WhoHisp 94
Espla (y Triay), Oscar 1886-1976 NewGrDO
Esplen, John Graham 1932- Who 94
Esplin, Da Lon 1951- WhoAmL 94
Esplin, Ian (George) 1914- Who 94
Espoile, Raul Hugo 1889-1958 NewGrDO
Esposito, Albert C. 1922- WhoAmP 93
Esposito, Albert Charles 1912- WhoAm 94
Esposito, Bonnie Lou 1947- WhoFI 94, WhoMW 93
Esposito, Cheryl Lynne 1964- WhoAmL 94
Esposito, Dennis Harry 1947- WhoAmL 94
Esposito, Frank, Jr. WhoAmP 93
Esposito, Giancarlo WhoHol 92
Esposito, Giancarlo 1958- IntMPA 94, WhoAm 94, WhoBlA 94
Esposito, Gianni d1974 WhoHol 92
Esposito, John Vincent 1946- WhoAmL 94
Esposito, Joseph John 1951- WhoAm 94
Esposito, Kristin Marie 1967- WhoFI 94
Esposito, Linda Hunter 1954- WhoMW 93
Esposito, Louis P., Jr. WhoAmP 93
Esposito, Mario John 1926- WhoAm 94
Esposito, Mark Mario 1958- WhoAmL 94
Esposito, Meade H. d1993 NewYTBS 93 [port]
Esposito, Nancy DrAPF 93
Esposito, Paul Andrew 1944- WhoAmP 93
Esposito, Philip Anthony 1942- WhoAm 94
Esposito, Rose Marie 1956- WhoAmL 94
Esposito, Theresa Harlow 1930- WhoAmP 93
Esposti, Piera Degli WhoHol 92
Espoy, Henry Marti 1917- WhoAm 94
Espree, Allen James 1941- WhoBlA 94
Espriu, Salvador 1913-1985 DcLB 134 [port]
Espy, Alphonso Michael 1953- WhoFI 94
Espy, Ben WhoAmP 93
Espy, Cecil Edward 1963- WhoBlA 94
Espy, Charles Clifford 1910- WhoAm 94
Espy, James William 1948- WhoFI 94, WhoScEn 94
Espy, Mark Joseph 1957- WhoMW 93
Espy, Michael WhoBlA 94
Espy, Michael 1953- AfrAmAl 6 [port]
Espy, Mike 1953- CngDr 93, ConBlB 6 [port], CurBio 93 [port], IntWW 93, WhoAm 94, WhoAmP 93, WhoFI 94
Espy, R. H. Edwin d1993 NewYTBS 93
Espy, Willard Richardson 1910- WhoAm 94
Espy, William Gray WhoHol 92
Espy-Wilson, Carol Yvonne 1957- WhoScEn 94
Esquea Guerrero, Emmanuel T. 1944- IntWW 93
Esquer, Cecilia D. 1942- WhoAmP 93
Esquer, Deborah Anne 1950- WhoWest 94
Esquerra, Manuel Romo 1943- WhoHisp 94
Esquerre, Jean Roland 1923- WhoBlA 94
Esquevin, Christian Raymond 1948- WhoWest 94
Esquibel, Edward Valdez 1928- WhoScEn 94
Esquibel, Lee E. 1934- WhoHisp 94
Esquinazi, Pablo David 1956- WhoScEn 94
Esquire, Arthur Seitz 1941- WhoAsA 94
Esquirol, Jean Etienne Dominique 1772-1840 EncSPD
Esquiroz, Margarita 1945- WhoHisp 94
Esquivel, Agerico Liwag 1932- WhoAm 94
Esquivel, Argelia Velez 1936- WhoBlA 94
Esquivel, Catarino 1933- WhoHisp 94
Esquivel, Joe WhoHisp 94
Esquivel, Laura NewYTBS 93 [port]
Esquivel, Manuel 1940- IntWW 93, Who 94
Esquivel, Rita WhoHisp 94
Esrati, David 1962- WhoMW 93
Esrey, Elizabeth Gove Goodier 1964- WhoFI 94
Esrey, William Todd 1940- WhoAm 94, WhoFI 94
Esrick, Jerald Paul 1941- WhoAm 94, WhoAmL 94
Essa, Lisa Beth 1955- WhoWest 94
Essaafi, M'Hamed 1930- IntWW 93, Who 94
Es-Said, Omar Salim 1952- WhoWest 94
Essame, Enid Mary Who 94
Essary, Loris DrAPF 93
Essayan, Michael 1927- Who 94
Essberger, Ruprecht 1923- IntWW 93
Essek, Rudolf d1941 WhoHol 92
Essel, Franz d1973 WhoHol 92
Essen, Louis 1908- Who 94
Essen, Viola d1961 WhoHol 92
Esser, Aristide Henri 1930- WhoAm 94, WhoScEn 94
Esser, Carl Eric 1942- WhoAm 94, WhoAmL 94
Esser, Frank Vincent 1939- WhoAm 94
Esser, Heinrich 1818-1872 NewGrDO
Esser, Hermin 1928- NewGrDO
Esser, Janet Brody WhoAmA 93
Esser, Karl Wright d1976 WhoHol 92
Esser, Otto 1917- IntWW 93
Esser, Peter d1970 WhoHol 92
Esser, Robin Charles 1935- Who 94
Esserman, Charles Howard 1958- WhoFI 94
Essert, Gary d1992 IntMPA 94N
Essery, David James 1938- Who 94
Essex, Earl of 1920- Who 94
Essex, David 1947- IntMPA 94, IntWW 93, WhoHol 92
Essex, Douglas Michael 1961- WhoScEn 94
Essex, Francis 1929- Who 94
Essex, Francis William 1916- Who 94
Essex, Harry J. 1915- IntMPA 94, WhoAm 94, WrDr 94
Essex, Jon d1986 WhoHol 92
Essex, Joseph Michael 1947- WhoAm 94
Essex, Myron Elmer 1939- WhoAm 94
Essex, Nathan Lee 1942- WhoAm 94
Essex, Saran 1948- WrDr 94
Essex, Terry 1946- WhoAmP 93
Essex, Wanda Elizabeth 1925- WhoMW 93
Essex-Cater, Antony John 1923- Who 94, WrDr 94
Essick, Raymond Brooke, III 1933- WhoAm 94
Essick, Robert N(ewman) 1942- ConAu 41NR
Essick, Robert Newman 1942- WhoAm 94
Essiet, Evaleen Johnson 1933- WhoBlA 94
Essig, Herman Frederick 1911- WhoMW 93
Essig, Nancy Claire 1939- WhoAm 94
Essig, Philippe Louis Charles Marie 1933- Who 94
Essler, Fred d1973 WhoHol 92
Essley, Roger Holmer 1949- WhoAmA 93
Esslin, Martin (Julius) 1918- WrDr 94
Esslin, Martin Julius 1918- Who 94
Essling, William Warren 1915- WhoMW 93
Esslinger, Anna Mae Linthicum 1912- WhoFI 94
Esslinger, Hartmut Heinrich 1944- WhoAm 94
Esslinger, John Thomas 1943- WhoAmL 94
Essman, Pansy Ellen 1918- WhoFI 94
Essman, Susie WhoHol 92
Essmyer, Michael Martin 1949- WhoAmL 94
Esson, (Thomas) Louis (Buvelot) 1878-1943 IntDcT 2
Essop, Ahmed 1931- WrDr 94
Esswood, Paul (Lawrence Vincent) 1942- NewGrDO

Eustace the Monk c. 1170-1217 *DcNaB MP*
Eustache, Jean d1981 *WhoHol 92*
Eustachio, Bartolomeo 1510?-1571 *EncDeaf*
Eustaquio, George Castro 1931- *WhoAmP 93*
Euster, Joanne Reed 1936- *WhoAm 94*
Eustice, Francis Joseph 1951- *WhoAm 94, WhoAmL 94*
Eustice, James Samuel 1932- *WhoAm 94*
Eustice, Robert Charles 1963- *WhoAmL 94*
Eustice, Russell Clifford 1919- *WhoAm 94, WhoFI 94*
Eustis, Albert Anthony 1921- *WhoAm 94*
Eustis, Helen (White) 1916- *WrDr 94*
Eustis, James R. 1945- *WhoAmL 94*
Eustis, Jeffrey Murdock 1947- *WhoAmL 94*
Eustis, Richmond Minor 1945- *WhoAmL 94*
Eustis, Robert Henry 1920- *WhoAm 94*
Eustis, William 1753-1825 *WhAmRev*
Euston, Earl of 1947- *Who 94*
Eustrel, Antony d1979 *WhoHol 92*
Evaige, Wanda Jo 1935- *WhoBlA 94*
Evan, William Martin 1922- *WhoAm 94*
Evancho, Joseph Andrew 1929- *WhoMW 93*
Evancho, Joseph William 1947- *WhoScEn 94*
Evangelatos, Daphne 1952- *NewGrDO*
Evangelista, Donato A. 1932- *WhoAm 94, WhoAmL 94, WhoFI 94*
Evangelista, James John 1952- *WhoFI 94*
Evangelista, Linda *IntWW 93*
Evangelista, Stella 1945- *WhoAsA 94*
Evangelisti, Robert 1954- *WhoMW 93*
Evanger, Arden Eide 1933- *WhoWest 94*
Evanger, Jacqueline Ruth 1926- *WhoAmP 93*
Evanier, David *DrAPF 93*
Evankovich, George Joseph 1930- *WhoFI 94, WhoWest 94*
Evano, Dennis Charles 1946- *WhoWest 94*
Evanoff, George C. 1931- *WhoAm 94*
Evanoff, Vlad 1916- *WrDr 94*
Evans *Who 94*
Evans, A. Briant 1909- *Who 94*
Evans, A. C. *WhoAmP 93*
Evans, Ada B. 1932- *WhoBlA 94*
Evans, Adeline Marie Lemelle 1939- *WhoAm 94*
Evans, Akwasi Rozelle 1948- *WhoBlA 94*
Evans, Alan 1930- *WrDr 94*
Evans, Alan Darrel 1939- *WhoAmP 93*
Evans, Alan George 1942- *WhoScEn 94*
Evans, Alan Roger 1933- *WhoFI 94*
Evans, Albert *WhoBlA 94*
Evans, Alfred Lee, Jr. 1940- *WhoAm 94*
Evans, Alfred Spring 1917- *WhoAm 94*
Evans, Alice *DrAPF 93*
Evans, Alice Catherine 1881-1975 *WorScD*
Evans, Alicia 1960- *WhoBlA 94*
Evans, Allen Donald 1956- *WhoAm 94*
Evans, Allen V. 1939- *WhoAmP 93*
Evans, Alun *Who 94*
Evans, (Thomas) Alun 1937- *Who 94*
Evans, Alun S. *Who 94*
Evans, Amanda Louise Elliot 1958- *Who 94*
Evans, Amos James 1922- *WhoBlA 94*
Evans, Andrew C. *IntMPA 94*
Evans, Angelo 1970- *WhoHol 92*
Evans, Anne 1939- *NewGrDO*
Evans, Anthony *Who 94*
Evans, Anthony (Adney) 1922- *Who 94*
Evans, (David) Anthony 1939- *Who 94*
Evans, Anthony (Howell Meurig) 1934- *Who 94*
Evans, Anthony Howard 1936- *WhoAm 94, WhoWest 94*
Evans, Anthony John 1930- *Who 94*
Evans, Anthony Thomas 1943- *Who 94*
Evans, Anton Nelson 1941- *WhoMW 93*
Evans, Art *WhoHol 92*
Evans, Arthur Bruce 1948- *WhoMW 93*
Evans, Arthur L. 1931- *WhoBlA 94*
Evans, Arthur Lee 1931- *WhoAm 94*
Evans, Audrey Elizabeth 1925- *WhoAm 94*
Evans, Augusta Jane 1835-1909 *BlmGWL*
Evans, Austin James 1920- *WhoAm 94*
Evans, Barry 1943- *IntMPA 94, WhoHol 92*
Evans, Barry Craig 1944- *WhoFI 94*
Evans, Barton, Jr. 1947- *WhoAm 94*
Evans, Bernard William 1934- *WhoAm 94, WhoWest 94*
Evans, Beverly Ann 1944- *WhoAmP 93, WhoWest 94*
Evans, Bill *DrAPF 93*
Evans, Bill 1920- *WhoAm 94*
Evans, Bill 1921-1985 *EncSF 93*
Evans, Bill 1940- *WhoAm 94*
Evans, Billy J. 1942- *WhoBlA 94*
Evans, Blackwell Bugg, Sr. 1927- *WhoAm 94*
Evans, Bob d1961 *WhoHol 92*
Evans, Bob 1944- *WhoAmA 93*
Evans, Bob Overton 1927- *WhoAm 94*
Evans, Brandon d1958 *WhoHol 92*
Evans, Brian P. 1950- *WhoAmL 94*
Evans, Briant *Who 94*
Evans, Bruce d1978 *WhoHol 92*
Evans, Bruce A. 1946- *WrDr 94*
Evans, Bruce David 1963- *WhoMW 93*
Evans, Bruce Dwight 1934- *WhoAm 94*
Evans, Bruce Haselton 1939- *WhoAmA 93*
Evans, Bruce Max 1937- *WhoFI 94*
Evans, Bruce Read *Who 94*
Evans, Burford Elonzo 1931- *WhoAmA 93*
Evans, Burtis Robbins 1925- *WhoWest 94*
Evans, Carole Yvonne Mims 1951- *WhoBlA 94*
Evans, Catherine Lee 1965- *WhoWest 94*
Evans, Cecile d1960 *WhoHol 92*
Evans, Chad (Arthur) 1951- *WrDr 94*
Evans, Charles *Who 94*
Evans, (Robert) Charles 1918- *Who 94*
Evans, Charles Albert 1912- *WhoAm 94*
Evans, Charles E. d1945 *WhoHol 92*
Evans, Charles E. 1938- *WhoAmP 93*
Evans, Charles Graham 1949- *WhoAmL 94*
Evans, Charles Hawes, Jr. 1940- *WhoAm 94*
Evans, Charles Wesley 1939- *WhoAmP 93*
Evans, Charlie Anderson 1945- *WhoScEn 94*
Evans, Charlotte A. *WhoBlA 94*
Evans, Cheryl Lynn 1950- *WhoBlA 94*
Evans, Christina Hambley *Who 94*
Evans, Christopher (D.) 1951- *EncSF 93*
Evans, Christopher Francis 1909- *Who 94*
Evans, Clay 1925- *WhoBlA 94*
Evans, Clifford d1985 *WhoHol 92*
Evans, Clifford Jessie 1923- *WhoAm 94*
Evans, Clive Ernest 1937- *Who 94*
Evans, Colin Rodney 1935- *Who 94*
Evans, Cooper *WhoAmP 93*
Evans, Craig 1949- *WhoFI 94*
Evans, Craig Vaughn 1953- *WhoMW 93*
Evans, Crecy Ann 1915- *WhoBlA 94*
Evans, Dale 1912- *WhoHol 92*
Evans, Daniel E. 1936- *WhoFI 94*
Evans, Daniel Fraley 1922- *WhoAm 94*
Evans, Daniel Fraley, Jr. 1949- *WhoAm 94, WhoAmL 94*
Evans, Daniel Jackson 1925- *IntWW 93, WhoAm 94, WhoAmP 93*
Evans, Daniel Scot 1953- *WhoAmP 93*
Evans, David 1935- *Who 94*
Evans, David 1937- *Who 94*
Evans, David (George) 1924- *Who 94*
Evans, David A. 1952- *WhoScEn 94*
Evans, David Alan Price 1927- *Who 94*
Evans, David Albert 1941- *WhoScEn 94*
Evans, David Allan *DrAPF 93*
Evans, David C. *WhoAm 94*
Evans, David Eifion 1911- *Who 94*
Evans, David Ellis 1930- *WrDr 94*
Evans, David Howard 1944- *Who 94*
Evans, David John 1935- *Who 94*
Evans, David Lawrence 1939- *WhoBlA 94*
Evans, David Lloyd C. *Who 94*
Evans, David Marshall 1937- *Who 94*
Evans, David Milne 1917- *Who 94*
Evans, David Myrddin 1946- *WhoScEn 94*
Evans, David Philip 1908- *Who 94*
Evans, David Richard John 1938- *Who 94*
Evans, David Stanley 1916- *WhoAm 94, WrDr 94*
Evans, David W. 1939- *WhoAmL 94*
Evans, David William 1963- *WhoMW 93*
Evans, David Wyke 1934- *IntWW 93*
Evans, Deanna Genelle 1943- *WhoMW 93*
Evans, Deborah Ann 1959- *WhoBlA 94*
Evans, DeeWitt Currie 1934- *WhoFI 94*
Evans, Denis James 1951- *WhoScEn 94*
Evans, Dennis Hyde 1939- *WhoAm 94, WhoScEn 94*
Evans, Derek *Who 94*
Evans, (John) Derek 1942- *Who 94*
Evans, Diana Powers 1928- *WhoAmP 93*
Evans, Dick 1941- *WhoAmA 93*
Evans, Dillon 1921- *WhoHol 92*
Evans, Don A. 1948- *WhoAm 94, WhoWest 94*
Evans, Donald 1946-1977 *WhoAmA 93N*
Evans, Donald Foster 1949- *WhoScEn 94*
Evans, Donald Gray 1940- *WhoAmL 94*
Evans, Donald John 1926- *WhoAm 94*
Evans, Donald Lee 1964- *WhoBlA 94*
Evans, Donald LeRoy 1933- *WhoMW 93*
Evans, Donald P(aul) 1930-1992 *ConAu 140*
Evans, Donna Browder *WhoBlA 94*
Evans, Dorsey 1930- *WhoBlA 94*
Evans, Douglas d1968 *WhoHol 92*
Evans, Douglas Hayward 1950- *WhoAmL 94*
Evans, Douglas McCullough 1925- *WhoAm 94*
Evans, Dwight 1954- *WhoAmP 93, WhoBlA 94*
Evans, Dwight Landis 1947- *WhoScEn 94*
Evans, E. Chris 1928- *WhoAmP 93*
Evans, E(dward) Everett 1893-1958 *EncSF 93*
Evans, Earl Alison, Jr. 1910- *WhoAm 94*
Evans, Eben 1920- *Who 94*
Evans, Edgar E. 1908- *WhoBlA 94*
Evans, Edith d1962 *WhoHol 92*
Evans, Edith d1976 *WhoHol 92*
Evans, Edward *WhoHol 92*
Evans, Edward Arthur 1895- *WhAm 10*
Evans, Edward Clark 1955- *WhoBlA 94*
Evans, Edward Lewis 1904- *Who 94*
Evans, Edward Parker 1942- *WhoAm 94*
Evans, Edward Spencer, Jr. 1943- *WhoScEn 94*
Evans, Edward Stanley Price 1925- *Who 94*
Evans, Edwin C. 1917- *IntWW 93*
Evans, Edwin Charles 1910- *WhoAm 94*
Evans, Edwin Curtis 1917- *WhoAm 94, WhoScEn 94*
Evans, Edwin Ellsworth 1950- *WhoAmL 94*
Evans, Eifion *Who 94*
Evans, Elizabeth *DrAPF 93*
Evans, Ellis *Who 94*
Evans, (David) Ellis 1930- *Who 94*
Evans, Ellis Dale 1934- *WhoAm 94*
Evans, Emrys *Who 94*
Evans, (William) Emrys 1924- *Who 94*
Evans, Ena Winifred 1938- *Who 94*
Evans, Eric *Who 94*
Evans, (Thomas) Eric 1928- *Who 94*
Evans, Eric J(ohn) 1945- *WrDr 94*
Evans, Ernestine D. 1917- *WhoHisp 94*
Evans, Ernestine Duran 1917- *WhoAmP 93*
Evans, Ersel Arthur 1922- *WhoAm 94*
Evans, Essi H. 1950- *WhoScEn 94*
Evans, Estelle d1985 *WhoHol 92*
Evans, Eva L. 1935- *WhoBlA 94*
Evans, Evan S. d1954 *WhoHol 92*
Evans, Evans *WhoHol 92*
Evans, F. Dean 1955- *WhoAmP 93*
Evans, F. Maurice 1930- *WhoAmP 93*
Evans, Fabyan Peter Leaf 1943- *Who 94*
Evans, Fay Jones 1909- *WhoAmP 93*
Evans, Francis Cope 1914- *WhoAm 94*
Evans, Francis Loring G. *Who 94*
Evans, Frank Edward 1923- *WhoAmP 93*
Evans, Franklin Bachelder 1922- *WhoAm 94*
Evans, Fred d1951 *WhoHol 92*
Evans, Frederick Anthony 1907- *Who 94*
Evans, G. Anne 1954- *WhoAmL 94*
Evans, Gareth (John) 1944- *Who 94*
Evans, Gareth John 1944- *IntWW 93*
Evans, Gary *WhoFI 94*
Evans, Gary William 1948- *WhoScEn 94*
Evans, Gene 1922- *WhoHol 92*
Evans, Gene 1924- *IntMPA 94*
Evans, George *DrAPF 93*
Evans, George Frederick 1922- *WhoScEn 94*
Evans, George Henry 1805-1856 *AmSocL*
Evans, George James 1944- *Who 94*
Evans, George Leonard 1931- *WhoScEn 94*
Evans, George Robert, Jr. 1931- *WhoAm 94*
Evans, Geraint 1922-1992 *AnObit 1992*
Evans, Geraint (Llewellyn) 1922-1992 *NewGrDO*
Evans, Geraint Llewellyn d1992 *IntWW 93N*
Evans, Geraint Llewellyn 1922-1992 *WhAm 10*
Evans, Gerald 1910- *EncSF 93*
Evans, Geraldine Ann 1939- *WhoMW 93*
Evans, Geri *WhoAmP 93*
Evans, Giles (Edwin) 1949-1988 *ConAu 141*
Evans, Glenn Preston 1964- *WhoFI 94*
Evans, Godfrey *Who 94*
Evans, (Thomas) Godfrey 1920- *Who 94*
Evans, Godfrey B. *WhoAmL 94*
Evans, Gordon Emil 1932- *WhoAmP 93*
Evans, Gordon John 1941- *WhoAmL 94*
Evans, Gregory James 1954- *WhoBlA 94*
Evans, Gregory Scott 1958- *WhoFI 94*
Evans, Gregory Thomas 1913- *WhoAm 94*
Evans, Grose 1916- *WhoAm 94, WhoAmA 93, WrDr 94*
Evans, Gwendolyn *WhoBlA 94*
Evans, Gwynfor 1912- *IntWW 93, Who 94*
Evans, H. Bradley, Jr. 1937- *WhoAm 94*
Evans, H. Dean 1929- *WhoAmP 93*
Evans, H. Gene 1941- *WhoAmP 93*
Evans, Harold (Matthew) 1928- *WrDr 94*
Evans, Harold Edward 1927- *WhoAm 94*
Evans, Harold J. 1921- *IntWW 93, WhoAm 94*
Evans, Harold Matthew 1928- *IntWW 93, Who 94*
Evans, Hasty *WhoAmP 93*
Evans, Haydn T. *Who 94*
Evans, Hazel Atkinson 1931- *WhoAmP 93*
Evans, Helen St. Clair d1927 *WhoHol 92*
Evans, Helena Phillips d1955 *WhoHol 92*
Evans, Henry 1918- *WhoAmA 93*
Evans, Henry 1934- *WhoAmP 93*
Evans, Herbert d1952 *WhoHol 92*
Evans, Hilary 1929- *ConAu 42NR*
Evans, Howard Ensign 1919- *WhoAm 94*
Evans, Hubert Carol 1921- *WhoAmP 93*
Evans, Hugh 1943- *WhoBlA 94*
Evans, Hugh E. 1934- *WhoAm 94*
Evans, Huw Prideaux 1941- *Who 94*
Evans, Hywel Eifion 1910- *Who 94*
Evans, I(drisyn) O(liver) 1894-1977 *EncSF 93*
Evans, Iain Richard 1951- *Who 94*
Evans, Ian *EncSF 93*
Evans, Ian Philip 1948- *Who 94*
Evans, J. Anthony 1938- *WhoFI 94*
Evans, J(ames) Ellis 1910- *Who 94*
Evans, Jack *WhoBlA 94*
Evans, Jack d1950 *WhoHol 92*
Evans, Jack 1953- *WhoAmP 93*
Evans, Jacqueline d1989 *WhoHol 92*
Evans, James *WhoAmP 93*
Evans, James 1801-1846 *EncNAR*
Evans, James 1932- *Who 94*
Evans, James Allan S. 1931- *WrDr 94*
Evans, James Carmichael 1900- *WhoBlA 94*
Evans, James Donald 1926- *Who 94*
Evans, James E. 1946- *WhoAmL 94*
Evans, James Earl 1929- *WhoFI 94*
Evans, James H. 1934- *WhoIns 94*
Evans, James Handel 1938- *WhoWest 94*
Evans, James Harold 1939- *WhoAm 94, WhoAmL 94, WhoAmP 93*
Evans, James Humphrey R. *Who 94*
Evans, James Hurlburt 1920- *WhoAm 94*
Evans, James L. 1954- *WhoBlA 94*
Evans, James Lee 1961- *WhoFI 94*
Evans, James Louis 1935- *WhoWest 94*
Evans, James R(ichard) 1908- *ConAu 141*
Evans, James Stanley 1921- *WhoAm 94, WhoFI 94*
Evans, James Stuart 1941- *WhoMW 93*
Evans, James Weldon 1926- *WhoAmP 93*
Evans, James William 1943- *WhoAm 94, WhoWest 94*
Evans, Jane 1944- *WhoFI 94*
Evans, Janelle Jo 1927- *WhoAmP 93*
Evans, Janice W. 1937- *WhoAmP 93*
Evans, Jed Reeder 1929- *WhoWest 94*
Evans, Jeremy David Agard 1936- *Who 94*
Evans, Jerry L. 1931- *WhoAmP 93*
Evans, Jerry Lee 1931- *WhoAm 94, WhoWest 94*
Evans, Jerry Norman *WhoAm 94*
Evans, Jesse 1937- *WhoAmP 93*
Evans, Jessie d1983 *WhoHol 92*
Evans, Jo Burt 1928- *WhoFI 94*
Evans, Joan 1934- *WhoHol 92*
Evans, Joe d1967 *WhoHol 92*
Evans, Joe d1973 *WhoHol 92*
Evans, Joe B. 1929- *WhoBlA 94*
Evans, Joel Raymond 1948- *WhoFI 94*
Evans, John *WhAmRev, Who 94*
Evans, John 1908- *WrDr 94*
Evans, John 1922- *WhoAmP 93*
Evans, John 1930- *Who 94*
Evans, John 1932- *WhoAm 94, WhoAmA 93*
Evans, (Henry) John 1930- *Who 94*
Evans, (Noel) John (Bebbington) 1933- *Who 94*
Evans, John Alan Maurice 1936- *Who 94*
Evans, John Alfred Eaton 1933- *Who 94*
Evans, John B. 1938- *WhoFI 94*
Evans, John David Gemmill 1942- *IntWW 93*
Evans, John Davies 1925- *Who 94*
Evans, John Derby 1944- *WhoFI 94*
Evans, John Erik 1934- *WhoIns 94*
Evans, John F. *WhoAm 94*
Evans, John Field 1928- *Who 94*
Evans, John G. *Who 94*
Evans, John James 1923- *WhoAm 94*
Evans, John Joseph 1940- *WhoFI 94*
Evans, John Kerr Q. *Who 94*
Evans, John Marten Llewellyn 1909- *Who 94*
Evans, John Mascal 1915- *Who 94*
Evans, John Maurice d1988 *WhoHol 92*
Evans, John Maurice 1936- *WhoAm 94*
Evans, John R. 1932- *WhoAmP 93*
Evans, John Robert 1929- *IntWW 93, Who 94, WhoAm 94, WhoScEn 94*
Evans, John Roger W. *Who 94*
Evans, John Stanley 1943- *Who 94*
Evans, John Thomas 1948- *WhoAmL 94*
Evans, John Vaughan 1933- *WhoAm 94, WhoScEn 94*
Evans, John Victor 1925- *WhoAmP 93*

Evans, John Wilson 1939- *WhoAmL 94*
Evans, John Yorath Gwynne 1922- *Who 94*
Evans, Jonathan *ConAu 43NR*
Evans, Jonathan 1936- *WrDr 94*
Evans, Jonathan Peter 1950- *Who 94*
Evans, Joseph D. 1946- *WhoAmL 94*
Evans, Josh 1971- *WhoHol 92*
Evans, Judith Futral *WhoAmA 93*
Evans, Judy Anne 1940- *WhoScEn 94*
Evans, Katherine d1692 *BlmGWL*
Evans, Kathy Lynn 1956- *WhoMW 93*
Evans, Kenneth Dawson 1915- *Who 94*
Evans, Kenneth R. 1938- *WrDr 94*
Evans, Lane 1951- *CngDr 93, WhoAm 94, WhoAmP 93, WhoMW 93*
Evans, Larry Melvyn 1932- *WhoAm 94, WhoWest 94*
Evans, Lawrence Boyd 1934- *WhoAm 94*
Evans, Lawrence Jack, Jr. 1921- *WhoAmL 94, WhoWest 94*
Evans, Lawrence Lee 1945- *WhoAmP 93*
Evans, Lee 1933- *WhoAm 94*
Evans, Lee 1947- *WhoBlA 94*
Evans, Leon, Jr. 1953- *WhoBlA 94*
Evans, Leon Edward, Jr. 1942- *WhoBlA 94*
Evans, LeRoy W. 1946- *WhoBlA 94*
Evans, Lillie R. 1913- *WhoBlA 94*
Evans, Linda 1942- *IntMPA 94, WhoAm 94*
Evans, Linda 1943- *WhoHol 92*
Evans, Linda Perryman 1950- *WhoAm 94*
Evans, Liz 1941- *WhoBlA 94*
Evans, Lloyd Russell, Jr. 1947- *WhoAmP 93*
Evans, Lloyd Thomas 1927- *IntWW 93, Who 94*
Evans, Loren Kenneth 1928- *WhoFI 94*
Evans, Lorenzo J. 1909- *WhoBlA 94*
Evans, Louise *WhoAm 94, WhoScEn 94*
Evans, Madelaine Glynne Dervel 1944- *Who 94*
Evans, Madge d1981 *WhoHol 92*
Evans, Margaret Ann 1947- *WhoMW 93*
Evans, Margarita Sawatzky 1930- *WhoMW 93*
Evans, Margie d1960 *WhoHol 92*
Evans, Mari *DrAPF 93, WhoBlA 94, WrDr 94*
Evans, Mari 1923- *AfrAmAl 6*
Evans, Mari-Lynn Currence 1959- *WhoFI 94*
Evans, Mark Armstrong 1940- *Who 94*
Evans, Mark C. 1952- *WhoAmL 94*
Evans, Marsha Jo Anne 1951- *WhoMW 93*
Evans, Martha *DrAPF 93*
Evans, Martin Frederic 1947- *WhoAm 94, WhoAmL 94*
Evans, Martin John 1941- *Who 94*
Evans, Mary Adetta 1909- *WhoBlA 94*
Evans, Mary Ann *BlmGWL*
Evans, Mary Arline 1946- *WhoAmL 94*
Evans, Mary Beth *WhoHol 92*
Evans, Mary Johnston 1930- *WhoAm 94*
Evans, Matthew 1941- *IntWW 93, Who 94*
Evans, Maude Jean 1931- *WhoMW 93*
Evans, Maureen Clare 1956- *WhoMW 93*
Evans, Maurice d1989 *WhoHol 92*
Evans, Maurice 1901-1989 *WhAm 10*
Evans, Max 1924- *WrDr 94*
Evans, Max Allen 1924- *WhoAm 94, WhoWest 94*
Evans, Max Jay 1943- *WhoAm 94, WhoWest 94*
Evans, Merle d1987 *WhoHol 92*
Evans, Michael *Who 94*
Evans, Michael 1922- *WhoHol 92*
Evans, (Thomas) Michael 1930- *Who 94*
Evans, Michael Dean 1953- *WhoFI 94*
Evans, Michael K(aye) 1938- *WrDr 94*
Evans, Michael Leigh 1941- *WhoScEn 94*
Evans, Michael Nordon 1915- *Who 94*
Evans, Mike 1951- *WhoHol 92*
Evans, Mike Allen 1961- *WhoAmP 93*
Evans, Milton L. 1936- *WhoBlA 94*
Evans, Minnie 1892-1987 *WhoAmA 93N*
Evans, Morgan *EncSF 93*
Evans, Morgan J. *WhoAm 94*
Evans, Mostyn *Who 94*
Evans, Mostyn 1925- *IntWW 93*
Evans, (Arthur) Mostyn 1925- *Who 94*
Evans, Muriel 1912?- *WhoHol 92*
Evans, Myra Lynn 1959- *WhoBlA 94*
Evans, Nancy d1963 *WhoHol 92*
Evans, Nancy 1915- *NewGrDO*
Evans, Neil B. 1947- *WhoAmP 93*
Evans, Newton Jasper, Jr. 1940- *WhoAmP 93*
Evans, Nigel Martin 1957- *Who 94*
Evans, Nolly Seymour 1927- *WhoAm 94*
Evans, Norman d1962 *WhoHol 92*
Evans, Oliver 1755-1819 *WorInv*
Evans, Orinda D. 1943- *WhoAm 94, WhoAmL 94*
Evans, Patricia E. 1946- *WhoBlA 94*
Evans, Patricia P. *WhoBlA 94*
Evans, Patrick Alexander Sidney 1943- *Who 94*
Evans, Paul 1950- *WhoScEn 94*
Evans, Paul M. 1954- *WhoWest 94*
Evans, Paul Vernon 1926- *WhoAmL 94, WhoWest 94*
Evans, Pauline D. 1922- *WhoScEn 94, WhoWest 94*
Evans, Peter d1989 *WhoHol 92*
Evans, Peter 1929- *Who 94*
Evans, Peter (Andrew) *WrDr 94*
Evans, Peter Angus 1929- *Who 94*
Evans, Peter Kenneth 1935- *WhoAm 94*
Evans, Peter Yoshio 1925- *WhoScEn 94*
Evans, Phillip L. 1937- *WhoBlA 94*
Evans, R. Daniel *DrAPF 93*
Evans, R. Mark 1953- *WhoMW 93*
Evans, R. Mont 1947- *WhoAmP 93*
Evans, Ralph Aiken 1924- *WhoAm 94*
Evans, Randall David 1951- *WhoWest 94*
Evans, Ray 1915- *IntMPA 94*
Evans, Raymond F., Jr. 1944- *WhoIns 94*
Evans, Reg *WhoHol 92*
Evans, Renee d1971 *WhoHol 92*
Evans, Rex d1969 *WhoHol 92*
Evans, Rhydwyn Harding d1993 *Who 94N*
Evans, Richard *WhoHol 92*
Evans, Richard 1923- *WhoAmA 93*
Evans, Richard (Mark) 1928- *Who 94*
Evans, Richard Alan 1934- *WhoAmP 93*
Evans, Richard Alexander 1965- *WhoScEn 94*
Evans, Richard I(sadore) 1922- *WrDr 94*
Evans, Richard James 1960- *WhoScEn 94*
Evans, Richard John 1947- *IntWW 93, Who 94*
Evans, Richard Lloyd 1935- *WhoWest 94*
Evans, Richard Mark 1928- *IntWW 93*
Evans, Robert *NewYTBS 93 [port]*
Evans, Robert 1927- *IntWW 93, Who 94*
Evans, Robert 1930- *IntMPA 94, WhoHol 92*
Evans, Robert, Jr. 1932- *WhoAm 94*
Evans, Robert Daryld 1962- *WhoWest 94*
Evans, Robert David 1945- *WhoAmL 94*
Evans, Robert George, Jr. 1953- *WhoFI 94, WhoMW 93*
Evans, Robert Graves 1944- *WhoAmA 93*
Evans, Robert J. 1930- *WhoAm 94*
Evans, Robert James 1914- *WhoAm 94*
Evans, Robert John 1909- *WhoWest 94*
Evans, Robert John Weston 1943- *IntWW 93, Who 94*
Evans, Robert Leonard 1917- *WhoMW 93*
Evans, Robert Noel 1922- *Who 94*
Evans, Robert Oran 1946- *WhoBlA 94*
Evans, Robert Owen 1919- *WrDr 94*
Evans, Robert S. 1948- *WhoAmL 94*
Evans, Robert Sheldon 1944- *WhoAm 94, WhoFI 94*
Evans, Robert Vincent 1958- *WhoFI 94, WhoScEn 94, WhoWest 94*
Evans, Robley Dunglison 1907- *WhoAm 94, WhoScEn 94*
Evans, Roderick *Who 94*
Evans, (David) Roderick 1946- *Who 94*
Evans, Rodney Earl 1939- *WhoFI 94*
Evans, Roger 1951- *WhoAm 94, WhoAmL 94*
Evans, Roger Kenneth 1947- *Who 94*
Evans, Roger Lynwood 1928- *WhoFI 94, WhoMW 93, WhoScEn 94*
Evans, Roger Michael 1960- *WhoScEn 94*
Evans, Roger W. *Who 94*
Evans, Ronald Allen 1940- *WhoAm 94, WhoFI 94, WhoWest 94*
Evans, Ronald Wayne 1927- *WhoAmP 93*
Evans, Rowland, Jr. 1921- *WhoAm 94, WhoAmP 93, WrDr 94*
Evans, Roxanne J. 1952- *WhoBlA 94*
Evans, Roy Lyon 1931- *Who 94*
Evans, Rudulph 1879-1960 *WhoAmA 93N*
Evans, Russell Wilmot 1922- *Who 94*
Evans, Ruthana Wilson 1932- *WhoBlA 94*
Evans, Samuel London 1902- *WhoBlA 94*
Evans, Sara M(argaret) 1943- *WrDr 94*
Evans, Sara Margaret *WhoMW 93*
Evans, Simon John 1937- *Who 94*
Evans, Slayton Alvin, Jr. 1943- *WhoBlA 94*
Evans, Spofford L. 1919- *WhoBlA 94*
Evans, Stephen Arter 1941- *WhoWest 94*
Evans, Sticks 1923- *WhoBlA 94*
Evans, Tabor 1927- *WrDr 94*
Evans, Tenniel 1926- *WhoHol 92*
Evans, Terence Thomas 1940- *WhoAmL 94*
Evans, Thelma Jean Mathis 1944- *WhoAm 94*
Evans, Therman E. 1944- *WhoBlA 94*
Evans, Thomas 1925- *WhoBlA 94*
Evans, Thomas Chives Newton 1947- *WhoAm 94, WhoFI 94*
Evans, Thomas Dowling 1942- *WhoAm 94, WhoFI 94, WhoWest 94*
Evans, Thomas Edgar, Jr. 1940- *WhoWest 94*
Evans, Thomas William 1930- *WhoAm 94*
Evans, Timothy C. 1943- *WhoAmP 93, WhoBlA 94*
Evans, Timothy Monroe 1945- *WhoWest 94*
Evans, Tom R. 1943- *WhoAmA 93*
Evans, Tommy Nicholas 1922- *WhoAm 94*
Evans, Trevor 1927- *Who 94*
Evans, Trevor Heiser 1909- *WhoAm 94*
Evans, Trevor John 1947- *Who 94*
Evans, Van Michael 1916- *WhoAm 94*
Evans, Vernon D. 1950- *WhoBlA 94*
Evans, Victor Miles 1939- *WhoAm 94*
Evans, Victoria Regina 1963- *WhoHisp 94*
Evans, Vincent *Who 94*
Evans, (William) Vincent (John) 1915- *Who 94*
Evans, Vincent Tobias 1955- *WhoBlA 94*
Evans, Wallace Rockwell, Jr. 1914- *WhoScEn 94*
Evans, Walter Reed 1921- *WhoFI 94*
Evans, Warren Cleage 1948- *WhoBlA 94*
Evans, Warren D. *WhoAmP 93*
Evans, Warren Felt 1817-1889 *DcAmReB 2*
Evans, Wayne Edward 1962- *WhoScEn 94*
Evans, Wayne Lewis 1954- *WhoAmL 94*
Evans, Webb 1913- *WhoBlA 94*
Evans, Wilbur d1987 *WhoHol 92*
Evans, Will d1931 *WhoHol 92*
Evans, Willa Dale 1916- *WhoAmP 93*
Evans, William Andrew 1939- *Who 94*
Evans, William C. 1899- *WhoBlA 94*
Evans, William Clayton 1944- *WhoBlA 94*
Evans, William David 1949- *Who 94*
Evans, William Davidson, Jr. 1943- *WhoAmL 94*
Evans, William E. 1931- *WhoBlA 94*
Evans, William Earl, Jr. 1956- *WhoAmL 94*
Evans, William Ellis 1952- *WhoAmL 94*
Evans, William Frederick 1957- *WhoAm 94*
Evans, William John 1929-1980 *AmCulL*
Evans, William Lee 1924- *WhoAm 94*
Evans, William McKee 1923- *WrDr 94*
Evans, William Neal 1950- *WhoWest 94*
Evans, William Thomas 1941- *WhoWest 94*
Evans, William Wilson 1932- *WhoAm 94*
Evans, Wynford *Who 94*
Evans, (John) Wynford 1934- *Who 94*
Evans-Anfom, Emmanuel 1919- *Who 94*
Evans-Bevan, Martyn Evan 1932- *Who 94*
Evans-Dodd, Theora Anita 1945- *WhoBlA 94*
Evansen, Virginia B(esaw) *WrDr 94*
Evans-Freke *Who 94*
Evans-Freke, Stephen Ralfe 1952- *WhoAm 94*
Evans Le Blanc, Candace Kay 1958- *WhoWest 94*
Evans-Lombe, Edward (Christopher) 1937- *Who 94*
Evans-McNeill, Elona Anita 1945- *WhoBlA 94*
Evanson, Barbara Gibbons 1944- *WhoAmP 93*
Evanson, Barbara Jean 1944- *WhoMW 93*
Evanson, Dennis B. 1956- *WhoAmL 94*
Evanson, Edith d1980 *WhoHol 92*
Evanson, Elizabeth Moss 1934- *WhoMW 93*
Evanson, Paul John 1941- *WhoAm 94*
Evans-Tranumn, Shelia 1951- *WhoBlA 94*
Evanzz, Karl 1953- *BlkWr 2, ConAu 140*
Evaristi, Marcella 1953- *ConDr 93*
Evarts, Charles McCollister 1931- *WhoAm 94*
Evarts, George William 1936- *WhoFI 94*
Evarts, Jeremiah 1781-1831 *EncNAR*
Evarts, Prescott, Jr. *DrAPF 93*
Evarts, William Maxwell, Jr. 1925- *WhoAm 94*
Evatt, Elizabeth Andreas 1933- *Who 94*
Evaul, William H., Jr. 1949- *WhoAmA 93*
Evdokimova, Eva 1948- *IntDcB [port], WhoAm 94*
Eve *Who 94*
Eve, Arthur O. 1933- *WhoAmP 93, WhoBlA 94*
Eve, Christina M. 1917- *WhoBlA 94*
Eve, Sarah 1749?-1774 *BlmGWL*
Evege, Walter L., Jr. 1943- *WhoBlA 94*
Eveillard, Jean-Marie 1960- *WhoAm 94*
Evein, Bernard 1929- *IntDcF 2-4*
Eveland, Johnny Leroy 1948- *WhoMW 93*
Eveland, Laverne Kent 1940- *WhoWest 94*
Eveleigh, Edward Walter 1917- *Who 94*
Eveleigh, Geoffrey Charles 1912- *Who 94*
Eveleigh, Nicolas c. 1748-1791 *WhAmRev*
Eveleigh, Virgil William 1931- *WhoAm 94*
Eveling, (Harry) Stanley 1925- *ConDr 93, WrDr 94*
Evelti, Mary M. 1920- *WhoAmP 93*
Evelyn, Douglas Everett 1941- *WhoAm 94*
Evelyn, Gwyneth 1925- *WhoAm 94*
Evelyn, John 1591-1664 *DcNaB MP*
Evelyn, John 1601-1685 *DcNaB MP*
Evelyn, John 1620-1706 *BlmGEL*
Evelyn, Judith d1967 *WhoHol 92*
Evelyn, Mary 1634-1709 *BlmGWL*
Evelyn, (John) Michael d1992 *Who 94N*
Evelyn, (John) Michael 1916-1992 *ConAu 140*
Evelyn And Her Magic Violin *WhoHol 92*
Even, Francis Alphonse 1920- *WhoAm 94*
Even, James A. *WhoIns 94*
Even, Jan 1950- *WhoAm 94*
Even, Randolph M. 1943- *WhoAmL 94*
Even, Robert Lawrence 1929- *WhoAmA 93*
Even, Robert Lawrence 1932- *WhoAm 94*
Evenbeck, Scott Edward 1946- *WhoMW 93*
Evennett, David Anthony 1949- *Who 94*
Evennett, Wallace d1973 *WhoHol 92*
Eveno, Bertrand 1944- *IntWW 93*
Evens, Michelle Jeanette 1964- *WhoMW 93*
Evens, Ronald Gene 1939- *WhoAm 94, WhoMW 93*
Evensen, Alf John 1938- *WhoFI 94*
Evensen, Jens 1917- *IntWW 93*
Evenson, Dennis David 1946- *WhoAmP 93*
Evenson, Kenneth M. 1932- *WhoScEn 94*
Evenson, Merle Armin 1934- *WhoAm 94*
Evenson, Michael Donald 1961- *WhoScEn 94*
Evenson, S. Jeanne 1938- *WhoFI 94, WhoWest 94*
Evenstad, Kenneth L. 1943- *WhoMW 93*
Everard, Christopher E. W. *Who 94*
Everard, David Charles 1940- *Who 94*
Everard, Robin (Charles) 1939- *Who 94*
Everard, Timothy John 1929- *Who 94*
Everbach, Otto George 1938- *WhoAm 94, WhoAmL 94*
Everdale, John *WhoIns 94*
Everdell, William Romeyn 1941- *WhoAm 94*
Everding, August 1928- *IntWW 93, NewGrDO*
Everding, Robert George 1945- *WhoWest 94*
Evered, David Charles 1940- *IntWW 93*
Evered, J. Erich 1953- *WhoFI 94*
Everest, Allan S. 1913- *WrDr 94*
Everest, Barbara d1968 *WhoHol 92*
Everest, David Anthony 1926- *Who 94*
Everest, Harvey Pettit 1895- *WhAm 10*
Everett, Ardell Tillman 1909-1988 *WhAm 10*
Everett, Bernard Jonathan 1943- *Who 94*
Everett, C. Curtis 1930- *WhoAm 94, WhoAmL 94*
Everett, Carl Bell 1947- *WhoAm 94, WhoAmL 94*
Everett, Carl Nicholas 1926- *WhoFI 94*
Everett, Chad 1936- *WhoHol 92*
Everett, Chad 1937- *IntMPA 94*
Everett, Charles William Vogt 1949- *Who 94*
Everett, Christopher Harris Doyle 1933- *Who 94*
Everett, David N. 1946- *WhoAmL 94*
Everett, Deborah Stuart 1951- *WhoMW 93*
Everett, Douglas Hugh 1916- *IntWW 93, Who 94, WrDr 94*
Everett, Durward R., Jr. 1925- *WhoAm 94*
Everett, Eileen *Who 94*
Everett, Elbert Kyle 1946- *WhoFI 94*
Everett, Eugenia Zink 1908- *WhoWest 94*
Everett, Francine *WhoHol 92*
Everett, Graham *DrAPF 93*
Everett, Hobart Ray, Jr. 1949- *WhoWest 94*
Everett, Howard Cheston 1909- *WhoWest 94*
Everett, J. Richard 1936- *WhoBlA 94*
Everett, Jack Veeder 1921- *WhoMW 93*
Everett, James Joseph 1955- *WhoAmL 94, WhoWest 94*
Everett, James William, Jr. 1957- *WhoAmL 94, WhoFI 94*
Everett, Jess Walter 1962- *WhoScEn 94*
Everett, Joann Marie *DrAPF 93*
Everett, John Prentis, Jr. 1941- *WhoAmL 94*
Everett, Karen J. 1926- *WhoMW 93*
Everett, Karin Anita 1961- *WhoMW 93*
Everett, Kay *WhoAmP 93*
Everett, Kay 1941- *WhoBlA 94*
Everett, Kenny 1944- *WhoHol 92*
Everett, Len G. *WhoAmA 93N*
Everett, Mark Allen 1928- *WhoAm 94*
Everett, Mary O. 1876-1948 *WhoAmA 93N*
Everett, Michael Thomas 1949- *WhoFI 94*
Everett, Mike 1948- *WhoAmP 93*

Everett, Oliver William 1943- *Who 94*
Everett, Pamela Irene 1947- *WhoAmL 94, WhoFI 94, WhoWest 94*
Everett, Percival L. 1933- *WhoBlA 94*
Everett, Percival L. 1956- *BlkWr 2*
Everett, Ralph B. 1951- *WhoBlA 94*
Everett, Ralph Bernard 1951- *WhoAmP 93*
Everett, Robert William 1947- *WhoScEn 94*
Everett, Robinson O. 1928- *CngDr 93*
Everett, Robinson Oscar 1928- *WhoAm 94, WhoAmL 94*
Everett, Ronald Emerson 1937- *WhoMW 93*
Everett, Royice Bert 1946- *WhoScEn 94*
Everett, Rupert 1959- *IntMPA 94, WhoHol 92*
Everett, Rupert 1960?- *ConAu 142, IntWW 93*
Everett, Stephen Edward 1958- *WhoWest 94*
Everett, Terry 1937- *CngDr 93, WhoAm 94, WhoAmP 93*
Everett, Thomas Gregory 1964- *WhoBlA 94*
Everett, Thomas Henry Kemp 1932- *Who 94*
Everett, Thomas Stewart 1942- *WhoFI 94*
Everett, Timmy d1977 *WhoHol 92*
Everett, Todd *WhoHol 92*
Everett, Warren Sylvester 1910- *WhoAm 94*
Everett, William Arlie 1962- *WhoMW 93*
Everett, Woodrow Wilson 1937- *WhoAm 94*
Evergon 1946- *WhoAmA 93*
Evergood, Philip 1901-1973 *WhoAmA 93N*
Everhard, Nancy *WhoHol 92*
Everhart, Denise *WhoAmP 93*
Everhart, Don, II 1949- *WhoAmA 93*
Everhart, Francis Grover, Jr. 1947- *WhoScEn 94*
Everhart, Leon Eugene 1928- *WhoWest 94*
Everhart, Rex 1920- *WhoAm 94, WhoHol 92*
Everhart, Robert Phillip 1936- *WhoMW 93*
Everhart, Roger Dean 1956- *WhoMW 93*
Everhart, Thomas Eugene 1932- *WhoAm 94, WhoScEn 94, WhoWest 94*
Everidge, Mary Jim 1930- *WhoAmP 93*
Everill, Richard Harold 1942- *WhoMW 93*
Everingham, Douglas Nixon 1923- *IntWW 93*
Everingham, Harry Towner 1908- *WhoWest 94*
Everingham, James Theodore 1939- *WhoAm 94*
Everingham, Millard 1912- *WhoAmA 93N*
Everist, Barbara 1949- *WhoAmP 93*
Everitt, Alan Milner 1926- *Who 94, WrDr 94*
Everitt, Alice Lubin 1936- *WhoAmL 94*
Everitt, Anthony Michael 1940- *IntWW 93, Who 94*
Everitt, Cheryl Anne 1948- *WhoWest 94*
Everitt, George Bain 1914- *WhoAm 94*
Everitt, Henry Olin, III 1963- *WhoScEn 94*
Everitt, William Howard 1940- *Who 94*
Everling, Ulrich 1925- *IntWW 93*
Everman, Welch D. *DrAPF 93*
Evernden, Margery (Gulbransen) 1916- *WrDr 94*
Everroad, John D. 1940- *WhoAm 94, WhoAmL 94*
Evers, Ann d1987 *WhoHol 92*
Evers, (James) Charles 1922- *HisWorL*
Evers, James Charles 1922- *WhoAmP 93, WhoBlA 94*
Evers, Jason 1927- *WhoHol 92*
Evers, Judith Ann 1939- *WhoMW 93*
Evers, Larry 1946- *WrDr 94*
Evers, Martin Louis 1957- *WhoScEn 94*
Evers, Medgar 1925-1963 *AfrAmAl 6 [port], HisWorL*
Evers, Medgar Wiley 1926-1963 *AmSocL [port]*
Evers, Myrlie *WhoBlA 94*
Evers, Robert Allen 1945- *WhoAm 94*
Evers, Walter 1914-1990 *WhAm 10*
Eversley, David Edward Charles 1921- *Who 94*
Eversley, Frederick John 1941- *WhoAm 94, WhoAmA 93*
Eversole, Kellye Anne 1958- *WhoAmP 93*
Eversole, Robyn Harbert 1971- *SmATA 74 [port]*
Everson, David E., Jr. 1944- *WhoAmL 94*
Everson, Deborah Sue 1952- *WhoAmL 94*
Everson, Diane Louise 1953- *WhoMW 93*
Everson, Frederick (Charles) 1910- *Who 94*
Everson, Joan Carol 1960- *WhoMW 93*
Everson, John Andrew 1933- *Who 94*
Everson, Leonard Charles 1923- *WhoAm 94*
Everson, Martin Joseph 1948- *WhoAmL 94*
Everson, Rachel Higgins d1993 *NewYTBS 93 [port]*
Everson, Richard H. 1945- *WhoAmP 93*
Everson, Ronald (Gilmour) 1903-1992 *WrDr 94N*
Everson, Steven Lee 1950- *WhoAmL 94*
Everson, William *DrAPF 93*
Everson, William (Oliver) 1912- *WrDr 94*
Everson, William K. 1929- *IntMPA 94*
Everson, William Oliver 1912- *WhoAm 94*
Everstine, Gordon Carl 1943- *WhoScEn 94*
Evert, Chris 1954- *BuCMET [port]*
Evert, Chris(tine) Marie 1954- *IntWW 93*
Evert, Christine Marie 1954- *Who 94, WhoAm 94*
Evert, John Andrew, Jr. 1917- *WhoWest 94*
Evert, Militiades 1939- *IntWW 93*
Evert, Ray Franklin 1931- *WhoMW 93, WhoScEn 94*
Everton, Marta Ve 1926- *WhoAm 94*
Everton, Paul d1948 *WhoHol 92*
Everts, Connor 1926- *WhoAm 94, WhoAmA 93*
Everwine, Peter (Paul) 1930- *WrDr 94*
Every, George 1909- *WrDr 94*
Every, Henry (John Michael) 1947- *Who 94*
Every, Russel B. 1924- *WhoFI 94*
Eves, David Charles Thomas 1942- *Who 94*
Eves, Jeffrey P. 1946- *WhoFI 94*
Eves, Jesse Parvin 1894- *WhAm 10*
Evesham, Epiphanius 1570-c. 1634 *DcNaB MP*
Evett, Kenneth Warnock 1913- *WhoAmA 93*
Evett, Malcolm 1942- *WhoWest 94*
Evigan, Greg *WhoAm 94*
Evigan, Greg 1953- *IntMPA 94*
Evigan, Greg 1954- *WhoHol 92*
Evilo *WhoAmA 93*
Evin, Claude 1949- *IntWW 93*
Evinrude, Ole 1877-1934 *WorInv*
Evison, Frank Foster 1922- *IntWW 93*
Evison, Pat *WhoHol 92*
Evison, (Helen June) Patricia 1924- *Who 94*
Evita d1952 *WhoHol 92*
Evliya, Celebi 1611-1684 *WhWE*
Evnin, Anthony Basil 1941- *WhoAm 94, WhoFI 94*
Evoy, John Joseph 1911- *WhoAm 94*
Evren, Kenan 1918- *IntWW 93*
Evrigenis, John Basil 1929- *WhoWest 94*
Evslin, Bernard d1993 *NewYTBS 93*
Evslin, Bernard 1922-1993 *ConAu 142, SmATA 77*
Evstatieva, Stefka 1947- *NewGrDO, WhoAm 94*
Evtukhov, Vasyl Ivanovych 1948- *LoBiDrD*
Evtushenko, Evgenii (Alexandrovich) 1933- *ConWorW 93*
Ewald, Carl 1856-1908 *EncSF 93*
Ewald, Douglas R. *WhoAmP 93*
Ewald, Elin Lake *WhoAmA 93*
Ewald, Johann von 1744-1813 *AmRev, WhAmRev*
Ewald, Johanna d1961 *WhoHol 92*
Ewald, Kitty Marie 1956- *WhoMW 93*
Ewald, Rex Alan 1951- *WhoAmL 94*
Ewald, Robert Charles 1940- *WhoAm 94*
Ewald, Robert Frederick 1924- *WhoFI 94, WhoIns 94, WhoMW 93*
Ewald, Robert Hansen 1947- *WhoFI 94*
Ewald, William Bragg, Jr. 1925- *WhoAm 94*
Ewalt, Henry Ward 1940- *WhoAmL 94*
Ewan, George Thomson 1927- *WhoAm 94*
Ewan, Joseph Andorfer 1909- *WhoAm 94, WhoMW 93*
Ewan, Richard Colin 1934- *WhoMW 93*
Ewan, William Kenneth 1943- *WhoAmL 94*
Ewankowich, Stephen Frank, Jr. 1966- *WhoScEn 94*
Ewans, Martin Kenneth 1928- *Who 94*
Ewart, Claire 1958- *SmATA 76 [port]*
Ewart, Florence Maud 1864-1949 *NewGrDO*
Ewart, Gavin (Buchanan) 1916- *WrDr 94*
Ewart, Gavin Buchanan 1916- *IntWW 93, Who 94, WhoAm 94*
Ewart, (William) Ivan (Cecil) 1919- *Who 94*
Ewart, John *WhoHol 92*
Ewart-Biggs, Baroness d1992 *Who 94N*
Ewart-Biggs, Baroness 1929- *WhoWomW 91*
Ewbank, Anthony (Bruce) 1925- *Who 94*
Ewbank, Henry Lee 1924- *WhoWest 94*
Ewbank, Inga-Stina 1932- *Who 94*
Ewbank, Michael Henry 1930- *Who 94*
Ewbank, Thomas Peters 1943- *WhoFI 94, WhoMW 93*
Ewbank, Walter Frederick 1918- *Who 94*
Ewbank, Weeb *ProFbHF [port]*
Ewel, Katherine Carter 1944- *WhoScEn 94*
Ewell, A. Ben, Jr. 1941- *WhoAmL 94*
Ewell, Allen Elmer, Jr. 1960- *WhoScEn 94*
Ewell, Miranda Juan 1948- *WhoAm 94, WhoWest 94*
Ewell, P. Lamont *WhoWest 94*
Ewell, Raymond W. 1928- *WhoBlA 94*
Ewell, Tom 1909- *IntMPA 94, WhoHol 92*
Ewell, Vincent Fletcher 1943- *WhoAm 94*
Ewell, Wallace Edmund 1942- *WhoFI 94, WhoScEn 94*
Ewell, Yvonne Amaryllis 1927- *WhoBlA 94*
Ewen, David 1907-1985 *NewGrDO*
Ewen, H.I. 1922- *WhoAm 94, WhoScEn 94*
Ewen, Paterson 1925- *IntWW 93, WhoAmA 93*
Ewen, Peter d1993 *Who 94N*
Ewen, Petra Barrera 1937- *WhoHisp 94*
Ewens, John Qualtrough d1992 *Who 94N*
Ewer, David 1954- *WhoAmP 93*
Ewer, Tom Keightley 1911- *Who 94*
Ewers, Anne *WhoWest 94*
Ewers, Arlen Branson 1940- *WhoMW 93*
Ewers, Hanns Heinz 1871-1943 *EncSF 93*
Ewers, James Benjamin, Jr. 1948- *WhoBlA 94*
Ewers, John Canfield 1909- *WhoAm 94*
Ewers, Patricia O'Donnell 1935- *WhoAm 94*
Ewers, R. Darrell 1933- *WhoAm 94, WhoFI 94*
Ewert, Alan 1949- *WhoWest 94*
Ewert, David Norfleet 1948- *WhoMW 93*
Ewert, Quentin Albert 1915- *WhoAmL 94*
Ewick, Charles Ray 1937- *WhoAm 94*
Ewig, Carl Stephen 1945- *WhoScEn 94*
Ewin, David Ernest Thomas F. *Who 94*
Ewing *Who 94*
Ewing, Alastair *Who 94*
Ewing, (Robert) Alastair 1909- *Who 94*
Ewing, Alexander 1814-1873 *DcNaB MP*
Ewing, Alexander Cochran 1931- *WhoAm 94*
Ewing, Bayard 1916-1991 *WhoAmA 93N*
Ewing, Benjamin Baugh 1924- *WhoAm 94*
Ewing, Channing Lester 1927- *WhoAm 94*
Ewing, Charles Boal, Jr. 1930- *WhoAm 94, WhoFI 94*
Ewing, Craig Michael 1964- *WhoScEn 94*
Ewing, David Charles 1942- *WhoMW 93*
Ewing, David Walkley 1923- *WhoAm 94, WrDr 94*
Ewing, Dean Edgar 1932- *WhoWest 94*
Ewing, Donna Marie 1936- *WhoMW 93*
Ewing, Edgar Louis 1913- *WhoAm 94, WhoAmA 93*
Ewing, Edwin S., Jr. 1924- *WhoIns 94*
Ewing, Elizabeth Cameron 1906- *WrDr 94*
Ewing, Finis 1773-1841 *DcAmReB 2*
Ewing, Frank Crockett 1951- *WhoAm 94*
Ewing, Frank Marion 1915- *WhoAm 94*
Ewing, Frederick R. *EncSF 93*
Ewing, George H. 1925- *WhoAm 94*
Ewing, Gordon 1912-1990 *WhAm 10*
Ewing, J. Benjamin 1931- *WhoAmP 93*
Ewing, Jack Robert 1947- *WhoWest 94*
Ewing, James 1736-1805 *WhAmRev*
Ewing, James Francis 1962- *WhoScEn 94*
Ewing, James Melvin 1956- *WhoBlA 94*
Ewing, Jenny *EncSF 93*
Ewing, John H. 1918- *WhoAmP 93*
Ewing, John Harwood 1944- *WhoMW 93*
Ewing, John Isaac 1924- *WhoAm 94*
Ewing, John Kirby 1923- *WhoAm 94, WhoFI 94*
Ewing, John R. 1917- *WhoBlA 94*
Ewing, Joseph Neff, Jr. 1925- *WhoAm 94*
Ewing, Juliana Horatia 1841-1885 *BlmGWL*
Ewing, Kathy 1937- *WhoAm 94*
Ewing, Ky Pepper, Jr. 1935- *WhoAm 94, WhoAmL 94*
Ewing, Lynn Moore, Jr. 1930- *WhoAm 94*
Ewing, Mamie Hans 1939- *WhoBlA 94*
Ewing, Margaret Anne 1945- *Who 94, WhoWomW 91*
Ewing, Maria (Louise) 1950- *NewGrDO*
Ewing, Maria Louise *WhoAm 94*
Ewing, Maria Louise 1950- *IntWW 93, Who 94*
Ewing, Mary Eileen 1926- *WhoMW 93*
Ewing, Meredyth Hanway 1895- *WhAm 10*
Ewing, Patrick 1962- *BasBi, WhoBlA 94*
Ewing, Patrick Aloysius 1962- *WhoAm 94*
Ewing, Randy L. 1944- *WhoAmP 93*
Ewing, Raymond C. 1936- *WhoAmP 93*
Ewing, Raymond Charles 1936- *WhoAm 94*
Ewing, Raymond Peyton 1925- *WhoFI 94, WhoMW 93*
Ewing, Richard Edward 1946- *WhoWest 94*
Ewing, Richard Tucker 1918- *WhoAm 94*
Ewing, Robert 1922- *WhoAm 94, WhoAmL 94*
Ewing, Robert Clark 1957- *WhoAmL 94*
Ewing, Rodney Charles 1946- *WhoScEn 94*
Ewing, Roger 1942- *WhoHol 92*
Ewing, Russ 1933- *WhoBlA 94*
Ewing, Russell Charles, II 1941- *WhoWest 94*
Ewing, Samuel Daniel, Jr. 1938- *WhoAm 94, WhoBlA 94, WhoFI 94*
Ewing, Sidney Alton 1934- *WhoAm 94*
Ewing, Stephen E. 1944- *WhoFI 94*
Ewing, Theodore Bode 1942- *WhoAmP 93*
Ewing, Thomas W. 1935- *CngDr 93, WhoAm 94, WhoAmL 94, WhoAmP 93, WhoMW 93*
Ewing, Wallace Kelley 1932- *WhoMW 93*
Ewing, Wayne Turner 1933- *WhoAm 94*
Ewing, William Barton 1938- *WhoAmP 93*
Ewing, William Hickman, Jr. 1942- *WhoAm 94*
Ewing, William James 1936- *WhoBlA 94*
Ewing, William Maurice 1906-1974 *WorScD*
Ewing, Winifred Margaret 1929- *IntWW 93, Who 94, WhoWomW 91*
Ewing Of Kirkford, Baron 1931- *Who 94*
Ewing-Wilson, Deborah Louise 1955- *WhoMW 93*
Ewins, David John 1942- *Who 94*
Ewins, Peter David 1943- *Who 94*
Ewles, Dana Adrian 1947- *WhoMW 93*
Ewoldt, Elda Mae 1934- *WhoAmP 93*
Eworth, Hans fl. 1540-1573 *DcNaB MP*
Ewusie, Joseph Yanney 1927- *Who 94*
Ewy, Gordon Allen 1933- *WhoAm 94*
Exarchos, Antonios 1932- *IntWW 93*
Exe, David Allen 1942- *WhoFI 94, WhoMW 93, WhoScEn 94*
Exetastes 1932- *WrDr 94*
Exeter, Archdeacon of *Who 94*
Exeter, Bishop of 1929- *Who 94*
Exeter, Dean of *Who 94*
Exeter, Marquess of 1935- *Who 94*
Exler, Samuel *DrAPF 93*
Exley, Charles Errol, Jr. 1929- *IntWW 93*
Exley, Frederick *DrAPF 93*
Exley, Frederick 1929-1992 *AnObit 1992*
Exley, Sheck *WhoScEn 94*
Exmouth, Viscount 1940- *Who 94*
Exner, Adam *Who 94*
Exon, J. James 1921- *CngDr 93, WhoAmP 93*
Exon, J(ohn) James 1921- *IntWW 93*
Exon, John James 1921- *WhoAm 94, WhoMW 93*
Explorabilis *EncSF 93*
Exposito, Daisy *WhoHisp 94*
Exton, Clive 1930- *ConDr 93, Who 94*
Exton, Clive (Jack Montague) 1930- *WrDr 94*
Exton, Rodney Noel 1927- *Who 94*
Extreme *ConMus 10 [port]*
Exum, James Gooden, Jr. 1935- *WhoAm 94, WhoAmL 94, WhoAmP 93*
Exum, Nathaniel *WhoAmP 93*
Exum, Thurman McCoy 1947- *WhoBlA 94*
Eyadema, (Etienne) Gnassingbe 1937- *IntWW 93*
Eybel, Carl Eugene 1943- *WhoMW 93*
Eyberg, Donald Theodore, Jr. 1944- *WhoAm 94, WhoMW 93*
Eybers, Elisabeth c. 1915- *BlmGWL*
Eybler, Joseph Leopold, Elder von 1765-1846 *NewGrDO*
Eyck, Frank 1921- *WrDr 94*
Eyckmans, Luc A.F. 1930- *IntWW 93*
Eyde, Richard Husted 1928-1990 *WhAm 10*
Eyde, Samuel *WorInv*
Eyen, Tom 1941-1991 *ConDr 93, WhAm 10*
Eyer, Bruce Jarrett 1941- *WhoWest 94*
Eyer, Michael John 1947- *WhoWest 94*
Eyer, Richard 1945- *WhoHol 92*
Eyer, Robert 1948- *WhoHol 92*
Eyerly, Jeannette Hyde 1908- *TwCYAW*
Eyerman, Thomas Jude 1939- *WhoAm 94*
Eyers, Patrick Howard Caines 1933- *Who 94*
Eykhoff, Pieter 1929- *IntWW 93, WhoScEn 94*
Eyler, Edward Eugene 1955- *WhoScEn 94*
Eyler, James R. 1942- *WhoAmL 94*
Eyman, Earl Duane 1925- *WhoAm 94*
Eyman, Richard Harrison 1930- *WhoAm 94*
Eyman, Richard Kenneth 1931- *WhoAm 94*
Eynon, John Marles 1923- *Who 94*

Eynon, Robert 1941- *WrDr 94*
Eyraud, Achille *EncSF 93*
Eyraud, Francis-Charles 1931- *IntWW 93*
Eyre, Annette *WrDr 94*
Eyre, Brian Leonard 1933- *Who 94*
Eyre, Charles Petrie 1817-1902
    DcNaB MP
Eyre, Edward John 1815-1901 *WhWE*
Eyre, Elizabeth 1926- *WrDr 94*
Eyre, Elizabeth 1927- *WrDr 94*
Eyre, Graham (Newman) 1931- *Who 94*
Eyre, Ivan 1935- *IntWW 93, WhoAm 94,*
    WhoAmA 93
Eyre, James (Ainsworth Campden Gabriel)
    1930- *Who 94*
Eyre, Patrick Giles Andrew 1940- *Who 94*
Eyre, Paul P. 1947- *WhoAm 94,*
    WhoAmL 94
Eyre, Peter 1942- *ConAu 140, WhoHol 92*
Eyre, Reginald (Edwin) 1924- *Who 94*
Eyre, Reginald John 1931- *WhoWest 94*
Eyre, Richard 1943- *IntWW 93*
Eyre, Richard Charles Hastings 1943-
    Who 94
Eyre, Richard Montague Stephens 1929-
    Who 94
Eyre, S. Robert 1922- *WrDr 94*
Eyre, William H., Jr. 1951- *WhoIns 94*
Eyres, Harry 1958- *WrDr 94*
Eyres Monsell *Who 94*
Eyrich, Henry George 1934- *WhoMW 93*
Eyrich, Henry Theodore 1933-
    WhoWest 94
Eyring, Edward Marcus 1931-
    WhoScEn 94
Eysenck, H(ans) J(urgen) 1916- *WrDr 94*
Eysenck, Hans Jurgen 1916- *IntWW 93,*
    Who 94
Eysenck, Michael (William) 1944-
    WrDr 94
Eysenck, Michael William 1944- *Who 94*
Eyskens, Mark 1933- *IntWW 93*
Eysmont, Zbigniew 1950- *IntWW 93*
Eysseleln, Viktor Ernst 1951-
    WhoWest 94
Eyster, Franklin Spangler, II 1941-
    WhoAm 94
Eyster, Mary Elaine 1935- *WhoAm 94*
Eysymontt, Jerzy 1937- *IntWW 93*
Eytan, Walter 1910- *IntWW 93*
Eythe, William d1957 *WhoHol 92*
Eyton, Anthony John Plowden 1923-
    IntWW 93, Who 94
Eyton, John Trevor 1934- *WhoAm 94,*
    WhoFI 94
Ezeilo, James Okoye Chukuka 1930-
    Who 94
Ezekiel, Nissim 1924- *WrDr 94*
Ezell, Eugene Mark 1941- *WhoAmP 93*
Ezell, Katherine Warthen 1946-
    WhoAmL 94
Ezell, Kenneth Pettey, Jr. 1949-
    WhoAmL 94
Ezell, William Alexander 1924-
    WhoBlA 94
Ezelle, Curtis 1921- *WhoAmP 93*
Ezelle, Robert Eugene 1927- *WhoAm 94*
Ezersky, William Martin 1951-
    WhoAmL 94
Ezhaya, Joseph Bernard 1943- *WhoFI 94*
Eziashi, Maynard *WhoHol 92*
Eziemefe, Godslove Ajenavi 1955-
    WhoBlA 94
Ezin, Jean-Pierre Onvehoun 1944-
    WhoScEn 94
Ezra, Baron 1919- *Who 94*
Ezra, David A. 1947- *WhoAm 94,*
    WhoAmL 94, WhoWest 94
Ezra, Derek 1919- *IntWW 93*
Ezrati, Milton Joseph 1947- *WhoFI 94*
Ezratty, Harry Aaron 1933- *WhoAmL 94*
Ezzard, Martha M. 1938- *WhoAmP 93*
Ezzell, Ben Roach 1943- *WhoWest 94*
Ezzell, Peter Q. 1947- *WhoAmL 94*

F

Fabian, Leonard William 1923- *WhoAm 94*

**F(ord), Lisa Collado 1944- *WhoAmA 93*
**Fa, Angie *WhoAsA 94*
**Faal, Edirissa M. O. 1954- *WhoAmL 94*
**Faalevao, Aviata Fano 1946- *WhoAmP 93*
**Faas, Ekbert 1938- *WrDr 94*
**Faassen, Willem d1978 *WhoHol 92*
**Faatz, Jeanne Ryan 1941- *WhoAmP 93, WhoWest 94, WhoWomW 91*
**Fabares, Shelley *WhoAm 94*
**Fabares, Shelley 1944- *IntMPA 94, WhoHol 92*
**Fabbri(-Mulder), Inez 1831-1909 *NewGrDO*
**Fabbri, Anna Maria fl. 1708-1723 *NewGrDO*
**Fabbri, Anne R. *WhoAmA 93*
**Fabbri, Brian John 1944- *WhoAm 94*
**Fabbri, Diego 1911-1980 *IntDcT 2*
**Fabbri, Fabio 1933- *IntWW 93*
**Fabbri, Franca 1935- *NewGrDO*
**Fabbri, Guerrina 1866 1946 *NewGrDO*
**Fabbrini, Giuseppe d1708 *NewGrDO*
**Fabe, Robert 1917- *WhoAmA 93*
**Fabel, Donald Criston 1897- *WhAm 10*
**Fabel, Thomas Lincoln 1946- *WhoAm 94, WhoAmL 94*
**Fabel, Warren L. 1933- *WhoIns 94*
**Fabela, Augie K., Sr. *WhoHisp 94*
**Fabelo, Roberto F. 1945- *WhoHisp 94*
**Fabend, Firth Haring *DrAPF 93*
**Fabens, Andrew Lawrie, III 1942- *WhoAm 94, WhoAmL 94*
**Faber, Adele 1928- *WhoAm 94*
**Faber, Bonita M. 1948- *WhoMW 93*
**Faber, Charles d1983 *WhoHol 92*
**Faber, David Alan 1942- *WhoAm 94, WhoAmL 94*
**Faber, David James Christian 1961- *Who 94*
**Faber, Erwin d1989 *WhoHol 92*
**Faber, Georges 1926- *IntWW 93*
**Faber, John 1918- *WrDr 94*
**Faber, John Henry 1918- *WhoAm 94*
**Faber, Julian Tufnell 1917- *Who 94*
**Faber, Leslie d1929 *WhoHol 92*
**Faber, Michael Leslie Ogilvie 1929- *Who 94*
**Faber, Michael R. 1953- *WhoAmL 94*
**Faber, Michael Warren 1943- *WhoAm 94, WhoAmL 94*
**Faber, Neil 1938- *WhoAm 94*
**Faber, Peter Lewis 1938- *WhoAm 94, WhoAmL 94*
**Faber, Richard (Stanley) 1924- *Who 94*
**Faber, Robertoh *DrAPF 93*
**Faber, Ron 1933- *WhoHol 92*
**Faber, Sandra Moore 1944- *WhoAm 94, WhoScEn 94*
**Faber, Thomas Erle 1927- *Who 94*
**Fabert, Jacques 1925- *WhoAmA 93*
**Fabian 1940- *WhoHol 92*
**Fabian, Andrew Christopher 1948- *Who 94*
**Fabian, Ava 1964- *WhoHol 92*
**Fabian, Francoise 1932- *WhoHol 92*
**Fabian, Heather Lynn 1969- *WhoMW 93*
**Fabian, Jeanne 1946- *WhoFI 94*
**Fabian, Jerome Francis 1943- *WhoFI 94*
**Fabian, John M. *WhoAm 94, WhoScEn 94*
**Fabian, John McCreary 1939- *WhoWest 94*
**Fabian, Larry Louis 1940- *WhoAm 94*
**Fabian, Leonard Jay 1946- *WhoWest 94*

**Fabian, Leonard William 1923- *WhoAm 94*
**Fabian, Olga *WhoHol 92*
**Fabian, (Andrew) Paul 1930- *Who 94*
**Fabian, Stephen E. 1930- *EncSF 93*
**Fabian Fabiano, Diane 1952- *WhoAmA 93*
**Fabiani, Dante Carl 1917- *IntWW 93, WhoAm 94*
**Fabiani, Simonetta *IntWW 93*
**Fabiano, John G. 1945- *WhoAmL 94*
**Fabietti, Victor Armando 1920- *WhoFI 94*
**Fabila, Jose Andres 1955- *WhoHisp 94*
**Fabilli, Mary *DrAPF 93*
**Fabio *NewYTBS 93 [port]*
**Fabio c. 1961- *News 93 [port]*
**Fabis, Ronald Bruce 1934- *WhoMW 93*
**Fabisch, Gale Warren 1950- *WhoFI 94*
**Fabius, Laurent 1946- *IntWW 93, Who 94*
**Fabray, Nanette 1920- *IntMPA 94, WhoHol 92*
**Fabre, Fred Ruffin 1939- *WhoFI 94*
**Fabre, Raoul Francois 1925- *WhoScEn 94*
**Fabre, Saturnin d1961 *WhoHol 92*
**Fabrega, Jorge 1922- *IntWW 93*
**Fabre-Ramirez, Miguel Juan 1950- *WhoAmP 93*
**Fabres, Oscar 1895-1961 *WhoAmA 93N*
**Fabri, Annibale Pio 1697-1760 *NewGrDO*
**Fabri, Candace J. 1949- *WhoAmL 94*
**Fabri, Luca c. 1740-1769 *NewGrDO*
**Fabri, Ralph 1894-1975 *WhoAmA 93N*
**Fabri, Zoltan 1917- *IntWW 93*
**Fabricand, Burton Paul 1923- *WhoAm 94*
**Fabricant, Arthur E. 1935- *WhoAm 94*
**Fabricant, Jill Diane *WhoScEn 94*
**Fabricant, Michael Louis David 1950- *Who 94*
**Fabricant, Neil 1937- *WhoAmL 94*
**Fabricant, Solomon 1906-1989 *WhAm 10*
**Fabrici, Girolamo 1537-1619 *WorScD*
**Fabricio, Roberto C. 1946- *WhoHisp 94*
**Fabricius, Fritz 1919- *IntWW 93*
**Fabricius, Sara Cecilia Margareta Gjorwell *BlmGWL*
**Fabrick, Howard David 1938- *WhoAm 94*
**Fabrikant, Craig Steven 1952- *WhoScEn 94*
**Fabrikant, Ilya Iosifovich 1949- *WhoMW 93*
**Fabris, Hubert Jakob 1926- *WhoMW 93*
**Fabris, Jacopo 1689-1761 *NewGrDO*
**Fabris, James A. 1938- *WhoAm 94*
**Fabritiis, Oliviero (Carlo) de *NewGrDO*
**Fabrizi, Aldo d1990 *WhoHol 92*
**Fabrizi, Franco *WhoHol 92*
**Fabrizi, Mario d1963 *WhoHol 92*
**Fabrizi, Vincenzo 1764-1812? *NewGrDO*
**Fabrizio, John Arthur, Jr. 1923- *WhoAmP 93*
**Fabrizius, Peter *ConAu 142*
**Fabrizius, Peter 1909- *WrDr 94*
**Fabry, John R. 1963- *WhoAmL 94*
**Fabry, Joseph B. 1909- *WrDr 94*
**Fabrycky, Wolter Joseph 1932- *WhoAm 94, WhoScEn 94*
**Fabrycy, Mark Zdzislaw 1922- *WhoAm 94*
**Fabunmi, James Ayinde 1950- *WhoScEn 94*
**Fabyan, E. Joseph 1951- *WhoMW 93*
**Faccenda, Philip John 1929- *WhoAm 94*
**Facchetti, Giacinto 1942- *WorESoc*
**Facchiano, Ferdinando 1927- *IntWW 93*

**Facchinelli, Lucia fl. 1724-1739 *NewGrDO*
**Facchinello, Lena Patricia 1925- *WhoMW 93*
**Facci, Domenico (Aurelio) 1916- *WhoAmA 93*
**Faccini, Ernest Carlo 1949- *WhoScEn 94*
**Faccinto, Victor Paul 1945- *WhoAm 94, WhoAmA 93*
**Faccio, Adele 1920- *WhoWomW 91*
**Faccio, Franco 1840-1891 *NewGrDO*
**Faccio, Rina *BlmGWL*
**Facco, Giacomo c. 1680-1753 *NewGrDO*
**Face, Albert Ray 1919- *WhoAmP 93*
**Face, Wayne Bruce 1942- *WhoFI 94*
**Facemyer, Karen L. 1954- *WhoAmP 93*
**Facer, Roger Lawrence Lowe 1933- *Who 94*
**Facey, Brenda Lee 1948- *WhoMW 93*
**Facey, John Abbott 1926- *WhoIns 94*
**Facey, Karlyle Frank 1926- *WhoFI 94*
**Facey, Martin Kerr 1948- *WhoAmA 94*
**Faches, William George 1928- *WhoAm 94*
**Fachet, William F., Jr. 1943- *WhoFI 94*
**Fachin Schiavi, Silvana 1938- *WhoWomW 91*
**Fachnie, Hugh Douglas 1952- *WhoFI 94*
**Facio, Gonzalo J. 1918- *IntWW 93*
**Facione, Peter Arthur 1944- *WhoAm 94*
**Fack, Robbert 1917- *Who 94*
**Fackenheim, Emil L(udwig) 1916- *WrDr 94*
**Fackler, Benjamine Lloyd 1926- *WhoAm 94*
**Fackler, Donald A., Jr. 1955- *WhoWest 94*
**Fackler, Ernest Carl, III 1943- *WhoAmP 93*
**Fackler, John Paul, Jr. 1934- *WhoAm 94*
**Fackler, Martin Luther 1933- *WhoAm 94, WhoScEn 94*
**Fackler, Walter D. d1993 *NewYTBS 93*
**Fackler, Walter David 1921- *WhoAm 94*
**Facos, James *DrAPF 93*
**Factor, Max, III 1945- *WhoAm 94, WhoAmL 94, WhoWest 94*
**Factor, Ronda Ellen 1953- *WhoScEn 94*
**Factor, Silas 1920- *WrDr 94*
**Faddeev, Ludwig D. *WhoScEn 94*
**Fadden, Delmar McLean 1941- *WhoScEn 94, WhoWest 94*
**Fadden, Eileen Ann 1943- *WhoFI 94*
**Fadden, Genevieve d1959 *WhoHol 92*
**Fadden, Tom d1980 *WhoHol 92*
**Faddeyev, Ludvig Dmitriyevich 1934- *IntWW 93, WhoScEn 94*
**Fadeev, Gennady Matveevich 1937- *LoBiDrD*
**Fadeev, Nikolai Sergeevich 1933- *LoBiDrD*
**Fadel, Georges Michel 1954- *WhoScEn 94*
**Fadeley, Edward Norman 1929- *WhoAm 94, WhoAmL 94, WhoAmP 93, WhoWest 94*
**Fadeley, Herbert John, Jr. 1922-1988 *WhAm 10*
**Fadeley, Nancie Peacocke 1930- *WhoAmP 93*
**Fadely, James Philip 1953- *WhoMW 93*
**Fadem, Barbara H. 1943- *WhoScEn 94*
**Fadem, Lloyd Robert 1951- *WhoFI 94*
**Faden, Lawrence Steven 1942- *WhoAmA 93*
**Faden, William 1749-1836 *DcNaB MP*
**Fader, Bruce E. 1948- *WhoAmL 94*

**Fader, Daniel Nelson 1930- *WhoAm 94*
**Fader, Ellen Strahs 1952- *WhoAm 94*
**Fader, Henry Conrad 1946- *WhoAm 94, WhoAmL 94*
**Fader, Seymour Jeremiah 1923- *WhoFI 94*
**Fader, Shirley Sloan *WhoAm 94*
**Faderan, Mary Agnes 1956- *WhoMW 93*
**Faderman, Lillian 1940- *BlmGWL, GayLL*
**Fadeyechev, Nikolai 1933- *IntDcB [port]*
**Fadeyechev, Nikolay Borisovich 1933- *IntWW 93*
**Fadeyev, Aleksandr 1901-1956 *TwCLC 53 [port]*
**Fadim, James B. 1943- *WhoAmL 94*
**Fadiman, Clifton *WhoAm 94*
**Fadiman, Clifton 1904- *WhoHol 92, WrDr 94*
**Fadulu, Sunday O. 1940- *WhoBlA 94*
**Fadum, Ralph Eigil 1912- *WhoAm 94*
**Faecher, Marc Stephen 1964- *WhoAmL 94*
**Faecke, Peter 1940- *IntWW 93*
**Faerstein, Howard *DrAPF 93*
**Faessler, Edwin Joseph 1944- *WhoMW 93*
**Faeth, Gerard Michael 1936- *WhoAm 94, WhoScEn 94*
**Faeth, Lisa Ellen 1955- *WhoScEn 94*
**Faeth, Paul Alfred 1928- *WhoMW 93*
**Fafian, Joseph, Jr. 1939- *WhoAm 94, WhoIns 94*
**Fagaly, William Arthur 1938- *WhoAm 94, WhoAmA 93*
**Fagan, Alanna 1939- *WhoAmA 93*
**Fagan, Barney d1937 *WhoHol 92*
**Fagan, Brian Murray 1936- *WrDr 94*
**Fagan, Cary 1957- *WrDr 94*
**Fagan, Cyril 1896-1970 *AstEnc*
**Fagan, Garth 1940- *WhoAm 94*
**Fagan, H(enry) A(llan) 1889-1963 *EncSF 93*
**Fagan, Harold Leonard 1920- *WhoBlA 94*
**Fagan, James H. *WhoAmP 93*
**Fagan, Kathy *DrAPF 93*
**Fagan, Patrick Feltrim 1935- *Who 94*
**Fagan, Renny 1956- *WhoAmP 93*
**Fagan, Sheila M. 1956- *WhoMW 93*
**Fagan, Thomas Perry 1932- *WhoAm 94*
**Fagan, Wayne Irwin 1943- *WhoAm 94, WhoFI 94*
**Fagan-Pryor, Ellen Catherine 1956- *WhoMW 93*
**Fagans, Karl P. 1942- *WhoFI 94*
**Fagbayi, Mutiu Olutoyin 1953- *WhoBlA 94*
**Fagbohun, C. Funsho 1958- *WhoMW 93*
**Fage, John Donnelly 1921- *Who 94, WrDr 94*
**Fage, Mary *BlmGWL*
**Fagelson, Harvey J. 1938- *WhoWest 94*
**Fagen, Donald 1948- *WhoAm 94*
**Fagen, Leslie Gordon 1950- *WhoAm 94, WhoAmL 94*
**Fagen, Richard Rees 1933- *WhoAm 94*
**Fager, Charles Anthony 1924- *WhoAm 94*
**Fager, Charles J. 1936- *WhoAmA 93*
**Fagerbakke, Bill *WhoHol 92*
**Fagerberg, Dixon, Jr. 1909- *WhoFI 94, WhoWest 94*
**Fagerberg, Roger Richard 1935- *WhoAm 94, WhoAmL 94, WhoMW 93*

Fagerhol, Magne Kristoffer 1935- *WhoScEn 94*
Fagersten, Gary George 1951- *WhoFI 94*
Faget, Maxime 1921- *WorInv*
Fagg, Gary Thomas 1948- *WhoIns 94*
Fagg, George G. *WhoAmP 93*
Fagg, George Gardner 1934- *WhoAm 94, WhoAmL 94*
Fagg, Harrison Grover 1931- *WhoAmP 93*
Fagg, Russell 1960- *WhoWest 94*
Fagg, Russell Charles 1960- *WhoAmP 93*
Fagg, William Harrison 1924- *WhoScEn 94*
Fagge, John William Frederick 1910- *Who 94*
Faggin, Federico 1941- *WhoAm 94*
Faggioli, Michelangelo 1666-1733 *NewGrDO*
Faggioni, Piero 1936- *NewGrDO*
Faghri, Ardeshir 1959- *WhoScEn 94*
Fagin, Claire M. *NewYTBS 93 [port]*
Fagin, Claire Mintzer *WhoAm 94*
Fagin, Claire Mintzer 1926- *IntWW 93*
Fagin, Darryl Hall 1942- *WhoBlA 94*
Fagin, David Kyle 1938- *WhoAm 94, WhoWest 94*
Fagin, Henry 1913- *WhoAm 94*
Fagin, Larry *DrAPF 93*
Fagin, Richard 1935- *WhoAm 94*
Fagnan, Marie-Antoinette d1770 *BlmGWL*
Fago, (Francesco) Nicola 1677-1745 *NewGrDO*
Fagoaga, Isidoro 1895-1976 *NewGrDO*
Fagot, Joseph Burdell 1917- *WhoAm 94*
Fagot, Robert Frederick 1921- *WhoAm 94*
Fagundes, Joseph Marvin, III 1953- *WhoAmL 94*
Fagundes Telles, Lygia *ConWorW 93*
Fagundo, Ana Maria 1938- *DcLB 134 [port], WhoAm 94, WhoWest 94*
Fahd Ibn Abdul Aziz 1923- *IntWW 93*
Fahey, David (Allen) 1948- *WrDr 94*
Fahey, David Michael 1937- *WhoMW 93*
Fahey, Helen F. *WhoAmL 94*
Fahey, James Edward 1953- *WhoFI 94*
Fahey, Jeff *IntMPA 94*
Fahey, Jeff 1956- *WhoHol 92*
Fahey, John Joseph 1945- *Who 94*
Fahey, John Leslie 1924- *WhoScEn 94*
Fahey, Joseph Francis, Jr. 1925- *WhoAm 94*
Fahey, Marcella Clifford 1934- *WhoAmP 93*
Fahey, Michael G. 1943- *WhoAmP 93*
Fahey, Myrna d1973 *WhoHol 92*
Fahey, Paul Farrell 1942- *WhoScEn 94*
Fahey, Peter Matthew 1946- *WhoFI 94*
Fahey, Reem Jarrar 1965- *WhoMW 93*
Fahey, Richard Paul 1944- *WhoAm 94, WhoMW 93*
Fahey, Thomas M. 1951- *WhoAmL 94*
Fahey, William Kelly 1952- *WhoAmL 94*
Fahien, Leonard August 1934- *WhoAm 94*
Fahim, Mostafa Safwat 1931- *WhoMW 93, WhoScEn 94*
Fahlen, Charles C. 1939- *WhoAmA 93*
Fahlgren, Herbert Smoot 1930- *WhoAm 94*
Fahlman, Betsy Lee 1951- *WhoAmA 93*
Fahlstrom, Oyvind 1928-1976 *WhoAmA 93N*
Fahmi, Hussein *WhoHol 92*
Fahmy, Ismail 1922- *IntWW 93, WrDr 94*
Fahmy, Mohamed Ali 1920- *IntWW 93*
Fahn, Abraham 1916- *WrDr 94*
Fahn, Jay 1949- *WhoFI 94*
Fahn, Stanley 1933- *WhoAm 94*
Fahner, Susan Patricia 1964- *WhoMW 93*
Fahner, Tyrone C. 1942- *WhoAm 94, WhoAmL 94*
Fahning, Melvyn Luverne 1936- *WhoScEn 94*
Fahrbach, Ruth C. *WhoAmP 93*
Fahrenheit, Daniel Gabriel 1686-1736 *WorInv*
Fahrenkopf, Frank J., Jr. 1939- *WhoAmP 93*
Fahrenkopf, Frank Joseph, Jr. 1939- *WhoAm 94*
Fahrenkrug, Randy Donald 1957- *WhoMW 93*
Fahrenthold, Eric Paul 1952- *WhoScEn 94*
Fahringer, Catherine Hewson 1922- *WhoAm 94*
Fahrnbruch, Dale E. 1924- *WhoAm 94, WhoAmL 94, WhoAmP 93, WhoMW 93*
Fahrney, Merry d1974 *WhoHol 92*
Fahrney, Milton d1941 *WhoHol 92*
Fahrni, Fritz 1942- *IntWW 93*
Fahs, Sophia Blanche Lyon 1876-1978 *DcAmReB 2*
Fa-Hsien 319-414 *WhWE*
Fahy, Christopher *DrAPF 93*
Fahy, Edward Joseph d1989 *WhAm 10*
Fahy, Janet M. 1959- *WhoFI 94*
Fahy, John J. 1954- *WhoAmL 94*
Faier, James Michael 1960- *WhoMW 93*
Faiers, Ted 1908-1985 *WhoAmA 93N*
Faig, Wolfgang 1939- *WhoScEn 94*
Faigen, Martha S. 1953- *WhoAmL 94*
Faignant, John Paul 1953- *WhoAmL 94*
Faiks, Jan 1945- *WhoAmP 93*
Failde, Augusto A. *WhoHisp 94*
Failey, George Leo, Jr. 1928- *WhoAm 94*
Failing, George Edgar 1912- *WhoAm 94*
Failinger, Marie Anita 1952- *WhoAmL 94*
Failla, Patricia McClement 1925- *WhoAm 94*
Failla, Richard C. d1993 *NewYTBS 93 [port]*
Faillard, Hans 1924- *IntWW 93*
Failoni, Sergio 1890-1948 *NewGrDO*
Failor, William Ned 1950- *WhoFI 94*
Faiman, Peter *IntMPA 94*
Faiman, Robert Neil 1923- *WhoAm 94*
Fain, Constance Frisby 1949- *WhoBlA 94*
Fain, Jay Lindsey 1950- *WhoFI 94*
Fain, Joel Maurice 1953- *WhoAm 94, WhoAmL 94*
Fain, John d1970 *WhoHol 92*
Fain, John Nicholas 1934- *WhoAm 94, WhoScEn 94*
Fain, Karen Kellogg 1940- *WhoWest 94*
Fain, Paul Kemp, Jr. *WhoAm 94, WhoFI 94*
Fain, Richard David 1947- *WhoAm 94*
Fain, Sammy d1989 *WhoHol 92*
Fain, Sammy 1902-1989 *WhAm 10*
Fainberg, Anthony 1944- *WhoScEn 94*
Faini, Anna Maria fl. 1719-1744 *NewGrDO*
Fainlight, Ruth *DrAPF 93*
Fainlight, Ruth 1931- *BlmGEL, WrDr 94*
Fainsilber, Adrien 1932- *IntWW 93*
Faint, John Anthony Leonard 1942- *Who 94*
Fainter, Lynda Jean 1947- *WhoMW 93*
Fainter, Robert A. 1942-1978 *WhoAmA 93N*
Faintich, Stephen Robert 1963- *WhoScEn 94*
Fair, Charles Maitland 1916- *WhoScEn 94*
Fair, Darwin *WhoBlA 94*
Fair, Dick d1982 *WhoHol 92*
Fair, Donald Robert Russell 1916- *Who 94*
Fair, Elinor d1957 *WhoHol 92*
Fair, Frank T. 1929- *WhoBlA 94*
Fair, George R. 1949- *WhoAmL 94*
Fair, Hudson Randolph 1953- *WhoMW 93*
Fair, James Rutherford, Jr. 1920- *WhoAm 94, WhoScEn 94*
Fair, Jean Everhard 1917- *WhoAm 94*
Fair, Michael 1946- *WhoAmP 93*
Fair, Mike 1942- *WhoAmP 93*
Fair, Norman Arnold 1945- *WhoIns 94*
Fair, Patricia Anne 1952- *WhoAmP 93*
Fair, Richard Barton 1942- *WhoAm 94*
Fair, Robert James 1919- *WhoAm 94*
Fair, Rodney Dale 1956- *WhoWest 94*
Fair, Ronald *DrAPF 93*
Fair, Ronald L. 1932- *WhoBlA 94*
Fair, Talmadge Willard 1939- *WhoBlA 94*
Fair, William Robert 1935- *WhoAm 94*
Fairall, Richard Snowden 1927- *WhoScEn 94*
Fairbairn, Brooke *Who 94*
Fairbairn, (James) Brooke 1930- *Who 94*
Fairbairn, Bruce *WhoHol 92*
Fairbairn, David 1924- *Who 94*
Fairbairn, David Eric 1917- *Who 94*
Fairbairn, David Ritchie 1934- *Who 94*
Fairbairn, Douglas 1926- *WrDr 94*
Fairbairn, Douglas Foakes 1919- *Who 94*
Fairbairn, John Sydney 1934- *IntWW 93, Who 94*
Fairbairn, Joyce 1939- *WhoWomW 91*
Fairbairn, Stephen Carl 1960- *WhoWest 94*
Fairbairn of Fordell, Nicholas (Hardwick) 1933- *Who 94*
Fairbairns, Zoe 1948- *BlmGEL*
Fairbairns, Zoe (Ann) 1948- *EncSF 93, WrDr 94*
Fairbairns, Zoe Ann 1948- *BlmGWL*
Fairbank, Alfred John 1895-1982 *DcNaB MP*
Fairbank, Christopher *WhoHol 92*
Fairbank, John K(ing) 1907-1991 *WrDr 94N*
Fairbank, John King 1907-1991 *WhAm 10*
Fairbank, Robert Harold 1948- *WhoAm 94*
Fairbank, William Martin 1917-1989 *WhAm 10*
Fairbanks, Bill d1945 *WhoHol 92*
Fairbanks, David Weston 1961- *WhoFI 94*
Fairbanks, Douglas d1939 *WhoHol 92*
Fairbanks, Douglas, Jr. 1907- *WhoHol 92*
Fairbanks, Douglas, Jr. 1909- *IntMPA 94*
Fairbanks, Douglas (Elton) 1909- *Who 94*
Fairbanks, Douglas Elton, Jr. 1909- *IntWW 93, WhoAm 94*
Fairbanks, Flobelle d1969 *WhoHol 92*
Fairbanks, Frank *WhoAmP 93*
Fairbanks, Frank Bates 1930- *WhoAm 94*
Fairbanks, Fred d1927 *WhoHol 92*
Fairbanks, Harold Vincent 1915- *WhoAm 94*
Fairbanks, Jerry 1904- *IntMPA 94*
Fairbanks, Jonathan Leo 1933- *WhoAm 94, WhoAmA 93*
Fairbanks, Lucille 1920- *WhoHol 92*
Fairbanks, Madeleine d1989 *WhoHol 92*
Fairbanks, Marion d1974? *WhoHol 92*
Fairbanks, Mary Kathleen 1948- *WhoFI 94, WhoScEn 94, WhoWest 94*
Fairbanks, Richard M., III 1941- *WhoAmP 93*
Fairbanks, Richard Monroe 1912- *WhoAm 94*
Fairbanks, Richard Monroe, III 1941- *WhoAm 94, WhoAmL 94*
Fairbanks, Robert Alvin 1944- *WhoAmL 94*
Fairbanks, Robert Gean 1950- *WhoMW 93*
Fairbanks, Russell Norman 1919- *WhoAm 94*
Fairbanks, William J. 1931- *WhoIns 94*
Fairbrother, Kenneth Archie 1957- *WhoMW 93*
Fairbrother, Sydney d1941 *WhoHol 92*
Fairburn, Charles Edward 1887-1945 *DcNaB MP*
Fairburn, Eleanor 1928- *WrDr 94*
Fairchild, Arvid Pershing 1925- *WhoWest 94*
Fairchild, Beatrice Magdoff 1916- *WhoAm 94*
Fairchild, Bob 1943- *WhoAmP 93*
Fairchild, David Lawrence 1946- *WhoAm 94*
Fairchild, Deborah West 1952- *WhoMW 93*
Fairchild, Gary Lee 1943- *WhoAm 94, WhoAmL 94*
Fairchild, Henry Brant, III 1945- *WhoMW 93*
Fairchild, John Burr 1927- *WhoAm 94*
Fairchild, Joseph Jerome 1949- *WhoAmP 93*
Fairchild, Joseph Virgil, Jr. 1933- *WhoAm 94, WhoFI 94*
Fairchild, Margaret *WhoHol 92*
Fairchild, May 1872-1959 *WhoAmA 93N*
Fairchild, Morgan 1950- *IntMPA 94, WhoHol 92*
Fairchild, Ray d1918 *WhoHol 92*
Fairchild, Raymond Eugene 1923- *WhoAm 94*
Fairchild, Raymond Francis 1946- *WhoAmL 94*
Fairchild, Robert Charles 1921- *WhoAm 94*
Fairchild, Roger *WhoAmP 93*
Fairchild, Russell H. 1947- *WhoAmP 93*
Fairchild, Samuel Wilson 1954- *WhoAm 94*
Fairchild, Thomas E. 1912- *WhoAm 94, WhoAmL 94, WhoMW 93*
Fairchild, William 1918- *IntMPA 94*
Fair Cloth, Duncan 1928- *WhoAm 94*
Faircloth, Larry V. 1948- *WhoAmP 93*
Faircloth, Lauch 1928- *CngDr 93*
Faircloth, McLauchlin *WhoAmP 93*
Faircloth, Sean 1960- *WhoAmP 93*
Fairclough, Anthony John 1924- *IntWW 93, Who 94*
Fairclough, Ellen Louks 1905- *Who 94*
Fairclough, John (Whitaker) 1930- *Who 94*
Fairclough, John Whitaker 1930- *IntWW 93*
Fairclough, Michael J. 1944- *WhoAmL 94*
Fairclough, Wilfred 1907- *Who 94*
Faire, Virginia d1948 *WhoHol 92*
Faire, Virginia Brown d1980 *WhoHol 92*
Faire, Zabrina *WrDr 94*
Faires, Ross N. 1934- *WhoFI 94*
Fairey, Michael John 1933- *Who 94*
Fairfax *Who 94*
Fairfax, Ann 1936- *WrDr 94*
Fairfax, Betty d1962 *WhoHol 92*
Fairfax, Bryan d1802 *WhAmRev*
Fairfax, James d1961 *WhoHol 92*
Fairfax, James Oswald 1933- *Who 94*
Fairfax, John 1930- *WrDr 94*
Fairfax, Lance d1974 *WhoHol 92*
Fairfax, Lettice d1948 *WhoHol 92*
Fairfax, Robert d1965 *WhoHol 92*
Fairfax, Thomas, Lord 1693-1781 *WhAmRev*
Fairfax, Vincent Charles d1993 *IntWW 93N, Who 94N*
Fairfax, Vincent Charles 1909- *IntWW 93*
Fairfax-Lucy, Edmund (John William Hugh Cameron-Ramsay-) 1945- *Who 94*
Fairfax Of Cameron, Lord 1956- *Who 94*
Fairfield, Betty Elaine Smith 1927- *WhoAm 94*
Fairfield, Darrell 1935- *WrDr 94*
Fairfield, John *DrAPF 93*
Fairfield, John Denis 1955- *WhoMW 93*
Fairfield, Lesley 1949- *WrDr 94*
Fairfield, Mary Ellen 1949- *WhoAmL 94*
Fairfield, Richard Thomas 1937- *WhoAmA 93*
Fairgrieve, (Thomas) Russell 1924- *Who 94*
Fairhall, Allen 1909- *Who 94*
Fairhaven, Baron 1936- *Who 94*
Fairhurst, Charles 1929- *WhoAm 94*
Fairleigh, Karen Evelyn 1965- *WhoWest 94*
Fairleigh, Marlane Paxson 1939- *WhoFI 94*
Fairleigh, Runa 1945- *WrDr 94*
Fairless, Benjamin Franklin 1890-1962 *EncABHB 9 [port]*
Fairley, Henry Barrie 1927- *WhoAm 94*
Fairley, James S(tewart) 1940- *WrDr 94*
Fairley, John (Alexander) 1939- *WrDr 94*
Fairley, John Alexander *Who 94*
Fairley, Richard L. 1933- *WhoBlA 94*
Fairlie, Alison Anna Bowie d1993 *Who 94N*
Fairlie, Hugh d1993 *Who 94N*
Fairlie-Cuninghame, William Henry 1930- *Who 94*
Fairman, Austin d1964 *WhoHol 92*
Fairman, Jarrett Sylvester 1939- *WhoFI 94*
Fairman, Jimmy W. 1948- *WhoBlA 94*
Fairman, Joan Alexandra 1935- *WrDr 94*
Fairman, Joel Martin 1929- *WhoAm 94*
Fairman, John Abbrey 1949- *WhoBlA 94*
Fairman, Marc P. 1945- *WhoAmL 94*
Fairman, Paul W. 1916-1977 *EncSF 93*
Fairobent, Douglas Kevin 1951- *WhoScEn 94*
Fairtlough, Gerard Howard 1930- *Who 94*
Fairweather, Claude Cyril 1906- *Who 94*
Fairweather, David G. 1945- *WhoIns 94*
Fairweather, Denys Vivian Ivor 1927- *Who 94*
Fairweather, Edwin Arthur 1916- *WhoWest 94*
Fairweather, Eric John 1942- *Who 94*
Fairweather, Frank Arthur 1928- *Who 94*
Fairweather, John C. 1952- *WhoAm 94*
Fairweather, Patrick (Stanislaus) 1936- *Who 94*
Fairweather, Robert Gordon Lee 1923- *WhoAm 94*
Fairweather, Sally H. 1917- *WhoAmA 93*
Faisal, I 1883?-1933 *HisWorL [port]*
Faisal, II 1935-1958 *HisWorL [port]*
Faison, Derek E. 1948- *WhoBlA 94*
Faison, Frankie *WhoHol 92*
Faison, Frankie 1949- *WhoBlA 94*
Faison, Helen Smith 1924- *WhoBlA 94*
Faison, John W. 1908- *WhoBlA 94*
Faison, Lee Vell 1933- *WhoAmP 93*
Faison, Ollie William, Jr. 1947- *WhoAmL 94*
Faison, Samson Lane, Jr. 1907- *WhoAmA 93*
Faison, Sandy *WhoHol 92*
Faison, Seth Shepard 1924- *WhoAm 94*
Faison, Sharon Gail 1955- *WhoBlA 94*
Faison, Thurman Lawrence 1938- *WhoBlA 94*
Faison, W. Mack 1945- *WhoAmL 94*
Faiss, Robert Dean 1934- *WhoAmL 94*
Fait, George A. 1926- *WhoIns 94*
Faith, Adam 1940- *IntWW 93, WhoHol 92*
Faith, Dolores 1942- *WhoHol 92*
Faith, (Irene) Sheila 1928- *Who 94*
Faithfull, Baroness 1910- *Who 94*
Faithfull, Emily 1835-1895 *DcNaB MP*
Faithfull, Lucy 1910- *WhoWomW 91*
Faithfull, Marianne 1946- *WhoHol 92*
Faitz, Ann Paula 1951- *WhoAmL 94*
Faivelson, Baruch N. d1993 *NewYTBS 93*
Faivre d'Arcier, Bernard 1944- *IntWW 93*
Faiz, Asif 1947- *WhoFI 94*
Fajans, Jack 1922- *WhoAm 94*
Fajans, Stefan Stanislaus 1918- *WhoAm 94*
Fajardo, Ben *WhoAsA 94*
Fajardo, Frank Torres 1949- *WhoHisp 94*
Fajardo, Frederick Joseph 1935- *WhoFI 94*
Fajardo, Jorge Elias 1942- *WhoHisp 94*
Fajardo, Juan Ramon, Jr. 1958- *WhoHisp 94*
Fajardo, Julius Escalante 1959- *WhoScEn 94*
Fajardo, Katharine Lynn 1951- *WhoAm 94*
Fajardo, Peter *WhoAsA 94*

Fajardo-Acosta, Fidel 1960- WhoHisp 94
Fajardo L-G, Luis Felipe 1927- WhoHisp 94
Fajer, Francisco Javier Garcia NewGrDO
Fajt, Gregory C. 1954- WhoAmP 93

Fakhoury, Rachid IntWW 93
Fakhrid-Deen, Nashid Abdullah 1949- WhoBlA 94
Fakir, Abdul 1935- See Four Tops, The ConMus 11
Fakley, Dennis Charles 1924- Who 94
Fakunle, Funmilayo BlmGWL
Fala, Herman C. 1949- WhoAm 94, WhoAmL 94
Falabella, John M. d1993 NewYTBS 93
Falagan-Girona, Mildred 1950- WhoHisp 94
Falana, Lola 1942- WhoHol 92
Falana, Lola 1943- WhoBlA 94
Falaniko, Frank, Jr. 1956- WhoAsA 94
Falardeau, Ernest Rene 1928- WhoWest 94
Falb, Peter Lawrence 1936- WhoAm 94
Falbe, Mary Lynn Marie 1958- WhoFI 94
Falber, Harold Julius 1946- WhoFI 94
Falcao, Armando Ribeiro 1920- IntWW 93
Falci, Kenneth J. WhoScEn 94
Falck, Colin 1934- WrDr 94
Falck, Maria J. 1962- WhoMW 93
Falco, Charles Maurice 1948- WhoWest 94
Falco, Edward DrAPF 93
Falco, Edward 1948- WrDr 94
Falco, Joao BlmGWL
Falco, Louis d1993 NewYTBS 93 [port]
Falco, Maria Josephine 1932- WhoAm 94
Falco, Michele 1688?-c. 1732 NewGrDO
Falcon, Angelo WhoHisp 94
Falcon, (Marie) Cornelie 1812-1897 NewGrDO [port]
Falcon, David 1946- Who 94
Falcon, Dora 1936- WhoHisp 94
Falcon, Ellen ConTFT 11
Falcon, Joseph A. WhoScEn 94
Falcon, Lidia 1935- BlmGWL
Falcon, Louis Albert 1932- WhoAm 94
Falcón, Luis M. 1955- WhoHisp 94
Falcon, Mark 1940- WrDr 94
Falcon, Michael Gascoigne 1928- IntWW 93, Who 94
Falcon, Norman Leslie 1904- Who 94
Falcón, Rafael 1947- WhoHisp 94
Falcon, Raymond Jesus, Jr. 1953- WhoAmL 94, WhoFI 94
Falcon, Ruth 1946- NewGrDO
Falcone, Alfonso Benjamin WhoAm 94, WhoWest 94
Falcone, Anthony 1952- WhoFI 94
Falcone, Carmine 1946- WhoWest 94
Falcone, Charles Anthony 1942- WhoFI 94
Falcone, Frank S. 1940- WhoAm 94
Falcone, Nola Maddox 1939- WhoAm 94, WhoFI 94
Falcone, Philip Francis 1929- WhoWest 94
Falcone, Sebastian Anthony 1927- WhoAm 94
Falconer, Alexander 1940- Who 94
Falconer, Charles Leslie 1951- Who 94
Falconer, David Duncan 1940- WhoAm 94
Falconer, Douglas (William) 1914- Who 94
Falconer, Douglas Scott 1913- IntWW 93, Who 94
Falconer, Kenneth EncSF 93
Falconer, Lee N. EncSF 93
Falconer, Peter Serrell 1916- Who 94
Falconer, Sovereign EncSF 93
Falconer, William 1732-1769 BlmGEL
Falconetti d1946 WhoHol 92
Falconi, Arturo d1934 WhoHol 92
Falconieri, John V(incent) 1920- WrDr 94
Falconnet, Francoise-Cecile de Chaumont 1738-1819 BlmGWL
Falcucci, Franca 1926- IntWW 93, WhoWomW 91
Faldbakken, Knut EncSF 93
Faldbakken, Knut (Robert) 1941- ConWorW 93
Faldo, Nicholas Alexander 1957- Who 94
Faldo, Nick 1957- IntWW 93, News 93-3 [port]
Faleomavaega, Eni F. H. CngDr 93, WhoAmP 93
Faleomavaega, Eni F. H. 1943- WhoAm 94
Faleomavaega, Eni Faauaa Hunkin, Jr. 1943- WhoAsA 94
Falero, Frank 1937- WhoWest 94
Fales, Haliburton, II 1919- WhoAm 94
Fales, Henry Marshall 1927- WhoScEn 94
Fales, Susan WhoBlA 94
Faletau, 'Inoke Fotu 1937- IntWW 93, Who 94
Faletti, Richard Joseph 1922- WhoAm 94
Falewicz, Magdalena 1946- NewGrDO
Faley, Richard Scott 1947- WhoAmL 94
Faley, Robert Lawrence 1927- WhoFI 94, WhoScEn 94, WhoWest 94
Falfan, Alfredo 1936- WhoAmA 93
Falgiano, Victor Joseph 1957- WhoScEn 94, WhoWest 94
Falick, Abraham Johnson 1920- WhoWest 94
Falick, James 1936- WhoAm 94
Falicov, Leopoldo Maximo 1933- IntWW 93, WhoAm 94, WhoWest 94
Falik, William A. 1846- WhoAmL 94
Falik, Yury Alexandrovich 1936- NewGrDO
Falin, Valentin Mikhailovich 1926- IntWW 93
Falino, Francis Joseph 1970- WhoHisp 94
Falise, Michel 1931- IntWW 93
Falit, Harvey Harris 1942- WhoMW 93
Falk, Arnold Charles, III 1943- WhoFI 94
Falk, Bennett 1943- WhoAmL 94
Falk, Bernard Henry 1926- WhoAm 94
Falk, Candace 1947- WrDr 94
Falk, Conrad Robert 1935- WhoAm 94
Falk, David B. 1950- WhoAm 94
Falk, Dean 1944- WhoScEn 94
Falk, Edgar Alan 1932- WhoAm 94
Falk, Eugene Hannes 1913- WhoAm 94
Falk, Eugene L. 1943- WhoAm 94, WhoFI 94
Falk, Harvey L. 1934- WhoFI 94
Falk, I. Lee 1947- WhoAm 94
Falk, James Harvey, Sr. 1938- WhoAm 94, WhoAmL 94
Falk, Joel 1945- WhoScEn 94
Falk, John Carl 1938- WhoMW 93
Falk, Julia S. 1941- WhoAm 94
Falk, Karl L. 1911-1988 WhAm 10
Falk, Lauren Weissman 1959- WhoAmL 94
Falk, Lee 1924- WrDr 94
Falk, Lee Harrison WhoAm 94
Falk, Lianne WhoHol 92
Falk, Marcia DrAPF 93
Falk, Marshall Allen 1929- WhoMW 93
Falk, Michael Philip 1953- WhoAmL 94
Falk, Michelle Ona 1957- WhoFI 94
Falk, Peter 1927- IntMPA 94, WhoAm 94, WhoCom, WhoHol 92
Falk, Richard Sands, Jr. 1941- WhoAm 94
Falk, Robert Barclay, Jr. 1945- WhoScEn 94
Falk, Robert Hardy 1948- WhoAmL 94, WhoFI 94
Falk, Roger (Salis) 1910- Who 94
Falk, Rossella WhoHol 92
Falk, Signi Lenea 1906- WrDr 94
Falk, Stanley Lawrence 1927- WrDr 94
Falk, Steven Mitchell 1961- WhoScEn 94
Falk, William James 1952- WhoAm 94, WhoAmL 94
Falk, Ze'ev W(ilhelm) 1923- ConAu 42NR, WrDr 94
Falkenberg, Mary Ann Theresa 1931- WhoFI 94, WhoMW 93
Falkenberg, William Stevens 1927- WhoWest 94
Falkenburg, Bob 1926- BuCMET
Falkenburg, Jinx 1919- WhoHol 92
Falkender, Baroness 1932- Who 94, WhoWomW 91
Falkenstein, Claire WhoAmA 93
Falkenstein, Julius d1933 WhoHol 92
Falkenstein, Karin Edith 1950- WhoMW 93
Falker, John Richard 1940- WhoAm 94
Falkie, Thomas Victor 1934- WhoAm 94
Falkiner, Edmond (Charles) 1938- Who 94
Falkingham, Donald Herbert 1918- WhoScEn 94
Falkingham, John Norman 1917- Who 94
Falkirk, Richard 1929- WrDr 94
Falkland, Master of 1963- Who 94
Falkland, Viscount 1935- Who 94
Falkmer, Karin Gunnel 1936- WhoWomW 91
Falkner, Bobbie E. WhoBlA 94
Falkner, Frank Tardrew 1918- WhoAm 94
Falkner, James George 1952- WhoFI 94, WhoWest 94
Falkner, (Donald) Keith 1900- IntWW 93, Who 94
Falkner, William Carroll 1954- WhoAmL 94
Falkouski, Richard John, Jr. 1954- WhoFI 94
Falkow, Stanley 1934- WhoWest 94
Falkowitz, Daniel 1936- WhoAm 94
Falkowski, Patricia Ann 1947- WhoFI 94
Falkum, Craig Clifford 1947- WhoMW 93
Falkus, Hugh Edward Lance 1917- Who 94
Fall, Aminata Sow 1941- ConWorW 93
Fall, Brian (James Proetel) 1937- Who 94
Fall, Brian James Proetel 1937- IntWW 93
Fall, David William 1948- Who 94
Fall, Harry H. 1920- WhoMW 93
Fall, Ibrahima 1942- IntWW 93
Fall, Kine Kirama BlmGWL
Fall, Leo(pold) 1873-1925 NewGrDO
Fall, Medoune 1919- IntWW 93
Fall, Timothy Lee 1960- WhoAmL 94
Falla (y Matheu), Manuel (Maria) de (los Dolores) 1876-1946 NewGrDO
Falla, Enrique C. 1939- WhoHisp 94
Falla, Enrique Crabb 1939- WhoAm 94, WhoFI 94
Falla, Paul Stephen 1913- Who 94
Fallaci, Oriana 1930- BlmGWL, IntWW 93, WhoAm 94
Fallam, Robert fl. 167-?- WhWE
Falldin, (Nils Olof) Thorbjorn 1926- IntWW 93
Fallding, Harold Joseph 1923- WhoAm 94
Falle, Daisy Carolyne 1940- WhoAm 94
Falle, Sam 1919- Who 94
Falleder, Arnold E. DrAPF 93
Fallek, Andrew Michael 1956- WhoAmL 94
Fallender, Deborah WhoHol 92
Faller, Donald E. 1927- WhoAm 94
Faller, Marion 1941- WhoAmA 93
Faller, Rhoda Dianne Grossberg 1946- WhoAmL 94
Faller, Susan Grogan 1950- WhoAm 94, WhoAmL 94
Fallert, Herbert C. 1936- WhoAmP 93
Fallet, George 1920- WhoScEn 94
Falletta, Jo Ann 1954- WhoAm 94, WhoWest 94
Falletta, John Matthew 1940- WhoAm 94, WhoScEn 94
Fallin, Daniel Paul 1955- WhoFI 94
Fallin, James Holder 1945- WhoAmP 93
Fallin, Joseph Price, Jr. 1947- WhoAmP 93
Fallin, Mary C. 1954- WhoAmP 93
Fallin, Pat Finley 1941- WhoAmP 93
Fallis, Albert Murray 1907- WhoAm 94
Fallis, Alexander Graham 1940- WhoAm 94
Fallis, Laurence S. DrAPF 93
Fallis, Stephen James 1942- WhoAmL 94
Fallon, Charles d1936 WhoHol 92
Fallon, Christopher Chaffee, Jr. 1948- WhoAm 94
Fallon, Daniel 1938- WhoAm 94
Fallon, David Michael 1946- WhoScEn 94
Fallon, Ed WhoAmP 93
Fallon, Gabriel d1980 WhoHol 92
Fallon, George ConAu 42NR
Fallon, Hazel Rosemary Who 94
Fallon, Ivan Gregory 1944- Who 94
Fallon, Jill Ellen 1945- WhoAmL 94
Fallon, John Golden 1946- WhoAm 94
Fallon, John Joseph 1923- WhoAmL 94
Fallon, Joseph Anthony 1941- WhoAmP 93
Fallon, Kristine K. 1949- WhoMW 93
Fallon, Louis Fleming, Jr. 1950- WhoScEn 94
Fallon, Martin Who 94
Fallon, Martin 1939- WrDr 94
Fallon, Michael DrAPF 93
Fallon, Michael 1952- Who 94
Fallon, Michael P. 1941- WhoHisp 94
Fallon, Padraic Matthew 1946- Who 94
Fallon, Peter 1931- Who 94
Fallon, Peter 1951- WrDr 94
Fallon, Richard Gordon 1923- WhoAm 94
Fallon, Stephen Francis 1956- WhoHisp 94, WhoIns 94
Fallon, Tina K. 1917- WhoAmP 93
Fallon, Tom DrAPF 93
Falloon, John H. IntWW 93
Falloppio, Gabriele 1523-1562 EncDeaf
Fallows, Albert Bennett 1928- Who 94
Fallows, James M(ackenzie) 1949- ConAu 43NR
Fallows, James Mackenzie 1949- WhoAm 94, WrDr 94
Falls, Arthur GrandPre 1901- WhoMW 93
Falls, C. Frank 1934- WhoAmP 93
Falls, Charles Buckles 1874-1959 WhoAmA 93N
Falls, Douglas A. 1952- WhoIns 94
Falls, Edward Joseph 1920- WhoAm 94
Falls, Elsa Queen 1942- WhoScEn 94
Falls, Joseph Francis 1928- WhoAm 94
Falls, Kathleene Joyce 1949- WhoMW 93
Falls, Marilyn Lee 1949- WhoAm 94
Falls, Olive Moretz 1934- WhoAm 94
Falls, Raymond Leonard, Jr. 1929-1991 WhAm 10
Falls, Robert Arthur 1954- WhoMW 93
Falls, William Wayne 1947- WhoAm 94
Fallside, Frank d1993 Who 94N
Falmar, Leslie Karen 1961- WhoHisp 94
Falmouth, Earl of 1630-1665 DcNaB MP
Falmouth, Viscount 1919- Who 94
Faloon, William Wassell 1920- WhoAm 94
Falquez-Certain, Miguel Angel 1948- WhoHisp 94
Falret, Jean-Pierre 1794-1870 EncSPD
Falret, Jules-Philippe-Joseph 1824-1902 EncSPD
Falsetta, Vincent Mario 1949- WhoAmA 93
Falsetto, Mario 1950- WhoAmA 93
Falsey, John ConTFT 11
Falsey, John Henry, Jr. 1951- WhoAm 94
Falsgraf, William Wendell 1933- WhoAm 94, WhoAmL 94
Falstad, William James 1934- WhoAmP 93
Falstein, Eugene I. 1908-1989 WhAm 10
Falstein, Louis DrAPF 93
Falstrom, Kenneth Edward 1946- WhoAmL 94
Falter, John 1910-1982 WhoAmA 93N
Falter, Robert Gary 1945- WhoAm 94
Falter, Vincent Eugene 1932- WhoAm 94
Falter-Barns, Suzanne 1958- ConAu 141
Falterman, Darrell John WhoIns 94
Falthammar, Carl-Gunne 1931- IntWW 93
Faltin, Bruce Charles 1947- WhoWest 94
Faltings, Gerd 1954- WhoAm 94
Faludi, Susan 1959- CurBio 93 [port]
Faludi, Susan C. WhoAm 94
Falvey, Patrick Joseph 1927- WhoAm 94, WhoAmL 94
Falvey, William Patrick 1946- WhoAmL 94
Falwell, Jerry 1933- AmSocL
Falwell, Jerry L. 1933- IntWW 93, WhoAm 94
Falwell, Robert V. 1948- WhoAmP 93
Falzarano, L. Domenic 1940- WhoAmP 93
Falzon, Michael 1945- IntWW 93
Falzone, Anthony Joseph 1942- WhoMW 93
Falzone, Michael Paul 1957- WhoAmL 94
Famiglietti, Nancy Zima 1956- WhoFI 94
Family Doctor, A 1908- WrDr 94
Famularo, John M. 1946- WhoAmL 94
Fan, Ada Mei 1953- WhoAsA 94
Fan, Carol C. WhoAsA 94
Fan, Chang-Yun 1918- WhoAsA 94
Fan, Changxin 1931- WhoScEn 94
Fan, Chien 1930- WhoAsA 94
Fan, David P. 1942- WhoMW 93
Fan, Hua-Tzu 1963- WhoMW 93
Fan, Hung Y. 1947- WhoAm 94, WhoWest 94
Fan, J.D. Jiangdi 1941- WhoScEn 94
Fan, Jiaxiang 1924- WhoScEn 94
Fan, Ky 1914- WhoAm 94
Fan, Liang-Shih 1947- WhoAsA 94
Fan, Tian-You 1939- WhoScEn 94
Fan, Xiyun WhoScEn 94
Fanaka, Jamaa 1942- WhoBlA 94
Fan Baojun 1940- WhoPRCh 91 [port]
Fancelli, Giuseppe 1833-1887 NewGrDO
Fancher, Evelyn Pitts WhoBlA 94
Fancher, Hampton 1938- WhoHol 92
Fancher, Jane S(uzanne) 1952- EncSF 93
Fancher, Michael Reilly 1946- WhoAm 94, WhoWest 94
Fancher, Rick 1953- WhoAmL 94
Fancher, Robert Burney 1940- WhoAm 94
Fancher, Robert T. 1954- WrDr 94
Fanchi, Peter A. 1950- WhoAmL 94
Fan Chongyan WhoPRCh 91 [port]
Fanciullo, William Patrick 1953- WhoAmL 94
Fancutt, Walter 1911- WrDr 94
Fandel, John DrAPF 93
Fando (Rais), Urbano 1855-1909? NewGrDO
Fandrich, Lamont H. 1951- WhoWest 94
Fane Who 94
Fane, Bron EncSF 93
Fane, Bron 1935- WrDr 94
Fane, David Anthony Thomas d1993 NewYTBS 93 [port]
Fane, Harry Frank Brien d1993 Who 94N
Fane, John NewGrDO
Fane, Julian 1927- WrDr 94
Fane, Julian (Charles) 1927- EncSF 93
Fane, Lawrence 1933- WhoAmA 93
Fanelli, Joseph James 1924- WhoFI 94
Fane Trefusis Who 94
Fanfani, Amintore 1908- IntWW 93
Fang, Cheng-Shen 1936- WhoAsA 94
Fang, Chunchang 1955- WhoScEn 94
Fang, Fabian Tien-Hwa 1929- WhoAsA 94
Fang, Florence WhoAsA 94
Fang, Florence S. WhoAsA 94
Fang, Frank F. 1930- WhoAsA 94
Fang, Frank Fu 1930- WhoAm 94
Fang, James WhoAsA 94
Fang, Jin Bao 1934- WhoAsA 94
Fang, John Ta-Chuan 1925-1992 WhoAsA 94N

Fang, Joong 1923- *WhoAm 94*
Fang, Joseph Pe Yong 1911- *WhoScEn 94*
Fang, Louis Li-Yeh 1963- *WhoAsA 94*
Fang, Ming M. 1955-1993 *WhoAsA 94N*
Fang, Pen Jeng 1931- *WhoAm 94, WhoAsA 94, WhoScEn 94*
Fang, Shu-Cherng 1952- *WhoScEn 94*
Fang, Yue 1960- *WhoScEn 94*
Fang, Zhaoqiang 1939- *WhoMW 93*
Fanger, Bradford Otto 1956- *WhoScEn 94*
Fanger, Donald Lee 1929- *WhoAm 94*
Fang Fukang *WhoPRCh 91*
Fang Guoxiong 1945?- *WhoPRCh 91*
Fang Hui *WhoPRCh 91 [port]*
Fangio, Juan Manuel 1911- *IntWW 93*
Fang Jiade *WhoPRCh 91*
Fang Jizhong 1923- *WhoPRCh 91 [port]*
Fang Jun 1904- *WhoPRCh 91*
Fang Lizhi 1936- *IntWW 93, WhoPRCh 91 [port]*
Fangmeier, Delmar Dean 1932- *WhoWest 94*
Fang Ming *WhoPRCh 91*
Fangor, Voy 1922- *WhoAmA 93*
Fang Qi 1920- *WhoPRCh 91*
Fang Qiang 1909- *WhoPRCh 91 [port]*
Fang Rongxin 1912- *WhoPRCh 91 [port]*
Fang Shaoyi 1911- *WhoPRCh 91 [port]*
Fang Sheng 1930?- *WhoPRCh 91 [port]*
Fang Shouxian *WhoPRCh 91 [port]*
Fang Shouxian 1932- *IntWW 93*
Fang Shu 1962- *WhoPRCh 91 [port]*
Fang Tianqi *WhoPRCh 91*
Fan Guoxiang *WhoPRCh 91*
Fang Weizhong 1928- *IntWW 93, WhoPRCh 91 [port]*
Fang Xiao *WhoPRCh 91*
Fang Yi 1916- *IntWW 93, WhoPRCh 91 [port]*
Fang Zengxian 1931- *WhoPRCh 91 [port]*
Fang Zhangshun 1934- *WhoPRCh 91 [port]*
Fan Hsu, Rita Lai-Tai 1945- *WhoWomW 91*
Fan Jin 1919- *WhoPRCh 91 [port]*
Fan Jingyi *WhoPRCh 91*
Fanjul, Alfonso *WhoHisp 94*
Fanjul, Andres *WhoHisp 94*
Fanjul, Jose *WhoHisp 94*
Fanjul, Rafael James, Jr. 1963- *WhoScEn 94*
Fankhanel, Edward H. 1958- *WhoHisp 94*
Fankhanel, K. Jane 1946- *WhoAmL 94*
Fankhauser, Allen 1950- *WhoAmL 94*
Fankhauser, Angeline 1936- *WhoWomW 91*
Fankhauser, Mark A. 1952- *WhoAmL 94*
Fan Lian 1919- *WhoPRCh 91 [port]*
Fan Muhan *WhoPRCh 91*
Fann, Al Louis 1925- *WhoBlA 94*
Fanner, Peter Duncan 1926- *Who 94*
Fannin, David Cecil 1946- *WhoAmL 94*
Fannin, Paul Jones 1907- *WhoAmP 93*
Fannin, William Richard 1951- *WhoWest 94*
Fanning, Barry Hedges 1950- *WhoAm 94*
Fanning, David 1755-1825 *AmRev, WhAmRev*
Fanning, Delvin Seymour 1931- *WhoAm 94*
Fanning, Edmund 1739-1818 *AmRev, WhAmRev [port]*
Fanning, Edmund 1769-1841 *WhWE*
Fanning, Eleanor 1949- *WhoAmL 94*
Fanning, Ellis Vinal, Jr. 1935- *WhoAmP 93*
Fanning, Frank d1934 *WhoHol 92*
Fanning, George Francis d1946 *WhoHol 92*
Fanning, John Harold 1916-1990 *WhAm 10*
Fanning, John Patton 1934- *WhoAmP 93*
Fanning, Katherine Woodruff 1927- *WhoAm 94*
Fanning, Kenneth James 1947- *WhoAmP 93*
Fanning, Margaret Beverly 1937- *WhoAm 94*
Fanning, Nathaniel 1755-1805 *WhAmRev*
Fanning, Robert Allen 1931- *WhoAm 94*
Fanning, Ronald Heath 1935- *WhoMW 93, WhoScEn 94*
Fanning, William Henry, Jr. 1917- *WhoScEn 94*
Fanning, William James 1927- *WhoAm 94*
Fanning, William Lincoln 1893- *WhAm 10*
Fanny-Dell 1939- *WhoWest 94*
Fano, Robert Mario 1917- *WhoAm 94*
Fano, Ugo 1912- *IntWW 93, WhoAm 94*
Fanone, Joseph Anthony 1949- *WhoAm 94, WhoAmL 94*
Fanos, John G. 1926- *WhoAmP 93*
Fanos, Kathleen Hilaire 1956- *WhoMW 93*
Fanos, William R. 1953- *WhoAmL 94*
Fan Qinzhen *WhoPRCh 91*
Fan Rongkang 1929- *WhoPRCh 91 [port]*
Fanseen, James Foster 1928- *WhoAm 94*
Fanshawe, Ann 1625-1680 *BlmGWL*
Fanshawe, Thomas Evelyn 1918- *Who 94*
Fanshawe Of Richmond, Baron 1927- *Who 94*
Fanshel, David 1923- *WhoAm 94*
Fanslow, Julia Earleen 1939- *WhoWest 94*
Fant, Clyde Edward, Jr. 1934- *WhoAm 94*
Fant, Douglas Vernon 1952- *WhoAmL 94*
Fant, Ennis Maurice 1961- *WhoAmP 93*
Fant, Joseph Lewis, III 1928- *WhoAm 94*
Fant, Lester G., III 1941- *WhoAm 94*
Fanta, Paul Edward 1921- *WhoAm 94*
Fantaci, James Michael 1946- *WhoAm 94*
Fantaschini, Ennio *WhoHol 92*
Fantasia, Mary E. 1919- *WhoAmP 93*
Fantasia, Nick *WhoAmP 93*
Fante, John 1909-1983 *DcLB 130 [port]*
Fante, Ronald Louis 1936- *WhoAm 94*
Fanthorpe, R(obert) L(ionel) 1935- *EncSF 93*
Fanthorpe, R(obert) Lionel 1935- *WrDr 94*
Fanthorpe, U. A. 1929- *BlmGWL*
Fanthorpe, U(rsula) A(skham) 1929- *WrDr 94*
Fantl, Susan *DrAPF 93*
Fanton, Jonathan Foster 1943- *WhoAm 94*
Fantoni, Barry (Ernest) 1940- *WrDr 94*
Fantoni, Barry Ernest 1940- *Who 94*
Fantoni, Sergio 1930- *WhoHol 92*
Fantozzi, Maria Marchetti *NewGrDO*
Fantozzi, Peggy Ryone 1948- *WhoAm 94*
Fantozzi, Tony 1933- *IntMPA 94*
Fantroy, Lloyd Nathaniel 1958- *WhoAmL 94*
Fantry, Catherine Huber 1948- *WhoAmP 93*
Fanuele, Michael Anthony 1938- *WhoAm 94, WhoFI 94, WhoScEn 94*
Fanus, Pauline Rife 1925- *WhoAm 94*
Fan Weitang *WhoPRCh 91*
Fanwick, Ernest 1926- *WhoAm 94*
Fan Zeng 1938- *WhoPRCh 91 [port]*
Fapohunda, Babatunde Olusegun 1952- *WhoScEn 94*
Farabaugh, Eugene Francis 1940- *WhoAmL 94*
Farabaugh, Kenneth Michael, Jr. 1946- *WhoFI 94*
Farabee, Ray 1932- *WhoAmP 93*
Farabow, Ford Franklin, Jr. 1938- *WhoAm 94*
Faracca, Michael Patrick 1958- *WhoScEn 94*
Farach-Carson, Mary Cynthia 1958- *WhoScEn 94*
Faracy, Stephanie *ConTFT 11, WhoHol 92*
Faraday, Bruce John 1919- *WhoAm 94, WhoScEn 94*
Faraday, Michael 1791-1867 *WorInv [port], WorScD [port]*
Farag, Shawky Abdelmonem 1939- *WhoMW 93*
Faragasso, Jack 1929- *WhoAmA 93*
Farage, Donald J. *WhoAm 94, WhoAmL 94*
Farah, fmr. Empress of Iran *IntWW 93*
Farah, Abdulrahim Abby 1919- *IntWW 93*
Farah, Benjamin Frederick 1956- *WhoAmL 94*
Farah, Caesar Elie 1929- *WhoAm 94*
Farah, Jameel *WhoHol 92*
Farah, Joseph Francis 1954- *WhoAm 94*
Farah, Nuruddin 1945- *BlkWr 2, WrDr 94*
Farah, Tawfic Elias 1946- *WhoWest 94*
Faraldo, Claude *WhoHol 92*
Faraldo, Daniel *WhoHol 92*
Faranda, John Paul 1957- *WhoFI 94, WhoWest 94*
Farao, Lucia Victoria 1927- *WhoHisp 94*
Faraone, Juana 1940- *WhoHisp 94*
Fararo, Thomas John 1933- *WhoAm 94*
Farazdel, Abbas 1943- *WhoScEn 94*
Farb, Edith Himel 1928- *WhoAm 94*
Farber, Amanda 1957- *WhoAmA 93*
Farber, Bart *IntMPA 94*
Farber, Bernard 1922- *WhoAm 94, WhoWest 94*
Farber, Bernard John 1948- *WhoAmL 94, WhoMW 93*
Farber, Deborah 1949- *WhoAmA 93*
Farber, Dennis H. 1946- *WhoAmA 93*
Farber, Donald Clifford 1923- *WhoAmL 94*
Farber, Emmanuel 1918- *WhoAm 94*
Farber, Eugene Mark 1917- *WhoScEn 94*
Farber, Evan Ira 1922- *WhoAm 94*
Farber, Isadore E. 1917- *WhoAm 94*
Farber, Jackie 1927- *WhoAm 94*
Farber, John J. 1925- *WhoAm 94, WhoFI 94*
Farber, Marvin 1901-1980 *ConAu 42NR*
Farber, Matthew Eban 1953- *WhoMW 93*
Farber, Maya M. 1936- *WhoAmA 93*
Farber, Neal Mark 1950- *WhoScEn 94*
Farber, Norma 1909-1984 *SmATA 75 [port]*
Farber, Paul Lawrence 1944- *WhoWest 94*
Farber, Seymour Morgan 1912- *WhoAm 94*
Farber, Steven Glenn 1946- *WhoAmL 94, WhoWest 94*
Farber, Thomas *DrAPF 93*
Farber, Viola Anna 1931- *WhoAm 94*
Farberman, Harold 1929- *NewGrDO*
Farberman, Harold 1930- *WhoAm 94*
Farbes, Hubert A., Jr. 1948- *WhoAmL 94*
Farbrother, Barry John 1943- *WhoMW 93*
Farbstein, Leonard *WhoAmP 93*
Farca, Marie C. 1935- *EncSF 93*
Farcus, Joseph Jay 1944- *WhoScEn 94*
Farebrother, Violet d1969 *WhoHol 92*
Fareed, Abdul Sabur *IntWW 93*
Fareed, Ahmed Ali 1932- *WhoMW 93*
Farell, Cesar Gustavo 1961- *WhoHisp 94*
Farella, Frank Eugene 1929- *WhoAmL 94*
Farell Cubillas, Arsenio 1921- *IntWW 93*
Farely, Alison 1937- *WrDr 94*
Faremo, Grete 1955- *WhoWomW 91*
Farenthold, Frances Tarlton 1926- *WhoAm 94*
Farentino, James 1938- *IntMPA 94, WhoAm 94, WhoHol 92*
Farer, Tom Joel 1935- *WhoAm 94*
Fares, William O. 1942- *WhoAmA 93*
Farese, Lawrence Anthony 1952- *WhoAm 94, WhoAmL 94*
Farese, Thomas Richard 1949- *WhoFI 94*
Farewell, Patricia *DrAPF 93*
Farfan-Ramirez, Lucrecia *WhoHisp 94*
Fargas, Antonio 1943- *WhoHol 92*
Fargas, Antonio 1946- *IntMPA 94*
Fargas, Laura *DrAPF 93*
Farge, Annie 1937- *WhoHol 92*
Farge, Yves Marie 1939- *WhoScEn 94*
Fargher, Lawrence Leroy 1932- *WhoAmP 93*
Fargher, Matthew *WhoHol 92*
Fargis, Paul McKenna 1939- *WhoAm 94*
Fargnoli, Gregory E. 1966- *WhoScEn 94*
Fargnoli, Patricia *DrAPF 93*
Fargo, Howard L. 1928- *WhoAmP 93*
Fargo, James 1938- *IntMPA 94*
Fargo, Louis James 1938- *WhoAm 94*
Fargo, Wilson D. 1944- *WhoAmL 94*
Farha, William Farah 1908- *WhoAm 94*
Farhat, Carol S. *WhoWest 94*
Farhat, Debbie Daly 1954- *WhoAmP 93*
Farhat, Vince Lee 1966- *WhoWest 94*
Farhataziz 1932- *WhoAsA 94*
Farhi, Jean Claude 1940- *WhoAmA 93*
Farho, James Henry, Jr. 1924- *WhoScEn 94*
Faria, Antonio F. 1948- *WhoHisp 94*
Faria, Gilberto 1942- *WhoHisp 94*
Faria, Joseph L. 1947- *WhoAmP 93*
Farian, Babette S. 1916- *WhoAmA 93*
Farias, Anna Maria 1952- *WhoHisp 94*
Farias, Edward J. *WhoHisp 94*
Farias, Fred, III 1957- *WhoHisp 94, WhoScEn 94*
Farias, Jesse 1945- *WhoHisp 94*
Farias, Ramiro, Jr. 1949- *WhoHisp 94*
Faricy, Raymond White, Jr. 1934- *WhoAmP 93*
Faricy, Richard Thomas 1928- *WhoAm 94*
Faricy, Robert L 1926- *WrDr 94*
Faries, McIntyre 1896- *WhAm 10, WhoAmP 93*
Farin, Lisa Schulke 1958- *WhoWest 94*
Farina, Carolyn 1964- *WhoHol 92*
Farina, Dennis 1944- *IntMPA 94, WhoHol 92*
Farina, John G. 1951- *WhoIns 94*
Farina, Lissette M. 1965- *WhoHisp 94*
Farina, Mimi 1945- *WhoHol 92*
Farina, Peter R. 1946- *WhoAm 94*
Farina, Philip 1953- *WhoMW 93*
Farina, Richard d1966 *WhoHol 92*
Farina, Sandy 1955- *WhoHol 92*
Farinacci, Jorge A. 1924- *WhoHisp 94*
Farinella, Paul James 1926- *WhoAm 94*
Farinelli 1705-1782 *NewGrDO [port]*
Farinelli, Giuseppe 1769-1836 *NewGrDO*
Farinelli, Jean L. 1946- *WhoAm 94*
Faringdon, Baron 1937- *Who 94*
Farinholt, Larkin Hundley 1905-1990 *WhAm 10*
Faris, Brunel De Bost 1937- *WhoAmA 93*
Faris, Charles Oren 1924- *WhoFI 94*
Faris, Elmer L. 1914- *WhoAmP 93*
Faris, Frank Edgar 1919- *WhoAm 94*
Faris, Jane Theresa Cantwell 1931- *WhoAmP 93*
Faris, Mustapha 1933- *IntWW 93*
Faris, Peter Kinzie 1943- *WhoAmA 93*
Farisani, Tshenuwani Simon 1947- *BlkWr 2*
Farish, Donald J(ames) 1942- *WrDr 94*
Farish, Terry *DrAPF 93*
Farison, James Blair 1938- *WhoAm 94*
Fariss, Bruce Lindsay 1934- *WhoAm 94*
Fariss, James Lee, Jr. 1934- *WhAm 10*
Faris-Stockem, Debbie Anne 1955- *WhoWest 94*
Farjeon, Herbert d1972 *WhoHol 92*
Farjeon, J(oseph) Jefferson 1883-1955 *EncSF 93*
Farkas, Abraham Krakauer 1947- *WhoWest 94*
Farkas, Charles Michael 1951- *WhoFI 94*
Farkas, Daniel Frederick 1933- *WhoScEn 94*
Farkas, Edward Barrister 1954- *WhoAm 94, WhoScEn 94*
Farkas, Ferenc 1905- *IntWW 93, NewGrDO*
Farkas, Gyorgy-Miklos 1941- *WhoScEn 94*
Farkas, Julius 1958- *WhoMW 93, WhoScEn 94*
Farkas, Odon 1851-1912 *NewGrDO*
Farkas, Paul Stephen 1952- *WhoScEn 94*
Farkas, Robin Lewis 1933- *WhoAm 94*
Farkas, Thomas 1937- *WhoMW 93, WhoScEn 94*
Farkas, Todd Ellis 1952- *WhoAmL 94*
Farland, Eugene Hector 1918- *WhoWest 94*
Farleigh, Lynn 1942- *WhoHol 92*
Farley, Andrew Newell 1934- *WhoAm 94*
Farley, Barbara Suzanne 1949- *WhoAmL 94*
Farley, Blanche *DrAPF 93*
Farley, Bruce A. 1943- *WhoAmP 93*
Farley, Carol 1936- *WrDr 94*
Farley, Carole 1946- *IntWW 93, WhoAm 94*
Farley, Carole (Ann) 1946- *NewGrDO*
Farley, Daniel W. 1955- *WhoAm 94, WhoAmL 94*
Farley, Donald B. 1935- *WhoAmP 93*
Farley, Dot d1971 *WhoHol 92*
Farley, Edward John 1934- *WhoAm 94*
Farley, Edward Raymond, Jr. 1918- *WhoAm 94*
Farley, Eugene Joseph 1950- *WhoFI 94*
Farley, Eugene Shedden, Jr. 1927- *WhoAm 94*
Farley, Frances *WhoAmP 93*
Farley, Francis James Macdonald 1920- *IntWW 93, Who 94*
Farley, Frank Frederic 1912- *WhoWest 94*
Farley, Frederick d1978 *WhoHol 92*
Farley, George Edward 1929- *WhoAmP 93*
Farley, George Francis 1947- *WhoWest 94*
Farley, Glenn Francis 1953- *WhoWest 94*
Farley, Harriet 1813-1907 *BlmGWL*
Farley, Henry Edward 1930- *Who 94*
Farley, Hugh Thomas 1931- *WhoAmP 93*
Farley, James d1947 *WhoHol 92*
Farley, James Bernard 1930- *WhoAm 94, WhoFI 94*
Farley, James Duncan 1926- *WhoAm 94*
Farley, James Newton 1928- *WhoAm 94*
Farley, James Parker 1924- *WhoAm 94*
Farley, James Thomas 1925- *WhoAm 94*
Farley, Jennie (Tiffany Towle) 1932- *WrDr 94*
Farley, Jerry Vincent 1939- *WhoMW 93*
Farley, John J., III 1942- *CngDr 93*
Farley, John Joseph 1920- *WhoAm 94*
Farley, John Joseph, III 1942- *WhoAm 94, WhoAmL 94*
Farley, John Michael 1930- *WhoAm 94*
Farley, John Michael 1932- *WhoAm 94*
Farley, Joseph McConnell 1927- *WhoAm 94, WhoFI 94*
Farley, Joseph P., Sr. *WhoAmP 93*
Farley, Kathleen Murphy 1936- *WhoAmP 93*
Farley, Leon Alex 1935- *WhoAm 94*
Farley, Lillian d1987 *WhoHol 92*
Farley, Lloyd Edward 1915- *WhoMW 93*
Farley, Margaret Mary 1926- *WhoAm 94*
Farley, Martin Birtell 1958- *WhoScEn 94*
Farley, Martyn Graham 1924- *Who 94*
Farley, Mary-Rose Christine *Who 94*
Farley, Matthew 1944- *WhoAmL 94*
Farley, Morgan d1988 *WhoHol 92*
Farley, Nicolette Suzanne 1963- *WhoMW 93*
Farley, Paul 1960- *WhoAmL 94*
Farley, Paul Emerson 1930- *WhoAm 94*
Farley, Peggy Ann 1947- *WhoAm 94, WhoFI 94*
Farley, Philip Judson 1916- *WhoAm 94*
Farley, Ralph Milne 1887-1963 *EncSF 93*
Farley, Rob *Who 94*
Farley, Robert Donald 1941- *WhoAm 94*
Farley, Robert Hugh 1950- *WhoMW 93*
Farley, Robert Joseph 1898- *WhAm 10*
Farley, Rosemary Carroll 1952- *WhoScEn 94*
Farley, Teresa *WhoHol 92*
Farley, Terrence Michael 1930- *WhoAm 94, WhoFI 94*
Farley, Thomas T. 1934- *WhoAmL 94, WhoFI 94, WhoWest 94*

Faulkner, (James) Dennis (Compton) 1926- Who 94
Faulkner, Dexter Harold 1937- WhoWest 94
Faulkner, Douglas 1929- Who 94
Faulkner, Edward WhoHol 92
Faulkner, Edwin Jerome 1911-1992 WhAm 10
Faulkner, Eric (Odin) 1914- Who 94
Faulkner, Eric Odin 1914- IntWW 93
Faulkner, Frank 1946- WhoAmA 93
Faulkner, Frank David 1915- WhoScEn 94
Faulkner, Frank M. 1946- WhoAm 94
Faulkner, Geanie WhoBlA 94
Faulkner, Howard J. 1945- WrDr 94
Faulkner, Hugh (Branston) 1916- Who 94
Faulkner, Hugh Charles 1912- Who 94
Faulkner, J. Hugh 1933- IntWW 93
Faulkner, James 1948- WhoHol 92
Faulkner, James Morison 1898- WhAm 10
Faulkner, James Vincent, Jr. 1944- WhoAmL 94
Faulkner, Jerry A. 1936- WhoIns 94
Faulkner, Jerry Allen 1936- WhoAm 94
Faulkner, John d1940 WhoHol 92
Faulkner, John Arthur 1923- WhoAm 94
Faulkner, John Richard Hayward 1941- Who 94
Faulkner, Juanita Smith 1935- WhoAm 94
Faulkner, Julia Ellen 1957- WhoAm 94
Faulkner, Kady B. 1901-1977 WhoAmA 93N
Faulkner, L. Jeanie 1954- WhoFI 94
Faulkner, Larry Ray 1944- WhoAm 94
Faulkner, Leonard Anthony Who 94
Faulkner, Lloyd C. 1926- WhoAm 94, WhoScEn 94
Faulkner, Maurice Ervin 1912- WhoWest 94
Faulkner, Mike 1949- WhoFI 94
Faulkner, Patricia Anne 1944- WhoAmP 93
Faulkner, Ralph d1987 WhoHol 92
Faulkner, Ray N. 1906-1975 WhoAmA 93N
Faulkner, Rex Lynn 1962- WhoAmL 94
Faulkner, Richard Oliver 1946- Who 94
Faulkner, Scot MacDonald 1953- WhoAmP 93
Faulkner, Sewell Ford 1924- WhoAm 94, WhoWest 94
Faulkner, Stephanie WhoHol 92
Faulkner, Teresa Ann 1958- WhoMW 93
Faulkner, Trader 1930- WhoHol 92
Faulkner, Walter Thomas 1928- WhoAm 94, WhoAmL 94
Faulkner, William 1897-1962 RfGShF
Faulkner, William 1897-1968 IntDcF 2-4
Faulkner, William Cuthbert 1897-1962 AmCulL [port]
Faulkner, Winthrop Waldron 1931- WhoAm 94
Faulkner Of Downpatrick, Lady 1925- Who 94
Faulknor, (Chauncey) Cliff(ord Vernon) 1913- WrDr 94
Faulks, Esmond James 1946- Who 94
Faulks, Peter Ronald 1917- Who 94
Faulks, Sebastian 1953- WrDr 94
Faulks, Sebastian Charles 1953- Who 94
Faull, David Wenlock 1929- Who 94
Faull, Ellen 1918- NewGrDO
Faull, James Edward 1945- WhoFI 94
Faulstich, Albert Joseph 1910- WhoAm 94, WhoFI 94
Faulstich, James R. 1933- WhoAm 94
Faulstich, Janet K. 1942- WhoAmP 93
Faulwell, Gerald Edward 1942- WhoAm 94
Faumuina, Ioane, Sr. WhoAmP 93
Faunce, Mark David 1967- WhoScEn 94
Faunce, Sarah Cushing 1929- WhoAmA 93
Faunce, William Dale 1947- WhoScEn 94
Fauntleroy, John Douglass, Sr. 1920-1989 WhAm 10
Fauntroy, Walter E. 1933- AfrAmAl 6, WhoAmP 93, WhoBlA 94
Fauques, Marianne-Agnes Pillement, Dame de 1721-1773 BlmGWL
Faur, Peter John 1949- WhoMW 93
Faure, Francois Michel 1947- WhoScEn 94
Faure, Gabriel 1845-1924 NewGrDO
Faure, Gunter 1934- WhoAm 94
Faure, Jean-Baptiste 1830-1914 NewGrDO [port]
Faure, John Edward 1956- WhoAmP 93
Faure, Maurice Henri 1922- IntWW 93
Faure, Raymond d1972 WhoHol 92
Faure, Roland 1926- IntWW 93
Faurer, Louis 1916- WhoAm 94, WhoAmA 93
Fauri, Eric Joseph 1942- WhoAmL 94
Fauroux, Roger 1926- IntWW 93
Fausch, David Arthur 1935- WhoAm 94
Fauset, Ian David 1943- Who 94
Fauset, Jessie Redmon 1882-1961 BlmGWL
Fausett, (William) Dean 1913- WhoAmA 93
Fausett, Lynn 1894-1977 WhoAmA 93N
Fausett, Robert Julian 1923- WhoScEn 94
Fausold, Martin Luther 1921- WhoAm 94
Faussett, Jimmy, Jr. d1940 WhoHol 92
Faust, A. Donovan 1919- WhoAm 94
Faust, David E. 1942- WhoAmL 94
Faust, Deborah C. 1951- WhoAmL 94
Faust, Frederick 1892-1944 TwCLC 49 [port]
Faust, Hazel Lee d1973 WhoHol 92
Faust, Irvin DrAPF 93
Faust, Irvin 1924- WrDr 94
Faust, James E. WhoAm 94
Faust, James Wille 1949- WhoAmA 93
Faust, Jeff Allen 1966- WhoMW 93
Faust, Joe Clifford 1957- EncSF 93
Faust, John Roosevelt, Jr. 1932- WhoAm 94
Faust, John William, Jr. 1922- WhoAm 94, WhoScEn 94
Faust, Marcus G. 1953- WhoAm 94
Faust, Martin d1943 WhoHol 92
Faust, Naomi F. DrAPF 93
Faust, Naomi Flowe WhoBlA 94
Faust, Robert McNeer 1939- WhoAm 94
Faust, Victoria 1944- WhoAmA 93
Faust, William Paul 1929- WhoAmP 93
Faustina NewGrDO
Faustini, Giovanni 1615-1651 NewGrDO
Faustini, Marco dc. 1675 NewGrDO
Faustman, Erik d1961 WhoHol 92
Fausto 1905-1939 WorESoc
Fausto-Gil, Fidel 1955- WhoHisp 94
Fautsko, Timothy Frank 1945- WhoWest 94
Fauvelle, Michael Henry 1920- Who 94
Fauver, John William 1921- WhoAm 94
Fauver, Scribner L. 1931- WhoAmP 93
Fauvet, Jacques 1914- IntWW 93
Favalaro, Rene WorInv
Favalora, John Clement 1935- WhoAm 94
Favaro, Dennis Ray 1961- WhoAmL 94
Favaro, Mary Kaye Asperheim 1934- WhoScEn 94
Favart, Charles-Simon 1710-1792 NewGrDO
Favart, Edmee 1885-1941 NewGrDO
Favart, Marie-Justine-Benoite 1727-1772 NewGrDO [port]
Favell, Anthony Rowland 1939- Who 94
Favero, Kenneth Edward 1946- WhoScEn 94
Favero, Mafalda 1903-1981 NewGrDO
Faversham, Alec d1955 WhoHol 92
Faversham, Philip d1982 WhoHol 92
Faversham, William d1940 WhoHol 92
Favier, Jean 1932- IntWW 93
Favila, Rodolfo Gomez 1951- WhoHisp 94
Faville, Curtis DrAPF 93
Faville, James Donald 1934- WhoWest 94
Favorite, Felix 1925- WhoAm 94
Favors, Kathryne Taylor 1924- WhoBlA 94
Favors, Malachi 1937- WhoAm 94
Favre, Alexandre Jean 1911- WhoScEn 94
Favre, Alexandre Jean Auguste 1911- IntWW 93
Favreau, Donald Francis 1919- WhoAm 94
Favreau, Irene B. 1950- WhoAmP 93
Favreau, Joseph Lucien Gilles WhoAm 94
Favretto, Richard J. 1941- WhoAm 94
Favrholdt, David Cornaby 1931- IntWW 93
Favro, Murray 1940- WhoAmA 93
Favrot, Henri Mortimer, Jr. 1930- WhoFI 94
Faw, Barbara Ann 1936- WhoBlA 94
Faw, Duane Leslie 1920- WhoAm 94, WhoWest 94
Faw, Melvin Lee 1925- WhoAm 94
Faw, Richard Earl 1936- WhoScEn 94
Fawbush, Andrew Jackson 1946- WhoAm 94, WhoAmL 94
Fawbush, Wayne H. 1944- WhoAmP 93
Fawcett, Bill 1947- EncSF 93
Fawcett, Charles d1922 WhoHol 92
Fawcett, Christopher Babcock 1951- WhoFI 94
Fawcett, Colin 1923- Who 94
Fawcett, David Blakley, Jr. 1927- WhoAm 94
Fawcett, Don Wayne 1917- IntWW 93, WhoAm 94, WhoWest 94
Fawcett, Dwight Winter 1927- WhoAm 94
Fawcett, E(dward) Douglas 1866-1960 EncSF 93
Fawcett, Edgar 1847-1904 EncSF 93
Fawcett, Eric d1972 WhoHol 92
Fawcett, F(rank) Dubrez 1891-1968 EncSF 93
Fawcett, Farrah 1947- IntMPA 94, WhoHol 92
Fawcett, Fausto EncSF 93
Fawcett, Frank Conger 1934- WhoAm 94
Fawcett, George d1939 WhoHol 92
Fawcett, George, Mrs. d1945 WhoHol 92
Fawcett, Gordon W. d1993 NewYTBS 93
Fawcett, Howard Hoy 1916- WhoFI 94, WhoScEn 94
Fawcett, James Davidson 1933- WhoMW 93
Fawcett, John Harold 1929- Who 94
Fawcett, John Thomas 1943- WhoAm 94
Fawcett, Kay-Tee Who 94
Fawcett, Kenneth James 1936- WhoMW 93
Fawcett, Millicent Garrett 1847-1929 HisWorL [port]
Fawcett, Nancy Drudge 1936- WhoAmP 93
Fawcett, Percy Harrison 1867-c. 1925 WhWE
Fawcett, Quinn 1942- WrDr 94
Fawcett, Richard Steven 1948- WhoMW 93
Fawcett, Robert 1903-1967 WhoAmA 93N
Fawcett, Robert Earl, Jr. 1931- WhoAm 94
Fawcett, Sherwood Luther 1919- WhoAm 94
Fawcett, Susan C. DrAPF 93
Fawcett, William d1974 WhoHol 92
Fawcus, Graham Ben 1937- Who 94
Fawcus, (Robert) Peter 1915- Who 94
Fawcus, Simon James David 1938- Who 94
Fawdon, Michele WhoHol 92
Fawdry, Marguerite 1912- WrDr 94
Fawell, Beverly 1930- WhoAmP 93
Fawell, Beverly Jean 1930- WhoMW 93
Fawell, Harris W. 1929- CngDr 93, WhoAm 94, WhoAmP 93, WhoMW 93
Fawell, Thomas William 1951- WhoMW 93
Faw Faw, William fl. 1800- EncNAR
Fawkes, Randol (Francis) 1924- Who 94
Fawkes, Wally 1924- Who 94
Fawley, John Jones 1921- WhoAm 94
Fawsett, Patricia Combs 1943- WhoAm 94, WhoAmL 94
Fawson, Jay 1929- WhoAmP 93
Fawver, J. Jay 1940- WhoAmP 93
Fax, Elton 1909- AfrAmAl 6 [port]
Fax, Elton C. 1909- WhoBlA 94
Fax, Elton Clay 1909- BlkWr 2, ConAu 43NR, WhoAmA 93
Fax, Jesslyn d1975 WhoHol 92
Faxon, Brad WhoAm 94
Faxon, Jack 1936- WhoAmP 93
Faxon, Lavinia SmATA 74
Faxon, Thomas Baker 1924- WhoAm 94, WhoAmL 94
Fay, Abbott Eastman 1926- WhoWest 94
Fay, Albert Hill 1911- WhoAm 94
Fay, Allen 1934- WrDr 94
Fay, Brendan d1975 WhoHol 92
Fay, Conner Martindale 1929- WhoAm 94
Fay, David B. 1950- WhoAm 94
Fay, Donald B. WhoAmP 93
Fay, Dorothy WhoHol 92
Fay, Edgar Stewart 1908- Who 94
Fay, Elsie d1927 WhoHol 92
Fay, Etienne 1770-1845 NewGrDO
Fay, Florence d1928 WhoHol 92
Fay, Frank d1961 WhoHol 92
Fay, Frank 1897-1961 WhoCom
Fay, Frederic Albert 1911- WhoAm 94
Fay, Gaby d1973 WhoHol 92
Fay, Hugh d1926 WhoHol 92
Fay, Jack d1928 WhoHol 92
Fay, James d1987 WhoHol 92
Fay, James Alan 1923- WhoAm 94
Fay, John J., Jr. 1927- WhoAmP 93
Fay, Jonas 1737-1818 WhAmRev
Fay, Julie DrAPF 93
Fay, Kevin John 1960- WhoAmL 94
Fay, Mark J. 1957- WhoFI 94
Fay, Maude 1878-1964 NewGrDO
Fay, Maureen A. WhoAm 94
Fay, Meagen WhoHol 92
Fay, Michael Who 94
Fay, (Humphrey) Michael (Gerard) 1949- Who 94
Fay, Michael Leo 1949- WhoAm 94, WhoAmL 94
Fay, Ming G. 1943- WhoAmA 93
Fay, Olive d1977 WhoHol 92
Fay, Patrick J. 1916- IntMPA 94
Fay, Peter Carlyle 1958- WhoMW 93
Fay, Peter T. WhoAmP 93
Fay, Peter Thorp 1929- WhoAm 94, WhoAmL 94
Fay, Peter Ward 1924- WhoAm 94
Fay, Raymond Charles 1947- WhoAm 94, WhoAmL 94
Fay, Regan Joseph 1948- WhoAm 94, WhoAmL 94
Fay, Richard James 1935- WhoWest 94
Fay, Robert Clinton 1936- WhoAm 94, WhoScEn 94
Fay, Robert Jesse 1920- WhoAm 94
Fay, Robert W. 1940- WhoAmP. 93
Fay, Robert Woods 1946- WhoFI 94
Fay, Terrence Michael 1953- WhoAm 94
Fay, Thomas A. 1927- WhoAm 94
Fay, Thomas Frederic 1940- WhoAm 94, WhoAmP 93
Fay, Toni G. 1947- WhoBlA 94
Fay, W. G. d1974 WhoHol 92
Fay, Wilbur M. 1904-1959 WhoAmA 93N
Fay, William M. 1945- CngDr 93
Fay, William Michael WhoAm 94, WhoAmL 94
Fayad, Nabil Mohamed 1947- WhoScEn 94
Fayard, Calvin C., Jr. 1943- WhoAmP 93
Fayat, Henri 1908- IntWW 93
Faye, Alice 1912- WhoHol 92
Faye, Frances WhoHol 92
Faye, Herbie d1980 WhoHol 92
Faye, Irma d1976 WhoHol 92
Faye, Jean Pierre 1925- IntWW 93
Faye, Joey 1909- WhoCom
Faye, Joey 1910- WhoHol 92
Faye, Julia d1966 WhoHol 92
Fayed, Mohamed 1933- IntWW 93
Fayer, Steve 1935- WrDr 94
Fayers, Norman Owen 1945- Who 94
Fayerweather, John 1922- WhoAm 94
Fayette, J.B. EncSF 93
Fayez, Mohamad al-Ali al- 1937- IntWW 93
Fayhee, Michael R. 1948- WhoAm 94, WhoAmL 94
Faylauer, Adolph d1961 WhoHol 92
Faylen, Frank d1985 WhoHol 92
Fayne, Irwin J. 1954- WhoAmL 94
Fayonsky, James Leon 1935- WhoFI 94
Fayrer, John (Lang Macpherson) 1944- Who 94
Fay-Schmidt, Patricia Ann 1941- WhoWest 94
Fayssoux, Peter 1745-1795 WhAmRev
Fazakerly, George W. 1941- WhoAmL 94
Fazan, Eleanor 1930- WhoHol 92
Fazenda, Louise d1962 WhoHol 92
Fazio, Anthony Lee 1937- WhoFI 94, WhoMW 93
Fazio, Evelyn M. WhoAm 94
Fazio, Peter Victor, Jr. 1940- WhoAm 94, WhoAmL 94, WhoMW 93
Fazio, Ronald C. 1944- WhoIns 94
Fazio, Vic 1942- CngDr 93, WhoAm 94, WhoWest 94
Fazio, Victor H. 1942- WhoAmP 93
Fazio, Victor Warren 1940- WhoAm 94
Fazio, Xavier WhoAmL 94
Fazzini, Georgia Carol 1946- WhoWest 94
Fazzino, Alex J. 1923- WhoAmP 93
Fazzone, David A. 1940- WhoAm 94
Fea, William Wallace d1993 Who 94N
Feachem, Richard George Andrew 1947- Who 94
Feagin, Robert Douglas, III 1937- WhoAmL 94
Feagin, Susan Louise 1948- WhoMW 93
Feagles, Gail Winter 1951- WhoAm 94
Feagles, Gerald Franklin 1934- WhoMW 93
Feagles, Robert West 1920- WhoFI 94
Feagley, Michael Rowe 1945- WhoAm 94, WhoAmL 94
Fealy, James R. 1967- WhoAmP 93
Fealy, Margaret d1955 WhoHol 92
Fealy, Maude d1971 WhoHol 92
Fear, Daniel E. 1949- WhoAmA 93
Fear-Fenn, Marcia Bell 1952- WhoMW 93
Fearing, John T. 1916- WhoBlA 94
Fearing, Kenneth 1902-1961 EncSF 93
Fearing, William Kelly 1918- WhoAmA 93
Fearn, Dean Henry 1943- WhoWest 94
Fearn, James E., Jr. 1945- WhoBlA 94
Fearn, James Ernest, Jr. 1945- WhoAmL 94
Fearn, Jeffrey Charles 1960- WhoScEn 94
Fearn, John Martin 1916- Who 94
Fearn, John (Francis) Russell 1908-1960 EncSF 93
Fearn, (Patrick) Robin 1934- Who 94
Fearn, Ronald Cyril (Ronnie) 1931- Who 94
Fearn, Sheila 1940- WhoHol 92
Fearn-Banks, Kathleen 1941- WhoBlA 94
Fearnot, Neal Edward 1953- WhoMW 93
Fearon, George R. 1943- WhoAmL 94
Fearon, Lee Charles 1938- WhoScEn 94, WhoWest 94
Fearon, Peter (Shaun) 1942- WrDr 94
Fearons, George Hadsall 1927- WhoIns 94
Fears, Emery Lewis, Jr. 1925- WhoBlA 94
Fears, Peggy WhoHol 92
Fears, Tom ProFbHF [port]
Fears, William Earl 1920- WhoAmP 93
Feast, Michael 1946- WhoHol 92
Feast, Michael William 1926- IntWW 93
Feast, William James 1938- WhoScEn 94
Feaster, LaVerne Williams 1926- WhoBlA 94

Feaster, Robert *DrAPF 93*
Feaster, Robert K. *WhoAm 94*
Feaster, S. Edward 1942- *WhoFI 94*
Feates, Francis Stanley 1932- *Who 94*
Feather, John Pliny 1947- *Who 94*
Feather, Lawrence Steven 1955- *WhoWest 94*
Feather, Leonard (Geoffrey) 1914- *WrDr 94*
Feather, Mark Randolph 1955- *WhoAmL 94*
Featherly, Henry Frederick 1930- *WhoAmL 94*
Featherly, William d1925 *WhoHol 92*
Featherman, Bernard 1929- *WhoAm 94, WhoFI 94*
Featherman, Sandra 1934- *WhoMW 93*
Featherston, C. Moxley 1914- *CngDr 93*
Featherstonaugh, Henry Gordon 1917- *WhoMW 93*
Featherstone, Bruce Alan 1953- *WhoAm 94, WhoAmL 94*
Featherstone, David Byrum 1945- *WhoAmA 93*
Featherstone, Hugh Robert 1926- *Who 94*
Featherstone, John Douglas Bernard 1944- *WhoAm 94*
Featherstone, Vane d1948 *WhoHol 92*
Featherstonhaugh, James Duane 1944- *WhoAmL 94*
Feaver, Douglas David 1921- *WhoAm 94, WhoWest 94*
Feaver, Douglas Russell 1914- *Who 94*
Feaver, George A. 1937- *WhoAm 94, WhoWest 94*
Feaver, John Clayton 1911- *WhoAm 94*
Feaver, William (Andrew) 1942- *WrDr 94*
Feaver, William Andrew 1942- *Who 94*
Feazell, Thomas Lee 1937- *WhoAm 94, WhoAmL 94, WhoFI 94*
Febiger, Christian 1746-1796 *AmRev, WhAmRev*
Febland, Harriet *WhoAmA 93*
Febres Cordero Rivadeneira, Leon *IntWW 93*
Fecher, Conrad Christopher 1946- *WhoFI 94*
Fecher, Constance 1911- *WrDr 94*
Fechner, Robert Eugene 1936- *WhoAm 94*
Fecht, Lorene 1949- *WhoMW 93*
Fechtel, Vince, Jr. *WhoAmP 93*
Fechtel, Vincent John 1936- *WhoAmL 94*
Fechteler, William M. 1896-1967 *HisDcKW*
Fechter, Claudia Zieser 1931- *WhoAmA 93*
Feck, Luke Matthew 1935- *WhoAm 94*
Feczko, William Albert 1937- *WhoAm 94*
Fedak, Mitchel George 1952- *WhoScEn 94*
Fedalen, Richard J. 1939- *WhoIns 94*
Fedchenko, Aleksey Pavlovich 1844-1873 *WhWE*
Fedchenko, Olga 1845-1921 *WhWE*
Fedden, (Adye) Mary 1915- *Who 94*
Fedder, Norman Joseph 1934- *WrDr 94*
Fedders, John Michael 1941- *WhoAm 94*
Feddoes, Sadie C. *WhoBlA 94*
Fedele, Daniele Teofilo *NewGrDO*
Fedele, Michael C. *WhoAmP 93*
Fedele, Philip A. 1939- *WhoAmP 93*
Fedeli, Frederick 1931-1989 *WhAm 10*
Fedeli, Giuseppe fl. 1680-1733 *NewGrDO*
Fedeli, Ruggiero c. 1665-1722 *NewGrDO*
Fedelle, Estelle *WhoAmA 93*
Feder, Allan Appel 1931- *WhoAm 94*
Feder, Arthur A. 1927- *WhoAm 94*
Feder, Ben 1923- *WhoAmA 93*
Feder, Bernard 1924- *WrDr 94*
Feder, Daniel Seth 1962- *WhoAmL 94*
Feder, Harold Abram 1932- *WhoAm 94*
Feder, Harry Simon 1953- *WhoFI 94*
Feder, Joseph 1932- *WhoMW 93*
Feder, Martin Elliott 1951- *WhoMW 93*
Feder, Penny Joy 1949- *WhoAmA 93*
Feder, Robert 1930- *WhoAmL 94*
Feder, Robert 1956- *WhoAm 94*
Feder, Saul E. 1943- *WhoAm 94, WhoFI 94*
Federe, Marion 1919- *WhoAmA 93*
Federici, Anthony Nicholas 1937- *WhoAmP 93*
Federici, Tony 1937- *WhoWest 94*
Federici, Vincenzo 1764-1826 *NewGrDO*
Federici, William R. *WhoAmP 93*
Federici, William Vito 1931- *WhoAm 94*
Federico, Andrew John 1950- *WhoAmL 94*
Federico, Domenic 1941- *WhoFI 94*
Federico, Gene 1918- *WhoAm 94*
Federico, Gennaro Antonio c. 1726-c. 1743 *NewGrDO*
Federico, Gloria Cabralez 1953- *WhoHisp 94*
Federico, Hugo A. 1947- *WhoHisp 94*
Federico, James Joseph, Jr. 1946- *WhoAmP 93*
Federico, Joe, Jr. 1935- *WhoHisp 94*
Federighi, Christine M. 1949- *WhoAmA 93*
Federle, Louis Anthony 1948- *WhoFI 94*
Federman, Daniel David 1928- *WhoAm 94*
Federman, Nicolas 1501-1542 *WhWE*
Federman, Raymond *DrAPF 93*
Federman, Raymond 1928- *ConAu 43NR, WhoAm 94, WrDr 94*
Federman, Steven Robert 1949- *WhoMW 93*
Federn, Paul 1871-1950 *EncSPD*
Federspiel, Birgitte *WhoHol 92*
Federspiel, Thomas Holger 1935- *IntWW 93*
Fedewa, Lawrence John 1937- *WhoAm 94, WhoFI 94*
Fedida, Sam 1918- *Who 94*
Fedirko, Pavel Stefanovich 1932- *IntWW 93*
Fedje, Neil Thomas 1938- *WhoFI 94*
Fedor, Allan John 1947- *WhoAmL 94*
Fedor, George Matthew, III 1967- *WhoScEn 94*
Fedorchak, Diana Rachelle 1945- *WhoWest 94*
Fedorchak, Timothy Hill 1958- *WhoFI 94*
Fedorchik, Bette Joy Winter 1953- *WhoAm 94*
Fedorenko, Nikolay Prokofiyevich 1917- *IntWW 93*
Fedorenko, Nikolay Trofimovich 1912- *IntWW 93*
Fedorko, Charles Andrew, Jr. 1947- *WhoWest 94*
Fedorochko, William, Jr. 1940- *WhoAm 94*
Fedoroff, Nina Vsevolod 1942- *WhoAm 94*
Fedorov, Boris Grigorevich 1958- *LoBiDrD*
Fedorov, Boris Grigorievich 1958- *IntWW 93*
Fedorov, Nikolai Vasilevich 1958- *LoBiDrD*
Fedorov, Nikolai Vasilievich 1958- *IntWW 93*
Fedorov, Svyatoslav Nikolaevich 1927- *IntWW 93, LoBiDrD*
Fedorov, Valentin Petrovich 1939- *LoBiDrD*
Fedorova, Sophia 1879-1963 *IntDcB [port]*
Fedorovitch, Sophie 1893-1953 *IntDcB [port]*
Fedorowicz, J(an) K(rzysztof) 1949- *WrDr 94*
Fedorowicz, Jane 1955- *WhoScEn 94*
Fedoruk, Sylvia O. 1927- *WhoWest 94*
Fedoseyev, Vladimir Ivanovich 1932- *IntWW 93*
Fedosov, Yevgeny Aleksandrovich 1929- *IntWW 93*
Fedota, Mark Clarke 1944- *WhoAmL 94*
Fedotov, Mikhail Aleksandrovich 1949- *IntWW 93, LoBiDrD*
Fedotov, Sergey Aleksandrovich 1931- *IntWW 93*
Fedrick, Geoffrey Courtis 1937- *Who 94*
Fee, Geraldine Julia 1937- *WhoScEn 94*
Fee, Gerard Wayne Cowle 1933- *WhoAm 94*
Fee, Melinda 1945- *WhoHol 92*
Fee, Thomas 1928- *WhoAm 94*
Fee, Thomas J. 1931- *WhoAmP 93*
Fee, Vickie d1975 *WhoHol 92*
Feehan, Patrick Augustine 1829-1902 *DcAmReB 2*
Feehan, Thomas Joseph 1924- *WhoAm 94*
Feeherry, Anthony M. 1947- *WhoAmL 94*
Feeks, J. Michael 1942- *WhoAm 94*
Feeley, Gregory 1955- *EncSF 93, WrDr 94*
Feeley, Henry Joseph, Jr. 1940- *WhoAm 94, WhoFI 94*
Feeley, James Terence 1950- *WhoAm 94*
Feeley, John Paul 1918- *WhoAm 94*
Feeley, Kevin F. 1962- *WhoFI 94*
Feeley, Malcolm M(cCollum) 1942- *ConAu 142*
Feeley, Michael F. 1953- *WhoAmP 93*
Feeley, Paul 1913-1966 *WhoAmA 93N*
Feeley, Sharon Denise 1949- *WhoMW 93*
Feeley, Theresa Gouvin 1947- *WhoAmP 93*
Feelings, Muriel Grey 1938- *WhoBlA 94*
Feelings, Thomas 1933- *WhoBlA 94*
Feely, John Joseph 1954- *WhoAmL 94*
Feeman, James Frederic 1922- *WhoScEn 94*
Feemster, John Arthur 1939- *WhoBlA 94*
Feeney, Craig Michael 1956- *WhoScEn 94*
Feeney, David Wesley 1938- *WhoAm 94*
Feeney, Don Joseph, Jr. 1948- *WhoMW 93*
Feeney, Floyd Fulton 1933- *WhoAmL 94*
Feeney, John Robert 1950- *WhoAm 94*
Feeney, Mark 1957- *WhoAm 94*
Feeney, Matthew Paul 1957- *WhoAmL 94*
Feeney, Patricia Sharon 1948- *WhoFI 94*
Feeney, Robert Earl 1913- *WhoScEn 94*
Feeney, Sandra Benedict 1936- *WhoAmA 93*
Feeney, Tom 1958- *WhoAmP 93*
Feenker, Cherie Diane 1950- *WhoAmL 94*
Feeny, Max Howard 1928- *Who 94*
Feeny, Thomas *DrAPF 93*
Feer, Charles Lewis 1960- *WhoWest 94*
Feerick, Bob 1920- *BasBi*
Feerick, Donald Joseph, Jr. 1965- *WhoAmL 94*
Feerick, John David 1936- *WhoAmL 94*
Fees, James Richard 1931- *WhoFI 94*
Fees, John T. 1967- *WhoWest 94*
Fees, Nancy Fardelius 1950- *WhoWest 94*
Feeser, Larry James 1937- *WhoAm 94*
Feferman, Solomon 1928- *WhoAm 94*
Feffer, Gerald Alan 1942- *WhoAm 94, WhoAmL 94*
Feffer, Paul Evan 1921- *WhoFI 94*
Fefferman, Charles Louis 1949- *WhoScEn 94*
Feggans, Edward L. 1919- *WhoBlA 94*
Feghali, Jandira 1957- *WhoWomW 91*
Fegley, Kenneth Allen 1923- *WhoAm 94*
Feheley, Lawrence Francis 1946- *WhoAmL 94*
Feher, George 1924- *IntWW 93, WhoAm 94, WhoScEn 94*
Feher, Joseph 1908-1987 *WhoAmA 93N*
Fehl, Barry Dean 1957- *WhoScEn 94*
Fehl, Philipp P. 1920- *WhoAmA 93, WrDr 94*
Fehlberg, Richard Allen 1939- *WhoMW 93*
Fehlberg, Robert Erick 1926- *WhoAm 94*
Fehler, Gene 1940- *SmATA 74 [port]*
Fehling, Jurgen 1885-1968 *NewGrDO*
Fehlner, Thomas Patrick 1937- *WhoAm 94, WhoScEn 94*
Fehmiu, Bekim 1932- *WhoHol 92*
Fehnel, Edward Adam 1922- *WhoAm 94*
Fehr, Basil Henry Frank 1912- *Who 94*
Fehr, Gregory Paris 1943- *WhoFI 94*
Fehr, J. Will 1926- *WhoAm 94, WhoWest 94*
Fehr, Kenneth Manbeck 1928- *WhoAm 94*
Fehr, Larry Michael 1952- *WhoWest 94*
Fehr, Lola Mae 1936- *WhoAm 94*
Fehr, Rudi 1911- *IntMPA 94*
Fehr, Walter Ronald 1939- *WhoAm 94*
Fehrenbach, Charles Max 1914- *IntWW 93*
Fehrenbach, T(heodore) R(eed) 1925- *WrDr 94*
Fehrenbacher, Don Edward 1920- *WhoAm 94, WrDr 94*
Fehrer, Steven Craig 1951- *WhoWest 94*
Fehribach, Ronald Steven 1949- *WhoWest 94*
Fehring, Anne Elizabeth 1954- *WhoMW 93*
Fehrmann, Waltraut Gerlinde 1959- *WhoWest 94*
Fehrs, Richard Francis 1933- *WhoFI 94*
Feibel, Frederick Arthur 1942- *WhoFI 94*
Feibelman, Peter Julian 1942- *WhoAm 94*
Feibusch, Hans 1898- *Who 94*
Feicht, Georg d1964 *WhoHol 92*
Feichter, Patton L. 1945- *WhoAmP 93*
Feichtinger, Mark Rudolph 1948- *WhoAm 94, WhoAmL 94*
Feichtner, John David 1930- *WhoWest 94*
Feick, Paul Alden 1939- *WhoWest 94*
Feidelson, Charles N., Jr. d1993 *NewYTBS 93*
Feiden, Karyn L. 1954- *ConAu 140*
Feiffer, Jules 1929- *IntWW 93, WhoAm 94, WhoAmA 93, WrDr 94*
Feiffer, Jules (Ralph) 1929- *ConDr 93*
Feig, Paul *WhoHol 92*
Feig, Stephen Arthur 1937- *WhoAm 94, WhoWest 94*
Feig, Terrence Lee 1949- *WhoFI 94*
Feigelson, Philip 1925- *WhoAm 94*
Feigen, Richard L. 1930- *WhoAm 94, WhoAmA 93*
Feigenbaum, Abraham Samuel 1929- *WhoScEn 94*
Feigenbaum, Armand Vallin 1920- *WhoAm 94, WhoFI 94*
Feigenbaum, Bob 1948- *WhoAmP 93*
Feigenbaum, Clifford Scott 1961- *WhoWest 94*
Feigenbaum, Edward A(lbert) 1936- *WrDr 94*
Feigenbaum, Edward Albert 1936- *WhoAm 94, WhoScEn 94*
Feigenbaum, Edward D. 1958- *WhoAmL 94*
Feigenbaum, Harvey 1933- *WhoAm 94*
Feigenbaum, Jay Lawrence 1952- *WhoAmP 93*
Feigenbaum, Larry J. 1947- *WhoFI 94*
Feigenbaum, Mitchell Jay 1944- *WhoScEn 94*
Feighan, Edward Farrell 1947- *WhoAm 94, WhoAmP 93*
Feight, Theodore J. 1946- *WhoFI 94*
Feigin, Barbara Sommer 1937- *WhoAm 94, WhoFI 94*
Feigin, Dorothy L. 1904-1969 *WhoAmA 93N*
Feigin, Marsha 1948- *WhoAmA 93*
Feigin, Ralph David 1938- *WhoAm 94*
Feigl, Dorothy Marie 1938- *WhoAm 94*
Feigl, Hugo 1890-1961 *WhoAmA 93N*
Feigon, Lee 1945- *WrDr 94*
Feikema, Feike 1912- *WhoAm 94, WrDr 94*
Feikens, John 1917- *WhoAm 94, WhoMW 93*
Feikens, Robert Houwing 1955- *WhoAmL 94*
Feil, Linda Mae 1948- *WhoFI 94, WhoWest 94*
Feil, Paul Arnold 1922- *WhoAmP 93*
Feild, Kay Carol 1938- *WhoAmP 93*
Feilden, Bernard (Melchior) 1919- *Who 94*
Feilden, Bernard Melchior 1919- *IntWW 93*
Feilden, Geoffrey Bertram Robert 1917- *IntWW 93, Who 94*
Feilden, Henry (Wemyss) 1916- *Who 94*
Feilding *Who 94*
Feilding, Viscount 1970- *Who 94*
Feiler, Herta d1970 *WhoHol 92*
Feiler, Jo Alison 1951- *WhoAm 94*
Feiler, William S. 1946- *WhoAmL 94*
Feiman, Thomas E. 1940- *WhoAm 94*
Fein, B(arbara) R. 1941- *WhoAmA 93*
Fein, Bernard 1908- *WhoAm 94*
Fein, Cheri *DrAPF 93*
Fein, Irving Ashley 1911- *WhoAm 94*
Fein, Leah Gold 1910- *WhoAm 94*
Fein, Linda Ann 1949- *WhoMW 93*
Fein, Marvin Abrams 1938- *WhoAmL 94*
Fein, Marvin Michael 1923-1990 *WhAm 10*
Fein, Rashi 1926- *IntWW 93*
Fein, Richard J. *DrAPF 93*
Fein, Richard J 1929- *WrDr 94*
Fein, Roger Gary 1940- *WhoAm 94, WhoAmL 94, WhoMW 93*
Fein, Ronald Lawrence 1943- *WhoAm 94*
Fein, Scott Norris 1949- *WhoAmL 94*
Fein, Seymour Howard 1948- *WhoAm 94*
Fein, Stanley 1919- *WhoAmA 93*
Fein, Thomas Paul 1946- *WhoMW 93*
Fein, William 1933- *WhoAm 94, WhoScEn 94, WhoWest 94*
Feinberg, David B. 1956- *GayLL, WrDr 94*
Feinberg, David Erwin 1922- *WhoAm 94*
Feinberg, Edward Burton 1945- *WhoAm 94*
Feinberg, Elen *WhoAmA 93*
Feinberg, Eugene Alexander 1954- *WhoAm 94*
Feinberg, Evgueniy Lvovich 1912- *IntWW 93*
Feinberg, Gerald 1933-1992 *WhAm 10, WrDr 94N*
Feinberg, Glenda Joyce 1948- *WhoMW 93*
Feinberg, Herbert 1926- *WhoAm 94*
Feinberg, Irwin L. 1916- *WhoAm 94*
Feinberg, Jean 1948- *WhoAmA 93*
Feinberg, Kenneth Roy 1945- *WhoAm 94, WhoAmL 94*
Feinberg, Lawrence Bernard 1940- *WhoAm 94*
Feinberg, Lee F. 1947- *WhoAmP 93*
Feinberg, Leonard 1914- *WhoAm 94, WrDr 94*
Feinberg, Martin Robert 1942- *WhoAm 94*
Feinberg, Mortimer Robert 1922- *WhoAm 94*
Feinberg, Norman Maurice 1934- *WhoFI 94*
Feinberg, Paul H. 1938- *WhoAm 94*
Feinberg, Peter Eric 1949- *Who 94*
Feinberg, Renee 1940- *ConAu 42NR*
Feinberg, Richard 1947- *WhoMW 93*
Feinberg, Richard Alan 1947- *WhoWest 94*
Feinberg, Richard E. *WhoAm 94*
Feinberg, Robert Edward 1935- *WhoAm 94*
Feinberg, Robert Ira 1956- *WhoAm 94, WhoAmL 94*
Feinberg, Robert S. 1934- *WhoAm 94, WhoFI 94*
Feinberg, Rosa Castro 1939- *WhoHisp 94*
Feinberg, Samuel 1908- *WhoAm 94*
Feinberg, Walter 1937- *WhoAm 94*
Feinberg, Wilfred *WhoAmP 93*
Feinberg, Wilfred 1920- *WhoAm 94, WhoAmL 94*
Feinblatt, Ebria *WhoAmA 93N*
Feinblum, Barnet Mark 1947- *WhoFI 94*
Feind, Barthold 1678-1721 *NewGrDO*

Feindel, William Howard 1918- *WhoAm 94*
Feinendegen, Ludwig E. 1927- *IntWW 93*
Feinendegen, Ludwig Emil 1927- *WhoScEn 94*
Feiner, Alexander 1928- *WhoAm 94*
Feiner, Joel S. 1938- *WhoAm 94*
Feingerts, Sandra Mills 1946- *WhoAmL 94*
Feingold, Bonnie F. 1942- *WhoMW 93*
Feingold, Daniel Leon 1958- *WhoFI 94, WhoMW 93, WhoScEn 94*
Feingold, David Sidney 1922- *WhoAm 94*
Feingold, Eugene 1931- *WrDr 94*
Feingold, Mark Lawrence 1963- *WhoScEn 94*
Feingold, Russell 1953- *CngDr 93*
Feingold, Russell D. 1953- *IntWW 93, WhoAmP 93*
Feingold, Russell Dana 1953- *WhoAm 94, WhoMW 93*
Feingold, S. Norman *WrDr 94*
Feingold, S. Norman 1914- *WhoAm 94*
Feinhals, Fritz 1869-1940 *NewGrDO*
Feinhandler, Edward Sanford 1948- *WhoWest 94*
Feininger, Andreas B. L. 1906- *WhoAmA 93*
Feininger, Andreas Bernhard Lyonel 1906- *WhoAm 94*
Feininger, T. Lux 1910- *WhoAmA 93*
Feininger, Theodore Lux 1910- *WhoAm 94*
Feinman, Alvin *DrAPF 93*
Feinman, Stephen E. 1932- *WhoAmA 93*
Feinstein, Alan 1941- *IntMPA 94, WhoHol 92*
Feinstein, Alan Shawn 1931- *WhoAm 94*
Feinstein, Allen Lewis 1929- *WhoAm 94*
Feinstein, Allen S. 1955- *WhoAmL 94*
Feinstein, Alvan Richard 1925- *IntWW 93, WhoAm 94, WhoScEn 94*
Feinstein, Bernice d1993 *NewYTBS 93*
Feinstein, Charles Hilliard 1932- *IntWW 93, Who 94*
Feinstein, David 1946- *WhoWest 94, WrDr 94*
Feinstein, Dianne 1933- *CngDr 93, IntWW 93, News 93-3, WhoAm 94, WhoWest 94*
Feinstein, Dianne Goldman 1933- *WhoAmP 93*
Feinstein, Elaine 1930- *BlmGEL, BlmGWL, WrDr 94*
Feinstein, Fred Ira 1945- *WhoAm 94, WhoAmL 94*
Feinstein, John 1956- *WrDr 94*
Feinstein, Joseph 1925- *WhoAm 94*
Feinstein, Martin 1921- *NewGrDO, WhoAm 94*
Feinstein, Michael 1956- *ConTFT 11*
Feinstein, Michael 1957- *WhoHol 92*
Feinstein, Miles Roger 1941- *WhoAmL 94*
Feinstein, Otto 1930- *WhoAmP 93*
Feinstein, Paul Louis 1955- *WhoAmL 94*
Feinstein, Richard Bruce 1945- *WhoAmL 94*
Feinstein, Roni *WhoAmA 93*
Feinstein, Roni 1954- *WrDr 94*
Feintuch, Richard David 1952- *WhoAmL 94*
Feir, Dorothy Jean 1929- *WhoAm 94, WhoMW 93*
Feir, Scott Eugene 1964- *WhoWest 94*
Feirson, Steven B. 1950- *WhoAm 94*
Feirstein, Frederick *DrAPF 93*
Feirstein, Frederick 1940- *WhoAm 94*
Feirstein, Janice 1942- *WhoFI 94*
Feisel, Lyle Dean 1935- *WhoAm 94*
Feiss, Carl Lehman 1907- *WhoAm 94*
Feiss, George James, III 1950- *WhoFI 94, WhoWest 94*
Feist, Gene 1930- *WhoAm 94*
Feist, Harold E. 1945- *WhoAmA 93*
Feist, Harry d1963 *WhoHol 92*
Feist, John Wilson 1936- *WhoAmL 94*
Feist, Leonard 1910- *WhoAm 94*
Feist, Michael Alan 1958- *WhoAmL 94*
Feist, Warner David 1909- *WhoAmA 93*
Feist, William Charles 1934- *WhoMW 93*
Feit, Eugene P. 1948- *WhoAm 94, WhoAmL 94*
Feit, Glenn M. 1929- *WhoAm 94, WhoAmL 94*
Feit, Michael 1928- *WhoFI 94, WhoMW 93*
Feit, Michael Dennis 1942- *WhoWest 94*
Feit, Theodore 1930- *WhoFI 94*
Feitel, Babara d1993 *NewYTBS 93*
Feitelberg, Susan Francis 1962- *WhoFI 94*
Feitelson, Helen Lundeberg *WhoAmA 93*
Feitelson, Jerald Stuart 1953- *WhoWest 94*
Feitelson, Lorser 1898-1978 *WhoAmA 93N*
Feith, Kathy Lynn 1956- *WhoFI 94*
Feitler, Robert 1930- *WhoAm 94*
Feito, Jose 1929- *WhoAm 94*
Feitshans, Buzz *IntMPA 94*
Feitshans, Fred Rollin 1937- *WhoAm 94*
Feitshans, Ilise Levy 1957- *WhoAmL 94*
Fei Xiaotong 1910- *IntWW 93, WhoPRCh 91 [port]*
Fei Zhirong *WhoPRCh 91*
Fei Ziwen *WhoPRCh 91*
Fejes, Claire 1920- *WhoAmA 93*
Fekete, Brian 1955- *WhoAmA 93*
Fekete, George Otto *WhoAmL 94*
Fekete, Gyula *EncSF 93*
Fekete, Janos 1918- *IntWW 93*
Fekety, Robert 1929- *WhoMW 93*
Fekner, John 1950- *WhoAmA 93*
Fekter, Maria Theresia 1956- *WhoWomW 91*
Fel, Marie 1713-1794 *NewGrDO*
Felak, Richard Peter 1945- *WhoScEn 94*
Feland, Gary 1939- *WhoAmP 93*
Felber, Rene 1933- *IntWW 93*
Felberg, David Edward 1957- *WhoWest 94*
Felch, Charles H., Sr. 1926- *WhoAmP 93*
Felch, William Campbell 1920- *IntWW 93, WhoAm 94*
Felcher, Peter L. 1939- *WhoAm 94*
Felcman, Judith 1941- *WhoScEn 94*
Feld, Alan David 1936- *WhoAm 94*
Feld, Augusta 1919- *WhoAmA 93*
Feld, Bernard T. 1919-1993 *NewYTBS 93 [port]*
Feld, Daniel Elias 1947- *WhoAmL 94*
Feld, Eliot 1942- *IntDcB [port], WhoAm 94, WhoHol 92*
Feld, Fritz 1900- *IntMPA 94, WhoAm 94, WhoHol 92*
Feld, Fritz 1900-1993 *NewYTBS 93 [port]*
Feld, Jonathan S. 1952- *WhoAm 94*
Feld, Joseph 1919- *WhoAm 94, WhoFI 94*
Feld, Joseph, Sr. 1933- *WhoFI 94*
Feld, Karen Irma 1947- *WhoAm 94*
Feld, Lawrence S. 1942- *WhoAmL 94*
Feld, Marian Parry *WhoAmA 93*
Feld, Michael Stephen 1940- *WhoAm 94*
Feld, Myron Xane 1915- *WhoWest 94*
Feld, Ross *DrAPF 93*
Feld, Stuart Paul 1935- *WhoAmA 93*
Feld, Thomas Robert 1944- *WhoAm 94*
Feld, Werner J 1910- *WrDr 94*
Feld, Werner Joachim 1910- *WhoAm 94*
Feldary, Eric d1968 *WhoHol 92*
Feldaverd, Nicholas Edward, III 1949- *WhoWest 94*
Feldbaek, Ole 1936- *IntWW 93*
Feldbaum, Alan Bruce 1956- *WhoAmL 94*
Feldberg, Chester Ben 1939- *WhoAm 94*
Feldberg, Meyer 1942- *WhoAm 94, WhoFI 94*
Feldberg, Michael Svetkey 1951- *WhoAm 94, WhoAmL 94*
Feldberg, Sumner Lee 1924- *WhoAm 94, WhoFI 94*
Feldberg, Wilhelm Siegmund 1900- *Who 94*
Feldbrill, Victor 1924- *WhoAm 94*
Feldbusch, Eric 1922- *NewGrDO*
Feldbusch, Michael F. 1951- *WhoMW 93*
Feldcamp, Larry Bernard 1938- *WhoAm 94, WhoAmL 94*
Felde, Martin Lee 1951- *WhoAm 94*
Felden, Tamara 1953- *WhoMW 93*
Feldenkreis, George 1935- *WhoHisp 94*
Felder, Cain Hope 1943- *WhoBlA 94*
Felder, Clarence *WhoHol 92*
Felder, David W. 1945- *WrDr 94*
Felder, Harvey 1955- *WhoBlA 94*
Felder, Jerome Solon *WhAm 10*
Felder, John Gressette 1944- *WhoAmP 93*
Felder, Loretta Kay 1956- *WhoBlA 94*
Felder, Michael Otis 1962- *WhoBlA 94*
Felder, Myrna 1941- *WhoAmL 94*
Felder, Raoul Lionel 1934- *WhoAmL 94, WhoFI 94*
Felder, Thomas E. *WhoBlA 94*
Felder, Tyree Preston, II 1927- *WhoBlA 94*
Felder, Willie W. 1927- *WhoAmP 93*
Felder-Hoehne, Felicia Harris *WhoBlA 94*
Felderman, Eric *DrAPF 93*
Feldgrill-Zankel, Ruth 1942- *WhoWomW 91*
Feldhaus, Paul A. 1926- *WhoAmA 93*
Feldhaus, Stephen Martin 1945- *WhoAm 94, WhoAmL 94*
Feldhof, Gerd 1931- *NewGrDO*
Feldhouse, Lynn Alexandra 1951- *WhoMW 93*
Feldhusen, Hazel J. 1928- *WhoMW 93*
Feldhusen, John F. 1926- *ConAu 141*
Feldhusen, John Frederick 1926- *WhoAm 94*
Feldkamp, Frederick L. 1945- *WhoAmL 94*
Feldkamp, Janet Kay 1956- *WhoAmL 94*
Feldkamp, Marcia Lynn 1952- *WhoWest 94*
Feldman, Adrienne Arsht 1942- *WhoAm 94*
Feldman, Alan *DrAPF 93*
Feldman, Albert Joseph 1929- *WhoAm 94*
Feldman, Allan Roy 1945- *WhoFI 94*
Feldman, Andrea d1972 *WhoHol 92*
Feldman, Annette Young 1916- *WhoWest 94*
Feldman, Arbraham Jehiel 1893- *WhAm 10*
Feldman, Arthur Mitchell 1942- *WhoAmA 93*
Feldman, Basil 1926- *Who 94*
Feldman, Bella *WhoAmA 93*
Feldman, Ben d1993 *NewYTBS 93*
Feldman, Ben 1912- *WhoFI 94*
Feldman, Bruce Alan 1959- *WhoScEn 94*
Feldman, Bruce Allen 1941- *WhoScEn 94*
Feldman, Burton Gordon 1911- *WhoAm 94*
Feldman, Charles 1924- *WhoScEn 94*
Feldman, Charles Franklin 1945- *WhoAmL 94*
Feldman, Clarice Rochelle 1941- *WhoAm 94*
Feldman, Corey *WhoHol 92*
Feldman, Corey 1971- *IntMPA 94*
Feldman, Daniel L(ee) 1949- *WrDr 94*
Feldman, Daniel Lee 1949- *WhoAmP 93*
Feldman, David Lewis 1951- *ConAu 140*
Feldman, David Scott 1963- *WhoAmL 94*
Feldman, Edmund Burke 1924- *WhoAm 94, WhoAmA 93*
Feldman, Edward S. 1929- *IntMPA 94*
Feldman, Edythe d1971 *WhoHol 92*
Feldman, Egal 1925- *WhoAm 94*
Feldman, Elaine Bossak 1926- *WhoAm 94, WhoScEn 94*
Feldman, Felix 1919- *WhoScEn 94*
Feldman, Franklin 1927- *WhoAm 94, WhoAmA 93*
Feldman, Fredric Joel 1940- *WhoWest 94*
Feldman, Gary Jay 1942- *WhoAm 94*
Feldman, Gary Marc 1953- *WhoScEn 94*
Feldman, Gerald D(onald) 1937- *WrDr 94*
Feldman, Gilbert 1931- *WhoMW 93*
Feldman, Gladys d1974 *WhoHol 92*
Feldman, Gordon 1928- *WhoAm 94*
Feldman, H. Larry 1941- *WhoAm 94*
Feldman, Harris Joseph 1942- *WhoMW 93*
Feldman, Hervey Allen 1937- *WhoAm 94, WhoFI 94*
Feldman, Howard S. *WhoFI 94*
Feldman, Ira S. 1943- *WhoAm 94*
Feldman, Irving *DrAPF 93*
Feldman, Irving 1928- *WhoAm 94*
Feldman, Irving (Mordecai) 1928- *WrDr 94*
Feldman, Jacob Alex 1954- *WhoScEn 94*
Feldman, Jay N. 1936- *WhoAm 94, WhoAmL 94*
Feldman, Jeffrey C. 1953- *WhoAmP 93*
Feldman, Jerome Myron 1935- *IntWW 93, WhoAm 94*
Feldman, Jill 1952- *NewGrDO*
Feldman, Joel Martin 1941- *WhoAm 94, WhoAmL 94*
Feldman, Joel Shalom 1949- *WhoAm 94*
Feldman, Kathleen Ann *WhoScEn 94*
Feldman, Lester 1948- *WhoWest 94*
Feldman, Louis Arnold 1941- *WhoWest 94*
Feldman, Mark B. 1935- *WhoAm 94*
Feldman, Mark Russel 1949- *WhoAm 94*
Feldman, Martin L. C. 1934- *WhoAm 94, WhoAmL 94, WhoAmP 93*
Feldman, Marty d1982 *WhoHol 92*
Feldman, Marty 1933-1982 *WhoCom*
Feldman, Marvin d1993 *NewYTBS 93 [port]*
Feldman, Marvin 1927- *WhoAm 94*
Feldman, Marvin Herschel 1945- *WhoFI 94*
Feldman, Matthew 1919- *WhoAmP 93*
Feldman, Michael 1926- *IntWW 93*
Feldman, Michael Brent 1956- *WhoAmP 93*
Feldman, Michel J. 1943- *WhoAmL 94*
Feldman, Morton 1926-1987 *NewGrDO*
Feldman, Murray Dov *WhoAmL 94*
Feldman, Myer 1917- *IntWW 93, WhoAm 94*
Feldman, Richard David 1949- *WhoAmL 94*
Feldman, Richard Jay 1952- *WhoAmP 93*
Feldman, Robert C. 1948- *WhoAmL 94*
Feldman, Robert C. 1956- *WhoAm 94, WhoFI 94*
Feldman, Robert George 1933- *WhoAm 94*
Feldman, Roger Bruce 1939- *WhoAm 94*
Feldman, Roger David 1943- *WhoAm 94, WhoAmL 94*
Feldman, Roger David 1945- *WhoAm 94, WhoAmL 94*
Feldman, Roger Lawrence 1949- *WhoAmA 93*
Feldman, Ronald *WhoAmA 93*
Feldman, Ronald 1938- *WhoAm 94*
Feldman, Ronald Arthur 1938- *WhoAm 94*
Feldman, Ruth *DrAPF 93*
Feldman, Ruth Duskin 1934- *ConAu 43NR, WhoMW 93*
Feldman, Samuel Mitchell 1933- *WhoAm 94*
Feldman, Scott M. 1942- *WhoAm 94, WhoAmL 94*
Feldman, Stanley 1930- *Who 94*
Feldman, Stanley G. *WhoAmP 93*
Feldman, Stanley George 1933- *WhoAm 94, WhoAmL 94, WhoWest 94*
Feldman, Stephen 1944- *WhoAm 94*
Feldman, Stephen M. 1948- *WhoAmL 94*
Feldman, Thomas Myron 1950- *WhoAm 94*
Feldman, Walter (Sidney) 1925- *WhoAmA 93*
Feldman, Walter Sidney 1925- *WhoAm 94*
Feldman, William Robert 1951- *WhoAmL 94*
Feldmann, Annette *DrAPF 93*
Feldmann, Edward George 1930- *WhoAm 94, WhoScEn 94*
Feldmann, Henry 1896- *WhAm 10*
Feldmann, Herman Fred 1935- *WhoScEn 94*
Feldmann, John H., III 1949- *WhoAmL 94*
Feldmann, Judith Gail 1938- *WhoMW 93*
Feldmann, Mark Ernst 1948- *WhoAmL 94*
Feldmann, R. Scott 1961- *WhoWest 94*
Feldmann, Shirley Clark 1929- *WhoAm 94*
Feldmar, Gabriel Gabor 1947- *WhoScEn 94*
Feldmiller, George E. 1946- *WhoAm 94, WhoAmL 94*
Feldon, Barbara 1933- *WhoHol 92*
Feldon, Barbara 1941- *IntMPA 94*
Feldon, Joan Sorge 1932- *WhoMW 93*
Feldschreiber, Harvey 1946- *WhoAmL 94*
Feldshuh, Tovah 1949- *WhoHol 92*
Feldshuh, Tovah 1952- *ConTFT 11*
Feldshuh, Tovah 1953- *IntMPA 94*
Feldshuh, Tovah S. 1952- *WhoAm 94*
Feldsien, Lawrence Frank 1939- *WhoScEn 94*
Feldstein, Alan R. 1944- *WhoAmL 94*
Feldstein, Albert B. *EncSF 93*
Feldstein, Albert B. 1925- *WhoAm 94*
Feldstein, Charles Robert 1922- *WhoMW 93*
Feldstein, Jay Eric 1955- *WhoAmL 94*
Feldstein, Joel Robert 1942- *WhoAm 94*
Feldstein, Martin Stuart 1939- *IntWW 93, Who 94, WhoAm 94, WhoFI 94*
Feldstein, Paul Joseph 1933- *WhoAm 94*
Feldstein, Richard 1945- *WhoMW 93*
Feldstein, Stanley 1930- *WhoScEn 94*
Feldstein Soto, Luis A. 1960- *WhoHisp 94*
Feldt, Allan Gunnar 1932- *WhoMW 93*
Feldt, David Allan 1957- *WhoMW 93*
Feldt, John Harrell 1940- *WhoAm 94*
Feldt, Kjell-Olof 1931- *IntWW 93*
Feldt, Robert Hewitt 1934- *WhoAm 94*
Feldt, Robert Junior 1929- *WhoMW 93*
Feldtmose, John Nielsen 1941- *WhoAm 94*
Feleciano, Paul, Jr. 1942- *WhoAmP 93, WhoHisp 94*
Felfe, Peter Franz 1939- *WhoAm 94*
Felgenhauer, H. R. *DrAPF 93*
Felger, Ralph William 1919- *WhoAm 94, WhoMW 93*
Felice, Cynthia 1942- *WrDr 94*
Felice, Cynthia (Lindgren) 1942- *EncSF 93*
Felice, Nicholas R. 1927- *WhoAmP 93*
Felice, Stephen Paul 1961- *WhoFI 94*
Felicella, Frank George 1946- *WhoAm 94*
Felicetti, Daniel A. 1942- *WhoAm 94*
Felici, Alessandro 1742-1772 *NewGrDO*
Felici, Angelo 1919- *IntWW 93*
Feliciana, Jerrye Brown 1951- *WhoBlA 94*
Feliciano, Humphrey 1957- *WhoFI 94*
Feliciano, Jose 1945- *ConMus 10 [port], WhoAm 94, WhoHisp 94*
Feliciano, Jose C. 1950- *WhoHisp 94*
Feliciano, Jose Celso 1950- *WhoAm 94*
Feliciano, José R. 1956- *WhoHisp 94*
Feliciano, Juan G. 1951- *WhoHisp 94*
Feliciano, Raul *WhoHisp 94*
Feliciano, Richard 1953- *WhoFI 94*
Feliciano, Tomas Bonilla *WhoAmP 93*
Feliciano, Valentin Delgado, Jr. 1943- *WhoHisp 94*
Feliciano, Wilma 1946- *WhoHisp 94*
Feliciotti, Enio 1926- *WhoFI 94*
Felicita, James Thomas 1947- *WhoWest 94*
Felinski, William Walter 1953- *WhoFI 94*
Felisky, Barbara Rosbe 1938- *WhoAmA 93*
Feliu, David Noel 1957- *WhoAmL 94*
Felix, Arthur, Jr. 1945- *WhoHisp 94*
Felix, Daniel Mendiola 1950- *WhoHisp 94*

Felix, David 1918- WhoAm 94
Felix, Dudley E. WhoBlA 94
Felix, Fred WhoHisp 94
Felix, George d1949 WhoHol 92
Felix, Junior Francisco 1967- WhoHisp 94
Felix, Kelvin Edward 1933- WhoAm 94
Felix, Maria 1914- WhoHol 92
Felix, Patricia Jean 1941- WhoFI 94
Felix, Raul 1938- WhoHisp 94
Felix, Ray 1930- BasBi
Felix, Richard J. 1942- WhoHisp 94
Felix, Richard James 1944- WhoFI 94, WhoWest 94
Felix, Robin 1954- WhoWest 94
Felix, Ted Mark 1947- WhoFI 94
Feliz, Luis Rafael 1967- WhoWest 94
Felker, David Larry 1940- WhoAmA 93
Felker, David Roland 1957- WhoFI 94
Felker, G. Stephen 1951- WhoFI 94
Felker, Harry WhoAmP 93
Felker, James M. 1939- WhoAm 94
Felker, Joseph B. 1926- WhoBlA 94
Felker, Ken 1943- WhoAmL 94
Felker, Martin Roy 1947- WhoWest 94
Felker, Peter WhoScEn 94
Felker, Robert Stratton 1942- WhoAmL 94
Felkner, William Jack 1963- WhoFI 94
Felknor, Bruce Lester 1921- WhoAm 94
Fell, Alison 1944- BlmGEL, BlmGWL [port]
Fell, Anthony 1914- Who 94
Fell, Barry 1917- WhoScEn 94, WrDr 94
Fell, David 1943- Who 94
Fell, Fraser M. 1928- WhoFI 94
Fell, Frederick Victor 1910- WhoAm 94
Fell, Gilbert Allen 1941- WhoMW 93
Fell, James Carlton 1943- WhoScEn 94
Fell, James F. 1944- WhoAm 94, WhoAmL 94
Fell, John 1721-1798 WhAmRev
Fell, Katherine Christine 1948- WhoWest 94
Fell, Margaret 1614-1702 BlmGWL
Fell, Norman 1924- IntMPA 94, WhoHol 92
Fell, Richard Taylor 1948- Who 94
Fell, Robert 1921- IntWW 93, Who 94
Fellegi, Ivan Peter 1935- WhoAm 94
Felleman, George P. 1941- WhoAmL 94
Fellenstein, Cora Ellen Mullikin 1930- WhoMW 93
Feller, Benjamin E. 1947- WhoFI 94
Feller, Bob 1918- WhoHol 92
Feller, Carlos 1925- NewGrDO
Feller, Catherine WhoHol 92
Feller, David E. 1916- WhoAm 94
Feller, Dennis Rudolph 1941- WhoScEn 94
Feller, Howard 1953- WhoAm 94
Feller, Lloyd Harris 1942- WhoAm 94, WhoAmL 94
Feller, Marc A. 1949- WhoAmL 94
Feller, Michel WhoHol 92
Feller, Robert L. 1919- WhoAmA 93
Feller, Robert Livingston 1919- WhoAm 94
Feller, Robert S., Sr. WhoWest 94
Feller, Robert William Andrew 1918- WhoAm 94
Feller, William Frank 1925- WhoScEn 94
Feller, Winthrop Bruce 1950- WhoScEn 94
Fellerman, Linden Jan 1956- WhoFI 94
Fellers, James Davison 1913- WhoAm 94, WhoAmL 94
Fellers, James Davison, Jr. 1948- WhoAm 94
Fellers, Raymond 1923- WhoAm 94
Fellers, Rhonda Gay 1955- WhoAmL 94, WhoFI 94
Fellgett, Peter Berners 1922- IntWW 93, Who 94
Fellhauer, David E. 1939- WhoAm 94
Fellin, Octavia Antoinette 1913- WhoWest 94
Felling, Darrell Edward WhoAmP 93
Felling, Donna M. WhoAmP 93
Fellingham, David Andrew 1937- WhoFI 94, WhoMW 93
Fellingham, Warren Luther, Jr. 1934- WhoMW 93
Fellini, Federico 1920- IntMPA 94, IntWW 93, Who 94, WhoAm 94, WhoHol 92
Fellini, Federico 1920-1993 NewYTBS 93 [port], News 94-2
Fellman, Daniel R. 1943- IntMPA 94
Fellman, John Keegan 1952- WhoWest 94
Fellman, Nat D. 1910- IntMPA 94
Fellman, Philip Vos 1951- WhoWest 94
Fellman, Richard Mayer 1935- WhoAmP 93
Fellner, Baruch Abraham 1944- WhoAm 94
Fellner, Fritz 1922- IntWW 93
Fellner, Michael Josef 1936- WhoAm 94
Fellner, Michael Joseph 1949- WhoMW 93
Fellner, Peter John 1943- Who 94
Fellner-Feldegg, Hugo Robert 1923- WhoScEn 94
Fellowes Who 94
Fellowes, Frederick Gale, Jr. 1930- WhoAm 94
Fellowes, Peter DrAPF 93
Fellowes, Robert 1941- Who 94
Fellowes, Rockcliffe d1950 WhoHol 92
Fellows, Alice 1935- WhoAmA 93
Fellows, Catherine WrDr 94
Fellows, Deborah Lynne WhoAmA 93
Fellows, Derek Edward 1927- Who 94
Fellows, Don WhoHol 92
Fellows, Donald Matthew 1955- WhoWest 94
Fellows, Edith 1923- WhoHol 92
Fellows, Edward Frank 1930- Who 94
Fellows, Fred 1934- WhoAmA 93
Fellows, George Wesley 1945- WhoIns 94
Fellows, Henry David, Jr. 1954- WhoAmL 94
Fellows, Jeffrey Keith 1940- Who 94
Fellows, Jerry Kenneth 1946- WhoAm 94, WhoAmL 94
Fellows, John Walter 1938- Who 94
Fellows, Larry Dean 1934- WhoWest 94
Fellows, Otis (Edward) 1908-1993 ConAu 141
Fellows, Otis Edward d1993 NewYTBS 93 [port]
Fellows, Robert Ellis 1933- WhoAm 94, WhoMW 93, WhoScEn 94
Fells, Ian 1932- IntWW 93, Who 94
Felman, Jyl Lynn DrAPF 93
Felman, Shoshana BlmGWL
Felmley, Jerry John 1933- WhoWest 94
Felmly, Bruce W. 1947- WhoAmL 94
Felmy, Hansjorg 1931- WhoHol 92
Felper, David Michael 1954- WhoAmL 94
Felperin, Howard (Michael) 1941- WrDr 94
Felrice, Barry 1945- WhoAmP 93
Fels, C. P. 1912-1991 WhoAmA 93N
Fels, Nicholas Wolff 1943- WhoAm 94, WhoAmL 94
Fels, Rendigs 1917- WhoAm 94
Felsen, Jerry 1940- WhoFI 94
Felsen, Leopold B. 1924- WhoAm 94
Felsen, Rosamund 1934- WhoAmA 93
Felsenfeld, Gary 1929- WhoAm 94
Felsenstein, Walter 1901-1975 NewGrDO
Felsenthal, Carol Judith 1949- WhoMW 93
Felsenthal, Steven Altus 1949- WhoAmL 94, WhoMW 93
Felsher, Murray 1936- WhoScEn 94
Felstehausen, Herman Henry 1936- WhoMW 93
Felstein, Ivor 1933- WrDr 94
Felt, Edward d1928 WhoHol 92
Felt, Irving Mitchell 1910- WhoAm 94
Felt, James Patterson 1950- WhoWest 94
Felt, James Wright 1926- WhoWest 94
Felt, Julia Kay 1941- WhoAmL 94
Felt, Paul S. 1947- WhoAmL 94
Feltch, Brent A. 1931- WhoAmP 93
Feltenstein, Harry David, Jr. 1920- WhoAm 94
Felter, Edwin Lester, Jr. 1941- WhoAmL 94
Felter, James Warren 1943- WhoAmA 93, WhoWest 94
Felter, John Kenneth 1950- WhoAm 94
Felter, June Marie 1919- WhoAmA 93
Feltey, Kathryn Margaret 1954- WhoMW 93
Felthous, Alan Robert 1944- WhoScEn 94
Feltner, William Clayton 1958- WhoWest 94
Felton, Ann Shirey 1941-1992 WhoBlA 94N
Felton, B. DrAPF 93
Felton, Charles B., Jr. 1936- WhoAmP 93
Felton, Dorothy Wood 1929- WhoAmP 93
Felton, Felix d1972 WhoHol 92
Felton, Gordon H. 1925- WhoAm 94
Felton, Guy Page, III 1937- WhoFI 94
Felton, Happy d1964 WhoHol 92
Felton, James A. 1919- WhoBlA 94
Felton, James A. 1945- WhoBlA 94
Felton, James Edward, Jr. 1932- WhoBlA 94
Felton, Jean Spencer 1911- WhoAm 94
Felton, John Walter 1929- WhoAm 94
Felton, Jule Wimberly, Jr. 1932- WhoAm 94
Felton, Katherine White 1949- WhoFI 94
Felton, Norman Francis 1913- WhoAm 94
Felton, Otis Leverna 1946- WhoBlA 94
Felton, Robert Stayton 1928- WhoIns 94
Felton, Samuel Page 1919- WhoWest 94
Felton, Verna d1966 WhoHol 92
Felton, Warren Locker, II 1925- WhoAm 94
Felton, Zora Belle 1930- WhoBlA 94
Felton-Elkins, Nancy Palm 1939- WhoFI 94, WhoMW 93
Feltovich, Paul John 1947- WhoMW 93
Felts, Diana J. DrAPF 93
Felts, Jean Carole 1933- WhoFI 94
Felts, William Robert, Jr. 1923- IntWW 93, WhoAm 94
Feltus, Alan 1943- WhoAmA 93
Feltus, James, Jr. 1921- WhoBlA 94
Feltus, Kay WhoHol 92
Feltwell, John 1948- ConAu 142
Felty, Kriss Delbert 1954- WhoAmL 94
Feltz, Charles Henderson 1916- WhoScEn 94
Felver, Charles Stanley 1916- WrDr 94
Felzenberg, Leonard Jerome 1933- WhoAmP 93
Felzke, Robert Harold 1929- WhoAmP 93
Femelidi, Volodymyr Olexandrovych 1905-1933 NewGrDO
Femling, Jean DrAPF 93
Femminella, Charles J., Jr. 1938- WhoFI 94
Fen, Allan Ming 1957- WhoAsA 94
Fenady, Andrew J. 1928- IntMPA 94
Fenaroli, Fedele 1730-1818 NewGrDO
Fenby, Eric (William) 1906- WrDr 94
Fenby, Eric William 1906- IntWW 93, Who 94
Fenby, Jonathan 1942- Who 94
Fenchel, Eric S. 1959- WhoFI 94
Fenchel, Tom Michael 1940- IntWW 93
Fenci, Renzo 1914- WhoAmA 93
Fendall, Neville Rex Edwards 1917- IntWW 93, Who 94
Fendall, Percy EncSF 93
Fendell, Jonas J. WhoAmA 93
Fendelman, Helaine 1942- WhoAm 94
Fender, Brian Edward Frederick 1934- IntWW 93, Who 94
Fender, Clarence Leo 1909-1991 WhAm 10
Fender, Freddy WhoHol 92
Fender, Freddy 1937- WhoAm 94, WhoHisp 94
Fender, Leo 1909-1991 ConMus 10 [port]
Fenderson, Caroline Houston 1932- WhoScEn 94
Fenderson, Reginald d1986 WhoHol 92
Fendler, Janos Hugo 1937- WhoAm 94
Fendler, Oscar 1909- WhoAm 94, WhoAmL 94, WhoAmP 93
Fendler, Sherman Gene 1947- WhoAmL 94
Fendrich, Roger Paul 1943- WhoAm 94
Fendrick, Alan Burton 1933- WhoAm 94, WhoFI 94
Fenech, Edwige WhoHol 92
Fenech, Joseph C. 1950- WhoAmL 94, WhoMW 93
Fenech-Adami, Edward 1934- IntWW 93, Who 94
Fenello, Michael John 1916- WhoAm 94
Fenelon, Francois de Pons de Salignac de la Mothe- 1651-1715 GuFrLit 2
Fenelon, Kenneth B. 1948- WhoAmL 94
Fenemore, Hilda WhoHol 92
Feneuille, Serge Jean Georges 1940- IntWW 93
Feng, Albert S. 1944- WhoMW 93
Feng, Anita N. DrAPF 93
Feng, Guofu Jeff 1957- WhoAsA 94
Feng, Hsien Wen 1928- WhoScEn 94
Feng, Jonathan Lee 1967- WhoAsA 94
Feng, Joseph Shao-Ying 1948- WhoWest 94
Feng, Paul Chi-Chia 1952- WhoMW 93
Feng, Theo-dric 1953- WhoAsA 94
Feng, Tse-Yun WhoAsA 94
Feng, Tse-yun 1928- WhoAm 94
Feng, Xin 1951- WhoAsA 94
Feng Dashi 1915- WhoPRCh 91 [port]
Feng Depei 1907- IntWW 93, WhoPRCh 91 [port]
Feng Duan WhoPRCh 91
Feng Duan 1923- IntWW 93
Fenger, Joan Cruff 1927- WhoAmP 93
Fenger, Manfred 1928- WhoAm 94
Fenger Moller, Grethe 1941- IntWW 93
Feng Guodong 1948- WhoPRCh 91
Feng He 1931- IntWW 93
Feng Hongda 1930- WhoPRCh 91
Feng Jiannan 1942?- WhoPRCh 91 [port]
Feng Jicai 1942?- WhoPRCh 91 [port]
Feng Jical 1942- ConWorW 93
Feng Jinsong 1934- IntWW 93, WhoPRCh 91 [port]
Feng Jinwen 1924- IntWW 93, WhoPRCh 91 [port]
Feng Jixin WhoPRCh 91
Feng Jun 1949- WhoPRCh 91 [port]
Feng Kang 1920- IntWW 93, WhoPRCh 91
Feng Keng 1907-1931 BlmGWL
Feng Lanming WhoPRCh 91
Feng Lanrui 1920- IntWW 93, WhoPRCh 91
Fengler, John Peter 1928- WhoAm 94
Feng Lida WhoPRCh 91 [port]
Feng Ling'an 1925- WhoPRCh 91 [port]
Feng Mu 1919- WhoPRCh 91 [port]
Feng Qing 1956- WhoPRCh 91 [port]
Feng Qiyong WhoPRCh 91 [port]
Feng Sutao 1906- WhoPRCh 91 [port]
Feng Tianshun 1921- WhoPRCh 91 [port]
Feng Tiyun 1925- WhoPRCh 91 [port]
Feng Wenbin 1911- WhoPRCh 91 [port]
Feng Xianming WhoPRCh 91 [port]
Feng Yaozong WhoPRCh 91
Feng Yidai 1913- WhoPRCh 91
Feng Yin 1921- WhoPRCh 91 [port]
Feng Ying 1962- WhoPRCh 91 [port]
Feng Ying 1963- IntWW 93
Feng Youlan 1895- WhoPRCh 91 [port]
Feng Yousong 1924- WhoPRCh 91 [port]
Feng Yuanjun 1900-1974 BlmGWL
Feng Yuanwei 1930- WhoPRCh 91 [port]
Feng Yunhe 1898- WhoPRCh 91 [port]
Feng Yuzhong WhoPRCh 91
Feng Zhi 1905- WhoPRCh 91 [port]
Feng Zhijun 1937- WhoPRCh 91 [port]
Feng Zhimao 1934- WhoPRCh 91 [port]
Feng Zhongpu BlmGWL
Feng Zizhi 1935- WhoPRCh 91 [port]
Fenhalls, Richard Dorian 1943- Who 94
Fenhaus, Louann Elta 1934- WhoMW 93
Fenical, Marlin E. 1907-1983 WhoAmA 93N
Fenichel, Norman Stewart 1924- WhoAm 94
Fenichel, Richard Lee 1925- WhoAm 94
Feniger, Jerome Roland, Jr. 1927- WhoAm 94
Fenimore, George Wiley 1921- WhoAm 94
Feninger, Claude 1926- WhoAm 94
Fenley, David A. 1954- WhoAmL 94
Fenlon, Jack 1940- WhoAmP 93
Fenn, Charles 1907- WrDr 94
Fenn, Dan Huntington, Jr. 1923- WhoAmP 93
Fenn, (Frances) Elizabeth 1914- WhoAmA 93
Fenn, Henry Courtensy 1894- WhAm 10
Fenn, Ingemund 1907- IntWW 93
Fenn, Jimmy O'Neil 1937- WhoScEn 94
Fenn, Lionel EncSF 93
Fenn, Nicholas (Maxted) 1936- Who 94
Fenn, Nicholas M. 1936- IntWW 93
Fenn, Ormon William, Jr. 1927- WhoAm 94
Fenn, Otto d1993 NewYTBS 93
Fenn, Raymond Wolcott, Jr. 1922- WhoAm 94
Fenn, Sherilyn 1964- WhoHol 92
Fenn, Sherilyn 1965- WhoAm 94
Fenn, Sherilynn 1965- IntMPA 94
Fenn, William Hartley 1955- WhoMW 93
Fenn, William P. d1993 NewYTBS 93
Fennario, David WrDr 94
Fennario, David 1947- ConDr 93, IntDcT 2
Fennebresque, John C. 1947- WhoAmL 94
Fennell, (John) Desmond (Augustine) 1933- Who 94
Fennell, Diane Marie 1944- WhoFI 94, WhoWest 94
Fennell, John Lister Illingworth 1918-1992 WrDr 94N
Fennell, Thomas E. 1950- WhoAm 94
Fennelly, Jane Corey 1942- WhoAm 94
Fennelly, Maura Ann 1962- WhoAmL 94
Fennelly, Parker d1988 WhoHol 92
Fennelly, Tony 1945- ConAu 43NR
Fennelly, Vincent M. 1920- IntMPA 94
Fennema, Owen Richard 1929- WhoAm 94, WhoScEn 94
Fenneman, George 1919- IntMPA 94
Fenner, Carol 1929- WrDr 94
Fenner, Derrick Steven 1967- WhoBlA 94
Fenner, Frank John 1914- IntWW 93, Who 94, WrDr 94
Fenner, James R. 1919- WrDr 94
Fenner, Peggy 1922- Who 94
Fenner, Peggy Edith 1922- WhoWomW 91
Fenner, Peter David 1936- WhoAm 94
Fenner, Roger T(heedham) 1943- WrDr 94
Fenner, Suzan Ellen 1947- WhoAm 94, WhoAmL 94
Fenner, Walter d1947 WhoHol 92
Fennessy, Edward 1912- Who 94
Fennessy, John James 1933- WhoAm 94
Fennessy, Timothy Bruce 1957- WhoAmL 94
Fenney, Roger Johnson 1916- Who 94
Fennick, Daniel Martin 1954- WhoAmL 94
Fenning, Lisa Hill 1952- WhoAm 94, WhoAmL 94, WhoWest 94
Fenninger, Leonard Davis 1917- WhoAm 94
Fenno, Jack 1911- WrDr 94
Fenno, Jenny fl. 1791- BlmGWL
Fenno, Richard Francis, Jr. 1926- WhoAm 94

Ferguson, Sheila Alease 1955- *WhoScEn 94*
Ferguson, Shellie Alvin 1943- *WhoBlA 94*
Ferguson, Sherlon Lee 1949- *WhoBlA 94*
Ferguson, Sherman E. 1944- *WhoBlA 94*
Ferguson, Stephen 1947- *WhoAm 94*
Ferguson, Susan Katharine Stover 1944- *WhoScEn 94*
Ferguson, Suzanne Carol 1939- *WhoAm 94*
Ferguson, Tamara *WhoMW 93*
Ferguson, Tee 1950- *WhoAmP 93*
Ferguson, Thomas Crooks 1933- *WhoAm 94*
Ferguson, Thomas Edward 1928- *WhoAmP 93*
Ferguson, Thomas George 1941- *WhoAm 94*
Ferguson, Thomas H. *WhoAm 94*
Ferguson, Thomas Jeffrey 1955- *WhoWest 94*
Ferguson, Thomas Joseph 1956- *WhoAmL 94*
Ferguson, Tracy Heiman 1910- *WhoAm 94*
Ferguson, W. J. d1930 *WhoHol 92*
Ferguson, Ward P. 1931- *WhoAmP 93*
Ferguson, Warren John 1920- *WhoAm 94, WhoAmL 94, WhoWest 94*
Ferguson, Whitworth, III 1954- *WhoAmL 94*
Ferguson, Wilfred 1917- *WhoAmP 93*
Ferguson, Wilkie Demeritte, Jr. 1939- *WhoBlA 94*
Ferguson, William *DrAPF 93*
Ferguson, William Charles 1930- *WhoAm 94, WhoFI 94*
Ferguson, William M(cDonald) 1917- *ConAu 41NR*
Ferguson, William McDonald 1917- *WhoAm 94*
Ferguson, Zeb 1875-1908
See Zeb and Zarrow *WhoCom*
Ferguson Davie, Antony (Francis) 1952- *Who 94*
Ferguson-Smith, Malcolm Andrew 1931- *IntWW 93, Who 94*
Fergusson, Adam (Dugdale) 1932- *Who 94*
Fergusson, Elizabeth Graeme 1737-1801 *BlmGWL*
Fergusson, Ewen (Alastair John) 1932- *Who 94*
Fergusson, Ewen Alastair John 1932- *IntWW 93*
Fergusson, Frances Daly 1944- *WhoAm 94*
Fergusson, James H. H. C. *Who 94*
Fergusson, Robert 1750-1774 *BlmGEL*
Fergusson, Robert George 1911- *WhoAm 94, WhoWest 94*
Fergusson of Kilkerran, Charles 1931- *Who 94*
Fergus-Thompson, Gordon 1952- *IntWW 93*
Ferholt, Eleanore Heusser *WhoAmA 93*
Feria, Abraham H. 1946- *WhoHisp 94*
Feria, Bernabe Francis 1949- *WhoMW 93*
Feria, Floridano 1937- *WhoHisp 94*
Feric, Gordan 1961- *WhoScEn 94*
Fericano, Paul *DrAPF 93*
Ferin, Michel Jacques 1939- *WhoScEn 94*
Ferino, Christopher Kenneth 1961- *WhoFI 94, WhoMW 93*
Feriola, James Philip 1925- *WhoAmA 93*
Ferkel, Larry Ralph 1950- *WhoAmL 94*
Ferkenhoff, Robert J. 1942- *WhoAm 94, WhoFI 94*
Ferkingstad, Susanne M. 1955- *WhoMW 93*
Ferlan, Arthur 1922- *WhoAmP 93*
Ferland, Barbara 1919- *BlmGWL*
Ferland, E. James 1942- *WhoAm 94, WhoFI 94*
Ferland, Roger K. 1947- *WhoAm 94, WhoAmL 94*
Ferling, Lawrence *ConAu 41NR*
Ferlinghetti, Lawrence *DrAPF 93*
Ferlinghetti, Lawrence 1919- *WhoAm 94*
Ferlinghetti, Lawrence 1920- *IntWW 93, WrDr 94*
Ferlinghetti, Lawrence (Mendes-Monsanto) 1919- *ConDr 93*
Ferlinghetti, Lawrence (Monsanto) 1919?- *ConAu 41NR*
Ferlinz, Jack 1942- *WhoAm 94*
Ferlita, Ernest 1927- *WrDr 94*
Ferm, Anders 1938- *IntWW 93*
Ferm, David G. *WhoAm 94*
Ferm, Robert Livingston 1931- *WhoAm 94*
Ferm, Robert M. 1948- *WhoAmL 94*
Ferm, Vergil Harkness 1924- *WhoAm 94*
Ferman, Edward L(ewis) 1937- *EncSF 93*
Ferman, Harriet Arlene *WhoAmP 93*
Ferman, Irving 1919- *WhoFI 94*
Ferman, James Alan 1930- *Who 94*
Ferman, Joseph W(olfe) 1906-1974 *EncSF 93*
Fermanian, Thomas Walter 1950- *WhoMW 93*
Fermat, Pierre de 1601-1665 *WorScD*
Fermi, Enrico 1901-1954 *WorScD [port]*
Fermin, Felix Jose 1963- *WhoHisp 94*
Fermony, Matthias Alexis de Roche c. 1737- *AmRev*
Fermor, Patrick Michael Leigh 1915- *IntWW 93, Who 94*
Fermor-Hesketh *Who 94*
Fermoso Garcia, Julio 1948- *IntWW 93*
Fermoy, Baron 1967- *Who 94*
Fermoy, Dowager Lady d1993 *Who 94N*
Fermoy, Lady d1993 *NewYTBS 93*
Fermoy, Matthias Alexis Roche de 1737- *WhAmRev*
Fern, Alan Maxwell 1930- *WhoAm 94, WhoAmA 93*
Fern, Arnold R. d1993 *NewYTBS 93*
Fern, Carole Lynn 1958- *WhoAmL 94*
Fern, Fanny *BlmGWL*
Fern, Frederick Harold 1954- *WhoAmL 94*
Fern, Fritzie d1932 *WhoHol 92*
Fern, Martin D. 1943- *WhoAmL 94*
Fernald, Charles Edward 1902-1990 *WhAm 10*
Fernald, David Gordon 1923-1990 *WhAm 10*
Fernald, George Herbert, Jr. 1926- *WhoAm 94*
Fernald, Harold Allen 1932- *WhoAm 94*
Fernald, Helen Elizabeth 1891-1964 *WhoAmA 93N*
Fernald, James Michael 1964- *WhoScEn 94*
Fernald, Russell Dawson 1941- *WhoAm 94*
Fernald, Willard Barker 1923- *WhoMW 93*
Fernan, Mary Brigid 1958- *WhoAmL 94*
Fernandel d1971 *WhoHol 92*
Fernandel 1903-1971 *WhoCom*
Fernandes, Alvaro fl. 144-?- *WhWE*
Fernandes, Angelo 1913- *Who 94*
Fernandes, Angelo Innocent 1913- *IntWW 93*
Fernandes, Eugenie 1943- *SmATA 77 [port]*
Fernandes, Gary Joe 1943- *WhoAm 94, WhoFI 94*
Fernandes, George 1930- *IntWW 93*
Fernandes, Miguel 1949- *WhoHol 92*
Fernandes, Nascimento d1956 *WhoHol 92*
Fernandes, Pedro Infante 1957- *WhoHisp 94*
Fernandes, Prabhavathi Bhat 1949- *WhoScEn 94*
Fernandes Salling, Lehua 1949- *WhoAmP 93, WhoHisp 94, WhoWest 94*
Fernandez, Abel A. 1952- *WhoHisp 94*
Fernandez, Adolfo, Jr. 1951- *WhoAmP 93, WhoHisp 94*
Fernandez, Albert Bades *WhoHisp 94*
Fernandez, Alberto F. 1952- *WhoHisp 94*
Fernandez, Alberto Miguel 1958- *WhoHisp 94*
Fernandez, Alex 1969- *WhoHisp 94*
Fernandez, Alfonso 1951- *WhoHisp 94*
Fernandez, Alfred P. 1934- *WhoHisp 94*
Fernandez, Alfredo Jose 1957- *WhoMW 93*
Fernandez, Alvaro Alfonso 1938- *WhoHisp 94*
Fernandez, Andres Jose 1940- *WhoHisp 94*
Fernandez, Aymara 1960- *WhoHisp 94*
Fernandez, Benedict Joseph, III 1936- *WhoHisp 94*
Fernandez, Benito R. *WhoHisp 94*
Fernandez, Bijou d1961 *WhoHol 92*
Fernandez, Carlos H. 1938- *WhoHisp 94*
Fernandez, Carlos Jesus 1951- *WhoHisp 94*
Fernandez, Carlos M. 1953- *WhoHisp 94*
Fernandez, Carol 1949- *WhoHisp 94*
Fernandez, Carole Fragoza 1941- *WhoHisp 94*
Fernandez, Castor A. *WhoHisp 94*
Fernandez, Castor A. 1943- *WhoAm 94*
Fernández, Celestino 1949- *WhoHisp 94*
Fernandez, Charlene Ramos 1955- *WhoHisp 94*
Fernandez, Charles M. *WhoHisp 94*
Fernandez, Chico *WhoHisp 94*
Fernandez, Constantino Francisco, Jr. 1941- *WhoHisp 94*
Fernandez, Daniel *DrAPF 93*
Fernandez, Dennis Lee 1963- *WhoMW 93*
Fernandez, Dolores M. 1944- *WhoHisp 94*
Fernandez, Dominique 1929- *IntWW 93*
Fernandez, Doria Goodrich 1958- *WhoHisp 94*
Fernandez, Eduardo B. 1936- *WhoHisp 94*
Fernandez, Edward R. *WhoHisp 94*
Fernandez, Emilio d1986 *WhoHol 92*
Fernández, Enrique *WhoHisp 94*
Fernandez, Erasto *WhoHisp 94*
Fernandez, Esther *WhoHol 92*
Fernandez, Eugenia 1957- *WhoHisp 94*
Fernandez, Eustasio, Jr. 1919- *WhoHisp 94*
Fernandez, Federico Antonio 1940- *WhoHisp 94*
Fernandez, Felix d1966 *WhoHol 92*
Fernandez, Ferdinand F. *WhoAmP 93*
Fernandez, Ferdinand Francis 1937- *WhoAm 94, WhoAmL 94, WhoHisp 94, WhoWest 94*
Fernandez, Fernando Lawrence 1938- *WhoHisp 94, WhoScEn 94*
Fernandez, Fidel Juan 1959- *WhoHisp 94*
Fernandez, Filiberto *WhoHisp 94*
Fernandez, Frances *WhoHisp 94*
Fernandez, Frances Garcia 1960- *WhoAmL 94*
Fernandez, Francisco *WhoHisp 94*
Fernández, Francisco Waldo 1912- *WhoHisp 94*
Fernández, Frank *WhoHisp 94*
Fernandez, George M. d1923 *WhoHol 92*
Fernandez, Gigi 1964- *WhoHisp 94*
Fernandez, Gilbert, Jr. 1938- *WhoHisp 94*
Fernández, Gilbert G. 1936- *WhoHisp 94*
Fernandez, Giselle *WhoHisp 94*
Fernandez, Guillermo G. *WhoHisp 94*
Fernandez, Gustavo Antonio 1944- *WhoHisp 94*
Fernandez, Happy 1939- *WhoAmP 93*
Fernández, Harida 1973- *WhoHisp 94*
Fernandez, Hector R. C. 1937- *WhoHisp 94*
Fernandez, Henry A. 1949- *WhoAm 94*
Fernandez, Henry Anthony 1949- *WhoHisp 94*
Fernández, Iris Virginia 1955- *WhoHisp 94*
Fernandez, J. M. *WhoHisp 94*
Fernandez, Jack Eugene, Sr. 1930- *WhoHisp 94*
Fernandez, James 1955- *WhoHisp 94*
Fernandez, Jeffrey Everard 1958- *WhoMW 93*
Fernandez, John 1935- *WhoHisp 94*
Fernandez, John Anthony 1940- *WhoHisp 94*
Fernandez, John D. 1947- *WhoHisp 94*
Fernandez, John Peter 1941- *WhoBlA 94*
Fernandez, Jon Jeffrey 1948- *WhoHisp 94*
Fernandez, Jorge Antonio 1944- *WhoHisp 94*
Fernandez, Jorge L. *WhoHisp 94*
Fernandez, Jose *WhoHisp 94*
Fernández, José B. 1948- *WhoHisp 94*
Fernandez, Jose Luis *WhoHisp 94*
Fernandez, Jose Ramon, Jr. 1944- *WhoHisp 94*
Fernandez, Jose Walfredo 1955- *WhoAm 94, WhoAmL 94*
Fernandez, Joseph A. 1935- *WhoAm 94, WhoHisp 94*
Fernandez, Juan *WhoHol 92*
Fernandez, Juan Carlos *WhoHisp 94*
Fernandez, Julian, Jr. *WhoHisp 94*
Fernandez, Leticia 1956- *WhoHisp 94*
Fernandez, Lillian 1954- *WhoHisp 94*
Fernandez, Linda Flawn 1943- *WhoFI 94*
Fernandez, Liz 1959- *WhoHisp 94*
Fernandez, Lloyd *WhoHisp 94*
Fernandez, Louis, Jr. *WhoHisp 94*
Fernandez, Louis Anthony 1939- *WhoHisp 94*
Fernandez, Louise Ann 1953- *WhoHisp 94*
Fernandez, Luis F. 1951- *WhoHisp 94*
Fernández, Luis Felipe 1958- *WhoHisp 94*
Fernandez, Manuel B. 1925- *WhoHisp 94*
Fernandez, Manuel G. *WhoHisp 94*
Fernandez, Manuel Jose 1946- *WhoHisp 94*
Fernandez, Manuel Joseph 1939- *WhoHisp 94*
Fernandez, Maria Alba 1936- *WhoHisp 94*
Fernandez, Maria Isabel 1953- *WhoHisp 94*
Fernandez, Mariano H. 1939- *WhoHisp 94*
Fernandez, Mark Antonio 1960- *WhoHisp 94*
Fernandez, Marlene *WhoHisp 94*
Fernández, Mary Joe 1971- *WhoHisp 94*
Fernandez, Matilde *WhoWomW 91*
Fernandez, Michael A. 1956- *WhoHisp 94*
Fernandez, Miguel Angel 1939- *WhoFI 94*
Fernandez, Mildred *WhoHisp 94*
Fernandez, Nelson *WhoHisp 94*
Fernandez, Nestor A., Sr. *WhoHisp 94*
Fernandez, Nino J. *WhoHisp 94*
Fernandez, Nino Joseph 1941- *WhoFI 94*
Fernandez, Noella *WhoHisp 94*
Fernández, Nohema del Carmen 1944- *WhoHisp 94*
Fernandez, Nuria Icel 1955- *WhoMW 93*
Fernandez, Oscar Lorenzo 1897-1948 *NewGrDO*
Fernandez, Pedro A. *WhoHisp 94*
Fernandez, Rafael Ludovino 1948- *WhoHisp 94*
Fernandez, Ramiro A. 1951- *WhoHisp 94*
Fernandez, Ramon d1962 *WhoHol 92*
Fernandez, Ramon 1958- *WhoHisp 94*
Fernández, Ramón S. 1934- *WhoHisp 94*
Fernandez, Raul A. 1945- *WhoHisp 94*
Fernandez, Rene 1961- *WhoMW 93, WhoScEn 94*
Fernandez, Ricardo, III 1970- *WhoHisp 94*
Fernandez, Ricardo Jesus 1953- *WhoHisp 94*
Fernandez, Ricardo R. 1940- *WhoAm 94, WhoHisp 94*
Fernandez, Robert I. 1956- *WhoHisp 94*
Fernandez, Roberta *WhoHisp 94*
Fernandez, Roberto G. 1951- *WhoHisp 94*
Fernandez, Rodney E. 1945- *WhoHisp 94*
Fernandez, Rodolfo 1940- *WhoHisp 94*
Fernández, Roger Rodriguez 1934- *WhoHisp 94*
Fernandez, Rolando Manuel 1963- *WhoFI 94*
Fernandez, Roy d1927 *WhoHol 92*
Fernandez, Roy M., Sr. *WhoHisp 94*
Fernandez, Roy M., Jr. *WhoHisp 94*
Fernandez, Ruben D. 1949- *WhoHisp 94*
Fernandez, Ruben Mark 1954- *WhoHisp 94*
Fernandez, Rudy 1960- *WhoHisp 94*
Fernandez, Rudy M., Jr. 1948- *WhoHisp 94*
Fernandez, Sally Garza 1958- *WhoHisp 94*
Fernandez, Secundino, Jr. 1942- *WhoHisp 94*
Fernandez, Theresa M. *WhoHisp 94*
Fernandez, Thomas L. 1930- *WhoHisp 94*
Fernandez, Tomas I. 1925- *WhoHisp 94*
Fernandez, Tomas Isidro 1925- *WhoAm 94*
Fernandez, Tony *WhoHisp 94*
Fernandez, Tony 1962- *WhoAm 94, WhoBlA 94, WhoHisp 94*
Fernandez, Valentin, Jr. 1953- *WhoHisp 94*
Fernandez, Wilfredo 1961- *WhoHisp 94*
Fernandez, Wilhelmenia 1947- *WhoHol 92*
Fernandez, Zandra Luz 1954- *WhoHisp 94*
Fernandez, Zenaida 1954- *WhoHisp 94*
Fernandez-Armesto, Felipe (Fermin Ricardo) 1950- *ConAu 142*
Fernández-Baca, David Fernando 1959- *WhoHisp 94*
Fernandez-Baca, Jaime A. 1954- *WhoHisp 94*
Fernandez Caballero, Manuel *NewGrDO*
Fernandez Chardiet, Miguel *WhoHisp 94*
Fernandez Cubas, Cristina 1945- *BlmGWL*
Fernandez De Cordoba, Francisco *WhWE*
Fernandez de Moratin, Leandro 1760-1828 *IntDcT 2*
Fernandez-Esteva, Frank 1931- *WhoHisp 94*
Fernández-Franco, Sonia M. 1938- *WhoHisp 94*
Fernandez-Guerra, Jorge 1952- *NewGrDO*
Fernandez Haar, Ana Maria 1951- *WhoHisp 94*
Fernández-Jiménez, Juan 1946- *WhoHisp 94*
Fernández-Madrid, Félix 1927- *WhoHisp 94*
Fernandez Maldonado Solari, Jorge 1922- *IntWW 93*
Fernandez-Martinez, Jose 1930- *WhoScEn 94*
Fernandez Miranda, Jorge 1950- *WhoScEn 94*
Fernandez Morales, Juana *BlmGWL*
Fernandez-Moran, Humberto 1924- *WhoScEn 94*
Fernandez-Morera, Dario *WhoHisp 94*
Fernandez-Muro, Jose Antonio 1920- *IntWW 93*
Fernández-Obregón, Adolfo Carlos 1951- *WhoHisp 94*
Fernández Olmos, Margarite 1949- *WhoHisp 94*
Fernandez Ordonez, Francisco d1992 *IntWW 93N*
Fernandez Pacheco, Ismael *WhoAmP 93, WhoHisp 94*
Fernandez-Palmer, Lydia *WhoHisp 94*
Fernandez-Pol, Blanca Dora 1932- *WhoScEn 94*
Fernandez-Pol, Jose Alberto 1943- *WhoScEn 94*
Fernandez-Quincoces, Guillermo J. 1947- *WhoAmL 94*
Fernandez-Repollet, Emma D. 1951- *WhoScEn 94*

Fernandez Retamar, Roberto 1930- IntWW 93
Fernandez Sanz, Matilde 1950- IntWW 93
Fernandez Shaw (y Iturralde), Guillermo 1893-1965 NewGrDO
Fernandez Shaw, Carlos 1865-1911 NewGrDO
Fernandez-Shaw, Carlos M(anuel) 1924- ConAu 140
Fernandez Stigliano, Ariel 1957- WhoScEn 94
Fernández-Torriente, Gastón F. 1924- WhoHisp 94
Fernandez-Torrijos, Vivian 1966- WhoHisp 94
Fernandez-Vazquez, Antonio A. 1949- WhoHisp 94
Fernandez-Velazquez, Juan R. 1936- WhoHisp 94
Fernandez-Velazquez, Juan Ramon 1936- WhoAm 94
Fernandez-Zayas, Marcelo R. 1938- WhoHisp 94
Fernando, Cecil T. 1924- WhoScEn 94
Fernando, Chitra BlmGWL
Fernando, Gilda Cordero 1930- BlmGWL
Fernando, Harindra Joseph 1955- WhoScEn 94
Fernando, Nicholas Marcus Who 94
Fernando, Nicholas Marcus 1932- IntWW 93
Fernando, Thusew Samuel 1906- IntWW 93
Fernando-Lewis, Sonia Gabriel 1954- WhoMW 93
Fernbach, John R. d1993 NewYTBS 93
Fernea, Robert Alan 1932- WhoAm 94
Ferneau, Philip James 1962- WhoAmL 94
Ferner, David Charles 1933- WhoMW 93
Ferner, Thomas Alan 1965- WhoMW 93
Fernex, Solange 1934- WhoWomW 91
Ferneyhough, Brian John Peter 1943- IntWW 93, Who 94
Ferng, Douglas Ming-Haw 1945- WhoMW 93
Ferngren, Gary Burt 1942- WhoWest 94
Fernholz, Erhard Robert 1941- WhoFI 94
Fernholz, Eunice Charlotte 1927- WhoAmP 93
Ferni, Carolina 1839-1926 NewGrDO
Fernicola, Gregory Anthony 1957- WhoAmL 94
Fernicola, Nilda Alicia Gallego Gandara 1931- WhoScEn 94
Fernie, Eric Campbell 1939- Who 94
Fernie, John Chipman 1945- WhoAmA 93
Fernie, John Donald 1933- WhoAm 94
Ferniel, Daniel d1976 WhoHol 92
Ferni-Germano, Virginia 1849-1934 NewGrDO
Ferniot, Jean 1918- IntWW 93
Fernos-Isern, Antonio 1895- WhAm 10
Fernous, Louis Ferdinand, Jr. 1938- WhoAm 94, WhoFI 94
Ferns, Pat Agnes 1941- WhoWest 94
Fernsler, John Paul 1940- WhoAm 94
Fernyhough, Bernard 1932- Who 94
Fernyhough, Ernest d1993 Who 94N
Feroce, Giovanni 1968- WhoAmP 93
Feron, David Snyder 1932- WhoAm 94
Feron, Elizabeth 1797-1853 NewGrDO
Feroz, Ehsan Habib 1952- WhoFI 94, WhoMW 93
Feroze, Rustam Moolan 1920- Who 94
Ferra, Lorraine DrAPF 93
Ferrá, Max 1937- WhoHisp 94
Ferracuti, Stefano Eugenio 1958- WhoScEn 94
Ferradas, Renaldo 1932- WhoHisp 94
Ferraday, Lisa WhoHol 92
Ferradini, Antonio 1718?-1779 NewGrDO
Ferragallo, Roger John 1923- WhoWest 94
Ferragut, Rene WhoHisp 94
Ferraguti Vallerini, Isa 1942- WhoWomW 91
Ferraioli, Armando 1949- WhoFI 94
Ferrall, Raymond (Alfred) 1906- Who 94
Ferrall, Victor Eugene, Jr. 1936- WhoAm 94, WhoMW 93
Ferrand, Jean C. 1930- WhoAm 94
Ferrandez, Gloria d1970 WhoHol 92
Ferrandini, Giovanni Battista c. 1710-1791 NewGrDO
Ferrando, Anne Kathleen 1968- WhoFI 94
Ferrando, Raymond 1912- WhoScEn 94
Ferrani, Cesira 1863-1943 NewGrDO
Ferranti, Sebastian Basil Joseph Ziani de Who 94
Ferrar, Harold 1935- WrDr 94
Ferrar, Nicholas BlmGEL
Ferrara, Abel HorFD
Ferrara, Abel 1951- IntMPA 94
Ferrara, Arthur Vincent 1930- WhoAm 94, WhoFI 94
Ferrara, Donna WhoAmP 93
Ferrara, Francis Xavier 1956- WhoAmL 94
Ferrara, Jackie WhoAmA 93
Ferrara, Peter Biagio, Jr. 1951- WhoAm 94
Ferrara, Peter J. 1955- WhoAmP 93
Ferrara, Peter Joseph 1955- WhoAm 94
Ferrara, Ralph C. 1945- WhoAm 94, WhoAmL 94
Ferrara, Stephane WhoHol 92
Ferrara, Stephen Arthur 1940- WhoAm 94
Ferrara, Thomas Charles 1951- WhoFI 94
Ferrare, Ashley WhoHol 92
Ferrare, Cristina 1950- WhoHol 92
Ferrarelli, Rina DrAPF 93
Ferrarese, Adriana c. 1760-1800? NewGrDO
Ferrari, Alberto Mario 1927- WhoFI 94
Ferrari, Benedetto 1603?-1681 NewGrDO
Ferrari, David G. 1944- WhoAmP 93
Ferrari, Domenic J. WhoAmP 93
Ferrari, Domenico 1940- WhoAm 94, WhoWest 94
Ferrari, Donna Mae 1931- WhoFI 94, WhoWest 94
Ferrari, Febo 1865- WhoAmA 93N
Ferrari, Francesco fl. 1624?-1683? NewGrDO
Ferrari, Francesco Gonella di NewGrDO
Ferrari, Gabrielle 1851?-1921 NewGrDO
Ferrari, Giacomo Gotifredo 1763?-1842 NewGrDO
Ferrari, Isabella WhoHol 92
Ferrari, Marianne 1946- WhoWest 94
Ferrari, Mary DrAPF 93
Ferrari, Michael David 1945- WhoMW 93
Ferrari, Michael Richard, Jr. 1940- WhoAm 94, WhoMW 93
Ferrari, Patricia 1942- WhoAmL 94
Ferrari, R(onald) L(eslie) 1930- WrDr 94
Ferrari, Raquel d1978 WhoHol 92
Ferrari, Richard Francis 1944- WhoAmP 93
Ferrari, Richard Harold 1956- WhoFI 94
Ferrari, Robert Joseph 1936- WhoAm 94
Ferrari, Serafino (Amedeo) de NewGrDO
Ferrari, Virginio Luig 1937- WhoAmA 93
Ferrari-Fontana, Edoardo 1878-1936 NewGrDO
Ferrario, Carlo 1833-1907 NewGrDO
Ferrario, Joseph A. 1926- WhoAm 94, WhoWest 94
Ferraris, Fred DrAPF 93
Ferraris, Ina Maria 1882-1971 NewGrDO
Ferrari Trecate, Luigi 1884-1964 NewGrDO
Ferraro, Anthony Michael, Sr. 1935- WhoAmP 93
Ferraro, Arnaldo A. 1936- WhoAmP 93
Ferraro, Arthur Kevin 1934- WhoWest 94
Ferraro, Betty M. 1925- WhoAmP 93
Ferraro, Charles Domenic 1913- WhoMW 93
Ferraro, Charles Michael 1955- WhoIns 94
Ferraro, Geraldine 1935- WhoWomW 91
Ferraro, Geraldine A. 1935- WhoAmP 93
Ferraro, Geraldine Anne 1935- IntWW 93, WhoAm 94
Ferraro, John WhoHisp 94
Ferraro, John 1924- WhoAmP 93
Ferraro, John Ralph 1918- WhoAm 94
Ferraro, Joseph 1944- WhoAmL 94
Ferraro, Michael Thomas 1957- WhoFI 94
Ferraro, Richard Edward 1924- WhoAmP 93
Ferraro, Vincent 1947- WhoScEn 94
Ferrars, E. X. 1907- WrDr 94
Ferrars, Elizabeth 1907- WrDr 94
Ferrat, Jacques Jean 1910- WrDr 94
Ferrata, Giuseppe 1865-1928 NewGrDO
Ferraud, Anna Bellinzani 1657-1740 BlmGWL
Ferrazza, Carl J. 1920- IntMPA 94
Ferrazzi, Ferruccio 1891- IntWW 93
Ferre, Antonio Luis 1934- WhoAm 94, WhoFI 94, WhoHisp 94
Ferre, Antonio R. WhoHisp 94
Ferré, Frederick 1933- WrDr 94
Ferre, Gianfranco 1944- IntWW 93, WhoAm 94
Ferré, Helen Aguirre 1957- WhoHisp 94
Ferre, Leo d1993 NewYTBS 93
Ferre, Luis A. 1904- WhoAmP 93, WhoHisp 94
Ferré, M. Isolina 1914- WhoHisp 94
Ferre, Maurice Antonio 1935- WhoHisp 94
Ferre, Rosario 1942?- ConWorW 93, WhoHisp 94
Ferrebee, Thomas G. 1937- WhoBlA 94
Ferree, David Arthur 1952- WhoAmL 94
Ferree, David Curtis 1943- WhoScEn 94
Ferree, Thurman Thomas WhoAmP 93
Ferreira, Armando Thomas 1932- WhoAm 94, WhoAmA 93, WhoHisp 94
Ferreira, Daniel Alves 1944- WhoMW 93
Ferreira, Francis Joseph, Jr. 1938- WhoAmP 93
Ferreira, Jay Michael 1967- WhoScEn 94
Ferreira, Jesse T. 1917- WhoAmP 93
Ferreira, Jo Ann Jeanette Chanoux 1943- WhoFI 94
Ferreira, Jose, Jr. 1956- WhoAm 94, WhoFI 94
Ferreira, Judith Anne 1940- WhoWest 94
Ferreira, Maria Luisa Lourenco 1936- WhoWomW 91
Ferreira, Paulo Alexandre 1964- WhoMW 93, WhoScEn 94
Ferreira, Penelope Anne Simoes 1939- WhoAmL 94
Ferreira, Procopio d1979 WhoHol 92
Ferreira de la Cerda, Bernarda 1595-1644 BlmGWL
Ferreira Falcon, Magno 1936- WhoScEn 94
Ferreira Veiga, Jose Augusto NewGrDO
Ferreira-Worth, Deirdre Charlyn 1958- WhoWest 94
Ferreiro, Claudio Eduardo 1939- WhoHisp 94
Ferrel, Cipriano WhoHisp 94
Ferrel, William 1817-1891 WorScD
Ferrell, Ben 1937- WrDr 94
Ferrell, Catherine (Klemann) 1947- WhoAmA 93
Ferrell, Charles Stewart 1949- WhoAm 94, WhoAmL 94
Ferrell, Conchata 1943- IntMPA 94, WhoHol 92
Ferrell, Conchata Galen 1943- WhoAm 94
Ferrell, Daniel Lee 1949- WhoWest 94
Ferrell, David Lee 1937- WhoAm 94
Ferrell, Frank 1940- WrDr 94
Ferrell, James Edwin 1939- WhoMW 93
Ferrell, James Ellsworth, Jr. 1955- WhoWest 94
Ferrell, Jane d1952 WhoHol 92
Ferrell, Joe C. 1947- WhoAmP 93
Ferrell, John Frederick 1942- WhoAm 94
Ferrell, Milton Morgan, Jr. 1951- WhoAmL 94
Ferrell, Nancy Warren 1932- WhoWest 94
Ferrell, Rebecca V. 1955- WhoScEn 94
Ferrell, Robert Hugh 1921- WhoAm 94
Ferrell, Rosie E. 1915- WhoBlA 94
Ferrell, Tyra WhoBlA 94
Ferrell, Wayne Edward, Jr. 1946- WhoAmL 94
Ferrell, William Garland, Jr. 1955- WhoScEn 94
Ferrelo, Bartolome 1499-1548 WhWE
Ferren, John 1905-1970 WhoAmA 93N
Ferren, John Maxwell 1937- WhoAm 94, WhoAmL 94, WhoAmP 93
Ferrendelli, James Anthony 1936- WhoAm 94
Ferrentino, Carl Thomas 1951- WhoAmL 94
Ferreol, Andrea WhoHol 92
Ferrer, Betzaida 1943- WhoHisp 94
Ferrer, Concepcio 1938- WhoWomW 91
Ferrer, Elizabeth V. 1955- WhoHisp 94
Ferrer, Esteban A. 1925- WhoAm 94
Ferrer, Fernando 1950- WhoHisp 94
Ferrer, Gloria Esther 1952- WhoHisp 94
Ferrer, John David 1944- WhoHisp 94
Ferrer, Jose 1909- WhoHol 92
Ferrer, Jose 1912-1992 AnObit 1992, ConTFT 11
Ferrer, Jose Vicente 1912-1992 WhAm 10
Ferrer, Lupita 1952- WhoHol 92
Ferrer, Marie Irene 1915- WhoAm 94
Ferrer, Mayra Ivelisse WhoHisp 94
Ferrer, Mel 1917- IntMPA 94, WhoHol 92
Ferrer, Miguel WhoHisp 94
Ferrer, Miguel 1954- IntMPA 94
Ferrer, Miguel 1955- WhoHol 92
Ferrer, Miguel Antonio 1938- WhoAm 94
Ferrer, Rafael 1933- WhoAmA 93
Ferrer, Roberto Sanchez NewGrDO
Ferrera, Arthur Rodney 1916- WhoAm 94
Ferrera, Karen Ruth 1956- WhoAmL 94
Ferrera, Kenneth Grant 1945- WhoAm 94
Ferrera, Robert James 1937- WhoAm 94
Ferreri, Vito Richard 1949- WhoAmL 94
Ferrero, Anna Maria 1931- WhoHol 92
Ferrero, Danton d1987 WhoHol 92
Ferrero, Guillermo E. 1954- WhoHisp 94
Ferrero, Lorenzo 1951- NewGrDO
Ferrero, Louis Peter 1942- WhoAm 94, WhoFI 94, WhoMW 93
Ferrero, Martin WhoHol 92
Ferrero, Thomas Paul 1951- WhoScEn 94
Ferrers, Earl 1929- Who 94
Ferrers, Helen d1943 WhoHol 92
Ferrer Salat, Carlos IntWW 93
Ferret, Ege WhoHol 92
Ferretti, Dante ConTFT 11
Ferretti, Jacopo 1784-1852 NewGrDO
Ferrey, Edgar Eugene 1920-1988 WhAm 10
Ferrey, Marie Esperanza 1964- WhoHisp 94
Ferreyra, Guillermo S. 1953- WhoHisp 94
Ferreyra, Mariana 1962- WhoMW 93
Ferri, Alessandra 1963- IntDcB [port]
Ferri, Alessandra 1964- WhoHol 92
Ferri, Alessandra Maria 1963- WhoAm 94
Ferri, Baldassare 1610-1680 NewGrDO
Ferriar, John 1761-1815 EncSPD
Ferrie, Alexander Martin 1923- Who 94
Ferriell, Peter Paul 1955- WhoMW 93
Ferrier, Johan Henri Eliza 1910- IntWW 93
Ferrier, Joseph John 1959- WhoScEn 94
Ferrier, Kathleen (Mary) 1912-1953 NewGrDO
Ferrier, Loretta Jean 1937- WhoAm 94
Ferrier, Noel 1930- WhoHol 92
Ferrier, Richard Delahide 1948- WhoAmP 93
Ferrier, Robert Patton 1934- Who 94
Ferrier, Susan 1782-1854 BlmGWL
Ferrier, Susan Edmonstone 1782-1854 BlmGEL
Ferries, John Charles 1937- WhoAm 94, WhoFI 94
Ferrigno, Lou 1951- WhoHol 92
Ferrigno, Robert 1948?- ConAu 140
Ferril, Thomas Hornsby 1896- WhAm 10
Ferrin, Allan Wheeler 1921- WhoAm 94
Ferring, David EncSF 93
Ferrini, James Thomas 1938- WhoAm 94
Ferrini, Vincent DrAPF 93
Ferris Who 94
Ferris, Audrey 1909- WhoHol 92
Ferris, Barbara 1942- WhoHol 92
Ferris, Barton Purdy, Jr. 1940- WhoAm 94
Ferris, Benjamin Greeley, Jr. 1919- WhoAm 94
Ferris, Charles Daniel 1933- WhoAm 94, WhoAmP 93
Ferris, Clifford Duras 1935- WhoAm 94
Ferris, Daniel B. 1947- WhoAmA 93
Ferris, Ernest Joseph 1932- WhoAm 94
Ferris, Evelyn Scott WhoAmL 94, WhoWest 94
Ferris, Francis (Mursell) 1932- Who 94
Ferris, Frederick Joseph 1920- WhoAm 94
Ferris, George Mallette 1894-1992 WhAm 10
Ferris, George Mallette, Jr. 1927- WhoAm 94
Ferris, Grey F. WhoAmP 93
Ferris, J. David 1937- WhoIns 94
Ferris, Jack Lester 1945- WhoMW 93
Ferris, James Leonard 1944- WhoAm 94
Ferris, James Peter 1932- WhoAm 94
Ferris, Joseph Edward 1929- WhoMW 93
Ferris, (Carlisle) Keith 1929- WhoAmA 93
Ferris, Leo d1993 NewYTBS 93
Ferris, Melton 1916-1988 WhAm 10
Ferris, Michael James 1944- WhoFI 94
Ferris, Monk 1931-1992 WrDr 94N
Ferris, Paul 1929- WrDr 94
Ferris, Paul Frederick 1929- Who 94
Ferris, Robert Albert 1942- WhoAm 94
Ferris, Robert Edmund 1918- WhoAm 94
Ferris, Ronald Curry Who 94
Ferris, Ronald Curry 1945- WhoAm 94, WhoWest 94
Ferris, Russell James, II 1938- WhoWest 94
Ferris, Theodore Vincent 1919- WhoScEn 94
Ferris, Thomas Francis 1930- WhoAm 94
Ferris, Timothy 1944- WrDr 94
Ferris, Virginia Rogers WhoAm 94
Ferris, Walter V. 1930- WhoAmL 94
Ferris, Warren Angus 1810-1873 WhWE
Ferris, William (R.) 1942- WrDr 94
Ferris, William L. 1941- WhoIns 94
Ferris, William Michael 1948- WhoAmL 94
Ferriss, Abbott Lamoyne 1915- WrDr 94
Ferriss, David Platt 1919- WhoAm 94
Ferriter, Clare 1913- WhoAmA 93
Ferriter, John Pierce 1938- WhoAm 94
Ferriter, Warren Joseph 1938- WhoAm 94, WhoFI 94
Ferritor, Daniel E. 1939- WhoAm 94
Ferriz, Miguel Angel d1967 WhoHol 92
Ferro, Anthony J. WhoHisp 94
Ferro, Benedict WhoHisp 94
Ferro, Jorge 1948- WhoHisp 94
Ferro, Ramon 1941- WhoHisp 94
Ferro, Robert (Michael) 1941-1988 GayLL
Ferro, Simón WhoHisp 94
Ferro, Simon 1953- WhoAmL 94, WhoAmP 93
Ferro, Walter WhoAmA 93
Ferro, Walter 1925- WhoAm 94
Ferrone, Dan WhoHol 92
Ferrone, Patrick Francis 1919- WhoMW 93
Ferrone, Soldano 1940- WhoAm 94
Ferro-Nyalka, Ruth Rudys 1930- WhoMW 93
Ferroud, Pierre-Octave 1900-1936 NewGrDO

Ferrucci, Raymond Vincent 1926- *WhoAm 94*
Ferry, Alexander 1931- *Who 94*
Ferry, Andrew Peter 1929- *WhoAm 94*
Ferry, Bryan 1945- *WhoAm 94*
Ferry, David *DrAPF 93*
Ferry, David Keane 1940- *WhoAm 94*
Ferry, Donald E. 1932- *WhoAm 94*
Ferry, Donald J. *WhoAmP 93*
Ferry, James Allen 1937- *WhoAm 94*
Ferry, Joan Evans 1941- *WhoFI 94*
Ferry, John Douglass 1912- *IntWW 93, WhoAm 94, WhoScEn 94, WrDr 94*
Ferry, John Yeoman 1953- *WhoAmP 93*
Ferry, Joseph Vincent, Jr. 1947- *WhoFI 94*
Ferry, Michael Alan 1955- *WhoAmL 94*
Ferry, Miles Yeoman 1932- *WhoAm 94, WhoAmP 93*
Ferry, Richard Michael 1937- *WhoAm 94, WhoFI 94, WhoWest 94*
Ferry, Thomas Edward 1955- *WhoMW 93*
Ferry, Thomas Spencer, Jr. 1956- *WhoMW 93*
Ferry, Wilbur Hugh 1910- *WhoAm 94*
Ferry, William Curran 1949- *WhoIns 94*
Fersen, Hans Axel, Count von 1755-1810 *WhAmRev [port]*
Fersht, Alan Roy 1943- *IntWW 93, Who 94*
Fershtman, Julie Ilene 1961- *WhoAmL 94, WhoMW 93*
Ferslew, Kenneth Emil 1953- *WhoScEn 94*
Ferson, Lu Ann 1935- *WhoMW 93*
Ferst, Jeanne Rolfe 1918- *WhoAmP 93*
Ferst, Walter B. 1951- *WhoAmL 94*
Ferte, Denis Pierre Jean Papillon de la *NewGrDO*
Fertig, Howard *WhoAm 94*
Fertig, Ralph David Hays 1930- *WhoAmP 93*
Fertig, Ted Brian O'Day 1937- *WhoWest 94*
Fertik, Ira J. 1940- *WhoAm 94*
Fertner, Antoni 1950- *WhoScEn 94*
Ferugheli, Paul J. 1956- *WhoIns 94*
Ferwerda, Jan Annette 1954- *WhoMW 93*
Fery, John Bruce 1930- *IntWW 93, WhoAm 94, WhoFI 94, WhoWest 94*
Ferzacca, William 1927- *WhoMW 93*
Ferzetti, Gabriele 1925- *WhoHol 92*
Ferziger, Joel Henry 1937- *WhoWest 94*
Fesanio, Merindo *NewGrDO*
Fesca, Friedrich (Ernst) 1789-1826 *NewGrDO*
Fescemyer, Howard William 1957- *WhoScEn 94*
Feschenko, Alexander *WhoScEn 94*
Fesco, Edward J. 1930- *WhoMW 93*
Fesh, Robert M. 1937- *WhoAmP 93*
Fesh, Stephen James, Jr. 1943- *WhoAmP 93*
Feshbach, Herman 1917- *IntWW 93, WhoAm 94, WhoScEn 94*
Feshbach, Murray 1929- *ConAu 140*
Feshbach, Norma Deitch 1926- *WhoAm 94*
Feshbach, Seymour 1925- *WhoAm 94*
Fesko, Timothy *WhoAmP 93*
Feskoe, Gaffney Jon 1949- *WhoAm 94, WhoFI 94*
Fesler, David Richard 1928- *WhoAm 94*
Fesler, Donald C. 1948- *WhoAmL 94*
Fesperman, John T(homas) 1925- *WrDr 94*
Fesq, Lorraine Mae 1957- *WhoScEn 94, WhoWest 94*
Fess, Philip Eugene 1931- *WhoAm 94*
Fessenden, Ann T. 1951- *WhoAmL 94*
Fessenden, Anne Lathrop *DrAPF 93*
Fessenden, Daniel J. *WhoAmP 93*
Fessenden, Reginald Aubrey 1866-1932 *WorInv*
Fessey, Mereth Cecil 1917- *Who 94*
Fessler, Ann Helene 1949- *WhoAmA 93*
Fessler, Donald Francis 1931- *WhoFI 94*
Fessler, Richard Donald 1943- *WhoAmP 93*
Fessler, Thomas Allan 1957- *WhoAmL 94*
Fest, Thorrel Brooks 1910- *WhoAm 94*
Festa (Maffei), Francesca 1778-1835 *NewGrDO*
Festa, Roger Reginald 1950- *WhoAm 94, WhoMW 93*
Fetchit, Stepin d1985 *WhoHol 92*
Fetchit, Stepin 1896-1985 *WhoCom*
Fetchit, Stepin 1902-1985 *AfrAmAl 6*
Fetchko, Peter J. 1943- *WhoAm 94, WhoAmA 93*
Feth, Frederick Charles 1938- *WhoWest 94*
Fetherston, Shaun M. 1966- *WhoIns 94*
Fetherston-Dilke, Charles Beaumont 1921- *Who 94*
Fetherston-Dilke, Mary Stella 1918- *Who 94*
Fetherstone, Eddie d1965 *WhoHol 92*
Fetis, Francois-Joseph 1784-1871 *NewGrDO*
Fetler, Andrew *DrAPF 93*
Fetler, Andrew 1925- *WhoAm 94*
Fetler, Paul 1920- *WhoAm 94*
Fetner, Robert Henry 1922- *WhoAm 94*
Fetridge, Bonnie-Jean Clark 1915- *WhoAm 94, WhoMW 93*
Fetridge, Clark Worthington 1946- *WhoAm 94, WhoAmP 93, WhoMW 93*
Fetridge, William Harrison 1906- *WhoAmP 93*
Fetridge, William Harrison 1906-1989 *WhAm 10*
Fetscher, Iring 1922- *IntWW 93*
Fetscher, Paul George William 1945- *WhoAm 94*
Fett, Eugene Werner 1932- *WhoAm 94*
Fett, William F. 1918- *WhoAmA 93*
Fetter, Alexander Lees 1937- *WhoAm 94*
Fetter, Frank Whitson 1899-1991 *WhAm 10*
Fetter, Richard Elwood 1923- *WhoAm 94*
Fetter, Robert Barclay 1924- *WhoAm 94*
Fetter, Steve 1959- *WhoScEn 94*
Fetter, Steven Michael 1952- *WhoMW 93*
Fetter, Theodore Henry 1906- *WhoAm 94*
Fetter, Trevor 1960- *WhoFI 94*
Fetter, Victor Peter, III 1968- *WhoFI 94*
Fetterman, James C. 1947- *WhoAmL 94*
Fetterolf, Charles Frederick 1928- *IntWW 93*
Fetters, Karl Leroy 1909-1990 *EncABHB 9*
Fetters, Norman Craig, II 1942- *WhoAm 94*
Fetters, Thomas Torrence 1938- *WhoFI 94*
Fetting, Fritz 1926- *WhoScEn 94*
Fetting, Rainer 1949- *IntWW 93, WhoAmA 93*
Fettinger, George Edgar 1929- *WhoAmP 93*
Fettiplace, Robert 1946- *Who 94, WhoMW 93, WhoScEn 94*
Fettweis, Alfred Leo Maria 1926- *IntWW 93*
Fettweis, Gunter Bernhard Leo 1924- *IntWW 93, WhoScEn 94*
Fettweis, Robert J. 1947- *WhoAmL 94*
Fetz, Anita 1957- *WhoWomW 91*
Fetzer, Brian Charles 1950- *WhoAmL 94*
Fetzer, David Guy 1951- *WhoWest 94*
Fetzer, Edward Frank 1940- *WhoAm 94*
Fetzer, James Henry 1940- *WhoMW 93*
Fetzer, John E. 1901- *IntMPA 94*
Fetzer, John Earl 1901-1991 *WhAm 10*
Fetzer, Mark Stephen 1950- *WhoAmL 94*
Feucht, Donald Lee 1933- *WhoAm 94, WhoScEn 94*
Feuchtenberger, William Pence 1930- *WhoAmP 93*
Feuchtersleben, Ernst, Freiherr von 1806-1849 *DcLB 133 [port]*
Feuchtersleben, Ernst von 1806-1849 *EncSPD*
Feuchtwang, Thomas Emanuel 1930- *WhoAm 94*
Feuer, Cy 1911- *WhoAm 94*
Feuer, Debra *WhoHol 92*
Feuer, Henry 1912- *WhoAm 94*
Feuer, Jerold 1945- *WhoAmL 94*
Feuer, Joseph N. 1940- *WhoAmP 93*
Feuer, Robert A. 1941- *WhoAmP 93*
Feuerbach, Ludwig 1804-1872 *DcLB 133 [port]*
Feuerbach, Ludwig (Andreas) 1804-1872 *EncEth*
Feuerberg, Mark Stanley 1942- *WhoFI 94*
Feuerherd, Victor Edmond 1925- *WhoFI 94*
Feuerherm, Kurt K. 1925- *WhoAmA 93*
Feuerlein, Willy John Arthur 1911- *WhoAm 94*
Feuerman, Carol Jeannne 1945- *WhoAmA 93*
Feuermann, Claudio A. *WhoHisp 94*
Feuerstein, Alan Ricky 1950- *WhoAmL 94*
Feuerstein, Donald Martin 1937- *WhoAm 94, WhoAmL 94*
Feuerstein, Georg 1947- *WhoWest 94*
Feuerstein, Georg W 1947- *WrDr 94*
Feuerstein, Herbert 1927- *WhoFI 94*
Feuerstein, Howard M. 1939- *WhoAm 94*
Feuerstein, Marcy Berry 1950- *WhoWest 94*
Feuerstein, Martin 1924- *WhoAmP 93*
Feuerstein, Roberta 1950- *WhoAmA 93*
Feuerstein, Ronald A. 1947- *WhoAmL 94*
Feuerwerker, Albert 1927- *WhoAm 94, WrDr 94*
Feuerzeig, Henry Louis 1938- *WhoAm 94*
Feuge, Oskar 1861-1913 *NewGrDO*
Feuille, Richard Harlan 1920- *WhoAm 94*
Feuillere, Edwige 1907- *WhoHol 92*
Feuillere, Edwige 1910- *IntWW 93*
Feuillere, Edwige 1943- *Who 94*
Feuillet, Christian Patrice 1948- *WhoScEn 94*
Feuillet, Raoul Auger c. 1660-1710 *IntDcB [port]*
Feulner, Edwin John, Jr. 1941- *WhoAm 94, WhoAmP 93, WhoFI 94, WhoScEn 94*
Feulner, Melvin Joseph 1948- *WhoMW 93*
Feury, Peg d1985 *WhoHol 92*
Feusier, Norman d1945 *WhoHol 92*
Feusner, LeRoy Carroll 1945- *WhoScEn 94*
Feussner, Alfred d1969 *WhoHol 92*
Feustking, Friedrich Christian 1678-1739 *NewGrDO*
Feuvrel, Sidney Leo, Jr. 1948- *WhoAmL 94*
Feversham, Baron 1945- *Who 94*
Fevery, Patrick Edmond 1955- *WhoWest 94*
Fevrier, Henry 1875-1957 *NewGrDO*
Fevurly, Keith Robert 1951- *WhoAmL 94*
Few, Benjamin Ferguson 1894- *WhAm 10*
Few, James Cecil 1930- *WhoAmA 93*
Few, William 1748-1828 *WhAmRev*
Few, William P. 1943- *WhoAmL 94*
Fewel, Harriett 1943- *WhoAmL 94*
Fewell, Charles Kenneth, Jr. 1943- *WhoAmL 94, WhoFI 94*
Fewell, Kenneth Robert 1948- *WhoIns 94*
Fewell, Richard 1937- *WhoBlA 94*
Fey, Dorothy *WhoAm 94*
Fey, Gary Michael 1945- *WhoFI 94*
Fey, Harold Edward 1898-1990 *WhAm 10*
Fey, John Theodore 1917- *WhoAm 94*
Fey, Robert Michael 1942- *WhoWest 94*
Fey, Thomas H. 1954- *WhoAmP 93*
Feydeau, Georges (-Leon-Jules-Marie) 1862-1921 *IntDcT 2 [port]*
Feyder, Jacques d1948 *WhoHol 92*
Feyder, Jean 1947- *IntWW 93*
Feyerabend, Paul K(arl) 1924- *WrDr 94*
Feyerabend, Paul Karl 1924- *WhoAm 94*
Feyh, Nancy Jean 1939- *WhoMW 93*
Feyide, Meshach Otokiti 1926- *IntWW 93*
Feyl, Susan 1947- *WhoScEn 94*
Feynman, Richard P. d1988 *NobelP 91N*
Feynman, Richard Phillips 1918- *IntWW 93*
Feynman, Richard Phillips 1918-1988 *WorScD [port]*
Feyzioglu, Turhan 1922- *IntWW 93*
Fezandie, (Ernest) Clement 1865-1959 *EncSF 93*
Ffitch, George Norman 1929- *Who 94*
Ffolkes, Marco Rodgers 1953- *WhoFI 94*
Ffolkes, Robert (Francis Alexander) 1943- *Who 94*
Ffolliott, Gladys d1928 *WhoHol 92*
Fforde, John Standish 1921- *IntWW 93, Who 94*
Ffowcs Williams, John Eirwyn 1935- *Who 94*
Ffrangcon-Davies, Gwen 1896- *WhoHol 92*
Ffrench, Baron 1956- *Who 94*
Ffrench-Davis, Ricardo 1936- *IntWW 93*
Ffytche, Timothy John 1936- *Who 94*
Fiacc, Padraic 1924- *WrDr 94*
Fiad, Roberto Eduardo 1958- *WhoHisp 94*
Fiala, David Marcus 1946- *WhoAmL 94, WhoMW 93*
Fiala, Marie L. 1952- *WhoAmL 94*
Fialer, Philip Anthony 1938- *WhoAm 94, WhoWest 94*
Fialko, Nathan 1881- *EncSF 93*
Fialkoff, Jay R. 1951- *WhoAm 94, WhoAmL 94*
Fialkov, Herman 1922- *WhoAm 94*
Fialkow, Philip Jack 1934- *WhoAm 94, WhoWest 94*
Fialkow, Steven 1943- *WhoFI 94*
Fialkowski, Barbara *DrAPF 93*
Fiamengo, Marya 1926- *BlmGWL*
Fiandach, Edward Louis 1953- *WhoAmL 94*
Fiander, Lewis 1938- *WhoHol 92*
Fiasconaro, Gregorio 1915- *NewGrDO*
Fibak, Wojtek 1952- *BuCMET*
Fibich, Howard Raymond 1932- *WhoAm 94*
Fibich, Zdenek (Antonin Vaclav) 1850-1900 *NewGrDO*
Fibiger, John Andrew 1932- *WhoAm 94, WhoWest 94*
Fibonacci, Leonardo c. 1170-c. 1230 *WorScD*
Fica, Juan 1949- *WhoScEn 94*
Ficalora, Joseph Paul 1957- *WhoScEn 94*
Ficano, Robert A. 1952- *WhoMW 93*
Ficano, Robert Anthony 1952- *WhoAmP 93*
Ficaro, Michael A. 1947- *WhoAmL 94*
Fichenberg, Robert Gordon 1920- *WhoAm 94*
Fichman, Fred *EncSF 93*
Fichman, Mark 1952- *WhoScEn 94*
Fichte, Johann Gottlieb 1762-1814 *EncEth*
Fichtel, Carl Edwin 1933- *WhoAm 94*
Fichtel, Dennis James 1952- *WhoFI 94*
Fichtel, Rudolph Robert 1915- *WhoAm 94*
Fichtenau, Heinrich 1912- *IntWW 93*
Fichter, George S. 1922-1993 *WrDr 94N*
Fichter, Herbert Francis 1920- *WhoAmA 93*
Fichter, John W. 1935- *WhoAmP 93*
Fichter, Joseph 1908- *ConAu 41NR*
Fichter, Joseph H. 1908- *WhoAm 94*
Fichter, Robert W. 1939- *WhoAmA 93*
Fichthorn, Luke Eberly, III 1941- *WhoAm 94*
Fichtner, Jay Sheldon 1926- *WhoAmL 94*
Fick, Earl Dean 1944- *WhoFI 94*
Fick, Gary Warren 1943- *WhoAm 94*
Fick, Gerhardt N. 1942- *WhoMW 93*
Fick, Walter Henry 1951- *WhoMW 93*
Ficken, Bruce W. 1948- *WhoAmL 94*
Ficker, Robin *WhoAmP 93*
Fickert, Kurt J 1920- *WrDr 94*
Fickert, Rob 1951- *WhoMW 93*
Fickett, Bob H. 1924- *WhoAmP 93*
Fickett, Edward Hale 1918- *WhoAm 94*
Fickett, Lewis Perley, Jr. 1926- *WhoAmP 93*
Fickett, Mary 1927- *WhoHol 92*
Fickinger, Wayne Joseph 1926- *WhoAm 94, WhoFI 94*
Fickle, Dorothy Helen 1921- *WhoMW 93*
Fickle, Stanley C. 1944- *WhoAmL 94*
Fickle, William Dick 1943- *WhoAmL 94, WhoMW 93*
Ficklen, Jack Howells 1911-1980 *WhoAmA 93N*
Fickler, Arlene 1951- *WhoAmL 94*
Fickling, Benjamin William 1909- *Who 94*
Fickling, William Arthur, Jr. 1932- *WhoAm 94*
Ficks, F. Lawrence 1930- *WhoFI 94*
Ficks, R. Snowden *EncSF 93*
Fidanza, Giovanni 1939- *WhoAm 94, WhoFI 94*
Fiddes, James Raffan 1919- *Who 94*
Fiddick, Paul William 1949- *WhoAm 94*
Fiddick, Peter Ronald 1938- *Who 94*
Fiddler, Adam 1865-1959 *EncNAR*
Fiddler, Jack c. 1820-1907 *EncNAR*
Fiddler, Joseph c. 1856-1909 *EncNAR*
Fidel, Howard Francis 1950- *WhoFI 94*
Fidel, Joseph A. 1923- *WhoAmP 93, WhoHisp 94*
Fidell, Linda Selzer 1942- *WhoScEn 94*
Fides, Peter Jon, II 1951- *WhoAmL 94*
Fidis, Coventine 1947- *WhoHisp 94*
Fidjestol, Bjarne 1937- *IntWW 93*
Fidler, Carol Ann 1942- *WhoMW 93*
Fidler, Charles Robert 1964- *WhoMW 93*
Fidler, Jan 1927- *Who 94*
Fidler, Jimmie d1988 *WhoHol 92*
Fidler, Ronald Wayne 1932- *WhoAmL 94*
Fidler, Spencer D. 1944- *WhoAmA 93*
Fidler-Simpson, John Cody *Who 94*
Fiebach, H. Robert 1939- *WhoAm 94, WhoAmL 94*
Fiebelman, Kenneth Franklin 1941- *WhoAmP 93*
Fiebert, Erik 1957- *WhoFI 94*
Fiebiger, James Russell 1941- *WhoFI 94*
Fiebiger, Stephen Charles 1958- *WhoAmL 94*
Fiebrink, Mark Edward 1951- *WhoIns 94*
Fiedeler, Hans *ConAu 141*
Fiedler, Bobbi 1937- *WhoAmP 93, WhoWomW 91*
Fiedler, Fred E 1922- *WrDr 94*
Fiedler, Fred Edward 1922- *WhoAm 94*
Fiedler, Harold Joseph 1924- *WhoAm 94*
Fiedler, Jean *DrAPF 93*
Fiedler, John *IntMPA 94*
Fiedler, John 1925- *WhoHol 92*
Fiedler, John Amberg 1941- *WhoFI 94, WhoWest 94*
Fiedler, Laurie W. 1960- *WhoAmL 94*
Fiedler, Lee N. 1940- *WhoAm 94, WhoFI 94*
Fiedler, Leigh Allan 1930- *WhoMW 93*
Fiedler, Leslie A. *DrAPF 93*
Fiedler, Leslie A(aron) 1917- *EncSF 93, WrDr 94*
Fiedler, Leslie Aaron 1917- *WhoAm 94*
Fiedler, Patrick James 1953- *WhoAm 94*
Fiedler, Robert Max 1945- *WhoMW 93, WhoScEn 94*
Fiedler, Sally A. *DrAPF 93*
Fiegen, Kristie K. *WhoAmP 93*
Fieger, Geoffrey Nels 1950- *NewYTBS 93 [port]*
Fiel, Maxine Lucille *WhoAm 94*
Field, A. J. 1924- *WhoAm 94*
Field, Alexander d1971 *WhoHol 92*
Field, Alexander James 1949- *WhoFI 94, WhoScEn 94, WhoWest 94*

Field, Andrea Bear 1949- *WhoAm 94, WhoAmL 94*
Field, Anne 1926- *Who 94*
Field, Arnold 1917- *Who 94*
Field, Arthur Norman 1935- *WhoAm 94*
Field, Barry John Anthony 1946- *Who 94*
Field, Ben d1939 *WhoHol 92*
Field, Betty d1973 *WhoHol 92*
Field, Carol Hart 1940- *WhoWest 94*
Field, Charles William 1934- *WhoWest 94*
Field, Chelsea *WhoHol 92*
Field, Christopher Alan 1965- *WhoWest 94*
Field, Crystal 1940- *WhoHol 92*
Field, Cyrus Adams 1902- *WhoAm 94*
Field, D. M. 1938- *WrDr 94*
Field, Dave *WhoHol 92*
Field, David (McLucas) 1944- *WrDr 94*
Field, David M. *IntMPA 94*
Field, Dorothy 1926- *WhoScEn 94*
Field, Edward *DrAPF 93*
Field, Edward 1924- *WrDr 94*
Field, Ellen 1952- *WhoAmP 93*
Field, Eugene 1850-1895 *DcLB 140 [port]*
Field, Frances *WhoAmP 93*
Field, Francis Edward 1923- *WhoScEn 94*
Field, Frank 1942- *Who 94, WrDr 94*
Field, Fred Howard 1928- *WhoWest 94*
Field, Frederick Gorham, Jr. 1932- *WhoAmP 93*
Field, Frederick V(anderbilt) 1905- *WrDr 94*
Field, Gans T. *EncSF 93*
Field, Geoffrey William 1941- *Who 94*
Field, George d1925 *WhoHol 92*
Field, George Brooks 1929- *WhoAm 94, WhoScEn 94*
Field, George Sydney 1905- *WhoAm 94*
Field, Gladys d1920 *WhoHol 92*
Field, Harold David, Jr. 1927- *WhoAm 94*
Field, Helen 1951- *IntWW 93, NewGrDO*
Field, Henry Augustus, Jr. 1928- *WhoAm 94*
Field, Henry Frederick 1941- *WhoAm 94*
Field, Hermann Haviland 1910- *WhoAm 94, WrDr 94*
Field, Ian Trevor 1933- *Who 94*
Field, James Bernard 1926- *WhoAm 94*
Field, Jeffrey Frederic 1954- *WhoWest 94*
Field, Jill Margaret 1934- *Who 94*
Field, Joanna 1900- *WrDr 94*
Field, John *Who 94*
Field, John 1921-1991 *IntDcB [port]*
Field, (Edward) John 1936- *Who 94*
Field, John Douglas 1964- *WhoScEn 94*
Field, John Edwin 1936- *Who 94*
Field, John Louis 1930- *WhoAm 94*
Field, Joseph Myron 1932- *WhoAm 94*
Field, Karen Ann 1936- *WhoMW 93*
Field, Kathleen d1980 *WhoHol 92*
Field, Kathleen Cottrell 1955- *WhoAmL 94*
Field, Lawrence Jeffrey 1955- *WhoAmL 94*
Field, Lyman 1914- *WhoAm 94, WhoAmA 93*
Field, Madalynne *WhoHol 92*
Field, Malcolm (David) 1937- *Who 94*
Field, Malcolm David 1937- *IntWW 93*
Field, Margaret 1923- *WhoHol 92*
Field, Mark G(eorge) 1923- *WrDr 94*
Field, Marshall 1941- *WhoAm 94*
Field, Marshall Hayward 1930- *Who 94*
Field, Mary *WhoHol 92*
Field, Michael *BlmGWL*
Field, Michael Robert 1945- *WhoMW 93*
Field, Michael Stanley 1940- *WhoFI 94, WhoScEn 94*
Field, Michael Walter 1948- *IntWW 93, Who 94*
Field, Morton Richard 1923- *WhoWest 94*
Field, Nathaniel 1587-1633 *BlmGEL*
Field, Noel Macdonald, Jr. 1934- *WhoAm 94*
Field, Norman d1956 *WhoHol 92*
Field, Peter 1926- *WhoAmP 93*
Field, Philip Sidney 1942- *WhoAmA 93*
Field, Rachel 1894-1942 *BlmGWL*
Field, Richard Alan 1947- *Who 94*
Field, Richard Clark 1940- *WhoAm 94, WhoAmL 94*
Field, Richard Jeffrey 1941- *WhoWest 94*
Field, Richard Sampson 1931- *WhoAmA 93*
Field, Robert Edward 1945- *WhoAm 94, WhoAmL 94, WhoFI 94, WhoMW 93*
Field, Robert Eugene 1946- *WhoScEn 94*
Field, Robert Isaac 1952- *WhoAmL 94*
Field, Robert Steven 1949- *WhoMW 93*
Field, Robert Warren 1944- *WhoAm 94, WhoScEn 94*
Field, Sally 1946- *IntMPA 94, WhoAm 94, WhoHol 92*
Field, Saul 1912-1987 *WhoAmA 93N*
Field, Shirley Ann 1936- *WhoHol 92*
Field, Shirley-Anne 1938- *IntMPA 94*
Field, Sid d1950 *WhoHol 92*
Field, Stanley *DrAPF 93*
Field, Steven Philip 1951- *WhoScEn 94*
Field, Sylvia 1901- *WhoHol 92*
Field, Ted *IntMPA 94, WhoAm 94*
Field, Virginia 1917- *WhoHol 92*
Field, Walter d1976 *WhoHol 92*
Field, William Bruce 1941- *WhoAmP 93*
Field, William James 1909- *Who 94*
Field, William Stephenson 1929- *WhoAm 94*
Fieldbinder, A. Christine 1951- *WhoMW 93*
Fielden, C. Franklin, III 1946- *WhoWest 94*
Fielden, Frank 1915- *Who 94*
Fielder, Barbara Lee 1942- *WhoWest 94*
Fielder, Cecil Grant 1963- *WhoAm 94, WhoBlA 94, WhoMW 93*
Fielder, Charles Robert 1943- *WhoAm 94, WhoFI 94*
Fielder, Fred Charles 1933- *WhoBlA 94*
Fielder, Leslie A. 1917- *IntWW 93*
Fielder, Mildred 1913- *WrDr 94*
Field-Fisher, Thomas Gilbert 1915- *Who 94*
Fieldhammer, Eugene Louis 1925- *WhoScEn 94*
Fieldhouse, Brian 1933- *Who 94*
Fieldhouse, David K(enneth) 1925- *WrDr 94*
Fieldhouse, David Kenneth 1925- *Who 94*
Fieldhouse, David Kenneth 1927- *IntWW 93*
Fieldhouse, John 1928-1992 *AnObit 1992*
Fielding, A(lexander) W(allace) 1918- *WrDr 94*
Fielding, Allen Fred 1943- *WhoAm 94*
Fielding, Colin (Cunningham) 1926- *Who 94*
Fielding, Edward d1945 *WhoHol 92*
Fielding, Elizabeth May 1917- *WhoAm 94, WhoAmP 93*
Fielding, Fenella 1930- *WhoHol 92*
Fielding, Fenella Marion 1934- *Who 94*
Fielding, Fred F. 1939- *WhoAmP 93*
Fielding, Fred Fisher 1939- *WhoAm 94*
Fielding, Harold Preston 1930- *WhoFI 94, WhoWest 94*
Fielding, Henry 1707-1754 *BlmGEL [port], IntDcT 2, NewGrDO*
Fielding, Herbert U. 1923- *WhoAmP 93*
Fielding, Herbert Ulysses 1923- *WhoBlA 94*
Fielding, Ivor Rene 1942- *WhoAm 94*
Fielding, Joy 1945- *ConAu 43NR*
Fielding, Judith L. 1938- *WhoAmL 94*
Fielding, Leslie 1932- *IntWW 93, Who 94*
Fielding, Marjery d1988 *WhoHol 92*
Fielding, Marjorie d1956 *WhoHol 92*
Fielding, Nigel G(oodwin) 1950- *WrDr 94*
Fielding, Paul N. *WhoAmP 93*
Fielding, Raymond 1931- *WrDr 94*
Fielding, Richard Walter 1933- *Who 94*
Fielding, Romaine d1927 *WhoHol 92*
Fielding, Ronald Herbert 1949- *WhoFI 94*
Fielding, Ronald Roy 1961- *WhoMW 93, WhoScEn 94*
Fielding, Sarah 1710-1768 *BlmGEL, BlmGWL*
Fielding, Stuart 1939- *WhoAm 94, WhoScEn 94*
Fielding, Xan 1918- *WrDr 94*
Fieldman, Leon 1926- *WhoAm 94*
Fieldman, Wayne Lyle 1944- *WhoMW 93*
Fields, Alan *IntMPA 94*
Fields, Alva Dotson 1929- *WhoBlA 94*
Fields, Annie Adams 1834-1915 *BlmGWL*
Fields, Anthony Lindsay Austin 1943- *WhoAm 94*
Fields, Benny d1959 *WhoHol 92*
Fields, Bernard Nathan 1938- *WhoAm 94, WhoScEn 94*
Fields, Bertram Harris 1929- *WhoAm 94*
Fields, Bessie Marie Williams 1940- *WhoAm 94*
Fields, Bill 1949- *WhoFI 94*
Fields, Brenda Joyce *WhoBlA 94*
Fields, C. Virginia 1946- *WhoAmP 93*
Fields, Chip 1952- *WhoHol 92*
Fields, Cleo 1962- *CngDr 93, WhoAm 94, WhoAmP 93, WhoBlA 94*
Fields, Curtis Grey 1933- *WhoFI 94, WhoMW 93*
Fields, Darrel Rex 1925- *WhoWest 94*
Fields, David C. 1937- *WhoAmP 93*
Fields, David Clark 1937- *WhoAm 94*
Fields, Debbi *ConAu 140*
Fields, Debra J. 1956- *ConAu 140*
Fields, Dennis H. 1945- *WhoAmP 93*
Fields, Dexter L. 1944- *WhoBlA 94*
Fields, Dorothy d1974 *WhoHol 92*
Fields, Douglas Philip 1942- *WhoAm 94*
Fields, Earl Grayson 1935- *WhoBlA 94*
Fields, Edward E. 1918- *WhoBlA 94*
Fields, Ellis Kirby 1917- *WhoAm 94, WhoScEn 94*
Fields, Ewaugh Finney *WhoBlA 94*
Fields, Freddie 1923- *IntMPA 94, WhoAm 94*
Fields, Fredrica H. 1912- *WhoAmA 93*
Fields, Gracie d1979 *WhoHol 92*
Fields, Henry Michael 1946- *WhoAm 94, WhoAmL 94*
Fields, Hugh G. 1930- *WhoAmP 93*
Fields, Inez C. *WhoBlA 94*
Fields, Jack E. 1952- *WhoAmL 94*
Fields, Jack M., Jr. 1952- *CngDr 93, WhoAmP 93*
Fields, Jack Milton, Jr. 1952- *WhoAm 94*
Fields, Joseph Newton, III 1949- *WhoScEn 94*
Fields, Julia *DrAPF 93*
Fields, Kathy 1947- *WhoHol 92*
Fields, Kenneth 1962- *WhoBlA 94*
Fields, Kim 1969- *WhoBlA 94, WhoHol 92*
Fields, Larkin W. *WhoIns 94*
Fields, Leo 1928- *WhoAm 94*
Fields, Lew d1941 *WhoHol 92*
Fields, Lew 1867-1941 *See* Weber and Fields *WhoCom*
Fields, Lloyd L. 1957- *WhoAmP 93*
Fields, M. Joan 1934- *WhoBlA 94*
Fields, Mitchell 1901-1966 *WhoAmA 93N*
Fields, Paul Robert 1919- *WhoAm 94*
Fields, R. Wayne 1941- *WhoWest 94*
Fields, Ralph Raymond 1907- *WhoAm 94*
Fields, Renee Christine 1953- *WhoMW 93*
Fields, Richard A. 1950- *WhoBlA 94*
Fields, Rick *DrAPF 93*
Fields, Robert *WhoHol 92*
Fields, Robert Charles 1920- *WhoAm 94*
Fields, Robert Ernest, III 1958- *WhoAmL 94*
Fields, Samuel Bennie 1925- *WhoBlA 94*
Fields, Savoynne Morgan 1950- *WhoBlA 94*
Fields, Scott (Gary) 1956- *WrDr 94*
Fields, Shep d1981 *WhoHol 92*
Fields, Sidney d1975 *WhoHol 92*
Fields, Spencer D. 1959- *WhoFI 94*
Fields, Stanley d1941 *WhoHol 92*
Fields, Stanley 1930- *WhoBlA 94*
Fields, Stuart Howard 1943- *WhoFI 94*
Fields, Suzanne Bregman 1936- *WhoAm 94*
Fields, Terence 1937- *Who 94*
Fields, Theodore 1922- *WhoAm 94*
Fields, Thomas Eric 1948- *WhoAmP 93*
Fields, Tommy d1988 *WhoHol 92*
Fields, Tony Dean *WhoHol 92*
Fields, Totie 1930-1978 *WhoCom*
Fields, Verna d1982 *IntDcF 2-4 [port]*
Fields, Victor Hugo 1907- *WhoBlA 94*
Fields, W. C. d1946 *WhoHol 92*
Fields, W.C. 1880-1946 *WhoCom [port]*
Fields, Wayne 1942- *WrDr 94*
Fields, Wendy Lynn 1946- *WhoAm 94*
Fields, William Albert 1939- *WhoAm 94*
Fields, William Alexander 1959- *WhoScEn 94*
Fields, William Hudson, III 1934- *WhoAm 94*
Fields, William I., Jr. 1944- *WhoBlA 94*
Fields, William Jay 1936- *WhoAm 94, WhoFI 94*
Fieldsend, John Charles Rowell 1921- *IntWW 93, Who 94*
Fieleke, Norman Siegfried 1932- *WhoAm 94*
Fielstra, Helen Adams 1921- *WhoAm 94*
Fienberg, Karen Dana 1966- *WhoWest 94*
Fienberg, Stephen Elliott 1942- *WhoAm 94*
Fiene, Alicia W. 1919-1961 *WhoAmA 93N*
Fiene, Ernest 1894-1965 *WhoAmA 93N*
Fiennes *Who 94*
Fiennes, Celia 1662-1741 *BlmGWL, DcNaB MP, WhWE*
Fiennes, Maurice (Alberic Twisleton-Wykeham-) 1907- *Who 94*
Fiennes, Oliver William Twisleton-Wykeham- 1926- *Who 94*
Fiennes, Ralph *IntWW 93*
Fiennes, Ranulph (Twisleton-Wykeham-), Sir 1944- *WrDr 94*
Fiennes, Ranulph Twisleton-Wykeham- 1944- *IntWW 93, Who 94*
Fiennes-Clinton *Who 94*
Fier, Elihu 1931- *WhoAm 94*
Fierce, Hughlyn F. *WhoBlA 94*
Fierce, Milfred C. 1937- *WhoBlA 94*
Fierer, Joshua Allan 1937- *WhoAm 94*
Fierheller, George Alfred 1933- *WhoAm 94*
Fiering, Norman Sanford 1935- *WhoAm 94*
Fierke, Thomas Garner 1948- *WhoAmL 94*
Fierla, Linda Lea 1951- *WhoMW 93*
Fierman, Gerald Shea 1924- *WhoFI 94, WhoScEn 94*
Fiero, Emilie L. 1889-1974 *WhoAmA 93N*
Fiero, Gloria K. 1939- *WhoAmA 93*
Fiero, Patricia G. *WhoAmP 93*
Fierro, Alex 1927- *WhoHisp 94*
Fierro, Paul *WhoHol 92*
Fierros, Juan Enrique 1951- *WhoHisp 94*
Fierros, Mario 1926- *WhoHisp 94*
Fierst, Glen Allen 1937- *WhoMW 93*
Fierstein, Harvey *IntWW 93*
Fierstein, Harvey 1954- *GayLL, IntMPA 94, WhoHol 92*
Fierstein, Harvey (Forbes) 1954- *ConDr 93, IntDcT 2, WrDr 94*
Fierstein, Harvey Forbes 1954- *WhoAm 94*
Fierstein, Ira 1952- *WhoAmL 94*
Fies, James David 1950- *WhoMW 93*
Fiesta, Lorenzo Eddrada 1950- *WhoWest 94*
Fiester, Clark George 1934- *WhoAm 94*
Fietsam, Robert Charles 1927- *WhoFI 94, WhoMW 93*
Fife, Duke of 1929- *Who 94*
Fife, Barbara J. *WhoAmP 93*
Fife, Bernard 1915- *WhoAm 94, WhoFI 94*
Fife, Dennis Jensen 1945- *WhoWest 94*
Fife, Edward H. 1942- *WhoAm 94*
Fife, Eugene Vawter 1940- *WhoAm 94, WhoFI 94*
Fife, Jerry Leo 1948- *WhoWest 94*
Fife, John Douglas, Jr. 1955- *WhoFI 94*
Fife, Jonathan Donald 1941- *WhoAm 94*
Fife, William Franklin 1921- *WhoAm 94*
Fife, William J., Jr. 1938- *WhoAm 94, WhoFI 94, WhoScEn 94*
Fife, Wilmer Krafft 1933- *WhoScEn 94*
Fifer, Edith Mary Caldwell *WhoMW 93*
Fifer, Ken *DrAPF 93*
Fifer, Samuel 1950- *WhoAm 94, WhoAmL 94*
Fifferi, Lauro *NewGrDO*
Fifield, Christopher G(eorge) 1945- *WrDr 94*
Fifield, Esther L. *WhoAmP 93*
Fifield, Russell Hunt 1914- *WhoAm 94*
Fifield, William O. 1946- *WhoAm 94, WhoAmL 94*
Fiflis, Ted J. 1933- *WhoAm 94*
Fifner, Douglas Karl 1953- *WhoAmL 94*
Fifoot, Paul Ronald Ninnes 1928- *Who 94*
Figa, Phillip Sam 1951- *WhoAmL 94*
Figard, Steve David 1954- *WhoMW 93*
Figaro, Mark O. 1921- *WhoBlA 94*
Figdor, Peter 1941- *WhoAmL 94*
Figen, I. Sevki 1924- *WhoScEn 94*
Figes, Eva 1932- *BlmGEL, BlmGWL, WrDr 94*
Figg, Leonard (Clifford William) 1923- *Who 94*
Figg, Mary 1934- *WhoAmP 93*
Figg, William Carl, Jr. 1949- *WhoWest 94*
Figge, F. J., II *WhoAm 94*
Figge, Frederick Henry, Jr. 1934- *WhoAm 94, WhoFI 94*
Figgess, John (George) 1909- *Who 94*
Figgie, Harry E., Jr. 1923- *WhoAm 94, WhoFI 94*
Figgins, David Forrester 1929- *WhoAm 94*
Figgins, Letha Arlene 1916- *WhoMW 93*
Figgis, Anthony St. John Howard 1940- *Who 94*
Figgis, Arthur Lenox 1918- *Who 94*
Figgis, Brian Norman 1930- *IntWW 93*
Figgis, N.P. 1939- *EncSF 93*
Figlar, Anita Wise 1950- *WhoFI 94*
Figley, Charles Ray 1944- *WhoScEn 94*
Figley, Melvin Morgan 1920- *WhoAm 94*
Figliola, Richard Stephen 1952- *WhoScEn 94*
Figman, Elliot *DrAPF 93*
Figman, Max d1952 *WhoHol 92*
Figman, Oscar d1930 *WhoHol 92*
Fignar, Eugene Michael 1946- *WhoAmL 94*
Fignar, Rosemary Casey 1945- *WhoFI 94*
Figner, Medea *NewGrDO*
Figner, Nikolay Nikolayevich 1857-1918 *NewGrDO*
Figueira, Thomas J. 1948- *ConAu 142*
Figueiredo, Cynthia Marston 1954- *WhoWest 94*
Figueiredo, Elisio de 1940- *IntWW 93*
Figueiredo, Hubert Fernandes 1958- *WhoWest 94*
Figueiredo, Joao Baptista de 1918- *IntWW 93*
Figueredo, Danilo H. 1951- *WhoHisp 94*
Figueroa, Adolfo 1941- *IntWW 93*
Figueroa, Alfredo *WhoHisp 94*
Figueroa, Angel Luis 1959- *WhoHisp 94*
Figueroa, Angela *WhoHisp 94*
Figueroa, Angelo 1957- *WhoHisp 94*
Figueroa, Antonio *WhoHisp 94*
Figueroa, Benito, Jr. 1947- *WhoHisp 94*
Figueroa, Betsie 1960- *WhoHisp 94*
Figueroa, Daphne Elizabeth 1960- *WhoHisp 94*

Figueroa, Darryl Lynette 1959- WhoHisp 94
Figueroa, Edna WhoHisp 94
Figueroa, Enrique Esquivel 1951- WhoHisp 94
Figueroa, Gabriel 1907- IntDcF 2-4
Figueroa, Ivan WhoAmP 93
Figueroa, J. Fernando 1957- WhoHisp 94
Figueroa, John 1949- WhoHisp 94
Figueroa, John (Joseph Maria) 1920- WrDr 94
Figueroa, John Emanuel 1947- WhoHisp 94
Figueroa, John J(oseph Maria) 1920- BlkWr 2
Figueroa, José Alcides 1962- WhoHisp 94
Figueroa, Jose-Angel DrAPF 93
Figueroa, Juan A. 1953- WhoHisp 94
Figueroa, Juan Alberto 1953- WhoAmP 93
Figueroa, Juan Manuel 1949- WhoScEn 94
Figueroa, Julian 1943- WhoHisp 94
Figueroa, Liz 1951- WhoHisp 94
Figueroa, Manuel 1959- WhoHisp 94
Figueroa, Mario WhoHisp 94
Figueroa, Michael Otto 1943- WhoWest 94
Figueroa, Nicholas 1933- WhoAmL 94, WhoHisp 94
Figueroa, Octavio Alfonso 1949- WhoHisp 94
Figueroa, Octavio D., Jr. 1942- WhoHisp 94
Figueroa, Pablo 1938- WhoHisp 94
Figueroa, Pedro Luis 1963- WhoHisp 94
Figueroa, Raul 1946- WhoHisp 94
Figueroa, Raymond 1947- WhoAmP 93, WhoHisp 94
Figueroa, Roberto WhoHisp 94
Figueroa, Samuel I. 1955- WhoHisp 94
Figueroa, Sandra 1946- WhoHisp 94
Figueroa, Sandra L. WhoHisp 94
Figueroa Chapel, Ramon DrAPF 93
Figueroa-Orozco, Victor WhoHisp 94
Figueroa-Otero, Iván 1944- WhoHisp 94
Figueroa-Sarriera, Heidi Judith 1958- WhoHisp 94
Figuhr, Reuben Richard 1896- WhAm 10
Figuli, Margita 1909- BlmGWL
Figures, Colin (Frederick) 1925- Who 94
Figures, Michael 1947- WhoBlA 94
Figures, Michael A. 1947- WhoAmP 93
Figures, Thomas H. 1944- WhoBlA 94
Figwer, Jozef Jacek 1928- WhoScEn 94
Fiigen, Bruce G. d1993 NewYTBS 93
Fiil, Niels Peter 1941- IntWW 93
Fikani, Richard Thomas 1964- WhoWest 94
Fike, Edward Lake 1920- WhoAm 94, WhoWest 94
Fike, Larry Lynn 1942- WhoWest 94
Fikentscher, Wolfgang 1928- IntWW 93
Fikre-Selassie, Wogderess IntWW 93
Filali, Abdellatif 1928- IntWW 93
Filan, Patrick J. 1956- WhoAmL 94
Filardi, Edward V. 1944- WhoAmL 94
Filardo, Leonor 1944- IntWW 93
Filardo, Thomas Wesley 1945- WhoMW 93
Filaret IntWW 93
Filaret, Metropolitan 1929- LoBiDrD
Filatov, Sergei Aleksandrovich 1936- LoBiDrD
Filatov, Sergey Alexandrovich 1936- IntWW 93
Filatova, Ludmila Pavlovna 1935- IntWW 93
Filauri, Antonio d1964 WhoHol 92
Filbert, William Jennings 1865-1944 EncABHB 9 [port]
Filbin, Gerald Joseph 1951- WhoScEn 94
Filbin, Thomas DrAPF 93
Filbinger, Hans Karl 1913- IntWW 93
Filby, P. William 1911- WrDr 94
Filby, Percy William 1911- WhoAm 94
Filby, William Charles Leonard 1933- Who 94
Filchner, Wilhelm 1877-1957 WhWE
Filchock, Ethel WhoAm 94, WhoMW 93
Fildes, Audrey WhoHol 92
File, Joseph 1923- WhoScEn 94
Filean, Arthur S. 1938- WhoIns 94
Filene, Edward Albert 1860-1937 AmSocL [port]
Filener, Millard Lee 1946- WhoFI 94, WhoWest 94
Filenko, Volodymyr Pylypovych 1955- LoBiDrD
Filer, Denis Edwin 1932- Who 94
Filer, Elizabeth Ann 1923- WhoAm 94
Filer, Kelvin Dean 1955- WhoBlA 94
Filer, Lloyd Jackson, Jr. 1919- WhoAm 94
Filer, (Douglas) Roger 1942- Who 94
Fileri, Philip R. 1952- WhoAmL 94
Filerman, Gary Lewis 1936- WhoAm 94
Filerman, Michael Herman 1938- WhoAm 94
Files, Gordon Louis 1912- WhoAmL 94, WhoWest 94
Files, Lawrence Burke 1961- WhoWest 94
Files, Mark Willard 1941- WhoFI 94
Filiatrault, Andre WhoScEn 94
Filice, Gregory Alan 1947- WhoMW 93
Filing, Nicholas A. 1947- WhoIns 94
Filip, Henry 1920- WhoWest 94
Filip, Joseph Stuart 1947- WhoAmP 93
Filipacchi, Daniel 1928- IntWW 93
Filipas, Magdalena WhoWomW 91
Filipek, Linda Susan 1953- WhoMW 93
Filipenko, Aleksandr Vasilevich 1950- LoBiDrD
Filipiak, Francis Leonard 1938- WhoAm 94
Filipo, Liufau WhoAmP 93
Filipov, Grisha 1919- IntWW 93
Filipovic, Augustin 1931- WhoAmA 93
Filipowski, Richard E. 1923- WhoAmA 93
Filippelli, Ronald Lee 1938- WhoAm 94
Filippeschi, Mario 1907-1979 NewGrDO
Filippine, Edward Louis 1930- WhoAm 94, WhoAmL 94, WhoMW 93
Filippini, Giovanna 1952- WhoWomW 91
Filippini, Ronald Daniel 1947- WhoFI 94
Filippini, Rosa 1954- WhoWomW 91
Filippo, Eduardo de IntDcT 2
Filippone, Vincent A. 1935- WhoFI 94
Filippone Steinbrick, Gay 1960- WhoScEn 94
Filippov, Petr Sergeevich 1945- LoBiDrD
Filippuzzi, Richard Alan 1959- WhoWest 94
Filipski, Alan James 1946- WhoWest 94
Filipski, Jeff DrAPF 93
Filisko, Frank Edward 1942- WhoAm 94, WhoScEn 94
Filkin, Elizabeth 1940- Who 94
Filkin, Geoffrey Who 94
Filkin, (David) Geoffrey (Nigel) 1944- Who 94
Filkosky, Josefa 1933- WhoAmA 93
Fill, Dennis C. 1929- WhoFI 94
Fill, Gerald A. Andrew 1938- WhoAmP 93
Fillbrook, Thomas George 1949- WhoMW 93
Filleborn, Daniel 1841-1904 NewGrDO
Filler, Gary B. WhoAm 94, WhoFI 94, WhoWest 94
Filler, John Nicholas 1951- WhoAmL 94
Filler, Robert 1923- WhoAm 94
Filler, Ronald 1957- WhoAmL 94
Filler, Ronald Howard 1948- WhoAm 94, WhoAmL 94
Fillerup, Mel 1924- WhoAmA 93
Fillerup, Melvin McDonald 1924- WhoWest 94
Fillet, Mitchell Harris 1948- WhoAm 94, WhoFI 94
Filleul, Jeanne 1424-1498 BlmGWL
Filleul, Peter Amy 1929- Who 94
Filley, Bette Elaine 1933- WhoWest 94
Filley, Laurence Duane 1932- WhoWest 94
Fillicaro, Barbara Jean WhoMW 93
Filling, Richard Rice 1932- WhoAmP 93
Fillingham, Lou Ann 1955- WhoFI 94
Fillingham, Patricia DrAPF 93
Fillin-Yeh, Susan WhoAmA 93
Fillion, Paul R. 1920- WhoAmP 93
Fillios, Louis Charles 1923- WhoAm 94
Fillioud, Georges 1929- IntWW 93
Fillius, Milton Franklin, Jr. 1922- WhoAm 94
Fillmore, Charles Sherlock 1854-1948 DcAmReB 2
Fillmore, Clyde d1946 WhoHol 92
Fillmore, Myrtle Page 1845-1931 DcAmReB 2
Fillmore, Nellie d1942 WhoHol 92
Fillmore, Peter Arthur 1936- WhoAm 94
Fillmore, Russell d1950 WhoHol 92
Fillmore, William L. WhoWest 94
Fillyaw, Leonard David 1939- WhoBlA 94
Filmon, Gary Albert 1942- IntWW 93, WhoAm 94, WhoMW 93
Filmus, Michael Roy 1943- WhoAmA 93
Filmus, Stephen I. 1948- WhoAmA 93
Filmus, Tully 1908- WhoAmA 93
Filner, Bob 1942- CngDr 93, WhoAmP 93
Filner, Bob 1943- WhoAm 94, WhoWest 94
Filomeno, Julio 1954- WhoHisp 94
Filon, Sidney Philip Lawrence 1905- Who 94
Filosa, Gary Fairmont Randolph, II 1931- WrDr 94
Filosa, Gary Fairmont Randolph V., II 1931- WhoAm 94, WhoFI 94, WhoWest 94
Filosa, Renato IntWW 93
Fils, Numes d1972 WhoHol 92
Filshin, Gennadiy Innokentyevich 1931- IntWW 93
Filson, Al d1925 WhoHol 92
Filson, Brent DrAPF 93
Filson, Ronald Coulter 1946- WhoAm 94
Filston, Howard Church 1935- WhoAm 94
Filstrup, E. Christian 1942- WhoAm 94
Filter, Eunice M. 1940- WhoAm 94, WhoFI 94
Filtzer, Hyman 1901-1967 WhoAmA 93N
Filz, Charles Joseph 1925- WhoWest 94
Fimbres, Gabrielle M. 1963- WhoHisp 94
Fimbres, Martha M. 1948- WhoHisp 94
Fimbres, Richard Gonzales 1954- WhoHisp 94
Fimple, Dennis WhoHol 92
Fina, Jack d1968 WhoHol 92
Fina, Paul Joseph 1959- WhoAmL 94
Fina, Thomas Witmer 1924- WhoAmP 93
Finaish, Fathi Ali 1954- WhoScEn 94
Finaish, Mohamed 1936- IntWW 93
Finale, Frank Louis DrAPF 93
Finam, John WhoMW 93
Finamore, Barbara Anne 1954- WhoAmL 94
Finamore, John Francis 1951- WhoMW 93
Finan, Ellen Cranston 1951- WhoWest 94
Finan, Joseph Lawrence, Jr. 1949- WhoFI 94
Finan, Richard H. 1934- WhoAmP 93
Finan, Timothy James 1953- WhoAm 94
Finan, W. Timothy 1950- WhoAmP 93
Finarelli, Margaret G. 1946- WhoAm 94
Finas, Lucette 1921- BlmGWL
Finazzi, Filippo 1706?-1776 NewGrDO
Finberg, Alan Robert 1927- WhoAm 94
Finberg, Barbara Denning 1929- WhoAm 94
Finberg, Donald Richard 1931- WhoAm 94
Finberg, James Michael 1958- WhoAmL 94
Finberg, Laurence 1923- WhoAm 94
Fincastle, Viscount 1946- Who 94
Fincato, Laura 1950- WhoWomW 91
Finch, Anne 1660-1720 BlmGWL
Finch, Annie DrAPF 93
Finch, C. Herbert 1931- WhoAm 94
Finch, Caleb Ellicott 1939- WhoAm 94, WhoWest 94
Finch, Carolyn-Bogart 1938- WhoAm 94
Finch, Charles Baker 1920- WhoAm 94
Finch, Christopher 1939- WrDr 94
Finch, Edward Ridley, Jr. 1919- WhoAm 94, WhoAmL 94
Finch, Flora d1940 WhoHol 92
Finch, Flora 1869-1940 See Bunny and Finch WhoCom
Finch, Flora 1947- WhoWest 94
Finch, Floyd Raymond, Jr. 1953- WhoAmL 94, WhoAmP 93
Finch, George Goode 1937- WhoMW 93
Finch, Gregory Martin 1951- WhoBlA 94
Finch, Harold Bertram, Jr. 1927- WhoAm 94, WhoFI 94
Finch, Herman Manuel 1914- WhoAm 94
Finch, James Robert 1964- WhoAmP 93
Finch, James Stuart 1948- WhoAmL 94
Finch, Janet M. 1950- WhoBlA 94
Finch, Janet Mitchell 1950- WhoAm 94
Finch, Jeremiah Stanton 1910- WhoAm 94
Finch, Jon 1941- WhoHol 92
Finch, Jon 1942- IntMPA 94
Finch, Jon Nicholas 1943- IntWW 93
Finch, Matthew 1921- WrDr 94
Finch, Merton 1921- WrDr 94
Finch, Michael Paul 1946- WhoAm 94, WhoAmL 94
Finch, Pearl Lamm 1927- WhoAmP 93
Finch, Peter d1977 WhoHol 92
Finch, Peter 1947- WrDr 94
Finch, Raymond Lawrence 1940- WhoAm 94, WhoBlA 94
Finch, Robert (Duer Claydon) 1900- WrDr 94
Finch, Robert Hutchison 1925- WhoAmP 93
Finch, Robert Jonathan 1955- WhoMW 93
Finch, Roger 1937- ConAu 140
Finch, Rogers Burton 1920- WhoAm 94
Finch, Ronald Corydon 1934- WhoAmL 94
Finch, Ronald M., Jr. 1932- WhoAm 94
Finch, Ruth Woodward 1916- WhoAmA 93
Finch, Sheila (Rosemary) 1935- EncSF 93
Finch, Stephen Clark 1929- Who 94
Finch, Stuart McIntyre 1919- WhAm 10
Finch, Thomas Wesley 1946- WhoWest 94
Finch, Walter Goss Gilchrist 1918- WhoAm 94
Finch, Warren Irvin 1924- WhoWest 94
Finch, William George Harold 1897-1990 WhAm 10
Finch, William H. 1924- WhoBlA 94
Fincham, Francis D. 1954- ConAu 140
Fincham, Frank D. ConAu 140
Fincham, John Robert Stanley 1926- IntWW 93, Who 94
Fincher, Beatrice González 1941- WhoHisp 94
Fincher, Cameron Lane 1926- WhoAm 94
Fincher, Daryl Wayne 1962- WhoScEn 94
Fincher, John Albert 1911- WhoAm 94
Fincher, John H. 1941- WhoAmA 93
Fincher, W. W., Jr. WhoAmP 93
Finch Hatton Who 94
Finch-Knightley Who 94
Finck, August von 1930- IntWW 93
Finck, Furman J. 1900- WhoAmA 93
Finck, Kevin William 1954- WhoAmL 94, WhoWest 94
Finck, Werner d1978 WhoHol 92
Fincke, Gary DrAPF 93
Finckenstein, Stefan, Reichsgraf Finck von 1961- IntWW 93
Fincun, Jeffrey D. 1946- WhoAmL 94
Finder, Theodore Roosevelt 1914- WhoAm 94
Finder-Stone, Patricia Ann 1929- WhoMW 93
Findlater, John 1944- WhoHol 92
Findlay, Alastair Donald Fraser 1944- Who 94
Findlay, David B., Jr. 1933- WhoAmA 93
Findlay, David W. 1946- WhoWest 94
Findlay, Donald Russell 1951- Who 94
Findlay, Eric Fraser 1926- WhoFI 94
Findlay, Helen T. 1909-1992 WhoAmA 93N
Findlay, Ian Herbert Fyfe 1918- IntWW 93, Who 94
Findlay, James Allen 1943- WhoAmA 93
Findlay, John d1918 WhoHol 92
Findlay, John Wilson 1915- WhoAm 94, WhoScEn 94
Findlay, Michael Alistair 1945- WhoAm 94
Findlay, Robert B. WhoFI 94
Findlay, Ruth d1949 WhoHol 92
Findlay, Theodore Bernard 1939- WhoAm 94
Findlay, Thomas d1941 WhoHol 92
Findlay, Walstein C., Jr. 1903- WhoAm 94
Findler, Nicholas Victor 1930- WhoWest 94
Findley, Carter Vaughn 1941- WhoMW 93
Findley, Delpha Yoder 1930- WhoMW 93
Findley, Don Aaron 1926- WhoAm 94
Findley, F. A. 1918- WhoAmP 93
Findley, Hazel Winifred Rockwell 1911- WhoAmP 93
Findley, James Smith 1926- WhoAm 94, WhoScEn 94
Findley, Martha Jean 1945- WhoMW 93
Findley, Paul 1921- WhoAm 94, WhoAmP 93
Findley, Samuel Augustus 1958- WhoFI 94
Findley, Timothy 1930- ConAu 42NR, WrDr 94
Findley, William Nichols 1914- WhoAm 94
Findley, William Ray, Jr. 1920- WhoMW 93
Findling, David Martin 1960- WhoScEn 94
Findon, Walter d1957 WhoHol 92
Findorff, Robert Lewis 1929- WhoFI 94
Fine, Anne 1947- Who 94, WhoAm 94, WrDr 94
Fine, Arthur I. 1937- WhoAm 94
Fine, Arthur Kenneth 1937- WhoAmL 94
Fine, Barry Kenneth 1938- WhoFI 94
Fine, Bernard J. 1926- WhoAm 94
Fine, Bob 1949- WhoFI 94
Fine, Charles Leon 1932- WhoAm 94
Fine, David Jeffrey 1950- WhoAm 94
Fine, Donald I. 1922- IntWW 93
Fine, Donald Irving 1922- WhoAm 94
Fine, Howard Alan 1941- WhoAm 94, WhoFI 94
Fine, Howard Floyd 1950- WhoAmL 94
Fine, James Allen 1934- WhoFI 94
Fine, Jane 1958- WhoAmA 93
Fine, Joseph Loyd, Jr. 1937- WhoAmP 93
Fine, Jud 1944- WhoAmA 93
Fine, Kit 1946- IntWW 93
Fine, Larry d1975 WhoHol 92
Fine, Larry 1902-1975 See Three Stooges, The WhoCom
Fine, Lawrence B. 1951- WhoAm 94
Fine, Lawrence Jay 1945- WhoAm 94, WhoMW 93
Fine, Marlene Rosen DrAPF 93
Fine, Max 1908-1989 WhAm 10
Fine, Michael Joseph 1937- WhoAm 94
Fine, Milton 1926- WhoAm 94, WhoFI 94
Fine, Morris Eugene 1918- WhoAm 94
Fine, Morton Samuel 1916- WhoScEn 94
Fine, Perle 1905-1988 WhoAmA 93N
Fine, Rana Arnold 1944- WhoAm 94
Fine, Reuben 1914-1993 NewYTBS 93 [port]
Fine, Richard Isaac 1940- WhoAm 94, WhoAmL 94, WhoFI 94, WhoWest 94

FitzAlan-Howard, Bennett-Thomas Henry Robert 1955- *WhoFI 94*
Fitzalan-Howard, Michael 1916- *Who 94*
Fitz-Allen, Adelaide d1935 *WhoHol 92*
Fitzball, Edward 1792-1873 *NewGrDO*
Fitz-Boodle, George Savage *BlmGEL*
Fitzclarence *Who 94*
Fitzer, Herbert Clyde 1910- *Who 94*
Fitzgeoffrey, John c. 1206-1258 *DcNaB MP*
Fitzgeorge, Harold James 1924- *WhoAm 94*
FitzGeorge-Balfour, (Robert George) Victor 1913- *Who 94*
Fitzgeorge-Parker, Tim 1920- *WrDr 94*
Fitzgerald *Who 94*
Fitz Gerald, A. Gregory *DrAPF 93*
Fitzgerald, Anthony Michael 1944- *WhoAmL 94*
Fitzgerald, Astrid 1938- *WhoAmA 93*
Fitzgerald, Barry d1961 *WhoHol 92*
Fitzgerald, Carol E. *WhoAmP 93*
Fitzgerald, Carrie Eugenia 1929- *WhoBlA 94*
Fitzgerald, Charles Patrick d1992 *IntWW 93N*
Fitzgerald, Charles Patrick 1902- *WrDr 94*
Fitzgerald, Charlotte Diane 1949- *WhoBlA 94*
Fitzgerald, Cissy d1941 *WhoHol 92*
Fitzgerald, Daniel Louis 1955- *WhoFI 94*
Fitzgerald, Daniel Patrick 1916- *Who 94*
Fitzgerald, Daniel Peter 1959- *WhoMW 93*
Fitzgerald, David William 1963- *WhoMW 93*
Fitz-Gerald, Desmond John Villiers 1937- *Who 94*
Fitzgerald, Edmond James 1912-1989 *WhAm 10*
Fitzgerald, Edmund B. 1926- *IntWW 93*
Fitzgerald, Edmund Bacon 1926- *WhoAm 94*
Fitzgerald, Edmund J. 1912-1989 *WhoAmA 93N*
Fitzgerald, Edward d1942 *WhoHol 92*
FitzGerald, Edward 1809-1893 *BlmGEL*
FitzGerald, Edward Browne 1934- *WhoAmL 94*
Fitzgerald, Edward Earl 1919- *WhoAm 94*
Fitzgerald, Ella 1918- *AfrAmAl 6 [port], IntWW 93, WhoAm 94, WhoBlA 94, WhoHol 92*
Fitzgerald, Ellen *WrDr 94*
Fitzgerald, Ernest Abner 1925- *WhoAm 94, WrDr 94*
Fitzgerald, Eugene Francis 1925- *WhoAm 94*
Fitzgerald, F(rancis) Scott (Key) 1896-1940 *RfGShF*
Fitzgerald, Frances 1940- *IntWW 93, WrDr 94*
Fitzgerald, Francis Scott Key 1896-1940 *AmCulL*
Fitzgerald, Frank 1929- *Who 94*
Fitzgerald, Frank Moore 1955- *WhoAmP 93*
Fitzgerald, Garret 1926- *IntWW 93, Who 94, WrDr 94*
FitzGerald, George (Peter Maurice) 1917- *Who 94*
Fitzgerald, Gerald Dennis 1939- *WhoMW 93*
Fitzgerald, Gerald Edward 1941- *Who 94*
Fitzgerald, Gerald Francis 1925- *WhoAm 94*
Fitzgerald, Gerald Loftus 1907- *Who 94*
Fitzgerald, Geraldine 1913- *WhoAm 94*
Fitzgerald, Geraldine 1914- *IntMPA 94, WhoHol 92*
Fitzgerald, Harold Kenneth 1921- *WhoAm 94*
Fitzgerald, Harriet 1904-1984 *WhoAmA 93N*
Fitzgerald, Herbert H. 1928- *WhoBlA 94*
Fitzgerald, Howard David 1938- *WhoBlA 94*
Fitzgerald, Hugh *EncSF 93*
Fitzgerald, J. Edward 1923-1977 *WhoAmA 93N*
Fitzgerald, James d1919 *WhoHol 92*
Fitzgerald, James Alfred, Jr. 1956- *WhoFI 94, WhoMW 93*
Fitzgerald, James Edward 1894- *WhAm 10*
Fitzgerald, James Edward 1947- *WhoAmL 94*
Fitzgerald, James Francis 1926- *WhoAm 94, WhoMW 93*
Fitzgerald, James Martin 1920- *WhoAmL 94, WhoWest 94*
Fitzgerald, James Michael *WhoAmP 93*
Fitzgerald, James Michael 1929- *WhoFI 94, WhoMW 93*
Fitzgerald, James Patrick 1946- *WhoAmL 94*
Fitzgerald, James Richard 1939- *WhoAm 94*
FitzGerald, James W. *WhoAm 94*
Fitzgerald, Janet Anne 1935- *WhoAm 94*
Fitzgerald, Janet Marie 1943- *WhoAm 94*
FitzGerald, Jerry 1936- *WhoWest 94*
Fitzgerald, John *WhAmRev*
Fitzgerald, John Charles, Jr. 1941- *WhoFI 94*
Fitzgerald, John E. 1920- *WhoAmL 94*
Fitzgerald, John Edmund 1923- *WhoAm 94, WhoScEn 94*
FitzGerald, John Edward, III 1945- *WhoAmL 94*
Fitzgerald, John Morgan 1922- *WhoAmL 94*
Fitzgerald, John W. *WhoAm 94*
Fitzgerald, John Warner 1924- *WhoAm 94, WhoAmP 93*
Fitzgerald, Joseph Michael, Jr. 1943- *WhoAmL 94*
Fitzgerald, Judith Klaswick 1948- *WhoAm 94, WhoAmL 94*
Fitzgerald, Kevin W. 1950- *WhoAmP 93*
Fitzgerald, Laurine Elisabeth 1930- *WhoAm 94*
Fitz-Gerald, Lewis 1959- *WhoHol 92*
Fitzgerald, Lillian d1947 *WhoHol 92*
Fitzgerald, Loretta Cieutat 1959- *WhoWest 94*
Fitzgerald, Michael 1951- *Who 94*
Fitzgerald, Michael Anthony 1944- *WhoAm 94, WhoFI 94*
FitzGerald, Michael Fleming 1955- *WhoFI 94*
FitzGerald, Michael Frederick Clive 1936- *Who 94*
Fitzgerald, Michael L. 1951- *WhoAmP 93*
Fitzgerald, Michael Lee 1951- *WhoAm 94, WhoMW 93*
Fitzgerald, Miranda F. 1947- *WhoAmL 94*
Fitzgerald, Neil d1982 *WhoHol 92*
Fitzgerald, Nuala *WhoHol 92*
Fitzgerald, Oscar P., IV 1943- *WhoAm 94*
Fitzgerald, Patricia Dunn 1944- *WhoAmP 93*
Fitzgerald, Patrick John 1928- *Who 94*
Fitzgerald, Penelope 1916- *BlmGWL*
Fitzgerald, Penelope (Mary Knox) 1916- *WrDr 94*
Fitzgerald, Penelope Mary 1916- *IntWW 93, Who 94*
Fitzgerald, Peter G. 1960- *WhoAmP 93*
Fitzgerald, Peter Gosselin 1960- *WhoMW 93*
Fitzgerald, Peter Hanley 1929- *IntWW 93*
FitzGerald, Presiley Lamorna *Who 94*
Fitzgerald, Raymond Richard 1921- *WhoAm 94*
FitzGerald, Richard Joseph, Jr. 1930- *WhoAm 94*
Fitzgerald, Richard Patrick 1950- *WhoWest 94*
Fitzgerald, Robert Hannon, Jr. 1942- *WhoAm 94, WhoScEn 94*
Fitzgerald, Robert Lynn 1939- *WhoWest 94*
Fitzgerald, Robert Maurice 1942- *WhoAm 94*
Fitz-Gerald, Roger Miller 1935- *WhoAm 94*
Fitzgerald, Roosevelt 1941- *WhoBlA 94*
Fitzgerald, Roy Lee 1911- *WhoBlA 94*
Fitzgerald, Sheryl Cunningham 1955- *WhoMW 93*
Fitzgerald, Stephen Arthur 1938- *IntWW 93*
FitzGerald, Sylvia Mary Denise 1939- *Who 94*
FitzGerald, Thomas Joe 1941- *WhoMW 93*
Fitzgerald, Thomas Robert 1959- *WhoFI 94*
Fitzgerald, Thomas Rollins 1922- *WhoAm 94*
Fitzgerald, Tikhon 1932- *WhoAm 94, WhoWest 94*
Fitzgerald, Vincent James 1950- *WhoWest 94*
Fitzgerald, Walter d1976 *WhoHol 92*
Fitzgerald, Walter George 1936- *WhoFI 94*
Fitzgerald, Wendy Anton 1957- *WhoAmL 94*
Fitzgerald, William *EncSF 93*
Fitzgerald, William Allingham 1937- *WhoAm 94, WhoFI 94*
Fitzgerald, William B. *WhoBlA 94*
Fitzgerald, William Brendan 1936- *WhoWest 94*
Fitzgerald, William F. 1936- *WhoScEn 94*
FitzGerald, William Henry G. 1909- *WhoAm 94*
Fitzgerald, William Henry Gerald 1909- *IntWW 93*
Fitzgerald, William Terry 1951- *WhoAmL 94*
Fitzgerald, Zelda 1900-1948 *BlmGWL*
Fitzgerald, Zelda Sayre 1900-1948 *TwCLC 52 [port]*
Fitzgerald-Lombard, Charles 1941- *Who 94*
Fitzgibbon, (Robert Louis) Constantine (Lee-Dillon) 1919-1983 *EncSF 93*
FitzGibbon, Daniel Harvey 1942- *WhoAm 94, WhoAmL 94*
FitzGibbon, John Phillips, Jr. 1948- *WhoFI 94*
FitzGibbon, Louis Theobald Dillon 1925- *Who 94*
Fitz-Gibbon, Ralph Edgerton c. 1904- *EncSF 93*
FitzGibbon, (Joanne Eileen) Theodora (Winifred) 1916- *WrDr 94*
Fitzgibbons, James M. 1934- *WhoFI 94*
FitzGilbert, Constance fl. 12th cent.- *BlmGWL*
Fitzhamon, Lewin d1961 *WhoHol 92*
FitzHarris, Viscount 1946- *Who 94*
Fitzharris, Edward d1974 *WhoHol 92*
Fitzharris, Joseph Charles 1946- *WhoMW 93*
Fitzhenry, Robert Irvine 1918- *WhoAm 94*
Fitzherbert *Who 94*
FitzHerbert, Giles Eden 1935- *Who 94*
FitzHerbert, Richard (Ranulph) 1963- *Who 94*
Fitzherbert-Brockholes, Michael John 1920- *Who 94*
Fitzhugh, David Michael 1946- *WhoAm 94, WhoAmL 94*
Fitzhugh, Howard Naylor 1909-1992 *WhoBlA 94N*
Fitzhugh, Kathryn 1950- *WhoAmL 94*
Fitzhugh, Kathryn Corrothers 1950- *WhoBlA 94*
Fitzhugh, Louise 1928-1974 *BlmGWL*
Fitzhugh, Peregrine *WhAmRev*
Fitzhugh, Venita d1920 *WhoHol 92*
Fitzhugh, William 1741-1809 *WhAmRev*
Fitzhugh, William Wyvill, Jr. 1914- *WhoAm 94*
Fitzjohn, John c. 1240-1275 *DcNaB MP*
Fitz-Maurice *Who 94*
Fitzmaurice, George d1940 *WhoHol 92*
Fitzmaurice, George 1877-1963 *IntDcT 2*
Fitzmaurice, Laurence Dorset 1938- *WhoAm 94*
Fitzmaurice, Michael d1967 *WhoHol 92*
Fitzmaurice, Michael William 1939- *WhoScEn 94*
Fitzpatrick, Albert E. 1928- *WhoBlA 94*
Fitzpatrick, B. Edward *WhoBlA 94*
Fitzpatrick, Charles R. 1938- *WhoIns 94*
Fitzpatrick, Cheryl Lynn 1955- *WhoMW 93*
Fitzpatrick, Christine Morris 1920- *WhoMW 93*
FitzPatrick, David Beatty 1920- *Who 94*
Fitzpatrick, Dennis Michael 1945- *WhoWest 94*
Fitzpatrick, (Geoffrey Richard) Desmond 1912- *IntWW 93, Who 94*
Fitzpatrick, Donald Keith 1934- *WhoAm 94*
Fitzpatrick, Duross 1934- *WhoAm 94, WhoAmL 94*
Fitzpatrick, Eileen Tabata 1944- *WhoAsA 94*
FitzPatrick, Francis James 1916- *WhoAmL 94, WhoFI 94*
Fitzpatrick, Garrett Joseph 1949- *WhoAm 94*
Fitzpatrick, Gilbert Lawrence 1930- *WhoAm 94*
Fitzpatrick, Harold Francis 1947- *WhoAmL 94, WhoFI 94*
Fitzpatrick, James d1980 *WhoHol 92*
Fitzpatrick, James Bernard 1930- *Who 94*
Fitzpatrick, James David 1938- *WhoAm 94*
Fitzpatrick, James Franklin 1933- *WhoAm 94*
Fitzpatrick, John (Bernard) 1929- *Who 94*
Fitzpatrick, John Henry 1956- *WhoAm 94*
Fitzpatrick, John Hitchcock 1923- *WhoAmP 93*
Fitzpatrick, John J. 1918- *WhoAm 94*
Fitzpatrick, John J. 1943- *WhoAmP 93*
Fitzpatrick, John Leo 1922- *WhoAmP 93*
Fitzpatrick, John Ronald 1923- *Who 94*
Fitzpatrick, Joseph Cyril 1909- *WhoAmA 93*
Fitzpatrick, Joseph Mark 1925- *WhoAmL 94*
Fitzpatrick, Joseph T. *WhoAmP 93*
Fitzpatrick, Judith 1941- *WhoAm 94*
Fitzpatrick, Julia C. d1985 *WhoBlA 94N*
Fitzpatrick, Kate *WhoHol 92*
Fitzpatrick, Kerri Lynn 1968- *WhoMW 93*
FitzPatrick, Kevin *DrAPF 93*
Fitzpatrick, Margaret Doyle 1952- *WhoAmL 94*
Fitzpatrick, Mark 1968- *WhoAm 94*
Fitzpatrick, Mary Alice 1956- *WhoMW 93*
Fitzpatrick, Michael J. 1950- *WhoAmP 93*
Fitzpatrick, Neil *WhoHol 92*
Fitzpatrick, Paul Early 1897- *WhAm 10*
Fitzpatrick, Peter 1906- *WhoAmL 94*
Fitzpatrick, Rosalyn M. 1911- *WhoAmP 93*
Fitzpatrick, Sean Kevin 1941- *WhoAm 94, WhoFI 94*
Fitzpatrick, Thomas c. 1799-1854 *WhWE*
Fitzpatrick, Thomas Bernard 1919- *WhoAm 94, WhoScEn 94*
Fitzpatrick, Thomas M. 1944- *WhoAmP 93*
Fitzpatrick, Thomas Mark 1951- *WhoAm 94, WhoAmL 94*
Fitzpatrick, Tony 1949- *ConAu 140*
Fitzpatrick, Vincent (dePaul, III) 1950- *WrDr 94*
Fitzpatrick, Whitfield Westfeldt 1942- *WhoAmL 94*
Fitzpatrick, William Henry 1908- *WhoAm 94*
Fitzpatrick, William Peter 1961- *WhoAmP 93*
FitzRoy *Who 94*
Fitzroy, Augustus Henry *WhAmRev*
FitzRoy, Charles (Patrick Hugh) 1957- *WrDr 94*
Fitzroy, Emily d1954 *WhoHol 92*
Fitzroy, Forrest Shands 1945- *WhoAmL 94*
Fitzroy, Louis d1947 *WhoHol 92*
Fitzroy, Margaret Cullington *WhoHol 92*
Fitzroy, Nancy deLoye 1927- *WhoAm 94*
Fitzroy, Robert 1805-1865 *WhWE*
FitzRoy Newdegate *Who 94*
Fitzsimmons, Bob 1939-1993 *NewYTBS 93 [port]*
Fitzsimmons, Cotton 1931- *BasBi, WhoAm 94, WhoWest 94*
Fitzsimmons, James Joseph 1908- *WhoAmA 93N*
Fitzsimmons, John Patrick 1964- *WhoScEn 94*
Fitzsimmons, Joseph John 1934- *WhoAm 94, WhoMW 93*
Fitzsimmons, Lisa Lynn 1964- *WhoWest 94*
FitzSimmons, Richard M. 1924- *WhoAm 94*
Fitzsimmons, Richard Stewart 1950- *WhoAmP 93*
Fitzsimmons, Robert 1863-1917 *DcNaB MP*
Fitzsimmons, Robert Patrick 1952- *WhoAmL 94, WhoAmP 93*
Fitzsimmons, Sophie Sonia 1943- *WhoAm 94, WhoScEn 94*
Fitzsimmons, Thomas *DrAPF 93*
Fitzsimmons, Timothy 1952- *WhoFI 94*
Fitzsimmons, Tom 1947- *WhoHol 92*
Fitzsimmons, William Kennedy d1992 *Who 94N*
Fitzsimonds, Carol Strause 1951- *WhoAmA 93*
Fitzsimonds, Roger Leon 1938- *WhoAm 94, WhoFI 94*
Fitzsimons, Anthony *Who 94*
Fitzsimons, Charles *WhoHol 92*
FitzSimons, Christopher 1964- *WhoScEn 94*
Fitzsimons, Donald Jeffery 1959- *WhoMW 93*
Fitzsimons, George K. 1928- *WhoAm 94, WhoMW 93*
Fitzsimons, James Thomas 1928- *Who 94*
Fitzsimons, P. Anthony 1946- *Who 94*
Fitzsimons, Patrick S. 1930- *WhoAm 94, WhoWest 94*
Fitzsimons, Ruth Marie d1989 *WhAm 10*
Fitzsimons, Thomas 1741-1811 *WhAmRev*
Fitzsimons, Tom Scott 1953- *WhoFI 94*
Fitzstephens, Donna Marie 1966- *WhoScEn 94*
Fitzthomas, Thomas dc. 1276 *DcNaB MP*
Fitzthumb, Ignaz *NewGrDO*
Fitzwalter, Baron 1914- *Who 94*
Fitzwater, Marlin 1942- *IntWW 93, WhoAm 94*
Fitzwater, Marsha Dean 1950- *WhoWest 94*
Fitzwater, Max Marlin 1942- *WhoAmP 93*
Fitzwater, Sidney Allen 1953- *WhoAm 94, WhoAmL 94*
Fitzwilliam, William *WhWE*
Fiume, Orazio 1908-1976 *NewGrDO*
Fiumefreddo, Charles A. 1933- *WhoAm 94, WhoFI 94*
Five, Billy 1952- *WrDr 94*
Five, Kaci Kullmann 1951- *IntWW 93*
Fives, Christopher Thomas 1957- *WhoFI 94*
Fix, George Arthur 1925- *WhoAmP 93*
Fix, Helen Herrink 1922- *WhoAmP 93*
Fix, John Neilson 1937- *WhoAm 94*
Fix, John Robert 1934- *WhoAmA 93*
Fix, Meyer 1906- *WhoAmL 94*
Fix, Paul d1983 *WhoHol 92*

Fix, Wilbur James 1927- *WhoAm 94, WhoWest 94*
Fixel, Lawrence *DrAPF 93*
Fixman, Marshall 1930- *IntWW 93, WhoAm 94, WhoScEn 94, WhoWest 94*
Fix-Romlow, Jeanne Kay 1947- *WhoWest 94*
Fizdale, Richard *WhoAm 94, WhoFI 94, WhoMW 93*
Fizeau, Armand-Hippolyte-Louis 1819-1896 *WorScD*
Fjelde, Rolf (Gerhard) 1926- *WrDr 94*
Fjerdingstad, Ejnar Jules 1937- *WhoScEn 94*
Fjordbotten, Edwin LeRoy 1938- *WhoWest 94*
Fjoslien, Dave 1936- *WhoAmP 93*
Flaagan, Odell D. 1938- *WhoAmP 93*
Flaccus, Edward 1921- *WhoAm 94*
Flach, Victor H. 1929- *WhoAm 94, WhoAmA 93, WhoWest 94*
Flachsbart, Peter George 1944- *WhoWest 94*
Flack, Audrey L. 1931- *WhoAmA 93*
Flack, Bertram Anthony 1924- *Who 94*
Flack, Charles Haynes 1927- *WhoAmL 94*
Flack, Harley Eugene 1943- *WhoBlA 94*
Flack, James Monroe 1913-1989 *WhAm 10*
Flack, Jerry D(avid) 1943- *WrDr 94*
Flack, Joe Fenley 1921- *WhoAm 94*
Flack, Joe Fenley, Jr. 1951- *WhoAmL 94*
Flack, John Robert 1942- *Who 94*
Flack, Roberta 1939- *AfrAmAl 6, WhoAm 94, WhoBlA 94, WhoHol 92*
Flacks, Erwin 1926- *WhoWest 94*
Flacks, Louis Michael 1937- *WhoScEn 94*
Flaco, El *DrAPF 93*
Fladeland, Betty 1919- *WhoAm 94, WrDr 94*
Flading, John Joseph 1960- *WhoFI 94*
Fladung, Jerome F. *WhoAmP 93*
Fladung, Nanette Copple 1964- *WhoMW 93*
Fladung, Richard Denis 1953- *WhoAmL 94*
Flagan, Richard Charles 1947- *WhoAm 94, WhoScEn 94*
Flagello, Ezio (Domenico) 1931- *NewGrDO*
Flagello, Ezio Domenico 1932- *WhoAm 94*
Flagello, Nicolas (Oreste) 1928- *NewGrDO*
Flaget, Benedict Joseph 1763-1850 *DcAmReB 2*
Flagg, Barry David 1962- *WhoFI 94*
Flagg, Cynthia Platt 1948- *WhoAmL 94*
Flagg, David 1937- *WhoAmP 93*
Flagg, E. Alma W. 1918- *WhoBlA 94*
Flagg, Fannie 1941?- *ConTFT 11, WhoHol 92*
Flagg, Francis 1898?-1946 *EncSF 93*
Flagg, J. Thomas 1917- *WhoBlA 94*
Flagg, James Montgomery d1960 *WhoHol 92*
Flagg, James Montgomery 1877-1960 *WhoAmA 93N*
Flagg, Jeanne Bodin 1925- *WhoAm 94*
Flagg, John William Hawkins 1929- *Who 94*
Flagg, Michael James 1958- *WhoAm 94*
Flagg, Norman Lee 1932- *WhoWest 94*
Flagg, Raymond Osbourn 1933- *WhoScEn 94*
Flagg, Robert Finch 1933- *WhoScEn 94*
Flagg, Ronald Simon 1953- *WhoAm 94*
Flagg, Steve *WhoHol 92*
Flaggs, George, Jr. 1953- *WhoAmP 93*
Flagle, Charles Denhard 1919- *WhoAm 94*
Flagle, Charles Lawrence 1949- *WhoScEn 94*
Flagler, Robert Loomis 1940- *WhoFI 94*
Flagler, Terrence 1964- *WhoBlA 94*
Flagler, William Lawrence 1922- *WhoWest 94*
Flagstad, Kirsten d1962 *WhoHol 92*
Flagstad, Kirsten (Malfrid) 1895-1962 *NewGrDO [port]*
Flahavin, Marian Joan *WhoAmA 93*
Flaherty, Ann Marie 1964- *WhoFI 94*
Flaherty, Brian J. 1965- *WhoAmP 93*
Flaherty, Brian P. 1953- *WhoAmL 94*
Flaherty, Charles Frances, Jr. 1938- *WhoAmP 93*
Flaherty, Charles Francis 1938- *WhoAm 94*
Flaherty, David T. *WhoAmP 93*
Flaherty, Doug *DrAPF 93*
Flaherty, Eugene Dewey 1898- *WhAm 10*
Flaherty, Francis X. 1947- *WhoAmP 93*
Flaherty, Francis Xavier 1947- *WhoAm 94*
Flaherty, James Joseph 1930- *WhoAmL 94*
Flaherty, Joe *WhoHol 92*
Flaherty, Joe 1936?-1983 *ConAu 141*
Flaherty, John Edmund 1948- *WhoAm 94*
Flaherty, John Edward, Jr. 1945- *WhoAm 94, WhoAmL 94*
Flaherty, John Joseph 1932- *WhoAm 94, WhoFI 94*
Flaherty, John P. *WhoAmP 93*
Flaherty, John P., Jr. 1931- *WhoAm 94, WhoAmL 94*
Flaherty, Larry Paul 1943- *WhoWest 94*
Flaherty, Mark G. 1949- *WhoAmL 94*
Flaherty, Mary Diana 1953- *WhoWomW 91*
Flaherty, Michael Francis 1936- *WhoAmP 93*
Flaherty, Michael Paul 1945- *WhoAm 94*
Flaherty, Nancy H. *WhoAmP 93*
Flaherty, Pat d1970 *WhoHol 92*
Flaherty, Patrick J. *WhoAmP 93*
Flaherty, Peter F. 1925- *WhoAmP 93*
Flaherty, Ray *ProFbHF*
Flaherty, Robert Edward 1948- *WhoAmP 93*
Flaherty, Roberta D. 1947- *WhoMW 93*
Flaherty, Susan Sweeney 1949- *WhoMW 93*
Flaherty, Tina Santi *WhoAm 94, WhoFI 94*
Flaherty, Virginia Chatfield 1921- *WhoAmP 93*
Flaherty, William E. 1933- *WhoFI 94*
Flahiff, George Bernard 1905-1989 *WhAm 10*
Flaiano, Ennio 1910-1972 *IntDcF 2-4*
Flaig, Robert B. 1941- *WhoAmL 94*
Flaim, Stephen Frederick 1948- *WhoWest 94*
Flake, Floyd H. 1945- *CngDr 93, WhoAmP 93, WhoBlA 94*
Flake, Floyd Harold 1945- *WhoAm 94*
Flake, Nancy Aline 1956- *WhoBlA 94*
Flakes, Larry Joseph 1947- *WhoBlA 94*
Flakne, Dawn Gayle 1959- *WhoScEn 94*
Flakoll, Timothy John 1959- *WhoMW 93*
Flam, Jack *DrAPF 93*
Flam, Jack D. 1940- *WhoAmA 93*
Flam, Jack Donald 1940- *WhoAm 94*
Flamand, Paul Henri 1909- *IntWW 93*
Flamant, Georges d1990 *WhoHol 92*
Flamer, John H., Jr. 1938- *WhoBlA 94*
Flaming, Iretha Mae 1935- *WhoMW 93*
Flaming, Wade A 1965- *WhoWest 94*
Flamm, Bryce Conway 1927- *WhoAmP 93*
Flamm, Daniel Lawrence 1943- *WhoWest 94*
Flamm, Donald 1899- *WhoFI 94*
Flamm, Leonard Nathan 1943- *WhoAmL 94*
Flamm, Melvin Daniel, Jr. 1934- *WhoWest 94*
Flamm, Walter H., Jr. 1947- *WhoAmL 94*
Flammarion, (Nicholas) Camille 1842-1925 *EncSF 93*
Flammarion, Charles-Henri 1946- *IntWW 93*
Flammer, George Herbert 1947- *WhoAmL 94*
Flamson, Richard Joseph, III 1929-1991 *WhAm 10*
Flamsteed, John *WorInv*
Flanagan, Barbara *WhoAm 94*
Flanagan, Barry 1941- *IntWW 93, Who 94, WhoAmA 93*
Flanagan, Bud d1968 *WhoHol 92*
Flanagan, Christie Stephen 1938- *WhoAm 94*
Flanagan, Deborah Mary 1956- *WhoAmL 94*
Flanagan, Dennis 1919- *WhoAm 94*
Flanagan, Dorothy Belle *ConAu 141*
Flanagan, E. Michael 1948- *WhoAmA 93*
Flanagan, Edward J. d1925 *WhoHol 92*
Flanagan, Edward S. 1950- *WhoAmP 93*
Flanagan, Eugene John Thomas 1923- *WhoAm 94*
Flanagan, Fionnula 1941- *WhoHol 92*
Flanagan, Fionnula Manon 1941- *WhoAm 94*
Flanagan, Francis Dennis 1912- *WhoAm 94*
Flanagan, Frederick James 1941- *WhoScEn 94*
Flanagan, Harry Paul 1933- *WhoMW 93*
Flanagan, Hugh d1925 *WhoHol 92*
Flanagan, James Henry, Jr. 1934- *WhoAmL 94, WhoWest 94*
Flanagan, James Loton *WhoAm 94, WhoScEn 94*
Flanagan, James Loton 1925- *IntWW 93*
Flanagan, James Philip 1954- *WhoAmP 93*
Flanagan, John Anthony 1942- *WhoAmL 94*
Flanagan, John F. 1898-1952 *WhoAmA 93N*
Flanagan, John J. 1961- *WhoAmP 93*
Flanagan, John Michael 1946- *WhoAm 94*
Flanagan, John Theodore 1906- *WhoAm 94*
Flanagan, Joseph Charles 1938- *WhoAm 94*
Flanagan, Joseph Patrick 1938- *WhoAm 94, WhoFI 94, WhoMW 93*
Flanagan, Joseph Patrick, Jr. 1924- *WhoAm 94, WhoAmL 94*
Flanagan, Joye Boggs 1927- *WhoAmP 93*
Flanagan, Judith Ann 1950- *WhoFI 94*
Flanagan, L. Martin 1932- *WhoAmL 94*
Flanagan, Latham, Jr. 1936- *WhoWest 94*
Flanagan, Margaret Ann 1955- *WhoMW 93*
Flanagan, Markus *WhoHol 92*
Flanagan, Martha Lang 1942- *WhoAm 94*
Flanagan, Michael 1943- *WhoAmA 93*
Flanagan, Michael Charles 1954- *WhoAmL 94*
Flanagan, Michael Gerard 1953- *WhoAmL 94*
Flanagan, Michael Joseph 1946- *Who 94*
Flanagan, Michael Perkins 1944- *WhoAmL 94*
Flanagan, Mike 1950- *WrDr 94*
Flanagan, Natalie Smith 1913- *WhoAmP 93*
Flanagan, Neil d1986 *WhoHol 92*
Flanagan, Patrick Anthony 1938- *WhoAmP 93*
Flanagan, Peter J. 1930- *WhoIns 94*
Flanagan, Rebecca d1938 *WhoHol 92*
Flanagan, Richard *DrAPF 93*
Flanagan, Robert *DrAPF 93*
Flanagan, Robert B., Sr. 1929- *WhoBlA 94*
Flanagan, Robert J. 1945- *WhoFI 94*
Flanagan, Robert Lawrence 1945- *WhoAmP 93*
Flanagan, Sarah G. 1951- *WhoAmL 94*
Flanagan, T. Earl, Jr. 1937- *WhoBlA 94*
Flanagan, Thomas (James Bonner) 1923- *WrDr 94*
Flanagan, Thomas James *WhoWest 94*
Flanagan, Thomas James Bonner 1923- *WhoAm 94*
Flanagan, Thomas Patrick *WhoAm 94*
Flanagan, Tommy 1930- *AfrAmAl 6*
Flanagan, Tommy Lee 1930- *WhoAm 94*
Flanagan, Van Kent 1945- *WhoAm 94*
Flanagan, William, (Jr.) 1923-1969 *NewGrDO*
Flanagan, William J. *WhoAmL 94*
Flanagin, Neil 1930- *WhoAm 94*
Flanagin, Patrick Henry 1948- *WhoAmP 93*
Flanary, Donald Herbert, Jr. 1949- *WhoAmL 94*
Flanders, Allen F. 1945- *WhoWest 94*
Flanders, David A. 1939- *WhoAmP 93*
Flanders, Dennis 1915- *Who 94*
Flanders, Donald Hargis 1924- *WhoFI 94*
Flanders, Dwight Prescott 1909- *WhoFI 94, WhoMW 93*
Flanders, Ed 1934- *WhoHol 92*
Flanders, Edward Paul 1934- *WhoAm 94*
Flanders, George James 1960- *WhoWest 94*
Flanders, Harry E. 1912- *WhoAmP 93*
Flanders, Helen Driver 1947- *WhoAm 94*
Flanders, Henry Jackson, Jr. 1921- *WhoAm 94*
Flanders, Jane *DrAPF 93*
Flanders, John W., Sr. 1927- *WhoAmP 93*
Flanders, Michael d1975 *WhoHol 92*
Flanders, Peggy *DrAPF 93*
Flanders, Raymond Alan 1929- *WhoMW 93*
Flanders, Scott Nelson 1956- *WhoAm 94*
Flandro, Millie L. 1954- *WhoAmP 93*
Flanery, Gail *WhoAmA 93*
Flanery, Lori Hudson 1965- *WhoAmL 94*
Flanigan, Alan *WhoAmP 93*
Flanigan, Alan H. *WhoAm 94*
Flanigan, Donna Marie Herring 1957- *WhoWest 94*
Flanigan, James Joseph 1936- *WhoAm 94, WhoFI 94, WhoWest 94*
Flanigan, Jeanne Marie 1946- *WhoAm 94*
Flanigan, Peter Magnus 1923- *WhoAm 94*
Flanigan, Richard D. 1941- *WhoAmP 93*
Flanigan, Robert Daniel, Jr. 1949- *WhoFI 94*
Flanigan, William Joseph 1930- *WhoAm 94*
Flanigen, Edith Marie *WhoScEn 94*
Flannagan, Benjamin Collins, IV 1927- *WhoAmL 94*
Flannagan, William Marvin, Jr. 1961- *WhoMW 93*
Flannelly, Kevin J. 1949- *WhoFI 94, WhoScEn 94, WhoWest 94*
Flannelly, Laura T. 1952- *WhoScEn 94, WhoWest 94*
Flanner, Janet 1892-1978 *BlmGWL, GayLL*
Flannery, Anne Catherine 1951- *WhoAm 94*
Flannery, Brian Paul 1948- *WhoScEn 94*
Flannery, Ellen Joanne 1951- *WhoAm 94, WhoAmL 94*
Flannery, Harry Audley 1947- *WhoAmL 94*
Flannery, John Philip, II 1946- *WhoAmL 94*
Flannery, John Sean Patrick 1958- *WhoFI 94*
Flannery, Joseph Patrick 1932- *IntWW 93, WhoAm 94*
Flannery, Kent V. *WhoScEn 94*
Flannery, Martin Henry 1918- *Who 94*
Flannery, Mary Ann 1939- *WhoMW 93*
Flannery, Nancy Gail 1951- *WhoIns 94*
Flannery, Peter 1951- *ConDr 93*
Flannery, Susan 1943- *WhoHol 92*
Flannery, Thomas 1919- *WhoAmA 93*
Flannery, Thomas A. 1918- *CngDr 93*
Flannery, Thomas Aquinas 1918- *WhoAm 94, WhoAmL 94*
Flannery, Wilbur Eugene 1907- *WhoScEn 94*
Flannery, William Jackson, Jr. 1944- *WhoAmL 94*
Flannigan, J. J. 1968- *WhoBlA 94*
Flannigan, Sandra F. 1946- *WhoMW 93*
Flansburg, James Sherman 1932- *WhoAm 94*
Flansburgh, Earl Robert 1931- *WhoAm 94, WhoFI 94, WhoScEn 94*
Flapan, Jan 1943- *WhoMW 93*
Flaschen, Evan Daniel 1957- *WhoAmL 94*
Flaschen, Steward Samuel 1926- *WhoAm 94, WhoFI 94*
Flaskamp, Ruth Ehmen Staack 1927- *WhoMW 93*
Flaskamp, William Davidson 1924- *WhoAm 94*
Flaskegaard, Richard Lee 1953- *WhoFI 94*
Flaster, Richard Joel 1943- *WhoAmL 94*
Flateau, Georges d1953 *WhoHol 92*
Flateau, John 1950- *WhoBlA 94*
Flaten, Betty Arlene 1938- *WhoAmP 93*
Flaten, Mark Douglas 1959- *WhoWest 94*
Flaten, Robert A. 1934- *WhoAm 94, WhoAmP 93*
Flath, Shirley 1950- *WhoMW 93*
Flather, Baroness *Who 94*
Flather, Gary Denis *Who 94*
Flatley, Guy 1934- *WhoAm 94*
Flatley, Lawrence Edward 1950- *WhoAm 94, WhoAmL 94*
Flatness, Mary Linda 1942- *WhoMW 93*
Flato, William Roeder, Jr. 1945- *WhoFI 94*
Flatt, Adrian Ede 1921- *WhoAm 94*
Flatt, Carter J. 1943- *WhoIns 94*
Flatt, Elmer E. *WhoAmP 93*
Flatt, Ernest Orville 1918- *WhoAm 94*
Flatt, Michael Oliver 1938- *WhoWest 94*
Flatte, Michael Edward 1967- *WhoScEn 94, WhoWest 94*
Flatte, Stanley Martin 1940- *WhoAm 94*
Flatters, Paul-Xavier 1832-1881 *WhWE*
Flattery, Paul Charles 1935- *WhoAmL 94*
Flattery, Thomas L. 1922- *IntMPA 94*
Flattery, Thomas Long 1922- *WhoAm 94, WhoAmL 94*
Flattmann, Alan Raymond 1946- *WhoAmA 93*
Flatts, Barbara Ann 1951- *WhoBlA 94*
Flaubert, Gustave 1821-1880 *BlmGEL, RfGShF*
Flaum, Joel M. *WhoAmP 93*
Flaum, Joel Martin 1936- *WhoAm 94, WhoAmL 94*
Flaum, Marshall Allen *WhoAm 94*
Flaum, Mayer d1990 *WhoHol 92*
Flaum, Sander Allen 1937- *WhoAm 94, WhoFI 94*
Flaus, John *WhoHol 92*
Flavell, Geoffrey 1913- *Who 94*
Flavell, Richard Anthony 1945- *IntWW 93, Who 94*
Flavell, Richard Bailey 1943- *Who 94*
Flavelle, (Joseph) David (Ellsworth) 1921- *Who 94*
Flavigny, Marie de 1805-1876 *BlmGWL*
Flavin, Dan 1933- *IntWW 93, WhoAmA 93*
Flavin, Glennon P. 1916- *WhoAm 94, WhoMW 93*
Flavin, James d1976 *WhoHol 92*
Flavin, Nancy Ann 1950- *WhoAmP 93*
Flax, Alexander Henry 1921- *WhoAm 94*
Flax, Martin Howard 1928- *WhoAm 94*
Flaxen, David William 1941- *Who 94*
Flaxer, Carl 1918- *WhoWest 94*
Flaxman, David 1939- *WhoAmL 94*
Flaxman, Howard Richard 1948- *WhoAm 94, WhoAmL 94*
Flaxman, John P. 1934- *IntMPA 94*
Flaxman, Kenneth N. 1948- *WhoAmL 94*
Fleagle, John Gwynn 1948- *WhoAm 94*
Fleagle, Patrick Elvin 1951- *WhoAmP 93*
Fleagle, Robert Guthrie 1918- *WhoWest 94*
Fleary, George McQuinn 1922- *WhoBlA 94*

Fletcher, Bramwell d1988 WhoHol 92
Fletcher, Cathy Ann 1949- WhoFI 94
Fletcher, Charles Montague 1911- Who 94
Fletcher, Cliff WhoBlA 94
Fletcher, Cliff 1935- WhoAm 94
Fletcher, Clifton Maurice 1935- WhoAmP 93
Fletcher, Colin 1922- WhoAm 94, WrDr 94
Fletcher, Craig Steven 1967- WhoFI 94, WhoScEn 94
Fletcher, Cyril 1913- WhoHol 92
Fletcher, David Quentin 1946- WhoScEn 94
Fletcher, Denise Koen 1948- WhoAm 94
Fletcher, Dexter WhoHol 92
Fletcher, Donald Warren 1929- WhoWest 94
Fletcher, Douglas Baden 1925- WhoAm 94
Fletcher, Dusty d1954 WhoHol 92
Fletcher, Edward Abraham 1924- WhoAm 94
Fletcher, Frank Alan 1939- WhoFI 94
Fletcher, Geoffrey Bernard Abbott 1903- Who 94
Fletcher, Geoffrey Scowcroft Who 94
Fletcher, George U. EncSF 93
Fletcher, Gilbert Hungerford 1911-1992 WhAm 10
Fletcher, Giles 1549?-1611 BlmGEL
Fletcher, Giles (the Younger) 1585-1623 BlmGEL
Fletcher, Glen Edward 1951- WhoBlA 94
Fletcher, Harry George, III 1941- WhoAm 94
Fletcher, Homer Lee 1928- WhoAm 94, WhoWest 94
Fletcher, Howard R. 1924- WhoBlA 94
Fletcher, Hugh Alasdair 1947- IntWW 93
Fletcher, Jack d1990 WhoHol 92
Fletcher, James Allen 1947- WhoWest 94
Fletcher, James Andrew 1945- WhoAm 94, WhoBlA 94
Fletcher, James C., Jr. 1934- WhoBlA 94
Fletcher, James Chipman 1919- WhoAmP 93
Fletcher, James Chipman 1919-1991 WhAm 10
Fletcher, James L. 1943- WhoAm 94, WhoAmL 94
Fletcher, James Muir Cameron 1914- IntWW 93, Who 94
Fletcher, James Warren 1943- WhoAm 94
Fletcher, Jeffrey Edward 1948- WhoScEn 94
Fletcher, Jerry Lee 1942- WhoWest 94
Fletcher, Joel Lafayette, Jr. 1897- WhAm 10
Fletcher, John 1579-1625 BlmGEL, IntDcT 2
Fletcher, John Antony 1918- Who 94
Fletcher, John Caldwell 1931- WhoAm 94
Fletcher, John Edwin 1941- Who 94
Fletcher, John Gould, Mrs. WhAm 10
Fletcher, John Lynn 1925- WhoScEn 94
Fletcher, John Sheidley 1953- WhoAm 94, WhoAmL 94
Fletcher, John Walter James 1937- WrDr 94
Fletcher, Joseph Smith 1863-1935 EncSF 93
Fletcher, Judith Ann 1943- WhoWest 94
Fletcher, Kim 1927- WhoWest 94
Fletcher, Lawrence d1970 WhoHol 92
Fletcher, Leland Vernon 1946- WhoAm 94, WhoAmA 93, WhoWest 94
Fletcher, Leroy Stevenson 1936- WhoAm 94, WhoScEn 94
Fletcher, Leslie 1906- Who 94
Fletcher, Leslie 1922- Who 94
Fletcher, Lester WhoHol 92
Fletcher, Louisa Adaline 1919- WhoBlA 94
Fletcher, Louise 1934- IntMPA 94, WhoHol 92
Fletcher, Louise 1936- WhoAm 94
Fletcher, Lucille 1912- WrDr 94
Fletcher, Malcolm Stanley 1936- Who 94
Fletcher, Marilyn Lowen DrAPF 93
Fletcher, Marjorie DrAPF 93
Fletcher, Marjorie Helen (Kelsey) 1932- Who 94
Fletcher, Mary Lee WhoFI 94
Fletcher, Milton Eric 1949- WhoBlA 94
Fletcher, Neil 1944- Who 94
Fletcher, Neville Horner 1930- IntWW 93
Fletcher, Norman WhoAmP 93
Fletcher, Norman S. WhoAm 94, WhoAmL 94
Fletcher, Ora d1920 WhoHol 92
Fletcher, Oscar Jasper, Jr. 1938- WhoAm 94
Fletcher, Page WhoHol 92
Fletcher, Paul Louie 1930- WhoFI 94
Fletcher, Paul Thomas 1912- Who 94
Fletcher, Peter Carteret 1916- Who 94
Fletcher, Philip B. WhoFI 94, WhoMW 93
Fletcher, Philip John 1946- Who 94
Fletcher, Phineas 1582-1650 BlmGEL
Fletcher, Randol Beryle 1957- WhoAmP 93
Fletcher, Raymond Russwald, Jr. 1929- WhoAm 94
Fletcher, Richard Alexander 1944- WrDr 94
Fletcher, Riley Eugene 1912- WhoAmL 94
Fletcher, Robert 1920- WhoAm 94
Fletcher, Robert E. 1938- WhoBlA 94
Fletcher, Robert Hillman 1940- WhoAm 94
Fletcher, Robin Anthony 1922- Who 94
Fletcher, Ronald 1921-1992 ConAu 42NR, WrDr 94N
Fletcher, Ronald Darling 1933- WhoAm 94
Fletcher, Ronald Stanley 1937- Who 94
Fletcher, Stuart Barron 1945- Who 94
Fletcher, Suzanne Wright 1940- WhoAm 94
Fletcher, Sylvester James 1934- WhoBlA 94
Fletcher, Tex d1987 WhoHol 92
Fletcher, Thomas William 1924- WhoAmP 93
Fletcher, Tyrone P. 1939- WhoBlA 94
Fletcher, Valerie J. 1951- WhoAmA 93
Fletcher, Virginia Carol 1944- WhoAmP 93
Fletcher, W. Fred 1928- WhoAmP 93
Fletcher, Winona Lee 1926- WhoBlA 94
Fletcher, Winston 1937- ConAu 42NR
Fletcher-Cook, Graham 1963- WhoHol 92
Fletcher-Cooke, Charles (Fletcher) 1914- Who 94
Fletcher the Elder, Giles 1546-1611 DcLB 136
Fletcher-Vane Who 94
Fletcher-Wynn, Valree 1922- WhoBlA 94
Flett, Nancy Jo W. 1936- WhoAmP 93
Flettner, Marianne 1933- WhoAm 94, WhoWest 94
Flettrich, Alvin Schaaf, Jr. 1944- WhoScEn 94
Flettrich, Carl Flaspoller 1948- WhoScEn 94
Fleu, Dorris Bell d1955 WhoHol 92
Fleur, Mary Louise 1951- WhoAmL 94
Fleurant, Gerdes 1939- WhoBlA 94
Fleuriet, Kenneth R. 1968- WhoAmP 93
Fleuriot De Langle, Paul-Antoine-Marie 1744-1787 WhWE
Fleury, Francois Louis Teissedre de 1749- AmRev
Fleury, Lorraine M. 1936- WhoAmP 93
Fleury, Marquis de Teissedre de WhAmRev
Fleury, Paul Aime 1939- WhoScEn 94
Fleury, Richard E. 1946- WhoAmP 93
Fleury, Thomas L. 1960- WhoAmP 93
Flew, Antony (Garrard Newton) 1923- WrDr 94
Flew, Antony Garrard Newton 1923- Who 94
Flewellen, Icabod 1916- WhoBlA 94
Flexner, Abraham 1866-1959 AmSocL
Flexner, James Thomas 1908- IntWW 93, WhoAm 94, WhoAmA 93, WrDr 94
Flexner, Louis Barkhouse 1902- WhoAm 94
Flexner, Stuart B. 1928-1990 WrDr 94N
Flexner, Stuart Berg 1928-1990 WhAm 10
Fleyshman, Veniamin Iosifovich 1913-1941 NewGrDO
Flichel, Eugene Anthony 1943- WhoAm 94
Flick, Carl 1926- WhoAm 94
Flick, John Edmond 1922- WhoAm 94
Flick, Lawrence F., II 1959- WhoFI 94
Flick, Loren Douglas 1955- WhoWest 94
Flick, Mary Jane 1958- WhoMW 93
Flick, Pat C. d1955 WhoHol 92
Flick, Paul John 1943- WhoAmA 93
Flick, Robbert 1939- WhoAmA 93
Flick, Robert J. 1944- WhoAmP 93
Flick, Sol E. 1915- WhoAm 94
Flick, Thomas Michael 1954- WhoAm 94, WhoMW 93
Flick, Warren Edmond 1943- WhoFI 94
Flick, William Fredrick 1940- WhoScEn 94, WhoWest 94
Flickenschild, Elisabeth d1977 WhoHol 92
Flicker, Ted 1930- WhoAm 94
Flicker, Theodore J. 1930- WhoHol 92
Flickinger, Charles John 1938- WhoAm 94
Flickinger, Harry Harner 1936- WhoAm 94, WhoAmL 94
Flickinger, Joe Arden 1949- WhoWest 94
Flickinger, Thomas L. 1939- WhoAm 94
Flieder, John Joseph 1936- WhoAm 94
Flieder, Stephen Eric 1959- WhoMW 93
Flieg, Helmut ConWorW 93
Fliegel, Ernie, Mrs. d1966 WhoHol 92
Fliegel, Leslie 1912-1968 WhoAmA 93N
Flieger, Howard Wentworth 1909- WhoAm 94
Flier, Michael S. 1941- WrDr 94
Flier, Michael Stephen 1941- WhoAm 94
Fliess, Peter Joachim 1915- WrDr 94
Fliether, Herbert 1911- NewGrDO
Fligg, James Edward 1936- WhoFI 94
Fligg, Loren L. 1940- WhoIns 94
Fligstein, Neil 1951- WrDr 94
Flimm, Jurgen 1941- IntWW 93
Findall, Jacqueline 1932- Who 94
Flinders, Mathew 1774-1814 WhWE
Flinders, Neil J 1934- WrDr 94
Flindt, Flemming 1936- IntDcB
Flindt, Flemming Ole 1936- IntWW 93
Flink, Hugo d1947 WhoHol 92
Flink, Jane Duncan 1929- WhoMW 93
Flinkstrom, Henry Allan 1933- WhoFI 94
Flinn, Charles Gallagher 1938- WhoAmL 94
Flinn, David Lynnfield 1943- WhoFI 94
Flinn, David R. 1937- WhoAm 94, WhoScEn 94
Flinn, Edward Ambrose, III 1931-1989 WhAm 10
Flinn, Eugene C. DrAPF 93
Flinn, James Edwin 1934- WhoMW 93
Flinn, John C. 1917- IntMPA 94
Flinn, Michael de Vlaming 1941- WhoFI 94
Flinn, Michael J. 1949- WhoAm 94, WhoAmL 94
Flinn, Michael Joseph 1958- WhoFI 94
Flinn, Monroe Lawrence 1917- WhoAmP 93
Flinn, Patricia Ellen DrAPF 93
Flinn, Patrick L. 1942- WhoAm 94, WhoFI 94
Flinn, Paul Anthony 1926- WhoScEn 94
Flinn, Roberta Jeanne 1947- WhoFI 94, WhoWest 94
Flinn, Thomas Hance 1922- WhoFI 94
Flinner, Dora 1940- WhoWomW 91
Flint, Anthony Patrick Fielding 1943- Who 94
Flint, Betty Margaret 1920- WrDr 94
Flint, Daniel Waldo Boone 1926- WhoAm 94, WhoAmL 94
Flint, David 1919- Who 94
Flint, George Squire 1930- WhoAm 94
Flint, Gordon B. 1919- WhoAmP 93
Flint, Hazel d1959 WhoHol 92
Flint, Helen d1967 WhoHol 92
Flint, Homer Eon 1892-1924 EncSF 93
Flint, Janet Altic 1935- WhoAmA 93
Flint, Joe 1948- WhoWest 94
Flint, John 1918- WrDr 94
Flint, John E. 1930- WhoAm 94
Flint, John Edgar 1930- WrDr 94
Flint, Kenneth Allen 1940- WhoFI 94
Flint, Kenneth C(ovey), Jr. 1947- ConAu 140
Flint, Lou Jean 1934- WhoWest 94
Flint, Mark Addison 1946- WhoAm 94
Flint, Mary Frances 1950- WhoBlA 94
Flint, Mary Louise 1949- WhoScEn 94
Flint, Michael Frederick 1932- Who 94
Flint, Myles Edward 1933- WhoAm 94
Flint, Rachael H. Who 94
Flint, Roland DrAPF 93
Flint, Russ 1944- SmATA 74
Flint, Sam d1980 WhoHol 92
Flint, Willis Wolfschmidt 1936- WhoWest 94
Flint-Shipman, Piers d1984 WhoHol 92
Flippen, Frances Morton WhoBlA 94
Flippen, Greg 1950- WhoBlA 94
Flippen, Jay C. d1971 WhoHol 92
Flipper, Henry O. 1856?-1940 AfrAmAl 6 [port]
Flippin, Lucy Lee WhoHol 92
Flippo, Ronnie G. 1937- WhoAmP 93
Flipse, John Edward 1921- WhoAm 94
Flipse, Mathew Jay 1896- WhAm 10
Fliri, Franz 1918- IntWW 93
Flisowski, Zdobyslaw 1932- IntWW 93
Fliss, Albert Edward, Jr. 1959- WhoScEn 94
Fliss, Raphael M. 1930- WhoAm 94, WhoMW 93
Flitcraft, Richard Kirby, II 1920- WhoAm 94, WhoFI 94
Flitman, Stephen Samuel 1966- WhoScEn 94
Flitner, Andreas 1922- IntWW 93
Flittie, Clifford Gilliland 1924- WhoAm 94
Flittie, John H. WhoIns 94
Flittie, John Howard 1936- WhoAm 94, WhoFI 94
Flocchini, Richard James 1939- WhoWest 94
Floccuzio, Luana 1960- WhoMW 93
Floch, Herve Alexander 1908- WhoScEn 94
Floch, Joseph 1895-1977 WhoAmA 93N
Floch, Martin Herbert 1928- WhoAm 94
Floch, Morton Hugh 1934- WhoFI 94
Floch-Baillet, Daniele Luce 1948- WhoScEn 94
Flock, Robert Ashby 1914- WhoWest 94
Flodine, Lloyd Randall 1946- WhoWest 94
Floersheim, Robert Bruce 1967- WhoScEn 94
Floersheimer, Walter D. 1900-1989 WhAm 10
Floeter, Kent 1937- WhoAmA 93
Floethe, Richard 1901-1988 WhoAmA 93N
Flogstad, Kjartan 1944- ConWorW 93
Flohn, Hermann 1912- IntWW 93
Floirat, Sylvain 1899-1993 NewYTBS 93
Flom, Edward Leonard 1929- WhoAm 94, WhoFI 94
Flom, Edward Lewis 1932- WhoMW 93
Flom, Gerald Trossen 1930- WhoAm 94
Flom, Joseph Harold 1923- WhoAm 94
Flom, Mark Alan 1955- WhoMW 93
Flomenhaft, Eleanor 1933- WhoAmA 93
Flon, Suzanne 1923- WhoHol 92
Flono, Fannie 1952- WhoBlA 94
Flood, A. L. WhoAm 94, WhoFI 94
Flood, Charles Bracelen 1929- WrDr 94
Flood, Daniel J. 1903- WhoAmP 93
Flood, David Andrew 1955- Who 94
Flood, Edward C. 1944-1985 WhoAmA 93N
Flood, Eugene, Jr. WhoBlA 94
Flood, Harold William 1922- WhoScEn 94
Flood, James Tyrrell 1934- WhoWest 94
Flood, Joan Moore 1941- WhoAmL 94
Flood, John Edward 1925- Who 94
Flood, John H. WhoAmP 93
Flood, John Martin 1939- Who 94
Flood, Michael Donovan 1949- Who 94
Flood, Michael Patrick 1962- WhoWest 94
Flood, Norman 1935- WrDr 94
Flood, Randolph Gene 1950- WhoAmP 93
Flood, Richard Sidney 1943- WhoAmA 93
Flood, Shearlene Davis 1938- WhoBlA 94
Flood, Verle Dennis 1924- WhoMW 93
Floody, Roger Roy 1927- WhoMW 93
Flooglebuckle, Al 1948- ConLC 76
Flook, Gary Raymond 1954- WhoMW 93
Flook, Maria DrAPF 93
Floor, Richard Earl 1940- WhoAm 94
Floquet, Etienne Joseph 1748-1785 NewGrDO
Flor, Loy Lorenz 1919- WhoScEn 94, WhoWest 94
Flora, Bert Howard 1957- WhoMW 93
Flora, Edward Benjamin 1929- WhoAm 94
Flora, Eric S. 1951- WhoWest 94
Flora, George Claude 1923- WhoAm 94
Flora, Jairus Dale, Jr. 1944- WhoAm 94
Flora, James (Royer) 1914- WrDr 94
Flora, James Royer 1914- WhoAmA 93
Flora, Jennifer Beach 1955- WhoWest 94
Flora, John Gerald 1936- WhoMW 93
Flora, Joseph M(artin) 1934- WrDr 94
Flora, Joseph Martin 1934- WhoAm 94
Flora, Kent Allen 1944- WhoMW 93
Flora, Maria Joan 1949- WhoAmL 94
Flora, William 1755-1820 WhAmRev
Florakis, Charilaos Ioannoy 1914- IntWW 93
Florance, Colden l'Hommedieu Ruggles 1931- WhoAm 94
Florath, Albert d1957 WhoHol 92
Flore, Jeanne fl. 16th cent.- BlmGWL
Florea, John 1916- IntMPA 94
Florea, Walter Graydon, Jr. 1954- WhoMW 93
Florelle d1974 WhoHol 92
Florelle, Odette 1898-1974 NewGrDO
Florence, Alexander Taylor 1940- Who 94
Florence, Eric Sheldon 1964- WhoFI 94
Florence, Frank Edward 1943- WhoWest 94
Florence, Jerry DeWayne 1948- WhoBlA 94
Florence, Johnny C. 1930- WhoBlA 94
Florence, Joseph Howard 1932- WhoWest 94
Florence, Kenneth James 1943- WhoAmL 94, WhoWest 94
Florence, Lucy Mae 1942- WhoFI 94
Florence, Myla Carol 1944- WhoAm 94
Florence, Paul Smith 1931- WhoMW 93
Florence, Verena Magdalena 1946- WhoWest 94
Florentino, Leila San Jose WhoAsA 94
Florentino, Leona 1849-1884 BlmGWL
Florentino, Vincent 1948- WhoIns 94
Florentz, Jean-Louis 1947- IntWW 93
Flores, Alberto Mares 1951- WhoHisp 94
Flores, Alberto Sierra 1956- WhoHisp 94
Flores, Alex 1959- WhoHisp 94
Flores, Alfonso J. 1949- WhoHisp 94
Flores, Alfred, Jr. 1958- WhoHisp 94
Flores, Alice Faye 1943- WhoHisp 94
Flores, Alma 1960- WhoHisp 94
Flores, Antonio R. 1947- WhoHisp 94

Flynn, Richard *DrAPF 93*
Flynn, Richard James 1928- *WhoAm 94, WhoAmL 94, WhoFI 94*
Flynn, Richard Jerome 1924- *WhoAm 94*
Flynn, Robert *DrAPF 93*
Flynn, Robert (Lopez) 1932- *WrDr 94*
Flynn, Robert Francis 1948- *WhoFI 94*
Flynn, Sharon Ann 1955- *WhoFI 94*
Flynn, Thomas *Who 94*
Flynn, Thomas Charles 1950- *WhoFI 94*
Flynn, Thomas Geoffrey 1937- *WhoAm 94*
Flynn, Thomas Joseph 1936- *WhoAm 94*
Flynn, Thomas Joseph 1947- *WhoFI 94*
Flynn, Thomas Lee 1946- *WhoAmL 94*
Flynn, Thomas Patrick 1924- *WhoAm 94*
Flynn, Thomas R. 1940- *WhoScEn 94*
Flynn, William Edward 1938- *WhoAmP 93*
Flynn, William Frederick 1952- *WhoAmL 94*
Flynn, William J. 1932- *WhoIns 94*
Flynn, William J., Jr. 1933- *WhoAmP 93*
Flynn, William Joseph 1926- *WhoAm 94, WhoIns 94*
Flynn, William Joseph, Jr. 1949- *WhoAmP 93*
Flynn, William Thomas 1916- *WhoScEn 94*
Flynn, William Thomas 1947- *WhoIns 94*
Flynn, Wilson Paul 1926- *WhoAmP 93*
Flynn Currie, Barbara 1940- *WhoWomW 91*
Flynn Peterson, Kathleen A. 1954- *WhoAmL 94*
Flynt, Candace *DrAPF 93*
Flynt, Clifton William 1953- *WhoFI 94, WhoMW 93, WhoScEn 94*
Flynt, Crisp B. 1949- *WhoAmP 93*
Flynt, John J., Jr. 1914- *WhoAmP 93*
Flynt, Larry Claxton 1942- *WhoAm 94*
Flys, Carlos Ricardo 1963- *WhoHisp 94*
Flythe, Jerry Kent 1954- *WhoFI 94*
Flythe, Starkey, Jr. *DrAPF 93*
FM-2030 *WrDr 94*
Fo, Dario *IntWW 93*
Fo, Dario 1926- *ConWorW 93, IntDcT 2 [port], Who 94*
Foa, Conrad Mario 1941- *WhoFI 94*
Foa, Joseph Victor 1909- *WhoAm 94*
Foakes, Reginald Anthony 1923- *Who 94*
Foale, Colin Henry 1930- *Who 94*
Foale, Marion Ann 1939- *IntWW 93*
Foard, Douglas W. 1939- *WhoAm 94*
Foard, Frederick Carter 1945- *WhoBlA 94*
Foard, Susan Lee 1938- *WhoAm 94*
Fobbe, Franz Caspar 1948- *WhoScEn 94*
Fobbs, Joan Merna 1943- *WhoAm 94*
Fobbs, Kevin 1954- *WhoBlA 94*
Fobes, John Edwin 1918- *IntWW 93*
Fobes, Melcher Prince 1911- *WhoMW 93*
Foccart, Jacques 1913- *IntWW 93*
Foch, Ferdinand 1851-1929 *HisWorL [port]*
Foch, Nina 1924- *IntMPA 94, WhoAm 94, WhoHol 92, WhoWest 94*
Focht, John Arnold, Jr. 1923- *WhoAm 94*
Focht, Michael Harrison 1942- *WhoAm 94*
Focht, Michael Harrison, Jr. 1965- *WhoAmL 94*
Focht, Theodore Harold 1934- *WhoAmL 94*
Focke, Katharina 1922- *IntWW 93*
Focke, Paul Everard Justus 1937- *Who 94*
Fockler, Herbert Hill 1922- *WhoAm 94, WhoFI 94*
Focks, Dana Alan 1948- *WhoScEn 94*
Fodden, Simon R. 1944- *WrDr 94*
Foden-Pattinson, Peter Lawrence d1992 *Who 94N*
Foderaro, Anthony Harolde 1926- *WhoAm 94*
Fodiman, Aaron Rosen 1937- *WhoFI 94*
Fodor, Eugene 1905-1991 *WhAm 10*
Fodor, Eugene Nicholas 1950- *WhoAm 94*
Fodor, Gabor Bela 1915- *WhoAm 94*
Fodor, George Emeric 1932- *WhoScEn 94*
Fodor, Susanna Serena 1950- *WhoAm 94, WhoAmL 94*
Fodor-Mainvielle, Josephine 1789-1870 *NewGrDO*
Fodrea, Carolyn Wrobel 1943- *WhoAm 94, WhoMW 93*
Fodstad, Harald 1940- *WhoScEn 94*
Fody, Edward Paul 1947- *WhoScEn 94*
Foe, Elizabeth *WhoScEn 94*
Foehl, Edward Albert 1942- *WhoAm 94, WhoFI 94*
Foehringer, George Brian 1958- *WhoFI 94*
Foehrkolb, Susan Mary 1948- *WhoMW 93*
Foell, Darrell William 1935- *WhoMW 93*
Foell, Earl William 1929- *WhoAm 94*
Foell, Laura Lee 1957- *WhoAmP 93*
Foell, Ronald R. 1929- *WhoFI 94*
Foell, Wesley Kay 1935- *WhoAm 94*
Foerch, James Steele 1946- *WhoMW 93*
Foerst, John George, Jr. 1927- *WhoFI 94*
Foerster, Anton 1837-1926 *NewGrDO*
Foerster, Bernd 1923- *WhoAm 94*
Foerster, Conrad Louis 1938- *WhoScEn 94*
Foerster, James Fredrick 1951- *WhoMW 93*
Foerster, Josef Bohuslav 1859-1951 *NewGrDO*
Foerster, Richard *DrAPF 93*
Foerster, Urban Michael, III 1952- *WhoAm 94*
Foersterling, Jay 1957- *WhoMW 93*
Foex, Pierre 1935- *Who 94*
Foflygen, Ronald Wayne 1944- *WhoWest 94*
Fofonoff, Nicholas Paul 1929- *WhoAm 94*
Foft, John William 1928- *WhoAm 94*
Fogam, Margaret Hanorah *WhoBlA 94*
Fogarassy, Helen *DrAPF 93*
Fogarty, Charles Joseph 1955- *WhoAmP 93*
Fogarty, Christopher Winthrop 1921- *Who 94*
Fogarty, Daniel P. 1924- *WhoAmP 93*
Fogarty, Edward Michael 1948- *WhoAmL 94*
Fogarty, Gerald Philip 1939- *WhoAm 94*
Fogarty, Jack V. *IntMPA 94*
Fogarty, John Patrick Cody 1958- *WhoAmL 94*
Fogarty, John Thomas 1929- *WhoAm 94*
Fogarty, John Thomas 1940- *WhoAm 94*
Fogarty, Katrina Sibley Park 1920- *WhoFI 94*
Fogarty, Michael Patrick 1916- *Who 94, WrDr 94*
Fogarty, Michael Thomas 1950- *WhoAmL 94*
Fogarty, Raymond W. 1957- *WhoAmP 93*
Fogarty, Robert Stephen 1938- *WhoAm 94*
Fogarty, William Martin, Jr. 1935- *WhoAm 94*
Fogas, Bruce Scott 1959- *WhoMW 93*
Fogden, Michael Ernest George 1936- *Who 94*
Fogel, Aaron *DrAPF 93*
Fogel, Adelaide Forst 1915- *WhoAmL 94*
Fogel, Alan Dale 1945- *WhoWest 94*
Fogel, Daniel Mark *DrAPF 93*
Fogel, David Alan 1942- *WhoAmP 93*
Fogel, Henry 1942- *WhoAm 94*
Fogel, Irving Martin 1929- *WhoAm 94, WhoFI 94, WhoScEn 94*
Fogel, Jacquelyn Jean 1951- *WhoMW 93*
Fogel, Joan Cathy 1943- *WhoAmL 94*
Fogel, Johann Christoph *NewGrDO*
Fogel, Paul David 1949- *WhoAm 94*
Fogel, Richard *WhoAmL 94*
Fogel, Robert W. *NewYTBS 93 [port]*
Fogel, Robert W. 1926- *Who 94*
Fogel, Robert William 1926- *IntWW 93, WhoAm 94, WhoMW 93, WrDr 94*
Fogel, Seymour d1993 *NewYTBS 93*
Fogel, Seymour 1911-1984 *WhoAmA 93N*
Fogel, Steven Marc 1958- *WhoWest 94*
Fogel, Vladimir d1929 *WhoHol 92*
Fogelberg, Daniel Grayling 1951- *WhoAm 94*
Fogelberg, Paul Alan 1951- *WhoMW 93*
Fogelholm, Markus 1946- *IntWW 93*
Fogelman, Martin 1928- *WhoAm 94*
Fogelman, Morris Joseph 1923- *WhoAm 94*
Fogelnest, Robert 1946- *WhoAmL 94*
Fogelson, Andrew 1942- *IntMPA 94*
Fogelson, David 1903- *WhoAm 94*
Fogelson, E. E. d1987 *WhoHol 92*
Fogelson, Raymond David 1933- *WhoAm 94*
Fogelsonger, Ned Raymond 1947- *WhoFI 94*
Fogerty, James Edward 1945- *WhoMW 93*
Fogerty, Thomas Richard 1941-1990 *WhAm 10*
Fogg, Alan 1921- *Who 94*
Fogg, Blaine Viles 1940- *WhoAm 94*
Fogg, Brian Jeffrey 1963- *WhoWest 94*
Fogg, Cyril Percival 1914- *Who 94*
Fogg, George Kephart 1947- *WhoAm 94*
Fogg, Gordon Elliott 1919- *IntWW 93, Who 94, WrDr 94*
Fogg, Joseph Graham, III 1946- *WhoAm 94*
Fogg, Mark Thomas 1954- *WhoMW 93*
Fogg, Monica *WhoAmA 93*
Fogg, Orian d1923 *WhoHol 92*
Fogg, Rebecca Snider 1949- *WhoAmA 93*
Fogg, Richard Lloyd 1937- *WhoAm 94*
Foggie, Charles H. 1912- *WhoBlA 94*
Foggie, Charles Herbert 1912- *WhoAm 94*
Foggon, George 1913- *Who 94*
Foggs, Edward L. *WhoAm 94*
Foggs, Edward L. 1934- *WhoBlA 94*
Foggs, Joyce D. 1930- *WhoBlA 94*
Fogh-Andersen, Poul 1913- *IntWW 93*
Foght, James Loren 1936- *WhoAm 94*
Fogle, Homer William, Jr. 1948- *WhoScEn 94*
Fogle, James 1936- *WrDr 94*
Fogle, James Lee 1950- *WhoAmL 94*
Fogleman, Guy 1924- *WhoAmP 93*
Fogleman, Guy Carroll 1955- *WhoScEn 94*
Fogleman, John Albert 1911- *WhoAm 94, WhoAmP 93*
Fogleman, Julian Barton 1920- *WhoAm 94*
Fogleman, Ronald Robert 1942- *WhoAm 94*
Foglesong, Paul David 1949- *WhoScEn 94*
Foglietta, Thomas M. 1928- *CngDr 93, WhoAmP 93*
Foglietta, Thomas Michael 1928- *WhoAm 94*
Fognani, John Dennis 1950- *WhoAm 94, WhoAmL 94*
Fogo, Donald Peter *WhoAmP 93*
Fogt, Howard W., Jr. 1942- *WhoAm 94, WhoAmL 94*
Fohl, Timothy 1934- *WhoAm 94*
Fohr, Jenny *WhoAmA 93*
Fohrman, Burton H. 1939- *WhoAm 94*
Foighel, Isi 1927- *IntWW 93*
Foignet, Charles Gabriel 1750-1836 *NewGrDO*
Foignet, Francois 1782-1845 *NewGrDO*
Foisie, Philip Manning 1922- *WhoAm 94*
Foix, J.V. 1893-1987 *DcLB 134 [port]*
Fojtik, Jan 1928- *IntWW 93*
Fok, Agnes Kwan 1940- *WhoAsA 94*
Fok, Henry Ying Tung *WhoPRCh 91*
Fok, Samuel Shiu-Ming 1926- *WhoAsA 94, WhoWest 94*
Fok, Thomas Dso Yun 1921- *WhoAm 94, WhoFI 94, WhoMW 93*
Fok, Yu-Si 1932- *WhoAsA 94*
Fokes, William B. *WhoIns 94*
Fokin, Vitold Pavlovych 1932- *IntWW 93, LoBiDrD*
Fokine, Mikhail 1880-1942 *IntDcB [port]*
Folan, Lorcan Michael 1960- *WhoScEn 94*
Foland, William James 1947- *WhoAmL 94*
Foland, Willis James 1947- *WhoAm 94*
Folberg, Harold Jay 1941- *WhoAm 94*
Folchetti, J. Robert 1934- *WhoScEn 94*
Folda, Jaroslav (Thayer), III 1940- *WhoAmA 93*
Foldes, Francis Ferenc 1910- *WhoScEn 94*
Foldes, Lucien Paul 1930- *Who 94*
Foldes, Peter *EncSF 93*
Foldi, Andrew Harry 1926- *WhoAm 94*
Folds, Charles Weston 1910- *WhoAm 94*
Foldvari, Istvan 1945- *WhoScEn 94*
Foletta, Tony d1980 *WhoHol 92*
Foley, Baron 1923- *Who 94*
Foley, Arvil Eugene 1924- *WhoScEn 94*
Foley, Bill d1981 *WhoHol 92*
Foley, Brian Charles 1910- *Who 94*
Foley, Brian T. 1959- *WhoAmL 94*
Foley, Daniel Edmund 1926- *WhoAm 94, WhoFI 94, WhoWest 94*
Foley, Daniel Joseph 1943- *WhoAm 94*
Foley, Daniel Ronald 1941- *WhoAm 94*
Foley, Deborah Ann 1954- *WhoMW 93*
Foley, Dennis Donald 1923-1988 *WhAm 10*
Foley, Dorance Vincent 1900-1988 *WhAm 10*
Foley, Dorothy Louise 1964- *WhoAmL 94*
Foley, Dorothy Swartz *WhoAmA 93*
Foley, Edward Joseph 1933- *WhoAm 94*
Foley, Edward W. 1937- *WhoIns 94*
Foley, Eileen 1918- *WhoAmP 93*
Foley, Ellen 1952- *WhoHol 92*
Foley, Fenton James, Jr. 1942- *WhoAmL 94*
Foley, George Bernard 1950- *WhoFI 94*
Foley, Helen A. 1953- *WhoAmP 93*
Foley, Hugh Smith 1939- *Who 94*
Foley, Jack *DrAPF 93*
Foley, Jack 1940- *BasBi, WhoAm 94*
Foley, James *IntMPA 94*
Foley, James David 1942- *WhoAm 94, WhoScEn 94*
Foley, James M. *WhoAmP 93*
Foley, James Patrick 1953- *WhoAmP 93*
Foley, James Thomas 1910-1990 *WhAm 10*
Foley, Jeffrey Young 1951- *WhoWest 94*
Foley, Joe d1955 *WhoHol 92*
Foley, Johanna Mary 1945- *Who 94*
Foley, John Joseph 1948- *WhoAmL 94*
Foley, John Miles 1947- *WhoMW 93*
Foley, John Paul 1939- *Who 94*
Foley, John Porter, Jr., Mrs. 1908- *WhoAm 94*
Foley, Joseph Bernard 1929- *WhoAm 94*
Foley, Joseph Lawrence 1953- *WhoAm 94*
Foley, Julie Hanahan 1963- *WhoMW 93*
Foley, June 1944- *TwCYAW*
Foley, Kathleen M. 1944- *WhoScEn 94*
Foley, Kathy Kelsey 1952- *WhoAmA 93*
Foley, Kevin 1950- *WhoIns 94*
Foley, Leo Thomas 1928- *WhoAmP 93, WhoMW 93*
Foley, Lewis Michael 1938- *WhoAm 94*
Foley, Lila A. 1925- *WhoHisp 94*
Foley, (Mary) Louise Munro 1933- *WrDr 94*
Foley, Lucille C. 1936- *WhoAmP 93*
Foley, Mark 1954- *WhoAmP 93*
Foley, Martha 1897-1977 *See* Burnett, Whit 1899-1973 *DcLB 137*
Foley, Martin James 1946- *WhoAm 94*
Foley, Maurice (Anthony) 1925- *Who 94*
Foley, Michael Francis 1946- *WhoAm 94*
Foley, Noel *Who 94*
Foley, (Thomas John) Noel 1914- *Who 94*
Foley, Patricia Jean 1956- *WhoFI 94*
Foley, Patrick Joseph 1930- *WhoAm 94, WhoIns 94*
Foley, Patrick Joseph 1934- *WhoAmP 93*
Foley, Patrick Martin 1930- *WhoAm 94*
Foley, Patrick Michael 1958- *WhoWest 94*
Foley, Paula Jean 1959- *WhoMW 93*
Foley, Peter Michael 1947- *WhoAm 94, WhoAmL 94*
Foley, Ralph M. 1940- *WhoAmP 93*
Foley, Ralph Morton 1940- *WhoMW 93*
Foley, Red d1968 *WhoHol 92*
Foley, Richard 1580-1657 *DcNaB MP*
Foley, Richard, Jr. 1949- *WhoAmP 93*
Foley, Ridgway Knight, Jr. 1937- *WhoAm 94*
Foley, Robert Matthew 1943- *WhoAmL 94*
Foley, Roger D. 1917- *WhoAmL 94, WhoWest 94*
Foley, Ronald E. 1945- *WhoIns 94*
Foley, Ronald F. 1950- *WhoAmP 93*
Foley, Ronald Graham Gregory 1923- *Who 94*
Foley, Stephen Joseph, Jr. 1956- *WhoAmL 94*
Foley, Thomas 1942- *WhoAm 94*
Foley, Thomas C. 1952- *WhoAm 94, WhoFI 94*
Foley, Thomas Joseph 1941- *WhoWest 94*
Foley, Thomas Michael 1943- *WhoAm 94, WhoWest 94*
Foley, Thomas S. 1929- *CngDr 93, NewYTBS 93 [port]*
Foley, Thomas Stephen 1929- *IntWW 93, Who 94, WhoAm 94, WhoAmP 93, WhoWest 94*
Foley, Timothy Albert 1947- *WhoAmA 93*
Foley, Timothy Francis 1942- *WhoFI 94*
Foley, Walter P. 1936- *WhoIns 94*
Foley, William Edward 1911-1990 *WhAm 10*
Foley, William Thomas 1911-1992 *WhAm 10*
Folgate, Homer Emmett, Jr. 1920- *WhoAm 94*
Folger, Fred, Jr. *WhoAmP 93*
Folger, Henry Clay 1857-1930 *DcLB 140 [port]*
Foli, A(llan) J(ames) 1835-1899 *NewGrDO*
Foligno, Angela da c. 1248-1304 *BlmGWL*
Folingsby, Kenneth *EncSF 93*
Folinsbee, Robert Edward 1917- *WhoAm 94*
Folio, Lorenzo 1938- *WhoAm 94*
Folisi, Joseph Charles 1948- *WhoMW 93*
Foljambe *Who 94*
Folk, Ernest L., III 1930-1989 *WhAm 10*
Folk, Frank Stewart 1932- *WhoBlA 94*
Folk, George Edgar, Jr. 1914- *WhoScEn 94*
Folk, James 1948- *WhoAm 94*
Folk, Robert Louis 1925- *WhoAm 94*
Folk, Roger Maurice 1936- *WhoAm 94*
Folk, Thomas Robert 1950- *WhoAm 94*
Folk, William R. 1944- *WhoMW 93*
Folkens, Alan Theodore 1936- *WhoScEn 94*
Folker, Cathleen Ann 1956- *WhoMW 93*
Folkers, Karl 1906- *IntWW 93*
Folkers, Karl August 1906- *WhoAm 94, WhoScEn 94, WorScD*
Folkers, Kimberly Kay 1960- *WhoMW 93*
Folkerts, Dennis Michael 1960- *WhoScEn 94*
Folkerts, Kenneth Lee 1950- *WhoMW 93*
Folkerts, Mark Allen 1956- *WhoWest 94*
Folkestone, Viscount 1955- *Who 94*
Folkinga, Celia Gould 1957- *WhoAmP 93*
Folkins, John William 1948- *WhoScEn 94*
Folkman, David H. 1934- *WhoAm 94*
Folkman, Moses Judah 1933- *WhoAm 94, WhoScEn 94*
Folkman, Steven Lee 1952- *WhoScEn 94*
Folks, Francis Neil 1939- *WhoScEn 94*
Folks, J. Leroy 1929- *WhoAm 94*
Folks, John M. 1948- *WhoAmP 93*
Folks, Leslie Scott 1955- *WhoBlA 94*
Folkus, Dan 1946- *WhoAmA 93*
Follansbee, Dorothy Leland 1911- *WhoAm 94*

Follansbee, William Uhler 1859-1939 EncABHB 9 [port]
Follesdal, Dagfinn 1932- IntWW 93, WhoAm 94
Follett, Brian (Keith) 1939- Who 94
Follett, James 1939- EncSF 93, WrDr 94
Follett, Jean Frances 1917-1991 WhoAmA 93N
Follett, Ken 1949- EncSF 93, IntWW 93
Follett, Ken(neth Martin) 1949- WrDr 94
Follett, Kenneth Martin 1949- WhoAm 94
Follett, Mary Vierling 1917- WhoMW 93
Follett, Robert J. R. 1928- WhoAmP 93
Follett, Robert John Richard 1928- WhoAm 94, WhoMW 93
Follett, Ronald Francis 1939- WhoAm 94
Follett, Roy Hunter 1935- WhoAm 94, WhoWest 94
Folley, Clyde H. 1927- WhoAm 94, WhoFI 94
Folley, Gregory Scott 1959- WhoMW 93
Follick, Edwin Duane 1935- WhoAmL 94, WhoFI 94, WhoWest 94
Follin-Jones, Elizabeth DrAPF 93
Follman, Dorothy Major 1932- WhoAm 94
Follmer, Paul L. WhoBlA 94
Follo, Carl R. 1944- WhoIns 94
Folloni, Deborah Ann Marie 1955- WhoAmL 94
Follows, Megan 1969- WhoHol 92
Folmar, Emory WhoAm 94
Folmar, Emory M. 1930- WhoAmP 93
Folmar, Joel Michael 1936- WhoAmP 93
Folmar, Larry John 1942- WhoAmL 94
Folsey, George c. 1898-1988 IntDcF 2-4
Folsey, George 1939- IntMPA 94
Folsom, Fran M. 1894- WhAm 10
Folsom, Franklin Brewster 1907- WhoAm 94, WrDr 94
Folsom, Fred Gorham, III 1945- WhoAmA 93
Folsom, Henry R. 1913- WhoAmP 93
Folsom, James, Jr. 1949- WhoAm 94
Folsom, James Elisha, Jr. 1949- WhoAmP 93
Folsom, John Roy 1918- WhoAm 94
Folsom, Lowell Edwin 1947- WhoMW 93
Folsom, Nathaniel 1726-1790 WhAmRev
Folsom, Richard Gilman 1907- WhoAm 94
Folsom, Rose 1953- WhoAmA 93
Folsom, Sallie Stark 1930- WhoAmP 93
Folsom, Victor Clarence 1909- WhoAmL 94
Folsom, Willis F. 1825-c. 1894 EncNAR
Folster, David 1937- WrDr 94
Folter, Roland 1943- WhoFI 94
Foltinek, Herbert 1930- IntWW 93
Folts, David Jacob 1958- WhoMW 93
Folts, Franklin Ertes 1893- WhAm 10
Foltz, Clinton Henry 1936- WhoAm 94
Foltz, Donald Joseph 1933- WhoWest 94
Foltz, Jack L. WhoAmL 94
Foltz, Kim d1993 NewYTBS 93
Foltz, Rodger Lowell 1934- WhoAm 94
Foltz-Gray, Dorothy DrAPF 93
Folwell, Denis d1971 WhoHol 92
Folz, Carol Ann 1951- WhoFI 94, WhoMW 93
Folz, Kathleen Louise WhoMW 93
Folzenlogen, P. D. 1939- WhoAm 94
Folz-Steinacker, Sigrid 1941- WhoWomW 91
Fomby, Thomas Blake 1947- WhoFI 94
Fomin 1929- WrDr 94
Fomin, Yevstigney Ipat'yevich 1761-1800 NewGrDO
Fomon, Samuel Joseph 1923- WhoAm 94
Fomufod, Antoine Kofi 1940- WhoBlA 94
Fonash, Stephen Joseph 1941- WhoAm 94, WhoScEn 94
Foncello, Martin John, Jr. 1952- WhoFI 94
Foncha, John Ngu 1916- IntWW 93
Fonck, Eugene Jason 1954- WhoScEn 94
Fonda, Bridget WhoAm 94
Fonda, Bridget 1963- WhoHol 92
Fonda, Bridget 1964- IntMPA 94
Fonda, Henry d1982 WhoHol 92
Fonda, Henry Jaynes 1905-1982 AmCulL [port]
Fonda, Jane 1937- IntMPA 94, IntWW 93, WhoAm 94, WhoHol 92, WrDr 94
Fonda, Peter 1939- IntMPA 94, WhoHol 92
Fondahl, John Walker 1924- WhoAm 94, WhoScEn 94
Fondaw, Ron 1954- WhoAmA 93
Fondiller, Robert 1916- WhoAm 94
Fondots, David John 1963- WhoWest 94
Fondren, Harold M. 1922- WhoAmA 93
Fondren, Larry E. 1947- WhoIns 94
Foner, Eric 1943- WhoAm 94, WrDr 94
Foner, Henry Joseph 1919- WhoAmP 93
Foner, Philip S. 1910- WhoAm 94, WrDr 94
Foner, Simon 1925- WhoAm 94
Fones, William H. D. 1917- WhoAmP 93
Fonfara, John W. WhoAmP 93
Fong, April Ann WhoAsA 94
Fong, Benson d1987 WhoHol 92
Fong, Bernard W. D. 1926- WhoAm 94
Fong, Bernard Wah Doung 1926- WhoAsA 94
Fong, Brian WhoHol 92
Fong, Carl S. 1959- WhoWest 94
Fong, Charlen WhoAsA 94
Fong, Dewey WhoAsA 94
Fong, Eva Chow 1939- WhoAsA 94
Fong, Gary Curtis 1963- WhoAm 94
Fong, Glenn Randall 1955- WhoAsA 94
Fong, Harold Michael 1938- WhoAm 94, WhoAmL 94, WhoAsA 94, WhoWest 94
Fong, Harry H. S. 1935- WhoAsA 94
Fong, Herbert S. 1939- WhoAsA 94
Fong, Hiram 1906- IntWW 93
Fong, Hiram L. 1906- WhoAm 94, WhoFI 94, WhoWest 94
Fong, Hiram Leong 1906- WhoAmP 93, WhoAsA 94
Fong, Ivan Kenneth 1961- WhoAmL 94
Fong, J Craig 1955- WhoAsA 94
Fong, Jack Sun-Chik 1941- WhoAsA 94
Fong, Joshua 1924- WhoAsA 94
Fong, Julita Angela 1933- WhoWest 94
Fong, Kai Meng 1960- WhoAsA 94
Fong, Kam WhoHol 92
Fong, Kevin M. 1955- WhoAmL 94
Fong, Kevin Murray 1955- WhoAsA 94
Fong, Leo WhoHol 92
Fong, Leslie Kaleiopu Wah Cheong 1946- WhoAmL 94
Fong, Mary Helena 1924- WhoAsA 94
Fong, Matthew K. 1953- WhoAsA 94
Fong, Nelson C. 1944- WhoAsA 94
Fong, Peter 1924- WhoAm 94
Fong, Peter C. K. 1955- WhoAm 94, WhoAmL 94
Fong, Raymond 1955- WhoAsA 94
Fong, Thomas Y. K. 1949- WhoAsA 94
Fong, Wang-Fun 1947- WhoScEn 94
Fong-Torres, Ben 1945- WhoAsA 94
Fong-Torres, Shirley 1946- WhoAsA 94
Fong Wong, Nellie Kut-Man 1949- WhoWomW 91
Fonkalsrud, Eric Walter 1932- WhoAm 94
Fonken, Gerhard Joseph 1928- WhoAm 94, WhoScEn 94
Fonne, Hiram A. 1932- WhoMW 93
Fonner, David Kent 1957- WhoAmL 94
Fonrose, Harold Anthony 1925- WhoBlA 94
Fons, August Marion, III 1951- WhoWest 94
Fons, Michael Patrick 1959- WhoScEn 94
Fonseca, Aloysius (Joseph) 1915-1991 WrDr 94N
Fonseca, James Francis 1923- WhoHisp 94
Fonseca, Juan E. 1919- WhoHisp 94
Fonseca, Orlando R. WhoAmP 93, WhoHisp 94
Fonseca, Santiago V. 1936- WhoHisp 94
Fonseca-C., Horacio R. 1940- WhoHisp 94
Fonss, Olaf d1949 WhoHol 92
Font, Roberto d1981 WhoHol 92
Fonta, Caroline 1957- WhoScEn 94
Fontaine, Andre 1921- IntWW 93
Fontaine, Andre Lucien Georges 1921- Who 94
Fontaine, Arnold Anthony 1962- WhoScEn 94
Fontaine, Athanas Paul 1905-1989 WhAm 10
Fontaine, E. Joseph WhoAmA 93
Fontaine, Eddie 1934- WhoHol 92
Fontaine, Edward Paul 1936- WhoAm 94
Fontaine, Frank d1978 WhoHol 92
Fontaine, Hippolyte WorInv
Fontaine, Joan 1917- IntMPA 94, WhoHol 92
Fontaine, John C. WhoAmL 94, WhoFI 94
Fontaine, John Clovis 1931- WhoAm 94
Fontaine, Lilian d1975 WhoHol 92
Fontaine, Maurice Alfred 1904- IntWW 93
Fontaine, Nicole Claude Marie 1942- WhoWomW 91
Fontaine, Pierre-Francois-Leonard 1762-1853 NewGrDO
Fontaine, Tony d1974 WhoHol 92
Fontaines, Comtesse de d1730 BlmGWL
Fontan, Gabrielle d1959 WhoHol 92
Fontana, Alessandro 1936- WhoScEn 94
Fontana, Anthony Jerome, Jr. 1950- WhoAmP 93
Fontana, Bill Patrick 1947- WhoAmA 93
Fontana, D(orothy) C(atherine) 1939- EncSF 93
Fontana, David A. 1947- WhoScEn 94
Fontana, Ferdinando 1850-1919 NewGrDO
Fontana, Gabriele 1957- NewGrDO
Fontana, Gary L. 1946- WhoAm 94
Fontana, Giacinto fl. 1712-1735 NewGrDO
Fontana, Giovanni Angelo 1944- IntWW 93
Fontana, Girolamo d1714 NewGrDO
Fontana, John Arthur 1955- WhoFI 94
Fontana, Mario H. 1933- WhoScEn 94
Fontana, Mars Guy 1910-1988 WhAm 10
Fontana, Peter Robert 1935- WhoScEn 94
Fontana, Robert Edward 1915- WhoAm 94
Fontana, Thomas M(ichael) 1951- WrDr 94
Fontana, Vincent Robert 1939- WhoAm 94
Fontane, Theodor 1819-1898 DcLB 129 [port]
Fontanel, Genevieve WhoHol 92
Fontanesi, Francesco 1751-1795 NewGrDO
Fontanet, Alvaro L. 1940- WhoHisp 94
Fontanez, Angel Gabriel 1960- WhoHisp 94
Fontanez, Dale W. 1967- WhoHisp 94
Fontanges, Vicomte de 1740-1822 WhAmRev
Fontanive, Lynn Marie WhoMW 93
Fontanne, Lynn d1983 WhoHol 92
Fontanne, Lynn 1887-1983 AmCulL
Fontannini, Clare d1984 WhoAmA 93N
Fontayne, K. Nicole WhoBlA 94
Fonte, Moderata 1555-1592 BlmGWL
Fontein, Frederik M. WhoIns 94
Fontelieu, Stocker WhoHol 92
Fontenay, Charles L(ouis) 1917- EncSF 93, WrDr 94
Fontendot, Elvin Clemence 1952- WhoAmP 93
Fontenele, Maria Luiza Menezes 1942- WhoWomW 91
Fontenelle, Bernard le Bovier, sieur de 1657-1757 GuFrLit 2
Fontenelle, Bernard le Bovier de 1657-1757 NewGrDO
Fontenelle, Bernard Le Bovyer De 1657-1757 EncSF 93
Fontenelle, Louisa 1769-1799 NewGrDO
Fontenelle, Lucien c. 1800-c. 1840 WhWE
Fontenot, Chester J. 1950- ConAu 43NR
Fontenot, Herman 1963- WhoBlA 94
Fontenot, Ken DrAPF 93
Fontenot, Louis K. 1918- WhoBlA 94
Fontenot, Mary Alice 1910- WrDr 94
Fontenot-Jamerson, Berlinda 1947- WhoBlA 94
Fontes, Brian F. 1950- WhoHisp 94
Fontes, Montserrat 1940- WhoHisp 94, WrDr 94
Fontes, Patricia J. 1936- WhoAm 94
Fontes, Wayne 1939- WhoAm 94, WhoMW 93
Fontette de Sommery, Mademoiselle fl. 18th cent.- BlmGWL
Fonteyn, Margot d1991 WhoHol 92
Fonteyn, Margot 1919-1991 IntDcB [port]
Fonteyn De Arias, Margot 1919-1991 WhAm 10
Fontheim, Claude G.B. 1955- WhoAmL 94, WhoFI 94
Fonvielle, William Harold 1943- WhoAm 94, WhoBlA 94
Fonville, Danny D. WhoBlA 94
Fonville, Dee DrAPF 93
Fonvizin, Denis Ivanovich 1745-1792 IntDcT 2
Foo, Charles 1922- WhoAsA 94
Foo, Lee Tung d1966 WhoHol 92
Foo, Wing d1953 WhoHol 92
Foody, Jan Petkus 1935- WhoFI 94
Fookes, Janet (Evelyn) 1936- Who 94
Fookes, Janet Evelyn 1936- WhoWomW 91
Foolery, Tom 1947- WhoAmA 93
Fools Crow, Frank c. 1891-1989 EncNAR
Foon, Dennis 1951- WrDr 94
Foonberg, Jay G. 1935- WhoAmL 94
Foong, Nicolai Yein 1960- WhoAsA 94
Foosaner, Judith 1940- WhoAmA 93
Foose, Robert James 1938- WhoAmA 93
Fooshee, Malcolm 1898-1989 WhAm 10
Foot, Baron 1909- Who 94
Foot, David 1929- WrDr 94
Foot, David Lovell 1939- Who 94
Foot, Geoffrey (James) 1915- Who 94
Foot, Michael 1913- Who 94, WrDr 94
Foot, Michael Colin 1935- Who 94
Foot, Michael David Kenneth Willoughby 1946- Who 94
Foot, Michael Mackintosh 1913- IntWW 93
Foot, Michael Richard Daniell 1919- Who 94, WrDr 94
Foot, Paul Mackintosh 1937- Who 94
Foot, Philippa Ruth 1920- IntWW 93, Who 94
Foote, Brian Lynn 1963- WhoWest 94
Foote, Christopher Spencer 1935- WhoAm 94
Foote, Courtenay d1925 WhoHol 92
Foote, David Ward, Jr. 1958- WhoFI 94, WhoMW 93
Foote, Douglas Dean 1945- WhoWest 94
Foote, Edward L. 1928- WhoAm 94
Foote, Edward Thaddeus, II 1937- WhoAm 94, WhoAmL 94
Foote, Emerson 1906- WhAm 10
Foote, Evelyn Patricia 1930- WhoAm 94
Foote, Geoffrey 1950- WrDr 94
Foote, Hallie 1953- WhoHol 92
Foote, Henry Robert Bowreman 1904- Who 94
Foote, Herbert N., Sr. 1934- WhoAmP 93
Foote, Horton 1916- IntMPA 94, WhoAm 94, WrDr 94
Foote, Horton, Jr. 1956- WhoHol 92
Foote, (Albert) Horton, (Jr.) 1916- ConDr 93
Foote, Howard Reed 1936- WhoAmA 93
Foote, James Maxwell 1941- WhoAm 94
Foote, Jim Edward, Jr. 1954- WhoWest 94
Foote, Joe Stephen 1949- WhoAmP 93, WhoMW 93
Foote, John, Jr. d1968 WhoAmA 93N
Foote, Lona d1993 NewYTBS 93
Foote, Margie Ellen 1929- WhoAmP 93
Foote, Martha Louisa 1957- WhoAmL 94
Foote, Mary Hallock 1847-1938 BlmGWL
Foote, Paul Sheldon 1946- WhoFI 94, WhoWest 94
Foote, Peter Godfrey 1924- Who 94
Foote, Richard Merrill 1953- WhoMW 93
Foote, Richard Van 1930- WhoAmL 94
Foote, Robert Hutchinson 1922- WhoAm 94
Foote, Samuel 1721?-1777 IntDcT 2
Foote, Shelby DrAPF 93
Foote, Shelby 1916- WhoAm 94, WrDr 94
Foote, Sherrill Lynne 1940- WhoFI 94, WhoMW 93
Foote, Simon James 1958- WhoScEn 94
Foote, Timothy Gilson 1926- WhoAm 94
Foote, W. David 1940- WhoFI 94
Foote, Warren Edgar 1935- WhoScEn 94
Foote, Will Howe 1874-1965 WhoAmA 93N
Foote, William Chapin 1951- WhoFI 94
Foote, Yvonne 1949- WhoBlA 94
Footer, Samuel Joseph 1930- WhoWest 94
Foote-Smith, Elizabeth DrAPF 93
Footitt, Hilary 1948- WrDr 94
Footman, Charles Worthington Fowden 1905- Who 94
Footman, Gordon Elliott 1927- WhoWest 94
Foots, James (William) 1916- IntWW 93, Who 94
Foottit, Anthony Charles 1935- Who 94
Fopp, Michael Anton 1947- Who 94
Foppa, Giuseppe Maria 1760-1845 NewGrDO
Foraboschi, Franco Paolo 1932- WhoScEn 94
Foraker, David Alan 1956- WhoAmL 94, WhoWest 94
Foraker, Lois WhoHol 92
Foran, Arthur d1967 WhoHol 92
Foran, David John 1937- WhoMW 93
Foran, Dick d1979 WhoHol 92
Foran, John Francis 1930- WhoAmP 93
Foran, Kenneth Lawrence 1941- WhoAmP 93
Foran, Mary d1981 WhoHol 92
Foran, Thomas Aquinas 1924- WhoAm 94
Foraste, Roland 1938- WhoScEn 94
Forbes Who 94
Forbes, Lord 1918- Who 94
Forbes, Master of 1946- Who 94
Forbes, Viscount 1981- Who 94
Forbes, Alastair (Granville) 1908- Who 94
Forbes, Alexander 1882- EncSF 93
Forbes, Allan Louis 1928- WhoAm 94
Forbes, Amy Ruth 1959- WhoAmL 94
Forbes, Anthony David Arnold William 1938- Who 94
Forbes, Arthur Lee, III 1928- WhoAmL 94
Forbes, Barbara WhoAm 94
Forbes, Bo Crosby 1964- WhoScEn 94
Forbes, Brenda 1909- WhoHol 92
Forbes, Bryan 1926- IntMPA 94, IntWW 93, Who 94, WhoAm 94, WhoHol 92, WrDr 94
Forbes, Calvin DrAPF 93
Forbes, Calvin 1945- WhoBlA 94
Forbes, Christopher 1950- WhoAm 94, WhoFI 94
Forbes, Colin WrDr 94
Forbes, Colin 1928- Who 94
Forbes, Daniel 1931- WrDr 94
Forbes, David 1945- IntMPA 94
Forbes, David Craig 1938- WhoAm 94, WhoWest 94
Forbes, David Richard 1944- WhoIns 94
Forbes, Donald James 1921- Who 94
Forbes, Donna Marie 1929- WhoAmA 93
Forbes, Edward Coyle 1915- WhoAm 94, WhoFI 94

Forbes, Edward W. 1873-1969 *WhoAmA 93N*
Forbes, Elizabeth 1924- *NewGrDO*
Forbes, Esther 1891-1967 *TwCYAW*
Forbes, Franklin Sim 1936- *WhoAm 94*
Forbes, Fred Alden, Jr. 1946- *WhoFI 94*
Forbes, Freddie d1952 *WhoHol 92*
Forbes, George 1849-1936 *DcNaB MP*
Forbes, George Hay 1821-1875 *DcNaB MP*
Forbes, George L. 1931- *WhoBlA 94*
Forbes, Gilbert Burnett 1915- *WhoAm 94, WhoScEn 94*
Forbes, Gordon Maxwell 1930- *WhoAm 94*
Forbes, Graham John Thomson 1951- *Who 94*
Forbes, Hamish (Stewart) 1916- *Who 94*
Forbes, Harland C(lement) 1898-1990 *WhAm 10*
Forbes, Ian 1914- *Who 94*
Forbes, Jack D. 1934- *WhoAm 94*
Forbes, James c. 1731-1780 *WhAmRev*
Forbes, James 1923- *Who 94*
Forbes, James Randy 1952- *WhoAmP 93*
Forbes, James Wendell 1923- *WhoAm 94*
Forbes, Jerry Wayne 1941- *WhoScEn 94*
Forbes, John 1950- *WrDr 94*
Forbes, John Allison 1922- *WhoAmA 93*
Forbes, John Douglas 1910- *WhoAm 94*
Forbes, John Edward 1925- *WhoFI 94*
Forbes, John Morrison 1925- *Who 94*
Forbes, John Ripley 1913- *WhoAm 94*
Forbes, John Stuart 1936- *Who 94*
Forbes, Kenneth Albert Faucher 1922- *WhoScEn 94, WhoWest 94*
Forbes, Leonard 1940- *WhoWest 94*
Forbes, Malcolm Stevenson 1919-1990 *WhAm 10*
Forbes, Malcolm Stevenson, Jr. 1947- *WhoAm 94, WhoAmP 93, WhoFI 94*
Forbes, Mary d1974 *WhoHol 92*
Forbes, Mary Elizabeth d1964 *WhoHol 92*
Forbes, Meriel 1913- *WhoHol 92*
Forbes, Milton Lester 1930- *WhoMW 93*
Forbes, Morton Gerald 1938- *WhoAmL 94*
Forbes, Nancy Ann 1959- *WhoFI 94*
Forbes, Nanette *Who 94*
Forbes, Norman d1932 *WhoHol 92*
Forbes, Peter 1942- *WhoAm 94*
Forbes, Ralph d1951 *WhoHol 92*
Forbes, Richard E. 1915- *WhoAm 94*
Forbes, Richard Mather 1916- *WhoAm 94*
Forbes, Richard Sinatra d1979 *WhoHol 92*
Forbes, Ross William 1949- *WhoWest 94*
Forbes, Scott *WhoHol 92*
Forbes, (Deloris) Stanton 1923- *WrDr 94*
Forbes, Stephen W. 1942- *WhoIns 94*
Forbes, Thayne John 1938- *Who 94*
Forbes, Theodore McCoy, Jr. 1929- *WhoAm 94*
Forbes, Thomas Rogers 1911-1988 *WhAm 10*
Forbes, Timothy Carter 1953- *WhoAm 94*
Forbes, Walter Alexander 1942- *WhoAm 94, WhoFI 94*
Forbes, William Frederick Eustace 1932- *Who 94*
Forbes, William (Daniel) Stuart- 1935- *Who 94*
Forbes-Leith of Fyvie, Andrew (George) 1929- *Who 94*
Forbes of Craigievar, John (Alexander Cumnock) 1927- *Who 94*
Forbes-Richardson, Helen Hilda 1950- *WhoMW 93*
Forbes-Robertson, Eric d1935 *WhoHol 92*
Forbes-Robertson, Frank d1947 *WhoHol 92*
Forbes-Robertson, J. d1937 *WhoHol 92*
Forbes-Robertson, John *WhoHol 92*
Forbes-Robertson, Peter *WhoHol 92*
Forbes-Sempill *Who 94*
Forbis, Bryan Lester 1957- *WhoMW 93*
Forbis, James Edwin 1931- *WhoAmP 93*
Forbis, Jim S. 1950- *WhoFI 94*
Forbis, John W. 1939- *WhoAmP 93*
Forbis, Richard George 1924- *WhoAm 94, WhoWest 94*
Forbus, Ina B. *WrDr 94*
Forbus, Wiley Davis 1894- *WhAm 10*
Forcade, Billy Stuart 1946- *WhoAmL 94*
Force, Floyd Charles d1947 *WhoHol 92*
Force, Juliana R. d1948 *WhoAmA 93N*
Force, Ken *WhoHol 92*
Force, Pierre Marie 1958- *WhoFI 94*
Force, Robert 1934- *WhoAm 94*
Force, Roland Wynfield 1924- *WhoAm 94, WhoAmA 93*
Force, Ronald Wayne 1941- *WhoAm 94*
Forcese, Dennis Philip 1941- *WhoAm 94*
Forche, Carolyn *DrAPF 93*
Forché, Carolyn (Louise) 1950- *WrDr 94*
Forchelli, Jeffrey David 1947- *WhoAmL 94*
Forcheskie, Carl S. 1927- *WhoAm 94*
Forchetti, Richard E. 1946- *WhoIns 94*
Forchhammer, Jes 1934- *IntWW 93*
Forchheimer, Otto Louis 1926- *WhoAm 94*
Forcht, Karen Anne 1944- *WhoAm 94*
Forcier, Gerald Raymond 1928- *WhoAmP 93*
Forcier, James Robert 1950- *WhoWest 94*
Forcier, Richard Charles 1941- *WhoAm 94*
Forcinio, Hallie Eunice 1952- *WhoMW 93*
Forcione, Alban Keith 1938- *WrDr 94*
Ford, Adam 1940- *Who 94*
Ford, Aileen W. 1934- *WhoBlA 94*
Ford, Albert S. 1929- *WhoBlA 94*
Ford, Alec George 1926- *WrDr 94*
Ford, Andrew (Russell) 1943- *Who 94*
Ford, Andrew Thomas 1944- *WhoAm 94*
Ford, Anthony *Who 94*
Ford, (John) Anthony 1938- *Who 94*
Ford, Antoinette 1941- *WhoBlA 94*
Ford, Antony 1944- *Who 94*
Ford, Ashley Lloyd 1939- *WhoAm 94, WhoMW 93*
Ford, Ashton *EncSF 93*
Ford, Ausbra 1935- *WhoBlA 94*
Ford, Barbara *WrDr 94*
Ford, Barry *WhoHol 92*
Ford, Benjamin d1986 *WhoHol 92*
Ford, Benjamin Thomas 1925- *Who 94*
Ford, Bette 1929- *WhoHol 92*
Ford, Betty Bloomer 1918- *WhoAm 94, WhoWest 94*
Ford, Boris 1917- *Who 94, WrDr 94*
Ford, Bowles C. 1911- *WhoBlA 94*
Ford, Brian J. 1939- *WhoScEn 94*
Ford, Brian John 1939- *WrDr 94*
Ford, Brinsley *Who 94*
Ford, (Richard) Brinsley 1908- *Who 94*
Ford, Bruce (Edwin) 1956- *NewGrDO*
Ford, Byron Milton 1939- *WhoScEn 94*
Ford, Carl d1982 *WhoHol 92*
Ford, Carolyn 1953- *WhoAmP 93*
Ford, Cathy 1952- *BlmGWL*
Ford, Cecil d1980 *WhoHol 92*
Ford, Charles 1936- *WhoBlA 94*
Ford, Charles Edmund 1912- *Who 94*
Ford, Charles Henri *DrAPF 93*
Ford, Charles Henri 1913- *GayLL, WhoAmA 93N, WrDr 94*
Ford, Charles Nathaniel 1940- *WhoMW 93*
Ford, Charles Reed 1931- *WhoAmP 93*
Ford, Charles Willard 1938- *WhoAm 94*
Ford, Chris 1949- *WhoAm 94*
Ford, Clarence Quentin 1923- *WhoAm 94*
Ford, Claudette d1933 *WhoHol 92*
Ford, Claudette Franklin 1942- *WhoBlA 94*
Ford, Clifford 1947- *NewGrDO*
Ford, Clyde Gilpin 1933- *WhoScEn 94*
Ford, Colin John 1934- *Who 94*
Ford, Constance d1993 *NewYTBS 93 [port]*
Ford, Constance 1923?-1993 *ConTFT 11*
Ford, Constance 1925- *WhoHol 92*
Ford, Daniel (Francis) 1931- *WrDr 94*
Ford, Danny R. 1952- *WhoAmP 93*
Ford, David d1983 *WhoHol 92*
Ford, David 1936- *WrDr 94*
Ford, David (Robert) 1935- *Who 94*
Ford, David Clayton 1949- *WhoAmP 93*
Ford, David Frank 1948- *Who 94*
Ford, David Leon, Jr. 1944- *WhoBlA 94*
Ford, David Robert 1935- *IntWW 93*
Ford, Deborah Lee 1945- *WhoBlA 94*
Ford, Deborah Mae 1950- *WhoMW 93*
Ford, Dennis Harcourt 1954- *WhoScEn 94*
Ford, Dexter 1917- *WhoAm 94*
Ford, Donald A. 1928- *WhoBlA 94*
Ford, Donald Hainline 1906- *WhoAm 94*
Ford, Donald Herbert 1926- *WhoAm 94*
Ford, Donald James 1930- *WhoAm 94*
Ford, Donis W. *DrAPF 93*
Ford, Douglas (William Cleverley) 1914- *WrDr 94*
Ford, Douglas Albert 1917- *Who 94*
Ford, Douglas Moret *EncSF 93*
Ford, Douglas William C. *Who 94*
Ford, Edward 1930- *WhoAmP 93*
Ford, Edward (William Spencer) 1910- *Who 94*
Ford, Eileen Otte 1922- *WhoAm 94*
Ford, Elaine *DrAPF 93*
Ford, Elbur *BlmGWL, ConAu 140, SmATA 74*
Ford, Elbur 1906-1993 *WrDr 94N*
Ford, Eleanor Clay 1896-1976 *WhoAmA 93N*
Ford, Ellen Hodson 1913- *WhoAm 94, WhoMW 93*
Ford, Emory A. 1940- *WhoAm 94*
Ford, Ernest (A. Clair) 1858-1919 *NewGrDO*
Ford, Evern D. 1952- *WhoBlA 94*
Ford, Faith 1964- *ConTFT 11, WhoHol 92*
Ford, Fenton d1938 *WhoHol 92*
Ford, Ford B. 1922- *WhoAmP 93*
Ford, Ford Barney 1922- *WhoAm 94*
Ford, Ford Madox 1873-1939 *BlmGEL [port], EncSF 93*
Ford, Francis d1953 *WhoHol 92*
Ford, Franklin Lewis 1920- *WhoAm 94*
Ford, Fred, Jr. 1930- *WhoBlA 94*
Ford, Frederick Ross 1936- *WhoMW 93*
Ford, Freeman Arms 1941- *WhoWest 94*
Ford, Garrett *EncSF 93*
Ford, Gary Henry 1952- *WhoMW 93*
Ford, Gary L. 1944- *WhoBlA 94*
Ford, Geoffrey *Who 94*
Ford, Geoffrey (Harold) 1923- *Who 94*
Ford, (Martin) Geoffrey 1942- *Who 94*
Ford, George Burt 1923- *WhoAm 94*
Ford, George H(arry) 1914- *WrDr 94*
Ford, George Johnson 1916- *Who 94*
Ford, George Washington, III 1924- *WhoBlA 94*
Ford, Gerald R. 1913- *WhoAmP 93*
Ford, Gerald Rudolph 1913- *Who 94*
Ford, Gerald Rudolph, Jr. 1913- *IntWW 93, WhoAm 94, WhoWest 94*
Ford, Geraldine Bledsoe *WhoBlA 94*
Ford, Gertrude *DrAPF 93*
Ford, Gillian Rachel 1934- *Who 94*
Ford, Glenn 1916- *IntMPA 94, WhoAm 94, WhoHol 92*
Ford, Glyn *Who 94*
Ford, (James) Glyn 1950- *Who 94*
Ford, Gordon Buell, Jr. 1937- *WhoAm 94, WhoFI 94, WhoMW 93, WrDr 94*
Ford, Gregory Clay 1955- *WhoFI 94*
Ford, Harold E. 1945- *CngDr 93*
Ford, Harold Eugene 1945- *WhoAm 94, WhoAmP 93, WhoBlA 94*
Ford, Harold Frank 1915- *Who 94*
Ford, Harold Warner 1915- *WhoWest 94*
Ford, Harrison d1957 *WhoHol 92*
Ford, Harrison 1942- *IntMPA 94, IntWW 93, WhoAm 94, WhoHol 92*
Ford, Harry Xavier 1921- *WhoAmA 93*
Ford, Helen d1982 *WhoHol 92*
Ford, Henry 1863-1947 *AmSocL [port], WorInv [port]*
Ford, Herbert (Paul) 1927- *WrDr 94*
Ford, Hilary 1922- *WrDr 94*
Ford, Hilda Eileen 1924- *WhoBlA 94*
Ford, Hugh 1913- *IntWW 93, Who 94*
Ford, James Allan 1920- *Who 94, WrDr 94*
Ford, James Carlton 1937- *WhoWest 94*
Ford, James Dayton 1924-1988 *WhAm 10*
Ford, James Henry, Jr. 1931- *WhoAm 94*
Ford, James W. *WhoBlA 94*
Ford, James W. 1922- *WhoBlA 94*
Ford, Jan *WhoHol 92*
Ford, Jean *WhoAmP 93*
Ford, Jean Elizabeth 1923- *WhoMW 93*
Ford, Jerry Lee 1940- *WhoAm 94, WhoMW 93*
Ford, Jesse Hill 1928- *WhoAm 94*
Ford, Jesse Hill, Jr. 1928- *WrDr 94*
Ford, Jill Hunsberger 1950- *WhoAmL 94*
Ford, Jimmie Richard 1936- *WhoFI 94*
Ford, Joan Elizabeth *DrAPF 93*
Ford, Joe M. 1937- *WhoAmP 93*
Ford, Joe T. 1937- *WhoAmP 93*
Ford, Joe Thomas 1937- *WhoAm 94*
Ford, John d1973 *WhoHol 92*
Ford, John 1586?-c. 1639 *IntDcT 2*
Ford, John 1586-1640? *BlmGEL*
Ford, John 1895-1973 *AmCulL*
Ford, John 1950- *WhoAmA 93*
Ford, John (Archibald) 1922- *Who 94*
Ford, John Archibald 1922- *IntWW 93*
Ford, John Charles 1942- *WhoAm 94, WhoFI 94*
Ford, John Gilmore *WhoAm 94, WhoAmA 93*
Ford, John M. 1957- *EncSF 93*
Ford, John Newton 1942- *WhoAmP 93, WhoBlA 94*
Ford, John Stephen 1957- *WhoFI 94*
Ford, John T., Jr. 1953- *WhoWest 94*
Ford, Johnny 1942- *WhoBlA 94*
Ford, Johnny, Sr. 1942- *WhoAmP 93*
Ford, Joseph 1914- *WhoAm 94*
Ford, Joseph Francis d1993 *Who 94N*
Ford, Joseph Raymond 1949- *WhoAm 94*
Ford, Judith Ann 1935- *WhoAm 94, WhoFI 94*
Ford, Judith Donna 1935- *WhoBlA 94*
Ford, Kathleen *DrAPF 93*
Ford, Kay Louise 1944- *WhoFI 94*
Ford, Keith John 1944- *WhoAmP 93*
Ford, Kenneth A. 1949- *WhoBlA 94*
Ford, Kenneth William 1926- *WhoAm 94*
Ford, Kirk *ConAu 43NR*
Ford, Kirk 1923- *WrDr 94*
Ford, L. H. *WhoAm 94*
Ford, Larry John 1941- *WhoFI 94*
Ford, Lee Ellen 1917- *WhoAmL 94, WhoScEn 94, WrDr 94*
Ford, Len d1972 *ProFbHF*
Ford, Lettie d1936 *WhoHol 92*
Ford, Lincoln Edmond 1938- *WhoMW 93*
Ford, Linda Lou 1948- *WhoAm 94*
Ford, Loretta C. 1920- *WhoAm 94, WhoScEn 94*
Ford, Louis H. 1935- *WhoAmP 93*
Ford, Louis Henry 1914- *WhoMW 93*
Ford, Lucille Garber 1921- *WhoAm 94*
Ford, Lucy Karen 1954- *WhoWest 94*
Ford, Luther L. 1931- *WhoBlA 94*
Ford, Lynette Rae 1945- *WhoAmP 93*
Ford, Marcella Woods *WhoBlA 94*
Ford, Maria *WhoHol 92*
Ford, Marion George, Jr. 1937- *WhoBlA 94*
Ford, Marlene Lynch 1954- *WhoAmP 93*
Ford, Mary Alice 1935- *WhoAmP 93*
Ford, Mary Elizabeth 1953- *WhoScEn 94*
Ford, Mary Spencer Jesse 1948- *WhoScEn 94*
Ford, Michael Q. 1949- *WhoWest 94*
Ford, Michael Raye 1945- *WhoAm 94, WhoAmL 94*
Ford, Michael W. 1938- *WhoAm 94*
Ford, Mick *WhoHol 92*
Ford, Morgan 1911- *CngDr 93*
Ford, Nancy Howard 1942- *WhoBlA 94*
Ford, Nancy Louise 1935- *WhoAm 94*
Ford, Nancy M. *WhoAmP 93*
Ford, Newell F. 1912-1989 *WhAm 10*
Ford, Patrick Joseph 1941- *WhoWest 94*
Ford, Patrick Kildea 1935- *WhoAm 94*
Ford, Paul d1976 *WhoHol 92*
Ford, Peter *Who 94*
Ford, Peter 1930- *Who 94*
Ford, (John) Peter 1912- *Who 94*
Ford, Peter C. 1941- *WhoScEn 94*
Ford, Peter George Tipping 1931- *Who 94*
Ford, Peter William 1947- *Who 94*
Ford, Petronella 1946- *WhoHol 92*
Ford, Phil *WhoHol 92*
Ford, Phil 1956- *BasBi*
Ford, Philip d1976 *WhoHol 92*
Ford, R(obert) A(rthur) D(ouglass) 1915- *ConAu 41NR, WrDr 94*
Ford, Raymond Eustace 1898- *Who 94*
Ford, Richard *DrAPF 93*
Ford, Richard 1944- *IntWW 93, WrDr 94*
Ford, Richard Christian 1961- *WhoWest 94*
Ford, Richard D. 1935- *WhoBlA 94*
Ford, Richard Earl 1933- *WhoAm 94*
Ford, Richard Edmond 1927- *WhoAm 94*
Ford, Richard Irving 1941- *WhoAm 94*
Ford, Rita d1993 *NewYTBS 93 [port]*
Ford, Robert *WhoAmP 93*
Ford, Robert (Cyril) 1923- *Who 94*
Ford, Robert A.D. *ConAu 41NR*
Ford, Robert Arthur Douglass 1915- *IntWW 93*
Ford, Robert Barney 1944- *WhoAm 94, WhoAmL 94*
Ford, Robert Benjamin, Jr. 1935- *WhoBlA 94*
Ford, Robert Blackman 1924- *WhoBlA 94*
Ford, Robert David 1956- *WhoAmL 94*
Ford, Robert Elden 1945- *WhoScEn 94*
Ford, Robert Joseph 1955- *WhoFI 94*
Ford, Robert Louis 1949- *WhoAm 94*
Ford, Robert Stanley 1929- *Who 94*
Ford, Robert Webster 1923- *Who 94*
Ford, Roger Hayes 1956- *WhoFI 94*
Ford, Ross d1988 *WhoHol 92*
Ford, Roy Arthur 1925- *Who 94*
Ford, Russell William 1947- *WhoWest 94*
Ford, Ruth 1920- *WhoHol 92*
Ford, Sarah Ann 1951- *WhoBlA 94*
Ford, Seabury Hurd 1902- *WhoAmL 94*
Ford, Silas M. 1937- *WhoFI 94*
Ford, Steven 1956- *WhoHol 92*
Ford, Sue Marie *WhoScEn 94*
Ford, Tennessee Ernie 1919-1991 *WhAm 10*
Ford, Thomas Jeffers 1930- *WhoFI 94*
Ford, Thomas Patrick 1918- *WhoAm 94*
Ford, Thomas Sparks 1944- *WhoFI 94*
Ford, Timothy Alan 1951- *WhoAmP 93*
Ford, Vernon N. 1945- *WhoBlA 94*
Ford, Victor Lavann 1955- *WhoScEn 94*
Ford, Victoria 1946- *WhoWest 94*
Ford, Virginia 1914- *WhoBlA 94*
Ford, Wallace d1966 *WhoHol 92*
Ford, Wallace L., II 1950- *WhoBlA 94*
Ford, Wallace Roy 1937- *WhoWest 94*
Ford, Walton 1960- *WhoAmA 93*
Ford, Wendell H. 1924- *CngDr 93, WhoAmP 93*
Ford, Wendell Hampton 1924- *IntWW 93, WhoAm 94*
Ford, Wilbur Leonard, Jr. 1937- *WhoAmP 93*
Ford, Wilfred Franklin 1920- *Who 94*
Ford, William *DrAPF 93*
Ford, William Clay 1925- *IntWW 93, WhoAm 94, WhoMW 93*
Ford, William D. 1927- *CngDr 93*
Ford, William David 1927- *WhoAm 94, WhoAmP 93, WhoMW 93*
Ford, William F. 1936- *WhoAm 94*

Ford, William Francis 1925- *WhoAm 94*
Ford, William L., Jr. 1941- *WhoBlA 94*
Ford, William R. 1933- *WhoBlA 94*
Ford, Yancey William, Jr. 1940- *WhoFI 94*
Ford-Choyke, Phyllis *DrAPF 93*
Forde, Arthur 1876- *WhoHol 92*
Forde, Brinsley *WhoHol 92*
Forde, Eugenie d1940 *WhoHol 92*
Forde, Florrie d1940 *WhoHol 92*
Forde, Fraser Philip, Jr. 1943- *WhoBlA 94*
Forde, Hal d1955 *WhoHol 92*
Forde, Harold McDonald 1916- *Who 94*
Forde, Henry deBoulay 1933- *IntWW 93*
Forde, James Albert 1927- *WhoBlA 94*
Forde, Jessica *WhoHol 92*
Forde, (Mary Marguerite) Leneen 1935- *Who 94*
Forde, Stanley d1929 *WhoHol 92*
Forde, Victoria d1964 *WhoHol 92*
Forde-Johnston, James 1927- *WrDr 94*
Fordemwalt, James Newton 1932- *WhoWest 94*
Forder, Anthony 1925- *WrDr 94*
Forder, Charles Robert 1907- *Who 94, WrDr 94*
Forder, Kenneth John 1925- *Who 94*
Fordham, John of c. 1340-1425 *DcNaB MP*
Fordham, Christopher Columbus, III 1926- *WhoAm 94*
Fordham, David Craig 1959- *WhoAmP 93*
Fordham, Jefferson Barnes 1905- *WhoAm 94*
Fordham, John Jeremy 1933- *Who 94*
Fordham, Larry Richard 1947- *WhoMW 93*
Fordham, Monroe 1939- *WhoBlA 94*
Fordham, Paul T. 1917- *WhoAmP 93*
Fordham, Sharon Ann 1952- *WhoFI 94*
Fordice, Daniel Kirkwood, Jr. 1934- *WhoAm 94*
Fordice, Kirk 1934- *WhoAmP 93*
Fording, Edmund Howard, Jr. 1937- *WhoAm 94*
Fordred, Dorice d1980 *WhoHol 92*
Ford-Robertson, Francis Calder d1993 *Who 94N*
Ford Slack, P.J. 1952- *WhoMW 93*
Fordtran, John Satterfield 1931- *WhoAm 94, WhoScEn 94*
Fordyce, Edward Winfield, Jr. 1941- *WhoAm 94*
Fordyce, James Clarence 1937- *WhoFI 94*
Fordyce, James Stuart 1931- *WhoScEn 94*
Fordyce, Samuel Wesley 1927- *WhoScEn 94*
Fore, Allen Gene 1965- *WhoMW 93*
Fore, Claude Harvel, III 1957- *WhoScEn 94*
Fore, Henrietta Holsman *WhoAm 94*
Fore, Scott Eugene 1954- *WhoAmL 94, WhoMW 93*
Fore, Stephanie Anne 1962- *WhoMW 93*
Foree, Jack Clifford 1935- *WhoBlA 94*
Forehand, Jennie Meador 1935- *WhoAmP 93*
Forehand, Margaret P. 1951- *WhoAm 94*
Forehand, Vernon Thomas, Jr. 1947- *WhoAmP 93*
Forehand, Winfred Brian 1945- *WhoAmP 93*
Forell, David Charles 1947- *WhoAm 94*
Forell, George Wolfgang 1919- *WhoAm 94*
Forella, June B. 1927- *WhoAmP 93*
Foreman, Anne N. 1947- *WhoAm 94*
Foreman, Carl 1914-1984 *IntDcF 2-4 [port]*
Foreman, Carol Lee Tucker 1938- *WhoAm 94*
Foreman, Christopher H. 1925- *WhoBlA 94*
Foreman, Dale M. 1948- *WhoAmP 93*
Foreman, Dale Melvin 1948- *WhoWest 94*
Foreman, Dave 1947?- *EnvEnc*
Foreman, David Bruce 1947- *WhoMW 93*
Foreman, Deborah *WhoHol 92*
Foreman, Dennis I. 1945- *WhoAm 94, WhoAmL 94*
Foreman, Doyle 1933- *WhoBlA 94*
Foreman, Edward Rawson 1939- *WhoAm 94, WhoAmL 94*
Foreman, George *NewYTBS 93 [port], WhoAm 94*
Foreman, George Edward 1949- *WhoBlA 94*
Foreman, Harold W. 1938- *WhoAmP 93*
Foreman, James Davis 1925- *WhAm 10*
Foreman, James Louis 1927- *WhoAm 94, WhoAmL 94, WhoMW 93*
Foreman, Jeff 1951- *WhoAmP 93*
Foreman, John 1925-1992 *AnObit 1992*
Foreman, John C. d1992 *IntMPA 94N*
Foreman, John Daniel 1940- *WhoFI 94*
Foreman, John Richard 1952- *WhoAm 94, WhoMW 93*
Foreman, Joyce B. 1948- *WhoBlA 94*
Foreman, Laura *WhoAm 94, WhoAmA 93*
Foreman, Lucille Elizabeth 1923- *WhoBlA 94*
Foreman, Michael 1938- *ChlLR 32 [port], Who 94, WrDr 94*
Foreman, Michael Marcellus 1941- *WhoAmP 93*
Foreman, Philip (Frank) 1923- *Who 94*
Foreman, Richard 1937- *ConDr 93, WhoAm 94, WrDr 94*
Foreman, S. Beatrice 1917- *WhoBlA 94*
Foreman, Stephen 1807-1881 *EncNAR*
Foreman, Thomas Alexander 1930- *WhoAm 94*
Forer, Anne U. *DrAPF 93*
Forer, Arthur H. 1935- *WhoAm 94*
Forer, Bertram Robin 1914- *WhoScEn 94*
Forer, Lucille Kremith *WhoWest 94*
Forero De Saade, Maria Teresa 1939- *IntWW 93*
Forese, James John 1935- *WhoAm 94, WhoFI 94*
Foresman, James Buckey 1935- *WhoMW 93, WhoScEn 94*
Forest, Antonia *WrDr 94*
Forest, Bill d1960 *WhoHol 92*
Forest, Carl Anthony 1940- *WhoAmL 94, WhoScEn 94*
Forest, Dial 1910- *WrDr 94*
Forest, Doris Elizabeth 1936- *WhoAm 94*
Forest, Eva Brown 1941- *WhoWest 94*
Forest, Frank d1976 *WhoHol 92*
Forest, Herman Silva 1921- *WhoAm 94*
Forest, Jean-Claude *EncSF 93*
Forest, Jean Kurt 1909-1975 *NewGrDO*
Forest, Jim 1941- *WrDr 94*
Forest, Karl d1944 *WhoHol 92*
Forest, Mark 1933- *WhoHol 92*
Forest, Michael *WhoHol 92*
Forest, Philip Earle 1931- *WhoFI 94*
Foresta, Merry 1949- *WhoAmA 93*
Forester, Baron 1938- *Who 94*
Forester, Bernard I. 1928- *WhoAm 94, WhoFI 94*
Forester, C(ecil) S(cott) 1899-1966 *EncSF 93*
Forester, David Roger 1953- *WhoScEn 94*
Forester, Erica Simms 1942- *WhoAm 94*
Forester, Jean Martha Brouillette 1934- *WhoFI 94*
Forester, John Gordon, Jr. 1933- *WhoAm 94*
Forester, Karl S. 1940- *WhoAm 94, WhoAmL 94*
Forester, Russell 1920- *WhoAm 94, WhoAmA 93*
Forester-Kinzer, Mary Grise 1938- *WhoMW 93*
Foresti, Roy, Jr. 1925- *WhoAm 94*
Forestier, Danielle 1943- *WhoWest 94*
Forestier-Walker, Michael (Leolin) 1949- *Who 94*
Foret, L. Palmer 1952- *WhoAmL 94*
Forey, William Francis 1961- *WhoMW 93*
Foreyt, John P(aul) 1943- *ConAu 41NR*
Forfar, John Oldroyd 1916- *Who 94*
Forgacs, Otto Lionel 1931- *WhoFI 94, WhoScEn 94*
Forgan, David Waller 1933- *WhoAm 94, WhoWest 94*
Forgan, Elizabeth Anne Lucy 1944- *Who 94*
Forge, Andrew Murray 1923- *Who 94, WhoAmA 93*
Forgeot, Jean 1915- *IntWW 93*
Forger, Robert Durkin 1928- *WhoAm 94*
Forgey, Tom 1939- *WhoAmP 93*
Forghani, Bagher 1936- *WhoWest 94*
Forgione, Pascal D., Jr. *WhoAm 94*
Forgnone, Robert 1936- *WhoAm 94, WhoAmL 94*
Forgue, Stanley Vincent 1916- *WhoAm 94*
Forgues, Jorge Paul 1955- *WhoFI 94*
Forgy, Lawrence *WhoAmP 93*
Forker, Charles R(ush) 1927- *WrDr 94*
Forker, David *WhoIns 94*
Forker, Olan Dean 1928- *WhoAm 94*
Forkert, Clifford Arthur 1916- *WhoWest 94*
Forks, Thomas Paul 1952- *WhoAm 94, WhoScEn 94*
Forland, Scott Thomas 1961- *WhoAmL 94*
Forlani, Arnaldo 1925- *IntWW 93*
Forlano, Anthony 1936- *WhoAm 94*
Forlines, Holli Angel 1961- *WhoFI 94*
Forlini, Frank John, Jr. 1941- *WhoMW 93, WhoScEn 94*
Form, Fredric Allan 1942- *WhoFI 94*
Forman, Alice 1931- *WhoAmA 93*
Forman, Arthur Harvey 1952- *WhoAmL 94*
Forman, Beth Rosalyne 1949- *WhoFI 94, WhoMW 93*
Forman, Bruce Harlan 1951- *WhoFI 94*
Forman, Carol *WhoHol 92*
Forman, Charles William 1916- *WhoAm 94, WrDr 94*
Forman, David 1745-1797 *WhAmRev*
Forman, David C. 1936- *WhoFI 94*
Forman, Denis 1917- *IntMPA 94, Who 94*
Forman, Donald T. 1932- *WhoAm 94*
Forman, Edgar Ross 1923- *WhoAm 94*
Forman, Ethel d1977 *WhoHol 92*
Forman, George Whiteman 1919- *WhoAm 94*
Forman, Graham Neil 1930- *Who 94*
Forman, H(enry) Chandlee d1991 *WhAm 10*
Forman, Howard C. 1946- *WhoAmP 93*
Forman, Howard I. 1917- *WhoAmP 93*
Forman, Howard Irving 1917- *WhoAm 94*
Forman, James 1928- *HisWorL*
Forman, James D(ouglas) 1932- *EncSF 93*
Forman, James Douglas 1932- *ConAu 42NR*
Forman, James Ross, III 1947- *WhoAmL 94*
Forman, Jay Douglas 1945- *WhoMW 93*
Forman, Jerome A. 1934- *IntMPA 94*
Forman, Joan *WrDr 94*
Forman, Joey d1982 *WhoHol 92*
Forman, John Denis *Who 94*
Forman, John Denis 1917- *IntWW 93*
Forman, Joseph Charles 1931- *WhoAm 94*
Forman, Kenneth Warner 1925- *WhoAmA 93*
Forman, Leonard P. 1945- *WhoAm 94*
Forman, Linda Helaine 1943- *WhoMW 93*
Forman, Michael Bertram 1921- *Who 94*
Forman, Milos 1932- *IntMPA 94, IntWW 93, Who 94, WhoAm 94, WhoHol 92*
Forman, Nigel *Who 94*
Forman, (Francis) Nigel 1943- *Who 94*
Forman, Paula *WhoAm 94, WhoFI 94*
Forman, Peter Gerald 1946- *WhoFI 94*
Forman, Peter Vandyne 1958- *WhoAmP 93*
Forman, Richard Allan 1939- *WhoFI 94*
Forman, Richard T. T. 1935- *WhoAm 94*
Forman, Richard Thomas 1935- *WhoWest 94*
Forman, Roy 1931- *Who 94*
Forman, Saul Zundel 1942- *WhoMW 93*
Forman, Steven Lawrence 1958- *WhoMW 93*
Forman, Tamara 1947- *WhoFI 94*
Forman, Tom d1926 *WhoHol 92*
Forman, Tom d1951 *WhoHol 92*
Formanek, Peter Raemin 1943- *WhoFI 94*
Formartine, Viscount 1983- *Who 94*
Formby, Bent Clark 1940- *WhoWest 94*
Formby, George d1961 *WhoHol 92*
Formby, Jim Earn 1920- *WhoAmP 93*
Formby, Mark S. 1956- *WhoAmP 93*
Formby, Myles Landseer 1901- *Who 94*
Formeller, Daniel Richard 1949- *WhoAmL 94*
Formes, Carl, Jr. d1939 *WhoHol 92*
Formes, Karl Johann 1815-1889 *NewGrDO*
Formica, Mercedes 1918- *BlmGWL*
Formica, Salvatore 1927- *IntWW 93*
Formichi, Cesare 1883-1949 *NewGrDO*
Formicola, John Joseph 1941- *WhoAmA 93*
Formigoni, Roberto 1947- *IntWW 93*
Formo, Jerome Lionel 1915- *WhoMW 93*
Formston, Clifford 1907- *Who 94*
Fornaciari, Gilbert Martin 1946- *WhoMW 93*
Fornara, Charles William 1935- *WhoAm 94, WrDr 94*
Fornaroli, Cia 1888-1954 *IntDcB [port]*
Fornarotto, Felicia Agnes 1957- *WhoFI 94*
Fornarotto, Michelle Lorraine 1966- *WhoAmL 94*
Fornas, Leander 1925- *WhoAmA 93*
Fornasari, Luciano c. 1815-1850? *NewGrDO*
Fornatto, Elio Joseph 1928- *WhoAm 94, WhoMW 93, WhoScEn 94*
Fornay, Alfred R., Jr. *WhoBlA 94*
Fornell, Eddy *WhoHisp 94*
Fornell, Roger Charles 1951- *WhoFI 94*
Fornelli, Joseph 1943- *WhoAmA 93*
Forner, Elmira *WhoAmP 93*
Forneris, Jeanne M. 1953- *WhoAmL 94*
Fornes, Candace Rae 1964- *WhoMW 93*
Fornes, Maria Irene 1930- *ConDr 93, IntDcT 2, WhoAm 94, WhoHisp 94, WrDr 94*
Forness, Steven Robert 1939- *WhoAm 94*
Forney, George David, Jr. 1940- *WhoAm 94*
Forney, J. F. *WhoAmP 93*
Forney, Mary Jane 1949- *WhoBlA 94*
Forney, Robert Clyde 1927- *WhoAm 94*
Forni, Patricia Rose 1932- *WhoAm 94*
Fornia, Rita 1878-1922 *NewGrDO*
Fornos, Werner H. 1933- *CurBio 93 [port]*
Fornshell, Dave Lee 1937- *WhoAm 94, WhoMW 93*
Foronjy, Richard *WhoHol 92*
Forquet, Philippe 1943- *WhoHol 92*
Forres, Baron 1946- *Who 94*
Forrest, Alan d1941 *WhoHol 92*
Forrest, Alexander 1849-1901 *WhWE*
Forrest, Alvane M. 1916- *WhoBlA 94*
Forrest, Arthur d1933 *WhoHol 92*
Forrest, Belford d1938 *WhoHol 92*
Forrest, Christine *WhoHol 92*
Forrest, Christopher Patrick 1946- *WhoAmA 93*
Forrest, David 1924- *WrDr 94*
Forrest, Edgar H. 1916- *WhoAmP 93*
Forrest, Edwin 1806-1872 *AmCulL*
Forrest, Frederic 1936- *IntMPA 94, WhoAm 94*
Forrest, Frederic 1943- *WhoHol 92*
Forrest, Geoffrey 1909- *Who 94*
Forrest, Geoffrey Cornish 1898- *Who 94*
Forrest, Hamilton 1901-1963 *NewGrDO*
Forrest, Helen 1919- *WhoHol 92*
Forrest, Henry J. *EncSF 93*
Forrest, Henry J. 1933- *WhoFI 94*
Forrest, Herbert Emerson 1923- *WhoAm 94, WhoAmL 94, WhoFI 94*
Forrest, Irene *WhoHol 92*
Forrest, James Taylor 1919- *WhoAmA 93*
Forrest, John 1847-1918 *WhWE*
Forrest, John Richard 1943- *Who 94*
Forrest, John Samuel d1992 *IntWW 93N, Who 94N*
Forrest, Katherine V. *BlmGWL*
Forrest, Katherine V(irginia) 1939- *GayLL, WrDr 94*
Forrest, Kenton Harvey 1944- *WhoWest 94*
Forrest, Kevin Richard 1959- *WhoMW 93*
Forrest, Leon 1937- *BlkWr 2, WrDr 94*
Forrest, Leon Richard 1937- *WhoBlA 94*
Forrest, Lottie Pickford d1936 *WhoHol 92*
Forrest, Mabel d1967 *WhoHol 92*
Forrest, Maryann *EncSF 93*
Forrest, Melba June 1931- *WhoMW 93*
Forrest, Patrick *Who 94*
Forrest, (Andrew) Patrick (McEwen) 1923- *IntWW 93, Who 94*
Forrest, Richard (Stockton) 1932- *WrDr 94*
Forrest, Robert Edwin 1949- *WhoAmL 94*
Forrest, Robin Whyte 1933- *Who 94*
Forrest, Ronald (Stephen) 1923- *Who 94*
Forrest, Sally 1928- *WhoHol 92*
Forrest, Sidney 1918- *WhoAm 94*
Forrest, Stephen 1958- *WhoMW 93*
Forrest, Steve 1924- *WhoHol 92*
Forrest, Steve 1925- *IntMPA 94*
Forrest, Steven 1949- *AstEnc*
Forrest, Suzanne Sims 1926- *WhoAm 94, WhoWest 94*
Forrest, Uriah 1756-1805 *WhAmRev*
Forrest, William d1989 *WhoHol 92*
Forrest, William George Grieve 1925- *Who 94, WrDr 94*
Forrest, William Ivon Norman 1914- *Who 94*
Forrest, William L. 1948- *WhoMW 93*
Forrestal, Patrick George 1945- *WhoMW 93*
Forrestal, Robert Patrick 1931- *WhoAm 94*
Forrestall, Thomas De Vany 1936- *WhoAmA 93*
Forrest-Carter, Audrey Faye 1956- *WhoBlA 94*
Forrester, Alan McKay 1940- *WhoFI 94, WhoMW 93*
Forrester, Charles Howard 1928- *WhoAmA 93*
Forrester, David Michael 1944- *Who 94*
Forrester, Duncan B(aillie) 1933- *WrDr 94*
Forrester, Duncan Baillie 1933- *Who 94*
Forrester, Eugene Priest 1926- *WhoFI 94*
Forrester, Frederick d1952 *WhoHol 92*
Forrester, Gary 1946- *WhoAmP 93*
Forrester, Giles Charles Fielding 1939- *Who 94*
Forrester, Helen 1919- *BlmGWL, WrDr 94*
Forrester, Ian Stewart 1945- *Who 94*
Forrester, J. Owen 1939- *WhoAm 94, WhoAmL 94*
Forrester, James *WhoAmP 93*
Forrester, Jay W. 1918- *WorInv*
Forrester, Jay Wright 1918- *WhoAm 94*
Forrester, John 1949- *ConAu 141*
Forrester, John Paul 1953- *WhoAm 94*
Forrester, John Stuart 1924- *Who 94*
Forrester, Larry L. 1944- *WhoIns 94*
Forrester, Leslie Ann 1958- *WhoAmL 94*
Forrester, Maureen (Kathleen Stuart) 1930- *NewGrDO*
Forrester, Michael 1917- *Who 94*
Forrester, Patricia Tobacco 1940- *WhoAmA 93*
Forrester, Peter Garnett 1917- *Who 94*
Forrester, Rex (Desmond) 1928- *WrDr 94*

Forrester, Rosemary Wellington 1953- WhoMW 93
Forrester, William Donald 1931- WhoAm 94, WhoFI 94
Forrester, William Ray 1911- WrDr 94
Forrester, William Ray, Jr. 1943- WhoAmL 94
Forrester-Paton, Douglas Shaw 1921- Who 94
Forrow, Brian Derek 1927- WhoAm 94
Forsbach, Jack Alan 1932- WhoWest 94
Forsberg, Charles Alton 1944- WhoWest 94
Forsberg, David Carl 1930- WhoAm 94
Forsberg, Dennis Patrick 1942- WhoMW 93
Forsberg, Franklin S. WhoAmP 93
Forsberg, (Charles) Gerald 1912- Who 94, WrDr 94
Forsberg, Kevin John 1934- WhoAm 94
Forsberg, Roy Walter 1937- WhoAm 94
Forsberg, Theodore John 1946- WhoAmL 94
Forsch, Frederick D. d1993 NewYTBS 93
Forsch, Robert d1948 WhoHol 92
Forsdale, Louis 1922- WhoAm 94, WhoWest 94
Forsee, Joe Brown 1949- WhoAm 94
Forsell, (Carl) John (Jacob) 1868-1941 NewGrDO
Forsen, Harold Kay 1932- WhoAm 94, WhoScEn 94
Forsen, K. Sture 1932- IntWW 93
Forseth, Lynn Marie 1956- WhoMW 93
Forsgren, John H., Jr. 1946- WhAm 10, WhoAm 94
Forsh, Ol'ga Dmitrievna 1873-1961 BlmGWL
Forshaw, Peter 1936- Who 94
Forslund, Constance 1950- WhoHol 92
Forslund, Thomas Odell 1951- WhoWest 94
Forsman, Alpheus Edwin 1941- WhoAmL 94
Forsman, Avis Clapper 1931- WhoAmL 94
Forsman, Chuck 1944- WhoAmA 93, WhoWest 94
Forsman, Dan WhoAm 94
Forsman, Harry d1933 WhoHol 92
Forson, Norman Ray 1929- WhoAm 94
Forss, Kent John 1959- WhoMW 93
Forssander, Paul Richard 1944- WhoFI 94, WhoScEn 94, WhoWest 94
Forssell, Borje Andreas 1939- WhoScEn 94
Forst, Brian Edward 1942- WhoFI 94
Forst, Edmund Charles, Jr. 1961- WhoMW 93
Forst, Judith Doris 1943- WhoAm 94
Forst, Marion Francis 1910- WhoAm 94
Forst, Willi d1980 WhoHol 92
Forstadt, Joseph Lawrence 1940- WhoAm 94
Forstadt, Matthew James 1946- WhoAmL 94
Forstater, Mark 1943- IntMPA 94
Forstchen, William R WrDr 94
Forstchen, William R. 1950- EncSF 93
Forste, Norman Lee 1935- WhoWest 94
Forstel, Gertrude 1880-1950 NewGrDO
Forster, Alan Moir 1940- WhoAm 94
Forster, Archibald (William) 1928- Who 94
Forster, Arnold 1912- WhoAm 94
Forster, Bruce Alexander 1948- WhoFI 94, WhoScEn 94, WhoWest 94
Forster, Cecil R. 1911- WhoBlA 94
Forster, Cecil R., Jr. 1943- WhoBlA 94
Forster, Charles Ian Kennerley 1911- Who 94
Forster, Cornelius Aloysius Philip d1993 NewYTBS 93
Forster, Cornelius Philip 1919- WhoAm 94
Forster, Daniel Grant 1960- WhoWest 94
Forster, Dianna Ruth 1937- WhoAmP 93
Forster, Donald 1920- Who 94
Forster, Donald Murray 1929- Who 94
Forster, E. M. 1879-1970 BlmGEL [port], ConLC 77 [port]
Forster, E(dward) M(organ) 1879-1970 EncSF 93, GayLL, NewGrDO, RfGShF
Forster, Eric Brown 1917- Who 94
Forster, Eric Gad 1941- WhoWest 94
Forster, Eric Otto 1918- WhoAm 94
Forster, Francis Michael 1912- WhoAm 94
Forster, Garey James 1950- WhoAmP 93
Forster, Homer W. 1944- WhoFI 94
Forster, James Francis 1956- WhoAmL 94
Forster, Johann Georg Adam 1754-1794 WhWE
Forster, Johann Reinhold 1729-1798 WhWE
Forster, John Fredrick, Jr. 1942- WhoAm 94, WhoAmL 94
Forster, Julian 1918- WhoAm 94
Forster, Kathrine 1960- WhoHol 92
Forster, Kurt Walter 1935- WhoAm 94
Forster, Leonard Wilson 1913- Who 94
Forster, Leslie Stewart 1924- WhoAm 94
Forster, Margaret 1938- BlmGWL, IntWW 93, Who 94, WrDr 94
Forster, Merlin Henry 1928- WhoAm 94
Forster, Michael Lockwood 1950- WhoScEn 94
Forster, Neil Milward 1927- Who 94
Forster, Norvela d1993 Who 94N
Forster, Oliver (Grantham) 1925- Who 94
Forster, Oliver Grantham 1925- IntWW 93
Forster, Peter d1982 WhoHol 92
Forster, Peter Hans 1942- WhoFI 94, WhoMW 93
Forster, Robert 1941- IntMPA 94, WhoHol 92
Forster, Robert Elder, II 1919- WhoAm 94
Forster, Rudolf d1968 WhoHol 92
Forster, William (Edward Stanley) 1921- Who 94
Forsting, James L. 1948- WhoMW 93
Forstman, Henry Jackson 1929- WhoAm 94
Forstrom, June Rochelle 1932- WhoWest 94
Forsyte, Charles Who 94
Forsyth, Ben Ralph 1934- WhoWest 94
Forsyth, Bill 1946- IntMPA 94
Forsyth, Bill 1947- IntWW 93, Who 94
Forsyth, Bruce Who 94
Forsyth, Bruce 1928- WhoHol 92
Forsyth, Constance 1903-1987 WhoAmA 93N
Forsyth, Dale Marvin 1945- WhoMW 93
Forsyth, Drew WhoHol 92
Forsyth, Elliott Christopher 1924- IntWW 93
Forsyth, Frank WhoHol 92
Forsyth, Frederick IntWW 93
Forsyth, Frederick 1938- EncSF 93, WhoAm 94, WrDr 94
Forsyth, George Howard, Jr. 1901-1991 WhAm 10
Forsyth, Ilene H(aering) 1928- WhoAmA 93
Forsyth, Ilene Haering 1928- WhoAm 94
Forsyth, James (Law) 1913- ConDr 93, WrDr 94
Forsyth, James Lorin 1942- WhoWest 94
Forsyth, Jennifer Mary 1924- Who 94
Forsyth, John D. WhoAm 94, WhoMW 93
Forsyth, Joseph 1942- WhoAm 94
Forsyth, Keith William 1950- WhoScEn 94
Forsyth, Michael (de Jong) 1951- WrDr 94
Forsyth, Michael Bruce 1954- Who 94
Forsyth, Peter Taylor 1848-1921 DcNaB MP
Forsyth, Raymond Arthur 1928- WhoAm 94, WhoWest 94
Forsyth, Rosemary 1944- WhoHol 92
Forsyth, William Douglass 1909- Who 94
Forsythe, Charles 1928- WhoHol 92
Forsythe, Clifford 1929- Who 94
Forsythe, Donald John 1955- WhoAmA 93
Forsythe, Douglas 1913- WhoAmP 93
Forsythe, Earl Andrew 1904- WhoAm 94
Forsythe, Frank S. 1932- WhoFI 94
Forsythe, Henderson 1917- WhoAm 94, WhoHol 92
Forsythe, James Roy 1920- Who 94
Forsythe, John 1918- IntMPA 94, WhoAm 94, WhoHol 92
Forsythe, John Edward 1937- WhoAmP 93
Forsythe, (John) Malcolm 1936- Who 94
Forsythe, Mary MacCornack 1920- WhoAmP 93
Forsythe, Mimi d1952 WhoHol 92
Forsythe, Paddy Who 94
Forsythe, Patricia Hays WhoMW 93
Forsythe, Peter Winchell 1937- WhoAm 94
Forsythe, Robert Elliott 1949- WhoFI 94, WhoScEn 94
Forsythe, Ronald 1932- WrDr 94
Forsythe, William IntMPA 94, IntWW 93, WhoHol 92
Forsythe, William 1949- IntDcB [port]
Forsyth-Johnson, Bruce Joseph 1928- Who 94
Forsyth Of That Ilk, Alistair Charles William 1929- Who 94
Fort, Arthur Tomlinson, III 1931- WhoAm 94
Fort, Charles DrAPF 93
Fort, Charles (Hoy) 1874-1932 EncSF 93
Fort, Denise Douglas 1951- WhoAmL 94
Fort, Edward B. WhoBlA 94
Fort, Garrett 1900-1945 IntDcF 2-4
Fort, Gerald Marshall 1919- WhoWest 94
Fort, Ilene Susan 1949- ConAu 140
Fort, James Tomlinson 1928- WhoAm 94, WhoFI 94
Fort, Jane 1938- WhoBlA 94
Fort, Jean 1915- Who 94
Fort, Jeffrey C. 1950- WhoAm 94, WhoAmL 94
Fort, John Franklin, III 1941- WhoAm 94, WhoFI 94
Fort, Maeve Geraldine 1940- Who 94
Fort, Randall Martin 1956- WhoAm 94
Fort, Raymond Cornelius, Jr. 1938- WhoAm 94
Fort, Ronald E. 1947- WhoIns 94
Fort, Teresa Carol 1964- WhoMW 93
Fort, Timothy Lyman 1958- WhoAmL 94
Fort, Tomlinson 1932- WhoAm 94
Fort, Wilkinson Davis 1926- WhoAmP 93
Fort, William H. 1915- WhoBlA 94
Fortado, Michael George 1943- WhoAm 94
Fort-Brescia, Bernardo WhoHisp 94
Fort-Brescia, Bernardo 1951- IntWW 93
Fort-Brescia, Bernardo M. 1951- WhoAmA 93
Forte, Baron 1908- Who 94
Forte, Charles 1908- IntWW 93
Forte, Dieter 1935- IntDcT 2
Forte, Fabian WhoHol 92
Forte, Fabian 1943- IntMPA 94
Forte, Joe d1967 WhoHol 92
Forte, Johnie, Jr. 1936- WhoBlA 94
Forte, Johnnie, Jr. 1936- AfrAmG [port]
Forte, Michael B. 1952- WhoAmP 93
Forte, Minnie T. 1916- WhoBlA 94
Forte, Nick Apollo 1938- WhoHol 92
Forte, Patrick 1950- WhoBlA 94
Forte, Rocco (John Vincent) 1945- IntWW 93, Who 94
Forte, Stephen Michael 1955- WhoAmL 94
Forte, Vincent WhoHol 92
Forte, Wesley E. 1933- WhoIns 94
Forte, Wesley Elbert 1933- WhoAm 94
Forten, James 1766-1842 AfrAmAl 6
Fortenbach, Ray Thomas 1927- WhoAm 94
Fortenbaugh, Samuel Byrod, III 1933- WhoAm 94, WhoAmL 94, WhoFI 94
Fortenberry, Carol Lomax 1959- WhoFI 94
Fortenberry, Jeffrey Kenton 1957- WhoScEn 94
Fortenberry, Joe d1993 NewYTBS 93
Fortenberry, Louis W. WhoAmP 93
Fortenberry, Rick 1946- WhoAmP 93
Fortescue, Earl d1993 Who 94N
Fortescue, Earl 1951- Who 94
Fortescue, (John) Adrian 1941- Who 94
Fortescue, Kenneth WhoHol 92
Fortescue, Muriel WhoHol 92
Fortescue, Trevor Victor Norman 1916- Who 94
Fortescue, Viola d1953 WhoHol 92
Fortess, Karl E. 1907- WhoAmA 93
Fortess, Karl Eugene 1907- WhoAm 94
Forteviot, Baron d1993 Who 94N
Forteviot, Baron 1938- Who 94
Fortgang, Chaim Jacob 1947- WhoAmL 94
Forth, Eric 1944- Who 94
Forth, Kevin Bernard 1949- WhoAm 94, WhoFI 94, WhoWest 94
Forth, Stuart 1923- WhoAm 94
Forthaus, Lynn Marie 1962- WhoMW 93
Forti, Anton 1790-1859 NewGrDO
Forti, Helena 1884-1942 NewGrDO
Fortia de Piles, Alphonse-Toussaint-Joseph-Andre-Marie-Marseille, Comte de 1758-1826 NewGrDO
Fortier, D'Iberville 1926- WhoAm 94
Fortier, Herbert d1949 WhoHol 92
Fortier, Jean-Marie Who 94
Fortier, Jean-Marie 1920- IntWW 93, WhoAm 94
Fortier, John Bertram 1942- WhoAm 94
Fortier, L. Yves 1935- IntWW 93, WhoAm 94
Fortier, Nicole WhoHol 92
Fortier, Robert 1927- WhoHol 92
Fortier, Samuel John 1952- WhoAmL 94
Fortier, Theodore T., Sr. 1926- WhoBlA 94
Fortin, Claude Jean 1957- WhoMW 93
Fortin, Joseph Andre 1937- WhoAm 94, WhoScEn 94
Fortin, Raymond D. WhoAmL 94
Fortinberry, Glen W. d1993 NewYTBS 93 [port]
Fortinberry, Glen W. 1927- WhoAm 94
Fortinberry, Toxey Thomas 1908- WhoAmP 93
Fortini, Victor Scott 1962- WhoFI 94
Fortinsky, Jerome Steven 1962- WhoAmL 94
Fortis, Louis G. 1947- WhoAmP 93
Fortman, Marvin 1930- WhoAmL 94
Fortman, Richard Allen 1936- WhoMW 93
Fortmann, Dan ProFbHF [port]
Fortmann, Thomas Edward WhoAm 94
Fortna, Lixi 1913- WhoAmP 93
Fortner, Billie Jean WhoFI 94
Fortner, Brand Irving 1955- WhoMW 93
Fortner, Elliott 1942- WhoAm 94
Fortner, Hueston Gilmore 1959- WhoWest 94
Fortner, Joseph Gerald 1921- WhoAm 94
Fortner, Richard J. WhoScEn 94
Fortner, Robert Steven 1948- WhoMW 93
Fortner, Wolfgang 1907-1987 NewGrDO
Fortney, Anne Price 1944- WhoAm 94
Fortney, Diane Eline Osborn 1958- WhoFI 94
Fortney, Steven DrAPF 93
Fortnoff, Alyce Lee 1955- WhoMW 93
Fortsch, Johann Philipp 1652-1732 NewGrDO
Fortson, Edward Norval 1936- WhoAm 94
Fortson, Eleanor Ann 1904- WhoAmP 93
Fortson, Elnora Agnes 1943- WhoBlA 94
Fortson, Henry David, Jr. 1946- WhoBlA 94
Fortuin, Johannes Martinus H. 1927- WhoScEn 94
Fortuin, Thomas Mark d1993 NewYTBS 93
Fortuin, Thomas Mark 1946- WhoWest 94
Fortuna, Vicki Lynn 1955- WhoMW 93
Fortuna, William Frank 1948- WhoMW 93, WhoScEn 94
Fortunate Eagle, Adam c. 1931- EncNAR
Fortunati, Gian Francesco 1746-1821 NewGrDO
Fortunato, Buddy 1946- WhoAmP 93
Fortunato, Nancy 1941- WhoAmA 93
Fortunato, Peter DrAPF 93
Fortunato, Vincent James 1952- WhoFI 94
Fortune, Alvin V. 1935- WhoBlA 94
Fortune, Edmund d1939 WhoHol 92
Fortune, George 1935- NewGrDO
Fortune, Gwendoline Y. WhoBlA 94
Fortune, James Michael 1947- WhoWest 94
Fortune, Joanne C. 1941- WhoAmL 94
Fortune, Louise d1981 WhoHol 92
Fortune, Lowell 1941- WhoAmL 94
Fortune, Mary BlmGWL
Fortune, Michael Joseph 1922- WhoAm 94
Fortune, Patrick John 1947- WhoFI 94
Fortune, Philip Robert 1913- WhoAm 94
Fortune, Porter Lee, Jr. 1920- WhAm 10
Fortune, Richard Cordova 1940- WhoHisp 94
Fortune, Robert Russell 1916- WhoAm 94
Fortune, T. Thomas 1856-1928 AfrAmAl 6, ConBlB 6 [port]
Fortune, Terence John 1946- WhoAm 94
Fortune, William Lemcke 1912- WhoAm 94, WhoMW 93
Fortuner, Renaud 1944- WhoWest 94
Fortuño, Luis G. 1960- WhoHisp 94
Fortuno, Victor M. 1952- WhoAmL 94
Fortus, Daniel d1984 WhoHol 92
Forty, Arthur John 1928- Who 94
Forward, David Ross 1934- WhoAmP 93
Forward, DeWitt Arthur 1894- WhAm 10
Forward, Dorothy Elizabeth 1919- WhoAmL 94
Forward, Gordon E. WhoFI 94
Forward, Robert L. 1932- WrDr 94
Forward, Robert L(ull) 1932- EncSF 93
Forward, Robert Lull 1932- WhoAm 94
Forward, Susan WrDr 94
Forwell, George Dick 1928- Who 94
Forwood, Anthony 1917- WhoHol 92
Forwood, Dudley (Richard) 1912- Who 94
Forwood, Gareth 1945- WhoHol 92
Forwood, Nicholas James 1948- Who 94
Fory, Petronella 1946- WrDr 94
Foryst, Carole WhoAm 94
Forzani, Rinaldo, III 1958- WhoAmL 94
Forzano, Giovacchino 1884-1970 NewGrDO
Fosback, Norman George 1947- WhoAm 94
Fosberg, F. Raymond 1908-1993 NewYTBS 93
Fosbre, Paul Butler 1962- WhoFI 94
Fosburg, Richard Garrison 1930- WhoAm 94
Fosburgh, James Whitney 1910-1978 WhoAmA 93N
Fosburgh, Lacey d1993 NewYTBS 93 [port]
Fosburgh, Lacey 1942-1993 ConAu 140
Foscue, James E. WhoFI 94
Fosdick, Harry Emerson 1878-1969 DcAmReB 2
Fosdick, Sina G. d1983 WhoAmA 93N
Fosgate, David M., Sr. WhoAmP 93
Foshay, Harold d1953 WhoHol 92
Foshee, E. Crum 1937- WhoAmP 93
Foshee, Thuong Nguyen 1948- WhoAsA 94
Fosheim, Douglas G. WhoAmP 93

Fosheim, Jon R. 1923- *WhoAmP 93*
Fosholt, Sanford Kenneth 1915- *WhoAm 94*
Foskett, Daphne 1911- *WrDr 94*
Foskett, David Robert 1949- *Who 94*
Foskett, Douglas John 1918- *Who 94, WrDr 94*
Foskey, Carnell T. 1956- *WhoBlA 94*
Fosmire, Fred Randall 1926- *WhoAm 94*
Fosness, Irene Waugh 1906- *WhoAmP 93*
Foss, Charles R. 1945- *WhoMW 93*
Foss, Chris(topher) 1946- *EncSF 93*
Foss, Clive (Frank Wilson) 1939- *WrDr 94*
Foss, Clive Frank Wilson 1939- *WhoAm 94*
Foss, Darrell d1962 *WhoHol 92*
Foss, Donald John 1940- *WhoAm 94*
Foss, Frederic A. 1922- *WhoAmP 93*
Foss, George B., Jr. 1924- *WhoAmL 94*
Foss, Harlan Funston 1918- *WhoAm 94*
Foss, Jerry Carl 1954- *WhoMW 93*
Foss, Joe 1915- *WhoAm 94*
Foss, John Frank 1938- *WhoAm 94*
Foss, John William 1933- *WhoAm 94*
Foss, Judith C. *WhoAmP 93*
Foss, Kathleen 1925- *Who 94*
Foss, Kenelm d1963 *WhoHol 92*
Foss, Lukas 1922- *IntWW 93, NewGrDO, WhoAm 94*
Foss, Patricia H. *WhoAmP 93*
Foss, Phillip *DrAPF 93*
Foss, Ralph Scot 1945- *WhoFI 94, WhoScEn 94*
Foss, Richard John 1944- *WhoMW 93*
Foss, Thomas E. 1934-1989 *WhAm 10*
Fossa, Giulia *WhoHol 92*
Fossas, Rafael 1952- *WhoFI 94*
Fosse, Bob d1987 *WhoHol 92*
Fosse, Erwin Ray 1918- *WhoAm 94*
Fosse, James Alan 1955- *WhoWest 94*
Fosse, Nicole 1963- *WhoHol 92*
Fosseen, Neal Randolph 1908- *WhoWest 94*
Fossel, Peter VanBrunt 1945- *WhoAm 94*
Fossey, Brigitte 1945- *WhoHol 92*
Fossey, Brigitte 1947- *IntMPA 94*
Fossier, Mike Walter 1928- *WhoAm 94*
Fossier, Robert 1927- *IntWW 93*
Fossland, Joeann Jones 1948- *WhoFI 94, WhoWest 94*
Fossum, Jerry George 1943- *WhoAm 94*
Fossum, Robert H. 1923- *WrDr 94*
Fossum, Robert Merle 1938- *WhoAm 94, WhoScEn 94*
Fost, Paulette 1937- *WhoWomW 91*
Foster *Who 94*
Foster, Abiel 1735-1806 *WhAmRev*
Foster, Alan d1985 *WhoHol 92*
Foster, Alan Dean 1946- *EncSF 93, WrDr 94*
Foster, Alan Herbert 1925- *WhoAm 94*
Foster, Alfred Carville, Jr. 1932- *WhoAmP 93*
Foster, Allan (Bentham) 1926- *Who 94*
Foster, Alvin Garfield 1934- *WhoBlA 94*
Foster, Ami *WhoHol 92*
Foster, Andrew William 1944- *Who 94*
Foster, April 1947- *WhoAmA 93*
Foster, Art d1947 *WhoHol 92*
Foster, Arthur Key, Jr. 1933- *WhoAmL 94*
Foster, Arthur Rowe 1924- *WhoAm 94*
Foster, Barbara Melanie 1945- *WhoScEn 94*
Foster, Barry 1931- *WhoHol 92*
Foster, Basil d1959 *WhoHol 92*
Foster, Ben 1926- *WhoAmP 93*
Foster, Brendan 1948- *IntWW 93, Who 94*
Foster, Brian Lee 1938- *WhoWest 94*
Foster, Buddy 1957- *WhoHol 92*
Foster, Carl Oscar, Jr. 1926- *WhoBlA 94*
Foster, Cary D. 1951- *WhoAmP 93*
Foster, Catherine Rierson 1935- *WhoAm 94, WhoFI 94*
Foster, Cecil A. 1954- *WhoBlA 94*
Foster, Charles Allen 1941- *WhoAm 94, WhoAmL 94*
Foster, Charles Bradford, III 1947- *WhoAmL 94*
Foster, Charles Crawford 1941- *WhoAm 94, WhoAmL 94*
Foster, Charles Henry Wheelwright 1927- *WhoAm 94*
Foster, Christine 1943- *IntMPA 94*
Foster, Christopher (David) 1930- *Who 94*
Foster, Christopher David 1930- *IntWW 93*
Foster, Christopher Norman 1946- *Who 94*
Foster, Clyde 1931- *WhoBlA 94*
Foster, Constance B. 1946- *WhoAm 94*
Foster, Dale Warren 1950- *WhoAm 94, WhoFI 94*
Foster, David 1929- *IntMPA 94*
Foster, David Lee 1933- *WhoAm 94*
Foster, David Manning 1944- *WrDr 94*
Foster, David Mark 1932- *WhoAm 94*
Foster, David Ramsey 1920- *WhoFI 94, WhoWest 94*
Foster, David Raymond 1948- *WhoMW 93*
Foster, David Scott 1938- *WhoAm 94, WhoWest 94*
Foster, David William 1940- *WrDr 94*
Foster, Deborah Valrie 1955- *WhoBlA 94*
Foster, Delores Jackson 1938- *WhoBlA 94*
Foster, Dennis (Haley) 1931- *Who 94*
Foster, Dennis James 1952- *WhoAmL 94*
Foster, Derek 1937- *Who 94*
Foster, Dianne 1928- *WhoHol 92*
Foster, Don 1932- *WhoAmA 93*
Foster, Donald d1969 *WhoHol 92*
Foster, Donald Isle 1925- *WhoAmA 93*
Foster, Donald Michael Ellison 1947- *Who 94*
Foster, Donald W. 1950- *WrDr 94*
Foster, Donnie Ted 1948- *WhoAmP 93*
Foster, Douglas Layne 1944- *WhoMW 93*
Foster, Douglas Leroy 1931- *WhoBlA 94*
Foster, Dudley d1973 *WhoHol 92*
Foster, Dudley Edwards, Jr. 1935- *WhoWest 94*
Foster, E. C. 1939- *WhoAmP 93, WhoBlA 94*
Foster, Eddie d1989 *WhoHol 92*
Foster, Edson L. 1927- *WhoAm 94*
Foster, Edward, Sr. 1945- *WhoBlA 94*
Foster, Edward E. 1939- *WhoAm 94*
Foster, Edward Halsey 1942- *WrDr 94*
Foster, Edward John 1938- *WhoScEn 94*
Foster, Edward Joseph 1967- *WhoScEn 94*
Foster, Edward Paul 1945- *WhoFI 94, WhoScEn 94*
Foster, Elizabeth Read 1912- *WrDr 94*
Foster, Eric H., Jr. 1943- *WhoAm 94, WhoFI 94*
Foster, Eugene Lewis 1922- *WhoAm 94, WhoScEn 94*
Foster, Fern Allen 1921-1991 *WhAm 10*
Foster, Frances 1924- *WhoAm 94, WhoHol 92*
Foster, Frances Helen 1924- *WhoBlA 94*
Foster, Frances Smith 1944- *WhoBlA 94, WrDr 94*
Foster, Frank B., III 1928- *WhoBlA 94*
Foster, Frederick *ConAu 41NR*
Foster, Genevieve 1893-1979 *WhoAmA 93N*
Foster, George 1919- *WrDr 94*
Foster, George Arthur 1948- *WhoBlA 94*
Foster, George Arthur C. *Who 94*
Foster, George C(ecil) 1893- *EncSF 93*
Foster, George McClelland, Jr. 1913- *WhoAm 94, WhoWest 94*
Foster, George William, Jr. 1919- *WhoAm 94, WhoAmL 94*
Foster, Gladys M. 1927- *WhoBlA 94*
Foster, Gloria 1936- *WhoBlA 94, WhoHol 92*
Foster, Greg 1959- *WhoBlA 94*
Foster, Hal 1892-1982 *WhoAmA 93N*
Foster, Hannah Webster 1758-1840 *BlmGWL*
Foster, Helen d1982 *WhoHol 92*
Foster, Henry Louis 1925- *WhoAm 94*
Foster, Henry Wendell 1933- *WhoBlA 94*
Foster, Hugh Warren 1921- *WhoAm 94*
Foster, Ian Hampden 1946- *Who 94*
Foster, Irene Parks 1927- *WhoMW 93*
Foster, Iris 1944- *WrDr 94*
Foster, J(ames) A(nthony) 1932- *WrDr 94*
Foster, J. Morris d1966 *WhoHol 92*
Foster, Jacques Yves 1924- *WhoMW 93*
Foster, James, Jr. d1978 *WhoHol 92*
Foster, James Caldwell 1943- *WhoAm 94*
Foster, James Franklin *WhoMW 93*
Foster, James H. 1931- *WhoBlA 94*
Foster, James H. 1955- *WhoIns 94*
Foster, James Hadlei 1938- *WhoBlA 94*
Foster, James Henry 1930- *WhoAm 94*
Foster, James Henry 1933- *WhoAm 94, WhoFI 94*
Foster, James J. 1945- *WhoAmL 94*
Foster, James Joseph 1957- *WhoScEn 94*
Foster, James Leroy 1944- *WhoAmP 93*
Foster, James Reuben 1930- *WhoFI 94, WhoMW 93*
Foster, James Ronald 1938- *WhoWest 94*
Foster, James W., Sr. *WhoAmA 93N*
Foster, Janice Martin 1946- *WhoBlA 94*
Foster, Jeanne *DrAPF 93*
Foster, Jeanne 1930- *WrDr 94*
Foster, Jeannette Howard 1895-1981 *GayLL*
Foster, Jo Ann A. 1944- *WhoMW 93*
Foster, Jo Graham 1915- *WhoAmP 93*
Foster, Joan Mary 1923- *Who 94*
Foster, Joanna Katharine 1939- *Who 94*
Foster, Joanna Katherine 1939- *IntWW 93*
Foster, Joanne Mary 1946- *WhoMW 93*
Foster, Jodie 1962- *IntMPA 94, IntWW 93, WhoAm 94, WhoHol 92*
Foster, Joe B. 1934- *WhoAm 94*
Foster, Joe C., Jr. 1925- *WhoAm 94*
Foster, John (Gregory) 1927- *Who 94*
Foster, John Burt 1911- *WhoMW 93*
Foster, John Clayton 1935- *WhoAmP 93*
Foster, John Horace 1927- *WhoAm 94*
Foster, John McNeely 1949- *WhoAm 94*
Foster, John Merrill 1891- *WhAm 10*
Foster, John Robert 1916- *Who 94*
Foster, John Robert 1940- *WhoAmL 94, WhoWest 94*
Foster, John Stanton 1921- *WhoAm 94*
Foster, John Stuart, Jr. 1922- *WhoAm 94, WhoScEn 94*
Foster, John William 1921- *Who 94*
Foster, John Witherspoon 1948- *WhoAmL 94*
Foster, Jonathan Rowe 1947- *Who 94*
Foster, Joseph E. 1954- *WhoAmL 94*
Foster, Joy Via 1935- *WhoScEn 94*
Foster, Julia 1941- *WhoHol 92*
Foster, Julia 1944- *IntMPA 94*
Foster, Julian Francis Sherwood 1926- *WhoAm 94*
Foster, Jylla Moore *WhoBlA 94*
Foster, Katherine D. 1924- *WhoAmP 93*
Foster, Kathijoe 1955- *WhoMW 93*
Foster, Kathleen Adair 1948- *WhoAm 94*
Foster, Kathryn Briggs 1943- *WhoAmP 93*
Foster, Katrina *WhoHol 92*
Foster, Kenneth E. d1964 *WhoAmA 93N*
Foster, Kennith Earl 1945- *WhoScEn 94, WhoWest 94*
Foster, Kim Alan 1956- *WhoMW 93*
Foster, Kimberly 1961- *WhoHol 92*
Foster, Kirk Anthony 1959- *WhoScEn 94*
Foster, LaDoris J. 1933- *WhoBlA 94*
Foster, Lanny Gordon 1948- *WhoScEn 94*
Foster, Lawrence 1941- *IntWW 93, Who 94, WhoWest 94*
Foster, Lawrence (Thomas) 1941- *NewGrDO*
Foster, (William) Lawrence 1947- *WrDr 94*
Foster, Leslie D. *DrAPF 93*
Foster, Lester Anderson, Jr. 1929- *WhoFI 94*
Foster, Linda Ann 1956- *WhoScEn 94*
Foster, Linda Nemec *DrAPF 93*
Foster, Linda T. 1943- *WhoAmP 93*
Foster, Lloyd Bennett 1911- *WhoAmL 94*
Foster, Lloyd L. 1930- *WhoBlA 94*
Foster, Luther H. 1913- *WhoBlA 94*
Foster, Luther Hilton 1913- *WhoAm 94*
Foster, Lynn 1952- *WhoAmL 94*
Foster, Lynn Irma 1969- *WhoScEn 94*
Foster, Lynne 1937- *SmATA 74 [port]*
Foster, M(ichael) A(nthony) 1939- *EncSF 93, WrDr 94*
Foster, M. Joan *WhoAmL 94*
Foster, Maelee Thomson 1932- *WhoAmA 93*
Foster, Malcolm Burton 1931- *WrDr 94*
Foster, Maria Elena 1956- *WhoHisp 94*
Foster, Mark Edward 1948- *WhoAmL 94, WhoFI 94, WhoWest 94*
Foster, Mark Gardner 1914- *WhoMW 93*
Foster, Mark Robert 1961- *WhoFI 94*
Foster, Mark Stephen 1948- *WhoAm 94, WhoAmL 94*
Foster, Mark Wingate 1942- *WhoAmL 94*
Foster, Marta 1941- *WhoHisp 94*
Foster, Martha d1987 *WhoHol 92*
Foster, Mary 1951- *WhoAmA 93*
Foster, Mary Christine 1943- *WhoAm 94, WhoWest 94*
Foster, Mary Frazer 1914- *WhoWest 94*
Foster, Maurice David *IntMPA 94*
Foster, Meg 1948- *IntMPA 94, WhoHol 92*
Foster, Michael Thomas 1951- *WhoMW 93*
Foster, Michael William 1940- *WhoWest 94*
Foster, Mike 1955- *WhoAmP 93*
Foster, Mildred Thomas 1927- *WhoBlA 94*
Foster, Murphy James, Jr. 1930- *WhoAmP 93*
Foster, Nancy Marie 1941- *WhoScEn 94*
Foster, Nora R(akestraw) 1947- *ConAu 140*
Foster, Norman d1976 *WhoHol 92*
Foster, Norman (Robert) 1935- *Who 94*
Foster, Norman Holland 1934- *WhoScEn 94*
Foster, Norman Leslie 1909- *Who 94*
Foster, Norman Robert 1935- *IntWW 93, WhoAm 94*
Foster, Ottis Charles 1959- *WhoScEn 94*
Foster, Pamela Anne 1937- *WhoMW 93*
Foster, Paul 1931- *ConDr 93, WhoAm 94, WrDr 94*
Foster, Pearl D. 1922- *WhoBlA 94*
Foster, Peter *Who 94*
Foster, (John) Peter 1919- *Who 94*
Foster, Peter Beaufoy 1921- *Who 94*
Foster, Peter Martin 1924- *Who 94*
Foster, Phil d1985 *WhoHol 92*
Foster, Philip A. *WhoAmP 93*
Foster, Philip Carey 1947- *WhoAmP 93*
Foster, Phoebe d1975 *WhoHol 92*
Foster, Portia L. 1953- *WhoBlA 94*
Foster, Preston d1970 *WhoHol 92*
Foster, Randolph Courtney 1952- *WhoAm 94, WhoAmL 94*
Foster, Raunell H. 1938- *WhoBlA 94*
Foster, Raymond Keith 1945- *WrDr 94*
Foster, Richard *EncSF 93*
Foster, Richard 1938- *WhoAm 94*
Foster, Richard 1946- *WhoAmP 93*
Foster, Richard Anthony 1941- *Who 94*
Foster, Richard T. 1933- *WhoAmL 94*
Foster, Rita Dorn 1933- *WhoAm 94*
Foster, Robert 1943- *Who 94*
Foster, Robert (Sidney) 1913- *Who 94*
Foster, Robert Bates 1940- *WhoAmL 94*
Foster, Robert Carmichael 1941- *WhoAm 94*
Foster, Robert Davis 1929- *WhoBlA 94*
Foster, Robert Edwin 1962- *WhoScEn 94*
Foster, Robert Ernest 1955- *WhoMW 93*
Foster, Robert Fitzroy 1949- *Who 94*
Foster, Robert Francis 1926- *WhoAm 94*
Foster, Robert Lawson 1925- *WhoAm 94*
Foster, Robert Leon 1939- *WhoBlA 94*
Foster, Robert W. 1920- *WhoAmP 93*
Foster, Robert Watson 1926- *WhoAm 94*
Foster, Rockwood Hoar 1923- *WhoAmP 93*
Foster, Roger Sherman, Jr. 1936- *WhoAm 94, WhoScEn 94*
Foster, Ron *WhoHol 92*
Foster, Ronald G. 1941- *WhoFI 94*
Foster, Rosebud Lightbourn 1934- *WhoBlA 94*
Foster, Roy *Who 94*
Foster, Roy Allen 1960- *WhoBlA 94*
Foster, Ruth Mary 1927- *WhoFI 94, WhoWest 94*
Foster, Ruth Sullivan 1929- *WhoAmP 93*
Foster, Samuel R. 1932- *WhoAmP 93*
Foster, Simon 1933- *WrDr 94*
Foster, Stan *WhoHol 92*
Foster, Stephen C. 1941- *WhoAmA 93*
Foster, Stephen Collins 1826-1864 *AmCulL [port]*
Foster, Stephen Kent 1936- *WhoAm 94*
Foster, Stephen Roch 1964- *WhoScEn 94*
Foster, Steven 1957- *WrDr 94*
Foster, Steven Douglas 1945- *WhoAmA 93*
Foster, Susan *WhoHol 92*
Foster, Susanna 1924- *WhoHol 92*
Foster, Thomas Ashcroft 1934- *Who 94*
Foster, Thomas P. 1939- *WhoIns 94*
Foster, Tim 1957- *WhoAmP 93*
Foster, Twila Louise 1955- *WhoAmL 94*
Foster, V. Alyce 1909- *WhoBlA 94*
Foster, Verna Lavonne 1939- *WhoMW 93*
Foster, Vincent c. 1945-1993 *News 94-1*
Foster, Vincent W., Jr. d1993 *NewYTBS 93 [port]*
Foster, W(alter) Bert(ram) 1869-1929 *EncSF 93*
Foster, W. Douglas 1942- *WhoFI 94*
Foster, Walter Herbert, Jr. 1919- *WhoFI 94*
Foster, Wannie Paul 1938- *WhoWest 94*
Foster, Warren *IntDcF 2-4*
Foster, Wendell 1929- *WhoAmP 93*
Foster, William B. 1931- *WhoIns 94*
Foster, William Edwin 1930- *WhoAm 94*
Foster, William James, III 1953- *WhoWest 94*
Foster, William K. 1933- *WhoBlA 94*
Foster, William Patrick 1919- *WhoBlA 94*
Foster, William Walter 1922- *WhoAmP 93*
Foster, William Z. 1881-1961 *EncABHB 9 [port]*
Foster, William Zebulon 1881-1961 *AmSocL*
Foster-Brown, Roy Stephenson 1904- *Who 94*
Foster-Grear, Pamela 1957- *WhoBlA 94*
Foster-Heuer, Ann 1934- *WhoWomW 91*
Foster-Sutton, Stafford William Powell d1991 *IntWW 93N*
Fota, Constantin *IntWW 93*
Fota, Frank George 1921- *WhoMW 93*
Fotek, Jan 1928- *NewGrDO*
Foth, Bob *WhoAm 94*
Foth, Joan B. 1930- *WhoAmA 93*
Fothergill, Dorothy Joan 1923- *Who 94*
Fothergill, Jessie 1851-1891 *BlmGWL*
Fothergill, John Wesley, Jr. 1928- *WhoScEn 94*
Fothergill, Richard Humphrey Maclean 1937- *Who 94*
Foti, Margaret A. 1944- *WhoAm 94*
Foti, Steven M. 1958- *WhoAmP 93*
Foti, Veronique M. 1938- *ConAu 141*
Fotopoulos, Mimis d1986 *WhoHol 92*
Fotsch, Dan Robert 1947- *WhoWest 94*
Fottrell, Patrick 1933- *IntWW 93*
Fouad, Hussein Yehya 1939- *WhoWest 94*
Fouassier, Jean-Pierre 1947- *WhoScEn 94*

Foucault, Jean Bernard Leon 1819-1868 *WorInv, WorScD [port]*
Foucault, Michel 1926-1984 *BlmGEL, EncEth, GayLL*
Fouce, Frank d1962 *WhoHol 92*
Fouch, Stephanie Saunders 1947- *WhoAm 94*
Fouchard, Joseph James 1928- *WhoAm 94, WhoAmP 93*
Foudree, Bruce William 1947- *WhoAm 94, WhoAmL 94*
Foudree, Charles M. *WhoFI 94*
Fougere, Pierre d1921 *WhoHol 92*
Fougeron, Pierre Jacques 1927- *WhoAm 94*
Fougez, Anna d1966 *WhoHol 92*
Fought, Lorianne 1962- *WhoMW 93, WhoScEn 94*
Fought, Sheryl Kristine 1949- *WhoScEn 94*
Fougner, John V. 1953- *WhoFI 94*
Foukal, Donald Charles 1926- *WhoFI 94*
Foulds, Donald Duane 1925- *WhoAm 94*
Foulds, Elfrida Vipont 1902- *WrDr 94*
Foulds, (Hugh) Jon 1932- *Who 94*
Foulger, Byron d1970 *WhoHol 92*
Foulger, Keith 1925- *Who 94*
Foulis, Iain (Primrose Liston) 1937- *Who 94*
Foulk, David Wingerd 1939- *WhoMW 93*
Foulk, Grover C. 1926- *WhoAmP 93*
Foulk, Jack 1941- *WhoAmP 93*
Foulk, Robert d1989 *WhoHol 92*
Foulke, Edwin G., Jr. *WhoAmP 93*
Foulke, Edwin Gerhart, Jr. 1952- *WhoAm 94, WhoAmL 94, WhoFI 94*
Foulke, Sarah B. 1955- *WhoAmL 94*
Foulke, William Green 1912- *WhoAm 94*
Foulke, William Green, Jr. 1942- *WhoAm 94*
Foulkes, George 1942- *Who 94*
Foulkes, Llyn 1934- *WhoAm 94, WhoAmA 93*
Foulkes, Nigel (Gordon) 1919- *Who 94*
Foulkes, Nigel Gordon 1919- *IntWW 93*
Foulkes, (Albert) Peter 1936- *WrDr 94*
Foulkes, Richard (George) 1944- *ConAu 141*
Foulkes, William David 1935- *WhoScEn 94*
Foulks, Carl Alvin 1947- *WhoBlA 94*
Foulks Foster, Ivadale Marie 1922- *WhoBlA 94*
Foulston, John 1772-1842 *DcNaB MP*
Foundas, Georges 1924- *WhoHol 92*
Founds, Henry W. 1942- *WhoAm 94*
Fountain, Alan 1946- *Who 94*
Fountain, Freeman Percival 1921- *WhoWest 94*
Fountain, Jay M. 1943- *WhoAmL 94*
Fountain, L. H. 1913- *WhoAmP 93*
Fountain, Linda Kathleen 1954- *WhoFI 94*
Fountain, Peter Dewey, Jr. 1930- *WhoAm 94*
Fountain, Robert Roy, Jr. 1932- *WhoAm 94*
Fountain, Roger 1942- *WhoMW 93*
Fountain, Ronald Glenn 1939- *WhoAm 94*
Fountain, William David 1940- *WhoScEn 94*
Fountain, William Stanley 1920- *WhoBlA 94*
Fountos, William Joseph, III 1956- *WhoMW 93*
Fountoukidou, Parthena *WhoWomW 91*
Fouque, Karoline Freifrau de la Motte c. 1773-1831 *BlmGWL*
Fouquette, Martin John, Jr. 1930- *WhoWest 94*
Fouraker, Lawrence Edward 1923- *WhoAm 94*
Fourcade, Christian 1944- *WhoHol 92*
Fourcade, Jean-Pierre 1929- *IntWW 93, Who 94*
Fourcard, Inez Garey *WhoAmA 93*
Foureau, Fernand 1850-1914 *WhWE*
Fourest, Henry-Pierre 1911- *IntWW 93*
Fourestier, Louis (Felix Andre) 1892-1976 *NewGrDO*
Fourier, Jean-Baptiste Joseph 1768-1830 *WorScD*
Fournelle, Raymond Albert 1941- *WhoMW 93*
Fournet, Gerard Lucien 1923- *WhoScEn 94*
Fournet, Jean 1913- *NewGrDO*
Fournet, Robert Louis 1928- *WhoFI 94*
Fourney, Michael E. 1936- *WhoAm 94*
Fournie, Raymond Richard 1951- *WhoAmL 94*
Fournie, Robert G. 1920- *WhoAm 94*
Fournier, Alex 1924- *WhoAmA 93*
Fournier, Alexis Jean 1865-1948 *WhoAmA 93N*
Fournier, Bernard 1938- *Who 94*
Fournier, Collette V. 1952- *WhoBlA 94*
Fournier, Donald Frederick 1934- *WhoWest 94*
Fournier, Donald Joseph, Jr. 1962- *WhoScEn 94*
Fournier, Jacques 1929- *IntWW 93*
Fournier, Jean 1914- *Who 94*
Fournier, Jean Pierre 1941- *WhoScEn 94*
Fournier, Serge Raymond-Jean 1931- *WhoAm 94*
Fournier, Walter Frank 1912- *WhoFI 94, WhoWest 94*
Fourqueux, Madame de fl. 18th cent.- *BlmGWL*
Four Step Brothers, The *WhoHol 92*
Four Tops, The *ConMus 11 [port]*
Fourtouni, Eleni *DrAPF 93*
Fouse, Sarah Virginia 1948- *WhoMW 93*
Fousek, Frank Daniel 1913-1979 *WhoAmA 93N*
Foushee, Geraldine George 1947- *WhoBlA 94*
Foushee, Prevost Vest 1952- *WhoBlA 94*
Foushee, Sandra *DrAPF 93*
Fouss, James H. 1939- *WhoAm 94*
Foust, Larry 1928-1984 *BasBi*
Foust, Paul McClain 1929- *WhoAmP 93*
Foust, Robert S. 1941- *WhoAmP 93*
Foust, Rosanne Skibo 1964- *WhoWest 94*
Fouste, Donna H. 1944- *WhoAmL 94*
Fout, Larry Roy 1930- *WhoMW 93*
Foutch, Gary Lynn 1954- *WhoScEn 94*
Fouts, Daniel Francis 1951- *WhoAm 94*
Fouts, James Fremont 1918- *WhoFI 94, WhoScEn 94*
Fouts, James Ralph 1929- *WhoAm 94, WhoScEn 94*
Fou Ts'ong 1934- *IntWW 93, Who 94*
Fouty, Marvin Francis 1936- *WhoFI 94, WhoMW 93*
Foutz, Samuel Theodore 1945- *WhoBlA 94*
Fouyas, Methodios 1925- *Who 94*
Fow, Louis Fairchild 1939- *WhoMW 93*
Fowden, Leslie 1925- *IntWW 93, Who 94*
Fowells, Joseph Dunthorne Briggs 1916- *Who 94*
Fowinkle, Eugene W. 1934- *WhoAm 94*
Fowke, David (Frederick Gustavus) 1950- *Who 94*
Fowke, Edith 1913- *BlmGWL*
Fowke, Edith Margaret 1913- *WrDr 94*
Fowke, Edith Margaret Fulton 1913- *WhoAm 94*
Fowke, Philip Francis 1950- *IntWW 93*
Fowkes, Frederick Mayhew 1915-1991 *WhAm 10*
Fowkes, Margo Sarah Miller 1961- *WhoWest 94*
Fowkes, Richard O. 1946- *IntMPA 94*
Fowlds, Derek 1937- *WhoHol 92*
Fowle, Eleanor Cranston *WhoAmP 93*
Fowle, Frank Fuller 1908- *WhoAmL 94*
Fowle, Geraldine Elizabeth 1929- *WhoAmA 93*
Fowle, Susannah *WhoHol 92*
Fowler, Abe Neal 1939- *WhoAmP 93*
Fowler, Alan Bicksler 1928- *WhoAm 94*
Fowler, Alastair (David Shaw) 1930- *WrDr 94*
Fowler, Alastair David Shaw 1930- *Who 94*
Fowler, Alfred 1889- *WhoAmA 93N*
Fowler, Almeda d1964 *WhoHol 92*
Fowler, Art d1953 *WhoHol 92*
Fowler, Barbara Ann 1945- *WhoBlA 94*
Fowler, Barbara Hughes 1926- *WhoAm 94*
Fowler, Ben B. 1916-1990 *WhAm 10*
Fowler, Bertie d1941 *WhoHol 92*
Fowler, Beryl *Who 94*
Fowler, Betty Janmae 1925- *WhoAm 94*
Fowler, Brenda d1942 *WhoHol 92*
Fowler, Bruce Allen 1963- *WhoMW 93*
Fowler, Bruce Allen 1966- *WhoFI 94*
Fowler, Bruce Andrew 1945- *WhoAm 94*
Fowler, C. Thomas 1930- *WhoAm 94, WhoFI 94*
Fowler, Caleb L. *WhoAm 94, WhoFI 94*
Fowler, Cecile Ann 1920- *WhoScEn 94*
Fowler, Charles 1792-1867 *DcNaB MP*
Fowler, Charles Albert 1920- *WhoAm 94*
Fowler, Charles Allison Eugene 1921- *WhoAm 94*
Fowler, Christopher B. *Who 94*
Fowler, Clyde Bernard 1924- *WhoAmP 93*
Fowler, Conrad Murphree 1918- *WhoAm 94, WhoAmP 93*
Fowler, Daniel McKay 1950- *WhoAmL 94*
Fowler, David Wayne 1937- *WhoAm 94, WhoScEn 94*
Fowler, Dennis Houston 1924- *Who 94*
Fowler, Derek 1929- *Who 94*
Fowler, Don D. 1936- *WrDr 94*
Fowler, Don Dee 1936- *WhoWest 94*
Fowler, Don Wall 1944- *WhoAmL 94*
Fowler, Dona J. 1928- *WhoWest 94*
Fowler, Donald Lionel 1935- *WhoAmP 93*
Fowler, Donald Raymond 1926- *WhoAm 94, WhoAmL 94*
Fowler, Earle Cabell 1921- *WhoAm 94*
Fowler, Edwin Babbitt d1977 *WhoHol 92*
Fowler, Elaine Henderson 1950- *WhoAmL 94*
Fowler, Elbert Wentzell 1915- *WhoAmP 93*
Fowler, Eric Nicholas 1954- *WhoAmA 93*
Fowler, Floyd Earl 1937- *WhoScEn 94*
Fowler, Frank Eison 1946- *WhoAmA 93*
Fowler, Gene d1960 *WhoHol 92*
Fowler, Gene 1931- *WrDr 94*
Fowler, George J., III 1950- *WhoAmL 94, WhoHisp 94*
Fowler, George Selton, Jr. 1920- *WhoMW 93, WhoScEn 94*
Fowler, Gerald Teasdale d1993 *Who 94N*
Fowler, Gilbert L. 1949- *WhoAm 94*
Fowler, H. M., Sr. *WhoAmP 93*
Fowler, Hammond 1901- *WhoAmP 93*
Fowler, Harriet Whittemore 1946- *WhoAmA 93*
Fowler, Harry 1926- *IntMPA 94, WhoHol 92*
Fowler, Henry 1870-1938 *DcNaB MP*
Fowler, Henry Hamill 1908- *IntWW 93, Who 94, WhoAm 94, WhoAmP 93*
Fowler, Horatio Seymour 1919- *WhoAm 94*
Fowler, Hugh Charles 1926- *WhoAmP 93*
Fowler, Ian 1932- *Who 94*
Fowler, Jack W. 1931- *WhoFI 94*
Fowler, Jacob 1765-1850 *WhWE*
Fowler, James D., Jr. 1944- *WhoAm 94*
Fowler, James Daniel, Jr. 1944- *WhoBlA 94*
Fowler, James Edward 1931- *WhoAmL 94*
Fowler, James M. 1939- *WhoWest 94*
Fowler, James Robert 1943- *WhoMW 93*
Fowler, Jay Bradford *DrAPF 93*
Fowler, Jerry M. 1940- *WhoAmP 93*
Fowler, John d1952 *WhoHol 92*
Fowler, John D. 1931- *WhoBlA 94*
Fowler, John Francis 1925- *Who 94, WhoScEn 94*
Fowler, John J. *WhoAmP 93*
Fowler, John Moore 1949- *WhoAm 94, WhoFI 94*
Fowler, John Russell 1918- *WhoAm 94, WhoFI 94*
Fowler, John Wellington 1935- *WhoAm 94*
Fowler, Joseph W. d1993 *NewYTBS 93 [port]*
Fowler, Joseph William 1894- *WhAm 10*
Fowler, Karen Joy 1950- *EncSF 93*
Fowler, Leon, Jr. 1943- *WhoBlA 94*
Fowler, Leslie R. 1924- *WhoAmP 93*
Fowler, Linda Marilyn 1936- *WhoAmP 93*
Fowler, Mark Stapleton 1941- *WhoAm 94*
Fowler, Mary Jean 1934- *WhoAmA 93*
Fowler, Mel 1922- *WhoAmA 93*
Fowler, Mel (Walter) 1921- *WhoAmA 93N*
Fowler, Michael *Who 94*
Fowler, (Edward) Michael (Coulson) 1929- *IntWW 93, Who 94*
Fowler, Michael Ross 1960- *WhoAmL 94*
Fowler, Nancy Crowley 1922- *WhoScEn 94, WhoWest 94*
Fowler, Nancy Mary *WhoWest 94*
Fowler, Nathaniel Eugene 1922- *WhoWest 94*
Fowler, Noble Owen 1919- *WhoAm 94*
Fowler, Nola Faye 1934- *WhoFI 94*
Fowler, Norman *IntWW 93, Who 94*
Fowler, (Peter) Norman 1938- *IntWW 93, Who 94*
Fowler, Patricia Cervantes Romero 1944- *WhoHisp 94*
Fowler, Paul Raymond 1958- *WhoMW 93*
Fowler, Peter Howard 1923- *IntWW 93, Who 94*
Fowler, Peter James 1936- *Who 94*
Fowler, Peter Jon 1936- *Who 94*
Fowler, Peter Niles 1951- *WhoWest 94*
Fowler, Queen Dunlap *WhoBlA 94*
Fowler, R.S. 1932- *WhoWest 94*
Fowler, Raymond David 1944- *WhoAm 94*
Fowler, Richard Hindle 1910- *WrDr 94*
Fowler, Richard Nicholas 1946- *Who 94*
Fowler, Robert *WhoAmP 93*
Fowler, Robert Asa 1928- *Who 94, WhoAm 94*
Fowler, Robert Glen 1930- *WhoAm 94*
Fowler, Robert Howard 1926- *WhoAm 94*
Fowler, Robert Ramsay 1944- *WhoAm 94*
Fowler, Rollen Charles 1962- *WhoWest 94*
Fowler, Ronald Frederick 1910- *Who 94*
Fowler, Ronald Vincent 1955- *WhoWest 94*
Fowler, Russell Marcus 1915- *WhoFI 94*
Fowler, Stephen Eugene 1940- *WhoAm 94, WhoMW 93*
Fowler, Susan Michele 1952- *WhoFI 94, WhoMW 93*
Fowler, Sydney *EncSF 93*
Fowler, Thomas Benton, Jr. 1947- *WhoScEn 94*
Fowler, Thomas Kenneth 1931- *WhoAm 94, WhoScEn 94*
Fowler, Tillie 1942- *CngDr 93, WhoAmP 93*
Fowler, Tillie Kidd *WhoAm 94*
Fowler, Tom *WhoAmP 93*
Fowler, Vivian Delores 1946- *WhoFI 94*
Fowler, W. Wyche, Jr. 1940- *WhoAmP 93*
Fowler, Walton Berry 1946- *WhoFI 94*
Fowler, William Alfred 1911- *IntWW 93, Who 94, WhoAm 94, WhoScEn 94, WhoWest 94*
Fowler, William Dix 1940- *WhoAm 94, WhoFI 94*
Fowler, William E., Jr. 1921- *WhoBlA 94*
Fowler, William Mayo, Jr. 1926- *WhoScEn 94*
Fowler, William Wyche, Jr. 1940- *IntWW 93*
Fowler, Wyche, Jr. 1940- *WhoAm 94*
Fowler, Wyman Beall 1937- *WhoAm 94*
Fowler Howitt, William *Who 94*
Fowles, George Richard 1928- *WhoAm 94*
Fowles, Glenys 1947?- *NewGrDO*
Fowles, John 1926- *BlmGEL [port], DcLB 139 [port], IntWW 93, Who 94, WhoAm 94, WrDr 94*
Fowles, John (Robert) 1926- *EncSF 93*
Fowley, Douglas 1911- *IntMPA 94, WhoHol 92*
Fowlie, Eldon Leslie 1928- *WhoAm 94*
Fowlkes, Doretha P. 1944- *WhoBlA 94*
Fowlkes, Joe 1948- *WhoAmP 93*
Fowlkes, John Guy 1898- *WhAm 10*
Fowlkes, Nancy P. *WhoBlA 94*
Fowlkes, Nelson J. 1934- *WhoBlA 94*
Fox, Aileen 1907- *WrDr 94*
Fox, Alan 1920- *WrDr 94*
Fox, Alan Martin 1938- *Who 94*
Fox, Andrew Mark 1957- *WhoFI 94*
Fox, Anne Chisholm 1941- *WhoAmP 93*
Fox, Anthony 1924- *WrDr 94*
Fox, Arthur Charles 1926- *WhoAm 94*
Fox, Arthur Joseph, Jr. 1923- *WhoAm 94*
Fox, Arturo Angel 1935- *WhoAm 94*
Fox, Athena Lynn 1966- *WhoAmL 94*
Fox, Barbara Lee 1937- *WhoMW 93*
Fox, Barry Howard 1957- *WhoScEn 94*
Fox, Barry Jay 1956- *WhoWest 94*
Fox, Bernard *WhoHol 92*
Fox, Bernard Hayman 1917- *WhoAm 94*
Fox, Bernard Michael 1942- *WhoAm 94*
Fox, Brad 1947- *WhoWest 94*
Fox, Brenda Gail 1961- *WhoFI 94*
Fox, Brian Michael 1944- *Who 94*
Fox, Bryan Patrick 1958- *WhoWest 94*
Fox, Byron Neal 1948- *WhoAmL 94*
Fox, C(harles) P(hilip) 1913- *WrDr 94*
Fox, Carl Alan 1950- *WhoScEn 94*
Fox, Carol 1926-1981 *NewGrDO*
Fox, Charles Eldon, Jr. 1941- *WhoAm 94*
Fox, Charles Harold 1905-1979 *WhoAmA 93N*
Fox, Charles Ira 1940- *WhoAm 94*
Fox, Charles James 1749-1806 *AmRev, BlmGEL, WhAmRev*
Fox, Christine R. 1947- *WhoAmP 93*
Fox, Christopher 1957- *WhoScEn 94*
Fox, Christopher Gene 1952- *WhoWest 94*
Fox, Connie *DrAPF 93*
Fox, Connie 1932- *WrDr 94*
Fox, Cyril A., Jr. 1937- *WhoAm 94*
Fox, Daniel Michael 1938- *WhoAm 94, WhoScEn 94*
Fox, Daniel Wayne 1962- *WhoAmL 94, WhoMW 93*
Fox, David *WhoHol 92*
Fox, David Peter 1953- *WhoScEn 94*
Fox, David Wayne 1931- *WhoAm 94, WhoFI 94*
Fox, Dawne Marie 1948- *WhoFI 94*
Fox, Dean Frederick 1944- *WhoAm 94*
Fox, Donald Melville 1942- *WhoIns 94*
Fox, Donald Robert 1945- *WhoAmL 94*
Fox, Donald Thomas 1929- *WhoAm 94, WhoAmL 94*
Fox, Donald William 1922- *WhoAmP 93*
Fox, (Charles) Douglas 1840-1921 *DcNaB MP*
Fox, Douglas Allan 1927- *WhoAm 94*
Fox, Douglas Brian 1947- *WhoAm 94*
Fox, Edward 1937- *IntMPA 94, IntWW 93, Who 94, WhoHol 92*
Fox, Edward A. 1936- *WhoAm 94*
Fox, Edward Hanton 1945- *WhoAm 94, WhoAmL 94*
Fox, Edward Inman 1933- *WhoAm 94*
Fox, Edward M. 1959- *WhoAmL 94*
Fox, Elaine Saphier 1934- *WhoAmL 94*
Fox, Eleanor Mae Cohen 1936- *WhoAm 94*
Fox, Elizabeth *DrAPF 93*
Fox, Emile 1953- *WhoScEn 94*
Fox, Emmet 1886-1951 *DcAmReB 2*
Fox, Everett V. 1915- *WhoBlA 94*
Fox, Flo 1945- *WhoAmA 93*
Fox, Frances Farnsworth 1928- *WhoAmP 93*

Fox, Frances Juanice 1916- *WhoWest 94*
Fox, Francis Haney 1933- *WhoAm 94, WhoAmL 94*
Fox, Francis Henry 1923- *WhoAm 94*
Fox, Franklyn d1967 *WhoHol 92*
Fox, Fred d1949 *WhoHol 92*
Fox, Gardner F(rancis) 1911-1986 *EncSF 93*
Fox, Geoffrey *DrAPF 93*
Fox, Geoffrey Charles 1944- *WhoAm 94*
Fox, George 1624-1691 *BlmGEL, DcAmReB 2, HisWorL [port]*
Fox, Gerald Lynn 1942- *WhoAm 94*
Fox, Gloria L. *WhoAmP 93*
Fox, Gordon D. 1961- *WhoAmP 93*
Fox, Grace d1946 *WhoHol 92*
Fox, Hamilton Phillips, III 1945- *WhoAm 94, WhoAmL 94*
Fox, Hanna *DrAPF 93*
Fox, Harry d1959 *WhoHol 92*
Fox, Hazel Mary 1928- *Who 94, WhoAmL 94*
Fox, Hazel Metz 1921-1989 *WhAm 10*
Fox, Henry H. Bucky 1942- *WhoAm 94*
Fox, Howard Neal 1946- *WhoAmA 93*
Fox, Howard Tall, Jr. 1920- *WhoAm 94*
Fox, Huckleberry 1975- *WhoHol 92*
Fox, Hugh *DrAPF 93*
Fox, Hugh (Bernard) 1932- *WrDr 94*
Fox, Irving 1910- *WhoHol 92*
Fox, J. Bradley *WhoAmP 93*
Fox, Jack 1940- *WhoWest 94*
Fox, Jack Jay 1916- *WhoAm 94*
Fox, Jacob Logan 1921- *WhoAm 94*
Fox, James 1939- *IntMPA 94, IntWW 93, Who 94, WhoHol 92*
Fox, James Carroll 1928- *WhoAm 94, WhoAmL 94*
Fox, James Carroll 1932- *WhoScEn 94*
Fox, James F. 1932- *WhoMW 93*
Fox, James Frederick 1917- *WhoAm 94*
Fox, James Gahan 1943- *WhoAm 94*
Fox, James M. *DrAPF 93*
Fox, James Robert 1950- *WhoAmL 94*
Fox, Janet *WhoHol 92*
Fox, Jean DeWitt 1918- *WhoAm 94*
Fox, Jeanne Jones 1929- *WhoBlA 94*
Fox, Jeannine Elise 1946- *WhoFI 94*
Fox, Jeff *WhoAmP 93*
Fox, Jeffrey James 1956- *WhoAmP 93*
Fox, Jerry *WhoHol 92*
Fox, Jimmie d1974 *WhoHol 92*
Fox, Joan Phyllis 1945- *WhoScEn 94*
Fox, Joel David 1949- *WhoWest 94*
Fox, John *ConAu 141, Who 94*
Fox, John d1984 *WhoHol 92*
Fox, John 1927- *WhoAmA 93*
Fox, John, Jr. d1919 *WhoHol 92*
Fox, (Anthony) John 1946- *Who 94*
Fox, John Bayley, Jr. 1936- *WhoAm 94*
Fox, John David 1929- *WhoAm 94*
Fox, John Jacob 1874-1944 *DcNaB MP*
Fox, John Reid 1951- *WhoMW 93*
Fox, John Wayne 1947- *WhoAmP 93*
Fox, Jon D. 1947- *WhoAmP 93*
Fox, Joseph Carl 1941- *WhoScEn 94*
Fox, Joseph Carter 1939- *WhoAm 94, WhoFI 94*
Fox, Joseph Leland 1938- *WhoAm 94, WhoWest 94*
Fox, Josephine d1953 *WhoHol 92*
Fox, Judith Hoos 1949- *WhoAmA 93*
Fox, Karl A(ugust) 1917- *WrDr 94*
Fox, Karl August 1917- *WhoAm 94, WhoScEn 94*
Fox, Kenneth 1929- *WhoAm 94*
Fox, Kenneth L. 1917- *WhoAm 94, WhoWest 94*
Fox, Kenneth Lambert 1927- *Who 94*
Fox, Kerry *WhoHol 92*
Fox, Langton Douglas 1917- *Who 94*
Fox, Lawrence 1932- *WhoAm 94*
Fox, Lawrence, III 1947- *WhoAm 94*
Fox, Lawrence J. 1943- *WhoAm 94, WhoAmL 94*
Fox, Len 1905- *WrDr 94*
Fox, Leon 1951- *WhoAmL 94*
Fox, Levi 1914- *WrDr 94*
Fox, Liam 1961- *Who 94*
Fox, Lincoln H. 1942- *WhoAmA 93*
Fox, Lloyd Allan 1945- *WhoAmL 94*
Fox, Lorraine Esther 1941- *WhoWest 94*
Fox, Lucas
See Motorhead *ConMus 10*
Fox, Lucia *DrAPF 93*
Fox, M(ichael) W. 1937- *WrDr 94*
Fox, Marcus *Who 94*
Fox, (John) Marcus 1927- *Who 94*
Fox, Marian Cavender 1947- *WhoScEn 94*
Fox, Mark Richard 1953- *WhoAmL 94*
Fox, Marvin c. 1936- *EncNAR*
Fox, Mary Catherine 1956- *WhoAmP 93*
Fox, Marye Anne 1947- *WhoAm 94*
Fox, Matthew *NewYTBS 93 [port]*
Fox, Matthew Ignatius 1934- *WhoAm 94*
Fox, Maurice Sanford 1924- *IntWW 93, WhoAm 94, WhoScEn 94*
Fox, Michael *WhoHol 92*
Fox, Michael Allen 1948- *WhoAmP 93*
Fox, Michael David 1937- *WhoAm 94, WhoAmA 93*
Fox, Michael J. 1961- *IntMPA 94, IntWW 93, WhoAm 94, WhoHol 92*
Fox, Michael John 1921- *Who 94*
Fox, Michael John 1942- *Who 94*
Fox, Michael Vass 1940- *WhoAm 94*
Fox, Michael W. 1950- *WhoAm 94, WhoAmL 94*
Fox, Michael Wilson 1937- *WhoAm 94, WhoScEn 94*
Fox, Michelle A. 1949- *WhoAmL 94*
Fox, Mickey d1987 *WhoHol 92*
Fox, Milton E. 1926- *WhoAmP 93*
Fox, Milton S. 1904-1971 *WhoAmA 93N*
Fox, Muriel 1928- *WhoAm 94*
Fox, Murray *Who 94*
Fox, (Henry) Murray 1912- *IntWW 93, Who 94*
Fox, N. Sean 1960- *WhoMW 93*
Fox, Patricia Sain 1954- *WhoMW 93*
Fox, Paul (Leonard) 1925- *Who 94*
Fox, Paul Leonard 1925- *IntWW 93*
Fox, Paul T. 1953- *WhoAm 94, WhoAmL 94*
Fox, Paul Walter 1949- *WhoAm 94, WhoAmL 94*
Fox, Paula *DrAPF 93*
Fox, Paula 1923- *TwCYAW, WhoAm 94, WrDr 94*
Fox, Pearl *WhoAmA 93*
Fox, Peter *WhoHol 92*
Fox, Peter Douglas 1948- *WhoMW 93*
Fox, Peter Kendrew 1949- *IntWW 93*
Fox, Randee Susan 1952- *WhoWest 94*
Fox, Reeder Rodman 1934- *WhoAm 94*
Fox, Regina Kiely d1993 *NewYTBS 93*
Fox, Renee Claire 1928- *IntWW 93, WhoAm 94*
Fox, Richard 1947- *IntMPA 94*
Fox, Richard A. 1929- *IntMPA 94*
Fox, Richard Edwin 1948- *WhoAmL 94*
Fox, Richard Henry 1938- *WhoAm 94*
Fox, Richard K., Jr. 1925- *WhoBlA 94*
Fox, Richard Lorain 1946- *WhoWest 94*
Fox, Richard Romaine 1934- *WhoScEn 94*
Fox, Richard Shirley 1943- *WhoAm 94*
Fox, Rick 1952- *WhoAmP 93*
Fox, Robert 1938- *Who 94, WrDr 94*
Fox, Robert August 1937- *WhoAm 94, WhoWest 94*
Fox, Robert Charles 1968- *WhoMW 93*
Fox, Robert Kriegbaum 1907- *WhoAm 94*
Fox, Robert McDougall 1939- *Who 94*
Fox, Robert R. *DrAPF 93*
Fox, Robert Trench 1937- *Who 94*
Fox, Robert William 1934- *WhoAm 94*
Fox, Roberta 1943- *WhoAmP 93*
Fox, Robin 1934- *WrDr 94*
Fox, Robin James L. *Who 94*
Fox, Ronald Ernest 1936- *WhoAm 94*
Fox, Ronald Forrest 1943- *WhoAm 94, WhoScEn 94*
Fox, Rose d1966 *WhoHol 92*
Fox, Roy 1920- *Who 94*
Fox, Ruth W. *Who 94*
Fox, Sally G. 1951- *WhoAmP 93*
Fox, Sam 1929- *WhoAm 94, WhoMW 93*
Fox, Samuel 1908- *WrDr 94*
Fox, Samuel Mickle, III 1923- *WhoAm 94*
Fox, Samuel Middleton 1856-1941 *EncSF 93*
Fox, Shayle Phillip 1934- *WhoAmL 94*
Fox, Sheila 1947- *WhoAm 94*
Fox, Shelley Zapara 1952- *WhoWest 94*
Fox, Sidney d1942 *WhoHol 92*
Fox, Sidney Albert 1898- *WhAm 10*
Fox, Sidney Walter 1912- *WhoAm 94, WorScD*
Fox, Sonny *WhoHol 92*
Fox, Stan 1952- *WhoAm 94*
Fox, Stephen R 1945- *WrDr 94*
Fox, Stuart Ira 1945- *WhoScEn 94, WhoWest 94*
Fox, Sylvan 1928- *WhoAm 94*
Fox, Ted 1954- *WrDr 94*
Fox, Terrence S. 1940- *WhoFI 94*
Fox, Terry Alan 1943- *WhoAmA 93*
Fox, Thomas Charles 1944- *WhoAm 94*
Fox, Thomas E., Jr. 1963- *WhoBlA 94*
Fox, Thomas George 1942- *WhoAm 94, WhoWest 94*
Fox, Thomas Walton 1923- *WhoAm 94*
Fox, Timothy Joseph 1951- *WhoFI 94*
Fox, Vernon Brittain 1916- *WhoAm 94*
Fox, Virginia d1982 *WhoHol 92*
Fox, Wallace 1920- *Who 94*
Fox, William 1879-1952 *IntDcF 2-4 [port]*
Fox, William, Jr. 1926- *WhoMW 93*
Fox, William Charles, III 1958- *WhoMW 93*
Fox, William F., Jr. 1942- *IntWW 93*
Fox, William J. d1993 *NewYTBS 93*
Fox, William K., Sr. 1917- *WhoBlA 94*
Fox, William L. *DrAPF 93*
Fox, William Price 1926- *ConAu 19AS [port]*
Fox, William Templeton 1932- *WhoAm 94*
Fox, Winifred Marjorie *Who 94*
Foxall, Colin 1947- *Who 94*
Foxall, Martha Jean 1931- *WhoBlA 94*
Foxall, Raymond 1916- *WrDr 94*
Fox-Andrews, James Roland Blake 1922- *Who 94*
Fox Bassett, Nigel 1929- *IntWW 93, Who 94*
Foxe, Earle d1973 *WhoHol 92*
Foxe, John 1516-1587 *BlmGEL*
Foxe, John 1517-1587 *DcLB 132 [port]*
Foxe, Luke 1586-c. 1635 *WhWE*
Foxell, Clive Arthur Peirson 1930- *Who 94*
Foxell, Nigel 1931- *WrDr 94*
Foxen, Gene Louis 1936- *WhoFI 94*
Foxen, Kathe Marlene 1964- *WhoMW 93*
Foxen, Richard William 1927- *WhoAm 94*
Fox-Freund, Barbara Susan 1949- *WhoFI 94*
Fox-Genovese, Elizabeth 1941- *WrDr 94*
Fox-Genovese, Elizabeth Ann 1941- *WhoAm 94*
Foxhoven, Jerry Ray 1952- *WhoAmL 94*
Foxhoven, Michael John 1949- *WhoFI 94, WhoWest 94*
Foxlee, James Brazier 1921- *Who 94*
Foxley, Alejandro 1939- *IntWW 93*
Foxley, William Coleman 1935- *WhoWest 94*
Foxley-Norris, Christopher (Neil) 1917- *Who 94*
Foxman, Abraham H. *WhoAm 94*
Foxman, Bruce Mayer 1942- *WhoAm 94*
Foxon, David Fairweather 1923- *Who 94*
Foxon, Harold Peter 1919- *Who 94*
Fox-Strangways *Who 94*
Foxton, Edwin Frederick 1914- *Who 94*
Foxwell, Ivan 1914- *IntMPA 94*
Foxwell, Julia Elena 1944- *WhoHisp 94*
Foxworth, Eugene D., Jr. 1927- *WhoAmP 93*
Foxworth, Jo *WhoAm 94*
Foxworth, John Edwin, Jr. 1932- *WhoAm 94, WhoMW 93*
Foxworth, Robert 1941- *IntMPA 94, WhoHol 92*
Foxworth, Robert Heath 1941- *WhoAm 94*
Foxx, Daniel LeRoy, Jr. 1939- *WhoWest 94*
Foxx, Elizabeth *WhoHol 92*
Foxx, Jack 1943- *WrDr 94*
Foxx, Redd 1922- *WhoHol 92*
Foxx, Redd 1922-1991 *AfrAmAl 6 [port], WhAm 10, WhoBlA 94N, WhoCom*
Foxx, Richard Michael 1944- *WhoScEn 94*
Foy, Benny Earl 1948- *WhoFI 94*
Foy, Bryan d1977 *WhoHol 92*
Foy, Charles d1984 *WhoHol 92*
Foy, Charles Daley 1923- *WhoAm 94*
Foy, Eddie d1928 *WhoHol 92*
Foy, Eddie, Jr. d1983 *WhoHol 92*
Foy, Eddie, III *WhoHol 92*
Foy, Edward Donald 1952- *WhoMW 93*
Foy, Herbert Miles, III 1945- *WhoAm 94, WhoAmL 94*
Foy, Lewis W. 1915- *EncABHB 9*
Foy, Madeline d1988 *WhoHol 92*
Foy, Mary d1987 *WhoHol 92*
Foy, Richard d1947 *WhoHol 92*
Foy, Thomas Patrick 1951- *WhoAmP 93*
Foy, Thomas Paul 1914- *WhoAmP 93*
Foye, Laurance Vincent 1925- *WhoAm 94*
Foye, Thomas Harold 1930- *WhoAm 94*
Foye-Eberhardt, Ladye Antoinette 1943- *WhoBlA 94*
Foyer, Eddie d1934 *WhoHol 92*
Foyil, James Douglas 1952- *WhoAmL 94*
Foyle, Christina Agnes Lilian *Who 94*
Foyle, Christina Agnes Lilian 1911- *IntWW 93*
Foyle, Dolores Hartley 1928- *WhoAmP 93*
Foyo, George William 1946- *WhoHisp 94*
Foyt, Anthony Joseph, Jr. 1935- *WhoAm 94*
Foyt, Arthur George 1937- *WhoAm 94*
Fozard, John William 1928- *IntWW 93, Who 94, WhoAm 94*
Fra, Dahli-Sterne 1895- *WhoAmA 93*
Frabel, Hans Godo 1941- *WhoAmA 93*
Frabotta, Biancamaria 1947- *BlmGWL*
Fracanzani, Carlo 1935- *IntWW 93*
Fracchia, Pearl Garza 1950- *WhoHisp 94*
Fracci, Carla *WhoHol 92*
Fracci, Carla 1936- *IntDcB [port]*
Frace, Charles Lewis 1926- *WhoAmA 93*
"Frack" d1979 *WhoHol 92*
Frack, Joseph E. 1948- *WhoIns 94*
Frackman, Noel 1930- *WhoAmA 93*
Frackman, Richard Benoit 1923- *WhoAm 94*
Frackman, Russell Jay 1946- *WhoAm 94, WhoAmL 94*
Frade, Peter Daniel 1946- *WhoAm 94*
Fradenburg, Louise Olga 1953- *ConAu 142*
Fradetal, Marcel 1908- *IntDcF 2-4*
Fradette, Richard E. 1954- *WhoAmL 94*
Fradkin, David Barry 1941- *WhoWest 94*
Fradkin, David Milton 1931- *WhoAm 94*
Fradkov, Valery Eugene 1954- *WhoScEn 94*
Fradley, Frederick Macdonell 1924- *WhoAm 94*
Fraeb, Henry d1841 *WhWE*
Fraedrich, Royal Louis 1931- *WhoAm 94*
Fraenkel, George Kessler 1921- *WhoAm 94*
Fraenkel, Jack R 1932- *WrDr 94*
Fraenkel, Jeffrey Andrew 1955- *WhoAmA 93*
Fraenkel, Ludwig Edward 1927- *Who 94*
Fraenkel, Naomi 1920- *BlmGWL*
Fraenkel, Peter Maurice 1915- *Who 94*
Fraenkel, Stephen Joseph 1917- *WhoAm 94*
Fraenkel-Conrat, Heinz 1910- *IntWW 93, WorScD*
Fraga, Elaina Martina 1947- *WhoHisp 94*
Fraga, Juan R. 1924- *WhoHisp 94*
Fraga, Luis *WhoHisp 94*
Fraga, Lupe *WhoHisp 94*
Fraga, Rosa *WhoHisp 94*
Fraga Iribarne, Manuel 1922- *IntWW 93, Who 94*
Fragale, Ron 1950- *WhoAmP 93*
Frager, Albert S. 1922- *WhoAm 94*
Frager, Norman 1936- *WhoAm 94*
Fragner, Matthew Charles 1954- *WhoAm 94*
Fragnito, Robert C. 1946- *WhoAmP 93*
Frago, William S. 1942- *WhoAm 94, WhoFI 94*
Fragola, Anthony *DrAPF 93*
Fragos, Berrien *DrAPF 93*
Frago-Zito, Ivy Marie 1956- *WhoFI 94*
Fraguela, Javier *WhoHisp 94*
Fraguela, Rafael José 1955- *WhoHisp 94*
Fraher, David J. *DrAPF 93*
Frahm, Donald R. 1932- *WhoIns 94*
Frahm, Donald Robert 1932- *WhoAm 94, WhoFI 94*
Frahm, Lorinda S. 1965- *WhoFI 94*
Frahm, Sheila 1945- *WhoAmP 93, WhoMW 93*
Frahm, Veryl Harvey, Jr. 1948- *WhoScEn 94*
Frahmann, Dennis George 1953- *WhoWest 94*
Fraiberg, Lawrence Phillip 1921- *WhoAm 94*
Fraiche, Donna DiMartino 1951- *WhoAmL 94*
Fraidin, Stephen 1939- *WhoAm 94, WhoAmL 94*
Frailey, Stephen A. 1957- *WhoAmA 93*
Fraiman, Genevieve Lam 1928- *WhoAm 94, WhoAmL 94*
Frair, Wayne Franklin 1926- *WhoScEn 94*
Fraise, Eugene 1932- *WhoAmP 93*
Fraiser, John J., Jr. *WhoAmP 93*
Fraitag, Leonard Alan 1961- *WhoScEn 94, WhoWest 94*
Frake, Charles Oliver 1930- *WhoAm 94*
Fraker, Anne Turner 1946- *WhoMW 93*
Fraker, Barbara J. 1950- *WhoMW 93*
Fraker, M. Suzanne 1945- *WhoFI 94*
Fraker, Mark Arnott 1944- *WhoWest 94*
Fraker, William A. 1923- *IntDcF 2-4, IntMPA 94*
Frakes, George Edward 1932- *WhoWest 94, WrDr 94*
Frakes, Lawrence Wright 1951- *WhoAm 94, WhoScEn 94*
Frakes, Phillip E. 1929- *WhoIns 94*
Frakes, Rod Vance 1930- *WhoAm 94*
Frakes, William B. 1952- *ConAu 141*
Fraknoi, Andrew 1948- *WhoAm 94, WhoScEn 94, WhoWest 94*
Fraleigh, John Walter 1945- *WhoMW 93*
Fraley, David K. 1952- *WhoAmA 93*
Fraley, Elwin Eugene 1934- *WhoAm 94*
Fraley, Leonie Jeanne 1941- *WhoMW 93*
Fraley, Ralph Reed 1945- *WhoAm 94, WhoMW 93*
Fraley, Ruth Ann 1942- *WhoAmL 94*
Fralick, Fred d1958 *WhoHol 92*
Frame, Alistair (Gilchrist) 1929- *Who 94*
Frame, Alistair Gilchrist 1929- *IntWW 93*
Frame, Clarence George 1918- *WhoAm 94*
Frame, Cynthia Solt *DrAPF 93*
Frame, David William 1934- *Who 94*
Frame, Donald Murdoch 1911- *WrDr 94*
Frame, Frank Riddell 1930- *IntWW 93, Who 94*
Frame, Janet 1924- *BlmGEL [port], IntWW 93, WrDr 94*
Frame, Janet (Paterson) 1924- *RfGShF*
Frame, Janet (Patterson) 1924- *EncSF 93*

Frame, Janet Paterson 1924- BlmGWL [port]
Frame, John 1950- WhoAmA 93
Frame, John McElphatrick 1939- WhoWest 94
Frame, John Timothy 1930- Who 94, WhoAm 94
Frame, Leonard W. 1917- WhoWest 94
Frame, Robert (Aaron) 1924- WhoAmA 93
Frame, Ronald 1953- WrDr 94
Frame, Ronald William Sutherland 1953- Who 94
Frame, Russell William 1929- WhoAm 94
Frame, Ted Ronald 1929- WhoWest 94
Framery, Nicolas Etienne 1745-1810 NewGrDO
Framme, Lawrence Henry, III 1949- WhoAmP 93
Frampton, Elon Wilson 1924- WhoMW 93
Frampton, George Thomas 1917- WhoAm 94
Frampton, George Thomas, Jr. 1944- WhoAm 94
Frampton, Hollis 1936-1984 ConAu 141, WhoAmA 93N
Frampton, (George Vernon) Meredith 1894-1984 DcNaB MP
Frampton, Paul Howard 1943- WhoAm 94
Frampton, Peter 1950- WhoAm 94, WhoHol 92
Franaho, Susan M. 1946- WhoMW 93
Franca, Celia 1921- IntDcB [port], WhoAm 94
Franca, Jose-Augusto 1922- IntWW 93
Francaix, Jean 1912- NewGrDO
France, Anatole 1844-1924 EncSF 93
France, Arnold William 1911- Who 94
France, Beatrice Murdock WhoAmP 93
France, Belinda Takach 1964- WhoAmL 94, WhoFI 94
France, C. V. d1949 WhoHol 92
France, Christopher (Walter) 1934- Who 94
France, Claude d1928 WhoHol 92
France, David 1959- ConAu 140
France, Edward Augustine, Jr. 1937- WhoAm 94
France, Erwin A. 1938- WhoBlA 94
France, Frederick Doug, Jr. 1953- WhoBlA 94
France, John Lyons 1933- WhoWest 94
France, Joseph David 1953- WhoAm 94, WhoFI 94
France, Linda 1958- ConAu 141
France, Newell Edwin 1927- WhoAm 94
France, Peter 1935- Who 94
France, Richard 1930- WhoHol 92
France, Richard Thomas 1938- Who 94
France, Ruth 1913-1968 BlmGWL
France, Samuel Ewing Hill 1925- WhoScEn 94
France, Tab DrAPF 93
France, Valerie Edith 1935- Who 94
Francen, Victor d1977 WhoHol 92
Frances, Harriette Anton WhoAmA 93
Frances, Stephen (Daniel) 1917-1989 EncSF 93
Francesca c. 13th cent.- See Paolo c. 13th cent.- BlmGEL
Francescatti, Zino Rene 1902-1991 WhAm 10
Franceschi, Ernest Joseph, Jr. 1957- WhoAmL 94, WhoWest 94
Franceschini, Giovanni Battista 1662?-1732 NewGrDO
Francese, Angela 1950- WhoWomW 91
Francesina NewGrDO
Franch, Richard Thomas 1942- WhoAm 94, WhoAmL 94
Franchere, Gabriel 1786-1863 WhWE
Franchetti, Alberto 1860-1942 NewGrDO
Franchetti, Arnold d1993 NewYTBS 93
Franchetti, Arnold 1909- NewGrDO
Franchi, Anna 1866-1954 BlmGWL
Franchi, Carlo 1743?-1779? NewGrDO
Franchi, Franco WhoHol 92
Franchi, Jorge 1965- WhoHisp 94
Franchi, Rafael L. 1927- WhoHisp 94
Franchi, Sergio d1990 WhoHol 92
Franchini, Gene Edward 1935- WhoAm 94, WhoAmL 94, WhoAmP 93, WhoWest 94
Franchini, Teresa d1972 WhoHol 92
Franchot, Peter 1947- WhoAmP 93
Franci, Benvenuto 1891-1985 NewGrDO
Franci, Carlo 1927- NewGrDO
Francia, Luis H. F. 1945- WhoAsA 94
Francillo-Kaufmann, Hedwig 1878-1948 NewGrDO
Francine, Anne 1917- WhoHol 92
Francine, Jean-Nicolas de 1662-1735 NewGrDO
Franciosa, Anthony 1928- IntMPA 94, WhoAm 94, WhoHol 92
Francis, I 1494-1547 HisWorL [port]
Francis, Albert W. 1952- WhoMW 93
Francis, Alec B. d1934 WhoHol 92
Francis, Alexandria Stephanie 1952- WhoAm 94
Francis, Ann d1983 WhoHol 92
Francis, Anne 1930- WhoHol 92
Francis, Anne 1932- IntMPA 94
Francis, Arlene 1908- IntMPA 94, WhoHol 92
Francis, Bevo 1932- BasBi
Francis, Bill Dean 1929- WhoAmA 93
Francis, C. D. E. 1916- WrDr 94
Francis, Charles d1973 WhoHol 92
Francis, Charles Andrew 1940- WhoAm 94, WhoScEn 94
Francis, Charles S. L. 1943- WhoBlA 94
Francis, Cheryl Margaret 1949- WhoBlA 94
Francis, Clare 1946- WrDr 94
Francis, Clare Mary 1946- Who 94
Francis, Clive 1946- WhoHol 92
Francis, Connie 1938- ConMus 10 [port], IntMPA 94, WhoHol 92
Francis, Dale Lyman 1917-1992 WhAm 10
Francis, Darryl Robert 1912- WhoAm 94
Francis, Delma J. 1953- WhoBlA 94
Francis, Dennis P. 1943- WhoIns 94
Francis, Derek d1984 WhoHol 92
Francis, Dick IntWW 93
Francis, Dick d1949 WhoHol 92
Francis, Dick 1920- ConAu 42NR, Who 94, WhoAm 94, WrDr 94
Francis, Dorothy Brenner 1926- WrDr 94
Francis, E. Aracelis 1939- WhoBlA 94
Francis, Edith V. WhoBlA 94
Francis, Edward Howel 1924- Who 94
Francis, Edward Reginald 1929- Who 94
Francis, Emile Percy 1926- WhoAm 94
Francis, Eugene WhoHol 92
Francis, Eulalie Marie WhoScEn 94
Francis, Eve d1980 WhoHol 92
Francis, Faith Ellen 1929- WhoScEn 94
Francis, Freddie 1917- HorFD [port], IntDcF 2-4 [port], IntMPA 94, WhoAm 94
Francis, Gilbert H. 1930- WhoBlA 94
Francis, Gwyn Jones 1930- Who 94
Francis, H. E. DrAPF 93
Francis, H(erbert) E(dward), Jr. 1924- WrDr 94
Francis, Harry McDonald, Jr. 1933- WhoAm 94
Francis, Henry Minton 1922- WhoBlA 94
Francis, Ivor d1986 WhoHol 92
Francis, James 1968- WhoBlA 94
Francis, James Delbert 1947- WhoAm 94
Francis, James L. 1943- WhoBlA 94
Francis, Jan 1951- WhoHol 92
Francis, Jean Thickens 1943- WhoAmA 93
Francis, Jerome Leslie 1941- WhoAmL 94
Francis, John Elbert 1937- WhoMW 93
Francis, John Michael 1939- Who 94
Francis, Joseph 1801-1893 WorInv
Francis, Joseph A. 1923- WhoBlA 94
Francis, Josiah c. 1770-1818 EncNAR
Francis, Kay d1968 WhoHol 92
Francis, Kennon Thompson 1945- WhoScEn 94
Francis, Kevin 1949- IntMPA 94
Francis, Larry 1933- WhoAm 94
Francis, Laurie (Justice) 1918- Who 94
Francis, Livingston S. 1929- WhoBlA 94
Francis, Madison Ke, Jr. 1945- WhoAmA 93
Francis, Marc Baruch 1934- WhoWest 94
Francis, Marion David 1923- WhoAm 94, WhoMW 93
Francis, Mary Frances Van Dyke 1925- WhoFI 94
Francis, Matthew (Charles) 1956- WrDr 94
Francis, Merrill Richard 1932- WhoAm 94, WhoAmL 94
Francis, Nicky d1960 WhoHol 92
Francis, Noel d1959 WhoHol 92
Francis, Norman Who 94
Francis, (William) Norman 1921- Who 94
Francis, Norman C. WhoBlA 94
Francis, Olin d1952 WhoHol 92
Francis, Owen 1912- Who 94
Francis, Patrick John 1964- WhoBlA 94
Francis, Paul 1953- WrDr 94
Francis, Peter WhoAmA 93
Francis, Peter Brereton 1953- Who 94
Francis, Peter David 1934- WhoAmL 94, WhoAmP 93, WhoWest 94
Francis, Philip 1740-1818 WhAmRev
Francis, Philip Hamilton 1938- WhoAm 94
Francis, Ray William, Jr. 1927- WhoBlA 94
Francis, Raymond d1987 WhoHol 92
Francis, Richard 1945- WrDr 94
Francis, Richard H. 1945- EncSF 93
Francis, Richard Haudiomont 1925- WhoAm 94
Francis, Richard L. 1919- WhoBlA 94
Francis, Richard Mark 1947- Who 94
Francis, Richard Norman 1949- WhoWest 94
Francis, Richard Stanley Who 94
Francis, Richard Stanley 1920- IntWW 93
Francis, Richard Trevor Langford d1992 IntWW 93N
Francis, Robert d1955 WhoHol 92
Francis, Robert Allen 1957- WhoMW 93
Francis, Robert Anthony 1950- Who 94
Francis, Robert Thomas 1935- WhoMW 93
Francis, Ronald Bernard 1964- WhoBlA 94
Francis, Sam 1923- IntWW 93, WhoAm 94, WhoAmA 93
Francis, Samuel Todd 1947- WhoAm 94
Francis, Sandra d1981 WhoHol 92
Francis, Shirley Ann 1934- WhoAmP 93
Francis, Talton Loe 1924- WhoAm 94
Francis, Thomas Edward 1933- WhoAmP 93
Francis, Timothy Duane 1956- WhoScEn 94, WhoWest 94
Francis, Tom 1951- WhoAmA 93
Francis, William Who 94
Francis, (Horace) William (Alexander) 1926- Who 94
Francis, William Kevin 1965- WhoScEn 94
Francis, William Lancelot 1906- Who 94
Francis, Wilma WhoHol 92
Francisci Di Baschi, Marco 1920- IntWW 93
Francisco, Anthony M. 1960- WhoBlA 94
Francisco, Betty d1950 WhoHol 92
Francisco, Curtis Scott 1951- WhoFI 94
Francisco, Edgar Wiggin, III 1930- WhoAm 94
Francisco, Emiliano Alonzo 1908?- WhoAsA 94
Francisco, James L. 1937- WhoAm 94, WhoMW 93
Francisco, James Lee 1937- WhoAmP 93
Francisco, Joseph Salvadore, Jr. 1955- WhoBlA 94, WhoMW 93
Francisco, Juan, Jr. 1952- WhoHisp 94
Francisco, Julia M. 1947- WhoAmP 93
Francisco, Kenneth Dale 1941- WhoAmP 93
Francisco, Marcia Madora 1958- WhoBlA 94
Francisco, Patricia Weaver DrAPF 93
Francisco, Peter c. 1760-1831 AmRev, WhAmRev
Francisco, Stephen Roy 1956- WhoHisp 94
Francisco, Wayne Markland 1943- WhoFI 94, WhoWest 94
Franciscus, James d1991 WhoHol 92
Franciscus, James Grover 1934-1991 WhAm 10
Francis Joseph, I 1830-1916 HisWorL [port]
Francis of Assisi 1182-1226 HisWorL [port]
Francis of Assisi, St. 1181?-1226 EnvEnc
Francis Xavier WhWE
Franck, Ardath Amond 1925- WhoMW 93, WhoScEn 94
Franck, Cesar(-Auguste-Jean-Guillaume-Hubert) 1822-1890 NewGrDO
Franck, Edouard IntWW 93
Franck, Frederick 1909- WrDr 94
Franck, Frederick S. 1909- WhoAmA 93
Franck, Frederick Sigfred 1909- WhoAm 94
Franck, Johann Wolfgang 1644?-c. 1710 NewGrDO
Franck, John L. d1920 WhoHol 92
Franck, Michael 1932- WhoAm 94, WhoAmL 94
Franck, Raoul d1984 WhoHol 92
Franck, Thomas Martin 1931- WhoAm 94, WhoAmL 94, WrDr 94
Franck, Violet M. 1949- ConAu 140
Franck, Walter d1961 WhoHol 92
Francka, Catherine Cantwell 1937- WhoAmP 93
Francke, Albert, III 1934- WhoAm 94
Francke, Gloria Niemeyer 1922- WhoAm 94
Francke, Linda Bird 1939- WhoAm 94
Franckel, Philip Leslie 1953- WhoAmL 94
Franckenstein, Clemens (Erwein Heinrich Karl Bonaventura), Freiherr von und zu 1875-1942 NewGrDO
Franckiewicz, Victor John, Jr. 1954- WhoAmP 93
Francklin, Michael 1733-1782 AmRev
Francklin, (Mavourn Baldwin) Philip 1913- Who 94
Francklyn, Christopher Steward 1957- WhoScEn 94
Francks, Don 1932- WhoHol 92
Franc-Nohain 1872-1934 NewGrDO
Franco, Adolfo Alberto 1956- WhoAmL 94
Franco, Adolfo Mariano 1922- WhoHisp 94
Franco, Angel 1951- WhoHisp 94
Franco, Annemarie Woletz 1933- WhoAm 94
Franco, Anthony M. 1933- WhoAm 94, WhoFI 94
Franco, Armando 1935- WhoHisp 94
Franco, Barbara 1945- WhoAmA 93
Franco, Charles, Sr. WhoHisp 94
Franco, Francisco 1892-1975 HisWorL [port]
Franco, Gloria Lopez WhoHisp 94
Franco, Herminia d1984 WhoHol 92
Franco, Hernán R. 1942- WhoHisp 94
Franco, Itamar Augusto Cautiero 1931- IntWW 93
Franco, Jesus 1930- HorFD
Franco, Jorge 1929- WhoWest 94
Franco, Jose, Jr. 1966- WhoHisp 94
Franco, José Antonio, III 1950- WhoHisp 94
Franco, Juan N. 1949- WhoHisp 94
Franco, Juan Roberto 1937- WhoHisp 94
Franco, Julio 1961- WhoHisp 94
Franco, Julio Cesar 1961- WhoAm 94, WhoBlA 94
Franco, Madeleine 1949- WhoWest 94
Franco, Maurice 1950- WhoWest 94
Franco, Paul Roy 1947- WhoHisp 94
Franco, Philip Anthony 1953- WhoAm 94, WhoAmL 94
Franco, Philip Joseph 1922- WhoFI 94
Franco, Ralph Abraham 1921- WhoAmL 94
Franco, Ramon WhoHol 92
Franco, Ramón Luis 1963- WhoHisp 94
Franco, Robert John 1932- WhoAmA 93N
Franco, Ruben 1947- WhoHisp 94
Franco, Rudolph Lopez 1929- WhoHisp 94
Franco, Thomas S. WhoIns 94
Franco, Veronica 1546-1591 BlmGWL
Franco, Victor 1937- WhoAm 94
Franco, Victor Manuel 1949- WhoHisp 94
Francoeur, Francois 1698-1787 NewGrDO
Francoeur, Louis-Joseph 1738-1804 NewGrDO
Francoeur, Robert Thomas 1931- WrDr 94
Francois, Christian WhoHol 92
Francois, Emmanuel Saturnin 1938- WhoBlA 94
Francois, Francis Bernard 1934- WhoAm 94, WhoFI 94
Francois, Jacques 1920- WhoHol 92
Francois, Louise von 1817-1893 BlmGWL, DcLB 129 [port]
Francois, Terry A. 1921- WhoBlA 94
Francois, Theodore Victor 1938- WhoBlA 94
Francois, William Armand 1942- WhoAm 94, WhoFI 94
Francois de Sales GuFrLit 2
Francois-Poncet, Jean Andre 1928- IntWW 93, Who 94
Francome, John 1952- Who 94
Franco Nogueira, Alberto 1918-1993 NewYTBS 93
Franczek, James Clement, Jr. 1946- WhoAmL 94
Frandina, Philip Frank 1928- WhoScEn 94
Frandsen, Lloyd 1948- WhoAmP 93
Frane, James Thomas 1942- WhoScEn 94
Franer, Charles William 1934- WhoMW 93
Franetovic, Vjekoslav 1946- WhoMW 93, WhoScEn 94
Franey, Billy d1940 WhoHol 92
Franey, Ros(alind) 1946- WrDr 94
Frang, Jerry Lee 1946- WhoMW 93
Frangakis, Gerassimos P. 1940- WhoScEn 94
Frangella, Luis 1944- WhoAmA 93N
Frangiossi, Catterina fl. 1683-1689 NewGrDO
Frangopol, Dan Mircea 1946- WhoWest 94
Frangopoulos, Zissimos A. 1944- WhoFI 94
Frangos, James George 1934- WhoAm 94
Frangsmyr, Tore 1938- IntWW 93
Franjieh, Suleiman d1992 IntWW 93N
Franjieh, Suleiman 1910-1992 AnObit 1992
Frank, A. Scott ConTFT 11
Frank, Alan 1922- WhoWest 94
Frank, Alan Donald 1917- Who 94
Frank, Albert Bernard 1939- WhoMW 93
Frank, Alfred Swift, Jr. 1924- WhoAmP 93
Frank, Allan d1979 WhoHol 92
Frank, Alvin R. 1927- WhoMW 93
Frank, Amalie Julianna 1933- WhoAm 94
Frank, André Gunder 1929- WrDr 94
Frank, Andrew Who 94
Frank, (Robert) Andrew 1964- Who 94

Frank, Anne 1929-1945 *Au&Arts 12 [port], BlmGWL*
Frank, Anne(lies Marie) 1929-1945 *TwCYAW*
Frank, Anthony Melchior 1931- *WhoAm 94, WhoFI 94*
Frank, Arthur J. 1946- *WhoAmL 94*
Frank, Barbara d1976 *WhoHol 92*
Frank, Barney 1940- *CngDr 93, WhoAm 94, WhoAmP 93*
Frank, Barry H. 1938- *WhoAmL 94*
Frank, Ben d1990 *WhoHol 92*
Frank, Bernard 1913- *WhoAm 94, WhoAmL 94*
Frank, Bernard Alan 1931- *WhoAmL 94*
Frank, Bruce Howard 1937- *WhoFI 94*
Frank, Carl d1972 *WhoHol 92*
Frank, Charles *Who 94*
Frank, Charles 1947- *WhoHol 92*
Frank, (Frederick) Charles 1911- *IntWW 93, Who 94*
Frank, Charles R(aphael, Jr.) 1937- *WrDr 94*
Frank, Charles Raphael, Jr. 1937- *WhoAm 94*
Frank, Charles William, Jr. 1922- *WhoAmA 93*
Frank, Christian d1967 *WhoHol 92*
Frank, Christopher Lynd 1949- *WhoScEn 94*
Frank, Claudia Pat 1936- *WhoAmP 93*
Frank, Craig Allen 1953- *WhoMW 93*
Frank, Curtiss E. 1904-1990 *WhAm 10*
Frank, David 1940- *WhoAmA 93*
Frank, David George 1953- *WhoFI 94*
Frank, Dieter 1930- *WhoAm 94*
Frank, Don J. 1937- *WhoAmP 93*
Frank, Donald Herbert 1931- *WhoWest 94*
Frank, Donna 1957- *WhoWest 94*
Frank, Douglas (George Horace) 1916- *Who 94*
Frank, Edgar Gerald 1931- *WhoAm 94*
Frank, Elizabeth 1945- *WhoAm 94*
Frank, Ernst 1847-1889 *NewGrDO*
Frank, Eugene Martin 1944- *WhoMW 93*
Frank, Eugene Maxwell 1907- *WhoAm 94*
Frank, Evelyn R. d1993 *NewYTBS 93*
Frank, F. Alexander 1916- *WhoAm 94*
Frank, Frederick 1932- *WhoAm 94*
Frank, Gary 1951- *WhoHol 92*
Frank, Gary A. 1953- *CngDr 93*
Frank, George Andrew 1938- *WhoAmL 94*
Frank, George Willard 1923- *WhoAm 94*
Frank, Gerald Duane 1948- *WhoWest 94*
Frank, Gerald Wendel 1923- *WhoAmP 93*
Frank, Gerold 1907- *WhoAm 94*
Frank, Harold Roy 1924- *WhoAm 94*
Frank, Harriet, Jr. *ConTFT 11*
Frank, Harvey 1930- *WhoAm 94*
Frank, Harvey 1944- *WhoFI 94*
Frank, Helen (Goodzeit) 1930- *WhoAmA 93*
Frank, Helmar Gunter 1933- *WhoScEn 94*
Frank, Helmut J. 1922- *WrDr 94*
Frank, Hilda Rhea Kaplan 1939- *WhoAm 94*
Frank, Horst 1929- *WhoHol 92*
Frank, Ilya Mikhailovich 1908-1990 *WhAm 10, WhoScEn 94*
Frank, Irwin Norman 1927- *WhoAm 94*
Frank, Isaiah 1917- *WhoAm 94*
Frank, J. Herbert d1926 *WhoHol 92*
Frank, J. Louis 1936- *WhoAm 94*
Frank, Jacob 1936- *WhoAmL 94*
Frank, James Aaron 1954- *WhoAm 94*
Frank, James Stuart 1945- *WhoAmL 94*
Frank, Jean Brown *WhoMW 93*
Frank, Jeffrey *DrAPF 93*
Frank, Jeffrey 1965- *WhoHol 92*
Frank, Jerome David 1909- *WhoAm 94*
Frank, Joanna 1941- *WhoHol 92*
Frank, John d1961 *WhoHol 92*
Frank, John LeRoy 1952- *WhoAmL 94*
Frank, John Paul 1917- *WhoAm 94*
Frank, John V. 1936- *WhoMW 93*
Frank, Jonathan Edward 1952- *WhoFI 94*
Frank, Jonny J. 1954- *WhoAmL 94*
Frank, Joseph (Nathaniel) 1918- *WrDr 94*
Frank, Joseph Elihu 1934- *WhoAmL 94*
Frank, Joseph Nathaniel 1918- *WhoAm 94*
Frank, Karl H. 1944- *WhoScEn 94*
Frank, Lawrence Robert 1944- *WhoWest 94*
Frank, Lloyd 1925- *WhoAm 94, WhoAmL 94*
Frank, Lorraine Weiss 1923- *WhoAmP 93*
Frank, Martin 1947- *WhoAm 94*
Frank, Mary 1933- *WhoAm 94*
Frank, Mary Lou Bryant 1952- *WhoScEn 94*
Frank, Melvin 1913-1988 *IntDcF 2-4*
Frank, Meredith Rose 1949- *WhoMW 93*
Frank, Michael M. 1937- *WhoAm 94*
Frank, Michael Victor 1947- *WhoScEn 94*
Frank, Milton d1993 *NewYTBS 93*
Frank, Morton 1912-1989 *WhAm 10*
Frank, Nancy G. 1943- *WhoAmP 93*
Frank, Pat (Harry Hart) 1907-1964 *EncSF 93*
Frank, Patricia Anne 1929- *WhoAmP 93*
Frank, Paul 1918- *IntWW 93*
Frank, Paul Addison 1895- *WhAm 10*
Frank, Paul Sardo, Jr. 1936- *WhoScEn 94*
Frank, Paul Theodore 1876-1958 *WhoAmA 93N*
Frank, Peter *DrAPF 93*
Frank, Peter Solomon 1950- *WhoAmA 93*
Frank, Philip Lawrence 1931- *WhoFI 94*
Frank, Richard *WhoHol 92*
Frank, Richard A. 1936- *WhoAmP 93*
Frank, Richard Calhoun 1930- *WhoAm 94*
Frank, Richard Horton, Jr. 1928- *WhoAmL 94*
Frank, Richard L. 1931- *WhoBlA 94*
Frank, Richard Sanford 1931- *WhoAm 94*
Frank, Richard Stephen 1940- *WhoScEn 94*
Frank, Robert Allen 1932- *WhoAm 94, WhoFI 94*
Frank, Robert Allen 1950- *WhoAm 94, WhoFI 94*
Frank, Robert G(regg), Jr. 1943- *WrDr 94*
Frank, Robert Joseph 1939- *WhoWest 94*
Frank, Robert Worth, Jr. 1914- *WhoAm 94*
Frank, Ronald Edward 1933- *WhoAm 94, WhoFI 94*
Frank, Ronald W. 1947- *WhoAm 94, WhoAmL 94, WhoFI 94*
Frank, Ruby Merinda 1920- *WhoFI 94*
Frank, Sanders Thalheimer 1938- *WhoAm 94, WhoMW 93, WhoScEn 94*
Frank, Sandra Kaye 1941- *WhoMW 93*
Frank, Scott 1960?- *ConTFT 11*
Frank, Sheldon *DrAPF 93*
Frank, Stanley Donald 1932- *WhoAm 94, WhoFI 94*
Frank, Stephanie Ann 1963- *WhoMW 93*
Frank, Stephen Ira 1942- *WhoMW 93*
Frank, Stephen Richard 1942- *WhoWest 94*
Frank, Steve 1954- *WhoAmP 93*
Frank, Steven Neil 1947- *WhoScEn 94*
Frank, Stuart 1934- *WhoAm 94*
Frank, Thaisa *DrAPF 93*
Frank, Theodore David 1941- *WhoAm 94*
Frank, Thomas Edward 1939- *WhoFI 94*
Frank, Thomas Paul 1956- *WhoMW 93*
Frank, Tony *WhoHol 92*
Frank, Victor H., Jr. 1927- *WhoAm 94*
Frank, Will d1925 *WhoHol 92*
Frank, William Charles 1940- *WhoAm 94*
Frank, William Fielding 1944- *WhoAm 94, WhoFI 94*
Frank, William George 1898- *WhAm 10*
Frank, William Nelson 1953- *WhoFI 94*
Frank, William Pendleton 1941- *WhoFI 94*
Frankau, Gilbert 1884-1952 *EncSF 93*
Frankau, Ronald d1951 *WhoHol 92*
Franke, Charles Henry 1933- *WhoAm 94*
Franke, Christopher *DrAPF 93*
Franke, Constant d1943 *WhoHol 92*
Franke, Daniel David 1965- *WhoWest 94*
Franke, David Parker 1965- *WhoFI 94*
Franke, Egon 1913- *IntWW 93*
Franke, Frederick Rahde 1918- *WhoAm 94*
Franke, George Edward 1936- *WhoScEn 94*
Franke, Herbert 1914- *IntWW 93*
Franke, Herbert W(erner) 1927- *EncSF 93*
Franke, Hilmar 1946- *WhoScEn 94*
Franke, John Charles 1937- *WhoMW 93*
Franke, John Jacob, Jr. 1930- *WhAm 10*
Franke, Lee E. *DrAPF 93*
Franke, Linda Frederick 1947- *WhoAmL 94*
Franke, Maripat Kemps 1960- *WhoMW 93*
Franke, Richard Homer 1937- *WhoWest 94*
Franke, Richard James 1931- *WhoAm 94, WhoFI 94*
Franke, Steven Wesley 1954- *WhoFI 94*
Franke, William Augustus 1937- *WhoAm 94*
Franke, William Birrell 1894- *WhAm 10*
Frankel, A. Steven 1942- *WhoWest 94*
Frankel, Alona 1937- *WrDr 94*
Frankel, Arnold J. 1922- *WhoAm 94*
Frankel, Art *WhoHol 92*
Frankel, Arthur 1928- *WhoAm 94*
Frankel, Barbara Brown 1928- *WhoScEn 94*
Frankel, Benjamin Harrison 1930- *WhoAm 94*
Frankel, Bonnie *NewYTBS 93 [port]*
Frankel, Charles James, III 1944- *WhoFI 94*
Frankel, Dextra 1924- *WhoAmA 93*
Frankel, Donald Leon 1931- *WhoAm 94*
Frankel, Douglas K. 1963- *WhoFI 94*
Frankel, Edward Irwin 1941- *WhoWest 94*
Frankel, Ellen 1951- *WrDr 94*
Frankel, Ernst Gabriel 1923- *WhoAm 94*
Frankel, Fanchon d1937 *WhoHol 92*
Frankel, Francine Ruth 1935- *WhoAm 94*
Frankel, Gene 1923- *WhoAm 94*
Frankel, Herbert *Who 94*
Frankel, (Sally) Herbert 1903- *Who 94*
Frankel, Irwin 1919- *WhoScEn 94*
Frankel, James Burton 1924- *WhoAmL 94*
Frankel, Jeffrey Alexander 1952- *WhoAm 94*
Frankel, Kenneth Mark 1940- *WhoAm 94, WhoScEn 94*
Frankel, Lois J. 1948- *WhoAmP 93*
Frankel, Martin Richard 1943- *WhoAm 94, WhoFI 94*
Frankel, Marvin 1924- *WhoAm 94*
Frankel, Marvin E. 1920- *WhoAm 94*
Frankel, Max 1930- *IntWW 93, WhoAm 94*
Frankel, Michael Henry 1939- *WhoAm 94*
Frankel, Michael S. 1946- *WhoAm 94, WhoScEn 94, WhoWest 94*
Frankel, Otto (Herzberg) 1900- *Who 94*
Frankel, Otto Herzberg 1900- *IntWW 93*
Frankel, Paul Herzberg d1992 *Who 94N*
Frankel, Robert F. 1943- *WhoAmP 93*
Frankel, Sally Herbert 1903- *IntWW 93*
Frankel, Sandor 1943- *WrDr 94*
Frankel, Saul Jacob 1917- *WhoAm 94*
Frankel, Sherman 1922- *WhoAm 94, WhoScEn 94*
Frankel, Stanley Arthur 1918- *WhoAm 94, WhoFI 94*
Frankel, Stephen H. 1963- *WhoAmL 94*
Frankel, William 1917- *Who 94*
Franken, Edmund Anthony, Jr. 1936- *WhoAm 94*
Franken, Hendrik 1936- *IntWW 93*
Franken, Steve 1932- *WhoHol 92*
Frankenberg, Dirk 1937- *WhoScEn 94*
Frankenberg, Robert Clinton 1911- *WhoAmA 93*
Frankenberger, Bertram, Jr. 1933- *WhoAm 94*
Frankenberger, Glenn Frances 1968- *WhoScEn 94*
Frankenburg, Richard James 1929- *WhoAmP 93*
Frankenhaeuser, Marianne 1925- *IntWW 93, WhoScEn 94*
Frankenheim, Samuel 1932- *WhoAm 94, WhoFI 94*
Frankenheimer, John 1930- *EncSF 93, IntMPA 94*
Frankenheimer, John Michael 1930- *IntWW 93, WhoAm 94*
Frankenstein, Alfred Victor 1906-1981 *WhoAmA 93N*
Frankenthaler, Helen 1928- *AmCulL, IntWW 93, WhoAm 94, WhoAmA 93*
Franker, Stephen Grant 1949- *WhoMW 93*
Frankeur, Paul d1974 *WhoHol 92*
Frankevich, Yevgeniy Leonidovich 1930- *IntWW 93*
Frankforter, Weldon DeLoss 1920- *WhoAm 94*
Frankfurter, Alfred d1965 *WhoAmA 93N*
Frankfurter, Jack 1929- *WhoAmA 93*
Frankham, David *WhoHol 92*
Frankham, Harold Edward 1911- *Who 94*
Frankhouser, Floyd Richard 1944- *WrDr 94*
Frankhouser, Homer Sheldon, Jr. 1927- *WhoAm 94, WhoFI 94*
Frankiewicz, Marcia Jean 1947- *WhoAm 94, WhoFI 94, WhoMW 93*
Franking, Holly Mae 1944- *WhoMW 93*
Frankish, Brian Edward 1943- *WhoWest 94*
Frankl, Daniel Richard 1922- *WhoAm 94*
Frankl, Kenneth Richard 1924- *WhoAm 94*
Frankl, Peter 1935- *IntWW 93, Who 94*
Frankl, Razelle *WhoFI 94*
Frankl, Razelle 1932- *WrDr 94*
Frankl, Spencer Nelson 1933- *WhoAm 94*
Frankl, Steven Kenneth 1944- *WhoAm 94*
Frankl, Viktor E. 1905- *WhoAm 94*
Frankl, William Stewart 1928- *WhoAm 94, WhoScEn 94*
Frankland *Who 94*
Frankland, Edward 1825-1899 *WorScD*
Frankland, Mark 1934- *ConAu 43NR*
Frankland, Noble *Who 94*
Frankland, (Anthony) Noble 1922- *Who 94, WrDr 94*
Frankle, Edward Alan 1946- *WhoAmL 94*
Frankle, Philip 1913-1968 *WhoAmA 93N*
Franklin, Albert Andrew Ernst 1914- *Who 94*
Franklin, Alberta d1976 *WhoHol 92*
Franklin, Alexander John 1921- *WrDr 94*
Franklin, Alfred Alton, Jr. 1947- *WhoFI 94*
Franklin, Allen D. 1945- *WhoBlA 94*
Franklin, Aretha 1942- *AfrAmAl 6 [port], IntWW 93, WhoAm 94, WhoBlA 94, WhoHol 92*
Franklin, Barbara 1940- *IntWW 93*
Franklin, Barbara Braemer 1938- *WhoAmL 94*
Franklin, Barbara Hackman 1940- *WhoAm 94*
Franklin, Barbara Kipp 1943- *WhoFI 94*
Franklin, Benjamin 1706-1790 *AmRev, EncSPD, HisWorL [port], WhAmRev [port], WorInv [port], WorScD [port]*
Franklin, Benjamin 1925- *WhoAmL 94*
Franklin, Benjamin 1934- *WhoBlA 94*
Franklin, Benjamin Barnum 1944- *WhoAm 94, WhoFI 94, WhoMW 93*
Franklin, Benjamin Edward 1922- *WhoBlA 94*
Franklin, Benjamin Nolan 1946- *WhoAmP 93*
Franklin, Bernard W. *WhoBlA 94*
Franklin, Billy Joe 1940- *WhoAm 94*
Franklin, Blake Timothy 1942- *WhoAm 94*
Franklin, Bonnie 1944- *IntMPA 94, WhoHol 92*
Franklin, Bonnie Gail 1944- *WhoAm 94*
Franklin, Bruce Walter 1936- *WhoAmL 94, WhoMW 93*
Franklin, Calvin G. 1929- *AfrAmG [port]*
Franklin, Carl C. 1922- *WhoAmP 93*
Franklin, Carole R. 1933- *WhoAmA 93*
Franklin, Cathy Lou Hinson 1950- *WhoWest 94*
Franklin, Charles E. 1938- *WhoAm 94*
Franklin, Charles Scothern 1937- *WhoAm 94*
Franklin, Clarence d1967 *WhoAmA 93N*
Franklin, Clarence Frederick 1945- *WhoBlA 94*
Franklin, Costella M. 1932- *WhoBlA 94*
Franklin, Curtis U., Jr. 1929- *WhoBlA 94*
Franklin, David 1908-1973 *NewGrDO*
Franklin, David Lee 1943- *WhoFI 94, WhoScEn 94*
Franklin, David M. 1943- *WhoBlA 94*
Franklin, David Michael 1940- *WhoAmL 94*
Franklin, Deborah Read Rogers 1708-1774 *BlmGWL*
Franklin, Diane *WhoHol 92*
Franklin, Dolores Mercedes *WhoBlA 94*
Franklin, Don *WhoHol 92*
Franklin, Don 1931- *WhoAmA 93*
Franklin, Don 1960- *WhoBlA 94*
Franklin, Donald Bruce 1942- *WhoFI 94*
Franklin, Edgar 1879- *EncSF 93*
Franklin, Edward Ward 1926- *WhoAm 94*
Franklin, Eric (Alexander) 1910- *Who 94*
Franklin, Eugene T., Jr. 1945- *WhoBlA 94*
Franklin, Eve 1954- *WhoAmP 93*
Franklin, Floyd 1929- *WhoBlA 94*
Franklin, Frederic *WhoAm 94*
Franklin, Frederic 1914- *IntDcB [port]*
Franklin, Frederick Russell 1929- *WhoAm 94, WhoAmL 94, WhoMW 93*
Franklin, Gayle Jessup 1957- *WhoBlA 94*
Franklin, Gene Farthing 1927- *WhoAm 94, WhoScEn 94*
Franklin, George Charles 1935- *WhoAm 94*
Franklin, George Henry 1923- *Who 94*
Franklin, Gilbert Alfred 1919- *WhoAmA 93*
Franklin, Gloria *WhoHol 92*
Franklin, Gordon Herbert 1933- *Who 94*
Franklin, Grant L. 1918- *WhoBlA 94*
Franklin, H. Allen 1945- *WhoFI 94*
Franklin, H. Bruce 1934- *EncSF 93*
Franklin, Hannah 1937- *WhoAmA 93*
Franklin, Hardy R. 1929- *WhoBlA 94*
Franklin, Harold A. *WhoBlA 94*
Franklin, Herbert Lehman, Jr. 1940- *WhoAmP 93*
Franklin, Herman 1935- *WhoBlA 94*
Franklin, Howard David 1953- *WhoScEn 94*
Franklin, Hugh d1986 *WhoHol 92*
Franklin, Irene d1941 *WhoHol 92*
Franklin, Irene 1876-1941 *WhoCom*
Franklin, J. E. *DrAPF 93*
Franklin, J. E. 1937- *WhoBlA 94*
Franklin, James Craig 1958- *WhoWest 94*
Franklin, James Robert 1951- *WhoAm 94*
Franklin, James Russell 1944- *WhoAmP 93*
Franklin, Jane 1792-1875 *WhWE*
Franklin, Janet Marie 1958- *WhoWest 94*
Franklin, Jeffrey Alan 1964- *WhoAmL 94*
Franklin, Jim William 1935- *WhoWest 94*
Franklin, Joe 1926- *WrDr 94*
Franklin, Joe 1927- *WhoHol 92*
Franklin, Joel Nicholas 1930- *WhoAm 94*
Franklin, John *Who 94*

Franklin, John 1786-1847 WhWE
Franklin, (William) John 1927- Who 94
Franklin, John H(ope) 1915- WrDr 94
Franklin, John Hope 1915- AfrAmAl 6 [port], AmSocL, BlkWr 2, ConBlB 5 [port], IntWW 93, WhoAm 94, WhoBlA 94
Franklin, John Orland 1939- WhoAmL 94
Franklin, John Patrick WhoWest 94
Franklin, Jon Daniel 1942- WhoAm 94, WhoWest 94
Franklin, Jude Eric 1943- WhoAm 94
Franklin, Julian Harold 1925- WhoAm 94
Franklin, Keith Barry 1954- WhoScEn 94
Franklin, Keith Jerome 1963- WhoScEn 94
Franklin, Kenneth Linn 1923- WhoAm 94
Franklin, Kenneth Ronald 1932- WhoAm 94
Franklin, Kerry 1926- WrDr 94
Franklin, Larry Daniel 1942- WhoAm 94
Franklin, Leonard 1914- WhoAmL 94
Franklin, Linda Campbell 1941- WrDr 94
Franklin, Marc Adam 1932- WhoAm 94
Franklin, Margaret Lavona Barnum 1905- WhoMW 93
Franklin, Margery Bodansky 1933- WhoAm 94
Franklin, Marjorie A. 1935- WhoMW 93
Franklin, Marshall 1929- WhoWest 94
Franklin, Martha d1929 WhoHol 92
Franklin, Martha Lois 1956- WhoBlA 94
Franklin, Michael (David Milroy) 1927- Who 94
Franklin, Michael Harold 1923- IntMPA 94, WhoAm 94
Franklin, Michael Len 1965- WhoFI 94
Franklin, Miles 1879-1954 BlmGWL [port]
Franklin, Milton B., Jr. 1950- WhoBlA 94
Franklin, Miriam WhoHol 92
Franklin, Murray Joseph 1922- WhoAm 94
Franklin, Nancy Jo 1963- WhoScEn 94
Franklin, Nick 1943- WhoAmP 93
Franklin, Oliver St. Clair, Jr. 1945- WhoBlA 94
Franklin, Pamela 1949- WhoHol 92
Franklin, Pamela 1950- IntMPA 94
Franklin, Patt 1962- WhoAmA 93
Franklin, Percy 1926- WhoBlA 94
Franklin, Phyllis 1932- WhoAm 94
Franklin, Ralph William 1937- WhoAm 94
Franklin, Raoul Norman 1935- IntWW 93, Who 94
Franklin, Renty Benjamin 1945- WhoBlA 94
Franklin, Richard 1934- WhoAmP 93
Franklin, Richard 1948- IntMPA 94
Franklin, Richard 1949- HorFD [port]
Franklin, Richard Arnold 1956- WhoWest 94
Franklin, Richard Langdon 1925- WrDr 94
Franklin, Richard Mark 1947- WhoAm 94, WhoMW 93
Franklin, Robert A. IntMPA 94
Franklin, Robert Blair 1919- WhoWest 94
Franklin, Robert Brewer 1937- WhoAm 94
Franklin, Robert Charles 1936- WhoFI 94
Franklin, Robert Drury 1935- WhoFI 94
Franklin, Robert M(ichael) 1954- WrDr 94
Franklin, Robert McFarland 1943- WhoAm 94
Franklin, Robert Michael 1954- WhoBlA 94
Franklin, Robert Stambaugh 1942- WhoAm 94
Franklin, Robert Vernon, Jr. 1926- WhoBlA 94
Franklin, Ronald Vincent 1952- WhoMW 93
Franklin, Rosa WhoAmP 93
Franklin, Rosalind Elsie 1920-1958 DcNaB MP, WorScD
Franklin, Rupert d1939 WhoHol 92
Franklin, Samuel Harvey 1928- WrDr 94
Franklin, Scott Harrison 1954- WhoWest 94
Franklin, Shirley Clarke 1945- WhoBlA 94
Franklin, Sidney d1931 WhoHol 92
Franklin, Sidney d1976 WhoHol 92
Franklin, Stanley Phillip 1931- WhoAm 94
Franklin, Thomas Doyal, Jr. 1941- WhoScEn 94
Franklin, Tom WhoHol 92
Franklin, Walt DrAPF 93
Franklin, Warren WhoAm 94
Franklin, Warwick Orlando 1938- IntWW 93
Franklin, Wayne L. 1955- WhoBlA 94
Franklin, Wayne Leonard 1955- WhoMW 93
Franklin, William 1731-1813 AmRev, WhAmRev
Franklin, William Alfred 1916- Who 94
Franklin, William B. 1948- WhoBlA 94
Franklin, William Bruce 1956- WhoFI 94
Franklin, William Emery 1933- WhoAm 94
Franklin, William P. 1953- WhoFI 94
Franklin, William Webster 1941- WhoAmP 93
Franklyn, Beth d1956 WhoHol 92
Franklyn, Fredric d1989 WhoHol 92
Franklyn, Irwin d1966 WhoHol 92
Franklyn, Leo d1975 WhoHol 92
Franklyn, William 1926- WhoHol 92
Franklyn-Robbins, John WhoHol 92
Franko, Bernard Vincent 1922- WhoAm 94
Franko, Joseph R. 1946- WhoWest 94
Franko, Lawrence George 1942- WhoFI 94
Frankovich, George Richard 1920- WhoAm 94
Frankovich, Mike 1910- WhoHol 92
Frankovich, Mike J. 1910-1992 WhAm 10
Frankovitch, Mike 1910-1992 AnObit 1992
Frankowiak, James Raymond 1946- WhoAm 94
Frankowski, Charles J. 1945- WhoWest 94
Frankowski, Leo A. 1943- EncSF 93
Franks, Baron d1992 IntWW 93N, Who 94N
Franks, Allen 1936- WhoMW 93
Franks, Arthur Temple 1920- Who 94
Franks, Bob 1951- CngDr 93
Franks, C. Ronald WhoAmP 93
Franks, Cecil Simon 1935- Who 94
Franks, Charles Leslie 1934- WhoAm 94
Franks, Chloe 1963- WhoHol 92
Franks, David 1720-1793 WhAmRev
Franks, David Brian 1958- WhoAmL 94
Franks, David Salisbury 1743-1793 WhAmRev
Franks, Desmond Gerald Fergus 1928- Who 94
Franks, Dick Who 94
Franks, Everlee Gordon 1931- WhoBlA 94
Franks, Gary A. 1953- AfrAmAl 6, WhoBlA 94
Franks, Gary Alvin 1953- WhoAm 94, WhoAmP 93
Franks, Helen 1934- WrDr 94
Franks, Herbert Hoover 1934- WhoAmL 94, WhoMW 93
Franks, Herschel Pickens 1930- WhoAmL 94
Franks, Hollis Berry 1916- WhoFI 94
Franks, Isaac 1759-1822 WhAmRev
Franks, J. Robert 1937- WhoAm 94
Franks, Janice 1950- WhoAmL 94
Franks, Jerry d1971 WhoHol 92
Franks, John Gerald 1905- Who 94
Franks, Jon Michael 1941- WhoAmL 94
Franks, Julius, Jr. 1922- WhoBlA 94
Franks, Lewis E. 1931- WhoAm 94
Franks, Lucinda Laura 1946- WhoAm 94
Franks, Martin Davis 1950- WhoAmP 93
Franks, Michael Lee 1954- WhoAmP 93
Franks, Oliver 1905- HisDcKW
Franks, Oliver (Shewell) 1905-1992 CurBio 93N
Franks, Oliver Shewell 1985-1992 AnObit 1992
Franks, Paul Todd 1962- WhoScEn 94
Franks, Robert D. 1951- WhoAm 94, WhoAmP 93
Franks, Ronald Dwyer 1946- WhoAm 94
Franks, Stephen G. 1950- WhoIns 94
Franks, Suzan L. R. 1949- WhoAmP 93
Franks, Trent 1957- WhoAmP 93
Franks, Vaudry Lee 1921- WhoAmP 93
Franksen, Robert Wells 1962- WhoMW 93
Frankum, James Edward 1921- WhoAm 94
Frankum, Ronald Bruce 1935- WhoAmP 93, WhoScEn 94
Frann, Mary 1944- WhoHol 92
Frano, Andrew Joseph 1953- WhoAmL 94
Fransen, Curt Alan 1957- WhoAmL 94
Fransen, Roger Charles 1949- WhoAmL 94
Fransioli, Thomas Adrian 1906- WhoAmA 93
Franson, Carl Irvin 1934- WhoWest 94
Franson, Paul Oscar, III 1941- WhoAm 94, WhoFI 94
Fransson, Torsten Henry 1949- WhoScEn 94
Franta, William Roy 1942- WhoAm 94
Frantisak, Frank 1933- WhoFI 94
Frantz, Andrew Gibson 1930- WhoAm 94
Frantz, Charles 1925- WhoAm 94
Frantz, Dalies d1965 WhoHol 92
Frantz, Dean Leslie 1919- WhoMW 93, WhoScEn 94
Frantz, Ferdinand 1906-1959 NewGrDO
Frantz, Jack Thomas 1939- WhoAm 94, WhoFI 94
Frantz, Joe B. d1993 NewYTBS 93
Frantz, Joe B. 1917- WrDr 94
Frantz, John Corydon 1926- WhoAm 94
Frantz, Justus IntWW 93
Frantz, Leroy, Jr. 1927- WhoAmP 93
Frantz, Martin 1952- WhoAmP 93
Frantz, Michael Jennings 1951- WhoAm 94, WhoAmL 94
Frantz, Ray William, Jr. 1923- WhoAm 94
Frantz, Robert Lewis 1925- WhoAm 94
Frantz, Stephen Richard 1958- WhoMW 93
Frantz, Welby Marion 1912- WhoAm 94
Frantzen, Allen J. 1947- WrDr 94
Frantzen, Allen John 1947- WhoMW 93
Frantzen, Henry Arthur 1942- WhoAm 94
Frantzen, Jeffrey Alan 1953- WhoMW 93
Frantzides, Constantine Themis 1950- WhoScEn 94
Frantzve, Jerri Lyn 1942- WhoFI 94
Franval, Jean WhoHol 92
Franyo, Richard Louis 1944- WhoAm 94, WhoFI 94
Franz, Arthur 1920- IntMPA 94, WhoHol 92
Franz, Craig Joseph 1953- WhoScEn 94
Franz, Daniel Thomas 1949- WhoFI 94, WhoMW 93
Franz, Dennis 1944- WhoHol 92
Franz, Donald Eugene, Jr. 1944- WhoAm 94, WhoFI 94
Franz, Eduard d1983 WhoHol 92
Franz, Frank Andrew 1937- WhoAm 94
Franz, Herbert 1908- IntWW 93
Franz, John E. 1929- WhoScEn 94
Franz, Joseph d1970 WhoHol 92
Franz, Keith S. 1954- WhoAmP 93
Franz, Kevin Gerhard 1953- Who 94
Franz, Kevin John 1962- WhoMW 93
Franz, Lydia Millicent Truc 1924- WhoFI 94
Franz, Paul 1876-1950 NewGrDO
Franz, Robert Warren 1924- WhoAm 94
Franz, Steven Mark 1962- WhoMW 93
Franz, William Scott 1957- WhoWest 94
Franzblau, Carl 1934- WhoAm 94
Franze, Harold Paul 1955- WhoFI 94
Franzen, Gayle M. 1945- WhoAm 94
Franzen, Hugo Friedrich 1934- WhoScEn 94
Franzen, Janice Marguerite Gosnell 1921- WhoAm 94
Franzen, Jonathan DrAPF 93
Franzen, Lavern Gerhard 1926- WhoAm 94
Franzen, Peter 1943- WhoFI 94
Franzen, Russell Bernard 1955- WhoAm 94
Franzen, Ulrich J. 1921- IntWW 93, WhoAm 94
Franzia, Joseph Stephen 1942- WhoWest 94
Franzke, Hans-Hermann 1927- WhoScEn 94
Franzke, Richard Albert 1935- WhoAm 94, WhoAmL 94
Franzkowski, Rainer 1935- WhoFI 94
Franzl, Ferdinand 1767-1833 NewGrDO
Franzmann, Albert Wilhelm 1930- WhoAm 94
Franzmeier, Donald Paul 1935- WhoAm 94
Franzoni, Charles M. 1932- WhoAmP 93
Franzos, Karl Emil 1848-1904 DcLB 129 [port]
Frapan, Ilse 1849-1908 BlmGWL
Frappia, Linda Ann 1946- WhoWest 94
Frappier, Armand 1904- IntWW 93
Frappier, Armand 1904-1991 WhAm 10
Frappier, Cara Munshaw 1942- WhoMW 93
Frappier, Gilles 1931- WhoAm 94
Frary, Dayne Lee 1949- WhoWest 94
Frary, Karen Marie 1955- WhoMW 93
Frary, Michael 1918- WhoAmA 93
Frary, Richard Spencer 1924- WhoAm 94, WhoWest 94
Frasca, Joanne M. 1953- WhoAm 94
Frasca, Mary d1973 WhoHol 92
Frasch, Brian Bernard 1956- WhoAmL 94
Fraschini, Gaetano 1816-1887 NewGrDO
Frasconi, Antonio 1919- WhoAmA 93
Frase, Richard Stockwell 1945- WhoAmL 94
Fraser Who 94
Fraser, Baron 1945- IntWW 93
Fraser, Alasdair MacLeod 1946- Who 94
Fraser, Alex d1956 WhoHol 92
Fraser, Alvardo M. 1922- WhoBlA 94
Fraser, Andrea R. 1965- WhoAmA 93
Fraser, Angus (McKay) 1928- Who 94
Fraser, Angus Simon James 1945- Who 94
Fraser, Anthea WrDr 94
Fraser, Anthony Walkinshaw 1934- Who 94
Fraser, Antonia 1932- IntWW 93, Who 94, WhoAm 94, WrDr 94
Fraser, Bernard William 1941- IntWW 93
Fraser, Bill d1987 WhoHol 92
Fraser, Bruce (Donald) 1910-1993 ConAu 142
Fraser, Bruce Donald d1993 Who 94N
Fraser, Campbell IntWW 93, Who 94
Fraser, Campbell 1923- WhoAm 94
Fraser, (James) Campbell 1923- IntWW 93, Who 94
Fraser, Catherine Anne 1947- WhoWest 94
Fraser, Charles (Annand) 1928- Who 94
Fraser, Charles Elbert 1929- WhoAm 94
Fraser, Colin Angus Ewen 1918- Who 94
Fraser, Conon 1930- WrDr 94
Fraser, Constance d1973 WhoHol 92
Fraser, Cosmo Lyle 1950- WhoWest 94
Fraser, D. Ian 1931- WhoIns 94
Fraser, David (William) 1920- Who 94
Fraser, David Charles 1942- WhoFI 94
Fraser, David William 1944- WhoAm 94
Fraser, Derek 1940- Who 94
Fraser, Donald Alexander Stuart 1925- WhoAm 94
Fraser, Donald Blake 1910- Who 94
Fraser, Donald Boyd, Jr. 1961- WhoAmL 94
Fraser, Donald C. 1941- WhoAm 94
Fraser, Donald Hamilton 1929- Who 94
Fraser, Donald MacKay 1924- WhoAm 94, WhoAmP 93, WhoMW 93
Fraser, Donald Ross 1927- WhoAmP 93
Fraser, Dorothy (Rita) 1926- Who 94
Fraser, Douglas 1910- WrDr 94
Fraser, Douglas (Ferrar) 1929-1982 WhoAmA 93N
Fraser, Douglas Andrew 1916- IntWW 93
Fraser, Earl Donald 1912- WhoWest 94
Fraser, Earl W., Jr. 1947- WhoBlA 94
Fraser, Edward Who 94
Fraser, (James) Edward 1931- Who 94
Fraser, Elizabeth WhoHol 92
Fraser, Everett MacKay 1921- WhoAmL 94
Fraser, George Broadrup 1914- WhoAm 94
Fraser, George C. 1945- WhoBlA 94
Fraser, George MacDonald 1925- Who 94, WrDr 94
Fraser, Harry d1974 WhoHol 92
Fraser, Harry 1937- WrDr 94
Fraser, Helen WhoHol 92
Fraser, Henry S. 1900- WhoAm 94
Fraser, Hugh WhoHol 92
Fraser, Hugh Vincent d1993 Who 94N
Fraser, Ian 1901- Who 94
Fraser, Ian (James) 1923- Who 94
Fraser, Ian Edward 1920- Who 94
Fraser, Ian Watson 1907- Who 94, WrDr 94
Fraser, James (David) 1924- Who 94
Fraser, James Cavender 1941- WhoAm 94
Fraser, James Owen Arthur 1937- Who 94
Fraser, James S. d1943 WhoHol 92
Fraser, Jane 1924- WrDr 94
Fraser, Jane Marian 1950- WhoScEn 94
Fraser, Jean Ethel 1923-1991 WhoBlA 94N
Fraser, John 1931- WhoHol 92
Fraser, John Allen 1931- IntWW 93, Who 94, WhoAm 94
Fraser, John Denis 1934- Who 94
Fraser, John Foster 1930- WhoAm 94, WhoFI 94
Fraser, John Keith 1922- WhoAm 94
Fraser, John Stewart 1931- Who 94
Fraser, John Wayne 1944- WhoFI 94
Fraser, Joseph T., Jr. 1898- WhAm 10
Fraser, Karen WhoAmP 93
Fraser, Kathleen DrAPF 93
Fraser, Kathleen 1937- WrDr 94
Fraser, Kathleen Joy 1937- WhoAm 94
Fraser, Kenneth John Alexander 1929- Who 94
Fraser, Kenneth William, Jr. 1937- WhoAm 94, WhoFI 94
Fraser, Laura G. 1889-1966 WhoAmA 93N
Fraser, Leo W. 1926- WhoAmP 93
Fraser, Leon Allison 1921- WhoBlA 94
Fraser, Liz 1933- WhoHol 92
Fraser, Malcolm Who 94
Fraser, Malcolm 1869-1949 WhoAmA 93N
Fraser, (John) Malcolm 1930- IntWW 93, Who 94
Fraser, Malcolm James, Jr. 1952- WhoMW 93, WhoScEn 94
Fraser, Margot 1936- WrDr 94
Fraser, Marion Anne 1932- Who 94
Fraser, Mark D. 1951- WhoWest 94
Fraser, Mark Robert 1953- WhoWest 94
Fraser, Mary Ann 1959- SmATA 76 [port]
Fraser, Mary Edna 1952- WhoAmA 93
Fraser, Michael Neely 1960- WhoMW 93
Fraser, Morris 1941- WrDr 94

Fraser, Moyra 1923- *WhoHol 92*
Fraser, Neale 1933- *BuCMET*
Fraser, Paterson *Who 94*
Fraser, (Henry) Paterson 1907- *Who 94*
Fraser, Peter Marshall 1918- *IntWW 93, Who 94*
Fraser, Phyllis 1917- *WhoHol 92*
Fraser, Raymond (Joseph) 1941- *WrDr 94*
Fraser, Rhonda Beverly 1960- *WhoBlA 94*
Fraser, Richard d1971 *WhoHol 92*
Fraser, Robert (H.) 1947- *WrDr 94*
Fraser, Robert Burchmore 1928- *WhoAm 94*
Fraser, Robert Charles 1932- *WhoFI 94*
Fraser, Robert Donald Bruce 1924- *IntWW 93*
Fraser, Robert Gordon 1921- *WhoAm 94*
Fraser, Rodger Alvin 1944- *WhoBlA 94*
Fraser, Ronald 1930- *WhoHol 92*
Fraser, Ronald (Angus) 1930- *WrDr 94*
Fraser, Ronald (Arthur) 1888-1974 *EncSF 93*
Fraser, Ronald Petrie 1917- *Who 94*
Fraser, (Thomas) Russell (Cumming) 1908- *Who 94*
Fraser, Russell A(lfred) 1927- *WrDr 94*
Fraser, Russell Alfred 1927- *WhoAm 94*
Fraser, Shelagh 1923- *WhoHol 92*
Fraser, Simon 1726-1782 *AmRev, WhAmRev*
Fraser, Simon 1729-1777 *AmRev, WhAmRev*
Fraser, Simon 1738-1813 *AmRev, WhAmRev*
Fraser, Simon 1776-1862 *WhWE*
Fraser, Simon William Hetherington 1951- *Who 94*
Fraser, Stanley Charles 1951- *WhoFI 94, WhoMW 93*
Fraser, Sylvia 1935- *BlmGWL*
Fraser, Thomas Augustus, Jr. 1915-1989 *WhAm 10*
Fraser, Thomas Edwards 1944- *WhoBlA 94*
Fraser, Thomas Jefferson 1932- *WhoAmP 93*
Fraser, Troy L. 1949- *WhoAmP 93*
Fraser, Veronica Mary 1933- *Who 94*
Fraser, W. Hamish 1941- *WrDr 94*
Fraser, William (Kerr) 1929- *Who 94*
Fraser, William James 1921- *Who 94*
Fraser, William Kerr 1929- *IntWW 93*
Fraser, William Neil 1932- *WhoAm 94*
Fraser McLuskey, James *Who 94*
Fraser Of Carmyllie, Baron 1945- *Who 94*
Fraser Of Kilmorack, Baron 1915- *IntWW 93, Who 94*
Fraser-Reid, Bertram Oliver 1934- *WhoAm 94, WhoScEn 94*
Fraser-Simson, Harold 1872-1944 *NewGrDO*
Fraser-Smith, Elizabeth Birdsey 1938- *WhoAm 94*
Fraser-Tytler, Christian Helen 1897- *Who 94*
Frasher, Jim 1930- *WhoHol 92*
Frasi, Giulia fl. 1742-1772 *NewGrDO*
Frasier, Ernest P. 1954- *WhoFI 94*
Frasier, Gary W. 1937- *WhoAm 94, WhoWest 94*
Frasier, George Ernest 1942- *WhoWest 94*
Frasier, Jim 1940- *WhoAmP 93*
Frasier, Leroy B. 1910- *WhoBlA 94*
Frasier, Mary Mack 1938- *WhoBlA 94*
Frasier, Ralph Kennedy 1938- *WhoAmL 94, WhoBlA 94*
Frassinelli, Guido Joseph 1927- *WhoScEn 94, WhoWest 94*
Frasure, Evan 1951- *WhoAmP 93*
Frasure, Robert C. 1942- *WhoAm 94, WhoAmP 93*
Frasyniuk, Wladyslaw 1954- *IntWW 93*
Fratcher, William Franklin 1913-1992 *WhAm 10, WrDr 94N*
Fratellini, Annie *WhoHol 92*
Fratello, Michael Robert 1947- *WhoAm 94, WhoMW 93*
Frater, Alexander 1937- *ConAu 140, WrDr 94*
Frater, Hal 1909- *WhoAmA 93*
Frater, Robert William Mayo 1928- *WhoAm 94*
Frateschi, Lawrence Jan 1952- *WhoMW 93*
Frati, Luigi 1943- *WhoScEn 94*
Fratianno, Aladena James d1993 *NewYTBS 93 [port]*
Fratini, Georgina Carolin 1931- *IntWW 93*
Fratt, Charles Kennedy Poe 1931-1988 *WhAm 10*
Frattali, Rose E. 1931- *WhoIns 94*
Fratti, Laura Dubman d1992 *NewYTBS 93*
Fratti, Mario 1927- *ConDr 93, WrDr 94*
Fratz, D(onald) Douglas 1952- *EncSF 93*
Frauchiger, Fritz A. 1941- *WhoAmA 93*
Frauchiger, Fritz Arnold 1941- *WhoWest 94*
Frauen, Kurt Herman 1925- *WhoAmL 94*
Frauenfelder, Hans 1922- *WhoAm 94, WhoScEn 94*
Frauenglas, Robert A. *DrAPF 93*
Frauens, Marie 1902- *WhoMW 93*
Fraughton, Edward James 1939- *WhoAmA 93*
Fraumann, Willard George 1948- *WhoAm 94*
Fraumeni, Joseph F., Jr. 1933- *WhoAm 94, WhoScEn 94*
Fraunfelder, Doug Lee 1953- *WhoMW 93*
Fraunfelder, Frederick Theodore 1934- *WhoAm 94, WhoWest 94*
Fraunhofer, Joseph von 1787-1826 *WorInv*
Fraustita d1988 *WhoHol 92*
Frausto, Antonio R. d1954 *WhoHol 92*
Frausto, Marco Antonio 1950- *WhoHisp 94*
Frautschi, Steven Clark 1933- *WhoAm 94, WhoScEn 94, WhoWest 94*
Frautschi, Timothy Clark 1937- *WhoAm 94*
Frautschi, Walter Albert 1901- *WhoAm 94*
Frawley, Daniel S. 1943- *WhoAmP 93*
Frawley, Daniel Seymour 1943- *WhoAm 94*
Frawley, James *ConTFT 11*
Frawley, James 1937- *IntMPA 94*
Frawley, Patrick Joseph, Jr. 1923- *WhoAm 94*
Frawley, Robert Donald 1947- *WhoAmL 94, WhoFI 94*
Frawley, Sean Paul 1940- *WhoAm 94*
Frawley, Thomas Francis 1919- *WhoAm 94*
Frawley, William d1966 *WhoHol 92*
Frawley, William 1887-1966 *WhoCom*
Fray, Lionel Louis 1935- *WhoAm 94*
Frayer, William Edward 1947- *WhoMW 93*
Frayling, Christopher John 1946- *Who 94*
Frayling, Nicholas Arthur 1944- *Who 94*
Frayn, Claire *Who 94*
Frayn, Michael 1933- *BlmGEL, ConDr 93, EncSF 93, IntDcT 2 [port], IntWW 93, Who 94, WrDr 94*
Frayne, David 1934- *Who 94*
Frayne, David Patrick 1965- *WhoWest 94*
Frayne, Frank L. d1938 *WhoHol 92*
Frayser, Michael Keith 1966- *WhoScEn 94*
Fraysse, Jean-Pierre 1930- *IntWW 93*
Fraysse-Cazalis, Jacqueline Paulette Marguerite 1947- *WhoWomW 91*
Frayssinet, Daniel Fernand 1956- *WhoWest 94*
Fraze, Candida *DrAPF 93*
Fraze, Denny T. 1940- *WhoAmA 93*
Frazee, Jane d1985 *WhoHol 92*
Frazee, Mary Ann 1934- *WhoAmP 93*
Frazee, Robert C. 1928- *WhoAmP 93*
Frazee, Rowland C. 1921- *IntWW 93*
Frazee, Ruth *WhoHol 92*
Frazee, (Charles) Steve 1909- *WrDr 94*
Frazen, Laurence Michael 1958- *WhoAmL 94*
Frazer, Alex d1958 *WhoHol 92*
Frazer, Andrew 1928- *WrDr 94*
Frazer, Cloyce Clemon 1919- *WhoWest 94*
Frazer, Dan *WhoHol 92*
Frazer, Eva Louise 1957- *WhoBlA 94*
Frazer, Jack Winfield 1924- *WhoAm 94*
Frazer, James (Nisbet), Jr. 1949- *WhoAmA 93*
Frazer, James G. 1854-1941 *BlmGEL*
Frazer, John Howard 1924- *WhoAm 94*
Frazer, John Paul 1914- *WhoAm 94*
Frazer, John Thatcher 1932- *WhoAmA 93*
Frazer, Malcolm John 1931- *Who 94*
Frazer, Nimrod Thompson 1929- *WhoAm 94, WhoFI 94*
Frazer, Nitra d1979 *WhoHol 92*
Frazer, Robert d1944 *WhoHol 92*
Frazer, Ron d1983 *WhoHol 92*
Frazer, Rupert *WhoHol 92*
Frazer, Shamus 1912- *EncSF 93*
Frazer, Simon 1729-1777 *AmRev*
Frazetta, Frank 1928- *EncSF 93, WhoAm 94*
Frazier, A. D., Jr. 1944- *WhoAm 94*
Frazier, Adolphus Cornelious *WhoAmP 93, WhoBlA 94*
Frazier, Arthur 1914- *WrDr 94*
Frazier, Audrey Lee 1927- *WhoBlA 94*
Frazier, Bernard Joseph 1954- *WhoFI 94*
Frazier, Charles Douglas 1939- *WhoBlA 94*
Frazier, Chet June 1924- *WhoAm 94*
Frazier, Dan E., Sr. 1949- *WhoBlA 94*
Frazier, Dennis Allen 1955- *WhoAmP 93*
Frazier, Donald Tha, Sr. 1935- *WhoAm 94*
Frazier, Douglas Byron 1957- *WhoFI 94*
Frazier, Douglas N. *WhoAmL 94*
Frazier, Edward O'Neil 1946- *WhoAmP 93*
Frazier, Eufaula Smith 1924- *WhoBlA 94*
Frazier, Eugene Richard 1947- *WhoAm 94*
Frazier, Frances Curtis 1948- *WhoBlA 94*
Frazier, Francis *EncNAR*
Frazier, Francis Marie 1932- *WhoAmP 93*
Frazier, Francis Philip *EncNAR*
Frazier, George 1943- *WhoAmL 94*
Frazier, Henry B., III 1934- *WhoAmP 93*
Frazier, Henry Bowen, III 1934- *WhoAm 94, WhoAmL 94*
Frazier, Herman Ronald 1954- *WhoBlA 94*
Frazier, Hillman Terome 1950- *WhoAmP 93*
Frazier, Ian 1951- *WrDr 94*
Frazier, Jack Mynter Hoyt 1954- *WhoAmL 94*
Frazier, Jimmy Leon 1939- *WhoBlA 94*
Frazier, Joe 1944- *WhoAm 94, WhoBlA 94, WhoHol 92*
Frazier, John *WhoAmP 93*
Frazier, John Lionel Devin 1932- *WhoAm 94*
Frazier, John Phillip 1939- *WhoAm 94*
Frazier, John Warren 1913- *WhoAm 94*
Frazier, Jordan *WhoBlA 94*
Frazier, Joseph Norris 1925- *WhoBlA 94*
Frazier, Julie A. 1962- *WhoBlA 94*
Frazier, Keith David 1960- *WhoAmL 94*
Frazier, Kenneth 1867-1949 *WhoAmA 93N*
Frazier, Kimberlee Gonterman 1953- *WhoFI 94, WhoMW 93, WhoScEn 94*
Frazier, Lawrence Alan 1936- *WhoIns 94*
Frazier, Lee Rene 1946- *WhoBlA 94*
Frazier, Leon 1932- *WhoBlA 94*
Frazier, LeRoy 1946- *WhoAm 94*
Frazier, Leslie Antonio 1959- *WhoBlA 94*
Frazier, Leslie Bryn 1965- *WhoWest 94*
Frazier, Lincoln B. 1905- *WhoAmP 93*
Frazier, Owsley B. 1935- *WhoAm 94, WhoFI 94*
Frazier, Pamela *WrDr 94*
Frazier, Paul D. 1922- *WhoAmA 93*
Frazier, Pauline Clarke 1936- *WhoBlA 94*
Frazier, Peggy Kaluz 1943- *WhoAmP 93*
Frazier, Ramona Yancey 1941- *WhoBlA 94*
Frazier, Ranta A. 1915- *WhoBlA 94*
Frazier, Ray Jerrell 1943- *WhoBlA 94*
Frazier, Regina Jollivette 1943- *WhoBlA 94*
Frazier, Reginald Lee 1934- *WhoBlA 94*
Frazier, Richard Williams 1922-1983 *WhoAmA 93N*
Frazier, Rick C. 1936- *WhoBlA 94*
Frazier, Robert (Alexander) 1951- *EncSF 93*
Frazier, Ron 1942- *WhoHol 92*
Frazier, Ronald Gerald, Jr. 1965- *WhoScEn 94*
Frazier, Sheila 1948- *WhoHol 92*
Frazier, Sheila E. 1948- *IntMPA 94*
Frazier, Simon 1729-1777 *AmRev*
Frazier, Thomas Alexander 1894- *WhAm 10*
Frazier, Thomas Edward 1958- *WhoMW 93*
Frazier, Walt 1945- *BasBi, WhoAm 94, WhoBlA 94*
Frazier, Walter Ronald 1939- *WhoFI 94*
Frazier, William A. 1908- *WhoAm 94*
Frazier, William James 1942- *WhoBlA 94*
Frazier, Wynetta Artricia 1942- *WhoBlA 94*
Frazier-Ellison, Vicki L. 1963- *WhoBlA 94*
Frazier-Tsai, Karen Lynne 1952- *WhoAm 94*
Frazin, Gladys d1939 *WhoHol 92*
Frazza, George S. 1934- *WhoAmL 94*
Frazzetta, Thomas H. 1934- *WhoAm 94*
Frazzi, Vito 1888-1975 *NewGrDO*
Freaney, Vincent 1945- *WhoIns 94*
Frears, Stephen 1941- *IntMPA 94*
Frears, Stephen Arthur 1941- *IntWW 93, Who 94*
Freas, Frank Kelly 1922- *WhoAm 94, WhoWest 94*
Freas, (Frank) Kelly 1922- *EncSF 93*
Freauf, Elizabeth S. 1936- *WhoAmP 93*
Freberg, Stan 1926- *WhoCom, WhoHol 92*
Freberg, Stanley 1926- *WhoAm 94*
Freborg, Layton *WhoAmP 93*
Freccia, Massimo 1906- *IntWW 93*
Frech, Bruce 1956- *WhoScEn 94*
Frechet, Maurice-Rene 1878-1973 *WorScD*
Frechette, Ernest Albert 1918- *WhoAm 94*
Frechette, Mark d1975 *WhoHol 92*
Frechette, Myles Robert Rene 1936- *WhoAmP 93*
Frechette, Peter *WhoHol 92*
Frechette, Peter Loren 1937- *WhoAm 94*
Frechette, Roland A. 1927- *WhoAmP 93*
Frechette, Roland L. 1936- *WhoAmP 93*
Frechette, Van Derck 1916- *WhoAm 94, WhoScEn 94*
Freckelton, Sondra 1936- *WhoAmA 93*
Freckleton, Jon Edward 1939- *WhoFI 94*
Frecon, Alain Jean-Christian 1946- *WhoAm 94*
Freda, Aldo 1921- *WhoAmP 93*
Fredd, Chester Arthur *WhoBlA 94*
Frede, Michael 1940- *Who 94*
Frede, Richard *DrAPF 93*
Fredegund c. 550-597 *HisWorL*
Fredell, Gail 1951- *WhoAmA 93*
Fredenthal, David 1914-1958 *WhoAmA 93N*
Fredenthal, Ruth Ann 1938- *WhoAmA 93*
Frederici, Blanche d1933 *WhoHol 92*
Frederici, C. Carleton 1938- *WhoAmL 94*
Frederick, I 1123-1190 *HisWorL [port]*
Frederick, II 1194-1250 *HisWorL [port]*
Frederick, II 1712-1786 *NewGrDO*
Frederick, Anne Del 1963- *WhoMW 93*
Frederick, Beebe Ray, Jr. 1938- *WhoAmP 93*
Frederick, Cassandra c. 1741-1779? *NewGrDO*
Frederick, Charles Boscawen 1919- *Who 94*
Frederick, Clay Bruce 1948- *WhoScEn 94*
Frederick, David Charles 1951- *WhoFI 94*
Frederick, Deloras Ann 1942- *WhoAmA 93*
Frederick, Dolliver H. 1944- *WhoAm 94*
Frederick, Doyle Grimes 1935- *WhoAm 94*
Frederick, Earl James 1927- *WhoAm 94*
Frederick, Edward Charles 1930- *WhoAm 94*
Frederick, Edward Russell 1913- *WhoScEn 94*
Frederick, Eugene Wallace 1927- *WhoAmA 93N*
Frederick, Freddie Burke d1986 *WhoHol 92*
Frederick, Gay Marcille 1960- *WhoMW 93*
Frederick, George Francis 1937- *WhoFI 94*
Frederick, Glenn Douglas 1940- *WhoFI 94*
Frederick, Hal *WhoHol 92*
Frederick, Helen 1945- *WhoAmA 93*
Frederick, James Paul 1943- *WhoScEn 94*
Frederick, Joseph Francis, Jr. 1933- *WhoAm 94, WhoFI 94*
Frederick, K. C. *DrAPF 93*
Frederick, Kathleen Anne 1950- *WhoMW 93*
Frederick, Keith Richard 1969- *WhoWest 94*
Frederick, Lafayette 1923- *WhoAm 94*
Frederick, Lloyd Randall 1921- *WhoMW 93*
Frederick, Lynne 1953- *WhoHol 92*
Frederick, Marcel Sal 1926- *WhoAmP 93*
Frederick, Melvin Lyle 1929- *WhoAmP 93*
Frederick, Norman L., Jr. 1965- *WhoScEn 94*
Frederick, Pauline d1938 *WhoHol 92*
Frederick, Pauline d1990 *WhAm 10*
Frederick, Randall D. *WhoAmP 93*
Frederick, Raymond Joseph 1948- *WhoMW 93*
Frederick, Richard 1954- *WhoAmP 93*
Frederick, Robert Rice 1926- *IntWW 93*
Frederick, Ronald David 1966- *WhoScEn 94*
Frederick, Samuel Adams 1946- *WhoAmL 94*
Frederick, Saradell Ard *WhoAmA 93*
Frederick, Vicki 1954- *WhoHol 92*
Frederick, Virginia Fiester *WhoWomW 91*
Frederick, Virginia Fiester 1916- *WhoAmP 93, WhoMW 93*
Frederick, Willard Drawn, Jr. 1934- *WhoAmP 93*
Frederick, William d1931 *WhoHol 92*
Frederick, William Sherrad 1938- *WhoAm 94*
Fredericks, Barry Irwin 1936- *WhoAmL 94*
Fredericks, Beverly Magnuson 1928- *WhoAmA 93*
Fredericks, Charles d1970 *WhoHol 92*
Fredericks, Dale E. *WhoAm 94, WhoAmL 94*
Fredericks, Francis 1935- *WhoAmP 93*
Fredericks, Frank 1909- *WrDr 94*
Fredericks, Henry St. Clair 1942- *WhoAm 94*
Fredericks, Kay Louise 1943- *WhoMW 93*
Fredericks, Leroy Owen 1924- *WhoBlA 94*
Fredericks, Marshall Maynard 1908- *WhoAm 94, WhoAmA 93, WhoMW 93*
Fredericks, Norman John 1914- *WhoAm 94*

Fredericks, Patricia Ann 1941- *WhoWest 94*
Fredericks, Robert Joseph 1934- *WhoFI 94*
Fredericks, Sharon Kay 1942- *WhoMW 93*
Fredericks, Stephen Mark 1950- *WhoMW 93*
Fredericks, Ward Arthur 1939- *WhoAm 94, WhoFI 94, WhoWest 94*
Fredericks, Wayne 1917- *WhoAm 94*
Fredericks, Wesley Charles, Jr. 1948- *WhoAm 94, WhoAmL 94, WhoFI 94*
Frederickson, Arman Frederick 1918- *WhoAm 94*
Frederickson, Arthur Robb 1941- *WhoScEn 94*
Frederickson, Charles Richard 1938- *WhoFI 94, WhoWest 94*
Frederickson, David J. 1944- *WhoAmP 93*
Frederickson, Dennis R. 1939- *WhoAmP 93*
Frederickson, Dennis Russel 1939- *WhoMW 93*
Frederickson, H. Gray, Jr. 1937- *IntMPA 94*
Frederickson, Horace George 1937- *WhoAm 94*
Frederickson, John Marcus 1941- *WhoFI 94*
Frederickson, Keith Alvin 1925- *WhoAm 94*
Frederickson, Lyle L. 1905- *WhoAmP 93*
Frederickson, Vance O. 1928- *WhoIns 94*
Frederick the Great, II 1712-1786 *HisWorL [port]*
Fredericton, Bishop of 1932- *Who 94*
Frederiksen, Marilynn Elizabeth Conners 1949- *WhoAm 94*
Frederikson, Edna *DrAPF 93*
Frederking, Traugott Heinrich Karl 1926- *WhoWest 94*
Fredette, Raymond David 1954- *WhoAm 94*
Fredette, Richard Chester 1934- *WhoAm 94*
Fredga, Arne 1902- *IntWW 93*
Fredine, Clarence Gordon 1909- *WhoScEn 94*
Fredlund, Ray 1925- *WhoAmP 93*
Fredman, Alice G(reen) 1924-1993 *ConAu 141*
Fredman, Alice Green d1993 *NewYTBS 93*
Fredman, Berna Warner 1944- *WhoAmL 94*
Fredman, Faiya R. 1925- *WhoAmA 93*
Fredman, Howard S. 1944- *WhoAmL 94*
Fredman, Myer 1932- *NewGrDO*
Fredman, Samuel George 1924- *WhoAmP 93*
Fredman, Stephen *DrAPF 93*
Fredmann, Martin 1943- *WhoAm 94, WhoWest 94*
Fredrick, Earl E., Jr. 1929- *WhoBlA 94*
Fredrick, Laurence William 1927- *WhoAm 94*
Fredricks, Anthony Theo 1910- *WhoWest 94*
Fredricks, Edgar John 1942- *WhoAmP 93*
Fredricks, Richard 1933- *WhoAm 94*
Fredricksen, Cleve Laurance 1941- *WhoAm 94*
Fredrickson, Arthur Allan 1923- *WhoAm 94*
Fredrickson, Daniel Alan *WhoAmA 93*
Fredrickson, Donald Sharp 1924- *IntWW 93, WhoAm 94, WhoAmP 93*
Fredrickson, George Marsh 1934- *WhoAm 94*
Fredrickson, Lawrence Thomas 1928- *WhoAm 94*
Fredrickson, Leigh Harry 1939- *WhoMW 93*
Fredrickson, Lola Jean 1945- *WhoFI 94, WhoMW 93*
Fredrickson, Sharon Wong 1956- *WhoMW 93*
Fredrickson, Vance O. 1928- *WhoFI 94*
Fredrik, Burry 1925- *WhoAm 94*
Fredriksen, Carolyn Myers 1952- *WhoMW 93*
Fredston, Arthur Howard 1929- *WhoAm 94, WhoAmL 94*
Free, Alfred Henry 1913- *WhoMW 93, WhoScEn 94*
Free, Ann Cottrell *WhoAm 94*
Free, E. LeBron 1940- *WhoAmL 94*
Free, Helen M. 1923- *WhoAm 94, WhoMW 93, WhoScEn 94*
Free, Kenneth A. 1936- *WhoBlA 94*
Free, Mary Moore 1933- *WhoScEn 94*
Free, Ray D. 1910- *WhoAmP 93*
Free, Ross Vincent 1943- *WhoScEn 94*
Free, William Albert 1929- *WhoWest 94*
Free, William Augustus, Sr. 1898- *WhAm 10*
Free, William John 1943- *WhoAm 94, WhoAmL 94*
Free, World B. 1953- *BasBi, WhoBlA 94*
Freear, Louie d1939 *WhoHol 92*
Freeark, Robert James 1927- *WhoAm 94*
Freeberg, Don 1924- *WhoFI 94*
Freeborn, Henry F. d1957 *WhoHol 92*
Freeborn, Joann Lee *WhoAmP 93*
Freeborn, Michael D. 1946- *WhoAmL 94*
Freeborn, Richard (Harry) 1926- *WrDr 94*
Freeburg, Richard Gorman 1938- *WhoFI 94*
Freed, Aaron David 1922- *WhoAm 94*
Freed, Alan d1965 *WhoHol 92*
Freed, Alvyn Mark 1913- *WhoWest 94*
Freed, Arthur 1894-1973 *IntDcF 2-4 [port]*
Freed, Bert 1919- *WhoAm 94, WhoHol 92*
Freed, Charles 1926- *WhoAm 94*
Freed, David 1936- *WhoAmA 93*
Freed, David Clark 1936- *WhoAm 94*
Freed, DeBow 1925- *WhoAm 94*
Freed, Doris Jonas d1993 *NewYTBS 93 [port]*
Freed, Douglass Lynn 1944- *WhoAmA 93*
Freed, Edmond Lee 1935- *WhoScEn 94*
Freed, Edwin Dreese 1920- *WhoMW 93*
Freed, Elaine Eilers 1934- *WhoAmP 93, WhoWest 94*
Freed, Eric Robert 1950- *WhoWest 94*
Freed, Ernest Bradfield 1908- *WhoAmA 93N*
Freed, Hermine 1940- *WhoAmA 93*
Freed, Hirsh 1910- *WhoAm 94*
Freed, Howard A. 1926- *WhoAmP 93*
Freed, Jack Herschel 1938- *WhoAm 94*
Freed, James Ingo 1930- *WhoAm 94*
Freed, Karl Frederick 1942- *WhoAm 94, WhoScEn 94*
Freed, Kathryn E. *WhoAmP 93*
Freed, Kenneth Alan 1957- *WhoAmL 94*
Freed, Lazar *WhoHol 92*
Freed, Linda Ames 1936- *WhoMW 93*
Freed, Linda Rae 1957- *WhoWest 94*
Freed, Lynn *DrAPF 93*
Freed, Lynn Ruth 1945- *WrDr 94*
Freed, Marcia 1948- *WhoWest 94*
Freed, Murray Monroe 1924- *WhoAm 94*
Freed, Ray *DrAPF 93*
Freed, Rita Evelyn 1952- *WhoAm 94*
Freed, Rona *WhoHol 92*
Freed, Sam 1948- *WhoHol 92*
Freed, Stanley Arthur 1927- *WhoAm 94*
Freed, Walter 1951- *WhoAmP 93*
Freed, William 1902-1984 *WhoAmA 93N*
Freedberg, A. Stone 1908- *WhoAm 94*
Freedberg, David Adrian 1948- *Who 94*
Freedberg, Irwin Mark 1931- *WhoAm 94*
Freedberg, Sydney Joseph 1914- *IntWW 93, WhoAm 94, WhoAmA 93, WrDr 94*
Freedenberg, Paul 1943- *WhoAmP 93*
Freedgood, Anne Goodman 1917- *WhoAm 94*
Freedland, Michael 1934- *WrDr 94*
Freedland, Richard Allan 1931- *WhoAm 94*
Freedley, Vinton d1969 *WhoHol 92*
Freedman, Albert Z. *WhoAm 94*
Freedman, Alfred Mordecai 1917- *WhoScEn 94*
Freedman, Allen Royal 1940- *WhoAm 94*
Freedman, Amelia 1940- *Who 94*
Freedman, Anita 1927- *WhoAmP 93*
Freedman, Anthony Stephen 1945- *WhoAm 94, WhoAmP 93*
Freedman, Audrey Willock 1929- *WhoFI 94*
Freedman, Barbara Louise 1938- *WhoWest 94*
Freedman, Barbara S. 1952- *WhoMW 93*
Freedman, Bart Joseph 1955- *WhoAmL 94, WhoWest 94*
Freedman, Ben d1987 *WhoHol 92*
Freedman, Charles 1925- *Who 94*
Freedman, Charles 1941- *WhoAm 94*
Freedman, Daniel X. d1993 *NewYTBS 93*
Freedman, Daniel X. 1921-1993 *ConAu 141*
Freedman, David Amiel 1938- *WhoAm 94*
Freedman, David Noel 1922- *WhoAm 94, WhoMW 93*
Freedman, Dawn Angela 1942- *Who 94*
Freedman, Deborah Eileen 1953- *WhoFI 94*
Freedman, Deborah S. 1947- *WhoAmA 93*
Freedman, Ellis Joseph 1921- *WhoAmL 94*
Freedman, Eric 1949- *WhoMW 93*
Freedman, Eugene M. 1932- *WhoAm 94, WhoFI 94*
Freedman, Frank Harlan 1924- *WhoAm 94*
Freedman, Gerald M. 1943- *WhoAm 94, WhoAmL 94*
Freedman, Gregg 1957- *WhoWest 94*
Freedman, Harry 1922- *WhoAm 94*
Freedman, Helen E. *WhoAmL 94*
Freedman, Howard Martin 1953- *WhoFI 94*
Freedman, Jacqueline *WhoAmA 93*
Freedman, James Oliver 1935- *WhoAm 94*
Freedman, Jerome 1916- *WhoAm 94*
Freedman, Jerrold 1942- *IntMPA 94*
Freedman, Joel 1948- *WhoIns 94*
Freedman, Jonathan Borwick 1950- *WhoAm 94*
Freedman, Joseph 1923- *WhoFI 94*
Freedman, Joyce Beth 1945- *WhoMW 93*
Freedman, Judith 1939- *WhoAmP 93*
Freedman, Kenneth David 1947- *WhoAmL 94*
Freedman, Laurence Stuart 1948- *WhoScEn 94*
Freedman, Lawrence David 1948- *Who 94*
Freedman, Louis 1917- *Who 94*
Freedman, Louis Martin 1947- *WhoScEn 94*
Freedman, Maurice 1904- *WhoAmA 93N*
Freedman, Mervin Burton 1920- *WhoAm 94, WrDr 94*
Freedman, Michael Hartley 1951- *WhoAm 94, WhoScEn 94, WhoWest 94*
Freedman, Monroe Henry 1928- *WhoAm 94, WhoAmL 94*
Freedman, Nancy 1920- *EncSF 93, WrDr 94*
Freedman, Philip 1926- *WhoAm 94*
Freedman, Randall Lee 1948- *WhoAmL 94*
Freedman, Robert *DrAPF 93*
Freedman, Robert Louis 1940- *WhoAm 94, WhoAmL 94*
Freedman, Ronald 1917- *IntWW 93, WhoAm 94, WrDr 94*
Freedman, Russell (Bruce) 1929- *TwCYAW*
Freedman, Russell Bruce 1929- *WhoAm 94*
Freedman, Samuel 1908- *Who 94*
Freedman, Samuel Orkin 1928- *WhoAm 94*
Freedman, Samuel Sumner 1927- *WhoAmP 93*
Freedman, Sandra Warshaw 1943- *WhoAm 94, WhoAmP 93*
Freedman, Stanley 1921- *WhoWest 94*
Freedman, Stanley Arnold 1922- *WhoAm 94*
Freedman, Stanley Marvin 1923- *WhoAm 94*
Freedman, Theodore Levy 1947- *WhoAm 94*
Freedman, Walter 1914- *WhoAm 94*
Freedman, William Mark 1946- *WhoAm 94, WhoAmL 94*
Freedom, Nancy 1932- *WhoWest 94*
Freeh, Edward James 1925- *WhoAm 94*
Freeh, Louis J. 1950- *News 94-2 [port], WhoAm 94, WhoAmL 94*
Freeh, Louis Joseph 1950- *NewYTBS 93 [port], WhoAmP 93*
Freehill, Maurice F. 1915- *WhoAm 94*
Freehling, Allen Isaac 1932- *WhoWest 94*
Freehling, Daniel Joseph 1950- *WhoAm 94, WhoAmL 94*
Freehling, Harold George, Jr. 1947- *WhoMW 93*
Freehling, Norman 1905- *WhoAm 94*
Freehling, Paul Edward 1938- *WhoAm 94*
Freehling, Stanley Maxwell 1924- *WhoAm 94*
Freehling, Willard Maxwell 1913- *WhoAm 94*
Freehling, William W(ilhartz) 1935- *WrDr 94*
Freehling, William Wilhartz 1935- *WhoAm 94*
Freel, Aleta d1935 *WhoHol 92*
Freeland, Charles 1940- *WhoAmL 94*
Freeland, Darryl Creighton 1939- *WhoWest 94*
Freeland, Emile Charroppin 1896- *WhAm 10*
Freeland, James M. Jackson 1927- *WhoAm 94, WhoAmL 94*
Freeland, John Chester, III 1950- *WhoScEn 94*
Freeland, John Redvers 1927- *Who 94*
Freeland, Kevin Paul 1957- *WhoFI 94*
Freeland, Mary Graham *Who 94*
Freeland, Michael Willis 1941- *WhoAm 94, WhoAmL 94*
Freeland, Patricia L. 1944- *WhoAmL 94*
Freeland, Robert Frederick 1919- *WhoWest 94*
Freeland, Robert Lenward, Jr. 1939- *WhoBlA 94*
Freeland, Russell L. 1929- *WhoBlA 94*
Freeland, Shawn Ericka 1968- *WhoBlA 94*
Freeland, T. Paul 1916-1988 *WhAm 10*
Freeland, William Lee 1929- *WhoAmA 93*
Freeling, Nicolas 1927- *Who 94, WrDr 94*
Freels, Willard Dudley 1924- *WhoAmP 93*
Freeman, Al d1956 *WhoHol 92*
Freeman, Al, Jr. 1934- *AfrAmAl 6, IntMPA 94, WhoHol 92*
Freeman, Albert Cornelius, Jr. *WhoBlA 94*
Freeman, Albert E. 1931- *WhoAm 94, WhoScEn 94*
Freeman, Anne Hobson *DrAPF 93*
Freeman, Antoinette Rosefeldt 1937- *WhoAmL 94*
Freeman, Arny d1986 *WhoHol 92*
Freeman, Arthur 1925- *WhoAm 94*
Freeman, Arthur J. 1930- *WhoMW 93*
Freeman, Barbara C(onstance) 1906- *WrDr 94*
Freeman, Barbara M. 1947- *WrDr 94*
Freeman, Bernardus fl. 1700- *EncNAR*
Freeman, Beth Labson 1953- *WhoAmP 93*
Freeman, Bill 1938- *WrDr 94*
Freeman, Bob A. 1926- *WhoAm 94*
Freeman, Brian S. 1967- *WhoScEn 94*
Freeman, Bryant C. 1931- *WhoMW 93*
Freeman, C. 1933- *WhoAmP 93*
Freeman, Carolyn Ruth 1950- *WhoAm 94*
Freeman, Catherine 1931- *Who 94*
Freeman, Catherine Elaine 1956- *WhoMW 93*
Freeman, Charles E. *WhoAmL 94, WhoMW 93*
Freeman, Charles Eldridge 1933- *WhoBlA 94*
Freeman, Charles W., Jr. 1943- *WhoAmP 93*
Freeman, Charles Wellman, Jr 1943- *IntWW 93*
Freeman, Clarence Calvin 1923- *WhoAm 94*
Freeman, Clifford Echols, Jr. 1959- *WhoFI 94*
Freeman, Corinne 1926- *WhoAm 94, WhoAmP 93*
Freeman, Corwin Stuart, Jr. 1947- *WhoMW 93*
Freeman, Daniel Herbert, Jr. 1945- *WhoScEn 94*
Freeman, Darlene Marie 1951- *WhoHisp 94*
Freeman, David 1927- *WhoAmL 94, WhoWest 94*
Freeman, David 1944- *WhoAm 94, WhoFI 94*
Freeman, David 1945- *ConDr 93*
Freeman, David 1952- *NewGrDO*
Freeman, David (Edgar) 1945- *WrDr 94*
Freeman, David Calvin, Sr. 1942- *WhoBlA 94*
Freeman, David Charles 1952- *Who 94*
Freeman, David Forgan 1918- *WhoAm 94*
Freeman, David John 1928- *Who 94*
Freeman, David John 1948- *WhoAmL 94*
Freeman, David L. 1937- *WhoAmA 93*
Freeman, David Laurence 1946- *WhoScEn 94*
Freeman, David Lynn 1924- *WhoAm 94*
Freeman, Davis 1923- *WrDr 94*
Freeman, Devery *DrAPF 93*
Freeman, Dewayne 1955- *WhoAmP 93*
Freeman, Diane S. *WhoBlA 94*
Freeman, Dick *WhoAm 94, WhoWest 94*
Freeman, Don 1908-1978 *ChlLR 30 [port]*
Freeman, Don 1909-1978 *WhoAmA 93N*
Freeman, Donald Cary 1938- *WhoWest 94*
Freeman, Donald Chester, Jr. 1930- *WhoAm 94*
Freeman, Donald Wilford 1929- *WhoFI 94*
Freeman, Edward Anderson 1914- *WhoBlA 94*
Freeman, Edward C. *WhoBlA 94*
Freeman, Edward C. 1906- *WhoAmP 93*
Freeman, Elaine Lavalle 1929- *WhoAm 94*
Freeman, Elizabeth Anne 1958- *WhoAm 94*
Freeman, Ernest Allan 1932- *Who 94*
Freeman, Ernest Michael 1937- *Who 94*
Freeman, Ernest Robert 1933- *WhoAm 94*
Freeman, Eugene Edward 1952- *WhoScEn 94*
Freeman, Evelyn 1940- *WhoBlA 94*
Freeman, Frankie M. 1916- *WhoBlA 94*
Freeman, Gaylord 1910-1991 *WhAm 10*
Freeman, George Clemon, Jr. 1929- *WhoAm 94, WhoAmL 94*
Freeman, George Vincent 1911- *Who 94*
Freeman, Gertrude 1927- *WhoAmA 93*
Freeman, Gill Sherryl 1949- *WhoAmL 94*
Freeman, Gillian 1929- *ConAu 43NR, WrDr 94*
Freeman, Gordon Russel 1930- *WhoScEn 94*
Freeman, Graham P. M. 1946- *WhoAm 94*
Freeman, Graydon LaVerne 1904- *WhoAm 94*
Freeman, Gregory Bruce 1956- *WhoBlA 94*
Freeman, Habern *WhoAmP 93*
Freeman, Harold P. 1933- *WhoBlA 94*
Freeman, Harold Webber 1899- *Who 94*
Freeman, Harry Boit, Jr. 1926-1990 *WhAm 10*

Freeman, Harry Louis 1932- *WhoAm 94, WhoFI 94*
Freeman, Harry Lynwood 1920- *WhoAm 94*
Freeman, Henry McCall 1947- *WhoAm 94*
Freeman, Herbert 1925- *WhoAm 94*
Freeman, Herbert James 1941- *WhoWest 94*
Freeman, Houghton 1921- *WhoIns 94*
Freeman, Hovey Thomas 1894- *WhAm 10*
Freeman, Howard d1967 *WhoHol 92*
Freeman, Howard Edgar 1929-1992 *WhAm 10*
Freeman, Howard Lee, Jr. 1935- *WhoAm 94*
Freeman, Hugh James 1947- *WhoAm 94*
Freeman, Hugh Lionel 1929- *Who 94*
Freeman, Ira Henry 1906- *WhoAm 94*
Freeman, J. E. *WhoHol 92*
Freeman, James A. 1945- *WhoIns 94*
Freeman, James Atticus, III 1947- *WhoAmL 94*
Freeman, James David 1958- *WhoFI 94*
Freeman, James Robin *Who 94*
Freeman, James William 1946- *WhoAmP 93*
Freeman, Jane 1885-1963 *WhoAmA 93N*
Freeman, Jeff(rey Vaughn) 1946- *WhoAmA 93*
Freeman, Jo 1945- *WrDr 94*
Freeman, Joan 1941- *WhoHol 92*
Freeman, Joe Bailey 1937- *WhoFI 94*
Freeman, Joel 1922- *IntMPA 94*
Freeman, John *Who 94*
Freeman, John 1666-1736 *NewGrDO*
Freeman, John 1915- *IntWW 93*
Freeman, John Allen 1912- *Who 94*
Freeman, John Anthony 1937- *Who 94*
Freeman, John F. 1957- *WhoAmP 93*
Freeman, John Mark 1933- *WhoAm 94*
Freeman, John Philip Hawk 1951- *WhoMW 93*
Freeman, Jordan d1781 *WhAmRev*
Freeman, Joseph William 1914- *Who 94*
Freeman, Joyce 1927- *WhoAmP 93*
Freeman, Judson, Jr. 1943- *WhoAm 94, WhoAmL 94*
Freeman, Karen Arline 1947- *WhoMW 93*
Freeman, Kathleen *WhoHol 92*
Freeman, Kathryn 1956- *WhoAmA 93*
Freeman, Kenneth David 1906- *WhAm 10*
Freeman, Kenneth Donald 1912- *WhoBlA 94*
Freeman, Kerlin, Jr. 1930- *WhoBlA 94*
Freeman, Kester St. Clair, Jr. 1944- *WhoAm 94*
Freeman, Kristi Tubbs 1963- *WhoWest 94*
Freeman, Larry Leroy 1934- *WhoFI 94*
Freeman, (Harry) Lawrence 1869-1954 *NewGrDO*
Freeman, Lee Allen, Jr. 1940- *WhoAm 94*
Freeman, Lelabelle Christine 1923- *WhoBlA 94*
Freeman, Leonard Murray 1937- *WhoAm 94*
Freeman, Leslie Gordon 1935- *WhoAm 94*
Freeman, Linton Clarke 1927- *WhoAm 94*
Freeman, Louis McDaniel 1940- *WhoAm 94*
Freeman, Louis S. 1940- *WhoAm 94, WhoAmL 94*
Freeman, Lucy 1916- *WrDr 94*
Freeman, Mallory Bruce 1938- *WhoAmA 93*
Freeman, Marianne *WhoAmP 93*
Freeman, Marie Joyce 1934- *Who 94*
Freeman, Marjorie Kler 1929- *WhoScEn 94*
Freeman, Mark 1908- *WhoAm 94, WhoAmA 93*
Freeman, Martin 1944- *WhoWest 94*
Freeman, Marvin 1963- *WhoBlA 94*
Freeman, Mary E(leanor) Wilkin 1852-1930 *RfGShF*
Freeman, Mary E. Wilkins 1852-1930 *BlmGWL*
Freeman, Mary Lamb *DrAPF 93*
Freeman, Mary Louise 1941- *WhoAmP 93*
Freeman, Maurice d1953 *WhoHol 92*
Freeman, McKinley Howard, Sr. 1920- *WhoBlA 94*
Freeman, Meredith Norwin 1920- *WhoAm 94*
Freeman, Michael Alexander Reykers 1931- *IntWW 93, Who 94*
Freeman, Michael O. 1948- *WhoAmP 93*
Freeman, Michael Stuart 1946- *WhoAm 94*
Freeman, Michael T. 1946- *WhoFI 94*
Freeman, Mickey *WhoHol 92*
Freeman, Milton Malcolm Roland 1934- *WhoAm 94*
Freeman, Milton Victor 1911- *WhoAm 94, WhoAmL 94, WhoFI 94*
Freeman, Mona 1926- *WhoHol 92*
Freeman, Montine McDaniel 1915- *WhoAm 94*

Freeman, Morgan 1937- *AfrAmAl 6 [port], IntMPA 94, IntWW 93, WhoAm 94, WhoBlA 94, WhoHol 92*
Freeman, Morton S. 1912- *WhoAm 94*
Freeman, Myrna Faye 1939- *WhoFI 94*
Freeman, Nancy Leigh 1960- *WhoWest 94*
Freeman, Nathaniel 1741-1827 *WhAmRev*
Freeman, Neal Blackwell 1940- *WhoAm 94*
Freeman, Neil 1948- *WhoFI 94, WhoWest 94*
Freeman, Nelson R. 1924- *WhoBlA 94*
Freeman, Norman E., Sr. 1950- *WhoBlA 94*
Freeman, Orville Lothrop 1918- *IntWW 93, WhoAmP 93*
Freeman, Palmer, Jr. 1944- *WhoAmP 93*
Freeman, Pam 1946- *WhoHol 92*
Freeman, Patricia Elizabeth 1924- *WhoWest 94*
Freeman, Paul *WhoHol 92*
Freeman, Paul 1916- *Who 94*
Freeman, Paul D. 1936- *WhoBlA 94*
Freeman, Paul Illife *Who 94*
Freeman, Peter Craig 1956- *WhoAm 94*
Freeman, Peter Sunderlin 1944- *WhoFI 94*
Freeman, Philip Conrad, Jr. 1937- *WhoAm 94*
Freeman, Preston Garrison 1933- *WhoBlA 94*
Freeman, Ralph 1911- *IntWW 93, Who 94*
Freeman, Ralph Carter *WhoAm 94, WhoWest 94*
Freeman, Ralph McKenzie 1902-1990 *WhAm 10*
Freeman, Raymond 1932- *IntWW 93, Who 94*
Freeman, Raymond Lee 1919- *WhoAm 94*
Freeman, Richard Austin 1862-1943 *DcNaB MP*
Freeman, Richard C. 1926- *WhoAm 94*
Freeman, Richard Dean 1928- *WhoFI 94*
Freeman, Richard Francis 1934- *WhoFI 94*
Freeman, Richard Gavin 1910- *Who 94*
Freeman, Richard J. 1950- *WhoFI 94*
Freeman, Richard Merrell 1921- *WhoAm 94, WhoAmP 93*
Freeman, Robert *WhoAmA 93*
Freeman, Robert L. 1934- *WhoAmP 93*
Freeman, Robert Lee *WhoBlA 94*
Freeman, Robert Lee 1939- *WhoAmA 93*
Freeman, Robert Louis 1956- *WhoAmP 93*
Freeman, Robert Mallory 1941- *WhoAm 94, WhoFI 94*
Freeman, Robert Schofield 1935- *WhoAm 94*
Freeman, Robert Turner, Jr. 1918- *WhoAm 94, WhoBlA 94*
Freeman, Roger A 1904- *WrDr 94*
Freeman, Roger Adolph 1904-1991 *WhAm 10*
Freeman, Roger Norman 1942- *Who 94*
Freeman, Roland L. *WhoAmA 93*
Freeman, Ronald J. 1947- *WhoBlA 94*
Freeman, Ruby E. 1921- *WhoBlA 94*
Freeman, Ruges R. 1917- *WhoBlA 94*
Freeman, Russell Adams 1932- *WhoAm 94, WhoAmL 94*
Freeman, Sarah (Caroline) 1940- *WrDr 94*
Freeman, Shirley Ann 1930- *WhoAmP 93*
Freeman, Shirley Walker 1951- *WhoBlA 94*
Freeman, Simon (David) 1952- *WrDr 94*
Freeman, Stella d1936 *WhoHol 92*
Freeman, Stewart Howard 1941- *WhoAmL 94*
Freeman, Susan Maud 1950- *WhoAm 94, WhoAmL 94*
Freeman, Susan Tax 1938- *WhoAm 94*
Freeman, Theodore H., Jr. 1950- *WhoBlA 94*
Freeman, Thomas d1821 *WhWE*
Freeman, Thomas 1925- *WrDr 94*
Freeman, Thomas F. 1920- *WhoBlA 94*
Freeman, Thomas G. 1937- *WhoAmP 93*
Freeman, Thomas G., II 1945- *WhoAm 94*
Freeman, Tina 1951- *WhoAmA 93*
Freeman, Todd Ira 1953- *WhoAmL 94*
Freeman, Tom M. 1952- *WhoAm 94*
Freeman, Tony *WrDr 94*
Freeman, Travis 1925- *WhoAmP 93*
Freeman, Val LeRoy 1926- *WhoWest 94*
Freeman, Vernie Edward, II 1961- *WhoAmL 94*
Freeman, Vivian L. 1927- *WhoAmP 93*
Freeman, Vivian Lois 1927- *WhoWest 94*
Freeman, Walter 1895-1972 *EncSPD*
Freeman, Walter Eugene 1928- *WhoBlA 94*
Freeman, William d1932 *WhoHol 92*
Freeman, William A. 1943- *WhoFI 94*
Freeman, William Ernest, Jr. 1913- *WhoAm 94*
Freeman, William M. 1926- *WhoAmP 93, WhoBlA 94*

Freeman, William T. *DrAPF 93*
Freeman Allen, Geoffrey 1922- *WrDr 94*
Freeman-Appelbaum, Margery *WhoAmA 93*
Freeman-Grenville *Who 94*
Freeman-Grenville, Greville Stewart Parker 1918- *WrDr 94*
Freeman-Mitford, Rupert d1939 *WhoHol 92*
Freemantle, Brian (Harry) 1936- *ConAu 43NR, WrDr 94*
Freeman-Wilson, Karen Marie 1960- *WhoBlA 94*
Freemont, James McKinley 1942- *WhoBlA 94*
Freeny, Patrick Clinton 1942- *WhoAm 94*
Freer, Charles Edward Jesse 1901- *Who 94*
Freer, Coburn 1939- *WhoAm 94*
Freer, Eleanor Everest 1864-1942 *NewGrDO*
Freer, Howard Mortimer 1904-1960 *WhoAmA 93N*
Freer, John Herschel 1938- *WhoAm 94*
Freer, Lyle Leroy 1925- *WhoAmP 93*
Freer, Robert (William George) 1923- *Who 94*
Freer, Robert Elliott, Jr. 1941- *WhoAm 94, WhoAmL 94*
Freericks, Mary *DrAPF 93*
Freerksen, Enno 1910- *IntWW 93*
Frees, Paul d1985 *WhoHol 92*
Frees, Paul 1920-1986 *WhoCom*
Freese, Frank E. 1940- *WhoIns 94*
Freese, George E., Jr. 1920- *WhoAmP 93*
Freese, Katherine 1957- *WhoMW 93*
Freese, Mathias B. *DrAPF 93*
Freese, Raymond William 1934- *WhoMW 93*
Freese, Richard 1937- *WhoAmP 93*
Freese, Sigrid Halvorson 1939- *WhoAmP 93*
Freese, Stephen J. 1960- *WhoAmP 93*
Freese, Uwe Ernest 1925- *WhoAm 94*
Freeson, Reginald 1926- *Who 94*
Freestone, Thomas Lawrence 1938- *WhoWest 94*
Freeth, Denzil Kingson 1924- *Who 94*
Freeth, Douglas Duncan 1935- *WhoAm 94*
Freeth, Gordon 1914- *IntWW 93, Who 94*
Freeth, John 1731-1808 *DcNaB MP*
Freeth, Peter Stewart 1938- *Who 94*
Freeze, James Donald 1932- *WhoAm 94*
Freeze, Roy Allan 1939- *WhoAm 94*
Frega, Patrick R. 1945- *WhoAmL 94*
Fregia, Darrell Leon 1949- *WhoBlA 94*
Fregia, Ray 1948- *WhoBlA 94*
Fregoli, Leopoldo d1936 *WhoHol 92*
Fregosi, James Louis 1942- *WhoAm 94*
Fregoso, Thomas G. 1958- *WhoHisp 94*
Frehlich, Rodney George 1952- *WhoScEn 94*
Frehner, Walter *IntWW 93*
Frei, Emil, III 1924- *WhoAm 94*
Frei, Ephraim Heinrich 1912- *IntWW 93*
Frei, Michael Clark 1946- *WhoFI 94*
Freiberg, Jeffrey Joseph 1960- *WhoScEn 94*
Freiberg, Joseph Albert 1898- *WhAm 10*
Freiberg, Lowell Carl 1939- *WhoAm 94*
Freiberger, Walter Frederick 1924- *WhoAm 94, WhoFI 94, WhoScEn 94*
Freibert, Pat 1936- *WhoAmP 93, WhoWomW 91*
Freibott, George August 1954- *WhoFI 94, WhoScEn 94, WhoWest 94*
Freid, Jacob *WhoAm 94*
Freid, James Martin 1965- *WhoScEn 94*
Freidank, c. 1170-c. 1233 *DcLB 138*
Freidberg, Sidney 1914- *WhoAm 94, WhoAmL 94*
Freidel, Frank d1993 *NewYTBS 93*
Freidel, Frank (Burt, Jr.) 1916-1993 *ConAu 140*
Freidenbergs, Ingrid 1944- *WhoScEn 94*
Freidheim, Cyrus F., Jr. 1935- *WhoAm 94*
Freidin, John 1941- *WhoAmP 93*
Freidkin, Evgenii S. 1948- *WhoScEn 94*
Freidson, Eliot Lazarus 1923- *WhoAm 94*
Freier, Bruce 1955- *WhoMW 93*
Freier, Tom *WhoAmP 93*
Freiermuth, Mark Robert 1958- *WhoWest 94*
Freifeld, Eric 1919- *WhoAmA 93N*
Freiheit, Clayton Fredric 1938- *WhoAm 94, WhoWest 94*
Freiherr von Kleydorff, Ludwig Otto Alex 1926- *WhoAm 94*
Freiherr von Kleydorff, Ludwig Otto Alexander 1926- *WhoFI 94*
Freij, Bishara Joudeh 1954- *WhoMW 93*
Freije, Philip Charles 1944- *WhoAmL 94*
Freil, Raymond d1939 *WhoHol 92*
Freilich, Irvin M. 1949- *WhoAmL 94*
Freilich, Jeff 1948- *WhoAm 94*
Freilich, Joan Sherman 1941- *WhoFI 94*

Freilich, Michael L. 1912-1975 *WhoAmA 93N*
Freilich, Robert H. 1936- *WhoAmL 94*
Freilich, Samuel d1993 *NewYTBS 93*
Freilicher, Jane 1924- *WhoAm 94, WhoAmA 93*
Freilicher, Melvyn *DrAPF 93*
Freilicher, Morton 1931- *WhoAm 94*
Freiligrath, Ferdinand 1810-1876 *DcLB 133 [port]*
Freilinger, James Edward 1939- *WhoFI 94*
Freiman, Charles Visvald 1932- *WhoAm 94*
Freiman, David Burl 1947- *WhoAm 94*
Freiman, David Galland 1911- *WhoAm 94*
Freiman, Paul E. 1932- *WhoFI 94*
Freiman, Robert J. 1917-1991 *WhoAmA 93N*
Freimark, Bob 1922- *WhoAmA 93*
Freimark, Jeffrey Philip 1955- *WhoAm 94, WhoFI 94*
Freimark, Robert 1922- *WhoAm 94*
Freind, Stephen F. 1944- *WhoAmP 93*
Freinkel, Norbert 1926-1989 *WhAm 10*
Freinkel, Ruth Kimmelstiel 1926- *WhoAm 94*
Freire, Daniel G. 1964- *WhoAmL 94*
Freireich, Donna L. 1948- *WhoIns 94*
Freireich, Emil J 1927- *WhoAm 94*
Freiria, Evaristo, Jr. 1929-1989 *WhAm 10*
Freis, James Henry 1944- *WhoAm 94*
Freise, Earl Jerome 1935- *WhoWest 94*
Freise, Eric Louis 1951- *WhoAmL 94*
Freisen, Gil *WhoBlA 94*
Freiser, Lawrence M. 1942- *WhoAmL 94*
Freishtat, Harvey W. 1946- *WhoAm 94, WhoAmL 94*
Freisinger, Randall R. *DrAPF 93*
Freiss, Stephane *WhoHol 92*
Freitag, Edward George 1946- *WhoAmL 94*
Freitag, Frederick Gerald 1952- *WhoMW 93*
Freitag, Harlow 1936- *WhoAm 94*
Freitag, Peter Roy 1943- *WhoFI 94, WhoScEn 94, WhoWest 94*
Freitag, Robert Frederick 1920- *WhoAm 94, WhoScEn 94*
Freitag, Wolfgang Martin 1924- *WhoAm 94, WhoAmA 93*
Freitas, Antoinette Juni 1944- *WhoFI 94*
Freitas, Frederico (Guedes) de 1902-1980 *NewGrDO*
Freitas, Robert Archibald, Jr. 1952- *WhoWest 94*
Freitas, Stephen Joseph 1958- *WhoWest 94*
Freitas Do Amaral, Diogo *IntWW 93*
Freivalds, Laila *WhoWomW 91*
Freivalds, Laila 1942- *IntWW 93*
Freizer, Louis A. 1931- *WhoAm 94, WhoFI 94*
Frejacques, Claude 1924- *IntWW 93*
Freksa, Friedrich *EncSF 93*
Freleng, Friz 1906- *IntDcF 2-4, IntMPA 94*
Frelich, Phyllis 1944- *WhoAm 94*
Frelick, Linden Frederick 1938- *WhoAm 94*
Freling, Richard Alan 1932- *WhoAm 94*
Frelinger, Jeffrey Allen 1948- *WhoAm 94*
Frelinghuysen, Frederick 1753-1804 *WhAmRev*
Frelinghuysen, Joseph S. 1912- *WrDr 94*
Frelinghuysen, Rodney P. 1946- *WhoAmP 93*
Frelinghuysen, Theodorus Jacobus 1692-1748? *DcAmReB 2*
Frelow, Robert Dean 1932- *WhoBlA 94*
Frelow, Robert Lee, Jr. 1966- *WhoBlA 94*
Fremans, Mlle. fl. 1721-1743 *NewGrDO*
Fremantle *Who 94*
Fremantle, John Tapling 1927- *Who 94*
Fremault, Anita *WhoHol 92*
Fremaux, Louis Joseph Felix 1921- *IntWW 93, Who 94*
Fremgen, James Morgan 1933- *WrDr 94*
Fremlin, Celia 1914- *WrDr 94*
Fremon, David Kent 1949- *WhoMW 93*
Fremont, Alfred d1930 *WhoHol 92*
Fremont, Alicia Ann 1959- *WhoMW 93*
Fremont, Ernest Hoar, Jr. 1925- *WhoAmL 94*
Fremont, John Charles 1813-1890 *HisWorL [port], WhWE [port]*
Fremont, Thierry 1963- *WhoHol 92*
Fremont-Smith, Marion R. 1926- *WhoAm 94*
Fremont-Smith, Thayer 1931- *WhoAm 94*
Fremouw, Edward Joseph 1934- *WhoAm 94*
Fremstad, Olive 1871-1951 *NewGrDO*
Frenaud, Andre 1907- *ConWorW 93*
French *Who 94*
French, Alfred 1916- *IntWW 93, WrDr 94*
French, Alfred Dexter 1943- *WhoScEn 94*

French, Alice 1850-1934 *BlmGWL*
French, Anne 1956- *BlmGWL*
French, Anthony Philip 1920- *Who 94, WhoAm 94, WhoScEn 94*
French, Arthur *WhoHol 92*
French, Arthur Leeman, Jr. 1940- *WhoFI 94*
French, Barbara Conner 1926- *WhoAmP 93*
French, Bert d1924 *WhoHol 92*
French, Bevan Meredith 1937- *WhoAm 94*
French, Bruce Hartung 1915- *WhoAm 94*
French, Cecil Charles John 1926- *Who 94*
French, Charles Ezra 1923- *WhoAm 94*
French, Charles Ferris, Jr. 1918- *WhoAm 94*
French, Charles K. d1952 *WhoHol 92*
French, Charles Stacy 1907- *IntWW 93, WhoAm 94*
French, Christopher James Saunders 1925- *Who 94*
French, Clarence Levi, Jr. 1925- *WhoAm 94, WhoFI 94, WhoWest 94*
French, Curtis Edwin 1941- *WhoFI 94*
French, Daniel Chester 1850-1931 *AmCulL*
French, David *DrAPF 93*
French, David 1939- *ConDr 93, IntDcT 2, WrDr 94*
French, David 1947- *Who 94*
French, David Heath 1918- *WhoAm 94, WhoWest 94*
French, David Rowthorne 1937- *Who 94*
French, Dennis Donald 1954- *WhoAm 94*
French, Dorothy Fay 1951- *WhoAmL 94*
French, Douglas Charles 1944- *Who 94*
French, Edward Ronald 1937- *WhoScEn 94*
French, Edwige 1948- *WhoHol 92*
French, Eunice Pelafigue 1938- *WhoAm 94*
French, Fiona 1944- *SmATA 75, WrDr 94*
French, George d1961 *WhoHol 92*
French, George Wesley 1928- *WhoBlA 94*
French, Georgine Louise 1934- *WhoWest 94*
French, Glendon Everett, Jr. 1934- *WhoAm 94*
French, Hadley Mack 1952- *WhoMW 93*
French, Harold d1982 *WhoHol 92*
French, Harold Stanley 1921- *WhoAm 94, WhoFI 94*
French, Helen d1917 *WhoHol 92*
French, Henry Pierson, Jr. 1934- *WhoFI 94*
French, Henry William 1910- *Who 94*
French, Howard W. 1957- *WhoBlA 94*
French, Hugh d1976 *WhoHol 92*
French, James J. 1926- *WhoBlA 94*
French, Jay Michael 1963- *WhoMW 93*
French, Joan *DrAPF 93*
French, John, III 1932- *WhoAm 94, WhoAmL 94, WhoFI 94*
French, John Dwyer 1933- *WhoAm 94, WhoAmL 94*
French, John Henry, Jr. 1911- *WhoAm 94*
French, Joseph Henry 1928- *WhoBlA 94*
French, Joseph Jordan, Jr. 1931- *WhoAm 94, WhoAmL 94*
French, Judson Cull 1922- *WhoAm 94, WhoScEn 94*
French, Kenneth Ronald 1954- *WhoAm 94*
French, Kenny R. 1958- *WhoAmP 93*
French, Layne Bryan 1950- *WhoAm 94, WhoAmL 94*
French, Leigh 1945- *WhoHol 92*
French, Leslie 1904- *WhoHol 92*
French, Leslie Richard 1904- *Who 94*
French, Linda Jean 1947- *WhoAm 94*
French, Lisa 1953- *WhoIns 94*
French, Lloyd A. d1950 *WhoHol 92*
French, Lyle Albert 1915- *WhoAm 94*
French, Marilyn 1929- *BlmGWL, IntWW 93, WhoAm 94, WrDr 94*
French, Mary fl. 1703- *BlmGWL*
French, MaryAnn 1952- *WhoBlA 94*
French, Michael Bruce 1954- *WhoFI 94*
French, Michael C. 1943- *WhoAmL 94*
French, Neil Desha 1922- *WhoFI 94*
French, Neville Arthur Irwin 1920- *Who 94*
French, Norma d1989 *WhoHol 92*
French, Paul *EncSF 93, SmATA 74, TwCYAW*
French, Paul 1920-1992 *ConLC 76 [port]*
French, Philip (Neville) 1933- *WrDr 94*
French, Philip Franks 1932- *WhoAm 94, WhoFI 94*
French, Philip Neville 1933- *Who 94*
French, R(oger) K(enneth) 1938- *ConAu 42NR*
French, Ray 1927- *WhoAmP 93*
French, Ray H. 1919- *WhoAmA 93*
French, Raymond 1920- *WhoAm 94*
French, Raymond Douglas 1918- *WhoFI 94*

French, Richard Frederic 1915- *WhoAm 94*
French, Robert O. d1981 *WhoHol 92*
French, Robert P. 1919- *WhoAmP 93, WhoBlA 94*
French, Robert Warren 1911- *WhoAm 94*
French, Simon 1957- *TwCYAW, WrDr 94*
French, Stanley George 1933- *WhoAm 94*
French, Stephen Warren 1934- *WhoAmA 93, WhoWest 94*
French, Susan *WhoHol 92*
French, Ted d1978 *WhoHol 92*
French, Thomas McGuinness 1934- *WhoAmL 94*
French, Valerie d1990 *WhoHol 92*
French, Victor d1989 *WhAm 10, WhoHol 92*
French, Warren B., Jr. 1923- *WhoAmP 93*
French, Warren G. 1922- *WrDr 94*
French, William Cullen 1951- *WhoMW 93*
French, William Harold 1926- *WhoAm 94*
French, William J. 1942- *WhoScEn 94*
French, William James 1945- *WhoMW 93*
Frend, William (Hugh Clifford) 1916- *WrDr 94*
Frend, William Hugh Clifford 1916- *IntWW 93, Who 94*
Freneau, Philip Morin 1752-1832 *AmCulL, WhAmRev*
Frenger, Paul Fred 1946- *WhoScEn 94*
Freni, Mirella 1935- *IntWW 93, NewGrDO, WhoAm 94*
Frenkel, Daniil Grigor'yevich 1906-1984 *NewGrDO*
Frenkel, Eugene Phillip 1929- *WhoAm 94, WhoScEn 94*
Frenkel, James R. 1948- *EncSF 93*
Frenkel, Michael 1936- *WhoAm 94, WhoAmL 94*
Frenkel, Steven I. 1964- *WhoAmL 94*
Frenkiel, Richard Henry 1943- *WhoScEn 94*
Frensley, A. C. *WhoAmP 93*
Frenster, John Henry 1928- *WhoWest 94*
Frentz, Nick Andrew 1963- *WhoAmL 94*
Frenz, Bertram Anton 1945- *WhoScEn 94*
Frenz, Dorothy Ann 1954- *WhoScEn 94*
Frenz, Paul D. 1941- *WhoAmL 94*
Frenzel, Charles Alfon 1940- *WhoWest 94*
Frenzel, Otto N., III 1930- *WhoAm 94*
Frenzel, William Eldridge 1928- *WhoAmP 93*
Frenzer, Peter F. 1934- *WhoIns 94*
Frenzer, Peter Frederick 1934- *WhoAm 94, WhoFI 94*
Frere, James Arnold 1920- *Who 94*
Frere, Jean 1919- *IntWW 93*
Frere, John Edward 1947- *WhoAm 94*
Frere, John Hookham 1769-1846 *BlmGEL*
Frere, Maurice Herbert 1932- *WhoAm 94, WhoScEn 94*
Frere, Richard Tobias 1938- *Who 94*
Frere, S(heppard) S(underland) 1916- *WrDr 94*
Frere, Sheppard Sunderland 1916- *IntWW 93, Who 94*
Frerichs, Donald L. 1931- *WhoAmP 93*
Frerichs, Ernest Sunley 1925- *WhoAm 94*
Frerichs, Kent Elmer 1946- *WhoAmP 93*
Frerichs, Ruth Colcord *WhoAmA 93*
Frerichs, Wayne Marvin 1933- *WhoMW 93*
Frerichs Doderer, Minnette 1923- *WhoWomW 91*
Freron, Elie-Catherine 1718-1776 *GuFrLit 2*
Freschl, (Giovanni) Domenico c. 1630-1710 *NewGrDO*
Fresco, Jacques Robert 1928- *WhoAm 94*
Fresco, Robert M. 1928- *IntMPA 94*
Frese, Edward Scheer, Jr. 1944- *WhoFI 94*
Frese, Walter Wenzel 1909- *WhoAm 94*
Fresen, Gary W. 1953- *WhoAmL 94*
Fresh, Edith McCullough 1942- *WhoBlA 94*
Freshwater, Donald Cole 1924- *Who 94*
Freshwater, Michael Felix 1948- *WhoAm 94, WhoScEn 94*
Freshwater, Paul Ross 1941- *WhoMW 93*
Fresiello, Deborah Ann 1964- *WhoFI 94*
Fresnay, Pierre d1975 *WhoHol 92*
Fresnel, Augustin Jean 1788-1827 *WorScD*
Fresno, Fernando d1949 *WhoHol 92*
Fresno, Leonides 1927- *WhoHisp 94*
Fresno Larrain, Juan Francisco 1914- *IntWW 93*
Freso, Tibor 1918-1967 *NewGrDO*
Frésquez, Edward J. *WhoHisp 94*
Fresquez, Ernest C. 1955- *WhoHisp 94*
Fresquez, Ralph E. 1934- *WhoHisp 94*
Frésquez, Sonny *WhoHisp 94*
Fresson, Bernard 1933- *WhoHol 92*
Freston, Thomas E. 1945- *WhoFI 94*
Freter, Mark Allen 1947- *WhoWest 94*
Frets, Barbara J. *WhoAmA 93*

Fretter, T. H. 1946- *WrDr 94*
Fretter, William Bache 1916-1991 *WhAm 10*
Fretthold, Timothy Jon 1949- *WhoAm 94, WhoAmL 94, WhoFI 94*
Fretwell, Carl Quention, II 1951- *WhoBlA 94*
Fretwell, Elbert Kirtley, Jr. 1923- *WhoAm 94*
Fretwell, Elizabeth *Who 94*
Fretwell, Elizabeth 1920- *NewGrDO*
Fretwell, Estil Van 1952- *WhoAmP 93*
Fretwell, (Major) John (Emsley) 1930- *Who 94*
Fretwell, John Emsley 1930- *IntWW 93*
Fretwell, Lincoln Darwin 1944- *WhoWest 94*
Fretwell, Nancy Houx 1944- *WhoAmP 93*
Freud, Anna 1895- *WhAm 10*
Freud, Clement (Raphael) 1924- *Who 94*
Freud, Clement (Raphael), Sir 1924- *WrDr 94*
Freud, Lucian 1922- *IntWW 93, Who 94*
Freud, Nicholas S. 1942- *WhoAmL 94*
Freud, Sigmund *BlmGWL*
Freud, Sigmund 1856-1939 *BlmGEL, EncSPD, TwCLC 52 [port]*
Freud, Sophie 1924- *WrDr 94*
Freudberg, Seth D. 1959- *WhoIns 94*
Freudenberger, C(arlton) Dean 1930- *WrDr 94*
Freudenberger, Herbert Justin 1926- *WhoAm 94, WrDr 94*
Freudenberger, Herman 1922- *WhoAm 94, WrDr 94*
Freudenburg, William R. 1951- *WhoMW 93, WhoScEn 94*
Freudenheim, Jo L. 1952- *WhoScEn 94*
Freudenheim, Milton B. 1927- *WhoAm 94*
Freudenheim, Nina *WhoAmA 93*
Freudenheim, Tom Lippmann 1937- *WhoAm 94, WhoAmA 93*
Freudenstein, Ferdinand 1926- *WhoAm 94, WhoScEn 94*
Freudenthal, Ralph Ira 1940- *WhoScEn 94*
Freudenthal, Steven F. 1949- *WhoAmP 93*
Freudenthal, Steven Franklin 1949- *WhoAm 94*
Freudmann, Axel I. 1946- *WhoIns 94*
Freund, Charles Gibson 1923- *WhoAm 94*
Freund, Doris Isabelle 1920- *WhoAmP 93*
Freund, Eckhard 1940- *WhoAm 94, WhoScEn 94*
Freund, Emma Frances 1922- *WhoAm 94, WhoScEn 94*
Freund, Fred A. 1928- *WhoAm 94*
Freund, Fredric S. 1930- *WhoAm 94, WhoFI 94*
Freund, Gerald 1930- *WhoAm 94*
Freund, Harry Louis 1905- *WhoAmA 93*
Freund, James Coleman 1934- *WhoAm 94, WhoAmL 94*
Freund, Karl 1890-1969 *HorFD [port], IntDcF 2-4 [port]*
Freund, Lambert Ben 1942- *WhoAm 94, WhoScEn 94*
Freund, Mitchell David 1953- *WhoAm 94*
Freund, Morton 1900-1990 *WhAm 10*
Freund, Paul Abraham 1908-1992 *WhAm 10*
Freund, Pepsi 1938- *WhoAmA 93*
Freund, Philip 1909- *WrDr 94*
Freund, Richard L. 1921- *WhoAm 94*
Freund, Ronald S. 1934- *WhoAm 94*
Freund, Tibor 1910- *WhoAmA 93*
Freund, Will Frederick 1916- *WhoAmA 93*
Freund, William Curt 1926- *WhoAm 94*
Freundlich, August L. 1924- *WhoAmA 93*
Freund-Rosenthal, Miriam Kottler 1906- *IntWW 93*
Frevert, Donald Kent 1950- *WhoScEn 94, WhoWest 94*
Frevert, James Wilmot 1922- *WhoFI 94*
Frew, Bud L. 1933- *WhoFI 94*
Frew, Henry Lorimer 1933- *WhoWest 94*
Frew, Patricia A. 1953- *WhoAmP 93*
Frewer, Glyn (Mervyn Louis) 1931- *WrDr 94*
Frewer, Matt 1958- *IntMPA 94, WhoHol 92*
Frewin, Anthony 1947- *EncSF 93*
Frey, Albert 1903- *WhoAm 94*
Frey, Albert Wesley 1898- *WhAm 10*
Frey, Andrew Lewis 1938- *WhoAm 94*
Frey, Arno d1961 *WhoHol 92*
Frey, Barbara Louise 1952- *WhoAmA 93*
Frey, Betty Jean 1914- *WhoWest 94*
Frey, Callie d1948 *WhoHol 92*
Frey, Charles Frederick 1929- *WhoAm 94*
Frey, Christian Miller 1923- *WhoAm 94*
Frey, Dale Franklin 1932- *WhoAm 94, WhoFI 94*
Frey, Donald Nelson 1923- *WhoAm 94*
Frey, Donald Peter 1967- *WhoMW 93*
Frey, Edward John 1910-1988 *WhAm 10*
Frey, Eric d1988 *WhoHol 92*
Frey, Erwin F. 1892-1967 *WhoAmA 93N*

Frey, Francesca *WhoAsA 94*
Frey, Frederick August 1938- *WhoAm 94*
Frey, Frederick James 1950- *WhoIns 94*
Frey, Gerard Louis 1914- *WhoAm 94*
Frey, Glenn *WhoHol 92*
Frey, Glenn 1948- *WhoAm 94*
Frey, Harley Harrison, Jr. 1920- *WhoMW 93*
Frey, Herman S. 1920- *WhoAm 94, WhoFI 94*
Frey, Jacob Benjamin 1875-1957 *EncNAR*
Frey, James McKnight 1932- *WhoAm 94*
Frey, James N. *EncSF 93*
Frey, John Thomas 1957- *WhoAmL 94*
Frey, Joseph Richard 1897-1990 *WhAm 10*
Frey, Kenneth O. *WhoAmP 93*
Frey, Laura Marie 1958- *WhoMW 93*
Frey, Leonard d1988 *WhoHol 92*
Frey, Martin Alan 1939- *WhoAm 94*
Frey, Maurice d1993 *NewYTBS 93*
Frey, Nathaniel d1970 *WhoHol 92*
Frey, Paul 1942- *NewGrDO*
Frey, Robert G. *WhoAmP 93*
Frey, Robert Imbrie 1943- *WhoAm 94, WhoFI 94*
Frey, Robert Mark 1928- *WhoAmL 94*
Frey, Robert Mark 1954- *WhoMW 93*
Frey, Sami 1937- *WhoHol 92*
Frey, Stuart Macklin 1925- *WhoAm 94*
Frey, Viola 1933- *WhoAmA 93*
Frey, William Carl 1930- *WhoAm 94*
Freyberg, Baron d1993 *Who 94N*
Freyberg, Baron 1970- *Who 94*
Freyberg, Dale Wayne 1927- *WhoScEn 94*
Freyberg, Paul 1923- *WrDr 94*
Freyberg, Paul (Richard) 1923-1993 *ConAu 141*
Freyberger, Manfred d1981 *WhoHol 92*
Freycinet, Louis-Claude De Saulces De 1779-1842 *WhWE*
Freyd, Peter John 1936- *WhoAm 94*
Freyd, William Pattinson 1933- *WhoAm 94, WhoFI 94*
Freydberg, Margaret Howe *DrAPF 93*
Freydis fl. 100-?- *WhWE*
Freyer, Achim 1934- *NewGrDO*
Freyer, Charles C. 1947- *WhoAmL 94*
Freyermuth, Clifford L. *WhoScEn 94*
Freymann, Raymond Florent 1952- *WhoScEn 94*
Freymann, Vance Gordon King 1959- *WhoFI 94*
Freymiller, Mary Jean 1933- *WhoMW 93*
Freymond, Jacques 1911- *IntWW 93*
Freymuth, Peter 1936- *WhoWest 94*
Freyndlikh, Alisa Brunovna 1934- *IntWW 93*
Freyre, Ernesto, Jr. 1942- *WhoHisp 94*
Freyre, Frank 1948- *WhoMW 93*
Freyss, David 1933- *WhoAm 94*
Freytag, Donald Ashe 1937- *WhoAm 94*
Freytag, Gustav 1816-1895 *DcLB 129 [port]*
Freytag, Lucy 1941- *WhoAmP 93*
Freytag, Richard Arthur 1933- *WhoFI 94*
Freytag, Sharon Nelson 1943- *WhoAmL 94*
Frezza, Bernard, Jr. 1952- *WhoAmP 93*
Frezza, Robert 1956- *EncSF 93*
Frezzolini, Erminia 1818-1884 *NewGrDO*
Frezzolini, Giuseppe 1789-1861 *NewGrDO*
Fri, Robert Wheeler 1935- *WhoAm 94, WhoAmP 93*
Friant, Charles 1890-1947 *NewGrDO*
Friar, Kimon d1993 *NewYTBS 93*
Friar, Kimon 1911-1993 *ConAu 141*
Friar, Martha Jane 1952- *WhoAmL 94*
Frias, Christina R. 1938- *WhoHisp 94*
Frias, Francisco M. *WhoHisp 94*
Frias, Jaime Luis 1933- *WhoAm 94*
Frias, Linda *WhoHisp 94*
Frias, Louis A. *WhoHisp 94*
Frias, Louis Jaime 1946- *WhoHisp 94*
Frias, Luz Maria 1962- *WhoHisp 94*
Frias, Rafael *WhoAmP 93*
Friauf, Katherine Elizabeth 1956- *WhoFI 94*
Friaz, Guadalupe Mendez 1953- *WhoHisp 94*
Fribec, Kresimir 1908- *NewGrDO*
Friberg, Arnold 1913- *WhoAmA 93, WhoWest 94*
Friberg, John E. 1942- *WhoAmL 94*
Friberth, Carl 1736-1816 *NewGrDO*
Fribley, Jack M. 1948- *WhoAmL 94*
Fribourg, Michel *WhoAm 94, WhoFI 94*
Fribourgh, James Henry 1926- *WhoAm 94, WhoScEn 94*
Fricano, John C. d1993 *NewYTBS 93*
Fricano, John Charles 1930- *WhoFI 94*
Fricano, Tom S. 1930- *WhoAmA 93*
Fricano, Tom Salvatore 1930- *WhoWest 94*
Fricci, Antonietta 1840-1912 *NewGrDO*
Frichot, Sylvette *WhoWomW 91*
Frick 1915- *WhoWest 94*

Friedman, Josh(ua M.) 1941- *ConAu 140*
Friedman, Joshua M. 1941- *WhoAm 94*
Friedman, Jules Daniel 1928- *WhoWest 94*
Friedman, K. Bruce 1929- *WhoAm 94*
Friedman, Ken *DrAPF 93*
Friedman, Ken 1949- *WhoAmA 93*
Friedman, Kenneth Michael 1945- *WhoScEn 94*
Friedman, Kenneth Todd *WhoWest 94*
Friedman, Kinky *WrDr 94*
Friedman, Lawrence Jacob 1940- *WhoMW 93*
Friedman, Lawrence M. 1930- *WhoAm 94, WrDr 94*
Friedman, Lawrence Meir 1930- *ConAu 43NR*
Friedman, Lawrence Milton 1945- *WhoIns 94*
Friedman, Lawrence Samuel 1953- *WhoScEn 94*
Friedman, Lewis Richard 1941- *WhoAmL 94*
Friedman, Linda A. 1952- *WhoAm 94, WhoAmL 94*
Friedman, Louis Frank 1941- *WhoAm 94*
Friedman, Lyman Guettel 1918- *WhoAmL 94*
Friedman, Lynn 1933- *WhoMW 93*
Friedman, Maralyn *DrAPF 93*
Friedman, Marcia *WhoAm 94*
Friedman, Marion 1918- *WhoScEn 94*
Friedman, Mark 1932- *WhoScEn 94*
Friedman, Mark J. 1952- *WhoAmL 94*
Friedman, Martin 1925- *WhoAm 94, WhoAmA 93*
Friedman, Martin Burton 1927- *WhoAm 94*
Friedman, Marvin Ross *WhoAmA 93*
Friedman, Maurice Stanley 1921- *WhoAm 94*
Friedman, Max 1953- *WhoAmL 94*
Friedman, Melvin 1930- *WhoAm 94*
Friedman, Melvin J. 1928- *WrDr 94*
Friedman, Melvin Jack 1928- *WhoAm 94*
Friedman, Meyer 1910- *WhoAm 94*
Friedman, Michael 1949- *WhoAmP 93*
Friedman, Michael Howard 1944- *WhoWest 94*
Friedman, Michael Jan 1955- *EncSF 93*
Friedman, Michael Lee 1947- *WhoMW 93*
Friedman, Michael Phillip 1951- *WhoAmL 94*
Friedman, Mickey 1944- *WhoAm 94*
Friedman, Miles 1950- *WhoAm 94*
Friedman, Milton 1912- *AmSocL [port], IntWW 93, Who 94, WhoAm 94, WhoFI 94, WhoWest 94, WrDr 94*
Friedman, Morton Lee 1932- *WhoAm 94*
Friedman, Moshe 1936- *WhoScEn 94*
Friedman, Murray 1926- *WhoAm 94, WhoAmP 93*
Friedman, Myles Ivan 1924- *WhoAm 94*
Friedman, Nancy Bengis *DrAPF 93*
Friedman, Neal Joel 1940- *WhoAmL 94*
Friedman, Neil Stuart 1934- *WhoFI 94*
Friedman, Norman *DrAPF 93*
Friedman, Norman 1925- *WrDr 94*
Friedman, Paul *DrAPF 93*
Friedman, Paul 1931- *WhoAm 94*
Friedman, Paul 1937- *WrDr 94*
Friedman, Paul D. 1953- *WhoAmP 93*
Friedman, Paul Jay 1937- *WhoAm 94*
Friedman, Paul Lawrence 1944- *WhoAm 94, WhoAmL 94*
Friedman, Paula Naomi 1939- *WhoWest 94*
Friedman, Peter *WhoHol 92*
Friedman, Philip (J.) *ConAu 141*
Friedman, Philip Harvey 1941- *WhoScEn 94*
Friedman, Ralph 1904- *WhAm 10*
Friedman, Ralph 1922- *WhoAm 94*
Friedman, Raymond 1922- *WhoAm 94*
Friedman, Reuben Isidore 1946- *WhoAmL 94*
Friedman, Richard *DrAPF 93*
Friedman, Richard Everett 1942- *WhoAm 94*
Friedman, Richard Harry 1952- *WhoAmL 94*
Friedman, Richard Lee 1950- *WhoMW 93*
Friedman, Richard S. 1944- *WhoAmL 94*
Friedman, Robert 1947- *WhoAm 94*
Friedman, Robert G. 1945- *WhoAmL 94*
Friedman, Robert Jay 1948- *WhoScEn 94*
Friedman, Robert Jeffrey 1957- *WhoFI 94*
Friedman, Robert L. 1930- *IntMPA 94*
Friedman, Robert L. 1943- *WhoFI 94*
Friedman, Robert Laurence 1943- *WhoAm 94, WhoAmL 94*
Friedman, Robert Lee 1930- *WhoAm 94*
Friedman, Robert Michael 1950- *WhoAm 94, WhoAmL 94, WhoFI 94*
Friedman, Robert Morris 1932- *WhoScEn 94*
Friedman, Robert N. *WhoFI 94*
Friedman, Robert Sidney 1927- *WhoAm 94*
Friedman, Ronald Marvin 1930- *WhoAm 94, WhoScEn 94*
Friedman, Roselyn L. 1942- *WhoAm 94*
Friedman, Rosemary 1929- *WrDr 94*
Friedman, Roy *DrAPF 93*
Friedman, S. L. *DrAPF 93*
Friedman, Sabra *WhoAmA 93*
Friedman, Sally Ceila 1932- *WhoAmA 93*
Friedman, Samuel Selig 1935- *WhoAm 94, WhoAmL 94*
Friedman, Sander Berl 1927- *WhoScEn 94*
Friedman, Sanford *DrAPF 93*
Friedman, Saul Robert 1946- *WhoAmL 94*
Friedman, Scott Edward 1958- *WhoAmL 94*
Friedman, Seymour Mark 1917- *IntMPA 94*
Friedman, Sharon Mae 1943- *WhoScEn 94*
Friedman, Sheila Natasha Simrod *DrAPF 93*
Friedman, Shelly Arnold 1949- *WhoAm 94, WhoScEn 94, WhoWest 94*
Friedman, Sonya *DrAPF 93*
Friedman, Stanley 1922- *WhoWest 94*
Friedman, Stanley 1925- *WhoAm 94, WhoMW 93*
Friedman, Stanley David 1930- *WhoAmL 94*
Friedman, Stanley Joseph 1928-1992 *WhAm 10*
Friedman, Stephen 1937- *IntMPA 94*
Friedman, Stephen James 1938- *WhoAm 94, WhoAmL 94, WhoFI 94*
Friedman, Steven 1945- *WhoAm 94*
Friedman, Steven Lewis 1946- *WhoAm 94, WhoAmL 94*
Friedman, Steven M. 1955- *WhoAm 94, WhoFI 94*
Friedman, Sue Tyler 1925- *WhoFI 94*
Friedman, Sydney M. 1916- *WhoAm 94*
Friedman, Terry B. 1949- *WhoAmP 93*
Friedman, Thomas L(oren) 1953- *WrDr 94*
Friedman, Tod H. 1962- *WhoAmL 94*
Friedman, Townsend B., Jr. 1940- *WhoAmP 93*
Friedman, Victor Stanley 1933- *WhoAm 94*
Friedman, Wilbur Harvey 1907- *WhoAm 94*
Friedman, Will Joel 1950- *WhoWest 94*
Friedman, William Hersh 1938- *WhoAm 94*
Friedman, Yaakov Yosef 1897-1993 *NewYTBS 93*
Friedmann, Adolph Edward 1922- *WhoFI 94*
Friedmann, David Scott 1964- *WhoMW 93*
Friedmann, Elizabeth 1941- *ConAu 142*
Friedmann, Emerich Imre 1921- *WhoAm 94, WhoScEn 94*
Friedmann, Jacques-Henri 1932- *Who 94*
Friedmann, John 1926- *ConAu 41NR*
Friedmann, Mark Alan 1960- *WhoMW 93*
Friedmann, Paul 1933- *WhoScEn 94*
Friedmann, Peretz Peter 1938- *WhoAm 94, WhoWest 94*
Friedmann, Shraga d1970 *WhoHol 92*
Friedmann, Thomas *DrAPF 93*
Friedmann, Yohanan 1936- *WrDr 94*
Friedman Phillips, Pauline 1918- *WhoAm 94*
Friednash, Douglas Jay 1962- *WhoAmP 93*
Friedner, Lewis R. 1956- *WhoAmP 93*
Friedrich, II *NewGrDO*
Friedrich, Charles H., III 1947- *WhoAmL 94*
Friedrich, Charles William 1943- *WhoMW 93*
Friedrich, Christopher Andrew 1956- *WhoScEn 94*
Friedrich, Dwight P. 1913- *WhoAmP 93*
Friedrich, Gotz 1930- *NewGrDO*
Friedrich, John *WhoHol 92*
Friedrich, Paul *DrAPF 93*
Friedrich, Paul 1927- *WhoAm 94, WrDr 94*
Friedrich, Robert Edmund 1918- *WhoAm 94*
Friedrich, Rose Marie 1941- *WhoFI 94, WhoMW 93*
Friedrich, Stephen Miro 1932- *WhoAm 94*
Friedrich, W. 1805?-1879? *NewGrDO*
Friedrich, William M. 1949- *WhoAmL 94*
Friedrich, William R. 1943- *WhoAmL 94*
Friedrich-Patterson, Evelyn Beth 1953- *WhoFI 94*
Friedrichs, Betty Josephine 1960- *WhoWest 94*
Friedrichs, Fritz 1849-1918 *NewGrDO*
Friedrich von Hausen c. 1171-1190 *DcLB 138 [port]*
Friedt, James P. 1942- *WhoAmL 94*
Friel, Arthur O(lney) 1885-1959 *EncSF 93*
Friel, Bernard Preston 1930- *WhoAm 94*
Friel, Brian 1929- *ConDr 93, IntDcT 2, IntWW 93, Who 94, WhoAm 94, WrDr 94*
Friel, Daniel Denwood, Sr. 1920- *WhoAm 94*
Friel, Thomas J., Jr. 1951- *WhoAmL 94*
Friel, Thomas Patrick 1943- *WhoAm 94*
Frieling, Gerald Harvey, Jr. 1930- *WhoAm 94*
Frieling, Leonard Ira 1951- *WhoAmL 94*
Frieling, Thomas Jerome 1953- *WhoAm 94*
Friels, Colin *IntMPA 94*
Friels, Colin 1954- *WhoHol 92*
Frieman, Edward Allan 1926- *WhoAm 94, WhoWest 94*
Friemann, Witold 1889-1977 *NewGrDO*
Friemel, Jerome L. 1932- *WhoAmP 93*
Friend, Alexander Lloyd 1960- *WhoScEn 94*
Friend, Amy Susan 1958- *WhoAmP 93*
Friend, Archibald Gordon 1912- *Who 94*
Friend, Barbara *DrAPF 93*
Friend, Bernard Ernest 1924- *Who 94*
Friend, Brian Edward 1959- *WhoFI 94*
Friend, Cynthia M. 1955- *WhoAm 94, WhoScEn 94*
Frien D., David 1899-1978 *WhoAmA 93N*
Friend, David Robert 1956- *WhoWest 94*
Friend, Ed *EncSF 93*
Friend, Edward Armand 1921- *WhoAmL 94*
Friend, Edward Malcolm, Jr. *WhoAm 94*
Friend, Edward Malcolm, III 1946- *WhoAm 94, WhoAmL 94*
Friend, Helen Margaret 1931- *WhoMW 93*
Friend, Jed 1958- *WhoWest 94*
Friend, Jonathan Joseph 1955- *WhoAm 94*
Friend, Kelsey E. 1922- *WhoAmP 93*
Friend, Lionel 1945- *IntWW 93, NewGrDO, Who 94*
Friend, Louise d1976 *WhoHol 92*
Friend, Oscar J(erome) 1897-1963 *EncSF 93*
Friend, Patricia M. 1931- *WhoAmA 93*
Friend, Peter Michael *WhoAm 94*
Friend, Philip 1915- *WhoHol 92*
Friend, Phyllis (Muriel) 1922- *Who 94*
Friend, Rex Duane 1954- *WhoAmL 94*
Friend, Richard Henry 1953- *Who 94*
Friend, Robert *DrAPF 93*
Friend, Robert 1913- *WrDr 94*
Friend, Robert Nathan 1930- *WhoMW 93*
Friend, Ronald 1943- *WhoAmL 94*
Friend, Theodore Wood, III 1931- *WhoAm 94*
Friend, Walter William, Jr. 1920-1989 *WhAm 10*
Friend, William Benedict 1931- *WhoAm 94*
Friend, William C. *WhoAmP 93*
Friend, William Kagay 1946- *WhoAm 94*
Friendly, Fred W. 1915- *IntMPA 94, IntWW 93, WhoAm 94, WrDr 94*
Friendly, Lynda E. *WhoAm 94*
Friermood, Elisabeth H(amilton) 1903-1992 *WrDr 94N*
Frierson, Charles Davis, III 1932- *WhoAmP 93*
Frierson, Daniel K. 1942- *WhoFI 94*
Frierson, Harry L., Jr. *WhoAmP 93*
Frierson, Herb *WhoAmP 93*
Fries, Arthur Lawrence 1937- *WhoFI 94*
Fries, Charles W. 1928- *IntMPA 94*
Fries, David Samuel 1945- *WhoWest 94*
Fries, Donald E. 1943- *WhoIns 94*
Fries, Donald Eugene 1943- *WhoAm 94*
Fries, Gregory Thomas 1966- *WhoFI 94*
Fries, James Franklin 1938- *WhoAm 94*
Fries, James Lawrence 1932- *WhoAm 94*
Fries, Joseph Michael 1937- *WhoAm 94*
Fries, Kenny *DrAPF 93*
Fries, Lita Linda 1942- *WhoWest 94*
Fries, Marilyn Sibley 1945- *WhoMW 93*
Fries, Maureen Holmberg 1931- *WhoAm 94*
Fries, Otto H. d1938 *WhoHol 92*
Fries, Richard James 1940- *Who 94*
Fries, Robert Francis 1911- *WhoAm 94*
Fries, Sharon Lavonne 1959- *WhoBlA 94*
Friese, George Ralph 1936- *WhoAm 94, WhoFI 94*
Friese, Nancy Marlene 1948- *WhoAmA 93*
Friese, Robert Charles 1943- *WhoAm 94, WhoAmL 94, WhoWest 94*
Friesecke, Raymond Francis 1937- *WhoAm 94, WhoFI 94, WhoWest 94*
Friesel, Claude Wayne 1935- *WhoWest 94*
Friesel, Evyatar 1930- *WrDr 94*
Friesen, Henry George 1934- *WhoAm 94, WhoScEn 94*
Friesen, Oris Dewayne 1940- *WhoWest 94*
Friesen, Richard Aldon 1928- *WhoAm 94*
Friesen, Wolfgang Otto 1942- *WhoAm 94*
Frieser, Cordula 1950- *WhoWomW 91*
Friesner, Esther M. 1951- *ConAu 41NR*
Friesz, Donald Stuart 1929- *WhoWest 94*
Friesz, Ray Lee 1930- *WhoAmA 93*
Frietsche, Antonietta *NewGrDO*
Frietze, José Victor 1943- *WhoHisp 94*
Friez, Rick Earl 1945- *WhoWest 94*
Frieze, Alan Michael 1945- *WhoScEn 94*
Frieze, Harold Delbert 1943- *WhoAmL 94*
Friganza, Trixie d1955 *WhoHol 92*
Frigel, Per 1750-1842 *NewGrDO*
Frigerio, Alejandro 1955- *WhoFI 94*
Frigerio, Charles Straith 1957- *WhoAmL 94*
Frigerio, Ezio 1930- *NewGrDO*
Frigerio, Ismael 1955- *WhoHisp 94*
Frigerio, Ronald Joseph 1940- *WhoAmP 93*
Frigge, Thomas Richard 1952- *WhoMW 93*
Friggebo, Birgit 1941- *IntWW 93, WhoWomW 91*
Friggens, A. *EncSF 93*
Friggens, Thomas George 1949- *WhoAm 94, WhoMW 93*
Frigo, James Peter Paul 1942- *WhoFI 94*
Frigoletto, Fredric David, Jr. 1933- *WhoAm 94*
Frigon, Henry Frederick 1934- *WhoFI 94*
Frigon, Judith Ann 1945- *WhoWest 94*
Frihd, Gertrud d1984 *WhoHol 92*
Friis, Erik J(ohan) 1913- *WrDr 94*
Friis, Erik Johan 1913- *WhoAm 94*
Friis, Henning Kristian 1911- *IntWW 93*
Friman, Alice *DrAPF 93*
Frimer, Norman E. d1993 *NewYTBS 93 [port]*
Frimerman, Leslie 1943- *WhoAm 94*
Friml, (Charles) Rudolf 1879-1972 *NewGrDO*
Frimmer, Paul Norman 1945- *WhoAm 94, WhoAmL 94*
Frimpong-Ansah, Jonathan Herbert 1930- *IntWW 93*
Frinak, Sheila Jo 1963- *WhoScEn 94*
Frindall, Bill 1939- *WrDr 94*
Frindall, William Howard 1939- *Who 94*
Frings, Manfred Servatius 1925- *WhoMW 93*
Frink, Elisabeth d1993 *IntWW 93N*
Frink, Elisabeth 1930- *IntWW 93*
Frink, Elisabeth 1930-1993 *NewYTBS 93*
Frink, Elisabeth Jean d1993 *Who 94N*
Frink, Frederick T. 1920- *WhoAmP 93*
Frink, Jno. Spence 1930- *WhoIns 94*
Frink, John Spencer 1930- *WhoBlA 94*
Frink, Ronald Murice 1959- *WhoBlA 94*
Frink, Samuel H. 1944- *WhoBlA 94*
Frink Reed, Caroliese Ingrid 1949- *WhoBlA 94*
Frinsko, F. Paul 1939- *WhoAmL 94*
Frinta, Mojmir Svatopluk 1922- *WhoAmA 93*
Frinton, Freddie d1968 *WhoHol 92*
Friou, George Jacob 1919- *WhoAm 94*
Fripp, Alfred Thomas 1899- *Who 94*
Fris, Maria d1961 *WhoHol 92*
Frisari, Girolamo fl. 1678-1686 *NewGrDO*
Frisbee, Don Calvin 1923- *WhoAm 94, WhoWest 94*
Frisbee, John Lee 1943- *WhoAm 94*
Frisbee, Lee *DrAPF 93*
Frisbie, Curtis Lynn, Jr. 1943- *WhoAm 94, WhoAmL 94*
Frisbie, Marlene Ann 1955- *WhoMW 93*
Frisby, Audrey Mary *Who 94*
Frisby, David Henry 1951- *WhoMW 93*
Frisby, Herbert Russell, Jr. 1950- *WhoAm 94, WhoAmL 94*
Frisby, James Curtis 1930- *WhoAm 94*
Frisby, Mildred d1939 *WhoHol 92*
Frisby, Robert W. 1920- *WhoAmP 93*
Frisby, Roger Harry Kilbourne 1921- *Who 94*
Frisby, Terence 1932- *ConDr 93, Who 94, WrDr 94*
Frisch, Fred I. 1935- *WhoFI 94*
Frisch, Harry David 1954- *WhoAm 94, WhoAmL 94*
Frisch, Harry Lloyd 1928- *WhoAm 94, WhoScEn 94*
Frisch, Henry F. 1947- *WhoAmL 94*
Frisch, Henry Jonathan 1944- *WhoAm 94*
Frisch, Ivan Thomas 1937- *WhoScEn 94*
Frisch, Jonathan David 1963- *WhoWest 94*
Frisch, Joseph 1921- *WhoAm 94*
Frisch, Karl (Ritter) von 1886-1982 *ConAu 42NR*
Frisch, Kurt Charles 1918- *WhoScEn 94*
Frisch, Max (Rudolf) 1911-1991 *IntDcT 2*
Frisch, Max Rudolf 1911-1991 *WhAm 10*
Frisch, Otto Robert *WorScD*
Frisch, Robert A. 1931- *WhoAm 94*
Frisch, Robert Emile 1925- *WhoAm 94*
Frisch, Rose Epstein 1918- *WhoAm 94*
Frisch, Sidney 1899-1987 *WhAm 10*

Frischenmeyer, Michael Leo 1951- WhoFI 94
Frischenschlager, Friedhelm 1943- IntWW 93
Frisches, Axel d1956 WhoHol 92
Frischknecht, Lee Conrad 1928- WhoAm 94, WhoWest 94
Frischkorn, David Ephraim Keasbey, Jr. 1951- WhoFI 94
Frischling, Carl 1937- WhoAm 94
Frischmann, Donald W. 1921- WhoIns 94
Frischmann, Wilem William Who 94
Frischmuth, Barbara 1941- BlmGWL
Frischmuth, Johann Christian 1741-1790 NewGrDO
Frischmuth, Robert Alfred 1940- WhoFI 94
Friscia, John Scott 1958- WhoAmL 94
Frisco, Joe d1958 WhoHol 92
Frisco, Joe 1890-1958 WhoCom
Frisco, Louis Joseph 1923- WhoAm 94
Frisell, Sonja 1937- NewGrDO
Frisell, Wilhelm Richard 1920- WhoAm 94
Frisell-Schroder, Sonja Bettie 1937- WhoAm 94
Frishe, Jim 1946- WhoAmP 93
Frishkoff, Patricia Ann 1944- WhoWest 94
Frishkoff, Paul WhoWest 94
Frishman, Dan WhoHol 92
Frishman, Eileen Steinberg 1946- WhoWest 94
Frishmuth, Harriet Whitney 1880-1979 WhoAmA 93N
Frisina, Gary Anthony 1949- WhoFI 94
Frisina, Robert Dana 1955- WhoAm 94
Frisinger, Haakan H. J. 1928- IntWW 93
Frisk, Ruth Davis 1916- WhoMW 93
Frisman, Roger Lawrence 1952- WhoMW 93
Frison, Lee A. 1941- WhoBlA 94
Frison, Paul Maurice 1937- WhoAm 94
Frisque, Alvin Joseph 1923- WhoAm 94
Frisque, Gilles 1943- WhoScEn 94
Frisse, Ronald Joseph 1966- WhoScEn 94
Frist, Thomas Fearn 1910- WhoAm 94
Frist, Thomas Fearn, Jr. 1938- WhoAm 94, WhoFI 94
Frist, William H. 1952- WrDr 94
Fristad, Mary Antonette 1959- WhoMW 93
Fristedt, Hans 1943- WhoFI 94
Fristoe, John Robert 1941- WhoMW 93
Friswold, Fred Ravndahl 1937- WhoAm 94
Fritch, Charles E. c. 1920- EncSF 93
Fritch, Le Ann 1937- WhoAmP 93
Fritcher, Earl Edwin 1923- WhoScEn 94, WhoWest 94
Fritchie, Barbara d1989 WhoHol 92
Frith, Anthony Ian Donald 1929- Who 94
Frith, David Edward John 1937- Who 94
Frith, Donald Alfred 1918- Who 94
Frith, Douglas Kyle 1931- WhoAmL 94
Frith, Edward Leslie 1919- Who 94
Frith, Francis 1822-1898 DcNaB MP
Frith, Leslie d1961 WhoHol 92
Frith, Margaret WhoAm 94
Frith, Richard Michael Cokayne 1949- Who 94
Frith, Royce Herbert 1923- WhoAm 94
Frith, Tom d1945 WhoHol 92
Fritsch, Albert J(oseph) 1933- WrDr 94
Fritsch, Billy Dale, Jr. 1956- WhoFI 94
Fritsch, Bruno 1926- ConAu 41NR
Fritsch, Elizabeth 1940- Who 94
Fritsch, Willy d1973 WhoHol 92
Fritsche, Claudia 1952- IntWW 93
Fritsche, Thomas Richard 1951- WhoWest 94
Fritschel, Ted C. 1932- WhoAmP 93
Fritschler, A. Lee 1937- WhoAm 94
Fritter, Randy Joe 1955- WhoAmP 93
Fritton, Karl Andrew 1955- WhoAmL 94
Fritts, Harold Clark 1928- WhoAm 94, WhoScEn 94
Fritts, Harry Washington, Jr. 1921- WhoAm 94
Fritts, John Frederick 1934- WhoAm 94
Fritts, Jon Mark 1961- WhoWest 94
Fritts, Mary Bahr 1938- WrDr 94
Fritz, Bruce Morrell 1947- WhoAm 94
Fritz, Cecil Morgan 1921- WhoAm 94, WhoFI 94
Fritz, Charles Eugene 1926- WhoMW 93
Fritz, Edward William 1953- WhoScEn 94
Fritz, George H. 1919- WhoAmP 93
Fritz, Harry 1937- WhoAmP 93
Fritz, Hillary Jane 1956- WhoFI 94
Fritz, Jack Wayne 1927- WhoAm 94
Fritz, James Sherwood 1924- WhoAm 94
Fritz, Jean 1915- TwCYAW, WrDr 94
Fritz, Jean Guttery 1915- WhoAm 94
Fritz, Jock Thane 1952- WhoMW 93
Fritz, Mary G. 1938- WhoAmP 93
Fritz, Moses Kelly 1904- WhoBlA 94
Fritz, Rene Eugene, Jr. 1943- WhoAm 94
Fritz, Roger Jay 1928- WhoAm 94
Fritz, Ruth Ann 1931- WhoAmP 93
Fritz, Samuel 1653-1728 WhWE
Fritz, Terrence Lee 1943- WhoFI 94
Fritz, Thomas G. 1946- WhoAmL 94
Fritz, Thomas Vincent 1934- WhoAm 94, WhoFI 94
Fritz, Walter Helmut 1929- IntWW 93
Fritz, William Warren 1943- WhoAm 94
Fritze, James Lyle, Sr. 1959- WhoFI 94
Fritzell, Erik Kenneth 1946- WhoMW 93
Fritzell, Peter A(lgren) 1940- WrDr 94
Fritzell, Peter Algren 1940- WhoMW 93
Fritzeri, Alessandro Mario Antonio NewGrDO
Fritzhand, Gary I. 1943- WhoAmL 94
Fritzhand, Marek d1992 IntWW 93N
Fritzke, Audrey Elmere 1933- WhoAm 94
Fritzlen, Thomas L., Jr. 1945- WhoAm 94, WhoFI 94
Fritzler, Gerald J. 1953- WhoAmA 93
Fritzler, Gerald John 1953- WhoWest 94
Fritzsche, Allan W. 1895- WhAm 10
Fritzsche, David J. 1940- WhoWest 94
Fritzsche, Hellmut 1927- WhoAm 94, WhoScEn 94
Frizzel, Teresa R. WhoWest 94
Frizzel, Terry 1927- WhoAmP 93
Frizzell, David Nason WhoAmP 93
Frizzell, Edward William 1946- Who 94
Frizzell, Lefty 1928-1975 ConMus 10 [port]
Frizzell, Lou d1979 WhoHol 92
Frizzell, William Kenneth 1928- WhoAm 94
Frizzelle, Nolan 1921- WhoAmP 93
Frobe, Gert d1988 WhoHol 92
Frobisher, Martin 1535-1594 WhWE [port]
Frock, Edmond Burnell 1910-1991 WhAm 10
Frock, J. Daniel 1940- WhoAm 94
Frodsham, Anthony Freer 1919- Who 94
Frodsham, John David 1930- IntWW 93
Froe, Dreyfus Walter 1914- WhoBlA 94
Froe, Otis David 1912- WhoBlA 94
Froeb, Donald Forrest 1930- WhoAmL 94
Froebe, Gerald Allen 1935- WhoAm 94, WhoAmL 94
Froehlich, Anne Liese 1923- WhoAmP 93
Froehlich, Fritz Edgar 1925- WhoAm 94, WhoScEn 94
Froehlich, Harold Vernon 1932- WhoAm 94, WhoAmP 93
Froehlich, Laurence Alan 1951- WhoAmL 94
Froehlich, Robert Elmer 1942- WhoFI 94, WhoWest 94
Froehlich, Virgil WhoFI 94
Froehlke, Robert Frederick 1922- WhoAm 94
Froelich, Cezar M. 1946- WhoAmL 94
Froelich, Frederick Karl 1946- WhoFI 94
Froelich, Jerome Joseph, Jr. 1943- WhoAmL 94
Froelich, Jerry Walter 1957- WhoWest 94
Froelich, Paul 1897- WhoAmA 93N
Froelich, Susan G. 1951- WhoMW 93
Froelich, Wolfgang Andreas 1927- WhoAm 94
Froelker, Jim 1949- WhoAmP 93
Froemming, Herbert Dean 1936- WhoAm 94
Froes, Walter J. d1958 WhoHol 92
Froeschle, Robert Edward 1918- WhoAm 94
Froese, Robert 1945- EncSF 93
Froese, Victor 1940- WhoAm 94
Froessl, Horst Waldemar 1929- WhoScEn 94
Froewiss, Kenneth Clark 1945- WhoAm 94
Froggatt, Leslie (Trevor) 1920- IntWW 93, Who 94
Froggatt, Peter 1928- Who 94
Frohberg, Regina 1783-1850 BlmGWL
Frohbieter-Mueller, Jo 1934- WhoMW 93
Frohlich, Albrecht 1916- IntWW 93, Who 94
Frohlich, Edward David 1931- WhoAm 94
Frohlich, Jurg Martin 1946- WhoScEn 94
Frohlich, Kenneth 1945- WhoIns 94
Frohlich, Kenneth R. 1945- WhoAm 94
Frohlichstein, Alan 1953- WhoMW 93
Frohlichstein, David Lee 1956- WhoFI 94
Frohling, Edwards S. 1942- WhoAm 94
Frohman, Lawrence Asher 1935- WhoAm 94
Frohman, Roland H. 1928- WhoBlA 94
Frohnen, Richard Gene 1930- WhoWest 94
Frohnmayer, David Braden 1940- WhoAm 94, WhoAmL 94, WhoAmP 93, WhoWest 94
Frohnmayer, John Edward 1942- IntWW 93, WhoAm 94
Frohock, Fred Manuel 1937- WhoAm 94
Frohock, Joan 1939- WhoAm 94
Frohring, Paul Robert WhoAm 94
Froid de Mereaux, Nicolas-Jean Le NewGrDO
Froines, John 1939- HisWorL
Froisland, James Michael 1950- WhoFI 94
Froissart, Jean c. 1337-c. 1410 BlmGEL
Frolich, Gustav d1987 WhoHol 92
Frolich, Henriette 1768-1833 BlmGWL
Frolick, Patricia Mary 1923- WhoAm 94
Frolik, Charles Alan 1945- WhoMW 93
Frolik, Lawrence Anton 1944- WhoAmL 94
Froling, Ewa WhoHol 92
Frolov, Ivan Timofeyevich 1929- IntWW 93
Frolov, Konstantin Vasilievitch 1932- WhoScEn 94
Frolov, Konstantin Vasilyevich 1932- IntWW 93
Frolov, Markian Petrovich 1892-1944 NewGrDO
From, Alvin 1943- WhoAmP 93
From, Arthur Harvey Leigh 1936- WhoMW 93
Froman, Ann WhoAm 94
Froman, Ann 1942- WhoAmA 93
Froman, Jane d1980 WhoHol 92
Froman, Margarita 1890-1970 IntDcB [port]
Froman, Ramon Mitchell 1908-1980 WhoAmA 93N
Froman, Sandra Sue 1949- WhoAm 94, WhoAmL 94
Fromanteel, Ahasuerus 1607-1693 DcNaB MP
Fromberg, Gerald 1925-1977 WhoAmA 93N
Fromberg, Malcolm Hubert 1935- WhoAmL 94
Fromberg, Robert DrAPF 93
Fromboluti, Iona WhoAmA 93
Fromboluti, Sideo 1920- WhoAmA 93
Frome, Michael 1920- WrDr 94
Frome, Milton d1989 WhoHol 92
Fromentin, Christine Anne 1953- WhoAmA 93
Froment-Meurice, Henri 1923- IntWW 93
Fromer, Irene Claire d1993 NewYTBS 93
Fromewick, Richard G. 1944- WhoAmL 94
Fromhagen, Carl, Jr. 1926- WhoAm 94, WhoScEn 94
Fromholz, Haley James 1938- WhoAm 94, WhoAmL 94
Fromkes, Saul d1991 WhAm 10
Fromkin, Victoria Alexandra 1923- WhoAm 94
Fromlet, K. Hubert 1947- WhoScEn 94
Fromm, Alfred 1905- WhoAm 94
Fromm, Arno Henry 1902-1991 WhAm 10
Fromm, David 1939- WhoAm 94
Fromm, Eli 1939- WhoAm 94, WhoScEn 94
Fromm, Erika 1910- WhoAm 94
Fromm, Erwin Frederick 1933- WhoFI 94
Fromm, Hans Walther Herbert 1919- IntWW 93
Fromm, Henry Gordon 1911- WhoAm 94
Fromm, Jeffery Bernard 1947- WhoAmL 94
Fromm, Joseph 1920- WhoAm 94
Fromm, Joseph L. 1930- WhoFI 94
Fromm, Paul Oliver 1923- WhoAm 94
Fromm, Winfield Eric 1918- WhoAm 94
Fromme, Friedrich Karl 1930- IntWW 93
Frommelt, Jeffrey James 1940- WhoAm 94
Frommer, Henry 1943- WhoAm 94, WhoFI 94
Frommer, Peter Leslie 1932- WhoAm 94
Frommhold, Walter 1921- WhoScEn 94
Fromm-Reichmann, F. 1890-1957 EncSPD
Fromowitz, Allen 1948- WhoFI 94
Fromstein, Mitchell S. 1928- IntWW 93, WhoAm 94, WhoFI 94
Froncek-Rankin, Teresa P. WhoIns 94
Frondizi, Arturo 1908- IntWW 93
Frondoni, Angelo 1808?-1891 NewGrDO
Fronek, David N. 1943- WhoAm 94, WhoAmL 94
Fronek, Joseph E 1951- WhoWest 94
Fronk, William Joseph 1925- WhoAm 94
Front, Marshall Bernard 1937- WhoMW 93
Frontai, Jean d1988 WhoHol 92
Frontiere, Dominic 1931- IntMPA 94
Frontiere, Georgia WhoAm 94, WhoWest 94
Frontz, Leslie 1950- WhoAmA 93
Fronza Crepaz, Lucia 1955- WhoWomW 91
Frood, Alan Campbell 1926- Who 94
Froom, William Watkins 1915- WhoAm 94
Froomkin, Joseph 1927- WhoFI 94
Froos, Sylvia WhoHol 92
Frosch, Aaron R. 1924-1989 WhAm 10
Frosch, Robert Alan 1928- WhoAm 94, WhoFI 94, WhoScEn 94
Froseth, Glen WhoAmP 93
Frosh, Brian E. 1946- WhoAmP 93
Fross, Roger Raymond 1940- WhoAm 94
Frossard, Andre 1915- IntWW 93
Frossard, Charles (Keith) 1922- Who 94
Frossi, Paolo 1921- WhoScEn 94
Frost, A. Corwin 1934- WhoFI 94
Frost, Abraham Edward Hardy 1918- Who 94
Frost, Alan d1982 WhoHol 92
Frost, Albert Edward 1914- Who 94
Frost, Barbara Sherry 1948- WhoAmL 94
Frost, Brian Reginald Thomas 1926- WhoMW 93
Frost, Brian Standish 1958- WhoAmL 94
Frost, Carol DrAPF 93
Frost, Celestine DrAPF 93
Frost, Chester R. 1939- WhoAm 94
Frost, David 1939- WhoCom
Frost, David (Paradine) 1939- Who 94, WrDr 94
Frost, David Paradine 1939- IntWW 93, WhoAm 94
Frost, Douglas Van Anden 1910-1989 WhAm 10
Frost, Earle Wesley 1899- WhoAm 94
Frost, Edmund Bowen 1942- WhoAm 94, WhoAmL 94
Frost, Ellen Louise 1945- WhoAm 94
Frost, Everett L. 1942- WhoWest 94
Frost, Felicia Dodee 1956- WhoFI 94
Frost, Frederick George, Jr. 1907-1991 WhAm 10
Frost, George 1720-1796 WhAmRev
Frost, George 1935- Who 94
Frost, Gerald Philip Anthony 1943- Who 94
Frost, Gualter 1628-1652 DcNaB MP
Frost, Horace Wier 1893- WhAm 10
Frost, Hugh A. 1926- WhoBlA 94
Frost, J. Ormond 1927- WhoAm 94
Frost, Jack Martin 1928- WhoScEn 94
Frost, James Arthur 1918- WhoAm 94
Frost, James E. WhoMW 93
Frost, Jason 1952- EncSF 93
Frost, Jeffrey Michael Torbet 1938- Who 94
Frost, Jerry William 1940- WhoAm 94
Frost, Joe Lindell 1933- WhoAm 94
Frost, John 1912-1993 NewYTBS 93
Frost, John Dutton d1993 Who 94N
Frost, John Elliott 1924- WhoFI 94, WhoScEn 94
Frost, John Kingsbury 1922-1990 WhAm 10
Frost, John Wesley, II 1942- WhoAmL 94
Frost, Jonas Martin 1942- WhoAm 94, WhoAmP 93
Frost, Julianne Louise 1958- WhoMW 93
Frost, Kid WhoHisp 94
Frost, Linda Smith 1956- IntMPA 94
Frost, Lindsay WhoHol 92
Frost, Margaret Anne 1935- WhoFI 94, WhoMW 93
Frost, Mark WhoAm 94
Frost, Mark C. ConTFT 11
Frost, Martin 1942- CngDr 93
Frost, Michael Edward 1941- Who 94
Frost, Monica McAsey 1959- WhoMW 93
Frost, Norma W. 1927- WhoAmP 93
Frost, Norman Cooper 1923- WhoAm 94
Frost, O(rcutt) W(illiam) 1926- WrDr 94
Frost, Olivia Pleasants WhoBlA 94
Frost, Philip M. 1948- WhoAmL 94
Frost, Phyllis Irene 1917- Who 94
Frost, Rainer Lindon Cullum 1957- WhoAmL 94
Frost, Richard DrAPF 93
Frost, Robert 1874-1963 AmCulL
Frost, Robert 1939- WhoAm 94
Frost, Robert Edwin 1932- WhoAm 94
Frost, Ronald Edwin 1936- Who 94
Frost, Rose 1950- WhoMW 93
Frost, Ryker 1945- WrDr 94
Frost, S. D. 1930- WhoAmP 93
Frost, S. David 1930- WhoAm 94
Frost, S. Newell 1935- WhoWest 94
Frost, Sadie WhoHol 92
Frost, Stanley 1942- WhoAmL 94, WhoWest 94
Frost, Stanley Brice 1913- WrDr 94
Frost, Stanley F. 1942- WhoAmP 93
Frost, Stuart Homer 1925- WhoAmA 93
Frost, Susan Cooke 1949- WhoScEn 94
Frost, Sydney Who 94
Frost, (Thomas) Sydney 1916- Who 94
Frost, Terence 1915- Who 94
Frost, Terry 1906- WhoHol 92
Frost, Thomas Clayborne 1927- WhoAm 94
Frost, Thomas Pearson 1933- IntWW 93, Who 94
Frost, Warren WhoHol 92
Frost, William Henry 1930- WhoBlA 94
Frost, William Lee 1926- WhoAm 94
Frost, Wilson WhoAmP 93, WhoBlA 94

Frost, Winston Lyle 1958- WhoAmL 94
Frostic, Gwen 1906- WhoMW 93
Frothingham, Octavius Brooks 1822-1895 DcAmReB 2
Frothingham, Thomas Eliot 1926- WhoAm 94
Frouchtben, Bernard 1878-1956 WhoAmA 93N
Froude, James Anthony 1818-1894 NinCLC 43 [port]
Froude, William 1810-1879 WorInv
Froula, James DeWayne 1945- WhoAm 94
Frova, Andrea Fausto 1936- WhoScEn 94
Frowein, Jochen Abraham 1934- IntWW 93
Frowick, Robert Holmes 1929- WhoAm 94
Frowick, Roy Halston WhAm 10
Froy, Martin 1926- Who 94
Frucht, Harold 1953- WhoScEn 94
Fruchtenbaum, Edward 1948- WhoAm 94, WhoFI 94
Fruchter, Benjamin 1914- WrDr 94
Fruchter, Jonathan Sewell 1945- WhoWest 94
Fruchthendler, Fred Barry 1951- WhoWest 94
Fruchtman, Milton A. IntMPA 94
Fruchtman, Milton Allen WhoAm 94
Frudakis, Anthony P. 1953- WhoAmA 93
Frudakis, Evangelos William 1921- WhoAm 94, WhoAmA 93
Frudakis, Gerd Hesness 1952- WhoAmA 93
Frudakis, Zenos 1951- WhoAmA 93
Frudakis, Zenos Antonios 1951- WhoAm 94
Fruechtenicht, Thomas Eric 1940- WhoAmP 93
Frueckert, Rolf Herbert 1945- WhoFI 94
Frueh, Joanna 1948- WhoAmA 93
Fruehling, Rosemary Therese 1933- WhoMW 93
Fruehwald, Edwin Scott 1955- WhoAmL 94
Fruehwald, Kristin G. 1946- WhoAm 94, WhoAmL 94
Fruehwald, Michael R. 1948- WhoAmL 94
Fruet, William 1933- HorFD
Fru-Fru BlmGWL
Frug, Gerald E. 1939- WhoAm 94
Frugoli, Amadeo 1932- IntWW 93
Frugoni, Carlo Innocenzo 1692-1768 NewGrDO
Fruh, Eugen 1914- IntWW 93
Fruhauf, Aline 1907-1978 WhoAmA 93N
Fruhbeck De Burgos, Rafael 1933- IntWW 93, WhoAm 94
Fruin, Robert Cornelius 1925- WhoAm 94
Fruin, Roger Joseph 1915- WhoAmL 94
Fruin, Stephen 1949- WhoAmL 94
Fruin, W. Mark 1943- ConAu 140
Fruit, Karen Brezina 1959- WhoMW 93
Fruit, Melvyn Herschel 1937- WhoAm 94
Fruitman, Frederick Howard 1950- WhoFI 94
Fruitt, Paul N. 1931- WhoAm 94
Frum, Barbara 1937-1992 AnObit 1992
Frum, Carlos M. 1945- WhoHisp 94
Frumerie, (Per) Gunnar (Fredrik) de 1908-1987 NewGrDO
Frumkes, Herbert M. 1926- WhoFI 94
Frumkes, Lewis Burke DrAPF 93
Frumkes, Melvyn Benjamin 1929- WhoAmL 94
Frumkin, Allan 1926- IntWW 93, WhoAm 94, WhoAmA 93
Frumkin, Gene DrAPF 93
Frumkin, Gene 1928- WhoWest 94, WrDr 94
Frungillo, Nicholas Anthony, Jr. 1960- WhoFI 94
Frush, James Carroll, Jr. 1930- WhoWest 94
Fruth, Terence Melling 1938- WhoAmL 94
Fruton, Joseph S(tewart) 1912- WrDr 94
Fruton, Joseph Stewart 1912- IntWW 93
Fruzzetti, Oreste Giorgio 1938- WhoScEn 94
Fry, Albert Joseph 1937- WhoAm 94
Fry, Charles George 1936- WhoMW 93
Fry, Christine L. 1943- WhoMW 93
Fry, Christopher 1907- BlmGEL, ConDr 93, IntDcT 2, IntWW 93, Who 94, WrDr 94
Fry, Clarence Herbert 1926- WhoAm 94
Fry, Craig R. 1952- WhoAmP 93
Fry, Darrell 1963- WhoBlA 94
Fry, Darryl Diamond 1939- WhoFI 94
Fry, David Stow 1949- WhoAmL 94
Fry, Donald C. WhoAmP 93
Fry, Donald Lewis 1924- WhoAm 94, WhoMW 93
Fry, Donald Owen 1921- WhoAm 94
Fry, Donald William d1992 Who 94N
Fry, Doris Hendricks 1918- WhoAm 94
Fry, Earl H. 1947- WhoAm 94
Fry, Edward 1925- WrDr 94
Fry, Edward Donald, II 1956- WhoAmP 93
Fry, Edward F. 1935-1992 WhoAmA 93N
Fry, Elizabeth 1780-1845 HisWorL [port]
Fry, Elizabeth H. W. 1951- WhoAmL 94
Fry, George Sinclair 1936- WhoWest 94
Fry, Hayden 1929- WhoAm 94
Fry, Ian Kelsey 1923- Who 94
Fry, James Wilson 1939- WhoAm 94
Fry, John 1922- Who 94
Fry, John 1930- WhoAm 94
Fry, Jonathan Michael 1937- IntWW 93, Who 94
Fry, K. Edward 1943- WhoAmP 93
Fry, Leroy F. 1918- WhoAmP 93
Fry, Leslie McGee 1913- WhoAmP 93
Fry, Linda Sue 1961- WhoAm 94, WhoWest 94
Fry, Louis Edwin, Jr. 1928- WhoAm 94, WhoBlA 94
Fry, Malcolm Craig 1928- WhoAm 94
Fry, Margaret (Louise) 1931- Who 94
Fry, Marion Golda 1932- IntWW 93
Fry, Maxwell John 1944- WhoAm 94
Fry, Meredith Warren 1924- WhoFI 94
Fry, Michael Graham 1934- WhoAm 94
Fry, Morton Harrison, II 1946- WhoAmL 94
Fry, Peter Derek 1931- Who 94
Fry, Peter George Robin Plantagenet S. Who 94
Fry, Philip Michael 1965- WhoMW 93
Fry, Richard Henry 1900- Who 94
Fry, Ronald Ernest 1925- Who 94
Fry, Rosalie K(ingsmill) 1911-1992 WrDr 94N
Fry, Roy Henry 1931- WhoMW 93
Fry, Shirley 1927- BuCMET [port]
Fry, Simon 1947- WhoBlA 94
Fry, Stephen John 1957- IntWW 93, Who 94
Fry, Thomas 1717?-1772 DcNaB MP
Fry, William Finley, Jr. 1924- WrDr 94
Fry, William Frederick 1921- WhoAm 94
Fry, William Gordon 1909- Who 94
Fry, William Henry 1813-1864 NewGrDO
Fry, William Norman H. Who 94
Fryar, Fred Eric 1962- WhoAmL 94
Fryar, Irving Dale 1962- WhoBlA 94
Fryback, William Max 1921- WhoAmP 93
Fryberg, Abraham 1901- Who 94
Fryberger, Betsy G. 1935- WhoAmA 93
Fryberger, Theodore Kevin 1950- WhoScEn 94
Fryburger, Vernon Ray, Jr. 1918- WhoAm 94
Fryczkowski, Andrzej Witold 1939- WhoMW 93, WhoScEn 94
Fryd, David Steven 1950- WhoScEn 94
Frydman, Paul 1906- WhoMW 93
Frye, Billy Eugene 1933- WhoAm 94
Frye, Charles A(nthony) 1946- BlkWr 2
Frye, Charles Alton 1936- WhoAmP 93
Frye, Charles Anthony 1946- WhoBlA 94
Frye, Clayton Wesley, Jr. 1930- WhoFI 94
Frye, David 1934- WhoCom
Frye, David Scott 1955- WhoIns 94
Frye, Dwight d1943 WhoHol 92
Frye, Ellen DrAPF 93
Frye, F. Kytle, III 1947- WhoAmL 94
Frye, Frank L. d1935 WhoHol 92
Frye, Helen Jackson 1930- WhoAm 94, WhoAmL 94, WhoWest 94
Frye, Henry E. 1932- WhoAm 94, WhoAmL 94, WhoAmP 93, WhoBlA 94
Frye, John H., Jr. 1908- WhoAm 94
Frye, John William, III 1929- WhoAm 94
Frye, Joseph 1711-1794 WhAmRev
Frye, Judith Eleen Minor WhoAm 94, WhoFI 94, WhoWest 94
Frye, Keith Nale 1941- WhoAm 94
Frye, Mary Barnard 1963- WhoFI 94
Frye, Michael John Ernest 1945- Who 94
Frye, Nadine Grace WhoBlA 94
Frye, (Herman) Northrop 1912-1991 WhAm 10
Frye, Patrick Michael 1957- WhoFI 94
Frye, Paul Edward 1948- WhoAmL 94
Frye, Raymond Eugene 1961- WhoScEn 94
Frye, Reginald Stanley 1936- WhoBlA 94
Frye, Richard Arthur 1948- WhoAmL 94
Frye, Richard Nelson 1920- IntWW 93, WhoAm 94, WrDr 94
Frye, Robert Edward 1936- WhoBlA 94
Frye, Roland (Mushat) 1921- WrDr 94
Frye, Roland Mushat 1921- WhoAm 94
Frye, Roland Mushat, Jr. 1950- WhoAmL 94
Frye, Steven Wayne 1954- WhoWest 94
Frye, Virgil WhoHol 92
Frye, Wilbur Wayne 1933- WhoAm 94
Frye, William IntMPA 94
Frye, William Charles 1937- WhoAmL 94
Frye, William S. 1924- AfrAmG [port]
Frye, William Sinclair 1924- WhoBlA 94
Fryefield, Peter Jay 1949- WhoAmL 94
Fryer, Appleton 1927- WhoFI 94
Fryer, David Richard 1936- Who 94
Fryer, Edwin S. 1947- WhoAm 94, WhoAmL 94
Fryer, Eric WhoHol 92
Fryer, Geoffrey 1927- IntWW 93, Who 94
Fryer, Gladys Constance 1923- WhoWest 94
Fryer, John Stanley 1937- WhoAm 94
Fryer, Jonathan 1950- WrDr 94
Fryer, Judith Dorothy 1950- WhoAm 94, WhoAmL 94
Fryer, Lester K. WhoAmP 93
Fryer, Patricia 1948- WhoWest 94
Fryer, Robert Samuel 1931- WhoMW 93
Fryer, Robert Sherwood 1920- WhoAm 94
Fryer, Thomas Waitt, Jr. 1936- WhoAm 94
Fryer, Wilfred George d1993 Who 94N
Fryer, William B. 1949- WhoAmL 94
Frykberg, W. Randolph 1947- WhoMW 93
Frykenberg, Robert E(ric) 1930- WrDr 94
Frykenberg, Robert Eric 1930- WhoAm 94
Frykman, John H(arvey) 1932- ConAu 43NR
Frym, Gloria DrAPF 93
Fryman, David Travis 1969- WhoAm 94, WhoMW 93
Fryman, Louis William 1935- WhoAm 94, WhoAmL 94
Fryman, Virgil Thomas, Jr. 1940- WhoAmL 94
Frymer, Murry 1934- WhoAm 94, WhoWest 94
Frymire, Richard L. 1931- WhoAmP 93
Fryrear, Donald William 1936- WhoScEn 94
Fryt, Michael David 1955- WhoAmL 94
Fryt, Monte Stanislaus 1949- WhoFI 94, WhoScEn 94, WhoWest 94
Fry-Wendt, Sherri Diane 1958- WhoMW 93, WhoScEn 94
Fryxell, David Allen 1956- WhoAm 94
Fryxell, Karl Joseph 1953- WhoWest 94
Fryzuk, Michael Daniel 1952- WhoAm 94, WhoScEn 94
Fthenakis, Emanuel John 1928- WhoAm 94
Fthenakis, Vasilis 1951- WhoScEn 94
Ftizgerald, Joseph Michael 1952- WhoFI 94
Fu, Albert Joseph 1959- WhoScEn 94
Fu, Gang 1956- WhoScEn 94
Fu, Jyun-Horng 1959- WhoAsA 94
Fu, Karen K. 1940- WhoAsA 94
Fu, Karen King-Wah 1940- WhoAm 94
Fu, Kuan-Chen 1933- WhoAsA 94
Fu, LiMin 1953- WhoAsA 94
Fu, Michael Chung-Shu 1962- WhoAsA 94
Fu, Paul Chung, Jr. 1969- WhoAsA 94
Fu, Paul S. 1932- WhoAsA 94
Fu, Peter K. 1959- WhoAsA 94
Fu, Shou-Cheng Joseph 1924- WhoAsA 94, WhoScEn 94
Fu, Tina C. 1939- WhoAsA 94
Fu, Yuan Chin 1930- WhoScEn 94
Fua, Giorgio 1919- IntWW 93
Fuad, Kutlu Tekin 1926- Who 94
Fuavai, Te'O WhoAmP 93
Fubini, Eugene Ghiron 1913- WhoAm 94
Fuca, Juan De 1536-1602 WhWE
Fucaloro, Anthony Frank 1943- WhoWest 94
Fuccello, Tom d1993 NewYTBS 93 [port]
Fucci, Joseph Leonard 1950- WhoFI 94
Fucci, Linda Dean 1947- WhoFI 94
Fuchigami, Leslie Hirao 1942- WhoScEn 94
Fu Chongbi WhoPRCh 91
Fuchs, Alfred Herman 1932- WhoAm 94
Fuchs, Anke 1937- IntWW 93, WhoWomW 91
Fuchs, Anna-Riitta 1926- WhoAm 94
Fuchs, Anna Rupertina 1657-1722 BlmGWL
Fuchs, Anton von 1849-1925 NewGrDO
Fuchs, Beth Ann 1963- WhoScEn 94
Fuchs, Daniel DrAPF 93
Fuchs, Daniel d1993 NewYTBS 93
Fuchs, Daniel 1909- WrDr 94
Fuchs, Daniel 1909-1993 ConAu 142, DcLB Y93N [port]
Fuchs, Elaine V. 1950- WhoAm 94, WhoMW 93
Fuchs, Eugen 1893-1971 NewGrDO
Fuchs, Ewald Franz 1939- WhoAm 94
Fuchs, Fritz 1918- WhoAm 94
Fuchs, Hanno 1928- WhoAm 94
Fuchs, Ignacije NewGrDO
Fuchs, James A. 1943- WhoMW 93
Fuchs, James E. 1927- WhoFI 94
Fuchs, Jay R. 1955- WhoIns 94
Fuchs, Jerome Herbert 1922- WhoFI 94
Fuchs, Joseph Herman 1917- WhoAmP 93
Fuchs, Joseph Louis 1931- WhoAm 94
Fuchs, Josephine S. 1935- WhoAmP 93
Fuchs, Laszlo Jehoshua 1949- WhoScEn 94
Fuchs, Lawrence Howard 1927- WhoAm 94
Fuchs, Leo 1911- WhoHol 92
Fuchs, Leo L. 1929- IntMPA 94
Fuchs, Lucy 1935- WrDr 94
Fuchs, Marta 1898-1974 NewGrDO
Fuchs, Martin I. 1952- WhoAm 94, WhoAmL 94
Fuchs, Mary Tharsilla 1912- WhoAmA 93
Fuchs, Michael 1946- IntMPA 94
Fuchs, Michael J. 1946- WhoAm 94, WhoFI 94
Fuchs, Nancy Kathleen 1961- WhoMW 93
Fuchs, Olivia Anne Morris 1949- WhoAmL 94
Fuchs, Owen George 1951- WhoFI 94, WhoScEn 94
Fuchs, Peter Cornelius 1936- WhoWest 94
Fuchs, Robert 1847-1927 NewGrDO
Fuchs, Rodney Goeth 1938- WhoFI 94
Fuchs, Roland John 1933- WhoAm 94, WhoScEn 94, WhoWest 94
Fuchs, Sheldon James WhoScEn 94
Fuchs, Thomas 1942- WhoWest 94
Fuchs, Victor R(obert) 1924- ConAu 41NR
Fuchs, Victor Robert 1924- IntWW 93, WhoAm 94, WhoFI 94, WhoWest 94
Fuchs, Vivian, Sir 1908- WrDr 94
Fuchs, Vivian (Ernest) 1908- Who 94
Fuchs, Vivian Ernest 1908- IntWW 93
Fuchsberger, Joachim 1927- WhoHol 92
Fudenberg, Herman Hugh 1928- WhoAm 94
Fudge, Alan 1944- WhoHol 92
Fudge, Ann Marie WhoBlA 94
Fudge, Ann Marie 1951- WhoAm 94
Fudge, Edward William 1944- WhoAmL 94
Fudge, Jack D. 1934- WhoAm 94
Fudge, Joe Allen 1939- WhoAmP 93
Fudge, Mary Ann 1947- WhoMW 93
Fudim, Allan 1945- WhoAmL 94
Fudro, Stanley J. 1918- WhoAmP 93
Fuegi, John 1936- WhoAm 94, WrDr 94
Fuehrer, Mark Edwin DrAPF 93
Fuenning, Esther Renate WhoAm 94
Fuenning, Samuel Isaiah 1916- WhoMW 93
Fueno, Takayuki 1931- WhoScEn 94
Fuente, D. I. 1946- WhoFI 94
Fuentealba, Victor William 1922- WhoAm 94
Fuentes, Alejandro Alberto 1957- WhoHisp 94
Fuentes, Augusto Sanchez WhoAmP 93
Fuentes, Carlos 1928- ConWorW 93, HispLC [port], IntWW 93, RfGShF, Who 94, WhoAm 94, WhoHisp 94
Fuentes, Carlos 1929- EncSF 93
Fuentes, Carmen A. 1965- WhoWest 94
Fuentes, Daisy 1966- WhoHisp 94
Fuentes, Eduardo Sanchez de NewGrDO
Fuentes, Elia Ivonne WhoHisp 94
Fuentes, Ernesto WhoHisp 94
Fuentes, Ernesto Venegas 1947- WhoHisp 94
Fuentes, Fernando Luis 1952- WhoHisp 94
Fuentes, Francisco 1946- WhoHisp 94
Fuentes, Giorgio 1756-1821 NewGrDO
Fuentes, Gloria Hernandez 1950- WhoHisp 94
Fuentes, Humberto WhoHisp 94
Fuentes, John WhoHisp 94
Fuentes, Leopoldo C. 1949- WhoHisp 94
Fuentes, Manuel 1955- WhoHisp 94
Fuentes, Martha Ayers 1923- WhoAm 94
Fuentes (y) Matons, Laureano 1825-1898 NewGrDO
Fuentes, Pete Acosta 1952- WhoHisp 94
Fuentes, Philip K. 1956- WhoHisp 94
Fuentes, R. Alan 1949- WhoHisp 94
Fuentes, Roberto EncSF 93
Fuentes, Tina Guerrero 1949- WhoHisp 94
Fuentes, Virginia d1956 WhoHol 92
Fuentes-chao, René WhoHisp 94
Fuentevilla, Manuel Edward 1923- WhoScEn 94
Fuentez, Lucio 1944- WhoHisp 94
Fuerbringer, Alfred Ottomar 1903- WhoAm 94
Fuerbringer, Ernst-Fritz d1988 WhoHol 92
Fuerniss, Gloria Villasana 1949- WhoHisp 94
Fuerst, Jean Stern 1919- WhoBlA 94
Fuerst, Shirley Miller 1928- WhoAmA 93
Fuerst, Steven Bernard 1945- WhoAm 94
Fuerstenau, Douglas Winston 1928- WhoAm 94, WhoWest 94
Fuerstenburg, Paul W. 1875-1953 WhoAmA 93N

Fuertes (y Piqueras), Mariano Soriano *NewGrDO*
Fuertes, Gloria 1918- *BlmGWL*
Fuertes, Raul A. 1940- *WhoHisp 94*
Fuess, Billings Sibley, Jr. 1928- *WhoFI 94*
Fuest, Robert 1927- *HorFD [port], IntMPA 94*
Fuetterer, Werner *WhoHol 92*
Fufuka, Natika Njeri Yaa 1952- *WhoMW 93*
Fufuka, Tika N.Y. 1952- *WhoBlA 94*
Fuga, Sandro 1906- *NewGrDO*
Fugal, Jared Widdison 1963- *WhoWest 94*
Fugard, Athol 1932- *ConLC 80 [port], IntWW 93, Who 94, WhoHol 92, WrDr 94*
Fugard, (Harold) Athol (Lannigan) 1932- *ConDr 93, IntDcT 2 [port]*
Fugard, Athol Harold 1932- *WhoAm 94*
Fugard, Michael Teape 1933- *Who 94*
Fugard, Sheila 1932- *BlmGWL*
Fugate, Douglas Brown 1906-1988 *WhAm 10*
Fugate, Edward 1956- *WhoMW 93*
Fugate, Ivan Dee 1928- *WhoFI 94*
Fugate, Jack Millard 1927- *WhoMW 93*
Fugate, Joe Kemp 1931- *WhoMW 93*
Fugate, Judith 1956- *WhoAm 94*
Fugate, Wilbur Lindsay 1913- *WhoAm 94*
Fugate-Wilcox, Terry 1944- *WhoAm 94*
Fugazy, Louis V. d1993 *NewYTBS 93*
Fugazzi, Paul Anthony 1959- *WhoFI 94*
Fuge, Charles 1966- *SmATA 74 [port]*
Fugelberg, Nancy Jean 1947- *WhoMW 93*
Fugere, Lucien 1848-1935 *NewGrDO*
Fugere, Paul 1851-c. 1910 *NewGrDO*
Fuget, Charles Robert 1929- *WhoBlA 94*
Fuget, Henry Eugene 1925- *WhoBlA 94*
Fugett, Jean S., Jr. *WhoBlA 94*
Fugh, John L. 1934- *WhoAsA 94*
Fugh, John Liu 1934- *WhoAm 94, WhoAmL 94*
Fugiel, Frank Paul 1950- *WhoFI 94*
Fugina, Peter X. *WhoAmP 93*
Fugita, Stephen Susumu 1943- *WhoAsA 94*
Fugler, Michael Roy 1949- *WhoAmL 94*
Fuguet, Howard K. 1937- *WhoAm 94*
Fu Hao 1916- *IntWW 93, WhoPRCh 91 [port]*
Fuhlrodt, Norman Theodore 1910- *WhoFI 94, WhoWest 94*
Fuhr, Grant 1962- *WhoAm 94*
Fuhr, Grant Scott 1962- *WhoBlA 94*
Fuhr, Samuel E. 1918-1990 *WhoBlA 94N*
Fuhrer, Arthur K. 1926- *WhoAm 94, WhoAmL 94*
Fuhriman, Robert Lee 1940- *WhoWest 94*
Fuhrman, Bruce Livermore 1936- *WhoWest 94*
Fuhrman, Charles Andrew 1933- *WhoAm 94*
Fuhrman, Esther 1939- *WhoAmA 93*
Fuhrman, Frederick Alexander 1915- *WhoAm 94*
Fuhrman, Jed Alan 1956- *WhoWest 94*
Fuhrman, Kendall Nelson 1962- *WhoWest 94*
Fuhrman, Kenneth Wayne 1932- *WhoMW 93*
Fuhrman, Kevin Daniel 1965- *WhoWest 94*
Fuhrman, Linn 1944- *WhoAmP 93*
Fuhrman, Ralph Edward 1909- *WhoAm 94*
Fuhrman, Robert Alexander 1925- *IntWW 93, WhoAm 94, WhoWest 94*
Fuhrman, Steve *WhoAmP 93*
Fuhrmann, Charles J., II 1945- *WhoAm 94, WhoFI 94*
Fuhrmann, Debora Josephine 1957- *WhoMW 93*
Fuhrmann, Horst 1926- *IntWW 93, WhoScEn 94*
Fuhrmann, Mark E. 1953- *WhoAmL 94*
Fuhs, Georg Wolfgang 1932- *WhoScEn 94*
Fuhs, Henry G. 1941- *WhoAmP 93*
Fuhs, Wendy L. 1950- *WhoAm 94, WhoMW 93*
Fuiava, Michael *WhoAmP 93*
Fuimaono, Lutu Tenari 1930- *WhoAmP 93*
Fu Jie 1935- *WhoPRCh 91 [port]*
Fujii, Akira 1942- *WhoScEn 94*
Fujii, Hironori Aliga 1944- *WhoScEn 94*
Fujii, Jack Koji 1940- *WhoAsA 94*
Fujii, Keishi 1939- *WhoAm 94, WhoFI 94*
Fujii, Kiyo 1921- *WhoWest 94*
Fujii, Kozo 1951- *WhoScEn 94*
Fujii, Masayuki 1958- *WhoScEn 94*
Fujikawa, Denson Gen 1942- *WhoAsA 94*
Fujikawa, Gyo 1908- *SmATA 76 [port]*
Fujikawa, Jerry d1983 *WhoHol 92*
Fujiki, Marjorie 1954- *WhoAsA 94*
Fujimatsu, Tadao 1935- *WhoAsA 94*
Fujime, Yukihiro 1945- *WhoScEn 94*
Fujimori, Alberto Kenyo 1939- *IntWW 93*
Fujimori, Masamichi 1921- *IntWW 93*
Fujimori, Yoshiaki 1951- *WhoMW 93*
Fujimoto, Gregg Takashi 1951- *WhoFI 94, WhoWest 94*
Fujimoto, Isao 1933- *WhoAsA 94*
Fujimoto, Jack *WhoAsA 94*
Fujimoto, James G. 1957- *WhoAm 94, WhoAsA 94*
Fujimoto, James Randall 1954- *WhoAsA 94*
Fujimoto, Robert I. *WhoAsA 94*
Fujimoto, Takao 1931- *IntWW 93*
Fujimoto, Wilfred Yorio 1940- *WhoAsA 94*
Fujimura, Robert Kanji 1933- *WhoAsA 94*
Fujimura, Robert Kiyoshi 1959- *WhoAsA 94*
Fujinami, Takao 1932- *IntWW 93*
Fujioka, John 1925- *WhoHol 92*
Fujioka, Masao 1924- *IntWW 93*
Fujioka, Roger Sadao 1938- *WhoAm 94, WhoScEn 94*
Fujioka, Takashi 1946- *WhoAsA 94*
Fujita, Eiichi 1922- *WhoScEn 94*
Fujita, Hiroyuki 1952- *IntWW 93*
Fujita, James Hiroshi 1958- *WhoWest 94*
Fujita, Kenji 1955- *WhoAmA 93*
Fujita, Shigeji 1929- *WhoAm 94*
Fujita, Sumi 1933- *WhoWomW 91*
Fujita, Tetsuya Theodore 1920- *WhoAm 94, WhoScEn 94*
Fujita, Tsuneo 1933- *WhoScEn 94*
Fujita, Yoshio 1908- *IntWW 93*
Fujitani, Martin Tomio 1968- *WhoScEn 94, WhoWest 94*
Fujiwara, Kamatari d1985 *WhoHol 92*
Fujiwara, Michinaga 966-1028 *HisWorL [port]*
Fujiwara, Theresa *WhoAsA 94*
Fujiyama, Naraichi 1915- *Who 94*
Fukae, Kensuke 1926- *WhoAm 94*
Fukai, Masani 1927- *WhoAsA 94*
Fukai, Yuh 1934- *WhoScEn 94*
Fuks, Zvi Y. 1936- *WhoAm 94*
Fukuda, Haruko 1946- *WrDr 94*
Fukuda, Ichiro 1940- *WhoScEn 94*
Fukuda, Morimichi 1929- *WhoScEn 94*
Fukuda, Naomi Nobuko 1963- *WhoWest 94*
Fukuda, Steven Ken 1952- *WhoScEn 94*
Fukuda, Takeo 1905- *IntWW 93*
Fukuhara, Henry 1913- *WhoAmA 93, WhoAsA 94, WhoWest 94*
Fukui, George Masaaki 1921- *WhoScEn 94*
Fukui, Hatsuaki 1927- *WhoAm 94, WhoFI 94, WhoScEn 94*
Fukui, Kenichi 1918- *IntWW 93, Who 94, WhoAm 94, WhoScEn 94*
Fukui, Nobu 1942- *WhoAmA 93*
Fukui, Yasuo 1951- *WhoScEn 94*
Fukui, Yasuyuki 1934- *WhoScEn 94*
Fukui, Yoshio 1942- *WhoMW 93*
Fu Kuiqing 1920- *WhoPRCh 91 [port]*
Fu Kuiqing, Lieut.-Gen. 1920- *IntWW 93*
Fukukawa, Shinji 1932- *IntWW 93*
Fukumoto, Benjamin I. 1938- *WhoWest 94*
Fukumoto, Bert Ken 1955- *WhoAmL 94*
Fukumoto, Geal S. 1961- *WhoFI 94*
Fukumoto, Leslie Satsuki 1955- *WhoAmL 94*
Fukumoto, Neal Susumu 1958- *WhoScEn 94*
Fukunaga, Carol A. 1947- *WhoAmP 93*
Fukunaga, Keinosuke 1930- *WhoAm 94, WhoAsA 94*
Fukurai, Hiroshi 1954- *WhoAsA 94*
Fukushima, Barbara Naomi 1948- *WhoFI 94*
Fukushima, Eiichi 1936- *WhoAsA 94*
Fukushima, Joji 1927- *IntWW 93*
Fukutake, Tadashi 1917- *WrDr 94*
Fukuyama, Francis *WhoAsA 94*
Fukuyama, Francis 1952- *ConAu 140*
Fukuyama, Tohru 1948- *WhoScEn 94*
Fukuyama, Yukio 1928- *WhoScEn 94*
Fukuzumi, Naoyoshi 1924- *WhoScEn 94*
Fulbeck, Kip 1965- *WhoAsA 94*
Fulbright, Dennis Wayne 1952- *WhoScEn 94*
Fulbright, J(ames) William 1905- *Who 94, WrDr 94*
Fulbright, James William 1905- *WhoAm 94, WhoAmP 93*
Fulbright, John William 1952- *WhoWest 94*
Fulbright, (James) William 1905- *IntWW 93*
Fulcher, Carolyn Jean 1956- *WhoFI 94*
Fulcher, Derick Harold 1917- *Who 94*
Fulcher, James William 1941- *WhoMW 93*
Fulchino, Paul Edward 1946- *WhoAm 94*
Fulci, Francesco Paolo 1931- *IntWW 93*
Fulci, Lucio 1927- *HorFD*
Fulco, Armand John 1932- *WhoAm 94, WhoWest 94*
Fulco, Frank 1908- *WhoAmP 93*
Fulco, Jose Roque 1927- *WhoAm 94*
Fulcomer, James Joseph 1943- *WhoAmP 93*
Fulcomer, Virginia Ann 1916- *WhoMW 93*
Fuld, Fred, III 1952- *WhoFI 94*
Fuld, James Jeffrey 1916- *WhoAm 94*
Fuld, Richard Severin, Jr. 1946- *WhoAm 94, WhoFI 94*
Fuld, Stanley H. 1903- *WhoAm 94*
Fuld, Steven Alan 1963- *WhoFI 94*
Fulda, Michael 1939- *WhoScEn 94*
Fulde, Walter John 1935- *WhoWest 94*
Fuldheim, Dorothy 1893-1989 *WhAm 10*
Fulero, Solomon M. 1950- *WhoScEn 94*
Fulford, David 1925- *WhoHol 92*
Fulford, John Hurtman 1895- *WhAm 10*
Fulford, Mark Lansing 1948- *WhoAmL 94*
Fulford, Robert John 1923- *Who 94*
Fulford, William James 1949- *WhoAmP 93*
Fulgenzi, Benjamin 1925- *WhoFI 94, WhoMW 93*
Fulger, Holly *WhoHol 92*
Fulgham, Roietta Goodwin 1948- *WhoBlA 94*
Fulghum, Brice Elwin 1919- *WhoFI 94*
Fulghum, Robert *WrDr 94*
Fulghum, Robert L. 1937- *WhoAm 94*
Fulginiti, Vincent 1931- *WhoAm 94*
Fulgoni, Gian Marc 1948- *WhoAm 94*
Fulham, Bishop Suffragan of 1931- *Who 94*
Fulham, Gerard Aquinas 1920-1990 *WhAm 10*
Fu Limin 1936- *WhoPRCh 91 [port]*
Fulk, Paul Frederick 1935- *WhoMW 93*
Fulk, Roscoe Neal 1916- *WhoAm 94*
Fulkerson, William Measey, Jr. 1940- *WhoAm 94, WhoWest 94*
Fulkes, Jean Aston *WhoMW 93*
Fulks, James Arthur 1946- *WhoWest 94*
Fulks, Joe 1921-1976 *BasBi*
Fulks, Robert Grady 1936- *WhoAm 94*
Fulks, Sarah Jane 1914- *WhoAm 94*
Fullagar, Paul David 1938- *WhoAm 94*
Fullagar, William Watts 1914- *WhoAm 94*
Fullam, John P. 1921- *WhoAm 94, WhoAmL 94*
Fullem, L. Robert 1929- *WhoAm 94*
Fullen, Dave Christian 1951- *WhoMW 93*
Fullen, Floyd Russell 1938- *WhoAmP 93*
Fullenkamp, Ronald Joseph 1941- *WhoFI 94*
Fullenweider, Donn Charles 1935- *WhoAmL 94*
Fuller, Alfred Worcester 1923- *WhoAm 94*
Fuller, Almyra Oveta 1955- *WhoBlA 94*
Fuller, Alvarado M(ortimer) 1851- *EncSF 93*
Fuller, Anne Elizabeth Havens 1932- *WhoAm 94*
Fuller, Arthur Orpen 1926- *IntWW 93*
Fuller, Barbara *WhoHol 92*
Fuller, Benjamin Franklin 1922- *WhoAm 94*
Fuller, Blair *DrAPF 93*
Fuller, Bobby d1966 *WhoHol 92*
Fuller, Brian Leslie 1936- *Who 94*
Fuller, (Richard) Buckminster 1895-1983 *WorInv [port]*
Fuller, Charles 1939- *AfrAmAl 6 [port], WhoAm 94, WhoBlA 94, WrDr 94*
Fuller, Charles (H.), Jr. 1939- *IntDcT 2*
Fuller, Charles (H., Jr.) 1939- *ConDr 93*
Fuller, Charles (Henry, Jr.) 1939- *BlkWr 2*
Fuller, Charles Edward 1887-1968 *DcAmReB 2*
Fuller, Charles Patrick 1964- *WhoMW 93*
Fuller, Clem d1961 *WhoHol 92*
Fuller, Craig L. 1951- *WhoAmP 93*
Fuller, Craig Lawrence 1951- *WhoAm 94*
Fuller, Curtis D. 1934- *WhoBlA 94*
Fuller, Curtis G. 1912-1961 *WhAm 10*
Fuller, D. Ward 1945- *WhoFI 94*
Fuller, David Otis, Jr. 1939- *WhoAmL 94*
Fuller, David Ralph 1932- *WhoAmL 94*
Fuller, Dewey C. 1934- *WhoBlA 94*
Fuller, Diana 1931- *WhoAmA 93*
Fuller, Dianna Lynn 1963- *WhoAmL 94*
Fuller, Don Edgar 1928- *WhoAmP 93*
Fuller, Doris Jean 1945- *WhoBlA 94*
Fuller, E. Bert 1898- *WhoAmP 93*
Fuller, Edmund 1914- *WrDr 94*
Fuller, Edward d1979 *WhoHol 92*
Fuller, Edwin Daniel 1945- *WhoAm 94, WhoFI 94*
Fuller, Elizabeth 1775-1856 *BlmGWL*
Fuller, Emily Rutgers 1941- *WhoAmA 93*
Fuller, Ernie Cecil 1962- *WhoFI 94*
Fuller, Frances d1980 *WhoHol 92*
Fuller, Gary Albert 1941- *WhoWest 94*
Fuller, Gary Lee 1955- *WhoAmP 93*
Fuller, Gene N. 1946- *WhoAmL 94*
Fuller, Geoffrey Herbert 1927- *Who 94*
Fuller, Glenn R. 1946- *WhoAm 94, WhoWest 94*
Fuller, Gloria Ann 1952- *WhoBlA 94*
Fuller, Harold David 1937- *WhoBlA 94*
Fuller, Harry Laurance 1938- *WhoAm 94, WhoFI 94, WhoMW 93*
Fuller, Haynes R. 1928- *WhoAmP 93*
Fuller, Howard *WhoMW 93*
Fuller, Irene d1945 *WhoHol 92*
Fuller, Jack (William) 1946- *WrDr 94*
Fuller, Jack Glendon, Jr. 1923- *WhoAm 94*
Fuller, Jack Lewis 1945- *WhoBlA 94*
Fuller, Jack William 1946- *WhoAm 94, WhoMW 93*
Fuller, Jackson Franklin 1920- *WhoAm 94*
Fuller, Jacqualyn Gist 1942- *WhoMW 93*
Fuller, James B. 1949- *WhoAmP 93*
Fuller, James Chester Eedy 1927- *WhoAm 94*
Fuller, James J. 1946- *WhoBlA 94*
Fuller, James Richard 1961- *WhoMW 93*
Fuller, James William 1940- *WhoWest 94*
Fuller, Jay B. 1961- *WhoMW 93*
Fuller, Jean (Violet) Overton 1915- *ConAu 42NR, WrDr 94*
Fuller, Jeffrey P. 1950- *WhoAmA 93*
Fuller, Jesse d1976 *WhoHol 92*
Fuller, Joan D. 1928- *WhoAm 94*
Fuller, John (Bryan Munro) 1917- *Who 94*
Fuller, John (Harold) 1916- *WrDr 94*
Fuller, John (Leopold) 1937- *WrDr 94*
Fuller, John (William Fleetwood) 1936- *Who 94*
Fuller, John Charles 1937- *WhoAmA 93*
Fuller, John Garsed Campbell 1930- *WhoAm 94*
Fuller, John Grant 1913- *WhAm 10*
Fuller, John Joseph 1931- *WhAm 10*
Fuller, John Langworthy 1910-1992 *WhAm 10*
Fuller, John Leopold 1937- *Who 94*
Fuller, John Williams 1940- *WhoMW 93*
Fuller, Karon Kathleen 1941- *WhoMW 93*
Fuller, Kathryn Scott 1946- *WhoAm 94, WhoScEn 94*
Fuller, Kenneth C. *WhoAmP 93*
Fuller, Kenneth Roller 1913- *WhoAm 94*
Fuller, Kevin Rice 1958- *WhoAmL 94*
Fuller, Lance 1928- *WhoHol 92*
Fuller, Larry 1938- *WhoAm 94*
Fuller, Lawrence Arthur 1949- *WhoAmL 94*
Fuller, Lawrence Joseph 1914- *WhoAm 94*
Fuller, Lawrence Robert 1941- *WhoMW 93*
Fuller, Lee Dennison 1910- *WhoMW 93*
Fuller, Leslie d1948 *WhoHol 92*
Fuller, Loie d1928 *WhoHol 92*
Fuller, Margaret d1952 *WhoHol 92*
Fuller, Margaret 1810-1850 *BlmGWL*
Fuller, Mark Adin, Jr. 1933- *WhoAm 94, WhoFI 94*
Fuller, Mark Everett 1958- *WhoAmL 94*
Fuller, Martin J. 1947- *WhoIns 94*
Fuller, Mary d1973 *WhoHol 92*
Fuller, Mary 1922- *WhoAmA 93*
Fuller, Mary Falvey 1941- *WhoWest 94*
Fuller, Mary Louise 1949- *WhoMW 93*
Fuller, Maurice DeLano, Jr. 1930- *WhoAm 94*
Fuller, Melvin Stuart 1931- *WhoAm 94*
Fuller, Meta Vaux Warrick 1877-1968 *AfrAmAl 6, WhoAmA 93N*
Fuller, Michael Jeffrey 1953- *WhoMW 93*
Fuller, Michael John 1932- *Who 94*
Fuller, Millard Dean 1935- *WhoAm 94*
Fuller, Nancy Belle 1948- *WhoWest 94*
Fuller, Norvell Ricardo 1953- *WhoBlA 94*
Fuller, Olive *WhoHol 92*
Fuller, Penny 1940- *WhoHol 92*
Fuller, Perry Lucian 1922- *WhoAm 94, WhoAmL 94*
Fuller, R. Buckminster 1895-1983 *WhoAmA 93N*
Fuller, Reggie Paul 1952- *WhoMW 93*
Fuller, Reginald Horace 1915- *WhoAm 94, WrDr 94*
Fuller, Richard 1804-1876 *DcAmReB 2*
Fuller, Richard Buckminster, Jr. 1895-1983 *AmSocL*
Fuller, Richard Eugene 1897-1976 *WhoAmA 93N*
Fuller, Richard Milton 1933- *WhoScEn 94*
Fuller, Robert 1933- *WhoHol 92*
Fuller, Robert Earl 1938- *WhoWest 94*
Fuller, Robert Ferrey 1929- *WhoAm 94*
Fuller, Robert Gorham, Jr. 1938- *WhoAmL 94*
Fuller, Robert Kenneth 1942- *WhoWest 94*
Fuller, Robert Leander 1943- *WhoAmL 94, WhoFI 94*
Fuller, Ron 1948- *WhoAmP 93*
Fuller, Rosalinde d1982 *WhoHol 92*
Fuller, Roy 1912- *BlmGEL*
Fuller, Roy (Broadbent) 1912-1991 *WrDr 94N*
Fuller, Sam 1911- *WhoHol 92*

Fuller, Samuel 1912- IntMPA 94, WhoAm 94
Fuller, Samuel Ashby 1924- WhoAm 94, WhoAmL 94
Fuller, Samuel Henry, III 1946- WhoAm 94
Fuller, Sarah Margaret 1810-1850 AmSocL, DcAmReB 2
Fuller, Simon William John 1943- Who 94
Fuller, Stephen Herbert 1920- WhoAm 94
Fuller, Steven Craig 1961- WhoMW 93
Fuller, Stuart Mitchell 1960- WhoMW 93
Fuller, Sue WhoAm 94, WhoAmA 93
Fuller, Terry Ray 1953- WhoAmL 94
Fuller, Theodore 1918- WhoAm 94
Fuller, Thomas Ralph 1927- WhoFI 94
Fuller, Thomas S. 1934- WhoBlA 94
Fuller, Toria WhoHol 92
Fuller, Tracy Annette 1962- WhoFI 94
Fuller, Wallace Hamilton 1915- WhoAm 94
Fuller, Walter Lelus, III 1951- WhoFI 94
Fuller, Wanda 1938- WhoAmP 93
Fuller, Wanda Lou 1938- WhoMW 93
Fuller, Wayne Arthur 1931- WhoAm 94
Fuller, Wayne Maurice 1946- WhoFI 94
Fuller, Wayne P. 1932- WhoAmP 93
Fuller, William Dean 1947- WhoWest 94
Fuller, William Henry, Jr. 1962- WhoAm 94
Fuller, William P. WhoAmP 93
Fuller, William Richard 1920- WhoMW 93
Fuller, William Roger 1949- WhoWest 94
Fuller, William Sidney 1931- WhoAm 94
Fullerton, Alexander (Fergus) 1924- WrDr 94
Fullerton, Charles Michael 1932- WhoWest 94
Fullerton, Charles William 1917- WhoAm 94
Fullerton, Darren Scott 1965- WhoMW 93
Fullerton, Fiona 1955- WhoHol 92
Fullerton, Gail 1927- WrDr 94
Fullerton, Gail Jackson 1927- WhoAm 94, WhoWest 94
Fullerton, Jesse Wilson 1947- WhoScEn 94
Fullerton, Lawrence Rae 1952- WhoAmL 94
Fullerton, Mary WhoAmA 93
Fullerton, Melanie 1962- WhoHol 92
Fullerton, Mollie Hays WhoAm 94
Fullerton, Peter George Patrick Downing 1930- Who 94
Fullerton, Philippa Stevenson 1949- WhoAm 94
Fullerton, R. Donald 1931- IntWW 93, WhoAm 94, WhoFI 94
Fullerton, Robert Victor 1918- WhoAm 94
Fullerton, Thomas Mankin, Jr. 1959- WhoFI 94
Fullerton, William Hugh 1939- IntWW 93, Who 94
Fullilove, Don WhoHol 92
Fullilove, Paul A., Sr. 1916- WhoBlA 94
Fulling, Rusty Lee 1967- WhoMW 93
Fullmer, Daniel Warren 1922- WhoAm 94, WhoWest 94
Fullmer, David R. 1931- WhoAm 94
Fullmer, Donald Kitchen 1915- WhoWest 94
Fullmer, Harold Milton 1918- WhoAm 94
Fullmer, Joseph Anthony, Jr. 1943- WhoWest 94
Fullmer, Paul 1934- WhoAm 94
Fullmer, Ronald K. WhoAmP 93
Fullmer, Steven Mark 1956- WhoFI 94, WhoWest 94
Fullmer, Terry Lloyd 1939- WhoWest 94
Fullwood, Brent Lanard 1963- WhoBlA 94
Fullwood, Harlow, Jr. 1941- WhoBlA 94
Fulmer, Hugh Scott 1928- WhoAm 94
Fulmer, Kevin Michael 1968- WhoScEn 94
Fulmer, Michael Clifford 1954- WhoFI 94, WhoMW 93
Fulmer, Ronald Calhoun 1945- WhoAmP 93
Fulmer, Vincent Anthony 1927- WhoAm 94
Fulop, Milford 1927- WhoAm 94
Fulp, James Alan 1951- WhoFI 94
Fulrath, Irene 1945- WhoFI 94
Fuls-Richie, Elva Stout 1924- WhoWest 94
Fulthorpe, Henry Joseph 1916- Who 94
Fulton, Alice DrAPF 93
Fulton, Alice Bordwell 1952- WhoScEn 94
Fulton, Barbara Jane 1952- WhoMW 93
Fulton, Burt J. 1925- WhoAmL 94
Fulton, Chandler Montgomery 1934- WhoAm 94
Fulton, Christopher Cuyler 1948- WhoWest 94
Fulton, Cyrus James 1873-1949 WhoAmA 93N
Fulton, Darrell Nelson 1946- WhoFI 94, WhoMW 93, WhoScEn 94
Fulton, (Edmund) Davie 1916- Who 94
Fulton, Donald Lee 1935- WhoBlA 94
Fulton, Eileen 1934- WhoHol 92
Fulton, Fred Franklin 1920- WhoAmA 93
Fulton, Fred W. 1949- WhoAmL 94
Fulton, Hamish 1946- WhoAmA 93
Fulton, Jack E. 1939- WhoAmA 93
Fulton, James Franklin 1930- WhoAm 94
Fulton, James Murdock 1914-1989 WhAm 10
Fulton, Janet Schwartz 1952- WhoMW 93
Fulton, Jessie Lee d1983 WhoHol 92
Fulton, Joan WhoHol 92
Fulton, John 1902-1966 IntDcF 2-4
Fulton, John Francis 1933- Who 94
Fulton, Julie 1960- WhoHol 92
Fulton, Katherine Nelson 1955- WhoAm 94
Fulton, Len DrAPF 93
Fulton, Len 1934- WhoAm 94
Fulton, Maude d1950 WhoHol 92
Fulton, Norman Robert 1935- WhoFI 94, WhoWest 94
Fulton, Patsy Jo 1934- WhoMW 93
Fulton, Paul 1934- WhoAm 94, WhoFI 94
Fulton, Rad WhoHol 92
Fulton, Richard 1921- WhoAm 94
Fulton, Richard Alsina 1926- WhoAm 94
Fulton, Richard Delbert 1945- WhoWest 94
Fulton, Richard Harmon 1927- WhoAmP 93
Fulton, Richard T. 1948- WhoAm 94
Fulton, Rikki WhoHol 92
Fulton, Robert 1765-1815 WorInv
Fulton, Robert Andrew 1944- Who 94
Fulton, Robert Brank 1911- WhoAmP 93
Fulton, Robert D. 1929- WhoAmP 93
Fulton, Robert Henry 1926- WhoBlA 94
Fulton, Robert Lester 1926- WhoAm 94
Fulton, Robin 1937- WrDr 94
Fulton, Sandy Michael 1943- WhoAm 94
Fulton, Thomas Benjamin 1918- WhoAm 94
Fulton, Tony E. 1951- WhoAmP 93
Fulton, Wendy WhoHol 92
Fults, Daniel Webster, III 1953- WhoWest 94
Fultz, Clair Ervin 1911- WhoAm 94
Fultz, Dave 1921- WhoAm 94
Fultz, Philip Nathaniel 1943- WhoFI 94, WhoWest 94
Fultz, Robert Edward 1941- WhoAmL 94
Fulweiler, Howard Wells 1932- WhoAm 94
Fulweiler, Patricia Platt 1923- WhoFI 94
Fulweiler, Spencer Biddle 1913- WhoFI 94
Fulwiler, Robert Neal 1937- WhoAm 94
Fulwood, Sam, III 1956- WhoBlA 94
Fumagalli, Barbara Merrill 1926- WhoAm 94, WhoAmA 93
Fumagalli Carulli, Ombretta (Battistina) 1944- WhoWomW 91
Fumelh, Madame de fl. 18th cent.- BlmGWL
Fumento, Rocco DrAPF 93
Fumento, Rocco 1923- WrDr 94
Fumerton, Patricia ConAu 140
Fumo, Vincent J. 1943- WhoAmP 93
Funaba, Masatomi 1938- WhoScEn 94
Funabiki, Jon 1949- WhoAsA 94
Funabiki, Ryuhei 1931- WhoScEn 94
Funada, Hajime IntWW 93
Funahashi, Akira 1928- WhoMW 93, WhoScEn 94
Funahashi, Masao 1913- IntWW 93
Funai, Helen WhoHol 92
Funari, John H. 1929- WhoAm 94
Funcke, Liselotte 1918- IntWW 93
Fundenberg, Herman Hugh 1928- WhoScEn 94
Funderburg, I. Owen 1924- WhoBlA 94
Funderburk, David 1944- WhoAmP 93
Funderburk, David B. 1944- WhoAm 94
Funderburk, Henry Hanly, Jr. 1931- WhoAm 94
Funderburk, Kenneth Leroy 1936- WhoAmP 93
Funderburk, Raymond 1944- WhoAmL 94
Funderburk, William Watson 1931- WhoBlA 94
Fundingsland, Lynn Omar 1948- WhoMW 93
Fundora, Thomas 1935- WhoAmA 93
Funegard, Erik Gustaf 1950- WhoMW 93
Fung, Adrian Kin-Chiu 1936- WhoAm 94
Fung, Bing M. 1939- WhoAsA 94
Fung, Daniel Yee Chak 1942- WhoAsA 94
Fung, Dennis Lung 1940- WhoAsA 94
Fung, Gordon L. 1951- WhoAsA 94
Fung, Henry C. 1939- WhoAsA 94
Fung, Henry Chong 1939- WhoScEn 94
Fung, Ho-Leung 1943- WhoAm 94, WhoAsA 94
Fung, Hung-Gay 1955- WhoAsA 94
Fung, K. C. 1955- WhoFI 94
Fung, Kee-Ying 1948- WhoAsA 94, WhoScEn 94
Fung, Kenneth Ping-Fan 1911- Who 94
Fung, Lance Michael 1963- WhoAm 94
Fung, Shun C. 1943- WhoAsA 94
Fung, Sui An 1922- WhoAsA 94
Fung, Sun-Yiu 1932- WhoAsA 94
Fung, Sun-Yiu Samuel 1932- WhoScEn 94, WhoWest 94
Fung, Victor K. IntWW 93
Fung, Willie d1945 WhoHol 92
Fung, Yuan-Cheng Bertram 1919- WhoAm 94, WhoAsA 94, WhoScEn 94
Fung-Chen-Pen, Emma Solaita 1951- WhoAm 94
Funge, Robert DrAPF 93
Fungoni, Papebrochio NewGrDO
Funicello, Annette 1942- WhoHol 92
Funk, Alfred d1993 NewYTBS 93
Funk, Charlotte M. 1934- WhoAmA 93
Funk, Cyril Reed, Jr. 1928- WhoAm 94
Funk, David Albert 1927- WhoAm 94, WhoAmL 94
Funk, Everett Eugene 1933- WhoMW 93
Funk, Frank E. 1923- WhoAm 94
Funk, Irving M. 1945- WhoAmL 94
Funk, James William, Jr. 1947- WhoMW 93
Funk, John William 1937- WhoAm 94
Funk, Lisa Averill 1957- WhoMW 93
Funk, Milton Albert 1918- WhoWest 94
Funk, Paul Edward 1940- WhoAm 94
Funk, Peter V. K. 1921- WhoAm 94
Funk, Robert Norris 1930- WhoAm 94, WhoAmA 93, WhoWest 94
Funk, Robert Walter 1926- WhoWest 94
Funk, Roger L. 1934- WhoAmA 93
Funk, Roland Vernon Terry 1945- WhoAmL 94
Funk, Sherman Maxwell 1925- WhoAm 94, WhoAmP 93
Funk, Susan Ellen 1951- WhoFI 94
Funk, Verne J. 1932- WhoAmA 93
Funk, William Henry 1933- WhoAm 94
Funke, Cheryl Husa 1955- WhoWest 94
Funke, Gosta Werner 1906- IntWW 93
Funken, Karl-Heinz 1953- WhoScEn 94
Funkhouser, Elmer Newton, Jr. 1916- WhoAm 94
Funkhouser, Erica DrAPF 93
Funkhouser, Erica 1949- WrDr 94
Funkhouser, Lawrence William 1921- WhoAm 94
Funkhouser, Paul William 1952- WhoFI 94
Funkhouser, Richard 1917- WhoAmP 93
Funk Orsini, Paula Ann 1956- WhoScEn 94
Funn, Carlton A., Sr. 1932- WhoBlA 94
Funn, Courtney Harris 1941- WhoBlA 94
Funnell, Augustine 1952- EncSF 93
Funnell, Kevin Joseph 1949- WhoAmL 94
Funseth, Robert Lloyd Eric Martin 1926- WhoAm 94
Funsten, Herbert Oliver, III 1962- WhoScEn 94
Funston, Gary Stephen 1951- WhoWest 94
Funston, Keith 1910-1992 AnObit 1992
Funt, Allen 1914- IntMPA 94, WhoHol 92
Fuoco, Philip Stephen 1946- WhoAmL 94
Fuoco, Sofia 1830-1916 IntDcB [port]
Fu Qifeng 1941- IntWW 93
Fuqua, Charlie d1971 WhoHol 92
Fuqua, Don 1933- WhoAm 94, WhoAmP 93
Fuqua, John Brooks 1918- WhoAm 94, WhoFI 94
Fuqua, Robert EncSF 93
Fuqua, Robert Edward 1943- WhoAm 94
Fuqua, Thomas Edward 1942- WhoAmP 93
Fuqua, Wilbur d1953 WhoHol 92
Fu Quanyou 1930- IntWW 93, WhoPRCh 91 [port]
Fur, Lajos 1930- IntWW 93
Furan, Rodney Luke Leroy 1927- WhoWest 94
Furbay, John Harvey 1903- WhoAm 94
Furbay, Walter M. 1920- WhoFI 94
Furbee, Carol Widmer 1942- WhoMW 93
Furbee, Louanna 1937- WhoMW 93
Furber, Bradley Bolton 1964- WhoAmL 94
Furber, Edward Parker 1898- WhAm 10
Furber, Robert c. 1674-1756 DcNaB MP
Furber, (Frank) Robert 1921- Who 94
Furbringer, Ernst Fritz d1988 WhoHol 92
Furbush, David Malcolm 1954- WhoAm 94, WhoAmL 94
Furchtgott, David Grover 1955- WhoScEn 94
Furcolo, Foster 1917- WhoAmP 93
Furcon, John Edward 1942- WhoMW 93
Furda, Gregory H. 1946- WhoAm 94, WhoAmL 94
Furdeck, Constance 1929- WhoAmP 93
Furen, Walter Enoch 1930- WhoWest 94
Furer, Arthur Carl Othmar 1920- IntWW 93
Furer, Stanford Arthur 1916- WhoWest 94
Furer-Haimendorf, Christoph von 1909- Who 94
Furet, Francois 1927- IntWW 93
Furetiere, Antoine 1619-1688 GuFrLit 2
Furey, Barney d1938 WhoHol 92
Furey, Deborah Ann 1966- WhoScEn 94
Furey, Dorothy 1940- WhoHisp 94
Furey, Gerard DrAPF 93
Furey, James A. d1930 WhoHol 92
Furey, James Joseph 1938- WhoFI 94
Furey, James Michael 1927- WhoAmL 94
Furey, Lewis WhoHol 92
Furey, Linda Ann 1958- WhoAmL 94
Furey, Michael EncSF 93
Furey, Michael K. 1949- WhoAmL 94
Furey, Patrick Dennis 1954- WhoAmL 94
Furey, Robert L. 1941- WhoScEn 94
Furey, Sherman Francis, Jr. 1919- WhoAmL 94
Furfine, Earl Michael 1962- WhoFI 94
Furgason, Maiya Kathryn 1944- WhoAm 94
Furgason, Robert Roy 1935- WhoAm 94
Furgeson, William Royal 1941- WhoAmL 94
Furgler, Kurt 1924- IntWW 93
Furgol, Edward Mackie 1955- WhoAm 94
Furgurson, Ernest Baker, Jr. 1929- WhoAm 94
Furia, Philip (G.) 1943- WrDr 94
Furia, Philip George 1943- WhoMW 93
Furie, Sidney J. 1933- IntMPA 94
Furiga, Richard Daniel 1935- WhoAm 94, WhoScEn 94
Furigay, Rodolfo Lazo 1938- WhoAm 94
Furimsky, Stephen, Jr. 1924- WhoWest 94
Furino, Antonio WhoAm 94
Furlane, Mark Elliott 1949- WhoAm 94
Furlanetto, Ferruccio 1949- NewGrDO
Furlaud, Richard Mortimer 1923- IntWW 93
Furlong, Charles Richard 1950- WhoAm 94
Furlong, Edward V., Jr. 1937- WhoAm 94
Furlong, George Morgan, Jr. 1931- WhoAm 94
Furlong, Monica 1930- Who 94
Furlong, Monica (Mavis) 1930- TwCYAW
Furlong, Nadine Mary 1945- WhAm 10
Furlong, Patrick David 1948- WhoMW 93
Furlong, Robert Joseph 1954- WhoMW 93
Furlong, Robert Stafford 1904- Who 94
Furlong, Ronald (John) Who 94
Furlonger, Robert William 1921- Who 94
Furlough, Joyce Lynn 1961- WhoBlA 94
Furlow, Mack Vernon, Jr. 1931- WhoAm 94
Furlow, Mary Beverley 1933- WhoWest 94
Furlow, Rita WhoAmP 93
Furman, Anthony Michael 1934- WhoAm 94, WhoFI 94
Furman, Arthur F., Mrs. WhoAmA 93
Furman, David Stephen 1945- WhoAmA 93, WhoWest 94
Furman, Deane Philip 1915- WhoAm 94
Furman, Hezekiah Wyndol Carroll 1922- WhoAm 94, WhoAmL 94
Furman, Howard 1938- WhoAmL 94
Furman, James B. 1937- WhoBlA 94
Furman, James Merle 1932- WhoAm 94
Furman, Laura DrAPF 93
Furman, Laura 1945- ConAu 18AS [port]
Furman, Richard 1755-1825 DcAmReB 2
Furman, Robert Howard 1918- WhoAm 94
Furman, Roger d1983 WhoHol 92
Furman, Roy Lance 1939- WhoAm 94, WhoFI 94
Furman, Samuel Elliott 1932- WhoAm 94
Furman, Stan 1932- WhoAmP 93
Furmanski, Philip 1946- WhoAm 94
Furmansky, Bert Sol 1945- WhoWest 94
Furmston, Bentley Edwin 1931- Who 94
Furmston, Michael Philip 1933- Who 94
Furnas, David William 1931- WhoAm 94, WhoScEn 94
Furnas, Howard Earl 1919- WhoAm 94
Furnas, Joseph Chamberlain 1905- WhoAm 94
Furneaux, Henry Morrice 1954- WhoScEn 94
Furneaux, Tobias 1735-1781 WhWE
Furneaux, Yvonne 1928- WhoHol 92
Furnell, Raymond 1935- Who 94
Furner, Derek Jack 1921- Who 94
Furness, Viscount 1929- Who 94
Furness, Alan Edwin 1937- Who 94
Furness, Betty 1916- IntMPA 94, WhoAm 94, WhoHol 92
Furness, Deborra-Lee WhoHol 92
Furness, Peter John 1956- WhoAmL 94
Furness, Rex L. 1923- WhoAmP 93
Furness, Robin Who 94

Furness, Simon John 1936- *Who 94*
Furness, Stephen (Roberts) 1933- *Who 94*
Furney, Linda Jeanne 1947- *WhoAmP 93, WhoWomW 91*
Furnier, Vincent 1948- *WhoAm 94*
Furnish, Victor Paul 1931- *WrDr 94*
Furnish, Zelma M. 1927- *WhoAmP 93*
Furniss, Delma 1934- *WhoAmP 93*
Furniss, Harry d1925 *WhoHol 92*
Furniss, Peter 1919- *Who 94*
Furniss, Susan West 1924- *WhoAmP 93*
Furnival, George Mitchell 1908- *WhoAm 94, WhoWest 94*
Furnival Jones, (Edward) Martin 1912- *Who 94*
Furnweger, Karen 1951- *WhoMW 93*
Furphy, Daniel Gene 1951- *WhoFI 94*
Furr, James William, Jr. 1938- *WhoFI 94 ,*
Furr, Jim 1939- *WhoAmA 93*
Furr, Olin Fayrell, Jr. 1943- *WhoAmL 94*
Furr, Quint Eugene 1921- *WhoAm 94, WhoFI 94*
Furr, Warwick Rex, II 1940- *WhoAmL 94*
Furrer, John Rudolf 1927- *WhoAm 94, WhoFI 94*
Furrh, Lemuel Christopher 1921- *WhoAmP 93*
Furry, Elda *WhoHol 92*
Fursch-Madi, Emma 1847-1894 *NewGrDO*
Fursdon, Francis William Edward 1925- *Who 94*
Furse, Elizabeth 1936- *CngDr 93, WhoAm 94, WhoAmP 93, WhoWest 94*
Furse, James Robert 1939- *WhoAm 94*
Furse, Jill d1944 *WhoHol 92*
Furse, Judith d1974 *WhoHol 92*
Fursikov, Andrei Vladimirovich 1945- *WhoScEn 94*
Fursland, Richard Curtis 1948- *WhoAm 94, WhoFI 94*
Furst, Arthur 1914- *WhoAm 94, WhoWest 94*
Furst, Austin O. *IntMPA 94*
Furst, Errol Kenneth 1946- *WhoAm 94*
Furst, George 1918- *WhoScEn 94*
Furst, Janos Kalman 1935- *IntWW 93*
Furst, Lilian R(enee) 1931- *WrDr 94*
Furst, Lilian Renee 1931- *WhoAm 94*
Furst, Norma Fields 1931- *WhoAm 94*
Furst, Patricia Ann *WhoIns 94*
Furst, Ronald Terrence 1949- *WhoWest 94*
Furst, Stephen 1954- *WhoHol 92*
Furst, Stephen Andrew 1951- *Who 94*
Furst, William d1993 *NewYTBS 93*
Furste, Wesley Leonard, II 1915- *WhoAm 94, WhoMW 93, WhoScEn 94*
Furstenberg, Princess Ira *WhoHol 92*
Furstman, Shirley Elsie Daddow 1930- *WhoFI 94*
Furter, William Frederick 1931- *WhoAm 94*
Furth, Frederick Paul 1934- *WhoAm 94, WhoAmP 93*
Furth, George 1932- *ConDr 93, WhoAm 94, WhoHol 92, WrDr 94*
Furth, Harold Paul 1930- *IntWW 93, WhoScEn 94*
Furth, John Jacob 1929- *WhoAm 94*
Furth, Warren Wolfgang 1928- *IntWW 93*
Furthman, Jules 1888-1966 *IntDcF 2-4 [port]*
Furtinger, Zvonimir *EncSF 93*
Furtner, Joe d1965 *WhoHol 92*
Furtney, Diane *DrAPF 93*
Furton, George C. *WhoAmP 93*
Furtwangler, Albert (J.) 1942- *ConAu 41NR*
Furtwangler, Virginia *DrAPF 93*
Furtwangler, Virginia W(alsh) 1932- *ConAu 41NR*
Furtwangler, (Gustav Heinrich Ernst Martin) Wilhelm 1886-1954 *NewGrDO*
Furubotn, Eirik Grundtvig 1923- *WhoAm 94*
Furuhata, Taketo 1930- *WhoAm 94, WhoFI 94*
Furuichi, Susumu 1931- *WhoScEn 94*
Furukawa, Fred M. 1932- *WhoAsA 94*
Furukawa, John Kazuya 1955- *WhoWest 94*
Furukawa, Larry Kiyoshi 1952- *WhoAsA 94*
Furukawa, Theodore Paul 1944- *WhoAsA 94*
Furumoto, Horace Wataru 1931- *WhoAm 94*
Furuta, Harry *WhoAsA 94*
Furuta, Karin L. 1963- *WhoAsA 94*
Furuta, Otto K. 1943- *WhoAsA 94*
Furuta, Richard K. 1953- *WhoAsA 94*
Furuta, Soichi 1927- *WhoAsA 94*
Furutani, Warren *WhoAsA 94*
Furuto, David Masaru 1945- *WhoWest 94*
Furuto, Sharlene Bernice Choy Lin 1947- *WhoAsA 94*
Furuya, Tsutomu 1928- *WhoScEn 94*

Furuzan 1935- *BlmGWL*
Fury, Billy d1983 *WhoHol 92*
Fury, Ed *WhoHol 92*
Fury, Loretta *WhoHol 92*
Fusai, Ippolito fl. 1661-1696 *NewGrDO*
Fusaro, Ramon Michael 1927- *WhoAm 94*
Fusciardi, Katherine 1965- *WhoMW 93*
Fusco, Andrew G. 1948- *WhoAm 94, WhoAmL 94, WhoFI 94*
Fusco, Angelo 1953- *WhoAmP 93*
Fusco, Anthony Salvatore 1954- *WhoFI 94*
Fusco, Carole Lynn 1954- *WhoMW 93*
Fusco, Giovanni 1906-1968 *IntDcF 2-4*
Fusco, John *WhoAmP 93*
Fusco, Laurie S. 1941- *WhoAmA 93*
Fusco, Louis Michael 1949- *WhoAmP 93*
Fusco, Penny Plummer 1968- *WhoScEn 94*
Fusco, Peter Richard 1945- *WhoAmA 93*
Fusco, Yolanda 1922- *WhoAmA 93*
Fuscone, Richard M. 1951- *WhoFI 94*
Fuse, Bobby LeAndrew, Jr. 1952- *WhoBlA 94*
Fusek, Serena *DrAPF 93*
Fuselier, Louis Alfred 1932- *WhoAm 94, WhoAmL 94*
Fusfeld, Daniel Roland 1922- *WhoAm 94*
Fusfeld, Irving Sidney 1893- *WhAm 10*
Fusi, Juan Pablo 1945- *IntWW 93*
Fusier-Gir, Jeanne d1974 *WhoHol 92*
Fusin, Kate 1943- *WrDr 94*
Fusina, Alessandro Eugenio 1937- *WhoAm 94*
Fuson, Anne Beaty 1928- *WhoAmP 93*
Fuson, Ben(jamin) W(illis) 1911- *WrDr 94*
Fuson, Douglas Finley 1944- *WhoAm 94, WhoAmL 94*
Fuss, Johann Evangelist *NewGrDO*
Fusscas, J. Peter *WhoAmP 93*
Fussell, Aaron E. *WhoAmP 93*
Fussell, Catharine Pugh 1919- *WhoAm 94*
Fussell, Paul 1895- *WhAm 10*
Fussell, Paul 1924- *IntWW 93, WhoAm 94, WrDr 94*
Fussell, Paul Stephen 1958- *WhoScEn 94*
Fussell, Robert Foreman 1938- *WhoAm 94, WhoAmL 94*
Fussell, Ronald Moi 1956- *WhoFI 94*
Fussenegger, Gertrud 1912- *BlmGWL*
Fussey, David Eric 1943- *Who 94*
Fussichen, Kenneth 1950- *WhoMW 93, WhoScEn 94*
Fussiner, Howard 1923- *WhoAmA 93*
Fussl, Karl Heinz 1924- *NewGrDO*
Fussner, Frank Smith 1920- *WrDr 94*
Fuste, Jose Antonio 1943- *WhoAm 94, WhoAmL 94*
Fuster, Jaime B. 1941- *WhoAmP 93, WhoHisp 94*
Fuster, Valentin 1943- *WhoAm 94*
Fusz, Janos 1777-1819 *NewGrDO*
Futai, Masamitsu 1940- *WhoScEn 94*
Futas, Elizabeth Dorothy 1944- *WhoAm 94*
Futch, Archer Hamner 1925- *WhoWest 94*
Futch, Edward 1911- *WhoBlA 94*
Futch, Howard E. 1928- *WhoAmP 93*
Futcher, Hugh *WhoHol 92*
Futcher, Jane P. 1947- *SmATA 76 [port]*
Futcher, Palmer Howard 1910- *WhoAm 94*
Futernick, Kenneth David 1953- *WhoScEn 94*
Futey, Bohdan A. 1939- *CngDr 93, WhoAm 94, WhoAmL 94*
Futia, Leo R. 1919- *WhoIns 94*
Futia, Leo Richard 1919- *WhoAm 94*
Fu Tianlin 1946- *IntWW 93, WhoPRCh 91 [port]*
Fu Tieshan 1931- *IntWW 93, WhoPRCh 91 [port]*
Futoran, Herbert S. 1942- *WhoIns 94*
Futrell, Ashley Brown, Jr. 1956- *WhoAmP 93*
Futrell, Basil Lee 1937- *WhoAm 94*
Futrell, John William 1935- *WhoAm 94*
Futrell, Mary Alice Hatwood 1940- *WhoAm 94*
Futrell, Mary Hatwood 1940- *WhoBlA 94*
Futrell, Nancy Nielson 1947- *WhoScEn 94*
Futrell, Robert Frank 1917- *WhoFI 94*
Futrelle, Jacques 1875-1912 *EncSF 93*
Futter, Ellen Victoria 1949- *WhoAm 94*
Futter, Victor 1919- *WhoAm 94, WhoAmL 94*
Futterman, Dorothea Hardt 1955- *WhoWest 94*
Futterman, Jack 1933- *WhoAm 94, WhoFI 94*
Futuyma, Douglas Joel 1942- *WhoAm 94*
Fux, Johann Joseph c. 1660-1741 *NewGrDO*
Fu Xishou 1930- *WhoPRCh 91 [port]*
Fu Xishou 1931- *IntWW 93*
Fu Xuewen 1903- *WhoPRCh 91 [port]*

Fu Yuantian *WhoPRCh 91*
Fuzak, Victor Thaddeus 1926- *WhoAm 94, WhoAmL 94*
Fuzelier, Louis 1672-1752 *NewGrDO*
Fuzesi, Stephen, Jr. 1948- *WhoAm 94*
Fuzhenko, Ivan Vasilevich 1937- *LoBiDrD*
Fybel, Richard D. 1946- *WhoAm 94, WhoAmL 94*
Fye, Paul McDonald 1912-1988 *WhAm 10*
Fye, Rodney Wayne 1928- *WhoWest 94*
Fye, W. Bruce, III 1946- *WhoAm 94*
Fyfe, George Lennox 1941- *Who 94*
Fyfe, H(orace) B(owne) 1918- *EncSF 93*
Fyfe, Jo Suzanne (Storch) 1941- *WhoAmA 93*
Fyfe, Maria 1938- *Who 94, WhoWomW 91*
Fyfe, Richard Warren 1942- *WhoScEn 94*
Fyfe, Rita Marie 1960- *WhoMW 93*
Fyfe, William Arthur 1916- *WhoAmP 93*
Fyfe, William Sefton 1927- *IntWW 93, Who 94, WhoAm 94, WhoScEn 94*
Fyfe, William Stevenson 1935- *Who 94*
Fyffe, Les *WhoScEn 94*
Fyffe, Will d1947 *WhoHol 92*
Fyfield, Frances 1948- *WrDr 94*
Fyge, Sarah 1669?-1722? *BlmGWL*
Fygi, Eric J. *WhoAmL 94*
Fyjis-Walker, Richard Alwyne 1927- *Who 94*
Fyke, Kenneth John 1940- *WhoAm 94*
Fykes, Leroy Matthews, Jr. 1945- *WhoBlA 94*
Fyler, Carl John 1921- *WhoMW 93*
Fyodorova, Victoria 1946- *WhoHol 92*
Fyodorova, Zoya d1981 *WhoHol 92*
Fysh *EncSF 93*
Fysh, Robert Michael 1940- *Who 94*
Fyson, J(enny) G(race) 1904- *WrDr 94*

G

Gaa, Peter Charles 1955- *WhoScEn 94*
Gaab, Michael Robert 1947- *WhoScEn 94*
Gaafar, Sayed Mohammed 1924- *WhoAm 94*
Gaal, Franciska d1972 *WhoHol 92*
Gaal, John 1952- *WhoAm 94, WhoAmL 94*
Gaalova, Barbara Kanzler 1953- *WhoFI 94*
Gaan, Margaret 1914- *WrDr 94*
Gaar, Gillian G. 1959- *ConAu 142*
Gaar, Marilyn Audrey Wiegraffe 1946- *WhoMW 93*
Gaar, Norman Edward 1929- *WhoAmL 94, WhoMW 93*
Gaard, Greta 1960- *ConAu 140*
Gaard, Thomas J. 1939- *WhoIns 94*
Gaarder, Marie 1935- *WhoAm 94*
Gaba, Marianne *WhoHol 92*
Gabaldón, Benjamín Alfonso 1926- *WhoHisp 94*
Gabaldón, Julia K. 1947- *WhoHisp 94*
Gabaldon, Theresa Ann 1954- *WhoHisp 94*
Gabaldon, Tony *WhoAmP 93*
Gabaldon, Tony 1930- *WhoHisp 94*
Gabarro, John Joseph 1939- *WhoAm 94*
Gabathuler, Erwin 1933- *Who 94*
Gabay, Donald D. 1935- *WhoIns 94*
Gabay, Donald David 1935- *WhoAm 94*
Gabb, (William) Harry 1909- *Who 94*
Gabbai, Alexandre *WhoScEn 94*
Gabbai, Moni E. 1943- *WhoIns 94*
Gabbard, Douglas, II 1952- *WhoAmL 94*
Gabbard, G. N. *DrAPF 93*
Gabbard, Glen Owens 1949- *WhoAm 94*
Gabbert, Lyndon Jay 1958- *WhoMW 93*
Gabbin, Alexander Lee 1945- *WhoBlA 94*
Gabbin, Joanne Veal 1946- *WhoBlA 94*
Gabbour, Iskandar 1929- *WhoAm 94*
Gabe, Ron *WhoAmA 93*
Gabel, Creighton 1931- *WhoAm 94*
Gabel, Edward Alexander 1947- *WhoIns 94*
Gabel, Frederick Daniel, Jr. 1938- *WhoIns 94*
Gabel, George DeSaussure, Jr. 1940- *WhoAm 94, WhoAmL 94, WhoFI 94*
Gabel, Johannes Karl 1952- *WhoAm 94*
Gabel, Katherine 1938- *WhoAm 94*
Gabel, Krystal Leigh 1964- *WhoMW 93*
Gabel, Martin d1986 *WhoHol 92*
Gabel, Michael Wayne 1951- *WhoAmL 94*
Gabel, Patricia 1949- *WhoAmL 94*
Gabel, Ronald Glen 1937- *WhoFI 94*
Gabel, Scilla 1937- *WhoHol 92*
Gabeler-Brooks, Jo 1931- *WhoAmA 93*
Gabelli, Mario J. *WhoAm 94, WhoFI 94*
Gabelman, John Warren 1921- *WhoWest 94*
Gabelnick, Henry Lewis 1940- *WhoScEn 94*
Gaber, Elsie Jean Kins 1952- *WhoMW 93*
Gaber, Robert 1923- *WhoScEn 94*
Gaberino, John Anthony, Jr. 1941- *WhoAmL 94*
Gaberman, Harry 1913- *WhoAmL 94, WhoFI 94*
Gaberman, Judith *DrAPF 93*
Gaberson, Howard Axel 1931- *WhoWest 94*
Gabert, Alex W. *WhoHisp 94*

Gabet, Stephen J. *WhoAmP 93*
Gabhart, Ann 1947- *ConAu 142, SmATA 75 [port]*
Gabichvadze, Revaz Kondrat'yevich 1913- *NewGrDO*
Gabin, George Joseph 1931- *WhoAmA 93*
Gabin, Jean d1976 *WhoHol 92*
Gabinski, Theris M. 1938- *WhoAmP 93*
Gable, Carl Irwin 1939- *WhoAm 94*
Gable, Carol Brignoli 1945- *WhoAm 94*
Gable, Christopher *IntWW 93*
Gable, Christopher 1940- *IntDcB [port], WhoHol 92*
Gable, Clark d1960 *WhoHol 92*
Gable, Fred Burnard 1929- *WhoAm 94*
Gable, G. Ellis 1905- *WhoAm 94*
Gable, Jack d1967 *WhoHol 92*
Gable, John Clark 1961- *WhoHol 92*
Gable, John Oglesby 1944- *WhoAmA 93*
Gable, John Starrett 1946- *WhoMW 93*
Gable, June *WhoHol 92*
Gable, Karen Elaine 1939- *WhoMW 93*
Gable, Robert Elledy 1934- *WhoAm 94, WhoAmP 93, WhoFI 94*
Gable, Robert S. 1934- *WhoScEn 94*
Gable, Robert William, Jr. 1939- *WhoScEn 94*
Gable, Thomas D. 1942- *WhoAmL 94*
Gablehouse, Timothy Reuben 1951- *WhoAmL 94*
Gablentz, Otto von der 1930- *IntWW 93*
Gabler, Mirko 1951- *SmATA 77 [port]*
Gabler, Robert Charles 1960- *WhoAmL 94*
Gabler, Robert Clair 1933- *WhoWest 94*
Gabler, William Joseph 1952- *WhoAmL 94*
Gabler-Hover, Janet A. 1953- *WrDr 94*
Gablik, Suzi 1934- *WhoAmA 93, WrDr 94*
Gabo, Naum 1890-1977 *WhoAmA 93N*
Gabor, Al *DrAPF 93*
Gabor, Billy 1922- *BasBi*
Gabor, Dennis 1900-1979 *WorInv*
Gabor, Eva 1919- *WhoHol 92*
Gabor, Frank 1918- *WhoFI 94, WhoIns 94*
Gabor, Jeffrey Alan 1942- *WhoFI 94*
Gabor, Zsa Zsa 1917- *WhoHol 92*
Gabor, Zsa Zsa 1918- *IntMPA 94*
Gabovich, Mikhail 1905-1965 *IntDcB [port]*
Gabovitch, Steven Alan 1953- *WhoAmL 94*
Gabovitch, William 1922- *WhoAmL 94*
Gabre-Medhin, Tsegaye (Kawessa) 1936?- *BlkWr 2*
Gabre-Sellassie, Zewde 1926- *IntWW 93*
Gabria, Joanne Bakaitis 1945- *WhoFI 94*
Gabrick, Robert William 1940- *WhoMW 93*
Gabridge, Michael Gregory 1943- *WhoAm 94*
Gabriel, Astrik Ladislas 1907- *WhoAm 94*
Gabriel, Benjamin Moses 1931- *WhoBlA 94*
Gabriel, Charles Alvin 1928- *WhoAm 94*
Gabriel, D. Bruce 1954- *WhoAmL 94*
Gabriel, Daniel *DrAPF 93*
Gabriel, Dennis R. 1950- *WhoHisp 94*
Gabriel, Eberhard John 1942- *WhoAmL 94*
Gabriel, Edward Michael 1950- *WhoAm 94*

Gabriel, Eileen M. 1951- *WhoIns 94*
Gabriel, Ethel d1967 *WhoHol 92*
Gabriel, Hannelore *WhoAmA 93*
Gabriel, Israel El 1944- *WhoWest 94*
Gabriel, Jean d1977 *WhoHol 92*
Gabriel, John 1931- *WhoHol 92*
Gabriel, Joyce Valeria 1937- *WhoMW 93*
Gabriel, Jüri (Evald) 1940- *WrDr 94*
Gabriel, Kathryn (Ann) 1955- *ConAu 140*
Gabriel, Larry E. 1946- *WhoAmP 93*
Gabriel, Michael 1927- *WhoWest 94*
Gabriel, Michael 1940- *WhoAm 94*
Gabriel, Michal 1960- *IntWW 93*
Gabriel, Mordecai Lionel 1918- *WhoAm 94*
Gabriel, Peter 1950- *IntWW 93, WhoAm 94, WhoHol 92*
Gabriel, Philip L(ouis) 1918-1993 *ConAu 141*
Gabriel, Rennie 1948- *WhoFI 94, WhoWest 94*
Gabriel, Richard Weisner 1949- *WhoAmL 94*
Gabriel, Robert 1931- *WhoAm 94*
Gabriel, Roger Eugene 1929- *WhoAm 94, WhoFI 94*
Gabriele, Vincenzo 1948- *WhoFI 94*
Gabrielian, Armen 1940- *WhoWest 94*
Gabrielides, Andreas 1949- *IntWW 93*
Gabrielli, Caterina 1730-1796 *NewGrDO*
Gabrielli, Domenico 1651-1690 *NewGrDO*
Gabrielli, Laetitia *WhoHol 92*
Gabrielli, Nicolo 1814-1891 *NewGrDO*
Gabrielse, Edward Jerome 1942- *WhoFI 94*
Gabrielsen, Carol Ann 1951- *WhoMW 93*
Gabrielsen, Holger d1956 *WhoHol 92*
Gabrielsen, Paul Thomas 1929- *WhoWest 94*
Gabrielson, Dave *WhoAmP 93*
Gabrielson, Ira Wilson 1922- *WhoAm 94*
Gabrielson, Shirley Gail 1934- *WhoWest 94*
Gabrielson, Walter Oscar 1935- *WhoAmA 93*
Gabrilove, Jacques Lester 1917- *WhoAm 94*
Gabrilovich, Yevgeny 1899-1993 *NewYTBS 93*
Gabrio, Gabriel d1946 *WhoHol 92*
Gabrovsky, Peter Nicolaev 1944- *WhoWest 94*
Gabrynowicz, Joanne Irene 1949- *WhoAmL 94*
Ga-bu-long 1926- *WhoPRCh 91 [port]*
Gaburo, Kenneth d1993 *NewYTBS 93*
Gaburo, Kenneth (Louis) 1926- *NewGrDO*
Gaburo, Virginia Hommel 1938- *WhoAmL 94*
Gabussi, Rita c. 1815-1891 *NewGrDO*
Gabussi, Vincenzo 1800-1846 *NewGrDO*
Gabutti, Alberto 1960- *WhoScEn 94*
Gaby, Daniel M. 1933- *WhoAm 94*
Gaby, Frank d1945 *WhoHol 92*
Gaby Lee 1930- *WhoAm 94*
Gac, Frank David 1951- *WhoWest 94*
Gaccione, Anthony Salvatore 1898- *WhAm 10*
Gacem, Debra Ann 1955- *WhoMW 93*
Gach, Gary G. *DrAPF 93*
Gach, George 1909- *WhoAmA 93*

Gachette, Louise Foston 1911- *WhoBlA 94*
Gachot, Charles Artur Jacques 1931- *WhoFI 94*
Gaci, Pjeter 1931- *NewGrDO*
Gacic, Radisa 1938- *IntWW 93*
Gacioch, Michael Theodore, Jr. 1955- *WhoFI 94*
Gackle, William Frederick 1927- *WhoAmP 93*
Gackstetter, Dean Duane 1929- *WhoMW 93*
Gacon-Dufor, Marie Armande Jeanne 1753-1835? *BlmGWL*
Gacono, Carl B. 1954- *WhoWest 94*
Gad, Lance Stewart 1945- *WhoFI 94*
Gad, Robert K., III 1946- *WhoAm 94, WhoAmL 94*
Gad, Rose 1968- *IntDcB*
Gadal, Louis Stephen 1936- *WhoWest 94*
Gadallah, Leslie 1939- *EncSF 93*
Gadamer, Hans Georg 1900- *EncEth, IntWW 93*
Gadberry, Wayne Ronald 1946- *WhoFI 94*
Gadbois, Richard A., Jr. 1932- *WhoAm 94, WhoAmL 94, WhoWest 94*
Gadbury, John 1627-1704 *AstEnc*
Gadd, Jack *WhoAmP 93*
Gadd, John 1925- *Who 94*
Gadd, L. Damon d1993 *NewYTBS 93*
Gadd, Renee 1908- *WhoHol 92*
Gadd, (John) Staffan 1934- *Who 94*
Gadda Conti, Piero 1902- *IntWW 93*
Gaddafi, Mu'ammar Muhammad al- 1942- *IntWW 93*
Gaddafi, Wanis *IntWW 93*
Gaddam, Encik Kasitah bin 1947- *IntWW 93*
Gaddes, (John) Gordon 1936- *Who 94*
Gaddes, Richard 1942- *NewGrDO, WhoAm 94*
Gaddis, John Lewis 1941- *WhoAm 94*
Gaddis, M. Francis 1920- *WhoScEn 94*
Gaddis, Mary Peabody 1927- *WhoMW 93*
Gaddis, Paul Otto 1924- *WhoAm 94*
Gaddis, Sarah 1955?- *ConAu 142*
Gaddis, Vincent Hayes 1913- *WrDr 94*
Gaddis, William *DrAPF 93*
Gaddis, William 1922- *IntWW 93, WhoAm 94, WrDr 94*
Gaddis Rose, Marilyn 1930- *WhoAm 94, WrDr 94*
Gaddy, Beatrice 1933- *WhoBlA 94*
Gaddy, Bob L. 1940- *WhoFI 94*
Gaddy, Carolyn C. 1910- *WhoAmP 93*
Gaddy, Christopher Royal 1960- *WhoMW 93*
Gaddy, James Leoma 1932- *WhoAm 94, WhoScEn 94*
Gaddy, M. Gordon 1936- *WhoIns 94*
Gaddy, Oscar Lee 1932- *WhoAm 94*
Gaddy, Robert Joseph 1924- *WhoAm 94*
Gade, Henry *EncSF 93*
Gade, Marvin Francis 1924- *WhoAm 94*
Gad-el-Hak, Mohamed 1945- *WhoScEn 94*
Gadell, James David 1949- *WhoAmP 93*
Gaden, Elmer Lewis, Jr. 1923- *WhoAm 94*
Gadgil, Gangadhar (Gopal) 1923- *RfGShF*
Gadgil, Vithal Narhar 1928- *IntWW 93*
Gadke, Karen 1934- *WhoMW 93*
Gadney, Reg 1941- *WrDr 94*

Gadol, Nancy 1949- WhoWest 94
Gadol, Peter 1964- WrDr 94
Gadola, Paul V. 1929- WhoAm 94, WhoAmL 94
Gadomski, Robert Eugene 1947- WhoAm 94
Gadsby, Edward Northup, Jr. 1935- WhoAm 94
Gadsby, (Gordon) Neville 1914- Who 94
Gadsby, Robin Edward 1939- WhoAm 94, WhoFI 94
Gadsden, Christopher 1724-1805 WhAmRev
Gadsden, Christopher Henry 1946- WhoAmL 94
Gadsden, Eugene Hinson 1912- WhoBlA 94
Gadsden, Nathaniel J., Jr. 1950- WhoBlA 94
Gadsden, Peter (Drury Haggerston) 1929- Who 94
Gadsden, Peter Drury Haggerston 1929- IntWW 93
Gadsden, Richard Hamilton 1925- WhoAm 94
Gadsden, Thomas P. 1949- WhoAm 94, WhoAmL 94
Gadski, Johanna 1872-1932 NewGrDO
Gadson, Rosetta E. 1938- WhoBlA 94
Gadzhibekov, Uzeir (Abdul Huseyn) NewGrDO
Gadzhiev, Gadis Abdullaevich 1953- LoBiDrD
Gadzhiyev, Dzhevdet NewGrDO
Gadzinski, Barbara Ann 1955- WhoMW 93
Gaebler, (Gerhard Otto) Rainer 1938- IntWW 93
Gaebler, Richard H. 1930- WhoIns 94
Gaede, Anton Henry, Jr. 1939- WhoAm 94
Gaede, Ruth Ann 1952- WhoMW 93
Gaehtgens, Thomas Wolfgang 1940- IntWW 93
Gaeng, Paul Ami 1924- WhoAm 94
Gaenzl, Kurt (Friedrich) 1946- WrDr 94
Gaer, Evdokiya Aleksandrovna 1934- WhoWomW 91
Gaerlan, Pureza Flor Monzon 1933- WhoScEn 94
Gaertner, Alfred Ludwig 1953- WhoScEn 94
Gaertner, Christopher Wolfgang 1962- WhoAm 94
Gaertner, Donell J. 1932- WhoAm 94, WhoMW 93
Gaertner, Gary M. WhoAmL 94
Gaertner, James Leo 1943- WhoMW 93
Gaertner, Ken DrAPF 93
Gaertner, Richard Francis 1933- WhoAm 94, WhoScEn 94
Gaertner, Wolfgang Wilhelm 1929-1989 WhAm 10
Gaess, Roger DrAPF 93
Gaeta, Federico Carlos Arejola 1951- WhoWest 94
Gaeta, Gerald 1955- WhoHisp 94
Gaeta, Michael A. 1945- WhoMW 93
Gaeta, Vincent Ettore 1963- WhoScEn 94
Gaetano d1793? NewGrDO
Gaetano, Angela Maria 1964- WhoHisp 94
Gaetano, Cortesi 1912- IntWW 93
Gaete Rojas, Sergio 1939- IntWW 93
Gaeth, M. Ben 1921- WhoAmP 93
Gaeth, Matthew Ben 1921- WhoMW 93
Gaeuman, John Victor 1932- WhoMW 93
Gaff, Brian Michael 1962- WhoFI 94
Gaff, Jerry Gene 1936- WhoAm 94
Gaffar, Abdul 1940- WhoScEn 94
Gaffarello NewGrDO
Gaffey, Thomas Michael, Jr. 1934- WhoAm 94
Gaffey, William Robert 1924- WhoMW 93
Gaffin, Gerald Eliot 1932- WhoAmL 94
Gaffin, Melanie 1973- WhoHol 92
Gaffke, Howard William 1918- WhoAmP 93
Gaffney Who 94
Gaffney, Donald Lee 1952- WhoAmL 94
Gaffney, Edward McGlynn 1941- WhoAmL 94, WhoMW 93
Gaffney, Elizabeth DrAPF 93
Gaffney, Floyd 1930- WhoBlA 94
Gaffney, Francis Michael 1940- WhoAm 94, WhoAmL 94
Gaffney, Gary Robert 1955- WhoMW 93
Gaffney, James Anthony 1928- Who 94
Gaffney, Jane Ellen 1949- WhoMW 93
Gaffney, John F. 1934- WhoAmP 93
Gaffney, John W. 1930- WhoBlA 94
Gaffney, Leslie Gale 1951- WhoBlA 94
Gaffney, Liam 1911- WhoHol 92
Gaffney, Mark William 1951- WhoAmL 94
Gaffney, Mary Louise WhoBlA 94
Gaffney, Michael Scully 1928- WhoAm 94, WhoFI 94
Gaffney, Patrick Michael 1951- WhoScEn 94
Gaffney, Paul Cotter 1917- WhoAm 94
Gaffney, Paul Golden, II 1946- WhoAm 94
Gaffney, Robert 1931- IntMPA 94
Gaffney, Robert J. 1944- WhoAmP 93
Gaffney, Thomas 1915- WhoAm 94
Gaffney, Thomas Daniel 1933- WhoBlA 94
Gaffney, Thomas Edward 1930- WhoAm 94
Gaffney, Thomas Francis 1945- WhoAm 94
Gafford, Charlotte DrAPF 93
Gafforini, Elisabetta c. 1772-1810? NewGrDO
Gaffrey, Marc Scott 1962- WhoAmL 94
Gafney, Harry D. 1943- WhoAm 94
Gafny, Arnon 1932- IntWW 93
Gagarin, Dennis Paul 1952- WhoWest 94
Gage, Viscount 1932- Who 94
Gage, Ben d1978 WhoHol 92
Gage, Berkeley (Everard Foley) 1904- Who 94
Gage, Beverly Anne 1934- WhoAmP 93
Gage, Calvin William 1929- WhoAm 94
Gage, Carl Webster 1955- WhoAmP 93
Gage, Charles Quincey 1946- WhoAm 94
Gage, Delwyn 1930- WhoAmP 93
Gage, Delwyn Orin 1930- WhoWest 94
Gage, E. Dean 1942- WhoAm 94
Gage, Edwin C., III 1940- WhoAm 94, WhoFI 94
Gage, Erford d1945 WhoHol 92
Gage, Frances M. 1924- WhoAmA 93
Gage, Fred Kelton 1925- WhoAm 94
Gage, Gaston Hemphill 1930- WhoAmL 94
Gage, George Henry 1924- WhoFI 94
Gage, Harlow W. 1911- IntWW 93
Gage, John 1937- WhoAm 94
Gage, Lois Waite 1922- WhoMW 93
Gage, Nathaniel Lees 1917- IntWW 93, WhoAm 94
Gage, Patrick 1942- WhoAm 94
Gage, Peter William 1937- IntWW 93
Gage, Robert 1885- WhAm 10
Gage, Robert Jeffrey 1951- WhoAm 94, WhoAmL 94
Gage, Ruth Elva 1940- WhoAmP 93
Gage, S. R. 1945- WrDr 94
Gage, Sharen Swartz 1951- WhoAm 94, WhoAmL 94
Gage, Thomas 1719?-1787 AmRev
Gage, Thomas 1721-1787 WhAmRev
Gage, Thomas Underwood 1960- WhoAmP 93
Gage, Tommy Wilton 1935- WhoAm 94
Gage, Warren Austin 1949- WhoFI 94
Gage, William Allen, Jr. 1962- WhoAmL 94
Gage, William Marcus 1938- Who 94
Gage, Wilson 1922- WrDr 94
Gagewin c. 1850-1919 EncNAR
Gagge, A. Pharo d1993 NewYTBS 93
Gaggero, Joseph James 1927- Who 94
Gaggini, John Edmund 1949- WhoAm 94, WhoAmL 94
Gaggioli, Nestor Gustavo 1940- WhoScEn 94
Gaggioli, Richard Arnold 1934- WhoAm 94
Gaggiotti, Pellegrino fl. 1714-1758 NewGrDO
Gagliano, Frank 1931- WrDr 94
Gagliano, Frank (Joseph) 1931- ConDr 93
Gagliano, Frank Joseph 1931- WhoAm 94
Gagliano, Gerard Anthony 1954- WhoWest 94
Gagliano, Marco da 1582-1643 NewGrDO
Gagliano, S. Thomas 1931- WhoAmP 93
Gagliardi, Lee Parsons 1918- WhoAm 94, WhoAmL 94
Gagliardi, Pat 1950- WhoAmP 93
Gagliardi, Raymond Alfred 1922- WhoScEn 94
Gagliardi, Ugo Oscar 1931- WhoAm 94, WhoScEn 94
Gagliardo, John G. 1933- WrDr 94
Gagliardo, Victor Arthur 1957- WhoScEn 94
Gaglione, Frank T. 1944- WhoAmL 94
Gagne, Paul Ernest 1946- WhoAm 94
Gagne, Peter Joseph 1941- WhoAmL 94
Gagnebin, Albert P. 1909- IntWW 93
Gagnebin, Albert Paul 1909- WhoAm 94
Gagneur, Marie-Louise 1832-1902 BlmGWL
Gagnier, Bruce 1941- WhoAmA 93
Gagnier, Holly WhoHol 92
Gagnon, Charles 1934- WhoAmA 93
Gagnon, Charles Eugene 1934- WhoAmA 93
Gagnon, Craig Alan 1960- WhoAmP 93
Gagnon, Craig William 1940- WhoAm 94
Gagnon, Edith Morrison 1909- WhoAm 94
Gagnon, Edouard 1918- IntWW 93
Gagnon, Eugene L. 1943- WhoAmP 93
Gagnon, Jean-Marie 1933- IntWW 93
Gagnon, Jean Paul 1941- WhoMW 93
Gagnon, John Harvey 1946- WhoScEn 94
Gagnon, Margaret Ann Callahan 1952- WhoWest 94
Gagnon, Rene A. d1979 WhoHol 92
Gagnon, Stewart Walter 1949- WhoAm 94, WhoAmL 94
Gagnon, Wayne Joseph 1949- WhoWest 94
Gago, Jenny WhoHisp 94
Gagosian, Larry WhoAm 94
Gagosian, Robert B. 1944- WhoAm 94
Gaguine, Benito 1912- WhoAm 94
Gahagan, Helen d1980 WhoHol 92
Gahagan, James (Edward), Jr. 1927- WhoAmA 93
Gahagan, James Edward, Jr. 1927- WhoAm 94
Gahagan, Marilyn Ann 1949- WhoMW 93
Gahagan, Michael Barclay 1943- Who 94
Gahagan, Thomas Gail 1938- WhoScEn 94
Gahagan, Walter Hamer d1993 NewYTBS 93
Gahan, Kathleen Mason 1940- WhoWest 94
Gahan, Peter Brian 1933- WhoScEn 94
Gahlinger, Shardith Dean 1961- WhoMW 93
Gahmberg, Carl G. 1942- IntWW 93
Gahuni dc. 1857 EncNAR
Gai, Eliezer 1944- WhoAm 94
Gai, Madge E. 1944- WhoAmP 93
Gaia, Pam WhoAmP 93
Gaiber, Lawrence Jay 1960- WhoFI 94, WhoWest 94
Gaiber, Maxine Diane 1949- WhoWest 94
Gaich, Sharon Denise 1961- WhoMW 93
Gaidar, Egor Timurovich 1956- LoBiDrD
Gaidar, Yegor IntWW 93
Gaige, Russell d1974 WhoHol 92
Gail, Barbara 1933- WrDr 94
Gail, Max 1943- IntMPA 94
Gail, Max 1944- WhoHol 92
Gail, Maxwell Trowbridge, Jr. 1943- WhoAm 94
Gail, Otto Willi 1896-1956 EncSF 93
Gail, Sanford R. 1943- WhoAmL 94
Gail, (Edmee) Sophie 1775-1819 NewGrDO
Gailey, Charles Franklin, Jr. 1926- WhoFI 94
Gailhard, Andre(-Charles-Samson) 1885-1966 NewGrDO
Gailhard, Pierre 1848-1918 NewGrDO
Gailis, Janis 1909-1975 WhoAmA 93N
Gailitis, Karlis 1936- LoBiDrD
Gailius, Gilbert Keistutis 1931- WhoAm 94, WhoFI 94
Gaillard, Bernard 1944- WhoBlA 94
Gaillard, George Siday, III 1941- WhoFI 94
Gaillard, John Palmer, Jr. 1920- WhoAm 94
Gaillard, Mary Katharine 1939- WhoAm 94, WhoScEn 94, WhoWest 94
Gaillard, Ralph C., Sr. 1943- WhoBlA 94
Gaillard, Slim d1991 WhoHol 92
Gailys, John M. 1941- WhoFI 94
Gaiman, Neil (Richard) 1960- EncSF 93, WrDr 94
Gaimard, Joseph-Paul 1796-1858 WhWE
Gain, Jeffrey W. WhoMW 93
Gainer, Andrew A. 1919- WhoBlA 94
Gainer, Carl E. WhoAmP 93
Gainer, Carol Lee 1942- WhoAmP 93
Gainer, Cindy 1962- SmATA 74
Gainer, Frank Edward 1938- WhoBlA 94
Gainer, Glen B. 1960- WhoAmP 93
Gainer, Glen B., Jr. 1927- WhoAmP 93
Gainer, John F. 1954- WhoBlA 94
Gainer, Leila Josephine 1948- WhoFI 94
Gainer, Ruby Jackson WhoBlA 94
Gaines, Adriane Theresa 1947- WhoBlA 94
Gaines, Alan Jay 1942- WhoAmA 93
Gaines, Alan McCulloch 1938- WhoAm 94
Gaines, Alexander Pendleton 1910- WhAm 10
Gaines, Atwood Dwight 1945- WhoMW 93
Gaines, Ava Candace 1963- WhoBlA 94
Gaines, Boyd 1953- WhoHol 92
Gaines, Clarence E., Sr. 1923- WhoBlA 94
Gaines, Clarence L. 1914- WhoBlA 94
Gaines, Corey Yasuto 1965- WhoBlA 94
Gaines, Cristina E. 1946- WhoHisp 94
Gaines, Donna 1951- WrDr 94
Gaines, Edythe J. 1922- WhoBlA 94
Gaines, Ernest J. DrAPF 93, WhoAm 94
Gaines, Ernest J. 1933- AfrAmAl 6, WhoBlA 94, WrDr 94
Gaines, Ernest J(ames) 1933- BlkWr 2, ConAu 42NR, TwCYAW
Gaines, Francis Pendleton, III 1944- WhoAm 94, WhoAmL 94
Gaines, Frank D. 1934- WhoAmP 93
Gaines, Frederick DrAPF 93
Gaines, H. Michael 1945- WhoIns 94
Gaines, Herschel Davis 1942- WhoBlA 94
Gaines, Howard Clarke 1909- WhoAm 94, WhoAmL 94, WhoWest 94
Gaines, Howard Rudolph 1953- WhoAmL 94
Gaines, Irving David 1923- WhoAmL 94
Gaines, James Edwin, Jr. 1938- WhoAm 94
Gaines, James Russell 1947- WhoAm 94
Gaines, John A., Sr. 1941- WhoBlA 94
Gaines, John Adrian 1955- WhoWest 94
Gaines, Jon Christopher 1968- WhoFI 94
Gaines, Kay Heeren 1943- WhoMW 93
Gaines, Kenneth R. 1943- WhoAm 94, WhoAmL 94
Gaines, Lee d1987 WhoHol 92
Gaines, Leonard WhoHol 92
Gaines, Leslie Doran 1912- WhoBlA 94
Gaines, Ludwell Ebersole 1927- WhoAm 94
Gaines, Manyles B., Jr. 1938- WhoBlA 94
Gaines, Mark L. WhoAmP 93
Gaines, Mary E. WhoBlA 94
Gaines, Natalie Mallie WhoAm 94
Gaines, Oscar Cornell 1954- WhoBlA 94
Gaines, Paul Laurence, Sr. 1932- WhoBlA 94
Gaines, Peter Mathew 1951- WhoAm 94
Gaines, Ray D. 1932- WhoBlA 94
Gaines, Richard d1975 WhoHol 92
Gaines, Richard Kendall 1947- WhoBlA 94
Gaines, Robert Darryl 1951- WhoAmL 94, WhoMW 93
Gaines, Robert E. 1923- WhoAmP 93
Gaines, Robert Martin 1931- WhoAmL 94
Gaines, Samuel Stone 1938- WhoBlA 94
Gaines, Sedalia Mitchell 1917- WhoBlA 94
Gaines, Sylvester, Jr. 1921- WhoBlA 94
Gaines, Thurston Lenwood, Jr. 1922- WhoBlA 94
Gaines, Tyler Belt 1924- WhoAmL 94, WhoMW 93
Gaines, Victor Pryor 1939- WhoBlA 94
Gaines, Weaver Henderson 1943- WhoAmL 94, WhoFI 94
Gaines, William Chester 1933- WhoAm 94, WhoMW 93
Gaines, William M. 1922-1992 AnObit 1992
Gaines, William Maxwell 1922-1992 WhAm 10
Gaines, William Robert 1927- WhoAmA 93
Gainey, Leonard Dennis, II 1927- WhoBlA 94
Gainey, Micajah WhAmRev
Gainey, Robert Michael 1953- WhoAm 94
Gainford, Baron 1921- Who 94
Gainham, Rachel 1922- Who 94
Gainham, Sarah 1922- WrDr 94
Gainor, Thomas Edward 1933- WhoAm 94
Gainous, Fred Jerome 1947- WhoAm 94
Gains, Courtney WhoHol 92
Gainsborough, Earl of 1923- Who 94
Gainsborough, George Fotheringham 1915- Who 94
Gainsborough, Michael 1938- Who 94
Gainsbourg, Charlotte 1972- WhoHol 92
Gainsbourg, Serge d1991 WhoHol 92
Gainsbourg, Serge 1928-1991 WhAm 10
Gainsburg, Roy Ellis 1932- WhoAm 94
Gainsford, Ian Derek 1930- Who 94
Gaintner, John Richard 1936- WhoAm 94, WhoScEn 94
Gainuse, Alexandrina 1932- WhoWomW 91
Gair, George Frederick 1926- IntWW 93, Who 94
Gairdner, John Smith 1925- WhoAm 94
Gairy, Eric Matthew 1922- IntWW 93, Who 94
Gaisford, John Scott 1934- Who 94
Gaisser, Julia Haig 1941- WhoAm 94
Gaitan, Antonio C., Jr. 1933- WhoHisp 94
Gaitán, Fernando J., Jr. WhoHisp 94
Gaitan, Fernando J., Jr. 1948- WhoAm 94, WhoAmL 94, WhoAmL 94, WhoMW 93
Gaitan, Ramon 1934- WhoHisp 94
Gaite, Carmen Martin ConWorW 93
Gaither, Alonzo Smith 1903- WhoBlA 94
Gaither, Cornelius E. 1928- WhoBlA 94
Gaither, Dorothy B. 1941- WhoBlA 94
Gaither, Edmund B. 1944- WhoAmA 93, WhoBlA 94
Gaither, James C. 1937- WhoAm 94
Gaither, James W., Jr. 1954- WhoBlA 94
Gaither, Jerry Lee 1956- WhoFI 94
Gaither, John F. 1949- WhoAm 94, WhoAmL 94
Gaither, John F., Jr. WhoAm 94

Gaither, John Francis 1918- WhoAm 94, WhoFI 94
Gaither, John Stokes 1944- WhoAm 94, WhoFI 94
Gaither, M. Magalene Dulin 1928- WhoAmP 93
Gaither, Magalene Dulin 1928- WhoBlA 94
Gaither, Richard A. 1939- WhoBlA 94
Gaither, Thomas W. 1938- WhoBlA 94
Gaither, William Samuel 1932- WhoAm 94
Gaito, Constantino 1878-1945 NewGrDO
Gaitonde, Sunil Sharadchandra 1960- WhoScEn 94
Gaius, Saimon 1920- Who 94
Gajardo, Joel WhoHisp 94
Gajdos, George John 1951- WhoAmL 94
Gajdosik, Richard Lee 1949- WhoWest 94
Gajdusek, D. Carleton 1923- WorScD
Gajdusek, D(aniel) Carleton 1923- WrDr 94
Gajdusek, Daniel Carleton 1923- IntWW 93, Who 94, WhoAm 94, WhoScEn 94
Gajec, John Joseph 1918- WhoMW 93
Gajec, Lucile Cruz WhoHisp 94
Gaje Ghale 1922- Who 94
Gajendar, Nandigam 1940- WhoAsA 94
Gaji-Zade, Khikmet Abdul-Ragim Olgy 1954- LoBiDrD
Gajjar, Jagdish Trikamji 1940- WhoAsA 94
Gajotti, Pellegrino NewGrDO
Gakov, Vladimir 1951- EncSF 93
Gal, Aaron 1955- WhoScEn 94
Gal, David 1946- WhoScEn 94
Gal, Hans 1890-1987 NewGrDO
Gala (Vetasco), Antonio 1936- ConWorW 93
Gala, Andrew Roman 1959- WhoAmL 94
Gala, Richard Robert 1935- WhoMW 93
Galabru, Michel WhoHol 92
Galaburda, Albert Mark 1948- WhoAm 94
Galadari, Abdel-Wahab 1938- IntWW 93
Galainena, Mariano Luis 1922- WhoHisp 94
Galambos, Barbara Bramley 1954- WhoMW 93
Galambos, Benjamin NewGrDO
Galambos, John Thomas 1921- WhoAm 94
Galambos, Suzanne Julia 1927- WhoWest 94
Galambos, Theodore Victor 1929- WhoAm 94, WhoScEn 94
Galan, Cristobal 1630?-1684 NewGrDO
Galán, Héctor WhoHisp 94
Galan, Juan Arturo, Jr. 1944- WhoHisp 94
Galán, Nely 1964- WhoHisp 94
Galan Alvarez, Victor J. 1933- WhoHisp 94
Galane, Morton Robert 1926- WhoAm 94, WhoAmL 94, WhoWest 94
Galanis, George J. WhoAmP 93
Galanis, John William 1937- WhoAmL 94
Galanopoulos, Kelly 1952- WhoScEn 94
Galanos, James 1924- IntWW 93, WhoAm 94
Galant, Herbert Lewis 1928- WhoAm 94
Galant, Lisa Marie 1965- WhoMW 93
Galante, Jane Hohfeld 1924- WrDr 94
Galante, Joseph Anthony, Jr. 1947- WhoScEn 94
Galante, Marlene 1952- WhoMW 93
Galante, Pierre 1909- WrDr 94
Galanter, Eugene 1924- WhoAm 94
Galanter, Marc 1941- WhoAm 94
Galanter, Robert Allen 1945- WhoAmL 94
Galanter, Ruth WhoAmP 93
Galarraga, Andres Jose 1961- WhoAm 94, WhoHisp 94, WhoWest 94
Galarza, Gabino E. 1941- WhoHisp 94
Galas, David John 1944- WhoScEn 94
Galask, Rudolph Peter 1935- WhoAm 94
Galassi, Jonathan DrAPF 93
Galassi, Jonathan White 1949- WhoAm 94
Galassini, Timothy Robert 1963- WhoFI 94
Galasso, Francis Salvatore 1931- WhoAm 94
Galat, Bernard F. 1950- WhoFI 94
Galati, Frank Joseph 1943- WhoAm 94
Galati, Michael Anthony 1930- WhoIns 94
Galatianos, Gus A. 1947- WhoFI 94
Galatte-Howard, Gail Ann 1959- WhoFI 94, WhoMW 93
Galatz, Henry Francis 1947- WhoAmL 94
Galatzer-Levy, Robert Milton 1944- WhoMW 93
Galaxan, Sol EncSF 93
Galazka, Jacek Michal 1924- WhoAm 94
Galazov, Akhsarbek Khadzhimurzaevich 1929- LoBiDrD
Galazzo, Jorge Luis 1956- WhoWest 94
Galban, Ventura NewGrDO
Galbert de Campistron, Jean NewGrDO
Galbis, Ignacio R. M. WhoHisp 94
Galbis, Ignacio Ricardo Maria 1931- WhoWest 94
Galbis, Ricardo 1936- WhoHisp 94
Galbraith Who 94
Galbraith, Evan Griffith 1928- WhoAm 94, WhoAmP 93
Galbraith, J. Kenneth 1908- IntWW 93
Galbraith, James 1947- WhoAmL 94
Galbraith, James Hunter 1925- Who 94
Galbraith, James Kenneth 1952- WhoAm 94
Galbraith, James Marshall 1942- WhoAm 94
Galbraith, James Ronald 1936- WhoFI 94
Galbraith, Jean 1906- WrDr 94
Galbraith, John Allen 1923- WhoAmP 93
Galbraith, John Kenneth 1908- AmSocL, Who 94, WhoAm 94, WhoAmP 93, WrDr 94
Galbraith, John Robert 1935- WhoFI 94
Galbraith, John Robert 1938- WhoWest 94
Galbraith, John Semple 1916- WhoAm 94
Galbraith, John William 1921- WhoAm 94
Galbraith, Lissa Ruth 1954- WhoScEn 94
Galbraith, Marie W. WhoAmP 93
Galbraith, Nanette Elaine Gerks 1928- WhoScEn 94
Galbraith, Neil 1911- Who 94
Galbraith, Nicol Spence 1927- IntWW 93
Galbraith, Peter W. WhoAm 94
Galbraith, Peter Woodard 1950- WhoAmP 93
Galbraith, Richard Anthony 1950- WhoAm 94
Galbraith, Ruth Ellen 1959- WhoMW 93
Galbraith, Ruth Legg 1923- WhoAm 94
Galbraith, Samuel Laird 1945- Who 94
Galbraith, Tom 1944- WhoAmL 94
Galbraith, William Campbell 1935- Who 94
Galbreath, Anthony Dale 1954- WhoBlA 94
Galbreath, Gary John 1950- WhoScEn 94
Galbreath, Harry Curtis 1965- WhoBlA 94
Galbut, Martin Richard 1946- WhoAmL 94, WhoWest 94
Gal-Chen, Tzvi 1941- WhoScEn 94
Galdikas, Birute WhoScEn 94
Gale, Alice d1941 WhoHol 92
Gale, Andrew Guy 1959- WhoWest 94
Gale, Bob 1951- IntMPA 94, WrDr 94
Gale, Christine Ann 1953- WhoAmL 94
Gale, Connie Ruth 1946- WhoAmL 94
Gale, Daniel Bailey 1933- WhoWest 94
Gale, David WhoHol 92
Gale, Dorothy d1978 WhoHol 92
Gale, Eddra WhoHol 92
Gale, Edwin John 1943- WhoAmL 94
Gale, Elizabeth 1948- NewGrDO
Gale, Ernest Frederick 1914- IntWW 93, Who 94
Gale, Fay Who 94
Gale, (Gwendoline) Fay 1932- Who 94
Gale, Fournier Joseph, III 1944- WhoAmL 94
Gale, George 1919- IntMPA 94
Gale, George Alexander 1906- Who 94, WhoAm 94
Gale, George Daniel, Jr. 1943- WhoScEn 94
Gale, Gladys d1948 WhoHol 92
Gale, Gwendoline Fay 1932- IntWW 93
Gale, Jean d1984 WhoHol 92
Gale, John 1929- Who 94
Gale, June WhoHol 92
Gale, Laura Roy 1959- WhoMW 93
Gale, Lillian d1972 WhoHol 92
Gale, Maradel Krummel 1939- WhoWest 94
Gale, Marguerite d1948 WhoHol 92
Gale, Mary Ellen 1940- WhoAmL 94
Gale, Michael 1932- Who 94
Gale, Michael R. 1952- WhoAmP 93
Gale, Michael Sadler 1919- Who 94
Gale, Neil Jan 1960- WhoMW 93
Gale, Pamela Lynn Beckman 1945- WhoMW 93
Gale, Paul L. 1950- WhoAmL 94
Gale, Paula Jane 1946- WhoAm 94
Gale, Peggy 1944- WhoAmA 93
Gale, Randall Glenn 1952- WhoAmL 94
Gale, Robert Lee 1919- WhoAm 94
Gale, Robert Peter 1945- WhoAm 94
Gale, Roger James 1943- Who 94
Gale, Stephan Marc 1952- WhoScEn 94
Gale, Steven Hershel 1940- WhoAm 94
Gale, Thomas Martin 1926- WhoAm 94
Gale, Vi DrAPF 93
Gale, Walter Rasin 1878-1959 WhoAmA 93N
Gale, William Henry 1905- WhoAm 94
Gale, William Henry 1915- WhoAmA 93
Gale, Zona DrAPF 93
Gale, Zona 1874-1938 IntDcT 2
Galea, Louis 1948- IntWW 93
Galeana, Frank H. 1929- WhoHisp 94
Galeazza, Marc Thomas 1962- WhoScEn 94
Galecke, Robert Michael 1942- WhoAm 94
Galecki, Johnny WhoHol 92
Galeen, Henrik d1949 WhoHol 92
Galeen, Henrik 1882-1949 IntDcF 2-4
Galeener, Frank Lee 1936- WhoAm 94, WhoWest 94
Galef, Andrew G. 1932- WhoAm 94, WhoFI 94
Galef, Andrew Geoffrey 1932- WhoAm 94, WhoFI 94, WhoWest 94
Galef, Sandra R. WhoAmP 93
Galeffi, Carlo 1882-1961 NewGrDO
Galehouse, Daniel Christian 1949- WhoMW 93
Galella, Ronald Edward 1931- WhoAm 94
Galen fl. 2nd cent.- BlmGEL
Galen c. 130-c. 200 WorScD
Galen, Elaine 1928- WhoAmA 93
Galenson, Walter 1914- WrDr 94
Galento, Tony d1979 WhoHol 92
Galeotti, Steven 1952- WhoFI 94
Galeotti, Vincenzo 1733-1816 IntDcB
Galer, Mary Jane 1924- WhoAmP 93
Galerati, Caterina fl. 1701-1721 NewGrDO
Gales, James 1922- WhoBlA 94
Gales, Kathleen Emily 1927- Who 94
Gales, Robert Robinson 1941- WhoAmL 94
Gales, Samuel Joel 1930- WhoWest 94
Galeyev, Albert Abubakirovich 1940- IntWW 93, WhoScEn 94
Galfo, Armand James 1924- WhoAm 94
Galgoczi, Erszebet 1930-1989 BlmGWL [port]
Galiardo, John William 1933- WhoAm 94, WhoAmL 94
Galiatsatos, Vassilios 1958- WhoMW 93, WhoScEn 94
Galiazzo, Connie C. WhoAmP 93
Galib, Eudaldo Baez WhoAmP 93
Galiber, Joseph L. 1924- WhoBlA 94
Galiber, Joseph Lionel 1924- WhoAmP 93
Galib-Frangie, Jussef M. 1938- WhoAmP 93
Galician, Mary-Lou 1946- WhoAm 94
Galie, Louis Michael 1945- WhoAm 94, WhoFI 94
Galifianakis, Nick 1928- WhoAmP 93
Galil, Uzia 1925- WhoAm 94
Galilea, Susana 1962- WhoHisp 94
Galilei, Galileo WorInv
Galileo 1564-1642 WorInv
Galileo Galilei 1564-1642 BlmGEL, WorScD [port]
Galimi, Dominick Joseph 1945- WhoFI 94
Galin, Aleksandr 1942- IntWW 93
Galin, Lydia WhoHol 92
Galin, Miles A. 1932- WhoAm 94
Galina, G. A. 1870?-1942 BlmGWL
Galindez, Emilio 1943- WhoHisp 94
Galindo, Beatriz 1474?-1534 BlmGWL
Galindo, Cezar 1954- WhoHisp 94
Galindo, Christian Anze 1941- WhoFI 94
Galindo, Donald Vernon 1925- WhoWest 94
Galindo, Eileen 1966- WhoHisp 94
Galindo, Felipe 1957- WhoHisp 94
Galindo, Lazaro 1940- WhoHisp 94
Galindo, Miguel Angel 1960- WhoScEn 94
Galindo, Nacho d1973 WhoHol 92
Galindo, Pedro d1989 WhoHol 92
Galindo, Rafael WhoHisp 94
Galindo, Ramon Gracia 1921- WhoHisp 94
Galindo, Xiomara Inez 1961- WhoHisp 94
Galindo-Elvira, Carlos 1967- WhoHisp 94
Galinee, Rene De Brehant De WhWE
Galinsky, Dennis Lee 1948- WhoMW 93
Galinsky, Gotthard Karl 1942- WhoAm 94
Galinsky, Karl 1942- WrDr 94
Galinsky, Norman 1942- WhoAmA 93
Galioto, Frank Martin, Jr. 1942- WhoAm 94
Galioto, Salvatore DrAPF 93
Galipeau, Jacques WhoHol 92
Galipeau, Steven Arthur 1948- WhoWest 94
Galitzine, Leo d1969 WhoHol 92
Galjaard, Hans 1935- IntWW 93
Galkin, Elliott Washington 1921-1990 WhAm 10
Galkin, Robert Theodore 1926- WhoFI 94
Gall, Charles A. 1950- WhoAmL 94
Gall, Donald Alan 1934- WhoScEn 94, WhoWest 94
Gall, Elizabeth Benson 1944- WhoMW 93
Gall, Eric Papineau 1940- WhoAm 94, WhoScEn 94
Gall, Graham Alexander Edward 1936- WhoAm 94
Gall, Helen Louise 1930- WhoMW 93
Gall, Henderson Alexander 1927- Who 94
Gall, Jeffrey 1950- NewGrDO
Gall, John R. 1945- WhoAmL 94
Gall, Joseph Grafton 1928- IntWW 93, WhoAm 94
Gall, Lenore Rosalie 1943- WhoBlA 94
Gall, Louise von 1815-1855 DcLB 133 [port]
Gall, Martin 1944- WhoAm 94
Gall, Maryann Baker 1945- WhoAm 94, WhoAmL 94
Gall, Meredith Damien 1942- WhoAm 94
Gall, Patience Beth 1936- WhoMW 93
Gall, Sally M. DrAPF 93
Gall, Sandy Who 94
Gall, Sandy 1927- WrDr 94
Gall, Thomas Mitchell 1942- Who 94
Gall, Walter George 1929- WhoWest 94
Gall, Yvonne 1885-1972 NewGrDO
Galla, Tito d1979 WhoHol 92
Gallacher, Baron 1920- Who 94
Gallacher, Bernard 1949- Who 94
Gallacher, Hugh 1903-1957 WorESoc [port]
Gallacher, John 1931- Who 94
Gallacher, Tom 1934- ConDr 93, WrDr 94
Gallager, Mike John 1945- WhoBlA 94
Gallager, Robert Gray 1931- WhoAm 94, WhoScEn 94
Gallagher 1947- WhoCom
Gallagher, Abisola Helen 1950- WhoBlA 94
Gallagher, Alissa Marie 1959- WhoMW 93
Gallagher, Anne Porter 1950- WhoFI 94
Gallagher, Bernard Patrick 1910-1989 WhAm 10
Gallagher, Betsy Ellwanger 1952- WhoAmL 94
Gallagher, Brad K. 1944- WhoIns 94
Gallagher, Brian A. 1957- WhoAmP 93
Gallagher, Carole 1950- ConAu 142, WhoAmA 93
Gallagher, Charles Woodworth 1959- WhoAmL 94
Gallagher, Christina Annastacia 1955- WhoAmL 94
Gallagher, Cynthia 1972- WhoAmA 93
Gallagher, Daniel Francis 1948- WhoAm 94, WhoAmL 94
Gallagher, Daniel J. 1947- WhoAmL 94
Gallagher, Daniel P., Jr. 1951- WhoAm 94, WhoAmL 94
Gallagher, David Kent 1931- WhoWest 94
Gallagher, Dennis Joseph 1939- WhoAmP 93, WhoWest 94
Gallagher, Ed d1929 WhoHol 92
Gallagher, Edward 1973-1929 See Gallagher and Shean WhoCom
Gallagher, Edward Joseph 1952- WhoScEn 94
Gallagher, Edward Patrick 1944- Who 94
Gallagher, Edward Peter 1951- WhoAm 94
Gallagher, Elizabeth 1953- WhoAmL 94
Gallagher, Francis Heath 1905- Who 94
Gallagher, Gary W(illiam) 1950- WrDr 94
Gallagher, Gerald Raphael 1941- WhoAm 94
Gallagher, Glen d1960 WhoHol 92
Gallagher, Helen 1926- WhoHol 92
Gallagher, Helen M. 1965- WhoAm 94
Gallagher, Hubert R. 1907- WhoAm 94
Gallagher, Hugh Gregory 1932- WhoAm 94
Gallagher, J. Jack, Jr. WhoAmP 93
Gallagher, James C. 1945- WhoAmL 94
Gallagher, James J. A. 1927- WhoAmP 93
Gallagher, James P. WhoAm 94
Gallagher, James Roswell 1903- WrDr 94
Gallagher, James Wes 1911- WhoAm 94
Gallagher, Joan Shodder 1941- WhoScEn 94
Gallagher, Joel Wayne 1945- WhoFI 94
Gallagher, John Bentley 1894- WhAm 10
Gallagher, John Donald d1981 WhoHol 92
Gallagher, John Francis WhoAm 94
Gallagher, John Pirie 1916- WhoAm 94
Gallagher, John Robert, Jr. 1941- WhoMW 93
Gallagher, John S. T. WhoAm 94
Gallagher, John Sill, III 1947- WhoAm 94
Gallagher, Joseph Francis 1926- WhoAm 94
Gallagher, Kathleen Ellen 1949- WhoAmA 93
Gallagher, Kenna Who 94
Gallagher, (Francis George) Kenna 1917- Who 94
Gallagher, Kent Grey 1933- WhoMW 93
Gallagher, Kevin M. 1932- WhoIns 94
Gallagher, Lindy Allyn 1954- WhoFI 94
Gallagher, Maire Teresa 1933- Who 94

Galt, Barry J. 1933- *WhoFI 94*
Galt, Galan *WhoHol 92*
Galt, Jack E. 1923- *WhoAmP 93*
Galt, John 1779-1839 *BlmGEL, RfGShF*
Galt, John Kirtland 1920- *WhoAm 94, WhoWest 94*
Galt, John William 1940- *WhoAm 94*
Galter, Irene 1934- *WhoHol 92*
Galterio, Lou 1942- *NewGrDO*
Galterio, Louis 1951- *WhoFI 94, WhoScEn 94*
Galtieri, Leopoldo Fortunato 1926- *IntWW 93*
Galton, Francis 1822-1911 *WorScD*
Galton, Raymond Percy 1930- *Who 94*
Galton, Valerie Anne 1934- *WhoAm 94*
Galtung, Johan 1930- *IntWW 93*
Galun, Esra 1927- *IntWW 93*
Galuppi, Antonio dc. 1780 *NewGrDO*
Galuppi, Baldassare 1706-1785 *NewGrDO*
Galuszka, Frank Richard 1947- *WhoAmA 93*
Galvan, Eddie 1927- *WhoHisp 94*
Galvan, Elias Gabriel 1938- *WhoAm 94*
Galvan, Jesus Gerrero *WhoAmA 93N*
Galvan, Jose Manuel 1952- *WhoHisp 94*
Galvan, Juan Manuel 1952- *WhoHisp 94*
Galvan, Manuel P. 1949- *WhoHisp 94*
Galvan, Noemi Ethel 1939- *WhoHisp 94*
Galvan, Robert J. 1921- *WhoHisp 94*
Galvan, Roberto A. *DrAPF 93*
Galvan, Ventura fl. 1762-1773 *NewGrDO*
Galvan, William de *WhAmRev*
Galvan-Carroll, Mary Grace 1958- *WhoHisp 94*
Galvani, Ciro d1956 *WhoHol 92*
Galvani, Dino d1960 *WhoHol 92*
Galvani, Giacomo 1825-1889 *NewGrDO*
Galvani, Luigi 1737-1798 *WorScD [port]*
Galvani, Paul B. 1938- *WhoAm 94, WhoAmL 94*
Galvano, Mauro *WhoHisp 94*
Galvany, Maria 1878-1944 *NewGrDO*
Galvao, Louis Alberto 1949- *WhoWest 94*
Galvao, Patricia 1910-1962 *BlmGWL*
Galvao Filho, Orlando 1940- *IntWW 93*
Galvarriato, Eulalia 1905- *BlmGWL*
Galveas, Ernane 1922- *IntWW 93*
Galves, Fred Anthony 1961- *WhoAmL 94*
Gálvez, Arnaldo E. 1940- *WhoHisp 94*
Galvez, Bernardo de 1746-1786 *AmRev, WhAmRev*
Galvez, Jorge F. 1940- *WhoHisp 94*
Galvez, Jose de 1726-1786 *AmRev*
Galvez, Jose de 1729-1786 *WhAmRev*
Galvez, William 1945- *WhoWest 94*
Galvin, Bernard Vincent Joseph 1933- *Who 94*
Galvin, Brendan *DrAPF 93*
Galvin, Brendan 1938- *WrDr 94*
Galvin, Charles Edward, Jr. 1960- *WhoWest 94*
Galvin, Charles O'Neill 1919- *WhoAmL 94*
Galvin, Christopher B. 1951- *WhoAm 94, WhoFI 94*
Galvin, Elias *WhoWest 94*
Galvin, Emma Corinne 1909- *WhoBlA 94*
Galvin, Fred 1936- *WhoMW 93*
Galvin, Gerald T. 1942- *WhoWest 94*
Galvin, Jene Maurice 1943- *WhoAmP 93*
Galvin, John Richard 1960- *WhoAmL 94*
Galvin, John Rogers 1929- *IntWW 93, Who 94, WhoAm 94*
Galvin, Joseph F. 1942- *WhoAmL 94*
Galvin, Madeline Sheila 1948- *WhoAmL 94, WhoFI 94*
Galvin, Martin *DrAPF 93*
Galvin, Martin Jay 1949- *WhoAmL 94*
Galvin, Matthew Reppert 1950- *WhoMW 93*
Galvin, Michael *WhoAmP 93*
Galvin, Michael John, Jr. 1930- *WhoAm 94, WhoAmL 94*
Galvin, Michael Paul 1952- *WhoFI 94*
Galvin, Patrick 1927- *WrDr 94*
Galvin, Patrick G. 1926- *WhoAmP 93*
Galvin, Robert J. 1938- *WhoAmL 94*
Galvin, Robert W. 1922- *IntWW 93, WhoAm 94, WhoFI 94, WhoScEn 94*
Galvin, Thomas F. d1993 *NewYTBS 93 [port]*
Galvin, Thomas John 1932- *WhoAm 94*
Galvin, William C. *WhoAmP 93*
Galvin, William F. *WhoAmP 93*
Galway, Viscount 1922- *Who 94*
Galway, James 1939- *IntWW 93, Who 94, WhoAm 94*
Galway, Robert Conington 1920- *WrDr 94*
Galway And Kilmacduagh, Bishop of 1929- *Who 94*
Galwey, Geoffrey (Valentine) 1912- *WrDr 94*
Galy, Maurice d1993 *NewYTBS 93*
Galyon, Luther Anderson, III 1946- *WhoAmL 94*
Galysh, Robert Alan 1954- *WhoFI 94, WhoMW 93, WhoScEn 94*
Gam, Alexander d1981 *WhoHol 92*
Gam, Paul Jonathan 1959- *WhoAsA 94*
Gam, Rita 1928- *WhoHol 92*
Gama, Vasco Da c. 1460-1524 *WhWE*
Gamache, Albert *WhoAmP 93*
Gamache, Joey *WhoHisp 94*
Gamache, Kathleen Anne 1956- *WhoAmL 94*
Gamache, Richard Donald 1935- *WhoFI 94*
Gamarnik, Moisey Yankelevich 1936- *WhoScEn 94*
Gamassi, Mohamed Abdul Ghani al- 1921- *IntWW 93*
Gamba, John Jerome 1944- *WhoFI 94*
Gamba, Tomas F. 1951- *WhoAmL 94*
Gambal, David 1931- *WhoAm 94*
Gambara, Veronica 1485-1550 *BlmGWL*
Gambardella, Rosemary *WhoAm 94, WhoAmL 94*
Gambardella, William V. 1960- *WhoAmP 93*
Gambarelli, Maria d1990 *WhoHol 92*
Gambari, Ibrahim Agboola 1944- *IntWW 93*
Gambarini, Grazia Lavinia 1942- *WhoScEn 94*
Gambaro, Ernest Umberto 1938- *WhoWest 94*
Gambaro, Griselda 1928- *BlmGWL, ConWorW 93, IntDcT 2*
Gambarov, Isa Yunis ogly 1957- *IntWW 93*
Gambarov, Isa Yusif Ogly 1957- *LoBiDrD*
Gambee, Dave 1937- *BasBi*
Gambee, Eleanor Brown 1904- *WhoAm 94*
Gambee, Robert Rankin 1942- *WhoAm 94, WhoFI 94*
Gambero, Darrell J. *WhoIns 94*
Gambet, Daniel George 1929- *WhoAm 94*
Gambier, Dominique 1947- *IntWW 93*
Gambier, James 1723-1789 *AmRev, WhAmRev*
Gambill, Bruce Warren 1930- *WhoAmP 93*
Gambill, Calvin 1924- *WhoAmP 93*
Gambill, Malcolm W. *WhoAm 94, WhoFI 94*
Gambill, Michael Arthur 1943- *WhoFI 94*
Gambill, Norman Paul 1941- *WhoMW 93*
Gambill, Robert 1955- *NewGrDO*
Gambill, Sue *DrAPF 93*
Gambill, Terry A. 1942- *WhoMW 93*
Gambina, Ralph d1981 *WhoHol 92*
Gambino, Jerome James 1925- *WhoAm 94, WhoWest 94*
Gambino, Robert William 1926- *WhoAm 94*
Gambino, Salvatore Raymond 1926- *WhoAm 94*
Gamble, Alvan 1916- *WhoFI 94*
Gamble, Andrew Michael 1947- *WrDr 94*
Gamble, Bertin Clyde 1891- *WhAm 10*
Gamble, Cameron C. *WhoAmL 94*
Gamble, David (Hugh Norman) 1966- *Who 94*
Gamble, Douglas Irvin 1953- *WhoMW 93*
Gamble, E. James 1929- *WhoAm 94, WhoAmL 94*
Gamble, Ed 1943- *WrDr 94*
Gamble, Eva M. 1952- *WhoBlA 94*
Gamble, Francoise Yoko 1962- *WhoScEn 94*
Gamble, Fred d1939 *WhoHol 92*
Gamble, George Clinton 1910- *WhoAm 94*
Gamble, Harry T. *WhoAm 94*
Gamble, Janet Helen 1917- *WhoBlA 94*
Gamble, John B., Jr. 1949- *WhoAmL 94*
Gamble, John Reeves, Jr. 1922- *WhoAmP 93*
Gamble, Josias Christopher 1778-1848 *DcNaB MP*
Gamble, Kathryn Elizabeth 1915- *WhoAmA 93*
Gamble, Kenneth 1943- *WhoBlA 94*
Gamble, Kenneth L. 1941- *WhoBlA 94*
Gamble, Kevin Douglas 1965- *WhoBlA 94*
Gamble, Lee St. Clair 1954- *WhoWest 94*
Gamble, Margaret Jones *WhoAmP 93*
Gamble, Oscar Charles 1949- *WhoBlA 94*
Gamble, Ralph d1966 *WhoHol 92*
Gamble, Robert Lewis 1947- *WhoBlA 94*
Gamble, Ron 1933- *WhoAmP 93*
Gamble, Theodore Robert, Jr. 1953- *WhoFI 94*
Gamble, Tracy Joseph 1954- *WhoAm 94*
Gamble, Warburton d1945 *WhoHol 92*
Gamble, Wilbert 1932- *WhoBlA 94*
Gamble, Wilbur T., III 1959- *WhoAmP 93*
Gamble, William Belser, Jr. 1925- *WhoAm 94*
Gamble, William F. 1950- *WhoBlA 94*
Gamblin, Noriko 1956- *WhoAsA 94*
Gambling, William Alexander 1926- *IntWW 93, Who 94, WhoScEn 94*
Gamboa, Alejandro 1948- *WhoHisp 94*
Gamboa, Anthony H. 1942- *WhoHisp 94*
Gamboa, Darlene 1948- *WhoHisp 94*
Gamboa, Elias d1959 *WhoHol 92*
Gamboa, Erasmo 1941- *WhoHisp 94*
Gamboa, George Charles 1923- *WhoAm 94, WhoWest 94*
Gamboa, Harry, Jr. 1951- *WhoHisp 94*
Gamboa, John C. 1941- *WhoHisp 94*
Gamboa, Reymundo *DrAPF 93*
Gamboa, Theodore David 1951- *WhoHisp 94*
Gambon, Marie Anne 1952- *WhoWest 94*
Gambon, Michael 1940- *IntMPA 94, WhoHol 92*
Gambon, Michael John 1940- *IntWW 93, Who 94*
Gamboni, Ciro Anthony 1940- *WhoAm 94*
Gambrell, David Henry 1929- *IntWW 93, WhoAm 94, WhoAmP 93*
Gambrell, James Bruton, III 1926- *WhoAm 94*
Gambrell, Richard Donald, Jr. 1931- *WhoAm 94, WhoScEn 94*
Gambrell, Thomas Ross 1934- *WhoWest 94*
Gambuti, Gary, Jr. 1937- *WhoAm 94*
Gamby, Lawrence Edward 1964- *WhoWest 94*
Gamedze, A. B. 1921- *IntWW 93*
Gamelli, Richard L. 1949- *WhoScEn 94*
Gamer, Henry d1989 *WhoHol 92*
Gamer, Nancy Crews 1937- *WhoWest 94*
Gamer, Robert Emanuel 1938- *WhoMW 93*
Gamerith, Gernot 1953- *WhoScEn 94*
Gameros, L. Ignacio 1939- *WhoHisp 94*
Gamerra, Giovanni de *NewGrDO*
Games, Abram 1914- *Who 94*
Games, David Edgar 1938- *IntWW 93*
Gamet, Donald Max 1916- *WhoAm 94, WhoFI 94*
Gamey, Ronald Kenneth 1945- *WhoAm 94, WhoFI 94*
Gámez, Antonio 1955- *WhoHisp 94*
Gamez, Kathy Joe 1956- *WhoHisp 94*
Gamez, Peter 1966- *WhoHisp 94*
Gamez, Robert 1968- *WhoHisp 94*
Gamidov, Iskander Mejid Ogly 1948- *LoBiDrD*
Gamin, Mark Andrew 1952- *WhoAmL 94*
Gaminara, Albert William 1913- *Who 94*
Gamkrelidze, Thomas Valerianovich 1929- *IntWW 93*
Gamlen, James Eli, Jr. 1950- *WhoScEn 94*
Gamlin, Lionel d1967 *WhoHol 92*
Gamm, Carol Amy 1967- *WhoMW 93*
Gamm, Gordon Julius 1939- *WhoAmL 94*
Gamm, Stanford Ralph 1917- *WhoWest 94*
Gammage, Robert Alton 1938- *WhoAm 94, WhoAmL 94, WhoAmP 93*
Gammal, Albert Abraham, Jr. 1928- *WhoAmP 93*
Gammans, James Patrick 1952- *WhoScEn 94*
Gammelgaard, Lars P. 1945- *IntWW 93*
Gammell, Gloria Ruffner 1948- *WhoFI 94, WhoWest 94*
Gammell, James Gilbert Sydney 1920- *Who 94*
Gammell, John Frederick 1921- *Who 94*
Gammell, Robin *WhoHol 92*
Gammell, Stephen 1943- *WrDr 94*
Gammell, Wayne William 1940- *WhoMW 93*
Gammie, Anthony Petrie 1934- *WhoAm 94, WhoFI 94*
Gammie, George 1898- *WhAm 10*
Gammie, Gordon Edward 1922- *Who 94*
Gammill, Darryl Curtis 1950- *WhoFI 94, WhoWest 94*
Gammill, John Stewart 1923- *WhoIns 94*
Gammill, Kenneth M. 1943- *WhoAmL 94*
Gammill, Lee M., Jr. 1934- *WhoIns 94*
Gammill, Lee Morgan, Jr. 1934- *WhoAm 94, WhoFI 94*
Gammill, Noreen d1988 *WhoHol 92*
Gammon, Catherine *DrAPF 93*
Gammon, E. Ann 1933- *WhoAmP 93*
Gammon, Elinor W. 1944- *WhoAmL 94*
Gammon, James *IntMPA 94, WhoHol 92*
Gammon, James Alan 1934- *WhoAm 94*
Gammon, Janice Carlene 1946- *WhoAmP 93*
Gammon, Juanita-La Verne *WhoAmA 93*
Gammon, Malcolm Ernest, Sr. 1947- *WhoFI 94*
Gammon, Reginald Adolphus 1921- *WhoAmA 93, WhoBlA 94*
Gammon, Samuel Rhea, III 1924- *WhoAm 94*
Gammon, Timothy Edward 1947- *WhoFI 94*
Gammon, William Hunter 1948- *WhoAmL 94*
Gamon, Hugh Wynell 1921- *Who 94*
Gamoran, Abraham Carmi 1926-1991 *WhAm 10*
Gamota, Daniel Roman 1965- *WhoScEn 94*
Gamota, George 1939- *WhoAm 94*
Gamow, George 1904-1968 *EncSF 93, WorScD [port]*
Gampu, Ken *WhoHol 92*
Gamron, W. Anthony 1948- *WhoAm 94*
Gamroth, Arthur Paul 1930- *WhoFI 94*
Gams, Sylvia S. 1943- *WhoAmP 93*
Gamsakhurdia, Zviad Konstantinovich 1939- *IntWW 93, LoBiDrD*
Gamse, Alan N. 1942- *WhoAmL 94*
Gamsky, Neal Richard 1931- *WhoMW 93*
Gamson, Annabelle 1928- *WhoAm 94*
Gamson, Bernard William 1917- *WhoAm 94*
Gamson, William A(nthony) 1934- *WrDr 94*
Gamson, Zelda Finkelstein 1936- *WhoAm 94*
Gamst, Frederick Charles 1936- *WrDr 94*
Gamwell, Lynn 1943- *WhoAmA 93*
Gamzatov, Rasul Gamzatovich 1923- *IntWW 93*
Gan, Chester d1959 *WhoHol 92*
Gan, Elena Andreevna 1814-1842 *BlmGWL*
Gan, Felisa So 1943- *WhoScEn 94*
Gan, Jose C. 1933- *WhoAsA 94*
Gan, Leong-Huat 1945- *WhoScEn 94*
Ganapathy, Jayanthi 1954- *WhoMW 93*
Ganapol, Barry Douglas 1944- *WhoAm 94*
Ganas, Perry Spiros 1937- *WhoAm 94*
Ganbaatar, Adyagiin 1959- *IntWW 93*
Ganbold, Davaadorjiin 1957- *IntWW 93*
Gan Bolin 1935- *WhoPRCh 91*
Gance, Abel d1981 *WhoHol 92*
Gancer, Donald Charles 1933- *WhoAm 94*
Gancher, David Arthur 1943- *WhoAm 94*
Ganci, James J. 1943- *WhoFI 94*
Ganczarczyk, Jerzy Jozef 1928- *WhoAm 94*
Gandal, Larry N. 1939- *WhoAmL 94*
Gandar, Leslie Walter 1919- *Who 94*
Gandara, Carmen 1900-1977 *BlmGWL*
Gandara, Daniel 1948- *WhoAmL 94, WhoHisp 94*
Gandara, Jose Raul de la 1957- *WhoHisp 94*
Gandeactena, Catherine d1673 *EncNAR*
Gandee, John Stephen 1909- *Who 94*
Gandel, Earl David 1934- *WhoAm 94*
Gander, Forrest *DrAPF 93*
Gander, John Edward 1925- *WhoAm 94*
Gandert, Miguel Adrian 1956- *WhoAmA 93*
Gandevia, Bryan Harle 1925- *WrDr 94*
Gandhi, Arun Manilal 1934- *WhoAsA 94*
Gandhi, Bharat R. 1942- *WhoAm 94*
Gandhi, Homi D. *WhoAsA 94*
Gandhi, Indira 1917-1984 *HisWorL [port]*
Gandhi, Maneka *WhoWomW 91*
Gandhi, Maneka Anand 1956- *IntWW 93*
Gandhi, Manmohan Purushottam 1901- *Who 94*
Gandhi, Mihir Jitendra 1960- *WhoWest 94*
Gandhi, Mohandas 1869-1948 *HisWorL [port]*
Gandhi, Mohandas Kamarchand 1869-1948 *EncEth*
Gandhi, Mohandas Karamchand 1869-1948 *EnvEnc*
Gandhi, Mukesh P. 1964- *WhoAsA 94*
Gandhi, Natwar Mohan 1940- *WhoAsA 94*
Gandhi, Om Parkash 1934- *WhoAm 94, WhoScEn 94, WhoWest 94*
Gandhi, Prashant P. 1965- *WhoAsA 94*
Gandhi, Shailesh Ramesh 1960- *WhoScEn 94*
Gandhi, Suketu Ramesh 1959- *WhoScEn 94*
Gandhi, Vikram H. 1945- *WhoAsA 94*
Gandhi, Vikram Ijatrai 1960- *WhoAsA 94*
Gandia, Aldo Ray 1958- *WhoHisp 94*
Gandois, Jean Guy Alphonse 1930- *IntWW 93*
Gandolf, Raymond L. 1930- *WhoAm 94*
Gandon, Yves 1899- *EncSF 93*
Gandsey, Louis John 1921- *WhoScEn 94, WhoWest 94*
Gandurski, Ronald Edward 1941- *WhoMW 93*
Gandusio, Antonio d1951 *WhoHol 92*
Gandy, Charles David 1949- *WhoAm 94*
Gandy, Christopher Thomas 1917- *Who 94*
Gandy, David Stewart 1932- *Who 94*
Gandy, Gerald Larmon 1941- *WhoScEn 94*
Gandy, H. Conway 1934- *WhoAmL 94*
Gandy, James Thomas 1952- *WhoScEn 94*
Gandy, Roland A., Jr. 1924- *WhoBlA 94*
Gandy, Ronald Herbert 1917- *Who 94*
Gandy, William Gerald 1949- *WhoAmL 94*
Gane, Barrie Charles 1935- *Who 94*

Gane, Michael 1927- *Who 94*
Gane, Nolan d1915 *WhoHol 92*
Ganek, Dorothy Skeados 1946- *WhoAmA 93*
Ganelin, Charles V. 1950- *WhoMW 93*
Ganelin, Vyacheslav Shevelevich 1944- *IntWW 93*
Ganelius, Tord Hjalmar 1925- *IntWW 93*
Ganellin, Charon Robin 1934- *IntWW 93, Who 94*
Ganesan, Ann Katharine 1933- *WhoAm 94*
Ganesh, Orekonde 1941- *WhoMW 93*
Ganet, Abner S. 1925- *WhoAmP 93*
Ganev, Stoyan *IntWW 93*
Ganey, James Hobson 1944- *WhoBlA 94*
Ganey, Terry Joseph 1948- *WhoAm 94*
Ganfield, David Russ, II 1959- *WhoAmL 94*
Gan Fuxi 1938- *WhoPRCh 91*
Gang, Stephen R. 1951- *WhoAm 94*
Gang, Stuart Worthington 1928- *WhoMW 93*
Gangal, Shiva Shanker 1934- *WhoAsA 94*
Gangemi, Columbus Rudolph, Jr. 1947- *WhoAm 94*
Gangemi, Kenneth *DrAPF 93*
Ganger, Robert Mondell 1903-1992 *WhAm 10*
Gangle, Sandra Smith 1943- *WhoAmL 94*
Gangloff, Deborah 1952- *WrDr 94*
Gangopadhyay, Chitta R. 1934- *WhoAsA 94*
Gangopadhyay, Sunita Bhardwaj 1964- *WhoScEn 94*
Gangstad, John Erik 1948- *WhoAm 94, WhoAmL 94*
Gangulee, Amitava 1941- *WhoAsA 94*
Ganguly, Ashit Kumar 1934- *WhoScEn 94*
Ganguly, Jibamitra 1938- *WhoAsA 94*
Ganguly, Suman 1942- *WhoAsA 94*
Gan Guoping *WhoPRCh 91*
Gangwal, Rakesh 1953- *WhoAsA 94*
Gangware, Edgar Brand, Jr. 1922- *WhoMW 93*
Gangwere, Heather Hendry 1964- *WhoWest 94*
Gani, Joseph Mark 1924- *IntWW 93, WhoAm 94*
Gani, Shafiqul 1946- *IntWW 93*
Ganick, Nicholas *EncSF 93*
Ganilau, Penaia d1993 *NewYTBS 93 [port]*
Ganilau, Penaia Kanatabatu 1918- *IntWW 93, Who 94*
Ganina, Maiia Anatolievna 1927- *BlmGWL*
Ganios, Tony 1960- *WhoHol 92*
Ganis, Sidney M. 1940- *IntMPA 94*
Gan Ku 1924- *WhoPRCh 91 [port]*
Ganley, Beatrice *DrAPF 93*
Ganley, Gladys Dickens 1929- *ConAu 41NR*
Ganley, James Powell 1937- *WhoAm 94*
Ganley, Oswald Harold 1929- *ConAu 41NR, WhoAm 94*
Ganley, Paul Mullin 1939- *WhoAmL 94*
Gann, Donald L. 1940- *WhoAmP 93*
Gann, Ernest K(ellogg) 1910-1991 *EncSF 93, WrDr 94N*
Gann, Ernest Kellogg 1910-1991 *WhAm 10*
Gann, Gregory Charles 1950- *WhoFI 94*
Gann, Lewis Henry 1924- *WrDr 94*
Gann, Pamela Brooks 1948- *WhoAmL 94*
Gann, William D. 1878-1955 *EncSF 93*
Gannam, John 1907-1965 *WhoAmA 93N*
Gannatal, Joseph Paul 1955- *WhoWest 94*
Gannaway, Nancy Harrison 1929- *WhoBlA 94*
Ganne, (Gustave) Louis 1862-1923 *NewGrDO*
Gannett, Ann Cole 1916- *WhoAmP 93*
Gannett, Deborah *WhAmRev*
Gannett, Ezra Stiles 1801-1871 *DcAmReB 2*
Gannett, Robert T. 1917- *WhoAmP 93*
Gannett, Ruth Stiles 1923- *WrDr 94*
Gannon, Alice H. 1954- *WhoIns 94*
Gannon, Ann Ida 1915- *WhoAm 94*
Gannon, Frances Virginia 1929- *WhoWest 94*
Gannon, Jane Frances 1964- *WhoScEn 94*
Gannon, Jerome Aylward 1935- *WhoAm 94*
Gannon, John 1950- *WhoAmP 93*
Gannon, John Sexton 1927- *WhoAmL 94*
Gannon, Lanie E. *WhoAmA 93*
Gannon, Leo J. 1950- *WhoAmP 93*
Gannon, Mary Carol 1944- *WhoAm 94*
Gannon, Michael Robert 1958- *WhoScEn 94*
Gannon, Paul J. *WhoAmP 93*
Gannon, Richard Galen 1950- *WhoAmP 93*
Gannon, Robert P. *WhoFI 94*
Gannon, Thomas P. 1943- *WhoAmP 93*
Gann-Wick, Lisa Marie 1966- *WhoMW 93*
Gano, John 1924- *WhoAm 94, WhoAmL 94*
Gano, Lila 1949- *SmATA 76 [port]*
Ganoe, Charles Stratford 1929- *WhoAm 94*
Ganoe, George Grant 1950- *WhoScEn 94*
Ganong, William Francis 1924- *WhoAm 94*
Ganong, William Francis, III 1951- *WhoAm 94, WhoScEn 94*
Ganoung, Richard *WhoHol 92*
Ganoza-Becker, Maria Clelia 1937- *WhoAm 94*
Gans, Bernard R. 1948- *WhoAmL 94*
Gans, Bruce Merrill 1947- *WhoMW 93*
Gans, Bruce Michael *DrAPF 93*
Gans, Carl 1923- *WhoAm 94, WhoMW 93*
Gans, Carol Butchko 1954- *WhoMW 93*
Gans, Dennis Joseph 1949- *WhoFI 94*
Gans, Eric L. 1941- *WrDr 94*
Gans, Eric Lawrence 1941- *WhoWest 94*
Gans, Erna Irene *WhoFI 94, WhoMW 93*
Gans, Herbert J. 1927- *WhoAm 94*
Gans, Herbert J(ulius) 1927- *WrDr 94*
Gans, Lucy C. 1949- *WhoAmA 93*
Gans, Manfred 1922- *WhoFI 94*
Gans, Roger Frederick 1941- *WhoAm 94*
Gans, Samuel Myer 1925- *WhoFI 94*
Gans, Sharon 1942- *WhoHol 92*
Gans, Walter Gideon 1936- *WhoAmL 94, WhoFI 94*
Ganseforth, Monika 1940- *WhoWomW 91*
Ganser, Sigbert J. M. 1853-1931 *EncSPD*
Gansevoort, Leonard 1751-1810 *WhAmRev*
Gansevoort, Peter 1749-1812 *AmRev, WhAmRev [port]*
Ganshof Van Der Meersch, Walter 1900- *IntWW 93*
Gansinger, James Michael 1945- *WhoWest 94*
Gansler, Jacques Singleton 1934- *WrDr 94*
Gansovsky, Sever (Feliksovich) 1918-1990 *EncSF 93*
Ganstrom, Linda Marie 1958- *WhoMW 93*
Gansz, David C.D. *DrAPF 93*
Gant, Donald Ross 1928- *WhoAm 94, WhoFI 94*
Gant, George Arlington Lee 1941- *WhoAm 94*
Gant, Harry *WhoAm 94*
Gant, Harry d1967 *WhoHol 92*
Gant, Horace Zed 1914- *WhoAmL 94*
Gant, John 1944- *Who 94*
Gant, Joseph Erwin, Jr. 1912- *WhoAmP 93*
Gant, Joseph Erwin, III 1940- *WhoAmL 94*
Gant, Norman Ferrell, Jr. 1939- *WhoAm 94*
Gant, Phillip M., III 1949- *WhoBlA 94*
Gant, Phyllis *BlmGWL*
Gant, Raymond Leroy 1961- *WhoBlA 94*
Gant, Richard *ConAu 43NR, WhoHol 92*
Gant, Richard 1936- *WrDr 94*
Gant, Ron 1965- *WhoAm 94*
Gant, Ronald Edwin 1965- *WhoBlA 94*
Gant, Wanda Adele 1949- *WhoBlA 94*
Gant, William M. 1939- *WhoAmP 93*
Gantcher, Nathan 1940- *WhoAm 94, WhoFI 94*
Gantenbein, Rex Earl 1950- *WhoWest 94*
Ganter, Bernard J. 1928- *WhoAm 94*
Gantin, Bernardin 1922- *IntWW 93*
Gantman, Geraldine Ann 1945- *WhoFI 94*
Gantner, Carrillo Baillieu 1944- *IntWW 93*
Gantry, Donald d1985 *WhoHol 92*
Gantt, David F. 1941- *WhoAmP 93*
Gantt, Gloria 1945- *WhoBlA 94*
Gantt, Harvey *WhoAmP 93*
Gantt, Harvey Bernard 1943- *WhoBlA 94*
Gantt, Walter N. 1921- *WhoBlA 94*
Gantz, Ann Cushing 1935- *WhoAmA 93*
Gantz, Bruce Jay 1946- *WhoAm 94, WhoMW 93*
Gantz, Carroll Melvin 1931- *WhoAm 94*
Gantz, David Alfred 1942- *WhoAm 94, WhoAmL 94*
Gantz, John G., Jr. 1948- *WhoFI 94, WhoIns 94*
Gantz, Kenneth F(ranklin) 1905- *EncSF 93*
Gantz, Nancy Rollins 1949- *WhoWest 94*
Gantz, Norman J. 1947- *WhoAmL 94*
Gantz, Richard Alan 1946- *WhoAm 94, WhoMW 93*
Gantz, Suzi Grahn 1954- *WhoMW 93*
Gantz, Wilbur H., III 1937- *IntWW 93*
Gantzer, John Carroll 1947- *WhoWest 94*
Gantzer, Mary Lou 1950- *WhoMW 93*
Ganulin, Neil 1948- *WhoAmL 94*
Gan Xiangmeng *WhoPRCh 91*
Ganz, Barbara Carol 1949- *WhoWest 94*
Ganz, Bruno 1941- *IntMPA 94, WhoHol 92*
Ganz, David 1948- *WhoFI 94*
Ganz, David L. 1951- *WhoAmL 94*
Ganz, Erwin M. 1929- *WhoAm 94*
Ganz, Felix 1959- *WhoFI 94*
Ganz, Howard L. 1942- *WhoAm 94*
Ganz, Lowell 1948- *ConTFT 11, IntMPA 94, WhoAm 94*
Ganz, Molly Rose 1950- *WhoMW 93*
Ganz, Peter Felix 1920- *Who 94*
Ganz, Samuel 1911- *WhoAm 94*
Ganz, Sol d1993 *NewYTBS 93*
Ganz, Sylvia Squires *WhoAmA 93*
Ganz, Tony *IntMPA 94*
Ganz, William I. 1951- *WhoScEn 94*
Ganzarain, Mirentxu 1957- *WhoAmA 93*
Ganzarolli, Wladimiro 1932- *NewGrDO*
Ganzel, Teresa *WhoHol 92*
Ganzert, R. J. d1987 *WhoHol 92*
Gan Zhijian 1927- *IntWW 93, WhoPRCh 91 [port]*
Ganzhorn, Jack d1956 *WhoHol 92*
Ganzi, Victor Frederick 1947- *WhoAmL 94*
Gan Ziyu 1929- *IntWW 93, WhoPRCh 91 [port]*
Ganzl, Kurt (Friedrich) 1946- *NewGrDO*
Gan Zongrong *WhoPRCh 91*
Ganzoni *Who 94*
Ganzuri, Kamal Al- 1933- *IntWW 93*
Gao, Chun Xin 1958- *WhoMW 93*
Gao, Hong-Bo 1961- *WhoScEn 94*
Gao, Hong Wen 1945- *WhoScEn 94*
Gao, Jiali 1962- *WhoAsA 94*
Gao, Yi-Tian 1959- *WhoScEn 94*
Gao Changli *WhoPRCh 91*
Gao Chao *WhoPRCh 91*
Gao De *WhoPRCh 91*
Gao Dengbang 1915- *WhoPRCh 91 [port]*
Gao Dezhan 1932- *IntWW 93, WhoPRCh 91 [port]*
Gao Dezheng *WhoPRCh 91*
Gao Di 1927- *WhoPRCh 91 [port]*
Gao Fenglian 1964- *WhoPRCh 91 [port]*
Gao Guanhua 1919- *WhoPRCh 91 [port]*
Gao Houliang *WhoPRCh 91*
Gao Huanchang 1924- *WhoPRCh 91 [port]*
Gao Jianzhong *WhoPRCh 91*
Gao Jingde 1922- *IntWW 93, WhoPRCh 91 [port]*
Gao Liang *WhoPRCh 91 [port]*
Gao Lingyun 1918- *WhoPRCh 91 [port]*
Gao Lulin *WhoPRCh 91*
Gao Min 1970- *WhoPRCh 91 [port]*
Gaon, Solomon 1912- *Who 94*
Gaona, Tomás M. 1922- *WhoHisp 94*
Gao Rui *WhoPRCh 91*
Gaos, Vicente 1919-1980 *DcLB 134 [port]*
Gao Shangquan 1929- *IntWW 93, WhoPRCh 91 [port]*
Gao Shouyao *WhoPRCh 91*
Gao Shuchun *WhoPRCh 91*
Gao Tian 1917- *WhoPRCh 91 [port]*
Gao Tianzheng *WhoPRCh 91*
Gao Tianzheng, Maj.-Gen. 1931- *IntWW 93*
Gao Tingyao *WhoPRCh 91*
Gao Wen 1929- *WhoPRCh 91 [port]*
Gao Xiaosheng 1928- *WhoPRCh 91 [port]*
Gao Xiaoxia 1919- *WhoPRCh 91 [port]*
Gao Xingjian 1940- *WhoPRCh 91*
Gao Xingmin *WhoPRCh 91 [port]*
Gao Xiu 1918- *WhoPRCh 91 [port]*
Gao Yan 1942- *IntWW 93, WhoPRCh 91 [port]*
Gao Yang 1909- *WhoPRCh 91 [port]*
Gao Yi 1916- *WhoPRCh 91*
Gao Ying 1929- *IntWW 93, WhoPRCh 91 [port]*
Gao Yisheng *IntWW 93*
Gao Youxi 1920- *IntWW 93*
Gao Yunjia *WhoPRCh 91*
Gao Zhanxiang 1935- *IntWW 93, WhoPRCh 91 [port]*
Gao Zhengmin *WhoPRCh 91*
Gao Zhenjia 1929- *WhoPRCh 91 [port]*
Gao Zhenning 1929- *WhoPRCh 91 [port]*
Gao Zi 1947- *WhoPRCh 91 [port]*
Gapes, Michael John 1952- *Who 94*
Gaples, Harry Seraphim 1935- *WhoAm 94*
Gaponov-Grekhov, Andrey Viktorovich 1926- *IntWW 93, WhoScEn 94*
Gaposchkin, Peter John Arthur 1940- *WhoWest 94*
Gapp, Paul John 1928-1992 *WhAm 10*
Gappa, Judith M. *WhoMW 93*
Gara, Otto Gabriel *WhoAmL 94*
Garabedian, Charles 1923- *WhoAmA 93*
Garabedian, Charles, Jr. 1943- *WhoScEn 94*
Garabedian, Paul R. 1927- *IntWW 93*
Garabedian, Paul Roesel 1927- *WhoAm 94*
Garafalo, Sebastian Joseph 1932- *WhoAmP 93*
Garafola, Lynn 1946- *WrDr 94*
Garagiola, Joe 1926- *WhoAm 94*
Garai, Gabor 1951- *WhoAm 94, WhoAmL 94*
Garai, Toma 1935- *WhoWest 94*
Garaikoetxea Urriza, Carlos 1939- *IntWW 93*
Garajalde, Fernando Alberto 1953- *WhoFI 94*
Garamendi, John R. 1945- *WhoAmP 93*
Garance, Dominick 1912- *WhoAm 94*
Garand, Christopher Pierre 1947- *WhoIns 94*
Garang, John 1943- *IntWW 93*
Garas, Kaz 1940- *WhoHol 92*
Garas, Klara 1919- *IntWW 93*
Garasa, Angel d1976 *WhoHol 92*
Garat, Henry d1959 *WhoHol 92*
Garat, (Dominique) Pierre (Jean) 1762-1823 *NewGrDO*
Garaudy, Roger Jean Charles 1913- *IntWW 93*
Garavaglia, Ferruccio d1912 *WhoHol 92*
Garavaglia, Maria Pia 1947- *WhoWomW 91*
Garavel, Paul James 1958- *WhoAmP 93*
Garavelli, John Stephen 1947- *WhoAm 94*
Garaveo, Onorato d1956 *WhoHol 92*
Garay, Alon A. 1957- *WhoWest 94*
Garay, Antonio Francisco 1947- *WhoHisp 94*
Garay, José Manuel 1965- *WhoHisp 94*
Garay, Joseph Paul 1949- *WhoFI 94*
Garay, Val Christian 1942- *WhoHisp 94*
Garayalde, Allen *WhoHisp 94*
Garayua, Mary Isa 1945- *WhoHisp 94*
Garb, Andrew Steven 1942- *WhoAm 94, WhoAmL 94*
Garba, Edward Aloysius 1921- *WhoAm 94*
Garba, Joseph Nanven 1943- *IntWW 93*
Garbacz, Gerald George 1936- *WhoAm 94*
Garbacz, Patricia Frances 1941- *WhoMW 93*
Garbacz, Ron Rand 1938- *WhoFI 94*
Garbaczewski, Daniel Frank 1950- *WhoMW 93*
Garbarino, Joseph William 1919- *WhoAm 94, WhoWest 94*
Garbarino, Robert Paul 1929- *WhoAmL 94*
Garbark, Melvin D. 1930- *WhoMW 93*
Garbaty, Eugene L. d1966 *WhoAmA 93N*
Garbaty, Marie Louise 1910- *WhoAm 94, WhoAmA 93*
Garbe, Charlotte 1929- *WhoWomW 91*
Garbe, William 1948-1989 *WhoAmA 93N*
Garber, Alan Joel 1943- *WhoAm 94*
Garber, Alan S. 1950- *WhoAmL 94*
Garber, Barry L. 1930- *WhoAmL 94*
Garber, Betty Kahn 1950- *WhoMW 93*
Garber, Charles Nelson 1947- *WhoFI 94*
Garber, Charles Stedman, Jr. 1943- *WhoAm 94, WhoFI 94*
Garber, Daniel 1880-1958 *WhoAmA 93N*
Garber, Daniel Elliot 1949- *WhoAm 94*
Garber, David J. 1949- *WhoMW 93*
Garber, Eugene K. *DrAPF 93*
Garber, Harry Douglas 1928- *WhoAm 94, WhoFI 94*
Garber, James Noble, II 1933- *WhoAmL 94*
Garber, Jan d1977 *WhoHol 92*
Garber, Jerold Allan 1942- *WhoWest 94*
Garber, Joseph R(ene) 1943- *WrDr 94*
Garber, Matthew 1956- *WhoHol 92*
Garber, Morris Joseph 1912- *WhoWest 94*
Garber, Philip E. 1949- *WhoAm 94, WhoAmL 94*
Garber, Richard Ian 1950- *WhoMW 93*
Garber, Robert Edward 1949- *WhoAm 94*
Garber, Samuel Baugh 1934- *WhoAm 94, WhoFI 94, WhoMW 93*
Garber, Sheldon 1920- *WhoMW 93*
Garber, Stanley J. 1941- *WhoAmL 94*
Garber, Terri 1960- *WhoHol 92*
Garber, Victor 1949- *WhoHol 92*
Garber, Zev 1941- *WhoWest 94*
Garberding, Larry Gilbert 1938- *WhoAm 94, WhoFI 94, WhoMW 93*
Garbers, Christoph Friedrich 1929- *IntWW 93*
Garbers, David Lorn 1944- *WhoScEn 94*
Garbett, Bryson *WhoAmP 93*
Garbey, Barbaro 1957- *WhoBlA 94*
Garbin, Albeno Patrick 1932- *WhoAm 94*
Garbin, Edoardo 1865-1943 *NewGrDO*
Garbis, Andrew Nicholas 1936- *WhoFI 94*
Garbis, Marvin Joseph 1936- *WhoAm 94, WhoAmL 94*
Garbisch, Bernice Chrysler *WhoAmA 93N*
Garbisch, Edgar William 1899-1979 *WhoAmA 93N*
Garbo, Greta d1990 *WhoHol 92*
Garbo, Greta 1905-1990 *AmCulL [port], WhAm 10*
Garbo, Norman 1919- *EncSF 93*
Garbo, Sven d1967 *WhoHol 92*
Garbona, Edgar *WhoHisp 94*
Garbose, Doris Rhoda 1924- *WhoAmP 93*

Garbus, Martin 1934- *WrDr 94*
Garbus, Martin Solomon 1934- *WhoAmL 94*
Garbutt, Eugene James 1925- *WhoAm 94, WhoAmL 94*
Garbutt, Frank A. d1947 *WhoHol 92*
Garbutt, Janice Lovoos *WhoAmA 93*
Garbutt, John Thomas 1929- *WhoMW 93*
Garby, Lee Hawkins, Mrs. 1890- *EncSF 93*
Garcelon, John Herrick 1957- *WhoScEn 94*
Garces, Francisco 1934- *IntWW 93*
Garces, Francisco Tomas Hermenegildo 1738-1781 *WhWE*
Garces, Isabel d1981 *WhoHol 92*
Garces, Mauricio d1989 *WhoHol 92*
Garces, Rich 1971- *WhoHisp 94*
Garcetti, Gilbert I. *WhoAmL 94*
Garchie, Peter Lynn 1957- *WhoAmL 94*
Garchik, Leah Lieberman 1945- *WhoAm 94*
Garchik, Morton Lloyd 1929- *WhoAmA 93*
Garcia, A. C. *WhoAmP 93*
Garcia, Adalberto Carlos 1954- *WhoHisp 94*
Garcia, Adalberto Moreno 1943- *WhoHisp 94*
Garcia, Adolfo Ramon 1948- *WhoAm 94, WhoAmL 94, WhoHisp 94*
Garcia, Adriana 1941- *WhoHisp 94*
Garcia, Albert B. 1944- *WhoHisp 94*
Garcia, Alberto *WhoHisp 94*
Garcia, Alberto 1930- *WhoHisp 94*
Garcia, Alberto, Jr. 1930- *WhoHisp 94*
Garcia, Alberto A. 1945- *WhoHisp 94*
Garcia, Alberto Ureta 1926- *WhoHisp 94*
Garcia, Alexander 1919- *WhoAm 94*
Garcia, Alfonso E., Sr. 1933- *WhoHisp 94*
Garcia, Alfred R. 1957- *WhoHisp 94*
Garcia, Alfred Robert 1957- *WhoWest 94*
Garcia, Alfredo *WhoHisp 94*
Garcia, Alicia Rangel 1964- *WhoHisp 94*
Garcia, Allan d1938 *WhoHol 92*
Garcia, Alma *WhoHisp 94*
Garcia, Amando S., Sr. 1934- *WhoHisp 94*
Garcia, Andres 1948- *WhoHisp 94*
Garcia, Andrew E., Sr. *WhoHisp 94*
Garcia, Andy 1956- *IntMPA 94, IntWW 93, WhoAm 94, WhoHisp 94, WhoHol 92*
Garcia, Angel Cintron *WhoAmP 93*
Garcia, Anna *WhoHisp 94*
Garcia, Anthony Edward 1951- *WhoHisp 94*
Garcia, Antonio Agustin 1959- *WhoScEn 94*
Garcia, Antonio E. 1901- *WhoHisp 94*
Garcia, Antonio E. 1924- *WhoHisp 94*
Garcia, Antonio José 1959- *WhoHisp 94*
Garcia, Antonio M. 1946- *WhoHisp 94*
Garcia, Arcenio A., Sr. 1947- *WhoAmP 93*
Garcia, Arcenio Arturo, Sr. 1947- *WhoHisp 94*
Garcia, Ariel Antonio 1953- *WhoHisp 94*
Garcia, Armando *WhoHisp 94*
Garcia, Armando 1931- *WhoHisp 94*
Garcia, Armando 1951- *WhoHisp 94*
Garcia, Arnold, Jr. 1948- *WhoHisp 94*
Garcia, Arnulfo 1946- *WhoHisp 94*
Garcia, Arnulfo, Jr. 1948- *WhoHisp 94*
Garcia, Arthur 1924- *Who 94*
Garcia, Arturo 1914- *Who 94*
Garcia, Bernardo Alejandro 1941- *WhoHisp 94*
Garcia, Bernardo Mario 1964- *WhoAmL 94*
Garcia, Bernardo Ramon 1956- *WhoHisp 94*
Garcia, Blanche 1946- *WhoHisp 94*
Garcia, Carlos *WhoHisp 94*
Garcia, Carlos 1967- *WhoHisp 94*
Garcia, Carlos Arturo 1935- *WhoHisp 94*
Garcia, Carlos E. *WhoHisp 94*
Garcia, Carlos Emilio 1942- *WhoHisp 94*
Garcia, Carlos Ernesto 1936- *WhoHisp 94*
Garcia, Carlos Fernando 1953- *WhoHisp 94*
Garcia, Carmen M. *WhoHisp 94*
Garcia, Casimiro Gilbert 1930- *WhoWest 94*
Garcia, Castelar Medardo 1942- *WhoAmL 94*
Garcia, Catalina Esperanza 1944- *WhoHisp 94*
Garcia, Cecilia R. *WhoHisp 94*
Garcia, Celso-Ramon 1921- *WhoAm 94, WhoHisp 94*
Garcia, Cesar *WhoHisp 94*
Garcia, Clara L. 1948- *WhoHisp 94*
Garcia, Conrad, Jr. *WhoHisp 94*
Garcia, Cordelia Villarreal 1951- *WhoHisp 94*
Garcia, Crisostomo Bautista 1948- *WhoFI 94*
Garcia, Crispin, Jr. 1945- *WhoHisp 94*
Garcia, Cristina 1958- *ConAu 141, WhoHisp 94*
Garcia, Cristina 1959- *ConLC 76 [port]*
Garcia, Curt Jonathan 1960- *WhoWest 94*
Garcia, Damaso Domingo 1957- *WhoHisp 94*
Garcia, Daniel, Jr. 1944- *WhoHisp 94*
Garcia, Daniel Albert 1946- *WhoHisp 94*
Garcia, Daniel P. 1947- *WhoHisp 94*
Garcia, Daniel Ray 1953- *WhoHisp 94*
Garcia, Danny 1954- *WhoHisp 94*
Garcia, David *WhoHisp 94*
Garcia, David H. 1949- *WhoHisp 94*
Garcia, David J. *WhoHisp 94*
Garcia, David Joseph 1946- *WhoHisp 94*
Garcia, David M. 1956- *WhoHisp 94*
Garcia, David Richard 1953- *WhoHisp 94*
Garcia, Dawn E. 1959- *WhoHisp 94*
Garcia, Delano J. *WhoAmP 93, WhoHisp 94*
Garcia, Dennis *WhoHisp 94*
Garcia, Dennis R. 1954- *WhoHisp 94*
Garcia, Domingo 1940- *WhoHisp 94*
Garcia, Domingo 1958- *WhoScEn 94*
Garcia, Domingo A. 1958- *WhoHisp 94*
Garcia, Domingo Alberto 1958- *WhoAmP 93*
Garcia, Donald Adolph 1936- *WhoHisp 94*
Garcia, Eddie 1970- *WhoHol 92*
Garcia, Edith V. 1931- *WhoAmP 93*
Garcia, Edna I. *WhoAmP 93*
Garcia, Eduardo 1964- *WhoHisp 94*
Garcia, Edward 1958- *WhoHisp 94*
Garcia, Edward Coronado 1946- *WhoHisp 94*
Garcia, Edward J. 1928- *WhoAm 94, WhoAmL 94, WhoHisp 94, WhoWest 94*
Garcia, Edwin E. *WhoAmP 93*
Garcia, Edwin E. 1955- *WhoHisp 94*
Garcia, Edwina 1944- *WhoAmP 93, WhoHisp 94*
Garcia, Efraim S. 1931- *WhoHisp 94*
Garcia, Eleuterio M. 1943- *WhoHisp 94*
Garcia, Elias *WhoHisp 94*
Garcia, Eligio, Jr. 1939- *WhoHisp 94*
Garcia, Elizabeth Mildred 1956- *WhoHisp 94*
Garcia, Elsa Laura 1954- *WhoHisp 94*
Garcia, Elvira Elena 1938- *WhoHisp 94*
Garcia, Enildo Albert 1932- *WhoHisp 94*
Garcia, Enrique A. 1947- *WhoHisp 94*
Garcia, Ernest Eugene 1946- *WhoAmP 93, WhoHisp 94*
Garcia, Ernest Victor 1948- *WhoScEn 94*
Garcia, Ernie Rudolfo 1948- *WhoHisp 94*
Garcia, Esther 1945- *WhoHisp 94*
Garcia, Eugene Nicholas 1925- *WhoHisp 94*
Garcia, Eva 1950- *WhoHisp 94*
Garcia, Evelyn 1952- *WhoHisp 94*
Garcia, Evelyn Jasso 1948- *WhoHisp 94*
Garcia, Everardo *WhoHisp 94*
Garcia, F. Chris 1940- *WhoAm 94, WhoHisp 94*
Garcia, Felix M. *WhoHisp 94*
Garcia, Fernando *WhoHisp 94*
Garcia, Florencio Oscar 1934- *WhoWest 94*
Garcia, Frances 1941- *WhoHisp 94*
Garcia, Frances Josephine 1938- *WhoHisp 94*
Garcia, Francisco A. 1956- *WhoHisp 94*
Garcia, Francisco Cesareo, III 1946- *WhoHisp 94*
Garcia, Francisco Jose 1920- *WhoHisp 94*
Garcia, Frank d1993 *NewYTBS 93 [port]*
Garcia, Frank 1924- *WhoAmA 93*
Garcia, Frank C. 1924- *WhoHisp 94*
Garcia, Frank T. 1948- *WhoAmL 94*
Garcia, Gabriel 1952- *WhoHisp 94*
Garcia, George Florencio 1942- *WhoHisp 94*
Garcia, Gerald *WhoHisp 94*
Garcia, Gilbert 1945- *WhoHisp 94*
Garcia, Gustavo *WhoHisp 94*
Garcia, Guy D. 1955- *WhoHisp 94*
Garcia, H. F. 1925- *WhoHisp 94*
Garcia, Harry G. *WhoHisp 94*
Garcia, Hector *WhoHisp 94*
Garcia, Hector Gomez 1931- *WhoHisp 94*
Garcia, Hector H. 1930- *WhoHisp 94*
Garcia, Héctor Perez 1914- *WhoHisp 94*
Garcia, Hector Santos 1957- *WhoHisp 94*
Garcia, Henry d1970 *WhoHol 92*
Garcia, Henry F. 1943- *WhoHisp 94*
Garcia, Herlinda 1944- *WhoHisp 94*
Garcia, Hermán S. 1950- *WhoHisp 94*
Garcia, Hipolito Frank 1925- *WhoAm 94, WhoAmL 94, WhoHisp 94*
Garcia, Ignacio Razon 1953- *WhoAmL 94*
Garcia, Isidro *WhoHisp 94*
Garcia, Israel 1937- *WhoHisp 94*
Garcia, Iva *WhoHisp 94*
Garcia, J. A. *WhoHisp 94*
Garcia, James 1932- *WhoHisp 94*
Garcia, Jane C. *WhoHisp 94*
Garcia, Jasper 1939- *WhoAmP 93*
Garcia, Javier N. 1948- *WhoHisp 94*
Garcia, Jerry 1942- *WhoAm 94, WhoHisp 94*
Garcia, Jess *WhoHisp 94*
Garcia, Jesus 1941- *WhoHisp 94*
Garcia, Jesus Alvaro, Jr. 1948- *WhoHisp 94*
Garcia, Jesús Enrique 1946- *WhoHisp 94*
Garcia, Jesus G. *WhoHisp 94*
Garcia, Jesus G. 1956- *WhoAmP 93*
Garcia, Joaquin 1940- *WhoHisp 94*
Garcia, Joe Baldemar 1942- *WhoHisp 94*
Garcia, Joe G., Jr. 1946- *WhoHisp 94*
Garcia, Joe Manuel, Jr. 1952- *WhoHisp 94*
Garcia, John 1917- *WhoHisp 94*
Garcia, John 1950- *WhoHisp 94*
Garcia, John A. *WhoHisp 94*
Garcia, John Anthony 1955- *WhoHisp 94*
Garcia, John C. 1944- *WhoHisp 94*
Garcia, John F. 1964- *WhoHisp 94*
Garcia, John Martin 1949- *WhoHisp 94*
Garcia, Jorge Jesus 1955- *WhoHisp 94*
Garcia, Jorge Logan 1950- *WhoHisp 94*
Garcia, Jorge Luis 1953- *WhoAmP 93*
Garcia, Jose *WhoHisp 94*
Garcia, Jose Bautista 1966- *WhoHisp 94*
Garcia, José D., Jr. 1936- *WhoHisp 94*
Garcia, José F. 1928- *WhoHisp 94*
Garcia, Jose-Guadalupe Villarreal 1947- *WhoHisp 94*
Garcia, José Guillermo 1959- *WhoHisp 94*
Garcia, Jose Heriberto 1952- *WhoAmL 94*
Garcia, Jose Joel 1946- *WhoHisp 94*
Garcia, José Luis 1960- *WhoHisp 94*
Garcia, Jose Luix 1949- *WhoMW 93*
Garcia, Jose Mauricio Nunes 1767-1830 *NewGrDO*
Garcia, Jose Pablo Moncayo *NewGrDO*
Garcia, Jose Zebedeo 1945- *WhoAmP 93, WhoHisp 94, WhoWest 94*
Garcia, Josefina M. 1906- *WhoHisp 94*
Garcia, Joseph 1962- *WhoHisp 94*
Garcia, Joseph, Jr. 1941- *WhoHisp 94*
Garcia, Joseph E. 1950- *WhoHisp 94*
Garcia, Joseph Guadalupe 1931- *WhoHisp 94*
Garcia, Josie Alaniz 1946- *WhoHisp 94*
Garcia, Juan Andres 1967- *WhoHisp 94*
Garcia, Juan C. 1944- *WhoHisp 94*
Garcia, Juan Carlos 1945- *WhoMW 93*
Garcia, Juan Carlos 1961- *WhoHisp 94*
Garcia, Juan Castanon 1949- *WhoHisp 94*
Garcia, Juan F. 1950- *WhoHisp 94*
Garcia, Juan G. 1933- *WhoHisp 94*
Garcia, Juan Manuel 1953- *WhoHisp 94*
Garcia, Juan Ramon 1947- *WhoHisp 94*
Garcia, Juanita *WhoHisp 94*
Garcia, Juanita Garcia 1934- *WhoHisp 94*
Garcia, Juliet Villarreal 1949- *WhoHisp 94*
Garcia, Julio H. *WhoHisp 94*
Garcia, Julio Ralph, Sr. 1932- *WhoHisp 94*
Garcia, Kerry J. 1952- *WhoHisp 94*
Garcia, Kwame N. 1946- *WhoBlA 94*
Garcia, Laura Diana 1961- *WhoHisp 94*
Garcia, Lauro *WhoHisp 94*
Garcia, Lawrence Dean 1936- *WhoHisp 94*
Garcia, Lawrence R. 1951- *WhoHisp 94*
Garcia, Len *WhoIns 94*
Garcia, Leo A. *WhoHisp 94*
Garcia, Lino, Jr. 1934- *WhoHisp 94*
Garcia, Lionel Gonzalo 1935- *WhoHisp 94*
Garcia, Lloyd Bert 1957- *WhoWest 94*
Garcia, Louie Joe 1954- *WhoHisp 94*
Garcia, Louis *WhoHisp 94*
Garcia, Louis Lawrence 1947- *WhoFI 94*
Garcia, Louis R. 1931- *WhoIns 94*
Garcia, Luis Alonzo 1954- *WhoHisp 94*
Garcia, Luis Cesareo 1949- *WhoAmL 94*
Garcia, Luis M. *WhoHisp 94*
Garcia, Luis R. 1949- *WhoHisp 94*
Garcia, Luis Rene, Jr. 1945- *WhoHisp 94*
Garcia, Lydia Maria 1936- *WhoHisp 94*
Garcia, Magdalena *WhoHisp 94*
Garcia, Manuel, Jr. *WhoHisp 94*
Garcia, Manuel (del Populo Vicente Rodriguez) 1775-1832 *NewGrDO [port]*
Garcia, Manuel (Patricio Rodriguez) 1805-1906 *NewGrDO*
Garcia, Manuel Blas 1942- *WhoHisp 94*
Garcia, Manuel J. *WhoHisp 94*
Garcia, Marc Anthony 1962- *WhoAm 94*
Garcia, Margaret A. 1950- *WhoHisp 94*
Garcia, Margaret Louise 1963- *WhoHisp 94*
Garcia, Maria 1955- *WhoHisp 94*
Garcia, Maria S. T. *WhoHisp 94*
Garcia, Mario, Jr. 1959- *WhoHisp 94*
Garcia, Mario T. 1944- *WhoHisp 94*
Garcia, Marlene Linares 1956- *WhoHisp 94*
Garcia, Marta Irma 1946- *WhoWest 94*
Garcia, Mary Ann 1937- *WhoHisp 94*
Garcia, Mary Dolores 1949- *WhoHisp 94*
Garcia, Mary Inez 1931- *WhoAmP 93*
Garcia, Mary Jane 1936- *WhoHisp 94*
Garcia, Mary Jane M. 1936- *WhoAmP 93*
Garcia, Mary Jane Madrid 1936- *WhoWest 94*
Garcia, Marz John 1937- *WhoAmP 93*
Garcia, Melva Ybarra 1950- *WhoHisp 94*
Garcia, Michael *WhoHisp 94*
Garcia, Michael John 1948- *WhoHisp 94*
Garcia, Michael T. *WhoHisp 94*
Garcia, Miguel A., Jr. 1952- *WhoHisp 94*
Garcia, Miguel Angel 1938- *WhoHisp 94*
Garcia, Mildred 1952- *WhoHisp 94*
Garcia, Neftalí G. 1943- *WhoHisp 94*
Garcia, Nicolas A., III 1932- *WhoHisp 94*
Garcia, Nicolas Bruce 1961- *WhoHisp 94*
Garcia, Nicole *WhoHol 92*
Garcia, Nora *WhoHisp 94*
Garcia, Norma G. 1950- *WhoHisp 94*
Garcia, Ofelia *WhoHisp 94*
Garcia, Ofelia 1941- *WhoAmA 93*
Garcia, Olga Cháidez 1957- *WhoHisp 94*
Garcia, Olivia 1953- *WhoHisp 94*
Garcia, Orlando 1952- *WhoHisp 94*
Garcia, Orlando L. 1952- *WhoAmP 93*
Garcia, Oscar Manuel 1950- *WhoHisp 94*
Garcia, Oscar Nicolas 1936- *WhoAm 94, WhoHisp 94*
Garcia, Otto Luis 1947- *WhoHisp 94*
Garcia, Patricia A. 1956- *WhoAmL 94*
Garcia, Pauline J. 1948- *WhoHisp 94*
Garcia, Pedro Ivan 1947- *WhoScEn 94*
Garcia, Pedro Vasquez 1937- *WhoHisp 94*
Garcia, Peter 1930- *WhoHisp 94*
Garcia, Peter Angel 1960- *WhoHisp 94*
Garcia, Peter C. *WhoHisp 94*
Garcia, Peter C. 1951- *WhoHisp 94*
Garcia, Priscilla *WhoHol 92*
Garcia, Rafael I. 1955- *WhoHisp 94*
Garcia, Rafael Jorge 1933- *WhoScEn 94*
Garcia, Rafael Wilson 1943- *WhoHisp 94*
Garcia, Rahn Howard 1953- *WhoWest 94*
Garcia, Ralph, Jr. 1943- *WhoHisp 94*
Garcia, Raquel Elena 1946- *WhoHisp 94*
Garcia, Raul *WhoAmP 93*
Garcia, Raúl A. 1949- *WhoHisp 94*
Garcia, Raul C. 1946- *WhoHisp 94*
Garcia, Raul P., Jr. 1947- *WhoHisp 94*
Garcia, Ray 1960- *WhoHisp 94*
Garcia, Raymond E. 1941- *WhoHisp 94*
Garcia, Raymond Lloyd 1942- *WhoScEn 94*
Garcia, René 1939- *WhoHisp 94*
Garcia, René Luis 1945- *WhoHisp 94*
Garcia, Ricardo Alberto 1946- *WhoHisp 94*
Garcia, Ricardo H. *WhoHisp 94*
Garcia, Ricardo J. 1947- *WhoHisp 94*
Garcia, Ricardo Romano 1938- *WhoHisp 94*
Garcia, Rich *WhoHisp 94*
Garcia, Richard *WhoHisp 94*
Garcia, Richard Amado 1941- *WhoHisp 94*
Garcia, Richard Louis 1952- *WhoScEn 94*
Garcia, Rick *WhoHisp 94*
Garcia, Rita Zamora 1937- *WhoHisp 94*
Garcia, Robert 1933- *WhoAmP 93*
Garcia, Robert Allen 1952- *WhoHisp 94*
Garcia, Robert George 1956- *WhoHisp 94*
Garcia, Robert L. 1948- *WhoHisp 94*
Garcia, Robert N. 1937- *WhoAmP 93*
Garcia, Robert S. *WhoHisp 94*
Garcia, Robert Stanley 1958- *WhoHisp 94*
Garcia, Roberto *WhoHisp 94*
Garcia, Rod *WhoHisp 94*
Garcia, Rodolfo, Jr. 1963- *WhoAmP 93, WhoHisp 94*
Garcia, Roland, Jr. 1958- *WhoHisp 94*
Garcia, Roland B. *WhoHisp 94*
Garcia, Ronald Samuel 1962- *WhoHisp 94*
Garcia, Rose *WhoHisp 94*
Garcia, Rose Marie 1959- *WhoHisp 94*
Garcia, Ruben *WhoHisp 94*
Garcia, Rudolph 1951- *WhoAm 94, WhoAmL 94*
Garcia, Rudy 1963- *WhoHisp 94*
Garcia, Rupert 1941- *WhoAmA 93*
Garcia, Sam *WhoHisp 94*
Garcia, Sam 1957- *WhoHisp 94*
Garcia, Santos 1947- *WhoHisp 94*
Garcia, Sara d1980 *WhoHol 92*
Garcia, Sheila *WhoHisp 94*
Garcia, Sid 1959- *WhoHisp 94*
Garcia, Silas T. *WhoAmP 93*
Garcia, Stella *WhoHol 92*
Garcia, Stephen Gregory 1947- *WhoWest 94*
Garcia, Stephen Trinidad 1944- *WhoHisp 94*
Garcia, Susana 1956- *WhoHisp 94*
Garcia, Sylvia R. 1950- *WhoHisp 94*
Garcia, Teofilo 1942- *WhoHisp 94*
Garcia, Terry Donato 1953- *WhoAmL 94*
Garcia, Thomas David 1967- *WhoHisp 94*
Garcia, Wanda *WhoHisp 94*
Garcia, William Burres 1940- *WhoBlA 94*
Garcia, William T. 1958- *WhoHisp 94*

Garcia, Yvonne 1949- *WhoHisp 94*
Garcia, Yvonne 1956- *WhoHisp 94*
Garcia Anoveros, Jaime 1932- *IntWW 93*
Garcia-Araiza, Leonardo R. 1947- *WhoHisp 94*
Garcia Arias, Ludivina 1945- *WhoWomW 91*
Garcia-Ayvens, Francisco *WhoHisp 94*
Garcia-Bárcena, Yanira E. 1950- *WhoHisp 94*
Garcia-Barrera, Gloria 1952- *WhoHisp 94*
Garcia-Berry, Abelardo A. 1921- *WhoHisp 94*
Garcia-Borras, Thomas 1926- *WhoWest 94*
Garcia-Bunuel, Luis 1931- *WhoWest 94*
Garcia-Cartagena, Esther 1945- *WhoHisp 94*
Garcia-Cisneros, Florencio 1924- *WhoHisp 94*
Garcia-Clyne, Sonia 1957- *WhoHisp 94*
Garcia De Jalon, Alejandro Bedox 1925- *WhoHisp 94*
Garcia de Oteyza, Juan 1962- *WhoHisp 94*
Garcia-Diaz, Alberto 1945- *WhoHisp 94*
Garcia Diez, Juan Antonio 1940- *IntWW 93*
Garcia Fajer, Francisco Javier 1730-1809 *NewGrDO*
Garcia-Ferraz, Nereyda 1954- *WhoHisp 94*
Garcia Fusté, Tomas *WhoHisp 94*
Garcia-Godoy, Franklin 1952- *WhoHisp 94*
Garcia-Gómez, Jorge 1937- *WhoHisp 94*
Garcia-Granados, Sergio Eduardo 1942- *WhoAm 94, WhoFI 94*
Garcia-Gregory, Jorge A. 1946- *WhoHisp 94*
Garcia Gutierrez, Antonio 1813-1884 *NewGrDO*
Garcia-Kone, Anna Y. 1953- *WhoHisp 94*
Garcia Lopez, Estela 1966- *WhoHisp 94*
Garcia Lorca, Federico 1898-1936 *GayLL, IntDcT 2, NewGrDO, TwCLC 49 [port]*
Garcia Mansilla, Eduardo 1871-1930 *NewGrDO*
Garcia-Manzanedo, Hector 1926- *WhoHisp 94*
Garcia Marquez, Gabriel *Who 94*
Garcia Marquez, Gabriel 1928- *ConWorW 93, HispLC [port], IntWW 93, RfGShF*
Garcia Marquez, Gabriel Jose 1928- *WhoAm 94*
Garcia Marruz, Fina 1923- *BlmGWL*
Garcia Martinez, Hernando 1942- *WhoScEn 94*
Garcia Martinez, Ricardo Javier 1943- *WhoScEn 94*
Garcia Millán, Angel 1953- *WhoHisp 94*
Garcia Morales, Adelaida *BlmGWL*
Garcia-Moran, Manuel 1935- *WhoScEn 94*
Garcia-Nakata, Lorraine 1950- *WhoHisp 94*
Garcia Nieto, Jose 1914- *IntWW 93*
Garcia-Núñez, Fernando 1944- *WhoHisp 94*
Garcia-Oliva, Manolo 1938- *WhoHisp 94*
Garcia Oller, Jose Luis 1923- *WhoAm 94, WhoHisp 94*
Garcia Pacheco, Fabian c. 1725-c. 1808 *NewGrDO*
Garcia-Palmieri, Mario Ruben 1927- *WhoHisp 94*
Garcia-Parra, Jaime 1931- *Who 94*
Garcia-Pedrosa, José R. 1946- *WhoHisp 94*
Garcia-Pedrosa, Jose Ramon 1946- *WhoAmL 94*
Garcia Pelaez, Raul 1922- *IntWW 93*
Garcia-Pena, Roberto 1910- *IntWW 93*
Garcia Perez, Alan 1949- *IntWW 93*
Garcia Pinto, Magdalena 1943- *WhoHisp 94*
Garcia Prado, Judith *WhoHisp 94*
Garcia-Prats, Joseph A. 1944- *WhoHisp 94*
Garcia-Ramirez, Lucky May 1961- *WhoHisp 94*
Garcia Ramirez, Sergio 1938- *IntWW 93*
Garcia-Rangel, Sara Marina 1939- *WhoHisp 94*
Garcia-Rill, Edgar Enrique 1948- *WhoAm 94, WhoScEn 94*
Garcia-Rios, Jose M. 1957- *WhoHisp 94*
Garcia-Rodriguez, Sergio 1961- *WhoHisp 94*
Garcia-Rosaly, Leticia 1949- *WhoHisp 94*
Garcia Santiago, Ramon *WhoHisp 94*
Garcia-Serrano, Maria Victoria 1959- *WhoHisp 94*
Garcia-Torres, Francisco Jose 1945- *WhoHisp 94*
Garcia Vargas, Joaquin d1993 *NewYTBS 93*
Garcia Vargas, Julian 1946- *IntWW 93*
Garcia-Verdugo, Luisa 1960- *WhoHisp 94*
Garcia-Witkowski, Phyllis Josephine 1934- *WhoWest 94*
Garcia Yebra, Valentin 1917- *IntWW 93*
Garcin, Henri 1929- *WhoHol 92*
Garcin, Laurent fl. 170-?- *NewGrDO*
Garcisanz, Isabel 1934- *NewGrDO*
Garczewski, Ronald James 1969- *WhoScEn 94*
Gard, Beverly J. 1940- *WhoAmP 93, WhoMW 93*
Gard, Curtis Eldon 1921- *WhoAm 94*
Gard, Janice *TwCYAW*
Gard, Janice 1902- *WrDr 94*
Gard, John 1963- *WhoAmP 93*
Gard, Joyce 1911- *WrDr 94*
Gard, Robert (Joseph) 1927- *NewGrDO*
Gard, Robert Edward 1910-1992 *ConAu 140, SmATA 74*
Gard, (Sanford) Wayne 1899-1986 *ConAu 43NR*
Garda, Robert Allen 1939- *WhoAm 94*
Gardam, David Hill 1922- *Who 94*
Gardam, Jane 1928- *SmATA 76 [port], TwCYAW, WrDr 94*
Gardam, Jane Mary *Who 94*
Gardaphe, Fred L(ouis) 1952- *WrDr 94*
Gardaphe, Fred Louis 1952- *WhoMW 93*
Gardar Svarsson *WhWE*
Garde, Anand Madhav 1945- *WhoScEn 94*
Garde, Betty d1989 *WhoHol 92*
Garde, John Charles 1961- *WhoAmL 94*
Garde, Pierre de *NewGrDO*
Gardea, Aili Tapio 1964- *WhoHisp 94*
Gardebring, Sandra S. *WhoAmL 94, WhoAmP 93*
Gardel, Carlos d1935 *WhoHol 92*
Gardel, Maximilien 1741-1787 *IntDcB*
Gardel, Pierre 1758-1840 *IntDcB [port]*
Gardel, Pierre Gabriel 1758-1840 *NewGrDO*
Gardella, David Edward 1944- *WhoWest 94*
Gardella, Hazel L. 1915- *WhoAmP 93*
Gardella, Libero Anthony 1935- *WhoAm 94*
Gardella, Tess d1950 *WhoHol 92*
Gardelli, Lamberto 1915- *IntWW 93, NewGrDO*
Gardeman, Geneva E. *WhoAmP 93*
Garden, Bruce 1936- *WrDr 94*
Garden, Donald J. *EncSF 93*
Garden, Edward (James Clarke) 1930- *WrDr 94*
Garden, Mary d1967 *WhoHol 92*
Garden, Mary 1874-1967 *AmCulL, NewGrDO [port]*
Garden, Nancy 1938- *SmATA 77 [port], TwCYAW, WrDr 94*
Garden, Timothy 1944- *Who 94*
Gardener, Andrew Todd 1958- *WhoFI 94*
Gardenfors, Peter 1949- *IntWW 93*
Gardenhire, Donald Paul 1955- *WhoWest 94*
Gardenhire, Gary Wayne 1945- *WhoAmP 93*
Gardenia, Vincent d1992 *IntMPA 94N*
Gardenia, Vincent 1921-1992 *WhAm 10*
Gardenia, Vincent 1922- *WhoHol 92*
Gardenia, Vincent 1922-1992 *AnObit 1992, ConTFT 11*
Gardenier, John Stark, II 1937- *WhoAm 94*
Gardenier, Turkan Kumbaraci 1941- *WhoAm 94*
Gardent, Paul 1921- *IntWW 93*
Gardes, Renee d1972 *WhoHol 92*
Gardi, Francesco 1760?-c. 1810 *NewGrDO*
Gardin, John George, II 1949- *WhoWest 94*
Gardin, Vladimir d1965 *WhoHol 92*
Gardiner, Anthony Morris 1945- *WhoFI 94*
Gardiner, Carl W. d1993 *NewYTBS 93*
Gardiner, D. Bruce 1942- *WhoWest 94*
Gardiner, Donald Andrew 1922- *WhoAm 94*
Gardiner, Donald K. 1939- *WhoIns 94*
Gardiner, Donald Kent 1939- *WhoAm 94*
Gardiner, Duncan *Who 94*
Gardiner, (John) Duncan (Broderick) 1937- *Who 94*
Gardiner, E. Nicholas P. 1939- *WhoAm 94, WhoFI 94*
Gardiner, George (Arthur) 1935- *Who 94*
Gardiner, George L. 1933- *WhoBlA 94*
Gardiner, Helen (Louisa) 1901- *Who 94*
Gardiner, Henry Gilbert 1927- *WhoAmA 93*
Gardiner, John 1747-1808 *WhAmRev*
Gardiner, John Andrew 1937- *WhoMW 93*
Gardiner, John Eliot 1943- *IntWW 93, NewGrDO, Who 94*
Gardiner, John Ralph 1946- *Who 94*
Gardiner, Joseph William Fawsitt 1920- *WhoAm 94*
Gardiner, Judith Kegan 1941- *WhoMW 93*
Gardiner, Keith Mattinson 1933- *WhoAm 94*
Gardiner, Lester Raymond, Jr. 1931- *WhoAmL 94*
Gardiner, Lora Jean *DrAPF 93*
Gardiner, Nancy Elizabeth 1964- *WhoWest 94*
Gardiner, Ormsin Sornmoonpin 1934- *WhoMW 93*
Gardiner, Patrick 1922- *WrDr 94*
Gardiner, Patrick Lancaster 1922- *Who 94*
Gardiner, Peter Dod Robin 1927- *Who 94*
Gardiner, Peter R. 1949- *IntMPA 94*
Gardiner, Reginald d1980 *WhoHol 92*
Gardiner, Robert (Kweku Atta) 1914- *Who 94*
Gardiner, Robert Kweku Atta 1914- *IntWW 93*
Gardiner, T. Michael 1946- *WhoAmA 93*
Gardiner, Victor Alec 1929- *Who 94*
Gardiner, William Cecil, Jr. 1933- *WhoAm 94*
Gardiner, William Douglas Haig 1917- *WhoAm 94*
Gardiner-Scott, William 1906- *Who 94*
Gardini, Raul d1993 *Who 94N*
Gardini, Raul 1933- *IntWW 93*
Gardinier, Suzanne *DrAPF 93*
Gardino, Vincent Anthony 1953- *WhoFI 94*
Gardiol, Rita Mazzetti *WhoMW 93*
Gardner *Who 94*
Gardner, A. Barclay 1930- *WhoWest 94*
Gardner, Alvin Frederick 1920- *WhoAm 94*
Gardner, Amelia d1947 *WhoHol 92*
Gardner, Andrew Bradford 1937- *WhoAmA 93*
Gardner, Andrew M. 1959- *WhoAmL 94*
Gardner, Ann *WhoAmA 93*
Gardner, Ann 1937- *WhoAmP 93*
Gardner, Antony John 1927- *Who 94*
Gardner, Arnold Burton 1930- *WhoAm 94*
Gardner, Arthur 1910- *WhoHol 92*
Gardner, Audrey V. 1946- *WhoScEn 94*
Gardner, Autrey Thaddeus, Jr. 1939- *WhoWest 94*
Gardner, Ava d1990 *WhoHol 92*
Gardner, Ava 1922-1990 *WhAm 10*
Gardner, Barbara *WhoAmP 93*
Gardner, Bernard 1931- *WhoAm 94*
Gardner, Bettiann 1930- *WhoFI 94*
Gardner, Bettye J. *WhoBlA 94*
Gardner, Booth 1936- *WhoAmP 93*
Gardner, Bradford Arthur 1949- *WhoFI 94*
Gardner, (Robert) Brian 1931- *WrDr 94*
Gardner, Brian E. 1952- *WhoAm 94, WhoAmL 94*
Gardner, Brother Dave 1926-1983 *WhoCom*
Gardner, Bruce D. *WhoAmL 94*
Gardner, Bruce D. 1951- *WhoIns 94*
Gardner, Bruce Lynn 1942- *WhoScEn 94*
Gardner, Caleb 1739-1806 *WhAmRev*
Gardner, Carroll F. 1934- *WhoAmP 93*
Gardner, Caryn Sue 1960- *WhoAmL 94*
Gardner, Cedric Boyer 1946- *WhoBlA 94*
Gardner, Charles d1924 *WhoHol 92*
Gardner, Charles Olda 1919- *WhoAm 94, WhoMW 93*
Gardner, Charlotte A. 1931- *WhoAmP 93*
Gardner, Clyde Edward 1931- *WhoFI 94, WhoScEn 94, WhoWest 94*
Gardner, Colin R. 1952- *WhoAmA 93*
Gardner, Colin Raymond 1952- *WhoWest 94*
Gardner, Connie Louise 1947- *WhoMW 93*
Gardner, Cyril d1942 *WhoHol 92*
Gardner, Dale Ray 1946- *WhoAmL 94*
Gardner, Dave d1983 *WhoHol 92*
Gardner, David Edward 1923- *WhoAm 94*
Gardner, David John 1953- *WhoFI 94*
Gardner, David Pierpont 1933- *IntWW 93, Who 94, WhoAm 94*
Gardner, Donald LaVere 1930- *WhoAm 94*
Gardner, Dorsey Robertson 1942- *WhoAm 94*
Gardner, Douglas Bruce B. *Who 94*
Gardner, Douglas Frank 1943- *Who 94*
Gardner, Ed d1963 *WhoHol 92*
Gardner, Edward (Lucas) 1912- *Who 94*
Gardner, Edward Clinton 1920- *WrDr 94*
Gardner, Edward G. *WhoAm 94, WhoFI 94*
Gardner, Edward G. 1925- *WhoBlA 94*
Gardner, Erle Stanley 1889-1970 *EncSF 93*
Gardner, Evelyn Mae 1944- *WhoMW 93*
Gardner, Everette Shaw, Jr. 1944- *WhoAm 94*
Gardner, Frank W. 1923- *WhoBlA 94*
Gardner, Gary Edward 1952- *WhoAmL 94, WhoMW 93*
Gardner, George Henry 1897- *WhAm 10*
Gardner, George Peabody 1917- *WhoAm 94*
Gardner, Gregory Allen 1958- *WhoScEn 94*
Gardner, Harold Wayne 1935- *WhoMW 93*
Gardner, Harrison 1928- *WhoMW 93*
Gardner, Helen d1968 *WhoHol 92*
Gardner, Helen 1908-1986 *BlmGWL*
Gardner, Henry L. 1944- *WhoBlA 94*
Gardner, Herb(ert) 1934- *ConDr 93, WrDr 94*
Gardner, Herbert 1921- *Who 94*
Gardner, Homer Jay 1942- *WhoWest 94*
Gardner, Howard Alan 1920- *WhoAm 94*
Gardner, Howard Earl 1943- *WhoAm 94, WhoScEn 94*
Gardner, Howard Garry 1943- *WhoMW 93*
Gardner, Hoyt Devane 1923- *WhoAmP 93*
Gardner, Hugh C., III 1943- *WhoAmL 94*
Gardner, Hunter d1952 *WhoHol 92*
Gardner, Hy d1989 *WhoHol 92*
Gardner, Hy 1908-1989 *WhAm 10*
Gardner, J. Neal 1944- *WhoAmL 94*
Gardner, J. Stephen 1944- *WhoAmL 94*
Gardner, Jack d1929 *WhoHol 92*
Gardner, Jack d1955 *WhoHol 92*
Gardner, Jack d1977 *WhoHol 92*
Gardner, Jackie Randolph 1930- *WhoBlA 94*
Gardner, Jake 1947- *NewGrDO*
Gardner, James 1907- *Who 94*
Gardner, James Albert 1943- *WhoAm 94*
Gardner, James Carson 1933- *WhoAmP 93*
Gardner, James Harkins 1943- *WhoAm 94, WhoFI 94*
Gardner, James Jesse 1932- *Who 94*
Gardner, James K. 1943- *WhoAmL 94*
Gardner, Jay D. *WhoAmL 94*
Gardner, Jeremy 1932- *WrDr 94*
Gardner, Jerome *EncSF 93*
Gardner, Jerome 1932- *WrDr 94*
Gardner, Jerry Dean 1939- *WhoAm 94*
Gardner, Jewelle Baker 1925- *WhoFI 94*
Gardner, Jill Andria 1967- *WhoMW 93*
Gardner, Jill Christopher 1948- *WhoAm 94*
Gardner, Jim 1946- *WhoAmP 93*
Gardner, Joan 1914- *WhoHol 92*
Gardner, Joan A. 1933- *WhoAmA 93*
Gardner, John 1926- *EncSF 93*
Gardner, John 1933-1982 *EncSF 93*
Gardner, John (Champlin, Jr.) 1933-1982 *RfGShF*
Gardner, John (Edmund) 1926- *WrDr 94*
Gardner, John (Linton) 1917- *NewGrDO*
Gardner, John Frederick 1953- *WhoMW 93*
Gardner, John Linton 1917- *Who 94*
Gardner, John M. 1942- *WhoAmL 94*
Gardner, John Pickens, Jr. 1952- *WhoAmP 93*
Gardner, John R. 1937- *WhoIns 94*
Gardner, John Reed, II 1925- *WhoIns 94*
Gardner, John Robert 1937- *WhoAm 94, WhoFI 94*
Gardner, John William 1912- *IntWW 93, Who 94, WhoAm 94, WhoAmP 93*
Gardner, Joseph 1752-1794 *WhAmRev*
Gardner, Joseph Elden 1923- *WhoMW 93*
Gardner, Joseph Eugene 1946- *WhoAmP 93*
Gardner, Joseph Henry 1935- *WhoMW 93*
Gardner, Joseph Lawrence 1933- *WhoAm 94*
Gardner, Kathleen D. 1947- *WhoAm 94, WhoAmL 94*
Gardner, Kathryn Ann 1956- *WhoAmL 94*
Gardner, Kenneth Burslam 1924- *IntWW 93, Who 94*
Gardner, Kevin R. 1954- *WhoAmL 94*
Gardner, LaMaurice Holbrook 1936- *WhoBlA 94*
Gardner, Leonard Burton, II 1927- *WhoAm 94, WhoWest 94*
Gardner, Leonard Foster 1921- *WhoAmP 93*
Gardner, Lewis *DrAPF 93*
Gardner, Lloyd Calvin, Jr. 1934- *WhoAm 94*
Gardner, Loman Ronald 1938- *WhoBlA 94*
Gardner, Lora Jean 1964- *WhoMW 93*
Gardner, Marjorie Hyer 1923-1991 *WhAm 10*
Gardner, Marsha Lou Stull 1942- *WhoWest 94*
Gardner, Marshall Allen 1940- *WhoFI 94*
Gardner, Martin 1914- *EncSF 93*
Gardner, Michael Leopold George 1946- *WhoScEn 94*
Gardner, Miriam *GayLL*
Gardner, Miriam 1930- *WrDr 94*
Gardner, Murray Briggs 1929- *WhoAm 94*
Gardner, Nancy d1973 *WhoHol 92*

Gardner, Noel *EncSF 93*
Gardner, Nord Arling 1923- *WhoFI 94, WhoWest 94*
Gardner, Norman Keith Ayliffe 1925- *Who 94*
Gardner, Paul F. 1930- *WhoAmP 93*
Gardner, Paul Jay 1929- *WhoAm 94*
Gardner, Peter D. 1927-1989 *WhAm 10*
Gardner, Peter Jaglom 1958- *WhoFI 94*
Gardner, Phyllis Ann 1937- *WhoAmP 93*
Gardner, Piers *Who 94*
Gardner, (James) Piers 1954- *Who 94*
Gardner, R. H. 1918- *WhoAm 94*
Gardner, Ralph Bennett 1919- *Who 94*
Gardner, Ralph D. 1923- *WrDr 94*
Gardner, Ralph David 1923- *WhoAm 94*
Gardner, Randall 1958- *WhoAmP 93*
Gardner, Ray Dean, Jr. 1954- *WhoAmL 94*
Gardner, Richard d1972 *WhoHol 92*
Gardner, Richard A. 1931- *WrDr 94*
Gardner, Richard Alan 1931- *WhoAm 94*
Gardner, Richard Hartwell 1934- *WhoAm 94*
Gardner, Richard Kent 1928- *WhoAm 94*
Gardner, Richard Lavenham 1943- *IntWW 93, Who 94*
Gardner, Richard Newton 1927- *IntWW 93, WhoAm 94, WhoAmP 93*
Gardner, Rita *WhoHol 92*
Gardner, Robert Alexander 1944- *WhoWest 94*
Gardner, Robert Dickson Robertson 1924- *Who 94*
Gardner, Robert Earl 1919- *WhoAmA 93*
Gardner, Robert Joseph 1924- *WhoMW 93*
Gardner, Robert Meade 1927- *WhoFI 94, WhoMW 93*
Gardner, Robert Scott, Jr. 1958- *WhoMW 93*
Gardner, Robin Pierce 1934- *WhoAm 94, WhoScEn 94*
Gardner, Ronald Bruce 1944- *WhoFI 94*
Gardner, Russell Heuer 1944- *WhoAmL 94*
Gardner, Russell Menese 1920- *WhoAm 94, WhoAmL 94*
Gardner, Samuel C. 1931- *WhoBlA 94*
Gardner, Sandra *DrAPF 93*
Gardner, Shayle d1945 *WhoHol 92*
Gardner, Sheila 1933- *WhoAmA 93*
Gardner, Stanley 1934- *WhoScEn 94*
Gardner, Stephen *DrAPF 93*
Gardner, Stephen K. 1949- *WhoAmL 94*
Gardner, Steve *WhoAmP 93*
Gardner, Steven Leslie 1950- *WhoAmL 94*
Gardner, Susan Ross 1941- *WhoAmA 93*
Gardner, Thomas Dunstan 1951- *WhoMW 93*
Gardner, Thomas Earle 1938- *WhoAm 94*
Gardner, Thomas F. 1945- *WhoAmL 94*
Gardner, W. Booth 1936- *IntWW 93*
Gardner, Walter Everett 1940- *WhoAmP 93*
Gardner, Warner Winslow 1909- *WhAm 10, WhoAm 94*
Gardner, Warren Henry 1895- *WhAm 10*
Gardner, Warren Joseph, Jr. 1951- *WhoFI 94*
Gardner, Wilford Robert 1925- *IntWW 93, WhoScEn 94, WhoWest 94*
Gardner, Willard Hale 1925- *WhoAmP 93, WhoFI 94, WhoWest 94*
Gardner, William Albert, Jr. 1939- *WhoAm 94*
Gardner, William Allen 1942- *WhoAm 94, WhoScEn 94*
Gardner, William E., Jr. d1991 *WhoBlA 94N*
Gardner, William Earl 1928- *WhoAm 94*
Gardner, William George 1945- *WhoAm 94*
Gardner, William John 1940- *WhoMW 93*
Gardner, William Leonard 1942- *WhoAm 94*
Gardner, William Maving 1914- *Who 94*
Gardner, William Michael 1932- *WhoAm 94*
Gardner, William Michael 1948- *WhoAm 94, WhoAmP 93*
Gardner, Winston W., Jr. 1938- *WhoAmP 93*
Gardner-Medwin, Robert Joseph 1907- *Who 94*
Gardner Of Parkes, Baroness 1927- *Who 94, WhoWomW 91*
Gardom, Garde Basil 1924- *Who 94, WhoAm 94*
Gardon, John Leslie 1928- *WhoScEn 94*
Gardoni, Italo 1821-1882 *NewGrDO*
Gardons, S. S. 1926- *WrDr 94*
Gardoqui, Diego *AmRev*
Garducci, Tommaso *NewGrDO*
Gardyn, George Edwards 1928- *WhoHisp 94*
Gare, Nene 1919- *BlmGWL*
Gareau, Joseph H. 1947- *WhoIns 94*
Gareffa, Peter M(ichael) 1952- *ConAu 43NR*
Garegg, Per Johan 1933- *WhoScEn 94*
Gareis, Robert J. 1936- *WhoAm 94*
Garel, Leo 1917- *WhoAmA 93*
Garelick, Martin 1924- *WhoAm 94*
Garel-Jones, (William Armand Thomas) Tristan 1941- *Who 94*
Garelli, Jacques *ConWorW 93*
Garet, Jedd 1955- *WhoAmA 93*
Garey, Donald Lee 1931- *WhoAm 94, WhoFI 94, WhoScEn 94, WhoWest 94*
Garey, Kerry Anne 1957- *WhoWest 94*
Garey, Pat 1932- *WhoAmA 93*
Garey, Terry A. *DrAPF 93*
Garff, Robert H. *WhoAmP 93*
Garfield, Allen 1939- *IntMPA 94, WhoHol 92*
Garfield, Bernard Howard 1924- *WhoAm 94*
Garfield, Brian (F. W.) 1939- *WrDr 94*
Garfield, Brian Wynne 1939- *WhoAm 94*
Garfield, Ernest 1932- *WhoAmP 93*
Garfield, Eugene 1925- *WhoAm 94*
Garfield, Genie May 1921- *WhoWest 94*
Garfield, Gerald 1946- *WhoAm 94, WhoAmL 94*
Garfield, Howard Michael 1942- *WhoAmL 94, WhoWest 94*
Garfield, Joan Barbara 1950- *WhoMW 93*
Garfield, Johanna *DrAPF 93*
Garfield, John d1952 *WhoHol 92*
Garfield, John David 1943- *WhoHol 92*
Garfield, Julie 1946- *WhoHol 92*
Garfield, Leon 1921- *ConAu 41NR, SmATA 76 [port], TwCYAW, Who 94, WrDr 94*
Garfield, Leslie Jerome 1932- *WhoFI 94*
Garfield, Nancy Ellen 1954- *WhoMW 93*
Garfield, Nancy Jane 1947- *WhoMW 93*
Garfield, Robert Edward 1955- *WhoAm 94*
Garfin, Louis 1917- *WhoAm 94*
Garfinkel, Barry Herbert 1928- *WhoAm 94, WhoAmL 94*
Garfinkel, David 1930- *WhAm 10*
Garfinkel, Harmon Mark 1933- *WhoAm 94, WhoScEn 94*
Garfinkel, Herbert 1920- *WhoAm 94*
Garfinkel, Jane E. 1952- *WhoAmL 94*
Garfinkel, Marvin 1929- *WhoAmL 94*
Garfinkel, Neil B. 1964- *WhoAmL 94*
Garfinkel, Patricia *DrAPF 93*
Garfinkel, Philip 1926-1992 *WhAm 10*
Garfinkle, Devra 1956- *WhoScEn 94*
Garfinkle, Louis 1928- *IntMPA 94*
Garfitt, Alan 1920- *Who 94*
Garfitt, Roger 1944- *WrDr 94*
Garforth, Francis William 1917- *WrDr 94*
Garfunkel, Art 1941- *IntWW 93, WhoAm 94*
Garfunkel, Art 1942- *IntMPA 94, WhoHol 92*
Garg, Anupam K. 1956- *WhoScEn 94*
Garg, Arun 1947- *WhoAsA 94*
Garg, Devendra 1948- *WhoAm 94, WhoAsA 94*
Garg, Devendra Prakash 1934- *WhoAm 94, WhoScEn 94*
Garg, Mridula 1938- *BlmGWL*
Garg, Prem 1944- *WhoAsA 94*
Garg, Rajinder P. 1942- *WhoAsA 94*
Garg, Ramesh Chandra 1943- *WhoAsA 94*
Garg, Umesh 1953- *WhoAsA 94, WhoMW 93*
Garg, Vijay Kumar 1963- *WhoAsA 94*
Gargan, Edward d1964 *WhoHol 92*
Gargan, Jack T. d1958 *WhoHol 92*
Gargan, Thomas Joseph 1952- *WhoWest 94*
Gargan, William d1979 *WhoHol 92*
Gargana, John Joseph, Jr. 1931- *WhoAm 94*
Gargano, Amil *WhoAm 94*
Gargano, Charles A. *WhoAmP 93*
Gargaro, Ernest Joseph, Jr. 1947- *WhoFI 94*
Gargaro, Eugene A., Jr. 1942- *WhoAmL 94*
Garges, Susan 1953- *WhoAm 94*
Gargiulo, Andrea Weiner 1946- *WhoAmL 94*
Gargiulo, Franca 1962- *WhoWest 94*
Gargiulo, Gerald John 1934- *WhoScEn 94*
Gargiulo, Louis 1950- *WhoAmP 93*
Gargiulo, Terenzio 1905-1972 *NewGrDO*
Garhart, Martin J. 1946- *WhoAmA 93*
Garibaldi, Antoine Michael 1950- *WhoBlA 94*
Garibaldi, Giuseppe 1807-1882 *HisWorL [port]*
Garibaldi, Louis *WhoScEn 94*
Garibaldi, Marie L. 1934- *WhoAmP 93*
Garibaldi, Marie Louise 1934- *WhoAmL 94*
Garibaldi, Peter P. 1931- *WhoAmP 93*
Garibaldi, Ricciotti 1847-1924 *HisWorL*
Garibay, Emilio d1965 *WhoHol 92*
Garibay, Javier *WhoHisp 94*
Garibay, Joseph Michael 1960- *WhoScEn 94*
Garibay-Gutierrez, Luis 1916- *WhoAm 94*
Garig, Scott Allen 1955- *WhoWest 94*
Garimella, Suresh Venkata 1963- *WhoScEn 94*
Garin, Geoffrey Douglas 1953- *WhoAm 94*
Garin, Marita *DrAPF 93*
Garin, Michael *WhoHol 92*
Garing, John Seymour 1930- *WhoAm 94*
Garing, William Henry 1910- *Who 94*
Garinger, Louis Daniel *WhoAm 94*
Garino, Terry Joseph 1960- *WhoWest 94*
Garis, Howard R(oger) 1873-1962 *EncSF 93*
Garisa, Antonio d1989 *WhoHol 92*
Garison, Lynn Lassiter 1954- *WhoFI 94*
Garitano, Rita *DrAPF 93*
Garko, Gianni *WhoHol 92*
Garland, Basil 1920- *Who 94*
Garland, Bennett 1939- *WrDr 94*
Garland, Beverly 1930- *IntMPA 94, WhoHol 92*
Garland, Carl Wesley 1929- *WhoAm 94*
Garland, Caroline Mary 1938- *WhoWest 94*
Garland, Chuck 1898-1971 *BuCMET*
Garland, Edward d1980 *WhoHol 92*
Garland, Frances Vaughan 1924- *WhoAmP 93*
Garland, Franklin d1945 *WhoHol 92*
Garland, Garfield Garrett 1945- *WhoFI 94, WhoWest 94*
Garland, Geoff 1926- *WhoHol 92*
Garland, George David 1926- *IntWW 93*
Garland, (Hannibal) Hamlin 1860-1940 *RfGShF*
Garland, Hannibal Hamlin 1860-1940 *AmCulL [port]*
Garland, Harry Thomas 1947- *WhoScEn 94*
Garland, Hazel Barbara 1913- *WhoBlA 94*
Garland, James Boyce 1920- *WhoAmL 94*
Garland, James Wilson, Jr. 1933- *WhoAm 94*
Garland, John William 1944- *WhoAmL 94*
Garland, Joseph A. *WhoAmP 93*
Garland, Judy d1969 *WhoHol 92*
Garland, Marie Tarvin 1943- *WhoAmP 93*
Garland, Nicholas Withycombe 1935- *Who 94*
Garland, Patrick 1935- *IntWW 93*
Garland, Patrick Ewart 1935- *Who 94*
Garland, Patrick Neville 1929- *Who 94*
Garland, Peter *Who 94*
Garland, (Frederick) Peter (Collison) 1912- *Who 94*
Garland, Peter Bryan 1934- *Who 94*
Garland, Phyllis T. 1935- *WhoBlA 94*
Garland, Ray Lucian 1934- *WhoAmP 93*
Garland, Richard d1969 *WhoHol 92*
Garland, Richard Roger 1958- *WhoAmL 94*
Garland, Robert Raymond 1949- *WhoMW 93*
Garland, Sara Gay 1946- *WhoAmP 93*
Garland, Sylvia Dillof 1919- *WhoAm 94, WhoAmL 94*
Garland, Thomas Jack, Sr. 1934- *WhoAmP 93*
Garland, Victor 1934- *IntWW 93*
Garland, (Ransley) Victor 1934- *Who 94*
Garland, William James 1948- *WhoAm 94*
Garland, Winston Kinnard 1964- *WhoBlA 94*
Garlett, Marti Watson 1945- *WhoWest 94*
Garlette, William Henry Lee 1951- *WhoAm 94*
Garlick, George Frederick John 1919- *Who 94*
Garlick, James Graham 1936- *WhoAmP 93*
Garlick, John 1921- *Who 94*
Garlick, Kenneth John 1916- *Who 94*
Garlick, Raymond 1926- *WrDr 94*
Garlid, Kermit Leroy 1929- *WhoAm 94*
Garling, David John Haldane 1937- *Who 94*
Garlinghouse, David Michael 1957- *WhoAmL 94*
Garlington, Lee *WhoHol 92*
Garlinski, Jozef 1913- *WrDr 94*
Garlo, Olgierd Casimir 1919- *WhoMW 93*
Garlock, Gabriella Lynn 1964- *WhoMW 93*
Garlough, William Glenn 1924- *WhoAm 94, WhoFI 94, WhoWest 94*
Garly, Edward d1938 *WhoHol 92*
Garmaise, Freda 1928- *WrDr 94*
Garmaker, Dick 1932- *BasBi*
Garman, David K. 1957- *WhoAmP 93*
Garman, Ed 1914- *WhoAmA 93*
Garman, Mary Minnette 1932- *WhoAmP 93*
Garman, Merle Edward, Jr. 1942- *WhoFI 94*
Garman, Teresa A. 1937- *WhoAmP 93*
Garman, Teresa Agnes 1937- *WhoMW 93*
Garman, Willard Hershel 1912- *WhoAm 94*
Garmatis, Iakovos *WhoAm 94, WhoMW 93*
Garment, Suzanne 1946- *ConAu 142*
Garmer, William Robert 1946- *WhoAmL 94*
Garmes, Lee 1898-1978 *IntDcF 2-4 [port]*
Garmey, Ronald 1937- *WhoAmP 93*
Garmezy, Norman 1918- *WhoAm 94*
Garmire, Elsa Meints 1939- *WhoScEn 94, WhoWest 94*
Garmoyle, Viscount 1965- *Who 94*
Garms, Walter Irving, Jr. 1925-1989 *WhAm 10*
Garn, Edwin Jacob 1932- *IntWW 93, WhoAm 94, WhoAmP 93*
Garn, Kevin S. 1955- *WhoAmP 93*
Garn, Stanley Marion 1922- *IntWW 93, WhoAm 94, WhoMW 93*
Garnaut, Ross Gregory 1946- *IntWW 93*
Garne, Gaston *EncSF 93*
Garner, Alan 1934- *EncSF 93, TwCYAW, Who 94, WrDr 94*
Garner, Alan (Francis) 1950- *WrDr 94*
Garner, Albert Headden 1955- *WhoAm 94*
Garner, Alto Luther 1916- *WhoAm 94*
Garner, Anthony (Stuart) 1927- *Who 94*
Garner, Archibald 1904-1970 *WhoAmA 93N*
Garner, Bryan Andrew 1958- *WhoAmL 94*
Garner, Carlene Ann 1945- *WhoWest 94*
Garner, Charles 1931- *WhoBlA 94*
Garner, Charles William 1939- *WhoAm 94*
Garner, Dale Mark 1957- *WhoFI 94*
Garner, Daniel C. 1950- *WhoAmL 94*
Garner, Don d1958 *WhoHol 92*
Garner, Donald K. 1944- *WhoAm 94, WhoAmL 94*
Garner, Douglas Russell 1953- *WhoScEn 94*
Garner, Edward, Jr. 1942- *WhoBlA 94*
Garner, Edward Markley, II 1949- *WhoAm 94*
Garner, Erroll 1921-1977 *AfrAmAl 6*
Garner, Frederic Francis d1993 *Who 94N*
Garner, Frederick Leonard 1920- *Who 94*
Garner, Geraldine 1946- *WhoMW 93*
Garner, Graham *EncSF 93*
Garner, Grayce Scott 1922- *WhoBlA 94*
Garner, Harvey Louis 1926- *WhoAm 94*
Garner, Helen 1942- *BlmGWL, WrDr 94*
Garner, Jac Buford 1954- *WhoFI 94*
Garner, James 1928- *IntMPA 94, IntWW 93, WhoAm 94, WhoHol 92*
Garner, James Parent 1923- *WhoAm 94*
Garner, Jasper Henry Barkdoll 1921- *WhoScEn 94*
Garner, Jay Montgomery 1938- *WhoAm 94*
Garner, Jennifer Leigh 1959- *WhoMW 93*
Garner, Jim D. 1963- *WhoAmP 93*
Garner, Jim David 1963- *WhoMW 93*
Garner, John Charles 1949- *WhoWest 94*
Garner, John Donald 1931- *Who 94*
Garner, John Michael 1935- *WhoAm 94*
Garner, John W. 1924- *WhoBlA 94*
Garner, June Brown 1923- *WhoBlA 94*
Garner, La Forrest Dean 1933- *WhoBlA 94*
Garner, Lon L. 1927- *WhoBlA 94*
Garner, Lynn Evan 1941- *WhoWest 94*
Garner, Marcellus Craig, Jr. 1948- *WhoAmL 94*
Garner, Marie G. 1924- *WhoAmP 93*
Garner, Mary E. *WhoBlA 94*
Garner, Mary Martin *WhoAmL 94*
Garner, Maurice Richard 1915- *Who 94*
Garner, Melvin C. 1941- *WhoBlA 94*
Garner, Michael Scott 1939- *Who 94*
Garner, Mildred Maxine 1919- *WhoAm 94*
Garner, Nadine *WhoHol 92*
Garner, Nathan Warren 1944- *WhoBlA 94*
Garner, Patrick Lynn 1950- *WhoScEn 94*
Garner, Paul Trantham 1951- *WhoFI 94*
Garner, Peggy Ann d1984 *WhoHol 92*
Garner, Phil 1949- *WhoAm 94, WhoMW 93*
Garner, Richard Warren 1948- *WhoIns 94*
Garner, Robert Dale 1933- *WhoAm 94*
Garner, Robert Edward Lee 1946- *WhoAm 94*
Garner, Rolf *EncSF 93*
Garner, Samuel Paul 1910- *WhoAm 94*
Garner, Thomas L. 1930- *WhoBlA 94*
Garner, Val Z. 1932- *WhoAmP 93*
Garner, Velvia M. 1941- *WhoBlA 94*
Garner, Wayne 1951- *WhoAmP 93*
Garner, Wendell (Richard) 1921- *WrDr 94*
Garner, Wendell Richard 1921- *IntWW 93, WhoAm 94*
Garner, William 1920- *WrDr 94*

Garner, William Darrell 1933- *WhoFI 94*
Garnes, Delbert Franklin 1943- *WhoScEn 94*
Garnes, William A. 1924- *WhoBlA 94*
Garnet, A. H. 1926- *WrDr 94*
Garnet, Henry Highland c. 1815-1882 *AmSocL, DcAmReB 2*
Garnett, Angelica 1918- *WrDr 94*
Garnett, Bernard E. 1940- *WhoBlA 94*
Garnett, David 1892-1981 *EncSF 93*
Garnett, David S. 1947- *EncSF 93*
Garnett, Edward 1868-1936 *EncSF 93*
Garnett, Eve d1991 *TwCYAW*
Garnett, Eve C. R. *WrDr 94*
Garnett, Gale *WhoHol 92*
Garnett, Ian David Graham 1944- *Who 94*
Garnett, Jess 1924- *WhoAmP 93*
Garnett, John *Who 94*
Garnett, (William) John (Poulton Maxwell) 1921- *Who 94*
Garnett, Julia Charity *Who 94*
Garnett, Kevin Mitchell 1950- *Who 94*
Garnett, Marion Winston 1919- *WhoAm 94, WhoAmL 94, WhoBlA 94*
Garnett, Richard 1835-1906 *EncSF 93*
Garnett, Richard (Duncan Carey) 1923- *WrDr 94*
Garnett, Ronald Leon 1945- *WhoBlA 94*
Garnett, Stanley Iredale, II 1943- *WhoAm 94*
Garnett, Tay d1977 *WhoHol 92*
Garnett, Thomas Ronald 1915- *Who 94*
Garnett, William 1916- *WhoAm 94*
Garnett, William Ashford 1916- *WhoAmA 93*
Garnette, Booker Thomas 1930- *WhoBlA 94*
Garnham, Percy Cyril Claude 1901- *IntWW 93, Who 94, WrDr 94*
Garnier, Edward Henry 1952- *Who 94*
Garnier, John 1934- *Who 94*
Garnier, Marie-Joseph-Francois 1839-1873 *WhWE*
Garnier, Olivier Pierre 1959- *WhoFI 94*
Garnier, Robert c. 1545-1590 *GuFrLit 2*
Garnier, Robert Charles 1916- *WhoAm 94*
Garnock, Viscount 1990- *Who 94*
Garnsey, Clarke Henderson 1913- *WhoAmA 93*
Garnsey, David Arthur 1909- *Who 94*
Garnsworthy, Lewis Samuel 1922- *IntWW 93*
Garofalo, James Anthony 1955- *WhoFI 94*
Garofano, Giuseppe 1944- *IntWW 93*
Garoian, Charles Richard 1943- *WhoAmA 93*
Garon, Claude Francis 1942- *WhoScEn 94, WhoWest 94*
Garon, Marco *EncSF 93*
Garon, Norman d1975 *WhoHol 92*
Garon, Pauline d1965 *WhoHol 92*
Garon, Philip Stephen 1947- *WhoAm 94, WhoAmL 94*
Garou, Louis P. 1953- *WrDr 94*
Garoufalis, Angelo George 1929- *WhoFI 94*
Garouste, Gerard 1946- *IntWW 93*
Garoutte, Bill Charles 1921- *WhoAm 94*
Garpow, James Edward 1944- *WhoAm 94, WhoFI 94*
Garr, Carl Robert 1927- *WhoAm 94, WhoFI 94*
Garr, Eddie d1956 *WhoHol 92*
Garr, Lawrence David 1945- *WhoAm 94*
Garr, Louis J., Jr. 1939- *WhoAm 94*
Garr, Louis Joseph, Jr. 1939- *WhoAmL 94*
Garr, Teri 1945- *WhoCom, WhoHol 92*
Garr, Teri 1949- *IntMPA 94*
Garr, Teri Ann 1952- *WhoAm 94*
Garrahan, Paul Jamison 1928- *WhoWest 94*
Garrahy, J. Joseph 1930- *WhoAmP 93*
Garralaga, Martin d1981 *WhoHol 92*
Garrard, Don 1929- *NewGrDO*
Garrard, Don Edward Burdett *WhoAm 94*
Garrard, Lancelot Austin d1993 *Who 94N*
Garrard, Lancelot Austin 1904-1993 *ConAu 140, WrDr 94N*
Garrard, Mary DuBose 1937- *WhoAmA 93*
Garrard, Richard 1937- *Who 94*
Garrard, Rose 1946- *IntWW 93*
Garrard, Timothy F(rancis) 1943- *WrDr 94*
Garrard, William c. 1510-1571 *DcNaB MP*
Garratt, Graham 1935- *WhoAm 94*
Garratt, Herbert William 1864-1913 *DcNaB MP*
Garratty, George 1935- *WhoScEn 94*
Garraty, John A., Jr. 1949- *WhoAmL 94*
Garraway, Michael Oliver 1934- *WhoBlA 94*
Garraway, William 1617-1701 *DcNaB MP*
Garrelick, Joel Marc 1941- *WhoScEn 94*
Garrels, John Carlyle 1914- *Who 94*
Garret, Paula Lyn 1951- *WhoAm 94*
Garretson, Donald Everett 1921- *WhoAm 94*
Garretson, Henry David 1929- *WhoAm 94, WhoScEn 94*
Garretson, Owen Loren 1912- *WhoWest 94*
Garretson, Robert Mark 1951- *WhoWest 94*
Garretson, Steven Michael 1950- *WhoWest 94*
Garrett, Aline M. 1944- *WhoBlA 94*
Garrett, Anne Marie 1963- *WhoMW 93*
Garrett, Anthony David 1928- *Who 94*
Garrett, Betty 1919- *IntMPA 94, WhoHol 92*
Garrett, Betty Lou 1930- *WhoMW 93*
Garrett, Cain, Jr. 1942- *WhoBlA 94*
Garrett, Charlcie H. d1978 *WhoHol 92*
Garrett, Charles Geoffrey Blythe 1925- *WhoAm 94, WhoScEn 94*
Garrett, Charlotte *DrAPF 93*
Garrett, Cheryl Ann 1946- *WhoBlA 94*
Garrett, Christopher Arthur 1961- *WhoMW 93*
Garrett, Darrell Eugene 1959- *WhoFI 94*
Garrett, David William 1962- *WhoAmL 94*
Garrett, Dennis Andrew 1940- *WhoAm 94, WhoWest 94*
Garrett, Devry W. 1949- *WhoAmL 94*
Garrett, Duane B. 1947- *WhoAmL 94*
Garrett, E. Reid 1946- *WhoAmL 94*
Garrett, E. Scott 1959- *WhoAmP 93*
Garrett, E. Wyman 1933- *WhoBlA 94*
garrett, evvy *DrAPF 93*
Garrett, Florence Rome 1912- *WrDr 94*
Garrett, Fredda d1976 *WhoHol 92*
Garrett, George *DrAPF 93*
Garrett, George 1929- *DcLB 130 [port]*
Garrett, George (Palmer) 1929- *ConAu 42NR*
Garrett, George (Palmer, Jr.) 1929- *WrDr 94*
Garrett, George Palmer, Jr. 1929- *WhoAm 94*
Garrett, Godfrey John 1937- *Who 94*
Garrett, Gordon Henderson 1937- *WhoAmL 94*
Garrett, Guy Thomas 1932-1988 *WhAm 10*
Garrett, Guy Thomas, Jr. 1932- *WhoAm 94, WhoBlA 94*
Garrett, H. Lawrence 1939- *IntWW 93*
Garrett, H. Lawrence, III 1939- *WhoAmP 93*
Garrett, Hank *WhoHol 92*
Garrett, Helen Blue 1933- *WhoAmP 93*
Garrett, Helen Marie *WhoAmP 93*
Garrett, Henry Edmund Melvill Lennox 1924- *Who 94*
Garrett, J. Patrick 1943- *WhoAm 94*
Garrett, J. Richard 1945- *WhoIns 94*
Garrett, James Edward, Jr. 1959- *WhoBlA 94*
Garrett, James Henry, Jr. 1961- *WhoScEn 94*
Garrett, James Joseph 1939- *WhoAm 94*
Garrett, Jasper Patrick 1943- *WhoAmL 94*
Garrett, Jerry Dale 1940- *WhoAm 94*
Garrett, Joan 1953- *WhoWest 94*
Garrett, Joao Baptista da Silva Leitao de Almeida 1799-1854 *IntDcT 2*
Garrett, John Laurence 1931- *Who 94*
Garrett, Joseph Edward 1943- *WhoScEn 94*
Garrett, Joy d1993 *NewYTBS 93 [port]*
Garrett, Joyce F. 1931- *WhoBlA 94*
Garrett, K. Michael 1948- *WhoAmL 94*
Garrett, Larry Carlton 1950- *WhoFI 94*
Garrett, Lawrence G., Jr. 1942- *IntMPA 94*
Garrett, Leif 1961- *WhoHol 92*
Garrett, Lesley 1955- *NewGrDO*
Garrett, Leslie *DrAPF 93*
Garrett, Louis Henry 1960- *WhoBlA 94*
Garrett, Marilyn Ruth 1957- *WhoMW 93*
Garrett, Mary Elizabeth 1937- *WhoAmP 93*
Garrett, Maxie 1931- *WhoAmP 93*
Garrett, Melvin Alboy 1936- *WhoBlA 94*
Garrett, Michael d1990 *WhoHol 92*
Garrett, Naomi M. 1906- *WhoBlA 94*
Garrett, Nathan Taylor 1931- *WhoBlA 94*
Garrett, Nola *DrAPF 93*
Garrett, Norman Anthony 1947- *WhoMW 93*
Garrett, Patsy *WhoHol 92*
Garrett, Paul C. 1946- *WhoBlA 94*
Garrett, Pearson Beverly 1895- *WhAm 10*
Garrett, Peter
See Midnight Oil *ConMus 11*
Garrett, (Gordon) Randall (Phillip) 1927- *WrDr 94*
Garrett, (Gordon) Randall (Phillip David) 1927-1987 *EncSF 93*
Garrett, Raymond (William) 1900- *Who 94*
Garrett, Reginald Hooker 1939- *WhoAm 94*
Garrett, Richard 1920- *WrDr 94*
Garrett, Richard Anthony 1918- *Who 94*
Garrett, Richard G. 1948- *WhoAmL 94*
Garrett, Robert 1937- *WhoAm 94*
Garrett, Robert Dean 1933- *WhoFI 94, WhoMW 93*
Garrett, Robert Stephens 1937- *WhoWest 94*
Garrett, Romeo Benjamin 1910- *WhoBlA 94*
Garrett, Ruby Grant 1941- *WhoBlA 94*
Garrett, Sam d1989 *WhoHol 92*
Garrett, Sandy 1943- *WhoAmP 93*
Garrett, Shirley Gene 1944- *WhoAm 94, WhoMW 93*
Garrett, Stephen 1922- *WhoAmA 93*
Garrett, Stuart Grayson *WhoAmA 93*
Garrett, Suzanne Thornton 1960- *WhoScEn 94*
Garrett, Sylvester 1911- *WhoAm 94*
Garrett, Terence 1929- *Who 94*
Garrett, Thaddeus, Jr. 1948- *WhoBlA 94*
Garrett, Theodore Louis 1943- *WhoAm 94, WhoAmL 94*
Garrett, Thomas H., III 1945- *WhoAmL 94*
Garrett, Thomas John 1927- *Who 94*
Garrett, Tim 1951- *WhoAmP 93*
Garrett, Tom 1954- *WhoAmP 93*
Garrett, Virginia Bonner 1922- *WhoAmP 93*
Garrett, Wilbur Eugene 1930- *WhoAm 94*
Garrett, William Edward d1993 *Who 94N*
Garrett, William Jerry, Jr. 1962- *WhoWest 94*
Garrett Anderson, Elizabeth 1836-1917 *HisWorL [port]*
Garrett Harshaw, Karla 1955- *WhoBlA 94*
Garretto, Leonard Anthony, Jr. 1925- *WhoFI 94*
Garrett-Perry, Nanette Dawn 1968- *WhoScEn 94*
Garrettson, Freeborn 1752-1827 *DcAmReB 2*
Garrick, David 1717-1779 *BlmGEL [port], NewGrDO*
Garrick, John 1902- *WhoHol 92*
Garrick, Rian *WhoHol 92*
Garrick, Richard d1962 *WhoHol 92*
Garrick, Ronald 1940- *Who 94*
Garrick, Thomas S. 1966- *WhoBlA 94*
Garrido (Vargas), Pablo 1905-1982 *NewGrDO*
Garrido, Augie *WhoAm 94, WhoWest 94*
Garrido, Jose A., Jr. 1953- *WhoHisp 94*
Garrido, Plinio Luis 1948- *WhoHisp 94*
Garrido Perez, Mercedes 1956- *WhoScEn 94*
Garrier, Jo Ann Ross 1960- *WhoMW 93*
Garriga, Julio 1955- *WhoHisp 94*
Garriga, Mark *WhoAmP 93*
Garrigan, Kristine Ottesen 1939- *WhoMW 93*
Garrigan, Richard Thomas 1938- *WhoAm 94, WhoMW 93*
Garrigan, William Henry, III 1954- *WhoMW 93*
Garrigle, William Aloysius 1941- *WhoAmL 94*
Garrigo, Jose R. 1936- *WhoHisp 94*
Garrigues, Beverly Jean 1942- *WhoWest 94*
Garrigues, Gayle Lynne 1955- *WhoAmL 94, WhoWest 94*
Garrigues, Malvina *NewGrDO*
Garrigues, Suzanne 1945- *WhoAmA 93*
Garrigus, Charles B(yford) 1914- *WrDr 94*
Garrigus, Charles Byford 1914- *WhoWest 94*
Garrigus, Upson Stanley 1917- *WhoAm 94*
Garrincha 1933- *WorESoc [port]*
Garrioch, Alfred Campbell 1848-1934 *EncNAR*
Garrioch, (William) Henry 1916- *Who 94*
Garriott, Owen Kay 1930- *WhoAm 94*
Garris, Jacalen J. 1963- *WhoAmL 94*
Garris, Sidney Reginald 1922- *WhoWest 94*
Garrish, Theodore John 1943- *WhoAm 94*
Garrison, Althea 1940- *WhoAm 94, WhoAmP 93*
Garrison, Barbara 1931- *WhoAmA 93*
Garrison, Betty Bernhardt 1932- *WhoWest 94*
Garrison, Bruce 1950- *ConAu 141*
Garrison, Charles Eugene 1943- *WhoMW 93*
Garrison, Clayton 1921- *WhoAm 94*
Garrison, Daniel H. 1937- *WrDr 94*
Garrison, David *DrAPF 93*
Garrison, David Earl *WhoAmA 93*
Garrison, Dee 1934- *WrDr 94*
Garrison, Edwin Ronald 1897- *WhAm 10*
Garrison, Elizabeth Jane 1952- *WhoAmA 93*
Garrison, Esther F. 1922- *WhoBlA 94*
Garrison, Eve 1908- *WhoAmA 93*
Garrison, F. Sheridan *WhoAm 94, WhoFI 94, WhoWest 94*
Garrison, Frederick *TwCYAW*
Garrison, Gene K. *WhoAmA 93*
Garrison, Guy Grady 1927- *WhoAm 94*
Garrison, James Harvey 1842-1931 *DcAmReB 2*
Garrison, James Robert 1955- *WhoAmL 94*
Garrison, Jane Gayle 1951- *WhoAm 94*
Garrison, Jesse Janes 1901- *WhoAmA 93N*
Garrison, Jewell K. 1946- *WhoBlA 94*
Garrison, Jim 1922-1992 *AnObit 1992*
Garrison, Jim (C.) 1921- *WrDr 94*
Garrison, John Raymond 1938- *WhoAm 94*
Garrison, Jon 1944- *NewGrDO*
Garrison, Jordan Muhammad, Jr. 1956- *WhoBlA 94*
Garrison, Joseph *DrAPF 93*
Garrison, Kathleen Marie 1954- *WhoWest 94*
Garrison, Larry Richard 1951- *WhoMW 93*
Garrison, Lester Boyd 1948- *WhoWest 94*
Garrison, Lisa *DrAPF 93*
Garrison, Lloyd Kirkham 1897- *WhAm 10*
Garrison, Mabel 1886-1963 *NewGrDO*
Garrison, Mark Joseph 1930- *WhoAm 94*
Garrison, Michael d1966 *WhoHol 92*
Garrison, Omar V 1913- *WrDr 94*
Garrison, Paul Cornell 1935- *WhoMW 93*
Garrison, Paul F. 1929- *WhoFI 94*
Garrison, Peggy *DrAPF 93*
Garrison, Pitser Hardeman 1912- *WhoAmL 94*
Garrison, Preston Jones 1942- *WhoAm 94*
Garrison, Ray Harlan 1922- *WhoAm 94, WhoMW 93*
Garrison, Richard Christopher 1948- *WhoAm 94*
Garrison, Robert E., Jr. 1923- *WhoBlA 94*
Garrison, Robert Frederick 1936- *WhoAm 94*
Garrison, Sean 1937- *WhoHol 92*
Garrison, Thomas Edmond 1922- *WhoAmP 93*
Garrison, Thomas S. 1952- *WhoWest 94*
Garrison, Truitt B. 1936- *WhoAm 94*
Garrison, U. Edwin 1928- *WhoAm 94, WhoFI 94, WhoWest 94*
Garrison, Walter R. 1926- *WhoAm 94*
Garrison, William Lloyd 1805-1879 *AmSocL, HisWorL [port]*
Garrison, William Lloyd 1939- *WhoMW 93*
Garrison, William Louis 1924- *WhoAm 94*
Garrison, Zina 1963- *BuCMET, IntWW 93, WhoBlA 94*
Garrison-Corbin, Patricia Ann 1947- *WhoBlA 94*
Garrison-Jackson, Zina 1963- *WhoAm 94*
Garrison-Jackson, Zina Lynna 1963- *WhoBlA 94*
Garrity, Donald Lee 1927- *WhoAm 94*
Garrity, Harry d1928 *WhoHol 92*
Garrity, John Joseph 1955- *WhoAmP 93*
Garrity, Juan David 1961- *WhoHisp 94*
Garrity, Keith R. *WhoMW 93*
Garrity, Monique P. 1941- *WhoBlA 94*
Garrity, Paul Gerard 1923- *WhoFI 94*
Garrity, Robert T. 1949- *WhoAmP 93*
Garrity, Rodman Fox 1922- *WhoAm 94*
Garrity, Thomas Joseph 1960- *WhoFI 94*
Garrity, Vincent Francis, Jr. 1937- *WhoAm 94*
Garrity, Wendell Arthur, Jr. 1920- *WhoAmL 94*
Garro, Elena 1920- *BlmGWL, ConWorW 93*
Garrod, Dorothy Anne Elizabeth 1892-1968 *DcNaB MP*
Garrod, (John) Martin (Carruthers) 1935- *Who 94*
Garron, Marco *EncSF 93*
Garrone, Gabriel Marie 1901- *IntWW 93*
Garrop, Barbara Ann 1941- *WhoWest 94*
Garrot, Patricia Mary 1938- *WhoMW 93*
Garrott, Homer L. 1914- *WhoBlA 94*
Garrott, Idamae 1916- *WhoAmP 93*
Garrou, John L. W. 1943- *WhoAmL 94*
Garrow, David J. 1953- *WrDr 94*
Garrow, David Jeffries 1953- *WhoAm 94*
Garruto, John Anthony 1952- *WhoFI 94, WhoWest 94*
Garruto, Michelle Bartok 1961- *WhoFI 94, WhoWest 94*
Garry, Charles d1939 *WhoHol 92*
Garry, Charles R. 1909-1991 *WhAm 10*
Garry, Claude d1918 *WhoHol 92*
Garry, Joe d1954 *WhoHol 92*
Garry, John Thomas, II 1923- *WhoAmL 94*
Garry, Robert Campbell d1993 *Who 94N*

Garry, Stacey Lynne 1952- *WhoWest 94*
Garry, Vincent Ferrer 1937- *WhoScEn 94*
Garry, William James 1944- *WhoAm 94*
Garsh, Eleanor Susan 1947- *WhoAm 94, WhoAmL 94*
Garsh, Thomas Burton 1931- *WhoAm 94, WhoWest 94*
Garshelis, David Lance 1953- *WhoScEn 94*
Garshnek, Victoria 1957- *WhoWest 94*
Garside, Anthony David 1950- *WhoWest 94*
Garside, Charles Roger 1948- *Who 94*
Garside, (Pamela) Jane 1936- *Who 94*
Garside, John d1958 *WhoHol 92*
Garside, John 1941- *Who 94*
Garside, John Rushforth, II 1935- *WhoAm 94*
Garside, Larry Joe 1943- *WhoWest 94*
Garside, Marlene Elizabeth 1933- *WhoFI 94*
Garside, Roger Ramsay 1938- *Who 94*
Garside, Steven L. 1957- *WhoWest 94*
Garske, Jay Toring 1936- *WhoScEn 94, WhoWest 94*
Garson, Arnold Hugh 1941- *WhoAm 94, WhoWest 94*
Garson, Bill *DrAPF 93*
Garson, Clee *EncSF 93*
Garson, Greer 1906- *WhoHol 92*
Garson, Greer 1908- *IntMPA 94, Who 94, WhoAm 94*
Garson, John *WhoHol 92*
Garson, Paul 1946- *EncSF 93*
Garson, Robin William 1921- *Who 94*
Garson, William Jeffrey 1946- *WhoAmL 94*
Garst, David Blackburn 1943- *WhoIns 94*
Garst, Elizabeth 1951- *WhoMW 93*
Garst, Richard Sylvester 1936- *WhoAmP 93*
Garstang, Roy Henry 1925- *WhoAm 94, WhoWest 94*
Garsten, Joel Jay 1948- *WhoScEn 94*
Garston, Gerald Drexler 1925- *WhoAm 94, WhoAmA 93*
Gart, Murray Joseph 1924- *WhoAm 94*
Gartel, Laurence M. 1956- *WhoAmA 93*
Garten, Bill *DrAPF 93*
Garten, Cliff 1954- *WhoAmA 93*
Garten, David B. 1952- *WhoAm 94, WhoAmL 94*
Garten, George Scott 1942- *WhoMW 93*
Garten, Wayne Philip 1952- *WhoFI 94*
Gartenberg, Seymour Lee 1931- *WhoAm 94, WhoFI 94*
Gartenhaus, Solomon 1929- *WhoAm 94*
Garth, Adam 1966- *WhoAmL 94*
Garth, Bryant Geoffrey 1949- *WhoAm 94, WhoAmL 94*
Garth, David d1988 *WhoHol 92*
Garth, George d1819 *WhAmRev*
Garth, John 1894-1971 *WhoAmA 93N*
Garth, Leonard I. 1921- *WhoAm 94, WhoAmL 94*
Garth, Otis d1955 *WhoHol 92*
Garth, Samuel 1661-1719 *BlmGEL*
Garth, Will *EncSF 93*
Garthoff, Raymond L(eonard) 1929- *WrDr 94*
Garthoff, Raymond Leonard 1929- *WhoAmP 93*
Garthwaite, William 1906- *Who 94*
Gartlan, Joseph V., Jr. 1925- *WhoAmP 93*
Gartland, Eugene Charles, Jr. 1950- *WhoMW 93*
Gartland, John C. 1940- *WhoAmP 93*
Gartland, John Joseph 1918- *WhoAm 94*
Gartland, William Joseph, Jr. 1941- *WhoAm 94*
Gartler, Stanley Michael 1923- *WhoWest 94*
Gartley, Markham Ligon 1944- *WhoAmP 93*
Gartling, David Keith 1947- *WhoScEn 94*
Gartner, Alan P. 1935- *WhoAm 94*
Gartner, Chloe Maria 1916- *WrDr 94*
Gartner, Dale W. 1943- *WhoAmP 93*
Gartner, Daniel Lee 1945- *WhoMW 93*
Gartner, Harold Henry, III 1948- *WhoAmL 94, WhoWest 94*
Gartner, Joseph Charles 1945- *WhoFI 94*
Gartner, Lawrence Mitchel 1933- *WhoAm 94*
Gartner, Michael Alfred 1959- *WhoAm 94*
Gartner, Michael G. 1938- *IntMPA 94*
Gartner, Michael Gay 1938- *WhoAm 94, WhoMW 93*
Gartner, Murray 1922- *WhoAm 94*
Gartner, W. Joseph 1928- *WhoFI 94*
Garton, George Alan 1922- *IntWW 93, Who 94*
Garton, John Henry 1941- *Who 94*
Garton, John Leslie 1916- *Who 94*
Garton, Robert Dean 1933- *WhoAmP 93, WhoMW 93*
Garton, Thomas William 1947- *WhoAm 94, WhoAmL 94*
Garton, William Reginald Stephen 1912- *Who 94*
Garton Ash, Timothy *WrDr 94*
Gartrell, Bernadette A. 1945- *WhoBlA 94*
Gartrell, Joseph Lee 1961- *WhoWest 94*
Gartrell, Luther R. 1940- *WhoBlA 94*
Garts, James Rufus, Jr. 1949- *WhoAmL 94*
Gartz, Paul Ebner 1946- *WhoScEn 94, WhoWest 94*
Garufi, Bianca 1920- *BlmGWL*
Garvagh, Baron 1920- *Who 94*
Garve, Andrew 1908- *WrDr 94*
Garvens, Ellen *WhoAmA 93*
Garver, Fanny 1927- *WhoAmA 93*
Garver, Frederick Merrill 1945- *WhoFI 94, WhoMW 93*
Garver, George Holdt 1946- *WhoAmL 94*
Garver, Kathy 1948- *WhoHol 92*
Garver, Lori Beth 1961- *WhoAm 94*
Garver, Newton 1928- *ConAu 142*
Garver, Oliver Bailey, Jr. 1925- *WhoAm 94, WhoWest 94*
Garver, Richard Alvin 1956- *WhoFI 94*
Garver, Robert S. 1942- *WhoAm 94*
Garver, Robert Vernon 1932- *WhoAm 94*
Garver, Theodore Meyer 1929- *WhoAm 94*
Garver, Thomas H. 1934- *WhoAmA 93*
Garver, Thomas Haskell 1934- *WhoAm 94*
Garver, Walter Raymond 1927- *WhoAmA 93*
Garverick, Pamela L. 1949- *WhoFI 94*
Garvey, Anthony James 1947- *WhoFI 94*
Garvey, Charles Carter, Jr. 1947- *WhoAmL 94*
Garvey, Daniel Cyril 1940- *WhoScEn 94*
Garvey, Doris Burmester 1936- *WhoWest 94*
Garvey, Ed d1939 *WhoHol 92*
Garvey, Ellen Gruber *DrAPF 93*
Garvey, Eugene F. 1933- *WhoAmP 93*
Garvey, Evelyn Jewel 1931- *WhoWest 94*
Garvey, Gerald Thomas 1935- *WhoAm 94*
Garvey, J. Kevin 1942- *WhoAmL 94*
Garvey, James Anthony 1923- *WhoAm 94*
Garvey, James Francis 1957- *WhoScEn 94*
Garvey, James Sutherland 1922- *WhoAmP 93*
Garvey, Jeanne W. *WhoAmP 93*
Garvey, Joanne Marie 1935- *WhoAm 94*
Garvey, John Charles 1921- *WhoAm 94*
Garvey, John Leo 1927- *WhoAm 94*
Garvey, Justine Spring 1922- *WhoScEn 94, WhoWest 94*
Garvey, Lillian Batlin d1993 *NewYTBS 93*
Garvey, Marcus 1887-1940 *AfrAmAl 6, HisWorL [port]*
Garvey, Marcus Mosiah 1887-1940 *AmSocL [port], DcAmReB 2*
Garvey, Margaret S. 1947- *WhoAmL 94*
Garvey, Michael J. 1953- *WhoAm 94, WhoAmL 94*
Garvey, Michael Steven 1950- *WhoScEn 94*
Garvey, Richard Anthony 1950- *WhoAm 94, WhoAmL 94*
Garvey, Richard J. 1945- *WhoAm 94, WhoAmL 94*
Garvey, Rita *WhoAmP 93*
Garvey, Robert Robey, Jr. 1921- *WhoAm 94*
Garvey, Steve(n Patrick) 1948- *WrDr 94*
Garvey, Terence Brian 1952- *WhoAmL 94*
Garvey, Thomas 1936- *Who 94*
Garvin, Andrew Paul 1945- *WhoAm 94*
Garvin, Anita 1907- *WhoHol 92*
Garvin, Anthony O. 1947- *WhoAmL 94*
Garvin, Clifton C., Jr. 1921- *IntWW 93*
Garvin, Clifton Canter, Jr. 1921- *Who 94*
Garvin, Harold Whitman 1924- *WhoAmP 93*
Garvin, Jonathan 1932- *WhoBlA 94*
Garvin, Mildred Barry 1929- *WhoAmP 93, WhoBlA 94*
Garvin, Richard M(cClellan) 1934- *EncSF 93*
Garvin, Thomas Michael 1935- *WhoFI 94*
Garvin, Vail Pryor 1942- *WhoAm 94*
Garway, William 1617-1701 *DcNaB MP*
Garwin, Richard L. 1928- *IntWW 93*
Garwin, Richard Lawrence 1928- *WhoAm 94*
Garwood, Audrey 1927- *WhoAmA 93*
Garwood, Douglas Leon 1944- *WhoMW 93*
Garwood, Ellen Clayton *WhoAmP 93*
Garwood, Ellen Clayton d1993 *NewYTBS 93 [port]*
Garwood, John *WhoHol 92*
Garwood, John Delvert 1915- *WhoAm 94*
Garwood, (Miriam) Margaret 1927- *NewGrDO*
Garwood, Thomas Chason, Jr. 1944- *WhoAmL 94, WhoFI 94*
Garwood, Victor Paul 1917- *WhoAm 94*
Garwood, William d1950 *WhoHol 92*
Garwood, William Everett 1919- *WhoScEn 94*
Garwood, William L. 1931- *WhoAmP 93*
Garwood, William Lockhart 1931- *WhoAm 94, WhoAmL 94*
Gary, Benjamin Walter, Jr. 1934- *WhoAm 94*
Gary, Charles Lester 1917- *WhoAm 94*
Gary, Dorothy Hales 1917- *WhoAmA 93*
Gary, Elbert H. 1845-1927 *EncABHB 9 [port]*
Gary, Harold d1984 *WhoHol 92*
Gary, James Frederick 1920- *WhoAm 94, WhoFI 94*
Gary, Jan 1925- *WhoAmA 93*
Gary, John 1932- *WhoAm 94, WhoHol 92*
Gary, John Godfrey, Jr. 1943- *WhoAmP 93*
Gary, Lawrence Edward 1939- *WhoBlA 94*
Gary, Leon, Jr. 1941- *WhoAmL 94*
Gary, Lesley *Who 94*
Gary, Lorraine 1937- *IntMPA 94, WhoHol 92*
Gary, Marc 1952- *WhoAm 94*
Gary, Melvin L. 1938- *WhoBlA 94*
Gary, Nancy Elizabeth 1937- *WhoAm 94*
Gary, Raymond D. 1908-1993 *NewYTBS 93*
Gary, Richard David 1949- *WhoAm 94, WhoAmL 94*
Gary, Richard N. 1943- *WhoAmL 94*
Gary, Robert W. 1938- *WhoIns 94*
Gary, Roger Vanstrom 1946- *WhoAmP 93, WhoFI 94*
Gary, Romain 1914-1980 *EncSF 93*
Gary, Stuart Hunter 1946- *WhoAmL 94*
Gary, T. Bart 1953- *WhoAmL 94*
Gary, Walter Joseph 1944- *WhoScEn 94*
Gary, Willie E. *WhoBlA 94*
Gary, Wyndham Lewis 1916-1989 *WhAm 10*
Garza, Angie 1948- *WhoHisp 94*
Garza, Anita Hernandez 1936- *WhoHisp 94*
Garza, Antoinette 1939- *WhoHisp 94*
Garza, Antonio O., Jr. *WhoHisp 94*
Garza, Augustine 1944- *WhoHisp 94*
Garza, Betty V. *WhoHisp 94*
Garza, Carlos *WhoHisp 94*
Garza, Carlos, Jr. 1944- *WhoHisp 94*
Garza, Carmen Lomas *WhoHisp 94*
Garza, Cipriano *WhoHisp 94*
Garza, Cutberto 1947- *WhoHisp 94*
Garza, Cyndy 1956- *WhoHisp 94*
Garza, Daniel *DrAPF 93*
Garza, Diva *WhoHisp 94*
Garza, Edmund T. 1943- *WhoHisp 94*
Garza, Edward 1947- *WhoHisp 94*
Garza, Emilio M. 1947- *WhoAmP 93, WhoHisp 94*
Garza, Emilio Miller 1947- *WhoAm 94, WhoAmL 94*
Garza, Enola 1953- *WhoHisp 94*
Garza, Eva d1966 *WhoHol 92*
Garza, Federico, Jr. 1958- *WhoHisp 94*
Garza, Federico G. 1932- *WhoHisp 94*
Garza, Fidencio Gustavo, Jr. 1932- *WhoHisp 94*
Garza, Francisco Xavier 1952- *WhoHisp 94*
Garza, G. Jaime *WhoHisp 94*
Garza, Geoffrey Rene 1964- *WhoHisp 94*
Garza, Jaime R. 1954- *WhoHisp 94*
Garza, Jaime René 1941- *WhoHisp 94*
Garza, Javier *WhoHisp 94*
Garza, Javier Joaquin 1955- *WhoHisp 94*
Garza, Jim S. 1949- *WhoHisp 94*
Garza, Jose G. 1932- *WhoHisp 94*
Garza, Jose Leyva 1942- *WhoHisp 94*
Garza, Juan 1944- *WhoHisp 94*
Garza, Juanita Elizondo 1939- *WhoHisp 94*
Garza, Lalo *WhoHisp 94*
Garza, Lloyd *WhoHisp 94*
Garza, M. Antoinette 1939- *WhoHisp 94*
Garza, Marco *WhoHisp 94*
Garza, Margarito *WhoHisp 94*
Garza, Margarito P. *WhoHisp 94*
Garza, Maria C. 1959- *WhoHisp 94*
Garza, Maria Luisa *WhoHisp 94*
Garza, Martin Edward 1965- *WhoHisp 94*
Garza, Melita Marie *WhoHisp 94*
Garza, Oliver P. 1941- *WhoHisp 94*
Garza, Oscar 1955- *WhoHisp 94*
Garza, Oscar H., Jr. 1947- *WhoHisp 94*
Garza, Patricia Lara *WhoHisp 94*
Garza, Rachel Delores 1952- *WhoHisp 94*
Garza, Raymond Robles 1931- *WhoHisp 94*
Garza, Raymond T. *WhoHisp 94*
Garza, Raynaldo T. 1957- *WhoHisp 94*
Garza, Reynaldo G. 1915- *WhoAm 94, WhoAmL 94, WhoHisp 94*
Garza, Richard Robert 1947- *WhoHisp 94*
Garza, Rick Earnest 1952- *WhoHisp 94*
Garza, Robert *WhoHisp 94*
Garza, Robert 1957- *WhoHisp 94*
Garza, Roberto 1942- *WhoHisp 94*
Garza, Roberto G. 1943- *WhoHisp 94*
Garza, Roberto Jesus 1934- *WhoAm 94, WhoHisp 94*
Garza, Roberto Montes 1951- *WhoHisp 94*
Garza, Roberto P. 1941- *WhoHisp 94*
Garza, Rogelio Cantú 1946- *WhoHisp 94*
Garza, Rosario 1950- *WhoHisp 94*
Garza, Roy 1951- *WhoHisp 94*
Garza, Ruben A. *WhoHisp 94*
Garza, Rubén Cesar, Sr. 1935- *WhoHisp 94*
Garza, Salvador, Jr. 1955- *WhoHisp 94*
Garza, San Juanita 1955- *WhoHisp 94*
Garza, Thomas A. 1962- *WhoHisp 94*
Garza, Thomas F. 1965- *WhoHisp 94*
Garza, Thomas Jesus 1958- *WhoHisp 94*
Garza, Trini *WhoHisp 94*
Garza, Vicki 1932- *WhoAmP 93*
Garza, William Alfred 1950- *WhoHisp 94*
Garza, Ygnacio *WhoHisp 94*
Garza, Ygnacio 1953- *WhoAmP 93*
Garza, Yolanda 1955- *WhoHisp 94*
Garza, Yolanda Cruz 1944- *WhoHisp 94*
Garza-Adame, Maria Dolores 1946- *WhoHisp 94*
Garza-Góngora, Sara R. *WhoHisp 94*
Garzarelli, Elaine Marie 1951- *WhoAm 94, WhoFI 94*
Garza Schmilewski, Diva *WhoHisp 94*
Garzia, Francesco Saverio *NewGrDO*
Garzia, Ricardo Francisco 1926- *WhoMW 93*
Garzia, Samuel Angelo 1920- *WhoAm 94*
Garzio, Angelo C. 1922- *WhoAmA 93*
Garzione, John Edward 1950- *WhoScEn 94*
Garzoli, Silvia L. *WhoHisp 94*
Garzon-Blanco, Armando 1941- *WhoAmA 93*
Gasaway, Laura Nell 1945- *WhoAmL 94*
Gasbarro, Pasco, Jr. 1944- *WhoAm 94*
Gascar, Pierre 1916- *IntWW 93*
Gasch, Manning 1943- *WhoAm 94, WhoAmL 94*
Gasch, Oliver 1906- *CngDr 93*
Gasch, Pauline Diana *Who 94*
Gaschen, Francis Allan 1950- *WhoAmP 93*
Gaschler, Thomas Friedrich 1960 *WhoMW 93*
Gasco, Alberto 1938- *WhoScEn 94*
Gascoigne, Bamber 1935- *Who 94, WrDr 94*
Gascoigne, George 1539-1577 *BlmGEL, DcLB 136 [port]*
Gascoigne, John 1951- *WrDr 94*
Gascoigne, Paul 1967- *WorESoc*
Gascoigne, Paul John 1967- *IntWW 93*
Gascoigne, Stanley 1914- *Who 94*
Gascon, Jean d1988 *WhoHol 92*
Gascoyne, David 1916- *BlmGEL*
Gascoyne, David (Emery) 1916- *WrDr 94*
Gascoyne, Joel 1650-1705 *DcNaB MP*
Gascoyne-Cecil, Robert 1830-1903 *HisWorL [port]*
Gasdia, Cecilia 1960- *NewGrDO*
Gash, Frederick d1993 *NewYTBS 93*
Gash, Joe 1941- *WrDr 94*
Gash, Jonathan 1933- *WrDr 94*
Gash, Lauren Beth *WhoAmP 93*
Gash, Lauren Beth 1960- *WhoAmL 94, WhoMW 93*
Gash, Norman 1912- *IntWW 93, Who 94, WrDr 94*
Gasich, Welko Elton 1922- *WhoAm 94, WhoFI 94*
Gasior, James Mark 1959- *WhoFI 94*
Gasior, Walter David, Jr. 1952- *WhoMW 93*
Gasiorkiewicz, Eugene Anthony 1950- *WhoAmL 94*
Gasiorowicz, Stephen George 1928- *WhoAm 94*
Gasiorowska, Xenia d1989 *WhAm 10*
Gask, Daphne Irvine Prideaux 1920- *Who 94*
Gaskell, Carolyn Suzanne 1954- *WhoAm 94*
Gaskell, Colin Simister 1937- *Who 94*
Gaskell, Elizabeth 1810-1865 *BlmGWL, RfGShF*
Gaskell, Elizabeth Cleghorn 1810-1865 *BlmGEL [port]*
Gaskell, Holbrook 1813-1909 *DcNaB MP*
Gaskell, Jane 1941- *EncSF 93, WrDr 94*
Gaskell, (John) Philip (Wellesley) 1926- *Who 94, WrDr 94*
Gaskell, Richard (Kennedy Harvey) 1936- *Who 94*
Gaskell, Robert Eugene 1912- *WhoAm 94*
Gaskell, Robert Weyand 1945- *WhoScEn 94*
Gaskell, Sonia 1904-1974 *IntDcB [port]*
Gaskill, Charles d1943 *WhoHol 92*
Gaskill, David Abram 1894- *WhAm 10*
Gaskill, Herbert Leo 1923- *WhoWest 94*

Gaskill, Robert Clarence 1931- *AfrAmG [port]*
Gaskill, William 1930- *IntWW 93, Who 94*
Gaskin, Catherine 1929- *Who 94, WrDr 94*
Gaskin, Felicia 1943- *WhoAm 94, WhoScEn 94*
Gaskin, Frances Christian 1936- *WhoBlA 94*
Gaskin, J(ohn) C(harles) A(ddison) 1936- *WrDr 94*
Gaskin, Jeanine 1945- *WhoBlA 94*
Gaskin, Leonard O. 1920- *WhoBlA 94*
Gaskin, Leroy 1924- *WhoBlA 94*
Gaskin, Maxwell 1921- *Who 94*
Gaskins, Douglas Kenneth 1951- *WhoAm 94*
Gaskins, H. Rex 1958- *WhoScEn 94*
Gaskins, Louise Elizabeth 1930- *WhoBlA 94*
Gaslini, Giorgio 1929- *NewGrDO*
Gasowski, Ronald Edward 1941- *WhoWest 94*
Gaspar, Gary J. 1949- *WhoIns 94*
Gaspar, Laszlo *EncSF 93*
Gaspar, Peter Paul 1935- *WhoAm 94*
Gaspar, Rogelio G. 1965- *WhoWest 94*
Gaspard, Marcus Stuart 1948- *WhoAmP 93*
Gaspard, Patrice T. 1954- *WhoBlA 94*
Gaspari, Giovanni Paolo 1712-1775 *NewGrDO*
Gaspari, Remo 1921- *IntWW 93*
Gaspari, Russell Arthur 1941- *WhoAm 94*
Gasparini, Domenico Maria Angiolo *NewGrDO*
Gasparini, Francesco 1661-1727 *NewGrDO*
Gasparini, Quirino 1721-1778 *NewGrDO*
Gasparotto, Renso 1952- *WhoScEn 94*
Gasparovic, Ivan 1941- *IntWW 93*
Gasparro, Frank 1909- *WhoAm 94, WhoAmA 93*
Gasper, George, Jr. 1939- *WhoMW 93*
Gasper, Jo Ann 1946- *WhoAm 94*
Gasper, Louis 1911- *WhoWest 94*
Gasper, Ruth Eileen 1934- *WhoFI 94, WhoMW 93*
Gasper-Galvin, Lee DeLong 1956- *WhoScEn 94*
Gasperoni, Emil, Sr. 1926- *WhoFI 94*
Gasperoni, John Lino 1951- *WhoWest 94*
Gass, Arthur Edward 1931- *WhoScEn 94*
Gass, Clinton Burke 1920- *WhoAm 94*
Gass, Craig Nelson 1945- *WhoFI 94*
Gass, Gertrude Zemon *WhoMW 93*
Gass, Ian (Graham) 1926-1992 *WrDr 94N*
Gass, Ian Graham d1992 *IntWW 93N, Who 94N*
Gass, James Ronald 1924- *Who 94*
Gass, Lee Alan 1958- *WhoFI 94*
Gass, Manus M. 1928- *WhoAm 94*
Gass, Raymond William 1937- *WhoAmL 94*
Gass, Susan Mary 1943- *WhoMW 93*
Gass, Tyler Evan 1948- *WhoScEn 94*
Gass, William (Howard) 1924- *WrDr 94*
Gass, William H. *DrAPF 93*
Gass, William H. 1924- *ShSCr 12 [port], WhoAm 94*
Gassel, Philip Michael 1947- *WhoAm 94, WhoAmL 94*
Gassen, Joseph Albert 1926- *WhoAm 94*
Gassendi, Pierre 1592-1655 *GuFrLit 2*
Gasser, Henry Martin 1909-1981 *WhoAmA 93N*
Gasser, Wilbert Warner, Jr. 1923- *WhoAm 94*
Gassere, Eugene Arthur 1930- *WhoAm 94*
Gassier, Edouard 1820-1872 *NewGrDO*
Gassler, David K. 1954- *WhoFI 94*
Gassler, Frank Henry 1951- *WhoAm 94*
Gassman, Alan Scott 1959- *WhoAmL 94*
Gassman, Lewis 1910- *Who 94*
Gassman, Victor Alan 1935- *WhoFI 94, WhoWest 94*
Gassman, Vittorio 1922- *IntMPA 94, IntWW 93, WhoHol 92*
Gassmann, Florian Leopold 1729-1774 *NewGrDO*
Gassmann, Henry 1927- *WhoAmP 93*
Gassner, Dennis *ConTFT 11*
Gasson, (Gordon) Barry 1935- *Who 94*
Gasson, John Gustav Haycraft 1931- *Who 94*
Gast, Alice P. *WhoScEn 94*
Gast, Carolyn Bartlett (Lutz) 1929- *WhoAmA 93*
Gast, Dwight V. *WhoAmA 93*
Gast, Harry T., Jr. 1920- *WhoAmP 93*
Gast, Kelly P. 1922- *WrDr 94*
Gast, Michael Carl 1930- *WhoAmA 93*
Gast, Nancy Lou 1941- *WhoWest 94*
Gast, Peter 1854-1918 *NewGrDO*
Gast, Robert Gale 1931- *WhoAm 94*
Gastaldi, Jerome 1945- *WhoAmA 93*
Gastaut, Henri Jean 1915- *IntWW 93*
Gaster, Theodor 1906-1992 *AnObit 1992*
Gastil, Richard Walter, Jr. 1953- *WhoWest 94*
Gastil, Russell Gordon 1928- *WhoAm 94*
Gastineau, Clifford Felix 1920- *WhoAm 94*
Gastineau, Michael Keith 1957- *WhoIns 94*
Gaston, Arnett W. 1938- *WhoBlA 94*
Gaston, Bill 1927- *WrDr 94*
Gaston, Cito 1944- *CurBio 93 [port], WhoAm 94, WhoBlA 94*
Gaston, Don F. *WhoAm 94*
Gaston, Edwin Willmer, Jr. 1925- *WrDr 94*
Gaston, George d1937 *WhoHol 92*
Gaston, Gerald N. *WhoIns 94*
Gaston, Henry Victor 1943- *WhoAmP 93*
Gaston, Hugh Philip 1910- *WhoFI 94, WhoMW 93, WhoScEn 94*
Gaston, Jerry Collins 1940- *WhoScEn 94*
Gaston, Joseph Alexander 1928- *WhoBlA 94*
Gaston, Karl Kuntis 1929- *WhoMW 93*
Gaston, Linda Saulsby 1947- *WhoBlA 94*
Gaston, Mack Charles 1940- *AfrAmG [port], WhoAm 94, WhoBlA 94, WhoWest 94*
Gaston, Marilyn Hughes 1939- *WhoBlA 94*
Gaston, Minnie L. 1909- *WhoBlA 94*
Gaston, William James 1927- *WrDr 94*
Gaston, William W. 1926- *IntWW 93*
Gastoni, Lisa 1935- *WhoHol 92*
Gastrock, Phil d1956 *WhoHol 92*
Gastwirt, Lawrence E. 1936- *WhoScEn 94*
Gastwirth, Donald Edward 1944- *WhoAm 94*
Gastwirth, Joseph Lewis 1938- *WhoAm 94*
Gaswirth, Ronald M. 1944- *WhoAm 94, WhoAmL 94*
Gasymov, Tofig Masim Ogly 1938- *LoBiDrD*
Gat, Joel R. 1926- *IntWW 93*
Gatch, Lee 1909-1968 *WhoAmA 93N*
Gatch, Milton McCormick, Jr. 1932- *WhoAm 94, WrDr 94*
Gatchell, Howell Lamborn, Jr. 1948- *WhoFI 94*
Gatdula, Francisco Ric 1958- *WhoAsA 94*
Gatehouse, Graham Gould 1935- *Who 94*
Gatehouse, Robert Alexander 1924- *Who 94*
Gatell, Jose Maria 1951- *WhoScEn 94*
Gately, Alexander Patrick 1949- *WhoFI 94, WhoWest 94*
Gately, David F. *WhoAmP 93*
Gately, George 1928- *WhoAm 94*
Gately, Mark Donohue 1952- *WhoAm 94, WhoAmL 94*
Gately, Maurice Kent 1946- *WhoScEn 94*
Gatenby, Greg 1950- *WrDr 94*
Gates, Albert 1908- *WrDr 94*
Gates, Audrey Castine 1937- *WhoBlA 94*
Gates, Beatrix *DrAPF 93*
Gates, Bill 1955- *News 93-3 [port]*
Gates, Bruce Clark 1940- *WhoScEn 94*
Gates, Carolyn 1935- *WhoAmP 93*
Gates, Charles Cassius 1921- *WhoAm 94, WhoFI 94, WhoWest 94*
Gates, Clifford E., Jr. 1946- *WhoBlA 94*
Gates, Clifton W. 1923- *WhoBlA 94, WhoMW 93*
Gates, Crawford Marion 1921- *WhoAm 94*
Gates, Daryl Francis 1926- *WhoWest 94*
Gates, David 1947?- *ConAu 140*
Gates, David Allan 1946- *WhoAm 94, WhoAmL 94*
Gates, Harry Irving 1934- *WhoAmA 93*
Gates, Henry Louis 1950- *WrDr 94*
Gates, Henry Louis, Jr. 1950- *BlkWr 2, WhoAm 94, WhoBlA 94*
Gates, Horatio 1728-1806 *AmRev, WhAmRev [port]*
Gates, Hugh H. *WhoAmP 93*
Gates, Jacquelyn Knight 1951- *WhoBlA 94*
Gates, James David 1927- *WhoAm 94*
Gates, James Lloyd, Jr. 1957- *WhoAmL 94*
Gates, James Steven 1959- *WhoAmL 94*
Gates, Jan Ellen 1953- *WhoWest 94*
Gates, Jay Rodney 1945- *WhoAmA 93*
Gates, Jeff S. *WhoAmA 93*
Gates, Jimmie Earl 1956- *WhoBlA 94*
Gates, Jodie *WhoAm 94*
Gates, John W., III 1939- *WhoIns 94*
Gates, Karla Diane 1952- *WhoWest 94*
Gates, L. Keith *WhoAmP 93*
Gates, Larry 1915- *WhoAm 94, WhoHol 92*
Gates, Lawrence Stuart 1934- *WhoAmL 94*
Gates, Leslie Clifford 1918- *WhoAm 94*
Gates, Mahlon Eugene 1919- *WhoAm 94*
Gates, Marshall De Motte, Jr. 1915- *IntWW 93*
Gates, Marshall DeMotte, Jr. 1915- *WhoAm 94, WhoScEn 94*
Gates, Martina Marie 1957- *WhoMW 93*
Gates, Marvin 1929- *WhoScEn 94*
Gates, Maxine d1990 *WhoHol 92*
Gates, Michael Andrew 1946- *WhoMW 93*
Gates, Milo Sedgwick 1923- *WhoAm 94, WhoFI 94*
Gates, Moine R. 1940- *WhoAmP 93*
Gates, Nancy 1924- *WhoHol 92*
Gates, Nina Jane 1947- *WhoBlA 94*
Gates, Norman T(immins) 1914- *WrDr 94*
Gates, Otis A., III 1935- *WhoBlA 94*
Gates, Paul Edward 1945- *WhoBlA 94*
Gates, Paul W(allace) 1901- *WrDr 94*
Gates, Philip Don 1937- *WhoAm 94*
Gates, Philomene (A.) 1918- *WrDr 94*
Gates, Phyllis *WhoHol 92*
Gates, Rebecca Twilley 1932- *WhoAmP 93*
Gates, Richard Daniel 1942- *WhoAm 94*
Gates, Rick *WhoHol 92*
Gates, Robert Clare 1951- *WhoAmP 93*
Gates, Robert E. 1920- *WhoAmP 93*
Gates, Robert M. *Who 94*
Gates, Robert M. 1943- *IntWW 93, WhoAmP 93*
Gates, Ronald Cecil 1923- *Who 94*
Gates, Ruth d1966 *WhoHol 92*
Gates, Scott Allan 1956- *WhoMW 93*
Gates, Stephen Frye 1946- *WhoAm 94, WhoAmL 94*
Gates, Theodore Allan, Jr. 1933- *WhoWest 94*
Gates, Theodore Ross 1918- *WhoAm 94*
Gates, Thomas Edward 1953- *WhoScEn 94*
Gates, Thomas Michael 1943- *WhoBlA 94*
Gates, Thomas Paul 1941- *WhoAmA 93*
Gates, Walter Edward 1946- *WhoFI 94*
Gates, William H. 1925- *WhoAm 94*
Gates, William H. 1955- *WorInv*
Gates, William Henry 1955- *IntWW 93*
Gates, William Henry, III 1955- *WhoAm 94, WhoFI 94, WhoScEn 94, WhoWest 94*
Gates, William S. 1944- *WhoIns 94*
Gates, William Simon 1944- *WhoFI 94*
Gateson, Marjorie d1977 *WhoHol 92*
Gatewood, Algie C. 1951- *WhoBlA 94*
Gatewood, Barbara J. 1954- *WhoMW 93*
Gatewood, Buford Echols 1913- *WhoMW 93, WhoScEn 94*
Gatewood, James C. *WhoAmP 93*
Gatewood, Joseph Todd 1964- *WhoAmL 94*
Gatewood, Judith Anne 1944- *WhoFI 94*
Gatewood, Lucian B. 1945- *WhoBlA 94*
Gatewood, Maud 1934- *WhoAmA 93*
Gatewood, Tela Lynne *WhoAmL 94*
Gatewood, Wallace Lavell 1946- *WhoBlA 94*
Gatewood, Willard Badgett, Jr. 1931- *WhoAm 94*
Gatford, Ian 1940- *Who 94*
Gath, Philip C. 1947- *WhoAm 94*
Gathe, Joseph C. 1929- *WhoBlA 94*
Gathercole, John Robert 1937- *Who 94*
Gathers, George Roger 1936- *WhoWest 94*
Gathorne-Hardy *Who 94*
Gathorne-Hardy, Jonathan 1933- *WrDr 94*
Gathright, Howard T. 1935- *WhoAmL 94*
Gathright, John Byron, Jr. 1933- *WhoAm 94*
Gati, Frank 1938- *WhoWest 94*
Gati, William Eugene 1959- *WhoFI 94*
Gatje, Robert Frederick 1927- *WhoAm 94*
Gatland, Kenneth William 1924- *WrDr 94*
Gatley, Donald Perkins 1932- *WhoScEn 94*
Gatley, William Stuart, Sr. 1932- *WhoWest 94*
Gatliff, Frank d1990 *WhoHol 92*
Gatlin, Daniel G. 1957- *WhoWest 94*
Gatlin, Elissa L. 1948- *WhoBlA 94*
Gatlin, Fred 1948- *WhoAmP 93, WhoMW 93*
Gatlin, Jerry *WhoHol 92*
Gatlin, John C(hristian) 1897- *WhAm 10*
Gatlin, Karen Pauline Boe 1942- *WhoAmL 94*
Gatlin, Ken 1940- *WhoWest 94*
Gatlin, Larry Alan 1950- *WhoScEn 94*
Gatlin, Larry Wayne 1948- *WhoAm 94*
Gatlin, Michael Gerard 1956- *WhoAmL 94*
Gatling, Chris Raymond 1967- *WhoBlA 94*
Gatling, Eva Ingersoll 1912- *WhoAmA 93*
Gatling, Patricia Lynn 1960- *WhoBlA 94*
Gatling, Richard Jordan 1818-1903 *WorInv*
Gatos, Harry Constantine 1921- *WhoAm 94*
Gatos, Stephanie 1935- *WrDr 94*
Gatrell, John d1981 *WhoHol 92*
Gatrell, Marion Thompson 1909- *WhoAmA 93N*
Gatrell, Robert Morris 1906-1982 *WhoAmA 93N*
Gatrousis, Christopher 1928- *WhoWest 94*
Gatski, Frank *ProFbHF*
Gatski, Ron Bernard 1935- *WhoAmP 93*
Gatson, Wilina Ione 1925- *WhoBlA 94*
Gatt, Colin 1934- *Who 94*
Gatt, Lawrence 1941- *IntWW 93*
Gatta, Antonio fl. 1763-1771 *NewGrDO*
Gattaz, Yvon 1925- *IntWW 93*
Gattegno, Jean 1935- *IntWW 93*
Gatten, Tom *DrAPF 93*
Gattey, Charles Neilson 1921- *WrDr 94*
Gatti, Armand 1924- *ConWorW 93*
Gatti, Carlo 1876-1965 *NewGrDO*
Gatti, Daniel Jon 1946- *WhoAmL 94, WhoWest 94*
Gatti, Daute *ConWorW 93*
Gatti, Gabriella 1916- *NewGrDO*
Gatti, Guido M(aggiorino) 1892-1973 *NewGrDO*
Gatti, Luigi (Maria Baldassare) 1740-1817 *NewGrDO*
Gatti, Theobaldo di c. 1650-1727 *NewGrDO*
Gatti-Casazza, Giulio 1869-1940 *NewGrDO*
Gattie, Erma Charlotte 1961- *WhoAm 94*
Gatting, Michael William 1957- *IntWW 93*
Gattis, James Ralph 1944- *WhoFI 94*
Gattison, Kenneth Clay 1964- *WhoBlA 94*
Gatto, Joseph Daniel 1956- *WhoFI 94*
Gatto, Louis Constantine 1927- *WhoAm 94*
Gatto, Paul Anthony 1929- *WhoAmA 93*
Gatto, Rose Marie 1931- *WhoAmA 93*
Gatty, Margaret 1809-1873 *BlmGWL*
Gatty, Trevor Thomas 1930- *Who 94*
Gatward, James 1957- *IntMPA 94*
Gatward, (Anthony) James 1938- *Who 94*
Gatza, James 1933- *WhoIns 94*
Gatzke, Judith 1941- *WhoMW 93*
Gau, John Glen Mackay 1940- *Who 94*
Gaubert, Philippe 1879-1941 *NewGrDO*
Gaubert, Ronald Joseph 1946- *WhoFI 94*
Gauch, Eugene William, Jr. 1922- *WhoAm 94*
Gauch, Matthew Donald 1963- *WhoWest 94*
Gauch, Ronald W. 1938- *WhoAmP 93*
Gaucher, Yves 1934- *WhoAmA 93*
Gauci, Victor J. 1931- *IntWW 93*
Gaudard, Pierre 1927- *WhoAmA 93*
Gaudard, Thierry M. 1957- *WhoAm 94*
Gaudet, Douglas A. 1954 *WhoIns 94*
Gaudet, Edward John *WhoFI 94*
Gaudette, Francis J. d1993 *NewYTBS 93*
Gaudiani, Claire Lynn 1944- *WhoAm 94*
Gaudichaud-Beaupre, Charles 1789-1854 *WhWE*
Gaudieri, Alexander V. J. 1940- *WhoAm 94, WhoAmA 93*
Gaudieri, Millicent Hall 1941- *WhoAm 94*
Gaudin, Edward Clark 1931- *WhoAmP 93*
Gaudin, Marguerite 1909- *WhoAmA 93N*
Gaudin, Stephane d1993 *NewYTBS 93*
Gaudio, Antonio dal fl. 1669-1682 *NewGrDO*
Gaudio, Tony 1885-1951 *IntDcF 2-4*
Gaudion, Donald Alfred 1913- *WhoAm 94*
Gaudreau, Jules Oscar, Jr. 1961- *WhoFI 94*
Gaudreau, Russell A., Jr. 1943- *WhoAm 94, WhoAmL 94*
Gaudry, Roger 1913- *IntWW 93, Who 94, WhoAm 94*
Gauen, Patrick Emil 1950- *WhoAm 94*
Gauer, Donald L. 1932- *WhoIns 94*
Gauff, Joseph F., Jr. 1939- *WhoBlA 94*
Gauge, Alexander d1960 *WhoHol 92*
Gauger, Michele Roberta 1949- *WhoMW 93*
Gauger, Rick *EncSF 93*
Gaugh, Harry F. d1992 *WhoAmA 93N*
Gaughan, Dennis Charles 1955- *WhoAmL 94*
Gaughan, Eugene Francis 1945- *WhoAm 94*
Gaughan, Jack 1930-1985 *EncSF 93*
Gaughan, John Anthony 1947- *WhoAmP 93*
Gaughan, Norbert F. 1921- *WhoAm 94, WhoMW 93*
Gaughan, Vincent, Sr. d1993 *NewYTBS 93*
Gaughan, Vincent Michael 1919- *WhoFI 94*
Gauguin, Lorraine d1974 *WhoHol 92*
Gaukler, George 1936- *WhoAmP 93*
Gauld, William Wallace 1919- *Who 94*
Gaulden, Jimmiee Lewis 1952- *WhoFI 94*

Gauldie, Enid Elizabeth 1928- *WrDr 94*
Gauldin, Charles Alan 1959- *WhoAmL 94*
Gauldin, Michael Glen 1954- *WhoAm 94*
Gaule, Wendy Anne 1959- *WhoAmL 94*
Gaulin, Jean 1942- *Who 94, WhoFI 94*
Gaulke, Earl H. 1927- *WhoMW 93*
Gaulke, Mary Florence 1923- *WhoWest 94*
Gaull, Gerald Edward 1930- *WhoAm 94*
Gaulle, Charles de 1890-1970 *HisWorL [port]*
Gault, Charles Alexander 1908- *Who 94*
Gault, David Hamilton 1928- *Who 94*
Gault, Donald Eiker 1923- *WhoScEn 94*
Gault, John Franklin 1936- *WhoFI 94*
Gault, Judith *WhoHol 92*
Gault, Marian Holness 1934- *WhoBlA 94*
Gault, N. L., Jr. 1920- *WhoAm 94*
Gault, Robert Mellor 1945- *WhoAm 94, WhoAmL 94*
Gault, Ronald T. *WhoBlA 94*
Gault, Stanley Carleton 1926- *WhoAm 94, WhoFI 94, WhoMW 93*
Gault, Terrell Wilson 1951- *WhoWest 94*
Gault, Thomas Munro 1938- *Who 94*
Gault, William Campbell 1910- *WrDr 94*
Gault, Willie James 1960- *WhoBlA 94*
Gaulter, Derek Vivian 1924- *Who 94*
Gaultier, Henry d1972 *WhoHol 92*
Gaultier, Jean-Paul 1952- *IntWW 93*
Gaultiere, Kristi Southard 1965- *WhoWest 94*
Gaultney, John Orton 1915- *WhoAm 94, WhoFI 94*
Gaultney, Lawrence Doka 1956- *WhoMW 93*
Gaumer, Dale Jackson 1936- *WhoMW 93*
Gaumont, Leon 1864-1946 *IntDcF 2-4*
Gaunaurd, Guillermo C. 1940- *WhoAm 94, WhoScEn 94*
Gaunce, Michael Paul 1949- *WhoMW 93*
Gaunt, Graham 1933- *WrDr 94*
Gaunt, Janet Lois 1947- *WhoAmL 94, WhoWest 94*
Gaunt, Jonathan Robert 1947- *Who 94*
Gaunt, Mary 1861-1942 *BlmGWL*
Gaunt, Peter *ConAu 42NR*
Gaunt, Valerie 1933- *WhoHol 92*
Gaunt, William 1937- *WhoHol 92*
Gaunt, William L. 1945- *WhoAmL 94*
Gauntier, Gene d1966 *WhoHol 92*
Gauntlett, David Allan 1954- *WhoAmL 94*
Gauquelin, Francoise 1929- *AstEnc*
Gauquelin, Michel 1928-1991 *AstEnc*
Gaus, Gunter 1929- *IntWW 93*
Gausden, Ronald 1921- *Who 94*
Gauss, Carl Friedrich 1777-1855 *WorInv, WorScD*
Gaustad, Edwin Scott 1923- *WhoAm 94*
Gaustad, John Eldon 1938- *WhoAm 94*
Gaustad, Richard Dale 1952- *WhoWest 94*
Gaut, Norman Eugene 1937- *WhoAm 94*
Gaut, Slim d1964 *WhoHol 92*
Gautheret, Roger 1910- *IntWW 93*
Gauthier, Dan 1963- *WhoHol 92*
Gauthier, Jacqueline d1982 *WhoHol 92*
Gauthier, Jon Lawrence 1962- *WhoScEn 94*
Gauthier, Mary Elizabeth 1917- *WhoMW 93*
Gauthier, Ninon 1943- *WhoAmA 93*
Gauthier, Suzanne d1988 *WhoHol 92*
Gauthier, Suzanne Anita 1948- *WhoAmA 93*
Gauthier, Tina Lee 1953- *WhoWest 94*
Gauthier, Wendell Haynes 1943- *WhoAmL 94*
Gauthier, Xaviere 1942- *BlmGWL*
Gautier, Axel 1942-1993 *NewYTBS 93 [port]*
Gautier, Dick 1937- *WhoAm 94*
Gautier, Dick 1939- *WhoHol 92*
Gautier, Eduardo Emilio 1927- *WhoHisp 94*
Gautier, (Jean-Francois-)Eugene 1822-1878 *NewGrDO*
Gautier, George J. 1952- *WhoFI 94*
Gautier, Judith 1846-1917 *BlmGWL*
Gautier, Michel *WhoHol 92*
Gautier, Pierre 1642?-1696 *NewGrDO*
Gautier, Theophile 1811-1872 *IntDcB*
Gautier, William Louis 1938- *WhoAmL 94*
Gautier-Smith, Peter Claudius 1929- *Who 94*
Gautreaux, Marcelian Francis, Jr. 1930- *WhoAm 94*
Gautreaux, Timothy Martin *DrAPF 93*
Gautrey, Peter 1918- *Who 94*
Gautschi, Walter 1927- *WhoAm 94*
Gauvain, Timothy John Lund 1942- *Who 94*
Gauvenet, Andre Jean 1920- *WhoScEn 94*
Gauvey, Susan K. 1948- *WhoAm 94, WhoAmL 94*
Gauvin, Claude E. 1939- *WhoAmA 93*
Gauvin, Michel 1919- *IntWW 93*
Gauvin, William Henry 1913- *IntWW 93*
Gauvreau, N. Paul 1948- *WhoAmP 93*
Gauvreau, Robert George 1948- *WhoAmA 93*
Gava, Antonio 1930- *IntWW 93*
Gavac, Donna Broderick 1926- *WhoWest 94*
Gavagan, Margaret d1949 *WhoHol 92*
Gavalas, Alexander Beary 1945- *WhoAmA 93*
Gavaldon, Edward Adolph 1945- *WhoHisp 94*
Gavaler, Judith Ann Stohr Van Thiel *WhoScEn 94*
Gavan, James Anderson 1916- *WhoAm 94*
Gavande, Sampat A. 1936- *WhoAsA 94*
Gavande, Sampat Anand 1936- *WhoScEn 94*
Gavaskar, Sunil 1949- *IntWW 93, WrDr 94*
Gavaskar, Sunil Manohar 1949- *Who 94*
Gavazzeni, Gianandrea 1909- *NewGrDO*
Gavazzeni, Gianandrea 1919- *IntWW 93*
Gavazzi, Aladino A. 1922- *WhoAm 94*
Gaveaux, Pierre 1760-1825 *NewGrDO*
Gavelis, Jonas Rimvydas 1950- *WhoScEn 94*
Gaven, Jean 1922- *WhoHol 92*
Gavenda, John David 1933- *WhoAm 94*
Gavenus, Edward Richard 1932- *WhoAm 94*
Gaver, Chasen *DrAPF 93*
Gavey, James Edward 1942- *WhoFI 94*
Gavezzotti, Angelo 1944- *WhoScEn 94*
Gavian, Peter Wood 1932- *WhoFI 94*
Gavin, Austin 1909- *WhoAm 94*
Gavin, Catherine 1907- *WrDr 94*
Gavin, Donald Glenn 1942- *WhoAmL 94*
Gavin, Elizabeth 1938- *WhoAmP 93*
Gavin, Gene *WhoAmP 93*
Gavin, Herbert James 1921- *WhoAm 94*
Gavin, James John, Jr. 1922- *WhoAm 94*
Gavin, James M. 1907-1990 *WhAm 10*
Gavin, James Merricks Lewis 1911- *Who 94*
Gavin, James Raphael, III 1945- *WhoBlA 94*
Gavin, John 1928- *WhoHol 92*
Gavin, John 1932- *IntMPA 94, IntWW 93*
Gavin, John Anthony Golenor 1932- *WhoHisp 94*
Gavin, John J. 1920- *WhoAmP 93*
Gavin, John Neal 1946- *WhoAm 94*
Gavin, L. Katherine *WhoBlA 94*
Gavin, Louis Brooks 1907- *WhoAmL 94*
Gavin, Mary Jane 1941- *WhoMW 93*
Gavin, Paula Lance 1945- *WhoHisp 94*
Gavin, Robert Michael, Jr. 1940- *WhoAm 94*
Gavin, T. Edward 1922- *WhoFI 94*
Gavin, Thomas *DrAPF 93*
Gavina, Pedro L. *WhoHisp 94*
Gavinski, Thomas Sylvester 1953- *WhoMW 93*
Gaviria Trujillo, Cesar *IntWW 93*
Gavish, Bezalel 1945- *WhoAm 94*
Gavish, Yeshayahu 1925- *IntWW 93*
Gavito, Letty G. *WhoHisp 94*
Gavito, Olga Leticia 1951- *WhoHisp 94*
Gavlock, Eugene Harlan 1925- *WhoFI 94*
Gavras, Constantin 1933- *WhoAm 94*
Gavrilov, Andrei Vladimirovich 1955- *IntWW 93*
Gavrilov, Yury Vasilevich 1953- *LoBiDrD*
Gavrity, John D. 1940- *WhoIns 94*
Gavrity, John Decker 1940- *WhoAm 94*
Gavron, Robert 1930- *Who 94*
Gavronsky, Serge *DrAPF 93*
Gavronsky, Serge 1932- *WrDr 94*
Gavzy, William Breier 1950- *WhoFI 94*
Gaw, R. Steven 1957- *WhoMW 93*
Gaw, Robert Steven 1957- *WhoAmP 93*
Gawain Poet *BlmGEL*
Gawalt, Gerard Wilfred 1943- *WhoAm 94, WhoAmL 94*
Gawande, Atul A. 1965- *WhoAsA 94*
Gawarecki, Carolyn Ann *WhoAmA 93*
Gawf, John Lee 1922- *WhoAm 94*
Gawienowski, Anthony Michael 1959- *WhoMW 93*
Gawron, Jean Mark 1953- *EncSF 93*
Gawrylowicz, Henry Thaddeus 1928- *WhoScEn 94*
Gawsworth, John 1912-1970 *EncSF 93*
Gawthorne, Peter d1962 *WhoHol 92*
Gawthrop, Robert Smith, III 1942- *WhoAm 94, WhoAmL 94*
Gaxton, William d1963 *WhoHol 92*
Gay, (John) 1685-1732 *IntDcT 2*
Gay, Alden d1979 *WhoHol 92*
Gay, Aleda Susan 1951- *WhoMW 93*
Gay, Amelia 1905- *WrDr 94*
Gay, Anne 1952- *EncSF 93*
Gay, Arthur F. d1993 *NewYTBS 93*
Gay, Benjamin 1916- *WhoBlA 94*
Gay, Betsy 1927- *WhoAmA 93*
Gay, Birdie Spivey 1918- *WhoBlA 94*
Gay, Carl Lloyd 1950- *WhoAmL 94*
Gay, Charles d1950 *WhoHol 92*
Gay, David Braxton 1957- *WhoFI 94*
Gay, David Earl 1944- *WhoMW 93*
Gay, David Holden 1954- *WhoFI 94, WhoScEn 94*
Gay, Eddie C. 1940- *WhoBlA 94*
Gay, Elizabeth Dershuck *WhoAmA 93*
Gay, Emil Laurence 1923- *WhoAm 94, WhoFI 94*
Gay, Geoffrey Charles Lytton 1914- *IntWW 93, Who 94*
Gay, George Wilsmore 1913- *Who 94*
Gay, Greg Allen 1952- *WhoAmP 93*
Gay, Helen Parker 1920- *WhoBlA 94*
Gay, Inez d1975 *WhoHol 92*
Gay, J. Drew *EncSF 93*
Gay, James 1918- *WhoAmL 94*
Gay, James F. 1942- *WhoBlA 94*
Gay, Joan Dabkowski 1940- *WhoAmP 93*
Gay, John 1685-1732 *BlmGEL, NewGrDO*
Gay, John 1924- *IntMPA 94*
Gay, John H. 1928- *BlkWr 2*
Gay, John William 1951- *WhoMW 93*
Gay, Kathlyn R 1930- *WrDr 94*
Gay, Kathlyn Ruth 1930- *WhoMW 93*
Gay, Leslie N., Jr. d1993 *NewYTBS 93*
Gay, Maisie d1945 *WhoHol 92*
Gay, Maria 1879-1943 *NewGrDO*
Gay, Marie-Louise 1952- *WrDr 94*
Gay, Peter 1923- *IntWW 93, WhoAm 94, WrDr 94*
Gay, Peter (Jack) 1923- *ConAu 41NR*
Gay, Richard Leslie 1950- *WhoWest 94*
Gay, Robert Derril 1939- *WhoAm 94*
Gay, Sarah Elizabeth 1950- *WhoAmL 94*
Gay, Sophie 1776-1852 *BlmGWL*
Gay, Theodis *WhoAmP 93*
Gay, Thomas Paul 1950- *WhoAmL 94*
Gay, Walter d1936 *WhoHol 92*
Gay, William 1955- *WhoBlA 94*
Gay, William Ingalls 1926- *WhoAm 94*
Gayan, Anil Kumarsingh 1948- *IntWW 93*
Gayarre, Julian (Sebastian) 1844-1890 *NewGrDO*
Gayas-Jungwirth, I(rene) *WhoAmA 93*
Gay-Bryant, Claudine Moss 1915- *WhoScEn 94*
Gaydar, Yegor Timurovich 1956- *IntWW 93*
Gaydon, Alfred Gordon 1911- *IntWW 93, Who 94, WrDr 94*
Gaydos, Joseph Matthew 1926- *WhoAmP 93*
Gaydos, Michael Edward, IV 1956- *WhoFI 94*
Gaydos, Tim 1941- *WhoAmA 93*
Gaydos, William John 1953- *WhoMW 93*
Gaye fl. 1676-1681 *NewGrDO*
Gaye, Albie d1965 *WhoHol 92*
Gaye, Amadou Karim 1913- *IntWW 93*
Gaye, Gregory 1900- *WhoHol 92*
Gaye, Howard d1955 *WhoHol 92*
Gaye, Lisa *WhoHol 92*
Gaye, Lisa 1935- *WhoHol 92*
Gaye, Marvin d1984 *WhoHol 92*
Gaye, Marvin 1939-1984 *AfrAmAl 6 [port]*
Gayer, Alan J. *WhoAm 94*
Gayer, Catherine 1937- *NewGrDO*
Gayer, Echlin d1926 *WhoHol 92*
Gayer, John Harrison 1919- *WhoAm 94*
Gaylaird, Christopher *WhoWest 94*
Gayle, Addison 1932-1991 *WhAm 10*
Gayle, Addison, Jr. 1932-1991 *WhoBlA 94N*
Gayle, Crystal *WhoAm 94*
Gayle, Emma 1928- *WrDr 94*
Gayle, Gibson, Jr. 1926- *WhoAm 94*
Gayle, Helene Doris 1955- *WhoBlA 94*
Gayle, Henry K. 1910- *EncSF 93*
Gayle, Irving Charles 1920-1983 *WhoBlA 94N*
Gayle, Jackie 1928- *WhoCom*
Gayle, Jackie 1929- *WhoHol 92*
Gayle, Joseph Central, Jr. 1942- *WhoScEn 94*
Gayle, Lucille Jordan 1920- *WhoBlA 94*
Gayle, Monica *WhoHol 92*
Gayle, Shaun Lanard 1962- *WhoAm 94*
Gayles, Franklin Johnson *WhoBlA 94*
Gayles, Joseph Nathan, Jr. *WhoAm 94*
Gayles, Joseph Nathan Webster, Jr. 1937- *WhoBlA 94*
Gayles, Lindsey, Jr. 1953- *WhoBlA 94*
Gayles-Felton, Anne Richardson 1923- *WhoBlA 94*
Gayle-Thompson, Delores J. 1938- *WhoBlA 94*
Gayley, James 1855-1920 *EncABHB 9 [port]*
Gaylin, Ned L. 1935- *WhoAm 94*
Gaylin, Willard 1925- *WhoAm 94, WrDr 94*
Gaylor, Adolph Darnell 1950- *WhoBlA 94*
Gaylor, Diane Marie 1938- *WhoMW 93*
Gaylor, Donald Hughes 1926- *WhoAm 94, WhoScEn 94*
Gaylor, James Leroy 1934- *WhoScEn 94*
Gaylor, Walter 1913- *WhoWest 94*
Gaylord, Albert Stanley 1942- *WhoAmL 94, WhoWest 94*
Gaylord, Edson I. *WhoScEn 94*
Gaylord, Edward Lewis 1919- *WhoAm 94, WhoFI 94*
Gaylord, Ellihue, Sr. 1922- *WhoBlA 94*
Gaylord, Frank Chalfant, II 1925- *WhoAmA 93*
Gaylord, Mary Fletcher 1915- *WhoAmP 93*
Gaylord, Mitch 1961- *WhoHol 92*
Gaylord, Norman Grant 1923- *WhoAm 94*
Gaylord, Randall Keenan 1957- *WhoAmL 94*
Gaylord, Robert Stephen 1933- *WhoScEn 94*
Gaylord, Sanford Fred 1923- *WhoAm 94*
Gay-Lussac, Joseph Louis 1778-1850 *WorScD [port]*
Gayman, Benjamin Franklin 1947- *WhoAmL 94*
Gaymon, Nicholas Edward 1928- *WhoBlA 94*
Gayne, Clifton Alexander, Jr. 1912-1971 *WhoAmA 93N*
Gayner, Esther K. 1914- *WhoAm 94*
Gaynes, George 1917- *WhoHol 92*
Gaynor, Dean Scott 1964- *WhoFI 94, WhoWest 94*
Gaynor, Florence Small d1993 *NewYTBS 93 [port]*
Gaynor, Harry J. 1921- *WrDr 94*
Gaynor, James M., Jr. 1943- *WhoAm 94, WhoAmL 94*
Gaynor, Janet d1984 *WhoHol 92*
Gaynor, Joseph 1925- *WhoAm 94, WhoScEn 94, WhoWest 94*
Gaynor, Kevin Allen 1948- *WhoAm 94*
Gaynor, Mitzi 1930- *WhoHol 92*
Gaynor, Mitzi 1931- *IntMPA 94*
Gaynor, Ronald Kevin 1952- *WhoWest 94*
Gaynor, Ruth d1919 *WhoHol 92*
Gaynor, Vere Egerton 1947- *WhoMW 93*
Gayoom, Maumoon Abdul 1937- *IntWW 93*
Gayoso, Antonio 1939- *WhoHisp 94*
Gayre of Gayre and Nigg, Robert *Who 94*
Gayre of Gayre and Nigg, Robert 1907- *WrDr 94*
Gayson, Eunice 1931- *WhoHol 92*
Gaythwaite, John William 1948- *WhoScEn 94*
Gayton, Bertram *EncSF 93*
Gayton, Gary D. 1933- *WhoBlA 94*
Gayton, Joseph W. *WhoHisp 94*
Gayton, Nelson 1963- *WhoHisp 94*
Gayton, Ronald B. 1938- *WhoHisp 94*
Gazabaev, Chakhit 1949- *LoBiDrD*
Gazda, Walter Edward, Jr. 1955- *WhoFI 94*
Gazdar, Gerald James Michael 1950- *Who 94*
Gaze, Gwen *WhoHol 92*
Gaze, Nigel Raymond 1943- *WhoScEn 94*
Gaze, R(aymond) Michael 1927- *WrDr 94*
Gaze, Raymond Michael 1927- *IntWW 93, Who 94*
Gazeley, Barbara Joan 1955- *WhoAmL 94*
Gazelle, Wendy *WhoHol 92*
Gazenko, Oleg Georgievich 1918- *IntWW 93*
Gazinski, Benon 1953- *WhoScEn 94*
Gazit, Shlomo 1926- *IntWW 93*
Gazouleas, Panagiotis J. 1927- *WhoAm 94*
Gaztambide (y Garbayo), Joaquin (Romualdo) 1822-1870 *NewGrDO*
Gaztambide, Mario F. 1945- *WhoHisp 94*
Gaztambide, Mario Francisco, Jr. 1945- *WhoAmP 93*
Gaztambide, Peter *WhoHisp 94*
Gazzaniga, Giuseppe 1743-1818 *NewGrDO*
Gazzaniga, Marietta 1824-1884 *NewGrDO*
Gazzar, Abdel Hadi el 1925- *IntWW 93*
Gazzara, Ben 1930- *IntMPA 94, WhoAm 94, WhoHol 92*
Gazzard, Roy James Albert 1923- *Who 94*
Gazzo, Michael V. 1923- *WhoHol 92*
Gazzola, Charles David 1957- *WhoAmL 94*
Gazzoli, John Joseph, Jr. 1947- *WhoAm 94, WhoAmL 94*
Gbeho, James Victor 1935- *IntWW 93*
Gbewonyo, Sylvestre Kwadzo 1942- *WhoFI 94*
Gbezera-Bria, Michel 1946- *IntWW 93*
Gdlyan, Telman Khorenovich 1940- *IntWW 93, LoBiDrD*
Gdowski, Walter J. 1946- *WhoIns 94*
Ge, Guang Ping 1934- *WhoScEn 94*
Ge, Li-Feng 1947- *WhoScEn 94*
Ge, Weikun 1942- *WhoScEn 94*
Geach, Christine 1930- *WrDr 94*

Geach, Gertrude Elizabeth Margaret Who 94
Geach, Peter (Thomas) 1916- IntWW 93
Geach, Peter Thomas 1916- Who 94
Geadelmann, Patricia Lou WhoMW 93
Geaga, Jaime V. 1953- WhoAsA 94
Geake, Raymond Robert 1936- WhoAmP 93, WhoMW 93
Gealt, Adelheid Maria 1946- WhoAm 94
Gealt, Adelheid Medicus 1946- WhoAmA 93
Gealy, Douglas Edward 1960- WhoMW 93
Gealy, Fred Daniel 1894- WhAm 10
Gealy, Stephen Scott 1952- WhoAmL 94
Gean, Donald H. WhoAmP 93
Geanakoplos, Deno John 1916- WhoAm 94
Geaney, Dennis J(oseph) 1914-1992 ConAu 140
Geannopulos, Nicholas George 1930- WhoAm 94
Gear, Charles William 1935- WhoAm 94
Gear, Josephine 1938- WhoAmA 93
Gear, Kathleen O'Neal 1954- EncSF 93
Gear, Luella d1980 WhoHol 92
Gear, Michael Frederick Who 94
Gear, Sara Moreau 1941- WhoAmP 93, WhoWomW 91
Gear, W. Michael 1955- EncSF 93
Gear, William 1915- Who 94
Gearan, Mark D. WhoAm 94, WhoAmP 93
Geare, John Cullen 1949- WhoWest 94
Gearen, John J. 1943- WhoAm 94, WhoAmL 94
Gearhart, Jane Annette Simpson 1918- WhoAmL 94, WhoWest 94
Gearhart, Marilyn Kaye 1950- WhoMW 93
Gearhart, Marvin 1927- WhoAm 94
Gearhart, May WhoAmA 93N
Gearhart, Robert James, Jr. 1961- WhoWest 94
Gearhart, Sally Miller 1931- EncSF 93
Gearhart, Thomas Lee 1942- WhoAm 94
Gearheart, Bill R 1928- WrDr 94
Gearon, John Michael 1934- WhoAm 94
Gearring, Joel Kenneth 1936- WhoBlA 94
Gearty, Edward Joseph 1923- WhoAm 94, WhoAmP 93
Geary, Anthony 1947- IntMPA 94, WhoHol 92
Geary, Bud d1946 WhoHol 92
Geary, Clarence Butler 1912- WhoBlA 94
Geary, David Leslie 1947- WhoAm 94, WhoFI 94
Geary, Joseph Emmett, Jr. 1939- WhoMW 93
Geary, Maine WhoHol 92
Geary, Patricia (Carol) 1951- WrDr 94
Geary, Paul c. 1961- See Extreme ConMus 10
Geary, Warren Truman 1923- WhoFI 94
Geballe, Ronald 1918- WhoAm 94
Geballe, Theodore Henry 1920- WhoAm 94
Ge Baoquan 1913- WhoPRCh 91
Gebauer, Phyllis DrAPF 93
Gebb, Sheldon A. 1935- WhoAm 94
Gebber, Gerard Lincoln 1939- WhoMW 93
Gebbia, Karen Marie 1958- WhoAmL 94, WhoWest 94
Gebbia, Robert James 1947- WhoFI 94
Gebbie, Katharine Blodgett 1932- WhoScEn 94
Gebbie, Kristine c. 1944- News 94-2 [port]
Gebbie, Kristine M. WhoAmP 93
Gebbie, Kristine Moore 1943- WhoAm 94, WhoScEn 94, WhoWest 94
Gebel, Franz Xaver 1787-1843? NewGrDO
Gebel, Georg 1709-1755 NewGrDO
Gebelein, Richard Stephen 1946- WhoAm 94, WhoAmP 93
Gebel-Williams, Gunther 1934- WhoAm 94
Geber, Anthony 1919- WhoAm 94
Geber, Hana 1910- WhoAmA 93N
Gebert, Carl Junior 1937- WhoWest 94
Gebhard, Bob WhoAm 94, WhoWest 94
Gebhard, David 1927- WhoAm 94, WhoAmA 93
Gebhard, David Fairchild 1925- WhoScEn 94
Gebhard, Roger Lee 1945- WhoMW 93
Gebhardt, Frank d1951 WhoHol 92
Gebhardt, Fred 1925- IntMPA 94
Gebhardt, George M. d1919 WhoHol 92
Gebhardt, Joseph Davis 1946- WhoAmP 93
Gebhardt, Robert Charles 1937- WhoAmL 94
Gebhardt, Roland 1939- WhoAmA 93
Gebhart, Albert d1950 WhoHol 92
Gebhart, Carl Grant 1926- WhoAm 94
Gebler, Carlo (Ernest) 1954- WrDr 94
Gébler, Ernest 1915- WrDr 94
Ge Bo WhoPRCh 91
Gebuhr, Otto d1954 WhoHol 92
Gecau, Kimani J. 1947- WhoBlA 94
Gecht, Martin Louis 1920- WhoAm 94
Gechtoff, Sonia 1926- WhoAm 94, WhoAmA 93
Geck, Francis Joseph 1900- WhoAmA 93, WhoMW 93
Geckle, George Leo, III 1939- WhoAm 94
Geckle, Robert Alan 1944- WhoAm 94
Geckler, Richard Delph 1918- WhoAm 94
Ge Cuilin 1930- BlmGWL
Geczik, Ronald Joseph 1933- WhoScEn 94
Gedda, Nicolai 1925- IntWW 93
Gedda, Nicolai (Harry Gustaf) 1925- NewGrDO
Geddes, Baron 1937- Who 94
Geddes, Alexander MacIntosh 1934- Who 94
Geddes, Barbara Sheryl 1944- WhoWest 94
Geddes, Charles Lynn 1928- WhoWest 94
Geddes, Ford Irvine 1913- IntWW 93, Who 94
Geddes, Gary 1940- ConAu 140, WrDr 94
Geddes, George WhAmRev
Geddes, Jane 1960- WhoAm 94
Geddes, LaDonna McMurray 1935- WhoMW 93
Geddes, LaNelle Evelyn 1935- WhoAm 94
Geddes, Leslie Alexander 1921- WhoAm 94
Geddes, Michael Dawson 1944- Who 94
Geddes, Paul 1922- WrDr 94
Geddes, Reay Who 94
Geddes, (Anthony) Reay (Mackay) 1912- Who 94
Geddes, Robert 1923- WhoAm 94
Geddes, Robert C. 1927- WhoAmP 93
Geddes, Robert Dale 1938- WhoAm 94, WhoAmL 94
Geddes, William George Nicholson 1913- Who 94
Geddie, John Jay 1937- WhoAmP 93
Geddie, Lemuel Gray, Jr. 1945- WhoAmL 94
Geddie, Thomas Edwin 1930- WhoFI 94
Geddy, Vernon Meredith, Jr. 1926- WhoAm 94
Gede, Thomas Frederick 1948- WhoAmP 93
Gedeon 1929- LoBiDrD
Gedeon, Lucinda Heyel 1947- WhoAmA 93
Gedgaudas, Eugene 1924- WhoAm 94
Gedge, Pauline 1945- BlmGWL
Gedike, Alexander Fyodorovich 1877-1957 NewGrDO
Gedlen, James Martin 1946- WhoAmL 94
Gedling, Donnie 1939- WhoAmP 93
Gedling, Raymond 1917- Who 94
Gedrick, Jason 1965- WhoHol 92
Geduld, Emanuel Edward 1943- WhoFI 94
Geduld, Harry M(aurice) 1931- ConAu 42NR
Geduldig, Alfred 1936- WhoAm 94
Gee, Al 1942- WhoBlA 94
Gee, Anthony Hall 1948- Who 94
Gee, Arthur 1937- WhoAsA 94
Gee, Charlotte IntMPA 94
Gee, Chuck Yim 1933- WhoFI 94, WhoWest 94
Gee, David Charles Laycock 1947- Who 94
Gee, David Stephenson 1944- Who 94
Gee, Dolly M. 1959- WhoAsA 94
Gee, Earl Justin 1953- WhoAmP 93
Gee, Edwin Austin 1920- IntWW 93
Gee, Elwood Gordon 1944- WhoAm 94
Gee, Gayle Catherine 1934- WhoAmP 93
Gee, Geoffrey 1910- IntWW 93, Who 94
Gee, George d1959 WhoHol 92
Gee, Gregory Williams 1948- WhoAm 94
Gee, Helen WhoAmA 93
Gee, James David 1934- WhoAm 94
Gee, James Gilliam 1896- WhAm 10
Gee, Juliet Leslie 1954- WhoAmL 94
Gee, Li-Lan WhoAmA 93
Gee, Maggie 1948- BlmGWL, EncSF 93
Gee, Maggie (Mary) 1948- WrDr 94
Gee, Matthew Lane 1959- WhoAmL 94
Gee, Maurice (Gough) 1931- EncSF 93, RfGShF, WrDr 94
Gee, Montgomery M. 1948- WhoAsA 94
Gee, Norman F. 1940- WhoAsA 94
Gee, Richard 1942- Who 94
Gee, Robert LeRoy 1926- WhoAm 94, WhoMW 93
Gee, Robert W. WhoAsA 94
Gee, Shirley 1932- ConDr 93, WrDr 94
Gee, Steven Mark 1953- Who 94
Gee, Terry W. 1940- WhoAmP 93
Gee, Thomas Gibbs WhoAmP 93
Gee, Thomas Gibbs 1925- WhoAm 94
Gee, Timothy Hugh 1936- Who 94
Gee, Virginia Catherine 1941- WhoAsA 94
Gee, Walter 1927- WhoAmP 93
Gee, William Rowland, Jr. 1940- WhoBlA 94
Gee, Yun 1906-1963 WhoAmA 93N
Gee, Zand F. 1955- WhoAsA 94
Geefen, Terence John 1921- Who 94
Geehan, Robert William 1909-1990 WhAm 10
Geehr, Richard S. 1938- WrDr 94
Geeker, Nicholas Peter 1944- WhoAm 94
Geelan, Peter Brian Kenneth 1929-1992 WhAm 10
Geelong, Bishop of Who 94
Geens, Andre 1941- IntWW 93
Geens, Gaston 1931- IntWW 93
Geentiens, Gaston Petrus, Jr. 1935- WhoFI 94
Geer, Charles Edward 1952- WhoMW 93
Geer, Ellen 1941- WhoHol 92
Geer, Jack Charles 1927- WhoAm 94
Geer, James Hamilton 1924- WhoAm 94
Geer, James Hamilton, Jr. 1948- WhoAmL 94
Geer, John Farr 1930- WhoAm 94
Geer, John William 1952- WhoFI 94
Geer, Kevin 1954- WhoHol 92
Geer, Lennie d1989 WhoHol 92
Geer, Raleigh WhoHol 92
Geer, Ronald Lamar 1926- WhoAm 94
Geer, Stephen DuBois 1930- WhoAm 94
Geer, Will d1978 WhoHol 92
Geerdes, James 1924- WhoAm 94
Geering, Ian Walter 1947- Who 94
Geering, R(onald) G(eorge) 1918- WrDr 94
Geerlings, Gerald Kenneth 1897- WhoAm 94, WhoAmA 93
Geerlings, Peter Johannes 1939- WhoScEn 94
Geers, Thomas Lange 1939- WhoAm 94
Geertsma, Robert Henry 1929- WhoAm 94
Geertz, Clifford 1926- IntWW 93
Geertz, Clifford (James) 1926- WrDr 94
Geertz, Clifford James 1926- WhoAm 94
Geesaman, Donald Franklin 1949- WhoMW 93
Geeseman, Robert George 1944- WhoAmL 94
Geesey, Titus Cornelius 1893-1969 WhoAmA 93N
Geeslin, Bailey M. 1938- WhoAm 94
Geeslin, Lee Gaddis 1920- WhoAmA 93
Geeson, Judy 1948- IntMPA 94, WhoHol 92
Geeson, Sally WhoHol 92
Geewax, John Julius 1956- WhoFI 94
Geffe, Kent Lyndon 1957- WhoMW 93
Geffen, David NewYTBS 93 [port]
Geffen, David 1943- IntMPA 94, IntWW 93, WhoAm 94
Geffen, Sidney d1986 WhoHol 92
Geffert, Harry 1934- WhoAmA 93
Geffner, Deborah 1953- WhoHol 92
Geffner, Donna Sue 1946- WhoAm 94
Gefke, Henry Jerome 1930- WhoAm 94
Gefter, Judith Michelman WhoAmA 93
Gefter, Mikhail Yakovlevich 1918- IntWW 93, LoBiDrD
Gefter, William Irvin 1915- WhoAm 94
Gegauff, Paul d1983 WhoHol 92
Gegauff, Paul 1922-1983 IntDcF 2-4
Gegesi Kiss, Pal 1900- IntWW 93
Geghman, Yahya Hamoud 1934- IntWW 93
Ge Guilin 1941- WhoPRCh 91
Geh, Hans-Peter 1934- IntWW 93
Geha, Alexander Salim 1936- WhoAm 94, WhoMW 93
Geha, Joseph (A.) 1944- WrDr 94
Gehl, Eugene Othmar 1923- WhoAm 94
Gehlert, Donald Richard 1958- WhoScEn 94
Gehlhoff, Walter 1922- IntWW 93
Gehling, Michael Paul WhoFI 94, WhoScEn 94
Gehlsen, Troy Reynold 1967- WhoMW 93
Gehm, David Eugene 1952- WhoMW 93
Gehm, Denise Charlene 1951- WhoAm 94
Gehman, Bruce Lawrence 1937- WhoScEn 94
Geho, Walter Blair 1939- WhoScEn 94
Ge Hongsheng 1931- IntWW 93, WhoPRCh 91
Gehot, Joseph 1756-c. 1820 NewGrDO
Gehr, Mary WhoAm 94
Gehr, Mary (Ray) WhoAmA 93
Gehr, Thomas Yeats, Jr. 1953- WhoMW 93
Gehrels, Jurgen Carlos 1935- Who 94
Gehres, Eleanor Agnew Mount 1932- WhoWest 94
Gehres, James 1932- WhoAmL 94, WhoWest 94
Gehres, Walter Arnold 1920- WhoAmP 93
Gehrig, Edward Harry 1925- WhoAm 94
Gehrig, James Joseph 1921- WhoAmP 93
Gehrig, Leo Joseph 1918- WhoAm 94
Gehrig, Lou d1941 WhoHol 92
Gehrig, Michael Ford 1947- WhoAmL 94
Gehring, David Austin 1930- WhoAm 94, WhoScEn 94
Gehring, Frederick William 1925- WhoAm 94, WhoMW 93
Gehring, George Joseph, Jr. 1931- WhoScEn 94, WhoWest 94
Gehring, George Michael 1958- WhoWest 94
Gehring, Gillian Anne 1941- IntWW 93
Gehring, Perry James 1936- WhoAm 94
Gehring, Richard Webster 1927- WhoScEn 94
Gehring, Ronald Kent 1941- WhoAmL 94
Gehring, Ted WhoHol 92
Gehring, Walter Jakob 1939- IntWW 93
Gehringer, Charlie 1903-1993 NewYTBS 93 [port]
Gehringer, Richard George 1949- WhoAm 94, WhoFI 94
Gehrke, Allen Charles 1934- WhoAm 94
Gehrke, Charles William 1917- WhoAm 94
Gehrke, Douglas Edward 1957- WhoMW 93
Gehrke, Karen Marie 1940- WhoMW 93
Gehrke, Robert James 1940- WhoWest 94
Gehrlein, Michael Timothy 1966- WhoScEn 94
Gehrung, Jean d1938 WhoHol 92
Gehry, Frank O(wen) 1929- WhoAmA 93
Gehry, Frank Owen 1929- AmCulL, IntWW 93, WhoAm 94
Gehrz, Robert Douglas 1944- WhoMW 93
Gehrz, Robert Gustave 1915- WhoAm 94
Geib, George Winthrop 1939- WhoMW 93
Geib, Philip Oldham 1921- WhoAm 94
Geibel, Emanuel 1815-1884 DcLB 129 [port]
Geiduschek, E(rnest) Peter 1928- IntWW 93
Geiduschek, Ernest Peter 1928- WhoAm 94
Geier, Chester S. 1921-1991 EncSF 93
Geier, George 1918- WhoAm 94
Geier, Gerhard 1935- WhoScEn 94
Geier, James Aylward Develin 1925- WhoAm 94, WhoMW 93
Geier, James Thomas 1959- WhoMW 93
Geier, Joan Austin DrAPF 93
Geier, Mark Robin 1948- WhoAm 94
Geier, Philip Henry, Jr. 1935- WhoAm 94, WhoFI 94
Geiersbach, Ronald Paul 1952- WhoAmL 94
Geigel, Kenneth Francis 1938- WhoHisp 94
Geiger, Alexander 1950- WhoAmL 94
Geiger, Allen Richard 1951- WhoWest 94
Geiger, Daniel Jay 1949- WhoScEn 94
Geiger, David Nathaniel 1933- WhoBlA 94
Geiger, Edith Rogers 1912- WhoAmA 93
Geiger, Elizabeth De Chamisso WhoAmA 93N
Geiger, Gene Edward 1928- WhoAm 94
Geiger, Glenn Charles 1952- WhoAm 94
Geiger, Hans Wilhelm WorInv
Geiger, Hans Wilhelm 1882-1945 WorScD
Geiger, Helmut 1928- IntWW 93
Geiger, Herman d1966 WhoHol 92
Geiger, James Norman 1932- WhoAmL 94
Geiger, Joseph Francis 1941- WhoFI 94
Geiger, Ken 1958- WhoAm 94
Geiger, Louis Charles 1921- WhoScEn 94
Geiger, Louis George 1913- WhoAm 94
Geiger, Mark Watson 1949- WhoAm 94, WhoFI 94
Geiger, Michaela 1943- WhoWomW 91
Geiger, Phillip Neil 1956- WhoAmA 93
Geiger, Randall L. 1949- WhoAm 94
Geiger, Raymond Aloysius 1910- WhoAm 94
Geiger, Richard Eugene 1943- WhoMW 93
Geiger, Richard Lawrence 1917- WhoAm 94, WhoFI 94
Geiger, Robert Keith 1923- WhoAm 94
Geiger, Victor Alan 1948- WhoAm 94
Geihs, Frederick Siegfried 1935- WhoAm 94, WhoAmL 94, WhoFI 94, WhoWest 94
Geijo, Fernando Antonio 1955- WhoScEn 94
Geiken, Alan Richard 1923- WhoWest 94
Geikie, James Murdoch 1839-1915 DcNaB MP
Geiman, J. Robert 1931- WhoAm 94, WhoAmL 94, WhoMW 93
Geis, Bernard 1909- WhoAm 94
Geis, Duane Virgil 1923- WhoAm 94
Geis, Gerald E. 1933- WhoAmP 93
Geis, Gilbert Lawrence 1925- WhoAm 94

Geis, Jerome Arthur 1946- *WhoAm 94, WhoAmL 94*
Geis, Milton Arthur 1926- *WhoAmA 93*
Geis, Norman Winer 1925- *WhoAm 94*
Geis, Richard E(rwin) 1927- *EncSF 93*
Geise, Harry Fremont 1920- *WhoFI 94, WhoScEn 94*
Geise, Richard Allen 1945- *WhoScEn 94*
Geise, Sugar d1988 *WhoHol 92*
Geisel, Cameron Meade, Jr. 1937- *WhoAm 94*
Geisel, Charles Edward 1927- *WhoScEn 94*
Geisel, Ernesto 1907- *IntWW 93*
Geisel, Harold Walter 1947- *WhoAm 94*
Geisel, Henry Jules 1947- *WhoAmL 94*
Geisel, Martin Simon 1941- *WhoAm 94, WhoFI 94*
Geisel, Robert Carl 1920- *WhoAmP 93*
Geisel, Thedor Seuss 1904-1991 *WhoAmA 93N*
Geisel, Theodor Seuss 1904-1991 *SmATA 75 [port], WhAm 10, WrDr 94N*
Geiselhart, Lorene Annetta 1929- *WhoMW 93*
Geiselman, Paula Jeanne 1944- *WhoAm 94*
Geisendorfer, James Vernon 1929- *WhoMW 93*
Geisendorfer, Julius d1953 *WhoHol 92*
Geisenheimer, Emile J. 1947- *WhoAm 94*
Geiser, Elizabeth Able 1925- *WhoAm 94*
Geisert, Arthur (Frederick) 1941- *WrDr 94*
Geisert, Arthur Frederick 1941- *WhoAmA 93*
Geisert, Wayne Frederick 1921- *WhoAm 94*
Geishecker, John Andrew, Jr. 1937- *WhoFI 94*
Geisinger, James S. 1953- *WhoFI 94*
Geisinger, Kurt Francis 1951- *WhoAm 94*
Geisler, Ernest Keith, Jr. 1931- *WhoAm 94*
Geisler, Hans Emanuel 1935- *WhoAm 94, WhoMW 93*
Geisler, Jerry Hubert 1934- *WhoAmP 93*
Geisler, Jonathan David 1949- *WhoAm 94*
Geisler, Linus Sebastian 1934- *WhoScEn 94*
Geisler, Nathan David 1946- *WhoFI 94*
Geisler, Norman (Leo) 1932- *WrDr 94*
Geisler, Paul 1856-1919 *NewGrDO*
Geisler, Phyllis Muriel 1924- *WhoWest 94*
Geisler, Rosemary P. 1947- *WhoFI 94*
Geismar, Ludwig Leo 1921- *WrDr 94*
Geismar, Richard Lee 1927- *WhoAm 94*
Geismar, Thomas H. 1931- *WhoAm 94*
Geiss, Janice Marie 1950- *WhoAmL 94*
Geiss, Johannes 1926- *IntWW 93*
Geissbuhler, Arnold 1897- *WhoAmA 93*
Geissbuhler, Stephan 1942- *WhoAm 94*
Geissert, Katy 1926- *WhoAmP 93*
Geissinger, Frederick Wallace 1945- *WhoAm 94, WhoFI 94*
Geissinger, John Blank 1906-1991 *WhAm 10*
Geissler, Heiner 1930- *IntWW 93*
Geissler, Johann Heinrich Wilhelm 1815-1879 *WorInv*
Geissman, Mary Joan 1939- *WhoAmP 93*
Geist, Bill *ConAu 140*
Geist, George F. 1955- *WhoAmP 93*
Geist, Harold 1916- *WrDr 94*
Geist, Jacob Myer 1921-1991 *WhAm 10*
Geist, Jerry Douglas 1934- *WhoWest 94*
Geist, Jill Marie 1959- *WhoMW 93*
Geist, Karin Ruth Tammeus Mcphail 1938- *WhoWest 94*
Geist, Richard A. 1944- *WhoAmP 93*
Geist, Sidney 1914- *WhoAmA 93*
Geist, William E. 1945?- *ConAu 140*
Geistfeld, Ronald Elwood 1933- *WhoAm 94, WhoMW 93*
Geistringer, Marie 1836-1903 *NewGrDO*
Geistweidt, Gerald 1948- *WhoAmP 93*
Geitel, Hans *WorInv*
Geitel, Hans Friedrich 1855-1923 *WorScD*
Geitgey, Doris Arlene 1920- *WhoAm 94*
Geithner, Paul Herman, Jr. 1930- *WhoAm 94*
Geiwitz, James 1938- *WhoScEn 94*
Gejdenson, Sam 1948- *CngDr 93, WhoAm 94, WhoAmP 93*
Ge Ji 1929- *WhoPRCh 91*
Gekas, George 1930- *CngDr 93*
Gekas, George William 1930- *WhoAm 94, WhoAmP 93*
Gekht, Yury Grigorevich 1943- *LoBiDrD*
Gekiere, Madeleine *WhoAmA 93*
Gelatt, Charles Daniel 1918- *WhoAm 94, WhoMW 93*
Gelb, Arthur 1924- *WhoAm 94*
Gelb, Arthur 1937- *WhoAm 94, WhoScEn 94*
Gelb, Bruce S. 1927- *WhoAmP 93*
Gelb, Harold Seymour 1920- *WhoAm 94*
Gelb, Jan 1906-1978 *WhoAmA 93N*
Gelb, Joseph Donald 1923- *WhoAmL 94, WhoFI 94*
Gelb, Joseph W. 1938- *WhoAm 94*
Gelb, Judith Anne 1935- *WhoAm 94, WhoAmL 94*
Gelb, Leslie Howard 1937- *WhoAm 94, WhoAmP 93*
Gelb, Michael H. *WhoScEn 94*
Gelb, Richard Lee 1924- *WhoAm 94, WhoFI 94, WhoScEn 94*
Gelb, Richard Mark 1947- *WhoAmL 94*
Gelb, Victor 1926- *WhoAm 94*
Gelbach, Martha Harvey 1913- *WhoAm 94*
Gelband, Henry 1936- *WhoAm 94*
Gelbard, Fernando 1940- *IntWW 93*
Gelbard, Robert S. *WhoAmP 93*
Gelbard, Robert Sidney 1944- *WhoAm 94*
Gelbart, Abe 1911- *WhoAm 94, WhoScEn 94*
Gelbart, Larry 1925- *IntMPA 94, WhoAm 94, WrDr 94*
Gelbart, Larry 1928- *ConDr 93, IntWW 93*
Gelbein, Jay Joel 1949- *WhoFI 94*
Gelber, Don Jeffrey 1940- *WhoAm 94, WhoAmL 94, WhoWest 94*
Gelber, Herbert D. *WhoAmP 93*
Gelber, Herbert Donald 1932- *WhoAm 94*
Gelber, Jack 1932- *ConDr 93, ConLC 79 [port], IntDcT 2, WhoAm 94, WrDr 94*
Gelber, Louise Carp 1921- *WhoAmP 93*
Gelber, Robert Cary 1951- *WhoAmL 94*
Gelber, Samuel 1929- *WhoAmA 93*
Gelboin, Harry Victor 1929- *WhoScEn 94*
Geldart, Clarence d1935 *WhoHol 92*
Geldart, Donald James Wallace 1938- *WhoAm 94*
Gelder, James R. *WhoIns 94*
Gelder, John William 1933- *WhoAm 94*
Gelder, Michael Graham 1929- *Who 94*
Gelderblom-Lankhout, Hanneke M. 1936- *WhoWomW 91*
Gelderman, Carol (Wettlaufer) 1935- *WrDr 94*
Geldermann Hails, Barbara *WhoAmA 93*
Geldmacher, Robert Carl 1917- *WhoAm 94*
Geldof, Bob 1954- *IntWW 93, Who 94*
Geldon, Fred Wolman 1946- *WhoAmL 94*
Ge Le *WhoPRCh 91*
Gelehrter, Thomas David 1936- *WhoAm 94, WhoScEn 94*
Gelenberg, Alan Jay 1944- *WhoWest 94*
Gelernt, Irwin M. 1935- *WhoScEn 94*
Geleta, Greg *DrAPF 93*
Gelfan, Gregory 1950- *IntMPA 94*
Gelfand, Israel Moiseyevich 1913- *IntWW 93*
Gelfand, Ivan 1927- *WhoAm 94, WhoFI 94, WhoMW 93*
Gelfand, M. David 1949- *WhoAm 94*
Gelfand, Morris Arthur 1908- *WhoAm 94*
Gelfand, Neal 1944- *WhoAm 94*
Gelfman, Robert William 1932- *WhoAm 94*
Gelfond, Rhoda *DrAPF 93*
Gelfond, Stuart Howard 1962- *WhoAmL 94*
Gelhaus, Robert Joseph 1941- *WhoAmL 94*
Gelhorn, Martha *DrAPF 93*
Gelin, Daniel 1921- *WhoHol 92*
Gelin, Daniel Yves 1921- *IntWW 93*
Gelin, Franklin Charles 1945- *WhoWest 94*
Gelin, Nicolas 1726-c. 1779 *NewGrDO*
Gelinas, David L. 1951- *WhoAmP 93*
Gelinas, Gratien 1909- *IntDcT 2, IntWW 93*
Gelinas, Isabelle *WhoHol 92*
Gelinas, John Gerald 1929- *WhoAm 94*
Gelinas, Marc Adrien 1947- *WhoAm 94, WhoFI 94*
Gelinas, Paul Joseph 1914- *WhoScEn 94*
Gelinas, Robert William 1931- *WhoAmA 93*
Gelineau, Louis Edward 1928- *WhoAm 94*
Gelinske, Michelle Marie 1968- *WhoMW 93*
Geliot, Michael 1933- *NewGrDO*
Gelis, James Viron 1959- *WhoMW 93*
Gell, Philip George Houthem 1914- *Who 94*
Gellatly, Michael *WhoAmA 93*
Gellenbeck, Benno d1974 *WhoHol 92*
Geller, A. Neal 1943- *WhoAm 94*
Geller, Brian L. 1948- *IntMPA 94*
Geller, Bruce d1981 *WhoHol 92*
Geller, Daniel Lee 1951- *WhoMW 93*
Geller, Esther 1921- *WhoAm 94, WhoAmA 93*
Geller, Gary Neil 1954- *WhoScEn 94*
Geller, Harold Arthur 1954- *WhoFI 94, WhoScEn 94*
Geller, Jay Hardie 1946- *WhoAmL 94*
Geller, Jeffrey Lawrence 1953- *WhoFI 94*
Geller, Kenneth Steven 1947- *WhoAm 94, WhoAmL 94*
Geller, Margaret Joan 1947- *WhoScEn 94*
Geller, Matthew 1954- *WhoAmA 93*
Geller, Robert James 1937- *WhoAm 94, WhoFI 94*
Geller, Ronald Gene 1943- *WhoAm 94, WhoScEn 94*
Geller, Ruth *DrAPF 93*
Geller, Sandra R. 1949- *WhoAmL 94*
Geller, Seymour 1921- *WhoAm 94*
Geller, Steven Anthony 1958- *WhoAmP 93*
Gellermann, Henry 1912- *WhoAm 94*
Gellert, George Geza 1938- *WhoAm 94*
Gellert, Michael Erwin 1931- *WhoAm 94*
Gellert, Vance F. *WhoAmA 93*
Gelles, Harry 1934- *WhoAm 94*
Gelles, Richard James 1946- *WhoAm 94*
Gellhorn, Alfred 1913- *WhoAm 94*
Gellhorn, Ernest Albert Eugene 1935- *WhoAm 94, WhoAmL 94*
Gellhorn, Martha *IntWW 93*
Gellhorn, Martha c. 1908- *AmSocL, WrDr 94*
Gellhorn, Peter 1912- *Who 94*
Gellhorn, Walter 1906- *WhoAm 94*
Gelli, Bianca 1933- *WhoWomW 91*
Gellineau, Victor Marcel, Jr. 1942- *WhoBlA 94*
Gellis, Abraham J. d1993 *NewYTBS 93*
Gellis, Barrie *DrAPF 93*
Gellis, Roberta (Leah Jacobs) 1927- *WrDr 94*
Gellis, Sandy L. *WhoAmA 93*
Gellis, Sydney Saul 1914- *WhoAm 94*
Gellise, Mary Yvonne 1934- *WhoAm 94*
Gellman, Gloria Gae Seeburger Schick 1947- *WhoFI 94, WhoWest 94*
Gellman, Isaiah 1928- *WhoScEn 94*
Gellman, Jacob *WhAm 10*
Gellman, Nancy Joan 1945- *WhoAmL 94*
Gellman, Yale H. 1934- *WhoAm 94*
Gell-Mann, Murray 1929- *IntWW 93, Who 94, WhoAm 94, WhoScEn 94, WhoWest 94, WorScD, WrDr 94*
Gellner, Ernest (André) 1925- *WrDr 94*
Gellner, Ernest Andre 1925- *IntWW 93, Who 94*
Gelman, Aleksandr Isaakovich 1933 *IntWW 93*
Gelman, Andrew Richard 1946- *WhoAmL 94*
Gelman, David Graham 1926- *WhoAm 94*
Gelman, Kiminko 1966- *WhoHol 92*
Gelman, Larry *WhoHol 92*
Gelman, Larry 1930- *WhoAm 94*
Gelman, Liebe Kazan *DrAPF 93*
Gelman, Mark Lloyd 1959- *WhoAmL 94*
Gelman, Milton 1914-1991 *WhoAmA 93N*
Gelmis, Joseph Stephan 1935- *WhoAm 94*
Gelpi, Albert 1931- *WrDr 94*
Gelpi, Albert Joseph 1931- *WhoAm 94*
Gelpi, Barbara Charlesworth 1933- *WhoAm 94*
Gelpi, C. James 1940- *WhoAmL 94*
Gelpi, Michael Anthony 1940- *WhoWest 94*
Gelpi, William R. 1937- *WhoHisp 94*
Gelsi, Frederick A. *WhoAmP 93*
Gelston, David 1744-1828 *WhAmRev*
Gelston, John Herbert 1949- *WhoScEn 94*
Gelston, Mortimer Ackley 1920- *WhoAmP 93*
Gelt, Howard B. *WhoAmP 93*
Geltman, Edward A. 1946- *WhoAm 94*
Geltman, Lily 1903- *WhoAmA 93*
Geltner, Danita Sue 1952- *WhoAmA 93*
Geltner, Frank Joseph, Jr. 1941- *WhoWest 94*
Geltner, Peter Benjamin 1943- *WhoWest 94*
Geltrude, Daniel John 1965- *WhoFI 94*
Geltser, Ekaterina 1876-1962 *IntDcB [port]*
Geltz, Charles Gottlieb 1896- *WhAm 10*
Geltzer, Robert Lawrence 1945- *WhoAm 94*
Geltzer, Sheila Simon *WhoAm 94*
Gelven, Michael Paul 1946- *WhoFI 94*
Gem, Louis-Adolphe *NewGrDO*
Gem, Richard David Harvey 1945- *Who 94*
Gemayel, Amin 1942- *IntWW 93*
Gemelli, Enrico d1926 *WhoHol 92*
Gemery, Henry Albert 1930- *WhoAm 94*
Gemescu, Virginia *WhoWomW 91*
Gemier, Firmin d1933 *WhoHol 92*
Gemignani, Joseph Adolph 1932- *WhoAm 94, WhoAmL 94*
Gemignani, Michael Caesar 1938- *WhoAm 94*
Geminn, Walter Lawrence, Jr. 1959- *WhoScEn 94*
Gemma, Giuliano 1938- *WhoHol 92*
Gemma, John P. 1939- *WhoIns 94*
Gemma, Peter B., Jr. 1950- *WhoAmP 93*
Gemma, Peter Benedict, Jr. 1950- *WhoFI 94*
Gemmell, David A. 1948- *EncSF 93*
Gemmell, Don 1903- *WhoHol 92*
Gemmell, Joseph Paul 1935- *WhoAm 94*
Gemmell, Kathleen *DrAPF 93*
Gemmell-Akalis, Bonni Jean 1950- *WhoMW 93*
Gemmett, Robert James 1936- *WhoAm 94*
Gemmill, Elizabeth H. 1945- *WhoAmL 94*
Gemmill, Robert Andrew 1911- *WhAm 10*
Gemora, Charlie d1961 *WhoHol 92*
Gems, Jonathan (Malcolm Frederick) 1952- *ConDr 93*
Gems, Pam 1925- *BlmGEL, BlmGWL, WrDr 94*
Gems, (Iris) Pam(ela) 1925- *ConDr 93*
Gemsa, Diethard 1937- *WhoScEn 94*
Gemser, Laura *WhoHol 92*
Gen, Martin 1926- *WhoFI 94*
Gen, Nikolai Leonidovich 1958- *LoBiDrD*
Genabith, Richard Carl 1946- *WhoAmL 94*
Genalo, Robert James 1954- *WhoFI 94*
Genaro, Donald Michael 1932- *WhoFI 94, WhoScEn 94*
Genaro, Joseph M. 1930- *WhoHisp 94*
Genaro, Tony *WhoHol 92*
Genauer, Emily *WhoAmA 93, WrDr 94*
Genberg, Ira 1947- *WhoAmL 94*
Gencarelli, Jane B. 1929- *WhoAmP 93*
Gencer, Leyla 1924- *NewGrDO*
Genco, Ralph Joseph 1947- *WhoMW 93*
Genco, Robert Joseph 1938- *WhoAm 94*
Gendece, Brian 1956- *IntMPA 94*
Gendel, Eugene B. 1948- *WhoWest 94*
Gendel, Mike d1985 *WhoHol 92*
Gendell, Gerald Stanleigh 1929- *WhoAm 94*
Gendelman, Howard Eliot 1954- *WhoScEn 94*
Genders, Roger Alban Marson 1919- *Who 94*
Gendreau-Massaloux, Michele 1944- *IntWW 93*
Gendron, Francois-Eric *WhoHol 92*
Gendron, Joseph Saul 1938- *WhoAmP 93*
Gendron, Pierre d1956 *WhoHol 92*
Genee, Adeline 1878-1970 *IntDcB [port]*
Genee, (Franz Friedrich) Richard 1823-1895 *NewGrDO*
Geneen, Harold Sydney 1910- *IntWW 93*
Genega, Paul *DrAPF 93*
Genega, Stanley G. *WhoScEn 94*
Genel, Myron 1936- *WhoAm 94, WhoScEn 94*
Gener, Jose M. *WhoHisp 94*
Generali, Pietro 1773-1832 *NewGrDO*
General Idea *WhoAmA 93*
Generes, Tasker 1942- *WhoHisp 94*
Generous, Eric Yves Jacques 1960- *WhoFI 94*
Genesen, Judith Levin 1932- *WhoAm 94*
Genesen, Louis 1926- *WhoAm 94*
Genest, Emile *WhoHol 92*
Genest, Jacques 1919- *WhoAm 94*
Genest, Veronique *WhoHol 92*
Genet *GayLL*
Genet, Jean d1986 *WhoHol 92*
Genet, Jean 1910-1986 *GayLL, IntDcT 2 [port]*
Genet, Jean Pierre 1942- *WhoScEn 94*
Genetet, Bernard 1931- *WhoScEn 94*
Genetski, Robert James 1942- *WhoAm 94*
Geneville, Geoffrey de d1314 *DcNaB MP*
Genevois, Simone *WhoHol 92*
Geng, Shu 1942- *WhoAsA 94*
Geng, Thomas William 1958- *WhoAmP 93*
Geng Biao 1909- *WhoPRCh 91 [port]*
Genge, Kenneth Lyle *Who 94*
Genge, Mark 1927- *Who 94*
Genge, Paul d1988 *WhoHol 92*
Genge, William Harrison 1923- *WhoAm 94, WhoFI 94*
Gengel, Gary Paul 1959- *WhoAmL 94*
Geng Gengshan *WhoPRCh 91*
Genghis Khan c. 1162-1227 *HisWorL [port], WhWE*
Gengler, M. Jeanne 1912- *WhoAm 94*
Gengor, Virginia Anderson 1927- *WhoFI 94, WhoWest 94*
Geniat, Gilberte d1986 *WhoHol 92*
Geniat, Marcelle d1959 *WhoHol 92*
Geniesse, Robert John 1929- *WhoAm 94*
Genillard, Robert Louis 1929- *IntWW 93*
Genin, Roland 1927- *WhoAm 94, WhoFI 94*
Genini, Ronald Walter 1946- *WhoWest 94*
Genis, Vladimir I. 1946- *WhoScEn 94*
Geniusz, Robert Myles 1948- *WhoAmA 93*
Genk, Lori A. 1957- *WhoIns 94*
Genkin, Barry Howard 1949- *WhoAm 94, WhoAmL 94*
Genkin, Jonathan 1957- *WhoAmA 93*
Genkin, Steven S. 1957- *WhoAmL 94*
Genkins, Gabriel 1928- *WhoAm 94*

Georges, (Philip) Telford 1923- Who 94
Georgesco, Victor 1948- WhoFI 94
Georgescu, Florin 1953- IntWW 93
Georgescu, Peter Andrew 1939- IntWW 93, WhoAm 94, WhoFI 94
Georgescu, Valeriu C. d1993 NewYTBS 93
Georgeson, Tom WhoHol 92
Georges-Picot, Olga 1944- WhoHol 92
Georgi, Yvonne 1903-1975 IntDcB [port]
Georgiade, Nicholas George 1918- WhoAm 94
Georgiades, Gabriel George 1956- WhoWest 94
Georgiades, William Den Hartog 1925- WhoAm 94
Georgiadis, Nicholas 1925- NewGrDO
Georgiana, John Thomas 1942- WhoMW 93, WhoScEn 94
Georgieff, Gregory 1942- WhoFI 94
Georgine, Robert A. WhoIns 94
Georgine, Robert Anthony 1932- WhoAm 94
Georgius, John R. 1944- WhoAm 94, WhoFI 94
Georgopapadakos, Michael Agis 1947- WhoFI 94
Georgopoulos, Maria 1949- WhoAm 94
Gephardt, Richard A. 1941- NewYTBS 93 [port]
Gephardt, Richard Andrew 1941- IntWW 93, WhoAm 94, WhoAmP 93, WhoMW 93
Gephardt, Richrd A. 1941- CngDr 93
Geppaart, Chris P. A. 1931- IntWW 93
Geppert, Edward James, Jr. 1947- WhoMW 93
Geppert, Walter 1939- IntWW 93
Gepponi, Angelo 1911- WhoAmA 93
Ger, Shaw-Shyong 1959- WhoFI 94, WhoWest 94
Geraci, F. Phillip 1931- WhoAm 94
Geraci, Lucian Arthur 1923- WhoAmA 93
Geraghty, Carmelita d1966 WhoHol 92
Geraghty, Jeanne WhoAmP 93
Geraghty, Kenneth George 1950- WhoAm 94
Geraghty, Tom d1945 WhoHol 92
Geraghty, Tom d1985 WhoHol 92
Geraint, Baron 1925- Who 94
Gerald, Ara d1957 WhoHol 92
Gerald, Arthur Thomas, Jr. 1947- WhoBlA 94
Gerald, Barry 1934- WhoAm 94
Gerald, Gilberto Ruben 1950- WhoBlA 94
Gerald, Helen IntMPA 94
Gerald, Jim d1958 WhoHol 92
Gerald, John Bart DrAPF 93
Gerald, Melvin Douglas, Sr. 1942- WhoBlA 94
Gerald, Michael Charles 1939- WhoAm 94
Gerald, Nash Ogden 1946- WhoScEn 94
Gerald, William 1918- WhoBlA 94
Geraldo, Manuel Robert 1950- WhoBlA 94
Geraldson, Jodi Lynn 1965- WhoFI 94
Geraldson, Raymond I. 1911- WhoAm 94
Geraldson, Raymond I., Jr. 1940- WhoAmL 94, WhoMW 93
Geran, Joseph, Jr. 1945- WhoAmA 93, WhoBlA 94
Gerard, Baron 1949- Who 94
Gerard, Charles WhoHol 92
Gerard, Conrad Alexandre 1729-1790 AmRev, WhAmRev [port]
Gerard, Emanuel 1932- WhoAm 94
Gerard, Fred N. 1930- WhoAmL 94
Gerard, Geoffrey Who 94
Gerard, (William) Geoffrey 1907- Who 94
Gerard, Gil 1940- WhoHol 92
Gerard, Gil 1943- IntMPA 94
Gerard, James Wilson 1935- WhoAm 94
Gerard, Jean B. S. 1938- WhoAmP 93
Gerard, Jean Broward Shevlin 1938- WhoAm 94
Gerard, Jim DrAPF 93
Gerard, Jules Bernard 1929- WhoAm 94
Gerard, Kenneth Foster 1953- WhoFI 94
Gerard, Lillian 1914- IntMPA 94
Gerard, Mark Edward 1952- WhoScEn 94
Gerard, Paula (Renison) 1907-1991 WhoAmA 93N
Gerard, Philip DrAPF 93
Gerard, Philip C. 1946- WhoAm 94, WhoAmL 94
Gerard, Philip R. 1913- IntMPA 94
Gerard, Ralph Joseph 1948- WhoMW 93
Gerard, Rolf 1909- NewGrDO
Gerard, Ronald 1925- Who 94
Gerard, Roy Dupuy 1931- WhoAm 94
Gerard, Stephen Stanley 1936- WhoAmL 94
Gerard, Susan WhoAmP 93
Gerard, Teddie d1942 WhoHol 92
Gerard, W. Gene 1932- WhoAm 94, WhoFI 94
Gerard, Whitney Ian 1934- WhoAm 94
Gerardi, Roy G., Jr. 1948- WhoScEn 94
Gerardia, Helen WhoAmA 93N
Gerardino de Benítez, Nivia 1932- WhoHisp 94
Gerard-Pearse, John Roger Southey 1924- Who 94
Geras, Adele (Daphne) 1944- TwCYAW
Geras, Adele (Daphne Weston) 1944- WrDr 94
Geras, Norman (Myron) 1943- WrDr 94
Gerasch, Alfred d1955 WhoHol 92
Gerasch, Thomas Ernest 1949- WhoScEn 94
Geraschenko, Victor Vladimirovich 1937- IntWW 93
Gerashchenko, Viktor Vladimirovich 1937- LoBiDrD
Gerasimov, Gennadi Ivanovich 1930- IntWW 93
Gerasimov, Gennady Ivanovich 1930- LoBiDrD
Gerasimov, Sergei d1985 WhoHol 92
Gerasimov, Valentin Pavlovich 1940- LoBiDrD
Gerassi, John 1931- WrDr 94
Gerathy, E. Carroll 1915- WhoAm 94
Geray, Steven d1973 WhoHol 92
Gerba, Charles Peter 1945- WhoAm 94, WhoScEn 94, WhoWest 94
Gerbarg, Darcy 1949- WhoAmA 93
Gerber, Albert B. 1913- WhoAmL 94
Gerber, Arthur Mitchell 1940- WhoScEn 94
Gerber, Barbara Ann Witter 1934- WhoAm 94
Gerber, Barry Eldon 1942- WhoWest 94
Gerber, Beth Ellen 1956- WhoMW 93
Gerber, Carl Joseph 1934- WhoMW 93
Gerber, Dan DrAPF 93
Gerber, Dan(iel Frank) 1940- ConAu 41NR
Gerber, David IntMPA 94
Gerber, Douglas E 1933- WrDr 94
Gerber, Douglas Earl 1933- WhoAm 94
Gerber, Edward F. 1932- WhoAmL 94
Gerber, Elizabeth Daniel 1940- WhoAmP 93
Gerber, Eugene J. 1931- WhoAm 94, WhoMW 93
Gerber, Heinz Joseph 1924- WhoAm 94
Gerber, Joel 1940- CngDr 93, WhoAm 94, WhoAmL 94
Gerber, John C(hristian) 1908- WrDr 94
Gerber, John Christian 1908- WhoAm 94, WhoMW 93
Gerber, John Jay 1914-1991 WhAm 10
Gerber, Lawrence 1940- WhoAm 94
Gerber, Louis Emil 1930- WhoAm 94, WhoAmL 94
Gerber, Lucille D. 1952- WhoMW 93
Gerber, Merrill Joan DrAPF 93
Gerber, Merrill Joan 1938- WrDr 94
Gerber, Michael Albert 1939- WhoScEn 94
Gerber, Michael H. 1944- IntMPA 94
Gerber, Murray A. WhoAm 94
Gerber, Robert Evan 1947- WhoAm 94, WhoAmL 94
Gerber, Roger Alan 1939- WhoAm 94
Gerber, Sanford Edwin 1933- WhoAm 94
Gerber, Seymour 1920- WhoAm 94
Gerber, Thomas William 1921-1991 WhAm 10
Gerber, William 1908- WrDr 94
Gerber, William Kenton 1954- WhoAm 94
Gerberding, Bette Jean 1933- WhoMW 93
Gerberding, Greta Elaine 1960- WhoAmL 94
Gerberding, Miles Carston 1930- WhoAm 94, WhoAmL 94
Gerberding, William Passavant 1929- WhoAm 94, WhoWest 94
Gerberg, Eugene Jordan 1919- WhoAm 94
Gerberg, Judith Levine 1940- WhoFI 94
Gerberich, William Warren 1935- WhoAm 94
Gerberick, M. Ekola DrAPF 93
Gerberry, Ronald Vincent 1953- WhoAmP 93
Gerbi, Susan Alexandra 1944- WhoAm 94
Gerbie, Albert Bernard 1927- WhoAm 94
Gerbino, John 1941- WhoAm 94
Gerbitz, Lois Lynn 1954- WhoMW 93
Gerbner, George 1919- WhoAm 94
Gerbracht 1924- WhoWest 94
Gerbracht, Bob 1924- WhoAmA 93
Gerbracht, Terry Lynne 1955- WhoFI 94
Gerchen, David Kenneth 1955- WhoMW 93
Gerchick, Mark L. 1952- WhoAmL 94
Gerde, Carlyle Noyes 1946- WhoAmL 94
Gerdemann, James Wessel 1921- WhoAm 94
Gerdener, John Gerhard 1949- WhoFI 94
Gerdes, Craig Michael 1966- WhoMW 93
Gerdes, David A. 1942- WhoAmP 93
Gerdes, David Alan 1942- WhoAmL 94
Gerdes, Ingeborg 1938- WhoAmA 93
Gerdes, Neil Wayne 1943- WhoAm 94, WhoMW 93
Gerdes, Ralph Donald 1951- WhoMW 93
Gerdine, Leigh 1917- WhoAm 94, WhoMW 93
Gerding, Benjamin Franklin, III 1916- WhoFI 94
Gerding, Donna Ethel 1922- WhoAmP 93
Gerding, Thomas Graham 1930- WhoScEn 94
Gerdt, Elisaveta 1891-1975 IntDcB
Gerdt, Pavel 1844-1917 IntDcB
Gerdts, Abigail Booth 1937- WhoAmA 93
Gerdts, William H. 1929- WhoAmA 93
Gerdts, William Henry 1929- WhoAm 94
Gere, James Monroe 1925- WhoAm 94
Gere, John Arthur Giles 1921- Who 94
Gere, Richard 1949- IntMPA 94, IntWW 93, Who 94, WhoAm 94, WhoHol 92
Gereighty, Andrea S. DrAPF 93
Gerek, William Michael 1950- WhoAm 94
Geremek, Bronislaw 1932- IntWW 93
Geren, Brenda L. 1950- WhoFI 94
Geren, Gerald S. 1939- WhoAmL 94, WhoFI 94
Geren, Pete WhoAmP 93
Geren, Pete 1952- CngDr 93
Geren, Preston 1952- WhoAm 94
Geren, Preston Murdoch, Jr. 1923- WhoAm 94
Gerenday, Laci Anthony De 1911- WhoAmA 93
Gerentz, Sven 1921- IntWW 93
Geret, Georges WhoHol 92
Gerety, Peter Leo 1912- WhoAm 94
Gerety, Robert John 1939- WhoAm 94
Gerety, Tom 1946- WhoAm 94
Gerfen, Henry James 1940- WhoAm 94
Gergacz, John William 1950- WhoMW 93
Gergely, John 1919- WhoScEn 94
Gergely, Mihaly EncSF 93
Gergely, Peter 1936- WhoScEn 94
Gergely, Tomas 1943- WhoScEn 94
Gergen, David 1942- News 94-1 [port]
Gergen, David Richmond 1942- NewYTBS 93 [port], WhoAm 94
Gerges, Abraham G. 1934- WhoAmP 93
Gergess, Antoine Nicolas 1965- WhoScEn 94
Gergiannakis, Anthony Emmanuel 1935- WhoAm 94, WhoWest 94
Gergiev, Valery Abesalomovich 1953- IntWW 93
Gergis, Samir Danial 1933- WhoAm 94, WhoMW 93
Gergiyev, Valery (Abissalovich) 1953- NewGrDO
Gerhard, Derek James 1927- Who 94
Gerhard, Harry E., Jr. 1925- WhoFI 94
Gerhard, Lee Clarence 1937- WhoAm 94, WhoScEn 94
Gerhard, Roberto 1896-1970 NewGrDO
Gerhardi, William 1895-1977 EncSF 93
Gerhardinger, Peter F. 1957- WhoScEn 94
Gerhardsen, Tove Strand 1946- IntWW 93
Gerhardt, Claudia Jay Sadler 1947- WhoMW 93
Gerhardt, Dan W. WhoAmP 93
Gerhardt, Douglas L. WhoScEn 94
Gerhardt, Glenn Rodney 1923- WhoFI 94
Gerhardt, Ida (Gardina Margaretha) 1905- BlmGWL
Gerhardt, Jon Stuart 1943- WhoAm 94, WhoScEn 94
Gerhardt, Lillian Noreen 1932- WhoAm 94
Gerhardt, Paul Louis 1935- WhoFI 94
Gerhardt, Philipp 1921- WhoAm 94, WhoMW 93
Gerhardt, Rosario Alejandrina 1953- WhoScEn 94
Gerhart, Eugene Clifton 1912- WhoAm 94, WhoAmL 94
Gerhart, Frederick John 1946- WhoAm 94, WhoAmL 94
Gerhart, James Basil 1928- WhoAm 94
Gerhart, Peter Milton 1945- WhoAm 94
Gerhart, Ursula Caroline 1927- WhoAm 94
Gerhold, William Henry 1929- WhoAmA 93
Gericke, Paul William 1924- WhoAm 94
Gericke, Philip Otto 1936- WhoWest 94
Gerig, Abner F. 1907- WhoMW 93
Gerig, Roy Nofziger 1947- WhoWest 94
Gerike, Ann Elizabeth 1933- WhoAm 94
Gerike, Ernest Luther 1917- WhoMW 93
Ge-ri-le-tu WhoPRCh 91
Geriner, Richard Martin 1940- WhoFI 94
Geringer, James E. 1944- WhoAmP 93
Geringer, Susan Diane 1954- WhoWest 94
Gerin-Lajoie, Guy 1928- WhoAmA 93
Gerischer, Heinz 1919- IntWW 93
Gerjuoy, Edward 1918- WhoAm 94
Gerkan, Meinhard von IntWW 93
Gerke, Harold Edward 1912- WhoAmP 93
Gerken, George Manz 1933- WhoScEn 94
Gerken, Jeffrey David 1949- WhoMW 93
Gerken, John Raymond, Jr. 1926- WhoAmP 93
Gerken, Robert William Frank 1932- Who 94
Gerken, Walter Bland 1922- WhoAm 94, WhoWest 94
Gerking, Shelby Delos, Jr. 1918- WhoAm 94
Gerl, Barbara 1770-1806 NewGrDO
Gerl, Franz Xaver 1764-1827 NewGrDO
Gerl, James WhoAmP 93
Gerlach, Christopher S. 1952- WhoAmA 93
Gerlach, Don R. 1932- WrDr 94
Gerlach, Franklin Theodore 1935- WhoAmL 94
Gerlach, G. Donald 1933- WhoAm 94
Gerlach, Gary G. 1945- WhoAm 94
Gerlach, James William 1955- WhoAmP 93
Gerlach, John DrAPF 93
Gerlach, John B. 1927- WhoFI 94
Gerlach, Larry R(euben) 1941- WrDr 94
Gerlach, Luther Paul 1930- WhoAm 94
Gerlach, Manfred 1928- IntWW 93
Gerlach, Rebecca Anne 1956- WhoMW 93
Gerlach, Robert C. 1948- WhoAmL 94
Gerlach, Robert Louis 1940- WhoAm 94, WhoScEn 94
Gerlach, Scott B. 1948- WhoIns 94
Gerlach, Thurlo Thompson 1916- WhoScEn 94
Gerlache De Gomery, Adrien-Victor-Joseph, Baron De 1866-1934 WhWE
Gerlick, Helen J. 1931- WhoWest 94
Gerling, Gerard Michael 1939- WhoScEn 94
Gerling, Max Otto 1945- WhoMW 93
Gerling, William Curtis 1937- WhoAmP 93
Gerlits, Francis Joseph 1931- WhoAm 94, WhoAmL 94
Gerlitz, Curtis Neal 1944- WhoFI 94, WhoMW 93
Gerlitz, Dennis Eugene 1937- WhoIns 94
Gerlt, Joseph Luther 1934- WhoMW 93
Germain, Claire Madeleine 1951- WhoAmL 94
Germain, George Sackville 1716-1785 AmRev, WhAmRev [port]
Germain, Gerald 1942- WhoAm 94, WhoFI 94
Germain, Paul 1920- IntWW 93
Germain, Regina 1961- WhoAmL 94
Germain, Sophie 1776-1831 WorScD
Germain Cutler, Lynn 1938- WhoWomW 91
Germaine, Mary 1933- WhoHol 92
German, Aleksey Georgievich 1938- IntWW 93
German, Edward 1862-1936 NewGrDO
German, Edward Cecil 1921- WhoAmL 94
German, G. Michael 1952- WhoAmL 94
German, John George 1921- WhoAm 94
German, Marjorie DaCosta 1932- WhoScEn 94
German, Norman DrAPF 93
German, Norton Isaiah 1933- WhoScEn 94
German, Randall Michael 1946- WhoAm 94, WhoScEn 94
German, Ronald Stephen 1946- WhoAm 94
German, William 1919- WhoAm 94, WhoWest 94
Germane, Gayton Elwood 1920- WhoAm 94
Germani, Fernando 1906- IntWW 93
Germann, Richard Paul 1918- WhoAm 94, WhoFI 94, WhoMW 93
Germann, Steven James 1947- WhoAm 94
Germano, Arthur Charles 1951- WhoFI 94
Germano, Carmen Peter 1924- WhoMW 93
Germano, Guido 1959- WhoWest 94
Germano, Peter B. EncSF 93
Germano, Thomas 1963- WhoAmA 93
Germano, William Paul 1950- WhoAm 94
Germanotta, Jeffrey Steven 1958- WhoFI 94, WhoMW 93
German Reed, Thomas NewGrDO
Germany, Albert 1942- WhoBlA 94
Germany, Daniel Monroe 1937- WhoAm 94
Germany, Sylvia Marie Armstrong 1950- WhoBlA 94
Germeshausen, Kenneth Joseph 1907-1990 WhAm 10
Germi, Pietro d1974 WhoHol 92
Germino, Felix Joseph 1930- WhoMW 93, WhoScEn 94
Germond, Jack 1928- WrDr 94
Germonprez, Valerie d1988 WhoHol 92

Germscheid, Thomas Joseph 1954- WhoAmL 94
Gernaat, John WhoAmP 93
Gernand, Bradley Elton 1964- WhoAm 94
Gerner, Frank Matthew 1961- WhoScEn 94
Gerner, Ken DrAPF 93
Gernes, Julius E. 1939- WhoAmL 94
Gernes, Sonia DrAPF 93
Gernhardt, Henry Kendall 1932- WhoAmA 93
Gernsbacher, Morton Ann 1955- WhoMW 93
Gernsback, Hugo 1884-1967 DcLB 137 [port], EncSF 93
Gernsheim, Helmut (Erich Robert) 1913- WrDr 94
Gernsheim, Helmut Erich Robert 1913- IntWW 93, Who 94
Gerntholz, Gereld F. 1936- WhoAmP 93
Gerntholz, Gereld Felix 1936- WhoMW 93
Gero, Anthony George 1936- WhoFI 94
Gero, George d1993 NewYTBS 93
Gerold, Herman d1920 WhoHol 92
Geroltu WhoPRCh 91
Gerome, Raymond WhoHol 92
Geron, George Henry 1944- WhoAmP 93
Geronimo 1829-1909 HisWorL [port]
Gerosa, Peter Norman 1928- Who 94
Gerow, Edwin Mahaffey 1931- WhoAm 94
Gerow, James A. 1911- WhoAmP 93
Gerpheide, John Henry 1925- WhoWest 94
Gerra, Ralph A., Jr. 1948- WhoAm 94, WhoAmL 94
Gerra, Rosa A. WhoHisp 94
Gerrald, Kathy 1944- WhoAmP 93
Gerrard, A. J. 1944- WrDr 94
Gerrard, Alfred Horace 1899- Who 94
Gerrard, Basil Harding 1919- Who 94
Gerrard, Charles 1887- WhoHol 92
Gerrard, David Keith Robin 1939- Who 94
Gerrard, Douglas d1950 WhoHol 92
Gerrard, Gene d1971 WhoHol 92
Gerrard, John 1944- WrDr 94
Gerrard, John Henry 1920- Who 94
Gerrard, Keith 1935- WhoAm 94
Gerrard, Neil Francis 1942- Who 94
Gerrard, Peter Noel 1930- Who 94
Gerrard, Ronald Tilbrook 1918- Who 94
Gerrard-Wright, Richard Eustace John 1930- Who 94
Gerrare, Wirt 1862- EncSF 93
Gerratana, Theresa Bielinski 1949- WhoAmP 93
Gerretsen, Thom 1952- WhoMW 93
Gerringer, Robert d1989 WhoHol 92
Gerrish, Brian Albert 1931- WhoAm 94, WrDr 94
Gerrish, Catherine Ruggles 1911- WhoFI 94
Gerrish, Flo WhoHol 92
Gerrish, Hollis G. 1907- WhoAm 94, WhoFI 94
Gerritsen, Hendrik Jurjen 1927- WhoAm 94
Gerritsen, Mary Ellen 1953- WhoAm 94
Gerritson, Lisa 1957- WhoHol 92
Gerrity, Daniel Wallace 1948- WhoFI 94
Gerrity, Frank, II 1918- WhoAm 94
Gerrity, Thomas P. 1941- WhoAm 94, WhoFI 94
Gerrodette, Charles Everett 1934- WhoWest 94
Gerrold, David 1944- EncSF 93, WrDr 94
Gerroll, Daniel 1951- WhoHol 92
Gerron, Kurt d1944 WhoHol 92
Gerry, Alex WhoHol 92
Gerry, Elbridge 1744-1814 WhAmRev [port]
Gerry, Elbridge Thomas 1908- WhoAm 94
Gerry, Elbridge Thomas, Jr. 1933- WhoAm 94, WhoFI 94
Gerry, John Francis 1925- WhoAm 94, WhoAmL 94
Gerry, Joseph John 1928- WhoAm 94
Gerry, Martin Hughes, IV 1943- WhoAm 94, WhoAmP 93
Gers, Harvey 1947- WhoMW 93
Gers, Seymour 1931- WhoAm 94
Gersami DrAPF 93
Gersao, Teolinda 1940- BlmGWL [port]
Gersch, Harold Arthur 1922- WhoAm 94, WhoScEn 94
Gerschbacher, Corine Marie 1961- WhoFI 94
Gersh, Bill 1943- WhoAmA 93
Gersh, David Lewis 1942- WhoAm 94, WhoAmL 94
Gershator, David DrAPF 93
Gershator, Phillis DrAPF 93
Gershbein, Leon Lee 1917- WhoAm 94, WhoMW 93
Gershel, Alan M. 1951- WhoAmL 94
Gershengorn, Marvin Carl WhoAm 94, WhoScEn 94
Gershenson, Alan C. 1947- WhoAmL 94
Gershenson, Harry 1902- WhoAm 94
Gershevitch, Ilya 1914- IntWW 93, Who 94
Gershgoren, Sid DrAPF 93
Gershman, Carl Samuel 1943- WhoAm 94
Gershon, Karen ConAu 141
Gershon, Karen 1923- WrDr 94
Gershon, Michael David 1938- WhoAm 94
Gershon, Nina 1940- WhoAm 94, WhoAmL 94
Gershon, Norm 1947- WhoAmP 93
Gershon, William I. 1934- WhoMW 93
Gershowitz, Michael Victor 1942- WhoMW 93
Gershoy, Eugenie 1901-1983 WhoAmA 93N
Gershwin, George d1937 WhoHol 92
Gershwin, George 1898-1937 AmCulL, ConMus 11 [port], NewGrDO
Gershwin, Ira 1896-1983 AmCulL, ConMus 11 [port], NewGrDO
Gersie, Michael H. 1948- WhoIns 94
Gerson, Alan Gerald 1944- WhoAmL 94
Gerson, Betty Lou WhoHol 92
Gerson, Carol Roberts 1948- WhoMW 93
Gerson, Corinne DrAPF 93
Gerson, David 1953- WhoAmP 93, WhoFI 94
Gerson, Donald Franklin 1946- WhoMW 93
Gerson, Elliot F. 1952- WhoIns 94
Gerson, Elliot Francis 1952- WhoAm 94
Gerson, Eva d1959 WhoHol 92
Gerson, Gary Stanford 1945- WhoMW 93
Gerson, Irwin Conrad 1930- WhoAm 94
Gerson, Jerome Howard 1928- WhoAm 94, WhoAmL 94
Gerson, John Henry Cary 1945- Who 94
Gerson, Lowell Walter 1942- WhoMW 93
Gerson, Mark 1921- IntWW 93
Gerson, Mauricio 1953- WhoHisp 94
Gerson, Michael Joel 1951- WhoWest 94
Gerson, Paul d1957 WhoHol 92
Gerson, Ralph Joseph 1949- WhoAm 94, WhoAmL 94
Gerson, Robert Walthall 1935- WhoAm 94
Gerson, Stuart Michael 1944- WhoAm 94, WhoAmL 94
Gersony, Welton Mark 1931- WhoAm 94
Gersovitz, Sarah Valerie WhoAmA 93
Gerst, Hilde W. WhoAmA 93
Gerst, Paul Howard 1927- WhoAm 94
Gerst, Steven Richard 1958- WhoFI 94, WhoScEn 94
Gerstacker, Friedrich 1816-1872 DcLB 129 [port]
Gerstad, John d1981 WhoHol 92
Gerstein, David Brown 1936- WhoAm 94, WhoFI 94
Gerstein, David Steven 1951- WhoAmA 93
Gerstein, Ellen WhoHol 92
Gerstein, Esther 1924- WhoAm 94
Gerstein, Hilda Kirschbaum 1911- WhoFI 94
Gerstein, Irving R. 1942- WhoFI 94
Gerstein, Manny 1939- WhoAmL 94
Gerstein, Mark Bender 1966- WhoScEn 94
Gerstel, Martin Stephen 1941- WhoFI 94
Gersten, Berta d1972 WhoHol 92
Gersten, Jerome William 1917- WhoAm 94
Gerstenberg, Frank Eric 1941- Who 94
Gerstenberg, Richard Charles 1909- Who 94
Gerstenberger, Dean Lee 1948- WhoWest 94
Gerstenberger, Donna 1929- WrDr 94
Gerstenberger, Donna Lorine 1929- WhoAm 94
Gerstenhaber, Ronald Alan 1947- WhoAmP 93
Gerstenmaier, John Herbert 1916-1991 WhAm 10
Gerster, Etelka 1855-1920 NewGrDO
Gerster, Florian 1949- IntWW 93
Gerster, Ottmar 1897-1969 NewGrDO
Gerster, Robert Gibson 1945- WhoAm 94
Gerstle, Frank d1970 WhoHol 92
Gerstler, Amy DrAPF 93
Gerstman, George Henry 1939- WhoAmL 94
Gerstman, Sharon Stern 1952- WhoAmL 94
Gerstmann, Elan 1960- WhoAmL 94
Gerstmayr, John Wolfgang 1949- WhoAm 94
Gerstner, John Joseph 1946- WhoMW 93
Gerstner, Kurt B. 1957- WhoAmL 94
Gerstner, Lou 1942- News 93 [port]
Gerstner, Louis Vincent, Jr. 1942- IntWW 93, NewYTBS 93 [port], WhoAm 94, WhoFI 94
Gerstner, Robert William 1934- WhoAm 94, WhoMW 93, WhoScEn 94
Gert, Bernard 1934- WhoAm 94
Gert, Valeska d1978 WhoHol 92
Gertenbach, Robert Frederick 1923- WhoAm 94
Gerth, Brian Edward 1959- WhoMW 93
Gerth, Donald R. 1928- IntWW 93
Gerth, Donald Rogers 1928- WhoAm 94, WhoWest 94
Gerth, Ruth d1952 WhoAmA 93N
Gertig, June Munford 1943- WhoAm 94
Gertis, Neill Allan 1943- WhoFI 94, WhoScEn 94
Gertler, Alfred Martin 1922- WhoAm 94
Gertler, Menard M. 1919- WhoAm 94, WhoScEn 94
Gertrud von Helfta 1256-1302 BlmGWL
Gertsyk, Adelaida Kazimirovna 1870-1925 BlmGWL
Gertych, Zbigniew 1922- IntWW 93, Who 94
Gertz, Alison 1966-1992 AnObit 1992
Gertz, David Lee 1950- WhoFI 94, WhoWest 94
Gertz, Elmer 1906- ConAu 42NR, WhoAm 94, WhoMW 93
Gertz, Irving 1915- IntMPA 94
Gertz, Jami 1965- IntMPA 94, WhoHol 92
Gertzman, Stephen F. 1946- WhoAmL 94
Gerulaitis, Vitas 1954- BuCMET
Geruson, Richard J. 1957- ConAu 140
Gervais, C(harles) H(enry) 1946- WrDr 94
Gervais, Charles-Hubert 1671-1744 NewGrDO
Gervais, Darwin 1921- WhoFI 94
Gervais, Floyd 1931- WhoAmP 93
Gervais, Generose 1919- WhoAm 94
Gervais, Glen C. 1961- WhoAmP 93
Gervais, John Lewis d1798 WhAmRev
Gervais, Marcel Who 94
Gervais, Michel 1944- WhoAm 94
Gervais, Paul Nelson 1947- WhoAm 94, WhoFI 94
Gervasi, Anne 1947- WhoScEn 94
Gervasi, Frank 1895- WhAm 10
Gerville-Reache, Jeanne 1882-1915 NewGrDO
Gervin, Derrick Eugene 1963- WhoBlA 94
Gervin, George 1952- BasBi, WhoBlA 94
Gervin, Les Stephen 1948- WhoWest 94
Gervinus, Georg Gottfried 1805-1871 DcLB 133 [port]
Gervis Meyrick Who 94
Gerwel, Gert Johannes (Jakes) 1947- IntWW 93
Gerwick, Ben Clifford, Jr. 1919- WhoAm 94
Gerwick-Brodeur, Madeline Carol 1951- WhoWest 94
Gerwin, Ann Wham 1949- WhoAmL 94
Gerwin, Brenda Isen 1939- WhoAm 94
Gerwin, Gary Mark 1955- WhoWest 94
Gerwin, Leslie Ellen 1950- WhoAmL 94
Gery, John DrAPF 93
Gery, Michael E. WhoAmP 93
Gery, Robert Lucian W. Who 94
Gerzina, Gretchen (Aletha) Holbrook 1950- ConAu 140
Gerzso, Gunther 1915- WhoAmA 93
Gesang Doje WhoPRCh 91
Gesang Doje 1936- IntWW 93
Gesch, Roy (George) 1920- WrDr 94
Gescheidle, Randal Alan 1956- WhoWest 94
Gescheidle, Robert Heath 1959- WhoWest 94
Gesell, Gerhard A. d1993 NewYTBS 93 [port]
Geselowitz, David Beryl 1930- WhoScEn 94
Geshell, Richard Steven 1943- WhoWest 94
Ge Shiying WhoPRCh 91
Geske, Norman Albert 1915- WhoAmA 93
Geskin, Ernest Samuel 1935- WhoScEn 94
Gesler, Alan Edward 1945- WhoAmL 94
Gesmer, Henry 1912- WhoAm 94, WhoAmL 94
Gesner, Carol 1922- WrDr 94
Gess, Albin Horst 1942- WhoAmL 94, WhoScEn 94, WhoWest 94
Gess, Denise 1952- WrDr 94
Gess, Nicholas Michael 1955- WhoAmL 94
Gessel, David Jacob 1966- WhoWest 94
Gessel, Stanley Paul 1916- WhoAm 94, WhoWest 94
Gessel, Van Craig 1950- WhoWest 94
Gessner, Adrienne d1987 WhoHol 92
Gessner, Charles Herman 1938- WhoAm 94
Gessner, Lynne 1919- WrDr 94
Gessner, Michael DrAPF 93
Gessner, Richard DrAPF 93
Gessner, Robert Valentine 1948- WhoMW 93
Gessow, Alfred 1922- WhoAm 94
Gest, Howard 1921- WhoAm 94, WhoScEn 94
Gest, Howard David 1952- WhoAm 94
Gest, Inna d1965 WhoHol 92
Gest, Kathryn Waters 1947- WhoAm 94
Gest, Robbie Dale 1964- WhoScEn 94
Gesteland, Robert Charles 1930- WhoAm 94
Gestetner, David 1937- Who 94, WhoFI 94
Gestetner, Jonathan 1940- Who 94
Gestewitz, Friedrich Christoph 1753-1805 NewGrDO
Geston, Mark DrAPF 93
Geston, Mark S(ymington) 1946- EncSF 93, WrDr 94
Geszty, Sylvia 1934- NewGrDO
Getchell, Earle Duncan 1916- WhoAmP 93
Getchey, Ronald D. 1949- WhoAmL 94
Gethers, Peter DrAPF 93
Gethin, Richard (Joseph St. Lawrence) 1949- Who 94
Gething, Richard Templeton 1911- Who 94
Ge Tingsui 1913- WhoPRCh 91
Getis, Arthur 1934- WhoAm 94
Getler, Helen 1925- WhoAmA 93, WhoAmP 93
Getman, Julius (G.) 1931- ConAu 140
Getman, Willard Etheridge 1949- WhoAmL 94
Getnick, Neil Victor 1953- WhoAmL 94
Geto Boys, The ConMus 11 [port]
Getreu, Ian Edwin 1943- WhoWest 94
Getreu, Sanford 1930- WhoWest 94
Getreuer, Kurt Walter 1954- WhoWest 94
Getsi, Lucia C. DrAPF 93
Getsinger, Keith Robert 1964- WhoFI 94
Gettelfinger, Gerald Andrew 1935- WhoAm 94, WhoMW 93
Gettelman, Robin Claire 1952- WhoMW 93
Getten, Thomas Frank 1947- WhoAmL 94
Getter, Gregory R. 1950- WhoMW 93
Getter, Keith Edward 1962- WhoMW 93
Gettig, Martin Winthrop 1939- WhoScEn 94
Getting, Ivan Alexander 1912- WhoAm 94
Gettinger, William d1966 WhoHol 92
Gettings, Don E. 1923- WhoAmP 93
Gettleman, Jeffrey Warren 1946- WhoWest 94
Gettleman, Robert William 1943- WhoAmL 94
Gettler, Benjamin 1925- WhoAm 94, WhoMW 93
Gettler, Michael Leo 1952- WhoMW 93
Gettman, Lorraine WhoHol 92
Gettner, Alan Frederick 1941- WhoAmL 94
Getto, Ernest John 1944- WhoAm 94, WhoAmL 94
Getto, Virgil M. 1924- WhoAmP 93
Getty, Balthazar 1975- WhoHol 92
Getty, Carol Pavilack 1938- WhoAm 94
Getty, Donald 1933- IntWW 93
Getty, Donald Ross 1933- Who 94
Getty, Estelle 1923- IntMPA 94, WhoAm 94, WhoHol 92
Getty, Gordon Peter 1933- WhoAm 94
Getty, J. Paul 1892-1976 WhoAmA 93N
Getty, Jay d1967 WhoHol 92
Getty, Nilda Fernandez 1936- WhoAmA 93
Getz, Christina L. 1964- WhoMW 93
Getz, Don 1920- IntMPA 94
Getz, Donald d1993 IntMPA 94N
Getz, Ernest John 1918- WhoAm 94, WhoAmL 94
Getz, George Fulmer, Jr. 1908-1992 WhAm 10
Getz, Gregory John 1955- WhoAmL 94
Getz, Herbert A. WhoAmL 94
Getz, James Edward 1950- WhoAmL 94, WhoMW 93
Getz, John IntMPA 94
Getz, John 1947- WhoHol 92
Getz, Lowell Vernon 1932- WhoFI 94
Getz, Malcolm 1945- WhoAm 94
Getz, Morton Ernest 1930- WhoScEn 94
Getz, Solomon 1936- WhoFI 94
Getz, Stan 1927-1991 WhAm 10, WhoHol 92
Getzels, Jacob Warren 1912- WhoAm 94
Getzendanner, Susan 1939- WhoAm 94
Getzwiller, Polly 1924- WhoAmP 93
Geusic, Joseph Edward 1931- WhoScEn 94
Geuss, Gary George 1958- WhoAmL 94, WhoWest 94
Geva, Tamara 1904- WhoHol 92
Gevaert, Francois-Auguste 1828-1908 NewGrDO
Gevantman, Judith 1949- WhoAm 94
Geveden, Charles R. 1940- WhoAmP 93
Gevers, Marcia Bonita 1946- WhoAmL 94
Gevitz, Norman Jan 1948- WhoMW 93

Gewanter, Harry Lewis 1950- WhoAm 94
Gewartowski, James Walter 1930- WhoAm 94
Gewecke, Thomas H. 1944- WhoAm 94
Geweke, John Frederick 1948- WhoAm 94
Gewertz, Bruce Labe 1949- WhoAm 94
Gewertz, Kenneth A. WhoAmP 93
Gewertz, Martin Anson 1948- WhoAmL 94
Gewin, James W. 1940- WhoAm 94
Gewirth, Alan 1912- EncEth
Gewirtz, Elliot 1947- WhoAm 94
Gewirtz, Gerry 1920- WhoAm 94
Gewirtz, Paul D. 1947- WhoAm 94
Ge Wujue 1937- IntWW 93, WhoPRCh 91 [port]
Gex, Robert B., IV 1943- WhoAmL 94
Gex, Walter Joseph, III 1939- WhoAm 94, WhoAmL 94
Geye, Susan Marie 1954- WhoMW 93
Geyer, Barbara Ann 1940- WhoAmP 93
Geyer, Carolyn Kay Smith 1936- WhoMW 93
Geyer, Dennis Lynn 1950- WhoWest 94
Geyer, Edward B., Jr. 1929- WhoBlA 94
Geyer, Georgie Anne 1935- WhoAm 94, WrDr 94
Geyer, Harold Carl 1905- WhoAm 94
Geyer, Sidna Priest 1943- WhoMW 93
Geyer, Thomas Powick 1946- WhoAm 94
Geyman, John P 1931- WrDr 94
Geyman, John Payne 1931- WhoAm 94
Gezelter, Robert L. 1959- WhoScEn 94
Ge Zhicheng 1920- WhoPRCh 91 [port]
Gezurian, Dorothy Ellen 1956- WhoFI 94
Gfeller, Donna Kvinge 1959- WhoMW 93, WhoScEn 94
Ghadia, Suresh Kantilal 1948- WhoScEn 94
Ghafar Baba, Abdul 1925- IntWW 93
Ghaffar, Muhammad Abdul 1949- IntWW 93
Ghaffari, Abolghassem 1909- IntWW 93
Ghahramani, Bahador 1944- WhoFI 94
Ghai, Dharam Pal 1936- IntWW 93
Ghai, Om Prakash d1992 IntWW 93N
Ghaidan, Saadoun 1930- IntWW 93
Ghale, Subedar Gaje Who 94
Ghalem, Nadia BlmGWL
Ghali, Amin WhoScEn 94
Ghali, Anwar Youssef 1944- WhoScEn 94
Ghali, Boutros B. Who 94
Ghali, Boutros-Boutros 1922- WhoAm 94
Ghan, Linda (R.) 1947- SmATA 77 [port]
Ghandhi, Sorab K. 1928- WhoAsA 94
Ghandhi, Sorab Khushro 1928- WhoScEn 94
Ghanem, George 1961- WhoFI 94
Ghanem, Mohamed Hafez 1925- IntWW 93
Ghani, Ashraf Muhammad 1931- WhoFI 94, WhoScEn 94
Gharekhan, Chinmaya Rajaninath 1937- IntWW 93
Ghasimi, Mohammad Reza 1947- IntWW 93
Ghausi, Mohammed Shuaib 1930- WhoAm 94, WhoScEn 94
Ghazala, Mohamed Abdel Halim Abu IntWW 93
Ghazali, Salem 1944- WhoScEn 94
Ghazanfar, Shaikh Mohammed 1937- WhoWest 94
Ghazarian, Rouben 1956- WhoScEn 94
Ghazaryan, Yuri 1933- NewGrDO
Ghecas, Anthony George 1961- WhoAmP 93
Ghedini, Giorgio Federico 1892-1965 NewGrDO
Ghee, Marshall Douglas 1945- WhoAmP 93
Ghelderode, Michel de 1898-1962 IntDcT 2
Ghent, Donald Joseph, Jr. 1952- WhoFI 94
Ghent, Henri 1926- WhoAmA 93
Ghent, Henri Hermann 1926- WhoBlA 94
Ghent, Peer 1939- WhoFI 94
Ghent, Robert Maynard, Jr. 1956- WhoScEn 94
Gheorghe, Stefan IntWW 93
Gheorghiu, Ion (Alin) 1929- IntWW 93
Gheorghiu, Mihail Mihnea 1919- IntWW 93
Gheraieb, Abdelkrim 1935- Who 94
Gheraldi, Cesarina d1986 WhoHol 92
Gherardeschi, Filippo Maria 1738-1808 NewGrDO
Gherardi, Piero 1909-1971 IntDcF 2-4
Gherardini, Rinaldo 1657-1707? NewGrDO
Gherlein, Gerald Lee 1938- WhoAmL 94, WhoFI 94
Gherlein, John Harlan 1926- WhoAm 94
Gherlein, John Mills 1955- WhoAmL 94
Gherlone, Mildred Streeter 1925- WhoAmP 93
Gherman, Beverly 1934- WrDr 94
Ghermanoff, George d1965 WhoHol 92
Gherson, Adolph Randolph Albert 1928- IntWW 93
Gherty, John E. 1944- WhoAm 94, WhoFI 94, WhoMW 93
Ghetti, Bernardino Francesco 1941- WhoAm 94
Ghezal, Ahmed 1930- IntWW 93
Ghezzi, Bert(il W.) 1941- WrDr 94
Ghiara, Paolo 1958- WhoScEn 94
Ghiardi, James Domenic 1918- WhoAm 94
Ghiaurov, Nicolai 1929- IntWW 93, NewGrDO, WhoAm 94
Ghiglia, Lorenzo 1936- NewGrDO
Ghiglia, Oscar Alberto 1938- WhoAm 94
Ghigna, Charles DrAPF 93
Ghika, Nicolas 1906- IntWW 93
Ghikas, Panos George WhoAmA 93
Ghikas, Patience Haley WhoAmA 93
Ghim, Thad T. 1939- WhoAsA 94
Ghindia, George William 1958- WhoWest 94
Ghingher, John J., III 1944- WhoAmL 94
Ghini, Massimo WhoHol 92
Ghione, Emilio d1930 WhoHol 92
Ghiorso, Albert 1915- WorScD
Ghiselin, Brewster DrAPF 93
Ghiselin, Brewster 1903- WhoAm 94, WhoWest 94, WrDr 94
Ghisi, Federico 1901-1975 NewGrDO
Ghislanzoni, Antonio 1824-1893 NewGrDO
Ghiuselev, Nicola 1936- IntWW 93
Ghiuselev, Nikola NewGrDO
Ghiz, Joseph Atallah 1945- IntWW 93, Who 94
Ghizikis, Phaidon 1917- IntWW 93
Ghizoni, Cesar Celeste 1945- WhoScEn 94
Ghnassia, Jill Dix 1947- WhoAm 94
Gholson, General James, Jr. 1944- WhoBlA 94
Gholston, Betty J. 1942- WhoBlA 94
Ghorbal, Ashraf IntWW 93
Ghormley, Ralph McDougall 1927- WhoAm 94
Ghorpade, Ajit Kisanrao 1954- WhoScEn 94
Ghose, Rabindra Nath 1925- WhoAm 94, WhoFI 94
Ghose, Zulfikar DrAPF 93
Ghose, Zulfikar 1935- WrDr 94
Ghosh, Amal K. 1931- WhoAsA 94
Ghosh, Amitav 1956- WrDr 94
Ghosh, Amitava 1957- WhoAsA 94
Ghosh, Arun Kumar 1930- WhoFI 94, WhoScEn 94, WrDr 94
Ghosh, Asish 1935- WhoScEn 94
Ghosh, Bhaskar Kumar 1936- WhoAsA 94
Ghosh, Bivas Kanti 1954- WhoAsA 94
Ghosh, Chinmoy 1953- WhoAsA 94
Ghosh, Christopher Paul 1961- WhoAmP 93
Ghosh, Chuni Lal 1948- WhoScEn 94
Ghosh, Deepak Ranjan 1965- WhoScEn 94
Ghosh, Gautam 1950- IntWW 93
Ghosh, Kalyan K. 1938- WhoAsA 94
Ghosh, Kanchan 1966- WhoMW 93
Ghosh, Malathi 1947- WhoScEn 94
Ghosh, Nimai Kumar 1943- WhoAsA 94
Ghosh, Sid 1934- WhoScEn 94
Ghosh, Subhas 1944- WhoAsA 94
Ghosh, Subir 1950- WhoScEn 94
Ghosh, Sujan 1946- WhoAsA 94
Ghosh, Swapan Kumar 1942- WhoAsA 94
Ghoshal, Nani Gopal 1934- WhoAm 94
Ghostley, Alice 1926- IntMPA 94, WhoHol 92
Ghougassian, Joseph 1944- WhoAmP 93
Ghozali, Sid Ahmed 1937- IntWW 93
Ghrib, Mohamed 1943- IntWW 93
Ghrist, John Alton 1950- WhoFI 94
Ghurburrun, Beergoonath 1928- IntWW 93
Ghurburrun, Rabindrah 1929- Who 94
Giacalone, Frank Thomas 1951- WhoFI 94
Giacalone, Vito WhoAmA 93
Giacco, Alexander Fortunatus 1919- WhoAm 94, WhoFI 94, WhoScEn 94
Giacconi, Riccardo 1931- IntWW 93, WhoAm 94, WhoScEn 94
Giachello, Aida L. Maisonet 1945- WhoHisp 94
Giachetti, Fosco d1974 WhoHol 92
Giachetti, Gianfranco d1936 WhoHol 92
Giacobbe, Frederick W. 1943- WhoMW 93
Giacobbe, Maria 1928- BlmGWL
Giacoletto, Joseph Richard 1935- WhoFI 94
Giacoletto, Lawrence Joseph 1916- WhoAm 94
Giacolini, Earl L. WhoFI 94
Giacomelli, Geminiano c. 1692-1740 NewGrDO
Giacomelli, Giorgio 1930- IntWW 93
Giacometti, Annette d1993 NewYTBS 93
Giacometto, Leo A. 1962- WhoAmP 93
Giacomini, Giuseppe 1940- NewGrDO, WhoAm 94
Giacomo, Salvatore di NewGrDO
Giaconi, Luisa 1870-1908 BlmGWL
Giacopini, Dorene Mary 1960- WhoWest 94
Giacosa, (Giuseppe) 1847-1906 IntDcT 2
Giacosa, Giuseppe 1847-1906 NewGrDO
Giaever, Ivar 1929- IntWW 93, Who 94, WhoAm 94, WhoScEn 94, WorScD
Giai, Giovanni Antonio 1690-1764 NewGrDO
Giaimo, Robert N. 1919- WhoAmP 93
Gialanella, Donald G. 1956- WhoAmA 93
Gialanella, Philip Thomas 1930- WhoAm 94, WhoWest 94
Giallanza, Charles Philip 1950- WhoAmL 94
Giallelis, Stathis 1941- WhoHol 92
Gialleonardo, Victor 1928- WhoAm 94
Giallorenzi, Thomas Gaetano 1943- WhoAm 94, WhoScEn 94
Giam, Choo-Seng 1931- WhoAm 94, WhoAsA 94, WhoScEn 94
Giamatti, A. Bartlett 1938-1989 WhAm 10
Giambalvo, Louis WhoHol 92
Giambalvo, Vincent 1942- WhoAm 94
Giambertone, Paul WhoAmA 93
Giambra, Joel A. 1957- WhoAmP 93
Giambra, Leonard Michael 1941- WhoScEn 94
Giambrone, Timothy Paul 1957- WhoFI 94
Giambruni, Tio 1925-1971 WhoAmA 93N
Giammatteo, Hollis DrAPF 93
Giampietro, Isabel WhoAmA 93
Giampietro, Wayne Bruce 1942- WhoAm 94, WhoAmL 94
Giampoli, Roy Bruce 1952- WhoMW 93
Gian, Joe WhoHol 92
Gianakaris, Constantine John 1934- WrDr 94
Gianakos, Cristos 1934- WhoAmA 93
Gianakos, Irene 1954- WhoMW 93
Gianakos, Nicholas 1947- WhoScEn 94
Gianakos, Steve 1938- WhoAmA 93
Gianasi, Rick WhoHol 92
Giancola, Dennis James 1952- WhoMW 93
Giancola, Holly Harrington 1961- WhoFI 94
Giancotti, Francesca Romana 1956- WhoScEn 94
Gianelli, William Reynolds 1919- WhoAm 94
Gianforcaro, Beth Anne 1961- WhoMW 93
Giani, Nini 1904-1972 NewGrDO
Gianinno, Susan McManama 1948- WhoAm 94
Gianino, John Joseph 1935- WhoAm 94, WhoFI 94
Gianlorenzi, Nona Elena 1939- WhoAmA 93
Giannaros, Demetrios Spiros 1949- WhoScEn 94
Giannetti, Louis Daniel 1937- WhoAm 94
Giannetti, Ronald Armand 1946- WhoWest 94
Giannetti, Thomas Leonard 1947- WhoAm 94, WhoAmL 94
Giannettini, Antonio 1648-1721 NewGrDO
Giannetto, Randal J. WhoAmP 93
Giannini, A. James 1947- WhoMW 93, WhoScEn 94
Giannini, Cheryl WhoHol 92
Giannini, Cynthia WhoAm 94
Giannini, David DrAPF 93
Giannini, Dusolina 1902-1986 NewGrDO
Giannini, Ettore d1990 WhoHol 92
Giannini, Gabriel Maria 1905-1989 WhAm 10
Giannini, Giancarlo 1942- IntMPA 94, WhoHol 92
Giannini, Jill Marie 1966- WhoMW 93
Giannini, Matthew Carlo 1950- WhoAmL 94
Giannini, Valerio Louis 1938- WhoAm 94
Giannini, Vittorio 1903-1966 NewGrDO
Gianniny, Omer Allan, Jr. 1925- WhoAm 94
Giannis, Athanassios 1954- WhoScEn 94
Giannopoulos, Joanne WhoMW 93, WhoScEn 94
Gianoli, Paul DrAPF 93
Gianoulakis, John Louis 1938- WhoAmL 94
Giansante, Louis 1952- WhoAmL 94
Gianturco, Carolyn (Margaret) 1934- NewGrDO
Gianturco, Delio E. 1940- WhoAm 94
Gianturco, Maurizio Antonio 1928- WhoAm 94
Gianturco, Paola 1939- WhoFI 94
Gianviti, Francois Paul Frederic 1938- IntWW 93
Giap, Vo Nguyen IntWW 93
Giaquinta, Benjamin E. 1922- WhoAmP 93
Giardina, Denise DrAPF 93
Giardina, James Michael 1949- WhoWest 94
Giardina, Paul Anthony 1949- WhoAm 94
Giardina, Richard Cono 1944- WhoWest 94
Giardini, Felice (de) 1716-1796 NewGrDO
Giardini, Valerie Anne 1949- WhoFI 94
Giarrano, Thomas 1953- WhoFI 94
Giarrocco, Vincent John, Jr. 1958- WhoFI 94
Giarrusso, Giovanni 1939- WhoAm 94
Giarrusso, Michael Thomas 1955- WhoAmP 93
Giauque, Brent J. 1943- WhoAmL 94
Giauque, Gerald Stone 1941- WhoWest 94
Giauque, Richard Wayne 1936- WhoAmL 94
Giay, Giovanni Antonio NewGrDO
Gibala, Louise 1897- WhoAmA 93
Gibala, Ronald 1938- WhoAm 94
Gibaldi, Milo 1938- WhoAm 94
Gibans, James David 1930- WhoAm 94
Gibans, Nina Freedlander 1932- WhoMW 93
Gibault, Pierre 1737-1804 WhAmRev, WhWE
Gibb, Andrew Thomas Fotheringham 1947- Who 94
Gibb, Arthur 1908- WhoAmP 93
Gibb, Barry & Gibb, Maurice & Gibb, Robin WhoHol 92
Gibb, Barry 1946- WhoAm 94
See Also Bee Gees, The WhoHol 92
Gibb, Cynthia 1964- WhoHol 92
Gibb, Don WhoHol 92
Gibb, Francis Ross 1927- IntWW 93, Who 94
Gibb, Ian Pashley 1926- Who 94
Gibb, Lisa Jo Christenson 1961- WhoMW 93
Gibb, Maurice
See Gibb, Barry & Gibb, Maurice & Gibb, Robin WhoHol 92
Gibb, Maurice WhoHol 92
Gibb, Maurice 1949- WhoAm 94
See Also Bee Gees, The WhoHol 92
Gibb, Robert DrAPF 93
Gibb, Robin
See Gibb, Barry & Gibb, Maurice & Gibb, Robin WhoHol 92
Gibb, Robin WhoHol 92
Gibb, Robin 1949- WhoAm 94
See Also Bee Gees, The WhoHol 92
Gibb, Walter Frame 1919- Who 94
Gibbard, Allan (Fletcher) 1942- WrDr 94
Gibbard, Allan Fletcher 1942- IntWW 93
Gibbard, T.S.J. EncSF 93
Gibbens, Barnaby John 1935- Who 94
Gibbens, Linda Irene 1961- WhoWest 94
Gibberd, Kathleen 1897- WrDr 94
Gibbered, Eric Waters 1897-1972 WhoAmA 93N
Gibberson, William 1919- WhoHol 92
Gibbes, Emily V. 1915- WhoBlA 94
Gibbes, William Holman 1930- WhoAmL 94
Gibbings, Peter (Walter) 1929- Who 94
Gibbins, Bob 1936- WhoAmL 94
Gibbins, Ronald Charles Who 94
Gibble, Kenneth L(ee) 1941- WrDr 94
Gibble, Stephen Robert 1956- WhoAmP 93
Gibbon, Edward 1737-1794 BlmGEL
Gibbon, John (Houghton) 1917- Who 94
Gibbon, Lewis Grassic EncSF 93
Gibbon, Michael 1930- Who 94
Gibbons, Ayllene WhoHol 92
Gibbons, Barry J. 1946- WhoAm 94, WhoFI 94
Gibbons, Carroll d1954 WhoHol 92
Gibbons, Cedric 1893-1960 IntDcF 2-4 [port]
Gibbons, Celia Victoria Townsend 1911- WhoFI 94
Gibbons, Christopher 1615?-1676 NewGrDO
Gibbons, Dave 1949- EncSF 93
Gibbons, David Who 94
Gibbons, (John) David 1927- Who 94
Gibbons, Edward Francis 1949- WhoScEn 94
Gibbons, Floyd d1939 WhoHol 92
Gibbons, (Raphael) Floyd (Phillips) 1886-1939 EncSF 93
Gibbons, Hugh (James) 1937- WhoAmA 93
Gibbons, Ian Read 1931- IntWW 93, Who 94
Gibbons, James 1834-1921 DcAmReB 2
Gibbons, James A. 1944- WhoAmP 93
Gibbons, James Arthur 1944- WhoAmL 94, WhoWest 94

Gibbons, James Franklin 1931- *WhoAm 94*
Gibbons, James Mortimer, III 1957- *WhoWest 94*
Gibbons, Jennifer d1993 *NewYTBS 93*
Gibbons, John 1956- *WhoBlA 94*
Gibbons, John David *IntWW 93*
Gibbons, John Ernest 1940- *Who 94*
Gibbons, John Howard 1929- *WhoAm 94, WhoAmP 93, WhoScEn 94*
Gibbons, John Joseph 1924- *WhoAmL 94*
Gibbons, Joseph F. 1948- *WhoAmP 93*
Gibbons, Joseph John 1906- *WhoAm 94*
Gibbons, Julia Smith 1950- *WhoAm 94, WhoAmL 94*
Gibbons, Kenneth Harry 1931- *Who 94*
Gibbons, Leeza *WhoAm 94*
Gibbons, LeRoy 1937- *WhoWest 94*
Gibbons, Mark Hanley 1952- *WhoAmP 93*
Gibbons, Mark L. 1949- *WhoAmL 94*
Gibbons, Michael 1925- *WhoAmP 93*
Gibbons, Michael Eugene 1952- *WhoMW 93*
Gibbons, Michael Lawrence 1969- *WhoWest 94*
Gibbons, Michael Randolph 1959- *WhoMW 93*
Gibbons, Patrick Chandler 1943- *WhoAm 94, WhoMW 93*
Gibbons, Reginald *DrAPF 93*
Gibbons, Robert d1977 *WhoHol 92*
Gibbons, Robert Ebbert 1940- *WhoAm 94*
Gibbons, Robert J. 1945- *WhoIns 94*
Gibbons, Robert John 1944- *WhoAmL 94*
Gibbons, Robert Philip 1933- *WhoAm 94, WhoFI 94*
Gibbons, Ronald John 1932- *WhoAm 94*
Gibbons, Rose d1964 *WhoHol 92*
Gibbons, Sam 1920- *CngDr 93*
Gibbons, Sam M. 1920- *WhoAmP 93*
Gibbons, Samuel Melville 1920- *WhoAm 94*
Gibbons, (Edward) Stanley 1840-1913 *DcNaB MP*
Gibbons, Stella 1902-1989 *BlmGWL*
Gibbons, Thomas Michael 1925- *WhoAm 94, WhoFI 94*
Gibbons, Walter E. 1952- *WhoBlA 94*
Gibbons, William 1726-1800 *WhAmRev*
Gibbons, William Edward Doran 1948- *Who 94*
Gibbons, William John 1947- *WhoAm 94, WhoAmL 94*
Gibbons, William Reginald, Jr. 1947- *WhoAm 94, WhoMW 93*
Gibbs *Who 94*
Gibbs, Adrian 1954- *WhoHol 92*
Gibbs, Alan d1988 *WhoHol 92*
Gibbs, Alma G. 1914- *WhoBlA 94*
Gibbs, Alonzo (Lawrence) 1915-1992 *WrDr 94N*
Gibbs, Anthony Matthews 1933- *IntWW 93, WrDr 94*
Gibbs, Antoinette *NewYTBS 93 [port]*
Gibbs, Antony 1756-1815 *DcNaB MP*
Gibbs, Arland LaVerne 1916- *WhoMW 93*
Gibbs, Arnold James 1923- *WhoAmL 94*
Gibbs, Barbara *DrAPF 93*
Gibbs, Barbara 1950- *WhoAmA 93*
Gibbs, Barbara Kennedy 1950- *WhoAm 94, WhoWest 94*
Gibbs, C. Jeanean *DrAPF 93*
Gibbs, Cecil Armstrong 1889-1960 *NewGrDO*
Gibbs, Charles Melvin 1921- *Who 94*
Gibbs, Christine Gresham 1946- *WhoWest 94*
Gibbs, Dale L. 1923- *WhoMW 93*
Gibbs, Darryl *NewYTBS 93 [port]*
Gibbs, David *WhoAmP 93*
Gibbs, David 1944- *IntMPA 94*
Gibbs, David George 1925- *WhoAm 94*
Gibbs, Delbridge Lindley 1917-1992 *WhAm 10*
Gibbs, Elizabeth Dorothea 1955- *WhoScEn 94*
Gibbs, Elizabeth Villa 1935- *WhoAmP 93*
Gibbs, Eustace Hubert Beilby 1929- *Who 94*
Gibbs, Federic A. 1903-1992 *WhAm 10*
Gibbs, Frank P. 1925- *WhoAm 94*
Gibbs, Frederick Winfield 1932- *WhoAm 94*
Gibbs, Gerald Ernest d1992 *Who 94N*
Gibbs, Harry (Talbot) 1917- *IntWW 93, Who 94*
Gibbs, Irving d1955 *WhoHol 92*
Gibbs, James Alanson 1935- *WhoAm 94, WhoFI 94, WhoScEn 94*
Gibbs, James Howard 1929- *WhoAm 94, WhoFI 94*
Gibbs, James Lowell, Jr. 1931- *WhoAm 94*
Gibbs, Janet *DrAPF 93*
Gibbs, Jewelle Taylor 1933- *WhoBlA 94*
Gibbs, Joe Jackson 1940- *WhoAm 94*
Gibbs, John 1917- *Who 94*
Gibbs, John Patrick 1948- *WhoFI 94*
Gibbs, John Roger 1942- *WhoAmL 94*
Gibbs, Joseph d1921 *WhoHol 92*
Gibbs, Josiah Willard 1839-1903 *WorScD [port]*
Gibbs, June Nesbitt 1922- *WhoAm 94, WhoAmP 93*
Gibbs, Karen Patricia 1952- *WhoBlA 94*
Gibbs, Kenneth David 1957- *WhoFI 94*
Gibbs, L. James 1947- *WhoAmP 93*
Gibbs, Lancelot Richard 1934- *IntWW 93*
Gibbs, Lawrence B. 1938- *WhoAm 94*
Gibbs, Lewis 1891- *EncSF 93*
Gibbs, Lippman Martin 1938- *WhoAm 94, WhoAmL 94*
Gibbs, Lois 1951- *EnvEnc [port]*
Gibbs, Marla 1931- *IntMPA 94, WhoAm 94, WhoBlA 94*
Gibbs, Marla 1933- *WhoHol 92*
Gibbs, Martin 1922- *WhoAm 94, WhoScEn 94*
Gibbs, May 1877-1969 *BlmGWL*
Gibbs, Molly (Peel) 1912- *Who 94*
Gibbs, Oswald Moxley 1927- *Who 94*
Gibbs, Philip Stone 1943- *WhoMW 93*
Gibbs, R(onald) Darnley 1904- *WrDr 94*
Gibbs, Richard John 1943- *Who 94*
Gibbs, Richard John Hedley 1941- *Who 94*
Gibbs, Richard L. 1947- *WhoIns 94*
Gibbs, Richard Leslie 1927- *WhoAm 94, WhoFI 94*
Gibbs, Robert Harrison 1946- *WhoWest 94*
Gibbs, Robert Paton d1940 *WhoHol 92*
Gibbs, Roger Geoffrey 1934- *IntWW 93, Who 94*
Gibbs, Roland (Christopher) 1921- *Who 94*
Gibbs, Roland Christopher 1921- *IntWW 93*
Gibbs, Rosalyn Davenport 1936- *WhoAmL 94*
Gibbs, Sandra E. 1942- *WhoBlA 94*
Gibbs, Sarah Preble 1930- *WhoAm 94*
Gibbs, Sheila Shand c. 1930- *WhoHol 92*
Gibbs, Stephen 1920- *IntWW 93, Who 94*
Gibbs, Steven Howard 1961- *WhoMW 93*
Gibbs, Timothy 1966- *WhoHol 92*
Gibbs, Tom 1942- *WhoAmA 93*
Gibbs, Warmoth T. d1993 *NewYTBS 93*
Gibbs, Warmoth T. 1892-1993 *WhoBlA 94N*
Gibbs, William Eugene 1930- *WhoAm 94*
Gibbs, William Harold 1950- *WhoAm 94, WhoWest 94*
Gibbs, William Lee 1945- *WhoBlA 94*
Gibbs, Y. Gale 1946- *WhoAmA 93*
Gibby, Daniel Jay 1963- *WhoAmL 94*
Gibby, Mabel Enid Kunce 1926- *WhoAm 94, WhoScEn 94*
Gibeau, Marie 1950- *WhoWomW 91*
Gibelli, Lorenzo 1718-1812 *NewGrDO*
Gibeon, Leonard 1945- *WhoFI 94*
Giberson, Karl Willard 1957- *WhoScEn 94*
Gibert, Paul-Cesar 1717-1787 *NewGrDO*
Gibert, Peter 1942- *WhoHisp 94*
Gibian, George 1924- *WhoAm 94*
Gibian, Thomas George 1922- *WhoAm 94*
Gibin, Joao 1929?- *NewGrDO*
Giblett, Eloise Rosalie 1921- *WhoAm 94*
Giblett, Phylis Lee Walz 1945- *WhoWest 94*
Gibley, Christopher Paul 1966- *WhoWest 94*
Giblin, James Cross 1933- *SmATA 75 [port], WhoAm 94*
Giblin, Louis 1944- *WhoFI 94, WhoMW 93*
Giblin, Pamela M. 1946- *WhoAmL 94*
Giblin, Patrick David 1932- *WhoAm 94*
Giblon, Shirley T(enhouse) 1935- *WrDr 94*
Giblyn, Charles d1934 *WhoHol 92*
Gibney, Frank Bray 1924- *WhoAm 94, WhoWest 94*
Gibney, Kristen 1948- *WhoFI 94, WhoMW 93*
Gibney, Lawrence John 1932- *WhoIns 94*
Gibney, Louise d1986 *WhoHol 92*
Gibney, Rebecca *WhoHol 92*
Gibney, Robert L., Jr. 1947- *WhoAmL 94*
Gibori, Geula 1945- *WhoMW 93*
Gibraltar In Europe, Auxiliary Bishop of *Who 94*
Gibraltar In Europe, Bishop of 1945- *Who 94*
Gibraltar In Europe, Suffragan Bishop of 1936- *Who 94*
Gibran, Kahlil 1922- *WhoAm 94*
Gibran, Kahlil George 1922- *WhoAmA 93*
Gibson *Who 94*
Gibson, Baron 1916- *IntWW 93, Who 94*
Gibson, Alexander (Drummond) 1926- *NewGrDO, Who 94*
Gibson, Alexander Drummond 1926- *IntWW 93*
Gibson, Alison L. 1952- *WhoWest 94*
Gibson, Althea 1927- *AfrAmAl 6 [port], BuCMET [port], WhoAm 94, WhoBlA 94, WhoHol 92*
Gibson, Anne 1940- *Who 94*
Gibson, Antonio Marice 1962- *WhoBlA 94*
Gibson, Arthur 1943- *WrDr 94*
Gibson, Arthur Charles 1947- *WhoWest 94*
Gibson, Barry Joseph 1951- *WhoAm 94*
Gibson, Benedict S. 1946- *WhoAmA 93*
Gibson, Benjamin F. 1931- *WhoAm 94, WhoAmL 94, WhoBlA 94, WhoMW 93*
Gibson, Betty 1911- *SmATA 75*
Gibson, Betty M. 1938- *WhoBlA 94*
Gibson, Bruce 1953- *WhoAmP 93*
Gibson, Bynum 1949- *WhoAmP 93*
Gibson, Camille Mary 1937- *WhoAmP 93*
Gibson, Carlton Wayne 1934- *WhoAmP 93*
Gibson, Charles Colmery 1914- *WhoAm 94*
Gibson, Charles DeWolf 1943- *WhoAm 94*
Gibson, Charles E(dmund) 1916- *WrDr 94*
Gibson, Chrisman 1948- *WhoAmL 94*
Gibson, Christopher (Herbert) 1921- *Who 94*
Gibson, Clifford William 1933- *WhoScEn 94*
Gibson, Colin *EncSF 93*
Gibson, Connie Jean 1955- *WhoFI 94*
Gibson, Count Dillon,, Jr. 1921- *WhoAm 94*
Gibson, David 1922- *Who 94*
Gibson, David 1939- *Who 94*
Gibson, David Allen 1957- *WhoScEn 94*
Gibson, David Frederic 1942- *WhoWest 94*
Gibson, David Mark 1923- *WhoAm 94*
Gibson, Denice Yvonne 1955- *WhoWest 94*
Gibson, Derek 1945- *IntMPA 94*
Gibson, Donal 1958- *WhoHol 92*
Gibson, Donald B. 1933- *WhoBlA 94*
Gibson, Donald Bancroft 1928- *WhoAmP 93*
Gibson, Donald Cameron Ernest Forbes 1916- *Who 94*
Gibson, Douglas B. 1951- *WhoAm 94*
Gibson, Edward 1936- *EncSF 93*
Gibson, Edward Fergus 1937- *WhoAm 94*
Gibson, Edward G. *WhoAmA 93*
Gibson, Edward Lewis 1932- *WhoBlA 94*
Gibson, Eleanor Jack 1910- *IntWW 93, WhoAm 94, WhoScEn 94*
Gibson, Elisabeth Jane 1937- *WhoWest 94*
Gibson, Elizabeth Harris *WhoMW 93*
Gibson, Elvis Edward 1937- *WhoBlA 94*
Gibson, Ernest Gerard 1961- *WhoBlA 94*
Gibson, Ernest L., III 1945- *WhoFI 94*
Gibson, Ernest Robinson 1920- *WhoBlA 94*
Gibson, Ernest W., III 1927- *WhoAmP 93*
Gibson, Ernest Willard, III 1927- *WhoAmL 94*
Gibson, Everett Kay, Jr. 1940- *WhoAm 94*
Gibson, Floyd *EncSF 93*
Gibson, Floyd Robert 1910- *WhoAm 94, WhoAmL 94, WhoMW 93*
Gibson, Frank William Ernest 1923- *IntWW 93, Who 94*
Gibson, George 1747-1791 *WhAmRev*
Gibson, George 1904- *WhoAmA 93*
Gibson, George Edward 1909- *WhoMW 93*
Gibson, George Edward, Jr. 1958- *WhoFI 94*
Gibson, George M. 1934- *WhoAm 94*
Gibson, Gerald John 1944- *WhoScEn 94*
Gibson, Gordon Ronald 1929- *WhoScEn 94*
Gibson, Grace Evelyn Loving *DrAPF 93*
Gibson, Graeme 1934- *WrDr 94*
Gibson, (George) Granville 1936- *Who 94*
Gibson, Gregory A. 1948- *WhoBlA 94*
Gibson, Gregory James 1958- *WhoFI 94, WhoMW 93*
Gibson, Guadalupe 1917- *WhoHisp 94*
Gibson, Harold Leslie George 1917- *Who 94*
Gibson, Harris, Jr. 1936- *WhoBlA 94*
Gibson, Harry H. C. 1913- *WhoBlA 94*
Gibson, Helen d1977 *WhoHol 92*
Gibson, Henry 1935- *IntMPA 94, WhoHol 92*
Gibson, Hoot d1962 *WhoHol 92*
Gibson, Hugh 1918- *WhoAm 94, WhoAmL 94*
Gibson, Ian 1939- *WrDr 94*
Gibson, Jack 1920- *WhoAmP 93*
Gibson, James d1938 *WhoHol 92*
Gibson, James d1973 *WhoHol 92*
Gibson, James 1902-1992 *WhAm 10*
Gibson, James (Charles) 1919- *ConAu 41NR*
Gibson, James C. *ConAu 41NR*
Gibson, James D. 1938- *WhoAmA 93*
Gibson, James Edwin 1941- *WhoAm 94*
Gibson, James Isaac 1925- *WhoAmP 93*
Gibson, James John 1923- *WhoAm 94*
Gibson, James O. 1934- *WhoBlA 94*
Gibson, James Thomas, Jr. 1921- *WhoAm 94*
Gibson, Jane *WhoHol 92*
Gibson, Janet Marie 1959- *WhoMW 93*
Gibson, Jay 1950- *WhoAmP 93*
Gibson, Jeremy Allen 1962- *WhoAmL 94*
Gibson, Jerry Leigh 1930- *WhoAm 94*
Gibson, John d1971 *WhoHol 92*
Gibson, John 1740-1822 *WhAmRev*
Gibson, John A. *WhoBlA 94*
Gibson, John C. 1934- *WhoAmP 93*
Gibson, John Egan 1926- *WhoAm 94*
Gibson, John Peter 1929- *Who 94*
Gibson, John R. *WhoAmP 93*
Gibson, John Robert 1925- *WhoAm 94, WhoAmL 94, WhoMW 93*
Gibson, John Sibbald 1923- *Who 94*
Gibson, John Stuart 1958- *WhoAmA 93*
Gibson, John Thomas 1948- *WhoBlA 94*
Gibson, John Vernon Morice 1937- *WhoAmP 93*
Gibson, John Walter 1922- *Who 94*
Gibson, Johnnie M. M. 1949- *WhoBlA 94*
Gibson, Joseph 1916- *Who 94*
Gibson, Joseph David 1928- *Who 94*
Gibson, Joseph Edward 1893- *WhAm 10*
Gibson, Joseph Lee 1940- *WhoAmL 94*
Gibson, Joseph Whitton, Jr. 1922- *WhoAm 94*
Gibson, Josephine 1929- *WrDr 94*
Gibson, Julie *WhoHol 92*
Gibson, Kathleen Rita 1942- *WhoScEn 94*
Gibson, Kathy Halvey 1956- *WhoScEn 94*
Gibson, Kenneth d1972 *WhoHol 92*
Gibson, Kenneth Allen 1932- *ConBlB 6 [port], WhoBlA 94*
Gibson, Kenneth O., Sr. *WhoAmP 93*
Gibson, Laurie Ann 1962- *WhoWest 94*
Gibson, Leonard Young d1993 *Who 94N*
Gibson, Lois K. 1929- *WhoAmP 93*
Gibson, Margaret *DrAPF 93*
Gibson, Margaret d1964 *WhoHol 92*
Gibson, Margaret 1948- *BlmGWL*
Gibson, Mark Edwards 1955- *WhoMW 93*
Gibson, Mary Jane 1933- *WhoAmP 93, WhoWomW 91*
Gibson, Maurice 1960- *WhoBlA 94*
Gibson, McGuire 1938- *WhoAm 94*
Gibson, Mel 1956- *IntMPA 94, IntWW 93, WhoAm 94, WhoHol 92*
Gibson, Melvin Roy 1920- *WhoAm 94, WhoWest 94*
Gibson, Michael Addison 1943- *WhoAm 94, WhoScEn 94*
Gibson, Michael Bradford d1993 *Who 94N*
Gibson, Michael Denny 1947- *WhoMW 93*
Gibson, Michael John 1939- *Who 94*
Gibson, Mike d1993 *NewYTBS 93*
Gibson, Miles 1947- *WrDr 94*
Gibson, Morgan *DrAPF 93*
Gibson, Nell Braxton 1942- *WhoBlA 94*
Gibson, Norman d1976 *WhoHol 92*
Gibson, P. J. *DrAPF 93*
Gibson, P(atricia) J(oann) *BlkWr 2, ConAu 142*
Gibson, Patricia Ann 1942- *WhoMW 93*
Gibson, Paul, Jr. 1927- *WhoBlA 94*
Gibson, Paul Alexander 1941- *Who 94*
Gibson, Peggy Kathryn 1936- *WhoAm 94*
Gibson, Peter (Leslie) 1934- *IntWW 93, Who 94*
Gibson, Peter Cecil 1913- *Who 94*
Gibson, Pryor A. 1957- *WhoAmP 93*
Gibson, Quentin 1913- *WrDr 94*
Gibson, Quentin Howieson 1918- *Who 94, WhoAm 94*
Gibson, Ralph (Brian) 1922- *Who 94*
Gibson, Ralph H. 1939- *WhoAmA 93*
Gibson, Ralph Holmes 1939- *WhoAm 94*
Gibson, Ralph Milton 1923- *WhoBlA 94*
Gibson, Rankin MacDougal 1916- *WhoAm 94*
Gibson, Raymond Eugene 1924- *WhoAm 94*
Gibson, Raymond Novarro 1961- *WhoScEn 94*
Gibson, Reginald Oswald 1902-1983 *DcNaB MP*
Gibson, Reginald W. 1927- *CngDr 93*
Gibson, Reginald Walker 1927- *WhoAm 94, WhoAmL 94, WhoBlA 94*
Gibson, Rex 1931- *IntWW 93*
Gibson, Richard (Thomas) 1931- *BlkWr 2*
Gibson, Richard Ingram 1948- *WhoWest 94*
Gibson, Robert 1927- *WrDr 94*
Gibson, Robert 1935- *WhoAm 94, WhoBlA 94, WhoMW 93*
Gibson, Robert Alfred 1932- *WhoAmP 93*
Gibson, Robert Dennis 1942- *IntWW 93, Who 94*
Gibson, Robert Donald Davidson 1927- *Who 94*

Gibson, Robert Fisher 1906-1990 *WhAm 10*
Gibson, Robert Lee 1946- *WhoAm 94, WhoScEn 94*
Gibson, Robert Peter 1945- *WhoAm 94*
Gibson, Roger Fletcher, Jr. 1944- *WhoMW 93*
Gibson, Roland 1902- *WhoAmA 93N*
Gibson, Roy 1924- *IntWW 93, Who 94*
Gibson, Sam Thompson 1916- *WhoAm 94, WhoScEn 94*
Gibson, Sarah L. 1927- *WhoBlA 94*
Gibson, Scott Wilbert 1948- *WhoMW 93*
Gibson, Sonny *WhoHol 92*
Gibson, Stephen Lee 1942- *WhoAm 94, WhoAmL 94*
Gibson, Stephen M. *DrAPF 93*
Gibson, Stephen Miller 1952- *WhoFI 94*
Gibson, Terence Allen 1937- *Who 94*
Gibson, Thelma Jean 1934- *WhoAmP 93*
Gibson, Thomas d1993 *Who 94N*
Gibson, Thomas Fenner, III 1955- *WhoAm 94*
Gibson, Thomas Joseph 1935- *WhoAm 94, WhoFI 94*
Gibson, Thomas Richard 1942- *WhoFI 94*
Gibson, Treva Kay 1938- *WhoWest 94*
Gibson, Truman K., Jr. 1912- *WhoBlA 94*
Gibson, Virginia 1928- *WhoHol 92*
Gibson, Walter B(rown) 1897-1985 *EncSF 93*
Gibson, Walter Samuel 1932- *WhoAm 94, WhoAmA 93, WrDr 94*
Gibson, Warren Arnold 1941- *WhoBlA 94*
Gibson, Wilford Henry 1924- *Who 94*
Gibson, William *WhoAm 94*
Gibson, William 1914- *ConAu 42NR, ConDr 93, WhoAm 94, WrDr 94*
Gibson, William 1948- *Au&Arts 12 [port]*
Gibson, William (Ford) 1948- *EncSF 93, TwCYAW, WrDr 94*
Gibson, William B. 1938- *WhoAm 94*
Gibson, William C. *WhoAmP 93*
Gibson, William Charles 1959- *WhoScEn 94*
Gibson, William David 1925- *Who 94*
Gibson, William Edward 1944- *WhoAm 94*
Gibson, William F. 1933- *ConBlB 6 [port]*
Gibson, William Ford 1948- *WhoAm 94*
Gibson, William Francis 1952- *WhoAm 94*
Gibson, William Howard, Jr. 1941- *WhoBlA 94*
Gibson, William Lee 1949- *WhoFI 94*
Gibson, William M. 1934- *WhoBlA 94*
Gibson, William S. 1933- *WhoIns 94*
Gibson, William Shepard 1933- *WhoAm 94*
Gibson, William Willard 1897- *WhAm 10*
Gibson, William Willard, Jr. 1932- *WhoAm 94*
Gibson, Wynne d1987 *WhoHol 92*
Gibson, Yolanda 1944- *WhoWest 94*
Gibson, Yvonne *WhoWomW 91*
Gibson-Barboza, Mario 1918- *IntWW 93, Who 94*
Gibson-Craig-Carmichael, David Peter William 1946- *Who 94*
Gibson-Watt, Baron 1918- *Who 94*
Gick, Philip David 1913- *Who 94*
Gidaspov, Boris Veniaminovich 1933- *IntWW 93, LoBiDrD*
Gidda, Jaswant Singh 1946- *WhoAsA 94*
Gidden, Barry Owen Barton 1915- *Who 94*
Giddens, Anthony 1938- *Who 94*
Giddens, Bill 1957- *NewYTBS 93 [port]*
Giddens, Don Peyton 1940- *WhoAm 94, WhoScEn 94*
Giddens, James W. 1938- *WhoAmL 94*
Giddens, John Madison, Jr. 1962- *WhoScEn 94*
Giddens, Kenneth R. d1993 *NewYTBS 93 [port]*
Giddens, Paul Joseph 1944- *WhoFI 94, WhoMW 93*
Gidding, Nelson 1919- *ConAu 142*
Giddings, Clifford Frederick 1936- *WhoFI 94*
Giddings, Helen *WhoAmP 93*
Giddings, J. Calvin *WhoScEn 94*
Giddings, John Calvin 1930- *WrDr 94*
Giddings, Mark Steven 1955- *WhoFI 94*
Giddings, (Kenneth Charles) Michael 1920- *Who 94*
Giddings, Paula Jane 1947- *WhoBlA 94*
Giddins, Gary Mitchell 1948- *WhoAm 94*
Gide, Andre d1951 *WhoHol 92*
Gide, Andre 1869-1951 *BlmGEL, ShSCr 13 [port]*
Gide, Andre (Paul Guillaume) 1869-1951 *GayLL, RfGShF*
Gidel, Robert Hugh 1951- *WhoAm 94, WhoFI 94*
Gideon, Bond *WhoHol 92*
Gideon, Kenneth W. 1946- *WhoAmP 93*
Gideon, Kenneth Wayne 1946- *WhoAm 94, WhoAmL 94, WhoFI 94*
Gideon, Melville d1933 *WhoHol 92*
Gideon, Miriam 1906- *WhoAm 94*
Gideon, Patrick R. 1958- *WhoMW 93*
Gideon, Richard Walter 1928- *WhoFI 94*
Gideon-Hawke, Pamela Lawrence 1945- *WhoWest 94*
Gidh, Kedar Keshav 1967- *WhoScEn 94*
Gidley, John Lynn 1924- *WhoAm 94*
Gidley, Pamela 1965- *WhoHol 92*
Gidley, Thomas Dunne 1934- *WhoAmL 94*
Gidlow, Elsa 1898-1986 *GayLL*
Gidney, Calvin L. 1930- *WhoBlA 94*
Gidron, Richard D. 1938- *WhoBlA 94*
Gidwitz, Gerald 1906- *WhoAm 94, WhoFI 94, WhoMW 93*
Gidwitz, Ronald J. 1945- *WhoAm 94, WhoFI 94, WhoMW 93*
Giebisch, Gerhard Hans 1927- *WhoAm 94*
Giebner, Cara Rae 1940- *WhoMW 93*
Giedt, Bruce Alan 1937- *WhoAm 94*
Giedt, Walvin Roland 1905- *WhoWest 94*
Giedt, Warren Harding 1920- *WhoAm 94*
Giegerich, Thomas Anthony 1937- *WhoMW 93*
Giehse, Therese d1975 *WhoHol 92*
Giel, James Arthur, Jr. 1952- *WhoFI 94*
Gielen, Michael 1927- *NewGrDO*
Gielen, Michael Andreas 1927- *IntWW 93*
Gielgud, John *NewYTBS 93 [port]*
Gielgud, John 1904- *BlmGEL, IntMPA 94, WhoAm 94, WhoHol 92*
Gielgud, (Arthur) John 1904- *IntWW 93, Who 94*
Gielgud, (Arthur) John, Sir 1904- *WrDr 94*
Gielgud, Maina 1945- *IntDcB [port], Who 94*
Gielgud, Val d1981 *WhoHol 92*
Giem, Ross Nye, Jr. 1923- *WhoWest 94*
Gienow, Herbert Hans Walter 1926- *IntWW 93*
Gier, Audra May Calhoon 1940- *WhoAm 94, WhoMW 93, WhoScEn 94*
Gier, Karan Hancock 1947- *WhoScEn 94, WhoWest 94*
Gierasch, Stefan *WhoHol 92*
Gierbolini, Gilberto 1926- *WhoHisp 94*
Gierbolini-Ortiz, Gilberto 1926- *WhoAm 94, WhoAmL 94*
Gierek, Edward 1913- *IntWW 93*
Gierer, Vincent A., Jr. 1947- *WhoAm 94*
Giering, John Louis 1944- *WhoFI 94*
Giering, Richard Herbert 1929- *WhoMW 93*
Gierke, Craig Sherman 1950- *WhoAmP 93*
Gierke, H. F. 1943- *CngDr 93*
Gierke, Herman Fredrick, III 1943- *WhoAmL 94, WhoAmP 93*
Gierke, Sandra Jean 1937- *WhoMW 93*
Gierowski, Stefan 1925- *IntWW 93*
Giersbach, Walter C. 1897- *WhAm 10*
Giersch, Herbert 1921- *IntWW 93*
Gierson, James d1781 *AmRev*
Gierster, Hans 1925- *IntWW 93*
Giertz, J. Fred 1943- *WhoAm 94*
Gierut, Thomas Michael 1966- *WhoMW 93*
Gies, Jan d1993 *NewYTBS 93 [port]*
Gies, Martha *DrAPF 93*
Gies, Ronald Bruce 1965- *WhoFI 94*
Gies, Thomas Anthony 1930- *WhoAm 94*
Giesa, Michael William 1943- *WhoWest 94*
Giesbert, Franz-Olivier 1949- *IntWW 93*
Gieschen, Donald Werner 1924- *WhoWest 94*
Gieschen, Martin John 1918-1991 *WhoAmA 93N*
Giese, Clayton Frederick 1931- *WhoScEn 94*
Giese, David E. 1942- *WhoAmP 93*
Giese, Edgar William 1941- *WhoAmP 93*
Giese, Elizabeth Ann 1943- *WhoAmP 93*
Giese, Heiner 1944- *WhoAmL 94*
Giese, Theodore Lynn 1945- *WhoFI 94*
Giese, Warren Kenneth 1924- *WhoAmP 93*
Giese, William Herbert 1944- *WhoAm 94*
Giesecke, Charles Lewis 1761-1833 *DcNaB MP*
Giesecke, Gustav Ernst 1908- *WhoAm 94*
Giesecke, Leonard Frederick 1937- *WhoAm 94*
Gieseke, Johann Georg Carl Ludwig 1761-1833 *NewGrDO*
Gieseking, Hal E. 1932- *WrDr 94*
Giesel, James Austin 1960- *WhoAmL 94*
Gieseler, Daniel J., Jr. 1938- *WhoIns 94*
Gieseler, Eugene C. 1937- *WhoAm 94, WhoAmL 94*
Gieselman, Kenneth E. 1920- *WhoAmP 93*
Giesen, Arthur Rossa, Jr. 1932- *WhoAmP 93*
Giesen, Herman Mills 1928- *WhoFI 94, WhoScEn 94*
Giesen, John William 1928- *WhoAm 94*
Giesen, Richard Allyn 1929- *WhoAm 94*
Giesey, Harry George 1933- *WhoIns 94*
Giesie, Pamela Dee 1961- *WhoWest 94*
Gieske, Friedhelm 1928- *Who 94*
Giesler, Robert Alvin 1929- *WhoMW 93*
Giesser, Nancy Lynne 1942- *WhoMW 93*
Giessinger, Peter W. 1920- *WhoAmP 93*
Giesy, J(ohn) U(lrich) 1877-1948 *EncSF 93*
Gieve, (Edward) John (Watson) 1950- *Who 94*
Gievers, Karen A. 1949- *WhoAmL 94*
Gieysztor, Aleksander 1916- *IntWW 93*
Gifaldi, David 1950- *SmATA 76 [port]*
Giff, Patricia Reilly 1935- *ConAu 41NR*
Giffard *Who 94*
Giffard, Adam Edward 1934- *Who 94*
Giffard, Anna Marcella 1707-1777 *BlmGEL*
Giffard, Henry 1694-1772 *BlmGEL*
Giffard, (Charles) Sydney (Rycroft) 1926- *Who 94*
Giffen, Daniel Harris 1938- *WhoAm 94*
Giffen, John A. 1938- *IntWW 93, WhoAm 94, WhoFI 94*
Giffen, Lawrence Everett, Sr. 1923- *WhoMW 93*
Giffin, Gordon Davies 1949- *WhoAmP 93*
Giffin, Kenneth Neal 1944- *WhoAmP 93, WhoMW 93*
Giffin, Mary (Elizabeth) 1919- *WrDr 94*
Giffin, Reggie Craig 1942- *WhoAm 94, WhoAmL 94*
Giffin, Walter Charles 1936- *WhoAm 94, WhoWest 94*
Gifford, Baron 1940- *Who 94*
Gifford, Alan d1989 *WhoHol 92*
Gifford, Arthur Roy 1937- *WhoWest 94*
Gifford, Barry *DrAPF 93*
Gifford, Barry (Colby) 1946- *WrDr 94*
Gifford, Bernard R. 1943- *WhoBlA 94*
Gifford, Carol Lynn 1942- *WhoAmP 93*
Gifford, Charles Henry 1913- *IntWW 93*
Gifford, Charles Kilvert 1942- *WhoAm 94, WhoFI 94*
Gifford, Chuck 1933- *WhoAmP 93*
Gifford, Denis 1927- *WrDr 94*
Gifford, Donald Arthur 1945- *WhoAmL 94*
Gifford, Edward Stewart, Jr. 1907- *WrDr 94*
Gifford, Ernest Milton 1920- *WhoAm 94, WhoScEn 94*
Gifford, Frances 1920- *WhoHol 92*
Gifford, Frank *ProFbHF [port]*
Gifford, Frank 1930- *WhoHol 92*
Gifford, Frank Newton 1930- *WhoAm 94*
Gifford, George E. 1924- *WhoAm 94*
Gifford, Gerald Frederic 1939- *WhoScEn 94*
Gifford, Harry Cortland Frey 1919- *WhoAm 94*
Gifford, Helen (Margaret) 1935- *NewGrDO*
Gifford, (Charles) Henry 1913- *Who 94*
Gifford, J. Nebraska 1939- *WhoAmA 93*
Gifford, Janet Lynn 1960- *WhoAmL 94*
Gifford, John Irving 1930- *WhoMW 93*
Gifford, Kathie Lee 1953- *ConAu 142, WhoAm 94*
Gifford, Michael Brian 1936- *IntWW 93, Who 94*
Gifford, Nelson Sage 1930- *WhoAm 94, WhoFI 94*
Gifford, Patricia Louise 1945- *WhoMW 93*
Gifford, Peter
See Midnight Oil *ConMus 11*
Gifford, Porter William 1918- *WhoAm 94*
Gifford, Prosser 1929- *WhoAm 94*
Gifford, Ray Wallace, Jr. 1923- *WhoAm 94*
Gifford, Thomas (Eugene) 1937- *WrDr 94*
Gifford, Virginia Snodgrass 1936- *WhoAm 94*
Gifford, Wendy *WhoHol 92*
Gifford, William *DrAPF 93*
Gifford, William 1756-1826 *BlmGEL*
Gifford, William Henry, Jr. 1955- *WhoAmL 94*
Gifford, William Leo 1930- *WhoAmP 93*
Giffuni, Flora Baldini *WhoAmA 93*
Gifkins, Robert Cecil 1918- *WhoScEn 94*
Gift, Donn *WhoHol 92*
Gift, James J. *WhoScEn 94*
Gift, Roland *WhoHol 92*
Giftos, Elaine 1945- *WhoHol 92*
Giga, Yoshikazu 1955- *WhoScEn 94*
Giger, H.R. 1940- *EncSF 93*
Giger, Joyce Anne Newman 1950- *WhoAm 94*
Giger, Peter 1945- *WhoScEn 94*
Giggall, George Kenneth 1914- *Who 94*
Gigger, Helen C. 1944- *WhoBlA 94*
Gigger, Nathaniel Jay 1944- *WhoBlA 94*
Giggey, James Walker 1931- *WhoAm 94*
Gigler, Daniel Richard 1951- *WhoAmL 94*
Gigler, Joseph Herbert 1955- *WhoFI 94*
Gigli, Beniamino d1957 *WhoHol 92*
Gigli, Beniamino 1890-1957 *NewGrDO [port]*
Gigli, Clarice fl. 1682-1690 *NewGrDO*
Gigli, Gerolamo 1660-1722 *NewGrDO*
Gigli, Irma 1931- *WhoAm 94, WhoHisp 94, WhoScEn 94*
Giglio, Anthony P. *WhoAmP 93*
Giglio, Frank 1933- *WhoAmP 93*
Giglio, Joseph Charles, Jr. 1952- *WhoAmL 94*
Giglio, Nicki Sue 1951- *WhoMW 93*
Giglio, Steven Rene 1952- *WhoAmL 94*
Gigliotti, Frank Bruno 1896- *WhAm 10*
Gigliotti, Frank J. 1942- *WhoAmP 93*
Gigliotti, Joanne Marie 1945- *WhoAmA 93*
Gigliotti, Richard Joseph 1945- *WhoFI 94*
Gignac, Judith Ann 1939- *WhoAmP 93*
Giguere, Brenda Sue 1959- *WhoMW 93*
Giguiere, Michele Louise 1944- *WhoAmL 94*
Gigy, Mabel d1952 *WhoHol 92*
Gihwala, Dherendra Isver 1951- *WhoScEn 94*
Gijón y Robles, Rafael 1925- *WhoHisp 94*
Gijsen, Wim *EncSF 93*
Gikas, Paul William 1928- *WhoAm 94*
Gikow, Ruth 1913-1982 *WhoAmA 93N*
Gil, Antonio C. 1946- *WhoHisp 94*
Gil, Carlos B. 1937- *WhoHisp 94*
Gil, David Georg 1924- *WrDr 94*
Gil, Federico Guillermo 1915- *WhoAm 94, WrDr 94*
Gil, Francis Rene 1961- *WhoHisp 94*
Gil, Gilbert d1988 *WhoHol 92*
Gil, Guillermo *WhoAmL 94*
Gil, Gustavo 1950- *WhoHisp 94*
Gil, Irena Urszula *WhoWomW 91*
Gil, Janusz Andrzej 1951- *WhoScEn 94*
Gil, Lazier 1939- *WhoAm 94*
Gil, Libia Socorro 1947- *WhoAsA 94*
Gil, Lourdes 1951- *WhoHisp 94*
Gil, Luis A. 1950- *WhoHisp 94*
Gil, Mieczyslaw 1944- *IntWW 93*
Gil, Peter 1941- *WhoHisp 94*
Gil, Vincent *WhoHol 92*
Gil-Albert, Juan 1906- *DcLB 134 [port]*
Gilardi, Gilardo 1889-1963 *NewGrDO*
Gilardi, Richard D. 1936- *WhoFI 94*
Gilardoni, Domenico 1798-1831 *NewGrDO*
Gilb, Corinne Lathrop 1925- *WhoMW 93*
Gilb, Dagoberto *DrAPF 93*
Gilb, Dagoberto 1950- *WhoHisp 94*
Gilbane, Jean Ann 1923- *WhoAm 94*
Gilbane, Thomas F., Jr. 1947- *WhoFI 94*
Gilbane, William James 1908- *WhoFI 94*
Gilbart, Andrew James 1950- *Who 94*
Gilbart-Denham, Seymour Vivian 1939- *Who 94*
Gilberd, Bruce Carlyle *Who 94*
Gilberg, Arnold L. 1936- *WhoAm 94*
Gilberg, Kenneth Roy 1951- *WhoAmL 94*
Gilbert *Who 94*
Gilbert, Adam B. 1952- *WhoAmL 94*
Gilbert, Alan (Graham) 1944- *WrDr 94*
Gilbert, Alan David 1944- *Who 94*
Gilbert, Alan Jay 1951- *WhoAmL 94*
Gilbert, Albert C. 1924- *WhoBlA 94*
Gilbert, Albert Earl 1939- *WhoAmA 93*
Gilbert, Albert Francis 1937- *WhoAm 94, WhoMW 93*
Gilbert, Allan Arthur 1925- *WhoAm 94*
Gilbert, Anna 1916- *WrDr 94*
Gilbert, Anne Wieland 1927- *WhoAm 94*
Gilbert, Anthony (John) 1934- *NewGrDO*
Gilbert, Anthony Chapin 1937- *WhoAm 94*
Gilbert, Arnold Martin 1921- *WhoAmA 93*
Gilbert, Arthur C. *WhoAmP 93*
Gilbert, Arthur Charles 1926- *WhoScEn 94*
Gilbert, Arthur Charles Francis 1929- *WhoAm 94*
Gilbert, Arthur N. 1920- *IntMPA 94*
Gilbert, Benjamin 1755-1828 *WhAmRev*
Gilbert, Benjamin Franklin 1918- *WrDr 94*
Gilbert, Bentley Brinkerhoff 1924- *WrDr 94*
Gilbert, Bil 1927- *WrDr 94*
Gilbert, Billy d1971 *WhoHol 92*
Gilbert, Billy 1894-1971 *WhoCom*
Gilbert, Blaine Louis 1940- *WhoAmL 94*
Gilbert, Bob d1973 *WhoHol 92*
Gilbert, Bob 1939- *WhoAmP 93*
Gilbert, Bradley 1961- *WhoAm 94*
Gilbert, Bruce 1947- *IntMPA 94*
Gilbert, Celia *DrAPF 93*
Gilbert, Charles Breed, III 1922- *WhoAmP 93*
Gilbert, Charles D. 1949- *WhoScEn 94*
Gilbert, Charles Richard Alsop 1916- *WhoAm 94*
Gilbert, Christopher *DrAPF 93*

Gilkes, Arthur Gwyer 1915- WhoAmL 94, WhoMW 93
Gilkes, Cheryl Townsend 1947- WhoBlA 94
Gilkeson, Robert F. d1993 NewYTBS 93
Gilkey, Gordon Waverly 1912- WhoAm 94, WhoAmA 93, WhoWest 94
Gilkey, Otis Bernard 1966- WhoBlA 94
Gilkey, Richard Charles 1925- WhoAmA 93
Gilkey, William C. 1932- WhoBlA 94
Gilkie, Robert James 1935- WhoAmP 93
Gilkyson, Tony
See X ConMus 11
Gill, Ajit Singh 1933- WhoScEn 94
Gill, Allen Douglas 1946- WhoMW 93
Gill, Amory T. 1901-1966 BasBi
Gill, Anna Margherita Anya 1963- WhoScEn 94
Gill, Anthony (Keith) 1930- IntWW 93, Who 94
Gill, Anton 1948- WrDr 94
Gill, Ardian 1929- WhoIns 94
Gill, Ardian C. 1929- WhoAm 94
Gill, Atherton Leslie 1935- WhoWest 94
Gill, B. M. 1921- WrDr 94
Gill, Barbara A. WhoAmP 93
Gill, Bartholomew 1943- WrDr 94
Gill, Basil d1955 WhoHol 92
Gill, Benjamin Franklin 1917- WhoAm 94
Gill, Betty 1921- WhoAmP 93
Gill, Brendan DrAPF 93
Gill, Brendan 1914- IntWW 93, WhoAm 94, WrDr 94
Gill, Brian 1942- Who 94
Gill, Carole O'Brien 1946- WhoAm 94
Gill, Christopher John Fred 1936- Who 94
Gill, Clark Cyrus 1915- WhoAm 94
Gill, Clyde Dennis 1951- WhoMW 93
Gill, Cyril James 1904- Who 94
Gill, Daniel E. 1936- WhoAm 94, WhoFI 94
Gill, David 1928- Who 94
Gill, David (Lawrence William) 1934- WrDr 94
Gill, David Brian 1957- WhoAm 94
Gill, Donald George 1927- WhoAm 94
Gill, E. Ann 1951- WhoAm 94, WhoAmL 94
Gill, Elaine Goldman 1924- WhoWest 94
Gill, Elbert T., Jr. WhoAmP 93
Gill, Ernest Clark 1903-1992 WhAm 10
Gill, Florence d1965 WhoHol 92
Gill, Frederick James 1906-1974 WhoAmA 93N
Gill, Gail Stoorza 1943- WhoAm 94, WhoFI 94
Gill, Gary Lorin 1960- WhoAmP 93
Gill, Gene 1933- WhoAmA 93
Gill, George Norman 1934- WhoAm 94
Gill, George Wilhelm 1941- WhoWest 94
Gill, Gerald Lawson 1947- WhoFI 94
Gill, Gerald Robert 1948- WhoBlA 94
Gill, Gillian C(atherine) 1942- WrDr 94
Gill, Glenda Eloise 1939- WhoBlA 94
Gill, Harry 1922- Who 94
Gill, Henry Herr 1930- WhoAm 94
Gill, Henry Leonard 1939- WhoScEn 94
Gill, Ian Gordon 1919- Who 94
Gill, Jack 1930- Who 94
Gill, Jacqueline A. 1950- WhoBlA 94
Gill, Jane Pittenger 1932- WhoAmL 94, WhoWest 94
Gill, Jerry H. 1933- WrDr 94
Gill, John WhoHol 92
Gill, John 1732-1785 WhAmRev
Gill, John Joseph, Jr. 1943- WhoFI 94
Gill, John Ray 1953- WhoFI 94
Gill, Johnny 1967- WhoBlA 94
Gill, Keith Hubert 1929- WhoAmL 94
Gill, Kendall Cedric 1968- WhoBlA 94
Gill, Kenneth 1927- Who 94
Gill, (James) Kenneth 1920- Who 94
Gill, Kenneth Edward 1932- Who 94
Gill, Laverne McCain 1947- WhoBlA 94
Gill, Leonard William George 1918- Who 94
Gill, Louis John 1940- WhoAmP 93
Gill, Lyle Bennett 1916- WhoAmL 94, WhoMW 93
Gill, Malcolm Who 94
Gill, (George) Malcolm 1934- Who 94
Gill, Margaret Gaskins 1940- WhoAm 94
Gill, Margaret S. WhoAmP 93
Gill, Michael J. 1952- WhoAm 94
Gill, Mohammad Akram 1935- WhoScEn 94
Gill, Myrna Lakshmi 1943- WrDr 94
Gill, Patrick F. 1955- WhoAmP 93
Gill, Pete
See Motorhead ConMus 10
Gill, Peter 1939- ConDr 93, Who 94, WrDr 94
Gill, Raymond Joseph 1930- WhoAm 94
Gill, Rebecca LaLosh 1944- WhoWest 94
Gill, Richard Lawrence 1946- WhoAm 94, WhoAmL 94
Gill, Richard Thomas 1927- WhoAm 94
Gill, Robert B. 1931- WhoAm 94, WhoFI 94
Gill, Robert Lewis 1912- WhoBlA 94
Gill, Robert Stowe d1918 WhoHol 92
Gill, Robert Tucker 1946- WhoAmL 94
Gill, Robin Denys 1927- Who 94
Gill, Robin Morton 1944- Who 94
Gill, Rockne 1931- WhoAmL 94
Gill, Ronald Crispin 1916- WrDr 94
Gill, Rosa Underwood 1944- WhoBlA 94
Gill, Sam D. 1943- WrDr 94
Gill, Samuel A. 1932- WhoBlA 94
Gill, Sarah Prince 1728-1771 BlmGWL
Gill, Stanley Jensen 1929-1991 WhAm 10
Gill, Stanley Sanderson 1923- Who 94
Gill, Stephen Paschall 1938- WhoAm 94
Gill, Suzanne L(utz) 1941- WrDr 94
Gill, Thomas D., Jr. 1942- WhoAmL 94
Gill, Thomas James, III 1932- WhoAm 94
Gill, Thomas M. 1941- WhoIns 94
Gill, Thomas Steffen 1944- WhoWest 94
Gill, Tom d1971 WhoHol 92
Gill, Troy D. 1937- WhoBlA 94
Gill, Vince WhoAm 94
Gill, Walter Brent 1950- WhoAmL 94
Gill, William Albert, Jr. 1924- WhoAm 94
Gill, William Haywood 1929- WhoFI 94
Gill, William Nelson 1928- WhoAm 94, WhoScEn 94
Gill, William Robert 1920- WhoAm 94, WhoScEn 94
Gillam, Clifford Riggs 1897- WhAm 10
Gillam, Isaac Thomas, IV 1932- WhoWest 94
Gillam, James Kennedy 1922- WhoAm 94
Gillam, John B., III 1946- WhoAmP 93
Gillam, Max Lee 1926- WhoAm 94
Gillam, Patrick John 1933- IntWW 93, Who 94, WhoAm 94
Gillam, Penelope Ursula 1965- WhoFI 94
Gillam, Stanley George 1915- Who 94
Gillan, Cheryl Elise Kendall 1952- Who 94
Gillan, Ian 1945-
See Deep Purple ConMus 11
Gillan, Jeffrey Scott 1957- WhoMW 93
Gillan, Maria Mazziotti DrAPF 93
Gillanders, Lewis Alexander 1925- Who 94
Gillani, Noor Velshi 1944- WhoScEn 94
Gillard, Francis George 1908- IntWW 93, Who 94
Gillard, Peter McCann 1941-1988 WhAm 10
Gillard, Stuart WhoHol 92
Gillard, Stuart Thomas 1946- WhoAm 94
Gillaspie, Athey Graves, Jr. 1938- WhoScEn 94
Gill-Davies, Jane 1883- WhoHol 92
Gille, Philippe(-Emile-Francois) 1831-1901 NewGrDO
Gillean, Jack Ward 1956- WhoAmL 94
Gillece, James Patrick, Jr. 1944- WhoAm 94, WhoAmL 94
Gilleland, Richard A. WhoAm 94, WhoFI 94
Gillen, Howard William 1923- WhoScEn 94
Gillen, James Robert 1937- WhoAm 94, WhoAmL 94, WhoFI 94
Gillen, John 1947- WhoAmA 93
Gillen, William Albert 1914- WhoAm 94, WhoAmL 94
Gillenson, Lewis William 1918-1992 WhAm 10
Gillenwater, Jay Young 1933- WhoAm 94
Giller, Edward Bonfoy 1918- WhoAm 94, WhoWest 94
Giller, Norman Myer 1918- WhoAm 94, WhoFI 94
Giller, Walter 1927- WhoHol 92
Gillerman, Gerald 1924- WhoAmL 94
Gilles, Daniel 1917- IntWW 93
Gilles, Dennis Cyril 1925- Who 94
Gilles, Genevieve 1946- WhoHol 92
Gilles, Herbert Michael 1921- IntWW 93
Gilles, Herbert Michael Joseph 1921- Who 94
Gilles, Nancy WhoHol 92
Gillespie, Alastair William 1922- WhoAm 94
Gillespie, Alexander Joseph, Jr. 1923- WhoAm 94
Gillespie, Angus Kress 1942- WrDr 94
Gillespie, Anita Wright 1953- WhoMW 93
Gillespie, Arnold 1899-1978 IntDcF 2-4
Gillespie, Avon E. 1938- WhoBlA 94
Gillespie, Bonita 1951- WhoBlA 94
Gillespie, Bruce 1947- EncSF 93
Gillespie, Charles A., Jr. 1935- WhoAmP 93
Gillespie, Charles Anthony, Jr. 1935- IntWW 93
Gillespie, Cynthia K. d1993 NewYTBS 93
Gillespie, Cynthia K. 1941- WrDr 94
Gillespie, Cynthia K. 1941-1993 ConAu 140
Gillespie, Dana 1949- WhoHol 92
Gillespie, Daniel Curtis, Sr. 1922- WhoAm 94
Gillespie, David Ellis 1933- WhAm 10
Gillespie, David H. d1993 NewYTBS 93
Gillespie, Diane Filby 1943- WrDr 94
Gillespie, Dizzy 1917- CurBio 93 [port]
Gillespie, Dizzy 1917-1993 AfrAmAl 6 [port], CurBio 93N, NewYTBS 93 [port], WhAm 10, WhoBlA 94N
Gillespie, Dorothy Muriel 1920- WhoAmA 93
Gillespie, Edward d1918 WhoHol 92
Gillespie, Edward Malcolm 1935- WhoAm 94
Gillespie, Eugene 1922- WhoAmP 93
Gillespie, Gardest 1943- WhoAmP 93
Gillespie, Gardner F. 1945- WhoAmL 94
Gillespie, Gary Don 1943- WhoMW 93, WhoScEn 94
Gillespie, George Joseph, III 1930- WhoAm 94
Gillespie, Gerald (Ernest Paul) 1933- WrDr 94
Gillespie, Gerald Ernest Paul 1933- WhoAm 94
Gillespie, Gina 1952- WhoHol 92
Gillespie, Gregory Joseph 1936- WhoAmA 93
Gillespie, Gwain Homer 1931- WhoAm 94, WhoFI 94
Gillespie, Helen Davys 1954- WhoFI 94
Gillespie, Iain E. 1931- IntWW 93
Gillespie, Iain Erskine 1931- Who 94
Gillespie, Ian 1945- Who 94
Gillespie, J. Martin 1949- WhoFI 94, WhoMW 93
Gillespie, James Davis 1955- WhoAmL 94
Gillespie, James Howard 1917- WhoAm 94
Gillespie, James Laurence 1946- WhoMW 93
Gillespie, Jane Lee 1957- WhoAmP 93
Gillespie, Jerry WhoAmP 93
Gillespie, Joe Daniel 1947- WhoFI 94
Gillespie, John Birks d1993 IntWW 93N
Gillespie, John Birks 1917-1993 AmCulL [port]
Gillespie, John Fagan 1936- WhoFI 94
Gillespie, John Spence 1926- Who 94
Gillespie, John Thomas 1928- WhoAm 94
Gillespie, Joseph David 1951- WhoMW 93
Gillespie, Joseph Gerard 1939- WhoFI 94
Gillespie, Junetta DrAPF 93
Gillespie, Kingsley 1895- WhAm 10
Gillespie, L. Kay 1940- WhoWest 94
Gillespie, Marcia A. 1944- WhoBlA 94
Gillespie, Marilyn Iola 1940- WhoAmP 93
Gillespie, Mary Krempa 1941- WhoAm 94
Gillespie, Nellie Redd WhoAm 94
Gillespie, O. Stanley 1916- WhoAmP 93
Gillespie, Rena Harrell 1949- WhoBlA 94
Gillespie, Rhondda 1941- IntWW 93
Gillespie, Robert 1933- WhoHol 92
Gillespie, Robert B. WrDr 94
Gillespie, Robert Bruce 1953- WhoScEn 94
Gillespie, Robert James 1942- WhoAm 94, WhoFI 94
Gillespie, Robert Wayne 1944- WhoAm 94, WhoFI 94
Gillespie, Ronald James 1924- IntWW 93, Who 94, WhoAm 94
Gillespie, Rory Andrew 1956- WhoAm 94
Gillespie, Roxani Manou 1941- WhoAm 94
Gillespie, Sarah Ashman 1953- WhoAm 94
Gillespie, Shane Patrick 1968- WhoScEn 94
Gillespie, Thomas David 1939- WhoMW 93, WhoScEn 94
Gillespie, Thomas Francis, Jr. 1957- WhoFI 94
Gillespie, Thomas Stuart 1938- WhoAm 94
Gillespie, Thomas William 1928- WhoAm 94
Gillespie, William G. 1931- WhoBlA 94
Gillespie, William Hewitt 1905- Who 94
Gillet, Roland 1962- WhoScEn 94
Gillett, Charles 1915- WhoAm 94
Gillett, Charlie 1942- WrDr 94
Gillett, David Keith 1945- Who 94
Gillett, Edward 1915- WrDr 94
Gillett, Fran 1928- WhoAmP 93
Gillett, George Nield, Jr. 1938- WhoAm 94, WhoFI 94
Gillett, John Bledsoe 1927- WhoScEn 94
Gillett, Jonathan Newell 1941- WhoAm 94
Gillett, Margaret 1930- WrDr 94
Gillett, Robin (Danvers Penrose) 1925- Who 94
Gillett, Robin Danvers Penrose 1925- IntWW 93
Gillett, Victor William, Jr. 1932- WhoFI 94
Gillette, Anita 1936- WhoHol 92
Gillette, Bob 1923- WrDr 94
Gillette, Dean 1925- WhoAm 94
Gillette, Edward LeRoy 1932- WhoAm 94
Gillette, Frank C., Jr. WhoScEn 94
Gillette, Frankie Jacobs 1925- WhoBlA 94
Gillette, George William, Jr. d1957 WhoHol 92
Gillette, Gordon Edgar 1931- WhoAm 94
Gillette, Halbert Scranton 1922- WhoAm 94
Gillette, Harry d1977 WhoHol 92
Gillette, Hyde 1906- WhoAm 94
Gillette, Kevin Mark 1955- WhoAmP 93
Gillette, King Camp WorInv
Gillette, Lyra Stephanie 1930- WhoBlA 94
Gillette, Minnie 1929- WhoAmP 93
Gillette, Patricia K. 1951- WhoAmL 94
Gillette, Paul Crawford 1942- WhoAm 94
Gillette, Richard Gareth 1945- WhoWest 94
Gillette, Robert West 1934- WhoAmP 93
Gillette, Roger 1917- WhoScEn 94, WhoWest 94
Gillette, Ruth 1907- WhoHol 92
Gillette, Stanley C. WhoAm 94
Gillette, Susan Downs 1950- WhoAm 94, WhoFI 94
Gillette, W. Michael 1941- WhoAm 94, WhoAmL 94, WhoAmP 93, WhoWest 94
Gillette, William d1937 WhoHol 92
Gillette, William 1933- WhoAm 94
Gilley, Gary Edward 1950- WhoFI 94
Gilley, Mickey 1936- WhoHol 92
Gilley, Mickey Leroy 1936- WhoAm 94
Gilley, Sheridan (Wayne) 1945- WrDr 94
Gilley, Smith E. WhoAmP 93
Gillford, Lord 1960- Who 94
Gillham, Grant David 1957- WhoWest 94
Gillham, John Kinsey 1930- WhoAm 94
Gillham, Nicholas Wright 1932- WhoAm 94
Gillham, Robert 1938- WhoAm 94
Gilliam, Arleen Fain 1949- WhoBlA 94
Gilliam, Armon Louis 1964- WhoBlA 94
Gilliam, Bates McCluer 1918- WhoAmP 93
Gilliam, Burton WhoHol 92
Gilliam, Carroll Lewis 1929- WhoAm 94
Gilliam, David WhoHol 92
Gilliam, Dorothy Butler WhoAm 94, WhoBlA 94
Gilliam, Du-Bois Layfelt 1951- WhoBlA 94
Gilliam, Earl B. 1931- WhoBlA 94
Gilliam, Earl Ben 1931- WhoAm 94, WhoAmL 94, WhoWest 94
Gilliam, Fannie H. 1943- WhoAmL 94
Gilliam, Frank Delano WhoBlA 94
Gilliam, George Harrison 1942- WhoAmL 94, WhoAmP 93
Gilliam, Herman Arthur, Jr. 1943- WhoBlA 94
Gilliam, Jack 1956- WhoWest 94
Gilliam, Jackson Earle 1920- WhoAm 94
Gilliam, James Franklin 1915-1990 WhAm 10
Gilliam, James H., Sr. 1920- WhoBlA 94
Gilliam, James H., Jr. 1945- WhoAm 94, WhoAmL 94, WhoBlA 94, WhoFI 94
Gilliam, Jean Marie 1923- WhoAmP 93
Gilliam, John A. 1935- WhoAm 94
Gilliam, John Charles 1927- WhoAm 94
Gilliam, John Rally 1945- WhoBlA 94
Gilliam, Marvin L. 1941- WhoBlA 94
Gilliam, Mary 1928- WhoWest 94
Gilliam, Melvin Randolph 1921- WhoAm 94, WhoScEn 94
Gilliam, Michael C. 1948- WhoIns 94
Gilliam, Reginald Earl 1944- WhoAmP 93
Gilliam, Reginald Earl, Jr. 1944- WhoBlA 94
Gilliam, Robert M., Sr. 1926- WhoBlA 94
Gilliam, Roosevelt Sandy, Jr. 1932- WhoBlA 94
Gilliam, Sam 1933- AfrAmAl 6, WhoAm 94, WhoAmA 93
Gilliam, Sam, Jr. 1933- WhoBlA 94
Gilliam, Stu WhoHol 92
Gilliam, Terry 1940- IntMPA 94, Who 94, WhoHol 92
See Also Monty Python's Flying Circus WhoCom
Gilliam, Terry Vance 1940- IntWW 93, WhoAm 94
Gilliams, Tyrone 1941- WhoBlA 94
Gillian, Kay ConAu 142, -43NR
Gilliard, Joseph Wadus 1914- WhoBlA 94
Gilliat, Leslie 1917- IntMPA 94
Gilliat, Martin John d1993 Who 94N
Gilliatt, Neal 1917- WhoAm 94
Gilliatt, Penelope DrAPF 93, IntWW 93
Gilliatt, Penelope d1993 IntWW 93N, NewYTBS 93 [port], WrDr 94N
Gilliatt, Penelope (Ann Douglas) 1932- EncSF 93

Gilliatt, Penelope (Ann Douglass) 1932-1993 ConAu 141
Gilliatt, Penelope Ann Douglass Corner d1993 Who 94N
Gillibrand, Sydney 1934- Who 94
Gillice, Sondra Jupin WhoFI 94
Gillick, John 1916- Who 94
Gillick, John Edward 1945- WhoAm 94, WhoAmL 94
Gillick, Patrick 1937- WhoAm 94
Gillie, Christopher 1914- WrDr 94
Gillie, Dennis Lee 1952- WhoWest 94
Gillie, Jean d1949 WhoHol 92
Gillie, Michelle Francoise 1956- WhoScEn 94
Gillier, Jean-Claude 1667-1737 NewGrDO
Gillies, Donald Allastair 1931- WhoAm 94
Gillies, Donald Richard 1939- WhoAm 94
Gillies, (Maurice) Gordon 1916- Who 94
Gillies, John Arthur 1947- WhoWest 94
Gillies, Louis Archibald d1993 NewYTBS 93
Gillies, Mary Ann WhoAmA 93N
Gillies, Max WhoHol 92
Gillies, Patricia Ann 1929- WhoWest 94
Gillies, Thomas Daniel 1920- WhoAm 94
Gillies, Valerie 1948- WrDr 94
Gilligan, Carol WhoAm 94
Gilligan, Carol 1936- ConAu 142
Gilligan, Jerome P. 1953- WhoAmL 94
Gilligan, John Gerard 1949- WhoScEn 94
Gilligan, John P. 1949- WhoAmL 94
Gilligan, Lawrence George 1948- WhoMW 93
Gilligan, Louis F. 1943- WhoAmL 94
Gilligan, Mary Ann 1956- WhoAmL 94
Gilligan, Michael James 1944- WhoAm 94
Gilligan, Robert F. 1942- WhoAmP 93
Gilligan, Robert G. WhoAmP 93
Gilligan, William Lee 1924- WhoAmP 93
Gilligan-Ivanjack, Claudia Marlene 1947- WhoWest 94
Gillilan, William J, III 1946- WhoAm 94, WhoFI 94
Gilliland, Alexis A(rnaldus) 1931- EncSF 93, WrDr 94
Gilliland, David Who 94
Gilliland, (James Andrew) David 1937- Who 94
Gilliland, David Jervois Thetford 1932- Who 94
Gilliland, Hap 1918- WhoWest 94
Gilliland, Helen d1942 WhoHol 92
Gilliland, James Sevier 1933- WhoAm 94, WhoAmL 94
Gilliland, Jennifer Who 94
Gilliland, John Campbell, II 1945- WhoAmL 94
Gilliland, Mary DrAPF 93
Gilliland, Norman Paul 1949- WhoMW 93
Gilliland, Richard 1952- WhoHol 92
Gilliland, William Elton 1919- WhoAm 94
Gillin, Donald T. d1992 IntMPA 94N
Gillin, Hugh WhoHol 92
Gillin, John F. 1956- WhoScEn 94
Gillin, Malvin James, Jr. 1946- WhoAmL 94
Gillin, Peter G. 1943- WhoAmL 94
Gilling, John 1912-1984 HorFD [port]
Gilling, Lancelot Cyril Gilbert 1920- Who 94
Gilling, Lucille WhoAmA 93
Gilling, Rebecca WhoHol 92
Gillingham, Bryan Reginald 1944- WhoAm 94
Gillingham, (Francis) John 1916- Who 94
Gillingham, Michael John 1933- Who 94
Gillingham, Peter Llewellyn 1914- Who 94
Gillingham, Robert Fenton 1944- WhoAm 94
Gillingham, Stephen Thomas 1944- WhoAmL 94, WhoFI 94
Gillings, Walter 1912-1979 EncSF 93
Gillingwater, Claude d1939 WhoHol 92
Gillingwater, Denis Claude 1946- WhoAmA 93
Gillio, Vickie Ann 1948- WhoAmL 94
Gilliom, Judith Carr 1943- WhoAm 94
Gillion, Michael 1946- WhoAmL 94
Gillion, Walter Michael 1946- WhoAmP 93
Gillis, Ann 1927- IntMPA 94, WhoHol 92
Gillis, Bernard Benjamin Who 94
Gillis, Bernard Thomas 1931- WhoAm 94
Gillis, Bill d1946 WhoHol 92
Gillis, Carl L., Jr. 1917- WhoAmP 93
Gillis, Chester 1951- WrDr 94
Gillis, Christine Diest-Lorgion WhoFI 94
Gillis, Christopher d1993 NewYTBS 93 [port]
Gillis, Don 1912-1978 NewGrDO
Gillis, Donald Scott 1962- WhoFI 94
Gillis, Elizabeth 1960- WhoAmL 94
Gillis, Geoffrey Lawrence 1944- WhoAmL 94
Gillis, Hugh Marion, Sr. 1918- WhoAmP 93
Gillis, John Bond 1960- WhoAmL 94
Gillis, John L., Jr. 1939- WhoAmL 94
Gillis, John Simon 1937- WhoAm 94, WhoScEn 94, WhoWest 94
Gillis, Lee Elwood WhoAmP 93
Gillis, Marvin Bob 1920- WhoFI 94
Gillis, Menelaus Arthur 1935- WhoFI 94
Gillis, Nelson Scott 1953- WhoFI 94
Gillis, Paul Leonard 1953- WhoAm 94, WhoWest 94
Gillis, Shirley J. Barfield 1943- WhoBlA 94
Gillis, Steven 1953- WhoAm 94, WhoScEn 94
Gillis, Theresa M. 1949- WhoAmL 94
Gillis, Theresa McKinzy 1945- WhoBlA 94
Gillis, William Freeman 1948- WhoAm 94
Gillispie, Harold Leon 1933- WhoMW 93
Gillispie, Lucy Anthony 1928- WhoAmP 93
Gillispie, Robert J. 1943- WhoAmL 94
Gillispie, Steven Brian 1955- WhoWest 94
Gillispie, William Henry 1927- WhoBlA 94
Gillman, Arthur Emanuel 1927- WhoAm 94
Gillman, Barbara Seitlin 1937- WhoAmA 93
Gillman, Bernard Arthur 1927- Who 94
Gillman, Greta Joanne 1945- WhoWest 94
Gillman, Leonard 1917- WhoAm 94, WhoScEn 94
Gillman, Michael Joseph 1939- WhoAmL 94
Gillman, Peter (Charles) 1942- WrDr 94
Gillman, Richard DrAPF 93
Gillman, Richard 1931- WhoAm 94, WhoFI 94
Gillman, Sid ProFbHF
Gillmar, Stanley Frank 1935- WhoAm 94, WhoFI 94, WhoWest 94
Gillmer, Thomas Charles 1911- WhoScEn 94
Gillmor, Charles Stewart 1938- WhoAm 94
Gillmor, John Edward 1937- WhoAm 94
Gillmor, Karen L. 1948- WhoAmP 93
Gillmor, Karen Lako 1948- WhoMW 93
Gillmor, Paul E. 1939- CngDr 93, WhoAm 94, WhoMW 93
Gillmor, Paul Eugene 1939- WhoAmP 93
Gillmore, Alan David 1905- Who 94
Gillmore, Alver James 1947- WhoAmL 94
Gillmore, Alver James, III 1947- WhoAmP 93
Gillmore, David (Howe) 1934- Who 94
Gillmore, David Howe 1934- IntWW 93
Gillmore, Inez Haynes 1873-1970 EncSF 93
Gillmore, Margalo d1986 WhoHol 92
Gillmore, Parker EncSF 93
Gillmore, Robert 1946- WhoAm 94
Gillock, Edgar Hardin 1928- WhoAmP 93
Gillon, Adam 1921- WrDr 94
Gillon, Alexander AmRev
Gillon, Luc-Pierre-A. 1920- IntWW 93
Gillon, Raanan Evelyn Zvi 1941- Who 94
Gillooly, Craig Lewis 1960- WhoAmL 94
Gillooly, Edna Rae 1932- WhoAm 94
Gillot, Claude 1673-1722 NewGrDO
Gilloteaux, Jacques Jean-Marie Anthime 1944- WhoMW 93
Gil-Loyzaga, Pablo Enrique 1954- WhoScEn 94
Gills, Norbert d1920 WhoHol 92
Gillson, Roy Charles 1952- WhoFI 94
Gill Thompson, Norma N. 1920- WhoMW 93
Gillum, Ronald M. 1939- WhoBlA 94
Gilly, Dinh 1877-1940 NewGrDO
Gilly, Kennedy J., Jr. 1950- WhoAmL 94
Gilman, Ada d1921 WhoHol 92
Gilman, Alan B. 1930- WhoAm 94
Gilman, Alfred Goodman 1941- WhoAm 94, WhoScEn 94
Gilman, Arita d1986 WhoHol 92
Gilman, Benjamin A. 1922- CngDr 93, WhoAmP 93
Gilman, Benjamin Arthur 1922- WhoAm 94
Gilman, Charles Alan 1949- WhoAm 94, WhoAmL 94
Gilman, Charlotte Perkins 1860-1935 AmSocL [port], BlmGWL, EncSF 93, HisWorL [port], ShSCr 13 [port]
Gilman, Charlotte (Anna) Perkins (Stetson) 1860-1935 RfGShF
Gilman, Daniel Coit 1831-1908 AmSocL
Gilman, Daniel D. 1954- WhoMW 93
Gilman, David Alan 1933- WhoAm 94
Gilman, Donald W., Jr. 1945- WhoMW 93
Gilman, Dorothy 1923- WrDr 94
Gilman, Dugan DrAPF 93
Gilman, Fred d1988 WhoHol 92
Gilman, George G. 1936- WrDr 94
Gilman, George L. WhoAmP 93
Gilman, Harold John Wilde 1876-1919 DcNaB MP
Gilman, Herbert 1924-1990 WhAm 10
Gilman, James Russell 1956- WhoScEn 94
Gilman, John Joseph 1925- WhoAm 94
Gilman, John Taylor 1753-1828 WhAmRev
Gilman, Jonathan Charles 1953- WhoFI 94
Gilman, Kenneth B. WhoFI 94
Gilman, Marvin Stanley 1922- WhoAm 94
Gilman, Nelson Jay 1938- WhoAm 94
Gilman, Nicolas 1755-1814 WhAmRev
Gilman, Peter A. WhoAm 94
Gilman, Richard 1925- WhoAm 94, WrDr 94
Gilman, Richard Carleton 1923- WhoAm 94
Gilman, Rita Gail 1935- WhoAmL 94
Gilman, Robert Cham EncSF 93
Gilman, Robert Cham 1921- WrDr 94
Gilman, Ronald Lee 1942- WhoAm 94
Gilman, Sam d1985 WhoHol 92
Gilman, Sander Lawrence 1944- WhoAm 94
Gilman, Sheldon Glenn 1943- WhoAmL 94
Gilman, Sid 1932- WhoAm 94, WhoMW 93
Gilmartin, F. Thomas 1940- WhoAmA 93
Gilmartin, John A. 1942- WhoAm 94, WhoFI 94
Gilmartin, Malvern 1926- WhoScEn 94
Gilmartin, Michael Raymond 1952- WhoWest 94
Gilmartin, Platt Jay 1952- WhoWest 94
Gilmartin, Raymond V. 1941- WhoAm 94, WhoFI 94
Gilmartin, Robert E., III 1950- WhoAmL 94
Gilmer, Charles Thomas 1933- WhoAmP 93
Gilmer, Donald H. 1945- WhoAmP 93
Gilmer, Harry Wesley 1937- WhoAm 94
Gilmer, John Kelly, Jr. 1958- WhoFI 94
Gilmer, Robert 1938- WhoScEn 94
Gilmer, Thomas Edward, Jr. 1925- WhoAm 94
Gilmont, Ernest Rich 1929- WhoAm 94
Gilmor, Jane E. 1947- WhoAmA 93
Gilmore, Al Tony 1946- WhoBlA 94
Gilmore, Allan Emory 1924- WhoScEn 94
Gilmore, Allen Douglas 1947- WhoWest 94
Gilmore, Anthony EncSF 93
Gilmore, Art 1912- WhoAm 94
Gilmore, Artis 1948- BasBi, WhoBlA 94
Gilmore, Barney d1949 WhoHol 92
Gilmore, Billie d1931 WhoHol 92
Gilmore, Brian Terence 1937- Who 94
Gilmore, Bruce Philip 1948- WhoAmL 94
Gilmore, Carol Jacqueline Who 94
Gilmore, Carter 1926- WhoAmP 93
Gilmore, Carter C. 1926- WhoBlA 94
Gilmore, Charles Arthur 1919- WhoBlA 94
Gilmore, Charles Minot 1942- WhoFI 94
Gilmore, Clarence Percy 1926- WhoAm 94
Gilmore, David D. 1943- WrDr 94
Gilmore, Dennis 1949- WhoHol 92
Gilmore, Don E. 1928- WhoAmP 93
Gilmore, Douglas d1950 WhoHol 92
Gilmore, Edwin 1931- WhoBlA 94
Gilmore, Frank d1943 WhoHol 92
Gilmore, Gail V. 1950- NewGrDO
Gilmore, Gary R. 1950- WhoAmP 93
Gilmore, Gordon Ray 1935- WhoFI 94
Gilmore, H. William WhoAm 94
Gilmore, Harry WhoAm 94, WhoAmP 93
Gilmore, Helen d1947 WhoHol 92
Gilmore, Helen Carol WhoMW 93
Gilmore, Horace Weldon 1918- WhoAm 94, WhoAmL 94, WhoMW 93
Gilmore, James Stanley, Jr. 1926- WhoAm 94, WhoAmP 93
Gilmore, James Stuart, III 1949- WhoAmP 93
Gilmore, Jerry Carl 1933- WhoAm 94
Gilmore, Jesse Lee 1920- WhoAm 94
Gilmore, Jimmie Dale 1945- ConMus 11 [port]
Gilmore, John DrAPF 93
Gilmore, John (Norman) 1951- WrDr 94
Gilmore, John Allen Dehn 1947- WhoAmL 94
Gilmore, John T. 1935- WhoBlA 94
Gilmore, June Ellen 1927- WhoAm 94, WhoMW 93
Gilmore, Kathi 1944- WhoAm 94, WhoAmP 93, WhoMW 93
Gilmore, Lowell d1960 WhoHol 92
Gilmore, Mark, Jr. 1939- WhoAmP 93
Gilmore, Marshall 1931- WhoBlA 94
Gilmore, Mary 1865-1962 BlmGWL
Gilmore, Maurice Eugene 1938- WhoScEn 94
Gilmore, Michael Clinton 1954- WhoMW 93
Gilmore, Peter 1931- WhoHol 92
Gilmore, Richard G. 1927- WhoBlA 94, WhoFI 94
Gilmore, Robert Gordon WhoAm 94
Gilmore, Robert McKinley, Sr. 1952- WhoBlA 94
Gilmore, Robert Witter 1933- WhoMW 93
Gilmore, Roger 1932- WhoAm 94, WhoAmA 93
Gilmore, Rosalind E.J. 1937- IntWW 93
Gilmore, Rosalind Edith Jean 1937- Who 94
Gilmore, Sam d1981 WhoHol 92
Gilmore, Thomas David 1952- WhoScEn 94
Gilmore, Thomas Meyer 1942- WhoFI 94
Gilmore, Thomas Odell, Sr. 1936- WhoAmP 93
Gilmore, Timothy Jonathan 1949- WhoFI 94, WhoWest 94
Gilmore, Virginia d1986 WhoHol 92
Gilmore, Voit 1918- WhoAm 94
Gilmore, William Rhodes, II 1946- WhoAmP 93
Gilmore, William S. 1934- IntMPA 94
Gilmour Who 94
Gilmour, Alan Breck 1928- Who 94
Gilmour, Alexander Clement 1931- Who 94
Gilmour, Allan (Macdonald) 1916- Who 94
Gilmour, Allan Dana 1934- WhoAm 94, WhoMW 93
Gilmour, Barbara 1921- WrDr 94
Gilmour, Craddock Matthew 1909- WhoWest 94
Gilmour, Edward Ellis 1930- WhoAm 94
Gilmour, Faye G. d1984 WhoHol 92
Gilmour, Ian WhoHol 92
Gilmour, Jeff L. 1947- WhoAmP 93
Gilmour, John (Edward) 1912- Who 94
Gilmour, John C. 1939- WrDr 94
Gilmour, John H. d1922 WhoHol 92
Gilmour, Mavis Gwendolyn 1926- IntWW 93
Gilmour, Nigel Benjamin Douglas 1947- Who 94
Gilmour, Robert Arthur 1944- WhoAm 94
Gilmour, Sally 1921- IntDcB [port]
Gilmour Of Craigmillar, Baron 1926- IntWW 93, Who 94
Giloth-David, King R. 1940- WhoBlA 94
Gilpatric, Roswell Leavitt 1906- WhoAm 94
Gilpatrick, Janet Louise 1944- WhoAmP 93
Gilpin, Alan 1924- WrDr 94
Gilpin, Bruce Wyndham, Jr. 1965- WhoWest 94
Gilpin, Charles d1930 WhoHol 92
Gilpin, Charles 1878-1930 AfrAmAl 6
Gilpin, Clemmie Edward 1942- WhoBlA 94
Gilpin, Henry Edmund 1922- WhoAmA 93
Gilpin, John d1983 WhoHol 92
Gilpin, John 1930-1983 IntDcB [port]
Gilpin, Larry Vincent 1943- WhoAm 94
Gilpin, Laura 1891-1979 WhoAmA 93N
Gilreath, Coot, Jr. 1937- WhoBlA 94
Gilreath, Thomas LeRoy 1952- WhoFI 94
Gilreath, Warren Dean 1920- WhoAm 94
Gilrin, Theodore H. d1967 WhoAmA 93N
Gilroy, Beryl 1924- BlmGWL
Gilroy, Beryl (Agatha) 1924- BlkWr 2
Gilroy, Frank 1925- IntMPA 94
Gilroy, Frank D. DrAPF 93
Gilroy, Frank D(aniel) 1925- ConDr 93, WrDr 94
Gilroy, Frank Daniel 1925- WhoAm 94
Gilroy, Tracy Anne Hunsaker 1959- WhoAmL 94, WhoMW 93
Gilroy Bevan, David Who 94
Gilruth, Robert Rowe 1913- IntWW 93, WhoAm 94, WhoScEn 94
Gilse, Jan van 1881-1944 NewGrDO
Gilsenan, Michael Dermot Cole 1940- Who 94
Gilsinan, James Francis, III 1945- WhoAm 94
Gilson, Arnold Leslie 1931- WhoFI 94, WhoScEn 94
Gilson, Barbara EncSF 93
Gilson, Charles (James Louis) 1878-1943 EncSF 93
Gilson, Earl Arthur 1923- WhoAmP 93
Gilson, Estelle DrAPF 93
Gilson, Giles 1942- WhoAmA 93
Gilson, Jerome 1931- WhoAm 94
Gilson, Nigel Langley 1922- Who 94
Gilson, Paul 1865-1942 NewGrDO
Gilson, Tom d1962 WhoHol 92
Gilson, W. E., Jr. 1936- WhoIns 94
Gilstein, Jacob Burrill 1923- WhoAm 94
Giltinan, Celia Elaine 1956- WhoMW 93

Giltner, Otis Beryl 1931- WhoFI 94
Gilton, Donna L. 1950- WhoBlA 94
Gilven, Hezekiah 1927- WhoBlA 94
Gilway, Barry John 1945- WhoIns 94
Gilwee, Jon Devak 1952- WhoWest 94
Gilyard, Clarence, Jr. WhoHol 92
Gilyeat, Ian Rhys 1959- WhoWest 94
Gilzow, Homer Floyd, Jr. 1950- WhoFI 94, WhoMW 93
Gim, H. W. d1973 WhoHol 92
Gimaro, Christopher Andrew 1964- WhoFI 94
Gimat, Jean-Joseph Sourbader de 1743- WhAmRev
Gimbel, Alfred Adolf 1944- WhoWest 94
Gimbel, Allen Mark 1956- WhoAm 94
Gimbel, John 1922-1992 WrDr 94N
Gimbel, Louis S., III 1929- WhoAmP 93
Gimbel, Madeleine Esther 1944- WhoAmL 94
Gimbel, Norman WhoAm 94
Gimbel, R. Nicholas 1951- WhoAmL 94
Gimbel, Roger 1925- IntMPA 94
Gimblett, Max(well) 1935- WhoAmA 93
Gimbrone, Michael Anthony, Jr. 1943- WhoAm 94
Gimbutas, Marija 1921- WhoAm 94
Gimenez (y Bellido), Jeronimo 1854-1923 NewGrDO
Giménez, Carlos 1954- WhoHisp 94
Gimenez, Eduardo 1940- NewGrDO
Gimenez, Jose Raul 1955- WhoHisp 94
Gimenez, Raul 1950- NewGrDO
Gimenez-Porrata, Alfonso 1937- WhoHisp 94
Gimeno, Andres 1937- BuCMET
Gimeno, Emil 1921- WhoHisp 94
Gimferrer, Pere 1945- IntWW 93
Gimferrer, Pere (Pedro) 1945- DcLB 134 [port]
Gimingham, Charles Henry 1923- Who 94
Gimma, Joseph Anthony 1907-1990 WhAm 10
Gimmarro, Steven Paul 1959- WhoMW 93
Gimmestad, Michael Jon 1943- WhoWest 94
Gimpel, Erica 1965- WhoHol 92
Gimpel, Jakob d1989 WhoHol 92
Gimpel, Rodney Frederick 1953- WhoScEn 94
Gimson, Ernest William 1864-1919 DcNaB MP
Gimson, George Stanley 1915- Who 94
Gin, Jackson 1934- WhoMW 93
Gin, Jerry B. 1943- WhoAsA 94
Ginader, George Hall 1933- WhAm 10
Ginaitt, Peter T. 1960- WhoAmP 93
Ginalski, Mark 1960- WhoWest 94
Ginanni, Maria 1892-1953 BlmGWL
Ginastera, Alberto (Evaristo) 1916-1983 NewGrDO
Ginder, John Matthew 1961- WhoScEn 94
Gindin, James 1926- WrDr 94
Gindin, William Howard 1931- WhoAm 94, WhoAmL 94
Gindlesberger, Pamela Ann 1958- WhoMW 93
Ginensky, Amy B. 1953- WhoAm 94, WhoAmL 94
Giner, Salvador 1934- IntWW 93
Gines, Ralph Junior 1933- WhoAmP 93
Ging, Jack 1934- WhoHol 92
Gingell, John 1925- Who 94
Gingell, Laurie William Albert 1925- Who 94
Gingell, Robert Arthur 1923- WhoAmL 94
Ginger, Ann F(agan) 1925- WrDr 94
Ginger, Phyllis Ethel 1907- Who 94
Gingerich, Owen Jay 1930- WhoAm 94
Gingerich, Philip Derstine 1946- WhoAm 94, WhoScEn 94
Gingerich, Richard Geoffrey Warmington 1948- WhoFI 94
Gingher, Marianne DrAPF 93
Gingher, Robert (S.) 1945- ConAu 141
Gingiss, Benjamin Jack 1911- WhoAm 94
Gingiss, Randall Jon 1945- WhoAmL 94
Gingl, Manfred 1948- WhoFI 94
Gingold, Dan IntMPA 94
Gingold, Dennis Marc 1949- WhoAm 94, WhoAmL 94, WhoFI 94
Gingold, George Norman 1939- WhoAm 94
Gingold, Harlan Bruce 1946- WhoAmL 94
Gingold, Helene d1926 WhoHol 92
Gingold, Hermione d1987 WhoHol 92
Gingras, Gustave 1918- WhoAm 94
Gingrich, Arnold 1903-1976 DcLB 137 [port]
Gingrich, John Thomas 1964- WhoWest 94
Gingrich, Newt 1943- CngDr 93, IntWW 93, WhoAmP 93
Gingrich, Newt(on Leroy) 1943- WrDr 94
Gingrich, Newton Leroy 1943- WhoAm 94
Gingrich-Petersen, Carolyn Ashcraft WhoAm 94
Giniecki, Kathleen Anne 1966- WhoScEn 94
Giniger, Henry 1922-1993 NewYTBS 93 [port]
Giniger, Kenneth Seeman 1919- WhoAm 94
Ginjaar, Nelly Jeanne 1931- WhoWomW 91
Ginley, Thomas J. 1938- WhoAm 94
Ginn, David 1951- WhoAmP 93
Ginn, H. Rand 1942- WhoWest 94
Ginn, Howard d1926 WhoHol 92
Ginn, John Charles 1937- WhoAm 94
Ginn, Richard Van Ness 1943- WhoAm 94
Ginn, Robert Martin 1924- WhoAm 94, WhoMW 93
Ginn, Ronald Bryan 1934- WhoAmP 93
Ginn, Ronn 1933- WhoAm 94
Ginn, Sam L. 1937- WhoAm 94, WhoFI 94, WhoWest 94
Ginna, Robert Emmett, Jr. 1925- IntMPA 94
Ginnett, Robert Charles 1947- WhoScEn 94
Ginnetti, John P. 1945- WhoIns 94
Ginnever, Charles 1931- WhoAmA 93
Ginolfi, James J. 1955- WhoAmP 93
Ginorio, Angela Beatriz 1947- WhoHisp 94
Ginoza, William 1914- WhoScEn 94
Ginsberg, Allen DrAPF 93
Ginsberg, Allen 1926- AmCulL, ConAu 41NR, GayLL, IntWW 93, WhoAm 94, WhoHol 92, WrDr 94
Ginsberg, Barry Howard 1945- WhoAm 94
Ginsberg, Benjamin 1947- WhoAm 94
Ginsberg, David Lawrence 1932- WhoAm 94
Ginsberg, Donald Maurice 1933- WhoScEn 94
Ginsberg, Edward 1917- WhoAm 94, WhoMW 93
Ginsberg, Ernest 1931- WhoAm 94, WhoAmL 94
Ginsberg, Frank Charles 1944- WhoAm 94
Ginsberg, Harold Louis 1903-1990 WhAm 10
Ginsberg, Harold Samuel 1917- WhoAm 94
Ginsberg, Hersh Meier 1928- WhoAm 94
Ginsberg, Leon Herman 1936- WhoAm 94
Ginsberg, Lewis Robbins 1932- WhoAm 94
Ginsberg, Myron 1943- WhoScEn 94
Ginsberg, Myron David 1939- WhoAm 94, WhoScEn 94
Ginsberg, Ronald Erwin 1946- WhoAmP 93
Ginsberg, Sidney 1920- IntMPA 94
Ginsberg-Fellner, Fredda 1937- WhoAm 94, WhoScEn 94
Ginsburg, Allen J. 1944- WhoAmL 94
Ginsburg, Ann 1932- WhoAm 94
Ginsburg, Carl DrAPF 93
Ginsburg, Charles David 1912- WhoAm 94, WhoAmL 94, WhoFI 94
Ginsburg, Daniel Alan 1961- WhoFI 94
Ginsburg, David 1921- Who 94
Ginsburg, David 1952- WhoAm 94
Ginsburg, Douglas H. WhoAmP 93
Ginsburg, Douglas Howard 1946- CngDr 93, WhoAm 94, WhoAmL 94
Ginsburg, Edward S. 1948- WhoAm 94, WhoAmL 94
Ginsburg, Ellin Louis WhoAm 94, WhoFI 94
Ginsburg, Estelle 1924- WhoAmA 93
Ginsburg, Faye D(iana) 1952- WrDr 94
Ginsburg, Gerald J. 1930- WhoAm 94
Ginsburg, Iona Horowitz 1931- WhoAm 94
Ginsburg, Lawrence David 1947- WhoAm 94
Ginsburg, Lewis S. 1914- IntMPA 94
Ginsburg, Lucien WhAm 10
Ginsburg, Marcus 1915- WhoAm 94
Ginsburg, Martin David 1932- WhoAm 94
Ginsburg, Max 1931- WhoAmA 93
Ginsburg, Mirra 1919- EncSF 93
Ginsburg, Norton Sydney 1921- WhoAm 94
Ginsburg, Ruth Bader 1933- CngDr 93, News 93 [port], WhoAm 94, WhoAmL 94, WhoAmP 93
Ginsburg, Ruth Joan Bader 1933- NewYTBS 93 [port]
Ginsburg, Seymour 1927- WhoAm 94, WhoWest 94
Ginsburg, Sigmund G. 1937- WhoAm 94
Ginsburgh, Robert Neville 1923- WhAm 10
Ginsburgs, George 1932- WrDr 94
Ginsky, Marvin H. 1930- WhoAm 94, WhoAmL 94, WhoFI 94
Gintautas, Jonas 1938- WhoAm 94, WhoScEn 94
Ginter, James Lee 1945- WhoAm 94
Gintoft, Ethel Margaret WhoMW 93
Ginty, Robert 1948- WhoHol 92
Gintzler, Janice Mae 1951- WhoMW 93
Ginyard, J. C. d1978 WhoHol 92
Ginza, Joey Darrel d1987 WhoHol 92
Ginzberg, Eli 1911- IntWW 93, WhoAm 94, WrDr 94
Ginzberg, Louis 1873-1953 DcAmReB 2
Ginzburg, Aleksandr Ilyich 1936- IntWW 93
Ginzburg, Evgeniia Semenovna 1896-1980 BlmGWL
Ginzburg, Lidia Yakovlevna d1990 IntWW 93N
Ginzburg, Lidiia Iakovlevna 1902-1990 BlmGWL
Ginzburg, Natalia 1916-1991 BlmGWL [port]
Ginzburg, Natalia Levi 1916-1991 WhAm 10
Ginzburg, Ralph 1929- WhoAm 94
Ginzburg, Rubin 1930- WhoAm 94
Ginzburg, Vitaly Lazarevich 1916- IntWW 93
Ginzburg, Yankel 1945- WhoAm 94
Ginzburg, Yankel (Jacob) 1945- WhoAmA 93
Ginzel, Andrew 1954- WhoAmA 93
Ginzel, Roland 1921- WhoAmA 93
Ginzton, Edward Leonard 1915- IntWW 93, WhoAm 94
Giobbi, Edward Giacchino 1926- WhoAm 94
Giobbi, Edward Gioachino 1926- WhoAmA 93
Giocondi, Gino J. 1931- WhoFI 94
Gioello, Debbie 1935- WhoAmA 93
Gioffre, Bruno Joseph 1934- WhoAmL 94
Gioi, Vivi d1975 WhoHol 92
Gioia, Angelo Joseph 1951- WhoMW 93
Gioia, Anthony Alfred 1934- WhoMW 93
Gioia, Dana DrAPF 93
Gioia, (Michael) Dana 1950- WrDr 94
Gioia, Gaetano c. 1760-1826 NewGrDO
Gioia, Philip Joseph 1946- WhoFI 94
Gioia, Ted 1957- WhoWest 94
Gioiella, Russell Michael 1954- WhoAmL 94
Gioioso, Joseph Vincent 1939- WhoMW 93
Giolitti, Alessandro 1955- WhoScEn 94
Giolitti, Antonio 1915- IntWW 93, Who 94
Giolitto, Barbara WhoMW 93
Giolitto, Barbara A. WhoAmP 93
Giometti, Gulio Mario 1960- WhoFI 94, WhoMW 93
Giomini, Marcello 1939- WhoScEn 94
Gionfriddo, Maurice Paul 1931- WhoScEn 94
Gionfriddo, Paul 1953- WhoAmP 93
Gior, Fino 1936- WhoFI 94
Giorda, Marcello d1960 WhoHol 92
Giordan, Andre Jean Pierre Henri 1946- WhoScEn 94
Giordanella, Frank 1959- WhoAmL 94
Giordani, Giuseppe 1751-1798 NewGrDO
Giordani, Tommaso c. 1730-1806 NewGrDO
Giordano, Andrew Anthony 1932- WhoAm 94, WhoWest 94
Giordano, Anthony Bruno 1915- WhoAm 94
Giordano, August Thomas 1923- WhoAm 94
Giordano, Clara 1924- WhoAmP 93
Giordano, Domiziana WhoHol 92
Giordano, Gary S. 1950- WhoAmP 93
Giordano, Gerard Raymond 1946- WhoWest 94
Giordano, Greg Joe 1960- WhoAmA 93
Giordano, John Read 1937- WhoAm 94
Giordano, Joseph, Jr. 1946- WhoAmP 93
Giordano, Joseph, Jr. 1953- WhoFI 94
Giordano, Larry F. 1945- WhoAmP 93
Giordano, Lawrence Francis 1953- WhoAmL 94
Giordano, Michele 1930- IntWW 93
Giordano, Nicholas Anthony 1943- WhoAm 94, WhoFI 94
Giordano, Paul Gregory 1956- WhoAmL 94, WhoWest 94
Giordano, Richard Vincent 1934- IntWW 93, Who 94, WhoAm 94
Giordano, Saverio P. 1943- WhoAm 94
Giordano, Serafino 1936- WhoFI 94
Giordano, Tony 1939- WhoAm 94
Giordano, Umberto (Menotti Maria) 1867-1948 NewGrDO
Giordano-McCanless, Angela Maria 1965- WhoWest 94
Giorgi, E. J. 1921- WhoAmP 93
Giorgi, Eleonora WhoHol 92
Giorgi, Elsie Agnes 1911- WhoAm 94
Giorgi-Belloc, Teresa NewGrDO
Giorgini, Aristodemo 1879-1937 NewGrDO
Giorgio, Paul Joseph 1950- WhoAmP 93
Giorgio, Todd Donald 1960- WhoScEn 94
Giorgio, William d1980 WhoHol 92
Giorgi-Righetti, Geltrude NewGrDO
Giorno, John DrAPF 93
Giorno, John 1936- WhoAmA 93
Giorza, Paolo 1832-1914 NewGrDO
Giosa, Nicola de NewGrDO
Gioseffi, Daniela DrAPF 93
Giotti, Cosimo 1759-1830 NewGrDO
Giovacchini, Peter Louis 1922- WhoAm 94, WhoMW 93, WhoScEn 94
Giovacchini, Robert Peter 1928- WhoAm 94
Giovanardi, Nicolo 1661-1729 NewGrDO
Giovanelli, Riccardo 1946- WhoAm 94
Giovanetti, Kevin Louis 1953- WhoScEn 94
Giovanni 1949- WhoAmA 93
Giovanni, Nikki DrAPF 93
Giovanni, Nikki 1943- AfrAmAl 6, BlkWr 2, BlmGWL, ConAu 41NR, TwCYAW, WhoAm 94, WhoBlA 94
Giovanni, Nikki (Yolande C., Jr.) 1943- WrDr 94
Giovannini, Pietro fl. 1779-1786 NewGrDO
Giovannitti, Len DrAPF 93
Giovenco, John V. 1936- WhoFI 94
Giovine, Giulio 1947- WhoFI 94
Giovo, Nicola NewGrDO
Gipe, Florence Meda 1896- WhAm 10
Gipe, George 1933-1986 EncSF 93
Gipe, Lawrence 1962- WhoAmA 93
Gipp, Chuck 1947- WhoAmP 93
Gippin, Robert Malcolm 1948- WhoAm 94
Gippius, Zinaida Nikolaevna 1869-1945 BlmGWL
Gipps, Jonathan Henry William 1947- Who 94
Gippsland, Bishop of 1929- Who 94
Gips, C. L. Terry 1945- WhoAmA 93
Gips, Edward U. 1922- WhoAm 94
Gips, Walter Fuld, Jr. 1920- WhoAm 94
Gipson, Arthur A. 1935- WhoBlA 94
Gipson, Bernard Franklin, Sr. 1921- WhoBlA 94
Gipson, Francis E., Sr. 1923- WhoBlA 94
Gipson, Fred(erick Benjamin) 1908-1973 TwCYAW
Gipson, Gordon 1914- WhoAm 94, WhoWest 94
Gipson, Lovelace Preston, II 1942- WhoBlA 94
Gipson, Mack, Jr. 1931- WhoBlA 94
Gipson, Reve WhoBlA 94
Gipson, Robert Malone 1939- WhoAm 94
Gipstein, Milton Fivenson 1951- WhoAmL 94, WhoWest 94
Gipstein, Robert Malcolm 1936- WhoWest 94
Gir EncSF 93
Gira, Catherine Russell 1932- WhoAm 94
Giral, Angela 1935- WhoHisp 94
Giraldi, Robert Nicholas 1939- WhoAm 94
Giraldo, Cesar A. WhoHisp 94
Giraldo, Rene WhoHisp 94
Giraldoni, Eugenio 1871-1924 NewGrDO
Giraldoni, Leone 1824-1897 NewGrDO
Girand, James Fields 1937- WhoFI 94
Girard, Bill 1936- WhoAmA 93
Girard, G. Tanner 1952- WhoMW 93
Girard, (Charles) Jack 1951- WhoAmA 93
Girard, Jacques 1940- WhoAm 94
Girard, James Emery 1945- WhoAm 94
Girard, James Louis 1953- WhoAmP 93
Girard, James P. DrAPF 93
Girard, James Preston 1944- WhoMW 93
Girard, Joseph d1949 WhoHol 92
Girard, Leonard Arthur 1942- WhoAm 94
Girard, Louis Joseph 1919- WhoAm 94
Girard, Nettabell 1938- WhoAm 94, WhoAmL 94
Girard, Remy WhoHol 92
Girard, Rene Noel 1923- IntWW 93, WhoAm 94
Girard, Robert David 1946- WhoAm 94, WhoAmL 94
Girard-diCarlo, David Franklin 1943- WhoAm 94, WhoAmL 94
Girardeau, Arnett E. 1929- WhoAmP 93
Girardeau, Isabella fl. 1709-1712 NewGrDO
Girardeau, Marvin Denham 1930- WhoAm 94, WhoWest 94
Girardi, Alexander 1850-1918 NewGrDO [port]
Girardin, Burton Lee 1934- WhoMW 93
Girardin, David Walter 1951- WhoWest 94
Girardin, Delphine de 1804-1855 BlmGWL
Girardin, Ray WhoHol 92

Girardot, Annie 1931- IntMPA 94, WhoHol 92
Girardot, Annie Suzanne 1931- IntWW 93
Girardot, Etienne d1939 WhoHol 92
Girardot, Hippolyte WhoHol 92
Girards, James Edward 1963- WhoAmL 94
Giraud, Andre Louis Yves 1925- IntWW 93
Giraud, Bernadette WhoHol 92
Giraud, Claude WhoHol 92
Giraud, Fiorello 1868-1928 NewGrDO
Giraud, Francois-Joseph d1788? NewGrDO
Giraud, Jean 1938- EncSF 93
Giraud, Marthe NewGrDO
Giraud, Michel 1929- IntWW 93
Giraud, Octavio d1958 WhoHol 92
Giraud, Raymond Dorner 1920- WhoAm 94
Giraud, Roland WhoHol 92
Giraudais, Francois Chesnard De La WhWE
Giraudeau, Bernard WhoHol 92
Giraudeau, Jean 1916- NewGrDO
Giraudet, Michele 1945- WhoScEn 94
Giraudier, Antonio 1926- WhoAmA 93
Giraudier, Antonio A., Jr. 1926- WhoHisp 94
Giraudoux, Jean (Hippolyte) 1882-1944 IntDcT 2
Girault, Thomas Lackey 1893- WhAm 10
Giray, I. Safa 1931- IntWW 93
Girden, Eugene Lawrence 1930- WhoAm 94
Girdler, Tom M. 1877-1965 EncABHB 9 [port]
Girdler, William, Jr. 1947-1978 HorFD
Girdlestone, Cuthbert M(orton) 1895-1975 NewGrDO
Girdwood, Ronald Haxton 1917- IntWW 93, Who 94
Gire, Sharon L. 1944- WhoAmP 93
Gire, Sharon Lee 1944- WhoMW 93
Girelli (Aquilar), Antonia Maria fl. 1752-1773 NewGrDO
Girgenti, John Alexander 1947- WhoAmP 93
Girgus, Joan Stern 1942- WhoAm 94
Giri, Jagannath 1933- WhoAsA 94, WhoMW 93
Giri, Tulsi 1926- IntWW 93
Giribaldi, Tomas 1847-1930 NewGrDO
Girling, Bettie Joyce Moore 1930- WhoAm 94
Girling, John (Lawrence Scott) 1926- WrDr 94
Girling, Robert George William, III 1929- WhoFI 94
Giro, Anna (Maddalena) c. 1710-1748? NewGrDO
Giro, Manuel 1848-1916 NewGrDO
Giro, R. (R. Gironda) 1936- WhoAmA 93
Girod, Frank Paul 1908- WhoWest 94
Girod, Fred 1951- WhoAmP 93
Girolami, Paul 1926- IntWW 93, Who 94
Giron, Fabio 1931- WhoHisp 94
Girón, José Alberto 1948- WhoHisp 94
Giron, Robert LeRoy 1952- WhoHisp 94
Gironda, A. John, III 1956- WhoScEn 94
Gironda, R. WhoAmA 93
Girone, Maria Elena 1939- WhoHisp 94
Girone, Vito Anthony 1910- WhoAm 94
Girotta, Mario 1939- WhoHol 92
Girotti, Massimo 1918- WhoHol 92
Girouard, Kenneth 1955- WhoScEn 94
Girouard, Mark 1931- Who 94, WrDr 94
Giroud, Francoise BlmGWL
Giroud, Francoise 1916- IntWW 93
Giroust, Francois 1737-1799 NewGrDO
Giroux, E. X. 1924- WrDr 94
Giroux, Jackie WhoHol 92
Giroux, Lee d1973 WhoHol 92
Giroux, Robert 1914- WhoAm 94
Giroux, Robert-Jean-Yvon 1939- WhoAm 94
Girovich, Mark Jacob 1934- WhoFI 94
Girth, Marjorie Louisa 1939- WhoAm 94
Girtman, Gregory Iverson 1956- WhoScEn 94
Girton, Lance 1942- WhoWest 94
Girty, Simon 1741-1818 AmRev, WhAmRev
Girvigian, Raymond 1926- WhoAm 94, WhoWest 94
Girvin, Eb Carl 1917- WhoAm 94
Girvin, Gary Edward 1951- WhoAmP 93
Girvin-Quirk, Susan 1950- WhoMW 93
Girzone, Joseph 1930- WhoAm 94
Girzone, Joseph F(rancis) 1930- SmATA 76 [port], WrDr 94
Gisbert, Nelson 1946- WhoHisp 94
Gisborough, Baron 1927- Who 94
Giscard D'Estaing, Francois 1926- IntWW 93
Giscard D'Estaing, Valery 1926- IntWW 93, Who 94
Giscombe, C. S. DrAPF 93
Gish, Annabeth IntMPA 94
Gish, Annabeth 1970- WhoHol 92
Gish, Dorothy d1968 WhoHol 92
Gish, Lillian d1993 IntMPA 94N
Gish, Lillian 1893-1993 ConTFT 11, CurBio 93N, NewYTBS 93 [port], News 93
Gish, Lillian 1896- IntMPA 94
Gish, Lillian 1899- WhoHol 92
Gish, Lillian (Diana) 1896?-1993 ConAu 140
Gish, Lillian Diana d1993 IntWW 93N, Who 94N
Gish, Mary d1948 WhoHol 92
Gish, Nancy K. 1942- WrDr 94
Gish, Norman Richard 1935- WhoAm 94
Gish, Robert F. 1940- WrDr 94
Gish, Robert Franklin 1940- WhoWest 94
Gish, Sheila WhoHol 92
Gislason, Eric Arni 1940- WhoAm 94, WhoMW 93
Gislason, Gylfi Th. 1917- IntWW 93
Gismondi, Celeste fl. 1725-1734 NewGrDO
Giso, Frank, III 1949- WhoAm 94, WhoAmL 94
Gisriel, Michael 1951- WhoAmP 93
Gissel, L. Henry, Jr. 1939- WhoAm 94
Gissendanner, John M. 1939- WhoBlA 94
Gisser, Michael Victor 1957- WhoAmL 94, WhoFI 94
Gissing, Bruce 1931- WhoAm 94, WhoFI 94
Gissing, George 1857-1903 DcLB 135 [port]
Gissing, George Robert 1857-1903 BlmGEL
Gissler, Sigvard Gunnar, Jr. 1935- WhoAm 94, WhoMW 93
Gist, Carole Anne-Marie WhoBlA 94
Gist, Christopher c. 1706-1759 WhWE
Gist, George Reinecker 1919- WhoMW 93
Gist, Herman C. WhoAmP 93
Gist, Howard Battle, Jr. 1919- WhoAm 94
Gist, J. Fred 1951- WhoAmL 94
Gist, Jack Lee 1953- WhoWest 94
Gist, Jessie M. Gilbert 1925- WhoBlA 94
Gist, Karen Wingfield 1950- WhoBlA 94
Gist, Lewis Alexander, Jr. 1921- WhoBlA 94
Gist, Mordecai 1743-1792 WhAmRev [port]
Gist, Nathaniel d1796 WhAmRev
Gist, Robert 1924- WhoHol 92
Gitch, David William 1939- WhoWest 94
Gite, Lloyd Anthony 1951- WhoBlA 94
Githiga, John Gatungu 1942- WhoBlA 94
Githii, Ethel Waddell WhoBlA 94
Gitin, David DrAPF 93
Gitin, Maria DrAPF 93
Gitler, Samuel Carlos 1933- WhoAm 94
Gitlin, Chris 1933- WhoAmP 93
Gitlin, H. Joseph 1932- WhoAmL 94
Gitlin, Michael 1943- WhoAmA 93
Gitlin, Todd DrAPF 93
Gitlin, Todd 1943- WhoWest 94, WrDr 94
Gitlin-Petlak, Laura 1957- WhoAmL 94
Gitlitz, David Martin 1942- WhoAm 94
Gitlitz, Melvin Hyman 1940- WhoScEn 94
Gitlow, Abraham Leo 1918- WhoAm 94
Gitlow, Stanley Edward 1926- WhoScEn 94
Gitner, Deanne 1944- WhoAm 94
Gitner, Geoffrey P. 1944- WhoAm 94, WhoAmL 94
Gitner, Gerald L. 1945- WhoAm 94
Gitnick, Gary Lee 1939- WhoWest 94
Gitnik, Paul J. 1960- WhoFI 94
Gitt, Cynthia E. 1946- WhoAmL 94
Gitt, Steven Mark 1960- WhoMW 93
Gittelman, Marc Jeffrey 1947- WhoAm 94
Gittelsohn, Roland B 1910- WrDr 94
Gittelson, Bernard 1918- WhoAm 94
Gittelson, June WhoHol 92
Gittens, James Philip 1952- WhoBlA 94
Gitter, Allan Reinhold 1936- WhoAm 94, WhoAmL 94
Gitter, Max 1943- WhoAm 94, WhoAmL 94
Gitterman, Alex WhoAm 94
Gitterman, Jeffrey Lewis 1965- WhoFI 94
Gittes, Franklin M. 1947- WhoAmL 94
Gittes, Ruben Foster 1934- WhoAm 94, WhoScEn 94
Gittess, Ronald Marvin 1937- WhoAm 94
Gittinger, D. Wayne 1933- WhoAm 94
Gittings, Clare (St. Quentin) 1954- WrDr 94
Gittings, Harold John 1947- Who 94
Gittings, Robert 1911-1992 AnObit 1992
Gittings, Robert (William Victor) 1911- WrDr 94
Gittings, Robert (William Victor) 1911-1992 ConAu 43NR
Gittleman, Arthur Paul 1941- WhoWest 94
Gittleman, Gary V. 1945- WhoAmL 94
Gittleman, Morris 1912- WhoFI 94, WhoScEn 94
Gittleman, Sol 1934- WhoAm 94
Gittler, Joseph B. 1912- WrDr 94
Gittler, Joseph Bertram 1912- WhoAm 94
Gittler, Robert d1978 WhoHol 92
Gittler, Steven 1926- WhoAmL 94
Gittlin, Arthur Sam 1914- WhoAm 94, WhoFI 94
Gittus, John Henry 1930- Who 94
Giudice, Eugene Michael 1964- WhoMW 93
Giuffrida, Alfred John 1951- WhoAmL 94
Giuffrida, Tom A. 1946- WhoAm 94
Giuggio, John P. d1993 NewYTBS 93
Giuggio, John Peter 1930- WhoFI 94
Giuglini, Antonio 1827-1865 NewGrDO
Giuliani, Alex 1927- WhoAmP 93
Giuliani, Cecilia c. 1760-1792? NewGrDO
Giuliani, Eleanor Regina 1949- WhoScEn 94
Giuliani, Peter 1907- WhoAmP 93
Giuliani, Rudolph 1944- News 94-2 [port], WhoAmP 93
Giuliani, Rudolph W. NewYTBS 93 [port]
Giuliani, Rudolph W. 1944- WhoAm 94
Giuliano, Concetto Richard 1935- WhoWest 94
Giulianti, Mara Selena 1944- WhoAm 94, WhoAmP 93
Giulietti, James D. WhoAmP 93
Giulini, Carlo Maria 1914- IntWW 93, NewGrDO, Who 94
Giunchigliani, Chris 1954- WhoAmP 93
Giunta, Anthony John 1928- WhoAmP 93
Giunta, Joseph 1951- WhoMW 93
Giuranna, Bruno 1933- IntWW 93
Giurescu, Dinu C. 1927- IntWW 93
Giurgiutiu, Victor 1949- WhoScEn 94
Gius, Julius 1911- WhoAm 94
Giusti, George WhAm 10
Giusti, George d1990 WhoAmA 93N
Giusti, Gino Paul 1927- WhoAm 94, WhoFI 94
Giusti, Girolamo fl. 1729-c. 1735 NewGrDO
Giusti, Joseph Paul 1935- WhoAm 94
Giusti, Luigi NewGrDO
Giusti, Robert George 1937- WhoAm 94
Giusti, William Roger 1947- WhoAm 94, WhoAmL 94
Giustinelli, Giuseppi fl. 1762-1769 NewGrDO
Giuvo, Nicola c. 1680-1748? NewGrDO
Givan, Boyd Eugene WhoAm 94
Givan, Richard M. 1921- WhoAmP 93
Givan, Richard Martin 1921- WhoAm 94, WhoAmL 94, WhoMW 93
Givant, Philip Joachim 1935- WhoFI 94, WhoWest 94
Givas, Thomas Peter 1957- WhoAmL 94
Givaudan, Ben Trested, III 1936- WhoAm 94
Given, David Eli 1938- WhoMW 93
Given, Edward Ferguson 1919- Who 94
Given, Kenna Sidney 1938- WhoAm 94
Given, Phyllis WhoAmP 93
Given, Ronald B. 1952- WhoAm 94
Givenchy 1927- WhoAm 94
Givenchy, Hubert de 1927- IntWW 93
Givens, Arthur A., Jr. 1936- WhoAmP 93
Givens, Charles J. 1942?- ConAu 140
Givens, Clementina M., Sister 1921- WhoBlA 94
Givens, David W. 1932- WhoAm 94, WhoMW 93
Givens, Donovahn Heston 1930- WhoBlA 94
Givens, Douglas Randall 1944- WhoMW 93
Givens, E. Terrian 1930- WhoBlA 94
Givens, Ernest P. 1964- WhoBlA 94
Givens, Henry, Jr. WhoBlA 94
Givens, Jack Rodman 1928- WhoAmL 94
Givens, Jeanne WhoAmP 93
Givens, John Kenneth 1940- WhoAm 94
Givens, Joshua Edmond 1953- WhoBlA 94
Givens, Ken 1947- WhoAmP 93
Givens, Lawrence 1938- WhoBlA 94
Givens, Leonard D. 1943- WhoAmL 94
Givens, Leonard David 1943- WhoBlA 94
Givens, Paul Edward 1934- WhoAm 94
Givens, Paul Ronald 1923- WhoAm 94
Givens, Richard Ayres 1932- WhoAmL 94
Givens, Robin WhoAm 94
Givens, Robin 1964- IntMPA 94, WhoHol 92
Givens, Robin 1965- WhoBlA 94
Givens, Rocelious 1928- WhoBlA 94
Givens, Ron D. 1952- WhoAmP 93
Givens, Roy E. 1929- WhoAmP 93
Givens, Stephen Bruce 1952- WhoScEn 94
Givens, William L. 1940- WhoWest 94
Givens, Willie Alan 1938- Who 94
Givhan, Mercer A., Jr. 1943- WhoBlA 94
Givhan, Robin Deneen 1964- WhoBlA 94
Givins, Abe, Jr. 1951- WhoBlA 94
Givins, Robert C(artwright) 1845-1915 EncSF 93
Givler, Leroy Ernest 1964- WhoFI 94
Givney, Kathryn d1978 WhoHol 92
Givot, George d1984 WhoHol 92
Givray, Henry Steven 1953- WhoMW 93
Gizouli, Dafallah IntWW 93
Gizzi, Domenico c. 1680-1758 NewGrDO
Gizzi, Michael DrAPF 93
Gizziello NewGrDO
Gjaerevoll, Olav 1916- IntWW 93
Gjedde, Albert Hellmut 1946- WhoScEn 94
Gjellerup, Pia 1959- WhoWomW 91
Gjerde, Andrea Jo 1955- WhoScEn 94
Gjerde, Bjartmar 1931- IntWW 93
Gjerde, Kristina Maria 1957- WhoAmL 94
Gjerstad, Diane A. 1957- WhoAmP 93
Gjertsen, Astrid 1928- IntWW 93
Gjertsen, O. Gerard 1932- WhoAm 94
Gjertson, Stephen Arthur 1949- WhoAmA 93
Gjesteby, Kari 1947- IntWW 93, WhoWomW 91
Gjonnes, Jon Kjell 1931- IntWW 93
Gjovig, Bruce Quentin 1951- WhoAm 94, WhoFI 94, WhoMW 93, WhoScEn 94
Glabe, Elmer Frederick 1911- WhoMW 93
Glacel, Barbara Pate 1948- WhoFI 94
Glachant, Antoine-Charles 1770-1851 NewGrDO
Glad, Dain Sturgis 1932- WhoScEn 94, WhoWest 94
Glad, John 1941- WrDr 94
Glad, Paul E. B. 1950- WhoAmL 94
Glad, Paul Wilbur 1926- WhoAm 94
Glad, Suzanne Lockley 1929- WhoWest 94
Gladchun, Lawrence L. 1950- WhoAm 94, WhoAmL 94
Gladden, Brenda Winckler 1943- WhoBlA 94
Gladden, Dean Robert 1953- WhoMW 93
Gladden, James Walter, Jr. 1940- WhoAm 94
Gladden, Joseph Rhea, Jr. 1942- WhoAmL 94, WhoFI 94
Gladden, Major P. 1935- WhoBlA 94
Gladden, Robert Wiley 1958- WhoFI 94
Gladden, Solomon Washington 1836-1918 AmSocL, DcAmReB 2
Gladding, Nicholas C. 1945- WhoAm 94, WhoAmL 94
Gladding, Peter Norris 1963- WhoFI 94
Glade, William Patton, Jr. 1929- WhoAm 94
Gladeck, Joseph M., Jr. 1950- WhoAmP 93
Glader, Mats Lennart 1945- WhoScEn 94
Gladfelter, Wilbert Eugene 1928- WhoScEn 94
Gladieux, Bernard Louis 1907- WhoAm 94
Gladilin, Anatoliy Tikhonovich 1935- IntWW 93
Glading, Jan DrAPF 93
Gladis, Jay 1949- WhoAm 94, WhoAmL 94
Gladki, Hanna Zofia 1933- WhoScEn 94
Gladkovsky, Arseny Pavlovich 1894-1945 NewGrDO
Gladner, Marc Stefan 1952- WhoAmL 94, WhoWest 94
Gladney, John Hanser 1948- WhoMW 93
Gladney, Marcellious 1949- WhoBlA 94
Gladney, William Beckett 1896- WhAm 10
Gladson, Guy Allen, Jr. 1928- WhoAmL 94
Gladstein, Martin Keith 1957- WhoScEn 94
Gladstone, Arthur M. 1921- WrDr 94
Gladstone, Barbara WhoAmA 93
Gladstone, Dana WhoHol 92
Gladstone, David Arthur Steuart 1935- IntWW 93, Who 94
Gladstone, Herbert Jack 1924- WhoAm 94
Gladstone, Kim Diane 1957- WhoAmL 94, WhoMW 93
Gladstone, Lee 1914- WhoMW 93
Gladstone, M. J. 1923- WhoAmA 93
Gladstone, Maggie 1921- WrDr 94
Gladstone, Milton 1914-1992 WhAm 10
Gladstone, Richard Bennett 1924- WhoAm 94
Gladstone, Stuart M. 1946- WhoAmL 94
Gladstone, (Erskine) William 1925- IntWW 93, Who 94
Gladstone, William Ewart 1809-1898 BlmGEL, HisWorL [port]
Gladstone, William Louis 1931- WhoAm 94
Gladstone, William Sheldon, Jr. 1923- WhoAm 94
Gladwell, Beatrice Howard 1914- WhoAmP 93
Gladwell, Dennis A. 1943- WhoAmL 94

Gladwell, Graham Maurice Leslie 1934- *WhoAm 94*
Gladwin, Derek Oliver 1930- *Who 94*
Gladwin, Joe d1987 *WhoHol 92*
Gladwin, John Warren 1942- *Who 94*
Gladwyn, Baron 1900- *IntWW 93, Who 94*
Gladwyn, Lord 1900- *WrDr 94*
Gladysz, John Andrew 1952- *WhoWest 94*
Glaenzer, Richard Howard 1933- *WhoScEn 94*
Glahe, Fred R. 1934- *WrDr 94*
Glahn, Wilbur A., III 1947- *WhoAmL 94*
Glaister, Lesley (G.) 1956- *WrDr 94*
Glaisyer, Hugh 1930- *Who 94*
Glaman, Eugenie Fish 1872-1956 *WhoAmA 93N*
Glamann, Kristof 1923- *IntWW 93, Who 94*
Glamis, Lord 1986- *Who 94*
Glamis, Walter *EncSF 93*
Glammack, George 1919- *BasBi*
Glamorgan, Earl of 1989- *Who 94*
Glancy, Alfred Robinson, III 1938- *WhoAm 94, WhoMW 93*
Glancy, Diane *DrAPF 93*
Glancy, Diane 1941- *WrDr 94*
Glancy, Michael 1950- *WhoAmA 93*
Glancy, Nicholas Ray 1955- *WhoAmL 94*
Glancy, Ruth F(ergusson) 1948- *ConAu 141*
Glancy, Thomas Xavier, Jr. 1955- *WhoAmL 94*
Glancy, Walter John 1942- *WhoAm 94*
Glancz, Ronald Robert 1943- *WhoAm 94*
Glandine, Viscount 1967- *Who 94*
Glang, Gabriele *DrAPF 93*
Glanstein, Joel Charles 1940- *WhoAmL 94*
Glanton, Lydia Jackson 1909- *WhoBlA 94*
Glanton, Pam 1947- *WhoAmP 93*
Glanton, Richard H. 1946- *WhoAm 94, WhoAmL 94*
Glanton, Richard Howard 1946- *WhoAmP 93*
Glanton, Sadye Lyerson 1900- *WhoBlA 94*
Glantz, David M. 1942- *WrDr 94*
Glantz, Gina Stritzler 1943- *WhoAmP 93*
Glantz, Kalman 1937- *WrDr 94*
Glantz, Wendy Newman 1956- *WhoAmL 94*
Glantzman, Judy 1956- *WhoAmA 93*
Glanusk, Baron 1917- *Who 94*
Glanville, Alec William 1921- *Who 94*
Glanville, Brian 1931- *DcLB 139 [port]*
Glanville, Brian (Lester) 1931- *WrDr 94*
Glanville, Brian Lester 1931- *Who 94*
Glanville, Cecil E. 1925- *WhoBlA 94*
Glanville, Evelyn Boyd 1924- *AfrAmAl 6*
Glanville, James William 1923-1992 *WhAm 10*
Glanville, Jeffrey Alan 1965- *WhoMW 93*
Glanville, Jerry 1941- *WhoAm 94*
Glanville, Robert Edward 1950- *WhoAm 94, WhoAmL 94*
Glanville Brown, William *Who 94*
Glanville-Hicks, Peggy 1912-1990 *NewGrDO, WhAm 10*
Glanville-Jones, Thomas *Who 94*
Glanz, Andrea E. 1952- *WhoAmA 93*
Glanz, Barbara Anne 1943- *WhoMW 93*
Glanz, Karen 1953- *WrDr 94*
Glanzer, Murray 1922- *WhoScEn 94*
Glanzer, Seymour 1926- *WhoAm 94*
Glarner, Fritz 1899-1972 *WhoAmA 93N*
Glasauer, Franz Ernst 1930- *WhoAm 94*
Glasberg, Laurence Brian 1943- *WhoAm 94*
Glasberg, Meyer Samuel 1916- *WhoAmL 94*
Glasberg, Paula Drillman 1939- *WhoAm 94, WhoFI 94*
Glasby, (Alfred) Ian 1931- *Who 94*
Glasby, John S(tephen) 1928- *EncSF 93*
Glasco, Anita L. 1942- *WhoBlA 94*
Glasco, Joseph M. 1925- *WhoAmA 93*
Glasco, Joseph Milton 1925- *WhoAm 94*
Glasco, Kimberly *WhoAm 94*
Glascoff, Donald G., Jr. 1945- *WhoAmL 94*
Glase, Peter J. 1941- *WhoAmL 94*
Glaser, Alvin 1932- *WhoFI 94*
Glaser, Arthur Henry 1947- *WhoAmL 94*
Glaser, Bruce 1933- *WhoAmA 93*
Glaser, Claude Edward, Jr. 1919- *WhoAm 94*
Glaser, Daniel 1918- *WhoAm 94*
Glaser, David 1919- *WhoAmA 93*
Glaser, Donald A. 1926- *WorInv*
Glaser, Donald Arthur 1926- *IntWW 93, Who 94, WhoAm 94, WhoScEn 94, WhoWest 94*
Glaser, Douglas Edward 1951- *WhoFI 94*
Glaser, Elton *DrAPF 93*
Glaser, Franz (Joseph) 1798-1861 *NewGrDO*
Glaser, Gilbert Herbert 1920- *WhoAm 94*
Glaser, Harold 1924- *WhoAm 94*
Glaser, Isabel Joshlin *DrAPF 93*
Glaser, Jennifer Backer 1963- *WhoMW 93*
Glaser, John William 1933- *WhoWest 94*
Glaser, Joseph Bernard 1925- *WhoAm 94*
Glaser, Kurt 1914- *WrDr 94*
Glaser, Lillian d1969 *WhoHol 92*
Glaser, Luis 1932- *WhoAm 94*
Glaser, Lulu d1958 *WhoHol 92*
Glaser, Michael S. *DrAPF 93*
Glaser, Milton 1929- *WhoAm 94, WhoAmA 93*
Glaser, Norman Dale 1921- *WhoAmP 93*
Glaser, Paul Michael 1943- *IntMPA 94, WhoHol 92*
Glaser, Peter Edward 1923- *WhoAm 94*
Glaser, Ralph Thomas 1943- *WhoMW 93*
Glaser, Richard A. 1952- *WhoAmL 94*
Glaser, Robert Edward 1935- *WhoAm 94*
Glaser, Robert Joy 1918- *IntWW 93, WhoAm 94*
Glaser, Robert Leonard 1929- *WhoAm 94*
Glaser, Ronald 1939- *WhoAm 94*
Glaser, Steven Jay 1957- *WhoAmL 94*
Glaser, Vaughn d1958 *WhoHol 92*
Glaser, Vera Romans *WhoAm 94*
Glaser, William 1940- *WhoAmP 93*
Glaser, William Arnold 1925- *WrDr 94*
Glasgow, Archbishop of *Who 94*
Glasgow, Earl of 1939- *Who 94*
Glasgow, Provost of *Who 94*
Glasgow, Douglas G. *WhoBlA 94*
Glasgow, Ellen 1873-1945 *BlmGWL*
Glasgow, Ellen Anderson Gholson 1873-1945 *AmCulL*
Glasgow, Gil *WhoHol 92*
Glasgow, J. C. 1947- *WhoScEn 94*
Glasgow, James Alan 1945- *WhoAmL 94*
Glasgow, Jesse Edward 1923- *WhoAm 94*
Glasgow, Lukman 1935-1988 *WhoAmA 93N*
Glasgow, Norman Milton 1922- *WhoAmL 94*
Glasgow, Paul T. 1946- *WhoAmL 94*
Glasgow, Robert Joe 1942- *WhoAmP 93*
Glasgow, Robert Morris, III 1964- *WhoFI 94*
Glasgow, Robert Russell 1952- *WhoMW 93*
Glasgow, Roger A. 1942- *WhoAmL 94*
Glasgow, Vaughn Leslie 1944- *WhoAm 94, WhoAmA 93*
Glasgow, Willene Graythen 1939- *WhoFI 94*
Glasgow, William Jacob 1946- *WhoAm 94, WhoAmL 94, WhoFI 94*
Glasgow And Galloway, Bishop of 1959- *Who 94*
Glasgow And Galloway, Dean of *Who 94*
Glashausser, Suellen 1945- *WhoAmA 93*
Glasheen, Charles R. 1942- *WhoAmL 94*
Glashow, Sheldon L. 1932- *WorScD*
Glashow, Sheldon Lee 1932- *IntWW 93, Who 94, WhoAm 94, WhoScEn 94*
Glasier, Alice Geneva *WhoAmA 93*
Glasier, Alice Geneva 1903- *WhoAm 94, WhoWest 94*
Glaskin, G(erald) M(arcus) 1923- *EncSF 93, WrDr 94*
Glasman, Michael Morris 1956- *WhoScEn 94*
Glasner, Ann K. *DrAPF 93*
Glaspell, Susan 1876-1948 *BlmGWL*
Glaspell, Susan (Keating) 1882?-1948 *IntDcT 2*
Glaspie, April C. *WhoAmP 93*
Glasrud, Bruce Alden 1940- *WhoAm 94, WhoWest 94*
Glasrud, Clarence A 1911- *WrDr 94*
Glass, Alastair Malcolm 1940- *WhoAm 94*
Glass, Alexander Jacob 1933- *WhoAm 94*
Glass, Amanda 1948- *WrDr 94*
Glass, Andrew *WrDr 94*
Glass, Andrew James 1935- *WhoAm 94*
Glass, Anthony Trevor 1940- *Who 94*
Glass, Arnold Lewis 1951- *WhoScEn 94*
Glass, Betty Dunn 1935- *WhoAmP 93*
Glass, Carson McElyea 1915- *WhoAm 94*
Glass, Daniel S. *WhoAm 94, WhoFI 94*
Glass, David Carter 1930- *WhoAm 94*
Glass, David D. 1935- *WhoAm 94, WhoFI 94*
Glass, David Eugene 1956- *WhoScEn 94*
Glass, Dennis R. 1949- *WhoIns 94*
Glass, Dorothy F. *WhoAmA 93*
Glass, Douglas B. 1949- *WhoAmL 94*
Glass, Edward Brown 1913- *Who 94*
Glass, Everett d1966 *WhoHol 92*
Glass, Fred Stephen 1940- *WhoAmL 94*
Glass, Frederick M. d1993 *NewYTBS 93*
Glass, Gaston d1965 *WhoHol 92*
Glass, Gerald Damon 1967- *WhoBlA 94*
Glass, H(iram) Bentley 1906- *IntWW 93*
Glass, Henry Peter 1911- *WhoAm 94*
Glass, Herbert 1934- *WhoAm 94*
Glass, Hugh c. 1780-1833 *WhWE*
Glass, Irvine Israel 1918- *WhoAm 94*
Glass, James 1928- *WhoBlA 94*
Glass, James Clifford 1937- *WhoWest 94*
Glass, Jesse, Jr. *DrAPF 93*
Glass, Joanna 1936- *BlmGWL*
Glass, Joanna (McClelland) 1936- *ConAu 43NR*
Glass, John Derek 1941- *WhoAm 94*
Glass, Kenneth Edward 1940- *WhoAm 94*
Glass, Laurel Ellen 1923- *WhoAm 94*
Glass, Lawrence David *WhoMW 93*
Glass, M. Milton d1993 *NewYTBS 93 [port]*
Glass, Malcolm *DrAPF 93*
Glass, Margaret Smyllie 1946- *WhoAm 94*
Glass, Michael 1945- *WhoAm 94*
Glass, Michael L. 1945- *WhoAmA 93*
Glass, Milton Louis 1929- *WhoAm 94*
Glass, Myrtle d1945 *WhoHol 92*
Glass, Ned d1984 *WhoHol 92*
Glass, Norman Jeffrey 1946- *Who 94*
Glass, Philip 1937- *AmCulL, IntWW 93, NewGrDO, Who 94, WhoAm 94*
Glass, Robert David 1922- *WhoAmP 93*
Glass, Robert Davis 1922- *WhoAm 94, WhoAmL 94, WhoBlA 94*
Glass, Ron 1945- *WhoHol 92*
Glass, Ronald 1945- *WhoBlA 94*
Glass, Ronald L. 1946- *WhoAm 94*
Glass, Ronald Lee 1946- *WhoAm 94*
Glass, Seamon *WhoHol 92*
Glass, Stanford Lee 1934- *WhoAm 94*
Glass, Thomas 1945- *WhoAmP 93*
Glass, Thomas Graham, Jr. 1926- *WhoScEn 94*
Glass, Torrey Allen 1952- *WhoFI 94*
Glass, Virginia M. 1927- *WhoBlA 94*
Glass, Wendy D. 1925- *WhoAmA 93*
Glasscock, C. Edward 1943- *WhoAmL 94*
Glasscock, Gary M. 1951- *WhoAm 94*
Glasscock, James Samuel 1931- *WhoAmP 93*
Glasscock, John Lewis 1928- *Who 94*
Glasscock, Kent *WhoAmP 93*
Glasscock, Sarah (Jean) 1952- *WrDr 94*
Glasse, John Howell 1922- *WhoAm 94*
Glasse, Robert M. d1993 *NewYTBS 93*
Glasse, Robert Marshall 1929-1993 *ConAu 140*
Glasse, Thomas Henry 1898- *Who 94*
Glasser, Charles Edward 1940- *WhoWest 94*
Glasser, Farrell C. 1944- *WhoAmL 94*
Glasser, Ira Saul 1938- *WhoAm 94, WhoAmL 94*
Glasser, Israel d1993 *NewYTBS 93*
Glasser, Israel Leo 1924- *WhoAm 94, WhoAmL 94*
Glasser, James J. 1934- *WhoAm 94, WhoFI 94*
Glasser, Joseph 1925- *WhoAm 94*
Glasser, Joshua David 1961- *WhoScEn 94*
Glasser, Melvin Allan 1915- *WhoAm 94*
Glasser, Norma Penchansky 1941- *WhoAmA 93*
Glasser, Otto John 1918- *WhoAm 94*
Glasser, Paul Harold 1929- *WhoAm 94*
Glasser, Perry *DrAPF 93*
Glasser, Stephen Paul 1940- *WhoAm 94*
Glasser, William 1925- *WhoWest 94*
Glasser, Wolfgang Gerhard 1941- *WhoScEn 94*
Glassett, Tim Scott 1956- *WhoAmL 94, WhoWest 94*
Glassford, Wilfred *EncSF 93*
Glassgold, Alfred Emanuel 1929- *WhoAm 94*
Glassgold, I. Leon 1923- *WhoAm 94*
Glassgow, Edwin John 1945- *Who 94*
Glassgow, M. Edward 1934- *WhoAmP 93*
Glassheim, Eliot Alan 1938- *WhoAmP 93*
Glassick, Charles Etzweiler 1931- *WhoAm 94*
Glassman, Abraham 1933- *WhoAmP 93*
Glassman, Alexander Howard 1934- *WhoAm 94*
Glassman, Armand Barry 1938- *WhoAm 94, WhoScEn 94*
Glassman, Arthur Joseph 1948- *WhoWest 94*
Glassman, Bruce 1961- *SmATA 76*
Glassman, Caroline D. *WhoAmP 93*
Glassman, Caroline Duby 1922- *WhoAm 94, WhoAmL 94*
Glassman, Edward 1929- *WhoAm 94*
Glassman, George Morton 1935- *WhoScEn 94*
Glassman, Gerald Seymour 1932- *WhoAm 94, WhoFI 94*
Glassman, Herbert Haskel 1919- *WhoAm 94*
Glassman, Howard Theodore 1934- *WhoAm 94*
Glassman, Irvin 1923- *WhoAm 94, WhoScEn 94*
Glassman, James Kenneth 1947- *WhoAm 94*
Glassman, Jerome Martin 1919- *WhoAm 94*
Glassman, Jon David 1944- *WhoAm 94, WhoAmP 93*
Glassman, Lawrence S. 1953- *WhoScEn 94*
Glassman, Lee Douglas 1966- *WhoAmL 94*
Glassman, Ronald M. 1937- *WrDr 94*
Glassman, Stanley Alan 1945- *WhoAm 94*
Glassman, Steven J. 1944- *WhoAm 94, WhoAmL 94*
Glassmeyer, Edward 1915- *WhoAm 94*
Glassmeyer, James Milton 1928- *WhoScEn 94*
Glassmire, Gus d1946 *WhoHol 92*
Glassmoyer, Thomas Parvin 1915- *WhoAm 94, WhoAmL 94*
Glassner, Barry 1952- *WhoAm 94, WrDr 94*
Glassock, Richard James 1934- *WhoAm 94, WhoScEn 94*
Glasson, Linda 1947- *WhoFI 94*
Glasson, Lloyd 1931- *WhoAm 94, WhoAmA 93*
Glasspole, Florizel (Augustus) 1909- *Who 94*
Glasspole, Florizel Augustus 1909- *IntWW 93*
Glasstone, Samuel 1897- *WhAm 10*
Glatfelter, Philip Henry, III 1916- *WhoAm 94*
Glatman-Stein, Marcia 1944- *WhoAm 94*
Glatt, Linnea 1949- *WhoAmA 93*
Glatt, Michael D. 1942- *WhoAm 94*
Glatthaar, Joseph T(homas) 1957- *ConAu 142*
Glatzer, Jeffrey L. 1944- *WhoAmL 94*
Glatzer, Robert Anthony 1932- *WhoFI 94, WhoWest 94*
Glauber, Michael A. 1943- *WhoAm 94*
Glauberman, Melvin L. 1927- *WhoAmL 94*
Glaubinger, Lawrence David 1925- *WhoFI 94*
Glaude, Stephen A. 1954- *WhoBlA 94*
Glauert, Audrey Marion 1925- *Who 94*
Glaug, Frank Steven 1957- *WhoMW 93*
Glaum, Louise d1970 *WhoHol 92*
Glauner, Alfred William 1936- *WhoAm 94*
Glauser, Mark Nelson 1957- *WhoScEn 94*
Glauthier, T. James 1944- *WhoAm 94*
Glaves Smith, Frank William 1919- *Who 94*
Glaviano, Vincent Valentino 1920- *WhAm 10*
Glavin, A. Rita Chandellier 1937- *WhoAmL 94*
Glavin, James Edward 1923- *WhoAm 94*
Glavin, James Henry, III 1931- *WhoAmL 94, WhoAmP 93*
Glavin, William F. 1932- *IntWW 93*
Glavin, William Francis 1932- *Who 94, WhoAm 94*
Glavine, Tom 1966- *WhoAm 94*
Glavopoulos, Christos Dimitrios 1958- *WhoScEn 94*
Glawe, Lloyd Neil 1932- *WhoScEn 94*
Glaz, Hertha 1908- *NewGrDO*
Glaze, Andrew *DrAPF 93*
Glaze, Andrew Louis 1920- *WrDr 94*
Glaze, Bob 1927- *WhoAmP 93*
Glaze, Eleanor *DrAPF 93*
Glaze, Michael John Carlisle 1935- *Who 94*
Glaze, Peter d1983 *WhoHol 92*
Glaze, Robert Pinckney 1933- *WhoAm 94*
Glaze, Thomas A. 1938- *WhoAmL 94*
Glaze, Tim Leon 1951- *WhoMW 93*
Glaze, Tom 1938- *WhoAm 94, WhoAmP 93*
Glazebrook, Carla Rae 1958- *WhoWest 94*
Glazebrook, (Reginald) Mark 1936- *Who 94*
Glazebrook, Philip 1937- *WrDr 94*
Glazer, Barry David 1948- *WhoAm 94*
Glazer, Benjamin 1887-1956 *IntDcF 2-4*
Glazer, Donald Jack 1942- *WhoAm 94*
Glazer, Donald Wayne 1944- *WhoAm 94, WhoAmL 94*
Glazer, Edward Louis 1946- *WhoAm 94, WhoAmL 94*
Glazer, Esther *WhoAm 94*
Glazer, Frederic Jay 1937- *WhoAm 94*
Glazer, Gary Mark 1950- *WhoScEn 94*
Glazer, Guilford 1921- *WhoWest 94*
Glazer, Jack Henry 1928- *WhoAmL 94*
Glazer, Jane *DrAPF 93*
Glazer, Larry Sylvester 1939- *WhoFI 94*
Glazer, Laurence Charles 1945- *WhoAm 94*
Glazer, Martin A. 1946- *WhoAmL 94*
Glazer, Michael 1940- *WhoAmL 94*
Glazer, Michael H. 1948- *WhoAm 94, WhoAmL 94*
Glazer, Miriyam Myra 1945- *WhoWest 94*
Glazer, Nathan 1923- *IntWW 93, WhoAm 94, WrDr 94*
Glazer, Rea Helene 1944- *WhoWest 94*
Glazer, Richard C. 1942- *WhoAmL 94*

Glazer, Ronald Barry 1943- *WhoAm 94, WhoAmL 94*
Glazer, Steven Donald 1948- *WhoAmL 94*
Glazer, William *IntMPA 94*
Glazer, William Frank 1965- *WhoAmL 94*
Glazev, Sergei Yurevich 1961- *LoBiDrD*
Glazier, Kenneth M. 1948- *WhoAmL 94*
Glazier, Loss Pequeño *WhoHisp 94*
Glazier, Lyle *DrAPF 93*
Glazier, Robert Carl 1927- *WhoAm 94*
Glazier, Stephen Charles 1950- *WhoAmL 94*
Glazier, Stephen Davey 1949- *WhoMW 93*
Glaz'iev, Sergey Yurievich 1961- *IntWW 93*
Glazko, Anthony Joachim 1914- *WhoMW 93, WhoScEn 94*
Glazner, Greg(ory Allen) 1958- *ConAu 142*
Glazner, Raymond Charles *WhoAm 94*
Glazunov, Aleksandr 1865-1936 *IntDcB*
Glazunov, Andrey fl. 183-?-184-? *WhWE*
Glazunov, Ilya Sergeyevich 1930- *IntWW 93*
Gleason, Abbott 1938- *WhoAm 94*
Gleason, Adda d1971 *WhoHol 92*
Gleason, Alfred M. 1930- *WhoFI 94, WhoWest 94*
Gleason, Andrew Mattei 1921- *IntWW 93, WhoAm 94*
Gleason, Daniel J. 1944- *WhoAmL 94*
Gleason, Darlene Harriette 1933- *WhoMW 93*
Gleason, David *WhoAmP 93*
Gleason, Douglas 1916- *WhoAm 94*
Gleason, Douglas Renwick 1956- *WhoWest 94*
Gleason, Eliza 1909- *WhoBlA 94*
Gleason, Frederick G(rant) 1848-1903 *NewGrDO*
Gleason, Gerald Wayne 1911- *WhoAmL 94, WhoMW 93*
Gleason, Harold Anthony 1945- *WhoFI 94*
Gleason, Jackie d1987 *WhoHol 92*
Gleason, Jackie 1916-1987 *WhoCom [port]*
Gleason, James d1959 *WhoHol 92*
Gleason, James Mullaney 1948- *WhoAmL 94*
Gleason, Jean Berko 1931- *WhoAm 94*
Gleason, Jean Wilbur 1943- *WhoAm 94, WhoAmL 94, WhoFI 94*
Gleason, Joanna 1950- *WhoAm 94, WhoHol 92*
Gleason, Joe Duncan 1879-1959 *WhoAmA 93N*
Gleason, John James 1941- *WhoAm 94*
Gleason, John Martin 1907- *WhoAm 94*
Gleason, John Patrick, Jr. 1941- *WhoAm 94*
Gleason, Judith *DrAPF 93*
Gleason, Larry 1938- *IntMPA 94*
Gleason, Lucille d1947 *WhoHol 92*
Gleason, Maurice Francis 1909- *WhoBlA 94*
Gleason, Norman Dale 1943- *WhoAm 94*
Gleason, Paul *WhoHol 92*
Gleason, Philip Wayne 1943- *WhoAmP 93*
Gleason, Ralph Newton 1922- *WhoAm 94*
Gleason, Robert A., Sr. 1909- *WhoAmP 93*
Gleason, Robert Davis 1935- *WhoAmP 93*
Gleason, Robert Willard 1932- *WhoAm 94*
Gleason, Russell d1945 *WhoHol 92*
Gleason, Thomas Clifford 1953- *WhoScEn 94*
Gleason, Thomas Daues 1936- *WhoAm 94*
Gleason, Thomas W. 1900- *WhoFI 94*
Gleason, Thomas W. 1900-1992 *AnObit 1992*
Gleason, Thomas W(illiam) 1900-1992 *CurBio 93N*
Gleason, William F., Jr. *WhoAmL 94*
Gleave, John T 1917- *WrDr 94*
Gleave, T(homas) P(ercy) 1908-1993 *ConAu 141*
Gleaves, Edwin Sheffield 1936- *WhoAm 94*
Gleazer, Edmund John, Jr. 1916- *WhoAm 94*
Gleberman, Morton Jerome 1931- *WhoWest 94*
Glebov, George d1960 *WhoHol 92*
Glebov, Igor *NewGrDO*
Gleckler, Robert d1939 *WhoHol 92*
Gleckner, Robert F(rancis) 1925- *WrDr 94*
Gleckner, Robert Francis 1925- *WhoAm 94*
Gledhill, Anthony John 1938- *Who 94*
Gledhill, Barton LeVan 1936- *WhoWest 94*
Gledhill, David Anthony 1934- *IntWW 93, Who 94*
Gledhill, Nicholas *WhoHol 92*
Glee, George, Jr. 1938- *WhoBlA 94*
Gleed, William H. 1933- *WhoIns 94*
Glees, Anthony 1948- *WrDr 94*
Gleeson, Anthony Murray 1938- *Who 94*
Gleeson, Austin Michael 1938- *WhoAm 94*
Gleeson, James William 1920- *Who 94*
Gleeson, Jeremy Michael 1953- *WhoWest 94*
Gleeson, Paul Francis 1941- *WhoAm 94, WhoAmL 94*
Gleeson, Redmond *WhoHol 92*
Glegg, John B. *Who 94*
Gleich, Gerald Joseph 1931- *WhoAm 94, WhoScEn 94*
Gleich, Walter A. 1924- *IntWW 93*
Gleichauf, John George 1933- *WhoScEn 94*
Gleichert, Gregg Charles 1948- *WhoFI 94, WhoMW 93*
Gleichman, John Alan 1944- *WhoMW 93, WhoScEn 94*
Gleichman, Pamela Walton 1944- *WhoAmP 93*
Gleick, James 1954- *WhoAm 94*
Gleijeses, Mario 1955- *WhoAm 94, WhoFI 94*
Gleim, James Mac 1934- *WhoAm 94*
Gleim, Jeffrey Eugene 1956- *WhoScEn 94*
Gleiman, Lubomir 1923- *WhoAm 94*
Gleiss, Henry Weston 1928- *WhoAmL 94, WhoMW 93*
Gleisser, Marcus David 1923- *WhoAm 94*
Gleissner, Heinrich 1927- *Who 94*
Gleissner, Stephen Gregory 1962- *WhoMW 93*
Gleitze, Mercedes 1900-1979 *DcNaB MP*
Gleitzman, Morris 1953- *WrDr 94*
Gleixner, Richard Anthony 1955- *WhoScEn 94*
Glekel, Jeffrey Ives 1947- *WhoAm 94, WhoAmL 94*
Gleklen, Donald Morse 1936- *WhoAm 94*
Glemp, Jozef 1929- *IntWW 93*
Glemser, Oskar Max 1911- *IntWW 93*
Glen, Alexander (Richard) 1912- *Who 94*
Glen, Alexander Richard 1912- *IntWW 93*
Glen, Alice Esther 1881-1940 *BlmGWL*
Glen, Archibald 1909- *Who 94*
Glen, Archie d1966 *WhoHol 92*
Glen, Duncan (Munro) 1933- *WrDr 94*
Glen, Emilie *DrAPF 93*
Glen, Frank Grenfell 1933- *WrDr 94*
Glen, Henry 1739-1814 *WhAmRev*
Glen, Iain 1961- *WhoHol 92*
Glen, John 1932- *IntMPA 94*
Glen, William 1778-1849 *DcNaB MP*
Glenamara, Baron 1912- *IntWW 93, Who 94*
Glenapp, Viscount 1943- *Who 94*
Glenarthur, Baron 1944- *Who 94*
Glencer, Suzanne Thomson 1942- *WhoScEn 94*
Glenconner, Baron 1926- *Who 94*
Glencross, David 1936- *Who 94*
Glendening, Everett Austin 1929- *WhoAm 94*
Glendenning, Candace *WhoHol 92*
Glendenning, Carol P. 1953- *WhoAmL 94*
Glendenning, Don Mark 1953- *WhoAmL 94*
Glendevon, Baron 1912- *Who 94*
Glendining, Alan 1924- *Who 94*
Glendinning, Ernest d1936 *WhoHol 92*
Glendinning, Ethel *WhoHol 92*
Glendinning, James Garland 1919- *Who 94*
Glendinning, Peter 1951- *WhoAmA 93*
Glendinning, Victoria 1937- *IntWW 93, Who 94*
Glendon, Frank d1937 *WhoHol 92*
Glendower, Rose 1925- *WrDr 94*
Glendyne, Baron 1926- *Who 94*
Glen Haig, Mary (Alison) 1918- *Who 94*
Glenister, Brian Frederick 1928- *WhoScEn 94*
Glenister, Tony William Alphonse 1923- *Who 94*
Glenn, Albert H. 1922- *WhoFI 94*
Glenn, Andrea Poutasse 1951- *WhoMW 93*
Glenn, Archibald *IntWW 93, Who 94*
Glenn, (Joseph Robert) Archibald 1911- *IntWW 93, Who 94*
Glenn, Belinda 1963- *WhoWest 94*
Glenn, Cecil E. 1938- *WhoBlA 94*
Glenn, Charles Owen 1938- *IntMPA 94*
Glenn, Cleta Mae 1921- *WhoAmL 94*
Glenn, Constance White 1933- *WhoAmA 93, WhoWest 94*
Glenn, Daniel O. 1942- *WhoWest 94*
Glenn, David Wright 1943- *WhoAm 94, WhoFI 94*
Glenn, Dennis Eugene 1948- *WhoBlA 94*
Glenn, Donald d1958 *WhoHol 92*
Glenn, Edward C., Jr. 1922- *WhoBlA 94*
Glenn, Forrest d1954 *WhoHol 92*
Glenn, Gary Richard 1958- *WhoWest 94*
Glenn, Gene W. 1928- *WhoAmP 93*
Glenn, Gerald Marvin 1942- *WhoAm 94*
Glenn, Guy Charles 1930- *WhoWest 94*
Glenn, James 1937- *WhoAm 94*
Glenn, James D., Jr. 1934- *WhoAmL 94, WhoWest 94*
Glenn, James Francis 1928- *WhoAm 94*
Glenn, Jerry Hosmer, Jr. 1938- *WhoAm 94*
Glenn, John 1921- *CngDr 93*
Glenn, John H(erschel), Jr. 1921- *Who 94*
Glenn, John Herschel, Jr. 1921- *IntWW 93, WhoAm 94, WhoAmP 93, WhoMW 93, WhoScEn 94*
Glenn, John M. *WhoAmL 94*
Glenn, Karen *DrAPF 93*
Glenn, Kevin J. 1951- *WhoAmL 94*
Glenn, Lawrence Randolph 1938- *WhoAm 94*
Glenn, Lucia Howarth 1930- *WhoWest 94*
Glenn, Mark William 1953- *WhoScEn 94*
Glenn, Mel 1943- *TwCYAW*
Glenn, Michael Douglas 1940- *WhoAm 94*
Glenn, Norval Dwight 1933- *WhoAm 94*
Glenn, Patricia Campbell 1942- *WhoBlA 94*
Glenn, Paul Dale 1947- *WhoAmL 94*
Glenn, Peter G. 1943- *WhoAm 94*
Glenn, Ramona Martin 1931- *WhoAmP 93*
Glenn, Raymond d1974 *WhoHol 92*
Glenn, Richard M. C., III 1943- *WhoAmL 94*
Glenn, Robert Edward 1944- *WhoAm 94*
Glenn, Rogers 1930- *WhoScEn 94*
Glenn, Roland Douglas *WhoAm 94, WhoScEn 94*
Glenn, Ronald Fedric 1943- *WhoAmP 93*
Glenn, Roy d1971 *WhoHol 92*
Glenn, Roy Johnson 1920- *WhoFI 94*
Glenn, Scott 1941- *WhoHol 92*
Glenn, Scott 1942- *ConTFT 11, IntMPA 94, WhoAm 94*
Glenn, Steven Claude 1947- *WhoFI 94*
Glenn, Thomas Michael 1940- *WhoAm 94, WhoWest 94*
Glenn, Valerie Rose 1954- *WhoWest 94*
Glenn, Wayne Eugene 1924- *WhoAm 94, WhoFI 94*
Glenn, William Wallace Lumpkin 1914- *WhoAm 94*
Glenn, Wynola 1932- *WhoBlA 94*
Glennan, T. Keith 1905- *IntWW 93*
Glennen, Robert Eugene, Jr. 1933- *WhoAm 94, WhoMW 93*
Glenner, George Geiger 1927- *WhoWest 94*
Glenner, Richard Allen 1934- *WhoMW 93*
Glennie, Angus James Scott 1950- *Who 94*
Glennie, Evelyn Elizabeth Ann 1965- *IntWW 93, Who 94*
Glennon, Bert 1893-1967 *IntDcF 2-4*
Glennon, Harrison Randolph, Jr. 1914- *WhoAm 94*
Glennon, James Joseph 1942- *WhoFI 94*
Glennon, James M. 1942- *IntMPA 94*
Glennon, Thomas Manchester 1954- *WhoWest 94*
Glenny, Lyman Albert 1918- *WhoAm 94*
Glenny, Robert Joseph Ervine 1923- *Who 94*
Glentoran, Baron 1912- *Who 94*
Glentworth, Viscount 1963- *Who 94*
Glentz, Joseph Louis 1955- *WhoMW 93*
Glenville, Peter 1913- *WhoHol 92*
Glenville, Shaun d1968 *WhoHol 92*
Glerum, Charles Lively 1953- *WhoAmL 94*
Glerum, John C. 1950- *WhoFI 94*
Gleser, Goldine Cohnberg 1915- *WhoMW 93*
Gleske, Leonhard 1921- *IntWW 93*
Glesmann, Sylvia Maria 1923- *WhoAmA 93*
Gless, Sharon *WhoAm 94*
Gless, Sharon 1943- *IntMPA 94, WhoHol 92*
Glessing, Molly d1971 *WhoHol 92*
Glessner, David Arthur 1953- *WhoMW 93*
Glester, John William 1946- *Who 94*
Gleue, Lorine Anna 1926- *WhoMW 93*
Glezer, Nechemia 1910- *WhoAmA 93*
Glezos, Matthews 1927- *WhoAm 94*
Gliauda, Jurgis 1906- *WrDr 94*
Glick, Allan H. 1938- *WhoAm 94*
Glick, Cynthia Susan 1950- *WhoAmL 94, WhoMW 93*
Glick, Deborah J. *WhoAmP 93*
Glick, Earl A. 1930- *WhoAm 94*
Glick, Edward Bernard 1929- *WrDr 94*
Glick, Garland Wayne 1921- *WhoAm 94*
Glick, Hyman J. 1904- *IntMPA 94*
Glick, Ian Bernard 1948- *Who 94*
Glick, J. Leslie 1940- *WhoAm 94*
Glick, John H. 1943- *WhoAm 94, WhoScEn 94*
Glick, John P. 1938- *WhoAmA 93*
Glick, Joseph d1978 *WhoHol 92*
Glick, Leslie Alan 1946- *WhoAm 94, WhoAmL 94*
Glick, Michael Andrew 1958- *WhoScEn 94*
Glick, Milton Don 1937- *WhoWest 94*
Glick, Neal B. 1951- *WhoAm 94*
Glick, Paula Florence *WhoAmA 93*
Glick, Philip Milton 1905- *WhoAm 94*
Glick, Phyllis *IntMPA 94*
Glick, Richard Myron 1952- *WhoAm 94, WhoAmL 94*
Glick, Ruth Burtnick 1942- *WhoAm 94*
Glick, Stanley 1947- *WhoWest 94*
Glick, Steven Marc 1947- *WhoFI 94, WhoWest 94*
Glick, Warren W. 1927- *WhoAm 94*
Glick-Colquitt, Karen Lynne 1945- *WhoMW 93*
Glickenhaus, Sarah Brody 1919- *WhoAm 94, WhoFI 94*
Glickfeld, Carole L. *DrAPF 93*
Glicklich-Rosenberg, Lucille Barash 1926- *WhoMW 93*
Glickman, Albert Seymour 1923- *WhoAm 94*
Glickman, Arthur 1923- *WhoAmA 93*
Glickman, Carl David 1926- *WhoAm 94*
Glickman, Dan 1944- *CngDr 93*
Glickman, Daniel Robert 1944- *WhoAm 94, WhoAmP 93, WhoMW 93*
Glickman, Franklin Sheldon 1929- *WhoAm 94*
Glickman, Harry 1924- *WhoAm 94, WhoWest 94*
Glickman, Louis 1933- *WhoAm 94*
Glickman, Marlene 1936- *WhoFI 94*
Glickman, Maurice 1906- *WhoAmA 93N*
Glickman, Norman J. 1942- *WrDr 94*
Glickman, Robert Morris 1939- *WhoAm 94*
Glickman, Ronald C. 1956- *WhoAmP 93*
Glicksberg, Charles Irving 1900- *WrDr 94*
Glicksman, Arvin Sigmund 1924- *WhoAm 94*
Glicksman, Jay 1953- *WhoWest 94*
Glicksman, Martin Eden 1937- *WhoAm 94, WhoScEn 94*
Glicksman, Maurice 1928- *WhoAm 94*
Glicksman, Russell Allen 1939- *WhoAm 94*
Glickson, Andrew Asher 1949- *WhoAmP 93*
Glickstein, Eileen Agard 1948- *WhoAm 94*
Glickstein, Howard Alan 1929- *WhoAmL 94*
Glickstein, Karen Rose 1962- *WhoAmL 94*
Glickstein, Steven 1952- *WhoAm 94*
Glidden, Allan Hartwell 1920- *WhoAm 94*
Glidden, Bruce 1928- *WhoScEn 94*
Glidden, Carlos *WorInv*
Glidden, John Redmond 1936- *WhoAm 94*
Glidden, Joseph Farwell *WorInv*
Glidden, Lloyd Sumner, Jr. 1922- *WhoAm 94*
Glidden, Robert Burr 1936- *WhoAm 94*
Gliddon, John d1990 *WhoHol 92*
Glidewell, Iain (Derek Laing) 1924- *IntWW 93, Who 94*
Gliebe, Veronica Maria 1958- *WhoFI 94*
Glieberman, Herbert Allen 1930- *WhoAm 94, WhoAmL 94, WhoMW 93*
Gliedman, Marvin L. 1929- *WhoAm 94*
Gliege, John Gerhardt 1948- *WhoAmL 94*
Glier, Ingeborg Johanna 1934- *WhoAm 94*
Glier, Mike 1953- *WhoAmA 93*
Glier, Reyngol'd Moritsevich 1874?-1956 *NewGrDO*
Gliewe, Unada G. 1927- *WrDr 94*
Gligorov, Kiro 1917- *IntWW 93*
Glikes, Erwin Arno 1937- *WhoAm 94*
Glimcher, Arnold *NewYTBS 93 [port]*
Glimcher, Arnold B. 1938- *WhoAm 94, WhoAmA 93*
Glimcher, Melvin Jacob 1925- *WhoAm 94, WhoScEn 94*
Glimm, Adele *DrAPF 93*
Glimm, James Gilbert 1934- *WhoAm 94, WhoScEn 94*
Glimm, James Y(ork) 1942- *WrDr 94*
Glimmerveen, Ulco 1958- *WrDr 94*
Glin, Knight of *Who 94*
Glindeman, Henry Peter, Jr. 1924- *WhoAm 94*
Gliner, Erast Boris 1923- *WhoScEn 94*
Glines, Carroll Vane, Jr. 1920- *WhoAm 94*
Glines, Ellen d1951 *WhoAmA 93N*
Glines, Stephen Ramey 1952- *WhoScEn 94*
Glines, Victor Leroy 1895- *WhAm 10*
Glinka, Mikhail Ivanovich 1804-1857 *NewGrDO*
Glinska, Teofila 1765?-1799 *BlmGWL*
Glinsky, Vincent 1895-1975 *WhoAmA 93N*

Glisky, Elizabeth Louise 1941- *WhoScEn 94*
Glismann, Diane Duffy 1935- *WhoWest 94*
Glissant, Edouard 1928- *ConWorW 93*
Glissant, Edouard Mathieu 1928- *WhoAm 94*
Glisson, Jackie 1954- *WhoAmP 93*
Glistrup, Mogens 1926- *IntWW 93*
Glitman, Karen Micouela 1963- *WhoAmP 93*
Glitman, Maynard W. *WhoAmP 93*
Glitman, Maynard Wayne 1933- *IntWW 93*
Glitz, Dohn George 1936- *WhoAm 94*
Glitz, Donald Robert 1944- *WhoFI 94*
Glixon, David Morris 1908- *WhoAm 94*
Gloag, Ann Heron 1942- *Who 94*
Gloag, Helena *WhoHol 92*
Gloag, John 1896-1981 *EncSF 93*
Gloag, Julian 1930- *WrDr 94*
Gloag, William Murray 1865-1934 *DcNaB MP*
Gloak, Graeme Frank 1921- *Who 94*
Glober, George Edward, Jr. 1944- *WhoAmL 94*
Globoke, Joseph Raymond 1955- *WhoMW 93*
Globus, Dorothy Twining *WhoAmA 93*
Globus, Yoram *IntMPA 94*
Globus, Yoram 1943- *IntWW 93*
See Also Golan, Menahem 1929- *IntDcF 2-4*
Glock, Charles Young 1919- *WhoAm 94*, *WhoWest 94*
Glock, Marvin David 1912- *WhoAm 94*, *WrDr 94*
Glock, William (Frederick) 1908- *Who 94*
Glock, William Frederick 1908- *IntWW 93*
Glocker, Theodore Wesley, Jr. 1925- *WhoAm 94*
Glocker, Theodore William 1953- *WhoAmL 94*
Glockner, Peter G. 1929- *WhoAm 94*
Glockner, William Daniel, Jr. 1963- *WhoWest 94*
Glodeanu, Liviu 1938-1978 *NewGrDO*
Glodis, William J., Jr. 1934- *WhoAmP 93*
Glodowski, Robert John 1946- *WhoFI 94*
Gloeggler, Tony *DrAPF 93*
Gloger, Betty Ruth 1931- *WhoMW 93*
Glomazic-Lekovic, Stanka 1924- *WhoWomW 91*
Glomb, Diana *WhoAmP 93*, *WhoWest 94*
Glommen, Harvey Hamilton 1928- *WhoMW 93*
Glomset, Daniel Anders 1913- *WhoAm 94*
Gloor, Christopher Barta 1949- *WhoFI 94*
Gloor, Robert Louis 1940- *WhoAmP 93*
Glori, Ann d1977 *WhoHol 92*
Gloria, Madalena da 1672-176-? *BlmGWL*
Glorig, Ostor 1919- *WhoAmA 93*
Glos, Margaret Beach 1936- *WhoAm 94*
Glosband, Daniel Martin 1944- *WhoAm 94*, *WhoAmL 94*
Glosch, Carl Wilhelm 1731?-1809 *NewGrDO*
Gloss, Molly 1944- *WrDr 94*
Glossbrenner, Alfred Stroup 1901- *EncABHB 9 [port]*
Glossbrenner, Ernestine Viola 1932- *WhoAmP 93*
Glosser, James William 1931- *WhoAm 94*
Glosser, Jeffrey Mark 1936- *WhoAm 94*, *WhoAmL 94*
Glosser, William Louis 1929- *WhoAm 94*, *WhoAmL 94*
Glossop, Peter 1928- *IntWW 93*, *NewGrDO*, *Who 94*
Glossop, Reginald 1880- *EncSF 93*
Glossop, Ronald John 1933- *WhoMW 93*
Gloster, Elizabeth 1949- *Who 94*
Gloster, Hugh Morris 1911- *WhoBlA 94*
Gloster, Jesse E. 1915- *WhoBlA 94*
Gloster, John 1922- *Who 94*
Gloster, John Gaines 1928- *WhoBlA 94*
Glosup, Lorene 1911- *WhoAm 94*
Glosz, Rosemary d1963 *WhoHol 92*
Gloth, Alec Robert 1927- *WhoFI 94*
Glotta, Ronald Delon 1941- *WhoAmL 94*
Glotzer, Albert 1908- *WrDr 94*
Glotzer, David *DrAPF 93*
Gloucester, Archdeacon of *Who 94*
Gloucester, Bishop of 1935- *Who 94*
Gloucester, Dean of *Who 94*
Gloucester, Duke of 1944- *Who 94R*
Gloucester, Earl of c. 1291-1347 *DcNaB MP*
Gloucester, H.R.H. The Duke of 1944- *IntWW 93*
Gloudeman, Joseph Floyd 1935- *WhoAm 94*
Glover, Agnes W. 1925- *WhoBlA 94*
Glover, Alan Harney 1949- *WhoAmP 93*
Glover, Anthony Richard 1944- *WhoScEn 94*
Glover, Anthony Richard Haysom 1934- *Who 94*
Glover, Archibald F. 1902-1991 *WhoBlA 94N*
Glover, Arthur Lewis, Jr. 1912- *WhoBlA 94*
Glover, Bernard E. 1933- *WhoBlA 94*
Glover, Billy Joe 1938- *WhoAmP 93*
Glover, Bobby L. 1936- *WhoAmP 93*
Glover, Brian 1934- *WhoHol 92*
Glover, Bruce *WhoHol 92*
Glover, Celestie Jane 1964- *WhoWest 94*
Glover, Chester Artis 1954- *WhoBlA 94*
Glover, Clarence Ernest, Jr. 1956- *WhoBlA 94*
Glover, Clifford Clarke 1913- *WhoAm 94*
Glover, Conrad Nathan 1895- *WhAm 10*
Glover, Corey
See Living Colour *News 93-3*
Glover, Crispin 1964- *IntMPA 94*
Glover, Crispin 1965- *WhoHol 92*
Glover, Crispin Hellion 1964- *WhoAm 94*
Glover, Danny 1947- *AfrAmAl 6 [port]*, *IntMPA 94*, *WhoAm 94*, *WhoBlA 94*, *WhoHol 92*
Glover, David Val 1932- *WhoMW 93*
Glover, Delone Bradford 1924- *WhoAmP 93*
Glover, Denise M. 1952- *WhoBlA 94*
Glover, Diana M. 1948- *WhoBlA 94*
Glover, Donald H. 1918- *WhoAmP 93*
Glover, Donald Robert *WhoAm 94*
Glover, Edmund d1978 *WhoHol 92*
Glover, Eric 1935- *Who 94*
Glover, Everett William, Jr. 1948- *WhoScEn 94*
Glover, Fred William 1937- *WhoAm 94*, *WhoScEn 94*
Glover, Gilbert Louis 1921- *WhoAmP 93*
Glover, Gleason 1934- *WhoBlA 94*
Glover, Hamilton 1937- *WhoBlA 94*
Glover, Hilda Weaver 1933- *WhoAm 94*
Glover, Imogene Davison 1924- *WhoAmP 93*
Glover, James (Malcolm) 1929- *IntWW 93*, *Who 94*
Glover, James Todd 1939- *WhoMW 93*
Glover, Jane (Alison) 1949- *NewGrDO*
Glover, Jane Alison 1949- *IntWW 93*, *Who 94*
Glover, Janet Reaveley 1912- *WrDr 94*
Glover, Jimmy Ray 1945- *WhoAmP 93*
Glover, John 1732-1794 *AmRev*
Glover, John 1732-1797 *WhAmRev [port]*
Glover, John 1817-1902 *DcNaB MP*
Glover, John 1944- *IntMPA 94*, *WhoHol 92*
Glover, John L. 1943- *WhoAmP 93*
Glover, John Neville 1913- *Who 94*
Glover, Jon 1943- *WrDr 94*
Glover, Judith 1943- *WrDr 94*
Glover, Julian 1935- *WhoHol 92*
Glover, Kara *WhoHol 92*
Glover, Karen E. 1950- *WhoAm 94*, *WhoAmL 94*
Glover, Keith 1946- *Who 94*
Glover, Kenneth Elijah 1952- *WhoBlA 94*
Glover, Kenneth Frank 1920- *Who 94*
Glover, Linda F. 1951- *WhoBlA 94*
Glover, Lisa Marie 1963- *WhoMW 93*
Glover, Maggie Wallace 1948- *WhoAmP 93*
Glover, Michael James Kevin 1940- *IntWW 93*
Glover, Myles Howard 1928- *Who 94*
Glover, Norman James 1929- *WhoAm 94*
Glover, Paul W. 1947- *WhoIns 94*
Glover, Paul Williams, III 1947- *WhoAm 94*
Glover, Peter James 1913- *Who 94*
Glover, Richard 1712-1785 *BlmGEL*
Glover, Robert 1936- *WhoAmA 93*
Glover, Robert Finlay 1917- *Who 94*
Glover, Robert G. 1931- *WhoBlA 94*
Glover, Roger 1954-
See Deep Purple *ConMus 11*
Glover, Ruth Champion 1926- *WhoAmP 93*
Glover, Sarah L. 1954- *WhoBlA 94*
Glover, Savion 1973- *WhoHol 92*
Glover, Stephen Charles Morton 1952- *Who 94*
Glover, Trevor David 1940- *Who 94*
Glover, Victor (Joseph Patrick) 1932- *Who 94*
Glover, Victor Norman 1948- *WhoBlA 94*
Glover, William Harper 1911- *WhoAm 94*
Glover, William James 1924- *Who 94*
Glovka, Richard Paul 1937- *WhoAm 94*
Glovsky, Alan *WhoAmA 93*
Glovsky, Susan G. L. 1955- *WhoAmL 94*
Glowacki, Richard Chester 1932- *WhoAm 94*
Glowatch, David Joseph 1966- *WhoFI 94*
Glower, Donald Duane 1926- *WhoAm 94*, *WhoMW 93*
Glowienka, Emerine Frances 1920- *WhoWest 94*
Glowinski, Roland 1937- *WhoAm 94*
Glowner, M. Lee d1923 *WhoHol 92*
Glowski, Susan Kathleen 1947- *WhoMW 93*
Gloyd, Lawrence Eugene 1932- *WhoAm 94*, *WhoFI 94*
Gloyna, Earnest Frederick 1921- *WhoAm 94*, *WhoScEn 94*
Glube, Constance Rachelle 1931- *WhoAm 94*
Glubok, Shirley (Astor) *ConAu 43NR*
Gluck, Alma 1884-1938 *NewGrDO*
Gluck, Christoph Willibald, Ritter von 1714-1787 *NewGrDO*
Gluck, Dale Richard 1952- *WhoWest 94*
Gluck, Hazel Frank 1933- *WhoAmP 93*
Gluck, Heidi 1944- *WhoAmA 93*
Gluck, Henry 1928- *WhoFI 94*
Gluck, Louise *DrAPF 93*
Gluck, Louise 1943- *BlmGWL*, *ConLC 81 [port]*, *WrDr 94*
Gluck, Louise Elisabeth 1943- *WhoAm 94*
Gluck, Matthew 1942- *WhoAmL 94*
Gluck, Tereze *DrAPF 93*
Gluckel von Hameln 1645-1724 *BlmGWL*
Gluckstein, Fritz Paul 1927- *WhoAm 94*
Gluckstern, Robert Leonard 1924- *WhoAm 94*
Glue, George Thomas 1917- *Who 94*
Gluhman, Joseph Walter 1934- *WhoAmA 93*
Gluhman, Margaret A. *WhoAmA 93*
Glumer, Claire von 1825-1906 *BlmGWL*
Glusband, Steven Joseph 1947- *WhoAmL 94*
Glushenko, Yevgeniya Konstatinovna 1952- *IntWW 93*
Glushien, Morris P. 1909- *WhoAm 94*
Glushko, Victor 1946- *WhoScEn 94*, *WhoWest 94*
Glushkovsky, Adam Pavlovich 1793-c. 1870 *IntDcB*
Gluska, Aharon *WhoAmA 93*
Glut, Don(ald) F. 1944- *WrDr 94*
Glut, Donald F(rank) 1944- *EncSF 93*
Gluth, Robert C. 1924- *WhoFI 94*
Gluyas, Constance 1920- *WrDr 94*
Gluys, Charles Byron 1928- *WhoFI 94*
Glyde, Henry George 1906- *WhoAmA 93*
Glyn *Who 94*
Glyn, Alan 1918- *Who 94*
Glyn, Anthony (Geoffrey Leo Simon) 1922- *Who 94*, *WrDr 94*
Glyn, Elinor d1943 *WhoHol 92*
Glyn, Hilary B. 1916- *Who 94*
Glyn, Neva Carr d1975 *WhoHol 92*
Glyn, Richard (Lindsay) 1943- *Who 94*
Glyndwr, Owain 1354?-1416? *BlmGEL*
Glynias, Stefan J. 1946- *WhoAmL 94*
Glyn Jones, Richard 1946- *EncSF 93*
Glynn, A(nthony) A(rthur) 1929- *EncSF 93*
Glynn, Alan Anthony 1923- *Who 94*
Glynn, Arthur Lawrence 1916- *WhoAm 94*
Glynn, Carlin 1940- *IntMPA 94*, *WhoAm 94*, *WhoHol 92*
Glynn, Edward 1935- *WhoAm 94*
Glynn, Gary Allen 1946- *WhoAm 94*
Glynn, Gerard Francis 1963- *WhoAmL 94*
Glynn, Ian Michael 1928- *IntWW 93*, *Who 94*
Glynn, James Vincent 1938- *WhoIns 94*
Glynn, John Joseph, Jr. 1941- *WhoAmP 93*
Glynn, Leonard M. 1948- *WrDr 94*
Glynn, Thomas P. 1946- *WhoAm 94*
Glynn, Thomas V. 1944- *WhoAmL 94*
Glynne, Howell 1906-1969 *NewGrDO*
Glynne, Mary d1954 *WhoHol 92*
Gmelch, George 1944- *WrDr 94*
Gmelch, Sharon (Bohn) 1947- *WrDr 94*
Gmelin, Johann Georg 1709-1755 *WhWE*
Gmelin, Leopold *WorScD*
Gmirya, Boris Romanovich *NewGrDO*
Gn, Thye-Wee 1962- *WhoAsA 94*
Gnaedinger, Mary 1898-1976 *EncSF 93*
Gnam, Adrian 1940- *WhoWest 94*
Gnanadesikan, Ramanathan 1932- *WhoAsA 94*
Gnanam, A. 1932- *IntWW 93*
Gnarowski, Michael 1934- *WrDr 94*
Gnass, Fritz d1958 *WhoHol 92*
Gnat, Raymond Earl 1932- *WhoAm 94*, *WhoMW 93*
Gnatt, Poul Rudolph 1923- *IntWW 93*
Gnecchi, Vittorio 1876-1954 *NewGrDO*
Gnecco, Francesco c. 1769-1810? *NewGrDO*
Gnecco, Louis T. 1945- *WhoHisp 94*
Gnehm, Edward, Jr. *WhoAmP 93*
Gnehm, Edward W., Jr. 1944- *IntWW 93*, *WhoAm 94*
Gnehm, Max Willi 1943- *WhoWest 94*
Gneuss, Helmut (Walter Georg) 1927- *ConAu 141*
Gneuss, Helmut Walter Georg 1927- *IntWW 93*
Gnichtel, William Van Orden 1934- *WhoAm 94*, *WhoAmL 94*
Gniewek, Raymond Louis 1947- *WhoAm 94*
Gnirk, Lloyd Allen 1952- *WhoMW 93*
Gnodtke, Carl F. 1936- *WhoAmP 93*
Go, Daniel Y. 1958- *WhoAsA 94*
Go, Howard T. 1933- *WhoAsA 94*
Go, Mateo Lian Poa 1918- *WhoAsA 94*
Go, Robert A. 1955- *WhoMW 93*
Go, Vay Liang Wong 1938- *WhoWest 94*
Goacher, Rosanne Elaine 1948- *WhoFI 94*
Goad, Anne Laine *WhoAmA 93*
Goad, (Edward) Colin (Viner) 1914- *Who 94*
Goad, Janet Deniece 1960- *WhoMW 93*
Goad, Judy Ann 1946- *WhoAmP 93*
Goad, Linda May 1948- *WhoAm 94*
Goad, Nolen E. 1941- *WhoAmP 93*
Goade, Ann Marie 1955- *WhoAmL 94*
Goaley, Donald Joseph 1935- *WhoIns 94*
Goans, Judy Winegar 1949- *WhoAmL 94*
Goates, Delbert Tolton 1932- *WhoWest 94*
Goay, Michael Song-Chye 1964- *WhoWest 94*
Gobar, Alfred Julian 1932- *WhoAm 94*, *WhoFI 94*, *WhoWest 94*
Gobar, Sally Randall 1933- *WhoWest 94*
Gobatti, Stefano 1852-1913 *NewGrDO*
Gobbato, Angelo (Mario Giulio) 1943- *NewGrDO*
Gobbi, Tito d1984 *WhoHol 92*
Gobbi, Tito 1913-1984 *NewGrDO [port]*
Gobbo, James (Augustine) 1931- *Who 94*
Gobel, Franz Xaver *NewGrDO*
Gobel, George d1991 *WhoHol 92*
Gobel, George 1919-1991 *WhoCom*
Gobel, George Leslie 1919-1991 *WhAm 10*
Gobel, John Henry 1926- *WhoAm 94*
Gobel, Steven 1955- *WhoMW 93*
Gober, Hans Joachim 1931- *WhoScEn 94*
Gober, Hershel W. 1936- *WhoAm 94*, *WhoAmP 93*
Gobert, Boy d1986 *WhoHol 92*
Gobets, Dennis Richard 1955- *WhoWest 94*
Gobie, Henry Macaulay 1911- *WhoAm 94*
Gobin, Gabriel *WhoHol 92*
Goble, Danney 1946- *WrDr 94*
Goble, Edward Earl 1938- *WhoAmP 93*
Goble, Elise Joan H. 1932- *WhoWest 94*
Goble, George G. 1929- *WhoAm 94*
Goble, Gerald Leroy, Jr. 1953- *WhoAmP 93*
Goble, John Frederick 1925- *Who 94*
Goble, Neil 1933- *EncSF 93*
Goble, Paul 1933- *WhoAm 94*
Goble, Paul John 1964- *WhoWest 94*
Goble, Willis Rhoads, Jr. 1954- *WhoAmL 94*
Gobrecht, Heinrich Friedrich 1909- *WhoScEn 94*
Goburdhun, Jagdishwar 1946- *IntWW 93*
Gobuzas, Aldona M. *WhoAmA 93*
Gochberg, Thomas Joel 1939- *WhoAm 94*
Gochenour, Edwin A. 1952- *WhoAmP 93*
Gochnauer, Richard Wallis 1949- *WhoAm 94*
Gochoco, Jose Luis 1952- *WhoWest 94*
Gocial, Tammy Marie 1965- *WhoMW 93*
Gock, Terry Sai-Wah 1951- *WhoWest 94*
Gocke, David Joseph 1933- *WhoAm 94*
Gockel, John Raymond 1947- *WhoFI 94*
Gockley, David 1943- *NewGrDO*
Godager, Jane Ann 1943- *WhoWest 94*
Godara, Lal Chand 1952- *WhoScEn 94*
Godard, Benjamin (Louis Paul) 1849-1895 *NewGrDO*
Godard, Donald Wesley 1947- *WhoWest 94*
Godard, James McFate 1907- *WhoAm 94*
Godard, Jean-Luc 1930- *CurBio 93 [port]*, *IntMPA 94*, *IntWW 93*, *Who 94*, *WhoAm 94*, *WhoHol 92*
Godbee, John F. 1926- *WhoAmP 93*
Godbee, Thomasina D. 1946- *WhoBlA 94*
Godber, Geoffrey Chapham 1912- *Who 94*
Godber, George (Edward) 1908- *Who 94*
Godber, John (Harry) 1956- *ConDr 93*, *WrDr 94*
Godber, Noel (Lambert) 1881- *EncSF 93*
Godbold, Albert 1895- *WhAm 10*
Godbold, Donald Horace 1928- *WhoBlA 94*
Godbold, E(dward) Stanly, Jr. 1942- *WrDr 94*
Godbold, Francis Stanley 1943- *WhoAm 94*, *WhoFI 94*
Godbold, Gene Hamilton 1936- *WhoAmL 94*
Godbold, Geoff 1935- *IntMPA 94*
Godbold, Jake M. *WhoAmP 93*
Godbold, James Homer, Jr. 1947- *WhoScEn 94*
Godbold, John Cooper 1920- *WhoAm 94*, *WhoAmL 94*
Godbold, N. Terry 1948- *WhoIns 94*

Goetzke, Ronald Richard 1933- *WhoIns 94*
Goetzl, Thomas Maxwell 1943- *WhoAmA 93*
Goetzmann, Harry Edward, Jr. 1937- *WhoAm 94, WhoFI 94*
Goeudevert, Daniel 1942- *IntWW 93*
Goewey, Gordon Ira 1924- *WhoAm 94*
Goeyvaerts, Karel (August) 1923- *NewGrDO*
Goez, J. L. 1939- *WhoHisp 94*
Goff *Who 94*
Goff, Charles Wesley, Jr. 1940- *WhoAm 94*
Goff, Donald L. 1947- *WhoAmP 93*
Goff, Harold Milton 1947- *WhoScEn 94*
Goff, Harry Russell 1915- *WhoAm 94*
Goff, James Albert 1941- *WhoAm 94*
Goff, John Samuel 1931- *WhoWest 94*
Goff, Kenneth Alan 1941- *WhoScEn 94*
Goff, Kenneth Wade 1928- *WhoAm 94*
Goff, Lila Johnson 1944- *WhoAm 94, WhoMW 93*
Goff, Mark Scott 1947- *WhoMW 93*
Goff, Martyn 1923- *Who 94, WrDr 94*
Goff, Norris d1978 *WhoHol 92*
Goff, Norvel 1949- *WhoAmP 93*
Goff, Philip Bruce 1953- *IntWW 93*
Goff, R. Michael 1949- *WhoFI 94*
Goff, Robert (William Davis-) 1955- *Who 94*
Goff, Robert Burnside 1924- *WhoAm 94*
Goff, Robert Edward 1952- *WhoFI 94*
Goff, Thomas Jefferson 1907- *WhoAmA 93*
Goff, Wilhelmina Delores 1940- *WhoBlA 94*
Goff, Wilmer Scott 1923- *WhoMW 93*
Goffart, Walter Andre 1934- *WhoAm 94*
Goffe, Art *WhoAmP 93*
Goffe, William Arthur 1929- *WhoAm 94, WhoAmL 94*
Goffe, William Gregory 1949- *WhoAm 94*
Goffen, Rona 1944- *WhoAm 94*
Goffi, Richard James 1963- *WhoScEn 94*
Goffinet, Jeffrey Alan 1959- *WhoAmL 94*
Goffinet, Serge 1959- *WhoScEn 94*
Goffman, Daniel Stephen 1954- *WhoMW 93*
Goffman, Erving 1922-1988 *EncSPD*
Goffman, Judy *WhoAmA 93*
Goffman, Thomas Edward 1953- *WhoScEn 94*
Goffman, William 1924- *WhoAm 94, WhoScEn 94*
Goff Of Chieveley, Baron 1926- *IntWW 93, Who 94*
Goforth, Charles Preston 1950- *WhoAmL 94, WhoWest 94*
Goforth, Charles Wayne 1931- *WhoAmP 93*
Goforth, Ellen 1926- *WrDr 94*
Goforth, Mary Elaine 1922- *WhoMW 93*
Goforth, Nathan Dan 1951- *WhoWest 94*
Goforth, Raymond Reed 1968- *WhoWest 94*
Goforth, William Clements 1937- *WhoAmL 94*
Gofrank, Frank Louis 1918- *WhoAm 94*
Gofron, Kazimierz Jan 1962- *WhoScEn 94*
Gofton, E. Story d1939 *WhoHol 92*
Gogan, Catherine Mary 1959- *WhoScEn 94*
Gogan, Gerald William 1941- *WhoMW 93*
Gogan, James Wilson 1938- *WhoFI 94*
Gogarty, William Barney 1930- *WhoAm 94, WhoWest 94*
Gogate, Kamalakar Chintaman 1940- *WhoScEn 94*
Gogerty, David Calvin 1934- *WhoFI 94*
Goggin, Joseph Robert 1926- *WhoFI 94*
Goggin, Margaret Knox 1919- *WhoAm 94*
Goggin, Noreen Louise 1954- *WhoScEn 94*
Goggins, Horace 1929- *WhoBlA 94*
Goggins, John Francis 1933- *WhoAm 94*
Gogick, Kathleen Christine 1945- *WhoAm 94*
Gogisgi *DrAPF 93*
Goglia, Charles A., Jr. 1931- *WhoAmL 94*
Gogo, Gregory 1943- *WhoAmL 94*
Gogoberidze, Lana Levanovna 1928- *IntWW 93*
Gogol (Ianovskii), Nikolai (Vasil'evich) 1809-1852 *RfGShF*
Gogol (Yanovsky), Nikolai (Vasilevich) 1809-1852 *IntDcT 2*
Gogol, Nikolai *EncSF 93*
Gogol, Nikolai Vasilyevich 1809-1852 *BlmGEL*
Gogol, Nikolay Vasil'yevich 1809-1852 *NewGrDO*
Gogolin, Marilyn Tompkins 1946- *WhoWest 94*
Gogorza, Patricia (Gahagan) De 1936- *WhoAmA 93*
Gogreve, Donald Joseph 1950- *WhoFI 94*
Gogue, Wilma S. 1961- *WhoMW 93*
Goguen, Emile J. *WhoAmP 93*
Goguen, John Marc 1967- *WhoFI 94*
Goguen, Joseph Amadee 1941- *Who 94*
Gogulski, Paul 1938- *WhoScEn 94*
Goh, Anthony Li-Shing 1954- *WhoMW 93*
Goh, Ben K. 1961- *WhoAsA 94*
Goh, David S. 1941- *WhoAsA 94*
Gohagan, John Kenneth 1939- *WhoScEn 94*
Gohagen, Omar *EncSF 93*
Goh Chok Tong 1941- *IntWW 93, Who 94*
Goheen, David Wade 1920- *WhoWest 94*
Goheen, Ellen Rozanne 1944- *WhoAmA 93*
Goheen, Harry Earl 1915-1989 *WhAm 10*
Goheen, Robert (Francis) 1919- *WrDr 94*
Goheen, Robert F. 1919- *WhoAmP 93*
Goheen, Robert Francis 1919- *IntWW 93, Who 94, WhoAm 94*
Gohel, Jayvantsinhji (Kayaji) 1915- *Who 94*
Gohil, Pratapsinh 1950- *WhoMW 93*
Goh Keng Swee 1918- *IntWW 93*
Gohlke, Florence Margaret 1914- *WhoAmP 93*
Gohlke, Frank William 1942- *WhoAm 94, WhoAmA 93*
Gohn, Sandra P. 1951- *WhoAmL 94*
Goicouria, Pedro A. *WhoHisp 94*
Goimbault, Odette *WhoHol 92*
Goin, Olive Bown 1912- *WhoWest 94*
Goin, Peter *WhoAmA 93*
Goin, Peter Jackson 1951- *WhoWest 94*
Goines, Betty d1929 *WhoHol 92*
Goines, Donald 1937?-1974 *ConLC 80 [port]*
Goines, Leonard 1934- *WhoBlA 94*
Going, David Louis 1958- *WhoAmL 94*
Going, Frederica d1959 *WhoHol 92*
Going, Jo 1947- *WhoAmA 93*
Going, Margaret Mary 1921- *IntWW 93*
Going, Richard Fuller 1896- *WhAm 10*
Going, Robert Neil 1951- *WhoAmP 93*
Going, William Thornbury 1915- *WhoAm 94*
Goings, Ralph 1928- *WhoAm 94, WhoAmA 93*
Goins, Frances Floriano 1950- *WhoAm 94*
Goins, John Clement 1896- *WhAm 10*
Goins, Mary G. 1929- *WhoBlA 94*
Goins, N. Walter *WhoBlA 94*
Goins, Richard Anthony 1950- *WhoAm 94, WhoAmL 94*
Goins, Sharon Elizabeth 1950- *WhoAmL 94*
Goiporia, Maneck Nadirshaw 1932- *IntWW 93*
Goishi, Dean M. 1943- *WhoAsA 94*
Goizueta, Roberto 1931- *IntWW 93*
Goizueta, Roberto C. 1931- *WhoHisp 94*
Goizueta, Roberto Crispulo 1931- *WhoAm 94, WhoFI 94*
Goizueta, Roberto Segundo 1954- *WhoHisp 94*
Gojmerac-Leiner, Georgia *DrAPF 93*
Goka, Richard Shunji 1947- *WhoWest 94*
Gokarn, Vijay Murlidhar 1953- *WhoScEn 94*
Gokceli, Yasar Kemal *ConWorW 93*
Gokey, Franklin Charles 1916- *WhoIns 94*
Gokieli, Vano Rafailovich 1899-1972 *NewGrDO*
Gol, Jean 1942- *IntWW 93*
Gola, Jose d1939 *WhoHol 92*
Gola, Tom 1933- *BasBi*
Golab, Michael F. 1950- *WhoAmL 94*
Golab, Wlodzimierz Andrzej 1938- *WhoScEn 94*
Golan, Gila *WhoHol 92*
Golan, Martin *DrAPF 93*
Golan, Menahem 1929- *IntDcF 2-4, IntMPA 94, IntWW 93*
Golan, Stephen Leonard 1951- *WhoAm 94*
Goland, Martin 1919- *WhoAm 94, WhoScEn 94*
Golant, Victor Evgen'evich 1928- *WhoScEn 94*
Golant, William 1937- *WrDr 94*
Golany, Gideon Salomon 1928- *WhoAm 94*
Golarz, Raymond John 1940- *WhoMW 93*
Golashesky, Chrysa Zofia 1957- *WhoFI 94*
Golaski, Nicholas John 1954- *WhoScEn 94*
Golbin, Andree 1923- *WhoAmA 93*
Golbraykh, Isaak German 1935- *WhoScEn 94*
Golchan, Frederic *IntMPA 94*
Golcuklu, Ahmet Feyyaz 1926- *IntWW 93*
Gold, Aaron Alan 1919- *WhoAm 94*
Gold, Alan B. 1917- *WhoAm 94*
Gold, Alan Stephen 1944- *WhoAm 94, WhoAmL 94*
Gold, Albert 1916- *WhoAm 94, WhoAmA 93*
Gold, Alison Leslie 1945- *WrDr 94*
Gold, Anne Marie 1949- *WhoWest 94*
Gold, Arnold Henry 1932- *WhoAm 94*
Gold, Arthur 1917- *WrDr 94*
Gold, Arthur 1917-1990 *WhAm 10*
Gold, Arthur (Abraham) 1917- *Who 94*
Gold, Bela 1915- *WhoAm 94*
Gold, Bernard 1930- *WhoAm 94*
Gold, Betty d1987 *WhoHol 92*
Gold, Brandy 1977- *WhoHol 92*
Gold, Carol Sapin *WhoAm 94*
Gold, Daniel Howard 1942- *WhoScEn 94*
Gold, Edgar 1934- *WhoAm 94*
Gold, Edward *DrAPF 93*
Gold, Edward David 1941- *WhoAm 94, WhoAmL 94*
Gold, Emanuel R. 1935- *WhoAmP 93*
Gold, Ernest 1921- *IntMPA 94*
Gold, Fay Helfand 1907- *WhoAmA 93*
Gold, George Myron 1935- *WhoAm 94, WhoAmL 94*
Gold, Gerald Seymour 1931- *WhoAm 94*
Gold, H(orace) L(eonard) 1914- *EncSF 93, WrDr 94*
Gold, Harold Arthur 1929- *WhoAm 94, WhoAmL 94*
Gold, Harold B. 1955- *WhoAmL 94*
Gold, Herbert *DrAPF 93*
Gold, Herbert 1924- *WrDr 94*
Gold, Herman *DrAPF 93*
Gold, I. Randall 1951- *WhoAmL 94*
Gold, Ivan *DrAPF 93*
Gold, Jack 1930- *IntWW 93, Who 94*
Gold, James Paul 1944- *WhoAm 94*
Gold, Jay Alexander 1950- *WhoMW 93*
Gold, Jay D. 1942- *WhoAm 94*
Gold, Jeffrey Mark 1945- *WhoAm 94, WhoFI 94*
Gold, Jimmy d1967 *WhoHol 92*
Gold, John (Joseph Manson) 1925- *Who 94*
Gold, Jonathan Peter 1961- *WhoFI 94*
Gold, Joseph 1912- *IntWW 93, Who 94*
Gold, Joseph 1930- *WhoAm 94, WhoScEn 94*
Gold, Judith Hammerling 1941- *WhoAm 94*
Gold, Judith Z. 1952- *WhoAmL 94*
Gold, Kenneth Arthur 1954- *WhoFI 94*
Gold, Laurence Stephen 1936- *WhoAm 94, WhoAmL 94*
Gold, Lee Kevin 1958- *WhoMW 93*
Gold, Leonard Singer 1934- *WhoAm 94*
Gold, Lorne W. 1928- *WhoAm 94, WhoScEn 94*
Gold, Martha B. *WhoAmA 93*
Gold, Martin Elliot 1946- *WhoAm 94, WhoAmL 94*
Gold, Marvin Harold 1915- *WhoWest 94*
Gold, Melvyn d1993 *IntMPA 94N*
Gold, Michael Nathan 1952- *WhoWest 94*
Gold, Neil D. 1948- *WhoAmL 94*
Gold, Noe 1947- *WhoAm 94*
Gold, Norman Myron 1930- *WhoAm 94*
Gold, Peter Frederick 1945- *WhoAm 94, WhoAmL 94*
Gold, Phil 1936- *IntWW 93, WhoAm 94, WhoScEn 94*
Gold, Philip William 1944- *WhoScEn 94*
Gold, Phradie Kling 1933- *WhoFI 94*
Gold, Richard Horace 1935- *WhoAm 94*
Gold, Richard N. 1945- *WhoFI 94*
Gold, Rick L. 1946- *WhoWest 94*
Gold, Robert Arthur 1923- *WhoWest 94*
Gold, Robin Belsky 1959- *WhoMW 93*
Gold, Sandra Orenberg 1937- *WhoAm 94*
Gold, Sharon Cecile 1949- *WhoAmA 93*
Gold, Shirley Jeanne 1925- *WhoAmP 93, WhoWest 94*
Gold, Simeon 1949- *WhoAm 94, WhoAmL 94*
Gold, Stanley P. 1942- *WhoAm 94, WhoFI 94, WhoWest 94*
Gold, Stephen Charles 1915- *Who 94*
Gold, Steven J(ames) 1955- *ConAu 141*
Gold, Steven Michael 1953- *WhoAmL 94*
Gold, Stuart Walter 1949- *WhoAm 94, WhoAmL 94*
Gold, Sylviane 1948- *WhoAm 94*
Gold, Thomas 1920- *IntWW 93, Who 94, WhoAm 94, WorScD*
Gold, Todd 1958- *WrDr 94*
Gold, Tracey 1969- *WhoHol 92*
Gold, Vera Johnson 1951- *WhoFI 94, WhoWest 94*
Goldanskii, Vitalii Iosifovich 1923- *IntWW 93, WhoScEn 94*
Goldaper, Gabriele Gay 1937- *WhoWest 94*
Goldbart, Paul Mark 1960- *WhoScEn 94*
Goldbarth, Albert *DrAPF 93*
Goldbarth, Albert 1948- *WrDr 94*
Goldbaum, Michael Henry 1939- *WhoScEn 94*
Goldbeck, George P. 1925- *WhoIns 94*
Goldbeck, Robert Arthur, Jr. 1950- *WhoScEn 94, WhoWest 94*
Goldberg, Abraham 1923- *IntWW 93, Who 94*
Goldberg, Alan Joel 1943- *WhoAmL 94*
Goldberg, Alan Marvin 1939- *WhoAm 94*
Goldberg, Alan S. 1942- *WhoAmL 94*
Goldberg, Albert Levi 1898- *WhAm 10*
Goldberg, Arnold Herbert 1933- *WhoAmA 93*
Goldberg, Arnold Irving 1929- *WhoAm 94, WhoScEn 94*
Goldberg, Arthur Abba 1940- *WhoAm 94, WhoFI 94*
Goldberg, Arthur H. 1942- *WhoAm 94, WhoFI 94*
Goldberg, Arthur Joseph 1908- *WhAm 10*
Goldberg, Arthur Lance 1950- *WhoWest 94*
Goldberg, Arthur Lewis 1939- *WhoAm 94*
Goldberg, Arthur M. *WhoAm 94, WhoFI 94*
Goldberg, Aubrey 1940- *WhoAmL 94*
Goldberg, Avram Jacob 1930- *WhoAm 94*
Goldberg, Avrum M. 1943- *WhoAm 94, WhoAmL 94*
Goldberg, Barbara *DrAPF 93*
Goldberg, Bert Harvey 1949- *WhoFI 94*
Goldberg, Bertram J. 1942- *WhoAm 94*
Goldberg, Bertrand 1913- *IntWW 93, WhoAm 94*
Goldberg, Billy B. 1915- *WhoAmP 93*
Goldberg, Burton David 1927- *WhoMW 93*
Goldberg, Daniel L. 1946- *WhoAmL 94*
Goldberg, David 1934- *WhoAmL 94*
Goldberg, David Alan 1933- *WhoAm 94*
Goldberg, David Bryan 1954- *WhoScEn 94, WhoWest 94*
Goldberg, David Charles 1940- *WhoAm 94*
Goldberg, David Gerard 1947- *Who 94*
Goldberg, David Meyer 1933- *WhoAm 94*
Goldberg, David Theo 1952- *WhoWest 94*
Goldberg, Deborah Ann 1955- *WhoMW 93*
Goldberg, Dennis Ian 1948- *WhoMW 93*
Goldberg, Edward David 1921- *IntWW 93*
Goldberg, Edward Davidow 1921- *WhoAm 94*
Goldberg, Edward L. 1940- *WhoAm 94, WhoFI 94*
Goldberg, Edward Morris 1931- *WhoWest 94*
Goldberg, Elias 1887-1978 *WhoAmA 93N*
Goldberg, Erwin 1930- *WhoScEn 94*
Goldberg, Fred 1921- *IntMPA 94*
Goldberg, Fred Sellmann 1941- *WhoAm 94, WhoWest 94*
Goldberg, Gary David 1944- *WhoAm 94*
Goldberg, Gary Syd 1948- *WhoAmP 93*
Goldberg, Gerald Jay *DrAPF 93*
Goldberg, Glenn 1953- *WhoAmA 93*
Goldberg, Harold Howard 1924- *WhoScEn 94*
Goldberg, Harold Philip 1939- *WhoAmL 94*
Goldberg, Harold Seymour 1925- *WhoAm 94, WhoScEn 94*
Goldberg, Harry Finck 1936- *WhoAm 94*
Goldberg, Harvey 1940- *WhoFI 94*
Goldberg, Herman R. 1915- *WhoAmP 93*
Goldberg, Herman Raphael 1915- *WhoAm 94*
Goldberg, Homer Beryl 1924- *WhoAm 94*
Goldberg, Howard A. 1945- *WhoAmL 94*
Goldberg, Howard D. d1993 *NewYTBS 93*
Goldberg, Icchok Ignacy 1916- *WhoAm 94*
Goldberg, Irving Hyman 1926- *WhoAm 94*
Goldberg, Irving Loeb 1906- *WhoAm 94, WhoAmL 94*
Goldberg, Ivan Baer 1939- *WhoFI 94*
Goldberg, Ivan D. 1934- *WhoAm 94*
Goldberg, Jacob 1926- *WhoAm 94*
Goldberg, James K. 1945- *WhoAmL 94*
Goldberg, Janet E. 1951- *WhoAmL 94*
Goldberg, Jay 1933- *WhoAmL 94*
Goldberg, Jay Lenard 1939- *WhoAm 94, WhoAmL 94*
Goldberg, Jim *WhoAmA 93*
Goldberg, Jocelyn Hope Schnier 1953- *WhoFI 94*
Goldberg, Joel Henry 1945- *WhoAmL 94*
Goldberg, Jolande Elisabeth 1931- *WhoAmL 94*
Goldberg, Jonathan Jacob 1947- *Who 94*
Goldberg, Joseph 1950- *WhoAmL 94*
Goldberg, Judith 1947- *WhoAmA 93*
Goldberg, Judy Hiller 1933- *WhoWest 94*
Goldberg, Kenneth Yigael 1961- *WhoWest 94*
Goldberg, Kirsten Boyd 1963- *WhoScEn 94*
Goldberg, Larry Joel 1951- *WhoAmL 94*
Goldberg, Lawrence Irwin 1940- *WhoAm 94*
Goldberg, Lea 1911-1978 *BlmGWL [port]*

Goldberg, Lee Winicki 1932- *WhoFI 94, WhoWest 94*
Goldberg, Leon Isadore 1926-1989 *WhAm 10*
Goldberg, Leonard 1934- *ConTFT 11, IntMPA 94, WhoAm 94, WhoFI 94*
Goldberg, Leslie Roberta *WhoWest 94*
Goldberg, Lester *DrAPF 93*
Goldberg, Lewis Robert 1932- *WhoScEn 94*
Goldberg, Louis 1908- *WrDr 94*
Goldberg, Luella Gross 1937- *WhoAm 94*
Goldberg, Marc David 1944- *WhoFI 94*
Goldberg, Marc Evan 1957- *WhoFI 94*
Goldberg, Mark Arthur 1934- *WhoWest 94*
Goldberg, Mark Joel 1941- *WhoAm 94, WhoAmL 94*
Goldberg, Martin 1930- *WhoAm 94*
Goldberg, Marvin Allen 1943- *WhoAmL 94*
Goldberg, Melvin A. *WhoAm 94*
Goldberg, Melvin Arthur 1923- *WhoAm 94*
Goldberg, Melvyn Ralph 1948- *WhoMW 93*
Goldberg, Michael 1924- *WhoAm 94, WhoAmA 93*
Goldberg, Michael Arthur 1941- *WhoAm 94, WhoFI 94, WhoWest 94*
Goldberg, Michael Mitchell 1924- *WhoFI 94*
Goldberg, Morris 1928- *WhoWest 94*
Goldberg, Morton Edward 1932- *WhoAm 94*
Goldberg, Morton Falk 1937- *WhoAm 94, WhoScEn 94*
Goldberg, Myra *DrAPF 93*
Goldberg, Myron Allen 1942- *WhoScEn 94*
Goldberg, Neil A. 1947- *WhoAm 94, WhoAmL 94*
Goldberg, Norman Albert 1918- *WhoAm 94, WhoMW 93*
Goldberg, Norman Lewis 1906-1982 *WhoAmA 93N*
Goldberg, Pamela Winer 1955- *WhoFI 94*
Goldberg, Paul (Boris) 1959- *WrDr 94*
Goldberg, Ray Allan 1926- *WhoAm 94, WhoScEn 94*
Goldberg, Reiner 1939- *NewGrDO*
Goldberg, Richard Robert 1941- *WhoAm 94, WhoAmL 94*
Goldberg, Richard W. 1927- *CngDr 93, WhoAm 94, WhoAmL 94*
Goldberg, Rita Maria 1933- *WhoAm 94*
Goldberg, Robert D. 1951- *WhoAmP 93*
Goldberg, Robert M. 1941- *WhoAmL 94*
Goldberg, Robert N. 1953- *WhoWest 94*
Goldberg, Ronald David 1938- *WhoAmL 94*
Goldberg, Roselee *WhoAmA 93*
Goldberg, Rube d1970 *WhoHol 92*
Goldberg, Samuel 1925- *WhoAm 94*
Goldberg, Samuel 1928- *WhoFI 94*
Goldberg, Samuel Irving 1923- *WhoAm 94, WhoMW 93*
Goldberg, Samuel Louis d1991 *IntWW 93N*
Goldberg, Samuel Louis 1926- *WrDr 94*
Goldberg, Sandra Gail 1940- *WhoAmP 93*
Goldberg, Seth A. 1953- *WhoAm 94*
Goldberg, Sherman I. *WhoAmL 94*
Goldberg, Sidney 1931- *WhoAm 94, WhoFI 94*
Goldberg, Stanley Irwin 1934- *WhoFI 94*
Goldberg, Stanley Joshua 1939- *WhoAmL 94*
Goldberg, Stephanie Benson 1951- *WhoAm 94*
Goldberg, Steven F. 1950- *WhoIns 94*
Goldberg, Steven H. 1941- *WhoAmL 94*
Goldberg, Steven Selig 1950- *WhoAmL 94*
Goldberg, Susan April 1947- *WhoAm 94, WhoAmL 94*
Goldberg, Szymon d1993 *NewYTBS 93*
Goldberg, Vicki Comm 1945- *WhoMW 93*
Goldberg, Victor Joel 1933- *WhoAm 94, WhoFI 94*
Goldberg, Whoopi *IntWW 93, WhoBlA 94*
Goldberg, Whoopi 1949- *AfrAmAl 6 [port], IntMPA 94, WhoAm 94, WhoCom [port]*
Goldberg, Whoopi 1955- *News 93-3 [port], WhoHol 92*
Goldberg, William K. 1954- *WhoScEn 94*
Goldberger, Alan Steven 1949- *WhoAmL 94*
Goldberger, Arthur Earl, Jr. *WhoScEn 94*
Goldberger, Arthur Stanley 1930- *WhoAm 94, WhoFI 94*
Goldberger, Avriel H. 1928- *ConAu 140*
Goldberger, Blanche Rubin 1914- *WhoAm 94*
Goldberger, Charles Arthur 1939- *WhoAmL 94*
Goldberger, George Stefan 1947- *WhoFI 94*
Goldberger, Marvin Leonard 1922- *IntWW 93, Who 94*
Goldberger, Paul Jesse 1950- *WhoAm 94*
Goldberger, Stephen A. *WhoAm 94*
Goldberg-Kent, Susan 1944- *WhoAm 94, WhoMW 93*
Goldblatt, Barry Lance 1945- *WhoFI 94*
Goldblatt, David Ira 1937- *WhoAm 94*
Goldblatt, Hal Michael 1952- *WhoWest 94*
Goldblatt, Harold d1982 *WhoHol 92*
Goldblatt, Simon *Who 94*
Goldblatt, Stanford Jay 1939- *WhoAm 94*
Goldblatt, Steven Harris 1947- *WhoAmL 94*
Goldblith, Samuel Abraham 1919- *WhoAm 94*
Goldbloom, Richard Ballon 1924- *WhoAm 94*
Goldbloom, Victor Charles 1923- *WhoAm 94*
Goldblum, Jeff 1952- *IntMPA 94, IntWW 93, WhoAm 94, WhoHol 92*
Goldby, Frank 1903- *Who 94*
Golde, David William 1940- *WhoAm 94*
Goldeen, Dorothy A. 1948- *WhoAmA 93*
Goldemberg, Isaac *DrAPF 93*
Goldemberg, Isaac 1945- *WhoHisp 94*
Goldemberg, Jose *WhoScEn 94*
Golden, Annie 1952- *WhoHol 92*
Golden, Arthur F. 1946- *WhoAm 94, WhoAmL 94*
Golden, Arthur Ivanhoe 1926- *WhoBlA 94*
Golden, Balfour Henry 1922- *WhoFI 94*
Golden, Bob d1979 *WhoHol 92*
Golden, Bruce Paul 1943- *WhoAm 94*
Golden, Carole Ann 1942- *WhoScEn 94*
Golden, Christopher Anthony 1937- *WhoAm 94, WhoAmL 94*
Golden, Cornelius Joseph, Jr. 1948- *WhoAmL 94*
Golden, Daniel Lewis 1913- *WhoAmL 94*
Golden, David Edward 1932- *WhoAm 94*
Golden, Donald Leon 1940- *WhoBlA 94*
Golden, Eddie d1983 *WhoHol 92*
Golden, Edward Scott 1955- *WhoAmL 94*
Golden, Elliott 1926- *WhoAmL 94*
Golden, Eloise Elizabeth 1938- *WhoMW 93*
Golden, Eunice *WhoAmA 93*
Golden, Eve 1957- *WrDr 94*
Golden, Evelyn Davis 1951- *WhoBlA 94*
Golden, Francis St. Clair 1936- *Who 94*
Golden, Fred Stephan 1945- *WhoFI 94*
Golden, Gail Kadison *DrAPF 93*
Golden, Geoffrey *WhoHol 92*
Golden, Gerald Samuel 1935- *WhoAm 94*
Golden, Grace Lydia d1993 *Who 94N*
Golden, Gregg Hannan Stewart 1953- *WhoAmL 94*
Golden, Herbert L. *IntMPA 94*
Golden, Howard Ira 1946- *WhoAmL 94*
Golden, Jacqueline Audry 1935- *WhoAmP 93*
Golden, Jerome B. 1917- *IntMPA 94*
Golden, John Dennis 1954- *WhoAmL 94*
Golden, John F. 1949- *WhoAm 94*
Golden, John Joseph, Jr. 1943- *WhoFI 94, WhoScEn 94*
Golden, John Matthew 1895- *WhAm 10*
Golden, Joseph Aaron 1940- *WhoAmL 94*
Golden, Judith 1934- *WhoAm 94, WhoAmA 93*
Golden, Julius 1929- *WhoWest 94*
Golden, Leon 1930- *WhoAm 94*
Golden, Leslie Morris 1943- *WhoScEn 94*
Golden, Libby *WhoAm 94, WhoAmA 93*
Golden, Louie 1940- *WhoBlA 94*
Golden, Louis Joseph 1952- *WhoFI 94*
Golden, Marita 1950- *BlkWr 2, ConAu 42NR, WhoBlA 94*
Golden, Mark 1948- *WrDr 94*
Golden, Marvin Darnell 1955- *WhoBlA 94*
Golden, Michael 1913- *WhoHol 92*
Golden, Michael 1942- *WhoAm 94, WhoAmL 94, WhoAmP 93, WhoWest 94*
Golden, Mike *DrAPF 93*
Golden, Milton M. 1915- *WhoAm 94*
Golden, Morton J. 1929- *WhoAmA 93*
Golden, Myron 1947- *WhoBlA 94*
Golden, Nancy Felice 1950- *WhoFI 94*
Golden, Olive Fuller *WhoHol 92*
Golden, Pat 1951- *IntMPA 94*
Golden, Paul A. 1918- *WhoAmP 93*
Golden, R. Vance, III 1947- *WhoAmL 94*
Golden, Renny 1937- *ConAu 142*
Golden, Reynold Stephen 1937- *WhoScEn 94*
Golden, Robert Bennett 1948- *WhoFI 94, WhoMW 93*
Golden, Robert Charles 1946- *WhoAm 94, WhoFI 94*
Golden, Rolland Harve 1931- *WhoAmA 93*
Golden, Ronald Allen 1944- *WhoBlA 94*
Golden, Ruth Fuller d1931 *WhoHol 92*
Golden, Samuel Lewis 1921- *WhoBlA 94*
Golden, Terence C. 1944- *WhoAm 94*
Golden, Thomas Fuller 1942- *WhoAmL 94*
Golden, Tim Robert 1954- *WhoAmP 93*
Golden, Timothy Christopher 1956- *WhoScEn 94*
Golden, Webster Lee 1944- *WhoAmL 94*
Golden, William B. *WhoAmP 93*
Golden, William C. 1936- *WhoAm 94*
Golden, William R., Jr. 1946- *WhoAm 94*
Golden, William Theodore 1909- *WhoAm 94*
Golden, Willie L. 1952- *WhoBlA 94*
Golden, Wilson 1948- *WhoAmL 94*
Golden, Woodrow Wilson, Jr. 1948- *WhoAmP 93*
Goldenberg, Andrew Avi 1945- *WhoAm 94*
Goldenberg, Barbara L. 1952- *WhoMW 93*
Goldenberg, Charles Bruce 1950- *WhoWest 94*
Goldenberg, Charles Lawrence 1933- *WhoAm 94, WhoFI 94*
Goldenberg, David Milton 1938- *WhoAm 94, WhoScEn 94*
Goldenberg, Elizabeth Leigh 1963- *WhoFI 94*
Goldenberg, Eric Mark 1956- *WhoMW 93*
Goldenberg, George 1929- *WhoAm 94, WhoFI 94*
Goldenberg, Gerald Joseph 1933- *WhoAm 94*
Goldenberg, Ronald Edwin 1931- *WhoAm 94*
Goldenberg, Sam d1945 *WhoHol 92*
Goldenberg, Sherri Roberta 1964- *WhoAm 94*
Goldenberg, Steven Paul 1946- *WhoAmL 94*
Goldenberg, Susan 1944- *WrDr 94*
Golden Gate Quartet *WhoHol 92*
Goldenhersh, Joseph Herman 1914-1992 *WhAm 10*
Goldense, Bradford Lincoln 1955- *WhoFI 94*
Goldensohn, Barry *DrAPF 93*
Goldensohn, Lorrie *DrAPF 93*
Goldenson, Leonard H. 1905- *IntMPA 94*
Goldenson, Robert M 1908- *WrDr 94*
Goldenweiser, Alexander (Borisovich) 1875-1961 *NewGrDO*
Golderman, Cynthia R. *DrAPF 93*
Goldey, James Mearns 1926- *WhoAm 94*
Goldfarb, Bernard Sanford 1917- *WhoAm 94, WhoAmL 94, WhoFI 94, WhoMW 93*
Goldfarb, Bob 1961- *WhoFI 94*
Goldfarb, David 1917- *WhoAmP 93*
Goldfarb, Donald 1941- *WhoAm 94*
Goldfarb, I. Jay 1933- *WhoWest 94*
Goldfarb, Irene Dale 1929- *WhoFI 94*
Goldfarb, Martin 1938- *WhoAm 94*
Goldfarb, Marvin Al 1928- *WhoScEn 94*
Goldfarb, Muriel Bernice 1920- *WhoFI 94*
Goldfarb, Reuven *DrAPF 93*
Goldfarb, Richard Charles 1946- *WhoScEn 94*
Goldfarb, Robert Lawrence 1951- *WhoFI 94*
Goldfarb, Robert Stanley 1943- *WhoAm 94*
Goldfarb, Ronald (Lawrence) 1933- *WrDr 94*
Goldfarb, Ronald B. *WhoScEn 94*
Goldfarb, Ronald Lawrence 1933- *WhoAm 94*
Goldfarb, Russell M 1934- *WrDr 94*
Goldfarb, Sidney *DrAPF 93*
Goldfarb, Timothy Moore 1949- *WhoAm 94*
Goldfarb, Warren David 1949- *WhoAm 94*
Goldfeder, Anna d1993 *NewYTBS 93*
Goldfein, Alan *DrAPF 93*
Goldfeld, Stephen Michael 1940- *WhoAm 94, WhoFI 94*
Goldfield, Alfred Sherman 1939- *WhoAm 94*
Goldfield, Edward L. 1930- *WhoAmA 93*
Goldfield, Edwin David 1918- *WhoAm 94*
Goldfield, Emily Dawson 1947- *WhoFI 94*
Goldfield, Joseph 1918- *WhoScEn 94*
Goldfine, Beatrice 1923- *WhoAmA 93*
Goldfine, Howard 1932- *WhoAm 94*
Goldfine, Miriam 1933- *WhoAm 94*
Goldfinger, Eliot 1950- *WhoAmA 93*
Goldfus, Donald Wayne 1934- *WhoAm 94, WhoFI 94*
Goldgar, Arnold Benjamin 1957- *WhoMW 93*
Goldgar, Bertrand Alvin 1927- *WhoAm 94*
Goldgar, Corinne Hartman 1928- *WhoMW 93*
Goldhaber, Gerald Martin 1944- *WhoAm 94*
Goldhaber, Gerson 1924- *WhoAm 94, WhoScEn 94*
Goldhaber, Gertrude Scharff 1911- *IntWW 93, WhoAm 94, WhoScEn 94*
Goldhaber, Jacob Kopel 1924- *WhoAm 94*
Goldhaber, Maurice 1911- *IntWW 93, WhoAm 94, WhoScEn 94*
Goldhirsh, Bernard A. 1940- *WhoAm 94*
Goldhurst, William 1929- *WhoAm 94*
Goldiamond, Israel 1919- *WhoAm 94*
Goldie, Peter 1955- *WhoScEn 94*
Goldie, Peter Lawrence 1946- *Who 94*
Goldie, Ray Robert 1920- *WhoAmL 94, WhoWest 94*
Goldie, Wyndham d1957 *WhoHol 92*
Goldin, Alan Gary 1942- *WhoAm 94*
Goldin, Amy 1926-1978 *WhoAmA 93N*
Goldin, Augusta 1906- *WrDr 94*
Goldin, Barbara Diamond 1946- *WhoAm 94, WrDr 94*
Goldin, Barry Ralph 1942- *WhoScEn 94*
Goldin, Claudia 1946- *ConAu 142*
Goldin, Claudia Dale 1946- *WhoAm 94*
Goldin, Daniel 1940- *WhoAm 94*
Goldin, Daniel S. 1940- *CurBio 93 [port], IntWW 93, WhoScEn 94*
Goldin, Judah 1914- *WhoAm 94*
Goldin, Kenneth Lee 1936- *WhoMW 93*
Goldin, Leon 1923- *WhoAm 94, WhoAmA 93*
Goldin, Martin Bruce 1938- *WhoMW 93*
Goldin, Milton 1927- *WhoAm 94*
Goldin, Nan R. 1953- *WhoAmA 93*
Goldin, Robert Allen, Sr. 1939- *WhoMW 93*
Goldin, Sidney d1937 *WhoHol 92*
Goldin, Sol 1909- *WhoAm 94*
Goldin, Stephen *DrAPF 93*
Goldin, Stephen 1947- *EncSF 93, WrDr 94*
Goldina, Miriam d1979 *WhoHol 92*
Golding, Arthur 1536?-1605 *BlmGEL*
Golding, Arthur 1536-1606 *DcLB 136*
Golding, Brage 1920- *WhoAm 94*
Golding, Bruce 1947- *IntWW 93*
Golding, Charles William 1931- *WhoAm 94*
Golding, Cornelius E. 1947- *WhoIns 94*
Golding, George Earl 1925- *WhoWest 94*
Golding, John 1929- *Who 94*
Golding, John 1931- *Who 94*
Golding, John (Simon Rawson) 1921- *Who 94*
Golding, John Anthony 1920- *Who 94*
Golding, Llin *WhoWomW 91*
Golding, Llinos 1933- *Who 94*
Golding, Louis 1895-1958 *EncSF 93*
Golding, Martin Philip 1930- *WhoAm 94*
Golding, Monica *Who 94*
Golding, (Cecilie) Monica 1902- *Who 94*
Golding, Peter 1947- *WrDr 94*
Golding, Raymund Marshall 1935- *Who 94, WrDr 94*
Golding, Stuart Samuel 1917-1988 *WhAm 10*
Golding, Susan *WhoAmP 93*
Golding, Susan 1945- *WhoAm 94*
Golding, Terence Edward 1932- *Who 94*
Golding, William 1911- *BlmGEL*
Golding, William 1911-1993 *ConLC 81 [port], NewYTBS 93 [port]*
Golding, William (Gerald) 1911- *EncSF 93, IntWW 93*
Golding, William (Gerald) 1911-1993 *ConAu 141, CurBio 93N, TwCYAW*
Golding, William (Gerald), Sir 1911-1993 *WrDr 94N*
Golding, William Gerald d1993 *Who 94N*
Golding, William Gerald 1924- *WhoWest 94*
Goldingay, John 1942- *Who 94*
Goldis, Sy 1928- *WhoAm 94*
Goldmacher, Jeffery Allan 1956- *WhoFI 94*
Goldman, Aaron 1913- *WhoAm 94*
Goldman, Alan Ira 1937- *WhoAm 94*
Goldman, Albert 1927- *WrDr 94*
Goldman, Alfred Emmanuel 1925- *WhoAm 94*
Goldman, Allan Bailey 1937- *WhoAm 94*
Goldman, Allen Marshall 1937- *WhoAm 94, WhoScEn 94*
Goldman, Alvin Lee 1938- *WhoAm 94*
Goldman, Ann Sepe *WhoFI 94*
Goldman, Antony John 1940- *Who 94*
Goldman, Ari L. 1949- *ConAu 140*
Goldman, Arnold (Melvyn) 1936- *WrDr 94*
Goldman, Arnold Ira 1945- *WhoScEn 94*
Goldman, Arthur Joseph 1934- *WhoMW 93*
Goldman, Benjamin Edward 1940- *WhoAm 94*
Goldman, Bernard d1966 *WhoHol 92*
Goldman, Bernard 1928- *WhoAm 94*
Goldman, Bert Arthur 1929- *WhoAm 94*
Goldman, Berthold 1913- *IntWW 93*
Goldman, Bo 1932- *IntMPA 94*
Goldman, Bobbie *DrAPF 93*
Goldman, Brian Arthur 1946- *WhoAm 94*
Goldman, Charles Norton 1932- *WhoAm 94*

Goldman, Charles R(emington) 1930- *WrDr 94*
Goldman, Charles Remington 1930- *WhoScEn 94*
Goldman, Clifford Alan 1943- *WhoAm 94*
Goldman, Clint Paul *WhoAm 94*
Goldman, Danny *WhoHol 92*
Goldman, Don Steven 1950- *WhoWest 94*
Goldman, Donald A. 1947- *WhoAm 94*
Goldman, Donald Howard 1942- *WhoAm 94*
Goldman, E. S. *DrAPF 93*
Goldman, Edmund 1906- *IntMPA 94*
Goldman, Edward Bruce 1943- *WhoAmL 94*
Goldman, Edward M. *DrAPF 93*
Goldman, Ellen Suzanne 1953- *WhoAmL 94*
Goldman, Emma 1869-1940 *AmSocL, WomPubS*
Goldman, Ernest Harold 1922- *WhoScEn 94*
Goldman, Eugene I. 1951- *WhoAm 94*
Goldman, Francisco *WhoHisp 94*
Goldman, Francisco 1955- *ConLC 76 [port]*
Goldman, Gary Craig 1951- *WhoAmL 94*
Goldman, George David 1923- *WhoAm 94*
Goldman, Gerald 1934- *WhoAmP 93*
Goldman, Gerald 1944- *WhoAmL 94*
Goldman, Gerald Hillis 1947- *WhoAm 94*
Goldman, Henry Maurice 1911-1991 *WhAm 10*
Goldman, Israel David 1936- *WhoAm 94, WhoScEn 94*
Goldman, Jack 1937- *WhoAmP 93*
Goldman, Jack Leslie 1935- *WhoMW 93*
Goldman, James 1927- *ConDr 93, WhoAm 94, WrDr 94*
Goldman, Jamie Lee 1957- *WhoFI 94*
Goldman, Jane *IntMPA 94*
Goldman, Jay 1930- *WhoAm 94*
Goldman, Jerry Stephen 1951- *WhoAmL 94*
Goldman, Joel J. 1940- *WhoAm 94, WhoAmL 94*
Goldman, Joel S. 1942- *WhoAm 94, WhoAmL 94*
Goldman, Joseph Elias 1923- *WhoAm 94*
Goldman, Judith *WhoAmA 93*
Goldman, Judy *DrAPF 93*
Goldman, Lawrence Saul 1942- *WhoAmL 94*
Goldman, Leo 1920- *WhoAm 94*
Goldman, Leonard Manuel 1925- *WhoAm 94, WhoScEn 94*
Goldman, Lester 1942- *WhoAmA 93*
Goldman, Lloyd *DrAPF 93*
Goldman, Louis Budwig 1948- *WhoAm 94, WhoAmL 94*
Goldman, Marshall I(rwin) 1930- *WrDr 94*
Goldman, Marvin 1928- *WhoAm 94*
Goldman, Matt 1961- *WhoAmA 93*
Goldman, Michael *DrAPF 93*
Goldman, Michael F. 1939- *IntMPA 94*
Goldman, Moe 1909- *BasBi*
Goldman, Murray Abraham 1937- *WhoAm 94*
Goldman, Nancy Joan Kramer 1953- *WhoAm 94*
Goldman, Nathan Carliner 1950- *WhoAmL 94*
Goldman, Norman Lewis 1933- *WhoAm 94*
Goldman, Patricia Ann 1942- *WhoAm 94, WhoAmP 93, WhoFI 94*
Goldman, Paul *WhoAmP 93*
Goldman, Peter 1929- *WhoScEn 94*
Goldman, Rachel Bok 1937- *WhoAmA 93, WhoMW 93*
Goldman, Ralph 1919-1977 *WhAm 10*
Goldman, Ralph Frederick 1928- *WhoAm 94*
Goldman, Ralph Morris 1920- *WhoAm 94*
Goldman, Richard Lurie 1925- *WhoAmL 94*
Goldman, Robert Irving 1932- *WhoAm 94, WhoFI 94*
Goldman, Roger L. 1941- *ConAu 142*
Goldman, Roy Lawrence 1954- *WhoAmL 94*
Goldman, Samuel 1912- *IntWW 93, Who 94*
Goldman, Sheldon 1939- *WhoAm 94*
Goldman, Shepard *IntMPA 94*
Goldman, Simon 1913- *WhoAm 94*
Goldman, Stanford 1907- *WhoAm 94*
Goldman, Stephen H. *EncSF 93*
Goldman, Steven Jason 1947- *WhoAmL 94, WhoFI 94*
Goldman, Virginia Veronica 1919- *WhoAmP 93*
Goldman, William *DrAPF 93*
Goldman, William 1931- *IntDcF 2-4, IntMPA 94, IntWW 93, WhoAm 94, WrDr 94*
Goldman, William M. 1946- *WhoAm 94, WhoAmL 94*
Goldman, Yale E. *WhoScEn 94*
Goldman-Carter, Janice Lynn 1954- *WhoAmL 94*
Goldmann, Morton Aaron 1924- *WhoAm 94*
Goldmann, Nahum 1948- *WhoScEn 94*
Goldmann, Peter D. 1953- *WhoFI 94*
Goldmark, Karl 1830-1915 *NewGrDO*
Goldmark, Peter Carl 1906-1977 *WorInv*
Goldmark, Peter Carl, Jr. 1940- *WhoAm 94*
Goldner, Charles d1955 *WhoHol 92*
Goldner, Harriet J. 1949- *WhoMW 93*
Goldner, Janet 1952- *WhoAmA 93*
Goldner, Sheldon Herbert 1928- *WhoAm 94*
Goldoni, Carlo 1707-1793 *IntDcT 2, NewGrDO*
Goldoni, Lelia 1937- *WhoHol 92*
Goldovsky, Boris 1908- *WhoAm 94*
Goldowsky, Barbara *DrAPF 93*
Goldowsky, Noah 1909- *WhoAmA 93N*
Goldreich, Gloria *DrAPF 93*
Goldreich, Joseph Daniel 1925- *WhoScEn 94*
Goldreich, Peter 1939- *IntWW 93*
Goldreich, Peter Martin 1939- *WhoScEn 94*
Goldrein, Neville Clive *Who 94*
Goldrick, John Richard 1929- *WhoAm 94*
Goldring, Elizabeth 1945- *WhoAmA 93*
Goldring, Harold Benjamin 1929- *WhoFI 94*
Goldring, John Bernard 1944- *Who 94*
Goldring, Mary Sheila *Who 94*
Goldring, Nancy Deborah 1945- *WhoAmA 93*
Goldring, Norman Max 1937- *WhoAm 94, WhoMW 93*
Goldring, Patrick (Thomas Zachary) 1921- *WrDr 94*
Golds, Anthony Arthur 1919- *IntWW 93, Who 94*
Goldsack, Alan Raymond 1947- *Who 94*
Goldsack, John Redman 1932- *Who 94*
Goldsamt, Bonnie Blume 1946- *WhoAmL 94*
Goldsberry, Richard Eugene 1956- *WhoFI 94, WhoScEn 94*
Goldsberry, Ronald Eugene 1942- *WhoBlA 94*
Goldsberry, Steven 1949- *WrDr 94*
Goldsborough, James Oliver 1936- *ConAu 142, WhoWest 94*
Goldsborough, Robert 1733-1788 *WhAmRev*
Goldsborough, Robert Gerald 1937- *WhoAm 94*
Goldsby, Richard Allen 1934- *WhoScEn 94*
Goldsby, W. Dean, Sr. *WhoBlA 94*
Goldscheider, Sidney 1920- *WhoAm 94*
Goldschmid, Harvey Jerome 1940- *WhoAm 94, WhoAmL 94*
Goldschmidt, Adalbert von 1848-1906 *NewGrDO*
Goldschmidt, Arthur Eduard, Jr. 1938- *WhoAm 94*
Goldschmidt, Bernd 1950- *WhoScEn 94*
Goldschmidt, Berthold 1903- *IntWW 93, NewGrDO*
Goldschmidt, Bertrand 1912- *IntWW 93*
Goldschmidt, Charles 1921- *WhoAm 94*
Goldschmidt, Lucien 1912- *WhoAmA 93*
Goldschmidt, Lynn Harvey 1951- *WhoAm 94*
Goldschmidt, Neil Edward 1940- *IntWW 93, WhoAmP 93*
Goldschmidt, Richard Benedict *WorScD*
Goldschmidt, Robert Alphonse 1937- *WhoAm 94*
Goldschmidt, Victor W. 1936- *WhoHisp 94*
Goldschmidt, Yaaqov 1927- *WrDr 94*
Goldsen, Bruce I. 1959- *WhoMW 93*
Goldsen, Susan Eva 1963- *WhoMW 93*
Goldsholle, Gerry Harvey 1940- *WhoAmL 94*
Goldsleger, Cheryl 1951- *WhoAmA 93*
Goldsmith, Alexander Benedict Hayum 1960- *Who 94*
Goldsmith, Alexander Kinglake 1938- *Who 94*
Goldsmith, Ann *DrAPF 93*
Goldsmith, Arthur 1926- *WrDr 94*
Goldsmith, Arthur Austin 1926- *WhoAm 94*
Goldsmith, Barbara *DrAPF 93, WhoAm 94, WrDr 94*
Goldsmith, Barbara 1931- *WhoAmA 93*
Goldsmith, Benedict Isaac 1916- *WhoAmA 93*
Goldsmith, Billy Joe 1933- *WhoAm 94*
Goldsmith, Bram 1923- *WhoAm 94*
Goldsmith, Caroline Lerner *WhoAmA 93*
Goldsmith, Cele 1933- *EncSF 93*
Goldsmith, Clifford Henry 1919- *WhoAm 94*
Goldsmith, Clio 1957- *WhoHol 92*
Goldsmith, Donald Alan 1943- *WhoAm 94, WhoAmL 94*
Goldsmith, Donald William 1943- *WhoWest 94*
Goldsmith, Edward Rene David 1928- *Who 94*
Goldsmith, Elsa M. 1920- *WhoAmA 93*
Goldsmith, Ethel Frank 1919- *WhoMW 93*
Goldsmith, Frederica *DrAPF 93*
Goldsmith, Harry Sawyer 1929- *WhoAm 94*
Goldsmith, Harvey 1946- *IntWW 93*
Goldsmith, Howard *DrAPF 93*
Goldsmith, Howard 1943- *EncSF 93*
Goldsmith, Howard 1945- *WhoAm 94*
Goldsmith, Jack Landman 1910- *WhoAm 94*
Goldsmith, James (Michael) 1933- *Who 94*
Goldsmith, James Michael 1933- *IntWW 93*
Goldsmith, Jan *WhoAmP 93*
Goldsmith, Janet Jane 1942- *WhoAm 94*
Goldsmith, Jeanette Erlbaum *DrAPF 93*
Goldsmith, Jerry 1929- *IntDcF 2-4, IntMPA 94, WhoAm 94*
Goldsmith, John Anton 1951- *WhoAm 94*
Goldsmith, John D. 1951- *WhoAmL 94*
Goldsmith, John Stuart 1924- *Who 94*
Goldsmith, Julian Royce 1918- *WhoAm 94*
Goldsmith, Karen Lee 1946- *WhoAmL 94*
Goldsmith, Kathleen Mawhinney 1957- *WhoFI 94*
Goldsmith, Lawrence Charles 1916- *WhoAmA 93*
Goldsmith, Lee Selig 1939- *WhoAm 94*
Goldsmith, Lowell Alan 1938- *WhoAm 94, WhoScEn 94*
Goldsmith, Lynn 1948- *ConAu 142*
Goldsmith, Marianne 1948- *WhoWest 94*
Goldsmith, Mark Allan 1952- *WhoAmL 94*
Goldsmith, Mark L. 1936- *WhoAm 94*
Goldsmith, Martin H. 1947- *WhoAm 94*
Goldsmith, Martin M. 1913- *IntMPA 94*
Goldsmith, Mary Helen M. 1933- *WhoScEn 94*
Goldsmith, Michael Allen 1946- *WhoScEn 94*
Goldsmith, Mortimer Michael 1950- *WhoFI 94*
Goldsmith, Morton Ralph 1882-1971 *WhoAmA 93N*
Goldsmith, Nancy Carrol 1940- *WhoFI 94*
Goldsmith, Oliver 1730-1774 *BlmGEL [port], IntDcT 2*
Goldsmith, Paul Felix 1948- *WhoAm 94*
Goldsmith, Peter Henry 1950- *Who 94*
Goldsmith, Philip 1930- *Who 94*
Goldsmith, Richard Norman 1943- *WhoAm 94, WhoAmL 94*
Goldsmith, Robert Frederick Kinglake 1907- *Who 94*
Goldsmith, Robert Hillis 1911-1992 *WhAm 10*
Goldsmith, Robert Holloway 1930- *WhoAm 94, WhoFI 94, WhoWest 94*
Goldsmith, Robert Lewis 1928- *WhoAm 94*
Goldsmith, Ruth 1924- *WhoAmP 93*
Goldsmith, Scott K. 1950- *WhoAmL 94*
Goldsmith, Sidney 1930- *WhoAm 94*
Goldsmith, Stanley Alan 1956- *WhoAmL 94*
Goldsmith, Stanley Joseph 1937- *WhoAm 94*
Goldsmith, Stephen 1946- *WhoAm 94, WhoAmP 93, WhoMW 93*
Goldsmith, Steven Robert 1954- *WhoWest 94*
Goldsmith, Walter D. 1944- *WhoAmL 94*
Goldsmith, Walter Kenneth 1938- *Who 94*
Goldsmith, Werner 1924- *WhoAm 94*
Goldsmith, William Wallace 1893- *WhAm 10*
Goldsmith, Willis Jay 1947- *WhoAm 94, WhoAmL 94*
Goldson, Alfred Lloyd *WhoScEn 94*
Goldson, Alfred Lloyd 1946- *WhoBlA 94*
Goldspiel, Arnold Nelson 1949- *WhoFI 94*
Goldstaub, Anthony (James) 1949- *Who 94*
Goldstaub, Jane Hilary *Who 94*
Goldstein, Abraham S. 1925- *IntWW 93, WhoAm 94, WrDr 94*
Goldstein, Alfred 1926- *Who 94*
Goldstein, Alfred George 1932- *WhoAm 94, WhoMW 93*
Goldstein, Allan B. 1948- *WhoAm 94*
Goldstein, Allan Leonard 1937- *WhoAm 94, WhoScEn 94*
Goldstein, Alvin 1929- *WhoAm 94*
Goldstein, Andrew Lee 1959- *WhoAmL 94*
Goldstein, Arthur S. 1948- *WhoAmL 94*
Goldstein, Avram 1919- *IntWW 93, WhoAm 94*
Goldstein, Barry Bruce 1947- *WhoWest 94*
Goldstein, Bennett Howard 1950- *WhoAmL 94*
Goldstein, Bernard 1929- *WhoAm 94*
Goldstein, Bernard David 1939- *WhoAm 94*
Goldstein, Bernard Herbert 1907- *WhoAm 94*
Goldstein, Bruce 1944- *WhoAmL 94*
Goldstein, Burton Jack 1930- *WhoAm 94*
Goldstein, Carl 1938- *WhoAmA 93, WrDr 94*
Goldstein, Charles Arthur 1936- *WhoAm 94, WhoAmL 94*
Goldstein, Charles Barry *WhoAmA 93*
Goldstein, Charles H. 1939- *WhoAm 94*
Goldstein, Charles Henry 1938- *WhoAm 94*
Goldstein, Daniel Joshua 1950- *WhoAmA 93*
Goldstein, David 1870-1958 *DcAmReB 2*
Goldstein, David Arthur 1934- *WhoScEn 94*
Goldstein, David Baird 1951- *WhoWest 94*
Goldstein, David Louis 1957- *WhoMW 93*
Goldstein, Dora Benedict 1922- *WhoAm 94*
Goldstein, E. Ernest 1918- *WhoAm 94*
Goldstein, Edward 1923- *WhoAm 94*
Goldstein, Edward David 1927- *WhoAm 94*
Goldstein, Edward W. 1942- *WhoAmL 94*
Goldstein, Elliott 1915- *WhoAm 94*
Goldstein, Fern 1935- *WhoAmA 93*
Goldstein, Frank Robert 1943- *WhoAm 94, WhoAmL 94*
Goldstein, Franklin 1928- *WhoAm 94*
Goldstein, Fred 1924- *WhoAm 94*
Goldstein, Gerald 1931- *WhoAm 94*
Goldstein, Gladys *WhoAmA 93*
Goldstein, Harvey 1939- *WrDr 94*
Goldstein, Howard 1933- *WhoAmA 93*
Goldstein, Howard Bernard 1943- *WhoFI 94*
Goldstein, Howard Sheldon 1952- *WhoAmL 94*
Goldstein, Howard Warren 1949- *WhoAm 94, WhoAmL 94*
Goldstein, Imre 1938- *ConAu 140*
Goldstein, Irving 1938- *WhoFI 94*
Goldstein, Irving Robert 1916- *WhoScEn 94*
Goldstein, Irving Solomon 1921- *WhoAm 94*
Goldstein, Irwin Joseph 1929- *WhoScEn 94*
Goldstein, Jack 1938- *WhoAm 94, WhoFI 94*
Goldstein, Jack 1945- *WhoAmA 93*
Goldstein, Jack Charles 1942- *WhoAmL 94*
Goldstein, Jacob Herman 1915- *WhoAm 94*
Goldstein, Jacob Louis 1923- *WhoAmP 93*
Goldstein, Jeffrey L. 1950- *ConTFT 11*
Goldstein, Jenette 1960- *WhoHol 92*
Goldstein, Jennie d1960 *WhoHol 92*
Goldstein, Jerome 1931- *WrDr 94*
Goldstein, Jerome Arthur 1941- *WhoAm 94*
Goldstein, Jerome Charles 1935- *WhoAm 94*
Goldstein, Jerome S. 1940- *WhoAm 94*
Goldstein, Jerry Robert 1947- *WhoAmL 94*
Goldstein, Joan Delano *Who 94*
Goldstein, Joel 1938- *WhoScEn 94*
Goldstein, Jonathan 1943- *WhoAm 94*
Goldstein, Jonathan Amos 1929- *WhoAm 94, WrDr 94*
Goldstein, Joseph 1923- *WhoAm 94, WrDr 94*
Goldstein, Joseph Irwin 1939- *WhoAm 94*
Goldstein, Joseph Leonard 1940- *IntWW 93, Who 94, WhoAm 94, WhoScEn 94*
Goldstein, Julius 1918- *WhoAmA 93*
Goldstein, Kenneth B. 1949- *WhoAmL 94*
Goldstein, Kurt 1878-1965 *EncSPD*
Goldstein, Laurence *DrAPF 93*
Goldstein, Lionel Alvin 1932- *WhoFI 94*
Goldstein, Lisa 1953- *EncSF 93*
Goldstein, Louis L. 1913- *WhoAmP 93*
Goldstein, Louis Lazarus 1913- *WhoAm 94*
Goldstein, Manfred 1927- *WhoFI 94*
Goldstein, Marcia Landweber 1952- *WhoAm 94, WhoAmL 94*
Goldstein, Marion *DrAPF 93*
Goldstein, Mark *WhoAm 94*
Goldstein, Mark 1957- *WhoAmL 94*

Goldstein, Mark David 1947- WhoAm 94
Goldstein, Mark Kingston Levin 1941- WhoScEn 94
Goldstein, Mark L. 1950- WhoAmL 94
Goldstein, Marvin Emanuel 1938- WhoAm 94, WhoScEn 94
Goldstein, Marvin Mark 1944- WhoAm 94, WhoAmL 94
Goldstein, Maxine Shapiro 1926- WhoAmP 93
Goldstein, Melvyn C. 1938- WhoAm 94, WhoMW 93
Goldstein, Menek 1924- WhoAm 94
Goldstein, Michael WhoAm 94, WhoFI 94, WhoHol 92
Goldstein, Michael 1939- Who 94
Goldstein, Michael B. 1943- WhoAm 94, WhoAmL 94
Goldstein, Michael Gerald 1946- WhoAm 94, WhoAmL 94
Goldstein, Michael Saul 1944- WhoWest 94
Goldstein, Milton 1914- WhoAm 94, WhoAmA 93
Goldstein, Milton 1926- IntMPA 94
Goldstein, Morris 1945- WhoAm 94
Goldstein, Murray 1925- WhoAm 94, WhoScEn 94
Goldstein, N. Linda 1953- WhoAmL 94
Goldstein, Nathan 1927- WhoAmA 93
Goldstein, Norm 1939- WhoAm 94
Goldstein, Norman 1934- WhoWest 94
Goldstein, Norman R. 1944- WhoAm 94
Goldstein, Norman Robert 1928- WhoAm 94
Goldstein, Paul 1943- WhoAm 94
Goldstein, Paul Henry 1936- WhoMW 93
Goldstein, Peggy R. 1921- WhoAm 94
Goldstein, Richard A. 1942- WhoAm 94, WhoFI 94
Goldstein, Richard David 1957- WhoAmL 94
Goldstein, Richard Jay 1928- WhoAm 94, WhoMW 93, WhoScEn 94
Goldstein, Robert Arnold 1941- WhoAm 94
Goldstein, Robert Justin 1947- WrDr 94
Goldstein, Robin 1952- WrDr 94
Goldstein, Rubin 1933- WhoScEn 94
Goldstein, Samuel R. 1918- WhoAm 94
Goldstein, Scott Bruce 1956- WhoAmL 94
Goldstein, Sheldon 1951- WhoAmA 93
Goldstein, Sidney 1927- WhoAm 94, WrDr 94
Goldstein, Simon 1935- WhoWest 94
Goldstein, Simon Alfred 1935- Who 94
Goldstein, Stanley P. 1934- WhoAm 94, WhoFI 94
Goldstein, Stanley Philip 1923- WhoAm 94
Goldstein, Steve WhoHol 92
Goldstein, Steven 1950 WhoAm 94, WhoAmL 94
Goldstein, Steven Alan 1954- WhoScEn 94
Goldstein, Steven Edward 1948- WhoWest 94
Goldstein, Steven Jay 1951- WhoAmL 94
Goldstein, Stuart Wolf 1931- WhoAmL 94, WhoWest 94
Goldstein, Sylvia Beatrice 1919- WhoAmL 94
Goldstein, Thomas 1944- WhoAmL 94
Goldstein, Walter Elliott 1940- WhoAm 94, WhoScEn 94
Goldstein, William M. 1942- WhoWest 94
Goldstein, William Marks 1935- WhoAm 94
Goldstein-Jackson, Kevin 1946- WrDr 94
Goldstein-Jackson, Kevin Grierson 1946- Who 94
Goldstick, Thomas Karl 1934- WhoAm 94
Goldstine, Abner D. 1929- WhoAm 94
Goldstine, Herman Heine 1913- IntWW 93, WhoAm 94
Goldstine, Jonathan Heine 1959- WhoFI 94
Goldstine, Robert David 1932- WhoMW 93
Goldstine, Stephen Joseph 1937- WhoAm 94
Goldston, Barbara M. Harral 1937- WhoAm 94, WhoFI 94, WhoWest 94
Goldston, Nathaniel R., III 1938- WhoBlA 94
Goldston, Ralph Peter 1929- WhoBlA 94
Goldston, Stephen Eugene 1931- WhoAm 94
Goldston, William D., Jr. WhoAmP 93
Goldstone, Adrienne Willa 1953- WhoAmL 94
Goldstone, David Joseph 1929- Who 94
Goldstone, Hilary F. 1947- WhoAmP 93
Goldstone, James 1931- IntMPA 94
Goldstone, Jeffrey 1933- IntWW 93, Who 94, WhoAm 94, WhoScEn 94
Goldstone, Jerry 1940- WhoWest 94
Goldstone, Leonard Clement 1949- Who 94
Goldstone, Mark Lewis 1959- WhoAmL 94
Goldstone, Peter Walter 1926- Who 94
Goldstone, Philip David 1950- WhoScEn 94
Goldstone, Richard J. 1938- IntWW 93
Goldstone, Robert 1952- WhoIns 94
Goldstone, Sanford 1926- WhoAm 94
Goldstone, Steven F. 1946- WhoAm 94, WhoAmL 94
Goldstrand, Dennis Joseph 1952- WhoFI 94, WhoWest 94
Goldstucker, Eduard 1913- IntWW 93
Goldsworthy, Ian Francis 1943- Who 94
Goldsworthy, John d1958 WhoHol 92
Goldsworthy, Peter 1951- WrDr 94
Goldsworthy, Robert Flood, Jr. 1943- WhoAmP 93
Goldsworthy, (Arthur) Stanley 1926- Who 94
Goldszer, Bath-Sheba 1932- WhoAmA 93
Goldthorpe, Brian Lees d1992 Who 94N
Goldthorpe, Brian Lees 1933- IntWW 93
Goldthorpe, John Clifford 1931- WhoAm 94
Goldthorpe, John Harry 1935- IntWW 93, Who 94
Goldthwait, Bob 1958- WhoHol 92
Goldthwait, Bob 1962- WhoAm 94, WhoCom
Goldthwait, Bobcat 1962- IntMPA 94
Goldthwaite, Richard A(llen) 1933- WrDr 94
Goldwasser, Edwin Leo 1919- WhoAm 94
Goldwasser, Eugene 1922- WhoAm 94, WhoMW 93
Goldwasser, Gary H. 1941- WhoAmL 94
Goldwasser, Judith Wax 1944- WhoMW 93
Goldwasser, Thomas 1939- WrDr 94
Goldwater, Barry, Jr. 1938- WhoAmP 93
Goldwater, Barry M(orris) 1909- Who 94, WrDr 94
Goldwater, Barry Morris 1909- IntWW 93, WhoAm 94, WhoAmP 93, WhoWest 94
Goldwater, John L. 1916- WrDr 94
Goldwater, John Leonard 1916- WhoAm 94
Goldwater, Leonard John 1903-1992 WhAm 10
Goldwater, Marilyn 1927- WhoAmP 93
Goldwater, Robert 1907-1973 WhoAmA 93N
Goldweitz, Saul 1920- WhoAm 94
Goldwin, Robert (Allen) 1922- WrDr 94
Goldwin, Robert A. 1922- WhoAmP 93
Goldwitz, Susan DrAPF 93
Goldwyn, Samuel 1882-1974 AmCulL
Goldwyn, Samuel 1884-1974 IntDcF 2-4 [port]
Goldwyn, Samuel, Jr. 1926- IntMPA 94
Goldwyn, Samuel John, Jr. 1926- WhoAm 94
Goldwyn, Tony 1960- ConTFT 11, WhoHol 92
Goldy, Daniel Louis 1915- WhoAmP 93
Golecki, Ilan WhoScEn 94
Goleizovsky, Kasyan 1892-1970 IntDcB
Golembeski, Jerome John 1931- WhoAm 94
Golembiovsky, Igor Nesterovich 1935- IntWW 93
Golembiovsky, Igor Nestorovich 1936- LoBiDrD
Goleminov, Marin 1908- NewGrDO
Golemon, Albert Sidney 1904-1991 WhAm 10
Golemon, Ronald Kinnan 1938- WhoAm 94, WhoAmL 94
Goler, Michael David 1952- WhoAmL 94
Goler, Robert 1956- WhoAmA 93
Goler, Robert I. 1956- WhoMW 93
Golerkansky, Peter Joseph 1950- WhoScEn 94
Goley, Mary Anne 1945- WhoAmA 93
Golgi, Camillo 1843-1926 WorScD [port]
Goliday, Willie V. 1956- WhoBlA 94
Goliger, Nancy 1948- IntMPA 94
Goligher, John Cedric 1912- Who 94
Golightly, Danold Wayne 1941- WhoScEn 94
Golightly, Lena Mills WhoAm 94, WhoBlA 94
Golightly, Max Chatterton 1924- WhoAm 94
Golightly, Trueman Harlan 1897-1988 WhAm 10
Goligorski, Eduardo EncSF 93
Golijanin, Danilo M. 1952- WhoScEn 94
Golikov, Vyacheslav Mikhailovich 1952- LoBiDrD
Golin, Alvin 1929- WhoAm 94
Golin, Milton 1921- WhoMW 93
Golinkin, Joseph Webster 1896-1977 WhoAmA 93N
Golinkin, Scott Gordon 1952- WhoAmL 94
Golino, Carlo Luigi 1913-1991 WhAm 10
Golino, Valeria 1966- IntMPA 94, WhoHol 92
Golis, Paul Robert 1954- WhoAmL 94
Golisciani, Enrico 1848-1919 NewGrDO
Golishev, Efim 1897-1970 NewGrDO
Goliti, Melissa Nan 1960- WhoWest 94
Golitsyn, Georgiy 1935- WhoScEn 94
Golitz, Loren Eugene 1941- WhoAm 94, WhoWest 94
Goll, Claire 1891-1977 BlmGWL
Goll, Karen Marie WhoMW 93
Goll, Paulette Susan 1947- WhoMW 93
Goll, Peter 1947- WhoAmP 93
Goll, Sherrie Markin 1946- WhoAmP 93
Gollahalli, Subramanyam Ramappa 1942- WhoAsA 94
Gollaher, Michael Monroe 1953- WhoAmP 93
Gollancz, Livia Ruth 1920- Who 94
Golland, Jo d1987 WhoHol 92
Golledge, Reginald George 1937- WhoWest 94
Golleher, George 1948- WhoFI 94
Goller, Sue Lynne 1961- WhoMW 93
Gollin, Albert Edwin 1930- WhoAm 94
Gollin, Alfred M. 1926- Who 94
Gollin, Joshua A. 1905- WhoAmA 93N
Gollin, Rita K. 1928- ConAu 140
Gollin, Stuart Allen 1941- WhoAm 94
Gollin, Susanne Merle 1953- WhoAm 94
Gollner, Joseph Edward Lawrence 1937- WhoAm 94
Gollner, Marie Louise 1932- WhoAm 94
Gollner, Theodor 1929- IntWW 93
Gollob, Herman Cohen 1930- WhoAm 94
Gollobin, Leonard Paul 1928- WhoAm 94
Gollong, Paul Bernhard Werner 1916- WhAm 10
Gollott, Thomas Arlin 1935- WhoAmP 93
Gollub, Jerry WhoAm 94
Gollwitzer, Helmut d1993 NewYTBS 93
Golm, Ernest d1962 WhoHol 92
Golm, Lisa d1964 WhoHol 92
Golmanavich, Jerald Leo 1948- WhoFI 94
Golob, David Lawrence 1966- WhoFI 94
Golodner, Adam Marc 1959- WhoAmL 94, WhoWest 94
Golodner, Jack 1931- WhoAm 94
Gologorsky, Steven Phillip 1962- WhoFI 94
Golomb, Barry 1924- WhoAmL 94
Golomb, Frederick Martin 1924- WhoAm 94, WhoScEn 94
Golomb, Harvey Morris 1943- WhoAm 94
Golomb, James Douglas 1949- WhoMW 93
Golomb, Richard Moss 1958- WhoAmL 94
Golomb, Solomon Wolf 1932- WhoAm 94
Golombek, Harry 1911- Who 94
Golomski, William Arthur WhoAm 94
Golomstock, Igor (Naumovitch) 1929- WrDr 94
Golonka, Arlene 1936- WhoHol 92
Goloschokin, Alexander Isaac 1965- WhoMW 93
Golovchenko, Jene Andrew 1946- WhoScEn 94
Golovine, Serge 1924- IntDcB [port]
Golovnev, Anatoly Andreevich 1942- LoBiDrD
Golovnin, Vasily Mikhailovich 1776-1831 WhWE
Golovnya, Anatoli 1900-1982 IntDcF 2-4
Golpaygani, Mohammed Riza d1993 NewYTBS 93
Golphin, Vincent F. A. 1952- WhoBlA 94
Golson, George Barry 1944- WhoAm 94
Golsong, Dominique 1955- WhoAmL 94
Golsong, Heribert 1927- IntWW 93
Golt, Sidney 1910- Who 94
Golten, Robert Joseph 1933- WhoAmL 94
Golter, Harry 1924- WhoAm 94
Goltz, Christel 1912- NewGrDO
Goltz, H. A. 1924- WhoAmP 93
Goltz, Robert William 1923- WhoAm 94, WhoWest 94
Goltz, Sonia May 1959- WhoMW 93
Goltzman, David 1944- WhoAm 94
Golu, Mihai 1934- IntWW 93
Golub, Alan 1939- WhoAm 94, WhoFI 94
Golub, Barry Eric 1957- WhoIns 94
Golub, Gene Howard 1932- WhoAm 94, WhoScEn 94
Golub, Harvey 1939- IntWW 93, WhoAm 94, WhoFI 94
Golub, Howard Victor 1945- WhoAm 94, WhoAmL 94, WhoFI 94
Golub, Leon 1922- IntWW 93, WhoAmA 93
Golub, Leon Albert 1922- WhoAm 94
Golub, Lewis 1931- WhoAm 94
Golub, Neil 1937- WhoFI 94
Golub, Peter Richard 1952- WhoAm 94
Golub, Stephen Bruce 1941- WhoAm 94
Golub, Thomas A. WhoIns 94
Golub, William 1904-1992 WhAm 10
Golub, William Weldon 1914- WhoAm 94, WhoAmL 94
Golubeff, Gregory d1958 WhoHol 92
Golubic, Theodore 1928- WhoAmA 93
Golubic, Theodore Roy 1928- WhoWest 94
Golubitsky, Martin 1945- ConAu 140
Golubitsky, Martin Aaron 1945- WhoScEn 94
Golubock, Harvey Lewis 1942- WhoAm 94
Golubski, Joseph Frank 1953- WhoMW 93, WhoScEn 94
Golusin, Millard R. 1947- WhoMW 93
Golz, James F. 1947- WhoIns 94
Gom, Leona 1946- BlmGWL
Goma, Louis Sylvain 1941- IntWW 93
Gomard, Bernhard 1926- IntWW 93
Gombell, Minna d1973 WhoHol 92
Gomberg, Edith S. Lisansky 1920- WhoAm 94
Gomberg, Henry Jacob 1918- WhoAm 94
Gomberg, Sydelle WhoAm 94
Gomberville, Marin Le Roy, sieur de 1599-1674 GuFrLit 2
Gombler, Willy Hans 1941- WhoScEn 94
Gombocz, Erich Alfred 1951- WhoWest 94
Gombojav, Damdingiyn 1919- IntWW 93
Gombosuren, Tserenpiliin 1943- IntWW 93
Gombrich, Ernst (Hans Josef) 1909- IntWW 93, Who 94
Gombrich, Ernst (Hans Josef), Sir 1909- WrDr 94
Gombrich, Richard Francis 1937- Who 94
Gombrowicz, Witold 1904-1969 IntDcT 2
Gomer, Anne Olah 1928- WhoMW 93
Gomer, Robert 1924- IntWW 93, WhoAm 94, WhoScEn 94
Gomersall, Earl Raymond 1930- WhoAm 94
Gomersall, Stephen John 1948- Who 94
Gomery, Adrien-Victor-Joseph WhWE
Gomes (de Araujo junior), Joao 1868-1963 NewGrDO
Gomes, Alfredo (de Freitas) Dias 1922- IntDcT 2
Gomes, (Antonio) Carlos 1836-1896 NewGrDO
Gomes, Diogo 1440-1482 WhWE
Gomes, Edward Clayton, Jr. 1933- WhoMW 93
Gomes, Eliezer d1979 WhoHol 92
Gomes, Elza d1984 WhoHol 92
Gomes, Estevao c. 1474-c. 1538 WhWE
Gomes, Fernao fl. 147-?- WhWE
Gomes, Francisco da Costa 1914- IntWW 93
Gomes, Henriqueta Godinho WhoWomW 91
Gomes, Joao Fernando Pereira 1960- WhoScEn 94
Gomes, Maria Fernandes 1950- WhoFI 94
Gomes, Norman Vincent 1914- WhoFI 94, WhoScEn 94
Gomes, Peter John 1942- WhoAm 94, WhoBlA 94
Gomes, Pietro NewGrDO
Gomes, Socorro 1952- WhoWomW 91
Gomes, Wayne Reginald 1938- WhoAm 94
Gomes de Araujo, Joao 1846-1943 NewGrDO
Gomez, Adelina Marquez 1930- WhoHisp 94
Gomez, Adelina S. WhoHisp 94
Gomez, Alain Michel 1938- IntWW 93
Gomez, Alfred WhoHisp 94
Gomez, Alfredo C. 1939- WhoHisp 94
Gomez, Andy Santiago 1954- WhoHisp 94
Gomez, Antonio A. 1945- WhoHisp 94
Gomez, Armelio Juan 1947- WhoHisp 94
Gomez, Augie d1966 WhoHol 92
Gomez, Aurelia F. 1937- WhoHisp 94
Gomez, Basil Anthony, Jr. 1936- WhoHisp 94
Gomez, Ben WhoHisp 94
Gómez, Carlos R. 1937- WhoHisp 94
Gomez, Carmen 1957- WhoHisp 94
Gomez, Charles Lawrence 1934- WhoHisp 94
Gomez, Cynthia Ann 1958- WhoHisp 94
Gomez, Daniel J. 1926- WhoBlA 94
Gomez, David Frederick 1940- WhoAmL 94, WhoWest 94
Gomez, Dennis Craig 1948- WhoBlA 94
Gomez, Eduardo 1930- WhoHisp 94
Gomez, Edward Casimiro 1938- WhoAm 94, WhoHisp 94
Gomez, Elias Galvan 1934- WhoHisp 94
Gomez, Elsa 1938- WhoHisp 94
Gómez, Ernesto Alvarado 1946- WhoHisp 94
Gomez, Faustino 1935- WhoHisp 94
Gomez, Fausto B. 1954- WhoHisp 94
Gómez, Francis D. 1941- WhoHisp 94

Gomez, Francis Dean 1941- *WhoAm 94, WhoFI 94*
Gomez, George *WhoHisp 94*
Gomez, George 1958- *WhoAmP 93*
Gomez, Guillermo G. 1933- *WhoHisp 94*
Gomez, Isabel 1941- *WhoHisp 94*
Gomez, Jaime Armando *WhoHisp 94*
Gomez, Jaime G. 1932- *WhoScEn 94*
Gomez, James H. 1949- *WhoHisp 94*
Gomez, Jesus Albert 1954- *WhoHisp 94*
Gomez, Jewelle *DrAPF 93*
Gomez, Jewelle 1948- *BlkWr 2, ConAu 142, GayLL*
Gomez, Jill *IntWW 93, Who 94*
Gomez, Jill 1942- *NewGrDO*
Gomez, John 1961- *WhoHisp 94*
Gomez, John R., Sr. 1923- *WhoHisp 94*
Gomez, Jorge Luis 1964- *WhoHisp 94*
Gómez, José Félix 1949- *WhoHisp 94*
Gomez, Jose Pantaleon, III 1956- *WhoHisp 94*
Gomez, Judy M. 1949- *WhoAmP 93*
Gomez, Kevin Lawrence Johnson 1950- *WhoBlA 94*
Gomez, Larry *WhoAmL 94*
Gomez, Lawrence J. 1946- *WhoHisp 94*
Gomez, Lawrence T. 1940- *WhoHisp 94*
Gomez, Leo 1967- *WhoHisp 94*
Gomez, Leonel, Jr. 1965- *WhoHisp 94*
Gómez, LeRoy Marcial 1934- *WhoHisp 94*
Gomez, Louis Salazar 1939- *WhoWest 94*
Gomez, Luis Maria *IntWW 93*
Gomez, Luis Oscar 1943- *WhoAm 94, WhoHisp 94*
Gomez, Madeleine-Angelique Poisson, Dame Gabriel de 1684-1770 *BlmGWL*
Gomez, Manuel *WhoHisp 94*
Gomez, Manuel Rodriguez 1928- *WhoAm 94*
Gomez, Marga 1959- *WhoHisp 94*
Gómez, Margaret Juarez 1944- *WhoHisp 94*
Gomez, Margarita 1940- *WhoHisp 94*
Gomez, Maria Rosario 1941- *WhoHisp 94*
Gomez, Mario J. 1956- *WhoHisp 94*
Gomez, Martin *WhoWest 94*
Gomez, Martin J. 1951- *WhoHisp 94*
Gomez, Mary Louise 1950- *WhoHisp 94*
Gomez, Michael 1942- *WhoHisp 94*
Gomez, Mike 1951- *WhoHisp 94*
Gomez, Mirta 1953- *WhoAmA 93*
Gomez, Orlando A. *WhoHisp 94*
Gomez, Oscar C. 1946- *WhoHisp 94*
Gomez, Paul 1957- *WhoHisp 94*
Gomez, Pedro Judas 1962- *WhoHisp 94*
Gomez, Pete *WhoHisp 94*
Gomez, Pietro *NewGrDO*
Gomez, Raul 1948- *WhoHisp 94*
Gomez, Reynaldo A. 1949- *WhoHisp 94*
Gomez, Ricardo Eduardo 1938- *WhoHisp 94*
Gomez, Richard *WhoHisp 94*
Gomez, Richard A., Sr. 1954- *WhoHisp 94*
Gomez, Robert Pastor, II 1948- *WhoHisp 94*
Gomez, Rod J. *WhoHisp 94*
Gomez, Romel Del Rosario 1960- *WhoScEn 94*
Gomez, Ronald J. 1934- *WhoAmP 93*
Gómez, Rudolph *WhoHisp 94*
Gomez, Rudolph Vasquez 1944- *WhoHisp 94*
Gomez, Ruth 1938- *WhoHisp 94*
Gomez, Salvador *WhoHisp 94*
Gomez, Sharon Jeanneene 1954- *WhoHisp 94*
Gomez, Stephen Jesus 1957- *WhoHisp 94*
Gomez, Thomas *WhoHisp 94*
Gomez, Thomas d1971 *WhoHol 92*
Gomez, Tom Philip 1954-1993 *WhoHisp 94N*
Gomez, Tony *WhoHisp 94*
Gomez, Victor J. 1941- *WhoHisp 94*
Gómez-Baisden, Gladys Esther 1943- *WhoHisp 94*
Gomezbeck, El Tal d1989 *WhoHol 92*
Gomez-Bethke, Irene Marie 1935- *WhoHisp 94*
Gomez-Calderon, Javier 1948- *WhoHisp 94*
Gomez de Avellaneda, Gertrudis 1814-1873 *BlmGWL*
Gómez Gil, Alfredo 1936- *WhoHisp 94*
Gómez-Martínez, José Luis 1943- *WhoHisp 94*
Gomez-Mejia, Luis R. 1949- *WhoHisp 94*
Gomez Ojea, Carmen 1945- *BlmGWL*
Gomez Palacio, Enrique 1947- *WhoHisp 94*
Gomezplata, Albert 1930- *WhoHisp 94*
Gomez-Quinones, Juan *DrAPF 93, WhoHisp 94*
Gomez-Quintero, Ela R. *WhoHisp 94*
Gomez-Quiroz, Juan 1939- *WhoHisp 94*
Gomez-Quiroz, Juan Manuel 1939- *WhoAmA 93*
Gomez-Rodriguez, Manuel 1940- *WhoAm 94, WhoHisp 94*
Gómez Rosa, Alexis 1950- *WhoHisp 94*
Gomez-Sicre, Jose 1916-1991 *WhoAmA 93N*
Gomez-Tellez, Ignacio 1939- *WhoHisp 94*
Gomez-Tumpkins-Preston, Cheryl Annette 1954- *WhoHisp 94*
Gómez-Vega, Ibis del Carmen 1952- *WhoHisp 94*
Gomi, Yasumasa *WhoAm 94, WhoFI 94, WhoWest 94*
Gomide, Fernando de Mello 1927- *WhoScEn 94*
Gomillion, Charles Goode 1900- *WhoBlA 94*
Gomis y Colomer, Jose Melchor 1791-1836 *NewGrDO*
Gomm, Richard Culling C. *Who 94*
Gomme, Robert Anthony 1930- *Who 94*
Gomola, Maria *WhoWomW 91*
Gomory, Ralph Edward 1929- *IntWW 93, WhoAm 94, WhoScEn 94*
Gompers, Samuel 1850-1924 *AmSocL [port], HisWorL [port]*
Gompertz, (Arthur John) Jeremy 1937- *Who 94*
Gomperz, Paul Andreas 1937- *WhoFI 94*
Gomringer, Eugen 1925- *IntWW 93*
Gomulka, Wladyslaw 1905-1982 *HisWorL [port]*
Gona, Ophelia Delaine 1936- *WhoBlA 94*
Gonano, Aulo Ivo 1952- *WhoAmP 93*
Goncalves, Fatima *WhoHisp 94*
Goncalves, Olga 193-?- *BlmGWL*
Goncalves, Vasco dos Santos 1921- *IntWW 93*
Goncalves, Vinicius A. 1961- *WhoFI 94*
Goncalves da Silva, Cylon Eudoxio Tricot 1946- *WhoScEn 94*
Goncarovs, Gunti 1956- *WhoScEn 94*
Gonchigdorj, Radnaasumbreliin 1954- *IntWW 93*
Goncourt, Edmond Louis Antonine Huot de 1822-1896 *BlmGEL*
Goncourt, Jules Alfred Huot de 1830-1870 *BlmGEL*
Goncz, Arpad 1922- *ConWorW 93, IntWW 93*
Goncz, Douglas Dana 1959- *WhoScEn 94*
Gonda, David Joel 1950- *WhoMW 93*
Gonda, Igor 1947- *WhoScEn 94*
Gonda, Jan 1905- *IntWW 93*
Gondek, John Richard 1959- *WhoScEn 94*
Gondek, Therese Marie 1950- *WhoMW 93*
Gonder, Sharon 1943- *WhoMW 93*
Gonderman, Robert Frank 1959- *WhoAmL 94*
Gondinet, (Pierre-)Edmond(-Julien) 1828-1888 *NewGrDO*
Gonella, Francesco fl. 1794-1812 *NewGrDO*
Gonet, Judith Janu 1947- *WhoMW 93*
Gong, Prince 1833-1898 *HisWorL*
Gong, Edmond Joseph 1930- *WhoAm 94*
Gong, Ginny 1948- *WhoAsA 94*
Gong, Henry, Jr. 1947- *WhoWest 94*
Gong, Jin Kang 1957- *WhoAsA 94*
Gong, Mamie Poggio 1951- *WhoWest 94*
Gong, Yitai 1941- *WhoScEn 94*
Gonga, Dawilli 1946- *WhoBlA 94*
Gongaware, Donald Francis 1935- *WhoFI 94*
Gong Benyan 1927- *IntWW 93, WhoPRCh 91 [port]*
Gong Dafei *WhoPRCh 91*
Gong Daxi 1936- *WhoPRCh 91 [port]*
Gong Li *WhoPRCh 91 [port]*
Gong Liu 1927- *WhoPRCh 91 [port]*
Gongora, Leonel *WhoAmA 93*
Gongora-Trejos, Enrique 1931- *WhoScEn 94*
Gong Pinmei 1901- *WhoPRCh 91*
Gong Pusheng 1913- *IntWW 93*
Gong Pusheng 1917?- *WhoPRCh 91 [port]*
Gong Shiping 1944- *WhoPRCh 91*
Gong-tang-cang *WhoPRCh 91*
Gong Xianyong 1942- *WhoPRCh 91 [port]*
Gong Xue 1954- *WhoPRCh 91 [port]*
Gong Yuzhi 1929- *WhoPRCh 91 [port]*
Gong Zirong 1914- *WhoPRCh 91 [port]*
Goñi, Paul 1929- *WhoHisp 94*
Gonick, Catherine *DrAPF 93*
Gonick, Harvey Craig 1930- *WhoAm 94*
Gonick, Paul 1930- *WhoAm 94*
Gonne, Maud c. 1865-1953 *HisWorL [port]*
Gonne, Maud Edith 1866-1953 *DcNaB MP*
Gonnella, Nina Celeste 1953- *WhoAm 94*
Gonnering, Russell Stephen 1949- *WhoMW 93, WhoScEn 94*
Gonor, Robert F. 1949- *WhoIns 94*
Gonsalez, Giuseppe fl. c. 1900-1935 *NewGrDO*
Gonsalves, June Miles 1939- *WhoBlA 94*
Gonsalves, Robert Arthur 1935- *WhoScEn 94*
Gonsalves, Roy *DrAPF 93*
Gonso, Harry L. 1948- *WhoAmL 94*
Gonson, S. Donald 1936- *WhoAm 94*
Gontcharova, Nathalie 1881-1962 *IntDcB*
Gonthier, Charles Doherty 1928- *WhoAm 94*
Gontier, Jean Roger 1927- *WhoScEn 94*
Gontrum, Peter Baer 1932- *WhoWest 94*
Gonya, Donald Alan 1934- *WhoAmL 94*
Gonya, Patrice Yeager 1951- *WhoFI 94*
Gonye, Laszlo K. 1922- *WhoIns 94*
Gonynor, Francis James 1959- *WhoAmL 94*
Gonyo, Jeffrey Myron 1963- *WhoAmL 94*
Gonzaga, Pietro 1751-1831 *NewGrDO*
Gonzaga Family *NewGrDO*
Gonzales, A. Nick 1946- *WhoHisp 94*
Gonzales, Alberto R. 1955- *WhoHisp 94*
Gonzales, Alex D. 1927- *WhoHisp 94*
Gonzales, Alexander J. 1954- *WhoAmL 94*
Gonzales, Alexis 1931- *WhoAm 94*
Gonzales, Alexis, Brother 1931- *WhoHisp 94*
Gonzales, Alfred *WhoHisp 94*
Gonzales, Alphonse Charles 1951- *WhoMW 93*
Gonzales, Andrés Antonio 1947- *WhoHisp 94*
Gonzales, Anthony Ralph 1959- *WhoFI 94*
Gonzales, Aurora H. 1932- *WhoHisp 94*
Gonzales, Betty J. *WhoHisp 94*
Gonzales, Bridget Anneliese 1960- *WhoHisp 94*
Gonzales, Carlotta 1910- *WhoAmA 93*
Gonzales, Cesar A. 1952- *WhoHisp 94*
Gonzales, Ciriaco Q. 1933- *WhoHisp 94*
Gonzales, Claire 1959- *WhoHisp 94*
Gonzales, Dalmacio 1945- *NewGrDO*
Gonzales, David Fidel 1943- *WhoHisp 94*
Gonzales, Diana España 1947- *WhoHisp 94*
Gonzales, Dorothy 1943- *WhoHisp 94*
Gonzales, Eduardo 1954- *WhoHisp 94*
Gonzales, Edward 1947- *WhoHisp 94*
Gonzales, Eloisa Aragon 1952- *WhoHisp 94*
Gonzales, Emory Thomas 1951- *WhoHisp 94*
Gonzales, Felipe 1946- *WhoHisp 94*
Gonzales, Francisco 1947- *WhoHisp 94*
Gonzales, Frank *WhoHisp 94*
Gonzales, Gilberto d1954 *WhoHol 92*
Gonzales, Irma E. 1948- *WhoHisp 94*
Gonzales, Isabel *WhoHisp 94*
Gonzales, J. Luis 1963- *WhoHisp 94*
Gonzales, Jake, Jr. 1928- *WhoHisp 94*
Gonzales, James Lawrence 1947- *WhoHisp 94*
Gonzales, Jerry Puente 1947- *WhoHisp 94*
Gonzales, Jimmy d1971 *WhoHol 92*
Gonzales, Joe *WhoHisp 94*
Gonzales, Joe 1949- *WhoHisp 94*
Gonzales, Joe Anthony 1957- *WhoHisp 94*
Gonzales, John *WhoAmP 93*
Gonzales, John Edmond 1924- *WhoAm 94*
Gonzales, José *WhoHisp 94*
Gonzales, Joseph M. *WhoHisp 94*
Gonzales, Juan L., Jr. 1945- *WhoHisp 94*
Gonzales, Leo 1943- *WhoHisp 94*
Gonzales, Lily L. *WhoHisp 94*
Gonzales, Liz 1957- *WhoHisp 94*
Gonzales, Lorenzo Tomas 1949- *WhoHisp 94*
Gonzales, Manuel, Jr. 1954- *WhoHisp 94*
Gonzales, Manuel Garcia 1943- *WhoHisp 94*
Gonzales, Martin A. 1952- *WhoHisp 94*
Gonzales, Michael David 1951- *WhoHisp 94*
Gonzales, Myrtle d1918 *WhoHol 92*
Gonzales, Nancy Alderete 1948- *WhoAmP 93*
Gonzales, Nick, Jr. 1937- *WhoMW 93*
Gonzales, Nita *WhoHisp 94*
Gonzales, Pablo 1949- *WhoHisp 94*
Gonzales, Pancho 1928- *WhoHisp 94*
Gonzales, Pedro Antonio 1930- *WhoHisp 94*
Gonzales, Phillip B. 1946- *WhoHisp 94*
Gonzales, Rafael Alfred 1951- *WhoWest 94*
Gonzales, Rebecca 1946- *WhoHisp 94*
Gonzales, Rebecca Ann 1966- *WhoHisp 94*
Gonzales, Rene 1961- *WhoHisp 94*
Gonzales, Richard A. 1944- *WhoHisp 94*
Gonzales, Richard Alonzo 1928- *WhoHisp 94*
Gonzales, Richard Daniel 1959- *WhoWest 94*
Gonzales, Richard Joseph 1950- *WhoWest 94*
Gonzales, Richard L. *WhoWest 94*
Gonzales, Richard L. 1938- *WhoHisp 94*
Gonzales, Richard Robert 1945- *WhoWest 94*
Gonzales, Richard S. 1954- *WhoHisp 94*
Gonzales, Rick 1959- *WhoHisp 94*
Gonzales, Robert E. 1936- *WhoAmP 93*
Gonzales, Roberta Marie *WhoHisp 94*
Gonzales, Ron *WhoAmP 93*
Gonzales, Ron 1951- *WhoHisp 94*
Gonzales, Ron 1954- *WhoHisp 94*
Gonzales, Severiano H. 1942- *WhoHisp 94*
Gonzales, Stanley James 1929- *WhoHisp 94*
Gonzales, Stephanie 1950- *WhoAm 94, WhoAmP 93, WhoHisp 94, WhoWest 94*
Gonzales, Stephen Elliott 1955- *WhoAmP 93*
Gonzales, Steve T. 1962- *WhoHisp 94*
Gonzales, Thomas 1940- *WhoHisp 94*
Gonzales, Thomas A. *WhoHisp 94*
Gonzales, Tomasa Calixta 1948- *WhoHisp 94*
Gonzales-Berry, Erlinda Viola 1942- *WhoHisp 94*
Gonzales-Kimbrough, Marcia Joan 1953- *WhoHisp 94*
Gonzales Posada, Luis 1945- *IntWW 93*
Gonzales Rogers, Donna Jean 1959- *WhoHisp 94*
Gonzales-Thornell, Consuelo *WhoHisp 94*
Gonzalez, A. C. *WhoHisp 94*
Gonzalez, Aida Argentina 1940- *WhoHisp 94*
Gonzalez, Al *WhoAmP 93*
Gonzalez, Alan Francis 1951- *WhoAmL 94*
Gonzalez, Alberto 1947- *WhoHisp 94*
Gonzalez, Alejandro 1960- *WhoHisp 94*
Gonzalez, Alex Ramon 1932- *WhoHisp 94*
Gonzalez, Alexander 1945- *WhoHisp 94*
Gonzalez, Alexander G. 1952- *WhoHisp 94*
Gonzalez, Alfonso 1944- *WhoHisp 94*
Gonzalez, Alfonso, Jr. 1938- *WhoHisp 94*
Gonzalez, Alfred Phillip 1951- *WhoHisp 94*
Gonzalez, Alfredo *WhoHisp 94*
Gonzalez, Alicia Cristina 1947- *WhoWest 94*
Gonzalez, Andrew Manuel 1927- *WhoHisp 94*
González, Angela 1947- *WhoHisp 94*
González, Angelo 1943- *WhoHisp 94*
Gonzalez, Annabella Quintanilla 1941- *WhoHisp 94*
Gonzalez, Antonio Erman 1935- *IntWW 93*
González, Arleen Caballero 1957- *WhoHisp 94*
Gonzalez, Armando L. *WhoHisp 94*
Gonzalez, Arnie 1949- *WhoHisp 94*
Gonzalez, Arthur Padilla 1954- *WhoAmA 93*
Gonzalez, Atanacio Barrera, III 1941- *WhoHisp 94*
Gonzalez, Avelino Juan 1951- *WhoHisp 94*
Gonzalez, Bernardo Antonio 1950- *WhoHisp 94*
Gonzalez, Bryan B. *WhoHisp 94*
Gonzalez, Caleb 1929- *WhoHisp 94*
Gonzalez, Cambell 1918- *WhoBlA 94*
Gonzalez, Carlos *WhoHisp 94*
Gonzalez, Carlos A. 1956- *WhoHisp 94*
Gonzalez, Carlos Alberto 1958- *WhoHisp 94*
Gonzalez, Carlos F. 1948- *WhoHisp 94*
González, Carlos Juan 1945- *WhoHisp 94*
Gonzalez, Carlos Manuel 1946- *WhoHisp 94*
Gonzalez, Catherine Gunsalus 1934- *WrDr 94*
González, Celedonio 1923- *WhoHisp 94*
González, César Augusto 1931- *WhoHisp 94*
Gonzalez, Charles A. 1945- *WhoHisp 94*
Gonzalez, Conrado A. 1945- *WhoHisp 94*
González, Constantino Jose 1956- *WhoHisp 94*
Gonzalez, Crispin, Jr. 1936- *WhoHisp 94*
González, Cristina 1951- *WhoHisp 94*
Gonzalez, Dale V. *WhoHisp 94*
Gonzalez, Daniel J. 1946- *WhoHisp 94*
Gonzalez, Dario R. 1953- *WhoHisp 94*
Gonzalez, David Alfonso 1962- *WhoScEn 94*
Gonzalez, David John 1951- *WhoHisp 94*
Gonzalez, David Lawrence 1957- *WhoHisp 94*
Gonzalez, David R. 1944- *WhoHisp 94*
González, Deena J. 1952- *WhoHisp 94*
Gonzalez, Diana 1946- *WhoHisp 94*
Gonzalez, Diane Kathryn 1947- *WhoMW 93*
Gonzalez, Donaciano E. 1947- *WhoHisp 94*
Gonzalez, Edgar 1924- *WhoHisp 94*
Gonzalez, Edgar R. 1957- *WhoHisp 94*
Gonzalez, Eduardo *WhoHisp 94*
Gonzalez, Edward, Jr. 1931- *WhoHisp 94*

Good, Michael Robert 1961- *WhoWest 94*
Good, Norma Lee 1932- *WhoMW 93*
Good, Robert Alan 1922- *WhoAm 94, WhoScEn 94*
Good, Robert J. *WhoAmP 93*
Good, Ronald D'Oyley d1992 *Who 94N*
Good, Roy Sheldon 1924- *WhoFI 94*
Good, Ruth *DrAPF 93*
Good, Sheldon Fred 1933- *WhoMW 93*
Good, Steven Loren 1956- *WhoAmL 94*
Good, Thomas Arnold 1925- *WhoWest 94*
Good, Thomas Lindall 1943- *WhoAm 94*
Good, Timothy Jay 1947- *WhoMW 93*
Good, Virginia Johnson 1919- *WhoFI 94*
Good, Walter Raymond 1924- *WhoAm 94*
Good, Willa W. 1915- *WhoBlA 94*
Good, William Allen 1949- *WhoAm 94*
Goodacre, Glenna 1939- *WhoAmA 93*
Goodacre, Kenneth 1910- *Who 94*
Goodacre, Peter Eliot 1945- *Who 94*
Goodale, Cecil Paul d1992 *Who 94N*
Goodale, James Campbell 1933- *WhoAm 94*
Goodale, Toni Krissel 1941- *WhoAm 94*
Goodall, Anthony Charles 1916- *Who 94*
Goodall, (Arthur) David (Saunders) 1931- *IntWW 93, Who 94*
Goodall, David William 1914- *Who 94*
Goodall, Frances Louise 1915- *WhoFI 94, WhoScEn 94, WhoWest 94*
Goodall, Frederique Vincent 1959- *WhoMW 93*
Goodall, Grace d1940 *WhoHol 92*
Goodall, H(arold) L(loyd), Jr. 1952- *WrDr 94*
Goodall, Hurley 1927- *WhoAmP 93*
Goodall, Hurley Charles, Sr. 1927- *WhoBlA 94*
Goodall, Jackson Wallace, Jr. 1938- *WhoAm 94, WhoWest 94*
Goodall, Jane 1934- *ConAu 43NR, IntWW 93, WhoScEn 94, WrDr 94*
Goodall, Leon Steele 1925- *WhoIns 94*
Goodall, Leonard Edwin 1937- *WhoAm 94*
Goodall, Maurice John 1928- *Who 94*
Goodall, Newman 1896- *WhAm 10*
Goodall, Peter 1920- *Who 94*
Goodall, Reginald 1901-1990 *NewGrDO*
Goodart, Nan L. 1938- *WhoAmL 94*
Goodbird, Edward 1869-1938 *EncNAR*
Goodbody, John Collett 1915- *WhAm 10*
Goodbred, Ray Edward 1929- *WhoAmA 93*
Good-Brown, Sue Ann 1960- *WhoWest 94*
Goodby, James Eugene 1929- *WhoAmP 93*
Goodby, Jeffrey *WhoWest 94*
Goodchild, David Hicks 1926- *Who 94*
Goodchild, David Lionel Napier 1935- *Who 94*
Goodchild, George 1885-1969 *EncSF 93*
Goodchild, John Charles, Jr. 1945- *WhoAm 94*
Goodchild, Marianne *Who 94*
Goodchild, Michael *WhoScEn 94*
Goodchild, Peter Robert Edward 1939- *Who 94*
Goodchild, Robert Marshall 1933- *WhoAm 94*
Goodchild, Ronald Cedric Osbourne 1910- *Who 94*
Goodchild, Sidney 1903- *Who 94*
Goodden, Randall Lee 1951- *WhoMW 93*
Goodden, Robert Yorke 1909- *Who 94*
Goode, Andrea Horrocks 1957- *WhoWest 94*
Goode, Anthony William 1944- *IntWW 93*
Goode, Barry Paul 1948- *WhoAmL 94*
Goode, Calvin C. 1927- *WhoAmP 93, WhoBlA 94*
Goode, (Penelope) Cary (Anne) 1947- *Who 94*
Goode, Chris K. 1963- *WhoBlA 94*
Goode, Clement Tyson 1929- *WhoAm 94*
Goode, David Ronald 1941- *WhoAm 94, WhoFI 94*
Goode, George Ray 1930- *WhoBlA 94*
Goode, Harry C., Jr. 1938- *WhoAmP 93*
Goode, Jack d1971 *WhoHol 92*
Goode, James (Arthur) 1924-1992 *ConAu 140*
Goode, James Edward 1943- *WhoBlA 94*
Goode, James Francis 1944- *WhoMW 93*
Goode, James Moore 1939- *WhoAm 94*
Goode, Joe 1937- *WhoAmA 93*
Goode, John Martin 1934- *WhoAm 94*
Goode, Mal 1908- *AfrAmAl 6*
Goode, Malvin R. 1908- *WhoBlA 94*
Goode, Mark Bernard 1951- *WhoFI 94*
Goode, Richard 1916- *WrDr 94*
Goode, Richard Benjamin 1916- *WhoAm 94*
Goode, Richard Stephen 1943- *WhoAm 94*
Goode, Royston Miles 1933- *Who 94*
Goode, Stephen Hogue 1924- *WhoAm 94*
Goode, Victor M. 1947- *WhoBlA 94*
Goode, Virgil Hamlin, Jr. 1946- *WhoAmP 93*
Goode, W. Wilson *WhoAmP 93*
Goode, W. Wilson 1938- *AfrAmAl 6 [port], WhoAm 94, WhoBlA 94*
Goode, Wayne 1937- *WhoAmP 93*
Goodeagle, Mrs. fl. 1890- *EncNAR*
Goodell, Brian Wayne 1942- *WhoAm 94*
Goodell, Christina Marie 1959- *WhoAm 94*
Goodell, George Sidney 1921- *WhoAm 94*
Goodell, Horace Grant 1925- *WhoAm 94*
Goodell, John Dewitte 1909- *WhoFI 94, WhoMW 93, WhoScEn 94*
Goodell, Larry *DrAPF 93*
Goodell, Sol 1906- *WhoAm 94*
Goodell, Warren Franklin 1924- *WhoAm 94*
Goodelman, Aaron J. 1891-1978 *WhoAmA 93N*
Goodelman, Ruth 1914- *WhoAmA 93*
Gooden, C. Michael *WhoBlA 94*
Gooden, Cherry Ross 1942- *WhoBlA 94*
Gooden, Dwight Eugene 1964- *WhoAm 94, WhoBlA 94*
Gooden, Pamela Joyce 1954- *WhoAmL 94*
Gooden, Robert 1949- *WhoScEn 94*
Gooden, Samuel Ellsworth 1916- *WhoBlA 94*
Gooden, Winston Earl *WhoBlA 94*
Goodenough, Anthony Michael 1941- *Who 94*
Goodenough, Cecilia Phyllis 1905- *Who 94*
Goodenough, Frederick Roger 1927- *Who 94*
Goodenough, J. B. *DrAPF 93*
Goodenough, John Bannister 1922- *Who 94, WhoAm 94*
Goodenough, Keith 1956- *WhoAmP 93*
Goodenough, Richard (Edmund) 1925- *Who 94*
Goodenough, Ward Hunt 1919- *IntWW 93, WhoAm 94, WrDr 94*
Goodenow, Rita M. R. 1943- *WhoAmP 93*
Gooders, John 1937- *WrDr 94*
Goodes, Melvin Russell 1935- *IntWW 93, WhoAm 94, WhoFI 94, WhoScEn 94*
Goodeve, Grant 1952- *WhoHol 92*
Goodey, Ila Marie 1948- *WhoAm 94, WhoWest 94*
Goodfellow, Brent H. 1940- *WhoAmP 93*
Goodfellow, Mark Aubrey 1931- *Who 94*
Goodfellow, Peter Neville 1951- *Who 94*
Goodfellow, Rosalind Erica 1927- *Who 94*
Goodfield, (Gwyneth) June 1927- *WrDr 94*
Goodfriend, Herbert Jay 1926- *WhoAm 94, WhoAmL 94*
Goodger, John Verne 1936- *WhoAm 94*
Goodhart, Lady 1939- *Who 94*
Goodhart, Charles Albert Eric 1936- *Who 94*
Goodhart, (Hilary Charles) Nicholas 1919- *Who 94*
Goodhart, Philip (Carter) 1925- *Who 94*
Goodhart, Robert (Anthony Gordon) 1948- *Who 94*
Goodhart, William (Howard) 1933- *Who 94*
Goodhartz, Gerald 1938- *WhoAmL 94*
Goodheart, Clyde Raymond 1931- *WhoMW 93*
Goodheart, Eugene 1931- *WhoAm 94, WrDr 94*
Goodheart, Lawrence B. 1944- *WrDr 94*
Goodhew, Howard Ralph, Jr. 1923- *WhoMW 93*
Goodhew, Richard Henry *Who 94*
Goodhew, Victor (Henry) 1919- *Who 94*
Goodhue, Bertram Grosvenor 1869-1924 *AmCulL*
Goodhue, Mary B. *WhoAmP 93*
Goodhue, Mary Brier 1921- *WhoAm 94*
Goodhue, Peter Ames 1931- *WhoScEn 94*
Goodhue, Sarah Whipple 1641-1681 *BlmGWL*
Goodhue, Thomas W. 1949- *ConAu 142*
Goodhue, Tracey 1943- *WrDr 94*
Goodin, Sallie (Brown) 1953- *SmATA 74 [port]*
Goodin, Vera-Jane 1955- *WhoMW 93*
Goodine, Linda Adele 1958- *WhoAmA 93*
Gooding, Anthony James Joseph S. *Who 94*
Gooding, Charles Arthur 1936- *WhoAm 94*
Gooding, Charles Thomas 1931- *WhoAm 94, WhoScEn 94*
Gooding, Cuba, Jr. *WhoBlA 94*
Gooding, Judson 1926- *WhoAm 94, WrDr 94*
Gooding, Karen Marie 1948- *WhoMW 93*
Gooding, Keith Horace 1913- *Who 94*
Gooding, LeAnna Dillon 1949- *WhoMW 93*
Gooding, Michael John 1949- *WhoMW 93*
Gooding, Philip Curtis 1958- *WhoMW 93*
Goodings, Allen 1925- *Who 94*
Goodison, Alan (Clowes) 1926- *Who 94*
Goodison, Lorna 1947- *BlmGWL, ConAu 142*
Goodison, Lorna (Gaye) 1947- *WrDr 94*
Goodison, Nicholas (Proctor) 1934- *Who 94*
Goodison, Nicholas Proctor 1934- *IntWW 93*
Goodison, Robin Reynolds 1912- *Who 94*
Goodkin, Michael Jon 1941- *WhoAm 94*
Goodkin, Richard E. 1953- *ConAu 141*
Goodkind, Conrad George 1944- *WhoAm 94*
Goodkind, John Morton 1934- *WhoScEn 94*
Goodkind, Louis William 1914- *WhoAm 94*
Goodlad, Alastair (Robertson) 1943- *Who 94*
Goodlad, John I. 1920- *ConAu 43NR, WrDr 94*
Goodlad, John Inkster 1920- *WhoAm 94*
Goodland, John I. 1920- *IntWW 93*
Goodland, Judith Mary 1938- *Who 94*
Goodlatte, Robert W. 1952- *CngDr 93*
Goodlatte, Robert William 1952- *WhoAm 94, WhoAmP 93*
Goodlett, Berry Christopher 1931- *WhoAmP 93*
Goodlett, Carlton B. 1914- *WhoAmP 93, WhoBlA 94*
Goodliffe, Michael d1976 *WhoHol 92*
Goodling, William F. *CngDr 93*
Goodling, William F. 1927- *WhoAm 94*
Goodling, William Franklin 1927- *WhoAmP 93*
Goodloe, Celestine Wilson 1954- *WhoBlA 94*
Goodloe, John Duncan, IV 1935- *WhoAm 94*
Goodman, Baron 1913- *Who 94*
Goodman, Adrienne Joy 1948- *WhoAmP 93*
Goodman, Alan Noel 1934- *WhoScEn 94*
Goodman, Alfred 1920- *WhoAm 94*
Goodman, Alfred (Grant) 1920- *NewGrDO*
Goodman, Alfred Nelson 1945- *WhoAmL 94*
Goodman, Allan H. 1950- *WhoAmL 94*
Goodman, Allen Charles 1947- *WhoAm 94*
Goodman, Alvin S. 1925- *WhoAm 94*
Goodman, Andrew d1993 *NewYTBS 93 [port]*
Goodman, Andrew 1907-1993 *CurBio 93N*
Goodman, Arnold Abraham 1913- *IntWW 93*
Goodman, Arthur H. 1935- *WhoAmP 93*
Goodman, Barbara 1932- *Who 94*
Goodman, Barbara Joan 1950- *WhoWest 94*
Goodman, Beatrice May 1933- *WhoWest 94*
Goodman, Benjamin 1904- *WhoAm 94, WhoAmA 93*
Goodman, Benjamin David 1909-1986 *AmCulL [port]*
Goodman, Benny d1986 *WhoHol 92*
Goodman, Bernard 1923- *WhoAm 94*
Goodman, Bertram 1904- *WhoAmA 93*
Goodman, Bruce Gerald 1948- *WhoAm 94*
Goodman, Bruce J. 1941- *WhoFI 94*
Goodman, Calvin Jerome 1922- *WhoAmA 93*
Goodman, Carol 1945- *WhoAm 94, WhoAmL 94*
Goodman, Carolyn 1956- *WhoAm 94*
Goodman, Charles David 1928- *WhoMW 93*
Goodman, Charles Schaffner 1916- *WhoAm 94*
Goodman, Charles Schaffner, Jr. 1949- *WhoFI 94*
Goodman, Charles Thomas 1954- *WhoAmP 93*
Goodman, Charlotte Margolis 1934- *WrDr 94*
Goodman, Corey Scott 1951- *WhoScEn 94*
Goodman, Daniel 1957- *WhoScEn 94*
Goodman, David *Who 94*
Goodman, (John) David (Whitlock) 1932- *Who 94*
Goodman, David Barry Poliakoff 1942- *WhoAm 94*
Goodman, David Bryan 1953- *WhoAm 94, WhoWest 94*
Goodman, David R. 1946- *WhoFI 94*
Goodman, David Wayne 1945- *WhoScEn 94*
Goodman, David Z. *IntMPA 94*
Goodman, Dean *WhoHol 92*
Goodman, Dewitt Stetten 1930-1991 *WhAm 10*
Goodman, Dody 1915- *WhoHol 92*
Goodman, Donald C. 1927- *WhoAm 94*
Goodman, Donald Joseph 1922- *WhoMW 93, WhoScEn 94*
Goodman, Elinor Mary 1946- *Who 94*
Goodman, Elizabeth Ann 1950- *WhoAm 94, WhoAmL 94*
Goodman, Ellen (Holtz) 1941- *WrDr 94*
Goodman, Ellen Holtz 1941- *WhoAm 94*
Goodman, Elliot R 1923- *WrDr 94*
Goodman, Elliot Raymond 1923- *WhoAm 94*
Goodman, Elliott Irvin 1934- *WhoAm 94*
Goodman, Eric 1953- *ConAu 141*
Goodman, Erik David 1944- *WhoAm 94, WhoScEn 94*
Goodman, Erika *WhoAm 94*
Goodman, Ernest Monroe 1955- *WhoFI 94*
Goodman, Evan Besey 1940- *WhoMW 93*
Goodman, Florence Jeanne 1922- *WhoAmA 93*
Goodman, Gary A. 1948- *WhoAm 94*
Goodman, Gary Alan 1947- *WhoAm 94, WhoAmL 94, WhoMW 93*
Goodman, Geoffrey George 1921- *Who 94*
Goodman, George D. 1940- *WhoBlA 94*
Goodman, George Jerome Waldo 1930- *WhoAm 94*
Goodman, Gordon d1960 *WhoHol 92*
Goodman, Gwendolyn Ann 1955- *WhoWest 94*
Goodman, Harold 1926- *WhoScEn 94*
Goodman, Harold S. 1937- *WhoAm 94*
Goodman, Helen 1939- *WhoAmA 93*
Goodman, Henry Maurice 1934- *WhoAm 94*
Goodman, Herbert Irwin 1923- *WhoAm 94, WhoScEn 94*
Goodman, Howard *Who 94*
Goodman, (Robert) Howard 1928- *Who 94*
Goodman, Howard Alan 1955- *WhoScEn 94*
Goodman, Hubert Thorman 1933- *WhoMW 93, WhoScEn 94*
Goodman, Ivy *DrAPF 93*
Goodman, James A. 1936- *WhoAm 94, WhoAmL 94*
Goodman, James Anthony 1936- *WhoAmP 93*
Goodman, James Arthur, Sr. 1933- *WhoBlA 94*
Goodman, James Neil 1929- *WhoAmA 93*
Goodman, Jane Yager 1923- *WhoMW 93*
Goodman, Janis G. 1951- *WhoAmA 93*
Goodman, Jess Thompson 1936- *WhoFI 94*
Goodman, Joel Warren 1933- *WhoAm 94*
Goodman, John 1952- *IntMPA 94, WhoAm 94, WhoHol 92*
Goodman, John Francis Bradshaw 1940- *Who 94*
Goodman, Jonathan 1933- *WrDr 94*
Goodman, Jordan Elliot 1954- *WhoAm 94*
Goodman, Joseph Champion 1937- *WhoAm 94*
Goodman, Joseph Wilfred 1936- *WhoAm 94, WhoScEn 94, WhoWest 94*
Goodman, Karen Lacerte 1946- *WhoFI 94*
Goodman, Ken(neth Hunt) 1950- *WhoAmA 93*
Goodman, Kevin R. 1964- *WhoFI 94*
Goodman, Lawrence Eugene 1920- *WhoAm 94, WhoScEn 94*
Goodman, Lee d1988 *WhoHol 92*
Goodman, Lenn Evan 1944- *WhoWest 94*
Goodman, Leon 1935- *WhoFI 94*
Goodman, Linda *WhoAm 94*
Goodman, Lindsey Alan 1957- *WhoFI 94*
Goodman, Louis Allan 1943- *WhoAm 94*
Goodman, Louis Wolf 1942- *WrDr 94*
Goodman, Madeleine Joyce 1945- *WhoWest 94*
Goodman, Major Merlin 1938- *WhoAm 94*
Goodman, Marian 1928- *WhoAmA 93*
Goodman, Mark 1946- *WhoAmA 93*
Goodman, Mark N. 1952- *WhoAmL 94, WhoWest 94*
Goodman, Marlene Kay 1951- *WhoMW 93*
Goodman, Martin R. 1943- *WhoAm 94, WhoAmL 94*
Goodman, Mary A. 1934- *WhoWest 94*
Goodman, Matthew Samuel 1947- *WhoScEn 94*
Goodman, Max A. 1924- *WhoAm 94*
Goodman, Melinda *DrAPF 93*
Goodman, Michael A. 1903-1991 *WhAm 10*
Goodman, Michael Bradley 1930- *Who 94*
Goodman, Michael Frederick 1951- *WhoFI 94*
Goodman, Michael G. 1946- *WhoWest 94*
Goodman, Michael Jack 1931- *Who 94*
Goodman, Mitchell *DrAPF 93*
Goodman, Morris 1925- *WhoAm 94, WhoMW 93*
Goodman, Morse Lamb 1917- *Who 94*
Goodman, Murray 1928- *WhoWest 94*
Goodman, Myrna Marcia 1936- *WhoMW 93*
Goodman, (Henry) Nelson 1906- *WrDr 94*

Goodman, Norman 1934- *WhoAm 94*
Goodman, Norton Victor 1936- *WhoAm 94*
Goodman, Paul 1911-1972 *ConDr 93, DcLB 130 [port]*
Goodman, Percival 1904-1989 *WhAm 10*
Goodman, Perry 1932- *Who 94*
Goodman, Philip Jay 1946- *WhoAmL 94*
Goodman, Raymond John 1916- *IntWW 93*
Goodman, Richard 1945- *WrDr 94*
Goodman, Richard Shalem *WhoAmL 94*
Goodman, Robert Cedric 1956- *WhoWest 94*
Goodman, Robert Merwin 1945- *WhoAm 94, WhoFI 94*
Goodman, Robert O., Jr. 1956- *WhoBlA 94*
Goodman, Roger B 1919- *WrDr 94*
Goodman, Roland Alfred 1933- *WhoAm 94*
Goodman, Roy M. 1930- *WhoAmP 93*
Goodman, Roy Matz 1930- *WhoAm 94*
Goodman, Russell Brian 1945- *WhoWest 94*
Goodman, Sam Richard 1930- *WhoAm 94, WhoFI 94, WhoWest 94*
Goodman, Samuel J. 1942- *WhoAmL 94*
Goodman, Sidney 1936- *WhoAmA 93*
Goodman, Stanley 1931- *WhoAm 94*
Goodman, Stanley Leonard 1920- *WhoAm 94*
Goodman, Stephen H. 1944- *WhoAm 94*
Goodman, Stephen Kent 1949- *WhoWest 94*
Goodman, Stephen Murry 1940- *WhoAmL 94*
Goodman, Stuart Lauren 1938- *WhoAm 94*
Goodman, Terence James 1950- *WhoWest 94*
Goodman, Thomas Andrew 1954- *WhoAm 94*
Goodman, Toby Ray 1948- *WhoAm 94, WhoAmP 93*
Goodman, William Alfred 1961- *WhoScEn 94*
Goodman, William Beehler 1923- *WhoAm 94*
Goodman, William I. 1919- *WhoAm 94*
Goodman, William Lee 1946- *WhoWest 94*
Goodman, William R., III 1952- *WhoAmP 93*
Goodman, William Richard 1930- *WhoFI 94*
Goodman, William Wolf 1917- *WhoAmP 93*
Goodman, Willian Henry 1943- *WhoFI 94*
Goodner, Carol 1904- *WhoHol 92*
Goodner, Dwight Benjamin 1913- *WhoAm 94*
Goodner, Homer Wade 1929- *WhoScEn 94*
Goodner, John Green *WhoAmP 93*
Goodner, John Ross, Jr. 1927- *WhoAm 94*
Goodness, Richard Grayson 1955- *WhoMW 93*
Goodnick, Paul Joel 1950- *WhoScEn 94*
Goodnick, Stephen Marshall 1955- *WhoScEn 94*
Goodnight, Patricia Ann 1947- *WhoAmP 93*
Goodnight, Susan Ina 1938- *WhoWest 94*
Goodno, Kevin P. 1962- *WhoAmP 93*
Goodnough, Robert 1923- *WhoAmA 93*
Goodnow, Frank A. 1923- *WhoAmA 93*
Goodnow, Gordon James, Jr. 1947- *WhoWest 94*
Goodover, Pat M. 1916- *WhoAmP 93*
Goodpaster, Andrew Jackson 1915- *IntWW 93, Who 94, WhoAm 94*
Goodpasture, H(enry) McKennie 1929- *WrDr 94*
Goodreds, John Stanton 1934- *WhoAm 94*
Goodrich, Alan Owens 1958- *WhoAmL 94*
Goodrich, Charles W. d1931 *WhoHol 92*
Goodrich, Chris 1956- *WrDr 94*
Goodrich, Craig Robert 1949- *WhoScEn 94, WhoWest 94*
Goodrich, David 1941- *Who 94*
Goodrich, David Charles 1926- *WhoScEn 94*
Goodrich, Deborah *WhoHol 92*
Goodrich, Donald Wells 1898- *WhAm 10*
Goodrich, Dorthee *WhoAmP 93*
Goodrich, Edna d1971 *WhoHol 92*
Goodrich, Elizur 1734-1797 *WhAmRev*
Goodrich, Frances 1891-1984 *IntDcF 2-4*
Goodrich, Gail 1943- *BasBi [port]*
Goodrich, George Herbert 1925- *WhoAm 94*
Goodrich, Glenn A. 1925- *WhoAmP 93*
Goodrich, Harold Thomas 1931- *WhoBlA 94*
Goodrich, Henry Calvin 1920- *WhoAm 94*
Goodrich, Herbert Funk, Jr. 1942- *WhoAm 94, WhoAmL 94*
Goodrich, James F. *WhoAmP 93*
Goodrich, James Tait 1946- *WhoScEn 94*
Goodrich, James W. 1939- *WhoAmA 93*
Goodrich, James William 1939- *WhoAm 94*
Goodrich, Jeffrey Clay 1958- *WhoWest 94*
Goodrich, John Bernard 1928- *WhoAm 94, WhoAmL 94*
Goodrich, Julian R. 1943- *WhoAmP 93*
Goodrich, Kenneth Paul 1933- *WhoAm 94*
Goodrich, Leland Matthew 1899-1990 *WhAm 10*
Goodrich, Leon Raymond 1936- *WhoAm 94*
Goodrich, Louis d1945 *WhoHol 92*
Goodrich, M. Keith *WhoAm 94, WhoFI 94*
Goodrich, Maurice Keith 1935- *WhoAm 94, WhoFI 94*
Goodrich, Nathaniel Herman 1914- *WhoAm 94*
Goodrich, Norma Lorre 1917- *WhoAm 94*
Goodrich, Patricia *DrAPF 93*
Goodrich, Philip Harold Ernest *Who 94*
Goodrich, Robert Emmett 1940- *IntMPA 94*
Goodrich, Thelma E. 1933- *WhoBlA 94*
Goodrich, Thomas Michael 1945- *WhoAm 94, WhoAmL 94, WhoFI 94*
Goodricke, John 1708-1789 *DcNaB MP*
Goodridge, Alan Gardner 1937- *WhoAm 94, WhoMW 93*
Goodridge, Allan D. 1936- *WhoAm 94*
Goodridge, Henry Edmund 1797-1864 *DcNaB MP*
Goodridge, Lawrence Wayne 1941- *WhoAmA 93*
Goodridge, Noel Herbert Alan 1930- *Who 94, WhoAm 94*
Goodridge, Sehon Sylvester 1937- *Who 94*
Goodridge, Tracy Rochelle 1965- *WhoAmP 93*
Goodrow, Garry *WhoHol 92*
Goodsell, David Scott, Jr. 1961- *WhoWest 94*
Goodsman, James Melville 1947- *Who 94*
Goodson, Annie Jean *WhoBlA 94*
Goodson, Ernest Jerome 1953- *WhoBlA 94*
Goodson, Frances Elizabeth *WhoBlA 94*
Goodson, Frederick Brian 1938- *Who 94*
Goodson, James Abner, Jr. 1921- *WhoBlA 94*
Goodson, Leroy Beverly 1933- *WhoBlA 94*
Goodson, Louie Aubrey, Jr. 1922- *WhoAm 94*
Goodson, Mark d1992 *IntMPA 94N*
Goodson, Mark 1915-1992 *AnObit 1992, ConTFT 11, CurBio 93N*
Goodson, Mark (Weston Lassam) 1925- *Who 94*
Goodson, Martin L., Jr. 1943- *WhoBlA 94*
Goodson, Michael John 1937- *Who 94*
Goodson, Raymond Eugene 1935- *WhoAm 94, WhoFI 94*
Goodson, Richard Carle, Jr. 1945- *WhoFI 94, WhoScEn 94*
Goodson-Wickes, Charles 1945- *Who 94*
Goodspeed, Barbara 1919- *WhoAm 94*
Goodspeed, Edgar Johnson 1871-1962 *DcAmReB 2*
Goodspeed, Scott Winans 1954- *WhoAm 94, WhoFI 94*
Goodstein, Aaron E. 1942- *WhoAmL 94*
Goodstein, Barnett Maurice 1921- *WhoAm 94*
Goodstein, David Louis 1939- *WhoAm 94*
Goodstein, Richard George 1947- *WhoFI 94*
Goodstein, Sanders Abraham 1918- *WhoMW 93*
Goodstein-Shapiro, F. 1931- *WhoAmA 93*
Goodstone, Edward H. 1934- *WhoIns 94*
Goodstone, Edward Harold 1934- *WhoAm 94*
Goodstone, Rosemary Ann 1947- *WhoMW 93*
Goodtimes, Art *DrAPF 93*
Goodwill, Margaret 1950- *WhoAmA 93*
Goodwill, Margaret Jane 1950- *WhoAm 94*
Goodwillie, Eugene William, Jr. 1941- *WhoAm 94*
Goodwin, Albert 1906- *Who 94*
Goodwin, Alfred Theodore 1923- *WhoAm 94, WhoAmL 94, WhoAmP 93, WhoWest 94*
Goodwin, Angela *WhoHol 92*
Goodwin, Barbara A. 1938- *WhoAm 94*
Goodwin, Bernard 1907- *WhoAm 94*
Goodwin, Bill d1958 *WhoHol 92*
Goodwin, Bill 1942- *WhoAmP 93*
Goodwin, Bruce Kesseli 1931- *WhoAm 94*
Goodwin, Claude Elbert 1910- *WhoAm 94*
Goodwin, Craufurd David 1934- *WhoAm 94*
Goodwin, Dale Eugene 1955- *WhoWest 94*
Goodwin, David George 1957- *WhoScEn 94*
Goodwin, Della McGraw 1931- *WhoBlA 94*
Goodwin, Dennis Michael 1950- *WhoBlA 94*
Goodwin, Donald Edward 1949- *WhoBlA 94*
Goodwin, Donald William 1931- *WhoAm 94*
Goodwin, Dorothy C. 1914- *WhoAmP 93*
Goodwin, Douglas Ira 1946- *WhoAm 94*
Goodwin, E. Marvin 1936- *WhoBlA 94*
Goodwin, Earl 1911- *WhoAmP 93*
Goodwin, Eric Thomson 1913- *Who 94*
Goodwin, Eugene D. *ConAu 41NR*
Goodwin, Evelyn Louise 1949- *WhoBlA 94*
Goodwin, Felix L. 1919- *WhoBlA 94*
Goodwin, Frank Erik 1954- *WhoScEn 94*
Goodwin, Frederick King 1936- *WhoAm 94, WhoScEn 94*
Goodwin, Geoffrey (Lawrence) 1916- *WrDr 94*
Goodwin, Geoffrey Lawrence 1916- *Who 94*
Goodwin, George E. 1941- *WhoAmP 93*
Goodwin, George Edward 1924- *WhoAmP 93*
Goodwin, George Evans 1917- *WhoAm 94*
Goodwin, Greta Hall *WhoAmP 93*
Goodwin, Guy 1940- *WhoAmA 93*
Goodwin, Harold 1902- *WhoHol 92*
Goodwin, Harold 1917- *WhoHol 92*
Goodwin, Harry Eugene 1922- *WhoAm 94*
Goodwin, Hugh Wesley 1921- *WhoBlA 94*
Goodwin, Irwin 1929- *WhoScEn 94*
Goodwin, James d1980 *WhoHol 92*
Goodwin, James Osby 1939- *WhoBlA 94*
Goodwin, Jean McClung 1946- *WhoAm 94*
Goodwin, Jesse Francis 1929- *WhoBlA 94*
Goodwin, Joe William 1928- *WhoAmP 93*
Goodwin, John Forrest 1918- *IntWW 93, Who 94*
Goodwin, John Robert 1929- *WhoAmL 94, WhoWest 94*
Goodwin, Joseph Robert 1942- *WhoAmP 93*
Goodwin, Kathleen Watson 1940- *WhoAmP 93*
Goodwin, Kathrin Joan 1967- *WhoMW 93*
Goodwin, Kelly Oliver Perry 1911- *WhoBlA 94*
Goodwin, Kemper 1906- *WhoAm 94*
Goodwin, Ken(neth Leslie) 1934- *WrDr 94*
Goodwin, Larry 1945- *WhoAmP 93*
Goodwin, Laurel 1941- *WhoHol 92*
Goodwin, Leonard George 1915- *IntWW 93, Who 94*
Goodwin, Louis Payne 1922- *WhoAmA 93*
Goodwin, Martin David 1964- *WhoBlA 94*
Goodwin, Maryellen 1965- *WhoAmP 93*
Goodwin, Matthew (Dean) 1929- *Who 94*
Goodwin, Mercedier Cassandra de Freitas *WhoBlA 94*
Goodwin, Michael 1945- *WhoHol 92*
Goodwin, Michael 1949- *ConAu 141*
Goodwin, Michael Raymond 1950- *WhoMW 93*
Goodwin, Nancy Lee 1940- *WhoAm 94*
Goodwin, Nat C. d1919 *WhoHol 92*
Goodwin, Neil 1951- *Who 94*
Goodwin, Noel *Who 94*
Goodwin, (Trevor) Noel 1927- *Who 94*
Goodwin, Norma J. 1937- *WhoBlA 94*
Goodwin, Norman J. 1913- *WhoAmP 93*
Goodwin, Paul 1919- *WhoAm 94*
Goodwin, Paul Beale 1938- *WhoAmL 94, WhoMW 93*
Goodwin, Peter Austin 1929- *Who 94*
Goodwin, Phillip Hugh 1940- *WhoAm 94*
Goodwin, Ralph Roger 1917- *WhoAm 94*
Goodwin, Richard 1934- *IntMPA 94*
Goodwin, Richard Clarke 1949- *WhoScEn 94*
Goodwin, Richard Hale 1910- *WhoAm 94*
Goodwin, Richard Murphey 1913- *Who 94*
Goodwin, Robert d1983 *WhoHol 92*
Goodwin, Robert Cabaniss 1898- *WhAm 10*
Goodwin, Robert Daniel, Jr. 1950- *WhoAmP 93*
Goodwin, Robert Delmege 1920- *WhoAm 94*
Goodwin, Robert Kerr 1948- *WhoBlA 94*
Goodwin, Robert T., Sr. 1915- *WhoBlA 94*
Goodwin, Rodney Keith Grove 1944- *WhoAm 94*
Goodwin, Rolf Ervine 1956- *WhoAmL 94*
Goodwin, Ronald 1925- *IntMPA 94*
Goodwin, Ruby d1961 *WhoHol 92*
Goodwin, Ruby Berkley 1903-1961 *BlkWr 2*
Goodwin, Sandra Joan 1937- *WhoWest 94*
Goodwin, Stephen *DrAPF 93*
Goodwin, Stephen Robert 1948- *WhoBlA 94*
Goodwin, Suzanne 1916- *WrDr 94*
Goodwin, Thomas Jones 1968- *WhoBlA 94*
Goodwin, Todd 1931- *WhoAm 94*
Goodwin, Trevor W(alworth) 1916- *WrDr 94*
Goodwin, Trevor Walworth 1916- *IntWW 93, Who 94*
Goodwin, Vaughn Allen 1968- *WhoBlA 94*
Goodwin, Vickie Lee 1948- *WhoAmP 93*
Goodwin, Warren Herbert 1925- *WhoAmP 93*
Goodwin, Willard Elmer 1915- *WhoAm 94*
Goodwin, William Dean 1937- *WhoFI 94*
Goodwin, William Maxwell 1939- *WhoAm 94*
Goodwin, William Olin 1945- *WhoFI 94*
Goodwin, William Pierce, Jr. 1949- *WhoBlA 94*
Goodwine, James K., Jr. 1930- *WhoWest 94*
Goodwins, Leslie d1969 *WhoHol 92*
Goodwyn, Kendall Wirt 1911-1990 *WhAm 10*
Goody, Joan 1935- *WhoAm 94*
Goody, Joan Edelman 1935- *IntWW 93*
Goody, John R(ankine) 1919- *WrDr 94*
Goody, John Rankine 1919- *Who 94*
Goody, Launcelot John 1908- *Who 94*
Goody, Richard Mead 1921- *WhoAm 94*
Goodyear, Austin 1919- *WhoAm 94*
Goodyear, Charles 1800-1860 *WorInv [port]*
Goodyear, Frank H., Jr. 1944- *WhoAmA 93*
Goodyear, Frank Henry, Jr. 1944- *WhoAm 94*
Goodyear, Jack Dale 1935- *WhoScEn 94*
Goodyear, John H(enry), III 1941- *ConAu 41NR*
Goodyear, John L. 1930- *WhoAmA 93*
Goodyear, John Lake 1930- *WhoAm 94*
Goodyear, Julie Ann 1956- *WhoMW 93*
Goodyer, Ian Michael 1949- *Who 94*
Goodykoontz, Bess d1990 *WhAm 10*
Goodykoontz, Charles Alfred 1928- *WhoAm 94*
Googasian, George Ara 1936- *WhoAm 94, WhoAmL 94*
Googe, Barnabe 1540-1594 *DcLB 132*
Googins, Robert R. 1937- *WhoIns 94*
Googins, Robert Reville 1937- *WhoAm 94*
Gook, Sade 1904-1977 *See* Vic and Sade *WhoCom*
Gook, Victor 1883-1957 *See* Vic and Sade *WhoCom*
Gookin, Daniel 1612-1686? *EncNAR*
Gookin, Thomas Allen Jaudon 1951- *WhoWest 94*
Gookin, William Scudder 1914- *WhoScEn 94, WhoWest 94*
Gookins, Elmer Franklin 1940- *WhoFI 94*
Goolagong, Evonne 1951- *BuCMET [port]*
Goold, Baron 1934- *Who 94*
Goold, Florence Charlotte 1925- *WhoMW 93*
Goold, Florence Wilson 1912- *WhoMW 93*
Goold, George (Leonard) 1923- *Who 94*
Goold, J. William 1953- *WhoAmP 93*
Goold, St. Leger 1853-1909 *BuCMET*
Goold-Adams, Richard John Moreton 1916- *Who 94*
Goolden, Richard d1981 *WhoHol 92*
Gooley, Charles E. 1953- *WhoBlA 94*
Goolkasian, Aram Richard 1924- *WhoAm 94*
Goolrick, Robert Mason 1934- *WhoAmL 94*
Goolsbee, Charles Thomas 1935- *WhoAm 94, WhoAmL 94, WhoFI 94*
Goolsby, Tony 1933- *WhoAmP 93*
Gooneratne, Tilak Eranga 1919- *Who 94*
Gooneratne, (Malini) Yasmine 1935- *ConAu 41NR*
Goonetilleke, Albert 1936- *IntWW 93*
Goonetilleke, D(evapriya) C(hitra) R(anjan) A(lwis) 1938- *WrDr 94*
Goonrey, Charles W. *WhoAmL 94*
Goons, The *WhoCom*
Goor, E. Patricia 1935- *WhoWest 94*
Goor, Ronald Stephen 1940- *WhoAm 94*
Goorey, Nancy Jane 1922- *WhoAm 94*
Goorney, Howard 1921- *WhoHol 92*
Goorwitz, Allen *WhoHol 92*
Goos, Bernd *IntWW 93*
Goos, Roger Delmon 1924- *WhoAm 94, WhoScEn 94*
Goosby, Zuretti L. 1922- *WhoBlA 94*
Goose c. 1835-1915 *EncNAR*
Gooskens, Robert Henricus Johannus 1948- *WhoScEn 94*
Goossen, Duane A. 1955- *WhoAmP 93*
Goossen, Eugene Coons 1920- *WhoAmA 93*
Goossen, Jacob Frederic 1927- *WhoAm 94*
Goossens, (Aynsley) Eugene 1893-1962 *NewGrDO*
Goostree, Robert Edward 1923- *WhoAm 94, WhoAmL 94*
Goott, Alan Franklin 1947- *WhoAmL 94*
Goott, Daniel 1919- *WhoAm 94*

Gootzeit, Jack Michael 1924- *WhoAm 94*
Gopal, Pradip Goolab 1957- *WhoScEn 94*
Gopal, Raj 1942- *WhoScEn 94*
Gopal, Ram *WhoHol 92*
Gopal, Sarvepalli 1923- *IntWW 93, Who 94, WrDr 94*
Gopalakrishna, K. V. 1944- *WhoAsA 94*
Gopalakrishnan, Bhaskaran 1960- *WhoScEn 94*
Gopalan, Coluthur 1918- *Who 94*
Gopalan, Muhundan 1960- *WhoScEn 94*
Gopikanth, M. L. 1954- *WhoAsA 94*
Gopnik, Adam 1956- *WhoAm 94*
Gopon, Gene George 1944- *WhoIns 94*
Gopon, Leon Michael 1941- *WhoMW 93*
Goppel, Alfons *IntWW 93N*
Goppelt, John Walter 1924- *WhoScEn 94*
Gopstein, Israel 1940- *WhoAmL 94*
Gopu, Vijaya K.A. 1949- *WhoAm 94*
Gora, Claudio *WhoHol 92*
Gorai, Dinesh Chandra *Who 94*
Gorai, Dinesh Chandra 1934- *IntWW 93*
Goralski, Robert 1928-1988 *WhAm 10*
Goran, Morris 1916- *WrDr 94*
Gorans, Gerald Elmer 1922- *WhoAm 94, WhoFI 94, WhoWest 94*
Goranson, Harvey Edward 1952- *WhoScEn 94*
Goransson, Bengt 1932- *IntWW 93*
Goranzon, Marie *WhoHol 92*
Gorard, Anthony John 1927- *Who 94*
Goray, Narayan Ganesh 1907- *IntWW 93, Who 94*
Gorbachev, Mikhail 1931- *HisWorL [port]*
Gorbachev, Mikhail Sergeevich 1931- *LoBiDrD*
Gorbachev, Mikhail Sergeyevich 1931- *IntWW 93, NobelP 91 [port], Who 94*
Gorbachev, Raisa (Maksimovna) 1934?- *ConAu 141*
Gorbachev, Raisa Maksimovna 1934- *IntWW 93*
Gorbacheva, Raisa Maksimovna 1934- *WhoWomW 91*
Gorbanevskaia, Natalia (Evgen'evna) 1936- *ConWorW 93*
Gorbanevskaia, Natal'ia Evgen'evna 1936- *BlmGWL*
Gorbanevskaya, Natalya *ConWorW 93*
Gorbaty, Martin Leo 1942- *WhoScEn 94*
Gorbold, Robert Reese 1952- *WhoAmL 94*
Gorbunovs, Anatolijs 1942- *LoBiDrD*
Gorbunovs, Anatoliys 1942- *IntWW 93*
Gorcey, Bernard d1955 *WhoHol 92*
Gorcey, David d1984 *WhoHol 92*
Gorcey, David 1921- *See* East Side Kids *WhoCom*
Gorcey, Elizabeth *WhoHol 92*
Gorcey, Leo d1969 *WhoHol 92*
Gorcey, Leo 1917-1969 *WhoCom*
Gorcheff, Nick A. 1958- *WhoMW 93*
Gorchov, Ron 1930- *WhoAmA 93*
Gorczynski, Dale Michael 1950- *WhoAmP 93*
Gordan, Andrew Leb 1923- *WhoMW 93*
Gordan, Gilbert Saul 1916- *WhoAm 94*
Gordeler, Karl 1884-1945 *HisWorL*
Gorden, Fred A. 1940- *WhoBlA 94*
Gorden, Fred Augustus 1940- *AfrAmG [port]*
Gorden, Gene Lenard 1954- *WhoMW 93*
Gorden, Michael Lee 1957- *WhoFI 94*
Gorden, Phillip *WhoAm 94*
Gorden, Stephen Arthur 1926- *WhoWest 94*
Gordenker, Hendrik William Paul 1959- *WhoAmL 94*
Gordenker, Leon 1923- *WhoAm 94*
Gorder, Cheryl Marie 1952- *WhoWest 94*
Gorder, Clayton J. 1936-1987 *WhoAmA 93N*
Gorder, Steven F. 1951- *WhoAm 94*
Gorder, William E. *WhoAmP 93*
Gordes, Joel N. 1946- *WhoAmP 93*
Gordesky, Morton 1929- *WhoAmL 94*
Gordey, Michel 1913- *IntWW 93*
Gordeyev, Vyacheslav Mikhailovich 1948- *IntWW 93*
Gordievsky, Oleg 1938- *ConAu 140*
Gordigiani, Antonio dc. 1824 *NewGrDO*
Gordigiani, Giovanni Battista 1795-1871 *NewGrDO*
Gordigiani, Luigi 1806-1860 *NewGrDO*
Gordigiani Family *NewGrDO*
Gordilho, Regina Helena Costa 1933- *WhoWomW 91*
Gordimer, Nadine 1923- *BlmGEL, BlmGWL, IntWW 93, NobelP 91 [port], RfGShF, TwCYAW, Who 94, WhoAm 94, WrDr 94*
Gordin, Dean Lackey 1935- *WhoAm 94*
Gordin, Misha 1946- *WhoAmA 93*
Gordin, Sidney 1918- *WhoAmA 93*
Gordis, David Moses 1940- *WhoAm 94*
Gordis, Enoch 1931- *WhoAm 94*
Gordis, Joshua Haim 1960- *WhoScEn 94*
Gordis, Leon 1934- *WhoAm 94*
Gordis, Robert 1908- *WrDr 94*
Gordis, Robert 1908-1992 *WhAm 10*
Gordley, Marilyn Classe 1929- *WhoAmA 93*
Gordley, Metz Tranbarger 1932- *WhoAmA 93*
Gordly, Avel 1947- *WhoAmP 93*
Gordner, John R. 1962- *WhoAmP 93*
Gordon *Who 94*
Gordon, Aaron Z. 1929- *WhoBlA 94*
Gordon, Adoniram Judson 1836-1895 *DcAmReB 2*
Gordon, Al *WhoAmP 93*
Gordon, Albert F. 1934- *WhoAmA 93*
Gordon, Albert Hamilton 1901- *WhoAm 94*
Gordon, Alex 1922- *IntMPA 94*
Gordon, Alexander c. 1692-1754? *NewGrDO*
Gordon, Alexander 1752-1799 *DcNaB MP*
Gordon, Alexander 1841-1931 *DcNaB MP*
Gordon, Alexander H., II 1944- *WhoBlA 94*
Gordon, Alexander John 1917- *Who 94*
Gordon, Alice Jeannette Irwin 1934- *WhoMW 93*
Gordon, Allan M. 1933- *WhoBlA 94*
Gordon, Allen 1948- *WhoAmP 93*
Gordon, Andrew C. L. D. *Who 94*
Gordon, Andrew S. 1949- *WhoAm 94, WhoAmL 94*
Gordon, Angus Neal, Jr. 1919- *WhoAm 94*
Gordon, Anthony Robert 1959- *WhoWest 94*
Gordon, Arnold Mark 1937- *WhoAmL 94*
Gordon, Arthur Ernest 1902-1989 *WhAm 10*
Gordon, Aubrey Abraham 1925- *Who 94*
Gordon, Audrey Kramen 1935- *WhoMW 93*
Gordon, Barbara C. 1935- *WhoAmP 93*
Gordon, Barry 1948- *WhoHol 92*
Gordon, Barry (Lewis John) 1934- *WrDr 94*
Gordon, Barry Joel 1945- *WhoAm 94*
Gordon, Bart 1949- *CngDr 93*
Gordon, Barton Jennings 1949- *WhoAm 94, WhoAmP 93*
Gordon, Basil 1932- *WhoAm 94*
Gordon, Benjamin J., Jr. 1932- *WhoAmP 93*
Gordon, Bernard 1922- *WhoAm 94*
Gordon, Bert d1974 *WhoHol 92*
Gordon, Bert I. *EncSF 93, IntMPA 94*
Gordon, Bertha Comer 1916- *WhoBlA 94*
Gordon, Beverly 1948- *WhoMW 93*
Gordon, Bobby 1913- *WhoHol 92*
Gordon, Bonnie *DrAPF 93*
Gordon, Bonnie Heather 1952- *WhoAm 94*
Gordon, Boyd 1926- *Who 94*
Gordon, Brian William 1926- *Who 94*
Gordon, Brock Bingham 1934- *WhoAmL 94*
Gordon, Bruce 1916- *WhoHol 92*
Gordon, Bruce 1929- *IntMPA 94*
Gordon, Bruce S. 1946- *WhoBlA 94*
Gordon, C. Henry d1940 *WhoHol 92*
Gordon, Carl *WhoHol 92*
Gordon, Carl Jackson, Jr. 1944- *WhoAmP 93*
Gordon, Carl Rufus 1932- *WhoBlA 94*
Gordon, Caroline 1895- *BlmGWL*
Gordon, Caroline 1895-1981 *RfGShF*
Gordon, Charles *IntMPA 94*
Gordon, Charles 1905- *WhoAm 94*
Gordon, Charles (Addison Somerville Snowden) 1918- *Who 94*
Gordon, Charles C. 1944- *WhoAmL 94*
Gordon, Charles D. 1934- *WhoBlA 94*
Gordon, Charles Eugene 1938- *WhoBlA 94*
Gordon, Charles F. *DrAPF 93*
Gordon, Charles Franklin 1921- *WhoBlA 94*
Gordon, Charles George 1833-1885 *HisWorL [port]*
Gordon, Charles Robert 1935- *WhoAmP 93*
Gordon, Christine Constance 1963- *WhoWest 94*
Gordon, Claire *WhoHol 92*
Gordon, Clarke *WhoHol 92*
Gordon, Claude Eugene 1916- *WhoWest 94*
Gordon, Clifford Wesley *WhoBlA 94*
Gordon, Coco *DrAPF 93*
Gordon, Colin d1972 *WhoHol 92*
Gordon, Conrad J. 1937- *WhoAm 94*
Gordon, Corey Lee 1956- *WhoAmL 94*
Gordon, Craig Jeffrey 1953- *WhoMW 93, WhoScEn 94*
Gordon, Cyrus H. 1908- *Who 94*
Gordon, Cyrus Herzl 1908- *WhoAm 94, WrDr 94*
Gordon, Dane Rex 1925- *WhoAm 94*
Gordon, Daniel *WhoHol 92*
Gordon, Darrell R. 1926- *WhoBlA 94*
Gordon, David *EncSF 93*
Gordon, David 1936- *WhoAm 94*
Gordon, David Eliot 1949- *WhoAm 94*
Gordon, David Jamieson 1947- *WhoAm 94*
Gordon, David Sorrell 1941- *Who 94*
Gordon, David Stott 1951- *WhoAmL 94*
Gordon, David Zevi 1943- *WhoAmL 94*
Gordon, Deborah Hannes 1946- *WrDr 94*
Gordon, Derek E. 1954- *WhoBlA 94*
Gordon, Desmond Spencer 1911- *Who 94*
Gordon, Dexter d1990 *WhoHol 92*
Gordon, Dexter 1923-1989 *AfrAmAl 6 [port]*
Gordon, Dexter 1923-1990 *ConMus 10 [port]*
Gordon, Dexter Keith 1923-1990 *WhAm 10*
Gordon, Diana Russell 1938- *WhoAm 94*
Gordon, Diane 1919- *WrDr 94*
Gordon, Don 1926- *IntMPA 94, WhoHol 92*
Gordon, Donald *EncSF 93*
Gordon, Donald 1924- *WrDr 94*
Gordon, Donald 1930- *IntWW 93*
Gordon, Donald (Ramsay) 1929- *WrDr 94*
Gordon, Donald C(raigie) 1911- *WrDr 94*
Gordon, Donald Edward 1931- *WhoAmA 93N*
Gordon, Donald Howard 1954- *WhoWest 94*
Gordon, Dorothy 1919- *WhoHol 92*
Gordon, Douglas *Who 94, WhoHol 92*
Gordon, (Robert) Douglas 1936- *Who 94*
Gordon, Edgar George 1924- *WhoAmL 94*
Gordon, Edmund W. 1921- *WhoBlA 94*
Gordon, Edmund Wyatt 1921- *WhoScEn 94*
Gordon, Edward 1930- *WhoAm 94*
Gordon, Edward 1948- *WhoAmP 93*
Gordon, Edward Earl 1949- *WhoMW 93*
Gordon, Edward R. d1938 *WhoHol 92*
Gordon, Edwin Jason 1952- *WhoBlA 94*
Gordon, Elaine 1931- *WhoWomW 91*
Gordon, Elaine Y. 1931- *WhoAmP 93*
Gordon, Eldridge Elmer, Jr. 1952- *WhoFI 94*
Gordon, Ellen Rubin *WhoAm 94, WhoMW 93*
Gordon, Eric A(rthur) 1945- *WrDr 94*
Gordon, Ernest 1916- *WhoAm 94, WrDr 94*
Gordon, (Alexander) Esme d1993 *Who 94N*
Gordon, Ethel E(dison) 1915- *WrDr 94*
Gordon, Ethel M. 1911- *WhoBlA 94*
Gordon, Eugene Andrew 1917- *WhoAm 94, WhoAmL 94*
Gordon, Eugene Irving 1930- *WhoAm 94*
Gordon, Eve *WhoHol 92*
Gordon, Ezra 1921- *WhoAm 94*
Gordon, Fannetta Nelson 1919- *WhoBlA 94*
Gordon, Francis 1928- *WhoAmP 93*
Gordon, Frank Wallace 1935- *WhoAm 94*
Gordon, Frank X. *WhoAmP 93*
Gordon, Frank X., Jr. 1929- *WhoAmL 94*
Gordon, Fred *DrAPF 93*
Gordon, Gale 1906- *IntMPA 94, WhoHol 92*
Gordon, Gavin d1970 *WhoHol 92*
Gordon, Gavin d1983 *WhoHol 92*
Gordon, George *ConAu 140*
Gordon, George Angier 1853-1929 *DcAmReB 2*
Gordon, George N. 1926- *WrDr 94*
Gordon, George Stanwood, Jr. 1935- *WhoScEn 94*
Gordon, Gerald *Who 94, WhoHol 92*
Gordon, (Cosmo) Gerald (Maitland) 1945- *Who 94*
Gordon, Gerald Henry 1929- *Who 94*
Gordon, Gerald Timothy *DrAPF 93*
Gordon, Gilbert 1933- *WhoAm 94*
Gordon, Giles 1940- *DcLB 139 [port]*
Gordon, Giles (Alexander Esme) 1940- *ConAu 43NR, WrDr 94*
Gordon, Giles Alexander Esme 1940- *Who 94*
Gordon, Glen Charles d1977 *WhoHol 92*
Gordon, Glen E. 1935-1992 *WhAm 10*
Gordon, Glenna Jo 1968- *WhoMW 93*
Gordon, Gloria d1962 *WhoHol 92*
Gordon, Gloria c. 1937- *WhoHol 92*
Gordon, Gordon 1906- *WrDr 94*
Gordon, Grant d1972 *WhoHol 92*
Gordon, Gray d1976 *WhoHol 92*
Gordon, Hal d1946 *WhoHol 92*
Gordon, Hannah 1941- *ConTFT 11, WhoHol 92*
Gordon, Hannah Cambell Grant 1941- *Who 94*
Gordon, Hannah Elizabeth 1920- *WhoAmP 93*
Gordon, Harold d1959 *WhoHol 92*
Gordon, Harold John 1896- *WhAm 10*
Gordon, Harris d1947 *WhoHol 92*
Gordon, Harrison J. 1950- *WhoAmL 94*
Gordon, Harry d1948 *WhoHol 92*
Gordon, Harry H. 1938- *WhoIns 94*
Gordon, Hayes 1920- *WhoHol 92*
Gordon, Helen A. 1923- *WhoBlA 94*
Gordon, Helen Heightsman 1932- *WhoWest 94*
Gordon, Helmut Albert 1908- *WhoScEn 94*
Gordon, Herman 1925- *WhoAmL 94, WhoFI 94*
Gordon, Howard Lyon 1930- *WhoFI 94*
Gordon, Hugh Sangster, Jr. 1949- *WhoWest 94*
Gordon, Huntley d1956 *WhoHol 92*
Gordon, Ian Alistair 1908- *Who 94, WrDr 94*
Gordon, Irvin H. 1912- *WhoAmP 93*
Gordon, Irving Martin 1926- *WhoMW 93*
Gordon, Jack 1953- *WhoFI 94*
Gordon, Jack D. 1922- *WhoAmP 93*
Gordon, Jack David 1922- *WhoAm 94*
Gordon, Jacqueline Regina 1964- *WhoScEn 94*
Gordon, Jacques Nicholas 1956- *WhoAm 94*
Gordon, Jaimy *DrAPF 93*
Gordon, Jaimy 1944- *ConAu 140, WhoAm 94*
Gordon, James d1941 *WhoHol 92*
Gordon, James 1739-1810 *WhAmRev*
Gordon, James Braund 1911- *WhoAm 94*
Gordon, James Charles Mellish 1941- *Who 94*
Gordon, James Edward 1788?-1864 *DcNaB MP*
Gordon, James Fleming 1918-1990 *WhAm 10*
Gordon, James Houston 1946- *WhoAmP 93*
Gordon, James Power 1928- *WhoScEn 94*
Gordon, James Roycroft 1898- *WhAm 10*
Gordon, James S. 1941- *WhoAmL 94*
Gordon, James Stuart 1936- *Who 94*
Gordon, Janine M. 1946- *WhoAm 94, WhoFI 94*
Gordon, Jay Andre 1954- *WhoFI 94*
Gordon, Jay Fisher 1926- *WhoAm 94*
Gordon, Jeanne 1884-1952 *NewGrDO*
Gordon, Jeanne Brown *WhoAmP 93*
Gordon, Jeffrey I. 1948- *WhoAm 94*
Gordon, Jeffrey Sheppard 1942- *WhoAm 94, WhoAmL 94*
Gordon, Joel Charles 1929- *WhoAm 94*
Gordon, Joel Ethan 1930- *WhoAm 94*
Gordon, John 1912-1978 *WhoAmA 93N*
Gordon, John (William) 1925- *WrDr 94*
Gordon, John Bennett 1947- *WhoAm 94, WhoAmL 94*
Gordon, John Charles 1939- *WhoAm 94*
Gordon, John Edward 1941- *WhoAmL 94*
Gordon, John Fraser 1916- *WrDr 94*
Gordon, John Keith 1940- *Who 94*
Gordon, John Leo 1933- *WhoAm 94*
Gordon, John Lynn 1933- *WhoWest 94*
Gordon, John S. 1946- *WhoAmA 93*
Gordon, John Siesel 1946- *WhoMW 93*
Gordon, Jonathan David 1949- *WhoAm 94*
Gordon, Joseph Cooper 1959- *WhoAmP 93*
Gordon, Joseph Elwell 1921- *WhoAm 94*
Gordon, Joseph G., II 1945- *WhoBlA 94*
Gordon, Joseph Harold 1909- *WhoAm 94, WhoAmL 94, WhoWest 94*
Gordon, Joseph Wallace 1957- *WhoScEn 94*
Gordon, Josephine *WhoAmA 93*
Gordon, Joy L. 1933- *WhoAmA 93*
Gordon, Judith *WhoFI 94, WhoWest 94*
Gordon, Julia Swayne d1933 *WhoHol 92*
Gordon, Julian 1936- *WhoFI 94*
Gordon, Julie Peyton 1940- *WhoAm 94, WhoMW 93*
Gordon, Karen Ann 1957- *WhoMW 93*
Gordon, Karen Elizabeth *WhoWest 94*
Gordon, Katharine 1916- *WrDr 94*
Gordon, Katherine H. 1948- *WhoWomW 91*
Gordon, Kathryn Lee 1947- *WhoWest 94*
Gordon, Keith 1961- *IntMPA 94, WhoHol 92*
Gordon, Keith (Lyndell) 1906- *Who 94*
Gordon, Kenneth E., Jr. 1942- *WhoAmL 94*
Gordon, Kenneth Ira 1959- *WhoAmL 94*
Gordon, Kenneth Marshall 1950- *WhoAmP 93*
Gordon, Kirpal *DrAPF 93*
Gordon, Kitty d1974 *WhoHol 92*
Gordon, Lancaster 1962- *WhoBlA 94*
Gordon, Larry David 1938- *WhoMW 93*
Gordon, Larry Jean 1926- *WhoAm 94*
Gordon, Lawrence 1936- *IntMPA 94, WhoAm 94*
Gordon, Lawrence J. 1953- *WhoAmL 94*
Gordon, Leo 1922- *WhoHol 92*
Gordon, Leon d1960 *WhoHol 92*
Gordon, Leonard 1935- *WhoAm 94, WhoWest 94*
Gordon, Leonard Victor 1917- *WhoAm 94*

Gordon, Levan 1933- *WhoBlA 94*
Gordon, Lewis Alexander 1937- *WhoFI 94*
Gordon, Lincoln 1913- *WhoAm 94*
Gordon, Linda 1940- *WhoMW 93*
Gordon, Lionel Eldred Peter S. *Who 94*
Gordon, Lisa *WhoHol 92*
Gordon, Lois G. 1938- *WrDr 94*
Gordon, Lois Goldfein 1938- *WhoAm 94*
Gordon, Lois Jackson 1932- *WhoBlA 94*
Gordon, Lorne Bertram 1945- *WhoAm 94*
Gordon, Lou 1908- *WrDr 94*
Gordon, Louis 1946- *WhoWest 94*
Gordon, Lyndall (Felicity) 1941- *ConAu 141*
Gordon, MacDonnell *DrAPF 93*
Gordon, Mack d1959 *WhoHol 92*
Gordon, Malcolm Stephen 1933- *WhoAm 94*
Gordon, Margaret Shaughnessy 1910- *WhoAm 94, WhoWest 94*
Gordon, Marian d1927 *WhoHol 92*
Gordon, Marianne 1944- *WhoHol 92*
Gordon, Marilyn 1940- *WhoWest 94*
Gordon, Marjorie *WhoAm 94, WhoHol 92*
Gordon, Mark *WhoHol 92*
Gordon, Mark Elliott 1956- *WhoScEn 94*
Gordon, Marshall 1937- *WhoAm 94*
Gordon, Martin 1939- *WhoAm 94, WhoAmA 93*
Gordon, Marvin Jay 1946- *WhoWest 94*
Gordon, Mary *DrAPF 93*
Gordon, Mary d1963 *WhoHol 92*
Gordon, Mary 1949- *BlmGWL*
Gordon, Mary (Catherine) 1949- *WrDr 94*
Gordon, Mary Catherine 1949- *WhoAm 94*
Gordon, Mary McDougall 1929- *WhoAm 94, WrDr 94*
Gordon, Maude Turner d1940 *WhoHol 92*
Gordon, Max 1903-1989 *WhAm 10*
Gordon, Maxie S., Sr. 1910- *WhoBlA 94*
Gordon, Maxwell 1910-1982 *WhoAmA 93N*
Gordon, Maxwell 1921- *WhoAm 94, WhoFI 94*
Gordon, Michael d1993 *IntMPA 94N, NewYTBS 93*
Gordon, Michael 1953- *WhoAmL 94*
Gordon, Michael Duane 1949- *WhoMW 93*
Gordon, Michael John Caldwell 1948- *Who 94*
Gordon, Michael Mackin 1950- *WhoAm 94*
Gordon, Michael Robert 1947- *WhoAmP 93*
Gordon, Mildred d1993 *NewYTBS 93*
Gordon, Mildred 1923- *Who 94, WhoWomW 91*
Gordon, Millard Verne *EncSF 93*
Gordon, Milton A. 1912-1990 *WhAm 10*
Gordon, Milton A. 1935- *WhoBlA 94*
Gordon, Milton Andrew 1935 *WhoAm 94, WhoWest 94*
Gordon, Milton G. 1922- *WhoAm 94, WhoWest 94*
Gordon, Milton Paul 1930- *WhoAm 94*
Gordon, Myron L. 1918- *WhoAmL 94, WhoMW 93*
Gordon, Nadia *Who 94*
Gordon, Neil *EncSF 93*
Gordon, Nicholas 1928- *WhoAm 94*
Gordon, Nicole Ann 1954- *WhoAm 94*
Gordon, Noele d1985 *WhoHol 92*
Gordon, Nora d1970 *WhoHol 92*
Gordon, Norman Botnick 1921- *WhoAm 94*
Gordon, P(atrick) S(cott) 1953- *WhoAmA 93*
Gordon, Pamela Ann 1947- *WhoAmL 94*
Gordon, Pamela Joan 1936- *Who 94*
Gordon, Patrick W. *Who 94*
Gordon, Paul *DrAPF 93*
Gordon, Paul d1929 *WhoHol 92*
Gordon, Paul David 1941- *WhoFI 94*
Gordon, Paul John 1921- *WhoAm 94*
Gordon, Paul Perry 1927- *WhoAmP 93*
Gordon, Peter H. 1948- *WrDr 94*
Gordon, Peter Lowell 1953- *WhoWest 94*
Gordon, Peter Macie 1919- *Who 94*
Gordon, Philip B. 1885-1948 *EncNAR*
Gordon, Phillip 1943- *WhoAm 94, WhoAmL 94*
Gordon, Priscilla Stuart 1955- *WhoWest 94*
Gordon, Rena Joyce 1936- *WhoAm 94*
Gordon, Rex 1917- *EncSF 93, WrDr 94*
Gordon, Richard d1956 *WhoHol 92*
Gordon, Richard 1921- *Who 94, WrDr 94*
Gordon, Richard 1925- *IntMPA 94*
Gordon, Richard 1950- *WhoAmL 94*
Gordon, Richard A. *EncSF 93*
Gordon, Richard Edwards 1922- *WhoAm 94, WhoScEn 94*
Gordon, Richard H. *WhoAm 94*
Gordon, Richard Lewis 1934- *WhoAm 94*
Gordon, Richard M. Erik 1949- *WhoFI 94*
Gordon, Richard Warner 1969- *WhoScEn 94*
Gordon, Robert d1971 *WhoHol 92*
Gordon, Robert fl. 177-?- *WhWE*
Gordon, Robert Allen, Jr. 1951- *WhoAm 94, WhoAmL 94*
Gordon, Robert Anthony Eagleson 1952- *Who 94*
Gordon, Robert Boyd 1929- *WhoAm 94*
Gordon, Robert Charles Frost 1920- *WhoAmP 93*
Gordon, Robert Edward 1925- *WhoAm 94*
Gordon, Robert Eugene 1932- *WhoWest 94*
Gordon, Robert Fitzgerald 1928- *WhoBlA 94*
Gordon, Robert Frederick *WhoAm 94*
Gordon, Robert James 1932- *Who 94*
Gordon, Robert James 1940- *WhoAm 94*
Gordon, Robert Jay 1942- *WhoAm 94*
Gordon, Robert Jay 1949- *WhoMW 93*
Gordon, Robert L. 1941- *WhoBlA 94*
Gordon, Robert Lynn 1935- *WhoAm 94*
Gordon, Robert Rae 1954- *WhoAmL 94*
Gordon, Robert Wilson d1993 *Who 94N*
Gordon, Roger L. *WhoAm 94, WhoFI 94, WhoWest 94*
Gordon, Ronald *Who 94*
Gordon, (Archibald) Ronald (McDonald) 1927- *Who 94*
Gordon, Ronald Eugene 1946- *WhoBlA 94*
Gordon, Ronald John 1954- *WhoHisp 94*
Gordon, Ronnie Roslyn 1923- *WhoScEn 94*
Gordon, Roy d1978 *WhoHol 92*
Gordon, Roy Gerald 1940- *WhoAm 94, WhoScEn 94*
Gordon, Roy Turner d1972 *WhoHol 92*
Gordon, Russell Talbert 1936- *WhoAmA 93*
Gordon, Ruth d1985 *WhoHol 92*
Gordon, Ruth Vida 1926- *WhoWest 94*
Gordon, Samuel Neal 1950- *WhoMW 93*
Gordon, Sara J. 1937- *WhoFI 94*
Gordon, Sarah (Ann) 1944- *WrDr 94*
Gordon, Seymour 1929- *WhoMW 93*
Gordon, Shana *WhoAm 94*
Gordon, Sheila 1927- *WrDr 94*
Gordon, Siamon 1938- *Who 94*
Gordon, Sidney 1917- *Who 94*
Gordon, Spike *EncSF 93*
Gordon, Stephen Maurice 1942- *WhoAm 94*
Gordon, Steven B. 1948- *WhoScEn 94*
Gordon, Steven Eric 1960- *WhoWest 94*
Gordon, Steven Jeffrey 1958- *WhoScEn 94*
Gordon, Steven Joe 1956- *WhoFI 94*
Gordon, Steven Stanley 1919- *WhoAm 94*
Gordon, Stewart 1914- *WrDr 94*
Gordon, Stewart George 1937- *WhoAm 94*
Gordon, Stuart 1946- *HorFD [port]*
Gordon, Stuart 1947- *ConTFT 11, EncSF 93, WrDr 94*
Gordon, Susan 1950- *WhoHol 92*
Gordon, Sydney Jeter 1946- *WhoWest 94*
Gordon, Thomas 1918- *WrDr 94*
Gordon, Thomas 1967- *WhoBlA 94*
Gordon, Thomas Christian, Jr. 1915- *WhoAm 94*
Gordon, Timothy d1993 *NewYTBS 93*
Gordon, Tina *WhoAmA 93*
Gordon, Vera d1948 *WhoHol 92*
Gordon, Vera Kate *Who 94*
Gordon, Violet 1907- *WhoAmA 93*
Gordon, Vivian V. 1934- *WhoBlA 94*
Gordon, Vivian V(erdell) 1934- *BlkWr 2*
Gordon, Walter 1907- *WhoAm 94*
Gordon, Walter Carl, Jr. 1927- *WhoBlA 94*
Gordon, Walter Kelly 1930- *WhoAm 94*
Gordon, Walter Lear, III 1942- *WhoBlA 94*
Gordon, Wendell Chaffee 1916- *WhoAm 94*
Gordon, Wendy Jane *WhoAmL 94*
Gordon, William 1728-1807 *WhAmRev*
Gordon, William A. 1940- *WhoAm 94*
Gordon, William A. 1950- *WrDr 94*
Gordon, William Edwin 1918- *IntWW 93, WhoAm 94*
Gordon, William George 1931- *WhoAmP 93*
Gordon, William Howat Leslie 1914- *Who 94*
Gordon, William Richard 1913- *WhoAm 94*
Gordon, Winfield James 1926- *WhoBlA 94*
Gordon-Brown, Alexander Douglas 1927- *Who 94*
Gordon-Cumming, Alexander Roualeyn 1924- *Who 94*
Gordon Cumming, William Gordon 1928- *Who 94*
Gordon Davies, John *Who 94*
Gordon-Dillard, Joan Yvonne 1955- *WhoBlA 94*
Gordon-Duff, Thomas Robert 1911- *Who 94*
Gordone, Charles 1925- *WrDr 94*
Gordone, Charles 1927- *WhoAm 94, WhoHol 92*
Gordone, Charles (Edward) 1925- *ConDr 93*
Gordone, Charles Edward 1925- *WhoBlA 94*
Gordon-Finlayson, Robert 1916- *Who 94*
Gordoni, Arthur d1966 *WhoHol 92*
Gordon Jones, Edward 1914- *Who 94*
Gordon-Lennox *Who 94*
Gordon Lennox, Bernard Charles 1932- *Who 94*
Gordon Lennox, Nicholas Charles 1931- *Who 94*
Gordons 1906- *WrDr 94*
Gordon-Shelby, Lurdys Marie 1963- *WhoBlA 94*
Gordon-Sinclair, John 1962- *WhoHol 92*
Gordon-Smith, David Gerard 1925- *Who 94*
Gordonsmith, John Arthur Harold 1942- *WhoAm 94*
Gordon-Smith, Ralph d1993 *IntWW 93N, Who 94N*
Gordon-Smith, Ralph 1905- *IntWW 93*
Gordy, Berry 1929- *IntMPA 94, WhoAm 94*
Gordy, Berry, Jr. 1929- *AfrAmAl 6, WhoBlA 94*
Gordy, Desiree D'Laura 1956- *WhoBlA 94*
Gordy, Laura Belle 1930- *WhoAmP 93*
Gordy, Robert P. 1933-1986 *WhoAmA 93N*
Gordy, Roy d1981 *WhoHol 92*
Gordy, Stephen Ellison 1920- *WhoAmP 93*
Gore *Who 94*
Gore, Al 1948- *CngDr 93*
Gore, Al(bert, Jr.) 1948- *ConAu 142*
Gore, Albert, Jr. 1948- *EnvEnc [port], IntWW 93, Who 94, WhoAm 94, WhoAmP 93*
Gore, Albert Jackson, Jr. 1960- *WhoFI 94*
Gore, Arthur 1868-1928 *BuCMET*
Gore, Barry Maurice 1944- *WhoAm 94*
Gore, Blinzy L. 1921- *WhoBlA 94*
Gore, Bryan Frank 1938- *WhoWest 94*
Gore, Catherine 1799-1861 *BlmGWL*
Gore, Catherine Grace Frances 1799-1861 *BlmGEL*
Gore, David Alan 1947- *WhoAmA 93*
Gore, David Curtiss 1964- *WhoFI 94*
Gore, David L. 1937- *WhoBlA 94*
Gore, David Lee 1937- *WhoAmL 94, WhoMW 93*
Gore, Donald Ray 1936- *WhoAm 94, WhoMW 93*
Gore, Frederick John Pym 1913- *IntWW 93, Who 94*
Gore, James William 1953- *WhoScEn 94*
Gore, Jefferson Anderson 1943- *WhoAmA 93*
Gore, John 1730-1790 *WhWE*
Gore, John Michel 1955- *WhoBlA 94*
Gore, Joseph A. *WhoBlA 94*
Gore, Ken 1911- *WhoAmA 93*
Gore, Lesley 1946- *WhoHol 92*
Gore, Logan Melville, III 1949- *WhoMW 93*
Gore, Louise 1925- *WhoAmP 93*
Gore, Mary Elizabeth 1948- *ConAu 142*
Gore, Michael 1951- *IntMPA 94*
Gore, Michael Edward John 1935- *Who 94*
Gore, Michael Lee 1960- *WhoAmL 94*
Gore, Paul Annesley 1921- *Who 94*
Gore, Richard (Ralph St. George) 1954- *Who 94*
Gore, Rosa d1941 *WhoHol 92*
Gore, St. John *Who 94*
Gore, (Francis) St. John (Corbet) 1921- *Who 94*
Gore, Samuel Marshall 1927- *WhoAmA 93*
Gore, Samuel Thomas 1933- *WhoAmP 93*
Gore, Sandy *WhoHol 92*
Gore, Spencer 1850-1906 *BuCMET*
Gore, Susan Belinda 1949- *WhoMW 93*
Gore, Thomas Gavin 1939- *WhoWest 94*
Gore, Tipper *ConAu 142, NewYTBS 93 [port]*
Gore, Tipper 1948- *WhoAm 94*
Gore, Tom 1946- *WhoAmA 93*
Gore, Walter 1910-1979 *IntDcB [port]*
Gore, Wilbert Lee 1912-1986 *WhAm 10*
Gore, William Jay 1924- *WhoAm 94*
Gore-Booth, Angus (Josslyn) 1920- *Who 94*
Gore-Booth, Constance 1868-1927 *DcNaB MP*
Gore-Booth, David Alwyn 1943- *Who 94*
Gore-Booth, Eva 1870-1926 *BlmGWL*
Gore-Booth, Eva Selina 1870-1926 *DcNaB MP*
Gorecki, Henryk Mikolaj 1933- *IntWW 93*
Gorecki, Jan 1926- *WhoAm 94*
Goree, Gary Paul 1951- *WhoAmA 93*
Goree, Janie Glymph 1921- *WhoBlA 94*
Gore-Langton *Who 94*
Gorelick, Jamie Shona 1950- *WhoAm 94, WhoAmL 94*
Gorelick, Jeffrey Bruce 1955- *WhoScEn 94*
Gorelick, Shirley 1924- *WhoAmA 93*
Gorelik, Alexander 1964- *WhoWest 94*
Gorell, Baron 1927- *Who 94*
Goren, Alexander Mircea 1940- *WhoAm 94*
Goren, Arnold Louis *WhoAm 94*
Goren, Charles Henry 1901-1991 *WhAm 10*
Goren, Howard Joseph 1941- *WhoScEn 94*
Goren, Judith *DrAPF 93*
Goren, Roger 1950- *WhoFI 94*
Goren, Shlomo 1917- *IntWW 93*
Goren, Steven Eliot 1960- *WhoAmL 94*
Gorena, Sam Luis 1958- *WhoHisp 94*
Gorenberg, Charles Lloyd 1938- *WhoFI 94*
Gorenberg, Norman Bernard 1923- *WhoScEn 94, WhoWest 94*
Goreniuc, Mircea C. Paul 1942- *WhoAmA 93*
Gorenstein, David G. 1945- *WhoScEn 94*
Gorenstein, Shirley Slotkin 1928- *WhoAm 94*
Gorenz, David John 1958- *WhoMW 93*
Gorer, Geoffrey (Edgar) 1905-1985 *EncSF 93*
Gores, Christopher Merrel 1943- *WhoAm 94, WhoAmL 94*
Gores, Gary Gene 1940- *WhoMW 93*
Gores, Joe 1931- *WrDr 94*
Gores, Joseph Nicholas 1931- *WhoAm 94*
Gores, Landis 1919-1991 *WhAm 10*
Gores, Thomas C. 1948- *WhoAmL 94*
Goretta, Claude 1929- *IntWW 93*
Gorev, Nikolay Nikolayevich d1992 *IntWW 93N*
Gorey, Edward (St. John) 1925- *WrDr 94*
Gorey, Edward St. John 1925- *WhoAm 94*
Gorfinkel, Marc Paul 1954- *WhoAmL 94*
Gorgas, William Crawford *WorScD*
Gorgeous George d1963 *WhoHol 92*
Gorges, Heinz August 1913- *WhoFI 94*
Gorham, Bradford 1935- *WhoAmP 93*
Gorham, David L. 1932- *WhoAm 94*
Gorham, Eville 1925- *WhoAm 94, WhoMW 93, WhoScEn 94*
Gorham, Frank DeVore, Jr. 1921- *WhoAm 94*
Gorham, Michael 1907- *WrDr 94*
Gorham, Nathaniel 1738-1796 *WhAmRev*
Gorham, Robin Stuart 1939- *Who 94*
Gorham, Sarah *DrAPF 93*
Gorham, Sidney 1870-1947 *WhoAmA 93N*
Gorham, Thelma Thurston 1913-1992 *WhoBlA 94N*
Gorham, William 1930 *WhoAm 94*
Gorham, William Hartshorne 1933- *WhoAm 94*
Goria, Giovanni 1943- *IntWW 93*
Gorin, George 1925- *WhoAm 94*
Gorin, Igor d1982 *WhoHol 92*
Gorin, Ralph Edgar 1948- *WhoWest 94*
Gorin, Robert Seymour 1935- *WhoAmL 94*
Gorin, William 1908- *WhoAm 94*
Goring, David Arthur Ingham 1920- *WhoAm 94*
Goring, Hermann 1893-1946 *HisWorL [port]*
Goring, Marius 1912- *ConTFT 11, IntMPA 94, IntWW 93, Who 94, WhoHol 92*
Goring, Peter Allan Elliott 1943- *WhoAm 94*
Goring, William (Burton Nigel) 1933- *Who 94*
Goring, William S. 1943- *WhoBlA 94*
Goring Thomas, Arthur *NewGrDO*
Gorinson, Stanley M. 1945- *WhoAm 94*
Goritz, Otto 1873-1929 *NewGrDO*
Gor'kii, Maksim 1868-1936 *RfGShF*
Gorky, Arshile 1905-1948 *AmCulL*
Gorky, Maxim *ConAu 141*
Gorky, Maxim d1936 *WhoHol 92*
Gorky, Maxim 1868-1936 *IntDcT 2*
Gorla, Rama S. R. 1941- *WhoAsA 94*
Gorlach, Manfred *ConAu 140*
Gorland, Ronald Kent 1944- *WhoAm 94*
Gorland, Scott Lance 1949- *WhoAm 94*
Gorley Putt, Samuel *Who 94*
Gorlin, Cathy Ellen 1953- *WhoAmL 94*
Gorlin, Richard 1926- *WhoAm 94*
Gorlin, Robert James 1923- *WhoAm 94*
Gormalley, Joan Patricia 1938- *WhoAmP 93*
Gorman, Alvin Larry 1933- *WhoAm 94*
Gorman, Barbara Rose 1945- *WhoWest 94*
Gorman, Benjamin Frank 1931- *WhoFI 94*
Gorman, Bertha Gaffney 1940- *WhoBlA 94*

Gotovchits, Georgy Olexandrovich 1935- *WhoScEn 94*
Gotschalk, Felix C. 1929- *EncSF 93, WrDr 94*
Gotschlich, Emil Claus 1935- *WhoAm 94, WhoScEn 94*
Gotshall, Jan Doyle 1942- *WhoFI 94*
Gotshall, Mark Edward 1960- *WhoMW 93*
Gotsopoulos, Barbara Lynn 1948- *WhoFI 94*
Gott, Barbara d1944 *WhoHol 92*
Gott, Edwin Hays 1908-1986 *EncABHB 9 [port]*
Gott, George *DrAPF 93*
Gott, Haydn 1946- *Who 94*
Gott, J. Richard, III 1947- *WhoAm 94, WhoScEn 94*
Gott, James L. 1933- *WhoFI 94*
Gott, Jerry D. 1940- *WhoMW 93*
Gott, Karel 1939- *IntWW 93*
Gott, Raymond Eugene 1940- *WhoWest 94*
Gott, Richard (Willoughby) 1938- *WrDr 94*
Gott, Richard Willoughby 1938- *Who 94*
Gott, Robert Dean 1946- *WhoAmP 93*
Gott, Rodney C. d1993 *NewYTBS 93*
Gott, Wesley Atlas 1942- *WhoMW 93*
Gotta, Alexander Walter 1935- *WhoAm 94, WhoScEn 94*
Gotte, Klaus 1932- *IntWW 93*
Gotte, Rose 1938- *WhoWomW 91*
Gottenborg, David Andrew 1955- *WhoWest 94*
Gotter, (Johann) Friedrich Wilhelm 1746-1797 *NewGrDO*
Gottesman, Callman 1909- *WhoAmL 94*
Gottesman, David Sanford 1926- *WhoAm 94*
Gottesman, Irving Isadore 1930- *WhoAm 94, WhoScEn 94*
Gottesman, Michael Marc 1946- *WhoAm 94, WhoScEn 94*
Gottesman, Roy Tully 1928- *WhoAm 94*
Gottesman, S.D. *EncSF 93*
Gottesman, Scott 1957- *WhoIns 94*
Gottesman, Stuart 1949- *IntMPA 94*
Gottfredson, Don Martin 1926- *WhoAm 94*
Gottfredson, Gary Don 1947- *WhoScEn 94*
Gottfredson, Mark Alan 1957- *WhoFI 94*
Gottfried, Benjamin Frank 1939- *WhoFI 94*
Gottfried, Brian 1952- *BuCMET*
Gottfried, Byron Stuart 1934- *WhoAm 94*
Gottfried, David Scott 1962- *WhoScEn 94*
Gottfried, Eugene Leslie 1929- *WhoAm 94, WhoScEn 94, WhoWest 94*
Gottfried, Gilbert 1955- *WhoCom, WhoHol 92*
Gottfried, Ira Sidney 1932- *WhoAm 94*
Gottfried, Keith Evan 1966- *WhoFI 94*
Gottfried, Kurt 1929- *WhoAm 94, WhoScEn 94*
Gottfried, Leon Albert 1925- *WhoAm 94*
Gottfried, Richard Norman 1947- *WhoAmP 93*
Gottfried von Strassburg dc. 1230 *DcLB 138 [port]*
Gottheimer, George M., Jr. 1933- *WhoIns 94*
Gotthelf, Jeremias 1797-1854 *DcLB 133 [port]*
Gotthoffer, Lance 1949- *WhoAmL 94*
Gottieb, Alan M. 1947- *WhoAm 94*
Gottier, Richard Chalmers 1918- *WhoAm 94*
Gottlander, Robert Jan Lars 1956- *WhoFI 94, WhoMW 93, WhoScEn 94*
Gottleib, Carl *WhoHol 92*
Gottleib, Franz Michael 1948- *WhoWest 94*
Gottler, Archie d1959 *WhoHol 92*
Gottlieb, Abraham Arthur 1937- *WhoAm 94, WhoScEn 94*
Gottlieb, Adolph 1903-1974 *WhoAmA 93N*
Gottlieb, Alan Merril 1947- *WhoWest 94*
Gottlieb, Allen Sandford 1928- *WhoAm 94*
Gottlieb, Amy *DrAPF 93*
Gottlieb, (Maria) Anna (Josepha Francisca) 1774-1856 *NewGrDO*
Gottlieb, Annie 1946- *WrDr 94*
Gottlieb, Arnold 1926- *WhoScEn 94*
Gottlieb, Bernard 1913- *Who 94*
Gottlieb, Carl 1938- *IntMPA 94*
Gottlieb, Carla 1912- *WhoAmA 93*
Gottlieb, Daniel Seth 1954- *WhoAmL 94*
Gottlieb, Darcy *DrAPF 93*
Gottlieb, Edward 1910- *WhoAm 94*
Gottlieb, Elaine *DrAPF 93*
Gottlieb, Gidon Alain Guy 1932- *WhoAm 94*
Gottlieb, H. David 1956- *WhoScEn 94*
Gottlieb, Hinko 1886- *EncSF 93*
Gottlieb, James R. 1947- *WhoAmP 93*
Gottlieb, James Rubel 1947- *WhoAmL 94*
Gottlieb, Jane Ellen 1954- *WhoAm 94*
Gottlieb, Jerrold Howard 1946- *WhoAm 94*
Gottlieb, Jonathan W. 1959- *WhoAmL 94*
Gottlieb, Joseph Abraham 1918- *WhoAm 94*
Gottlieb, Julius Judah 1919- *WhoScEn 94*
Gottlieb, Leon Herbert 1927- *WhoWest 94*
Gottlieb, Leonard Solomon 1927- *WhoAm 94, WhoScEn 94*
Gottlieb, Lester M. 1932- *WhoFI 94*
Gottlieb, Marilyn 1942- *WhoAm 94*
Gottlieb, Morton Edgar 1921- *WhoAm 94*
Gottlieb, Moshe 1948- *WhoScEn 94*
Gottlieb, Paul 1935- *IntWW 93, WhoAm 94*
Gottlieb, Paul Mitchel 1954- *WhoAmL 94*
Gottlieb, Peter 1930- *NewGrDO*
Gottlieb, Richard Douglas 1942- *WhoAm 94, WhoMW 93*
Gottlieb, Robert Adams 1931- *IntWW 93, Who 94, WhoAm 94*
Gottlieb, Sanford 1926- *WhoAmP 93*
Gottlieb, Sheldon Fred 1932- *WhoAm 94*
Gottlieb, Sherry Gershon 1948- *WhoWest 94*
Gottlieb, Shirle Sherman 1930- *WhoWest 94*
Gottlieb, Theodore *WhoCom, WhoHol 92*
Gottman, Wendell Alan 1942- *WhoMW 93*
Gottmann, Jean 1915- *Who 94, WhoAm 94*
Gottmann, Jean-Iona 1915- *IntWW 93*
Gotto, Antonio Marion, Jr. 1935- *WhoAm 94*
Gottovi, Karen Elizabeth 1941- *WhoAmP 93*
Gottron, Francis Robert, III 1953- *WhoMW 93*
Gottschalg, Melvin G. 1921- *WhoAmP 93*
Gottschalk, Alexander 1932- *WhoAm 94*
Gottschalk, Alfred 1930- *WhoAm 94, WhoMW 93*
Gottschalk, Arthur William 1952- *WhoAm 94*
Gottschalk, Carl William 1922- *IntWW 93, WhoAm 94*
Gottschalk, Charles Max 1928- *WhoAm 94*
Gottschalk, Ferdinand d1944 *WhoHol 92*
Gottschalk, Frank Klaus 1932- *WhoAm 94, WhoFI 94*
Gottschalk, Fritz 1937- *WhoAmA 93*
Gottschalk, Gerhard 1935- *IntWW 93*
Gottschalk, Joachim d1941 *WhoHol 92*
Gottschalk, John Simison 1912- *WhoAm 94*
Gottschalk, Kurt William 1952- *WhoScEn 94*
Gottschalk, Laura Riding 1901-1991 *WrDr 94N*
Gottschalk, Louis A(ugust) 1916- *ConAu 41NR*
Gottschalk, Louis August 1916- *WhoAm 94, WhoWest 94*
Gottschalk, Louis Moreau 1829-1869 *AfrAmAl 6 [port], AmCulL, NewGrDO*
Gottschalk, Mary Therese 1931- *WhoAm 94*
Gottschalk, Max Jules 1909- *WhoAmA 93, WhoWest 94*
Gottschalk, Stephen Elmer 1947- *WhoAm 94, WhoAmL 94*
Gottschalk, Thomas A. 1942- *WhoAm 94, WhoAmL 94*
Gottschalk, Walter Helbig 1918- *WhoScEn 94*
Gottschall, Edward M(aurice) 1915- *WrDr 94*
Gottschall, Edward Maurice 1915- *WhoAm 94*
Gottsched, Luise Adelgunde Victorie 1713-1762 *BlmGWL*
Gottschlich, Gary William 1946- *WhoAm 94*
Gottshall, Franklin H. 1902-1992 *WrDr 94N*
Gottsman, Earl Eugene 1946- *WhoAm 94*
Gottstein, Barnard Jacob 1925- *WhoFI 94, WhoWest 94*
Gottstein, Barney J. *WhoAmP 93*
Gottwald, Bruce Cobb 1933- *WhoAm 94*
Gottwald, Bruce Cobb, Jr. 1957- *WhoAm 94*
Gottwald, Floyd Dewey, Jr. 1922- *WhoAm 94, WhoFI 94*
Gottwald, John D. 1954- *WhoFI 94*
Gottwald, Klement 1896-1953 *HisWorL [port]*
Gottzein, Eveline 1931- *WhoScEn 94*
Goty, Mici d1946 *WhoHol 92*
Götz, Ignacio L. 1933- *WrDr 94*
Gotze, Heinz 1912- *IntWW 93*
Gotzoyannis, Stavros Eleutherios 1933- *WhoScEn 94*
Goubeau, Vincent De Paul 1898- *WhAm 10*
Gouda, Moustafa Abdel-Hamid 1942- *WhoFI 94*
Goudal, Jetta d1985 *WhoHol 92*
Goudelock, Carol V. 1938- *WhoWest 94*
Goudev, Vladimir Victorovich 1940- *IntWW 93*
Goudie, Andrew Shaw 1945- *Who 94*
Goudie, James *Who 94*
Goudie, (Thomas) James (Cooper) 1942- *Who 94*
Goudie, John Carrick 1919- *Who 94*
Goudie, William Henry 1916- *Who 94*
Goudinoff, Peter *WhoAmP 93*
Goudreau, Barry 1951- *See* Boston *ConMus 11*
Goudvis, Bertha 1876-1966 *BlmGWL*
Goudy, Andrew James 1943- *WhoBlA 94*
Goudy, James Joseph Ralph 1952- *WhoFI 94, WhoMW 93, WhoScEn 94*
Goudy, Josephine Gray 1925- *WhoMW 93*
Gouesbet, Gerard 1947- *WhoScEn 94*
Gouge, Susan Cornelia Jones 1924- *WhoAm 94, WhoScEn 94*
Gouge-Gericke, Dory 1956- *WhoWest 94*
Gougelman, Paul Reina 1951- *WhoAmL 94*
Gougeon, Joel 1943- *WhoAmP 93*
Gougeon, Len (G.) 1947- *WrDr 94*
Gouges, Marie Gouze 1755-1793 *BlmGWL*
Gouges, Marie-Olympe de 1748-1793 *HisWorL*
Gough, Viscount 1941- *Who 94*
Gough, Barry Morton 1938- *IntWW 93*
Gough, Brandon *Who 94*
Gough, (Charles) Brandon 1937- *Who 94*
Gough, Carolyn Harley 1922- *WhoAm 94*
Gough, Cecil Ernest Freeman 1911- *Who 94*
Gough, Denis Ian 1922- *WhoAm 94*
Gough, Douglas Owen 1941- *Who 94*
Gough, Georgia Belle 1920- *WhoAmA 93*
Gough, Harrison Gould 1921- *WhoAm 94, WhoScEn 94, WhoWest 94*
Gough, Hugh Rowlands 1905- *IntWW 93, Who 94*
Gough, Janet 1940- *Who 94*
Gough, John d1968 *WhoHol 92*
Gough, John Francis 1934- *WhoAm 94, WhoAmL 94*
Gough, Kathleen 1925- *WhoAm 94*
Gough, Lloyd d1984 *WhoHol 92*
Gough, Michael 1917- *IntMPA 94, IntWW 93, WhoHol 92*
Gough, Michael John 1939- *WhoIns 94*
Gough, Pauline Bjerke 1935- *WhoAm 94*
Gough, Richard 1635-1723 *DcNaB MP*
Gough, Robert Alan 1931- *WhoAmA 93*
Gough, Walter C. 1943- *WhoBlA 94*
Gough, William (John) 1945- *WrDr 94*
Gough, William Cabot 1930- *WhoWest 94*
Gough-Calthorpe *Who 94*
Gougher, Ronald Lee 1939- *WhoFI 94*
Gougis, Lorna Gail 1948- *WhoBlA 94*
Gouhier, Henri Gaston 1898- *IntWW 93*
Gouilloud, Michel 1930- *WhoFI 94*
Gouin, Francis R. 1938- *WhoAm 94*
Gouin, Serge 1943- *WhoAm 94*
Gouin, Warner Peter 1954- *WhoMW 93, WhoScEn 94*
Gouke, Cecil Granville 1928- *WhoFI 94, WhoMW 93*
Goukouni Oueddei *IntWW 93*
Goulard, Guy Yvon 1940- *WhoAm 94*
Goulart, Ron(ald Joseph) 1933- *EncSF 93, WrDr 94*
Goulazian, Peter Robert 1939- *WhoAm 94*
Goulbourne, Donald Samuel, Jr. 1950- *WhoBlA 94*
Gould *Who 94*
Gould, Alan *EncSF 93*
Gould, Alan d1980 *WhoHol 92*
Gould, Alan Brant 1938- *WhoAm 94*
Gould, Alan I. 1940- *WhoAmL 94*
Gould, Alan J. d1993 *NewYTBS 93*
Gould, Allan (Mendel) 1944- *WrDr 94*
Gould, Alvin R. 1922- *WhoAm 94*
Gould, Arthur Irwin 1929- *WhoAm 94*
Gould, Bernard Albert 1912-1988 *WhAm 10*
Gould, Billy d1950 *WhoHol 92*
Gould, Bruce Allan 1938- *WhoAm 94*
Gould, Bryan 1939- *WrDr 94*
Gould, Bryan Charles 1939- *IntWW 93, Who 94*
Gould, Cecil (Hilton Monk) 1918- *WrDr 94*
Gould, Cecil Hilton Monk 1918- *Who 94*
Gould, Celia R. 1957- *WhoAmP 93*
Gould, Charles F. 1932- *WhoAmP 93*
Gould, Charles Perry 1909- *WhoAm 94*
Gould, Clio LaVerne 1919- *WhoWest 94*
Gould, David 1940- *WhoAm 94*
Gould, David John 1949- *Who 94*
Gould, Donald (William) 1919- *Who 94*
Gould, Donald Everett 1932- *WhoAm 94, WhoFI 94, WhoScEn 94*
Gould, Donald Paul 1958- *WhoWest 94*
Gould, Dorothy *WhoHol 92*
Gould, Edward John Humphrey 1943- *Who 94*
Gould, Edwin Sheldon 1926- *WhoAm 94*
Gould, Elliott 1938- *IntMPA 94, IntWW 93, WhoAm 94, WhoHol 92*
Gould, F(rancis) Carruthers 1844-1925 *EncSF 93*
Gould, F(rederick) J(ames) 1855-1938 *EncSF 93*
Gould, Frank William 1937- *Who 94*
Gould, Gail Ruth *Who 94*
Gould, Gary Howard 1938- *WhoAmP 93*
Gould, Geraldine Jimenez 1943- *WhoHisp 94*
Gould, Glenn Hunting 1949- *WhoFI 94*
Gould, Gordon 1920- *WhoAm 94, WhoScEn 94, WorInv*
Gould, Gypsy d1966 *WhoHol 92*
Gould, Harold 1923- *IntMPA 94, WhoAm 94, WhoHol 92*
Gould, Harry Edward, Jr. 1938- *WhoAm 94, WhoFI 94*
Gould, Herbert J. 1927- *WhoWest 94*
Gould, Howard d1938 *WhoHol 92*
Gould, Irving 1919- *WhoFI 94*
Gould, Jack 1914-1993 *NewYTBS 93 [port]*
Gould, Jack Lee d1977 *WhoHol 92*
Gould, James A. 1922- *WrDr 94*
Gould, James L. 1945- *WrDr 94*
Gould, James Spencer 1922- *WhoAm 94, WhoFI 94*
Gould, Jason 1966- *WhoHol 92*
Gould, Jay Martin 1915- *WhoAm 94*
Gould, Jean d1993 *NewYTBS 93*
Gould, Jean R(osalind) 1909-1993 *ConAu 142, SmATA 77*
Gould, John Charles d1993 *Who 94N*
Gould, John Howard 1929- *WhoAmA 93*
Gould, John Philip, Jr. 1939- *WhoAm 94, WhoFI 94, WhoMW 93*
Gould, John Wiley 1939- *WhoAm 94, WhoAmL 94*
Gould, Joseph d1993 *IntMPA 94N, NewYTBS 93*
Gould, Judith 1945- *WrDr 94*
Gould, Judith 1952- *WrDr 94*
Gould, Karen Keel 1946- *WhoAmA 93*
Gould, Kenneth B. 1955- *WhoAmL 94*
Gould, Kenneth Lance 1938- *WhoAm 94*
Gould, Lawrence McKinley 1896- *WhAm 10*
Gould, Lewis Jerome 1932- *WhoAmL 94*
Gould, Lewis Ludlow 1939- *WhoAm 94*
Gould, Lois *DrAPF 93, WrDr 94*
Gould, Loyal Norman 1927- *WhoAm 94*
Gould, Marilyn 1928- *SmATA 76 [port]*
Gould, Martha B. 1931- *WhoAm 94, WhoWest 94*
Gould, Michael Alan 1954- *WhoAmL 94*
Gould, Michael Lee 1949- *WhoMW 93*
Gould, Milton Samuel 1909- *WhoAm 94*
Gould, Morton 1913- *IntWW 93, WhoAm 94, WhoHol 92*
Gould, Nathaniel 1661-1728 *DcNaB MP*
Gould, Paston d1783 *WhAmRev*
Gould, Patricia 1924- *Who 94*
Gould, Peter (Robin) 1932- *WrDr 94*
Gould, Peter Robin 1932- *WhoAm 94*
Gould, Philip 1922- *WhoAmA 93*
Gould, Phillip L. 1937- *WhoAm 94, WhoMW 93, WhoScEn 94*
Gould, R. Budd 1937- *WhoAmP 93*
Gould, Richard A. *WhoAmP 93*
Gould, Richard Allan 1939- *WhoAm 94*
Gould, Robert 1935- *Who 94*
Gould, Robert R. *WhoAmP 93*
Gould, Roberta *DrAPF 93*
Gould, Ronald 1945- *WhoAmL 94*
Gould, Roy Walter 1927- *WhoAm 94*
Gould, Sandra *WhoHol 92*
Gould, Sid *WhoHol 92*
Gould, Stefanie Caryn 1969- *WhoMW 93*
Gould, Stephen 1909- *WhoAmA 93*
Gould, Stephen Jay *NewYTBS 93 [port]*
Gould, Stephen Jay 1941- *IntWW 93, WhoAm 94, WrDr 94*
Gould, Steven (Charles) 1955- *ConAu 140*
Gould, Syd S. 1912- *WhoFI 94*
Gould, Terry Allen 1942- *WhoAmL 94*
Gould, Thomas William 1914- *Who 94*
Gould, Warren Howard 1946- *WhoAmL 94*
Gould, Wesley Larson 1917- *WhoAm 94*
Gould, William d1960 *WhoHol 92*
Gould, William B(enjamin, IV) 1936- *WrDr 94*
Gould, William Benjamin, IV 1936- *WhoBlA 94*
Gould, William Drum 1897- *WhAm 10*
Gould, William F. 1939- *WhoIns 94*
Goulden, (Peter) John 1941- *Who 94*
Goulden, Joseph C 1934- *WrDr 94*

Goulden, Joseph Chesley 1934- WhoAm 94
Goulder, Gerald Polster 1953- WhoFI 94
Gouldey, Glenn Charles 1952- WhoFI 94, WhoMW 93
Goulding, Alf d1972 WhoHol 92
Goulding, Edmund d1959 WhoHol 92
Goulding, (Ernest) Irvine 1910- Who 94
Goulding, Ivis d1973 WhoHol 92
Goulding, Lingard Who 94
Goulding, (William) Lingard (Walter) 1940- Who 94
Goulding, Marrack Irvine 1936- IntWW 93, Who 94
Goulding, Merrill Keith 1933- WhoScEn 94
Goulding, Nora 1944- WhoAm 94
Goulding, Paul Edmund 1934- WhoAmP 93
Goulding, Ray d1990 WhoHol 92
Goulding, Raymond Walter 1922-1990 WhAm 10
Gould-Kardell, Maxine Lubow 1942- WhoFI 94, WhoWest 94
Gould Of Potternewton, Baroness 1932- Who 94
Gould-Porter, Arthur E. d1987 WhoHol 92
Goulds, Peter J. 1948- WhoAmA 93
Gouldthorpe, Kenneth Alfred Percival 1928- WhoAm 94, WhoWest 94
Gouled Aptidon, Hassan 1916- IntWW 93
Goulet, Charles Ryan 1927- WhoAm 94
Goulet, Claude 1925- WhoAmA 93
Goulet, Cynthia Wagner 1957- WhoAmL 94
Goulet, Denis Andre 1931- WhoAm 94
Goulet, Harvey E., Jr. 1941- WhoAmP 93
Goulet, John DrAPF 93
Goulet, Kevin 1963- WhoMW 93
Goulet, Lorrie 1925- WhoAm 94, WhoAmA 93
Goulet, Maurice 1932- WhoAmP 93
Goulet, Robert NewYTBS 93 [port]
Goulet, Robert 1933- IntMPA 94, WhoHol 92
Goulet, Robert Gerard 1933- WhoAm 94
Goulet, William Dawson 1941- WhoAm 94, WhoWest 94
Goulian, Mehran 1929- IntWW 93
Goulianos, Konstantin 1935- WhoAm 94, WhoScEn 94
Goulstone, (Thomas Richard) Kerry 1936- Who 94
Goulter, Barbara ConAu 141
Goulty, Alan Fletcher 1947- Who 94
Gouma-Peterson, Thalia 1933- ConAu 140, WhoAmA 93
Gounaris, Anne Demetra 1924- WhoAm 94
Gounaris, Elias 1941- Who 94
Gounelle De Pontanel, Hugues 1903- IntWW 93
Gounley, Dennis Joseph 1950- WhoAmL 94
Gounod, Charles-Francois 1818-1893 NewGrDO
Goupil, Jeanne WhoHol 92
Goupy, Jacques Louis 1934- WhoScEn 94
Goupy, Joseph 1689-1768 NewGrDO
Gourad Hamadou, Barkad IntWW 93
Gouraige, Herve 1950- WhoAmL 94
Gouran, Dennis Stephen 1941- WhoAm 94
Gouras, Peter 1930- WhoAm 94
Gourdeau, Raymond H. 1936- WhoAmP 93
Gourdie, Tom 1913- WrDr 94
Gourdin, Edward Orval (Ned) 1897-1966 AfrAmG
Gourdine, Delcie Southall DrAPF 93
Gourdine, Meredith Charles 1929- WorInv
Gourdine, Simon Peter 1940- WhoAm 94, WhoBlA 94
Gourdon, Alain 1928- IntWW 93
Gourevitch, Jacqueline 1933- WhoAmA 93
Gourevitch, Peter Alexis 1943- WhoAm 94
Gourevitch, Victor 1925- WhoAm 94
Gouri, Haim ConWorW 93
Gourisse, Daniel 1939- IntWW 93
Gourlay, David 1922- WrDr 94
Gourlay, Ian Who 94
Gourlay, (Basil) Ian (Spencer) 1920- Who 94
Gourlay, Janet Who 94
Gourlay, Simon (Alexander) 1934- Who 94
Gourley, Dick R. 1944- WhoAm 94
Gourley, James Leland 1919- WhoAm 94
Gourley, James Walter, III 1941- WhoFI 94
Gourley, Meryl d1981 WhoHol 92
Gourley, Paul Lee 1952- WhoScEn 94
Gourley, Ronald Robert 1919- WhoAm 94
Gournay, Marie de Jars 1565?-1645 BlmGWL
Gournay, Marie-Fanny 1926- WhoWomW 91
Gourvitz, Elliot Howard 1945- WhoAmL 94
Gouse, S. William, Jr. 1931- WhoAm 94, WhoAmP 93
Gousha, Richard Paul 1923- WhoAm 94
Gouskos, John Theodore 1949- WhoMW 93
Goutard, Noel 1931- IntWW 93
Gouterman, Martin Paul 1931- WhoAm 94
Goutman, Dolya 1918- WhoAmA 93
Gouvion, Jean Baptiste 1747-1792 WhAmRev
Gouw, Cynthia Gie-Kiok 1963- WhoAsA 94
Gouwens, Dale Roger 1953- WhoMW 93
Gouyon, Paul 1910- IntWW 93
Gouyon, Paul Cardinal 1910- WhoAm 94
Gouyou Beauchamps, Xavier 1937- IntWW 93
Govan, Francis Hawks 1916- WhoAmA 93
Govan, Gladys Vernita Mosley 1918- WhoWest 94
Govan, Jerry N., Jr. WhoAmP 93
Govan, Lawrence (Herbert) 1919- Who 94
Govan, Reginald C. 1953- WhoBlA 94
Govan, Reginald Charles 1953- WhoAmL 94
Govan, Ronald M. 1931- WhoBlA 94
Govan, Sandra Yvonne 1948- WhoBlA 94
Gove, Gilbert English 1932- WhoAm 94, WhoAmL 94
Gove, Philip Babcock 1902- EncSF 93
Gove, Samuel Kimball 1923- WhoAm 94
Gover, Alan Shore 1948- WhoAm 94, WhoAmL 94
Gover, James Edwin 1940- WhoAm 94
Gover, Mildred d1947 WhoHol 92
Gover, Raymond Lewis 1927- WhoAm 94
Gover, (John) Robert 1929- WrDr 94
Govett, William John Romaine 1937- Who 94
Govi, O. 1929- WrDr 94
Govier, George Wheeler 1917- WhoScEn 94
Govier, Katherine 1948- BlmGWL
Govier, William Charles 1936- WhoAm 94
Govil, Narendra Kumar 1940- WhoAsA 94
Govindarajulu, Zakkula 1933- WhoAsA 94
Govindjee 1933- WhoAm 94, WhoAsA 94, WhoMW 93, WhoScEn 94
Gow, Andrew Sydenham Farrar 1886-1978 DcNaB MP
Gow, Haven Bradford 1950- WhoAsA 94
Gow, Jack Frank 1920- WhoFI 94
Gow, Jane (Elizabeth) 1944- Who 94
Gow, John Stobie 1933- Who 94
Gow, Leonard Maxwell H. Who 94
Gow, Linda Yvonne Cherwin 1948- WhoFI 94
Gow, Michael Who 94
Gow, Michael 1955- ConDr 93
Gow, (James) Michael 1924- IntWW 93, Who 94
Gow, Neil 1932- Who 94
Gow, Ronald d1993 NewYTBS 93
Gow, Ronald 1897-1993 ConAu 141, ConDr 93, WrDr 94N
Gow, Wendy Who 94
Gow, William Connell 1909- Who 94
Gowan, James 1925- IntWW 93
Gowan, Joseph Patrick, Jr. 1939- WhoFI 94
Gowans, Alan 1923- WhoAmA 93, WrDr 94
Gowans, Gregory Who 94
Gowans, (Urban) Gregory 1904- Who 94
Gowans, James (Learmonth) 1924- Who 94
Gowans, James Learmonth 1924- IntWW 93
Gowans, James Palmer 1930- Who 94
Gowans, James R. 1929- WhoAmP 93
Gowans, William Rory, Mrs. WhAm 10
Gowar, Norman William 1940- Who 94
Goward, Mary Anne 1805-1899 NewGrDO
Goward, Russell 1935- WhoAmP 93
Goward, Russell A. 1935- WhoBlA 94
Gowda, Deve Javare 1918- Who 94
Gowda, Narasimhan Ramaiah 1949- WhoFI 94
Gowdy, Curt WhoHol 92
Gowdy, Curt 1919- IntMPA 94
Gowdy, Curtis 1919- WhoAm 94
Gowdy, David Clive 1946- Who 94
Gowdy, Franklin Brockway 1945- WhoAm 94
Gowdy, Miriam Betts 1928- WhoAm 94
Gowdy, Peter David 1963- WhoWest 94
Gowdy, Robert C. 1943- WhoIns 94
Gowen, George W. 1929- WhoAmL 94
Gowen, Nancy Adele 1934- WhoMW 93
Gowen, Richard Joseph 1935- WhoAm 94, WhoFI 94, WhoScEn 94
Gowenlock, Brian Glover 1926- Who 94
Gowens, Walter, II 1954- WhoFI 94
Gower Who 94
Gower, Bob G. 1937- WhoAm 94, WhoFI 94
Gower, David Ivon 1957- IntWW 93
Gower, Dortha Sue 1936- WhoMW 93
Gower, Godfrey Philip d1992 Who 94N
Gower, Harold Edward 1940- WhoFI 94
Gower, Iris 1939- WrDr 94
Gower, Jim Who 94
Gower, John 1330?-1408 BlmGEL
Gower, John Clark 1941- WhoAmP 93
Gower, John Hugh 1925- Who 94
Gower, Laurence Cecil Bartlett 1913- Who 94
Gower, Thomas Charles 1926- WhoAmP 93
Gower Isaac, Anthony John Who 94
Gowetz, Irene 1907-1988 WhAm 10
Gowing, Delmer Charles, III 1943- WhoAm 94, WhoAmL 94
Gowing, Lawrence (Burnett), Sir 1918-1991 WrDr 94N
Gowing, Margaret Mary 1921- Who 94, WrDr 94
Gowing, Noel Frank Collett 1917- Who 94
Gowland, Gibson d1951 WhoHol 92
Gowland, John Stafford 1898- EncSF 93
Gowland, Mary Lee DrAPF 93
Gowlland, (George) Mark 1943- Who 94
Gowon, Yakubu 1934- IntWW 93, Who 94
Gowrie, Earl of 1939- Who 94
Gowrie, Alexander Patrick Greysteil Hore-Ruthven, Rt. Hon. The Earl of 1939- IntWW 93
Goy, David John Lister 1949- Who 94
Goya, Mona d1961 WhoHol 92
Goya, Tito d1985 WhoHol 92
Goyal, Megh R. 1949- WhoAsA 94
Goyal, Raj Kumar 1937- WhoAm 94
Goyal, Ramesh Kumar 1948- WhoMW 93
Goyal, Suresh 1960- WhoAsA 94
Goyan, Michael Donovan 1938- WhoAm 94
Goyco, Rafael WhoHisp 94
Goycochea, Sergio 1963- WorESoc
Goyco-Graziani, Ana Nisi WhoAmP 93
Goyder, Daniel George 1938- Who 94
Goyder, George Armin 1908- Who 94, WrDr 94
Goyemido, Genevieve WhoWomW 91
Goyer, Jean-Pierre 1932- IntWW 93
Goyer, Robert Andrew 1927- WhoAm 94
Goyer, Robert Stanton 1923- WhoAm 94
Goyer, Virginia L. 1942- WhoFI 94
Goyette, Geoffrey Robert 1948- WhoFI 94, WhoMW 93
Goyle, Rajinder Kumar 1945- WhoScEn 94
Goyne, Roderick A. 1949- WhoAm 94, WhoAmL 94
Goytisolo (Gay), Luis 1935- ConWorW 93
Goytisolo, Agustin de 1924- WhoHisp 94
Goytisolo, Jose Agustin 1928- DcLB 134 [port]
Goytisolo, Juan 1931- ConWorW 93, HispLC [port]
Goz, Harry WhoHol 92
Goza, Franklin William 1955- WhoMW 93
Gozani, Tsahi 1934- WhoAm 94, WhoScEn 94, WhoWest 94
Gozenpud, Abram Akimovich 1908- NewGrDO
Gozney, Richard Hugh Turton 1951- Who 94
Gozon, Jozsef Stephan 1933- WhoAm 94, WhoMW 93
Gozon, Richard C. 1938- WhoAm 94, WhoFI 94
Gozonsky, Edwin S. 1930- WhoFI 94
Gozum, Marvin Enriquez 1960- WhoScEn 94
Gozzi, Carlo 1720-1806 IntDcT 2 [port], NewGrDO
Gozzi, Patricia 1950- WhoHol 92
Graaf, Regnier de 1641-1673 WorScD
Graaff, de Villiers 1913- IntWW 93, Who 94
Graaff, Johannes de WhAmRev
Graarud, Gunnar 1886-1960 NewGrDO
Graba, Jayson L. WhoAmP 93
Grabach, John R. 1880-1981 WhoAmA 93N
Grabar, Oleg 1929- WhoAm 94
Grabarklewics Miroslawa, Kasimiera WhoWomW 91
Grabarz, Donald Francis 1941- WhoWest 94
Grabarz, Joseph S., Jr. 1956- WhoAmP 93
Grabau, Charles M. 1948- WhoHisp 94
Grabau, Larry J. 1954- WhoAm 94
Grabbe, Christian Dietrich 1801-1836 DcLB 133 [port], IntDcT 2
Grabe, William O. 1938- WhoFI 94
Grabeel, Nancy G. 1957- WhoAmP 93
Grabel, Susan 1942- WhoAmA 93
Grabemann, Karl W. 1929- WhoAm 94
Graber, Ben 1948- WhoAmP 93
Graber, Doris Appel 1923- WhoAm 94
Graber, Edward Alex 1914- WhoAm 94
Graber, Harris David 1939- WhoFI 94
Graber, Pierre 1908- IntWW 93
Graber, Robert Bates 1950- WhoMW 93
Graber, Steve Laszlo 1960- WhoMW 93
Graber, Steven Wayne 1950- WhoAmL 94
Graber, Susan P. 1949- WhoAm 94, WhoAmL 94, WhoAmP 93, WhoWest 94
Graber, Thomas M. 1917- WhoAm 94
Graber, Vincent James 1931- WhoAmP 93
Graber, William Raymond 1943- WhoFI 94
Grabewska, Danuba WhoWomW 91
Grabham, Anthony (Herbert) 1930- Who 94
Grabiel, Julio 1946- WhoHisp 94
Grabien, Deborah EncSF 93
Grabill, Jim DrAPF 93
Grabill, Paul E. DrAPF 93
Grabiner, Anthony Stephen 1945- Who 94
Grabinski, Carol Joanne 1941- WhoMW 93
Grable, Betty d1973 WhoHol 92
Grable, Edward E. 1926- WhoAm 94
Grable, Reginald Harold 1917- WhoMW 93
Grabley, Ursula d1977 WhoHol 92
Grabner, George John 1918- WhoAm 94
Grabo, Anders P. 1950- WhoIns 94
Graboski, Thomas Walter 1947- WhoAm 94
Grabosky, Terri Jo 1949- WhoMW 93
Grabow, Raymond John 1932- WhoAmL 94
Grabow, Stephen Harris 1943- WhoAm 94
Grabowski, Chester Adam 1946- WhoAm 94
Grabowski, Elizabeth 1940- WhoFI 94
Grabowski, Janice Lynn 1948- WhoMW 93
Grabowski, Michael Joseph 1961- WhoMW 93
Grabowski, Norman WhoHol 92
Grabowski, Richard W. 1951- WhoIns 94
Grabowski, Roger J. 1947- WhoAm 94
Grabowski, Sandra Reynolds 1943- WhoMW 93
Grabowsky, Craig 1957- WhoScEn 94
Graboys, George 1932- WhoAm 94
Grabscheld, William Henry 1931- WhoFI 94
Grabske, William John 1943- WhoAm 94
Graburn, Nelson Hayes Henry 1936- WhoAm 94
Grace, Augusto F. WhoAmP 93
Grace, Brian Guiles 1942- WhoAmL 94
Grace, Carol c. 1921- WhoHol 92
Grace, Charles Brown, Jr. 1934- WhoAm 94
Grace, Charles Emmanuel 1881-1960 DcAmReB 2
Grace, Colleen 1951- WhoAmL 94
Grace, David Joseph 1946- WhoAmL 94
Grace, Dick d1965 WhoHol 92
Grace, Dixie Lee 1948- WhoMW 93
Grace, Eugene G. 1876-1960 EncABHB 9 [port]
Grace, George DrAPF 93
Grace, George William 1921- WhoScEn 94
Grace, H. David 1936- WhoAm 94
Grace, Helen Kennedy 1935- WhoAm 94
Grace, Horace R. 1943- WhoBlA 94
Grace, J. Peter 1913- IntWW 93, WhoAm 94, WhoFI 94
Grace, James Martin 1943- WhoAm 94
Grace, Jason Roy 1936- WhoAm 94
Grace, John Eugene 1931- WhoAm 94
Grace, John Kenneth 1945- WhoAm 94
Grace, John Ross 1943- WhoAm 94
Grace, John Wiliam 1927- WhoAm 94
Grace, John William 1921- WhoWest 94
Grace, Julianne Alice 1937- WhoAm 94
Grace, Marcellus 1947- WhoBlA 94
Grace, Marcia Bell 1937- WhoAm 94
Grace, Mark Eugene 1964- WhoAm 94, WhoMW 93
Grace, Michael Judd 1957- WhoScEn 94
Grace, Nickolas 1949- WhoHol 92
Grace, Oliver Russell 1909-1992 WhAm 10
Grace, Patricia 1937- BlmGWL
Grace, Patricia (Frances) 1937- RfGShF, WrDr 94
Grace, Richard Anthony 1944- WhoFI 94
Grace, Richard Edward 1930- WhoAm 94, WhoMW 93
Grace, Robert Charles 1957- WhoMW 93
Grace, Robert M., Jr. 1947- WhoAmL 94
Grace, Sue WhoAmP 93
Grace, Sweet Daddy 1881-1960 AfrAmAl 6
Grace, Thomas Paul 1946- WhoAm 94
Gracey, Douglas Robert 1936- WhoAm 94
Gracey, Howard 1935- Who 94
Gracey, James Steele 1927- WhoAm 94
Gracey, John Halliday 1925- Who 94
Gracey, Robert William 1941- WhoFI 94

Grant, William A., Jr. 1937- *WhoAm 94, WhoFI 94*
Grant, William Bruce 1953- *WhoFI 94*
Grant, William Downing 1917- *WhoAm 94*
Grant, William Frederick 1924- *WhoAm 94*
Grant, William Packer, Jr. 1942- *WhoFI 94*
Grant, William Robert 1925- *WhoAm 94*
Grant, William W. 1934- *WhoBlA 94*
Grant, William West, III 1932- *WhoAm 94, WhoWest 94*
Grant, Wilmer, Jr. 1940- *WhoBlA 94*
Grant-Adamson, Lesley (Heycock) 1942- *WrDr 94*
Grantchester, Baron 1921- *Who 94*
Granter, Sharon Savoy 1940- *WhoMW 93*
Grant-Ferris *Who 94*
Grantham, Bishop Suffragan of 1942- *Who 94*
Grantham, Charles *WhoBlA 94*
Grantham, Charles Edward 1950- *WhoScEn 94*
Grantham, Dewey Wesley 1921- *WhoAm 94*
Grantham, George Leighton 1920- *WhoAm 94*
Grantham, Jared James 1936- *WhoScEn 94*
Grantham, Joseph Michael, Jr. 1947- *WhoFI 94*
Grantham, Pamela Maas 1962- *WhoAmL 94, WhoMW 93*
Grantham, Richard Robert 1927- *WhoAm 94*
Grantham, Roy Aubrey 1926- *Who 94*
Grantley, Baron 1923- *Who 94*
Grantley, Robert Clark 1948- *WhoBlA 94*
Grant of Dalvey, Patrick Alexander Benedict 1953- *Who 94*
Grant of Monymusk, Archibald 1954- *Who 94*
Grants, Valdis 1942- *WhoFI 94, WhoMW 93*
Grant-Suttie, (George) Philip *Who 94*
Granville *Who 94*
Granville, Earl 1918- *Who 94*
Granville, Audrey d1972 *WhoHol 92*
Granville, Austyn *EncSF 93*
Granville(-)Barker, Harley 1877-1946 *IntDcT 2 [port]*
Granville, Bernard d1936 *WhoHol 92*
Granville, Bonita d1988 *WhoHol 92*
Granville, Charlotte d1942 *WhoHol 92*
Granville, Joan d1974 *WhoHol 92*
Granville, Keith 1910-1990 *WhAm 10*
Granville, Louise d1968 *WhoHol 92*
Granville, Sydney d1959 *WhoHol 92*
Granville, Taylor d1923 *WhoHol 92*
Granville, William, Jr. 1940- *WhoBlA 94*
Granville Barker, Harley 1877-1946 *BlmGEL*
Granville Of Eye, Baron 1899- *Who 94*
Granville Slack, George *Who 94*
Granz, Marianne 1942- *WhoWomW 91*
Granzow, Paul H. 1927- *WhoAm 94, WhoFI 94*
Grape, Oliver *ConAu 43NR*
Grapes, Jack *DrAPF 93*
Grapewin, Charles d1956 *WhoHol 92*
Grapin, Jacqueline G. 1942- *WhoAm 94*
Grapner-Mitchell, Pamela Kay 1946- *WhoMW 93*
Grappelli, Stephane 1908- *ConMus 10 [port], IntWW 93, Who 94, WhoAm 94*
Grapski, Ladd Raymond 1942- *WhoAm 94*
Graser, Merle Lawrence 1929- *WhoAm 94*
Grasgreen, Martin 1925- *IntMPA 94*
Grashof, August Edward 1932- *WhoAm 94*
Grashow, James Bruce 1942- *WhoAmA 93*
Grasmick, Nancy S. *WhoAm 94*
Grass, Alan Brian 1942- *WhoAmL 94*
Grass, Alexander 1927- *WhoAm 94, WhoFI 94*
Grass, George Mitchell, IV 1957- *WhoWest 94*
Grass, Gunter 1927- *IntWW 93*
Grass, Gunter (Wilhelm) 1927- *ConWorW 93, IntDcT 2*
Grass, Gunter Wilhelm 1927- *Who 94*
Grass, Judith Ellen 1953- *WhoScEn 94*
Grass, Patty Patterson *WhoAmA 93*
Grassby, Bertram d1953 *WhoHol 92*
Grasse, Francois-Joseph-Paul 1722-1788 *AmRev*
Grasse, Francois Joseph Paul, Comte de 1722-1788 *WhAmRev [port]*
Grasse, John M., Jr. 1927- *WhoScEn 94*
Grasselle, Harry Otto d1979 *WhoHol 92*
Grasselli, Jeanette Gecsy 1928- *WhoAm 94, WhoScEn 94*
Grasselli, Robert Karl 1930- *WhoAm 94*
Grasser, George Robert 1939- *WhoAm 94*
Grasshoff, Alex *WhoAm 94*
Grasshoff, Alex 1930- *IntMPA 94*
Grassi, Cecilia c. 1740-c. 1782 *NewGrDO*
Grassi, Ellen Elizabeth 1949- *WhoFI 94*
Grassi, James Edward 1943- *WhoWest 94*
Grassi, Joseph A(ugustus) 1922- *ConAu 41NR*
Grassi, Joseph F. 1949- *WhoAmL 94*
Grassi, Marco 1934- *WhoAmA 93*
Grassia, Thomas Charles 1946- *WhoAmL 94*
Grassian, Vicki Helene 1959- *WhoScEn 94*
Grassie, Charles Wesley, Jr. 1952- *WhoAmP 93*
Grassini, Josephina (Maria Camilla) 1773-1850 *NewGrDO*
Grassle, Karen 1944- *WhoHol 92*
Grassley, Charles E. 1933- *CngDr 93, IntWW 93, WhoAmP 93*
Grassley, Charles Ernest 1933- *WhoAm 94, WhoMW 93*
Grassmuck, George Ludwig 1919- *WhoAm 94*
Grasso, Doris (Ten-Eyck) 1914- *WhoAmA 93*
Grasso, Giovanni d1930 *WhoHol 92*
Grasso, Jack 1927- *WhoAmA 93*
Grasso, Mary Ann 1952- *IntMPA 94, WhoAm 94, WhoWest 94*
Grasso, Patricia Gaetana 1940- *WhoScEn 94*
Grasso, Richard A. *WhoAm 94, WhoFI 94*
Grasso, Salvatore Fortunato 1945- *WhoAmA 93*
Grasz, Leonard Steven 1961- *WhoAmL 94*
Gratacap, Louis Pope 1851-1917 *EncSF 93*
Gratch, Serge 1921- *WhoAm 94, WhoScEn 94*
Grate, Isaac, Jr. 1952- *WhoBlA 94*
Grathwohl, Susan Maria *DrAPF 93*
Gratias, Arthur Louis 1920- *WhoAmP 93*
Graton, Milton Stanley 1908- *WhoFI 94*
Grattan, Donald Henry 1926- *Who 94*
Grattan, Henry 1746-1820 *HisWorL [port]*
Grattan, Patricia Elizabeth 1944- *WhoAm 94*
Grattan-Bellew, Henry Charles 1933- *Who 94*
Grattan-Cooper, Sidney 1911- *Who 94*
Grattet, Paul Maurice 1936- *WhoWest 94*
Gratton, Patrick John Francis 1933- *WhoFI 94*
Gratus, Jack 1935- *WrDr 94*
Gratwick, John 1918- *Who 94*
Gratwick, John 1923- *WhoAm 94*
Gratwick, Stephen 1924- *Who 94*
Gratz, Barnard 1738-1811 *WhAmRev*
Gratz, Leopold 1929- *IntWW 93*
Gratz, Michael 1740-1811 *WhAmRev*
Gratz, Pauline 1924- *WhoAm 94*
Gratz, Rebecca 1781-1869 *DcAmReB 2*
Gratz, W. W. *WhoAmP 93*
Gratzek, Michael Henry 1950- *WhoMW 93*
Gratzer, George Andrew 1936- *WhoAm 94*
Gratzios, Agamemnon 1922- *IntWW 93*
Grau, Frederick Vahlcamp 1902-1990 *WhAm 10*
Grau, John Michael 1952- *WhoAm 94*
Grau, Juan *WhoHisp 94*
Grau, Marcy Beinish 1950- *WhoFI 94*
Grau, Maurice 1849-1907 *NewGrDO*
Grau, Raphael Anthony 1963- *WhoScEn 94*
Grau, Shirley Ann *DrAPF 93*
Grau, Shirley Ann 1929- *BlmGWL, WhoAm 94, WrDr 94*
Grau, Thomas Paul 1960- *WhoMW 93*
Graubard, Ann Wolfe *WhoAmA 93*
Graubard, Mark 1904-1992 *WrDr 94N*
Graubard, Seymour 1911- *WhoAm 94*
Graubard, Stephen Richards 1924- *WhoAm 94*
Graubart, Jeffrey Lowell 1940- *WhoWest 94*
Graue, Louis Geoffrey 1951- *WhoWest 94*
Grauer, Ben d1977 *WhoHol 92*
Grauer, Douglas Dale 1956- *WhoMW 93*
Grauer, Gladys 1923- *WhoAmA 93*
Grauer, Manfred 1945- *WhoScEn 94*
Grauer, Sherry 1939- *WhoAmA 93*
Grauer, Stuart Robert 1950- *WhoWest 94*
Grauert, Johannes 1930- *IntWW 93*
Graule, Raymond Siegfried 1932- *WhoScEn 94*
Graulty, Reynaldo 1948- *WhoAmP 93*
Grauman, Sid d1950 *WhoHol 92*
Graumann, Karl d1948 *WhoHol 92*
Graun, Carl Heinrich 1703?-1759 *NewGrDO*
Graupe, Daniel 1934- *WhoAm 94*
Graupe-Pillard, Grace *WhoAmA 93*
Graupner, (Johann) Christoph 1683-1760 *NewGrDO*
Grausam, Jeffrey Leonard 1943- *WhoAm 94, WhoAmL 94*
Grausman, Philip 1935- *WhoAmA 93*
Grautoff, Ferdinand Heinrich 1871-1935 *EncSF 93*
Gravatt, Eugene Michael 1952- *WhoFI 94*
Grave, Walter Wyatt 1901- *IntWW 93, Who 94*
Gravel, Camille F., Jr. 1915- *WhoAmP 93*
Gravel, Geary 1951- *EncSF 93*
Gravel, Mike 1930- *IntWW 93, WhoAmP 93*
Gravel, Tina Marie 1960- *WhoFI 94*
Gravelle, James Francis 1943- *WhoAmL 94*
Gravelle, Karen 1942- *WrDr 94*
Gravelle, Pierre 1941- *WhoAm 94*
Gravely, Jane Candace 1952- *WhoScEn 94*
Gravely, Melvin J. 1940- *WhoBlA 94*
Gravely, Samuel L., Jr. 1922- *AfrAmAl 6, ConBlB 5 [port], WhoBlA 94*
Gravely, Samuel Lee 1922- *AfrAmG [port]*
Gravenberg, Eric Von 1950- *WhoBlA 94*
Gravenstein, Joachim Stefan 1925- *WhoAm 94*
Graver, Elizabeth 1964- *WrDr 94*
Graver, Jack Edward 1935- *WhoAm 94, WhoScEn 94*
Graver, Lawrence Stanley 1931- *WhoAm 94, WrDr 94*
Gravers, Steve d1978 *WhoHol 92*
Graves, Baron 1911- *Who 94*
Graves, Allene 1952- *WhoBlA 94*
Graves, Anna Marie 1959- *WhoAmL 94*
Graves, Austin Taylor 1908-1991 *WhAm 10*
Graves, Benjamin Barnes 1920- *WhoAm 94*
Graves, Benjamin Kelly, Jr. 1955- *WhoFI 94*
Graves, Bradford 1939- *WhoAmA 93*
Graves, C(harles) L(arcom) *EncSF 93*
Graves, Carol Kenney 1937- *WhoFI 94, WhoMW 93*
Graves, Carole A. 1938- *WhoBlA 94*
Graves, Charles E. 1931- *WhoAmP 93*
Graves, Clifford W. 1939- *WhoBlA 94*
Graves, Cody L. 1960- *WhoAmP 93*
Graves, Curtis M. 1938- *WhoBlA 94*
Graves, Douglas Bruce 1951- *WhoMW 93*
Graves, Earl G. 1935- *AfrAmAl 6 [port], WhoBlA 94*
Graves, Earl G., Jr. *WhoBlA 94*
Graves, Earl Gilbert 1935- *WhoAm 94, WhoFI 94*
Graves, Ernest d1983 *WhoHol 92*
Graves, Ernest, Jr. 1924- *WhoAm 94*
Graves, Forrest Wilson, Jr. 1945- *WhoMW 93*
Graves, Francis Porter, Jr. 1923- *WhoAmP 93*
Graves, Frank Xavier, Jr. *WhAm 10*
Graves, Fred Hill 1914- *WhoAm 94*
Graves, George d1949 *WhoHol 92*
Graves, Gerald William 1924- *WhoAmP 93*
Graves, H. Brice 1912- *WhoAm 94*
Graves, Harris Breiner 1928- *WhoMW 93, WhoScEn 94*
Graves, Howard Dwayne 1939- *WhoAm 94*
Graves, Irene Amelia 1906- *WhoBlA 94*
Graves, Jackie 1926- *WhoBlA 94*
Graves, James Francis 1951- *WhoMW 93*
Graves, James J. 1953- *WhoAm 94, WhoFI 94*
Graves, James Robinson 1820-1893 *DcAmReB 2*
Graves, Jerrell Loren *WhoMW 93*
Graves, Jerrod Franklin 1930- *WhoBlA 94*
Graves, Jesse d1949 *WhoHol 92*
Graves, Joan Page 1959- *WhoScEn 94*
Graves, John 1920- *WrDr 94*
Graves, John Clifford 1963- *WhoBlA 94*
Graves, John Fred, III 1945- *WhoScEn 94*
Graves, John W. d1978 *WhoAmA 93N*
Graves, Joseph Lewis, Jr. 1955- *WhoScEn 94, WhoWest 94*
Graves, Judson 1947- *WhoAm 94, WhoAmL 94*
Graves, Ka *WhoAmA 93*
Graves, Ka 1938- *WhoWest 94*
Graves, Kathryn d1977 *WhoHol 92*
Graves, Kenneth Robert 1942- *WhoAmA 93*
Graves, Lawrence Lester 1917- *WhoAm 94*
Graves, Lawrence Murray 1896- *WhAm 10*
Graves, Leon C. 1951- *WhoAmP 93*
Graves, Leslie Theresa 1956- *WhoBlA 94*
Graves, Linda Marie 1948- *WhoMW 93*
Graves, Lorraine Elizabeth 1957- *WhoAm 94*
Graves, Maitland 1902- *WhoAmA 93N*
Graves, Maureen Ann 1946- *WhoMW 93*
Graves, Michael 1934- *AmCulL, WhoAm 94, WhoAmA 93*
Graves, Michael A(rthur) R(oy) 1933- *WrDr 94*
Graves, Michael Leon, II 1970- *WhoScEn 94*
Graves, Morris 1910- *WhoAmA 93*
Graves, Morris Cole 1910- *WhoAm 94*
Graves, Nancy Stevenson *WhoAm 94*
Graves, Nancy Stevenson 1940- *WhoAmA 93*
Graves, Patrick Lee 1945- *WhoAmL 94*
Graves, Peter 1911- *IntMPA 94, WhoHol 92*
Graves, Peter 1926- *IntMPA 94, WhoAm 94, WhoHol 92*
Graves, Pirkko Maija-Leena 1930- *WhoAm 94*
Graves, Ralph d1977 *WhoHol 92*
Graves, Ray 1924- *WhoAm 94*
Graves, Ray Reynolds 1946- *WhoAm 94, WhoAmL 94, WhoBlA 94*
Graves, Raymond Lee 1928- *WhoBlA 94*
Graves, Robert 1895-1985 *BlmGEL*
Graves, Robert, Jr. d1954 *WhoHol 92*
Graves, Robert (Von Ranke) 1895-1985 *EncSF 93*
Graves, Robert Edward 1929- *WhoAmA 93*
Graves, Robert James 1957- *WhoMW 93*
Graves, Robert John 1945- *WhoScEn 94*
Graves, Robert Lawrence 1926- *WhoAm 94*
Graves, Roderick Lawrence 1959- *WhoBlA 94*
Graves, Roy Danner 1943- *WhoWest 94*
Graves, Roy Neil *DrAPF 93*
Graves, Rupert *WhoHol 92*
Graves, Rupert 1963- *IntMPA 94*
Graves, Ruth Parker 1934- *WhoAm 94*
Graves, Sam *WhoAmP 93*
Graves, Samuel 1713-1787 *AmRev, WhAmRev*
Graves, Sherman Teen 1905- *WhoBlA 94*
Graves, Stephen Matthew 1955- *WhoWest 94*
Graves, Teresa 1944- *WhoHol 92*
Graves, Thomas 1725-1802 *AmRev, WhAmRev*
Graves, Thomas Ashley, Jr. 1924- *WhoAm 94*
Graves, Thomas Browning 1932- *WhoFI 94*
Graves, Valerie *EncSF 93*
Graves, Valerie 1930- *WrDr 94*
Graves, Valerie Jo 1950- *WhoBlA 94*
Graves, Vashti Sylvia 1967- *WhoMW 93*
Graves, Wallace *DrAPF 93*
Graves, Wallace Billingsley 1922- *WhoAm 94*
Graves, Walter Albert 1920- *WhoAm 94*
Graves, William 1937- *WhoAmP 93*
Graves, William H(orace) 1898- *WhAm 10*
Graves, William P. E. 1926- *WhoAm 94*
Graves, William Preston 1953- *WhoAm 94, WhoAmP 93, WhoMW 93*
Gravet, Fernand d1970 *WhoHol 92*
Graveure, Louis 1888-1968 *NewGrDO*
Gravier, Charles *WhAmRev*
Gravina, Carla *WhoHol 92*
Gravina, Cesare 1858- *WhoHol 92*
Graving, Richard John 1929- *WhoAmL 94*
Grawemeyer, Joy 1934- *WhoMW 93*
Gray *Who 94*
Gray, Lord 1931- *Who 94*
Gray, Master of 1964- *Who 94*
Gray, Aisling Whitfield 1964- *WhoAmL 94*
Gray, Alasdair (James) 1934- *EncSF 93, WrDr 94*
Gray, Alasdair James 1934- *IntWW 93, Who 94*
Gray, Alexander d1975 *WhoHol 92*
Gray, Alexander Stuart 1905- *Who 94*
Gray, Alfred M. 1928- *IntWW 93*
Gray, Alfred Orren 1914- *WhoAm 94, WhoWest 94, WrDr 94*
Gray, Alice Wirth *DrAPF 93*
Gray, Allen Gibbs 1915- *WhoAm 94*
Gray, Alvin L. 1928- *WhoAm 94*
Gray, Andrew Aitken 1912- *Who 94*
Gray, Andrew Jackson 1924- *WhoBlA 94*
Gray, Angela 1915- *WrDr 94*
Gray, Anthony James 1936- *Who 94*
Gray, Anthony Rollin 1939- *WhoAm 94*
Gray, Archibald Duncan, Jr. 1938- *WhoAm 94*
Gray, Arnold d1936 *WhoHol 92*
Gray, Arnold L. 1954- *WhoAmL 94*
Gray, Arthur, Jr. fl. 1907- *EncNAR*
Gray, Arthur, Jr. 1922- *WhoAm 94*
Gray, Arvella 1906- *WhoHol 92*
Gray, Audrey Nesbitt 1920- *WhoMW 93*
Gray, Augustine Heard, Jr. 1936- *WhoAm 94*
Gray, Barbara E. *WhoAmP 93*
Gray, Barbara Jean 1926- *WhoAmP 93*
Gray, Barry Sherman 1916- *WhoAm 94*
Gray, Betty d1919 *WhoHol 92*

Gray, Billy d1978 *WhoHol 92*
Gray, Billy 1934- *WhoAmP 93*
Gray, Billy 1938- *WhoHol 92*
Gray, Billy Joe d1966 *WhoHol 92*
Gray, Brian Mark 1939- *WhoAmL 94*
Gray, Burl Bradley 1938- *WhoWest 94*
Gray, C. Boyden *WhoAmP 93*
Gray, C. Vernon 1939- *WhoBlA 94*
Gray, Carl Thomas 1943- *WhoMW 93*
Gray, Carlos Gibson 1937- *WhoMW 93*
Gray, Carol Coleman 1946- *WhoBlA 94*
Gray, Carol Hickson 1958- *WhoScEn 94*
Gray, Carol Joyce *WhoAm 94*
Gray, Carole 1940- *WhoHol 92*
Gray, Caroline 1930- *WrDr 94*
Gray, Charles 1928- *WhoHol 92*
Gray, Charles 1948- *WhoAmP 93*
Gray, Charles Agustus 1938- *WhoAm 94*
Gray, Charles Antony St. John 1942- *Who 94*
Gray, Charles Augustus 1928- *WhoFI 94*
Gray, Charles Buffum 1934- *WhoAm 94*
Gray, Charles Elmer 1919- *WhoAm 94*
Gray, Charles H. *WhoHol 92*
Gray, Charles Horace 1911- *Who 94*
Gray, Charles Ireland 1929- *Who 94*
Gray, Charles Jackson 1947- *WhoAm 94*
Gray, Charles Melvin 1944- *WhoMW 93*
Gray, Charles Robert 1952- *WhoAmL 94*
Gray, Christine 1922- *WhoBlA 94*
Gray, Christine Elaine 1964- *WhoMW 93*
Gray, Christopher 1694-1764 *DcNaB MP*
Gray, Christopher Donald 1951- *WhoScEn 94*
Gray, Clarence Cornelius, III 1917- *WhoBlA 94*
Gray, Clarence Jones 1908- *WhoAm 94, WhoFI 94*
Gray, Clayland Boyden 1943- *WhoAm 94*
Gray, Clayton 1918- *WrDr 94*
Gray, Cleve 1918- *WhoAm 94, WhoAmA 93*
Gray, Coleen 1922- *IntMPA 94, WhoHol 92*
Gray, Curme 1910-1980 *EncSF 93*
Gray, D. Wayne 1931- *WhoAm 94*
Gray, Danny Bruce 1956- *WhoAmP 93*
Gray, Daphne *WhoHol 92*
Gray, David 1914- *Who 94*
Gray, David 1927-1983 *BuCMET*
Gray, David Lawrence 1930- *WhoAm 94*
Gray, David Marshall 1947- *WhoScEn 94*
Gray, Denis Everett 1926- *Who 94*
Gray, Denis John Pereira 1935- *Who 94*
Gray, Diane 1941- *WhoAm 94*
Gray, Dolores 1924- *WhoHol 92*
Gray, Don 1935- *WhoAmA 93*
Gray, Donald d1978 *WhoHol 92*
Gray, Donald Allan 1964- *WhoWest 94*
Gray, Donald Clifford 1930- *Who 94*
Gray, Donald Lee 1948- *WhoScEn 94*
Gray, Donna Mae 1933- *WhoAm 94*
Gray, Donnee L. 1951- *WhoBlA 94*
Gray, Dorothy d1976 *WhoHol 92*
Gray, Dorothy Peyton 1943- *WhoBlA 94*
Gray, Dorothy Randall *DrAPF 93*
Gray, Douglas 1930- *IntWW 93, Who 94, WrDr 94*
Gray, Dulcie *Who 94*
Gray, Dulcie 1919- *IntMPA 94, WhoHol 92*
Gray, Dulcie 1920- *WrDr 94*
Gray, Duncan Montgomery, Jr. 1926- *WhoAm 94*
Gray, E. Arthur 1925- *WhoAmP 93*
Gray, E. George 1924- *IntWW 93*
Gray, Earl Haddon 1929- *WhoBlA 94*
Gray, Earnest 1957- *WhoBlA 94*
Gray, Eddie d1969 *WhoHol 92*
Gray, Edman Lowell 1939- *WhoAm 94, WhoMW 93*
Gray, Edmund Wesley 1928- *WhoWest 94*
Gray, Edward C. 1944-1989 *WhAm 10*
Gray, Edward George 1924- *Who 94*
Gray, Edward John 1930- *WhoAm 94*
Gray, Edward Wesley, Jr. 1946- *WhoBlA 94*
Gray, Elise N. 1936- *WhoAmA 93*
Gray, Elisha 1835-1901 *WorInv*
Gray, Elizabeth Janet *TwCYAW*
Gray, Elizabeth Janet 1902- *WrDr 94*
Gray, Elmon Taylor 1925- *WhoAmP 93*
Gray, Elspet 1929- *WhoHol 92*
Gray, Enid Maurine 1943- *WhoAm 94*
Gray, Erin 1951- *WhoHol 92*
Gray, Eve 1904- *WhoHol 92*
Gray, Festus Gail 1943- *WhoScEn 94*
Gray, Frances M. 1910- *WhoAm 94*
Gray, Francine du Plessix *DrAPF 93, WhoAm 94*
Gray, Francine du Plessix 1930- *WrDr 94*
Gray, Francis Campbell 1940- *WhoAm 94*
Gray, Frank C. *WhoMW 93*
Gray, Frank Truan 1920- *WhoAm 94*
Gray, Franklin Dingwall 1904-1990 *WhAm 10*
Gray, Fred David *WhoBlA 94*
Gray, Fred Ernest 1911- *WhoAmP 93*
Gray, Frederick Thomas, Jr. 1951- *WhoAm 94, WhoAmP 93*
Gray, Frederick William, III 1944- *WhoAm 94, WhoAmL 94*
Gray, Gary Gene 1940- *WhoScEn 94*
Gray, Gary James 1948- *WhoMW 93*
Gray, Gavin Campbell, II 1948- *WhoWest 94*
Gray, Gene d1950 *WhoHol 92*
Gray, Geoffrey Leicester 1905- *Who 94*
Gray, George d1967 *WhoHol 92*
Gray, George 1907- *WhoAm 94*
Gray, George, III 1945- *WhoWest 94*
Gray, George Allen 1918- *WhoMW 93*
Gray, George Thomas Alexander 1949- *Who 94*
Gray, George W., III 1945- *WhoBlA 94*
Gray, George William 1926- *IntWW 93, Who 94*
Gray, Gilbert 1928- *Who 94*
Gray, Gilda d1959 *WhoHol 92*
Gray, Glen d1963 *WhoHol 92*
Gray, Glenith Charlene 1948- *WhoAmP 93*
Gray, Gloria d1918 *WhoHol 92*
Gray, Gordon d1993 *NewYTBS 93 [port]*
Gray, Gordon 1905- *IntMPA 94*
Gray, Gordon Joseph d1993 *Who 94N*
Gray, Gordon Joseph 1910- *IntWW 93*
Gray, Gordon L. 1924- *WhoAm 94*
Gray, Gordon Thomas Seccombe 1911- *Who 94*
Gray, Gregory Edward 1954- *WhoWest 94*
Gray, Hanna Holborn 1930- *Who 94, WhoAm 94, WhoMW 93*
Gray, Hans Crete 1962- *WhoFI 94*
Gray, Harold 1894-1968 *WhoAmA 93N*
Gray, Harold James 1907- *Who 94, WrDr 94*
Gray, Harriette Ann d1987 *WhoHol 92*
Gray, Harrison 1711-1794 *WhAmRev*
Gray, Harry Barkus 1935- *IntWW 93, WhoAm 94, WhoScEn 94*
Gray, Harry J. 1919- *IntWW 93*
Gray, Harry Jack 1919- *WhoAm 94*
Gray, Harry Joshua 1924- *WhoAm 94*
Gray, Henry c. 1827-1861 *DcNaB MP*
Gray, Henry David 1908- *WhoAm 94, WhoWest 94*
Gray, Herbert E. 1931- *IntWW 93*
Gray, Herbert Harold, III 1953- *WhoAmL 94*
Gray, Hope Diffenderfer 1917- *WhoAm 94*
Gray, Horace Montgomery 1898- *WhAm 10*
Gray, Hugh 1916- *Who 94*
Gray, Ian 1951- *ConAu 142*
Gray, J. Charles 1932- *WhoAmL 94*
Gray, J. R. 1938- *WhoAmP 93*
Gray, Jabez d1950 *WhoAmA 93N*
Gray, Jack d1956 *WhoHol 92*
Gray, Jack 1927- *ConDr 93, WrDr 94*
Gray, Jack Charles 1931- *WhoMW 93*
Gray, James 1923- *WhoAm 94*
Gray, James Alexander 1920- *WhoAm 94*
Gray, James Austin, II 1946- *WhoBlA 94*
Gray, James Caldwell 1934- *WhoWest 94*
Gray, James E. *WhoBlA 94*
Gray, James Howard 1943- *WhoBlA 94*
Gray, James Joshua 1942- *WhoWest 94*
Gray, James Larry 1932- *WhoFI 94*
Gray, James Lee 1943- *WhoScEn 94*
Gray, James Martin 1851-1935 *DcAmReB 2*
Gray, James Patrick 1958- *WhoMW 93*
Gray, James Peyton 1943- *WhoAm 94*
Gray, James Randolph, III 1965- *WhoScEn 94*
Gray, James S. 1943- *WhoAm 94, WhoAmL 94*
Gray, James Samuel 1936- *WhoWest 94*
Gray, Jan Charles 1947- *WhoAmL 94, WhoFI 94, WhoWest 94*
Gray, Jay Kurtis 1964- *WhoAmL 94*
Gray, Jennifer d1962 *WhoHol 92*
Gray, Jennifer Ann 1949- *WhoBlA 94*
Gray, Jennifer Emily 1946- *WhoScEn 94*
Gray, Jerome Edmund 1959- *WhoAmL 94*
Gray, Jerry 1961- *WhoBlA 94*
Gray, Jim 1932- *WhoAmA 93*
Gray, Jo Anne Hastings 1921- *WhoAmP 93*
Gray, Joan Maurisse *WhoAmP 93*
Gray, Joanne S. 1943- *WhoBlA 94*
Gray, Joe d1971 *WhoHol 92*
Gray, John *Who 94*
Gray, John 1913- *Who 94*
Gray, John 1946- *ConDr 93, WrDr 94*
Gray, John, II 1956- *WhoAmP 93*
Gray, John (Archibald Browne) 1918- *Who 94*
Gray, John (Michael Dudgeon) 1913- *Who 94*
Gray, (Reginald) John 1916- *Who 94*
Gray, John Archibald Browne 1918- *IntWW 93*
Gray, John Augustus 1924- *WhoAm 94*
Gray, John B., Jr. 1951- *WhoIns 94*
Gray, John Bullard 1927- *WhoAm 94*
Gray, John Charles 1943- *WhoAmL 94*
Gray, John David 1928- *WhoAmP 93*
Gray, John Delton 1919- *WhoAm 94*
Gray, John Edmund 1922- *WhoAm 94*
Gray, John F. 1951- *WhoMW 93*
Gray, John Lathrop, III 1931- *WhoAm 94*
Gray, John Magnus 1915- *Who 94*
Gray, John Malcolm 1934- *IntWW 93, Who 94*
Gray, John Richard 1929- *Who 94*
Gray, John Stephens 1910-1991 *WhAm 10*
Gray, John Walker 1931- *WhoAm 94*
Gray, John Walton David 1936- *Who 94*
Gray, John Wylie 1935- *WhoAm 94*
Gray, Johnnie Lee 1953- *WhoBlA 94*
Gray, Johnny *WhoAm 94*
Gray, Joseph *Who 94*
Gray, Joseph William 1938- *WhoBlA 94*
Gray, Karen G. *WhoBlA 94*
Gray, Karla M. 1947- *WhoAmP 93*
Gray, Karla Marie *WhoAm 94, WhoAmL 94, WhoWest 94*
Gray, Keith A., Jr. 1947- *WhoBlA 94*
Gray, Kenneth D. *WhoBlA 94*
Gray, Kenneth D. 1944- *AfrAmG [port]*
Gray, Kenneth Eugene 1930- *WhoAm 94*
Gray, kenneth J. 1924- *WhoAmP 93*
Gray, Kenneth John 1919- *WhoAm 94*
Gray, Kenneth Walter 1939- *Who 94*
Gray, Kenneth Wayne 1944- *WhoFI 94, WhoScEn 94*
Gray, Kevin *WhoHol 92*
Gray, Kevin John 1951- *Who 94*
Gray, Laman A., Jr. 1940- *WhoAm 94*
Gray, Larry 1944- *WhoAmA 93*
Gray, Lawrence d1970 *WhoHol 92*
Gray, Leo Don d1966 *WhoHol 92*
Gray, Leon 1951- *WhoBlA 94*
Gray, Leonard W. 1942- *WhoAmP 93*
Gray, Linda d1963 *WhoHol 92*
Gray, Linda 1940- *IntMPA 94, WhoAm 94, WhoHol 92*
Gray, Linda Esther 1948- *NewGrDO, Who 94*
Gray, Lorna 1945- *WhoHol 92*
Gray, Louis Patrick 1916- *IntWW 93*
Gray, Lyons 1942- *WhoAmP 93*
Gray, Maceo 1940- *WhoBlA 94*
Gray, Mack d1981 *WhoHol 92*
Gray, Malcolm 1927-1993 *WrDr 94N*
Gray, Marcus J. 1936- *WhoBlA 94*
Gray, Margaret Ann 1950- *WhoFI 94*
Gray, Margaret Caroline 1913- *Who 94*
Gray, Margaret E(lla) 1956- *ConAu 141*
Gray, Margaret Edna 1931- *WhoAm 94*
Gray, Marie Elise 1914- *WhoAmA 93, WhoWest 94*
Gray, Marion d1975 *WhoHol 92*
Gray, Mark William 1916- *WhoMW 93*
Gray, Martin *Who 94*
Gray, (Hamish) Martin (Vincent) 1946- *Who 94*
Gray, Marvin Kenneth, Jr. 1958- *WhoFI 94*
Gray, Marvin Lee, Jr. 1945- *WhoAm 94, WhoAmL 94*
Gray, Marvin W. 1944- *WhoBlA 94*
Gray, Mary Terri 1961- *WhoFI 94*
Gray, Mary Wheat 1939- *WhoAm 94, WhoScEn 94*
Gray, Mattie Evans 1935- *WhoBlA 94*
Gray, Maurine d1981 *WhoHol 92*
Gray, Mayo L. *DrAPF 93*
Gray, Mel 1961- *WhoAm 94, WhoMW 93*
Gray, Melvin 1932- *WhoAm 94*
Gray, Merlyn Delorme 1931- *WhoMW 93*
Gray, Michael Kenneth 1958- *WhoFI 94*
Gray, Michael Stuart 1932- *Who 94*
Gray, Michael William 1962- *WhoMW 93*
Gray, Milner Connorton 1899- *Who 94*
Gray, Milton Hefter 1910- *WhoAm 94*
Gray, Monique Sylvaine *Who 94*
Gray, Moses W. 1937- *WhoBlA 94*
Gray, Myles McClure 1932- *WhoAm 94*
Gray, Myrtle Edwards 1914- *WhoBlA 94*
Gray, Nadia 1923- *WhoHol 92*
Gray, Naomi T. 1924- *WhoBlA 94*
Gray, Nicolete 1911- *WrDr 94*
Gray, Oriel 1920- *BlmGWL*
Gray, Oscar Shalom 1926- *WhoAm 94*
Gray, Pat *DrAPF 93*
Gray, Patience 1917- *ConAu 142*
Gray, Patricia 1946- *WhoAmP 93*
Gray, Patricia Ellen 1939- *WhoAm 94*
Gray, Patricia Joyce 1951- *WhoAmL 94, WhoWest 94*
Gray, Patricia Miele 1946- *WhoMW 93*
Gray, Patrick Wise 1953- *WhoAmL 94*
Gray, Patrick Worth *DrAPF 93*
Gray, Paul Edward 1932- *IntWW 93, Who 94, WhoAm 94*
Gray, Paul Richard Charles 1948- *Who 94*
Gray, Paul Wesley 1947- *WhoWest 94*
Gray, Pearl Spears 1945- *WhoBlA 94*
Gray, Peter 1926- *IntWW 93, Who 94*
Gray, Peter Francis 1937- *Who 94*
Gray, Peter Lawrence 1957- *WhoAmL 94*
Gray, Peter Stuart 1951- *WhoAmL 94*
Gray, Philip Burton 1957- *WhoAmL 94*
Gray, Philip Howard 1926- *WhoAm 94, WhoScEn 94, WhoWest 94*
Gray, Phyllis d1922 *WhoHol 92*
Gray, Phyllis Anne 1926- *WhoAm 94*
Gray, Rachel G. *WhoAmP 93*
Gray, Ralph 1915- *WhoAm 94*
Gray, Richard 1928- *WhoAm 94, WhoAmA 93*
Gray, (John) Richard 1929- *WrDr 94*
Gray, Richard Alexander, Jr. 1927- *WhoAm 94*
Gray, Richard Arden 1935- *WhoWest 94*
Gray, Richard Butler 1922- *WrDr 94*
Gray, Richard Charles, Jr. 1951- *WhoMW 93*
Gray, Richard Dennis 1951- *Who 94*
Gray, Richard Edwin, III 1950- *WhoAmL 94*
Gray, Richard Jerome 1961- *WhoWest 94*
Gray, Richard John 1944- *Who 94*
Gray, Richard Moss 1924- *WhoWest 94*
Gray, Richard Paul 1945- *Who 94*
Gray, Robert 1755-1806 *WhWE*
Gray, Robert 1928- *Who 94*
Gray, Robert 1945- *WrDr 94*
Gray, Robert (Archibald Speir) 1942- *WrDr 94*
Gray, Robert Beckwith 1912- *WhoScEn 94*
Gray, Robert Dean 1941- *WhoBlA 94*
Gray, Robert Donald 1924- *WhoFI 94, WhoWest 94*
Gray, Robert E. 1941- *AfrAmG [port], WhoBlA 94*
Gray, Robert Hugh 1931- *WhoAmA 93*
Gray, Robert Keith 1923- *IntWW 93, WhoAm 94, WhoFI 94*
Gray, Robert Linwood 1950- *WhoFI 94*
Gray, Robert Michael Ker *Who 94*
Gray, Robert Molten 1943- *WhoAm 94, WhoWest 94*
Gray, Robert R. 1910- *WhoBlA 94*
Gray, Robert Steele 1923- *WhoAm 94*
Gray, Robert Walker *Who 94*
Gray, Robert Ward 1916- *WhoAmA 93*
Gray, Robin 1924- *Who 94*
Gray, Robin 1944- *Who 94*
Gray, Robin (Trevor) 1940- *Who 94*
Gray, Robin McDowall 1931- *Who 94*
Gray, Robin Trevor 1940- *IntWW 93*
Gray, Rod *EncSF 93*
Gray, Roger d1959 *WhoHol 92*
Gray, Roger Ibbotson d1992 *Who 94N*
Gray, Ronald D. 1942- *WhoAm 94, WhoWest 94*
Gray, Ronald Frederick 1944- *WhoWest 94*
Gray, Ronald Loren 1964- *WhoWest 94*
Gray, Ruben L. 1938- *WhoBlA 94*
Gray, Russell 1908- *WrDr 94*
Gray, Sally 1916- *WhoHol 92*
Gray, Seymour 1911- *WhoAm 94, WrDr 94*
Gray, Sheila Hafter 1930- *WhoAm 94*
Gray, Sheldon 1938- *WhoAm 94*
Gray, Simon (James Holliday) 1936- *ConDr 93, IntDcT 2, WrDr 94*
Gray, Simon James Holliday 1936- *IntWW 93, Who 94*
Gray, Spalding *NewYTBS 93 [port]*
Gray, Spalding 1941- *ConDr 93, IntMPA 94, WhoAm 94, WhoHol 92, WrDr 94*
Gray, Stanley Randolph, Jr. 1958- *WhoScEn 94*
Gray, Stella d1956 *WhoHol 92*
Gray, Stephen 1666-1736 *WorScD*
Gray, Sterling Perkins, Jr. 1943- *WhoBlA 94*
Gray, Susan W. d1992 *NewYTBS 93*
Gray, Teresa Corinna Ubertis *BlmGWL*
Gray, Theodore Flint, Jr. 1939- *WhoScEn 94*
Gray, Theodore Milton 1927- *WhoAmP 93*
Gray, Thomas 1716-1771 *BlmGEL*
Gray, Thomas Alexander 1948- *WhoAmA 93*
Gray, Thomas Cecil 1913- *Who 94*
Gray, Thomas K. 1945- *IntMPA 94*
Gray, Thomas Stephen 1950- *WhoAm 94*
Gray, Timothy 1926- *WhoHol 92*
Gray, Tony 1922- *WrDr 94*
Gray, Truman Stretcher 1906-1992 *WhAm 10*
Gray, Valerie Hamilton 1959- *WhoBlA 94*
Gray, Veleka 1947- *WhoHol 92*
Gray, Verne Allen 1943- *WhoWest 94*
Gray, Vernon 1930- *WhoHol 92*
Gray, Victor 1917- *WrDr 94*
Gray, Virginia Hickman 1945- *WhoAm 94, WhoMW 93*
Gray, Walter Franklin 1929- *WhoAm 94*
Gray, Walter J. 1926- *WhoAmP 93*
Gray, Walter P., III 1952- *WhoWest 94*

Gray, Wellington Burbank 1919-1977 *WhoAmA 93N*
Gray, Wilfred Douglas 1937- *WhoBlA 94*
Gray, William (Hume) 1955- *Who 94*
Gray, William (Stevenson) 1928- *Who 94*
Gray, William Allan 1950- *WhoAmL 94*
Gray, William Crane 1835-1919 *EncNAR*
Gray, William Guerin 1948- *WhoAm 94*
Gray, William H., III 1941- *AfrAmAl 6 [port], WhoAm 94, WhoAmP 93, WhoBlA 94*
Gray, William Oxley 1914- *WhoAmL 94*
Gray, Willoughby 1916- *WhoHol 92*
Graybeal, Jack Daniel 1930- *WhoScEn 94*
Graybeal, Lynne Elizabeth 1956- *WhoWest 94*
Graybeal, Sidney Norman 1924- *WhoAm 94*
Graybill, David Wesley 1949- *WhoAm 94, WhoWest 94*
Graybill, Jan Leo 1958- *WhoFI 94*
Graybill, Joseph d1913 *WhoHol 92*
Grayburn, Susan T. 1955- *WhoAmL 94*
Grayck, Marcus Daniel 1927- *WhoAm 94*
Gray Debros, Winifred Marjorie *Who 94*
Graydon, Alexander 1752-1818 *WhAmRev*
Graydon, Allan 1898- *WhAm 10*
Graydon, Frank Drake 1921- *WhoAm 94*
Graydon, Michael (James) 1938- *IntWW 93, Who 94*
Graydon, Ruth *DrAPF 93*
Graydon, Wasdon, Jr. 1950- *WhoBlA 94*
Grayer, Jeffrey 1965- *WhoBlA 94*
Grayhack, John Thomas 1923- *WhoAm 94*
Graylin, John Cranmer 1921- *IntWW 93*
Gray-Little, Bernadette 1944- *WhoAm 94, WhoBlA 94*
Graylow, Richard Vernon 1940- *WhoAmL 94*
Gray-Morgan, LaRuth H. *WhoBlA 94*
Gray Of Contin, Baron 1927- *Who 94*
Grays, Mattelia Bennett 1931- *WhoBlA 94*
Graysmark, John *ConTFT 11*
Graysmith, Robert 1942- *ConAu 41NR, WhoAm 94*
Grayson, Albert Kirk 1935- *WhoAm 94*
Grayson, Barbara Ann 1954- *WhoBlA 94*
Grayson, Bette Rita 1947- *WhoAmL 94*
Grayson, Byron J., Sr. 1949- *WhoBlA 94*
Grayson, Cecil 1920- *IntWW 93, Who 94*
Grayson, Charles Jackson, Jr. 1923- *WhoAm 94*
Grayson, Clifford Prevost 1857-1951 *WhoAmA 93N*
Grayson, David S. 1943- *WhoMW 93*
Grayson, Deborah Eve *DrAPF 93*
Grayson, Edward Davis 1938- *WhoAm 94*
Grayson, Ellison Capers, Jr. 1928- *WhoFI 94, WhoWest 94*
Grayson, Elsie Michelle 1962- *WhoBlA 94*
Grayson, George W. 1938- *WhoAmP 93*
Grayson, George Wallace 1938- *WhoAmP 93*
Grayson, George Welton 1938- *WhoBlA 94*
Grayson, Gerald Herbert 1940- *WhoAm 94*
Grayson, Hal d1959 *WhoHol 92*
Grayson, Harry L. 1929- *WhoBlA 94*
Grayson, James Paul 1950- *WhoFI 94*
Grayson, Jennifer A. 1949- *WhoBlA 94*
Grayson, Jeremy (Brian Vincent) 1933- *Who 94*
Grayson, Jessie d1953 *WhoHol 92*
Grayson, John Allan 1930- *WhoAm 94*
Grayson, John N. 1932- *WhoBlA 94*
Grayson, John Richard 1925- *WhoMW 93*
Grayson, John Wesley 1941- *WhoWest 94*
Grayson, Kathryn 1922- *WhoHol 92*
Grayson, Kathryn 1923- *IntMPA 94*
Grayson, Lawrence Peter 1937- *WhoAm 94*
Grayson, Liane Kuhnsman 1956- *WhoMW 93*
Grayson, N. June 1927- *WhoAmP 93*
Grayson, Richard *DrAPF 93*
Grayson, Richard 1925- *WhoHol 92*
Grayson, Richard Andrew 1966- *WhoScEn 94*
Grayson, Robert Allen 1927- *WhoAm 94*
Grayson, Robert Larry 1947- *WhoFI 94*
Grayson, Russell Wayne 1953- *WhoAmL 94*
Grayson, Stanley Edward 1950- *WhoBlA 94*
Grayson, Susan Cubillas 1946- *WhoAm 94*
Grayson, Violet Elizabeth 1956- *WhoAmL 94*
Grayson, Walton George, III 1928- *WhoFI 94*
Grayson, William c. 1736-1790 *WhAmRev*
Grayson, William Jackson, Jr. 1930- *WhoFI 94*
Grayson, William P. d1993 *NewYTBS 93 [port]*
Grayson, Zachary Louis 1959- *WhoAmL 94*
Gray-Stoewsand, Lorraine Rae 1963- *WhoMW 93*
Grayston, J. Thomas 1924- *WhoAm 94*
Grayston, Kenneth 1914- *Who 94*
Grazda, Ed 1947- *WhoAmA 93*
Grazer, Brian *WhoAm 94*
Grazer, Brian 1951- *IntMPA 94*
Grazhdanin, Misha *ConAu 42NR*
Graziadei, William Daniel, III 1943- *WhoAm 94, WhoScEn 94*
Graziani, Edward C. *WhoAmP 93*
Graziani, Francesco 1828-1901 *NewGrDO*
Graziani, Leonard Joseph 1929- *WhoAm 94*
Graziani, Lodovico 1820-1885 *NewGrDO*
Graziani, Sante 1920- *WhoAmA 93*
Graziano, Catherine Elizabeth 1931- *WhoAmP 93*
Graziano, Charles Dominic 1920- *WhoMW 93*
Graziano, Craig Frank 1950- *WhoAmL 94*
Graziano, Frank *DrAPF 93*
Graziano, Joseph A. 1945- *WhoAm 94, WhoFI 94, WhoWest 94*
Graziano, Rocky d1990 *WhoHol 92*
Graziano, Vincent James 1933- *WhoMW 93*
Grazier, James *EncSF 93*
Grazin, Igor Nikolai 1952- *WhoAm 94*
Grazioli, Albert John, Jr. 1954- *WhoWest 94*
Graziosi, Franco *WhoHol 92*
Grcevic, Barbara Helen 1951- *WhoAmL 94*
Greacen, Edmund 1877-1949 *WhoAmA 93N*
Greacen, John Morley 1942- *WhoAmL 94*
Greager, William Edgar 1951- *WhoFI 94*
Greaney, James Robert 1922- *WhoFI 94*
Greaney, John M. *WhoAmP 93*
Greaney, John M. 1939- *WhoAmL 94*
Greaney, John Patrick 1956- *WhoScEn 94*
Greaney, Patrick Joseph 1939- *WhoAm 94, WhoFI 94*
Greanias, George 1948- *WhoAmP 93*
Greanias, Stanley Louis 1949- *WhoAm 94*
Greanias, Thomas George 1965- *WhoWest 94*
Grear, Effie C. 1927- *WhoBlA 94*
Grear, James Malcolm 1931- *WhoAmA 93*
Grear, William A. 1923- *WhoBlA 94*
Grearson, Brian James 1949- *WhoAmL 94*
Greaser, Constance Udean 1938- *WhoFI 94*
Greaser, Marion Lewis 1942- *WhoAm 94*
Greason, Arthur LeRoy, Jr. 1922- *WhoAm 94*
Greason, Murray Crossley, Jr. 1936- *WhoAm 94*
Greason, Staci *WhoHol 92*
Great, Don Charles 1951- *WhoWest 94*
Greatbatch, Wilson 1919- *WhoAm 94, WhoScEn 94, WorInv*
Great Gildersleeve, The 1908-1985 *WhoCom*
Greathead, David John 1931- *Who 94*
Greathead, James Henry 1844-1896 *DcNaB MP*
Greathouse, Walser S. d1966 *WhoAmA 93N*
Greaton, John 1741-1783 *WhAmRev*
Greatorex, Wilfred *EncSF 93*
Greatrex, Neil 1951- *Who 94*
Greaux, Cheryl Prejean 1949- *WhoBlA 94*
Greaver, Hanne 1933- *WhoAmA 93*
Greaver, Harry 1929- *WhoAm 94, WhoAmA 93, WhoWest 94*
Greaver, Joanne Hutchins 1939- *WhoScEn 94*
Greaves, Derrick 1927- *IntWW 93*
Greaves, Edith d1952 *WhoHol 92*
Greaves, Ian Alexander 1947- *WhoScEn 94*
Greaves, J. Randall 1955- *WhoAm 94, WhoFI 94*
Greaves, James L. 1943- *WhoAmA 93*
Greaves, James Louis 1943- *WhoAm 94*
Greaves, Jeffrey 1926- *Who 94*
Greaves, Malcolm Watson 1933- *Who 94*
Greaves, Margaret 1914- *WrDr 94*
Greaves, Melvyn Francis 1941- *Who 94*
Greaves, Nick 1955- *SmATA 77*
Greaves, William *WhoBlA 94, WhoHol 92*
Greaves, William Garfield *WhoAm 94*
Greaves, William Webster 1951- *WhoMW 93, WhoScEn 94*
Greaza, Walter d1973 *WhoHol 92*
Greb, Gordon Barry 1921- *WhoAm 94*
Greb, Richard Harold 1945- *WhoMW 93*
Grebe, Lynn Charles 1952- *WhoAmP 93*
Grebe, Michael W. *WhoAmP 93*
Grebe, Michael W. 1940- *WhoAmL 94*
Grebel, Lawrence Bovard 1951- *WhoAmL 94*
Greben, Stanley Edward 1927- *WhoAm 94*
Grebenc, Joseph D. 1958- *WhoScEn 94*
Grebenik, Eugene 1919- *Who 94*
Grebenshchikov, Boris 1953- *IntWW 93*
Greber, Jakob d1731 *NewGrDO*
Greber, Judith *DrAPF 93*
Greber, Robert Martin 1938- *WhoAm 94, WhoFI 94, WhoWest 94*
Greble, Thomas Charles 1949- *WhoAmL 94*
Grebner, Bernice Prill *WhoMW 93*
Grebner, Dennis William 1932- *WhoAm 94*
Grebner, Eugene Ernest 1931- *WhoScEn 94*
Grebner, Mark 1952- *WhoAmP 93*
Grebow, Edward 1949- *WhoAm 94*
Grebstein, Sheldon Norman 1928- *WhoAm 94, WrDr 94*
Grebus, Luis *NewGrDO*
Grech, Anthony Paul 1930-1990 *WhAm 10*
Grech, Joe Debono 1941- *IntWW 93*
Grechaninov, Alexander Tikhonovich 1864-1956 *NewGrDO*
Grecis, Nicola de *NewGrDO*
Greco, Anthony Joseph 1937- *WhoAmA 93*
Greco, Buddy 1926- *WhoHol 92*
Greco, Cosetta 1930- *WhoHol 92*
Greco, Emilio 1913- *IntWW 93*
Greco, Giuseppe 1929- *IntWW 93*
Greco, Ignazio J. 1961- *WhoIns 94*
Greco, Jose 1918- *WhoAm 94, WhoHol 92*
Greco, Joseph Dominic, Jr. 1955- *WhoAmL 94*
Greco, Juliette 1927- *WhoHol 92*
Greco, Michael S. 1942- *WhoAm 94, WhoAmL 94*
Greco, Peter d1985 *WhoHol 92*
Greco, Ralph Steven 1942- *WhoScEn 94*
Greco, Robert d1965 *WhoAmA 93N*
Greco, Stephen *DrAPF 93*
Greco, Stephen R. 1919- *WhoAmP 93*
Greco, Thomas G. 1944- *WhoScEn 94*
Greco, Thomas Henry, Jr. 1936- *WhoWest 94*
Grecsek, Matthew Thomas 1963- *WhoFI 94*
Grecy, Mlle. *NewGrDO*
Grede, William J. 1897-1989 *WhAm 10*
Greden, John Francis 1942- *WhoScEn 94*
Greeff-Andriessen, Pelagie 1860-1937 *NewGrDO*
Greehey, William Eugene 1936- *WhoAm 94, WhoFI 94*
Greek, Darold I. 1909- *WhoAm 94*
Greeley, Andrew (Moran) 1928- *WrDr 94*
Greeley, Andrew M(oran) 1928- *ConAu 43NR, EncSF 93*
Greeley, Andrew Moran 1928- *WhoAm 94, WhoMW 93*
Greeley, Charles Mathew 1941- *WhoAmA 93*
Greeley, Dana McLean 1908-1986 *DcAmReB 2*
Greeley, Evelyn d1975 *WhoHol 92*
Greeley, Horace 1811-1872 *AmSocL [port]*
Greeley, J. Sharon 1940- *WhoMW 93*
Greeley, Joseph May 1902- *WhoAm 94*
Greeley, Richard Folsom 1915- *WhoScEn 94*
Greeley, Robert Charles 1948- *WhoWest 94*
Greeley, Robert Emmett 1932- *WhoFI 94*
Greeley, Ronald 1939- *WhoWest 94*
Greeley, Sean McGovern 1961- *WhoFI 94*
Greeley, Valerie 1953- *ConAu 43NR*
Greeley, Walter Franklin 1931- *WhoAm 94*
Greely, Adolphus Washington 1844-1935 *WhWE*
Greely, Michael T. 1940- *WhoAmP 93*
Green, A. C. 1963- *WhoBlA 94*
Green, Aaron Alphonso 1946- *WhoBlA 94*
Green, Abel d1973 *WhoHol 92*
Green, Adolph 1915- *IntMPA 94, WhoAm 94, WhoHol 92, WrDr 94*
Green, Adolph 1918- *See* Comden, Betty 1919- *IntDcF 2-4*
Green, Al *WhoBlA 94*
Green, Al 1915- *WhoHol 92*
Green, Al 1946- *WhoAm 94, WhoBlA 94*
Green, Alan, Jr. 1925- *WhoAmP 93*
Green, Albert Edward *IntWW 93*
Green, Albert Edward 1912- *Who 94*
Green, Alfred E. d1960 *WhoHol 92*
Green, Allan (David) 1935- *Who 94*
Green, Allan Wright 1949- *WhoWest 94*
Green, Allison Anne 1936- *WhoMW 93*
Green, Alvin 1931- *WhoAm 94*
Green, Andrew Curtis 1936- *Who 94*
Green, Andrew Fleming 1941- *Who 94*
Green, Andrew M(alcolm) 1927- *WrDr 94*
Green, Andrew Wilson 1923- *WhoAm 94*
Green, Angelo Gray 1950- *WhoBlA 94*
Green, Anita Lorraine 1948- *WhoBlA 94*
Green, Anna 1933- *NewGrDO*
Green, Anna Katharine 1846-1935 *BlmGWL*
Green, Anne Louise 1961- *WhoMW 93*
Green, Anthony Eric Sandall 1939- *IntWW 93, Who 94*
Green, Art 1941- *WhoAmA 93*
Green, Arthur 1928- *Who 94*
Green, Arthur Edward Chase 1911- *Who 94*
Green, Arthur Jackson 1928- *Who 94*
Green, Arthur Nelson 1941- *WhoAm 94*
Green, Asa Norman 1929- *WhoAm 94*
Green, Ashbel 1928- *WhoAm 94*
Green, Barbara-Marie 1928- *WhoAm 94, WhoBlA 94*
Green, Barbara Strawn 1938- *WhoAm 94*
Green, Barry Spencer 1932- *Who 94*
Green, Benedict *Who 94*
Green, Benjamin *DrAPF 93*
Green, Benjamin 1813-1858 *DcNaB MP*
Green, Benjamin Louis 1951- *WhoFI 94*
Green, Bennett Donald 1950- *WhoFI 94*
Green, Benny 1927- *Who 94, WrDr 94*
Green, Bernard *WhoAm 94, WhoFI 94*
Green, Bernard 1887-1951 *WhoAmA 93N*
Green, Bernard 1925- *IntWW 93, Who 94*
Green, Bill 1929- *WhoAmP 93*
Green, Brenda Kay 1947- *WhoBlA 94*
Green, Brian Gerald 1954- *WhoFI 94, WhoWest 94*
Green, Brian Glenn 1951- *WhoMW 93*
Green, Bruce Allan 1948- *WhoAmP 93*
Green, Bryan S(tuart) W(estmacott) 1901-1993 *ConAu 140*
Green, Bryan Stuart Westmacott d1993 *Who 94N*
Green, Brynmor Hugh 1941- *Who 94*
Green, Burton d1922 *WhoHol 92*
Green, Calvin Coolidge 1931- *WhoBlA 94*
Green, Carol H. 1944- *WhoAm 94*
Green, Carolyn Louise 1950- *WhoBlA 94*
Green, Cathy A. 1960- *WhoIns 94*
Green, Cecil *WhoAmP 93*
Green, Cecil Howard 1900- *WhoAm 94*
Green, Celia (Elizabeth) 1935- *WrDr 94*
Green, Charles 1734-1771 *DcNaB MP*
Green, Charles A. *WhoBlA 94*
Green, Charles A. 1927- *WhoBlA 94*
Green, Charles Frederick 1930- *Who 94*
Green, Charles Stanley, III 1937- *WhoMW 93*
Green, Charlotte Kimball 1940- *WhoWest 94*
Green, Cheryl Delois 1958- *WhoAmL 94*
Green, Christina J. *DrAPF 93*
Green, Christopher Edward Wastie 1943- *Who 94*
Green, Cicero M., Jr. 1930- *WhoBlA 94*
Green, Cliff(ord) 1934- *WrDr 94*
Green, Clifford Scott 1923- *WhoAm 94, WhoAmL 94, WhoBlA 94*
Green, Clyde Octavious 1960- *WhoBlA 94*
Green, Consuella 1946- *WhoBlA 94*
Green, Curtis 1957- *WhoBlA 94*
Green, Curtis E. 1923- *WhoBlA 94*
Green, Cyril Kenneth 1931- *WhoWest 94*
Green, D(ennis) H(oward) 1922- *WrDr 94*
Green, Dale Monte 1922- *WhoAm 94*
Green, Dallas 1934- *WhoAm 94*
Green, Dan 1935- *IntWW 93, WhoAm 94*
Green, Daniel Fred 1947- *WhoWest 94*
Green, Danny 1903- *WhoHol 92*
Green, Darrell 1960- *WhoAm 94, WhoBlA 94*
Green, David *Who 94*
Green, David 1899- *WhoAm 94*
Green, David 1922- *WhoFI 94, WhoMW 93*
Green, (Gregory) David 1948- *Who 94*
Green, David Ferrell 1935- *WhoMW 93*
Green, David Headley 1936- *Who 94*
Green, David Henry 1921- *WhoAm 94*
Green, David Leo 1951- *WhoAmP 93*
Green, David Marvin 1932- *WhoScEn 94*
Green, David O. 1923- *WhoAm 94*
Green, David Oliver 1908- *WhoAmA 93*
Green, David Oliver, Jr. 1908- *WhoWest 94*
Green, David Richard 1964- *WhoScEn 94*
Green, David Thomas 1925- *WhoAm 94*
Green, David William 1942- *WhoMW 93*
Green, David William 1951- *WhoAm 94*
Green, Deborah Kennon 1951- *WhoBlA 94*
Green, Deborah Parkhurst 1954- *WhoMW 93*
Green, Denis d1954 *WhoHol 92*
Green, Denise G. 1946- *WhoAmA 93*
Green, Dennis *WhoAm 94*
Green, Dennis 1949- *ConBlB 5 [port], WhoBlA 94, WhoMW 93*
Green, Dennis Howard 1922- *Who 94*
Green, Dennis Joseph 1941- *WhoAm 94, WhoFI 94*
Green, Dennis O. 1940- *WhoBlA 94*
Green, Diane Patricia 1941- *WhoAmP 93*
Green, Don Wesley 1932- *WhoAm 94, WhoScEn 94*
Green, Donald Edward 1955- *WhoMW 93*
Green, Donald Hugh 1929- *WhoAm 94*

Green, Donald Ross 1924- WhoScEn 94, WrDr 94
Green, Donald Webb 1944- WhoAm 94
Green, Donna WhoAmP 93
Green, Dorothy d1961 WhoHol 92
Green, Dorothy d1963 WhoHol 92
Green, Dorothy 1915- BlmGWL
Green, Dorothy 1920- WhoHol 92
Green, Dorothy Selma 1929- WhoWest 94
Green, Douglas Foster 1947- WhoAmP 93
Green, Earl Leroy 1913- WhoAm 94
Green, Edward Anthony 1922- WhoAm 94
Green, Edward Crocker 1944- WhoScEn 94
Green, Edward Hartman, V 1962- WhoAmL 94
Green, Edward L. WhoBlA 94
Green, Eleanor Myers 1948- WhoAm 94
Green, Eliot Jonah 1965- WhoAmL 94
Green, Elisabeth Sara 1940- ConAu 42NR
Green, Elizabeth A(dine) H(erkimer) 1906- WrDr 94
Green, Elizabeth Lee 1911-1989 WhoBlA 94N
Green, Emily d1980 WhoHol 92
Green, Eric 1967- WhoBlA 94
Green, Ernest G. 1941- WhoBlA 94
Green, Evanna E. 1931- WhoAmP 93
Green, Fitzhugh 1917-1990 WhAm 10
Green, Flora Hungerford 1941- WhoAm 94
Green, Forrest F. 1915- WhoBlA 94
Green, Francis 1742-1809 WhAmRev
Green, Francis J. 1906- WhoWest 94
Green, Francis William 1920- WhoWest 94
Green, Frank Alan 1931- Who 94
Green, Frank Earl 1931- WhoMW 93
Green, Franklin D. 1933- WhoBlA 94
Green, Fraser 1955- WhoAm 94
Green, Fred E. d1940 WhoHol 92
Green, Fred Wallace 1945- WhoFI 94, WhoIns 94
Green, Fred William 1952- WhoWest 94
Green, Freddie d1987 WhoHol 92
Green, Frederick Chapman 1920- WhoBlA 94
Green, Frederick Pratt 1903- WrDr 94
Green, Friday Ann 1940- WhoFI 94
Green, Gabriel 1924- WhoWest 94
Green, Galen DrAPF 93
Green, Gareth Montraville 1931- WhoAm 94
Green, Gary Quentin 1942- WhoAmP 93
Green, Gaston Alfred, III 1966- WhoAm 94, WhoBlA 94, WhoWest 94
Green, Gene 1947- CngDr 93, WhoAm 94, WhoAmP 93
Green, Geoffrey DrAPF 93
Green, Geoffrey Hugh 1920- Who 94
Green, George D. 1943- WhoAmA 93
Green, George Dallas 1934- WhoAm 94
Green, George F. WhoAmP 93
Green, George Hugh 1911- Who 94
Green, George Joseph 1938- WhoAm 94
Green, George Norris 1939- WhoAmP 93
Green, Georgia Mae 1950- WhoBlA 94
Green, Gerald 1922- WhoAm 94, WrDr 94
Green, Gerald B. WhoAmP 93
Green, Gerald Walker 1945- WhoAm 94
Green, Geraldine D. 1938- WhoBlA 94
Green, Gerard Nicholas Valentine 1950- Who 94
Green, Gertrude Dorsey 1949- WhoAm 94
Green, Gilbert d1984 WhoHol 92
Green, Gloria J. 1954- WhoBlA 94
Green, Gordon Jay 1957- WhoAm 94
Green, Guy 1913- IntDcF 2-4 [port], IntMPA 94
Green, Guy (Stephen Montague) 1937- Who 94
Green, Guy Mervin Charles WhoAm 94
Green, Guy Stephen Montague 1937- IntWW 93
Green, H. F. d1979 WhoHol 92
Green, Hamilton 1934- IntWW 93
Green, Hannah DrAPF 93, TwCYAW
Green, Harold Daniel 1934- WhoMW 93
Green, Harold Paul 1922- WhoAmL 94
Green, Harry d1958 WhoHol 92
Green, Harry Western, II 1940- WhoAm 94
Green, Henry 1905-1973 BlmGEL, EncSF 93
Green, Henry Leonard 1931- WhoMW 93
Green, Hilarie Cattell 1959- WhoWest 94
Green, Hilary EncSF 93
Green, Holly Ann 1962- WhoMW 93
Green, Howard 1925- IntWW 93, WhoAm 94
Green, Howard Alan 1938- WhoFI 94
Green, Howard I. 1936- WhoWest 94
Green, Howard Peyton, III 1949- WhoAm 94
Green, Hubert 1946- WhoAm 94
Green, Hugh 1959- WhoBlA 94
Green, Hughie 1920- WhoHol 92
Green, Humphrey Christian 1924- Who 94
Green, Hylda d1988 WhoHol 92
Green, I.G. EncSF 93
Green, J. C. R. 1949- WrDr 94
Green, J. Paul 1929- ConAu 141
Green, Jack IntMPA 94
Green, Jack 1925- WhoWest 94
Green, Jack Allen 1945- WhoAm 94
Green, Jack Coulson 1941- WhoWest 94
Green, Jack Peter 1925- WhoAm 94
Green, Jacki E. 1950- WhoFI 94
Green, Jacob Carl 1957- WhoBlA 94
Green, James Anton 1949- WhoScEn 94
Green, James Collins 1921- WhoAmP 93
Green, James Craig 1933- WhoWest 94
Green, James Douglas 1921- WhoAmP 93
Green, James L. 1945- WhoBlA 94
Green, James Murney 1944- WhoMW 93
Green, James P., Jr. WhoAmP 93
Green, James R(obert) 1944- WrDr 94
Green, James Richard d1993 NewYTBS 93
Green, James Samuel 1947- WhoAm 94
Green, James Stuart 1945- WhoAmL 94
Green, James Weston 1913- WhoAm 94
Green, James Wyche 1915- WhoAm 94
Green, Jarvis R. 1953- WhoBlA 94
Green, Jay M. WhoFI 94
Green, Jean Balfour 1939- WhoMW 93
Green, Jeff 1954- WhoAmP 93
Green, Jeffrey 1946- AstEnc
Green, Jeffrey C. 1941- WhoAmL 94
Green, Jeffrey M. 1944- ConAu 140
Green, Jen EncSF 93
Green, Jerome Frederic 1928- WhoAm 94
Green, Jerrold David 1948- WhoWest 94
Green, Jerry Alan 1943- WhoWest 94
Green, Jerry Howard 1930- WhoFI 94, WhoMW 93
Green, Jerry Richard 1946- WhoAm 94
Green, Jersey Michael-Lee 1952- WhoAm 94, WhoAmL 94
Green, Jim 1936- WhoAmP 93
Green, Joan WhoAmP 93
Green, Joe fl. 1930-1950 EncNAR
Green, Joel Henry 1954- WhoWest 94
Green, John d1793 WhAmRev
Green, John 1787-1852 DcNaB MP
Green, John Alden 1925- WhoAm 94
Green, John Cawley 1910- WhoAm 94
Green, John Daniel 1964- WhoMW 93
Green, John David 1948- WhoMW 93, WhoScEn 94
Green, John Dennis Fowler 1909- Who 94
Green, John Edward 1937- Who 94
Green, John Joseph 1931- WhoAm 94
Green, John Kevin WhoAmP 93
Green, John Kevin 1949- WhoAmL 94
Green, John Lafayette, Jr. 1933- WhoAm 94, WhoMW 93
Green, John LaVerne 1962- WhoMW 93
Green, John Michael 1924- Who 94
Green, John Orne 1922- WhoAm 94
Green, John Raeburn 1894- WhAm 10
Green, John William 1942- WhoWest 94
Green, Johnny d1989 WhoHol 92
Green, Johnny 1908-1989 IntDcF 2-4
Green, Johnny 1933- BasBi
Green, Jonathan (William) 1939- WhoAmA 93
Green, Jonathan William 1939- WhoAm 94, WhoWest 94
Green, Jonathon 1948- WrDr 94
Green, Joseph 1905- IntMPA 94, WhoHol 92
Green, Joseph 1928- WhoAm 94, WhoScEn 94
Green, Joseph 1933- WhoAmP 93
Green, Joseph 1938- IntMPA 94
Green, Joseph, Jr. 1950- WhoBlA 94
Green, Joseph (Lee) 1931- EncSF 93, WrDr 94
Green, Joseph Barnet 1928- WhoAm 94, WhoScEn 94
Green, Joseph Martin 1925- WhoAm 94
Green, Joshua, III 1936- WhoAm 94, WhoFI 94, WhoWest 94
Green, Joyce 1928- WhoFI 94, WhoMW 93
Green, Joyce Hens 1928- CngDr 93, WhoAm 94, WhoAmL 94
Green, Judd d1932 WhoHol 92
Green, Judith 1936- WrDr 94
Green, Julia Lynne 1959- WhoFI 94
Green, Julian 1900- IntWW 93
Green, Julian Hartridge 1900- Who 94
Green, Julien 1900- ConLC 77 [port]
Green, Julien (Hartridge) 1900- ConWorW 93
Green, June Lazenby 1914- CngDr 93, WhoAm 94, WhoAmL 94
Green, Kate DrAPF 93
Green, Katherine Ann 1947- WhoAmL 94
Green, Kay 1927- ConAu 41NR
Green, Kenneth d1969 WhoHol 92
Green, Kenneth 1934- Who 94
Green, Kenneth W. WhoAmP 93
Green, Kerri 1967- WhoHol 92
Green, Kyle Mark 1951- WhoAmP 93
Green, Larry Alton 1948- WhoAm 94
Green, Larry Anthony 1952- WhoAmL 94
Green, Larry W. 1946- WhoBlA 94
Green, Laurence Alexander Who 94
Green, Lawrence 1938- WhoScEn 94
Green, Lawrence Raymond 1948- WhoAmL 94
Green, Lawrence Rodman 1946- WhoAmL 94
Green, Lawrence W(inter) 1940- ConAu 42NR
Green, Lawrence Winter 1940- WhoWest 94
Green, Lennis Harris 1940- WhoMW 93
Green, Leo Edward 1932- WhoAmP 93
Green, Leon, Jr. 1922- WhoAm 94
Green, Leon William 1925- WhoAm 94
Green, Leslie Claude 1920- WhoAm 94, WhoWest 94
Green, Leslie Leonard 1925- Who 94
Green, Lester L. 1941- WhoBlA 94
Green, Lewis Cox 1924- WhoAmL 94
Green, Liller 1928- WhoBlA 94
Green, Linda Lou 1946- WhoFI 94
Green, Litterial 1970- WhoBlA 94
Green, Lucinda Jane 1953- Who 94
Green, Malcolm 1942- Who 94
Green, Malcolm C. 1925- IntMPA 94
Green, Malcolm Leslie Hodder 1936- Who 94
Green, Malcolm Robert 1943- Who 94
Green, Marc Edward 1943- ConAu 42NR
Green, Marguerite 1922- WhoAm 94
Green, Marilyn Virginia 1948- WhoWest 94
Green, Mark 1917- Who 94
Green, Mark A. 1960- WhoAmP 93
Green, Mark Joseph 1945- WhoAm 94
Green, Marshall 1916- IntWW 93, WhoAm 94, WhoAmP 93
Green, Martin (Burgess) 1927- EncSF 93, WrDr 94
Green, Martin Leonard 1936- WhoAmA 93
Green, Martyn d1975 WhoHol 92
Green, Mary Eloise 1903- WhoMW 93
Green, Mary Georgina 1913- Who 94
Green, Matthew 1696-1737 BlmGEL
Green, Maurice 1926- WhoAm 94, WhoScEn 94
Green, Maurice Berkeley 1920- WhoScEn 94
Green, Maurice Richard 1922- WhoAm 94, WhoScEn 94
Green, Mayer Albert 1909- WhoScEn 94
Green, Melanie Jane 1968- WhoWest 94
Green, Meyra Jeanne 1946- WhoFI 94
Green, Michael Who 94
Green, (Edward) Michael (Bankes) 1930- Who 94
Green, Michael (Frederick) 1927- WrDr 94
Green, (Norman) Michael 1926- Who 94
Green, Michael Boris 1946- IntWW 93, Who 94
Green, Michael Dennis 1944- WhoMW 93
Green, Michael Frederick 1927- ConAu 41NR
Green, Michael Frederick 1939- Who 94
Green, Michael I. 1930- WhoWest 94
Green, Michael John 1941- Who 94
Green, Michael Philip 1947- IntWW 93, Who 94
Green, Michelle 1953- ConAu 140
Green, Mino 1927- Who 94
Green, Miriam d1981 WhoHol 92
Green, Mitzi d1969 WhoHol 92
Green, Morris 1922- WhoAm 94
Green, Morris Lee 1916- WhoWest 94
Green, Morton 1917- WhoMW 93
Green, Nancy Ann 1949- WhoAmL 94
Green, Nancy Elizabeth 1955- WhoAmA 93
Green, Nancy Loughridge 1942- WhoAm 94
Green, Neal Jeffrey 1964- WhoWest 94
Green, Neva Joyce 1933- WhoAmL 94
Green, Nigel d1972 WhoHol 92
Green, Norman Harry 1952- WhoWest 94
Green, Norman Kenneth 1924- WhoAm 94
Green, Norman Marston, Jr. 1932- WhoFI 94
Green, Norman Michael 1926- IntWW 93
Green, Nunsowe EncSF 93
Green, O. O. 1932- WrDr 94
Green, Oliver Francis, Jr. 1924- WhoAm 94
Green, Oliver Winslow 1930- WhoBlA 94
Green, Otis Andre 1964- WhoBlA 94
Green, Otis Michael 1945- WhoScEn 94
Green, Owen (Whitley) 1925- IntWW 93, Who 94
Green, Paul (Eliot) 1894-1981 ConDr 93, IntDcT 2
Green, Paul C. 1919- WhoIns 94
Green, Paul Cecil 1919- WhoWest 94
Green, Paul Eliot, Jr. 1924- WhoAm 94, WhoScEn 94
Green, Paula WhoAm 94
Green, Pauline 1948- Who 94, WhoWomW 91
Green, Peggy Meyers 1943- WhoAm 94
Green, Percy William Powlett 1912- Who 94
Green, Peter (James Frederick) 1924- IntWW 93, Who 94
Green, Peter (Morris) 1924- WrDr 94
Green, Peter Morris 1924- Who 94, WhoAm 94
Green, Philip Bevington 1933- WhoAm 94
Green, Phillip Dale 1954- WhoAm 94
Green, Phillip Freeman 1955- WhoWest 94
Green, Raymond A. 1944- WhoBlA 94
Green, Raymond Bert 1929- WhoAm 94, WhoAmL 94, WhoFI 94
Green, Raymond Silvernail 1915- WhoAm 94, WhoFI 94
Green, Raymond William 1940- WhoAm 94
Green, Reginald d1973 WhoHol 92
Green, Reuben H. 1934- WhoBlA 94
Green, Richard 1936- WhoAmL 94, WhoScEn 94, WrDr 94
Green, Richard Alan 1926- WhoAm 94
Green, Richard Calvin, Jr. 1954- WhoAm 94, WhoFI 94
Green, Richard Carter 1947- WhoBlA 94
Green, Richard James 1928- WhoAm 94
Green, Richard John 1944- WhoAm 94
Green, Richard Kevin 1957- WhoWest 94
Green, Richard Lancelyn Gordon 1953- WhoAm 94
Green, Richard Paul, II 1944- WhoMW 93
Green, Richard Steven 1953- WhoAmL 94
Green, Rickey 1954- WhoBlA 94
Green, Ricky 1954- BasBi
Green, Robert EncSF 93
Green, Robert Allen 1927- WhoAmP 93
Green, Robert B. 1941- WhoIns 94
Green, Robert Durham WhoAmP 93
Green, Robert Edward, Jr. 1932- WhoAm 94, WhoScEn 94
Green, Robert Frederick 1923- WhoMW 93, WhoScEn 94
Green, Robert James 1937- Who 94
Green, Robert L. 1933- WhoBlA 94
Green, Robert Lamar 1914- WhoAm 94, WhoScEn 94
Green, Robert Lamar, Jr. 1951- WhoAm 94
Green, Robert Leonard 1931- WhoAm 94
Green, Robert Leslie Stuart 1925- Who 94
Green, Robert S. 1927- WhoAm 94
Green, Robert Scott 1953- WhoAm 94, WhoWest 94
Green, Roger Curtis 1932- IntWW 93
Green, Roger J. 1944- WhoAmA 93
Green, Roger James 1944- WrDr 94
Green, Roger L. 1949- WhoAmP 93
Green, Roger (Gilbert) Lancelyn 1918-1987 EncSF 93
Green, Roland, Sr. 1940- WhoBlA 94
Green, Roland J(ames) 1944- EncSF 93
Green, Ron DrAPF 93
Green, Ronald Michael 1942- WhoAm 94
Green, Rose Basile 1914- WhoAm 94
Green, Roy 1957- WhoBlA 94
Green, Russell Peter 1942- WhoFI 94
Green, Ruth A. 1917- WhoBlA 94
Green, Ruth Milton 1924- WhoMW 93
Green, RuthAnn 1935- WhoMW 93
Green, Sam 1907- Who 94
Green, Samuel DrAPF 93
Green, Samuel, Jr. WhoBlA 94
Green, Samuel Isaac 1942- WhoScEn 94
Green, Sara Edmond 1954- WhoFI 94
Green, Saul 1925- WhoAm 94
Green, Scott E. 1951- WrDr 94
Green, Scott Elliott 1951- WhoAmP 93
Green, Sean Curtis 1970- WhoBlA 94
Green, Seth 1973- WhoHol 92
Green, Sharon 1942- EncSF 93
Green, Sharon Jordan 1948- WhoScEn 94
Green, Sharon V. WhoAmP 93
Green, Sharon Vincentine 1943- WhoMW 93
Green, Sheryl Anne 1952- WhoWest 94
Green, Shirley Moore 1933- WhoAm 94
Green, Sidney 1961- WhoBlA 94
Green, Sihugo 1934- BasBi
Green, Sonia Maria WhoHisp 94
Green, Stella Echave 1948- WhoHisp 94
Green, Stephen EncSF 93, Who 94
Green, (Edward) Stephen (Lycett) 1910- Who 94
Green, Stephen J(ohn) 1940- WrDr 94
Green, Sterling 1946- WhoBlA 94
Green, Steven J. 1945- WhoAm 94, WhoFI 94
Green, Steven Ray 1956- WhoAmP 93

Greenman, Herbert L. 1946- *WhoAmL 94*
Greenman, Jane Friedlieb 1950- *WhoAm 94*
Greenman, Jeremiah 1758-1828 *WhAmRev*
Greenman, John Frederick 1949- *WhoAm 94, WhoMW 93*
Greenman, Judith H. 1935- *WhoAm 94*
Greenman, Norman Lawrence 1923- *WhoAm 94*
Greeno, John Ladd 1949- *WhoAm 94*
Greenoak, Francesca 1946- *Who 94*
Greenock, Lord 1952- *Who 94*
Greenough, Beverly *Who 94*
Greenough, Walter Croan 1951- *WhoAm 94, WhoAmL 94*
Greenough, William Bates, III 1932- *WhoAm 94*
Greenough, William Croan 1914-1980 *WhAm 10*
Greenough, William Tallant 1944- *WhoAm 94, WhoMW 93*
Green-Price, Robert (John) 1940- *Who 94*
Greenquist, Brad *WhoHol 92*
Greenshields, Robert McLaren 1933- *Who 94*
Greensides, Ronald J. 1941- *WhoAmP 93*
Greenslade, Forrest Charles 1939- *WhoAm 94*
Greenslade, Roy 1946- *Who 94*
Greensmith, Edward William 1909- *'Vho 94*
Greensmith, Edwin Lloydd 1900- *Who 94*
Greenspan, Alan 1926- *IntWW 93, Who 94, WhoAm 94, WhoAmP 93, WhoFI 94*
Greenspan, Arnold Michael 1938- *WhoAm 94*
Greenspan, Bernard 1914- *WhoWest 94*
Greenspan, Daniel S. 1951- *WhoMW 93*
Greenspan, David 1956- *ConDr 93*
Greenspan, Deborah *WhoAm 94*
Greenspan, Donald 1928- *WhoAm 94*
Greenspan, Francis S. 1920- *WhoAm 94*
Greenspan, George, Mrs. 1900- *WhoAmA 93*
Greenspan, Harvey Philip 1933- *WhoAm 94*
Greenspan, Jay Scott 1959- *WhoAm 94*
Greenspan, Jeffrey Dov 1954- *WhoAmL 94*
Greenspan, John S. 1938- *WhoWest 94*
Greenspan, Leon Joseph 1932- *WhoAmL 94, WhoFI 94*
Greenspan, Michael Alan 1940- *WhoAm 94*
Greenspan-Margolis, June Rita Edelman 1934- *WhoAm 94*
Greenspon, Robert Alan 1947- *WhoAmL 94*
Greenspun, Adele Aron 1938- *SmATA 76 [port]*
Greenspun, H. M. Hank 1909-1989 *WhAm 10*
Greenstadt, Melvin 1918- *WhoAm 94*
Greenstein, Abraham Jacob 1949- *WhoAm 94*
Greenstein, Fred Irwin 1930- *WhoAm 94*
Greenstein, George 1940- *WrDr 94*
Greenstein, Ilise 1928- *WhoAmA 93N*
Greenstein, Jack 1915- *WrDr 94*
Greenstein, Jerome 1925- *WhoScEn 94*
Greenstein, Jesse Leonard 1909- *IntWW 93, WhoAm 94*
Greenstein, Julius Sidney 1927- *WhoAm 94, WhoMW 93*
Greenstein, Marla Nan 1957- *WhoAmL 94*
Greenstein, Martin Richard 1944- *WhoAm 94, WhoAmL 94*
Greenstein, Merle Edward 1937- *WhoFI 94, WhoWest 94*
Greenstein, Neil David 1954- *WhoAmL 94*
Greenstein, Robert M. 1946- *WhoAm 94, WhoAmP 93*
Greenstein, Ruth Louise 1946- *WhoAm 94*
Greenstock, Jeremy Quentin 1943- *Who 94*
Greenstone, J(ohn) David 1937-1990 *WhAm 10*
Greenstone, James Lynn 1943- *WhoAm 94*
Greenstone, Marion 1925- *WhoAmA 93*
Greenstreet, Mark *WhoHol 92*
Greenstreet, Robert Charles 1952- *WhoAm 94*
Greenstreet, Sydney d1954 *WhoHol 92*
Greentree, (William Wayne) Chris 1935- *Who 94*
Greenwald, Alan Frank 1944- *WhoAm 94*
Greenwald, Alice 1952- *WhoAmA 93*
Greenwald, Anthony Galt 1939- *WhoScEn 94*
Greenwald, Anton Carl 1947- *WhoScEn 94*

Greenwald, Carol Schiro 1939- *WhoAm 94*
Greenwald, Caroline Meyer 1936- *WhoAm 94*
Greenwald, Edward Harris 1920- *WhoFI 94*
Greenwald, G. Jonathan 1943- *ConAu 142*
Greenwald, Gerald 1935- *IntWW 93, WhoAm 94*
Greenwald, Gerald Bernard 1929- *WhoAm 94*
Greenwald, Gilbert Saul 1927- *WhoAm 94*
Greenwald, Harry J. *EncSF 93*
Greenwald, John Edward 1942- *WhoAm 94*
Greenwald, Linda *DrAPF 93*
Greenwald, Margaret Marie 1951- *WhoMW 93*
Greenwald, Maria Barnaby 1940- *WhoAmP 93*
Greenwald, Martin 1942- *WhoAm 94*
Greenwald, Milton 1919- *WhoAm 94*
Greenwald, Peter 1936- *WhoAm 94, WhoScEn 94*
Greenwald, Robert 1927- *WhoAm 94, WhoFI 94*
Greenwald, Robert 1948- *IntMPA 94*
Greenwald, Roger *DrAPF 93*
Greenwald, Sheila 1934- *TwCYAW*
Greenwald, Sheila Ellen 1934- *WhoAm 94*
Greenwald, Ted *WrDr 94*
Greenwall, Frank Koehler 1896- *WhAm 10*
Greenwalt, Clifford Lloyd 1933- *WhoFI 94*
Greenwalt, Lynn Adams 1931- *WhoAmP 93*
Greenwalt, Tibor J. 1914- *WrDr 94*
Greenwalt, Tibor Jack 1914- *IntWW 93, WhoAm 94*
Greenway, Baron 1941- *Who 94*
Greenway, Ann d1977 *WhoHol 92*
Greenway, Francis Howard 1777-1837 *DcNaB MP*
Greenway, Harry 1934- *Who 94*
Greenway, Hugh Davids Scott 1935- *WhoAm 94*
Greenway, John Robert 1946- *Who 94*
Greenway, John Selmes 1924- *WhoAm 94*
Greenway, Marlene Laura 1940- *WhoWest 94*
Greenway, Robert Glen 1932- *WhoWest 94*
Greenway, Tom d1985 *WhoHol 92*
Greenway, William *DrAPF 93*
Greenwell, Dora 1821-1882 *BlmGWL*
Greenwell, Edward (Bernard) 1948- *Who 94*
Greenwell, F. Gerald 1944- *WhoAmL 94*
Greenwell, Jeffrey *Who 94*
Greenwell, (Arthur) Jeffrey 1931- *Who 94*
Greenwell, Ronald Everett 1938- *WhoAm 94, WhoFI 94*
Greenwold, Warren Eldon 1923- *WhoAm 94*
Greenwood, Viscount 1914- *Who 94*
Greenwood, Allan N. *WhoAm 94*
Greenwood, Allen Harold Claude 1917- *Who 94*
Greenwood, Barbara 1940- *WrDr 94*
Greenwood, Bruce *WhoHol 92*
Greenwood, Caleb 1763-1850 *WhWE*
Greenwood, Charles H. 1933- *WhoBlA 94*
Greenwood, Charlotte d1978 *WhoHol 92*
Greenwood, Daphne T. 1949- *WhoAmP 93*
Greenwood, David 1957- *WhoBlA 94*
Greenwood, David A. 1946- *WhoAmL 94*
Greenwood, David Ernest 1937- *Who 94*
Greenwood, Donald Theodore 1923- *WhoMW 93*
Greenwood, Duncan Joseph 1932- *IntWW 93, Who 94*
Greenwood, Frank 1924- *WhoFI 94, WhoScEn 94*
Greenwood, Geoffrey Wilson 1929- *Who 94*
Greenwood, Gordon H. *WhoAmP 93*
Greenwood, Grace *BlmGWL*
Greenwood, Harriet Lois 1950- *WhoMW 93*
Greenwood, Harry Marshall, III 1934- *WhoWest 94*
Greenwood, Hubert d1950 *WhoHol 92*
Greenwood, James, III 1936- *WhoAmP 93*
Greenwood, James C. 1951- *CngDr 93*
Greenwood, James Charles 1951- *WhoAm 94, WhoAmP 93*
Greenwood, James Russell d1993 *Who 94N*
Greenwood, Jane 1934- *ConTFT 11*
Greenwood, Janet Kae Daly 1943- *WhoAm 94*
Greenwood, Jeffrey Michael 1935- *Who 94*
Greenwood, Jeremy John Denis 1942- *Who 94*
Greenwood, Joan d1987 *WhoHol 92*
Greenwood, Joan 1942- *WhoAmP 93*

Greenwood, Joen Elizabeth 1934- *WhoFI 94*
Greenwood, John 1760-1819 *WhAmRev*
Greenwood, John Edward Douglas 1923- *WhoFI 94*
Greenwood, John T. 1949- *WhoBlA 94*
Greenwood, Karen 1956- *WhoMW 93*
Greenwood, L. C. Henderson 1946- *WhoBlA 94*
Greenwood, Lawrence George 1921- *WhoAm 94*
Greenwood, Lee Melvin 1942- *WhoAm 94*
Greenwood, Lisa 1955- *BlmGWL*
Greenwood, M. R. C. 1943- *WhoScEn 94*
Greenwood, Marion 1909-1970 *WhoAmA 93N*
Greenwood, Mark A. *WhoAm 94*
Greenwood, Maryscott 1965- *WhoAmP 93*
Greenwood, Norman Neill 1925- *IntWW 93, Who 94, WrDr 94*
Greenwood, P. Nicholas 1945- *WhoAmL 94*
Greenwood, Peter Bryan *Who 94*
Greenwood, Peter Humphry 1927- *Who 94*
Greenwood, Richard M. 1947- *WhoAm 94, WhoFI 94, WhoWest 94*
Greenwood, Richard P. 1941- *WhoScEn 94*
Greenwood, Ronald 1921- *Who 94*
Greenwood, Ted 1930- *WrDr 94*
Greenwood, Theresa M. Winfrey 1936- *WhoBlA 94*
Greenwood, Thomas d1797 *NewGrDO*
Greenwood, Tim *WhoAmP 93*
Greenwood, Walter 1903-1974 *ConDr 93*
Greenwood, Wilbur Rowe, III 1941- *WhoWest 94*
Greenwood, William E. 1947- *WhoAm 94, WhoFI 94*
Greenwood, William Warren 1942- *WhoAm 94*
Greenwood, Winifred d1961 *WhoHol 92*
Greenya, Cyril James 1944- *WhoAm 94*
Greep, Linda Caryl 1947- *WhoWest 94*
Greer, Allen Curtis, II 1951- *WhoAm 94, WhoAmL 94*
Greer, Ann Lennarson 1944- *ConAu 43NR*
Greer, Bayless Lynn 1941- *WhoAmP 93*
Greer, Bernard Lewis, Jr. 1940- *WhoAm 94, WhoAmL 94*
Greer, Carl Crawford 1940- *WhoAm 94, WhoMW 93*
Greer, Charles Eugene 1945- *WhoAmL 94, WhoFI 94*
Greer, Clayton Andrew 1966- *WhoScEn 94*
Greer, Dabbs 1917- *WhoHol 92*
Greer, Dale R. 1950- *WhoFI 94*
Greer, Darrell Stephen 1949- *WhoWest 94*
Greer, David d1977 *WhoHol 92*
Greer, David Carr 1937- *WhoAmL 94, WhoMW 93*
Greer, David Clive 1937- *Who 94*
Greer, David Keith 1961- *WhoAmL 94*
Greer, David Llewellyn 1930- *WhoScEn 94*
Greer, David S. 1925- *WhoAm 94*
Greer, David Steven 1925- *IntWW 93*
Greer, Edward 1924- *AfrAmG [port], WhoBlA 94*
Greer, Edward Cooper 1957- *WhoScEn 94*
Greer, Edward G. d1993 *NewYTBS 93*
Greer, Germaine 1939- *BlmGWL [port], IntWW 93, Who 94, WhoAm 94, WrDr 94*
Greer, Gordon Bruce 1932- *WhoAm 94, WhoAmL 94, WhoFI 94*
Greer, Gordon Bruce, Jr. 1960- *WhoFI 94*
Greer, Gregory Scott 1958- *WhoFI 94*
Greer, Hal 1936- *BasBi [port], WhoBlA 94*
Greer, Howard Earl 1921- *WhoAm 94, WhoWest 94*
Greer, Ingrid d1981 *WhoHol 92*
Greer, J. Ronnie 1952- *WhoAmP 93*
Greer, James Alexander, II 1932- *WhoAm 94*
Greer, Jane 1924- *IntMPA 94, WhoHol 92*
Greer, Jane Ruth 1941- *WhoAmA 93*
Greer, John Sydney 1944- *WhoAmA 93*
Greer, John W. *WhoAmP 93*
Greer, Joseph Epps 1923- *WhoAm 94*
Greer, Julian d1928 *WhoHol 92*
Greer, Karyn Lynette 1962- *WhoBlA 94*
Greer, Melvin 1929- *WhoAm 94*
Greer, Michael 1943- *WhoHol 92*
Greer, Monte Arnold 1922- *WhoAm 94*
Greer, Norris E. 1945- *WhoAmL 94*
Greer, Pedro Jose, Jr. 1956- *WhoHisp 94*
Greer, R. Douglas 1942- *WhoScEn 94*
Greer, Randall Dewey 1951- *WhoAm 94*
Greer, Raymond White 1954- *WhoAmL 94, WhoFI 94*
Greer, Richard *EncSF 93*
Greer, Richard Ewing, Sr. 1935- *WhoWest 94*
Greer, Robert O., Jr. *DrAPF 93*

Greer, Robert O., Jr. 1944- *WhoBlA 94*
Greer, Scott (Allen) 1922- *ConAu 43NR*
Greer, Sonny d1982 *WhoHol 92*
Greer, Tee S., Jr. 1935- *WhoBlA 94*
Greer, Thomas H. 1942- *WhoAm 94, WhoBlA 94, WhoMW 93*
Greer, Thomas Hoag 1914- *WhoAm 94*
Greer, Thomas Vernon 1932- *WhoAm 94*
Greer, Tom 1846?-1904 *EncSF 93*
Greer, Walter (Marion) 1920- *WhoAmA 93*
Greer, Wesley Dwaine 1937- *WhoAmA 93*
Greeran, Judith Rae 1939- *WhoWest 94*
Greet, Ben d1936 *WhoHol 92*
Greet, Clare d1939 *WhoHol 92*
Greet, Kenneth Gerald 1918- *IntWW 93, Who 94, WrDr 94*
Greetham, (George) Colin 1929- *Who 94*
Greever, John 1934- *WhoWest 94*
Greeves, R. V. 1935- *WhoAmA 93*
Greevy (Tattan), Bernadette 1940- *NewGrDO*
Greevy, Bernadette *IntWW 93*
Grefe, Richard 1945- *WhoAm 94*
Grefe, Robert Herman 1941- *WhoFI 94*
Grefe, Rolland Eugene 1920- *WhoAm 94, WhoAmL 94*
Greffenius, Albert Julius 1924- *WhoAmL 94*
Gregg, Percy 1836-1889 *EncSF 93*
Grega, Lawrence Michael 1964- *WhoFI 94*
Gregan, Edmund Robert 1936- *WhoAm 94*
Gregan, John Patrick 1947- *WhoFI 94*
Greganti, Mac Andrew 1947- *WhoAm 94*
Greger, Debora *DrAPF 93*
Greger, Janet L. 1948- *IntWW 93*
Gregersen, Max A. 1951- *WhoScEn 94*
Gregerson, Byron Arnold 1942- *WhoIns 94*
Gregerson, Linda *DrAPF 93*
Gregerson, Ned Owen 1940- *WhoWest 94*
Gregerson, Richard O. *WhoAmP 93*
Gregg, Arnold d1936 *WhoHol 92*
Gregg, Arthur James 1928- *AfrAmG [port]*
Gregg, Bradley *WhoHol 92*
Gregg, Bruce Pendleton, Jr. 1938- *WhoFI 94*
Gregg, Charles Thornton 1927- *WhoAm 94*
Gregg, David, III 1933- *WhoFI 94*
Gregg, Davis Weinert 1918- *WhoAm 94, WrDr 94*
Gregg, Dick Hoskins, Jr. 1939- *WhoAmP 93*
Gregg, Donald P. 1927- *WhoAmP 93*
Gregg, Everley d1959 *WhoHol 92*
Gregg, Forrest *ProFbHF [port]*
Gregg, Forrest 1933- *WhoAm 94*
Gregg, Harrison, Jr. 1940- *WhoAmP 93*
Gregg, Harrison M., Jr. 1942- *WhoBlA 94*
Gregg, Hubert 1914- *WhoHol 92, WrDr 94*
Gregg, Hubert Robert Harry 1914- *Who 94*
Gregg, Hugh 1917- *WhoAm 94, WhoAmP 93*
Gregg, James D. 1947- *WhoAm 94, WhoAmL 94*
Gregg, Jay Mason 1951- *WhoMW 93*
Gregg, John Bailey 1922- *WhoMW 93*
Gregg, John Franklin 1943- *WhoAm 94*
Gregg, John Pennypacker 1947- *WhoAmL 94*
Gregg, John Richard 1954- *WhoAmP 93, WhoMW 93*
Gregg, John Robert *WorInv*
Gregg, Jon Mann 1943- *WhoAm 94, WhoAmL 94*
Gregg, Judd 1947- *CngDr 93, IntWW 93, WhoAm 94*
Gregg, Judd Alan 1947- *WhoAmP 93*
Gregg, Linda *DrAPF 93*
Gregg, Lucius Perry 1933- *WhoBlA 94*
Gregg, Lucius Perry, Jr. 1933- *WhoAm 94, WhoWest 94*
Gregg, Michael B. 1930- *WhoAm 94*
Gregg, Michael W. 1935- *WhoAm 94*
Gregg, Pauline *WrDr 94*
Gregg, Richard (Alexander) 1927- *WrDr 94*
Gregg, Richard Leo 1944- *WhoAm 94, WhoFI 94*
Gregg, Richard Nelson 1926-1986 *WhoAmA 93N*
Gregg, Robert E. 1960- *WhoHisp 94*
Gregg, Robert Edgar 1947- *WhoAm 94*
Gregg, Robert Lee 1932- *WhoMW 93*
Gregg, Robert Lem, Jr. 1921- *WhoAmP 93*
Gregg, Sidney John 1902- *WrDr 94*
Gregg, Virginia d1986 *WhoHol 92*
Gregg, Walter Emmor, Jr. 1941- *WhoAmL 94*
Greggs, Elizabeth May Bushnell 1925- *WhoWest 94*
Grego, Peter 1949- *WhoWest 94*

Grego-Heintz, Donna Marie 1956- *WhoWest 94*
Gregoire, Christine *WhoAmP 93*
Gregoire, Christine O. *WhoAm 94, WhoAmL 94, WhoWest 94*
Gregoire, Henri *IntWW 93*
Gregoire, Mathieu A. 1953- *WhoAmA 93*
Gregoire, Paul 1911- *IntWW 93, Who 94*
Gregoire, Paul Cardinal 1911- *WhoAm 94*
Gregoire, Pierre 1907- *IntWW 93*
Gregor, Arthur *DrAPF 93*
Gregor, Arthur 1923- *WrDr 94*
Gregor, Bohumil 1926- *NewGrDO*
Gregor, Clunie Bryan 1929- *WhoAm 94, WhoScEn 94*
Gregor, Dorothy Deborah 1939- *WhoAm 94*
Gregor, Eduard 1936- *WhoScEn 94, WhoWest 94*
Gregor, Harold Laurence 1929- *WhoAmA 93, WhoMW 93*
Gregor, Joseph 1888-1960 *NewGrDO*
Gregor, Jozsef 1940- *NewGrDO*
Gregor, Lee *EncSF 93*
Gregor, Marlene Pierce 1932- *WhoMW 93*
Gregor, Nora d1949 *WhoHol 92*
Gregor, Tibor Philip 1919- *WhoAm 94*
Gregora, Peter J. 1946- *WhoAmL 94*
Gregoratos, Gabriel 1929- *WhoWest 94*
Gregorian, Vartan 1934- *IntWW 93, WhoAm 94*
Gregorich, Barbara 1943- *ConAu 42NR*
Gregorich, Penny Denise 1968- *WhoMW 93*
Gregorio, John T. 1926- *WhoAmP 93*
Gregorio, Juan 1896-1971 *EncNAR*
Gregorio, Luis Justino Lopes 1929- *WhoAm 94*
Gregorio, Rose 1932- *WhoHol 92*
Gregorio, William 1945- *WhoAmP 93*
Gregorios, Paulos 1922- *IntWW 93*
Gregorios, Paulos Mar 1922- *WhoAm 94*
Gregoriou, Gregor Georg 1937- *WhoScEn 94*
Gregorious *Who 94*
Gregorius, Beverly June 1915- *WhoAm 94*
Gregoropoulos, John 1921- *WhoAmA 93*
Gregorsky, Frank William 1955- *WhoAmP 93*
Gregory *WhoWest 94*
Gregory, Lady 1852-1932 *IntDcT 2*
Gregory, VII c. 1020-1085 *HisWorL [port]*
Gregory, Alan Thomas 1925- *Who 94*
Gregory, Andre *WhoHol 92*
Gregory, Angela 1903-1990 *WhoAmA 93N*
Gregory, Arthur Stanley 1914- *WhoAm 94*
Gregory, Augusta 1852-1932 *BlmGEL, BlmGWL*
Gregory, Augustus Charles 1819-1905 *WhWE*
Gregory, Benji 1978- *WhoHol 92*
Gregory, Bernard Vincent 1926- *WhoBlA 94*
Gregory, Bettina Louise 1946- *WhoAm 94*
Gregory, Bill 1960- *WhoAmP 93*
Gregory, Bobby Lee 1938- *WhoAm 94*
Gregory, Bruce 1917- *WhoAmA 93*
Gregory, Bruce Nicholas 1938- *WhoScEn 94*
Gregory, Bruce Webster 1964- *WhoFI 94*
Gregory, Byron L. 1945- *WhoAm 94, WhoAmL 94*
Gregory, Calvin 1942- *WhoAm 94, WhoFI 94, WhoWest 94*
Gregory, Calvin Luther 1942- *WhoIns 94*
Gregory, Carole *DrAPF 93*
Gregory, Carolyn *DrAPF 93*
Gregory, Charles L. 1949- *WhoAmL 94*
Gregory, Chauncey Klugh 1963- *WhoAmP 93*
Gregory, Chester 1930- *WhoAmP 93*
Gregory, Cleburne E., III 1947- *WhoAmL 94*
Gregory, Clifford 1924- *Who 94*
Gregory, Conal Robert 1947- *Who 94*
Gregory, Connie Lee 1954- *WhoMW 93*
Gregory, Cynde *DrAPF 93*
Gregory, Cynthia 1946- *IntDcB [port]*
Gregory, Cynthia Kathleen 1946- *WhoAm 94*
Gregory, Dave
See XTC *ConMus 10*
Gregory, Dick 1932- *WhoAm 94, WhoAmP 93, WhoBlA 94, WhoCom, WhoHol 92, WrDr 94*
Gregory, Dora d1954 *WhoHol 92*
Gregory, E. John, Sr. 1919- *WhoHisp 94*
Gregory, Eleanor Anne *WhoWest 94*
Gregory, Ena 1908- *WhoHol 92*
Gregory, Fern Alexandra 1951- *WhoMW 93*
Gregory, Francis Thomas 1821-1888 *WhWE*
Gregory, Frederick Drew 1941- *AfrAmAl 6, WhoBlA 94*
Gregory, George G. 1932- *WhoAm 94, WhoAmL 94*
Gregory, George T. 1921- *WhoAmP 93*
Gregory, Gilbert E. *WhoAmP 93*
Gregory, Gus 1940- *WhoFI 94*
Gregory, Hardy, Jr. *WhoAmP 93*
Gregory, Herold La Mar 1923- *WhoAm 94*
Gregory, Holly Wanda Januszkiewicz 1956- *WhoAmL 94*
Gregory, Howard Verne 1918- *WhoMW 93*
Gregory, J. Dennis *BlkWr 2*
Gregory, Jackson V. 1941- *WhoAmP 93*
Gregory, James 1911- *WhoAm 94, WhoHol 92, WhoWest 94*
Gregory, James Michael 1935- *WhoAm 94*
Gregory, Joan 1930- *WhoAmA 93*
Gregory, John *EncSF 93*
Gregory, John 1879-1958 *WhoAmA 93N*
Gregory, John 1933- *WrDr 94*
Gregory, John Peter 1925- *Who 94*
Gregory, John R. 1918- *IntMPA 94*
Gregory, Joseph Tracy 1914- *WhoAm 94*
Gregory, Joseph Winfield 1965- *WhoAmL 94*
Gregory, Judith 1951- *WhoWest 94*
Gregory, Karl Dwight 1931- *WhoBlA 94*
Gregory, Kathleen Jordan *WhoHol 92*
Gregory, Kathrine Patricia 1952- *WhoFI 94*
Gregory, Keith Edward 1924- *WhoMW 93*
Gregory, Kenneth John 1938- *Who 94*
Gregory, Kirk Dennis 1954- *WhoMW 93*
Gregory, Kristiana 1951- *ConAu 141, SmATA 74 [port]*
Gregory, Laura Ann 1940- *WhoFI 94*
Gregory, Leslie Howard James 1915- *Who 94*
Gregory, Lewis Dean 1953- *WhoAmL 94*
Gregory, Lisa *ConAu 42NR*
Gregory, Mark 1965- *WhoHol 92*
Gregory, Mary *WhoHol 92*
Gregory, Mel Hyatt, Jr. 1936- *WhoAm 94*
Gregory, Michael *WhoHol 92*
Gregory, Michael Anthony 1925- *Who 94*
Gregory, Michael Samuel 1949- *WhoBlA 94*
Gregory, Michael Strietmann 1929- *WhoAm 94, WhoWest 94*
Gregory, Myra May 1912- *WhoFI 94*
Gregory, Nelson Bruce 1933- *WhoFI 94, WhoWest 94*
Gregory, Norman Wayne 1920- *WhoAm 94*
Gregory, Owen *EncSF 93*
Gregory, Patricia Jeanne 1951- *WhoMW 93, WhoScEn 94*
Gregory, Paul d1942 *WhoHol 92*
Gregory, Paul 1920- *WhoHol 92*
Gregory, Peter Roland 1946- *Who 94*
Gregory, Philip Lawrence, Jr. 1954- *WhoAmL 94*
Gregory, Philippa 1954- *WrDr 94*
Gregory, Richard Claxton 1932- *WhoBlA 94*
Gregory, Richard Hyde 1960- *WhoFI 94*
Gregory, Richard Langton 1923- *Who 94, WrDr 94*
Gregory, Richard Lee 1954- *WhoScEn 94*
Gregory, Rick Dean 1954- *WhoAmL 94*
Gregory, Rita Kay 1958- *WhoMW 93*
Gregory, Robert Alphonso 1935- *WhoBlA 94*
Gregory, Robert D. *DrAPF 93*
Gregory, Robert Scott 1954- *WhoScEn 94*
Gregory, Roger Lee 1953- *WhoBlA 94*
Gregory, Roger Michael 1939- *Who 94*
Gregory, Roland Charles Leslie *Who 94*
Gregory, Ronald 1921- *Who 94*
Gregory, Ross 1933- *WhoAm 94, WhoMW 93*
Gregory, Roy 1916- *Who 94*
Gregory, Roy 1935- *WrDr 94*
Gregory, Russell Arthur 1943- *WhoAm 94*
Gregory, Stan(ley Wayne) 1948- *WhoAmA 93*
Gregory, Stephan 1927- *WrDr 94*
Gregory, Stephen 1952- *WrDr 94*
Gregory, Steven 1953- *WrDr 94*
Gregory, Sylver K. 1973- *WhoBlA 94*
Gregory, Thea *WhoHol 92*
Gregory, Theodore Morris 1952- *WhoBlA 94*
Gregory, Theopalis K. 1952- *WhoAmP 93*
Gregory, Thomas Bradford 1944- *WhoMW 93, WhoScEn 94*
Gregory, Thomas Lang 1935- *WhoFI 94*
Gregory, Vance Peter, Jr. 1943- *WhoMW 93, WhoScEn 94*
Gregory, W. Larry 1950- *WhoScEn 94*
Gregory, Wanda Jean 1925- *WhoAmL 94*
Gregory, Waylande 1905-1971 *WhoAmA 93N*
Gregory, Will d1926 *WhoHol 92*
Gregory, William David 1960- *WhoWest 94*
Gregory, William Edgar 1910- *WhoWest 94*
Gregory, William Edward 1958- *WhoAmL 94*
Gregory, William N., Jr. 1929- *WhoIns 94*
Gregory, William Stanley 1949- *WhoAmL 94*
Gregory, Wilton D. 1947- *WhoBlA 94*
Gregory-Goodrum, Ellna Kay 1943- *WhoAmA 93*
Gregoryk, Michael David 1951- *WhoWest 94*
Gregory the Great, I c. 540-604 *HisWorL [port]*
Gregson, Baron 1924- *Who 94*
Gregson, John d1975 *WhoHol 92*
Gregson, Mary Poage 1910- *WhoAmP 93*
Gregson, Peter (Lewis) 1936- *Who 94*
Gregson, Peter Lewis 1936- *IntWW 93*
Gregson, William Derek Hadfield 1920- *Who 94*
Greguric, Franjo 1939- *IntWW 93*
Gregware, James Murray 1956- *WhoAm 94, WhoFI 94*
Greider, William (F.) *WrDr 94*
Greider, William (Harold) 1936- *ConAu 41NR*
Greif, Edward Louis 1909- *WhoAm 94, WhoFI 94*
Greif, Geoffrey L. 1949- *ConAu 140*
Greif, Joseph 1943- *WhoAmL 94*
Greif, Robert 1938- *WhoAm 94*
Greif, Steven Denis 1951- *WhoAmL 94*
Greifenstein, Frederick John 1946- *WhoWest 94*
Greiff, Barrie S(anford) 1935- *WrDr 94*
Greiffenberg, Catharina Regina von 1633-1694 *BlmGWL*
Greifinger, David Ross 1957- *WhoAmL 94*
Greig, Brian Strother 1950- *WhoAm 94, WhoAmL 94*
Greig, (Henry Louis) Carron 1925- *Who 94*
Greig, Doreen (Edith) 1917- *WrDr 94*
Greig, Henry Louis Carron 1925- *IntWW 93*
Greig, John *WhoAmP 93*
Greig, Robert d1958 *WhoHol 92*
Greig, Robert Thomson 1945- *WhoAm 94*
Greig, Thomas Currie 1931- *WhoAm 94*
Greig, William Harold 1951- *WhoAmL 94*
Greig, William Taber, Jr. 1924- *WhoAm 94*
Greigg, Ronald Edwin 1946- *WhoAmL 94*
Greigg, Stanley Lloyd 1931- *WhoAmP 93*
Greig of Eccles, James Dennis 1926- *Who 94*
Greil, Ralph H. 1947- *WhoAmL 94*
Greiling, Mindy 1948- *WhoAmP 93*
Greiling, Paul Theodore 1939- *WhoAm 94*
Greils, Howard Monroe 1947- *WhoWest 94*
Greilsheimer, James Gans 1937- *WhoAm 94*
Greiman, Alan J. 1931- *WhoAmP 93*
Greiman, April 1948- *WhoAm 94*
Grein, Jack Thomas 1862-1935 *BlmGEL*
Grein, Richard Frank 1932- *WhoAm 94*
Greindl, Josef d1993 *IntWW 93N*
Greindl, Josef 1912- *IntWW 93, NewGrDO*
Greiner, David Lee 1964- *WhoFI 94*
Greiner, G. Roger 1942- *WhoIns 94*
Greiner, Keith Allen 1940- *WhoAmP 93*
Greiner, Morris Esty, Jr. 1920- *WhoAm 94*
Greiner, Nicholas Frank 1947- *Who 94*
Greiner, Peter Charles 1938- *WhoAm 94*
Greiner, Richard C. 1953- *WhoAmL 94*
Greiner, Sandy *WhoAmP 93*
Greiner, Stephen W. 1944- *WhoAmL 94*
Greiner, Thomas Moseley 1961- *WhoScEn 94*
Greiner, Walter Albin Erhard 1935- *IntWW 93, WhoScEn 94*
Greiner, William Robert 1934- *WhoAm 94*
Greinke, Everett Donald 1929- *WhoAm 94*
Greis, Wayne Raymond 1942- *WhoMW 93*
Greisen, Kenneth Ingvard 1918- *WhoAm 94*
Greisler, Howard Parker 1950- *WhoAm 94*
Greisman, Harvey William 1948- *WhoFI 94*
Greissle, Hermann A. 1925-1991 *WhoAmA 93N*
Greist, Kim 1958- *IntMPA 94, WhoHol 92*
Greist, Mary Coffey 1947- *WhoAm 94*
Greitzer, Carol *WhoAmP 93*
Greitzer, Edward Marc 1941- *WhoAm 94, WhoScEn 94*
Greive, William Henry 1933- *WhoMW 93*
Greiving, Paul William 1957- *WhoFI 94*
Grejtak, Gena Renee 1962- *WhoMW 93*
Greki, Anna 1931-1966 *BlmGWL*
Grekova, I. 1907- *BlmGWL, ConWorW 93*
Grekova, Irina Nikolaevna 1907- *IntWW 93*
Grelinger, Wim d1977 *WhoHol 92*
Grella, Robert Alan 1939- *WhoIns 94*
Grelle, Lawrence E. 1943- *WhoAmL 94*
Grelle, Martin Glen 1954- *WhoAmA 93*
Grembowski, David Emil 1951- *WhoWest 94*
Grembowski, Eugene 1938- *WhoFI 94, WhoWest 94*
Gremillion, Curtis Lionel, Jr. 1924- *WhoAm 94, WhoScEn 94*
Gremillion, L. Todd 1947- *WhoAmL 94*
Gremmels, Marion Louise Chapman 1924-1987 *ConAu 142*
Gremont, Henri *NewGrDO*
Gren, Conrad Roger 1955- *WhoFI 94, WhoWest 94*
Grenald, Raymond 1928- *WhoAm 94*
Grenander, M. E. 1918- *WhoAm 94*
Grenard, Jack 1933- *WhoWest 94*
Grendell, Diane V. *WhoAmP 93*
Grendelmeier, Verena 1939- *WhoWomW 91*
Grendi, Ernest W. *WhoFI 94*
Grendler, Paul Frederick 1936- *WhoAm 94*
Grendon, Stephen *EncSF 93*
Grenell, Barbara 1944- *WhoAmA 93*
Grenell, James Henry 1924- *WhoAm 94*
Grenet, Eliseo d1950 *WhoHol 92*
Grenet, Francois Lupien c. 1700-1753 *NewGrDO*
Grenfell, Baron 1935- *Who 94*
Grenfell, Andree 1940- *Who 94*
Grenfell, George 1849-1906 *WhWE*
Grenfell, George Albert, Jr. 1941- *WhoWest 94*
Grenfell, Gloria Ross 1926- *WhoWest 94*
Grenfell, Joyce d1979 *WhoHol 92*
Grenfell, Julian Pascoe Francis St. Leger 1935- *IntWW 93*
Grenfell, Simon Pascoe 1942- *Who 94*
Grenfell-Baines, George 1908- *Who 94*
Grenga, Michelle Louise 1965- *WhoMW 93*
Grenier, Edward Joseph, Jr. 1933- *WhoAm 94, WhoAmL 94*
Grenier, Fernand 1927- *WhoAm 94, WhoScEn 94*
Grenier, Henry R. *WhoAmP 93*
Grenier, Jean-Marie Rene 1926- *IntWW 93*
Grenier, John Edward 1930- *WhoAmP 93*
Grenier, Judson A., Jr. 1930- *WhoWest 94*
Grenier, Peter Francis 1934- *Who 94*
Grenier, Zach 1954- *WhoHol 92*
Grenig, Jay Edward 1943- *WhoMW 93*
Grening, L. Keith 1957- *WhoFI 94*
Grenley, Aaron Lemuel 1946- *WhoWest 94*
Grenley, Gary Irving 1947- *WhoAmL 94*
Grenley, Philip 1912- *WhoScEn 94, WhoWest 94*
Grennan, Cynthia 1938- *WhoWest 94*
Grennan, Eamon *DrAPF 93*
Grennan, Eamon 1941- *WrDr 94*
Grennan, Jim 1933- *WhoAmL 94*
Grenon, Gregory *WhoAmA 93*
Grenquist, Peter Carl 1931- *WhoAm 94*
Grenser, Johann Friedrich 1758-1795 *NewGrDO*
Grenside, John (Peter) 1921- *Who 94*
Grensky, Ronald D. 1954- *WhoAmP 93*
Grenvallet *NewGrDO*
Grenville *Who 94*
Grenville, George 1712-1770 *WhAmRev [port]*
Grenville, John A. S. 1928- *WrDr 94*
Grenville, John Ashley Soames 1928- *Who 94*
Grenville, Kate 1950- *BlmGWL*
Grenville, Richard 1540-1591 *WhWE*
Grenville-Grey, Wilfrid Ernest 1930- *Who 94*
Grenyer, Herbert Charles 1913- *Who 94*
Grenz, Stanley J. 1950- *WhoAm 94*
Grenzebach, William Southwood 1945- *WhoScEn 94*
Greppin, John Aird Coutts 1937- *WhoAm 94*
Gresak, Jozef 1907-1987 *NewGrDO*
Gresens, James W. 1943- *WhoAmL 94*
Greseth, Mona *WhoAmP 93*
Gresham, (Geoffrey) Austin 1924- *Who 94*
Gresham, Donald 1956- *WhoBlA 94*
Gresham, Edith d1976 *WhoHol 92*
Gresham, Edward 1565-1613 *DcNaB MP*
Gresham, Gary Stuart 1951- *WhoAm 94*
Gresham, Glen Edward 1931- *WhoAm 94*
Gresham, James Arthur 1928- *WhoAm 94*
Gresham, John Kenneth *WhoAmP 93*
Gresham, Johnny, Jr. *WhoAmP 93*
Gresham, Louise Shane 1952- *WhoWest 94*
Gresham, Perry E(pler) 1907- *ConAu 42NR*
Gresham, Perry Epler 1907- *WhoAm 94*
Gresham, Robert Coleman 1917- *WhoAm 94, WhoAmP 93*

Gresham, Robert Lambert, Jr. 1943- *WhoWest 94*
Gresham, Sue Kratze 1940- *WhoMW 93*
Gresham, Timothy Ward 1953- *WhoAmL 94*
Gresham, Zane Oliver 1948- *WhoAm 94, WhoAmL 94*
Gresla, Eric C. 1960- *WhoMW 93*
Gresley, (Herbert) Nigel 1876-1941 *DcNaB MP*
Gresley, Stephen Clark 1940- *WhoMW 93*
Gresnick, Antoine-Frederic 1755?-1799 *NewGrDO*
Gresov, Boris Vladimir 1914- *WhoAm 94*
Gress, Edward Jules 1940- *WhoFI 94*
Gress, Elsa 1919-1989 *BlmGWL*
Gress, Googy *WhoHol 92*
Gress, Steve C. 1947- *WhoMW 93*
Gressak, Anthony Raymond, Jr. 1947- *WhoAm 94*
Gresse, Andre 1868-1937 *NewGrDO*
Gresse, Leon(-Pierre-Napoleon) 1845-1900 *NewGrDO*
Gressel, Michael L. 1902- *WhoAmA 93*
Gressens, June P. 1924- *WhoAmP 93*
Gressens, O. 1897- *WhAm 10*
Gresser, Herbert David 1930- *WhoScEn 94*
Gresser, Mark Geoffrey 1958- *WhoScEn 94*
Gresser, Seymour 1926- *WrDr 94*
Gresser, Seymour Gerald 1926- *WhoAmA 93*
Gressette, Lawrence M., Jr. 1932- *WhoFI 94*
Gresshoff, Peter Michael 1948- *WhoScEn 94*
Gressley, Gene Maurice 1931- *WhoAm 94*
Gressman, Eugene 1917- *WhoAm 94*
Gresso, Vernon Riddle 1927- *WhoFI 94*
Greswell, Jeaffreson Herbert 1916- *Who 94*
Gretchaninov, Alexandr Tikhonovich *NewGrDO*
Grether, David Maclay 1938- *WhoAm 94*
Gretler, Heinrich d1977 *WhoHol 92*
Gretry, Andre-Ernest-Modeste 1741-1813 *NewGrDO*
Gretry, Lucile 1772-1790 *NewGrDO*
Gretton, Baron 1975- *Who 94*
Gretton, Peter William d1992 *Who 94N*
Gretz, Stephen Randolph 1948- *WhoAm 94*
Gretzinger, James 1925- *WhoScEn 94*
Gretzinger, Ralph Edwin, III 1948- *WhoFI 94*
Gretzky, Wayne 1961- *WhoAm 94, WhoWest 94*
Greulich, Richard Curtice 1928- *WhoAm 94*
Greulich, Robert Charles 1958- *WhoFI 94*
Greve, Felix Paul (Berthold Friedrich) 1879-1948 *ConAu 141*
Greve, Guy Robert 1947- *WhoAmL 94, WhoMW 93*
Greve, John 1927- *Who 94*
Greve, John Henry 1934- *WhoAm 94, WhoScEn 94*
Greve, Lucius, II 1915- *WhoFI 94, WhoMW 93*
Grevengoed, Glenn Burdette 1959- *WhoAmL 94*
Grevill, Laurent *WhoHol 92*
Greville *Who 94*
Greville, Alice 1842-1903 *BlmGWL*
Greville, Edmond d1966 *WhoHol 92*
Greville, Fulke 1554-1628 *BlmGEL*
Greville, Phillip Jamieson 1925- *Who 94*
Grevisse, Fernand 1924- *IntWW 93*
Grew, Kimberly Ann 1962- *WhoMW 93*
Grew, Priscilla Croswell 1940- *WhoAm 94, WhoMW 93, WhoScEn 94*
Grew, Raymond Edward 1923- *WhoScEn 94*
Grew, Robert Ralph 1931- *WhoAmL 94, WhoFI 94*
Grewal, Harnam Singh 1937- *Who 94*
Grewal, Perminder Singh 1956- *WhoAsA 94*
Grewcock, William L. 1925- *WhoAm 94, WhoFI 94, WhoMW 93*
Grewe, John Mitchell 1938- *WhoAm 94*
Grewell, Judith Lynn 1945- *WhoMW 93*
Grewelle, Larry Allan 1937- *WhoFI 94*
Grey *Who 94*
Grey, Earl 1939- *Who 94*
Grey (Dudley), Jane 1537-1554 *BlmGWL [port]*
Grey, Alan Hartley 1925- *Who 94*
Grey, Alex V. 1953- *WhoAmA 93*
Grey, Anne 1907- *WhoHol 92*
Grey, Anthony 1938- *WrDr 94*
Grey, Anthony (Dysart) 1949- *Who 94*
Grey, Beryl 1927- *IntDcB [port], Who 94*
Grey, Beryl (Elizabeth) 1927- *WrDr 94*
Grey, Beryl Elizabeth 1927- *IntWW 93*
Grey, Brenda 1910- *WrDr 94*
Grey, Carol *EncSF 93*
Grey, Charles *EncSF 93*
Grey, Charles 1729-1807 *AmRev, WhAmRev*
Grey, Charles 1919- *WrDr 94*
Grey, Denise *WhoHol 92*
Grey, George 1812-1898 *WhWE*
Grey, Georges d1954 *WhoHol 92*
Grey, Georgina 1930- *WrDr 94*
Grey, (Constance) Gladys de *NewGrDO*
Grey, Gloria d1947 *WhoHol 92*
Grey, Henry 1849-1913 *EncABHB 9*
Grey, Henry 1954- *WhoAm 94*
Grey, Howard Alan 1932- *WhoWest 94*
Grey, Ian 1918- *WrDr 94*
Grey, J. David d1993 *NewYTBS 93*
Grey, J. David 1935- *WrDr 94*
Grey, J. David 1935-1993 *ConAu 140*
Grey, Jane d1944 *WhoHol 92*
Grey, Jane 1537-1554 *DcLB 132 [port]*
Grey, Jennifer 1960- *IntMPA 94, WhoHol 92*
Grey, Jerry 1926- *ConAu 43NR, WrDr 94*
Grey, Joel 1932- *IntMPA 94, WhoAm 94, WhoHol 92*
Grey, John Egerton 1929- *Who 94*
Grey, John St. John 1934- *Who 94*
Grey, Katherine d1950 *WhoHol 92*
Grey, Leonard d1918 *WhoHol 92*
Grey, Linda *IntWW 93, WhoAm 94, WhoFI 94*
Grey, Lita 1908- *WhoHol 92*
Grey, Madeline d1950 *WhoHol 92*
Grey, Nan d1993 *NewYTBS 93 [port]*
Grey, Nan 1918- *WhoHol 92*
Grey, Olga d1973 *WhoHol 92*
Grey, Richard E. *WhoAm 94, WhoFI 94*
Grey, Richard S. 1950- *WhoAmL 94*
Grey, Robert d1934 *WhoHol 92*
Grey, Robert Dean 1939- *WhoAm 94, WhoScEn 94, WhoWest 94*
Grey, Robert Waters *DrAPF 93*
Grey, Robin Douglas 1931- *Who 94*
Grey, Virginia 1917- *IntMPA 94, WhoHol 92*
Grey, Wilfrid Ernest G. *Who 94*
Grey Cloud, David 1840-1890 *EncNAR*
Grey Egerton, (Philip) John (Caledon) 1920- *Who 94*
Greyn, Clinton *WhoHol 92*
Grey Of Codnor, Baron 1903- *Who 94*
Grey Of Naunton, Baron 1910- *IntWW 93, Who 94*
Grey Owl 1888-1938 *ChlLR 32 [port]*
Greyson, Jerome 1927- *WhoWest 94*
Greytak, Lee Joseph 1949- *WhoFI 94*
Greytak, Thomas John 1940- *WhoAm 94*
Greywall, Mahesh Inder-Singh 1934- *WhoScEn 94*
Grey-Wilson, Christopher 1944- *WrDr 94*
Greze, Jean-Louis 1931- *WhoFI 94*
Gribben, Alan 1941- *WhoAm 94*
Gribbin, David James 1939- *WhoAmP 93*
Gribbin, David James, III 1939- *WhoAm 94*
Gribbin, John 1946- *EncSF 93*
Gribbin, Robert E., III 1946- *WhoAmP 93*
Gribbin, Thomas Edward 1953- *WhoMW 93*
Gribble, Arthur Stanley 1904- *Who 94*
Gribble, Christopher Blair 1962- *WhoFI 94*
Gribble, Harry Wagstaff d1981 *WhoHol 92*
Gribbon, Daniel McNamara 1917- *WhoAm 94*
Gribbon, Eddie d1965 *WhoHol 92*
Gribbon, Edward John 1943- *Who 94*
Gribbon, Harry d1961 *WhoHol 92*
Gribbon, Nigel St. George 1917- *Who 94*
Gribeauval, Jean Baptiste Vaquette de 1715-1789 *AmRev*
Gribin, Liz 1934- *WhoAmA 93*
Gribov, Alexei d1977 *WhoHol 92*
Gribov, Vladimir N. *WhoScEn 94*
Gribovicz, Lee Penn 1949- *WhoWest 94*
Gribow, Dale Seward 1943- *WhoAmL 94, WhoFI 94*
Griboyedov, Alexander Sergeyevich 1795-1829 *IntDcT 2 [port]*
Grice, George Daniel 1929- *WhoAm 94*
Gridban, Volsted *EncSF 93*
Gridban, Volsted 1919- *WrDr 94*
Grider, George William 1912- *WhAm 10*
Grider, Jay 1935- *WrDr 94*
Grider, Joseph Kenneth 1921- *WhoAm 94*
Grider, Kathy Jill 1954- *WhoMW 93*
Gridley, Baron 1906- *Who 94*
Gridley, Richard 1711-1796 *AmRev, WhAmRev*
Gridley, Sam *DrAPF 93*
Gridoux, Lucas d1952 *WhoHol 92*
Grieb, Kenneth J 1939- *WrDr 94*
Grieb, Kenneth Joseph *WhoMW 93*
Grieb, Robert William 1930- *WhoIns 94*
Griebel, Robert Donald 1930- *WhoMW 93*
Griebsch, Linda 1948- *WhoAmP 93*
Griech, Frederick G. 1944- *WhoFI 94*
Grieco, Joseph V. 1915- *WhoAmP 93*
Grieco, Paul Anthony 1944- *WhoAm 94*
Grieco, Richard 1964- *WhoHol 92*
Grieder, Jerome B. 1932- *WrDr 94*
Grieder, Terence 1931- *WhoAmA 93*
Griefen, John Adams 1942- *WhoAm 94, WhoAmA 93*
Grieg, Edvard (Hagerup) 1843-1907 *NewGrDO*
Grieg, (Johan) Nordahl (Brun) 1902-1943 *IntDcT 2*
Grieger, Gunter 1931- *WhoScEn 94*
Griego, Adán 1959- *WhoHisp 94*
Griego, Alfred Anthony 1943- *WhoHisp 94*
Griego, Charles 1951- *WhoAmP 93*
Griego, Charles James 1957- *WhoHisp 94*
Griego, Jose Sabino 1938- *WhoHisp 94*
Griego, Linda 1935- *WhoHisp 94*
Griego, Phil *WhoHisp 94*
Griego, Tony A. 1955- *SmATA 77*
Griego, Vincent E. 1940- *WhoHisp 94*
Griego Erwin, Diana 1959- *WhoHisp 94*
Griego Jones, Toni 1945- *WhoHisp 94*
Griem, Hans Rudolf 1928- *WhoAm 94, WhoScEn 94*
Griem, Helmut *WhoHol 92*
Griem, Helmut 1940- *IntMPA 94*
Grieman, Fred Joseph 1952- *WhoScEn 94*
Grieman, John Joseph 1944- *WhoAm 94*
Griepp, Milton Charles 1953- *WhoMW 93*
Grier, Arthur E., Jr. 1943- *WhoBlA 94*
Grier, Barbara G(ene Damon) 1933- *GayLL*
Grier, Bobby 1942- *WhoBlA 94*
Grier, Charles Crocker 1938- *WhoWest 94*
Grier, David Alan *WhoHol 92*
Grier, David Alan 1955- *IntMPA 94*
Grier, David Alan 1956- *WhoBlA 94*
Grier, Eldon (Brockwill) 1917- *WrDr 94*
Grier, Francis Ebenezer 1948- *WhoAmP 93*
Grier, George Edward 1934- *WhoAmP 93*
Grier, Harry Dobson Miller 1914-1972 *WhoAmA 93N*
Grier, Herbert Earl 1911- *WhoAm 94*
Grier, Jack Wesley 1930- *WhoAmP 93*
Grier, James Edward 1935- *WhoAm 94, WhoFI 94, WhoWest 94*
Grier, Jimmie d1959 *WhoHol 92*
Grier, John K. 1950- *WhoBlA 94*
Grier, Johnny 1947- *WhoBlA 94*
Grier, Joseph Williamson, Jr. 1915- *WhoAm 94, WhoAmL 94*
Grier, Katherine C. 1953- *WrDr 94*
Grier, Manton M. 1945- *WhoAmL 94*
Grier, Margot Edmands 1946- *WhoAmA 93*
Grier, Maurice Edward 1895- *WhAm 10*
Grier, Nathaniel 1918- *WhoScEn 94*
Grier, Pam 1949- *IntMPA 94, WhoHol 92*
Grier, Pamala S. *WhoBlA 94*
Grier, Patrick Arthur 1918- *Who 94*
Grier, Phillip Michael 1941- *WhoAm 94, WhoAmL 94*
Grier, Richard L. 1945- *WhoAmL 94*
Grier, Robert Dixon 1956- *WhoFI 94*
Grier, Roosevelt 1932- *WhoBlA 94*
Grier, Rosey 1932- *WhoBlA 94, WhoHol 92*
Grier, William E. 1933- *WhoFI 94*
Grierson, Michael (John Bewes) 1921- *Who 94*
Grierson, Patricia Minter *DrAPF 93*
Grierson, Philip 1910- *IntWW 93, Who 94, WrDr 94*
Grierson, Ronald (Hugh) 1921- *Who 94*
Grierson, Ronald Hugh 1921- *IntWW 93*
Grierson, William 1917- *WhoAm 94, WhoScEn 94*
Gries, David Joseph 1939- *WhoAm 94*
Gries, Don *WhoAmP 93*
Gries, John Paul 1911- *WhoAm 94*
Gries, Jonathan *WhoHol 92*
Griesa, Thomas Poole 1930- *WhoAm 94, WhoAmL 94*
Griesbach, Karl-Rudi 1916- *NewGrDO*
Griesche, Robert Price 1953- *WhoWest 94*
Griese, Bob *ProFbHF [port]*
Griese, Carol 1945- *Who 94*
Griese, John William, III 1955- *WhoScEn 94*
Griesedieck, Ellen 1948- *WhoAmA 93*
Griesemer, Allan David 1935- *WhoAm 94, WhoWest 94*
Griesemer, John N. *WhoAm 94*
Griesemer, Paul G. 1944- *WhoAmL 94*
Griesemer, Richard Allen 1929- *WhoAm 94*
Grieser, Emil 1926- *WhoAmP 93*
Griesheimer, John 1952- *WhoAmP 93*
Griesheimer, John E. 1952- *WhoMW 93*
Griesheimer, Ronald E. 1936- *WhoAmP 93*
Grieshober, William Edward 1942- *WhoFI 94*
Griesinger, Wilhelm 1817-1868 *EncSPD*
Griess, (Johann) Peter 1829-1888 *DcNaB MP*
Griesser, James Albert 1952- *WhoScEn 94*
Griessler, Franz Anton 1897-1974 *WhoAmA 93N*
Grieve, Hon. Lord 1917- *Who 94*
Grieve, Carlton Archibald, Jr. 1959- *WhoMW 93*
Grieve, Graham Robert 1946- *WhoScEn 94*
Grieve, Harold Walter 1901- *WhoWest 94*
Grieve, Leona Lee 1954- *WhoWest 94*
Grieve, Percy *Who 94*
Grieve, Pierson MacDonald 1927- *WhoAm 94, WhoFI 94, WhoMW 93*
Grieve, Robert 1910- *Who 94*
Grieve, Robert 1939- *WhoAmP 93*
Grieve, Thomas Alan 1948- *WhoAm 94*
Grieve, William Percival 1915- *Who 94*
Grieve, William Robertson *Who 94*
Grieves, David 1933- *Who 94*
Grieves, John Kerr 1935- *Who 94*
Grieves, Robert Belanger 1935- *WhoAm 94*
Griew, Stephen 1928- *Who 94*
Grifasi, Joe 1944- *WhoHol 92*
Grifell, Prudencia d1970 *WhoHol 92*
Griff, Alan *EncSF 93*
Griff, Irene Carol 1965- *WhoScEn 94*
Griffel, Kay 1940- *NewGrDO*
Griffen, Clyde Chesterman 1929- *WhoAm 94*
Griffen, Nannie d1925 *WhoHol 92*
Griffen, Vanessa 1952- *BlmGWL*
Griffen, Ward O., Jr. 1928- *WhoAm 94*
Griffenhagen, George Bernard 1924- *WhoAm 94*
Griffes, Donald L. 1931- *WhoAmP 93*
Griffeth, Paul Lyman 1919- *WhoAm 94*
Griffeth, Ronald Clyde 1935- *WhoAmL 94*
Griffeth, Ross John 1896- *WhAm 10*
Griffeth, Simone *WhoHol 92*
Griffey, Dick 1943- *WhoBlA 94*
Griffey, Ken, Sr. 1950- *WhoBlA 94*
Griffey, Ken, Jr. 1969- *News 94-1 [port], WhoAm 94, WhoBlA 94, WhoWest 94*
Griffey, Linda Boyd 1949- *WhoAmL 94*
Griffies, Ethel d1975 *WhoHol 92*
Griffin, Alfredo 1957- *WhoHisp 94*
Griffin, Anita Jane 1945- *WhoMW 93*
Griffin, Ann White *WhoBlA 94*
Griffin, Anthony (Templer Frederick Griffith) 1920- *IntWW 93, Who 94*
Griffin, Archie 1954- *WhoBlA 94*
Griffin, Arthur d1953 *WhoHol 92*
Griffin, Ben L., Jr. 1923- *WhoIns 94*
Griffin, Bertha L. 1930- *WhoBlA 94*
Griffin, Betty Sue 1943- *WhoBlA 94*
Griffin, Bob Franklin 1935- *WhoAm 94, WhoAmP 93, WhoMW 93*
Griffin, Bobby *WhoAmP 93*
Griffin, Bobby L. 1938- *WhoBlA 94*
Griffin, Booker 1938- *WhoBlA 94*
Griffin, Brian 1941- *EncSF 93*
Griffin, Bryant Wade 1915- *WhoAm 94, WhoAmL 94*
Griffin, Campbell Arthur, Jr. 1929- *WhoAm 94, WhoAmL 94*
Griffin, Carleton Hadlock 1928- *WhoAm 94*
Griffin, Carlton d1940 *WhoHol 92*
Griffin, Celine *WhoHol 92*
Griffin, Charles Kevin 1943- *WhoFI 94*
Griffin, Charles Lawrence, III 1948- *WhoAmP 93*
Griffin, Chris A. *WhoAmA 93*
Griffin, Christopher L. 1954- *WhoAmL 94*
Griffin, Clarence 1888-1973 *BuCMET*
Griffin, Clayton Houstoun 1925- *WhoAm 94*
Griffin, Craig Gerald 1956- *WhoFI 94*
Griffin, Cyrus 1748-1810 *WhAmRev*
Griffin, (Charles) David 1915- *Who 94*
Griffin, Deborah Seltzer 1949- *WhoAmL 94*
Griffin, Dennis Austin 1945- *WhoMW 93*
Griffin, DeWitt James 1914- *WhoAm 94, WhoFI 94, WhoScEn 94, WhoWest 94*
Griffin, Donald (Redfield) 1915- *IntWW 93*
Griffin, Donald R. 1915- *WrDr 94*
Griffin, Donald Redfield 1915- *WhoAm 94*
Griffin, Donald S. *WhoScEn 94*
Griffin, Donald Wayne 1937- *WhoAm 94, WhoFI 94*
Griffin, Edgar Allen 1907- *Who 94*
Griffin, Edna Westberry 1907- *WhoBlA 94*
Griffin, Edward Michael 1937- *WhoAm 94*
Griffin, Edwin H., Jr. 1935- *WhoScEn 94*
Griffin, Ervin Verome 1949- *WhoBlA 94*
Griffin, Eurich Z. 1938- *WhoAmL 94, WhoBlA 94*
Griffin, F. O'Neil 1926- *WhoAm 94*
Griffin, Frank d1953 *WhoHol 92*
Griffin, G. Edward 1931- *WhoAm 94*

Griffin, G. Lee 1938- *WhoAm 94, WhoFI 94*
Griffin, Gary Arthur 1937- *WhoFI 94*
Griffin, Gerald d1919 *WhoHol 92*
Griffin, Gregory O. *WhoBlA 94*
Griffin, (Arthur) Harry 1911- *WrDr 94*
Griffin, Harry Frederick 1951- *WhoFI 94*
Griffin, Herschel Emmett 1918- *WhoAm 94*
Griffin, Hugh C. 1943- *WhoAm 94, WhoAmL 94*
Griffin, J. David 1961- *WhoAmL 94*
Griffin, J. Philip, Jr. 1932- *WhoIns 94*
Griffin, Jacqueline J. 1942- *WhoAmP 93*
Griffin, James Anthony 1934- *WhoAm 94, WhoMW 93*
Griffin, James Bennett 1905- *IntWW 93, WhoAm 94*
Griffin, James D. 1929- *WhoAmP 93*
Griffin, James Donald 1929- *WhoAm 94*
Griffin, James Edward 1941- *WhoWest 94*
Griffin, James Edwin 1927- *WhoAm 94*
Griffin, James Ellis 1941- *WhoAmL 94*
Griffin, James Stafford 1917- *WhoBlA 94*
Griffin, James T. d1993 *NewYTBS 93*
Griffin, Jasper 1937- *IntWW 93, Who 94*
Griffin, Jean 1931- *WhoWest 94*
Griffin, Jean Latz 1943- *WhoAm 94*
Griffin, Jean Thomas 1937- *WhoBlA 94*
Griffin, Jim Tyson *WhoAmP 93*
Griffin, Jo Ann Thomas 1933- *WhoFI 94*
Griffin, John *Who 94*
Griffin, (Arthur) John (Stewart) 1924- *Who 94*
Griffin, John J., Jr. 1950- *WhoAmL 94*
Griffin, John James 1932- *WhoAmL 94*
Griffin, John Joseph, Jr. 1946- *WhoScEn 94*
Griffin, John Parry 1938- *Who 94*
Griffin, John W. 1948- *WhoAmL 94*
Griffin, John Wallace d1993 *NewYTBS 93*
Griffin, Johnny 1928- *AfrAmAl 6*
Griffin, Joseph Lawrence 1951- *WhoMW 93*
Griffin, Joseph Parker 1944- *WhoAm 94, WhoAmL 94*
Griffin, Josephine 1928- *WhoHol 92*
Griffin, Judith Ann 1948- *WhoAm 94*
Griffin, Katherine L. 1928- *WhoAmP 93*
Griffin, Kathleen C. *DrAPF 93*
Griffin, Keith B(roadwell) 1938- *WrDr 94*
Griffin, Keith Broadwell 1938- *Who 94, WhoAm 94*
Griffin, Kenneth James 1928- *Who 94*
Griffin, Kitty Colleen 1956- *WhoMW 93*
Griffin, L. Robert 1943- *WhoAmL 94*
Griffin, Larry D. *DrAPF 93*
Griffin, Leonard James, Jr. 1962- *WhoBlA 94*
Griffin, Lula Bernice 1949- *WhoBlA 94*
Griffin, Lynne *WhoHol 92*
Griffin, Mario *WhoHisp 94*
Griffin, Mark Adam 1960- *WhoAmL 94*
Griffin, Martin R. 1952- *WhoAmL 94*
Griffin, Marvin Anthony 1923- *WhoAm 94*
Griffin, Mary 1916- *WhoAm 94*
Griffin, Melanie Hunt 1949- *WhoFI 94*
Griffin, Merv 1925- *IntMPA 94, WhoHol 92*
Griffin, Merv(yn Edward), Jr. 1925- *WrDr 94*
Griffin, Merv Edward 1925- *WhoAm 94, WhoFI 94, WhoWest 94*
Griffin, Michael D. 1958- *WhoBlA 94*
Griffin, Michael Gary 1948- *WhoAmP 93*
Griffin, Michael Harold 1921- *Who 94*
Griffin, Michael J. 1933- *WhoAmP 93*
Griffin, Nancy Lien 1952- *WhoAmP 93*
Griffin, Oscar O'Neal, Jr. 1933 *WhoAm 94*
Griffin, P(auline) M. 1947- *ConAu 140, EncSF 93*
Griffin, Paul 1922- *Who 94*
Griffin, Paul R. 1950- *WhoAmL 94*
Griffin, Peni R(ae) 1961- *WrDr 94*
Griffin, Percy Lee 1945- *WhoBlA 94*
Griffin, Peter 1942- *WrDr 94*
Griffin, Phillip Stone 1938- *WhoAm 94*
Griffin, Ples Andrew 1929- *WhoBlA 94*
Griffin, Rachael S. d1983 *WhoAmA 93N*
Griffin, Redd F. 1938- *WhoAmP 93*
Griffin, Richard George, Jr. 1927- *WhoBlA 94*
Griffin, Richard Weldon 1954- *WhoWest 94*
Griffin, Robert d1960 *WhoHol 92*
Griffin, Robert Gregory 1953- *WhoAmL 94*
Griffin, Robert P. 1923- *IntWW 93*
Griffin, Robert Paul 1923- *WhoAm 94, WhoAmL 94, WhoAmP 93, WhoMW 93*
Griffin, Robert Thomas 1917- *WhoAm 94, WhoAmP 93*
Griffin, Ronald Charles 1943- *WhoBlA 94*
Griffin, Russell M(organ) 1943-1986 *EncSF 93*
Griffin, Ruth Lewin 1925- *WhoAmP 93*
Griffin, Scott 1938- *WhoAm 94*
Griffin, Susan *DrAPF 93*
Griffin, Sylvia Gail 1935- *WhoWest 94*
Griffin, Thomas Aquinas, Jr. 1927- *WhoFI 94*
Griffin, Thomas E., Jr. 1946- *WrDr 94*
Griffin, Thomas J. 1917- *WhoBlA 94*
Griffin, Thomas McLean 1922- *WhoAm 94*
Griffin, Thomas Norfleet, Jr. 1933- *WhoAm 94*
Griffin, Tom 1926- *WhoAm 94*
Griffin, Victor fl. 1906-1953 *EncNAR*
Griffin, Victor Gilbert Benjamin 1924- *IntWW 93, Who 94*
Griffin, Villard Stuart, Jr. 1937- *WhoAm 94*
Griffin, W. Boyd 1945- *WhoFI 94*
Griffin, Walter *DrAPF 93*
Griffin, Walter Joseph 1926- *WhoAmP 93*
Griffin, Walter Roland 1942- *WhoAmP 93*
Griffin, Wilfred Lee 1939- *WhoAmP 93*
Griffin, William Francis 1933- *WhoFI 94*
Griffin, William Joseph 1936- *WhoFI 94*
Griffin, William Lester Hadley 1918- *WhoAm 94*
Griffin, William Martin 1943- *WhoFI 94*
Griffin, William Mell, III 1957- *WhoAmL 94*
Griffin, William Ralph 1943- *WhoFI 94*
Griffin, William Stanley 1935- *WhoWest 94*
Griffin, William Thomas 1905-1992 *WhAm 10*
Griffin-Burrill, Kathleen R. F. 1924- *WhoAm 94*
Griffinger, Michael R. 1936- *WhoAm 94*
Griffini, Giacomo fl. 1692-1697 *NewGrDO*
Griffin-Johnson, Lorraine Antionette 1951- *WhoBlA 94*
Griffis, Anthony Eric 1950- *WhoAmL 94*
Griffis, Fletcher Hughes 1938- *WhoScEn 94*
Griffis, Nixon d1993 *NewYTBS 93*
Griffiss, James E(dward) 1928- *WrDr 94*
Griffith, Alan Richard 1941- *IntWW 93, WhoAm 94*
Griffith, Andy 1926- *IntMPA 94, WhoAm 94, WhoCom, WhoHol 92*
Griffith, Arthur Leonard 1920- *WrDr 94*
Griffith, Barbara J. 1935- *WhoBlA 94*
Griffith, Benjamin Woodward, Jr. 1922- *ConAu 42NR*
Griffith, Bezaleel Herold 1925- *WhoAm 94, WhoScEn 94*
Griffith, Bill 1941- *WrDr 94*
Griffith, Calvin Grant, III 1927- *WhoAmP 93*
Griffith, Carl David 1937- *WhoScEn 94, WhoWest 94*
Griffith, Carl Dean 1935- *WhoScEn 94*
Griffith, Charles Russell 1953- *WhoScEn 94*
Griffith, Clark Calvin, II 1941- *WhoAm 94*
Griffith, Corinne d1979 *WhoHol 92*
Griffith, D. W. d1948 *WhoHol 92*
Griffith, Daniel Boyd 1934- *WhoAm 94*
Griffith, Darrell 1958- *BasBi*
Griffith, Darrell Steven 1958- *WhoBlA 94*
Griffith, David J. 1946- *WhoAmL 94*
Griffith, David Wark 1875-1948 *AmCulL [port]*
Griffith, Donald Kendall 1933- *WhoAm 94, WhoAmL 94, WhoMW 93*
Griffith, Dotty 1949- *WhoAm 94*
Griffith, E. H. d1975 *WhoHol 92*
Griffith, Edward *WhoAmP 93*
Griffith, Edward, II 1948- *WhoAm 94, WhoAmL 94*
Griffith, Elwin Jabez 1938- *WhoAm 94, WhoBlA 94*
Griffith, Emlyn Irving 1923- *WhoAm 94, WhoAmL 94, WhoFI 94*
Griffith, Ernest Ralph 1928- *WhoAm 94*
Griffith, Evan Joseph, Jr. 1941- *WhoWest 94*
Griffith, Ezra 1942- *WhoBlA 94*
Griffith, F. Lee, III 1947- *WhoAm 94, WhoAmL 94*
Griffith, G. Larry 1937- *WhoAm 94*
Griffith, Garth Ellis 1928- *WhoAm 94*
Griffith, Gary Alan 1946- *WhoBlA 94*
Griffith, George 1857-1906 *EncSF 93*
Griffith, Gordon d1958 *WhoHol 92*
Griffith, Harry d1926 *WhoHol 92*
Griffith, Helen V(irginia) 1934- *WrDr 94*
Griffith, Howard Morgan 1958- *WhoAmL 94*
Griffith, Hugh d1980 *WhoHol 92*
Griffith, J. Gordon 1931- *WhoWest 94*
Griffith, Jack William 1929- *WhoAm 94*
Griffith, James 1919- *WhoHol 92*
Griffith, James Leigh 1951- *WhoAmL 94*
Griffith, James Lewis 1940- *WhoAmL 94*
Griffith, James William 1922- *WhoAm 94*
Griffith, Jerry Dice 1933- *WhoAm 94, WhoScEn 94*
Griffith, John A. 1936- *WhoBlA 94*
Griffith, John Aneurin Grey 1918- *Who 94*
Griffith, John Earl, Jr. 1953- *WhoAm 94, WhoAmL 94*
Griffith, John H. 1931- *WhoBlA 94*
Griffith, John Randall 1934- *WhoAm 94*
Griffith, John Vincent *WhoAm 94*
Griffith, Katherine d1921 *WhoHol 92*
Griffith, Katherine d1934 *WhoHol 92*
Griffith, Katherine Birgit 1960- *WhoMW 93*
Griffith, Katherine Scott 1942- *WhoFI 94*
Griffith, Kenneth 1921- *IntWW 93, Who 94, WhoHol 92*
Griffith, Kristin *WhoHol 92*
Griffith, Ladd Ray 1930- *WhoAm 94*
Griffith, Lawrence Stacey Cameron 1937- *WhoAm 94*
Griffith, Leonard *Who 94*
Griffith, (Arthur) Leonard 1920- *Who 94*
Griffith, Linda A. *WhoHol 92*
Griffith, Louis Oscar 1875-1956 *WhoAmA 93N*
Griffith, Mark Richard 1960- *WhoBlA 94*
Griffith, Mary 1800?-1877 *EncSF 93*
Griffith, Melanie *IntWW 93*
Griffith, Melanie 1957- *IntMPA 94, WhoAm 94, WhoHol 92*
Griffith, Michael *Who 94*
Griffith, (Edward) Michael (Wynne) 1933- *Who 94*
Griffith, Michael John 1949- *WhoAmL 94*
Griffith, Osbie Hayes 1938- *WhoAm 94*
Griffith, Owen Glyn 1922- *Who 94*
Griffith, Owen Wendell 1946- *WhoMW 93*
Griffith, Patricia Browning *DrAPF 93*
Griffith, Patrick Theodore 1962- *WhoScEn 94*
Griffith, Peter 1927- *WhoAm 94*
Griffith, Raymond d1957 *WhoHol 92*
Griffith, Raymond 1890-1957 *WhoCom*
Griffith, Reginald Wilbert 1930- *WhoBlA 94*
Griffith, Robert d1961 *WhoHol 92*
Griffith, Robert Charles 1939- *WhoScEn 94*
Griffith, Robert E. 1929- *WhoAmP 93*
Griffith, Robert Frederick 1911- *WhoAmP 93*
Griffith, Robert Keeffe 1951- *WhoAmL 94*
Griffith, Robert W. 1946- *WhoAmL 94*
Griffith, Roberta 1937- *WhoAmA 93*
Griffith, Stephen Loyal 1945- *WhoAm 94*
Griffith, Steve Campbell, Jr. 1933- *WhoAm 94, WhoAmL 94*
Griffith, Steven Franklin, Sr. 1948- *WhoAmL 94, WhoFI 94*
Griffith, Steven Lee 1960- *WhoScEn 94*
Griffith, Stewart Cathie d1993 *Who 94N*
Griffith, Susan Buffington 1956- *WhoMW 93*
Griffith, Thomas 1915- *IntWW 93*
Griffith, Thomas Gwynfor 1926- *WrDr 94*
Griffith, Thomas Ian 1960- *WhoHol 92*
Griffith, Thomas Lee, Jr. 1902- *WhoBlA 94*
Griffith, Tracy 1963- *WhoHol 92*
Griffith, Vera Victoria 1920- *WhoBlA 94*
Griffith, W. Kimball 1949- *WhoAmL 94*
Griffith, William Alexander 1922- *WhoAm 94*
Griffith, William E(dgar) 1920- *WrDr 94*
Griffith, William H. 1933- *WhoWest 94*
Griffith, William M. d1960 *WhoHol 92*
Griffith Edwards, James *Who 94*
Griffith Joyner, Florence *IntWW 93*
Griffith Joyner, Florence 1959- *WhoBlA 94*
Griffith-Joyner, Florence Delores 1959- *WhoAm 94, WhoWest 94*
Griffiths *Who 94*
Griffiths, Baron 1923- *IntWW 93, Who 94*
Griffiths, Alan Gordon 1952- *IntWW 93*
Griffiths, Allen Phillips 1927- *Who 94*
Griffiths, Ambrose *Who 94*
Griffiths, (Michael) Ambrose *Who 94*
Griffiths, Antony Vaughan 1951- *Who 94*
Griffiths, Arthur 1922- *Who 94*
Griffiths, Arthur R. *WhoAm 94*
Griffiths, Bede 1906- *IntWW 93*
Griffiths, Bede 1906-1993 *NewYTBS 93 [port]*
Griffiths, Bertie Bernard 1930- *WhoBlA 94*
Griffiths, Bruce (Fletcher) 1924- *Who 94*
Griffiths, Bryn(lyn David) 1933- *WrDr 94*
Griffiths, Daniel Edward 1917- *WhoAm 94*
Griffiths, David 1945- *WhoAmL 94*
Griffiths, David Arthur *EncSF 93*
Griffiths, David Howard 1922- *Who 94*
Griffiths, David Hubert 1940- *Who 94*
Griffiths, David John 1931- *Who 94*
Griffiths, David John 1956- *WhoFI 94*
Griffiths, David Laurence 1944- *Who 94*
Griffiths, David Neil 1935- *WhoAm 94*
Griffiths, David Nigel 1927- *Who 94*
Griffiths, Derek 1946- *WhoHol 92*
Griffiths, Edward 1929- *Who 94*
Griffiths, Eldon (Wylie) 1925- *Who 94*
Griffiths, Eldon Wylie 1925- *WhoWest 94*
Griffiths, George Langford 1929- *WhoAmP 93, WhoMW 93*
Griffiths, Geraldine *WhoHol 92*
Griffiths, Harold Morris 1926- *Who 94*
Griffiths, Helen 1939- *WrDr 94*
Griffiths, Howard 1938- *Who 94*
Griffiths, Howard 1947- *Who 94*
Griffiths, Hugh 1891-1954 *DcNaB MP*
Griffiths, Iorwerth David Ace *WhoAm 94, WhoWest 94*
Griffiths, Islwyn Owen 1924- *Who 94*
Griffiths, Jane d1975 *WhoHol 92*
Griffiths, Jane Jackson 1932- *WhoAmP 93*
Griffiths, John (C.) 1934- *EncSF 93*
Griffiths, John Calvert 1931- *Who 94*
Griffiths, John Charles 1934- *Who 94*
Griffiths, John Gwyn 1911- *WrDr 94*
Griffiths, John N. *Who 94*
Griffiths, John Pankhurst 1930- *Who 94*
Griffiths, John William Roger 1921- *Who 94*
Griffiths, Karen L. 1953- *WhoAmP 93*
Griffiths, Lawrence 1933- *Who 94*
Griffiths, Leslie John 1942- *Who 94*
Griffiths, Linda *WhoHol 92*
Griffiths, Linda 1956- *WrDr 94*
Griffiths, Lloyd Joseph 1941- *WhoAm 94*
Griffiths, Lucy *WhoHol 92*
Griffiths, Martha 1912- *WhoAmP 93, WhoWomW 91*
Griffiths, Nigel 1955- *Who 94*
Griffiths, Paul 1947- *WrDr 94*
Griffiths, Paul Anthony 1947- *Who 94*
Griffiths, Paul David 1953- *Who 94*
Griffiths, Peggy Strauss 1925- *WhoBlA 94*
Griffiths, Peter Anthony 1945- *Who 94*
Griffiths, Peter Denham 1927- *Who 94*
Griffiths, Peter Harry Steve 1928- *Who 94*
Griffiths, Peter John 1944- *Who 94*
Griffiths, Philip A. 1938- *IntWW 93*
Griffiths, Phillip A. 1938- *WhoAm 94, WhoScEn 94*
Griffiths, Richard 1947- *WhoHol 92*
Griffiths, Richard (Mathias) 1935- *WrDr 94*
Griffiths, Robert *Who 94*
Griffiths, (William) Robert 1948- *Who 94*
Griffiths, Robert Budington 1937- *WhoAm 94, WhoScEn 94*
Griffiths, Robert Pennell 1949- *WhoFI 94, WhoMW 93*
Griffiths, Roger Noel Price 1931- *Who 94*
Griffiths, Roy *Who 94*
Griffiths, (Ernest) Roy 1926- *Who 94*
Griffiths, Sally 1934- *WrDr 94*
Griffiths, Sian Meryl 1952- *Who 94*
Griffiths, Steve 1949- *WrDr 94*
Griffiths, Sylvia Preston 1924- *WhoAm 94*
Griffiths, Terry 1947- *IntWW 93*
Griffiths, Trevor 1913- *Who 94*
Griffiths, Trevor 1935- *BlmGEL, ConDr 93, IntDcT 2, IntWW 93, Who 94, WrDr 94*
Griffiths, Walter L. 1946- *WhoAmL 94*
Griffiths, William Arthur 1940- *Who 94*
Griffiths, William Harold 1943- *WhoWest 94*
Griffiths, William Perry 1937- *WhoAmA 93*
Griffiths, Winston James 1943- *Who 94*
Griffith-Smith, Barbara Taylor 1932- *WhoMW 93*
Griffiths Of Fforestfach, Baron 1941- *IntWW 93, Who 94*
Griffith Williams, John *Who 94*
Griffitts, Hannah 1727-1817 *BlmGWL*
Griffitts, James John 1912- *WhoScEn 94*
Griffitts, Keith Loyd 1942- *WhoFI 94*
Griffo, James Vincent, Jr. 1928- *WhoAm 94*
Griffy, Thomas Alan 1936- *WhoAm 94*
Grigaut, Paul L. d1969 *WhoAmA 93N*
Grigg, John (Edward Poynder) 1924- *Who 94, WrDr 94*
Grigg, William Clyde 1952- *WhoFI 94*
Grigg, William Humphrey 1932- *WhoAm 94, WhoFI 94*
Grigger, David John 1960- *WhoScEn 94*
Griggs, Anthony 1946- *WhoBlA 94*
Griggs, Anthony 1960- *WhoBlA 94*
Griggs, Gary Bruce 1943- *WhoScEn 94, WhoWest 94*
Griggs, Harry Kindell, Sr. 1910- *WhoBlA 94*
Griggs, Ian Macdonald 1928- *Who 94*
Griggs, James C. 1907- *WhoBlA 94*
Griggs, James Clifton, Jr. 1930- *WhoBlA 94*
Griggs, James Henry 1912-1989 *WhAm 10*

Griggs, John d1967 *WhoHol 92*
Griggs, John Robert 1949- *WhoMW 93*
Griggs, John W. 1924- *WhoBlA 94*
Griggs, John Wyeth 1947- *WhoAmL 94*
Griggs, Judith Ralph 1946- *WhoBlA 94*
Griggs, Leonard LeRoy, Jr. 1931- *WhoAm 94*
Griggs, Maitland Lee 1902-1989 *WhoAmA 93N*
Griggs, Mary 1904- *WrDr 94*
Griggs, Mildred Barnes 1942- *WhoBlA 94*
Griggs, Norman Edward 1916- *Who 94*
Griggs, Terry 1951- *ConAu 140*
Griggy, Kenneth Joseph 1934- *WhoAm 94*
Griglock, William John 1948- *WhoIns 94*
Grignan, Francoise-Marguerite, Comtesse de 1646-1705 *BlmGWL*
Grignaschi, Giancarlo 1926- *IntWW 93*
Grigor, Margaret Christian 1912-1981 *WhoAmA 93N*
Grigorcea, Adrian Gabriel 1965- *WhoAm 94*
Grigorescu, Dan 1931- *IntWW 93*
Grigoriadis, Mary 1942- *WhoAmA 93*
Grigoriev, Serge 1883-1968 *IntDcB [port]*
Grigorovich, Yuri 1927- *IntDcB [port]*
Grigorovich, Yuriy Nikolayevich 1927- *IntWW 93*
Grigsby, Calvin Burchard 1946- *WhoBlA 94*
Grigsby, Charles T. *WhoBlA 94*
Grigsby, Chester Poole, Jr. 1929- *WhoFI 94*
Grigsby, David P. 1949- *WhoBlA 94*
Grigsby, Gordon *DrAPF 93*
Grigsby, Henry Jefferson, Jr. 1930- *WhoAm 94*
Grigsby, James A. 1942- *WhoIns 94*
Grigsby, Jefferson Eugene, Jr. 1918- *WhoAm 94, WhoAmA 93, WhoBlA 94*
Grigsby, Jefferson Eugene, III 1944- *WhoBlA 94*
Grigsby, Lonnie Oscar 1939- *WhoAm 94, WhoFI 94*
Grigsby, Lucy Clemmons 1916- *WhoBlA 94*
Grigsby, Margaret Elizabeth 1923- *WhoAm 94, WhoBlA 94*
Grigsby, Marshall C. 1946- *WhoAm 94, WhoBlA 94*
Grigsby, Troy L., Sr. 1934- *WhoBlA 94*
Grigson, Geoffrey Douglas 1944- *Who 94*
Grigson, Sophie 1959- *Who 94*
Grigull, Ulrich 1912- *IntWW 93*
Grijalva, Carlos Vincent, Jr. 1950- *WhoHisp 94*
Grijalva, Joshua *WhoHisp 94*
Grijalva, Juan de 1489-1527 *WhWE*
Grijalva, Michelle Armijo 1953- *WhoHisp 94*
Grijalva, Raúl M. *WhoHisp 94*
Grijalva Mosquera, Victor Elias 1938- *WhoAm 94*
Grile, Dod *EncSF 93*
Griliches, Zvi 1930- *IntWW 93, WhoAm 94*
Grilikhes, Alexandra *DrAPF 93*
Grill, Lawrence J. 1936- *WhoAm 94*
Grill, Linda 1938- *WhoHisp 94*
Griller, David 1948- *WhoAm 94*
Griller, Gordon Moore 1944- *WhoAmL 94*
Griller, Sidney Aaron 1911- *Who 94*
Grillet, Alain R. *Who 94*
Grillo, Basil F. 1910- *IntMPA 94*
Grillo, Esther Angela 1954- *WhoAmA 93*
Grillo, Hermes Conrad 1923- *WhoAm 94*
Grillo, Joann Danielle 1939- *WhoAm 94*
Grillo, John 1942- *ConDr 93*
Grillo, Leo 1949- *WhoWest 94*
Grillo, Maria Angelica 1928- *WhoScEn 94*
Grillparzer, Franz 1791-1872 *DcLB 133 [port], IntDcT 2 [port], NewGrDO*
Grills, Michael Geoffrey 1937- *Who 94*
Grilly, Edward Rogers 1917- *WhoAmP 93, WhoWest 94*
Grim, Eugene Donald 1922- *WhoAm 94*
Grim, Frederick Earl 1946- *WhoFI 94*
Grim, John Norman 1933- *WhoWest 94*
Grim, Patricia Ann 1940- *WhoFI 94*
Grim, Samuel Oram 1935- *WhoAm 94*
Grima, Andrew Peter 1921- *Who 94*
Grimald, Nicholas c. 1519-c. 1562 *DcLB 136*
Grimaldi, Alan M. 1944- *WhoAmL 94*
Grimaldi, Alberto 1925- *IntMPA 94*
Grimaldi, Francesco Maria 1618-1663 *WorScD*
Grimaldi, Giovanni Francesco 1606-1680 *NewGrDO*
Grimaldi, Iliana d1962 *WhoHol 92*
Grimaldi, James Thomas 1928- *WhoFI 94*
Grimaldi, Leonard Nicholas 1942- *WhoFI 94*
Grimaldi, Nicholas Lawrence 1950- *WhoAm 94*
Grimaldi, Nicolo *NewGrDO*

Grimalt, Jose *WhoHisp 94*
Grimani, Vincenzo 1652?-1710 *NewGrDO*
Grimani Family *NewGrDO*
Grimaud, Michel (Robert) 1945-1993 *ConAu 142*
Grimault, Paul 1905- *IntDcF 2-4*
Grimball, William Heyward 1917- *WhoAm 94*
Grimble, Ian 1921- *WrDr 94*
Grimble, Reverend Charles James *ConAu 41NR*
Grime, Mark Stephen Eastburn 1948- *Who 94*
Grimes, Alan P 1919- *WrDr 94*
Grimes, Barbara Lauritzen 1945- *WhoAmP 93*
Grimes, Calvin M., Jr. *WhoBlA 94*
Grimes, Charles B., Jr. 1927- *WhoAm 94*
Grimes, Craig Alan 1956- *WhoScEn 94, WhoWest 94*
Grimes, Dale Mills 1926- *WhoAm 94*
Grimes, Darlene M. C. 1960- *WhoBlA 94*
Grimes, David Lynn 1947- *WhoAm 94*
Grimes, Don 1937- *IntWW 93*
Grimes, Douglas M. 1942- *WhoBlA 94*
Grimes, Duane 1957- *WhoAmP 93*
Grimes, Edward Clifford 1940- *WhoWest 94*
Grimes, Frances T. 1869-1963 *WhoAmA 93N*
Grimes, Frank *WhoHol 92*
Grimes, Gary 1955- *IntMPA 94, WhoHol 92*
Grimes, Gerald 1941- *WhoAmP 93*
Grimes, Howard Ray 1918- *WhoAm 94, WhoFI 94*
Grimes, Howard Warren 1922- *WhoAm 94*
Grimes, Hugh Gavin 1929- *WhoAm 94, WhoMW 93*
Grimes, James Gordon 1951- *WhoScEn 94*
Grimes, John Grayson 1935- *WhoAm 94*
Grimes, Joseph Edward 1941- *WhoWest 94*
Grimes, Joseph Rudolph 1923- *IntWW 93*
Grimes, Larry Bruce 1940- *WhoAm 94, WhoAmL 94*
Grimes, Margaret W. *WhoAmA 93*
Grimes, Margaret Whitehurst 1917- *WhoMW 93*
Grimes, Martha *WhoAm 94, WrDr 94*
Grimes, Mary June 1947- *WhoAmL 94*
Grimes, Nikki 1950- *WhoBlA 94*
Grimes, R. Dale 1953- *WhoAmL 94*
Grimes, Richard Allen 1929- *WhoFI 94, WhoScEn 94*
Grimes, Russell Newell 1935- *WhoAm 94*
Grimes, Ruth Elaine 1949- *WhoWest 94*
Grimes, Scott 1971- *WhoHol 92*
Grimes, Stephen H. 1927- *WhoAmP 93*
Grimes, Stephen Henry 1927- *WhoAm 94, WhoAmL 94*
Grimes, Tammy 1934- *IntMPA 94, WhoHol 92*
Grimes, Tom 1954- *ConAu 140*
Grimes, Tommy d1934 *WhoHol 92*
Grimes, Voni B. 1922- *WhoBlA 94*
Grimes, William Alvan 1911- *WhoAm 94, WhoAmL 94*
Grimes, William Winston 1927- *WhoBlA 94*
Grimes-Farrow, Dorothea D. 1952- *WhoFI 94*
Grimke, Angelina Emily 1805-1879 *BlmGWL, DcAmReB 2*
Grimke, Archibald Henry 1849-1930 *AmSocL*
Grimke, Charlotte L. Forten 1837-1914 *AmSocL*
Grimke, Charlotte L. Forten 1839-1914 *BlmGWL*
Grimke, Francis James 1850-1937 *AmSocL, DcAmReB 2*
Grimke, John F. 1752-1819 *WhAmRev*
Grimke, Sarah M. 1792-1873 *WomPubS*
Grimke, Sarah Moore 1792-1873 *AmSocL, BlmGWL, DcAmReB 2*
Grimke Weld, Angelina 1805-1879 *WomPubS*
Grimke Weld, Angelina Emily 1805-1879 *AmSocL*
Grimley, Jeffrey Michael 1957- *WhoAm 94*
Grimley, Liam Kelly 1936- *WhoAm 94*
Grimley, Oliver Fetterolf 1920- *WhoAmA 93*
Grimley, Robert Thomas 1930- *WhoAm 94*
Grimley Evans, John 1936- *Who 94*
Grimm, Ben Emmet 1924- *WhoAm 94*
Grimm, Curt David 1957- *WhoScEn 94*
Grimm, Daniel K. 1949- *WhoAm 94, WhoAmP 93, WhoWest 94*
Grimm, Donald E. 1930- *WhoFI 94*
Grimm, Friedrich Melchior, Baron von 1723-1807 *GuFrLit 2*
Grimm, Glenn Alan 1951- *WhoMW 93*

Grimm, Jacob 1785-1863 *BlmGEL*
Grimm, Jacob (Ludwig Karl) 1785-1863 *RfGShF*
Grimm, James R. 1935- *WhoAm 94*
Grimm, Larry Leon 1950- *WhoWest 94*
Grimm, Louis John 1933- *WhoAm 94*
Grimm, Lucille Davis 1929- *WhoAmA 93*
Grimm, Paula 1950- *WhoAm 94*
Grimm, Raymond Max 1924- *WhoAmA 93*
Grimm, Ruediger Ernst 1939- *WhoMW 93*
Grimm, Terry M. 1942- *WhoAm 94, WhoAmL 94*
Grimm, Victor E. 1937- *WhoAm 94*
Grimm, Wilhelm 1786-1859 *BlmGEL*
Grimm, Wilhelm (Karl) 1786-1859 *RfGShF*
Grimm, William Richard 1952- *WhoAm 94*
Grimm Brothers *NewGrDO*
Grimme, A. Jeannette 1921- *WhoMW 93*
Grimmeiss, Hermann Georg 1930- *IntWW 93, WhoScEn 94*
Grimmer, Gary G. 1950- *WhoAmL 94*
Grimmer, Harry Clinton 1935- *WhoAmP 93*
Grimmer, Margot 1944- *WhoAm 94, WhoMW 93*
Grimmer, Mineko 1949- *WhoAmA 93*
Grimmet, Alex J. 1928- *WhoMW 93*
Grimmett, Geoffrey Richard 1950- *Who 94*
Grimmett, Sadie A. 1932- *WhoBlA 94*
Grimmick, Henry William 1945- *WhoWest 94*
Grimond, Baron 1913- *Who 94*
Grimond, Lord d1993 *NewYTBS 93 [port]*
Grimond, Jo(seph) 1913- *WrDr 94*
Grimond, Joseph 1913- *IntWW 93*
Grimsbo, Raymond Allen 1948- *WhoScEn 94, WhoWest 94*
Grimsby, Bishop Suffragan of 1935- *Who 94*
Grimsey, Colin Robert 1943- *Who 94*
Grimshaw, Ewing Henry Wrigley 1911- *Who 94*
Grimshaw, James Albert, Jr. 1940- *WhoAm 94*
Grimshaw, Nicholas Thomas 1939- *IntWW 93, Who 94*
Grimshaw, Paul *WhoAm 94*
Grimsley, Ethelyne 1941- *WhoBlA 94*
Grimsley, James Alexander, Jr. 1921- *WhoAm 94*
Grimsley, Will Henry 1914- *WhoAm 94*
Grimstead, Hettie d1986 *WrDr 94N*
Grimston *Who 94*
Grimston, Viscount 1978- *Who 94*
Grimston Of Westbury, Baron 1925- *Who 94*
Grimthorpe, Baron 1915- *Who 94*
Grimthorpe, Lady 1925- *Who 94*
Grimwade, Andrew (Sheppard) 1930- *IntWW 93, Who 94*
Grimwade, Arthur Girling 1913- *WrDr 94*
Grimwade, John Girling 1920- *Who 94*
Grimwood, Herbert d1929 *WhoHol 92*
Grin, Alexander *EncSF 93*
Grinager, Alexander 1865-1949 *WhoAmA 93N*
Grinberg, Meyer Stewart 1944- *WhoAm 94*
Grinberg, Michel *ConWorW 93*
Grindal, Edmund 1519?-1583 *DcLB 132 [port]*
Grindall, Douglas Lynn 1946- *WhoMW 93*
Grindall, Emerson Jon 1938- *WhoScEn 94*
Grindberg, Alan K. 1932- *WhoAmP 93*
Grindberg, Thomas Carl 1957- *WhoAmP 93*
Grindberg, Tony *WhoAmP 93*
Grinde, Donald A(ndrew), Jr. 1946- *ConAu 141*
Grinde, Larry Hal 1948- *WhoAmP 93*
Grindea, Daniel 1924- *WhoAm 94, WhoFI 94, WhoScEn 94*
Grindea, Miron 1909- *Who 94*
Grindlay, Jonathan Ellis 1944- *WhoAm 94, WhoScEn 94*
Grindle, Art 1923- *WhoAmP 93*
Grindle, Robert J. 1934- *WhoAmP 93*
Grindon, John Evelyn 1917- *Who 94*
Grindrod, Helen Marjorie 1936- *Who 94*
Grindrod, John Basil Rowland 1919- *IntWW 93, Who 94*
Grindrod, Muriel (Kathleen) 1902- *WrDr 94*
Grindstaff, Bob Reynolds 1934- *WhoAmP 93*
Grindstaff, Elizabeth Ann 1955- *WhoWest 94*
Grine, Donald Reaville 1930- *WhoAm 94*
Grine, Florence May 1927- *WhoMW 93*
Grinell, Sheila 1945- *WhoAm 94*
Griner, Donald Burke 1941- *WhoScEn 94*

Griner, James Crawford 1942- *WhoMW 93*
Griner, Ned H. 1928- *WhoAmA 93*
Griner, Paul Francis 1933- *WhoAm 94*
Grinevskaia, Izabella Arkad'evna 1864-1944 *BlmGWL*
Gring, David M. 1945- *WhoAm 94*
Gringauz, Raisa 1932- *WhoWest 94*
Griniov, Vladimir Borisovych 1945- *LoBiDrD*
Grinker, Morton *DrAPF 93*
Grinker, Roy Richard d1993 *NewYTBS 93 [port]*
Grinling, Jasper Gibbons 1924- *Who 94*
Grinnage, Jack *WhoHol 92*
Grinnell, Alan Dale 1936- *WhoAm 94, WhoScEn 94*
Grinnell, David *EncSF 93*
Grinnell, John Erle 1896-1990 *WhAm 10*
Grinstead, Amelia Ann 1945- *WhoBlA 94*
Grinstead, Stanley (Gordon) 1924- *IntWW 93, Who 94*
Grinstead, William Carter, Jr. 1930- *WhoAm 94*
Grinstein, Gerald 1932- *WhoAm 94, WhoFI 94*
Grint, Edmund Thomas Charles 1904- *Who 94*
Grinyer, Peter Hugh 1935- *Who 94*
Grip *EncSF 93*
Grip, Carl Manfred, Jr. 1921- *WhoAm 94*
Grip, Robert H. 1929- *WhoAmP 93*
Gripe, Maria (Kristina) 1923- *SmATA 74 [port]*
Grippa, Anthony John 1945- *WhoIns 94*
Grippe, Florence (Berg) 1912- *WhoAmA 93*
Grippe, Peter 1912- *WhoAmA 93*
Grippi, Salvatore William 1921- *WhoAm 94, WhoAmA 93*
Gripshover, Mary Louise 1935- *WhoMW 93*
Grisanti, Eugene Philip 1929- *WhoAm 94, WhoFI 94*
Grisar, Albert 1808-1869 *NewGrDO*
Grisar, Johann Martin 1929- *WhoScEn 94*
Grischkowsky, Daniel Richard 1940- *WhoAm 94, WhoScEn 94*
Griscom, Thomas Cecil 1949- *WhoAm 94, WhoFI 94*
Grise, Wilma Marie 1937- *WhoMW 93*
Grisel, Louis d1928 *WhoHol 92*
Grisewood, Harman Joseph Gerard 1906- *Who 94*
Grisewood, Norman Curtis 1929- *WhoScEn 94*
Grisez, Germain 1929- *IntWW 93*
Grisham, Charles Milton 1947- *WhoAm 94*
Grisham, Deborah Alice 1951- *WhoMW 93*
Grisham, Joe Wheeler 1931- *WhoAm 94, WhoScEn 94*
Grisham, John 1955- *CurBio 93 [port], WhoAm 94, WrDr 94*
Grisham, John Conrad 1945- *WhoMW 93*
Grisham, Noel 1916- *WhoAmP 93*
Grisham, R. B. 1953- *WhoAmP 93*
Grisham, Richard Bond 1945- *WhoAmL 94*
Grisham, Robert Douglas 1926- *WhoAmL 94*
Grisham, Sandra Burns 1949- *WhoAmL 94, WhoFI 94*
Grisham, Thomas Woodruff 1949- *WhoFI 94*
Grisham, Wayne Richard 1923- *WhoAmP 93*
Grishin, Viktor 1914-1992 *AnObit 1992*
Grisi, Carlotta 1819-1899 *IntDcB [port]*
Grisi, Giuditta 1805-1840 *NewGrDO*
Grisi, Giulia 1811-1869 *NewGrDO [port]*
Grisi, Jeanmarie Conte 1958- *WhoAm 94*
Griskey, Richard George 1931- *WhoAm 94*
Grisko, Carolyn Marie 1953- *WhoMW 93*
Grismer, Raymond Leonard 1895- *WhAm 10*
Grisolia, Santiago 1923- *WhoMW 93, WhoScEn 94*
Grispino, Maria Genevieve 1954- *WhoFI 94*
Grissett, Willie James 1931- *WhoBlA 94*
Grissmer, John 1933- *IntMPA 94*
Grissom, Charles Buell 1959- *WhoScEn 94*
Grissom, Eugene Edward 1922- *WhoAmA 93*
Grissom, Freda Gill *WhoAmA 93*
Grissom, Garth Clyde 1930- *WhoAm 94*
Grissom, Gerald Homer 1951- *WhoAm 94*
Grissom, Joseph Carol 1931- *WhoAm 94*
Grissom, Ken 1945- *WrDr 94*
Grissom, Lee Alan 1942- *WhoAm 94, WhoFI 94*
Grissom, Marquis Dean 1967- *WhoAm 94, WhoBlA 94*

Grissom, Raymond Earl, Jr. 1943- *WhoScEn 94*
Grist, Arthur L. 1930- *WhoBlA 94*
Grist, Clarence Richard 1932- *WhoScEn 94*
Grist, Ian 1938- *Who 94*
Grist, John 1928- *WhoFI 94*
Grist, John Frank 1924- *Who 94*
Grist, Norman Roy 1918- *Who 94*
Grist, Raymond 1939- *WhoBlA 94*
Grist, Reri *WhoBlA 94*
Grist, Reri 1932- *AfrAmAl 6 [port], NewGrDO*
Grist, Robin Digby 1940- *Who 94*
Grist, Ronald *WhoBlA 94*
Grist, William Ladon 1938- *WhoAmP 93*
Griswell, J. Barry 1949- *WhoIns 94*
Griswold, A. J. 1905- *WhoBlA 94*
Griswold, Alexander Viets 1766-1843 *DcAmReB 2*
Griswold, Benjamin Howell, IV 1940- *WhoAm 94, WhoFI 94*
Griswold, David A. 1954- *WhoAmP 93*
Griswold, Denny *WhoAm 94*
Griswold, Erwin Nathaniel 1904- *IntWW 93, WhoAm 94, WhoAmL 94, WhoAmP 93*
Griswold, Francis Hopkinson 1904-1989 *WhAm 10*
Griswold, Frank Tracy, III 1937- *WhoAm 94, WhoMW 93*
Griswold, Gary Norris 1947- *WhoFI 94*
Griswold, Gerald W. 1938- *WhoIns 94*
Griswold, Grace d1927 *WhoHol 92*
Griswold, James d1935 *WhoHol 92*
Griswold, James B. 1946- *WhoAm 94, WhoAmL 94*
Griswold, Jerome 1947- *WrDr 94*
Griswold, Martha Kerfoot 1930- *WhoWest 94*
Griswold, Paul Michael 1945- *WhoMW 93*
Griswold, Putnam 1875-1914 *NewGrDO*
Griswold, Ralph Esty 1894- *WhAm 10*
Griswold, Valerie Anne 1962- *WhoAmL 94*
Griswold del Castillo, Richard A. 1942- *WhoHisp 94*
Gritsai, Alexei Michailovich 1914- *IntWW 93*
Gritsch, Eric W(alter) 1931- *WrDr 94*
Gritsi-Milliex, Tatiana 1920- *BlmGWL*
Gritton, Earl Thomas 1933- *WhoMW 93*
Gritton, Eugene Charles 1941- *WhoAm 94*
Gritzner, Jeffrey Allman 1941- *WhoScEn 94*
Grivas, Theodore 1922- *WhoAm 94*
Griver, Michael A. 1942- *WhoIns 94*
Grives, Steven 1951- *WhoHol 92*
Grivna, Edward Lewis 1956- *WhoScEn 94*
Grivna, Gordon Michael 1959- *WhoWest 94*
Grix, Henry M. 1948- *WhoAmL 94*
Grizi, Samir Amine 1942- *WhoFI 94*
Grizodubova, Valentina (Stepanovna) 1910?-1993 *CurBio 93N*
Grizodubova, Valentina S. d1993 *NewYTBS 93 [port]*
Grizzard, George 1928- *IntMPA 94, WhoAm 94, WhoHol 92*
Grizzard, Lewis 1946- *WrDr 94*
Grizzard, Lewis (M.), Jr. 1946- *WhoAm 94*
Grizzard, Robert Harold 1915- *WhoAmP 93*
Grizzle, Mary R. 1921- *WhoAmP 93*
Grmek, Dorothy Antonia 1930- *WhoMW 93*
Groark, Eunice 1938- *WhoAm 94, WhoAmP 93*
Groark, Thomas J., Jr. 1937- *WhoAm 94*
Groat, Carlton d1940 *WhoHol 92*
Groat, Dick 1930- *BasBi*
Groat, Hall Pierce 1932- *WhoAmA 93*
Groat, Hall Pierce, II 1967- *WhoAmA 93*
Groat, Kathleen Delores 1941- *WhoAmP 93*
Groat, Linda Noel 1946- *WhoMW 93*
Grob, Gerald N. 1931- *ConAu 42NR, WhoAm 94, WrDr 94*
Groban, Robert Sidney, Jr. 1948- *WhoAm 94, WhoAmL 94*
Grobe, Charles Stephen 1935- *WhoAm 94*
Grobe, Donald (Roth) 1929-1986 *NewGrDO*
Grobel, Lawrence 1947- *WrDr 94*
Grober, Matthew Scott 1959- *WhoWest 94*
Groberg, James Jay 1928- *WhoAm 94*
Grobler, Richard Victor 1936- *Who 94*
Grobman, Hulda Gross 1920- *WhoAm 94*
Grobman, Marc Ross 1947- *WhoFI 94*
Grob-Prandl, Gertrude 1917- *NewGrDO*
Grobschmidt, Richard A. 1948- *WhoAmP 93*
Grobstein, Clifford 1916- *WhoAm 94, WrDr 94*
Groby, Frank d1987 *WhoHol 92*
Groce, Ewin Petty 1953- *WhoAmL 94*
Groce, Herbert Monroe, Jr. 1929- *WhoBlA 94*
Groce, James Freelan 1948- *WhoFI 94, WhoScEn 94*
Groce, Joan Alice 1930- *WhoMW 93*
Groce, William Henry, III 1940- *WhoScEn 94*
Grochoski, Gregory Thomas 1946- *WhoFI 94*
Groch-Tochman, David Antone 1963- *WhoWest 94*
Grock 1880-1959 *WhoCom*
Grocott, Bruce Joseph 1940- *Who 94*
Grocott, Stephen Charles 1957- *WhoScEn 94*
Grocyn, William 1446?-1519 *BlmGEL*
Grodberg, Marcus Gordon 1923- *WhoScEn 94*
Grode, Murray T. *WhoIns 94*
Groden, Michael (Lewis) 1947- *WrDr 94*
Grodensky, Samuel 1894-1974 *WhoAmA 93N*
Grodin, Charles 1935- *IntMPA 94, WhoAm 94, WhoHol 92*
Grodin, Jay H. 1944- *WhoAmL 94*
Grodin, Richard A. *WhoAmP 93*
Grodins, Fred Sherman 1915-1989 *WhAm 10*
Grodnitzky, Alan Scot 1953- *WhoAm 94, WhoAmL 94*
Grodon, Roger Dean 1950- *WhoAmL 94*
Grodsky, Gerold Morton 1927- *WhoAm 94*
Grodsky, Sheila Taylor 1933- *WhoAmA 93*
Grody, Donald 1927- *WhoAm 94*
Grody, Kathryn 1948- *WhoHol 92*
Grody, Mark Stephen 1938- *WhoAm 94*
Grody, Wayne William 1952- *WhoWest 94*
Groebe, Hans 1916- *IntWW 93*
Groeben, Hans von der 1907- *IntWW 93*
Groebil, Werner 1915- *See* Frick and Frack *WhoCom*
Groebli, Werner Fritz 1915- *WhoAm 94, WhoWest 94*
Groedel, Burt Jay 1937- *WhoAmA 93*
Groeger, Joseph Herman 1925- *WhoAm 94*
Groell, Theophil 1932- *WhoAmA 93*
Groen, Alma de *IntDcT 2*
Groen, Alma de 1941- *BlmGWL*
Groenberg, Ake d1969 *WhoHol 92*
Groener, Dick *WhoAmP 93*
Groener, Harry 1951- *WhoHol 92*
Groeneveld, David Paul 1952- *WhoScEn 94*
Groenier, Ben d1977 *WhoHol 92*
Groening, Matt *NewYTBS 93 [port]*
Groening, Matt 1954- *WrDr 94*
Groening, Matthew 1954- *WhoAm 94*
Groening, William Andrew, Jr. 1912- *WhoAm 94*
Groeninger, Edward John 1947- *WhoWest 94*
Groenman, Louise S. 1940- *WhoWomW 91*
Groenman, Sjoerd 1913- *IntWW 93*
Groennert, Charles Willis 1937- *WhoAm 94*
Groennings, Sven Ole 1934- *WhoAm 94*
Groer, Hans Hermann 1919- *IntWW 93*
Groesch, John William, Jr. 1923- *WhoFI 94, WhoMW 93, WhoScEn 94*
Groeschel, August Herman 1908-1989 *WhAm 10*
Groethe, Reed 1952- *WhoAm 94*
Groetzinger, Jon, Jr. 1949- *WhoAm 94, WhoAmL 94*
Groff, Ben *DrAPF 93*
Groff, David Clark, Jr. 1946- *WhoAmL 94*
Groff, David Huston 1945- *WhoWest 94*
Groff, Jo Ann 1956- *WhoAmP 93*
Groff, Regis F. 1935- *WhoAmP 93, WhoBlA 94*
Groffrey, Frank Eden 1944- *WhoBlA 94*
Grogan, Alice Washington 1956- *WhoAmL 94, WhoFI 94*
Grogan, Clare 1962- *WhoHol 92*
Grogan, Edward Joseph 1959- *WhoScEn 94*
Grogan, Gerald 1884-1918 *EncSF 93*
Grogan, Hubert Joseph *WhoMW 93*
Grogan, Kenneth Augustine 1924- *WhoAm 94*
Grogan, Kevin 1948- *WhoAm 94, WhoAmA 93*
Grogan, Patricia 1962- *WhoAmP 93*
Grogan, Robert Harris 1933- *WhoAmL 94, WhoFI 94*
Grogan, Stanley Joseph, Jr. 1925- *WhoWest 94*
Grogan, Thomas Stephen 1951- *WhoFI 94*
Grogan, Timothy James 1940- *WhoAm 94*
Grogan, Vincent J. 1935- *WhoAmL 94*
Grogan, William Robert 1924- *WhoAm 94*
Grogger, Paula 1892-1984 *BlmGWL*
Groh, Clifford J., Sr. 1926- *WhoAm 94*
Groh, Clifford John, Sr. 1926- *WhoAmP 93*
Groh, David 1939- *WhoHol 92*
Groh, Gabor Gyula 1948- *WhoScEn 94*
Groh, Rupert James, Jr. 1933- *WhoAm 94, WhoAmL 94, WhoWest 94*
Grohskopf, Bernice *DrAPF 93, WrDr 94*
Groiss, Fred George 1936- *WhoAm 94*
Grojsman, Sophia *NewYTBS 93 [port]*
Grol, Anne Catherine 1931- *WhoWomW 91*
Grold, L. James 1932- *WhoWest 94*
Grollman, Thomas Bird 1939- *WhoWest 94*
Grom, Bogdan 1918- *WhoAmA 93*
Gromack, Alexander J. 1953- *WhoAmP 93*
Groman, Arthur 1914- *WhoAm 94, WhoAmL 94*
Groman, Neal Benjamin 1921- *WhoAm 94*
Groman, Richard Paul 1953- *WhoWest 94*
Groman, Robert Howard 1942- *WhoAmL 94*
Gromel, G. H., Jr. 1946- *WhoAmL 94*
Gromen, Richard John 1930- *WhoAm 94*
Gromov, Boris Vsevolodovich 1943- *IntWW 93, LoBiDrD*
Gromov, Feliks Nikolaevich 1937- *LoBiDrD*
Gromov, Felix Nikolaevich 1937- *IntWW 93*
Gromov, Mikhael 1943- *IntWW 93*
Gromyko, Anatoly Andreyevich 1932- *IntWW 93*
Gromyko, Andrei A. 1909-1989 *HisDcKW*
Gromyko, Andrey Andreyevich 1909-1989 *WhAm 10*
Gronamann, Sybilla *NewGrDO*
Gronau, Ernst d1938 *WhoHol 92*
Gronbeck, Bruce E(lliot) 1941- *WrDr 94*
Gronbeck, Christopher Elliott 1969- *WhoScEn 94*
Gronborg, Erik 1931- *WhoAmA 93*
Grondahl, Carol Harriet 1940- *WhoAmP 93*
Grondahl, Kirsti Kolle 1943- *IntWW 93*
Grondal, Benedikt 1924- *IntWW 93*
Gronemeyer, Jeffrey Michael 1963- *WhoWest 94*
Gronemus, Barbara 1931- *WhoAmP 93*
Groner, Beverly Anne *WhoAm 94, WhoAmL 94*
Groner, Lissy 1954- *WhoWomW 91*
Groner, Pat Neff 1920- *WhoAm 94*
Groner, Paul Stephen 1937- *WhoScEn 94*
Groner, Samuel Brian 1916- *WhoAm 94, WhoAmL 94*
Gronfein, William Philip 1947- *WhoMW 93*
Gronfeldt, Vibeke *EncSF 93*
Gronhaug, Arnold Conrad 1921- *Who 94*
Groninga, John Donald 1945- *WhoAmP 93*
Gronk 1954- *WhoAmA 93, WhoHisp 94*
Gronka, Martin Steven 1952- *WhoFI 94*
Gronli, John Victor 1932- *WhoWest 94*
Gronlier, Juan F. 1951- *WhoHisp 94*
Gronlier, Juan Francisco 1951- *WhoFI 94*
Gronlund, Scott Douglas 1959- *WhoScEn 94*
Gronning, Lloyd Joseph 1951- *WhoWest 94*
Gronow, David Gwilym Colin 1929- *Who 94*
Gronowicz, Antoni *DrAPF 93*
Gronquist, Carl Harry 1903-1991 *WhAm 10*
Gronstal, Michael E. 1950- *WhoAmP 93*
Groom, Dale 1912- *WhoAm 94*
Groom, Gary Lee 1946- *WhoAm 94, WhoMW 93*
Groom, James Haynes 1919- *WhoAmP 93*
Groom, John Miller 1936- *WhoAm 94*
Groom, John Patrick 1929- *Who 94*
Groom, (Arthur John) Pelham *EncSF 93*
Groom, Raymond John 1944- *Who 94*
Groom, Sam *WhoHol 92*
Groombridge, Walter Stanley 1913- *WhoAmA 93*
Groome, Reginald K. 1927- *WhoAm 94, WhoFI 94*
Groomes, Emrett W. 1930- *WhoBlA 94*
Groomes, Freddie Lang 1934- *WhoBlA 94*
Groomes, Gary 1955- *WhoHol 92*
Grooms, Harlan Hobart 1900-1991 *WhAm 10*
Grooms, Henry Randall 1944- *WhoBlA 94, WhoWest 94*
Grooms, John Merril 1957- *WhoScEn 94*
Grooms, Karen Victoria Morton 1956- *WhoBlA 94*
Grooms, Larry Willis 1945- *WhoAm 94*
Grooms, Red 1937- *WhoAm 94, WhoAmA 93*
Grooms-Curington, Talbert Lawrence, Sr. 1956- *WhoBlA 94*
Grooney, Ernest d1946 *WhoHol 92*
Groos, Arthur Bernhard, Jr. 1943- *WhoAm 94*
Groos, James Andrew 1943- *WhoMW 93*
Groot, Candice Beth 1954- *WhoAmA 93*
Groot, Huig de 1583-1645 *EncEth*
Groot, Per Soltoft 1924- *IntWW 93*
Grootenhuis, Peter 1924- *Who 94*
Groothaert, Jacques 1922- *IntWW 93*
Groover, Denmark, Jr. 1922- *WhoAmP 93*
Groover, Jan 1943- *WhoAmA 93*
Groover, Sandra Mae 1955- *WhoFI 94, WhoMW 93*
Gropius, Georg Walter Adolf 1883-1969 *AmCulL*
Gropp, Kenneth Ahlburn 1922- *WhoAmP 93*
Gropp, Louis Oliver 1935- *WhoAm 94*
Gropper, Allan Louis 1944- *WhoAm 94, WhoAmL 94*
Gropper, Cathy 1949- *WhoAmA 93*
Gropper, William 1897-1977 *WhoAmA 93N*
Groppo, Antonio fl. 1643-1667 *NewGrDO*
Gros, Andre 1908- *IntWW 93*
Gros, Francisco Roberto Andre 1942- *IntWW 93*
Gros, Francois 1925- *IntWW 93*
Gros, Marvin 1948- *WhoAmP 93*
Grosbard, Ulu 1929- *IntMPA 94, WhoAm 94*
Grosberg, Percy 1925- *Who 94*
Grosch, Laura 1945- *WhoAmA 93*
Grosch, Laura Dudley 1945- *WhoAm 94*
Groscost, Jeff *WhoAmP 93*
Grose, Alan 1937- *Who 94*
Grose, B. Donald 1943- *WhoAm 94*
Grose, Charles Frederick 1942- *WhoMW 93*
Grose, George Dennis 1953- *WhoWest 94*
Grose, Peter (Bolton) 1934- *WrDr 94*
Grose, Robert Freeman 1924- *WhoAm 94*
Grose, Thomas Lucius Trowbridge 1924- *WhoAm 94*
Grose, William Rush 1939- *WhoAm 94*
Groseclose, Everett Harrison 1938- *WhoAm 94*
Groseclose, John Robert 1938- *WhoAmP 93*
Groseclose, William Buell, III 1959- *WhoWest 94*
Groseilliers, Medard Chouart, Sieur Des 1618-c. 1697 *WhWE*
Grosfeld, Jay Lazar 1935- *WhoAm 94*
Grosfield, Lorents 1944- *WhoAmP 93*
Grosh, Michael Edward 1956- *WhoMW 93*
Groshans, Werner 1913-1986 *WhoAmA 93N*
Grosheim, Georg Christoph 1764-1841 *NewGrDO*
Groshek, Michael Dean 1932- *WhoAm 94*
Groshens, Jean-Claude 1926- *IntWW 93*
Grosholz, Emily *DrAPF 93*
Grosklaus, James G. 1935- *WhoFI 94*
Groskopf, John E. 1945- *WhoIns 94*
Grosky, William Irvin 1944- *WhoMW 93*
Grosland, Emery Layton 1929- *WhoAm 94*
Gros Louis, Kenneth Richard Russell 1936- *WhoAm 94, WhoMW 93*
Grosman, Alan M. 1935- *WhoAmL 94*
Gross, A. Christopher 1942- *WhoScEn 94*
Gross, Abraham 1928- *WhoAm 94*
Gross, Al 1918- *WhoAm 94*
Gross, Alice *WhoAmA 93*
Gross, Allen 1937- *WhoWest 94*
Gross, Allen Jeffrey 1948- *WhoAmL 94*
Gross, Arye *WhoHol 92*
Gross, Barbara L. 1960- *WhoWest 94*
Gross, Benny J. *WhoAmP 93*
Gross, Carol Jeanne 1930- *WhoMW 93*
Gross, Caroline Lord 1940- *WhoAm 94, WhoAmP 93*
Gross, Chaim 1904-1991 *WhAm 10, WhoAmA 93N*
Gross, Charles 1958- *WhoAmP 93*
Gross, Charles Gordon 1936- *WhoAm 94*
Gross, Charles Merrill 1935- *WhoAmA 93*
Gross, Charles Robert 1958- *WhoMW 93*
Gross, Charles Wayne 1930- *WhoAm 94*
Gross, Clark David 1952- *WhoWest 94*
Gross, David 1940- *ConAu 140*
Gross, David F. 1953- *WhoAmL 94*
Gross, David Lee 1943- *WhoAm 94*
Gross, Delbert L. 1950- *WhoAmP 93*
Gross, Dennis Michael 1947- *WhoScEn 94*
Gross, Dorothy-Ellen 1949- *WhoMW 93*
Gross, Earl 1899- *WhoAmA 93*
Gross, Edward *WhoAm 94*
Gross, Elissa Frances 1954- *WhoAmA 93*
Gross, Emma Rosalie 1943- *WhoWest 94*
Gross, Ernest Arnold 1906- *WhoAm 94*
Gross, Ernest R. 1906- *HisDcKW*
Gross, Ernie 1913- *WrDr 94*
Gross, Estelle Shane d1992 *WhoAmA 93N*
Gross, Fred W., Jr. 1911- *WhoAmP 93*
Gross, Fritz A. d1993 *NewYTBS 93 [port]*
Gross, Gene d1989 *WhoHol 92*
Gross, Hal Raymond 1914- *WhoAm 94*

Gross, Herbert Gerald 1916- *WhoScEn 94, WhoWest 94*
Gross, Hilvie Olson 1926- *WhoAmP 93*
Gross, Hugh *DrAPF 93*
Gross, Ira Kenneth 1946- *WhoAm 94*
Gross, Iris Lee 1941- *WhoAm 94*
Gross, Irwin Lee 1943- *WhoAm 94, WhoAmL 94*
Gross, James Dehnert 1929- *WhoAm 94*
Gross, James Howard 1941- *WhoAm 94*
Gross, James Irvan, Jr. 1956- *WhoWest 94*
Gross, Jeffrey Scott 1966- *WhoAmL 94*
Gross, Jenard Morris 1929- *WhoAm 94*
Gross, Jill Susan 1961- *WhoMW 93*
Gross, Joe L. W. *WhoAmP 93*
Gross, Joel 1951- *WrDr 94*
Gross, Joel Edward 1939- *WhoFI 94*
Gross, Johannes 1932- *IntWW 93*
Gross, Johannes Heinrich 1916- *ConAu 43NR*
Gross, John (Jacob) 1935- *WrDr 94*
Gross, John Birney 1924- *WhoAm 94*
Gross, John H. 1942- *WhoAmL 94*
Gross, John Jacob 1935- *IntWW 93, Who 94*
Gross, John Owen 1894- *WhAm 10*
Gross, Jonathan Light 1941- *WhoAm 94*
Gross, Joseph Francis 1932- *WhoAm 94, WhoWest 94*
Gross, Joseph Wallace 1945- *WhoAm 94*
Gross, Julia Ann 1957- *WhoMW 93*
Gross, Julie *WhoAmA 93*
Gross, Kaufman Kennard 1916- *WhoScEn 94*
Gross, Kenneth H. 1949- *IntMPA 94*
Gross, Larry Paul 1942- *WhoAm 94*
Gross, Laura Ann 1948- *WhoFI 94*
Gross, Leroy 1926- *WhoAm 94*
Gross, Leslie Jay 1944- *WhoAmL 94*
Gross, Leslie Pamela 1952- *WhoFI 94*
Gross, Liza Elisa 1957- *WhoHisp 94*
Gross, Lois Irene 1920- *WhoAmP 93*
Gross, Ludwik 1904- *IntWW 93, WhoAm 94, WrDr 94*
Gross, Marilyn A. 1937- *WhoAmA 93*
Gross, Martin Louis 1938- *WhoAmP 93*
Gross, Mary 1953- *IntMPA 94, WhoHol 92*
Gross, Mary Elizabeth 1957- *WhoMW 93*
Gross, Michael 1947- *IntMPA 94, WhoAm 94, WhoHol 92*
Gross, Michael Fred 1957- *WhoWest 94*
Gross, Michael Julius 1946- *WhoAmL 94*
Gross, Michael Lawrence 1940- *WhoAm 94, WhoScEn 94*
Gross, Miriam Marianna 1939- *Who 94*
Gross, Nahum David 1923- *IntWW 93*
Gross, Noel L. *WhoAmP 93*
Gross, Patrick Walter 1944- *WhoAm 94, WhoFI 94*
Gross, Paul 1902- *WhoAm 94*
Gross, Paul Allan 1937- *WhoAm 94*
Gross, Paul Hans 1931- *WhoScEn 94, WhoWest 94*
Gross, Paul Randolph 1928- *WhoAm 94*
Gross, Peter Alan 1938- *WhoAm 94, WhoScEn 94*
Gross, Peter Henry 1952- *Who 94*
Gross, Philip (John) 1952- *WrDr 94*
Gross, Rainer 1951- *WhoAmA 93*
Gross, Richard (Edmund) 1920- *WrDr 94*
Gross, Richard Alan 1949- *WhoAm 94*
Gross, Richard Edmund 1920- *WhoAm 94*
Gross, Richard Philip 1903- *WhoWest 94*
Gross, Robert 1930-1991 *WhAm 10*
Gross, Robert Alan 1945- *WhoAm 94*
Gross, Robert S. 1963- *WhoFI 94*
Gross, Ronald *DrAPF 93*
Gross, Ronald Martin *WhoAm 94, WhoFI 94*
Gross, Ruth Taubenhaus 1920- *WhoAm 94*
Gross, Samson Richard 1926- *WhoScEn 94*
Gross, Sandra Lerner *WhoAmA 93*
Gross, Seymour Paul 1930- *WhoScEn 94*
Gross, Sharon Ruth 1940- *WhoScEn 94*
Gross, Shirley Marie 1917- *WhoMW 93*
Gross, Sidney W. 1904- *WhoAm 94*
Gross, Solomon Joseph 1920- *Who 94*
Gross, Sophie Anne 1957- *WhoWest 94*
Gross, Stanislaw 1924- *WhoScEn 94*
Gross, Stanley Merhl 1953- *WhoMW 93*
Gross, Stephen Mark 1938- *WhoAm 94*
Gross, Steven 1946- *WhoFI 94*
Gross, Steven Ross 1946- *WhoAm 94*
Gross, Theodore Lawrence 1930- *WhoAm 94, WhoMW 93*
Gross, Thomas Edward 1948- *WhoWest 94*
Gross, Thomas Kenneth 1941- *WhoFI 94*
Gross, Thomas Paul 1949- *WhoScEn 94*
Gross, William Allen 1924- *WhoWest 94*
Gross, William H. 1944- *WhoIns 94*
Gross, William J. d1924 *WhoHol 92*
Gross, William Joseph 1932- *WhoMW 93*
Gross, William Spargo 1946- *WhoScEn 94*
Grossart, Angus McFarlane McLeod 1937- *Who 94*
Grossatesta, Gaetano c. 1700-1774? *NewGrDO*
Grossberg, David Burton 1956- *WhoScEn 94*
Grossberg, Jack 1927- *IntMPA 94*
Grossberg, Jake 1932- *WhoAmA 93*
Grossberg, Jeffrey Bart 1946- *WhoWest 94*
Grossberg, John Morris 1927- *WhoScEn 94*
Grossberg, Sidney Edward 1929- *WhoAm 94*
Grosschmid-Zsögöd, Geza Benjamin d1992 *Who 94N*
Grosse, C(arolyn Ann Gawarecki) 1931- *WhoAmA 93*
Grossenbacher-Schmid, Ruth 1936- *WhoWomW 91*
Grosser, Alfred 1925- *IntWW 93*
Grosser, Bernard Irving 1929- *WhoAm 94, WhoWest 94*
Grosser, Morton 1931- *SmATA 74 [port], WhoWest 94*
Grosser, Steven 1960- *WhoAmL 94*
Grosser, T.J. 1938- *WhoAm 94*
Grosset, Alexander Donald, Jr. 1932- *WhoFI 94*
Grosset, Jessica Ariane 1952- *WhoMW 93*
Grossetete, Ginger Lee 1936- *WhoWest 94*
Grossfeld, Michael L. 1955- *WhoFI 94, WhoScEn 94*
Grossfeld, Robert Michael 1943- *WhoScEn 94*
Grossfeld, Stan 1951- *WhoAm 94, WrDr 94*
Grosshandler, Vera Rosalie 1951- *WhoMW 93*
Grossheim, Elmer Ronald 1935- *WhoAmL 94*
Grossi, Carlo c. 1634-1688 *NewGrDO*
Grossi, Eleonora fl. 1868-1871 *NewGrDO*
Grossi, Francis Xavier, Jr. 1943- *WhoAm 94, WhoAmL 94*
Grossi, Francisco Vio 1943- *WhoAm 94*
Grossi, Giovanni Francesco 1653-1697 *NewGrDO*
Grossi, Olindo 1909- *WhoAm 94*
Grossi, Patrick S. 1942- *WhoAmP 93*
Grossi, Ralph Edward 1949- *WhoAm 94*
Grossi, Richard J. 1935- *WhoFI 94*
Grossi, William Anthony 1953- *WhoAmL 94, WhoMW 93*
Grossinger, Richard *DrAPF 93*
Grossinger, Richard (Selig) 1944- *ConAu 42NR*
Grossinger, Tania 1937- *WrDr 94*
Grosskopf, Suanne 1954- *WhoFI 94*
Grosskreutz, Joseph Charles 1922- *WhoAm 94, WhoMW 93, WhoScEn 94*
Grosskurth, Kurt d1975 *WhoHol 92*
Grosskurth, Phyllis 1924- *ConAu 42NR, WrDr 94*
Grossman, Allan I. 1945- *WhoAmL 94*
Grossman, Allen Neil 1946- *WhoFI 94*
Grossman, Allen R. *DrAPF 93*
Grossman, Alvin 1924- *WhoWest 94*
Grossman, Andrew J. *DrAPF 93*
Grossman, Barbara 1943- *WhoAmA 93*
Grossman, Bob 1956- *WhoAm 94*
Grossman, Burton Jay 1924-1990 *WhAm 10*
Grossman, Dan S. 1953- *WhoAm 94*
Grossman, Daniel J. 1963- *WhoAmL 94*
Grossman, David 1954- *ConWorW 93*
Grossman, David J. 1954- *WhoFI 94*
Grossman, Debra A. 1951- *WhoAm 94, WhoAmL 94*
Grossman, Edward G. *NewYTBS 93*
Grossman, Edward Jeffrey 1959- *WhoAmL 94*
Grossman, Elizabeth Korn 1923- *WhoAm 94*
Grossman, Elmer Roy 1929- *WhoAm 94*
Grossman, Ernie 1924- *IntMPA 94*
Grossman, Everett Philip 1924- *WhoFI 94*
Grossman, Florence *DrAPF 93*
Grossman, Frances Kaplan 1939- *WhoAm 94*
Grossman, Fredric James 1932- *WhoAm 94*
Grossman, Gary David 1954- *WhoScEn 94*
Grossman, Herschel I. 1939- *WhoAm 94*
Grossman, Howard K. 1950- *IntMPA 94*
Grossman, Irving d1964 *WhoHol 92*
Grossman, Irving 1926- *WhoAm 94*
Grossman, Jack 1925- *WhoAm 94*
Grossman, Jack Steven 1950- *WhoFI 94*
Grossman, Jacob S. 1930- *WhoAm 94, WhoScEn 94*
Grossman, James Richard 1952- *WhoMW 93*
Grossman, Janice 1949- *WhoAm 94*
Grossman, Jerome 1917- *WhoAmP 93*
Grossman, Jerome Barnett 1919- *WhoAm 94*
Grossman, Jerome Harvey 1939- *WhoAm 94*
Grossman, Jerome Kent 1953- *WhoAmL 94*
Grossman, Jerrold B. 1947- *WhoFI 94*
Grossman, Joan Delaney 1928- *WhoAm 94*
Grossman, Joanne Barbara 1949- *WhoAm 94*
Grossman, Joel Barry 1936- *WhoAm 94*
Grossman, John Henry, III 1945- *WhoAm 94*
Grossman, John Joseph 1924- *WhoAm 94*
Grossman, Karl (H.) 1942- *WrDr 94*
Grossman, Karl H. 1942- *WhoAm 94*
Grossman, Kenneth Cedric 1945- *WhoMW 93*
Grossman, Lawrence 1924- *WhoAm 94, WhoScEn 94*
Grossman, Lawrence Morton 1922- *WhoAm 94*
Grossman, Lisa Robbin 1952- *WhoMW 93*
Grossman, Ludwik 1835-1915 *NewGrDO*
Grossman, Martin *DrAPF 93*
Grossman, Martin Bernard 1961- *WhoScEn 94*
Grossman, Maurice 1907- *WhoWest 94*
Grossman, Maurice Kenneth 1927- *WhoAmA 93*
Grossman, Michael 1942- *WhoAm 94*
Grossman, Morton 1926- *WhoAmA 93*
Grossman, Morton Samuel 1926- *WhoAm 94*
Grossman, Nancy *WhoAm 94*
Grossman, Nancy 1940- *WhoAmA 93*
Grossman, Nathan 1914- *WhoScEn 94*
Grossman, Richard *DrAPF 93*
Grossman, Robert Allen 1941- *WhoFI 94*
Grossman, Robert George 1933- *WhoAm 94*
Grossman, Robert James 1936- *WhoWest 94*
Grossman, Robert L. 1954- *WhoAmL 94*
Grossman, Robert Lee 1957- *WhoMW 93*
Grossman, Ron *DrAPF 93*
Grossman, Ronald 1936- *WhoFI 94*
Grossman, Sanford 1929- *WhoAm 94, WhoAmL 94*
Grossman, Sanford Jay 1953- *WhoAm 94, WhoFI 94*
Grossman, Sebastian P. 1934- *WrDr 94*
Grossman, Sheldon 1940- *WhoAmA 93*
Grossman, Stephen Lewin 1935- *WhoAmL 94*
Grossman, Steven *WhoAmP 93*
Grossman, Stewart Fred 1947- *WhoAmL 94*
Grossman, Theodore Martin 1949- *WhoAm 94*
Grossman, Victor G. 1951- *WhoAmL 94*
Grossman, Wendy Marshall 1953- *WhoFI 94*
Grossman, William 1940- *WhoAm 94*
Grossman, Zoltan Charles 1962- *WhoMW 93*
Grossmann, Edith Searle 1863-1931 *BlmGWL*
Grossmann, Gustav Friedrich Wilhelm 1746?-1796 *NewGrDO*
Grossmann, Ignacio Emilio 1949- *WhoAm 94, WhoScEn 94*
Grossmann, Judith 1931- *BlmGWL*
Grossmann, Reinhardt 1931- *WrDr 94*
Grossmann, Reinhardt S. 1931- *ConAu 42NR*
Grossmann, Ronald Stanyer 1944- *WhoAmL 94*
Grossmith, Ena d1944 *WhoHol 92*
Grossmith, George d1935 *WhoHol 92*
Grossmith, George 1847-1912 *BlmGEL, NewGrDO*
Grossmith, Lawrence d1944 *WhoHol 92*
Grossmith, Robert (Anthony) 1954- *WrDr 94*
Grossmith, Weedon d1919 *WhoHol 92*
Grossmith, Weedon 1852-1919 *BlmGEL*
Grossnickle, Nevin Edwin 1950- *WhoMW 93*
Grosso, James Alan 1948- *WhoFI 94*
Grosso Romero, Gloria (Maria Teresa) 1936- *WhoWomW 91*
Grossweiner, Leonard Irwin 1924- *WhoAm 94*
Grosveld, Franklin Gerardus 1948- *Who 94*
Grosvenor *Who 94*
Grosvenor, Earl 1991- *Who 94*
Grosvenor, Gilbert Melville 1931- *WhoAm 94, WhoScEn 94*
Grosvenor, Richard 1584-1645 *DcNaB MP*
Grosvenor, Robert 1937- *WhoAmA 93*
Grosvenor, Verta Mae 1938- *BlkWr 2, ConAu 42NR, WhoBlA 94*
Grosvenor, Vertamae *DrAPF 93*
Grosz, Barbara Jean 1948- *WhoAm 94, WhoScEn 94*
Grosz, Elisabeth 1963- *WhoHol 92*
Grosz, George 1893-1959 *WhoAmA 93N*
Grosz, Mick *WhoAmP 93*
Grosz, Morton Eric 1944- *WhoAmL 94*
Grosz, Philip J. 1952- *WhoAm 94*
Grosz, Wilhelm 1894-1939 *NewGrDO*
Grot, Anton 1884-1974 *IntDcF 2-4*
Grote, David (G.) 1945- *WrDr 94*
Grotell, Maija 1899-1973 *WhoAmA 93N*
Groten, Barnet 1933- *WhoAm 94*
Grotenrath, Ruth 1912-1988 *WhoAmA 93N*
Grotewiel, Ken 1949- *WhoAmP 93, WhoMW 93*
Groth, Alexander Jacob 1932- *WhoAm 94*
Groth, Brian J. *DrAPF 93*
Groth, Bruno 1905-1991 *WhoAmA 93N*
Groth, James Arthur 1955- *WhoAmP 93*
Groth, Jon Quentin 1941- *WhoMW 93*
Groth, Klaus 1819-1899 *DcLB 129 [port]*
Groth, Patricia Celley *DrAPF 93*
Groth, Richard Lee 1946- *WhoAmP 93*
Grothaus, Pamela Sue 1958- *WhoFI 94, WhoMW 93*
Grothe, Susan K. 1962- *WhoMW 93*
Grotheer-Ridings, Patricia 1964- *WhoMW 93*
Grother, David Michael 1946- *WhoFI 94, WhoMW 93*
Grotius, Hugo 1583-1645 *EncEth, HisWorL [port]*
Grotjan, Harvey Edward, Jr. 1947- *WhoMW 93*
Groton, James Purnell 1927- *WhoAm 94*
Grotowski, Jerzy 1933- *BlmGEL, IntWW 93, WhoAm 94*
Grotrian, Philip Christian Brent 1935- *Who 94*
Grott, Geraldine 1941- *WhoMW 93*
Grotterod, Knut 1922- *WhoAm 94, WhoScEn 94*
Grotz, Dorothy Rogers *WhoAmA 93*
Grotzinger, Laurel Ann 1935- *WhoAm 94, WhoMW 93*
Grotzinger, Timothy Lee 1951- *WhoScEn 94*
Grouby, E. A., Jr. *WhoAmP 93*
Groues, Henri 1912- *IntWW 93*
Groues, Henri Antoine *Who 94*
Groult, Benoite 1920- *ConAu 142*
Groult, Benoite 1921- *BlmGWL*
Groult, Flora 1925- *BlmGWL*
Ground, (Reginald) Patrick 1932- *Who 94*
Grounds, Roger 1938- *WrDr 94*
Grounds, Stanley Paterson 1904- *Who 94*
Grounes, Mikael 1933- *WhoScEn 94*
Grous, John Joseph 1955- *WhoScEn 94*
Groussard, Serge 1921- *IntWW 93*
Grousset, Paschal *EncSF 93*
Groussman, Dean G. *WhoFI 94*
Groussman, Raymond G. 1935- *WhoAmL 94, WhoWest 94*
Grout, Donald J(ay) 1902-1987 *NewGrDO*
Grout, James 1927- *WhoHol 92*
Grout, Robert W. 1944- *WhoAmL 94*
Grove, Andrew S. 1936- *WhoAm 94, WhoFI 94, WhoWest 94, WrDr 94*
Grove, Brandon Hambright, Jr. 1929- *WhoAm 94*
Grove, Brian Allen 1960- *WhoFI 94*
Grove, Charles Gerald 1929- *Who 94*
Grove, Daniel 1923- *WhoBlA 94*
Grove, David Anthony 1941- *Who 94*
Grove, David Lavan 1937- *WhoAm 94, WhoAmL 94*
Grove, David Lawrence 1918- *WhoAm 94*
Grove, Dennis *Who 94*
Grove, (William) Dennis 1927- *Who 94*
Grove, Dudley Roulhac 1945- *WhoMW 93*
Grove, Edmund (Frank) 1920- *Who 94*
Grove, Edward Ryneal 1912- *WhoAmA 93*
Grove, Ewart Lester 1913- *WhoMW 93*
Grove, Fred(erick Herridge) 1913- *WrDr 94*
Grove, Frederick Philip *ConAu 141*
Grove, Frederick Philip 1897-1948 *EncSF 93*
Grove, Helen Harriet *WhoAm 94, WhoMW 93*
Grove, Henriette 1922- *BlmGWL*
Grove, Jack Stein 1951- *WhoScEn 94, WhoWest 94*
Grove, Jean Donner 1912- *WhoAmA 93*
Grove, Jean Donner 1912-1992 *WhAm 10*
Grove, John Scott 1927- *Who 94*
Grove, Kalvin Myron 1937- *WhoAm 94*
Grove, Myrna Jean 1949- *WhoMW 93*
Grove, Myrtle d1970 *WhoHol 92*
Grove, Peter J. *EncSF 93*
Grove, Richard Charles 1940- *WhoMW 93*
Grove, Russell Sinclair, Jr. 1939- *WhoAmL 94*
Grove, Samuel Harold 1925- *WhoAmA 93*
Grove, Trevor Charles 1945- *Who 94*

Grove, W. *EncSF 93*
Grove, Will O. 1915- *WrDr 94*
Grove, William Boyd 1929- *WhoAm 94*
Grove, William Johnson 1920- *WhoAm 94*
Grovender, Gladys Lovern 1921- *WhoMW 93*
Grovenor, Linda *WhoHol 92*
Grover, Allen d1993 *NewYTBS 93*
Grover, Derek James Langlands 1949- *Who 94*
Grover, Edward *WhoHol 92*
Grover, Eve Ruth 1929- *WhoAm 94*
Grover, Herbert Joseph 1937- *WhoAmP 93*
Grover, James Robb 1928- *WhoScEn 94*
Grover, Leonard d1926 *WhoHol 92*
Grover, Mark Donald 1955- *WhoScEn 94*
Grover, Norman LaMotte 1928- *WhoAm 94*
Grover, Philip 1929- *WrDr 94*
Grover, Phyllis Bradman 1924- *WhoAm 94*
Grover, Robert Lawrence 1910- *WhoAm 94*
Grover, Rosalind Redfern 1941- *WhoFI 94, WhoScEn 94*
Grover, William Herbert 1938- *WhoAm 94*
Groves, Bonnie *WhoAmP 93*
Groves, Charles d1955 *WhoHol 92*
Groves, Charles d1992 *IntWW 93N*
Groves, Charles 1915-1992 *AnObit 1992*
Groves, Charles Barnard 1915-1992 *WhAm 10*
Groves, Delores Ellis 1940- *WhoBlA 94*
Groves, Franklin Nelson 1930- *WhoAm 94*
Groves, Fred d1955 *WhoHol 92*
Groves, George H. 1944- *WhoAm 94*
Groves, George L., Jr. 1928- *WhoAm 94*
Groves, Georgina 1909- *WrDr 94*
Groves, Hannah Cutier 1868-1952 *WhoAmA 93N*
Groves, Harold Martin 1897- *WhAm 10*
Groves, Harry Edward 1921- *WhoBlA 94*
Groves, Hurst Kohler 1941- *WhoFI 94*
Groves, J(ohn) W(illiam) 1910- *EncSF 93*
Groves, James Lee 1950- *WhoWest 94*
Groves, James Martin 1934- *WhoAmP 93*
Groves, John Dudley 1922- *Who 94*
Groves, John Taylor, III 1943- *WhoAm 94, WhoScEn 94*
Groves, Michael 1936- *WhoAm 94*
Groves, Monica Renae 1959- *WhoMW 93*
Groves, Naomi Jackson *WhoAmA 93*
Groves, Ray John 1935- *WhoAm 94, WhoFI 94*
Groves, Richard Bebb 1933- *Who 94*
Groves, Robin *WhoHol 92*
Groves, Roderick Trimble 1936- *WhoMW 93*
Groves, Ronald Edward 1920- *Who 94*
Groves, Seli *SmATA 77*
Groves, Sharon Sue 1944- *WhoMW 93*
Groves, Sheridon Hale 1947- *WhoScEn 94, WhoWest 94*
Groves, Theodore Francis, Jr. 1941- *WhoAm 94*
Groves, Victor d1971 *WhoHol 92*
Groves, Wallace 1901-1988 *WhAm 10*
Groves, William Craig 1941- *WhoAmP 93*
Groves, William Jason 1946- *WhoAmL 94*
Grove-White, Robin Bernard 1941- *Who 94*
Grovlez, Gabriel (Marie) 1879-1944 *NewGrDO*
Grow, Lilly Yvonne 1944- *WhoAmP 93*
Grow, Michael Abbott 1947- *WhoAm 94, WhoAmL 94*
Grow, Philip William 1946- *WhoFI 94*
Grow, Richard Dennis 1942- *WhoAm 94, WhoAmL 94*
Grow, Robert Theodore 1948- *WhoFI 94, WhoScEn 94*
Growcott, Frank R. *WhoHol 92*
Growdon, Marcia Cohn 1945- *WhoAmA 93*
Growe, Joan Anderson 1935- *WhoAm 94, WhoAmP 93, WhoMW 93*
Growe, Sarah Jane 1939- *WrDr 94*
Grower, Russell d1958 *WhoHol 92*
Growick, Philip 1944- *WhoFI 94*
Groza, Alex 1926- *BasBi*
Groza, Joanna Raluca 1943- *WhoWest 94*
Groza, Lou *ProFbHF [port]*
Groza, Maria 1918- *WhoWomW 91*
Grua, Carlo Luigi Pietro c. 1665-1726 *NewGrDO*
Grua, Carlo Pietro c. 1700-1773 *NewGrDO*
Grua, Charles 1934- *WhoScEn 94*
Grub, Phillip Donald 1931- *WhoAm 94*
Gruba, Jim 1946- *WhoMW 93*
Gruba-McCallister, Frank Peter 1952- *WhoScEn 94*
Grubar, Francis Stanley 1924-1991 *WhoAmA 93N*
Grubb, David *WhoAmA 93*
Grubb, David 1951- *WhoAmP 93*
Grubb, David Conway 1944- *WhoScEn 94*
Grubb, David H. 1936- *WhoWest 94*
Grubb, Donald Hartman 1924- *WhoAm 94*
Grubb, Erica B. 1947- *WhoAmL 94*
Grubb, Floyd Dale 1949- *WhoAmP 93*
Grubb, George G. 1931- *WhoAm 94*
Grubb, Jay G. *WhoAmL 94*
Grubb, Lewis Craig 1954- *WhoFI 94*
Grubb, Norman Percy 1895- *WrDr 94*
Grubb, Pat Pincombe 1922-1977 *WhoAmA 93N*
Grubb, Peter John 1935- *Who 94*
Grubb, Robert *WhoHol 92*
Grubb, Robert Lynn 1927- *WhoAm 94, WhoFI 94, WhoScEn 94*
Grubb, William Francis X. 1944- *WhoAm 94*
Grubb, Wilson Lyon 1910- *WhoAm 94*
Grubbs, Donald Ray 1947- *WhoAm 94*
Grubbs, Donald Shaw, Jr. 1929- *WhoAm 94, WhoAmL 94, WhoFI 94*
Grubbs, Donell Roy 1961- *WhoAmL 94*
Grubbs, Elven Judson 1930- *WhoAm 94*
Grubbs, Jeffrey Thomas 1957- *WhoScEn 94*
Grubbs, Robert H. 1942- *WhoScEn 94*
Grubbs, Shelby Russell 1949- *WhoAmL 94*
Grubbs, Steven E. 1964- *WhoAmP 93*
Grubbs, Steven Eric 1964- *WhoMW 93*
Grubbstrom, Karl Robert William 1941- *WhoScEn 94*
Grube, Bernhard Adam 1715-1808 *EncNAR*
Grube, Dick DeWayne 1933- *WhoAm 94*
Grube, Elizabeth 1917- *WhoFI 94, WhoMW 93*
Grube, Joel William 1949- *WhoScEn 94*
Grube, Karl Bertram 1946- *WhoAm 94, WhoAmL 94*
Grube, Oden Montgomery 1946- *WhoAmP 93*
Gruben, Karl Taylor 1951- *WhoAmL 94*
Gruber, Aaronel Deroy *WhoAmA 93*
Gruber, Aaronel deRoy 1927- *WhoAm 94*
Gruber, Alan Richard 1927- *WhoAm 94*
Gruber, Andras 1954- *WhoWest 94*
Gruber, Aspasia 1948- *WhoIns 94*
Gruber, Fredric Francis 1931- *WhoAm 94*
Gruber, Gary John 1955- *WhoIns 94*
Gruber, George Michael 1951- *WhoFI 94*
Gruber, Ira Dempsey 1934- *WhoAm 94*
Gruber, J. Richard 1948- *WhoAmA 93*
Gruber, Jack 1931- *WhoScEn 94*
Gruber, Jack Alan 1943- *WhoScEn 94*
Gruber, John d1981 *WhoHol 92*
Gruber, John Balsbaugh 1935- *WhoAm 94, WhoScEn 94*
Gruber, John Edward 1936- *WhoMW 93*
Gruber, Kenneth Allen 1948- *WhoScEn 94*
Gruber, Loren Charles 1941- *WhoMW 93*
Gruber, Marianne *EncSF 93*
Gruber, Sheldon 1930- *WhoAm 94*
Gruber, William Paul 1932- *WhoAm 94*
Gruberg, Martin 1935- *WhoAm 94, WrDr 94*
Gruberova, Edita 1946- *NewGrDO*
Grubert, Carl Alfred 1911-1979 *WhoAmA 93N*
Grubich, Donald Nicholas 1934- *WhoMW 93*
Grubin, Brian Lee 1957- *WhoWest 94*
Grubin, Harold Lewis 1939- *WhoScEn 94*
Grubin, Sharon E. *WhoAmL 94*
Grubman, Wallace Karl 1928- *WhoAm 94*
Grucci, Felix James, Sr. d1993 *NewYTBS 93 [port]*
Gruccio-Thorman, Lillian Joan 1927- *WhoAmL 94*
Gruchacz, Robert S. 1929- *WhoAm 94*
Gruchalla, Michael Emeric 1946- *WhoScEn 94, WhoWest 94*
Grucza, Leo (Victor) 1935- *WhoAmA 93*
Grudin, Louis d1993 *NewYTBS 93 [port]*
Grudinina, Anna Kornilovna *WhoWomW 91*
Grudzinski, Chester Walter, Jr. 1956- *WhoAmL 94*
Grue, Eva Sue 1945- *WhoAmP 93*
Grue, Howard Wood 1927- *WhoAm 94*
Grue, Lee Meitzen *DrAPF 93*
Gruebele, Martin 1964- *WhoScEn 94*
Grueber, Johann 1623-1680 *WhWE*
Gruen, Armin 1944- *WhoScEn 94*
Gruen, Claude 1931- *WhoWest 94*
Gruen, David Henry 1929- *WhoAm 94*
Gruen, Erich S(tephen) 1935- *WrDr 94*
Gruen, Erich Stephen 1935- *WhoAm 94*
Gruen, Gerald Elmer 1937- *WhoAm 94*
Gruen, John 1926- *WhoAmA 93*
Gruen, Nina Jaffe 1933- *WhoWest 94*
Gruen, Robert 1913- *IntMPA 94*
Gruen, Shirley Schanen 1923- *WhoAmA 93*
Gruenbaum, Adolf 1923- *ConAu 43NR*
Gruenberg, Elliot Lewis 1918- *WhoAm 94*
Gruenberg, Erich 1924- *IntWW 93*
Gruenberg, Ernest Matsner 1915-1991 *WhAm 10*
Gruenberg, Gladys Walleman 1920- *WhoMW 93*
Gruenberg, Karl Walter 1928- *Who 94*
Gruenberg, Leonard S. 1913- *IntMPA 94*
Gruenberg, Louis 1884-1964 *NewGrDO*
Gruenberg, Mark Jonathan 1953- *WhoAm 94*
Gruenberg, Max F., Jr. 1943- *WhoAmP 93, WhoWest 94*
Gruenberg, Michael L. 1946- *WhoFI 94*
Gruenberger, Peter 1937- *WhoAm 94*
Gruenburg, Meir d1993 *NewYTBS 93*
Gruendel, Aileen Dopp 1939- *WhoMW 93*
Gruenes, David B. 1958- *WhoAmP 93*
Gruenfeld, Jay 1924- *WhoWest 94*
Gruenfeld, Lee 1950- *ConAu 142*
Gruenther, Sue Cory d1948 *WhoAmA 93N*
Gruenwald, George Henry 1922- *WhoAm 94, WhoFI 94, WhoWest 94*
Gruenwald, Mark Edward 1959- *WhoMW 93*
Gruenwald, Oskar 1941- *WhoWest 94*
Gruer, William E. 1937- *WhoFI 94*
Gruetter, Bryan William 1958- *WhoAmL 94*
Gruettner, Donald W. 1930- *WhoAm 94*
Gruff, Eric Stephen 1963- *WhoWest 94*
Gruffydd, (Robert) Geraint 1928- *Who 94*
Gruffydd, William John 1881-1954 *DcNaB MP*
Gruffydd Jones, Daniel *Who 94*
Grugel, Lee E. *WhoMW 93*
Grugel, Richard Nelson 1951- *WhoScEn 94*
Grugeon, John (Drury) 1928- *Who 94*
Gruger, Audrey Lindgren 1930- *WhoAmP 93*
Gruger, Edward Hart, Jr. 1928- *WhoScEn 94*
Gruger, Frederick R. 1871-1953 *WhoAmA 93N*
Gruhl, Andrea Morris 1939- *WhoFI 94*
Gruhl, Robert H. 1945- *WhoIns 94*
Gruhl, Robert Herbert 1945- *WhoAm 94, WhoFI 94*
Gruhl, Suzanne Swiderski 1946- *WhoFI 94*
Gruhn, Josephine 1927- *WhoAmP 93*
Gruhn, Robert Stephen 1938- *WhoMW 93*
Gruitza, Michael Cornell 1951- *WhoAmP 93*
Grujanac, Louis Ljubisa 1959- *WhoMW 93*
Grum, Clifford J. 1934- *WhoAm 94, WhoFI 94*
Grumbach, Argula von c. 1498-1563 *BlmGWL*
Grumbach, Doris *DrAPF 93*
Grumbach, Doris 1918- *BlmGWL, WhoAm 94, WrDr 94*
Grumbach, Doris (Isaac) 1918- *ConAu 42NR, GayLL*
Grumbach, George Jacques, Jr. 1941- *WhoAm 94*
Grumbach, Melvin Malcolm 1925- *IntWW 93, WhoAm 94*
Grumbacher, John Richard 1950- *WhoAm 94*
Grumbine, Edith Mae 1927- *WhoAmP 93*
Grumbine, R. Edward 1953- *ConAu 140*
Grumbles, John Leslie 1947- *WhoMW 93*
Grumbling, Hudson Virgil, Jr. 1936- *WhoWest 94*
Grumbo, Howard *WhoAmP 93*
Grumbold, Robert 1639-1720 *DcNaB MP*
Grumet, Martin 1954- *WhoScEn 94*
Grumet, Priscilla Hecht 1943- *WhoAm 94*
Grumley, Michael 1941- *WrDr 94*
Grummann, Paul H. d1950 *WhoAmA 93N*
Grummer, Elisabeth *IntWW 93N*
Grummer, Elisabeth 1911-1986 *NewGrDO*
Grun, Friederike 1836-1917 *NewGrDO*
Grunau, Herman Carl 1895- *WhAm 10*
Grunbaum, Adolf 1923- *WhoAm 94, WrDr 94*
Grunbaum, Fritz 1880- *WhoHol 92*
Grunbaum, Therese 1791-1876 *NewGrDO*
Grunberg, Patrick Ramon 1941- *WhoHisp 94*
Grunberg, Robert Leon Willy 1940- *WhoAm 94*
Grunberger, Dezider 1922- *WhoAm 94*
Grunberg-Manago, Marianne 1921- *IntWW 93*
Grunblatt, Mark 1957- *WhoAmL 94*
Grund, David Ira 1947- *WhoAmL 94*
Grund, Johanna-Christina 1934- *WhoWomW 91*
Grund, Leo d1978 *WhoHol 92*
Grund, Walter James, Jr. 1927- *WhoAm 94*
Grundbacher, Frederick John 1926- *WhoAm 94*
Grundberg, Andy 1947- *WhoAmA 93, WrDr 94*
Grundberg, Betty *WhoAmP 93*
Grundberg, Betty 1938- *WhoMW 93*
Grunder, Arthur Neil 1936- *WhoAm 94*
Grunder, Paul Edwin 1931- *WhAm 10*
Grunder, Robert Douglas 1953- *WhoWest 94*
Grundfest, Joseph A. 1951- *WhoAmP 93*
Grundfest, Joseph Alexander 1951- *WhoAm 94*
Grundgens, Gustav d1963 *WhoHol 92*
Grundhofer, John F. 1939- *WhoAm 94, WhoFI 94, WhoMW 93*
Grundman, Valentine Rock, Jr. 1932- *WhoAmL 94*
Grundmeyer, Douglas Lanaux 1948- *WhoAmL 94*
Grundstein, Nathan (David) 1913- *WrDr 94*
Grundstein, Nathan David 1913- *WhoAm 94*
Grundy, Betty Lou Bottoms 1940- *WhoAm 94*
Grundy, David Stanley 1943- *Who 94*
Grundy, J(ohn Owen) 1911-1985 *WhoAmA 93N*
Grundy, James Caldwell, Jr. 1923- *WhoAmP 93*
Grundy, Joan 1920- *WrDr 94*
Grundy, Kenneth William 1936- *WhoAm 94*
Grundy, (James) Milton 1926- *Who 94*
Grundy, Pamela C. 1962- *ConAu 140*
Grundy, Richard David 1937- *WhoScEn 94*
Grundy, Roy Rawsthorne 1930- *WhoMW 93*
Grundy, Stephanie Christine 1958- *Who 94*
Grune, George Vincent 1929- *WhoAm 94, WhoFI 94*
Grunebaum, Ernest Michael 1934- *WhoAm 94*
Gruner, George *WhoAmP 93*
Gruner, Olivier *WhoHol 92*
Grunert, Carl *EncSF 93*
Grunes, David Leon 1921- *WhoAm 94*
Grunes, Robert Lewis 1941- *WhoAm 94, WhoScEn 94*
Grunewald, Ann Mae 1933- *WhoAmP 93*
Grunewald, Gary Lawrence 1937- *WhoAm 94*
Grunewald, Gottfried 1675-1739 *NewGrDO*
Grunewald, Michael 1954- *WhoScEn 94*
Grunewald, Raymond Bernhard 1928- *WhoAmL 94*
Grunewalt, Pine 1937- *WrDr 94*
Grunfeld, Cyril 1922- *Who 94*
Grunfeld, Ernst *WhoFI 94*
Grunfeld, Frederic V 1929- *WrDr 94*
Grunfeld, Henry 1904- *IntWW 93, Who 94*
Grunig, James Elmer 1942- *WhoAm 94*
Gruning, Ilka d1964 *WhoHol 92*
Gruning, Wilhelm 1858-1942 *NewGrDO*
Gruninger, John E. 1939- *WhoIns 94*
Gruninger, Robert Martin 1937- *WhoScEn 94*
Grunke, Andrew Frederick 1946- *WhoScEn 94*
Grunn, (John) Homer 1880-1944 *NewGrDO*
Grunsell, Charles Stuart Grant 1915- *Who 94*
Grunseth, Jon Rieder 1945- *WhoAmP 93*
Grunsfeld, Ernest Alton, III 1929- *WhoAm 94*
Grunstad, Norman Lee 1939- *WhoWest 94*
Grunstein, Leonard 1952- *WhoAmL 94*
Grunt, Jerome Alvin 1923- *WhoAm 94*
Gruntman, Michael A. 1954- *WhoScEn 94*
Grunwald, Alfred 1884-1951 *NewGrDO*
Grunwald, Arnold Paul 1910- *WhoScEn 94*
Grunwald, Bryan Elliott 1943- *WhoWest 94*
Grunwald, Ernest 1923- *IntWW 93*
Grunwald, Ernest Max 1923- *WhoAm 94*
Grunwald, Henry Anatole 1922- *IntWW 93*
Grupe, Barbara A.P. 1943- *WhoAm 94*
Grupp, Carl Alf 1939- *WhoAm 94, WhoAmA 93*
Gruppe, Charles 1928- *WhoAmA 93*
Gruppe, Emil Albert 1896-1978 *WhoAmA 93N*
Gruppe, Karl Heinrich 1893-1982 *WhoAmA 93N*
Gruppen, Larry Dale 1955- *WhoScEn 94*
Gruppo, Leonard Quirico 1942- *WhoAmP 93*
Gruse, Gregory G. *WhoAmP 93*
Grusendorf, Kent 1939- *WhoAmP 93*
Grusenmeyer, David Clouse 1953- *WhoWest 94*

Guerrand, Jean-Rene d1993 NewYTBS 93
Guerrant, David Edward 1919- WhoAm 94
Guerra-Vela, Claudio 1945- WhoHisp 94
Guerrera, John F. 1925- WhoAmP 93
Guerrero (y Torres), Jacinto 1895-1951 NewGrDO
Guerrero, Andrés Gonzales, Jr. 1943- WhoHisp 94
Guerrero, Anthony R., Jr. 1945- WhoHisp 94
Guerrero, Antonio Moreno, Jr. 1950- WhoHisp 94
Guerrero, Carlos J. 1961- WhoHisp 94
Guerrero, Carlos Joel 1943- WhoHisp 94
Guerrero, Charles 1944- WhoHisp 94
Guerrero, Crispin Ideleon WhoAmP 93
Guerrero, Dan 1940- WhoHisp 94
Guerrero, Daniel G. 1951- WhoHisp 94
Guerrero, Dolores WhoHisp 94
Guerrero, Dolores 1941- WhoHisp 94
Guerrero, Edward Garcia 1932- WhoAmP 93
Guerrero, Gilbert, Jr. 1960- WhoHisp 94
Guerrero, Guillermo E. 1946- WhoHisp 94
Guerrero, Jose 1914- WhoAmA 93N
Guerrero, Jose 1914-1991 WhAm 10
Guerrero, Jose Alfredo 1963- WhoWest 94
Guerrero, José Luis 1958- WhoHisp 94
Guerrero, José Miguel 1958- WhoHisp 94
Guerrero, Juan Manuel 1954- WhoHisp 94
Guerrero, Juan N. 1946- WhoHisp 94
Guerrero, Juan T. WhoAmP 93
Guerrero, Lena 1957- WhoAmP 93, WhoHisp 94
Guerrero, Luis F. 1936- WhoHisp 94
Guerrero, Mario, Jr. 1962- WhoHisp 94
Guerrero, Omar Victor 1954- WhoHisp 94
Guerrero, Pedro 1956- WhoBlA 94, WhoHisp 94
Guerrero, Pedro R. Deleon WhoAmP 93
Guerrero, Raul 1945- WhoAmA 93
Guerrero, Raul Fernandez 1963- WhoHisp 94
Guerrero, Roberto 1958- WhoHisp 94
Guerrero-Anderson, Esperanza 1944- WhoHisp 94, WhoMW 93
Guerrero-Duby, Sara Frances 1954- WhoHisp 94
Guerrette, Richard Hector 1930- WhoFI 94
Guerri, Sergio 1905- IntWW 93
Guerri, William Grant 1921- WhoAm 94
Guerrini, Bernard A. 1947- WhoAmL 94
Guerrini, Guido 1890-1965 NewGrDO
Guerrise, Patrick P. 1943- WhoAm 94
Guerritore, Monica WhoHol 92
Guerrrero, Herman Tenorio 1948- WhoAmP 93
Guertin, Robert Gerald 1947- WhoFI 94
Guertin, Robert Powell 1939- WhoAm 94
Guertin, Therese Anne 1963- WhoMW 93
Guertler, Peter H. d1993 NewYTBS 93
Gu Erxiong WhoPRCh 91
Guesnerie, Charlotte-Marie-Anne Charbonniere de la 1710-1785 BlmGWL
Guesnerie, Roger Sylvain Maxime Auguste 1943- IntWW 93
Guess, Francis S. 1946- WhoAmP 93, WhoBlA 94
Guess, Gordon Blue 1936- WhoAmP 93
Guess, James David 1941- WhoAmL 94
Guessford, George d1968 WhoHol 92
Guest Who 94
Guest, Anthony Gordon 1930- Who 94, WrDr 94
Guest, Barbara DrAPF 93
Guest, Barbara 1920- WhoAm 94, WrDr 94
Guest, Buddy Ross 1920- WhoMW 93
Guest, Calvin Ray 1923- WhoAmP 93
Guest, Christopher 1948- IntMPA 94, WhoAm 94, WhoHol 92
Guest, Cynthia Jean 1963- WhoMW 93
Guest, Donald Britnor 1929- WhoFI 94
Guest, Douglas 1916- IntWW 93
Guest, Douglas Albert 1916- Who 94
Guest, Edgar A. d1959 WhoHol 92
Guest, Eric Ronald 1904- Who 94
Guest, George Howell 1924- IntWW 93, Who 94
Guest, Gerald Bentley 1936- WhoScEn 94
Guest, Harry 1932- WrDr 94
Guest, Henry Alan 1920- Who 94
Guest, Ivor (Forbes) 1920- ConAu 42NR, WrDr 94
Guest, Ivor Forbes 1920- Who 94
Guest, James Alfred 1940- WhoAm 94
Guest, John Rodney 1935- IntWW 93, Who 94
Guest, Judith DrAPF 93
Guest, Judith 1936- WrDr 94
Guest, Judith Ann 1936- WhoAm 94
Guest, Karl Macon 1915- WhoAm 94
Guest, Lance WhoHol 92
Guest, Lance 1960- IntMPA 94
Guest, Lynn 1939- WrDr 94
Guest, Maurice Mason 1906- WhAm 10
Guest, Melville Richard John 1943- Who 94
Guest, Michael Kurt 1949- WhoAmL 94
Guest, Nicholas WhoHol 92
Guest, Raymond Richard 1907-1991 WhAm 10
Guest, Raymond Richard, Jr. 1939- WhoAmP 93
Guest, Richard Eugene 1944- WhoWest 94
Guest, Robert H. 1916- WhoAmP 93
Guest, Robert Henry 1916- WhoAm 94
Guest, Tom R. 1952- WhoFI 94
Guest, Trevor George 1928- Who 94
Guest, Val IntMPA 94
Guest, Weldon S. 1947- WhoScEn 94
Guetary, Georges WhoHol 92
Gueterbock Who 94
Guethlein, William O. 1927- WhoAmL 94
Guette, Madame de la 1613-1676 BlmGWL
Guettel, Henry Arthur 1928- WhoAm 94
Guetz, Burton Walter 1951- WhoAmL 94
Guetzke, Thomas Lorin 1958- WhoMW 93
Guetzkow, Daniel Steere 1949- WhoAm 94, WhoScEn 94
Guetzkow, Harold 1915- WhoWest 94
Guetzloe, Douglas Micheal 1954- WhoAmP 93
Guevara, Anne Marie 1949- WhoWest 94
Guevara, Che 1928-1967 HispLC [port]
Guevara, Daniel Luis 1947- WhoHisp 94
Guevara, Ernesto 1928-1967 HisWorL [port]
Guevara, Esequiel C. 1953- WhoHisp 94
Guevara, Francisco Antonio 1924- WhoHisp 94
Guevara, Gilberto 1942- WhoHisp 94
Guevara, Gustavo, Jr. 1949- WhoHisp 94
Guevara, Jacinto 1956- WhoHisp 94
Guevara, Jose Luis WhoHisp 94
Guevara, Juan G. DrAPF 93
Guevara, Raúl Rubio 1954- WhoHisp 94
Guevara, Theresa Sabater 1947- WhoHisp 94
Guevara, Yingo 1931- WhoHisp 94
Guevara Arze, Walter 1911- IntWW 93
Guevara Piñero, Jose Luis 1931- WhoHisp 94
Gueymard, Louis 1822-1880 NewGrDO
Gueymard-Lauters, Pauline 1834-1876? NewGrDO
Guezennec, Yann Guillaume 1956- WhoScEn 94
Gu Fangzhou WhoPRCh 91
Guffey, Burnett 1905-1983 IntDcF 2-4 [port]
Guffey, Cary 1972- WhoHol 92
Guffey, George Robert 1932- WrDr 94
Guffin, Gilbert Lee 1906- WrDr 94
Gu Gan 1942- WhoPRCh 91 [port]
Gugas, Chris 1921- WhoMW 93
Gugel, Craig Thomas 1954- WhoAm 94, WhoFI 94
Gu Gengyu 1905- WhoPRCh 91 [port]
Gugenheim, Lawrence 1951- WhoFI 94
Guggenheim, Charles E. 1924- WhoAm 94
Guggenheim, Daniel 1856-1930 AmSocL
Guggenheim, Frederick Gibson 1935- WhoAm 94
Guggenheim, Harry Frank 1890-1971 WhoAmA 93N
Guggenheim, Meyer 1828-1905 AmSocL
Guggenheim, Peggy 1898-1979 WhoAmA 93N
Guggenheim, Richard E. 1913- WhoAm 94
Guggenheim, Simon 1867-1941 AmSocL
Guggenheim-Boucard, Alan Andre Albert Pa 1950- WhoWest 94
Guggenheimer, Heinrich Walter 1924- WhoAm 94
Guggenheimer, Richard Henry 1906-1977 WhoAmA 93N
Guggenhime, Richard Elias 1908-1988 WhAm 10
Guggenhime, Richard Johnson 1940- WhoAm 94, WhoAmL 94, WhoWest 94
Guglielmi, Giacomo 1782-c. 1820 See Guglielmi Family NewGrDO
Guglielmi, Louis O. 1906-1956 WhoAmA 93N
Guglielmi, Pietro Alessandro 1728-1804 NewGrDO
Guglielmi, Pietro Carlo 1772-1817 NewGrDO
Guglielmi Family NewGrDO
Guglielminetti, Amalia 1885-1941 BlmGWL
Guglielmini, Pietro Carlo NewGrDO
Guglielmino, Russell J. 1940- WhoAmL 94
Guglielmo, Tony WhoAmP 93
Guglielmo Ebreo c. 1420-c. 1481 IntDcB
Guglietta, Antonio 1956- WhoMW 93
Gugliotti, Robert Anthony 1960- WhoMW 93
Gu Gongxu 1907- WhoPRCh 91
Gu Gongxu 1908- IntWW 93
Guha, Phulrenu 1911- IntWW 93
Guhl, George d1943 WhoHol 92
Guhr, Karl (Wilhelm Ferdinand) 1787-1848 NewGrDO
Gu Hua 1942- IntWW 93, WhoPRCh 91 [port]
Gu Hui 1930- WhoPRCh 91 [port]
Gu Hui, Lieut.-Gen. 1930- IntWW 93
Gui, James Edmund 1928- WhoAm 94
Gui, Luigi 1914- IntWW 93
Gui, Vittorio 1885-1975 NewGrDO
Guibert, Elisabeth 1725-1788 BlmGWL
Guibert, Iliana WhoHisp 94
Guibert, Louise-Alexandrine, Comtesse de 1765?-1826 BlmGWL
Guicciardi, Francesco fl. 1705-1724 NewGrDO
Guice, Daniel D., Jr. 1953- WhoAmP 93
Guice, Gregory Charles 1952- WhoBlA 94
Guice, John Thompson 1923- WhoAm 94, WhoWest 94
Guice, Leroy 1944- WhoBlA 94
Guice, Raleigh Terry 1940- WhoBlA 94
Guice, Terry L. 1955- WhoAmP 93
Guichard, Henry d18th cent. NewGrDO
Guichard, Olivier Marie Maurice 1920- IntWW 93
Guichen, Luc Urbain de Bouexic, Comte de 1712-1790 WhAmRev
Guichet, Melody 1949- WhoAmA 93
Guida, Anthony James, Jr. 1961- WhoAmL 94
Guida, Dominick 1946- WhoAmA 93
Guida, James John 1957- WhoScEn 94
Guida, Pat 1929- WhoFI 94
Guida, Peter Matthew 1927- WhoAm 94
Guidacci, Margherita 1921- BlmGWL
Guidera, George Clarence 1942- WhoAmP 93
Guidera, John Victor 1950- WhoWest 94
Guidetti Serra, Bianca 1919- WhoWomW 91
Guidi, Francesco fl. 1841-1860 NewGrDO
Guidi, John Neil 1954- WhoScEn 94
Guidi, Robert d1977 WhoHol 92
Guido, Beatrix 1924- BlmGWL
Guido, Cecily Margaret 1912- WrDr 94
Guido, Michael Anthony 1954- WhoAmP 93, WhoMW 93
Guido, Robert Norman 1935- WhoAmP 93
Guido the Columnis BlmGEL
Guidry, Arreader Pleanna WhoBlA 94
Guidry, David 1957- WhoBlA 94
Guidry, Jessie P. 1941- WhoAmP 93
Guidry, John Michael 1962- WhoAmP 93
Guidry, Roman Antoine 1926- WhoAmP 93
Guidry-White, Carlette Denise 1968- WhoBlA 94
Guiducci, Armanda 1923- BlmGWL
Guiffre, Aldo WhoHol 92
Guiffre, Carlo WhoHol 92
Guignabodet, Liliane 1939- IntWW 93
Guigou, Elisabeth 1946- WhoWomW 91
Guigou, Elisabeth Alexandrine Marie 1946- IntWW 93
Guiher, James Morford, Jr. 1927- WhoAm 94
Guilak, Farshid 1964- WhoScEn 94
Guilarte, Pedro M. 1952- WhoHisp 94
Guilarte, Pedro Manuel 1952- WhoFI 94
Guilbault, Rose del Castillo 1952- WhoHisp 94
Guilbeau, Eric J. 1944- WhoScEn 94
Guilbert, Ann WhoHol 92
Guilbert, Lionel 1918- WhoAmP 93
Guilbert, Yvette d1944 WhoHol 92
Guilbert de Pixerecourt, Rene Charles NewGrDO
Guilboa, Amos 1912- WhoHisp 94
Guild, Alden 1929- WhoAm 94
Guild, Clark Joseph, Jr. 1921- WhoAm 94
Guild, Ivor Reginald 1924- Who 94
Guild, Lurelle Van Arsdale 1898- WhAm 10
Guild, Nancy 1925- WhoHol 92
Guild, Nelson Prescott 1928- WhoAm 94
Guild, Richard Samuel 1925- WhoFI 94
Guildford, Bishop of 1929- Who 94
Guildford, Dean of Who 94
Guiles, Fred Lawrence 1920- WrDr 94
Guiles, Jon Roger 1945- WhoAmP 93
Guilfoil, Thomas WhoAmP 93
Guilford, Earl of 1933- Who 94
Guilford, Andrew John 1950- WhoAm 94, WhoAmL 94
Guilford, Diane Patton 1949- WhoBlA 94
Guilfoyle, George H. 1913-1991 WhAm 10
Guilfoyle, James d1964 WhoHol 92
Guilfoyle, James Joseph 1956- WhoFI 94, WhoMW 93
Guilfoyle, John W. 1921-1989 WhAm 10
Guilfoyle, Margaret (Georgina Constance) 1926- Who 94
Guilfoyle, Margaret Georgina Constance 1926- IntWW 93
Guilfoyle, Paul WhoHol 92
Guilfoyle, Paul d1961 WhoHol 92
Guilfoyle, Richard J. 1935- WhoIns 94
Guilhaume, Philippe 1942- IntWW 93
Guill, John Russell 1959- WhoWest 94
Guillabert, Andre 1918- IntWW 93
Guillard, Nicolas-Francois 1752-1814 NewGrDO
Guillaud, Jean Louis 1929- IntWW 93
Guillaumat, Pierre 1909-1991 WhAm 10
Guillaume, Alfred Joseph, Jr. 1947- WhoBlA 94
Guillaume, Gilbert 1930- IntWW 93
Guillaume, Marnix Leo Karl 1938- WhoAm 94
Guillaume, Raymond Kendrick 1943- WhoAm 94
Guillaume, Robert 1927- WhoCom
Guillaume, Robert 1929- WhoHol 92
Guillaume, Robert 1937- IntMPA 94, WhoBlA 94
Guillaumont, Antoine Jean-Baptiste 1915- IntWW 93
Guillaumont, Robert 1933- WhoScEn 94
Guillebeaux, Tamara Elise WhoBlA 94
Guillem, Sylvie 1965- IntDcB [port], IntWW 93
Guillemette, Gloria Vivian 1929- WhoAm 94
Guillemin, Michel Pierre 1943- WhoScEn 94
Guillemin, Roger 1924- WorScD
Guillemin, Roger C. L. 1924- WhoAm 94, WhoScEn 94, WhoWest 94
Guillemin, Roger Charles Louis 1924- IntWW 93, Who 94
Guillemot, Agnes 1931- IntDcF 2-4
Guillen (y Batista), Nicolas (Cristobal) 1902- BlkWr 2
Guillén, Alfonso, Jr. 1949- WhoHisp 94
Guillen, Ana Magda WhoHisp 94
Guillen, Manuel E. WhoHisp 94
Guillen, Michael Arthur WhoScEn 94
Guillen, Nicolas 1902-1989 ConLC 79 [port], HispLC [port]
Guillen, Ozzie 1964- WhoAm 94, WhoHisp 94
Guillen, Tomás 1949- WhoHisp 94, WrDr 94
Guilleragues, Gabriel-Joseph de Lavergne, Vicomte de 1628-1685 GuFrLit 2
Guillermin, John 1925- IntMPA 94, IntWW 93
Guillermo, Tessie 1957- WhoAsA 94
Guillery, Rainer W. 1929- IntWW 93
Guillery, Rainer Walter 1929- Who 94, WhoAm 94
Guillet, James Edwin 1927- WhoAm 94
Guillet, Pernette du c. 1520-1545 BlmGWL
Guillevic, Eugene 1907- ConWorW 93, IntWW 93
Guillo, Magdalena 1940- BlmGWL
Guillory, Elcie WhoAmP 93
Guillory, Jack Paul 1938- WhoScEn 94
Guillory, Jeffery Michael 1966- WhoAmL 94
Guillory, John L. 1945- WhoBlA 94
Guillory, Julius James 1927- WhoBlA 94
Guillory, Keven 1953- WhoBlA 94
Guillory, Linda Semien 1950- WhoBlA 94
Guillory, William A. 1938- WhoBlA 94
Guillot, Patrick Carl 1945- WhoAmL 94
Guillou, Pierre John 1945- Who 94
Guilly, Richard Lester 1905- Who 94
Guilmain, Jacques 1926- WhoAmA 93
Guilmenot, Richard Arthur, III 1948- WhoBlA 94
Guilmette, Raymond Alfred 1946- WhoWest 94
Guiloff, Jorge Francisco 1952- WhoHisp 94
Guilpin, Everard c. 1572-1608? DcLB 136
Guimaraes, Elina 1904-1991 BlmGWL
Guimaraes, George Gomes 1944- WhoAm 94
Guimaraes, Marilu Segatto 1951- WhoWomW 91
Guimaraes Rosa, Joao 1908-1967 RfGShF
Guimard, Marie-Madeleine 1743-1816 IntDcB [port]
Guimary, Ramon Curtis 1929- WhoFI 94, WhoWest 94
Guimond, John Patrick 1927- WhoAm 94
Guimond, Richard Joseph 1947- WhoAm 94, WhoScEn 94
Guin, Don Lester 1940- WhoAmL 94, WhoFI 94
Guin, Junius Foy, Jr. 1924- WhoAm 94
Guin, Mark NewYTBS 93 [port]
Guin, Winford Harold 1926- WhoAm 94
Guin, Wyman (Woods) 1915- WrDr 94
Guin, Wyman (Woods) 1915-1989 EncSF 93

Guinan, Mary Elizabeth 1939- *WhoAm 94*
Guinan, Richard C., Jr. 1942- *WhoAmL 94*
Guinan, Texas d1933 *WhoHol 92*
Guinan, William Joseph 1948- *WhoAmL 94*
Guinart, Roque d1975 *WhoHol 92*
Guindon, Yvan 1951- *WhoAm 94*
Guinee, Rodger J. 1962- *WhoFI 94*
Guingona, Michael Patrick 1962- *WhoAsA 94*
Guinier, Andre Jean 1911- *IntWW 93*
Guinier, Carol Lani *WhoBlA 94*
Guinier, Ewart 1910-1990 *WhAm 10*
Guinier, Lani 1950- *NewYTBS 93 [port]*
Guinn, Charles Clifford, Jr. 1935- *WhoAmL 94*
Guinn, David Crittenden 1926- *WhoAm 94, WhoFI 94, WhoScEn 94*
Guinn, Janet Martin 1942- *WhoScEn 94*
Guinn, John Rockne 1936- *WhoAm 94*
Guinn, Kenny C. 1934- *WhoFI 94*
Guinn, Reuben Kent 1954- *WhoFI 94*
Guinn, Stanley Willis 1953- *WhoFI 94, WhoWest 94*
Guinness *Who 94*
Guinness, Alec 1914- *IntMPA 94, IntWW 93, Who 94, WhoAm 94, WhoCom, WhoHol 92*
Guinness, Bryan (Walter) 1905-1992 *WrDr 94N*
Guinness, Desmond 1931- *ConAu 141*
Guinness, Desmond (Walter) 1931- *Who 94*
Guinness, Howard (Christian Sheldon) 1932- *Who 94*
Guinness, James Edward Alexander Rundell 1924- *IntWW 93, Who 94*
Guinness, John Ralph Sidney 1935- *Who 94*
Guinness, Kenelm (Ernest Lee) 1928- *Who 94*
Guinness, Kenelm L. 1928- *WhoScEn 94*
Guinnessey, Kathleen M. 1960- *WhoFI 94*
Guinot, Luis, Jr. 1935- *WhoAm 94*
Guinouard, Donald Edgar 1929- *WhoWest 94*
Guinouard, Philip Andre 1960- *WhoWest 94*
Guinto-Juco, Estelita 1930- *WhoWomW 91*
Guinzburg, Adiel 1966- *WhoScEn 94*
Guinzburg, Frederick 1897-1978 *WhoAmA 93N*
Guiomar, Julien *WhoHol 92*
Guion, Robert Morgan 1924- *WhoScEn 94*
Guiot, Fernand *WhoHol 92*
Guiraud, Ernest 1837-1892 *NewGrDO*
Guiraudon, Julia 1873-1914? *NewGrDO*
Guirdham, Arthur 1905-1992 *WrDr 94N*
Guirrand, Jane *WhoHol 92*
Guirsch, James Franklin 1956- *WhoMW 93*
Guise, David Earl 1931- *WhoAm 94*
Guise, John (Grant) 1927- *Who 94*
Guise, Steven Lee 1946- *WhoAmL 94*
Guise, Thomas d1930 *WhoHol 92*
Guisewite, Cathy Lee 1950- *WhoAm 94*
Gui Shiyong 1934- *WhoPRCh 91 [port]*
Guist, Fredric Michael 1946- *WhoAm 94, WhoFI 94*
Guitano, Anton W. 1950- *WhoBlA 94*
Guitart, Agustin Ramon 1935- *WhoHisp 94*
Guitart, Jorge Miguel 1937- *WhoHisp 94*
Guitart, William *WhoHisp 94*
Guiton, Bonnie 1941- *WhoBlA 94*
Guiton, Bonnie F. 1941- *WhoAm 94*
Guitry, Genevieve d1964 *WhoHol 92*
Guitry, Sacha d1957 *WhoHol 92*
Guittard, Lawrence *WhoHol 92*
Guittarr, Dennis C. 1947- *WhoFI 94*
Guitti, Francesco 1605-c. 1645 *NewGrDO*
Guitton, Henri 1904- *IntWW 93*
Guitton, Jean Marie Pierre 1901- *IntWW 93*
Guitty, Madeleine d1936 *WhoHol 92*
Guivens, Norman Roy, Jr. 1957- *WhoScEn 94*
Guizar, Ricardo Diaz 1933- *WhoAm 94*
Guizar, Tito 1908- *WhoHol 92*
Guizot, Pauline 1773-1827 *BlmGWL*
Guizzo, Mary Lou 1954- *WhoMW 93*
Gujadhur, Radhamohun 1909- *Who 94*
Gu Jiaji *WhoPRCh 91*
Gu Jianfen *WhoPRCh 91*
Gu Jinchi 1932- *IntWW 93, WhoPRCh 91 [port]*
Gu Jingsheng *WhoPRCh 91*
Gu Jinping *WhoPRCh 91*
Gu Jinxin *WhoPRCh 91*
Gujral, Inder Kumar 1919- *IntWW 93*
Gu Junzheng *EncSF 93*
Gulager, Clu 1928- *IntMPA 94, WhoHol 92*
Gulak-Artemovsky, Semyon Stepanovich 1813-1873 *NewGrDO*
Gulan, Stephen Richard 1935- *WhoMW 93*
Gulati, Adarsh Kumar 1956- *WhoAsA 94*
Gulati, Akhilesh 1954- *WhoWest 94*
Gulati, Suresh Thakurdas 1936- *WhoScEn 94*
Gulbadam, Begum fl. 16th cent.- *BlmGWL*
Gulbenkian, Paul *WhoAm 94*
Gulbinowicz, Henryk Roman 1928- *IntWW 93*
Gulbrandson, L. C. 1922- *WhoAmP 93*
Gulbranson, Ellen 1863-1947 *NewGrDO*
Gulcher, Robert Harry 1925- *WhoAm 94*
Gulda, Edward James 1945- *WhoAm 94, WhoFI 94, WhoMW 93*
Guldager, Christine Lynn 1953- *WhoMW 93*
Guldberg, Ove 1918- *IntWW 93*
Gulden, Simon 1938- *WhoAm 94*
Guldimann, Till M. 1949- *WhoAm 94*
Guldner, Harold W. *WhoAmP 93*
Gulezian, Michael 1957- *WhoWest 94*
Gulick, Donna Marie 1956- *WhoFI 94*
Gulick, Henry G. *WhoIns 94*
Gulick, John 1924- *WhoAm 94*
Gulick, Luther (Halsey) 1892-1993 *CurBio 93N*
Gulick, Luther H. d1993 *NewYTBS 93 [port]*
Gulick, Peter Gregory 1950- *WhoMW 93*
Gulick, Peter VanDyke 1930- *WhoAmL 94*
Gulick, Stephen Millard 1948- *WhoAmP 93*
Gulick, Walter Lawrence 1927- *WhoAm 94*
Gulin, Angeles 1943- *NewGrDO*
Gu Linfang *WhoPRCh 91 [port]*
Gulino, Frank 1954- *WhoAmL 94*
Gulinson, Susan Kay 1956- *WhoAmL 94*
Gulis, Dean Alexander 1955- *WhoFI 94*
Gulka, John Matthew 1953- *WhoFI 94*
Gulkin, Harry 1927- *WhoAm 94*
Gulko, Edward 1950- *WhoFI 94*
Gulko, Paul Michael 1944- *WhoAm 94*
Gull, Paula Mae 1955- *WhoWest 94*
Gull, Ranger *EncSF 93*
Gull, Rupert (William Cameron) 1954- *Who 94*
Gullahorn, Jack W. 1948- *WhoAmL 94*
Gullan, Campbell d1939 *WhoHol 92*
Gulland, Eugene D. 1947- *WhoAm 94*
Gullander, Werner Paul 1908- *WhoAm 94*
Gullans, Charles *DrAPF 93*
Gullans, Charles (Bennett) 1929- *WrDr 94*
Gullans, Charles (Bennett) 1929-1993 *ConAu 141*
Gullans, Charles Bennett 1929-1993 *NewYTBS 93*
Gullapalli, Pratap 1959- *WhoScEn 94*
Gullatt, Jane *WhoAmP 93*
Gullattee, Alyce C. 1928- *WhoBlA 94*
Gulledge, Michael Stanley 1950- *WhoAmP 93*
Gulledge, Robert Ivan 1932- *WhoAmP 93*
Gulledge, Sandra Smith 1949- *WhoFI 94*
Gulledge, Yutana Ruth 1950- *WhoAmP 93*
Gullekson, Edwin Henry, Jr. 1935- *WhoMW 93*
Gullen, George E., III 1939- *WhoMW 93*
Gullen, John Douglas 1958- *WhoAmL 94*
Guller, Todd Jaime 1960- *WhoMW 93*
Gulleson, Pam *WhoAmP 93*
Gullet, Leon Estle 1930- *WhoMW 93*
Gulley, Girtha 1935- *WhoAmP 93*
Gulley, Joan Long 1947- *WhoAm 94*
Gulley, Wilbur P. 1948- *WhoAmP 93*
Gulley, Wilbur Paul, Jr. 1923- *WhoAm 94*
Gulley, Wilson 1937- *WhoBlA 94*
Gullichsen, Johan Erik 1936- *IntWW 93*
Gullick, Richard Warren 1958- *WhoMW 93*
Gullickson, Alvin 1940- *WhoAmP 93*
Gullickson, Dale Dean 1933- *WhoAmP 93*
Gullickson, Glenn, Jr. 1919- *WhoAm 94*
Gullickson, Roger Wayne 1938- *WhoAmP 93*
Gullickson, Tim 1951- *BuCMET*
Gullickson, Tom 1951- *BuCMET*
Gulling, Daniel Lee 1944- *WhoMW 93*
Gulling, Nick *WhoAmP 93*
Gullit, Ruud 1962- *WorESoc*
Gulliver, Dorothy 1908- *WhoHol 92*
Gulliver, James Gerald 1930- *Who 94*
Gulliver, John William 1951- *WhoAmL 94*
Gullotti, Antonino Pietro 1929- *IntWW 93*
Gullstrand, Allvar 1862-1930 *WorScD*
Gulluscio, Ronald John 1937- *WhoAmP 93*
Gully *Who 94*
Gully, Anthony Lacy 1938- *WhoAmA 93*
Gulmi, James Singleton 1946- *WhoAm 94*
Gulmi, Joseph 1947- *WhoAmL 94*
Gulotta, Victor 1954- *WhoFI 94*
Guloy, Pompeyo B., Jr. *WhoAsA 94*
Gulpilil, David 1954- *WhoHol 92*
Gulrajani, Ramesh Mulchand 1944- *WhoScEn 94*
Gulrajani, Robert B. 1953- *WhoAsA 94*
Gulson, DeLoris Anne 1940- *WhoMW 93*
Gulvin, David Horner 1934- *WhoAm 94*
Gulyas, Denes 1954- *IntWW 93, NewGrDO*
Guma, Greg William 1947- *WhoAm 94*
Gumaer, Elliott Wilder, Jr. 1933- *WhoAm 94*
Gu Maoxuan *WhoPRCh 91*
Gumbel, Bryant 1948- *AfrAmAl 6 [port], IntMPA 94*
Gumbel, Bryant Charles 1948- *IntWW 93, WhoAm 94, WhoBlA 94*
Gumbel, Greg 1946- *WhoBlA 94*
Gumberts, William A. 1912- *WhoAmA 93N*
Gumbiner, Kenneth Jay 1946- *WhoAm 94*
Gumbiner, Robert Louis 1923- *WhoAm 94, WhoFI 94*
Gumbinner, Paul S. 1942- *WhoAm 94*
Gumbleton, Thomas J. 1930- *WhoAm 94*
Gumbs, Godfrey Anthony 1948- *WhoScEn 94*
Gumbs, Oliver Sinclair 1913- *WhoBlA 94*
Gumbs, Philip N. 1923- *WhoBlA 94*
Gumede, Archiebald Jacob 1914- *IntWW 93*
Gumerman, George John 1936- *WhoScEn 94*
Gumerson, Jean Gilderhus 1923- *WhoAm 94*
Gu Ming 1919- *WhoPRCh 91 [port]*
Gumley, Frances Jane 1955- *Who 94*
Gummel, Hermann Karl 1923- *WhoAm 94*
Gummelt, Samuel 1944- *WhoAmA 93*
Gummer, Don 1946- *WhoAmA 93*
Gummer, Ellis Norman 1915- *Who 94*
Gummer, John Selwyn 1939- *IntWW 93, Who 94*
Gummer, Peter Selwyn 1942- *IntWW 93, Who 94, WhoAm 94, WhoFI 94*
Gummere, John 1928- *WhoAm 94, WhoFI 94, WhoIns 94*
Gummere, Walter Cooper 1917- *WhoAm 94*
Gummin, Barbara Hall 1955- *WhoWest 94*
Gumms, Emmanuel George, Sr. 1928- *WhoBlA 94*
Gumnick, James Louis 1930- *WhoScEn 94*
Gumnit, Robert Jerome 1931- *WhoMW 93*
Gump, Richard Anthony 1917- *WhoAm 94*
Gumpel, Glenn J. *WhoAm 94, WhoWest 94*
Gumpel, Hugh 1926- *WhoAmA 93*
Gumpel, Peter Eric 1955- *WhoAmL 94*
Gumper, Lindell Lewis 1947- *WhoScEn 94*
Gumpert, Emil 1895- *WhAm 10*
Gumpert, Gunther 1919- *WhoAm 94, WhoAmA 93*
Gumpert, Jon *IntMPA 94*
Gumpertz, Werner Herbert 1917- *WhoAm 94*
Gumperz, John J(oseph) 1922- *WrDr 94*
Gumpright, Herbert Lawrence, Jr. 1946- *WhoScEn 94*
Gumrukcuoglu, Rahmi Kamil 1927- *Who 94*
Gu Mu 1914- *IntWW 93, WhoPRCh 91 [port]*
Guna-Kasem, Pracha 1934- *IntWW 93*
Gunar, Lee Roy 1938- *WhoIns 94*
Gunaratne, Dhavalasri Shelton Abeywickreme 1940- *WhoAsA 94, WhoMW 93*
Gunasinghe, Siri 1925- *WhoAmA 93*
Gunby, John *WhAmRev*
Gunby Kelly, Carolyn 1954- *WhoFI 94*
Gund, Agnes *WhoAm 94*
Gund, Agnes 1938- *WhoAmA 93*
Gund, Christopher Michael 1968- *WhoMW 93*
Gund, George, III 1937- *WhoAm 94, WhoWest 94*
Gund, Gordon 1939- *WhoAm 94, WhoMW 93, WhoWest 94*
Gund, Peter Herman 1940- *WhoFI 94*
Gundareva, Natalia 1948- *WhoHol 92*
Gundelfinger, Ralph Mellow 1925- *WhoMW 93*
Gunderman, Karen M. 1951- *WhoAmA 93*
Gunderrode, Karoline von 1780-1806 *BlmGWL*
Gundersen, Martin A. 1940- *WhoScEn 94*
Gundersen, Wayne Campbell 1936- *WhoAm 94*
Gundersheimer, Herman (Samuel) 1903- *WhoAmA 93*
Gundersheimer, Karen 1939- *WrDr 94*
Gundersheimer, Werner Leonard 1937- *WhoAm 94*
Gunderson, Barry L. 1945- *WhoAmA 93*
Gunderson, Cleon Henry 1932- *WhoWest 94*
Gunderson, Donald Raymond 1942- *WhoScEn 94*
Gunderson, Edward Lynn 1952- *WhoScEn 94*
Gunderson, Elmer Millard 1929- *WhoAm 94, WhoAmP 93, WhoWest 94*
Gunderson, Gerald Axel 1940- *WhoAm 94*
Gunderson, Joanna *DrAPF 93*
Gunderson, Judith Keefer 1939- *WhoFI 94*
Gunderson, Karen 1943- *WhoAmA 93*
Gunderson, Keith *DrAPF 93*
Gunderson, Keith Howard 1955- *WhoMW 93*
Gunderson, Morley Kenneth 1945- *WhoFI 94*
Gunderson, Richard L. 1933- *WhoIns 94*
Gunderson, Robert Vernon, Jr. 1951- *WhoAm 94, WhoAmL 94*
Gunderson, Steve 1951- *CngDr 93*
Gunderson, Steve Craig 1951- *WhoAm 94, WhoAmP 93, WhoMW 93*
Gunderson, Ted Lee 1928- *WhoWest 94*
Gundlach, Frank Norman 1938- *WhoAm 94*
Gundlach, Heinz Ludwig 1937- *WhoAm 94, WhoFI 94*
Gundlach, Helen Fuchs 1892-1959 *WhoAmA 93N*
Gundlach, Robert 1926- *WorInv*
Gundlach, Scott Michael 1959- *WhoFI 94*
Gundlefinger, John Andre 1937- *WhoAmA 93*
Gundrum, James Richard 1929- *WhoAm 94*
Gundry, Inglis 1905- *NewGrDO*
Gundry, Jo Ann 1945- *WhoMW 93*
Gundry, Stanley N. 1937- *WhoAm 94*
Gundy, Frances Darnell 1947- *WhoMW 93*
Gundy, Jeff *DrAPF 93*
Gundy, Roy Nathaniel, Jr. 1967- *WhoBlA 94*
Guner, Osman Fatih 1956- *WhoWest 94*
Guney, Yilmaz d1984 *WhoHol 92*
Gungaadorj, Sharavyn 1935- *IntWW 93*
Gungah, Dwarkanath 1940- *IntWW 93*
Gungtamcang *WhoPRCh 91*
Gunia, Robert E. 1944- *WhoWest 94*
Gun-Munro, Sydney Douglas 1916- *Who 94*
Gunn, Alan 1940- *WhoAm 94*
Gunn, Albert Edward, Jr. 1933- *WhoAm 94*
Gunn, Alex M., Jr. 1928- *WhoBlA 94*
Gunn, Arthur Clinton 1942- *WhoBlA 94*
Gunn, Bill d1989 *WhoHol 92*
Gunn, Brian L. 1964- *WhoMW 93*
Gunn, Brooke 1946- *WrDr 94*
Gunn, Bunty Moffat 1923- *Who 94*
Gunn, Charles d1918 *WhoHol 92*
Gunn, Earl d1963 *WhoHol 92*
Gunn, Ellen 1951- *WhoAmA 93*
Gunn, Frank Michael 1956- *WhoAmP 93*
Gunn, George F., Jr. 1927- *WhoAm 94, WhoAmL 94*
Gunn, Giles Buckingham 1938- *WhoAm 94*
Gunn, Gladys 1937- *WhoBlA 94*
Gunn, Henry Martin 1898- *WhAm 10*
Gunn, James E(dwin) 1923- *EncSF 93, WrDr 94*
Gunn, James Edward 1938- *WhoAm 94*
Gunn, Jeannie 1870-1961 *BlmGWL*
Gunn, John (Currie) 1916- *Who 94*
Gunn, John Angus Livingston 1934- *Who 94*
Gunn, John Charles 1937- *IntWW 93, Who 94*
Gunn, John Humphrey 1942- *Who 94*
Gunn, Judy 1915- *WhoHol 92*
Gunn, Karen Sue 1951- *WhoAm 94*
Gunn, Marion Ballantyne 1947- *Who 94*
Gunn, Mary Elizabeth 1914- *WhoMW 93*
Gunn, Michael William 1945- *WhoAm 94, WhoFI 94*
Gunn, Moses d1993 *NewYTBS 93 [port]*
Gunn, Moses 1929- *IntMPA 94, WhoAm 94, WhoHol 92*
Gunn, Neil M(iller) 1891-1973 *EncSF 93*
Gunn, Paul James 1922- *WhoAmA 93*
Gunn, Peter Nicholson 1914- *Who 94*
Gunn, Richard *Who 94*
Gunn, (Alan) Richard 1936- *IntWW 93, Who 94*
Gunn, Robert Burns 1939- *WhoAm 94*
Gunn, Robert Dewey 1928- *WhoAm 94*
Gunn, Robert Louis 1931- *WhoAmP 93*
Gunn, Robert Murray 1927- *WhoAm 94*
Gunn, Robert Norman 1925- *IntWW 93, Who 94*
Gunn, Roderick James 1945- *WhoAm 94*
Gunn, Russell *WhoAmP 93*
Gunn, Steve *WhoAmP 93*
Gunn, Thom *DrAPF 93*

Gunn, Thom 1929- *BlmGEL, ConLC 81 [port]*
Gunn, Thom(son William) 1929- *GayLL, WrDr 94*
Gunn, Thomas Jeremy 1952- *WhoAmL 94*
Gunn, Thomas M. *WhoAm 94, WhoFI 94, WhoWest 94*
Gunn, Thomas Patrick d1943 *WhoHol 92*
Gunn, Thomson William 1929- *IntWW 93, Who 94, WhoAm 94*
Gunn, Vonda 1920- *WhoAmP 93*
Gunn, William (Archer) 1914- *Who 94*
Gunn, William Archer 1914- *IntWW 93*
Gunn, Willie Cosdena Thomas 1926- *WhoBlA 94*
Gunnars, Kristjana 1948- *BlmGWL*
Gunnarson, Arthur Bernard 1896- *WhAm 10*
Gunnarsson, Birgir Isleifur 1936- *IntWW 93*
Gunnarsson, Thorarinn 1957- *EncSF 93*
Gunnel, Joseph C., Sr. 1918- *WhoBlA 94*
Gunnell, Dale Ray 1936- *WhoAm 94*
Gunnell, (William) John 1933- *Who 94*
Gunnell, Sally 1966- *IntWW 93*
Gunnels, Doug 1948- *WhoAmP 93*
Gunnemann, Louis Herman 1910-1989 *WhAm 10*
Gunner, Lawrence George 1939- *WhoAmP 93*
Gunnerson, Robert Mark 1949- *WhoAm 94*
Gunness, Robert Charles 1911- *WhoAm 94*
Gunning, Brian Edgar Scourse 1934- *Who 94*
Gunning, Charles Theodore 1935- *Who 94*
Gunning, David Hall 1942- *WhoAm 94, WhoAmL 94*
Gunning, Francis Patrick 1923- *WhoAm 94*
Gunning, John Edward Maitland d1992 *Who 94N*
Gunning, John Thaddeus 1917- *WhoAm 94*
Gunning, Robert Clifford 1931- *WhoAm 94*
Gunning, Sally (Carlson) 1951- *ConAu 140*
Gunning, Steven Richard 1945- *WhoWest 94*
Gunnings, Thomas S. 1935- *WhoBlA 94*
Gunnison, Douglas 1944- *WhoAm 94*
Gunnison, John Williams 1812-1853 *WhWE*
Gunnlaugsson, Gordon Harvey 1944- *WhoAm 94*
Gunnoe, Nancy Lavenia 1921- *WhoFI 94*
Gunreth, Elizabeth d1948 *WhoHol 92*
Guns, Ronald A. 1948- *WhoAmP 93*
Gunsalus, Irwin C. 1912- *WhoAm 94, WhoMW 93*
Gunsalus, Irwin Clyde 1912- *IntWW 93*
Gunsberg, David B. 1949- *WhoAmL 94*
Gunsberg, Sheldon 1920- *IntMPA 94*
Gunsbourg, Raoul 1859-1955 *NewGrDO*
Gunsch, Michael Henry 1958- *WhoFI 94*
Gunsch, Ronald E. *WhoAmP 93*
Gunsett, Daniel J. 1948- *WhoAm 94, WhoAmL 94*
Gunshor, Ruth *WhoAmA 93*
Gunson, Ameral Blanche Tregurtha 1948- *IntWW 93*
Gunst, Peter Henrik 1944- *WhoAm 94, WhoAmL 94*
Gunst, Robert Allen 1948- *WhoFI 94*
Gunston, Bill *ConAu 42NR*
Gunston, Bill 1927- *WrDr 94*
Gunston, John (Wellesley) 1962- *Who 94*
Gunston, William Tudor 1927- *ConAu 42NR*
Gunstone, Frank Denby 1923- *WrDr 94*
Gunstream, Robby Dean 1951- *WhoWest 94*
Gunsul, Alan Lane Webster 1926- *WhoWest 94*
Gunsul, Brooks R. W. 1928- *WhoAm 94*
Guntaka, Ramareddy Venkata 1942- *WhoMW 93*
Gunter, Annie Laurie 1919- *WhoAmP 93*
Gunter, Bill 1934- *WhoAmP 93*
Gunter, Bradley Hunt 1940- *WhoFI 94*
Gunter, Carl N., Jr. 1938- *WhoAmP 93*
Gunter, Carolyn M. 1931- *WhoAmP 93*
Gunter, Cornelius d1990 *WhoHol 92*
Gunter, Emily Diane 1948- *WhoFI 94*
Gunter, Frank Elliott 1934- *WhoAm 94, WhoAmA 93*
Gunter, Gordon 1909- *WhoScEn 94*
Gunter, Horst 1913- *NewGrDO*
Gunter, John Brown, Jr. 1919- *WhoAm 94*
Gunter, John Forsyth 1938- *Who 94*
Gunter, John Richmond 1941- *WhoAm 94*
Gunter, Joseph Clifford, III 1943- *WhoAm 94, WhoAmL 94*
Gunter, Laurie 1922- *WhoBlA 94*
Gunter, Linda Hinkleman 1949- *WhoAmP 93*
Gunter, Michael Donwell 1947- *WhoAmL 94*
Gunter, Pete (Addison Yancey) 1936- *WrDr 94*
Gunter, Randel Harlan 1961- *WhoMW 93*
Gunter, Rick 1948- *WhoFI 94*
Gunter, Rickey Van 1944- *WhoAm 94*
Gunter, Robert L. 1945- *WhoAmL 94*
Gunter, Russell Allen 1950- *WhoAm 94, WhoAmL 94*
Gunter, William D., Jr. 1934- *WhoIns 94*
Gunter, William Dawson, Jr. 1934- *WhoAm 94*
Gunter, William Dayle, Jr. 1932- *WhoScEn 94, WhoWest 94*
Gunther, Carl d1951 *WhoHol 92*
Gunther, Carol L. *DrAPF 93*
Gunther, Charles F. 1933- *WhoAmA 93*
Gunther, Gary A. 1947- *WhoMW 93*
Gunther, George Lackman 1919- *WhoAmP 93*
Gunther, Gerald 1927- *WhoAm 94, WrDr 94*
Gunther, Gotthard *EncSF 93*
Gunther, Jack Disbrow 1908-1990 *WhAm 10*
Gunther, Jacob E., III *WhoAmP 93*
Gunther, Jane Perry 1916- *WhoAm 94*
Gunther, Julius 1818-1904 *NewGrDO*
Gunther, Leon 1939- *WhoAm 94*
Gunther, Marc 1951- *WhoAm 94*
Gunther, Marian Waclaw Jan 1923- *WhoMW 93, WhoScEn 94*
Gunther, Mizzi 1879-1961 *NewGrDO*
Gunther, Paul Benjamin 1947- *WhoMW 93*
Gunther, Richard Paul 1946- *WhoMW 93*
Gunther, Richard S. 1925- *WhoWest 94*
Gunther, Robert Jene 1955- *WhoMW 93*
Gunther, Timothy 1957- *WhoAm 94*
Gunther, William Edward 1948- *WhoScEn 94*
Guntheroth, Warren Gaden 1927- *WhoAm 94*
Gunthorpe, Uriel Derrick 1924- *WhoBlA 94*
Guntly, Gregory G. 1942- *WhoAm 94*
Guntly, Leon Arnold 1944- *WhoScEn 94*
Gunton, Bob 1945- *WhoHol 92*
Gunty, Morty d1984 *WhoHol 92*
Gunzberg, Roy S. d1987 *WhoHol 92*
Gunzenhauser, Gerard Ralph, Jr. 1960- *WhoAm 94*
Gunzenhauser, Stephen Charles 1942- *WhoAm 94*
Gunzo, Izawa 1940- *WhoScEn 94*
Guo, Chu 1933- *WhoScEn 94*
Guo, David 1952- *WhoAsA 94*
Guo, Dongyao 1935- *WhoScEn 94*
Guo, Hua *WhoAsA 94*
Guo, Hua 1962- *WhoScEn 94*
Guo, Xin Kang 1938- *WhoScEn 94*
Guo Benyu *WhoPRCh 91*
Guo Chang 1970- *WhoPRCh 91*
Guo Changming *WhoPRCh 91*
Guo Chaoren 1934- *IntWW 93, WhoPRCh 91 [port]*
Guo Chengji 1917- *WhoPRCh 91*
Guo Chu *WhoPRCh 91*
Guo-dao Duoji *WhoPRCh 91*
Guo Dezhi 1932- *WhoPRCh 91 [port]*
Guo Dongbo *WhoPRCh 91 [port]*
Guo Feng *WhoPRCh 91 [port]*
Guo Fengmin 1930- *IntWW 93, WhoPRCh 91 [port]*
Guo Hongtao 1904- *WhoPRCh 91 [port]*
Guo Ji *WhoPRCh 91*
Guo Jiading *WhoPRCh 91*
Guo Jian 1913- *WhoPRCh 91*
Guo Junyan *WhoPRCh 91*
Guo Kun *WhoPRCh 91 [port]*
Guo Linxiang 1914- *WhoPRCh 91 [port]*
Guo Linxiang, Gen. 1914- *IntWW 93*
Guo Liwen 1920- *IntWW 93, WhoPRCh 91 [port]*
Guo Musun 1920- *IntWW 93, WhoPRCh 91*
Guo Peihui *WhoPRCh 91 [port]*
Guo Pingtan 1933- *IntWW 93, WhoPRCh 91*
Guo Rongchan 1933- *WhoPRCh 91 [port]*
Guo Ruiren 1905- *WhoPRCh 91 [port]*
Guo Runlin 1940- *WhoPRCh 91*
Guo Shichang *WhoPRCh 91*
Guo Shicong *WhoPRCh 91*
Guo Shuyan 1935- *WhoPRCh 91 [port]*
Guo Songnian 1931- *WhoPRCh 91 [port]*
Guo Tao 1927- *WhoPRCh 91 [port]*
Guo Wei *WhoPRCh 91*
Guo Weicheng 1912- *WhoPRCh 91 [port]*
Guo Weicheng, Maj.-Gen. 1912- *IntWW 93*
Guo Weifan 1914- *WhoPRCh 91 [port]*
Guo Xiexian 1925- *IntWW 93, WhoPRCh 91*
Guo Xiuyi 1911- *WhoPRCh 91 [port]*
Guo Xiuzhen 1917- *WhoPRCh 91 [port]*
Guo Xuebo 1950- *WhoPRCh 91 [port]*
Guo Yizong 1940- *WhoPRCh 91 [port]*
Guo Yuehua 1956- *IntWW 93, WhoPRCh 91 [port]*
Guo Yuhuai 1934- *WhoPRCh 91 [port]*
Guo Yunzhong *WhoPRCh 91*
Guo Zhaolie 1924- *WhoPRCh 91*
Guo Zhenqian 1932- *WhoPRCh 91 [port]*
Guo Zhenquian 1932- *IntWW 93*
Guo Zhi 1925- *WhoPRCh 91 [port]*
Guo Ziheng *WhoPRCh 91*
Guo Zurong 1930- *WhoPRCh 91 [port]*
Gup, Benton Eugene 1936- *WhoAm 94*
Guppy, Nicholas (Gareth Lechmere) 1925- *WrDr 94*
Gupta, Ajay 1959- *WhoAsA 94*
Gupta, Ajay Kumar 1961- *WhoAsA 94*
Gupta, Amit 1962- *WhoAsA 94*
Gupta, Anand 1960- *WhoScEn 94*
Gupta, Anil K. 1949- *WhoAsA 94*
Gupta, Anil Kumar 1953- *WhoWest 94*
Gupta, Anil S. 1961- *WhoAsA 94*
Gupta, Arjun K. 1938- *WhoAsA 94*
Gupta, Arjun Kumar 1938- *WhoMW 93*
Gupta, Arun Premchand 1958- *WhoAsA 94*
Gupta, Ashok K. 1950- *WhoAsA 94*
Gupta, Ashwani Kumar 1948- *WhoAm 94, WhoAsA 94*
Gupta, Bhagwandas 1946- *WhoAsA 94*
Gupta, Bhupender S. 1937- *WhoAsA 94*
Gupta, Bimleshwar Prasad 1946- *WhoWest 94*
Gupta, Brij Mohanlal 1932- *WhoAsA 94*
Gupta, Chitranjan J. 1941- *WhoAsA 94*
Gupta, Dharam V. 1945- *WhoAsA 94, WhoScEn 94*
Gupta, Gian Chand 1939- *WhoAsA 94*
Gupta, Gopal Das 1946- *WhoScEn 94*
Gupta, Hem Chander 1931- *WhoMW 93, WhoScEn 94*
Gupta, Jatinder Nath Dass 1942- *WhoAsA 94*
Gupta, Jiwan D. 1940- *WhoAsA 94*
Gupta, Kailash Chandra 1943- *WhoMW 93*
Gupta, Kamla P. 1947- *WhoAsA 94*
Gupta, Kamla Prasad 1947- *WhoMW 93*
Gupta, Krishan L. 1946- *WhoAsA 94*
Gupta, Krishna Chandra 1948- *WhoAm 94*
Gupta, Kuldip Chand 1940- *WhoAm 94, WhoScEn 94*
Gupta, Madan Mohan 1936- *WhoAm 94*
Gupta, Madhu Sudan 1945- *WhoAm 94, WhoAsA 94*
Gupta, Manjula K. 1942- *WhoAsA 94*
Gupta, Naim C. 1933- *WhoAsA 94*
Gupta, Om Prakash K. 1926- *WhoAsA 94*
Gupta, Omprakash K. 1950- *WhoAsA 94*
Gupta, Pardeep K. 1958- *WhoAsA 94*
Gupta, Parveen P. 1957- *WhoAsA 94, WhoFI 94*
Gupta, Paul R. 1950- *WhoAm 94*
Gupta, Prabhat Kumar *WhoScEn 94*
Gupta, Pradeep Kumar 1944- *WhoAsA 94*
Gupta, Praveen K. 1957- *WhoMW 93*
Gupta, Raj Kumar 1943- *WhoAsA 94*
Gupta, Rajat Kumar 1948- *WhoAsA 94*
Gupta, Rajat Kumar 1960- *WhoAmL 94*
Gupta, Rajesh 1961- *WhoScEn 94, WhoWest 94*
Gupta, Rajeshwar Kumar 1931- *WhoAsA 94, WhoMW 93*
Gupta, Rajiv 1961- *WhoAsA 94*
Gupta, Rajiv Kumar 1964- *WhoAsA 94*
Gupta, Rakesh Kumar 1947- *WhoAsA 94*
Gupta, Ram Bihari 1954- *WhoAsA 94*
Gupta, Ramesh Chandra 1941- *WhoScEn 94*
Gupta, Ramesh K. 1953- *WhoAsA 94*
Gupta, Ratanlal N. 1931- *WhoAsA 94*
Gupta, Ravi Chandra 1956- *WhoFI 94*
Gupta, Rishab Kumar 1943- *WhoScEn 94*
Gupta, Ron Singh 1949- *WhoAsA 94*
Gupta, Samir 1965- *WhoAsA 94*
Gupta, Sanjay 1957- *WhoAsA 94*
Gupta, Sanjeev 1954- *WhoAsA 94*
Gupta, Santosh 1940- *WhoAsA 94*
Gupta, Saroj Lata 1948- *WhoAsA 94*
Gupta, Sudhir 1944- *WhoScEn 94*
Gupta, Sunil 1958- *WhoAsA 94*
Gupta, Sunil Kumar 1928- *IntWW 93*
Gupta, Suraj Narayan 1924- *WhoAm 94, WhoFI 94, WhoScEn 94*
Gupta, Surendra K. 1938- *WhoAsA 94*
Gupta, Surendra Kumar 1938- *WhoAm 94*
Gupta, Surendra Kumar 1944- *WhoAsA 94*
Gupta, Tapan K. 1941- *WhoAsA 94*
Gupta, Tarun 1957- *WhoFI 94*
Gupta, Tej R. 1942- *WhoAsA 94*
Gupta, Udayan 1950- *WhoAsA 94*
Gupta, Umesh Chandra 1937- *WhoScEn 94*
Gupta, Venu Gopal 1934- *WhoAsA 94*
Gupta, Vijay 1962- *WhoAsA 94*
Gupta, Vijay Kumar 1941- *WhoAm 94*
Gupta, Virendra K. 1932- *WhoAsA 94*
Gupta, Yogendra Mohan 1949- *WhoAsA 94*
Gupte, Shridhar 1933- *IntWW 93*
Guptill, James Daniel 1951- *WhoMW 93*
Guptill, Katharine Schuyler 1959- *WhoWest 94*
Guptill, Stephen Charles 1950- *WhoScEn 94*
Gupton, Guy Winfred, III 1949- *WhoAmL 94*
Gur, Batya *BlmGWL*
Gur, Mordechai 1930- *IntWW 93*
Gura, Eugen 1842-1906 *NewGrDO*
Gura, Hermann 1870-1944 *NewGrDO*
Gurak, Stanley Joseph 1949- *WhoWest 94*
Guralnick, Sidney Aaron 1929- *WhoAm 94, WhoScEn 94*
Guran, Yolanda Ileana 1946- *WhoWest 94*
Gurash, John Thomas 1910- *WhoAm 94, WhoWest 94*
Guravich, Dan 1918- *SmATA 74 [port]*
Gurbacs, John Joseph 1947- *WhoAmA 93*
Gurbaxani, Shyam H. M. 1928- *WhoWest 94*
Gurchenko, Ludmila Markovna 1935- *IntWW 93*
Gurchenko, Lyudmila 1935- *WhoHol 92*
Gurdon *Who 94*
Gurdon, John Bertrand 1933- *IntWW 93, Who 94*
Gureckis, Adam C., Sr. 1924- *WhoAmP 93*
Gurecky, Vaclav Matyas 1705?-1743 *NewGrDO*
Gurevich, David 1951- *ConAu 140*
Gurevich, Georgi Josifovich 1917- *IntWW 93*
Gurevich, Liubov'lakovleva 1866-1940 *BlmGWL*
Gurevitch, Arnold William 1936- *WhoAm 94*
Gurfein, Peter J. 1948- *WhoAm 94*
Gurfein, Richard Alan 1946- *WhoAmL 94*
Gurganus, Allan *DrAPF 93*
Gurganus, Allan 1947- *GayLL, WrDr 94*
Gurgin, Vonnie Ann 1940- *WhoAm 94, WhoScEn 94, WhoWest 94*
Gurgulino de Souza, Heitor 1928- *IntWW 93*
Gurholt-Wiese, Victoria Jean *WhoMW 93*
Guri, Haim 1923?- *ConWorW 93*
Gurian, Mal 1926- *WhoAm 94*
Gurian, Martin Edward 1943- *WhoScEn 94*
Gurian, Paul R. 1946- *IntMPA 94*
Guridi (Bidaola), Jesus 1886-1961 *NewGrDO*
Gurie, Sigrid d1969 *WhoHol 92*
Gurin, Arnold 1917-1991 *WhAm 10*
Gurin, Ellen d1972 *WhoHol 92*
Gurin, Meg *WhoAm 94*
Gurin, Richard Stephen 1940- *WhoAm 94*
Gurk, Paul *EncSF 93*
Gurland, Joseph 1923- *WhoAm 94*
Gurle, Leonard c. 1621-1685 *DcNaB MP*
Gurley, Dorothy J. 1931- *WhoBlA 94*
Gurley, Franklin Louis 1925- *WhoAm 94, WhoAmL 94, WhoFI 94*
Gurley, Helen Ruth 1939- *WhoBlA 94*
Gurley, Steven Harrison 1957- *WhoFI 94*
Gurley, William R. 1939- *WhoAmP 93*
Gurley Brown, Helen 1922- *IntWW 93*
Gurlitt, Manfred 1890-1973 *NewGrDO*
Gurnah, Abdulrazak 1948- *WrDr 94*
Gurne, Patricia Dorothy 1941- *WhoAmL 94*
Gurnee, Hal 1935- *WhoAm 94*
Gurnett, Donald Alfred 1940- *WhoAm 94, WhoMW 93*
Gurney, A(lbert) R(amsdell) 1930- *WrDr 94*
Gurney, A(lbert) R(amsdell), Jr. 1930- *ConDr 93*
Gurney, Albert Ramsdell 1930- *WhoAm 94*
Gurney, Christopher Scott 1965- *WhoAmP 93*
Gurney, Daniel Sexton 1931- *WhoAm 94, WhoWest 94*
Gurney, David *EncSF 93*
Gurney, Edmund d1925 *WhoHol 92*
Gurney, Edward John 1914- *WhoAmP 93*
Gurney, George 1939- *WhoAmA 93*
Gurney, Hugh Douglas 1937- *WhoAm 94*
Gurney, Ivor Bertie 1890-1937 *DcNaB MP*
Gurney, James 1958- *EncSF 93, SmATA 76*
Gurney, John Steven 1962- *SmATA 75 [port]*
Gurney, Leanne 1943- *WhoAmL 94*
Gurney, Mary Kathleen 1964- *WhoMW 93*
Gurney, Nicholas Bruce Jonathan 1945- *Who 94*
Gurney, Oliver Robert 1911- *IntWW 93, Who 94*
Gurney, Pamela Kay 1948- *WhoMW 93*

Gurney, Rachel WhoHol 92
Gurney, Samuel 1816-1882 DcNaB MP
Gurney, Susan Rothwell 1951- WhoAmA 93
Gurnis, Michael 1959- WhoMW 93, WhoScEn 94
Gurnitz, Robert Ned 1938- WhoAm 94, WhoMW 93
Gurnsey, Garrold Melvin 1937- WhoWest 94
Gurnsey, Kathleen W. WhoAmP 93
Gurnsey, Kathleen Wallace WhoWest 94
Gurnsey, Kitty 1927- WhoWomW 91
Guro, Elena Genrikhovna 1877-1913 BlmGWL
Gurr, A(ndrew) J(ohn) 1936- WrDr 94
Gurr, Clifton Lee 1932- WhoScEn 94
Gurr, David 1936- WrDr 94
Gurr, Lena 1897- WhAm 10
Gurr, Michael Ian 1939- Who 94
Gurr, Ted Robert 1936- WhoAm 94
Gurrola, Augustine E. WhoHisp 94
Gurrola, Robert James 1939- WhoHisp 94
Gurry, Francis Gerard 1951- WhoAmL 94, WhoFI 94
Gursky, Herbert 1930- WhoAm 94
Gursoy, Ahmet 1929- WhoAmA 93
Gurstel, Norman Keith 1939- WhoAmL 94
Gurtin, Morton Edward 1934- WhoAm 94
Gurtler, Jeffrey C. 1943- WhoIns 94
Gurule, Albert WhoAmP 93
Gurulé, Ernest WhoHisp 94
Gurule, Jimmy 1951- WhoAm 94, WhoHisp 94
Gurulé, José 1951- WhoHisp 94
Gurusiddaiah, Sarangamat 1937- WhoScEn 94
Gurvitch, Geraldine Wilma 1942- WhoAm 94
Gurvitz, Milton Solomon 1919- WhoAm 94
Gurwell, Stephen Lamar 1951- WhoFI 94
Gurwitch, Arnold Andrew 1925- WhoAm 94
Gurwitz-Hall, Barbara Ann 1942- WhoWest 94
Gury, Jeremy 1913- WhoAm 94
Gurzenda, Thaddeus J. 1922- WhoAmP 93
Gusberg, Saul Bernard 1913- WhoAm 94
Gusdon, John Paul, Jr. 1931- WhoScEn 94
Guse, Carol Ann 1952- WhoMW 93
Gusek, Todd Walter 1959- WhoMW 93, WhoScEn 94
Gusella, Ernest 1941- WhoAmA 93
Gusella, Mary Margaret 1948- WhoAm 94
Gusev, Petr 1904-1987 IntDcB [port]
Gusewelle, C. W. DrAPF 93
Gusewelle, Charles Wesley 1933- WhoAm 94
Gush, Jean Direzze WhoAmP 93
Gu Shanqing 1931- WhoPRCh 91 [port]
Gushee, Allison Taylor 1962- WhoFI 94
Gushee, Richard Bordley 1926- WhoAm 94
Gu Shenggu WhoPRCh 91
Gu Shifan WhoPRCh 91
Gushman, John Louis 1912- WhoAm 94
Guskin, Alan E. 1937- WhoAm 94, WhoMW 93
Guslyannikov, Vasily Dmitrievich 1949- LoBiDrD
Gusnard, Raymond Thomas 1926- WhoAm 94
Guss, Helen Joanne Foley 1937- WhoWest 94
Guss, Louis 1918- WhoHol 92
Guss, Paul Phillip 1956- WhoScEn 94
Gusse, Brian Raymond 1948- WhoWest 94
Gussin, Robert Zalmon 1938- WhoAm 94, WhoScEn 94
Gussow, Alan 1931- WhoAm 94, WhoAmA 93
Gussow, Don 1907-1992 WhAm 10
Gussow, Roy 1918- WhoAm 94, WhoAmA 93
Gussow, Sue Ferguson 1935- WhoAmA 93
Gussow, William Carruthers 1908- WhoAm 94
Gust, Gerald N. 1946- WhoAmP 93
Gust, Joyce Jane 1952- WhoMW 93
Gustafson, Albert Katsuaki 1949- WhoAmL 94, WhoFI 94
Gustafson, Alice Fairleigh 1946- WhoAmL 94
Gustafson, Bill 1930- WhoAmP 93
Gustafson, Carol 1925- WhoHol 92
Gustafson, Charles I. WhoAm 94
Gustafson, Charles Ivan 1931- WhoAm 94
Gustafson, Cheri Lynn 1968- WhoWest 94
Gustafson, Clark Charles 1953- WhoMW 93
Gustafson, Dan WhoAmP 93
Gustafson, David A(rthur) 1946- ConAu 141
Gustafson, David Harold 1935- WhoMW 93
Gustafson, David Harold 1940- WhoScEn 94
Gustafson, Donald Franklin 1934- WhoMW 93
Gustafson, Earl Bernard 1927- WhoAmL 94
Gustafson, Grant Bernard 1944- WhoWest 94
Gustafson, James E. 1946- WhoIns 94
Gustafson, Jim DrAPF 93
Gustafson, Jim 1938- WhoAmP 93
Gustafson, John Alfred 1925- WhoAm 94
Gustafson, Lawrence Raymond 1918- WhoAmL 94
Gustafson, Nancy 1956- NewGrDO
Gustafson, Paula 1941- WhoWest 94
Gustafson, Peter L. 1945- WhoAmL 94
Gustafson, Pier WhoAmA 93
Gustafson, Ralph 1909- WrDr 94
Gustafson, Ralph Barker 1909- WhoAm 94
Gustafson, Randall Lee 1947- WhoWest 94
Gustafson, Richard Alrick 1941- WhoAm 94
Gustafson, Richard Charles 1942- WhoAm 94
Gustafson, Sarah 1959- WhoAm 94
Gustafson, Steven Mark 1957- WhoMW 93
Gustafson, Tom 1949- WhoAmP 93
Gustafson, Winthrop Adolph 1928- WhoAm 94
Gustafsson, Alva d1926 WhoHol 92
Gustafsson, Borje Karl 1930- WhoAm 94
Gustafsson, Hans 1923- IntWW 93
Gustafsson, Lars (Erik Einar) 1936- ConWorW 93
Gustafsson, Lars Erik Einar 1936- IntWW 93, WhoAm 94
Gustafsson, Leif Axel 1940- IntWW 93
Gustafsson, Lennart Ake 1935- WhoAm 94
Gustainis, John Edward 1958- WhoFI 94
Gustav, V, King 1858-1950 BuCMET
Gustavino, Stephen Ray 1962- WhoScEn 94
Gustavson, Carl Gustav 1915- WhoAm 94
Gustavson, Dean Leonard 1924- WhoAm 94
Gustavson, Joan Ellen Carlson 1947- WhoWest 94
Gustavson, Karl-Henrik 1930- WhoScEn 94
Gustavson, Leland d1966 WhoAmA 93N
Gustavson, Mark Steven 1951- WhoAmL 94
Gustavson, Robert A. WhoWest 94
Gustavus, III 1746-1792 NewGrDO
Gustavus Adolphus 1594-1632 HisWorL [port]
Gustavus Vasa, I c. 1496-1560 HisWorL [port]
Guste, William Joseph 1922- WhoAmP 93
Gustin, Ann Winifred 1941- WhoScEn 94
Gustin, Arno Anthony 1906-1991 WhAm 10
Gustin, Christopher WhoAmA 93
Gustine, Franklin Johns 1931- WhoAmP 93
Gustine, Paul d1964 WhoHol 92
Gustman, Alan Leslie 1944- WhoAm 94
Guston, Philip 1913-1980 WhoAmA 93N
Gut, Rainer Emil 1932- IntWW 93
Gutche, Gene 1907- WhoAm 94
Gutek, Edward Philip 1941- WhoMW 93
Gutek, Gerald Lee 1935- WhoAm 94
Gutekunst, Richard Ralph 1926- WhoAm 94
Gutelius, Edward Warner 1922- WhoFI 94
Gutenberg, Beno WorScD
Gutenberg, Johannes c. 1395-c. 1468 WorInv [port]
Guterding, William F. 1952- WhoIns 94
Guterman, Sheryl Levine WhoAm 94
Gutermuth, Scott Alan 1953- WhoFI 94, WhoMW 93
Gutermuth, William D. 1952- WhoAmL 94
Guterson, David 1956- WrDr 94
Gutfeld, Norman E. 1911- WhoAm 94
Gutfreund, Herbert 1921- IntWW 93, Who 94
Gutfreund, John H. 1929- WhoAm 94
Gutfreund, John Halle 1929- Who 94
Guth, Alan Harvey 1947- IntWW 93, WhoAm 94, WhoScEn 94
Guth, Paul 1910- IntWW 93
Guth, Paul C. 1922- WhoAm 94, WhoAmL 94
Guth, Raymond WhoHol 92
Guth, Sherman Leon 1932- WhoAm 94
Guth, Theodore Etter 1954- WhoAm 94, WhoAmL 94
Guth, Wilfried 1919- IntWW 93
Guthardt, Helmut 1934- IntWW 93
Guthardt, Phyllis (Myra) 1929- Who 94
Guthart, Leo A. 1937- WhoFI 94
Guthe, Karl Frederick 1918- WhoMW 93
Gutheil-Schoder, Marie 1874-1935 NewGrDO
Gutheim, Frederick d1993 NewYTBS 93
Gutheim, Frederick 1908- WhoAm 94
Gutheim, Frederick 1908-1993 ConAu 142
Gutheim, Robert Julius 1911- WhoAm 94
Guthke, Karl Siegfried 1933- WhoAm 94
Guthman, Jack 1938- WhoAm 94
Guthman, Leo S. WhoAmA 93
Guthman, Sandra Polk 1944- WhoFI 94
Guthrie, Alfred Bertram, Jr. 1901-1991 WhAm 10
Guthrie, Arlo 1947- WhoHol 92
Guthrie, Bert 1932- WhoAmP 93
Guthrie, Bill Myers 1933- WhoFI 94
Guthrie, Carlton Lyons 1952- WhoBlA 94
Guthrie, Catherine S. Nicholson WhoAm 94
Guthrie, Charles (Ronald Llewelyn) 1938- Who 94
Guthrie, David Neal 1941- WhoWest 94
Guthrie, Diana Fern 1934- WhoMW 93
Guthrie, Donald Angus 1931- Who 94
Guthrie, Edgar King 1917- WhoWest 94
Guthrie, Edward Everett 1941- WhoAm 94
Guthrie, Frank Albert 1927- WhoAm 94, WhoScEn 94
Guthrie, Frederick 1924- NewGrDO
Guthrie, George Ralph 1928- WhoAm 94, WhoFI 94
Guthrie, H. Douglas 1949- WhoMW 93
Guthrie, Harvey Henry, Jr. 1924- WhoAm 94
Guthrie, Helen A. 1925- WhoAm 94
Guthrie, Henry Lee 1942- WhoMW 93
Guthrie, Hugh Delmar 1919- WhoScEn 94
Guthrie, James Bryan 1957- WhoWest 94
Guthrie, James Dalglish 1950- Who 94
Guthrie, James Williams 1936- WhoAm 94
Guthrie, Janet 1938- WhoAm 94
Guthrie, John Reiley 1921- WhoAm 94
Guthrie, John Robert 1942- WhoScEn 94
Guthrie, Judith K. 1948- WhoAm 94, WhoAmL 94
Guthrie, Kenneth MacGregor d1993 Who 94N
Guthrie, M. Philip 1945- WhoIns 94
Guthrie, Malcolm (Connop) 1942- Who 94
Guthrie, Marc D. WhoAmP 93
Guthrie, Mearl Raymond, Jr. 1922- WhoAm 94
Guthrie, Michael Who 94
Guthrie, (Garth) Michael 1941- Who 94
Guthrie, Michael J. 1950- WhoBlA 94
Guthrie, Michael Steele 1954- WhoMW 93, WhoScEn 94
Guthrie, Patricia Sue 1958- WhoAm 94, WhoWest 94
Guthrie, Randolph Hobson IntWW 93N
Guthrie, Randolph Hobson 1905-1989 WhAm 10
Guthrie, Randolph Hobson, Jr. 1934- WhoAm 94
Guthrie, Richard Alan 1935- WhoAm 94
Guthrie, Robert Baxter 1920- WhoFI 94
Guthrie, Robert Isles Loftus 1937- Who 94
Guthrie, Robert V. WhoBlA 94
Guthrie, Robert Val 1930- WhoAm 94, WhoScEn 94
Guthrie, Roy David 1934- Who 94
Guthrie, Roy David (Gus) 1934- IntWW 93
Guthrie, Russell Dale 1936- WhoScEn 94
Guthrie, Samuel WorScD
Guthrie, Shirley 1928- WhoAmP 93
Guthrie, Tyrone d1971 WhoHol 92
Guthrie, Tyrone 1900-1971 NewGrDO
Guthrie, Wallace Nessler, Jr. 1939- WhoAm 94
Guthrie, Woodrow Wilson 1912-1967 AmCulL, AmSocL [port]
Gutierrez, Adolfo E. WhoHisp 94
Gutierrez, Alberto F. WhoHisp 94
Gutierrez, Alfredo WhoAmP 93, WhoHisp 94
Gutierrez, Alfredo, Jr. 1932- WhoHisp 94
Gutiérrez, Ana Sol 1942- WhoHisp 94
Gutierrez, Andres 1953- WhoHisp 94
Gutierrez, Anthony 1961- WhoHisp 94
Gutierrez, Antonio 1939- WhoHisp 94
Gutierrez, Arturo F. WhoHisp 94
Gutierrez, Carl Tommy Cruz 1941- WhoAmP 93
Gutierrez, Carlos WhoHisp 94
Gutierrez, Carlos Jose 1927- IntWW 93
Gutierrez, Carlos M. WhoHisp 94
Gutierrez, David G. WhoHisp 94
Gutierrez, David Gregory 1954- WhoHisp 94
Gutierrez, David John 1963- WhoHisp 94
Gutierrez, Diego d1554 WhWE
Gutierrez, Donald Kenneth 1932- WhoHisp 94
Gutierrez, Emilio J. 1966- WhoHisp 94
Gutierrez, Eric-Steven 1960- WhoHisp 94
Gutierrez (y) Espinosa, Felipe 1825-1899 NewGrDO
Gutiérrez, Félix Frank 1943- WhoHisp 94
Gutiérrez, Fernando José WhoHisp 94
Gutierrez, Franklin 1948- WhoAmP 93
Gutierrez, Franklin Abel 1951- WhoHisp 94
Gutierrez, Fred A., Jr. 1951- WhoHisp 94
Gutierrez, Gabriel A. WhoHisp 94
Gutierrez, Gary George 1949- WhoHisp 94
Gutierrez, George A. 1954- WhoHisp 94
Gutierrez, George Armando 1932- WhoHisp 94
Gutierrez, Gerald A. 1954- WhoHisp 94
Gutierrez, Gerard V. 1924- WhoHisp 94
Gutierrez, Gloria 1943- WhoHisp 94
Gutierrez, Guillermo 1946- WhoHisp 94
Gutierrez, Gustavo 1928- IntWW 93, WhoAm 94
Gutiérrez, Heberto 1953- WhoHisp 94
Gutierrez, Hector, Jr. 1947- WhoHisp 94
Gutierrez, Henry Florentino 1948- WhoHisp 94
Gutierrez, Horacio Tomas WhoHisp 94
Gutierrez, Irma Guadalupe 1951- WhoHisp 94
Gutierrez, Isidore Aragon, Sr. 1935- WhoHisp 94
Gutierrez, Jack Allen 1951- WhoHisp 94
Gutierrez, Jaime P. WhoAmP 93
Gutierrez, Jaime P. 1949- WhoHisp 94
Gutierrez, Jay Jose 1951- WhoHisp 94
Gutiérrez, Jesús 1928- WhoHisp 94
Gutierrez, John R. 1952- WhoHisp 94
Gutierrez, Jose WhoHisp 94
Gutierrez, Jose Angel 1944- WhoHisp 94
Gutierrez, Jose Ramon 1936- WhoHisp 94
Gutierrez, Juan J. 1942- WhoHisp 94
Gutierrez, Julio Cesar 1920- IntWW 93
Gutiérrez, Linda 1955- WhoHisp 94
Gutierrez, Lino 1951- WhoAm 94
Gutierrez, Lisa Jean 1962- WhoHisp 94
Gutierrez, Lorraine Padilla 1925- WhoHisp 94
Gutierrez, Louis Felipe 1956- WhoFI 94
Gutierrez, Luis 1953- CngDr 93
Gutiérrez, Luis V. 1953 WhoHisp 94
Gutierrez, Luis V. 1956- WhoAm 94, WhoAmP 93, WhoMW 93
Gutiérrez, María Lourdes WhoHisp 94
Gutierrez, Mario R. 1917- IntWW 93
Gutierrez, Max, Jr. 1930- WhoHisp 94
Gutierrez, Myrna 1959- WhoHisp 94
Gutierrez, Nancy C. 1941- WhoHisp 94
Gutierrez, Orlando WhoHisp 94
Gutierrez, Orlando A. WhoHisp 94
Gutierrez, Oswald WhoHisp 94
Gutierrez, Pamela Jean Holbrook 1956- WhoMW 93
Gutierrez, Paul WhoHisp 94
Gutierrez, Peter Luis 1939- WhoHisp 94
Gutierrez, Ralph 1931- WhoHisp 94
Gutiérrez, Ralph Joseph 1945- WhoHisp 94
Gutiérrez, Ramón Arturo 1951- WhoHisp 94
Gutierrez, Raymond WhoHisp 94
Gutierrez, Renaldy Jose 1947- WhoAmL 94
Gutierrez, Robert P. WhoHisp 94
Gutierrez, Roberto 1936- WhoAmP 93, WhoHisp 94
Gutierrez, Rodolfo V. 1951- WhoHisp 94
Gutierrez, Rosendo 1932- WhoAmP 93
Gutierrez, Rosie Maria 1949- WhoHisp 94
Gutierrez, Rudolfo C., Jr. 1947- WhoHisp 94
Gutierrez, Rudolfo Valentino, Jr. 1960- WhoHisp 94
Gutierrez, Sally Valencia 1918- WhoHisp 94
Gutierrez, Sidney M. 1951- WhoHisp 94
Gutierrez, Sonia I. 1939- WhoHisp 94
Gutierrez, Ted A. 1940- WhoHisp 94
Gutierrez, Yezid 1936- WhoHisp 94
Gutierrez, Zaide Silvia 1959- WhoHol 92
Gutierrez Del Alamo, Rosa Conde 1947- IntWW 93
Gutiérrez de la Solana, Alberto 1913- WhoHisp 94
Gutierrez Keeton, Rebecca Lisa 1963- WhoWest 94
Gutierrez-Medina, Hector 1951- WhoWest 94
Gutierrez Mellado, Manuel 1912- IntWW 93
Gutierrez-Revuelta, Pedro 1949- WhoHisp 94
Gutierrez-Ryburn, Blanca Rosa 1962- WhoFI 94, WhoWest 94
Gutierrez-Santos, Luis Emiliano 1945- WhoAm 94
Gutierrez-Sloan, Esther 1953- WhoHisp 94

Gyllenhammar, Pehr Gustaf 1935-
  IntWW 93, Who 94, WhoAm 94,
  WhoFI 94
Gylseth, Doris Lillian Hanson 1934-
  WhoWest 94
Gyngell, Bruce 1929- *IntWW 93*
Gyngell, Kym *WhoHol 92*
Gynt, Greta 1916- *WhoHol 92*
Gyohten, Toyoo 1931- *ConAu 140,*
  IntWW 93
Gyongyossy, Leslie Laszlo 1932-
  WhoScEn 94
Gyp 1850-1932 *BlmGWL*
Gyra, Francis Joseph, Jr. 1914-
  WhoAmA 93
Gyrowetz, Adalbert 1763-1850 *NewGrDO*
Gys, Leda d1957 *WhoHol 92*
Gysbers, Norman Charles 1932-
  WhoAm 94
Gysel, James Michael 1946- *WhoMW 93*
Gyurkovics, Maria 1915-1973 *NewGrDO*
Gyuzelev, Nikola 1936- *NewGrDO*

H

Ha, Chong W. 1938- *WhoAsA 94*
Ha, Chong Wan 1938- *WhoFI 94, WhoWest 94*
Ha, Joseph Man-Kyung 1936- *WhoAsA 94*
Ha, Sam Bong 1954- *WhoScEn 94*
Ha, Sung Kyu 1960- *WhoScEn 94*
Haab, Larry David 1937- *WhoAm 94, WhoFI 94*
Haac, Oscar A. 1918- *WrDr 94*
Haack, Cynthia R. *WhoAmA 93*
Haack, David Wilford 1945- *WhoWest 94*
Haack, Dieter 1934- *IntWW 93*
Haack, Friedrich Wilhelm 1760-1827 *NewGrDO*
Haack, Kathe d1986 *WhoHol 92*
Haack, Richard Wilson 1935- *WhoFI 94, WhoMW 93*
Haack, Robert Allen 1952- *WhoScEn 94*
Haack, Sandra Jeanne 1952- *WhoMW 93*
Haack, Terry L. 1948- *WhoMW 93*
Haacke, Ewart Mark 1951- *WhoMW 93*
Haacke, Glenna K. 1956- *WhoMW 93*
Haacke, Hans Christoph 1936- *WhoAmA 93*
Haacke, Hans Christoph Carl 1936- *IntWW 93*
Haade, William d1966 *WhoHol 92*
Haag, Donald Richard 1943- *WhoMW 93*
Haag, Everett Keith 1928- *WhoAm 94*
Haag, Joel Edward 1962- *WhoMW 93, WhoScEn 94*
Haag, Philip S. 1951- *WhoAmL 94*
Haag, Rudolf 1922- *IntWW 93*
Haag, Walter Monroe, Jr. 1940- *WhoAm 94*
Haag, William George 1910- *WhoAm 94*
Haag, William Otto, Jr. 1942- *WhoAmP 93*
Haage, Robert Mitchell 1924- *WhoWest 94*
Haagen, Margarete d1966 *WhoHol 92*
Haagen, Paul Hess 1950- *WhoAmL 94*
Haagensen, Donald Albert 1945- *WhoAmL 94*
Haagen-Smit, Arie Jan 1900-1977 *EnvEnc*
Haagenson, Duard Dean 1941- *WhoAmP 93*
Haak, Harold Howard 1935- *WhoAm 94*
Haak, Jan Friedrich Wilhelm 1917- *IntWW 93*
Haak, John Ransford 1938- *WhoAm 94*
Haake, James *WhoHol 92*
Haake, Katharine *DrAPF 93*
Haake, Paul 1932- *WhoAm 94*
Haakenson, Marlan Herman 1937- *WhoAmP 93*
Haakenson, Philip Niel 1924- *WhoMW 93*
Haak-Frendscho, Mary 1956- *WhoMW 93*
Haal, Renee d1964 *WhoHol 92*
Haaland, Douglas 1952- *WhoWest 94*
Haan, Charles Thomas 1941- *WhoAm 94, WhoScEn 94*
Haan, Christopher Francis *Who 94*
Haan, Pieter de 1927- *IntWW 93*
Haar, Andrew John 1963- *WhoScEn 94*
Haar, Charlene Kay 1941- *WhoAmP 93*
Haar, Charles M(onroe) 1920- *WrDr 94*
Haar, Charles Monroe 1920- *WhoAm 94*
Haar, Francis 1908- *WhoAmA 93*
Haar, James 1929- *WrDr 94*
Haar, Tom 1941- *WhoAmA 93*

Haarder, Bertel 1944- *IntWW 93*
Haarlow, John B. 1946- *WhoAm 94, WhoAmL 94*
Haas, Anton Jacob, Jr. 1933- *WhoMW 93*
Haas, Barbara Dolores 1940- *WhoMW 93*
Haas, Betty Jane 1924- *WhoAmP 93*
Haas, Bradley Dean 1957- *WhoWest 94*
Haas, Carolyn Buhai 1926- *WhoAm 94*
Haas, David Colton 1931- *WhoScEn 94*
Haas, David I. 1955- *WhoAmL 94*
Haas, Deborah Lynn 1952- *WhoFI 94*
Haas, Dolly 1910- *WhoHol 92*
Haas, Dorothy *SmATA 17AS [port]*
Haas, Douglas Eric 1950- *WhoAm 94*
Haas, Edward Lee 1935- *WhoAm 94, WhoFI 94*
Haas, Eleanor A. *WhoFI 94*
Haas, Ellen *WhoAm 94, WhoAmP 93*
Haas, Eric Thomas 1952- *WhoAmL 94*
Haas, Ernst Bernard 1924- *WhoAm 94*
Haas, Felix 1921- *WhoAm 94*
Haas, Francis Joseph 1899-1953 *DcAmReB 2*
Haas, Frederick Carl 1936- *WhoAm 94, WhoFI 94*
Haas, Frederick Peter 1911- *WhoAm 94*
Haas, George Aaron 1919- *WhoAm 94*
Haas, George Edward 1948- *WhoAm 94*
Haas, Harold Murray 1925- *WhoAm 94*
Haas, Howard Green 1924- *WhoAm 94*
Haas, Hugo d1968 *WhoHol 92*
Haas, Jacqueline Crawford 1935- *WhoAmL 94*
Haas, James Wayne 1944- *WhoFI 94*
Haas, Jeffrey Edward 1949- *WhoScEn 94*
Haas, John C. 1934- *WhoAm 94*
Haas, Jonathan Stuart 1950- *WhoMW 93*
Haas, Joseph 1879-1960 *NewGrDO*
Haas, Joseph Alan 1950- *WhoAmL 94*
Haas, Joseph Marshall 1927- *WhoAm 94*
Haas, Kenneth B(rooks) 1898- *WhAm 10*
Haas, Kenneth Gregg 1943- *WhoAm 94*
Haas, Lester Carl 1913- *WhoAm 94*
Haas, Lukas 1976- *IntMPA 94, WhoHol 92*
Haas, Marc 1908-1990 *WhAm 10*
Haas, Marilyn Ann 1941- *WhoMW 93*
Haas, Mark 1955- *WhoMW 93*
Haas, Merrill Wilber 1910- *WhoAm 94*
Haas, Michael 1938- *WhoWest 94*
Haas, Michele Iris 1964- *WhoFI 94*
Haas, Nancy Carol 1951- *WhoWest 94*
Haas, Paul Raymond 1915- *WhoAm 94*
Haas, Pavel 1899-1944 *NewGrDO*
Haas, Peter E. 1918- *IntWW 93, WhoFI 94*
Haas, Raymond P. 1942- *WhoAmL 94*
Haas, Richard J. 1937- *WhoIns 94*
Haas, Richard John 1936- *IntWW 93, WhoAmA 93*
Haas, Richard Joseph 1928- *WhoMW 93*
Haas, Robert Donnell 1953- *WhoFI 94*
Haas, Robert Douglas 1942- *IntWW 93, WhoAm 94, WhoFI 94, WhoWest 94*
Haas, Robert John 1930- *WhoScEn 94*
Haas, Ronald Henry 1937- *WhoFI 94*
Haas, Samuel Douglas 1950- *WhoAm 94, WhoAmL 94*
Haas, Suzanne Newhouse 1945- *WhoFI 94, WhoMW 93*
Haas, Sylvia 1947- *WhoMW 93*
Haas, Thomas Joseph 1951- *WhoScEn 94*
Haas, Trice Walter 1932- *WhoScEn 94*

Haas, Walter A., Jr. 1916- *WhoAm 94, WhoWest 94*
Haas, Walter J. *WhoAm 94, WhoWest 94*
Haas, Ward John 1921- *WhoAm 94*
Haas, Warren James 1924- *WhoAm 94*
Haas, William Paul 1927- *WhoAm 94*
Haas-Berger, Ineke 1935- *WhoWomW 91*
Haase, Alfred d1960 *WhoHol 92*
Haase, Ashley Thomson 1939- *WhoAm 94, WhoScEn 94*
Haase, Donald Paul 1950- *WhoMW 93*
Haase, Gerald Martin 1947- *WhoWest 94*
Haase, Robert William 1950- *WhoWest 94*
Haase, Rod *WhoHol 92*
Haase, Susan Jo 1942- *WhoAmP 93*
Haase, William Edward 1943- *WhoAm 94*
Haasen, Peter 1927- *IntWW 93*
Haaseth, Ronald Carl 1952- *WhoWest 94*
Haass, Erwin Herman 1904- *WhoAm 94*
Haass, Richard Nathan 1951- *WhoAm 94*
Haavelmo, Trygve *IntWW 93*
Haavelmo, Trygve 1911- *NobelP 91 [port], Who 94*
Haavikko, Paavo (Juhani) 1931- *ConWorW 93*
Haavikko, Paavo Juhani 1931- *IntWW 93*
Haayen, Richard Jan 1924- *WhoAm 94*
Haba, Alois 1893-1973 *NewGrDO*
Haba, James *DrAPF 93*
Haba, Karel 1898-1972 *NewGrDO*
Habak, Philip Antione 1937- *WhoMW 93*
Habakkuk, Hrothgar John 1915- *IntWW 93*
Habakkuk, John (Hrothgar) 1915- *Who 94*
Habakkuk, John Hrothgar 1915- *WrDr 94*
Habash, George 1925- *IntWW 93*
Habash, Stephen J. 1951- *WhoAm 94*
Habbal, Fawaz 1948- *WhoFI 94*
Habbart, Ellisa Opstbaum 1959- *WhoAmL 94*
Habbel, Wolfgang R. 1924- *IntWW 93*
Habben, David Marshall 1952- *WhoScEn 94*
Habbestad, Kathryn Louise 1949- *WhoAm 94, WhoWest 94*
Habbick, Brian Ferguson 1939- *WhoAm 94*
Habeck, Fritz 1916- *IntWW 93*
Habecker, Eugene Brubaker 1946- *WhoAm 94*
Habedank, Gary L. 1944- *WhoFI 94*
Habeeb, Virginia Thabet *WhoAm 94*
Habegger, Alfred 1892- *EncNAR*
Habegger, Alfred (Carl) 1941- *WrDr 94*
Habeishi, Fred Gabriel 1945- *WhoFI 94*
Haben, John William 1956- *WhoFI 94, WhoMW 93*
Haben, Ralph H., Jr. *WhoAmP 93*
Habeneck, Francois-Antoine 1781-1849 *NewGrDO*
Habenicht, Wenda 1956- *WhoAmA 93*
Haber, Andrew Harold *WhoAmL 94*
Haber, Edgar 1932- *WhoAm 94*
Haber, Francis Colin 1920-1990 *WhAm 10*
Haber, Fritz 1868-1934 *WorInv*
Haber, Ira Joel 1947- *WhoAm 94, WhoAmA 93*
Haber, Jeffry Robert 1960- *WhoFI 94*
Haber, Joyce d1993 *NewYTBS 93*

Haber, Joyce 1932- *IntMPA 94, WhoAm 94*
Haber, Joyce 1932-1993 *ConAu 142*
Haber, Karen 1955- *EncSF 93*
Haber, Meryl Harold 1934- *WhoAm 94*
Haber, Michael S. 1948- *WhoAmL 94*
Haber, Paul 1936- *WhoScEn 94*
Haber, Paul Adrian Life 1920- *WhoScEn 94*
Haber, Ralph Norman 1932- *WhoAm 94*
Haber, Robert J. *WhoAm 94, WhoFI 94*
Haber, Warren H. 1941- *WhoAm 94*
Haberaecker, Heather Jean 1949- *WhoMW 93*
Haberer, Jean-Yves 1932- *IntWW 93*
Haberfeld, Gwyneth *Who 94*
Haberfield, Graham d1975 *WhoHol 92*
Habergritz, George Joseph 1909- *WhoAmA 93*
Haberland, David Lee 1960- *WhoFI 94*
Haberle, Joan *WhoAmP 93*
Haberle, Joan Baker *WhoAm 94*
Haberler, Gottfried 1900- *WrDr 94*
Haberlin, William Earl 1925- *WhoWest 94*
Haberman, Charles Morris 1927- *WhoScEn 94*
Haberman, Rex Stanley 1924- *WhoAmP 93, WhoMW 93*
Haberman, Richard 1945- *WrDr 94*
Haberman, Shelby Joel 1947- *WhoAm 94*
Habermann, A. Nico d1993 *NewYTBS 93*
Habermann, David Andrew 1957- *WhoScEn 94*
Habermann, Helen Margaret 1927- *WhoAm 94, WhoScEn 94*
Habermann, Norman 1933- *WhoAm 94, WhoFI 94*
Habermann, Ted Richard 1957- *WhoAmL 94*
Habermas, Jurgen 1929- *EncEth, IntWW 93*
Habermehl, Gerhard Georg 1931- *WhoScEn 94*
Habermeier, Jeurgen 1941- *WhoFI 94*
Habersham, James 1712-1775 *WhAmRev*
Habersham, John 1754-1799 *WhAmRev*
Habersham, Joseph 1751-1815 *WhAmRev [port]*
Habersham, Robert 1929- *WhoBlA 94*
Haberstroh, Richard David 1943- *WhoMW 93*
Habgood, Anthony John 1946- *Who 94, WhoAm 94*
Habgood, John Stapylton *Who 94*
Habgood, John Stapylton 1927- *IntWW 93, WrDr 94*
Habib, Fortuna Simcha 1963- *WhoAmL 94*
Habib, Philip Charles d1992 *IntWW 93N*
Habib, Philip Charles 1920-1992 *AnObit 1992, WhAm 10*
Habib-Deloncle, Michel 1921- *IntWW 93*
Habibi, Amil *EncSF 93*
Habibi, Hassan Ebrahim *IntWW 93*
Habibi, Imil 1919?- *ConWorW 93*
Habiby, Emile *ConWorW 93*
Habich, Eduard 1880-1960 *NewGrDO*
Habich, Matthias *WhoHol 92*
Habicht, Christian Herbert 1926- *WhoAm 94*
Habicht, F. Henry, II 1953- *WhoAmP 93*
Habicht, Frank Henry 1920- *WhoAm 94*

Habicht, Jean-Pierre 1934- *WhoAm 94*
Habicht, Werner 1930- *IntWW 93*
Habif, David Valentine 1939-1992
WhAm 10
Habig, Douglas Arnold 1946- *WhoFI 94*
Habig, Thomas Louis 1928- *WhoAm 94,
WhoFI 94*
Habiger, Richard J. 1941- *WhoAmL 94*
Habinck, Gale Ralph 1942- *WhoMW 93*
Hablutzel, Margo Lynn 1961-
WhoAmL 94
Hablutzel, Nancy Zimmerman 1940-
WhoAmL 94
Hablutzel, Philip Norman 1935-
WhoAmL 94, WhoFI 94, WhoMW 93
Habraken, Nicolaas John 1928-
IntWW 93
Habre, Hissene *IntWW 93*
Habre, Hissene 1942- *ConBlB 6 [port]*
Habsburg-Lothringen, Otto von 1912-
IntWW 93
Habsburgo, Inmaculada de *WhoHisp 94*
Haburn, William Bert 1933- *WhoFI 94*
Habush, Robert Lee 1936- *WhoAm 94,
WhoAmL 94, WhoMW 93*
Haby, Rene Jean 1919- *IntWW 93*
Habyarimana, Juvenal 1937- *IntWW 93*
Habymana, Bonaventure *IntWW 93*
Hacanson, Gordon Leroy 1915-
WhoAmP 93
Hacault, Antoine *Who 94*
Hacault, Antoine Joseph Leon 1926-
WhoAm 94, WhoAmP 93
Haccoun, David 1937- *WhoAm 94*
Hachette, Jean-Louis 1925- *IntWW 93*
Hachey, Thomas Eugene 1938-
WhoAm 94
Hachten, Richard Arthur, II 1945-
WhoMW 93
Hachten, William Andrews 1924-
WhoAm 94
Hack, Carole Mae 1942- *WhoAm 94*
Hack, George Donald 1926- *WhoMW 93*
Hack, Herman d1967 *WhoHol 92*
Hack, John Tilton 1913- *WhAm 10*
Hack, Linda 1949- *WhoAmL 94*
Hack, Patricia Y. 1926-
 See Hack, Phillip S. 1916- & Hack,
 Patricia Y. 1926- *WhoAmA 93*
Hack, Patricia Y. 1926- *WhoAmA 93*
Hack, Phillip S. 1916- & Hack, Patricia Y.
 1926- *WhoAmA 93*
Hack, Ronald Lee 1955- *WhoAmL 94*
Hack, Shelley 1948- *WhoHol 92*
Hack, Shelley 1952- *IntMPA 94*
Hack, Signe d1973 *WhoHol 92*
Hackam, Reuben 1936- *WhoAm 94*
Hackathorne, George d1940 *WhoHol 92*
Hackbarth, Dorothy Alice 1921-
WhoWest 94
Hackbirth, David William 1935-
WhoAm 94, WhoFI 94
Hackel, Emanuel 1925- *WhoAm 94,
WhoScEn 94*
Hackel, Mary Roeper 1933- *WhoMW 93*
Hackel-Sims, Stella Bloomberg 1926-
WhoAm 94
Hackeman, Calvin Leslie 1953- *WhoFI 94*
Hackemesser, Larry Gene 1950-
WhoScEn 94
Hacken, Stephen Ira 1954- *WhoMW 93*
Hackenbroch, Yvonne Alix 1912-
WhoAmA 93
Hacker, Alan Ray 1938- *Who 94*
Hacker, Andrew 1929- *ConAu 41NR,
WhoAm 94, WrDr 94*
Hacker, Benjamin T. 1935-
AfrAmG [port], WhoIns 94
Hacker, Benjamin Thurman 1935-
WhoBlA 94
Hacker, Charles R. 1920- *IntMPA 94*
Hacker, David Solomon 1925-
WhoScEn 94
Hacker, David Willson 1928-
WhoMW 93
Hacker, George Lanyon *Who 94*
Hacker, Jon Christopher 1950-
WhoAm 94
Hacker, Joseph *WhoHol 92*
Hacker, Kenneth Russell 1947-
WhoWest 94
Hacker, Maria d1963 *WhoHol 92*
Hacker, Marilyn *DrAPF 93*
Hacker, Marilyn 1942- *BlmGWL,
WrDr 94*
Hacker, Mark Gregory 1961- *WhoWest 94*
Hacker, Pat 1947- *WhoAmP 93*
Hacker, Paul 1946- *WhoAm 94*
Hacker, Rose 1906- *WrDr 94*
Hacker, Sabina Ann Gonzales 1957-
WhoHisp 94
Hackerman, Norman 1912- *WhoScEn 94*
Hackes, Peter *WhoHol 92*
Hackes, Peter Sidney 1924- *WhoAm 94*
Hacket, Albert 1900-
 See Goodrich, Frances 1891-1984
 IntDcF 2-4
Hackett, Albert 1900- *WhoHol 92*

Hackett, Barbara Kloka 1928-
WhoAm 94, WhoAmL 94, WhoMW 93
Hackett, Barry Dean 1964- *WhoBlA 94*
Hackett, Bobby d1976 *WhoHol 92*
Hackett, Brian 1911- *Who 94*
Hackett, Bruce Clayton 1938- *WhoAm 94,
WhoFI 94*
Hackett, Buddy 1924- *IntMPA 94,
WhoAm 94, WhoCom [port], WhoHol 92*
Hackett, Carol Ann Hedden 1939-
WhoAm 94, WhoScEn 94, WhoWest 94
Hackett, Cecil Arthur 1908- *Who 94,
WrDr 94*
Hackett, Charles d1942 *WhoHol 92*
Hackett, Charles 1889-1942 *NewGrDO*
Hackett, Claire *WhoHol 92*
Hackett, Dennis William 1929- *Who 94*
Hackett, Dwight Vernon 1945-
WhoAmA 93
Hackett, Earl Randolph 1932-
WhoAm 94, WhoScEn 94
Hackett, Florence d1954 *WhoHol 92*
Hackett, Hal d1967 *WhoHol 92*
Hackett, Harold 1878-1937 *BuCMET*
Hackett, James Edwin, Jr. 1943-
WhoIns 94
Hackett, James K. d1926 *WhoHol 92*
Hackett, Janette d1979 *WhoHol 92*
Hackett, Jim *WhoHol 92*
Hackett, Joan d1983 *WhoHol 92*
Hackett, John (Winthrop) 1910-
EncSF 93, WrDr 94
Hackett, John Byron 1933- *WhoAm 94*
Hackett, John Charles Thomas 1939-
Who 94
Hackett, John Francis 1956- *WhoAm 94*
Hackett, John Peter 1942- *WhoAm 94,
WhoWest 94*
Hackett, John Thomas 1932- *WhoAm 94*
Hackett, John Wilkins 1924- *Who 94*
Hackett, John Winthrop 1910-
IntWW 93, Who 94
Hackett, Joseph Leo 1937- *WhoScEn 94*
Hackett, Karl d1948 *WhoHol 92*
Hackett, Kevin James 1947- *WhoScEn 94*
Hackett, Kevin R. 1949- *WhoAm 94,
WhoAmL 94*
Hackett, Lillian d1973 *WhoHol 92*
Hackett, Luther Frederick 1933-
WhoAm 94
Hackett, Mickey *WhoAmA 93*
Hackett, Obra V. 1937- *WhoBlA 94*
Hackett, Pamela Jean Stegora 1963-
WhoMW 93
Hackett, Peter 1933- *Who 94*
Hackett, Philip *DrAPF 93*
Hackett, Randall Scott 1943- *WhoWest 94*
Hackett, Randall Winslow 1935-
WhoAm 94
Hackett, Raymond d1958 *WhoHol 92*
Hackett, Richard C. *WhoAmP 93*
Hackett, Robert John 1943- *WhoAm 94,
WhoAmL 94*
Hackett, Robert Moore 1936-
WhoScEn 94
Hackett, Roger Fleming 1922- *WhoAm 94*
Hackett, Rufus E. 1910- *WhoBlA 94*
Hackett, Samuel Everett 1877-
EncABHB 9
Hackett, Stanley Hailey 1945- *WhoAm 94,
WhoAmL 94*
Hackett, Wesley Phelps, Jr. 1939-
WhoAmL 94, WhoMW 93
Hackett, Wilbur L., Jr. 1949- *WhoBlA 94*
Hackett, William Bostock, III 1928-
WhoWest 94
Hackey, George Edward, Jr. 1948-
WhoBlA 94
Hackford, Taylor 1944- *IntMPA 94*
Hacking, Baron 1938- *Who 94*
Hacking, Anthony Stephen 1941- *Who 94*
Hacking, Ian MacDougall 1936-
IntWW 93
Hackl, Alphons J. *WhoAm 94*
Hackl, Donald John 1934- *WhoAm 94,
WhoMW 93*
Hackland, Sarah Ann *Who 94*
Hackler, John Byron, III 1925-
WhoAm 94
Hackler, Michael Lewis 1960- *WhoFI 94*
Hackler, Mitsuno Ishii *WhoAmA 93*
Hackler, Ronald Ervin 1940- *WhoMW 93*
Hackler, Ruth Ann 1924- *WhoAmP 93*
Hackley, Emma Azalia 1867-1922
AfrAmAl 6
Hackley, Lloyd Vincent 1940-
WhoAm 94, WhoBlA 94
Hacklin, Allan Dave 1943- *WhoAmA 93*
Hackman, Edward M. 1943- *WhoMW 93*
Hackman, Gene 1930- *IntMPA 94,
WhoHol 92*
Hackman, Gene 1931- *IntWW 93,
WhoHol 92*
Hackman, Karen Lee 1956- *WhoAmL 94*
Hackmann, Robert M. 1953- *WhoWest 94*
Hackmann, Frank Henry 1945-
WhoAmL 94, WhoMW 93
Hackney, Archdeacon of *Who 94*

Hackney, Anthony C. 1956- *WhoScEn 94*
Hackney, Arthur 1925- *Who 94*
Hackney, Clinton Porter 1952-
WhoAmP 93
Hackney, Francis Sheldon 1933-
NewYTBS 93 [port], WhoAm 94
Hackney, Howard Smith 1910-
WhoMW 93
Hackney, James Acra, III 1939-
WhoAm 94
Hackney, Joe 1945- *WhoAmP 93*
Hackney, Pearl *WhoHol 92*
Hackney, Robert Ward 1942-
WhoWest 94
Hackney, Rod(erick Peter) 1942- *WrDr 94*
Hackney, Roderick Peter 1942-
IntWW 93, Who 94
Hackney, Sheldon 1933- *WhoAmP 93*
Hackney, Virginia Howitz 1945-
WhoAm 94, WhoAmL 94
Hackney, William Pendleton 1924-
WhoAm 94
Hackney-Simmons, Mary Alice 1955-
WhoWest 94
Hacks, Peter 1928- *ConWorW 93,
IntDcT 2*
Hackwood, Susan 1955- *WhoAm 94,
WhoScEn 94*
Hackworth, David H. 1931- *WrDr 94*
Hackworth, Donald E. 1937- *WhoAm 94*
Hackworth, John Dennis 1937- *WhoFI 94*
Hackworth, Theodore James, Jr. 1926-
WhoWest 94
Hackworth, Timothy 1786-1850
DcNaB MP
Hackworth, Werter Shipp 1895-
WhAm 10
Hacquart, Carolus 1640-1700? *NewGrDO*
Hadani, Itzhak 1943- *WhoScEn 94*
Hadar, Mary 1945- *WhoAm 94*
Hadas, Elizabeth Chamberlayne 1946-
WhoAm 94, WhoWest 94
Hadas, Julia Ann 1945- *WhoMW 93*
Hadas, Pamela White 1946- *WhoAm 94*
Hadas, Rachel *DrAPF 93*
Hadas, Rachel 1948- *WrDr 94*
Hadaway, James Benjamin 1962-
WhoScEn 94
Hadba, Carlos Benjamin 1960-
WhoWest 94
Haddad, Abraham Herzl 1938-
WhoAm 94, WhoMW 93
Haddad, Benjamin Albert 1955-
WhoAmP 93
Haddad, Edmonde Alex 1931-
WhoWest 94
Haddad, Edward Raouf 1926-
WhoScEn 94, WhoWest 94
Haddad, Ernest Mudarri 1938-
WhoAm 94, WhoAmL 94
Haddad, Fred 1946- *WhoAmL 94*
Haddad, George Ilyas 1935- *WhoAm 94,
WhoMW 93, WhoScEn 94*
Haddad, George Richard 1918-
WhoAm 94
Haddad, Gladys Marylin 1930-
WhoMW 93
Haddad, Heskel Marshall 1930-
WhoAm 94, WhoScEn 94
Haddad, Inad 1953- *WhoMW 93,
WhoScEn 94*
Haddad, James Henry 1923- *WhoFI 94,
WhoScEn 94*
Haddad, Jamil Raouf 1923- *WhoAm 94*
Haddad, Jerrier Abdo 1922- *WhoAm 94*
Haddad, Robert John 1956- *WhoAmL 94*
Haddad, Sulaiman Ahmed el 1930-
IntWW 93
Haddaoui, Khalil 1937- *Who 94*
Haddaway, James David 1933- *WhoFI 94*
Haddeland, Peter James 1956-
WhoAmP 93
Hadden, Earl French 1946- *WhoWest 94*
Hadden, Eddie Raynord 1943-
WhoBlA 94
Hadden, John Alexander 1886- *WhAm 10*
Haddidi, Helmi El- 1925- *IntWW 93*
Haddington, Earl of 1941- *Who 94*
Haddix, Carol Ann 1946- *WhoAm 94*
Haddix, Charles E. 1915- *WhoAm 94*
Haddix, Michael 1961- *WhoBlA 94*
Haddix, Robert Allen 1964- *WhoWest 94*
Haddo, Earl of 1955- *Who 94*
Haddock, Frank E. 1938- *WhoFI 94*
Haddock, Fred T. 1919- *WhoAm 94,
WhoMW 93, WhoScEn 94*
Haddock, Harold, Jr. 1932- *WhoAm 94*
Haddock, John d1987 *WhoHol 92*
Haddock, John Ivan 1939- *WhoMW 93*
Haddock, Mable J. 1948- *WhoBlA 94*
Haddock, Randy Dean 1947-
WhoAmL 94
Haddock, Raymond Earl 1936-
WhoAm 94
Haddock, Robert Lynn 1945- *WhoAm 94,
WhoFI 94, WhoScEn 94*

Haddock, Ronald Wayne 1940-
WhoAm 94, WhoFI 94
Haddock, William F. d1969 *WhoHol 92*
Haddon, Celia 1944- *WrDr 94*
Haddon, Dayle 1949- *WhoHol 92*
Haddon, Harold Alan 1940- *WhoAm 94*
Haddon, James Francis 1954- *WhoBlA 94*
Haddon, Peter d1962 *WhoHol 92*
Haddon, Phoebe Anniese 1950-
WhoAmL 94
Haddon, Sam Ellis 1937- *WhoAm 94,
WhoAmL 94*
Haddon, Timothy John 1948-
WhoWest 94
Haddon-Cave, (Charles) Philip 1925-
IntWW 93, Who 94
Haddox, Arden Ruth Stewart 1930-
WhoMW 93
Haddox, Mari Kristine 1950-
WhoScEn 94
Haddox, Mark *WhoAm 94, WhoScEn 94*
Haddy, Francis John 1922- *WhoAm 94*
Haden, Charles 1937- *WhoAm 94*
Haden, Charles H., II 1937- *WhoAm 94,
WhoAmL 94*
Haden, Clovis Roland 1940- *WhoAm 94*
Haden, Eunice (Barnard) 1901-
WhoAmA 93
Haden, Mabel D. *WhoBlA 94*
Haden, Mabel Dole *WhoAmL 94*
Haden, Sara d1981 *WhoHol 92*
Haden, William Demmery 1909- *Who 94*
Haden, William R. *WhoWest 94*
Haden-Guest, Baron 1913- *Who 94*
Hader, Clementin *NewGrDO*
Hader, Elmer (Stanley) 1889-1973
WhoAmA 93N
Haderlein, Thomas M. 1935- *WhoAm 94*
Hadewych 13th cent.- *BlmGWL*
Hadfield, Antony 1936- *Who 94*
Hadfield, (Ellis) Charles (Raymond)
1909- *Who 94*
Hadfield, James Irvine Havelock 1930-
Who 94, WhoScEn 94
Hadfield, John *Who 94*
Hadfield, (Geoffrey) John 1923- *Who 94*
Hadfield, John Charles Heywood 1907-
Who 94
Hadfield, John Collingwood d1993
Who 94N
Hadfield, M. Gary 1935- *WhoScEn 94*
Hadfield, Michael Gale 1937-
WhoWest 94
Hadfield, Ronald 1939- *Who 94*
Hadfield, Ted Lee 1950- *WhoAmA 93*
Hadges, Thomas Richard 1948-
WhoWest 94
Hadid, Zaha *NewYTBS 93 [port]*
Hadidian, Dikran Yenovk 1920-
WhoAm 94
Hadingham, Evan 1951- *WrDr 94*
Hadingham, Reginald Edward Hawke
1915- *Who 94*
Hadipriono, Fabian Christy 1947-
WhoMW 93
Hadirca, Ion Dumitru 1949- *LoBiDrD*
Hadithi, Murtada al- *IntWW 93*
Hadjiapostolou, Nikolaos 1879-1941
NewGrDO
Hadjicostis, Andreas Nicholas 1948-
WhoScEn 94
Hadjiev, Parashkev 1912-1992 *NewGrDO*
Hadjikov, Lyuben Manolov 1939-
WhoScEn 94
Hadjiolov, Asen A. 1930- *IntWW 93*
Hadjistamov, Dimiter 1940- *WhoScEn 94*
Hadlee, Richard (John) 1951- *Who 94*
Hadlee, Richard John 1951- *IntWW 93*
Hadley, Arthur T(wining) 1924- *EncSF 93*
Hadley, David Allen 1936- *Who 94*
Hadley, Drummond *DrAPF 93*
Hadley, Elizabeth Harrison 1955-
WhoAmL 94
Hadley, Franklin *EncSF 93*
Hadley, Glen L. 1952- *WhoScEn 94*
Hadley, Graham Hunter 1944- *Who 94*
Hadley, Harlan Dwight 1928-
WhoWest 94
Hadley, Henry (Kimball) 1871-1937
NewGrDO
Hadley, Howard Alva, Jr. 1941-
WhoBlA 94
Hadley, Jerry 1952- *NewGrDO,
WhoAm 94*
Hadley, Joan *WrDr 94*
Hadley, John Bart 1942- *WhoFI 94*
Hadley, Lee 1934-
 See Irwin, Hadley *TwCYAW*
Hadley, Leila (E. B.) 1929- *WrDr 94*
Hadley, Leonard Albert 1911- *Who 94*
Hadley, Leonard Anson 1934-
WhoAm 94, WhoFI 94
Hadley, Marlin LeRoy 1931- *WhoAm 94*
Hadley, Mary 1949- *WhoScEn 94*
Hadley, Paul Burrest, Jr. 1955-
WhoWest 94
Hadley, Paul Ervin 1914- *WhoAm 94*
Hadley, Reed d1974 *WhoHol 92*

Hadley, Robert James 1938- *WhoAm 94*
Hadley, Rollin Van Nostrand 1927-1992 *WhAm 10, WhoAmA 93N*
Hadley, Stanton Thomas 1936- *WhoAm 94*
Hadley, Vickie Jean *WhoMW 93*
Hadley, William Keith 1928- *WhoAm 94, WhoWest 94*
Hadley, William Melvin 1942- *WhoWest 94*
Hadley-Garcia, George 1954- *WhoHisp 94*
Hadlick, Paul Emery, Jr. 1930- *WhoFI 94*
Hadlock, Channing M. *IntMPA 94*
Hadlock, John M. 1937- *WhoAm 94*
Hadlock, Wendell Stanwood 1911-1978 *WhoAmA 93N*
Hadlow, David Moore 1928- *WhoAm 94*
Hadnot, Thomas Edward 1944- *WhoBlA 94*
Hadnott, Bennie L. 1944- *WhoBlA 94*
Hadnott, Grayling 1950- *WhoBlA 94*
Hadow, Frank 1855-1946 *BuCMET*
Hadow, Gordon 1908- *Who 94*
Hadow, (Reginald) Michael 1915- *Who 94*
Hadrian 76-138 *HisWorL [port]*
Hadsel, Fred Latimer 1916- *WhoAmP 93*
Hadsell, Virginia Thompson 1921- *WhoWest 94*
Hadwiger, Don Frank 1930- *WhoAm 94*
Hadzi, Dimitri 1921- *WhoAmA 93*
Haebel, Robert Edward 1927- *WhoAm 94, WhoWest 94*
Haeberle, William Leroy 1922- *WhoFI 94, WhoMW 93*
Haeberlin, Heinrich Rudolf 1947- *WhoAm 94, WhoScEn 94*
Haebler, Ingrid 1926- *IntWW 93*
Haeckel, Ernst 1834-1919 *EnvEnc [port]*
Haeckel, Ernst Heinrich 1834-1919 *WorScD*
Haedo, Jorge Alberto 1945- *WhoFI 94, WhoHisp 94*
Haefele, Douglas Monroe 1952- *WhoMW 93*
Haefele, Edwin Theodore 1925- *WhoAm 94*
Haefeli, Charles d1955 *WhoHol 92*
Haeffele, Deborah 1954- *SmATA 76 [port]*
Haeffner, Johann Christian Friedrich 1759-1833 *NewGrDO*
Haefliger, Ernst 1919- *NewGrDO*
Haegele, John Ernest 1941- *WhoAm 94*
Haegelin, William Mark 1949- *WhoMW 93*
Haeger, Milton R. 1936- *WhoMW 93*
Haeger, Phyllis Marianna 1928- *WhoAm 94*
Haehnel, William Otto, Jr. 1924-1991 *WhAm 10*
Haelterman, Edward Omer 1918- *WhoAm 94*
Haemer, Carl D. 1946- *WhoAmP 93*
Haemmerlie, Frances Montgomery 1948- *WhoScEn 94*
Haen, Peter John 1938- *WhoWest 94*
Haendel, Ida 1928- *IntWW 93, Who 94*
Haenggi, Dieter Christoph 1960- *WhoScEn 94*
Haenicke, Diether Hans 1935- *WhoAm 94, WhoMW 93*
Haenlein, George Friedrich Wilhelm 1927- *WhoAm 94*
Haensel, Vladimir 1914- *WhoAm 94, WhoScEn 94*
Haenszel, William Manning 1910- *WhoAm 94*
Haentjes, Werner 1923- *NewGrDO*
Haerer, Carol 1933- *WhoAm 94, WhoAmA 93*
Haerer, Deane Norman 1935- *WhoFI 94*
Haering, Edwin Raymond 1932- *WhoAm 94*
Haering, Harold John 1930- *WhoAmP 93*
Haering, Rudolph Roland 1934- *WhoAm 94*
Haerle, Paul Raymond 1932- *WhoAm 94, WhoAmP 93*
Haertel, Charles Wayne 1937- *WhoMW 93*
Haertel, James C. 1957- *WhoFI 94*
Haesaert, Clara 1924- *BlmGWL*
Haesche, Arthur B., Jr. 1932- *WhoAmP 93*
Haeske, Horst 1925- *WhoAm 94*
Haessle, Jean-Marie Georges 1939- *WhoAm 94, WhoAmA 93*
Haessler, Greg D. 1950- *WhoIns 94*
Haessly, Jacqueline 1937- *WhoMW 93*
Haettenschwiller, Alphonse A. 1925- *WhoAmP 93*
Haeuser, Michael John 1943- *WhoAm 94*
Haeussermann, Walter 1914- *WhoScEn 94*
Hafen, Bruce Clark 1940- *WhoAm 94, WhoWest 94*
Hafen, Leroy R. 1893- *WhAm 10*
Hafer, Barbara *WhoAmP 93*
Hafer, Frederick Douglass 1941- *WhoAm 94*
Hafer, John J. *WhoAmP 93*
Hafer, Joseph Page 1941- *WhoAmL 94*
Haferkamp, Wilhelm 1923- *IntWW 93, Who 94*
Hafets, Richard Jay 1951- *WhoAm 94, WhoAmL 94*
Hafey, Edward Earl Joseph 1917- *WhoWest 94*
Hafez, Amin El 1911- *IntWW 93*
Haff, Barbara J. E. *WhoAmA 93*
Hafferman, William F. 1908- *WhoAmP 93*
Haffey, Antoinette 1948- *WhoMW 93*
Haffey, Jack 1945- *WhoAmP 93*
Haffey, Larry Joe 1943- *WhoMW 93*
Haffey, Richard Arthur 1953- *WhoAmP 93*
Haffner, Albert Edward 1907- *Who 94*
Haffner, Alden Norman 1928- *WhoAm 94*
Haffner, Alfred Loveland, Jr. 1925- *WhoAm 94, WhoAmL 94*
Haffner, Charles Christian, III 1928- *WhoAm 94*
Haffner, F. Kinsey 1948- *WhoAmL 94*
Haffner, Marlene Elisabeth 1941- *WhoAm 94*
Hafford, Arnold Albert 1957- *WhoAmL 94*
Hafford, Patricia Ann 1947- *WhoAm 94, WhoFI 94*
Hafgren, Lilly 1884-1965 *NewGrDO*
Hafif, Marcia 1929- *WhoAmA 93*
Hafner, Arthur Wayne 1943- *WhoAm 94*
Hafner, Dudley H. 1935- *WhoAm 94*
Hafner, Joseph A., Jr. 1944- *WhoAm 94, WhoFI 94*
Hafner, Kenneth John 1952- *WhoMW 93*
Hafner, Lars A. 1961- *WhoAmP 93*
Hafner, Lawrence Erhardt 1924- *WhoAm 94*
Hafner, Philipp 1735-1764 *NewGrDO*
Hafner, Theodore 1901-1990 *WhAm 10*
Hafner, Thomas Mark 1943- *WhoAm 94*
Hafner, Ursula 1943- *WhoWomW 91*
Hafors, Aina Birgitta 1934- *WhoScEn 94*
Hafrey, Leigh 1951- *ConAu 142*
Hafsia, Jalila *BlmGWL*
Hafstad, Lawrence R. d1993 *NewYTBS 93 [port]*
Haft, Marilyn Geisler 1943- *WhoAm 94, WhoAmL 94*
Hafter, Robert d1955 *WhoHol 92*
Haftl, Franklin Dale 1934- *WhoIns 94*
Haftmann, Werner 1912- *IntWW 93*
Haga, Antonia *WhoWomW 91*
Haga, Enoch John 1931- *WhoWest 94, WrDr 94*
Haga, Takehiko 1936- *WhoWest 94*
Hagan, Alfred Chris 1932- *WhoAm 94, WhoAmL 94, WhoWest 94*
Hagan, Ann Patricia 1955- *WhoAmL 94*
Hagan, Cliff 1931- *BasBi [port]*
Hagan, Dorothy Wermuth 1942- *WhoWest 94*
Hagan, Frederick 1918- *WhoAmA 93*
Hagan, Gary C. 1938- *WhoAmL 94*
Hagan, Gwenael Stephane 1960- *WhoBlA 94*
Hagan, Howard d1985 *WhoHol 92*
Hagan, James Garrison 1936- *WhoAmA 93*
Hagan, John Aubrey 1936- *WhoAm 94*
Hagan, John Charles, III 1943- *WhoAm 94*
Hagan, Joseph Henry 1935- *WhoAm 94*
Hagan, Kenneth James 1936- *WhoAm 94*
Hagan, Molly *WhoHol 92*
Hagan, Patrick Joseph 1959- *WhoMW 93*
Hagan, Randall Lee 1945- *WhoAm 94*
Hagan, Robert E. *WhoAmP 93*
Hagan, Robert F. *WhoAmP 93*
Hagan, Robert K. 1948- *WhoAm 94*
Hagan, Robert Leslie 1923- *WhoAm 94*
Hagan, Samuel Lewis 1950- *WhoAmL 94*
Hagan, Thomas Marion 1944- *WhoAmP 93*
Hagan, Wallace Woodrow 1913- *WhoAm 94*
Hagan, William Thomas 1918- *WhoAm 94*
Hagan, Willie James 1950- *WhoBlA 94*
Hagan-Harrell, Mary M. *WhoAmP 93*
Hagans, Karen Carter 1958- *WhoMW 93*
Hagans, Robert Frank 1926- *WhoAm 94*
Hagans, Robert Reginald, Jr. 1954- *WhoFI 94*
Hagar, Charles Frederick 1930- *WhoWest 94*
Hagar, Jack 1951- *WhoMW 93*
Hagar, Judith 1938- *WrDr 94*
Hagar, Judy Carol 1947- *WhoFI 94*
Hagar, William Gardner, III 1940- *WhoScEn 94*
Hagard, Spencer 1942- *Who 94*
Hagart-Alexander, Claud *Who 94*
Hagarty, Lois Sherman 1948- *WhoAmP 93*
Hagarty, Mark 1954- *WhoAmL 94*
Hagauer, Richard William 1928- *WhoAm 94*
Hagberg, Carl Thomas 1942- *WhoAm 94*
Hagberg, Charles Paul 1934- *WhoWest 94*
Hagberg, Chris Eric 1949- *WhoAmL 94*
Hagberg, Daniel Scott 1965- *WhoScEn 94*
Hagberg, Viola Wilgus 1952- *WhoAmL 94*
Hage, Jeffrey A. 1951- *WhoAmL 94*
Hage, Raymond Joseph 1943- *WhoAmA 93*
Hage, Stephen John 1943- *WhoWest 94*
Hagedorn, Diana *DrAPF 93*
Hagedorn, Donald James 1919- *WhoAm 94*
Hagedorn, Frank M. 1938- *WhoAmL 94*
Hagedorn, Henry Howard 1940- *WhoAm 94, WhoScEn 94*
Hagedorn, Jessica *DrAPF 93*
Hagedorn, Jessica Tarahata *BlmGWL*
Hagedorn, Jessica Tarahata 1949- *WhoAsA 94*
Hagedorn, Jurgen 1933- *IntWW 93*
Hagedorn, Robert, Jr. 1952- *WhoAmP 93, WhoWest 94*
Hagedorn, Thomas M. 1943- *WhoAmP 93*
Hagefstration, John E., Jr. 1961- *WhoAmL 94*
Hagegard, Hakon 1945- *NewGrDO*
Hagel, John, III 1950- *WhoFI 94*
Hagel, Raymond Charles 1916- *WhoAm 94*
Hagele, Mary Catherine 1942- *WhoMW 93*
Hagelin, John Samuel 1954- *WhoAmP 93, WhoMW 93, WhoScEn 94*
Hagelman, Charles William, Jr. 1920- *WhoAm 94*
Hagelstein, Robert Philip 1942- *WhoAm 94*
Hageman, Brian Charles 1952- *WhoScEn 94*
Hageman, Charles Lee 1935- *WhoAmA 93, WhoMW 93*
Hageman, Howard G(arberich) 1921-1992 *ConAu 140*
Hageman, James C. 1930- *WhoAmP 93*
Hageman, Jim Howard 1956- *WhoMW 93*
Hageman, Richard d1966 *WhoHol 92*
Hageman, Richard 1882-1966 *NewGrDO*
Hageman, Richard Harry 1917- *WhoAm 94*
Hagemann, Dolores Ann 1935- *WhoAmP 93, WhoFI 94, WhoMW 93, WhoScEn 94*
Hagen, Arthur Ainsworth 1933- *WhoAm 94*
Hagen, Bruce 1930- *WhoAmP 93, WhoMW 93*
Hagen, Carl I. 1944- *IntWW 93*
Hagen, Cecelia *DrAPF 93*
Hagen, Charles d1958 *WhoHol 92*
Hagen, Charles William, Jr. 1918- *WhoAm 94*
Hagen, Christopher Donald 1943- *WhoAmL 94*
Hagen, Craig 1965- *WhoAmP 93*
Hagen, Daniel Russell 1952- *WhoScEn 94*
Hagen, Edna Mae 1932- *WhoWest 94*
Hagen, Erica *WhoHol 92*
Hagen, George Leon 1924- *WhoAm 94*
Hagen, Glenn W. 1948- *WhoAmL 94, WhoFI 94*
Hagen, Helen Eugenia 1891-1964 *AfrAmAl 6*
Hagen, James Alfred 1932- *WhoAm 94, WhoFI 94*
Hagen, James Laurence 1957- *WhoFI 94*
Hagen, Jean d1977 *WhoHol 92*
Hagen, John G. 1941- *WhoMW 93*
Hagen, John P. 1908-1990 *WhAm 10*
Hagen, John William 1940- *WhoAm 94*
Hagen, Kevin *WhoHol 92*
Hagen, Kirk Dee 1953- *WhoWest 94*
Hagen, Lawrence Jacob 1940- *WhoMW 93, WhoScEn 94*
Hagen, Linda S. 1944- *WhoAmP 93*
Hagen, Orville West 1915- *WhoAmP 93*
Hagen, Paul Beo 1920- *WhoAm 94*
Hagen, R. E. 1933- *WhoAm 94*
Hagen, Richard E. 1937- *WhoAmP 93*
Hagen, Ronald Henry 1941- *WhoMW 93*
Hagen, Ross *WhoHol 92*
Hagen, Stephen James 1962- *WhoScEn 94*
Hagen, Thomas Bailey 1935- *WhoAm 94*
Hagen, Thomas Lynn 1954- *WhoMW 93*
Hagen, Uta 1919- *WhoHol 92, WrDr 94*
Hagen, Uta Thyra 1919- *IntWW 93, WhoAm 94*
Hagen, Victor W. Von *Who 94*
Hagenbruch, Charlotte d1968 *WhoHol 92*
Hagenbuch, John Jacob 1951- *WhoWest 94*
Hagenbuch, Rodney Dale *WhoWest 94*
Hagendorf, Stanley 1930- *WhoAmL 94*
Hagendorn, William 1925- *WhoAm 94*
Hagen-Frederiksen, Jan 1941- *WhoFI 94*
Hageniers, Omer Leon 1944- *WhoScEn 94*
Hagenlocker, Edward E. 1939- *WhoFI 94*
Hagens, William Joseph 1942- *WhoWest 94*
Hagenstein, Perry Reginald 1931- *WhoAm 94*
Hagenstein, William David 1915- *WhoAm 94, WhoScEn 94, WhoWest 94*
Hager, Charles Read 1937- *WhoAm 94*
Hager, Clay Steven 1958- *WhoAmL 94*
Hager, Clyde d1944 *WhoHol 92*
Hager, Elizabeth Sears 1944- *WhoAmP 93, WhoWomW 91*
Hager, Eugene Randolph 1930- *WhoWest 94*
Hager, Hellmut W. 1926- *WhoAmA 93*
Hager, Hellmut Wilhelm 1926- *WhoAm 94*
Hager, Henry G. *WhoAmP 93*
Hager, James 1953- *WhoAmP 93*
Hager, John Patrick 1936- *WhoAm 94*
Hager, John V. 1949- *WhoAmL 94*
Hager, Joseph C. 1944- *WhoBlA 94*
Hager, Kathy Elaine 1951- *WhoFI 94*
Hager, Kurt 1912- *IntWW 93*
Hager, Larry Stanley 1942- *WhoAm 94*
Hager, Leopold 1935- *NewGrDO*
Hager, Linda Wesseling 1941- *WhoMW 93*
Hager, Lowell Paul 1926- *WhoAm 94, WhoMW 93, WhoScEn 94*
Hager, Marlene Joyce 1941- *WhoAmP 93*
Hager, Orval O. 1918- *WhoAm 94*
Hager, Pamela Ann 1950- *WhoMW 93*
Hager, Paul Calvin 1931- *WhoAm 94*
Hager, Robert *WhoAm 94*
Hager, Robert Worth 1928- *WhoAm 94*
Hager, Roscoe Franklin 1941- *WhoBlA 94*
Hager, Stephen Mark 1949- *WhoMW 93*
Hager, Tom 1938- *WhoAmP 93*
Hager, Trent J. 1962- *WhoAmP 93*
Hagerla, Mark R. 1936- *WhoAmP 93*
Hagerman, Allen Reid 1951- *WhoAm 94*
Hagerman, Edward 1939- *WrDr 94*
Hagerman, Michael Charles 1951- *WhoAmL 94*
Hagerman, Peter Stanley 1939- *WhoAm 94*
Hagerman, Robert Lester 1940- *WhoFI 94*
Hagerson, Lawrence John 1931- *WhoFI 94*
Hagerstrand, Martin Alan 1911- *WhoAmA 93*
Hagerthy, Ron 1932- *WhoHol 92*
Hagerty, Julie 1955- *IntMPA 94, WhoHol 92*
Hagerty, Kim Louise 1956- *WhoWest 94*
Hagerty, Michael d1991 *WhoHol 92*
Hagerty, Paul James 1939- *WhoMW 93*
Hagerty, Polly Martiel 1946- *WhoWest 94*
Hagerty, William John Gell 1939- *Who 94*
Hagestadt, John Valentine 1938- *Who 94*
Hagey, Walter Rex 1909- *WhoFI 94*
Hagfors, Tor 1930- *WhoAm 94, WhoScEn 94*
Hagg, Barbara Ann 1931- *WhoAmP 93*
Hagg, Rexford A. *WhoAmP 93*
Haggander, Mari Anne 1951- *NewGrDO*
Haggar, Edmond Ralph 1916- *WhoFI 94*
Haggar, Paul *IntMPA 94*
Haggard, Forrest Deloss 1925- *WhoAm 94, WhoMW 93*
Haggard, H. Rider 1856-1925 *BlmGEL*
Haggard, H(enry) Rider 1856-1925 *EncSF 93*
Haggard, Joan Claire 1932- *WhoMW 93*
Haggard, Joel Edward 1939- *WhoAmL 94, WhoWest 94*
Haggard, Merle *NewYTBS 93 [port]*
Haggard, Merle 1937- *WhoHol 92*
Haggard, Merle Ronald 1937- *WhoAm 94*
Haggard, Paul 1907- *WrDr 94*
Haggard, Piers 1939- *ConTFT 11, HorFD, IntMPA 94*
Haggard, Stephen d1943 *WhoHol 92*
Haggard, William *Who 94*
Haggard, William 1907- *EncSF 93, WrDr 94*
Haggard, William 1907-1993 *DcLB Y93N [port]*
Haggard, William Henry 1920- *WhoScEn 94*
Haggard-Martinez, Donna Lynn 1952- *WhoFI 94*
Haggart, Alastair Iain MacDonald 1915- *IntWW 93, Who 94*
Haggart, Mary Elizabeth *Who 94*
Haggerston Gadsden, Peter Drury *Who 94*
Haggerty, Brian John 1945- *WhoIns 94*
Haggerty, Charles A. *WhoWest 94*
Haggerty, Dan 1943- *WhoHol 92*
Haggerty, David M. 1942- *WhoIns 94*
Haggerty, Don d1988 *WhoHol 92*
Haggerty, H. B. *WhoHol 92*
Haggerty, James C. 1954- *WhoAmL 94*
Haggerty, James J. 1936- *WhoAmP 93*

Hainline, Adrian, Jr. 1921- *WhoScEn 94*
Hainline, Forrest A., Jr. d1993 *NewYTBS 93*
Hainline, Forrest Arthur, Jr. 1918- *WhoFI 94*
Hainsworth, Brad E. 1935- *WhoWest 94*
Hainsworth, D(avid) R(oger) 1931- *ConAu 141*
Hainsworth, Gordon 1934- *Who 94*
Hainworth, Henry Charles 1914- *IntWW 93, Who 94*
Hair, Jay D. 1945- *CurBio 93 [port]*
Hair, Jay Dee 1945- *WhoAm 94, WhoScEn 94*
Hair, Jennie *DrAPF 93*
Hair, John 1941- *WhoBlA 94*
Hair, Kittie Ellen 1948- *WhoWest 94*
Hair, Mattox Strickland 1938- *WhoAmP 93*
Haire, James 1938- *WhoAm 94, WhoWest 94*
Haire, James R. *WhoAm 94, WhoMW 93*
Haire, James R. 1947- *WhoIns 94*
Haire, John Russell 1925- *WhoAm 94*
Haire, William J. 1944- *WhoAm 94*
Haire, Wilson John 1932- *ConDr 93, WrDr 94*
Hairell, melvin L. 1938- *WhoIns 94*
Hairston, Eddison R., Jr. 1933- *WhoBlA 94*
Hairston, George W. 1942- *WhoAm 94, WhoAmL 94*
Hairston, Happy 1942- *BasBi*
Hairston, Helen Covington 1937- *WhoMW 93*
Hairston, James Christopher 1960- *WhoFI 94*
Hairston, Jerry Wayne 1952- *WhoBlA 94*
Hairston, Jester *WhoBlA 94*
Hairston, Jester 1901- *WhoHol 92*
Hairston, Joseph Henry 1922- *WhoBlA 94*
Hairston, Margaret *WhoHol 92*
Hairston, Nelson George 1917- *WhoAm 94, WhoScEn 94*
Hairston, Oscar Grogan 1921- *WhoBlA 94*
Hairston, Otis L. 1918- *WhoBlA 94*
Hairston, Raleigh Daniel 1934- *WhoBlA 94*
Hairston, Rowena L. 1928- *WhoBlA 94*
Hairston, Thomas Joseph 1943- *WhoMW 93*
Hairston, William 1928- *WhoBlA 94, WhoHol 92*
Hairston, William (Russell, Jr.) 1928- *BlkWr 2*
Hairston, William Michael 1947- *WhoAm 94*
Hairston, William Russell, Jr. 1928- *WhoAm 94*
Hairstone, Marcus A. 1926- *WhoBlA 94*
Haisch, Bernhard Michael 1949- *WhoWest 94*
Haiser, Gary Martin 1945- *WhoFI 94*
Haislip, John *DrAPF 93*
Haist, David A. 1951- *WhoAmL 94*
Hait, Gershon 1927- *WhoAm 94*
Haithcock, Madeline *WhoAmP 93*
Haithem, Muhammad Ali 1940- *IntWW 93*
Haitink, Bernard 1929- *IntWW 93, Who 94*
Haitink, Bernard (Johann Herman) 1929- *NewGrDO*
Haitsma, Klaas Hayo 1962- *WhoMW 93*
Haitz, Henry Bernard, III 1964- *WhoMW 93*
Haizinger, Anton 1796-1869 *NewGrDO*
Haizlip, Henry Hardin, Jr. 1913- *WhoAm 94*
Hajah Rahmah Osman 1939- *WhoWomW 91*
Hajare, Raju Padmakar 1960- *WhoScEn 94*
Hajdu, Istvanne *WhoWomW 91*
Hajdys, Dorothy *NewYTBS 93 [port]*
Haje, Peter Robert 1934- *WhoAm 94, WhoAmL 94, WhoFI 94*
Hajek, Ann Elizabeth 1952- *WhoScEn 94*
Hajek, Francis Paul 1958- *WhoAmL 94*
Hajek, Jiri d1993 *NewYTBS 93 [port]*
Hajek, Jiri 1913- *IntWW 93*
Hajek, Otomar 1930- *WhoAm 94, WhoMW 93*
Hajek, Robert J., Sr. 1943- *WhoAmL 94, WhoFI 94, WhoMW 93*
Hajek, Thomas J. *WhoScEn 94*
Hajela, Prabhat 1956- *WhoAsA 94*
Hajian, Gerald 1940- *WhoScEn 94*
Hajibeyov, Uzeir (Abdul Huseyn) 1885-1948 *NewGrDO*
Hajim, Edmund A. 1936- *WhoFI 94*
Hajiya Kebar *WhoPRCh 91*
Hajiyani, Mehdi Hussain 1939- *WhoAsA 94*
Hajiyev, (Akhmet) Jevdet (Ismail) 1917- *NewGrDO*
Hajj, Ibrahim Nasri 1942- *WhoAm 94*
Hajjar, David P. *WhoScEn 94*
Hajjar, Katherine Amberson 1952- *WhoScEn 94*
Hajnal, John 1924- *IntWW 93, Who 94*
Hajos, Zoltan George 1926- *WhoScEn 94*
Hakala, Edith Marie 1942- *WhoAmP 93*
Hakala, Judyth Ann 1955- *WhoMW 93*
Hakala, Thomas John 1948- *WhoFI 94*
Hakansson, Lars-Ove 1937- *IntWW 93*
Hake, Edward fl. 1566-1604 *DcLB 136*
Hake, Erwin Ernst 1906- *WhoMW 93*
Hakeem, Muhammad Abdul 1945- *WhoWest 94*
Hakel, Milton Daniel, Jr. 1941- *WhoAm 94*
Haken, Wolfgang 1928- *WhoMW 93*
Hakim, Ali Hussein 1943- *WhoFI 94*
Hakim, George 1913- *IntWW 93*
Hakim, Louise Zalta 1922- *WhoFI 94*
Hakim, Raymond 1909-1980 *IntDcF 2-4*
Hakim, Robert 1907- *IntDcF 2-4*
Hakim, S. *DrAPF 93*
Hakim, Tawfiq al- 1898-1986 *EncSF 93*
Hakima, Mala'ika 1950- *WhoBlA 94*
Hakim-Elahi, Enayat 1934- *WhoScEn 94*
Hakimi, S. Louis 1932- *WhoAm 94*
Hakins, Dick d1990 *WhoHol 92*
Hakkanen, Matti Klaus Juhani 1936- *IntWW 93*
Hakkila, Eero Arnold 1931- *WhoScEn 94, WhoWest 94*
Hakkila, Jon Eric 1957- *WhoMW 93*
Hakkinen, Raimo Jaakko 1926- *WhoAm 94, WhoScEn 94*
Hakluyt, Richard 1522?-1616 *DcLB 136*
Hakluyt, Richard c. 1552-1616 *WhWE*
Hakluyt, Richard 1553?-1616 *BlmGEL*
Hakola, Hannu Panu Aukusti 1932- *WhoAm 94, WhoScEn 94*
Hakola, John Wayne 1932- *WhoScEn 94*
Haksar, Parmeshwar Narain 1913- *IntWW 93*
Halabi, Mohammed Ali el- 1937- *IntWW 93*
Halaby, Najeeb E. 1915- *WhoAm 94*
Halaby, Najeeb Elias 1915- *Who 94*
Halaby, Samia Asaad 1936- *WhoAm 94, WhoAmA 93*
Halahmy, Oded 1938- *WhoAmA 93*
Halam, Ann *EncSF 93*
Halam, Ann 1952- *TwCYAW, WrDr 94*
Halama, William A. 1940- *WhoAmL 94*
Halamandaris, Harry 1938- *WhoAm 94*
Halamandaris, Val John 1942- *WhoAm 94*
Halamova, Masa 1908-1986 *BlmGWL*
Halan, John Paul 1928- *WhoAm 94, WhoFI 94*
Halaris, Angelos 1942- *WhoAm 94*
Halas, Cynthia Ann 1961- *WhoFI 94*
Halas, George d1983 *ProFbHF [port]*
Halas, John 1912- *IntDcF 2-4, Who 94*
Halas, Richard Nicholas 1955- *WhoFI 94*
Halasa, Adel F. 1933- *WhoMW 93*
Halasi-Kun, George Joseph 1916- *WhoAm 94*
Halasi-Kun, Tibor 1914-1991 *WhAm 10*
Halaska, Robert H. 1940- *WhoAm 94*
Halasz, Laszlo 1905- *NewGrDO*
Halasz, Nicholas Alexis 1931- *WhoAm 94*
Halasz, Piri 1935- *WhoAmA 93*
Halasz, Sandor Viktor 1953- *WhoMW 93*
Halawi, Ibrahim 1938- *IntWW 93*
Halbach, David Allen 1931- *WhoAmA 93*
Halbedel, Elaine Marie 1951- *WhoWest 94*
Halbeisen, Quinlan 1928- *WhoMW 93*
Halberg, Arvo Kusta 1910- *WhoAm 94*
Halberg, Blake Dexter 1955- *WhoAmL 94*
Halberg, Charles C. 1942- *WhoAmP 93*
Halberg, Charles John August, Jr. 1921- *WhoAm 94, WhoScEn 94, WhoWest 94*
Halberg, G. Peter 1915- *WhoAm 94*
Halberg, Murray (Gordon) 1933- *Who 94*
Halberstam, David *NewYTBS 93 [port]*
Halberstam, David 1934- *WhoAm 94, WrDr 94*
Halberstam, Heini 1926- *WhoAm 94*
Halberstam, Isidore Meir 1945- *WhoScEn 94*
Halberstam, Malvina 1937- *WhoAm 94*
Halberstam, Michael J(oseph) 1932-1980 *EncSF 93*
Halbert, Chuck 1919- *BasBi*
Halbherr, Josef Anton 1947- *WhoWest 94*
Halbouty, Michel Thomas 1909- *WhoAm 94*
Halbrecht, Kenneth Ashley 1960- *WhoFI 94*
Halbreich, Kathy 1949- *WhoAm 94, WhoMW 93*
Halbrook, Anne-Mieke Platt *WhoAmA 93*
Halbrook, David McCall 1927- *WhoAmP 93*
Halbrook, Rita Robertshaw 1930- *WhoAmA 93*
Halbrooks, Darryl Wayne 1948- *WhoAmA 93*
Halbur, Lois Lorraine 1958- *WhoMW 93*
Halby, Anthony Wayne 1949- *WhoFI 94*
Halchak, Alyce Cesare 1949- *WhoAmL 94*
Halchuck, John Allan 1942- *WhoFI 94*
Haldane, Alexander 1800-1882 *DcNaB MP*
Haldane, Charlotte (Franken) 1894-1969 *EncSF 93*
Haldane, Frederick Duncan Michael 1951- *WhoScEn 94*
Haldane, George French 1940- *WhoScEn 94*
Haldane, J(ohn) B(urdon) S(anderson) 1892-1964 *EncSF 93*
Haldane, John Burdon Sanderson 1892-1964 *WorScD*
Haldar, Dipak 1937- *WhoAsA 94*
Haldeman, Charles Waldo, III 1936- *WhoScEn 94*
Haldeman, E. Barry 1944- *WhoAmL 94*
Haldeman, H. R. 1926-1993 *NewYTBS 93, News 94-2*
Haldeman, Harry R. 1926- *IntWW 93, WhoAm 94*
Haldeman, Jack C(arroll), II 1941- *EncSF 93*
Haldeman, Jack C(arroll, II) 1941- *WrDr 94*
Haldeman, Joe *DrAPF 93*
Haldeman, Joe 1943- *EncSF 93*
Haldeman, Joe (William) 1943- *WrDr 94*
Haldeman, Michael Davis 1947- *WhoWest 94*
Haldeman, Susan Ward 1951- *WhoAmL 94*
Haldimand, Frederick 1718-1791 *AmRev, WhAmRev*
Haldingham, Richard of fl. 1260-1278 *DcNaB MP*
Hale, Alan d1950 *WhoHol 92*
Hale, Alan, Jr. d1990 *WhoHol 92*
Hale, Allean Lemmon 1914- *WrDr 94*
Hale, Archie Douglas 1949- *WhoWest 94*
Hale, Barbara 1922- *IntMPA 94, WhoHol 92*
Hale, Barnaby d1964 *WhoHol 92*
Hale, Beverly Ann 1939- *WhoFI 94, WhoMW 93*
Hale, Binnie d1984 *WhoHol 92*
Hale, Bruce Donald 1933- *WhoWest 94*
Hale, Carl Dennis 1949- *WhoWest 94*
Hale, Cecil 1945- *WhoWest 94*
Hale, Chanin *WhoHol 92*
Hale, Charles Martin 1936- *WhoAm 94*
Hale, Charles Russell 1916- *WhoAm 94, WhoAmL 94*
Hale, Charlotte 1928- *WhoAm 94*
Hale, Clara 1905-1992 *AnObit 1992, CurBio 93N, News 93-3*
Hale, Clara McBride d1992 *WhoBlA 94N*
Hale, Claudia Joan 1937- *WhoWest 94*
Hale, Clayton W. 1941- *WhoAmP 93*
Hale, Creighton d1965 *WhoHol 92*
Hale, Cynthia Lynnette 1952- *WhoBlA 94*
Hale, Daniel Cudmore 1944- *WhoAmL 94*
Hale, Danny Lyman 1944- *WhoFI 94*
Hale, David C. 1964- *WhoAmP 93*
Hale, David Clovis 1964- *WhoMW 93*
Hale, Dean Edward 1950- *WhoWest 94*
Hale, Diana 1933- *WhoWest 94*
Hale, Don 1937- *WhoAmP 93*
Hale, Dorothy d1938 *WhoHol 92*
Hale, Doty Doherty 1938- *WhoAm 94*
Hale, Douglas 1929- *ConAu 140*
Hale, Earl F., Jr. 1945- *WhoAmL 94*
Hale, Edward Everett 1822-1909 *EncSF 93*
Hale, Edward Harned 1923- *WhoBlA 94*
Hale, Ernest A. 1920- *WhoAmP 93*
Hale, Fiona *WhoHol 92*
Hale, Ford R., Jr. 1918- *WhoFI 94*
Hale, Franc d1986 *WhoHol 92*
Hale, Gary Allen 1954- *WhoAmP 93*
Hale, Gene *WhoBlA 94*
Hale, Gene 1946- *WhoBlA 94*
Hale, Georgia d1985 *WhoHol 92*
Hale, Georgina 1943- *WhoHol 92*
Hale, Gerald G. 1953- *WhoAmP 93*
Hale, Hamilton Orin 1906- *WhoAm 94*
Hale, Harold 1937- *WhoAmP 93*
Hale, Hilton Ingram 1956- *WhoMW 93*
Hale, Irving 1932- *WhoFI 94*
Hale, Jack K. 1928- *WhoAm 94*
Hale, James Russell 1918- *WhoAm 94*
Hale, James Thomas 1940- *WhoAmL 94, WhoFI 94*
Hale, Janet Campbell *DrAPF 93*
Hale, Janice Ellen 1948- *WhoBlA 94*
Hale, Jean *WhoHol 92*
Hale, John d1947 *WhoHol 92*
Hale, John 1926- *ConDr 93, WrDr 94*
Hale, John (Rigby) 1923- *Who 94*
Hale, John Hampton 1924- *Who 94*
Hale, John Mark 1955- *WhoAmP 93*
Hale, John Rigby 1923- *IntWW 93*
Hale, Jonathan d1966 *WhoHol 92*
Hale, Joseph Rice 1935- *WhoAm 94*
Hale, Joseph Robert 1927- *WhoAmP 93*
Hale, Judson Drake, Sr. 1933- *WhoAm 94*
Hale, Kathleen 1898- *Who 94*
Hale, Keron *BlmGWL*
Hale, Kimberly Anice 1962- *WhoBlA 94*
Hale, Lance Mitchell 1956- *WhoAmL 94*
Hale, Lillian Westcott 1881-1963 *WhoAmA 93N*
Hale, Lola Miranda 1944- *WhoAmL 94*
Hale, Louis Dewitt 1917- *WhoAmP 93*
Hale, Louise Closser d1933 *WhoHol 92*
Hale, Lucretia Peabody 1820-1900 *BlmGWL*
Hale, Marcia L. *WhoAm 94*
Hale, Michael 1918- *WrDr 94*
Hale, Mona Walker *WhoAmP 93*
Hale, Monte 1921- *WhoHol 92*
Hale, Nancy 1908- *BlmGWL*
Hale, Nathan 1755-1776 *AmRev, WhAmRev [port]*
Hale, Nathan Cabot 1925- *WhoAmA 93*
Hale, Norman Morgan 1933- *Who 94*
Hale, Oron James 1902-1991 *WhAm 10*
Hale, Paul Nolen, Jr. 1941- *WhoScEn 94*
Hale, Phale D. 1915- *WhoBlA 94*
Hale, Raymond 1936- *Who 94*
Hale, Richard d1916 *WhoHol 92*
Hale, Richard d1981 *WhoHol 92*
Hale, Richard Lee 1930- *WhoAm 94*
Hale, Richard Stephen 1951- *WhoAmP 93*
Hale, Robert d1940 *WhoHol 92*
Hale, Robert d1977 *WhoHol 92*
Hale, Robert 1937- *NewGrDO*
Hale, Robert Beverly 1901- *WhoAmA 93N*
Hale, Robert Beverly 1901-1985 *ConAu 141*
Hale, Robert D(avid) 1928- *WrDr 94*
Hale, Roger Loucks 1934- *WhoAm 94, WhoMW 93*
Hale, Ron *WhoHol 92*
Hale, Ronald F. 1943- *WhoWest 94*
Hale, Russell Dean 1944- *WhoAmP 93*
Hale, Samuel 1917- *WhoAmP 93*
Hale, Sarah Josepha 1788-1879 *BlmGWL*
Hale, Seldon Houston 1948- *WhoFI 94*
Hale, Sonnie d1959 *WhoHol 92*
Hale, Violet Elaine *WhoWest 94*
Hale, Walter *WhoHol 92*
Hale, Walter Allen, III 1952- *WhoMW 93*
Hale, William Bryan, Jr. 1933- *WhoAm 94*
Haleck, Fiasili Puni *WhoAmP 93*
Halefoglu, Vahit M. 1919- *IntWW 93*
Halegua, Alfredo 1930- *WhoAmA 93, WhoHisp 94*
Haleman, Laura Rand 1946- *WhoAmA 93*
Halemane, Thirumala Raya 1953- *WhoAsA 94*
Haler, Lawrence Eugene 1951- *WhoWest 94*
Hales, Alfred Washington 1938- *WhoAm 94*
Hales, Antony John 1948- *IntWW 93, Who 94*
Hales, Daniel B. 1941- *WhoAm 94*
Hales, David Foster 1944- *WhoAm 94*
Hales, Edward Everette 1932- *WhoBlA 94*
Hales, Frederick David 1930- *Who 94*
Hales, H. Edward, Jr. 1944- *WhoAmL 94*
Hales, Janette Callister 1933- *WhoAmP 93*
Hales, Mary Ann 1953- *WhoBlA 94*
Hales, Nicholas *Who 94*
Hales, (Charles) Nicholas 1935- *Who 94*
Hales, Patricia Louise 1955- *WhoMW 93*
Hales, Peter Bacon 1950- *WrDr 94*
Hales, Robert Lynn 1927- *WhoWest 94*
Hales, Stephen 1677-1761 *WorScD*
Hales, Thomas *NewGrDO*
Hales, William Roy 1934- *WhoBlA 94*
Hales-Mabry, Celia Elaine 1946- *WhoMW 93*
Halevi, Emil Amitai 1922- *WhoScEn 94*
Halevi, Zev ben Shimon 1933- *WrDr 94*
Halevy, Abraham Hayim 1927- *WhoScEn 94*
Halevy, (Jacques-Francois-)Fromental (-Elie) 1799-1862 *NewGrDO*
Halevy, Ludovic 1834-1908 *NewGrDO*
Haley, Alex 1921-1992 *AfrAmAl 6 [port], AnObit 1992, ConLC 76 [port]*
Haley, Alex(ander Murray Palmer) 1921-1992 *BlkWr 2*
Haley, Alex (Palmer) 1921-1992 *WrDr 94N*
Haley, Alex Palmer 1921-1992 *WhAm 10*
Haley, Alexander Palmer 1921-1992 *WhoBlA 94N*
Haley, Bill d1981 *WhoHol 92*
Haley, Charles Lewis 1964- *WhoAm 94, WhoBlA 94*
Haley, Claude *EncSF 93*
Haley, Clifton Edward 1931- *WhoFI 94, WhoMW 93*
Haley, David Alan 1943- *WhoAm 94*
Haley, Donald C. 1928- *WhoBlA 94*
Haley, Earl Albert 1933- *WhoBlA 94*
Haley, Ed *WhoAmP 93*

Haley, Gail E. 1939- WhoAmA 93
Haley, Gail E(inhart) 1939- WrDr 94
Haley, Gail Einhart 1939- WhoAm 94
Haley, George 1929- WhoAm 94
Haley, George Brock, Jr. 1926- WhoAm 94
Haley, George Patrick 1948- WhoAm 94, WhoAmL 94
Haley, George Williford Boyce 1925- WhoAm 94, WhoAmP 93, WhoBlA 94, WhoFI 94
Haley, Jack d1979 WhoHol 92
Haley, Jack, Jr. 1933- IntMPA 94, WhoAm 94, WrDr 94
Haley, Jackie Earle 1961- WhoHol 92
Haley, James F., Jr. 1945- WhoAmL 94
Haley, James William 1943- WhoAmP 93
Haley, John C. 1929- IntWW 93
Haley, John Charles 1905-1991 WhoAmA 93N
Haley, John Charles 1929- WhoAm 94
Haley, John David 1924- WhoWest 94
Haley, John K. 1951- WhoFI 94
Haley, Johnetta Randolph WhoMW 93
Haley, Johnetta Randolph 1923- WhoBlA 94
Haley, Joseph William 1938- WhoAm 94
Haley, Keith Brian 1933- Who 94
Haley, Kenneth (Harold Dobson) 1920- WrDr 94
Haley, Kenneth Harold Dobson 1920- Who 94
Haley, Lucinda Jenkins 1956- WhoAmL 94
Haley, Maria Luisa Mabilangan WhoAsA 94
Haley, Nedom Angier 1943- WhoAmL 94
Haley, Pat WhoAmP 93
Haley, Patience E. WhoAmA 93
Haley, Paul R. 1953- WhoAmP 93
Haley, Priscilla J. 1926- WhoAmA 93
Haley, Priscilla Jane 1926- WhoAm 94
Haley, Robert D. 1893-1959 WhoAmA 93N
Haley, Robert E. 1946- WhoAmL 94
Haley, Roger Kendall 1938- WhoAm 94
Haley, Roy W. 1947- WhoAm 94, WhoFI 94
Haley, Sally 1908- WhoAmA 93
Haley, Sally Fulton 1908- WhoWest 94
Haley, Shirley Wilson 1923- WhoMW 93
Haley, Stephen B. 1942- WhoAm 94
Haley, Thomas John 1913- WhoWest 94
Haley, Vincent Peter 1931- WhoAm 94
Haley, Wayne William 1947- WhoIns 94
Haley-Oliphant, Ann Elizabeth 1957- WhoScEn 94
Half, Robert 1918- WhoAm 94, WhoFI 94
Halfacre, Frank Edward 1936- WhoBlA 94
Halfant, Gary D. 1953- WhoWest 94
Halfen, David 1924- WhoAm 94
Halff, Robert H. 1908- WhoAmA 93
Halff, Robert Hart 1908- WhoWest 94
Halford, Gary Ross 1937- WhoScEn 94
Halford, Michael Charles Kirkpatrick 1914- Who 94
Halford, Richard W. 1944- WhoAmP 93
Halford, Rob
See Judas Priest ConMus 10
Halford, Sharon Lee 1946- WhoWest 94
Halford-MacLeod, Aubrey Seymour 1914- Who 94
Halfpenny, Brian Norman 1936- Who 94
Halfpenny, James Carson 1947- WhoWest 94
Halfvarson, Lucille Robertson 1919- WhoMW 93
Halgren, Jack 1940- WhoAm 94
Halgren, Lee A. WhoMW 93
Haliburton, Thomas Chandler 1796-1865 RfGShF
Halibut, Edward EncSF 93
Halicki, H. B. d1989 WhoHol 92
Haliczer, James Solomon 1952- WhoAmL 94, WhoFI 94
Halidom, M.Y. EncSF 93
Halifax, Archbishop of 1922- Who 94
Halifax, Archdeacon of Who 94
Halifax, Earl of 1944- Who 94
Halikas, James Anastasio 1941- WhoMW 93
Halil, Rasiah 1956- BlmGWL
Halimi, Gisele 1927- BlmGWL
Halio, Jay Leon 1928- WhoAm 94
Haliw, Andrew Jerome, III 1946- WhoAm 94, WhoAmL 94
Halket, Thomas D. 1948- WhoAmL 94
Halkett, Alan Neilson 1931- WhoAm 94
Halkett, Ann 1623-1699 BlmGWL
Halki, John Joseph 1926- WhoAm 94
Halkias, Christos Constantine 1933- WhoFI 94, WhoScEn 94
Halkin, Hubert 1936- WhoAm 94
Halkin, Theodore 1924- WhoAmA 93
Halko, Joe 1940- WhoAmA 93
Halko, Joseph Anthony 1940- WhoWest 94
Halkyard, Edwin Milton 1934- WhoAm 94
Hall, A. M. 1948- WhoAmP 93
Hall, Adam Who 94, WrDr 94
Hall, Addie June 1930- WhoBlA 94
Hall, Adelaide d1993 NewYTBS 93 [port]
Hall, Adelaide 1904- WhoHol 92
Hall, Adrienne Ann WhoAm 94
Hall, Albert 1936- WhoAmP 93
Hall, Albert 1937- WhoHol 92
Hall, Albert 1959- WhoBlA 94
Hall, Albert Leander 1926- WhoAm 94
Hall, Albert Peter Who 94
Hall, Aleksander 1953- IntWW 93
Hall, Alexander d1968 WhoHol 92
Hall, Alfred Charles 1917- Who 94
Hall, Alfred Rupert 1920- IntWW 93, Who 94
Hall, Alton Jerome 1945- WhoBlA 94
Hall, Amelia d1984 WhoHol 92
Hall, Andrew Clifford 1944- WhoAm 94
Hall, Angus 1932- WrDr 94
Hall, Anna Maria Fielding 1800-1881 BlmGWL
Hall, Anthony d1988 WhoHol 92
Hall, Anthony Elmitt 1940- WhoWest 94
Hall, Anthony Michael 1968- IntMPA 94, WhoHol 92
Hall, Anthony Robert 1938- WhoAm 94
Hall, Anthony Stewart 1945- Who 94, WrDr 94
Hall, Anthony Vincent 1936- IntWW 93
Hall, Anthony W., Jr. 1944- WhoBlA 94
Hall, Anthony William 1951- Who 94
Hall, Anthony William, Jr. 1944- WhoAmP 93
Hall, Arch d1978 WhoHol 92
Hall, Arnold (Alexander) 1915- Who 94
Hall, Arnold Alexander 1915- IntWW 93, WhoAm 94
Hall, Arsenio 1955- WhoAm 94
Hall, Arsenio 1956- WhoBlA 94, WhoHol 92
Hall, Arsenio 1959- IntMPA 94, WhoCom
Hall, Arsenio 1960- AfrAmAl 6 [port]
Hall, Arthur Eugene, Jr. 1955- WhoFI 94
Hall, Arthur Herbert 1901- Who 94
Hall, Arthur Raymond, Jr. 1922- WhoAm 94
Hall, Austin c. 1885-1933 EncSF 93
Hall, Aylmer 1914- WrDr 94
Hall, Barbara 1960- TwCYAW, WrDr 94
Hall, Basil (Brodribb) 1918- Who 94
Hall, Ben L. WhoAmP 93
Hall, Benjamin Lewis, III 1956- WhoBlA 94
Hall, Bernadette 1945- BlmGWL
Hall, Bernard 1921- Who 94
Hall, Bernard 1925- WhoAm 94
Hall, Beth Shand 1946- WhoMW 93
Hall, Betty 1921- Who 94
Hall, Betty B. 1921- WhoAmP 93
Hall, Beverly Adele 1935- WhoAm 94
Hall, Billy d1944 WhoHol 92
Hall, Blaine H(ill) 1932- ConAu 140
Hall, Blake G. 1953- WhoAmP 93
Hall, Bobby Ray WhoAmP 93
Hall, Bonnie Baker 1944- WhoFI 94
Hall, Bonnie Green 1941- WhoAmP 93
Hall, Brad WhoHol 92
Hall, Brad Bailey 1951- WhoScEn 94
Hall, Bradley Mahlon 1958- WhoFI 94
Hall, Brian WhoHol 92
Hall, Brian Edward 1958- WhoBlA 94
Hall, Brian Keith 1941- WhoAm 94
Hall, Brinley Morgan 1912-1991 WhAm 10
Hall, Bronwyn Hughes 1945- WhoFI 94, WhoScEn 94, WhoWest 94
Hall, Bruce 1942- WhoAmL 94
Hall, Bruce Warren 1946- WhoFI 94
Hall, C(harles) William 1922- WhAm 10
Hall, Calvin 1941- WhoBlA 94
Hall, Cameron ConAu 141, SmATA 76
Hall, Cameron 1897- WhoHol 92
Hall, Cameron Parker 1898- WhAm 10
Hall, Carl Albin 1921- WhoAmA 93
Hall, Carl W. 1924- WrDr 94
Hall, Carl Wells, III 1947- WhoAmL 94
Hall, Carl William 1924- WhoAm 94, WhoScEn 94
Hall, Carlyle Washington, Jr. 1943- WhoAm 94
Hall, Carol Lynn 1947- WhoMW 93
Hall, Catherine (Mary) 1922- Who 94
Hall, Cecilia Vasquez 1947- WhoWest 94
Hall, Charles Adams 1949- WhoFI 94, WhoMW 93, WhoScEn 94
Hall, Charles Allan 1941- WhoAm 94, WhoScEn 94
Hall, Charles Allen 1933- WhoAm 94
Hall, Charles Edward 1933- WhoMW 93
Hall, Charles Ernest 1938- WhoFI 94
Hall, Charles Francis 1821-1871 WhWE
Hall, Charles Frederick 1920- WhoAm 94, WhoWest 94
Hall, Charles Harold 1934- WhoBlA 94
Hall, Charles L. d1940 EncNAR
Hall, Charles Martin 1863-1914 WorInv
Hall, Charles Potter, Jr. 1932- WhoAm 94
Hall, Charles Washington 1930- WhAm 10
Hall, Charlie d1959 WhoHol 92
Hall, Charlotte Hauch 1945- WhoAm 94
Hall, Cheryl Lynn 1951- WhoMW 93
Hall, Christine C. Iijima 1953- WhoBlA 94
Hall, Christopher 1944- WhoScEn 94
Hall, Christopher Eric 1951- WhoWest 94
Hall, Christopher George Longden 1956- WhoFI 94
Hall, Christopher Myles 1932- Who 94
Hall, Clarence Albert, Jr. 1930- WhoAm 94
Hall, Claude Hampton 1922- WhoAm 94
Hall, Cliff d1972 WhoHol 92
Hall, Clifford Charles 1953- WhoScEn 94
Hall, Conrad 1926- IntDcF 2-4, IntMPA 94, WhoAm 94
Hall, Cynthia Holcomb WhoAmP 93
Hall, Cynthia Holcomb 1929- WhoAm 94, WhoAmL 94, WhoWest 94
Hall, Dale Edward 1947- WhoScEn 94
Hall, Daniel A. 1933- WhoBlA 94
Hall, Daniel G. 1938- WhoIns 94
Hall, Darnell WhoBlA 94
Hall, Daryl 1949- WhoAm 94
Hall, David DrAPF 93
Hall, David 1916- WhoAm 94
Hall, David 1928- IntWW 93
Hall, David 1930- Who 94
Hall, David 1943- WhoAm 94
Hall, David 1947- WhoHol 92
Hall, David 1950- WhoBlA 94
Hall, David Anthony, Jr. 1945- WhoBlA 94
Hall, David C. 1943- ConAu 140
Hall, David Charles 1944- WhoAm 94
Hall, David Charles 1955- WhoWest 94
Hall, David Craig 1958- WhoAmL 94
Hall, David Edward 1940- WhoAm 94
Hall, David John 1942- Who 94
Hall, David Lee 1946- WhoScEn 94
Hall, David Locke 1955- ConAu 140
Hall, David M. 1928- AfrAmG [port]
Hall, David Max 1949- WhoAmL 94
Hall, David McKenzie 1928- WhoBlA 94
Hall, David Oakley 1935- IntWW 93, Who 94
Hall, David Stanley 1935- WhoWest 94
Hall, David W. 1947- WhoIns 94
Hall, Delilah Ridley 1953- WhoBlA 94
Hall, Delores WhoBlA 94
Hall, Delton Dwayne 1965- WhoBlA 94
Hall, Denis C. Who 94
Hall, Denis Whitfield 1913- Who 94
Hall, Dennis A. 1946- WhoAm 94
Hall, Derek Harry 1945- WhoAm 94
Hall, Desmond W(inter) 1909-1992 EncSF 93
Hall, Dewey Eugene 1932- WhoMW 93
Hall, Dick 1938- WhoAmP 93
Hall, Dolores Brown WhoBlA 94
Hall, Don d1993 NewYTBS 93
Hall, Don Alan 1938- WhoAm 94
Hall, Don Courtney 1937- WhoMW 93
Hall, Donald DrAPF 93
Hall, Donald d1948 WhoHol 92
Hall, Donald 1928- IntWW 93, WhoAm 94
Hall, Donald (Andrew, Jr.) 1928- WrDr 94
Hall, Donald (Percy) 1930- Who 94
Hall, Donald Joyce 1928- WhoAm 94, WhoFI 94
Hall, Donald M. 1920- WhoAmP 93
Hall, Donald Norman Blake 1944- WhoAm 94, WhoScEn 94, WhoWest 94
Hall, Donald R. 1944- WhoAmL 94
Hall, Dorothy d1953 WhoHol 92
Hall, Douglas (Basil) 1909- Who 94
Hall, Douglas E. 1943- WhoAmP 93
Hall, Douglas John 1928- WhoAm 94
Hall, Douglas N. 1930- WhoIns 94
Hall, Douglas Scott 1940- WhoAm 94
Hall, Dudley d1960 WhoHol 92
Hall, Duncan 1947- Who 94
Hall, Durward Gorham 1910- WhoAmP 93
Hall, Dwayne Allen 1958- WhoFI 94
Hall, E. Eugene 1932- WhoAm 94
Hall, Edna d1945 WhoHol 92
Hall, Edward 1497-1547 DcLB 132
Hall, Edward 1498?-1547 BlmGEL
Hall, Edward Clarence 1931-1991 WhoBlA 94N
Hall, Edward Michael d1993 Who 94N
Hall, Edward Thomas 1924- Who 94
Hall, Edward Twitchell 1914- WhoAm 94
Hall, Edwin Herbert 1855-1938 WorScD
Hall, Edwin Huddleston, Jr. 1935- WhoFI 94
Hall, Edwin King WhoAmL 94
Hall, Edwin L. 1949- WhoAmP 93
Hall, Elisa BlmGWL
Hall, Elizabeth 1929- SmATA 77 [port], WhoAm 94
Hall, Elizabeth K. 1924- WhoMW 93
Hall, Ella d1981 WhoHol 92
Hall, Elliott Sawyer 1938- WhoBlA 94, WhoFI 94
Hall, Ernest 1930- Who 94
Hall, Ernest E. 1901- WhAm 10
Hall, Ernest L. 1940- WhoAm 94
Hall, Ethel Harris 1928- WhoBlA 94
Hall, Eugene Curtis 1958- WhoBlA 94
Hall, Evan 1905- WrDr 94
Hall, Evelyn Alice 1945- WhoBlA 94
Hall, Frances EncSF 93
Hall, Francis Woodall 1918- Who 94
Hall, Francoise Puvrez 1932- WhoAm 94
Hall, Franklin Perkins 1938- WhoAmP 93
Hall, Fred, III 1945- WhoBlA 94
Hall, Freddie Lee, Jr. 1943- WhoWest 94
Hall, Frederick Keith 1930- WhoAm 94, WhoScEn 94
Hall, Gary Lee 1949- WhoAmL 94
Hall, Gaylord Alden 1949- WhoAm 94
Hall, Geoffrey Dana 1948- WhoAmP 93
Hall, Geoffrey Penrose Dickinson 1916- Who 94
Hall, Geoffrey Ronald 1928- Who 94
Hall, George Who 94
Hall, (Harold) George 1920- Who 94
Hall, George Atwater 1925- WhoAm 94
Hall, George B., Jr. 1948- WhoAmL 94
Hall, George Joseph, Jr. 1952- WhoScEn 94
Hall, George M. d1930 WhoHol 92
Hall, George Rumney 1937- Who 94
Hall, Geraldine d1970 WhoHol 92
Hall, Gimone 1940- WrDr 94
Hall, Glenn Allen 1955- WhoAmP 93, WhoMW 93
Hall, Gordon 1926- WhoAmP 93
Hall, Gordon R. 1926- WhoAm 94, WhoAmL 94, WhoWest 94
Hall, Grace Rosalie 1921- WhoScEn 94
Hall, Granville Stanley 1844-1924 AmSocL
Hall, Grayson d1985 WhoHol 92
Hall, Gregory Clark 1950- WhoWest 94
Hall, Gus 1910- WhoAm 94
Hall, H. Douglas DrAPF 93
Hall, H(ugh) Gaston 1931- WrDr 94
Hall, Hal(bert) W(eldon) 1941- EncSF 93
Hall, Hansel Crimiel 1929- WhoBlA 94, WhoMW 93
Hall, Harber Homer 1920- WhoAmP 93
Hall, Harold H. 1926-1991 WhAm 10
Hall, Harold L. WhoBlA 94
Hall, Harold Percival 1913- Who 94
Hall, Harold Robert 1935- WhoWest 94
Hall, Harvey WhoHol 92
Hall, Henry d1954 WhoHol 92
Hall, Henry Edgar 1928- IntWW 93, Who 94
Hall, Henry Lyon, Jr. 1931- WhoAm 94
Hall, Holly d1984 WhoHol 92
Hall, Homer L. 1939- WhoMW 93
Hall, Horace Eugene 1933- WhoFI 94
Hall, Horathel 1926- WhoBlA 94
Hall, Houghton Alexander 1936- WhoScEn 94
Hall, Howard d1921 WhoHol 92
Hall, Howard Harry 1933- WhoAmL 94
Hall, Howard Lewis 1963- WhoScEn 94
Hall, Howard Pickering 1915- WhoScEn 94, WhoWest 94
Hall, Howard Ralph 1919- WhoBlA 94
Hall, Howard Tracy 1919- WhoAm 94
Hall, Hubert Desmond 1925- Who 94
Hall, Hugh David 1931- WhoAm 94
Hall, Huntz 1919- WhoCom
Hall, Huntz 1920- WhoHol 92
Hall, Huntz (Henry) 1920- IntMPA 94
Hall, Hurley W. 1935- WhoAmP 93
Hall, J. Albert d1920 WhoHol 92
Hall, J(ohn) C(live) 1920- WrDr 94
Hall, J. M. WhoIns 94
Hall, Jack Gilbert 1927- WhoAm 94
Hall, Jack L. 1941- WhoBlA 94
Hall, James EncSF 93
Hall, James d1612 WhWE
Hall, James d1940 WhoHol 92
Hall, James 1761-1832 WorScD
Hall, James 1918- WrDr 94
Hall, James Alexander 1920- WhoAm 94
Hall, James Andrew 1935- ConAu 42NR
Hall, James Arthur, III 1944- WhoFI 94
Hall, James B(yron) 1918- ConAu 42NR, WrDr 94
Hall, James Baker DrAPF 93
Hall, James Byron DrAPF 93
Hall, James Carter 1958- WhoWest 94
Hall, James Curtis 1926- WhoAm 94
Hall, James E. 1933- WhoAm 94
Hall, James Frederick 1921- WhoAm 94
Hall, James Marcell 1951- WhoWest 94
Hall, James Parker 1906- WhoAm 94
Hall, James Reginald 1936- WhoBlA 94
Hall, James Reginald, Jr. 1936- AfrAmG [port]

Haller, (Victor) Albrecht von 1708-1777 *WorScD*
Haller, Archibald Orben 1926- *WhoAm 94, WhoMW 93, WhoScEn 94*
Haller, Bill 1950- *WrDr 94*
Haller, Calvin John 1925- *WhoAm 94*
Haller, Charles Edward 1924- *WhoAm 94*
Haller, Edwin Wolfgang 1936- *WhoScEn 94*
Haller, Emanuel 1927- *WhoAmA 93*
Haller, Ernest d1970 *WhoHol 92*
Haller, Ernest 1896-1970 *IntDcF 2-4 [port]*
Haller, Eugene Ernest 1943- *WhoScEn 94*
Haller, Gerald Joseph 1936- *WhoMW 93*
Haller, Gret 1947- *WhoWomW 91*
Haller, Hayden Abney 1950- *WhoAm 94*
Haller, Ivan 1934- *WhoScEn 94*
Haller, James R. 1935- *WhoAmL 94*
Haller, John C. 1945- *WhoAm 94*
Haller, Kenneth L. Lawrence 1922- *WhoAmP 93*
Haller, Ralph A. 1948- *WhoAm 94*
Haller, William Paul 1957- *WhoScEn 94*
Halleran, E(ugene) E(dward) 1905- *WrDr 94*
Hallerman, Victoria *DrAPF 93*
Hallet, Agnes d1954 *WhoHol 92*
Hallett, Albert d1935 *WhoHol 92*
Hallett, Carol 1937- *WhoAmP 93*
Hallett, Carol Boyd 1937- *WhoAm 94, WhoAmL 94*
Hallett, Cecil Walter 1899- *Who 94*
Hallett, Charles A(rthur) *ConAu 141*
Hallett, Charles Arthur, Jr. 1939- *WhoAm 94*
Hallett, Dean Charles 1958- *WhoWest 94*
Hallett, Douglas L. 1949- *WhoAmL 94*
Hallett, George Edward Maurice 1912- *Who 94*
Hallett, Graham 1929- *WrDr 94*
Hallett, Heather Carol 1949- *Who 94*
Hallett, John 1929- *WhoWest 94*
Hallett, Kenneth Victor 1956- *WhoAmL 94*
Hallett, Laurence S. 1957- *WhoIns 94*
Hallett, Mark 1943- *WhoAm 94, WhoScEn 94*
Hallett, Neil *WhoHol 92*
Hallett, Robert Steven 1946- *WhoMW 93*
Hallett, Robin 1926- *WrDr 94*
Hallett, Tom Wayne 1954- *WhoFI 94*
Hallett, Victor George Henry 1921- *Who 94*
Hallett, Wade Aaron 1964- *WhoFI 94*
Hallett, William Jared 1923- *WhoAm 94*
Halleux, Albert Martin Julien 1920- *WhoFI 94*
Halley, Anne *DrAPF 93*
Halley, Edmond 1656-1742 *WorScD*
Halley, Harry L(ee) S(tuart) 1894- *WhAm 10*
Halley, James Alfred 1948- *WhoScEn 94*
Halley, James Woods, Jr. 1938- *WhoAm 94, WhoMW 93*
Halley, Laurence *Who 94*
Halley, Peter 1953- *WhoAmA 93*
Halley, Susan Toland 1958- *WhoMW 93*
Hallgarten, Anthony Bernard Richard 1937- *Who 94*
Hallgarten, S(iegfried Salomon) F(ritz) 1902- *WrDr 94*
Hallgren, Richard Edwin 1932- *WhoAm 94, WhoScEn 94*
Hallgrimsson, Geir 1925- *IntWW 93*
Halli, H.R. *EncSF 93*
Halliburton, Jeanne d1986 *WhoHol 92*
Halliburton, Robert John 1935- *Who 94*
Halliburton, Warren J. 1924- *BlkWr 2, WhoBlA 94*
Hallick, Mary Paloumpis 1922- *WhoMW 93*
Hallick, Tom *WhoHol 92*
Halliday, Bryant *WhoHol 92*
Halliday, Dorothy *ConAu 43NR*
Halliday, Fred 1946- *Who 94*
Halliday, Gardner d1966 *WhoHol 92*
Halliday, Harriet Hudnut 1941- *WhoMW 93*
Halliday, Ian 1928- *WhoAm 94*
Halliday, Ian Francis 1927- *Who 94*
Halliday, Jackson d1966 *WhoHol 92*
Halliday, John d1947 *WhoHol 92*
Halliday, John Frederick 1942- *Who 94*
Halliday, John Meech 1936- *WhoAm 94, WhoWest 94*
Halliday, Joseph William 1938- *WhoAm 94*
Halliday, Lena d1937 *WhoHol 92*
Halliday, Michael Alexander Kirkwood 1925- *Who 94*
Halliday, Miriam *DrAPF 93*
Halliday, Nancy R. 1936- *WhoAmA 93*
Halliday, Nigel Vaux 1956- *ConAu 140*
Halliday, Norman Pryde 1932- *Who 94*
Halliday, Robert Taylor *Who 94*
Halliday, Roy (William) 1923- *Who 94*
Halliday, Roy Arthur 1934- *WhoWest 94*
Halliday, S. F. P. *Who 94*
Halliday, Stephen Mills 1927- *WhoMW 93*
Halliday, Walter John 1907- *WhoAm 94*
Halliday, William James, Jr. 1921- *WhoFI 94*
Halliday, William R(oss) 1926- *WrDr 94*
Halliday, William Ross 1926- *WhoAm 94, WhoScEn 94, WhoWest 94*
Halliday-Borkowski, Miriam *DrAPF 93*
Hallier, Gerard Edouard 1941- *WhoAm 94*
Hallier, Hans-Joachim 1930- *IntWW 93*
Halligan, Howard Ansel 1937- *WhoAm 94*
Halligan, James Edmund 1936- *WhoAm 94, WhoWest 94*
Halligan, Mike Lewis 1949- *WhoAmP 93*
Halligan, Robert F. 1925-1989 *WhAm 10*
Halligan, Roger John, Jr. 1948- *WhoMW 93*
Halligan, William d1957 *WhoHol 92*
Hallila, Bruce Allan 1950- *WhoScEn 94*
Hallin, Emily Watson 1919- *WrDr 94*
Hallin, Margareta 1931- *NewGrDO*
Hallinan, James D. 1959- *WhoFI 94*
Hallinan, John Cornelius 1919- *WhoMW 93, WhoScEn 94*
Hallinan, Joseph Thomas 1960- *WhoAm 94*
Hallinan, Lincoln *Who 94*
Hallinan, (Adrian) Lincoln 1922- *Who 94*
Hallinan, Mary Alethea *Who 94*
Hallinan, Maureen Theresa *WhoAm 94*
Hallinan, Nancy *DrAPF 93*
Hallinan, Vincent W. 1897-1992 *AnObit 1992*
Halling, Leonard William 1927- *WhoAm 94*
Hallingby, Paul, Jr. 1919- *WhoAm 94*
Hallisey, Jeremiah F. 1939- *WhoAmP 93*
Hallissey, Michael 1943- *WhoFI 94*
Halliwell, Brian 1930- *Who 94*
Halliwell, David 1936- *WrDr 94*
Halliwell, David (William) 1936- *ConDr 93*
Halliwell, Richard Edward Winter 1937- *Who 94*
Halliwell, Tony *EncSF 93*
Hall-Keith, Jaqueline Yvonne 1953- *WhoBlA 94*
Hallman, Donald U. *WhoIns 94*
Hallman, Dwayne Duncan 1962- *WhoIns 94*
Hallman, Gary L. 1940- *WhoAm 94*
Hallman, Gary Lee 1940- *WhoAmA 93*
Hallman, Grady Lamar, Jr. 1930- *WhoAm 94*
Hallman, H. Theodore, Jr. 1933- *WhoAmA 93*
Hallman, Harry M., Jr. 1934- *WhoAmP 93*
Hallman, Henry Theodore, Jr. 1933- *WhoAm 94*
Hallman, Leroy 1915- *WhoAmL 94*
Hallman, Ted *WhoAmA 93*
Hallman, Viola 1944- *IntWW 93*
Hallman, William P., Jr. 1942- *WhoAmL 94*
Hallmark, Donald Parker 1945- *WhoAmA 93*
Hallmark, R. Elaine 1942- *WhoAmL 94, WhoWest 94*
Hall-Matthews, Anthony Francis *Who 94*
Hallo, William W. 1928- *WrDr 94*
Hallo, William Wolfgang 1928- *WhoAm 94*
Hallock, C. Wiles, Jr. 1918- *WhoAm 94, WhoWest 94*
Hallock, James Anthony 1942- *WhoAm 94*
Hallock, John Wallace, Jr. 1946- *WhoAmP 93*
Hallock, Joseph Theodore 1921- *WhoAmP 93*
Hallock, Joseph Theodore Ted 1921- *WhoWest 94*
Hallock, Robert Wayne 1944- *WhoAmL 94*
Halloin, Samuel 1923- *WhoAmP 93*
Hallon, Gayle 1946- *Who 94*
Hallor, Edith d1971 *WhoHol 92*
Hallor, Ray d1944 *WhoHol 92*
Halloran, Bernard Thorpe 1931- *WhoAm 94*
Halloran, Daniel Edward 1939- *WhoMW 93*
Halloran, James Joseph 1929- *WhoAm 94*
Halloran, James Vincent, III 1942- *WhoFI 94, WhoWest 94*
Halloran, John A. 1946- *WhoAmL 94*
Halloran, Kathleen L. 1952- *WhoAm 94*
Halloran, Leo Augustine 1931- *WhoAm 94, WhoFI 94*
Halloran, Michael James 1941- *WhoAm 94, WhoAmL 94, WhoWest 94*
Halloran, Michael William 1947- *WhoFI 94*
Halloran, Richard Colby 1930- *WhoAm 94, WhoWest 94*
Halloran, Thomas James 1935- *WhoFI 94*
Halloran, William Frank 1934- *WhoAm 94*
Halloway, Maggie *WhoHol 92*
Hallowell, Ann 1938- *WhoAmP 93*
Hallowell, Benjamin (Carew) d1834 *WhAmRev*
Hallowell, Burton Crosby 1915- *WhoAm 94*
Hallowell, Robert Edward 1918- *WhoAm 94*
Hallowell, Roger 1910-1989 *WhAm 10*
Hallowell, Tommy 1960- *WrDr 94*
Hallowell, Walter Henry 1943- *WhoAm 94, WhoFI 94*
Hallowes, Odette Marie Celine 1912- *IntWW 93, Who 94*
Hallows, Michael Colin Lloyd 1941- *WhoAm 94*
Hallquist, Kevin Paul 1959- *WhoAmL 94*
Halls, Ethyl May d1967 *WhoHol 92*
Halls, Peter Conrad 1956- *WhoAmL 94*
Halls, Wilfred Douglas 1918- *WrDr 94*
Hall-Sheedy, Leslee Ann 1955- *WhoMW 93*
Hallstein, Ingeborg 1937- *NewGrDO*
Hallstrom, Ivar Christian 1826-1901 *NewGrDO*
Hallstrom, Lasse 1946- *IntWW 93*
Hallsworth, Ernest Gordon 1913- *Who 94*
Hallums, Benjamin F. 1940- *WhoBlA 94*
Hallus, Tak *EncSF 93*
Hallward, Bertrand Leslie 1901- *Who 94*
Hall Williams *Who 94*
Hallyday, David 1966- *WhoHol 92*
Hallyday, Johnny *NewYTBS 93 [port], WhoHol 92*
Halm, Margo Anne 1961- *WhoMW 93*
Halm, Martin *WhoHol 92*
Halmen, Pet(re) 1943- *NewGrDO*
Halmi, Robert 1924- *WhoAm 94*
Halmi, Robert, Sr. 1924- *IntMPA 94*
Halmos, Paul Richard 1916- *WhoAm 94*
Halmos, Peter 1943- *WhoAm 94*
Halnan, Patrick John 1925- *Who 94*
Halonen, Marilyn Jean 1941- *WhoAm 94*
Halonen, Tarja Kaarina 1943- *IntWW 93, WhoWomW 91*
Halop, Billy d1976 *WhoHol 92*
Halop, Billy 1920-1976 *See East Side Kids WhoCom*
Halop, Florence d1986 *WhoHol 92*
Halopoff, William Evon 1934- *WhoWest 94*
Halpenny, Diana Doris 1951- *WhoAmL 94*
Halpenny, Leonard Cameron 1915- *WhoWest 94*
Halper, Emanuel Barry 1933- *WhoAm 94, WhoAmL 94*
Halper, Harlan Richard 1958- *WhoAm 94*
Halper, Thomas 1942- *WhoAm 94*
Halperin, Bertrand Israel 1941- *IntWW 93, WhoAm 94*
Halperin, David A. *WhoAm 94*
Halperin, David M(artin) 1952- *ConAu 41NR*
Halperin, David Richard 1944- *WhoAm 94*
Halperin, Donald Marc 1945- *WhoAmP 93*
Halperin, Errol R. 1941- *WhoAmL 94*
Halperin, George Bennett 1926- *WhoAm 94*
Halperin, Irving *DrAPF 93*
Halperin, Jerome Arthur 1937- *WhoAm 94*
Halperin, Jerome Yale 1930- *WhoAm 94, WhoMW 93*
Halperin, Joan *DrAPF 93*
Halperin, John Jacob 1950- *WhoScEn 94*
Halperin, John Stephen 1942- *WhoAm 94*
Halperin, John William 1941- *WhoAm 94*
Halperin, Jonathan L. 1949- *WrDr 94*
Halperin, Joseph 1922- *WhoScEn 94*
Halperin, Joseph 1923- *WhoScEn 94*
Halperin, Mark W. *DrAPF 93*
Halperin, Mark Warren 1940- *WhoWest 94*
Halperin, Meyer d1993 *NewYTBS 93*
Halperin, Morton H. 1938- *NewYTBS 93 [port]*
Halperin, Nan d1963 *WhoHol 92*
Halperin, Richard E. 1954- *WhoAm 94*
Halperin, Richard George 1948- *WhoFI 94, WhoMW 93*
Halperin, Robert Milton 1928- *WhoAm 94*
Halperin, Samuel 1930- *WhoAm 94*
Halperin, Tulio 1926- *IntWW 93*
Halpern, Abraham Leon 1925- *WhoAm 94*
Halpern, Alvin Michael 1938- *WhoAm 94*
Halpern, Barry David 1949- *WhoAm 94, WhoAmL 94*
Halpern, Benjamin 1912- *WhAm 10*
Halpern, Bruce Peter 1933- *WhoAm 94, WhoScEn 94*
Halpern, Charles Robert 1939- *WhoAm 94*
Halpern, Daniel *DrAPF 93*
Halpern, Daniel 1945- *IntWW 93, WhoAm 94, WrDr 94*
Halpern, Dina d1989 *WhoHol 92*
Halpern, Georges Maurice 1935- *WhoWest 94*
Halpern, Jack 1925- *IntWW 93, Who 94, WhoAm 94, WhoMW 93, WhoScEn 94*
Halpern, James Bladen 1936- *WhoAm 94, WhoAmL 94*
Halpern, James S. 1945- *CngDr 93, WhoAm 94, WhoAmL 94*
Halpern, Jay *DrAPF 93*
Halpern, Jeffrey S. 1942- *WhoAmL 94*
Halpern, Joseph William 1954- *WhoAmL 94*
Halpern, Joseph Yehuda 1953- *WhoWest 94*
Halpern, Kevin Gregg 1948- *WhoAm 94*
Halpern, Laurence R. 1946- *WhoIns 94*
Halpern, Manfred 1924- *WhoAm 94*
Halpern, Marjorie Stela Agosin *BlmGWL*
Halpern, Nathan L. 1914- *WhoAmA 93*
Halpern, Nathan Loren 1914- *WhoAm 94*
Halpern, Nora R. 1960- *WhoAmA 93*
Halpern, Paul 1961- *ConAu 141*
Halpern, Philip Morgan 1956- *WhoAmL 94*
Halpern, Ralph (Mark) 1938- *IntWW 93, Who 94*
Halpern, Ralph Lawrence 1929- *WhoAm 94, WhoAmL 94*
Halpern, Richard I. 1949- *WhoAmL 94*
Halpern, Seymour 1915- *WhoAmP 93*
Halpern, Sheila A. 1940- *WhoAmL 94*
Halpern, Terry *WhoAm 94*
Halperson, Michael Allen 1946- *WhoFI 94*
Halpert, David H. 1946- *WhoAmL 94*
Halpert, Leonard Walter 1924- *WhoAm 94*
Halpert, Robert 1958- *WhoAmL 94*
Halpin, Anna Marie 1923- *WhoAm 94*
Halpin, Charles A. *Who 94*
Halpin, Charles Aime 1930- *WhoAm 94, WhoWest 94*
Halpin, Daniel William 1938- *WhoAm 94, WhoScEn 94*
Halpin, Kathleen Mary 1903- *Who 94*
Halpin, Luke 1947- *WhoHol 92*
Halpin, Mary Elizabeth 1951- *WhoMW 93*
Halpin, Patrick Goodchild 1953- *WhoAmP 93*
Halpin, Timothy Patrick 1960- *WhoWest 94*
Halprin, Albert 1947- *WhoAmL 94*
Halprin, Anna Schuman 1920- *WhoAm 94*
Halprin, Daria *WhoHol 92*
Halprin, Lawrence 1916- *WhoAm 94*
Halprin, Rick 1940- *WhoAmL 94*
Halsall, Eric 1920- *WrDr 94*
Halsan, Stuart A. *WhoAmP 93*
Halsband, Frances 1943- *WhoAm 94*
Halsbury, Earl of 1880-1943 *EncSF 93*
Halsbury, Earl of 1908- *IntWW 93, Who 94*
Halsema, Barbara Ann 1959- *WhoMW 93*
Halseth, Michael James 1944- *WhoAm 94*
Halsey, A(lbert) H(enry) 1923- *WrDr 94*
Halsey, Albert Henry 1923- *IntWW 93, Who 94*
Halsey, Brett 1933- *WhoHol 92*
Halsey, Brian Elliott 1942- *WhoAmA 93*
Halsey, (Henry) David 1919- *Who 94*
Halsey, Douglas Martin 1953- *WhoAmL 94*
Halsey, James Albert 1930- *WhoAm 94*
Halsey, John Walter Brooke 1933- *Who 94*
Halsey, Philip Hugh 1928- *Who 94*
Halsey, Richard Sweeney 1929- *WhoAm 94*
Halsey, William Melton 1915- *WhoAmA 93*
Halsey-Brandt, Greg *WhoWest 94*
Halsman, Philippe 1906-1979 *WhoAmA 93N*
Halstan, Margaret d1967 *WhoHol 92*
Halstead, Bruce Walter 1920- *WhoScEn 94*
Halstead, Bryon d1963 *WhoHol 92*
Halstead, Dirck S. 1936- *WhoAm 94*
Halstead, Donna 1947- *WhoAmP 93*
Halstead, Harry Moore 1918- *WhoAm 94*
Halstead, John G. H. 1922- *IntWW 93, WhoAm 94*
Halstead, John Irvin, II 1965- *WhoScEn 94*
Halstead, Lester Mark 1927- *WhoWest 94*
Halstead, Philip Hubert 1933- *WhoScEn 94*

Halstead, Ronald 1927- *IntWW 93, Who 94*
Halstead, Ronald Lawrence 1923- *WhoScEn 94*
Halstead, William B. 1949- *WhoFI 94*
Halsted, David Crane 1941- *WhoAm 94*
Halsted, John Mac Harg 1905-1990 *WhAm 10*
Halsted, Sharon Lea 1937- *WhoMW 93*
Halsted, William Stewart 1852-1922 *WorScD*
Halston 1932-1990 *WhAm 10*
Halstrom, Frederic Norman 1944- *WhoAmL 94*
Halstrom, Lasse 1946- *IntMPA 94*
Halter, Edmund John 1928- *WhoScEn 94*
Halter, Gary 1941- *WhoAmP 93*
Halter, Henry James, Jr. 1947- *WhoFI 94*
Halter, Jon Charles 1941- *WhoAm 94*
Halter, Marek 1936- *ConAu 140*
Halterman, Benjamin Ballard 1925- *WhoAmP 93*
Halterman, Dawn Helen 1966- *WhoMW 93*
Halterman, Harold Leland 1950- *WhoWest 94*
Halthon, John Louis 1943- *WhoMW 93*
Haltiner, Fred d1973 *WhoHol 92*
Haltiwanger, Robert Sidney, Jr. 1923- *WhoAm 94*
Haltom, Billy Reid 1945- *WhoAmL 94*
Haltom, Elbert Bertram, Jr. 1922- *WhoAm 94, WhoAmL 94*
Halton, Charles d1959 *WhoHol 92*
Halton, Michael *WhoHol 92*
Haltrecht, Monty 1932- *WrDr 94*
Halula, Madelon Clair 1955- *WhoScEn 94*
Halushynsky, George Dobroslav 1935- *WhoScEn 94*
Haluska, Edward J. 1916- *WhoAmP 93*
Haluska, George Joseph 1947- *WhoScEn 94*
Haluska, Loren Andrew 1924- *WhoMW 93*
Halva, Allen Keith 1913- *WhoAmL 94, WhoMW 93*
Halver, John Emil 1922- *IntWW 93, WhoAm 94*
Halverhout, Winn William 1953- *WhoAmL 94*
Halverson, Dionne Porter 1947- *WhoAmP 93*
Halverson, George Clarence 1914- *WhoAm 94*
Halverson, Harold Wendell 1926- *WhoAmP 93*
Halverson, Kenneth Shaffer 1933- *WhoAmP 93*
Halverson, Leslie Eugene d1953 *WhoHol 92*
Halverson, Richard C. 1916- *CngDr 93*
Halverson, Richard Christian 1916- *WhoAm 94*
Halverson, Richard Paul 1941- *WhoAm 94*
Halverson, Ronald T. 1936- *WhoAmP 93*
Halverson, Steven Thomas 1954- *WhoAmL 94, WhoWest 94*
Halverson, Sue 1946- *WhoAmL 94*
Halverson, Wendell Quelprud 1916- *WhoAm 94*
Halverstadt, Donald Bruce 1934- *WhoAm 94*
Halverstadt, Jonathan Scott 1952- *WhoAm 94, WhoWest 94*
Halverstadt, Robert Dale 1920- *WhoAm 94, WhoFI 94*
Halvorsen, David E. d1993 *NewYTBS 93*
Halvorsen, Einfrid 1931- *IntWW 93*
Halvorsen, Elspeth Colette 1929- *WhoAmA 93*
Halvorsen, Morrie Edward 1931- *WhoAm 94*
Halvorsen, Stanley Warren 1953- *WhoScEn 94*
Halvorsen, Thomas Glen 1954- *WhoScEn 94*
Halvorson, Alfred Rubin 1921- *WhoWest 94*
Halvorson, Ardell David 1945- *WhoAm 94, WhoScEn 94, WhoWest 94*
Halvorson, Gary Alfred 1949- *WhoMW 93, WhoScEn 94*
Halvorson, Harlyn Odell 1925- *WhoScEn 94*
Halvorson, Marilyn 1948- *WrDr 94*
Halvorson, Newman Thorbus, Jr. 1936- *WhoAm 94*
Halvorson, Rodney N. 1949- *WhoAmP 93*
Halvorson, Roger A. 1934- *WhoAmP 93*
Halvorson, William Arthur 1928- *WhoFI 94, WhoScEn 94*
Halward, Chris c. 1928- *WhoHol 92*
Halwig, Nancy Diane 1954- *WhoFI 94*
Halyard, Michele Yvette 1961- *WhoBlA 94*
Ham, Arlene Hansen 1936- *WhoAmP 93*
Ham, Bob *EncSF 93*

Ham, Bonnie Davis 1947- *WhoAmP 93*
Ham, Caroline Richardson 1927- *WhoAmP 93*
Ham, David Kenneth R. *Who 94*
Ham, Debra Newman 1948- *WhoBlA 94*
Ham, Donald Jamieson 1934- *WhoAmP 93*
Ham, Gary Martin 1940- *WhoWest 94*
Ham, George Eldon 1939- *WhoAm 94, WhoMW 93, WhoScEn 94*
Ham, Harry d1943 *WhoHol 92*
Ham, Inyong 1925- *WhoAm 94, WhoScEn 94*
Ham, Jack *ProFbHF*
Ham, James Milton 1920- *IntWW 93, Who 94, WhoAm 94, WhoScEn 94*
Ham, Jane Fay *WhoAmP 93*
Ham, Joe Strother, Jr. 1928- *WhoAm 94*
Ham, John Dudley Nelson 1902- *Who 94*
Ham, Lee Edward 1919- *WhoAm 94*
Ham, Leslie Gilmer 1930- *WhoAm 94*
Ham, Norman Douglas 1929- *WhoAm 94*
Ham, Richard 1923- *WhoAmP 93*
Ham, Wayne Albert 1938- *WrDr 94*
Hama, Mie *WhoHol 92*
Hamachek, John Walter 1948- *WhoFI 94*
Hamachek, Ross Frank 1942- *WhoAm 94*
Hamachek, Tod Russell 1946- *WhoAm 94, WhoWest 94*
Hamad, Abdul-Latif Yousef al- 1937- *IntWW 93*
Hamada, Hiroki 1952- *WhoScEn 94*
Hamada, Jin 1945- *WhoScEn 94*
Hamada, Keinosuke 1924- *WhoScEn 94*
Hamada, Nobuhiro A. 1944- *WhoScEn 94*
Hamada, Robert Seiji 1937- *WhoAm 94, WhoMW 93*
Hamade, Thomas Ali 1952- *WhoMW 93*
Hamady, Jack Ameen 1909- *WhoAm 94*
Hamady, Ron 1947- *IntMPA 94*
Hamady, Walter Samuel 1940- *WhoAmA 93*
Hamaguchi, Satoshi 1959- *WhoScEn 94*
Hamaguchi, Yozo 1909- *WhoAmA 93*
Hamai, James Yutaka 1926- *WhoWest 94*
Hamaker, Richard Franklin 1924- *WhoScEn 94*
Hamal, Henri 1744-1820 *NewGrDO*
Hamal, Jean-Noel 1709-1778 *NewGrDO*
Hamalainen, Pekka Kalevi 1938- *WhoAm 94, WhoMW 93*
Hamalainen, Tuulikki Katriina (Pia) 1940- *WhoWomW 91*
Hamama, Faten *WhoHol 92*
Hamamoto, Darrell Yoshito 1953- *WhoAsA 94*
Haman, Raymond William 1927- *WhoAm 94*
Haman, Sarah Armstrong 1949- *WhoWest 94*
Hamann, Deryl Frederick 1932- *WhoAmL 94*
Hamann, Kevin Robert 1962- *WhoMW 93*
Hamann, Lee H. 1952- *WhoAmL 94*
Hamann, Marilyn D. 1945- *WhoAmA 93*
Hamann, Norman Lee, Sr. 1936- *WhoMW 93*
Hamann, Sefton Davidson 1921- *IntWW 93*
Hamar, Diana Kathleen *WhoAmA 93*
Hamar, H. Jeffrey 1958- *WhoWest 94*
Hamari, Julia 1942- *IntWW 93, NewGrDO*
Hamarneh, Sami K. 1925- *IntWW 93*
Hamarneh, Sami Khalaf 1925- *WhoAm 94*
Hamasaki, Les 1939?- *WhoAsA 94*
Hamberg, Daniel 1924- *WhoAm 94*
Hamberg, Marcelle R. 1931- *WhoBlA 94*
Hamberlin, Emiel 1939- *WhoBlA 94*
Hambidge, Douglas Walter 1927- *IntWW 93, Who 94, WhoWest 94*
Hambleden, Dowager Viscountess 1904- *Who 94*
Hambleden, Viscount 1930- *Who 94*
Hamblen, Charles Hillen, Jr. 1917- *WhoAmP 93*
Hamblen, Derek Ivens Archibald 1917- *Who 94*
Hamblen, Donald Lee 1928- *WhoAmP 93*
Hamblen, John Wesley 1924- *WhoAm 94*
Hamblen, Karen A. *WhoAmA 93*
Hamblen, L. Jane 1949- *WhoAm 94, WhoAmL 94*
Hamblen, Lapsley Walker, Jr. 1926- *CngDr 93, WhoAm 94, WhoAmL 94*
Hamblet, Michael Jon 1940- *WhoMW 93*
Hambleton, George Blow Elliott 1929- *WhoAm 94, WhoFI 94*
Hambleton, Kenneth George 1937- *Who 94*
Hambleton, Richard A. 1954- *WhoAmA 93*
Hambleton, Thomas Edward 1911- *WhoAm 94*
Hamblett, Stephen 1934- *WhoAm 94*
Hamblett, Theora 1895- *WhoAmA 93N*

Hambley, Mark G. 1948- *WhoAmP 93*
Hamblin, Daniel Morgan 1942- *WhoScEn 94*
Hamblin, Jacob 1819-1886 *EncNAR*
Hamblin, Robert W(ayne) 1938- *WrDr 94*
Hambling, Gerry *ConTFT 11*
Hambling, Herbert Peter Hugh 1953- *WhoFI 94*
Hambling, (Herbert) Hugh 1919- *Who 94*
Hambling, Maggi 1945- *IntWW 93*
Hambling, Milton Herbert 1926- *WhoScEn 94*
Hambly, Barbara 1951- *EncSF 93*
Hambourg, Maria Morris 1949- *WrDr 94*
Hambraeus, Bengt 1928- *WhoAm 94*
Hambraeus, Birgitta 1930- *WhoWomW 91*
Hambrecht, William R. 1935- *WhoFI 94*
Hambrick, George Walter, Jr. 1922- *WhoAm 94*
Hambrick, Harold E., Jr. 1943- *WhoBlA 94*
Hambrick, Jackson Reid 1917- *WhoAm 94*
Hambrick, John Donald 1943- *WhoFI 94*
Hambrick, Marvin K. 1921- *WhoAm 94*
Hambrick, Patricia A. *WhoAmP 93*
Hambright, Robert John 1956- *WhoAmL 94*
Hambro, Charles Eric Alexander 1930- *IntWW 93, Who 94*
Hambro, Jocelyn Olaf 1919- *IntWW 93, Who 94*
Hambro, Richard Alexander 1946- *Who 94*
Hambro, Rupert Nicholas 1943- *IntWW 93, Who 94*
Hamburg, Beatrix Ann 1923- *WhoAm 94*
Hamburg, Charles Bruce 1939- *WhoAm 94, WhoAmL 94*
Hamburg, Dan 1948- *CngDr 93, WhoAmP 93*
Hamburg, Daniel 1948- *WhoAm 94, WhoWest 94*
Hamburg, David A. 1925- *WhoAm 94, WhoScEn 94*
Hamburg, Joseph 1922- *WhoAm 94*
Hamburg, Marian Virginia 1918- *WhoAm 94*
Hamburg, Roger Phillip 1934- *WhoMW 93*
Hamburger, Brian James 1963- *WhoMW 93*
Hamburger, Jean 1909-1992 *WhAm 10*
Hamburger, Jeffrey Allen 1947- *WhoFI 94*
Hamburger, Michael (Peter Leopold) 1924- *WrDr 94*
Hamburger, Michael Peter Leopold 1924- *IntWW 93, Who 94*
Hamburger, Philip 1914- *WrDr 94*
Hamburger, Philip Paul 1914- *WhoAm 94*
Hamburger, Richard James 1937- *WhoAm 94*
Hamburger, Sidney (Cyril) 1914- *Who 94*
Hamburger, Sydney K. 1935- *WhoAmA 93*
Hamburger, Viktor 1900- *WhoAm 94*
Hamby, A. Garth d1993 *NewYTBS 93*
Hamby, Alonzo L(ee) 1940- *WrDr 94*
Hamby, Alonzo Lee 1940- *WhoAm 94*
Hamby, James A. *DrAPF 93*
Hamby, Jeannette 1933- *WhoWest 94*
Hamby, Jeannette K. 1933- *WhoAmP 93*
Hamby, Michael E. 1952- *WhoIns 94*
Hamby, Peter Norman 1959- *WhoMW 93, WhoScEn 94*
Hamby, Roscoe Jerome 1919- *WhoBlA 94*
Hamda, Mohamed El Bedji 1934- *IntWW 93*
Hamdi, Imad d1984 *WhoHol 92*
Hameed, A. C. S. 1929- *IntWW 93*
Hameed, A. C. Shahul 1929- *Who 94*
Hameister, Lavon Louetta 1922- *WhoFI 94, WhoMW 93*
Hameka, Hendrik Frederik 1931- *WhoAm 94, WhoScEn 94*
Hamel, Dana Bertrand 1923- *WhoAm 94*
Hamel, David Charles 1953- *WhoScEn 94*
Hamel, Douglas E. 1951- *WhoAmL 94*
Hamel, Fred Meade 1943- *WhoAmL 94*
Hamel, Louis H., Jr. 1934- *WhoAm 94, WhoAmL 94*
Hamel, Louis Reginald 1945- *WhoFI 94, WhoMW 93*
Hamel, Mark Edwin 1953- *WhoAmL 94*
Hamel, Maurice 1941- *WhoAmP 93*
Hamel, Reginald 1931- *WhoAm 94*
Hamel, Robert Dean 1937- *WhoAmL 94*
Hamel, Rodolphe 1929- *WhoAm 94, WhoAmL 94, WhoFI 94*
Hamel, Veronica 1943- *IntMPA 94, WhoAm 94, WhoHol 92*
Hamel, William R. d1958 *WhoHol 92*
Hamelin, Clement d1957 *WhoHol 92*
Hamelin, Jean-Guy 1925- *WhoAm 94*
Hamelin, Louis-Edmond 1923- *IntWW 93*
Hamelin, Marcel 1937- *WhoAm 94*
Hamell, Patrick Joseph 1910- *WrDr 94*

Hamelmann, Norma Ruth 1944- *WhoMW 93*
Hamer, Charles James 1931- *WhoAmA 93*
Hamer, Fannie Lou 1917-1977 *AfrAmAl 6 [port], ConBlB 6 [port], HisWorL*
Hamer, Fannie Lou Townsend 1917-1977 *AmSocL*
Hamer, Gerald d1972 *WhoHol 92*
Hamer, H. E. Jean Jerome 1916- *IntWW 93*
Hamer, Jeffrey Michael 1949- *WhoFI 94*
Hamer, Jesse Dewey 1898- *WhAm 10*
Hamer, Judith Ann 1939- *WhoBlA 94*
Hamer, Rupert (James) 1916- *Who 94*
Hamer, Rupert James 1916- *IntWW 93*
Hamer, Rusty d1990 *WhoHol 92*
Hamer, Walter Jay 1907- *WhoScEn 94*
Hamerik, Asger 1843-1923 *NewGrDO*
Hamerik, Ebbe 1898-1951 *NewGrDO*
Hamerlik, Michael Francis 1961- *WhoAmP 93*
Hamermesh, Daniel Selim 1943- *WhoAm 94*
Hamermesh, Morton 1915- *WhoAm 94, WhoMW 93, WhoScEn 94*
Hamerow, Theodore Stephen 1920- *WhoAm 94*
Hamerslough, Walter Scott 1935- *WhoWest 94*
Hamerstrom, Frances 1907- *WhoMW 93*
Hamerton, John Laurence 1929- *WhoAm 94, WhoScEn 94*
Hamerton-Kelly, Robert Gerald 1938- *WhoWest 94*
Hames, Carl Martin 1938- *WhoAmA 93*
Hames, Clifford Moffett 1926- *WhoAm 94*
Hames, Curtis Gordon 1920- *WhoAm 94*
Hames, Gary Lawrence 1945- *WhoMW 93*
Hames, William Lester 1947- *WhoAmL 94*
Hamid, Michael 1934- *WhoAm 94*
Hamid, Salah 1924- *IntWW 93*
Hamid, Syed Halim 1953- *WhoScEn 94*
Hamidi *WhoPRCh 91*
Hamidjaja, Wiriadi Willy 1962- *WhoFI 94, WhoWest 94*
Hamil, David Alexander 1908- *WhoAmP 93*
Hamill, Allen William 1948- *WhoAm 94*
Hamill, Brian *WhoHol 92*
Hamill, Bruce W. 1941- *WhoScEn 94*
Hamill, Carol 1953- *WhoScEn 94, WhoWest 94*
Hamill, Dorothy Stuart 1957- *WhoAm 94*
Hamill, Ethel 1910- *WrDr 94*
Hamill, James Paul 1944- *WhoAm 94*
Hamill, Janet *DrAPF 93*
Hamill, John *WhoHol 92*
Hamill, John P. 1940- *WhoAm 94*
Hamill, Judith Ellen 1953- *WhoMW 93*
Hamill, Lucille d1939 *WhoHol 92*
Hamill, Margaret Hudgens 1937- *WhoBlA 94*
Hamill, Mark 1951- *WhoAm 94, WhoWest 94*
Hamill, Mark 1952- *IntMPA 94, WhoHol 92*
Hamill, Patrick 1930- *Who 94*
Hamill, Pete 1935- *IntMPA 94, WhoAm 94, WhoHol 92*
Hamill, Robert L. 1927- *WhoMW 93*
Hamill, Sam *DrAPF 93*
Hamill, Tim J. 1942- *WhoAmA 93*
Hamilton *Who 94*
Hamilton, Duke of 1938- *Who 94*
Hamilton, Marquess of 1969- *Who 94*
Hamilton, A. C. 1918- *WhoAmP 93*
Hamilton, A(lbert) C(harles) 1921- *WrDr 94*
Hamilton, Adrian Walter 1923- *Who 94*
Hamilton, Adrianne Pauline U. *Who 94*
Hamilton, Alana *WhoHol 92*
Hamilton, Albert Charles 1921- *WhoAm 94*
Hamilton, Alexander 1755-1804 *HisWorL [port]*
Hamilton, Alexander 1757-1804 *AmRev, WhAmRev [port]*
Hamilton, Alexander Kenneth 1915- *Who 94*
Hamilton, Alexander Macdonald 1925- *Who 94*
Hamilton, Alfred Starr *DrAPF 93*
Hamilton, Alice 1869-1970 *AmSocL [port], HisWorL [port]*
Hamilton, Allan Corning 1921- *WhoAm 94*
Hamilton, Allen Emerson, Jr. 1935- *WhoWest 94*
Hamilton, Allen Philip 1937- *WhoFI 94, WhoWest 94*
Hamilton, Andrew J. 1941- *WhoAmL 94*
Hamilton, Anne Linnea 1949- *WhoFI 94*
Hamilton, Anthony Robert 1924-1988 *WhAm 10*

Hamilton, Archibald (Gavin) 1941-
Who 94
Hamilton, Art *WhoAmP 93, WhoBlA 94*
Hamilton, Arthur Campbell 1942- *Who 94*
Hamilton, Arthur N. 1917- *WhoBlA 94*
Hamilton, Arthur Richard C. *Who 94*
Hamilton, Aubrey J. 1927- *WhoBlA 94*
Hamilton, Bernard 1932- *WrDr 94*
Hamilton, Bernie 1929- *WhoHol 92*
Hamilton, Beth Alleman 1927-
WhoMW 93
Hamilton, Betty d1935 *WhoHol 92*
Hamilton, Beverly Lannquist 1946-
WhoAm 94
Hamilton, Big John d1984 *WhoHol 92*
Hamilton, Bill *WhoAm 94*
Hamilton, Bobby Wayne 1946- *WhoFI 94*
Hamilton, Bruce Ross 1930- *WhoAmP 93*
Hamilton, Carrie 1964- *WhoHol 92*
Hamilton, Cecil Austin 1950- *WhoFI 94*
Hamilton, Charles 1704-1786 *DcNaB MP*
Hamilton, Charles 1913- *WrDr 94*
Hamilton, Charles Edward, Jr. 1957-
WhoWest 94
Hamilton, Charles Henry 1903-
WhoAm 94
Hamilton, Charles Howard 1935-
WhoWest 94
Hamilton, Charles S. 1927- *WhoBlA 94*
Hamilton, Charles V(ernon) 1929-
BlkWr 2, ConAu 42NR
Hamilton, Charles Vernon 1929-
WhoBlA 94
Hamilton, Cheryl Louise 1951-
WhoMW 93
Hamilton, Christopher John 1947-
WhoFI 94
Hamilton, Cicely 1872-1952 *BlmGWL,
EncSF 93*
Hamilton, Clive *EncSF 93*
Hamilton, Clyde H. *WhoAmP 93*
Hamilton, Clyde Henry 1934- *WhoAm 94,
WhoAmL 94*
Hamilton, Curtis d1978 *WhoHol 92*
Hamilton, Dagmar Strandberg 1932-
WhoAm 94, WhoAmL 94
Hamilton, Daniel Stephen 1932-
WhoAm 94
Hamilton, Darden Cole 1956-
WhoWest 94
Hamilton, Darryl Quinn 1964-
WhoBlA 94
Hamilton, David (Peter) 1935- *NewGrDO*
Hamilton, David Lee 1937- *WhoAm 94*
Hamilton, David Mike 1951- *WhoWest 94*
Hamilton, David Wendell 1953-
WhoAm 94
Hamilton, Dewayne 1951- *WhoAmP 93*
Hamilton, Donald (Bengtsson) 1916-
WrDr 94
Hamilton, Donald Bengtsson 1916-
WhoAm 94, WhoWest 94
Hamilton, Donald Emery 1938-
WhoAm 94
Hamilton, Donald Reed 1947- *WhoAm 94*
Hamilton, Douglas Owens 1931- *Who 94*
Hamilton, Dran *WhoHol 92*
Hamilton, Dundas *Who 94*
Hamilton, (James) Dundas 1919- *Who 94*
Hamilton, Dwight Alan 1928-
WhoAmP 93
Hamilton, E. Douglas d1993 *NewYTBS 93*
Hamilton, Earl Jefferson 1899-1989
WhAm 10
Hamilton, Earle Grady, Jr. 1920-
WhoAm 94
Hamilton, Eben William 1937- *Who 94*
Hamilton, Edmond (Moore) 1904-1977
EncSF 93
Hamilton, Edward (Sydney) 1925- *Who 94*
Hamilton, Edward Marsh 1941-
WhoFI 94, WhoMW 93
Hamilton, Edward N., Jr. 1947-
WhoBlA 94
Hamilton, Edward Pierpont 1897-
WhAm 10
Hamilton, Edward Sylvester 1939-
WhoWest 94
Hamilton, Edwin 1936- *WhoBlA 94*
Hamilton, Elizabeth 1906- *WrDr 94*
Hamilton, Eugene Kenneth 1939-
WhoAmP 93
Hamilton, Florence d1919 *WhoHol 92*
Hamilton, Frank *WhoAmP 93*
Hamilton, Frank Moss 1930- *WhoAmA 93*
Hamilton, Franklin D. 1942- *WhoBlA 94*
Hamilton, Fred d1980 *WhoHol 92*
Hamilton, Gail *BlmGWL, DrAPF 93,
SmATA 77*
Hamilton, Gail 1911- *WrDr 94*
Hamilton, Gary Glen 1943- *WhoAm 94*
Hamilton, Gavin Francis 1930-
WhoWest 94
Hamilton, Gay *WhoHol 92*
Hamilton, George 1939- *IntMPA 94,
WhoHol 92*
Hamilton, George E., Jr. 1895-1990
WhAm 10

Hamilton, George Earl 1934- *WhoAmA 93*
Hamilton, George Gordon d1939
WhoHol 92
Hamilton, George Heard 1910- *Who 94,
WhoAm 94*
Hamilton, George "Spike" d1957
WhoHol 92
Hamilton, Grace Towns 1907-1992
WhoBlA 94N
Hamilton, Graeme Montagu 1934-
Who 94
Hamilton, Guy 1922- *IntMPA 94*
Hamilton, H(enry) G(lenn) 1895-
WhAm 10
Hamilton, H. J. Belton 1924- *WhoBlA 94*
Hamilton, Hale d1942 *WhoHol 92*
Hamilton, Harold Philip 1924-
WhoAm 94
Hamilton, Harry E. 1962- *WhoBlA 94*
Hamilton, Harry Lemuel, Jr. 1938-
WhoAm 94, WhoWest 94
Hamilton, Helen Packer 1927-
WhoAmP 93
Hamilton, Henry d1796 *WhAmRev*
Hamilton, Henry c. 1734-1796 *AmRev*
Hamilton, Howard Britton 1923-
WhoAm 94
Hamilton, Howard Laverne 1916-
WhoAm 94
Hamilton, Howard W. 1948- *WhoBlA 94*
Hamilton, Hugh Alexander 1929-
WhoAm 94
Hamilton, Hugh Gray Wybrants 1918-
Who 94
Hamilton, Iain (Ellis) 1922- *NewGrDO*
Hamilton, Iain Ellis 1922- *Who 94*
Hamilton, Ian 1938- *ConAu 41NR,
Who 94*
Hamilton, (Robert) Ian 1938- *WrDr 94*
Hamilton, Ian Robertson 1925- *Who 94*
Hamilton, J. Frank *WhoHol 92*
Hamilton, J. Richard 1929- *WhoAm 94*
Hamilton, Jack d1925 *WhoHol 92*
Hamilton, Jack Martin 1946- *WhoMW 93*
Hamilton, Jackson Douglas 1949-
WhoAmL 94
Hamilton, James 1918- *Who 94*
Hamilton, James (Arnot) 1923- *Who 94*
Hamilton, James A. 1944- *WhoAmL 94*
Hamilton, James Beckham 1920-
WhoAmP 93
Hamilton, James Dundas 1919-
IntWW 93
Hamilton, James E. 1935- *WhoAmP 93*
Hamilton, James G. 1939- *WhoBlA 94*
Hamilton, James Harold *WhoAmP 93*
Hamilton, James Joseph 1945-
WhoMW 93
Hamilton, James Marvie 1950-
WhoAm 94
Hamilton, James P. 1946- *WhoIns 94*
Hamilton, James Robertson 1921-
WrDr 94
Hamilton, James William 1932-
WhoAm 94
Hamilton, James William 1933-
WhoWest 94
Hamilton, Jane *WhoHol 92*
Hamilton, Jean Constance 1945-
WhoAm 94, WhoAmL 94, WhoMW 93
Hamilton, Jeff 1934- *WhoAmP 93*
Hamilton, Jerald 1927- *WhoAm 94,
WhoWest 94*
Hamilton, Joan 1950- *WhoAmP 93*
Hamilton, Joe Clay *WhoAmP 93*
Hamilton, Joel Raymond 1948-
WhoWest 94
Hamilton, John d1817 *AmRev, WhAmRev*
Hamilton, John d1958 *WhoHol 92*
Hamilton, John 1941- *Who 94*
Hamilton, John (Graham) 1910- *Who 94*
Hamilton, John Carl 1955- *WhoScEn 94*
Hamilton, John Dayton, Jr. 1934-
WhoAm 94, WhoBlA 94
Hamilton, John F. d1967 *WhoHol 92*
Hamilton, John Joslyn, Jr. 1949-
WhoBlA 94
Hamilton, John M. *WhoBlA 94*
Hamilton, John Mark, Jr. 1931-
WhoBlA 94
Hamilton, John Maxwell 1947- *WrDr 94*
Hamilton, John Ross 1924- *WhoAm 94*
Hamilton, Joseph H. d1965 *WhoHol 92*
Hamilton, Joseph Hants, Jr. 1932-
WhoAm 94
Hamilton, Joseph L. 1951- *WhoAmL 94*
Hamilton, Joseph Willard 1922-
WhoBlA 94
Hamilton, Juan B. 1945- *WhoAmA 93*
Hamilton, Judith Hall 1944- *WhoFI 94*
Hamilton, Karen Lee 1954- *WhoMW 93*
Hamilton, Kenneth 1948- *WhoAmP 93*
Hamilton, Kenneth (Morrison) 1917-
WrDr 94
Hamilton, Kim *WhoHol 92*
Hamilton, Kipp d1981 *WhoHol 92*
Hamilton, Kris Paul 1947- *WhoWest 94*
Hamilton, Laurel d1955 *WhoHol 92*

Hamilton, Lawrence White 1957-
WhoFI 94
Hamilton, Lee H. 1931- *CngDr 93*
Hamilton, Lee Herbert 1931- *WhoAm 94,
WhoAmP 93, WhoMW 93*
Hamilton, Leicester Forsyth 1893-
WhAm 10
Hamilton, Leo Richard 1927-
WhoAmP 93
Hamilton, Leonard *WhoBlA 94*
Hamilton, Leonard Derwent 1921-
WhoAm 94, WhoScEn 94
Hamilton, Linda 1956- *IntMPA 94,
WhoHol 92*
Hamilton, Linda Helen 1952-
WhoScEn 94
Hamilton, Lisa Tomalynn 1958-
WhoAmL 94
Hamilton, Lloyd d1953 *WhoHol 92*
Hamilton, Lois *WhoHol 92*
Hamilton, Lonnie, III 1927- *WhoAmP 93*
Hamilton, Loudon Pearson 1932- *Who 94*
Hamilton, Louis Peter 1956- *WhoMW 93*
Hamilton, Louise Virginia 1913-
WhoAmP 93
Hamilton, Lyman Critchfield, Jr. 1926-
WhoAm 94
Hamilton, Lynn 1930- *WhoBlA 94,
WhoHol 92*
Hamilton, Mahlon d1960 *WhoHol 92*
Hamilton, Malcolm Cowan 1938-
WhoAm 94
Hamilton, Malcolm William Bruce S.
Who 94
Hamilton, Marc d1987 *WhoHol 92*
Hamilton, Margaret d1985 *WhoHol 92*
Hamilton, Mark Alan 1960- *WhoMW 93*
Hamilton, Mark John 1953- *WhoMW 93*
Hamilton, Martha *Who 94*
Hamilton, Martin Alva 1939-
WhoWest 94
Hamilton, Mary (E.) 1927- *WrDr 94*
Hamilton, Mary Margaret *Who 94*
Hamilton, Max Chester 1918-
WhoMW 93
Hamilton, McKinley John 1921-
WhoBlA 94
Hamilton, Michael Aubrey 1918- *Who 94*
Hamilton, Michael Bruce 1939-
WhoScEn 94
Hamilton, Michael R. 1945- *WhoIns 94*
Hamilton, Michael Scott 1953-
WhoAm 94
Hamilton, Milton Holmes 1925-
WhoAmP 93
Hamilton, Milton Holmes, Sr. 1925-
WhoAm 94
Hamilton, Milton Hugh, Jr. 1932-
WhoAmP 93
Hamilton, Murray d1986 *WhoHol 92*
Hamilton, Myer Alan Barry K. *Who 94*
Hamilton, Nancy Beth 1948- *WhoMW 93*
Hamilton, Nancy Jeanne 1959-
WhoWest 94
Hamilton, Neil *Who 94*
Hamilton, Neil d1984 *WhoHol 92*
Hamilton, (Mostyn) Neil 1949- *Who 94*
Hamilton, Neil Alfred 1932- *WhoAm 94*
Hamilton, Nigel *NewYTBS 93 [port]*
Hamilton, Nigel 1944- *ConAu 41NR*
Hamilton, Nigel John Mawdesley 1938-
Who 94
Hamilton, North Edward Frederick D.
Who 94
Hamilton, Pat R. 1923- *WhoAmP 93*
Hamilton, Patricia Rose 1948-
WhoAmA 93
Hamilton, (Anthony Walter) Patrick
1904-1962 *EncSF 93*
Hamilton, Paul 1915- *WrDr 94*
Hamilton, Paul L. 1941- *WhoBlA 94*
Hamilton, Penny Rafferty 1948-
WhoWest 94
Hamilton, Perrin C. 1921- *WhoAmL 94*
Hamilton, Peter Bannerman 1946-
WhoAm 94
Hamilton, Peter Owen 1944- *WhoAm 94,
WhoFI 94*
Hamilton, Phanuel J. 1929- *WhoBlA 94*
Hamilton, Phillip 1952- *WhoAmP 93*
Hamilton, Phillip Douglas 1954-
WhoAmL 94
Hamilton, Phillip H. 1964- *WhoAmL 94*
Hamilton, Pierpont Morgan 1898-
WhAm 10
Hamilton, Priscilla 1927- *WrDr 94*
Hamilton, Rainy, Jr. 1956- *WhoBlA 94*
Hamilton, Ralph West 1933- *WhoAm 94*
Hamilton, Raymond 1950- *WhoBlA 94*
Hamilton, Richard *WhoHol 92*
Hamilton, Richard 1922- *IntWW 93,
Who 94*
Hamilton, (Robert Charles) Richard
(Caradoc) 1911- *Who 94*
Hamilton, Richard Alfred 1941-
WhoMW 93
Hamilton, Richard Caradoc *Who 94*

Hamilton, Richard Columbus 1943-
WhoAmP 93
Hamilton, Richard Daniel 1928-
WhoAm 94
Hamilton, Richard Graham 1932- *Who 94*
Hamilton, Richard Lee 1939- *WhoAm 94*
Hamilton, Robert Appleby, Jr. 1940-
WhoFI 94, WhoMW 93
Hamilton, Robert Burns 1949-
WhoScEn 94
Hamilton, Robert Lee 1935- *WhoWest 94*
Hamilton, Robert Morrison 1936-
WhoAm 94
Hamilton, Robert Paul 1957- *WhoAmL 94*
Hamilton, Robert William 1905- *Who 94*
Hamilton, Robert William 1939-
WhoAm 94
Hamilton, Robert Woodruff 1931-
WhoAm 94
Hamilton, Ross T. 1946- *WhoBlA 94*
Hamilton, Russell George, Jr. 1934-
WhoAm 94
Hamilton, Samuel Cartenius 1936-
WhoBlA 94
Hamilton, Scott 1953- *WhoAmL 94*
Hamilton, Scott Scovell 1958- *WhoAm 94,
WhoWest 94*
Hamilton, Shirley Siekmann 1928-
WhoMW 93
Hamilton, Stephen David Derwent 1952-
WhoAm 94
Hamilton, Stephen K. 1946- *WhoIns 94*
Hamilton, Stephen Stewart 1962-
WhoScEn 94
Hamilton, Steve *DrAPF 93*
Hamilton, Steven A. 1947- *WhoAmL 94*
Hamilton, Steven G. 1939- *WhoAmL 94*
Hamilton, Susan *Who 94*
Hamilton, Susan Owens 1951-
WhoAmL 94
Hamilton, Suzanna *WhoHol 92*
Hamilton, T. Earle 1905- *WhoAm 94*
Hamilton, Theophilus Elliott 1923-
WhoBlA 94
Hamilton, Thomas Herman 1931-
WhoAm 94, WhoFI 94
Hamilton, Thomas M. 1944- *WhoAm 94*
Hamilton, Thomas Mackin, Jr. 1944-
WhoAmL 94
Hamilton, Thomas Michael 1947-
WhoAm 94
Hamilton, Thomas Stewart 1911-
WhoAm 94
Hamilton, Thomas Woolman 1948-
WhoMW 93
Hamilton, Todd Cameron *EncSF 93*
Hamilton, Tony *WhoHol 92*
Hamilton, Virginia 1936- *BlkWr 2,
BlmGWL, WhoAm 94, WhoBlA 94*
Hamilton, Virginia (Esther) 1936-
EncSF 93, TwCYAW, WrDr 94
Hamilton, Virginia Mae 1946-
WhoMW 93, WhoScEn 94
Hamilton, Virginia Van der Veer 1921-
WhoAm 94
Hamilton, W. Paul C. 1938- *WhoAmA 93*
Hamilton, Wallis Sylvester 1911-
WhoScEn 94
Hamilton, Warren Bell 1925- *WhoAm 94*
Hamilton, Wilbur Wyatt 1931-
WhoBlA 94
Hamilton, William Berry, Jr. 1929-
WhoAm 94
Hamilton, William Donald 1936-
IntWW 93, Who 94, WhoScEn 94
Hamilton, William Frank 1939-
WhoAm 94
Hamilton, William Frederick, III 1943-
WhoWest 94
Hamilton, William Howard 1918-
WhoAm 94
Hamilton, William J., Jr. 1932-
WhoAmP 93
Hamilton, William McLean 1919-
IntWW 93
Hamilton, William Milton 1925-
WhoAm 94, WhoMW 93
Hamilton, William Nathan 1926-
WhoBlA 94
Hamilton, William Rowan 1805-1865
WorScD
Hamilton, William T. 1939- *WhoAm 94*
Hamilton, William Thomas 1822-1908
WhWE
Hamilton, William Winter 1917- *Who 94*
Hamilton, Willie L. 1941- *WhoAm 94,
WhoMW 93*
Hamilton-Dalrymple, Hew *Who 94*
Hamilton Depassier, Juan *IntWW 93*
Hamilton-Edwards, Gerald (Kenneth
Savery) 1906- *WrDr 94*
Hamilton Fraser, Donald *Who 94*
Hamilton-Jones, John 1926- *Who 94*
Hamilton Of Dalzell, Baron 1938- *Who 94*
Hamilton-Rahi, Lynda Darlene 1950-
WhoBlA 94
Hamilton-Russell *Who 94*
Hamilton-Smith *Who 94*

Hamister, Donald Bruce 1920- *WhoAm 94*
Hamiyeh, Adel 1940- *IntWW 93*
Hamlar, David Duffield, Sr. 1924- *WhoBlA 94*
Hamlar, Portia Y. T. 1932- *WhoBlA 94*
Hamlet, James Frank 1921- *AfrAmG [port], WhoBlA 94*
Hamlet, Joseph Frank 1934- *WhoAm 94*
Hamlet, Ova *EncSF 93*
Hamlet, Susan H. 1954- *WhoAmA 93*
Hamlett, Dale Edward 1921- *WhoAmA 93, WhoWest 94*
Hamlett, Dilys 1928- *WhoHol 92*
Hamlett, James Gordon *WhoFI 94, WhoScEn 94*
Hamlett, Ray 1933- *WhoAmP 93*
Hamley, Donald Alfred 1931- *Who 94*
Hamley-Clifford, Molly d1956 *WhoHol 92*
Hamlin, Alan Russell 1948- *WhoFI 94*
Hamlin, Albert T. 1926- *WhoBlA 94*
Hamlin, Arthur Henry 1942- *WhoBlA 94*
Hamlin, Arthur Tenney 1913- *WhoAm 94*
Hamlin, Dan William 1947- *WhoAm 94, WhoFI 94*
Hamlin, David W. 1952- *WhoBlA 94*
Hamlin, Don Auer 1934- *WhoFI 94*
Hamlin, Donald Walter 1936- *WhoWest 94*
Hamlin, Donna Marie 1954- *WhoAm 94*
Hamlin, Douglas Scott 1959- *WhoMW 93*
Hamlin, Edmund Martin, Jr. 1949- *WhoWest 94*
Hamlin, Ernest Lee 1943- *WhoBlA 94*
Hamlin, George d1986 *WhoHol 92*
Hamlin, George 1869-1923 *NewGrDO*
Hamlin, Harry 1951- *IntMPA 94, WhoHol 92*
Hamlin, Harry Robinson 1951- *WhoAm 94*
Hamlin, James Turner, III 1929- *WhoAm 94*
Hamlin, Kenneth Eldred, Jr. 1917- *WhoAm 94*
Hamlin, Kurt Wesley 1950- *WhoScEn 94*
Hamlin, Louise 1949- *WhoAmA 93*
Hamlin, Michael John 1930- *Who 94*
Hamlin, Robert Henry 1923- *WhoAm 94*
Hamlin, Roger Eugene 1945- *WhoAm 94, WhoMW 93*
Hamlin, Scott Jeffrey 1961- *WhoScEn 94*
Hamlin, Sonya B. *WhoAm 94*
Hamlin, Susan Elizabeth 1966- *WhoWest 94*
Hamlin, Thomas Leonard 1946- *WhoAm 94*
Hamlin, Vincent T. d1993 *NewYTBS 93*
Hamling, William L(awrence) 1921- *EncSF 93*
Hamlisch, Marvin 1944- *IntDcF 2-4, IntMPA 94, IntWW 93, NewGrDO, WhoAm 94*
Hamlyn, D(avid) W(alter) 1924- *WrDr 94*
Hamlyn, David Walter 1924- *Who 94*
Hamlyn, Paul (Bertrand) 1926- *Who 94*
Hamlyn, Paul Bertrand 1926- *IntWW 93*
Hamm, Barbara Lawanda 1957- *WhoBlA 94*
Hamm, Beth Creevy 1885-1958 *WhoAmA 93N*
Hamm, Charles (Edward) 1925- *NewGrDO*
Hamm, Charles John 1937- *WhoAm 94*
Hamm, David Bernard 1948- *WhoAm 94*
Hamm, Donald Ivan 1928- *WhoAm 94*
Hamm, George Ardeil 1934- *WhoWest 94*
Hamm, Lee *WhoAmP 93*
Hamm, Patricia Ann 1943- *WhoWest 94*
Hamm, Robert M. 1944- *WhoWest 94*
Hamm, Robert MacGowan 1950- *WhoScEn 94*
Hamm, Suzanne Margaret 1943- *WhoAm 94*
Hamm, Thomas Douglas 1957- *WhoMW 93*
Hamm, Vernon Louis, Jr. 1951- *WhoMW 93*
Hamm, William Giles 1942- *WhoWest 94*
Hamm, William Joseph 1910- *WhoAm 94*
Hammack, William Franklin 1949- *WhoAmL 94*
Hammack, William S. 1961- *WhoScEn 94*
Hammad, Alam E. 1949- *WhoFI 94*
Hammadi, Sadoon 1930- *IntWW 93*
Hammaker, Paul M. 1903- *WhoAm 94*
Hammam, M. Shawky 1919- *WhoMW 93*
Hammam, James Michael 1957- *WhoMW 93*
Hamman, Rodd Arthur 1953- *WhoAmL 94*
Hamman, Steven Roger 1946- *WhoWest 94*
Hammann, Chester A. 1948- *WhoIns 94*
Hammann, Lester Everett 1927- *WhoAm 94*
Hammarskjold, Dag 1905-1961 *HisWorL [port], HisDcKW*

Hammarskjold, Knut (Olof Hjalmar Akesson) 1922- *Who 94*
Hammarskjold, Knut Olof Hjalmar Akesson 1922- *IntWW 93*
Hamm-Brucher, Hildegard 1921- *WhoWomW 91*
Hamme, Duane Eugene 1939- *WhoFI 94*
Hamme, Richard Byron 1942- *WhoFI 94*
Hammel, Ernest Martin 1939- *WhoMW 93*
Hammel, Eugene Alfred 1930- *IntWW 93*
Hammel, Harold Theodore 1921- *WhoMW 93, WhoScEn 94*
Hammel, John Wingate 1943- *WhoAmL 94*
Hammel, Sheryl Marie 1949- *WhoMW 93*
Hammel-Davis, Donna P. 1947- *WhoBlA 94*
Hammell, Grandin Gaunt 1945- *WhoWest 94*
Hammer 1962- *WhoAm 94*
Hammer, Alan Ronald 1946- *WhoAmL 94*
Hammer, Alfred Emil 1925- *WhoAm 94, WhoAmA 93*
Hammer, Alvin *WhoHol 92*
Hammer, Armand 1898-1990 *WhAm 10, WhoAmA 93N*
Hammer, Ben *WhoHol 92*
Hammer, Bernard 1933- *WhoAmL 94*
Hammer, Carl 1914- *WhoAm 94*
Hammer, Charles Lawrence, Jr. 1922- *WhoAmP 93*
Hammer, Daniel William 1932- *WhoAm 94, WhoAmL 94*
Hammer, David Lindley 1929- *WhoAmL 94, WhoMW 93*
Hammer, Donald Arthur 1942- *WhoScEn 94*
Hammer, Donald Price 1921- *WhoAm 94*
Hammer, Elizabeth B. *WhoAmA 93*
Hammer, Emanuel F 1926- *WrDr 94*
Hammer, Emanuel Frederick 1926- *WhoAm 94*
Hammer, Fred d1939 *WhoHol 92*
Hammer, Gottlieb d1993 *NewYTBS 93*
Hammer, Harold Harlan 1920- *WhoAm 94, WhoFI 94*
Hammer, Jacob Myer 1927- *WhoAm 94*
Hammer, James Dominic George 1929- *Who 94*
Hammer, James Henry 1951- *WhoScEn 94*
Hammer, Jan Harold 1939- *WhoWest 94*
Hammer, John Henry, II 1943- *WhoMW 93*
Hammer, John Morgan 1913- *WhoScEn 94*
Hammer, Kearney Lee 1947- *WhoWest 94*
Hammer, M. C. 1962- *WhoBlA 94*
Hammer, Martha W. 1945- *WhoAmL 94*
Hammer, Mary Lou Simpson 1934- *WhoAmP 93*
Hammer, Patrick, Jr. *DrAPF 93*
Hammer, Raymond Jack 1920- *Who 94*
Hammer, Richard David 1946- *WhoMW 93*
Hammer, Robert Eugene 1931- *WhoMW 93*
Hammer, Roy Armand 1934- *WhoAm 94*
Hammer, Sanford S. 1935-1990 *WhAm 10*
Hammer, Susan *WhoAmP 93*
Hammer, Susan M. 1948- *WhoAmL 94*
Hammer, Susan W. 1938- *WhoAm 94, WhoWest 94*
Hammer, Thorvald Frederick 1893- *WhAm 10*
Hammer, Victor Karl d1967 *WhoAmA 93N*
Hammer, Wade Burke 1932- *WhoAm 94*
Hammer, Will d1957 *WhoHol 92*
Hammer, Zevulun 1936- *IntWW 93*
Hammerback, John Clark 1938- *WhoWest 94*
Hammerbeck, Christopher John Anthony 1943- *Who 94*
Hammerbeck, Wanda Lee 1945- *WhoAmA 93*
Hammerich, Asger *NewGrDO*
Hammerle, Fredric Joseph 1944- *WhoAm 94*
Hammerle, Gerlinde 1940- *WhoWomW 91*
Hammerling, Robert Charles 1934- *WhoAm 94*
Hammerly, Harry Allan 1934- *WhoAm 94*
Hammerman, Kenneth Jay 1945- *WhoWest 94*
Hammerman, Marc Randall 1947- *WhoMW 93*
Hammerman, Pat Jo 1953- *WhoAmA 93*
Hammerman, Stephen Lawrence 1938- *WhoAm 94, WhoAmL 94, WhoFI 94*
Hammerschmidt, Ben L. 1947- *WhoScEn 94*
Hammerschmidt, John Paul 1922- *WhoAm 94, WhoAmP 93*
Hammerschmidt, Judith L. 1954- *WhoAmP 93*

Hammerschmidt, Ronald Francis 1951- *WhoScEn 94*
Hammersley, Frederick 1919- *WhoAmA 93*
Hammersley, John Michael 1920- *IntWW 93, Who 94*
Hammersley, Peter Gerald 1928- *Who 94*
Hammerstein, Elaine d1948 *WhoHol 92*
Hammerstein, Oscar, I 1846-1919 *NewGrDO*
Hammerstein, Oscar, II d1960 *WhoHol 92*
Hammerstein, Oscar (Greeley Clendenning), II 1895-1960 *NewGrDO*
Hammerstrom, Beverly Swoish 1944- *WhoAmP 93, WhoMW 93*
Hammerton, John Alexander 1871-1949 *DcNaB MP*
Hammerton, Rolf Eric 1926- *Who 94*
Hammes, Gordon G. 1934- *IntWW 93, WhoAm 94, WhoScEn 94*
Hammes, John A. 1924- *WrDr 94*
Hammes, Karl 1896-1939 *NewGrDO*
Hammes, Michael Noel 1941- *IntWW 93*
Hammes, Terry Marie 1955- *WhoFI 94*
Hammesfahr, Robert Winter 1954- *WhoAm 94*
Hammett, Benjamin Cowles 1931- *WhoWest 94*
Hammett, Bryant O'Dare, Jr. 1956- *WhoAmP 93*
Hammett, Clifford (James) 1917- *Who 94*
Hammett, Dashiell 1894-1961 *BlmGEL*
Hammett, (Samuel) Dashiell 1894-1961 *ConAu 42NR, RfGShF*
Hammett, Harold George 1906- *Who 94*
Hammett, Olivia *WhoHol 92*
Hammett, Polly Horton 1930- *WhoAmA 93*
Hammett, Samuel Dashiell 1894-1961 *AmCulL [port]*
Hammett, Seth *WhoAmP 93*
Hammett, William M. H. 1944- *WhoAm 94, WhoFI 94*
Hammett, Willie Anderson 1945- *WhoBlA 94*
Hammick, Stephen (George) 1926- *Who 94*
Hammill, James F. 1943- *WhoAmL 94*
Hammill, R. Joseph 1942- *WhoAmP 93*
Hamming, Richard Wesley 1915- *WhoAm 94, WhoWest 94*
Hammitt, Frederick Gnichtel 1923-1989 *WhAm 10*
Hammock, Edward R. 1938- *WhoBlA 94*
Hammock, Jim 1933- *WhoAmP 93*
Hammock, John Calvin 1944- *WhoAm 94*
Hammock, Ted Lewis 1932- *WhoAmP 93*
Hammock, Virgil Gene 1938- *WhoAmA 93*
Hammon, Jupiter 1711-c. 1800 *WhAmRev*
Hammon, Jupiter 1720?-1800? *AfrAmAl 6*
Hammon, William McDowell 1904-1989 *WhAm 10*
Hammond, Allen Lee 1943- *WhoAm 94*
Hammond, Anthony Hilgrove 1940- *Who 94*
Hammond, Arthur 1904-1991 *NewGrDO*
Hammond, Benjamin Franklin 1934- *WhoBlA 94*
Hammond, Bill 1947- *WhoAmP 93*
Hammond, Bobby E., Jr. 1953- *WhoIns 94*
Hammond, Catherine Elizabeth 1909- *Who 94*
Hammond, Charles d1941 *WhoHol 92*
Hammond, Charles Ainley 1933- *WhoAm 94*
Hammond, Charles Bessellieu 1936- *WhoAm 94, WhoScEn 94*
Hammond, Charles Earl 1960- *WhoScEn 94*
Hammond, Clarke Randolph 1945- *WhoScEn 94*
Hammond, Dale 1947- *WhoIns 94*
Hammond, David Alan 1948- *WhoAm 94*
Hammond, David Greene 1913- *WhoAm 94*
Hammond, David R. 1954- *WhoAmL 94*
Hammond, Deanna Lindberg 1942- *WhoAm 94*
Hammond, Debra Lauren 1957- *WhoBlA 94*
Hammond, Donald Leroy 1927- *WhoAm 94*
Hammond, Dorothy d1950 *WhoHol 92*
Hammond, Earl Gullette 1926- *WhoScEn 94*
Hammond, Edward H. 1944- *WhoAm 94, WhoMW 93*
Hammond, Edwin Hughes 1919- *WhoAm 94*
Hammond, Eric Albert Barratt 1929- *Who 94*
Hammond, Frank d1941 *WhoHol 92*
Hammond, Frank Jefferson, III 1953- *WhoAmL 94*
Hammond, Frank Joseph 1919- *WhoAm 94*
Hammond, Freeman d1968 *WhoHol 92*

Hammond, Gale Thomas 1939- *WhoAmA 93*
Hammond, George Denman 1923- *WhoAm 94*
Hammond, George Simms 1921- *IntWW 93, WhoAm 94, WhoScEn 94*
Hammond, Gerald (Arthur Douglas) 1926- *WrDr 94*
Hammond, Glenn Barry, Sr. 1947- *WhoAmL 94*
Hammond, H. W. 1917- *WhoAmP 93*
Hammond, Harmony 1944- *WhoAmA 93*
Hammond, Harold Francis 1908- *WhoAm 94*
Hammond, Harold Logan 1934- *WhoAm 94, WhoMW 93, WhoScEn 94*
Hammond, Herb(ert L.) 1945- *ConAu 140*
Hammond, Herbert J. 1951- *WhoAmL 94*
Hammond, Howard David 1924- *WhoAm 94, WhoScEn 94*
Hammond, J. D. 1933- *WhoAm 94, WhoFI 94*
Hammond, J(ohn) R. 1933- *WrDr 94*
Hammond, James A. 1929- *WhoBlA 94*
Hammond, James Anthony 1936- *Who 94*
Hammond, James Matthew 1930- *WhoBlA 94*
Hammond, Jane 1937- *WrDr 94*
Hammond, Jane 1950- *WhoAmA 93*
Hammond, Jane Laura *WhoAm 94*
Hammond, Jay Sterner 1922- *WhoAmP 93*
Hammond, Jeffrey Alan 1969- *WhoMW 93*
Hammond, Jerome Jerald 1942- *WhoAm 94*
Hammond, Jimmy Martin 1944- *WhoAmP 93*
Hammond, Joan 1912- *IntWW 93*
Hammond, Joan (Hood) 1912- *NewGrDO, Who 94*
Hammond, John *WhoBlA 94*
Hammond, John 1955- *WhoHol 92*
Hammond, John Henry, Jr. 1910-1987 *AmCulL*
Hammond, John R. *WhoAmP 93*
Hammond, John William, V 1946- *WhoAmP 93*
Hammond, Johnie 1932- *WhoAmP 93*
Hammond, Judy McLain 1956- *WhoWest 94*
Hammond, Karen Smith 1954- *WhoFI 94*
Hammond, Kay d1980 *WhoHol 92*
Hammond, Kay d1982 *WhoHol 92*
Hammond, Keith *EncSF 93*
Hammond, Kenneth Ray 1951- *WhoBlA 94*
Hammond, Kenneth T. 1926- *WhoBlA 94N*
Hammond, Larry A. 1945- *WhoAmL 94*
Hammond, Leslie King 1944- *WhoAmA 93*
Hammond, Lewis Maynard 1918- *WhoWest 94*
Hammond, Lily Hardy 1859-1925 *DcAmReB 2*
Hammond, Lou Rena Charlotte 1939- *WhoAm 94*
Hammond, Mac *DrAPF 93*
Hammond, Mac 1926- *WrDr 94*
Hammond, Margaret 1949- *WhoAmL 94*
Hammond, (John) Martin 1944- *Who 94*
Hammond, Mary Elizabeth Hale 1942- *WhoAm 94*
Hammond, Mary Stewart *DrAPF 93*
Hammond, Melvin Alan Ray, Jr. 1949- *WhoBlA 94*
Hammond, Michael Harry Frank 1933- *Who 94*
Hammond, Michael Peter 1932- *WhoAm 94*
Hammond, Nanci Lynne *WhoHol 92*
Hammond, Natalie Hays 1904- *WhoAmA 93N*
Hammond, Nellie Handcock 1909- *WhoAmP 93*
Hammond, Nicholas 1950- *WhoHol 92*
Hammond, Nicholas (Geoffrey Lempriere) 1907- *WrDr 94*
Hammond, Nicholas Geoffrey Lempriere 1907- *IntWW 93, Who 94*
Hammond, Norman David Curle 1944- *Who 94, WhoAm 94*
Hammond, Patricia Flood 1948- *WhoAmL 94*
Hammond, Paul Young 1929- *WhoAm 94*
Hammond, Peter 1923- *IntMPA 94, WhoHol 92*
Hammond, Phyllis Baker 1930- *WhoAmA 93*
Hammond, R. Philip 1916- *WhoAm 94*
Hammond, Ralph *DrAPF 93*
Hammond, Red 1947- *WhoAmA 93*
Hammond, Richard Horace 1950- *WhoScEn 94*
Hammond, Rick L. 1951- *WhoIns 94*
Hammond, Robert Alexander, III 1930- *WhoAm 94*
Hammond, Robert Lee 1926- *WhoAm 94*

Hammond, Roger *WhoHol 92*
Hammond, Roy John William 1928- *Who 94*
Hammond, Roy Joseph 1929- *WhoAm 94*
Hammond, Russell Kenneth 1947- *WhoAmP 93*
Hammond, Ruth *DrAPF 93*
Hammond, S. Robert, Jr. 1947- *WhoAmL 94*
Hammond, Samuel 1757-1842 *WhAmRev*
Hammond, Sidney N. *WhoAmP 93*
Hammond, Steven Alan 1953- *WhoAm 94*
Hammond, Thomas c. 1600-1658 *DcNaB MP*
Hammond, Thomas T(aylor) 1920-1993 *ConAu 140*
Hammond, Ulysses Bernard 1951- *WhoBlA 94*
Hammond, Ulysses S., Jr. 1919- *WhoBlA 94*
Hammond, Virginia d1972 *WhoHol 92*
Hammond, W. Rodney 1946- *WhoBlA 94*
Hammond, William *WhoAm 94*
Hammond, William 1727-1793 *DcNaB MP*
Hammond, William Rogers 1920-1990 *WhAm 10*
Hammond-Chambers, (Robert) Alexander 1942- *Who 94*
Hammond Innes, Ralph 1913- *IntWW 93, Who 94, WrDr 94*
Hammond-Kominsky, Cynthia Cecelia 1957- *WhoMW 93*
Hammonds, Alfred 1937- *WhoBlA 94*
Hammonds, Cleveland, Jr. 1936- *WhoBlA 94*
Hammonds, Elizabeth Ann 1968- *WhoScEn 94*
Hammond-Stroud, Derek 1926- *NewGrDO, Who 94*
Hammons, David 1943- *WhoAmA 93*
Hammons, James Hutchinson 1934- *WhoAm 94*
Hammons, Mark Edgar 1950- *WhoAmP 93*
Hammons, Royce Mitchell 1945- *WhoFI 94*
Hammons, S. Paul 1942- *WhoAmL 94*
Hammontree, Marie 1913- *WrDr 94*
Hammura, Ryo *EncSF 93*
Hammurabi fl. c. 1792BC-1750BC *HisWorL [port]*
Hamner, Earl 1923- *IntMPA 94*
Hamner, Earl Henry, Jr. 1923- *WhoAm 94*
Hamner, Granville d1993 *NewYTBS 93*
Hamner, Homer Howell 1915- *WhoAm 94, WhoScEn 94, WhoWest 94*
Hamner, Reginald Turner 1939- *WhoAmL 94*
Hamner, W. Easley 1937- *WhoFI 94*
Hamnett, Katharine 1948- *IntWW 93*
Hamnett, Thomas Orlando 1930- *Who 94*
Hamod, Sam *DrAPF 93*
Hamolsky, Milton William 1921- *WhoAm 94*
Hamon, Lucienne *WhoHol 92*
Hamon, Richard Grady 1937- *WhoAm 94*
Hamo of Hythe c. 1275-1352 *DcNaB MP*
Hamori, Csaba 1948- *IntWW 93*
Hamos, Robert Eustace 1941- *WhoWest 94*
Hamovitch, Mitzi Berger 1924-1992 *ConAu 140*
Hamovitch, William 1922- *WhoAm 94*
Hamp, Eric Pratt 1920- *WhoAm 94*
Hampden *Who 94*
Hampden, Viscount 1937- *Who 94*
Hampden, Michael Dougherty 1940- *WhoAmL 94*
Hampden, Walter d1955 *WhoHol 92*
Hampe, Michael 1935- *IntWW 93*
Hampe, Michael (Hermann) 1935- *NewGrDO*
Hampel, Alvin 1927- *WhoAm 94*
Hampel, Leonard Anthony, Jr. 1939- *WhoAm 94*
Hampel, Robert Edward 1941- *WhoAm 94*
Hampel, Ronald Claus 1932- *IntWW 93, Who 94*
Hamper, Bruce Cameron 1955- *WhoScEn 94*
Hamper, Genevieve d1971 *WhoHol 92*
Hamper, Robert Joseph 1956- *WhoAm 94, WhoFI 94, WhoMW 93*
Hampl, Patricia *DrAPF 93*
Hampsch, George (Harold) 1927- *WrDr 94*
Hampshire, Margaret Grace 1918- *Who 94*
Hampshire, Michael John 1939- *Who 94*
Hampshire, Stuart 1914- *IntWW 93*
Hampshire, Stuart (Newton) 1914- *Who 94*
Hampshire, Stuart (Newton), Sir 1914- *WrDr 94*
Hampshire, Susan 1938- *WhoHol 92*
Hampshire, Susan 1941- *IntMPA 94*

Hampshire, Susan 1942- *IntWW 93, Who 94, WhoAm 94*
Hampson, Anne *WrDr 94*
Hampson, Elwyn Lloyd 1916- *Who 94*
Hampson, Ferdinand Charles 1947- *WhoAmA 93*
Hampson, Frank 1917-1985 *EncSF 93*
Hampson, Keith 1943- *Who 94*
Hampson, Norman 1922- *IntWW 93, Who 94, WrDr 94*
Hampson, Robert (Gavin) 1948- *WrDr 94*
Hampson, Robert George 1943- *WhoAmL 94*
Hampson, Stuart 1947- *Who 94*
Hampson, Thomas 1955- *NewGrDO*
Hampson, Thomas Meredith 1929- *WhoAm 94*
Hampson-Wiest, Coraline Marie 1934- *WhoFI 94*
Hampstead, Archdeacon of *Who 94*
Hampton, Baron 1925- *Who 94*
Hampton, Ambrose Gonzales, Jr. 1926- *WhoAmA 93*
Hampton, Antony Barmore 1919- *Who 94*
Hampton, Benjamin Bertram 1925- *WhoAm 94*
Hampton, Bill 1925-1977 *WhoAmA 93N*
Hampton, Bryan 1938- *Who 94*
Hampton, Charles Edwin 1948- *WhoAmL 94*
Hampton, Christopher 1946- *BlmGEL*
Hampton, Christopher (James) 1946- *ConDr 93, IntDcT 2 [port], WrDr 94*
Hampton, Christopher James 1946- *IntWW 93, Who 94*
Hampton, Crystal d1922 *WhoHol 92*
Hampton, Delon 1933- *WhoAm 94, WhoBlA 94*
Hampton, E. Lynn 1947- *WhoAm 94*
Hampton, Edwin Harrell 1928- *WhoBlA 94*
Hampton, Elwood 1924- *WhoBlA 94*
Hampton, Faith d1949 *WhoHol 92*
Hampton, Frank, Sr. 1923- *WhoBlA 94*
Hampton, George Mervyn 1928- *WhoAmP 93*
Hampton, Glen Richard 1948- *WhoMW 93*
Hampton, Gordon Francis 1912- *WhoAm 94*
Hampton, Grace 1937- *WhoAmA 93, WhoBlA 94*
Hampton, Grayce d1963 *WhoHol 92*
Hampton, Henry 1940- *ConBlB 6 [port]*
Hampton, Henry (Eugene, Jr.) 1940- *BlkWr 2*
Hampton, Henry Eugene, Jr. 1940- *WhoAm 94, WhoBlA 94*
Hampton, Hope d1982 *WhoHol 92*
Hampton, James 1936- *IntMPA 94, WhoHol 92*
Hampton, James Wilburn 1931- *WhoScEn 94*
Hampton, John 1926- *Who 94*
Hampton, John Lewis 1935- *WhoAm 94*
Hampton, John Vernon 1929- *WhoAmP 93*
Hampton, John W. 1918- *WhoAmA 93*
Hampton, Kenneth T. *WhoAmP 93*
Hampton, Lawrence Paul 1956- *WhoAmL 94*
Hampton, Leroy 1927- *WhoAm 94, WhoBlA 94*
Hampton, Lionel 1909- *AfrAmAl 6 [port]*
Hampton, Lionel 1913- *WhoHol 92*
Hampton, Lionel Leo 1908- *WhoBlA 94*
Hampton, Lionel Leo 1913- *WhoAm 94*
Hampton, Louise d1946 *WhoHol 92*
Hampton, Margaret Josephine 1935- *WhoAm 94*
Hampton, Mark Garrison 1923- *WhoAm 94*
Hampton, Matthew Joseph 1958- *WhoScEn 94*
Hampton, Michael Eugene 1955- *WhoBlA 94*
Hampton, Myra d1945 *WhoHol 92*
Hampton, Opal Jewell 1942- *WhoBlA 94*
Hampton, Paul 1937- *WhoHol 92*
Hampton, Philip McCune 1932- *WhoAm 94*
Hampton, Phillip Jewel 1922- *WhoAmA 93, WhoBlA 94*
Hampton, Phillip Michael 1932- *WhoAm 94*
Hampton, Ralph Clayton, Jr. 1934- *WhoAm 94*
Hampton, Rex Herbert 1918- *WhoAm 94*
Hampton, Robert K., Sr. 1919- *WhoFI 94*
Hampton, Robert L. 1947- *WhoBlA 94*
Hampton, Robert Wayne 1953- *WhoFI 94*
Hampton, Rodney 1969- *WhoBlA 94*
Hampton, Ronald Everett 1945- *WhoBlA 94*
Hampton, Sandra Dee Smith 1950- *WhoFI 94*
Hampton, Thomas Earle 1950- *WhoBlA 94*

Hampton, Thurman B. 1949- *WhoBlA 94*
Hampton, Trevor Richard Walker 1930- *Who 94*
Hampton, Verne Churchill, II 1934- *WhoAm 94*
Hampton, Wade c. 1751-1835 *WhAmRev*
Hampton, Wanda Kay Baker *WhoBlA 94*
Hampton, Wayne *WhoAmP 93*
Hampton, William (Albert) 1929- *WrDr 94*
Hampton, William C. 1956- *WhoWest 94*
Hampton, William Wade, III 1915- *WhoAm 94*
Hampton, Willie L. 1933- *WhoBlA 94*
Hamra, Sam F., Jr. 1932- *WhoAmP 93*
Hamre, Gary Leslie William 1939- *WhoMW 93*
Hamre, Leif 1914- *WrDr 94*
Hamren, Nancy Van Brasch 1947- *WhoWest 94*
Hamric, Laurence Mason 1948- *WhoAmL 94*
Hamric, Peggy 1940- *WhoAmP 93*
Hamrick, Brasil Ward, Jr. 1958- *WhoFI 94*
Hamrick, Burwell d1970 *WhoHol 92*
Hamrick, Joseph Eugene, Jr. 1954- *WhoWest 94*
Hamrick, Joseph Thomas 1921- *WhoAm 94, WhoFI 94*
Hamrick, Kenneth Edison 1923- *WhAm 10*
Hamrol, Lloyd 1937- *WhoAmA 93*
Hamstra, Stephen Arthur 1959- *WhoScEn 94*
Hamsun, Knut 1859-1952 *TwCLC 49 [port]*
Hamwee, Baroness 1947- *Who 94*
Hamwi, Richard Alexander 1947- *WhoAmA 93*
Ham-Ying, J. Michael 1956- *WhoBlA 94*
Hamylton Jones, Keith 1924- *Who 94*
Hamza, Ahmed Amin 1941- *IntWW 93*
Hamzaee, Reza Gholi 1951- *WhoMW 93*
Hamzah, Razaleigh *IntWW 93*
Hamzeh, Zaid 1932- *IntWW 93*
Hamzehee, Hossein Gholi 1956- *WhoScEn 94*
Hamzy, Joseph Amin 1915- *WhoAmP 93*
Han, Anna M. 1956- *WhoAsA 94*
Han, Byung Joon 1959- *WhoAsA 94*
Han, Chien-Pai 1936- *WhoAm 94, WhoAsA 94*
Han, Chingping Jim 1957- *WhoAsA 94, WhoScEn 94*
Han, Grace Yang 1941- *WhoAsA 94*
Han, In-Sop 1936- *WhoAsA 94*
Han, Ittah 1939- *WhoFI 94, WhoWest 94*
Han, Jaok 1930- *WhoAm 94, WhoAsA 94*
Han, Je-Chin 1946- *WhoAsA 94, WhoScEn 94*
Han, Jiawei 1949- *WhoScEn 94, WhoWest 94*
Han, Jinchen 1938- *WhoAsA 94*
Han, Kenneth N. 1938- *WhoAsA 94*
Han, Li-Ming 1953- *WhoWest 94*
Han, Lit S. 1925- *WhoAm 94*
Han, Maggie *WhoHol 92*
Han, Moo-Young 1934- *WhoAm 94, WhoAsA 94*
Han, Oksoo 1960- *WhoScEn 94*
Han, Ruijing 1963- *WhoScEn 94*
Han, Sang Hyun 1959- *WhoScEn 94*
Han, Sherman Hsiao-min 1948- *WhoAsA 94*
Han, Susan S. 1957- *WhoAsA 94*
Han, Weimin 1963- *WhoMW 93*
Han, Xianming Lance 1963- *WhoAsA 94, WhoMW 93*
Hanable, William Shannon 1938- *WhoWest 94*
Hanafan, Thomas Patrick 1947- *WhoAmP 93*
Hanafusa, Hidesaburo 1929- *WhoAm 94, WhoAsA 94, WhoScEn 94*
Hanahan, Donald James 1919- *WhoAm 94*
Hanahan, James Lake 1932- *WhoFI 94*
Hanai, Toshihiko 1941- *WhoScEn 94*
Han Aili 1937- *BlmGWL*
Han Aiping 1962- *WhoPRCh 91 [port]*
Hanami, Clement S. 1961- *WhoAsA 94*
Hanamirian, Varujan 1952- *WhoFI 94, WhoScEn 94*
Hanamura, Nihachiro *WhoAm 94, WhoFI 94*
Hanan, Joe John 1931- *WhoAm 94*
Hanan, Patrick Dewes 1927- *WhoAm 94*
Hananiya, Haldu A. 1942- *Who 94*
Hanard, Patricia Ann 1943- *WhoMW 93*
Hanau, Kenneth John, Jr. 1927- *WhoAm 94, WhoFI 94*
Hanauer, Joe Franklin 1937- *WhoAm 94, WhoWest 94*
Hanawalt, Philip Courtland 1931- *WhoAm 94, WhoWest 94*
Hanaway, Donald 1933- *WhoAmP 93*
Hanaway, Paul E. 1932- *WhoAmP 93*

Hanaway, Sandra K. 1934- *WhoAmP 93*
Han Bangyan 1931- *WhoPRCh 91*
Han Boping *WhoPRCh 91*
Hanbury, George Lafayette, II 1943- *WhoAm 94*
Hanbury, Hanmer (Cecil) 1916- *Who 94*
Hanbury, Harold Grenville 1898- *WrDr 94*
Hanbury, Harold Greville d1993 *Who 94N*
Hanbury, John (Capel) 1908- *Who 94*
Hanbury, Marshall E. 1944- *WhoAm 94*
Hanbury, Una 1909-1990 *WhAm 10*
Hanbury-Tenison, Richard 1925- *Who 94*
Hanbury-Tenison, Robin 1936- *WrDr 94*
Hanbury-Tension, Airling Robin 1936- *Who 94*
Hanbury-Tracy *Who 94*
Hance, Anthony James 1932- *WhoWest 94*
Hance, Harvey 1957- *WhoHisp 94*
Hance, James Henry, Jr. 1944- *WhoAm 94*
Hance, Kent 1942- *WhoAmP 93*
Hanchey, Janet Lynn 1956- *WhoAmA 93*
Hanchuruck, Stephen P. 1955- *WhoAmP 93*
Hancock, Allan G. 1935- *WhoAmP 93*
Hancock, Allen C. 1908- *WhoBlA 94*
Hancock, Alton Guy 1932- *WhoAmL 94*
Hancock, Barbara *WhoHol 92*
Hancock, Charles Cavanaugh, Jr. 1935- *WhoAm 94*
Hancock, Charles M. 1936- *WhoAmP 93*
Hancock, Charles Wilbourne 1924- *WhoAm 94*
Hancock, Christine *Who 94*
Hancock, David (John Stowell) 1934- *Who 94*
Hancock, Deana Lori 1961- *WhoMW 93*
Hancock, Don Ray 1948- *WhoScEn 94, WhoWest 94*
Hancock, Elisabeth Joy 1947- *Who 94*
Hancock, Ellen Marie 1943- *WhoAm 94, WhoFI 94*
Hancock, Emily Stone 1945- *WhoAm 94, WhoWest 94*
Hancock, Ethnea Mary 1937- *Who 94*
Hancock, Eugene Wilson White 1929- *WhoBlA 94*
Hancock, Gary C. 1951- *WhoAmP 93*
Hancock, Geoffrey Francis 1926- *Who 94*
Hancock, Geoffrey White 1946- *WhoAm 94*
Hancock, Gerre Edward 1934- *WhoAm 94*
Hancock, Gwendolyn Carter 1933- *WhoBlA 94*
Hancock, H(arrie) Irving 1868-1922 *EncSF 93*
Hancock, Harriet Daniels 1936- *WhoAmL 94*
Hancock, Herbert Jeffrey 1940- *WhoAm 94, WhoBlA 94*
Hancock, Herbie 1940- *AfrAmAl 6 [port], WhoHol 92*
Hancock, Ian (Robert) 1940- *ConAu 142*
Hancock, Ian Francis 1942- *WhoAm 94*
Hancock, James (A.) 1921- *ConAu 141*
Hancock, James Beaty *WhoMW 93, WhoScEn 94*
Hancock, James Hughes 1931- *WhoAm 94, WhoAmL 94*
Hancock, Joan Herrin 1930- *WhoFI 94, WhoMW 93*
Hancock, John *AmRev, WhoHol 92*
Hancock, John d1992 *WhAm 10, WhoBlA 94N*
Hancock, John 1737-1793 *HisWorL, WhAmRev [port]*
Hancock, John 1939- *IntMPA 94*
Hancock, John Allan 1940- *WhoFI 94*
Hancock, John C. 1938- *WhoScEn 94*
Hancock, John Coulter 1929- *WhoAm 94*
Hancock, John D. 1939- *WhoAm 94*
Hancock, John P., Jr. 1949- *WhoAmL 94*
Hancock, John Ray 1964- *WhoAmP 93*
Hancock, John Walker, III 1937- *WhoAm 94*
Hancock, Keith Jackson 1935- *Who 94*
Hancock, Kenneth G. d1993 *NewYTBS 93*
Hancock, Loni 1940- *WhoAm 94, WhoWest 94*
Hancock, Loni 1950- *WhoAmP 93*
Hancock, Malcolm Cyril 1936-1993 *ConAu 140*
Hancock, Marion Donald 1939- *WhoAm 94*
Hancock, Mark Edward 1945- *WhoFI 94*
Hancock, Mel 1929- *CngDr 93, WhoAm 94, WhoAmP 93, WhoMW 93*
Hancock, Michael Stephen 1917- *Who 94*
Hancock, Michael Thomas 1946- *Who 94*
Hancock, Newell Leslie 1943- *WhoWest 94*
Hancock, Norman 1916- *Who 94*
Hancock, P(ercy) E(llis) Thompson 1904- *Who 94*

Hancock, Prentis *WhoHol 92*
Hancock, Robert D., Jr. 1944- *WhoAmL 94*
Hancock, Robert Jack 1928- *WhoAm 94*
Hancock, Ronald John 1934- *Who 94*
Hancock, S. Lee 1955- *WhoAmL 94*
Hancock, Sheila *Who 94*
Hancock, Sheila 1933- *WhoHol 92*
Hancock, Stewart F., Jr. 1923- *WhoAmL 94*
Hancock, Stewart Freeman, Jr. 1923- *WhoAmP 93*
Hancock, Susan Hunter 1944- *WhoWest 94*
Hancock, Thomas 1786-1865 *WorInv*
Hancock, Thomas 1913- *WhoAm 94*
Hancock, Thomas Emerson 1949- *WhoScEn 94*
Hancock, Tony d1968 *WhoHol 92*
Hancock, V. Ray 1926- *WhoAmP 93*
Hancock, Valston Eldridge 1907- *Who 94*
Hancock, Walker (Kirtland) 1901- *WhoAmA 93*
Hancock, Walker Kirtland 1901- *WhoAm 94*
Hancock, Wayne M. *WhoAmL 94*
Hancock, William Frank, Jr. 1942- *WhoFI 94*
Hancock, William Geremain, Jr. 1943- *WhoAmP 93*
Hancock, William Glenn 1950- *WhoAm 94*
Hancock, William Marvin 1957- *WhoScEn 94*
Hancocks, David Morgan 1941- *WhoAm 94, WhoWest 94*
Hancox, David Robert 1951- *WhoFI 94*
Hancox, Ralph 1929- *WhoAm 94*
Hancox, Robert Ernest 1943- *WhoAm 94, WhoFI 94*
Hand, Bethlyn J. *IntMPA 94*
Hand, Brian Edward 1963- *WhoAm 94*
Hand, Cadet Hammond, Jr. 1920- *WhoAm 94, WhoScEn 94*
Hand, Edward 1744-1802 *WhAmRev*
Hand, Edward 1774-1802 *AmRev*
Hand, Elaine 1934- *WhoAmP 93*
Hand, Elbert O. 1939- *WhoAm 94, WhoFI 94*
Hand, Elizabeth 1957- *EncSF 93, WrDr 94*
Hand, Geoffrey David 1918- *Who 94*
Hand, Geoffrey Joseph Philip 1931- *Who 94, WrDr 94*
Hand, Herbert Hensley 1931- *WhoAm 94, WhoFI 94*
Hand, Joan Carole *DrAPF 93*
Hand, John 1926- *WhoAm 94*
Hand, John Lester 1947- *Who 94*
Hand, John Oliver 1941- *WhoAm 94, WhoAmA 93*
Hand, Jon Thomas 1963- *WhoBlA 94*
Hand, Kernan K. Skip 1945- *WhoAmP 93*
Hand, Molly Williams 1892-1951 *WhoAmA 93N*
Hand, Paul Edgar 1931- *WhoFI 94*
Hand, Perry A. 1945- *WhoAmP 93*
Hand, Peter James 1937- *WhoAm 94, WhoScEn 94*
Hand, Raymond W. 1928- *WhoAmP 93*
Hand, Robert E. 1947- *WhoAmL 94*
Hand, Robert S. 1942- *AstEnc*
Hand, Roger 1938- *WhoAm 94*
Hand, Stephen Block 1942- *WhoAmL 94*
Hand, William Brevard 1924- *WhoAmL 94*
Hand, William M. *WhoAmP 93*
Handal, Kenneth V. 1949- *WhoAmL 94*
Handberg, Irene Deak *WhoAm 94*
Handcock *Who 94*
Handel, Bernard 1926- *WhoFI 94*
Handel, David Jonathan 1946- *WhoAm 94, WhoMW 93*
Handel, George Frederick 1685-1759 *BlmGEL*
Handel, George Frideric 1685-1759 *NewGrDO*
Handel, Leo A. 1924- *IntMPA 94*
Handel, Michael I. 1942- *WrDr 94*
Handel, Morton Emanuel 1935- *WhoAm 94, WhoFI 94*
Handel, Peter H. 1937- *WhoAm 94*
Handel, Richard Craig 1945- *WhoAmL 94, WhoFI 94*
Handel, Stephen Edward 1942- *WhoAmL 94*
Handel, Ted M. 1954- *WhoAmL 94*
Handel, William Keating 1935- *WhoFI 94, WhoWest 94*
Handel, Yitzchak S. 1940- *WhoScEn 94*
Handell, Albert George 1937- *WhoAmA 93*
Handelman, Alice Roberta 1943- *WhoMW 93*
Handelman, Stanley Myron *WhoHol 92*
Handel-Mazzetti, Enrica von 1871-1955 *BlmGWL*
Handelsman, Harold S. 1946- *WhoAm 94, WhoFI 94*
Handelsman, Lawrence Marc 1945- *WhoAm 94*
Handelsman, M. Gene 1923- *WhoAm 94*
Handelsman, Mitchell M. 1954- *WhoScEn 94*
Han Depei *WhoPRCh 91*
Handey, Jack 1949- *ConAu 141*
Handford, (George) Clive *Who 94*
Handford, Jack 1917- *WhoWest 94*
Handford, Martin John 1956- *WhoAm 94*
Handforth, Ruth d1965 *WhoHol 92*
Handforth, Thomas S. 1897-1948 *WhoAmA 93N*
Handke, Peter *DrAPF 93*
Handke, Peter 1942- *ConWorW 93, IntDcT 2*
Handke-Schwarz, Libgart 1941- *IntWW 93*
Handl, Irene d1987 *WhoHol 92*
Handlan, Allen Layman 1947- *WhoAmL 94*
Handleman, David 1914- *WhoFI 94*
Handler, Adam Michael 1959- *WhoAmL 94*
Handler, Alan B. 1931- *WhoAm 94, WhoAmL 94, WhoAmP 93*
Handler, Arthur M. 1937- *WhoAm 94, WhoAmL 94*
Handler, Audrey 1934- *WhoAmA 93*
Handler, Audrey Solomon 1934- *WhoMW 93*
Handler, Carole Enid 1939- *WhoAm 94*
Handler, David 1952- *ConAu 141*
Handler, Elisabeth Helen 1944- *WhoAm 94*
Handler, Enid Irene 1932- *WhoScEn 94*
Handler, Evan 1961- *WhoHol 92*
Handler, George 1928- *WhoFI 94*
Handler, Harold Robert 1935- *WhoAm 94*
Handler, Jerome Sidney 1933- *WhoAm 94*
Handler, Lauren E. 1953- *WhoAmL 94*
Handler, Lawrence David 1945- *WhoAm 94*
Handler, Mark S. 1933- *WhoAm 94, WhoFI 94*
Handler, Milton 1903- *WhoAm 94*
Handler, Mimi 1934- *WhoAm 94*
Handler, Sidney 1932- *WhoAm 94*
Handler, Steven P. 1946- *WhoAm 94, WhoAmL 94*
Handler, T. Richard 1946- *WhoAmL 94*
Handlery, Paul Robert 1920- *WhoAm 94*
Handley, Anthony Michael 1936- *Who 94*
Handley, Carol Margaret 1929- *Who 94*
Handley, David John D. *Who 94*
Handley, Eric Walter 1926- *IntWW 93, Who 94, WrDr 94*
Handley, Gerald Matthew 1942- *WhoAmL 94*
Handley, Graham Roderick 1926- *WrDr 94*
Handley, Helen M. 1921- *WhoAmP 93*
Handley, Leon Hunter 1927- *WhoAm 94, WhoAmL 94*
Handley, Mark Thurston 1956- *WhoAmL 94*
Handley, Max (Adrian Robert) 1945- *EncSF 93*
Handley, Mike d1981 *WhoHol 92*
Handley, Thomas Lange 1949- *WhoMW 93*
Handley, Tommy d1949 *WhoHol 92*
Handley, Vernon George 1930- *IntWW 93, Who 94*
Handley-Taylor, Geoffrey 1920- *Who 94*
Handlin, Jim *DrAPF 93*
Handlin, Oscar 1915- *IntWW 93, Who 94, WhoAm 94*
Handman, Barbara Ann 1928- *WhoAmP 93*
Handman, Lou d1956 *WhoHol 92*
Handman, Toby d1981 *WhoHol 92*
Handon, Marshall R., Jr. 1937- *WhoBlA 94*
Handron, Deanne Westfall 1955- *WhoWest 94*
Hands, David Richard Granville 1943- *Who 94*
Hands, Rachel Indra 1961- *WhoMW 93*
Hands, Terence David 1941- *IntWW 93, Who 94, WhoAm 94*
Hands, William Arthur 1917- *WhAm 10*
Handschu, Barbara Ellen 1942- *WhoAmL 94*
Handschumacher, Albert Gustave 1918- *WhoAm 94, WhoWest 94*
Handsome Lake 1735-1815 *DcAmReB 2*
Handt, Herbert 1926- *NewGrDO*
Handville, Robert T. 1924- *WhoAmA 93*
Handwerker, A. M. 1928- *WhoFI 94, WhoScEn 94*
Handwerker, Sy 1933- *WhoMW 93*
Handworth, Elsie *WhoHol 92*
Handworth, Octavia d1979 *WhoHol 92*
Handy (Miller), Dorothy Antoinette 1930- *AfrAmAl 6*
Handy, Alice Warner 1948- *WhoAm 94*
Handy, Benny Ben 1937- *WhoAmP 93*
Handy, Charles Brian 1932- *Who 94*
Handy, Charles Brooks 1924- *WhoAm 94*
Handy, Delores 1947- *WhoBlA 94*
Handy, Drucilla 1924- *WhoMW 93*
Handy, Edward Otis, Jr. 1929- *WhoAm 94*
Handy, Floyd E. *WhoAmP 93*
Handy, James *WhoHol 92*
Handy, James R. 1954- *WhoAmP 93*
Handy, John Richard, III 1933- *WhoBlA 94*
Handy, Lillian B. *WhoBlA 94*
Handy, Lyman Lee 1919- *WhoAm 94*
Handy, Nicholas Charles 1941- *Who 94*
Handy, Nixeon Civille *DrAPF 93*
Handy, Richard Lincoln 1929- *WhoAm 94*
Handy, Robert Maxwell 1931- *WhoAm 94*
Handy, Rollo 1927- *WrDr 94*
Handy, Rollo Leroy 1927- *WhoAm 94, WhoFI 94*
Handy, W. C. d1958 *WhoHol 92*
Handy, William Christopher 1873-1958 *AfrAmAl 6 [port]*
Handy, William Russell 1950- *WhoMW 93*
Handy, William Talbot, Jr. 1924- *WhoAm 94, WhoBlA 94, WhoMW 93*
Handy-Miller, D. Antoinette 1930- *WhoBlA 94*
Handysides, Clarence d1931 *WhoHol 92*
Handzel, Patricia Reis 1936- *WhoAmP 93*
Handzel, Steven Jeffrey 1954- *WhoFI 94*
Handzlik, Jan Lawrence 1945- *WhoAm 94, WhoAmL 94, WhoWest 94*
Handzova, Viera 1931- *BlmGWL*
Hane, Mikiso 1922- *WhoAm 94*
Haneke, Ralph Adair 1927- *WhoFI 94*
Haneman, Howard Frederick 1928- *WhoAmP 93*
Haneman, Vincent Siering, Jr. 1924- *WhoWest 94*
Hanemann, Carl C. 1944- *WhoAmL 94*
Hanen, Andrew Scott 1953- *WhoAm 94, WhoAmL 94*
Hanenkrat, Frank Thomas 1939- *WhoAm 94*
Hanes, David Gordon 1941-1991 *WhAm 10*
Hanes, Donald Dean 1926- *WhoAmP 93*
Hanes, Frank Borden *DrAPF 93*
Hanes, Frank Borden 1920- *WhoAm 94, WrDr 94*
Hanes, James (Albert) 1924- *WhoAmA 93*
Hanes, James Henry 1922- *WhoAm 94*
Hanes, John G. 1936- *WhoAmP 93, WhoWest 94*
Hanes, John T. 1936- *WhoFI 94, WhoMW 93*
Hanes, Ralph Philip, Jr. 1926- *WhoAm 94*
Hanesian, Deran 1927- *WhoAm 94*
Haney, Anne *WhoHol 92*
Haney, Carol d1964 *WhoHol 92*
Haney, Darnel L. 1937- *WhoBlA 94*
Haney, Daryl *WhoHol 92*
Haney, David d1985 *WhoHol 92*
Haney, Don Lee 1934- *WhoBlA 94*
Haney, Enoch Kelly 1940- *WhoAmP 93*
Haney, Fred 1898- *WhAm 10*
Haney, Harold Levon 1929- *WhoWest 94*
Haney, J. Terrence 1933- *WhoAm 94*
Haney, James Stuart 1945- *WhoAmP 93*
Haney, Jim *WhoAmP 93*
Haney, Napoleon 1926- *WhoBlA 94*
Haney, Paul Dunlap 1911- *WhAm 10*
Haney, Raymond Lee 1939- *WhoFI 94*
Haney, Robert Locke 1928- *WhoFI 94, WhoWest 94*
Haney, William D., III 1945- *WhoAm 94, WhoAmL 94*
Haney, William Valentine Patrick 1925- *WrDr 94*
Hanf, James Alphonso 1923- *WhoWest 94*
Hanf, Noel E., Jr. 1940- *WhoAmL 94*
Hanff, Helene 1916- *Who 94, WrDr 94*
Hanfling, Phyllis Ann 1942- *WhoAmL 94*
Hanfmann, George M. A. 1911-1986 *WhoAmA 93N*
Hanford, Agnes Rutledge 1927- *WhoFI 94*
Hanford, Charles B. d1926 *WhoHol 92*
Hanford, Craig Bradley 1953- *WhoBlA 94*
Hanford, George Hyde 1920- *WhoAm 94*
Hanford, Mary *DrAPF 93*
Hanft, Helen 1937- *WhoHol 92*
Hanft, John D. 1943- *WhoIns 94*
Hanft, Jules d1936 *WhoHol 92*
Hanft, Ruth 1929- *IntWW 93*
Hanft, Ruth S. Samuels 1929- *WhoAm 94*
Han Fucai 1929- *WhoPRCh 91 [port]*
Han Fudong *WhoPRCh 91*
Han Fuyou *WhoPRCh 91 [port]*
Hang, Tru 1945- *WhoAsA 94*
Hangartner, Thomas Niklaus 1949- *WhoMW 93*
Hangen, Bruce Boyer 1947- *WhoAm 94, WhoMW 93*
Hangen, Welles d1970 *NewYTBS 93 [port]*
Hanger, Emmett Wilson, Jr. 1948- *WhoAmP 93*
Hanger, George c. 1751-1824 *AmRev, WhAmRev*
Hanger, William Sherwood 1945- *WhoMW 93*
Hang Faji 1946- *WhoPRCh 91 [port]*
Hangley, William Thomas 1941- *WhoAmL 94*
Hangsleben, John William 1959- *WhoMW 93*
Han Guang *WhoPRCh 91*
Han Guang 1912- *WhoPRCh 91 [port]*
Hang Yin 1944- *BlmGWL*
Hang Ying 1944- *IntWW 93, WhoPRCh 91 [port]*
Hanham, Harold John 1928- *IntWW 93, Who 94*
Hanham, Leonard Edward 1921- *Who 94*
Hanham, Michael (William) 1922- *Who 94*
Han Hongshu 1933- *WhoPRCh 91 [port]*
Han Huaizhi 1922- *WhoPRCh 91 [port]*
Han Huaizhi, Lieut.-Gen. 1922- *IntWW 93*
Hani, Chris d1993 *IntWW 93N*
Hani, Chris 1942- *IntWW 93*
Hani, Chris 1942-1993 *ConBlB 6 [port], News 93*
Hanifen, Richard Charles 1931- *WhoAm 94, WhoWest 94*
Hanifin, Timothy John 1931- *WhoAmL 94*
Hanigan, Lawrence 1925- *WhoAm 94*
Hanigan, Marvin Frank 1931- *WhoAm 94*
Hanigan, Thomas Edward, Jr. 1922-1991 *WhAm 10*
Hanin, Israel 1937- *WhoAm 94*
Hanin, Roger 1925- *IntWW 93, WhoHol 92*
Hanisch, Kathy Ann *WhoMW 93, WhoScEn 94*
Hanisko, John-Cyril Patrick 1937- *WhoMW 93, WhoScEn 94*
Han Jian 1957- *WhoPRCh 91 [port]*
Hank, Bernard J., Jr. 1929- *WhoAm 94*
Hanka, Erika 1905-1958 *IntDcB*
Hankamer, Jorge 1940- *WhoWest 94*
Hanke, Byron Reidt 1911- *WhoAm 94*
Hanke, David Robert 1952- *WhoMW 93*
Hanke, Henriette 1785-1862 *BlmGWL*
Hanke, Karl 1750-1803 *NewGrDO*
Hanke, Karl William, III 1958- *WhoMW 93*
Hanke, Lewis Ulysses 1905- *IntWW 93*
Han Kehua 1919- *WhoPRCh 91 [port]*
Hankel, Wilhelm 1929- *IntWW 93*
Hanken, Garrett L. 1948- *WhoAmL 94*
Hanken, James Carl 1939- *WhoAm 94*
Hankenson, Edward Craig, Jr. 1935- *WhoAm 94*
Hankerson, Barry *WhoHol 92*
Hankes, Harold Lee 1936- *WhoMW 93*
Hankes, Lester Valentine 1955- *WhoFI 94*
Hankes-Drielsma, Claude Dunbar 1949- *IntWW 93, Who 94*
Hanket, Mark John 1943- *WhoAm 94, WhoAmL 94*
Hankey, Baron 1905- *Who 94*
Hankey, Henry Arthur Alers 1914- *Who 94*
Hankey, Robert E. 1931- *WhoAmA 93*
Hankey, Robert Maurice Alers 1905- *IntWW 93*
Hankey, Ronald Shannon 1962- *WhoFI 94*
Hankin, Arthur W. 1943- *WhoAmL 94*
Hankin, Bernard Jacob 1913- *WhoAm 94*
Hankin, C(herry) A(nne) 1937- *WrDr 94*
Hankin, Elaine Krieger 1938- *WhoAm 94*
Hankin, Errol Patrick 1942- *WhoAm 94*
Hankin, Larry *WhoHol 92*
Hankin, Leonard J. 1917- *WhoAm 94*
Hankin, Mitchell Robert 1949- *WhoAmL 94*
Hankin, Noel Newton 1946- *WhoBlA 94*
Hankin, Robert Michael 1930- *WhoAm 94*
Hankins, Andrew Jay, Jr. 1942- *WhoBlA 94*
Hankins, Beverly Ann 1940- *WhoFI 94*
Hankins, (Frederick) Geoffrey 1926- *Who 94*
Hankins, Harold Charles Arthur 1930- *Who 94*
Hankins, Hesterly G., III 1950- *WhoBlA 94, WhoFI 94, WhoScEn 94, WhoWest 94*
Hankins, Irvin W., III 1946- *WhoAmL 94*
Hankins, Marie Garner 1943- *WhoMW 93*
Hankins, Raleigh Walter 1958- *WhoScEn 94*
Hankins, Shirley Williams 1931- *WhoAmP 93*
Hankins, Timothy Howard 1956- *WhoAmL 94*
Hankins, Winston H. 1932- *WhoIns 94*

Hankinson, Alan 1926- *WrDr 94*
Hankinson, Charlene Joy 1949-
WhoMW 93
Hankinson, James Floyd 1943-
WhoAm 94, WhoFI 94
Hankinson, Risdon William 1938-
WhoScEn 94
Hankis, Roy Allen 1943- *WhoMW 93*
Hankla, Cathryn *DrAPF 93*
Hankour, Rachid 1960- *WhoScEn 94*
Hanks, Alan R. 1939- *WhoAm 94,
WhoScEn 94*
Hanks, Bryan Cayce 1896- *WhAm 10*
Hanks, David Allen 1940- *WhoAmA 93*
Hanks, Eugene Ralph 1918- *WhoWest 94*
Hanks, Gary Arlin 1944- *WhoWest 94*
Hanks, Grace Mary 1954- *WhoAm 94*
Hanks, James Judge, Jr. 1943-
WhoAm 94, WhoAmL 94
Hanks, John Dennis 1948- *WhoAmP 93*
Hanks, Larry Lincoln 1943- *WhoAmP 93*
Hanks, Nancy 1927-1983 *WhoAmA 93N*
Hanks, Patrick Wyndham 1940- *Who 94*
Hanks, Robert J. 1943- *WhoFI 94*
Hanks, Robert Jack 1923- *WhoAm 94*
Hanks, Tom *IntWW 93*
Hanks, Tom 1956- *IntMPA 94,
WhoAm 94, WhoCom, WhoHol 92*
Hanle, Paul Arthur 1947- *WhoAm 94*
Hanlen, John (Garrett) 1922-
WhoAmA 93
Hanley, Aidan Alexander *DrAPF 93*
Hanley, Alyce A. 1933- *WhoAmP 93*
Hanley, Benjamin 1941- *WhoAmP 93*
Hanley, Charles 1920- *WhoAm 94*
Hanley, Clifford 1922- *WrDr 94*
Hanley, Dana Carlton 1962- *WhoAmP 93*
Hanley, Edward J. 1903-1982
EncABHB 9 [port]
Hanley, Frank 1930- *WhoAm 94,
WhoFI 94*
Hanley, Fred William 1939- *WhoWest 94*
Hanley, George T. 1945- *WhoAmP 93*
Hanley, Gerald (Anthony) 1916- *WrDr 94*
Hanley, Howard Granville 1909- *Who 94*
Hanley, J. Frank, II 1943- *WhoBlA 94*
Hanley, Jack 1952- *WhoAmA 93*
Hanley, James 1901-1985 *ConDr 93,
EncSF 93*
Hanley, James Michael 1920-
WhoAmP 93
Hanley, Jenny 1947- *WhoHol 92*
Hanley, Jeremy James 1945- *Who 94*
Hanley, Jimmy d1970 *WhoHol 92*
Hanley, John Francis 1955- *WhoAmP 93*
Hanley, John W., Jr. 1949- *WhoAmL 94*
Hanley, Joseph Andrew 1966-
WhoScEn 94
Hanley, Kevin Lance 1961- *WhoWest 94*
Hanley, Mark Stephen 1958- *WhoAmP 93*
Hanley, Michael (Bowen) 1918- *Who 94*
Hanley, Michelle Boucher 1958-
WhoScEn 94
Hanley, Paul Windsor 1944- *WhoFI 94*
Hanley, Peter Ronald 1939- *WhoAm 94*
Hanley, Priscilla Hobson 1950-
WhoAmP 93
Hanley, Robert, Jr. 1933- *WhoAm 94*
Hanley, Robert Francis 1924-1991
WhAm 10
Hanley, T. Edward d1969 *WhoAmA 93N*
Hanley, Thomas Francis, III 1951-
WhoAmL 94
Hanley, Thomas Patrick 1951-
WhoMW 93
Hanley, Thomas Richard 1945-
WhoAm 94
Hanley, William *DrAPF 93*
Hanley, William 1931- *ConDr 93,
WrDr 94*
Hanley, William B., Jr. d1959 *WhoHol 92*
Han Lili *WhoPRCh 91*
Hanlin, Hugh Carey 1925- *WhoAm 94*
Hanlin, Russell L. 1932- *WhoAm 94,
WhoFI 94*
Hanlon, Bert d1972 *WhoHol 92*
Hanlon, David G. 1935- *WhoAmP 93*
Hanlon, David Patrick 1944- *WhoFI 94*
Hanlon, Edward d1931 *WhoHol 92*
Hanlon, Emily *DrAPF 93*
Hanlon, Francis X. 1941- *WhoAmL 94*
Hanlon, James Allison 1937- *WhoAm 94*
Hanlon, John Joseph 1912-1988
WhAm 10
Hanlon, Neal B. 1945- *WhoAmP 93*
Hanlon, Robert Timothy 1937-
WhoAm 94
Hanlon, Tom d1970 *WhoHol 92*
Hanlon, Tom Allan 1945- *WhoAmP 93*
Hanmai Saori *WhoPRCh 91*
Han Meilin 1936- *IntWW 93,
WhoPRCh 91 [port]*
Hanmer, Don R. 1945- *WhoAmL 94*
Hanmer, Hiram R(upert) 1896- *WhAm 10*
Hanmer, John (Wyndham Edward) 1928-
Who 94
Hanmer, Stephen Read, Jr. 1933-
WhoAm 94

Hann, Derek William 1935- *Who 94*
Hann, Georg 1897-1950 *NewGrDO*
Hann, James 1933- *Who 94, WhoScEn 94*
Hann, James David 1931- *WhoAm 94*
Hann, Judith 1942- *SmATA 77 [port]*
Hann, Roy William, Jr. 1934- *WhoAm 94*
Hann, William Donald 1928-
WhoScEn 94
Hanna, Annette Adrian *WhoAmA 93*
Hanna, Betty d1976 *WhoHol 92*
Hanna, Carey McConnell 1941-
WhoAm 94
Hanna, Cassandra H. 1940- *WhoBlA 94*
Hanna, Colin Arthur 1946- *WhoFI 94*
Hanna, David *WhoScEn 94*
Hanna, Donald Eugene 1947-
WhoWest 94
Hanna, Eduardo Zacarias 1941-
WhoFI 94
Hanna, Frank Joseph 1939- *WhoFI 94*
Hanna, Franklyn d1931 *WhoHol 92*
Hanna, Geoffrey Chalmers 1920-
WhoAm 94
Hanna, George Parker 1918- *WhoScEn 94*
Hanna, George Verner, III 1943-
WhoAm 94, WhoAmL 94
Hanna, Harlington Leroy, Jr. 1951-
WhoBlA 94
Hanna, Harry Adolphus 1940-
WhoAm 94, WhoAmL 94
Hanna, Harry Mitchell 1936-
WhoAmL 94
Hanna, Jack (Bushnell) 1947- *ConAu 141,
SmATA 74 [port]*
Hanna, Jack Bushnell 1947- *WhoAm 94*
Hanna, Jerry Glenn 1946- *WhoAmP 93*
Hanna, John A. 1942- *WhoAm 94*
Hanna, John P. 1918- *WhoIns 94*
Hanna, Katherine 1913-1988
WhoAmA 93N
Hanna, Katherine Merritt 1953-
WhoAmP 93
Hanna, Mark Alan 1970- *WhoMW 93*
Hanna, Marsha L. 1951- *WhoMW 93*
Hanna, Martin Shad 1940- *WhoAm 94,
WhoAmP 93*
Hanna, Maxcy Grover, Jr. 1940-
WhoScEn 94
Hanna, Michael George, Jr. 1936-
WhoAm 94
Hanna, Mike 1953- *WhoAmP 93*
Hanna, Milford A. 1947- *WhoScEn 94*
Hanna, Nessim 1938- *WhoAm 94*
Hanna, Paul Dean, Jr. *WhoAmA 93*
Hanna, R. Philip d1957 *WhoHol 92*
Hanna, Ralph, III 1942- *WhoAm 94*
Hanna, Robert C. 1933- *WhoAm 94,
WhoFI 94*
Hanna, Robert Cecil 1937- *WhoAmL 94*
Hanna, Roberta Jones 1925- *WhoAm 94*
Hanna, Roland *WhoBlA 94*
Hanna, Stanley Sweet 1920- *WhoWest 94*
Hanna, Suzanne Louise 1953-
WhoMW 93
Hanna, Terry Ross 1947- *WhoAmL 94*
Hanna, Thomas King d1951
WhoAmA 93N
Hanna, Tom *DrAPF 93*
Hanna, W.C. 1910?- *EncSF 93*
Hanna, Willard A. d1993 *NewYTBS 93*
Hanna, William 1910- *IntDcF 2-4*
Hanna, William 1911- *IntMPA 94*
Hanna, William Brooks 1936- *WhoAm 94*
Hanna, William Denby 1910- *WhoAm 94*
Hanna, William Francis 1938-
WhoScEn 94
Hanna, William Johnson 1922-
WhoAm 94, WhoWest 94
Hanna, William Michael 1954-
WhoAmL 94
Hanna, William W. 1936- *WhoAm 94,
WhoFI 94*
Hannaford, Peter (Dor) 1932- *WrDr 94*
Hannaford, Peter Dor 1932- *WhoAm 94,
WhoFI 94*
Hannah, Barry *DrAPF 93*
Hannah, Barry 1942- *ConAu 43NR,
WhoAm 94, WrDr 94*
Hannah, Daryl 1960- *IntMPA 94,
IntWW 93, WhoAm 94, WhoHol 92*
Hannah, Duncan (Rathbun) 1952-
WhoAmA 93
Hannah, Hamner, III 1939- *WhoAm 94*
Hannah, Hubert H., Sr. 1920- *WhoBlA 94*
Hannah, James D. d1978 *WhoHol 92*
Hannah, John *ProFbHF, WhoHol 92*
Hannah, John H., Jr. *WhoAm 94,
WhoFI 94*
Hannah, John Junior 1923- *WhoAmA 93*
Hannah, John Robert, Sr. 1939-
WhoFI 94
Hannah, Kristin 1960- *ConAu 141*
Hannah, Leslie 1947- *Who 94*
Hannah, Mack H., Jr. *WhoBlA 94*
Hannah, Marc Regis 1956- *WhoBlA 94*

Hannah, Mary Elizabeth 1940-
WhoMW 93
Hannah, Mary-Emily 1936- *WhoAm 94*
Hannah, Melvin James 1938- *WhoBlA 94*
Hannah, Mosie R. 1949- *WhoBlA 94*
Hannah, Nicholas 1940- *IntWW 93*
Hannah, Norman Britton 1919-
WhoAm 94
Hannah, Page 1964- *WhoHol 92*
Hannah, Richards W. d1993
NewYTBS 93
Hannah, Robert Wesley 1931-
WhoScEn 94
Hannah, Stephen *WhoMW 93*
Hannah, Tom 1948- *WhoAmP 93*
Hannah, Wayne Robertson, Jr. 1931-
WhoAm 94
Hannah, William 1929- *Who 94*
Hannam, Charles Lewis 1925- *WrDr 94*
Hannam, John (Gordon) 1929- *Who 94*
Hannam, Michael Patrick Vivian 1920-
Who 94
Hannaman, George William, Jr. 1943-
WhoScEn 94
Hannan, Bradley 1935- *WhoMW 93*
Hannan, Chris(topher John) 1958-
ConDr 93
Hannan, Christie Phillip 1928-
WhoAm 94
Hannan, Edward James 1921- *WrDr 94*
Hannan, Edward John 1942- *WhoFI 94*
Hannan, Eilene 1946- *NewGrDO*
Hannan, Greg *DrAPF 93*
Hannan, Myles 1936- *WhoAm 94,
WhoAmL 94, WhoFI 94*
Hannan, Paul W. 1949- *WhoAmP 93*
Hannan, Robert Charles *EncSF 93*
Hannan, Robert William 1939-
WhoAm 94, WhoFI 94
Hannan, Wyota 1930- *WhoAmP 93*
Han Nanpeng 1932- *WhoPRCh 91 [port]*
Hannawalt, Willis Dale 1928- *WhoAm 94*
Hannay, Alastair 1932- *WrDr 94*
Hannay, David (Hugh Alexander) 1935-
Who 94
Hannay, David Hugh Alexander 1935-
IntWW 93
Hannay, Elizabeth Anne Scott 1942-
Who 94
Hannay, Felicity 1947- *WhoAmL 94*
Hannay, Janneka 1933- *WhoAmA 93*
Hannay, Norman Bruce 1921- *WhoAm 94*
Hannay, Roger (Durham) 1930-
NewGrDO
Hannay, William Mouat, III 1944-
WhoAm 94
Hann-Byrd, Adam *WhoHol 92*
Hanneford, Poodles d1967 *WhoHol 92*
Hannel, Rodger Dale 1951- *WhoMW 93*
Hannele, Pirkko *SmATA 76*
Hannema, Dirk 1953- *WhoScEn 94*
Hanneman, Elaine Esther 1928-
WhoMW 93
Hanneman, Frederick d1980 *WhoHol 92*
Hanneman, Jeff
See Slayer *ConMus 10*
Hanneman, Paul A. 1936- *WhoAmP 93*
Hanneman, Rodney Elton 1936-
WhoAm 94, WhoScEn 94
Hanneman, Timothy John 1950-
WhoScEn 94
Hannemann, Gus *WhoAmP 93*
Hannemann, Walter A. 1914- *IntMPA 94*
Hannen, Hermione d1983 *WhoHol 92*
Hannen, John Edward *Who 94*
Hannen, John Edward 1937- *WhoAm 94*
Hannen, Nicholas d1972 *WhoHol 92*
Hannen, Peter d1932 *WhoHol 92*
Hanner, Bob 1945- *WhoAmP 93*
Hanners, David *WhoAm 94*
Hannes, James Alan 1943- *WhoIns 94*
Hanni, Don Lamar 1926- *WhoAmP 93*
Han Nianlong 1910- *IntWW 93,
WhoPRCh 91 [port]*
Hannibal 247BC-183BC *HisWorL [port]*
Hannibal, Alice Priscilla 1916-
WhoBlA 94
Hannibal, Edward *DrAPF 93*
Hannibal, Edward L 1936- *WrDr 94*
Hannibal, Gary Eugene 1943-
WhoAmP 93
Hannibal, Joseph Harry 1945-
WhoAmA 93
Hannibalsson, Jon Baldvin 1939-
IntWW 93
Hannig, Gary 1952- *WhoAmP 93*
Hannigan, Alyson 1974- *WhoHol 92*
Hannigan, Frank 1931- *WhoAm 94*
Hannigan, James *Who 94*
Hannigan, James Edgar 1928- *Who 94*
Hannigan, Maurice J. 1941- *WhoWest 94*
Hannigan, Paul *DrAPF 93*
Hannigan, Thomas M. 1940- *WhoAmP 93*
Hannigan, Vera Simmons 1932-
WhoAm 94
Hanning, Gary William 1942- *WhoFI 94,
WhoScEn 94*

Hanning, Maurice F(rancis) 1894-
WhAm 10
Han Ningfu *WhoPRCh 91*
Hannington, Mary Lee 1960- *WhoMW 93*
Hannington, Walter 1896-1966
DcNaB MP
Hanno fl. 47-?BC- *WhWE*
Hanno, Beverly A. 1932- *WhoAmP 93*
Hannon, Brian Desmond Anthony *Who 94*
Hannon, Bruce R. 1934- *WhoAm 94*
Hannon, Bruce Michael 1934-
WhoMW 93
Hannon, Ezra 1926- *WrDr 94*
Hannon, John Robert 1945- *WhoAm 94,
WhoFI 94*
Hannon, Kemp *WhoAmP 93*
Hannon, Kevin P. 1949- *WhoIns 94*
Hannon, Lenn Lamar 1943- *WhoAmP 93*
Hannon, Timothy Patrick 1948-
WhoAmL 94
Hannon, Violet Marie 1943- *WhoMW 93*
Hannon, William Evans 1932- *WhoAm 94*
Hannon, William Joseph, Jr. 1934-
WhoFI 94
Hannover, Georg Wilhelm, Prinz von
1915- *IntWW 93*
Hannum, Alex 1923- *BasBi [port]*
Hannum, David Lawrence 1945-
WhoFI 94
Hannum, Gerald Luther 1915-
WhoAmP 93
Hannum, Gerald Luther Lou 1915-
WhoWest 94
Hannum, Robert John 1921- *WhoAmP 93*
Hanny, James Michael 1942-
WhoAmL 94
Hanold, Terrance 1912- *WhoAm 94*
Hanon, Bernard 1932- *IntWW 93,
Who 94*
Hanover, John David 1961- *WhoAmL 94*
Hanover, Stanley I. 1947- *WhoAmL 94*
Hanowell, Ernest Goddin 1920-
WhoWest 94
Hanower, Lee David 1959- *WhoAmL 94*
Han Peixin 1921- *IntWW 93,
WhoPRCh 91 [port]*
Han Pyo-Wook 1916- *HisDcKW*
Hanquet, Huberte 1926- *WhoWomW 91*
Hanrahan, Barbara 1939- *BlmGWL,
WrDr 94*
Hanrahan, Brian 1949- *Who 94*
Hanrahan, Patrick Jude 1954- *WhoFI 94*
Hanrahan, Richard Andrew 1946-
WhoAmP 93
Hanrahan, Robert Joseph 1932-
WhoAm 94
Hanrahan, Robert P. 1934- *WhoAmP 93*
Hanrahan, Susan Marie 1953-
WhoMW 93
Hanrahan, Thomas P. 1950- *WhoAm 94*
Hanrath, Linda Carol 1949- *WhoMW 93*
Hanratty, Carin Gale 1953- *WhoScEn 94*
Hanratty, Thomas Joseph 1926-
WhoAm 94
Hanray, Laurence d1947 *WhoHol 92*
Hanreddy, Joseph 1947- *WhoMW 93*
Hanreider, Wolfram F 1931- *WrDr 94*
Hanretta, Allan Gene 1930- *WhoWest 94*
Hanrott, Francis George Vivian 1921-
Who 94
Hans, Paul Charles 1946- *WhoFI 94*
Hans Adam, II 1945- *IntWW 93*
Hansan, Mary Anne 1961- *WhoAm 94*
Hansard, James William 1936-
WhoAm 94
Hansberry, Lorraine 1930-1965
*AfrAmAl 6 [port], BlmGWL,
ConBlB 6 [port]*
Hansberry, Lorraine (Vivian) 1930-1965
IntDcT 2
Hansberry-Moore, Virginia T. 1930-
WhoBlA 94
Hansbrough, John Fenwick 1945-
WhoScEn 94
Hansbury, John Garfield 1940-
WhoAmP 93
Hansbury, Stephan Charles 1946-
WhoAmL 94
Hansbury, Vivien H. 1927- *WhoBlA 94*
Hansch, Joachim Horst 1946-
WhoWest 94
Hanschen, Peter Walter 1945- *WhoAm 94*
Hanseid, Einar 1943- *IntWW 93*
Hansel, Howell d1917 *WhoHol 92*
Hansel, James Gordon 1937-
WhoScEn 94
Hansel, Paul George 1917- *WhoAm 94*
Hansel, Stephen Arthur 1947- *WhoAm 94,
WhoFI 94*
Hansel, William 1918- *WhoScEn 94*
Hansel, William Clayton 1917-
WhoAmP 93
Hansell, Dean 1952- *WhoAm 94*
Hansell, Edgar Frank 1937- *WhoAm 94*
Hansell, Ellen 1869-1937 *BuCMET*
Hansell, Freya *WhoAmA 93*
Hansell, John Royer 1931- *WhoAm 94*

Hansell, William Howard, Jr. 1937- *WhoAm 94*
Hanselman, Gregory L. 1952- *WhoAmP 93*
Hanselman, Richard Wilson 1927- *WhoAm 94, WhoFI 94*
Hanselmann, Fredrick Charles 1955- *WhoAmL 94*
Hansen, Alan Edward 1953- *WhoMW 93*
Hansen, Alan Lee 1951- *WhoScEn 94*
Hansen, Alicia 1952- *WhoAmP 93*
Hansen, Andrew Marius 1929- *WhoAm 94*
Hansen, Ann Natalie 1927- *WrDr 94*
Hansen, Arlen J. 1936- *WrDr 94*
Hansen, Arlen Jay 1936- *WhoWest 94*
Hansen, Armin Carl 1886-1957 *WhoAmA 93N*
Hansen, Arne Rae 1940-1992 *WhAm 10, WhoAmA 93N*
Hansen, Arthur Gene 1925- *WhoAm 94*
Hansen, Barbara (Joan) *WrDr 94*
Hansen, Barbara C. 1941- *IntWW 93*
Hansen, Barbara Caleen 1941- *WhoAm 94*
Hansen, Bennett Roy 1945- *WhoAm 94*
Hansen, Bent 1920- *IntWW 93*
Hansen, Bernard J. 1944- *WhoAmP 93*
Hansen, Bev 1944- *WhoAmP 93*
Hansen, Bobby J. 1926- *WhoAm 94, WhoFI 94*
Hansen, Brooks 1965- *WrDr 94*
Hansen, Carl R. 1926- *WhoAmP 93, WhoMW 93*
Hansen, Carol Baker *DrAPF 93*
Hansen, Caryl Jean 1929- *WhoWest 94*
Hansen, Chadwick 1926- *WrDr 94*
Hansen, Charles 1926- *WhoAm 94*
Hansen, Christian Andreas, Jr. 1926- *WhoAm 94*
Hansen, Christian Gregory 1957- *WhoScEn 94*
Hansen, Christopher Agnew 1934- *WhoAmL 94*
Hansen, Claire V. 1925- *WhoAm 94*
Hansen, Clifford Peter 1912- *IntWW 93, WhoAm 94, WhoAmP 93, WhoWest 94*
Hansen, Curtis LeRoy 1933- *WhoAm 94, WhoAmL 94, WhoWest 94*
Hansen, Dale J. 1939- *WhoScEn 94*
Hansen, David Dee 1947- *WhoAmP 93*
Hansen, David R. 1938- *WhoAmP 93*
Hansen, David Rasmussen 1938- *WhoAm 94, WhoAmL 94, WhoMW 93*
Hansen, Dennis S. 1942- *WhoAmP 93*
Hansen, Donald Curtis 1929- *WhoFI 94, WhoWest 94*
Hansen, Donald D. 1928- *WhoIns 94*
Hansen, Donald Marty 1935- *WhoMW 93*
Hansen, Donald W. 1924- *WhoAm 94*
Hansen, Donna Lauree 1939- *WhoMW 93*
Hansen, Edward Allen 1929- *WhoAm 94*
Hansen, Edward Daniel 1939- *WhoAmL 94, WhoAmP 93*
Hansen, Einar d1927 *WhoHol 92*
Hansen, Elisa Marie 1952- *WhoAm 94*
Hansen, Eric Ralph 1954- *WhoAmL 94*
Hansen, Finn 1945- *WhoScEn 94*
Hansen, Florence Marie Congiolosi 1934- *WhoWest 94*
Hansen, Frances Frakes *WhoAmA 93*
Hansen, Francis Eugene 1925- *WhoAm 94*
Hansen, Frederic J. 1946- *WhoWest 94*
Hansen, Gale *WhoHol 92*
Hansen, Gary Maynard 1949- *WhoAmL 94*
Hansen, Gaylen Capener 1921- *WhoAmA 93*
Hansen, Genevieve Evans 1931- *WhoFI 94*
Hansen, Grant Lewis 1921- *WhoAm 94*
Hansen, Gunnar *DrAPF 93*
Hansen, Gunnar 1947- *WhoHol 92*
Hansen, H. Jack 1922- *WhoAm 94, WhoFI 94, WhoMW 93*
Hansen, Hans d1962 *WhoHol 92*
Hansen, Harold John 1942- *WhoAmA 93*
Hansen, Herbert W. 1935- *WhoAm 94*
Hansen, Hugh Justin 1923- *WhoAm 94*
Hansen, J. Allan 1952- *WhoFI 94*
Hansen, James Douglas 1954- *WhoWest 94*
Hansen, James E. 1941- *WhoScEn 94*
Hansen, James Lee 1925- *WhoAm 94, WhoAmA 93, WhoWest 94*
Hansen, James V. 1932- *CngDr 93, WhoAm 94, WhoAmP 93, WhoWest 94*
Hansen, Jane 1946- *WhoMW 93*
Hansen, Janis *WhoHol 92*
Hansen, Jean Marie 1937- *WhoMW 93*
Hansen, Jim 1959- *WhoAmP 93*
Hansen, John Albert 1939- *WhoAmP 93*
Hansen, John D. 1933- *WhoAmP 93*
Hansen, John Herbert 1945- *WhoMW 93*
Hansen, John Leslie 1958- *WhoWest 94*
Hansen, John Paul 1928- *WhoMW 93*
Hansen, Jon *DrAPF 93*
Hansen, Jorgen Hartmann 1936- *WhoFI 94*
Hansen, Joseph *DrAPF 93*
Hansen, Joseph 1923- *GayLL, WrDr 94*
Hansen, Joseph Daniel 1945- *WhoAmL 94*
Hansen, Joyce 1942- *WrDr 94*
Hansen, Joyce (Viola) 1942- *BlkWr 2, ConAu 43NR*
Hansen, Joyce Viola 1942- *WhoBlA 94*
Hansen, Juanita d1961 *WhoHol 92*
Hansen, Karen Thornley 1945- *WhoFI 94*
Hansen, Karl 1950- *EncSF 93*
Hansen, Kathleen Ann 1954- *WhoMW 93*
Hansen, Kathryn Gertrude 1912- *WhoMW 93*
Hansen, Kenneth Russell 1926- *WhoWest 94*
Hansen, Kent Forrest 1931- *WhoAm 94*
Hansen, Kurt 1910- *IntWW 93*
Hansen, L(ouise) Taylor *EncSF 93*
Hansen, Larry Dean 1953- *WhoMW 93*
Hansen, Leland Joe 1944- *WhoFI 94*
Hansen, Leonard Joseph 1932- *WhoWest 94*
Hansen, Lorraine Sundal 1929- *WhoMW 93*
Hansen, Lowell C., II *WhoAmP 93*
Hansen, M. Reed 1929- *WhoAmP 93*
Hansen, Marijean 1953- *WhoFI 94*
Hansen, Marilyn Schooley 1947- *WhoMW 93*
Hansen, Mark Charles 1956- *WhoAmL 94*
Hansen, Martin Craig 1951- *WhoFI 94*
Hansen, Matilda 1929- *WhoWest 94*
Hansen, Matilda Anne 1929- *WhoAmP 93, WhoWomW 91*
Hansen, Max d1961 *WhoHol 92*
Hansen, Michael Roy 1953- *WhoScEn 94, WhoWest 94*
Hansen, Michael Wayne 1955- *WhoMW 93*
Hansen, Mick *WhoAmP 93*
Hansen, Miriam 1949- *WhoMW 93*
Hansen, Mogens Herman 1940- *IntWW 93*
Hansen, Morris H. d1990 *IntWW 93N*
Hansen, Nancy C. Urdahl 1940- *WhoWest 94*
Hansen, Nick Dane 1938- *WhoAm 94*
Hansen, Niels 1924- *IntWW 93*
Hansen, Nina *WhoHol 92*
Hansen, Ole Viggo 1934- *WhoMW 93*
Hansen, Orval 1926- *WhoAm 94*
Hansen, Orval Howard 1926- *WhoAmP 93*
Hansen, P. Gregers 1933- *IntWW 93*
Hansen, Partick Steven 1953- *WhoWest 94*
Hansen, Patricia Lea 1954- *WhoAmP 93*
Hansen, Patti 1956- *WhoHol 92*
Hansen, Paula Renee 1952- *WhoAm 94*
Hansen, Per Brinch 1938- *WhoAm 94, WhoScEn 94*
Hansen, Per Kristian 1932- *WhoAm 94, WhoFI 94*
Hansen, Peter 1921- *WhoHol 92*
Hansen, Peter James 1956- *WhoScEn 94*
Hansen, Poul Einer 1939- *ConAu 141*
Hansen, Ralph Holm 1923- *WhoAm 94*
Hansen, Randall Glenn 1946- *WhoWest 94*
Hansen, Rebonna Dale 1964- *WhoAmL 94*
Hansen, Richard Arthur 1941- *WhoAm 94*
Hansen, Richard Fred 1932- *WhoAm 94*
Hansen, Robert 1924- *WhoAmA 93*
Hansen, Robert Blaine 1925- *WhoAmP 93*
Hansen, Robert Clinton 1926- *WhoAm 94*
Hansen, Robert Dennis 1945- *WhoWest 94*
Hansen, Robert Gunnard 1939- *WhoWest 94*
Hansen, Robert J. 1940- *WhoScEn 94*
Hansen, Robert Joseph 1918- *WhoAm 94, WhoScEn 94*
Hansen, Robert Suttle 1918- *WhoAm 94*
Hansen, Robert Wayne 1911- *WhoAm 94*
Hansen, Robert William 1924- *WhoAm 94*
Hansen, Robyn L. 1949- *WhoAm 94, WhoAmL 94*
Hansen, Roderick Peter 1950- *WhoFI 94*
Hansen, Ron 1947- *WrDr 94*
Hansen, Ronald Gregory 1929- *WhoWest 94*
Hansen, Ross N. 1956- *WhoScEn 94*
Hansen, Sarah Eveleth (Campbell) 1917- *WhoAmA 93*
Hansen, Scott W. 1951- *WhoAmL 94*
Hansen, Shirley Jean 1928- *WhoScEn 94*
Hansen, Sigvard Theodore, Jr. 1935- *WhoWest 94*
Hansen, Stella Jean 1925- *WhoAmP 93*
Hansen, Steve D. *WhoAmP 93*
Hansen, Tom *DrAPF 93*
Hansen, Ursula 1935- *WhoWomW 91*
Hansen, Vern *WrDr 94*
Hansen, Victor 1903- *BasBi*
Hansen, W. Lee 1928- *WhoAm 94*
Hansen, Walter Eugene 1929- *WhoWest 94*
Hansen, Wayne Richard 1939- *WhoWest 94*
Hansen, Wayne W. 1942- *WhoAm 94, WhoAmL 94*
Hansen, Wendell Jay 1910- *WhoBlA 94, WhoFI 94, WhoMW 93*
Hansen, Will 1953- *WhoScEn 94*
Hansen, William d1975 *WhoHol 92*
Hansen, Zenon Clayton Raymond 1909-1990 *WhAm 10*
Hansenne, Michel 1940- *IntWW 93, Who 94*
Hansen-Rachor, Sharon Ann 1954- *WhoMW 93*
Hansen-Rivera, Carmen 1948- *WhoHisp 94*
Hanser, Mary Julia 1941- *WhoAm 94*
Hansey, Donald G. 1929- *WhoAmP 93*
Hansford, John Edgar 1922- *Who 94*
Hansford, Larry Clarence 1945- *WhoFI 94*
Han Shao Gong 1953- *IntWW 93, WhoPRCh 91 [port]*
Hanshaw, James Barry 1928- *WhoAm 94*
Han Shuying *WhoPRCh 91*
Hansler, Jeffrey Kurt 1957- *WhoWest 94*
Hanslick, Eduard 1825-1904 *NewGrDO*
Hanslip, Ann 1934- *WhoHol 92*
Hansmann, Ralph Emil 1918- *WhoAm 94*
Hansmeier, Barbara Jo 1954- *WhoMW 93*
Hansohm, Dirk Christian 1956- *WhoScEn 94*
Hanson, Baron 1922- *Who 94*
Hanson, Alexander Contee 1749-1806 *WhAmRev*
Hanson, Alfred Olaf 1914- *WhoMW 93*
Hanson, Allen Dennis 1936- *WhoAm 94, WhoFI 94*
Hanson, Angus Alexander 1922- *WhoAm 94*
Hanson, Ann H. 1935- *WhoAmP 93*
Hanson, Anne Coffin 1921- *WhoAm 94, WhoAmA 93*
Hanson, Anthony (Leslie Oswald) 1934- *Who 94*
Hanson, Arnold Philip 1924- *WhoAm 94*
Hanson, Bertram Speakman 1905- *Who 94*
Hanson, Brett Allen 1963- *WhoScEn 94*
Hanson, Brian John Taylor 1939- *Who 94*
Hanson, Bruce Eugene 1942- *WhoAmL 94, WhoFI 94, WhoMW 93*
Hanson, Bruce J. 1942- *WhoAmP 93*
Hanson, Carl Malmrose 1941- *WhoAm 94*
Hanson, Carol G. 1934- *WhoAmP 93*
Hanson, Charles *DrAPF 93*
Hanson, Charles Allen 1926- *WhoAmP 93*
Hanson, Charles Richard 1948- *WhoFI 94*
Hanson, Clifford R. 1936- *WhoIns 94*
Hanson, Curtis *IntMPA 94*
Hanson, Curtis Jay 1954- *WhoScEn 94*
Hanson, Dale 1942- *WhoAm 94, WhoFI 94, WhoWest 94*
Hanson, Dale S. 1938- *WhoAm 94*
Hanson, Darrell Roy 1954- *WhoAmP 93*
Hanson, David Alan 1956- *WhoScEn 94*
Hanson, David Bigelow 1946- *WhoAm 94, WhoFI 94*
Hanson, David George 1957- *Who 94*
Hanson, David James 1943- *WhoAmL 94*
Hanson, David Scott, Jr. 1946- *WhoAmP 93*
Hanson, Dennis Michael 1943- *WhoAm 94*
Hanson, Dennis Wayne 1948- *WhoWest 94*
Hanson, Derrick George 1927- *Who 94*
Hanson, Diane Charske 1946- *WhoFI 94*
Hanson, Donald E. 1926- *WhoAmP 93*
Hanson, Doris J. 1925- *WhoAmP 93*
Hanson, Duane 1925- *IntWW 93, WhoAmA 93*
Hanson, Duane Allen 1950- *WhoWest 94*
Hanson, Duane Elwood 1925- *WhoAm 94*
Hanson, Earl D. d1993 *NewYTBS 93*
Hanson, Earl D(orchester) 1927- *WrDr 94*
Hanson, Earl Dorchester 1927- *WhoAm 94*
Hanson, Elizabeth Meader 1684-1737 *BlmGWL*
Hanson, Erwin *WhoAmP 93*
Hanson, Eugene Bail 1895- *WhAm 10*
Hanson, Eugene Nelson 1917- *WhoAm 94*
Hanson, Floyd Bliss 1939- *WhoAm 94, WhoMW 93, WhoScEn 94*
Hanson, Gary A. 1954- *WhoAmL 94*
Hanson, Gary W. 1950- *WhoAmP 93*
Hanson, George Fulford 1916- *WhoAm 94*
Hanson, George Peter 1933- *WhoWest 94*
Hanson, Gerald Warner 1938- *WhoWest 94*
Hanson, Gilbert Nikolai 1936- *WhoAm 94*
Hanson, Gladys d1973 *WhoHol 92*
Hanson, H. S. 1926- *WhoAmP 93*
Hanson, Harold Palmer 1921- *WhoAm 94, WhoScEn 94*
Hanson, Heidi Elizabeth 1954- *WhoAm 94*
Hanson, Hilary Ruth 1963- *WhoWest 94*
Hanson, Howard (Harold) 1896-1981 *NewGrDO*
Hanson, Howard Paul 1950- *WhoWest 94*
Hanson, Hugh 1915- *WhoScEn 94*
Hanson, J. B. 1946- *WhoAmA 93*
Hanson, James Donald 1935- *Who 94*
Hanson, James Edward 1922- *IntWW 93*
Hanson, Jean Elizabeth 1949- *WhoAm 94, WhoAmL 94*
Hanson, Jeannine Lucille 1954- *WhoMW 93*
Hanson, Jeff O. 1958- *WhoAmP 93*
Hanson, Jerry 1943- *WhoAmP 93*
Hanson, Jerry Clinton 1939- *WhoAmL 94*
Hanson, Jerry J. *WhoAmP 93*
Hanson, Jim *DrAPF 93*
Hanson, Jo *WhoAm 94, WhoAmA 93*
Hanson, Joan Catherine 1965- *WhoMW 93*
Hanson, John *Who 94*
Hanson, John 1721-1783 *WhAmRev*
Hanson, (Charles) John 1919- *Who 94*
Hanson, John Gilbert 1938- *IntWW 93, Who 94*
Hanson, John J. 1922- *WhoAm 94, WhoAmL 94, WhoWest 94*
Hanson, John K. 1913- *WhoAm 94, WhoMW 93*
Hanson, John L. 1950- *WhoBlA 94*
Hanson, John M. 1932- *WhoAm 94, WhoScEn 94*
Hanson, John Mark 1955- *WhoScEn 94*
Hanson, John Norman 1945- *WhoAmL 94*
Hanson, John R. 1941- *WhoAmP 93*
Hanson, Joseph J. 1930- *WhoAm 94*
Hanson, Judy *WhoAmA 93*
Hanson, Karen 1947- *WhoMW 93*
Hanson, Kenneth *DrAPF 93*
Hanson, Kenneth Hamilton 1919- *WhoAmL 94*
Hanson, Kenneth Merrill 1940- *WhoScEn 94, WhoWest 94*
Hanson, Kenneth O. 1922- *WrDr 94*
Hanson, Kent Bryan 1954- *WhoAmL 94*
Hanson, Kermit Osmond 1916- *WhoAm 94*
Hanson, Kristine Weilbacker 1961- *WhoFI 94*
Hanson, LaMont Dix 1954- *WhoWest 94*
Hanson, Larry Keith 1932- *WhoAm 94, WhoWest 94*
Hanson, Lars d1965 *WhoHol 92*
Hanson, Lawrence 1936-1992 *WhoAmA 93N*
Hanson, Leila Fraser 1942- *WhoAm 94*
Hanson, Lowell Knute 1935- *WhoScEn 94*
Hanson, Lyle *WhoAmP 93*
Hanson, Marcy *WhoHol 92*
Hanson, Marian W. 1933- *WhoAmP 93*
Hanson, Maurice Francis 1907- *WhoAm 94*
Hanson, Monte R. 1956- *WhoMW 93*
Hanson, Neil 1923- *Who 94*
Hanson, Noel Rodger 1942- *WhoFI 94*
Hanson, Norma Lee 1930- *WhoAmP 93*
Hanson, Norman 1916- *WhoAmL 94*
Hanson, Orlin 1930- *WhoAmP 93*
Hanson, Paul d1940 *WhoHol 92*
Hanson, Paul David 1939- *WhoAm 94*
Hanson, Paul R. 1952- *WrDr 94*
Hanson, Paula E. 1944- *WhoAmP 93*
Hanson, Pauline *WrDr 94*
Hanson, Philip 1936- *WrDr 94*
Hanson, Philip Holton 1943- *WhoAmA 93*
Hanson, Raymond Lester 1912- *WhoAm 94*
Hanson, Richard A. 1946- *WhoAm 94*
Hanson, Richard Edwin 1931- *WhoAm 94, WhoScEn 94, WhoWest 94*
Hanson, Richard Winfield 1935- *WhoAm 94*
Hanson, Robert A. 1924- *IntWW 93*
Hanson, Robert Arthur 1924- *WhoAm 94, WhoMW 93*
Hanson, Robert Carl 1926- *WhoAm 94*
Hanson, Robert Duane 1935- *WhoAm 94*
Hanson, Robert Eugene 1947- *WhoAmP 93, WhoMW 93*
Hanson, Robert Frederick 1944- *WhoAmL 94*
Hanson, Robert James 1936- *WhoScEn 94*
Hanson, Robert Paul 1918-1987 *WhAm 10*
Hanson, Roger James 1927- *WhoAm 94*
Hanson, Roger Kvamme 1932- *WhoAm 94*
Hanson, Roland Stuart 1932- *WhoScEn 94*
Hanson, Ronald William 1950- *WhoAm 94, WhoAmL 94*
Hanson, Ronald Windell 1947- *WhoScEn 94*
Hanson, Samuel Lee 1939- *WhoAm 94*

Hanson, Scott T. 1966- WhoFI 94

Hanson, Selden Raymond 1918- WhoAmP 93

Hanson, Spook d1924 WhoHol 92

Hanson, Susan 1943- WhoHol 92

Hanson, Susan Easton 1943- WhoAm 94

Hanson, Susan Jane 1958- WhoFI 94

Hanson, Thomas Lawrence 1941- WhoMW 93

Hanson, Thomas S. 1939- WhoAmP 93

Hanson, Thor 1928- WhoAm 94

Hanson, Toni Jo 1949- WhoMW 93

Hanson, Vern WrDr 94

Hanson, Vern 1920- EncSF 93

Hanson, Vic(tor) J(oseph) WrDr 94

Hanson, Victor Henry, II 1930- WhoAm 94

Hanson, Wallace B. WhoAmP 93

Hanson, Walter Edmund 1916- WhoAm 94

Hanson, Walter Raymond 1931- WhoAmP 93

Hanson, William Bert 1923- WhoScEn 94

Hanson, William Cook 1909- WhoAmL 94

Hanson-Painton, Olivia Lou 1949- WhoScEn 94

Hanssen, Shirley Mae 1935- WhoFI 94

Hanssens, Charles-Louis(-Joseph) 1777-1852 NewGrDO

Hansson, Gunnar Claes 1951- WhoScEn 94

Hansteen, Henry B. 1904-1991 WhAm 10

Han Suyin 1917- IntWW 93, Who 94, WrDr 94

Hansvick, Christine L. 1949- WhoWest 94

Hantho, Charles Harold 1931- WhoAm 94, WhoFI 94

Hanthorn, Dennis Wayne 1951- WhoAm 94, WhoMW 93

Han Tianheng 1940- WhoPRCh 91 [port]

Han Tianshi WhoPRCh 91 [port]

Han Tianyao 1915- WhoPRCh 91 [port]

Hanton, Alastair Kydd 1926- Who 94

Hanton, Emile Michael WhoFI 94

Hanton, Scott Douglas 1963- WhoScEn 94

Hanus, Frantisek 1943- IntWW 93

Hanus, Jan 1915- NewGrDO

Hanus, Jerome 1940- WhoAm 94, WhoMW 93

Hanuschak, George Alan 1949- WhoAm 94

Hanushek, Eric Alan 1943- WhoAm 94

Hanuszkiewicz, Adam 1924- IntWW 93

Hanway, Donald Grant 1918- WhoAm 94

Hanway, H. Edward 1952- WhoIns 94

Hanway, John, III 1952- WhoFI 94

Hanworth, Viscount 1916- Who 94

Han Wudi 156BC-87BC HisWorL

Han Xin 1955- WhoPRCh 91

Han Xu 1924- IntWW 93, WhoPRCh 91 [port]

Han Yulin WhoPRCh 91

Han Yuqun WhoPRCh 91

Hanzak, Janice Chrisman 1944- WhoFI 94, WhoMW 93

Hanzalek, Astrid T. 1928- WhoAmP 93

Hanzalova, Drahomira 1931- WhoWomW 91

Hanzelik, Carl Harold 1945- WhoAmL 94

Han Zhengqing WhoPRCh 91

Han Zheyi 1914- WhoPRCh 91 [port]

Hanzlicek, C. G. DrAPF 93

Hanzlik, Alan Edward 1947- WhoAm 94

Hanzlik, Paul F. 1942- WhoAm 94, WhoAmL 94

Hanzlik, Rayburn DeMara 1938- WhoAm 94, WhoAmL 94, WhoAmP 93

Hao, Wei Min 1953- WhoWest 94

Hao Jan ConWorW 93

Hao Jianxiu 1935- IntWW 93, WhoPRCh 91 [port], WhoWomW 91

Hao Ran 1932- ConWorW 93, IntWW 93, WhoPRCh 91 [port]

Hao Tingzao WhoPRCh 91

Hao Yan WhoPRCh 91

Hao Yichun 1920- WhoPRCh 91 [port]

Haozous, Bob 1943- WhoAmA 93

Hapgood, David 1926- WrDr 94

Hapgood, Robert Derry 1928- WhoAm 94

Hapgood, Susan T. 1957- WhoAmA 93

Hapke, Paul Frederick 1922-1984 WhoAmA 93N

Hapner-Rockhill, Elizabeth 1957- WhoAmL 94

Happ, Harvey Heinz 1928- WhoAm 94

Happel, Henry William 1911-1990 WhAm 10

Happel, John 1908- WhoAm 94

Happel, Kenneth Malcolm 1949- WhoWest 94

Happer, William, Jr. 1939- WhoAm 94, WhoScEn 94

Happold, Edmund 1930- Who 94

Haq, Bilal Ul 1943- WhoAm 94, WhoScEn 94

Haq, Iftikhar Ul 1939- WhoScEn 94

Haqq, Khalida Ismail 1946- WhoBlA 94

Haque, M. Shamsul 1934- WhoAsA 94

Haque, Malika Hakim WhoAm 94, WhoMW 93

Haque, Zahur U. 1950- WhoAsA 94

Hara, Ernest Hideo 1909- WhoAm 94

Hara, George 1952- WhoFI 94

Hara, Kazuko 1935- NewGrDO

Hara, Keiko WhoAmA 93

Hara, Kenzaburo 1907- IntWW 93

Hara, Lloyd 1940?- WhoAsA 94

Hara, Masanori 1952- WhoScEn 94

Hara, Saburo 1928- WhoAsA 94

Hara, Setsuko WhoHol 92

Hara, Stanley Ikuo 1923- WhoAmP 93

Hara, Sumio 1911- IntWW 93

Hara, Yasuo 1934- WhoScEn 94

Harab, Elliot Peter 1948- WhoAmL 94

Harad, George Jay 1944- WhoWest 94

Harada, Shoza 1923- IntWW 93

Harada, Yoshiya 1934- WhoScEn 94

Harada Yasuko 1928- BlmGWL

Haraden, Jonathan 1744-1803 WhAmRev

Haragan, Donald Robert 1936- WhoAm 94

Harakas, Stanley Samuel 1932- WrDr 94

Haralampu, George Stelios 1925- WhoAm 94

Harald, V 1937- IntWW 93

Harald Hardraade, III 1015-1066 HisWorL [port]

Haraldseth, Leif 1929- IntWW 93

Haralick, Robert Martin 1943- WhoAm 94

Haralson, John Olen 1954- WhoScEn 94

Haralson, Kathleen Mary 1944- WhoMW 93

Haralson, Larry L. WhoBlA 94

Haramaki, Chiko 1925- WhoAsA 94

Haramundanis, Katherine Leonora 1937- WhoScEn 94

Haran, Maeve 1950- WrDr 94

Harand, Irene 1900-1975 HisWorL [port]

Harangozo, Gyula 1908-1974 IntDcB

Hara-Nielsen, Sylvia Ann 1948- WhoAsA 94

Harano, Ross Masao 1942- WhoAsA 94

Harapi, Tonin 1928-1992 NewGrDO

Harare, Archbishop of 1932- Who 94

Harare, Bishop of 1927- Who 94

Harareet, Haya 1933- WhoHol 92

Harari, Clement WhoHol 92

Harari, Hananiah 1912- WhoAm 94, WhoAmA 93

Harary, Frank 1921- WhoAm 94, WhoScEn 94

Harary, Keith 1953- WhoScEn 94

Harbach, William O. 1919- IntMPA 94

Harbart, Gertrude Felton 1908- WhoAmA 93

Harbaugh, Carl d1960 WhoHol 92

Harbaugh, Daniel Paul 1948- WhoAmL 94, WhoWest 94

Harbaugh, George Milton 1930- WhoAm 94

Harbaugh, John Warvelle 1926- WhoAm 94, WhoWest 94

Harbaugh, Lois Jensen 1942- WhoScEn 94

Harbaugh, William d1924 WhoHol 92

Harbeck, William H. 1955- WhoAmL 94

Harbeck, William James 1921- WhoAm 94, WhoFI 94

Harben, Hubert d1942 WhoHol 92

Harben, Joan d1953 WhoHol 92

Harben, Will(iam) N(athaniel) 1858-1919 EncSF 93

Harber, Loretta Michele 1954- WhoFI 94

Harber, Michael Eric 1965- WhoScEn 94, WhoWest 94

Harberger, Arnold C. 1924- WrDr 94

Harberger, Arnold Carl 1924- WhoAm 94, WhoMW 93

Harbert, Guy Morley, Jr. 1929- WhoAm 94

Harbert, Kenneth Ray 1947- WhoAm 94

Harberton, Viscount 1910- Who 94

Harbin, John Pickens 1917- WhoAm 94

Harbin, Raymond 1948- WhoAmP 93

Harbinson, Joel Cline 1954- WhoAmL 94

Harbinson, W(illiam) Allen 1941- EncSF 93

Harbison, Earle Harrison, Jr. 1928- IntWW 93, WhoAm 94, WhoFI 94

Harbison, Ed 1941- WhoAmP 93

Harbison, James Wesley, Jr. 1934- WhoAm 94

Harbison, John 1938- CurBio 93 [port], NewGrDO, WhoAm 94

Harbison, John Robert 1953- WhoAm 94, WhoWest 94

Harbison, Kent Gregory 1944- WhoAm 94

Harbison, Peter 1939- IntWW 93

Harbison, Samuel Alexander 1941- Who 94

Harbison, William 1922- Who 94

Harbison, William J. 1923- WhoAmP 93

Harbison, William James 1923- WhoAm 94, WhoAmL 94

Harbor, William H. 1920- WhoAmP 93

Harbord, Anne Marie 1954- WhoWest 94

Harbord, Carl d1958 WhoHol 92

Harbord-Hamond Who 94

Harbordt, Charles Michael 1942- WhoFI 94

Harborne, Peter Gale 1945- Who 94

Harbort, Robert Adolph, Jr. 1947- WhoScEn 94

Harbottle, Anthony Hall Harrison 1925- Who 94

Harbottle, (George) Laurence 1924- Who 94

Harbottle, Michael Neale 1917- Who 94, WrDr 94

Harbottle, Philip (James) 1941- EncSF 93

Harbou, Thea von 1888-1954 BlmGWL

Harbour, David Franklin, III 1942- WhoAmP 93

Harbour, Jerry Lee 1949- WhoWest 94

Harbrant, Robert Francis 1942- WhoAm 94

Harbron, Garrett Lee 1940- WhoMW 93

Harbuck, Edwin Charles 1934- WhoFI 94

Harburg, Edelaine Roden d1989 WhoHol 92

Harbury, Colin 1922- WrDr 94

Harbury, Henry Alexander 1927- WhoAm 94

Harbutt, Charles 1935- WhoAm 94, WhoAmA 93

Harchenhorn, V. Lanny WhoAmP 93

Harcleroad, Fred Farley 1918- WhoAm 94

Harclerode, Jack Edgar 1935- WhoAm 94

Harcourt, Geoffrey Colin 1931- IntWW 93, Who 94, WrDr 94

Harcourt, Geoffrey David 1935- Who 94

Harcourt, Glenn EncSF 93

Harcourt, H. Baxter 1924- WhoAmP 93

Harcourt, James d1951 WhoHol 92

Harcourt, Michael Franklin 1943- Who 94, WhoWest 94

Harcourt, Palma WrDr 94

Harcourt, Peggie d1916 WhoHol 92

Harcourt, Robert Neff 1932- WhoWest 94

Harcourt, William d1923 WhoHol 92

Harcourt-Smith, David 1931- Who 94

Harcrow, E. Earl 1954- WhoAmL 94

Harcus, Portia Gwen WhoAmA 93

Hard, Darlene 1936- BuCMET

Hardage, Page Taylor 1944- WhoAm 94, WhoFI 94, WhoScEn 94

Hardaker, Ian Alexander 1932- Who 94

Hardaway, Anfernee WhoBlA 94

Hardaway, Ernest, II 1938- WhoBlA 94

Hardaway, Francine Olman 1941- WhoWest 94

Hardaway, Jerry David 1951- WhoBlA 94

Hardaway, Robert Morris, III 1916- WhoAm 94

Hardaway, Thomas C. 1957- WhoAmP 93

Hardaway, Tim 1966- WhoAm 94, WhoWest 94

Hardaway, Timothy Duane 1966- WhoBlA 94

Hardaway, Yvonne Veronica 1950- WhoBlA 94

Hardbeck, George William 1925- WhoAm 94

Hardberger, Phillip Duane 1934- WhoAm 94

Hardcastle, Alan (John) 1933- Who 94

Hardcastle, Jack Donald 1933- Who 94

Hardcastle, James C. 1914- WhoBlA 94

Hardcastle, (Jesse) Leslie 1926- Who 94

Hardcastle, Michael 1933- WrDr 94

Hardcastle, Victoria WhoHol 92

Hardebeck, Beth Elaine 1958- WhoMW 93

Hardee, David Wyatt 1947- WhoAmL 94

Hardee, G. Wayne 1957- WhoAmL 94

Hardee, Larry Lee 1959- WhoFI 94

Hardee, William Covington 1919- WhoAm 94

Hardeman, Carole Hall WhoBlA 94

Hardeman, Charles Dwayne 1961- WhoAmP 93

Hardeman, James Anthony 1943- WhoBlA 94

Hardeman, Strotha E., Jr. 1929- WhoBlA 94

Harden, Acheson Adair, Jr. 1921- WhoAm 94

Harden, Alice Varnado 1948- WhoAmP 93

Harden, Arthur 1865-1940 WorScD

Harden, Blaine 1952- WrDr 94

Harden, Blaine Charles 1952- WhoAm 94

Harden, Bruce Donald Richard 1940- WhoAmP 93

Harden, Donald B. 1939- WhoAmL 94

Harden, Donald B(enjamin) 1901- WrDr 94

Harden, Donald Benjamin 1901- Who 94

Harden, Gary Martin 1955- WhoAmL 94

Harden, James Richard Edwards 1916- Who 94

Harden, Jon Bixby 1944- WhoAm 94

Harden, Lydia Dixon 1959- WhoAm 94

Harden, Marcia Gay 1959- WhoHol 92

Harden, Marvin WhoAm 94, WhoAmA 93, WhoBlA 94, WhoWest 94

Harden, Mary Louise 1942- WhoMW 93

Harden, O(leta) Elizabeth (McWhorter) 1935- WrDr 94

Harden, Oleta Elizabeth 1935- WhoAm 94

Harden, Patrick Alan 1936- WhoAm 94, WhoWest 94

Harden, Robert James 1952- WhoBlA 94

Harden, Robert T. 1960- WhoAmP 93

Harden, Vincent Louis 1955- WhoFI 94, WhoMW 93

Hardenberger, (Ulf) Hakan 1961- Who 94

Hardenbergh, Jacob Rutsen 1736-1790 WhAmRev

Hardenbrook, Yvonne Moore DrAPF 93

Hardenburg, Robert Earle 1919- WhoAm 94, WhoScEn 94

Hardenburger, Janice WhoAmP 93

Harder, Charles Mabry 1899-1959 WhoAmA 93N

Harder, Clark Andrew 1955- WhoAmP 93, WhoMW 93

Harder, Jesse J. WhoAmP 93

Harder, John E. 1930- WhoAm 94

Harder, Joseph C. 1916- WhoAmP 93

Harder, Kelsie Brown 1922- WhoAm 94

Harder, Kelsie T. 1942- WhoWest 94

Harder, Lewis Bradley 1918- WhoAm 94

Harder, Manfred 1937- IntWW 93

Harder, Michael Upham 1953- WhoWest 94

Harder, Robert Clarence 1929- WhoAm 94, WhoMW 93

Harder, Rodney WhoAmA 93

Harder, Rolf Peter 1929- WhoAm 94, WhoAmA 93

Harder, Ronald R. 1943- WhoIns 94

Harder, Ruel Tan 1946- WhoScEn 94

Harder, Sarah Snell 1937- WhoMW 93

Harder, Virgil Eugene 1923- WhoAm 94

Harders, Clarence Waldemar 1915- Who 94

Hardesty, C. Howard, Jr. 1922- WhoAm 94

Hardesty, David Carter, Jr. 1945- WhoAmL 94

Hardesty, Donald Lynn 1941- WhoWest 94

Hardesty, Egbert Railey 1915- WhoAm 94

Hardesty, Hiram Haines 1914- WhoAm 94

Hardesty, James Dunn 1946- WhoAm 94

Hardesty, Michael Robert 1952- WhoMW 93

Hardesty, Robert Lynch 1940- WhoAm 94

Hardesty, Shevawn Rae 1955- WhoFI 94

Hardesty, Thomas Fabian 1928- WhoAmP 93

Hardgrave, Phil 1950- WhoWest 94

Hardgrove, George Lind, Jr. 1933- WhoScEn 94

Hardgrove, James Alan 1945- WhoAm 94, WhoAmL 94

Hardie, Andrew Rutherford 1946- Who 94

Hardie, Archibald George 1908- Who 94

Hardie, Charles (Edgar Mathewes) 1910- Who 94

Hardie, Charles Edgar Mathewes 1910- IntWW 93

Hardie, Colin Graham 1906- Who 94

Hardie, Donald David Graeme 1936- Who 94

Hardie, Douglas (Fleming) 1923- Who 94

Hardie, Frank 1911- WrDr 94

Hardie, George Graham 1933- WhoAm 94, WhoWest 94

Hardie, James Hiller 1929- WhoAm 94

Hardie, Jeremy Who 94

Hardie, (Charles) Jeremy (Mawdesley) 1938- Who 94

Hardie, Kate WhoHol 92

Hardie, Keir 1856-1915 HisWorL [port]

Hardie, Miles Clayton 1924- Who 94

Hardie, Robert C. 1921- WhoAm 94

Hardie, Robert L., Jr. 1941- WhoBlA 94

Hardie, Russell d1973 WhoHol 92

Hardie, Sean 1947- WrDr 94

Hardiman, Joseph Raymond 1937- WhoAm 94, WhoFI 94

Hardiman, Phillip Thomas 1935- WhoBlA 94

Hardiman, Terrence 1937- WhoHol 92

Hardiman, Therese Anne 1956- WhoAmL 94

Hardin, Adlai Stevenson 1901-1989 WhAm 10

Hardin, Adlai Stevenson, Jr. 1937- WhoAm 94

Hardin, Adlais 1901-1989 WhoAmA 93N

Hardin, Boniface 1933- WhoBlA 94

Hardin, Charles Wheeler 1926- WhoAmP 93

Hardin, Clement 1916- WrDr 94

Hardin, Clifford M 1915- WrDr 94

Harper, Marion, Jr. 1916-1989 WhAm 10
Harper, Mary L. 1925- WhoBlA 94
Harper, Mary Starke 1919- WhoBlA 94
Harper, Matrid Thaisa 1949- WhoAm 94
Harper, Michael Henry, Jr. 1942- WhoAm 94
Harper, Michael John Kennedy 1935- WhoAm 94
Harper, Michael S. DrAPF 93
Harper, Michael S(teven) 1938- WrDr 94
Harper, Michael Steven 1938- WhoBlA 94
Harper, Mitchell Van 1956- WhoAmP 93
Harper, Neville W. WhoBlA 94
Harper, Oliver William, III 1953- WhoMW 93
Harper, Patricia Ann 1957- WhoMW 93
Harper, Patricia Mullaney 1932- WhoAmP 93
Harper, Paul WhoHol 92
Harper, Paul Church, Jr. 1920- WhoAm 94
Harper, Ralph Champlin 1916- WhoAm 94
Harper, Richard Henry 1950- WhoWest 94
Harper, Richard L. WhoAmP 93
Harper, Robert WhoAmP 93
Harper, Robert 1931- WhoHol 92
Harper, Robert Alexander 1924- WhoAm 94
Harper, Robert Allan 1915- WhoAm 94
Harper, Robert John, Jr. 1930- WhoScEn 94
Harper, Robert Lee 1920- WhoBlA 94
Harper, Robert Leslie 1939- WhoAm 94
Harper, Robert Levell 1942- WhoWest 94
Harper, Ron 1933- WhoHol 92
Harper, Ronald 1964- WhoBlA 94
Harper, Ronald J. 1945- WhoBlA 94
Harper, Rory EncSF 93
Harper, (John) Ross 1935- Who 94
Harper, Roy W. 1905- WhoAm 94, WhoAmP 93
Harper, Ruth B. 1927- WhoBlA 94
Harper, Ruth Bebe 1927- WhoAmP 93, WhoWomW 91
Harper, S. Birnie 1944- WhoAm 94
Harper, Samantha WhoHol 92
Harper, Sara J. 1926- WhoBlA 94
Harper, Sarah Elizabeth Grubbs WhoBlA 94
Harper, Shari Belafonte 1954- WhoBlA 94
Harper, Susan (Rice) 1943- ConAu 142
Harper, T. Errol 1947- WhoBlA 94
Harper, Tara K. 1961- ConAu 141
Harper, Taylor F. WhoAmP 93
Harper, Ted Alan 1947- WhoIns 94
Harper, Terry 1955- WhoBlA 94
Harper, Tess 1950- WhoHol 92
Harper, Tess 1952- IntMPA 94
Harper, Thelma Marie 1940- WhoAmP 93, WhoBlA 94
Harper, Thomas 1908-1989 WhAm 10
Harper, Tommy 1940- WhoBlA 94
Harper, Valerie 1940- IntMPA 94, WhoAm 94, WhoCom, WhoHol 92
Harper, Vera Jean 1925- WhoWest 94
Harper, Vincent EncSF 93
Harper, Virginia Alyson 1961- WhoAmL 94
Harper, Walter Edward, Jr. 1950- WhoBlA 94
Harper, Walter Joseph 1947- WhoAm 94, WhoFI 94, WhoMW 93
Harper, William 1944- WhoAmA 93
Harper, William C. 1944- WhoAm 94
Harper, William Rainey 1856-1906 DcAmReB 2
Harper, William Ronald 1944- Who 94
Harper, William Taylor 1893- WhAm 10
Harper, William Thomas, III 1956- WhoBlA 94
Harper, William Walter 1950- WhoMW 93
Harper Gow, (Leonard) Maxwell 1918- Who 94
Harper Woods, Pauline 1930- WhoWomW 91
Harpham, Virginia Ruth 1917- WhoAm 94
Harpham, William 1906- Who 94
Harpley, Sydney 1927-1992 AnObit 1992
Harpole, Joyce Ann 1951- WhoAmL 94
Harpool, Doug 1956- WhoAmP 93
Harpprecht, Klaus Christoph 1927- IntWW 93
Harps, William S. 1916- WhoBlA 94
Harpster, James Erving 1923- WhoAmL 94
Harpster, Robert Eugene 1930- WhoScEn 94
Harpum, Charles 1953- Who 94
Harr, Barbara DrAPF 93
Harr, Karl Gottlieb, Jr. 1922- WhoAm 94
Harr, Lawrence F. 1938- WhoIns 94
Harr, Lawrence Francis 1938- WhoAm 94
Harr, Lucy Loraine 1951- WhoAm 94
Harr, Milton Edward 1925- WhoMW 93
Harr, Silver d1968 WhoHol 92
Harr, Teri Ann 1960- WhoMW 93
Harradine, Archie d1974 WhoHol 92
Harrah, Robert E. d1993 NewYTBS 93
Harrah, Robert Eugene 1916- WhoAm 94
Harral, John Menteith 1948- WhoAm 94, WhoAmL 94
Harral McNally, Loretta Margaret 1957- WhoAmP 93
Harrawood, Paul 1928- WhoAm 94
Harre, Alan Frederick 1940- WhoAm 94, WhoMW 93
Harre, Rom 1927- WrDr 94
Harrel, P. Arley 1948- WhoAm 94, WhoAmL 94
Harreld, James Bruce 1950- WhoAm 94
Harrell, Andre WhoBlA 94
Harrell, Barbara Williams 1949- WhoScEn 94
Harrell, Charles Adair 1893- WhAm 10
Harrell, Charles H. WhoBlA 94
Harrell, David Edwin, Jr. 1930- WrDr 94
Harrell, Don W. 1938- WhoIns 94
Harrell, Douglas Gaines 1958- WhoScEn 94
Harrell, Edward Harding 1939- WhoAm 94
Harrell, Ernest James 1936- AfrAmG [port], WhoBlA 94
Harrell, H. Steve 1948- WhoBlA 94
Harrell, Henry Howze 1939- WhoAm 94, WhoFI 94
Harrell, Irene Burk 1927- WrDr 94
Harrell, James H. 1937- WhoAmP 93
Harrell, Limmie Lee, Jr. 1941- WhoAmL 94
Harrell, Lynn 1944- IntWW 93
Harrell, Lynn Morris 1944- Who 94, WhoAm 94, WhoWest 94
Harrell, Mack 1909-1960 NewGrDO
Harrell, Morris 1920- WhoAm 94
Harrell, Oscar W., Jr. WhoBlA 94
Harrell, Robert L. 1930- WhoBlA 94
Harrell, Robert S. 1952- WhoAmL 94
Harrell, Robert W., Jr. WhoAmP 93
Harrell, Robert Wesley, Jr. 1939- WhoAmP 93
Harrell, Roy G., Jr. 1944- WhoAmL 94
Harrell, Samuel Macy 1931- WhoAm 94, WhoFI 94, WhoMW 93
Harrell, Thomas Hicks 1951- WhoScEn 94
Harrell, William Edwin 1962- WhoBlA 94
Harrell, William H. 1946- WhoAmL 94
Harrelson, James P. WhoAmP 93
Harrelson, Walter Joseph 1919- WhoAm 94, WrDr 94
Harrelson, Woody 1961- IntMPA 94, WhoAm 94, WhoHol 92
Harrer, Gustave Adolphus 1924- WhoAm 94
Harrer, Heinrich 1912- Who 94
Harrhy, Eiddwen (Mair) 1949- NewGrDO
Harrhy, Eiddwen Mair 1949- Who 94
Harrich, Holda 1931- WhoWomW 91
Harrick, Jim WhoAm 94, WhoWest 94
Harries, Davyd 1937- WhoHol 92
Harries, Karsten 1937- WhoAm 94
Harries, Kathryn 1951- NewGrDO
Harries, Mags 1945- WhoAmA 93
Harries, Richard Douglas Who 94
Harries, Richard Douglas 1936- IntWW 93
Harriett, Judy Anne 1960- WhoScEn 94
Harriford, Daphne 1925- WrDr 94
Harrigan, Anthony Hart 1925- WhoAm 94
Harrigan, Edward 1844-1911 IntDcT 2
Harrigan, John Frederick 1925- WhoAm 94, WhoWest 94
Harrigan, John Thomas, Jr. 1929- WhoAm 94
Harrigan, Kenneth William J. 1927- WhoAm 94, WhoFI 94
Harrigan, Laura G. 1953- WhoAm 94
Harrigan, Lucille Frasca 1930- WhoAmP 93
Harrigan, Nedda d1989 WhoHol 92
Harrigan, Patrick J. 1941- ConAu 142
Harrigan, Richard George 1952- WhoMW 93
Harrigan, Rodney Emile 1945- WhoBlA 94
Harrigan, William d1966 WhoHol 92
Harrill, Bob E. 1930- WhoAmP 93
Harrill, Fred Falls 1948- WhoAmP 93
Harriman, Constance Bastine WhoAm 94
Harriman, Gerald Eugene 1924- WhoAm 94
Harriman, John Howland 1920- WhoAm 94, WhoAmP 93, WhoWest 94
Harriman, Katherine Jordan 1915- WhoAmP 93
Harriman, Malcolm Bruce 1950- WhoFI 94
Harriman, Morril Hilton, Jr. 1950- WhoAmP 93
Harriman, Pamela NewYTBS 93 [port], WhoAmP 93
Harriman, Pamela Digby Churchill 1920- IntWW 93, WhoAm 94
Harriman, Philip Darling 1937- WhoScEn 94
Harriman, Philip E. WhoAmP 93
Harriman, Richard Lee 1932- WhoMW 93
Harriman, W. Averell 1891-1986 HisDcKW
Harring, Dean K. 1951- WhoIns 94
Harringer, Olaf Carl 1919- WhoAm 94
Harrington, Earl of 1922- Who 94
Harrington, Alan DrAPF 93
Harrington, Alan 1919- EncSF 93
Harrington, Albert Blair 1914- Who 94
Harrington, Anthony Stephen 1941- WhoAm 94
Harrington, Arthur John 1950- WhoAmL 94
Harrington, Benjamin Franklin, III 1922- WhoAm 94
Harrington, Bob 1950-1992 WhAm 10
Harrington, Bruce Michael 1933- WhoAm 94
Harrington, Bryan Rulison 1953- WhoAmA 93
Harrington, Buck d1971 WhoHol 92
Harrington, C. Michael 1946- WhoAmL 94
Harrington, Carol A. 1953- WhoAm 94, WhoAmL 94
Harrington, Chestee Marie 1941- WhoAmA 93
Harrington, Curtis 1928- HorFD [port], IntMPA 94
Harrington, Daniel William 1938- WhoAmP 93
Harrington, Delphi 1942- WhoHol 92
Harrington, Donald Francis 1929- WhoAmL 94
Harrington, Donald James 1945- WhoAm 94
Harrington, Donald Szantho 1914- WhoAmP 93
Harrington, Edward Dennis, Jr. 1921- WhoAmP 93
Harrington, Edward F. 1933- WhoAm 94, WhoAmL 94
Harrington, Edward Michael 1928-1989 AmSocL
Harrington, Elaine Carolyn 1938- WhoBlA 94
Harrington, Fred Harvey 1912- WhoAm 94
Harrington, Gary 1953- WrDr 94
Harrington, Gary Burnes 1934- WhoFI 94
Harrington, George William 1929- WhoAm 94
Harrington, Gerald E. 1945- WhoBlA 94
Harrington, Glenn Lewis 1942- WhoFI 94, WhoWest 94
Harrington, Herbert H. 1946- WhoFI 94
Harrington, Illtyd 1931- Who 94
Harrington, James A. 1942- WhoMW 93
Harrington, James E., Jr. 1940- WhoAmL 94
Harrington, James Thomas 1949- WhoAmP 93
Harrington, James Timothy 1942- WhoAm 94, WhoAmL 94
Harrington, Jean Patrice WhoAm 94
Harrington, Jeremy Thomas 1932- WhoAm 94
Harrington, Jesse Moye, III 1940- WhoAm 94, WhoFI 94
Harrington, John d1945 WhoHol 92
Harrington, John Leo 1936- WhoAm 94
Harrington, John Leonard, Jr. 1955- WhoAm 94
Harrington, John Michael, Jr. 1921- WhoAm 94
Harrington, John Timothy 1921- WhoAm 94
Harrington, John Vincent 1919- WhoAm 94
Harrington, Joseph Francis 1938- WhoFI 94
Harrington, Joseph Julian 1919- WhoAmP 93
Harrington, Kate d1978 WhoHol 92
Harrington, Kent 1945- ConAu 141
Harrington, Kevin Paul 1951- WhoAmL 94
Harrington, Kurt Ross 1952- WhoFI 94
Harrington, LaMar 1917- WhoAm 94, WhoAmA 93
Harrington, Laura 1958- WhoHol 92
Harrington, Leonard 1922- WhoIns 94
Harrington, Lindsay Marvin 1944- WhoAmP 93
Harrington, (John) Malcolm 1942- Who 94
Harrington, Malcolm W. WhoAmP 93
Harrington, Marguerite Ann 1949- WhoFI 94
Harrington, Marion Ray 1924- WhoAm 94
Harrington, Marion Thomas 1901-1990 WhAm 10
Harrington, Mark Garland 1953- WhoWest 94
Harrington, Martin L. 1929- WhoAmP 93
Harrington, Maura Jaye 1964- WhoWest 94
Harrington, Michael 1928-1989 WhAm 10
Harrington, Michael James, Sr. 1945- WhoAmP 93
Harrington, Michael Joseph 1936- WhoAmP 93
Harrington, Nancy D. WhoAm 94
Harrington, Norman William 1948- WhoWest 94
Harrington, Pat 1929- IntMPA 94
Harrington, Pat, Sr. d1965 WhoHol 92
Harrington, Pat, Jr. 1929- WhoCom, WhoHol 92
Harrington, Patrick, Jr. WhoAm 94
Harrington, Patrick John 1949- Who 94
Harrington, Paul C. 1950- WhoAmP 93
Harrington, Paul W. 1934- WhoAmP 93
Harrington, Peter F. 1936- WhoAmP 93
Harrington, Peter Tyrus 1951- WhoFI 94
Harrington, Philip Leroy 1946- WhoBlA 94
Harrington, Randy WhoHol 92
Harrington, Robert Dudley, Jr. 1932- WhoFI 94
Harrington, Robert Evans 1962- WhoAmL 94
Harrington, Robert S. d1993 NewYTBS 93
Harrington, Roger Fuller 1925- WhoAm 94
Harrington, Rosemarie 1956- WhoMW 93
Harrington, Russell Doyne, Jr. 1944- WhoAm 94
Harrington, Thomas Barrett 1936- WhoAmL 94
Harrington, Thomas Daniel 1952- WhoFI 94
Harrington, Thomas Joseph 1935- WhoAm 94
Harrington, Thomas Neal 1953- WhoAmL 94
Harrington, Timothy J. 1918- WhoAm 94
Harrington, Walter Howard, Jr. 1926- WhoAmL 94, WhoWest 94
Harrington, William 1931- ConAu 42NR
Harrington, William Charles 1942- WhoAmA 93
Harrington, William David 1930- WhoFI 94
Harrington, William Fields 1920- WhoAm 94, WhoScEn 94
Harrington, William Palmer 1925- WhoScEn 94
Harrington, Zella Mason 1940- WhoBlA 94
Harrington-Lloyd, Jeanne Leigh WhoWest 94
Harriot, Thomas 1560-1621 DcLB 136 [port], WhWE, WorScD
Harris Who 94
Harris, Baron 1920- Who 94
Harris, Aaron 1930- WhoAm 94
Harris, Ace d1964 WhoHol 92
Harris, Addie 1940-1982 See Shirelles, The ConMus 11
Harris, Adrian Llewellyn 1950- Who 94
Harris, Al Carl 1956- WhoBlA 94
Harris, Alan d1980 WhoHol 92
Harris, Alan (James) 1916- Who 94
Harris, Albert d1981 WhoHol 92
Harris, Albert Edward 1927- IntWW 93
Harris, Albert J. 1908- WrDr 94
Harris, Alfred DrAPF 93
Harris, Alfred 1919- WhoAm 94
Harris, Alfred Peter 1932- WhoAmA 93, WhoMW 93
Harris, Allen 1929- WhoAm 94, WhoAmL 94
Harris, Anita 1942- WhoHol 92
Harris, Ann Birgitta Sutherland 1937- WhoAm 94
Harris, Ann S. WhoAm 94
Harris, Ann Sutherland 1937- WhoAmA 93
Harris, Anne Macintosh 1925- Who 94
Harris, Anthony (Travers Kyrle) 1918- Who 94
Harris, Anthony David 1941- Who 94
Harris, Anthony Geoffrey S. Who 94
Harris, Anthony John 1940- Who 94
Harris, Anthony Leonard 1935- Who 94
Harris, Archie Jerome 1950- WhoBlA 94
Harris, Arlene d1976 WhoHol 92
Harris, Arlene 1944- WhoAm 94
Harris, Arthur Horne 1931- WhoScEn 94
Harris, Arthur Leonard, III 1949- WhoBlA 94
Harris, Augustine 1917- IntWW 93, Who 94

Harris, Augustus (Henry Glossop) 1852-1896 *NewGrDO*
Harris, Aurand 1915- *WhoAm 94, WrDr 94*
Harris, Avaline True 1935- *WhoAm 94*
Harris, Averell d1966 *WhoHol 92*
Harris, Barbara 1935- *IntMPA 94, WhoAm 94*
Harris, Barbara Ann 1951- *WhoBlA 94*
Harris, Barbara C. 1930- *AfrAmAl 6 [port]*
Harris, Barbara Clemente 1931- *WhoBlA 94*
Harris, Barbara Clementine 1930- *WhoAm 94*
Harris, Barbara Hull 1921- *WhoWest 94*
Harris, Basil Vivian 1921- *Who 94*
Harris, Bayard Easter 1944- *WhoAmL 94*
Harris, Ben Jorj 1904-1957 *WhoAmA 93N*
Harris, Ben Maxwell 1923- *WhoAm 94*
Harris, Benjamin 1949- *WhoScEn 94*
Harris, Benjamin Harte, Jr. 1937- *WhoAm 94, WhoAmL 94*
Harris, Bernard A., Jr. *WhoBlA 94*
Harris, Bernice Eisen 1927- *WhoFI 94*
Harris, Bert J., Jr. 1919- *WhoAmP 93*
Harris, Betty Wright 1940- *WhoBlA 94*
Harris, Bill 1939- *WhoAmP 93*
Harris, Bob Lee 1938- *WhoMW 93*
Harris, Brad *WhoHol 92*
Harris, Brent Richard 1959- *WhoFI 94*
Harris, Brian *Who 94*
Harris, (Reginald) Brian 1934- *Who 94*
Harris, Brian Craig 1941- *WhoAmL 94*
Harris, Brian Nicholas 1931- *Who 94*
Harris, Brian Thomas 1932- *Who 94*
Harris, Bruce Eugene 1950- *WhoFI 94*
Harris, Bruce Fairgray 1921- *WrDr 94*
Harris, Bryant G. 1916- *WhoBlA 94*
Harris, Burnell 1954- *WhoBlA 94*
Harris, Burton Henry 1941- *WhoAm 94*
Harris, Burton M. 1938- *WhoAm 94*
Harris, Burtt *IntMPA 94*
Harris, Calvin D. 1941- *WhoBlA 94*
Harris, Carl Gordon 1936- *WhoBlA 94*
Harris, Carol R. 1954- *WhoBlA 94*
Harris, Caroline d1937 *WhoHol 92*
Harris, Carolyn Ann 1953- *WhoBlA 94*
Harris, Caspa L., Jr. 1928- *WhoBlA 94*
Harris, Cecil Rhodes 1923- *Who 94*
Harris, Charles *Who 94*
Harris, (Geoffrey) Charles (Wesson) 1945- *Who 94*
Harris, Charles Albert 1952- *WhoBlA 94*
Harris, Charles Burt 1940- *WhoMW 93*
Harris, Charles Cornelius 1951- *WhoBlA 94*
Harris, Charles Cox 1952- *WhoAmP 93*
Harris, Charles Dean 1958- *WhoMW 93*
Harris, Charles Edgar 1915- *WhoAm 94*
Harris, Charles Elmer 1922- *WhoAm 94*
Harris, Charles F. 1934- *WhoBlA 94*
Harris, Charles Frederick 1934- *WhoAm 94*
Harris, Charles Herbert S. *Who 94*
Harris, Charles Marcus 1943- *WhoAmL 94*
Harris, Charles Overton 1909-1990 *WhAm 10*
Harris, Charles R. d1993 *NewYTBS 93*
Harris, Charles Somerville 1950- *WhoBlA 94, WhoWest 94*
Harris, Charles Thomas 1943- *WhoAmL 94*
Harris, Charles Ward 1926- *WhoAm 94*
Harris, Charles Wesley 1929- *WhoBlA 94*
Harris, Charney Anita *WhoAmA 93*
Harris, Chauncy D(ennison) 1914- *WrDr 94*
Harris, Chauncy Dennison 1914- *IntWW 93, WhoAm 94, WhoMW 93, WhoScEn 94*
Harris, Cheryl Andrea 1967- *WhoBlA 94*
Harris, Chris 1948- *WhoAmP 93*
Harris, Christie 1907- *BlmGWL*
Harris, Christie (Lucy Irwin) 1907- *WrDr 94*
Harris, Christie (Lucy) Irwin 1907- *SmATA 74 [port]*
Harris, Christie Lucy 1907- *WhoAm 94, WhoWest 94*
Harris, Christopher 1933- *WhoAm 94*
Harris, Christopher Kirk 1951- *WhoAm 94*
Harris, Claire 1937- *BlmGWL*
Harris, Clare d1949 *WhoHol 92*
Harris, Clare Winger 1891-1968 *EncSF 93*
Harris, Clark Everett 1966- *WhoWest 94*
Harris, Claude *WhoWest 94*
Harris, Claude 1940- *WhoAmP 93*
Harris, Claude, Jr. 1940- *WhoAmL 94*
Harris, Clifton L. 1938- *WhoBlA 94*
Harris, Colin Cyril 1928- *WhoAm 94*
Harris, Conley 1943- *WhoAmA 93*
Harris, Cornelia 1963- *WhoBlA 94*
Harris, Craig 1952- *WhoMW 93*
Harris, Curtis Alexander 1956- *WhoBlA 94*
Harris, Cynthia *WhoHol 92*
Harris, Cynthia Julian 1953- *WhoBlA 94*
Harris, Cyril Manton *WhoAm 94*
Harris, D. George 1933- *WhoAm 94*
Harris, Daisy 1931- *WhoBlA 94*
Harris, Dale Benner 1914- *WhoAm 94*
Harris, Dale Ray 1937- *WhoAm 94, WhoAmL 94, WhoWest 94*
Harris, Dan Wayne 1950- *WhoFI 94*
Harris, Daniel, Jr. 1948- *WhoAmL 94*
Harris, Darryl Wayne 1941- *WhoAm 94, WhoWest 94*
Harris, David *WhoAmP 93, WhoHol 92*
Harris, David 1922- *Who 94*
Harris, David, Jr. 1931- *WhoBlA 94*
Harris, David Alan 1949- *WhoAm 94*
Harris, David Andrew 1934- *WhoMW 93*
Harris, David Anthony 1937- *Who 94*
Harris, David Ellsworth 1934- *WhoBlA 94*
Harris, David Henry 1924- *WhoAm 94*
Harris, David Jack 1948- *WhoAmA 93, WhoWest 94*
Harris, David Joel 1950- *WhoFI 94, WhoWest 94*
Harris, David L. 1948- *WhoAmL 94*
Harris, David L. 1952- *WhoBlA 94*
Harris, David Michael 1943- *Who 94*
Harris, David Philip 1937- *WhoMW 93*
Harris, David Russell 1930- *Who 94*
Harris, David Thomas 1956- *WhoWest 94*
Harris, Deborah Turner 1951- *WrDr 94*
Harris, Debra Coral 1953- *WhoWest 94*
Harris, Debra Lynne 1956- *WhoMW 93*
Harris, Dewey Lynn 1933- *WhoMW 93*
Harris, DeWitt O. 1944- *WhoBlA 94*
Harris, Diana R. *Who 94*
Harris, Diane Carol 1942- *WhoAm 94*
Harris, Dolores Ashley *WhoAmA 93*
Harris, Dolores M. 1930- *WhoBlA 94*
Harris, Don Navarro 1929- *WhoBlA 94*
Harris, Don Victor, Jr. 1921- *WhoAm 94, WhoAmL 94*
Harris, Donald 1931- *WhoAm 94*
Harris, Donald Bertram 1904- *Who 94*
Harris, Donald J. *WhoBlA 94*
Harris, Donald Ray 1938- *WhoAm 94*
Harris, Donald Stuart 1940- *WhoBlA 94*
Harris, Donald Wayne 1942- *WhoMW 93*
Harris, Dorothy Clark 1949- *WhoAm 94*
Harris, Dorothy D. 1935- *WhoAmA 93*
Harris, Dorothy Vilma 1936- *WhoHisp 94*
Harris, Douglas Allen 1942- *WhoBlA 94*
Harris, Douglas Clay 1939- *WhoAm 94, WhoFI 94*
Harris, Dudley Arthur 1925- *WrDr 94*
Harris, Earl 1922- *WhoBlA 94*
Harris, Earl Edward 1931- *WhoAm 94*
Harris, Earl L. *WhoAmP 93*
Harris, Earl L. 1941- *WhoBlA 94*
Harris, Ed 1950- *IntMPA 94, WhoHol 92*
Harris, Ed Jerome J. 1920- *WhoAmP 93*
Harris, Eddy Louis 1956- *WhoBlA 94*
Harris, Edmund Leslie 1928- *Who 94*
Harris, Edna Mae *WhoHol 92*
Harris, Edward A. 1946- *WhoWest 94*
Harris, Edward Allen 1950- *WhoAm 94*
Harris, Edward D., Jr. 1937- *WhoAm 94*
Harris, Edward E. 1933- *WhoBlA 94*
Harris, Edward Richard, Jr. 1928- *WhoAmP 93*
Harris, Edwin Cyrus 1940- *WhoAmP 93*
Harris, Elbert L. 1913- *WhoBlA 94*
Harris, Elihu Mason 1947- *WhoAm 94, WhoAmP 93, WhoBlA 94, WhoWest 94*
Harris, Elizabeth 1944- *WrDr 94*
Harris, Ellen Gandy 1910- *WhoAm 94*
Harris, Ellen Schwartz 1949- *WhoAmA 93*
Harris, Ellen W. 1948- *WhoAm 94, WhoAmL 94*
Harris, Elliott Stanley 1922- *WhoAm 94*
Harris, Elmer Beseler 1939- *WhoAm 94*
Harris, Elroy 1966- *WhoBlA 94*
Harris, Emily Katharine *DrAPF 93*
Harris, Emma Earl 1936- *WhoWest 94*
Harris, Emmylou 1947- *WhoAm 94, WhoHol 92*
Harris, Eric Albert 1920- *WhoWest 94*
Harris, Eric Nathan 1959- *WhoWest 94*
Harris, Eric William 1951- *WhoScEn 94*
Harris, Errol E(ustace) 1908- *ConAu 41NR*
Harris, Eugene Edward 1940- *WhoBlA 94*
Harris, Eugene Whitney 1964- *WhoMW 93*
Harris, Evelyn S. 1950- *WhoAmL 94*
Harris, F. Chandler 1914- *WhoWest 94*
Harris, Fletcher 1926- *WhoAmP 93*
Harris, Forrest Joseph 1916- *WhoAmP 93*
Harris, Fox d1988 *WhoHol 92*
Harris, Francis 1957- *WrDr 94*
Harris, Franco *ProFbHF [port]*
Harris, Franco 1950- *WhoBlA 94*
Harris, Frank *Who 94, WhoBlA 94*
Harris, Frank 1856-1931 *EncSF 93*
Harris, Frank 1934- *Who 94*
Harris, (Walter) Frank 1920- *Who 94*
Harris, Frank W. 1920- *WhoAmP 93*
Harris, Fred *WhoBlA 94*
Harris, Fred R. 1930- *WhoAm 94, WhoAmP 93, WrDr 94*
Harris, Frederick Allan 1941- *WhoWest 94*
Harris, Frederick George 1922- *WhoAm 94*
Harris, Freeman Cosmo 1935- *WhoBlA 94*
Harris, Gail B. 1953- *WhoAmL 94*
Harris, Gary Lynn 1953- *WhoBlA 94*
Harris, Gary M. 1943- *WhoWest 94*
Harris, Gene 1964- *WhoBlA 94*
Harris, Geoffrey (Herbert) 1914- *Who 94*
Harris, Geoffrey Wingfield 1913-1971 *DcNaB MP*
Harris, George d1986 *WhoHol 92*
Harris, George A. 1950- *WrDr 94*
Harris, George Bryan 1964- *WhoAmL 94*
Harris, George Dea 1945- *WhoBlA 94*
Harris, George E., Jr. 1955- *WhoWest 94*
Harris, Geraldine 1951- *WrDr 94*
Harris, Geraldine E. *WhoBlA 94*
Harris, Gil W. 1946- *WhoBlA 94*
Harris, Gladys Bailey 1947- *WhoBlA 94*
Harris, Gladys Marris 1965- *WhoMW 93*
Harris, Gleason Ray 1952- *WhoBlA 94*
Harris, Glen *WhoAm 94*
Harris, Glenn Anthony 1951- *WhoAmL 94*
Harris, Glenn H. 1919- *WhoAmP 93*
Harris, Gloriane 1947- *WhoAmA 93*
Harris, Gregory George 1951- *WhoAmL 94*
Harris, Gregory Scott 1955- *WhoAm 94*
Harris, Guy Hendrickson 1914- *WhoScEn 94*
Harris, H(enry) S(ilton) 1926- *WrDr 94*
Harris, Harcourt Glenties 1928- *WhoBlA 94*
Harris, Harold (Morris) 1915- *WrDr 94*
Harris, Harold (Morris) 1915-1993 *ConAu 142*
Harris, Harold Hart 1940- *WhoMW 93*
Harris, Harold Ross 1895- *WhAm 10*
Harris, Harold Stephen, Jr. 1955- *WhoAmL 94*
Harris, Harry 1919- *IntWW 93, Who 94*
Harris, Harvey Sherman 1915- *WhoAmA 93*
Harris, Hassel B. 1931- *WhoBlA 94*
Harris, Helen(a) (Barbara Mary) 1927- *WrDr 94*
Harris, Helen B. 1925- *WhoBlA 94*
Harris, Henry 1925- *IntWW 93, Who 94*
Harris, Henry Hiter, Jr. 1922- *WhoAm 94*
Harris, Henry William 1919- *WhoAm 94*
Harris, Henry Wood 1938- *WhoAm 94*
Harris, Herbert 1911- *WrDr 94*
Harris, Herbert Donald, Jr. 1932- *WhoAm 94*
Harris, Herbert E., II 1926- *WhoAmP 93*
Harris, Hollis Loyd 1931- *WhoAm 94, WhoFI 94*
Harris, Horatio Preston 1925- *WhoBlA 94*
Harris, Howard Alan 1939- *WhoScEn 94*
Harris, Howard Elliott 1943- *WhoAm 94*
Harris, Howard F. 1909- *WhoBlA 94*
Harris, Howard Hunter 1924- *WhoAm 94*
Harris, Howard Jeffrey 1949- *WhoWest 94*
Harris, Hugh Christopher Emlyn 1936- *Who 94*
Harris, Hugh Robert 1938- *WhoMW 93*
Harris, Ian (Cecil) 1910- *Who 94*
Harris, Ira Stephen 1945- *WhoScEn 94*
Harris, Irene Joyce 1926- *Who 94*
Harris, Irving 1927- *WhoAm 94*
Harris, Irving Brooks 1910- *WhoAm 94*
Harris, Isaac Henson 1912- *WhoAm 94*
Harris, J. Henry *EncSF 93*
Harris, J. Mervyn 1933- *WhoAmP 93*
Harris, J. Ollie 1913- *WhoAmP 93*
Harris, J. Robert, II 1944- *WhoBlA 94*
Harris, Jack *WhoBlA 94*
Harris, Jack H. 1931- *WhoAmP 93*
Harris, Jack Wolfred Ashford 1906- *Who 94*
Harris, Jacob George 1938- *WhoAm 94*
Harris, James *WhoBlA 94*
Harris, James 1746-1820 *WhAmRev*
Harris, James, III *WhoBlA 94*
Harris, James A. 1926- *WhoBlA 94*
Harris, James A., Jr. 1944- *WhoAmL 94*
Harris, James Andrew 1932- *WhoBlA 94*
Harris, James B. 1928- *IntMPA 94*
Harris, James C., II 1967- *WhoScEn 94*
Harris, James Dexter 1919- *WhoAm 94*
Harris, James E. 1946- *WhoBlA 94*
Harris, James Edward 1947- *WhoAmL 94*
Harris, James Franklin 1941- *WhoAm 94*
Harris, James G., Jr. 1931- *WhoBlA 94*
Harris, James Herman 1942- *WhoMW 93, WhoScEn 94*
Harris, James Howard 1961- *WhoMW 93*
Harris, James Martin 1928- *WhoAm 94*
Harris, James Michael 1951- *WhoAm 94*
Harris, James W. 1946- *WhoAm 94*
Harris, James Wilbur 1948- *WhoAmP 93*
Harris, Jana *DrAPF 93*
Harris, Jana 1947- *WrDr 94*
Harris, Janel Kay 1949- *WhoMW 93*
Harris, Jasper William 1935- *WhoBlA 94*
Harris, Jay Howard 1936- *WhoAm 94*
Harris, Jay Terrence 1948- *WhoBlA 94*
Harris, Jean E. 1947- *WhoAm 94, WhoAmL 94*
Harris, Jean Laney 1932- *WhoAmP 93*
Harris, Jean Louise 1931- *WhoAm 94, WhoBlA 94, WhoMW 93*
Harris, Jeanette G. 1934- *WhoBlA 94*
Harris, Jed Gilbert, Jr. 1954- *WhoAmP 93*
Harris, Jeffrey 1944- *WhoAm 94*
Harris, Jeffrey Sherman 1944- *WhoAm 94*
Harris, Jerilyn Rolinson 1942- *WhoWest 94*
Harris, Jerome C., Jr. 1947- *WhoBlA 94*
Harris, Jerome Sylvan 1909- *WhoAm 94*
Harris, Jerrold B. 1942- *WhoFI 94*
Harris, Jerry L. 1943- *WhoAmL 94*
Harris, Jesse Graham, Jr. 1926-1988 *WhAm 10*
Harris, Jim *WhoHol 92*
Harris, Jimmie 1945- *WhoBlA 94*
Harris, Jo Ann *WhoHol 92*
Harris, Joe Frank 1936- *WhoAm 94, WhoAmP 93*
Harris, Joe Newton 1946- *WhoWest 94*
Harris, Joel Bruce 1941- *WhoAm 94, WhoAmL 94*
Harris, Joel Chandler 1848-1908 *AmCulL, RfGShF*
Harris, John 1791-1873 *DcNaB MP*
Harris, John 1916-1991 *WrDr 94N*
Harris, John 1932- *Who 94*
Harris, John (Hulme) 1938- *Who 94*
Harris, John Beynon *EncSF 93*
Harris, John Charles 1936- *Who 94*
Harris, John Charles 1943- *WhoAm 94*
Harris, John Chester 1953- *WhoMW 93*
Harris, John Clifton 1935- *WhoBlA 94*
Harris, John Edward 1936- *WhoAm 94*
Harris, John Edwin 1932- *Who 94*
Harris, John Everett 1930- *WhoBlA 94*
Harris, John F(rederick) 1931- *WrDr 94*
Harris, John Frederick 1931- *Who 94*
Harris, John Frederick 1938- *Who 94*
Harris, John H. 1940 *WhoBlA 94*
Harris, John J. 1951- *WhoBlA 94*
Harris, John Kenneth 1948- *WhoAmL 94*
Harris, John Myron 1926- *WhoAmP 93*
Harris, John Percival 1925- *Who 94*
Harris, John Robert 1919- *IntWW 93, Who 94*
Harris, John William 1920- *WhoAm 94*
Harris, John Woods 1893- *WhoFI 94*
Harris, Johnson *EncSF 93*
Harris, Jonathan 1917- *WhoHol 92*
Harris, Jonathan 1921- *WrDr 94*
Harris, Jonathan R. 1950- *WhoAmL 94*
Harris, Jordan *WhoAm 94*
Harris, Joseph *DrAPF 93*
Harris, Joseph d1953 *WhoHol 92*
Harris, Joseph Benjamin 1920- *WhoBlA 94*
Harris, Joseph Elliot, II 1945- *WhoBlA 94*
Harris, Joseph John, III 1946- *WhoBlA 94*
Harris, Joseph McAllister 1929- *WhoMW 93, WhoScEn 94*
Harris, Joseph P. 1938- *WhoAmP 93*
Harris, Joseph Preston 1935- *WhoBlA 94*
Harris, Joseph R. 1937- *WhoBlA 94*
Harris, Joy *Who 94*
Harris, Joyce Jean 1928- *WhoFI 94*
Harris, Judith L. 1948- *WhoAmL 94*
Harris, Jules Eli 1934- *WhoAm 94, WhoScEn 94*
Harris, Julie *IntMPA 94*
Harris, Julie 1925- *IntMPA 94, IntWW 93, WhoHol 92*
Harris, Julie Ann 1925- *WhoAm 94*
Harris, Julius *WhoHol 92*
Harris, Julius 1940- *WhoBlA 94*
Harris, Jullian Hoke 1906-1987 *WhoAmA 93N*
Harris, K. David 1927- *WhoAm 94, WhoAmL 94, WhoAmP 93, WhoMW 93*
Harris, Karen Kostock 1942- *WhoFI 94*
Harris, Karen L. 1963- *WhoScEn 94*
Harris, Katherine d1927 *WhoHol 92*
Harris, Kathy B. 1948- *WhoFI 94*
Harris, Kay d1971 *WhoHol 92*
Harris, Keith Murray 1932- *Who 94*
Harris, Keith Stell 1952- *WhoWest 94*
Harris, Kenneth *Who 94*
Harris, Kenneth 1919- *IntWW 93*
Harris, (David) Kenneth 1919- *Who 94*
Harris, Kenneth Alfred 1949- *WhoFI 94*
Harris, Kenneth Kelley 1960- *WhoScEn 94*
Harris, Kenny D. 1950- *WhoAmP 93*
Harris, King William 1943- *WhoFI 94*
Harris, Kip King 1945- *WhoWest 94*
Harris, LaDonna Vita Crawford 1931- *AmSocL*
Harris, Lara *WhoHol 92*

Harris, William John 1928- *WhoAm 94*
Harris, William Joseph 1944- *WhoScEn 94*
Harris, William M. 1932- *WhoBlA 94*
Harris, William McKinley, Sr. 1941- *WhoBlA 94*
Harris, William North 1938- *WhoFI 94*
Harris, William R. 1915- *WhoBlA 94*
Harris, William Stanworth 1950- *WhoAmL 94*
Harris, William Theodore, Jr. 1949- *WhoAmL 94*
Harris, William Vernon 1938- *WhoAm 94*
Harris, William Wadsworth, II *WhoAmA 93*
Harris, Wilson *Who 94*
Harris, Wilson 1921- *BlmGEL*
Harris, (Theodore) Wilson 1921- *BlkWr 2, Who 94, WrDr 94*
Harris, Winifred 1880- *WhoHol 92*
Harris, Winifred Clarke 1924- *WhoBlA 94*
Harris, Wynonie d1969 *WhoHol 92*
Harris, Y. L. *DrAPF 93*
Harris, Yvette Renee 1957- *WhoScEn 94*
Harris, Zelema M. 1940- *WhoBlA 94*
Harris-Burland, J(ohn) B(urland) 1870-1926 *EncSF 93*
Harris-Ebohon, Altheria Thyra 1948- *WhoBlA 94*
Harris Jones, Mary 1830?-1930 *WomPubS*
Harris McKenzie, Ruth Bates 1919- *WhoBlA 94*
Harris Of Greenwich, Baron 1930- *Who 94*
Harris Of High Cross, Baron 1924- *IntWW 93, Who 94*
Harrison *Who 94*
Harrison, A. B. 1909- *WhoBlA 94*
Harrison, Adlene 1923- *WhoAmP 93*
Harrison, Aidan Timothy 1960- *WhoScEn 94*
Harrison, Albert Norman d1992 *Who 94N*
Harrison, Albertis Sydney, Jr. 1907- *WhoAmP 93*
Harrison, Alene *WhoWest 94*
Harrison, Algea Othella 1936- *WhoBlA 94*
Harrison, (William) Allan 1911- *WhoAmA 93N*
Harrison, Alonzo 1952- *WhoFI 94*
Harrison, Anna Jane 1912 *WhoAm 94, WhoScEn 94*
Harrison, Antony H. 1948- *WrDr 94*
Harrison, Barbara Grizzuti 1934- *WhoAm 94*
Harrison, Barry 1951- *WhoScEn 94*
Harrison, Beatrice Marie 1958- *WhoMW 93*
Harrison, Benjamin c. 1724-1791 *HisWorL*
Harrison, Benjamin 1726-1791 *WhAmRev*
Harrison, Benjamin Leslie 1928- *WhoAm 94*
Harrison, Bernard 1933- *WrDr 94*
Harrison, Beverly E. 1948- *WhoBlA 94*
Harrison, Bob 1927- *BasBi*
Harrison, Bob 1941- *WhoBlA 94*
Harrison, Booker David 1908- *WhoBlA 94*
Harrison, Boyd G., Jr. 1949- *WhoBlA 94*
Harrison, Brian *Who 94*
Harrison, (Alastair) Brian (Clarke) 1921- *Who 94*
Harrison, Brian Fraser 1918- *WrDr 94*
Harrison, Bryan Desmond 1931- *IntWW 93, Who 94*
Harrison, Bryan James 1947- *Who 94*
Harrison, Cameron Elias 1945- *Who 94*
Harrison, Carey d1957 *WhoHol 92*
Harrison, Carlos Enrique 1956- *WhoHisp 94*
Harrison, Carol L. 1946- *WhoBlA 94*
Harrison, Carole 1933- *WhoAmA 93*
Harrison, Carole Alberta 1942- *WhoWest 94*
Harrison, Cathryn 1959- *WhoHol 92*
Harrison, Charles Maurice 1927- *WhoAm 94, WhoAmL 94*
Harrison, Charles Victor 1907- *Who 94*
Harrison, Charles Wagner, Jr. 1913- *WhoAm 94, WhoScEn 94, WhoWest 94*
Harrison, Charlie J., Jr. 1932- *WhoBlA 94, WhoMW 93*
Harrison, Charlie James, Jr. 1932- *WhoAmP 93*
Harrison, Christine Delane 1947- *WhoMW 93*
Harrison, Claude William 1922- *Who 94*
Harrison, Clifford Joy, Jr. 1925- *WhoAm 94*
Harrison, Colin *Who 94*
Harrison, (Robert) Colin 1938- *Who 94*
Harrison, Constance Cary 1843-1920 *BlmGWL*
Harrison, Craig 1942- *EncSF 93*
Harrison, Craig Donald 1956- *WhoFI 94*

Harrison, Craig Royston 1933- *WhoWest 94*
Harrison, Dalton C. 1953- *WhoAmP 93*
Harrison, Daphne Duval 1932- *WhoBlA 94*
Harrison, David 1930- *IntWW 93, Who 94*
Harrison, David Lakin 1926- *WrDr 94*
Harrison, Delbert Eugene 1951- *WhoBlA 94*
Harrison, Denis Byrne 1917- *Who 94*
Harrison, Devin *DrAPF 93*
Harrison, Don Edmunds 1950- *WhoWest 94*
Harrison, Don K., Sr. 1933- *WhoBlA 94*
Harrison, Donald 1946- *WhoAm 94, WhoAmL 94*
Harrison, Donald (Frederick Norris) 1925- *Who 94*
Harrison, Donald Carey 1934- *WhoAm 94*
Harrison, Donald Richard 1947- *WhoAmP 93*
Harrison, Douglas A. 1949- *WhoAmL 94*
Harrison, Douglas Creese 1901- *Who 94*
Harrison, E. Hunter 1944- *WhoAm 94, WhoFI 94*
Harrison, Earl David 1932- *WhoAm 94, WhoAmL 94, WhoFI 94*
Harrison, Earle 1903- *WhoAm 94, WhoFI 94, WhoWest 94*
Harrison, Edward 1766-1838 *DcNaB MP*
Harrison, Edward Peter Graham 1948- *Who 94*
Harrison, Edward Robert 1919- *WhoAm 94*
Harrison, Edward Thomas, Jr. 1929- *WhoScEn 94*
Harrison, Edythe C. 1937- *WhoAmP 93*
Harrison, Elizabeth Fancourt *WrDr 94*
Harrison, Ellen Kroll 1946- *WhoAm 94, WhoAmL 94*
Harrison, Emma Louise 1918- *WhoBlA 94*
Harrison, Emmett Bruce, Jr. 1932- *WhoAm 94*
Harrison, Ernest (Thomas) 1926- *Who 94*
Harrison, Ernest Alexander 1937- *WhoBlA 94*
Harrison, Ernest Franklin 1929- *WhoAm 94*
Harrison, Ernest Thomas 1926- *IntWW 93*
Harrison, Ethel Mae 1931- *WhoWest 94*
Harrison, Everett F(alconer) 1902- *WrDr 94*
Harrison, Faye Venetia 1951- *WhoBlA 94*
Harrison, Francis Alexander Lyle 1910- *Who 94*
Harrison, Francis Anthony Kitchener 1914- *Who 94*
Harrison, Frank *Who 94*
Harrison, Frank 1913- *WhoAm 94*
Harrison, Frank 1940- *WhoAmP 93*
Harrison, Frank Joseph 1919- *WhoAmL 94*
Harrison, Fred Brian 1927- *Who 94*
Harrison, Frederick Joseph 1951- *WhoAmL 94, WhoAmP 93*
Harrison, George 1943- *IntMPA 94, IntWW 93, WhoAm 94, WhoHol 92*
Harrison, George Brooks 1940- *WhoAm 94*
Harrison, Gerald 1929- *WhoAm 94*
Harrison, Gilbert Warner 1940- *WhoAm 94*
Harrison, Gloria Gimma 1928- *WhoAm 94*
Harrison, Gloria Macías *WhoHisp 94*
Harrison, Gordon Ray 1931- *WhoAm 94*
Harrison, Gregory 1950- *WhoHol 92*
Harrison, Gregory 1952- *IntMPA 94, WhoAm 94*
Harrison, Gregory Alexander 1896- *WhAm 10*
Harrison, Gregory Arnold 1944- *WhoAm 94*
Harrison, Guy Newell 1946- *WhoAmL 94*
Harrison, Harold Edward 1908-1989 *WhAm 10*
Harrison, Harry 1925- *EncSF 93, WrDr 94*
Harrison, Harry Paul 1923- *WhoAmP 93, WhoBlA 94*
Harrison, Hattie N. 1928- *WhoAmP 93, WhoBlA 94*
Harrison, Hazel 1883-1969 *AfrAmAl 6*
Harrison, Helen Amy 1943- *WhoAmA 93*
Harrison, Helen Mayer *WhoAmA 93*
Harrison, Helga (Susan Barbara) 1923- *EncSF 93*
Harrison, Henry Starin 1930- *WhoAm 94*
Harrison, Ian Stewart 1919- *Who 94*
Harrison, Imelda *WhoHisp 94*
Harrison, J. Berry 1939- *WhoAmP 93*
Harrison, J. Frank, Jr. 1930- *WhoAm 94, WhoFI 94*
Harrison, J. Waller 1940- *WhoAmL 94*
Harrison, James *WorInv*
Harrison, James, Jr. 1930- *WhoBlA 94*

Harrison, James (Ernest) 1927- *ConAu 140*
Harrison, James H. 1951- *WhoAmP 93*
Harrison, James Harvey, Jr. 1927- *WhoFI 94*
Harrison, James Joshua, Jr. 1936- *WhoAm 94*
Harrison, James Ostelle 1920- *WhoScEn 94*
Harrison, James R. 1956- *WhoMW 93*
Harrison, James Thomas 1937- *WhoAm 94*
Harrison, James Wilburn 1918- *WhoScEn 94*
Harrison, Jean *WhoHol 92*
Harrison, Jeanette LaVerne 1948- *WhoBlA 94*
Harrison, Jeffrey *DrAPF 93*
Harrison, Jenilee 1960- *WhoHol 92*
Harrison, Jeremy Thomas 1935- *WhoAm 94*
Harrison, Jerry Calvin 1941- *WhoAm 94*
Harrison, Jessel Anidjah 1923- *Who 94*
Harrison, Jim *DrAPF 93*
Harrison, Jim 1937- *WrDr 94*
Harrison, Jimmie 1952- *WhoAmA 93*
Harrison, Jimmy d1977 *WhoHol 92*
Harrison, Joan 1909- *IntDcF 2-4*
Harrison, Joan S. d1993 *NewYTBS 93*
Harrison, Joe B. 1941- *WhoAmL 94*
Harrison, John 1693-1776 *WorInv*
Harrison, John (Albert Bews) 1921- *Who 94*
Harrison, John Alexander 1944- *WhoAm 94*
Harrison, John Armstrong 1915- *WhoAm 94*
Harrison, John Arthur 1936- *WhoAm 94*
Harrison, John Barron 1937- *WhoFI 94*
Harrison, John Clive 1937- *Who 94*
Harrison, John Conway 1913- *WhoAm 94, WhoAmL 94, WhoAmP 93, WhoWest 94*
Harrison, John F(letcher) C(lews) 1921- *WrDr 94*
Harrison, John Fletcher Clews 1921- *Who 94*
Harrison, John H. *Who 94*
Harrison, John Ray 1930- *WhoAmP 93*
Harrison, John Raymond 1933- *WhoAm 94*
Harrison, John Straton, Jr. 1956- *WhoFI 94*
Harrison, Joseph Gillis, Jr. 1950- *WhoHisp 94*
Harrison, Joseph Heavrin 1929- *WhoAmL 94*
Harrison, Joseph Robert, Jr. 1918- *WhoAmA 93*
Harrison, Joseph William 1931- *WhoAmP 93, WhoMW 93*
Harrison, Joseph Wylie 1937- *WhoAmP 93*
Harrison, Julia 1920- *WhoAmP 93*
Harrison, June d1974 *WhoHol 92*
Harrison, Karen A. 1947- *WhoMW 93*
Harrison, Kathleen 1892- *Who 94*
Harrison, Kathleen 1898- *WhoHol 92*
Harrison, Keith (Edward) 1932- *WrDr 94*
Harrison, Keith Michaele 1956- *WhoWest 94*
Harrison, Ken L. 1942- *WhoAm 94, WhoWest 94*
Harrison, Kenneth (Cecil) 1915- *WrDr 94*
Harrison, Kenneth Cecil 1915- *Who 94*
Harrison, Kenneth Lee 1955- *WhoFI 94*
Harrison, Lester 20th cent.- *BasBi*
Harrison, Linda 1946- *WhoHol 92*
Harrison, Lois Smith 1924- *WhoFI 94*
Harrison, Lorrin d1993 *NewYTBS 93*
Harrison, Lou 1917- *NewGrDO*
Harrison, Lou Silver 1917- *WhoAm 94*
Harrison, Lowell H 1922- *WrDr 94*
Harrison, Lyndon Henry Arthur 1947- *Who 94*
Harrison, M(ichael) John 1945- *EncSF 93, WrDr 94*
Harrison, Marcia Ann 1955- *WhoScEn 94*
Harrison, Marion Edwyn 1931- *WhoAm 94, WhoAmL 94*
Harrison, Marjorie Freeman 1952- *WhoAmP 93*
Harrison, Mark d1952 *WhoHol 92*
Harrison, Mark I. 1934- *WhoAm 94, WhoAmL 94*
Harrison, Mernoy Edward, Jr. 1947- *WhoBlA 94*
Harrison, Michael *Who 94, WhoHol 92*
Harrison, Michael 1907- *WrDr 94*
Harrison, Michael 1907-1991 *EncSF 93*
Harrison, Michael 1939- *Who 94*
Harrison, Michael 1940- *WhoAm 94*
Harrison, (George) Michael (Antony) 1925- *WhoAm 94*
Harrison, Michael (Guy Vicat) 1939- *Who 94*
Harrison, Michael Alexander 1936- *WhoWest 94*

Harrison, Michael Gregory 1941- *WhoAmL 94*
Harrison, Michael Jackson 1941- *Who 94*
Harrison, Michael James Harwood 1936- *Who 94*
Harrison, Michael Jay 1932- *WhoAm 94*
Harrison, Molly 1909- *Who 94*
Harrison, Mona K. d1957 *WhoHol 92*
Harrison, Monika Edwards 1949- *WhoAm 94*
Harrison, Moses W., II 1932- *WhoAmL 94, WhoAmP 93, WhoMW 93*
Harrison, Nancy 1923- *ConAu 142*
Harrison, Nell d1973 *WhoHol 92*
Harrison, Newton A. 1932- *WhoAmA 93*
Harrison, Noel 1934- *WhoHol 92*
Harrison, Orrin Lea, III 1949- *WhoAmL 94*
Harrison, Orval C. 1940- *WhoAmP 93*
Harrison, Otto R. *WhoAm 94, WhoFI 94*
Harrison, Pamela *DrAPF 93*
Harrison, Patricia de Stacy *WhoAm 94, WhoFI 94*
Harrison, Patrick George 1943- *WhoWest 94*
Harrison, Patrick Kennard 1928- *Who 94*
Harrison, Patrick Woods 1946- *WhoAmL 94*
Harrison, Paul Carter 1936- *BlkWr 2, WhoBlA 94*
Harrison, Pearl Lewis 1932- *WhoBlA 94*
Harrison, Peter 1716-1775 *AmCulL [port]*
Harrison, R. Reed, III 1948- *WhoFI 94*
Harrison, Ray 1928- *WhoAmP 93*
Harrison, Rebecca Newth *DrAPF 93*
Harrison, Rex d1990 *WhoHol 92*
Harrison, Rex Carey 1908-1990 *WhAm 10*
Harrison, Richard *Who 94, WhoHol 92*
Harrison, Richard 1920- *IntWW 93*
Harrison, Richard (John) 1920- *Who 94*
Harrison, (John) Richard 1921- *Who 94*
Harrison, Richard (John), Sir 1920- *WrDr 94*
Harrison, Richard B. d1935 *WhoHol 92*
Harrison, Richard B. 1864-1935 *AfrAmAl 6*
Harrison, Richard Donald 1923- *WhoAm 94*
Harrison, Richard Paul, Jr. 1960- *WhoMW 93*
Harrison, Richard Wayne 1944- *WhoAm 94, WhoAmL 94*
Harrison, Robert Drew 1923- *WhoAm 94*
Harrison, Robert H. 1745-1790 *WhAmRev*
Harrison, Robert Hunter 1929- *WhoScEn 94*
Harrison, Robert Michael 1945- *Who 94*
Harrison, Robert Vernon McElroy 1935- *WhoAm 94*
Harrison, Robert Victor 1951- *WhoScEn 94*
Harrison, Robert Walker, III 1941- *WhoBlA 94*
Harrison, Roger *Who 94*
Harrison, Roger 1938- *WrDr 94*
Harrison, (Desmond) Roger (Wingate) 1933- *Who 94*
Harrison, Roger G. 1943- *WhoAmP 93*
Harrison, Roger Gran 1943- *WhoAm 94*
Harrison, Ronald E. 1936- *WhoBlA 94*
Harrison, Ronald Gary 1941- *WhoAmP 93*
Harrison, Roscoe Conklin, Jr. 1944- *WhoBlA 94*
Harrison, Roslyn Siman 1935- *WhoAm 94*
Harrison, Rowland John Hill 1943- *IntWW 93*
Harrison, Roy M(ichael) 1948- *ConAu 140*
Harrison, Russell Edward 1921- *IntWW 93*
Harrison, S. David 1930- *WhoAm 94*
Harrison, Samuel Hughel 1956- *WhoAmL 94*
Harrison, Sarah 1946- *WrDr 94*
Harrison, Scott Patrick 1962- *WhoAmL 94*
Harrison, Selig Seidenman 1927- *WhoAm 94*
Harrison, Shirley Dindy 1951- *WhoBlA 94*
Harrison, Stephen Coplan 1943- *WhoAm 94*
Harrison, Stephen John 1966- *WhoAmP 93*
Harrison, Stephen Paul 1948- *WhoMW 93*
Harrison, Steven L. 1946- *WhoMW 93*
Harrison, Sue 1950- *WrDr 94*
Harrison, Susan 1938- *WhoHol 92*
Harrison, Susie Frances 1859-1935 *BlmGWL*
Harrison, Ted *Who 94*
Harrison, Terence 1933- *Who 94*
Harrison, Theophilus George 1907- *Who 94*
Harrison, Thomas F. 1942- *WhoAm 94*

Harrison, Thomas Galbraith 1895- WhAm 10
Harrison, Thomas James 1935- WhoAm 94
Harrison, Thomas L. 1947- WhoAm 94
Harrison, Tony 1931- WhoAmA 93
Harrison, Tony 1937- BlmGEL, ConDr 93, IntWW 93, NewGrDO, Who 94, WrDr 94
Harrison, Vernon d1992 WhoBlA 94N
Harrison, Vernon Lee, Jr. 1945- WhoAmL 94
Harrison, Walter 1921- Who 94
Harrison, Walter Andrew 1961- WhoFI 94
Harrison, Walter Ashley 1930- WhoScEn 94, WhoWest 94
Harrison, Warren 1951- WhoFI 94
Harrison, Wayne David 1953- IntWW 93
Harrison, Wendell Richard 1942- WhoBlA 94
Harrison, Wendy Jane Merrill 1961- WhoFI 94
Harrison, Willard W. 1937- WhoScEn 94
Harrison, William DrAPF 93
Harrison, William 1535-1593 DcLB 136
Harrison, William 1813-1868 NewGrDO
Harrison, William, Jr. WhAmRev
Harrison, William Burwell, Jr. 1943- WhoAm 94, WhoFI 94
Harrison, William Hardin 1933- WhoAm 94, WhoWest 94
Harrison, William Henry 1896-1990 WhAm 10
Harrison, William K., Jr. 1895-1987 HisDcKW
Harrison, William L. 1936- WhoIns 94
Harrison, William Neal 1933- WhoAm 94
Harrison, William Oliver, Jr. 1945- WhoAmL 94, WhoAmP 93, WhoFI 94
Harrison, William Ridgeway 1961- WhoWest 94
Harrison, William Wright 1915- WhoAm 94
Harrison-Church, Ronald James 1915- Who 94
Harrison-Hall, Michael Kilgour 1925- Who 94
Harrison-Johnson, Yvonne Elois 1939- WhoAm 94
Harrison-Jones, Lois WhoBlA 94
Harris-Pinkelton, Norma 1927- WhoBlA 94
Harriss, C(lement) Lowell 1912- WrDr 94
Harriss, Charles (Albert Edwin) 1862-1929 NewGrDO
Harriss, Cynthia Therese 1952- WhoAm 94
Harriss, Gerald Leslie 1925- IntWW 93, Who 94
Harriss, James Dozier 1951- WhoFI 94
Harrisville, Roy Alvin, III 1954- WhoMW 93
Harriton, Abraham 1893-1986 WhoAmA 93N
Harritt, Norman L. 1941- WhoAm 94, WhoFI 94
Harroch, Richard David 1953- WhoAm 94, WhoAmL 94
Harrod, Billy Joe 1933- WhoAm 94
Harrod, Charles Scott 1953- WhoWest 94
Harrod, Dominick Roy 1940- Who 94
Harrod, James 1742-1793 WhAmRev
Harrod, Lionel Alexander Digby 1924- Who 94
Harrod, Scott 1910- WhoAm 94
Harrod-Eagles, Cynthia 1948- WrDr 94
Harrold, Austin Leroy 1942- WhoBlA 94
Harrold, Bernard 1925- WhoAm 94, WhoAmL 94
Harrold, Jeffery Deland 1956- WhoBlA 94
Harrold, Kathryn 1950- IntMPA 94, WhoHol 92
Harrold, Lawrence A. 1952- WhoBlA 94
Harrold, Ronald Thomas 1933- WhoAm 94
Harrold, Roy Mealham 1928- Who 94
Harron, Charles d1915 WhoHol 92
Harron, Don(ald Hugh) 1924- ConDr 93, WrDr 94
Harron, Donald 1924- WhoHol 92
Harron, John d1939 WhoHol 92
Harron, Raymond Vincent 1963- WhoMW 93
Harron, Robert d1920 WhoHol 92
Harron, Tessie d1918 WhoHol 92
Harrop, Diane Glaser 1953- WhoFI 94, WhoWest 94
Harrop, Donald Bruce WhoWest 94
Harrop, Peter (John) 1926- Who 94
Harrop, Robert Daniel 1950- WhoAmL 94
Harrop, William Caldwell 1929- WhoAm 94, WhoAmP 93
Harroun, Ann Patricia 1935- WhoAmP 93
Harroun, Dorothy Sumner 1935- WhoAmA 93
Harrow, Kathryn d1987 WhoHol 92
Harrow, Lisa 1943- WhoHol 92
Harrow, Nancy WhoAm 94
Harrowby, Earl of 1922- Who 94
Harrower, Elizabeth 1928- BlmGWL, WrDr 94
Harrower, Pamela Jane 1958- WhoFI 94
Harruff, Lewis Gregory 1947- WhoScEn 94
Harry, Debbie 1945- WhoHol 92
Harry, Deborah Ann 1945- IntWW 93, WhoAm 94
Harry, J. S. 1939- WrDr 94
Harry, Jackee WhoBlA 94
Harry, Peter J. 1950- WhoAmL 94
Harry, Ralph Lindsay 1917- IntWW 93
Harry, Robert Hayden 1918- WhoAm 94
Harryhausen, Ray 1920- EncSF 93, IntDcF 2-4, IntMPA 94, IntWW 93
Harryhausen, Ray Frederick 1920- WhoAm 94
Harryman, Eva Marie 1914- WhoAmP 93
Harsanyi, Charles 1905-1973 WhoAmA 93N
Harsanyi, Janice 1929- WhoAm 94
Harsanyi, John Charles 1920- WhoAm 94
Harsanyi, Tibor 1898-1954 NewGrDO
Harsch, Joseph Close 1905- IntWW 93, Who 94
Harsdorf, James Ervin WhoAmP 93
Harsdorf, Sheila 1956- WhoAmP 93
Harsdorf, Sheila Eloise 1956- WhoMW 93
Harsdorffer, Georg Philipp 1607-1658 NewGrDO
Harsen, Edward Charles 1958- WhoWest 94
Harsent, David 1942- WrDr 94
Harsha, Philip Thomas 1942- WhoWest 94
Harsha, William H. 1921- WhoAmP 93
Harshaw, Margaret 1909- NewGrDO
Harshbarger, Dwight 1938- WhoAm 94
Harshbarger, John Carl 1936- WhoScEn 94
Harshbarger, Richard B. 1934- WhoAm 94
Harshbarger, Scott WhoAmP 93
Harshbarger, Scott 1941- WhoAm 94, WhoAmL 94
Harshman, Carl Leonard 1944- WhoMW 93
Harshman, Kemp Robert 1948- WhoAmP 93
Harshman, Marc DrAPF 93
Harshman, Morton Leonard 1932- WhoAm 94
Harshman, Raymond Brent 1948- WhoAmL 94
Harsney, Johanna Marie Offner 1914- WhoMW 93
Harstad, Kenneth Gunder 1939- WhoWest 94
Harston, Julian John Robert Clive 1942- Who 94
Hart, Agnes d1979 WhoAmA 93N
Hart, Alan 1935- Who 94
Hart, Alan Edward 1935- Who 94
Hart, Albert d1940 WhoHol 92
Hart, Albert E., Jr. 1945- WhoAmL 94
Hart, Alex Way 1940- WhoAm 94
Hart, Alexander Hendry 1916- Who 94
Hart, Allen M. 1925- WhoAmA 93
Hart, Alvin Leroy 1925- WhoAm 94
Hart, Anelay Colton Wright 1934- Who 94
Hart, (Margaret Eleanor) Anne ConAu 141
Hart, Anthony Who 94
Hart, (Thomas) Anthony (Alfred) 1940- Who 94
Hart, Anthony Bernard 1917- Who 94
Hart, Anthony John 1923- Who 94
Hart, Anthony Ronald 1946- Who 94
Hart, Arthur Alvin 1921- WhoAm 94
Hart, Barbara McCollum 1937- WhoBlA 94
Hart, Barry Thomas 1940- WhoScEn 94
Hart, Bettieanne Childers 1948- WhoAmP 93
Hart, Betty Miller 1918- WhoAm 94, WhoAmA 93
Hart, C. Allan 1909- WhoAm 94
Hart, Carolyn G(impel) 1936- ConAu 41NR, SmATA 74 [port], WrDr 94
Hart, Cecil William Joseph 1931- WhoAm 94, WhoMW 93
Hart, Charles 1630?-1683 BlmGEL
Hart, Charles 1869-1950 EncABHB 9 [port]
Hart, Charles (A.) 1940- WrDr 94
Hart, Charles Willard, Jr. 1928- WhoAm 94
Hart, Christina WhoHol 92
Hart, Christopher Alvin 1947- WhoAmP 93, WhoBlA 94
Hart, Claire Marie 1955- WhoAmP 93
Hart, Claudia 1955- WhoAmA 93
Hart, Clifford Harvey 1935- WhoAmL 94
Hart, Daniel Anthony 1927- WhoAm 94
Hart, David WhoHol 92
Hart, David Churchill 1940- WhoAm 94, WhoAmL 94, WhoFI 94
Hart, David M(ontgomery) 1927- WrDr 94
Hart, David Michael 1940- Who 94
Hart, David Paul 1933- WhoWest 94
Hart, Dean Evan 1957- WhoScEn 94
Hart, Derek O. d1986 WhoHol 92
Hart, Diane 1926- WhoHol 92
Hart, Dolores 1938- WhoHol 92
Hart, Donald 1933- Who 94
Hart, (Frank) Donald Who 94
Hart, Donald Larcum, Jr. 1955- WhoAmP 93
Hart, Donald Milton 1914- WhoAm 94
Hart, Donald Purple 1937- WhoAm 94, WhoWest 94
Hart, Doris 1925- BuCMET [port]
Hart, Dorothy WhoAm 94
Hart, Dorothy 1923- WhoHol 92
Hart, Edward E. 1927- WhoBlA 94
Hart, Edward L. DrAPF 93
Hart, Edward LeRoy 1916- WhoAm 94, WhoWest 94
Hart, Edward Richard 1945- WhoWest 94
Hart, Edwin James 1910- WhoAm 94
Hart, Eldon Charles 1915- WhoWest 94
Hart, Elizabeth Kaye 1943- WhoWest 94
Hart, Ellis EncSF 93
Hart, Elsie Faye 1920- WhoMW 93
Hart, Emily 1940- WhoBlA 94
Hart, Eric Mullins 1925- WhoAm 94
Hart, Evelyn 1956- IntDcB [port], WhoAm 94
Hart, F(rancis) Dudley 1909- Who 94
Hart, Florence d1960 WhoHol 92
Hart, Francis J(oseph) 1898- WhAm 10
Hart, Frank James 1947- WhoWest 94
Hart, Frank Thomas 1911- Who 94
Hart, Fred d1927 WhoHol 92
Hart, Frederick Donald 1915- WhoAm 94
Hart, Frederick Michael 1929- WhoAm 94
Hart, Fritz (Bennicke) 1874-1949 NewGrDO
Hart, Gary 1936- IntWW 93, WhoAmP 93
Hart, Gary K. 1943- WhoAmP 93
Hart, Gary W. 1936- WhoAm 94, WhoWest 94
Hart, George 1927- WhoAmP 93
Hart, George Vaughan 1911- Who 94
Hart, Gordon d1973 WhoHol 92
Hart, Graham Allan 1940- Who 94
Hart, Gurnee Fellows 1929- WhoAm 94
Hart, Guy William Pulbrook 1931- Who 94
Hart, H(erbert) L(ionel) A(dolphus) 1907- WrDr 94
Hart, H(erbert) L(ionel) A(dolphus) 1907-1992 ConAu 140
Hart, Harold Rudoff 1926- WhoBlA 94
Hart, Harvey 1928- IntMPA 94
Hart, Harvey 1928-1989 WhAm 10
Hart, Helen Mavis 1954- WhoScEn 94
Hart, Helen P. 1927- WhoMW 93
Hart, Herbert Lionel Adolphus d1992 IntWW 93N, Who 94N
Hart, Herbert Michael 1928- WhoAm 94
Hart, Horace Henry 1840-1916 DcNaB MP
Hart, Howard Franklin 1947- WhoAmL 94, WhoWest 94
Hart, Howard Roscoe, Jr. 1929- WhoAm 94
Hart, Ila Jo 1928- WhoAmP 93
Hart, Indian Jack d1974 WhoHol 92
Hart, Irl Lester WhoWest 94
Hart, Irving Harlow, III 1938- WhoWest 94
Hart, Jacob P. 1942- WhoAmL 94
Hart, Jacqueline D. WhoBlA 94
Hart, James David 1911-1990 WhAm 10
Hart, James Harlan 1934- WhoMW 93
Hart, James R. 1952- WhoAmP 93
Hart, James W., Jr. 1953- WhoAm 94
Hart, James Warren 1944- WhoAm 94
Hart, James Whitfield, Jr. 1935- WhoAm 94
Hart, Jay Albert Charles 1923- WhoMW 93
Hart, Jean Hardy 1942- WhoScEn 94
Hart, Jean MacAulay WhoWest 94
Hart, Jeffrey Allen 1947- WhoMW 93
Hart, Jerome Thomas 1932- WhoAmP 93
Hart, Joan G. 1947- WhoMW 93
Hart, Joanne DrAPF 93
Hart, Joe 1944- WhoAmP 93
Hart, John DrAPF 93, WhoHol 92
Hart, John 1711-1779 WhAmRev
Hart, John 1921- IntDcB
Hart, John 1924- WhoAm 94, WhoWest 94
Hart, John 1938- WrDr 94
Hart, John Amasa 1950- WhoScEn 94
Hart, John Clifton 1945- WhoAm 94, WhoAmL 94
Hart, John Edward 1946- WhoAmL 94
Hart, John Fincher 1937- WhoScEn 94
Hart, John Francis 1868- WhoAmA 93N
Hart, John Fraser 1924- WrDr 94
Hart, John Lewis 1931- WhoAm 94, WhoAmA 93, WhoWest 94
Hart, John Mason 1935- WrDr 94
Hart, John P. 1960- WhoAm 94
Hart, Jonathan (Locke) 1956- ConAu 142
Hart, Joseph d1921 WhoHol 92
Hart, Joseph H. 1931- WhoAm 94, WhoWest 94
Hart, Joseph Kirwin 1934- WhoMW 93
Hart, Judith 1924-1991 WrDr 94N
Hart, Julia Catherine 1796-1867 BlmGWL
Hart, Kay M. 1954- WhoAmP 93
Hart, Kenneth Nelson 1930- WhoAm 94
Hart, Kevin 1954- WrDr 94
Hart, Kitty Carlisle 1917- WhoAm 94
Hart, Larry Calvin 1942- WhoAm 94, WhoAmL 94
Hart, Larry Edward 1945- WhoAm 94
Hart, LeRoy Banks 1954- WhoFI 94
Hart, Lewis O. d1920 WhoHol 92
Hart, Linda WhoHol 92
Hart, Lorenz d1943 WhoHol 92
Hart, Loring Edward 1924- WhoAm 94
Hart, Louis d1972 WhoHol 92
Hart, Lynn Patricia 1954- WhoAmL 94
Hart, Mabel d1960 WhoHol 92
Hart, Margie WhoHol 92
Hart, Marian Griffith 1929- WhoWest 94
Hart, Mark L., Jr. 1943- WhoAmL 94
Hart, Mary WhoHol 92
Hart, Mary 1950- WhoAm 94
Hart, Mary 1951?- ConTFT 11
Hart, Mary S. 1957- WhoMW 93
Hart, Maurice d1978 WhoHol 92
Hart, Melissa A. 1962- WhoAmP 93
Hart, Michael 1928- Who 94
Hart, Michael 1938- IntWW 93, Who 94
Hart, Michael Christopher Campbell 1948- Who 94
Hart, Michael David 1951- WhoAmL 94
Hart, Michael John 1946- WhoWest 94
Hart, Michael T. 1943- WhoAmL 94
Hart, Mildred WhoBlA 94
Hart, Morgan Drake 1899- WhoAmA 93N
Hart, Moss IntDcT 2
Hart, Moss 1904-1961 AmCulL
Hart, Myer d1795 WhAmRev
Hart, N. Berne 1930- WhoWest 94
Hart, Nancy c. 1735- WhAmRev
Hart, Nancy c. 1735-1800 AmRev
Hart, Nathaniel Irwin 1930- WhoAm 94
Hart, Neal d1949 WhoHol 92
Hart, Nick 1925- WhoAmP 93
Hart, Noel A. 1927- WhoBlA 94
Hart, Oliver D'Arcy 1948- WhoAm 94
Hart, Oliver Simon D'Arcy 1948- Who 94
Hart, P(hilip) M(ontagu) D'Arcy 1900- Who 94
Hart, Pamela Heim 1946- WhoMW 93
Hart, Parker T. 1910- IntWW 93
Hart, Parker Thompson 1910- WhoAmP 93
Hart, Patrick Joseph 1925- WhoAm 94
Hart, Peter Who 94
Hart, (Everard) Peter 1925- Who 94
Hart, Phyllis 1942- WhoAmP 93
Hart, Phyllis D. 1942- WhoBlA 94
Hart, Raymond 1913- Who 94
Hart, Renee Ann WhoMW 93
Hart, Richard d1951 WhoHol 92
Hart, Richard Banner 1932- WhoAm 94, WhoAmL 94
Hart, Richard LaVerne 1929- WhoWest 94
Hart, Richard Nevel, Jr. 1940- WhoAm 94
Hart, Richard Odum 1927- WhoAmP 93
Hart, Richard Terance 1961- WhoMW 93
Hart, Richard Wesley 1933- WhoFI 94
Hart, Robert Camillus 1934- WhoAm 94, WhoAmL 94, WhoFI 94, WhoMW 93
Hart, Robert Gerald 1937- WhoScEn 94
Hart, Robert Gordon 1921- WhoAm 94, WhoAmA 93
Hart, Robert M. 1944- WhoAm 94, WhoAmL 94
Hart, Robert Mayes 1925- IntWW 93
Hart, Roderick P. 1945- WhoAm 94
Hart, Roger Dudley 1943- Who 94
Hart, Ronald Lee 1937- WhoFI 94
Hart, Ronald Leon 1937- WhoWest 94
Hart, Ronald O. 1942- WhoBlA 94
Hart, Ronald Wilson 1942- WhoAm 94
Hart, Roxanne 1952- WhoHol 92
Hart, Russ Allen 1946- WhoWest 94
Hart, Ruth d1952 WhoHol 92
Hart, Sharon Yvonne 1956- WhoMW 93
Hart, Stanley Robert 1935- IntWW 93, WhoAm 94, WhoScEn 94
Hart, Stephanie DrAPF 93
Hart, Stephen Harding 1908- WhoAm 94
Hart, Stephen John 1960- WhoWest 94
Hart, Steven Jay WhoFI 94
Hart, Sunshine d1930 WhoHol 92
Hart, Susan 1941- WhoHol 92
Hart, Teddy d1971 WhoHol 92

Hartmann, Ruth Annemarie 1936- *WhoMW 93*
Hartmann, Sadakichi d1944 *WhoHol 92*
Hartmann, Werner 1955- *WhoScEn 94*
Hartmann, William Edward 1916- *WhoAm 94*
Hartmann, William Herman 1931- *WhoAm 94*
Hartmann, William Kenneth 1939- *WhoAm 94*
Hartmann, William Morris 1939- *WhoMW 93*
Hartmann-Johnsen, Olaf Johan 1924- *WhoScEn 94*
Hartmann von Aue c. 1160-c. 1205 *DcLB 138 [port]*
Hartnack, Carl Edward 1916- *IntWW 93*
Hartnack, Justus 1912- *WrDr 94*
Hartnack, Paul Richard Samuel 1942- *Who 94*
Hartnell, Helen Elizabeth 1954- *WhoAmL 94*
Hartnell, William d1975 *WhoHol 92*
Hartness, Sandra Jean 1944- *WhoFI 94*
Hartnett, D. Paul 1927- *WhoAmP 93*
Hartnett, James Patrick 1924- *WhoAm 94*
Hartnett, Jane Ann 1947- *WhoFI 94*
Hartnett, John F. 1937- *WhoFI 94*
Hartnett, Michael 1941- *WrDr 94*
Hartnett, Michael Warren 1946- *WhoMW 93*
Hartnett, Thomas Forbes 1941- *WhoAmP 93*
Hartnett, Thomas Patrick 1942- *WhoAm 94*
Hartnett, Thomas Robert, III 1920- *WhoAmL 94*
Hartnett, Will Ford 1956- *WhoAmL 94, WhoAmP 93*
Hart-Nibbrig, Harold C. 1938- *WhoBlA 94*
Hartnoll, Mary Charmian 1939- *Who 94*
Hart of South Lanark, Baroness 1924- *WhoWomW 91*
Hartog, Dirk fl. 160-?- *WhWE*
Hartog, Harold Samuel Arnold 1910- *Who 94*
Hartog, Horald Samuel Arnold 1910- *IntWW 93*
Hartog, Jan de 1914- *IntWW 93*
Hartog, John, II 1936- *WhoAm 94*
Harton, Ernest H. 1936- *WhoIns 94*
Harton, Herbert Lynn 1961- *WhoFI 94*
Harton, John James 1941- *WhoAm 94, WhoFI 94*
Hartong, Mark Worthington 1958- *WhoScEn 94*
Hartop, Christopher F.T. 1957- *WhoAm 94*
Hartopp, John Edmund Cradock 1912- *Who 94*
Hartpence, Patricia Ann 1956- *WhoFI 94*
Hartquist, Edwin Eugene 1941- *WhoScEn 94*
Hartranft, John C. 1942- *WhoAmL 94*
Hartrick, Janice Kay 1952- *WhoAmL 94*
Hartridge, Jon 1934- *EncSF 93*
Hart-Román, Dennis J. 1960- *WhoHisp 94*
Hartsaw, William O. 1921- *WhoAm 94, WhoMW 93, WhoScEn 94*
Hartse, Denise Yvonne Durfee 1951- *WhoAmP 93*
Hartsell, Fletcher Lee, Jr. 1947- *WhoAmP 93*
Hartsell, Samuel David 1937- *WhoFI 94*
Hartsfield, Arnett L., Jr. 1918- *WhoBlA 94*
Hartsfield, Brent David 1956- *WhoScEn 94*
Hartsfield, Henry Warren, Jr. 1933- *WhoAm 94, WhoScEn 94*
Hartsfield, Howard C. 1926- *WhoBlA 94*
Hartshorn, Michael Philip 1936- *IntWW 93*
Hartshorn, Willis E. 1950- *WhoAmA 93*
Hartshorne, Charles 1897- *WhoAm 94, WrDr 94*
Hartshorne, Richard 1899- *WrDr 94*
Hartshorne, Thomas L 1935- *WrDr 94*
Hartsing, Ralph H., Sr. 1896- *WhAm 10*
Hartsock, Linda Sue 1940- *WhoAm 94*
Hartsoe, Joseph Robert 1954- *WhoAmL 94*
Hartson, Maurice J., III 1936- *WhoIns 94*
Hartsook, David L. 1948- *WhoIns 94*
Hartsook, Larry D. 1943- *WhoAm 94*
Hartsough, Gayla A. Kraetsch 1949- *WhoWest 94*
Hartsough, Walter Douglas 1924- *WhoAm 94*
Hartstein, Allan Mark 1947- *WhoScEn 94*
Hartstein, Jacob I. 1912-1991 *WhAm 10*
Hartston, William Roland 1947- *WrDr 94*
Hartsuck, Jean Ann 1939- *WhoAm 94*
Hartt, Frederick 1914-1991 *WhAm 10, WhoAmA 93N*
Hartt, Grover, III 1948- *WhoAmL 94*
Hartt, Julian N(orris) 1911- *WrDr 94*
Hartt, Julian Norris 1911- *WhoAm 94*
Hartt, Stanley Herbert 1937- *WhoFI 94*
Hartung, Christin 1941- *WhoAmP 93*
Hartung, Dorothy Allen 1903- *WhoWest 94*
Hartung, Frank Edwin 1940- *WhoAmP 93*
Hartung, Hans Heinrich Ernst 1904-1989 *WhAm 10*
Hartung, Harald 1932- *IntWW 93*
Hartung, Jon F. 1939- *WhoAmL 94*
Hartung, Lorraine E. 1944- *WhoHisp 94*
Hartung, Mary *WhoAmP 93, WhoWest 94*
Hartung, Thomas Frederick 1927- *WhoAmP 93*
Hartung, Walter Magnus 1907- *WhoAm 94*
Hartweger, Gordon Gravius 1939- *WhoAmL 94, WhoMW 93*
Hartwell, Baron 1911- *IntWW 93, Who 94*
Hartwell, Benjamin James 1908- *Who 94*
Hartwell, Brodrick William Charles Elwin 1909- *Who 94*
Hartwell, David G(eddes) 1941- *EncSF 93*
Hartwell, Eric 1915- *Who 94*
Hartwell, Erin *WhoAm 94*
Hartwell, George Kenneth 1891-1949 *WhoAmA 93N*
Hartwell, John Mowry 1929- *WhoMW 93*
Hartwell, Kathleen Irene 1951- *WhoMW 93*
Hartwell, Leland Harrison 1939- *WhoScEn 94*
Hartwell, (William) Michael Berry 1911- *ConAu 142*
Hartwell, Patricia Lochridge 1916- *WhoAmA 93*
Hartwell, Robert Carl 1961- *WhoScEn 94*
Hartwell, Samuel Adams 1930- *WhoFI 94*
Hartwell, Stephen 1916- *WhoAm 94*
Hartwick, Elbert Stuart 1903-1990 *WhAm 10*
Hartwick, Thomas Stanley 1934- *WhoWest 94*
Hartwig, Eugene Lawrence 1933- *WhoAm 94, WhoAmL 94*
Hartwig, Harvey L. 1943- *WhoIns 94*
Hartwig, Heinie 1939- *WhoAmA 93*
Hartwig, Larry Dean 1940- *WhoAm 94*
Hartwig, Robert Allen, Jr. 1958- *WhoWest 94*
Hartwig, Thomas Leo 1952- *WhoAm 94*
Hartwigsen, Christian Cornelius 1942- *WhoFI 94*
Hart Willard, Emma 1787-1870 *WomPubS*
Harty, Belford Donald, Jr. 1928- *WhoBlA 94*
Harty, Bernard Peter 1943- *Who 94*
Harty, James D. 1929- *WhoAm 94*
Harty, James Quinn 1925- *WhoAm 94*
Harty, Mark P. 1951- *WhoAmL 94*
Harty, Michael *Who 94*
Harty, Patricia 1941- *WhoHol 92*
Harty, Sheila Therese 1948- *WhoAm 94*
Hartz, Bradley Scott 1955- *WhoFI 94*
Hartz, Brian D. 1965- *WhoWest 94*
Hartz, Fred Robert 1933- *WhoAm 94*
Hartz, Harry J. 1925- *WhoFI 94*
Hartz, Jim 1940- *IntMPA 94*
Hartz, Renee Semo 1946- *WhoAm 94*
Hartz, Steven Edward Marshall 1948- *WhoAmL 94*
Hartzell, Andrew Cornelius, Jr. 1927- *WhoAm 94*
Hartzell, Charles R. 1941- *WhoAm 94, WhoScEn 94*
Hartzell, Harrison Criss, Jr. 1946- *WhoScEn 94*
Hartzler, Ed *WhoAmP 93*
Hartzler, Geoffrey Oliver 1946- *WhoMW 93*
Hartzler, Stanley James 1947- *WhoMW 93*
Hartzog, Ernest E. 1928- *WhoBlA 94*
Hartzog, George B., Jr. 1920- *IntWW 93*
Hartzog, Wendell L., Jr. 1951- *WhoAmP 93*
Haruda, Fred David 1950- *WhoWest 94*
Haruf, Kent *DrAPF 93*
Haruna, Alhaji *Who 94*
Harutunian, Albert Theodore, III 1955- *WhoAmL 94*
Harut'yunyan, Alexander Grigor 1920- *NewGrDO*
Harvanek, Robert Francis 1916- *WhoAm 94*
Harvard, Beverly Bailey 1950- *WhoBlA 94*
Harvard, Jack *WhoAmP 93*
Harvell, Michael Cleland 1946- *WhoAmL 94*
Harvell, Valeria Gomez 1958- *WhoBlA 94*
Harvest, Judith R. *WhoAmA 93*
Harvest, Rainbow *WhoHol 92*
Harvey *Who 94*
Harvey, Abner McGehee 1911- *WhoAm 94*
Harvey, Alan Frederick Ronald 1919- *Who 94*
Harvey, Albert C. *WhoAmL 94*
Harvey, Alexander, II 1923- *WhoAm 94, WhoAmL 94*
Harvey, Alison Margaret 1950- *WhoAmP 93*
Harvey, (William) Andre 1941- *WhoAmA 93*
Harvey, Andrew 1952- *NewYTBS 93 [port], WrDr 94*
Harvey, Anne Caroline Ballingall *Who 94*
Harvey, Anthony 1931- *IntMPA 94, IntWW 93, WhoHol 92*
Harvey, Anthony Ernest 1930- *Who 94*
Harvey, Anthony Peter 1940- *Who 94*
Harvey, Arthur Douglas 1916- *Who 94*
Harvey, Aubrey Eaton, III 1944- *WhoScEn 94*
Harvey, Barbara Fitzgerald 1928- *IntWW 93, Who 94*
Harvey, Benjamin Hyde 1908- *Who 94*
Harvey, Beverly Ann 1957- *WhoBlA 94*
Harvey, Billy V. 1932- *WhoAmP 93*
Harvey, Bob 1936- *WhoAmP 93*
Harvey, Brian Wilberforce 1936- *Who 94*
Harvey, Bryan Hugh 1914- *Who 94*
Harvey, Bryan Laurence 1937- *WhoAm 94, WhoScEn 94*
Harvey, Bryan Stanley 1963- *WhoAm 94*
Harvey, Calvin Rea 1943- *WhoAm 94, WhoAmL 94*
Harvey, Cannon Y. 1940- *WhoAmL 94*
Harvey, Caroline *Who 94*
Harvey, Caroline 1943- *WrDr 94*
Harvey, Charles Albert, Jr. 1949- *WhoAmL 94*
Harvey, Charles P., II 1947- *WhoAmP 93*
Harvey, Charles Richard Musgrave 1937- *Who 94*
Harvey, Clarence d1945 *WhoHol 92*
Harvey, Clarie Collins 1916- *WhoBlA 94*
Harvey, Colin Edwin 1944- *WhoAm 94*
Harvey, Colin Stanley 1924- *Who 94*
Harvey, Crete Bowman 1929- *WhoAmP 93*
Harvey, Curran Whitthorne, Jr. 1928- *WhoAm 94*
Harvey, Cynthia *WhoAm 94*
Harvey, Cynthia 1957- *IntDcB [port]*
Harvey, David 1935- *Who 94*
Harvey, David Christensen 1934- *WhoAmP 93*
Harvey, David Michael 1934- *WhoAmL 94*
Harvey, Denise M. 1954- *WhoBlA 94*
Harvey, Dermot 1941- *WhoAmA 93*
Harvey, Don *WhoHol 92*
Harvey, Don d1963 *WhoHol 92*
Harvey, Donald d1931 *WhoHol 92*
Harvey, Donald 1930- *WhoAm 94, WhoAmA 93, WhoWest 94*
Harvey, Donald Gilbert 1947- *WhoAmA 93*
Harvey, Donald Joseph 1922- *WhoAm 94*
Harvey, Donald Phillips 1924- *WhoAm 94*
Harvey, Douglas Stewart 1952- *WhoMW 93*
Harvey, Douglass Coate 1917- *WhoAm 94*
Harvey, Edward d1975 *WhoHol 92*
Harvey, Edwin Malcolm 1928- *WhoAm 94*
Harvey, Elaine Louise 1936- *WhoWest 94*
Harvey, Elizabeth Robyn 1946- *WhoWomW 91*
Harvey, Estella Jacqueline *Who 94*
Harvey, F. Barton, Jr. 1921- *WhoAm 94*
Harvey, F. Reese 1941- *WhoAm 94*
Harvey, Fletcher d1931 *WhoHol 92*
Harvey, Forrester d1945 *WhoHol 92*
Harvey, Frank d1981 *WhoHol 92*
Harvey, Frank (Laird) 1913-1981 *EncSF 93*
Harvey, Gabriel 1545?-1630 *BlmGEL*
Harvey, Gayle Ellen *DrAPF 93*
Harvey, George Burton 1931- *WhoAm 94, WhoFI 94*
Harvey, George Edwin 1938- *WhoAm 94*
Harvey, Georgette d1952 *WhoHol 92*
Harvey, Georgia d1960 *WhoHol 92*
Harvey, Gerald 1950- *WhoBlA 94*
Harvey, Glenn F. 1940- *WhoAm 94*
Harvey, Gregory Alan 1949- *WhoWest 94*
Harvey, H. Clark, Jr. 1942- *WhoAmL 94*
Harvey, Hal 1960- *WhoFI 94*
Harvey, Harold A. 1944- *WhoBlA 94*
Harvey, Harry d1985 *WhoHol 92*
Harvey, Harry, Jr. d1978 *WhoHol 92*
Harvey, Herbert Raymond 1931- *WhoMW 93*
Harvey, Herschel Ambrose, Jr. 1929- *WhoFI 94*
Harvey, J. Bruce 1942- *WhoAmP 93*
Harvey, J. R. 1937- *WhoFI 94*
Harvey, Jack d1954 *WhoHol 92*
Harvey, Jacqueline V. 1933- *WhoBlA 94*
Harvey, James *EncSF 93*
Harvey, James 1922- *WhoAm 94, WhoAmL 94, WhoAmP 93, WhoMW 93*
Harvey, James 1929- *WrDr 94*
Harvey, James Douglas 1929- *WhoAm 94*
Harvey, James Gerald 1934- *WhoWest 94*
Harvey, James Ross 1934- *WhoAm 94, WhoFI 94, WhoWest 94*
Harvey, James V. d1965 *WhoAmA 93N*
Harvey, Jane R. 1945- *WhoFI 94*
Harvey, Jean G. d1966 *WhoHol 92*
Harvey, Joan *DrAPF 93*
Harvey, Joan C. 1948- *WrDr 94*
Harvey, Joanne H. 1932- *WhoAm 94, WhoMW 93*
Harvey, John d1970 *WhoHol 92*
Harvey, John (Hooper) 1911- *WrDr 94*
Harvey, John Adriance 1930- *WhoAm 94*
Harvey, John Ashmore 1964- *WhoScEn 94*
Harvey, John B. 1938- *WrDr 94*
Harvey, John Collins 1923- *WhoAm 94*
Harvey, John Edgar 1920- *Who 94*
Harvey, John F(rederick) 1921- *WrDr 94*
Harvey, John Grover 1934- *WhoAm 94*
Harvey, John Marshall 1921- *WhoScEn 94*
Harvey, John Martin d1944 *WhoHol 92*
Harvey, Jonathan Dean 1939- *IntWW 93, Who 94*
Harvey, Jonathan Paul 1941- *WhoAmL 94*
Harvey, Joseph K. 1939- *WhoAmP 93*
Harvey, Joseph Paul, Jr. 1922- *WhoAm 94, WhoWest 94*
Harvey, Karen Lynne Garcia 1953- *WhoWest 94*
Harvey, Katherine Abler 1946- *WhoMW 93*
Harvey, Kathryn 1947- *WrDr 94*
Harvey, Kathryn Tinker 1924- *WhoAmP 93*
Harvey, Kenneth A. 1951- *WhoAmP 93*
Harvey, Kenneth George 1940- *Who 94*
Harvey, Kenneth Ray 1965- *WhoBlA 94*
Harvey, Kenneth Ricardo 1956- *WhoWest 94*
Harvey, Laurence d1973 *WhoHol 92*
Harvey, Lee F. d1950 *WhoHol 92*
Harvey, Leonard Patrick 1929- *Who 94*
Harvey, Leslie Leo 1926- *WhoFI 94*
Harvey, Lester Schley 1898- *WhAm 10*
Harvey, Lew d1953 *WhoHol 92*
Harvey, Lilian d1968 *WhoHol 92*
Harvey, Linda Joy 1957- *WhoBlA 94*
Harvey, Lorena Kay 1943- *WhoMW 93*
Harvey, Lottie d1948 *WhoHol 92*
Harvey, Louis-Charles 1945- *WhoBlA 94*
Harvey, Louis James 1948- *WhoScEn 94*
Harvey, M(ary) Elayn 1945- *EncSF 93*
Harvey, Marc Sean 1960- *WhoAmL 94, WhoWest 94*
Harvey, Marilyn d1973 *WhoHol 92*
Harvey, Mary Frances Clare 1927- *Who 94*
Harvey, Maurice Reginald 1957- *WhoBlA 94*
Harvey, Michael d1993 *NewYTBS 93*
Harvey, Michael Lee 1944- *WhoAm 94*
Harvey, Michael Llewellyn Tucker 1943- *Who 94*
Harvey, Monica M. 1948- *WhoMW 93*
Harvey, Morris d1944 *WhoHol 92*
Harvey, Morris Lane 1950- *WhoAmL 94*
Harvey, Neil 1938- *Who 94*
Harvey, Nicholas Barton 1961- *Who 94*
Harvey, Nigel 1916- *WrDr 94*
Harvey, Norma Baker 1943- *WhoBlA 94*
Harvey, Norman Ronald 1933- *WhoAm 94*
Harvey, P(aul) D(ean) A(dshead) 1930- *WrDr 94*
Harvey, Paul d1955 *WhoHol 92*
Harvey, Paul 1918- *WhoAm 94*
Harvey, Paul Dean Adshead 1930- *Who 94*
Harvey, Paul H. 1947- *Who 94*
Harvey, Paul W. 1957- *WhoWest 94*
Harvey, Peter 1922- *Who 94*
Harvey, (Brian) Peter 1951- *WrDr 94*
Harvey, Peter Kent 1946- *Who 94*
Harvey, Philip James Benedict 1915- *Who 94*
Harvey, Polly Jean c. 1970- *ConMus 11 [port]*
Harvey, Raymond 1950- *WhoBlA 94*
Harvey, Raymond Curtis 1950- *WhoAm 94*
Harvey, Richard Blake 1930- *WhoWest 94*
Harvey, Richard Dudley 1923- *WhoFI 94, WhoWest 94*
Harvey, Richard R. *WhoBlA 94*
Harvey, Robert Dixon Hopkins 1920- *WhoAm 94*
Harvey, Robert Lambart 1953- *Who 94*
Harvey, Robert Martin 1924- *WhoAmA 93*
Harvey, Robert Zell 1943- *WhoMW 93*

Harvey, Robin Elise 1952- *WhoAm 94, WhoAmL 94*
Harvey, Rodney 1967- *WhoHol 92*
Harvey, Ronald Edward 1955- *WhoMW 93*
Harvey, Ronald Gilbert 1927- *WhoAm 94*
Harvey, Rose Marie 1924- *WhoFI 94*
Harvey, Rupert d1954 *WhoHol 92*
Harvey, Stephen d1993 *NewYTBS 93*
Harvey, Stephen 1949-1993 *ConAu 140*
Harvey, Stewart Clyde 1921- *WhoWest 94*
Harvey, Thomas Cockayne 1918- *Who 94*
Harvey, Thomas F. 1938- *WhoAmL 94*
Harvey, Thomas J. 1939- *WhoAm 94*
Harvey, Tom *WhoHol 92*
Harvey, Trice Jeraine 1936- *WhoAmP 93*
Harvey, Van Austin 1926- *WhoAm 94*
Harvey, Wardelle G. 1926- *WhoBlA 94*
Harvey, Wayne Evan 1952- *WhoMW 93*
Harvey, William 1578-1657 *WorScD*
Harvey, William Brantley, Jr. 1930- *WhoAm 94, WhoAmP 93*
Harvey, William Burnett 1922- *WhoAm 94*
Harvey, William DuBee 1937- *WhoWest 94*
Harvey, William George 1932- *WhoWest 94*
Harvey, William Graeme 1947- *Who 94*
Harvey, William James, III 1912- *WhoBlA 94*
Harvey, William M. 1933- *WhoBlA 94*
Harvey, William R. 1941- *WhoBlA 94*
Harvey-Byrd, Patricia Lynn 1954- *WhoBlA 94*
Harveycutter, Robert Carey, Jr. 1952- *WhoAmP 93*
Harvey-Jamieson, Harvey Morro 1908- *Who 94*
Harvey-Jones, John (Henry) 1924- *ConAu 140, IntWW 93, Who 94*
Harvey Of Prestbury, Baron 1906- *Who 94*
Harvey Of Tasburgh, Baron 1921- *Who 94*
Harvie, John 1742-1807 *WhAmRev*
Harvie, Jonathan Alexander 1950- *Who 94*
Harvie, Peggy Ann 1936- *WhoMW 93*
Harvieux, Anne Marie 1945- *WhoAm 94*
Harvie-Watt, James 1940- *Who 94*
Harvill, Doris Holve 1936- *WhoWest 94*
Harvill, H. Doyle 1929- *WhoAm 94*
Harville, Mary Rich 1962- *WhoAmL 94*
Harvin, Alvin 1937- *WhoBlA 94*
Harvin, C. Alex, III 1950- *WhoAmP 93*
Harvin, David Tarleton 1945- *WhoAm 94, WhoAmL 94*
Harvin, Durant Kevin, III 1966- *WhoBlA 94*
Harvin, Edwin Lawrence 1898- *WhAm 10*
Harvin, Lucius H., III 1938- *WhoFI 94*
Harvin, William Charles 1919- *WhoAm 94*
Harvington, Baron 1907- *Who 94*
Harvit, Elliott William 1960- *WhoAmL 94*
Harvitt, Adrianne Stanley 1954- *WhoAmL 94*
Harvor, Beth 1936- *WrDr 94*
Harward, Byron L. 1949- *WhoAmP 93*
Harward, Donald *WhoAm 94*
Harward, Naomi Markee 1907- *WhoWest 94*
Harwayne, Frank 1920- *WhoIns 94*
Harwell, Aubrey Biggs 1942- *WhoAm 94, WhoAmL 94*
Harwell, B. Hicks 1933- *WhoAmP 93*
Harwell, Beth Halteman 1957- *WhoAmP 93*
Harwell, David W. 1932- *WhoAmP 93*
Harwell, David Walker 1932- *WhoAm 94, WhoAmL 94*
Harwell, Edwin Whitley 1929- *WhoAm 94*
Harwell, Tyler P. 1952- *WhoAmP 93*
Harwell, William Earnest 1918- *WhoAm 94*
Harwick, Betty Corinne Burns 1926- *WhoWest 94*
Harwick, Dennis Patrick 1949- *WhoAmL 94*
Harwick, Maurice 1933- *WhoAmL 94, WhoWest 94*
Harwit, Martin Otto 1931- *WhoAm 94, WhoScEn 94*
Harwood, Brian Dennis 1932- *WhoAm 94, WhoFI 94*
Harwood, Clifford B. *WhoAmP 93*
Harwood, (Henry) David 1938- *WrDr 94*
Harwood, Edward Dunning 1950- *WhoMW 93*
Harwood, Elizabeth (Jean) 1938-1990 *NewGrDO*
Harwood, Gwen 1920- *BlmGWL*
Harwood, Gwen(doline Nessie) 1920- *WrDr 94*
Harwood, Ivan Richmond 1939- *WhoAm 94, WhoScEn 94*
Harwood, Jerry 1926- *WhoAm 94*
Harwood, John d1944 *WhoHol 92*
Harwood, John B. 1952- *WhoAmP 93*
Harwood, John Simon 1960- *WhoScEn 94*
Harwood, John Warwick 1946- *Who 94*
Harwood, Kirk Edward 1964- *WhoScEn 94*
Harwood, Lee 1939- *ConAu 19AS [port], WrDr 94*
Harwood, Madeline Bailey 1914- *WhoAmP 93, WhoWomW 91*
Harwood, Richard Lee 1925- *WhoAm 94*
Harwood, Robin Louise 1958- *WhoScEn 94*
Harwood, Ronald 1934- *ConDr 93, IntMPA 94, Who 94, WrDr 94*
Harwood, Stanley 1926- *WhoAm 94, WhoAmP 93*
Harwood, Thomas Riegel 1926- *WhoScEn 94*
Harwood, Vanessa Clare 1947- *WhoAm 94*
Harwood, Virginia Ann 1925- *WhoMW 93*
Harwood-Baumel, Bernice *WhoAmA 93*
Harz, G. Michael 1951- *WhoWest 94*
Harzman, Leonard Alvin 1941- *WhoMW 93*
Hasan, Aqeel Khatib 1955- *WhoBlA 94*
Hasan, Mahmudul 1936- *IntWW 93*
Hasan, Rabiul *DrAPF 93*
Hasan, Syed E. 1939- *WhoAsA 94*
Hasan, Syed Eqbal 1939- *WhoMW 93*
Hasan, Waqar 1963- *WhoWest 94*
Hasani, Sinan 1922- *IntWW 93*
Hasanov, Hasan Aziz Ogly *IntWW 93*
Hasara, Karen 1940- *WhoAmP 93*
Hasay, George C. 1948- *WhoAmP 93*
Hasbrook, A. Howard 1913- *WhoScEn 94*
Hasbrouck, Ellsworth Eugene 1913- *WhoBlA 94*
Hasbrouck, Norman Gene 1952- *WhoAm 94*
Hascal, Lon d1932 *WhoHol 92*
Hascall, John 1941- *EncNAR*
Haschek-Hock, Wanda Maria 1949- *WhoMW 93*
Haschke, Paul Charles 1954- *WhoScEn 94*
Hasday, Robert Joel 1949- *WhoAm 94, WhoAmL 94*
Hase, David John 1940- *WhoAm 94*
Hase, Karl-Gunther von 1917- *IntWW 93*
Hase, William Louis 1945- *WhoMW 93*
Hase, Yuriko 1947- *WhoWomW 91*
Haseeb, Khair El-Din 1929- *IntWW 93*
Hasegawa, Akinori 1941- *WhoScEn 94*
Hasegawa, Hideki 1941- *WhoScEn 94*
Hasegawa, Jack Koichi 1944- *WhoAsA 94*
Hasegawa, Kenko 1916- *IntWW 93*
Hasegawa, Noriko *WhoAmA 93*
Hasegawa, Norishige 1907- *IntWW 93*
Hasegawa, Ryusuke 1940- *WhoScEn 94*
Hasegawa, Tadashi 1948- *WhoScEn 94*
Hasegawa, Takashi d1992 *IntWW 93N*
Hasek, Jaroslav 1883-1923 *RfGShF*
Haselbach, Anna Elizabeth 1942- *WhoWomW 91*
Haselby, Kenneth Aaron 1941- *WhoMW 93*
Haselden, Catherine Anderson 1957- *WhoAmL 94*
Haselden, Clyde LeRoy 1914- *WhoAm 94*
Haselden, Geoffrey Gordon 1924- *Who 94*
Haseldine, (Charles) Norman 1922- *Who 94*
Haseler, Stephen Michael Alan 1942- *Who 94*
Haseley, Susan L. 1959- *WhoIns 94*
Haselgrove, Dennis Cliff 1914- *Who 94*
Haselhurst, Alan Gordon Barraclough 1937- *Who 94*
Haselkorn, Robert 1934- *WhoAm 94*
Haselmann, John Philip 1940- *WhoAm 94, WhoFI 94*
Haselmayer, Louis August 1911- *WhoAm 94*
Haselmire, Michael Joseph 1940- *WhoWest 94*
Haseltine, Florence Pat 1942- *WhoAm 94, WhoScEn 94*
Haseltine, Herbert 1877-1962 *WhoAmA 93N*
Haseltine, James Lewis 1924- *WhoAm 94, WhoAmA 93*
Haseltine, Maury (Margaret Wilson) 1925- *WhoAmA 93*
Haselton, Britt Davis Liddicoat 1962- *WhoAmL 94*
Haselton, Forrest Ronald 1938- *WhoFI 94*
Haselton, Joseph Gerard 1963- *WhoAmL 94*
Haselton, Rick Thomas 1953- *WhoAmL 94*
Haselwood, Eldon LaVerne 1933- *WhoAm 94*
Haselwood, James Edward 1942- *WhoMW 93*
Hasen, Burt Stanley 1921- *WhoAmA 93*
Hasen, Burton Stanley 1921- *WhoAm 94*
Hasenberg, Thomas Charles 1958- *WhoScEn 94*
Hasenclever, Walter 1890-1940 *IntDcT 2*
Hasenmiller, Stephen J. 1949- *WhoIns 94*
Hasenoehrl, Daniel Norbert Francis 1929- *WhoWest 94*
Hasenohrl, Donald W. 1935- *WhoAmP 93*
Hasen-Sinz, Susan Katherine 1965- *WhoMW 93*
Haser, Charlotte 1784-1871 *NewGrDO*
Haserick, John Roger 1915- *WhoAm 94*
Hasford, Gustav *DrAPF 93*
Hasford, (Jerry) Gustav 1947-1993 *ConAu 140*
Hash, Joe Kevin 1957- *WhoWest 94*
Hash, John Frank 1944- *WhoAm 94*
Hasha, Dennis Lloyd 1953- *WhoScEn 94*
Hashem, Elaine M. 1940- *WhoAmP 93*
Hashemi-Yeganeh, Shahrokh 1958- *WhoScEn 94*
Hashian, John 1949- *See* Boston *ConMus 11*
Hashim, Edmund d1974 *WhoHol 92*
Hashim, Elinor Marie 1933- *WhoAm 94*
Hashim, George A. 1931- *WhoScEn 94*
Hashim, Jawad M. 1938- *IntWW 93*
Hashim, Khalidah 1945- *BlmGWL*
Hashim, Mustafa 1935- *WhoBlA 94*
Hashimi, Abdul Razzak el- *IntWW 93*
Hashimoto, Akira 1949- *WhoAsA 94*
Hashimoto, Andrew Ginji 1944- *WhoScEn 94*
Hashimoto, Clarice Y. 1954- *WhoAmP 93*
Hashimoto, Eiji 1931- *WhoAsA 94*
Hashimoto, Ken 1931- *WhoAsA 94*
Hashimoto, Kunio 1929- *WhoAm 94, WhoScEn 94*
Hashimoto, Lloyd Ken 1944- *WhoWest 94*
Hashimoto, Nobuyuki 1958- *WhoScEn 94*
Hashimoto, Rentaro 1930- *WhoAsA 94*
Hashimoto, Ryutaro 1937- *IntWW 93*
Hashimoto, Shiori 1952- *WhoScEn 94*
Hashimoto, Steven George 1953- *WhoAsA 94*
Hashimoto, Tsuneyuki 1950- *WhoScEn 94*
Hashiro, Brian Satoru 1953- *WhoWest 94*
Hashmi, (Aurangzeb) Alamgir 1951- *WrDr 94*
Hashmi, Farrukh Siyar 1927- *Who 94*
Hashmi, Mohammed Zafar 1956- *WhoAsA 94*
Hashmi, Sajjad Ahmad 1933- *WhoAm 94, WhoIns 94*
Hashmi, Sayed A. 1942- *WhoAsA 94*
Hasina Wajed, Sheikh *WhoWomW 91*
Hasior, Wladyslaw 1928- *IntWW 93*
Haskale, Hadassah *DrAPF 93*
Haskard, Cosmo (Dugal Patrick Thomas) 1916- *Who 94*
Haskayne, Richard Francis 1934- *WhoAm 94, WhoWest 94*
Haskel, Baron 1934- *Who 94*
Haskel, Leonhard d1923 *WhoHol 92*
Haskell, Al d1969 *WhoHol 92*
Haskell, Alene V. 1952- *WhoAmL 94*
Haskell, Arthur Jacob 1926- *WhoAm 94*
Haskell, Barbara 1946- *WhoAm 94, WhoAmA 93*
Haskell, Barry Geoffry 1941- *WhoAm 94, WhoScEn 94*
Haskell, Bob *WhoAmP 93*
Haskell, Charles Mortimer 1939- *WhoScEn 94*
Haskell, David *WhoHol 92*
Haskell, Donald McMillan 1932- *WhoAm 94, WhoAmL 94*
Haskell, Eric Todd 1950- *WhoWest 94*
Haskell, Floyd K. *WhoAmP 93*
Haskell, Francis 1928- *IntWW 93*
Haskell, Francis (James Herbert) 1928- *WrDr 94*
Haskell, Francis James Herbert 1928- *Who 94*
Haskell, Guy Henry 1956- *WhoMW 93*
Haskell, Jane 1923- *WhoAmA 93*
Haskell, John Henry Farrell, Jr. 1932- *WhoAm 94, WhoFI 94*
Haskell, Keith *Who 94*
Haskell, (Donald) Keith 1939- *Who 94*
Haskell, Molly 1939- *WrDr 94*
Haskell, Paul Gershon 1927- *WhoAm 94*
Haskell, Peter 1934- *WhoHol 92*
Haskell, Peter Abraham 1934- *WhoAm 94*
Haskell, Peter Thomas 1923- *Who 94*
Haskell, Thales Hastings 1834-1909 *EncNAR*
Haskell, Thomas Langdon 1939- *WhoAm 94*
Haskell, Valerie Kropotkin 1950- *WhoMW 93*
Haskell, William H. 1875-1952 *WhoAmA 93N*
Haskett, James Albert 1942- *WhoWest 94*
Haskin, Byron 1899-1984 *EncSF 93, IntDcF 2-4*
Haskin, Charles Wilson d1927 *WhoHol 92*
Haskin, Donald Lee 1945- *WhoAm 94*
Haskin, Donald Marcus 1920- *WhoAmA 93*
Haskin, Harry R. d1953 *WhoHol 92*
Haskin, Larry Allen 1934- *WhoScEn 94*
Haskin, Lawrence John 1951- *WhoAmL 94*
Haskin, Robert William, Jr. 1958- *WhoAmL 94*
Haskins, Anne *DrAPF 93*
Haskins, Caryl Parker 1908- *IntWW 93, WhoAm 94, WhoFI 94, WhoScEn 94*
Haskins, Cherry Anne *WhoAmP 93*
Haskins, Clem Smith 1943- *WhoBlA 94*
Haskins, Donald A. 1931- *WhoAmP 93*
Haskins, George Lee 1915- *WrDr 94*
Haskins, George Lee 1915-1991 *WhAm 10*
Haskins, James 1941- *WhoAm 94*
Haskins, James S. 1941- *BlkWr 2, TwCYAW, WhoBlA 94*
Haskins, James W., Jr. 1932- *WhoBlA 94*
Haskins, Jim *BlkWr 2*
Haskins, Jim 1941- *WrDr 94*
Haskins, John Franklin 1919-1991 *WhoAmA 93N*
Haskins, Joseph, Jr. *WhoBlA 94*
Haskins, Kristen Elizabeth 1944- *WhoMW 93*
Haskins, Larry Wayne 1948- *WhoAm 94*
Haskins, Lola *DrAPF 93*
Haskins, Marian McKeen 1954- *WhoWest 94*
Haskins, Michael Kevin 1950- *WhoBlA 94*
Haskins, Morice Lee, Jr. 1947- *WhoBlA 94*
Haskins, Perry Glen 1938- *WhoFI 94, WhoMW 93*
Haskins, Robert E. 1952- *WhoAmP 93*
Haskins, Sam 1926- *IntWW 93, Who 94*
Haskins, Sylvia Shaw Judson 1897- *WhAm 10*
Haskins, Terry E. 1955- *WhoAmP 93*
Haskins, William J. 1930- *WhoBlA 94*
Haskins, Yvonne B. 1938- *WhoBlA 94*
Haskowitz, Howard 1947- *WhoIns 94*
Hasl, Rudolph Carl 1942- *WhoAmL 94*
Haslam, Baron 1923- *Who 94*
Haslam, Alec (Leslie) 1904- *Who 94*
Haslam, Alfred Seale 1844-1927 *DcNaB MP*
Haslam, David William 1923- *Who 94*
Haslam, Geoffrey *Who 94*
Haslam, (William) Geoffrey 1914- *Who 94*
Haslam, Gerald *DrAPF 93*
Haslam, Gerald William 1937- *WrDr 94*
Haslam, John 1764-1844 *EncSPD*
Haslam, John Gordon 1932- *Who 94*
Haslam, Robert 1923- *IntWW 93*
Haslam, Robert Thomas, III 1946- *WhoAm 94*
Haslanger, Martin Frederick 1947- *WhoMW 93, WhoScEn 94*
Haslegrave, Herbert Leslie 1902- *Who 94, WrDr 94*
Haslegrave, Neville Crompton 1914- *Who 94*
Haslem, Jane N. 1934- *WhoAmA 93*
Hasler, Arthur Davis 1908- *IntWW 93*
Hasler, Geoff J. 1947- *WhoFI 94*
Haslett, John d1777 *WhAmRev*
Haslewood, Geoffrey Arthur Dering 1910- *Who 94*
Hasley, Michael A. 1941- *WhoIns 94*
Hasley, Ronald K. 1935- *WhoMW 93*
Hasling, Jill Freeman 1952- *WhoAm 94*
Hasling, Robert J. 1929- *WhoAmL 94*
Haslip, Joan 1912- *Who 94*
Hasluck, Nicholas 1942- *WrDr 94*
Hasluck, Paul (Meernaa Caedwalla) 1905-1993 *ConAu 140, WrDr 94N*
Hasluck, Paul Meernaa Caedwalla d1993 *IntWW 93N, Who 94N*
Haslund, Shannon Lee 1966- *WhoWest 94*
Haslup, Charles Le Roy, III 1941- *WhoAmL 94*
Hasner, Rolf Kaare 1919- *WhoFI 94*
Ha-So-De 1918- *WhoAmA 93*
Haspel, Arthur Carl 1945- *WhoAm 94, WhoScEn 94*
Haspel, Stanley Joel 1931- *WhoAm 94*
Hasper, John W. 1935- *WhoAmP 93*
Hasper, Kurt T., Jr. 1946- *WhoWest 94*
Hasquin, Herve 1942- *IntWW 93*
Hass, Anthony 1923-1992 *WhAm 10*
Hass, Charles John William 1934- *WhoAmL 94*
Hass, David Wayne 1960- *WhoWest 94*
Hass, Kenneth Charles 1958- *WhoMW 93*
Hass, Lawrence Joel 1946- *WhoAm 94*
Hass, Robert *DrAPF 93*
Hass, Robert 1941- *WrDr 94*
Hass, Sabine 1949- *NewGrDO*
Hassall, Cedric Herbert 1919- *Who 94*

Hassall, Christopher 1912-1963 *NewGrDO*
Hassall, Imogen d1980 *WhoHol 92*
Hassall, Tom Grafton 1943- *Who 94*
Hassall, William Owen 1912- *Who 94, WrDr 94*
Hassam, Frederick Childe 1859-1935 *AmCulL*
Hassan, II 1929- *IntWW 93*
Hassan, Aftab Syed 1952- *WhoFI 94, WhoScEn 94*
Hassan, Fred 1945- *WhoFI 94*
Hassan, Hosni Moustafa 1937- *WhoScEn 94*
Hassan, Ihab (Habib) 1925- *WrDr 94*
Hassan, Ihab Habib 1925- *ConAu 41NR, WhoAm 94*
Hassan, Jawad Ebrahim 1949- *WhoScEn 94*
Hassan, Jean-Claude Gaston 1954- *IntWW 93*
Hassan, Joshua (Abraham) 1915- *IntWW 93, WhoAm 94*
Hassan, Lois Mary 1949- *WhoMW 93*
Hassan, M. Zia 1933- *WhoAm 94, WhoMW 93*
Hassan, Mamoun Hamid 1937- *Who 94*
Hassan, Michael R. 1948- *WhoAmL 94*
Hassan, Mohammad Hassan 1956- *WhoScEn 94*
Hassan, Moulaye al- *IntWW 93*
Hassan, Sayed Abdullah El 1925- *Who 94*
Hassan, William Ephriam, Jr. 1923- *WhoAm 94*
Hassan, Yassin Abdel 1945- *WhoAm 94*
Hassan, Zurinah *BlmGWL*
Hassanali, Noor Mohamed 1918- *IntWW 93*
Hassanein, Khatab M. 1926- *WhoAm 94*
Hassanein, Richard C. 1951- *IntMPA 94*
Hassanein, Salah M. 1921- *IntMPA 94*
Hassan Ibn Talal, H.R.H. 1947- *IntWW 93*
Hassan Sharq, Mohammad 1925- *IntWW 93*
Hassard, Howard 1910- *WhoAm 94*
Hassberger, Richard L. *WhoIns*
Hasse, Clemens d1959 *WhoHol 92*
Hasse, Henry L. 1913-1977 *EncSF 93*
Hasse, Johann Adolf 1699?-1783 *NewGrDO*
Hasse, Margaret M. *DrAPF 93*
Hasse, O. E. d1978 *WhoHol 92*
Hassel, Kai-Uwe von 1913- *IntWW 93*
Hassel, Martin Lawrence 1955- *WhoMW 93*
Hasselbacher, Peter 1946- *WhoScEn 94*
Hasselbalch, Marilyn Jean 1930- *WhoMW 93*
Hasselfeldt, Gerda 1950- *IntWW 93, WhoWomW 91*
Hasselgren, Robert William 1949- *WhoIns 94*
Hasselhoff, David 1952- *IntMPA 94, WhoHol 92*
Hassell, Dennis Edward 1945- *WhoWest 94*
Hassell, Frances M. 1925- *WhoBlA 94*
Hassell, Frances Massey 1925- *WhoIns 94*
Hassell, George d1937 *WhoHol 92*
Hassell, Gerald L. 1951- *WhoAm 94*
Hassell, Hugh Robert 1945- *WhoWest 94*
Hassell, John David 1958- *WhoWest 94*
Hassell, Joyce Barnett 1932- *WhoAmP 93*
Hassell, Leroy R. 1955- *WhoAmP 93*
Hassell, Leroy Rountree 1955- *WhoAmL 94*
Hassell, Leroy Rountree, Sr. 1955- *WhoBlA 94*
Hassell, Mary Eloise McCain 1958- *WhoAmP 93*
Hassell, Michael Patrick 1942- *IntWW 93, Who 94*
Hassell, Morris William 1916- *WhoAmL 94*
Hassell, Peter Albert 1916- *WhoMW 93, WhoScEn 94*
Hasselman, Richard B. 1926- *WhoAm 94*
Hasselmans, Louis 1878-1957 *NewGrDO*
Hasselmeyer, Eileen Grace *WhoAm 94*
Hasselmo, Nils 1931- *IntWW 93, WhoAm 94, WhoMW 93*
Hasselquist, Maynard Burton 1919- *WhoAm 94, WhoAmL 94, WhoFI 94, WhoMW 93*
Hasselriis, Floyd Norbert 1922- *WhoScEn 94*
Hasselstrom, Linda *DrAPF 93*
Hassenfeld, Alan Geoffrey 1948- *WhoAm 94, WhoFI 94*
Hassenfeld, Stephen David 1942-1989 *WhAm 10*
Hasser, Christopher John 1968- *WhoMW 93*
Hassert, Brent *WhoAmP 93*
Hassert, Elizabeth Anne 1956- *WhoMW 93*

Hassett, Carol Alice 1947- *WhoAm 94*
Hassett, Francis (George) 1918- *Who 94*
Hassett, Francis George 1918- *IntWW 93*
Hassett, Jacquelyn Ann 1930- *WhoMW 93*
Hassett, Joseph Mark 1943- *WhoAm 94, WhoAmL 94*
Hassett, Lewis E. 1955- *WhoAmL 94*
Hassett, Marilyn 1947- *WhoHol 92*
Hassett, Ronald Douglas Patrick 1923- *Who 94*
Hassfurder, Leslie Jean 1943- *WhoMW 93*
Hassialis, Menelaos Dimitiou 1909- *WhoScEn 94*
Hassid, Sami 1912- *WhoAm 94*
Hasskamp, Kris 1951- *WhoAmP 93*
Hasslein, George Johann 1917- *WhoAm 94*
Hassler, Donald M. *DrAPF 93*
Hassler, Donald M(ackey) 1937- *WrDr 94*
Hassler, Donald M(ackey, II) 1937- *EncSF 93*
Hassler, Donald Mackey, II 1937- *WhoAm 94, WhoMW 93*
Hassler, Elaine *WhoAmP 93*
Hassler, Jon (Francis) 1933- *WrDr 94*
Hassler, Jon Francis 1933- *WhoMW 93*
Hassler, Kenneth W(ayne) 1932- *EncSF 93*
Hassler, Raymond Joseph *WhoMW 93*
Hassner, Alfred 1930- *WhoScEn 94*
Hasso, Signe 1915- *WhoHol 92*
Hasso, Signe Eleonora Cecilia 1915- *WhoAm 94*
Hassold, Ernest Christopher 1896- *WhAm 10*
Hasson, James Keith, Jr. 1946- *WhoAm 94, WhoAmL 94*
Hasson, Kirke Michael 1949- *WhoAm 94, WhoAmL 94*
Hasson, Maurice 1934- *IntWW 93*
Hasson, Nicole Denise 1963- *WhoBlA 94*
Hasson, Susan A. 1946- *WhoAmP 93*
Hassouna, Fred 1918- *WhoWest 94*
Hassrick, Peter H. 1941- *WhoAmA 93*
Hassrick, Peter Heyl 1941- *WhoAm 94, WhoWest 94*
Hast, Adele 1931- *WhoAm 94*
Hast, Malcolm Howard 1931- *WhoAm 94*
Hast, Robert 1945- *WhoScEn 94*
Hastad, Douglas Noel 1949- *WhoMW 93*
Hasten, Michael V. 1946- *WhoAm 94, WhoAmL 94*
Hastenteufel, Dieter 1939- *WhoAmA 93*
Hasterlo, John S. 1963- *WhoScEn 94*
Hastert, Dennis 1942- *WhoAm 94, WhoAmP 93, WhoMW 93*
Hastert, J. Dennis 1942- *CngDr 93*
Hastert, Robert Charles 1924- *WhoMW 93*
Hastert, Roger Joseph Leon 1929- *Who 94*
Hastie, Reid 1916-1987 *WhoAmA 93N*
Hastie, Robert Cameron 1933- *Who 94*
Hastie, Ronald Leslie 1941- *WhoMW 93*
Hastie, William H. 1904-1976 *AfrAmAl 6 [port]*
Hastie-Smith, Richard Maybury 1931- *Who 94*
Hastilow, Michael Alexander 1923- *Who 94*
Hasting, Glen Richard, II 1945- *WhoMW 93*
Hastings *Who 94*
Hastings, Baron 1912- *Who 94*
Hastings, Adrian Christopher 1929- *IntWW 93, Who 94*
Hastings, Alcee 1936- *WhoAmP 93*
Hastings, Alcee L. 1936- *CngDr 93*
Hastings, Alcee Lamar 1936- *WhoAm 94, WhoBlA 94*
Hastings, Alfred James 1938- *Who 94*
Hastings, Baird 1919- *WhoAm 94*
Hastings, Beverly 1944- *WrDr 94*
Hastings, Beverly 1945- *WrDr 94*
Hastings, Bob 1921- *WhoHol 92*
Hastings, Brooke 1946- *WrDr 94*
Hastings, Dan Thomas 1947- *WhoAmL 94*
Hastings, Don 1934- *IntMPA 94*
Hastings, Donald F. 1928- *WhoAm 94, WhoFI 94*
Hastings, Donald Francis 1934- *WhoAm 94*
Hastings, Edward Walton 1931- *WhoAm 94, WhoWest 94*
Hastings, Edwin Hamilton 1917- *WhoAmN 94*
Hastings, George Gordon *EncSF 93*
Hastings, Graham 1926- *WrDr 94*
Hastings, Harold Morris 1946- *WhoScEn 94*
Hastings, Henry d1963 *WhoHol 92*
Hastings, Hudson *EncSF 93*
Hastings, Joan King 1932- *WhoAmP 93*
Hastings, John A., Jr. 1954- *WhoAmP 93*

Hastings, John Woodland 1927- *WhoAm 94*
Hastings, Lawrence Vaeth 1919- *WhoAm 94, WhoAmL 94*
Hastings, Lois Jane 1928- *WhoAm 94*
Hastings, Mark Robert 1957- *WhoAmL 94*
Hastings, Max M(acdonald) 1945- *WrDr 94*
Hastings, Max Macdonald 1945- *IntWW 93, Who 94*
Hastings, Merrill George, Jr. 1922- *WhoWest 94*
Hastings, Michael 1938- *Who 94, WrDr 94*
Hastings, Michael (Gerald) 1938- *ConDr 93*
Hastings, Milo (Milton) 1884-1957 *EncSF 93*
Hastings, Nancy Peters *DrAPF 93*
Hastings, Peter G. *WhoAmP 93*
Hastings, Philip Kay 1922- *WhoAm 94*
Hastings, Phyllis (Dora Hodge) 1904- *WrDr 94*
Hastings, Phyllis Ann 1945- *WhoMW 93*
Hastings, Richard Norman 1941- *WhoAmP 93*
Hastings, Robert Eugene 1932- *WhoMW 93*
Hastings, Robert Paul 1933- *WrDr 94*
Hastings, Robert Pusey 1910- *WhoAm 94*
Hastings, S. Robert 1945- *WhoScEn 94*
Hastings, Stephen (Lewis Edmonstone) 1921- *Who 94*
Hastings, Stephen John 1961- *WhoMW 93*
Hastings, Warren 1732-1818 *HisWorL [port]*
Hastings, Warren 1889- *WhoHol 92*
Hastings, William C. 1921- *WhoAmP 93*
Hastings, William Charles 1921- *WhoAm 94, WhoAmL 94, WhoMW 93*
Hastings, Wilmot Reed 1935- *WhoAm 94*
Hastings Bass *Who 94*
Hastler, Russell Clifford, Jr. 1925- *WhoMW 93*
Haston, Raymond Curtiss, Jr. 1945- *WhoBlA 94*
Hastrich, Jerome Joseph 1914- *WhoAm 94, WhoWest 94*
Hasty, Frederick Emerson, III 1950- *WhoAmL 94*
Hasty, John C. 1930- *WhoAmP 93*
Hasty, Keith A. *WhoAmL 94*
Hasty, W. G., Sr. *WhoAmP 93*
Hasty, William Grady, Jr. 1947- *WhoAm 94, WhoAmL 94*
Haswell, Anthony 1756-1816 *WhAmRev*
Haswell, Carleton Radley 1939- *WhoAm 94*
Haswell, Chetwynd John Drake 1919- *WrDr 94*
Haswell, Ernest Bruce 1889-1965 *WhoAmA 93N*
Haswell, Frank I. 1918- *WhoAmP 93*
Haswell, Hollee 1948- *WhoAmA 93*
Haswell, (Anthony) James (Darley) 1922- *Who 94*
Haswell, Percy d1945 *WhoHol 92*
Haswell, T. Clayton 1949- *WhoAm 94*
Haszeldine, Robert Neville 1925- *IntWW 93, Who 94*
Hata, David M. 1947- *WhoAsA 94*
Hata, Donald Teruo, Jr. 1939- *WhoAsA 94*
Hata, Hiroaki 1940- *WhoAsA 94*
Hata, Koichi 1949- *WhoScEn 94*
Hata, Nadine Ishitani 1941- *WhoAsA 94*
Hata, Tsutomu *IntWW 93*
Hatada, Kazuyuki 1951- *WhoScEn 94*
Hatai, Thomas Henry 1937- *WhoWest 94*
Hatala, Mary Ann 1959- *WhoFI 94*
Hatanaka, Hiroshi 1932- *WhoScEn 94*
Hatanaka, Robert Ken 1953- *WhoFI 94*
Hatano, Akira 1911- *IntWW 93*
Hatano, Sadashi 1929- *WhoScEn 94*
Hatano, Yoshio 1932- *IntWW 93*
Hatar, Gyozo 1914- *ConWorW 93*
Hatayama, Rodney Ken 1950- *WhoAsA 94*
Hatch, Ardis Messick *DrAPF 93*
Hatch, Connie *WhoAmA 94*
Hatch, David Edwin 1939- *Who 94*
Hatch, David Lincoln 1910- *WhoAm 94*
Hatch, Dorothy L. *DrAPF 93*
Hatch, Edward William 1952- *WhoFI 94, WhoMW 93*
Hatch, Emily Nichols 1871-1959 *WhoAmA 93N*
Hatch, Francis Whiting, Jr. 1925- *WhoAmP 93*
Hatch, Frederick Henry 1864-1932 *DcNaB MP*
Hatch, George Clinton 1919- *WhoAm 94, WhoWest 94*
Hatch, Gerald *EncSF 93*
Hatch, Harold Arthur 1924- *WhoAm 94*

Hatch, Henry Clifford, Jr. 1916- *IntWW 93*
Hatch, Henry J. *WhoAm 94*
Hatch, Ike d1961 *WhoHol 92*
Hatch, Ira 1835- *EncNAR*
Hatch, Jack Gilchrist 1950- *WhoAmP 93*
Hatch, Jeffrey Scott 1964- *WhoScEn 94*
Hatch, John D. 1942- *WhoAmL 94*
Hatch, John Davis 1907- *WhoAm 94, WhoAmA 93, WhoWest 94*
Hatch, John W. 1919- *WhoAmA 93*
Hatch, Kenneth L. 1934- *WhoWest 94*
Hatch, Linda *WhoAmP 93*
Hatch, Mark Bruce 1959- *WhoScEn 94*
Hatch, Marshall, Mrs. 1918- *WhoAmA 93*
Hatch, Marshall Davidson 1932- *IntWW 93, Who 94*
Hatch, Mary 1935- *WhoAmA 93*
Hatch, Mary Gies 1913- *WhoAm 94*
Hatch, Mary Wendell Vander Poel 1919- *WhoScEn 94*
Hatch, Michael Alan 1948- *WhoAmP 93*
Hatch, Michael Ward 1949- *WhoAm 94, WhoAmL 94*
Hatch, Monroe W., Jr. 1933- *WhoAm 94*
Hatch, Nathan Orr 1946- *WhoAm 94*
Hatch, Orrin G. 1934- *CngDr 93*
Hatch, Orrin Grant 1934- *IntWW 93, WhoAm 94, WhoAmP 93, WhoWest 94*
Hatch, Pamela H. *WhoAmP 93*
Hatch, Pamela Post 1942- *WhoWest 94*
Hatch, Richard 1945- *WhoHol 92*
Hatch, Robert Frederick 1934- *WhoWest 94*
Hatch, Robert Noel 1932- *WhoAmL 94*
Hatch, Robert Norris 1914- *WhoAm 94*
Hatch, Robert Walter 1929- *WhoAm 94*
Hatch, Robert Winslow 1938- *WhoFI 94*
Hatch, Ronald Ray 1938- *WhoWest 94*
Hatch, Sinclair 1906-1989 *WhAm 10*
Hatch, Steven Graham 1951- *WhoFI 94, WhoWest 94*
Hatch, W. A. S. 1948- *WhoAmA 93*
Hatch, Wilda Gene 1917- *WhoAm 94*
Hatch, William H. 1947- *WhoAmP 93*
Hatch, William Riley d1925 *WhoHol 92*
Hatchadorian, Matthew J. 1941- *WhoAm 94*
Hatchadorian, Matthew Jack 1941- *WhoAmP 93*
Hatchard, Frederick Henry 1923- *Who 94*
Hatchel, Robert Eugene 1937- *WhoAmP 93*
Hatcher, Allen Edward 1944- *WhoAm 94*
Hatcher, (L.) Brower *WhoAmA 93*
Hatcher, Carolyn Clark 1938- *WhoFI 94*
Hatcher, Charles F. 1939- *WhoAmP 93*
Hatcher, Charles Ross, Jr. 1930- *WhoAm 94*
Hatcher, David Alton, Jr. 1946- *WhoWest 94*
Hatcher, Donald Lewis 1947- *WhoMW 93*
Hatcher, E. Porter, Jr. 1936- *WhoAmP 93*
Hatcher, Edward Luverne 1946- *WhoMW 93*
Hatcher, Ester L. 1933- *WhoBlA 94*
Hatcher, Glenn Edward 1944- *WhoMW 93*
Hatcher, Harlan Henthorne 1898- *WhAm 10*
Hatcher, Herbert John 1926- *WhoWest 94*
Hatcher, James Donald 1923-1991 *WhAm 10*
Hatcher, James F., Jr. d1993 *NewYTBS 93*
Hatcher, Jeffrey F. *WhoBlA 94*
Hatcher, Joe Branch 1936- *WhoAm 94*
Hatcher, (Melvyn) John 1942- *WrDr 94*
Hatcher, John Christopher 1946- *WhoWest 94*
Hatcher, John Woodville, Jr. 1944- *WhoAmP 93*
Hatcher, Lillian 1915- *WhoBlA 94*
Hatcher, Lizzie R. 1954- *WhoBlA 94*
Hatcher, Richard G. 1933- *WhoAmP 93*
Hatcher, Richard Gordon 1933- *WhoBlA 94*
Hatcher, Robert Douglas 1924- *WhoAm 94*
Hatcher, Robert V., III 1956- *WhoIns 94*
Hatcher, Teri *WhoHol 92*
Hatcher, Thomas Fountain 1931- *WhoMW 93*
Hatcher, William Augustus 1960- *WhoBlA 94*
Hatcher, William S. 1935- *WrDr 94*
Hatcher, William Spottswood 1935- *WhoAm 94*
Hatchett, Duayne 1925- *WhoAmA 93*
Hatchett, Edward Earl 1923- *WhoAm 94*
Hatchett, Elbert 1936- *WhoBlA 94*
Hatchett, Joseph W. 1932- *AfrAmAl 6, WhoAmP 93*
Hatchett, Joseph Woodrow 1932- *WhoAm 94, WhoAmL 94, WhoBlA 94*
Hatchett, Paul Andrew 1925- *WhoBlA 94*
Hatchett, William F. *WhoBlA 94*

Hauschka, Stephen Denison 1940- *WhoAm 94*
Hauschka, Theodore Spaeth 1908- *WhoAm 94*
Hausdorfer, Gary Lee 1946- *WhoWest 94*
Hause, Jesse Gilbert 1929- *WhoAm 94*
Hause, Norman Laurance 1922- *WhoWest 94*
Hausel, William Dan 1949- *WhoWest 94*
Hauselt, Denise Ann 1956- *WhoAmL 94*
Hauseman, David Nathaniel 1895- *WhAm 10*
Hausenfluck, Robert Dale 1947- *WhoAmP 93*
Hauser, Barbara R. 1945- *WhoAmL 94*
Hauser, Charles Newland McCorkle 1929- *WhoAm 94*
Hauser, Charlie Brady 1917- *WhoAmP 93, WhoBlA 94*
Hauser, Christopher George 1954- *WhoAmL 94*
Hauser, Daniel Eugene 1942- *WhoAmP 93*
Hauser, Erich 1930- *IntWW 93*
Hauser, Fay *WhoHol 92*
Hauser, Frank Ivor 1922- *Who 94*
Hauser, Franz 1794-1870 *NewGrDO*
Hauser, Fred P. 1937- *WhoAm 94, WhoFI 94*
Hauser, George 1922- *WhoScEn 94*
Hauser, Gustave M. 1929- *WhoAm 94*
Hauser, Harry Raymond 1931- *WhoAm 94*
Hauser, Heinrich d1956 *WhoHol 92*
Hauser, Helmut Otmar 1936- *WhoScEn 94*
Hauser, Jerry Lee 1950- *WhoAmP 93*
Hauser, John Reid 1938- *WhoAm 94*
Hauser, Joyce Roberta *WhoFI 94*
Hauser, Julius 1914- *WhoScEn 94*
Hauser, Kurt Francis 1955- *WhoScEn 94*
Hauser, Marianne *DrAPF 93*
Hauser, Marianne 1910- *WrDr 94*
Hauser, Michael George 1939- *WhoAm 94*
Hauser, Nancy McKnight 1909-1990 *WhAm 10*
Hauser, Paul Joseph 1942- *WhoFI 94*
Hauser, Paul R. 1917- *WhoMW 93*
Hauser, Philip M. 1909- *IntWW 93, WrDr 94*
Hauser, Ray Louis 1927- *WhoFI 94*
Hauser, Richard Alan 1943- *WhoAm 94, WhoAmL 94*
Hauser, Rita Eleanore Abrams 1934- *WhoAm 94*
Hauser, Robert J., Jr. *WhoAmP 93*
Hauser, Robert Mason 1942- *WhoAm 94*
Hauser, Rudolf 1909- *IntWW 93*
Hauser, Simon Petrus 1954- *WhoScEn 94*
Hauser, Stephen K. 1952- *WhoMW 93*
Hauser, Susan *DrAPF 93*
Hauser, William Barry 1939- *WhoAm 94*
Hauser, William Harold 1942- *WhoAmL 94*
Hauser, Wings *IntMPA 94, WhoHol 92*
Hauserman, William Foley 1919- *WhoAm 94*
Hausey, Robert Michael 1949- *WhoAmA 93*
Hausheer, Frederick Herman 1955- *WhoScEn 94*
Haushofer, Marlen 1920-1970 *BlmGWL*
Hausler, William John, Jr. 1926- *WhoAm 94, WhoMW 93*
Hausman, Alice 1942- *WhoAmP 93*
Hausman, Arthur Herbert 1923- *WhoAm 94*
Hausman, Bogumil 1956- *WhoScEn 94*
Hausman, Bruce 1930- *WhoAm 94*
Hausman, David Lawrence 1951- *WhoMW 93*
Hausman, Ethel d1993 *NewYTBS 93*
Hausman, Fred S. 1921- *WhoAmA 93*
Hausman, Gerald *DrAPF 93*
Hausman, Hershel Judah 1923- *WhoMW 93*
Hausman, Howard 1945- *WhoAm 94, WhoFI 94*
Hausman, Jerome Joseph 1925- *WhoAmA 93*
Hausman, Jerry Allen 1946- *WhoAm 94, WhoFI 94*
Hausman, Keith Lynn 1949- *WhoAm 94*
Hausman, Kenneth G. 1948- *WhoAmL 94*
Hausman, Michael *IntMPA 94*
Hausman, Richard Donald 1945- *WhoAmP 93*
Hausman, Samuel 1897-1992 *WhAm 10*
Hausman, Steven Jack 1945- *WhoScEn 94*
Hausman, William Ray 1941- *WhoAm 94, WhoMW 93*
Hausmann, Marianne Pisko *WhoAmA 93N*
Hausmann, William Dirk 1955- *WhoAmL 94*
Hausmann, Winifred Wilkinson 1922- *WrDr 94*

Hausner, Gideon Maks 1915-1990 *WhAm 10*
Hausner, Jerry *WhoHol 92*
Hauspurg, Arthur 1925- *IntWW 93*
Hausrath, Joan W. 1942- *WhoAmA 93*
Haussay, Nicole Colleson du 1713-1801 *BlmGWL*
Haussegger, Nicolas *WhAmRev*
Hausser, Robert Louis 1914- *WhoAm 94, WhoAmL 94*
Haussermann, Oscar William, Jr. 1921- *WhoAm 94*
Hausset, Nicole Colleson du 1713-1801 *BlmGWL*
Haussinger, Dieter Lothar 1951- *WhoScEn 94*
Haussler, Jerrilynn Reher 1946- *WhoMW 93*
Haussler, Richard d1964 *WhoHol 92*
Haussmann, Helmut 1943- *IntWW 93*
Haussmann, Norman Joseph 1940- *WhoWest 94*
Haussmann, Trudy Diane 1965- *WhoFI 94*
Hausvater, Alexander 1948- *WrDr 94*
Haut, Claire (Joan) *WhoAmA 93*
Hautaluoma, Jacob Edward 1933- *WhoWest 94*
Hautzig, Esther 1930- *TwCYAW, WrDr 94*
Hauver, Constance Longshore 1938- *WhoAm 94*
Hauxwell, Gerald Dean 1935- *WhoScEn 94*
Hauxwell, Hannah 1926- *ConAu 140*
Ha Van Lau 1918- *IntWW 93*
Havard, Cyril (William Holmes) 1925- *WrDr 94*
Havard, John David Jayne 1924- *Who 94*
Havard, John Francis 1909- *WhoWest 94*
Havard-Williams, Peter 1922- *Who 94*
Havas, Peter 1916- *WhoAm 94*
Havasy, Charles Kukenis 1970- *WhoScEn 94*
Havdala, Henri Salomon 1931- *WhoAm 94*
Havekost, Daniel John 1936- *WhoAm 94*
Havel, Jean Eugene Martial 1928- *WhoAm 94*
Havel, Jennifer *SmATA 74*
Havel, Joe d1932 *WhoHol 92*
Havel, John Edward 1950- *WhoScEn 94*
Havel, Joseph G. 1954- *WhoAmA 93*
Havel, Richard Joseph 1925- *IntWW 93, WhoAm 94, WhoScEn 94*
Havel, Richard W. 1946- *WhoAm 94, WhoAmL 94*
Havel, Vaclav 1936- *ConWorW 93, IntDcT 2 [port], IntWW 93, Who 94*
Havelange, Jean Marie Faustin Godefroid 1916- *IntWW 93*
Havelka, Thomas Edward 1947- *WhoMW 93*
Havell, Ernest Binfield 1861-1934 *DcNaB MP*
Havelock, Christine Mitchell 1924- *WhoAmA 93*
Havelock, Wilfrid (Bowen) 1912- *Who 94*
Havelock-Allan, Anthony 1904- *IntDcF 2-4 [port]*
Havelock-Allan, Anthony James Allan 1904- *Who 94*
Havelock-Allan, (Anthony) Mark (David) 1951- *Who 94*
Haveman, Jacqueline Ruth 1948- *WhoMW 93*
Haveman, Robert Henry 1936- *WhoMW 93, WrDr 94*
Havemann, Ernst 1918- *WrDr 94*
Havemeyer, Horace, Jr. 1914-1990 *WhAm 10*
Haven, Charna d1971 *WhoHol 92*
Haven, Edwin Jesse De *WhWE*
Haven, Gilbert 1821-1880 *DcAmReB 2*
Haven, Jens 1724-1796 *EncNAR*
Haven, Thomas Edward 1920- *WhoAm 94*
Haven, Thomas Kenneth 1906- *WhoAm 94*
Havener, Robert Dale 1930- *WhoAm 94*
Havens, Candace Jean 1952- *WhoFI 94, WhoWest 94*
Havens, Carl Bradford 1918- *WhoWest 94*
Havens, Charles W., III 1936- *WhoAm 94, WhoIns 94*
Havens, Charnell Thomas 1938- *WhoMW 93*
Havens, Deborah Lynne 1959- *WhoAm 94*
Havens, Harry Stewart 1935- *WhoAm 94*
Havens, James Dexter 1900-1960 *WhoAmA 93N*
Havens, Jan 1948- *WhoAmA 93*
Havens, John Franklin 1927- *WhoAm 94*
Havens, Kenneth Harold, Sr. 1930- *WhoWest 94*
Havens, Leston Laycock 1924- *ConAu 43NR, WhoAm 94*
Havens, Murray Clark 1932- *WhoAm 94*

Havens, Murry P. *WhoAmA 93N*
Havens, Oliver Hershman 1917- *WhoAm 94*
Havens, Richie 1941- *ConMus 11 [port], WhoHol 92*
Havens, Thomas R.H. 1939- *WhoWest 94*
Havens, Timothy Markle 1945- *WhoAm 94, WhoFI 94*
Havens, Walter Paul, Jr. 1911-1992 *WhAm 10*
Havens, William Westerfield, Jr. 1920- *WhoAm 94*
Haver, Christopher Sterling 1966- *WhoWest 94*
Haver, June 1926- *WhoHol 92*
Haver, Jurgen F. 1932- *WhoFI 94*
Haver, Phyllis d1960 *WhoHol 92*
Haver, Ronald d1993 *NewYTBS 93*
Haverland, Mark A. 1946- *WhoAmP 93*
Haverland, Richard Michael 1941- *WhoIns 94*
Havern, Robert A., III 1949- *WhoAmP 93*
Havers, Michael 1923-1992 *WhAm 10*
Havers, Nigel 1951- *IntMPA 94, IntWW 93, WhoHol 92*
Havers, Robert Michael Oldfield 1923-1992 *AnObit 1992*
Haversat, Lillian Kerr 1938- *WhoAmA 93*
Haverty, Grace Ligammari *WhoAmA 93*
Haverty, Harold V. 1930- *WhoAm 94, WhoFI 94*
Haverty, John Rhodes 1926- *WhoAm 94*
Haverty, Lawrence Joseph, Jr. 1944- *WhoFI 94*
Havery, Richard Orbell 1934- *Who 94*
Havewala, Noshir Behram 1938- *WhoScEn 94*
Havey, Lois Arlene 1935- *WhoMW 93*
Haviaras, Stratis *DrAPF 93*
Haviaras, Stratis 1935- *IntWW 93, WrDr 94*
Havice, Pamela A. 1957- *WhoMW 93*
Havier, J. Alex d1945 *WhoHol 92*
Havighurst, Alfred F 1904- *WrDr 94*
Havighurst, Alfred Freeman 1904-1991 *WhAm 10*
Havighurst, Clark Canfield 1933- *IntWW 93, WhoAm 94, WhoAmL 94*
Havighurst, Harold Canfield 1897- *WhAm 10*
Havighurst, Robert J. 1900-1991 *WhAm 10*
Havil, Anthony 1915- *WrDr 94*
Haviland, Bancroft Dawley 1925- *WhoAm 94*
Haviland, Camilla Klein 1926- *WhoAm 94*
Haviland, David Sands 1942- *WhoAm 94*
Haviland, Denis William Garstin Latimer 1910- *IntWW 93, WhoFI 94*
Haviland, James West 1911- *WhoAm 94*
Haviland, Rena d1954 *WhoHol 92*
Haviland, Robert Paul 1913- *WhoAm 94*
Havill, Juanita *DrAPF 93*
Havill, Juanita 1949- *SmATA 74 [port]*
Havill, Nancy Ches 1945- *WhoMW 93*
Havilland *Who 94*
Havinga, Nick *ConTFT 11*
Havis, Allan 1951- *ConDr 93*
Havlicek, Franklin J. 1947- *WhoAm 94, WhoFI 94*
Havlicek, John 1940- *BasBi, WhoAm 94*
Havlik, Michael Alexander 1956- *WhoMW 93*
Havlin, John Leroy 1950- *WhoMW 93*
Havner, Kerry Shuford 1934- *WhoScEn 94*
Havoc, June 1916- *IntMPA 94, WhoAm 94, WhoHol 92*
Havran, Martin Joseph 1929- *WhoAm 94, WrDr 94*
Havran, Wendy Lynn 1955- *WhoWest 94*
Havrilek, Christopher Moore 1959- *WhoScEn 94*
Havrilla, Robert Donald *WhoMW 93*
Hawaii, Bishop of *Who 94*
Hawarden, Viscount 1961- *Who 94*
Hawdon, Robin 1939- *WhoHol 92*
Hawe, David Lee 1938- *WhoFI 94*
Hawel, Rudolf *EncSF 93*
Hawerchuk, Dale *WhoAm 94*
Hawes, Alexander Boyd, Jr. 1947- *WhoAm 94*
Hawes, Bernadine Tinner 1950- *WhoBlA 94*
Hawes, Douglas Wesson 1932- *WhoAm 94*
Hawes, Grace Maxcy 1926- *WhoWest 94*
Hawes, Judy 1913- *WrDr 94*
Hawes, Louis 1931- *WhoAmA 93*
Hawes, Nancy Elizabeth 1944- *WhoScEn 94*
Hawes, Robert Dowell 1937- *WhoAm 94*
Hawes, Stephen 1475?-c. 1529 *DcLB 132*
Hawes, William 1785-1846 *NewGrDO*
Hawfield, W. B., Jr. 1947- *WhoAmP 93*

Hawk, Alex 1926- *WrDr 94*
Hawk, Alex 1939- *WrDr 94*
Hawk, Carl Curtis 1931-1989 *WhAm 10*
Hawk, Carole Lynn 1947- *WhoMW 93*
Hawk, Charles N., Jr. 1931- *WhoBlA 94*
Hawk, Charles Nathaniel, III 1957- *WhoBlA 94*
Hawk, Charles Silas 1953- *WhoScEn 94*
Hawk, Clark Wiliams 1936- *WhoScEn 94*
Hawk, Douglas James 1959- *WhoWest 94*
Hawk, George Wayne 1928- *WhoAm 94*
Hawk, Jeremy 1918- *WhoHol 92*
Hawk, Phillip Michael 1939- *WhoAm 94*
Hawk, Robert Dooley 1940- *WhoFI 94*
Hawk, Robert M. 1924- *WhoAmP 93*
Hawkanson, David Robert 1946- *WhoAm 94*
Hawke, Baron 1950- *Who 94*
Hawke, Bernard Ray 1946- *WhoAm 94*
Hawke, Ethan *WhoHol 92*
Hawke, Ethan 1970- *IntMPA 94*
Hawke, Gary Richard 1942- *WrDr 94*
Hawke, John Daniel, Jr. 1933- *WhoAm 94, WhoAmL 94*
Hawke, R. Jack 1941- *WhoAmP 93*
Hawke, Robert D. 1932- *WhoAmP 93*
Hawke, Robert James Lee 1929- *IntWW 93, Who 94*
Hawke, Roger Jewett 1935- *WhoAm 94*
Hawke, Rohn Olin d1967 *WhoHol 92*
Hawke, Ronald Samuel 1940- *WhoWest 94*
Hawke, Simon *DrAPF 93, EncSF 93*
Hawke, Simon 1951- *WrDr 94*
Hawken, Dinah 1943- *BlmGWL*
Hawken, Janet Grace 1952- *WhoWest 94*
Hawken, Lewis Dudley 1931- *Who 94*
Hawken, Susan 1966- *WhoMW 93*
Hawker, Dennis Gascoyne 1921- *Who 94*
Hawker, Graham Alfred 1947- *Who 94*
Hawker, John *WhoHol 92*
Hawker, Vanessa Kaye 1967- *WhoWest 94*
Hawkes, Carol Ann *WhoAm 94*
Hawkes, Christopher 1905-1992 *AnObit 1992*
Hawkes, (Charles Francis) Christopher d1992 *IntWW 93N*
Hawkes, David 1923- *Who 94*
Hawkes, Elizabeth H. 1943- *WhoAmA 93*
Hawkes, G. W. *DrAPF 93*
Hawkes, Glenn Rogers 1919- *WhoAm 94, WhoWest 94*
Hawkes, J(ohn) G(regory) 1915- *WrDr 94*
Hawkes, Jacquetta 1910- *EncSF 93, IntWW 93, Who 94, WrDr 94*
Hawkes, John *DrAPF 93*
Hawkes, John 1925- *IntWW 93, WhoAm 94*
Hawkes, John (Clendennin Burne, Jr.) 1925- *ConDr 93, WrDr 94*
Hawkes, John Gregory 1915- *Who 94*
Hawkes, Judith 1949- *WrDr 94*
Hawkes, Kevin 1959- *WrDr 94*
Hawkes, Michael John 1929- *Who 94*
Hawkes, Paul M. 1957- *WhoAmP 93*
Hawkes, Raymond 1920- *Who 94*
Hawkes, William S. 1945- *WhoAmL 94*
Hawkes, Zachary 1925- *WrDr 94*
Hawkesbury, Viscount 1972- *Who 94*
Hawkesworth, Eric (William) 1921- *WrDr 94*
Hawkesworth, John Stanley 1920- *Who 94*
Hawkesworth, (Thomas) Simon (Ashwell) 1943- *Who 94*
Hawkey, G. Michael 1941- *WhoAm 94, WhoAmL 94*
Hawkey, Philip A. 1946- *WhoAm 94, WhoWest 94*
Hawkin, Martin *EncSF 93*
Hawking, Stephen W. 1942- *WhoAm 94, WhoScEn 94*
Hawking, Stephen W(illiam) 1942- *WrDr 94*
Hawking, Stephen William 1942- *IntWW 93, Who 94, WorScD [port]*
Hawkins, Alberta Lee 1947- *WhoAmP 93*
Hawkins, Alma Mae 1904- *WhoWest 94*
Hawkins, Andre 1953- *WhoBlA 94*
Hawkins, Anne Hunsaker 1944- *ConAu 142*
Hawkins, Anthony Donald 1942- *Who 94*
Hawkins, Armis E. 1920- *WhoAmP 93*
Hawkins, Armis Eugene 1920- *WhoAm 94, WhoAmL 94*
Hawkins, Arthur 1943- *WhoAm 94, WhoFI 94*
Hawkins, Arthur (Ernest) 1913- *Who 94*
Hawkins, Arthur Michael 1942- *WhoFI 94*
Hawkins, Ashton 1937- *WhoAm 94*
Hawkins, Augustus F. 1907- *WhoAmP 93, WhoBlA 94*
Hawkins, Barbara 1947- *WhoAmA 93*
Hawkins, Barry Curtis 1943- *WhoAmL 94*
Hawkins, Barton A. *WhoAm 94*
Hawkins, Benjamin 1754-1816 *WhAmRev*
Hawkins, Benny F., Sr. 1931- *WhoBlA 94*

Hawkins, Bobbie Louise *DrAPF 93*
Hawkins, Brett William 1937- *WhoAm 94*
Hawkins, Calvin D. 1945- *WhoBlA 94*
Hawkins, Catherine Eileen 1939- *Who 94*
Hawkins, Charles Robert 1943- *WhoAmP 93*
Hawkins, Cheryl La Don 1958- *WhoBlA 94*
Hawkins, Christopher James 1937- *Who 94*
Hawkins, Coleman 1904-1969 *AfrAmAl 6, ConMus 11 [port]*
Hawkins, Coleman Randolph 1904-1969 *AmCulL*
Hawkins, Connie 1942- *BasBi, WhoBlA 94*
Hawkins, Daniel Ballou 1934- *WhoWest 94*
Hawkins, Darroll Lee 1948- *WhoScEn 94*
Hawkins, David Cartwright 1913- *WhoAm 94*
Hawkins, David Ramon 1927- *WhoWest 94*
Hawkins, David Richard 1937- *Who 94*
Hawkins, David Rollo, Sr. 1923- *WhoAm 94, WhoScEn 94*
Hawkins, Debra Lynn 1949- *WhoWest 94*
Hawkins, Dennis Patrick 1945- *WhoMW 93*
Hawkins, Desmond 1908- *Who 94*
Hawkins, Desmond Ernest 1919- *Who 94*
Hawkins, Dolores d1987 *WhoHol 92*
Hawkins, Donald Bruce 1956- *WhoAmP 93*
Hawkins, Donald Merton 1921- *WhoAm 94*
Hawkins, Donna Black 1944- *WhoAmP 93*
Hawkins, Dorisula Wooten 1941- *WhoBlA 94*
Hawkins, Edward Jackson 1927- *WhoAm 94, WhoAmL 94*
Hawkins, Eldridge 1940- *WhoBlA 94*
Hawkins, Eldridge Thomas Enoch 1940- *WhoAmP 93*
Hawkins, Eliot Dexter 1932- *WhoAm 94*
Hawkins, Eric William 1915- *Who 94*
Hawkins, Erick *WhoAm 94*
Hawkins, Erskine d1993 *NewYTBS 93*
Hawkins, Erskine Ramsay 1914- *WhoBlA 94*
Hawkins, Falcon Black, Jr. 1927- *WhoAm 94, WhoAmL 94*
Hawkins, Francis Glenn 1917- *WhoAm 94*
Hawkins, Frank Ernest 1904- *Who 94*
Hawkins, Gene *WhoBlA 94*
Hawkins, Gerald 1943- *WhoAmP 93*
Hawkins, Gerald Stanley 1928- *WrDr 94*
Hawkins, Harley Buford 1929- *WhoAmP 93*
Hawkins, Hersey R., Jr. 1965- *WhoBlA 94*
Hawkins, Howard Caesar 1956- *Who 94*
Hawkins, Howard P. 1900- *WhoBlA 94*
Hawkins, Howard R., Jr. 1950- *WhoAm 94, WhoAmL 94*
Hawkins, Humphrey Villiers Caesar d1993 *Who 94N*
Hawkins, Hunt *DrAPF 93*
Hawkins, J(esse) Mills 1898- *WhAm 10*
Hawkins, Jack d1973 *WhoHol 92*
Hawkins, Jack Wade 1934- *WhoAm 94*
Hawkins, Jacquelyn 1943- *WhoMW 93*
Hawkins, James 1939- *WhoBlA 94*
Hawkins, James Alexander, II 1929- *WhoAm 94*
Hawkins, James C. 1932- *WhoBlA 94*
Hawkins, James Douglas, Jr. 1959- *WhoScEn 94*
Hawkins, James Victor 1936- *WhoWest 94*
Hawkins, Jamesetta 1938- *WhoBlA 94*
Hawkins, Janet Lynn 1956- *WhoScEn 94*
Hawkins, Jasper Stillwell, Jr. 1932- *WhoAm 94*
Hawkins, Jimmy 1941- *WhoHol 92*
Hawkins, John 1532-1595 *WhWE*
Hawkins, John H., Jr. *WhoAmP 93*
Hawkins, John Morgan 1935- *WhoAmP 93*
Hawkins, John Russell, III 1949- *WhoBlA 94*
Hawkins, Joseph Elmer, Jr. 1914- *WhoAm 94, WhoMW 93, WhoScEn 94*
Hawkins, Joyce H. 1936- *WhoAmP 93*
Hawkins, Katherine Ann 1947- *WhoAm 94*
Hawkins, Kenneth Bruce 1947- *WhoAmP 93*
Hawkins, Kenneth Lee 1951- *WhoMW 93*
Hawkins, Kevin France 1959- *WhoWest 94*
Hawkins, Laetitia-Matilda 1759-1835 *DcNaB MP*
Hawkins, Laura 1951- *SmATA 74 [port]*
Hawkins, Lawrence C. 1919- *WhoBlA 94*
Hawkins, Linda *WhoHol 92*
Hawkins, Lionel Anthony 1933- *WhoFI 94, WhoMW 93*
Hawkins, Lonny W. 1956- *WhoWest 94*
Hawkins, Mark David 1960- *WhoFI 94*
Hawkins, Mary Bess 1951- *WhoMW 93*
Hawkins, Mary Ellen Higgins *WhoAmP 93*
Hawkins, Mary L. *WhoBlA 94*
Hawkins, Merrill Morris 1914- *WhoAm 94*
Hawkins, Michael D. 1945- *WhoAmP 93*
Hawkins, Michael Daly 1945- *WhoAm 94, WhoAmL 94*
Hawkins, Michael W. 1947- *WhoAmL 94*
Hawkins, Muriel A. 1946- *WhoBlA 94*
Hawkins, Myrtle H. *WhoAmA 93*
Hawkins, Neil Middleton 1935- *WhoAm 94*
Hawkins, Nicholas John 1957- *Who 94*
Hawkins, Osie d1993 *NewYTBS 93*
Hawkins, Osie 1913- *NewGrDO*
Hawkins, Osie Penman, Jr. 1913- *WhoAm 94*
Hawkins, Pamela Leigh Huffman 1950- *WhoScEn 94*
Hawkins, Paul (Lancelot) 1912- *Who 94*
Hawkins, Paula *IntWW 93, WhoAm 94*
Hawkins, Paula F. 1927- *WhoAmP 93*
Hawkins, Reginald A. 1923- *WhoBlA 94*
Hawkins, Richard Graeme 1941- *Who 94*
Hawkins, Richard Michael 1949- *WhoAmL 94*
Hawkins, Richard Stephen *Who 94*
Hawkins, Robert 1939- *WhoAmP 93*
Hawkins, Robert Garvin 1936- *WhoAm 94*
Hawkins, Robert Lee 1938- *WhoAmP 93, WhoFI 94, WhoWest 94*
Hawkins, Robert S. 1938- *WhoAmP 93*
Hawkins, Robert W. 1949- *WhoAmL 94*
Hawkins, Ronnie *WhoHol 92*
Hawkins, Scott Alexis 1954- *WhoAmL 94*
Hawkins, "Screamin'" Jay 1929- *WhoHol 92*
Hawkins, Shane V. 1957- *WhoScEn 94*
Hawkins, Stan 1955- *WhoAmP 93*
Hawkins, Steven Wayne 1962- *WhoBlA 94*
Hawkins, Theodore F. 1908- *WhoBlA 94*
Hawkins, Thomas Wilson, Jr. 1941- *WhoAmA 93*
Hawkins, Tom *DrAPF 93*
Hawkins, Tracey L. 1960- *WhoMW 93*
Hawkins, Trip *NewYTBS 93 [port]*
Hawkins, W. Whitley 1931- *WhoAm 94, WhoFI 94*
Hawkins, Walter Lincoln 1911- *WhoBlA 94*
Hawkins, Walter Lincoln 1911-1992 *WhAm 10*
Hawkins, Ward 1912-1990 *EncSF 93*
Hawkins, Wilbur *WhoAm 94*
Hawkins, William Andrew 1938- *WhoAmP 93*
Hawkins, William Douglas 1946- *WhoBlA 94*
Hawkins, William E. N. 1943- *WhoAm 94*
Hawkins, William F. 1931- *WhoAm 94*
Hawkins, William H., II 1948- *WhoAmL 94*
Hawkins, William R. *WhoIns 94*
Hawkins, Willis Moore 1913- *WhoAm 94*
Hawkinson, Carl E. 1947- *WhoAmP 93*
Hawkinson, Gary Michael 1948- *WhoAm 94*
Hawkinson, Marie C. 1927- *WhoAmP 93*
Hawkinson, Thomas Edwin 1952- *WhoMW 93*
Hawkley, Dan *WhoAmP 93*
Hawkrigg, Melvin Michael 1930- *WhoAm 94, WhoFI 94*
Hawks, Barrett Kingsbury 1938- *WhoAm 94*
Hawks, Charles Monroe d1951 *WhoHol 92*
Hawks, Frank d1938 *WhoHol 92*
Hawks, Howard Winchester 1896-1977 *AmCulL*
Hawks, James Wade 1957- *WhoMW 93*
Hawks, Jane Esther Hokanson 1955- *WhoMW 93*
Hawks, Katherine A. 1943- *WhoWest 94*
Hawks, William Harry, Jr. *WhoAmP 93*
Hawksley, John Callis d1993 *Who 94N*
Hawksley, (Philip) Warren 1943- *Who 94*
Hawksworth, David Leslie 1946- *Who 94*
Hawksworth, Marjorie *DrAPF 93*
Hawkwood, Allan *EncSF 93*
Hawley, Allen Burton d1925 *WhoHol 92*
Hawley, Anne 1943- *WhoAm 94*
Hawley, Barbara L. 1950- *WhoAmL 94*
Hawley, Daniel V. 1950- *WhoFI 94*
Hawley, Dennis James 1958- *WhoFI 94*
Hawley, Donald (Frederick) 1921- *Who 94*
Hawley, Donald Frederick 1921- *IntWW 93*
Hawley, Ellis Wayne 1929- *WhoAm 94*
Hawley, Frank Jordan, Jr. 1927- *WhoAm 94*
Hawley, Frederick William, III 1931- *WhoAm 94*
Hawley, Gideon 1727-1807 *EncNAR*
Hawley, H. Dudley d1941 *WhoHol 92*
Hawley, Henry Nicholas *Who 94*
Hawley, James Charles 1954- *WhoFI 94*
Hawley, John Joseph 1952- *WhoFI 94*
Hawley, John William 1932- *WhoWest 94*
Hawley, Joseph 1723-1788 *WhAmRev*
Hawley, Margaret Foote 1880-1963 *WhoAmA 93N*
Hawley, Mark Hiram d1986 *WhoHol 92*
Hawley, Nanci Elizabeth 1942- *WhoFI 94, WhoWest 94*
Hawley, Ormi d1942 *WhoHol 92*
Hawley, Philip Metschan 1925- *WhoAm 94, WhoFI 94, WhoWest 94*
Hawley, Phillip Eugene 1940- *WhoFI 94*
Hawley, R. Stephen *WhoAmP 93*
Hawley, Richard A 1945- *WrDr 94*
Hawley, Robert 1936- *IntWW 93, Who 94*
Hawley, Robert A. 1952- *WhoAmL 94*
Hawley, Robert Cross 1920- *WhoWest 94*
Hawley, Sandra Sue 1948- *WhoMW 93, WhoScEn 94*
Hawley, T. M. 1953- *ConAu 140*
Hawley, Thomas Alan 1955- *WhoAmP 93*
Hawley, Wanda d1963 *WhoHol 92*
Hawley, William E. d1976 *WhoHol 92*
Hawlicek, Hilde 1942- *WhoWomW 91*
Hawn, Goldie 1945- *IntMPA 94, IntWW 93, WhoAm 94, WhoCom [port], WhoHol 92*
Hawn, John d1964 *WhoHol 92*
Hawn, William Eugene 1941- *WhoAm 94*
Hawn Myers, Patricia Lynn 1968- *WhoWest 94*
Haworth, B. Coquill 1904- *WhoAmA 93N*
Haworth, Betsy Ellen 1924- *Who 94*
Haworth, Byron Allen 1907- *WhoAmP 93*
Haworth, Charles Ray 1943- *WhoAm 94, WhoAmL 94*
Haworth, Dale Keith 1924- *WhoAm 94*
Haworth, Daniel Thomas 1928- *WhoAm 94*
Haworth, James Chilton 1923- *WhoAm 94*
Haworth, Jill 1945- *WhoHol 92*
Haworth, John Leigh W. *Who 94*
Haworth, Larry Eugene 1946- *WhoWest 94*
Haworth, Lawrence Lindley 1926- *WhoAm 94*
Haworth, Leslie William 1943- *WhoFI 94*
Haworth, Lionel 1912- *IntWW 93, Who 94*
Haworth, Martha d1966 *WhoHol 92*
Haworth, Michael Elliott, Jr. 1928- *WhoAm 94*
Haworth, Peter 1889- *WhoAmA 93N*
Haworth, Philip 1927- *Who 94*
Haworth, Richard James 1943- *Who 94*
Haworth, Richard Thomas 1944- *WhoAm 94*
Haworth, Steven John 1965- *WhoMW 93*
Haworth, Ted d1993 *NewYTBS 93*
Haworth, Vinton d1970 *WhoHol 92*
Hawpe, David Vaughn 1943- *WhoAm 94*
Hawran, Paul William 1952- *WhoAm 94*
Hawrylewicz, Ervin John *WhoMW 93*
Hawrylyshyn, Bohdan Wolodymyr 1926- *WhoFI 94*
Haws, Henry H. *WhoAmP 93*
Haws, Janet A. 1939- *WhoMW 93*
Haws, Robert Dunn 1932- *WhoWest 94*
Hawse, Lionel A. 1942- *WhoAmL 94*
Hawse, Thomas J., III 1945- *WhoAmP 93*
Hawthorn, Christopher John 1936- *Who 94*
Hawthorne, Angel L. 1959- *WhoBlA 94*
Hawthorne, Bruce N. 1949- *WhoAmL 94*
Hawthorne, Dave *WhoHol 92*
Hawthorne, David d1942 *WhoHol 92*
Hawthorne, Douglas Bruce 1948- *WhoWest 94*
Hawthorne, Douglas Lawson 1942- *WhoAm 94*
Hawthorne, Frank Howard 1923- *WhoAm 94*
Hawthorne, Jack Gardner 1921- *WhoAmA 93*
Hawthorne, James Burns 1930- *Who 94*
Hawthorne, Kenneth B. *WhoAmP 93*
Hawthorne, Kenneth L. *WhoBlA 94*
Hawthorne, Lucia Shelia *WhoBlA 94*
Hawthorne, Marion Frederick 1928- *WhoAm 94, WhoScEn 94, WhoWest 94*
Hawthorne, Nan Louise 1952- *WhoWest 94*
Hawthorne, Nathaniel 1804-1864 *AmCulL, EncSF 93, RfGShF*
Hawthorne, Nathaniel 1943- *WhoBlA 94*
Hawthorne, Nigel 1929- *IntMPA 94, WhoHol 92*
Hawthorne, Nigel Barnard 1929- *IntWW 93, Who 94, WhoAm 94*
Hawthorne, Robert Alexander, Jr. 1937- *WhoAmP 93*
Hawthorne, Victor Morrison 1921- *WhoAm 94*
Hawthorne, William (Rede) 1913- *IntWW 93, Who 94*
Hawthorne, William Rede 1913- *WhoScEn 94*
Hawtin, Brian Richard 1946- *Who 94*
Hawtin, David Christopher 1943- *Who 94*
Hawtin, Michael Victor 1942- *Who 94*
Hawton, Hector 1901- *EncSF 93*
Hawton, Robert P. 1953- *WhoAm 94*
Hawtrey, Anthony d1954 *WhoHol 92*
Hawtrey, Charles d1923 *WhoHol 92*
Hawtrey, Charles d1988 *WhoHol 92*
Hawtrey, John Havilland Procter 1905- *Who 94*
Hawver, Dennis Arthur 1940- *WhoAm 94*
Hax, Arnoldo Cubillos 1936- *WhoAm 94*
Haxby, Donald Leslie 1928- *Who 94*
Haxel, Otto Philipp Leonhard 1909- *IntWW 93*
Haxo, Francis Theodore 1921- *WhoAm 94*
Haxton, Brooks *DrAPF 93*
Haxton, Brooks 1950- *WrDr 94*
Haxton, David 1943- *WhoAm 94, WhoAmA 93*
Haxton, Donovan Merle, Jr. 1941- *WhoScEn 94*
Haxton, Josephine Ayres 1921- *ConAu 41NR*
Haxton, Lori Ann 1958- *WhoMW 93*
Haxton, Richardson Ayres 1948- *WhoAmP 93*
Hay *Who 94*
Hay, Lord 1984- *Who 94*
Hay, A. John 1938- *WhoAmA 93*
Hay, Alexandra 1947- *WhoHol 92*
Hay, Alexandre 1919-1991 *WhAm 10*
Hay, Allan Stuart 1929- *Who 94, WhoAm 94*
Hay, Andrew Mackenzie 1928- *WhoFI 94, WhoWest 94*
Hay, Andrew Osborne 1945- *IntWW 93*
Hay, Arthur Thomas Erroll d1993 *Who 94N*
Hay, Austin *WhoHol 92*
Hay, Carla Humphrey 1942- *WhoMW 93*
Hay, Charles Richard 1950- *WhoAmL 94*
Hay, David (Osborne) 1916- *Who 94*
Hay, David (Russell) 1927- *Who 94*
Hay, David Russell 1927- *IntWW 93*
Hay, Dennis Lee 1958- *WhoAmL 94*
Hay, Denys 1915- *Who 94, WrDr 94*
Hay, Dick 1942- *WhoAmA 93*
Hay, Donald Peter 1944- *WhoMW 93*
Hay, Elizabeth (Jean) 1936- *WrDr 94*
Hay, Elizabeth Dexter 1927- *WhoAm 94, WhoScEn 94*
Hay, Eloise Knapp 1926- *WhoAm 94*
Hay, Frances Mary *Who 94*
Hay, Frederick Dale 1944- *WhoAm 94*
Hay, George 1922- *EncSF 93*
Hay, George Adam 1930- *Who 94*
Hay, George Austin 1915- *WhoAm 94, WhoAmA 93, WhoFI 94*
Hay, George D. d1968 *WhoHol 92*
Hay, Hamish (Grenfell) 1927- *Who 94*
Hay, Howard *WhoAm 94*
Hay, Howard Clinton 1944- *WhoAm 94, WhoAmL 94*
Hay, Ike 1944- *WhoAmA 93*
Hay, Jacob 1920- *EncSF 93*
Hay, James B. D. *Who 94*
Hay, Janet S. 1933- *WhoAmP 93*
Hay, Jess Thomas 1931- *WhoAmP 93, WhoFI 94*
Hay, Joel W. 1952- *WhoWest 94*
Hay, John 1838-1905 *HisWorL [port]*
Hay, John 1915- *WhoAm 94*
Hay, John 1928- *EncSF 93*
Hay, John Albert 1919- *Who 94*
Hay, John Anthony 1942- *Who 94*
Hay, John Duncan 1909- *Who 94*
Hay, John Erroll Audley 1935- *Who 94*
Hay, John Franklin 1934- *WhoMW 93*
Hay, John Leonard 1940- *WhoAmL 94, WhoWest 94*
Hay, John Thomas 1921- *WhoAm 94*
Hay, John Woods, Jr. 1905- *WhoFI 94, WhoWest 94*
Hay, Mary d1957 *WhoHol 92*
Hay, Melba Porter 1949- *WrDr 94*
Hay, Nick 1949- *WhoAmL 94*
Hay, (Helen) Olga *Who 94*
Hay, Raymond A. *IntWW 93*
Hay, Richard 1942- *Who 94*
Hay, Richard Carman 1921- *WhoScEn 94*
Hay, Richard Laurence 1929- *WhoAm 94, WhoWest 94*
Hay, Richard Le Roy 1926- *WhoAm 94*
Hay, Rick Vance 1949- *WhoMW 93*
Hay, Robert Arthur 1920- *Who 94*
Hay, Robert Colquhoun 1933- *Who 94*
Hay, Robert Dean 1921- *WhoAm 94*
Hay, Robert Pettus 1941- *WhoMW 93*

Hay, Robin William Patrick Hamilton 1939- *Who 94*
Hay, Ronald Frederick Hamilton 1941- *Who 94*
Hay, Russell J. 1940- *WhoAmP 93*
Hay, W(illiam) Delisle *EncSF 93*
Hay, Will d1949 *WhoHol 92*
Hay, William Charles 1935- *WhoAm 94, WhoWest 94*
Hay, William J. 1937- *WhoAmL 94*
Hay, William Thomson 1888-1949 *DcNaB MP*
Hay, William Winn 1934- *WhoAm 94, WhoWest 94*
Hayaishi, Osamu 1920- *IntWW 93, WhoScEn 94*
Hayakawa, Kan-Ichi 1931- *WhoAm 94, WhoScEn 94*
Hayakawa, Kiyoshi d1993 *NewYTBS 93*
Hayakawa, Noboru 1938- *WhoAsA 94*
Hayakawa, S. I. 1906-1992 *WhoAsA 94N*
Hayakawa, Samuel Ichiye *IntWW 93N*
Hayakawa, Samuel Ichiye 1906-1992 *AnObit 1992, WhAm 10*
Hayakawa, Satio d1992 *IntWW 93N*
Hayakawa, Sessue d1973 *WhoHol 92*
Hayakawa, Sidney Akira 1948- *WhoAsA 94*
Hayasaka, Fumio 1914-1955 *IntDcF 2-4*
Hayase, Joshua Yoshio 1925- *WhoAsA 94*
Hayashi, Alan T. 1954- *WhoWest 94*
Hayashi, Dennis Wayne 1952- *WhoAsA 94*
Hayashi, Edwin Kenichi 1942- *WhoAmP 93*
Hayashi, Elmer Kinji 1938- *WhoAsA 94*
Hayashi, Fumihiko 1930- *WhoAsA 94*
Hayashi, George Yoichi 1920- *WhoScEn 94*
Hayashi, Grant Shiuichi 1957- *WhoWest 94*
Hayashi, Hikaru 1931- *NewGrDO*
Hayashi, James Akira 1926- *WhoAsA 94*
Hayashi, Masato 1938- *WhoAsA 94*
Hayashi, Masumi 1945- *WhoAmA 93, WhoAsA 94*
Hayashi, Midori *WhoAsA 94*
Hayashi, Mie May 1962- *WhoAsA 94*
Hayashi, Mitsuhiko 1930- *WhoScEn 94*
Hayashi, Robert H. 1938- *WhoAsA 94*
Hayashi, Seigo 1943- *WhoAsA 94*
Hayashi, Shizuo 1922- *WhoScEn 94*
Hayashi, Tadao *WhoScEn 94*
Hayashi, Taikan *IntWW 93*
Hayashi, Taizo 1920- *WhoScEn 94*
Hayashi, Takao 1949- *WhoScEn 94*
Hayashi, Takemi 1938- *WhoScEn 94*
Hayashi, Tetsumaro 1929- *WhoAsA 94, WrDr 94*
Hayashi, Toshiko 1940- *WhoWomW 91*
Hayashi, William Yasuo 1941- *WhoAsA 94*
Hayashi, Yasuko 1948- *NewGrDO*
Hayashi, Yoshihiro 1940- *WhoScEn 94*
Hayashi, Yoshimi 1922- *WhoAmP 93*
Hayashi, Yoshiro 1927- *IntWW 93*
Hayashida, Charley Taketoshi 1918-1993 *WhoAsA 94N*
Hayashida, Frank 1933- *WhoAsA 94*
Hayashida, Ronald Hideo 1942- *WhoAsA 94*
Hayashida, Yukio 1915- *IntWW 93*
Hayashikawa, Doris S. 1943- *WhoAsA 94*
Hayashi Kyoko 1930- *BlmGWL*
Hayashi Mariko 1954- *BlmGWL*
Hayasi, Nisiki 1929- *WhoFI 94, WhoScEn 94*
Hayat, Gilbert Salomon 1944- *WhoFI 94*
Hayball, Frederick Ronald 1914- *Who 94*
Haycock, Edward 1790-1870 *DcNaB MP*
Haycock, Kate 1962- *SmATA 77 [port]*
Haycock, Kenneth Roy 1948- *WhoAm 94*
Haycraft, Anna 1932- *WrDr 94*
Haycraft, Anna Margaret 1932- *IntWW 93, Who 94*
Haycraft, Colin Berry 1929- *Who 94*
Haycraft, Howard 1905-1991 *WhAm 10*
Haycraft, John (Stacpoole) 1926- *WrDr 94*
Haycraft, John Stacpoole 1926- *Who 94*
Haydanek, Ronald Edward 1932- *WhoAm 94*
Haydar, Loutof Allah 1940- *Who 94*
Haydar, Mohammad Haydar 1931- *IntWW 93*
Haydari, Buland al- 1926- *ConWorW 93*
Hay Davison, Ian Frederic *Who 94*
Hayday, Anthony Victor 1930- *Who 94*
Haydee, Marcia *WhoHol 92*
Haydee, Marcia 1939- *IntDcB [port]*
Haydel, James V., Sr. *WhoBlA 94*
Haydel, Richard d1949 *WhoHol 92*
Hayden, Anna Tompson 1648-c. 1720 *BlmGWL*
Hayden, Bridget 1815-1890 *EncNAR*
Hayden, Carla Diane 1952- *WhoBlA 94*
Hayden, Cedric 1934- *WhoAmP 93*
Hayden, Dolores *DrAPF 93*
Hayden, Don *WhoHol 92*
Hayden, Donald E 1915- *WrDr 94*
Hayden, Eric William 1919- *WrDr 94*
Hayden, Esther Allen c. 1713-1758 *BlmGWL*
Hayden, Ferdinand Vandeveer 1829-1887 *WhWE*
Hayden, Frank *WhoBlA 94*
Hayden, Harold 1947- *WhoAmP 93*
Hayden, Harry d1955 *WhoHol 92*
Hayden, Henry Thomas 1941- *WhoWest 94*
Hayden, J. Charles d1943 *WhoHol 92*
Hayden, James d1983 *WhoHol 92*
Hayden, Jan Marie 1954- *WhoAmL 94*
Hayden, Jay Gary 1936- *WhoMW 93*
Hayden, John Carleton 1933- *WhoBlA 94*
Hayden, John Michael 1944- *IntWW 93*
Hayden, John Olin 1932- *WhoAm 94*
Hayden, Joseph A., Jr. 1944- *WhoAmL 94*
Hayden, Joseph P., Jr. 1929- *WhoIns 94*
Hayden, Joseph Page, Jr. 1929- *WhoAm 94*
Hayden, Karl *WhoHol 92*
Hayden, Lawrence Marie 1925- *WhoAm 94*
Hayden, Leroy Austin 1927- *WhoAmP 93*
Hayden, Leroy Robert, Jr. 1935- *WhoIns 94*
Hayden, Linda 1951- *WhoHol 92*
Hayden, Martin S. *WhoAmP 93*
Hayden, Martin Scholl 1912-1991 *WhAm 10*
Hayden, Mary *WhoHol 92*
Hayden, Melissa 1921- *WhoHol 92*
Hayden, Melissa 1923- *IntDcB [port]*
Hayden, Melva Joan 1956- *WhoAmL 94*
Hayden, Mike 1944- *WhoAmP 93*
Hayden, Naura *WhoHol 92*
Hayden, Neil Steven 1937- *WhoAm 94*
Hayden, Palmer C. 1893-1973 *WhoAmA 93N*
Hayden, Ralph Frederick 1922- *WhoAm 94, WhoFI 94*
Hayden, Raymond Paul 1939- *WhoAm 94, WhoAmL 94*
Hayden, Richard 1956- *WhoAmP 93*
Hayden, Richard Michael 1945- *WhoAm 94, WhoFI 94*
Hayden, Robert C., Jr. 1937- *WhoBlA 94*
Hayden, Robert E. 1913-1980 *AfrAmAl 6*
Hayden, Ron L. 1948- *WhoWest 94*
Hayden, Russell d1981 *WhoHol 92*
Hayden, Spencer James 1922- *WhoFI 94*
Hayden, Sterling d1986 *WhoHol 92*
Hayden, Thomas E(mmet) 1939- *ConAu 41NR*
Hayden, Thomas Emmett 1939- *AmSocL*
Hayden, Tom *ConAu 41NR*
Hayden, Tom 1939- *WhoAmP 93, WhoWest 94, WrDr 94*
Hayden, Tom 1940- *HisWorL [port]*
Hayden, Tony Martin 1957- *WhoWest 94*
Hayden, Vern Clarence 1937- *WhoFI 94*
Hayden, Vernon d1990 *WhoHol 92*
Hayden, Walter John 1951- *WhoScEn 94*
Hayden, William George 1933- *IntWW 93, Who 94*
Hayden, William Hughes 1940- *WhoBlA 94*
Hayden, William Joseph 1929- *Who 94*
Hayden, William Robert 1947- *WhoAm 94, WhoAmL 94*
Haydn, (Franz) Joseph 1732-1809 *NewGrDO*
Haydn, Michael 1737-1806 *NewGrDO*
Haydn, Richard d1985 *WhoHol 92*
Haydock, John d1918 *WhoHol 92*
Haydock, Robert, Jr. 1917- *WhoAmL 94*
Haydock, Ron d1977 *WhoHol 92*
Haydock, Walter James 1947- *WhoMW 93*
Haydon, Francis Edmund Walter 1928- *Who 94*
Haydon, Glen 1896- *WhAm 10*
Haydon, Harold (Emerson) 1909- *WhoAmA 93*
Haydon, Julie 1910- *WhoHol 92*
Haydon, LuAnn Marie 1951- *WhoMW 93*
Haydon, Robin 1920- *IntWW 93*
Haydon, Walter Robert 1920- *Who 94*
Haydu, Claire R. 1954- *WhoWest 94*
Haye, Clifford S. 1942- *WhoBlA 94*
Haye, Colvyn Hugh 1925- *IntWW 93, Who 94*
Haye, Helen d1957 *WhoHol 92*
Hayek, Carolyn Jean 1948- *WhoAm 94, WhoAmL 94*
Hayek, Friedrich A. von d1992 *NobelP 91N*
Hayek, Friedrich August (Von) 1899-1992 *WhAm 10*
Hayek, Friedrich August von 1899-1992 *AnObit 1992*
Hayek, Ignace Antoine, II 1910- *IntWW 93*
Hayek, John William 1941- *WhoAmL 94*
Hayek, Linda Marie 1951- *WhoMW 93*
Hayek, Nicolas G. 1928- *IntWW 93*
Hayek, William Edward 1947- *WhoAm 94*
Hayers, Sidney 1921- *HorFD*
Hayes, Agnes Thresa 1919- *WhoAmP 93*
Hayes, Alberta Phyllis Wildrick 1918- *WhoScEn 94*
Hayes, Albertine Brannum *WhoBlA 94*
Hayes, Alfred 1910-1989 *WhAm 10*
Hayes, Alice Bourke 1937- *WhoAm 94*
Hayes, Allison d1977 *WhoHol 92*
Hayes, Alvin, Jr. 1932- *WhoBlA 94*
Hayes, Andrew Patrick 1958- *WhoFI 94*
Hayes, Andrew Wallace 1939- *WhoScEn 94*
Hayes, Andrew Wallace, II 1939- *WhoAm 94*
Hayes, Ann *DrAPF 93*
Hayes, Ann Louise 1924- *WhoAm 94*
Hayes, Annamarie Gillespie 1931- *WhoBlA 94*
Hayes, Arthur C. *WhoAmP 93*
Hayes, Arthur Chester 1918- *WhoMW 93*
Hayes, Arthur Michael 1915- *WhoAm 94*
Hayes, Bernadene d1987 *WhoHol 92*
Hayes, Bernadette Marie *WhoMW 93*
Hayes, Bernardine Frances 1939- *WhoFI 94*
Hayes, Bill 1925- *WhoHol 92*
Hayes, Billie *WhoHol 92*
Hayes, Brenda Sue Nelson 1941- *WhoMW 93*
Hayes, Brent Charles 1971- *WhoWest 94*
Hayes, Brian 1929- *IntWW 93*
Hayes, Brian 1940- *Who 94*
Hayes, Brian (David) 1929- *Who 94*
Hayes, Brian Paul 1949- *WhoAm 94, WhoScEn 94*
Hayes, Burgain Garfield 1948- *WhoAmL 94*
Hayes, Byron Jackson, Jr. 1934- *WhoAm 94, WhoAmL 94, WhoWest 94*
Hayes, Catherine d1941 *WhoHol 92*
Hayes, Catherine 1825-1861 *NewGrDO*
Hayes, Charles 1943- *WhoBlA 94*
Hayes, Charles A. 1918- *WhoAmP 93, WhoBlA 94*
Hayes, Charles A. 1935- *WhoAm 94, WhoFI 94*
Hayes, Charles Austin 1946- *WhoFI 94*
Hayes, Charles Franklin, III 1932- *WhoScEn 94*
Hayes, Charles L. *DrAPF 93*
Hayes, Charles Langley 1939- *WrDr 94*
Hayes, Charles Lawton 1927- *WhoAm 94*
Hayes, Charles Leonard 1921- *WhoBlA 94*
Hayes, Charles Victor 1955- *WhoScEn 94*
Hayes, Charlie 1965- *WhoBlA 94*
Hayes, Christopher L. 1958- *ConAu 142*
Hayes, Claude (James) 1912- *Who 94*
Hayes, Claude Quinten Christopher 1945- *WhoWest 94*
Hayes, Colin Graham Frederick 1919- *Who 94*
Hayes, Curtiss Leo 1931- *WhoBlA 94*
Hayes, Cynthia Lela 1949- *WhoFI 94*
Hayes, David J. 1953- *WhoAm 94, WhoAmL 94*
Hayes, David John Arthur, Jr. 1929- *WhoAm 94, WhoAmL 94*
Hayes, David Kirk 1963- *WhoScEn 94*
Hayes, David M. 1942- *WhoAmL 94*
Hayes, David Michael 1943- *WhoAm 94, WhoAmL 94*
Hayes, David Vincent 1931- *WhoAm 94, WhoAmA 93*
Hayes, Davis 1950- *IntWW 93*
Hayes, Debra Troxell 1952- *WhoMW 93*
Hayes, Delbert J. 1935- *WhoFI 94*
Hayes, Denis 1944- *EnvEnc [port]*
Hayes, Denis A(llen) 1944- *WrDr 94*
Hayes, (Robert) Dennis 1952- *WrDr 94*
Hayes, Dennis Edward 1938- *WhoAm 94*
Hayes, Dennis Joseph 1934- *WhoAm 94*
Hayes, Derek Cumberland 1936- *WhoAm 94*
Hayes, Donald LeRaye 1939- *WhoAmP 93*
Hayes, Edward c. 1550-c. 1613 *DcNaB MP*
Hayes, Edward, Jr. 1947- *WhoBlA 94*
Hayes, Edwin Junius, Jr. 1932- *WhoAm 94*
Hayes, Eleanor Maxine 1954- *WhoBlA 94*
Hayes, Elizabeth A. 1957- *WhoAmP 93*
Hayes, Elvin 1945- *BasBi*
Hayes, Elvin E., Sr. 1945- *WhoBlA 94*
Hayes, Ernest M. 1946- *WhoWest 94*
Hayes, Evelyn *BlmGWL*
Hayes, Floyd Windom, III 1942- *WhoBlA 94*
Hayes, Francis Mahon 1930- *IntWW 93*
Hayes, Frank d1923 *WhoHol 92*
Hayes, Frederick William 1848-1918 *EncSF 93*
Hayes, Gaylon Curtis 1949- *WhoAmL 94*
Hayes, George d1967 *WhoHol 92*
Hayes, George d1969 *WhoHol 92*
Hayes, George Nicholas 1928- *WhoAmL 94*
Hayes, Gerald 1940- *WhoAmA 93*
Hayes, Gerald Joseph 1950- *WhoAm 94, WhoAmL 94*
Hayes, Gladys Lucille Allen 1913- *WhoFI 94*
Hayes, Gordon Glenn 1936- *WhoScEn 94, WhoWest 94*
Hayes, Grace d1989 *WhoHol 92*
Hayes, Graham Edmondson 1929- *WhoBlA 94*
Hayes, Gregory Michael 1954- *WhoWest 94*
Hayes, Guy Scull d1993 *NewYTBS 93*
Hayes, Harold Thomas Pace 1926-1989 *WhAm 10*
Hayes, Hazel *WhoHol 92*
Hayes, Helen d1993 *IntMPA 94N, IntWW 93N, Who 94N*
Hayes, Helen 1900- *IntMPA 94, WhoHol 92*
Hayes, Helen 1900-1993 *AmCulL, ConAu 140, ConTFT 11, CurBio 93N, NewYTBS 93 [port], News 93*
Hayes, Henry Clifton 1942- *WhoAmP 93*
Hayes, Ira M. d1956 *WhoHol 92*
Hayes, Isaac 1942- *AfrAmAl 6, ConMus 10 [port], WhoAm 94, WhoBlA 94, WhoHol 92*
Hayes, Isaac Israel 1832-1881 *WhWE*
Hayes, J. Harold, Jr. 1953- *WhoBlA 94*
Hayes, J. Kevin 1950- *WhoAmL 94*
Hayes, J. Michael 1946- *WhoAmL 94*
Hayes, Jacqueline Crement 1941- *WhoMW 93*
Hayes, James A. 1946- *CngDr 93*
Hayes, James Alison 1946- *WhoAm 94, WhoAmP 93*
Hayes, James B. *WhoAm 94, WhoFI 94*
Hayes, James Edward 1928- *WhoAm 94*
Hayes, James Franklin 1948- *WhoAmL 94*
Hayes, James J., Jr. 1947- *WhoAmL 94*
Hayes, James Mark 1958- *WhoAmL 94*
Hayes, James Martin 1924- *Who 94*
Hayes, James Ray 1946- *WhoFI 94*
Hayes, Janet Gray 1926- *WhoAm 94, WhoAmP 93*
Hayes, Janice Cecile Osgard 1941- *WhoAm 94*
Hayes, Jeanne 1942- *WhoWest 94*
Hayes, Jeffrey C. 1946- *WhoAmL 94*
Hayes, Jeremy Joseph James 1953- *Who 94*
Hayes, Jerome Arthur, III 1948- *WhoFI 94*
Hayes, Jerri *WhoHol 92*
Hayes, Jim *WhoBlA 94*
Hayes, Jimmy *WhoHol 92*
Hayes, Joan Eames 1916- *WhoAmP 93*
Hayes, Joe Black 1915- *WhoAmP 93*
Hayes, John (Osler Chattock) 1913- *Who 94*
Hayes, John (Trevor) 1929- *WrDr 94*
Hayes, John Bruton, Jr. 1942- *WhoAm 94, WhoFI 94*
Hayes, John C., III 1945- *WhoAmP 93*
Hayes, John D. 1947- *WhoFI 94*
Hayes, John Edward, Jr. 1937- *WhoAm 94, WhoFI 94, WhoMW 93*
Hayes, John Francis 1919- *WhoAm 94, WhoAmP 93*
Hayes, John Freeman 1926- *WhoAm 94*
Hayes, John Marion 1909- *WhoScEn 94*
Hayes, John Michael 1919- *IntDcF 2-4, IntMPA 94*
Hayes, John Patrick 1921- *WhoAm 94*
Hayes, John Patrick 1944- *WhoAm 94*
Hayes, John Patrick, Jr. 1949- *WhoAm 94*
Hayes, John Philip 1924- *IntWW 93, Who 94*
Hayes, John Trevor 1929- *IntWW 93, Who 94*
Hayes, John William 1945- *Who 94*
Hayes, Jonathan Michael 1962- *WhoBlA 94*
Hayes, Joseph d1781 *WhAmRev*
Hayes, Joseph (Arnold) 1918- *WrDr 94*
Hayes, Karen Wood 1935- *WhoAmP 93*
Hayes, Kirk M. 1936- *WhoIns 94*
Hayes, Larry B. 1939- *WhoAmL 94*
Hayes, Laura M. 1927- *WhoAmA 93*
Hayes, Laurence C. d1974 *WhoHol 92*
Hayes, Leola G. *WhoBlA 94*
Hayes, Lester 1955- *WhoBlA 94*
Hayes, Lewis Mifflin, Jr. 1941- *WhoAmL 94*
Hayes, Lind *WhoHol 92*
Hayes, Linda 1918- *WhoHol 92*
Hayes, Lorraine *WhoHol 92*
Hayes, M. M. M. *DrAPF 93*
Hayes, Maggie d1977 *WhoHol 92*
Hayes, Marilyn Jo 1934- *WhoWest 94*
Hayes, Marion LeRoy 1931- *WhoBlA 94*
Hayes, Mark Stephen 1946- *WhoAmL 94*
Hayes, Martin Joseph 1932- *WhoAmP 93*
Hayes, Mary Phyllis 1921- *WhoAm 94, WhoFI 94, WhoMW 93*
Hayes, Maureen Ann 1957- *WhoMW 93*

Hayes, Melvyn 1935- *WhoHol 92*
Hayes, Michael Cecil 1946- *WhoAmL 94*
Hayes, Michael D. 1951- *WhoAmP 93*
Hayes, Michele T. 1948- *WhoAmL 94*
Hayes, N. *ConAu 142*
Hayes, Nan *ConAu 142*
Hayes, Neil John 1951- *WhoAmL 94*
Hayes, Nicholas 1947- *WhoAmP 93*
Hayes, Norman Robert, Jr. 1948- *WhoAmL 94*
Hayes, Patricia 1910- *WhoHol 92*
Hayes, Patricia Ann 1944- *WhoAm 94*
Hayes, Patrick Timothy 1948- *WhoAmL 94*
Hayes, Paul d1969 *WhoHol 92*
Hayes, Paul Gordon 1934- *WhoAm 94*
Hayes, Paul Martin 1942- *WrDr 94*
Hayes, Peter Charles 1953- *WhoMW 93*
Hayes, Peter John 1942- *WhoAm 94*
Hayes, Peter Lind 1915- *IntMPA 94, WhoAm 94, WhoHol 92*
Hayes, Philip Harold 1940- *WhoAmP 93*
Hayes, Randy 1944- *WhoAmA 93*
Hayes, Rebecca Anne 1950- *WhoFI 94*
Hayes, Reginald d1953 *WhoHol 92*
Hayes, Richard C. 1938- *WhoBlA 94*
Hayes, Richard Johnson 1933- *WhoAm 94, WhoAmL 94*
Hayes, Robert Allen 1939- *WhoAmP 93*
Hayes, Robert Bruce 1925- *WhoAm 94*
Hayes, Robert C. *WhoAmP 93*
Hayes, Robert C. 1936- *WhoAmP 93*
Hayes, Robert Deming 1925- *WhoScEn 94*
Hayes, Robert E. 1933- *WhoAmP 93*
Hayes, Robert E. 1950- *WhoAmL 94*
Hayes, Robert Emmet 1920- *WhoAm 94*
Hayes, Robert Emmet 1951- *WhoAmP 93*
Hayes, Robert Francis 1941- *WhoAm 94*
Hayes, Robert Green 1936- *WhoScEn 94*
Hayes, Robert Herrick 1936- *WhoAm 94*
Hayes, Robert Mayo 1926- *WhoAm 94*
Hayes, Robert Wesley, Jr. 1952- *WhoAmP 93*
Hayes, Roger Peter 1945- *IntWW 93*
Hayes, Roland 1887-1977 *AfrAmAl 6*
Hayes, Roland Harris 1931- *WhoBlA 94*
Hayes, Ron 1931- *WhoHol 92*
Hayes, Sam d1958 *WhoHol 92*
Hayes, Samuel Banks, III 1936- *WhoAm 94*
Hayes, Samuel Linton, III 1935- *WhoAm 94*
Hayes, Samuel Perkins 1910- *WhoAm 94, WrDr 94*
Hayes, Sarah Hall 1934- *WhoAm 94*
Hayes, Scott Birchard 1926- *WhoAm 94*
Hayes, Shirley Ann 1955- *WhoWest 94*
Hayes, Stephen Kurtz 1949- *WhoMW 93*
Hayes, Stephen M. 1952- *WhoAmL 94*
Hayes, Stephen Thorne 1952- *WhoAmL 94*
Hayes, Stephen William d1978 *WhoHol 92*
Hayes, Susan Seaforth *WhoHol 92*
Hayes, Thomas A. 1943- *WhoIns 94*
Hayes, Thomas Jay, III 1914- *WhoAm 94*
Hayes, Thomas Moore, III 1952- *WhoAmL 94*
Hayes, Thomas W. 1945- *WhoAmP 93*
Hayes, Timothy George 1946- *WhoAmL 94*
Hayes, Timothy George 1954- *WhoAmL 94*
Hayes, Tom *WhoIns 94*
Hayes, Tua *WhoAmA 93*
Hayes, Vertis 1911- *WhoBlA 94*
Hayes, Vertis Clemon 1911- *WhoAm 94*
Hayes, Waldron Stanley, Jr. 1938- *WhoAm 94*
Hayes, Walter 1924- *Who 94*
Hayes, Webb Cook, III 1920- *WhoAm 94*
Hayes, Wendy Jennings 1942- *WhoMW 93*
Hayes, Wilbur Frank 1936- *WhoScEn 94*
Hayes, William 1913- *Who 94*
Hayes, William 1930- *Who 94*
Hayes, William Aloysius 1920- *WhoAm 94*
Hayes, William Christopher d1963 *WhoAmA 93N*
Hayes, William David 1961- *WhoAmL 94*
Hayes, William J. 1949- *WhoAmL 94*
Hayes, William Lamar 1935- *WhoWest 94*
Hayes, William S. d1988 *WhoHol 92*
Hayes-Bautista, David E. 1945- *WhoHisp 94*
Hayes-Deckebach, Jill Linette 1959- *WhoAmL 94*
Hayes-Giles, Joyce V. 1948- *WhoBlA 94*
Hayes-Jordan, Margaret 1943- *WhoBlA 94*
Hayflick, Leonard 1928- *WhoAm 94*
Hayford, Charles W. 1941- *WrDr 94*
Hayford, John Sargent 1940- *WhoAm 94*
Haygarth, Anthony 1945- *WhoHol 92*
Haygood, Atticus Greene 1839-1896 *DcAmReB 2*
Haygood, Paul M. 1942- *WhoAmL 94*
Haygood, Wil 1954- *BlkWr 2, ConAu 142, WhoBlA 94*
Hayhoe, Baron 1925- *Who 94*
Hayhoe, Frank George James 1920- *Who 94*
Hayhurst, James Frederick Palmer 1941- *WhoAm 94*
Hayhurst, Richard Allen 1948- *WhoAmL 94, WhoAmP 93*
Hayle, Grace d1963 *WhoHol 92*
Haylett, Margaret Wendy 1953- *WhoAm 94*
Hayling, William H. 1925- *WhoBlA 94*
Haylock, John (Mervyn) 1918- *WrDr 94*
Haym, Nicola Francesco 1678-1729 *NewGrDO*
Haym, Rudolf 1821-1901 *DcLB 129 [port]*
Haymaker, Carlton Luther, Jr. 1944- *WhoScEn 94*
Haymaker, William Jackson 1925- *WhoFI 94*
Hayman, A. Charles 1880- *WhoHol 92*
Hayman, Carol Bessent *DrAPF 93*
Hayman, Carol Bessent 1927- *WhoAm 94, WrDr 94*
Hayman, Cyd 1944- *WhoHol 92*
Hayman, David *WhoHol 92*
Hayman, David 1927- *WrDr 94*
Hayman, Harry 1917- *WhoAm 94*
Hayman, Helene (Valerie) 1949- *Who 94*
Hayman, Jeffrey Lloyd 1955- *WhoAm 94*
Hayman, John David Woodburn 1918- *Who 94*
Hayman, Lillian 1922- *WhoHol 92*
Hayman, Mitchell Brent 1964- *WhoFI 94*
Hayman, Richard Warren Joseph 1920- *WhoAm 94*
Hayman, Ronald 1932- *WrDr 94*
Hayman, Seymour 1914- *WhoAm 94*
Hayman, Walter Kurt 1926- *IntWW 93, Who 94, WrDr 94*
Hayman, Warren C. 1932- *WhoBlA 94*
Hayman, William Samuel d1993 *Who 94N*
Hayman-Joyce, Robert John 1940- *Who 94*
Haymer, Johnny d1989 *WhoHol 92*
Haymerle, Heinrich d1990 *IntWW 93N*
Haymes, Bob d1989 *WhoHol 92*
Haymes, Dick d1980 *WhoHol 92*
Haymes, Harmon Hayden 1927- *WhoAm 94*
Haymes, Robert C. 1931- *WhoAm 94*
Hay-Messick, Velma *WhoAmA 93*
Haymon, Alan *WhoBlA 94*
Haymon, Cynthia 1958- *NewGrDO*
Haymon, S(ylvia) T(heresa) 1918- *WrDr 94*
Haymond, J. Brent 1936- *WhoAmP 93, WhoWest 94*
Haymond, Paula J. 1949- *WhoAm 94*
Haymons, Dan Lester, Jr. 1936- *WhoAm 94*
Haymore, Tyrone 1947- *WhoBlA 94*
Hayn, Annette *DrAPF 93*
Hayna, Lois Beebe *DrAPF 93*
Hayne, David Mackness 1921- *WhoAm 94*
Hayne, Donald d1979 *WhoHol 92*
Hayne, Harriet 1922- *WhoAmP 93*
Hayne, Harriet Ann 1922- *WhoWest 94*
Hayne, Isaac 1745-1781 *WhAmRev*
Hayne, jack McVicar 1920- *WhoAmP 93*
Hayne, Sally Durner 1955- *WhoMW 93*
Hayner, Herman Henry 1916- *WhoAmL 94, WhoWest 94*
Hayner, J(ohn) Clifford 1893- *WhAm 10*
Hayner, Jeannette C. 1919- *WhoAmP 93*
Hayner, Jeannette Clare 1919- *WhoAm 94, WhoWest 94*
Haynes, Alphonso Worden *WhoBlA 94*
Haynes, Arden R. *WhoAm 94, WhoFI 94*
Haynes, Arden Ramon 1927- *IntWW 93*
Haynes, Arthur d1966 *WhoHol 92*
Haynes, Barbara Asche 1935- *WhoBlA 94*
Haynes, Boyd Withers, Jr. 1917- *WhoAm 94*
Haynes, Bradley 1954- *WhoAmP 93*
Haynes, Caleb Vance, Jr. 1928- *WhoAm 94, WhoWest 94*
Haynes, Clarence E. *WhoAmP 93*
Haynes, Daniel L. d1954 *WhoHol 92*
Haynes, David Francis 1926- *Who 94*
Haynes, David Nathan 1943- *WhoAmL 94*
Haynes, Deborah Gene 1954- *WhoMW 93, WhoScEn 94*
Haynes, Denys Eyre Lankester 1913- *Who 94*
Haynes, Desmond Leo 1956- *IntWW 93*
Haynes, Dick d1980 *WhoHol 92*
Haynes, Donald 1934-1988 *WhAm 10*
Haynes, Donald Kenneth 1934- *WhoMW 93*
Haynes, Douglas H. 1936- *WhoAmA 93*
Haynes, Douglas Martin 1922- *WhoAm 94*
Haynes, Duncan Harold 1945- *WhoScEn 94*
Haynes, Eleanor Louise *WhoBlA 94*
Haynes, Ernest Anthony 1922- *Who 94*
Haynes, Eugene, Jr. *WhoBlA 94*
Haynes, Frank *Who 94*
Haynes, Frank L., Jr. 1944- *WhoBlA 94*
Haynes, Frank Maurice 1935- *WhoFI 94*
Haynes, Gary Allen 1936- *WhoAm 94*
Haynes, Gene A. *WhoAmP 93*
Haynes, George E., Jr. 1920- *WhoBlA 94*
Haynes, George Edmund, Jr. 1912- *WhoBlA 94*
Haynes, George Edward 1910- *WhoAmA 93*
Haynes, Harold Eugene, Jr. 1956- *WhoScEn 94*
Haynes, Henry D. 1920-1971 *See* Homer and Jethro *WhoCom*
Haynes, Hilda d1986 *WhoHol 92*
Haynes, James Almand 1933- *WrDr 94*
Haynes, James Earl, Jr. 1943- *WhoFI 94*
Haynes, James H. 1953- *WhoBlA 94*
Haynes, Jean Reed 1949- *WhoAm 94, WhoAmL 94*
Haynes, Jeanne A. 1935- *WhoMW 93*
Haynes, Joe M. 1936- *WhoAmP 93*
Haynes, Joel Robert 1954- *WhoScEn 94*
Haynes, John K. *WhoBlA 94*
Haynes, John Kermit 1943- *WhoBlA 94*
Haynes, John Mabin 1928- *WhoAm 94*
Haynes, John Robert *EncSF 93*
Haynes, Jorge *WhoHisp 94*
Haynes, K. Gregory 1945- *WhoAmL 94*
Haynes, Karen Sue 1946- *WhoAm 94*
Haynes, Lemuel 1753-1833 *AfrAmAl 6 [port], WhAmRev*
Haynes, Leonard L., Jr. 1923- *WhoAm 94, WhoBlA 94*
Haynes, Leonard L., III 1947- *WhoAm 94, WhoBlA 94*
Haynes, Linda *WhoHol 92*
Haynes, Lloyd d1986 *WhoHol 92*
Haynes, Marcia Margaret 1931- *WhoMW 93*
Haynes, Marion E. 1935- *WhoFI 94*
Haynes, Marques 1917- *BasBi*
Haynes, Martha Patricia 1951- *WhoAm 94*
Haynes, Marti 1947- *WhoFI 94*
Haynes, Mary *DrAPF 93*
Haynes, Michael *WhoHol 92*
Haynes, Michael E. 1927- *WhoBlA 94*
Haynes, Michael James 1953- *WhoBlA 94*
Haynes, Moses Alfred 1921- *WhoAm 94*
Haynes, Nancy 1947- *WhoAmA 93*
Haynes, Neal J. 1912- *WhoBlA 94*
Haynes, Ora Lee 1925- *WhoBlA 94*
Haynes, Patricia Somerville 1956- *WhoBlA 94*
Haynes, Paul Duane 1942- *WhoMW 93*
Haynes, Peter 1925- *Who 94*
Haynes, R. 1934- *WhoAmA 93*
Haynes, R. Michael 1940- *WhoAm 94*
Haynes, Ray *WhoAmP 93*
Haynes, Renée Oriana *WrDr 94*
Haynes, Richard L. 1934- *WhoAmP 93*
Haynes, Robert *DrAPF 93*
Haynes, Robert Hall 1931- *WhoAm 94*
Haynes, Robert Vaughn 1929- *WhoAm 94*
Haynes, Roberta 1929- *WhoHol 92*
Haynes, Roy 1925- *AfrAmAl 6*
Haynes, Sherwood Kimball 1910-1990 *WhAm 10*
Haynes, Sue Blood 1939- *WhoBlA 94*
Haynes, Sybille (Edith) 1926- *WrDr 94*
Haynes, Thomas Morris 1918- *WhoAm 94*
Haynes, Tiger 1914- *IntMPA 94, WhoHol 92*
Haynes, Todd 1961- *WhoAm 94*
Haynes, Ulric St. Clair, Jr. 1931- *WhoAm 94, WhoBlA 94*
Haynes, Walter Wesley 1919- *WhoBlA 94*
Haynes, William Arthur 1947- *WhoWest 94*
Haynes, William Eli 1943- *WhoFI 94*
Haynes, William Ernest 1936- *WhoAmL 94*
Haynes, William J., Jr. 1949- *WhoBlA 94*
Haynes, William James, II 1958- *WhoAm 94, WhoAmL 94*
Haynes, Willie C., III 1951- *WhoBlA 94*
Haynes, Worth Edward 1942- *WhoBlA 94*
Haynes-Dixon, Margaret Rumer *Who 94*
Haynie, Howard Edward 1928- *WhoAm 94*
Haynie, Hugh 1927- *WhoAmA 93*
Haynie, Jim *WhoHol 92*
Haynie, Mary Donaldson 1923- *WhoAmP 93*
Haynie, Ron 1945- *WhoAmA 93*
Haynie, Thomas Powell, III 1932- *WhoAm 94*
Haynie, Tony Wayne 1955- *WhoAmL 94*
Haynsworth, Clement Furman, Jr. 1912-1989 *WhAm 10*
Haynsworth, Harry Jay, IV 1938- *WhoAm 94*
Hayo, George Edward, Jr. 1934- *WhoAm 94*
Hayob, John L. 1950- *WhoAmL 94*
Hayon, Elie M. 1932- *WhoAm 94*
Hayr, Kenneth (William) 1935- *Who 94*
Hayre, Ruth Wright *WhoBlA 94*
Hays, Cindy Shelton 1949- *WhoAmP 93*
Hays, David Arthur 1930- *WhoAm 94*
Hays, Diana Joyce Watkins 1945- *WhoFI 94*
Hays, Donald 1947- *WrDr 94*
Hays, Donald Osborne 1907- *WhoAm 94*
Hays, Elizabeth Loretta 1937- *WhoMW 93*
Hays, Frank Drury 1912- *WhoFI 94*
Hays, Glenn G., Mrs. 1895- *WhAm 10*
Hays, Herschel Martin 1920- *WhoFI 94, WhoScEn 94*
Hays, Howard H. 1917- *WhoAm 94, WhoWest 94*
Hays, J. Jefferson 1929- *WhoAmP 93*
Hays, James Emerson 1955- *WhoMW 93*
Hays, James Fred 1933- *WhoAm 94*
Hays, James Richard *WhoAmL 94*
Hays, Janice *DrAPF 93*
Hays, John *WhoAmP 93*
Hays, John Bruce 1937- *WhoWest 94*
Hays, Kathryn *WhoAm 94, WhoHol 92*
Hays, Kelley Ann 1960- *ConAu 142*
Hays, Lee d1981 *WhoHol 92*
Hays, Lewis W. 1914- *WhoAm 94*
Hays, Marguerite Thompson 1930- *WhoAm 94*
Hays, Marilyn Patricia 1935- *WhoMW 93*
Hays, Marion Steele 1925- *WhoAmP 93*
Hays, Mary 1760-1843 *BlmGWL, DcNaB MP*
Hays, Mary Ludwig c. 1754-1832 *WhAmRev [port]*
Hays, Michael DeWayne 1948- *WhoAm 94*
Hays, Patrick Gregory 1942- *WhoAm 94, WhoWest 94*
Hays, Patrick Henry 1947- *WhoAmP 93*
Hays, Paul B. 1935- *WhoScEn 94*
Hays, Paul M. 1946- *WhoAmP 93*
Hays, Peggy Ann 1948- *WhoMW 93*
Hays, Peter L. 1938- *WhoAm 94, WrDr 94*
Hays, Richard Martin 1927- *WhoAm 94, WhoFI 94*
Hays, Rick F. 1952- *WhoFI 94, WhoWest 94*
Hays, Robert *DrAPF 93*
Hays, Robert 1947- *IntMPA 94*
Hays, Robert 1948- *WhoHol 92*
Hays, Robert Alexander 1944- *WhoAmL 94*
Hays, Robert Davies 1927- *WhoAmL 94*
Hays, Ronald Jackson 1928- *IntWW 93, WhoAm 94, WhoScEn 94, WhoWest 94*
Hays, Ruth 1950- *WhoAm 94, WhoAmL 94*
Hays, Sidney Brooks 1931- *WhoAm 94*
Hays, Sindy Jean *WhoMW 93*
Hays, Steele 1925- *WhoAmL 94*
Hays, Thomas Chandler 1935- *WhoAm 94, WhoFI 94*
Hays, Thomas R. 1915- *WhoAm 94*
Hays, Todd Alan 1961- *WhoWest 94*
Hays, Will d1937 *WhoHol 92*
Hays, Will H. d1954 *WhoHol 92*
Hays, William R., III 1949- *WhoAmL 94*
Hays, Wilma Pitchford 1909- *WrDr 94*
Haysbert, Dennis *WhoBlA 94, WhoHol 92*
Haysbert, Raymond Victor 1920- *WhoFI 94*
Haysbert, Raymond Victor, Sr. 1920- *WhoBlA 94*
Hays Butler, Holly Lynn 1962- *WhoMW 93*
Haysel, A. R. d1954 *WhoHol 92*
Hayslett, John Paul 1935- *WhoAm 94*
Hayslett, Paul Joseph 1963- *WhoScEn 94*
Hayslett, Roderick James 1945- *WhoAm 94*
Hayslip, Le Ly 1950- *WhoAsA 94*
Haysom, Ian Richard 1949- *WhoAm 94, WhoWest 94*
Hayssen, Virginia 1951- *WhoScEn 94*
Haytaian, Garabed 1938- *WhoAmP 93*
Hayter, Baron 1911- *Who 94*
Hayter, Alethea (Catharine) 1911- *WrDr 94*
Hayter, Dianne 1949- *Who 94*
Hayter, James d1983 *WhoHol 92*
Hayter, John Samuel 1940- *WhoAm 94*
Hayter, Paul David Grenville 1942- *Who 94*
Hayter, Teresa 1940- *WrDr 94*
Hayter, William (Goodenough) 1906- *WrDr 94*
Hayter, William Goodenough 1906- *IntWW 93, Who 94*

Haythe, Winston McDonald 1940- *WhoAmL 94*
Haythorn, J. Denny 1947- *WhoAmL 94*
Haythorne, George Vickers 1909- *WrDr 94*
Haythorne, Joan 1915- *WhoHol 92*
Haythorne, John *Who 94*
Haythorne, Naomi Christine *Who 94*
Haythornthwaite, Philip John 1951- *ConAu 42NR, WrDr 94*
Haythornthwaite, Robert Morphet 1922- *WhoAm 94*
Haytipper, Nita d1930 *WhoHol 92*
Hayton, David John 1944- *Who 94*
Hayton, Jacob William 1926- *WhoAm 94*
Hayton, Lennie d1971 *WhoHol 92*
Hayton, William Leroy 1944- *WhoScEn 94*
Hayutin, David Lionel 1930- *WhoAm 94*
Hayutin, Marc I. 1944- *WhoAm 94, WhoAmL 94*
Hayward, Ann Stewart 1944- *WhoBlA 94*
Hayward, Anthony (William Byrd) 1927- *Who 94*
Hayward, Arthur D'Alanson 1946- *WhoWest 94*
Hayward, Brooke 1937- *WhoHol 92*
Hayward, Chard *WhoHol 92*
Hayward, Charles E. 1950- *WhoAm 94*
Hayward, Charles Winthrop 1927- *WhoAm 94*
Hayward, Chuck *WhoHol 92*
Hayward, Derek *Who 94*
Hayward, (John) Derek (Risdon) 1923- *Who 94*
Hayward, Edward Joseph 1943- *WhoAm 94, WhoAmL 94*
Hayward, Fredric Mark 1946- *WhoWest 94*
Hayward, George J. 1944- *WhoAmL 94*
Hayward, George Joel 1941- *WhoMW 93*
Hayward, George Victor 1918- *Who 94*
Hayward, Gerald William 1927- *Who 94*
Hayward, Harold 1920- *WhoFI 94*
Hayward, Jack (Arnold) 1923- *Who 94*
Hayward, Jack Ernest Shalom 1931- *Who 94*
Hayward, Jacqueline C. 1944- *WhoBlA 94*
Hayward, James 1943- *WhoAmA 93*
Hayward, James Lloyd 1948- *WhoMW 93*
Hayward, Jane 1918- *WhoAm 94, WhoAmA 93*
Hayward, Jane Elizabeth 1946- *Who 94*
Hayward, Jeffery J. 1960- *WhoAmP 93*
Hayward, Jim d1981 *WhoHol 92*
Hayward, John Tucker 1910- *WhoAm 94*
Hayward, Louis d1985 *WhoHol 92*
Hayward, Peter 1905- *WhoAmA 93*
Hayward, Richard d1964 *WhoHol 92*
Hayward, Richard (Arthur) 1910- *Who 94*
Hayward, Robert Antony 1949- *Who 94*
Hayward, Ronald 1917- *IntWW 93*
Hayward, Ronald George 1917- *Who 94*
Hayward, Ronald Hamilton 1927- *WhoAm 94*
Hayward, Ronald Harry 1944- *WhoFI 94*
Hayward, Rowland c. 1520-1593 *DcNaB MP*
Hayward, Stephen 1954- *WrDr 94*
Hayward, Steven Fredric 1958- *WhoWest 94*
Hayward, Susan d1975 *WhoHol 92*
Hayward, Thomas B. 1924- *IntWW 93*
Hayward, Thomas Zander, Jr. 1940- *WhoAm 94*
Hayward, Timothy Yeatman 1941- *WhoAmP 93*
Hayward, William Stephens *EncSF 93*
Hayward Ellen, Patricia Mae *Who 94*
Hayward Smith, Rodger 1943- *Who 94*
Hayward-Surry, Jeremy 1942- *WhoAm 94*
Haywood, Betty Jean 1942- *WhoAm 94*
Haywood, Billie d1979 *WhoHol 92*
Haywood, Bruce 1925- *WhoAm 94*
Haywood, Carolyn 1898-1990 *SmATA 75 [port]*
Haywood, Charles 1904- *WrDr 94*
Haywood, Chris *WhoHol 92*
Haywood, Eliza 1690?-1756 *BlmGWL*
Haywood, Eliza 1693?-1756 *BlmGEL*
Haywood, Eliza (Fowler) 1693?-1756 *EncSF 93*
Haywood, George Weaver 1952- *WhoBlA 94*
Haywood, Harold 1923- *Who 94*
Haywood, Helen Irene 1937- *WhoFI 94*
Haywood, Herbert Carlton 1931- *WhoAm 94, WhoScEn 94*
Haywood, Hiram H., Jr. 1921- *WhoBlA 94*
Haywood, L. Julian *WhoBlA 94*
Haywood, L. Julian 1927- *WhoAm 94*
Haywood, Lorna (Marie) 1939- *NewGrDO*
Haywood, Margaret A. 1912- *WhoBlA 94*
Haywood, Mark Francis 1949- *WhoAmL 94*
Haywood, Norcell D. 1935- *WhoBlA 94*
Haywood, Oliver Garfield 1911- *WhoAm 94*
Haywood, Richard Mowbray 1933- *WrDr 94*
Haywood, Robert Alan 1948- *WhoAmL 94*
Haywood, Roosevelt V., Jr. 1929- *WhoBlA 94*
Haywood, Spencer 1949- *BasBi, WhoBlA 94*
Haywood, Theodore Joseph 1929- *WhoAm 94*
Haywood, Thomas Charles Stanley 1911- *Who 94*
Haywood, Wardell 1928- *WhoBlA 94*
Haywood, William Dudley 1869-1928 *AmSocL [port]*
Haywood, William H. 1942- *WhoBlA 94*
Haywoode, M. Douglas 1938- *WhoBlA 94*
Hayworth, John David, Jr. 1958- *WhoWest 94*
Hayworth, Rita d1987 *WhoHol 92*
Hayworth, Robert Wilson, III 1963- *WhoFI 94*
Hayworth, Ruth A. 1930- *WhoAmP 93*
Hayzlett, Gary Keith 1941- *WhoAmP 93*
Hayzlett, Robert Ralph 1921- *WhoFI 94*
Hazama, Chuck *WhoAsA 94*
Hazama, Chuck 1932- *WhoAmP 93*
Hazan, Marcella Maddalena 1924- *WhoAm 94*
Hazard, Evan Brandao 1929- *WhoMW 93*
Hazard, Geoffrey Cornell, Jr. 1929- *WhoAm 94*
Hazard, Jack 1906- *WrDr 94*
Hazard, John Newbold 1909- *WhoAm 94, WhoAmL 94, WrDr 94*
Hazard, John Wharton 1912- *WhoAm 94*
Hazard, Jonathan 1744-c. 1824 *WhAmRev*
Hazard, Neil Livingstone 1952- *WhoAm 94*
Hazard, Robert Culver, Jr. 1934- *WhoAm 94, WhoFI 94*
Hazard, Stephen B. 1945- *WhoAmL 94*
Haze, Jonathan *WhoHol 92*
Haze, Stan *WhoHol 92*
Hazekamp, Nancy H. 1926- *WhoAmP 93*
Hazel, James R. C., Jr. 1940- *WhoFI 94, WhoMW 93*
Hazel, Joanie Beverly 1946- *WhoScEn 94, WhoWest 94*
Hazel, John Tilghman, Jr. 1930- *WhoAm 94*
Hazel, Joseph Ernest 1933- *WhoAm 94*
Hazel, Paul 1944- *EncSF 93*
Hazel, Robert *DrAPF 93*
Hazelbauer, Gerald Lee 1944- *WhoWest 94*
Hazeldine, James *WhoHol 92*
Hazelet, Luana 1944- *WhoMW 93*
Hazel-Ford, Tess Diane 1947- *WhoMW 93*
Hazelhoff, Robertus 1930- *IntWW 93*
Hazelhurst, Noni *WhoHol 92*
Hazell, Bertie 1907- *Who 94*
Hazell, Derna *WhoHol 92*
Hazell, Frank 1883- *WhoAmA 93N*
Hazell, Frederick Roy 1930- *Who 94*
Hazell, Hy d1970 *WhoHol 92*
Hazell, Quinton 1920- *Who 94*
Hazell, Robert John Davidge 1948- *Who 94*
Hazelrigg, George Arthur, Jr. 1939- *WhoScEn 94*
Hazeltine, Barrett 1931- *WhoAm 94, WhoScEn 94*
Hazeltine, Gerald Lester 1924- *WhoFI 94*
Hazeltine, Joyce *WhoAm 94, WhoAmP 93, WhoMW 93*
Hazeltine, Richard Deimel 1942- *WhoScEn 94*
Hazelton, Donald Ross 1943- *WhoMW 93*
Hazelton, Joe d1936 *WhoHol 92*
Hazelton, Penny Ann 1947- *WhoAmL 94*
Hazelton, Robert G. 1968- *WhoAmP 93*
Hazelwood, Harry, Jr. 1921- *WhoBlA 94*
Hazelwood, John A. 1938- *WhoAm 94*
Hazen, Eleanor Franklin 1939- *WhoAmP 93*
Hazen, Elizabeth 1885-1975 *WorScD*
Hazen, Joseph H. *WhoAmA 93*
Hazen, Moses 1733-1803 *AmRev, WhAmRev*
Hazen, Paul Mandeville 1941- *IntWW 93, WhoAm 94, WhoFI 94, WhoWest 94*
Hazen, Richard 1911-1990 *WhAm 10*
Hazen, Robert Miller 1948- *WhoAm 94*
Hazen, Ryan David 1960- *WhoMW 93*
Hazen, Steven Kelsey 1949- *WhoAm 94, WhoAmL 94*
Hazen, Wallace Richard 1934- *WhoAm 94*
Hazen, William Harris 1931- *WhoAm 94*
Hazewinkel, Michiel 1943- *WhoScEn 94*
Hazewinkel, Van 1943- *WhoWest 94*
Hazi, Vencel 1925- *Who 94*
Hazim, Ignace 1921- *IntWW 93*
Hazlehurst, Cameron 1941- *WrDr 94*
Hazlehurst, Franklin Hamilton 1925- *WhoAmA 93*
Hazlehurst, Robert Purviance, Jr. 1919- *WhoAm 94*
Hazlerigg, Baron 1910- *Who 94*
Hazlett, Bill d1948 *WhoHol 92*
Hazlett, David C. 1962- *WhoFI 94*
Hazlett, James Arthur 1917- *WhoAm 94*
Hazlett, James Stephen 1940- *WhoAm 94*
Hazlett, Mark A. 1948- *WhoAmL 94*
Hazlett, Paul Edward 1937- *WhoMW 93*
Hazlewood, Arthur Dennis 1921- *Who 94*
Hazlewood, Carl E. 1950- *WhoAmA 93*
Hazlewood, Frederick Samuel 1921- *Who 94*
Hazlewood, John c. 1726-1800 *WhAmRev*
Hazlewood, John 1924- *Who 94*
Hazlewood, Judith Evans 1930- *WhoAm 94*
Hazlewood, Lee *WhoHol 92*
Hazlewood-Brady, Anne *DrAPF 93*
Hazlitt, Don 1948- *WhoAmA 93*
Hazlitt, Henry 1894- *EncSF 93, IntWW 93*
Hazlitt, Henry 1894-1993 *ConAu 141, NewYTBS 93 [port]*
Hazlitt, William 1778-1830 *BlmGEL*
Hazners, Dainis *DrAPF 93*
Hazo, Samuel *DrAPF 93*
Hazo, Samuel (John) 1928- *WrDr 94*
Hazouri, Thomas L. 1944- *WhoAmP 93*
Hazzard, Frances Jane Osborn 1925- *WhoFI 94*
Hazzard, James 1955- *WhoAmP 93*
Hazzard, Mary *DrAPF 93*
Hazzard, Shirley *DrAPF 93*
Hazzard, Shirley 1931- *BlmGWL, IntWW 93, WhoAm 94, WrDr 94*
Hazzard, Terry Louis 1957- *WhoBlA 94*
Hazzard, Walt 1942- *BasBi*
Hazzard, Walter R. 1942- *WhoBlA 94*
Hazzard, William Russell 1936- *WhoAm 94*
Hazzard, Wilton *EncSF 93*
H. D. *GayLL*
H. D. 1886-1961 *BlmGWL [port]*
H'Doubler, Francis Todd, Jr. 1925- *WhoAm 94*
He, Chengjian 1957- *WhoScEn 94*
He, Duo-Min 1941- *WhoScEn 94*
He, Tian-Xiao 1954- *WhoMW 93*
He, Xing-Fei 1958- *WhoScEn 94, WhoWest 94*
Heacock, Don Roland 1928- *WhoBlA 94*
Heacock, Earl Larry 1935- *WhoScEn 94*
Heacock, Pamela Patricia 1960- *WhoAmL 94*
Heacock, Phillip Kaga 1938- *WhoFI 94*
Heacox, Russel Louis 1922- *WhoScEn 94*
Head, Viscount 1937- *Who 94*
Head, Adrian Herbert 1923- *Who 94*
Head, Alan Kenneth 1925- *IntWW 93, Who 94*
Head, Albon O., Jr. 1946- *WhoAmL 94*
Head, Allan Bruce 1944- *WhoAmL 94*
Head, Ann 1915- *TwCYAW*
Head, Audrey May 1924- *Who 94*
Head, Barbara Gamwell 1918- *WhoAmP 93*
Head, Bessie 1937-1986 *BlkWr 2, BlmGWL, RfGShF*
Head, Cecil Franklin 1906- *WhoAmA 93*
Head, Christopher Alan 1951- *WhoAmL 94*
Head, Dennis Alec 1925- *Who 94*
Head, Edith d1981 *WhoHol 92*
Head, Edith 1897-1981 *IntDcF 2-4 [port]*
Head, Edith 1927- *WhoBlA 94*
Head, Edward Dennis 1919- *WhoAm 94*
Head, Elizabeth 1930- *WhoAmL 94*
Head, Elizabeth Spoor 1928- *WhoScEn 94*
Head, Evelyn Harris Shields 1944- *WhoBlA 94, WhoFI 94, WhoMW 93*
Head, Francis (David Somerville) 1916- *Who 94*
Head, George Bruce 1931- *WhoAmA 93*
Head, George Lewis 1941- *WhoIns 94*
Head, George Steven 1952- *WhoIns 94*
Head, Glenn O. 1925- *WhoIns 94*
Head, Gregory Alan 1955- *WhoScEn 94*
Head, Gwen *DrAPF 93*
Head, Hayden Wilson, Jr. 1944- *WhoAm 94, WhoAmL 94*
Head, Helaine *WhoBlA 94*
Head, Howard 1914-1991 *WhAm 10*
Head, Ivan Leigh 1930- *WhoAm 94, WhoWest 94*
Head, J. Michael 1953- *WhoAm 94, WhoFI 94*
Head, James Thomas 1945- *WhoAmP 93*
Head, Joanne Crane 1930- *WhoAmP 93*
Head, John Francis, Jr. 1920- *WhoAm 94*
Head, Jonathan Frederick 1949- *WhoScEn 94*
Head, Julie Etta 1966- *WhoScEn 94*
Head, Kenneth Scott 1954- *WhoMW 93*
Head, Laura Dean 1948- *WhoBlA 94*
Head, Michael (Dewar) 1900-1976 *NewGrDO*
Head, Michael Edward 1936- *Who 94*
Head, Mildred Eileen 1911- *Who 94*
Head, Murray 1946- *WhoHol 92*
Head, Patrick James 1932- *WhoAm 94, WhoAmL 94*
Head, Philip John 1951- *Who 94*
Head, Raymond, Jr. 1921- *WhoBlA 94*
Head, Raymond (Victor) 1948- *WrDr 94*
Head, Robert G. *DrAPF 93*
Head, Robert William 1941- *WhoAmA 93*
Head, Roy Joe *WhoAmP 93*
Head, Samuel 1948- *WhoBlA 94*
Head, Thomas Floyd 1937- *WhoIns 94*
Head, Tim David 1946- *IntWW 93*
Head, Verna Silva 1914- *WhoAmP 93*
Head, William Carl 1951- *WhoAmL 94*
Head, William Iverson, Sr. 1925- *WhoAm 94, WhoFI 94, WhoScEn 94*
Headden, Susan M. *WhoMW 93*
Headding, Lillian Susan 1944- *WhoAm 94, WhoFI 94, WhoWest 94*
Headfort, Marquis of 1932- *Who 94*
Head-Gordon, Teresa Lyn 1960- *WhoScEn 94*
Headington, Christopher (John Magenis) 1930- *WrDr 94*
Headington, Christopher John Magenis 1930- *IntWW 93*
Headlam, Stewart Duckworth 1847-1924 *DcNaB MP*
Headlee, Raymond 1917- *WhoAm 94*
Headlee, Richard Harold 1930- *WhoAm 94, WhoFI 94, WhoIns 94*
Headlee, Rolland Dockeray 1916- *WhoAm 94, WhoWest 94*
Headley, Baron 1902- *Who 94*
Headley, Anne Renouf 1937- *WhoAm 94, WhoFI 94*
Headley, David Allen 1946- *WhoAmA 93*
Headley, De Costa Oneal 1946- *WhoBlA 94*
Headley, Elizabeth *TwCYAW*
Headley, Glennon C., Jr. 1947- *WhoIns 94*
Headley, John M. 1929- *WrDr 94*
Headley, Judy Anne 1942- *WhoWest 94*
Headley, Kathryn Wilma 1940- *WhoMW 93*
Headley, Nathan Leroy 1936- *WhoFI 94, WhoWest 94*
Headley, Oliver St. Clair 1942- *WhoScEn 94*
Headley, Shari 1963- *WhoHol 92*
Headley, Sherman Knight 1922-1988 *WhAm 10*
Headliner c. 1968- *See* Arrested Development *News 94-2*
Headly, Derek 1908- *Who 94*
Headly, Glenne 1955- *WhoHol 92*
Headly, Glenne 1957- *IntMPA 94*
Headly, Glenne Aimee 1958- *WhoAm 94*
Headman, Arlan Osmond, Jr. 1952- *WhoAmL 94*
Headrick, John Anderson 1931- *WhoFI 94*
Headrick, Jon C. 1943- *WhoIns 94*
Headrick, Linda Ann 1955- *WhoMW 93*
Headrick, Roger Lewis 1936- *WhoAm 94, WhoMW 93*
Headrick, Thomas Edward 1933- *WhoAm 94, WhoAmL 94*
Headstrom, Richard (Birger) 1902- *WrDr 94*
Heady, Ferrel 1916- *WhoAm 94, WhoWest 94*
Heady, Harold F(ranklin) 1916- *WrDr 94*
Heady, Judith Emily 1939- *WhoMW 93*
Heaf, Peter Julius Denison 1922- *Who 94*
Heafey, Edwin Austin, Jr. 1930- *WhoAm 94*
Heagy, Thomas Charles 1945- *WhoAm 94*
Heagy, William D. 1964- *SmATA 76 [port]*
Heal, Anthony Standerwick 1907- *Who 94*
Heal, Geoffrey Martin 1944- *WhoFI 94, WhoScEn 94*
Heal, Jane 1946- *WrDr 94*
Heal, Joan 1922- *WhoHol 92*
Heal, Oliver Standerwick 1949- *Who 94*
Heal, Penelope *EncSF 93*
Heal, Sylvia Lloyd 1942- *Who 94*
Heald, Anthony 1944- *IntMPA 94, WhoHol 92*
Heald, Bruce Day 1935- *WhoAm 94*
Heald, Darrel Verner 1919- *WhoAm 94*
Heald, Jack Wendell 1925- *WhoWest 94*
Heald, Mervyn 1930- *Who 94*
Heald, Morrell 1922- *WhoAm 94*
Heald, Oliver 1954- *Who 94*
Heald, Paul Francis 1944- *WhoScEn 94*
Heald, Suzette 1943- *WrDr 94*
Heald, Thomas Routledge 1923- *Who 94*
Heald, Tim(othy Villiers) 1944- *WrDr 94*
Healea, Monica d1993 *NewYTBS 93*
Healey, Baron 1917- *Who 94*
Healey, Lady 1918- *Who 94*
Healey, Anne *WhoAmP 93*
Healey, Anne 1955- *WhoMW 93*
Healey, Arthur H. *WhoAmP 93*

Healey, Ben(jamin James) 1908- *WrDr 94*
Healey, Charles Edward C. *Who 94*
Healey, Chris M. *WhoScEn 94*
Healey, Denis (Winston) 1917- *WrDr 94*
Healey, Denis Winston 1917- *IntWW 93*
Healey, Derek 1936- *NewGrDO*
Healey, Derek Edward 1936- *WhoAm 94*
Healey, Deryck John 1937- *Who 94*
Healey, Dorian *WhoHol 92*
Healey, E. J. 1924- *WhoAmP 93*
Healey, Ed d1978 *ProFbHF*
Healey, Edna May *Who 94*
Healey, Edward Hopkins 1925- *WhoAm 94, WhoMW 93*
Healey, Frank Henry 1924- *WhoAm 94*
Healey, James *WhoHol 92*
Healey, James Stewart 1931- *WhoAm 94*
Healey, John G. 1938- *WhoAm 94*
Healey, Kerry Murphy 1960- *WhoAmL 94*
Healey, Laurette Ann 1954- *WhoFI 94, WhoWest 94*
Healey, Lynne Kover *WhoAm 94*
Healey, Mary *WhoHol 92*
Healey, Michael Charles 1942- *WhoScEn 94*
Healey, Myron 1922- *WhoHol 92*
Healey, Peter F. 1942- *WhoAmL 94*
Healey, Philip B. 1921- *WhoAmP 93*
Healey, Robert Joseph 1925- *WhoAm 94*
Healey, Robert William 1947- *WhoMW 93*
Healey, Skip 1934- *WhoAmP 93*
Healey, Thomas George *WhoMW 93*
Healton, Bruce Carney 1955- *WhoFI 94, WhoMW 93, WhoScEn 94*
Healton, Donald Carney 1930- *WhoAm 94*
Healy, Alice Fenvessy 1946- *WhoAm 94*
Healy, Ann M. 1952- *WhoFI 94*
Healy, Anne Laura 1939- *WhoAmA 93*
Healy, Arthur K. D. 1902-1978 *WhoAmA 93N*
Healy, Barbara Anne 1951- *WhoFI 94, WhoWest 94*
Healy, Barbara Mary *WhoWest 94*
Healy, Bernadine P. 1944- *Who 94, WhoAm 94, WhoScEn 94*
Healy, Dan d1969 *WhoHol 92*
Healy, Daniel J. 1908- *WhoAmP 93*
Healy, David *WhoHol 92*
Healy, David Frank 1926- *WhoMW 93, WrDr 94*
Healy, David George 1949- *WhoFI 94*
Healy, Deborah Ann *WhoAmA 93*
Healy, Eloise Klein *DrAPF 93*
Healy, George William, III 1930- *WhoAm 94, WhoAmL 94*
Healy, Harold Harris, Jr. 1921- *WhoAm 94*
Healy, James Augustine 1830-1900 *AfrAmAl 6 [port], DcAmReB 2*
Healy, James Bruce 1947- *WhoWest 94*
Healy, James Casey 1956- *WhoAmL 94*
Healy, Jane Elizabeth 1949- *WhoAm 94*
Healy, Janet *WhoAm 94*
Healy, Jeremiah 1948- *WrDr 94*
Healy, John Francis 1926- *Who 94*
Healy, John T. *IntMPA 94*
Healy, Jonathan Lee 1945- *WhoAmP 93*
Healy, Joseph Francis, Jr. 1930- *WhoAm 94, WhoAmL 94, WhoFI 94*
Healy, Julia Schmitt 1947- *WhoAmA 93*
Healy, Katherine 1969- *WhoHol 92*
Healy, Kevin E. *WhoScEn 94*
Healy, Kieran John Patrick 1957- *WhoWest 94*
Healy, Marcia d1972 *WhoHol 92*
Healy, Mary 1918- *WhoAm 94, WhoHol 92*
Healy, Maurice Eugene 1933- *Who 94*
Healy, Michael T. 1943- *WhoAmL 94*
Healy, Michael W. 1946- *WhoAmP 93*
Healy, Nicholas Joseph 1910- *WhoAm 94, WhoAmL 94*
Healy, Patricia Colleen 1935- *WhoMW 93*
Healy, Raymond J(ohn) 1907- *EncSF 93*
Healy, Richard Joseph 1946- *WhoAmL 94*
Healy, Robert Danforth 1939- *WhoFI 94*
Healy, Robert E. d1993 *NewYTBS 93 [port]*
Healy, Robert Edward 1904- *WhoAm 94*
Healy, Sophia (Warner) 1938- *WrDr 94*
Healy, Steven Michael 1949- *WhoFI 94, WhoMW 93*
Healy, Ted *WhoCom*
Healy, Ted d1937 *WhoHol 92*
Healy, Theresa Ann 1932- *WhoAm 94, WhoAmP 93*
Healy, Theresa M. 1946- *WhoAmP 93*
Healy, Thomas H. 1922- *WhoAmL 94*
Healy, Thomas P., Jr. 1926- *WhoAmL 94*
Healy, Thomas William 1937- *IntWW 93*
Healy, Tim T. *Who 94*
Healy, Timothy S. 1923- *CurBio 93 [port]*
Healy, Timothy S. 1923-1992 *AnObit 1992, CurBio 93N, NewYTBS 93 [port]*
Healy, Timothy S(tafford) 1923-1992 *ConAu 140*
Healy, Walter 1910- *WhoAmP 93*
Healy, Walter F. X. 1941- *WhoAmL 94*
Healy, William Charles 1950- *WhoFI 94*
Healy, William James 1939- *WhoAmP 93*
Healy, William Kent 1930- *WhoAm 94*
Healy, William Paul 1916- *WhoAmL 94*
Healy, Winston, Jr. 1937- *WhoWest 94*
Healy-French, Florence Margaret 1921- *WhoWest 94*
Heaney, Gerald William 1918- *WhoAm 94, WhoAmL 94, WhoMW 93*
Heaney, Henry Joseph 1935- *Who 94*
Heaney, Leonard Martin 1906- *Who 94*
Heaney, Robert Proulx 1927- *WhoAm 94*
Heaney, Seamus 1939- *IntWW 93, WrDr 94*
Heaney, Seamus Justin 1939- *BlmGEL, Who 94, WhoAm 94*
Heaney, Timothy M. 1946- *WhoAmL 94*
Heaney, William Joseph 1943- *WhoAmP 93*
Heaney, William Matthew 1949- *WhoMW 93*
Heanley, Charles Laurence 1907- *Who 94*
Heap, Brian *Who 94*
Heap, (Robert) Brian 1935- *Who 94*
Heap, Desmond 1907- *Who 94, WrDr 94*
Heap, James C. 1935- *WhoAmP 93*
Heap, James Clarence *WhoMW 93, WhoScEn 94*
Heap, Jane *BlmGWL*
Heap, John Arnfield 1932- *Who 94*
Heap, Linda Sue 1952- *WhoMW 93*
Heap, Peter William 1935- *IntWW 93, Who 94*
Heap, Robert Brian 1935- *IntWW 93*
Heaphy, James Cullen, III 1952- *WhoWest 94*
Heaphy, John Merrill 1927- *WhoAm 94*
Heaps, Marvin Dale 1932- *WhoAm 94*
Heaps, Wilson A. 1896- *WhAm 10*
Heard, Alexander 1917- *WhoAm 94*
Heard, Anthony Hazlitt 1937- *WrDr 94*
Heard, Charles Stephen, Jr. 1936- *WhoAm 94*
Heard, Daphne d1983 *WhoHol 92*
Heard, Drew R. 1950- *WhoAmL 94*
Heard, Edwin Anthony 1926- *WhoAm 94*
Heard, Fred W. 1940- *WhoAmP 93*
Heard, Gerald 1889-1971 *EncSF 93*
Heard, H.F. *EncSF 93*
Heard, Herman Willie, Jr. 1961- *WhoBlA 94*
Heard, John 1946- *IntMPA 94, WhoHol 92*
Heard, John 1947- *WhoAm 94*
Heard, Keith G. 1956- *WhoAmP 93*
Heard, Lillian 1965- *WhoAmA 93*
Heard, Lonear Windham *WhoBlA 94*
Heard, Lynnette Michelle 1953- *WhoMW 93*
Heard, Manning Wright 1896- *WhAm 10*
Heard, Marian L. *WhoBlA 94*
Heard, Marstron 1897- *WhAm 10*
Heard, Nathan Cliff 1936- *WhoBlA 94*
Heard, Nathaniel *WhAmRev*
Heard, Paul W., Jr. *WhoAmP 93*
Heard, Peter Graham 1929- *Who 94*
Heard, Ronald Roy 1947- *WhoWest 94*
Heard, William Robert 1925- *WhoAm 94, WhoFI 94, WhoIns 94*
Hearin, William Jefferson 1909- *WhoAm 94*
Hearle, Douglas Geoffrey 1933- *WhoAm 94*
Hearle, Kevin *DrAPF 93*
Hearn, Ann *WhoHol 92*
Hearn, Anthony Clem 1937- *WhoWest 94*
Hearn, Barry Maurice William 1948- *Who 94*
Hearn, Charles Virgil 1930- *WhoWest 94*
Hearn, Chick 1922?- *BasBi*
Hearn, Clifford Burton, Jr. 1937- *WhoAmP 93*
Hearn, David A. 1957- *WhoIns 94*
Hearn, David Anthony 1929- *Who 94*
Hearn, Donald Peter 1947- *Who 94*
Hearn, Edell Midgett 1929- *WhoAm 94*
Hearn, Edward d1963 *WhoHol 92*
Hearn, Frank Wright d1993 *Who 94N*
Hearn, Fred d1923 *WhoHol 92*
Hearn, George Arthur *Who 94*
Hearn, George Henry 1927- *WhoAm 94*
Hearn, Guy *WhoHol 92*
Hearn, James Woodrow 1931- *WhoAm 94*
Hearn, John Patrick 1943- *Who 94, WhoMW 93*
Hearn, Joyce Camp *WhoAmP 93*
Hearn, Julia Knox d1976 *WhoHol 92*
Hearn, Kathleen K. 1947- *WhoAmL 94*
Hearn, Lew 1882- *WhoHol 92*
Hearn, M. F., Jr. 1938- *WhoAmA 93*
Hearn, Milton Thomas 1943- *WhoScEn 94*
Hearn, Otis 1917- *WrDr 94*
Hearn, Peter 1933- *WhoAm 94*
Hearn, Rosemary 1929- *WhoBlA 94, WhoMW 93*
Hearn, Ruby Puryear 1940- *WhoAm 94*
Hearn, Sam d1964 *WhoHol 92*
Hearn, Sharon Sklamba 1956- *WhoAmL 94*
Hearn, Timothy Tyrone 1955- *WhoMW 93*
Hearne, Earl 1956- *WhoBlA 94*
Hearne, George Archer 1934- *WhoAm 94, WhoMW 93*
Hearne, Graham James 1937- *IntWW 93, Who 94*
Hearne, John 1926- *WrDr 94*
Hearne, Peter Ambrose 1927- *Who 94*
Hearne, Reginald 1929- *WrDr 94*
Hearne, Richard d1979 *WhoHol 92*
Hearne, Samuel 1745-1792 *WhWE [port]*
Hearne, Stana Dresher 1926- *WhoWest 94*
Hearne, Stephen Zachary 1952- *WhoAm 94*
Hearne, Susan Lynn 1966- *WhoAmL 94*
Hearnes, Betty 1927- *WhoAmP 93*
Hearnes, Warren Eastman 1923- *IntWW 93, WhoAmP 93*
Hearn-Haynes, Theresa 1954- *WhoAmL 94*
Hearns, Thomas 1958- *IntWW 93, WhoAm 94, WhoBlA 94*
Hearon, Dennis James 1941- *WhoBlA 94*
Hearon, Shelby *DrAPF 93*
Hearon, Shelby 1931- *WhoAm 94, WrDr 94*
Hearon, William Montgomery 1914- *WhoWest 94*
Hearsey, Hyder Jung 1782-1840 *WhWE*
Hearst, Austine McDonnell 1928-1991 *WhAm 10*
Hearst, George Randolph, Jr. 1927- *IntWW 93, WhoAm 94*
Hearst, Gladys Whitley Henderson *WhoAm 94*
Hearst, John Eugene 1935- *WhoAm 94*
Hearst, Patricia Campbell 1954- *WrDr 94*
Hearst, Randolph Apperson 1915- *IntWW 93, WhoAm 94*
Hearst, Stephen 1919- *Who 94*
Hearst, William Randolph d1993 *Who 94N*
Hearst, William Randolph 1863-1951 *AmSocL*
Hearst, William Randolph, Jr. d1993 *IntWW 93N*
Hearst, William Randolph, Jr. 1908- *IntWW 93*
Hearst, William Randolph, Jr. 1908-1993 *CurBio 93N, NewYTBS 93 [port]*
Hearst, William Randolph, III 1949- *WhoAm 94, WhoWest 94*
Hearth, John Dennis Miles 1929- *Who 94*
Heartney, Eleanor 1954- *WhoAmA 93*
Heartney, Matthew Thomas 1953- *WhoAmL 94*
Heartz, Daniel 1928- *NewGrDO*
Heasel, John Frederick 1934- *WhoMW 93*
Heasley, John d1989 *WhoHol 92*
Heasley, Marla *WhoHol 92*
Heaslip, Richard George 1932- *Who 94*
Heaslip, William A. *WhoFI 94*
Heaster, Arlene L. 1958- *WhoAm 94*
Heater, Derek Benjamin 1931- *WrDr 94*
Heater, William Henderson 1928- *WhoMW 93*
Heath, Adrian Lewis Ross d1992 *IntWW 93N*
Heath, Angela *Who 94*
Heath, (Lettyce) Angela 1944- *Who 94*
Heath, Anthony Francis 1942- *Who 94*
Heath, Bernard Oliver 1925- *Who 94*
Heath, Bertha Clara 1909- *WhoBlA 94*
Heath, Brent Alan 1960- *WhoFI 94*
Heath, Catherine 1924-1991 *WrDr 94N*
Heath, Charles Chastain 1921- *WhoAmP 93*
Heath, Charles Dickinson 1941- *WhoAmL 94*
Heath, Comer, III 1935- *WhoBlA 94*
Heath, Dave 1931- *WhoAmA 93*
Heath, David C. 1940- *WhoAmA 93*
Heath, David Martin *WhoAmA 93*
Heath, Dody *WhoHol 92*
Heath, Douglas Hamilton 1925- *WhoAm 94*
Heath, Dwight B 1930- *WrDr 94*
Heath, Dwight Braley 1930- *WhoAm 94*
Heath, Edward (Richard George) 1916- *Who 94, WrDr 94*
Heath, Edward Peter 1914- *Who 94*
Heath, Edward Richard George 1916- *IntWW 93*
Heath, Gary Brian 1954- *WhoFI 94, WhoWest 94*
Heath, George Ross 1939- *WhoAm 94, WhoWest 94*
Heath, Gloria Whitton 1922- *WhoAm 94*
Heath, Gordon 1918- *WhoHol 92*
Heath, Gregory Ernest 1941- *WhoScEn 94*
Heath, Henry Wylde Edwards 1912- *Who 94*
Heath, Hunter, III 1942- *WhoWest 94*
Heath, James E. 1926- *WhoBlA 94*
Heath, James Lee 1939- *WhoAm 94*
Heath, James Milton 1948- *WhoIns 94*
Heath, John Baldwin 1924- *Who 94*
Heath, John Moore 1922- *Who 94*
Heath, Larman Jefferson, Jr. 1950- *WhoWest 94*
Heath, Linda Joyce 1944- *WhoMW 93*
Heath, Malcolm (Frederick) 1957- *WrDr 94*
Heath, Mariwyn Dwyer 1935- *WhoMW 93*
Heath, Mark 1927- *Who 94*
Heath, Martha J. 1946- *WhoAmP 93*
Heath, Maurice (Lionel) 1909- *Who 94*
Heath, Michael John 1935- *Who 94*
Heath, Michael Stuart 1940- *Who 94*
Heath, Oscar Victor Sayer 1903- *Who 94*
Heath, Percy 1923- *WhoAm 94*
Heath, Peter 1938- *EncSF 93*
Heath, Richard Eddy 1930- *WhoAm 94*
Heath, Richard Murray 1927- *WhoAm 94*
Heath, Richard Raymond 1929- *WhoAm 94*
Heath, Rod 1884-1936 *BuCMET*
Heath, Roger Charles 1943- *WhoAmP 93*
Heath, Roy A. K. 1926- *WrDr 94*
Heath, Roy A(ubrey) K(elvin) 1926- *BlkWr 2*
Heath, Royston *EncSF 93*
Heath, Samuel K. 1954- *WhoAmA 93*
Heath, Sandra 1944- *WrDr 94*
Heath, Ted d1969 *WhoHol 92*
Heath, Ted Harris 1951- *WhoScEn 94*
Heath, Timothy Gordon 1962- *WhoScEn 94*
Heath, Vernon H. 1929- *WhoFI 94*
Heath, Veronica 1927- *WrDr 94*
Heath, William *DrAPF 93*
Heath, William 1737-1814 *AmRev, WhAmRev*
Heath, William W(ebster) 1929- *WrDr 94*
Heath-Brown, David Rodney 1952- *Who 94*
Heathcoat Amory, Lady *Who 94*
Heathcoat-Amory, David Philip 1949- *Who 94*
Heathcoat Amory, Ian 1942- *Who 94*
Heathcock, Clayton Howell 1936- *WhoAm 94, WhoScEn 94, WhoWest 94*
Heathcock, Joe d1980 *WhoHol 92*
Heathcock, John Edwin 1937- *WhoMW 93*
Heathcock, John Herman 1943- *WhoFI 94*
Heathcote, Frederic Roger 1944- *Who 94*
Heathcote, Gilbert (Simon) 1913- *Who 94*
Heathcote, Michael Perryman 1927- *Who 94*
Heathcote, Steven 1964- *IntDcB*
Heathcote, Thomas d1986 *WhoHol 92*
Heathcote-Drummond-Willoughby *Who 94*
Heathcote-Smith, Clifford Bertram Bruce 1912- *Who 94*
Heather, Fred Doenges 1943- *WhoAm 94*
Heather, Jean 1921- *WhoHol 92*
Heather, Roy *WhoHol 92*
Heather, Stanley Frank 1917- *Who 94*
Heatherington, J. Scott 1919- *WhoAm 94*
Heatherley, Clifford d1937 *WhoHol 92*
Heatherly, David A. 1950- *WhoIns 94*
Heatherly, Henry Edward 1936- *WhoAm 94*
Heatherly, May *WhoHol 92*
Heatherton, Joey 1944- *IntMPA 94, WhoHol 92*
Heath-Stubbs, John (Francis Alexander) 1918- *IntWW 93, Who 94, WrDr 94*
Heatley, Brian Antony 1947- *Who 94*
Heatly, Peter 1924- *Who 94*
Heaton, Brian Thomas 1940- *IntWW 93*
Heaton, Charles Lloyd 1935- *WhoMW 93*
Heaton, Claude Edwin 1897- *WhAm 10*
Heaton, David 1923- *Who 94*
Heaton, E. Henry, Jr. 1954- *WhoAmP 93*
Heaton, Eric William 1920- *IntWW 93, WrDr 94*
Heaton, Frances Anne 1944- *Who 94*
Heaton, Hannah Cook 1721-1794 *BlmGWL*
Heaton, Janet N. 1936- *WhoAmA 93*
Heaton, Joe L. 1951- *WhoAmP 93*
Heaton, John Busby 1953- *WhoAmP 93*
Heaton, Ken L. *WhoAmP 93*
Heaton, Larry Cadwalder, II 1956- *WhoFI 94*
Heaton, Ralph Neville 1912- *Who 94*
Heaton, Tom 1928- *WrDr 94*
Heaton, William 1920- *Who 94*
Heaton, Yvo (Robert) Henniker- 1954- *Who 94*
Heaton-Ward, William Alan 1919- *Who 94, WrDr 94*
Heatter, Gabriel d1972 *WhoHol 92*

Hedricks, Cynthia Ann 1949- *WhoWest 94*
Hedstrom, Ana Lisa *WhoAmA 93*
Hedstrom, Kenneth Gerald 1939- *WhoWest 94*
Hedstrom, Mitchell Warren 1951- *WhoAm 94, WhoFI 94*
Hedstrom, Susan Lynne 1958- *WhoWest 94*
Hedstrom, Tina *WhoHol 92*
He Duoling 1948- *WhoPRCh 91 [port]*
Hedwall, Jeanette Nickel 1937- *WhoWest 94*
Hedyle fl. c. 3rd cent.BC- *BlmGWL*
Hee, Edward K. Y. 1933- *WhoAsA 94*
Hee, Hon-Chew 1906- *WhoAmA 93*
Heeb, Ben 1942- *WhoFI 94*
Heeb, Dan Laird 1950- *WhoMW 93*
Heeb, Louis F. *WhoFI 94*
Heebe, Frederick Jacob Regan 1922- *WhoAm 94, WhoAmL 94*
Heebner, Albert Gilbert 1927- *WhoAm 94*
Heebner, Charles Frederick 1938- *WhoWest 94*
Heebner, David Richard 1927- *WhoAm 94*
Heefner, William Frederick 1922- *WhoAm 94*
Heege, Robert Charles 1922- *WhoAmL 94*
Heeger, Alan Jay 1936- *WhoAm 94, WhoScEn 94*
Heeke, Dennis Henry 1927- *WhoAmP 93, WhoMW 93*
Heekin, James Robson, III 1949- *WhoAm 94, WhoFI 94*
Heekin, Valerie Anne 1953- *WhoWest 94*
Heeks, Willy 1951- *WhoAm 94, WhoAmA 93*
Heelan, Patrick Aidan 1926- *WhoAm 94*
Heemann, Paul Warren 1933- *WhoMW 93*
Heen, Leslie Alan 1961- *WhoAmL 94*
Heenan, Maurice 1912- *Who 94*
Heeps, William 1929- *Who 94*
Heer, David Macalpine 1930- *WhoAm 94, WrDr 94*
Heer, Donald Gary 1948- *WhoWest 94*
Heer, Edwin LeRoy 1938- *WhoFI 94*
Heer, Ewald 1930- *WhoWest 94*
Heer, Nicholas Lawson 1928- *WhoAm 94*
Heeramaneck, Nasil M. 1902-1971 *WhoAmA 93N*
Heere, Karen R. 1944- *WhoAm 94*
Heerens, Robert Edward 1915- *WhoAm 94*
Heerman, William R. 1933- *WhoIns 94*
Heermann, Gottlob Ephraim 1727-1815 *NewGrDO*
Heermann, Lauren James 1947- *WhoAmP 93*
Heermans, John Michael 1958- *WhoWest 94*
Heers, Arthur Frank 1944- *WhoWest 94*
Heertje, Arnold 1934- *WrDr 94*
Heerwagen, Elwood J., Jr. 1934- *WhoAmL 94*
Heerwagen, Paul K. 1895-1992 *WrDr 94N*
Hees, George H. 1910- *Who 94*
Hees, George Harris 1910- *IntWW 93, WhoAm 94*
Heeschen, Conrad *WhoAmP 93*
Heeschen, David Sutphin 1926- *IntWW 93, WhoAm 94*
Heeseman, Rex 1942- *WhoAmL 94*
Heeter, James A. 1948- *WhoAmL 94*
Hefestay, Jack 1947- *WhoAmP 93*
Heffelbower, Dwight Earl 1925- *WhoAm 94*
Heffelfinger, David Mark 1951- *WhoScEn 94, WhoWest 94*
Heffelfinger, Frank Peavey 1897- *WhAm 10*
Heffer, Richard 1946- *WhoHol 92*
Hefferan, Harry Howard, Jr. 1925- *WhoAmL 94*
Heffern, Debbi Marie 1956- *WhoMW 93*
Heffern, Gordon Emory 1924- *WhoAm 94*
Heffern, Richard Arnold 1950- *WhoWest 94*
Heffernan, James Vincent 1926- *WhoAm 94, WhoAmL 94*
Heffernan, John 1934- *WhoHol 92*
Heffernan, John Baptist 1894- *WhAm 10*
Heffernan, Joseph P. 1936- *WhoAmL 94*
Heffernan, Michael *DrAPF 93*
Heffernan, Michele Olga 1949- *WhoAmL 94*
Heffernan, Nathan Stewart 1920- *WhoAm 94, WhoAmL 94, WhoAmP 93, WhoMW 93*
Heffernan, Peter John 1945- *WhoAm 94*
Heffernan, Phillip Thomas, Jr. 1922- *WhoAm 94*
Heffernan, Thomas *DrAPF 93*
Heffernan, Wilbert Joseph 1932- *WhoAm 94*
Heffes, Harry 1939- *WhoAm 94*
Heffley, Wayne 1927- *WhoHol 92*
Hefflinger, David L. 1947- *WhoAmL 94*
Hefflinger, LeRoy Arthur 1935- *WhoWest 94*
Heffner, Carolyn Dee 1947- *WhoWest 94*
Heffner, Grover Chester 1919- *WhoAm 94*
Heffner, Herbert Floyd 1936- *WhoWest 94*
Heffner, Kyle T. *WhoHol 92*
Heffner, Mark B. *WhoAmP 93*
Heffner, Ralph H. 1938- *WhoAm 94, WhoFI 94*
Heffner, Richard D. 1925- *IntMPA 94*
Heffner, Richard Douglas 1925- *WhoAm 94*
Heffner, Richard Louis 1933- *WhoFI 94*
Heffron, Dorris 1944- *WrDr 94*
Heffron, Howard A. 1927- *WhoAm 94*
Heffron, Mary J. 1935- *WrDr 94*
Heffron, Richard T. 1930- *IntMPA 94*
Heffron, Walter Gordon 1925- *WhoScEn 94*
Hefley, James Carl 1930- *WhoMW 93*
Hefley, Joel 1935- *CngDr 93*
Hefley, Joel M. 1935- *WhoAm 94, WhoWest 94*
Hefley, Joel Maurice 1935- *WhoAmP 93*
Heflich, Robert Henry 1946- *WhoScEn 94*
Heflin, Alan Michael 1939- *WhoAmP 93*
Heflin, Frances 1922- *WhoHol 92*
Heflin, Howell 1921- *CngDr 93*
Heflin, Howell Thomas 1921- *WhoAm 94, WhoAmP 93*
Heflin, John F. 1941- *WhoBlA 94*
Heflin, Kate 1946- *WhoHol 92*
Heflin, Marrion 1963- *WhoBlA 94*
Heflin, Marta *WhoHol 92*
Heflin, Martin Ganier 1932- *WhoAm 94*
Heflin, Nora *WhoHol 92*
Heflin, Talmadge Loraine 1940- *WhoAmP 93*
Heflin, Tom Pat 1934- *WhoAmA 93*
Heflin, Van d1971 *WhoHol 92*
Hefner, Cassandra Jewell 1956- *WhoWest 94*
Hefner, Christie Ann 1952- *WhoAm 94, WhoFI 94*
Hefner, Elroy M. 1923- *WhoAmP 93*
Hefner, Harry Simon 1911- *WhoAmA 93*
Hefner, Hugh M. 1926- *DcLB 137 [port]*
Hefner, Hugh Marston 1926- *IntWW 93, WhoAm 94*
Hefner, James A. *WhoAm 94*
Hefner, James A. 1941- *WhoBlA 94*
Hefner, James Homer 1932- *WhoAm 94*
Hefner, Jerrie Lou 1957- *WhoMW 93*
Hefner, Jerry Ned 1944- *WhoScEn 94*
Hefner, Jerry W. 1949- *WhoAmP 93*
Hefner, Keith *WhoHol 92*
Hefner, Philip James 1932- *WhoAm 94, WhoMW 93*
Hefner, Robert Alan 1929- *WhoAm 94*
Hefner, W. G. 1930- *CngDr 93, WhoAm 94, WhoAmP 93*
Heft, James Lewis 1943- *WhoAm 94*
Heftel, Cecil 1924- *WhoAmP 93*
Hefter, Daniel S. 1956- *WhoMW 93*
Hefter, Gilbert Morris 1932- *WhoMW 93*
Hefter, Laurence Roy 1935- *WhoAm 94, WhoAmL 94*
Heftler, Thomas E. 1943- *WhoAmL 94*
Heftmann, Erich 1918- *WhoScEn 94*
Hefty, Duane Seymore 1923- *WhoFI 94*
He Fushuo *WhoPRCh 91*
Hegarty, Anthony Francis 1942- *IntWW 93*
Hegarty, Frances 1948- *WrDr 94*
Hegarty, George John 1948- *WhoAm 94, WhoWest 94*
Hegarty, John Kevin 1944- *Who 94*
Hegarty, Mary Frances 1950- *WhoAmL 94, WhoMW 93*
Hegarty, Seamus *Who 94*
Hegarty, Thomas Brendan 1943- *Who 94*
Hegarty, Thomas Joseph 1935- *WhoAm 94*
Hegarty, William Kevin 1926- *WhoAm 94*
Hegarty, William Patrick 1929- *WhoScEn 94*
Hegazy, Abdel Aziz Muhammad 1923- *IntWW 93*
Hegde, Ashok Narayan 1959- *WhoScEn 94*
Hegde, Rama Krishna 1927- *IntWW 93*
Hege, Gerald K. 1948- *WhoAmP 93*
Hege, Joe H., Jr. 1926- *WhoAmP 93*
Hegedus, L. Louis 1941- *WhoAm 94, WhoScEn 94*
Hegel, Carolyn Marie 1940- *WhoAm 94, WhoMW 93*
Hegel, Eduard 1911- *IntWW 93*
Hegel, Georg Wilhelm Friedrich 1770-1831 *EncEth*
Hegelmann, Julius 1921- *WhoAm 94*
Hegeman, Charles Oxford 1940- *WhoBlA 94*
Hegeman, Daniel Jay 1963- *WhoAmP 93*
Hegeman, George Downing 1938- *WhoAm 94, WhoMW 93*
Hegeman, James Alan 1943- *WhoAm 94, WhoFI 94*
Hegeman, Mary Theodore 1907- *WrDr 94*
Hegenberger, John 1947- *WrDr 94*
Hegenderfer, Jonita Susan 1944- *WhoAm 94, WhoMW 93*
Heger, Herbert Krueger 1937- *WhoAm 94*
Heger, Robert 1886-1978 *NewGrDO*
Hegg, Philip N. 1945- *WhoMW 93*
Hegge, Carolyn Ann 1954- *WhoAmL 94*
Heggen, Arthur W. 1945- *WhoIns 94*
Heggen, Ivar Nelson 1954- *WhoAmL 94*
Hegger, Wilber L. 1936- *WhoBlA 94*
Heggers, John Paul 1933- *WhoScEn 94*
Heggie, O. P. d1936 *WhoHol 92*
Heggie, Robah Gray, Jr. 1929- *WhoIns 94*
Heggie, Robert James 1913- *WhoAm 94*
Heggs, Geoffrey Ellis 1928- *Who 94*
Heggs, Owen L. 1942- *WhoAm 94, WhoAmL 94*
Heggs, Renee Fanny Madeleine 1929- *Who 94*
Hegi, Ursula *DrAPF 93*
Heginbotham, Christopher John 1948- *Who 94*
Heginbotham, Erland Howard 1931- *WhoAm 94*
Heginbotham, Jan Sturza 1954- *WhoAm 94*
Heginbotham, Wilfred Brooks 1924- *Who 94*
Hegland, David Leroy 1919- *Who 94*
Hegmon, Oliver Louis 1907- *WhoBlA 94*
Hegrenes, Jack Richard 1929- *WhoWest 94*
Hegstad, Kjell 1961- *WhoFI 94*
Hegstad, Michael James 1953- *WhoWest 94*
Hegstad, Roland Rex 1926- *WhoAm 94*
Hegstrom, June 1941- *WhoAmP 93*
He Guang *WhoPRCh 91 [port]*
He Guanghui 1929- *WhoPRCh 91 [port]*
He Guangwei *WhoPRCh 91*
He Guangyuan 1930- *IntWW 93, WhoPRCh 91 [port]*
He Guoqiang 1944- *WhoPRCh 91*
Hegwood, William Lewis 1918- *WhoBlA 94*
Hegyes, Robert 1951- *WhoHol 92*
Hegyi, Albert Paul 1944- *WhoAm 94*
Hegyi, Julius 1923- *WhoAm 94*
He Haixia 1908- *WhoPRCh 91 [port]*
He Hai Xia (Yin) 1908- *IntWW 93*
He Haoju 1922- *WhoPRCh 91 [port]*
Hehir, Peter *WhoHol 92*
Hehl, Lambert Lawrence 1924- *WhoAmP 93*
Hehmeyer, Alexander d1993 *NewYTBS 93 [port]*
Hehn, Lorne Frederick 1936- *WhoAm 94*
He Houhua *WhoPRCh 91*
He Huanfen 1925- *WhoPRCh 91 [port]*
Heiberg, Astrid Noklebye 1936- *WhoWomW 91*
Heiberg, Elisabeth 1945- *WhoMW 93*
Heiberg, Robert Alan 1943- *WhoAm 94, WhoAmL 94*
Hei Boli 1918- *IntWW 93, WhoPRCh 91 [port]*
Heichel, Gary Harold 1940- *WhoAm 94, WhoMW 93*
Heick, Carl William, III 1960- *WhoFI 94*
Heide, Florence Parry 1919- *WrDr 94*
Heide, Ola Mikal 1931- *IntWW 93*
Heide, Richard Thomas 1931- *WhoAmP 93*
Heidegger, John Jacob 1666-1749 *NewGrDO*
Heidegger, Martin 1889-1976 *EncEth*
Heidel, Frederick (H.) 1915- *WhoAmA 93*
Heidelbaugh, Norman Dale 1927- *WhoAm 94*
Heidelberg, Helen Susan Hatvani 1957- *WhoMW 93*
Heidelberger, Kathleen Patricia 1939- *WhoAm 94*
Heidelberger, Michael 1888-1991 *WhAm 10*
Heideman, Renita Kay 1952- *WhoMW 93*
Heidemann, Robert Albert 1936- *WhoAm 94*
Heiden, Bernhard 1910- *NewGrDO*
Heiden, Charles Kenneth 1925- *WhoAm 94*
Heiden, James Patrick 1961- *WhoMW 93*
Heiden, Thomas John 1945- *WhoAm 94, WhoAmL 94*
Heidenheim, Roger Stewart 1909- *WhoAm 94*
Heidenreich, Douglas Robert 1932- *WhoAm 94*
Heidenry, John 1939- *ConAu 142*
Heidepriem, Scott Nelson 1956- *WhoAmP 93*
Heider, Frederick 1917- *IntMPA 94*
Heider, Jon Vinton 1934- *WhoAm 94, WhoAmL 94, WhoFI 94*
Heider, Joseph Patrick 1954- *WhoFI 94*
Heider, Karl G(ustav) 1935- *WrDr 94*
Heider, Karl Gustav 1935- *WhoAm 94*
Heidersbach, Kathe 1897-1979 *NewGrDO*
Heidig, Elizabeth Anne 1959- *WhoAmL 94*
Heidinger, Sonia Lynn 1963- *WhoMW 93*
Heidke, Ronald Lawrence 1937- *WhoAm 94*
Heidler, John Charles 1936- *WhoMW 93*
Heidorn, Douglas Bruce 1957- *WhoScEn 94*
Heidrick, Gardner Wilson 1911- *WhoAm 94, WhoFI 94, WhoMW 93*
Heidrick, Patricia Anne 1942- *WhoMW 93*
Heidrick, R. Clarke, Jr. 1949- *WhoAmL 94*
Heidrick, Robert Lindsay 1941- *WhoAm 94, WhoFI 94*
Heidt, Ellen Virginia *WhoBlA 94*
Heidt, Horace d1986 *WhoHol 92*
Heidt, Jeffrey L. 1945- *WhoAmL 94*
Heidt, Raymond Joseph 1933- *WhoWest 94*
Heiferman, Marvin 1948- *WhoAmA 93*
Heifetz, Alan William 1943- *WhoAm 94, WhoAmL 94*
Heifetz, Hank *DrAPF 93*
Heifetz, Jascha d1987 *WhoHol 92*
Heifetz, Jascha 1901-1987 *AmCulL [port]*
Heigaard, William S. 1938- *WhoAmP 93*
Heigert, Hans A. 1925- *IntWW 93*
Heiges, Donald Russel 1910-1990 *WhAm 10*
Heiges, Jesse Gibson 1914-1991 *WhAm 10*
Heigh, Bruce Richard 1951- *WhoFI 94*
Heigh, Helene *WhoHol 92*
Heigham, James Crichton 1930- *WhoAm 94*
Height, Dorothy I. 1912- *AfrAmAl 6 [port], WhoBlA 94*
Height, Jean d1967 *WhoHol 92*
Heijermans, Herman 1864-1924 *IntDcT 2*
Heikal, Muhammed Hassanein 1923- *IntWW 93*
Heiken, Jay Paul 1952- *WhoMW 93*
Heikkinen, Raimo Allan 1955- *WhoScEn 94*
Heiknert, Carl-Axel d1981 *WhoHol 92*
Heil, Roberta Vickie 1950- *WhoMW 93*
Heil, Russell Howard 1942- *WhoFI 94*
Heiland, Juanita Marie 1942- *WhoHisp 94*
Heilborn, George Heinz 1935- *WhoFI 94*
Heilbron, David Michael 1936- *WhoAm 94*
Heilbron, Hilary Nora Burstein 1949- *Who 94*
Heilbron, J(ohn) L(ewis) 1934- *ConAu 41NR*
Heilbron, John L. 1934- *WhoAm 94*
Heilbron, Louis Henry 1907- *WhoAm 94*
Heilbron, Rose 1914- *Who 94*
Heilbroner, Robert L. *WrDr 94*
Heilbroner, Robert L. 1919- *EnvEnc [port], IntWW 93, WhoAm 94*
Heilbronn, Marie 1851-1886 *NewGrDO*
Heilbronner, Francois 1936- *IntWW 93*
Heilbrun, Carolyn 1926- *BlmGWL*
Heilbrun, Carolyn G. 1926- *CurBio 93 [port]*
Heilbrun, Carolyn G(old) 1926- *WrDr 94*
Heilbrun, Carolyn Gold 1926- *IntWW 93, WhoAm 94*
Heilbrun, James 1924- *WhoAm 94*
Heilbrunn, Jeffrey 1950- *WhoAm 94*
Heiles, Carl Eugene 1939- *WhoAm 94*
Heilicser, Bernard Jay 1947- *WhoMW 93, WhoScEn 94*
Heilig, George Harris, Jr. 1942- *WhoAmP 93*
Heilig, William Wright 1940- *WhoAm 94*
Heiligenstein, Christian E. 1929- *WhoAmL 94*
Heiliger, Bernhard 1915- *IntWW 93*
Heilman, Carl Edwin 1911- *WhoAm 94, WhoAmL 94, WhoFI 94*
Heilman, E. Bruce 1926- *WhoAm 94*
Heilman, Edward Guy 1945- *WhoAmL 94*
Heilman, John Edward 1936- *WhoFI 94*
Heilman, Marlin Grant 1919- *WhoWest 94*
Heilman, Pamela Davis 1948- *WhoAm 94, WhoAmL 94*
Heilman, Richard Dean 1937- *WhoAm 94*
Heilman, Robert B. 1906- *WrDr 94*
Heilman, Stephen Nale 1951- *WhoFI 94*
Heilman, Wayne John 1957- *WhoWest 94*
Heilmann, Christian Flemming 1936- *WhoAm 94*
Heilmeier, George Harry 1936- *WhoAm 94, WhoScEn 94*
Heilmeier, Lori A. 1969- *WhoWest 94*
Heiloms, May *WhoAm 94, WhoAmA 93*

He Kang 1923- *IntWW 93, WhoPRCh 91 [port]*
Hekmatyar, Gulbuddin *IntWW 93*
Helaissi, Abdulrahman Al- 1922- *Who 94*
Helander, Bruce Paul 1947- *WhoAm 94, WhoAmA 93*
Helander, Clifford John 1948- *WhoScEn 94*
Helander, Robert Charles 1932- *WhoAm 94*
Helbach, David W. 1948- *WhoAmP 93, WhoMW 93*
Helberg, Shirley Adelaide Holden *WhoAm 94*
Helbert, Clifford L. 1920- *WhoAm 94*
Helbling, Alison Marie 1959- *WhoMW 93*
Helburn, Isadore B. 1938- *WhoAm 94*
Helburn, Nicholas 1918- *WhoAm 94*
Helck, Peter 1893-1988 *WhoAmA 93N*
Helck, (Clarence) Peter 1893- *WhAm 10*
Held, Al 1928- *IntWW 93, WhoAm 94, WhoAmA 93*
Held, Alma M. d1988 *WhoAmA 93N*
Held, Anna d1918 *WhoHol 92*
Held, Colbert Colgate 1917- *WhoScEn 94*
Held, David *IntMPA 94*
Held, George Anthony 1949- *WhoScEn 94*
Held, Heinz Joachim 1928- *IntWW 93*
Held, James Robert 1961- *WhoFI 94*
Held, Jay Allen 1961- *WhoWest 94*
Held, Jerry E. 1949- *WhoAmL 94*
Held, Joe Roger 1931- *WhoAm 94*
Held, John, Jr. 1889-1958 *WhoAmA 93N*
Held, Jonathan, Jr. 1947- *WhoAmA 93*
Held, Julius S. 1905- *WhoAmA 93*
Held, Karl *WhoHol 92*
Held, Lila M. 1925- *WhoAm 94, WhoMW 93*
Held, Mark Lawrence 1944- *WhoFI 94*
Held, Martin 1908- *WhoHol 92*
Held, Michael Charles *WhoAmP 93, WhoMW 93*
Held, Michael Joseph 1948- *WhoMW 93*
Held, Paul G. 1960- *WhoScEn 94*
Held, Peter 1916- *WrDr 94*
Held, Philip 1920- *WhoAm 94, WhoAmA 93*
Held, Richard M. 1922- *IntWW 93*
Held, Virginia 1929- *WhoAm 94*
Held, Virginia P 1929- *WrDr 94*
Held, William James 1944- *WhoScEn 94*
Heldabrand, John *WhoHol 92*
Helde, Richard A. 1951- *WhoAmL 94*
Heldenbrand, David William 1950- *WhoScEn 94*
Heldenbrand, Marilyn Louise 1939- *WhoMW 93*
Helder, Bruce Alan 1953- *WhoMW 93*
Helder, David Ernest 1947- *WhoAmA 93*
Helder, Jan Pleasant, Jr. 1963- *WhoAmL 94*
Helding, Phillip G., Jr. 1955- *WhoMW 93*
Heldman, Alan Wohl 1936- *WhoAm 94, WhoAmL 94*
Heldman, Dennis R. 1938- *WhoAm 94*
Heldman, Dennis Ray 1938- *WhoScEn 94*
Heldman, Gladys 1922- *BuCMET*
Heldman, James Gardner 1949- *WhoAmL 94*
Heldman, Louis Marc 1949- *WhoAm 94*
Heldman, Paul W. *WhoAmL 94, WhoFI 94*
Heldman, Robert Keith 1938- *WhoMW 93*
Heldmuth, Osvald d1966 *WhoHol 92*
Heldreth, Leonard Guy 1939- *WhoAm 94, WhoMW 93*
Heldstab, John Christian 1940- *WhoAm 94*
Heldt, Carl A. 1944- *WhoAmL 94*
Heldt, Carl Randall 1925- *WhoAmA 93*
Heldt, Nicholas W. 1950- *WhoAmL 94*
Heldy, Fanny 1888-1973 *NewGrDO*
Hele, Beji 1948- *BlmGWL*
Hele, Desmond George K. *Who 94*
Hele, Ivor (Henry Thomas) 1912- *Who 94*
Hele, James Warwick 1926- *Who 94*
Hele, Thomas d' *NewGrDO*
Helen, Nils Gunnar 1918- *IntWW 93*
Helena *BlmGWL*
Heleniak, David W. 1945- *WhoAmL 94*
Heleringer, Bob 1951- *WhoAmP 93*
Helfand, Arthur E. 1935- *WhoAm 94*
Helfand, Eugene 1934- *WhoAm 94*
Helfand, Marvin Sheldon 1936- *WhoAmL 94*
Helfand, Mitchell J. 1952- *WhoMW 93*
Helfand, Thomas Roy 1952- *WhoAmL 94*
Helfend, Dennis d1988 *WhoHol 92*
Helfer, Gloria *WhoWomW 91*
Helfer, Michael Stevens 1945- *WhoAmL 94*
Helferich, William H. 1943- *WhoAmL 94*
Helfert, Erich Anton 1931- *WhoAm 94, WhoWest 94*
Helfferich, Friedrich G. 1922- *WhoAm 94*
Helfferich, Merritt Randolph 1935- *WhoWest 94*
Helfgott, Michael *WhoAmP 93*
Helfgott, Roy B. 1925- *WhoAm 94*
Helfgott, Samson 1939- *WhoAmL 94*
Helfman, Elizabeth S 1911- *WrDr 94*
Helfond, Riva *WhoAmA 93*
Helfond, Wendy Worrall 1963- *WhoWest 94*
Helford, Michael Cary 1956- *WhoFI 94*
Helford, Paul Quinn 1947- *WhoWest 94*
Helfrich, Thomas E. 1950- *WhoIns 94*
Helfrick, Albert Darlington 1945- *WhoScEn 94*
Helfrick, Edward W. 1928- *WhoAmP 93*
Helft, Jorge Santiago 1934- *IntWW 93*
Helgadottir, Gudrun 1935- *WhoWomW 91*
Helgadottir, Ragnhildur 1930- *IntWW 93*
Helgason, Dean Eugene 1940- *WhoWest 94*
Helgason, Jon 1931- *IntWW 93*
Helgason, Sigurdur 1927- *WhoAm 94, WhoScEn 94*
Helgenberger, Marg *WhoAm 94*
Helgenberger, Marg 1958- *WhoHol 92*
Helgerson, Henry M., Jr. 1952- *WhoAmP 93*
Helgerson, Richard 1940- *WhoWest 94*
Helgeson, Duane Marcellus 1930- *WhoWest 94*
Helgeson, John Paul 1935- *WhoMW 93, WhoScEn 94*
Helgesson, Lars-Ake 1941- *WhoAm 94*
Helguera, Pablo 1971- *WhoHisp 94*
Heliker, John 1909- *WhoAm 94*
Heliker, John Edward 1909- *WhoAmA 93*
He Liliang *WhoPRCh 91*
Helin, James Dennis 1942- *WhoAm 94*
Helinger, Michael Green 1947- *WhoScEn 94*
Helinski, Donald Raymond 1933- *IntWW 93, WhoAm 94, WhoScEn 94*
Helioff, Anne Graile *WhoAm 94, WhoAmA 93*
He Liwei 1954- *WhoPRCh 91 [port]*
Helker, Keith Philip 1952- *WhoWest 94*
Hell, Richard *DrAPF 93*
Hell, Theodor *NewGrDO*
Hellaby, (Frederick Reed) Alan 1926- *Who 94*
Helland, Douglas Rolf 1945- *WhoScEn 94*
Helland, George Archibald, Jr. 1937- *WhoAm 94, WhoFI 94*
Helland, Vivian 1921- *WhoAmP 93*
Hellawell, Robert 1928- *WhoAm 94*
Hellbaum, Harold 1926- *WhoAmP 93*
Helle, John Harold 1935- *WhoWest 94*
Helleiner, Gerald K(arl) 1936- *ConAu 140*
Helleiner, Gerald Karl 1936- *WhoAm 94*
Hellen, Marjorie *WhoHol 92*
Hellen, Paul Eric 1955- *WhoScEn 94*
Hellenbrand, Samuel Henry 1916- *WhoAm 94*
Hellenbrecht, Edward Paul 1942- *WhoScEn 94*
Hellendale, Robert 1917- *WhoAm 94*
Hellenga, Robert R. *DrAPF 93*
Hellenthal, Joan Elizabeth 1945- *WhoWest 94*
Hellenthal, S. Ronald 1949- *WhoWest 94*
Heller, Adam 1933- *WhoAm 94*
Heller, Ann Williams 1904-1988 *WhAm 10*
Heller, Anthony Ferdinand 1944- *WhoWest 94*
Heller, Arthur 1930- *WhoAm 94*
Heller, Austin Norman 1914- *WhoScEn 94*
Heller, Barry M. 1953- *WhoAmL 94*
Heller, Ben 1925- *WhoAmA 93*
Heller, Charles Andrew, Jr. 1929- *WhoFI 94*
Heller, Cindy 1934- *WhoHol 92*
Heller, Dan L. 1953- *WhoAmL 94*
Heller, Dean A. 1960- *WhoAmP 93*
Heller, Donald Franklin 1947- *WhoScEn 94*
Heller, Donald Herbert 1943- *WhoAmL 94, WhoWest 94*
Heller, Dorothy *WhoAmA 93*
Heller, Dorothy 1926- *WhoAm 94*
Heller, Edwin 1929- *WhoAm 94*
Heller, Erich 1911-1990 *WhAm 10*
Heller, F. Arnold 1945- *WhoAmL 94*
Heller, Francie Madeline 1944- *WhoFI 94*
Heller, Francis Howard 1917- *WhoAm 94*
Heller, Franklin 1911- *IntMPA 94*
Heller, Fred 1924- *WhoAm 94, WhoFI 94*
Heller, Frederick 1932- *WhoAm 94*
Heller, Fritz d1966 *WhoHol 92*
Heller, Goldie *WhoAmA 93*
Heller, H. Robert 1940- *WhoAmP 93*
Heller, Heinz Robert 1940- *WhoAm 94*
Heller, Henry B. 1941- *WhoAmP 93*
Heller, Irwin Marshal 1946- *WhoAm 94, WhoAmL 94*
Heller, Jack Isaac 1932- *WhoAm 94*
Heller, Jackie d1988 *WhoHol 92*
Heller, James Stephen 1950- *WhoAm 94*
Heller, Jan K. 1951- *WhoAmP 93*
Heller, Janet Ruth *DrAPF 93*
Heller, John Herbert 1921- *WhoAm 94*
Heller, John L., II 1953- *WhoFI 94, WhoMW 93*
Heller, John Leland, Jr. 1940- *WhoMW 93*
Heller, John Phillip 1923- *WhoScEn 94*
Heller, John Roderick, Jr. 1905-1989 *WhAm 10*
Heller, John Roderick, III 1937- *WhoAm 94*
Heller, Joseph *DrAPF 93*
Heller, Joseph 1923- *ConAu 42NR, ConDr 93, IntWW 93, TwCYAW, WhoAm 94, WrDr 94*
Heller, Joyce Marie Zarosky 1962- *WhoAmL 94*
Heller, Jules 1919- *WhoAm 94, WhoAmA 93, WhoWest 94*
Heller, Kenneth Jeffrey 1943- *WhoMW 93, WhoScEn 94*
Heller, Lawrence H. *WhoAmL 94*
Heller, Louis B. d1993 *NewYTBS 93 [port]*
Heller, Lowell Quin 1922- *WhoMW 93*
Heller, Mark 1914- *WrDr 94*
Heller, Martin 1925- *WhoAm 94*
Heller, Max M. 1919- *WhoAmP 93*
Heller, Maxwell 1881-1963 *WhoAmA 93N*
Heller, Michael *DrAPF 93*
Heller, Michael D 1937- *WrDr 94*
Heller, Mitchell Thomas 1948- *WhoAm 94*
Heller, Otto 1896-1970 *IntDcF 2-4*
Heller, Pamela 1954- *WhoAmA 93*
Heller, Paul 1914- *WhoAm 94*
Heller, Paul M. 1927- *IntMPA 94*
Heller, Paul Michael 1927- *WhoAm 94*
Heller, Philip 1952- *WhoAmL 94*
Heller, Philip Henri 1919- *WhAm 10*
Heller, Randee *WhoHol 92*
Heller, Reinhold August 1940- *WhoAm 94, WhoAmA 93*
Heller, Richard Elliot 1907- *WhoMW 93*
Heller, Robert (Gordon Barry) 1932- *WrDr 94*
Heller, Robert Leo 1919- *WhoAm 94*
Heller, Robert Martin 1942- *WhoAm 94, WhoAmL 94*
Heller, Ronald Gary 1946- *WhoAm 94*
Heller, Ronald Ian 1956- *WhoAm 94, WhoAmL 94, WhoFI 94, WhoWest 94*
Heller, Stanley J. 1941- *WhoMW 93*
Heller, Steve F. *DrAPF 93*
Heller, Susanna 1956- *WhoAmA 93*
Heller, Theodore F. 1942- *WhoIns 94*
Heller, William J. 1953- *WhoAmL 94*
Heller, William Russell 1920- *WhoAm 94*
Hellerich, Charles L. 1943- *WhoAmL 94*
Hellerman, Leo 1924- *WhoScEn 94*
Hellerman, Marvin Lawrence 1927- *WhoAm 94*
Hellerman, Richard Keith 1963- *WhoAmL 94*
Hellerstein, Alvin Kenneth 1933- *WhoAm 94*
Hellerstein, Herman K. d1993 *NewYTBS 93*
Hellerstein, Jerome Robert 1907- *WhoAm 94*
Helletsgruber, Luise c. 1898-1967 *NewGrDO*
Hellickson, Kazuko Sato 1947- *WhoWest 94*
Hellie, Richard 1937- *WhoAm 94, WhoMW 93, WrDr 94*
Hellier, Eric Jim 1927- *Who 94*
Helling, James T. 1946- *WhoAm 94*
Hellinga, Lotte 1932- *Who 94*
Hellinger, Mark d1947 *WhoHol 92*
Helliwell, David Leedom 1935- *WhoAm 94*
Helliwell, John Richard 1953- *Who 94*
Helliwell, Thomas McCaffree 1936- *WhoAm 94*
Hellman, Arthur David 1942- *WhoAm 94*
Hellman, Bonnie *WhoHol 92*
Hellman, Frederick Warren 1934- *WhoAm 94, WhoFI 94, WhoWest 94*
Hellman, Hal 1927- *WrDr 94*
Hellman, Harriet Louise 1950- *WhoScEn 94*
Hellman, Herbert Martin 1943- *WhoAm 94, WhoAmL 94*
Hellman, Jane Elizabeth 1934- *WhoMW 93*
Hellman, Jerome 1928- *IntMPA 94*
Hellman, Lillian 1905-1984 *AmCulL*
Hellman, Lillian 1906-1984 *BlmGWL*
Hellman, Lillian (Florence) 1905-1984 *ConDr 93, IntDcT 2 [port]*
Hellman, Louis M. 1908-1990 *WhAm 10*
Hellman, Monte 1932- *IntMPA 94*
Hellman, Peter Stuart 1949- *WhoAm 94, WhoFI 94*
Hellman, Samuel 1934- *WhoAm 94*
Hellman, Sheila *DrAPF 93*
Hellmann, Donald Charles 1933- *WhoAm 94*
Hellmann, Maximilian Joseph c. 1703-1763 *NewGrDO*
Hellmann, Norma Janelle 1949- *WhoAm 94*
Hellmann, Robert F. *WhoAmP 93*
Hellmer, Karl d1974 *WhoHol 92*
Hellmesberger, Georg 1830-1852 *NewGrDO*
Hellmesberger, Joseph 1855-1907 *NewGrDO*
Hellmold, Ralph O. 1940- *WhoAm 94*
Hellmuth, C. T. 1926- *WhoIns 94*
Hellmuth, George Francis 1907- *IntWW 93, WhoAm 94, WhoMW 93, WhoScEn 94*
Hellmuth, James Grant 1923- *WhoAmP 93*
Hellmuth, Theodore Henning 1949- *WhoAm 94, WhoAmL 94*
Hellmuth, William Frederick, Jr. 1920- *WhoAm 94*
Hellreich, Philip David 1941- *WhoWest 94*
Hellrigl, Andreas d1993 *NewYTBS 93*
Hellring, Bernard 1916-1991 *WhAm 10*
Hellstrom, Mats 1942- *IntWW 93*
Hellstrom, Ward 1930- *WrDr 94*
Hellsvik, Gun *IntWW 93*
Hellum, Barney d1935 *WhoHol 92*
Hellums, Jesse David 1929- *WhoAm 94*
Hellwarth, Robert Willis 1930- *WhoWest 94*
Hellwig, Fritz 1912- *IntWW 93*
Hellwig, Helmut Wilhelm 1938- *WhoScEn 94*
Hellwig, Renate 1940- *WhoWomW 91*
Helly, Walter Sigmund 1930- *WhoAm 94*
Hellyer, A(rthur) G(eorge) L(ee) 1902-1993 *ConAu 140*
Hellyer, Arthur *ConAu 140*
Hellyer, Arthur George Lee d1993 *Who 94N*
Hellyer, Arthur George Lee 1902-1993 *WrDr 94N*
Hellyer, Clement David 1914- *WhoAm 94*
Hellyer, Constance Anne 1937- *WhoWest 94*
Hellyer, Jill 1925- *WrDr 94*
Hellyer, Paul T 1923- *WrDr 94*
Hellyer, Paul Theodore 1923- *IntWW 93, Who 94*
Hellyer, Timothy Michael 1954- *WhoMW 93*
Helm, Anne 1939- *WhoHol 92*
Helm, Anny 1903- *NewGrDO*
Helm, Brigitte 1906- *WhoHol 92*
Helm, Charles George 1949- *WhoScEn 94*
Helm, Christa d1977 *WhoHol 92*
Helm, DeWitt Frederick, Jr. 1933- *WhoAm 94*
Helm, Donald Cairney 1937- *WhoAm 94*
Helm, Everett (Burton) 1913- *NewGrDO*
Helm, Fay 1913- *WhoHol 92*
Helm, Frances 1926- *WhoHol 92*
Helm, Frederick 1926- *WhoAm 94*
Helm, George Neville, III 1954- *WhoFI 94*
Helm, Hans 1934- *NewGrDO*
Helm, Hugh Barnett 1914- *WhoAmL 94*
Helm, James Ernest 1957- *WhoMW 93*
Helm, Joan Mary 1934- *WhoFI 94*
Helm, John F., Jr. 1900-1972 *WhoAmA 93N*
Helm, John Leslie 1921- *WhoScEn 94*
Helm, Joseph Burge 1931- *WhoAm 94*
Helm, June 1924- *WhoAm 94*
Helm, Leonard *WhAmRev*
Helm, Levon 1942- *WhoHol 92*
Helm, Lewis Marshall 1931- *WhoAm 94, WhoAmP 93*
Helm, Margie May 1894- *WhAm 10*
Helm, Olive 1937- *WhoMW 93*
Helm, Percy Ralph 1926- *WhoAm 94*
Helm, Robert G. 1949- *WhoAmP 93*
Helm, Robert Meredith 1917- *WhoAm 94*
Helm, Terry Allen 1951- *WhoMW 93*
Helman, Alfred Blair 1920- *WhoAm 94*
Helman, Eve *WhoAmA 93*
Helman, Gerald Bernard 1932- *WhoAm 94*
Helman, Joseph Arthur 1937- *WhoAm 94*
Helman, Nathaniel T. d1993 *NewYTBS 93*
Helman, Phoebe 1929- *WhoAmA 93*
Helman, Robert Alan 1934- *WhoAm 94*
Helman, Stephen Jody 1949- *WhoAmL 94*
Helmbold, F. Wilbur 1917-1989 *WhAm 10*
Helmbold, Nancy Pearce 1918- *WhoAm 94*
Helmbold, Richard 1950- *WhoWest 94*
Helmbold, William Ross 1947- *WhoAmL 94*

Henderson, Bernard Vere 1928- *Who 94*
Henderson, Bert d1939 *WhoHol 92*
Henderson, Bert Thomas 1949- *WhoAmP 93*
Henderson, Betty d1979 *WhoHol 92*
Henderson, Bill *WhoHol 92*
Henderson, Brian Edmond 1937- *WhoAm 94, WhoScEn 94*
Henderson, Bruce Doolin 1915- *WhAm 10*
Henderson, Carl L., Jr. 1945- *WhoBlA 94*
Henderson, Carlota Nuanez 1933- *WhoHisp 94*
Henderson, Charles 1937- *WhoBlA 94*
Henderson, Charles Brooke 1929- *WhoAm 94*
Henderson, Charles Edward 1939- *Who 94*
Henderson, Charles Joseph 1924- *Who 94*
Henderson, Charles Linscott, Jr. 1928- *WhoAmP 93*
Henderson, Charles Richmond 1848-1915 *DcAmReB 2*
Henderson, Charles W(illiam) 1948- *WrDr 94*
Henderson, Cheri Kaye 1947- *WhoBlA 94*
Henderson, Clayton P. 1954- *WhoAmP 93*
Henderson, Crawford, Sr. 1931- *WhoBlA 94*
Henderson, D. Rudolph 1921- *WhoBlA 94*
Henderson, Dan Fenno 1921- *WhoAm 94, WhoAmL 94, WrDr 94*
Henderson, Daniel Gardner 1941- *WhoScEn 94*
Henderson, David *DrAPF 93, Who 94, WhoBlA 94*
Henderson, David 1927- *WrDr 94*
Henderson, (Patrick) David 1927- *Who 94*
Henderson, David Allen 1948- *WhoAm 94*
Henderson, David Lee 1958- *WhoBlA 94*
Henderson, Del d1956 *WhoHol 92*
Henderson, Denys (Hartley) 1932- *IntWW 93, Who 94*
Henderson, Derek 1935- *Who 94*
Henderson, Derek Scott 1929- *Who 94*
Henderson, Dick d1958 *WhoHol 92*
Henderson, Dick 1927- *WhoAmP 93*
Henderson, Dickie d1985 *WhoHol 92*
Henderson, Don 1932- *WhoHol 92*
Henderson, Donald 1938- *WhoAm 94*
Henderson, Donald Ainslie 1928- *IntWW 93, WhoAm 94*
Henderson, Donald Bernard, Jr. 1949- *WhoAm 94*
Henderson, Donald Blanton 1949- *WhoAmP 93*
Henderson, Donald Wayne 1951- *WhoWest 94*
Henderson, Dorland John 1898- *WhoAm 94*
Henderson, Doug d1978 *WhoHol 92*
Henderson, Douglas Boyd 1935- *WhoAm 94, WhoAmL 94*
Henderson, Douglas James 1934- *WhoWest 94*
Henderson, Douglas John 1949- *Who 94*
Henderson, Douglas Mackay 1927- *Who 94*
Henderson, Dwight Franklin 1937- *WhoAm 94*
Henderson, Eddie L. 1932- *WhoBlA 94*
Henderson, Edward Chance 1916- *Who 94*
Henderson, Edward Firth 1917- *Who 94*
Henderson, Edward Shelton 1932- *WhoAm 94*
Henderson, Edwin Harold 1927- *WhoAm 94*
Henderson, Elmer W. 1913- *WhoBlA 94*
Henderson, Elvira *WhoHol 92*
Henderson, Erma L. 1917- *WhoBlA 94*
Henderson, Ernest, III 1924- *WhoAm 94*
Henderson, Eugene F. 1920- *WhoAmP 93*
Henderson, Eugene Leroy 1925- *WhoAm 94, WhoAmL 94, WhoMW 93*
Henderson, Everette L(on) 1896- *WhAm 10*
Henderson, F(rancis) M(artin) 1921- *WrDr 94*
Henderson, Fletcher 1897-1952 *AfrAmAl 6 [port]*
Henderson, Fletcher Hamilton 1897-1952 *AmCulL*
Henderson, Florence 1934- *WhoAm 94, WhoHol 92*
Henderson, Frank 1948- *WhoWest 94*
Henderson, Frank E. 1928- *WhoAmP 93*
Henderson, Frank Ellis 1928- *WhoAm 94, WhoAmL 94*
Henderson, Frank S., Jr. 1958- *WhoBlA 94*
Henderson, Freddye Scarborough 1917- *WhoBlA 94*
Henderson, Frederick Bishop 1941- *WhoAm 94*
Henderson, George 1932- *WhoAm 94, WhoBlA 94*
Henderson, George A. d1923 *WhoHol 92*
Henderson, George David Smith 1931- *Who 94*
Henderson, George Ervin 1947- *WhoAm 94, WhoAmL 94*
Henderson, George Kennedy Buchanan 1921- *Who 94*
Henderson, George Miller 1915- *WhoAm 94*
Henderson, George Patrick 1915- *Who 94, WrDr 94*
Henderson, Gerald 1956- *WhoBlA 94*
Henderson, Gerald Eugene 1928- *WhoBlA 94*
Henderson, Giles Ian 1942- *Who 94*
Henderson, Gordon 1957- *ConBlB 5 [port]*
Henderson, Gordon Desmond 1930- *WhoAmL 94*
Henderson, Grace d1944 *WhoHol 92*
Henderson, Greer F. 1932- *WhoIns 94*
Henderson, Hamish 1919- *WrDr 94*
Henderson, Harold Richard, Jr. 1942- *WhoAm 94*
Henderson, Harold W. 1948- *WhoAm 94*
Henderson, Harry Brinton, Jr. 1914- *WhoAm 94*
Henderson, Hazel 1933- *EnvEnc*
Henderson, Helena Naughton 1956- *WhoAmL 94*
Henderson, Henry Fairfax, Jr. 1928- *WhoBlA 94*
Henderson, Herbert H. *WhoBlA 94*
Henderson, Herschel Bradford 1929-1983 *WhAm 10*
Henderson, Hollis Allen *WhoWest 94*
Henderson, Horace Edward *WhoAm 94*
Henderson, Horace Edward 1917- *IntWW 93*
Henderson, Hubert Platt 1918- *WhoAm 94*
Henderson, Hugh C. 1930- *WhoBlA 94*
Henderson, I. D., Jr. 1929- *WhoBlA 94*
Henderson, Ian Dalton 1918- *Who 94*
Henderson, Isaiah Hilkiah, Jr. *WhoBlA 94*
Henderson, Ivo d1968 *WhoHol 92*
Henderson, Jack d1957 *WhoHol 92*
Henderson, Jack 1931- *WhoAm 94*
Henderson, Jack E. d1983 *WhoHol 92*
Henderson, Jack W. 1931- *WhoAmA 93*
Henderson, Jacob R. 1911- *WhoBlA 94*
Henderson, James, Jr. *WhoAmP 93*
Henderson, James Alan 1934- *WhoAm 94, WhoFI 94, WhoMW 93*
Henderson, James Alexander d1993 *NewYTBS 93 [port]*
Henderson, James Ewart 1923- *Who 94*
Henderson, James Forney 1921- *WhoAmL 94*
Henderson, James H. 1937- *WhoBlA 94*
Henderson, James H. M. 1917- *WhoBlA 94*
Henderson, James Harold 1948- *WhoFI 94, WhoMW 93*
Henderson, James Henry, Sr. 1925- *WhoBlA 94*
Henderson, James J., Sr. 1908- *WhoBlA 94*
Henderson, James Marvin 1921- *WhoAm 94*
Henderson, James R. 1919- *WhoBlA 94*
Henderson, James Robert *WhoBlA 94*
Henderson, James Sanford 1947- *WhoMW 93*
Henderson, James Thyne d1993 *Who 94N*
Henderson, Jeffrey Donn 1959- *WhoMW 93*
Henderson, Jo d1988 *WhoHol 92*
Henderson, Joan *Who 94*
Henderson, Joe 1937- *AfrAmAl 6, WhoAm 94*
Henderson, John Brown 1918- *WhoAm 94*
Henderson, John Clark 1951- *WhoFI 94*
Henderson, John Drews 1933- *WhoAm 94*
Henderson, John Goodchilde Norie 1945- *WhoScEn 94*
Henderson, John L. 1932- *WhoBlA 94*
Henderson, John Robert 1950- *WhoAmL 94*
Henderson, John Ronald 1920- *Who 94*
Henderson, John Stuart Wilmot 1919- *Who 94*
Henderson, John William 1945- *WhoAm 94*
Henderson, John Woodworth 1916- *WhoAm 94*
Henderson, Joseph Welles 1920- *WhoAm 94*
Henderson, Joyce Ann 1947- *WhoBlA 94*
Henderson, Karen LeCraft *CngDr 93, WhoAmP 93*
Henderson, Karen LeCraft 1944- *WhoAm 94, WhoAmL 94*
Henderson, Kathryn Luther *WhoMW 93*
Henderson, Kaye Neil 1933- *WhoScEn 94*
Henderson, Keith Pernell 1966- *WhoBlA 94*
Henderson, Kenneth Atwood 1905- *WhoFI 94*
Henderson, Kevin Scott 1956- *WhoMW 93*
Henderson, Larry Ray 1950- *WhoFI 94*
Henderson, Larry W. 1954- *WhoBlA 94*
Henderson, LaVell Merl 1917- *WhoWest 94*
Henderson, LeMon *WhoBlA 94*
Henderson, Lenneal Joseph, Jr. 1946- *WhoAm 94, WhoBlA 94*
Henderson, Leroy W., Jr. 1936- *WhoBlA 94*
Henderson, Leslie Edwin 1922- *Who 94*
Henderson, Lester Klerstead 1906- *WhoAmA 93N*
Henderson, Linda Dalrymple 1948- *WhoAmA 93*
Henderson, Linda Kay *WhoAmP 93*
Henderson, Lloyd D. 1945- *WhoBlA 94*
Henderson, Louis Clifton, Jr. 1937- *WhoAm 94*
Henderson, Loy W. 1892-1986 *HisDcKW*
Henderson, Lucile Kelling 1894-1990 *WhAm 10*
Henderson, Lucius d1947 *WhoHol 92*
Henderson, Lynn Allyson 1956- *WhoFI 94*
Henderson, Madeline Mary 1922- *WhoAm 94*
Henderson, Marcia d1987 *WhoHol 92*
Henderson, Marilyn Ann 1949- *WhoFI 94*
Henderson, Mark Alan *WhoAmP 93*
Henderson, Maureen McGrath 1926- *WhoAm 94*
Henderson, (Andrew) Maxwell 1908- *WrDr 94*
Henderson, Michael Dean 1961- *WhoMW 93*
Henderson, Michael Douglas 1932- *WhoWest 94*
Henderson, Michael Dudley 1952- *WhoFI 94*
Henderson, Michael John Glidden 1938- *Who 94*
Henderson, Mike *WhoAmA 93*
Henderson, Milton Arnold 1922- *WhoAm 94*
Henderson, Nannette S. 1946- *WhoBlA 94*
Henderson, Nicholas *IntWW 93, Who 94*
Henderson, (John) Nicholas 1919- *IntWW 93, Who 94, WrDr 94*
Henderson, Nigel Stuart d1993 *Who 94N*
Henderson, Patricia McGovern 1940- *WhoWest 94*
Henderson, Patrick David 1927- *IntWW 93, WrDr 94*
Henderson, Patrick Moran 1946- *WhoAmP 93*
Henderson, Paul *BlmGWL*
Henderson, Paul 1940- *Who 94*
Henderson, Paul Audine 1925- *WhoAm 94*
Henderson, Paul Bargas, Jr. 1928- *WhoAm 94*
Henderson, R. Michael 1944- *WhoAmL 94*
Henderson, Ralph Ernest 1899-1989 *WhAm 10*
Henderson, Ralph Hale 1937- *WhoAm 94*
Henderson, Ramona Estelle 1952- *WhoBlA 94*
Henderson, Remond 1952- *WhoBlA 94*
Henderson, Richard 1735-1785 *WhAmRev*
Henderson, Richard 1924- *WrDr 94*
Henderson, Richard 1928- *WhoAmP 93*
Henderson, Richard 1945- *IntWW 93, Who 94*
Henderson, Richard Ashley 1947- *WhoFI 94*
Henderson, Richard Martin 1934- *WhoScEn 94*
Henderson, Richard Yates 1931- *Who 94*
Henderson, Rickey Henley 1958- *WhoAm 94, WhoBlA 94, WhoWest 94*
Henderson, Robbin Legere 1942- *WhoAmA 93*
Henderson, Robbye R. 1937- *WhoBlA 94*
Henderson, Robbye Robinson 1937- *WhoAm 94*
Henderson, Robert 1904- *WhoHol 92*
Henderson, Robert Alistair 1917- *IntWW 93, Who 94*
Henderson, Robert Brumwell 1929- *Who 94*
Henderson, Robert Cameron 1940- *WhoAm 94, WhoFI 94*
Henderson, Robert Earl 1935- *WhoAm 94*
Henderson, Robert Ewart 1937- *Who 94*
Henderson, Robert Franklin, Jr. 1944- *WhoAm 94, WhoAmL 94*
Henderson, Robert G. 1918- *WhoAmP 93*
Henderson, Robert Jules 1943- *WhoAm 94*
Henderson, Robert Waugh 1920- *WhoAm 94*
Henderson, Roberta Marie 1929- *WhoMW 93*
Henderson, Roger Anthony 1943- *Who 94*
Henderson, Roger C. 1938- *WhoAm 94*
Henderson, Romeo Clanton 1915- *WhoBlA 94*
Henderson, Ronald Wilbur 1933- *WhoAm 94*
Henderson, Roy (Galbraith) 1899- *NewGrDO, Who 94*
Henderson, Ruth Faynella *WhoBlA 94*
Henderson, Sammy Wayne 1957- *WhoWest 94*
Henderson, Schuyler Kent 1945- *WhoAmL 94*
Henderson, Scott Edward 1946- *WhoAmL 94*
Henderson, Skitch 1918- *IntMPA 94, WhoAm 94*
Henderson, Spencer, III d1993 *NewYTBS 93*
Henderson, Stanley Dale 1935- *WhoAm 94*
Henderson, Stanley Lee 1909- *WhoBlA 94*
Henderson, Steffi d1967 *WhoHol 92*
Henderson, Stephen Douglas 1942- *WhoMW 93*
Henderson, Stephen E. 1925- *WhoBlA 94*
Henderson, Stephen Paul 1949- *WhoAmL 94*
Henderson, Surena Bissette 1935- *WhoAmP 93*
Henderson, Susan Ayleen 1945- *WhoAmL 94, WhoMW 93*
Henderson, Susan Cardin 1953- *WhoMW 93*
Henderson, Talbot V. d1946 *WhoHol 92*
Henderson, Ted d1962 *WhoHol 92*
Henderson, Terry Lynn Moreland 1953- *WhoWest 94*
Henderson, Thelton Eugene 1933- *WhoAm 94, WhoAmL 94, WhoBlA 94, WhoWest 94*
Henderson, Theresa Crittenden 1937- *WhoBlA 94*
Henderson, Thomas 1743-1824 *WhAmRev*
Henderson, Thomas Henry, Jr. 1939- *WhoAm 94, WhoAmL 94*
Henderson, Thomas James 1931- *WhoFI 94*
Henderson, Valton Darryl 1955- *WhoMW 93*
Henderson, Victor 1939- *WhoAmA 93*
Henderson, Victor Warren 1951- *WhoWest 94*
Henderson, Virginia Ruth McKinney 1932- *WhoBlA 94*
Henderson, W. Guy 1928- *WhoAm 94*
Henderson, W. Lecil, II 1958- *WhoAmP 93*
Henderson, Walter G. 1930- *WhoFI 94*
Henderson, Walter J. *WhoAmP 93*
Henderson, William 1748-1787 *WhAmRev*
Henderson, William (MacGregor) 1913- *Who 94*
Henderson, William Boyd 1928- *WhoAm 94, WhoScEn 94*
Henderson, William Boyd 1936- *WhoAm 94*
Henderson, William C. *DrAPF 93*
Henderson, William C., II 1941- *WhoBlA 94*
Henderson, William Charles 1941- *WhoAm 94*
Henderson, William Darryl 1938- *ConAu 140, WhoWest 94*
Henderson, William L 1927- *WrDr 94*
Henderson, William MacGregor 1913- *IntWW 93*
Henderson, William Otto 1904- *WrDr 94*
Henderson, William Ross 1936- *Who 94*
Henderson, William Weaver 1953- *WhoMW 93*
Henderson, Zenna 1917- *BlmGWL*
Henderson, Zenna 1917-1983 *EncSF 93*
Henderson-Dixon, Karen Sue 1946- *WhoAm 94, WhoWest 94*
Henderson-Holmes, Safiya *DrAPF 93*
Henderson-Nocho, Audrey J. 1959- *WhoBlA 94*
Henderson Of Brompton, Baron 1922- *Who 94*
Henderson Smith, Stephen Lane 1919- *WrDr 94*
Henderson-Stewart, David (James) 1941- *Who 94*
Hendin, David Bruce 1945- *WhoAm 94*
Hendl, Walter 1917- *WhoAm 94*
Hendler, Lawrence 1953- *WhoWest 94*
Hendler, Samuel I. 1922- *WhoAm 94*
Hendley, Ashley Preston, Jr. 1938- *WhoWest 94*
Hendley, Dan Lunsford 1938- *WhoAm 94*
Hendon, Lea Alpha 1953- *WhoBlA 94*
Hendon, Marvin Keith 1960- *WhoScEn 94*
Hendon, Rickey *WhoAmP 93*
Hendon, Robert Caraway 1912- *WhoAm 94*
Hendon, Robert Randall 1894-1986 *WhAm 10*
Hendren, Gary E. 1943- *WhoAm 94*

Hendren, Jimm Larry 1940- *WhoAm 94, WhoAmL 94*
Hendren, Jo Ann 1935- *WhoFI 94*
Hendren, Robert Lee, Jr. 1925- *WhoAm 94, WhoWest 94*
Hendrian, Dutch d1953 *WhoHol 92*
Hendrick, George 1929- *WhoAm 94*
Hendrick, Gerald Paul 1949- *WhoAm 94*
Hendrick, Hal Wilmans 1933- *WhoAm 94, WhoWest 94*
Hendrick, Howard H. 1954- *WhoAm 94*
Hendrick, Howard Hamlin 1954- *WhoAmP 93*
Hendrick, Irving Guilford 1936- *WhoAm 94*
Hendrick, James Pomeroy 1901-1990 *WhAm 10*
Hendrick, James T. 1942- *WhoAmL 94*
Hendrick, John Morton 1917- *WhoScEn 94*
Hendrick, Max, III 1944- *WhoAmL 94*
Hendricks, Arch d1964 *WhoHol 92*
Hendricks, B. L., Jr. 1918- *WhoAmP 93*
Hendricks, Barbara *WhoHol 92*
Hendricks, Barbara 1948- *AfrAmAl 6, ConMus 10 [port], IntWW 93, NewGrDO, WhoAm 94, WhoBlA 94*
Hendricks, Barkley L. 1945- *WhoBlA 94*
Hendricks, Barkley Leonnard 1945- *WhoAmA 93*
Hendricks, Beatrice E. *WhoBlA 94*
Hendricks, Ben, Sr. d1930 *WhoHol 92*
Hendricks, Ben, Jr. d1938 *WhoHol 92*
Hendricks, Brian James 1948- *WhoFI 94, WhoWest 94*
Hendricks, Calvin 1933- *WhAm 10*
Hendricks, Charles Henning 1917- *WhoAm 94*
Hendricks, Constance Smith 1953- *WhoBlA 94*
Hendricks, David Charles 1948- *WhoAmA 93*
Hendricks, Donald Duane 1931- *WhoAm 94*
Hendricks, Dudley d1942 *WhoHol 92*
Hendricks, Ed Jerald 1935- *WhoAm 94*
Hendricks, Edward David 1946- *WhoAm 94, WhoFI 94*
Hendricks, Edward Lee 1952- *WhoAmA 93*
Hendricks, Edwin Francis 1941- *WhoAmL 94*
Hendricks, Elrod Jerome 1940- *WhoBlA 94*
Hendricks, Fanny-Dell 1939- *WhoWest 94*
Hendricks, Geoffrey *DrAPF 93*
Hendricks, Geoffrey 1931- *WhoAmA 93*
Hendricks, George David, Sr. 1913- *WrDr 94*
Hendricks, James (Powell) 1938- *WhoAmA 93*
Hendricks, James Edwin 1935- *WhoAm 94*
Hendricks, James Powell 1938- *WhoAm 94*
Hendricks, James W. 1924- *WhoAmL 94*
Hendricks, John d1949 *WhoHol 92*
Hendricks, Jon 1921- *WhoBlA 94*
Hendricks, Katherine 1949- *WhoAmL 94*
Hendricks, Kyle James 1958- *WhoWest 94*
Hendricks, Larry D. 1936- *WhoAmP 93*
Hendricks, Leonard D. 1952- *WhoScEn 94*
Hendricks, Leta 1954- *WhoBlA 94*
Hendricks, Lloyd I. *WhoAmP 93*
Hendricks, Louis d1923 *WhoHol 92*
Hendricks, Malvin Leon, Sr. 1921- *WhoAmP 93*
Hendricks, Marvin B. 1951- *WhoBlA 94*
Hendricks, Noah d1973 *WhoHol 92*
Hendricks, Randal Arlan 1945- *WhoAmL 94*
Hendricks, Richard D. 1937- *WhoBlA 94*
Hendricks, Robert Michael 1943- *WhoFI 94*
Hendricks, Stanley Marshall, II 1952- *WhoFI 94*
Hendricks, Steven Aaron 1960- *WhoBlA 94*
Hendricks, Suzanne Haskins 1940- *WhoMW 93*
Hendricks, Ted *ProFbHF [port]*
Hendricks, Terry Joseph 1954- *WhoScEn 94*
Hendricks, William Lawrence 1929- *WhoAm 94*
Hendrickse, Helenard Joe (Alan) 1927- *IntWW 93*
Hendrickse, Ralph George 1926- *IntWW 93, Who 94*
Hendricksen, Holmes G. 1933- *WhoFI 94*
Hendrickson, Alan Bryce 1945- *WhoFI 94*
Hendrickson, Benjamin *WhoHol 92*
Hendrickson, Boyde W. 1945- *WhoAm 94*
Hendrickson, Brian Donald 1960- *WhoMW 93*
Hendrickson, Bruce C. 1930- *WhoIns 94*
Hendrickson, Bruce Carl 1930- *WhoAm 94*
Hendrickson, Charles John 1950- *WhoAm 94*
Hendrickson, Constance Marie McRight 1949- *WhoAm 94*
Hendrickson, Elizabeth Ann 1936- *WhoWest 94*
Hendrickson, Jeffrey Thomas 1944- *WhoAm 94*
Hendrickson, Jerome Orland 1918- *WhoAm 94, WhoFI 94*
Hendrickson, John L. 1947- *WhoAmL 94*
Hendrickson, John T., Jr. *WhoAmP 93*
Hendrickson, Kent Herman 1939- *WhoAm 94*
Hendrickson, Neal B. 1949- *WhoAmP 93*
Hendrickson, Philip Holmes 1931- *WhoFI 94*
Hendrickson, Robert A 1923- *WrDr 94*
Hendrickson, Robert Augustus 1923- *WhoAm 94, WhoAmL 94*
Hendrickson, Robert Charles 1952- *WhoAmL 94*
Hendrickson, Robert Frederick 1933- *WhoAm 94*
Hendrickson, Robert Jerome 1967- *WhoMW 93*
Hendrickson, Samuel Linus 1964- *WhoMW 93*
Hendrickson, Tom *WhoAmP 93*
Hendrickson, Wayne Arthur 1941- *WhoAm 94, WhoScEn 94*
Hendrickson, William George 1918- *WhoFI 94, WhoScEn 94*
Hendricks-Verdejo, Carlos Doel, Sr. 1959- *WhoHisp 94*
Hendrickx, Andrew George 1933- *WhoAm 94, WhoScEn 94*
Hendrickx, Leonard Henry 1953- *WhoWest 94*
Hendrie, Don, Jr. *DrAPF 93*
Hendrie, Ernest d1929 *WhoHol 92*
Hendrie, Gerald Mills 1935- *Who 94*
Hendrie, Joseph Mallam 1925- *WhoAm 94, WhoAmP 93, WhoScEn 94*
Hendrie, Robert Andrew Michie 1938- *Who 94*
Hendrieth, Brenda Lucille 1955- *WhoBlA 94*
Hendriks, A(rthur) L(emière) 1922- *WrDr 94*
Hendrikson, Anders d1965 *WhoHol 92*
Hendrix, B. G. 1922- *WhoAmP 93*
Hendrix, Connie 1942- *WhoAmA 93*
Hendrix, Daniel W. 1922- *WhoBlA 94*
Hendrix, Deborah Lynne 1961- *WhoBlA 94*
Hendrix, Dennis R. 1940- *WhoAm 94, WhoFI 94*
Hendrix, Dennis R. 1953- *WhoAmP 93*
Hendrix, Harville 1935- *WrDr 94*
Hendrix, James Easton 1941- *WhoAm 94*
Hendrix, Jimi d1970 *WhoHol 92*
Hendrix, Jimi 1942-1970 *AfrAmAl 6 [port], AmCulL*
Hendrix, Jon Richard 1938- *WhoAm 94*
Hendrix, Kenneth Allen 1959- *WhoScEn 94*
Hendrix, Louise Butts 1911- *WhoWest 94*
Hendrix, Lynn Parker 1951- *WhoAm 94*
Hendrix, Martha Raye 1939- *WhoBlA 94*
Hendrix, Michael Wayne 1960- *WhoFI 94*
Hendrix, Robert Elvin 1946- *WhoFI 94*
Hendrix, Ronald Wayne 1943- *WhoMW 93, WhoScEn 94*
Hendrix, Rufus Sam, Jr. 1949- *WhoAm 94*
Hendrix, Stephen C. 1941- *WhoFI 94*
Hendrix, Walker A. 1949- *WhoAmP 93*
Hendrix, Wanda d1981 *WhoHol 92*
Hendrixson, Peter S. 1947- *WhoAm 94, WhoAmL 94*
Hendron, Joseph Gerard 1932- *Who 94*
Hendry, Andrew Delaney *WhoAm 94, WhoAmL 94*
Hendry, Anita d1940 *WhoHol 92*
Hendry, Arnold William 1921- *Who 94*
Hendry, Charles 1959- *Who 94*
Hendry, David Forbes 1944- *Who 94*
Hendry, Diana 1941- *WrDr 94*
Hendry, George Orr 1937- *WhoAm 94*
Hendry, Gloria *WhoBlA 94*
Hendry, Gloria 1949- *WhoHol 92*
Hendry, Ian d1984 *WhoHol 92*
Hendry, John (Lovat) 1952- *WrDr 94*
Hendry, Joy (McLaggan) 1953- *WrDr 94*
Hendry, Len d1981 *WhoHol 92*
Hendry, Linda May 1957- *WhoWest 94*
Hendry, Robert Ryon 1936- *WhoAmL 94*
Hendry, Stephen Gordon 1969- *IntWW 93*
Hendry, Thomas 1929- *WrDr 94*
Hendry, Tom 1929- *ConDr 93*
Hendy, John Giles 1948- *Who 94*
Hendy, Scott Gary 1951- *WhoWest 94*
Henebry, Michael Stevens 1946- *WhoMW 93, WhoScEn 94*
Henegan, John Clark 1950- *WhoAmL 94*
Henegar, Dale L. *WhoAmP 93*
Heneghan, Shawn Patrick 1951- *WhoScEn 94*
Henehan, Joan 1959- *WhoScEn 94*
He Neng 1942- *WhoPRCh 91*
Henenlotter, Frank *HorFD*
Henes, Donna *DrAPF 93*
Henes, Donna 1945- *WhoAm 94, WhoAmA 93*
Henes, John Derek 1937- *Who 94*
Henes, Samuel Ernst 1937- *WhoAm 94*
Heney, Joseph Edward 1927- *WhoAm 94, WhoFI 94*
Heng, Donald James, Jr. 1944- *WhoAm 94*
Heng, Gerald C-W 1941- *WhoAmL 94*
Heng, Stanley Mark 1937- *WhoAm 94, WhoMW 93, WhoWest 94*
Hengehold, Barbara Ann Tiemann 1951- *WhoMW 93*
Hengesbaugh, Bernard L. 1946- *WhoIns 94*
Henggao, Ding 1931- *WhoScEn 94*
Henglein, Friedrich Arnim 1926- *WhoScEn 94*
Heng Samrin 1934- *IntWW 93*
Hengsbach, Franz 1910-1991 *WhAm 10*
Hengstler, Gary Ardell 1947- *WhoAm 94*
Henham, Ernest G(eorge) 1870- *EncSF 93*
Henham, John Alfred 1924- *Who 94*
Henick, Alfred 1925- *WhoFI 94*
Henick, Steven Titman 1942- *WhoFI 94*
Henie, Sonja d1969 *WhoHol 92*
Henig, Pinny 1954- *WhoFI 94*
Henig, Stanley 1939- *Who 94*
Henige, David Patrick 1938- *WhoMW 93*
Henikoff, Leo M., Jr. 1939- *WhoAm 94*
Heninger, George R. 1934- *WhoScEn 94*
Heninger, Kurt Allen 1950- *WhoMW 93*
Heninger, Simeon Kahn, Jr. 1922- *WhoAm 94*
Henington, David Mead 1929- *WhoAm 94*
Henis, Jay Myls Stuart 1938- *WhoScEn 94*
Henize, Karl G. 1926-1993 *NewYTBS 93 [port]*
Henize, Karl Gordon 1926- *WhoScEn 94*
Henk, Floyd Henry 1929- *WhoFI 94*
Henke, Bruce R. 1950- *WhoAmL 94*
Henke, David Leigh 1945- *WhoMW 93*
Henke, Emerson Overbeck 1916- *WhoAm 94*
Henke, Janice Carine 1938- *WhoMW 93*
Henke, Kristine Anne 1959- *WhoMW 93*
Henke, Michael John 1940- *WhoAm 94, WhoAmL 94*
Henke, Shauna Nicole 1966- *WhoWest 94*
Henke, Theodore Robert 1952- *WhoIns 94*
Henke, William Kurt 1957- *WhoAmL 94*
Henkel, Arthur John, Jr. 1945- *WhoAm 94, WhoFI 94*
Henkel, Cathy *WhoAm 94*
Henkel, Christian Johann 1950- *WhoScEn 94*
Henkel, Eloise Elizabeth 1923- *WhoMW 93*
Henkel, Jenny Marie 1952- *WhoAmP 93*
Henkel, Kathryn G. 1952- *WhoAm 94, WhoAmL 94*
Henkel, Konrad 1915- *IntWW 93*
Henkel, Lee H., Jr. 1928- *WhoAmP 93*
Henkel, Oliver Carl, Jr. 1936- *WhoAm 94*
Henkel, Paul 1754-1825 *DcAmReB 2*
Henkel, Steve 1933- *WrDr 94*
Henkel, William 1941- *WhoAm 94*
Henkels, Ellen Therese 1951- *WhoMW 93*
Henkels, Mark *WhoWest 94*
Henkels, Paul MacAllister 1924- *WhoAm 94, WhoFI 94*
Henken, Willard John 1927- *WhoAm 94*
Henker, Paul d1960 *WhoHol 92*
Henkes, Kevin 1960- *SmATA 76 [port]*
Henkes, Robert 1922- *WrDr 94*
Henkin, Howard H. 1926- *IntMPA 94*
Henkin, Louis 1917- *WhoAm 94, WhoAmL 94, WrDr 94*
Henkin, Robert Irwin 1930- *WhoAm 94, WhoScEn 94*
Henkle, James Lee 1927- *WhoAmA 93*
Henkle, Roger Black 1935-1991 *WhAm 10*
Henle, Christian-Peter 1938- *IntWW 93*
Henle, Fritz d1993 *NewYTBS 93*
Henle, Fritz 1909- *WhoAmA 93*
Henle, Fritz 1909-1993 *ConAu 140*
Henle, Guy 1920-1992 *WhAm 10*
Henle, Jorg Alexander 1934- *IntWW 93*
Henle, Peter 1919- *WhoAm 94*
Henle, Robert Athanasius 1924- *WhoScEn 94*
Henle, Robert John 1909- *WhoAm 94*
Henley, Baron 1953- *Who 94*
Henley, Arthur *WrDr 94*
Henley, Arthur 1921- *WhoAm 94*
Henley, Beth *BlmGWL*
Henley, Beth 1952- *ConDr 93, IntDcT 2, WhoAm 94, WhoHol 92, WrDr 94*
Henley, Carl R. 1955- *WhoBlA 94*
Henley, Charles *DrAPF 93*
Henley, David d1986 *WhoHol 92*
Henley, Don 1948- *WhoAm 94*
Henley, Douglas (Owen) 1919- *Who 94*
Henley, Douglas Owen 1919- *IntWW 93*
Henley, Edgar Floyd, Jr. 1940- *WhoAmP 93*
Henley, Elizabeth Becker 1952- *IntWW 93*
Henley, Ernest M(ark) 1924- *IntWW 93*
Henley, Ernest Mark 1924- *WhoAm 94, WhoScEn 94, WhoWest 94*
Henley, Everett Scott 1940- *WhoAm 94*
Henley, Henry Howard, Jr. 1921- *WhoAm 94*
Henley, Hobart d1964 *WhoHol 92*
Henley, J. Smith 1917- *WhoAm 94, WhoAmL 94*
Henley, Jeffrey O. *WhoFI 94*
Henley, Joan 1904- *WhoHol 92*
Henley, John Tannery 1921- *WhoAmP 93*
Henley, Joseph (Charles Cameron) 1909- *Who 94*
Henley, Joseph Oliver 1949- *WhoFI 94*
Henley, Kenneth James 1939- *WhoWest 94*
Henley, Michael Harry George 1938- *Who 94*
Henley, Patricia *DrAPF 93*
Henley, Richard James 1956- *WhoAm 94*
Henley, Robert Lee 1934- *WhoMW 93*
Henley, Terry Lew 1940- *WhoScEn 94*
Henley, Vernard W. 1929- *WhoBlA 94*
Henley, Vernard William 1929- *WhoAm 94*
Henley, Virginia 1935- *ConAu 41NR*
Henn, Carrie *WhoHol 92*
Henn, Charles Herbert 1931- *Who 94*
Henn, Fritz Albert 1941- *WhoAm 94, WhoScEn 94*
Henn, John Howard 1942- *WhoAmL 94*
Henn, Mary Ann *DrAPF 93*
Henn, Walter 1912- *IntWW 93*
Henn, William L. 1953- *WhoAmL 94*
Henne, James Earl 1947- *WhoAm 94*
Henneberg, Johann Baptist 1768-1822 *NewGrDO*
Henneberger, Lawrence Francis 1938- *WhoAm 94, WhoAmL 94*
Hennecke, Clarence R. d1969 *WhoHol 92*
Hennedy, Hugh *DrAPF 93*
Henneke, Edward George 1940- *WhoAmL 94*
Hennekinne, Loic 1940- *IntWW 93*
Hennell, Michael Murray 1918- *Who 94*
Hennelly, Edmund Paul 1923- *WhoAm 94, WhoAmL 94, WhoFI 94*
Hennelly, James Joseph 1950- *WhoAmL 94*
Hennelowa, Jozefa *WhoWomW 91*
Henneman, John Bell, Jr. 1935- *WhoAm 94*
Hennemeyer, Robert Thomas 1925- *WhoAm 94*
Hennen, Tom *DrAPF 93*
Hennepin, Louis c. 1640-1701 *EncNAR, WhWE*
Henner, Marilu 1952- *IntMPA 94, WhoAm 94, WhoHol 92*
Henner, William David 1949- *WhoWest 94*
Hennes, David Joseph 1952- *WhoFI 94*
Hennes, Robert Taft 1930- *WhoAm 94*
Hennessey, Alice Elizabeth 1936- *WhoFI 94*
Hennessey, Audrey Kathleen 1936- *WhoScEn 94*
Hennessey, David d1926 *WhoHol 92*
Hennessey, David Patrick 1950- *WhoFI 94*
Hennessey, Edward F. 1919- *WhoAmP 93*
Hennessey, Francis Xavier 1955- *WhoMW 93*
Hennessey, Frank Martin 1938- *WhoAm 94*
Hennessey, Gilbert Hall, Jr. 1916- *WhoAm 94*
Hennessey, Jean Lande 1927- *WhoAmP 93*
Hennessey, John A. d1920 *WhoHol 92*
Hennessey, John Philip *WhoAm 94, WhoFI 94*
Hennessey, John William, Jr. 1925- *WhoAm 94*
Hennessey, Mark *WhoHol 92*
Hennessey, Maurice Vincent 1927- *WhoAmP 93*
Hennessey, Neil William 1943- *WhoFI 94*
Hennessey, Peter J., Jr. 1920- *WhoIns 94*
Hennessey, Raymond Frank 1925- *WhoAmP 93, WhoFI 94*
Hennessey, Robert John 1941- *WhoAm 94*
Hennessey, Timothy F. *WhoAmP 93*
Hennessey, William John 1948- *WhoAm 94, WhoAmA 93, WhoMW 93*
Hennessy *Who 94*

Hennessy, Arthur Leo, Jr. 1925- *WhoAmP 93*
Hennessy, Christopher 1909- *Who 94*
Hennessy, Daniel Kraft 1941- *WhoAm 94, WhoAmL 94*
Hennessy, Dean McDonald 1923- *WhoAm 94, WhoAmL 94*
Hennessy, Edward L., Jr. 1928- *IntWW 93*
Hennessy, Ellen Anne 1949- *WhoAm 94, WhoAmL 94*
Hennessy, Felicia Plesic 1956- *WhoMW 93*
Hennessy, James (Patrick Ivan) 1923- *Who 94*
Hennessy, James Ernest 1933- *WhoAm 94*
Hennessy, John Basil 1925- *IntWW 93*
Hennessy, John Francis 1928-1989 *WhAm 10*
Hennessy, John Francis, III 1955- *WhoFI 94, WhoScEn 94*
Hennessy, John J(oseph) 1958- *ConAu 141*
Hennessy, John M. 1936- *WhoAm 94, WhoFI 94*
Hennessy, John Wyndham P. *Who 94*
Hennessy, Joseph H. 1937- *WhoAm 94, WhoAmL 94*
Hennessy, Madeleine *DrAPF 93*
Hennessy, Margaret Barrett 1952- *WhoFI 94, WhoMW 93*
Hennessy, Mary Brigid Teresa 1933- *Who 94*
Hennessy, Max 1916-1991 *WrDr 94N*
Hennessy, Michael d1981 *WhoHol 92*
Hennessy, Paul Kevin 1932- *WhoAm 94*
Hennessy, Peter 1947- *WrDr 94*
Hennessy, Peter John 1947- *Who 94*
Hennessy, Sumiko Tanaka *WhoAsA 94*
Hennessy, Thomas Anthony 1936- *WhoWest 94*
Hennessy, Thomas Christopher 1916- *WhoAm 94*
Hennessy, Wesley Joseph 1914-1991 *WhAm 10*
Hennesey, Gerald Craft 1921- *WhoAm 94, WhoAmA 93*
Hennet, Remy Jean-Claude 1955- *WhoScEn 94*
Henney, Christopher Scot 1941- *WhoWest 94*
Henney, Jane Ellen 1947- *WhoAm 94*
Henney, Raymond Wade 1958- *WhoAmL 94*
Hennig, Charles William 1949- *WhoScEn 94*
Hennig, Frederick E. 1932- *WhoAm 94, WhoFI 94*
Hennigan, James Michael 1943- *WhoAm 94, WhoAmL 94, WhoWest 94*
Hennigan, Patrick John 1945- *WhoAm 94*
Hennigan, Thomas Anthony 1954- *WhoWest 94*
Hennigar, David J. 1939- *WhoAm 94*
Henniger, David Thomas 1936- *WhoAmL 94*
Hennighausen, Fred H. 1924- *WhoAmL 94*
Henniker, Baron 1916- *Who 94*
Henniker, Adrian Chandos 1946- *Who 94*
Henniker, Florence 1855-1923 *DcLB 135 [port]*
Henniker Heaton, Yvo Robert *Who 94*
Henniker-Major *Who 94*
Henning, Barbara *DrAPF 93*
Henning, Doug 1947- *WhoAm 94*
Henning, Edward B(urk) 1922-1993 *ConAu 141*
Henning, Edward Burk 1922- *WhoAmA 93*
Henning, Edward Burk 1922-1993 *NewYTBS 93*
Henning, Eva 1920- *WhoHol 92*
Henning, George Thomas, Jr. 1941- *WhoAm 94*
Henning, Harry Leonard 1938- *WhoAm 94, WhoAmL 94, WhoMW 93*
Henning, Joel Frank 1939- *WhoAm 94, WhoAmL 94*
Henning, Josephine Terrell 1914- *WhoAmP 93*
Henning, Judy *WhoAmP 93*
Henning, Kathleen Ann 1963- *WhoScEn 94*
Henning, Linda Kaye 1944- *IntMPA 94*
Henning, Lisbeth Lee 1955- *WhoWest 94*
Henning, Mark G. 1953- *WhoAm 94*
Henning, Pat d1973 *WhoHol 92*
Henning, Paul 1911- *IntMPA 94*
Henning, Rachel 1826-1914 *BlmGWL*
Henning, Rudolf Ernst 1923- *WhoAm 94*
Henning, Susan June 1946- *WhoAm 94*
Henning, William Wilson 1946- *WhoFI 94*
Henninger, Daniel Paul 1946- *WhoAm 94*
Henninger, G(eorge) Ross 1898- *WhAm 10*
Henninger, Polly 1946- *WhoScEn 94*
Hennings, Dorothy Ann 1937- *WhoFI 94*
Hennings, Emmy 1885-1948 *BlmGWL*
Hennings, John d1933 *WhoHol 92*
Hennings, Kenneth Milton 1943- *WhoBlA 94*
Hennings, Richard Owen 1911- *Who 94*
Henningsen, Agnes 1868-1962 *BlmGWL*
Henningsen, Linda Joyce 1954- *WhoMW 93*
Henningsen, Peter, Jr. 1926- *WhoAm 94*
Henningsen, Victor William, Jr. 1924- *WhoAm 94, WhoFI 94*
Hennion, Carolyn Laird 1943- *WhoFI 94*
Hennion, Reeve Lawrence 1941- *WhoAm 94*
Hennis, Hugh Linwood, III 1954- *WhoMW 93*
Hennissart, Martha *WrDr 94*
Hennon, Charles Berdell 1947- *WhoMW 93*
Hennon, G. Joe 1939- *WhoMW 93*
Henreid, Monika *WhoHol 92*
Henreid, Paul d1992 *WhAm 10*
Henreid, Paul 1907- *WhoHol 92*
Henreid, Paul 1908-1992 *AnObit 1992*
Henrey, Bobby 1939- *WhoHol 92*
Henrey, Madeleine 1906- *WrDr 94*
Henrey, Robert, Mrs. 1906- *Who 94*
Henri, Adrian (Maurice) 1932- *WrDr 94*
Henri, Adrian Maurice 1932- *Who 94*
Henri, David C. *WhoAmL 94*
Henri, Robert 1865-1929 *AmCulL*
Henrich, Biff 1953- *WhoAmA 93*
Henrich, Dieter 1927- *IntWW 93*
Henrich, Judy Rea 1945- *WhoWest 94*
Henrichs, Albert Maximinus 1942- *WhoAm 94*
Henrick, Michael Francis 1948- *WhoAm 94, WhoAmL 94*
Henricksen, Ralf Christian 1907-1975 *WhoAmA 93N*
Henrickson, Eiler Leonard 1920- *WhoAm 94, WhoScEn 94, WhoWest 94*
Henrickson, Martha (Klein) 1942- *WhoAmA 93*
Henrickson, Paul Robert *WhoAmA 93*
Henrickson, Thomas 1944- *WhoAmA 93*
Henrie, Gary Ray 1953- *WhoAmL 94*
Henrie, Kim Barton 1951- *WhoWest 94*
Henriksen, Finn 1915- *WhoAmL 94*
Henriksen, Lance *WhoHol 92*
Henriksen, Lance 1943- *IntMPA 94*
Henriksen, Lars Michael 1964- *WhoMW 93*
Henriksen, Melvin 1927- *WhoWest 94*
Henriksen, Thomas Hollinger 1939- *WhoAm 94*
Henrikson, Lois Elizabeth 1921- *WhoAm 94, WhoFI 94*
Henrikson, Mathias *WhoHol 92*
Henriksson, Jan Hugo Lennart 1933- *WhoScEn 94*
Henriksson, Thomas Martin 1951- *WhoWest 94*
Henrion, Robert 1915- *IntWW 93*
Henriques, Diana Blackmon 1948- *WhoAm 94*
Henriques, Richard Henry Quixano 1943- *Who 94*
Henriquez, Andres Antonio 1947- *WhoHisp 94*
Henriquez, Francis *WhoHisp 94*
Henríquez, Nelson 1941- *WhoHisp 94*
Henrison, (Anne) Rosina (Elizabeth) 1902- *Who 94*
Henritze, Bette *WhoHol 92*
Henry, Monsieur fl. 1813-1849 *NewGrDO*
Henry, I 1100-1135 *BlmGEL*
Henry, II 1133-1189 *HisWorL [port]*
Henry, II 1154-1189 *BlmGEL*
Henry, III 1216-1272 *BlmGEL*
Henry, IV 1399-1413 *BlmGEL*
Henry, IV 1553-1610 *HisWorL [port]*
Henry, V 1387-1422 *HisWorL [port]*
Henry, V 1413-1422 *BlmGEL*
Henry, VI 1422-1461 *BlmGEL*
Henry, VII 1457-1509 *HisWorL [port]*
Henry, VII 1485-1509 *BlmGEL*
Henry, VIII 1491-1547 *HisWorL [port]*
Henry, VIII 1509-1547 *BlmGEL*
Henry, Aaron 1922- *HisWorL*
Henry, Aaron E. 1922- *WhoBlA 94*
Henry, Aaron Edd 1922- *WhoAmP 93*
Henry, Alan Pemberton 1949- *WhoAm 94*
Henry, Alan Ray 1941- *WhoAm 94*
Henry, Alberta 1920- *WhoBlA 94*
Henry, Alberta Hill 1920- *WhoAmP 93*
Henry, Alexander d1814 *WhWE*
Henry, Alexander 1739-1824 *WhWE*
Henry, Alice Katherine 1936- *WhoAmL 94*
Henry, Allen Duane 1964- *WhoMW 93*
Henry, Andre Armand 1934- *IntWW 93*
Henry, Andrew c. 1775-1833 *WhWE*
Henry, Beulah Louise *WorInv*
Henry, Bill 1918- *WhoHol 92*
Henry, Brent Lee 1947- *WhoBlA 94*
Henry, Brian James 1961- *WhoWest 94*
Henry, Bruce Edward 1952- *WhoMW 93*
Henry, Buck 1930- *IntDcF 2-4, IntMPA 94, WhoAm 94, WhoCom, WhoHol 92*
Henry, C. Brad 1963- *WhoAmP 93*
Henry, Carl F. H. 1913- *IntWW 93*
Henry, Carl Ferdinand Howard 1913- *WhoAm 94*
Henry, Carol *DrAPF 93*
Henry, Carol 1930- *WhoAmP 93*
Henry, Carolyn Mary 1964- *WhoAmL 94*
Henry, Catherine 1949- *WhoMW 93*
Henry, Cecil James, Jr. 1937- *WhoMW 93*
Henry, Charles E. 1935- *WhoBlA 94*
Henry, Charles E. 1958- *WhoAmP 93*
Henry, Charles Jay 1950- *WhoAm 94, WhoScEn 94*
Henry, Charles Joseph 1936- *WhoFI 94*
Henry, Charles Patrick 1947- *WhoBlA 94, WhoWest 94*
Henry, Charles Robert 1937- *WhoAm 94*
Henry, Charlotte d1980 *WhoHol 92*
Henry, Claudette 1947- *WhoAm 94, WhoAmP 93*
Henry, Clifford, Jr. 1928- *WhoAmP 93*
Henry, Creagh d1946 *WhoHol 92*
Henry, Cyrus A., Jr. 1931- *WhoIns 94*
Henry, Daniel Joseph 1945- *WhoBlA 94*
Henry, David 1925- *Who 94*
Henry, David Allen 1950- *WhoWest 94*
Henry, David Howe, II 1918- *WhoAm 94*
Henry, David Winston 1932- *WhoBlA 94*
Henry, Deanne *WhoHol 92*
Henry, Deborah Jane 1952- *WhoMW 93*
Henry, DeLysle Leon 1935- *WhoAmL 94, WhoFI 94, WhoMW 93*
Henry, Denis (Aynsley) 1917- *Who 94*
Henry, Denis (Robert Maurice) 1931- *Who 94*
Henry, Desmond Paul 1921- *WrDr 94*
Henry, DeWitt *DrAPF 93*
Henry, DeWitt (Pawling, II) 1941- *WrDr 94*
Henry, DeWitt Pawling, II 1941- *WhoAm 94*
Henry, Douglas Selph, Jr. 1926- *WhoAmP 93*
Henry, Edgerton L. 1936- *WhoAmP 93*
Henry, Edward Frank 1923- *WhoFI 94, WhoMW 93*
Henry, Edward LeRoy 1921- *WhoAm 94*
Henry, Edwin Maurice, Jr. 1930- *WhoAmL 94*
Henry, Egbert Winston 1931- *WhoBlA 94*
Henry, Emmaline 1931- *WhoHol 92*
Henry, Forest T., Jr. 1937- *WhoBlA 94*
Henry, Frank d1963 *WhoHol 92*
Henry, Frank Haywood 1913- *WhoBlA 94*
Henry, Franklin M. d1993 *NewYTBS 93*
Henry, Frederick Edward 1947- *WhoAm 94*
Henry, Gale d1972 *WhoHol 92*
Henry, Gary Norman 1961- *WhoScEn 94*
Henry, Geoffrey Arama 1940- *Who 94*
Henry, George Mark 1955- *WhoAmP 93*
Henry, Gerald T. *WhoAmP 93*
Henry, Gerrit *DrAPF 93*
Henry, Gerrit Van Keuren 1950- *WhoAmA 93*
Henry, Gloria 1925- *WhoHol 92*
Henry, Gloria 1946- *WhoWomW 91*
Henry, Gloria Jean Mullins 1952- *WhoMW 93*
Henry, Gregg *WhoHol 92*
Henry, Hank d1981 *WhoHol 92*
Henry, Harriet Putnam 1923- *WhoAmL 94*
Henry, Howard Ward 1927- *WhoWest 94*
Henry, Howell George 1948- *WhoScEn 94*
Henry, I. Patricia 1947- *WhoBlA 94*
Henry, James 1731-1804 *WhAmRev*
Henry, James Holmes 1911- *Who 94*
Henry, James M. 1945- *WhoAmP 93*
Henry, James R. *WhoAmP 93*
Henry, James T., Sr. 1910- *WhoBlA 94*
Henry, Jay d1951 *WhoHol 92*
Henry, Jean *WhoAmA 93*
Henry, John d1958 *WhoHol 92*
Henry, John 1750-1798 *WhAmRev*
Henry, John A. 1904-1991 *WhAm 10*
Henry, John Dunklin 1937- *WhoAm 94*
Henry, John Joseph 1758-1811 *WhAmRev*
Henry, John Philip 1946- *Who 94*
Henry, John Porter, Jr. 1911- *WhoAm 94*
Henry, John Raymond 1943- *WhoAmA 93*
Henry, John Thomas 1933- *WhoAm 94, WhoMW 93*
Henry, John W., Jr. 1929- *WhoBlA 94*
Henry, Joseph 1797-1878 *AmSocL, WorInv, WorScD [port]*
Henry, Joseph King 1948- *WhoBlA 94, WhoMW 93*
Henry, Joseph Louis 1924- *IntWW 93, WhoAm 94, WhoBlA 94*
Henry, Joseph Patrick 1925- *WhoMW 93, WhoScEn 94*
Henry, Joseph R. 1945- *WhoWest 94*
Henry, Joseph W. 1916- *WhoAmP 93*
Henry, Joyce *WhoAmP 93*
Henry, Justin 1971- *IntMPA 94, WhoHol 92*
Henry, Karen Hawley 1943- *WhoWest 94*
Henry, Karl H. 1936- *WhoBlA 94*
Henry, Kathleen Marie 1950- *WhoMW 93*
Henry, Keith Edward 1953- *WhoScEn 94*
Henry, Kent Douglas 1964- *WhoScEn 94*
Henry, Laurie *DrAPF 93*
Henry, Laurin L(uther) 1921- *ConAu 43NR*
Henry, Laurin Luther 1921- *WhoAm 94*
Henry, Leanne Joan 1960- *WhoScEn 94*
Henry, Lenny 1958- *WhoHol 92*
Henry, Loren Fred 1947- *WhoAm 94*
Henry, Louis 1784-1836 *IntDcB*
Henry, Lowman Scott 1957- *WhoAmP 93*
Henry, Maeve 1960- *ConAu 142, SmATA 75 [port]*
Henry, Marcelett Campbell 1928- *WhoBlA 94*
Henry, Margaret 1914- *WhoAm 94*
Henry, Marguerite *WhoAm 94, WrDr 94*
Henry, Marion *ConAu 141, EncSF 93, SmATA 76*
Henry, Mark Alan 1958- *WhoAmP 93*
Henry, Matthew James 1954- *WhoScEn 94*
Henry, Merton Goodell 1926- *WhoAmP 93*
Henry, Michael F. 1946- *WhoAmL 94*
Henry, Mike 1941- *WhoHol 92*
Henry, Mildred M. Dalton *WhoBlA 94*
Henry, Morriss M. 1931- *WhoAmP 93*
Henry, Nancy Louise 1940- *WhoAmP 93*
Henry, Nicholas Llewellyn 1943- *WhoAm 94*
Henry, Norman Whitfield, III 1943- *WhoScEn 94*
Henry, O. 1862-1910 *RfGShF*
Henry, Pat d1982 *WhoHol 92*
Henry, Patricia Jean 1929- *WhoAm 94*
Henry, Patrick 1736-1799 *AmRev, HisWorL [port], WhAmRev [port]*
Henry, Patrick G. 1939- *WhoAm 94*
Henry, Paul B. d1993 *NewYTBS 93 [port]*
Henry, Paul B. 1942- *CngDr 93*
Henry, Paul Brentwood 1942- *WhoAmP 93*
Henry, Paul James 1927- *WhoAm 94*
Henry, Peter York 1951- *WhoAmL 94, WhoFI 94*
Henry, Philip Lawrence 1940- *WhoWest 94*
Henry, Phillip Michael 1953- *WhoMW 93*
Henry, Pierre 1927- *IntWW 93*
Henry, Ragan A. 1934- *AfrAmAl 6, WhoAm 94*
Henry, Rebecca Ann 1961- *WhoMW 93*
Henry, Rene Arthur, Jr. 1933- *WhoAm 94*
Henry, Richard Anthony 1951- *WhoWest 94*
Henry, Richard Conn 1940- *WhoAm 94*
Henry, Richard Joseph 1954- *WhoWest 94*
Henry, Robert d1971 *WhoHol 92*
Henry, Robert 1933- *WhoAmA 93*
Henry, Robert Charles 1929- *WhoAmP 93*
Henry, Robert Clayton 1923- *WhoBlA 94*
Henry, Robert H. 1953- *WhoAmP 93*
Henry, Robert John 1950- *WhoAm 94, WhoAmL 94*
Henry, Ronald James Whyte 1940- *WhoAm 94*
Henry, Roy B. 1944- *WhoFI 94*
Henry, Roy Monroe 1939- *WhoFI 94, WhoMW 93*
Henry, Samuel Dudley 1947- *WhoBlA 94*
Henry, Samuel James 1936- *WhoAm 94*
Henry, Sara Corrington 1942- *WhoAmA 93*
Henry, Scott 1967- *WhoFI 94*
Henry, Shirley Ann 1937- *WhoWest 94*
Henry, Steven Carl 1948- *WhoAm 94*
Henry, Susan Armstrong 1946- *WhoAm 94*
Henry, Sylvia Diane 1938- *WhoAmP 93*
Henry, Taylor Hill, Jr. 1935- *WhoFI 94*
Henry, Terry Jay 1937- *WhoMW 93*
Henry, Theodore Lynn 1949- *WhoScEn 94*
Henry, Thomas 1934- *WhoBlA 94*
Henry, Thomas Cradock d1993 *Who 94N*
Henry, Tom Browne d1980 *WhoHol 92*
Henry, Trevor (Ernest) 1902- *Who 94*
Henry, Victor d1985 *WhoHol 92*
Henry, Virgil Dwight 1953- *WhoAmP 93*
Henry, Waights Gibbs, Jr. 1910-1989 *WhAm 10*
Henry, Walter L. 1941- *WhoAm 94, WhoWest 94*
Henry, Walter Lester, Jr. 1915- *WhoAm 94, WhoBlA 94*
Henry, Warren Elliott 1909- *WhoBlA 94*
Henry, Wayne Burton 1945- *WhoAm 94*
Henry, Wendy Ann *Who 94*
Henry, Wilbur d1952 *ProFbHF*
Henry, Will 1912- *WrDr 94*

Herbert, Victor Daniel 1927- *WhoScEn 94*
Herbert, Victor James 1917- *WhoAm 94*
Herbert, Walter William 1934- *IntWW 93, Who 94*
Herbert, William *EncSF 93*
Herbert, William Carlisle 1947- *WhoAmL 94*
Herbert, William Penry Millwarden 1921- *Who 94*
Herbert, William Valentine 1936- *IntWW 93*
Herbert, Zbigniew 1924- *ConWorW 93, IntWW 93*
Herbert-Jones, Hugh (Hugo) Jarrett 1922- *Who 94*
Herbich, John Bronislaw 1922- *WhoAm 94*
Herbig, George Howard 1920- *IntWW 93, WhoAm 94*
Herbig, Gunther 1931- *IntWW 93, WhoAm 94*
Herbison, Jean (Marjory) 1923- *Who 94*
Herbison, John Steve 1939- *WhoFI 94, WhoWest 94*
Herbison, Margaret McCrorie 1907- *Who 94*
Herbison, Priscilla Joan 1943- *WhoMW 93*
Herbison, Timothy Allen 1955- *WhoMW 93*
Herbits, Stephen Edward 1942- *WhoAm 94, WhoFI 94*
Herblock 1909- *WhoAm 94*
Herbolsheimer, Robert Tilton 1954- *WhoAmL 94*
Herbst, Arthur Lee 1931- *WhoAm 94*
Herbst, Axel 1918- *IntWW 93*
Herbst, David George 1952- *WhoFI 94*
Herbst, David W. 1952- *WhoAmL 94*
Herbst, Della Mae 1935- *WhoAmP 93*
Herbst, Edward Ian 1945- *WhoFI 94*
Herbst, Jan Francis 1947- *WhoAm 94*
Herbst, Jonathan D. 1946- *WhoAmL 94*
Herbst, Josephine 1892-1969 *BlmGWL*
Herbst, Judith 1947- *SmATA 74 [port]*
Herbst, Jurgen 1928- *WhoAm 94, WhoMW 93, WrDr 94*
Herbst, Marcia Anne 1948- *WhoAmP 93*
Herbst, Marie A. 1928- *WhoAmP 93*
Herbst, Robert LeRoy 1935- *WhoAm 94, WhoAmP 93*
Herbst, Todd Leslie 1952- *WhoAmL 94*
Herbster, James Richard 1941- *WhoFI 94*
Herbster, William Gibson 1933- *WhoAm 94*
Herbstreith, Yvonne Mae 1942- *WhoMW 93*
Herch, Frank Alan 1949- *WhoAm 94, WhoAmL 94*
Hercigonja, Nikola 1911- *NewGrDO*
Herck, Paul van *EncSF 93*
Hercules, David Michael 1932- *WhoAm 94, WhoScEn 94*
Hercules, Frank E. M. 1917- *WhoBlA 94*
Hercules, Ronald James 1950- *WhoMW 93*
Hercus, (Margaret) Ann 1942- *Who 94*
Hercus, Luise Anna 1926- *IntWW 93*
Hercus, Margaret Ann 1942- *IntWW 93*
Herczynski, Andrzej 1956- *WhoScEn 94*
Herd, Carla *WhoHol 92*
Herd, Frederick Charles 1915- *Who 94*
Herd, Harold S. 1918- *WhoAmP 93*
Herd, Harold Shields 1918- *WhoAmL 94, WhoMW 93*
Herd, John E. 1932- *WhoBlA 94*
Herd, Richard *WhoHol 92*
Herda, Thilo H. 1949- *WhoIns 94*
Herdan, Innes 1911- *ConAu 142*
Herdeg, Howard Brian 1929- *WhoWest 94*
Herdeg, Klaus 1937- *WrDr 94*
Herder, Johann Gottfried 1744-1803 *NewGrDO*
Herder, Robert H. *WhoMW 93*
Herder, Stephen Rendell 1928- *WhoAm 94*
Herding, Klaus 1939- *ConAu 140*
Herdle, Lee A. 1954- *WhoFI 94*
Herdman, (John) Mark (Ambrose) 1932- *Who 94*
Herdon, Christopher de Lancy 1928- *Who 94*
Herdrich, Norman Wesley 1942- *WhoAm 94, WhoWest 94*
Heredia, Luis 1951- *WhoHisp 94*
Hereford, Archdeacon of *Who 94*
Hereford, Bishop of 1935- *Who 94*
Hereford, Dean of *Who 94*
Hereford, Viscount 1932- *Who 94*
Hereford, Frank Loucks, Jr. 1923- *WhoAm 94*
Hereford, Sonnie Wellington, III 1931- *WhoBlA 94*
Hereman, Willy Alois Maria 1954- *WhoWest 94*
Heremans, Jean d1970 *WhoHol 92*

Heremans, Joseph Pierre 1953- *WhoScEn 94*
Heren, Louis 1919- *WrDr 94*
Heren, Louis Philip 1919- *Who 94*
Herenton, W. W. *WhoAmP 93*
Herenton, Willie W. 1940- *WhoBlA 94*
Herenton, Willie W. 1943- *WhoAm 94*
Hereward the Great fl. 11th cent.- *BlmGEL*
Herf, Charles W. 1944- *WhoAm 94*
Herfel, Gary L. 1942- *WhoAmL 94*
Herfield, Phyllis 1947- *WhoAmA 93*
Herford, Geoffrey Vernon Brooke 1905- *Who 94*
Herford, John A. 1946- *WhoAmL 94*
Herford, Will d1934 *WhoHol 92*
Herforth, Lieselott 1916- *IntWW 93*
Herft, Roger Adrian *Who 94*
Herge, Henry Curtis, Sr. 1905- *WhoAm 94*
Herge, J. Curtis 1938- *WhoAm 94, WhoAmL 94*
Hergenhan, Joyce 1941- *WhoFI 94*
Hergenhan, Kenneth William 1931- *WhoAm 94*
Hergenroeder, Henry Robert, Jr. 1943- *WhoAmP 93*
Herger, Wally 1945- *CngDr 93*
Herger, Wally W., Jr. 1945- *WhoAm 94, WhoAmP 93, WhoWest 94*
Hergert, David Joseph 1952- *WhoScEn 94*
Hergert, Richard Gary 1949- *WhoWest 94*
Herget, Victoria Jean 1951- *WhoFI 94*
Herguth, Robert John 1926- *WhoAm 94*
Heriat, Philippe d1971 *WhoHol 92*
Heric, John F. 1942- *WhoAmA 93*
Hericourt, Jenny d' *BlmGWL*
Herincx, Raimund 1927- *IntWW 93*
Herincx, Raimund (Frederick) 1927- *NewGrDO*
Hering, Doris Minnie 1920- *WhoAm 94*
Hering, Gerhard F. 1908- *IntWW 93*
Hering, Grant Barnitz 1936- *WhoAm 94*
Hering, Harry 1887-1967 *WhoAmA 93N*
Hering, Henry 1874-1949 *WhoAmA 93N*
Hering, Jurgen 1937- *IntWW 93*
Hering, Robert Gustave 1934- *WhoAm 94*
Hering, William Marshall 1940- *WhoWest 94*
Herington, Anita Dixon 1949- *WhoMW 93*
Herington, Cecil John 1924- *WhoAm 94*
Herington, Mary Ellen 1957- *WhoMW 93*
Herink, Richie 1932- *WhoFI 94*
Heriot, Alexander John 1914- *Who 94*
Heris, Toni 1932- *WhoAm 94*
Heritage, John Langdon 1931- *Who 94*
Heritage, Robert 1927- *Who 94*
Heritage, Thomas Charles 1908- *Who 94*
Heritier, Charles Andre 1931- *WhoScEn 94*
Herjulfsson, Bjarni fl. 98-?- *WhWE*
Herke, Horst W. 1931- *IntWW 93*
Herkes, Robert N. 1931- *WhoAmP 93*
Herkhuf *WhWE*
Herkimer, Allen Gillman, Jr. 1924- *WhoAm 94*
Herkimer, Nicholas d1777 *AmRev*
Herkimer, Nicholas 1728-1777 *WhAmRev [port]*
Herking, Ursula d1974 *WhoHol 92*
Herklots, Carl Alexander 1759-1830 *NewGrDO*
Herkner, Bernadette Kay 1947- *WhoMW 93*
Herkner-Ballance, Mildred Luella 1915- *WhoMW 93*
Herkness, Lindsay Coates, III 1943- *WhoAm 94*
Herkstroter, Cornelius Antonius Johannes 1937- *IntWW 93*
Herlach, Mark Dayton 1950- *WhoAmL 94*
Herland, Hugh c. 1330-1411 *DcNaB MP*
Herlands, E. Ward *DrAPF 93*
Herlands, Jonathan 1951- *WhoAmL 94*
Herle, William d1589? *DcNaB MP*
Herlea, Nicolae 1927- *NewGrDO*
Herlein, Lillian d1971 *WhoHol 92*
Herlie, Eileen 1919- *WhoHol 92*
Herlie, Eileen 1920- *Who 94*
Herlihy, David Joseph 1930-1991 *WhAm 10*
Herlihy, Ed *WhoHol 92*
Herlihy, Ernest Herbert 1895- *WhAm 10*
Herlihy, James Edward 1942- *WhoAm 94*
Herlihy, James Leo *DrAPF 93*
Herlihy, James Leo d1993 *NewYTBS 93 [port]*
Herlihy, James Leo 1927- *ConDr 93, WhoAm 94, WhoHol 92, WrDr 94*
Herlihy, Robert Edward 1931- *WhoAm 94*
Herlihy, Thomas Mortimer 1953- *WhoAmL 94*
Herlin, Jacques *WhoHol 92*
Herling, John 1905- *WhoAm 94*
Herling, Michael *WhoAm 94, WhoFI 94*

Herlinger, Daniel Robert 1946- *WhoAm 94, WhoWest 94*
Herlitzka, Ina Lynn 1955- *WhoFI 94, WhoMW 93*
Herlitzka, Roberto *WhoHol 92*
Herlocker, John Robert 1935- *WhoWest 94*
Herlong, Albert Sydney, Jr. 1909- *WhoAmP 93*
Herlong, D. C. *WhoFI 94*
Herlong, Henry Michael, Jr. 1944- *WhoAm 94, WhoAmL 94*
Herlth, Robert 1893-1962 *IntDcF 2-4*
Hermach, Francis Lewis 1917- *WhoAm 94*
Herman, Al d1958 *WhoHol 92*
Herman, Alan David 1947- *WhoAmA 93*
Herman, Alexis M. *WhoAm 94*
Herman, Alexis M. 1947- *WhoAmP 93, WhoBlA 94*
Herman, Andrea Maxine 1938- *WhoAm 94, WhoWest 94*
Herman, Barbara F. 1941- *WhoAm 94*
Herman, Barbara Helen 1950- *WhoScEn 94*
Herman, Bernard L. 1951- *ConAu 140*
Herman, Brian Joesph 1958- *WhoAmL 94*
Herman, Charles Jacob 1937- *WhoAmL 94*
Herman, Chester Joseph 1941- *WhoAm 94*
Herman, Chloe Anna 1937- *WhoFI 94, WhoMW 93*
Herman, Dennis Andrew 1946- *WhoIns 94*
Herman, Edith Carol 1944- *WhoAm 94, WhoFI 94*
Herman, George Adam 1928- *WhoWest 94*
Herman, George Edward 1920- *WhoAm 94*
Herman, George Richard 1925- *WrDr 94*
Herman, Grace *DrAPF 93*
Herman, Hank 1949- *WhoAm 94*
Herman, Harry Martin, III 1953- *WhoWest 94*
Herman, Herbert 1934- *WhoAm 94*
Herman, Irving Leonard 1920- *WhoAm 94*
Herman, James Richard 1924- *WhoAm 94*
Herman, James Wiley 1946- *WhoWest 94*
Herman, Jay d1928 *WhoHol 92*
Herman, Jerry *WhoAm 94*
Herman, Joan E. 1953- *WhoIns 94*
Herman, Joan Elizabeth 1953- *WhoAm 94*
Herman, Joanna *DrAPF 93*
Herman, John Hughes 1945- *WhoAmL 94*
Herman, John L., Jr. 1949- *WhoFI 94*
Herman, Josef 1911- *Who 94*
Herman, Judith Lewis 1942- *ConAu 142*
Herman, Katherine Belle 1963- *WhoAmA 93*
Herman, Kathleen Virgil 1942- *WhoBlA 94*
Herman, Kenneth 1927- *WhoAm 94*
Herman, Kenneth Beaumont 1944- *WhoAm 94*
Herman, Kenneth Neil 1954- *WhoAm 94*
Herman, Kurt 1930- *WhoFI 94*
Herman, Larry Marvin 1951- *WhoScEn 94*
Herman, Lloyd Eldred 1936- *WhoAmA 93*
Herman, Lynn Briggs 1956- *WhoAmP 93*
Herman, Mark B. 1933- *WhoAmP 93*
Herman, Michael Alan 1945- *WhoWest 94*
Herman, Michael Harry 1954- *WhoScEn 94, WhoWest 94*
Herman, Michelle *DrAPF 93*
Herman, Michelle 1955- *WrDr 94*
Herman, Milton d1951 *WhoHol 92*
Herman, Norman 1924- *IntMPA 94*
Herman, Paul *WhoHol 92*
Herman, Paula Lacey 1948- *WhoAm 94, WhoAmL 94*
Herman, Pee-Wee 1952- *IntMPA 94, WhoCom [port], WhoHol 92*
Herman, Peter Windley 1944- *WhoAmL 94*
Herman, Pinky 1905- *IntMPA 94*
Herman, Robert 1914- *WhoAm 94, WhoScEn 94*
Herman, Robert Dixon 1911-1990 *WhAm 10*
Herman, Robert Lewis 1927- *WhoAm 94, WhoFI 94*
Herman, Robert S. 1919- *WhoAm 94*
Herman, Roger 1947- *WhoAmA 93*
Herman, Roger Eliot 1943- *WhoAm 94*
Herman, Ronald Charles 1948- *WhoWest 94*
Herman, Roy Alan 1943- *WhoMW 93*
Herman, Russ Michel 1942- *WhoAmL 94*
Herman, Sarah Andrews 1952- *WhoAmL 94*
Herman, Sidney N. 1953- *WhoAm 94*
Herman, Stephen Allen 1943- *WhoAm 94, WhoAmL 94*

Herman, Stephen Charles 1951- *WhoAmL 94*
Herman, Stewart Winfield 1948- *WhoMW 93*
Herman, Theodore L. 1936- *WhoIns 94*
Herman, Timothy J. 1944- *WhoAmL 94*
Herman, Tommy d1972 *WhoHol 92*
Herman, Vic *WhoAmA 94*
Herman, Walter E., III 1943- *WhoAmL 94*
Herman, Wayne Delton 1964- *WhoMW 93*
Herman, William 1907-1992 *AnObit 1992*
Herman, William Elsworth 1948- *WhoScEn 94*
Herman, William Sparkes 1931- *WhoAm 94*
Herman, Woody d1987 *WhoHol 92*
Hermance, Lyle Herbert 1939- *WhoMW 93*
Hermanies, John Hans 1922- *WhoAm 94, WhoAmP 93*
Hermaniuk, Maxim 1911- *IntWW 93, WhoAm 94, WhoMW 93*
Herman-Michielsens, Lucienne 1926- *WhoWomW 91*
Hermann, Alexander Henry Baxter 1917- *Who 94*
Hermann, Allen Max 1938- *WhoAm 94*
Hermann, Betty Jo 1934- *WhoAmP 93*
Hermann, Donald F. 1921- *WhoAmP 93*
Hermann, Donald Harold James 1943- *WhoAmL 94, WhoFI 94, WhoMW 93*
Hermann, Edward Robert 1920- *WhoAm 94, WhoMW 93*
Hermann, Francis Xavier 1943- *WhoAmL 94*
Hermann, Irm *WhoHol 92*
Hermann, James Ray 1946- *WhoWest 94*
Hermann, John Arthur 1943- *WhoScEn 94*
Hermann, Joseph N. *WhoAmP 93*
Hermann, M(ildred) L. *WhoAmA 93*
Hermann, Paul David 1925- *WhoAm 94*
Hermann, Philip J. 1916- *WhoAm 94, WhoAmL 94*
Hermann, Philip J(ay) 1916- *ConAu 41NR*
Hermann, Robert Jay 1933- *WhoAm 94, WhoAmP 93*
Hermann, Robert John 1944- *WhoAm 94, WhoAmL 94*
Hermann, Robert Ringen 1923- *WhoAm 94*
Hermann, Roland 1936- *NewGrDO*
Hermann, Steven Istvan 1934- *WhoAm 94, WhoFI 94*
Hermann, Thomas George 1935- *WhoAmL 94*
Hermann, William Henry 1924- *WhoAm 94*
Hermannsson, Steingrimur 1928- *IntWW 93*
Hermanovski, Egils P. 1947-1992 *WhAm 10*
Hermans, Anna 1944- *WhoWomW 91*
Hermans, Christopher 1936- *IntWW 93*
Hermans, Colin Olmsted 1936- *WhoAm 94*
Hermans, Hubert John 1937- *WhoScEn 94*
Hermans, Willem Frederik 1921- *ConWorW 93*
Hermanson, Theodore Harry 1965- *WhoScEn 94*
Hermanson Ogilvie, Judith 1945- *WhoAm 94*
Hermanuz, Ghislaine *WhoBlA 94*
Hermaszewski, Miroslaw 1941- *IntWW 93*
Hermening, Kevin J. 1959- *WhoAmP 93*
Hermer, Julius 1933- *Who 94*
Hermes, John N. 1946- *WhoAmL 94*
Hermes, Marjory Ruth 1931- *WhoMW 93*
Hermes, Patricia 1936- *TwCYAW*
Hermes, Peter G. 1947- *WhoAmL 94*
Hermes, Suzanne Elizabeth 1947- *WhoWest 94*
Hermida, Israel Octavio 1940- *WhoHisp 94*
Hermine, Hilda d1975 *WhoHol 92*
Hermine's Midgets *WhoHol 92*
Herminghouse, Patricia Anne 1940- *WhoAm 94*
Hermo, Alfonso Davila 1931- *WhoHisp 94*
Hermodsson, Elisabet Hermine 1927- *BlmGWL*
Hermon, Bev 1933- *WhoAmP 93*
Hermon, John (Charles) 1928- *IntWW 93, Who 94*
Hermon, Peter Michael Robert 1928- *Who 94*
Hermon-Hodge *Who 94*
Hermon-Taylor, John 1936- *Who 94*
Hermosillo, Danny James 1962- *WhoHisp 94*
Hermosillo, Maria del Carmen 1950- *WhoHisp 94*
Hermsen, James R. 1945- *WhoAmL 94*

Hermsen, Robert William 1934- *WhoScEn 94*
Hermsen, Terry *DrAPF 93*
Hern, Joseph George, Jr. 1956- *WhoAmL 94*
Hern, Oliver, Jr. *WhoHisp 94*
Hern, Pepe *WhoHol 92*
Hern, William Richard 1921- *Who 94*
Hernadi, Gyula *EncSF 93*
Hernadi, Paul 1936- *ConAu 42NR*
Hernady, Bertalan Fred 1927- *WhoScEn 94*
Hernaman-Johnson, Francis 1879-1949 *EncSF 93*
Hernandez, Aileen Clarke 1926- *WhoBlA 94*
Hernandez, Albert L. 1924- *WhoHisp 94*
Hernandez, Albert P. 1948- *WhoHisp 94*
Hernandez, Alex *WhoHisp 94*
Hernández, Alfonso V. 1937- *WhoHisp 94*
Hernandez, Andres Ramon 1952- *WhoHisp 94*
Hernández, Andrew 1951- *WhoHisp 94*
Hernandez, Andrew Charles 1954- *WhoHisp 94*
Hernandez, Anna d1945 *WhoHol 92*
Hernandez, Anthony Louis 1947- *WhoAmA 93*
Hernandez, Anthony Wayne 1953- *WhoAmL 94*
Hernández, Antonia 1948- *WhoHisp 94*
Hernández, Antonio 1938- *WhoHisp 94*
Hernandez, Arturo 1947- *WhoHisp 94*
Hernandez, Augustin 1937- *WhoHisp 94*
Hernandez, Barbara *DrAPF 93*
Hernández, Benigno Carlos 1917- *WhoHisp 94*
Hernandez, Berta Esperanza 1952- *WhoAmL 94*
Hernandez, Carlos 1967- *WhoHisp 94*
Hernández, César 1959- *WhoHisp 94*
Hernandez, Christine 1951- *WhoAmP 93, WhoHisp 94*
Hernández, Cirilo C. 1929- *WhoHisp 94*
Hernandez, Cruz Guajardo 1942- *WhoAmP 93*
Hernandez, David Andrade 1935- *WhoHisp 94*
Hernandez, David P. 1936- *WhoHisp 94*
Hernandez, Diego Edyl 1934- *WhoHisp 94*
Hernandez, Edward 1946- *WhoHisp 94*
Hernandez, Encarnacion 1946- *WhoHisp 94*
Hernandez, Enrique 1951- *WhoHisp 94*
Hernandez, Ernest G. 1931- *WhoHisp 94*
Hernandez, Eva 1958- *WhoHisp 94*
Hernández, Evelyn 1958- *WhoHisp 94*
Hernandez, Felix, Jr. 1954- *WhoHisp 94*
Hernandez, Fernando Vargas 1939- *WhoAmL 94, WhoWest 94*
Hernández, Frances 1926- *WhoHisp 94*
Hernandez, Francis Xavier 1965- *WhoHisp 94*
Hernandez, Gary *WhoHisp 94*
Hernandez, Gary J. 1953- *WhoHisp 94*
Hernandez, George d1922 *WhoHol 92*
Hernandez, George S. 1934- *WhoHisp 94*
Hernandez, George Stephen, Jr. 1934- *WhoAmP 93*
Hernandez, Gilberto Juan 1943- *WhoFI 94*
Hernández, Gladys 1951- *WhoHisp 94*
Hernandez, Guillermo Villanueva 1954- *WhoHisp 94*
Hernandez, Hector *WhoHisp 94*
Hernandez, Hector Rene 1953- *WhoHisp 94*
Hernández, Henry O., Jr. 1956- *WhoHisp 94*
Hernández, Hilda *WhoHisp 94*
Hernandez, Humberto *WhoHisp 94*
Hernandez, Humberto 1949- *WhoHisp 94*
Hernández, Irene Beltrán 1945- *WhoHisp 94*
Hernandez, Irene C. *WhoHisp 94*
Hernández, Isabel C. 1959- *WhoHisp 94*
Hernandez, J. Luis *WhoHisp 94*
Hernandez, Jacqueline Charmaine 1960- *WhoAmL 94*
Hernandez, James, Jr. 1942- *WhoHisp 94*
Hernandez, James S. 1954- *WhoHisp 94*
Hernandez, Jennifer Lynn 1959- *WhoHisp 94*
Hernández, Jeremy 1966- *WhoHisp 94*
Hernandez, Jesus Navarro 1935- *WhoHisp 94*
Hernandez, Jesus Ramon 1938- *WhoHisp 94*
Hernandez, Jo Farb 1952- *WhoAm 94, WhoAmA 93, WhoWest 94*
Hernandez, Joe d1972 *WhoHol 92*
Hernandez, Joe George 1946- *WhoHisp 94*
Hernandez, Joe L. 1933- *WhoAmP 93*
Hernandez, Joe V. *WhoHisp 94*
Hernandez, Joel Rosario *WhoAmP 93*
Hernandez, John 1952- *WhoAmA 93*
Hernandez, John Peter 1940- *WhoScEn 94*
Hernández, John R. 1955- *WhoHisp 94*
Hernandez, John S. 1945- *WhoAmP 93*
Hernandez, John Stephen 1945- *WhoHisp 94*
Hernandez, John Whitlock 1929- *WhoAmP 93, WhoHisp 94*
Hernandez, José 1935- *WhoHisp 94*
Hernandez, Jose Alberto 1949- *WhoHisp 94*
Hernandez, Jose Amaro 1930- *WhoHisp 94*
Hernandez, Jose Antonio 1951- *WhoHisp 94*
Hernandez, Jose E. 1957- *WhoHisp 94*
Hernandez, Jose Manuel 1925- *WhoHisp 94*
Hernandez, Joseph 1935- *WhoHisp 94*
Hernandez, Joseph Anthony 1950- *WhoHisp 94*
Hernández, Juan Donaldo 1933- *WhoHisp 94*
Hernandez, Juan Josef Perez *WhWE*
Hernández, Juana Amelia *WhoHisp 94*
Hernandez, Juano d1970 *WhoHol 92*
Hernandez, Julio, Jr. 1920- *WhoHisp 94*
Hernandez, Justin Joseph 1952- *WhoHisp 94*
Hernandez, Keith 1953- *WhoHisp 94*
Hernandez, Leodoro 1930- *WhoHisp 94*
Hernandez, Leticia Sanchez-Mendoza 1956- *WhoHisp 94*
Hernandez, Librada 1955- *WhoHisp 94*
Hernandez, Lillian A. 1959- *WhoWest 94*
Hernández, Lisa 1962- *WhoHisp 94*
Hernandez, Louis Fernando 1952- *WhoHisp 94*
Hernandez, Luis Garcia 1941- *WhoHisp 94*
Hernandez, Luisa Josefina 1928- *BlmGWL, ConWorW 93, IntDcT 2*
Hernández, Luz Corpi 1945- *WhoHisp 94*
Hernandez, Mack Ray 1944- *WhoHisp 94*
Hernandez, Malu *WhoHisp 94*
Hernandez, Manny *WhoHisp 94*
Hernandez, Manuel 1936- *WhoHisp 94*
Hernández, Manuel, Jr. 1951- *WhoHisp 94*
Hernández, Marcos, Jr. 1950- *WhoHisp 94*
Hernandez, Margaret I. 1953- *WhoHisp 94*
Hernandez, Maria *WhoHisp 94*
Hernández, María A. 1949- *WhoHisp 94*
Hernandez, Marie-Theresa 1952- *WhoHisp 94*
Hernandez, Marlissa 1966- *WhoHisp 94*
Hernandez, Mary N. 1940- *WhoBlA 94*
Hernandez, Medardo Concepcion 1947- *WhoScEn 94*
Hernandez, Michael A. *WhoHisp 94*
Hernandez, Michael Bruington 1960- *WhoHisp 94*
Hernandez, Miguel 1910-1942 *DcLB 134 [port]*
Hernández, Miguel Angel, Jr. 1941- *WhoHisp 94*
Hernández, Miguel José 1938- *WhoHisp 94*
Hernandez, Mike *WhoAmP 93, WhoHisp 94*
Hernandez, Mike A. *WhoHisp 94*
Hernández, Milagros 1938- *WhoHisp 94*
Hernández, Nicolás, Jr. 1953- *WhoHisp 94*
Hernandez, Noel *WhoHisp 94*
Hernández, Onésimo 1925- *WhoHisp 94*
Hernandez, Paul F. 1954- *WhoHisp 94*
Hernandez, Pedro R., Jr. 1941- *WhoHisp 94*
Hernández, Peggy 1956- *WhoHisp 94*
Hernandez, Philip Anthony 1940- *WhoAmP 93, WhoHisp 94*
Hernandez, Ramon R. 1936- *WhoHisp 94*
Hernandez, Ramon Robert 1936- *WhoMW 93*
Hernandez, Randal J. 1959- *WhoHisp 94*
Hernandez, Raoul Emilio 1955- *WhoHisp 94*
Hernandez, Raul Antonio 1962- *WhoHisp 94*
Hernandez, Rene *WhoHisp 94*
Hernandez, Richard Froylan 1943- *WhoHisp 94*
Hernandez, Richard G. 1953- *WhoHisp 94*
Hernandez, Rick Mark 1966- *WhoWest 94*
Hernandez, Rita Rios 1953- *WhoHisp 94*
Hernandez, Robert Louis 1947- *WhoHisp 94*
Hernandez, Robert M. *WhoHisp 94*
Hernandez, Robert Michael 1945- *WhoAmP 93, WhoHisp 94*
Hernandez, Robert Michael 1953- *WhoAmP 93*
Hernandez, Roberto 1964- *WhoHisp 94*
Hernandez, Roberto F. 1948- *WhoHisp 94*
Hernandez, Roger, Jr. 1958- *WhoHisp 94*
Hernandez, Roger Emilio 1955- *WhoHisp 94*
Hernandez, Roland A. 1957- *WhoHisp 94*
Hernandez, Ronald J. *WhoHisp 94*
Hernandez, Ruben 1949- *WhoHisp 94*
Hernandez, Sam 1948- *WhoAmA 93, WhoHisp 94*
Hernandez, Samuel E. 1935- *WhoHisp 94*
Hernandez, Santiago 1947- *WhoHisp 94*
Hernandez, Sergio Anthony 1946- *WhoHisp 94*
Hernández, Sigfredo Augusto 1954- *WhoHisp 94*
Hernandez, Susan 1960- *WhoHisp 94*
Hernandez, Teme Paul 1919- *WhoHisp 94*
Hernandez, Teresa V. *WhoHisp 94*
Hernandez, Tony *WhoHisp 94*
Hernandez, Tony 1951- *WhoAmP 93*
Hernandez, Tony J. 1951- *WhoWest 94*
Hernandez, Victoria 1948- *WhoHisp 94*
Hernandez, Wanda Grace 1942- *WhoMW 93*
Hernandez, Wilbert Eduardo 1916- *WhoScEn 94*
Hernandez, William Hector, Jr. 1930- *WhoAm 94, WhoHisp 94*
Hernandez, Xavier 1965- *WhoHisp 94*
Hernandez Agosto, Miguel A. 1927- *WhoAmP 93*
Hernández-Agosto, Miguel Angel 1927- *WhoHisp 94*
Hernandez Alcerro, Jorge Ramon 1948- *IntWW 93*
Hernandez-Avila, Manuel Luis 1935- *WhoAm 94, WhoHisp 94*
Hernandez Balaguer, Carmen Rosa *WhoWomW 91*
Hernandez Cervantes, Hector 1923- *IntWW 93*
Hernandez Colon, Rafael 1936- *IntWW 93, WhoAmP 93, WhoHisp 94*
Hernandez-Cruz, Luis *WhoAmA 93*
Hernandez-Cruz, Luis 1936- *WhoAm 94*
Hernandez Cruz, Victor *DrAPF 93*
Hernández-Delgado, Julio Luis 1953- *WhoHisp 94*
Hernández de López, Ana María 1930- *WhoHisp 94*
Hernandez-Denton, Federico 1944- *WhoAm 94, WhoAmL 94, WhoAmP 93*
Hernández-G., Manuel de Jesús 1949- *WhoHisp 94*
Hernandez-Gonzalez, Gloria Maria 1959- *WhoAmL 94*
Hernández Jimenez, Consuelo *WhoHisp 94*
Hernandez Mancha, Antonio *IntWW 93*
Hernandez-Martich, Jose David 1955- *WhoScEn 94*
Hernández-Miyares, Julio Enrique 1931- *WhoHisp 94*
Hernandez-Morales, Roberto Eduardo 1931- *WhoHisp 94*
Hernández-Piñero, Sally *WhoHisp 94*
Hernandez-Ramos, Florence Dolores 1950- *WhoHisp 94*
Hernandez-Reyes, Victor 1936- *WhoHisp 94*
Hernández-Rivera, Andrés 1935- *WhoHisp 94*
Hernandez-Sanchez, Juan Longino 1928- *WhoScEn 94*
Hernandez-Schneider, Ana Maria 1959- *WhoHisp 94*
Hernandez-Serna, Isabel 1945- *WhoHisp 94*
Hernandez-Stephens, Racquel Coreen 1970- *WhoWest 94*
Hernandez Toledo, Rene Antonio 1943- *WhoHisp 94*
Hernández Torres, Zaida *WhoHisp 94*
Hernandez-Vallejo, Evelyn 1954- *WhoHisp 94*
Hernandez von Hoff, Gladys Amanda *WhoHisp 94*
Hernando (y Palomar), Rafael (Jose Maria) 1822-1888 *NewGrDO*
Herndon, Charles Harbison 1915- *WhoAm 94*
Herndon, Claude Nash 1916- *WhoAm 94*
Herndon, Craig Garris 1947- *WhoBlA 94*
Herndon, David N. *WhoScEn 94*
Herndon, Douglas Michael 1951- *WhoFI 94*
Herndon, Gloria E. 1950- *WhoBlA 94*
Herndon, Harold Thomas, Sr. 1937- *WhoBlA 94*
Herndon, James 1925- *WhoBlA 94*
Herndon, James Francis 1929- *WhoAm 94*
Herndon, James Henry 1938- *WhoAm 94, WhoScEn 94*
Herndon, Lance H. 1955- *WhoBlA 94*
Herndon, Larry Lee 1953- *WhoBlA 94*
Herndon, Mark *WhoAm 94*
Herndon, Phillip George 1951- *WhoBlA 94*
Herndon, Robert McCulloch 1935- *WhoAm 94*
Herndon, Roy Clifford 1934- *WhoScEn 94*
Herndon, Terry (Eugene) 1939- *WrDr 94*
Herndon, Terry Eugene 1939- *WhoAm 94*
Herndon, William d1990 *WhoHol 92*
Herne, Chrystal d1950 *WhoHol 92*
Herne, James A. 1839-1901 *IntDcT 2*
Herne, Joseph 1639-1699 *DcNaB MP*
Hernes, Gudmund 1941- *WhoScEn 94*
Herniman, Ronald George 1923- *Who 94*
Hernon, Joseph Martin, Jr. 1936- *WhoAm 94*
Hernon, Richard Francis 1940- *WhoScEn 94*
Hernstadt, Judith Filenbaum 1942- *WhoAm 94*
Hernton, Calvin *DrAPF 93*
Hernton, Calvin C. 1933- *WrDr 94*
Hernton, Calvin Coolidge *WhoBlA 94*
Hero, Alfred Olivier, III 1955- *WhoMW 93*
Hero, Peter Decourcy 1942- *WhoAmA 93*
Herod, James, Jr. *WhoAmP 93*
Herodotus fl. 5th cent.BC- *BlmGEL*
Herodotus c. 490BC-420BC *WhWE*
Herod the Great *BlmGEL*
Herod the Great 73BC-4BC *HisWorL*
Heroet, Antoine 1492-1568 *GuFrLit 2*
Herold, Edward William d1993 *NewYTBS 93 [port]*
Herold, Edward William 1907- *WhoAm 94*
Herold, (Louis Joseph) Ferdinand 1791-1833 *NewGrDO*
Herold, Karl Guenter 1947- *WhoAm 94, WhoAmL 94*
Herold, Ralph Elliott 1919- *WhoWest 94*
Herold, Vilhelm Kristoffer 1865-1937 *NewGrDO*
Heron, Conrad (Frederick) 1916- *Who 94*
Heron, David Winston 1920- *WhoAm 94*
Heron, Joyce d1980 *WhoHol 92*
Heron, Julian Briscoe, Jr. 1939- *WhoAmL 94*
Heron, Michael Gilbert 1934- *Who 94*
Heron, Patrick 1920- *IntWW 93, Who 94, WrDr 94*
Heron, Raymond 1924- *Who 94*
Heron, Robert 1927- *Who 94*
Heron, Timothy Edward 1948- *WhoMW 93*
Heron, Wesley David 1949- *WhoFI 94*
Heron, William 1742-1819 *WhAmRev*
Heron-Allen, Edward *EncSF 93*
Heron-Maxwell, Nigel (Mellor) 1944- *Who 94*
Hero of Alexandria fl. 1st cent.- *WorInv*
Herophilus 4th cent.BC- *WorScD*
Herophyle *BlmGWL*
Heroult, Paul Louis Touissant 1863-1914 *WorInv*
Heroux, Claude 1942- *IntMPA 94*
Heroy, Susan *DrAPF 93*
Heroy, William Bayard, Jr. 1915- *WhoAm 94*
Herpe, David A. 1953- *WhoAm 94, WhoAmL 94*
Herpel, George Lloyd 1921- *WhoAm 94*
Herpst, Martha Jane 1911- *WhoAmA 93N*
Herpst, Robert Dix 1947- *WhoAmL 94*
Herr, Dan *IntWW 93N*
Herr, Dan 1917-1990 *WhAm 10*
Herr, Earl Binkley, Jr. 1928- *WhoFI 94, WhoMW 93*
Herr, James Michael 1943- *WhoAmL 94*
Herr, John Christian 1948- *WhoScEn 94*
Herr, Judy Ann 1941- *WhoMW 93*
Herr, Kenneth Julian 1927- *WhoAm 94*
Herr, King G. 1907- *WhoMW 93*
Herr, Leonard Jay 1928- *WhoMW 93*
Herr, Michael 1940- *WrDr 94*
Herr, Peter Helmut Friederich 1951- *WhoFI 94*
Herr, Richard 1922- *WhoAm 94, WhoWest 94*
Herr, Stanley Sholom 1945- *WhoAmL 94*
Herrad von Landsberg c. 1130-1195 *BlmGWL*
Herran, Manuel A. *WhoHisp 94*
Herrand, Marcel d1953 *WhoHol 92*
Herrbach, William Frank 1946- *WhoAmL 94*
Herregat, Guy-Georges Jacques 1939- *WhoAm 94, WhoFI 94*
Herrell, Astor Yeary 1935- *WhoBlA 94*
Herren, Albert R. *WhoAmP 93*
Herren, Roger *WhoHol 92*
Herrera, Albert A. 1950- *WhoHisp 94*
Herrera, Alberto, Jr. 1947- *WhoMW 93*
Herrera, Alfred J. *WhoHisp 94*
Herrera, Bertha Garza de 1927- *WhoHisp 94*
Herrera, C. Andrea 1959- *WhoHisp 94*
Herrera, Carl *WhoHisp 94*
Herrera, Carlos E. 1957- *WhoHisp 94*
Herrera, Carmen 1915- *WhoAmA 93, WhoHisp 94*

Herrera, Carolina 1939- *WhoAm 94, WhoHisp 94*
Herrera, Danilo V. 1956- *WhoHisp 94*
Herrera, Eduardo Antonio 1953- *WhoHisp 94*
Herrera, Esau Ruiz 1950- *WhoHisp 94*
Herrera, Estela Maris 1943- *WhoHisp 94*
Herrera, Fermín 1947- *WhoHisp 94*
Herrera, Fidel Michael 1939- *WhoHisp 94*
Herrera, Francisco Rafael 1943- *WhoWest 94*
Herrera, Frank 1942- *WhoHisp 94*
Herrera, Frank G. 1943- *WhoHisp 94*
Herrera, George 1957- *WhoHisp 94*
Herrera, Hector H. 1934- *WhoHisp 94*
Herrera, Henry R. 1942- *WhoHisp 94*
Herrera, Herman Richard 1940- *WhoHisp 94*
Herrera, John *WhoAm 94, WhoWest 94*
Herrera, Jorge d1981 *IntDcF 2-4*
Herrera, Jorge Luis 1956- *WhoHisp 94*
Herrera, José Alvarez 1917- *WhoHisp 94*
Herrera, Joseph Q. 1949- *WhoHisp 94*
Herrera, Lemuel 1949- *WhoHisp 94*
Herrera, Lorenzo, Jr. 1948- *WhoHisp 94*
Herrera, Luciano de *AmRev*
Herrera, Luis *WhoHisp 94*
Herrera, Luis Alberto 1944- *WhoHisp 94*
Herrera, Luis Felipe 1922- *IntWW 93*
Herrera, Manuel G. *WhoHisp 94*
Herrera, Marina A. 1942- *WhoHisp 94*
Herrera, Mario A. 1948- *WhoHisp 94*
Herrera, Mónica María 1944- *WhoHisp 94*
Herrera, Pastor, Jr. 1945- *WhoHisp 94*
Herrera, Paul Fredrick 1948- *WhoAm 94*
Herrera, Peter 1953- *WhoHisp 94*
Herrera, Rafael C. 1934- *WhoHisp 94*
Herrera, Rene J. 1953- *WhoHisp 94*
Herrera, Richard Leo Salaz 1942- *WhoHisp 94*
Herrera, Robert Bennett 1913- *WhoWest 94*
Herrera, Rodimiro, Jr. 1944- *WhoHisp 94*
Herrera, Rosalinda G. 1948- *WhoHisp 94*
Herrera, Shirley Mae 1942- *WhoFI 94, WhoWest 94*
Herrera, Steve 1949- *WhoHisp 94*
Herrera, Steve J. 1943- *WhoHisp 94*
Herrera Caceres, Hector Roberto 1943- *IntWW 93*
Herrera Campins, Luis 1925- *IntWW 93*
Herrera Garrido, Francisca 1869-1950 *BlmGWL*
Herrera-Lavan, Mario Antonio 1931- *WhoHisp 94*
Herrera-Pérez, Shirley 1957- *WhoHisp 94*
Herrera-Sobek, Maria *WhoHisp 94*
Herrerías, Catalina 1948- *WhoHisp 94*
Herrerias, Paul Kevin 1955- *WhoWest 94*
Herrero, Brunildo Antonio 1934- *WhoHisp 94*
Herrero, Carmen A. 1960- *WhoHisp 94*
Herrero-Kunhardt, Susana 1945- *WhoHisp 94*
Herrero Rodriguez De Minon, Miguel 1940- *IntWW 93*
Herreros, Enrique, Sr. d1977 *WhoHol 92*
Herres, Phillip Benjamin 1941- *WhoAm 94*
Herres, Robert T. 1932- *WhoIns 94*
Herres, Robert Tralles 1932- *WhoAm 94*
Herrick, Alan Adair 1896- *WhAm 10*
Herrick, Bruce Hale 1936- *WhoAm 94*
Herrick, Bruce W. 1944- *WhoIns 94*
Herrick, Earl George 1938- *WhoWest 94*
Herrick, Elbert Charles 1919- *WhoScEn 94*
Herrick, Jack d1952 *WhoHol 92*
Herrick, James Allen 1954- *WhoMW 93*
Herrick, John Dennis 1932- *WhoAm 94*
Herrick, Joseph d1966 *WhoHol 92*
Herrick, Kathleen Magara 1943- *WhoMW 93*
Herrick, Kenneth Gilbert 1921- *WhoAm 94, WhoFI 94, WhoMW 93*
Herrick, Neal Q(uentin) 1927- *ConAu 43NR*
Herrick, Paul E. 1963- *WhoScEn 94*
Herrick, Robert d1982 *WhoHol 92*
Herrick, Robert 1591-1674 *BlmGEL*
Herrick, Robert 1868-1938 *EncSF 93*
Herrick, Robert Ford 1912- *WhoAm 94*
Herrick, Robert James 1943- *WhoMW 93*
Herrick, Robert Wallace 1963- *WhoWest 94*
Herrick, Stewart Thurston 1945- *WhoAmL 94*
Herrick, Thomas Edward 1958- *WhoScEn 94*
Herrick, Todd W. 1942- *WhoAm 94, WhoFI 94, WhoMW 93, WhoScEn 94*
Herrick, Tracy Grant 1933- *ConAu 42NR, WhoWest 94*
Herrick, William *DrAPF 93*
Herrick, William 1915- *WrDr 94*
Herrick, William Duncan 1941- *WhoAmL 94*
Herridge, Geoffrey Howard 1904- *IntWW 93, Who 94*
Herrier, Mark *WhoHol 92*
Herries, Edward Matthew 1969- *WhoScEn 94*
Herries, Michael Alexander Robert Young- 1923- *Who 94*
Herries, Michael Robert Young- 1923- *IntWW 93*
Herries Of Terregles, Lady 1938- *Who 94*
Herriford, Merle Baird 1919- *WhoBlA 94*
Herriford, Robert Levi, Sr. 1931- *WhoAm 94*
Herrin, Frances Sudomier 1914- *WhoMW 93*
Herrin, Lamar 1940- *ConAu 142*
Herrin, Michael Douglas 1966- *WhoAmL 94*
Herrin, Moreland 1922- *WhoAm 94*
Herring, Aggie d1939 *WhoHol 92*
Herring, Bernard Duane *WhoBlA 94*
Herring, Bruce E. 1934- *WhoScEn 94*
Herring, Charles David 1943- *WhoAmL 94*
Herring, Charles F., Jr. 1950- *WhoAmL 94*
Herring, (William) Conyers 1914- *IntWW 93*
Herring, Cyril Alfred 1915- *Who 94*
Herring, Dal Martin 1940- *WhoMW 93*
Herring, David Mayo 1929- *WhoFI 94*
Herring, Grover Cleveland 1925- *WhoAmL 94*
Herring, Jack William 1925- *WhoAm 94*
Herring, Jan 1923- *WhoAmA 93*
Herring, Jenny Lorna 1960- *WhoWest 94*
Herring, Jerone Carson 1938- *WhoAm 94, WhoAmL 94*
Herring, Jess d1953 *WhoHol 92*
Herring, Kenneth Lee 1954- *WhoScEn 94*
Herring, Larry Windell 1946- *WhoBlA 94*
Herring, Laura *WhoHisp 94, WhoHol 92*
Herring, Leonard, Jr. 1934- *WhoBlA 94*
Herring, Leonard Gray 1927- *WhoAm 94, WhoFI 94*
Herring, Lynn 1958- *WhoHol 92*
Herring, Michael Earl 1958- *WhoWest 94*
Herring, Paul George Colin 1943- *WhoScEn 94*
Herring, Raymond Mark 1952- *WhoAm 94, WhoMW 93*
Herring, Reuben 1922- *WhoAm 94*
Herring, Susan Weller 1947- *WhoAm 94*
Herring, Victoria L. 1947- *WhoAmL 94, WhoFI 94*
Herring, William Arthur 1948- *WhoAmA 93*
Herring, William Conyers 1914- *WhoAm 94*
Herring, William F. 1932- *WhoBlA 94*
Herringer, Frank Casper 1942- *WhoAm 94, WhoFI 94, WhoWest 94*
Herringman, Henry 1628-1704 *DcNaB MP*
Herrington, Arthur W. 1891-1970 *WhoAmA 93N*
Herrington, Daniel Robert 1946- *WhoScEn 94*
Herrington, Donald Francis 1943- *WhoFI 94*
Herrington, James Patrick 1950- *WhoMW 93*
Herrington, John 1939- *WhoAmP 93*
Herrington, John David, III 1934- *WhoAm 94*
Herrington, John S. 1939- *IntWW 93*
Herrington, John Stewart 1939- *WhoFI 94*
Herrington, Kenneth Frank, III 1950- *WhoFI 94*
Herrington, Nell Ray *WhoAmA 93N*
Herrington, Neva *DrAPF 93*
Herrington, Perry Lee 1951- *WhoBlA 94*
Herrington, Walter John 1928- *Who 94*
Herriot, James *Who 94*
Herriot, James 1916- *IntWW 93, TwCYAW, WhoAm 94, WrDr 94*
Herriott, Donald Richard 1928- *WhoAm 94*
Herriott, Frank Wilbur 1893- *WhAm 10*
Herritt, Linda S. 1950- *WhoAmA 93*
Herrity, Andrew Charles 1948- *WhoWest 94*
Herrlinger, Stephen Paul 1959- *WhoScEn 94*
Herrman, Marcia Kutz 1927- *WhoWest 94*
Herrmann, Arthur L. 1926- *WhoAmP 93*
Herrmann, Benjamin Edward 1919- *WhoAm 94*
Herrmann, Bernard 1911-1975 *IntDcF 2-4 [port], NewGrDO*
Herrmann, Cal C. 1930- *WhoWest 94*
Herrmann, Carl Procter 1947- *WhoFI 94*
Herrmann, Conrad Beadle 1960- *WhoWest 94*
Herrmann, Diana Chang *DrAPF 93*
Herrmann, Douglas J. 1941- *WhoAm 94*
Herrmann, Edward 1943- *IntMPA 94, WhoHol 92*
Herrmann, Edward Kirk 1943- *WhoAm 94*
Herrmann, George 1921- *WhoAm 94, WhoScEn 94, WhoWest 94*
Herrmann, John J., Jr. 1937- *WhoAmA 93*
Herrmann, Josef 1903-1955 *NewGrDO*
Herrmann, Judith Ann 1943- *WhoMW 93, WhoScEn 94*
Herrmann, Karl-Ernst 1936- *NewGrDO*
Herrmann, Lacy Bunnell 1929- *WhoAm 94, WhoFI 94*
Herrmann, Luke John 1932- *WrDr 94*
Herrmann, Mary Margaret 1950- *WhoAm 94*
Herrmann, R. Gene 1949- *WhoFI 94*
Herrmann, Siegfried 1926- *IntWW 93*
Herrmann, Stephen E. 1944- *WhoAmL 94*
Herrmann, Theo 1902-1977 *NewGrDO*
Herrmann, Thomas Anthony 1928- *WhoMW 93*
Herrmann, Walter 1930- *WhoAm 94, WhoScEn 94*
Herrmanns, Ralph 1933- *WrDr 94*
Herrmannsfeldt, William Bernard 1931- *WhoScEn 94*
Herrnstadt, Richard Lawrence 1926- *WhoAm 94*
Herrnstein, Richard Julius 1930- *WhoAm 94*
Herro, John Joseph 1945- *WhoFI 94*
Herrod, Donald 1930- *Who 94*
Herrold, Kenneth Frederick 1913- *WhoAm 94*
Herron, Andrew 1909- *IntWW 93, Who 94*
Herron, Bill *DrAPF 93*
Herron, Bruce Wayne 1954- *WhoBlA 94*
Herron, Carolivia *WhoBlA 94*
Herron, Carolivia 1947- *BlkWr 2, ConAu 141*
Herron, Cindy *WhoBlA 94*
Herron, Cindy c. 1966- *See* En Vogue *ConMus 10*
Herron, Cindy c. 1966- *See* En Vogue *News 94-1*
Herron, Edwin Hunter, Jr. 1938- *WhoFI 94*
Herron, Elizabeth C. *DrAPF 93*
Herron, Ellen Patricia 1927- *WhoAmL 94, WhoWest 94*
Herron, George Davis 1862-1925 *DcAmReB 2*
Herron, Henry 1911- *Who 94*
Herron, Jack R. 1933- *WhoAmP 93*
Herron, James Dudley 1936- *WhoAm 94*
Herron, James M. 1934- *WhoAm 94, WhoFI 94*
Herron, James Michael 1934- *WhoAmL 94*
Herron, Jeffery Rohn 1957- *WhoMW 93*
Herron, Orley R. 1933- *WhoAm 94*
Herron, Orley Rufus 1933- *WrDr 94*
Herron, Ronald James *IntWW 93*
Herron, Ronald James 1930- *Who 94*
Herron, Roy B. 1953- *WhoAmP 93*
Herron, Sidney Earl 1952- *WhoFI 94*
Herron, Stephen House 1925- *WhoAm 94*
Herron, Vernon M. 1928- *WhoBlA 94*
Herron, William 1933- *WrDr 94*
Herrstrom, David Sten *DrAPF 93*
Herrup, Karl 1948- *WhoScEn 94*
Herry-Leclerc, Jeanne *WhoHol 92*
Hersant, Robert Joseph Emile 1920- *IntWW 93*
Hersch, Dennis Steven 1947- *WhoAm 94, WhoAmL 94*
Hersch, Russell LeRoy 1916- *WhoMW 93*
Herschbach, Dudley Robert 1932- *IntWW 93, Who 94, WhoAm 94, WhoScEn 94*
Herschberger, Ruth *DrAPF 93*
Herschel, Caroline Lucretia 1750-1848 *WorScD*
Herschel, John *DrAPF 93*
Herschel, John Frederick William 1792-1871 *WorInv*
Herschel, William 1738-1822 *WorScD [port]*
Herschel, William James 1833-1917 *DcNaB MP*
Herschell, Baron 1923- *Who 94*
Herschensohn, Bruce 1932- *WhoAm 94*
Herscher, Susan Kay 1949- *WhoMW 93*
Herscher, Uri David 1941- *WhoWest 94*
Herschfield, Harry d1974 *WhoHol 92*
Herschfus, Leon *WhoAmP 93*
Herschler, David Elijah 1940- *WhoAmA 93*
Herschler, Edgar J. 1918-1990 *WhAm 10*
Herschler, Elijah David 1940- *WhoWest 94*
Herschler, Leslie Norman 1958- *WhoWest 94*
Herschler, Robert John 1923- *WhoAm 94*
Herschman, Jeffrey D. 1948- *WhoAmL 94*
Hersee, Carol 1958- *WhoHol 92*
Hersee, Rose 1845-1924 *NewGrDO*
Herseth, Ralph Lars *WhoAmP 93*
Hersey, David 1939- *ConTFT 11*
Hersey, David Floyd 1928- *WhoAm 94*
Hersey, David Kenneth 1939- *Who 94, WhoAm 94*
Hersey, Derek d1993 *NewYTBS 93*
Hersey, George Leonard 1927- *WhoAm 94, WhoAmA 93*
Hersey, Harold (Brainerd) 1893-1956 *EncSF 93*
Hersey, John *DrAPF 93*
Hersey, John d1993 *Who 94N*
Hersey, John 1914- *EncSF 93*
Hersey, John 1914-1993 *ConLC 81 [port], NewYTBS 93 [port]*
Hersey, John (Richard) 1914-1993 *ConAu 140, CurBio 93N, SmATA 76, WrDr 94N*
Hersey, John Richard d1993 *IntWW 93N*
Hersey, John Richard 1914-1993 *AmCulL*
Hersh, Barry Fred 1947- *WhoFI 94*
Hersh, Richard H. *WhoAm 94*
Hersh, Robert Michael 1940- *WhoAmL 94*
Hersh, Robert Tweed 1927- *WhoMW 93, WhoScEn 94*
Hersh, Seymour M. 1937- *WhoAm 94*
Hersh, Stephen Peter 1940- *WhoAm 94*
Hershan, Stella K. *DrAPF 93*
Hershatter, Richard Lawrence 1923- *WhoAmL 94*
Hershberger, David Allen 1944- *WhoFI 94*
Hershberger, Donald R. 1949- *WhoMW 93*
Hershberger, Jerry Richard 1951- *WhoMW 93*
Hershberger, John Douglas 1958- *WhoAmL 94*
Hershberger, John Wayne, II 1946- *WhoIns 94*
Hershberger, Larry D. 1944- *WhoIns 94*
Hershberger, Robert Glen 1936- *WhoWest 94*
Hershberger, Steven Kaye 1953- *WhoMW 93*
Hershberger, Winifred 1922- *WhoAmP 93*
Hershenov, Bernard Zion 1927- *WhoAm 94*
Hersher, Kurt Bernard 1928- *WhoFI 94*
Hersher, Richard Donald 1942- *WhoMW 93*
Hershey, Alfred Day 1908- *IntWW 93, Who 94, WhoAm 94, WhoScEn 94, WorScD*
Hershey, Arthur Duane 1937- *WhoAmP 93*
Hershey, Barbara *IntWW 93*
Hershey, Barbara 1948- *IntMPA 94, WhoAm 94, WhoHol 92*
Hershey, Colin Harry 1935- *WhoAm 94, WhoFI 94*
Hershey, Dale 1941- *WhoAm 94*
Hershey, Falls Bacon 1918- *WhoAm 94*
Hershey, Gerald Lee 1931- *WhoAm 94*
Hershey, H. Garland, Jr. 1940- *WhoAm 94*
Hershey, Milton *WorInv*
Hershey, Nathan 1930- *WhoAm 94, WhoAmL 94*
Hershey, Nona 1946- *WhoAm 94, WhoAmA 93*
Hershey, Olive *WrDr 94*
Hershey, Robert Lewis 1941- *WhoScEn 94*
Hershey-Abraham, Jane 1961- *WhoAmP 93*
Hershfield, Leo 1904-1979 *WhoAmA 93N*
Hershiser, Orel Leonard, IV 1958- *WhoAm 94, WhoWest 94*
Hershkovitz, Philip 1909- *WhoMW 93*
Hershkowitz, Noah 1941- *WhoAm 94*
Hershman, James Howard, Jr. 1947- *WhoAmP 93*
Hershman, Lynn Lester *WhoAm 94, WhoWest 94*
Hershman, Lynn Lester 1941- *WhoAmA 93*
Hershman, Marcie 1951- *ConAu 141*
Hershman, Mendes 1911-1992 *WhAm 10*
Hershman, Morris 1920- *EncSF 93*
Hershman, Scott Edward 1958- *WhoAmL 94*
Hershner, Robert Franklin, Jr. 1944- *WhoAm 94, WhoAmL 94*
Hersholt, Jean d1956 *WhoHol 92*
Hershon, Robert *DrAPF 93*
Herskovitz, Marshall 1952- *IntMPA 94*
Herskovitz, Sam Marc 1949- *WhoAmL 94*
Herskowitz, Carol A. *WhoAmP 93*
Herskowitz, Ira 1946- *WhoAm 94*
Herslip, Larry 1945- *WhoAmP 93*
Hersman, Ferd William 1922- *WhoFI 94*
Hersman, Marion Frank 1932- *WhoAm 94*
Hersom, Naomi Louisa 1927- *IntWW 93*
Hersov, Basil Edward 1926- *IntWW 93*

Hersrud, James Robert 1946- *WhoAmP 93*
Herst, Herman, Jr. 1909- *WhoAm 94*
Herstam, Chris 1949- *WhoAmP 93*
Herstand, Arnold *WhoAmA 93N*
Herstand, Theodore 1930- *WhoAm 94*
Herstein, Carl William 1953- *WhoAm 94*
Herstek, Maureen Crook 1948- *WhoAmP 93*
Hersztajn Moldau, Juan 1945- *WhoScEn 94*
Herte, Mary Charlotte 1951- *WhoAm 94*
Hertel, Curtis A. 1953- *WhoAmP 93*
Hertel, David C. 1953- *WhoAmL 94*
Hertel, Dennis M. 1948- *WhoAmP 93*
Hertel, Jay Alan 1962- *WhoMW 93*
Hertel, John R. 1940- *WhoAmP 93*
Hertel, Paul R., Jr. 1928- *WhoIns 94*
Hertel, Suzanne Marie 1937- *WhoFI 94*
Herter, Albert 1871-1950 *WhoAmA 93N*
Hertford, Bishop Suffragan of 1936- *Who 94*
Hertford, Marquess of 1930- *Who 94*
Hertfordshire, Bishop in *Who 94*
Herth, Kaye Ann 1945- *WhoMW 93*
Hertig, Arthur Tremain 1904-1990 *WhAm 10*
Herting, Robert Leslie 1929- *WhoAm 94*
Hertle, Frank *DrAPF 93*
Hertlein, Fred, III 1933- *WhoWest 94*
Hertneky, Randy Lee 1955- *WhoWest 94*
Herts, E. J. d1951 *WhoHol 92*
Hertweck, E. Romayne 1928- *WhoWest 94*
Hertz, Alfred 1872-1942 *NewGrDO*
Hertz, Arthur Herman 1933- *WhoAm 94*
Hertz, Daniel Leroy, Jr. 1930- *WhoScEn 94*
Hertz, David Bendel 1919- *WhoAm 94*
Hertz, David Michael 1954- *WhoMW 93*
Hertz, Harry Steven 1947- *WhoAm 94*
Hertz, Heinrich Rudolf 1857-1894 *EncDeaf, WorScD*
Hertz, Kenneth Theodore 1951- *WhoAm 94*
Hertz, Leon 1938- *WhoAm 94*
Hertz, Michal 1844-1918 *NewGrDO*
Hertz, Natalie Zucker 1934- *WhoAmL 94*
Hertz, Patricia Ritenour 1966- *WhoScEn 94*
Hertz, Richard A. 1940- *WhoAmA 93*
Hertz, Richard Cornell 1916- *WhoAm 94*
Hertz, Roy 1909- *IntWW 93, WhoAm 94*
Hertz, Rudolf Heinrich 1917- *WhoAm 94*
Hertz, Vivienne Lucas 1928- *WhoMW 93*
Hertz, Willard Joel 1924- *WhoAm 94*
Hertz, William 1923- *IntMPA 94*
Hertzberg, Abraham 1922- *WhoAm 94, WhoScEn 94, WhoWest 94*
Hertzberg, Alanson Lee 1945- *WhoWest 94*
Hertzberg, Arthur 1921- *WhoAm 94, WrDr 94*
Hertzberg, Harold Joel 1922- *WhoAmL 94, WhoWest 94*
Hertzberg, Hendrik 1943- *WhoAm 94*
Hertzberg, Michael A. 1944- *WhoAmL 94*
Hertzberg, Paul Stuart 1949- *WhoAm 94*
Hertzberg, Richard Lloyd 1963- *WhoAmL 94*
Hertzberg, Richard Warren 1937- *WhoAm 94*
Hertzberg, Robert Steven 1954- *WhoAmL 94*
Hertzberg, Rose 1912- *WhoAmA 93*
Hertzberg, Sidney 1913?- *BasBi*
Hertzberg, Stuart E. 1926- *WhoAmP 93*
Hertzberger, Herman 1932- *IntWW 93*
Hertzka, Theodor 1845-1924 *EncSF 93*
Hertzke, Allen D. 1950- *ConAu 141*
Hertzman, Gay Mahaffy 1931- *WhoAmA 93*
Hertzman, Phillip Alan 1946- *WhoWest 94*
Hertzog, James Barry Munnik 1866-1942 *HisWorL [port]*
Hertzog, Robert William 1939- *WhoScEn 94*
Hertzsprung, Ejnar 1873-1967 *WorScD*
Herve 1825-1892 *NewGrDO*
Herve, Edmond 1942- *IntWW 93*
Herve-Bazin, Jean-Pierre Marie 1911- *IntWW 93*
Herves, Madeline d1969 *WhoAmA 93N*
Hervey *Who 94*
Hervey, Billy T. 1937- *WhoBlA 94*
Hervey, Elizabeth c. 1748-1820? *BlmGWL*
Hervey, Grizelda d1980 *WhoHol 92*
Hervey, Harry d1951 *WhoHol 92*
Hervey, Homer Vaughan 1936- *WhoFI 94*
Hervey, Irene 1910- *WhoHol 92*
Hervey, Jason *WhoHol 92*
Hervey, John Bethell 1928- *Who 94*
Hervey, Maurice H. *EncSF 93*
Hervey, Michael 1914- *EncSF 93*
Hervey, Roger Blaise Ramsay 1934- *Who 94*
Hervey-Bathurst, F. *Who 94*
Hervey of Boreham c. 1228-1277 *DcNaB MP*
Herwarth Von Bittenfeld, Hans 1904- *IntWW 93*
Herwarth von Bittenfeld, Hans Heinrich 1904- *Who 94*
Herwegh, Emma 1817-1904 *BlmGWL*
Herwegh, Georg 1817-1875 *DcLB 133 [port]*
Herwig, Joan Emily 1943- *WhoMW 93*
Herwig, Rob 1935- *WrDr 94*
Herwitz, Carla B. 1932- *WhoAm 94*
Herz, Andrew Lee 1946- *WhoAmL 94*
Herz, Carl Samuel 1930- *WhoAm 94*
Herz, George Peter 1928- *WhoScEn 94*
Herz, Henriette 1764-1847 *BlmGWL*
Herz, Joachim 1924- *NewGrDO*
Herz, Josef Edward 1924- *WhoScEn 94*
Herz, Leonard 1931- *WhoAm 94*
Herz, Marvin Ira 1927- *WhoAm 94*
Herz, Michael Joseph 1936- *WhoAm 94, WhoWest 94*
Herz, Ralph d1921 *WhoHol 92*
Herzberg, Charles Francis 1924- *Who 94*
Herzberg, Dorothy Crews 1935- *WhoWest 94*
Herzberg, Frederick 1923- *WhoAm 94*
Herzberg, Gerhard 1904- *IntWW 93, Who 94, WhoAm 94, WhoScEn 94, WhoWest 94, WrDr 94*
Herzberg, Judith (Frieda Lina) 1934- *BlmGWL, ConWorW 93*
Herzberg, Peter Jay 1950- *WhoAm 94*
Herzberg, Sydelle Shulman 1933- *WhoAmL 94*
Herzberg, Thomas *WhoAmA 93*
Herzberger, Arthur Conrad 1917- *WhoAmP 93*
Herzberger, Eugene E. 1920- *WhoAm 94*
Herzbrun, David Joseph 1927- *WhoAm 94*
Herzbrun, Helene McKinsey d1984 *WhoAmA 93N*
Herzel, Leo 1923- *WhoAm 94*
Herzenberg, Arvid 1925- *WhoAm 94*
Herzenberg, Caroline Littlejohn 1932- *WhoAm 94*
Herzer, Richard Kimball 1931- *WhoAm 94, WhoWest 94*
Herzfeld, Charles Maria 1925- *WhoAm 94, WhoScEn 94*
Herzfeld, Guido d1923 *WhoHol 92*
Herzfeld, John *WhoHol 92*
Herzfeld, Will Lawrence 1937- *WhoBlA 94*
Herzfeld-Kimbrough, Ciby 1941- *WhoMW 93*
Herzig, Christopher d1993 *Who 94N*
Herzing, Alfred Roy 1958- *WhoWest 94*
Herzing, Henry George 1936- *WhoFI 94*
Herzinger, Charles d1953 *WhoHol 92*
Herzl, Theodor *EncSF 93*
Herzl, Theodr 1860-1904 *HisWorL [port]*
Herzlich, Harold J. *WhoAm 94*
Herzog, Ann Elizabeth 1960- *WhoMW 93*
Herzog, Arthur 1927- *WrDr 94*
Herzog, Arthur, (III) 1927- *EncSF 93*
Herzog, Arthur, III 1927- *WhoAm 94*
Herzog, Beverly Leah 1954- *WhoAm 94*
Herzog, Brigitte 1943- *WhoAmL 94*
Herzog, Catherine Anita 1960- *WhoScEn 94*
Herzog, Chaim 1918- *ConAu 42NR, IntWW 93, Who 94*
Herzog, David K. 1955- *WhoAmL 94*
Herzog, Emile *EncSF 93*
Herzog, Fred d1928 *WhoHol 92*
Herzog, Fred F. 1907- *WhoAm 94*
Herzog, John E. 1936- *WhoAm 94, WhoFI 94*
Herzog, John L. 1938- *WhoAmP 93*
Herzog, Lester Barry 1953- *WhoAmL 94*
Herzog, Maurice 1919- *IntWW 93*
Herzog, Peter Emilius 1925- *WhoAm 94*
Herzog, Raymond Edward 1923- *WhoWest 94*
Herzog, Richard Barnard 1939- *WhoAm 94*
Herzog, Werner 1942- *IntMPA 94, IntWW 93*
Herzog, Whitey 1931- *WhoAm 94, WhoWest 94*
Herzstein, Robert Erwin 1931- *WhoAm 94*
Hesburgh, Theodore M. 1917- *IntWW 93*
Hesch, Wilhelm 1860-1908 *NewGrDO*
Heschel, Abraham Joshua 1907-1972 *DcAmReB 2*
Heseltine, Michael (Ray Dibdin) 1933- *Who 94*
Heseltine, Michael Ray Dibdin 1933- *IntWW 93*
Heseltine, William (Frederick Payne) 1930- *Who 94*
Heselton, Corys M. 1905- *WhoAmP 93*
Heselton, Kenneth Emery 1943- *WhoScEn 94*
Heselton, Patricia Ann 1946- *WhoAm 94*
Hesford, Marie Dorothy 1948- *WhoMW 93*
Hesh, Joseph McLean 1954- *WhoWest 94*
He Shangchun *WhoPRCh 91*
He Shoulun 1926- *WhoPRCh 91 [port]*
Heskes, Scott Earle 1952- *WhoWest 94*
Hesketh d1987 *WhoAmA 93N*
Hesketh, Baron 1950- *Who 94*
Hesketh, Phoebe 1909- *WrDr 94*
Heskin, Thomas M. *WhoAmP 93*
Hesky, Olga (Lynford) 1912-1974 *EncSF 93*
Hesla, Stephen *DrAPF 93*
Heslam, (Mary) Noelle *Who 94*
Heslep, Robert Durham 1930- *WrDr 94*
Hesler, G. Christian d1989 *WhoHol 92*
Heslin, James J. 1916- *WhoAm 94*
Heslin, James William, Jr. 1944- *WhoIns 94*
Heslin, John Thomas 1927- *WhoFI 94*
Heslop, Charles d1966 *WhoHol 92*
Heslop, David Thomas 1932- *Who 94*
Heslop, Marvin S. *WhoAmP 93*
Heslop, Patricia Evona 1943- *WhoFI 94*
Heslop, Philip Linnell 1948- *Who 94*
Heslop, Terence Murray 1942- *WhoAm 94*
Heslop-Harrison, John 1920- *IntWW 93, Who 94*
Hesp, B. *WhoScEn 94*
Hespos, Richard Franklin 1934- *WhoAm 94*
Hess, Amy Morris 1947- *WhoAmL 94*
Hess, Ann Marie 1944- *WhoScEn 94*
Hess, Arin Lynd 1956- *WhoAmP 93*
Hess, Arthur 1927- *WhoAm 94*
Hess, Bartlett Leonard 1910- *WhoMW 93*
Hess, Benno 1922- *IntWW 93*
Hess, Bernard Andes, Jr. 1940- *WhoAm 94*
Hess, Betty Jane *WhoHol 92*
Hess, Carole E. 1942- *WhoAmP 93*
Hess, Cecil F. 1949- *WhoScEn 94*
Hess, Charles Edward 1931- *WhoAm 94, WhoScEn 94, WhoWest 94*
Hess, Daniel Bartlett 1940- *WhoAmP 93*
Hess, David *WhoHol 92*
Hess, David Bruce 1943- *WhoFI 94*
Hess, David Graham 1957- *WhoFI 94*
Hess, David W. 1942- *WhoAmP 93*
Hess, David Willard 1933- *WhoAm 94*
Hess, Dennis John 1940- *WhoAm 94*
Hess, Dick L. 1938- *WhoAmP 93*
Hess, Donald C. 1948- *WhoAm 94, WhoAmL 94*
Hess, Donald F. 1919- *WhoFI 94*
Hess, Donald K. 1930- *WhoAm 94*
Hess, Donald Lamparter 1938- *WhoMW 93*
Hess, Dorothy Haldeman 1941- *WhoWest 94*
Hess, Earl Hollinger 1928- *WhoAm 94, WhoScEn 94*
Hess, Edwin John 1933- *WhoAm 94*
Hess, Ellen Elizabeth 1908- *Who 94*
Hess, Emerson Garfield 1914- *WhoAmL 94*
Hess, Errol *DrAPF 93*
Hess, Eugene Lyle 1914- *WhoAm 94*
Hess, Evelyn Victorine 1926- *WhoAm 94*
Hess, Frederick Dana 1946- *WhoFI 94*
Hess, Frederick J. 1941- *WhoAm 94*
Hess, Gary R 1937- *WrDr 94*
Hess, Geoffrey LaVerne 1949- *WhoFI 94*
Hess, George Alfred 1938- *WhoMW 93*
Hess, George Franklin, II 1939- *WhoAmL 94*
Hess, George Paul 1926- *WhoAm 94*
Hess, George Robert 1941- *WhoAm 94*
Hess, Glen E. 1942- *WhoAmL 94*
Hess, Hans Ober 1912- *WhoAm 94*
Hess, Harry Hammond 1906-1969 *WorScD*
Hess, Henry Leroy, Jr. 1924- *WhoAm 94, WhoAmL 94, WhoWest 94*
Hess, Ida Irene 1910- *WhoMW 93, WhoScEn 94*
Hess, Joan *WrDr 94*
Hess, John Philip 1954- *WhoFI 94, WhoMW 93*
Hess, Jonathan Robert 1956- *WhoMW 93*
Hess, Joyce *WhoAmA 93*
Hess, Karl 1923- *WhoAmP 93*
Hess, Karl 1945- *WhoAm 94*
Hess, Karsten 1930- *WhoAm 94*
Hess, LaVerne Derryl 1933- *WhoScEn 94*
Hess, Lawrence Eugene, Jr. 1923- *WhoAmL 94*
Hess, Leon 1914- *WhoAm 94, WhoFI 94*
Hess, Leonard Wayne 1949- *WhoMW 93, WhoScEn 94*
Hess, Lester Clay, Jr. 1940- *WhoAmL 94*
Hess, Linda Candace 1952- *WhoScEn 94*
Hess, Lynn *DrAPF 93*
Hess, Margaret Johnston 1915- *WhoMW 93*
Hess, Marilyn Ann *WhoAmP 93*
Hess, Milton Siegmund 1941- *WhoAm 94*
Hess, Orvan W. *WhoAm 94*
Hess, P. Gregory 1946- *WhoAmL 94*
Hess, Patrick Henry 1931- *WhoAm 94*
Hess, Peter A. 1938- *WhoAm 94*
Hess, Peter E. 1959- *WhoAmL 94*
Hess, Rex Allen 1949- *WhoMW 93*
Hess, Richard Alfred 1926- *WhoWest 94*
Hess, Richard Cletus 1934-1991 *WhAm 10*
Hess, Richard Lowell 1951- *WhoWest 94*
Hess, Robert, Jr. 1957- *WhoFI 94, WhoMW 93*
Hess, Robert L 1932- *WrDr 94*
Hess, Robert Lee 1932-1992 *WhAm 10*
Hess, Robert Pratt 1942- *WhoAmL 94*
Hess, Roger Leroy 1914- *WhoAmP 93*
Hess, Ronald Andrew 1942- *WhoScEn 94*
Hess, Rudolph 1894-1987 *HisWorL [port]*
Hess, Scott 1955- *WhoAmA 93*
Hess, Sidney J., Jr. 1910- *WhoAm 94*
Hess, Sidney Wayne 1932- *WhoAm 94*
Hess, Sonya *DrAPF 93*
Hess, Stanford Donald 1943- *WhoAm 94*
Hess, Stanley William 1939- *WhoAmA 93*
Hess, Stephen 1933- *WhoAm 94*
Hess, Steven Charles 1948- *WhoAmL 94*
Hess, Ted Harold 1932- *WhoWest 94*
Hess, Thomas B. 1920-1978 *WhoAmA 93N*
Hess, Ulrich Edward 1940- *WhoScEn 94*
Hess, Victor Franz 1883-1964 *WorScD*
Hess, Werner 1914- *IntWW 93*
Hess, Wilford Moser 1934- *WhoWest 94*
Hess, William E. 1908- *WhoAmP 93*
Hess, William L. 1947- *WhoAmL 94*
Hess, Wilmot Norton 1926- *WhoAm 94, WhoScEn 94*
Hessayon, David Gerald 1928- *Who 94*
Hessberg, Rufus R. 1921- *WhoAm 94*
Hesse, Bradford William 1957- *WhoWest 94*
Hesse, Carolyn Sue 1949- *WhoAmL 94*
Hesse, Christian August 1925- *WhoAm 94, WhoScEn 94, WhoWest 94*
Hesse, Ernst Christian 1676-1762 *NewGrDO*
Hesse, Eva 1936-1972 *WhoAmA 93N*
Hesse, Gerhard Edmund 1908- *IntWW 93*
Hesse, Gregory Getty 1963- *WhoAmL 94*
Hesse, Hermann 1877-1962 *EncSF 93*
Hesse, Karen 1952- *SmATA 74 [port]*
Hesse, Martha 1942- *WhoAmP 93*
Hesse, Martha O. 1942- *WhoAm 94*
Hesse, Mary Brenda 1924- *Who 94, WrDr 94*
Hesse, Nancy Jane 1948- *WhoFI 94*
Hesse, Ruth 1936- *NewGrDO*
Hesse, Stephen Max 1948- *WhoAm 94*
Hesse, Thurman Dale 1938- *WhoMW 93, WhoScEn 94*
Hesse, William d1936 *WhoHol 92*
Hesse, William Blass 1948- *WhoFI 94*
Hesse, William R. 1914- *WhoAm 94, WhoFI 94*
Hesse, Zora *WhoAmP 93*
Hessel, John M. 1952- *WhoAmL 94*
Hessel, Stephane F. 1917- *IntWW 93*
Hesselbach, Walter 1915- *IntWW 93*
Hesselbein, Frances Richards *WhoAm 94*
Hesselink, Ann Patrice 1954- *WhoAm 94*
Hesselink, Ira John, Jr. 1928- *WhoMW 93*
Hessellund-Jensen, Peter Lykke 1945- *WhoAmL 94*
Hesseman, Howard 1940- *IntMPA 94, WhoAm 94, WhoHol 92*
Hessen, Margaret Trexler 1956- *WhoScEn 94*
Hessenland, Werner d1979 *WhoHol 92*
Hesser, James Edward 1941- *WhoAm 94, WhoScEn 94, WhoWest 94*
Hesser, Woodrow Cleveland 1918- *WhoAmP 93*
Hessert, Paul 1925- *WrDr 94*
Hessey, John Hamilton 1952- *WhoMW 93*
Hessing, Charles Francis 1953- *WhoFI 94*
Hession, Thomas D. *WhoAmP 93*
Hessler, Curtis Alan 1943- *WhoAm 94*
Hessler, David William 1932- *WhoAm 94*
Hessler, Gordon 1930- *HorFD [port], IntMPA 94*
Hessler, John d1993 *NewYTBS 93*
Hessler, William Gerhard 1926- *WhoMW 93*
Hesslewood, Tom d1959 *WhoHol 92*
Hesslund, Bradley Harry 1958- *WhoFI 94, WhoMW 93*
Hessman, Frederick William 1939- *WhoScEn 94*
Hesson, John Edward 1938- *WhoWest 94*
Hesson, Paul Anthony 1923- *WhoAm 94*
Hesson, William M., Jr. 1943- *WhoAmL 94*
Hestad, Bjorn Mark 1926- *WhoFI 94, WhoMW 93*
Hestand, Michele Gail Burris 1956- *WhoMW 93*
Hestenes, Roberta *WhoHisp 94*

Hester, Albert Lee 1932- *WhoAm 94*
Hester, Arthur C. 1942- *WhoBlA 94*
Hester, Clinton Monroe 1895- *WhAm 10*
Hester, Douglas Benjamin 1927- *WhoAm 94*
Hester, Eva B. *WhoAmP 93*
Hester, Gerald LeRoy 1928- *WhoWest 94*
Hester, Harvey d1967 *WhoHol 92*
Hester, Jack W. 1929- *WhoAmP 93*
Hester, James Francis 1953- *WhoMW 93*
Hester, James McNaughton 1924- *IntWW 93, WhoAm 94*
Hester, James Stephen 1952- *WhoAmL 94*
Hester, Joan L. 1932- *WhoAmP 93*
Hester, John Frear 1927- *Who 94*
Hester, Linda Hunt 1938- *WhoAm 94*
Hester, M. L. *DrAPF 93*
Hester, M(arvin) Thomas 1941- *WrDr 94*
Hester, Melvyn Francis 1938- *WhoBlA 94, WhoFI 94*
Hester, Norman Eric 1946- *WhoAm 94*
Hester, Patrick Joseph 1951- *WhoAmL 94*
Hester, Paul Finley 1935- *WhoAmP 93*
Hester, Randolph Thompson, Jr. 1944- *WhoAm 94*
Hester, Ronald Ernest 1936- *IntWW 93, Who 94*
Hester, Ross Wyatt 1924- *WhoFI 94*
Hester, Slew 1912-1993 *BuCMET*
Hester, Thomas Patrick 1937- *WhoAm 94, WhoAmL 94*
Hester, Thomas Roy 1946- *WhoAm 94*
Hester, William d1993 *NewYTBS 93 [port]*
Hester, William Francis 1937- *WhoAm 94*
Hesterberg, Trude d1967 *WhoHol 92*
Hesterman, Wilfred Otto 1927- *WhoAmP 93*
Heston, Charlton 1922- *WhoHol 92*
Heston, Charlton 1924- *IntMPA 94, IntWW 93, Who 94, WhoAm 94*
Heston, Fraser 1956- *WhoHol 92*
Heston, Joan *WhoAmA 93*
Heston, Michael A., Sr. 1933- *WhoAmP 93*
Heterick, Robert Cary, Jr. 1936- *WhoAmP 93*
Heth, Diana Sue 1948- *WhoMW 93*
Hethe, Hamo de c. 1275-1352 *DcNaB MP*
Hetherington, Alastair *Who 94*
Hetherington, (Hector) Alastair 1919- *IntWW 93, Who 94*
Hetherington, Arthur (Ford) 1911- *Who 94*
Hetherington, Arthur Ford 1911- *IntWW 93*
Hetherington, Burton Lee 1928- *WhoAmP 93*
Hetherington, Carleton *Who 94*
Hetherington, (Arthur) Carleton 1916- *Who 94*
Hetherington, Cheryl Keiko 1952- *WhoWest 94*
Hetherington, Derick Henry Fellowes d1992 *Who 94N*
Hetherington, John 1930- *WhoWest 94*
Hetherington, John Joseph 1947- *WhoAmL 94*
Hetherington, John Warner 1938- *WhoAm 94*
Hetherington, Thomas Chalmers 1926- *Who 94*
Hetherly, Katheryn Johnson 1928- *WhoAmL 94*
Hetland, James Lyman, Jr. 1925- *WhoAm 94, WhoMW 93*
Hetland, John Robert 1930- *WhoAm 94, WhoAmL 94, WhoFI 94, WhoWest 94*
Hetley, Geoffrey William 1961- *WhoAmL 94*
Hetlinger, John Stuart 1948- *WhoMW 93*
Hetman, Nicholas Wayne 1950- *WhoAmL 94*
Hetman, Vadym Petrovych 1935- *LoBiDrD*
Hetrick, David LeRoy 1927- *WhoScEn 94*
Hetsko, Cyril Francis 1911- *WhoAm 94, WhoAmL 94, WhoFI 94*
Hetsko, Cyril Michael 1942- *WhoMW 93*
Hetsko, Jeffrey Francis 1950- *WhoAmL 94*
Hett, Joan Margaret 1936- *WhoWest 94*
Hettche, L. Raymond 1938- *WhoAm 94, WhoScEn 94*
Hetterscheidt, Margaret Ellen 1932- *WhoMW 93*
Hettich, Arthur Matthias 1925- *WhoAm 94*
Hettich, Michael *DrAPF 93*
Hettinger, Mary Elizabeth 1960- *WhoWest 94*
Hettinger, Stephen Ray 1945- *WhoAmP 93*
Hettinger, Steve *WhoAm 94*
Hettinger, Todd Robert 1969- *WhoWest 94*
Hettlage, Karl Maria 1902- *IntWW 93*
Hettler, Paul *WhoAm 94*
Hettrick, George H. 1940- *WhoAm 94*
Hettrick, John Lord 1934- *WhoAm 94*
Hettrick, Lynn C. 1944- *WhoAmP 93*
Hetzel, Dennis Richard 1952- *WhoAm 94*
Hetzel, Donald Stanford 1941- *WhoScEn 94*
Hetzel, Frederick Armstrong 1930- *WhoAm 94*
Hetzel, Fredrick William 1946- *WhoWest 94*
Hetzel, Joseph Adam 1941- *WhoFI 94*
Hetzel, Jules *EncSF 93*
Hetzel, Phyllis Bertha Mabel 1918- *Who 94*
Hetzel, Ralph D. 1912- *IntMPA 94*
Hetzel, William Gelal 1933- *WhoAm 94, WhoFI 94*
Hetzler, Lisa Leanne 1949- *WhoWest 94*
Hetzler, Susan Elizabeth Savage 1947- *WhoMW 93*
Hetzron, Robert 1937- *WhoAm 94, WrDr 94*
Heuberger, David Michael 1959- *WhoMW 93*
Heuberger, Richard (Franz Joseph) 1850-1914 *NewGrDO*
Heuer, Ann Foster 1934- *WhoAmP 93*
Heuer, Arthur Harold 1936- *WhoAm 94, WhoMW 93*
Heuer, Gerald Arthur 1930- *WhoAm 94, WhoMW 93*
Heuer, Jeffrey G. 1942- *WhoAmL 94*
Heuer, Kenneth John 1927- *WhoAm 94*
Heuer, Margaret B. 1935- *WhoFI 94, WhoScEn 94*
Heuer, Martin 1934- *WhoFI 94*
Heuer, Marvin Arthur 1947- *WhoMW 93, WhoScEn 94*
Heuer, Michael Alexander 1932- *WhoAm 94*
Heuer, Robert Maynard, II 1944- *WhoAm 94*
Heuermann, Magda 1868- *WhoAmA 93N*
Heuertz, Sarah Jane 1950- *WhoAm 94*
Heuman, Donna Rena 1949- *WhoAmL 94, WhoWest 94*
Heumann, Scott Fredric 1951- *WhoAm 94*
Heunis, (Jan) Christiaan 1927- *IntWW 93*
Heurlin, Bruce R. 1947- *WhoAm 94*
Heusch, Clemens August 1932- *WhoAm 94*
Heuschele, Werner Paul 1929- *WhoAm 94, WhoWest 94*
Heusinger, Hans-Joachim 1925- *IntWW 93*
Heusser, Calvin John 1924- *WhoAm 94*
Heusser, Eleanore Elizabeth *WhoAmA 93*
Heuston, Robert Francis Vere 1923- *Who 94*
Hevesi, Alan G. 1940- *WhoAmP 93*
Hevesi, Ludwig *EncSF 93*
Hevesy, Gyorgy 1885-1966 *WorScD*
Hevia, Martha 1941- *WhoWest 94*
Hevier, Richard Scott 1957- *WhoAmP 93*
Hewak, Benjamin 1935- *WhoMW 93*
Heward, Anthony Wilkinson 1918- *Who 94*
Heward, Edmund Rawlings 1912- *Who 94*
Hewat, Alan V. *DrAPF 93*
Hewat, Alexander 1745-1829 *WhAmRev*
Hewat, William Brian 1936- *WhoAm 94, WhoFI 94*
He Wenzhi 1931- *WhoPRCh 91 [port]*
Hewer, Thomas Frederick 1903- *Who 94*
Hewes, Dorothy Walker 1922- *WhoWest 94*
Hewes, Henry 1917- *WhoAm 94*
Hewes, Jonathan William 1945- *WhoAmL 94*
Hewes, Joseph 1730-1779 *WhAmRev*
Hewes, Laurence Ilsley, Jr. 1902-1989 *WhAm 10*
Hewes, Laurence Ilsley, III 1933- *WhoAm 94*
Hewes, Richard David 1926- *WhoAmP 93*
Hewes, Robert Charles 1953- *WhoMW 93*
Hewes, Robin Anthony Charles 1945- *Who 94*
Hewes, William G., III 1961- *WhoAmP 93*
Hewetson, Christopher (Raynor) 1929- *Who 94*
Hewetson, Reginald Hackett d1993 *Who 94N*
Hewett, Arthur Edward 1935- *WhoAm 94, WhoAmL 94*
Hewett, Christopher 1922- *WhoHol 92*
Hewett, Dorothy 1923- *BlmGWL [port]*
Hewett, Dorothy (Coade) 1923- *ConDr 93, IntDcT 2 [port], WrDr 94*
Hewett, Ed A. d1993 *NewYTBS 93 [port]*
Hewett, Ouida Hewett 1933- *WhoAmP 93*
Hewett, Peter (John Smithson) 1931- *Who 94*
Hewett, Richard William 1923- *Who 94*
Hewing, Pernell Hayes 1933- *WhoBlA 94*
Hewins, Nancy d1978 *WhoHol 92*
Hewish, Antony 1924- *IntWW 93, Who 94, WorScD*
Hewit, Augustine Francis 1820-1897 *DcAmReB 2*
Hewitt *Who 94*
Hewitt, Alan d1986 *WhoHol 92*
Hewitt, Alison Hope 1915- *WrDr 94*
Hewitt, Anthony Victor 1943- *WhoMW 93*
Hewitt, Basil 1926- *WhoBlA 94*
Hewitt, Bill d1947 *ProFbHF*
Hewitt, Bob 1940- *BuCMET*
Hewitt, Brian 1950- *WhoAm 94*
Hewitt, C. Anne 1941- *WhoFI 94*
Hewitt, Carl Herbert 1952- *WhoAm 94*
Hewitt, Carol A. 1945- *WhoAmL 94*
Hewitt, Cecil Rolph *Who 94*
Hewitt, Charles Colby, III 1949- *WhoFI 94*
Hewitt, Charles Walworth 1943- *WhoFI 94*
Hewitt, Dennis Edwin 1944- *WhoAm 94*
Hewitt, Don S. 1922- *WhoAm 94*
Hewitt, Duncan Adams 1949- *WhoAmA 93*
Hewitt, Edwin 1920- *WhoAm 94, WhoWest 94*
Hewitt, Eric John 1919- *IntWW 93, Who 94*
Hewitt, Francis Anthony 1943- *Who 94*
Hewitt, Francis Ray 1936-1992 *WhoAmA 93N*
Hewitt, Frank Seaver 1941-1990 *WhAm 10*
Hewitt, Frankie Lea 1931- *WhoAm 94*
Hewitt, Gavin Wallace 1944- *Who 94*
Hewitt, Geof *DrAPF 93*
Hewitt, Geof 1943- *WrDr 94*
Hewitt, Geoffrey Frederick 1934- *Who 94*
Hewitt, George Henry Gordon 1912- *Who 94*
Hewitt, Graves Desha 1928- *WhoIns 94*
Hewitt, Harold 1908- *Who 94*
Hewitt, Harold 1917- *Who 94*
Hewitt, Harry Ronald 1920- *IntWW 93, Who 94*
Hewitt, Henry d1968 *WhoHol 92*
Hewitt, Henry H. 1941- *WhoAmL 94*
Hewitt, James 1770-1827 *NewGrDO*
Hewitt, James J. 1933- *WhoAm 94*
Hewitt, James Watt 1932- *WhoAm 94, WhoAmL 94, WhoFI 94, WhoMW 93*
Hewitt, Jerene Cline 1917- *WhoWest 94*
Hewitt, John H., Jr. 1924- *WhoBlA 94*
Hewitt, John Stringer 1939- *WhoScEn 94*
Hewitt, Karen Renee 1950- *WhoFI 94*
Hewitt, Kenneth *WhoScEn 94*
Hewitt, Lenox *Who 94*
Hewitt, (Cyrus) Lenox (Simson) 1917- *Who 94*
Hewitt, Lester L. 1942- *WhoAmL 94*
Hewitt, Martin 1960- *WhoHol 92*
Hewitt, Michael Earling 1936- *Who 94*
Hewitt, Nicholas 1945- *WrDr 94*
Hewitt, Nicholas Charles Joseph 1947- *Who 94*
Hewitt, Patricia Hope 1948- *Who 94*
Hewitt, Paul Buck 1949- *WhoAm 94*
Hewitt, Penelope Ann 1932- *Who 94*
Hewitt, Peter McGregor 1929- *Who 94*
Hewitt, Richard Thornton 1917- *Who 94*
Hewitt, Robert Lee 1934- *WhoAm 94*
Hewitt, Ronald Jerome 1932- *WhoBlA 94*
Hewitt, Stephen Geoffrey 1950- *Who 94*
Hewitt, Thomas Edward 1939- *WhoAm 94, WhoFI 94, WhoMW 93*
Hewitt, Thurman H. 1919- *WhoAmA 93*
Hewitt, Virginia d1986 *WhoHol 92*
Hewitt, Vivian Ann Davidson *WhoAm 94*
Hewitt, Vivian Davidson *WhoBlA 94*
Hewitt, William Harley 1954- *WhoFI 94*
Hewitt, William James 1944- *WhoWest 94*
Hewlett, Antoinette Payne *WhoBlA 94*
Hewlett, Arthur 1907- *WhoHol 92*
Hewlett, David *WhoHol 92*
Hewlett, Dial, Jr. 1948- *WhoBlA 94*
Hewlett, Everett Augustus, Jr. 1943- *WhoBlA 94*
Hewlett, Horace Wilson 1915- *WhoAm 94*
Hewlett, Richard Greening 1923- *WhoAm 94*
Hewlett, Stephen Owen 1944- *WhoAmP 93*
Hewlett, Sylvia Ann 1946- *WrDr 94*
Hewlett, William Redington 1913- *WhoAm 94, WhoScEn 94, WhoWest 94*
Hewlett-Davies, Janet Mary 1938- *Who 94*
Hewson, Donna Walters 1947- *WhoFI 94*
Hewson, John 1930- *WrDr 94*
Hewson, John 1946- *IntWW 93*
Hewson, John Robert 1946- *Who 94*
Hewson, Paul 1960- *WhoAm 94*
Hewston, Alfred d1947 *WhoHol 92*
Hexham And Newcastle, Auxiliary Bishop of *Who 94*
Hexham And Newcastle, Bishop of 1928- *Who 94*
He Xiang *WhoPRCh 91*
He Xiaohu 1950- *WhoPRCh 91 [port]*
Hexner, Ervin Paul 1893- *WhAm 10*
Hext, Harrington *EncSF 93*
Hext, Kathleen Florence 1941- *WhoAm 94, WhoWest 94*
Hextall, Ron 1964- *WhoAm 94*
Hexter, Jack H. 1910- *WhoAm 94*
Hexter, Maurice Beck 1891-1990 *WhAm 10*
Hexum, Jon-Erik d1984 *WhoHol 92*
Hey, Ernest 1912- *Who 94*
Hey, James Stanley 1909- *Who 94*
Hey, John Charles 1935- *WhoAm 94*
Hey, John Denis 1944- *Who 94*
Hey, Nigel Stewart 1936- *WhoWest 94*
Hey, Phillip H. *DrAPF 93*
Hey, Richard *EncSF 93*
Hey, Robert Pierpont 1935- *WhoAm 94*
Hey, Virginia *WhoHol 92*
Heybach, John Peter 1950- *WhoFI 94*
Heyborne, Robert Linford 1923- *WhoAm 94*
Heyburn, John G. 1948- *WhoAm 94*
Heyburn, John G., II 1948- *WhoAmL 94*
Heyburn, Weldon d1951 *WhoHol 92*
Heyck, Theodore Daly 1941- *WhoAmL 94, WhoWest 94*
Heyde, Christopher Charles 1939- *IntWW 93*
Heyde, Martha Bennett 1920- *WhoAm 94*
Heydebrand, Wolf Von 1930- *WhoAm 94*
Heyderman, Arthur Jerome 1946- *WhoMW 93, WhoScEn 94*
Heydman, Abby Maria 1943- *WhoWest 94*
Heydon, J(oseph) K(entigern) *EncSF 93*
Heydorn, Kaj 1931- *WhoScEn 94*
Heydrich, Reinhard 1904-1942 *HisWorL*
Heydron, Vicki Ann *EncSF 93*
Heydron, Vicki Ann 1945- *WrDr 94*
Heydt, Louis Jean d1960 *WhoHol 92*
Heyen, Beatrice J. 1925- *WhoMW 93, WhoScEn 94*
Heyen, William *DrAPF 93*
Heyen, William 1940- *WrDr 94*
Heyer, Carol 1950- *SmATA 74 [port], WrDr 94*
Heyer, Carol Ann 1950- *WhoWest 94*
Heyer, Georgette 1902-1974 *BlmGWL*
Heyer, John Henry, II 1946- *WhoAmL 94*
Heyer, Paul 1936- *WrDr 94*
Heyer, Paul Otto 1936- *WhoAm 94*
Heyerdahl, Thor 1914- *IntWW 93, Who 94, WhoScEn 94, WrDr 94*
Heyert, Martin David 1934- *WhoAm 94*
Heyes, Herbert d1958 *WhoHol 92*
Heygate, Richard John Gage 1940- *Who 94*
Heyhoe, David Charles Ross 1938- *Who 94*
Heyhoe Flint, Rachael 1939- *Who 94*
He Ying 1914- *IntWW 93, WhoPRCh 91 [port]*
He Yingqiang *WhoPRCh 91 [port]*
He Yixiang, Maj.-Gen. 1911- *IntWW 93*
Heykes, Nancy Nelson 1952- *WhoMW 93*
Heyking, Elisabeth von 1861-1925 *BlmGWL*
Heyl, Allen Van, Jr. 1918- *WhoScEn 94, WhoWest 94*
Heyl, Bernard Chapman 1905-1966 *WhoAmA 93N*
Heyland, James Reuben 1956- *WhoFI 94*
Heylen, Syd *WhoHol 92*
Heyler, Grover Ross 1926- *WhoAm 94*
Heylin, Angela Christine 1943- *IntWW 93*
Heylin, Clinton (M.) 1960- *WrDr 94*
Heym, Stefan 1913- *ConWorW 93, IntWW 93*
Heymair, Magdalena c. 1545-c. 1586 *BlmGWL*
Heyman, Abigail 1942- *WrDr 94*
Heyman, Allan 1921- *Who 94*
Heyman, Art 1941- *BasBi*
Heyman, Barton 1937- *WhoHol 92*
Heyman, George Harrison, Jr. 1916- *WhoAm 94*
Heyman, Harry Clinton 1924- *WhoAmP 93*
Heyman, Horace (William) 1912- *Who 94*
Heyman, Ira Michael 1930- *IntWW 93, WhoWest 94*
Heyman, Jacques 1925- *Who 94, WrDr 94*
Heyman, John 1933- *IntMPA 94*
Heyman, Josiah McC(onnell) 1958- *ConAu 140*
Heyman, Julius Scott 1960- *WhoScEn 94*
Heyman, Lawrence Murray 1932- *WhoAm 94, WhoAmA 93*
Heyman, Melvin Bernard 1950- *WhoScEn 94*
Heyman, Michael Gerald 1945- *WhoAmL 94*
Heyman, Ralph Edmond 1931- *WhoAm 94*
Heyman, Samuel J. 1939- *WhoAm 94, WhoFI 94*
Heyman, Steven 1952- *WhoAmA 93*

Hicks, H. Beecher, Jr. 1944- *WhoBlA 94*
Hicks, Henderson 1930- *WhoBlA 94*
Hicks, Henry Beecher, Sr. 1912- *WhoBlA 94*
Hicks, Henry Davies *IntWW 93N*
Hicks, Henry Davies 1915-1991 *WhAm 10*
Hicks, Herbert Ray 1939- *WhoMW 93*
Hicks, Hilly *WhoHol 92*
Hicks, Ingrid Diann 1958- *WhoBlA 94*
Hicks, Irle Raymond 1928- *WhoAm 94*
Hicks, Irvin 1938- *WhoAmP 93*
Hicks, J. Portis 1938- *WhoAmL 94*
Hicks, James Benton, III 1956- *WhoAmL 94*
Hicks, James Bradley 1959- *WhoFI 94*
Hicks, James Earl 1951- *WhoMW 93*
Hicks, James Hermann 1955- *WhoAmL 94*
Hicks, Jim Ray 1935- *WhoAmP 93*
Hicks, Jimmie Lee 1936- *WhoWest 94*
Hicks, Jocelyn Muriel 1937- *WhoScEn 94*
Hicks, John d1989 *NobelP 91N*
Hicks, John (Richard) 1904-1989 *WrDr 94N*
Hicks, John Charles 1928- *Who 94*
Hicks, John David 1945- *WhoAm 94*
Hicks, John O., III 1943- *WhoAmP 93*
Hicks, John Richard 1904-1989 *WhAm 10*
Hicks, John T. 1925- *WhoAmP 93*
Hicks, John Victor 1907- *WhoWest 94*
Hicks, Judith Eileen 1947- *WhoMW 93*
Hicks, Ken Carlyle 1953- *WhoAm 94*
Hicks, Kerry Douglas 1962- *WhoWest 94*
Hicks, Kevin *WhoHol 92*
Hicks, Larry R. 1943- *WhoAmL 94*
Hicks, Larry W. 1948- *WhoAmP 93*
Hicks, Lawrence Wayne 1940- *WhoAm 94, WhoFI 94*
Hicks, Leon Nathaniel 1933- *WhoAmA 93, WhoBlA 94*
Hicks, Leonard d1971 *WhoHol 92*
Hicks, Leslie 1952- *WhoWest 94*
Hicks, Leslie Hubert 1927- *WhoAm 94*
Hicks, Louis Charles, Jr. 1951- *WhoBlA 94*
Hicks, Lucile P. 1938- *WhoAmP 93*
Hicks, M. Elizabeth 1944- *WhoAm 94*
Hicks, Marion Lawrence, Jr. 1945- *WhoAm 94*
Hicks, Mark C., Jr. 1927- *WhoAmP 93*
Hicks, Mark Wayne 1951- *WhoFI 94*
Hicks, Marshall M. 1931- *WhoAm 94*
Hicks, Maryellen 1949- *WhoBlA 94*
Hicks, Maureen Patricia 1948- *Who 94, WhoWomW 91*
Hicks, Maxine Elliott 1908- *WhoHol 92*
Hicks, Michael *Who 94*
Hicks, (William) Michael (Ellis) 1928- *Who 94*
Hicks, Michael David 1958- *WhoScEn 94*
Hicks, Morris Alvin 1936- *WhoWest 94*
Hicks, Orton Havergal 1900- *WhoAm 94*
Hicks, Paul B., Jr. 1925- *WhoAm 94*
Hicks, Paul B., III 1956- *WhoAmP 93*
Hicks, Richard Emery 1954- *WhoMW 93*
Hicks, Richard R. 1931- *WhoBlA 94*
Hicks, Robert 1938- *Who 94*
Hicks, Robert Alvin 1932- *WhoWest 94*
Hicks, Robert G. d1993 *NewYTBS 93*
Hicks, Robert Miller 1925- *WhoAmP 93*
Hicks, Robin Edgcumbe 1942- *Who 94*
Hicks, Russell d1957 *WhoHol 92*
Hicks, Seymour d1949 *WhoHol 92*
Hicks, Sheila 1934- *WhoAmA 93*
Hicks, Sherman Gregory 1946- *WhoMW 93*
Hicks, Susan Lynn Bowman 1952- *WhoMW 93*
Hicks, Taylor M., Jr. 1944- *WhoAm 94, WhoAmL 94*
Hicks, Thomas *Who 94*
Hicks, Thomas Erasmo 1957- *WhoScEn 94*
Hicks, Thomas Howard 1946- *WhoAm 94*
Hicks, Timothy Gerald 1952- *WhoAmL 94, WhoAmP 93*
Hicks, Troy Lee 1932- *WhoMW 93*
Hicks, Tyler Gregory 1921- *WhoAm 94*
Hicks, Veronica Abena 1949- *WhoBlA 94*
Hicks, Walter Joseph 1935- *WhoScEn 94*
Hicks, Wayland R. 1942- *WhoAm 94, WhoFI 94*
Hicks, William Albert, III 1942- *WhoAm 94, WhoAmL 94*
Hicks, William H. 1925- *WhoBlA 94*
Hicks, William James 1948- *WhoBlA 94*
Hicks, William L. 1928- *WhoBlA 94*
Hicks, William Stanley 1945- *WhoMW 93*
Hicks, Willie J. d1991 *WhoBlA 94N*
Hicks, Willie Lee 1931- *WhoBlA 94*
Hicks-Bartlett, Sharon Theresa 1951- *WhoBlA 94*
Hicks Beach *Who 94*
Hickson, David L. 1945- *WhoAmL 94*
Hickson, Ernest Charles 1931- *WhoFI 94, WhoWest 94*
Hickson, Eugene, Sr. 1930- *WhoBlA 94*
Hickson, Harry L. 1940- *WhoAmL 94*
Hickson, Joan 1906- *WhoHol 92*
Hickson, Joan Bogle 1906- *WhoAm 94*
Hickson, Michael 1938- *Who 94*
Hickson, Robin Julian 1944- *WhoScEn 94*
Hickson, Sherman Ruben 1950- *WhoBlA 94*
Hickson, William F., Jr. 1936- *WhoBlA 94*
Hicyilmaz, Gay 1947- *SmATA 77, WrDr 94*
Hida, George Tiberiu 1946- *WhoScEn 94*
Hida, Miyoko 1941- *WhoWomW 91*
Hida, Takeyuki 1927- *WhoScEn 94*
Hidalgo, Alberto 1935- *WhoHisp 94*
Hidalgo, Carlos Alberto 1955- *WhoHisp 94*
Hidalgo, David Kent *WhoHisp 94*
Hidalgo, Edward 1912- *WhoAm 94, WhoAmL 94, WhoHisp 94*
Hidalgo, Elvira de 1892-1980 *NewGrDO*
Hidalgo, Hector J. 1954- *WhoAmP 93*
Hidalgo, Hilda *WhoHisp 94*
Hidalgo, James Michael 1951- *WhoHisp 94*
Hidalgo, Jesse Elilio 1950- *WhoWest 94*
Hidalgo, Juan 1614-1685 *NewGrDO*
Hidalgo, Miguel 1958- *WhoFI 94, WhoWest 94*
Hidalgo, Nitza Mercedes 1951- *WhoHisp 94*
Hidalgo, Rodrigo 1940- *WhoHisp 94*
Hidalgo-De Jesús, Amarilis 1962- *WhoHisp 94*
Hidayat, Sadik *RfGShF*
Hidayatullah, Mohammad 1905-1992 *WhAm 10*
Hidayatullah, Mohammed d1992 *IntWW 93N*
Hidden, Anthony Brian 1936- *Who 94*
Hidden, (Frederick) Norman 1913- *WrDr 94*
Hiddleston, Ronal Eugene 1939- *WhoWest 94*
Hide, Peter Nicholas 1944- *WhoAmA 93*
Hide, Raymond 1929- *IntWW 93, Who 94*
Hideaki, Okada 1935- *WhoScEn 94*
Hidegkuti, Nandor 1922- *WorESoc*
Hiden, Robert Battaile, Jr. 1933- *WhoAm 94, WhoAmL 94*
Hider, David James 1934- *Who 94*
Hider, William Oliver 1946- *WhoFI 94*
Hidore, John Junior 1932- *WhoAm 94*
Hidy, George Martel 1935- *WhoAm 94*
Hieatt, Allen Kent 1921- *WhoAm 94*
Hieatt, Constance B(artlett) 1928- *WrDr 94*
Hieatt, Constance Bartlett 1928- *WhoAm 94*
Hieber, George Frederick, II 1942- *WhoAmP 93*
Hiebert, D(avid) Edmond 1910- *WrDr 94*
Hiebert, Donald Lee 1943- *WhoMW 93*
Hiebert, Ernest 1941- *WhoScEn 94*
Hiebert, Erwin Nick 1919- *IntWW 93*
Hiebert, Ray Eldon 1932- *WhoAm 94*
Hieftje, Gary Martin 1942- *WhoScEn 94*
Hieken, Charles 1928- *WhoAmL 94*
Hiel, Clem 1952- *WhoWest 94*
Hielscher, Leo (Arthur) 1926- *Who 94*
Hielscher, Udo Artur 1939- *WhoAm 94, WhoFI 94*
Hiemstra, Roger 1938- *WhoAm 94*
Hienton, Diane DeBrosse 1948- *WhoAmL 94*
Hienton, James Robert 1951- *WhoAmL 94, WhoFI 94*
Hienton, Joseph P. 1946- *WhoAmL 94*
Hier, John A. 1951- *WhoMW 93*
Hier, Marshall David 1945- *WhoAmL 94*
Hier, Perry O. *WhoAmP 93*
Hieronymus, Clara Booth Wiggins 1913- *WhoAm 94*
Hieronymus, Edward Whittlesey 1943- *WhoAm 94, WhoAmL 94*
Hiers, Walter d1933 *WhoHol 92*
Hiesiger, Barbara *DrAPF 93*
Hiestand, Emily (L.) 1947- *WrDr 94*
Hiestand, John d1987 *WhoHol 92*
Hiestand, Nancy Laura 1956- *WhoScEn 94*
Hiester, Daniel 1747-1804 *WhAmRev*
Hiester, Joseph 1752-1832 *WhAmRev*
Hiestermann, Horst 1934- *NewGrDO*
Hiett, Edward Emerson 1922- *WhoAm 94*
Hietter, Paul Andrew 1962- *WhoMW 93*
Hift, Fred 1924- *IntMPA 94*
Higa 1938- *WhoAmA 93*
Higa, Kunihiko 1956- *WhoAsA 94*
Higa, Leslie Hideyasu 1925- *WhoAsA 94*
Higa, Ross Rikio 1959- *WhoAsA 94*
Higa, Tatsuo 1939- *WhoScEn 94*
Higa, Walter Hiroichi 1919- *WhoAsA 94*
Higaki, Tokutaro 1916- *IntWW 93*
Higashi, Kerwin Masuto 1961- *WhoAsA 94*
Higashida, Yoshisuke 1942- *WhoScEn 94*
Higashiguchi, Minoru 1930- *WhoScEn 94*
Higbee, Donald William 1931- *WhoFI 94*
Higbee, Joan Florence 1945- *WhoAm 94*
Higbee, John P. 1933- *WhoAmP 93*
Higbee, Paul Stanford 1953- *WhoMW 93*
Higby, Edward Julian 1939- *WhoFI 94, WhoScEn 94*
Higby, Gregory James 1953- *WhoAm 94*
Higby, James Harland 1946- *WhoAm 94*
Higby, Mary Jane d1986 *WhoHol 92*
Higby, Wayne 1943- *WhoAm 94*
Higby, (Donald) Wayne 1943- *WhoAmA 93*
Higby, Wilbur d1934 *WhoHol 92*
Higdon, Barbara J. 1930- *WhoAm 94*
Higdon, Bernice Cowan 1918- *WhoWest 94*
Higdon, Charles Anthony 1947- *WhoScEn 94*
Higdon, Charles Gregory 1947- *WhoAmP 93*
Higdon, David Leon 1939- *WhoAm 94*
Higdon, Ernest D. *WhoAm 94*
Higdon, Hal 1931- *WrDr 94*
Higdon, Polly Susanne 1942- *WhoAm 94, WhoAmL 94, WhoWest 94*
Higdon, Willie Junior 1924- *WhoAmP 93*
Higelin, Jacques *WhoHol 92*
Higganbotham, Susan Diane 1962- *WhoFI 94*
Higginbotham, A. Leon, Jr. 1928- *AfrAmAl 6 [port], WhoAm 94, WhoAmP 93, WhoBlA 94*
Higginbotham, Donald *WhoAmP 93*
Higginbotham, G. J. *WhoAmP 93*
Higginbotham, James David 1924- *WhoMW 93*
Higginbotham, Jay 1937- *WrDr 94*
Higginbotham, John Taylor 1947- *WhoAmL 94*
Higginbotham, Kenneth Day, Sr. 1928- *WhoBlA 94*
Higginbotham, Lloyd William 1934- *WhoScEn 94, WhoWest 94*
Higginbotham, Patrick Errol 1938- *WhoAm 94, WhoAmL 94, WhoAmP 93*
Higginbotham, Peyton Randolph 1902- *WhoBlA 94*
Higginbotham, Samuel Page 1916- *WhoAmP 93*
Higginbotham-Brooks, Renee 1952- *WhoBlA 94*
Higginbottom, Donald Noble 1925- *Who 94*
Higginbottom, Samuel Logan 1921- *WhoAm 94*
Higgins *Who 94*
Higgins, Aidan 1927- *WrDr 94*
Higgins, Alec Wilfred 1914- *Who 94*
Higgins, Andrew J. 1921- *WhoAmP 93*
Higgins, Andrew Jackson 1921- *WhoAm 94*
Higgins, Andrew James 1948- *Who 94*
Higgins, Ann d1978 *WhoHol 92*
Higgins, Anthony *WhoHol 92*
Higgins, Barbara Lorene 1947- *WhoMW 93*
Higgins, Bennett Edward 1931- *WhoBlA 94*
Higgins, Bill Edward 1961- *WhoWest 94*
Higgins, Charles Graham 1925- *WhoAm 94*
Higgins, Chester A., Sr. 1917- *WhoBlA 94*
Higgins, Chester Archer, Jr. 1946- *WhoBlA 94*
Higgins, Christopher (Thomas) 1914- *Who 94*
Higgins, Christopher Francis 1955- *Who 94*
Higgins, Claire *WhoHol 92*
Higgins, Clarence R., Jr. 1927- *WhoBlA 94*
Higgins, Cleo Surry 1923- *WhoBlA 94*
Higgins, Colin d1988 *WhoHol 92*
Higgins, Colin Kirk 1945- *Who 94*
Higgins, D. S(ydney) 1938- *WrDr 94*
Higgins, Daniel B. 1948- *WhoAmL 94*
Higgins, David d1936 *WhoHol 92*
Higgins, David M. 1944- *WhoAmL 94*
Higgins, Dick *DrAPF 93*
Higgins, Dick 1938- *WhoAm 94, WhoAmA 93, WrDr 94*
Higgins, (George) Edward 1930- *WhoAmA 93*
Higgins, Edward Aloysius 1931- *WhoAm 94, WhoMW 93*
Higgins, Edward C. d1983 *WhoHol 92*
Higgins, Edward Ferdinand, III *WhoAmA 93*
Higgins, Edward Koelling 1926- *WhoAmA 93*
Higgins, Eugene 1875-1958 *WhoAmA 93N*
Higgins, Francis Edward 1935- *WhoMW 93*
Higgins, Frank *DrAPF 93*
Higgins, Frank 1927- *Who 94*
Higgins, Frederick Benjamin, Jr. 1936- *WhoAm 94*
Higgins, Geoffrey Trevor 1932- *WhoAm 94*
Higgins, George Edward 1930- *WhoAm 94*
Higgins, George V. *DrAPF 93*
Higgins, George V(incent) 1939- *WrDr 94*
Higgins, George Vincent 1939- *IntWW 93, WhoAm 94*
Higgins, Harold Bailey 1922- *WhoAm 94*
Higgins, Harrison Scott 1945- *WhoFI 94*
Higgins, Harry Vincent 1855-1928 *NewGrDO*
Higgins, Jack *IntWW 93, Who 94*
Higgins, Jack 1929- *WhoAm 94*
Higgins, Jack 1939- *WrDr 94*
Higgins, Jack 1954- *WhoAm 94, WhoMW 93*
Higgins, James Bradley 1941- *WhoWest 94*
Higgins, James F. *WhoAm 94*
Higgins, James Henry 1916- *WhoAm 94*
Higgins, James Henry, III 1940- *WhoAm 94*
Higgins, James Joseph 1920- *WhoMW 93*
Higgins, Jay Francis 1945- *WhoAm 94*
Higgins, Jim S. 1932- *WhoAmP 93*
Higgins, Joanna 1945- *ConAu 141*
Higgins, Joe 1910- *WhoHol 92*
Higgins, John Andrew 1940- *Who 94*
Higgins, John C(layborn) 1934- *WrDr 94*
Higgins, John Christopher 1932- *Who 94*
Higgins, John Edward, Jr. 1939- *WhoAmL 94*
Higgins, John Joseph 1934- *WhoAm 94, WhoFI 94*
Higgins, John Patrick Basil d1993 *Who 94N*
Higgins, Jon Stanley 1941- *WhoWest 94*
Higgins, Kenneth Raymond 1915- *WhoAm 94*
Higgins, Kimberley Kay 1957- *WhoFI 94*
Higgins, Lawrence Martin 1952- *WhoAmL 94*
Higgins, Leslie Bradbury 1919- *WhoAmP 93*
Higgins, Linwood McIntire 1948- *WhoAmP 93*
Higgins, Margaret Tullar 1930- *WhoAmP 93*
Higgins, Marge 1931- *WhoAmP 93*
Higgins, Marguerite 1920-1966 *HisDcKW*
Higgins, Mary Lou 1926- *WhoAmA 93*
Higgins, Matthew Joseph 1938- *WhoAm 94*
Higgins, Michael 1922- *WhoHol 92*
Higgins, Michael 1941- *IntWW 93*
Higgins, Michael John 1935- *Who 94*
Higgins, Michael Salyards 1946- *WhoMW 93*
Higgins, Michael William 1957- *WhoWest 94*
Higgins, Nancy Carol 1951- *WhoMW 93*
Higgins, Nancy McCready 1951- *WhoAmL 94*
Higgins, Ora A. 1919- *WhoBlA 94*
Higgins, Paul Anthony 1964- *WhoWest 94*
Higgins, Paul R. 1944- *WhoAmP 93*
Higgins, Penny D. 1954- *WhoMW 93*
Higgins, Peter Matthew 1923- *Who 94*
Higgins, Peter Thomas 1943- *WhoFI 94, WhoScEn 94*
Higgins, Reynold Alleyne d1993 *Who 94N*
Higgins, Reynold Alleyne 1916- *WrDr 94*
Higgins, Reynold Alleyne 1916-1993 *ConAu 141*
Higgins, Richard J. *WhoScEn 94*
Higgins, Rita Ann 1955- *BlmGWL*
Higgins, Robert Arthur 1924- *WhoAm 94*
Higgins, Robert Frederick 1944- *WhoAmL 94*
Higgins, Robert J. 1941- *WhoAmL 94*
Higgins, Robert Louis 1919- *WhoAm 94*
Higgins, Robert Walter 1934- *WhoAm 94*
Higgins, Rod Dwayne 1960- *WhoBlA 94*
Higgins, Rosalyn 1937- *IntWW 93, Who 94, WrDr 94*
Higgins, Ross *WhoHol 92*
Higgins, Ruth Ann 1944- *WhoWest 94*
Higgins, Ruth Ellen 1945- *WhoMW 93*
Higgins, Sammie L. 1923- *WhoBlA 94*
Higgins, Sean Marielle 1968- *WhoBlA 94*
Higgins, Stann 1952- *WhoBlA 94*
Higgins, Stephen E. 1938- *WhoAm 94*
Higgins, Terence (Langley) 1928- *Who 94*
Higgins, Therese 1925- *WhoAm 94*
Higgins, Thomas A. 1932- *WhoAm 94, WhoAmL 94*
Higgins, Thomas David 1959- *WhoAmL 94*
Higgins, Thomas James 1945- *WhoAm 94, WhoAmP 93*
Higgins, Thomas Joseph 1899- *WrDr 94*
Higgins, Thomas P. 1950- *WhoAmL 94*
Higgins, Victor 1884-1949 *WhoAmA 93N*

Higgins, Wallace Winfield 1931- *WhoAmP 93*
Higgins, Wilfred Frank *Who 94*
Higgins, William Alleyne 1928- *Who 94*
Higgins, William Henry Clay, III 1908- *WhoAm 94*
Higginsen, Vy *WhoBlA 94*
Higginson, Francis 1586-1630 *DcAmReB 2*
Higginson, Gordon (Robert) 1929- *Who 94*
Higginson, James Jackson 1921- *WhoAm 94*
Higginson, Jerry Alden, Jr. 1957- *WhoFI 94*
Higginson, Jerry Cassim 1938- *WhoAmP 93*
Higginson, John 1922- *IntWW 93*
Higginson, John 1932- *WhoWest 94*
Higginson, Roy Patrick 1946- *WhoScEn 94*
Higginson, Stephen 1743-1828 *WhAmRev*
Higginson, Thomas Joseph 1940- *WhoFI 94*
Higginson, Thomas Lee 1920-1990 *WhAm 10*
Higginson, Thomas Wentworth Storrow 1823-1911 *AmSocL*
Higginson, William J. *DrAPF 93*
Higgs, Barry 1934- *Who 94*
Higgs, Brian James 1930- *Who 94*
Higgs, Craig DeWitt 1944- *WhoAmL 94*
Higgs, David Lawrence 1951- *WhoAmL 94*
Higgs, DeWitt A. 1907- *WhoAm 94*
Higgs, Frederick C. 1935- *WhoBlA 94*
Higgs, John H. 1934- *WhoAm 94*
Higgs, Lloyd Albert 1937- *WhoAm 94*
Higgs, Mary Ann Spicer 1951- *WhoBlA 94*
Higgs, Michael *Who 94*
Higgs, (John) Michael (Clifford) 1912- *Who 94*
Higgs, Peter Ware 1929- *IntWW 93, Who 94*
Higgs, Richard d1977 *WhoHol 92*
High, Charles C., Jr. 1942- *WhoAmL 94*
High, Claude, Jr. 1944- *WhoBlA 94*
High, Denny F. 1939- *WhoFI 94*
High, Freida 1946- *WhoBlA 94*
High, George Borman 1931- *WhoAm 94*
High, Kenneth M., Jr. 1946- *WhoAmL 94*
High, Philip E(mpson) 1914- *EncSF 93, WrDr 94*
High, Robert Gordon d1993 *NewYTBS 93 [port]*
High, S. Dale 1942- *WhoAm 94*
High, Steven S. 1956- *WhoAmA 93*
High, Suzanne Irene 1946- *WhoAmL 94, WhoMW 93*
High, Thomas W. 1947- *WhoAm 94, WhoWest 94*
High, Timothy Griffin 1949- *WhoAm 94, WhoAmA 93*
High, William Fray 1962- *WhoAmL 94*
Higham, Charles 1931- *WrDr 94*
Higham, Geoffrey Arthur 1927- *Who 94*
Higham, John 1920- *IntWW 93, WhoAm 94*
Higham, John Arthur 1952- *Who 94*
Higham, John Drew 1914- *Who 94*
Higham, Norman 1924- *Who 94*
Higham, Philip Roger Canning 1920- *Who 94*
Higham, Robert R. A. 1935- *WrDr 94*
Higham, Robin 1925- *WhoAm 94, WrDr 94*
Higham, Roger Stephen *WrDr 94*
Highberger, William Foster 1950- *WhoAm 94, WhoAmL 94*
Highby, Lowell John 1962- *WhoMW 93*
Highet, Gilbert Keith MacInnes 1933- *WhoAm 94*
Highet, Helen Clark *Who 94*
Highet, John 1918- *WrDr 94*
Highfield, Robert Edward 1930- *WhoAm 94*
Highfield, (John) Roger (Loxdale) 1922- *WrDr 94*
Highfill, Philip Henry, Jr. 1918- *WhoAm 94*
Highland, Cecil Blaine, Jr. 1918- *WhoAm 94*
Highland, Dora 1924- *WrDr 94*
Highland, Harold Joseph 1917- *WhoScEn 94*
Highland, Marilyn Rae Schnell 1956- *WhoWest 94*
Highland, Monica 1934- *WrDr 94*
Highlander, Richard William 1940- *WhoWest 94*
Highlen, Larry Wade 1936- *WhoMW 93*
Highlen, Pamela Sue 1946- *WhoMW 93*
Highleyman, Samuel Locke, III 1928- *WhoAm 94*
Highsmith, Alonzo Walter 1965- *WhoBlA 94*
Highsmith, Carlton L. *WhoBlA 94*
Highsmith, Charles Albert 1921- *WhoBlA 94*
Highsmith, Jasper Habersham 1940- *WhoFI 94*
Highsmith, Patricia 1921- *IntWW 93, Who 94*
Highsmith, (Mary) Patricia 1921- *GayLL, WrDr 94*
Highsmith, Shelby 1929- *WhoAm 94, WhoAmL 94*
Highstein, Jene 1942- *WhoAmA 93*
Hight, B. Boyd 1939- *WhoAm 94, WhoAmL 94*
Hight, Harold Philip 1924- *WhoWest 94*
Hightower, Allen Ross, Jr. 1946- *WhoAmP 93*
Hightower, Anthony *WhoBlA 94*
Hightower, Anthony 1961- *WhoAmP 93*
Hightower, Bryan d1978 *WhoHol 92*
Hightower, Caroline Warner 1935- *WhoAm 94*
Hightower, Charles H., III 1934- *WhoBlA 94*
Hightower, Dennis Fowler 1941- *WhoBlA 94*
Hightower, Edward Stewart 1940- *WhoBlA 94*
Hightower, Eloyce d1939 *WhoHol 92*
Hightower, Foyle Robert, Jr. 1941- *WhoAmP 93*
Hightower, Gail 1946- *AfrAmAl 6*
Hightower, Herma J. *WhoBlA 94*
Hightower, Jack English 1926- *WhoAm 94, WhoAmL 94, WhoAmP 93*
Hightower, James Howard *WhoBlA 94*
Hightower, Jesse Robert 1939- *WhoScEn 94*
Hightower, Jim 1943- *WhoAmP 93*
Hightower, John B. 1933- *IntWW 93, WhoAmA 93*
Hightower, John Brantley 1933- *WhoAm 94*
Hightower, Len 1955- *WhoWest 94*
Hightower, Lynn S. *ConAu 140*
Hightower, Michael *WhoBlA 94*
Hightower, Monteria 1929- *WhoBlA 94*
Hightower, Neil Hamilton 1940- *WhoAm 94*
Hightower, Stephen Lamar 1956- *WhoBlA 94*
Hightower, Willar H., Jr. 1943- *WhoBlA 94*
Hights, William E. *WhoBlA 94*
Highwater, Jamake *DrAPF 93, WhoAm 94*
Highwater, Jamake 1942- *WhoAmA 93, WrDr 94*
Highwater, Rosella 1920- *IntDcB [port]*
Higi, William L. 1933- *WhoAm 94, WhoMW 93*
Higinbotham, Betty Louise Wilson 1910-1992 *WhAm 10*
Higinbotham, William Alfred 1910- *WhoAm 94*
Higiro, Joy *BlmGWL*
Higley, Bruce Wadsworth 1928- *WhoAm 94*
Higley, David L. 1952- *WhoIns 94*
Higley, Leon George 1958- *WhoMW 93*
Higman, Graham 1917- *Who 94*
Hignett, H. R. d1959 *WhoHol 92*
Hignett, John Mulock 1934- *Who 94*
Hignett, Mary d1980 *WhoHol 92*
Hignett, Peter George 1925- *Who 94*
Hignett, Sean 1934- *WrDr 94*
Higonnet, Patrice (Louis-René) 1938- *WrDr 94*
Higson, Charles *ConAu 142*
Higson, Gordon Robert 1932- *Who 94*
Higton, Dennis John 1921- *Who 94*
Higuchi, Clayton T. 1948- *WhoAsA 94*
Higuchi, Wesley Kenji 1964- *WhoWest 94*
Higuera, Jesus 1950- *WhoHisp 94*
Higuera, Jonathan J. *WhoHisp 94*
Higuera, Ted 1958- *WhoHisp 94*
Hihara, Lloyd Hiromi 1961- *WhoAsA 94*
Hijikata, Takeshi 1915- *IntWW 93*
Hijuelos, Oscar 1951- *HispLC [port], WhoAm 94*
Hijuelos, Oscar J. 1951- *WhoHisp 94*
Hiken, Gerald 1927- *WhoHol 92*
Hikida, Robert Seiichi 1941- *WhoAsA 94*
Hikind, Dov 1950- *WhoAmP 93*
Hikmet, Nazim 1902?-1963 *ConAu 141*
Hilaire, Laurent 1963- *IntDcB*
Hilal, Ahmed Izzedin 1924- *IntWW 93*
Hilaly, Agha 1911- *IntWW 93, Who 94*
Hilary, David Henry Jephson 1932- *Who 94*
Hilary, Jennifer 1942- *WhoHol 92*
Hilary, Jerold Wayne 1953- *WhoAmL 94*
Hilbe, Alfred J. 1928- *IntWW 93*
Hilbe, Joseph Michael 1944- *WhoWest 94*
Hilberg, Raul 1926- *WrDr 94*
Hilberry, Conrad *DrAPF 93*
Hilberry, Conrad Arthur 1928- *WrDr 94*
Hilberry, John David 1932- *WhoFI 94*
Hilbert, Angelia Hulda 1949- *WhoMW 93*
Hilbert, Bernard Charles 1921- *WhoAm 94*
Hilbert, David 1862-1943 *WorScD*
Hilbert, Donna *DrAPF 93*
Hilbert, Paul J. 1949- *WhoAmP 93*
Hilbert, Peter Louis, Jr. 1952- *WhoAm 94, WhoAmL 94*
Hilbert, Richard A. 1947- *ConAu 142*
Hilbert, Robert Backus 1929- *WhoAm 94*
Hilbert, Robert Saul 1941- *WhoAm 94*
Hilbert, Stephen C. 1946- *WhoAm 94, WhoFI 94*
Hilboldt, James Sonnemann 1929- *WhoFI 94*
Hilboldt, Lisa *WhoHol 92*
Hilborn, John R. 1928- *WhoFI 94*
Hilborn, Kathy Faye 1952- *WhoMW 93*
Hilborn, Michael G. 1943- *WhoAm 94*
Hilborne, Thomas George, Jr. 1946- *WhoAmL 94*
Hilbrecht, Norman Ty 1933- *WhoAm 94, WhoAmP 93, WhoWest 94*
Hilburg, Alan Jay 1948- *WhoFI 94*
Hilburn, Earl Drayton 1920-1989 *WhAm 10*
Hilburn, John Charles 1946- *WhoFI 94, WhoScEn 94*
Hilby, Robert Allan 1957- *WhoFI 94*
Hild, Guy Marvin 1937- *WhoAmL 94*
Hild, Jack *GayLL*
Hild, John Henry 1931- *Who 94*
Hilda of Whitby 614-680 *BlmGWL*
Hildebidle, John *DrAPF 93*
Hildebrand, Carol Ilene 1943- *WhoWest 94*
Hildebrand, Connie Marie 1944- *WhoMW 93*
Hildebrand, Daniel Walter 1940- *WhoAmL 94*
Hildebrand, David Kent 1940- *WhoAm 94*
Hildebrand, Don Cecil 1943- *WhoFI 94, WhoWest 94*
Hildebrand, Edwin A. 1954- *WhoFI 94*
Hildebrand, Francis Begnaud 1915- *WhoAm 94*
Hildebrand, H(endrick) Edward 1895- *WhAm 10*
Hildebrand, Hilde d1976 *WhoHol 92*
Hildebrand, John 1949- *WrDr 94*
Hildebrand, John Frederick 1940- *WhoAm 94*
Hildebrand, John Grant 1942- *WhoAm 94*
Hildebrand, June Marianne 1930- *WhoAmA 93*
Hildebrand, Lo d1936 *WhoHol 92*
Hildebrand, Mal 1943- *WhoMW 93*
Hildebrand, Richard Allen 1916- *WhoBlA 94, WhoMW 93*
Hildebrand, Robert Ivan 1925- *WhoMW 93*
Hildebrand, Rodney d1962 *WhoHol 92*
Hildebrand, Roger Henry 1922- *WhoAm 94, WhoMW 93*
Hildebrand, Verna 1924- *WrDr 94*
Hildebrand, Verna Lee 1924- *WhoAm 94, WhoMW 93*
Hildebrand, William Clayton 1951- *WhoScEn 94*
Hildebrandt, Bradford Walter 1940- *WhoAm 94*
Hildebrandt, Frederick Dean, Jr. 1933- *WhoAm 94, WhoFI 94*
Hildebrandt, Greg 1939- *Au&Arts 12 [port]*
Hildebrandt, Greg Alan 1950- *WhoMW 93*
Hildebrandt, Henry Mark 1926- *WhoMW 93*
Hildebrandt, Lanny Ross 1954- *WhoAmP 93*
Hildebrandt, Peter Warren 1963- *WhoWest 94*
Hildebrandt, Theodore Ware 1922- *WhoAm 94*
Hildebrandt, Tim 1939- *Au&Arts 12 [port]*
Hildebrandt, William Albert 1917- *WhoAmA 93*
Hildebranski, Robert Joseph 1966- *WhoScEn 94*
Hildebrant, Andy McClellan 1929- *WhoScEn 94, WhoWest 94*
Hildebrant, Jeffrey P. 1953- *WhoAmL 94*
Hildegard von Bingen 1098?-1179 *BlmGWL*
Hilden, Jytte 1942- *WhoWomW 91*
Hildenbrand, Werner 1936- *IntWW 93*
Hilder, Rowland d1993 *Who 94N*
Hilder, Rowland 1905-1993 *SmATA 77*
Hilderbran, Harvey 1960- *WhoAmP 93*
Hilderbrandt, Donald Franklin, II 1939- *WhoAm 94*
Hilderbrandt, Howard Logan 1874-1958 *WhoAmA 93N*
Hildesheimer, Wolfgang 1916-1991 *WhAm 10*
Hildick, E(mund) W(allace) 1925- *WrDr 94*
Hilding, Jerel Lee 1949- *WhoAm 94*
Hildner, Ernest Gotthold, III 1940- *WhoAm 94, WhoScEn 94, WhoWest 94*
Hildner, Phillips Brooks, II 1944- *WhoAmL 94*
Hildreth, Carolyn June 1940- *WhoMW 93*
Hildreth, Charles Steven 1949- *WhoWest 94*
Hildreth, Clifford 1917- *WhoAm 94*
Hildreth, Earlene 1949- *WhoMW 93*
Hildreth, Eugene A. *IntWW 93*
Hildreth, Eugene A. 1924- *WhoAm 94*
Hildreth, Gladys Johnson 1933- *WhoBlA 94*
Hildreth, James Robert 1927- *WhoAm 94*
Hildreth, (Henry) Jan (Hamilton Crossley) 1932- *Who 94*
Hildreth, (Harold) John (Crossley) d1992 *Who 94N*
Hildreth, Joseph Alan 1947- *WhoAmA 93*
Hildreth, Patricia Yvonne 1934- *WhoMW 93*
Hildreth, Roland James 1926- *WhoAm 94*
Hildrew, Bryan 1920- *IntWW 93, Who 94*
Hildt, Barbara A. 1946- *WhoAmP 93*
Hildum, Donald Clayton 1930- *WhoMW 93*
Hildyard, David (Henry Thoroton) 1916- *Who 94*
Hile, Duane L. 1945- *WhoMW 93*
Hile, Matthew George 1953- *WhoScEn 94*
Hile, Norman Carter 1945- *WhoAm 94, WhoAmL 94*
Hileman, Charles Clemens, III 1924- *WhoAm 94*
Hileman, Linda Carol 1947- *WhoWest 94*
Hiler, Edward Allan 1939- *WhoAm 94, WhoScEn 94*
Hiler, Hilaire 1898-1966 *WhoAmA 93N*
Hiler, John Patrick 1953- *WhoAm 94, WhoAmP 93*
Hiles, Bradley Stephen 1955- *WhoAmL 94*
Hiles, John Clifford, III 1959- *WhoWest 94*
Hilf, Russell 1931- *WhoAm 94*
Hilfer, Anthony Channell 1936- *WhoAm 94*
Hilferdin, Franz 1710?-1768 *IntDcB*
Hilferding, Franz 1710?-1768 *IntDcB*
Hilfiger, Tommy 1952- *News 93-3 [port], WhoAm 94*
Hilfinger, Dean Farrar 1912- *WhoAm 94*
Hilgard, Ernest (Ropiequet) 1904- *WrDr 94*
Hilgard, Ernest Ropiequet 1904- *IntWW 93, WhoAm 94, WhoWest 94*
Hilgartner, Charles Andrew 1932- *WhoScEn 94*
Hilgartner, Margaret Wehr 1924- *WhoAm 94*
Hilgeman, Georgia Kay 1950- *WhoWest 94*
Hilgeman, Liese 1961- *WhoAmA 93*
Hilgenberg, Eve Brantly Handy 1942- *WhoAm 94*
Hilgenberg, Jay 1960- *WhoAm 94*
Hilgenberg, John Christian 1941- *WhoAm 94*
Hilgenfeld, Rolf 1954- *WhoScEn 94*
Hilgenkamp, Kathryn Darline 1952- *WhoMW 93*
Hilger, Robert D. 1936- *WhoMW 93*
Hilger, Wolfgang 1929- *IntWW 93*
Hilgermann, Laura 1867-1937 *NewGrDO*
Hilgert, Raymond Lewis 1930- *WhoAm 94*
Hilgert, Ronald Francis 1947- *WhoWest 94*
Hilinski, Chester C. 1917- *WhoAm 94*
Hilken, E. Gene *WhoAmP 93*
Hilker, Anne Katherine 1953- *WhoAmL 94*
Hilker, Walter Robert, Jr. 1921- *WhoAm 94, WhoAmL 94, WhoWest 94*
Hilkert, Robert Joseph 1958- *WhoScEn 94*
Hill *Who 94*
Hill, Viscount 1931- *Who 94*
Hill, A. Alan 1938- *WhoAmP 93*
Hill, Aaron 1685-1750 *NewGrDO*
Hill, Al d1954 *WhoHol 92*
Hill, Alan Geoffrey 1931- *Who 94*
Hill, Alan John Wills 1912- *Who 94*
Hill, Alastair Malcolm 1936- *Who 94*
Hill, Albert Bernard 1928- *WhoAmP 93*
Hill, Albert Gordon 1910- *WhoAm 94*
Hill, Alette Olin 1933- *WhoWest 94*
Hill, Alfred 1917- *WhoAm 94*
Hill, Alfred 1925- *WhoBlA 94*
Hill, Alfred (Francis) 1870-1960 *NewGrDO*
Hill, Alice Lorraine 1935- *WhoFI 94*
Hill, Allen *Who 94*
Hill, (Hugh) Allen (Oliver) 1937- *Who 94*
Hill, Allen M. 1945- *WhoFI 94*
Hill, Amy 1953?- *WhoAsA 94*
Hill, Andrew William 1937- *WhoAm 94, WhoBlA 94, WhoWest 94*

Hill, Anita 1956- *AfrAmAl 6 [port], ConBlB 5 [port], News 94-1 [port]*
Hill, Anita Carraway 1928- *WhoAmP 93*
Hill, Anita F. 1956- *WhoAm 94*
Hill, Anita Faye 1956- *WhoBlA 94*
Hill, Anita June 1946- *WhoBlA 94*
Hill, Anna Marie 1938- *WhoWest 94*
Hill, Annette Tillman 1937- *WhoBlA 94*
Hill, Anthony 1930- *IntWW 93*
Hill, Anthony, Sr. 1957- *WhoAmP 93*
Hill, Anthony Whiting 1930- *WhoWest 94*
Hill, Antony James de Villiers 1940- *Who 94*
Hill, Archibald Vivian 1886-1977 *WorScD*
Hill, Arthur d1932 *WhoHol 92*
Hill, Arthur 1922- *IntMPA 94, WhoAm 94, WhoHol 92*
Hill, Arthur (Alfred) 1920- *Who 94*
Hill, Arthur Burit 1922- *WhoBlA 94*
Hill, Arthur James 1948- *WhoAm 94, WhoBlA 94, WhoFI 94*
Hill, Austin Bradford 1897-1991 *WhAm 10*
Hill, Avery 1924- *WhoBlA 94*
Hill, Barbara Ann 1944- *WhoAm 94*
Hill, Barbara Ann 1950- *WhoBlA 94*
Hill, Ben d1969 *WhoHol 92*
Hill, Bennett David 1934- *WhoAm 94, WhoBlA 94*
Hill, Benny 1925- *WhoHol 92*
Hill, Benny 1925-1992 *AnObit 1992, ConTFT 11, WhoCom*
Hill, Bernard *WhoHol 92*
Hill, Bernard 1944- *IntMPA 94*
Hill, Bettie L. 1935- *WhoAmP 93*
Hill, Betty J. 1948- *WhoBlA 94*
Hill, Beverly Ellen 1937- *WhoMW 93*
Hill, Billy d1940 *WhoHol 92*
Hill, Billy 1947- *WhoBlA 94*
Hill, Bob *ConAu 42NR*
Hill, Boyd *WhoAmP 93*
Hill, Boyd H., Jr. 1931- *WhoAm 94*
Hill, Brenda P. 1963- *WhoFI 94*
Hill, Brian 1930- *Who 94*
Hill, Brian 1947- *WhoAm 94*
Hill, Brian (John) 1932- *Who 94*
Hill, Bruce Edward 1964- *WhoBlA 94*
Hill, Bruce Marvin 1935- *WhoAm 94, WhoMW 93, WhoScEn 94*
Hill, Calvin 1947- *WhoBlA 94*
Hill, Carl M. *WhoBlA 94*
Hill, Carl Reuben 1957- *WhoWest 94*
Hill, Carol *DrAPF 93*
Hill, Carol 1942- *WrDr 94*
Hill, Carol (DeChellis) 1942- *EncSF 93*
Hill, Carol S. 1962- *WhoMW 93*
Hill, Cathy Lynn 1964- *WhoMW 93*
Hill, Charles d1938 *WhoHol 92*
Hill, Charles Christopher 1948- *WhoAmA 93*
Hill, Charles E. 1945- *WhoAmL 94*
Hill, Charles Graham, Jr. 1937- *WhoAm 94*
Hill, Charlyn Ann 1956- *WhoMW 93*
Hill, Christopher *IntWW 93, Who 94*
Hill, (John Edward) Christopher 1912- *IntWW 93, Who 94, WrDr 94*
Hill, Christopher John 1945- *IntWW 93, Who 94*
Hill, Clara Grant 1928- *WhoBlA 94*
Hill, Clinton 1922- *WhoAm 94*
Hill, Clinton J. 1922- *WhoAmA 93*
Hill, Colin Arnold Clifford 1929- *Who 94*
Hill, Cornelius d1907 *EncNAR*
Hill, Craig 1927- *WhoHol 92*
Hill, Craig Livingston 1949- *WhoScEn 94*
Hill, Curtis T., Sr. 1929- *WhoBlA 94*
Hill, Cynthia D. 1952- *WhoBlA 94*
Hill, Dale 1950- *WhoAm 94*
Hill, Dale Eugene 1931- *WhoMW 93*
Hill, Dale Richard 1939- *WhoWest 94*
Hill, Dana 1964- *WhoHol 92*
Hill, Daniel A. 1898- *WhAm 10*
Hill, Daniel George 1956- *WhoIns 94*
Hill, Daniel Milton 1956- *WhoWest 94*
Hill, Danny Edward 1947- *WhoAmP 93*
Hill, Dave *WhoHol 92*
Hill, Dave 1958- *WrDr 94*
Hill, David 1946- *IntWW 93*
Hill, David 1954- *WhoBlA 94*
Hill, David Allan 1942- *WhoAm 94, WhoWest 94*
Hill, David F. 1956- *WhoIns 94*
Hill, David Francis 1955- *WhoFI 94*
Hill, David Keynes 1915- *Who 94*
Hill, David Kimball 1910- *WhoAmL 94, WhoMW 93*
Hill, David Lamar 1941- *WhoAmL 94*
Hill, David Lawrence 1919- *WhoFI 94, WhoScEn 94*
Hill, David Neil 1957- *Who 94*
Hill, David Rowland 1948- *Who 94*
Hill, David Warren 1946- *WhoAm 94*
Hill, David Wayne 1947- *WhoFI 94*
Hill, David William 1949- *WhoMW 93*
Hill, Deborah 1944- *WhoBlA 94*
Hill, Debra *IntMPA 94, IntWW 93*
Hill, Dennis D. 1941- *WhoAmL 94*
Hill, Dennis Odell 1953- *WhoBlA 94*
Hill, Dennis Patrick 1960- *WhoFI 94, WhoMW 93*
Hill, Denson 1939- *WhoAm 94*
Hill, Derek *Who 94*
Hill, (Arthur) Derek 1916- *IntWW 93, Who 94*
Hill, Derek Keith 1967- *WhoBlA 94*
Hill, Derek Leonard 1930-1989 *WhAm 10*
Hill, Dewey L. *WhoAmP 93*
Hill, Diane M. 1953- *WhoMW 93*
Hill, Diane Seldon 1943- *WhoAm 94*
Hill, Dianne 1955- *WhoBlA 94*
Hill, Donna *DrAPF 93*
Hill, Donna Marie 1957- *WhoFI 94*
Hill, Doris d1976 *WhoHol 92*
Hill, Dorothy 1907- *Who 94*
Hill, Dorothy Kent 1907- *WhoAmA 93N*
Hill, Douglas 1935- *WrDr 94*
Hill, Douglas (Arthur) 1935- *EncSF 93, TwCYAW*
Hill, Douglas E. 1939- *WhoAmP 93*
Hill, Draper 1935- *WhoAm 94, WhoAmA 93*
Hill, Drew 1956- *WhoBlA 94*
Hill, Dudley d1960 *WhoHol 92*
Hill, Dumond Peck 1923-1991 *WhAm 10*
Hill, E. Shelton 1903- *WhoBlA 94*
Hill, Earl McColl 1926- *WhoAm 94, WhoAmL 94, WhoWest 94*
Hill, Earlene H. *WhoAmP 93*
Hill, Earlene Hooper *WhoAm 94*
Hill, Ed 1937- *WhoAmA 93*
Hill, Edward Jeffrey 1953- *WhoWest 94*
Hill, Edward William 1952- *WhoMW 93*
Hill, Edwin Lee 1936- *WhoMW 93*
Hill, Elizabeth (Mary) 1900- *Who 94*
Hill, Elizabeth K. 1917- *WhoAmP 93*
Hill, Elizabeth Starr 1925- *WrDr 94*
Hill, Ellyn Askins 1907- *WhoBlA 94*
Hill, Elmer William 1947- *WhoMW 93*
Hill, Emily 1911-1988 *EncNAR*
Hill, Emita Brady 1936- *WhoMW 93*
Hill, Eric 1927- *WrDr 94*
Hill, Eric 1966- *WhoBlA 94*
Hill, Ernest 1915- *EncSF 93*
Hill, Ernestine 1900-1972 *BlmGWL*
Hill, Errol (Gaston) 1921- *ConDr 93, WrDr 94*
Hill, Errol Gaston 1921- *BlkWr 2, WhoAm 94, WhoBlA 94*
Hill, Esther P. 1922- *WhoBlA 94*
Hill, Eugene DuBose, Jr. 1926- *WhoWest 94*
Hill, Fannie E. *WhoBlA 94*
Hill, Felicity (Barbara) 1915- *Who 94*
Hill, Fern Barry d1981 *WhoHol 92*
Hill, Florence Bernice 1938- *WhoAmP 93*
Hill, Frances Baylor fl. 1797- *BlmGWL*
Hill, Francis Frederick 1908- *WhoAm 94*
Hill, Frank 1954- *WhoAmP 93*
Hill, Frank Whitney, Jr. 1914- *WhoAm 94*
Hill, Fred 1939- *WhoAmP 93*
Hill, Fred A. 1937- *WhoAmP 93*
Hill, Fredric William 1918- *WhoScEn 94*
Hill, G. Richard 1951- *WhoAmL 94*
Hill, Gary 1951- *WhoAmA 93*
Hill, Gary Dean 1952- *WhoMW 93*
Hill, Geoffrey 1932- *BlmGEL, WrDr 94*
Hill, Geoffrey (William) 1932- *IntWW 93, Who 94*
Hill, George d1945 *WhoHol 92*
Hill, George C. 1938- *WhoIns 94*
Hill, George C. 1939- *WhoBlA 94*
Hill, George Calvin 1925- *WhoBlA 94*
Hill, George Geoffrey David 1911- *Who 94*
Hill, George Hiram 1940- *WhoBlA 94*
Hill, George Jackson, III 1932- *WhoAm 94*
Hill, George James 1932- *WhoAm 94*
Hill, George Raymond 1925- *Who 94*
Hill, George Richard 1921- *WhoAm 94*
Hill, George Roy *WhoAm 94*
Hill, George Roy 1921- *IntMPA 94, IntWW 93*
Hill, George Snow 1898-1969 *WhoAmA 93N*
Hill, Gerald Wayne 1947- *WhoAmP 93*
Hill, Gertrude Beatrice 1943- *WhoBlA 94*
Hill, Gil *WhoAmP 93*
Hill, Gilbert 1932- *WhoBlA 94*
Hill, Gladys 1894- *Who 94*
Hill, Glenn *NewYTBS 93 [port]*
Hill, Gordon R. 1950- *WhoWest 94*
Hill, Gordon Tusquellas 1948- *WhoWest 94*
Hill, Grace Lucile Garrison 1930- *WhoAm 94*
Hill, Graham Roderick 1946- *WhoAm 94*
Hill, Graham Starforth 1927- *IntWW 93, Who 94*
Hill, Gregory Spencer 1950- *WhoAmL 94*
Hill, Gus d1937 *WhoHol 92*
Hill, H. Haverstock *EncSF 93*
Hill, Hallene d1966 *WhoHol 92*
Hill, Hannah, Jr. 1703-1714 *BlmGWL*
Hill, Harold Eugene 1918- *WhoAm 94, WhoWest 94*
Hill, Harold Nelson, Jr. 1930- *WhoAm 94*
Hill, Harold Wayne 1933-1988 *WhoAmA 93N*
Hill, Harold Woodrow, Jr. 1942- *WhoFI 94*
Hill, Harry d1993 *Who 94N*
Hill, Harry David 1944- *WhoWest 94*
Hill, Harry Gilbert 1946- *WhoAmP 93*
Hill, Harry James, Jr. 1943- *WhoAmP 93*
Hill, Henry *WhoBlA 94*
Hill, Henry, Jr. 1935- *WhoBlA 94*
Hill, Henry Allen 1933- *WhoAm 94, WhoScEn 94*
Hill, Henry Gordon 1921- *Who 94*
Hill, Henry Parker 1918- *WhoAm 94*
Hill, Herman Ray 1937- *WhoAmP 93*
Hill, Homer *WhoAmA 93N*
Hill, Howard d1975 *WhoHol 92*
Hill, Howard Hampton 1915- *WhoBlA 94*
Hill, Hugh Kenneth 1937- *WhoAm 94*
Hill, Hyacinthe 1920- *WhAm 10*
Hill, Ian
See Judas Priest *ConMus 10*
Hill, Ian Macdonald 1919- *Who 94*
Hill, Irving 1915- *WhoAmL 94*
Hill, Ivan Conrad 1906- *Who 94*
Hill, J. Reginald 1955- *WhoAmL 94*
Hill, J. Tweed *WhoAmA 93*
Hill, Jack d1972 *WhoHol 92*
Hill, Jack 1944- *WhoAmP 93*
Hill, Jack Douglas 1937- *WhoMW 93, WhoScEn 94*
Hill, Jack Y. d1963 *WhoHol 92*
Hill, Jacqueline R. 1940- *WhoBlA 94*
Hill, James *Who 94*
Hill, James 1734-1811 *WhAmRev*
Hill, James 1938- *IntMPA 94*
Hill, James, Jr. 1941- *WhoBlA 94*
Hill, (Stanley) James (Allen) 1926- *Who 94*
Hill, (Stanley) James (Ledger) 1911- *Who 94*
Hill, James A., Sr. 1934- *WhoBlA 94*
Hill, James A., Jr. 1947- *WhoBlA 94*
Hill, James Berry 1945- *WhoAmA 93*
Hill, James C., Jr. 1947- *WhoAmP 93*
Hill, James Clinkscales 1924- *WhoAm 94, WhoAmL 94*
Hill, James Dean 1923- *WhoAmP 93*
Hill, James Derek 1956- *WhoAmL 94*
Hill, James Edward 1926- *WhoFI 94*
Hill, James Frederick 1943- *Who 94*
Hill, James H. 1947- *WhoBlA 94*
Hill, James Howard 1947- *WhoMW 93*
Hill, James L. 1928- *WhoBlA 94*
Hill, James L. 1936- *WhoBlA 94*
Hill, James Lee 1941- *WhoBlA 94*
Hill, James O. 1937- *WhoBlA 94*
Hill, James P. *WhoAmP 93*
Hill, James Paul 1954- *WhoAmP 93*
Hill, James Robert 1960- *WhoFI 94*
Hill, James S. 1949- *WhoAmL 94*
Hill, James Scott 1924- *WhoAm 94*
Hill, James Stanley 1914- *WhoAm 94*
Hill, James Tomilson 1948- *WhoAm 94, WhoFI 94*
Hill, James William Thomas *Who 94*
Hill, Janet Elizabeth 1955- *WhoAmL 94*
Hill, Jeffrey J. 1948- *WhoAmP 93*
Hill, Jeffrey Ronald 1948- *WhoBlA 94*
Hill, Jeffrey Thomas 1963- *WhoFI 94*
Hill, Jeffry Russell 1943- *WhoAmL 94*
Hill, Jerome 1937- *WhoAmP 93*
Hill, (James) Jerome, II 1905- *WhoAmA 93N*
Hill, Jerry C. 1943- *WhoAm 94*
Hill, Jesse, Jr. *WhoBlA 94*
Hill, Jesse W. 1948- *WhoAmL 94*
Hill, Jim *WhoWest 94*
Hill, Jim 1938- *WhoAmP 93*
Hill, Jim 1947- *WhoAmP 93*
Hill, Jim Dan 1897- *WhAm 10*
Hill, Jimmie Dale 1933- *WhoAm 94*
Hill, Jimmy *Who 94*
Hill, Joan 1919- *WhoAmA 93*
Hill, Joe 1879-1915 *AmSocL [port]*
Hill, John *EncSF 93, TwCYAW*
Hill, John 1786-1855 *DcNaB MP*
Hill, John 1922- *Who 94*
Hill, John 1945- *WrDr 94*
Hill, John (Maxwell) 1914- *Who 94*
Hill, John Alexander 1907- *IntWW 93, WhoAm 94*
Hill, John Alfred Rowley 1940- *Who 94*
Hill, John Brian 1957- *WhoAmL 94*
Hill, John C. 1926- *WhoBlA 94*
Hill, John Cameron 1927- *Who 94*
Hill, John Christian 1936- *WhoScEn 94*
Hill, John Conner 1945- *WhoAmA 93*
Hill, John deKoven 1920- *WhoAm 94*
Hill, John Earl 1953- *WhoWest 94*
Hill, John Edward Bernard 1912- *Who 94*
Hill, John Hemmingson 1941- *WhoMW 93*
Hill, John Henry 1839-1922 *WhoAmA 93N*
Hill, John Howard 1940- *WhoAm 94, WhoAmL 94*
Hill, John L. 1923- *WhoAmP 93*
Hill, John Lawrence 1934- *Who 94*
Hill, John McGregor 1921- *IntWW 93, Who 94*
Hill, John Richard 1929- *Who 94*
Hill, John Rutledge, Jr. 1922- *WhoAm 94*
Hill, John S. 1957- *WhoIns 94*
Hill, John Steven 1957- *WhoFI 94*
Hill, John Walter 1942- *WhoMW 93*
Hill, John William 1812-1879 *WhoAmA 93N*
Hill, Johnny R. 1944- *WhoBlA 94*
Hill, Johnson 1937- *WrDr 94*
Hill, Jonathan Booth 1944- *WhoAm 94*
Hill, Jonathan Hopkin 1960- *Who 94*
Hill, Joseph Caldwell 1944- *WhoScEn 94*
Hill, Joseph Havord 1940- *WhoBlA 94*
Hill, Judith C. *WhoAmP 93*
Hill, Judith Deegan 1940- *WhoAmL 94, WhoWest 94*
Hill, Julia A. *WhoAmP 93*
Hill, Julia H. *WhoBlA 94*
Hill, Julius W. 1917- *WhoBlA 94*
Hill, Karl 1831-1893 *NewGrDO*
Hill, Kathleen *DrAPF 93*
Hill, Kathryn d1947 *WhoHol 92*
Hill, Keith *Who 94*
Hill, (Trevor) Keith 1943- *Who 94*
Hill, Keith Roland 1951- *WhoWest 94*
Hill, Kelvin Arthur Willoughby 1957- *WhoScEn 94*
Hill, Ken d1990 *WhoHol 92*
Hill, Kenneth 1937- *WhoAmP 93*
Hill, Kenneth D. 1938- *WhoBlA 94*
Hill, Kenneth Randal 1952- *WhoBlA 94*
Hill, Kenneth Wade 1965- *WhoBlA 94*
Hill, Kent 1957- *WhoBlA 94*
Hill, Kimberley *WhoHol 92*
Hill, Larkin Payne 1954- *WhoFI 94*
Hill, Larry Kyle 1950- *WhoAmP 93*
Hill, Lawrence Thorne 1947- *WhoBlA 94*
Hill, Len *Who 94*
Hill, Lenora Mae 1937- *WhoAm 94*
Hill, Leo 1937- *WhoBlA 94*
Hill, Leonard Michael 1968- *WhoFI 94*
Hill, Leslie Francis 1936- *Who 94*
Hill, Lewis Reuben 1924- *WhoFI 94*
Hill, Lloyd E(rnest) 1938- *ConAu 141*
Hill, Lonzell Ramon 1965- *WhoBlA 94*
Hill, Louis Allen, Jr. 1927- *WhoAm 94*
Hill, Louis G. 1924- *WhoAmP 93*
Hill, Lowell Dean 1930- *WhoAm 94*
Hill, Luther Lyons 1896- *WhAm 10*
Hill, Luther Lyons, Jr. 1922- *WhoAm 94*
Hill, Lution Buford, Jr. 1956- *WhoFI 94*
Hill, Malcolm R(onald) 1942- *WrDr 94*
Hill, Marcia d1947 *WhoHol 92*
Hill, Marcus Edward 1947- *WhoIns 94*
Hill, Margaret 1924- *WhoWomW 91*
Hill, Margaret C. 1924- *WhoAmP 93*
Hill, Mariana *WhoHol 92*
Hill, Mark C. 1951- *WhoAm 94, WhoAmL 94*
Hill, Mark Collins 1951- *WhoWest 94*
Hill, Martin Jude 1966- *WhoScEn 94*
Hill, Martyn Geoffrey 1944- *Who 94*
Hill, Marvin Lewis 1951- *WhoBlA 94*
Hill, Mary Alice 1938- *WhoBlA 94*
Hill, Mary Ann 1961- *WhoScEn 94*
Hill, May Will d1977 *WhoHol 92*
Hill, Megan Lloyd *WhoAmA 93*
Hill, Melvin James 1919- *WhoAm 94*
Hill, Mervyn E., Jr. 1947- *WhoBlA 94*
Hill, Michael *Who 94*
Hill, Michael 1945- *WhoAmP 93*
Hill, (Eliot) Michael 1935- *Who 94*
Hill, Michael Arthur 1949- *Who 94*
Hill, Michael Edward 1943- *WhoBlA 94*
Hill, Michael J. 1943- *WrDr 94*
Hill, Michael Ray 1944- *WhoMW 93*
Hill, Michael Richard 1948- *WhoAmP 93*
Hill, Michael William 1928- *IntWW 93, Who 94*
Hill, Mike *WhoAmP 93*
Hill, Milton King, Jr. 1926- *WhoAmL 94*
Hill, Miriam Helen 1953- *WhoMW 93*
Hill, Morris Gerard 1948- *WhoAmL 94*
Hill, Nancy Lou 1949- *WhoAmP 93*
Hill, Nathan Scott 1962- *WhoWest 94*
Hill, Nellie *DrAPF 93*
Hill, Norman Edward 1934- *WhoMW 93*
Hill, Norman Julius 1925- *WhoAm 94*
Hill, Norman S. 1933- *WhoBlA 94*
Hill, Odell V. 1942- *WhoAmP 93*
Hill, Oliver Falvey 1887-1968 *DcNaB MP*
Hill, Oliver W. 1907- *WhoBlA 94*
Hill, Oliver White, Sr. 1907- *WhoAmL 94*
Hill, Orion Alvah, Jr. 1920- *WhoAm 94*
Hill, Pamela 1920- *WrDr 94*
Hill, Pamela 1938- *WhoAm 94*
Hill, Pati *DrAPF 93*
Hill, Patricia Francine 1955- *WhoMW 93*
Hill, Patricia Jo 1944- *WhoMW 93*
Hill, Patricia Liggins 1942- *WhoBlA 94*
Hill, Patrick Ray 1950- *WhoScEn 94, WhoWest 94*
Hill, Paul Drennen 1941- *WhoAm 94*

Hill, Paul Gordon 1933- *WhoBlA 94*
Hill, Paul Mark 1953- *WhoMW 93*
Hill, Paul W. 1967- *WhoScEn 94*
Hill, Pearl M. 1949- *WhoBlA 94*
Hill, Peter 1933- *WhoAmA 93*
Hill, Peter Waverly 1953- *WhoAmL 94, WhoAmP 93*
Hill, Philip 1917- *WhoAmL 94*
Hill, Philip Ernest 1873-1944 *DcNaB MP*
Hill, Phyllis *WhoHol 92*
Hill, Polly 1914- *IntWW 93, Who 94*
Hill, Polly Knipp 1900-1990 *WhoAmA 93N*
Hill, Prescott F. 1934- *WhoIns 94*
Hill, Ralph Kelly 1952- *WhoAm 94*
Hill, Ramsay d1976 *WhoHol 92*
Hill, Ray 1959- *WhoAmP 93*
Hill, Ray Allen 1942- *WhoBlA 94*
Hill, Raymond A. 1922- *WhoBlA 94*
Hill, Raymond Joseph 1935- *WhoAm 94, WhoFI 94, WhoMW 93*
Hill, Rebecca *DrAPF 93*
Hill, Reginald (Charles) 1936- *WrDr 94*
Hill, Reuben Benjamin 1938- *WhoBlA 94*
Hill, Richard *WhoHol 92*
Hill, Richard Conrad 1918- *WhoScEn 94*
Hill, Richard Devereux 1919- *WhoAm 94*
Hill, Richard Earl 1929- *WhoAm 94*
Hill, Richard F. *DrAPF 93*
Hill, Richard Johnson 1925-1989 *WhAm 10*
Hill, Richard L. 1919- *WhoAmP 93*
Hill, Richard Lee 1931- *WhoMW 93*
Hill, Richard Nathaniel 1930- *WhoBlA 94*
Hill, Richard Wayne 1950- *WhoAmA 93*
Hill, Rick *WhoAmP 93*
Hill, Riley *WhoHol 92*
Hill, Robb B. 1957- *WhoIns 94*
Hill, Robert d1966 *WhoHol 92*
Hill, Robert (Charles Finch) 1937- *Who 94*
Hill, Robert A. *WhoBlA 94*
Hill, Robert A. 1943- *WrDr 94*
Hill, Robert Arthur 1961- *WhoAm 94*
Hill, Robert Bernard 1938- *WhoBlA 94*
Hill, Robert C(ecil) 1929- *ConAu 42NR*
Hill, Robert Colgrove, Jr. 1963- *WhoWest 94*
Hill, Robert Gardiner 1811-1878 *EncSPD*
Hill, Robert J., Jr. 1943- *WhoBlA 94*
Hill, Robert James 1951- *WhoScEn 94*
Hill, Robert John 1932- *WhoMW 93*
Hill, Robert K. 1917- *WhoBlA 94*
Hill, Robert Larry 1946- *WhoWest 94*
Hill, Robert Lee 1928- *IntWW 93, WhoAm 94, WhoScEn 94*
Hill, Robert Lewis 1934- *WhoBlA 94*
Hill, Robert Martin 1949- *WhoWest 94*
Hill, Robert Michael 1943- *WhoAmP 93*
Hill, Robert P. 1948- *WhoAmL 94*
Hill, Robert W. *DrAPF 93*
Hill, Robert Williamson 1936- *Who 94*
Hill, Robin 1955- *WhoAmA 93*
Hill, Robyn Lesley 1942- *WhoAm 94, WhoAmA 93, WhoMW 93*
Hill, Robyn Marcella 1951- *WhoAmL 94*
Hill, Roderick *Who 94*
Hill, (Edward) Roderick 1904- *Who 94*
Hill, Rodney 1921- *IntWW 93, Who 94*
Hill, Roger *EncSF 93*
Hill, Roger Eugene 1936- *WhoScEn 94, WhoWest 94*
Hill, Roger Wendell 1939- *WhoFI 94*
Hill, Rolla B. 1929- *WhoAm 94*
Hill, Ronald Charles 1948- *WhoScEn 94*
Hill, Rosalie A. 1933- *WhoBlA 94*
Hill, Rosalind Mary Theodosia 1908- *WrDr 94*
Hill, Rose 1914- *WhoHol 92*
Hill, Roy Kenneth Leonard 1924- *Who 94*
Hill, Rufus S. 1923- *WhoBlA 94*
Hill, Russell *EncSF 93*
Hill, Russell 1935- *ConAu 141*
Hill, Russell Gibson 1921- *WhoScEn 94*
Hill, Russell Gordon 1954- *WhoMW 93*
Hill, S. Richardson, Jr. 1923- *IntWW 93*
Hill, Sam 1918- *WhoBlA 94*
Hill, Samuel Richardson, Jr. 1923- *WhoAm 94*
Hill, Sandra Denise 1949- *WhoMW 93*
Hill, Sandra J. *WhoAmP 93*
Hill, Sandra Patricia 1943- *WhoBlA 94*
Hill, Selima (Wood) 1945- *WrDr 94*
Hill, Sonny 1936- *WhoBlA 94*
Hill, Starforth *Who 94*
Hill, (Ian) Starforth 1921- *Who 94*
Hill, Stephen S. 1951- *WhoAm 94*
Hill, Steven 1922- *WhoHol 92*
Hill, Steven Richard 1947- *WhoAm 94, WhoFI 94*
Hill, Stuart C. 1926- *WhoAmP 93*
Hill, Susan 1942- *BlmGEL [port], BlmGWL, DcLB 139 [port]*
Hill, Susan (Elizabeth) 1942- *WrDr 94*
Hill, Susan Elizabeth 1942- *IntWW 93, Who 94*
Hill, Suzanne Marie 1958- *WhoMW 93*
Hill, Sylvia Ione-Bennett 1940- *WhoBlA 94*
Hill, Terence 1941- *IntMPA 94, WhoHol 92*
Hill, Terrell Leslie 1917- *IntWW 93, WhoAm 94*
Hill, Thelma d1938 *WhoHol 92*
Hill, Thelma W. 1933- *WhoBlA 94*
Hill, Thomas *WhoHol 92*
Hill, Thomas 1960- *WrDr 94*
Hill, Thomas Allen 1958- *WhoAmL 94, WhoFI 94, WhoMW 93*
Hill, Thomas Bowen, III 1929- *WhoAm 94*
Hill, Thomas Clark 1946- *WhoAm 94, WhoAmL 94, WhoMW 93*
Hill, Thomas Glenn, III 1942- *WhoAm 94*
Hill, Thomas Stewart 1936- *WhoAm 94, WhoMW 93*
Hill, Thomas W. 1945- *WhoAmL 94*
Hill, Thomas William, Jr. 1924- *WhoAmL 94*
Hill, Tiny d1971 *WhoHol 92*
Hill, Tyrone 1968- *WhoBlA 94*
Hill, Val Lane 1956- *WhoMW 93*
Hill, Velma Murphy 1938- *WhoBlA 94*
Hill, Victor Ernst, IV 1939- *WhoAm 94*
Hill, Virginia d1966 *WhoHol 92*
Hill, Vonciel Jones 1948- *WhoBlA 94*
Hill, W. Clayton 1916- *WhoFI 94*
Hill, Walter 1942- *ConAu 140, IntMPA 94, WhoAm 94*
Hill, Walter A. 1946- *WhoAm 94*
Hill, Walter Earl 1941- *WhoAmP 93*
Hill, Walter Edward, Jr. 1931- *WhoScEn 94, WhoWest 94*
Hill, Warren Herbert 1937- *WhoMW 93*
Hill, Wayne Spencer, II 1964- *WhoFI 94*
Hill, Wendell T., Jr. 1924- *WhoBlA 94*
Hill, Wesley d1930 *WhoHol 92*
Hill, Whitmell 1743-1797 *WhAmRev*
Hill, William 1741-1816 *WhAmRev*
Hill, William 1903-1971 *DcNaB MP*
Hill, William Alexander 1946- *WhoAm 94, WhoAmL 94*
Hill, William Boyle *EncSF 93*
Hill, William Bradley, Jr. 1952- *WhoBlA 94*
Hill, William Charles 1917- *WhoAmP 93*
Hill, William David 1928- *WhoAmL 94*
Hill, William George 1940- *Who 94*
Hill, William Joseph 1924- *WrDr 94*
Hill, William Mansfield 1925- *WhoAmA 93*
Hill, William Randolph, Jr. 1936- *WhoBlA 94*
Hill, William Sephton 1926- *Who 94*
Hill, William Thomas 1925- *WhoAm 94*
Hill, Wills *WhAmRev*
Hill, Wilmer Bailey 1928- *WhoAm 94*
Hill, XaCadene Averyllis 1909- *WhoBlA 94*
Hillabrandt, Larry Lee 1947- *WhoFI 94*
Hillaby, John 1917- *IntWW 93, Who 94, WrDr 94*
Hillaire, Marcel d1988 *WhoHol 92*
Hillard, Carole *WhoAmP 93*
Hillard, Darla 1946- *WrDr 94*
Hillard, Paula Janine 1952- *WhoMW 93*
Hillard, Richard Arthur Loraine 1906- *Who 94*
Hillard, Robert Ellsworth 1917- *WhoAm 94*
Hillary, Edmund 1919- *Who 94*
Hillary, Edmund (Percival) 1919- *WrDr 94*
Hillary, Edmund Percival 1919- *IntWW 93, WhoScEn 94*
Hillary, Richard Hope 1919-1943 *DcNaB MP*
Hillberry, Benny Max 1937- *WhoAm 94*
Hillberry, Sheila Marie Stuehrenberg 1945- *WhoMW 93*
Hillcourt, William 1900-1992 *AnObit 1992*
Hille, Bertil 1940- *WhoAm 94*
Hille, Robert Arthur 1931- *WhoAm 94*
Hille, Stanley James 1937- *WhoAm 94*
Hillebrand, Jeffrey Henry 1954- *WhoAm 94*
Hillebrand, Julie Ann 1962- *WhoScEn 94*
Hillebrecht, Hildegard 1927- *NewGrDO*
Hillebrecht, Rudolf Friedrich Heinrich 1910- *IntWW 93*
Hillegas, Mark R. 1926- *EncSF 93*
Hillegas, Michael 1729-1804 *WhAmRev*
Hillegas, Shawn 1964- *WhoHisp 94*
Hillegas, William Joseph 1937- *WhoMW 93*
Hillegass, Christine Ann 1952- *WhoAm 94*
Hillegass, Clifton Keith 1918- *WhoAm 94*
Hillegonds, Paul Christie 1949- *WhoAmP 93*
Hillel, Daniel 1930- *WhoAm 94, WhoScEn 94*
Hillel, Shlomo 1923- *IntWW 93*
Hillelson, Jeffrey P. 1919- *WhoAmP 93*
Hillelson, Jeffrey Paul 1919- *WhoMW 93*
Hillemacher, Paul (Joseph Guillaume) 1852-1933 *NewGrDO*
Hillemacher, Paul-Lucien *NewGrDO*
Hilleman, Maurice Ralph 1919- *IntWW 93, WhoAm 94, WhoScEn 94*
Hillenbrand, Daniel A. 1923- *WhoAm 94, WhoFI 94*
Hillenbrand, Martin Joseph 1915- *IntWW 93, WhoAm 94*
Hillenbrand, W. August 1940- *WhoFI 94*
Hiller, Arthur 1923- *IntMPA 94, WhoAm 94*
Hiller, Betty R. 1925- *WhoAmA 93*
Hiller, Catherine *DrAPF 93*
Hiller, David D. 1953- *WhoAmL 94*
Hiller, Deborah Lewis 1947- *WhoAm 94, WhoAmL 94*
Hiller, Eric *DrAPF 93*
Hiller, Ferdinand (von) 1811-1885 *NewGrDO*
Hiller, Friedrich Adam c. 1767-1812 *NewGrDO*
Hiller, George Mew 1956- *WhoFI 94*
Hiller, Joan Vitek 1960- *WhoMW 93*
Hiller, Johann Adam 1728-1804 *NewGrDO*
Hiller, John Jaren 1969- *WhoAmP 93*
Hiller, John Richard 1953- *WhoMW 93*
Hiller, Lejaren 1924- *WrDr 94*
Hiller, Lejaren (Arthur, Jr.) 1924- *NewGrDO*
Hiller, Stanley, Jr. 1924- *WhoAm 94, WhoFI 94, WhoWest 94*
Hiller, Susan 1940- *IntWW 93*
Hiller, Wendy *IntWW 93, WhoAm 94*
Hiller, Wendy 1912- *IntMPA 94, Who 94, WhoHol 92*
Hiller, William Clark 1933- *WhoScEn 94*
Hillerbrand, Hans J(oachim) 1931- *WrDr 94*
Hillerbrand, Hans Joachim 1931- *WhoAm 94*
Hiller-Fry, William Norman 1923- *IntWW 93*
Hillerich, Imma 1954- *WhoWomW 91*
Hillerman, John 1932- *IntMPA 94, WhoHol 92*
Hillerman, Tony 1925- *ConAu 42NR, TwCYAW, WhoAm 94, WhoWest 94, WrDr 94*
Hillern, Wilhelmine von 1836-1916 *BlmGWL*
Hillers, Delbert Roy 1932- *WhoAm 94*
Hillers, Virginia Nerlin *WhoWest 94*
Hillert, Gloria Bonnin 1930- *WhoAm 94, WhoMW 93*
Hillery, John Maurice 1938- *WhoAmL 94*
Hillery, Mark Stephen 1951- *WhoScEn 94*
Hillery, Mary Jane Larato 1931- *WhoAm 94*
Hillery, Patrick John 1923- *IntWW 93, Who 94*
Hillery, Robert Charles 1933- *WhoScEn 94*
Hilles, Richard Kelley 1965- *WhoMW 93*
Hilles, Sharon Lee 1944- *WhoWest 94*
Hillestad, Charles Andrew 1945- *WhoAmL 94*
Hillestad, Donna Dawn 1938- *WhoMW 93*
Hillestad, Gertrude Delene 1929- *WhoMW 93*
Hillesum, Etty 1914-1943 *BlmGWL, TwCLC 49 [port]*
Hille Valle, Kristin 1944- *WhoWomW 91*
Hillgarth, J(ocelyn) N(igel) 1929- *WrDr 94*
Hillgren, Sonja Dorothy 1948- *WhoAm 94*
Hillhouse, James 1728-1816 *WhAmRev*
Hillhouse, (Robert) Russell 1938- *Who 94*
Hilliar, Charles 1949- *WhoWest 94*
Hilliard, Alicia Victoria 1949- *WhoBlA 94*
Hilliard, Asa G(rant), III 1933- *BlkWr 2*
Hilliard, Asa Grant, III 1933- *WhoBlA 94*
Hilliard, Craig Sterling 1955- *WhoAmP 93*
Hilliard, Dalton 1964- *WhoBlA 94*
Hilliard, Dana S. 1972- *WhoAmP 93*
Hilliard, Danny C. 1957- *WhoAmP 93*
Hilliard, David 1942- *BlkWr 2, ConAu 142*
Hilliard, David Craig 1937- *WhoAmL 94, WhoMW 93*
Hilliard, Delories *WhoBlA 94*
Hilliard, Earl F. 1942- *CngDr 93*
Hilliard, Earl Frederick 1942- *WhoAm 94, WhoAmP 93, WhoBlA 94*
Hilliard, Ernest d1947 *WhoHol 92*
Hilliard, Garrison L. *DrAPF 93*
Hilliard, General K. 1940- *WhoBlA 94*
Hilliard, Harriet 1914- *WhoHol 92*
Hilliard, Harry d1966 *WhoHol 92*
Hilliard, Hazel d1971 *WhoHol 92*
Hilliard, Jack Briggs 1931- *WhoMW 93*
Hilliard, Kirk Loveland, Jr. 1941- *WhoMW 93, WhoScEn 94*
Hilliard, Landon 1939- *WhoAm 94, WhoFI 94*
Hilliard, Mack, Mrs. d1963 *WhoHol 92*
Hilliard, Michael W. 1947- *WhoAmL 94*
Hilliard, Noel (Harvey) 1929- *WrDr 94*
Hilliard, Patricia 1916- *WhoHol 92*
Hilliard, Patsy Jo *WhoBlA 94*
Hilliard, R. Glenn 1943- *WhoIns 94*
Hilliard, Robert *WhoHol 92*
Hilliard, Robert Glenn 1943- *WhoAm 94*
Hilliard, Robert Lee Moore 1931- *WhoBlA 94*
Hilliard, Sam Bowers 1930- *WhoAm 94*
Hilliard, Sharen Anne 1942- *WhoMW 93*
Hilliard, William Alexander *WhoBlA 94*
Hilliard, William Arthur 1927- *WhoBlA 94*
Hilliard Hillman, Elsie 1925- *WhoWomW 91*
Hilliard-Jones, Amy *WhoBlA 94*
Hillias, Peg d1961 *WhoHol 92*
Hillie, Verna *WhoHol 92*
Hillier, Bevis 1940- *IntWW 93, Who 94, WrDr 94*
Hillier, Donald Edward 1947- *WhoIns 94*
Hillier, Jack Ronald 1912- *Who 94, WrDr 94*
Hillier, James *WorInv*
Hillier, James 1915- *WhoAm 94, WhoScEn 94*
Hillier, James Robert 1937- *WhoAm 94*
Hillier, Jim 1941- *WrDr 94*
Hillier, Malcolm Dudley 1936- *Who 94*
Hillier, Paul Douglas 1949- *Who 94*
Hillier, William Edward 1936- *Who 94*
Hillier-Fry, (William) Norman 1923- *Who 94*
Hillig, Terry Thomas 1945- *WhoMW 93*
Hilligoss, Martha M. 1928-1987 *WhoAmA 93N*
Hilliker, Donald Beckstett 1944- *WhoAmL 94*
Hillila, Bernhard Hugo Paul 1919- *WhoAm 94*
Hillion, Pierre Theodore Marie 1926- *WhoScEn 94*
Hillis, Arthur Henry Macnamara 1905- *Who 94*
Hillis, Bryan V. 1956- *ConAu 141*
Hillis, Elwood Haynes 1926- *WhoAmP 93*
Hillis, Ivory O., Jr. 1930- *WhoAmP 93*
Hillis, Margaret 1921- *WhoAm 94*
Hillis, Mark B. 1947- *WhoAm 94, WhoAmL 94*
Hillis, Richard K. 1936- *WhoAmA 93, WhoWest 94*
Hillis, Rick 1956- *WrDr 94*
Hillis, Robert Gregory 1959- *WhoFI 94*
Hillis, Stephen Kendall 1942- *WhoAmP 93*
Hillis, William Daniel 1933- *WhoAm 94*
Hillis, William Daniel 1956- *WhoScEn 94*
Hill-Jones, Kathleen Lois 1955- *WhoWest 94*
Hill-Lubin, Mildred Anderson 1933- *WhoBlA 94*
Hillman, Alex L. 1900-1968 *WhoAmA 93N*
Hillman, Allan P. 1946- *WhoAmL 94*
Hillman, Arthur Stanley 1945- *WhoAmA 93*
Hillman, Barry (Leslie) 1942- *WrDr 94*
Hillman, Bill 1922- *WhAm 10*
Hillman, Bones
See Midnight Oil *ConMus 11*
Hillman, Brenda *DrAPF 93*
Hillman, Carol Elizabeth 1947- *WhoMW 93*
Hillman, Cindy Kay 1956- *WhoMW 93*
Hillman, David Charles 1952- *WhoAmL 94*
Hillman, Douglas Woodruff 1922- *WhoAm 94, WhoAmL 94, WhoMW 93*
Hillman, Elizabeth 1942- *ConAu 142, SmATA 75 [port]*
Hillman, Ellis Simon 1928- *Who 94*
Hillman, Elsie Hilliard 1925- *WhoAmP 93*
Hillman, Gracia 1949- *WhoBlA 94*
Hillman, John Richard 1944- *Who 94*
Hillman, Joyce 1936- *WhoAmP 93, WhoMW 93*
Hillman, Lee Scott 1955- *WhoAm 94, WhoFI 94*
Hillman, Leon 1921- *WhoScEn 94*
Hillman, Lin 1948- *WhoMW 93*
Hillman, Melville Ernest Douglas 1926- *WhoAm 94*
Hillman, Michael d1941 *WhoHol 92*
Hillman, Milton Henry 1929- *WhoWest 94*
Hillman, Morton C. 1926- *WhoAmP 93*
Hillman, Richard Ephraim 1940- *WhoAm 94*
Hillman, Robert Edward 1933- *WhoScEn 94*
Hillman, Robert Kent 1939- *WhoMW 93*
Hillman, Robert Sandor 1939- *WhoAm 94*
Hillman, Roger Lewis 1944- *WhoAm 94, WhoAmL 94*

Hillman, Shelton B., Jr. 1944-
WhoAmL 94
Hillman, Sidney 1887-1946 AmSocL
Hillman, Stanley Eric Gordon 1911-
WhoAm 94, WhoMW 93
Hillman, Thomas J. 1955- WhoMW 93
Hillman, Tommy 1936- WhoFI 94
Hillman, William Bryon 1951- IntMPA 94
Hillman, William Chernick 1935-
WhoAm 94, WhoAmL 94
Hill-Norton, Baron 1915- Who 94
Hill-Norton, Nicholas (John) 1939-
Who 94
Hill Norton, Peter John 1915- IntWW 93
Hillock, Gerald A. WhoAmP 93
Hillpot, Billy d1985 WhoHol 92
Hillringhouse, Mark DrAPF 93
Hills, Alan Lee 1954- WhoWest 94,
Hills, Albert Freeman, III 1961-
WhoFI 94
Hills, Andrew Worth 1949- Who 94
Hills, Austin Edward 1934- WhoAm 94
Hills, Barrington William 1937- Who 94
Hills, Beverly WhoHol 92
Hills, Carla E. 1934- CurBio 93 [port]
Hills, Carla Anderson 1934- IntWW 93,
WhoAm 94, WhoAmL 94, WhoAmP 93,
WhoWomW 91
Hills, David Graeme Muspratt 1925-
Who 94
Hills, David Henry 1933- Who 94
Hills, Denis (Cecil) 1913- WrDr 94
Hills, (Eric) Donald 1917- Who 94
Hills, Frederic Wheeler 1934- WhoAm 94
Hills, George 1918- WrDr 94
Hills, Gillian WhoHol 92
Hills, Graham (John) 1926- IntWW 93,
Who 94
Hills, James Bricky 1944- WhoBlA 94
Hills, John Merrill 1944- WhoAm 94
Hills, Laura Coombs 1859-1952
WhoAmA 93N
Hills, Lee 1906- WhoAm 94
Hills, Linda Launey 1947- WhoWest 94
Hills, Patricia 1936- WhoAmA 93
Hills, Patricia Gorton Schulze 1936-
WhoAm 94
Hills, Patti Lynn 1953- WhoFI 94,
WhoMW 93
Hills, Philip James 1933- WrDr 94
Hills, Regina J. 1953- WhoAm 94,
WhoWest 94
Hills, Richard Edwin 1945- Who 94
Hills, Roderick M. 1931- WhoAm 94
Hills, Roderick Maltman 1931-
IntWW 93
Hills, Sandra Longman 1934-
WhoWest 94
Hills, Thomas Derrill 1944- WhoFI 94
Hillsberg, Jon G. 1946- WhoAmL 94
Hillsborough, Earl of 1959- Who 94
Hillsborough, Wills Hill, Earl of
1718-1793 WhAmRev
Hillsman, Gerald C. 1926- WhoBlA 94
Hillsman, Regina Onie 1955-
WhoScEn 94
Hill-Smith, Derek Edward 1922- Who 94
Hillsmith, Fannie 1911- WhoAmA 93
Hillsmith, Fannie L. 1911- WhoAm 94
Hill Smith, Marilyn 1952- IntWW 93,
NewGrDO
Hillstrom, Thomas Peter 1943- WhoFI 94
Hill-Trevor Who 94
Hillway, Tyrus 1912- WhoAm 94
Hill-Wood, David (Basil) 1926- Who 94
Hilly, James D. 1954- WhoAmL 94
Hillyard, Blanche Bingley 1863-1946
BuCMET
Hillyard, Ira William 1924- WhoAm 94
Hillyard, Lyle William 1940-
WhoAmP 93, WhoWest 94
Hillyard, Richie Doak 1961- WhoScEn 94
Hillyard, Steven D. 1949- WhoAmL 94
Hillyer, William Hudson 1928-
WhoAmP 93
Hilmas, Duane Eugene 1938-
WhoWest 94
Hilmes, Michele 1953- WrDr 94
Hilmy, Said Ibrahim 1953- WhoScEn 94
Hilpert, Bruce Emil 1950- WhoWest 94
Hilpert, Brunette Kathleen Powers 1909-
WhoMW 93
Hilpert, Dale W. WhoFI 94
Hilpert, Edward Theodore, Jr. 1928-
WhoAm 94, WhoAmL 94, WhoWest 94
Hilpert, Heinz d1967 WhoHol 92
Hilpman, Paul Lorenz 1932- WhoScEn 94
Hilsenrath, Joel Alan 1965- WhoFI 94,
WhoScEn 94
Hilsman, Roger 1919- IntWW 93,
WrDr 94
Hilson, Arthur Lee 1936- WhoBlA 94
Hilson, Douglas 1941- WhoAmA 93
Hilst, Hilda 1930- BlmGWL
Hilsum, Cyril 1925- IntWW 93, Who 94
Hilt, Robert Stephen 1944- WhoMW 93
Hiltabidle, William Orme, Jr. 1896-
WhAm 10

Hiltibran, Robert Comegys 1920-
WhoMW 93
Hitner, William Albert 1914-1991
WhAm 10
Hilton, Alice Mary 1936- WhoAm 94
Hilton, Andrew Carson 1928- WhoAm 94
Hilton, Anthony Victor 1946- Who 94
Hilton, Barron 1927- WhoAm 94,
WhoFI 94, WhoWest 94
Hilton, (Andrew John) Boyd 1944-
WrDr 94
Hilton, Brian James George 1940- Who 94
Hilton, Claude Meredith 1940-
WhoAm 94, WhoAmL 94
Hilton, Clifford Thomas 1934-
WhoAm 94
Hilton, Daisy d1969
See Hilton, Violet d1969 & Hilton, Daisy
d1969 WhoHol 92
Hilton, Daisy d1969 WhoHol 92
Hilton, David DrAPF 93
Hilton, Donald Dean 1930- WhoFI 94
Hilton, Donnette Louise 1935-
WhoAmP 94
Hilton, Eric Michael 1933- WhoFI 94
Hilton, Francesca WhoHol 92
Hilton, Frank d1932 WhoHol 92
Hilton, George WhoHol 92
Hilton, George Woodman 1925- WrDr 94
Hilton, Haran d1930 WhoHol 92
Hilton, James 1900-1954 EncSF 93
Hilton, James Gorton 1923- WhoAm 94
Hilton, James L. 1930- WhoAm 94
Hilton, Janet 1945- IntWW 93
Hilton, John Howard Who 94
Hilton, (Alan) John Howard 1942-
Who 94
Hilton, John Millard Thomas 1934-
Who 94
Hilton, John Robert 1908- Who 94
Hilton, Kenneth M. 1926- WhoIns 94
Hilton, Lester Elliot 1923- WhoAmP 93
Hilton, Linda Sue 1950- WhoMW 93
Hilton, Margery WrDr 94
Hilton, Nicola Mary Who 94
Hilton, Ordway 1913- WhoAm 94
Hilton, Paul 1950- WhoAmL 94
Hilton, Peter 1919- Who 94
Hilton, Peter (John) 1923- WrDr 94
Hilton, Peter John 1923- Who 94,
WhoAm 94
Hilton, Robert L. WhoIns 94
Hilton, Robert Parker, Sr. 1927-
WhoAm 94
Hilton, Rodney (Howard) 1916- WrDr 94
Hilton, Rodney Howard 1916- Who 94
Hilton, Ronald 1911- WrDr 94
Hilton, Stanley William, Jr. WhoBlA 94
Hilton, Suzanne 1922- WrDr 94
Hilton, Tanya WhoBlA 94
Hilton, Theodore Craig 1949-
WhoScEn 94
Hilton, Thomas Scott 1952- WhoAm 94
Hilton, Timothy T. 1952- WhoAmL 94
Hilton, Violet d1969 & Hilton, Daisy
d1969 WhoHol 92
Hilton, Walter d1396 BlmGEL
Hilton, William (Samuel) 1926- Who 94
Hilton, William Howard 1949- WhoFI 94,
WhoMW 93
Hilton Of Eggardon, Baroness 1936-
Who 94
Hilts, Alvin 1908- WhoAmA 93
Hilts, Earl T. 1946- WhoAmL 94
Hilty, Peter Daniel DrAPF 93
Hilty, Terrence Keith 1951- WhoScEn 94
Hilty, Thomas R. 1943- WhoAmA 93
Hiltz, Arnold Aubrey 1924- WhoScEn 94
Hilverding, Franz 1710?-1768 IntDcB
Hilverding van Wewen, Franz (Anton
Christoph) 1710?-1768 NewGrDO
Hilyard, David Franklin 1949-
WhoWest 94
Hilyard, James Emerson 1941- WhoFI 94
Hilyard, Tommy Lee 1948- WhoBlA 94
Him ConAu 43NR
Himathongkam, Thep 1942- WhoScEn 94
Himber, Richard d1966 WhoHol 92
Hime, James A. 1954- WhoAmL 94
Hime, Martin 1928- Who 94
Himelfarb, Richard Jay 1942- WhoAm 94,
WhoFI 94
Himelfarb, Stephen Roy 1954-
WhoAmL 94
Himelick, Alan Edward 1929-1991
WhAm 10
Himelstein, Morgan Y 1926- WrDr 94
Himelstein, Peggy Donn 1932- WhoAm 94
Himes, Anne L. 1948- WhoAmL 94
Himes, Chester 1909-1984
AfrAmAl 6 [port]
Himes, Chester (Bomar) 1909-1984
BlkWr 2
Himes, Geoffrey DrAPF 93
Himes, George Elliott 1922- WhoMW 93,
WhoScEn 94
Himes, J. Fraser 1944- WhoAmL 94

Himes, James Albert 1919- WhoAm 94
Himes, Jane Ann 1923- WhoAm 94
Himes, John WhoHol 92
Himes, Kenneth Alan 1937- WhoFI 94
Himes, Laurence Austin 1940-
WhoAm 94, WhoMW 93
Himes, Ruth Barnes 1946- WhoAmL 94
Himilco fl. 48-?BC- WhWE
Himle, Erik 1924- IntWW 93
Himmel, Friedrich Heinrich 1765-1814
NewGrDO
Himmel, Michael B. 1950- WhoAmL 94
Himmel, Robert Louis 1939- WhoMW 93
Himmelberg, Charles John, III 1931-
WhoAm 94, WhoMW 93
Himmelberg, Robert Franklin 1934-
WhoAm 94
Himmelblau, David Mautner 1923-
WhoAm 94, WhoScEn 94
Himmelein, Mark William 1957-
WhoMW 93
Himmelfarb, Gertrude 1922- IntWW 93,
WrDr 94
Himmelfarb, John David 1946-
WhoAm 94, WhoAmA 93
Himmelfarb, Milton 1918- WhoAm 94,
WrDr 94
Himmelfarb, Susan E. 1943- WhoMW 93
Himmelright, Robert John, Jr. 1926-
WhoAm 94
Himmler, Heinrich 1900-1945
HisWorL [port]
Himms-Hagen, Jean Margaret 1933-
WhoAm 94
Himonas, James Demosthenes, Jr. 1932-
WhoWest 94
Himsl, Mathias A. 1912- WhoAmP 93
Himsl, Mathias Alfred 1912- WhoWest 94
Himstead, Scott 1931- WhoAm 94
Himstedt, Ronald Eugene 1943-
WhoMW 93
Himsworth, Harold (Percival) 1905-
Who 94
Himsworth, Harold Percival 1905-
IntWW 93
Himsworth, Richard Lawrence 1937-
Who 94
Hinault, Bernard 1954- IntWW 93
Hinch, Andrew Lewis, Sr. 1919-
WhoBlA 94
Hinch, Gerald K. WhoAm 94
Hinch, Stephen Walter 1951- WhoWest 94
Hinch, William Harry 1919- WhoWest 94
Hinchcliff, Richard Henry, Jr. 1948-
WhoIns 94
Hinchcliffe, Peter Robert Mossom 1937-
IntWW 93, Who 94
Hinchey, Bruce Alan 1949- WhoAmP 93,
WhoWest 94
Hinchey, Deborah Marie 1954-
WhoWest 94
Hinchey, Maurice D. 1938- CngDr 93,
WhoAmP 93
Hinchey, Maurice D., Jr. 1938-
WhoAm 94
Hinchingbrooke, Viscount Who 94
Hinchley, John William 1871-1931
DcNaB MP
Hinchliff, James Thomas 1939- WhoFI 94
Hinchliff, Peter Bingham 1929- Who 94,
WrDr 94
Hinchliff, Stephen 1926- Who 94
Hinchliffe, David Martin 1948- Who 94
Hinck, Franklin Neil 1930- WhoWest 94
Hinck, Walter 1922- IntWW 93
Hinckle, Warren James, III 1938-
WhoAm 94
Hinckley, Alfred WhoHol 92
Hinckley, Allen C(arter) 1877-1954
NewGrDO
Hinckley, Barbara 1937- WrDr 94
Hinckley, Frank T. 1913- WhoAmP 93
Hinckley, Gordon B. 1910- WhoAm 94,
WhoWest 94
Hinckley, Gregory Keith 1946-
WhoAm 94, WhoWest 94
Hinckley, Helen 1903- WrDr 94N
Hinckley, Lynn Schellig 1944-
WhoScEn 94
Hinckley, Robert Craig 1947- WhoAm 94
Hinckley, Stuart Wadsworth 1953-
WhoAmP 94
Hinckley, William L. d1918 WhoHol 92
Hincks, John Winslow 1931- WhoAm 94
Hind, Greg William 1946- WhoWest 94
Hind, Harry William 1915- WhoAm 94,
WhoWest 94
Hind, Henry Youle 1823-1908 WhWE
Hind, John William Who 94
Hind, Kenneth 1920- Who 94
Hind, Kenneth Harvard 1949- Who 94
Hind, Steven DrAPF 93
Hinde, John Gordon 1939- WhoScEn 94
Hinde, Madeline 1949- WhoHol 92
Hinde, Robert Aubrey 1923- IntWW 93,
Who 94
Hinde, Thomas IntWW 93, Who 94
Hinde, Thomas 1926- WrDr 94

Hinde, Wendy 1919- WrDr 94
Hindemith, Paul 1895-1963 AmCulL,
IntDcB, NewGrDO
Hinden, Michael C. 1941- WhoMW 93
Hinden, Richard Adam 1954- WhoAm 94
Hinden, Stanley Jay 1927- WhoAm 94
Hindenburg, Paul von 1847-1934
HisWorL [port]
Hinderaker, Allen W. 1948- WhoAmL 94
Hinderaker, Ivan 1916- WhoAm 94
Hinderaker, John Hadley 1950-
WhoAm 94, WhoAmL 94
Hinderas, Natalie 1927-1987
ConBlB 5 [port]
Hinderliter, Richard Glenn 1936-
WhoScEn 94
Hindermann, Richard L. WhoIns 94
Hinders, Mark Karl 1963- WhoScEn 94
Hindes, Chuck 1942- WhoAmA 93
Hindes, Gary Eugene 1950- WhoFI 94
Hindle, Art WhoHol 92
Hindle, Edward Francis 1918-
WhoAmL 94
Hindley, Colin Boothman 1923- Who 94
Hindley, Estella Jacqueline 1948- Who 94
Hindley, Michael John 1947- Who 94
Hindley, Norman DrAPF 93
Hindley-Smith, David Dury 1916-
Who 94
Hindlip, Baron 1912- Who 94
Hindman, Darwin Alexander, Jr. 1933-
WhoAmL 94, WhoMW 93
Hindman, Don J. 1926- WhoAm 94
Hindman, Earl WhoHol 92
Hindman, Kenneth August 1950-
WhoAmL 94
Hindman, Kyle WhoAmP 93
Hindman, Larrie C. 1937- WhoAm 94,
WhoAmL 94
Hindman, Leslie Susan 1954- WhoMW 93
Hindman, Randall Kevin 1952- WhoFI 94
Hindman, Robert Joseph 1946-
WhoAmL 94
Hindman, William 1743-1822 WhAmRev
Hindmarch, Gladys 1940- BlmGWL
Hindmarsh, Frederick Bell 1919- Who 94
Hindmarsh, Irene 1923- Who 94
Hindo, Walid Afram 1940- WhoAm 94,
WhoMW 93, WhoScEn 94
Hinds, Barbara Marie 1949- WhoFI 94
Hinds, Ciaran WhoHol 92
Hinds, David Stewart 1939- WhoWest 94
Hinds, Douglas L. 1933- WhoAmP 93
Hinds, Frank Crossman 1930-
WhoScEn 94
Hinds, Gary E. WhoAmP 93
Hinds, Glester Samuel 1951- WhoFI 94,
WhoScEn 94
Hinds, James William 1966- WhoScEn 94
Hinds, Lennox S. WhoBlA 94
Hinds, Richard De Courcy 1941-
WhoAm 94
Hinds, Richard Ely 1936- WhoIns 94
Hinds, Samuel Archibald Anthony 1943-
IntWW 93
Hinds, Samuel S. d1948 WhoHol 92
Hinds, Susan Marie 1962- WhoFI 94
Hinds, Thomas Sheldon 1943- WhoAm 94
Hindson, William Stanley 1920- Who 94
Hindus, Milton 1916- WhoAm 94,
WrDr 94
Hindus, Darlene Clark 1947- WhoBlA 94
Hine, Daryl DrAPF 93
Hine, Daryl 1936- WhoAm 94, WrDr 94
Hine, Deirdre Joan 1937- Who 94
Hine, Edward, Jr. 1952- WhoAmP 93
Hine, James Spencer 1939- WhoAm 94
Hine, Lewis Wickes 1874-1940 AmSocL
Hine, Lorraine A. WhoAmP 93
Hine, Maynard Kiplinger 1907-
IntWW 93
Hine, Muriel EncSF 93
Hine, Patrick 1932- IntWW 93
Hine, Patrick (Bardon) 1932- Who 94
Hine, Robert V. 1921- WrDr 94
Hine, Robert Van Norden, Jr. 1921-
WhoAm 94
Hine, Robert Walter 1924- WhoAmP 93
Hineira, Arapera 1932- BlmGWL
Hineman, Kalo A. 1922- WhoAmP 93
Hiner, Glen Harold, Jr. 1934- WhoAm 94,
WhoFI 94
Hiner, Thomas Joseph 1960-
WhoMW 93, WhoScEn 94
Hinerfeld, Norman Martin 1929-
WhoAm 94
Hinerfeld, Robert Elliot 1934- WhoAm 94
Hinerfeld, Ruth J. 1930- WhoAm 94
Hinerfeld, Susan Hope Slocum 1936-
WhoWest 94
Hinerman, Philip Lee 1954- WhoAmL 94
Hines, Alan DrAPF 93
Hines, Andrew Hampton, Jr. 1923-
WhoAm 94
Hines, Angus Irving, Jr. 1923- WhoAm 94
Hines, Anna Grossnickle 1946-
WhoAm 94
Hines, Anthony Loring 1941- WhoAm 94

Hirono, Mazie Keiko 1947- *WhoWest 94*
Hirons, Montague (John David) 1916- *WrDr 94*
Hirooka, Masaaki 1931- *WhoScEn 94*
Hirooka, Tomoo 1907- *IntWW 93*
Hirose, Akira 1941- *WhoAm 94*
Hirose, Shin-Ichi 1913- *IntWW 93*
Hirose, Teruo Terry 1926- *WhoAm 94, WhoScEn 94*
Hiroshige, Ernie *WhoAsA 94*
Hiroshima, Koji Edmund 1924- *WhoAm 94*
Hirota, Dennis Isao 1940- *WhoWest 94*
Hirota, Jitsuya 1924- *WhoScEn 94*
Hirota, Minoru 1933- *WhoScEn 94*
Hiroyasu, Hiroyuki 1935- *WhoScEn 94*
Hiroyuki, Hashimoto 1938- *WhoScEn 94*
Hirozawa, Shurei 1919- *WhoWest 94*
Hirrel, Michael John 1951- *WhoAmL 94, WhoFI 94*
Hirsch, Allen I. 1943- *WhoAmL 94*
Hirsch, Allen Vernon 1953- *WhoAm 94*
Hirsch, Anthony T. 1940- *WhoWest 94*
Hirsch, Arlene Sharon 1951- *WhoMW 93*
Hirsch, Austin L. 1948- *WhoAmL 94*
Hirsch, Barry 1933- *WhoAm 94, WhoAmL 94*
Hirsch, Carl Herbert 1934- *WhoAm 94, WhoFI 94*
Hirsch, Charles Bronislaw 1919- *WhoAm 94*
Hirsch, Daniel *WhoHol 92*
Hirsch, Daniel 1940- *WhoAmL 94*
Hirsch, David Alan 1947- *WhoAmL 94*
Hirsch, David L. *WhoAm 94, WhoAmL 94*
Hirsch, E. D., Jr. 1928- *ConLC 79 [port]*
Hirsch, E(ric) D(onald), Jr. 1928- *WrDr 94*
Hirsch, Edward *DrAPF 93*
Hirsch, Edward 1950- *ConAu 42NR, WrDr 94*
Hirsch, Edward Mark 1950- *WhoAm 94*
Hirsch, Elroy *ProFbHF [port]*
Hirsch, Elroy 1924- *WhoHol 92*
Hirsch, Eric Donald, Jr. 1928- *WhoAm 94*
Hirsch, Gary D. *WhoAm 94, WhoFI 94*
Hirsch, Gary D. 1949- *WhoAm 94, WhoFI 94*
Hirsch, Gary Mark 1950- *WhoScEn 94*
Hirsch, George Aaron 1934- *WhoAm 94*
Hirsch, Georges-Francois 1944- *IntWW 93*
Hirsch, Gilah Yelin 1944- *WhoAm 94, WhoAmA 93*
Hirsch, Gordon 1943- *WhoMW 93*
Hirsch, Harold Seller 1907-1990 *WhAm 10*
Hirsch, Horst Eberhard 1933- *WhoAm 94*
Hirsch, Howard Carlyle 1896- *WhAm 10*
Hirsch, Ira J. *WhoScEn 94*
Hirsch, Irma Lou Kolterman 1934- *WhoMW 93*
Hirsch, J. Michael 1946- *WhoAmL 94*
Hirsch, Janis 1950- *ConTFT 11*
Hirsch, Jay G. 1930- *WhoAm 94*
Hirsch, Jeffrey 1950- *WhoAm 94, WhoAmL 94*
Hirsch, Jeffrey Allan 1950- *WhoAm 94, WhoAmL 94*
Hirsch, Jerome Seth 1948- *WhoAm 94, WhoAmL 94*
Hirsch, Jerry 1922- *WhoMW 93, WhoScEn 94*
Hirsch, John Stephen 1930-1989 *WhAm 10*
Hirsch, Joseph 1910-1981 *WhoAmA 93N*
Hirsch, Joseph Allen 1950- *WhoScEn 94*
Hirsch, Judd 1935- *ConTFT 11, IntMPA 94, IntWW 93, WhoAm 94, WhoHol 92*
Hirsch, Jules 1927- *WhoScEn 94*
Hirsch, June *DrAPF 93*
Hirsch, June Schaut 1925- *WhoMW 93*
Hirsch, Laurence Eliot 1945- *WhoAm 94, WhoFI 94*
Hirsch, Lawrence Leonard 1922- *WhoAm 94*
Hirsch, Leon 1927- *IntWW 93*
Hirsch, Leon Charles 1927- *WhoAm 94, WhoFI 94*
Hirsch, Les J. 1947- *WhoAmP 93*
Hirsch, Mark J. 1953- *WhoScEn 94*
Hirsch, Milton *WhoAmP 93*
Hirsch, Milton Charles 1952- *WhoAmL 94*
Hirsch, Morris William 1933- *WhoAm 94*
Hirsch, Nathaniel David M'ttron 1897- *WhAm 10*
Hirsch, Paul Frederick 1945- *WhoWest 94*
Hirsch, Peter (Bernhard) 1925- *Who 94*
Hirsch, Peter Bernhard 1925- *IntWW 93, WhoAm 94, WhoScEn 94*
Hirsch, Philip Francis 1925- *WhoAm 94*
Hirsch, Raymond Robert 1936- *WhoAm 94*
Hirsch, Richard Arthur 1925- *WhoAm 94, WhoScEn 94*
Hirsch, Robert 1929- *WhoHol 92*
Hirsch, Robert Bruce 1926- *WhoAm 94*
Hirsch, Robert Lee 1947- *WhoFI 94*
Hirsch, Robert Louis 1935- *WhoAm 94*
Hirsch, Robert Mallin *WhoAmL 94*
Hirsch, Robert Paul 1925- *IntWW 93*
Hirsch, Robert W. 1939- *WhoAm 94*
Hirsch, Robert William 1925- *WhoAm 94*
Hirsch, Roseann Conte 1941- *WhoAm 94*
Hirsch, Seev 1931- *WrDr 94*
Hirsch, Stefan 1899-1964 *WhoAmA 93N*
Hirsch, Steven A. 1955- *WhoAmL 94*
Hirsch, Steven Richard 1937- *Who 94*
Hirsch, Thomas Edward, III 1953- *WhoAm 94*
Hirsch, Walter 1917- *WhoFI 94, WhoScEn 94, WhoWest 94*
Hirsch, Warren Mitchell 1945- *WhoScEn 94*
Hirsch, Werner Z. 1920- *WrDr 94*
Hirsch, Werner Zvi 1920- *WhoAm 94*
Hirsch Ballin, Ernst 1950- *IntWW 93*
Hirschberg, Michael Eric 1952- *WhoWest 94*
Hirschberg, Vera Hilda 1929- *WhoAm 94*
Hirschboeck, John Karl 1946- *WhoAm 94*
Hirschfeld, Albert 1903- *WhoAm 94, WhoAmA 93*
Hirschfeld, Arlene F. 1944- *WhoAm 94*
Hirschfeld, Burt 1923- *WrDr 94*
Hirschfeld, Gerald Joseph 1921- *WhoAm 94, WhoWest 94*
Hirschfeld, Magnus 1868-1935 *GayLL*
Hirschfeld, Michael 1950- *WhoAm 94, WhoAmL 94*
Hirschfeld, Michael L. 1950- *WhoAmL 94*
Hirschfeld, Ronald Colman 1930- *WhoAm 94*
Hirschfelder, Joseph Oakland 1911-1990 *WhAm 10*
Hirschfield, Alan J. *IntWW 93, WhoFI 94, WhoWest 94*
Hirschfield, Alan J. 1935- *IntMPA 94*
Hirschfield, Jim *WhoAmA 93*
Hirschfield, Robert S. 1928- *WhoAm 94*
Hirschhorn, Austin 1936- *WhoAm 94*
Hirschhorn, Clive 1940- *WrDr 94*
Hirschhorn, Elizabeth Ann 1962- *WhoScEn 94, WhoWest 94*
Hirschhorn, Eric Leonard 1946- *WhoAm 94*
Hirschhorn, Howard H(arvey) 1931- *ConAu 42NR*
Hirschhorn, Joel Stephen 1939- *WhoScEn 94*
Hirschhorn, Joseph H. 1899-1981 *WhoAmA 93N*
Hirschhorn, Joyce Donen 1926- *WhoAm 94*
Hirschhorn, Kurt 1926- *WhoAm 94, WhoScEn 94*
Hirschhorn, Rochelle 1932- *WhoScEn 94*
Hirschi, John 1933- *WhoAmP 93*
Hirschl, Simon 1935- *WhoScEn 94*
Hirschler, Philip 1955- *WhoFI 94*
Hirschman, Albert Otto 1915- *IntWW 93, WhoAm 94, WhoFI 94*
Hirschman, Charles, Jr. 1943- *WhoWest 94*
Hirschman, Edward *EncSF 93*
Hirschman, Jack *DrAPF 93*
Hirschman, Jack 1933- *WrDr 94*
Hirschman, Shalom Zarach 1936- *WhoAm 94*
Hirschman, Sherman Joseph 1935- *WhoAmL 94, WhoMW 93*
Hirschmann, Franz Gottfried 1945- *WhoWest 94*
Hirschmann, Ralph Franz 1922- *WhoAm 94*
Hirschoff, Jon T. 1941- *WhoAmL 94*
Hirschowitz, Basil Isaac 1925- *WhoAm 94, WhoScEn 94*
Hirschy, Gordon Harold 1942- *WhoMW 93*
Hirschy, James Conrad 1938- *WhoScEn 94*
Hirsen, James L. 1950- *WhoWest 94*
Hirsh, Allan Thurman, Jr. 1920- *WhoAm 94*
Hirsh, Annette Marie 1921- *WhoAmA 93*
Hirsh, Ira Jean 1922- *WhoAm 94*
Hirsh, Norman Barry 1935- *WhoAm 94, WhoFI 94, WhoScEn 94, WhoWest 94*
Hirsh, Theodore William 1934- *WhoAm 94*
Hirshan, Leonard 1927- *IntMPA 94*
Hirshen, Sanford 1935- *WhoAm 94*
Hirshfeld, Alan 1951- *ConAu 141*
Hirshfield, Baron 1913- *Who 94*
Hirshfield, Jane *DrAPF 93*
Hirshfield, Pearl *WhoAmA 93*
Hirshfield, Richard *GayLL*
Hirshfield, Stuart 1941- *WhoAm 94, WhoAmL 94*
Hirshleifer, David Adam 1958- *WhoWest 94*
Hirshman, Harold Carl 1945- *WhoAm 94, WhoAmL 94*
Hirshon, Robert Edward 1948- *WhoAm 94, WhoAmL 94*
Hirshon, Sheldon Ira 1947- *WhoAm 94, WhoAmL 94*
Hirshorn, Anne Sue *DrAPF 93*
Hirshowitz, Melvin Stephen 1938- *WhoAmL 94*
Hirshson, Stanley Philip 1928- *WhoAm 94*
Hirshson, William Roscoe 1928- *WhoAm 94*
Hirson, Alice *WhoHol 92*
Hirson, Estelle *WhoWest 94*
Hirst, David (Cozens-Hardy) 1925- *Who 94*
Hirst, David Michael Geoffrey 1933- *Who 94*
Hirst, Heston Stillings 1915- *WhoAm 94*
Hirst, John Malcolm 1921- *Who 94*
Hirst, Jonathan William 1953- *Who 94*
Hirst, Michael (William) 1946- *Who 94*
Hirst, Omer Lee 1913- *WhoAmP 93*
Hirst, Paul Heywood 1927- *IntWW 93, Who 94*
Hirst, Paul Quentin 1946- *WrDr 94*
Hirst, Peter Christopher 1943- *WhoAm 94*
Hirst, Richard B. *WhoAmL 94*
Hirst, Rob
See Midnight Oil *ConMus 11*
Hirst, Rodney Julian 1920- *Who 94*
Hirst, Wilma Elizabeth *WhoAm 94, WhoWest 94*
Hirt, Al 1922- *IntMPA 94, WhoHol 92*
Hirt, Eleonore *WhoHol 92*
Hirth, John Price 1930- *WhoAm 94*
Hirth, Russell Julius 1924- *WhoWest 94*
Hiruki, Chuji 1931- *WhoAm 94, WhoScEn 94*
Hirzebruch, Friedrich Ernst Peter 1927- *IntWW 93*
Hisatomi, John A. 1945- *WhoAsA 94*
Hiscock, Dana W. 1945- *WhoAmL 94*
Hiscock, Richard Carson 1944- *WhoScEn 94*
Hiscocks, Charles Richard 1907- *Who 94*
Hiscocks, Patrick Dennis 1956- *WhoWest 94*
Hiscocks, (Charles) Richard 1907- *WrDr 94*
Hiscox, Robert Ralph Scrymgeour 1943- *Who 94*
Hise, Mark Allen 1950- *WhoWest 94*
Hisert, George A. 1944- *WhoAmL 94*
Hishon, Elizabeth Anderson 1944- *WhoAmL 94*
Hislop, George Steedman 1914- *Who 94*
Hislop, Ian David 1960- *Who 94*
Hislop, Joseph d1977 *WhoHol 92*
Hislop, Joseph 1884-1977 *NewGrDO*
Hislop, Joseph Dewar 1884-1977 *DcNaB MP*
Hislop, Julia Rose Catherine 1962- *ConAu 141, SmATA 74 [port]*
Hislop, Mervyn Warren 1937- *WhoAm 94*
Hisrich, Joseph C. *WhoAmP 93*
Hiss, Alger 1904- *Who 94*
Hiss, Roland Graham 1932- *WhoAm 94*
Hiss, Tony 1941- *WhoAm 94*
Histake, Suafaase'e Faipa *WhoAmP 93*
Hitam, Dato' Mohd. Yusof 1936- *IntWW 93*
Hitam, Musa bin 1934- *IntWW 93*
Hitch, Brian 1932- *Who 94*
Hitch, Charles Johnston 1910- *IntWW 93, WhoAm 94*
Hitch, Horace 1921- *WhoAm 94, WhoAmL 94*
Hitch, James T., III 1949- *WhoAm 94*
Hitch, Jean Leason 1918- *WhoAmA 93*
Hitch, Robert A. 1920- *WhoAmA 93*
Hitch, Robert Landis 1947- *WhoFI 94, WhoMW 93*
Hitch, Stewart 1940- *WhoAmA 93*
Hitchborn, James Brian 1938- *WhoAm 94, WhoFI 94*
Hitchcock, Alfred d1980 *WhoHol 92*
Hitchcock, Alfred Joseph 1899-1980 *AmCulL [port]*
Hitchcock, Anthony John Michael 1929- *Who 94*
Hitchcock, Bion Earl 1942- *WhoAmL 94*
Hitchcock, Christopher Brian 1947- *WhoFI 94, WhoScEn 94*
Hitchcock, Deborah J. *ConAu 141*
Hitchcock, Edward 1793-1864 *DcAmReB 2*
Hitchcock, Edward Keith 1941- *WhoIns 94*
Hitchcock, Edward Robert 1929- *IntWW 93, Who 94*
Hitchcock, Ethan Allen 1909- *WhoAm 94*
Hitchcock, George *DrAPF 93*
Hitchcock, George (Parks) 1914- *WrDr 94*
Hitchcock, Harold Bradford 1903- *WhoAm 94*
Hitchcock, Harold Ralph 1950- *WhoWest 94*
Hitchcock, Henry Russell 1903-1986 *WhoAmA 93N*
Hitchcock, J. Gareth 1914- *WhoAm 94, WhoAmL 94, WhoMW 93*
Hitchcock, Jane 1953- *WhoHol 92*
Hitchcock, John David 1909- *WhoWest 94*
Hitchcock, Karen Ruth 1943- *WhoAm 94*
Hitchcock, Keith d1966 *WhoHol 92*
Hitchcock, Lillian Dorothy Staw 1922- *WhoMW 93*
Hitchcock, Patricia 1932- *WhoHol 92*
Hitchcock, Raymond d1929 *WhoHol 92*
Hitchcock, Raymond (John) 1922- *EncSF 93*
Hitchcock, Raymond John 1922-1992 *WrDr 94N*
Hitchcock, Rex d1950 *WhoHol 92*
Hitchcock, Sharon Marie 1947- *WhoMW 93*
Hitchcock, Vernon Thomas 1919- *WhoWest 94*
Hitchcock, Walter d1917 *WhoHol 92*
Hitchcock, Walter Anson 1918- *WhoAm 94*
Hitchen, Brian 1936- *Who 94*
Hitchen, Harold, Jr. 1934- *WhoIns 94*
Hitchen, John David 1935- *Who 94*
Hitchens, Christopher 1949- *WrDr 94*
Hitchens, Christopher Eric 1949- *WhoAmP 93*
Hitchens, David William 1955- *WhoWest 94*
Hitchens, Gilbert Archibald Ford 1932- *Who 94*
Hitchens, Neal 1957- *ConAu 141*
Hitchens, William Richard 1953- *WhoAmL 94*
Hitchin, Aylwin Drakeford 1907- *Who 94*
Hitchin, Nigel James 1946- *Who 94*
Hitching, Alan Norman 1941- *Who 94*
Hitching, Harry James 1909- *WhoAm 94*
Hitchings, George H. 1905-
See Elion, Gertrude Belle 1918- *WorScD*
Hitchings, George H., Jr. 1905- *NobelP 91 [port]*
Hitchings, George Herbert 1905- *IntWW 93, Who 94, WhoAm 94, WhoScEn 94*
Hitchner, Carl H. 1940- *WhoAmL 94*
Hitchon, William Nicholas Guy 1957- *WhoMW 93*
Hite, Elinor Kirkland 1942- *WhoMW 93*
Hite, James Tillman, III 1938- *WhoAm 94*
Hite, Judson Cary 1939- *WhoMW 93*
Hite, Les d1962 *WhoHol 92*
Hite, Nancy Ursula 1956- *WhoBlA 94*
Hite, Robert d1981 *WhoHol 92*
Hite, Robert Griffith 1932- *WhoAmL 94*
Hite, Robert Wesley 1936- *WhoWest 94*
Hite, Shere D. *IntWW 93*
Hite, Shere D. 1942- *WhoAm 94*
Hite, Sid 1954- *ConAu 142, SmATA 75*
Hites, Ronald Atlee 1942- *WhoAm 94*
Hitler, Adolf 1889-1945 *HisWorL [port], TwCLC 53 [port]*
Hitlin, David George 1942- *WhoAm 94, WhoScEn 94, WhoWest 94*
Hitner, Chuck 1943- *WhoAmA 93*
Hitomi, Georgia Kay 1952- *WhoScEn 94*
Hitt, David Hamilton 1925- *WhoAm 94*
Hitt, John Craig, Jr. 1965- *WhoMW 93*
Hitt, Leo N. 1955- *WhoAm 94, WhoAmL 94*
Hitt, Mary Barton 1936- *WhoAmP 93*
Hitt, Patricia Reilly 1918- *WhoAmP 93*
Hitter, Joseph Ira 1944- *WhoAmL 94*
Hitti, Youssef Samir 1954- *WhoScEn 94*
Hittinger, William Charles 1922- *WhoAm 94*
Hittle, David William 1947- *WhoAmL 94*
Hittle, James D. 1915- *WhoAm 94*
Hittle, Richard Howard 1923- *WhoAm 94, WhoFI 94*
Hittmair, Hans Christoph 1928- *IntWW 93*
Hittmair, Otto 1924- *IntWW 93*
Hittner, Barry G. 1946- *WhoAmL 94*
Hittner, David 1939- *WhoAm 94, WhoAmL 94*
Hitz, C. Breck 1944- *WhoScEn 94*
Hitz, Duane E. 1939- *WhoMW 93*
Hitz, Frederick Porter 1939- *WhoAm 94*
Hitzig, Rupert 1942- *IntMPA 94*
Hiura, Alan 1951?- *WhoAsA 94*
Hively, Georgenia d1977 *WhoHol 92*
Hives, Baron 1913- *Who 94*
Hivnor, Robert (Hanks) 1916- *ConDr 93*
Hiwatashi, Koichi 1921- *WhoScEn 94*
Hix, David Matthew 1958- *WhoMW 93*
Hix, Don d1964 *WhoHol 92*
Hix, H. Edgar *DrAPF 93*
Hix, Harvey Lee 1960- *WhoMW 93*
Hix, Larry James 1947- *WhoWest 94*
Hixon, James Edward 1938- *WhoAm 94, WhoMW 93*

Hobson, Harold 1904- *WrDr 94*
Hobson, Harry E., Jr. 1948- *WhoMW 93*
Hobson, Harry Lee, Jr. 1929- *WhoAm 94*
Hobson, Herschel Lee 1945- *WhoAmL 94*
Hobson, Howard 1903- *BasBi*
Hobson, J(ohn) Allan 1933- *ConAu 140*
Hobson, James Richard 1897- *WhAm 10*
Hobson, James Richmond 1937- *WhoAm 94, WhoAmL 94, WhoFI 94*
Hobson, Jay Damon 1942- *WhoFI 94*
Hobson, John 1946- *Who 94*
Hobson, John Allan 1933- *WhoAm 94*
Hobson, Katherine Thayer 1889-1982 *WhoAmA 93N*
Hobson, Keith Lee 1958- *WhoMW 93, WhoScEn 94*
Hobson, Lawrence John d1993 *Who 94N*
Hobson, Mark Stephan 1950- *WhoWest 94*
Hobson, Paul d1666 *DcNaB MP*
Hobson, Peter 1944- *Who 94*
Hobson, Phillip Maurice 1942- *WhoAmP 93*
Hobson, Richard R. G. 1931- *WhoAmP 93*
Hobson, Robert R. 1930- *WhoBlA 94*
Hobson, Robert Wayne, II 1939- *WhoAm 94*
Hobson, Valerie 1917- *WhoHol 92*
Hobson, Valerie Babette Louise *Who 94*
Hobson, William D. 1908- *WhoBlA 94*
Hobson-Simmons, Joyce Ann 1947- *WhoBlA 94*
Hoburg, James Frederick 1946- *WhoAm 94, WhoScEn 94*
Hobuss, Jim J. 1955- *WhoWest 94*
Hoby, Margaret 1571-1633 *DcNaB MP*
Hoby, Margaret Dakins Devereux Sidney 1571-1633 *BlmGWL*
Hoby, Thomas 1530-1566 *DcLB 132*
Hoccleve, Thomas 1368-1426 *BlmGEL*
Hocevar, Gary 1951- *WhoAmP 93*
Hoch, Alan Randall 1948- *WhoWest 94*
Hoch, Edward D. *DrAPF 93*
Hoch, Edward D. 1930- *WrDr 94*
Hoch, Edward D(entinger) 1930- *EncSF 93*
Hoch, Edward Dentinger 1930- *WhoAm 94*
Hoch, Frank William 1921- *WhoFI 94*
Hoch, Frederic Louis 1920- *WhoAm 94*
Hoch, Orion 1928- *IntWW 93*
Hoch, Orion Lindel 1928- *WhoAm 94, WhoFI 94, WhoWest 94*
Hoch, Peggy Marie 1959- *WhoScEn 94*
Hoch, Rand 1955- *WhoAmP 93*
Hoch, Roland Franklin 1940- *WhoAm 94*
Hoch, Standley Howard *WhoFI 94*
Hoch, William Henry 1944- *WhoWest 94*
Hoch, Winton C. 1907-1979 *IntDcF 2-4*
Hochachka, Peter William 1937- *WhoScEn 94*
Hochbaum, Godfrey Martin 1916- *WhoAm 94*
Hochberg, Audrey G. *WhoAmP 93*
Hochberg, Bayard Zabdial 1932- *WhoAm 94*
Hochberg, D. Peter 1940- *WhoMW 93*
Hochberg, Fred Philip 1952- *WhoAm 94*
Hochberg, Frederick George 1913- *WhoFI 94, WhoWest 94*
Hochberg, Hans Heinrich, XIV 1843-1926 *NewGrDO*
Hochberg, Irving 1934- *WhoScEn 94*
Hochberg, Jerome A. 1933- *WhoAm 94*
Hochberg, Julian 1923- *WhoAm 94*
Hochberg, Mark S. 1947- *WhoScEn 94*
Hochberg, Ronald Mark 1955- *WhoAmL 94*
Hochberg, Scott 1953- *WhoAmP 93*
Hochberg, Sheldon E. 1943- *WhoAmL 94*
Hochberger, John Richard 1960- *WhoWest 94*
Hochberger, Simon 1912- *WhoAm 94*
Hochbrueckner, George J. 1938- *CngDr 93, WhoAm 94*
Hochbrueckner, George Joseph 1938- *WhoAmP 93*
Hoche, Philip Anthony 1906- *WhoAm 94*
Hochenegg, Leonhard 1942- *WhoScEn 94*
Hochgraf, Norman Nicolai 1931- *WhoScEn 94*
Hochhalter, Gordon Ray 1946- *WhoFI 94, WhoMW 93*
Hochhaus, Pernola Jean 1944- *WhoAmP 93*
Hochhauser, Marilyn Helsenrott 1928- *WhoAmA 93*
Hochhauser, Sheila 1951- *WhoAmP 93*
Hochhauser, Victor 1923- *Who 94*
Hochheimer, Frank Leo 1943- *WhoFI 94*
Hochheiser, Marilyn *DrAPF 93*
Hochhuth, Rolf 1931- *ConWorW 93, IntDcT 2, IntWW 93*
Ho Chi Minh 1890-1969 *HisWorL [port]*
Hochkammer, William O., Jr. 1945- *WhoAmL 94*
Hochman, Alan Robert 1950- *WhoAmL 94*
Hochman, Bruce B. 1955- *WhoAmL 94*
Hochman, Charles Bruce 1934- *WhoAm 94*
Hochman, Gloria 1943- *ConAu 141*
Hochman, Harry 1925- *WhoMW 93*
Hochman, Jeffrey J. 1952- *WhoAmL 94*
Hochman, Jiri 1926- *ConAu 141*
Hochman, Kenneth George 1947- *WhoAm 94, WhoAmL 94*
Hochman, Kitty *WhoAmA 93*
Hochman, Sandra 1936- *WrDr 94*
Hochmeister, Angela Beth 1958- *WhoAmL 94*
Hochmuth, Robert Milo 1939- *WhoAm 94*
Hochova, Dagmar 1926- *WhoWomW 91*
Hochreiter, Joseph Christian, Jr. 1955- *WhoFI 94*
Hochschild, Adam 1942- *WhoAm 94*
Hochschild, Carroll Shepherd 1935- *WhoWest 94*
Hochschild, Richard 1928- *WhoWest 94*
Hochschwender, Herman Karl 1920- *WhoAm 94, WhoFI 94*
Hochschwender, Karl Albert 1927- *WhoFI 94*
Hochstadt, Harry 1925- *WhoAm 94*
Hochstadt, Joy 1939- *WhoAm 94*
Hochstatter, Harold *WhoAmP 93*
Hochstein, Anatoly Boris 1932- *WhoAm 94*
Hochstein, Rolaine *DrAPF 93*
Hochster, Melvin 1943- *WhoAm 94, WhoScEn 94*
Hochstetler, Donald Dee 1946- *WhoMW 93*
Hochstetler, Mark Allen 1956- *WhoMW 93*
Hochstetler, T. Max 1941- *WhoAmA 93*
Hochstrasser, Donald Lee 1927- *WhoAm 94*
Hochstrasser, John Michael 1938- *WhoScEn 94*
Hochuli, Edward G. 1950- *WhoAmL 94*
Hochwaelder, Fritz 1911-1986 *ConAu 42NR*
Hochwald, Werner 1910-1989 *WhAm 10*
Hochwalder, Fritz 1911-1986 *IntDcT 2 [port]*
Hock, Delwin D. 1935- *WhoFI 94*
Hock, Emil d1944 *WhoHol 92*
Hock, Frederick Wyeth 1924- *WhoAmL 94*
Hock, Hans Henrich 1938- *WhoMW 93*
Hock, Mort *IntMPA 94*
Hock, Morton 1929- *WhoAm 94, WhoFI 94*
Hock, Winfield Fletcher, Jr. 1931- *WhoAmL 94*
Hockaday, Arthur (Patrick) 1926- *Who 94*
Hockaday, Hugh 1892-1968 *WhoAmA 93N*
Hockaday, Irvine O., Jr. 1936- *WhoAm 94, WhoFI 94, WhoMW 93*
Hockaday, Michael Leon 1955- *WhoAmL 94*
Hockaday, Shepard Lynn 1961- *WhoFI 94*
Hockby, Stephen *BlmGWL*
Hocke, Jean-Pierre 1938- *IntWW 93, Who 94*
Hockenberg, Harlan David 1927- *WhoAm 94*
Hockenhull, Arthur James Weston 1915- *Who 94*
Hockensmith, Robert Franklin, Jr. 1955- *WhoFI 94*
Hockensmith, Scott Franklin 1949- *WhoWest 94*
Hocker, Alexander *Who 94*
Hockert, Valerie Margaret 1950- *WhoMW 93*
Hockett, Bob 1925- *WhoAmP 93*
Hockett, Charles F(rancis) 1916- *WrDr 94*
Hockett, Charles Francis 1916- *WhoAm 94*
Hockett, Christopher Burch 1959- *WhoAmL 94*
Hockett, Curtis Fredrick 1934- *WhoFI 94*
Hockfeld, Marla Gail Gerecht 1965- *WhoWest 94*
Hockin, Thomas 1938- *IntWW 93*
Hockin, Thomas Alexander 1938- *WhoAm 94, WhoFI 94*
Hocking, Anthony 1938- *WrDr 94*
Hocking, Duncan John 1944- *WhoFI 94*
Hocking, Frederick Denison Maurice 1899- *Who 94*
Hocking, John Gilbert 1920- *WhoAm 94*
Hocking, Mary (Eunice) 1921- *WrDr 94*
Hocking, Philip Norman 1925- *Who 94*
Hockley, Anthony Heritage F. *Who 94*
Hockley, Raymond Alan 1929- *Who 94*
Hockman, Stephen Alexander 1947- *Who 94*
Hockney, David *NewYTBS 93 [port]*
Hockney, David 1937- *AmCulL, IntWW 93, NewGrDO, Who 94, WhoAm 94, WhoAmA 93, WhoWest 94*
Hocott, Joe Bill 1921- *WhoFI 94, WhoScEn 94*
Hocq, Nathalie 1951- *IntWW 93*
Hocquenghem, Guy 1946-1988 *GayLL*
Hoctor, Harriet d1977 *WhoHol 92*
Hocutt, Betty E. 1939- *WhoAmP 93*
Hocutt, Max Oliver 1936- *WhoAm 94*
Hodakov, Chaim Mordechai Aizik 1902-1993 *NewYTBS 93*
Hodapp, Don Joseph 1937- *WhoAm 94*
Hodapp, Larry Frank 1956- *WhoMW 93*
Hodapp, Leroy Charles 1923- *WhoAm 94*
Hodas, David 1951- *WhoAmL 94*
Hodavance, Robert S. 1941- *WhoAm 94*
Hodder, Bramwell William 1923- *Who 94*
Hodder, Kane 1955- *WhoHol 92*
Hodder, William Alan 1931- *WhoAm 94, WhoFI 94, WhoMW 93*
Hodder-Williams, (John) Christopher (Glazebrook) 1926- *EncSF 93, WrDr 94*
Hodder-Williams, Paul 1910- *Who 94*
Hoddeson, Lillian 1940- *WhoMW 93*
Hoddinott, Alfred Henry, Jr. 1938- *WhoAmL 94*
Hoddinott, Alun 1929- *IntWW 93, NewGrDO, Who 94*
Hoddinott, Anthony Paul 1942- *Who 94*
Hoddinott, Ira Seymour 1897- *WhAm 10*
Hoddinott, R(alph) F(ield) 1913- *WrDr 94*
Hoddy, George Warren 1905- *WhoAm 94*
Hoddy, Raymond Arthur 1921- *WhoAm 94*
Hodel, Donald Paul 1935- *IntWW 93, WhoAmP 93*
Hodes, Abram 1922- *WhoWest 94*
Hodes, Art 1904?-1993 *NewYTBS 93 [port]*
Hodes, Barney 1943- *WhoAmA 93*
Hodes, Barton L. 1940- *WhoAm 94*
Hodes, Bernard S. 1931- *WhoAm 94*
Hodes, Horace Louis 1907-1989 *WhAm 10*
Hodes, Jonathan Ezra 1956- *WhoScEn 94*
Hodes, Linda *WhoAm 94*
Hodes, Marion Edward 1925- *WhoAm 94*
Hodes, Mel 1943- *WhoAmP 93*
Hodes, Richard Michael 1953- *WhoScEn 94*
Hodes, Richard S. 1924- *WhoAmP 93*
Hodes, Robert Bernard 1925- *WhoAm 94*
Hodes, Scott 1937- *WhoAm 94, WhoAmL 94, WhoAmP 93*
Hodess, Arthur Bart 1950- *WhoScEn 94*
Hodgart, Matthew (John Caldwell) 1916- *EncSF 93, WrDr 94*
Hodgart, Matthew John Caldwell 1916- *Who 94*
Hodgden, Lavinia Richards 1920- *WhoAmP 93*
Hodgdon, Harry Edward 1946- *WhoAm 94*
Hodgdon, Herbert James 1924- *WhoAm 94*
Hodgdon, Shirley Lamson 1921- *WhoAmP 93*
Hodge, A. Winston *WhoAmP 93*
Hodge, Adele P. 1942- *WhoBlA 94*
Hodge, Alexander Mitchell 1916- *Who 94*
Hodge, Anne Harkness 1951- *WhoAm 94*
Hodge, Bobby Lynn 1956- *WhoScEn 94*
Hodge, Carleton Taylor 1917- *WhoAm 94*
Hodge, Charles 1797-1878 *DcAmReB 2*
Hodge, Charles Mason 1938- *WhoBlA 94*
Hodge, Cynthia Elois 1947- *WhoBlA 94*
Hodge, Derek M. 1941- *WhoBlA 94*
Hodge, Derek Michael 1941- *WhoAmP 93*
Hodge, Donald Jerome 1969- *WhoBlA 94*
Hodge, Donald Ray 1939- *WhoScEn 94*
Hodge, Dorothy W. (Scottie) 1940- *WhoAmA 93*
Hodge, Douglas *WhoHol 92*
Hodge, Douglas Kern 1956- *WhoMW 93*
Hodge, Elbert Clifton, Jr. 1943- *WhoAm 94, WhoAmL 94*
Hodge, Ernest Vance 1945- *WhoMW 93*
Hodge, Francis 1915- *WrDr 94*
Hodge, George Lowrance 1934- *WhoAm 94*
Hodge, Gregory Eiland 1960- *WhoAmL 94*
Hodge, James Blythe 1946- *WhoAmL 94*
Hodge, James Lee 1935- *WhoAm 94*
Hodge, James Robert 1927- *WhoAm 94*
Hodge, James William 1943- *Who 94*
Hodge, Jane Aiken 1917- *WrDr 94*
Hodge, John Dennis 1929- *Who 94*
Hodge, John Edward 1914- *WhoBlA 94*
Hodge, John R. 1893-1963 *HisDcKW*
Hodge, John Rowland 1913- *Who 94*
Hodge, Julian Stephen Alfred 1904- *Who 94*
Hodge, Lonnie *DrAPF 93*
Hodge, Margaret Eve 1944- *Who 94*
Hodge, Marguerite V. 1920- *WhoBlA 94*
Hodge, Merle 1944- *BlmGWL*
Hodge, Michael Doyle 1948- *WhoFI 94*
Hodge, Michael John Davy V. *Who 94*
Hodge, Norris 1927- *WhoBlA 94*
Hodge, P. W. *ConAu 42NR*
Hodge, Patricia *IntWW 93*
Hodge, Patricia 1946- *IntMPA 94, Who 94, WhoHol 92*
Hodge, Paul W(illiam) 1934- *ConAu 42NR*
Hodge, Paul William 1934- *WhoAm 94, WrDr 94*
Hodge, Philip Gibson, Jr. 1920- *WhoAm 94, WhoScEn 94*
Hodge, Philip Tully 1950- *WhoScEn 94*
Hodge, R. Garey 1937- *WhoAmA 93*
Hodge, Raymond Joseph 1922-1990 *WhAm 10*
Hodge, Robert Joseph 1937- *WhoFI 94*
Hodge, T. Shirby 1841-1926 *EncSF 93*
Hodge, Thomas E. *WhoAmP 93*
Hodge, Verne Antonio 1933- *WhoAm 94*
Hodge, W. J. *WhoBlA 94*
Hodge, William Anthony 1962- *WhoBlA 94*
Hodge, Winifred 1950- *WhoMW 93, WhoScEn 94*
Hodgell, Murlin Ray 1924- *WhoAm 94*
Hodgell, Robert Overman 1922- *WhoAm 94, WhoAmA 93*
Hodgeman, Edwin 1935- *WhoHol 92*
Hodgen, Maurice Denzil 1929- *WhoAm 94*
Hodges, Agil Earl 1933- *WhoAmL 94*
Hodges, Ann 1928- *WhoAm 94*
Hodges, Beverly Palmer 1960- *WhoFI 94*
Hodges, C(yril) Walter 1909- *Who 94, WrDr 94*
Hodges, Carolyn Richardson 1947- *WhoBlA 94*
Hodges, Clarence Eugene 1939- *WhoAm 94, WhoAmP 93, WhoBlA 94*
Hodges, Cother L. 1920- *WhoBlA 94*
Hodges, Craig 1960- *BasBi*
Hodges, Craig Anthony 1960- *WhoBlA 94*
Hodges, David Albert 1937- *WhoAm 94*
Hodges, David Julian 1944- *WhoBlA 94*
Hodges, Dewey Harper 1948- *WhoAm 94*
Hodges, Donald Clark 1923- *WrDr 94*
Hodges, Doris M. 1915- *WrDr 94*
Hodges, Eddie 1947- *WhoHol 92*
Hodges, Edwin Clair 1940- *WhoFI 94*
Hodges, Elaine Mary 1928- *Who 94*
Hodges, Elizabeth *DrAPF 93*
Hodges, Gerald 1925- *Who 94*
Hodges, H. Gaylord, Jr. 1941- *WhoIns 94*
Hodges, Harold Earl 1934-1989 *WhoBlA 94N*
Hodges, Harold T. 1936- *WhoAmP 93*
Hodges, Harry F. 1933- *WhoAm 94*
Hodges, Helene 1949- *WhoBlA 94*
Hodges, Hollis *DrAPF 93*
Hodges, Horace d1951 *WhoHol 92*
Hodges, James Clark 1935- *WhoScEn 94*
Hodges, James Hovis 1956- *WhoAmP 93*
Hodges, John Andrews *WhoAmL 94*
Hodges, John Hendricks 1914- *WhoAm 94*
Hodges, John O. 1944- *WhoBlA 94*
Hodges, Johnny d1970 *WhoHol 92*
Hodges, Joseph Gilluly, Jr. 1942- *WhoAmL 94, WhoWest 94*
Hodges, Joseph Thomas Charles 1932- *Who 94*
Hodges, Jot Holiver, Jr. 1932- *WhoAmL 94*
Hodges, Joy 1915- *WhoHol 92*
Hodges, Joyce E. *WhoAmP 93*
Hodges, Kaneaster, Jr. *WhoAmP 93*
Hodges, Kenneth Bryant, III 1965- *WhoAmL 94*
Hodges, Lew 1956- *Who 94*
Hodges, Lewis (Macdonald) 1918- *Who 94*
Hodges, Lillian Bernice 1939- *WhoBlA 94*
Hodges, Margaret 1911- *WrDr 94*
Hodges, Margaret Moore 1911- *SmATA 75 [port], WhoAm 94*
Hodges, Mark Willie 1923- *Who 94*
Hodges, Melvin Sancho 1940- *WhoBlA 94*
Hodges, Michael P. 1941- *WrDr 94*
Hodges, Nancy Hutton 1933- *WhoAmP 93*
Hodges, Pat *WhoHol 92*
Hodges, Patricia Ann 1954- *WhoBlA 94*
Hodges, Paul Joseph 1959- *WhoAm 94*
Hodges, Paul V., Jr. 1913- *WhoAmP 93*
Hodges, Ralph B. 1930- *WhoAm 94, WhoAmL 94*
Hodges, Ralph Byron 1930- *WhoAmP 93*
Hodges, Richard *WhoAmP 93*
Hodges, Richard Andrew 1952- *Who 94*
Hodges, Richard Edwin 1928- *WhoWest 94*
Hodges, Robert Edgar 1922- *WhoScEn 94*
Hodges, Robert H., Jr. 1944- *WhoAm 94, WhoAmL 94*
Hodges, Robert Hayne, Jr. 1944- *CngDr 93*

Hodges, Ronald Dexter 1944- *WhoAmL 94*
Hodges, Thomas Kent 1936- *WhoAm 94*
Hodges, Thompson Gene 1913- *WhoAm 94*
Hodges, Vernon Wray 1929- *WhoFI 94, WhoScEn 94*
Hodges, Virgil Hall 1936- *WhoBlA 94*
Hodges, William C. d1961 *WhoHol 92*
Hodges, William Terrell 1934- *WhoAm 94, WhoAmL 94*
Hodge-Spencer, Cheryl Ann 1952- *WhoScEn 94*
Hodgetts, Richard M(ichael) 1942- *WrDr 94*
Hodgetts, Robert Bartley 1918- *Who 94*
Hodgins, Daniel Stephen 1939- *WhoAmL 94*
Hodgins, Earl d1964 *WhoHol 92*
Hodgins, Jack 1938- *WrDr 94*
Hodgins, Jack Stanley 1938- *WhoAm 94, WhoWest 94*
Hodgins, Leslie d1927 *WhoHol 92*
Hodgins, Michael Minden 1912- *Who 94*
Hodgins, Norman Francis, Jr. 1952- *WhoFI 94*
Hodgkin, Alan (Lloyd) 1914- *ConAu 140, Who 94*
Hodgkin, Alan Lloyd 1914- *IntWW 93, WhoAm 94, WhoScEn 94, WorScD*
Hodgkin, Dorothy Crowfoot 1910- *IntWW 93, WhoScEn 94, WorScD [port]*
Hodgkin, Dorothy Mary Crowfoot 1910- *Who 94*
Hodgkin, Douglas Irving 1939- *WhoAmP 93*
Hodgkin, Howard 1932- *IntWW 93, Who 94*
Hodgkin, Jonathan Alan 1949- *Who 94*
Hodgkin, Robin A. 1916- *WrDr 94*
Hodgkins, Christopher Joseph 1957- *WhoAmP 93*
Hodgkins, David C. *EncSF 93*
Hodgkins, David John 1934- *Who 94*
Hodgkins, Frederick Crie 1946- *WhoFI 94*
Hodgkins, Rosalind Selma 1942- *WhoAmA 93*
Hodgkins, Sarah Perkins 1750?-1803 *BlmGWL*
Hodgkinson, Arthur Edward 1913- *Who 94*
Hodgkinson, Derek *Who 94*
Hodgkinson, (William) Derek 1917- *Who 94*
Hodgkinson, Terence William Ivan 1913- *Who 94*
Hodgkinson, William James 1939- *WhoAm 94, WhoFI 94*
Hodgkiss, Alan Geoffrey 1921- *WrDr 94*
Hodgman, David Renwick 1947- *WhoAm 94, WhoAmL 94*
Hodgman, Helen 1945- *WrDr 94*
Hodgman, Vicki Jean 1933- *WhoMW 93*
Hodgskin, Thomas 1787-1869 *DcNaB MP*
Hodgson, Adam Robin 1937- *Who 94*
Hodgson, Alfreda Rose d1992 *IntWW 93N*
Hodgson, Allan Archibald 1937- *WhoAm 94*
Hodgson, Arthur Brian 1916- *Who 94*
Hodgson, Arthur Clay 1907- *WhoAmL 94, WhoMW 93*
Hodgson, Carlton Roy 1930- *WhoBlA 94*
Hodgson, Clague Pitman 1946- *WhoMW 93*
Hodgson, Derek *Who 94*
Hodgson, (Walter) Derek (Thornley) 1917- *Who 94*
Hodgson, Ernest 1932- *WhoAm 94*
Hodgson, Esther Naomi 1915- *WhoAmP 93*
Hodgson, George Charles Day 1913- *Who 94*
Hodgson, Gordon Hewett 1929- *Who 94*
Hodgson, Gregory Bernard 1946- *WhoWest 94*
Hodgson, Howard Osmond Paul 1950- *Who 94*
Hodgson, Hugh 1893- *WhAm 10*
Hodgson, James 1925- *Who 94*
Hodgson, James Day 1915- *IntWW 93, WhoAmP 93*
Hodgson, James Stanley 1942- *WhoAm 94*
Hodgson, John Bury 1912- *Who 94*
Hodgson, John Derek 1931- *Who 94*
Hodgson, Kenneth P. 1945- *WhoFI 94, WhoScEn 94, WhoWest 94*
Hodgson, Laura d1980 *WhoHol 92*
Hodgson, Leyland d1949 *WhoHol 92*
Hodgson, Mary 1673?-c. 1718 *NewGrDO*
Hodgson, Maurice (Arthur Eric) 1919- *Who 94*
Hodgson, Maurice Arthur Eric 1919- *IntWW 93*
Hodgson, Morgan Day 1947- *WhoAm 94*
Hodgson, Patricia Anne 1947- *Who 94*
Hodgson, Paul Edmund 1921- *WhoAm 94*
Hodgson, Peter C. 1934- *WrDr 94*
Hodgson, Peter Edward 1928- *WrDr 94*
Hodgson, Peter John 1929- *WhoAm 94*
Hodgson, Phyllis 1909- *Who 94*
Hodgson, Reginald Hutchins, Jr. 1939- *WhoFI 94*
Hodgson, Richard 1917- *WhoAm 94*
Hodgson, Robin Granville 1942- *Who 94*
Hodgson, Stanley Ernest 1918- *Who 94*
Hodgson, Terence Harold Henry 1916- *Who 94*
Hodgson, Thomas R. 1941- *IntWW 93*
Hodgson, Thomas Richard 1941- *WhoAm 94, WhoMW 93*
Hodgson, Thomas Richard Burnham 1926- *Who 94*
Hodgson, Walter John Barry 1939- *WhoAm 94*
Hodgson, William Donald John 1923- *Who 94*
Hodgson, William Hope 1877-1918 *EncSF 93*
Hodgson-Brooks, Gloria J. 1942- *WhoBlA 94*
Hodiak, John d1955 *WhoHol 92*
Hodiak, Katrina *WhoHol 92*
Hodin, Josef Paul 1905- *IntWW 93, Who 94, WrDr 94*
Hodjat, Yahya 1950- *WhoMW 93*
Hodkin, Hedley 1902- *Who 94*
Hodkinson, Henry Malcolm 1931- *Who 94*
Hodkinson, Judith Marie *Who 94*
Hodkinson, Sydney Phillip 1934- *WhoAm 94*
Hodl, Eleonore 1944- *WhoWomW 91*
Hodley, Jane *WhoAmA 93*
Hodne, Thomas Harold, Jr. 1927- *WhoAm 94*
Hodnett, Richard McInnis 1956- *WhoWest 94*
Hodnik, David F. 1947- *WhoFI 94*
Hodo, Edward Douglas *WhoAm 94*
Hodosan, Roza *WhoWomW 91*
Hodosh, Ellen Keough 1951- *WhoMW 93*
Hodous, Robert Power 1945- *WhoAm 94*
Hodowal, John Raymond 1945- *WhoFI 94*
Hodrova, Daniela 1946- *BlmGWL*
Hodsoll, Francis S. M. 1938- *WhoAmP 93*
Hodson, Christine Ann 1951- *WhoWest 94*
Hodson, Daniel Houghton 1944- *Who 94*
Hodson, Darrel Leroy 1912-1986 *WhAm 10*
Hodson, Denys Fraser 1928- *Who 94*
Hodson, Frank 1921- *Who 94*
Hodson, Henry Vincent 1906- *IntWW 93, Who 94, WrDr 94*
Hodson, Jerry B. 1960- *WhoAmL 94*
Hodson, John 1946- *Who 94*
Hodson, Kenneth Joe 1913- *WhoAm 94*
Hodson, Michael (Robin Adderley) 1932- *Who 94*
Hodson, Nancy Perry 1932- *WhoWest 94*
Hodson, Thane Raymond 1953- *WhoAm 94*
Hodson, Thomas David Tattersall 1942- *Who 94*
Hodson, Thomas Scott 1948- *WhoAmL 94*
Hodson, Thomas William 1946- *WhoAm 94, WhoFI 94*
Hodson, William Alan 1935- *WhoAm 94*
Hodur, Francis 1866-1953 *DcAmReB 2*
Hodza, Fadil 1916- *IntWW 93*
Hoe, Johann Joachim fl. c. 1680-1730 *NewGrDO*
Hoe, Richard M. 1812-1886 *WorInv*
Hoe, Richard March 1939- *WhoFI 94*
Hoebel, Bartley Gore 1935- *WhoAm 94, WhoScEn 94*
Hoebel, E. Adamson d1993 *NewYTBS 93*
Hoebel, Edward Adamson 1906- *WhoAm 94*
Hoebel, Edward Adamson 1906-1993 *ConAu 142*
Hoechner, Carl Ludwig 1928- *WhoFI 94*
Hoechstetter, Daniel 1525-1581 *DcNaB MP*
Hoecker, David 1948- *WhoAm 94*
Hoecker, Thomas Ralph 1950- *WhoAm 94, WhoAmL 94*
Hoecker, Wayne H. 1939- *WhoAmL 94*
Hoefel, Roseanne Louise 1962- *WhoMW 93*
Hoefer, Bruce R., Jr. 1954- *WhoAmL 94*
Hoeffel, Joseph M., III 1950- *WhoAmP 93*
Hoefflin, Richard Michael 1949- *WhoAmL 94*
Hoefle, Barbara Jean 1946- *WhoFI 94*
Hoeflich, Charles Hitschler 1914- *WhoAm 94*
Hoeflin, Ronald Kent 1944- *WhoAm 94*
Hoefling, John Alan 1925- *WhoAm 94*
Hoefling, John William 1948- *WhoAmL 94*
Hoefling, Rudolf Joachim 1942- *WhoAm 94*
Hoeft, Arthur Peter 1945- *WhoWest 94*
Hoeft, Cynthia Ann 1955- *WhoWest 94*
Hoeft, Douglas L. *WhoAmP 93*
Hoeft, Elizabeth Bayless 1942- *WhoAm 94*
Hoeft, John Thomas 1947- *WhoAmL 94*
Hoeft, Julius Albert 1946- *WhoAm 94*
Hoeft, Marlene Linnea 1955- *WhoMW 93*
Hoeft, Robert D. *DrAPF 93*
Hoeft, Robert Gene 1944- *WhoAm 94, WhoMW 93*
Hoeft, Steven H. 1951- *WhoAm 94, WhoAmL 94*
Hoeg, Donald Francis 1931- *WhoAm 94*
Hoeg, Thomas E. 1953- *WhoIns 94*
Hoegger, Erhard Fritz 1924- *WhoScEn 94*
Hoegh, Annelise 1948- *WhoWomW 91*
Hoegh, Leo Arthur 1908- *WhoAmP 93*
Hoeh, Theodore J. 1946- *WhoIns 94*
Hoehn, Carola *WhoHol 92*
Hoehn, Elmer L. 1915- *WhoAm 94*
Hoehn, Harry 1918-1974 *WhoAmA 93N*
Hoehn, William Edwin 1937- *WhoAm 94*
Hoehnel, Ludwig Von 1857-1905? *WhWE*
Hoehner, Harold W. 1935- *WrDr 94*
Hoehner, John Frederic 1946- *WhoAmL 94*
Hoekema, David Andrew 1950- *WhoAm 94*
Hoekema, Susan Bosma 1951- *WhoAmL 94*
Hoekman, Alvin James 1935- *WhoAmP 93*
Hoekman, Guus 1913- *NewGrDO*
Hoekman, Johan Bernard 1931- *Who 94*
Hoekman, John Bernard (Joop) 1931- *IntWW 93*
Hoekstra, Gerald Richard 1947- *WhoMW 93*
Hoekstra, Peter 1953- *CngDr 93, WhoAm 94, WhoAmP 93, WhoMW 93*
Hoekwater, James Warren 1946- *WhoAm 94*
Hoel, David Gerhard 1939- *WhoAm 94, WhoScEn 94*
Hoel, Lester A. 1935- *WhoAm 94*
Hoelldobler, Bert(hold Karl) 1936- *WrDr 94*
Hoellen, John James 1914- *WhoAmL 94, WhoAmP 93*
Hoelscher, Joanna Louise 1937- *WhoMW 93*
Hoelscher, John Henry 1932- *WhoAm 94*
Hoelscher, Ludwig 1907- *IntWW 93*
Hoelscher, Maryann M. 1968- *WhoMW 93*
Hoelscher, Robert James 1952- *WhoAm 94*
Hoelter, Timothy K. 1946- *WhoAmL 94*
Hoeltge, Gerald Adrian 1945- *WhoMW 93*
Hoelzel, Kathleen M. 1943- *WhoAmP 93*
Hoelzer, Guy Andrew 1956- *WhoScEn 94*
Hoen, Linda Lee 1952- *WhoWest 94*
Hoenack, August Frederick 1908- *WhoAm 94*
Hoener, Arthur 1929- *WhoAmA 93*
Hoengen, Elisabeth *NewGrDO*
Hoenig, Gerald Jay 1944- *WhoAmL 94*
Hoenig, J 1916- *WrDr 94*
Hoenig, Lawrence L. 1949- *WhoAmL 94*
Hoenigswald, Henry M 1915- *WrDr 94*
Hoenigswald, Henry Max 1915- *WhoAm 94, WhoScEn 94*
Hoenmans, Paul John 1932- *WhoAm 94, WhoFI 94*
Hoepner, Theodore John 1941- *WhoAm 94*
Hoerbiger, Attila *WhoHol 92*
Hoerbiger, Paul d1981 *WhoHol 92*
Hoerig, Gerald Lee 1943- *WhoAm 94*
Hoerle, Richard William 1923- *WhoMW 93*
Hoerneman, Calvin A., Jr. 1940- *WhoMW 93*
Hoerner, Ed d1983 *WhoHol 92*
Hoerner, John Lee 1939- *Who 94*
Hoerner, Richard Norris 1896- *WhAm 10*
Hoerner, Robert Jack 1931- *WhoAm 94, WhoAmL 94*
Hoerni, Jean Amedee 1924- *WhoAm 94, WhoWest 94*
Hoerr, John P., (III) 1930- *WrDr 94*
Hoerr, Stanley Obermann 1909-1990 *WhAm 10*
Hoesing, Barbara Joan 1932- *WhoAmP 93*
Hoessle, Charles Herman 1931- *WhoAm 94, WhoMW 93*
Hoevel, Michael James 1944- *WhoWest 94*
Hoeveler, Sarah E. 1961- *WhoWest 94*
Hoeveler, William M. 1922- *WhoAm 94*
Hoewing, Mark Wesley 1956- *WhoAm 94*
Hoewing, Raymond L. 1932- *WhoAm 94*
Hoey, Allen *DrAPF 93*
Hoey, Catharine Letitia 1946- *Who 94*
Hoey, David Joseph 1967- *WhoScEn 94*
Hoey, Dennis d1960 *WhoHol 92*
Hoey, Edwin Anderson 1930- *WhoAm 94*
Hoey, Iris d1979 *WhoHol 92*
Hoey, James Joseph 1936- *WhoAm 94*
Hoey, John d1978 *WhoHol 92*
Hoey, Michael Dennis 1960- *WhoScEn 94*
Hoey, Rita Marie 1950- *WhoAm 94*
Hof, Liselotte Bertha 1937- *WhoAm 94*
Hof, Patrick Raymond 1960- *WhoScEn 94*
Hofacker, Erich Paul 1898- *WhAm 10*
Hofeldt, John W. 1920- *WhoAm 94*
Hofer, Charles Warren 1940- *WhoFI 94*
Hofer, Chris d1964 *WhoHol 92*
Hofer, Clifford Andrew 1911- *WhoAmP 93*
Hofer, Evelyn *WhoAmA 93*
Hofer, Ingrid (Ingeborg) *WhoAmA 93*
Hofer, Johanna *WhoHol 92*
Hofer, (Maria) Josepha 1758-1819 *NewGrDO*
Hofer, Judith K. *WhoAm 94*
Hofer, Lonnie Joe 1955- *WhoMW 93*
Hofer, Mark A. 1953- *WhoAmL 94*
Hofer, Myron Arms 1931- *WhoAm 94*
Hofer, Robert D. 1932- *WhoAmP 93*
Hofer, Roy Ellis 1935- *WhoAm 94*
Hoferer, Jeanne *WhoAmP 93*
Hofert, Jack 1930- *WhoWest 94*
Hoff, Benjamin 1946- *ConAu 142*
Hoff, Carl d1965 *WhoHol 92*
Hoff, Charles Worthington, III 1934- *WhoAm 94*
Hoff, Edwin Frank, Jr. 1938- *WhoScEn 94*
Hoff, Gerald Charles 1938- *WhoScEn 94*
Hoff, Gerhardt Michael 1930- *WhoAm 94, WhoIns 94*
Hoff, H. S. *ConAu 42NR*
Hoff, Harry Summerfield *Who 94*
Hoff, Harry Summerfield 1910- *WrDr 94*
Hoff, James Edwin 1932- *WhoAm 94, WhoMW 93*
Hoff, Joan 1937- *WrDr 94*
Hoff, John Scott 1946- *WhoAmL 94, WhoMW 93*
Hoff, Jonathan Morind 1955- *WhoAm 94, WhoAmL 94*
Hoff, Joseph Russel 1952- *WhoMW 93*
Hoff, Julian Theodore 1936- *WhoAm 94, WhoScEn 94*
Hoff, Magdalene 1940- *WhoWomW 91*
Hoff, Marcian E. 1937- *WorInv*
Hoff, Margo *WhoAmA 93*
Hoff, Margo 1912- *WhoAm 94*
Hoff, Mary (King) 1956- *SmATA 74*
Hoff, Nathaniel Hawthorne 1929- *WhoBlA 94*
Hoff, Nicholas John 1906- *WhoAm 94*
Hoff, Philip Henderson 1924- *WhoAmP 93*
Hoff, Renae 1951- *WhoAmL 94, WhoWest 94*
Hoff, Syd(ney) 1912- *WrDr 94*
Hoff, Sydney 1912- *WhoAm 94*
Hoff, Timothy 1941- *WhoAm 94, WhoAmL 94*
Hoff, William Bruce, Jr. 1932- *WhoAm 94*
Hoffa, Harlan Edward 1925- *WhoAm 94*
Hoffa, James Riddle 1913-c. 1975 *AmSocL*
Hoffa, Portland d1990 *WhoHol 92*
Hoffart, Marita B. *WhoMW 93*
Hoffay, Thomas Richard 1948- *WhoAmP 93*
Hoffbeck, Loren John 1932- *WhoMW 93*
Hoffberg, David Lawrence 1932- *WhoAm 94*
Hoffberg, Judith A. 1934- *WhoAmA 93, WhoWest 94*
Hoffberg, Steven Mark 1960- *WhoScEn 94*
Hoffberger, Bruce Silver 1948- *WhoIns 94*
Hoffberger, Jerold Charles 1919- *WhoAm 94*
Hoffbrand, (Allan) Victor 1935- *Who 94*
Hoffding, (Niels) Finn 1899- *NewGrDO*
Hoffe, Monckton d1951 *WhoHol 92*
Hoffeld, Jeffrey M. 1945- *WhoAmA 93*
Hoffenberg, Harvey *WhoAm 94*
Hoffenberg, Marvin 1914- *WhoAm 94*
Hoffenberg, Raymond 1923- *IntWW 93, Who 94*
Hoffenblum, Allan Ernest 1940- *WhoWest 94*
Hoffenstein, Samuel 1890-1947 *IntDcF 2-4*
Hoffer, Charles Russell 1929- *WhoAm 94*
Hoffer, James Brian 1956- *WhoScEn 94*
Hoffer, John Louis 1931- *WhoAm 94*
Hoffer, Paul 1895-1949 *NewGrDO*
Hoffer, Paul B. 1939- *WhoAm 94*
Hoffer, Robert Morrison 1921- *WhoAm 94*
Hoffer, Thomas William 1938- *WhoAm 94, WhoFI 94*
Hoffert, Frank, Jr. 1937- *WhoMW 93*
Hoffert, J. Stanley 1947- *WhoIns 94*
Hoffert, Martin Irving 1938- *WhoAm 94*
Hoffgen, Marga 1921- *NewGrDO*

Hoffheimer, Daniel Joseph 1950- *WhoAm 94, WhoAmL 94, WhoFI 94, WhoMW 93*
Hoffinger, Jack S. 1926- *WhoAmL 94*
Hoffius, Dirk Cornelius 1943- *WhoAm 94, WhoAmL 94*
Hoffleit, Ellen Dorrit 1907- *WhoAm 94, WhoScEn 94*
Hoffler, Richard Winfred, Jr. 1944- *WhoBlA 94*
Hofflund, Paul 1928- *WhoAmL 94, WhoWest 94*
Hoffman, Abbie d1989 *WhoHol 92*
Hoffman, Abbie 1936-1989 *HisWorL*
Hoffman, Abbott 1936-1989 *AmSocL [port]*
Hoffman, Adonis Edward 1954- *WhoAmL 94*
Hoffman, Alan B. 1946- *WhoAmL 94*
Hoffman, Alan Craig 1944- *WhoAmL 94, WhoMW 93*
Hoffman, Alan Jay 1948- *WhoAm 94, WhoAmL 94*
Hoffman, Alan Jerome 1924- *IntWW 93, WhoAm 94, WhoScEn 94*
Hoffman, Albert *WorScD*
Hoffman, Albert Edward, Jr. 1959- *WhoFI 94*
Hoffman, Alfred John 1917- *WhoAm 94*
Hoffman, Alice 1952- *WrDr 94*
Hoffman, Allan Augustus 1934- *WhoScEn 94*
Hoffman, Allan Sachs 1932- *WhoAm 94, WhoWest 94*
Hoffman, Arnold d1966 *WhoAmA 93N*
Hoffman, Arthur W(olf) 1921- *WrDr 94*
Hoffman, Arthur Wolf 1921- *WhoAm 94*
Hoffman, Avi 1958- *ConTFT 11*
Hoffman, Barbara A. 1940- *WhoAmP 93*
Hoffman, Barbara Jo 1952- *WhoMW 93*
Hoffman, Barbara Kriete 1963- *WhoMW 93*
Hoffman, Barry Paul 1941- *WhoAmL 94*
Hoffman, Basil *WhoHol 92*
Hoffman, Bern d1979 *WhoHol 92*
Hoffman, Bernard Douglas, Jr. 1957- *WhoScEn 94*
Hoffman, Carol Maree 1944- *WhoAmA 93*
Hoffman, Charles Fenno, III 1958- *WhoWest 94*
Hoffman, Charles Steven 1949- *WhoFI 94*
Hoffman, Charles Stuart 1958- *WhoScEn 94*
Hoffman, Christian Matthew 1944- *WhoAm 94, WhoAmL 94*
Hoffman, Christopher Warren 1963- *WhoFI 94*
Hoffman, Chuck 1938- *WhoAmP 93*
Hoffman, Clarence d1981 *WhoHol 92*
Hoffman, Clark Collins 1941- *WhoMW 93*
Hoffman, Craig Allan 1955- *WhoFI 94*
Hoffman, Cynthia L. 1949- *WhoAmP 93*
Hoffman, Daniel *DrAPF 93*
Hoffman, Daniel 1923- *WrDr 94*
Hoffman, Daniel Gerard 1923- *WhoAm 94*
Hoffman, Daniel Steven 1931- *WhoAm 94*
Hoffman, Darleane Christian 1926- *WhoAm 94, WhoScEn 94, WhoWest 94*
Hoffman, David d1961 *WhoHol 92*
Hoffman, David 1957- *WhoAmP 93*
Hoffman, David Alan 1947- *WhoAmL 94*
Hoffman, David John 1944- *WhoScEn 94*
Hoffman, Dolores Garcia 1936- *WhoHisp 94*
Hoffman, Donald Alfred 1936- *WhoAmL 94*
Hoffman, Donald David 1955- *WhoFI 94, WhoScEn 94, WhoWest 94*
Hoffman, Donald M. 1935- *WhoAm 94*
Hoffman, Douglas Raymond 1957- *WhoAmL 94*
Hoffman, Douglas W. 1944- *WhoAm 94*
Hoffman, Dustin 1937- *IntMPA 94, WhoHol 92*
Hoffman, Dustin Lee 1937- *IntWW 93, Who 94, WhoAm 94*
Hoffman, E. Leslie 1947- *WhoAm 94*
Hoffman, Eberhard d1957 *WhoHol 92*
Hoffman, Edward Fenno, III 1916-1991 *WhAm 10, WhoAmA 93N*
Hoffman, Edward George 1945- *WhoFI 94*
Hoffman, Edward Richard, III 1928- *WhoAm 94, WhoFI 94*
Hoffman, Edwin Philip 1942- *WhoAm 94, WhoFI 94, WhoMW 93*
Hoffman, Elaine Janet *WhoAmA 93*
Hoffman, Elaine Janet 1925- *WhoWest 94*
Hoffman, Elizabeth C. *WhoAmP 93*
Hoffman, Elmo Rogers 1935- *WhoAmL 94*
Hoffman, Eric 1952- *WhoAmA 93*
Hoffman, Eva 1945- *WrDr 94*
Hoffman, Eva Alfreda 1945- *WhoAm 94*
Hoffman, Ferdi d1989 *WhoHol 92*
Hoffman, Francois-Benoit(-Henri) 1760-1828 *NewGrDO*
Hoffman, Frank Thomas 1958- *WhoMW 93*
Hoffman, Franklin Thomas 1953- *WhoWest 94*
Hoffman, Frederick William, IV 1951- *WhoAmP 93*
Hoffman, Gary Michael 1946- *WhoAm 94, WhoAmL 94*
Hoffman, Gene 1927- *WhoAm 94*
Hoffman, Gene Louis 1932- *WhoAmP 93*
Hoffman, George Alan 1937- *WhoWest 94*
Hoffman, George W(alter) 1914-1990 *WhAm 10*
Hoffman, Gertrude W. d1966 *WhoHol 92*
Hoffman, Gloria Levy 1933- *WhoFI 94*
Hoffman, Grace 1921- *NewGrDO*
Hoffman, Grace 1925- *IntWW 93*
Hoffman, Harley Howard 1935- *WhoMW 93*
Hoffman, Harold Wayne 1930- *WhoAm 94*
Hoffman, Harry Z. 1908-1990 *WhoAmA 93N*
Hoffman, Helen Bacon 1930- *WhoAmA 93*
Hoffman, Howard d1969 *WhoHol 92*
Hoffman, Howard Stanley 1925- *WhoAm 94*
Hoffman, Irwin 1924- *WhoAm 94*
Hoffman, Jack Leroy 1922- *WhoAm 94*
Hoffman, Jack Westly 1950- *WhoFI 94*
Hoffman, James Irvie, III 1941- *WhoWest 94*
Hoffman, James Leo 1938- *WhoMW 93*
Hoffman, James Paul 1943- *WhoAmL 94, WhoMW 93*
Hoffman, James R. 1932- *WhoAm 94, WhoMW 93*
Hoffman, Jane 1910- *WhoHol 92*
Hoffman, Jason Paul 1968- *WhoWest 94*
Hoffman, Jay C. 1961- *WhoAmP 93*
Hoffman, Jeffry Edward 1965- *WhoMW 93*
Hoffman, Jerome A. 1938- *WhoAm 94*
Hoffman, Jerry Carl 1943- *WhoScEn 94*
Hoffman, Jerry Irwin 1935- *WhoMW 93*
Hoffman, Jill *DrAPF 93*
Hoffman, Joan Bentley 1946- *WhoMW 93*
Hoffman, JoAnn 1952- *WhoAmL 94*
Hoffman, Joel Elihu 1937- *WhoAm 94*
Hoffman, Joel Harvey 1953- *WhoAm 94*
Hoffman, John Ernest, Jr. 1934- *WhoAm 94*
Hoffman, John Fletcher 1946- *WhoAm 94*
Hoffman, John Francis 1947- *WhoAm 94, WhoAmL 94*
Hoffman, John Harry 1913- *WhoAmL 94, WhoMW 93*
Hoffman, John Raleigh 1926- *WhoAm 94*
Hoffman, John Raymond 1945- *WhoAm 94, WhoFI 94*
Hoffman, John Wayne 1947- *WhoWest 94*
Hoffman, Joseph 1909- *IntMPA 94*
Hoffman, Joseph Irvine, Jr. 1939- *WhoBlA 94*
Hoffman, Joyce N. 1952- *WhoIns 94*
Hoffman, Judith A. 1943- *WhoMW 93*
Hoffman, Julien Ivor Ellis 1925- *WhoAm 94*
Hoffman, Karla Leigh 1948- *WhoFI 94, WhoScEn 94*
Hoffman, Kenneth John 1964- *WhoMW 93*
Hoffman, Kevin William 1961- *WhoScEn 94*
Hoffman, Larry Gene 1933-1991 *WhoAmA 93N*
Hoffman, Larry J. 1930- *WhoAm 94*
Hoffman, Lawrence Wayne 1945- *WhoMW 93*
Hoffman, Lee 1932- *EncSF 93, WrDr 94*
Hoffman, Leonard Elbert, Jr. 1919- *WhoAmL 94*
Hoffman, Lyman F. 1950- *WhoAmP 93*
Hoffman, Malvina 1887-1966 *WhoAmA 93N*
Hoffman, Mandy Lippman 1956- *WhoAmA 93*
Hoffman, Manny *WhoAmP 93*
Hoffman, Marilyn Friedman *WhoAm 94, WhoAmA 93*
Hoffman, Marion Marie 1934- *WhoAmP 93*
Hoffman, Mark Leslie 1952- *WhoAmL 94*
Hoffman, Marsha K. 1961- *WhoMW 93*
Hoffman, Martin 1935- *WhoAmA 93*
Hoffman, Martin Leon 1924- *WhoAm 94*
Hoffman, Mary (Margaret) 1945- *WrDr 94*
Hoffman, Mary Catherine 1923- *WhoMW 93*
Hoffman, Mary Claire 1947- *WhoWest 94*
Hoffman, Maryhelen H. Paulick 1943- *WhoAm 94*
Hoffman, Mathew 1954- *WhoAm 94, WhoAmL 94*
Hoffman, Max, Jr. d1945 *WhoHol 92*
Hoffman, Merle Holly 1946- *WhoAm 94*
Hoffman, Michael Charles 1947- *WhoMW 93*
Hoffman, Michael E. 1942- *WhoAmA 93*
Hoffman, Michael Eugene 1942- *WhoAm 94*
Hoffman, Michael Gene 1952- *WhoFI 94*
Hoffman, Michael J 1939- *WrDr 94*
Hoffman, Michael Jerome 1939- *WhoAm 94, WhoWest 94*
Hoffman, Michael Joseph 1942- *WhoMW 93*
Hoffman, Michael Richard 1939- *IntWW 93, Who 94*
Hoffman, Michael William 1955- *WhoAmL 94*
Hoffman, Mitchell J. 1951- *WhoAmL 94*
Hoffman, Mitchell Wade 1954- *WhoFI 94*
Hoffman, Nanci L. 1948- *WhoIns 94*
Hoffman, Nancy 1944- *WhoAm 94, WhoAmA 93*
Hoffman, Nancy E. 1944- *WhoAmL 94*
Hoffman, Nathaniel A. 1949- *WhoAm 94*
Hoffman, Neil James 1938- *WhoAm 94, WhoAmA 93, WhoWest 94*
Hoffman, Oscar Allen 1920- *WhoAm 94*
Hoffman, Otto d1944 *WhoHol 92*
Hoffman, Patricia Ann 1962- *WhoMW 93*
Hoffman, Paul Felix 1941- *WhoAm 94, WhoScEn 94, WhoWest 94*
Hoffman, Paul Jerome 1923- *WhoScEn 94*
Hoffman, Paul Maxim Laurence 1942- *Who 94*
Hoffman, Paul Roger 1934- *WhoAm 94*
Hoffman, Paul Shafer 1933- *WhoAmL 94*
Hoffman, Peter Toll 1946- *WhoAm 94*
Hoffman, Philip Andrew 1931- *WhoAm 94, WhoFI 94, WhoMW 93*
Hoffman, Philip E. d1993 *NewYTBS 93*
Hoffman, Philip E. 1951- *WhoAmP 93*
Hoffman, Philip Edward 1951- *WhoMW 93*
Hoffman, Philip Guthrie 1915- *WhoAm 94*
Hoffman, Philip Joseph 1958- *WhoAmL 94*
Hoffman, Richard *DrAPF 93*
Hoffman, Richard Bruce 1947- *WhoAm 94*
Hoffman, Richard George 1949- *WhoMW 93, WhoScEn 94*
Hoffman, Richard H. 1935- *WhoAm 94*
Hoffman, Richard M. 1942- *WhoAm 94*
Hoffman, Richard Peter 1911- *WhoAmA 93*
Hoffman, Richard William 1918- *WhoAm 94*
Hoffman, Robert *WhoAmP 93*
Hoffman, Robert 1939- *WhoHol 92*
Hoffman, Robert B. 1945- *WhoAm 94, WhoAmL 94*
Hoffman, Robert B. 1947- *WhoIns 94*
Hoffman, Robert E. 1924- *WhoAmP 93*
Hoffman, Robert Howard 1956- *WhoFI 94*
Hoffman, Robert S. 1929- *WhoScEn 94*
Hoffman, Rodney Joseph 1950- *WhoWest 94*
Hoffman, Rolland Edward 1931- *WhoWest 94*
Hoffman, Ronald 1941- *WrDr 94*
Hoffman, Ronald 1945- *WhoAm 94*
Hoffman, Ronald Bruce 1939- *WhoAm 94*
Hoffman, Ronald Robert 1934- *WhoAm 94, WhoFI 94*
Hoffman, S. David 1922- *WhoAm 94*
Hoffman, S. Joseph 1920- *WhoAm 94*
Hoffman, Stan *WhoHol 92*
Hoffman, Stanley 1928- *WhoFI 94*
Hoffman, Stanley Harold 1917- *Who 94*
Hoffman, Stuart Kenneth 1949- *WhoAmL 94*
Hoffman, Sue Ellen 1945- *WhoMW 93*
Hoffman, Sue Ellen 1965- *WhoMW 93*
Hoffman, Susan Katz 1949- *WhoAm 94*
Hoffman, Thom *WhoHol 92*
Hoffman, Valerie Jane 1953- *WhoAm 94, WhoAmL 94*
Hoffman, W. Andrew, III 1954- *WhoAmL 94*
Hoffman, Walter Edward 1907- *WhoAm 94, WhoAmL 94*
Hoffman, Wayne Melvin 1923- *WhoAm 94, WhoWest 94*
Hoffman, Wendy Maureen 1950- *WhoWest 94*
Hoffman, William *DrAPF 93*
Hoffman, William 1925- *WhoAm 94*
Hoffman, William A. 1920- *WhoAmA 93*
Hoffman, William Charles 1919- *WhoWest 94*
Hoffman, William G. 1937- *WhoIns 94*
Hoffman, William Kenneth 1924- *WhoMW 93*
Hoffman, William M. *DrAPF 93*
Hoffman, William M. 1939- *ConDr 93, WhoAm 94, WrDr 94*
Hoffman, William McKinley, Jr. 1934- *WhoAmA 93*
Hoffman-Bright, Betty Ann 1921- *WhoAmP 93*
Hoffman-Ladd, Valerie Jon 1954- *WhoMW 93*
Hoffmann(-Onegin), Lilly *NewGrDO*
Hoffmann, Ann Marie 1930- *WrDr 94*
Hoffmann, Arnold, Jr. 1915-1991 *WhoAmA 93N*
Hoffmann, Bruce 1947- *WhoAmP 93*
Hoffmann, Carl 1881-1947 *IntDcF 2-4*
Hoffmann, Carol Tomb 1952- *WhoFI 94*
Hoffmann, Charles Wesley 1929- *WhoAm 94*
Hoffmann, Christoph Ludwig 1944- *WhoAm 94, WhoAmL 94*
Hoffmann, Donald 1933- *WhoAm 94, WrDr 94*
Hoffmann, E. T. A. 1776-1822 *ShSCr 13 [port]*
Hoffmann, E(rnst) T(heodor) A(madeus) 1776-1822 *EncSF 93, NewGrDO*
Hoffmann, E(rnst) T(heodore) A(madeus) 1776-1822 *RfGShF*
Hoffmann, Gary David 1947- *WhoAmA 93*
Hoffmann, Gunter Georg 1954- *WhoScEn 94*
Hoffmann, Gunther F. 1938- *WhoScEn 94*
Hoffmann, Howard M. 1941- *WhoAm 94, WhoAmL 94*
Hoffmann, Jon Arnold 1942- *WhoWest 94*
Hoffmann, Kathryn Ann 1954- *WhoWest 94*
Hoffmann, Leesa L. 1947- *WhoAmA 93*
Hoffmann, Leonard Hubert 1934- *Who 94*
Hoffmann, Louis Gerhard 1932- *WhoAm 94*
Hoffmann, Luc 1923- *IntWW 93*
Hoffmann, Malcolm A(rthur) 1912- *WrDr 94*
Hoffmann, Malcolm Arthur 1912- *WhoAm 94, WhoAmL 94*
Hoffmann, Manfred Walter 1938- *WhoFI 94*
Hoffmann, Martin Richard 1932- *WhoAm 94, WhoAmL 94, WhoFI 94*
Hoffmann, Michael Richard 1947- *WhoAmL 94*
Hoffmann, Nancy-Larraine 1947- *WhoAmP 93*
Hoffmann, Oskar *EncSF 93*
Hoffmann, Oswald Carl Julius 1913- *WhoAm 94*
Hoffmann, Otto Louis 1918- *WhoMW 93*
Hoffmann, Peggy 1910- *WrDr 94*
Hoffmann, Peter (Conrad Werner) 1930- *WrDr 94*
Hoffmann, Peter Conrad Werner 1930- *WhoAm 94*
Hoffmann, Roald *DrAPF 93*
Hoffmann, Roald 1937- *ConAu 142, IntWW 93, Who 94, WhoAm 94, WhoScEn 94*
Hoffmann, Robert Shaw 1929- *WhoAm 94*
Hoffmann, Stanley 1928- *WrDr 94*
Hoffmann, Thomas Russell 1933- *WhoAm 94*
Hoffmann, Tony Dale 1960- *WhoWest 94*
Hoffmann, William Frederick 1933- *WhoAm 94, WhoWest 94*
Hoffmeister, Bertram Meryl 1907- *Who 94*
Hoffmeister, Donald Frederick 1916- *WhoAm 94, WrDr 94*
Hoffmeister, Franz Anton 1754-1812 *NewGrDO*
Hoffmeister, Gerhart 1936- *WhoWest 94*
Hoffmeister, Jana Marie *WhoAm 94, WhoScEn 94*
Hoffmeyer, Erik 1924- *IntWW 93*
Hoffmeyer, William Frederick 1936- *WhoAmL 94*
Hoffmire, John Sherwood, III 1956- *WhoFI 94*
Hoffner, Serenus Paul 1946- *WhoAmP 93*
Hoffnung, Gerard 1925-1959 *DcNaB MP*
Hoffs, Susanna 1960- *WhoHol 92*
Hoffstot, Henry Phipps, Jr. 1917- *WhoAm 94*
Hoff-Wilson, Joan 1937- *WrDr 94*
Hoflehner, Rudolf 1916- *IntWW 93*
Hoflich, Lucie d1956 *WhoHol 92*
Hofman, Elaine 1937- *WhoAmP 93*
Hofman, Elaine D. 1937- *WhoWest 94*
Hofman, Kevin Dale 1958- *WhoAmL 94*
Hofman, Leonard John 1928- *WhoAm 94, WhoMW 93*
Hofman, Sam 1928- *WhoAmP 93*
Hofmann, Adele Dellenbaugh 1926- *WhoAm 94*
Hofmann, Alan Frederick 1931- *WhoAm 94, WhoWest 94*
Hofmann, Albert Josef 1933- *WhoScEn 94*
Hofmann, August Wilhelm von 1818-1892 *WorInv*
Hofmann, Dan J. 1945- *WhoWest 94*

Hofmann, Douglas Allan 1950- *WhoAm 94, WhoAmL 94*
Hofmann, Douglas William 1945- *WhoAmA 93*
Hofmann, Frieder Karl 1949- *WhoScEn 94, WhoWest 94*
Hofmann, Gert 1931- *IntWW 93*
Hofmann, Hans 1880-1966 *WhoAmA 93N*
Hofmann, Heinrich (Karl Johann) 1842-1902 *NewGrDO*
Hofmann, Henry Robert 1936- *WhoMW 93*
Hofmann, Isabella 1957- *WhoHol 92*
Hofmann, John Edward 1934- *WhoMW 93*
Hofmann, John Richard, Jr. 1922- *WhoAm 94*
Hofmann, Kay 1932- *WhoAmA 93*
Hofmann, Klaus 1911- *IntWW 93, WhoAm 94*
Hofmann, Ludwig 1895-1963 *NewGrDO*
Hofmann, Michael 1957- *WrDr 94*
Hofmann, Paul Bernard 1941- *WhoAm 94*
Hofmann, Peter 1944- *IntWW 93, NewGrDO*
Hofmann, Theo 1924- *WhoAm 94*
Hofmann, Werner 1928- *IntWW 93*
Hofmannsthal, Hugo von 1874-1929 *DramC 4 [port], IntDcT 2, NewGrDO*
Hofmeister, Paul Emil Julius 1909- *IntWW 93*
Hofmekler, Ori 1952- *IntWW 93*
Hofmeyr, Murray 1925- *IntWW 93*
Hofmeyr, Murray Bernard 1925- *Who 94*
Hofmo, Gunvor 1921- *BlmGWL*
Hofrichter, David Alan 1948- *WhoMW 93*
Hofrichter, Lawrence S. 1947- *WhoAmL 94*
Hofrova, Jarmila 1958- *WhoWomW 91*
Hofschneider, Heinz S. *WhoAmP 93*
Hofsepian, Sylvia A. 1932- *SmATA 74 [port]*
Hofsommer, Donovan Lowell 1938- *WhoMW 93*
Hofsoos, Emil 1896- *WhAm 10*
Hofstad, Alice May 1948- *WhoMW 93*
Hofstadter, Daniel Samuel 1958- *WhoScEn 94*
Hofstadter, Douglas (Richard) 1945- *WrDr 94*
Hofstadter, Douglas Richard 1945- *WhoAm 94, WhoScEn 94*
Hofstadter, Richard 1916-1970 *AmSocL*
Hofstadter, Robert d1990 *NobelP 91N*
Hofstadter, Robert 1915- *WorScD*
Hofstadter, Robert 1915-1990 *WhAm 10*
Hofstatter, Leopold 1902- *WhoAm 94*
Hofstead, James Warner 1913- *WhoFI 94*
Hofsted, Jolyon Gene 1942- *WhoAmA 93*
Hofstetter, Dana Lieberman 1957- *WhoAmL 94*
Hofstetter, Henry W 1914- *WrDr 94*
Hofstetter, Kenneth John 1940- *WhoAm 94*
Hofstra, Hendrik Jan 1904- *IntWW 93*
Hoft, Thomas Wesley 1957- *WhoAmL 94*
Hogan, Arthur James 1940- *WhoFI 94*
Hogan, Ben 1912- *WhoAm 94*
Hogan, Ben W. 1912- *IntWW 93*
Hogan, Beverly Wade 1951- *WhoBlA 94*
Hogan, Bosco *WhoHol 92*
Hogan, Brenda 1928- *WhoHol 92*
Hogan, Carolyn Ann 1944- *WhoBlA 94*
Hogan, Charles Carlton 1921- *WhoScEn 94*
Hogan, Clarence Lester 1920- *WhoAm 94, WhoScEn 94, WhoWest 94*
Hogan, Claude Hollis 1920- *WhoAm 94*
Hogan, Cliff *DrAPF 93*
Hogan, Curtis Jule 1926- *WhoAm 94, WhoFI 94, WhoWest 94*
Hogan, Dan d1978 *WhoHol 92*
Hogan, Daniel Bolten 1943- *WhoFI 94, WhoScEn 94*
Hogan, David Craig 1942- *WhoFI 94*
Hogan, David Earl 1949- *WhAm 10*
Hogan, Dennis Charles 1964- *WhoAmP 93*
Hogan, Desmond 1950- *WrDr 94*
Hogan, Dick *WhoHol 92*
Hogan, Earl d1944 *WhoHol 92*
Hogan, Edward Leo 1932- *WhoAm 94*
Hogan, Edward Robert 1939- *WhoFI 94*
Hogan, Edwin B. 1940- *WhoBlA 94*
Hogan, Ernest *EncSF 93*
Hogan, Fannie Burrell *WhoBlA 94*
Hogan, G. W. *WhoAmP 93*
Hogan, Gerald P. 1946- *WhoIns 94*
Hogan, Henry Algernon Vickers d1993 *Who 94N*
Hogan, Henry Leon, III 1920- *WhoAm 94*
Hogan, Ilona Modly 1947- *WhoAm 94*
Hogan, Jack 1929- *WhoHol 92*
Hogan, James B. 1919- *WhoAmP 93*
Hogan, James Carroll, Jr. 1939- *WhoBlA 94*
Hogan, James Charles 1936- *WhoAm 94*
Hogan, James Michael 1946- *WhoFI 94*
Hogan, James P. d1943 *WhoHol 92*
Hogan, James P(atrick) 1941- *EncSF 93, WrDr 94*
Hogan, John A. *WhoBlA 94*
Hogan, John Donald 1927- *WhoAm 94, WhoFI 94*
Hogan, John Edward *WhoAmP 93*
Hogan, John P. *WhoAm 94*
Hogan, John P. 1938- *WhoAmP 93*
Hogan, John Paul 1919- *WhoAm 94*
Hogan, Jonathan *WhoHol 92*
Hogan, Joseph Charles 1922- *WhoScEn 94*
Hogan, Joseph Thomas 1943- *WhoScEn 94*
Hogan, Judy *DrAPF 93*
Hogan, Katherine Ann 1951- *WhoAmL 94*
Hogan, Kay *DrAPF 93*
Hogan, Keith Procter 1945- *WhoMW 93*
Hogan, Linda *DrAPF 93*
Hogan, Linda 1947- *BlmGWL, WrDr 94*
Hogan, Lisa Beth 1964- *WhoAmL 94*
Hogan, Mark 1931- *WhoAm 94*
Hogan, Mervin Booth 1906- *WhoAm 94, WhoScEn 94, WhoWest 94*
Hogan, Michael *DrAPF 93, WhoHol 92*
Hogan, Michael 1898- *WhoHol 92*
Hogan, Michael Henry 1927- *Who 94*
Hogan, Michael James 1950- *WhoFI 94*
Hogan, Michael Martin 1947- *WhoAmL 94*
Hogan, Michael Ray 1953- *WhoMW 93*
Hogan, Michael Robert 1946- *WhoAm 94, WhoAmL 94, WhoWest 94*
Hogan, Michael Thomas 1957- *WhoFI 94*
Hogan, Pat d1966 *WhoHol 92*
Hogan, Patrick Colm 1957- *WrDr 94*
Hogan, Paul *IntWW 93*
Hogan, Paul 1939- *IntMPA 94, WhoHol 92*
Hogan, (Robert) Ray 1908- *WrDr 94*
Hogan, Robert *WhoHol 92*
Hogan, Robert (Goode) 1930- *ConAu 41NR, WrDr 94*
Hogan, Robert Henry 1926- *WhoAm 94*
Hogan, Robert J. *EncSF 93*
Hogan, Roscoe Benjamin, Jr. 1921- *WhoAmL 94*
Hogan, Rosemarie 1924- *WhoAmP 93*
Hogan, "Society Kid" d1962 *WhoHol 92*
Hogan, Stephen John 1951- *WhoScEn 94*
Hogan, Steven L. 1953- *WhoAm 94*
Hogan, Steven Ryan 1946- *WhoAmP 93*
Hogan, Terrence Patrick 1937- *WhoAm 94*
Hogan, Terry Michael 1946- *WhoMW 93*
Hogan, Thomas Dennis, III 1930- *WhoFI 94*
Hogan, Thomas E. *WhoAmP 93*
Hogan, Thomas F. 1938- *CngDr 93*
Hogan, Thomas Francis 1938- *WhoAm 94, WhoAmL 94*
Hogan, Thomas Harlan 1944- *WhoAm 94*
Hogan, Thomas John 1946- *WhoAm 94*
Hogan, Thomas V. 1936- *WhoFI 94*
Hogan, Timothy Mark 1953- *WhoMW 93*
Hogan, Velvin Reeves 1944- *WhoWest 94*
Hogan, William 1788-1848 *DcAmReB 2*
Hogan, William E., II 1942- *WhoBlA 94*
Hogan-Flynn, Amanda 1949- *WhoFI 94*
Hogans, William Robertson, III 1945- *WhoBlA 94*
Hoganson, Curtis Wendell 1955- *WhoScEn 94*
Hoganson, Jason *WhoHol 92*
Hogarth, Burne 1911- *WhoAm 94, WhoAmA 93, WhoWest 94*
Hogarth, George 1783-1870 *NewGrDO*
Hogarth, Grace 1905- *WrDr 94*
Hogarth, James 1914- *Who 94*
Hogarth, John M. 1931- *IntMPA 94*
Hogarth, Lionel d1946 *WhoHol 92*
Hogarth, Paul *Who 94*
Hogarth, (Arthur) Paul 1917- *IntWW 93, Who 94*
Hogarth, William 1697-1764 *BlmGEL*
Hogarty, R. Scott 1953- *WhoAmL 94*
Hogben, Peter Graham 1925- *Who 94*
Hogberg, Carl Gustav 1913- *WhoFI 94*
Hogbin, Stephen *WhoAmA 93*
Hogbin, Walter 1937- *Who 94*
Hoge, Bill *WhoAmP 93*
Hoge, Franz Joseph 1944- *WhoAm 94*
Hoge, James Fulton, Jr. 1935- *WhoAm 94*
Hoge, Marlin Boyd 1914- *WhoAm 94*
Hoge, Phyllis *DrAPF 93*
Hoge, Robert Wilson 1947- *WhoAmA 93*
Hoge, Warren M. 1941- *WhoAm 94*
Hogen, Marvis Thomas 1923- *WhoAmP 93*
Hogen, Philip N. 1944- *WhoAmP 93*
Hogendorn, Jan S(tafford) 1937- *ConAu 43NR*
Hogendorn, Jan Stafford 1937- *WrDr 94*
Hogenkamp, Henricus Petrus Cornelis 1925- *WhoAm 94*
Hogg *Who 94*
Hogg, Arthur (Ramsay) 1896- *Who 94*
Hogg, Christopher (Anthony) 1936- *Who 94*
Hogg, Christopher Anthony 1936- *IntWW 93*
Hogg, Curly d1974 *WhoHol 92*
Hogg, David Clarence 1921- *WhoAm 94*
Hogg, Douglas (Martin) 1945- *Who 94*
Hogg, Edward William L. *Who 94*
Hogg, Gilbert Charles 1933- *Who 94*
Hogg, Helen Sawyer 1905- *WorScD*
Hogg, Ian 1937- *WhoHol 92*
Hogg, Ian (Leslie Trower) 1911- *Who 94*
Hogg, James 1770-1835 *BlmGEL*
Hogg, James R. 1934- *WhoAm 94*
Hogg, John (Nicholson) 1912- *Who 94*
Hogg, John Nicholson 1912- *IntWW 93*
Hogg, Mary Claire 1947- *Who 94*
Hogg, Norman 1938- *Who 94*
Hogg, Peter Beauchamp 1924- *Who 94*
Hogg, Quintin (McGarel) 1907- *WrDr 94*
Hogg, Robert Lynn 1893- *WhAm 10*
Hogg, Robert Vincent, Jr. 1924- *WhoAm 94*
Hogg, Robin Ivor Trower 1932- *Who 94*
Hogg, Sarah Elizabeth Mary 1946- *IntWW 93, Who 94*
Hogg, Tony Jefferson 1925-1983 *WhAm 10*
Hoggard, James 1941- *WrDr 94*
Hoggard, Lara Guldmar 1915- *WhoAm 94*
Hoggard, William Zack, Jr. 1951- *WhoFI 94*
Hoggart, Richard 1918- *IntWW 93, Who 94, WrDr 94*
Hoggart, Simon David 1946- *Who 94*
Hoggatt, Clela Allphin 1932- *WhoAm 94, WhoWest 94*
Hogge, (Arthur) Michael (Lancelot) 1925- *Who 94*
Hogger, Henry George 1948- *Who 94*
Hogges, Ralph 1947- *WhoBlA 94*
Hoggett, Anthony John Christopher 1940- *Who 94*
Hoggett, Brenda Marjorie 1945- *Who 94*
Hogle, Ann Meilstrup 1927- *WhoAmA 93*
Hoglund, Annette M. *WhoAmP 93*
Hoglund, Ellis S. 1898- *WhAm 10*
Hoglund, John Andrew 1945- *WhoAmL 94*
Hoglund, Richard Frank 1933- *WhoAm 94*
Hoglund, William Elis 1934- *WhoAm 94*
Hogner, Don La Rue 1937- *WhoWest 94*
Hogness, John Rusten 1922- *WhoAm 94*
Hognestad, Eivind 1921- *WhoAm 94*
Hogoboom, Belford E. 1926- *WhoIns 94*
Ho-Gonzalez, William 1957- *WhoAsA 94, WhoHisp 94*
Hogrogian, Nonny 1932- *SmATA 74 [port]*
Hogsett, Joseph H. *WhoAm 94, WhoMW 93*
Hogsett, Joseph H. 1956- *WhoAmP 93*
Hogu, Barbara J. Jones 1938- *WhoBlA 94*
Hogue, Alexandre 1898- *WhoAmA 93*
Hogue, Bobby L. 1939- *WhoAmP 93*
Hogue, Cynthia *DrAPF 93*
Hogue, John Harold 1955- *WhoWest 94*
Hogue, L. Eades 1944- *WhoAmL 94*
Hogue, Roland d1958 *WhoHol 92*
Hogue, Terry Glynn 1944- *WhoAm 94, WhoAmL 94*
Hoguet, George R. 1947- *WhoFI 94*
Hoguet, Robert L., Jr. d1993 *NewYTBS 93 [port]*
Hoguet, Robert Louis 1908- *WhoAm 94*
Hogun, James d1781 *WhAmRev*
Hogwood, Christopher Jarvis Haley 1941- *IntWW 93, Who 94, WhoAm 94*
Hohage, Frederick William 1938- *WhoAm 94*
Hohenadel, John Herman 1950- *WhoFI 94*
Hohenberg, Charles Morris 1940- *WhoAm 94*
Hohenberg, John 1906- *WhoAm 94, WrDr 94*
Hohenberg, Pierre Claude 1934- *WhoAm 94*
Hohendahl, Peter Uwe 1936- *WhoAm 94*
Hohenemser, Christoph 1937- *WhoAm 94*
Hohenfellner, Peter 1939- *IntWW 93*
Hohenrath, William Edward 1922- *WhoAm 94*
Hohenstein, Kurt A. 1955- *WhoAmP 93*
Hohenstein, Kurt Alan 1955- *WhoMW 93*
Hohl, Arthur d1964 *WhoHol 92*
Hohl, Martin D. 1958- *WhoScEn 94*
Hohler, G. Robert *WhoAm 94*
Hohler, Henry Arthur Frederick 1911- *Who 94*
Hohlmayer, Earl J. 1921- *WhoWest 94*
Hohlov, Yuri Eugenievich 1954- *WhoScEn 94*
Hohman, A. J., Jr. 1934- *WhoAmL 94*
Hohman, James Joseph 1948- *WhoMW 93*
Hohmeyer, Olav Hans 1953- *WhoScEn 94*
Hohn, Edward Lewis 1933- *WhoWest 94*
Hohn, Harry G. 1932- *WhoIns 94*
Hohn, Harry George 1932- *WhoAm 94, WhoFI 94*
Hohn, Jane Rushford 1941- *WhoFI 94*
Hohn, Jayne Marie 1957- *WhoMW 93*
Hohn, Richard G. 1936- *WhoIns 94*
Hohner, Kenneth Dwayne 1934- *WhoFI 94, WhoWest 94*
Hohnhorst, John C. 1952- *WhoAmL 94*
Hohoff, Curt 1913- *IntWW 93*
Hoholik, Anthony Paul 1955- *WhoFI 94*
Ho Hon *WhoWomW 91*
Hohulin, Martin 1964- *WhoAmP 93*
Hoi, Samuel Chuen-Tsung *WhoAm 94*
Hoi, Samuel Chuen-Tsung 1958- *WhoAmA 93*
Hoiby, Lee 1926- *NewGrDO, WhoAm 94*
Hoie, Claus 1911- *WhoAmA 93*
Hoie, Helen Hunt *WhoAmA 93*
Hoikes, Mary Elizabeth 1940- *WhoAmL 94*
Hoiland, Andrew Calvin 1926- *WhoAm 94*
Hoines, David Alan 1946- *WhoAmL 94*
Hoiseth, Kolbjorn 1932- *NewGrDO*
Hoisington, David Harold 1946- *WhoMW 93*
Hoisington, Margaret Bray 1941- *WhoFI 94*
Hoisington, Richard Williams 1929- *WhoFI 94*
Hoit, Marc I. 1957- *WhoScEn 94*
Hoivik, Thomas Harry 1941- *WhoWest 94*
Hojman, David E(nrique) 1946- *ConAu 141*
Hojnacki, Jerome Louis 1947- *WhoScEn 94*
Hojo, Masashi 1952- *WhoScEn 94*
Hokama, Yoshitsugi 1926- *WhoAsA 94, WhoWest 94*
Hokana, Gregory Howard 1944- *WhoFI 94, WhoScEn 94, WhoWest 94*
Hokana, John M. 1953- *WhoAmP 93*
Hokanson, Alicia *DrAPF 93*
Hokanson, Hans 1925- *WhoAmA 93*
Hokanson, Mary-Alan *WhoHol 92*
Hokanson, Shirley Ann 1936- *WhoAmP 93*
Hoke, Dean Edward 1950- *WhoWest 94*
Hoke, Helen L. *ConAu 43NR*
Hoke, Martin 1952- *WhoAmP 93*
Hoke, Martin R. 1952- *CngDr 93*
Hoke, Martin Rossiter 1952- *WhoAm 94, WhoMW 93*
Hoke, S. Candice 1955- *WhoAmL 94*
Hokenson, David Leonard 1950- *WhoMW 93*
Hokenstad, Merl Clifford, Jr. 1936- *WhoAm 94*
Hokin, Lowell Edward 1924- *WhoAm 94, WhoMW 93, WhoScEn 94*
Hokoyama, J. D. 1945 *WhoAsA 94*
Hokr, Dorothy Irene 1923- *WhoAmP 93*
Hoks, Barbara L. 1955- *WhoHisp 94*
Hol, Wim Gerardus Jozef 1945- *WhoScEn 94*
Holabird, Jean 1946- *WhoAmA 93*
Holabird, John Augur, Jr. 1920- *WhoAm 94, WhoMW 93*
Holaday, Allan Gibson 1916- *WhoAm 94*
Holahan, Richard Vincent 1909- *WhoAm 94*
Holahan, Susan *DrAPF 93*
Holbach, Paul Henri Thiry, baron d' 1723-1789 *EncEth*
Holberg, Ludvig 1684-1754 *EncSF 93, IntDcT 2 [port]*
Holberg, Ralph Gans, Jr. 1908- *WhoAm 94, WhoAmL 94*
Holbert, Josef Paul 1936- *WhoWest 94*
Holbert, Raymond 1945- *WhoBlA 94*
Holbert, Sue Elisabeth 1935- *WhoAm 94*
Holbert, Theodore Frank 1921- *WhoAm 94*
Holberton, Philip Vaughan 1942- *WhoAm 94*
Holbik, Karel 1920- *WhoAm 94, WrDr 94*
Holbik, Thomas 1960- *WhoFI 94*
Holbo, Paul Sothe 1929- *WhoWest 94, WrDr 94*
Holborow, Eric John 1918- *Who 94*
Holborow, Jonathan 1943- *Who 94*
Holborow, Leslie Charles 1941- *IntWW 93, Who 94*
Holbrook, Anthony 1940- *WhoFI 94, WhoScEn 94*
Holbrook, Charles R., III 1938- *WhoAmP 93*
Holbrook, Clyde Amos 1911-1989 *WhAm 10*
Holbrook, David *WhoHol 92*
Holbrook, David (Kenneth) 1923- *ConAu 43NR, WrDr 94*
Holbrook, David D. *WhoIns 94*
Holbrook, David Kenneth 1923- *Who 94*

Holbrook, Donald Benson 1925- *WhoAm 94, WhoAmL 94, WhoFI 94*
Holbrook, Douglas Cowen 1934- *WhoAm 94*
Holbrook, Frank Malvin 1952- *WhoAmL 94*
Holbrook, Hal 1925- *IntMPA 94, WhoAm 94, WhoHol 92*
Holbrook, Hollis Howard 1909-1984 *WhoAmA 93N*
Holbrook, James Russell 1944- *WhoAmL 94, WhoWest 94*
Holbrook, John *DrAPF 93, EncSF 93*
Holbrook, John Scott, Jr. 1939- *WhoAm 94*
Holbrook, Lanny Robert 1946- *WhoAmP 93*
Holbrook, Lee Bruce 1950- *WhoAm 94*
Holbrook, Norma Jeannette 1939- *WhoMW 93*
Holbrook, Peter Greene 1940- *WhoAmA 93*
Holbrook, Robert G. 1917- *WhoAmP 93*
Holbrook, Robert Sumner 1932- *WhoAm 94*
Holbrook, Sidney John 1950- *WhoAmP 93*
Holbrook, Vivian Nicholas 1913- *WhoAmA 93*
Holbrooke, Joseph 1878-1958 *NewGrDO*
Holbrooke, Richard 1941- *WhoAmP 93, WrDr 94*
Holbrooke, Richard Charles Albert 1941- *WhoAm 94*
Holbrow, Charles Howard 1935- *WhoAm 94*
Holby, Kristin *WhoHol 92*
Holch, Eric Sanford 1948- *WhoAm 94*
Holck, Frederick H. George 1927- *WhoAm 94*
Holck, Manfred, Jr. 1930- *WrDr 94*
Holck, Richard William 1947- *WhoFI 94*
Holcomb, Alice (McCaffery) 1906-1977 *WhoAmA 93N*
Holcomb, C. E. *WhoAmP 93*
Holcomb, Constance L. 1942- *WhoFI 94*
Holcomb, Craig 1948- *WhoAmP 93*
Holcomb, Donald Frank 1925- *WhoAm 94*
Holcomb, George Ruhle 1927- *WhoAm 94*
Holcomb, Grant 1944- *WhoAmA 93*
Holcomb, Grant, III 1944- *WhoAm 94*
Holcomb, Jim 1945- *WhoAmP 93*
Holcomb, Kathryn *WhoHol 92*
Holcomb, Lyle Donald, Jr. 1929- *WhoAmL 94*
Holcomb, M. Staser 1932- *WhoAm 94, WhoIns 94*
Holcomb, Philo 1936- *WhoFI 94*
Holcomb, Sarah *WhoHol 92*
Holcomb, W. R. *WhoAmP 93*
Holcomb, William A. 1926- *WhoAm 94*
Holcombe, Anna Calluori 1952- *WhoAmA 93*
Holcombe, Blanche Keaton 1912- *WhoAmA 93N*
Holcombe, Cressie Earl, Jr. 1945- *WhoScEn 94*
Holcombe, Harry d1987 *WhoHol 92*
Holcombe, Henry c. 1690-c. 1750 *NewGrDO*
Holcombe, Herb d1970 *WhoHol 92*
Holcombe, Homer Wayne 1949- *WhoScEn 94*
Holcombe, R. Gordon, Jr. 1913- *WhoAmA 93*
Holcombe, Randall Gregory 1950- *WhoAm 94*
Holcombe, William Jones 1925- *WhoAm 94, WhoFI 94*
Holcroft, Peter (George Culcheth) 1931- *Who 94*
Holcroft, Thomas 1745-1809 *BlmGEL, IntDcT 2*
Holdar, Robert Martin 1949- *WhoScEn 94*
Holdaway, Ronald M. *WhoAm 94, WhoAmL 94*
Holdaway, Ronald M. 1934- *CngDr 93*
Holdcroft, Leslie Thomas 1922- *WhoWest 94*
Holden, A. C. 1935- *WhoAmP 93*
Holden, Aaron Charles 1942- *WhoBlA 94*
Holden, Anthony (Ivan) 1947- *WrDr 94*
Holden, Anthony Ivan 1947- *Who 94*
Holden, Arthur Cort d1993 *NewYTBS 93*
Holden, Basil Munroe 1913- *Who 94*
Holden, Bob *WhoAm 94, WhoMW 93*
Holden, Carol Helen 1942- *WhoAmP 93*
Holden, Dalby 1926- *WrDr 94*
Holden, David (Charles Beresford) 1915- *Who 94*
Holden, David Morgan 1938- *WhoAm 94*
Holden, Derek 1935- *Who 94*
Holden, Donald 1931- *ConAu 43NR, WhoAm 94, WhoAmA 93*
Holden, Edgar Howard 1914- *WhoAmP 93*
Holden, Edward 1916- *Who 94*
Holden, Eric George 1963- *WhoScEn 94*
Holden, Ernest Lloyd 1941- *WhoWest 94*
Holden, Fay d1973 *WhoHol 92*
Holden, Frederick Douglass, Jr. 1949- *WhoAm 94, WhoAmL 94*
Holden, George Fredric 1937- *WhoAm 94, WhoFI 94, WhoWest 94*
Holden, Glen A. *WhoAmP 93*
Holden, Gloria d1991 *WhoHol 92*
Holden, Harry d1944 *WhoHol 92*
Holden, Helene 1935- *BlmGWL*
Holden, J(ames) Milnes 1918-1992 *WrDr 94N*
Holden, James D. 1944- *WhoAmL 94*
Holden, James Phillip 1932- *WhoAm 94*
Holden, James Stuart 1914- *WhoAm 94, WhoAmL 94*
Holden, Jan 1931- *WhoHol 92*
Holden, Jeffrey Donald 1956- *WhoWest 94*
Holden, Joan 1939- *ConDr 93, WrDr 94*
Holden, John Bernard 1910- *WhoAm 94*
Holden, John David 1967- *Who 94*
Holden, John Reid 1913- *Who 94*
Holden, Jonathan *DrAPF 93*
Holden, Jonathan 1941- *WhoMW 93*
Holden, Joyce 1930- *WhoHol 92*
Holden, Kip 1952- *WhoBlA 94*
Holden, Matthew, Jr. 1931- *WrDr 94*
Holden, Melvin Lee *WhoAmP 93*
Holden, Melvin Lee 1952- *WhoBlA 94*
Holden, Michael John 1955- *WhoAmL 94*
Holden, Michelle Anderson 1957- *WhoFI 94*
Holden, Michelle Y. 1954- *WhoBlA 94*
Holden, Myretta *WhoAm 94*
Holden, Nate *WhoAmP 93, WhoBlA 94*
Holden, Norman Edward 1936- *WhoScEn 94*
Holden, Patrick Brian 1937- *Who 94*
Holden, Raymond Henry 1924- *WhoAm 94*
Holden, Raymond Thomas 1904- *WhoAm 94*
Holden, Rebecca *WhoHol 92*
Holden, Reta *WhoAmP 93*
Holden, Reuben Andrus 1918- *WhoAm 94*
Holden, Richard Mark 1950- *WhoFI 94*
Holden, Robert 1949- *WhoAmP 93*
Holden, Robert Watson 1936- *WhoMW 93*
Holden, Roberto 1925- *IntWW 93*
Holden, Ronald Michael 1942- *WhoWest 94*
Holden, Ruth *WhoHol 92*
Holden, Ruth Egri 1911- *WhoAmA 93*
Holden, Sandra Sue 1938- *WhoFI 94*
Holden, Scott *WhoHol 92*
Holden, Thomas 1896- *WhAm 10*
Holden, Tim 1957- *CngDr 93, WhoAm 94, WhoAmP 93*
Holden, Viola d1967 *WhoHol 92*
Holden, William d1932 *WhoHol 92*
Holden, William d1981 *WhoHol 92*
Holden, William Hoyt, Jr. *WhoAmL 94*
Holden, William P. 1933- *WhoAm 94*
Holden, William Vaughn 1949- *WhoFI 94*
Holden, William Willard 1958- *WhoWest 94*
Holden-Brown, Derrick 1923- *IntWW 93, Who 94, WhoFI 94*
Holder, Adrian Blair 1967- *WhoFI 94*
Holder, Angela Roddey 1938- *WhoAm 94*
Holder, Aubrey I. 1950- *WhoAmL 94*
Holder, Barbara *DrAPF 93*
Holder, Elaine Edith 1926- *WhoAm 94*
Holder, Eric H. 1951- *WhoAmL 94*
Holder, Geoffrey 1930- *AfrAmAl 6, WhoAm 94, WhoBlA 94, WhoHol 92*
Holder, Harold D. 1939- *WhoScEn 94*
Holder, Harold Douglas, Sr. 1931- *WhoAm 94*
Holder, (John) Henry 1928- *Who 94*
Holder, Howard Randolph, Sr. 1916- *WhoAm 94, WhoFI 94*
Holder, Ian Alan 1934- *WhoMW 93*
Holder, Idalia 1947- *WhoBlA 94*
Holder, James Ray 1943- *WhoMW 93*
Holder, Jennifer Lynn 1961- *WhoWest 94*
Holder, John 1939?- *WhoHol 92*
Holder, John, Jr. 1947-1985 *ConAu 42NR*
Holder, Julius H. 1918- *WhoBlA 94*
Holder, Kenneth Allen 1936- *WhoAmA 93*
Holder, Lee 1932- *WhoAm 94*
Holder, Paul (Davie) 1911- *Who 94*
Holder, Phillip *WhoHol 92*
Holder, Reuben D. 1923- *WhoBlA 94*
Holder, Richard Gibson *WhoAm 94, WhoFI 94*
Holder, Roy *WhoHol 92*
Holder, Sallie Lou 1939- *WhoAm 94*
Holder, Thomas Martin 1926- *WhoAm 94*
Holder, Tom 1940- *WhoAmA 93*
Holder, Virginia Mary 1942- *WhoFI 94, WhoMW 93*
Holder, Wesley McD. d1993 *NewYTBS 93*
Holder, William 17th cent.- *EncDeaf*
Holderfield, Marilyn Ida 1937- *WhoMW 93*
Holderman, Dennis Dee 1948- *WhoFI 94*
Holderman, James F., Jr. 1946- *WhoAm 94, WhoAmL 94, WhoMW 93*
Holderman, John Loran 1944- *WhoWest 94*
Holderman, Melanie 1954- *WhoMW 93*
Holderness, Baron 1920- *IntWW 93, Who 94*
Holderness, Algernon Sidney, Jr. 1938- *WhoAm 94, WhoAmL 94*
Holderness, George Malcolm 1937- *WhoAm 94*
Holderness, Richard William 1927- *Who 94*
Holderness, Susan Rutherford 1941- *WhoMW 93*
Holdgate, Martin W. 1931- *WrDr 94*
Holdgate, Martin Wyatt 1931- *IntWW 93, Who 94*
Holdgrafer, Marian Helen 1927- *WhoAmP 93*
Holdheim, William (Wolfgang) 1926- *WrDr 94*
Holding, Clyde 1931- *IntWW 93*
Holding, Harvey 1934- *WhoAm 94, WhoFI 94*
Holding, John Francis 1936- *Who 94*
Holding, Lewis R. 1927- *WhoAm 94, WhoFI 94*
Holding, Malcolm Alexander 1932- *Who 94*
Holding, Thomas d1929 *WhoHol 92*
Holdredge, Wayne David 1946- *WhoMW 93*
Holdreith, Jacob Matthew Anthony 1965- *WhoAmL 94*
Holdren, John Paul 1944- *WhoAm 94*
Holdren, Judd d1974 *WhoHol 92*
Holdridge, Barbara 1929- *WhoAm 94*
Holdridge, John H. 1924- *WhoAmP 93*
Holdridge, Lee 1944- *IntMPA 94*
Holdridge, William Ernest 1948- *WhoMW 93*
Holdstock, Robert P. 1948- *WrDr 94*
Holdstock, Robert P(aul) 1948- *EncSF 93*
Holdsworth, Albert Edward d1993 *Who 94N*
Holdsworth, Janet Nott 1941- *WhoAm 94, WhoScEn 94, WhoWest 94*
Holdsworth, John *Who 94*
Holdsworth, (Arthur) John (Arundell) 1915- *Who 94*
Holdsworth, Robert Leo, Jr. 1959- *WhoFI 94, WhoScEn 94*
Holdsworth, Trevor *Who 94*
Holdsworth, (George) Trevor 1927- *IntWW 93, Who 94*
Holdt, David *DrAPF 93*
Holdt, Leland LaMar Stark 1930- *WhoAm 94*
Holdwick, Frances Lillian 1947- *WhoAmP 93*
Hole, Derek Norman 1933- *Who 94*
Hole, Dorothy (Henrietta Field) *WrDr 94*
Hole, Frank 1931- *WhoAm 94*
Hole, Jonathan *WhoHol 92*
Ho-Le, Ken Khoa 1955- *WhoScEn 94*
Hole, Richard Douglas 1949- *WhoAm 94*
Hole, Richard Eugene, II 1937- *WhoAmP 93*
Hole, Robert Bruce 1943- *WhoWest 94*
Holeman, Becky Ann 1959- *WhoMW 93*
Holeman, Russell Kent 1957- *WhoFI 94*
Holen, Arlene *WhoAmP 93*
Holen, Norman Dean 1937- *WhoAmA 93*
Holender, Barbara D. *DrAPF 93*
Holender, Fred 1952- *WhoFI 94*
Holewinski, Kevin Patrick 1960- *WhoAmL 94*
Holewinski, Michael S. 1947- *WhoAmP 93*
Holford, Ingrid 1920- *WrDr 94*
Holford, John Morley 1909- *Who 94*
Holford, Robert Stayner 1808-1892 *DcNaB MP*
Holgaard, Conrad J. *WhoMW 93*
Holgate, Edwin Headley 1892-1977 *WhoAmA 93N*
Holgate, Harold Norman 1933- *Who 94*
Holgate, Ron 1937- *WhoHol 92*
Holgate, Sidney 1918- *Who 94*
Holgate, William 1906- *Who 94*
Holger-Madsen, Forrest d1943 *WhoHol 92*
Holguin, Alfonso Hudson 1931- *WhoAm 94*
Holguin, Cesar Alfonso 1958- *WhoHisp 94*
Holguin, Gerald Allen 1958- *WhoHisp 94*
Holguin, Gina 1959- *WhoHisp 94*
Holguin, Hector 1935- *WhoHisp 94*
Holguin, Librado Malacara 1957- *WhoScEn 94*
Holiday, Billie d1959 *WhoHol 92*
Holiday, Billie 1915-1959 *AfrAmAl 6 [port], AmCulL [port]*
Holiday, Edith Elizabeth 1952- *WhoAm 94*
Holiday, Harry, Jr. 1923- *IntWW 93*
Holiday, Hope *WhoHol 92*
Holiday, Patrick James 1947- *WhoMW 93*
Holien, Kim Bernard 1948- *WhoFI 94*
Holifield, Kam *DrAPF 93*
Holiga, Ludomil Andrew 1920- *WhoAm 94*
Holiman, Reid 1928- *WhoAmP 93*
Holinger, Richard *DrAPF 93*
Holinger, William *DrAPF 93*
Holinshed, Raphael d1580? *BlmGEL*
Holkar, Mo *EncSF 93*
Holker, John 1745-1822 *WhAmRev*
Holkeri, Harri Hermanni 1937- *IntWW 93*
Holl, Ann C. 1948- *WhoAmP 93*
Holl, Edwin G. *WhoAm 94, WhoAmP 93*
Holl, John William 1928- *WhoAm 94*
Holl, Julie Kawahara 1960- *WhoAsA 94*
Holl, Mary Katherine 1958- *WhoWest 94*
Holl, Paul Edward 1959- *WhoFI 94*
Holl, Steven Myron 1947- *WhoAm 94*
Holla, Kadambar Seetharam 1934- *WhoScEn 94*
Hollabaugh, Mark 1949- *WhoMW 93*
Holladay, Cary *DrAPF 93*
Holladay, Don G. 1944- *WhoAmL 94*
Holladay, Harlan H. 1925- *WhoAmA 93*
Holladay, Hugh Edwin 1923- *WhoAmP 93*
Holladay, James Frank 1922- *WhoAm 94*
Holladay, Wendell Gene 1925- *WhoAm 94*
Holladay, Wilhelmina Cole *WhoAmA 93*
Hollamby, Edward Ernest 1921- *Who 94*
Hollan, R. Susan 1920- *IntWW 93*
Holland, Agneiszka 1948- *NewYTBS 93 [port]*
Holland, Agnieszka 1948- *IntMPA 94, IntWW 93*
Holland, Albert, Jr. d1993 *NewYTBS 93*
Holland, Alfred Charles 1927- *Who 94*
Holland, Anthony *Who 94*
Holland, Anthony d1988 *WhoHol 92*
Holland, (John) Anthony 1938- *Who 94*
Holland, Arthur David 1913- *Who 94*
Holland, Arthur John 1918-1989 *WhAm 10*
Holland, Bert d1980 *WhoHol 92*
Holland, Beth *WhoAm 94*
Holland, Betty Lou 1931- *WhoHol 92*
Holland, Bobby Ray, Jr. 1952- *WhoAmP 93*
Holland, Bradford Wayne 1943- *WhoAm 94*
Holland, Brian Arthur 1935- *Who 94*
Holland, C. Maurice d1974 *WhoHol 92*
Holland, Cecelia *DrAPF 93*
Holland, Cecelia 1943- *EncSF 93*
Holland, Cecelia (Anastasia) 1943- *WrDr 94*
Holland, Cecil d1973 *WhoHol 92*
Holland, Charles 1909-1987 *NewGrDO*
Holland, Charles Donald 1921- *WhoAm 94, WhoFI 94*
Holland, Charles Edward 1940- *WhoFI 94, WhoScEn 94*
Holland, Charles Hepworth 1923- *IntWW 93*
Holland, Charles Malcolm, Jr. 1932- *WhoAm 94*
Holland, Christie Anna 1950- *WhoAm 94*
Holland, Christopher (John) 1937- *Who 94*
Holland, Clarence A. 1929- *WhoAmP 93*
Holland, Clifton Vaughan 1914- *Who 94*
Holland, Daniel Mark 1920-1991 *WhAm 10*
Holland, Daniel Stephen 1955- *WhoAmP 93*
Holland, Dave
See Judas Priest *ConMus 10*
Holland, David Cuthbert Lyall 1915- *Who 94*
Holland, David George 1925- *Who 94*
Holland, David Lee 1947- *WhoScEn 94*
Holland, David Michael 1946- *WhoIns 94*
Holland, David Thurston 1923- *WhoAm 94*
Holland, Derek 1950- *WhoAmP 93*
Holland, Dianna Gwin 1948- *WhoAm 94*
Holland, Donald Harry 1928- *WhoAmP 93*
Holland, Donald Reginald 1940- *WhoAm 94*
Holland, Dorothy *WhoHol 92*
Holland, Edna d1982 *WhoHol 92*
Holland, Edward *Who 94*
Holland, Edward McHarg 1939- *WhoAmP 93*
Holland, Edward Richard Charles 1925- *Who 94*
Holland, Einion *Who 94*
Holland, (Robert) Einion 1927- *Who 94*
Holland, Elizabeth Anne 1928- *WrDr 94*

Holland, Endesha Ida Mae 1944- *ConTFT 11*
Holland, (Robert) Eonion 1927- *IntWW 93*
Holland, Erik *WhoHol 92*
Holland, Ethel M. 1946- *WhoBlA 94*
Holland, Eugene, Jr. 1922- *WhoAm 94*
Holland, Eugene Paul 1935- *WhoFI 94, WhoMW 93*
Holland, Francis (Ross), Jr. 1927- *WrDr 94*
Holland, Frank Robert Dacre 1924- *Who 94*
Holland, Franklin B. 1946- *WhoAmL 94*
Holland, Fred Anthony 1955- *WhoAmL 94*
Holland, Gene Grigsby 1928- *WhoAm 94*
Holland, Geoffrey 1938- *Who 94*
Holland, Gilbert Strom 1918- *WhoAmP 93*
Holland, Gladys *WhoHol 92*
Holland, Guy (Hope) 1918- *Who 94*
Holland, H. Russel 1936- *WhoAm 94, WhoAmL 94, WhoWest 94*
Holland, Harold Herbert 1932- *WhoAm 94*
Holland, Harrison M(elsher) 1921- *ConAu 43NR*
Holland, Harry Charles 1937- *WhoAmA 93*
Holland, Heinrich Dieter 1927- *IntWW 93*
Holland, Henry Norman 1947- *WhoWest 94*
Holland, Hilary *WhoHol 92*
Holland, Hillman Randall 1950- *WhoAmA 93*
Holland, Hubert Brian 1904- *WhoAm 94*
Holland, Iris K. 1920- *WhoAmP 93*
Holland, Isabelle 1920- *Au&Arts 11 [port], WrDr 94*
Holland, Isabelle Christian 1920- *WhoAm 94*
Holland, J. Archibald *WhoBlA 94*
Holland, Jack K. 1945- *WhoAmL 94*
Holland, James 1754-1823 *WhAmRev*
Holland, James M. 1928- *WhoAmP 93*
Holland, James Paul 1948- *WhoAm 94*
Holland, James R 1944- *WrDr 94*
Holland, James Richard, Jr. 1943- *WhoAm 94*
Holland, James Ricks 1929- *WhoAm 94*
Holland, James Tulley 1940- *WhoAm 94*
Holland, Jan Dawid 1746-1827 *NewGrDO*
Holland, Janice 1913-1962 *WhoAmA 93N*
Holland, John *Who 94*
Holland, John 1603-1701 *DcNaB MP*
Holland, John 1900- *WhoHol 92*
Holland, John Adams 1952- *WhoAmL 94*
Holland, John B. 1932- *WhoFI 94*
Holland, John Ben 1932- *WhoAm 94*
Holland, John Charles Francis 1897-1956 *DcNaB MP*
Holland, John Deal 1937- *WhoFI 94*
Holland, John Lewis 1919- *WhoScEn 94*
Holland, John Lewis 1937- *Who 94*
Holland, John Madison 1927- *WhoAm 94*
Holland, John Philip 1840-1914 *WorInv*
Holland, John Ray 1933- *WhoAm 94, WhoWest 94*
Holland, Joseph Robert 1936- *WhoAmP 93*
Holland, Joy 1946- *WhoMW 93*
Holland, Ken 1934- *WhoAmP 93*
Holland, Kenneth (Lawrence) 1918- *Who 94*
Holland, Kenneth John 1918- *WhoAm 94, WhoWest 94*
Holland, Kevin John William C. *Who 94*
Holland, Koren Alayne 1963- *WhoScEn 94*
Holland, Kristina 1944- *WhoHol 92*
Holland, Laurence H. 1926- *WhoBlA 94*
Holland, Leo Laverne 1941- *WhoFI 94*
Holland, Louis Edward 1948- *WhoMW 93*
Holland, Lyman Faith, Jr. 1931- *WhoAm 94, WhoAmL 94*
Holland, Lynda (H.) 1959- *SmATA 77*
Holland, Major Leonard 1941- *WhoBlA 94*
Holland, Marvin Arthur 1930- *WhoAm 94, WhoAmL 94*
Holland, Max (Mendel) 1950- *WrDr 94*
Holland, Merle Susan 1945- *WhoAm 94*
Holland, Michael Francis 1944- *WhoAm 94, WhoFI 94*
Holland, Michael J. 1947- *WhoAmL 94*
Holland, Michael James 1950- *WhoScEn 94, WhoWest 94*
Holland, Michael Leo 1956- *WhoFI 94*
Holland, Mildred d1944 *WhoHol 92*
Holland, Miriam d1948 *WhoHol 92*
Holland, Norman James Abbott 1927- *Who 94*
Holland, Norman N 1927- *WrDr 94*
Holland, Patricia Marcus 1952- *WhoAm 94*
Holland, Peanuts d1979 *WhoHol 92*
Holland, Philip (Welsby) 1917- *Who 94*
Holland, Ralph d1939 *WhoHol 92*
Holland, Randy *WhoAmP 93*
Holland, Randy James 1947- *WhoAm 94, WhoAmL 94*
Holland, Reece 1956- *ConTFT 11*
Holland, Richard Joyner 1925- *WhoAmP 93*
Holland, Robert *DrAPF 93*
Holland, Robert c. 1283-1328 *DcNaB MP*
Holland, Robert Campbell 1923- *WhoAm 94*
Holland, Robert Carl 1925- *WhoAm 94*
Holland, Robert Dale 1928- *WhoAmL 94*
Holland, Robert Michael *WhoAmP 93*
Holland, Robert Thurl 1923- *WhoFI 94*
Holland, Robin Jean 1942- *WhoWest 94*
Holland, Robin W. 1953- *WhoBlA 94*
Holland, Samuel *WhAmRev*
Holland, Sheila (Coates) 1937- *WrDr 94*
Holland, Spencer H. 1939- *WhoBlA 94*
Holland, Stephen 1962- *EncSF 93*
Holland, Stuart (Kingsley) 1940- *Who 94*
Holland, Thomas 1908- *Who 94*
Holland, Thomas Powell 1942- *WhoAm 94*
Holland, Toby J. J., Jr. 1928- *WhoAmP 93*
Holland, Tom *HorFD, IntMPA 94*
Holland, Tom 1936- *WhoAm 94, WhoAmA 93, WhoWest 94*
Holland, Wallace E. 1926- *WhoBlA 94*
Holland, Walter Werner 1929- *Who 94*
Holland, Warner Lamoine 1933- *WhoAmL 94*
Holland, Willard Raymond, Jr. 1936- *WhoAm 94, WhoFI 94*
Holland, William E. 1940- *WhoAmL 94*
Holland, William Lynn 1947- *WhoFI 94*
Holland, William Meredith *WhoBlA 94*
Holland, William Ray 1938- *WhoFI 94*
Holland-Calbert, Mary Ann 1941- *WhoBlA 94*
Hollander, Adam d1984 *WhoHol 92*
Hollander, Adrian Willoughby 1941- *WhoMW 93*
Hollander, Anne 1930- *WrDr 94*
Hollander, Daniel 1939- *WhoAm 94*
Hollander, David 1949- *WhoAmL 94*
Hollander, David 1971- *WhoHol 92*
Hollander, Doris Ann 1941- *WhoMW 93*
Hollander, Edwin Paul 1927- *WhoAm 94*
Hollander, Gerhard Ludwig 1922- *WhoAm 94*
Hollander, Herbert I. 1924- *WhoAm 94*
Hollander, Jack *WhoHol 92*
Hollander, Jean *DrAPF 93*
Hollander, John *DrAPF 93*
Hollander, John 1929- *IntWW 93, WhoAm 94, WrDr 94*
Hollander, Lawrence Jay 1940- *WhoFI 94*
Hollander, Lorin 1944- *WhoAm 94*
Hollander, Mildred d1937 *WhoHol 92*
Hollander, Milton Bernard 1928- *WhoAm 94*
Hollander, Patricia Ann 1928- *WhoAmL 94*
Hollander, Richard Edward 1947- *WhoAm 94*
Hollander, Robert B., Jr. 1933- *WhoAm 94*
Hollander, Samuel 1937- *IntWW 93, WhoAm 94, WrDr 94*
Hollander, Stanley C(harles) 1919- *WrDr 94*
Hollander, Stanley Charles 1919- *WhoAm 94, WhoFI 94*
Hollander, Stephen James 1957- *WhoMW 93*
Hollander, Toby Edward 1931- *WhoAm 94*
Holland-Hibbert *Who 94*
Holland-Martin, Robert George 1939- *Who 94*
Holland-Martin, Rosamund Mary 1914- *Who 94*
Hollands, Graham Spencer 1942- *Who 94*
Hollands, John Henry 1929- *WhoAm 94*
Hollandsworth, James G., Jr. 1944- *WrDr 94*
Hollandsworth, Kenneth Peter 1934- *WhoFI 94*
Hollans, Irby Noah, Jr. 1930- *WhoAm 94*
Hollar, Constance 1881-1945 *BlmGWL*
Hollar, Milton Conover 1930- *WhoBlA 94*
Hollard, Michel d1993 *NewYTBS 93*
Hollatz, Mike C. 1962- *WhoMW 93*
Hollatz, Sarah Schoales 1944- *WhoWest 94*
Hollberg, William Bealer 1947- *WhoAmL 94*
Holldobler, Bert(hold Karl) 1936- *WrDr 94*
Holldobler, Berthold Karl 1936- *IntWW 93, WhoAm 94, WhoScEn 94*
Holle, Charles G(eorge) 1898-1989 *WhAm 10*
Holle, Matthias 1951- *NewGrDO*
Holle, Reginald Henry 1925- *WhoMW 93*
Holleb, Arthur Irving 1921- *WhoAm 94*
Holleb, Doris B. 1922- *WhoMW 93*
Holleman, Frank Sharp, III 1954- *WhoAmP 93*
Holleman, Paul Douglas 1931- *WhoAm 94*
Holleman, Robert Wood, Jr. 1931- *WhoWest 94*
Holleman, William Homer 1940- *WhoMW 93*
Hollemweguer, Enoc Juan 1947- *WhoScEn 94*
Hollenbach, Ruth *WhoAm 94*
Hollenback, Matthias 1752-1829 *WhAmRev*
Hollenbaugh, Henry Ritchey 1947- *WhoAmL 94*
Hollenbaugh, Kenneth M. 1934- *WhoWest 94*
Hollenbeck, Harold Capistran 1938- *WhoAmP 93*
Hollenbeck, Karen Fern 1943- *WhoAm 94*
Hollenbeck, L. D. 1939- *WhoAmP 93*
Hollenbeck, Mark John 1960- *WhoAmP 93*
Hollenbeck, Marynell 1939- *WhoMW 93*
Hollenbeck, Ralph Anthony 1925- *WhoAm 94*
Hollenbeck, William Royden 1949- *WhoMW 93*
Hollenberg, David Henry 1946- *WhoMW 93*
Hollenberg, Donna Krolik 1942- *ConAu 142*
Hollen-Bolmgren, Donna 1935- *WhoAmA 93*
Hollenden, Baron 1914- *Who 94*
Hollender, Alfred L. *IntMPA 94*
Hollender, John Edward 1941- *WhoFI 94*
Hollender, Louis Francois 1922- *IntWW 93*
Hollensbe, Ronda Lee 1953- *WhoMW 93*
Hollenshead, Robert Earl 1940- *WhoAmL 94, WhoMW 93*
Hollenweger, Walter Jacob 1927- *Who 94*
Holler, Gwen Lynn 1957- *WhoIns 94*
Holler, John Raymond 1918- *WhoScEn 94*
Holler, York (George) 1944- *NewGrDO*
Holleran, Andrew c. 1943- *GayLL*
Holleran, John W. 1954- *WhoAmL 94*
Holleran, Kevin Joseph 1951- *WhoAmL 94*
Holleran-Rivera, Maria *WhoHisp 94*
Hollerbach, Serge 1923- *WhoAmA 93*
Hollerer, Walter Friedrich 1922- *IntWW 93*
Hollerith, Herman 1860-1929 *WorInv*
Hollerith, Richard, Jr. 1926- *WhoAm 94*
Hollerman, Charles Edward 1929- *WhoAm 94*
Holles, Anthony d1950 *WhoHol 92*
Holles, Robert 1926- *WrDr 94*
Holles, William d1947 *WhoHol 92*
Holleweg dit Wegman, Willy 1934- *WhoFI 94*
Holley, Audrey Rodgers 1939- *WhoAmL 94*
Holley, Cyrus Helmer 1936- *WhoAm 94, WhoFI 94*
Holley, Edward Gailon 1927- *WhoAm 94, WrDr 94*
Holley, Edward R. *WhoScEn 94*
Holley, Irving Brinton, Jr. 1919- *WhoAm 94, WrDr 94*
Holley, James W., III *WhoAm 94, WhoAmP 93*
Holley, James W., III 1926- *WhoBlA 94*
Holley, Jim 1943- *WhoBlA 94*
Holley, Jimmy W. *WhoAmP 93*
Holley, Lauren Allana 1948- *WhoAm 94*
Holley, Lawrence Alvin 1924- *WhoAm 94*
Holley, Robert W. d1993 *IntWW 93N, NewYTBS 93 [port]*
Holley, Robert W(illiam) 1922-1993 *CurBio 93N*
Holley, Robert William d1993 *Who 94N*
Holley, Robert William 1922- *WorScD*
Holley, Ronald Victor 1931- *Who 94*
Holley, Sandra Cavanaugh 1943- *WhoBlA 94*
Holley, Sharon Yvonne 1949- *WhoBlA 94*
Holley, (William) Stephen 1920- *Who 94*
Holley, Sylvia A. 1942- *WhoAmP 93*
Holley, Vance Maitland 1941- *WhoBlA 94*
Holleyman, Robert Walker, II 1955- *WhoAmL 94*
Holli, Betsy Biggar 1933- *WhoMW 93*
Holli, Melvin George 1933- *WhoMW 93, WrDr 94*
Hollick, Baron 1945- *Who 94*
Holliday, Alfonso David 1931- *WhoBlA 94*
Holliday, Bertha Garrett 1947- *WhoBlA 94*
Holliday, Bill d1984 *WhoHol 92*
Holliday, Billie *WhoBlA 94*
Holliday, Doc, Jr. 1936- *WhoWest 94*
Holliday, Frances B. *WhoBlA 94*
Holliday, Frank, Jr. d1948 *WhoHol 92*
Holliday, Fred 1936- *WhoHol 92*
Holliday, Frederick (George Thomas) 1935- *Who 94*
Holliday, Gay 1936- *WhoAmP 93*
Holliday, Harry d1942 *WhoHol 92*
Holliday, Jennifer 1960- *WhoBlA 94*
Holliday, Jennifer Yvette 1960- *WhoAm 94*
Holliday, John Moffitt 1935- *WhoAm 94*
Holliday, Judith 1938- *WhoAmA 93*
Holliday, Judy d1965 *WhoHol 92*
Holliday, Judy 1922-1965 *WhoCom*
Holliday, Kene *WhoHol 92*
Holliday, Leslie John 1921- *Who 94*
Holliday, Linda Lorraine 1951- *WhoAmL 94*
Holliday, Marjorie d1969 *WhoHol 92*
Holliday, Melanie 1951- *NewGrDO*
Holliday, Polly 1937- *WhoHol 92*
Holliday, Polly Dean 1937- *WhoAm 94*
Holliday, Prince E. 1935- *WhoBlA 94*
Holliday, Robert Kelvin 1933- *WhoAmP 93*
Holliday, Robin 1932- *IntWW 93, Who 94*
Holliday, Thomas Edgar 1948- *WhoAm 94, WhoAmL 94*
Holliday-Hayes, Wilhelmina Evelyn *WhoBlA 94*
Hollien, Harry Francis 1926- *WhoAm 94*
Hollies, Norman Robert Stanley 1922-1989 *WhAm 10*
Hollifield, Christopher Stanford 1959- *WhoScEn 94*
Hollifield, Gordon R. *WhoAmP 93*
Holliger, Fred Lee 1948- *WhoWest 94*
Holliger, Heinz 1939- *IntWW 93, Who 94*
Holliman, Argie N. 1957- *WhoBlA 94*
Holliman, David L. 1929- *WhoBlA 94*
Holliman, Earl 1928- *IntMPA 94, WhoHol 92*
Holliman, Margaret Cloud 1930- *WhoAmP 93*
Hollimon, Stuart C. 1950- *WhoAmL 94*
Hollin, Betty A. 1956- *WhoFI 94*
Hollin, Kenneth Ronald 1948- *WhoBlA 94*
Hollin, Shelby W. 1925- *WhoAmL 94*
Hollindale, Peter 1936- *WrDr 94*
Hollingdale, Reginald John 1930- *WrDr 94*
Hollinger, Charlotte Elizabeth 1951- *WhoScEn 94*
Hollinger, David Albert 1941- *WhoWest 94*
Hollinger, Mannfred Alan 1939- *WhoScEn 94*
Hollinger, Paula Colodny 1940- *WhoAmP 93, WhoWomW 91*
Hollinghurst, Alan 1954- *GayLL*
Hollings, Ernest F. 1922- *CngDr 93, IntWW 93*
Hollings, Ernest Frederick 1922- *WhoAm 94, WhoAmP 93*
Hollings, (Alfred) Kenneth 1918- *Who 94*
Hollings, (George) Leslie 1923- *IntWW 93*
Hollings, Michael Richard 1921- *IntWW 93, Who 94*
Hollingshaus, John *WhoAmP 93*
Hollingshead, Joe Edgar 1946- *WhoAmA 93*
Hollingsworth, Alan Merrill 1920-1991 *WhAm 10*
Hollingsworth, Alfred d1926 *WhoHol 92*
Hollingsworth, Alfred Delano 1942- *WhoBlA 94*
Hollingsworth, Alvin Carl 1930- *WhoAmA 93*
Hollingsworth, Brian 1923- *WrDr 94*
Hollingsworth, Cornelia Ann 1957- *WhoMW 93, WhoScEn 94*
Hollingsworth, David Southerland *WhoScEn 94*
Hollingsworth, Dorothy Frances 1916- *Who 94*
Hollingsworth, Gary Mayes 1944- *WhoMW 93*
Hollingsworth, Harry d1947 *WhoHol 92*
Hollingsworth, Jack Waring 1924- *WhoAm 94*
Hollingsworth, John Alexander 1925- *WhoBlA 94*
Hollingsworth, John Mark 1951- *WhoAmL 94*
Hollingsworth, John Mark 1957- *WhoWest 94*
Hollingsworth, Joseph Rogers 1932- *WhoAm 94*
Hollingsworth, Laviza Davine 1962- *WhoAmP 93*
Hollingsworth, Margaret 1940- *BlmGWL, ConDr 93, WrDr 94*
Hollingsworth, Margaret Camille 1929- *WhoFI 94, WhoWest 94*
Hollingsworth, Martha Schmidt 1944- *WhoAmL 94*

Hollingsworth, Meredith Beaton 1941- WhoWest 94
Hollingsworth, Michael Charles 1946- Who 94
Hollingsworth, Paul M 1932- WrDr 94
Hollingsworth, Perlesta A. 1936- WhoBlA 94
Hollingsworth, Pierre 1931- WhoBlA 94
Hollingsworth, Robert Edgar 1918- WhoAm 94
Hollingsworth, Samuel Hawkins, Jr. 1922- WhoAm 94
Hollingsworth, Stanley 1924- NewGrDO
Hollington, James Edward 1949- WhoWest 94
Hollington, Richard R., Jr. 1932- WhoAmP 93
Hollington, Richard Rings, Jr. 1932- WhoAm 94
Hollingworth, Beverly A. 1935- WhoAmP 93
Hollingworth, Clare 1911- Who 94
Hollingworth, John Harold 1930- Who 94
Hollingworth, Peter John Who 94
Hollins, David Michael 1966- WhoAm 94
Hollins, Hubert Walter Elphinstone 1923- Who 94
Hollins, Joseph Edward 1927- WhoBlA 94
Hollins, Leroy 1945- WhoBlA 94
Hollins, Mitchell Leslie 1947- WhoAm 94, WhoAmL 94
Hollinshead, Ariel Cahill 1929- WhoAm 94
Hollinshead, Byron Sharpe, Jr. 1929- WhoAm 94
Hollinshead, Earl Darnell, Jr. 1927- WhoAmL 94, WhoFI 94
Hollis Who 94
Hollis, Anthony Barnard 1927- Who 94
Hollis, Charles Eugene, Jr. 1948- WhoAm 94
Hollis, Crispian Who 94
Hollis, (Roger Francis) Crispian Who 94
Hollis, Daniel Ayrton 1925- Who 94
Hollis, Daryl Joseph 1946- WhoAmL 94
Hollis, Dean 1960- WhoWest 94
Hollis, Donald Roger 1936- WhoAm 94
Hollis, Douglas 1948- WhoAmA 93
Hollis, Geoffrey Alan 1943- Who 94
Hollis, Gerald 1919- Who 94
Hollis, Howell, III 1948- WhoAmL 94
Hollis, Hylda d1961 WhoHol 92
Hollis, Jack B. d1940 WhoHol 92
Hollis, James Martin 1938- Who 94
Hollis, Jesse Kendrick, Jr. 1942- WhoAmP 93
Hollis, Jocelyn DrAPF 93
Hollis, Kathleen Sue 1955- WhoFI 94, WhoMW 93
Hollis, Mark C. 1934- WhoAm 94, WhoFI 94
Hollis, Mark D. 1908- WhoAm 94
Hollis, Mary Lee 1942- WhoBlA 94
Hollis, Meldon S., Jr. 1945- WhoBlA 94
Hollis, Michael R. WhoBlA 94
Hollis, Posy Who 94
Hollis, Reginald 1932- Who 94, WhoAm 94
Hollis, Sheila Slocum 1948- WhoAmL 94
Hollis, Stephanie 1946- ConAu 141
Hollis, William Frederick 1954- WhoScEn 94
Hollis, William S. 1930- WhoAm 94
Hollis-Allbritton, Cheryl Dawn 1959- WhoMW 93
Hollis Of Heigham, Baroness 1941- Who 94
Hollison, Robert Victor, Jr. 1947- WhoWest 94
Hollister, Alice d1973 WhoHol 92
Hollister, Bernard Claiborne 1938- WhoMW 93
Hollister, Charles Davis 1936- WhoAm 94, WhoScEn 94
Hollister, Charles Warren 1930- WhoAm 94
Hollister, David Clinton 1942- WhoAmP 93
Hollister, Floyd Hill 1937- WhoScEn 94
Hollister, Joseph Robert 1946- WhoFI 94
Hollister, Leo Edward 1920- WhoAm 94
Hollister, Leonard d1946 WhoHol 92
Hollister, Lynda Jeanne 1960- WhoMW 93
Hollister, Paul WhoAmA 93
Hollister, Ripley Robert 1955- WhoWest 94
Hollister, Valerie (Dutton) 1939- WhoAmA 93
Hollister, William Gray 1915- WhoAm 94
Hollman, Arthur 1923- Who 94
Hollman, Gary A. 1947- WhoAmL 94
Hollmann, Rudolf Werner 1931- WhoScEn 94
Hollmann, Werner d1933 WhoHol 92
Hollo, Anselm DrAPF 93
Hollo, Anselm 1934- ConAu 19AS [port]
Hollo, Anselm (Paul Alexis) 1934- WrDr 94
Hollo, Janos 1919- IntWW 93
Hollom, Jasper (Quintus) 1917- IntWW 93, Who 94
Holloman, Bridget WhoHol 92
Holloman, Haskell Andrew 1907- WhoAmL 94
Holloman, James Horace, Jr. 1946- WhoAmL 94
Holloman, John L. S., Jr. 1919- WhoBlA 94
Holloman, Steven William 1952- WhoMW 93
Holloman, Thaddeus Bailey 1955- WhoBlA 94
Hollon, Herbert Holstein 1936- WhoBlA 94
Hollon, William Eugene 1913- WhoAm 94
Holloran, Thomas Edward 1929- WhoAm 94
Holloway, Albert Curtis 1931- WhoBlA 94
Holloway, Ardith E. 1958- WhoBlA 94
Holloway, Baliol d1967 WhoHol 92
Holloway, Barry (Blyth) 1934- Who 94
Holloway, Brian EncSF 93
Holloway, Brian Douglass 1959- WhoBlA 94
Holloway, Bruce Keener 1912- WhoAm 94
Holloway, Bruce William 1928- IntWW 93
Holloway, Callon Wesley, Jr. 1953- WhoBlA 94
Holloway, Charles Arthur 1936- WhoAm 94
Holloway, Cindy 1960- WhoFI 94, WhoWest 94
Holloway, Clyde C. 1943- WhoAmP 93
Holloway, David 1924- WrDr 94
Holloway, David 1942- WhoAm 94
Holloway, David James 1943- WhoWest 94
Holloway, David Richard 1924- Who 94
Holloway, Derrick Robert Le Blond 1917- Who 94
Holloway, Donald Phillip 1928- WhoAm 94, WhoAmL 94, WhoFI 94, WhoMW 93
Holloway, Douglas Patrick 1938- WhoAm 94
Holloway, Douglas V. 1954- WhoBlA 94
Holloway, Edgar Austin 1925- WhoAm 94
Holloway, Edward L. WhoAmP 93
Holloway, Ernest Leon 1930- WhoBlA 94
Holloway, Ernestine 1930- WhoBlA 94
Holloway, Frank 1924- Who 94
Holloway, Fred Garrigus 1898- WhAm 10
Holloway, Frederick Reginald Bryn 1947- Who 94
Holloway, (Percival) Geoffrey 1918- WrDr 94
Holloway, George Allen, Jr. 1938- WhoWest 94
Holloway, Gordon Arthur 1938- WhoAmL 94
Holloway, H. Maxson d1966 WhoAmA 93N
Holloway, Harris M. 1949- WhoBlA 94
Holloway, Harry WhoScEn 94
Holloway, Harry (Albert) 1925- WrDr 94
Holloway, Harry Rex, Jr. 1930- WhoMW 93
Holloway, Herman, Jr. WhoAmP 93
Holloway, Herman M., Sr. 1922- WhoBlA 94
Holloway, Herman Monwell, Sr. 1922- WhoAmP 93
Holloway, Hiliary H. 1928- WhoBlA 94
Holloway, Hiliary Hamilton 1928- WhoAm 94, WhoAmL 94
Holloway, J. Mills 1924- WhoBlA 94
Holloway, James D. 1931- WhoAmP 93
Holloway, James Lemuel, III 1922- IntWW 93, WhoAm 94
Holloway, Jerome Knight 1923- WhoAm 94
Holloway, Jerry 1941- WhoBlA 94
Holloway, Joaquin Miller, Jr. 1937- WhoBlA 94
Holloway, John 1920- IntWW 93, Who 94, WrDr 94
Holloway, John Thomas 1922- WhoAm 94
Holloway, Julian 1944- WhoHol 92
Holloway, Karla F. C. 1949- ConAu 141
Holloway, Leonard Leveine 1923- WhoAm 94
Holloway, Mark 1917- WrDr 94
Holloway, Mark Albert 1961- WhoAmP 93
Holloway, Marvin Lawrence 1911- WhoAm 94
Holloway, Muriel 1927- WhoAmP 93
Holloway, Nathaniel Overton, Jr. 1926- WhoBlA 94
Holloway, Nigel 1953- WrDr 94
Holloway, Paul Fayette 1938- WhoAm 94, WhoScEn 94
Holloway, Paul Howard 1943- WhoScEn 94
Holloway, Reginald Eric 1932- Who 94
Holloway, Richard Allen 1941- WhoFI 94
Holloway, Richard Frederick Who 94
Holloway, Richard Frederick 1933- IntWW 93
Holloway, Richard Lawrence 1949- WhoMW 93
Holloway, Robert Anthony 1946- WhoFI 94, WhoWest 94
Holloway, Robert John 1921- WhAm 10
Holloway, Robert Ross 1934- WhoAm 94
Holloway, Robert Wester 1945- WhoWest 94
Holloway, Robin (Greville) 1943- NewGrDO
Holloway, Robin Greville 1943- IntWW 93, Who 94
Holloway, Robin Hugh Ferguson 1922- Who 94
Holloway, Stanley d1982 WhoHol 92
Holloway, Sterling d1992 IntMPA 94N
Holloway, Sterling 1905- WhoHol 92
Holloway, Sterling Price d1992 WhAm 10
Holloway, Sterling Price 1905-1992 AnObit 1992
Holloway, Steven Dion 1966- WhoMW 93
Holloway, W. E. d1952 WhoHol 92
Holloway, Wade Justin 1956- WhoFI 94
Holloway, William J., Jr. WhoAmP 93
Holloway, William J., Jr. 1923- WhoAm 94, WhoAmL 94, WhoWest 94
Holloway, William Jimmerson 1917- WhoAm 94
Holloway, William Wayne 1935- WhoMW 93
Hollowell, Bill 1928- WhoAmP 93
Hollowell, Donald L. 1917- WhoBlA 94
Hollowell, Johnny Laveral 1951- WhoBlA 94
Hollowell, Kenneth Lawrence 1945- WhoBlA 94
Hollowell, Melvin L. 1930- WhoBlA 94
Hollowell, Monte J. 1949- WhoScEn 94
Hollreiser, Heinrich 1913- NewGrDO
Hollstein, Richard W. 1945- WhoAmL 94
Hollweg, Ilse 1922-1990 NewGrDO
Hollweg, Werner 1936- NewGrDO
Holly, Buddy 1936-1959 AmCulL
Holly, David C. 1915- ConAu 142
Holly, Ella Louise 1949- WhoBlA 94
Holly, Ellen 1931- WhoHol 92
Holly, J. Hunter 1932- WrDr 94
Holly, James Douglas 1952- WhoWest 94
Holly, Jan Elise 1965- WhoWest 94
Holly, Joan Hunter 1932-1982 EncSF 93
Holly, John Durward, III 1950- WhoAm 94
Holly, Lauren 1966- WhoHol 92
Holly, Mary d1976 WhoHol 92
Hollyer, Arthur Rene 1938- WhoAmL 94
Hollyfield, Joe G. 1938- WhoScEn 94
Hollyfield, John Scoggins 1939- WhoAm 94
Hollywood, Jimmy d1955 WhoHol 92
Hollywood, John Matthew 1910- WhoAm 94
Hollywood, Ken d1983 WhoHol 92
Holm, (Else) Anne (Lise) 1922- TwCYAW
Holm, Audrey Christine 1929- WhoAm 94
Holm, Barbara J. WhoAmP 93
Holm, Bill 1925- WhoAmA 93
Holm, Carl Henry 1915- Who 94
Holm, Celeste 1919- ConTFT 11, IntMPA 94, WhoAm 94, WhoHol 92
Holm, Edith Muriel 1921- WhoAmP 93
Holm, Eleanor 1913- WhoHol 92
Holm, Elisabeth 1917- IntWW 93
Holm, Erik 1933- IntWW 93
Holm, Grete c. 1882-1920? NewGrDO
Holm, Hanya d1992 WhAm 10
Holm, Hanya 1893-1992 AnObit 1992, CurBio 93N
Holm, Ian 1931- IntMPA 94, IntWW 93, Who 94, WhoAm 94, WhoHol 92
Holm, Jeanne M(arjorie) 1921- WrDr 94
Holm, Jeanne Marjorie 1921- WhoAm 94
Holm, John Cecil d1981 WhoHol 92
Holm, Magda d1982 WhoHol 92
Holm, Milton W. WhoAmA 93
Holm, Renate 1931- NewGrDO
Holm, Richard 1912-1988 NewGrDO
Holm, Richard H. 1933- IntWW 93
Holm, Richard Hadley 1933- WhoScEn 94
Holm, Robert Arthur 1935- WhoAm 94
Holm, Ruth WhoAmP 93
Holm, Sonia d1974 WhoHol 92
Holm, Sven 1940- EncSF 93
Holm, Tryggve O. A. 1905- IntWW 93
Holman, Alvin T. 1948- WhoBlA 94
Holman, Arthur (Stearns) 1926- WhoAmA 93
Holman, Arthur Stearns 1926- WhoAm 94, WhoWest 94
Holman, Benjamin F. 1930- WhoBlA 94
Holman, Bob DrAPF 93
Holman, Bud George 1929- WhoAm 94
Holman, Calvin Morns 1931- WhoAmP 93
Holman, Cecilia d1981 WhoHol 92
Holman, Charles Richardson 1915- WhoAm 94
Holman, Clare WhoHol 92
Holman, Clyde Charles 1952- WhoAmP 93
Holman, Cranston William 1907- WhoAm 94
Holman, D. Miles 1947- WhoAmL 94
Holman, Dick d1955 WhoHol 92
Holman, Donald Reid 1930- WhoAm 94
Holman, Doris Ann 1924- WhoBlA 94
Holman, Ernest Wayne 1948- WhoAmP 93
Holman, Felice 1919- SmATA 17AS [port], TwCYAW, WrDr 94
Holman, Forest H. 1942- WhoBlA 94
Holman, Francis Wade, Jr. 1939- WhoAm 94
Holman, Halsted Reid 1925- WhoAm 94, WhoScEn 94, WhoWest 94
Holman, Harland Eugene 1914- WhoAm 94
Holman, Harry d1947 WhoHol 92
Holman, J. Alan 1947- WhoAmL 94
Holman, (Edward) James 1947- Who 94
Holman, James K. 1942- WhoAmP 93
Holman, James Lewis 1926- WhoMW 93
Holman, John (William) 1951- WrDr 94
Holman, John Foster 1946- WhoFI 94, WhoWest 94
Holman, John Leonard 1929- WhoAm 94
Holman, John P. 1949- WhoAmL 94
Holman, Kermit Layton 1935- WhoAm 94
Holman, Kingsley David 1922- WhoAmP 93
Holman, Kristina Sue 1958- WhoAmL 94
Holman, Larry Dean 1940- WhoFI 94
Holman, Libby d1971 WhoHol 92
Holman, Margaret Mezoff 1951- WhoAm 94
Holman, Michael S. 1942- WhoAmL 94
Holman, Nat 1896- BasBi
Holman, Newton 1946- WhoAmP 93
Holman, Paul David 1943- WhoWest 94
Holman, Ralph Theodore 1918- IntWW 93, WhoAm 94
Holman, Rex WhoHol 92
Holman, Robert 1936- WrDr 94
Holman, Robert 1952- ConDr 93
Holman, Robert L. 1947- WhoFI 94
Holman, Rodney A. 1960- WhoBlA 94
Holman, Tomlinson 1946- WhoAm 94
Holman, Victoria Gean 1950- WhoMW 93
Holman, Vincent d1962 WhoHol 92
Holman, William Baker 1925- WhoMW 93
Holman, William G. 1953- WhoFI 94
Holman, William Henry, Jr. 1930- WhoFI 94
Holman-Hunt, Diana 1913-1993 NewYTBS 93
Holmberg, Albert William, Jr. 1923- WhoAm 94
Holmberg, Angela Brown 1956- WhoWest 94
Holmberg, Branton Kieth 1936- WhoFI 94
Holmberg, David John 1950- WhoMW 93
Holmberg, Eric Robert Reginald 1917- Who 94
Holmberg, Eva Birgitta WhoScEn 94
Holmberg, John-Henri EncSF 93
Holmberg, Joyce WhoAmP 93, WhoWomW 91
Holmberg, Raymon E. 1943- WhoAmP 93
Holmberg, Richard Hjalmar 1925-1988 WhAm 10
Holmberg, Ronald K. 1932- WhoFI 94
Holmberg, Ruth Sulzberger 1921- WhoAm 94
Holmblad, Edward Charles 1894- WhAm 10
Holmboe, Vagn 1909- IntWW 93
Holme Who 94
Holme, Barbara Shaw 1946- WhoAmP 93
Holme, K. E. 1912- WrDr 94
Holme, Michael Walter 1918- Who 94
Holme, Richard Phillips 1941- WhoAm 94, WhoAmL 94
Holme, Thea d1980 WhoHol 92
Holme, Thomas Timings 1913- WhoAm 94
Holmen, Neil E. 1950- WhoAm 94
Holmen, Reynold Emanuel 1916- WhoScEn 94
Holme of Cheltenham, Baron 1936- IntWW 93, Who 94
Holmer, Alan F. WhoAmP 93
Holmer, Alan Freeman 1949- WhoAm 94
Holmer, Edwin Carl 1921- WhoAm 94
Holmer, Freeman 1917- WhoWest 94
Holmer, Paul Cecil Henry 1923- Who 94
Holmer, Paul L. 1916- WrDr 94

Holmes, A.R. *EncSF 93*
Holmes, Albert William, Jr. 1932- *WhoAm 94, WhoWest 94*
Holmes, Allen Cornelius 1920-1990 *WhAm 10*
Holmes, Alvin A. 1939- *WhoAmP 93*
Holmes, Alvin Adolf 1939- *WhoBlA 94*
Holmes, Ann Hitchcock 1922- *WhoAm 94*
Holmes, Anthony 1931- *Who 94*
Holmes, Arthur, Jr. 1931- *AfrAmG [port]*
Holmes, Arthur F(rank) 1924- *WrDr 94*
Holmes, Augusta (Mary Anne) 1847-1903 *NewGrDO*
Holmes, B(ryan) J(ohn) 1939- *WrDr 94*
Holmes, Barbara Deveaux 1947- *WhoMW 93*
Holmes, Barbara J. 1934- *WhoBlA 94*
Holmes, Barry Trevor 1933- *Who 94*
Holmes, Ben d1943 *WhoHol 92*
Holmes, Bert Otis E., Jr. 1921- *WhoAm 94*
Holmes, Bradley Paul 1953- *WhoAm 94, WhoBlA 94*
Holmes, Brian d1993 *Who 94N*
Holmes, Broox Garrett 1932- *WhoAm 94*
Holmes, Bruce Scott 1951- *WhoWest 94*
Holmes, Bruce T. *EncSF 93*
Holmes, Burton d1958 *WhoHol 92*
Holmes, Carl 1925- *WhoBlA 94*
Holmes, Carl 1929- *WhoBlA 94*
Holmes, Carl Dean 1940- *WhoMW 93*
Holmes, Carl Dean 1944- *WhoAmP 93*
Holmes, Carl Kenneth 1960- *WhoScEn 94*
Holmes, Carlton 1951- *WhoBlA 94*
Holmes, Charles Everett 1931- *WhoAmL 94*
Holmes, Charlotte *DrAPF 93*
Holmes, Christian R. 1946- *WhoAmP 93*
Holmes, Christopher Francis 1959- *WhoFI 94*
Holmes, Claire Coleman 1931- *WhoFI 94*
Holmes, Clifton 1932- *WhoAmP 93*
Holmes, Cloyd James 1939- *WhoBlA 94*
Holmes, Colgate Frederick 1935- *WhoAm 94*
Holmes, Cynthia Misao Bell 1949- *WhoMW 93*
Holmes, Dallas Scott 1940- *WhoAmL 94*
Holmes, Darrell 1921- *WhoAm 94*
Holmes, Darrell E. 1934- *WhoAmP 93*
Holmes, Darryl *DrAPF 93*
Holmes, David 1935- *Who 94*
Holmes, David Bruce 1952- *WhoWest 94*
Holmes, David Bryan 1936- *WhoAmA 93*
Holmes, David Farrell 1959- *WhoMW 93*
Holmes, David Lee 1955- *WhoWest 94*
Holmes, David Richard 1940- *WhoAm 94*
Holmes, David S., Jr. 1914- *WhoAmP 93, WhoBlA 94*
Holmes, David Valentine 1945- *WhoAmA 93*
Holmes, David Vivian 1926- *Who 94*
Holmes, Debbie 1948- *WhoMW 93*
Holmes, Doloris *DrAPF 93*
Holmes, Donald G. *WhoAmP 93*
Holmes, Donna Jean 1954- *WhoScEn 94*
Holmes, Dorothy E. 1943- *WhoBlA 94*
Holmes, Douglas J. 1932- *WhoAmP 93*
Holmes, Dwight Ellis 1938- *WhoAm 94*
Holmes, Dyer Brainerd 1921- *IntWW 93*
Holmes, E. Selean 1954- *WhoBlA 94*
Holmes, Edward d1977 *WhoHol 92*
Holmes, Edward W. 1941- *WhoScEn 94*
Holmes, Eileen Martinez 1952- *WhoHisp 94*
Holmes, Eleanor *WhoWomW 91*
Holmes, Ernest Shurtleff 1887-1960 *DcAmReB 2*
Holmes, Eugene 1934- *NewGrDO*
Holmes, Everlena M. 1934- *WhoBlA 94*
Holmes, Francis William 1929- *WhoAm 94*
Holmes, Frank (Wakefield) 1924- *Who 94*
Holmes, Fred Gillespie 1913- *WhoAm 94*
Holmes, Frederic Lawrence 1932- *WhoAm 94*
Holmes, Frederick Franklin 1932- *WhoMW 93*
Holmes, Gary Mayo 1943- *WhoBlA 94*
Holmes, Genta Hawkins 1940- *WhoAmP 93*
Holmes, Geoffrey Shorter 1928- *IntWW 93, Who 94, WrDr 94*
Holmes, George d1985 *WhoHol 92*
Holmes, George Arthur 1927- *IntWW 93, Who 94*
Holmes, George Dennis 1926- *Who 94*
Holmes, George Edward 1937- *WhoScEn 94*
Holmes, George M. 1929- *WhoAmP 93*
Holmes, Gerda *WhoHol 92*
Holmes, H.H. *EncSF 93*
Holmes, Hamilton Earl 1941- *WhoBlA 94*
Holmes, Harry Dadisman 1944- *WhoFI 94*
Holmes, Helen d1950 *WhoHol 92*
Holmes, Helen Bequaert 1929- *WhoAm 94*
Holmes, Henry Allen 1933- *WhoAm 94*
Holmes, Henry Anderson 1936- *WhoFI 94*
Holmes, Henry Sidney, III 1944- *WhoBlA 94*
Holmes, Herbert 1932- *WhoBlA 94*
Holmes, Ida Mae 1952- *WhoFI 94*
Holmes, Jack Edward 1941- *WhoMW 93*
Holmes, Jack M. d1950 *WhoHol 92*
Holmes, James 1919- *WhoAm 94*
Holmes, James Arthur, Jr. 1954- *WhoBlA 94*
Holmes, James Franklin 1945- *WhoBlA 94*
Holmes, James Frederick 1937- *WhoWest 94*
Holmes, James Hill, III 1935- *WhoAmL 94*
Holmes, James Parker 1940- *WhoFI 94*
Holmes, Jay Thorpe 1942- *WhoAm 94*
Holmes, Jerry 1957- *WhoBlA 94*
Holmes, Jerry Dell 1935- *WhoAm 94*
Holmes, John d1988 *WhoHol 92*
Holmes, John 1913- *WrDr 94*
Holmes, John 1921- *WrDr 94*
Holmes, John A. 1949- *WhoAmP 93*
Holmes, John Eaton 1951- *Who 94*
Holmes, John Ernest Raymond 1925- *Who 94*
Holmes, John Haynes 1879-1964 *DcAmReB 2*
Holmes, John Leonard 1931- *WhoAm 94*
Holmes, John Richard 1917- *WhoAm 94*
Holmes, John Sharp, Jr. *WhoAmP 93*
Holmes, John Steven, II 1961- *WhoMW 93*
Holmes, John Wentworth 1925- *Who 94*
Holmes, Kathryn Louise 1937- *WhoMW 93*
Holmes, Kenneth Charles 1934- *IntWW 93, Who 94*
Holmes, Kenneth E. 1942- *WhoIns 94*
Holmes, Kenneth Robert 1937- *WhoMW 93*
Holmes, Kenneth Soar 1912- *Who 94*
Holmes, Kirby Garrett 1933- *WhoAmP 93*
Holmes, Larry 1949- *IntWW 93, WhoAm 94, WhoBlA 94*
Holmes, Larry W. 1942- *WhoAmA 93*
Holmes, Leo S. 1919- *WhoBlA 94*
Holmes, Litdell Melvin, Jr. 1944- *WhoBlA 94*
Holmes, Lorene B. 1937- *WhoBlA 94*
Holmes, Louyco W. 1924- *WhoBlA 94*
Holmes, Lowell D. 1925- *WrDr 94*
Holmes, Madeleine Taylor d1987 *WhoHol 92*
Holmes, Margaret E. 1942- *WhoScEn 94*
Holmes, Marion 1940- *WhoBlA 94*
Holmes, Marjorie 1910- *WrDr 94*
Holmes, Marjorie Rose *WhoAm 94*
Holmes, Martin (Rivington) 1905- *WrDr 94*
Holmes, Mary Brown 1950- *WhoBlA 94*
Holmes, Mary C. *WhoAmP 93*
Holmes, Mary E. 1945- *WhoAmP 93*
Holmes, Mary Tavener 1954- *ConAu 141*
Holmes, Maurice (Andrew) 1911- *Who 94*
Holmes, Maurice Colston 1935- *Who 94*
Holmes, Melvin Almont 1919- *WhoAm 94*
Holmes, Michael Gene 1937- *WhoAm 94, WhoAmL 94*
Holmes, Michelle *WhoHol 92*
Holmes, Milton d1987 *WhoHol 92*
Holmes, Mimi 1956- *WhoMW 93*
Holmes, Miriam H. 1951- *WhoAm 94*
Holmes, Norman Leonard 1928- *WhoAm 94*
Holmes, Oliver L. 1946- *WhoAmL 94*
Holmes, Oliver Wendell 1809-1894 *AmCulL, WorScD*
Holmes, Patrick 1939- *Who 94*
Holmes, Paul Kinloch, Jr. 1915- *WhoAmL 94*
Holmes, Paul Kinloch, III 1951- *WhoAmP 93*
Holmes, Paul Luther 1919- *WhoWest 94*
Holmes, Paull 1943- *WhoWest 94*
Holmes, Pee Wee d1936 *WhoHol 92*
Holmes, Peter (Fenwick) 1932- *Who 94*
Holmes, Peter Douglas 1948- *WhoAm 94*
Holmes, Peter F. 1932- *IntWW 93*
Holmes, Peter Sloan 1942- *Who 94*
Holmes, Phillips d1942 *WhoHol 92*
Holmes, Pierre d1993 *NewYTBS 93 [port]*
Holmes, Polly Mudge 1923- *WhoAmP 93*
Holmes, Ralph d1945 *WhoHol 92*
Holmes, Randall Kent 1940- *WhoAm 94*
Holmes, Rapley d1928 *WhoHol 92*
Holmes, Raymond 1921- *WrDr 94*
Holmes, Rebecca Anne 1955- *WhoMW 93*
Holmes, Reed M. 1917- *WhoAm 94*
Holmes, Richard 1945- *WrDr 94*
Holmes, Richard Albert 1958- *WhoWest 94*
Holmes, Richard Bernard 1951- *WhoBlA 94*
Holmes, Richard Brooks 1959- *WhoScEn 94, WhoWest 94*
Holmes, Richard Gordon Heath 1945- *Who 94*
Holmes, Richard Hugh Morris 1925- *WhoAm 94*
Holmes, Richard W. 1923- *WhoAmP 93*
Holmes, Richard Winn 1923- *WhoAm 94, WhoAmL 94, WhoMW 93*
Holmes, Robert d1945 *WhoHol 92*
Holmes, Robert A. 1943- *WhoAmP 93, WhoBlA 94*
Holmes, Robert Allen 1947- *WhoAmL 94*
Holmes, Robert B., Jr. 1946- *WhoAmP 93*
Holmes, Robert C. 1945- *WhoBlA 94*
Holmes, Robert Ernest 1943- *WhoBlA 94*
Holmes, Robert Eugene 1928- *WhoWest 94*
Holmes, Robert Kathrone, Jr. 1952- *WhoBlA 94*
Holmes, Robert L., Jr. 1934- *WhoBlA 94*
Holmes, Robert Lawrence 1935- *WhoAm 94*
Holmes, Robert Lewis 1926- *WrDr 94*
Holmes, Robert V. 1938- *WhoAmP 93*
Holmes, Robert Wayne 1950- *WhoFI 94, WhoScEn 94, WhoWest 94*
Holmes, Robert Wendell 1966- *WhoFI 94*
Holmes, Robert William 1929- *WhoAm 94*
Holmes, Robin Edmond Kendall 1938- *Who 94*
Holmes, Roger de Lacy 1948- *Who 94*
Holmes, Sherie Bell Shortridge 1956- *WhoAmL 94*
Holmes, Stephen A. 1951- *WhoAmP 93*
Holmes, Stuart d1971 *WhoHol 92*
Holmes, Taylor d1959 *WhoHol 92*
Holmes, Thomas Hall 1918-1988 *WhAm 10*
Holmes, Thomas Joseph 1953- *WhoFI 94, WhoScEn 94, WhoWest 94*
Holmes, Thomas Leroy 1953- *WhoWest 94*
Holmes, Tracy 1902- *WhoHol 92*
Holmes, Troy Thomas 1963- *WhoFI 94*
Holmes, Vernon Harrison 1920- *WhAm 10*
Holmes, Walter John 1906- *WhoFI 94*
Holmes, Walter Stephen, Jr. 1919- *WhoAm 94*
Holmes, Wendell d1962 *WhoHol 92*
Holmes, Wendell P., Jr. 1922- *WhoBlA 94*
Holmes, Wendy (Diana H. Noyes) 1946- *WhoAmA 93*
Holmes, Willard *WhoAm 94, WhoAmA 93*
Holmes, William 1922- *Who 94*
Holmes, William 1940- *WhoBlA 94*
Holmes, William B. 1937- *WhoBlA 94*
Holmes, William Dee 1929- *WhoAm 94*
Holmes, William Ernest 1947- *WhoIns 94*
Holmes, William J. d1946 *WhoHol 92*
Holmes, William Neil 1927- *Who 94*
Holmes, Willie A. 1928- *WhoBlA 94*
Holmes, Willynda 1944- *WhoAmP 93*
Holmes, Wilma K. 1933- *WhoBlA 94*
Holmes, Zan W., Jr. *WhoBlA 94*
Holmes a Court *Who 94*
Holmes A Court, (Michael) Robert 1937-1990 *WhAm 10*
Holmes-Gore, Arthur d1915 *WhoHol 92*
Holmes-Gore, Dorothy d1977 *WhoHol 92*
Holmes Sellors, Patrick John *Who 94*
Holmgren, Edwin Surl 1934- *WhoAm 94*
Holmgren, John P. 1933- *WhoAmP 93*
Holmgren, Laton Earle 1915- *WhoAm 94*
Holmgren, Mark *DrAPF 93*
Holmgren, Mike 1948- *WhoAm 94, WhoMW 93*
Holmgren, Paul *WhoAm 94*
Holmgren, R. John 1897-1963 *WhoAmA 93N*
Holmgren, Roderick B. 1914- *WhoWest 94*
Holmlund, Lisa Lynne 1960- *WhoWest 94*
Holmpatrick, Baron 1955- *Who 94*
Holmquest, Donald Lee 1939- *WhoAm 94, WhoScEn 94*
Holmquist, Paul R. 1943- *WhoIns 94*
Holmquist, Walter Richard 1934- *WhoAm 94, WhoWest 94*
Holms, Billy d1984 *WhoHol 92*
Holmstead, Jeffrey R. 1960- *WhoAm 94*
Holmstrom, David Edwin Arthur 1943- *WhoFI 94*
Holmstrom, Lynda Lytle 1939- *WrDr 94*
Holmwood, James Morley 1937- *WhoAm 94*
Holo, Selma R. 1943- *WhoAmA 93*
Holo, Selma Reuben 1943- *WhoWest 94*
Holohan, Ronald Joseph 1942- *WhoMW 93*
Holohan, William A. 1928- *WhoAmP 93*
Holonyak, Nick, Jr. 1928- *WhoAm 94, WhoScEn 94*
Holoubek, Gustaw 1923- *IntWW 93*
Holoubek, Ladislav 1913- *NewGrDO*
Holoun, Harold Dean 1939- *WhoAmA 93*
Holovak, Mike *WhoAm 94*
Holovatyi, Serhii Petrovych 1954- *LngBDD*
Holoyda, Olha 1954- *WhoFI 94*
Holperin, James C. 1950- *WhoAmP 93*
Holquist, James Michael 1935- *WhoAm 94*
Holroyd, Emilie Adams 1931- *WhoAmP 93*
Holroyd, Frank (Martyn) 1935- *Who 94*
Holroyd, John Hepworth 1935- *Who 94*
Holroyd, Margaret *Who 94*
Holroyd, Michael 1935- *IntWW 93, WhoAm 94, WrDr 94*
Holroyd, Michael (de Courcy Fraser) 1935- *Who 94*
Holroyd, William Arthur Hepworth 1938- *Who 94*
Holroyd, William Casper *WhoAmP 93*
Holroyde, Geoffrey Vernon 1928- *Who 94*
Holsapple, Michael Eugene 1951- *WhoAmL 94*
Holsch, Robert Fred 1952- *WhoAmA 93*
Holschbach, Vernon W. 1926- *WhoAmP 93*
Holscher, Richard Harry 1928- *WhoAm 94*
Holschuh, (George) Fred 1902- *WhoAmA 93*
Holschuh, John David 1926- *WhoAm 94, WhoAmL 94, WhoMW 93*
Holschuh, John David, Jr. 1955- *WhoAmL 94*
Holsclaw, Robert Graydon 1934- *WhoAm 94*
Holsen, James Noble, Jr. 1924- *WhoAm 94*
Holsen, Robert Charles 1913- *WhoAm 94*
Holsendolph, Ernest 1935- *WhoBlA 94*
Holsey, Lilla G. 1941- *WhoBlA 94*
Holsey, William Fleming, Jr. 1923- *WhoBlA 94*
Holshouser, James E., Jr. 1934- *IntWW 93*
Holshouser, James Eubert, Jr. 1934- *WhoAmP 93*
Holshouser, Marion S. *WhoAmP 93*
Holsinger, James Wilson, Jr. 1939- *WhoAm 94*
Holsinger, W. Preston 1942- *WhoFI 94*
Holsinger, Wayne Townsend 1931- *WhoAm 94*
Holsinger, William H. 1952- *WhoAmP 93*
Holsopple, Ben Delbert 1951- *WhoFI 94*
Holst, Gustav(us Theodore von) 1874-1934 *NewGrDO*
Holst, Johan Jorgen 1937- *IntWW 93*
Holst, Per 1939- *IntWW 93*
Holst, Sanford 1946- *WhoWest 94*
Holst, Spencer *DrAPF 93*
Holst, Willem 1911- *WhoAm 94*
Holstad, Scott C. *DrAPF 93*
Holste, Thomas James 1943- *WhoAmA 93*
Holstead, George B. 1924- *WhoAmP 93*
Holstead, John Burnham 1938- *WhoAm 94*
Holsted, James Leon 1944- *WhoAmP 93*
Holstein, Franz von 1826-1878 *NewGrDO*
Holstein, Jay Allen 1938- *WhoAm 94*
Holstein, Jens Christian 1930- *WhoFI 94*
Holstein, John C. 1945- *WhoAmP 93*
Holstein, John Charles 1945- *WhoAm 94, WhoAmL 94, WhoMW 93*
Holstein, Marilyn Anne 1958- *WhoAm 94*
Holstein, Michael *DrAPF 93*
Holstein, Robert K. 1967- *WhoWest 94*
Holstein, William Kurt 1936- *WhoAm 94*
Holsten, Mark 1965- *WhoAmP 93*
Holstener-Jorgensen, Helge 1924- *IntWW 93*
Holster, Robert Marc 1946- *WhoAm 94*
Holsti, Kalevi J. 1935- *WrDr 94*
Holsti, Kalevi Jacque 1935- *WhoAm 94*
Holsti, Ole Rudolf 1933- *WhoAm 94, WrDr 94*
Holstine, Michael Joseph 1957- *WhoFI 94*
Holston, John Curtis 1939- *WhoAmP 93*
Holston, Sharon Smith 1945- *WhoAm 94*
Holstrom, Carleton Arthur 1935- *WhoAm 94*
Holsworth, William C. 1944- *WhoFI 94*
Holt, Aline G. 1942- *WhoBlA 94*
Holt, Andrea Renee 1962- *WhoFI 94*
Holt, Arthur Frederick 1914- *Who 94*
Holt, Ben 1956-1990 *AfrAmAl 6*
Holt, Bertha Merrill 1916- *WhoAm 94, WhoAmP 93*
Holt, Charlene 1940- *WhoHol 92*
Holt, Charles Asbury 1948- *WhoAm 94*
Holt, Charlotte Sinclair 1914-1990 *WhoAmA 93N*
Holt, Christopher Robert Vesey 1915- *Who 94*
Holt, Conrad G. *EncSF 93*
Holt, Constance 1924- *Who 94*
Holt, David 1927- *WhoHol 92*
Holt, David B. 1944- *WhoAmP 93*
Holt, David Earl 1928- *WhoAm 94*

Holt, Deloris Lenette WhoBlA 94
Holt, Dennis F. WhoAm 94
Holt, Donald A. 1932- WhoAm 94, WhoMW 93, WhoScEn 94
Holt, Donald Dale 1936- WhoAm 94
Holt, Donald Edward, Jr. 1945- WhoAm 94
Holt, Donald H. 1941- WhoBlA 94
Holt, Dorothy L. 1930- WhoBlA 94
Holt, Douglas Emerson 1944- WhoAmP 93
Holt, Douglas Eugene 1924- WhoAm 94
Holt, Drawdy Norton, Jr. 1922- WhoAmP 93
Holt, Edward Allen 1946- WhoWest 94
Holt, Edward James 1942- WhoMW 93
Holt, Edwin d1920 WhoHol 92
Holt, Edwin J. WhoBlA 94
Holt, Eleanor Louise 1928- WhoAmP 93
Holt, Elizabeth Manners 1939- WhoScEn 94
Holt, Emily Newman DrAPF 93
Holt, Emogene 1927- WhoAmP 93
Holt, Essie W. WhoBlA 94
Holt, Frank Brett 1948- WhoMW 93
Holt, Frank Ross 1920- WhoScEn 94
Holt, Fred D. 1931- WhoBlA 94
Holt, Gene Allan 1957- WhoMW 93
Holt, Georgin L. 1934- WhoAm 94
Holt, Gerald Wayne 1935- WhoMW 93
Holt, Glen Edward 1939- WhoAm 94, WhoMW 93
Holt, Grace S. 1922- WhoBlA 94
Holt, Harold 1926- WhoAmP 93
Holt, Helen d1927 WhoHol 92
Holt, Helen Keil 1937- WhoAm 94
Holt, Jack Who 94
Holt, Jack d1951 WhoHol 92
Holt, Jack, Jr. 1929- WhoAmP 93
Holt, Jack W. 1936- WhoIns 94
Holt, Jack Wilson, Jr. 1929- WhoAm 94, WhoAmL 94
Holt, James (Clarke) 1922- Who 94
Holt, James Clarke 1922- IntWW 93, WrDr 94
Holt, James D. 1940- WhoAmP 93
Holt, James Franklin 1927- WhoWest 94
Holt, James Richard, Jr. 1958- WhoIns 94
Holt, James Stokes, III 1927- WhoBlA 94
Holt, Janet Louvau 1929- WhoWest 94
Holt, Jany WhoHol 92
Holt, Jason d1989 WhoHol 92
Holt, Jeanne Gleason 1937- WhoAmP 93
Holt, Jennifer 1920- WhoHol 92
Holt, Joe D. 1940- WhoAmP 93
Holt, John 1721-1784 WhAmRev
Holt, John B. 1915- WhoAm 94
Holt, John Bayley 1912- Who 94
Holt, John J. 1931- WhoBlA 94
Holt, John Lapworth 1912- Who 94
Holt, John Manly 1925- WhoMW 93
Holt, John Michael 1935- Who 94
Holt, John Riley 1918- Who 94
Holt, Jonathan Turner 1949- WhoAm 94
Holt, Judd 1941- ConAu 141
Holt, Kenneth Charles 1948- WhoBlA 94
Holt, Lee WhoAmP 93
Holt, Leo E. 1927- WhoBlA 94
Holt, Leon Conrad, Jr. 1925- WhoAm 94
Holt, Leroy 1967- WhoBlA 94
Holt, Louise 1924- WhoAmA 93
Holt, Marcia Chadwick 1936- WhoAmL 94
Holt, Maria Glen WhoAmP 93
Holt, Marjorie Sewell 1920- WhoAm 94, WhoAmP 93
Holt, Mark WhoAmP 93
Holt, Martha A. 1945- WhoAmA 93
Holt, Mary Who 94
Holt, Maude R. 1949- WhoBlA 94
Holt, Michael (Paul) 1929- WrDr 94
Holt, Mikel L. 1952- WhoBlA 94
Holt, Milton 1952- WhoAmP 93
Holt, Nancy Louise 1938- WhoAm 94, WhoAmA 93
Holt, Nick d1979 WhoHol 92
Holt, Patricia Lester 1944- WhoAm 94
Holt, Patrick 1912- WhoHol 92
Holt, Peter Malcolm 1918- IntWW 93, Who 94
Holt, Peter Rolf 1930- WhoAm 94
Holt, Philetus Havens, III 1928- WhoAm 94
Holt, Richard WhoHol 92
Holt, Richard Anthony Appleby 1920- Who 94
Holt, Richard D. 1942- WhoAmL 94
Holt, Robert Anthony 1967- WhoMW 93
Holt, Robert Ezell 1957- WhoFI 94
Holt, Robert LeRoi 1920- WhoAm 94
Holt, Robert Theodore 1928- WhoAm 94
Holt, Rochelle Lynn DrAPF 93
Holt, Ronald Lee 1952- WhoAmL 94
Holt, Roy James 1947- WhoMW 93
Holt, Scott W. 1948- WhoAmP 93
Holt, Seth 1923-1971 HorFD
Holt, Stephen S. 1940- WhoAm 94
Holt, Thad 1898- WhAm 10
Holt, Tim d1973 WhoHol 92
Holt, Tim 1945- WhoAmP 93
Holt, Timothy A. 1953- WhoIns 94
Holt, Timothy Arthur 1953- WhoAm 94
Holt, Tom 1961- WrDr 94
Holt, Veityа Eileene 1962- WhoBlA 94
Holt, Victoria BlmGWL, ConAu 140, SmATA 74, WhoAm 94
Holt, Victoria 1906-1993 WrDr 94N
Holt, Will WhoHol 92
Holt, William E. 1945- WhoAmL 94
Holt, William Henry 1939- WhoScEn 94
Holt, William Stull 1896- WhAm 10
Holt, Worthe Seymour 1929- WhoMW 93
Holtan, Boyd DeVere 1928- WhoAm 94
Holtan, Ramer B., Jr. 1944- WhoAmL 94
Holtan, Ruth Iona Tweeten 1924- WhoAmP 93
Holtan, Stanford Eugene 1921- WhoAmP 93
Holtby, Douglas Martin 1947- WhoAm 94
Holtby, Kenneth Fraser 1922- WhoAm 94
Holtby, Robert Tinsley 1921- Who 94, WrDr 94
Holtby, Winifred 1898-1935 BlmGWL, DcNaB MP, EncSF 93
Holte, Clarence L. 1909-1993 NewYTBS 93
Holte, Debra Leah 1952- WhoAm 94
Holten, Cort Conway 1950- WhoMW 93
Holten, James Joseph 1940- WhoFI 94, WhoMW 93
Holten, Knud EncSF 93
Holten, Samuel 1738-1816 WhAmRev
Holten, Virginia Lois Zewe 1938- WhoWest 94
Holter, Arlen Rolf 1946- WhoAm 94, WhoMW 93
Holter, Don Wendell 1905- WhoAm 94
Holter, Marvin Rosenkrantz 1922- WhoAm 94
Holtfreter, Johannes d1992 IntWW 93N
Holtfreter, Johannes Friedrich Karl 1901-1992 WhAm 10
Holth, Fredrik Davidson 1940- WhoAmL 94
Holth, Henry Albert 1927- WhoWest 94
Holtham, Carmen Gloria 1922- Who 94
Holthaus, Thomas Anthony 1941- WhoMW 93
Holthus, Rita May 1928- WhoAmP 93
Holthusen, Hans Egon 1913- IntWW 93
Holtkamp, Dorsey Emil 1919- WhoAm 94, WhoMW 93
Holtkamp, James Arnold 1949- WhoAm 94, WhoAmL 94
Holtkamp, Larry Joseph 1949- WhoMW 93
Holtkamp, Ronald W. 1952- WhoIns 94
Holtman, Donald Richard 1936- WhoAmL 94
Holtman, Mark Steven 1949- WhoScEn 94
Holtman, William J. 1921- WhoFI 94
Holt-Ochsner, Liana Kay 1958- WhoScEn 94
Holton, A. Linwood, Jr. 1923- IntWW 93, WhoAm 94, WhoAmP 93
Holton, Charles R. 1950- WhoAm 94, WhoAmL 94
Holton, Earl D. 1934- WhoAm 94, WhoFI 94
Holton, Gerald 1922- IntWW 93, WhoAm 94
Holton, Mark WhoHol 92
Holton, Michael 1927- Who 94
Holton, Michael David 1961- WhoBlA 94
Holton, Priscilla Browne 1921- WhoBlA 94
Holton, Raymond William 1929- WhoAm 94
Holton, Richard Henry 1926- WhoAm 94
Holton, Robert Page 1938- WhoAm 94
Holton, Thomas Ashley 1941- WhoAmL 94
Holton, William Chester 1939- WhoWest 94
Holton, William Coffeen 1930- WhoAm 94
Holton, William Milne 1931- WhoAm 94
Holtsberg, Philip Alan 1952- WhoAmL 94
Holtsinger, Edgar M. 1922- WhoAmP 93
Holtvedt, John R. 1920- WhoAmP 93
Holt-White, W(illiam Edward Bradden) 1878- EncSF 93
Holt-Wilkerson, Deborah Marie 1953- WhoMW 93
Holty, Carl Robert 1900-1973 WhoAmA 93N
Holtz, Abel WhoHisp 94
Holtz, Alan Steffen, Sr. 1922- WhoMW 93
Holtz, Carolyn A. 1952- WhoMW 93
Holtz, Daniel Martin 1959- WhoHisp 94
Holtz, Edgar Wolfe 1922- WhoAm 94, WhoAmL 94
Holtz, Gilbert Joseph 1924- WhoFI 94
Holtz, Glenn Edward 1938- WhoAm 94, WhoFI 94, WhoMW 93
Holtz, Itshak Jack 1925- WhoAmA 93
Holtz, James Otto 1935- WhoMW 93
Holtz, Joseph Norman 1930- WhoWest 94
Holtz, Lou d1980 WhoHol 92
Holtz, Louis Leo 1937- WhoAm 94, WhoMW 93
Holtz, Noel 1943- WhoScEn 94
Holtz, Paul Roscoe 1933- WhoAmP 93
Holtz, Robert Earl 1933- WhoMW 93
Holtz, Sidney 1925- WhoAm 94
Holtz, Tenen d1971 WhoHol 92
Holtz, Tobenette 1930- WhoScEn 94
Holtzapfel, Patricia Kelly 1948- WhoWest 94
Holtzapple, Mark Thomas 1956- WhoScEn 94
Holtzberg, Frederic 1922- WhoScEn 94
Holtzclaw, Joyce Madelyn Irene 1956- WhoWest 94
Holtzendorf, Louis-Casimir, Baron de 1728- WhAmRev
Holtzer, Alfred Melvin 1929- WhoAm 94, WhoMW 93
Holtzer, Marilyn Emerson 1938- WhoMW 93
Holtzman, Abraham 1921- WrDr 94
Holtzman, Alexander 1924- WhoAm 94
Holtzman, Elizabeth 1941- WhoAm 94
Holtzman, Ellen A. 1952- WhoAm 94
Holtzman, Gary Yale 1936- WhoAm 94
Holtzman, Jeffrey Kent 1955- WhoMW 93
Holtzman, Richard Beves 1927- WhoScEn 94
Holtzman, Robert Arthur 1929- WhoAm 94
Holtzman, Roberta Lee 1938- WhoMW 93
Holtzman, Wayne H(arold) 1923- IntWW 93
Holtzman, Wayne Harold 1923- WhoAm 94, WhoScEn 94, WrDr 94
Holtzmann, Howard Marshall 1921- WhoAm 94, WhoAmL 94
Holtzschue, Karl Bressem 1938- WhoAm 94, WhoAmL 94
Holub, Elaine Nathanson 1949- WhoWest 94
Holub, Gregory Steven 1950- WhoAm 94
Holub, Martin 1938- WhoAm 94
Holub, Maureen Agnes 1961- WhoMW 93
Holub, Miroslav 1923- ConWorW 93, IntWW 93
Holub, Robert Frantisek 1937- WhoScEn 94, WhoWest 94
Holubar, Alan d1925 WhoHol 92
Holve, Leslie Martin 1926- WhoWest 94
Holveck, David P. 1945- WhoScEn 94
Holveck, Jack 1943- WhoAmP 93
Holveck, Norvell 1945- WhoFI 94
Holverson, Harmon E. 1924- WhoAm 94
Holverson, John 1946- WhoAmA 93
Holvey, Samuel Boyer 1935- WhoAmA 93
Holvoe, Maria WhoHol 92
Holway, James Colin 1927- WhoFI 94
Holway, Richard Alvah 1955- WhoFI 94
Holwell, Peter 1936- Who 94
Holwell, Richard J. 1946- WhoAmL 94
Holwill, Richard N. 1945- WhoAmP 93
Holy, Ladislav 1933- ConAu 141
Holy, Ondrej Frantisek c. 1747-1783 NewGrDO
Holy Anchoress of Mansfield, The fl. 15th cent.- BlmGWL
Holy Dance, Robert d1972 EncNAR
Holyer, Ernie M. 1925- WrDr 94
Holyfield, Evander WhoAm 94, WhoBlA 94
Holyfield, Evander 1962- ConBlB 6 [port], CurBio 93 [port]
Holyoke, Edward Augustus 1908- WhoMW 93
Holyoke, Mary Vial 1737-1802 BlmGWL
Holywood, John c. 1200-1244? WhWE
Holz, Harold A. 1925- WhoAm 94
Holz, Harry George 1934- WhoAm 94, WhoAmL 94
Holz, Michael Harold 1942- WhoAmL 94
Holz, Richard Lee WhoAmL 94
Holz, Robert Kenneth 1930- WhoAm 94
Holzach, Robert 1922- IntWW 93, Who 94
Holzapfel, Christina Marie 1942- WhoAm 94
Holzbach, James Francis 1936- WhoScEn 94
Holzbach, Raymond Thomas 1929- WhoAm 94, WhoMW 93, WhoScEn 94
Holzbauer, Ignaz (Jakob) 1711-1783 NewGrDO
Holzberg, Harvey Alan 1938- WhoAm 94
Holzel, David Benjamin 1958- WhoAm 94
Holzel, Gustav 1813-1883 NewGrDO
Holzendorf, Betty S. 1939- WhoAmP 93, WhoBlA 94
Holzer, Arnim Sanchez 1959- WhoFI 94
Holzer, Edwin 1933- WhoAm 94
Holzer, Erika 1935- ConAu 141
Holzer, Hans WhoAm 94
Holzer, Jane 1940- WhoHol 92
Holzer, Jenny 1950- IntWW 93, WhoAmA 93
Holzer, Joe C. 1951- WhoAmL 94
Holzer, Thomas Lequear 1944- WhoAm 94, WhoWest 94
Holzgang, David Allan 1941- WhoWest 94
Holzhausen, Carl Johan EncSF 93
Holzheauser, Steve 1953- WhoAmP 93
Holzhey, Charles Steven 1936- WhoMW 93
Holzman, D. Keith 1936- WhoAm 94
Holzman, David Carl 1953- WhoScEn 94
Holzman, Dennis Tilden DrAPF 93
Holzman, Eric 1949- WhoAmA 93
Holzman, Franklyn D(unn) 1918- WrDr 94
Holzman, Franklyn Dunn 1918- WhoAm 94
Holzman, Howard Eugene 1934- WhoAm 94
Holzman, Jacquelin WhoAm 94
Holzman, James Louis 1949- WhoAmL 94
Holzman, Lew DrAPF 93
Holzman, Malcolm 1940- WhoAm 94
Holzman, Philip Seidman 1922- WhoAm 94, WhoScEn 94
Holzman, Red 1920- BasBi
Holzman, Robert Stuart 1907- WhoAm 94
Holzner, Burkart 1931- WhoAm 94
Holzschuh, Frank Paul 1947- WhoFI 94
Hom, Harry Lee, Jr. 1942- WhoAsA 94
Hom, Jimmy Lee 1958- WhoAmL 94
Hom, Kathleen B. 1947- WhoAsA 94
Hom, Marlon Kau 1947- WrDr 94
Hom, Mei-Ling 1951- WhoAsA 94
Hom, Peter Wah 1951- WhoAsA 94
Hom, Richard Yee 1950- WhoWest 94
Hom, Rose 1949?- WhoAsA 94
Hom, Theresa Maria 1957- WhoMW 93, WhoScEn 94
Hom, Wayne Chiu 1967- WhoScEn 94
Homaldo fl. 19th cent.- EncNAR
Homan, Cynthia Leslie WhoMW 93
Homan, David Carl 1956- WhoAmL 94
Homan, Gary Rex 1951- WhoMW 93
Homan, Gerlof 1930- WhoMW 93
Homan, John Vincent 1927- Who 94
Homan, Mildred Haerther 1922- WhoAmP 93
Homan, Paul M. 1940- WhoAm 94
Homan, Ralph D. 1928- WhoAmP 93
Homan, Ralph William 1951- WhoFI 94, WhoWest 94
Homan, Richard F. 1924- WhoAmP 93
Homan, Thomas Buckhurst 1921- Who 94
Homans, George Caspar 1910- Who 94
Homans, George Caspar 1910-1989 WhAm 10
Homans, Peter 1930- WhoAm 94, WrDr 94
Homans, Robert d1947 WhoHol 92
Homar, Lorenzo 1913- WhoAmA 93
Homberger, Eric 1942- WrDr 94
Homburg, Jeffrey Allan 1957- WhoScEn 94, WhoWest 94
Homburger, Freddy 1916- WhoAm 94
Home Who 94
Home, Earl of Who 94
Home, Alex(ander Frederick) Douglas 1903- WrDr 94
Home, Anna Margaret 1938- Who 94
Home, Cecil BlmGWL
Home, George 1920- Who 94
Home, John Gavin M. Who 94
Home, William (Dundas) 1968- Who 94
Home, William Douglas 1912-1992 AnObit 1992, ConDr 93, WrDr 94N
Home-Gall, Edward Reginald EncSF 93
Home-Gall, William Benjamin 1861-1936 EncSF 93
Homeier, Skip 1930- IntMPA 94, WhoHol 92
Homelson, Rochelle 1954- WhoAmP 93
Home Of The Hirsel, Baron 1903- IntWW 93, Who 94
Homer BlmGEL, NewGrDO
Homer fl. c. 800BC- EncSF 93
Homer, Arthur DrAPF 93
Homer, Arthur B. 1896-1972 EncABHB 9 [port]
Homer, Barry Wayne 1950- WhoAm 94
Homer, Julia Naomi 1951- WhoAm 94
Homer, Louise (Dilworth) 1871-1947 NewGrDO
Homer, Ronald A. 1947- WhoBlA 94
Homer, Thomas J. 1947- WhoAmP 93, WhoMW 93
Homer, William Innes 1929- WhoAm 94, WhoAmA 93, WrDr 94
Homer, Winslow 1836-1910 AmCulL [port]
Homer and Jethro WhoCom
Home Robertson, John David 1948- Who 94
Homes, A. M. DrAPF 93

Homes, A(my) M. *WrDr 94*
Homestead, Susan 1937- *WhoAm 94, WhoWest 94*
Homewood, Elizabeth Holmes Nash 1948- *WhoMW 93*
Homeyer, Howard C. 1933- *WhoAm 94*
Homick, Daniel John 1947- *WhoAmL 94*
Homitzky, Peter 1942- *WhoAmA 93*
Homma, Kazufumi 1943- *WhoAmA 93*
Homma, Morio 1930- *WhoScEn 94*
Homme, Marc S. 1949- *WhoWest 94*
Hommel, Daniel Jay 1955- *WhoWest 94*
Hommes, Frits Aukustinus 1934- *WhoAm 94, WhoScEn 94*
Hommrich, Denis E. 1945- *WhoAmP 93*
Homolka, Calvin Dean, II 1950- *WhoMW 93*
Homolka, Oscar d1978 *WhoHol 92*
Hompson, Davi Det 1939- *WhoAmA 93*
Homulos, Peter Stephen 1948- *WhoAm 94*
Homze, Edward Lee 1930- *WhoMW 93*
Homziak, Jurij 1948- *WhoScEn 94*
Hon, Andrew 1953- *WhoAsA 94*
Hon, David Nyok-Sai 1974- *WhoAsA 94*
Hon, Jean Marie d1955 *WhoHol 92*
Hon, Ralph Clifford 1903- *WhoAmL 94*
Hon, Wilma Joy 1934- *WhoAmP 93*
Honablue, Richard Riddick 1948- *WhoBlA 94*
Honaker, Jimmie Joe 1939- *WhoAmL 94*
Honaker, Richard Henderson 1951- *WhoAmP 93, WhoWest 94*
Honaman, J. Craig 1943- *WhoAm 94*
Honaman, June N. 1920- *WhoAmP 93*
Honami, Shinji 1945- *WhoScEn 94*
Honan, James Terry 1946- *WhoAm 94*
Honan, Kevin G. *WhoAmP 93*
Honan, Park 1928- *WrDr 94*
Honan, Tras 1930- *WhoWomW 91*
Honan, William Holmes 1930- *WhoAm 94*
Honan, William Joseph, III 1945- *WhoAmL 94*
Honavar, Vasant Gajanan 1960- *WhoMW 93, WhoScEn 94*
Honbo, Clayton K. 1938- *WhoWest 94*
Honda, Allen Shigeru 1947- *WhoAsA 94*
Honda, Frank d1924 *WhoHol 92*
Honda, Herbert Junji 1927- *WhoAmP 93*
Honda, Hiroshi 1950- *WhoScEn 94*
Honda, Ishiro d1993 *NewYTBS 93*
Honda, Margaret 1961- *WhoAmA 93*
Honda, Maya 1955- *WhoAsA 94*
Honda, Michael M. 1941- *WhoAsA 94*
Honda, Natsuo 1930- *WhoScEn 94*
Honda, Shigeru Irwin 1927- *WhoAsA 94*
Honda, Soichiro 1906-1991 *WhAm 10*
Honda, Toshio 1956- *WhoScEn 94*
Hondeghem, Luc M. 1944- *WhoScEn 94*
Honderich, Beland Hugh 1918- *WhoAm 94, WhoFI 94*
Honderich, Edgar Dawn Ross 1933- *Who 94*
Honderich, John Allen 1946- *WhoAm 94*
Honderich, Ted 1933- *WrDr 94*
Hondros, Ernest Demetrios 1930- *IntWW 93, Who 94*
Hone, David 1928- *Who 94*
Hone, Joseph 1937- *WrDr 94*
Hone, Michael Stuart 1936- *Who 94*
Hone, Ralph *Who 94*
Hone, (Herbert) Ralph d1992 *Who 94N*
Hone, (Herbert) Ralph 1896- *IntWW 93*
Hone, Robert Monro 1923- *Who 94*
Honea, Franklin Ivan 1931- *WhoScEn 94*
Honecker, Erich 1912- *IntWW 93*
Honecker, George J. *DrAPF 93*
Honecker, Margot 1927- *IntWW 93*
Honegger, Arthur d1955 *WhoHol 92*
Honegger, Arthur 1892-1955 *IntDcB, IntDcF 2-4, NewGrDO*
Honegger, Fritz 1917- *IntWW 93*
Honemann, Daniel Henry 1929- *WhoAm 94*
Honer, Paul Edward *WhoFI 94*
Honey, Michael 1941- *Who 94*
Honey, Richard Churchill 1924- *WhoAm 94*
Honey, Robert John 1936- *Who 94*
Honey, William B. 1942- *WhoAmL 94*
Honeychurch, Denis Arthur 1946- *WhoAmL 94*
Honeycombe, Gordon *Who 94*
Honeycombe, Gordon 1936- *WrDr 94*
Honeycombe, (Ronald) Gordon 1936- *Who 94*
Honeycombe, Robert (William Kerr) 1921- *Who 94*
Honeycombe, Robert William Kerr 1921- *IntWW 93*
Honeycutt, Andrew E. 1942- *WhoBlA 94*
Honeycutt, George Leonard 1936- *WhoAm 94*
Honeycutt, Kathleen 1941- *WhoAmP 93*
Honeycutt, Michael Allen 1962- *WhoScEn 94*
Honeyman, Brenda 1926- *WrDr 94*
Honeyman, Charles Mark 1949- *WhoAmL 94*
Honeyman, Janice Lynne 1949- *IntWW 93*
Honeyman, John c. 1729-1822 *AmRev*
Honeyman, John c. 1730-1823 *WhAmRev*
Honeysett, Martin 1943- *Who 94*
Honeystein, Karl 1932- *WhoAm 94*
Honeywell, Charles F. 1898- *WhAm 10*
Honeywell, Larry Gene 1935- *WhoAm 94, WhoMW 93*
Honeywell, Mark G. 1944- *WhoAmL 94*
Hong, Carl *WhoAsA 94*
Hong, Daniel Chonghan 1956- *WhoAsA 94*
Hong, Frances 1933- *WhoAsA 94*
Hong, George K. *WhoAsA 94*
Hong, Glenn Thomas 1954- *WhoAsA 94*
Hong, Gong-Soog 1950- *WhoAsA 94*
Hong, Howard V. 1912- *WrDr 94*
Hong, Howard Vincent 1912- *WhoAm 94*
Hong, Il Sik 1948- *WhoAsA 94*
Hong, Ilyoo Barry 1957- *WhoAsA 94*
Hong, James *WhoHol 92*
Hong, James Ming 1940- *WhoAm 94, WhoFI 94*
Hong, Jin Sung 1958- *WhoAsA 94*
Hong, John Song Yook 1944- *WhoAsA 94*
Hong, Kenneth 1967- *WhoAsA 94*
Hong, Lily Toy 1958- *SmATA 76 [port], WhoAsA 94*
Hong, Norman G. Y. 1947- *WhoWest 94*
Hong, Peter Lee 1956- *WhoMW 93*
Hong, Richard 1929- *WhoAm 94, WhoScEn 94*
Hong, Rose Lee 1946- *WhoMW 93*
Hong, Ryang H. 1933- *WhoAsA 94*
Hong, S. K. *WhoAsA 94*
Hong, S. Theodore 1930- *WhoAsA 94*
Hong, Se June 1944- *WhoAm 94*
Hong, Sebong 1949- *WhoAmL 94*
Hong, Seng Muy 1957- *WhoMW 93*
Hong, Shuguang 1954- *WhoAsA 94*
Hong, Suk Ki 1928- *WhoAsA 94*
Hong, Sung Ok 1931- *WhoAsA 94*
Hong, Tae-Shik 1934- *IntWW 93*
Hong, Waun Ki 1942- *WhoScEn 94*
Hong, Weihu 1956- *WhoAsA 94*
Hong, Wilson S. 1934- *IntMPA 94*
Hong, Yong Shik 1932- *WhoScEn 94*
Hong, Yoopyo 1949- *WhoAsA 94*
Hong, Zuu-Chang 1942- *WhoScEn 94*
Hong Chaosheng 1920- *WhoPRCh 91*
Hongen, Elisabeth 1906- *NewGrDO*
Hong Fuzeng 1932- *WhoPRCh 91*
Hong Guofan 1939- *WhoPRCh 91 [port]*
Hong Jiade *WhoPRCh 91*
Hong Jiawei 1936- *WhoPRCh 91*
Hong Jing 1917- *WhoPRCh 91 [port]*
Hongladarom, Sunthorn 1912- *IntWW 93, Who 94*
Hong Lin *WhoPRCh 91*
Hongo, Garrett (Kaoru) 1951- *WrDr 94*
Hongo, Garrett Kaoru *DrAPF 93*
Hongo, Garrett Kaoru 1951- *WhoAsA 94*
Hongo-Whiting, Valerie Ann 1953- *WhoWest 94*
Hong Qian 1909- *IntWW 93*
Hongsermeier, Martin Karl 1953- *WhoWest 94*
Hong Xuezhi 1913- *WhoPRCh 91 [port]*
Hong Xuezhi, Gen. 1913- *IntWW 93*
Hong Yi 1924- *WhoPRCh 91 [port]*
Hong Yongshi *WhoPRCh 91 [port]*
Hong Yuncheng *WhoPRCh 91*
Honig, Arnold 1928- *WhoAm 94*
Honig, Barbara J. 1933- *WhoAmP 93*
Honig, Barry Hirsh 1941- *WhoAm 94*
Honig, Bill 1937- *WhoAm 94*
Honig, Donald *DrAPF 93*
Honig, Edwin *DrAPF 93*
Honig, Edwin 1919- *IntWW 93, WhoAm 94, WrDr 94*
Honig, Eleanor D. *WhoAmA 93*
Honig, Frederick 1912- *Who 94*
Honig, George Raymond 1936- *WhoAm 94*
Honig, Lawrence Sterling 1953- *WhoScEn 94, WhoWest 94*
Honig, Lucy *DrAPF 93*
Honig, Mervin 1920- *WhoAmA 93*
Honigman, David M. 1955- *WhoAmP 93*
Honigmann, Ernst Anselm Joachim 1927- *Who 94*
Honikman, Larry Howard 1936- *WhoScEn 94*
Honjo, Masako 1948- *WhoAmA 93*
Honma, Shigemi 1920- *WhoAsA 94*
Honnef, Klaus 1939- *ConAu 142*
Honnold, John Otis, Jr. 1915- *WhoAm 94, WhoAmL 94*
Honor, Edward 1933- *AfrAmG [port]*
Honor, Noel Evans 1948- *WhoMW 93*
Honore, Antony Maurice 1921- *Who 94*
Honore, Charles E. 1934- *AfrAmG [port]*
Honore, Stephan LeRoy 1938- *WhoBlA 94*
Honoré, Tony 1921- *WrDr 94*
Honour, Hugh 1927- *WrDr 94*
Honour, (Patrick) Hugh 1927- *Who 94*
Honri, Percy d1953 *WhoHol 92*
Honri, Peter 1929- *WrDr 94*
Honton, Edward Jude 1955- *WhoWest 94*
Honton, Margaret *DrAPF 93*
Honts, Charles Robert 1953- *WhoScEn 94*
Honywood, Filmer (Courtenay William) 1930- *Who 94*
Hoo, Joe-Jie 1944- *WhoAsA 94*
Hoobler, James Ferguson 1938- *WhoAmP 93*
Hoobler, Sibley Worth 1911- *WhoAm 94*
Hoobler, Thomas 1944?- *EncSF 93*
Hood *Who 94*
Hood, Viscount 1914- *Who 94*
Hood, Ann 1956- *WrDr 94*
Hood, Archibald Andrew 1922- *WhoAmP 93*
Hood, Basil 1864-1917 *NewGrDO*
Hood, Bruce 1936- *WrDr 94*
Hood, Carroll V. 1936- *WhoAmP 93*
Hood, Charles Hurlburt 1938- *WhoAm 94*
Hood, Charles McKinley, Jr. 1936- *WhoBlA 94*
Hood, Christopher 1943- *WrDr 94*
Hood, Clifford Firoved 1894-1978 *EncABHB 9 [port]*
Hood, Darla *WhoCom*
Hood, Darla d1979 *WhoHol 92*
Hood, Denise Page 1952- *WhoBlA 94*
Hood, Dennis Carl 1937- *WhoMW 93*
Hood, Don *WhoHol 92*
Hood, Donald Curtis 1944- *WhoAmL 94*
Hood, Dorothy *WhoAmA 93*
Hood, Douglas Crary 1932- *WhoMW 93, WhoScEn 94*
Hood, E. James 1947- *WhoAmP 93*
Hood, Earl Edward 1940- *WhoAmL 94*
Hood, Earl James 1947- *WhoAmL 94, WhoMW 93*
Hood, Edward Exum, Jr. 1930- *WhoAm 94, WhoFI 94*
Hood, Elizabeth F. 1930-1991 *WhoBlA 94N*
Hood, Ethel Painter 1908-1982 *WhoAmA 93N*
Hood, Fred H. 1926- *WhoAmP 93*
Hood, Gary Allen 1943- *WhoAmA 93*
Hood, George W. 1869-1949 *WhoAmA 93N*
Hood, Graham Stanley 1936- *WhoAmA 93*
Hood, Harold 1931- *WhoAmP 93, WhoBlA 94*
Hood, Harold (Joseph) 1916- *Who 94*
Hood, Hugh (John Blagdon) 1928- *RfGShF, WrDr 94*
Hood, Jacqueline Ann Nitz 1954- *WhoWest 94*
Hood, James 1930- *WhoMW 93*
Hood, James 1948- *Who 94*
Hood, James Matthew, Jr. 1934- *WhoAmP 93*
Hood, Joe Don 1936- *WhoWest 94*
Hood, John 1924- *Who 94*
Hood, John B. 1944- *WhoAmL 94*
Hood, Joseph, Sr. d1965 *WhoHol 92*
Hood, Joseph M. 1942- *WhoAmL 94*
Hood, Jospeh M. 1942- *WhoAm 94*
Hood, Kenneth Dean 1953- *WhoAmP 93*
Hood, Lamartine Frain 1937- *WhoAm 94, WhoScEn 94*
Hood, Leroy Edward 1938- *IntWW 93, WhoAm 94, WhoScEn 94*
Hood, Lois Sage 1933- *WhoAmP 93*
Hood, Louise B. 1916- *WhoAmP 93*
Hood, Lucy Jane 1953- *WhoMW 93*
Hood, Lynley (Jane) 1942- *WrDr 94*
Hood, Martin Sinclair Frankland 1917- *WrDr 94*
Hood, Mary Bryan 1938- *WhoAm 94, WhoAmA 93*
Hood, Mary Dullea 1947- *WhoAmL 94*
Hood, Michael A. 1949- *WhoAmL 94*
Hood, Michael James 1946- *WhoWest 94*
Hood, Michael Lee 1959- *WhoMW 93*
Hood, Miki *WhoHol 92*
Hood, Morag 1942- *WhoHol 92*
Hood, Morris, Jr. 1934- *WhoAmP 93, WhoBlA 94*
Hood, Neil 1943- *Who 94*
Hood, Nicholas *Who 94, WhoAmP 93*
Hood, Nicholas 1923- *WhoBlA 94*
Hood, (William) Nicholas 1935- *Who 94*
Hood, Noel d1979 *WhoHol 92*
Hood, Peter *DrAPF 93*
Hood, Raymond Mathewson 1881-1934 *AmCulL*
Hood, Raymond W. 1936- *WhoBlA 94*
Hood, Raymond Walter 1936- *WhoAmP 93*
Hood, (Thomas) Richard *WhoAmA 93*
Hood, Richard A. 1950- *WhoMW 93*
Hood, Robert c. 1800-1821 *WhWE*
Hood, Robert E. 1936- *WhoBlA 94*
Hood, Robert H., Jr. *WhoFI 94*
Hood, Robert Holmes 1944- *WhoAmL 94*
Hood, Roger Grahame 1936- *Who 94*
Hood, Ronald Lee 1945- *WhoMW 93*
Hood, Ruth P. *WhoAmP 93*
Hood, Samuel 1724-1816 *AmRev, WhAmRev*
Hood, Samuel Harold 1926- *Who 94*
Hood, Sinclair *Who 94*
Hood, (Martin) Sinclair (Frankland) 1917- *Who 94*
Hood, Thomas 1799-1845 *BlmGEL*
Hood, Walter Kelly 1928- *WhoAmA 93*
Hood, William Boyd, Jr. 1932- *WhoAm 94*
Hood, William Clarence 1921- *IntWW 93, WhoAm 94*
Hood, William R. 1923- *WhoAmP 93*
Hood, William Wayne, Jr. 1941- *WhoAmL 94*
Hooe, John Robert, III 1952- *WhoAmP 93*
Hoof, Jef Van 1886-1959 *NewGrDO*
Hoofman, Cliff 1943- *WhoAmP 93*
Hoog, Patrick Edward 1954- *WhoAmL 94*
Hoog, Thomas William 1939- *WhoAmP 93*
Hoogenboom, Ari Arthur 1927- *WhoAm 94*
Hoogestraat, Jane *DrAPF 93*
Hoogland, Robert Frederics 1955- *WhoAmL 94*
Hooglandt, Jan Daniel 1926- *IntWW 93*
Hoogsteden, Aloysius Franciscus 1936- *WhoFI 94*
Hoogwerf, Byron James 1945- *WhoMW 93*
Hook, Charles Ruffin 1880-1963 *EncABHB 9 [port]*
Hook, Cornelius Henry 1929- *WhoFI 94*
Hook, David Morgan Alfred 1931- *Who 94*
Hook, Edward Watson, Jr. 1924- *WhoAm 94*
Hook, Frances A. 1912-1981 *WhoAmA 93N*
Hook, Harold Swanson 1931- *WhoAm 94, WhoFI 94, WhoIns 94*
Hook, James 1746-1827 *NewGrDO*
Hook, Jerry B. 1937- *WhoAm 94*
Hook, John Burney 1928- *WhoAm 94*
Hook, Julian Lee 1959- *WhoMW 93*
Hook, Mary Julia 1947- *WhoAm 94, WhoAmL 94*
Hook, Peter *NewYTBS 93 [port]*
Hook, Peter 1956- *See* New Order *ConMus 11*
Hook, Ralph Clifford, Jr. 1923- *WhoAm 94, WhoFI 94, WhoWest 94*
Hook, Ross Sydney 1917- *Who 94*
Hook, Sidney 1902-1989 *WhAm 10*
Hook, Vivian Yuan-Wen Ho 1953- *WhoScEn 94*
Hook, Walter 1919- *WhAm 10*
Hook, William Franklin 1935- *WhoMW 93*
Hookano, Thomas E. 1946- *WhoAm 94*
Hooke, Robert 1635-1703 *WorInv, WorScD*
Hooke, Roger LeBaron 1939- *WhoAm 94*
Hooker, Charlie 1953- *IntWW 93*
Hooker, Cheryl Mazzariello 1950- *WhoAmP 93*
Hooker, David Joseph 1950- *WhoAm 94, WhoAmL 94*
Hooker, Douglas Randolf 1954- *WhoBlA 94*
Hooker, Eric H. *WhoBlA 94*
Hooker, Hugh d1987 *WhoHol 92*
Hooker, James Todd 1946- *WhoMW 93*
Hooker, Jeremy 1941- *WrDr 94*
Hooker, John (Williamson) 1932- *WrDr 94*
Hooker, John Lee 1917- *WhoAm 94, WhoBlA 94*
Hooker, Joseph Dalton 1817-1911 *WhWE*
Hooker, Michael Ayerst 1923- *Who 94*
Hooker, Michael Kenneth 1945- *WhoAm 94*
Hooker, Morna Dorothy 1931- *Who 94, WrDr 94*
Hooker, Odessa Walker 1930- *WhoBlA 94*
Hooker, Richard 1553?-1600 *BlmGEL*
Hooker, Richard 1554-1600 *DcLB 132 [port]*
Hooker, Richard Alfred 1951- *WhoAm 94*
Hooker, Robert James 1942- *WhoAmL 94*
Hooker, Ronald George 1921- *Who 94*
Hooker, Son d1974 *WhoHol 92*
Hooker, Thomas 1586-1647 *DcAmReB 2*
Hooker, Van Dorn 1921- *WhoAm 94*
Hooker, Wade Stuart, Jr. 1941- *WhoAmL 94*
Hooker, William *DrAPF 93*
Hookham, Eleanor King *WhoAmA 93*
Hooks, Bell *BlkWr 2*
hooks, bell 1952- *ConBlB 5 [port]*
Hooks, Benjamin L. 1925- *AfrAmAl 6 [port]*
Hooks, Benjamin Lawson *WhoAmP 93*
Hooks, Benjamin Lawson 1925- *WhoAm 94, WhoBlA 94*

Hooks, Benjamin Lawson, Jr. 1925- AmSocL
Hooks, Charles Vernon 1930- WhoAmA 93
Hooks, David 1920- WhoHol 92
Hooks, Earl J. 1927- WhoAmA 93
Hooks, Frances Dancy 1927- WhoBlA 94
Hooks, George Bardin 1945- WhoAmP 93
Hooks, Geri 1935- WhoAmA 93
Hooks, Gregory M. 1953- ConAu 141
Hooks, James Byron, Jr. 1933- WhoBlA 94
Hooks, Jan 1957- WhoHol 92
Hooks, Kevin 1958- IntMPA 94, WhoHol 92
Hooks, Linda 1952- WhoHol 92
Hooks, Michael Anthony 1950- WhoBlA 94
Hooks, Mose Yvonne Brooks WhoBlA 94
Hooks, Robert 1937- IntMPA 94, WhoHol 92
Hooks, Robert Keith 1929- Who 94
Hooks, Tommy Louis 1936- WhoAmP 93
Hooks, William Henry 1953- WhoMW 93
Hookway, Harry (Thurston) 1921- Who 94
Hookway, Harry Thurston 1921- IntWW 93
Hool, Lance 1948- IntMPA 94
Hoolahan, Anthony Terence 1925- Who 94
Hoole, Alan Norman 1942- Who 94
Hoole, Arthur (Hugh) 1924- Who 94
Hoole, John George Aldick 1951- Who 94
Hoole, William Stanley 1903-1990 WhAm 10
Hooley, Christopher 1928- IntWW 93, Who 94
Hooley, Darlene 1939- WhoAmP 93
Hooley, Ernest Terah 1859-1947 DcNaB MP
Hooley, Frank Oswald 1923- Who 94
Hooley, James Robert 1932- WhoAm 94
Hooley, John Rouse 1927- Who 94
Hooley, Madeline d1977 WhoHol 92
Hooley, Robert Childs 1927- WhoAm 94
Hoon, Geoffrey William 1953- Who 94
Hoontrakul, Sommai 1918- IntWW 93
Hoop, Bernard 1939- WhoScEn 94
Hooper, Baroness 1939- Who 94, WhoWomW 91
Hooper, Anthony 1937- Who 94
Hooper, Anthony Sidney Colchester 1943- IntWW 93
Hooper, Arthur W., Jr. 1944- WhoAmL 94
Hooper, Arthur William 1919- WhoAm 94
Hooper, Ben Walter, II 1939- WhoAmP 93
Hooper, Biff 1952- WrDr 94
Hooper, Billy Ernest 1931- WhoAm 94
Hooper, Blake Howard 1922- WhoAm 94
Hooper, Carl Glenn 1936- WhoFI 94
Hooper, Catherine Evelyn 1939- WhoWest 94
Hooper, Charles German 1911- Who 94
Hooper, Chauncey M. 1894-1966 AfrAmG
Hooper, Chester Douglas 1941- WhoAmL 94
Hooper, David A. 1954- WhoFI 94
Hooper, David Lynn 1957- WhoAmL 94
Hooper, Don 1945- WhoAm 94, WhoAmP 93
Hooper, Edwin Bickford 1937- WhoWest 94
Hooper, Ewan 1935- WhoHol 92
Hooper, Gary Raymond 1946- WhoBlA 94
Hooper, Gerald F. 1923- WhoBlA 94
Hooper, Gerry Don 1941- WhoFI 94
Hooper, Henry Olcott 1935- WhoAm 94, WhoWest 94
Hooper, Ian 1941- WhoAm 94
Hooper, Jack Meredith 1928- WhoAmA 93
Hooper, James William 1937- WhoAm 94
Hooper, Jay Francis 1950- WhoFI 94
Hooper, Jere Mann 1933- WhoAm 94
Hooper, John Allen 1922- WhoAm 94
Hooper, John Edward 1926- WhoScEn 94
Hooper, John William 1926-1989 WhAm 10
Hooper, Judith 1949- WrDr 94
Hooper, Kay WrDr 94
Hooper, Leonard (James) 1914- Who 94
Hooper, Lucien Obed 1896- WhAm 10
Hooper, Maureen Brett 1927- SmATA 76 [port]
Hooper, Meredith Jean 1939- WrDr 94
Hooper, Michele J. 1951- WhoBlA 94
Hooper, Noel Barrie 1931- Who 94
Hooper, Patricia DrAPF 93
Hooper, Paul Franklin 1938- WhoWest 94
Hooper, Perry O., Jr. 1925- WhoAmP 93
Hooper, Peter 1919- WrDr 94N
Hooper, Richard 1939- Who 94
Hooper, Richard William 1953- WhoMW 93
Hooper, Robert Dale 1956- WhoMW 93
Hooper, Roy B., Jr. 1947- WhoAmP 93
Hooper, Susan Jeanne 1950- WhoMW 93
Hooper, Thomas Fredrick, III 1958- WhoAmP 93
Hooper, Tobe IntMPA 94
Hooper, Tobe 1943- HorFD [port]
Hooper, Virginia R. Fite 1917- WhoAmP 93
Hooper, Wayne Nelson 1944- WhoAm 94
Hooper, William 1742-1790 WhAmRev
Hoopes, David Craig 1942- WhoAmP 93
Hoopes, David S. 1928- ConAu 42NR
Hoopes, Isabella WhoHol 92
Hoopes, Janet Louise 1923- WhoAm 94
Hoopes, John Wilton 1958- WhoMW 93
Hoopes, Kathleen Ann 1957- WhoMW 93
Hoopes, Lorenzo Neville 1913- WhoAm 94
Hoopes, Lorna Elizabeth Slade 1957- WhoAmP 93
Hoopes, Sidney Lou 1944- WhoWest 94
Hoopes, Spencer Wendell 1947- WhoWest 94
Hoopes, Townsend Walter 1922- WhoAm 94
Hoopes, Walter Ronald 1933- WhoAm 94
Hoopis, Harry Peter 1947- WhoMW 93
Hoopman, Harold DeWaine 1920- IntWW 93
Hoops, Alan 1947- WhoAm 94, WhoFI 94, WhoWest 94
Hoops, Arthur d1916 WhoHol 92
Hoops, William D. 1942- WhoAmL 94
Hoops, William James 1957- WhoWest 94
Hoornstra, Edward H. 1921- WhoAm 94
Hoort, Steven Thomas 1949- WhoAm 94
Hoose, Fred d1952 WhoHol 92
Hoosier Hot Shots, The WhoHol 92
Hoosin, Janice 1942- WhoMW 93
Hooson, Baron 1925- Who 94
Hoot, William John 1916- WhoAm 94
Hooten, Peter WhoHol 92
Hooten, William Foster, Jr. 1926- WhoMW 93
Hootkin, Pamela Nan 1947- WhoAm 94
Hootkins, William WhoHol 92
Hootman, Harry Edward 1933- WhoScEn 94
Hootnick, Laurence R. 1942- WhoFI 94, WhoWest 94
Hooton, Bruce Duff 1928- WhoAmA 93
Hoover, Allan d1993 NewYTBS 93
Hoover, David A. 1939- WhoAmP 93
Hoover, David Carlson 1950- WhoAmL 94
Hoover, Donald Brunton 1930- WhoWest 94
Hoover, Donald Elwyn 1954- WhoMW 93
Hoover, Donald Leroy 1952- WhoFI 94
Hoover, Dwight Wesley 1926- WhoAm 94, WrDr 94
Hoover, Felix A. 1949- WhoBlA 94
Hoover, Francis Louis 1913- WhoAm 94, WhoAmA 93
Hoover, George Schweke 1935- WhoAm 94
Hoover, H. M. 1935- Au&Arts 11 [port]
Hoover, H(elen) M(ary) 1935- EncSF 93, TwCYAW, WrDr 94
Hoover, Herbert 1874-1964 HisWorL [port]
Hoover, Herbert William, Sr. 1928- WhoScEn 94
Hoover, Herbert William, Jr. 1918- IntWW 93, Who 94
Hoover, Howard S., Jr. WhoAm 94
Hoover, Jerri 1950- WhoAmP 93
Hoover, Jesse 1918- WhoBlA 94
Hoover, John Elwood 1924- WhoAm 94
Hoover, John Jay 1919- WhoAmA 93
Hoover, Kenneth H. 1896- WhAm 10
Hoover, Kenneth R(ay) 1940- WrDr 94
Hoover, Lola Mae 1947- WhoFI 94
Hoover, Lynn Colburn 1937- WhoMW 93
Hoover, Mae 1938- WhoAmP 93
Hoover, Marie Louise (Rochon) 1895-1976 WhoAmA 93N
Hoover, Mark Herbert 1947- WhoMW 93
Hoover, Paul DrAPF 93
Hoover, Paul 1946- ConAu 141
Hoover, Pearl Rollings 1924- WhoWest 94
Hoover, Phil WhoHol 92
Hoover, Richard WhoAm 94
Hoover, Robert Cleary 1928- WhoFI 94, WhoWest 94
Hoover, Roderick P., Jr. 1954- WhoIns 94
Hoover, Roland Armitage 1929- WhoAm 94
Hoover, Russell James 1940- WhoAm 94
Hoover, Susan DrAPF 93
Hoover, Theressa 1925- WhoBlA 94
Hoover, Thomas Warren 1932- WhoAmP 93
Hoover, Walter Boyd 1898-1989 WhAm 10
Hoover, William Henry WorInv
Hoover, William Leichliter 1944- WhoAm 94
Hoover, William Ray 1930- WhoAm 94, WhoFI 94, WhoWest 94
Hoover, William Walter 1932- WhoAmP 93
Hoovler, Michele Millison 1954- WhoFI 94
Hooykaas, Reijer 1906- IntWW 93
Hopcraft, Arthur 1932- WrDr 94
Hopcroft, George William 1927- Who 94
Hope Who 94
Hope, Rt. Hon. Lord 1938- IntWW 93, Who 94
Hope, A(lec) D(erwent) 1907- WrDr 94
Hope, Adrian Price Webley d1992 Who 94N
Hope, Akua Lezli DrAPF 93
Hope, Alan 1933- Who 94
Hope, Alec Derwent 1907- IntWW 93
Hope, Ammie Deloris 1946- WhoScEn 94
Hope, Anastasia Louise 1954- WhoFI 94
Hope, Bob 1903- ConAu 43NR, IntMPA 94, IntWW 93, Who 94, WhoAm 94, WhoCom [port], WhoHol 92, WrDr 94
Hope, Christopher 1944- Who 94
Hope, Christopher (David Tully) 1944- WrDr 94
Hope, Clarence Caldwell, Jr. d1993 NewYTBS 93
Hope, Colin Frederick Newton 1932- Who 94
Hope, David Who 94
Hope, David Michael Who 94
Hope, David Michael 1940- IntWW 93
Hope, Diana d1942 WhoHol 92
Hope, Douglas Olerich 1934- WhoAm 94
Hope, Evelyn d1966 WhoHol 92
Hope, Frank Lewis, Jr. 1930- WhoAm 94
Hope, Garland Howard 1911- WhoAm 94
Hope, Gary WhoHol 92
Hope, George Marion 1938- WhoScEn 94
Hope, Gerri Danette 1956- WhoWest 94
Hope, Gloria d1976 WhoHol 92
Hope, Harry 1926- IntMPA 94
Hope, Henry Radford 1905-1989 WhAm 10
Hope, James Arthur David Who 94
Hope, James Dennis, Sr. 1948- WhoScEn 94
Hope, James Franklin 1917- WhoFI 94
Hope, Jim d1975 WhoHol 92
Hope, John (Carl Alexander) 1939- Who 94
Hope, Judith H. 1939- WhoAmP 93
Hope, Judith Richards 1940- WhoAm 94
Hope, Julius Caesar 1932- WhoBlA 94
Hope, Laura Lee EncSF 93
Hope, Laura Lee 1949- WrDr 94
Hope, Laurence Frank 1918- Who 94
Hope, Lawrence Latimer 1939- WhoAm 94
Hope, Leslie WhoHol 92
Hope, Maidie d1937 WhoHol 92
Hope, Marcus Laurence Hulbert 1942- Who 94
Hope, Margaret WrDr 94
Hope, Marie H. 1927- WhoBlA 94
Hope, Marjorie (Cecelia) 1923- WrDr 94
Hope, Maurice 1951- IntWW 93
Hope, Michael S. 1942- WhoAm 94
Hope, Peter Who 94
Hope, (Charles) Peter 1912- Who 94
Hope, Richard WhoHol 92
Hope, Richard Oliver 1939- WhoBlA 94
Hope, Robert Holms-Kerr d1993 Who 94N
Hope, Ronald 1921- WrDr 94
Hope, Ronald Arthur 1956- WhoAmL 94
Hope, Samuel Howard 1946- WhoAm 94
Hope, Stephen D. 1947- WhoAmL 94
Hope, Thomas Walker 1920- WhoAm 94
Hope, Vida d1962 WhoHol 92
Hope, Warren T. 1944- WhoIns 94
Hope, William WhoHol 92
Hope, William Duane 1935- WhoAm 94
Hope-Dunbar, David 1941- Who 94
Hope Johnstone Who 94
Hope-Jones, Ronald Christopher 1920- Who 94
Hope-Morley Who 94
Hopen, Herbert John 1934- WhoAm 94, WhoScEn 94
Hopes, David Brendan DrAPF 93
Hope-Simpson, Jacynth (Ann) 1930- WrDr 94
Hopetoun, Earl of 1969- Who 94
Hope-Wallace, (Dorothy) Jaqueline 1909- Who 94
Hopewell, John Prince 1920- Who 94
Hopewell, Luz Araoz WhoHisp 94
Hopf, Hans d1993 NewYTBS 93
Hopf, Hans 1916- NewGrDO
Hopf, James F. 1961- WhoAmL 94
Hopfenbeck, George Martin, Jr. 1929- WhoAm 94
Hopfield, Jessica F. 1964- WhoScEn 94
Hopfield, John Joseph 1933- WhoAm 94, WhoScEn 94, WhoWest 94
Hopgood, Alan WhoHol 92
Hopgood, James F. 1943- WhoAm 94
Ho Ping WhoPRCh 91
Hopken, Arvid Niclas, Friherr von 1710-1778 NewGrDO
Hopkin, Bryan Who 94
Hopkin, (William Aylsham) Bryan 1914- Who 94
Hopkin, David (Armand) 1922- Who 94
Hopkin, John Raymond 1935- Who 94
Hopkins, Alan Cripps Nind 1926- Who 94
Hopkins, Albert E., Sr. 1928- WhoBlA 94
Hopkins, Andrew Jay 1964- WhoWest 94
Hopkins, Anthony 1937- IntMPA 94, IntWW 93, WhoHol 92
Hopkins, Anthony (Philip) 1937- Who 94
Hopkins, Anthony Philip 1937- Who 94, WhoAm 94
Hopkins, Anthony Strother 1940- Who 94
Hopkins, Antony 1921- IntWW 93, NewGrDO, Who 94, WrDr 94
Hopkins, B(ernice Elizabeth) 1926- WhoAmA 93
Hopkins, Barry L. 1943- WhoBlA 94
Hopkins, Ben d1941 WhoHol 92
Hopkins, Bert Earl 1902-1989 WhAm 10
Hopkins, Bo 1942- IntMPA 94, WhoHol 92
Hopkins, Bob d1962 WhoHol 92
Hopkins, Bruce Richard 1941- WhoAmL 94
Hopkins, Budd 1931- WhoAm 94, WhoAmA 93
Hopkins, Carl Edward 1912- WhoAm 94
Hopkins, Cecilia Ann 1922- WhoWest 94
Hopkins, Charles Peter, II 1953- WhoAm 94, WhoAmL 94, WhoFI 94
Hopkins, Charmaine L. 1946- WhoBlA 94
Hopkins, David Rex Eugene 1930- Who 94
Hopkins, Dianne McAfee 1944- WhoBlA 94
Hopkins, Donald J. 1947- WhoAm 94, WhoAmL 94
Hopkins, Donald Ray 1936- WhoAmL 94, WhoBlA 94
Hopkins, Donald Roswell 1941- WhoAm 94
Hopkins, Douglas Charles 1950- WhoScEn 94
Hopkins, Douglas Edward d1992 Who 94N
Hopkins, Edna J. 1924- WhoBlA 94
Hopkins, Edward Curtis 1922- WhoAmP 93
Hopkins, Edward Donald 1937- WhoAm 94
Hopkins, Edwina Weiskittel 1947- WhoWest 94
Hopkins, Elizabeth Ann 1941- Who 94
Hopkins, Emma Curtis 1853-1925 DcAmReB 2
Hopkins, Ernest Loyd 1930- WhoBlA 94
Hopkins, Esek 1718-1801 AmRev
Hopkins, Esek 1718-1802 WhAmRev
Hopkins, Esther Arvilla 1926- WhoBlA 94
Hopkins, Everett Harold 1912- WhoAm 94
Hopkins, Frederick Gowland 1861-1947 WorScD [port]
Hopkins, Gayle P. 1941- WhoBlA 94
Hopkins, George 1958- WhoAmP 93
Hopkins, George Emil 1937- WrDr 94
Hopkins, George Mathews Marks 1923- WhoAm 94, WhoAmL 94
Hopkins, Gerald Frank 1943- WhoFI 94
Hopkins, Gerard Manley 1844-1889 BlmGEL, DcNaB MP
Hopkins, Glen Eugene, Jr. 1949- WhoAmP 93
Hopkins, Godfrey Thurston 1913- IntWW 93
Hopkins, Grover Prevatte 1933- WhoAm 94, WhoAmP 93
Hopkins, Harold WhoHol 92
Hopkins, Harold Horace 1918- IntWW 93, Who 94
Hopkins, Harrison DrAPF 93
Hopkins, Harry 1913- WrDr 94
Hopkins, Henry Tyler 1928- WhoAmA 93, WhoWest 94
Hopkins, Jack Walker 1930- WhoAm 94, WhoAmP 93, WhoMW 93
Hopkins, Jacques Vaughn 1930- WhoAm 94
Hopkins, James EncSF 93
Hopkins, James Clarence 1930- WhoFI 94
Hopkins, James S. R. S. Who 94
Hopkins, Jasper 1936- WrDr 94
Hopkins, Jeannette E. 1922- WhoAm 94
Hopkins, Joan WhoHol 92
Hopkins, John d1570 See Sternhold, Thomas d1549 DcLB 132
Hopkins, John 1931- Who 94
Hopkins, John (Richard) 1931- ConDr 93, WrDr 94
Hopkins, John Abel, Jr. 1897- WhAm 10

Hopkins, John Burroughs 1742-1796 *AmRev, WhAmRev*
Hopkins, John David 1933- *WhoBlA 94*
Hopkins, John David 1938- *WhoAm 94, WhoAmL 94*
Hopkins, John Orville 1930- *WhoBlA 94*
Hopkins, John S., III 1943- *WhoAm 94*
Hopkins, Judith Owen 1952- *WhoAm 94*
Hopkins, Julian *Who 94*
Hopkins, (Richard) Julian 1940- *Who 94*
Hopkins, Kaitlin *NewYTBS 93 [port]*
Hopkins, Keith *Who 94*
Hopkins, Keith 1934- *WrDr 94*
Hopkins, (Morris) Keith 1934- *Who 94*
Hopkins, Kendal Coles 1908-1991 *WhoAmA 93N*
Hopkins, Kenneth R. 1922- *WhoAmA 93*
Hopkins, Kevin L. 1959- *WhoAmL 94*
Hopkins, Kevin R. 1954- *WhoAmP 93*
Hopkins, Larry Jones 1933- *WhoAmP 93*
Hopkins, Lee Bennett 1938- *WhoAm 94, WrDr 94*
Hopkins, Leroy Taft, Jr. 1942- *WhoBlA 94*
Hopkins, Linda 1925- *WhoHol 92*
Hopkins, Lyman 1907- *WrDr 94*
Hopkins, Mark 1802-1887 *DcAmReB 2*
Hopkins, Mark Lee 1939- *WhoAm 94*
Hopkins, Mark Willard 1958- *WhoScEn 94*
Hopkins, Michael John 1935- *IntWW 93, Who 94*
Hopkins, Miriam d1972 *WhoHol 92*
Hopkins, Muriel-Beth Norbrey 1951- *WhoAmL 94*
Hopkins, Myrtle B. 1933- *WhoAmP 93*
Hopkins, Paul Jeffrey 1940- *WhoAm 94*
Hopkins, Paul Nathan 1952- *WhoWest 94*
Hopkins, Pauline Elizabeth 1859-1930 *BlkWr 2, ConAu 141*
Hopkins, Perea M. 1931- *WhoBlA 94*
Hopkins, Peter 1911- *WhoAmA 93*
Hopkins, Philip Joseph 1954- *WhoWest 94*
Hopkins, R. Howard 1939- *WhoIns 94*
Hopkins, Raymond Frederick 1939- *WhoAm 94*
Hopkins, Robert Arthur 1920- *WhoScEn 94, WhoWest 94*
Hopkins, Robert E. 1929- *WhoAmP 93*
Hopkins, Robert Elliott 1931- *WhoMW 93*
Hopkins, Ronald Herbert 1941- *WhoWest 94*
Hopkins, Roy *WhoAmP 93*
Hopkins, Russell 1932- *Who 94*
Hopkins, Sam d1982 *WhoHol 92*
Hopkins, Samuel 1721-1803 *DcAmReB 2*
Hopkins, Samuel 1753-1819 *WhAmRev*
Hopkins, Samuel 1913- *WhoAm 94*
Hopkins, Sarah Winnemucca c. 1844-1891 *BlmGWL*
Hopkins, Shirley Knight *WhoHol 92*
Hopkins, Sidney Arthur 1932- *Who 94*
Hopkins, Speed Elliott 1948- *WhoAm 94*
Hopkins, Stephen 1707-1785 *WhAmRev*
Hopkins, Stephen Davis 1907- *WhoWest 94*
Hopkins, Telma 1948- *WhoBlA 94, WhoHol 92*
Hopkins, Terri 1949- *WhoAmA 93*
Hopkins, Theodore J. 1940- *WhoAmL 94*
Hopkins, Thomas David 1939- *WhoWest 94*
Hopkins, Thomas Duvall 1942- *WhoAm 94, WhoScEn 94*
Hopkins, Thomas Franklin *WhoBlA 94*
Hopkins, Thomas Gene 1932- *WhoAm 94, WhoFI 94*
Hopkins, Thomas Matthews 1927- *WhoAm 94*
Hopkins, Thomas Moore 1952- *WhoFI 94*
Hopkins, Vashti Edythe Johnson 1924- *WhoBlA 94*
Hopkins, Wes 1961- *WhoBlA 94*
Hopkins, William A. 1943- *WhoBlA 94*
Hopkins, William Benjamin, Sr. 1922- *WhoAmP 93*
Hopkinson *Who 94*
Hopkinson, Albert Cyril 1911- *Who 94*
Hopkinson, Barnabas John 1939- *Who 94*
Hopkinson, Charles 1869-1962 *WhoAmA 93N*
Hopkinson, David Albert 1935- *Who 94*
Hopkinson, David Hugh 1930- *Who 94*
Hopkinson, David Hugh Laing 1926- *Who 94*
Hopkinson, Deborah 1952- *SmATA 76 [port]*
Hopkinson, Francis 1737-1791 *WhAmRev*
Hopkinson, Giles 1931- *Who 94*
Hopkinson, Harold I. 1918- *WhoAmA 93*
Hopkinson, John Charles Oswald Rooke 1931- *Who 94*
Hopkinson, John Edmund 1924- *Who 94*
Hopkinson, Ralph Galbraith 1913- *Who 94*
Hopkinson, Shirley Lois 1924- *WhoWest 94*
Hopkirk, Joyce *Who 94*
Hopman, Harry 1906-1985 *BuCMET*
Hopmann, David E. 1943- *WhoAmL 94*
Hopmann, Philip Terrence 1942- *WhoAm 94*
Hopmeier, Michael Jonathon 1965- *WhoScEn 94*
Hopp, Anthony J. 1945- *WhoAm 94*
Hopp, Daniel Frederick 1947- *WhoAm 94, WhoAmL 94, WhoFI 94*
Hopp, Donald L. 1945- *WhoAmP 93*
Hopp, Julius 1819-1885 *NewGrDO*
Hopp, Nancy Smith 1943- *WhoMW 93*
Hopp, Richard A. 1946- *WhoAmL 94*
Hopp, Steven J. 1948- *WhoAmL 94*
Hoppe, Arthur (Watterson) 1925- *WrDr 94*
Hoppe, Arthur Watterson 1925- *WhoAm 94*
Hoppe, Charles W. 1935- *WhoAm 94*
Hoppe, Emil Otto 1878-1972 *DcNaB MP*
Hoppe, Marianne 1911- *WhoHol 92*
Hoppe, Matthias 1952- *SmATA 76 [port]*
Hoppe, Peter Christian 1942- *WhoAm 94*
Hoppe, Richard A. 1944- *WhoAmL 94*
Hoppe, Rudolf Reinhold Otto 1922- *WhoScEn 94*
Hoppe, Thomas J. 1957- *WhoAmP 93*
Hoppe, Wolfgang 1933- *WhoAm 94*
Hoppel, Jimmy Jack 1884-1969 *EncNAR*
Hoppel, Robert Gerald, Jr. 1921- *WhoAmL 94*
Hoppel, Thomas O'Marah 1937- *WhoScEn 94*
Hoppensteadt, Frank Charles 1938- *WhoAm 94, WhoScEn 94*
Hoppensteadt, Jon Kirk 1959- *WhoWest 94*
Hopper, Arthur Frederick 1917- *WhoScEn 94*
Hopper, Cecil Harold *WhoAm 94*
Hopper, Cornelius Lenard 1934- *WhoBlA 94*
Hopper, David Henry 1927- *WhoAm 94*
Hopper, David Lee 1953- *WhoWest 94*
Hopper, De Wolf d1935 *WhoHol 92*
Hopper, Dennis 1936- *IntMPA 94, IntWW 93, WhoAm 94, WhoHol 92*
Hopper, Edward 1882-1967 *AmCulL, WhoAmA 93N*
Hopper, Frank d1941 *WhoHol 92*
Hopper, Frank J. 1924- *WhoAmA 93*
Hopper, Frederick Ernest 1919- *Who 94*
Hopper, Grace 1906-1992 *AnObit 1992*
Hopper, Grace M. 1906-1992 *WhAm 10*
Hopper, Grace Murray 1906-1992 *WorInv*
Hopper, Hal d1970 *WhoHol 92*
Hopper, Hedda d1966 *WhoHol 92*
Hopper, Jack Rudd 1937- *WhoScEn 94*
Hopper, John D. 1923- *WhoAmP 93*
Hopper, John Dowl, Jr. 1946- *WhoBlA 94*
Hopper, Jon d1968 *WhoAmA 93N*
Hopper, Kevin Andrew 1962- *WhoScEn 94*
Hopper, Lloyd Wade 1956- *WhoAmL 94*
Hopper, Marianne Seward 1904- *WhoAmA 93N*
Hopper, Michelle Marie 1956- *WhoMW 93*
Hopper, Nancy Jane 1937- *WhoMW 93*
Hopper, Robert William 1945- *WhoAm 94*
Hopper, Sally *WhoWest 94*
Hopper, Sally H. 1934- *WhoAmP 93*
Hopper, Stephen Rodger 1949- *WhoAm 94*
Hopper, Taylor Lincoln 1933- *WhoAmP 93*
Hopper, Thomas A., Jr. 1959- *WhoAmP 93*
Hopper, Victoria 1909- *WhoHol 92*
Hopper, Walter Everett 1915- *WhoAm 94, WhoAmL 94, WhoFI 94*
Hopper, Wilbert Hill 1933- *WhoAm 94, WhoFI 94, WhoWest 94*
Hopper, Wilbert Hill (Bill) 1933- *IntWW 93*
Hopper, William d1970 *WhoHol 92*
Hopper, William Joseph 1929- *Who 94*
Hopper Inc *WhoAmA 93*
Hoppert, Gloria Jean 1949- *WhoMW 93, WhoScEn 94*
Hoppes, Alice Faye 1939- *WhoBlA 94*
Hoppes, Gary Jon 1946- *WhoMW 93*
Hoppes, Harrison Neil 1935- *WhoScEn 94*
Hoppes, Lowell E. 1913- *WhoAmA 93*
Hoppe-Selyer, Ernst Felix 1825-1895 *WorScD*
Hopping, Louis Melbert 1900-1987 *WhAm 10*
Hopping, Richard Lee 1928- *WhoAm 94*
Hopping, Wade Lee 1931- *WhoAmL 94*
Hopping, William Russell 1947- *WhoFI 94, WhoWest 94*
Hopple, Richard Van Tromp, Jr. 1947- *WhoAm 94*
Hoppmeyer, Calvin Carl, Jr. 1960- *WhoScEn 94*
Hoppock, Robert 1901- *WrDr 94*
Hopps, Raymond, Jr. 1949- *WhoFI 94*
Hopps, Sidney Bryce 1934- *WhoAm 94*
Hopson, Dennis 1965- *WhoBlA 94*
Hopson, Edwin Sharp 1945- *WhoAmL 94*
Hopson, Everett George 1922- *WhoAmL 94*
Hopson, Harold Theodore, II 1937- *WhoBlA 94*
Hopson, James Warren 1946- *WhoAm 94*
Hopson, Janet Louise 1950- *WhoScEn 94*
Hopson, Joyce Sue 1950- *WhoAmP 93*
Hopson, Kevin Mathew 1959- *WhoScEn 94*
Hopson, Melvin Clarence 1937- *WhoBlA 94*
Hopson, R. Keith 1950- *WhoAmL 94*
Hopson, Robert Melburn 1942- *WhoAmL 94*
Hopson, Violet *WhoHol 92*
Hopstetter, Robert Arthur 1962- *WhoFI 94*
Hopthrow, Harry Ewart d1992 *Who 94N*
Hoptner, Richard 1921- *WhoAmA 93*
Hopton, Russell d1945 *WhoHol 92*
Hopton, Walter de c. 1235-1296 *DcNaB MP*
Hopwood, Anthony George 1944- *Who 94*
Hopwood, David Alan 1933- *IntWW 93, Who 94, WhoScEn 94*
Hopwood, Howard H. 1945- *WhoAmL 94*
Hopwood, John L. 1942- *WhoAmL 94*
Hoque, Enamul 1951- *WhoAsA 94*
Horace 65BC-8BC *BlmGEL*
Horacek, Joseph, III 1941- *WhoAmL 94*
Horack, Thomas Borland 1946- *WhoAm 94*
Horad, Sewell D., Sr. 1922- *WhoBlA 94*
Horadam, Alwyn Francis 1923- *WrDr 94*
Horahan, Edward Bernard, III 1951- *WhoAm 94*
Horak, Gerry 1949- *WhoAmP 93*
Horak, Jan-Christopher 1951- *WhoAm 94*
Horak, Jiri 1924- *IntWW 93*
Horakova, Zdenka Zahutova 1925- *WhoAm 94*
Horam, John Rhodes 1939- *Who 94*
Horan, Forbes Trevor 1905- *Who 94*
Horan, Harold Eugene 1927- *WhoAm 94*
Horan, Hume Alexander 1934- *WhoAm 94*
Horan, James d1967 *WhoHol 92*
Horan, John J. 1920- *WhoAm 94*
Horan, John Patrick 1952- *WhoAm 94*
Horan, Justin Thomas 1927- *WhoAm 94*
Horan, Leo Gallaspy 1925- *WhoAm 94*
Horan, Mary Ann Theresa 1936- *WhoWest 94*
Horan, Michael Francis 1942- *WhoAmP 93*
Horan, R. Kevin 1950- *WhoAmP 93*
Horan, R. Thomas 1948- *WhoMW 93*
Horan, Robert 1928- *WhoAm 94*
Horan, Stephen Francis 1933- *WhoWest 94*
Horan, William F., Jr. *WhoAmP 93*
Horat, Heinz 1948- *ConAu 141*
Horbaczewski, Henry Zygmunt 1950- *WhoAmL 94*
Horbal, Koryne Emily 1937- *WhoAmP 93*
Horbaly, Robert S. 1945- *WhoAmL 94*
Horbatuck, Suzanne Marie 1964- *WhoScEn 94*
Horbowski, Mieczyslaw Apolinary 1849-1937 *NewGrDO*
Horch, Louis L. 1889-1979 *WhoAmA 93N*
Horcher, Albert 1959- *WhoFI 94*
Horcher, Paul V. *WhoAmP 93*
Horchow, Samuel Roger 1928- *WhoAm 94*
Hord, Brian Howard 1934- *Who 94*
Hord, Donal 1902-1966 *WhoAmA 93N*
Hord, Frederick (Lee) 1941- *BlkWr 2*
Hord, Frederick Lee 1941- *WhoBlA 94*
Hord, Noel Edward 1946- *WhoBlA 94*
Horde, Gaither Wilson 1926- *WhoAmP 93*
Hordell, Michael A. 1948- *WhoAmL 94*
Hordeman, Agnes Marie 1929- *WhoFI 94*
Horden, John 1828-1893 *EncNAR*
Horden, John Robert Backhouse *Who 94*
Horder, Baron 1910- *Who 94*
Horder, John Plaistowe 1919- *Who 94*
Horder, Mervyn 1910- *WrDr 94*
Horder, Richard A. 1946- *WhoAmL 94*
Hordern, (Alfred) Christopher (Willoughby) *Who 94*
Hordern, Michael 1911- *IntMPA 94, WhoHol 92*
Hordern, Michael (Murray) 1911- *Who 94*
Hordern, Michael Murray 1911- *IntWW 93*
Hordern, Peter (Maudslay) 1929- *Who 94*
Hore, John Edward 1929- *WhoAm 94, WhoFI 94*
Hore, Marlene Carole 1944- *WhoAm 94*
Horecker, Bernard L. 1914- *IntWW 93*
Horecker, Bernard Leonard 1914- *WhoAm 94*
Horecky, Paul L. 1913- *WrDr 94*
Horel, Martha Travis 1955- *WhoAmP 93*
Horen, Jeffrey Harry 1949- *WhoMW 93*
Horenstein, Cynthia Ann 1961- *WhoAmL 94*
Horenstein, Jascha 1898-1973 *NewGrDO*
Hore-Ruthven *Who 94*
Horgan, Betty d1956 *WhoHol 92*
Horgan, Cornelius Oliver 1944- *WhoAm 94*
Horgan, Dean K. 1944- *WhoAmP 93*
Horgan, John Joseph 1921- *WhoAmL 94*
Horgan, Patrick *WhoHol 92*
Horgan, Paul *DrAPF 93*
Horgan, Paul 1903- *IntWW 93, WhoAm 94, WrDr 94*
Horgan, Peter James 1949- *WhoScEn 94*
Horgan, Thomas R. 1953- *WhoAmP 93*
Horger, Edgar Olin, III 1937- *WhoAm 94*
Horgos, Robert P. *WhoAmP 93*
Horhn, John *WhoAmP 93*
Hori, Kosuke *IntWW 93*
Hori, Margaret Ann 1951- *WhoMW 93*
Hori, Tom Nichi 1940- *WhoAsA 94*
Hori, Yukio 1927- *WhoScEn 94*
Hori, Yutorio Claude 1945- *WhoAsA 94*
Horikoshi, Teizo 1898- *IntWW 93*
Horisberger, Don Hans 1951- *WhoMW 93*
Horita, Karen Keiko 1952- *WhoAmP 93*
Horiuchi, Atsushi 1929- *WhoAm 94, WhoScEn 94*
Horiuchi, Chikamasa Paul 1906- *WhoAsA 94*
Horiuchi, Gen 1964- *WhoAm 94*
Horiuchi, Glenn *WhoAsA 94*
Horiuchi, Paul 1906- *WhoAsA 94*
Horiuchi, Paul C. 1906- *WhoAmA 93*
Horiuchi, Randy 1954- *WhoAmP 93*
Horiuchi, Toshio 1918- *IntWW 93*
Horkey, Frank James 1955- *WhoFI 94*
Horkey, William Richard 1925- *WhoAm 94*
Horkowitz, Sylvester Peter 1921- *WhoScEn 94*
Horky, Karel 1909-1988 *NewGrDO*
Horky, Reginald Patrick 1952- *WhoFI 94, WhoMW 93*
Horlak, E.E. *EncSF 93*
Horlander, Nelle P. 1929- *WhoAmP 93*
Horler, Sydney 1888-1954 *EncSF 93*
Horlick, Edwin John 1925- *Who 94*
Horlick, Gary Norman 1947- *WhoAm 94, WhoAmL 94*
Horlick, John (James Macdonald) 1922- *Who 94*
Horlick, Ted *Who 94*
Horlock, Henry Wimburn Sudell 1915- *Who 94*
Horlock, John Harold 1928- *IntWW 93, Who 94, WrDr 94*
Horman, Edmund C. d1993 *NewYTBS 93 [port]*
Hormats, Robert David 1943- *WhoAm 94, WhoAmP 93*
Hormozi, Farrokh Zad 1937- *WhoFI 94*
Hormuth, Jo 1955- *WhoAmA 93*
Horn, Alan 1943- *IntMPA 94*
Horn, Alan Bowes d1992 *Who 94N*
Horn, Andrew Warren 1946- *WhoAmL 94*
Horn, Bruce 1946- *WhoAmA 93*
Horn, Camilla 1906- *WhoHol 92*
Horn, Charles Edward 1786-1849 *NewGrDO*
Horn, Charles Frederick 1924- *WhoAmP 93*
Horn, Charles G. 1939- *WhoAm 94, WhoFI 94*
Horn, Charles M. 1951- *WhoAm 94*
Horn, Christian Friedrich 1927- *WhoAm 94, WhoFI 94*
Horn, David C. 1952- *WhoAmL 94*
Horn, David D. 1941- *WhoIns 94*
Horn, David Dinsmore 1941- *WhoAm 94*
Horn, Deborah Sue 1954- *WhoAm 94*
Horn, Donald H. 1945- *WhoAmP 93*
Horn, Donald Paul 1955- *WhoMW 93*
Horn, Donna Kay 1951- *WhoMW 93*
Horn, Ellen M. 1965- *WhoAmL 94*
Horn, Ernst 1774-1848 *EncSPD*
Horn, Everett Byron, Jr. 1927- *WhoAmL 94, WhoIns 94*
Horn, Francis H. 1908- *IntWW 93*
Horn, Francis Henry 1908- *WhoAm 94*
Horn, Gabriel 1927- *IntWW 93, Who 94*
Horn, Gayle Patricia 1943- *WhoMW 93*
Horn, Gilbert *WhoWest 94*
Horn, Gyula 1932- *IntWW 93*
Horn, Heinz *Who 94*
Horn, Heinz 1930- *IntWW 93*
Horn, Hoye 1934- *WhoAmP 93*
Horn, James H. 1919- *WhoIns 94*
Horn, James Nathan 1941- *WhoAmP 93*
Horn, Janet 1950- *WhoScEn 94*
Horn, Jennie A. 1945- *WhoAsA 94*
Horn, Jennifer Ruth 1965- *WhoMW 93*

Horsley, (Beresford) Peter (Torrington) 1921- *Who 94*
Horsley, Richard D. 1942- *WhoAm 94*
Horsley, Stephen Daril 1947- *Who 94*
Horsley, Teri Lynne 1961- *WhoMW 93*
Horsley, Waller Holladay 1931- *WhoAm 94, WhoAmL 94*
Horsley, William Freeman 1939- *WhoAmL 94*
Horsma, David August 1940- *WhoWest 94*
Horsman, David A. Elliott 1932- *WhoAm 94, WhoFI 94*
Horsman, Dorothea (Jean) 1918- *Who 94*
Horsman, Greg 1963- *IntDcB [port]*
Horsman, James Deverell 1935- *WhoWest 94*
Horsman, Malcolm 1933- *Who 94*
Horsman, Michael John 1949- *Who 94*
Horsman, Reginald 1931- *WhoAm 94, WhoMW 93, WrDr 94*
Horsnell, Horace 1882-1949 *EncSF 93*
Horst, Bruce Everett 1921- *WhoAm 94, WhoMW 93*
Horst, Nancy Carroll 1933- *WhoMW 93*
Horstadius, Sven (Otto) 1898- *IntWW 93*
Horstman, Andrew W. 1951- *WhoAmL 94*
Horstman, Carol Bellhouse 1953- *WhoWest 94*
Horstman, Herman Gerhard 1898- *WhAm 10*
Horstmann, Dorothy Millicent 1911- *WhoAm 94*
Horstmann, James Douglas 1933- *WhoAm 94*
Horstmeyer, John A. *WhoFI 94*
Horszowski, Mieczyslaw 1892-1993 *NewYTBS 93 [port]*
Hort, James Fenton 1926- *Who 94*
Horta, Maria Teresa 1937- *BlmGWL*
Horten, Carl Frank 1914- *WhoAm 94*
Hortensia fl. 1st cent.BC- *BlmGWL*
Hortmanowicz, Zygmunt 1938- *IntWW 93*
Horton, Alexander Romeo 1923- *IntWW 93*
Horton, Azariah c. 1715-1777 *EncNAR*
Horton, Barbara *DrAPF 93*
Horton, Bernard Francis 1916- *WhoAm 94*
Horton, Bruce M. 1934- *WhoIns 94*
Horton, Carl E., Sr. 1944- *WhoBlA 94*
Horton, Carrell Peterson 1928- *WhoBlA 94*
Horton, Clara d1976 *WhoHol 92*
Horton, Clarence Pennington 1910- *WhoBlA 94*
Horton, Claude Wendell 1915- *WhoAm 94*
Horton, Clay 1957- *WhoAmP 93*
Horton, Dana Earl 1956- *WhoMW 93*
Horton, Dollie Bea Dixon 1942- *WhoBlA 94*
Horton, Donna Alberg 1935- *WhoScEn 94*
Horton, Earle C. 1943- *WhoBlA 94*
Horton, Edward Everett d1970 *WhoHol 92*
Horton, Elliott Argue, Jr. 1926- *WhoAm 94*
Horton, Eric William 1929- *Who 94*
Horton, Ethan Shane 1962- *WhoAm 94, WhoWest 94*
Horton, Finis Gene 1953- *WhoFI 94*
Horton, Frank 1919- *WhoAm 94, WhoAmL 94, WhoAmP 93*
Horton, Frank E 1939- *WrDr 94*
Horton, Frank Elba 1939- *IntWW 93, WhoAm 94, WhoMW 93*
Horton, Gary Bruce 1943- *WhoAm 94, WhoFI 94*
Horton, Gary William 1940- *WhoAmP 93*
Horton, George Moses 1797-1883? *AfrAmAl 6*
Horton, Gerald Talmadge 1934- *WhoAm 94*
Horton, Gloria Dee 1961- *WhoFI 94*
Horton, Gordon T. *EncSF 93*
Horton, Granville Eugene 1927- *WhoScEn 94*
Horton, Helen *WhoHol 92*
Horton, Herschella *WhoAmP 93*
Horton, Horace Robert 1935- *WhoAm 94*
Horton, Jack 1955- *WhoAmP 93*
Horton, Jack King 1916- *IntWW 93, WhoWest 94*
Horton, Jacklyn M. *WhoAmL 94*
Horton, James Robert 1928- *WhoAmL 94*
Horton, James T. 1918-1986 *WhoBlA 94N*
Horton, James Wright 1919- *WhoAm 94, WhoAmL 94*
Horton, Janice S. 1945- *WhoAmP 93*
Horton, Jared C. 1924- *WhoAm 94*
Horton, Jeffrey Roland 1958- *WhoMW 93*
Horton, Jerry Lee 1944- *WhoAmP 93*
Horton, Joanne Barbara 1932- *WhoHol 92*
Horton, John Alden 1920- *WhoAm 94*
Horton, John Edward 1930- *WhoAm 94*
Horton, John Tod 1928- *WhoAm 94*
Horton, Johnny d1960 *WhoHol 92*
Horton, Larkin, Jr. 1939- *WhoBlA 94*
Horton, Larnie G. *WhoBlA 94*
Horton, Larry Bruce 1942- *WhoAmL 94, WhoFI 94*
Horton, Lawrence Stanley 1926- *WhoWest 94*
Horton, Lemuel Leonard 1936- *WhoBlA 94*
Horton, Leonard Mead 1906-1989 *WhAm 10*
Horton, Leslie James 1912- *WhoFI 94, WhoMW 93*
Horton, Louisa 1924- *WhoHol 92*
Horton, Louise *DrAPF 93*
Horton, Lynn C. *WhoAmP 93*
Horton, Madeline Mary 1939- *WhoFI 94*
Horton, Madelyn (Stacey) 1962- *SmATA 77*
Horton, Marguerite Letitia 1917- *WhoWest 94*
Horton, Matthew Bethell 1946- *Who 94*
Horton, Michael L. 1961- *WhoFI 94, WhoWest 94*
Horton, Michael Scott 1964- *WrDr 94*
Horton, Myles 1905-1990 *ConAu 140*
Horton, Odell 1929- *WhoAm 94, WhoAmL 94, WhoBlA 94*
Horton, Paul B 1916- *WrDr 94*
Horton, Paul Bradfield 1920- *WhoAm 94, WhoAmL 94, WhoFI 94*
Horton, Peter *IntMPA 94*
Horton, Peter 1953- *WhoHol 92*
Horton, Raymond Anthony 1960- *WhoBlA 94*
Horton, Robert 1870- *WhoHol 92*
Horton, Robert 1924- *IntMPA 94, WhoHol 92*
Horton, Robert Baynes 1939- *IntWW 93, Who 94, WhoAm 94*
Horton, Robert Carlton 1926- *WhoAm 94, WhoAmP 93*
Horton, Russell *WhoHol 92*
Horton, Sherman D. *WhoAm 94, WhoAmP 93*
Horton, Sherman D., Jr. 1931- *WhoAmL 94*
Horton, Stella Jean 1944- *WhoBlA 94*
Horton, Susanne Pamela 1957- *WhoWest 94*
Horton, Thomas Edward, Jr. 1935- *WhoAm 94*
Horton, Thomas P. *WhoFI 94*
Horton, Thomas R. 1926- *WhoAm 94, WhoFI 94*
Horton, Wilfred Henry 1918- *WhoScEn 94*
Horton, William Alan 1955- *WhoScEn 94*
Horton, William Arnold 1945- *WhoScEn 94*
Horton, William David, Jr. 1953- *WhoScEn 94*
Horton, William Harrison 1942- *WhoAm 94*
Horton, William Noble 1948- *WhoFI 94*
Horton, William Russell 1931- *WhoAm 94*
Horton, Willie Wattison 1942- *WhoBlA 94*
Horton-LaForce, Tina Margaret 1961- *WhoAmL 94*
Horty, John Francis 1928- *WhoAmL 94*
Horusitzky, Zoltan 1903-1985 *NewGrDO*
Horvat, Branko 1928- *IntWW 93*
Horvat, Laura Jean 1947- *WhoMW 93*
Horvath, Betty 1927- *WrDr 94*
Horvath, Brooke Kenton 1953- *WhoMW 93*
Horvath, Charles d1978 *WhoHol 92*
Horvath, Csaba 1930- *WhoAm 94, WhoScEn 94*
Horvath, Diana Meredith 1963- *WhoScEn 94*
Horvath, Ian 1946-1990 *WhAm 10*
Horvath, Joan Catherine 1959- *WhoScEn 94*
Horvath, John, Jr. *DrAPF 93*
Horvath, Joseph John 1936- *WhoAm 94, WhoAmL 94*
Horvath, Juliana 1948- *WhoMW 93*
Horvath, Louis J. 1928- *WhoAmP 93*
Horvath, Odon (Josef) von 1901-1938 *IntDcT 2*
Horvath, Polly 1957- *WrDr 94*
Horvath, Terrence Michael 1961- *WhoWest 94*
Horvath, Vincent Victor 1942- *WhoScEn 94*
Horvath, Waltraud 1957- *WhoWomW 91*
Horvay, Martha J. 1949- *WhoAmA 93*
Horvitz, Howard Robert 1947- *WhoAm 94*
Horvitz, Michael John 1950- *WhoAm 94, WhoAmL 94*
Horvitz, Paul Michael 1935- *WhoAm 94*
Horvitz, Richard A. 1944- *WhoMW 93*
Horvitz, Suzanne Joan *WhoAmA 93*
Horwath, Leslie Kathleen 1953- *WhoAm 94*
Horwich, Alan 1948- *Who 94*
Horwich, Allan 1944- *WhoAm 94, WhoAmL 94*
Horwich, Franklin M. 1960- *WhoWest 94*
Horwich, George 1924- *WhoAm 94*
Horwin, Leonard 1913- *WhoAmL 94, WhoWest 94*
Horwitch, Marilyn Dolores 1927- *WhoMW 93*
Horwitt, Max Kenneth 1908- *WhoAm 94*
Horwitt, Will 1934-1985 *WhoAmA 93N*
Horwitz, Alan Fredrick 1944- *WhoAm 94, WhoMW 93, WhoScEn 94*
Horwitz, Allan Barry 1947- *WhoFI 94*
Horwitz, Barbara Ann 1940- *WhoAm 94, WhoWest 94*
Horwitz, Barry 1957- *WhoFI 94*
Horwitz, Channa 1932- *WhoAmA 93*
Horwitz, David A. *WhoScEn 94*
Horwitz, David Larry 1942- *WhoScEn 94*
Horwitz, Donald Paul 1936- *WhoAm 94*
Horwitz, Ethan 1952- *WhoAmL 94*
Horwitz, Harry 1927- *WhoAm 94*
Horwitz, Irwin Daniel 1920- *WhoAm 94*
Horwitz, Joshua Mark 1963- *WhoAmL 94*
Horwitz, Kurt d1974 *WhoHol 92*
Horwitz, Lawrence David 1939- *WhoAm 94*
Horwitz, Orville 1909- *WhoAm 94*
Horwitz, Paul 1938- *WhoAm 94*
Horwitz, Ralph Irving 1947- *WhoAm 94*
Horwitz, Rita 1933- *WhoMW 93*
Horwitz, Ronald M. 1938- *WhoAm 94*
Horwitz, Samuel 1918- *WhoAmP 93*
Horwitz, Sol 1920- *IntMPA 94*
Horwitz, Susan Band *WhoScEn 94*
Horwitz, Tony 1958- *ConAu 140*
Horwitz, William J. 1946- *WhoMW 93*
Horwood, Louise Pierce d1993 *NewYTBS 93*
Horwood, Owen Pieter Faure 1916- *IntWW 93, Who 94*
Horwood, William 1944- *ConAu 141*
Horyn, Mykhailo Mykhailovych 1930- *LngBDD*
Hosack, Robert E. 1911- *WhoAmP 93*
Hosain, Attia 1913- *BlmGWL [port]*
Hosbach, Howard Daniel 1931-1990 *WhAm 10*
Hose, John Horsley 1928- *Who 94*
Hosek, James Robert 1944- *WhoFI 94*
Hoselton, Steven Dale 1961- *WhoAmL 94*
Hoseman, Daniel 1935- *WhoAmL 94*
Hosemann, C. Delbert, Jr. 1947- *WhoAm 94, WhoAmL 94*
Hosenball, S. Neil *WhoAm 94*
Hoseney, Russell Carl 1934- *WhoScEn 94*
Hosford, Marylou 1920- *WhoHol 92*
Hoshelle, Marjorie d1989 *WhoHol 92*
Hoshi, Katsuo Kai 1933- *WhoWest 94*
Hoshi, Mineo 1950- *WhoAsA 94*
Hoshi, Shin'ichi 1926- *EncSF 93*
Hoshiko, Michael *WhoAsA 94*
Hosick, Howard Lawrence 1943- *WhoAm 94*
Hosie, James Findlay 1913- *Who 94*
Hosie, Stanley William 1922- *WhoFI 94, WhoWest 94*
Hosie, William Carlton 1936- *WhoAm 94, WhoFI 94, WhoWest 94*
Hosier, Gerald Douglas 1941- *WhoAmL 94*
Hosier, Harry 1750?-1806 *DcAmReB 2*
Hosier, John 1928- *Who 94*
Hosier, Peter 1919- *WrDr 94*
Hosken, Richard Bruce 1942- *WhoScEn 94*
Hoskens, Jane Fenn 1694- *BlmGWL*
Hosker, Gerald Albery 1933- *Who 94*
Hosker, Rayford Peter, Jr. 1943- *WhoAm 94*
Hoskin, Anne Eleanore 1924- *WhoAmP 93*
Hoskin, Gregory Keith 1939- *WhoAmL 94*
Hosking, Barbara Nancy 1926- *Who 94*
Hosking, Geoffrey Alan 1942- *IntWW 93, Who 94*
Hosking, John Everard 1929- *Who 94*
Hoskins, Alice Elizabeth 1934- *WhoWest 94*
Hoskins, Allen d1980 *WhoHol 92*
Hoskins, Bob 1942- *IntMPA 94, IntWW 93, WhoAm 94, WhoHol 92*
Hoskins, Brian John 1945- *Who 94*
Hoskins, David LeRoy 1945- *WhoAmL 94*
Hoskins, Geraldine 1940- *WhoAm 94*
Hoskins, John Allen 1942- *WhoAmL 94*
Hoskins, John H. 1934- *WhoAm 94*
Hoskins, L. Claron 1940- *WhoScEn 94*
Hoskins, Lowell 1927-1990 *WhAm 10*
Hoskins, Richard Jerold 1945- *WhoAm 94, WhoAmL 94*
Hoskins, Robert 1933- *EncSF 93, WrDr 94*
Hoskins, Robert William 1942- *Who 94*
Hoskins, W. Lee 1941- *WhoAm 94, WhoMW 93*
Hoskins, William John 1940- *WhoAm 94, WhoScEn 94*
Hoskins, William Keller 1935- *WhoAm 94*
Hoskins Clark, Tempy M. 1938- *WhoBlA 94*
Hoskyns, Benedict (Leigh) 1928- *Who 94*
Hoskyns, John (Austin Hungerford Leigh) 1927- *Who 94*
Hoskyns, John Austin Hungerford Leigh 1927- *IntWW 93*
Hosler, Charles Luther, Jr. 1924- *WhoAm 94*
Hosler, Russell John 1906- *WhoAm 94*
Hosman, Sharon 1939- *WhoMW 93*
Hosmane, Narayan Sadashiv 1948- *WhoScEn 94*
Hosmane, Ramachandra S. 1944- *WhoAsA 94*
Hosmer, Bradley Clark 1937- *WhoAm 94, WhoWest 94*
Hosmer, Bradley Edwin 1940- *WhoAm 94*
Hosmer, Craig 1959- *WhoAmP 93*
Hosmer, Titus 1737-1780 *WhAmRev*
Hosni, Mohammad Hosein 1955- *WhoScEn 94*
Hosni, Naguib 1928- *IntWW 93*
Hosoda, Kichizo 1912- *IntWW 93*
Hosokawa, Fumiko 1947- *WhoAsA 94*
Hosokawa, Morihiro 1938- *NewYTBS 93 [port], News 94-1 [port]*
Hosokawa, William K. 1915- *WhoAm 94, WhoAsA 94*
Hospers, John 1918- *WhoAm 94*
Hospital, Janette Turner 1942- *BlmGWL [port]*
Hospital, Maria Carolina 1957- *WhoHisp 94*
Hospodor, Andrew Thomas 1937- *WhoAm 94, WhoScEn 94*
Hoss, Selim al- 1930- *IntWW 93*
Hossain, A. L. F. 1956- *WhoMW 93*
Hossain, Akram Mohammed 1951- *WhoMW 93*
Hossain, Anwar 1944- *IntWW 93*
Hossain, Begum Rokeya Sakhawat *BlmGWL*
Hossain, Kemaluddin 1923- *IntWW 93*
Hossain, Shah Moazzem 1939- *IntWW 93*
Hossein, Robert 1927- *IntWW 93, WhoHol 92*
Hossenfeldt, Vera d1967 *WhoHol 92*
Hossler, David J. 1940- *WhoAmP 93*
Hossler, David Joseph 1940- *WhoAmL 94, WhoWest 94*
Host, Stig 1926- *WhoAm 94*
Hostage, John Brayne Arthur 1952- *WhoAmL 94*
Hosten, Adrian *WhoBlA 94*
Hoster, Anne d1954 *WhoHol 92*
Hostetler, Daniel Lee 1951- *WhoMW 93*
Hostetler, Dave 1951- *WhoWest 94*
Hostetler, H. Richard 1942- *WhoAmP 93*
Hostetler, Jeff W. 1961- *WhoAm 94, WhoWest 94*
Hostetler, Jeptha Ray 1939- *WhoMW 93*
Hostetler, Karl Yoder 1939- *WhoScEn 94, WhoWest 94*
Hostetter, Amos Barr, Jr. 1937- *WhoAm 94*
Hostetter, Gene Huber 1939- *WhAm 10*
Hostetter, H. Clyde 1925- *WhoWest 94*
Hostetter, James William 1948- *WhoMW 93*
Hostettler, Stephen John 1931- *WhoAm 94*
Hosticka, Carl 1944- *WhoAmP 93*
Hosticka, Carl J. 1944- *WhoWest 94*
Hostinsky, Otakar 1847-1910 *NewGrDO*
Hostler, Charles Warren 1919- *WhoAm 94, WhoAmP 93*
Hostnik, Charles Rivoire 1954- *WhoAmL 94, WhoWest 94*
Hoston, Germaine A. 1954- *WhoBlA 94*
Hostrop, Richard W 1925- *WrDr 94*
Hostrop, Richard Winfred 1925- *WhoWest 94*
Hotaling, Ada E. 1953- *WhoHisp 94*
Hotaling, Arthur d1938 *WhoHol 92*
Hotaling, Frank d1977 *WhoHol 92*
Hotaling, John James 1947- *WhoAmP 93*
Hotaling, Robert Bachman 1918- *WhoMW 93*
Hotchkies, Barry 1945- *WhoAm 94*
Hotchkis, Joan 1930- *WhoHol 92*
Hotchkis, Preston 1893- *WhAm 10*
Hotchkiss, Andra Ruth 1946- *WhoAm 94*
Hotchkiss, Anita Ruth 1937- *WhoAmL 94*
Hotchkiss, Benjamin Berkeley 1826-1885 *WorInv*
Hotchkiss, Bill *DrAPF 93*
Hotchkiss, Bruce A. 1935- *WhoAmP 93*
Hotchkiss, Edward Stanley 1963- *WhoAmL 94*
Hotchkiss, Eugene, III 1928- *WhoAm 94, WhoMW 93*
Hotchkiss, Henry Washington 1937- *WhoFI 94*

Hotchkiss, Judy Cohen 1940- *WhoAmP 93*
Hotchkiss, Ralf David 1947- *WhoAm 94*
Hotchkiss, Rollin Douglas 1911- *IntWW 93, WhoAm 94*
Hotchkiss, Vivian Evelyn 1956- *WhoWest 94*
Hotchkiss, Wesley Akin 1919- *WhoBlA 94*
Hotchkiss, William Rouse 1937- *WhoWest 94*
Hotchkiss, Winchester Fitch 1928- *WhoAm 94*
Hotchner, A(aron) E(dward) 1920- *WrDr 94*
Hotchner, Aaron Edward 1920- *WhoAm 94*
Hoteley, Mae d1954 *WhoHol 92*
Hotelling, Harold 1945- *WhoAm 94, WhoFI 94*
Hotelling, Katsuko Tsurukawa *WhoAsA 94*
Hotes, Robert William 1942- *WhoScEn 94*
Hoth, Steven Sergey 1941- *WhoAm 94, WhoAmL 94*
Hotham, Baron 1940- *Who 94*
Hotham, Gary *DrAPF 93*
Hotham, Richard 1722-1799 *DcNaB MP*
Hotham, William 1736-1813 *WhAmRev*
Hothfield, Baron 1939- *Who 94*
Hotle, Jackie Lee 1939- *WhoWest 94*
Hotson, John Hargrove 1930- *WrDr 94*
Hotson, John Leslie 1897-1992 *AnObit 1992*
Hotson, Leslie d1992 *IntWW 93N, Who 94N*
Hotspur 1364-1403 *BlmGEL*
Hotta, Gina H. *WhoAsA 94*
Hottel, Hoyt Clarke 1903- *IntWW 93, WhoAm 94*
Hottenstein, Evelyn K. 1948- *WhoFI 94*
Hotter, Hans 1909- *IntWW 93, NewGrDO [port], Who 94*
Hottinger, John Creighton 1945- *WhoAmL 94, WhoAmP 93, WhoMW 93*
Hottman, Carol Lee 1949- *WhoMW 93*
Hottois, Lawrence Daniel 1933- *WhoAm 94*
Hotung, Joseph (Edward) 1930- *Who 94*
Hotvedt, Kris J. 1943- *WhoAmA 93*
Hotvedt, Kris Joanna 1943- *WhoWest 94*
Hotz, Henry Palmer 1925- *WhoAm 94, WhoScEn 94, WhoWest 94*
Hotz, Robert Henry 1944- *WhoAm 94, WhoFI 94*
Hotze, Charles Wayne 1919- *WhoAm 94*
Hou, Chi Ming 1924-1991 *WhAm 10*
Hou, Guang Kun 1941- *WhoScEn 94*
Hou, Hsiao-hsien 1947- *IntWW 93*
Hou, Jiashi 1955- *WhoScEn 94*
Hou, Jin Chuan 1954- *WhoScEn 94*
Hou, William Chen-Nan 1955- *WhoAsA 94*
Houart-Brown, Mary Lou 1956- *WhoMW 93*
Hou Baolin 1916- *WhoPRCh 91 [port]*
Houbolt, John Cornelius 1919- *WhoAm 94*
Houbregs, Bob 1932- *BasBi*
Houchen, Joan Carol 1930- *WhoAmP 93*
Houchin, John Frederick, Sr. 1945- *WhoFI 94*
Houchins, Daniel Thomas 1955- *WhoMW 93*
Houchins, Larry *WhoAmL 94*
Houchins, Wiley Jack 1955- *WhoMW 93*
Houck, C. T. 1930- *WhoAmP 93*
Houck, Calvin Bryan 1896- *WhAm 10*
Houck, Charles d1981 *WhoHol 92*
Houck, Charles Weston 1933- *WhoAm 94, WhoAmL 94*
Houck, Cory-Jeanne 1960- *WhoAmP 93*
Houck, James I. 1941- *WhoAm 94*
Houck, John Burton 1928- *WhoAm 94*
Houck, John Candee 1931- *WhoAm 94*
Houck, John Roland 1923- *WhoAm 94*
Houck, Lewis Daniel, Jr. 1932- *WhoFI 94*
Houck, R. Edward 1950- *WhoAmP 93*
Houck, Sharon Lu Thomas 1952- *WhoFI 94*
Houck, William Russell 1926- *WhoAm 94*
Houck, William S., Jr. 1929- *WhoAmP 93*
Houdar de la Motte, Antoine-Charles de 1672-1731 *GuFrLit 2*
Houdashelt, Derrel Wilbur 1925- *WhoWest 94*
Houde, Germain *WhoHol 92*
Houdek, Robert G. 1940- *WhoAm 94, WhoAmP 93*
Houdetot, Comtesse de 1730?-1813 *BlmGWL*
Houdin, Michel-Gabriel d1802 *WhAmRev*
Houdini, Harry d1926 *WhoHol 92*
Houédard, (Pierre-)Sylvester, dom 1924- *WrDr 94*
Houel, Patrick 1942- *WhoAm 94*
Hou Fu *WhoPRCh 91*
Hougen, Jon Torger 1936- *WhoAm 94*
Hough, Aubrey Johnston, Jr. 1944- *WhoAm 94*
Hough, Bruce *WhoAmP 93*
Hough, Charlotte 1924- *WrDr 94*
Hough, David *WhoHol 92*
Hough, Eldred Wilson 1916-1990 *WhAm 10*
Hough, George Hubert 1921- *Who 94*
Hough, Jack Van Doren 1920- *WhoScEn 94*
Hough, Jennine 1948- *WhoAmA 93*
Hough, John 1941- *HorFD, IntMPA 94*
Hough, John Patrick 1928- *Who 94*
Hough, Julia Marie *Who 94*
Hough, Lawrence A. *WhoAm 94, WhoFI 94*
Hough, Lindy *DrAPF 93*
Hough, Lucile Young 1949- *WhoFI 94*
Hough, Maxine *WhoAmP 93*
Hough, Michael 1928- *WrDr 94*
Hough, Nanette 1933- *WhoWest 94*
Hough, Peter A. 1954- *ConAu 142*
Hough, Ralph Degnan 1943- *WhoAmP 93*
Hough, Richard 1922- *IntWW 93*
Hough, Richard (Alexander) 1922- *WrDr 94*
Hough, Richard Alexander 1922- *Who 94*
Hough, Richard T. 1923- *WhoFI 94*
Hough, Robert Alan 1959- *WhoFI 94*
Hough, S(tan) B. *EncSF 93*
Hough, S(tanley) B(ennett) 1917- *WrDr 94*
Hough, Stephen 1961- *Who 94*
Hough, Stephen Andrew Gill 1961- *IntWW 93*
Hough, Steven Hedges 1938- *WhoAmL 94, WhoWest 94*
Hough, Thomas Henry Michael 1933- *WhoAm 94, WhoAmL 94*
Hougham, John William 1937- *Who 94*
Hougham, Norman Russell 1937- *WhoMW 93*
Houghtaling, Colleen J. *DrAPF 93*
Houghtaling, Pamela Ann 1949- *WhoFI 94*
Houghtlen, Frances Elizabeth 1945- *WhoMW 93*
Houghton *Who 94*
Houghton, Alan Nourse 1924- *WhoAm 94*
Houghton, Alfred Thomas d1993 *Who 94N*
Houghton, Amo 1926- *CngDr 93*
Houghton, Amory, Jr. *IntWW 93N*
Houghton, Amory, Jr. 1926- *WhoAm 94, WhoAmP 93*
Houghton, Arthur A., Jr. 1906-1990 *WhoAmA 93N*
Houghton, Arthur Amory, Jr. 1906-1990 *WhAm 10*
Houghton, Barbara Jean 1947- *WhoAmA 93*
Houghton, Barrie 1941- *WhoHol 92*
Houghton, Brian Thomas 1931- *Who 94*
Houghton, Charles G., Jr. d1993 *NewYTBS 93*
Houghton, Charles Norris 1909- *WhoAm 94*
Houghton, Claude 1889-1961 *EncSF 93*
Houghton, Daniel c. 1740-1791 *WhWE*
Houghton, David Drew 1938- *WhoAm 94*
Houghton, Donald Cary 1946- *WhoAm 94*
Houghton, Eric 1930- *WrDr 94*
Houghton, Herbert 1920- *Who 94*
Houghton, James *WhoHol 92*
Houghton, James Richardson 1936- *IntWW 93, WhoAm 94, WhoFI 94, WhoScEn 94*
Houghton, John 1922- *Who 94*
Houghton, John 1931- *IntWW 93*
Houghton, John (Theodore) 1931- *Who 94*
Houghton, Katharine 1945- *WhoAm 94, WhoHol 92, WrDr 94*
Houghton, Raymond Carl, Jr. 1947- *WhoScEn 94*
Houghton, Robert Dyer 1912- *Who 94*
Houghton, Rodney Norman 1938- *WhoAm 94*
Houghton, (William) Stanley 1881-1913 *IntDcT 2*
Houghton, Timothy *DrAPF 93*
Houghton, William I. *WhoAmP 93*
Houghton, Woods Edward 1956- *WhoScEn 94*
Houghton, Woodson Plyer 1893-1990 *WhAm 10*
Houghton Of Sowerby, Baron 1898- *IntWW 93, Who 94*
Houglum, Peggy Ann 1948- *WhoWest 94*
Hougron, Jean (Marcel) 1923- *IntWW 93*
Hou Guangjiong *WhoPRCh 91 [port]*
Hou Guangjiong 1905- *IntWW 93*
Hou Jie 1931- *IntWW 93, WhoPRCh 91 [port]*
Hou Jingru 1902- *WhoPRCh 91 [port]*
Houk, Arlene Helen 1962- *WhoMW 93*
Houk, Billie Gene 1948- *WhoAmP 93*
Houk, Edwynn L. 1952- *WhoAmA 93*
Houk, Kendall Newcomb 1943- *WhoAm 94, WhoWest 94*
Houk, Nancy Mia 1940- *WhoAm 94*
Houk, Pamela P. 1935- *WhoAmA 93*
Houk, Robert Samuel 1952- *WhoScEn 94*
Houk, Vernon Neal 1929- *WhoAm 94*
Houlahan, Thomas G. 1963- *WhoAmP 93*
Houlbrooke, Ralph (A.) 1944- *WrDr 94*
Hould, Ra *WhoHol 92*
Houlden, (James) Leslie 1929- *Who 94*
Houlder, John Maurice 1916- *Who 94*
Houlding, Virginia H. 1953- *WhoWest 94*
Houldsworth, Richard (Thomas Reginald) 1947- *Who 94*
Houle, Cyril O 1913- *WrDr 94*
Houle, Daniel d1989 *WhoHol 92*
Houle, Frances Anne 1952- *WhoAm 94*
Houle, Joseph Adrien 1928- *WhoAm 94, WhoWest 94*
Houle, Joseph E. 1930- *WhoAm 94*
Houle, Philip P. *WhoAmL 94*
Houlette, Forrest Thomas 1954- *WhoMW 93*
Houley, Robert D. 1927- *WhoAmP 93*
Houlihan, Charles Daniel, Jr. 1953- *WhoAmL 94*
Houlihan, David Paul 1937- *WhoAm 94*
Houlihan, Dennis J. 1949- *WhoAmP 93*
Houlihan, Gerald John 1943- *WhoAm 94, WhoAmL 94*
Houlihan, Hilda Imelio 1937- *WhoAm 94*
Houlihan, Jane Kopp 1961- *WhoMW 93*
Houlihan, Patricia Powell 1947- *WhoFI 94*
Houlihan, Patrick T. 1942- *WhoAmA 93*
Houlihan, Patrick Thomas 1942- *WhoWest 94*
Houlihan, Robert Alan 1938- *WhoIns 94*
Houlne, Lois Lamoreaux 1910- *WhoMW 93*
Houlsby, Guy Tinmouth 1954- *Who 94*
Hoult, Peter John 1943- *WhoAm 94*
Houmann, Borge Kruuse 1902- *IntWW 93*
Houn, Franklin W 1920- *WrDr 94*
Houn, Fred Wei-han 1957- *WhoAsA 94*
Hounschell, John Charles 1955- *WhoMW 93*
Hounsell, Mark L. 1952- *WhoAmP 93*
Hounsell, William J. 1943- *WhoAmP 93*
Hounsfield, Godfrey *WorInv*
Hounsfield, Godfrey (Newbold) 1919- *Who 94*
Hounsfield, Godfrey Newbold 1919- *IntWW 93, WhoScEn 94*
Hountras, Peter Timothy 1927- *WhoAm 94*
Houphouet-Boigny, Felix 1905- *IntWW 93*
Houphouet-Boigny, Felix 1905-1993 *NewYTBS 93 [port]*
Houpis, Constantine Harry 1922- *WhoAm 94, WhoMW 93*
Houpis, Harry Louis Francis 1954- *WhoWest 94*
Houpt, Jeffrey Lyle 1941- *WhoAm 94*
Houpt, Stanley Robert, Jr. 1946- *WhoFI 94*
Houran, James Patrick 1969- *WhoScEn 94*
Hourani, A. H. *ConAu 140*
Hourani, Albert d1993 *NewYTBS 93*
Hourani, Albert (Habib) 1916?-1993 *ConAu 140*
Hou Renzhi 1911- *WhoPRCh 91 [port]*
Hourigan, David R. 1947- *WhoAmP 93*
Hourigan, Patrick John 1966- *WhoFI 94*
Houri-Pasotti, Myriam *BlmGWL*
Hou Runyu 1945- *IntWW 93, WhoPRCh 91*
Housch, Paul Toby 1956- *WhoAmL 94*
Housden, James Alan George 1904- *Who 94*
Housden, Peter James 1950- *Who 94*
House, Billy d1961 *WhoHol 92*
House, Carleen Faye 1950- *WhoMW 93*
House, Carolyn Joyce 1952- *WhoBlA 94*
House, Chandler d1982 *WhoHol 92*
House, Charles Raymond 1945- *WhoAmP 93*
House, Charles Staver 1908- *WhoAm 94*
House, Dana *WhoHol 92*
House, David (George) 1922- *Who 94*
House, David George 1922- *IntWW 93*
House, David L. 1943- *WhoAm 94, WhoFI 94, WhoWest 94*
House, Diane Jean 1948- *WhoMW 93*
House, Donald Lee, Sr. 1941- *WhoAm 94*
House, Edward Mandell 1858-1938 *EncSF 93*
House, Edwin Wesley 1939- *WhoAm 94*
House, Eric *WhoHol 92*
House, Ernest Robert 1937- *WhoWest 94*
House, Francis Harry 1908- *Who 94*
House, Frank Owen 1927-1989 *WhAm 10*
House, George Michael 1955- *WhoWest 94*
House, Gloria 1941- *BlkWr 2, ConAu 41NR*
House, Jack d1963 *WhoHol 92*
House, James Charles, Jr. 1902- *WhoAmA 93N*
House, James E. *WhoBlA 94*
House, John Peter Humphry 1945- *Who 94*
House, John W. 1941- *WhoScEn 94*
House, Joseph W. 1931- *WhoIns 94*
House, Karen Elliott 1947- *WhoAm 94*
House, Karen Sue 1958- *WhoWest 94*
House, Kevin N. 1957- *WhoBlA 94*
House, Leo Brandybuck 1954- *WhoWest 94*
House, Lon William 1952- *WhoScEn 94*
House, Marguerite *WhoHol 92*
House, Mary Corbin 1925- *WhoAmP 93*
House, Millard L. 1944- *WhoBlA 94*
House, Newton d1948 *WhoHol 92*
House, Peter Kyle 1965- *WhoWest 94*
House, Phillip Mercel 1962- *WhoFI 94*
House, R(ichard) C(alvin) 1927- *ConAu 142*
House, Robert William 1920- *WhoAm 94*
House, Robert William 1927- *WhoAm 94*
House, Roland Mark 1961- *WhoWest 94*
House, Ron *WhoHol 92*
House, Roy C. 1917- *WhoAm 94*
House, Son c. 1902-1988 *ConMus 11 [port]*
House, Suda Kay 1951- *WhoAmA 93*
House, Ted 1959- *WhoAmP 93*
House, Vincent F. 1938- *WhoAmP 93*
House, William Michael 1945- *WhoAm 94, WhoAmP 93*
Household, Geoffrey 1900-1988 *EncSF 93*
Household, Humphrey (George West) 1906- *WrDr 94*
Householder, Lucille Bejarano 1938- *WhoHisp 94*
Housel, Jerry Winters 1912- *WhoAm 94, WhoAmP 93*
Houseman, Alexander Randolph 1920- *Who 94*
Houseman, Donna Jean 1951- *WhoMW 93*
Houseman, Gerald L. 1939- *WhoMW 93*
Houseman, John d1988 *WhoHol 92*
Houseman, John 1902-1988 *IntDcF 2-4*
Houser, Allan C. 1914- *WhoAmA 93*
Houser, Caroline Mae *WhoAmA 93*
Houser, Charles William 1946- *WhoMW 93*
Houser, Daniel Edwin 1953- *WhoFI 94*
Houser, Donald Eugene 1948- *WhoFI 94*
Houser, Donald Russell 1941- *WhoScEn 94*
Houser, Douglas Guy 1935- *WhoAm 94*
Houser, Gerald Burnett 1951- *WhoWest 94*
Houser, Harold Byron 1921- *WhoAm 94*
Houser, Hubert *WhoAmP 93*
Houser, Jerry 1952- *WhoHol 92*
Houser, Jim 1928- *WhoAmA 93*
Houser, John Edward 1928- *WhoAmL 94*
Houser, Martha Jean 1928- *WhoMW 93*
Houser, Vincent Paul 1943- *WhoScEn 94*
Houser, William Douglas 1921- *WhoAm 94*
Houseworth, Richard Court 1928- *WhoAm 94*
Housewright, Artemis Skevakis 1927- *WhoAmA 93*
Housewright, Riley Dee 1913- *WhoAm 94*
Housewright, Wiley L. 1913- *ConAu 140*
Housewright, Wiley Lee 1913- *WhoAm 94*
Housh, Tedrick Addison, Jr. 1936- *WhoAmL 94*
Houshiary, Shirazeh 1955- *IntWW 93*
Housholder, Glenn Tholen 1925- *WhoScEn 94*
Hou Shujun 1927- *WhoPRCh 91 [port]*
Housinger, Warren Donald 1937- *WhoMW 93*
Houskeeper, Barbara 1922- *WhoAmA 93*
Houslay, Miles Douglas 1950- *IntWW 93*
Housley, Charles Edward 1939- *WhoAm 94*
Housley, Phil F 1964- *WhoAm 94*
Housley-Anthony, Mary Pat 1944- *WhoMW 93*
Housman, A. E. 1859-1936 *BlmGEL*
Housman, A(lfred) E(dward) 1859-1936 *GayLL*
Housman, Arthur d1942 *WhoHol 92*
Housman, Arthur Lloyd 1928-1990 *WhAm 10*
Housman, Laurence 1865-1959 *EncSF 93*
Housman, Russell F. 1928- *WhoAmA 93*
Housner, George William 1910- *WhoAm 94, WhoScEn 94*
Housner, Robert William 1949- *WhoMW 93*
Houssemayne du Boulay, (Edward Philip) George 1922- *Who 94*
Houssemayne du Boulay, Roger (William) 1922- *Who 94*
Houstecky, Miroslav 1926- *Who 94*
Houston, Agnes Wood 1920- *WhoBlA 94*

Houston, Alfred Dearborn 1940- *WhoAm 94*
Houston, Alice V. *WhoBlA 94*
Houston, Allan *WhoBlA 94*
Houston, Aubrey Claud D. *Who 94*
Houston, Billie d1955 *WhoHol 92*
Houston, Birgie Ann 1951- *WhoMW 93*
Houston, Bruce 1937- *WhoAmA 93*
Houston, Byron 1969- *WhoBlA 94*
Houston, Cecil J(ames) 1943- *WrDr 94*
Houston, Charles Hamilton 1895-1950 *AfrAmAl 6*
Houston, Cisco d1961 *WhoHol 92*
Houston, Cissy *WhoBlA 94*
Houston, Clarence Stuart 1927- *WhoWest 94*
Houston, Clyde d1977 *WhoHol 92*
Houston, Connie T. *WhoAmP 93*
Houston, Corinne P. 1922- *WhoBlA 94*
Houston, David d1993 *NewYTBS 93*
Houston, David 1929- *Who 94*
Houston, David 1938- *EncSF 93, WhoHol 92*
Houston, David John 1952- *WhoAmL 94*
Houston, David R. 1936- *WhoBlA 94*
Houston, Devin Burl 1957- *WhoMW 93, WhoScEn 94*
Houston, Dick 1943- *SmATA 74 [port]*
Houston, Donald 1924- *WhoHol 92*
Houston, Donald L. 1934-1988 *WhAm 10*
Houston, Douglas White 1950- *WhoAm 94*
Houston, E. James, Jr. 1939- *WhoAm 94, WhoFI 94*
Houston, Elizabeth Reece Manasco 1935- *WhoWest 94*
Houston, George d1944 *WhoHol 92*
Houston, Glyn 1926- *WhoHol 92*
Houston, Harry Rollins 1928- *WhoWest 94*
Houston, Howard Edwin 1910- *WhoAm 94*
Houston, Ivan J. 1925- *WhoBlA 94, WhoIns 94*
Houston, Ivan James 1925- *WhoAm 94*
Houston, J. Gorman, Jr. 1933- *WhoAmP 93*
Houston, James A. 1921- *SmATA 17AS [port], WhoAmA 93*
Houston, James A(rchibald) 1921- *SmATA 74 [port], TwCYAW, WrDr 94*
Houston, James Archibald 1921- *WhoAm 94*
Houston, James Caldwell 1917- *Who 94*
Houston, James D. *DrAPF 93*
Houston, James D 1933- *WrDr 94*
Houston, James Gorman, Jr. 1933- *WhoAm 94, WhoAmL 94*
Houston, Jamie Giles, III 1952- *WhoAmL 94*
Houston, Jane Hunt 1919- *WhoWest 94*
Houston, Jean d1965 *WhoHol 92*
Houston, Jeanne Wakatsuki 1934- *WhoAsA 94*
Houston, John Albert 1914- *WhoAm 94, WhoWest 94*
Houston, John Coates, Jr. 1909- *WhoAm 94*
Houston, John F. 1952- *WhoScEn 94*
Houston, John Michael 1944- *WhoAmP 93*
Houston, John Stewart *WhoAmA 93*
Houston, Johnny L. 1941- *WhoBlA 94*
Houston, Johnny Lee 1941- *WhoAm 94*
Houston, Karl LaVon 1964- *WhoFI 94*
Houston, Ken *ProFbHF*
Houston, Kenneth Ray 1944- *WhoBlA 94*
Houston, Les *WhoAmP 93*
Houston, Lillian S. 1946- *WhoBlA 94*
Houston, Marsh S. 1918- *WhoBlA 94*
Houston, Mary Etta (King) 1912- *WhoAmA 93*
Houston, Melba Jean 1943- *WhoMW 93*
Houston, Neal J. 1926- *WhoAmP 93*
Houston, Paul David 1944- *WhoAm 94, WhoWest 94*
Houston, Peyton *DrAPF 93*
Houston, Peyton Hoge 1910- *WhoAm 94*
Houston, R. B. 1935- *WrDr 94*
Houston, Renee d1980 *WhoHol 92*
Houston, Robert *DrAPF 93*
Houston, Sam 1793-1863 *HisWorL [port]*
Houston, Samuel Lee 1951- *WhoAm 94*
Houston, Seawadon Lee 1942- *WhoBlA 94*
Houston, Simpson Pete 1942- *WhoMW 93*
Houston, Stanley Dunsmore 1930- *WhoAm 94*
Houston, Thomas Dewey 1930- *WhoScEn 94*
Houston, Velina Hasu 1957- *WhoAsA 94*
Houston, W. Eugene 1920- *WhoBlA 94*
Houston, W. Robert 1928- *WrDr 94*
Houston, Wade *WhoBlA 94*
Houston, Whitney 1963- *AfrAmAl 6, IntWW 93, WhoAm 94, WhoBlA 94*
Houston, William Churchill c. 1746-1788 *WhAmRev*
Houston, William DeBoise 1940- *WhoBlA 94*
Houston, William Robert Montgomery 1922- *WhoMW 93*
Houstoun, Feather O'Connor 1946- *WhoAmP 93*
Houstoun, John 1744-1796 *WhAmRev*
Houstoun, Lawrence Orson, Jr. 1929- *WhoAm 94*
Houstoun, William 1755-1813 *WhAmRev*
Houstoun-Boswall, (Thomas) Alford 1947- *Who 94*
Houtchens, Barnard 1911- *WhoAm 94*
Houtchens, Robert Austin, Jr. 1953- *WhoAm 94*
Houthakker, Hendrik Samuel 1924- *IntWW 93, WhoAm 94, WhoFI 94*
Houtman, Cornelius c. 1540-1599 *WhWE*
Houtman, Frederik 1571-1627 *WhWE*
Houts, Larry Lee 1942- *WhoMW 93*
Houts, Marshall d1993 *NewYTBS 93*
Houts, Marshall Wilson 1919- *WhoAm 94*
Houtsma, Peter C. 1951- *WhoAmL 94*
Houtte, Jean van 1907- *IntWW 93*
Houtz, Duane Talbott 1933- *WhoAm 94*
Houvouras, Richard Paul 1949- *WhoAmP 93*
Hou Xianglin 1912- *WhoPRCh 91 [port]*
Hou Xueyu 1912- *WhoPRCh 91 [port]*
Hou Xun *WhoPRCh 91*
Hou Ying *WhoPRCh 91*
Houze, Gerald Lucian, Jr. 1936- *WhoScEn 94*
Houze, Jeneice Carmel 1938- *WhoBlA 94*
Hou Zhitong *WhoPRCh 91*
Hou Zhiying *WhoPRCh 91*
Hou Zongbin 1929- *IntWW 93, WhoPRCh 91 [port]*
Hovanec, B. Michael 1952- *WhoScEn 94*
Hovanec, George A., Jr. 1953- *WhoAmL 94*
Hovanec, Timothy Arthur 1956- *WhoScEn 94*
Hovanesian, Joseph Der 1930- *WhoAm 94*
Hovanessian, Shahen Alexander 1931- *WhoAm 94*
Hovannes, John 1904-1973 *WhoAmA 93N*
Hovannisian, Richard G. 1932- *WhoAm 94, WrDr 94*
Hovatter, Kurt Eugene 1954- *WhoWest 94*
Hovda, Theodore J. 1951- *WhoAmP 93*
Hovde, A. J. *DrAPF 93*
Hovde, Carl Frederick 1926- *WhoAm 94*
Hovde, F. Boyd 1934- *WhoAmL 94*
Hovde, Frederick Russell 1955- *WhoAmL 94*
Hovden, Scott Stephen 1953- *WhoFI 94*
Hovdesven, Arne 1928- *WhoAm 94*
Hove, Andrew C., Jr. 1934- *WhoAmP 93*
Hove, Andrew Christian 1934- *WhoAm 94, WhoFI 94*
Hove, Brian E. 1961- *WhoWest 94*
Hove, Howard Joseph 1925- *WhoAmP 93*
Hovell, Larry L. *WhoBlA 94*
Hovell, William Hilton 1786-1875 *WhWE*
Hovell-Thurlow-Cumming-Bruce *Who 94*
Hoven, Adrian d1981 *WhoHol 92*
Hoven, Helmert Frans van den 1923- *Who 94*
Hover, Charles S., Jr. *WhoAmP 93*
Hover, John Calvin, II 1943- *WhoAm 94*
Hovers, Johannes 1943- *IntWW 93*
Hoversten, Ellsworth Gary 1941- *WhoMW 93*
Hovet, Rodney Phillip 1956- *WhoMW 93*
Hovet, Thomas, Jr. 1923-1989 *WhAm 10*
Hovey, Alan Edwin, Jr. 1933- *WhoFI 94*
Hovey, Ann 1914- *WhoHol 92*
Hovey, E. Paul 1908- *WrDr 94*
Hovey, Fred 1868-1945 *BuCMET*
Hovey, James Clark 1948- *WhoAmP 93*
Hovey, Judith Kay 1941- *WhoMW 93*
Hovey, Justus Allan, Jr. 1922- *WhoAm 94*
Hovey, Tim d1989 *WhoHol 92*
Hovey, Walter Read 1949-1982 *WhoAmA 93N*
Hoveyda, Fereydoun 1924- *IntWW 93*
Hovgard, Carl 1905-1989 *WhAm 10*
Hovhaness, Alan 1911- *NewGrDO, WhoAm 94*
Hovhanisian, Edgar (Sergey) 1930- *NewGrDO*
Hovhanissian, Hratchia 1919- *IntWW 93*
Hovick, Louise d1970 *WhoHol 92*
Hovin, Arne William 1922- *WhoAm 94*
Hovind, David J. 1940- *WhoFI 94, WhoWest 94*
Hoving, John Hannes Forester 1923- *WhoAm 94, WhoFI 94*
Hoving, Thomas 1931- *IntWW 93, Who 94, WhoAm 94, WhoAmA 93*
Hoving, Walter 1897-1989 *WhAm 10*
Hovis, James Brunton 1922- *WhoAm 94, WhoAmL 94, WhoWest 94*
Hovis, John Herbert 1944- *WhoAm 94, WhoFI 94*
Hovis, Larry *WhoHol 92*
Hovis, Lorraine June 1924- *WhoAmP 93*
Hovis, Raymond Leader 1934- *WhoAmL 94*
Hovnanian, H. Philip 1920- *WhoAm 94, WhoScEn 94*
Hovorka, Robert L(eo), Jr. 1955- *EncSF 93*
Hovsepian, Leon 1915- *WhoAmA 93*
How, George M. d1993 *NewYTBS 93*
Howald, John William 1935- *WhoAmL 94*
Howard *Who 94*
Howard, A(rthur) E(llsworth) Dick 1933- *WrDr 94*
Howard, Adam Coleman *WhoHol 92*
Howard, Alan 1937- *WhoHol 92*
Howard, Alan (Mackenzie) 1937- *Who 94*
Howard, Alan Charles 1944- *WhoMW 93*
Howard, Alan Mackenzie 1937- *IntWW 93*
Howard, Alex T., Jr. 1924- *WhoAm 94, WhoAmL 94*
Howard, Alexander Edward 1909- *Who 94*
Howard, Allan D. 1949- *WhoAmP 93*
Howard, Alyssa 1941- *WrDr 94*
Howard, Andrea *WhoHol 92*
Howard, Andree 1910-1968 *IntDcB [port]*
Howard, Angela Kay 1964- *WhoAmL 94*
Howard, Ann 1936- *IntWW 93, NewGrDO, Who 94*
Howard, Anne *WhoHol 92*
Howard, Anthony Michell 1934- *IntWW 93, Who 94*
Howard, Arliss 1954- *WhoHol 92*
Howard, Arliss 1955- *IntMPA 94*
Howard, Art d1963 *WhoHol 92*
Howard, Arthur 1910- *WhoHol 92*
Howard, Arthur Ellsworth Dick 1933- *WhoAm 94*
Howard, Aubrey J. 1945- *WhoBlA 94*
Howard, Aughtum Luciel Smith 1906- *WhoScEn 94*
Howard, Barbara *WhoHol 92*
Howard, (Helen) Barbara 1926- *WhoAmA 93*
Howard, Barbara Sue Mesner 1944- *WhoAm 94*
Howard, Ben *DrAPF 93, WhoHol 92*
Howard, Bernadette Bunny 1956- *WhoMW 93*
Howard, Bernard Eufinger 1920- *WhoAm 94, WhoScEn 94*
Howard, Bert d1958 *WhoHol 92*
Howard, Billie Jean 1950- *WhoBlA 94*
Howard, Boothe d1936 *WhoHol 92*
Howard, Bradford Reuel 1957- *WhoWest 94*
Howard, Brian 1951- *NewGrDO*
Howard, Brian 1967- *WhoBlA 94*
Howard, Brie *WhoHol 92*
Howard, C. Stephen 1940- *WhoAmL 94*
Howard, Calvin Johnson 1947- *WhoBlA 94*
Howard, Carl Michael 1920- *WhoAm 94*
Howard, Carolyn J. B. *WhoAmP 93*
Howard, Cecil 1888-1956 *WhoAmA 93N*
Howard, Cecil Ray 1937- *WhoAmA 93*
Howard, Charles d1947 *WhoHol 92*
Howard, Charles 1630-1713 *DcNaB MP*
Howard, Charles 1919- *WhoAm 94*
Howard, Charles Beecher 1897- *WhAm 10*
Howard, Christian *Who 94*
Howard, (Rosemary) Christian 1916- *Who 94*
Howard, Christopher Holm 1956- *WhoWest 94*
Howard, Christopher John 1932- *Who 94*
Howard, Christopher Philip 1947- *WhoWest 94*
Howard, Clark *DrAPF 93*
Howard, Clark 1934- *WrDr 94*
Howard, Clint 1959- *WhoHol 92*
Howard, Constance d1980 *WhoHol 92*
Howard, Constance (Mildred) 1910- *WrDr 94*
Howard, Corliss Mays 1927- *WhoBlA 94*
Howard, Curly d1952 *WhoHol 92*
Howard, Curly 1903-1952 *See* Three Stooges, The *WhoCom*
Howard, Cy d1993 *IntMPA 94N*
Howard, Cy 1915-1993 *NewYTBS 93 [port]*
Howard, Daggett Horton 1917- *WhoAm 94, WhoAmL 94*
Howard, Dalton J., Jr. *WhoBlA 94*
Howard, Dan F. 1931- *WhoAmA 93*
Howard, Darnley William 1957- *WhoBlA 94*
Howard, David *WhoAmA 93*
Howard, David d1941 *WhoHol 92*
Howard, David 1839-1916 *DcNaB MP*
Howard, David 1937- *WhoAm 94*
Howard, David E. 1952- *WhoAm 94*
Howard, David King 1949- *WhoFI 94*
Howard, David M. 1928- *WrDr 94*
Howard, David S. *WhoHol 92*
Howard, Dean Denton 1927- *WhoAm 94*
Howard, Deborah Ann 1950- *WhoAmL 94*
Howard, Desmond *WhoAm 94*
Howard, Desmond Kevin 1970- *WhoBlA 94*
Howard, Donald 1927- *Who 94*
Howard, Donald R. 1928- *WhoBlA 94*
Howard, Donald Roy 1927- *WhAm 10*
Howard, Donald Searcy 1928- *WhoAm 94, WhoFI 94*
Howard, Donivan Richard 1937- *WhoScEn 94*
Howard, Earle 1926- *WhoAmP 93*
Howard, Eddy d1963 *WhoHol 92*
Howard, Edmund Bernard Carlo 1909- *Who 94*
Howard, Edward *Who 94*
Howard, (Hamilton) Edward (de Coucey) 1915- *Who 94*
Howard, Edward Allen 1931- *WhoMW 93*
Howard, Edward L. 1926- *WhoAmP 93*
Howard, Edward M. d1946 *WhoHol 92*
Howard, Edward T., III 1942- *WhoBlA 94*
Howard, Elizabeth 1950- *WhoAm 94*
Howard, Elizabeth Fitzgerald 1927- *BlkWr 2, SmATA 74 [port], WhoBlA 94*
Howard, Elizabeth Jane 1923- *IntWW 93, Who 94, WrDr 94*
Howard, Ellen 1943- *WrDr 94*
Howard, Ellen D. 1929- *WhoBlA 94*
Howard, Ernest B. d1993 *NewYTBS 93*
Howard, Esther d1965 *WhoHol 92*
Howard, Eugene d1965 *WhoHol 92*
Howard, Florence d1954 *WhoHol 92*
Howard, Frances d1976 *WhoHol 92*
Howard, Frances Minturn *DrAPF 93*
Howard, Frederick *WhAmRev*
Howard, Gene C. 1926- *WhoAmP 93*
Howard, Gene Claude 1926- *WhoAm 94*
Howard, George 1935- *WrDr 94*
Howard, George, Jr. 1924- *WhoAm 94, WhoAmL 94, WhoBlA 94*
Howard, George Harmon 1934- *WhoFI 94, WhoWest 94*
Howard, George S., Jr. 1952- *WhoAmL 94*
Howard, George Sallade 1903- *WhoAm 94*
Howard, George W. d1928 *WhoHol 92*
Howard, Gertrude d1934 *WhoHol 92*
Howard, Glen 1942- *WhoBlA 94*
Howard, Glen 1956- *WhoBlA 94*
Howard, Glen Scott 1950- *WhoAm 94, WhoAmL 94*
Howard, Glenn L. *WhoAmP 93*
Howard, Glennies Fay 1949- *WhoFI 94*
Howard, Gregory Charles 1947- *WhoAmL 94*
Howard, Gwendolyn Julius 1932- *WhoBlA 94*
Howard, Harold d1944 *WhoHol 92*
Howard, Harold Lloyd 1927- *WhoAmP 93*
Howard, Harry Clay 1929- *WhoAm 94*
Howard, Harry Nicholas 1902- *IntWW 93*
Howard, (John) Hayden *EncSF 93*
Howard, Helen d1927 *WhoHol 92*
Howard, Helen Addison 1904- *WrDr 94*
Howard, Helen Arlene 1927- *WhoAm 94*
Howard, Henry *WhoAmP 93*
Howard, Henry L. 1930- *WhoBlA 94*
Howard, Hildegarde 1901- *WhoAm 94*
Howard, Howell J., Jr. 1938- *WhoBlA 94*
Howard, Hubert Wendell 1927- *WhoAm 94*
Howard, Hugh Charles 1929- *WhoMW 93*
Howard, Humbert L. 1915- *WhoAmA 93*
Howard, Humbert Lincoln 1915- *WhoBlA 94*
Howard, Irene d1981 *WhoHol 92*
Howard, Ivan *EncSF 93*
Howard, J. Daniel 1943- *WhoAmP 93*
Howard, J. T. 1936- *WhoAmP 93*
Howard, J. Woodford, Jr. 1931- *WhoAm 94, WrDr 94*
Howard, Jack *Who 94*
Howard, Jack 1924- *WhoAm 94*
Howard, Jack Rohe 1910- *IntWW 93, WhoAm 94*
Howard, James Boag 1915- *Who 94*
Howard, James D. 1932- *WhoAmP 93*
Howard, James Griffiths 1927- *Who 94*
Howard, James Joseph, III 1935- *WhoFI 94, WhoMW 93*
Howard, James L. 1918- *WhoBlA 94*
Howard, James Merriam, Jr. 1922- *WhoAm 94*
Howard, James Newton *IntMPA 94*
Howard, James Webb 1925- *WhoAm 94, WhoFI 94, WhoWest 94*
Howard, Jane (Temple) 1935- *WrDr 94*
Howard, Jane Osburn 1926- *WhoWest 94*
Howard, Jason *WhoHol 92*
Howard, Jean 1919- *WhoHol 92*
Howard, Jean C. *DrAPF 93*
Howard, Jeffrey Hjalmar 1944- *WhoAm 94, WhoAmL 94*
Howard, Jeffrey R. *WhoAmL 94, WhoAmP 93*
Howard, Jennifer *WhoHol 92*
Howard, Jerome Edward 1933- *WhoFI 94*
Howard, Jo Ann 1937- *WhoWest 94*
Howard, Joan Alice 1929- *WhoAm 94*
Howard, Joan E. 1951- *ConAu 141*

Howard, Joe d1961 *WhoHol 92*
Howard, Joel L. 1941- *WhoFI 94*
Howard, John *WhoAmP 93, WhoHol 92*
Howard, John 1913- *WhoHol 92*
Howard, John Addison 1921- *WhoAm 94*
Howard, John Anthony 1950- *WhoAm 94*
Howard, John Arnold 1915- *WhoAm 94*
Howard, John Brigham 1912- *WhoAm 94*
Howard, John Eager 1752-1827 *AmRev, WhAmRev [port]*
Howard, John Hazel, Jr. 1946- *WhoMW 93*
Howard, John James 1923- *Who 94*
Howard, John Lindsay 1931- *WhoAm 94*
Howard, John Loring 1935- *WhoFI 94*
Howard, John Milton 1944- *WhoAmL 94*
Howard, John Robert 1933- *WhoBlA 94*
Howard, John Tasker 1911- *WhoAm 94*
Howard, John Winston 1939- *IntWW 93, Who 94*
Howard, John Zollie 1897- *WhAm 10*
Howard, Joseph Clemens 1922- *WhoAm 94, WhoAmL 94, WhoBlA 94*
Howard, Joseph H. 1912- *WhoBlA 94*
Howard, Joseph Harvey 1931- *WhoAm 94*
Howard, Joyce 1922- *WhoHol 92*
Howard, Jules Joseph, Jr. 1943- *WhoBlA 94*
Howard, Julia Craven 1944- *WhoAmP 93*
Howard, Karen Lynn 1967- *WhoWest 94*
Howard, Kathleen d1956 *WhoHol 92*
Howard, Kathleen 1880-1956 *NewGrDO*
Howard, Kathleen 1947- *WhoFI 94, WhoMW 93*
Howard, Katsuyo Kunugi 1945- *WhoWest 94*
Howard, Keith 1944- *WhoAmL 94*
Howard, Keith L. 1940- *WhoBlA 94*
Howard, Ken 1944- *IntMPA 94, WhoHol 92*
Howard, Kenneth *Who 94*
Howard, (James) Kenneth 1932- *Who 94*
Howard, Kenneth Calvin, Jr. 1947- *WhoAm 94*
Howard, Kenneth Irwin 1932- *WhoScEn 94*
Howard, Kenneth John 1946- *WhoWest 94*
Howard, Kevyn Major *WhoHol 92*
Howard, Kingston L. d1993 *NewYTBS 93*
Howard, Kingston Lee 1929- *WhoAm 94*
Howard, Lauren R. 1945- *WhoAmL 94*
Howard, Laurence Edward 1934- *WhoAmL 94, WhoMW 93*
Howard, Lawrence Cabot 1925- *WhoAm 94, WhoBlA 94*
Howard, Lee Milton 1922- *WhoAm 94*
Howard, Leon *WhoBlA 94*
Howard, Leon W., Jr. 1935- *WhoBlA 94*
Howard, Leonard Henry d1993 *Who 94N*
Howard, Leslie d1943 *WhoHol 92*
Howard, Leslie Kenyatta 1950- *WhoBlA 94*
Howard, Lewis d1951 *WhoHol 92*
Howard, Lewis Spilman 1930- *WhoAmL 94*
Howard, Lillie Pearl 1949- *WhoBlA 94, WhoMW 93*
Howard, Linda 1934- *WhoAmA 93*
Howard, Linda 1950- *WrDr 94*
Howard, Linwood E. 1954- *WhoBlA 94*
Howard, Lisa *WhoHol 92*
Howard, Lisa d1965 *WhoHol 92*
Howard, Louis T. 1923- *WhoAmP 93*
Howard, Louise Ernestine 1880-1969 *DcNaB MP*
Howard, Lucia Fakonas 1951- *WhoAmL 94*
Howard, Lytia Ramani 1950- *WhoBlA 94*
Howard, M(ichael) C. 1945- *ConAu 142*
Howard, M. Francine 1939- *WhoAm 94*
Howard, M. W., Jr. 1946- *WhoBlA 94*
Howard, Malcolm Jones 1939- *WhoAm 94, WhoAmL 94, WhoAmP 93*
Howard, Mamie R. 1946- *WhoBlA 94*
Howard, Margaret 1938- *Who 94*
Howard, Margie Eileen 1950- *WhoAmL 94*
Howard, Marie 1956- *WrDr 94*
Howard, Marjorie *WhoHol 92*
Howard, Mark Alan 1952- *WhoWest 94*
Howard, Mary d1989 *WhoHol 92*
Howard, Mary 1907-1991 *WrDr 94N*
Howard, Mary 1915- *WhoHol 92*
Howard, Matthew Aloysius 1940- *WhoFI 94*
Howard, Maureen 1930- *WrDr 94*
Howard, Mellie Rendon 1934- *WhoAmP 93*
Howard, Melvin 1935- *IntWW 93, WhoAm 94, WhoFI 94*
Howard, Michael *WhoHol 92*
Howard, Michael 1941- *IntWW 93, Who 94*
Howard, Michael (Eliot) 1922- *Who 94, WrDr 94*
Howard, Michael Eliot 1922- *IntWW 93*
Howard, Michael Joseph 1951- *WhoFI 94, WhoMW 93*
Howard, Michael Newman 1947- *Who 94*
Howard, Michael R. 1945- *WhoIns 94*
Howard, Michael Stockwin 1922- *Who 94*
Howard, Milton L. 1927- *WhoBlA 94*
Howard, Moe d1975 *WhoHol 92*
Howard, Moe 1897-1975 *See* Three Stooges, The *WhoCom*
Howard, Moses William, Jr. 1946- *WhoAm 94*
Howard, Murray 1914- *WhoAm 94, WhoFI 94, WhoWest 94*
Howard, Nancy E. 1951- *WhoAmL 94*
Howard, Nathan Southard 1941- *WhoAm 94*
Howard, Noni *DrAPF 93*
Howard, Norah d1968 *WhoHol 92*
Howard, Norman 1947- *WhoBlA 94*
Howard, Norman Leroy 1930- *WhoBlA 94*
Howard, Osbie L., Jr. 1943- *WhoBlA 94*
Howard, Patricia 1937- *WrDr 94*
Howard, Paul Lawrence, Jr. 1951- *WhoBlA 94*
Howard, Paul Noble, Jr. 1922- *WhoAm 94*
Howard, Paula Walton Ollick 1944- *WhoMW 93*
Howard, Peter d1968 *WhoHol 92*
Howard, Peter 1925- *Who 94*
Howard, Peter Milner 1937- *Who 94*
Howard, Philip (Nicholas Charles) 1933- *WrDr 94*
Howard, Philip Martin 1939- *WhoFI 94, WhoMW 93*
Howard, Philip Nicholas Charles 1933- *Who 94*
Howard, Pierre *WhoAm 94*
Howard, Pierre 1943- *WhoAmP 93*
Howard, R. Craig 1945- *WhoAmL 94*
Howard, Rance *WhoHol 92*
Howard, Randall K. 1943- *WhoAmL 94*
Howard, Randolph L. 1946- *WhoAmL 94*
Howard, Ray F. 1945- *WhoBlA 94*
Howard, Raymond Monroe, Sr. 1921- *WhoBlA 94*
Howard, Richard *DrAPF 93*
Howard, Richard 1929- *WhoAm 94, WrDr 94*
Howard, Richard Ralston, II 1948- *WhoFI 94, WhoScEn 94*
Howard, Richard Raymond, II 1963- *WhoFI 94*
Howard, Richard Turner 1935- *WhoAm 94*
Howard, Robert 1939- *Who 94*
Howard, Robert A. 1922- *WhoAmA 93*
Howard, Robert Allen 1944- *WhoAmP 93*
Howard, Robert Berry, Jr. 1916- *WhoBlA 94*
Howard, Robert Boardman 1896-1983 *WhoAmA 93N*
Howard, Robert Campbell, Jr. 1951- *WhoAmL 94, WhoWest 94*
Howard, Robert Clark 1931- *WhoFI 94*
Howard, Robert E(rvin) 1906-1936 *EncSF 93*
Howard, Robert Elliott 1933- *WhoAm 94*
Howard, Robert Franklin 1932- *WhoAm 94, WhoScEn 94*
Howard, Robert Miller 1919- *WhoAm 94*
Howard, Robert P. 1955- *WhoScEn 94*
Howard, Robert Staples 1924- *WhoAm 94, WhoWest 94*
Howard, Roger 1938- *ConDr 93, WrDr 94*
Howard, Ron 1954- *ConTFT 11, IntMPA 94, IntWW 93, WhoAm 94, WhoHol 92*
Howard, Ronald 1916- *WhoHol 92*
Howard, Ronald Claude 1902- *Who 94*
Howard, Russell Duane 1956- *WhoScEn 94*
Howard, Ruth d1944 *WhoHol 92*
Howard, Sally Purnell 1943- *WhoAmP 93*
Howard, Samuel 1710-1782 *NewGrDO*
Howard, Samuel H. 1939- *WhoBlA 94*
Howard, Samuel Hunter, Jr. 1953- *WhoAmP 93*
Howard, Sandy 1927- *IntMPA 94, WhoAm 94*
Howard, Sharon Effatt 1957- *WhoAmL 94*
Howard, Shemp d1955 *WhoHol 92*
Howard, Shemp 1895-1955 *WhoCom*
Howard, Sherwin Ward 1936- *WhoWest 94*
Howard, Shirley d1988 *WhoHol 92*
Howard, Shirley M. 1935- *WhoBlA 94*
Howard, Sidney 1891-1939 *IntDcF 2-4*
Howard, Sidney (Coe) 1891-1939 *IntDcT 2*
Howard, Stanley Louis 1948- *WhoAm 94*
Howard, Steven J. 1971- *WhoAmP 93*
Howard, Susan 1943- *WhoHol 92*
Howard, Susan Carol Pearcy 1954- *WhoScEn 94*
Howard, Susan E. 1961- *WhoBlA 94*
Howard, Susanne C. 1951- *WhoAmL 94*
Howard, Sydney d1946 *WhoHol 92*
Howard, Tanya Millicent 1968- *WhoBlA 94*
Howard, Theodore Walter 1942- *WhoAm 94*
Howard, Thomas Bailey, Jr. 1928- *WhoFI 94*
Howard, Thomas Clement 1943- *WhoMW 93*
Howard, Tom *WhoHol 92*
Howard, Tom d1955 *WhoHol 92*
Howard, Trevor d1988 *WhoHol 92*
Howard, Troy *EncSF 93*
Howard, Vance F. 1937- *WhoIns 94*
Howard, Vance Francis 1937- *WhoFI 94*
Howard, Vanessa *WhoHol 92*
Howard, Vanessa 1955- *BlkWr 2*
Howard, Vera Gouke *WhoBlA 94*
Howard, Victor 1923- *WhoWest 94*
Howard, Victor Carl 1952- *WhoAmP 93*
Howard, Vince *WhoHol 92*
Howard, Vincent d1946 *WhoHol 92*
Howard, Vivian Gordon 1923- *WhoBlA 94*
Howard, Volney Ward, Jr. 1941- *WhoWest 94*
Howard, W. O. *WhoAmP 93*
Howard, Walter d1922 *WhoHol 92*
Howard, Walter Boivin 1927- *WhoAmP 93*
Howard, Walter Burke 1916- *WhoAm 94*
Howard, Walter Egner 1917- *WhoWest 94*
Howard, Warda d1943 *WhoHol 92*
Howard, Warren F. *EncSF 93*
Howard, Wendy d1972 *WhoHol 92*
Howard, William d1944 *WhoHol 92*
Howard, William Barker, Jr. 1956- *WhoFI 94*
Howard, William Brian 1926- *Who 94*
Howard, William Dotson 1964- *WhoBlA 94*
Howard, William Gates, Jr. 1941- *WhoAm 94*
Howard, William H., III 1951- *WhoAmL 94*
Howard, William Herbert 1953- *WhoAm 94*
Howard, William J. 1923- *WhoFI 94*
Howard, William Jack 1922- *WhoAm 94*
Howard, William Matthew 1934- *WhoAm 94, WhoWest 94*
Howard, William R. *NewYTBS 93 [port]*
Howard, Willie d1949 *WhoHol 92*
Howard, Willie 1886-1949 *WhoCom*
Howard-Carter, Theresa 1929- *WhoAm 94*
Howard De Walden, Baron 1912- *Who 94*
Howard-Dobson, Patrick John 1921- *Who 94*
Howard-Drake, Jack Thomas Arthur 1919- *Who 94*
Howard-Hill, Trevor Howard 1933- *WhoAm 94*
Howard-Johnston, Clarence Dinsmore 1903- *Who 94*
Howard-Lawson, John (Philip) 1934- *Who 94*
Howard Nichols, Clarina 1810-1885 *WomPubS*
Howard Of Penrith, Baron 1905- *Who 94*
Howards, Joyzele Toby 1935- *WhoMW 93*
Howards, Stuart S. 1937- *WhoAm 94*
Howard-Vyse, Edward Dacre d1992 *Who 94N*
Howard-Williams, Jeremy 1922- *WrDr 94*
Howarth, Alan Thomas 1944- *Who 94*
Howarth, Clifford 1925- *WhoAmP 93*
Howarth, David 1912- *WrDr 94*
Howarth, David H. 1936- *WhoAm 94*
Howarth, Donald 1931- *ConDr 93, WrDr 94*
Howarth, Elgar 1935- *IntWW 93, NewGrDO, Who 94*
Howarth, George Edward 1949- *Who 94*
Howarth, (James) Gerald (Douglas) 1947- *Who 94*
Howarth, Jack d1984 *WhoHol 92*
Howarth, Leslie 1911- *IntWW 93, Who 94*
Howarth, Nigel John Graham 1936- *Who 94*
Howarth, Patrick (John Fielding) 1916- *WrDr 94*
Howarth, Peter James 1935- *Who 94*
Howarth, Robert F., Jr. 1944- *WhoAm 94, WhoAmL 94*
Howarth, Robert Lever 1927- *Who 94*
Howarth, Robert Lewis *WhoAmP 93*
Howarth, Shirley Reiff 1944- *WhoAmA 93*
Howarth, T(homas) E(dward) B(rodie) 1914-1988 *ConAu 141*
Howarth, Thomas 1914- *IntWW 93*
Howarth, Thomas 1921- *WhoAm 94*
Howarth, William (Louis) 1940- *WrDr 94*
Howat, Clark *WhoHol 92*
Howat, Gerald (Malcolm David) 1928- *WrDr 94*
Howat, Henry Taylor 1911- *Who 94*
Howat, John Keith 1937- *WhoAm 94, WhoAmA 93*
Howatch, Susan 1940- *IntWW 93, WrDr 94*
Howatson, Marianne 1948- *WhoAm 94, WhoFI 94*
Howatt, Helen Clare 1927- *WhoWest 94*
Howbert, Edgar Charles 1937- *WhoAm 94*
Howd, Isobel 1928- *Who 94*
Howd, Robert Allen 1944- *WhoWest 94*
Howden, David Gordon 1937- *WhoScEn 94*
Howden, Frederick Michael 1953- *WhoWest 94*
Howden, Timothy Simon 1937- *IntWW 93, Who 94*
Howdy, Clyde d1969 *WhoHol 92*
Howe *Who 94*
Howe, Earl 1951- *Who 94*
Howe, Albert Berry, Jr. 1917- *WhoAmP 93*
Howe, Allen 1918- *Who 94*
Howe, Art 1946- *WhoAm 94*
Howe, Ben Steventon 1935- *WhoAmP 93*
Howe, Brian Leslie 1936- *IntWW 93, Who 94*
Howe, Bruce Iver 1936- *WhoAm 94*
Howe, Burton Brower 1936- *WhoScEn 94*
Howe, Carroll Victor 1923- *WhoAm 94, WhoFI 94*
Howe, Charles Bryan 1935- *WhoAmP 93*
Howe, Christopher Barry 1937- *Who 94*
Howe, Daniel Bo 1944- *WhoScEn 94*
Howe, Daniel Walker 1937- *Who 94, WhoAm 94*
Howe, David Nathan 1941- *WhoFI 94, WhoMW 93*
Howe, David S. 1944- *WhoAmL 94*
Howe, Deborah d1978 *WhoHol 92*
Howe, Denis 1927- *Who 94*
Howe, Dennis 1940- *WhoAmP 93*
Howe, Derek Andrew 1934- *Who 94*
Howe, Dianne Shelden 1949- *WhoAm 94*
Howe, Doris (Kathleen) *WrDr 94*
Howe, Dorothy *WhoHol 92*
Howe, Drayton Ford, Jr. 1931- *WhoAmL 94, WhoWest 94*
Howe, Edwin Alberts, Jr. 1939- *WhoAmL 94*
Howe, Elias 1819-1867 *WorInv*
Howe, Elspeth Rosamund Morton *Who 94*
Howe, Eric James 1931- *Who 94*
Howe, Fanny *DrAPF 93*
Howe, Fanny 1940- *BlmGWL, WrDr 94*
Howe, Fisher 1914- *WhoAm 94*
Howe, Florence 1929- *WhoAm 94*
Howe, Frederic Clemson 1867-1940 *AmSocL*
Howe, G(eorge) Melvyn 1920- *Who 94*
Howe, Gary Woodson 1936- *WhoAm 94, WhoMW 93*
Howe, Geoffrey Leslie 1924- *Who 94*
Howe, George 1900- *WhoHol 92*
Howe, George Edward 1925- *Who 94*
Howe, Gordon 1928- *WhoAm 94*
Howe, Graham Lloyd 1950- *WhoAm 94*
Howe, Harold, II 1918- *IntWW 93*
Howe, Herbert Marshall 1912- *WhoAm 94*
Howe, Hugh Philip 1932- *WhoAm 94*
Howe, Irving 1920- *AmSocL*
Howe, Irving 1920-1993 *ConAu 141, CurBio 93N, NewYTBS 93 [port], WrDr 94N*
Howe, Jack 1911- *Who 94*
Howe, James 1946- *WrDr 94*
Howe, James Everett 1930- *WhoAm 94, WhoFI 94*
Howe, James Murray 1924- *WhoAm 94*
Howe, James Tarsicius 1924- *WhoAm 94, WhoFI 94*
Howe, James Wong 1899-1976 *IntDcF 2-4 [port]*
Howe, Jas. Murray 1924- *WhoAmL 94*
Howe, John Francis 1944- *Who 94*
Howe, John Frederick George 1930- *Who 94*
Howe, John Kingman 1945- *WhoMW 93*
Howe, John Perry 1910- *WhoAm 94*
Howe, John Prentice, III 1943- *WhoAm 94, WhoFI 94, WhoScEn 94*
Howe, John William Alexander 1920- *Who 94*
Howe, Jonathan Thomas 1940- *WhoAm 94, WhoAmL 94*
Howe, Jonathan Trumbull 1935- *WhoAm 94*
Howe, Joseph William 1930- *WhoWest 94*
Howe, Josephine Mary O'C. *Who 94*
Howe, Julia Ward 1819-1910 *AmSocL [port], BlmGWL*
Howe, Juliette Coupain 1944- *WhoScEn 94*
Howe, Katherine L. Mallet d1957 *WhoAmA 93N*
Howe, Kimberly Palazzo 1958- *WhoMW 93*
Howe, Lawrence 1921- *WhoAm 94*
Howe, Marie Elizabeth 1939- *WhoAmP 93*
Howe, Mark Lee 1965- *WhoWest 94*

Howe, Martha Morgan 1945- *WhoAm 94, WhoScEn 94*
Howe, Martin 1936- *Who 94*
Howe, Mary Kristin 1947- *WhoWest 94*
Howe, Muriel *WrDr 94*
Howe, Neil 1951- *WrDr 94*
Howe, Nelson H., II 1953- *WhoAmL 94*
Howe, Nelson S. 1935- *WhoAmA 93*
Howe, Oscar 1915- *WhoAmA 93*
Howe, Oscar 1915-1983 *WhoAmA 93N*
Howe, Ralph W., III 1954- *WhoAmP 93*
Howe, Richard 1726-1799 *WhAmRev [port]*
Howe, Richard Cuddy 1924- *WhoAm 94, WhoAmL 94, WhoAmP 93, WhoWest 94*
Howe, Richard J. 1928- *IntWW 93*
Howe, Richard Lord 1726-1799 *AmRev*
Howe, Richard Rives 1942- *WhoAm 94, WhoAmL 94*
Howe, Robert 1732-1786 *AmRev, WhAmRev [port]*
Howe, Robert Melvin 1939- *WhoAm 94, WhoFI 94*
Howe, Robert Wilson 1932- *WhoAm 94*
Howe, Robin 1908- *WrDr 94*
Howe, Ronald d1961 *WhoHol 92*
Howe, Ronald William 1932- *Who 94*
Howe, Ruth-Arlene W. 1933- *WhoBlA 94*
Howe, Samuel Gridley 1801-1876 *AmSocL*
Howe, Stanley Merrill 1924- *WhoAm 94, WhoFI 94, WhoMW 93*
Howe, Stephen Douglas 1948- *Who 94*
Howe, Susan *BlmGWL, DrAPF 93, WrDr 94*
Howe, Tina 1937- *ConDr 93, WrDr 94*
Howe, Walter d1957 *WhoHol 92*
Howe, Walter Charles, Jr. 1934- *WhoAm 94*
Howe, Warren Billings 1940- *WhoWest 94*
Howe, Wesley Jackson 1921- *WhoAm 94, WhoFI 94*
Howe, William 1729-1814 *AmRev, WhAmRev*
Howe, William Hugh 1928- *WhoMW 93*
Howell, Baron 1923- *Who 94*
Howell, Alfred Hunt 1912- *WhoAm 94*
Howell, Alice d1961 *WhoHol 92*
Howell, Allen Windsor 1949- *WhoAmL 94*
Howell, Alvin Harold 1908- *WhoAm 94*
Howell, Amaziah, III 1948- *WhoBlA 94*
Howell, Anthony 1945- *WrDr 94*
Howell, Arthur 1918- *WhoAm 94, WhoAmL 94*
Howell, Bailey 1937- *BasBi*
Howell, Barbara *DrAPF 93*
Howell, Barbara Fennema 1924- *WhoAm 94*
Howell, Benjamin Franklin, Jr. 1917- *WhoAm 94*
Howell, Bette 1920- *WrDr 94*
Howell, Bobby B. *WhoAmP 93*
Howell, C. Thomas 1966- *IntMPA 94, WhoHol 92*
Howell, Charles David 1957- *WhoWest 94*
Howell, Charles Maitland 1914- *WhoAm 94, WhoScEn 94*
Howell, Chester Thomas 1937- *WhoBlA 94*
Howell, Christopher *DrAPF 93*
Howell, Claude Flynn 1915- *WhoAmA 93*
Howell, Connie Rae 1952- *WhoMW 93*
Howell, David 1747-1824 *WhAmRev*
Howell, David (Arthur Russell) 1936- *WrDr 94*
Howell, David Arthur Russell 1936- *IntWW 93, Who 94*
Howell, Donald Lee 1935- *WhoAm 94, WhoAmL 94, WhoFI 94*
Howell, Dorothy J(ulia) 1940- *ConAu 142*
Howell, Edward d1986 *WhoHol 92*
Howell, Elizabeth (Mitch) Coon 1932- *WhoAmA 93*
Howell, Evelyn Michael Thomas 1913- *Who 94*
Howell, Everette Irl 1914- *WhoAm 94*
Howell, F(rancis) Clark 1925- *WrDr 94*
Howell, Forrest Franklin 1954- *WhoMW 93*
Howell, Francis Clark 1925- *IntWW 93, WhoAm 94*
Howell, Gareth 1935- *Who 94*
Howell, George Bedell 1919- *WhoAm 94, WhoMW 93*
Howell, George Cook, III 1956- *WhoAmL 94*
Howell, George F. *DrAPF 93*
Howell, George Washington 1927- *WhoAm 94*
Howell, Gerald T. 1914- *WhoBlA 94*
Howell, Gwynne (Richard) 1938- *NewGrDO*
Howell, Gwynne Richard 1938- *Who 94*
Howell, H. Scott 1929- *WhoFI 94*
Howell, Hannah Johnson 1905-1988 *WhoAmA 93N*
Howell, Harley Thomas 1937- *WhoAm 94, WhoAmL 94, WhoFI 94*
Howell, Henry Evans, Jr. 1920- *WhoAmP 93*
Howell, Hoke *WhoHol 92*
Howell, Jack Lynn 1943- *WhoFI 94*
Howell, James Burt, III 1933- *WhoFI 94*
Howell, James Edwin 1928- *WhoAm 94*
Howell, James F. 1934- *WhoAmP 93*
Howell, James Theodore 1919- *WhoAm 94*
Howell, Janet Denison 1944- *WhoAmP 93*
Howell, Janice Hopkins 1942- *WhoWest 94*
Howell, Joel DuBose 1953- *WhoAm 94, WhoMW 93*
Howell, Joel Walter, III 1949- *WhoAmL 94*
Howell, John Bernard Lloyd 1926- *Who 94*
Howell, John Christian 1924- *WrDr 94*
Howell, John E. 1946- *WhoAmL 94*
Howell, John Floyd 1932- *WhoAm 94*
Howell, John Frederick 1941- *Who 94*
Howell, John McDade 1922- *WhoAm 94*
Howell, John Michael 1933- *WhoMW 93*
Howell, John Reid 1936- *WhoAm 94, WhoScEn 94*
Howell, Joseph M., III 1946- *WhoFI 94*
Howell, Joyce Ann 1955- *WhoAmL 94*
Howell, Kenneth 1917- *WhoHol 92*
Howell, Kenneth Walter 1909- *Who 94*
Howell, Laurence A. 1943- *WhoBlA 94*
Howell, Llewellyn Donald 1940- *WhoWest 94*
Howell, Lloyd 1923- *Who 94*
Howell, Lottice d1982 *WhoHol 92*
Howell, Malqueen 1949- *WhoBlA 94*
Howell, Margaret 1946- *IntWW 93*
Howell, Mary Elizabeth 1942- *WhoFI 94*
Howell, Mary L. 1952- *WhoAm 94*
Howell, Max 1915- *WhoAmP 93*
Howell, Max Don 1887-1967 *EncABHB 9*
Howell, Michael Edward 1933- *IntWW 93, Who 94*
Howell, Norbert Allen 1951- *WhoMW 93*
Howell, Norman Gary 1949- *WhoIns 94*
Howell, Orvie Leon 1931- *WhoMW 93*
Howell, Patrick Leonard 1942- *Who 94*
Howell, Paul (Philip) 1917- *WrDr 94*
Howell, Paul Frederic 1951- *Who 94*
Howell, Paul Neilson 1918- *WhoAm 94, WhoFI 94*
Howell, Paul Philip 1917- *Who 94*
Howell, Peter Adrian 1941- *Who 94*
Howell, Rachel 1961- *WhoBlA 94*
Howell, Ralph Frederic 1923- *Who 94*
Howell, Ralph Rodney 1931- *WhoAm 94, WhoScEn 94*
Howell, Raymond Gary 1947- *WhoMW 93*
Howell, Richard 1754-1802 *WhAmRev*
Howell, Richard Paul, Sr. 1927- *WhoAm 94, WhoScEn 94*
Howell, Richard S. 1935- *WhoAmP 93*
Howell, Robert J., Jr. 1935- *WhoBlA 94*
Howell, Robert Thomas, Jr. 1942- *WhoAm 94, WhoAmL 94, WhoFI 94*
Howell, Robert Wayne 1916- *WhoAm 94*
Howell, Roger, Jr. 1936-1989 *WhAm 10*
Howell, Scott *EncSF 93*
Howell, Scott Newell 1953- *WhoAmP 93, WhoWest 94*
Howell, Sharon Marie 1950- *WhoBlA 94*
Howell, Stephen Barnard 1944- *WhoWest 94*
Howell, Steven Gordon 1953- *WhoAm 94, WhoAmL 94*
Howell, Terry Allen 1947- *WhoScEn 94*
Howell, Thomas 1944- *WhoAm 94*
Howell, Thomas Edwin 1918- *WhoAm 94*
Howell, Vincent Wyatt 1953- *WhoBlA 94*
Howell, Virginia Tier 1910- *WrDr 94*
Howell, W. Nathaniel 1939- *WhoAmP 93*
Howell, Warren Richardson 1912-1984 *DcLB 140 [port]*
Howell, Wesley Grant, Jr. 1937- *WhoAm 94*
Howell, Wilbur Samuel 1904-1992 *WhAm 10*
Howell, William Ashley, III 1949- *WhoAmL 94, WhoFI 94*
Howell, William B. 1932- *WhoBlA 94*
Howell, William Everett 1956- *WhoScEn 94*
Howell, William Haywood 1956- *WhoWest 94*
Howell, William J. 1946- *WhoIns 94*
Howell, William James 1943- *WhoAmP 93*
Howell, William Joseph 1946- *WhoFI 94*
Howell, William Page 1952- *WhoFI 94*
Howell, William Robert 1936- *WhoAm 94, WhoFI 94*
Howell, Willie R. 1926- *WhoBlA 94*
Howells *Who 94*
Howells, Anne 1941- *NewGrDO, Who 94*
Howells, Anne Elizabeth 1941- *IntWW 93*
Howells, Eric (Waldo Benjamin) 1933- *Who 94*
Howells, Gwyn 1918- *IntWW 93, Who 94*
Howells, John Gwilym 1918- *WrDr 94*
Howells, Kim Scott 1946- *Who 94*
Howells, Ursula 1922- *IntMPA 94, WhoHol 92*
Howells, William Dean 1837-1920 *AmCulL, AmSocL, EncSF 93*
Howells, William White 1908- *IntWW 93, WhoAm 94, WrDr 94*
Howe Of Aberavon, Baron 1926- *IntWW 93, Who 94*
Howe Of Aberavon, Lady 1932- *Who 94*
Hower, Edward *DrAPF 93*
Hower, Frank Beard, Jr. 1928- *WhoAm 94*
Hower, Philip Leland 1934- *WhoScEn 94*
Hower, Robert K. 1947- *WhoAmA 93*
Howerd, Frankie 1922- *WhoHol 92*
Howerton, Clarence d1975 *WhoHol 92*
Howerton, George 1905- *WhoAm 94*
Howerton, Helen V. 1933- *WhoAm 94*
Howerton, Robert Melton 1957- *WhoScEn 94*
Howerton, Tina Marie 1961- *WhoMW 93*
Howery, C. Kenneth 1950- *WhoFI 94*
Howes, Alfred S. 1917- *WhoAm 94, WhoFI 94, WhoIns 94*
Howes, Barbara *DrAPF 93*
Howes, Barbara 1914- *WrDr 94*
Howes, Benjamin Durward, III 1922- *WhoAm 94*
Howes, Bobby d1972 *WhoHol 92*
Howes, Brian Thomas 1957- *WhoAmL 94, WhoMW 93*
Howes, Christopher Kingston 1942- *Who 94*
Howes, Edith Annie 1872-1954 *BlmGWL*
Howes, Gloria *WhoAmP 93, WhoWest 94*
Howes, James Guerdon *WhoAm 94*
Howes, Jane *EncSF 93*
Howes, Kenneth Ronald 1935- *WhoMW 93*
Howes, Lorraine de Wet 1933- *WhoAm 94*
Howes, Mary 1941- *BlmGWL*
Howes, Reed d1964 *WhoHol 92*
Howes, Royce Bucknam 1950- *WhoAmA 93*
Howes, Sally Ann *Who 94*
Howes, Sally Ann 1930- *WhoHol 92*
Howes, Trevor Denis *WhoScEn 94*
Howett, John 1926- *WhoAmA 93*
Howe-Weintraub, Melody Raedell 1959- *WhoAmP 93*
Howey, John Richard 1933- *WhoAm 94*
Howe Yoon Chong 1923- *IntWW 93*
Howick Of Glendale, Baron 1937- *Who 94*
Howie *Who 94*
Howie, Archibald 1934- *IntWW 93, Who 94*
Howie, J. Robert 1929- *IntWW 93*
Howie, James (William), Sir 1907- *Who 94*
Howie, John Garvie Robertson 1937- *Who 94*
Howie, John Mackintosh 1936- *Who 94*
Howie, John Robert 1946- *WhoAm 94, WhoAmL 94*
Howie, Robert Andrew 1923- *Who 94*
Howie Of Troon, Baron 1924- *Who 94*
Howison, George Everett 1944- *WhoFI 94*
Howitt, Andrew Wilson 1960- *WhoScEn 94*
Howitt, Anthony Wentworth 1920- *Who 94*
Howitt, David Andrew 1953- *WhoWest 94*
Howitt, John Newton 1885-1958 *WhoAmA 93N*
Howitt, W(illiam) Fowler 1924- *Who 94*
Howker, Janni 1957- *TwCYAW*
Howkins, John 1907- *Who 94*
Howkins, John Anthony 1945- *Who 94*
Howl, Marcia Yvonne *EncSF 93*
Howland, Lord 1962- *Who 94*
Howland, Allen Hathaway 1921- *WhoFI 94*
Howland, Beth 1947- *WhoHol 92*
Howland, Bette *DrAPF 93*
Howland, Bette 1937- *WhoAm 94*
Howland, Edith d1949 *WhoAmA 93N*
Howland, Garth 1887-1950 *WhoAmA 93N*
Howland, Glenn Cornelius 1956- *WhoAmL 94*
Howland, Grafton Dulany 1943- *WhoFI 94*
Howland, Joan Sidney 1951- *WhoAmL 94*
Howland, Jobyna d1936 *WhoHol 92*
Howland, John Hudson, Sr. 1915- *WhoAmP 93*
Howland, Joseph Emery 1918- *WhoWest 94*
Howland, Kinnaird 1944- *WhoAmL 94*
Howland, Murray Shipley, Jr. 1911- *WhoAm 94*
Howland, Olin d1959 *WhoHol 92*
Howland, Paul 1948- *WhoScEn 94*
Howland, Peter McKinnon 1956- *WhoWest 94*
Howland, Richard 1934- *WhoAmP 93*
Howland, Richard Henry 1925-1990 *WhAm 10*
Howland, Richard Hubbard 1910- *WhoAmA 93*
Howland, Richard Moulton 1940- *WhoAmL 94*
Howland, Willard J. 1927- *WhoAm 94*
Howland, William Goldwin Carrington 1915- *Who 94, WhoAm 94*
Howland, William Stapleton 1919- *WhoAm 94*
Howle, C. Tycho 1949- *WhoFI 94*
Howlett, Anthony Douglas 1924- *Who 94*
Howlett, Carolyn Svrluga 1914- *WhoAm 94, WhoAmA 93*
Howlett, D(onald) Roger 1945- *WhoAmA 93, WrDr 94*
Howlett, Dale L. *WhoAmP 93*
Howlett, Donald Roger 1945- *WhoFI 94*
Howlett, Duncan 1906- *WrDr 94*
Howlett, Geoffrey (Hugh Whitby) 1930- *Who 94*
Howlett, Jack 1912- *Who 94*
Howlett, Joan *DrAPF 93*
Howlett, John David 1952- *WhoWest 94*
Howlett, Joseph 1943- *WhoAmP 93*
Howlett, Michael Joseph, Jr. 1948- *WhoAmL 94*
Howlett, Neil 1934- *NewGrDO*
Howlett, Neville Stanley 1927- *Who 94*
Howlett, Noel d1984 *WhoHol 92*
Howlett, Robert Glasgow 1906-1988 *WhAm 10*
Howlett, Ronald William 1928- *Who 94*
Howlett, Timothy H. 1948- *WhoAmL 94*
Howley, James McAndrew 1928- *WhoAmL 94*
Howley, Richard 1740-1784 *WhAmRev*
Howlin, Brendan 1958- *IntWW 93*
Howling, Alan Arthur 1958- *WhoScEn 94*
Howlin' Wolf 1910-1976 *AfrAmAl 6, AmCulL*
Howman, John Hartley 1918- *IntWW 93*
Howman, Karl 1953- *WhoHol 92*
Howorth, David Bishop 1947- *WhoAm 94, WhoAmL 94*
Howorth, Lucy Somerville *WhoAm 94, WhoAmL 94*
Howren, Charles Gresham 1941- *WhoAmP 93*
Howrey, Edward F. 1903- *WhoAm 94*
Howrey, Eugene Philip 1937- *WhoAm 94*
Howrey, Linda McKay 1953- *WhoMW 93*
Howrigan, D. Francis 1917- *WhoAmP 93*
Howsden, Arley Levern 1926- *WhoAmP 93*
Howse, Charles Melvin 1945- *WhoFI 94*
Howse, Ernest Marshall 1902- *WrDr 94*
Howse, Ernest Marshall (Frazer) 1902- *ConAu 43NR*
Howse, Humphrey Derek 1919- *Who 94*
Howse, Jennifer Louise 1945- *WhoAm 94*
Howse, Robert Davis 1908- *WhoAm 94*
Howsley, Richard Thornton 1948- *WhoWest 94*
Howsmon, Alan Johnston 1934- *WhoMW 93*
Howson, Bruce K. 1942- *WhoIns 94*
Howson, Emma *NewGrDO*
Howson, George 1886-1936 *DcNaB MP*
Howson, Robert E. 1932- *WhoAm 94, WhoFI 94*
Howting, Richard Michael 1949- *WhoAm 94, WhoFI 94*
Howze, Dorothy J. 1923- *WhoBlA 94*
Howze, James Dean 1930- *WhoAmA 93*
Howze, Joseph Lawson 1923- *WhoBlA 94*
Howze, Joseph Lawson Edward 1923- *WhoAm 94*
Howze, Karen Aileen 1950- *WhoAm 94, WhoBlA 94*
Hoxie, Al d1982 *WhoHol 92*
Hoxie, Hart *WhoHol 92*
Hoxie, Jack d1965 *WhoHol 92*
Hoxie, Joel P. 1948- *WhoAm 94*
Hoxie, Ralph Gordon 1919- *WhoAm 94, WhoFI 94*
Hoxie, Timothy Gordon 1960- *WhoAmL 94*
Hoxie, William Elwin 1956- *WhoFI 94*
Hoxsey, Betty June 1923- *WhoAmP 93*
Hoxter, Curtis Joseph 1922- *WhoAm 94*
Hoy, Claire 1940- *ConAu 140*
Hoy, Cyrus Henry 1926- *WhoAm 94*
Hoy, David 1913- *Who 94*
Hoy, David Couzens 1944- *WrDr 94*
Hoy, George Philip 1937- *WhoMW 93*
Hoy, Harold H. 1941- *WhoAmA 93*
Hoy, Harold Joseph 1934- *WhoAm 94*
Hoy, Linda 1946- *TwCYAW, WrDr 94*
Hoy, Marjorie Ann 1941- *WhoAm 94, WhoScEn 94*
Hoy, Nina *ConAu 140, SmATA 75*
Hoy, Rex Bruce 1928- *WhoAmP 93*
Hoy, Robert *WhoHol 92*

Hoy, Suellen 1942- *WhoMW 93*
Hoy, William Ivan 1915- *WhoAm 94*
Hoyal, Dorothy 1918- *WhoAmA 93*
Hoye, John T. *WhoAmP 93*
Hoye, Robert Earl 1931- *WhoScEn 94*
Hoye, Walter B. 1930- *WhoBlA 94*
Hoye, Walter B., II 1956- *WhoBlA 94*
Hoye, Walter Brisco 1930- *WhoWest 94*
Hoyem, Andrew *DrAPF 93*
Hoyem, Andrew 1935- *WrDr 94*
Hoyem, Andrew Lewison 1935- *WhoAm 94*
Hoyem, Tom 1941- *IntWW 93*
Hoyer, Carl Ivan 1930- *WhoIns 94*
Hoyer, Eugene Richard 1940- *WhoAmP 93*
Hoyer, Harvey Conrad 1907- *WhoAm 94*
Hoyer, Steny H. 1939- *CngDr 93*
Hoyer, Steny Hamilton 1939- *WhoAm 94, WhoAmP 93*
Hoyer, Stephen 1955- *WhoMW 93*
Hoyers, Anna Ovena 1584-1655 *BlmGWL*
Hoyes, Thomas 1935- *Who 94*
Hoying, James William 1957- *WhoFI 94*
Hoyland, John 1934- *IntWW 93, Who 94*
Hoyland, Michael (David) 1925- *WrDr 94*
Hoyle, Classie 1936- *WhoBlA 94*
Hoyle, David W. 1939- *WhoAmP 93*
Hoyle, (Eric) Douglas (Harvey) 1930- *Who 94*
Hoyle, Eric 1931- *Who 94*
Hoyle, Fred 1915- *EncSF 93, IntWW 93, Who 94, WorScD, WrDr 94*
Hoyle, Frederick James 1918- *Who 94*
Hoyle, Geoffrey 1941- *EncSF 93*
Hoyle, Geoffrey 1942- *WrDr 94*
Hoyle, John Douglas 1943- *WhoAm 94*
Hoyle, Lawrence Truman, Jr. 1938- *WhoAmL 94*
Hoyle, Sally Georgette 1957- *WhoMW 93*
Hoyle, Susan 1953- *Who 94*
Hoyle, Trevor 1940- *ConAu 142, EncSF 93, WrDr 94*
Hoyle, William Vinton, Jr. 1949- *WhoAmL 94*
Hoyles, J(ames) Arthur 1908- *WrDr 94*
Hoyme, Chad Earl 1933- *WhoAm 94*
Hoyne, Andrew Thomas 1947- *WhoAmL 94*
Hoyne, Thomas Temple 1875-1946 *EncSF 93*
Hoynes, Louis LeNoir, Jr. 1935- *WhoAm 94, WhoAmL 94, WhoFI 94*
Hoynoski, Bruce William 1955- *WhoMW 93*
Hoyos, (Fabriciano) Alexander 1912- *Who 94*
Hoyos, Rodolfo d1983 *WhoHol 92*
Hoyt, Arthur d1953 *WhoHol 92*
Hoyt, Bradley Arthur 1953- *WhoFI 94*
Hoyt, Bradley James 1949- *WhoFI 94*
Hoyt, Brooks Pettingill 1929- *WhoAm 94, WhoAmL 94*
Hoyt, Charlee Van Cleve 1936- *WhoFI 94*
Hoyt, Charles King 1938- *WhoFI 94*
Hoyt, Clark Freeland 1942- *WhoAm 94*
Hoyt, Clegg d1967 *WhoHol 92*
Hoyt, David Lemire 1951- *WhoAm 94*
Hoyt, David Richard 1950- *WhoAm 94*
Hoyt, Don A. *DrAPF 93*
Hoyt, Earl Edward, Jr. 1936- *WhoAm 94*
Hoyt, Edwin P. *DrAPF 93*
Hoyt, Ellen 1933- *WhoAmA 93*
Hoyt, Frances Weston 1908- *WhoAmA 93*
Hoyt, Frank Russell 1916- *WhoAm 94*
Hoyt, Helen d1979 *WhoHol 92*
Hoyt, Henry Hamilton 1895-1990 *WhAm 10*
Hoyt, Henry Hamilton, Jr. 1927- *WhoAm 94, WhoFI 94*
Hoyt, Herbert Austin Aikins 1937- *WhoAm 94*
Hoyt, Irvin N. 1941- *WhoAmL 94*
Hoyt, Jack Wallace 1922- *WhoWest 94*
Hoyt, James Lawrence 1943- *WhoAm 94*
Hoyt, John 1904- *WhoHol 92*
Hoyt, John Arthur 1932- *WhoAm 94*
Hoyt, Julia d1955 *WhoHol 92*
Hoyt, Kathleen Clark 1942- *WhoAmP 93*
Hoyt, Kenneth Boyd 1924- *WhoAm 94*
Hoyt, Kenneth M. 1948- *WhoAm 94, WhoAmL 94*
Hoyt, Leo d1937 *WhoHol 92*
Hoyt, Linda Jane 1955- *WhoAmP 93*
Hoyt, Mary Finch *WhoAm 94*
Hoyt, Mont Powell 1940- *WhoAm 94*
Hoyt, Monty 1944- *WhoAm 94*
Hoyt, Nelly Schargo 1920- *WhoAm 94*
Hoyt, Norris 1935- *WhoAmP 93*
Hoyt, Richard *WhoHol 92*
Hoyt, Richard 1941- *WrDr 94*
Hoyt, Robert Emmet 1923- *WhoAm 94*
Hoyt, Robert Joseph 1934-1988 *WhAm 10*
Hoyt, Seth *WhoAm 94*
Hoyt, Stanley Charles 1929- *WhoScEn 94*
Hoyt, Thomas L., Jr. 1941- *WhoBlA 94*
Hoyt, Whitney F. 1910-1980 *WhoAmA 93N*
Hoyt, William Vernor 1937- *WhoAm 94*
Hoyte, Arthur Hamilton 1938- *WhoBlA 94*
Hoyte, Hugh Desmond 1929- *IntWW 93, Who 94*
Hoyte, James Sterling 1944- *WhoBlA 94*
Hoyte, Lenon Holder 1905- *WhoBlA 94*
Hrabal, Bohumil 1914- *ConWorW 93, IntWW 93, RfGShF*
Hrabovsky, Leonid (Oleksandrovych) 1935- *NewGrDO*
Hrabowski, Freeman Alphonsa, III 1950- *WhoBlA 94*
Hracho, Lawrence John 1948- *WhoAmL 94*
Hrachovina, Frederick Vincent 1926- *WhoAm 94*
Hranitzky, E. Burnell 1941- *WhoScEn 94*
Hrawi, Elias 1930- *IntWW 93*
Hrazanek, Richard J. 1937- *WhoIns 94*
Hrdy, Sarah Blaffer 1946- *WhoAm 94, WhoWest 94*
Hresan, Sally L. 1946- *WhoAm 94*
Hribal, C. J. *DrAPF 93*
Hribar, John Peter, Sr. 1936- *WhoWest 94*
Hribar, Lawrence Joseph 1960- *WhoScEn 94*
Hric, Paul J. 1926- *WhoAmP 93*
Hrimaly, Vojtech 1842-1908 *NewGrDO*
Hrinko, Daniel Dean 1955- *WhoMW 93*
Hriskevich, Michael Edward 1926- *WhoAm 94*
Hristic, Stevan 1885-1958 *NewGrDO*
Hritz, George F. 1948- *WhoAmL 94*
Hrivnak, Pavel 1931- *IntWW 93*
Hron, Michael G. 1945- *WhoAm 94, WhoAmL 94*
Hrones, John Anthony 1912- *WhoAm 94*
Hrones, Stephen Baylis 1942- *WhoAmL 94*
Hrosvit *IntDcT 2*
Hrotsvitha (of Gandersheim) c. 935-c. 973 *IntDcT 2*
Hrotsvith von Gandersheim c. 935-c. 973 *BlmGWL*
Hrouda, Barthel 1929- *IntWW 93*
Hruba, Vera *WhoHol 92*
Hrubes, Donna Bleich 1940- *WhoMW 93*
Hrubes, Marvin R. 1944- *WhoAmP 93*
Hruby, Frank M. 1918- *WhoAm 94*
Hruby, Margarete d1948 *WhoHol 92*
Hrudey, Steve E. *WhoScEn 94*
Hrusinsky, Rudolf *WhoHol 92*
Hruska, Alan *EncSF 93*
Hruska, Alan J. 1933- *WhoAm 94*
Hruska, Elias N. *DrAPF 93*
Hruska, Roman Lee 1904- *WhoAm 94, WhoAmP 93*
Hruska, Ronald John, Jr. 1955- *WhoMW 93*
Hrut, Christopher Boleslaw 1958- *WhoFI 94, WhoWest 94*
Hrycak, Michael Paul 1959- *WhoAmL 94*
Hrycak, Peter 1923- *WhoAm 94, WhoFI 94, WhoScEn 94*
Hryciw, Roman D. 1958- *WhoScEn 94*
Hrydziusko, Wesley J. 1931- *WhoAmP 93*
Hsi, Bartholomew P. 1925- *WhoAsA 94*
Hsi, David C. 1928- *WhoAsA 94*
Hsi, David Ching Heng 1928- *WhoAm 94*
Hsia, Judith Ann 1954- *WhoAsA 94*
Hsia, Judo Jeoudao 1947- *WhoAsA 94*
Hsia, Lisa 1958- *WhoAsA 94*
Hsia, Martin Edgar 1957- *WhoAmL 94*
Hsia, Richard C. 1948- *WhoIns 94*
Hsia, Yuchuek 1944- *WhoAsA 94*
Hsia, Yukun 1941- *WhoAsA 94*
Hsiao, Benjamin S. 1958- *WhoAsA 94*
Hsiao, Chin 1935- *WhoAmA 93*
Hsiao, Fei-bin 1953- *WhoScEn 94*
Hsiao, Feng 1919- *WhoAsA 94*
Hsiao, Joan Hsi-Min 1965- *WhoAsA 94*
Hsiao, Julia *WhoAsA 94*
Hsiao, Margaret Sheng-Mei 1956- *WhoAsA 94*
Hsiao, Ming-Yuan 1954- *WhoMW 93, WhoScEn 94*
Hsiao, Mu-Yue 1933- *WhoAm 94*
Hsiao, Peter 1960- *WhoAmL 94*
Hsiao, Sidney C. 1905-1989 *WhoAsA 94N*
Hsiao, Tony An-Jen 1958- *WhoAsA 94*
Hsiao, Tyzen 1938- *WhoAsA 94*
Hsiao, William C. 1936- *WhoAm 94, WhoAsA 94, WhoScEn 94*
Hsie, Abraham Wuhsiung 1940- *WhoAsA 94*
Hsieh, Brian 1964- *WhoAsA 94*
Hsieh, Carl Chia-Fong 1939- *WhoAsA 94*
Hsieh, Chung-cheng 1954- *WhoAsA 94*
Hsieh, Cynthia C. 1961- *WhoAsA 94*
Hsieh, Daniel Sebastian 1964- *WhoAsA 94*
Hsieh, Dean Shui-Tien 1948- *WhoAsA 94*
Hsieh, Dennis P. H. 1937- *WhoAm 94*
Hsieh, Durwynne 1963- *WhoAsA 94*
Hsieh, Franklin 1947- *WhoAsA 94*
Hsieh, Hsin-Neng 1947- *WhoAsA 94*
Hsieh, Jeanette L. 1943- *WhoAsA 94*
Hsieh, Jui Sheng 1921- *WhoAm 94*
Hsieh, Li-Ping 1941- *WhoAsA 94*
Hsieh, Michael Thomas 1958- *WhoFI 94*
Hsieh, Philip Po-Fang 1934- *WhoAsA 94*
Hsieh, Rudy Ru-Pin 1950- *WhoFI 94*
Hsieh, Tom *WhoAmP 93, WhoAsA 94*
Hsieh, Wen-jen 1955- *WhoAsA 94*
Hsieh, Winston Wen-sun 1935- *WhoAsA 94*
Hsieh, You-Lo 1953- *WhoAsA 94*
Hsieh Fang 1904- *HisDcKW*
Hsin, Chen-Chung 1947- *WhoAsA 94*
Hsin, Liang Yih 1939- *WhoAsA 94*
Hsin, Victor Jun-Kuan 1945- *WhoFI 94*
Hsing, Rodney W. 1962- *WhoAsA 94*
Hsiung, Gueh Djen 1918- *WhoAsA 94*
Hsiung, Robert Yuan Chun 1935- *WhoAm 94*
Hsu, Albert Yutien 1922- *WhoAsA 94*
Hsu, Bertrand Dahung 1933- *WhoScEn 94*
Hsu, Cathy H. C. 1962- *WhoAsA 94*
Hsu, Charles Fu-Jen 1920- *WhoAsA 94*
Hsu, Charles Jui-cheng 1930- *WhoAsA 94, WhoFI 94*
Hsu, Chen-Chi 1935- *WhoAsA 94*
Hsu, Cheng 1951- *WhoScEn 94*
Hsu, Cheng-Tzu Thomas 1941- *WhoAm 94, WhoScEn 94*
Hsu, Chieh Su 1922- *WhoAm 94, WhoAsA 94, WhoScEn 94, WhoWest 94*
Hsu, Chien-Yeh 1963- *WhoScEn 94*
Hsu, Ching-yu 1898- *WhoAm 94*
Hsu, Cho-yun 1930- *WhoAm 94*
Hsu, Chung Yi 1944- *WhoScEn 94*
Hsu, Donald K. 1947- *WhoAsA 94*
Hsu, Evelyn 1953?- *WhoAsA 94*
Hsu, Frank H. 1935- *WhoAsA 94*
Hsu, George Chi-Yung 1945- *WhoAsA 94*
Hsu, Hsiu-Sheng 1931- *WhoAsA 94*
Hsu, Hsiung 1920- *WhoAm 94*
Hsu, Immanuel C. Y. 1923- *WhoAsA 94*
Hsu, Immanuel Chung Yueh 1923- *WhoAm 94*
Hsu, John J. 1919- *WhoAm 94*
Hsu, John Tseng Hsin 1931- *WhoAm 94*
Hsu, John Tseng-Hsiu 1931- *WhoAsA 94*
Hsu, John Y. 1938- *WhoAsA 94*
Hsu, Jong-Ping 1939- *WhoAsA 94*
Hsu, Jong-Pyng 1951- *WhoAsA 94*
Hsu, Julie Man-ching 1933- *WhoScEn 94*
Hsu, Kenneth Hsuehchia 1950- *WhoAsA 94*
Hsu, Kenneth Jinghwa 1929- *IntWW 93*
Hsu, Konrad Chang 1901- *WhoAsA 94*
Hsu, Laura Ling 1939- *WhoAsA 94*
Hsu, Liang-Chi 1931- *WhoAsA 94*
Hsu, Margaretha *WhoAsA 94*
Hsu, Mei-Ling 1932- *WhoAsA 94*
Hsu, Merlin 1954- *WhoAsA 94*
Hsu, Ming Chen 1924- *WhoAm 94*
Hsu, Ming-Yu 1925- *WhoScEn 94*
Hsu, Nai-chao 1927- *WhoAsA 94*
Hsu, Paul 1949- *WhoAsA 94*
Hsu, Peter Cheazone 1951- *WhoScEn 94*
Hsu, Ping 1957- *WhoAsA 94*
Hsu, Robert C. 1937- *ConAu 141*
Hsu, Robert Ying 1926- *WhoAsA 94*
Hsu, Roger Y. K. 1927- *WhoAm 94, WhoFI 94*
Hsu, Samuel 1947- *WhoAsA 94*
Hsu, Shaw Ling 1948- *WhoAsA 94*
Hsu, Shu-Dean 1943- *WhoWest 94*
Hsu, Stephen Charles 1960- *WhoAsA 94*
Hsu, Stephen M. 1943- *WhoAsA 94*
Hsu, Steven Hua-Sheng 1943- *WhoMW 93*
Hsu, Thomas Tseng-Chuang 1933- *WhoAm 94*
Hsu, Timothy 1952- *WhoAsA 94*
Hsu, Tse-Chi 1936- *WhoAsA 94*
Hsu, Yu-Chin 1958- *WhoWest 94*
Hsu, Yu Chu 1930- *WhoAsA 94*
Hsu, Yuan-Hsi 1945- *WhoAsA 94*
Hsu, Zuey-Shin 1930- *WhoScEn 94*
Hsuan-Tsang c. 600-664 *WhWE*
Hsu Ching-Chung 1907- *IntWW 93*
Hsueh, Chun-tu *WhoAsA 94*
Hsueh, Chun-tu 1922- *WhoAm 94*
Hsueh, Nancy 1939-1991 *WhoHol 92*
Hsueh, Yi-Fun 1964- *WhoAsA 94*
Hsui, Albert Tong-Kwan 1945- *WhoAsA 94*
Hsun Tzu 3rd cent.BC- *EncEth*
Hsu Shui-Teh 1931- *IntWW 93*
Hsu Tzu-Chiu 1920- *IntWW 93*
Hu, Albert Ke-Jeng 1961- *WhoAsA 94*
Hu, Bambi 1945- *WhoAsA 94*
Hu, Bei-Lok Bernard 1947- *WhoAsA 94*
Hu, Can Beven 1949- *WhoAsA 94*
Hu, Chao Hsiung 1939- *WhoAsA 94*
Hu, Chenming 1947- *WhoAm 94, WhoAsA 94*
Hu, Chi Chung 1927- *WhoAmA 93*
Hu, Chi Yu 1933- *WhoAm 94, WhoAsA 94, WhoWest 94*
Hu, Chia-Ren 1939- *WhoAsA 94*
Hu, Daniel Ching 1944- *WhoAsA 94*
Hu, Edna Gertrude Fenske 1922- *WhoWest 94*
Hu, Jane H. 1940- *WhoAsA 94*
Hu, Jimmy *WhoAsA 94, WhoHisp 94*
Hu, John Chih-An 1922- *WhoWest 94*
Hu, John Nan-Hai 1936- *WhoAsA 94*
Hu, Joseph Chi-Ping 1946- *WhoAm 94, WhoFI 94*
Hu, Joseph Kai Ming 1953- *WhoAsA 94*
Hu, Mary Lee 1943- *WhoAmA 93, WhoWest 94*
Hu, Paul Y. 1938- *WhoAsA 94*
Hu, Senqi 1952- *WhoScEn 94*
Hu, Sheng-Cheng 1940- *WhoAm 94*
Hu, Shiu-Lok 1949- *WhoAsA 94*
Hu, Steve Seng-Chiu 1922- *WhoAm 94, WhoAsA 94, WhoScEn 94*
Hu, Sze-Tsen 1914- *WhoAm 94*
Hu, Tsay-Hsin Gilbert 1956- *WhoScEn 94*
Hu, Wayne 1944- *WhoAsA 94*
Hu, Ximing 1946- *WhoScEn 94*
Hua, Li Min *DrAPF 93*
Hua, Li Min 1936- *WrDr 94*
Hua, Lulin *WhoScEn 94*
Hua, Tong-Wen 1929- *WhoScEn 94*
Huaco, George Arthur 1927- *WhoWest 94*
Huacuja, Manlio 1959- *WhoWest 94*
Huacuja, Yvonne Tamara 1948- *WhoHisp 94*
Hua Guofeng 1920- *IntWW 93*
Hua Guofeng 1921- *WhoPRCh 91 [port]*
Huai Guomo 1932- *WhoPRCh 91 [port]*
Hua Junwu 1915- *WhoPRCh 91 [port]*
Hua Liankui 1928- *WhoPRCh 91 [port]*
Hua Liming *WhoPRCh 91*
Huang, Alice Shih-Hou 1939- *WhoAsA 94*
Huang, Arnold *WhoAsA 94*
Huang, Barney Kuo-Yen 1931- *WhoAsA 94*
Huang, C.-T. James 1948- *WhoAsA 94*
Huang, Chaofu 1959- *WhoAsA 94*
Huang, Charles 1947- *WhoAsA 94*
Huang, Charles Chi-Jen 1947- *WhoFI 94*
Huang, Chau-Ting 1939- *WhoAsA 94*
Huang, Cheng-Cher 1947- *WhoAsA 94, WhoMW 93*
Huang, Cheng-Chi 1941- *WhoAsA 94*
Huang, Chi-chiang 1949- *WhoAsA 94*
Huang, Chi-Lung Dominic 1930- *WhoAsA 94, WhoMW 93*
Huang, Chien Chang 1931- *WhoAm 94, WhoWest 94*
Huang, Chin-pao 1941- *WhoAsA 94*
Huang, Denis K. 1925- *WhoAsA 94, WhoScEn 94*
Huang, Edwin I-Chuen 1933- *WhoScEn 94*
Huang, Eng-Shang 1940- *WhoScEn 94*
Huang, Eugene Yuching 1917- *WhoAm 94, WhoAsA 94, WhoMW 93, WhoScEn 94*
Huang, Feng Hou 1930- *WhoAsA 94*
Huang, Francis Fu-Tse 1922- *WhoAm 94, WhoWest 94*
Huang, Garng Morton 1951- *WhoAsA 94*
Huang, George Wenhong 1936- *WhoAsA 94*
Huang, H. K. 1939- *WhoWest 94*
Huang, H. T. *WhoAsA 94*
Huang, Hua-Feng 1935- *WhoAm 94*
Huang, Huey-Wen 1940- *WhoAsA 94*
Huang, I-Ning 1939- *WhoAsA 94*
Huang, Ian *WhoAsA 94*
Huang, Jack J. T. 1952- *WhoAsA 94*
Huang, Jacob Wen-Kuang 1935- *WhoAsA 94*
Huang, Jamin 1951- *WhoAsA 94*
Huang, Jason Jianzhong 1965- *WhoScEn 94*
Huang, Jen-Tzaw 1938- *WhoWest 94*
Huang, Jennming Stephen 1947- *WhoAsA 94*
Huang, Jiann-Shiun 1954- *WhoAsA 94*
Huang, Jim Jay 1946- *WhoScEn 94*
Huang, Jin 1946- *WhoAsA 94*
Huang, John Shiao-Shih 1940- *WhoAsA 94*
Huang, Joseph Chen-Huan 1933- *WhoScEn 94*
Huang, Joseph Chi Kan 1938- *WhoAsA 94*
Huang, Joseph T. 1962- *WhoAsA 94*
Huang, Joyce L. 1943- *WhoAsA 94*
Huang, Ju-Chang 1941- *WhoAsA 94, WhoScEn 94*
Huang, Jung-chang 1935- *WhoAsA 94*
Huang, Kee Chang 1917- *WhoAm 94, WhoAsA 94*
Huang, Ken Shen 1937- *WhoAsA 94*
Huang, Kerson 1928- *WhoAm 94*
Huang, Ko-Hsing 1953- *WhoAsA 94*
Huang, Kun Lien 1953- *WhoWest 94*
Huang, Lena Grace 1950- *WhoMW 93*
Huang, Liang Hsiung 1939- *WhoAsA 94*
Huang, Mei Qing 1942- *WhoScEn 94*
Huang, Ming-Hui 1951- *WhoAsA 94*
Huang, Nai-Chien 1932- *WhoAsA 94*

Huang, Pan Ming 1934- *WhoAm 94, WhoScEn 94, WhoWest 94*
Huang, Pei 1928- *WhoAsA 94*
Huang, Peisen Simon 1962- *WhoScEn 94*
Huang, Pien Chien 1931- *WhoAm 94*
Huang, Ray (Jen-yu) 1918- *ConAu 43NR*
Huang, Rayson Lisung 1920- *IntWW 93, Who 94*
Huang, Samuel T. 1939- *WhoAsA 94*
Huang, Shan-Jen Chen 1951- *WhoAsA 94*
Huang, Shih-Wen 1936- *WhoAsA 94*
Huang, Sung-cheng 1944- *WhoScEn 94, WhoWest 94*
Huang, Thomas Shi-Tao 1936- *WhoAm 94*
Huang, Thomas Tao-shing 1939- *WhoAm 94, WhoAsA 94*
Huang, Thomas W. 1941- *WhoAsA 94*
Huang, Thomas Weishing 1941- *WhoAmL 94*
Huang, Tseng 1925- *WhoAsA 94*
Huang, Victor Tsangmin 1951- *WhoAsA 94, WhoMW 93*
Huang, Wei-chiao 1955- *WhoAsA 94*
Huang, Wei-Sung Wilson 1956- *WhoAsA 94*
Huang, Weifeng 1930- *WhoAsA 94*
Huang, William H. 1947- *WhoAsA 94*
Huang, Wuu-Liang 1944- *WhoAsA 94*
Huang, Xun-Cheng 1946- *WhoAsA 94*
Huang, Yang-Tung 1955- *WhoScEn 94*
Huang, Yasheng 1960- *WhoAsA 94*
Huang, Yong Kang 1947- *WhoMW 93*
Huang, Zhen 1951- *WhoAsA 94*
Huang, Zhen-Fen 1956- *WhoAsA 94*
Huang, Zhi-Yong 1962- *WhoScEn 94*
Huang An-Lun 1949- *IntWW 93, WhoPRCh 91 [port]*
Huang Anren 1924- *IntWW 93*
Huang Baosheng *WhoPRCh 91*
Huang Baoyao *WhoPRCh 91*
Huang Baozhang 1937- *WhoPRCh 91 [port]*
Huang Bingwei 1913- *IntWW 93, WhoPRCh 91*
Huang Binxin *WhoPRCh 91*
Huang Changxi 1929- *WhoPRCh 91 [port]*
Huang Chao 1928- *WhoPRCh 91 [port]*
Huang Da 1925- *IntWW 93, WhoPRCh 91*
Huang Daneng 1916- *WhoPRCh 91 [port]*
Huang Daoqi 1924- *WhoPRCh 91 [port]*
Huang Daqing *WhoPRCh 91*
Huang Demao 1919- *IntWW 93*
Huang Dingchen 1901- *WhoPRCh 91 [port]*
Huang Diyan *WhoPRCh 91*
Huang Dufeng 1913- *IntWW 93, WhoPRCh 91 [port]*
Huang Fanzhang 1931- *IntWW 93*
Huang Feng 1930- *WhoPRCh 91 [port]*
Huang Ganying 1921- *IntWW 93, WhoPRCh 91 [port]*
Huang Guanyu 1945- *WhoPRCh 91 [port]*
Huang Hai *EncSF 93*
Huang Hanyun 1930- *WhoPRCh 91*
Huang Hua 1913- *IntWW 93, WhoPRCh 91 [port]*
Huang Huai 1939- *WhoPRCh 91*
Huang Huang 1933- *IntWW 93, WhoPRCh 91 [port]*
Huang Huihui 1960- *WhoPRCh 91*
Huang Huiqun *WhoPRCh 91*
Huang Jia 1921- *WhoPRCh 91 [port]*
Huang Jiahua *WhoPRCh 91*
Huang Jian 1927- *WhoPRCh 91 [port]*
Huang Jianmo *WhoPRCh 91*
Huang Jichun *WhoPRCh 91 [port]*
Huang Jingbo 1919- *IntWW 93, WhoPRCh 91 [port]*
Huang Jiqing 1904- *WhoPRCh 91 [port]*
Huang Jishu *WhoPRCh 91*
Huang Ju 1938- *IntWW 93, WhoPRCh 91 [port]*
Huang Jun 1914- *WhoPRCh 91 [port]*
Huang Junjun 1937- *WhoPRCh 91 [port]*
Huang Keli 1910- *WhoPRCh 91*
Huang Kewei 1907- *IntWW 93*
Huang Kun 1919- *IntWW 93, WhoPRCh 91 [port]*
Huang Kunyi *WhoPRCh 91 [port]*
Huang Liang 1920- *WhoPRCh 91*
Huang Liangchen 1912- *WhoPRCh 91 [port]*
Huang Luobin *WhoPRCh 91*
Huang Nai 1917- *WhoPRCh 91 [port]*
Huang Qifan 1951- *WhoPRCh 91*
Huang Qihan 1912- *WhoPRCh 91 [port]*
Huang Qingyun 1920- *BlmGWL*
Huang Qitao *WhoPRCh 91*
Huang Qizao 1933- *WhoPRCh 91 [port]*
Huang Qizhang *WhoPRCh 91 [port]*
Huang Runhua 1923- *WhoPRCh 91 [port]*
Huang Shikang *WhoPRCh 91*
Huang Shiming 1934- *WhoPRCh 91 [port]*
Huang Shuhuai *WhoPRCh 91*
Huang Shunxing 1923- *WhoPRCh 91 [port]*
Huang Shuqin 1940- *WhoPRCh 91 [port]*
Huang Suning 1950- *WhoPRCh 91*
Huang Tifei 1905- *WhoPRCh 91 [port]*
Huang Weilu 1916- *IntWW 93, WhoPRCh 91 [port]*
Huang Weiyuan 1921- *WhoPRCh 91 [port]*
Huang Xiandu 1907- *WhoPRCh 91 [port]*
Huang Xiaomin 1970- *WhoPRCh 91 [port]*
Huang Xinbai *WhoPRCh 91 [port]*
Huang Xinchuan 1928- *WhoPRCh 91 [port]*
Huang Xinting 1913- *WhoPRCh 91 [port]*
Huang Yicheng 1926- *WhoPRCh 91 [port]*
Huang Yijun 1915- *WhoPRCh 91*
Huang Yongyu 1924- *IntWW 93, WhoPRCh 91 [port]*
Huang Yuan 1905- *WhoPRCh 91*
Huang Yujun *WhoPRCh 91*
Huang Yukun 1917- *WhoPRCh 91 [port]*
Huang Yun *WhoPRCh 91*
Huang Yuzhang *WhoPRCh 91 [port]*
Huang Zhendong *WhoPRCh 91*
Huang Zhengqing 1903- *WhoPRCh 91 [port]*
Huang Zhicheng 1952- *WhoPRCh 91 [port]*
Huang Zhigang 1916- *WhoPRCh 91 [port]*
Huang Zhihong 1965- *WhoPRCh 91 [port]*
Huang Zhiliang *WhoPRCh 91*
Huang Zhizhen 1920- *IntWW 93, WhoPRCh 91 [port]*
Huang Zhou 1925- *IntWW 93, WhoPRCh 91 [port]*
Huang Zongdao 1921- *WhoPRCh 91 [port]*
Huang Zongjiang 1921- *WhoPRCh 91 [port]*
Huang Zongying 1925- *BlmGWL, IntWW 93, WhoPRCh 91 [port]*
Huang Zuolin 1906- *WhoPRCh 91 [port]*
Huan Han-ching *IntDcT 2*
Huan-jue-cai-lang 1929- *WhoPRCh 91 [port]*
Huant, Ernest Albin Camille 1905- *IntWW 93*
Huan Yushan *WhoPRCh 91*
Hua Sanchuan 1930- *WhoPRCh 91 [port]*
Hua Shoujun *WhoPRCh 91*
Huayta Nunez, Wilfredo *IntWW 93*
Hua Zhongyi *WhoPRCh 91*
Huband, Frank Louis 1938- *WhoAm 94*
Hubarenko, Vitaly Serhiyovych 1924- *NewGrDO*
Hubata, Robert 1942- *WhoWest 94*
Hubay, Charles Alfred 1918- *WhAm 10*
Hubay, Jeno 1858-1937 *NewGrDO*
Hubback, Eva Marian 1886-1949 *DcNaB MP*
Hubbard *Who 94*
Hubbard, Alan R. 1944- *WhoAmP 93*
Hubbard, Amos B. 1930- *WhoBlA 94*
Hubbard, Ann Louise Cox 1943- *WhoAm 94*
Hubbard, Arnette Rhinehart *WhoBlA 94*
Hubbard, Arthur Thornton 1941- *WhoAm 94, WhoScEn 94*
Hubbard, Bessie Renee 1961- *WhoScEn 94*
Hubbard, Bruce Alan 1948- *WhoBlA 94*
Hubbard, Calvin L. 1940- *WhoBlA 94*
Hubbard, Carroll, Jr. 1937- *WhoAmP 93*
Hubbard, Charles D. 1876-1951 *WhoAmA 93N*
Hubbard, Charles Ronald 1933- *WhoScEn 94, WhoWest 94*
Hubbard, Charles W. 1943- *WhoIns 94*
Hubbard, Darrell 1966- *WhoBlA 94*
Hubbard, David *Who 94*
Hubbard, (Richard) David (Cairns) 1936- *Who 94*
Hubbard, David Allan 1928- *WhoAm 94*
Hubbard, Dean Leon 1939- *WhoAm 94*
Hubbard, Donald 1926- *WhoWest 94*
Hubbard, Dorthy Stuart 1925- *WhoAmP 93*
Hubbard, Elizabeth *WhoAm 94, WhoHol 92*
Hubbard, Elizabeth Louise 1949- *WhoAmL 94, WhoMW 93*
Hubbard, Elizabeth Wright 1896- *WhAm 10*
Hubbard, Fred Leonhardt 1940- *WhoMW 93*
Hubbard, Freddie 1938- *WhoBlA 94*
Hubbard, Frederick Dewayne 1938- *WhoAm 94*
Hubbard, Gardiner Greene 1822-1897 *EncDeaf*
Hubbard, Grant Robert, II 1950- *WhoFI 94, WhoMW 93*
Hubbard, Gregory Scott 1948- *WhoWest 94*
Hubbard, Harold Mead 1924- *WhoScEn 94*
Hubbard, Harry 1924- *WhoAmP 93*
Hubbard, Harvey Hart 1921- *WhoAm 94*
Hubbard, Herbert Hendrix 1922- *WhoAm 94, WhoAmL 94*
Hubbard, Howard James 1938- *WhoAm 94*
Hubbard, Howard Leland 1931- *WhoAm 94*
Hubbard, Hylan T., III 1947- *WhoBlA 94*
Hubbard, Jack *WhoHol 92*
Hubbard, James Madison, Jr. *WhoBlA 94*
Hubbard, James W. 1948- *WhoAmP 93*
Hubbard, Jean P. 1917- *WhoBlA 94*
Hubbard, Jeremiah 1837-1915 *EncNAR*
Hubbard, Jesse Donald 1920- *WhoAm 94*
Hubbard, John d1988 *WhoHol 92*
Hubbard, John 1931- *IntWW 93, WhoAmA 93*
Hubbard, John Ingram 1930- *IntWW 93*
Hubbard, John Laird 1935- *WhoFI 94*
Hubbard, John Lewis 1947- *WhoAm 94*
Hubbard, John Morris 1916- *WhoMW 93*
Hubbard, John Perry 1903-1990 *WhAm 10*
Hubbard, John Randolph 1918- *WhoAm 94*
Hubbard, Josephine Brodie 1938- *WhoBlA 94*
Hubbard, Julia Faye 1948- *WhoAm 94*
Hubbard, Kenneth Dean 1934- *WhoAm 94*
Hubbard, Kenneth Gene 1949- *WhoMW 93, WhoScEn 94*
Hubbard, L(afayette) Ron(ald) 1911-1986 *EncSF 93*
Hubbard, Lafayette Ronald 1911-1986 *DcAmReB 2*
Hubbard, Lulu Mae d1966 *WhoHol 92*
Hubbard, Marilyn French 1946- *WhoBlA 94*
Hubbard, Mark Randall 1955- *WhoWest 94*
Hubbard, Michael Joseph 1942- *Who 94*
Hubbard, Paul Leonard 1942- *WhoBlA 94*
Hubbard, Paul Stancyl, Jr. 1931- *WhoAm 94*
Hubbard, Peter Lawrence 1946- *WhoAmL 94*
Hubbard, Phil 1956- *WhoBlA 94*
Hubbard, Phillip *WhoAmP 93, WhoHisp 94*
Hubbard, Randall Dee 1935- *WhoAm 94, WhoFI 94*
Hubbard, Reginald T. *WhoBlA 94*
Hubbard, Richard L. 1943- *WhoAmL 94*
Hubbard, Richard M. 1941- *WhoAmP 93*
Hubbard, Richard Ward 1929- *WhoWest 94*
Hubbard, Robert d1977 *ProFbHF*
Hubbard, Robert 1928- *WhoAmA 93*
Hubbard, Rose Lucille 1961- *WhoAmL 94*
Hubbard, Ruth 1924- *ConAu 41NR, WhoAm 94*
Hubbard, Ruth 1942- *WhoAm 94*
Hubbard, Samuel T., Jr. 1950- *WhoFI 94*
Hubbard, Stanley, Sr 1940- *WhoBlA 94*
Hubbard, Stanley Eugene 1897- *WhoAm 94*
Hubbard, Stanley Stub 1933- *WhoAm 94, WhoMW 93*
Hubbard, Susan *DrAPF 93*
Hubbard, Thomas Edwin 1944- *WhoAmL 94, WhoFI 94*
Hubbard, Thomas Foy 1898- *WhAm 10*
Hubbard, Thomas K. 1956- *WrDr 94*
Hubbard, Tom d1974 *WhoHol 92*
Hubbard, Walter T. 1924- *WhoBlA 94*
Hubbard, William Bogel 1940- *WhoAm 94*
Hubbard, William C. 1952- *WhoAm 94, WhoAmL 94*
Hubbard, William Neill, Jr. 1919- *WhoAm 94*
Hubbard, Z. Dianne 1950- *WhoMW 93*
Hubbard-Miles, Peter Charles 1927- *Who 94*
Hubbe, Henry Ernest 1932- *WhoFI 94*
Hubbe, Nikolaj *WhoAm 94*
Hubbe, Nikolaj 1967- *IntDcB [port]*
Hubbel, Michael Robert 1954- *WhoFI 94*
Hubbell, Billy James 1949- *WhoAmL 94*
Hubbell, Carl d1988 *WhoHol 92*
Hubbell, Douglas Osborne 1952- *WhoScEn 94*
Hubbell, Ernest 1914- *WhoAm 94, WhoAmL 94*
Hubbell, Floyd Allan 1948- *WhoWest 94*
Hubbell, George Loring, Jr. 1894-1990 *WhAm 10*
Hubbell, Henry Salem 1870-1949 *WhoAmA 93N*
Hubbell, James Windsor, Jr. 1922- *WhoAm 94*
Hubbell, John Howard 1925- *WhoAm 94*
Hubbell, Robert Newell 1931- *WhoWest 94*
Hubbell, Theodore Huntington 1897-1989 *WhAm 10*
Hubbell, Webster L. *WhoAmP 93*
Hubbell, Webster L. 1948- *WhoAmL 94*
Hubbert, Cork *WhoHol 92*
Hubbert, Marion King 1903-1989 *WhAm 10*
Hubble, Don Wayne 1939- *WhoAm 94, WhoFI 94*
Hubble, Edwin 1889-1953 *WorScD [port]*
Hubble, Roger Martin 1954- *WhoMW 93*
Hubbs, Arden Perry, II 1946- *WhoFI 94*
Hubbs, Clark 1921- *WhoAm 94, WhoScEn 94*
Hubbs, Donald Harvey 1918- *WhoAm 94*
Hubbs, Ronald M. 1908- *WhoFI 94, WhoMW 93*
Hubel, David Hunter 1926- *IntWW 93, Who 94, WhoAm 94, WhoScEn 94*
Hubel, Kenneth Andrew 1927- *WhoMW 93*
Huben, Brian David 1962- *WhoAmL 94, WhoWest 94*
Huben, Dolores Quevedo 1951- *WhoHisp 94*
Hubenthal, Karl Samuel 1917- *WhoAmA 93*
Hu Benyao 1933- *WhoPRCh 91*
Huber, Alberta 1917- *WhoAm 94*
Huber, Allan J. 1929- *WhoFI 94*
Huber, Antje Charlotte 1924- *IntWW 93*
Huber, Billie d1965 *WhoHol 92*
Huber, Brian Edward 1954- *WhoScEn 94*
Huber, Charles d1960 *WhoHol 92*
Huber, Clayton Lloyd 1955- *WhoFI 94*
Huber, Colleen Adlene 1927- *WhoWest 94*
Huber, David Lawrence 1937- *WhoScEn 94*
Huber, Don Lawrence 1928- *WhoAm 94*
Huber, Douglas Crawford 1939- *WhoScEn 94*
Huber, Franz Xaver 1755-1814 *NewGrDO*
Huber, Fred Dale 1898- *WhAm 10*
Huber, Gary Arthur 1944- *WhoScEn 94*
Huber, Gregory B. 1956- *WhoAmP 93*
Huber, Gusti d1993 *NewYTBS 93 [port]*
Huber, Gusti 1914- *WhoHol 92*
Huber, Hans 1852-1921 *NewGrDO*
Huber, Harold d1959 *WhoHol 92*
Huber, J. Neil, Jr. 1943- *WhoAmL 94*
Huber, Jack T *WrDr 94*
Huber, Joan Althaus 1925- *WhoAm 94*
Huber, Joan Joyce 1941- *WhoFI 94*
Huber, John David 1946- *WhoAm 94*
Huber, John Henry, III 1946- *WhoScEn 94*
Huber, John Michael 1947- *WhoAm 94*
Huber, John Michael 1958- *WhoFI 94*
Huber, Joseph Fowler 1946- *WhoFI 94*
Huber, Karl 1915- *IntWW 93*
Huber, Katherine Jeanne 1958- *WhoMW 93*
Huber, Kimberly Lynn 1968- *WhoMW 93*
Huber, Klaus 1924- *NewGrDO*
Huber, Linda Ruth 1955- *WhoWest 94*
Huber, Louis Anthony, III 1952- *WhoAmL 94*
Huber, Marie 1695-1753 *BlmGWL*
Huber, Martha Lu 1937- *WhoMW 93*
Huber, Norman Fred 1935- *WhoWest 94*
Huber, Norman King 1926- *WhoWest 94*
Huber, Paul Edward 1939- *WhoAm 94*
Huber, Paul William 1951- *WhoMW 93, WhoScEn 94*
Huber, Peter C. 1930- *WhoFI 94*
Huber, Raymond Stewart 1957- *WhoAmP 93*
Huber, Richard Leslie 1936- *WhoAm 94*
Huber, Richard Miller 1922- *WrDr 94*
Huber, Rita Norma 1931- *WhoAmP 93, WhoMW 93*
Huber, Robert 1937- *IntWW 93, NobelP 91 [port], Who 94, WhoScEn 94*
Huber, Robert Daniel 1922- *WhoAmP 93*
Huber, Robert John 1935- *WhoScEn 94*
Huber, Robert T. 1920- *WhoAmP 93*
Huber, Ronald R. 1947- *WhoFI 94*
Huber, Therese 1764-1829 *BlmGWL*
Huber, Thomas John 1969- *WhoMW 93*
Huber, Thomas Martin 1919- *WhoAm 94*
Huber, Thomas P. 1936- *WhoAmL 94*
Huber, Wayne Charles 1941- *WhoWest 94*
Huberdeau, Gustave 1874-1945 *NewGrDO*
Hubert, Anne M. *See* Hubert, Edgar F. & Hubert, Anne M. *WhoAmA 93*
Hubert, Anne M. *WhoAmA 93*
Hubert, Cam 1938- *WrDr 94*
Hubert, Edgar F. & Hubert, Anne M. *WhoAmA 93*
Hubert, Elisabeth (Michele Adelaide Marie) 1956- *WhoWomW 91*
Hubert, Frank d1966 *WhoHol 92*
Hubert, Frank William Rene 1915- *WhoAm 94*
Hubert, Harold d1916 *WhoHol 92*
Hubert, Helen Betty 1950- *WhoAm 94*
Hubert, Janet *WhoHol 92*
Hubert, Jean-Luc 1960- *WhoFI 94, WhoMW 93*
Hubert, Jim *DrAPF 93*

Hudspeth, John Robert 1938- WhoFI 94
Hudspeth, Stephen Mason 1947- WhoAm 94, WhoAmL 94
Hudspeth, William Jean 1935- WhoScEn 94
Hudy, John Joseph 1956- WhoScEn 94
Hue, Georges (Adolphe) 1858-1948 NewGrDO
Huebler, Douglas 1924- WhoAmA 93
Huebling, Craig 1935- WhoHol 92
Huebner, Emily A. Draper 1951- WhoMW 93
Huebner, Fredrick D. 1955- WrDr 94
Huebner, Harlan Pierce 1927- WhoAm 94
Huebner, Herbert d1972 WhoHol 92
Huebner, Jay Stanley 1939- WhoAm 94
Huebner, John Stephen 1940- WhoAm 94, WhoScEn 94
Huebner, Michael Denis 1941- Who 94
Huebner, Rosemarita 1932- WhoAmA 93
Huebner, Suzanne M. 1958- WhoFI 94
Huebsch, Robert P. 1949- WhoAm 94, WhoAmL 94
Huebscher, Fred 1960- WhoWest 94
Hueca, Angel Marrero 1946- WhoAmP 93
Hueca, Manuel Marrero WhoAmP 93
Hueffer, Ford Madox EncSF 93
Hueffer, Francis 1843-1889 NewGrDO
Huefner, Ronald Joseph 1941- WhoFI 94
Huefner, Sue Hamilton Pike 1940- WhoWest 94
Hueg, William Frederick 1924- WhoMW 93
Huehn, Julius 1904-1971 NewGrDO
Huelbig, Larry Leggett 1944- WhoAm 94, WhoAmL 94
Huelke, Donald Fred 1930- WhoAm 94, WhoScEn 94
Huelman, Joanne B. 1938- WhoAmP 93
Huels, Patrick 1949- WhoAmP 93
Huelsman, Joanne B. 1938- WhoMW 93
Huelsmann, Craig Thomas 1968- WhoMW 93
Huemer, Christina Gertrude 1947- WhoAmA 93
Huenefeld, Fred, Jr. 1929- WhoAmP 93
Huenefeld, Thomas Ernst 1937- WhoFI 94
Huenemann, Ruben Henry 1909- WhoAm 94
Huening, Walter Carl, Jr. 1923- WhoAm 94, WhoScEn 94
Huenink, Jeffrey C. 1956- WhoAmP 93
Huereque, Cynthia Patricia 1947- WhoHisp 94
Huerta, Albert 1943- WhoHisp 94
Huerta, Baldemar 1937- WhoAm 94
Huerta, Benito 1952- WhoHisp 94
Huerta, Dolores Fernandez 1930- WhoHisp 94
Huerta, Elmer Emilio 1952- WhoHisp 94
Huerta, Joe M. 1940- WhoHisp 94
Huerta, Joseph 1925- WhoHisp 94
Huerta, Michael Peter 1958- WhoHisp 94
Huerta, Ramon 1924- WhoAmP 93, WhoHisp 94
Huerta, Rodolfo Guzman d1984 WhoHol 92
Huerta, Ventura Perez 1933- WhoHisp 94
Huerta Diaz, Ismael 1916- IntWW 93
Huesca, Robert Thomas 1959- WhoHisp 94
Hueser, Roberta Jean 1932- WhoMW 93
Huesman, Jacqueline d1978 WhoHol 92
Huestis, Charles Benjamin 1920- WhoAm 94
Huestis, Douglas William 1925- WhoWest 94
Huestis, Marilyn Ann 1948- WhoScEn 94
Huestis, Russell d1964 WhoHol 92
Hueston, Frederick d1961 WhoHol 92
Hueston, Oliver David 1941- WhoBlA 94
Huet, David Richard 1961- WhoAmL 94
Huet, Jacqueline d1986 WhoHol 92
Huet, Marie-Helene Jaqueline 1944- WhoAm 94
Huet, Philippe Emile Jean 1920- IntWW 93
Huet, Pierre 1920- IntWW 93
Huet, Pierre-Daniel 1630-1721 GuFrLit 2
Huete, Stephen Marc 1955- WhoHisp 94
Hueter, James Warren 1925- WhoAmA 93, WhoWest 94
Huether, Richard G. 1948- WhoFI 94
Huether, Robert WhoAmP 93
Huetig, Roger Dean 1947- WhoAmP 93, WhoMW 93
Hueting, Juergen 1956- WhoScEn 94
Huett, Donald Ray, Jr. 1951- WhoMW 93
Huetteman, Raymond Theodore, Jr. 1929- WhoAm 94
Huetter, Glenn A., Jr. 1965- WhoAmL 94
Huettner, Richard Alfred 1927- WhoAm 94, WhoAmL 94, WhoFI 94, WhoScEn 94
Huey, Beverly Messick 1961- WhoScEn 94
Huey, Florence Greene 1872-1961 WhoAmA 93N
Huey, Hamilton Gregg, III 1953- WhoMW 93
Huey, Helen 1944- WhoAmP 93
Huey, Jolene W. WhoAsA 94
Huey, Joseph Wistar, III 1938- WhoFI 94
Huey, Mark C. DrAPF 93
Huey, Robert H. 1943- WhoAmL 94
Huey, Ward Ligon, Jr. 1938- WhoAm 94, WhoFI 94
Huf, Carol Elinor 1940- WhoMW 93
Hufana, Alejandrino G 1926- WrDr 94
Hufbauer, Gary Clyde 1939- WhoAm 94
Huff, Barbara A. 1929- WrDr 94
Huff, Brent WhoHol 92
Huff, Charles William 1955- WhoScEn 94
Huff, Clarence Ronald 1945- WhoAm 94
Huff, Dale Eugene 1930- WhoWest 94
Huff, David Charles 1950- WhoWest 94
Huff, David L. WhoAm 94
Huff, David Richard 1948- WhoMW 93
Huff, Forrest d1947 WhoHol 92
Huff, Gary D. 1950- WhoAmL 94
Huff, Gayle Compton 1956- WhoFI 94, WhoMW 93
Huff, Gene 1929- WhoAmP 93
Huff, Howard Lee 1941- WhoAmA 93
Huff, Janice Wages 1960- WhoBlA 94
Huff, John David 1952- WhoMW 93
Huff, John Gardner 1951- WhoAmP 93
Huff, Kenneth O. 1926- WhoWest 94
Huff, Laura Weaver 1930- WhoAmA 93
Huff, Leon Alexander 1942- WhoBlA 94
Huff, Louis Andrew 1949- WhoBlA 94
Huff, Louise d1973 WhoHol 92
Huff, Lula Lunsford 1949- WhoBlA 94
Huff, Marilyn L. 1951- WhoAm 94, WhoAmL 94, WhoWest 94
Huff, Marsha E. 1946- WhoAmL 94
Huff, Norman Thomas 1940- WhoMW 93
Huff, Paul Emlyn 1916- WhoAm 94
Huff, R. Randall 1940- WhoAmL 94
Huff, Ralph Richard 1944- WhoAmP 93
Huff, Richard D. 1947- WhoAmL 94
Huff, Ricky Wayne 1953- WhoWest 94
Huff, Robert DrAPF 93
Huff, Robert 1945- WhoAmA 93
Huff, Ronald Garland 1930- WhoScEn 94
Huff, Sam ProFbHF [port]
Huff, Sheila Lindsey 1951- WhoMW 93
Huff, Sheila Minor 1947- WhoMW 93
Huff, Stanley Eugene 1918- WhoAm 94
Huff, Steven D. 1951- WhoAmL 94
Huff, Steven S. 1941- WhoAmL 94
Huff, Thomas Ellis 1949- WhoAmP 93
Huff, W. Ray 1935- WhoAmP 93
Huff, Welcome Rex Anthony 1967- WhoScEn 94, WhoWest 94
Huff, William 1920- WhoBlA 94
Huff, William Braid 1950- WhoAm 94
Huff, William Henry, III 1937- WhoIns 94
Huff, William Jennings 1919- WhoAmL 94
Huff, William S. 1934- WhoAm 94
Huffaker, Gregory Dorian, Jr. 1944- WhoAmL 94
Huffaker, John Boston 1925- WhoAmL 94
Huffer, Dan L. 1937- WhoAm 94, WhoFI 94
Hufferd, Linda M. 1963- WhoMW 93
Huffine, Coy Lee 1924- WhoAm 94, WhoMW 93
Huffington, Arianna Stassinopoulos 1950- WrDr 94
Huffington, Michael 1947- CngDr 93, WhoAm 94, WhoAmP 93, WhoWest 94
Huffington, Roy Michael 1917- WhoAm 94, WhoAmP 93
Huffinley, Beryl 1926- Who 94
Huffman, Alice A. 1936- WhoAmP 93
Huffman, Arlie Curtis, Jr. 1942- WhoWest 94
Huffman, Bill S. 1924- WhoAmP 93
Huffman, Carl Augustus 1951- WhoMW 93
Huffman, D. C., Jr. WhoScEn 94
Huffman, David d1985 WhoHol 92
Huffman, Delia Gonzalez 1953- WhoHisp 94
Huffman, Delton Cleon, Jr. 1943- WhoAm 94
Huffman, Donald Wise 1927- WhoAmP 93
Huffman, Doris R. WhoAmP 93
Huffman, Doug
See Boston ConMus 11
Huffman, Edgar Joseph 1939- WhoAm 94, WhoWest 94
Huffman, Gregory Scott Combest 1946- WhoAm 94
Huffman, Harry Dale 1943- WhoAmP 93
Huffman, Henry Samuel 1926- WhoScEn 94
Huffman, James Thomas William 1947- WhoAm 94
Huffman, Kenneth Alan 1941- WhoScEn 94
Huffman, Laurence M. 1949- WhoAmL 94
Huffman, Leslie, Jr. 1929- WhoAm 94
Huffman, Linda Rae 1946- WhoWest 94
Huffman, Nancy Cook 1951- WhoMW 93
Huffman, Nona Gay 1942- WhoWest 94
Huffman, Odell Hampton 1923- WhoAmP 93
Huffman, Patricia Ann 1936- WhoMW 93
Huffman, Randall A. 1946- WhoAmL 94
Huffman, Robert Allen, Jr. 1950- WhoAmL 94
Huffman, Robert K. 1947- WhoAmL 94
Huffman, Robert Merle 1931- WhoMW 93
Huffman, Robert Vern 1957- WhoFI 94
Huffman, Rufus C. 1927- WhoBlA 94
Huffman, Sarilee Shesol 1949- WhoMW 93
Huffnagle, Norman Parmley 1941- WhoFI 94, WhoWest 94
Hufford, David Prinz 1938- WhoMW 93
Huffstetler, Palmer Eugene 1937- WhoAm 94, WhoAmL 94, WhoFI 94
Huffstickler, Albert DrAPF 93
Huffstodt, Karen WhoAm 94
Hufnagel, Charles Anthony 1916-1989 WhAm 10
Hufnagel, Frederick B. 1878-1954 EncABHB 9 [port]
Hufnagel, Henry Bernhardt 1942- WhoFI 94
Hufnagle, Kevin Brian 1956- WhoFI 94
Hufnagle, Paul C. 1936- WhoAmP 93
Hufschmidt, Maynard Michael 1912- WhoAm 94
Hufsey, Billy WhoHol 92
Hufstedler, Jon Edward 1937- WhoAm 94
Hufstedler, Seth Martin 1922- WhoAm 94
Hufstedler, Shirley Mount 1925- WhoAm 94
Huftalen, Lisa Freeman 1953- WhoFI 94
Hufton, Jeffrey Raymond 1964- WhoScEn 94
Hufton, Olwen Who 94
Hu Fuguo 1937- IntWW 93, WhoPRCh 91 [port]
Hug, Carl Casmir, Jr. 1936- WhoAm 94
Hug, Michel 1930- IntWW 93
Hug, Procter, Jr. 1931- WhoAmP 93
Hug, Procter Ralph, Jr. 1931- WhoAm 94, WhoAmL 94, WhoWest 94
Hug, Richard Ernest 1935- WhoAm 94
Hug, Rudolf Peter 1944- WhoScEn 94
Huge, August Frederick, Jr. 1923- WhoFI 94
Hugel, Charles E. 1928- WhoAm 94, WhoFI 94
Huger, Benjamin 1746-1779 WhAmRev
Huger, Bernard C. 1945- WhoAmL 94
Huger, Daniel 1741-1799 WhAmRev
Huger, Francis 1751-1811 WhAmRev
Huger, Isaac 1743-1797 WhAmRev
Huger, James E. WhoBlA 94
Huger, John 1744-1804 WhAmRev
Huggard, Ernest Douglas 1933- WhoFI 94
Huggard, John Parker 1945- WhoAmL 94
Huggard, Richard James 1935- WhoScEn 94
Huggett, Douglas Clare 1935- WhoMW 93
Huggett, Frank Edward 1924- WrDr 94
Huggett, Richard 1929- WrDr 94
Hugghins, Ernest Jay 1920- WhoAm 94
Huggins Who 94
Huggins, Alan (Armstrong) 1921- Who 94
Huggins, Charles B. 1901- IntWW 93, Who 94
Huggins, Charles Brenton 1901- WhoAm 94, WhoMW 93, WhoScEn 94
Huggins, Charles Edward 1929-1990 WhAm 10
Huggins, Charlotte Susan Harrison 1933- WhoMW 93
Huggins, Clarence L. 1926- WhoBlA 94
Huggins, David WhoAm 94, WhoFI 94
Huggins, George d1959 WhoHol 92
Huggins, Hazel Renfroe 1908- WhoBlA 94
Huggins, Hosiah, Jr. 1950- WhoAm 94, WhoBlA 94
Huggins, James Anthony 1953- WhoScEn 94
Huggins, James Bernard 1950- WhoAmP 93
Huggins, John Joseph 1958- WhoWest 94
Huggins, Kenneth Herbert d1993 Who 94N
Huggins, Linda Johnson 1950- WhoBlA 94
Huggins, Nathan Irvin 1927-1989 WhAm 10
Huggins, Peter Jeremy William Who 94
Huggins, Robert Gene 1938- WhoAmP 93
Huggins, Rollin Charles, Jr. 1931- WhoAm 94
Huggins, Roy 1914- IntMPA 94
Huggins, Victor, Jr. 1936- WhoAmA 93
Huggins, Waymond C. 1927- WhoAmP 93
Huggins, William 1824-1910 WorScD
Huggins, William Herbert 1919- WhoAm 94
Huggins-McLean, Yvonne 1950- WhoAmL 94
Huggler, Tom 1945- WhoMW 93
Hugh, Edwin Charles d1979 WhoHol 92
Hugh, George M. WhoAm 94, WhoFI 94, WhoWest 94
Hugh, Gregory Joseph 1942- WhoMW 93
Hughes Who 94
Hughes, Baron 1911- Who 94
Hughes, Alan Richard 1936- WhoAm 94
Hughes, Alfred Clifton 1932- WhoAm 94
Hughes, Allan Bebout 1924- WhoAm 94, WhoWest 94
Hughes, Allen 1921- WhoAm 94
Hughes, Allen Lee ConTFT 11
Hughes, Andrew Scott 1965- WhoAmL 94
Hughes, Aneurin Rhys 1937- Who 94
Hughes, Anita Lillian 1938- WhoBlA 94
Hughes, Ann WhoAmP 93
Hughes, Ann Hightower 1938- WhoAm 94
Hughes, Anthony Philip Gilson 1948- Who 94
Hughes, Anthony Vernon 1936- IntWW 93
Hughes, Antony Elwyn 1941- Who 94
Hughes, Arleigh Bruce 1930- WhoScEn 94
Hughes, Arthur d1982 WhoHol 92
Hughes, Arthur H. WhoAmP 93
Hughes, Arwel 1909-1988 NewGrDO
Hughes, Author E. 1929- WhoAm 94, WhoWest 94
Hughes, Barbara Bradford 1941- WhoMW 93
Hughes, Barnard 1915- IntMPA 94, WhoAm 94, WhoHol 92
Hughes, Bernice Ann 1959- WhoBlA 94
Hughes, Beverly 1949- WhoAmA 93
Hughes, Blake 1914- WhoAm 94
Hughes, Bradley Richard 1954- WhoFI 94, WhoWest 94
Hughes, Brenda 1919- WrDr 94
Hughes, Brendan WhoHol 92
Hughes, Byron William 1945- WhoAmL 94
Hughes, C. Gethin B. WhoWest 94
Hughes, Carl D. WhoBlA 94
Hughes, Carl Wilson 1914- WhoAm 94
Hughes, Carol 1915- WhoHol 92
Hughes, Carolyn J. Fairweather DrAPF 93
Hughes, Carolyn S. 1921- WhoHisp 94
Hughes, Carolyn Sue 1945- WhoMW 93
Hughes, Catherine IntWW 93
Hughes, Catherine Eva 1933- Who 94
Hughes, Catherine Liggins 1947- WhoBlA 94
Hughes, Charles E. 1931- WhoIns 94
Hughes, Charles Wilson 1946- WhoWest 94
Hughes, Christine Georgette 1946- WhoAm 94
Hughes, Cledwyn IntWW 93
Hughes, Colin Anfield 1930- WrDr 94
Hughes, D. T. SmATA 77
Hughes, Daniel DrAPF 93
Hughes, Daniel Webster 1926- WhoBlA 94
Hughes, David 1967- WhoAmP 93
Hughes, David (Collingwood) 1936- Who 94
Hughes, David (John) 1930- WrDr 94
Hughes, David Glyn 1928- Who 94
Hughes, David H. d1974 WhoHol 92
Hughes, David Henry 1942- WhoFI 94
Hughes, David John 1930- Who 94
Hughes, David Michael 1939- WhoAm 94
Hughes, David Morgan 1926- Who 94
Hughes, David Treharne Dillon 1931- Who 94
Hughes, Davis 1910- Who 94
Hughes, Dean 1943- SmATA 77 [port], TwCYAW
Hughes, Delos Dyson 1934- WhoAm 94
Hughes, Dennis (Talbot) EncSF 93
Hughes, Derek 1934- WhoIns 94
Hughes, Donald Kenneth 1933- WhoAmP 93
Hughes, Donald Lewellyn 1957- WhoWest 94
Hughes, Donald R. 1929- WhoAm 94, WhoFI 94
Hughes, Donna Lundin 1949- WhoBlA 94
Hughes, Dorothy B. d1993 NewYTBS 93
Hughes, Dorothy B(elle) 1904-1993 ConAu 141, WrDr 94N
Hughes, Dralene Kay 1957- WhoMW 93
Hughes, Dusty 1947- ConDr 93, WrDr 94
Hughes, Edsel 1923- WhoAmP 93
Hughes, Edward (Stuart Reginald) 1919- Who 94
Hughes, Edward John 1913- WhoAm 94, WhoAmA 93, WhoWest 94

Hughes, Edward John 1944- *WhoWest 94*
Hughes, Edward Joseph 1937- *WhoAmP 93*
Hughes, Edward P. *EncSF 93*
Hughes, Edward Stuart Reginald 1919- *IntWW 93*
Hughes, Edward Stuart Reginald, Sir 1919- *WrDr 94*
Hughes, Edward T. 1920- *WhoAm 94*
Hughes, Edwin Cutter, Jr. 1943- *WhoAm 94, WhoAmL 94*
Hughes, Edwin Lawson 1924- *WhoFI 94*
Hughes, Eleanor June *WhoMW 93*
Hughes, Elinor Lambert 1906- *WhoAm 94*
Hughes, Elizabeth 1928- *WrDr 94*
Hughes, Elizabeth Phillips 1851-1925 *DcNaB MP*
Hughes, Ernelle Combs 1918- *WhoBlA 94*
Hughes, Essie Meade 1908- *WhoBlA 94*
Hughes, Estelene Dial 1936- *WhoAmP 93*
Hughes, Eugene Morgan 1934- *WhoAm 94, WhoWest 94*
Hughes, Everett Clark 1904- *WhoAm 94*
Hughes, F. Marion 1948- *WhoAmL 94*
Hughes, Finola 1960- *WhoHol 92*
Hughes, Francis 1666?-1744 *NewGrDO*
Hughes, Fred George 1915- *WhoAm 94*
Hughes, G. Philip *WhoAmP 93*
Hughes, G. Philip 1953- *WhoAm 94*
Hughes, Gareth d1965 *WhoHol 92*
Hughes, Geoffrey 1944- *WhoHol 92*
Hughes, George 1937- *Who 94*
Hughes, George David 1930- *WhoAm 94*
Hughes, George Farant, Jr. 1923- *WhoFI 94*
Hughes, George Melvin 1938- *WhoBlA 94*
Hughes, George Michael 1939- *WhoAm 94, WhoAmL 94*
Hughes, George Morgan 1925- *Who 94*
Hughes, George Vincent 1930- *WhoBlA 94*
Hughes, George Wendell 1929- *WhoAm 94*
Hughes, Gervase (Alfred Booth) 1905- *NewGrDO*
Hughes, Glenn Vernon 1927- *WhoWest 94*
Hughes, Glyn 1935- *WrDr 94*
Hughes, Glyn Tegai 1923- *Who 94*
Hughes, Grace-Flores 1946- *WhoAm 94*
Hughes, Greg A. 1955- *WhoAmL 94*
Hughes, H. David 1947- *WhoAmL 94*
Hughes, H. Richard 1926- *IntWW 93*
Hughes, H. Stuart 1916- *WrDr 94*
Hughes, Harold Everett 1922- *WhoAmP 93*
Hughes, Harold Hasbrouck, Jr. 1930- *WhoAm 94*
Hughes, Harry Roe 1926- *WhoAm 94, WhoAmL 94, WhoAmP 93*
Hughes, Harvey L. 1909- *WhoBlA 94*
Hughes, Hazel d1974 *WhoHol 92*
Hughes, Heather 1954- *WrDr 94*
Hughes, Helen *WhoHol 92*
Hughes, Helen 1928- *IntWW 93*
Hughes, Herbert Delauney 1914- *Who 94*
Hughes, Hollis Eugene, Jr. 1943- *WhoBlA 94*
Hughes, Howard 1905-1976 *IntDcF 2-4 [port]*
Hughes, Howard 1938- *Who 94*
Hughes, Ian Frank 1940- *WhoScEn 94*
Hughes, Ieuan Arwel 1944- *Who 94*
Hughes, Ingrid *DrAPF 93*
Hughes, Isaac Sunny 1944- *WhoBlA 94*
Hughes, J. Anthony d1970 *WhoHol 92*
Hughes, J. Michael 1944- *WhoAmL 94*
Hughes, J. Peter 1924- *WhoMW 93*
Hughes, Jack (William) 1916- *Who 94*
Hughes, James 1919- *WhoMW 93*
Hughes, James Arthur 1939- *WhoFI 94, WhoScEn 94, WhoWest 94*
Hughes, James Charles 1944- *WhoAm 94*
Hughes, James Ernest 1927- *Who 94*
Hughes, James F. *WhoAmP 93*
Hughes, James Langston 1902-1967 *AmCulL [port]*
Hughes, James Paul 1920- *WhoAm 94*
Hughes, James Sinclair 1934- *WhoFI 94*
Hughes, Jerome Michael 1929- *WhoAm 94, WhoAmP 93, WhoMW 93*
Hughes, Jerry M. 1944- *WhoAmP 93*
Hughes, Jimmy Franklin, Sr. 1952- *WhoBlA 94*
Hughes, Joe Kenneth 1927- *WhoAm 94*
Hughes, John *IntMPA 94, Who 94*
Hughes, John 1677-1720 *NewGrDO*
Hughes, John 1925- *Who 94*
Hughes, (Edgar) John 1947- *Who 94*
Hughes, (Robert) John 1930- *Who 94*
Hughes, John A(nthony) 1941- *WrDr 94*
Hughes, John Chester 1924- *Who 94*
Hughes, John Dennis 1927- *Who 94*
Hughes, John Farrell 1946- *WhoAm 94, WhoFI 94*
Hughes, John G. 1930- *WhoIns 94*
Hughes, John George *Who 94*
Hughes, John Harold 1936- *WhoWest 94*
Hughes, John Joseph 1797-1864 *DcAmReB 2*
Hughes, John Lawrence 1925- *IntWW 93*
Hughes, John Pinnington- 1942- *Who 94*
Hughes, John Richard Poulton 1920- *Who 94*
Hughes, John Russell 1928- *WhoAm 94, WhoScEn 94*
Hughes, John Taylor 1908- *Who 94*
Hughes, John Vance 1946- *WhoAm 94*
Hughes, John W. *WhoAm 94*
Hughes, John William 1926- *WhoAmP 93*
Hughes, Johnnie Lee 1924- *WhoBlA 94*
Hughes, Jonathan Roberts Tyson 1928-1992 *WhAm 10*
Hughes, Joseph D. 1910- *WhoAm 94*
Hughes, Joyce A. 1940- *WhoBlA 94*
Hughes, Joyce Anne 1940- *WhoMW 93*
Hughes, Judith M. 1941- *WrDr 94*
Hughes, Judith Markham 1941- *WhoWest 94*
Hughes, Judy Lynne 1939- *WhoAmP 93*
Hughes, Katharine Kostbade 1956- *WhoMW 93*
Hughes, Katherine Dodson 1960- *WhoMW 93*
Hughes, Kathleen 1928- *IntMPA 94, WhoHol 92*
Hughes, Kathleen Allison Barnhart 1955- *WhoAmL 94*
Hughes, Kathleen Ann 1953- *WhoAmL 94*
Hughes, Keith L. 1944- *WhoAmL 94*
Hughes, Keith William 1946- *WhoAm 94, WhoFI 94*
Hughes, Ken 1922- *IntMPA 94*
Hughes, Kevin Michael 1952- *Who 94*
Hughes, Kevin Peter 1943- *WhoAm 94, WhoAmL 94*
Hughes, Kieran Patrick 1959- *WhoAmL 94*
Hughes, Kirsten *WhoHol 92*
Hughes, L. Wearen 1952- *WhoAmL 94*
Hughes, Langston 1902-1967 *AfrAmAl 6 [port], Au&Arts 12 [port]*
Hughes, (James) Langston 1902-1967 *GayLL, IntDcT 2, RfGShF*
Hughes, (James Mercer) Langston 1902-1967 *TwCYAW*
Hughes, Larry Neal 1941- *WhoMW 93*
Hughes, Laurel Ellen 1952- *WhoScEn 94*
Hughes, Lawrence Edward 1922- *WhoAmP 93*
Hughes, Leonard S., Jr. 1926- *WhoBlA 94*
Hughes, Leslie Ernest 1932- *IntWW 93, Who 94*
Hughes, Lewis Harry 1945- *Who 94*
Hughes, Linda J. 1950- *WhoAm 94, WhoWest 94*
Hughes, Linda Renate 1947- *WhoAmL 94*
Hughes, Lloyd d1958 *WhoHol 92*
Hughes, Lois June Hulme 1941- *WhoMW 93*
Hughes, Louis R. 1949- *IntWW 93*
Hughes, Louis Ralph 1949- *Who 94*
Hughes, Loyd Ray 1940- *WhoWest 94*
Hughes, Lyman G. 1945- *WhoAmL 94*
Hughes, Lynn Nettleton 1941- *WhoAm 94, WhoAmL 94*
Hughes, Lyric 1953- *WhoMW 93*
Hughes, Malcolm Kenneth 1943- *WhoAm 94*
Hughes, Mamie F. 1929- *WhoBlA 94*
Hughes, Marcia Marie 1949- *WhoAmL 94*
Hughes, Margaret Eileen 1943- *WhoAm 94, WhoAmL 94, WhoWest 94*
Hughes, Marie Sharon 1955- *WhoFI 94*
Hughes, Marija Matich *WhoAm 94, WhoAmL 94*
Hughes, Mark 1953- *WhoAmP 93*
Hughes, (William) Mark d1993 *Who 94N*
Hughes, Mark Lee 1960- *WhoScEn 94*
Hughes, Martin *WhoHisp 94*
Hughes, Martin 1922- *WhoAmP 93*
Hughes, Mary Beth 1919- *WhoHol 92*
Hughes, Mary Elizabeth 1940- *WhoAm 94*
Hughes, Mary Gray *DrAPF 93*
Hughes, Mary Katherine 1949- *WhoAmL 94, WhoWest 94*
Hughes, Matilda 1922- *WrDr 94*
Hughes, Michael H. 1954- *WhoIns 94*
Hughes, Michael Joseph 1951- *WhoMW 93*
Hughes, Michael Scott 1958- *WhoMW 93*
Hughes, Michael Wayne 1957- *WhoScEn 94*
Hughes, Michaela Kelly *WhoAm 94*
Hughes, Monica 1925- *BlmGWL, EncSF 93, WrDr 94*
Hughes, Monica (Ince) 1925- *TwCYAW*
Hughes, Nigel Howard 1937- *Who 94*
Hughes, Norah Ann O'Brien 1948- *WhoAm 94*
Hughes, Patricia E. 1940- *WhoMW 93*
Hughes, Patrick Henry 1942- *WhoIns 94*
Hughes, Paul *Who 94*
Hughes, (Harold) Paul 1926- *Who 94*
Hughes, Paul G. 1947- *WhoAmL 94*
Hughes, Paul Lucien 1938- *WhoAmA 93*
Hughes, Peter *Who 94*
Hughes, (David Evan) Peter 1932- *Who 94*
Hughes, Peter Thomas 1949- *Who 94*
Hughes, Philip Arthur Booley *Who 94*
Hughes, Phillip Samuel 1917- *WhoAm 94*
Hughes, Phillip William 1926- *WrDr 94*
Hughes, (James) Quentin 1920- *WrDr 94*
Hughes, R. John 1930- *WrDr 94*
Hughes, Ralph M. *WhoAmP 93*
Hughes, Randall L. 1940- *WhoAmL 94*
Hughes, Randy *WhoAmP 93*
Hughes, Ray Harrison 1924- *WhoAm 94*
Hughes, Richard 1900-1976 *BlmGEL*
Hughes, Richard 1909-1992 *AnObit 1992*
Hughes, Richard Charles 1915- *Who 94*
Hughes, Richard Douglas 1951- *WhoWest 94*
Hughes, Richard Drew 1957- *WhoFI 94*
Hughes, Richard Gene 1939- *WhoMW 93*
Hughes, Richard Holland 1947- *WrDr 94*
Hughes, Richard J(oseph) 1909-1992 *CurBio 93N*
Hughes, Rick L. 1960- *WhoMW 93*
Hughes, Robert 1932- *Who 94*
Hughes, Robert (Studley Forrest) 1938- *WrDr 94*
Hughes, Robert Edward 1924- *WhoAm 94*
Hughes, Robert Gurth 1951- *Who 94*
Hughes, Robert Harrison 1917- *WhoAm 94*
Hughes, Robert J. 1944- *WhoAmL 94*
Hughes, Robert Lachlan 1944- *WhoAm 94, WhoWest 94*
Hughes, Robert Merrill 1936- *WhoFI 94, WhoWest 94*
Hughes, Robert N. 1938- *WhoIns 94*
Hughes, Robert Neal 1938- *WhoFI 94*
Hughes, Robert Powell 1940- *WhoIns 94*
Hughes, Robert S. F. 1938- *WhoAmA 93*
Hughes, Robert Studley Forrest 1938- *Who 94, WhoAm 94*
Hughes, Robert Valentine 1943- *Who 94*
Hughes, Robin d1989 *WhoHol 92*
Hughes, Rochford *Who 94*
Hughes, (Sidney Weetman) Rochford 1914- *Who 94*
Hughes, Roddy 1891- *WhoHol 92*
Hughes, Rodney H. 1925- *WhoAmP 93*
Hughes, Roger K. *WhoWest 94*
Hughes, Ronald Frederick 1927- *Who 94*
Hughes, Ronald Joseph 1956- *WhoMW 93*
Hughes, Ronald LeRoy 1943- *WhoAm 94*
Hughes, Roy d1928 *WhoHol 92*
Hughes, Royston John 1925- *Who 94*
Hughes, Rush d1958 *WhoHol 92*
Hughes, Ruth Pierce 1919- *WhoMW 93*
Hughes, Sarah Gillette 1947- *WhoFI 94*
Hughes, Sean Patrick Francis 1941- *IntWW 93, Who 94*
Hughes, Sharon Mary 1952- *WhoFI 94*
Hughes, Shirley 1927- *Who 94, WrDr 94*
Hughes, Simon Henry Ward 1951- *Who 94*
Hughes, Sophie *DrAPF 93*
Hughes, Spencer Edward, Jr. 1933- *WhoFI 94*
Hughes, Spike (Patrick Cairns) 1908-1987 *NewGrDO*
Hughes, Stanley John 1918- *WhoAm 94*
Hughes, Stephen Skipsey 1952- *Who 94*
Hughes, Steve Michael 1942- *WhoAmP 93*
Hughes, Steven Jay 1948- *WhoAmL 94*
Hughes, Steven Michael 1955- *WhoWest 94*
Hughes, Suzanne Helen 1944- *WhoAmP 93*
Hughes, T. Arthur d1953 *WhoHol 92*
Hughes, Ted 1930- *BlmGEL, EncSF 93, IntWW 93, PoeCrit 7 [port], TwCYAW, Who 94, WhoAm 94, WrDr 94*
Hughes, Teresa P. 1932- *WhoAmP 93*
Hughes, Terry *ConTFT 11*
Hughes, Thomas Gerald, Jr. 1942- *WhoAmP 93*
Hughes, Thomas Joseph 1926- *WhoAm 94*
Hughes, Thomas Joseph 1943- *WhoAm 94, WhoScEn 94*
Hughes, Thomas Lowe 1925- *Who 94, WhoAm 94*
Hughes, Thomas McKenny 1832-1917 *DcNaB MP*
Hughes, Thomas Parke 1923- *WhoAm 94*
Hughes, Thomas W. 1951- *WhoAmL 94*
Hughes, Thomas William 1950- *WhoScEn 94*
Hughes, Tony 1890- *WhoHol 92*
Hughes, Tresa *WhoHol 92*
Hughes, Trevor (Poulton) 1925- *Who 94*
Hughes, Trevor Denby L. *Who 94*
Hughes, Vester Thomas, Jr. 1928- *WhoAm 94, WhoAmL 94*
Hughes, Victor *Who 94*
Hughes, (Harold) Victor 1926- *Who 94*
Hughes, Vincent 1956- *WhoAmP 93, WhoBlA 94*
Hughes, W. James 1944- *WhoWest 94*
Hughes, Walter Jones 1941- *WhoFI 94, WhoMW 93*
Hughes, Walter Thompson 1930- *WhoAm 94*
Hughes, Wendy *WhoHol 92*
Hughes, William 1910- *Who 94*
Hughes, William (Taylor) 1936- *WrDr 94*
Hughes, William Anthony 1921- *WhoAm 94*
Hughes, William Dillon 1900- *Who 94*
Hughes, William Frank 1930- *WhoAm 94*
Hughes, William Franklin, Jr. 1913- *WhoAm 94*
Hughes, William J. 1932- *CngDr 93*
Hughes, William James 1935- *WhoAmP 93*
Hughes, William John 1932- *WhoAm 94, WhoAmP 93*
Hughes, William L. 1952- *WhoWest 94*
Hughes, William Lewis 1926- *WhoAm 94*
Hughes, William Young 1940- *Who 94*
Hughes, Winifred Shirley 1927- *WhoAm 94*
Hughes, Yvonne d1950 *WhoHol 92*
Hughes, Zach 1928- *EncSF 93*
Hughes, Zack 1928- *WrDr 94*
Hughesdon, Charles Frederick 1909- *Who 94*
Hughes Jones, Nevin Campbell 1923- *Who 94*
Hughes-Morgan, David (John) 1925- *Who 94*
Hughes-Young *Who 94*
Hughey, David V. *DrAPF 93*
Hughey, James F., Jr. 1945- *WhoAmL 94*
Hughey, Kirk 1940- *WhoAmA 93*
Hughey, Richard Kohlman 1934- *WhoAmL 94*
Hughff, Victor William 1931- *Who 94*
Hughitt, Jeremiah Keefe 1930- *WhoAm 94, WhoFI 94*
Hugh-Jones, Wynn Normington 1923- *Who 94*
Hughs, Mary Geraldine 1929- *WhoWest 94*
Hughs, Richard Earl 1936- *WhoAm 94*
Hugh Smith, Andrew (Colin) 1931- *Who 94*
Hugh Smith, Andrew Colin 1931- *IntWW 93*
Hugh Smith, Henry Owen 1937- *Who 94*
Hughson, Mary Helen 1965- *WhoScEn 94*
Hughston, Jess 1923- *WhoAmP 93*
Hughston, Thomas Leslie, Jr. 1943- *WhoAmP 93*
Hughto, Darryl Leo 1943- *WhoAmA 93*
Hughto, Margie A. 1944- *WhoAmA 93*
Hugi, Maurice G. *EncSF 93*
Hugill, John 1930- *Who 94*
Hugill, Michael James 1918- *Who 94*
Hugill, Stan(ley James) 1906-1992 *WrDr 94N*
Hugin, Adolph Charles Eugene 1907- *WhoAm 94, WhoAmL 94, WhoFI 94*
Hugler, Edward C. 1950- *WhoAm 94, WhoFI 94*
Hugley, Carolyn F. 1958- *WhoAmP 93*
Hugo, Bruce 1945- *WhoAmP 93*
Hugo, Joan (Dowey) 1930- *WhoAmA 93*
Hugo, John (Mandeville) 1899- *Who 94*
Hugo, John Adam 1873-1945 *NewGrDO*
Hugo, Laurence 1917- *WhoHol 92*
Hugo, Mauritz d1974 *WhoHol 92*
Hugo, Norman Eliot 1933- *WhoAm 94*
Hugo, Victor(-Marie) 1802-1885 *BlmGEL, IntDcT 2 [port], NewGrDO*
Hugo of Bury St Edmunds fl. 1130- *DcNaB MP*
Hugoson, Gene 1945- *WhoAmP 93*
Hugstad, Paul Steven 1943- *WhoAm 94*
Huguenel, Edward David 1954- *WhoScEn 94*
Huguenin, George Richard 1937- *WhoFI 94*
Hugueny, Sharon 1944- *WhoHol 92*
Huguet, Josefina 1871-1951 *NewGrDO*
Huguez, Michael D. *WhoHisp 94*
Hugunin, James Richard 1947- *WhoAmA 93*
Hugus, Z. Zimmerman, Jr. 1923- *WhoAm 94*
Huh, Billy K. 1958- *WhoAsA 94*
Hu Han *IntWW 93*
Huhne, Christopher 1954- *WrDr 94*
Hu Hong 1918- *IntWW 93, WhoPRCh 91 [port]*
Huhs, John I. 1944- *WhoAm 94, WhoAmL 94*
Huhta, James Kenneth 1937- *WhoAm 94*
Hui, Chiu Shuen 1942- *WhoMW 93*
Hui, Pat 1943- *WhoAmA 93*
Hui, Sek Wen 1935- *WhoAsA 94*
Huibregtse, Jayne Lynnor 1952- *WhoMW 93*
Huie, Ben Terrell 1947- *WhoMW 93*

Humphrey, George Magoffin 1890-1970
EncABHB 9 [port]
Humphrey, George Magoffin, II 1942-
WhoAm 94
Humphrey, Gordon J. 1940- *WhoAmP 93*
Humphrey, Gordon John 1940-
IntWW 93
Humphrey, Harry d1947 *WhoHol 92*
Humphrey, Howard C. 1933- *WhoAm 94,*
WhoFI 94
Humphrey, Howard Clark *WhoIns 94*
Humphrey, Howard John 1940-
WhoBlA 94
Humphrey, Howard S., Sr. 1905-
WhoAmP 93
Humphrey, Hubert Grant 1910-1992
WhoBlA 94N
Humphrey, Hubert H(oratio) 1911-1978
ConAu 43NR
Humphrey, Hubert Horatio, III 1942-
WhoAm 94, WhoAmL 94, WhoAmP 93,
WhoMW 93
Humphrey, Jack Weldon d1967
WhoAmA 93N
Humphrey, James 1939- *WrDr 94*
Humphrey, James A. *WhoAmP 93*
Humphrey, James Philip 1921-
WhoBlA 94
Humphrey, Jennifer *DrAPF 93*
Humphrey, John Julius 1926-
WhoWest 94
Humphrey, John Peters 1905- *IntWW 93*
Humphrey, John Sparkman 1941-
WhoFI 94
Humphrey, Judy Lucille 1949-
WhoAmA 93
Humphrey, Karen 1945- *WhoAmP 93*
Humphrey, Karen Michael 1945-
WhoAm 94, WhoWest 94
Humphrey, Kathryn Britt 1923-
WhoBlA 94
Humphrey, Kathryn J. 1953- *WhoAmL 94*
Humphrey, Leonard Claude 1928-
WhoScEn 94
Humphrey, Lucie King 1911-
WhoAmP 93
Humphrey, Margo 1942- *WhoBlA 94*
Humphrey, Marian J. *WhoBlA 94*
Humphrey, Marion Andrew 1949-
WhoBlA 94
Humphrey, Mark *WhoHol 92*
Humphrey, Mary Ann 1943- *WrDr 94*
Humphrey, Neil Darwin 1928-
WhoAm 94
Humphrey, Nene 1947- *WhoAmA 93*
Humphrey, Orral d1929 *WhoHol 92*
Humphrey, Paul *DrAPF 93*
Humphrey, Philip Strong 1926-
WhoAm 94, WhoMW 93, WhoScEn 94
Humphrey, Richard Pryor, Jr.
WhoAmP 93
Humphrey, Robert Charles 1961-
WhoBlA 94
Humphrey, Robert Jennings 1952-
WhoAm 94
Humphrey, S. L. 1941- *WhoAmA 93*
Humphrey, Shirley J. 1937- *WhoAmP 93*
Humphrey, Sonnie *WhoBlA 94*
Humphrey, Todd John 1961- *WhoMW 93*
Humphrey, Todd Mitchell 1961-
WhoFI 94
Humphrey, Watts Sherman 1927-
WhoAm 94
Humphrey, William *DrAPF 93*
Humphrey, William d1942 *WhoHol 92*
Humphrey, William 1924- *WrDr 94*
Humphrey, William Albert 1927-
WhoAm 94, WhoFI 94
Humphrey, William Gerald 1904- *Who 94*
Humphreys, Arthur Leslie Charles 1917-
Who 94
Humphreys, B. V. 1927- *WrDr 94*
Humphreys, Cecil d1947 *WhoHol 92*
Humphreys, Charles 1714-1786
WhAmRev
Humphreys, Colin John 1941- *Who 94*
Humphreys, David 1752-1818
WhAmRev [port]
Humphreys, David John 1936-
WhoAm 94
Humphreys, David Leroy 1941-
WhoMW 93
Humphreys, Dick d1977 *WhoHol 92*
Humphreys, Edward Maurice 1952-
WhoMW 93
Humphreys, Edwin Coleman, Jr. 1919-
WhoAmP 93
Humphreys, Emyr (Owen) 1919- *WrDr 94*
Humphreys, Emyr Owen 1919- *Who 94*
Humphreys, J. R. *DrAPF 93*
Humphreys, James, Jr. 1748-1810
WhAmRev
Humphreys, James Burnham 1941-
WhoAm 94
Humphreys, James Charles 1934-
IntWW 93
Humphreys, James F. 1948- *WhoAmP 93*
Humphreys, James W. 1915- *WhoAm 94*

Humphreys, Janet *Who 94*
Humphreys, John Henry d1992 *Who 94N*
Humphreys, Joseph Roy 1938-
WhoWest 94
Humphreys, Josephine *DrAPF 93*
Humphreys, Josephine 1945- *WhoAm 94*
Humphreys, Keith Wood 1934- *Who 94*
Humphreys, Kenneth King 1938-
WhoAm 94
Humphreys, Kenneth William 1916-
Who 94
Humphreys, Lloyd Girton 1913-
WhoAm 94
Humphreys, Lynn Marie 1962-
WhoWest 94
Humphreys, Michael Edward 1953-
WhoFI 94
Humphreys, Mildred *WhoAmP 93*
Humphreys, Myles *Who 94*
Humphreys, (Raymond Evelyn) Myles
1925- *Who 94*
Humphreys, Olliver (William) 1902-
Who 94
Humphreys, Olliver William 1902-
IntWW 93
Humphreys, Priscilla Faith 1912-
WhoAmP 93, WhoWomW 91
Humphreys, Robert, Jr. 1932- *WhoIns 94*
Humphreys, Robert Arthur 1907- *Who 94*
Humphreys, Robert Lee 1924-
WhoAm 94, WhoFI 94
Humphreys, Robert Russell 1938-
WhoAm 94
Humphreys, Roberta Marie 1944-
WhoMW 93
Humphries, Barry *Who 94*
Humphries, Barry 1934- *WhoHol 92*
Humphries, (John) Barry 1934-
IntWW 93, Who 94
Humphries, Bee d1970 *WhoHol 92*
Humphries, Charles, Jr. 1943- *WhoBlA 94*
Humphries, Charlotte Anne 1955-
WhoMW 93
Humphries, David Ernest 1937- *Who 94*
Humphries, Frederick S. 1935-
WhoBlA 94
Humphries, Gerald *WhoHol 92*
Humphries, Gerard William 1928-
Who 94
Humphries, J. Bob 1946- *WhoAmL 94*
Humphries, James Donald, III 1944-
WhoAmL 94
Humphries, James Nathan 1958-
WhoBlA 94
Humphries, Jay 1962- *WhoBlA 94*
Humphries, Joan Ropes 1928-
WhoScEn 94
Humphries, John Anthony Charles 1925-
Who 94
Humphries, John Charles Freeman 1937-
Who 94
Humphries, John O'Neal 1931-
WhoAm 94
Humphries, Paula G. *WhoBlA 94*
Humphries, Stanley, Jr. 1946-
WhoWest 94
Humphries, T. W. *WhoAmP 93*
Humphries, Tessa *WhoHol 92*
Humphries, Weldon R. 1937- *WhoAm 94,*
WhoFI 94
Humphries, William Darlington 1927-
WhoFI 94
Humphries, William R. *WhoAmP 93*
Humphry, Derek 1930- *ConAu 41NR*
Humphry, Derek John 1930- *WhoWest 94*
Humphry, James, III 1916- *WhoAm 94*
Humphrys, Francis Henry 1879-1971
DcNaB MP
Humphrys, John 1943- *Who 94*
Humphrys, Leslie George 1921- *WrDr 94*
Humpleby, Twyla Jean 1933-
WhoAmP 93
Humpreys, Geoffrey 1921- *WrDr 94*
Humpton, Richard c. 1733-1804
WhAmRev
Humza, Amir d1993 *NewYTBS 93*
Hunault, Joan Burton 1950- *WhoMW 93*
Huncke, Herbert E(dwin) 1915- *WrDr 94*
Hundertmark, Lothar *NewGrDO*
Hundertwasser, Friedensreich 1928-
IntWW 93
Hundhausen, Robert John 1916-
WhoScEn 94, WhoWest 94
Hundley, Dennis Carl 1955- *WhoFI 94*
Hundley, Hot Rod 1934- *BasBi [port]*
Hundley, John Thomas 1948-
WhoAmL 94
Hundley, John Walker 1899-1990
WhAm 10
Hundley, Norris C., Jr. 1935- *WrDr 94*
Hundley, Norris Cecil, Jr. 1935-
WhoAm 94
Hundt, Paul Robert 1939- *WhoAmL 94*
Hundt, Reed Eric 1948- *WhoAm 94*
Huneke, William Lester 1954-
WhoAmP 93
Huneycutt, Alice Ruth 1951- *WhoAmL 94*
Hung, Chao-Shun 1942- *WhoAsA 94*

Hung, Chih-Cheng 1954- *WhoAsA 94*
Hung, George Kit 1947- *WhoScEn 94*
Hung, James Chen 1929- *WhoAm 94,*
WhoAsA 94
Hung, Ken 1947- *WhoAsA 94*
Hung, Kuen-Shan 1938- *WhoAsA 94,*
WhoScEn 94
Hung, Paul P. 1933- *WhoAsA 94*
Hung, Paul Porwen 1933- *WhoScEn 94*
Hung, Ru J. 1934- *WhoAm 94,*
WhoAsA 94, WhoScEn 94
Hung, Stephen Chifeng 1941- *WhoAsA 94*
Hung, Tin-Kan 1936- *WhoAm 94,*
WhoAsA 94
Hung, William Mo-Wei 1940-
WhoScEn 94
Hung, Yen-Wan 1944- *WhoAsA 94*
Hungate, Mark Edward 1951-
WhoAmL 94
Hungate, William Leonard 1922-
WhoAm 94, WhoAmL 94, WhoAmP 93,
WhoMW 93
Hunger, Anna *EncSF 93*
Hunger, Herbert 1914- *IntWW 93*
Hunger, John David 1941- *WhoFI 94*
Hungerford, Constance Cain 1948-
WhoAmA 93
Hungerford, David A. d1993
NewYTBS 93
Hungerford, David Samuel 1938-
WhoAm 94
Hungerford, Ed Vernon, III 1939-
WhoAm 94
Hungerford, Gary A. 1948- *WhoFI 94,*
WhoIns 94
Hungerford, Herbert Eugene 1918-
WhoScEn 94
Hungerford, John Girdlestone 1905-
WhoAm 94
Hungerford, Robert L., Sr. 1916-
WhoAmP 93
Hung Wah Michael Poon 1942-
WhoAmA 93
Hunhoff, Bernie P. 1951- *WhoAmP 93*
Hunia, Edward Mark 1946- *WhoAm 94*
Hunig, Siegfried Helmut 1921- *IntWW 93*
Hunigan, Earl 1929- *WhoBlA 94*
Hunigan, JoAnn 1948- *WhoMW 93*
Huni-Mihaczek, Felice 1891-1976
NewGrDO
Huning, Deborah Gray 1950- *WhoAm 94,*
WhoWest 94
Hunisak, John Michael 1944-
WhoAmA 93
Hunke, Ramon L. 1932- *WhoFI 94*
Hunkele, Lester Martin, III 1947-
WhoAm 94
Hunker, Henry L. 1924- *WrDr 94*
Hunkin, Tim(othy) Mark Trelawney
1950- *WrDr 94*
Hunking, Loila Belcher 1939-
WhoAmP 93
Hunkins, Francis Peter 1938- *WhoAm 94*
Hunkins, Raymond Breedlove 1939-
WhoAmL 94
Hunkler, Dennis 1943- *WhoAmA 93*
Hunlede, Ayi Houenou 1925- *IntWW 93*
Hunley, W. Helen 1920- *WhoWest 94*
Hunn, Dorothy Fegan 1928- *WhoBlA 94*
Hunn, Jack (Kent) 1906- *Who 94*
Hunn, Myron Vernon 1926- *WhoBlA 94*
Hunnicutt, Gayle 1943- *IntMPA 94*
Hunnicutt, Arthur d1979 *WhoHol 92*
Hunnicutt, Benjamin Kline 1943-
WrDr 94
Hunnicutt, Charles Alvin 1950-
WhoAm 94, WhoAmP 93
Hunnicutt, Ellen *DrAPF 93*
Hunnicutt, Gayle 1943- *WhoHol 92*
Hunnicutt, Richard Pearce 1926-
WhoScEn 94, WhoWest 94
Hunnicutt, Robert William 1954-
WhoWest 94
Hunningher, Benjamin 1903-1991
WhAm 10
Hunnings, (Thomas) Neville March
1929- *WrDr 94*
Hunnisett, Roy Frank 1928- *Who 94*
Hunsaker, Floyd B. 1915- *WhoWest 94*
Hunsaker, Fred R. 1939- *WhoAmP 93*
Hunsaker, Richard Kendall 1960-
WhoAmL 94
Hunsaker, Scott 1952- *WhoAmL 94*
Hunsberger, Bruce *DrAPF 93*
Hunsberger, Charles Wesley 1929-
WhoAm 94, WhoWest 94
Hunsberger, Robert Earl 1947-
WhoWest 94
Hunsdon Of Hunsdon, Baron *Who 94*
Hun Sen 1950- *IntWW 93*
Hunsicker, Harold Yundt 1914-
.*WhoScEn 94*
Hunsicker, J. Freedley, Jr. 1943-
WhoAmL 94
Hunsinger, Doyle J. 1947- *WhoFI 94*
Hunstad, Robert Edward 1940-
WhoAm 94, WhoIns 94
Hunstein, Carol 1944- *WhoAmL 94*

Hunstein, Carol W. *WhoAmP 93*
Hunsucker, Robert Dean 1925-
WhoAm 94
Hunsucker, Robert Dudley 1930-
WhoWest 94
Hunsworth, John Alfred 1921- *Who 94*
Hunt *Who 94*
Hunt, Baron 1910- *IntWW 93, Who 94*
Hunt, Alan Charles 1941- *Who 94*
Hunt, Albert R. 1942- *WhoAm 94*
Hunt, Angela Elwell 1957- *ConAu 142,*
SmATA 75 [port]
Hunt, Ann Elizabeth 1948- *WhoMW 93*
Hunt, Annette *WhoHol 92*
Hunt, Arthur James 1915- *Who 94*
Hunt, Barbara Ann *WhoBlA 94*
Hunt, Bernice Kohn 1920- *WrDr 94*
Hunt, Betty Syble 1919- *WhoBlA 94*
Hunt, Bob *ConAu 141*
Hunt, Bobby Ray 1941- *WhoAm 94*
Hunt, Brenda Rena 1960- *WhoMW 93*
Hunt, Bruce J. 1956- *WrDr 94*
Hunt, Bryan 1947- *WhoAm 94,*
WhoAmA 93
Hunt, Carl C. 1936- *WhoFI 94*
Hunt, Caroline Rose 1923- *IntWW 93*
Hunt, Charles Amoes 1950- *WhoBlA 94*
Hunt, Charles Brownlow, Jr. 1916-
WhoAm 94
Hunt, Charles Butler 1906- *WhoAm 94,*
WhoScEn 94
Hunt, Charles Edward 1953- *WhoScEn 94*
Hunt, Christina Lee 1959- *WhoAmL 94*
Hunt, Christopher John 1937- *Who 94*
Hunt, (Julian) Courtenay *WhoAmA 93*
Hunt, Darrold Victor 1941- *WhoBlA 94*
Hunt, Darwin Paul 1926- *WhoScEn 94*
Hunt, David *WhoHol 92*
Hunt, David (Wathen Stather) 1913-
Who 94, WrDr 94
Hunt, David Brian 1962- *WhoWest 94*
Hunt, David Claude 1957- *WhoMW 93*
Hunt, David Curtis 1935- *WhoAmA 93*
Hunt, David D. 1957- *WhoAmL 94*
Hunt, David Evans 1953- *WhoAmL 94*
Hunt, David Ford 1931- *WhoAm 94,*
WhoAmL 94
Hunt, David James Fletcher 1942-
IntWW 93, Who 94
Hunt, David Roderic Notley 1947-
Who 94
Hunt, David Wathen Stather 1913-
IntWW 93
Hunt, Deborah L. *DrAPF 93*
Hunt, Derek Simpson 1939- *Who 94*
Hunt, Desmond Charles 1918- *Who 94*
Hunt, Donald F. *WhoAm 94*
Hunt, Donald Frederick 1930- *Who 94*
Hunt, Donald R. 1921- *WhoAm 94*
Hunt, Donald Samuel 1938- *WhoAm 94*
Hunt, Donnell Ray 1926- *WhoAm 94,*
WhoScEn 94
Hunt, Douglas A. 1945- *WhoAmP 93*
Hunt, E(verette) Howard 1918- *WrDr 94*
Hunt, Earl Busby 1933- *WhoAm 94*
Hunt, Edgar Hubert 1909- *WrDr 94*
Hunt, Edward *WhoBlA 94*
Hunt, Edward H 1939- *WrDr 94*
Hunt, Effie Neva 1922- *WhoAm 94*
Hunt, Eleanor d1981 *WhoHol 92*
Hunt, Eugene 1948- *WhoBlA 94*
Hunt, Everett Clair 1928- *WhoAm 94*
Hunt, F(lorence) V(ance) *WrDr 94*
Hunt, Francesca 1920- *WrDr 94*
Hunt, Frank Bouldin 1915- *WhoAm 94*
Hunt, Franklin Griggs 1930- *WhoAm 94*
Hunt, Frederick Talley Drum, Jr. 1947-
WhoFI 94
Hunt, Gareth 1943- *WhoHol 92*
Hunt, George Andrew 1949- *WhoAmL 94*
Hunt, George G. 1935- *WhoIns 94*
Hunt, Gil 1919- *WrDr 94*
Hunt, Gilbert Adams *Who 94*
Hunt, Gill *EncSF 93*
Hunt, Gladys M. 1926- *WrDr 94*
Hunt, Gordon 1934- *WhoAm 94*
Hunt, Gregory Lynn 1947- *WhoAm 94*
Hunt, H. Guy 1933- *WhoAmP 93*
Hunt, Harold Keith 1938- *WhoAm 94*
Hunt, Harold Ray 1945- *WhoScEn 94*
Hunt, Heber Truman 1928- *WhoWest 94*
Hunt, Helen 1963- *IntMPA 94,*
WhoAm 94, WhoHol 92
Hunt, Henry George Bonavia- 1847-1917
DcNaB MP
Hunt, (Henry) Holman 1924- *Who 94*
Hunt, Howard Francis 1918- *WhoAm 94*
Hunt, Hugh 1911-1993 *ConAu 141*
Hunt, Hugh Sydney d1993 *Who 94N*
Hunt, Hugh Sydney 1911- *IntWW 93*
Hunt, Irene 1907- *TwCYAW, WrDr 94*
Hunt, Isaac 1742-1809 *WhAmRev*
Hunt, Isaac Cosby, Jr. 1937- *WhoBlA 94*
Hunt, J(oseph) McVicker 1906-1991
WhAm 10, WrDr 94N
Hunt, J. Roy 1884- *IntDcF 2-4*
Hunt, Jacob Tate 1916- *WhoAm 94*
Hunt, Jake c. 1860-c. 1910 *EncNAR*

Hunt, James Who 94
Hunt, James d1993 NewYTBS 93 [port]
Hunt, James, Jr. 1944- WhoBlA 94
Hunt, (Patrick) James 1943- Who 94
Hunt, James B., Jr. 1937- CurBio 93 [port]
Hunt, James Baxter, Jr. 1937- IntWW 93, WhoAm 94, WhoAmP 93
Hunt, James Calvin 1925- WhoAm 94
Hunt, James H., Jr. 1948- WhoScEn 94
Hunt, James K. 1951- WhoFI 94
Hunt, James L. 1942- WhoAmL 94
Hunt, James Leonard 1938- WhoAmP 93
Hunt, James Simon Wallis d1993 Who 94N
Hunt, James Simon Wallis 1947- IntWW 93
Hunt, Janell E. 1950- WhoAmP 93
Hunt, Janet Ross 1952- WhoScEn 94
Hunt, Jay d1932 WhoHol 92
Hunt, Jeffrey Brian 1958- WhoMW 93
Hunt, Jimmy 1939- WhoHol 92
Hunt, Joe 1919-1944 BuCMET
Hunt, Joe Harold 1925- WhoAm 94
Hunt, John (Leonard) 1929- Who 94
Hunt, John Bankson 1956- WhoAmP 93
Hunt, John David 1925- WhoAm 94
Hunt, John E. 1908-1989 WhAm 10
Hunt, John Edwin 1918- WhoAm 94, WhoFI 94
Hunt, John J. 1922- WhoAmP 93
Hunt, John Maitland 1932- Who 94
Hunt, John Stephen 1935- WhoMW 93
Hunt, John Wesley 1927- WhoAm 94
Hunt, Johnnie B. 1924- WhoFI 94
Hunt, Jonathan Lucas 1938- IntWW 93
Hunt, Joseph Francis 1941- WhoAm 94
Hunt, Judy WhoAmP 93
Hunt, Julian Charles Roland 1941- Who 94
Hunt, June Dawn 1951- WhoAmP 93
Hunt, Kenneth 1914- Who 94
Hunt, Kenneth Charles 1949- WhoAmL 94
Hunt, Kevan 1937- Who 94
Hunt, Lamar ProFbHF
Hunt, Lamar 1932- BuCMET, WhoAm 94, WhoMW 93
Hunt, Lawrence Halley, Jr. 1943- WhoAm 94, WhoAmL 94, WhoMW 93
Hunt, Leigh 1784-1859 BlmGEL [port]
Hunt, (James Henry) Leigh 1784-1859 NewGrDO
Hunt, Linda 1945- IntMPA 94, WhoAm 94, WhoHol 92
Hunt, Lynn 1878-1960 WhoAmA 93N
Hunt, Lynn (Avery) 1945- WrDr 94
Hunt, Madge d1935 WhoHol 92
Hunt, Malcolm Peter John 1938- Who 94
Hunt, Mark Alan 1949- WhoAm 94
Hunt, Marsha WhoHol 92
Hunt, Marsha 1917- IntMPA 94, WhoHol 92
Hunt, Marsha 1946- BlkWr 2
Hunt, Martin Robert 1942- Who 94
Hunt, Martita d1969 WhoHol 92
Hunt, Maurice 1943- WhoBlA 94
Hunt, Maurice William 1936- Who 94
Hunt, Michael O'Leary 1935- WhoMW 93
Hunt, Nan DrAPF 93
Hunt, Nicholas (John Streynsham) 1930- Who 94
Hunt, Nicholas Streynsham 1930- IntWW 93
Hunt, Norman Charles 1918- Who 94
Hunt, Norman Edwin 1916- WhoAm 94
Hunt, O'Neal 1914- WhoBlA 94
Hunt, Patricia Jacqueline 1961- WhoScEn 94
Hunt, Patricia Joan WrDr 94
Hunt, Pee Wee d1979 WhoHol 92
Hunt, Peter 1928- IntMPA 94
Hunt, Peter 1945- SmATA 76 [port]
Hunt, Peter (Leonard) 1945- WrDr 94
Hunt, Peter H. 1938- IntMPA 94
Hunt, Peter Huls 1938- WhoAm 94
Hunt, Peter John 1933- IntWW 93, Who 94
Hunt, Philip Alexander 1949- Who 94
Hunt, Philip Bodley 1916- Who 94
Hunt, Philip George 1957- WhoScEn 94
Hunt, Pierre 1925- IntWW 93
Hunt, Portia L. 1947- WhoBlA 94
Hunt, R. Samuel, III 1941- WhoAmP 93
Hunt, R(ichard) W(illiam) 1908-1979 ConAu 141
Hunt, Ralph WhoAmP 93
Hunt, Ray Lee 1943- WhoFI 94
Hunt, Rea M. d1961 WhoHol 92
Hunt, Rex (Masterman) 1926- Who 94
Hunt, Rex Masterman 1926- IntWW 93
Hunt, Richard 1935- AfrAmAl 6, ConBlB 6 [port], WhoAm 94
Hunt, Richard Bruce 1927- Who 94
Hunt, Richard C. 1942- WhoAmL 94
Hunt, Richard Henry 1912- Who 94
Hunt, Richard Howard 1935- WhoAmA 93, WhoBlA 94
Hunt, Robert (Frederick) 1918- Who 94
Hunt, Robert (William Gainer) 1923- WrDr 94
Hunt, Robert Alan 1935- Who 94
Hunt, Robert Chester 1923- WhoFI 94, WhoMW 93
Hunt, Robert G. 1957- WhoMW 93
Hunt, Robert Gordon, Jr. 1927- WhoWest 94
Hunt, Robert James 1921- WhoAmA 93
Hunt, Robert Michael 1948- WhoFI 94
Hunt, Robert S. 1951- WhoBlA 94
Hunt, Robert Weldon 1935- WhoAm 94
Hunt, Robert William 1947- WhoWest 94
Hunt, Roger WhoAmP 93
Hunt, Roger 1935- Who 94
Hunt, Roger Schermerhorn 1943- WhoAm 94
Hunt, Roland Charles Colin 1916- Who 94
Hunt, Ronald Duncan 1935- WhoAm 94, WhoScEn 94
Hunt, Ronald Forrest 1943- WhoAm 94, WhoAmL 94
Hunt, Ronald Joseph 1951- WhoBlA 94
Hunt, Ross Stuart 1959- WhoFI 94
Hunt, Sam 1946- WrDr 94
Hunt, Samuel D. 1933- WhoBlA 94
Hunt, Samuel Pancoast, III 1943- WhoAm 94
Hunt, Samuel William 1942- WhoAmP 93
Hunt, Stoker 1939- WrDr 94
Hunt, Stuart W., Sr. 1927- WhoAmP 93
Hunt, Sue Whittington 1952- WhoFI 94
Hunt, Terence 1943- Who 94
Hunt, Theodore William 1909- WhoScEn 94
Hunt, Thomas Cavanaugh 1944- WhoFI 94
Hunt, Tim Who 94
Hunt, (Richard) Tim(othy) 1943- Who 94
Hunt, Timothy Arthur 1949- WhoWest 94
Hunt, Vincent Robert 1934- WhoAm 94
Hunt, Violet 1866-1942 TwCLC 53 [port]
Hunt, Virgil 1911- WhoMW 93
Hunt, Virginia 1935- WhoWest 94
Hunt, Walter 1796-1859 WorInv
Hunt, Walter Kenneth, III 1953- WhoAm 94
Hunt, Walter L. 1941- WhoAm 94
Hunt, Wanda 1944- WhoAmP 93
Hunt, Warren Who 94
Hunt, (William) Warren 1909- Who 94
Hunt, Wayne Wolf Robe (Kewa-Tse-She) 1905-1977 WhoAmA 93N
Hunt, William DrAPF 93
Hunt, William E. WhoAmP 93
Hunt, William E. 1923- WhoHol 92
Hunt, William E., Sr. 1923- WhoAm 94, WhoAmL 94, WhoWest 94
Hunt, William Edward 1921- WhoAm 94
Hunt, William J. 1946- WhoIns 94
Hunt, William Morris 1824-1879 AmCulL
Hunt, Willie 1941- IntMPA 94
Hunt, Willis B., Jr. WhoAmL 94, WhoAmP 93
Hunt, Wilson Price c. 1782-1842 WhWE
Hunt-Davis, Miles Garth 1938- Who 94
Hunte, Beryl Eleanor WhoAm 94
Hunte, Joseph Alexander 1917- Who 94
Hunte, Otto d1960 IntDcF 2-4
Hunten, Donald Mount 1925- IntWW 93, WhoAm 94, WhoScEn 94
Hunter Who 94
Hunter, Hon. Lord 1913- Who 94
Hunter, Alan 1912- Who 94
Hunter, Alan (James Herbert) 1922- WrDr 94
Hunter, Alan Graham 1934- WhoScEn 94
Hunter, Alastair WhoHol 92
Hunter, Alberta d1984 WhoHol 92
Hunter, Alexander (Albert) 1920- Who 94
Hunter, Alexander Freeland Cairns 1939- Who 94
Hunter, Alistair John 1936- Who 94
Hunter, Andrew 1751-1823 WhAmRev
Hunter, Andrew Robert Frederick 1943- Who 94
Hunter, Anthony George Weaver 1916- Who 94
Hunter, Anthony Rex Who 94
Hunter, Archibald MacBride 1906-1991 WrDr 94N
Hunter, Archie Louis 1925-1992 WhoBlA 94N
Hunter, Barry Russell 1927- Who 94
Hunter, Bill WhoHol 92
Hunter, Bill d1967 WhoHol 92
Hunter, Brian Ronald 1968- WhoBlA 94
Hunter, Bruce F. 1933- WhoAmP 93
Hunter, Bynum Merritt 1925- WhoAm 94
Hunter, Cecil Thomas 1925- WhoBlA 94
Hunter, Charles A. 1926- WhoBlA 94
Hunter, Charles David 1929- WhoAm 94, WhoFI 94
Hunter, Clarence WhoAmP 93
Hunter, Clarence Henry 1925- WhoBlA 94
Hunter, Colin d1968 WhoHol 92
Hunter, Dale Rodney 1955- WhoBlA 94
Hunter, David 1941- WhoBlA 94
Hunter, David Lee 1933- WhoBlA 94
Hunter, David Wittmer 1928- WhoAm 94
Hunter, Deanna Kay 1958- WhoAmP 93
Hunter, Deanna Lorraine 1946- WhoBlA 94
Hunter, Debora 1950- WhoAmA 93
Hunter, Donald 1934- WhoFI 94
Hunter, Donald Forrest 1934- WhoAmL 94, WhoMW 93
Hunter, Douglas Lee 1948- WhoFI 94, WhoMW 93
Hunter, Duncan 1948- CngDr 93, WhoAmP 93
Hunter, Duncan Lee 1948- WhoAm 94, WhoWest 94
Hunter, Durant Adams 1948- WhoFI 94
Hunter, E. Waldo EncSF 93
Hunter, Earle Leslie, III 1929- WhoAm 94
Hunter, Eddie 1888-1974 AfrAmAl 6
Hunter, Edgar Hayes 1914- WhoAm 94
Hunter, Edna d1920 WhoHol 92
Hunter, Edwin Ford, Jr. 1911- WhoAm 94, WhoAmL 94
Hunter, Edwina Earle 1943- WhoBlA 94
Hunter, Elijah WhAmRev
Hunter, Elizabeth 1934- WrDr 94
Hunter, Elizabeth Ives-Valsam 1945- WhoAm 94
Hunter, Elmo Bolton 1915- WhoAm 94, WhoAmL 94, WhoMW 93
Hunter, Elza Harris 1908- WhoBlA 94
Hunter, Eric J. 1930- WrDr 94
Hunter, Evan 1926- EncSF 93, IntWW 93, Who 94, WhoAm 94, WrDr 94
Hunter, Forrest Walker 1950- WhoAm 94, WhoAmL 94
Hunter, Frances S. 1928-1992 WhoBlA 94N
Hunter, Francis Tipton 1896- WhoAmA 93N
Hunter, Frank 1894-1981 BuCMET
Hunter, Fred WhoAmP 93, WhoWest 94
Hunter, Frederick Douglas 1940- WhoBlA 94
Hunter, George d1945 WhoHol 92
Hunter, George fl. 180-?- WhWE
Hunter, George L. 1932- WhoAmP 93
Hunter, Gertrude T. 1926- WhoBlA 94
Hunter, Glenn d1945 WhoHol 92
Hunter, (James) Graham 1901-1988 WhAm 10
Hunter, Hal Edward, Jr. 1921- WhoAmP 93
Hunter, Harlen Charles 1940- WhoAm 94
Hunter, Harold V. 1917- WhoAmP 93
Hunter, Harrison d1923 WhoHol 92
Hunter, Holly 1958- IntMPA 94, WhoAm 94, WhoHol 92
Hunter, Howard J., Jr. 1946- WhoAmP 93
Hunter, Howard Jacque, Jr. 1946- WhoBlA 94
Hunter, Howard William 1907- WhoAm 94
Hunter, Hugh Trapnell 1959- WhoAmL 94
Hunter, Ian d1975 WhoHol 92
Hunter, Ian (Bruce Hope) 1919- Who 94
Hunter, Ian Alexander 1939- Who 94
Hunter, Ian Gerald Adamson 1944- Who 94
Hunter, Ian Murray 1917- Who 94
Hunter, Irby B. 1940- WhoBlA 94
Hunter, Ivy Joe 1966- WhoBlA 94
Hunter, J(ames) Paul 1934- WrDr 94
Hunter, J. Reese 1927- WhoAmP 93
Hunter, Jack Corbett 1930- WhoAmP 93
Hunter, Jack D(ayton) 1921- WrDr 94
Hunter, Jack Duval 1937- WhoAm 94, WhoAmL 94
Hunter, Jackie d1951 WhoHol 92
Hunter, James 1817-1881 EncNAR
Hunter, James Alexander 1928- WhoAm 94
Hunter, James Austen, Jr. 1941- WhoAm 94, WhoAmL 94
Hunter, James Galbraith, Jr. 1942- WhoAm 94, WhoAmL 94, WhoMW 93
Hunter, James Mackiell 1946- WhoBlA 94
Hunter, James Nathaniel, II 1943- WhoBlA 94
Hunter, James Paul 1934- WhoAm 94
Hunter, Jeffrey d1969 WhoHol 92
Hunter, Jeffrey L. 1955- WhoMW 93
Hunter, Jerry E. 1938- WhoAm 94, WhoFI 94
Hunter, Jerry L. 1942- WhoBlA 94
Hunter, Jerry M. 1952- WhoAmL 94
Hunter, Jim 1939- WrDr 94
Hunter, John 1728-1793 WorInv
Hunter, John 1915- Who 94
Hunter, John 1921- Who 94
Hunter, John, Jr. 1925- WhAm 10
Hunter, John Alfred 1921- WhoAm 94
Hunter, John Davidson WhoBlA 94
Hunter, John Garvin 1947- Who 94
Hunter, John H. 1934- WhoAmA 93
Hunter, John Murray 1920- Who 94
Hunter, John Nathaniel 1929- WhoWest 94
Hunter, John Oswald Mair Who 94
Hunter, John Robert 1936- WhoAm 94
Hunter, John Robert, Jr. 1936- WhoAmP 93
Hunter, John Stuart 1923- WhoAm 94
Hunter, John W. 1934- WhoBlA 94
Hunter, K. C. 1968- WhoMW 93
Hunter, Kaki 1956- WhoHol 92
Hunter, Keith Robert 1936- Who 94
Hunter, Kenneth Who 94
Hunter, Kenneth d1961 WhoHol 92
Hunter, Kenneth 1946- WhoAm 94
Hunter, (Adam) Kenneth (Fisher) 1920- Who 94
Hunter, Kenneth Eugene 1943- WhoFI 94
Hunter, Kenneth F. 1926- WhoAmP 93
Hunter, Kenneth James 1944- WhoAm 94
Hunter, Kent Robert 1947- WhoMW 93
Hunter, Kermit Houston 1910- WhoAm 94
Hunter, Kim 1922- IntMPA 94, WhoAm 94, WhoHol 92
Hunter, Kristin DrAPF 93
Hunter, Kristin 1931- WrDr 94
Hunter, Kristin 1937- WhoBlA 94
Hunter, Kristin (Elaine) 1931- TwCYAW
Hunter, Larry Dean 1950- WhoAm 94, WhoAmL 94
Hunter, Larry Lee 1938- WhoFI 94, WhoScEn 94
Hunter, Laurence Colvin 1934- Who 94
Hunter, Lawrence J. WhoAmP 93
Hunter, Leonard LeGrande, III 1940- WhoAmA 93
Hunter, Linda Mason 1946- WhoMW 93
Hunter, Lindsey WhoBlA 94
Hunter, Lloyd Thomas 1936- WhoBlA 94
Hunter, Lorie Ann 1969- WhoMW 93
Hunter, Lynn 1947- WhoWomW 91
Hunter, M. Penelope 1954- WhoWest 94
Hunter, Margaret Blake 1913- WhoAmP 93
Hunter, Margaret King 1919- WhoAm 94
Hunter, Matthew ConAu 140
Hunter, Matthew 1934- WhoAm 94, WhoFI 94
Hunter, Maurice d1966 WhoHol 92
Hunter, Mel 1927- WhoAmA 93
Hunter, Melvin Eugene 1946- WhoWest 94
Hunter, Michael 1941- WhoAm 94
Hunter, Michael (Cyril William) 1949- WrDr 94
Hunter, Michael James 1956- WhoAmP 93
Hunter, Mollie 1922- WrDr 94
Hunter, (Maureen) Mollie 1922- TwCYAW
Hunter, Muir Vane Skerrett 1913- Who 94
Hunter, Nancy Quintero 1961- WhoScEn 94
Hunter, Norman (George Lorimer) 1899- EncSF 93, WrDr 94
Hunter, Norman L. 1932- WhoBlA 94
Hunter, Oliver Clifford, Jr. 1935- WhoBlA 94
Hunter, Pamela 1919- Who 94
Hunter, Patrick J. 1929- WhoBlA 94
Hunter, Paul DrAPF 93
Hunter, Paul 1954- WhoAmA 93
Hunter, Philip d1982 WhoHol 92
Hunter, Philip Brown 1909- Who 94
Hunter, Philip John 1939- Who 94
Hunter, R. Haze 1924- WhoAmP 93
Hunter, Raymond Thomas 1942- WhoFI 94
Hunter, Richard d1962 WhoHol 92
Hunter, Richard C. 1939- WhoBlA 94
Hunter, Richard Edward 1919- WhoAm 94
Hunter, Richard Grant, Jr. 1938- WhoFI 94, WhoScEn 94
Hunter, Richard Samford, Jr. 1954- WhoAmL 94
Hunter, Richard William 1954- WhoWest 94
Hunter, Rita 1933- Who 94
Hunter, Rita (Nellie) 1933- NewGrDO
Hunter, Robert WhoAmP 93
Hunter, Robert C. 1944- WhoAmP 93
Hunter, Robert Charles 1948- WhoFI 94
Hunter, Robert Dean 1928- WhoAmP 93
Hunter, Robert Dean 1951- WhoAmL 94
Hunter, Robert Douglas 1928- WhoAmA 93
Hunter, Robert Douglas 1944- WhoMW 93
Hunter, Robert E. 1940- WhoAmP 93
Hunter, Robert Fabio 1960- WhoScEn 94
Hunter, Robert Grams 1927- WhoAm 94
Hunter, Robert Howard 1929- WhoAmA 93
Hunter, Robert J. 1934- WhoBlA 94
Hunter, Robert John 1933- IntWW 93

Hunter, Robert Madison, Jr. 1951- *WhoWest 94*
Hunter, Robert N., Jr. 1947- *WhoAmL 94*
Hunter, Ronald 1947- *WhoHol 92*
Hunter, Ronald V. 1944- *WhoAm 94, WhoFI 94*
Hunter, Ross 1916- *IntDcF 2-4, IntMPA 94*
Hunter, Ross 1924- *WhoHol 92*
Hunter, Ross 1926- *WhoAm 94*
Hunter, S.L. *EncSF 93*
Hunter, Sally Anne 1947- *WhoMW 93*
Hunter, Sally Irene 1936- *WhoMW 93*
Hunter, Sam 1923- *WhoAm 94, WhoAmA 93, WrDr 94*
Hunter, Steven L. 1953- *WhoAm 94*
Hunter, Tab 1931- *IntMPA 94, WhoHol 92*
Hunter, Teola P. 1933- *WhoAmP 93, WhoBlA 94*
Hunter, Terryl *DrAPF 93*
Hunter, Theodore Paul 1951- *WhoAmL 94, WhoWest 94*
Hunter, Thom Hugh 1918- *WhoAm 94*
Hunter, Thomas *WhoHol 92*
Hunter, Thomas D. 1948- *WhoAmL 94*
Hunter, Thomas Harrison 1913- *WhoAm 94*
Hunter, Thomas Willard 1915- *WhoWest 94*
Hunter, Tim *IntMPA 94*
Hunter, Todd d1968 *WhoHol 92*
Hunter, Todd 1953- *WhoAmP 93*
Hunter, Tony 1943- *IntWW 93, Who 94, WhoAm 94*
Hunter, Tony Wayne 1960- *WhoBlA 94*
Hunter, Tracey Lou 1966- *WhoBlA 94*
Hunter, Tricia 1952- *WhoAmP 93*
Hunter, Virginia *WhoHol 92*
Hunter, W. Raymond 1944- *WhoAmL 94*
Hunter, Walter Raymond 1953- *WhoWest 94*
Hunter, Willard Bowen 1944- *WhoMW 93*
Hunter, William Andrew 1913- *WhoBlA 94*
Hunter, William Armstrong 1953- *WhoAmP 93*
Hunter, William Dennis 1943- *WhoAm 94, WhoAmL 94*
Hunter, William Hill 1916- *Who 94*
Hunter, William Jay, Jr. 1944- *WhoAm 94*
Hunter, William John 1937- *Who 94*
Hunter, William L. 1936- *WhoBlA 94*
Hunter, William Morgan 1923- *WhoAm 94*
Hunter, William Schmidt 1931- *WhoFI 94, WhoScEn 94*
Hunter, Willie, Jr. 1949- *WhoAm 94*
Hunter-Blair, Edward (Thomas) 1920- *Who 94*
Hunter Blair, Pauline Clarke 1921- *WhoAm 94*
Hunter-Gault, Charlayne *WhoBlA 94*
Hunter-Gault, Charlayne 1942- *BlkWr 2, ConAu 141, ConBlB 6 [port]*
Hunter Green, Antoinette Velories 1931- *WhoFI 94*
Hunter Johnston, David Alan 1915- *Who 94*
Hunter-Lattany, Kristin Eggleston 1931- *WhoBlA 94*
Hunter Of Newington, Baron 1915- *IntWW 93, Who 94*
Hunter Smart, Norman *Who 94*
Hunter Smart, (William) Norman 1921- *Who 94*
Hunter-Stiebel, Penelope *WhoAm 94, WhoAmA 93*
Hunter-Tod, John (Hunter) 1917- *Who 94*
Huntford, Roland 1927- *ConAu 142*
Hunting, Anne Ritchie 1944- *WhoWest 94*
Hunting, (Lindsay) Clive 1925- *Who 94*
Hunting, (Henry) Gardner 1872-1958 *EncSF 93*
Hunting, (Charles) Patrick (Maule) d1993 *Who 94N*
Hunting, Richard Hugh 1946- *Who 94*
Hunting, Ward Martin 1923- *WhoAmP 93*
Huntingdon, Archdeacon of *Who 94*
Huntingdon, Bishop Suffragan of 1932- *Who 94*
Huntingdon, Earl of 1948- *Who 94*
Huntingfield, Baron 1915- *Who 94*
Hunting Horse c. 1846-1953 *EncNAR*
Huntington, A. Montgomery d1967 *WhoAmA 93N*
Huntington, A. Ronald 1921- *WhoAm 94*
Huntington, Anna V. Hyatt 1876-1973 *WhoAmA 93N*
Huntington, Anne Huntington 1740?-1790 *BlmGWL*
Huntington, Benjamin 1736-1800 *WhAmRev*
Huntington, Charles Ellsworth 1919- *WhoAm 94*
Huntington, Curtis Edward 1942- *WhoAm 94*

Huntington, Cynthia *DrAPF 93*
Huntington, David Mack Goode 1926- *WhoAm 94*
Huntington, Earl Lloyd 1929- *WhoAm 94*
Huntington, Ebenezer 1754-1834 *WhAmRev*
Huntington, Frederic Dan 1819-1904 *DcAmReB 2*
Huntington, Henry E. 1850-1927 *DcLB 140 [port]*
Huntington, Hillard Griswold 1944- *WhoFI 94, WhoScEn 94, WhoWest 94*
Huntington, Jabez 1719-1786 *WhAmRev*
Huntington, James Cantine, Jr. 1928- *WhoAm 94*
Huntington, Jedediah 1743-1818 *AmRev, WhAmRev*
Huntington, Jim 1941- *WhoAmA 93*
Huntington, John W. 1910-1976 *WhoAmA 93N*
Huntington, Margaret Wendell 1867-1958 *WhoAmA 93N*
Huntington, Mark Kenneth 1965- *WhoMW 93*
Huntington, Perry Katherine 1947- *WhoFI 94*
Huntington, R. Danny 1949- *WhoAmL 94*
Huntington, Samuel 1731-1796 *WhAmRev*
Huntington, Samuel Phillips 1927- *WhoAm 94, WrDr 94*
Huntington, Stephen N. 1943- *WhoAmL 94*
Huntington, William Reed 1838-1909 *DcAmReB 2*
Huntington, Wright d1916 *WhoHol 92*
Huntington-Whiteley, Hugo (Baldwin) 1924- *Who 94*
Huntley, Charles William 1913- *WhoAm 94*
Huntley, Chet d1974 *WhoHol 92*
Huntley, Dan *DrAPF 93*
Huntley, David C. 1930- *WhoAmA 93*
Huntley, Diane E. 1946- *WhoMW 93*
Huntley, Donald Wayne 1942- *WhoAmL 94*
Huntley, Douglas Spencer 1947- *WhoAmP 93*
Huntley, Fred d1931 *WhoHol 92*
Huntley, James Robert 1923- *WhoAm 94, WrDr 94*
Huntley, Luray d1919 *WhoHol 92*
Huntley, Mark Edward 1950- *WhoScEn 94, WhoWest 94*
Huntley, Raymond d1990 *WhoHol 92*
Huntley, Richard Frank 1926- *WhoBlA 94*
Huntley, Robert C., Jr. 1932- *WhoAmP 93*
Huntley, Robert Joseph 1924- *WhoWest 94*
Huntley, Robert Ross 1926- *WhoAm 94*
Huntley, Thomas 1938- *WhoAmP 93*
Huntley, Victoria Hutson 1900-1971 *WhoAmA 93N*
Huntley-Wright, Betty 1911- *WhoHol 92*
Huntly, Marquess of 1944- *Who 94*
Hunt Of Tanworth, Baron 1919- *IntWW 93, Who 94*
Hunton, Benjamin L. *AfrAmG*
Hunton, Donald Bothen 1927- *WhoAm 94*
Hunton, Jerry Floyd 1950- *WhoAmP 93*
Hunton, Richard Edwin 1924- *WrDr 94*
Huntoon, Abby E. 1951- *WhoAmA 93*
Huntoon, Robert Brian 1927- *WhoFI 94, WhoScEn 94*
Huntress, Betty Ann 1932- *WhoFI 94, WhoMW 93*
Huntress, Mary d1933 *WhoHol 92*
Huntress, Wesley Theodore, Jr. 1942- *WhoAm 94, WhoScEn 94*
Huntsberger, Jeffrey R. 1954- *WhoAmL 94*
Huntsberger, Michael William 1955- *WhoWest 94*
Huntsinger, Fritz Roy 1935- *WhoAm 94*
Huntsman, Benjamin 1704-1776 *WorInv*
Huntsman, Edward Loyd 1951- *WhoWest 94*
Huntsman, John M., Jr. 1960- *WhoAmP 93*
Huntsman, Jon M. 1937- *WhoAm 94, WhoAmP 93*
Huntsman, Jon Meade, Jr. 1960- *WhoAm 94*
Huntsman, Peter William 1935- *Who 94*
Huntwork, James R. 1948- *WhoAm 94, WhoAmL 94*
Huntwork, John C. 1948- *WhoAmP 93*
Huntzicker, William Edward 1946- *WhoMW 93*
Hununwe dc. 1890 *EncNAR*
Hunzicker, Warren John 1920- *WhoAm 94, WhoIns 94*
Hunziker, Robert McKee 1932- *WhoAm 94*
Huo Da *BlmGWL*
Huo Maozheng 1921- *WhoPRCh 91 [port]*
Huo Mingguang 1921- *WhoPRCh 91 [port]*

Huon De Kermadec, Jean-Michel 1748-1793 *WhWE*
Huong, Tran Van *IntWW 93*
Huo Shilian 1911- *IntWW 93*
Huo Shilian 1914?- *WhoPRCh 91 [port]*
Huot, Juliette *WhoHol 92*
Huot, Rachel Irene 1950- *WhoAm 94, WhoScEn 94*
Huot, Robert 1935- *WhoAmA 93*
Huotari, Bernice M. 1940- *WhoAmP 93*
Huo Yingdong 1923- *WhoPRCh 91 [port]*
Huo Yuping *WhoPRCh 91*
Hupe, Robert Martin 1964- *WhoAmL 94*
Hupert, Lillian Elizabeth 1950- *WhoMW 93*
Hupfeld, Stanley Francis 1944- *WhoAm 94*
Hu Ping 1930- *IntWW 93, WhoPRCh 91 [port]*
Hupp, Dennis Lee 1951- *WhoAmP 93*
Hupp, Frederick Duis 1938- *WhoAmA 93*
Hupp, Harry L. 1929- *WhoAm 94, WhoAmL 94, WhoWest 94*
Hupp, Jack Scott 1930- *WhoAm 94*
Hupp, Patricia Ellen 1950- *WhoAm 94*
Huppenthal, John J. 1954- *WhoAmP 93*
Hupper, John Roscoe 1925- *WhoAm 94*
Huppert, Elizabeth *WhoHol 92*
Huppert, Herbert Eric 1943- *IntWW 93, Who 94*
Huppert, Isabelle 1955- *IntMPA 94, WhoHol 92*
Huppert, Isabelle Anne 1953- *IntWW 93*
Huppert, Peggy Ann 1958- *WhoMW 93*
Huprich, Clifford Lester 1948- *WhoFI 94*
Hupy, Art 1924- *WhoAmA 93*
Huq, Muhammad Shamsul 1910- *IntWW 93*
Huq, Shamsul 1931- *IntWW 93*
Hu Qiaomu d1992 *IntWW 93N*
Hu Qiaomu 1912- *WhoPRCh 91 [port]*
Hu Qiheng 1934- *WhoPRCh 91 [port]*
Hu Qili 1929- *IntWW 93, WhoPRCh 91 [port]*
Hur, John Chonghwan 1931- *WhoAsA 94*
Hur, Sonja Vegdahl 1956- *WhoMW 93*
Hura, Patricia Teresa 1945- *WhoMW 93*
Hurabiell, John Philip, Sr. 1947- *WhoAm 94, WhoWest 94*
Huras, William David 1932- *WhoAm 94, WhoMW 93*
Hurches, Carlos E. *WhoHisp 94*
Hurd, Byron Thomas 1933- *WhoAm 94, WhoMW 93*
Hurd, Carl Bently 1919- *WhAm 10*
Hurd, Charles Dewitt 1897- *WhAm 10*
Hurd, Charles W. 1946- *WhoAm 94, WhoAmL 94*
Hurd, Cuthbert C. 1911- *WhoAm 94*
Hurd, David James, Jr. 1950- *WhoBlA 94*
Hurd, Douglas (Richard) 1930- *EncSF 93, Who 94*
Hurd, Douglas Richard 1930- *IntWW 93*
Hurd, G. David 1929- *WhoAm 94, WhoFI 94, WhoIns 94, WhoMW 93*
Hurd, Gale Anne 1955- *EncSF 93, IntMPA 94*
Hurd, Hugh *WhoHol 92*
Hurd, J. Nicholas 1942- *WhoAm 94*
Hurd, James L. P. 1945- *WhoBlA 94*
Hurd, Jerrie W. *DrAPF 93*
Hurd, John Earl 1945- *WhoMW 93*
Hurd, John Gavin 1914- *WhoAmP 93*
Hurd, John Owen 1946- *WhoMW 93*
Hurd, John R. 1942- *WhoAmL 94*
Hurd, Joseph Elbert 1942- *WhoAm 94*
Hurd, Joseph Kindall, Jr. 1938- *WhoBlA 94*
Hurd, Michael 1928- *NewGrDO*
Hurd, Michael John 1928- *WrDr 94*
Hurd, Paul Gemmill 1946- *WhoAmL 94*
Hurd, Peter 1904- *WhoAmA 93N*
Hurd, R. Edgar 1931- *WhoFI 94*
Hurd, Richard Nelson 1926- *WhoAm 94*
Hurd, Suzanne Sheldon 1939- *WhoAm 94, WhoScEn 94*
Hurd, William Charles 1947- *WhoBlA 94*
Hurdis, Everett Cushing 1918- *WhoScEn 94*
Hurdle, Hortense O. McNeil 1925- *WhoBlA 94*
Hurdle, Velma B. Brooks 1931- *WhoBlA 94*
Huret, Barry S. 1938- *WhoFI 94*
Hurewitz, Florence K. *WhoAmA 93*
Hurewitz, Jacob Coleman 1914- *WhoAm 94*
Hurford, Christopher John 1931- *IntWW 93*
Hurford, Gary Thomas 1936- *WhoFI 94*
Hurford, John Boyce 1938- *WhoAm 94*
Hurford, Peter (John) 1930- *Who 94*
Hurford, Peter John 1930- *IntWW 93*
Hurkos, Peter d1988 *WhoHol 92*
Hurland-Buning, Agnes 1926- *WhoWomW 91*
Hurlbert, Robert P. 1944- *WhoAm 94, WhoAmL 94*

Hurlbert, Roger William 1941- *WhoAm 94, WhoWest 94*
Hurlburt, Gladys d1988 *WhoHol 92*
Hurlburt, Harley Ernest 1943- *WhoScEn 94*
Hurlburt, Thomas 1808-1873 *EncNAR*
Hurlbut, Cornelius Searle, Jr. 1906- *WrDr 94*
Hurlbut, Geraldine 1933- *WhoMW 93*
Hurlbut, Kaatje *DrAPF 93*
Hurlbut, Robert Harold 1935- *WhoFI 94*
Hurlbut, Robert St. Clair 1924- *WhoAm 94*
Hurlebusch, Conrad Friedrich c. 1696-1765 *NewGrD*
Hurley, Alec d1913 *WhoHol 92*
Hurley, Alfred Francis 1928- *IntWW 93, WhoAm 94*
Hurley, Brian Xavier 1951- *WhoAm 94*
Hurley, Charles 1958- *WhoAmP 93*
Hurley, Cheryl Joyce 1947- *WhoAm 94*
Hurley, Denis Eugene 1915- *IntWW 93*
Hurley, Denis R. 1937- *WhoAm 94, WhoAmL 94*
Hurley, Denzil H. 1949- *WhoAmA 93*
Hurley, Donald Bertrand 1950- *WhoFI 94*
Hurley, Edward Timothy 1869-1950 *WhoAmA 93N*
Hurley, Elizabeth 1966- *WhoHol 92*
Hurley, Eric Glen 1959- *WhoMW 93*
Hurley, Francis T. 1927- *WhoAm 94, WhoWest 94*
Hurley, Frank Thomas, Jr. 1924- *WhoAm 94, WhoFI 94*
Hurley, Geoffrey Kevin 1948- *WhoAm 94*
Hurley, George
　See fIREHOSE ConMus 11
Hurley, Grady Schell 1954- *WhoAmL 94*
Hurley, Harry James, Jr. 1926- *WhoAm 94*
Hurley, James Donald, Jr. 1935- *WhoFI 94*
Hurley, James Edward, Jr. 1952- *WhoBlA 94*
Hurley, James Richardson 1932- *WhoAmP 93*
Hurley, James Vincent 1934- *WhoAmL 94, WhoWest 94*
Hurley, John d1978 *WhoHol 92*
Hurley, John 1928- *WrDr 94*
Hurley, John G. 1938- *WhoMW 93*
Hurley, John Joseph 1946- *WhoFI 94*
Hurley, John W. 1933- *WhoAmP 93*
Hurley, Julia d1927 *WhoHol 92*
Hurley, Katherine Torkelsen 1921- *WhoAmP 93*
Hurley, Laurence Harold 1944- *WhoAm 94, WhoScEn 94*
Hurley, Lawrence Eugene 1925- *WhoAmP 93*
Hurley, Lawrence Joseph 1946- *WhoAmL 94*
Hurley, Linda Kay 1951- *WhoAm 94*
Hurley, Margaret E. *WhoAmP 93*
Hurley, Mark Joseph 1919- *WhoAm 94, WhoWest 94*
Hurley, Marlene Emogene 1938- *WhoFI 94, WhoWest 94*
Hurley, Mary E. *WhoAmP 93*
Hurley, Maureen *DrAPF 93*
Hurley, Michael Anthony 1923- *IntWW 93*
Hurley, Morris Elmer, Jr. 1920- *WhoAm 94*
Hurley, Patrick Joseph 1941- *WhoAmP 93*
Hurley, Patrick Mason 1912- *WhoAm 94*
Hurley, Richard Keith 1956- *WhoScEn 94*
Hurley, Robert Joseph 1932- *WhoAm 94*
Hurley, Rosalinde 1929- *IntWW 93, Who 94*
Hurley, Samuel Clay, III 1936- *WhoAm 94*
Hurley, Thomas Daniel 1961- *WhoScEn 94*
Hurley, Thomas G. *DrAPF 93*
Hurley, Timothy J. 1951- *WhoAmL 94*
Hurley, William James, Jr. 1924- *WhoMW 93*
Hurley, William Joseph 1939- *WhoAm 94, WhoFI 94*
Hurley, Wilson 1924- *WhoAmA 93*
Hurlimann, Hans 1918- *IntWW 93*
Hurlock, James Bickford 1933- *WhoAm 94, WhoAmL 94*
Hurlock, Madeline d1989 *WhoHol 92*
Hurlock, Roger W. 1912- *IntMPA 94*
Hurlstone, Robert William 1952- *WhoAmA 93*
Hurmence, Belinda 1921- *SmATA 77 [port]*
Hurn, David 1934- *IntWW 93*
Hurn, Douglas d1974 *WhoHol 92*
Hurn, Roger 1938- *IntWW 93*
Hurn, (Francis) Roger 1938- *Who 94*
Hurndall, Richard d1984 *WhoHol 92*
Hurnik, Ilja 1922- *IntWW 93, NewGrDO*
Huron, Bishop of 1938- *Who 94*

Huron, Roderick Eugene 1934- *WhoAm 94*
Hurowitz, Bertram Donald 1932- *WhoMW 93*
Hurrell, Ann Patricia 1942- *WhoWest 94*
Hurrell, Anthony (Gerald) 1927- *Who 94*
Hurrell, Frederick Charles 1928- *Who 94*
Hurry, Leslie 1909-1978 *NewGrDO*
Hursey, James Samuel 1931- *WhoBlA 94*
Hursh, John R. 1943- *WhoAmP 93*
Hursh, Judy Ann Lopez 1945- *WhoAmP 93*
Hursh, Lynn Wilson 1953- *WhoAmL 94*
Hurskainen-Leppanen, Sinikka 1951- *WhoWomW 91*
Hurson, D. Joseph 1954- *WhoAmL 94*
Hurson, John Adams *WhoAmP 93*
Hurson, Michael 1941- *WhoAmA 93*
Hurst, Amanda Cady 1951- *WhoMW 93*
Hurst, Beverly J. 1933- *WhoBlA 94*
Hurst, Bobby 1953- *WhoAmP 93*
Hurst, Brandon d1947 *WhoHol 92*
Hurst, Charles Jackson 1941- *WhoAm 94*
Hurst, Christina Marie 1955- *WhoAm 94*
Hurst, Christon James 1954- *WhoScEn 94*
Hurst, Cleveland, Jr. 1939- *WhoBlA 94*
Hurst, David 1926- *WhoHol 92*
Hurst, Deborah 1946- *WhoWest 94*
Hurst, Dennis Michael 1951- *WhoAmP 93*
Hurst, Fannie d1968 *WhoHol 92*
Hurst, Fannie 1889-1968 *BlmGWL*
Hurst, George 1926- *Who 94*
Hurst, Gerald Barry 1933- *WhoAmP 93*
Hurst, Gregory Squire 1947- *WhoAm 94*
Hurst, H. Rex 1939- *WhoIns 94*
Hurst, Harrell Emerson 1949- *WhoScEn 94*
Hurst, Henry Ronald Grimshaw 1919- *Who 94*
Hurst, James Willard 1910- *WhoAm 94, WrDr 94*
Hurst, John Emory, Jr. 1928- *WhoAm 94*
Hurst, John Gilbert 1927- *Who 94*
Hurst, John L., III 1939- *WhoAm 94, WhoFI 94*
Hurst, Kenneth Thurston 1923- *WhoAm 94*
Hurst, Lee Edwin, III 1956- *WhoAmP 93*
Hurst, Leland Lyle 1930- *WhoAm 94*
Hurst, Lionel Alexander 1950- *IntWW 93*
Hurst, Lynn 1955- *WhoAmA 93*
Hurst, Margaret Anne 1957- *WhoAmL 94*
Hurst, Mark W. 1951- *WhoAmP 93*
Hurst, Michael Owen 1955- *WhoScEn 94*
Hurst, Michael William 1947- *WhoScEn 94*
Hurst, Nicholas Richard 1938- *WhoAm 94*
Hurst, Paul d1953 *WhoHol 92*
Hurst, Peter Thomas 1942- *Who 94*
Hurst, Phillip Gordon 1951- *WhoFI 94*
Hurst, Ralph N. 1918- *WhoAmA 93*
Hurst, Rick 1946- *WhoHol 92*
Hurst, Robert 1915- *Who 94*
Hurst, Robert Jay 1945- *WhoAm 94, WhoFI 94*
Hurst, Robert L., Jr. *WhoBlA 94*
Hurst, Robert Thomas, Jr. 1953- *WhoAmP 93*
Hurst, Rodney Lawrence 1944- *WhoBlA 94*
Hurst, Sharleene Page 1959- *WhoAmP 93*
Hurst, Susan A. 1959- *WhoAmL 94*
Hurst, Veronica 1931- *WhoHol 92*
Hurst, William Ryan 1965- *WhoMW 93*
Hurston, Zora Neale 1891?-1960 *TwCYAW*
Hurston, Zora Neale c. 1901-1960 *BlmGWL [port], RfGShF*
Hurston, Zora Neale 1903-1960 *AfrAmAl 6 [port]*
Hurt, Charles Edward 1930- *WhoAmL 94*
Hurt, Charlie Deuel, III 1950- *WhoAm 94, WhoWest 94*
Hurt, Daniel I. 1951- *WhoFI 94*
Hurt, George Richard 1946- *WhoScEn 94*
Hurt, James E. 1928- *WhoBlA 94*
Hurt, James Riggins 1934- *WhoAm 94*
Hurt, John 1940- *ConTFT 11, IntMPA 94, IntWW 93, Who 94, WhoHol 92*
Hurt, John Vincent 1940- *WhoAm 94*
Hurt, Katha 1947- *WhoAmP 93*
Hurt, Louis T., Sr. 1938- *WhoBlA 94*
Hurt, Mary d1976 *WhoHol 92*
Hurt, Mary Beth 1947- *WhoHol 92*
Hurt, Mary Beth 1948- *IntMPA 94*
Hurt, Nancy S. 1959- *WhoAmL 94*
Hurt, Robert H. 1943- *WhoAmP 93*
Hurt, Susanne M. *WhoAmA 93*
Hurt, William 1950- *IntMPA 94, IntWW 93, WhoAm 94, WhoHol 92*
Hurt, William Holman 1927- *WhoAm 94*
Hurtado, Albert L. 1946- *WrDr 94*
Hurtado, Ciro 1954- *WhoHisp 94*
Hurtado, I. Jay 1943- *WhoHisp 94*
Hurtado Larrea, Oswaldo 1940- *IntWW 93*
Hurtarte, Susana Peñalosa 1946- *WhoHisp 94*
Hurte, Leroy E. 1915- *WhoBlA 94*
Hurteau, Gilles David 1928- *WhoAm 94*
Hurteau, William James 1943- *WhoAm 94*
Hurter, Arthur Patrick *WhoAm 94*
Hurter, Ferdinand 1844-1898 *DcNaB MP*
Hurtgen, Peter Joseph 1941- *WhoAm 94*
Hurtgen, Peter Nicholas 1962- *WhoFI 94*
Hurtig, Martin Russell 1929- *WhoAmA 93*
Hurtubise, Jacques 1939- *WhoAmA 93*
Hurtubise, Mark 1948- *WhoWest 94*
Hurtuk, Edward Alan 1953- *WhoAmL 94*
Hurvich, Leo M. 1910- *IntWW 93*
Hurvich, Leo Maurice 1910- *WhoAm 94*
Hurvitz, Arthur Isaac 1939- *WhoAm 94*
Hurwicz, Leonid 1917- *WhoAm 94, WhoFI 94, WhoMW 93, WhoScEn 94*
Hurwitch, Jonathan William 1955- *WhoScEn 94*
Hurwitz, Charles Edwin 1940- *WhoAm 94, WhoFI 94, WhoScEn 94*
Hurwitz, Edward *WhoAmP 93*
Hurwitz, Ellen Stiskin 1942- *WhoAm 94*
Hurwitz, Emanuel 1919- *IntWW 93*
Hurwitz, Gary Alan 1950- *WhoAmL 94*
Hurwitz, Henry, Jr. 1918-1992 *WhAm 10*
Hurwitz, Jerard 1928- *IntWW 93*
Hurwitz, Johanna *DrAPF 93*
Hurwitz, Johanna 1937- *SmATA 18AS [port], TwCYAW*
Hurwitz, Johanna (Frank) 1937- *WrDr 94*
Hurwitz, Johanna Frank 1937- *WhoAm 94*
Hurwitz, Lawrence Neal 1939- *WhoAm 94*
Hurwitz, Leo 1909-1991 *WhAm 10*
Hurwitz, Mark Henry 1951- *WhoFI 94*
Hurwitz, Michael H. 1955- *WhoAmA 93*
Hurwitz, Sidney J. 1932- *WhoAmA 93*
Hurwitz, Sol 1932- *WhoAm 94*
Hurwitz, Vivian Ronald 1926- *Who 94*
Hurwood, Bernhardt J. 1926-1987 *ConAu 43NR*
Hurwood, Bernhardt J(ackson) 1926-1987 *EncSF 93*
Hus, Jan c. 1369-1415 *HisWorL [port]*
Husa, Karel Jaroslav 1921- *WhoAm 94*
Husain, Abul Basher M. *Who 94*
Husain, Maqbool Fida 1915- *IntWW 93*
Husain, Mazhar 1949- *WhoFI 94*
Husain, Mustafa Mahmood 1956- *WhoAsA 94*
Husain, Syed Shahid 1932- *WhoAm 94*
Husain, Taqdir 1929- *WhoAm 94*
Husak, Emil J. 1930- *WhoAmP 93*
Husak, Gustav 1913-1991 *WhAm 10*
Husar, Emile 1915- *WhoScEn 94*
Husar, John Paul 1937- *WhoAm 94, WhoMW 93*
Husar, Rudolf Bertalan 1941- *WhoScEn 94*
Husarik, Ernest Alfred 1941- *WhoMW 93*
Husayin Siyabayefu 1939- *WhoPRCh 91*
Husband, Bertram Paul 1950- *WhoAmL 94*
Husband, John Michael 1952- *WhoAm 94, WhoAmL 94*
Husband, Richard Lorin, Sr. 1931- *WhoAm 94, WhoFI 94*
Husband, Rick Douglas 1957- *WhoWest 94*
Husband, Thomas Mutrie 1936- *Who 94*
Husband, William Swire 1939- *WhoMW 93*
Husby, Anita Kay 1950- *WhoMW 93*
Husby, Donald Evans 1927- *WhoAm 94*
Husby, Jean Ann 1960- *WhoMW 93*
Husch, Gerhard (Heinrich Wilhelm Fritz) 1901-1984 *NewGrDO*
Huse, Diane Marie 1944- *WhoMW 93, WhoScEn 94*
Huseboe, Arthur Robert 1931- *WhoMW 93*
Huseboe, Doris Louise 1933- *WhoMW 93*
Husebye, Terry L. 1945- *WhoAmA 93*
Husemann, Anthony James 1955- *WhoScEn 94*
Husemann, Robert William 1931- *WhoAm 94*
Husen, Torsten 1916- *IntWW 93*
Huser, Richard Allan 1954- *WhoAmL 94*
Husfloen, Kyle Douglas 1949- *WhoAm 94*
Hush, Lisabeth *WhoHol 92*
Hush, Noel Sydney 1924- *Who 94*
Hushen, John W. 1935- *WhoAm 94*
Hu Sheng 1917- *WhoPRCh 91 [port]*
Hu Sheng 1918- *IntWW 93*
Hu Shi 1891-1962 *HisWorL*
Hu Shihua 1912- *WhoPRCh 91*
Hushing, William Collins 1918- *WhoAm 94*
Hushlak, Gerald 1945- *WhoAmA 93*
Hushon, John Daniel 1945- *WhoAm 94*
Hu Shujian *WhoPRCh 91*
Husick, Lawrence Alan 1958- *WhoAmL 94*
Husimi, Kodi 1909- *IntWW 93*
Husing, Ted d1962 *WhoHol 92*
Husk, Donald Estel 1925- *WhoMW 93*
Huskey, Harry Douglas 1916- *WhoAm 94, WhoWest 94*
Huskey, Herbert 1916- *WhoAmP 93*
Huskey, Larry C. 1944- *WhoAmP 93*
Huskey, William Jerome 1936- *WhoAmP 93*
Huskins, Joseph Patterson 1908- *WhoAmP 93*
Huskisson, Robert Andrews 1923- *Who 94*
Husky, Ferlin 1927- *WhoHol 92*
Huslid, Martin Johannes 1931- *IntWW 93*
Huslig, Mary Ann 1947- *WhoMW 93*
Husman, Catherine Bigot 1943- *WhoAm 94, WhoFI 94, WhoIns 94*
Husmann, Michael E. 1947- *WhoAmL 94*
Husmann, Ron 1937- *WhoHol 92*
Husni, Daoud 1870-1937 *NewGrDO*
Huson, Paul 1942- *WrDr 94*
Hu Songjie 1932- *WhoPRCh 91 [port]*
Huss, Charles Maurice 1946- *WhoWest 94*
Huss, Edward Carl 1950- *WhoMW 93*
Huss, Sandy *DrAPF 93*
Huss, Walter 1918- *WhoAmP 93*
Huss, William Lee 1956- *WhoMW 93*
Hussain, Fazle 1943- *WhoAsA 94*
Hussain, Karamat 1926- *Who 94*
Hussain, Mohammed Mustafa 1948- *IntWW 93*
Hussain, Mukhtar 1950- *Who 94*
Hussain, Riaz 1937- *WhoAsA 94*
Hussain, Syed Musarrat 1962- *WhoMW 93*
Hussain, Syeda Abida *WhoWomW 91*
Hussar, Daniel Alexander 1941- *WhoAm 94*
Hussein, Sharif 1853-1931 *HisWorL [port]*
Hussein, Abdirizak Haji 1924- *IntWW 93*
Hussein, Abdul-Aziz 1921- *IntWW 93*
Hussein, Abdullah 1931- *ConWorW 93*
Hussein, Ahmed Dia 1941- *WhoAm 94, WhoFI 94*
Hussein, Carlessia Amanda 1936- *WhoBlA 94*
Hussein, Mansour 1923- *IntWW 93*
Hussein, Saddam *IntWW 93*
Hussein, Waris 1938- *ConTFT 11, IntMPA 94*
Hussein bin Talal 1935- *Who 94*
Hussein Ibn Talal 1935- *IntWW 93*
Hussenot, Olivier d1978 *WhoHol 92*
Husser, John Edward 1951- *WhoMW 93*
Husserl, Consuelo R. 1948- *WhoHisp 94*
Husserl, Edmund (Gustav Albrecht) 1859-1938 *EncEth*
Husserl, Fred E. 1946- *WhoHisp 94*
Hussey, Charles E., II 1933- *WhoAm 94*
Hussey, Daniel James 1947- *WhoAmP 93*
Hussey, David Bradford 1960- *WhoWest 94*
Hussey, Dyneley 1893-1972 *NewGrDO*
Hussey, Gemma 1938- *IntWW 93*
Hussey, Jimmy d1930 *WhoHol 92*
Hussey, Joan Mervyn *Who 94*
Hussey, John *WhoHol 92*
Hussey, John B. *WhoAm 94, WhoAmP 93*
Hussey, Mark 1956- *WrDr 94*
Hussey, Marmaduke James 1923- *IntWW 93, Who 94*
Hussey, Obed 1792-1860 *WorInv*
Hussey, Olivia 1951- *IntMPA 94, WhoHol 92*
Hussey, Richard Francis 1956- *WhoAmL 94*
Hussey, Robert D. *WhoAmP 93*
Hussey, Robert E., Jr. *WhoAmP 93*
Hussey, Ruth 1914- *WhoHol 92*
Hussey, Susan Katharine 1939- *Who 94*
Hussey, Thomas 1741-1803 *WhAmRev*
Hussey, Ward MacLean 1920- *WhoAm 94*
Hussey, William Bertrand 1915- *WhoAm 94*
Husson, Philippe Jean Louis Marie 1927- *IntWW 93*
Hust, Bruce Kevin 1957- *WhoAmL 94*
Hustad, Thomas Pegg 1945- *WhoFI 94, WhoMW 93*
Husted, Beverly d1975 *WhoHol 92*
Husted, John Edwin 1915- *WhoAm 94*
Husted, Ralph Waldo 1911- *WhoAm 94*
Husted, Russell Forest 1950- *WhoMW 93, WhoScEn 94*
Huster, Francis *WhoHol 92*
Hustoles, Mary Jo 1952- *WhoMW 93*
Hustoles, Paul John 1952- *WhoAm 94, WhoMW 93*
Hustoles, Thomas Paul *WhoAm 94*
Huston, Anjelica 1951- *ConTFT 11, IntMPA 94, IntWW 93, WhoAm 94, WhoHol 92*
Huston, Beatrice Louise 1932- *WhoAm 94*
Huston, Brett Alan 1948- *WhoAmL 94*
Huston, Carol *WhoHol 92*
Huston, Charles Lukens 1856-1951 *EncABHB 9 [port]*
Huston, Charles Lukens, Jr. 1906-1982 *EncABHB 9 [port]*
Huston, Danny 1962- *IntMPA 94*
Huston, DeVerille Anne 1947- *WhoAm 94*
Huston, Edwin Allen 1938- *WhoAm 94, WhoFI 94*
Huston, Fred John 1929- *WhoScEn 94*
Huston, Harriette Irene Otwell *WhoWest 94*
Huston, Harris Hyde 1907- *WhoAm 94*
Huston, Jeffrey Charles 1951- *WhoMW 93, WhoScEn 94*
Huston, John d1987 *WhoHol 92*
Huston, John Charles 1927- *WhoAm 94, WhoAmL 94, WhoWest 94*
Huston, John Lewis 1919- *WhoAm 94*
Huston, John Wilson 1925- *WhoAm 94*
Huston, Josephine d1967 *WhoHol 92*
Huston, Kathleen Marie 1944- *WhoAm 94, WhoMW 93*
Huston, Kenneth Dale 1936- *WhoWest 94*
Huston, Kent Allen 1944- *WhoMW 93*
Huston, Margo 1943- *WhoAm 94*
Huston, Mervyn J(ames) 1912- *WrDr 94*
Huston, Michael E. 1948- *WhoIns 94*
Huston, Michael Joe 1942- *WhoAm 94, WhoAmL 94*
Huston, Michelle Madeliene 1965- *WhoMW 93*
Huston, Norman Earl 1919- *WhoAm 94*
Huston, Patricia *WhoHol 92*
Huston, Perry Clark 1933- *WhoAmA 93*
Huston, Philip d1980 *WhoHol 92*
Huston, Rima 1941- *WhoScEn 94*
Huston, Steven Craig 1954- *WhoAmL 94*
Huston, Ted Laird 1943- *WhoAm 94*
Huston, Thelma Diane 1956- *WhoHisp 94*
Huston, Tony *WhoHol 92*
Huston, Virginia 1925- *WhoHol 92*
Huston, Walter d1950 *WhoHol 92*
Huston-Collicott, Terri Lynn 1959- *WhoWest 94*
Hustvedt, Siri 1955- *ConLC 76 [port]*
Huszar, Arlene Celia 1952- *WhoAmL 94*
Huszar-Puffy, Karl d1942 *WhoHol 92*
Huszka, Jeno 1875-1960 *NewGrDO*
Huszti, Joseph Bela 1936- *WhoWest 94*
Hut, Piet 1952- *WhoScEn 94*
Huta, Henry Nicholaus 1947- *WhoFI 94, WhoScEn 94*
Hutasingh, Prakob 1912- *IntWW 93*
Hutchcraft, A. Stephens, Jr. 1930- *WhoFI 94, WhoWest 94*
Hutchcroft, Kevin 1964- *WhoAmP 93*
Hutchence, Michael 1960- *WhoHol 92*
Hutchens, Ann 1936- *WhoAmP 93*
Hutchens, Charles Kenneth 1947- *WhoAmL 94*
Hutchens, Don Derrel 1948- *WhoAmP 93*
Hutchens, John Kennedy 1905- *WhoAm 94*
Hutchens, John Oliver 1914- *WhoAm 94*
Hutchens, Michael D. 1960- *WhoAmL 94*
Hutchens, Tyra Thornton 1921- *WhoAm 94*
Hutcheon, Cifford Robert 1913- *WhoFI 94, WhoScEn 94*
Hutcheon, Duncan Elliot 1922- *WhoAm 94*
Hutcheon, Linda (Ann) 1947- *WrDr 94*
Hutcheon, Peter David 1943- *WhoAmL 94*
Hutcherson, Bernice B. R. 1925- *WhoBlA 94*
Hutcherson, Bobby 1941- *WhoAm 94*
Hutcherson, Christopher Alfred 1950- *WhoWest 94*
Hutcherson, Karen Fulghum 1951- *WhoScEn 94*
Hutcheson, David d1976 *WhoHol 92*
Hutcheson, Francis 1694-1746 *EncEth*
Hutcheson, James Sterling 1919- *WhoAm 94, WhoAmL 94*
Hutcheson, Janet Reid 1934- *WhoAm 94*
Hutcheson, Jerry Dee 1932- *WhoWest 94*
Hutcheson, Joseph Chappell, III 1907- *WhoAm 94*
Hutcheson, Larry 1942- *WhoAmP 93*
Hutcheson, Mark Andrew 1942- *WhoAm 94, WhoAmL 94*
Hutcheson, Philip Charles 1948- *WhoScEn 94*
Hutcheson, Thad T., Jr. 1941- *WhoAm 94*
Hutcheson, Thomas Taliaferro 1948- *WhoAmL 94*
Hutchin, Kenneth Charles 1908- *WrDr 94*
Hutchings, Andrew William Seymour 1907- *Who 94*
Hutchings, Brian LaMar 1915- *WhoAm 94*
Hutchings, Dale 1954- *WhoWest 94*
Hutchings, George Henry 1922- *WhoAm 94*
Hutchings, Gregory Frederick *Who 94*
Hutchings, John Barrie 1941- *WhoAm 94*
Hutchings, La Vere 1918- *WhoAmA 93*
Hutchings, Marjorie Clyde 1922- *WhoAmP 93*
Hutchings, Peter Lounsbery 1943- *WhoAm 94, WhoFI 94*

Huxley, Aldous 1894-1963 *Au&Arts 11 [port], BlmGEL [port], ConLC 79 [port], EncSF 93, NewGrDO*
Huxley, Aldous (Leonard) 1894-1963 *TwCYAW*
Huxley, Andrew Fielding 1917- *IntWW 93, Who 94, WhoAm 94, WhoScEn 94*
See Also Hodgkin, Alan Lloyd 1914- *WorScD*
Huxley, Anthony J(ulian) 1920-1992 *ConAu 140*
Huxley, Anthony Julian d1992 *Who 94N*
Huxley, Anthony Julian 1920- *WrDr 94*
Huxley, Brian 1931- *Who 94*
Huxley, Elspeth 1907- *BlmGWL*
Huxley, Elspeth (Josceline) 1907- *WrDr 94*
Huxley, Elspeth Josceline 1907- *IntWW 93, Who 94*
Huxley, George Leonard 1932- *IntWW 93, Who 94, WrDr 94*
Huxley, Gervas, Mrs. *Who 94*
Huxley, Hugh Esmor 1924- *IntWW 93, Who 94, WhoAm 94, WhoScEn 94*
Huxley, Keith 1933- *Who 94*
Huxley, Paul 1938- *Who 94*
Huxley, Peter Arthur 1926- *Who 94*
Huxley, Rick *WhoHol 92*
Huxley, Thomas Henry 1825-1895 *BlmGEL*
Huxstep, Emily Mary 1906- *Who 94*
Huxtable, Ada Louise *IntWW 93, WhoAm 94, WhoAmA 93*
Huxtable, Ada Louise 1921- *WrDr 94*
Huxtable, Anthony 1808-1883 *DcNaB MP*
Huxtable, Charles Richard 1931- *Who 94*
Huxtable, (William) John (Fairchild) 1912-1990 *WrDr 94N*
Huxtable, Judy *WhoHol 92*
Hu Yadong *WhoPRCh 91*
Hu Yamei *WhoPRCh 91*
Huyck, Willard *IntMPA 94*
Huydecoper, Jonkheer (Jan Louis) Reinier 1922- *IntWW 93*
Huydecoper, (Jan Louis) Reinier 1922- *Who 94*
Huyett, Daniel Henry, III 1921- *WhoAm 94, WhoAmL 94*
Huyett, Pat 1951- *WhoMW 93*
Huygens, Christiaan 1629-1695 *WorInv, WorScD [port]*
Huygens, Remmert William 1932- *WhoAm 94*
Huygens, Robert Burchard Constantijn 1931- *IntWW 93*
Huyghe, Patrick 1952- *WrDr 94*
Huyghe, Rene 1906- *IntWW 93, Who 94*
Huyghue, Michael *WhoBlA 94*
Huyghues-des-Etages, Jacques 1923- *IntWW 93*
Hu Yimin *WhoPRCh 91*
Hu Yizhou 1928- *IntWW 93, WhoPRCh 91 [port]*
Huyler, Jean Wiley 1935- *WhoAm 94*
Huynh, Alex Vu 1968- *WhoScEn 94*
Huynh, Boi-Hanh 1946- *WhoAsA 94*
Huynh, Dung Thiet 1953- *WhoAsA 94*
Huynh, Emmanuelle 1947- *WhoAsA 94*
Huynh, Nam Hoang 1949- *WhoScEn 94*
Huynh Ngoc, Phien 1944- *WhoScEn 94*
Huyot, Robert d1993 *NewYTBS 93*
Huysman, Arlene Weiss 1929- *WhoAm 94, WhoScEn 94*
Huyssen, Andreas 1942- *WhoAm 94*
Hu Yunlong *WhoPRCh 91 [port]*
Huzar, Eleanor Goltz 1922- *WhoAm 94*
Huzel, Dieter Karl 1912- *WhoScEn 94*
Hu Zhide *WhoPRCh 91*
Hu Zhiguang 1930- *WhoPRCh 91 [port]*
Hu Ziang 1897- *WhoPRCh 91 [port]*
Hvass, Charles Thomas, Jr. 1950- *WhoAmL 94*
Hvass, Sheryl Ramstad *WhoAmL 94*
Hveding, Vidkunn 1921- *IntWW 93*
Hvistendahl, Joyce Kilmer 1918- *WhoAm 94*
Hvorostovsky, Dmitry 1962- *NewGrDO*
Hwa, Jesse Chia-Hsi 1924- *WhoAsA 94*
Hwa, Terence Tai-Li 1964- *WhoScEn 94*
Hwang, Ange 1961- *WhoAsA 94*
Hwang, Charles C. 1930- *WhoAsA 94*
Hwang, Cherng-Jia 1937- *WhoAsA 94*
Hwang, Ching-Lai 1929- *WhoAsA 94*
Hwang, Chong F. 1958- *WhoAsA 94*
Hwang, Cordelia Jong 1942- *WhoScEn 94, WhoWest 94*
Hwang, Danny Pang 1936- *WhoScEn 94*
Hwang, David Henry 1957- *ConDr 93, DramC 4 [port], WhoAm 94, WhoAsA 94, WrDr 94*
Hwang, Dennis B. K. 1949- *WhoAsA 94*
Hwang, Dennis John 1955- *WhoAmL 94*
Hwang, Enoch Oi-Kee 1959- *WhoAsA 94*
Hwang, Guann-Jiun 1951- *WhoAsA 94*
Hwang, Henry Y. 1929- *WhoAsA 94*
Hwang, Hi Sook 1929- *WhoAsA 94*
Hwang, Hsin-Ginn 1953- *WhoAsA 94*
Hwang, Ivy 1957- *WhoAsA 94*
Hwang, Jenn-Shin 1956- *WhoScEn 94*
Hwang, John C. 1940- *WhoAsA 94*
Hwang, Kou Mau 1940- *WhoWest 94*
Hwang, Kwang Seo 1946- *WhoMW 93*
Hwang, Mark I. 1956- *WhoAsA 94*
Hwang, Nen-chen Richard 1957- *WhoAsA 94*
Hwang, Roland 1949- *WhoAsA 94*
Hwang, Shin Ja Joo 1943- *WhoAsA 94*
Hwang, Shoi Yean 1931- *WhoAsA 94*
Hwang, Shyshung 1938- *WhoAsA 94, WhoScEn 94*
Hwang, Suein Lim 1968- *WhoAsA 94*
Hwang, Te-Long 1943- *WhoAsA 94*
Hwang, Wei-Yuan 1949- *WhoAsA 94*
Hwang, William Gaong 1949- *WhoAsA 94*
Hwang, Woei-Yann Pauchy 1948- *WhoScEn 94*
Hwang, Woonbong 1958- *WhoScEn 94*
Hwang, Xochitl 1956- *WhoAsA 94*
Hwu, Peter S. 1966- *WhoAsA 94*
Hwu, Reuben Jih-Ru 1954- *WhoScEn 94*
Hyam, Michael Joshua 1938- *Who 94*
Hyam, Ronald 1936- *WrDr 94*
Hyams, Daisy Deborah 1912- *Who 94*
Hyams, Edward S(olomon) 1910-1975 *EncSF 93*
Hyams, Harold 1943- *WhoAmL 94*
Hyams, Harriet 1929- *WhoAmA 93*
Hyams, Joe 1923- *WhoAm 94, WrDr 94*
Hyams, John d1940 *WhoHol 92*
Hyams, Joseph 1926- *IntMPA 94*
Hyams, Leila d1977 *WhoHol 92*
Hyams, Peter 1943- *IntMPA 94*
Hyatali, Isaac (Emanuel) 1917- *Who 94*
Hyatt, Charles 1908- *BasBi*
Hyatt, Clayton d1932 *WhoHol 92*
Hyatt, Daniel Ray 1948- *WhoAmP 93*
Hyatt, David Eric 1957- *WhoScEn 94*
Hyatt, David Hudson 1941- *WhoFI 94*
Hyatt, Herman d1968 *WhoHol 92*
Hyatt, Herman Wilbert, Sr. 1926- *WhoBlA 94*
Hyatt, Joel Z. 1950- *WhoAm 94*
Hyatt, John Wesley 1837-1920 *WorInv*
Hyatt, Kenneth Ernest 1940- *WhoAm 94*
Hyatt, Walter Jones 1918- *WhoScEn 94*
Hyatt King, Alexander *Who 94*
Hybl, William Joseph 1942- *WhoAmL 94, WhoWest 94*
Hybridge, John 1948- *WhoWest 94*
Hyde, Lord 1976- *Who 94*
Hyde, Alan Litchfield 1928- *WhoAm 94, WhoAmL 94*
Hyde, Alice Bach 1939- *WhoAmA 93*
Hyde, Anthony 1946- *WrDr 94*
Hyde, Charles H. 1914- *WhoFI 94*
Hyde, Christopher 1949- *EncSF 93*
Hyde, Clarence Brodie, II 1937- *WhoAm 94*
Hyde, David Rowley 1929- *WhoAm 94*
Hyde, Dayton O. 1925- *WrDr 94*
Hyde, Douglas Gaylord 1943- *WhoAm 94*
Hyde, Eleanor *DrAPF 93*
Hyde, Eleanor 1915- *WrDr 94*
Hyde, G(eorge) Osmond 1898- *WhAm 10*
Hyde, Helen Yvonne 1947- *Who 94*
Hyde, Henry Baldwin 1915- *WhoFI 94*
Hyde, Henry J. 1924- *CngDr 93*
Hyde, Henry John 1924- *WhoAm 94, WhoAmP 93, WhoMW 93*
Hyde, Henry Van Zile, Jr. 1936- *WhoAmP 93*
Hyde, Herbert Lee 1925- *WhoAmP 93*
Hyde, Howard Laurence 1957- *WhoAmL 94*
Hyde, Jacquelyn *WhoHol 92*
Hyde, James Franklin 1903- *WhoScEn 94*
Hyde, John Michael 1930- *WhoAm 94*
Hyde, John Paul 1934- *WhoAm 94*
Hyde, Jonathan *WhoHol 92*
Hyde, Joseph R., III 1942- *WhoFI 94*
Hyde, Lawrence Henry, Jr. 1924- *WhoAm 94*
Hyde, Lawrence Layton 1930- *WhoMW 93*
Hyde, Margaret O(ldroyd) 1917- *SmATA 76 [port]*
Hyde, Margaret Sheila 1945- *Who 94*
Hyde, Mary Morley Crapo 1912- *WhoAm 94*
Hyde, Michael 1908- *WrDr 94*
Hyde, Norris J. 1924- *WhoAmP 93*
Hyde, Robert Burke, Jr. 1928- *WhoAm 94*
Hyde, Robin 1906-1939 *BlmGWL*
Hyde, Scott 1926- *WhoAmA 93*
Hyde, Shelley *EncSF 93*
Hyde, Steven Charles 1962- *WhoMW 93*
Hyde, Steven Robert 1949- *WhoFI 94, WhoMW 93*
Hyde, Stuart Wallace 1923- *WhoAm 94*
Hyde, Tommy 1916- *IntMPA 94*
Hyde, W(illiam) Leonard *Who 94*
Hyde, Wallace Nathaniel 1923- *WhoAmP 93*
Hyde, Walter 1875-1951 *NewGrDO*
Hyde, William R. 1923- *WhoBlA 94*
Hyde-Jackson, Maxine Deborah 1949- *WhoBlA 94*
Hyden, Dorothy Louise 1948- *WhoMW 93*
Hyden, Glen Warren 1961- *WhoAmP 93*
Hyde-Parker, Richard William *Who 94*
Hyde-Price, Adrian 1957- *ConAu 140*
Hyder, Alan *EncSF 93*
Hyder, Ghulam Muhammad Ali 1953- *WhoMW 93, WhoScEn 94*
Hyder, Monte Lee 1936- *WhoScEn 94*
Hyder, Qurratulain *ConWorW 93*
Hyder, Qurratulain 1927- *BlmGWL*
Hyder, Robert Lee 1910- *WhoAmP 93*
Hydes, David d1958 *WhoHol 92*
Hyde-White, Alex 1958- *WhoHol 92*
Hyde-White, Wilfrid d1991 *WhoHol 92*
Hyde-White, Wilfrid 1903-1991 *ConTFT 11, WhAm 10*
Hydrisko, Stanley Joseph 1927- *WhoFI 94*
Hyem, David Wayne 1962- *WhoFI 94*
Hyer, Charles Terry 1946- *WhoScEn 94*
Hyer, Frank Perry 1897- *WhAm 10*
Hyer, Frederick L., Jr. 1940- *WhoIns 94*
Hyer, Frederick Lewis, Jr. 1940- *WhoFI 94*
Hyer, Laura Jane 1956- *WhoFI 94*
Hyer, Martha 1924- *IntMPA 94, WhoHol 92*
Hyer, William Glasser Thomas 1921- *WhoMW 93*
Hyett, Barbara Helfgott *DrAPF 93*
Hyett, Doyle Gregory 1948- *WhoFI 94*
Hygeburg fl. 8th cent.- *BlmGWL*
Hykan, Robert Allen 1952- *WhoAmL 94*
Hykin, Mark Lazar 1943- *WhoFI 94*
Hyla, James Franklin 1945- *WhoScEn 94*
Hylan, Don d1968 *WhoHol 92*
Hyland, Barbara C. 1943- *WhoAmP 93*
Hyland, Catherine *WhoHol 92*
Hyland, Diana d1977 *WhoHol 92*
Hyland, Douglas K. S. 1949- *WhoAm 94, WhoAmA 93*
Hyland, Frances 1927- *WhoHol 92*
Hyland, Geoffrey Fyfe *WhoAm 94*
Hyland, John P. 1928- *WhoIns 94*
Hyland, Laurie Zoe 1939- *WhoFI 94*
Hyland, Lawrence Avison 1897-1989 *WhAm 10*
Hyland, Penelope 1953- *WhoWest 94*
Hyland, Robert Francis, Jr. d1992 *WhAm 10*
Hyland, (Henry) Stanley 1914- *WrDr 94*
Hyland, Thomas Patrick 1964- *WhoFI 94*
Hyland, Thomas Robert 1932- *WhoAmL 94*
Hyland, Thomas Walter 1943- *WhoAm 94, WhoAmL 94*
Hyland, Timothy Randall 1960- *WhoAmL 94*
Hyland, William Francis 1923- *WhoAm 94, WhoAmP 93*
Hyland, William George 1929- *WhoAm 94*
Hylander, Walter Raymond, Jr. 1924- *WhoScEn 94*
Hylands, Scott 1943- *WhoHol 92*
Hylden, Thomas 1946- *WhoAm 94, WhoAmL 94*
Hyle, Charles Thomas 1961- *WhoFI 94*
Hylen, Timothy William 1947- *WhoFI 94*
Hyler, Adam *WhAmRev*
Hyler, Lora Lee 1959- *WhoBlA 94*
Hylko, James Mark 1961- *WhoScEn 94*
Hylton, Baron 1932- *Who 94*
Hylton, Andrea Lamarr 1965- *WhoBlA 94*
Hylton, Hannelore Menke 1936- *WhoAm 94*
Hylton, Jack d1965 *WhoHol 92*
Hylton, Jane d1979 *WhoHol 92*
Hylton, Kenneth N. 1929- *WhoBlA 94*
Hylton, Richard d1962 *WhoHol 92*
Hylton, Taft H. 1936- *WhoBlA 94*
Hylton, Thomas James 1948- *WhoAm 94*
Hylton, Tracy 1922- *WhoAmP 93*
Hylton-Foster, Baroness 1908- *Who 94, WhoWomW 91*
Hyman, Alan Barry 1947- *WhoAm 94, WhoAmL 94*
Hyman, Albert Lewis 1923- *WhoAm 94, WhoScEn 94*
Hyman, (Robert) Anthony 1928- *WrDr 94*
Hyman, Betty Harpole 1938- *WhoFI 94*
Hyman, Bruce Malcolm 1943- *WhoAm 94, WhoScEn 94*
Hyman, Earle 1926- *AfrAmAl 6 [port], ConTFT 11, WhoAm 94, WhoBlA 94, WhoHol 92*
Hyman, Harold M(elvin) 1924- *WrDr 94*
Hyman, Isabelle 1930- *WhoAmA 93*
Hyman, Jerome Elliot 1923- *WhoAm 94, WhoAmL 94*
Hyman, Joe 1921- *IntWW 93, Who 94*
Hyman, John Allen 1961- *WhoFI 94*
Hyman, Kevin Michael 1950- *WhoFI 94, WhoWest 94*
Hyman, Leonard Stephen 1940- *WhoFI 94, WhoScEn 94*
Hyman, Leslie Gaye 1952- *WhoScEn 94*
Hyman, Lester Samuel 1931- *WhoAm 94*
Hyman, Linda, 1940- *WhoAmA 93*
Hyman, Mark J. 1916- *WhoBlA 94*
Hyman, Michael Bruce 1952- *WhoAmL 94*
Hyman, Milton 1905- *WhoAm 94*
Hyman, Milton Bernard 1941- *WhoAm 94, WhoAmL 94*
Hyman, Miranda *EncSF 93*
Hyman, Miranda 1950- *WrDr 94*
Hyman, Montague Allan 1941- *WhoAmL 94*
Hyman, Morton Peter 1936- *WhoAm 94, WhoFI 94*
Hyman, Paul G., Jr. 1952- *WhoAmL 94*
Hyman, Paula Ellen *WhoAm 94*
Hyman, Phyllis *WhoBlA 94*
Hyman, Ralph Alan 1928- *WhoAm 94*
Hyman, Randy Ellen *WhoAmL 94*
Hyman, Robert d1934 *WhoHol 92*
Hyman, Robin Philip 1931- *Who 94*
Hyman, Roger Alan 1943- *WhoFI 94*
Hyman, Roger David 1957- *WhoAmL 94*
Hyman, Ronald T(erry) 1933- *WrDr 94*
Hyman, Scott David 1960- *WhoScEn 94*
Hyman, Seymour 1927- *WhoAm 94*
Hyman, Seymour Charles 1919- *WhoAm 94*
Hyman, Sigmund M. 1921- *WhoFI 94*
Hyman, Terry Mac 1951- *WhoAmP 93*
Hyman, Terry Stanton 1946- *WhoAmL 94*
Hyman, Timothy 1946- *IntWW 93*
Hymel, Gary Gerard 1933- *WhoAm 94*
Hymer, Martha Nell 1956- *WhoMW 93*
Hymer, Warren d1948 *WhoHol 92*
Hymes, Dell Hathaway 1927- *WhoAm 94, WhoScEn 94*
Hymes, Jesse 1939- *WhoBlA 94*
Hymes, Robert Wayne 1956- *WhoMW 93*
Hymes, William Henry 1921- *WhoBlA 94*
Hymes, William Russell 1927- *WhoAmL 94*
Hymoff, Edward 1924-1992 *WhAm 10*
Hymowitz, Theodore 1934- *WhoAm 94, WhoMW 93*
Hynan, Linda Susan 1953- *WhoScEn 94*
Hynd, Ronald 1931- *IntDcB, Who 94*
Hynd, Ronald, Mrs. *Who 94*
Hynde, Chrissie 1951- *CurBio 93 [port]*
Hynds, Joseph Johnson, Jr. 1950- *WhoFI 94*
Hyne, C(harles) J(ohn) Cutcliffe (Wright) 1866-1944 *EncSF 93*
Hyne, James Bissett 1929- *WhoAm 94*
Hynek, C. Duke 1943- *WhoMW 93*
Hynek, Frederick James 1944- *WhoWest 94*
Hynes, Ann Patricia *Who 94*
Hynes, Carolyn E. 1925- *WhoAmP 93*
Hynes, Frank M. 1940- *WhoAmP 93*
Hynes, Garry 1953- *IntWW 93*
Hynes, Hugh Bernard Noel 1917- *WhoAm 94*
Hynes, John Dennis 1936- *WhoAmL 94*
Hynes, John Thomas 1933- *WhoMW 93*
Hynes, Mary Ann 1947- *WhoAm 94*
Hynes, Nancy Ellen 1956- *WhoScEn 94*
Hynes, Richard Olding 1944- *Who 94, WhoAm 94, WhoScEn 94*
Hynes, Samuel 1924- *IntWW 93, WhoAm 94, WrDr 94*
Hynes, Terence Michael 1954- *WhoAm 94, WhoAmL 94*
Hynes-Longendorfer, Lillian Margaret 1939- *WhoMW 93*
Hynninen, Jorma 1941- *NewGrDO*
Hynning, Clifford J(ames) 1913-1990 *WhAm 10*
Hynson, Carroll Henry, Jr. 1936- *WhoBlA 94*
Hynson, Joseph *WhAmRev*
Hypatia 370-415 *BlmGWL*
Hypatia of Alexandria 370-415 *WorInv*
Hyrne, Edmund 1748-1783 *WhAmRev*
Hyser, Joyce 1955- *WhoHol 92*
Hyslop *Who 94*
Hyslop, David Johnson 1942- *WhoMW 93*
Hyslop, Gary Lee 1944- *WhoMW 93*
Hyslop, James Telfer 1916- *Who 94*
Hyslop, Wade A., Jr. *WhoAmP 93*
Hyslop, William Arthur 1946- *WhoAm 94*
Hyson, Charles David 1915- *WhoAm 94*
Hyson, Dorothy 1915- *WhoHol 92*
Hyson, Jean 1933- *WhoAmA 93*
Hyson, Kevin 1951- *IntMPA 94*
Hytche, William P. 1927- *WhoBlA 94*
Hytche, William Percy 1927- *WhoAm 94*
Hyter, Micheal C. 1957- *WhoBlA 94*
Hytha, Robert J. 1928- *WhoAm 94, WhoFI 94*
Hythe, Hamo of c. 1275-1352 *DcNaB MP*
Hytier, Adrienne Doris *WhoAm 94*
Hytner, Benet Alan 1927- *Who 94*
Hytner, Nicholas 1956- *NewGrDO*
Hytner, Nicholas Robert 1956- *IntWW 93, Who 94*

Hytten, Olaf d1955 *WhoIIol 92*
Hyuga, Hosai 1906- *IntWW 93*
Hyun, Bong Hak 1922- *WhoAsA 94*
Hyun, Kun Sup 1937- *WhoAsA 94*
Hyun, Peter 1906- *WrDr 94*
Hyun, Peter 1906-1993 *ConAu 142*
Hyvrard, Jeanne *BlmGWL*
   ConWorW 93

I

Iacangelo, Peter August 1948- *WhoWest 94*
Iachello, Francesco *WhoScEn 94*
Iachetti, Rose Maria Anne 1931- *WhoWest 94*
Iachini, John Gilbert 1952- *WhoFI 94*
Iacobell, Frank Peter 1937- *WhoAm 94, WhoMW 93*
Iacobelli, John Louis 1931- *WhoFI 94*
Iacobelli, Mark Anthony 1957- *WhoMW 93*
Iacobellis, Sam Frank 1929- *WhoAm 94, WhoFI 94*
Iacobucci, Frank 1937- *WhoAm 94*
Iacobucci, Guillermo Arturo 1927- *WhoFI 94, WhoScEn 94*
Iacocca, Lee 1924- *WhoFI 94*
Iacocca, Lee (Lido Anthony) 1924- *WrDr 94*
Iacocca, Lee A. 1924- *IntWW 93*
Iacocca, Lido Anthony 1924- *WhoAm 94, WhoFI 94, WhoMW 93*
Iacone, Marge 1943- *WhoFI 94*
Iacono, James Michael 1925- *WhoScEn 94*
Iacoponi, Michael Joseph 1959- *WhoScEn 94*
Iacovou, Georgios 1938- *IntWW 93*
Iacurto, Francesco 1908- *WhoAmA 93*
Iadavaia, Elizabeth Ann 1960- *WhoFI 94*
Iademarco, Michael Francis 1960- *WhoMW 93*
Iafrate, Al Anthony 1966- *WhoAm 94*
Iakovidis, Spyros Eustace 1923- *WhoAm 94*
Iakovos *WhoAm 94, WhoMW 93*
Iakovos 1911- *WhoAm 94*
Iakovos, Archbishop 1911- *IntWW 93*
Iamele, Richard Thomas 1942- *WhoAmL 94, WhoWest 94*
Iams, Charles Gary 1950- *WhoMW 93*
Iams, Walter Roger 1942- *WhoMW 93*
Ian, Scott
    See Anthrax *ConMus 11*
Ianacone, Samuel Joseph, Jr. 1947- *WhoAm 94*
Iandoli, Claire Cecelia 1957- *WhoAmL 94*
Iannaccone, Carmine A. 1951- *WhoAm 94, WhoAmL 94*
Iannaccone, Michael 1962- *WhoFI 94*
Iannacone, Salvatore Joseph, III 1955- *WhoFI 94*
Iannella, Egidio 1921- *IntWW 93*
Iannetta, Scott Kimon 1943- *WhoWest 94*
Iannetti, Pasquale Francesco Paolo 1940- *WhoAmA 93*
Ianni, Francis Alphonse 1931- *WhoAm 94*
Ianni, Francis Anthony James 1929- *WhoAm 94*
Ianni, Lawrence Albert 1930- *WhoMW 93*
Ianni, Ronald William 1935- *IntWW 93, WhoAm 94*
Iannicelli, Joseph 1929- *WhoScEn 94*
Iannitelli, Susan 1953- *WhoAmP 93*
Iannone, Dorothy 1933- *WhoAmA 93*
Iannone, James R. 1947- *WhoAmP 93*
Iannotti, Lawrence William 1929- *WhoAm 94*
Iannucci, Salvatore J. 1927- *IntMPA 94*
Iannuzzi, Daniel Andrew 1934- *WhoAm 94*
Iannuzzi, John Nicholas 1935- *WhoAm 94, WhoAmL 94, WrDr 94*

Ianziti, Adelbert John 1927- *WhoFI 94, WhoScEn 94, WhoWest 94*
Iapalucci, Samuel H. 1952- *WhoFI 94*
Iaquinta, Leonard Phillip 1944- *WhoMW 94*
Iaquinto, Joseph Francis 1946- *WhoScEn 94*
Iatesta, John Michael 1944- *WhoAmL 94*
Iavicoli, Mario Anthony 1939- *WhoAm 94, WhoAmP 93*
Iba, Hank 1904- *BasBi*
Iba, Henry d1993 *NewYTBS 93 [port]*
Ibaceta, Herminia D. 1933- *WhoHisp 94*
Ibáñez, Manuel L. 1935- *WhoHisp 94*
Ibanez, Manuel Luis 1935- *WhoAm 94*
Ibanez, Maria Elena *WhoHisp 94*
Ibáñez, Richard *WhoHisp 94*
Ibanez, Sara de 1909-1971 *BlmGWL*
Ibarbourou, Juana de 1895-1979 *BlmGWL*
Ibarguen, Alberto 1944- *WhoAm 94, WhoAmL 94, WhoHisp 94*
Ibarra, Francisco De c. 1530-1575 *WhWE*
Ibarra, Jesse Daniel, Jr. 1918- *WhoHisp 94*
Ibarra, Oscar 1952- *WhoHisp 94*
Ibarra-Perez, Renato del Carmen 1945- *WhoHisp 94*
Ibarria, Antonio *WhoHisp 94*
Ibata, Koichi 1947- *WhoScEn 94*
Ibayashi, Tsuguio 1931- *WhoScEn 94*
Ibbetson, Arthur 1922- *IntMPA 94*
Ibbotson, Eva 1925- *ConAu 43NR*
Ibbotson, Eva (Maria Charlotte Michele Wiesner) 1925- *WrDr 94*
Ibbotson, Frank d1944 *WhoHol 92*
Ibbotson, Lancelot William Cripps 1909- *Who 94*
Ibbotson, Peter Stamford 1943- *Who 94*
Ibbott, Alec 1930- *Who 94*
Ibbott, Geoffrey Stephen 1949- *WhoScEn 94*
Ibbs, (John) Robin 1926- *IntWW 93, Who 94*
Ibbs, Ronald d1990 *WhoHol 92*
Ibegbu, Chris Chidozie 1957- *WhoScEn 94*
Ibekwe, Dan Onwura 1919- *IntWW 93*
Ibekwe, Lawrence Anene 1952- *WhoBlA 94*
Ibelema, Minabere 1952- *WhoBlA 94*
Iben, Icko, Jr. 1931- *WhoAm 94, WhoMW 93, WhoScEn 94*
Iben, Miriam Genevieve Fett 1937- *WhoMW 93*
Ibendahl, Jean Ayres 1918- *WhoMW 93*
Iberall, Arthur Saul 1918- *WhoAm 94, WhoWest 94*
Ibers, James Arthur 1930- *IntWW 93, WhoAm 94, WhoScEn 94*
Ibert, Jacques 1890-1962 *IntDcF 2-4*
Ibert, Jacques (Francois Antoine) 1890-1962 *NewGrDO*
Ibert, Lloyd *IntMPA 94*
Iberville, Pierre Le Moyne, Sieur D' 1661-1706 *WhWE*
Ibiam, (Francis) Akanu 1906- *Who 94*
Ibiam, Francis Akanu 1906- *IntWW 93*
Ibieta, Gabriella 1953- *WhoHisp 94*
Ibingira, Grace *BlmGWL*
Ibn Battuta, Abu Abd-Allah Muhammad 1304-1377 *WhWE*
Ibn Fadlan, Ahmad fl. 92-?- *WhWE*

Ibn Hawqal, Abu Al-Qasim Ibn Ali Alnasibi fl. 94-?-97-? *WhWE*
Ibn Jubayr, Abu Al-Hasan Muhammad 1145-1217 *WhWE*
Ibn Rusta, Abu Ali Ahmad fl. 90-?- *WhWE*
Ibn-Saud, Abd Al-Aziz 1880-1953 *HisWorL [port]*
Ibrahim, A. Mahammad 1953- *WhoFI 94*
Ibrahim, Abdullah 1934- *WhoBlA 94*
Ibrahim, Abu al-Qassim Mohammed 1937- *IntWW 93*
Ibrahim, Encik Anwar bin 1947- *IntWW 93*
Ibrahim, Fayez Barsoum 1929- *WhoScEn 94*
Ibrahim, Hassan Hamdi 1925- *IntWW 93*
Ibrahim, Izzat 1942- *IntWW 93*
Ibrahim, Kamarulazizi 1959- *WhoScEn 94*
Ibrahim, Kashim 1910- *IntWW 93, Who 94*
Ibrahim, Mamdouh H. 1946- *WhoMW 93*
Ibrahim, Mohammad Fathy Kahlil 1946- *WhoScEn 94*
Ibrahim, Mounir Boshra 1947- *WhoScEn 94*
Ibrahim, Sami *ConAu 141*
Ibrahim, Sid Moulay Abdullah 1918- *IntWW 93*
Ibrahimov, Mirza Azhdar oglu 1911- *IntWW 93*
Ibsen, Henrik 1828-1906 *BlmGEL [port], NewGrDO, TwCLC 52 [port]*
Ibsen, Henrik (Johan) 1828-1906 *ConAu 141, IntDcT 2 [port]*
Ibsen, Kenneth Howard 1931- *WhoWest 94*
Ibuka, Masaru 1908- *IntWW 93*
Ibur, Jane Ellen *DrAPF 93*
Ibuse, Masuji 1898-1993 *NewYTBS 93*
Ibuse Masuji 1898-1993 *ConAu 141, ConWorW 93*
Icahn, Carl C. 1936- *IntWW 93, WhoAm 94, WhoFI 94*
Icaza, Carmen de 1899- *BlmGWL*
Ice, Anne-Mare 1945- *WhoBlA 94*
Ice, George Gary 1950- *WhoWest 94*
Ice, Noel Carlysle 1951- *WhoAmL 94*
Ice, Richard Joseph 1961- *WhoMW 93*
Ice, Ruth *DrAPF 93*
Ice, Sue Harper 1934- *WhoAmP 93*
Ice Cube *AfrAmAl 6*
Ice Cube c. 1969- *ConMus 10 [port], WhoBlA 94*
Ice Cube 1970- *WhoAm 94*
Iceland, William Frederick 1924- *WhoFI 94*
Iceman, Sharon Lorraine 1953- *WhoMW 93*
Icenogle, Ronald Dean 1951- *WhoWest 94*
Ice-T *WhoAm 94, WhoBlA 94*
Ice-T 1958?- *ConBlB 6 [port]*
Ichaso, León *WhoHisp 94*
Ichel, David W. 1953- *WhoAmL 94*
Ichiishi, Tatsuro 1943- *WhoAm 94*
Ichikawa, Kon 1915- *IntWW 93*
Ichikawa, Wayne 1954- *WhoWest 94*
Ichikawa, Yoshio 1914- *WhoFI 94*
Ichiki, Andy M. 1932- *WhoAmL 94*
Ichimura, Tohju 1931- *WhoScEn 94*
I-Ching 634-695? *WhWE*
Ichino, Yoko *WhoAm 94*

Ichiyama, Dennis Yoshihide 1944- *WhoAm 94*
Ichiye, Takashi 1921- *WhoAsA 94*
Ichord, Richard H., Jr. 1926-1992 *AnObit 92*
Ickes, Gary R. 1944- *WhoAmP 93*
Ickes, Harold McEwen 1939- *WhoAmP 93*
Ickes, William 1947- *WhoScEn 94*
Ickes, William Alan 1956- *WhoFI 94*
Ida, Shoichi 1941- *WhoAmA 93*
Idaherma *WhoAmA 93*
Idalie, Heinric, Mme. *Who 94*
Idan, Moshe 1957- *WhoScEn 94*
Idaszak, Jerome Joseph 1945- *WhoAm 94*
Idavoy, Connie 1949- *WhoHisp 94*
Iddesleigh, Earl of 1932- *Who 94*
Iddings, Kathleen *DrAPF 93*
Ide, Judith Hope 1943- *WhoAmP 93*
Ide, Letitia d1993 *NewYTBS 93*
Ide, Robert D. 1951- *WhoAmP 93*
Ide, Roy William, III 1940- *WhoAm 94, WhoAmL 94*
Ide, Toshi 1958- *WhoWest 94*
Idelsohn, Sergio Rodolfo 1947- *WhoScEn 94*
Ideman, James M. 1931- *WhoAm 94, WhoAmL 94, WhoWest 94*
Iden, Sheldon 1933- *WhoAmA 93*
Idiens, Dale 1942- *Who 94*
Iding, Allan Earl 1939- *WhoAmL 94*
Idinopulos, Thomas A. 1935- *ConAu 141*
Idle, Dunning, V 1959- *WhoWest 94*
Idle, Eric 1943- *IntMPA 94, WhoAm 94, WhoCom, WhoHol 92*
Idleman, Lee Hillis 1933- *WhoFI 94*
Idler, David Richard 1923- *WhoAm 94*
Idnani, Kamal M. 1948- *WhoAsA 94*
Idol, James Daniel, Jr. 1928- *WhoAm 94*
Idol, John L(ane), Jr. 1932- *ConAu 140*
Idris, Yusuf *EncSF 93*
Idris, Yusuf 1927-1991 *RfGShF*
Idrisi, Abu Abd-Allah Muhammad Al-Sharif Al- 1099-1166 *WhWE*
Idzik, Daniel Ronald 1935- *WhoAm 94*
Idzik, Frank Michael 1927- *WhoAmP 93*
Idzik, Mark Michael 1954- *WhoAmP 93*
Idzik, Martin Francis 1942- *WhoAm 94*
Idzikowski, Stanislas 1894-1977 *IntDcB [port]*
Ieng Sary *IntWW 93*
Iennaco, John Joseph 1964- *WhoScEn 94*
Ierardi, Stephen John 1960- *WhoWest 94*
Ieremia, Talolvao Fa'afetai *WhoAmP 93*
Ievers, Frank George Eyre 1910- *Who 94*
Ievers, John Augustine 1912- *Who 94*
Ieyoub, Richard P. *WhoAmP 93*
Ieyoub, Richard Phillip 1944- *WhoAm 94, WhoAmL 94*
Ifft, Edward Milton 1937- *WhoScEn 94*
Iffy, Leslie 1925- *WhoAm 94, WhoScEn 94*
Igasaki, Masao, Jr. 1925- *WhoAm 94*
Igasaki, Paul 1955- *WhoAsA 94*
Igdalsky, Zviah *WhoHol 92*
Ige, David Y. 1957- *WhoAmP 93*
Ige, Marshall Kaoru 1954- *WhoAmP 93*
Iger, Robert 1951- *IntMPA 94*
Iger, Robert A. *NewYTBS 93 [port]*
Iger, Robert A. 1951- *WhoAm 94, WhoWest 94*
Iggers, Georg G(erson) 1926- *WrDr 94*
Iggers, Georg Gerson 1926- *WhoAm 94*

Indik, Bernard Paul 1932- *WhAm 10*
Indik, Martin Karl 1958- *WhoAmL 94*
Indira, Princess d1979 *WhoHol 92*
Indiviglia, Salvatore Joseph 1919- *WhoAm 94, WhoAmA 93*
Indoe, William F. 1942- *WhoAmL 94*
Indrisano, John d1968 *WhoHol 92*
Indurain, Miguel 1964- *News 94-1 [port]*
Indursky, Arthur 1943- *WhoAmL 94*
Indy, (Paul Marie Theodore) Vincent d' 1851-1931 *NewGrDO*
Inescort, Elaine d1964 *WhoHol 92*
Inescort, Frieda d1976 *WhoHol 92*
Ineson, Robert Earl 1957- *WhoFI 94*
Inez, Colette *DrAPF 93*
Inez, Colette 1931- *WhoAm 94, WrDr 94*
Inez, Mike
See Alice in Chains *ConMus 10*
Infanger, Ray E. 1924- *WhoAmP 93*
Infante, Cruz d1987 *WhoHol 92*
Infante, Donald Richard 1937- *WhoWest 94*
Infante, E. Anthony *WhoHisp 94*
Infante, Ettore Ferrari 1938- *WhoAm 94*
Infante, G. Cabrera *ConWorW 93*
Infante, Gabriel A. 1945- *WhoHisp 94*
Infante, Pedro d1957 *WhoHol 92*
Infanti, Angelo *WhoHol 92*
Infiesta, Felix *WhoHisp 94*
Infusino, Achille Francis 1953- *WhoFI 94, WhoMW 93*
Infusino, Jeffrey Scott 1950- *WhoAm 94*
Infuso, Joseph 1927- *WhoFI 94*
Ing, Dean 1931- *EncSF 93, WrDr 94*
Ing, Dean Charles 1931- *WhoScEn 94*
Ing, Dennis Roy 1947- *WhoFI 94, WhoWest 94*
Ing, Lawrence N. C. 1941- *WhoAsA 94*
Ing, Malcolm Ross 1934- *WhoAsA 94*
Ingalls, Bernice d1987 *WhoHol 92*
Ingalls, Don 1928- *IntMPA 94*
Ingalls, Eve 1936- *WhoAmA 93*
Ingalls, Jeremy *DrAPF 93*
Ingalls, Jeremy 1911- *WhoAm 94, WhoWest 94, WrDr 94*
Ingalls, Joyce 1950- *WhoHol 92*
Ingalls, Mabel Satterlee d1993 *NewYTBS 93*
Ingalls, Marie C. *WhoAmP 93*
Ingalls, Rachel 1941- *WrDr 94*
Ingalls, Robert Lynn 1934- *WhoAm 94*
Ingamells, John 1934- *IntWW 93*
Ingamells, John Anderson Stuart 1934- *Who 94*
Ingate, Mary 1912- *WrDr 94*
Ingber, Barbara 1932- *WhoAmA 93*
Ingber, Donald Elliot 1956- *WhoScEn 94*
Ingber, Marc Stuart 1950- *WhoScEn 94*
Inge, George Patrick Francis 1941- *Who 94*
Inge, M. Thomas 1936- *WrDr 94*
Inge, Milton Thomas 1936- *WhoAm 94*
Inge, Peter (Anthony) 1935- *IntWW 93, Who 94*
Inge, William d1973 *WhoHol 92*
Inge, William c. 1260-1322 *DcNaB MP*
Inge, William (Motter) 1913-1973 *ConDr 93, IntDcT 2 [port]*
Inge, William Motter 1913-1973 *AmCulL*
Ingebritsen, Steven Eric 1956- *WhoWest 94*
Inge-Innes-Lillingston, George David 1923- *Who 94*
Ingel, Florence Courtney 1963- *WrDr 94*
Ingelman-Sundberg, Axel 1910- *IntWW 93*
Ingelow, Jean 1820-1897 *BlmGWL*
Ingels, Jack Edward 1942- *WhoAm 94, WhoFI 94, WhoScEn 94*
Ingels, Marty 1936- *IntMPA 94, WhoAm 94, WhoHol 92*
Ingeman, Jerry Andrew 1950- *WhoMW 93*
Ingemunson, Dallas C. 1938- *WhoAmP 93*
Ingen Housz, Jan 1730-1799 *WorScD*
Inger, George Roe 1933- *WhoMW 93*
Ingerman, Michael Leigh 1937- *WhoFI 94, WhoWest 94*
Ingerman, Peter Zilahy 1934- *WhoScEn 94*
Ingersoll, Andrew Perry 1940- *WhoWest 94*
Ingersoll, Donald Paul 1944- *WhoMW 93*
Ingersoll, Gail Laura 1949- *WhoMW 93*
Ingersoll, Jared 1749-1822 *WhAmRev*
Ingersoll, John Gregory 1948- *WhoWest 94*
Ingersoll, Paul Mills 1928- *WhoAm 94*
Ingersoll, Ralph McAllister 1900-1985 *AmSocL*
Ingersoll, Robert Green 1833-1899 *DcAmReB 2*
Ingersoll, Robert Stephen 1914- *WhoAm 94*
Ingersoll, William d1936 *WhoHol 92*
Ingersoll, William Boley 1938- *WhoAmL 94, WhoFI 94*
Ingestre, Viscount 1978- *Who 94*
Ingham, Barrie *WhoHol 92*
Ingham, Bernard 1932- *IntWW 93, Who 94*
Ingham, Cranford A. *WhoAm 94, WhoFI 94*
Ingham, Daniel 1926- *WrDr 94*
Ingham, David R. 1942- *WhoScEn 94*
Ingham, Elaine Ruth 1952- *WhoScEn 94*
Ingham, Frederick *EncSF 93*
Ingham, John Henry d1992 *Who 94N*
Ingham, Kenneth 1921- *Who 94, WrDr 94*
Ingham, Norman William 1934- *WhoMW 93*
Ingham, R(ichard) A(rnison) 1935- *WrDr 94*
Ingham, Richard Gerald 1948- *WhoAmL 94*
Ingham, Stuart Edward 1942- *Who 94*
Ingham, Tom (Edgar) 1942- *WhoAmA 93*
Inghelbrecht, D(esire)-E(mile) 1880-1965 *NewGrDO*
Inghilleri, Giovanni 1894-1959 *NewGrDO*
Inghram, Mark Gordon 1919- *IntWW 93, WhoAm 94*
Ingilby, Joan Alicia 1911- *WrDr 94*
Ingilby, Thomas (Colvin William) 1955- *Who 94*
Ingle, Cress Stuart *WhoAmP 93*
Ingle, Henry Thomas 1943- *WhoAm 94*
Ingle, James Chesney, Jr. 1935- *WhoAm 94, WhoScEn 94, WhoWest 94*
Ingle, James Edward 1931- *WhoFI 94*
Ingle, John David 1940- *WhoAmL 94*
Ingle, John Ide 1919- *WhoAm 94*
Ingle, John S. 1933- *WhoAmA 93*
Ingle, Joseph B. 1946- *WrDr 94*
Ingle, Morton Blakeman 1942- *WhoAm 94, WhoFI 94*
Ingle, Red d1965 *WhoHol 92*
Ingle, Robert D. 1939- *WhoAm 94, WhoWest 94*
Ingle, Robert P. 1933- *WhoFI 94*
Ingle, Tom 1920-1973 *WhoAmA 93N*
Ingleby, Viscount 1926- *Who 94*
Ingledow, Anthony Brian 1928- *Who 94*
Ingledue, Scott Leroy 1949- *WhoMW 93*
Inglefield-Watson, John (Forbes) 1926- *Who 94*
Inglehart, Lorretta Jeannette 1947- *WhoScEn 94*
Ingles, James H. 1944- *WhoAm 94*
Ingles, Jose D. 1912- *IntWW 93*
Inglese, Anthony Michael Christopher 1951- *Who 94*
Inglewood, Baron 1951- *Who 94*
Inglewood, Kathleen 1876- *BlmGWL*
Inglis (Kello), Esther 1571-1624 *BlmGWL*
Inglis, Andrew Franklin 1920- *WhoAm 94*
Inglis, Bob *WhoAmP 93*
Inglis, Bob 1959- *CngDr 93*
Inglis, Brian 1916-1993 *WrDr 94N*
Inglis, Brian (St. John) 1916-1993 *ConAu 140*
Inglis, Brian St. John d1993 *Who 94N*
Inglis, Brian Scott 1924- *Who 94*
Inglis, Charles 1734-1816 *WhAmRev*
Inglis, David Rittenhouse 1905- *WhoAm 94*
Inglis, Elizabeth *WhoHol 92*
Inglis, George Bruton 1933- *Who 94*
Inglis, Ian Grahame 1929- *Who 94*
Inglis, James *WhoAm 94*
Inglis, James Craufuird Roger 1925- *Who 94*
Inglis, Kenneth Stanley 1929- *IntWW 93, Who 94*
Inglis, Robert Alexander 1918- *Who 94*
Inglis, Robert D 1959- *WhoAm 94*
Inglis, Sara *WhoHol 92*
Inglis-Jones, Nigel John 1935- *Who 94*
Inglis of Glencorse, Roderick (John) 1936- *Who 94*
Ingman, Charles William 1953- *WhoAmL 94*
Ingman, David Charles 1928- *Who 94*
Ingman, Nicholas 1948- *WrDr 94*
Ingman, Richard Wilson 1944- *WhoFI 94, WhoMW 93*
Ingold, Catherine White 1949- *WhoAm 94*
Ingold, Cecil Terence 1905- *Who 94*
Ingold, Keith Usherwood 1929- *IntWW 93, Who 94, WhoAm 94, WhoScEn 94*
Ingoldsby, Thomas M. 1945- *WhoAm 94*
Ingraham, Barton L(ee) 1930- *ConAu 43NR*
Ingraham, Edward Clarke, Jr. 1922- *WhoAm 94*
Ingraham, Hubert Alexander 1947- *IntWW 93*
Ingraham, Joe McDonald 1903-1990 *WhAm 10*
Ingraham, John Wright 1930- *WhoAm 94, WhoFI 94*
Ingraham, Karen Whitacre 1948- *WhoMW 93*
Ingraham, Leah Mae 1938- *WhoMW 93*
Ingraham, Lloyd d1956 *WhoHol 92*
Ingram, Adam Paterson 1947- *Who 94*
Ingram, Alvin John 1914- *IntWW 93, WhoAm 94*
Ingram, Alyce *DrAPF 93*
Ingram, Amber Rose 1960- *WhoMW 93*
Ingram, Bruce Guy 1943- *WhoFI 94*
Ingram, Cecil D. 1932- *WhoAmP 93, WhoWest 94*
Ingram, Charles Clark, Jr. 1916- *WhoAm 94*
Ingram, Charles William 1956- *WhoAmP 93*
Ingram, Colin 1936- *WhoWest 94*
Ingram, Dan *NewYTBS 93 [port]*
Ingram, David Christopher 1953- *WhoMW 93*
Ingram, David John Edward 1927- *IntWW 93, Who 94*
Ingram, David Stanley 1941- *Who 94*
Ingram, Denny Ouzts, Jr. 1929- *WhoAm 94, WhoAmL 94*
Ingram, Derek Thynne 1925- *WrDr 94*
Ingram, Earl Girardeau 1936- *WhoBlA 94*
Ingram, Edward John W. *Who 94*
Ingram, Eldridge B. 1949- *WhoBlA 94*
Ingram, Gary John 1933- *WhoAmP 93*
Ingram, George Conley 1930- *WhoAm 94, WhoAmL 94*
Ingram, Helen Q. 1932- *WhoAmP 93*
Ingram, Jack d1969 *WhoHol 92*
Ingram, James *WhoAm 94, WhoBlA 94*
Ingram, James 195-?- *ConMus 11 [port]*
Ingram, James (Herbert Charles) 1966- *Who 94*
Ingram, James Charles 1928- *IntWW 93*
Ingram, James E. 1941- *WhoAmL 94*
Ingram, James William, Jr. 1938- *WhoBlA 94*
Ingram, Judith 1926- *WhoAmA 93*
Ingram, Kathleen Annie *Who 94*
Ingram, Kenneth F. 1929- *WhoAmP 93*
Ingram, Kenneth Frank 1929- *WhoAm 94, WhoAmL 94*
Ingram, Kevin *WhoBlA 94*
Ingram, Lafayette N., III 1940- *WhoAmP 93*
Ingram, Lance *NewGrDO*
Ingram, LaVerne Dorothy 1955- *WhoBlA 94*
Ingram, Lawrence Warren 1921- *WhoAm 94*
Ingram, Maria *DrAPF 93*
Ingram, Michael d1976 *WhoHol 92*
Ingram, Nathaniel Hawthorne 1918- *WhoAmP 93*
Ingram, Paul 1934- *Who 94*
Ingram, Peggy Joyce 1943- *WhoWest 94*
Ingram, Peter Henry 1954- *WhoMW 93*
Ingram, Phillip M. 1945- *WhoBlA 94*
Ingram, Randy Jan 1956- *WhoMW 93*
Ingram, Rex d1950 *WhoHol 92*
Ingram, Rex d1969 *WhoHol 92*
Ingram, Rex 1895-1969 *AfrAmAl 6 [port], ConBlB 5 [port]*
Ingram, Riley E. 1941- *WhoAmP 93*
Ingram, Robert B. 1936- *WhoBlA 94*
Ingram, Robert Bruce 1940- *WhoAmL 94*
Ingram, Robert Edward Lee 1932- *WhoWest 94*
Ingram, Robert L. 1930- *WhoAmP 93*
Ingram, Robert Palmer 1917- *WhoAm 94*
Ingram, Robina Elaine 1956- *WhoWest 94*
Ingram, Samuel William, Jr. 1933- *WhoAm 94, WhoAmL 94*
Ingram, Stanley Edward 1922- *Who 94*
Ingram, Valerie J. 1959- *WhoBlA 94*
Ingram, Vernon M. 1924- *IntWW 93*
Ingram, Vernon Martin 1924- *Who 94, WrDr 94*
Ingram, W. Kent 1942- *WhoAmP 93*
Ingram, William Austin 1924- *WhoAm 94, WhoWest 94*
Ingram, William B. 1935- *WhoBlA 94*
Ingram, William Thomas, III 1937- *WhoScEn 94*
Ingram, Winifred 1913- *WhoBlA 94*
Ingram-Grant, Edith Jacqueline 1942- *WhoBlA 94*
Ingrams *Who 94*
Ingrams, Doreen (Constance) 1906- *WrDr 94*
Ingrams, Richard 1937- *WrDr 94*
Ingrams, Richard Reid 1937- *IntWW 93, Who 94*
Ingrand, Henry 1908- *IntWW 93*
Ingrao, Jerold Kenneth 1947- *WhoWest 94*
Ingrao, Pietro 1915- *IntWW 93*
Ingrassia, Ciccio *WhoHol 92*
Ingrassia, Giovanni 1510-1580 *EncDeaf*
Ingrassia, Paul Joseph 1950- *WhoAm 94*
Ingress Bell, Philip *Who 94*
Ingrey, Derek *EncSF 93*
Ingrey, Paul Bosworth 1939- *WhoIns 94*
Ingrid, Charles *EncSF 93*
Ingrody, Pamela Theresa 1962- *WhoScEn 94*
Ingrow, Baron 1917- *Who 94*
Ingrum, Adrienne G. 1954- *WhoBlA 94*
Ingstad, Helge Marcus 1899- *IntWW 93*
Ingster, Boris 1913- *IntMPA 94*
Ingstrup, Ole Michaelsen 1941- *WhoAm 94*
Ingvarsson, Ingvi S. 1924- *IntWW 93*
Ingwersen, Martin Lewis 1919- *WhoAm 94*
Inhofe, James M. 1934- *CngDr 93, WhoAm 94*
Inhofe, James Mountain 1934- *WhoAmP 93*
Inigo, Rafael Madrigal 1932- *WhoAm 94*
Injeyan, Seta L. 1946- *WhoAmA 93*
Ink, Claude 1928- *IntWW 93*
Ink, Dwight A. 1922- *WhoAm 94*
Inkeles, Alex 1920- *IntWW 93, WhoAm 94, WhoWest 94*
Inkin, Geoffrey (David) 1934- *Who 94*
Inkley, John James, Jr. 1945- *WhoAm 94, WhoAmL 94*
Inkley, Scott Russell 1921- *WhoAm 94*
Inkley, Scott Russell, Jr. 1952- *WhoAm 94*
Ink Spots, The *WhoHol 92*
Inkster, Juli 1960- *WhoAm 94*
Inkster, Norma 1936- *WhoWest 94*
Inkster, Norman David 1938- *WhoAm 94*
Inlow, Edgar Burke 1915- *WhoAm 94*
Inlow, Rush Osborne 1944- *WhoWest 94*
Inman, Bobby Ray 1931- *NewYTBS 93 [port], WhoAm 94, WhoAmP 93*
Inman, Claudia Jean 1942- *WhoFI 94, WhoWest 94*
Inman, Cullen Langdon 1933- *WhoScEn 94*
Inman, Daniel John 1947- *WhoAm 94, WhoScEn 94*
Inman, Derek Arthur 1937- *Who 94*
Inman, Edward Oliver 1948- *Who 94*
Inman, Edward S., III 1960- *WhoAmP 93*
Inman, Elizabeth Murray Campbell Smith c. 1724-1785 *BlmGWL*
Inman, Harry Ansel 1924- *WhoAm 94*
Inman, Herbert 1917- *Who 94*
Inman, James Carlton, Jr. 1945- *WhoScEn 94*
Inman, Marianne Elizabeth 1943- *WhoMW 93*
Inman, Mary Lou 1925- *WhoAmP 93*
Inman, Pauline Winchester 1904-1990 *WhoAmA 93N*
Inman, Robert (Anthony) 1931- *WrDr 94*
Inman, Roger 1915- *Who 94*
Inman, Ross Banks 1931- *WhoAm 94*
Inman, Will *DrAPF 93*
Inman, William Peter 1936- *WhoAm 94*
Inman-Campbell, Gail 1956- *WhoAmL 94*
Inn, Frank *WhoHol 92*
Innanen, Larry John 1950- *WhoAm 94*
Innaurato, Albert 1947- *ConDr 93*
Innaurato, Albert 1948- *WrDr 94*
Innaurato, Albert Francis 1947- *WhoAm 94*
Innerbichler, Nicholas R. *WhoHisp 94*
Innerst, Preston Eugene 1927- *WhoAm 94*
Innes, Alistair Campbell M. *Who 94*
Innes, David Lyn 1941- *WhoAm 94*
Innes, Evan *EncSF 93*
Innes, Evan 1928- *WrDr 94*
Innes, Fergus Munro 1903- *Who 94*
Innes, George 1938- *WhoHol 92*
Innes, Hammond *IntWW 93, Who 94*
Innes, Hammond 1913- *WrDr 94*
Innes, Jean d1978 *WhoHol 92*
Innes, Jean 1932- *WrDr 94*
Innes, John Phythian, II 1934- *WhoAm 94, WhoFI 94*
Innes, Kenneth Frederick, III 1950- *WhoAmL 94*
Innes, Maughan William 1922- *Who 94*
Innes, Michael *Who 94*
Innes, Michael 1906- *WrDr 94*
Innes, Peter (Alexander Berowald) 1937- *Who 94*
Innes, Robert Mann 1926- *Who 94*
Innes, Sheila Miriam 1931- *Who 94*
Innes, William Alexander Disney 1910- *Who 94*
Innes, William James Alexander 1934- *Who 94*
Innes-Ker *Who 94*
Innes of Coxton, David (Charles Kenneth Gordon) 1940- *Who 94*
Innes of Edingight, Malcolm (Rognvald) 1938- *Who 94*
Innes Of Edingight, Malcolm Rognvald 1938- *IntWW 93*
Inness, George 1825-1894 *AmCulL*
Inness-Brown, Elizabeth *DrAPF 93*
Innis, Richard Joseph 1946- *WhoAm 94, WhoAmL 94*
Innis, Robert E(dward) 1941- *WrDr 94*
Innis, Roy 1934- *AfrAmAl 6 [port], ConBlB 5 [port]*
Innis, Roy Emile Alfredo 1934- *AmSocL, IntWW 93, WhoAm 94, WhoBlA 94*
Inniss, Charles Evans 1935- *WhoBlA 94*

Inniss, Clifford (de Lisle) 1910- *Who 94*
Innocent, III 1161-1216 *HisWorL [port]*
Innocent, Harold 1933-1993 *NewYTBS 93*
Innocent, Harold 1935- *WhoHol 92*
Innocenti, Antonio 1915- *IntWW 93*
Innocenti, Luigi 1923- *IntWW 93*
Inoguchi, Takashi 1944- *WrDr 94*
Inokuma, Genichiro d1993 *NewYTBS 93*
Inokuti, Mitio 1933- *WhoAsA 94*
Inonu, Erdal 1926- *IntWW 93*
Inos, Joseph S. 1947- *WhoAmP 93*
Inose, Hiroshi 1927- *IntWW 93*
Inoshiro, Honda 1911- *HorFD*
Inoue, Akihiko 1958- *WhoFI 94*
Inoue, Kazuko 1946- *WhoAmA 93*
Inoue, Michael Shigeru 1936- *WhoAsA 94, WhoScEn 94*
Inoue, Shinya 1921- *WhoAm 94, WhoScEn 94*
Inoue, Takao 1957- *WhoScEn 94*
Inoue, Takashi *IntWW 93*
Inoue, Takeshi 1932- *WhoScEn 94*
Inoue, Yasushi 1907-1991 *WhAm 10*
Inoue, Yoshio 1929- *WhoScEn 94*
Inouye, Charles Shiro 1954- *WhoAsA 94*
Inouye, Daniel K. 1924- *CngDr 93, WhoAsA 94*
Inouye, Daniel Ken 1924- *IntWW 93, WhoAm 94, WhoAmP 93, WhoWest 94*
Inouye, David William 1950- *WhoAm 94, WhoScEn 94*
Inouye, Kaoru 1906- *IntWW 93*
Inouye, Minoru 1924- *IntWW 93*
Inouye, Richard Saburo 1953- *WhoAsA 94*
Insall, Donald William 1926- *Who 94*
Insanally, Samuel Rudolph 1936- *IntWW 93*
Insanguine, Giacomo (Antonio Francesco Paolo Michele) 1728-1795 *NewGrDO*
Insch, James Ferguson 1911- *Who 94*
Insdorf, Annette 1950- *IntMPA 94*
Insel, Michael S. 1947- *WhoAm 94, WhoAmL 94*
Inselberg, Diane Erskine Hunt 1944- *WhoAmL 94*
Inselberg, Rachel 1934- *WhoMW 93*
Inselman, Laura Sue 1944- *WhoAm 94*
Inserra, Ben Anthony 1937- *WhoFI 94*
Inskeep, Kenneth Hayes 1957- *WhoAmL 94*
Inskeep, Leroy G. 1948- *WhoAmL 94*
Inskeep, Robert Forman 1944- *WhoWest 94*
Inskip *Who 94*
Inslee, Jay 1951- *CngDr 93*
Inslee, Jay R. 1951- *WhoAm 94, WhoAmP 93, WhoWest 94*
Insler, Stanley 1937- *WhoAm 94*
Insley, Lillian Dorothy 1929- *WhoAmP 93*
Insley, Will 1929- *WhoAm 94, WhoAmA 93*
Insole, Douglas John 1926- *Who 94*
Instone, John Clifford 1924- *WhoAm 94*
Intemann, Robert Louis 1938- *WhoAm 94*
Interlenghi, Antonella 1961- *WhoHol 92*
Interlenghi, Franco 1930- *WhoHol 92*
Intili, Thomas Joseph 1959- *WhoAmL 94*
Intilli, Sharon Marie 1950- *WhoAm 94*
Intrater, Cheryl Watson Waylor 1943- *WhoMW 93*
Intriere, Anthony Donald 1920- *WhoWest 94*
Intriligator, Devrie Shapiro *WhoAm 94, WhoScEn 94, WhoWest 94*
Intriligator, Marc Steven 1952- *WhoAmL 94*
Intriligator, Michael David 1938- *IntWW 93, WhoAm 94*
Inui, Harumi 1934- *WhoWomW 91*
Inui, Thomas Spencer 1943- *WhoAm 94, WhoWest 94*
Inukai, Kyohei 1913- *WhoAmA 93*
Inverarity, Robert Bruce 1909- *WhoAmA 93*
Inverforth, Baron 1966- *Who 94*
Inverness, Provost of *Who 94*
Invernizio, Carolina 1858-1916 *BlmGWL*
Inverso, Marlene Joy 1942- *WhoWest 94*
Inverso, Peter 1938- *WhoAmP 93*
Inverurie, Lord 1976- *Who 94*
Inwood, Steve *WhoHol 92*
Inyamah, Nathaniel Ginikanwa N. 1934- *WhoBlA 94*
Inyang, Hilary Inyang 1959- *WhoScEn 94*
Inzenga (y Castellanos), Jose 1828-1891 *NewGrDO*
Inzetta, Mark Stephen 1956- *WhoAmL 94*
Inzunza, Ralph *WhoHisp 94*
Ioannides, George X. 1924- *IntWW 93*
Iodice, Elaine 1947- *WhoScEn 94*
Iodice, Joanna DiMeno 1953- *WhoAm 94*
Iodice, Ruth G. *DrAPF 93*
Ioffe, Boris Lazarevich 1926- *IntWW 93*
Iona, Mario 1917- *WhoAm 94*
Ione *BlkWr 2*
Ione, Carole *DrAPF 93*
Ione, Carole 1937- *BlkWr 2*
Ionesco, Eugene 1909?- *IntDcT 2*
Ionesco, Eugene 1912?- *ConWorW 93, IntWW 93, Who 94, WhoAm 94*
Ionescu, George Ghita 1913- *Who 94*
Ionescu, Ghita 1913- *WrDr 94*
Ionescu Tulcea, Cassius 1923- *WhoAm 94, WhoMW 93, WhoScEn 94*
Ionnescu, Demetriu G. *EncSF 93*
Ioppolo, Frank Sebastian 1942- *WhoAmL 94*
Iordanidou, Maria 1897- *BlmGWL*
Iorgulescu, Jorge 1935- *WhoAm 94*
Iorio, Adrian J. 1879-1957 *WhoAmA 93N*
Iorio, Ralph Arthur 1925- *WhoAm 94*
Ioseliani, Dzhaba *IntWW 93*
Iosifescu, Marius Vicentiu Viorel 1936- *IntWW 93*
Iosue, Carmine 1945- *WhoAm 94*
Iott, Wallace D. 1915- *WhoFI 94*
Iotti, Leonilde 1920- *WhoWomW 91*
Iovannisci, David Mark *WhoScEn 94*
Iovenko, Michael 1930- *WhoAm 94, WhoAmL 94*
Iovine, Carmine P. 1943- *WhoScEn 94*
Ip, Henrietta Man-Hing 1947- *WhoWomW 91*
Ip, John H. 1960- *WhoScEn 94*
Ipcar, Dahlov 1917- *WhoAm 94, WhoAmA 93*
Ipousteguy, (Jean Robert) 1920- *WhoAmA 93*
Ippen, Erich Peter 1940- *WhoAm 94*
Ippolito, Angelo 1922- *WhoAm 94, WhoAmA 93*
Ippolitov-Ivanov, Mikhail Mikhaylovich 1859-1935 *NewGrDO*
Ipsen, Bodil d1964 *WhoHol 92*
Ipsen, D. C. 1921- *WrDr 94*
Ipsen, Ernest L. 1869-1951 *WhoAmA 93N*
Ipsen, Grant R. 1932- *WhoAmP 93*
Ipsen, Grant Ruel 1932- *WhoWest 94*
Ipsen, Henry W. 1944- *WhoAmL 94*
Ipsen, Kent Forrest 1933- *WhoAm 94, WhoAmA 93*
Ipsen, Poul Janus 1936- *WhoAmA 93*
Ipswich, Archdeacon of *Who 94*
Ipswich, Bishop of *Who 94*
Ipswich, Viscount 1978- *Who 94*
Iqbal, S. Mohammed 1932- *WhoAsA 94*
Iqbal, Zafar 1941- *WhoScEn 94*
Iqbal, Zafar 1946- *WhoAm 94, WhoAsA 94*
Iqbal, Zafar Mohd 1938- *WhoMW 93, WhoScEn 94*
Iradier, Sebastian 1809-1865 *NewGrDO*
Irahola, Rene C. 1928- *WhoHisp 94*
Irala, Domingo Martinez De 1486?-1557 *WhWE*
Iran, Empress of *IntWW 93*
Irani, Jamshed Jiji 1936- *IntWW 93*
Irani, Ray R. 1935- *IntWW 93, WhoAm 94, WhoFI 94, WhoWest 94*
Irani, Raymond Reza 1928- *WhoAm 94*
Iranyi, Ladislaus Anthony 1923-1987 *WhAm 10*
Irateba c. 1814-1878 *WhWE*
Irato, Angela Jo 1965- *WhoFI 94*
Iravanchy, Shawn 1965- *WhoScEn 94*
Irby *Who 94*
Irby, Galven 1921- *WhoBlA 94*
Irby, Holt 1937- *WhoAmL 94*
Irby, Kenneth *DrAPF 93*
Irby, Kenneth 1936- *WrDr 94*
Irby, Kenneth Lee 1936- *WhoMW 93*
Irby, Nathan C., Jr. 1931- *WhoAmP 93*
Irby, Peyton S., Jr. 1944- *WhoAmL 94*
Irby, Ray 1918- *WhoBlA 94*
Irby, Stuart Charles, Jr. 1923- *WhoAm 94*
Iredale, Nancy L. 1947- *WhoAmL 94*
Iredale, Peter 1932- *Who 94*
Iredale, Randle W. 1929- *IntWW 93*
Iredale, Roger Oliver 1934- *Who 94*
Iredell, James 1751-1799 *WhAmRev*
Iredell, Russell 1889-1959 *WhoAmA 93N*
Irelan, John Ralph Smiley 1935- *WhoAm 94*
Irelan, Robert Withers 1937- *WhoFI 94*
Ireland, Andrew P. 1930- *WhoAmP 93*
Ireland, Anthony d1957 *WhoHol 92*
Ireland, Barbara M. *WhoAmP 93*
Ireland, David 1927- *EncSF 93, WrDr 94*
Ireland, Donovan Edward 1913- *WhoAmP 93*
Ireland, Emory 1944- *WhoAmL 94*
Ireland, Frank Edward 1913- *Who 94*
Ireland, George Ring 1956- *WhoFI 94*
Ireland, Herbert Orin 1919- *WhoAm 94*
Ireland, Jill d1990 *WhoHol 92*
Ireland, Joe C. *DrAPF 93*
Ireland, John 1838-1918 *DcAmReB 2*
Ireland, John 1914- *WhoHol 92*
Ireland, John 1914-1992 *AnObit 1992*
Ireland, Kathy *WhoHol 92*
Ireland, Kathy 1963- *WhoAm 94*
Ireland, Kevin (Mark) 1933- *WrDr 94*
Ireland, Lynda 1950- *WhoBlA 94*
Ireland, Michael Joseph 1961- *WhoAmL 94*
Ireland, Norma Olin 1907- *WhoAm 94*
Ireland, Norman Charles 1927- *IntWW 93, Who 94*
Ireland, Patricia 1945- *WhoAm 94*
Ireland, Patrick 1935- *WhoAm 94, WhoAmA 93*
Ireland, Patrick Gault de C. *Who 94*
Ireland, Ralph Leonard 1901-1990 *WhAm 10*
Ireland, Robert Abner, Jr. 1918- *WhoWest 94*
Ireland, Robert Livingston, III 1920- *WhoAm 94*
Ireland, Roderick Louis 1944- *WhoBlA 94*
Ireland, Ronald David 1925- *Who 94*
Ireland, Timothy F. 1958- *WhoAmP 93*
Irell, Lawrence Elliott 1912- *WhoAm 94*
Iremonger, Lucille 1921- *BlmGWL*
Iremonger, Thomas Lascelles Isa Shandon Valiant 1916- *Who 94*
Irena 1912- *WhoAmA 93*
Irenas, Joseph Eron 1940- *WhoAm 94, WhoAmL 94*
Irene d1962 *WhoHol 92*
Irene 1901-1962 *IntDcF 2-4 [port]*
Irene, Eugene Arthur 1941- *WhoAm 94*
Irene of Athens c. 752-803 *HisWorL [port]*
Irens, Alfred Norman 1911- *Who 94*
Ireson, Gordon Worley 1906- *Who 94*
Ireson, William Grant 1915-1989 *WhAm 10*
Ireton, Barrie Rowland 1944- *Who 94*
Ireton, Thomas Francis 1940- *WhoAm 94*
Irey, Charlotte York 1918- *WhoAm 94*
Irey, Nelson Sumner 1911- *WhoAm 94*
Irfan, Muhammad 1928- *WhoScEn 94*
Irgon, Joseph 1919- *WhoScEn 94*
Iri, Masao 1933- *WhoScEn 94*
Iriani, Abdul Karim al- *IntWW 93*
Iribarren, Norma Carmen 1938- *WhoHisp 94*
Iribarren Borges, Ignacio 1912- *IntWW 93*
Irick, Troy D. 1963- *WhoMW 93*
Irigaray, Luce 1930- *BlmGWL*
Irigoin, Jean 1920- *IntWW 93*
Irigonegaray, Pedro Luis 1948- *WhoHisp 94*
Irigoyen, Fructuoso Rascon 1949- *WhoHisp 94*
Irigoyen, Matilde M. 1949- *WhoHisp 94*
Irigoyen, Sal A. 1954- *WhoHisp 94*
Irimescu, Ion 1903- *IntWW 93*
Irino, Yoshiro 1921-1980 *NewGrDO*
Irion, Arthur Lloyd 1918- *WhoAm 94*
Irion, Joan K. 1953- *WhoAmL 94*
Irion, Mary Jean *DrAPF 93*
Irion, Mary Jean 1922- *WrDr 94*
Irion, Terry L. 1948- *WhoAmL 94*
Irions, Charles Carter 1929- *WhoAm 94*
Iris, Esperanza d1962 *WhoHol 92*
Irish, George Butler 1944- *WhoAm 94*
Irish, James Richard 1946- *WhoAm 94*
Irish, Jerry Arthur 1936- *WhoWest 94*
Irish, Leon Eugene 1938- *WhoAm 94*
Irish, Ned 1905-1982 *BasBi*
Irish, Ronald (Arthur) 1913- *Who 94*
Irish, Tom 1929- *WhoHol 92*
Iriye, Akira 1934- *WhoAm 94*
Irizarry, Balvino *WhoHisp 94*
Irizarry, Carmen 1956- *WhoHisp 94*
Irizarry, Carmen P. 1957- *WhoHisp 94*
Irizarry, Fernando *WhoHisp 94*
Irizarry, Herminio 1952- *WhoHisp 94*
Irizarry, John 1946- *WhoHisp 94*
Irizarry, Victor *WhoHisp 94*
Irizarry-Graziani, Carmen 1948- *WhoHisp 94*
Irizarry-Paoli, Julio A. 1955- *WhoHisp 94*
Irmagean 1947- *WhoBlA 94*
Irmak, Sadi 1904- *IntWW 93*
Irmen, J. Douglas 1947- *WhoAmL 94*
Irminger, Charles W. 1956- *WhoFI 94*
Irminger, Ginny Lynn 1954- *WhoFI 94*
Irobe, Yoshiaki 1911- *IntWW 93*
Irok, Leo Moggie Anak 1941- *IntWW 93*
Ironbiter, Suzanne Potter *DrAPF 93*
Iron Maiden *ConMus 10 [port]*
Irons, Edward D. *WhoBlA 94*
Irons, George Vernon 1902- *WhoAm 94*
Irons, Jeremy 1948- *IntMPA 94, IntWW 93, Who 94, WhoHol 92*
Irons, Jeremy John 1948- *WhoAm 94*
Irons, Neil L. 1936- *WhoAm 94*
Irons, Norman 1941- *Who 94*
Irons, Richard K. d1993 *NewYTBS 93*
Irons, Sandra Jean 1940- *WhoBlA 94*
Irons, Sue 1943- *WhoBlA 94*
Irons, William George 1933- *WhoAm 94, WhoMW 93*
Irons, William V. 1943- *WhoAmP 93*
Ironside, Baron 1924- *Who 94*
Ironside, Michael 1949- *WhoHol 92*
Iron Thunderhorse 1950- *WrDr 94*
Irr, Joseph David 1934- *WhoScEn 94*
Irrthum, Henri Emile 1947- *WhoFI 94, WhoScEn 94*
Irsay, James Steven 1959- *WhoAm 94, WhoMW 93*
Irsay, Robert 1923- *WhoAm 94, WhoMW 93*
Irsfeld, John H. *DrAPF 93*
Irsfeld, John Henry 1937- *WhoWest 94*
Irshaidat, Salah 1919- *IntWW 93*
Iruvanti, Pran Rao 1957- *WhoScEn 94*
Irvan, Ernie *WhoAm 94*
Irvan, Robert P. *WhoIns 94*
Irvin, Ben Leroy 1935- *WhoAmL 94*
Irvin, Byron Edward 1966- *WhoBlA 94*
Irvin, Charles Leslie 1935- *WhoBlA 94*
Irvin, George William 1940- *WhoScEn 94*
Irvin, Helen Arlene 1932- *WhoMW 93*
Irvin, John 1940- *IntMPA 94*
Irvin, Lynda Elare 1950- *WhoMW 93*
Irvin, Mark Christopher 1955- *WhoWest 94*
Irvin, Melvin, Jr. 1942- *WhoAmP 93*
Irvin, Michael Jerome 1966- *WhoAm 94*
Irvin, Michael P. 1950- *WhoAmL 94*
Irvin, Milton M. *WhoBlA 94*
Irvin, Monford Merrill 1919- *WhoBlA 94*
Irvin, Patricia Louise 1955- *WhoAmL 94*
Irvin, Rea 1881-1972 *WhoAmA 93N*
Irvin, Regina Lynette 1963- *WhoBlA 94*
Irvin, Robert Andrew 1948- *WhoAmP 93*
Irvin, Robert D. 1951- *WhoAm 94*
Irvin, Sally A. 1949- *WhoAmL 94*
Irvin, Samuel M. 1812-1887 *EncNAR*
Irvin, Thomas *WhoAmP 93*
Irvin, Tinsley H. 1933- *WhoIns 94*
Irvin, Tinsley Hoyt 1933- *WhoAm 94, WhoFI 94*
Irvin, William Adolf 1873-1952 *EncABHB 9 [port]*
Irvine *Who 94*
Irvine, Alan Montgomery 1926- *Who 94*
Irvine, Betty Jo 1943- *WhoAmA 93*
Irvine, Carolyn Lenette 1947- *WhoBlA 94*
Irvine, David Robert 1943- *WhoAmP 93*
Irvine, Donald Hamilton 1935- *Who 94*
Irvine, Frances L. 1940- *WhoAmP 93*
Irvine, Freeman Raymond, Jr. 1931- *WhoBlA 94*
Irvine, George 1948- *WhoAm 94*
Irvine, Gerard Sutherland 1913- *Who 94*
Irvine, Gretchen Kranz 1946- *WhoMW 93*
Irvine, James Eccles Malise 1925- *Who 94*
Irvine, Janice M. 1951- *WrDr 94*
Irvine, Jerry Andrew 1958- *WhoWest 94*
Irvine, John 1914- *Who 94*
Irvine, John Alexander 1947- *WhoAm 94, WhoAmL 94*
Irvine, John Ferguson 1920- *Who 94*
Irvine, John Henry 1951- *WhoScEn 94*
Irvine, John Maxwell 1939- *IntWW 93, Who 94*
Irvine, Mary Elizabeth 1913- *WhoAmP 93*
Irvine, Michael Fraser 1939- *Who 94*
Irvine, Mori 1955- *WhoAmL 94*
Irvine, Murray *Who 94*
Irvine, (John) Murray 1924- *Who 94*
Irvine, Norman Forrest 1922- *Who 94*
Irvine, Ralstone Robert 1898- *WhAm 10*
Irvine, Reed John 1922- *WhoAm 94*
Irvine, Robin d1933 *WhoHol 92*
Irvine, Robin (Orlando Hamilton) 1929- *Who 94*
Irvine, Robin Francis 1950- *Who 94*
Irvine, Robin Orlando Hamilton 1929- *IntWW 93*
Irvine, Thomas Francis, Jr. 1922- *WhoAm 94, WhoScEn 94*
Irvine, Vernon Bruce 1943- *WhoWest 94*
Irvine, William 1741-1804 *AmRev, WhAmRev*
Irvine, William Burriss 1925- *WhoFI 94*
Irvine Of Lairg, Baron 1940- *Who 94*
Irving, A. Marshall 1929- *WhoFI 94*
Irving, Amy 1953- *ConTFT 11, IntMPA 94, IntWW 93, WhoAm 94, WhoHol 92*
Irving, Andrew 1950- *WhoAmL 94*
Irving, Anna Duer 1873-1957 *WhoAmA 93N*
Irving, Charles d1981 *WhoHol 92*
Irving, Charles (Graham) *Who 94*
Irving, Clarence Larry, Jr. 1955- *WhoBlA 94*
Irving, Clifford *Who 94*
Irving, Clifford 1930- *WrDr 94*
Irving, (Edward) Clifford 1914- *Who 94*
Irving, Donald J. 1933- *WhoAmA 93*
Irving, Douglas Dorset 1944- *WhoScEn 94*
Irving, Edward 1927- *IntWW 93, Who 94, WhoAm 94*
Irving, Ellis 1902- *WhoHol 92*
Irving, Ethel d1963 *WhoHol 92*
Irving, Euclid A. 1952- *WhoAmL 94*
Irving, Frederick 1921- *WhoAmP 93*
Irving, George d1961 *WhoHol 92*
Irving, George S. 1922- *WhoHol 92*
Irving, George Steven 1922- *WhoAm 94*
Irving, George Washington, III 1940- *WhoAm 94*

Ives, Richard *DrAPF 93*
Ives, Richard Lee 1951- *WhoWest 94*
Ives, Robert Edward 1954- *WhoFI 94*
Ives, Ronn Brian 1950- *WhoAm 94*
Ives, Timothy Read 1928- *WhoAmP 93*
Ives, W. M. *WhoAmP 93*
Ives, William Charles 1933- *WhoAmP 93*
Ivester, Melvin Douglas 1947-
    WhoAm 94, WhoFI 94
Ivester, Robert Donald 1932- *WhoFI 94*
Ivey, Dana 1942- *WhoHol 92*
Ivey, David M. 1949- *WhoAmL 94*
Ivey, Donald Glenn 1922- *WhoAm 94*
Ivey, Elizabeth S. 1935- *WhoAm 94*
Ivey, Horace Spencer 1931- *WhoBlA 94*
Ivey, James Burnett 1925- *WhoAm 94,
    WhoAmA 93*
Ivey, Jean Eichelberger 1923- *NewGrDO,
    WhoAm 94*
Ivey, John Kemmerer 1961- *WhoAmL 94*
Ivey, Judith 1951- *CurBio 93 [port],
    IntMPA 94, WhoAm 94, WhoHol 92*
Ivey, Mark, III 1935- *WhoBlA 94*
Ivey, Michael 1968-
    See Basehead *ConMus 11*
Ivey, Michael Wayne 1964- *WhoFI 94*
Ivey, Rebecca 1965- *WhoBlA 94*
Ivey, Richard Macaulay 1925- *WhoAm 94*
Ivey, Robert Carl 1939- *WhoAm 94*
Ivey, Stephen David 1953- *WhoAmL 94*
Ivey, William James 1944- *WhoAm 94*
Ivie, Charles C. 1947- *WhoAmL 94*
Ivie, Leslie Todd 1960- *WhoFI 94*
Ivie, Russell Lyn 1953- *WhoWest 94*
Ivins, Marsha S. 1951- *WhoScEn 94*
Ivins, Molly *WhoAm 94*
Ivins, Molly c. 1942- *News 93 [port]*
Ivins, Orville Rush 1950- *WhoWest 94*
Ivins, Perry d1963 *WhoHol 92*
Ivins, William M., Jr. 1881-1961
    WhoAmA 93N
Ivison, David Malcolm 1936- *Who 94*
Ivo, Tommy 1936- *WhoHol 92*
Ivogun, Maria, Marquis d' 1891-1987
    NewGrDO
Ivon, Louis W. 1934- *WhoAmP 93*
Ivory, Brian Gammell 1949- *Who 94*
Ivory, Carolyn Kay 1944- *WhoBlA 94*
Ivory, Ellis Lorenzo 1953- *WhoMW 93*
Ivory, James 1928- *IntMPA 94*
Ivory, James Francis 1928- *IntWW 93,
    Who 94, WhoAm 94*
Ivory, Ming Marie 1949- *WhoAm 94*
Ivory, Peter B. C. B. 1927- *WhoAm 94*
Ivry, Alfred Lyon 1935- *WhoAm 94*
Ivry, Paul Xavier Desire 1829-1903
    NewGrDO
Ivsic, Mathieu Michel 1934- *WhoFI 94*
Ivy, Benjamin Franklin, III 1936-
    WhoFI 94
Ivy, Conway Gayle 1941- *WhoAm 94,
    WhoFI 94, WhoMW 93*
Ivy, Edward Everett 1913- *WhoScEn 94*
Ivy, James E. 1937- *WhoBlA 94*
Ivy, L. H. 1930- *WhoAmP 93*
Iwahashi, Satoshi 1949- *WhoAsA 94*
Iwai, Thomas Yoshio, Jr. 1949-
    WhoWest 94
Iwai, Wilfred Kiyoshi 1941- *WhoAmL 94*
Iwakura, Yoshio 1914- *WhoScEn 94*
Iwamasa, Ken 1943- *WhoAmA 93*
Iwamoto, Masakazu 1948- *WhoScEn 94*
Iwamoto, Ralph Shigeto 1927-
    WhoAmA 93
Iwamoto, Satori 1958- *WhoAsA 94*
Iwan, Dafydd 1943- *IntWW 93*
Iwan, Wilfred Dean 1935- *WhoAm 94*
Iwanaga-Penrose, Margaret *WhoAsA 94*
Iwanski, Myron Leonard 1950-
    WhoScEn 94
Iwao, Sumiko 1935- *ConAu 141*
Iwasaki, Iwao 1929- *WhoAsA 94*
Iwasaki, Junzo *IntWW 93*
Iwasaki, Ronald Seiji 1947- *WhoAsA 94*
Iwasaki, Toshio 1921- *WhoScEn 94*
Iwase, Randall Y. 1947- *WhoAsA 94*
Iwase, Randy 1947- *WhoAmP 93*
Iwashimizu, Yukio 1943- *WhoScEn 94*
Iwashita, Takeki 1931- *WhoScEn 94*
Iwata, Brian A. 1948- *WhoAsA 94*
Iwata, Brian Anthony 1948- *WhoScEn 94*
Iwata, Jan Lei 1959- *WhoAm 94*
Iwata, Jerry T. 1937- *WhoAsA 94*
Iwata, Kazuaki *WhoScEn 94*
Iwata, Kazuo 1910- *WhoScEn 94*
Iwata, Masakazu 1917- *WrDr 94*
Iwata, Paul Yoshio 1951- *WhoAsA 94*
Iwataki, David Michael 1954- *WhoAsA 94*
Iwataki, Miya 1944- *WhoAsA 94*
Iwatani, Yoshinori 1952- *WhoScEn 94*
Iwerks, Ub 1901-1971 *IntDcF 2-4*
Iwicki, Matthew Lawrence 1964-
    WhoAmL 94
Iwinski, James Phillip 1960- *WhoMW 93*
Ix, Robert Edward 1929- *WhoAm 94,
    WhoFI 94*
Iyanaga, Shokichi 1906- *IntWW 93*

Iyengar, Doreswamy Raghavachar 1930-
    WhoAsA 94
Iyengar, Sudharsan Rengaswamy 1961-
    WhoMW 93
Iyer, Ananth. V. 1960- *WhoAsA 94*
Iyer, Easwar S. 1949- *WhoAsA 94*
Iyer, Hariharaiyer Mahadeva 1931-
    WhoAsA 94, WhoWest 94
Iyer, Poorni Ramchandran 1961-
    WhoScEn 94
Iyer, Prem Shankar 1936- *WhoAsA 94*
Iyer, Ram Ramaswamy 1953- *WhoAsA 94*
Iyer, Ravishankar Krishnan 1949-
    WhoAsA 94, WhoMW 93
Iyer, Siddharth Pico 1957- *WhoAsA 94*
Iyoda, Mitsuhiko 1943- *WhoScEn 94*
Izant, Robert James, Jr. 1921- *WhoAm 94*
Izard, John 1923- *WhoAm 94*
Izard, Ralph 1742-1804 *WhAmRev*
Izatt, Jerald Ray 1928- *WhoAm 94*
Izay, Jo Roybal *WhoHisp 94*
Izay, Victor *WhoHol 92*
Izeboud, Pieternella Johanna 1949-
    WhoWomW 91
Izen, Steven Henry 1958- *WhoMW 93*
Izenour, George Charles 1912- *WhoAm 94*
Izenour, Steven 1940- *WhoAm 94*
Izenstark, Joseph Louis 1919- *WhoAm 94*
Izetbegovic, Alija 1925?- *CurBio 93 [port],
    IntWW 93*
Izmailov, Gerasim Alekseyevich fl.
    177-?-179-? *WhWE*
Izmerov, Nikolay Fedotovich 1927-
    IntWW 93
Izquierdo, Ricardo 1955- *WhoHisp 94*
Izquierdo Arija, Maria del Pilar 1935-
    WhoWomW 91
Izquierdo-Mora, Luis A. 1931-
    WhoHisp 94
Izquierdo Rojo, Maria 1946-
    WhoWomW 91
Izquierdo Stella, Jose G. *WhoHisp 94*
Izquierdo-Tejido, Pedro 1926-
    WhoHisp 94
Izrael, Yuri Antonievich 1930- *IntWW 93*
Izu, Masat 1939- *WhoMW 93*
Izuka, Kunio 1939- *WhoAmA 93*
Izumi, Kiyoshi 1921- *WhoAmA 93*
Izumigawa, Wallace Minoru 1953-
    WhoAsA 94
Izvitskaya, Isolda d1971 *WhoHol 92*
Izzo, Lucio 1932- *IntWW 93*
Izzo, Mary Alice 1953- *WhoWest 94*
Izzo, Michael J., Jr. 1944- *WhoAmL 94*
Izzo, Thomas J. 1942- *WhoAmP 93*
Izzo d'Amico, Fiamma 1964- *NewGrDO*

J

Jaar, Alfredo 1956- *WhoAmA 93*
Jaarsma-Buijserd, Ria (Maria) F. 1942- *WhoWomW 91*
Jaatteenmaki, Anneli Tuulikki 1955- *WhoWomW 91*
Jabagi, Habib Daoud 1922- *WhoScEn 94*
Jabara, Francis Dwight 1924- *WhoAm 94*
Jabara, Larry Edward 1953- *WhoMW 93*
Jabara, Michael Dean 1952- *WhoAm 94, WhoWest 94*
Jabara, Paul c. 1948-1992 *AnObit 1992*
Jabavu, Davidson Don Tengo 1885-1959 *BlkWr 2*
Jabavu, Noni 1919- *BlmGWL [port]*
Jabbar, Kareem Abdul *BlkWr 2*
Jabbour, George Moussa 1949- *WhoFI 94*
Jaber, Diana Abu *ConAu 142*
Jaberg, Eugene Carl 1927- *WhoMW 93*
Jabin, Marvin 1929- *WhoFI 94*
Jabine, Thomas B(oyd) 1925- *ConAu 141*
Jablokov, Alexander 1956- *ConAu 142, EncSF 93*
Jablon, Cara Star 1943- *WhoAmL 94*
Jablon, Steven I. 1949- *WhoAmL 94*
Jablons, Beverly *DrAPF 93*
Jablonske, William Joseph 1934- *WhoMW 93*
Jablonski, Henryk 1909- *IntWW 93*
Jablonski, James Arthur 1942- *WhoAmL 94*
Jablonski, Jon Steven 1951- *WhoAmL 94*
Jablonski, Michael Joseph *WhoMW 93*
Jablonski, Wanda Mary d1992 *WhAm 10*
Jablonsky, David 1938- *WrDr 94*
Jablonsky, Harvey Julius 1909-1989 *WhAm 10*
Jablow, Martha M(oraghan) 1944- *ConAu 43NR*
Jablowsky, Albert Isaac 1944- *WhoScEn 94*
Jabra, Jabra Ibrahim 1920- *ConWorW 93*
Jabre, Eddy-Marco 1948- *WhoScEn 94*
Jaccottet, Philippe 1925- *ConWorW 93*
Jacey, Charles Frederick, Jr. 1936- *WhoAm 94, WhoFI 94*
Jache, Albert William 1924- *WhoAm 94, WhoMW 93*
Jachim, Anthony d1978 *WhoHol 92*
Jachino, Carlo 1887-1971 *NewGrDO*
Jachna, Joseph D. 1935- *WhoAm 94*
Jachna, Joseph David 1935- *WhoAmA 93*
Jack, Alieu (Sulayman) 1922- *Who 94*
Jack, Bonnie Lee 1945- *WhoAmP 93*
Jack, Dana Crowley 1945- *ConAu 141*
Jack, David 1924- *Who 94*
Jack, David (Emmanuel) 1918- *Who 94*
Jack, David M. *Who 94*
Jack, Glen Robert 1895- *WhAm 10*
Jack, Hans-Martin 1955- *WhoMW 93*
Jack, Homer A. d1993 *NewYTBS 93*
Jack, Homer A(lexander) 1916-1993 *ConAu 142, CurBio 93N*
Jack, Ian (Robert James) 1923- *WrDr 94*
Jack, Ian Grant 1945- *Who 94*
Jack, Ian Robert James 1923- *Who 94*
Jack, James E. 1941- *WhoAm 94, WhoFI 94*
Jack, Kenneth Henderson 1918- *IntWW 93, Who 94*
Jack, Lynn d1993 *NewYTBS 93*
Jack, Malcolm Roy 1946- *Who 94*
Jack, Michael *Who 94*
Jack, (John) Michael 1946- *Who 94*

Jack, Nancy Rayford 1939- *WhoAm 94*
Jack, Raymond Evan 1942- *Who 94*
Jack, Richard d1952 *WhoAmA 93N*
Jack, Robert Barr 1928- *Who 94*
Jack, Stephen *WhoHol 92*
Jack, Steven Bruce 1960- *WhoScEn 94*
Jack, T. C. d1954 *WhoHol 92*
Jack, William Hugh 1929- *Who 94*
Jack, William Irvine 1935- *WhoWest 94*
Jackall, Robert *WrDr 94*
Jackaman, Michael Clifford John *IntWW 93*
Jackaman, Michael Clifford John 1935- *Who 94*
Jackard, Jerald Wayne *WhoAmA 93*
Jackee *WhoBlA 94*
Jackel, Lawrence *WhoAm 94*
Jackel, Richard 1926- *WhoHol 92*
Jackel, Simon Samuel 1917- *WhoFI 94*
Jackendoff, Nathaniel 1919- *WhoAm 94*
Jackendoff, Ray Saul 1945- *WhoAm 94*
Jacker, Corinne 1933- *WrDr 94*
Jacker, Corinne Litvin 1933- *WhoAm 94*
Jacket, Barbara Jean 1935- *WhoBlA 94*
Jackie, Bill d1954 *WhoHol 92*
Jackiw, Roman 1939- *WhoAm 94*
Jackle, Karen Dee 1945- *WhoFI 94*
Jackley, Nat d1988 *WhoHol 92*
Jacklich, Joel 1948- *WhoWest 94*
Jacklin, Anthony 1944- *Who 94*
Jacklin, Pamela Leslie 1945- *WhoAm 94, WhoAmL 94*
Jacklin, Tony 1944- *IntWW 93*
Jacklin, William 1943- *Who 94*
Jacklin, William Thomas 1940- *WhoMW 93*
Jackling, Roger Tustin 1943- *Who 94*
Jackman, Adrian Frederick 1954- *WhoFI 94*
Jackman, Henry Newton Rowell 1932- *WhoAm 94*
Jackman, Jay Myron 1939- *WhoWest 94*
Jackman, Lawrence Ervin 1941- *WhoMW 93*
Jackman, Lloyd Miles 1926- *WhoAm 94*
Jackman, Michele 1942- *WhoWest 94*
Jackman, Robert Alan 1939- *WhoAm 94*
Jackman, Stuart (Brooke) 1922- *WrDr 94*
Jackman, Sydney Wayne 1925- *WrDr 94*
Jacko 1959- *WhoHol 92*
Jacko, George G. 1959- *WhoAmP 93*
Jackobs, Joseph Alden 1917- *WhoMW 93*
Jackobs, Miriam Ann 1940- *WhoAm 94*
Jackont, Amnon 1948- *WrDr 94*
Jackovich, Victor *WhoAm 94, WhoAmP 93*
Jackowiak, Patricia 1959- *WhoAmL 94*
Jacks, Brian Paul 1943- *WhoWest 94*
Jacks, Hector Beaumont 1903- *Who 94*
Jacks, Jean-Pierre Georges Yves 1948- *WhoScEn 94*
Jacks, L. P. 1860-1955 *DcLB 135 [port]*
Jacks, Oliver 1920- *WrDr 94*
Jacks, Richard Nelson 1938- *WhoWest 94*
Jacks, Thomas Richard 1946- *WhoFI 94*
Jacks, Ulysses 1937- *WhoBlA 94*
Jackson, A. B. 1925-1981 *WhoAmA 93N*
Jackson, Acy Lee 1937- *WhoBlA 94*
Jackson, Ada Jean Work 1935- *WhoBlA 94*
Jackson, Agnes Moreland 1930- *WhoBlA 94*
Jackson, Alan *WhoAm 94*

Jackson, Alan Robert 1936- *Who 94*
Jackson, Alan William 1950- *WhoFI 94*
Jackson, Albert Leslie Samuel 1918- *Who 94*
Jackson, Albert Smith 1927- *WhoWest 94*
Jackson, Albert Stanton, Jr. 1949- *WhoAmP 93*
Jackson, Alexander Cosby Fishburn 1903- *Who 94*
Jackson, Alexander Young 1882-1974 *WhoAmA 93N*
Jackson, Alfred Thomas 1937- *WhoBlA 94*
Jackson, Allen Keith 1932- *WhoAm 94*
Jackson, Alphonse, Jr. 1927- *WhoAmP 93, WhoBlA 94*
Jackson, Alterman 1948- *WhoBlA 94*
Jackson, Alvin B., Jr. 1961- *WhoBlA 94*
Jackson, Andrew 1767-1845 *HisWorL [port], WhAmRev*
Jackson, Andrew 1945- *WhoBlA 94*
Jackson, Andrew Dudley 1943- *WhoAmL 94*
Jackson, Andrew Preston 1947- *WhoBlA 94*
Jackson, Ann d1956 *WhoAmA 93N*
Jackson, Anna Mae 1934- *WhoBlA 94*
Jackson, Anne *WhoAm 94*
Jackson, Anne 1926- *IntMPA 94, WhoHol 92*
Jackson, Anne R. 1937- *WhoAm 94*
Jackson, Annie Hurlburt 1877- *WhoAmA 93N*
Jackson, Anthony 1926- *WrDr 94*
Jackson, Art Eugene, Sr. 1941- *WhoBlA 94*
Jackson, Arthur D., Jr. 1942- *WhoBlA 94*
Jackson, Arthur James 1943- *WhoBlA 94*
Jackson, Arthur Roszell 1949- *WhoBlA 94*
Jackson, Aubrey N. 1926- *WhoBlA 94*
Jackson, Audrey Nabors 1926- *WhoBlA 94*
Jackson, Ava Nicola 1957- *WhoBlA 94*
Jackson, Barry 1938- *WhoHol 92*
Jackson, Barry Trevor 1936- *Who 94*
Jackson, Barry Wendell 1930- *WhoAmP 93*
Jackson, Basil 1920?- *EncSF 93*
Jackson, Belford Darrell 1938- *WhoMW 93*
Jackson, Belle 1935- *WrDr 94*
Jackson, Benita Marie 1956- *WhoBlA 94*
Jackson, Bennie, Jr. 1947- *WhoScEn 94*
Jackson, Bernard H. *WhoBlA 94*
Jackson, Betty 1947- *Who 94*
Jackson, Betty 1949- *IntWW 93*
Jackson, Betty Eileen 1925- *WhoWest 94*
Jackson, Betty Jane 1925- *WhoAmP 93*
Jackson, Betty L. Deason 1927- *WhoFI 94, WhoMW 93*
Jackson, Beverley Joy Jacobson 1928- *WhoWest 94*
Jackson, Beverly Anne 1947- *WhoBlA 94*
Jackson, Beverly Joyce 1955- *WhoBlA 94*
Jackson, Bill D. 1937- *WhoAm 94, WhoMW 93*
Jackson, Billy Morrow 1926- *WhoAm 94, WhoAmA 93*
Jackson, Blyden 1910- *WhoAm 94, WhoBlA 94*
Jackson, Bo *ConAu 141*
Jackson, Bo 1962- *WhoAm 94, WhoMW 93, WhoWest 94*

Jackson, Bo (Vincent Edward) 1962- *WhoBlA 94*
Jackson, Bobby L. 1945- *WhoBlA 94*
Jackson, Bobby Rand 1931- *WhoAm 94*
Jackson, Bradley A. 1949- *WhoAmL 94*
Jackson, Brandon Donald 1934- *Who 94*
Jackson, Brenda Susan 1950- *WhoMW 93*
Jackson, Brendan (James) 1935- *Who 94*
Jackson, Brian 1931- *IntMPA 94*
Jackson, Bruce Leslie *WhoAm 94*
Jackson, Burnett Lamar, Jr. 1928- *WhoBlA 94*
Jackson, C. Bernard 1927- *WhoBlA 94*
Jackson, C. D. 1902-1964 *HisDcKW*
Jackson, Carl Robert 1928- *WhoAm 94, WhoMW 93, WhoScEn 94*
Jackson, Carmault Benjamin, Jr. 1924- *WhoAm 94*
Jackson, Carol E. *WhoAmL 94, WhoMW 93*
Jackson, Caroline Frances 1946- *Who 94, WhoWomW 91*
Jackson, Carolyn Prewitt 1955- *WhoMW 93*
Jackson, Catherine Galloway 1945- *WhoMW 93*
Jackson, Celia S. 1958- *WhoHisp 94*
Jackson, Charles Clark 1952- *WhoAm 94, WhoAmL 94*
Jackson, Charles E. 1944- *WhoBlA 94*
Jackson, Charles E., Sr. 1938- *WhoBlA 94*
Jackson, Charles Edward 1943- *WhoAmP 93*
Jackson, Charles Ellis 1930- *WhoBlA 94*
Jackson, Charles Ian 1935- *WhoAm 94*
Jackson, Charles N., II 1931- *WhoBlA 94*
Jackson, Charles Richard, Jr. 1929- *WhoBlA 94*
Jackson, Charles Thomas *WorScD*
Jackson, Charles Wayne 1930- *WhoFI 94*
Jackson, Chris 1968- *BasBi*
Jackson, Chris Wayne 1969- *WhoBlA 94*
Jackson, Christopher Murray 1935- *Who 94*
Jackson, Clarence H. 1924- *WhoBlA 94*
Jackson, Claude 1942- *WhoBlA 94*
Jackson, Clinton 1954- *WhoBlA 94*
Jackson, Clyde O(wen) 1928- *WrDr 94*
Jackson, Clyde Wilson 1936- *WhoAmP 93*
Jackson, Coleman Lewis 1950- *WhoAmL 94*
Jackson, Colette d1969 *WhoHol 92*
Jackson, Cora May 1928- *WhoAmP 93*
Jackson, Cornelia Pinkney *WhoBlA 94*
Jackson, Curtis M. 1938- *WhoBlA 94*
Jackson, Curtis Maitland 1933- *WhoAm 94, WhoMW 93, WhoScEn 94*
Jackson, Cynthia L. 1954- *WhoAmL 94*
Jackson, D. Michael 1949- *WhoScEn 94*
Jackson, Dale d1961 *WhoHol 92*
Jackson, Dale Edward 1950- *WhoAm 94*
Jackson, Dan *WhoHol 92*
Jackson, Daniel 1954- *WrDr 94*
Jackson, Daniel David 1959- *WhoFI 94*
Jackson, Daniel Francis 1925- *WhoAm 94*
Jackson, Daniel Wyer 1929- *WhoFI 94*
Jackson, Daphne Diana 1933- *Who 94*
Jackson, Darnell 1955- *WhoBlA 94*
Jackson, Darrell *WhoAmP 93*
Jackson, Darrell Duane 1965- *WhoBlA 94*
Jackson, Darren Richard 1964- *WhoMW 93*
Jackson, Darrin Jay 1963- *WhoBlA 94*

Jackson, Daryl Sanders 1937- *IntWW 93*
Jackson, David 1747-1801 *WhAmRev*
Jackson, David 1946- *WhoAm 94*
Jackson, David A. 1924- *WhoAm 94, WhoMW 93*
Jackson, David Cooper 1931- *Who 94, WrDr 94*
Jackson, David E. d1837 *WhWE*
Jackson, David Gordon 1936- *WhoMW 93*
Jackson, David Lee 1946- *WhoMW 93*
Jackson, David Munro 1925- *WhoAm 94*
Jackson, David Pingree 1931- *WhoAm 94*
Jackson, David Robert 1945- *WhoWest 94*
Jackson, David Samuel 1940- *WhoBlA 94*
Jackson, Dempster McKee 1930- *WhoAm 94*
Jackson, Denise 1953- *WhoBlA 94*
Jackson, Dennis Lee 1937- *WhoBlA 94*
Jackson, Dennis R. 1946- *WhoMW 93*
Jackson, Derrick Zane 1955- *WhoBlA 94*
Jackson, Desreta *WhoHol 92*
Jackson, Devon d1984 *WhoHol 92*
Jackson, Dillon Edward 1945- *WhoAmL 94*
Jackson, Don Merrill 1913- *WhoAm 94, WhoAmL 94*
Jackson, Donald Ernest 1947- *WhoMW 93*
Jackson, Donald J. 1943- *WhoBlA 94*
Jackson, Donald Kenneth 1944- *WhoAm 94, WhoFI 94*
Jackson, Donald Richard 1938- *WhoFI 94*
Jackson, Dorothea E. *WhoBlA 94*
Jackson, Dorothy R. *WhoBlA 94*
Jackson, Douglas Stanley 1954- *WhoAmP 93*
Jackson, Douglas Webster 1949- *WhoScEn 94*
Jackson, Duane 1942- *WhoWest 94*
Jackson, Durward Pressley 1940- *WhoWest 94*
Jackson, E. F. 1919- *WrDr 94*
Jackson, Earl, Jr. 1938- *WhoBlA 94, WhoScEn 94*
Jackson, Earl C. 1933- *WhoBlA 94*
Jackson, Earl J. 1943- *WhoBlA 94*
Jackson, Earl K., Sr. 1938-1982 *WhoBlA 94N*
Jackson, Earline 1943- *WhoBlA 94*
Jackson, Eddie d1980 *WhoHol 92*
Jackson, Edgar Newton, Jr. 1959- *WhoBlA 94*
Jackson, Edward *Who 94*
Jackson, (John) Edward 1925- *Who 94*
Jackson, Edward Gardner 1942- *WhoAmP 93*
Jackson, Edward R. 1942- *WhoBlA 94*
Jackson, Edward W. 1915-1992 *WhoBlA 94N*
Jackson, Edwin L. 1930- *WhoScEn 94*
Jackson, Edwin Sydney 1922- *IntWW 93*
Jackson, Elaine *ConAu 43NR*
Jackson, Elaine 1929- *WrDr 94*
Jackson, Elijah 1947- *WhoBlA 94*
Jackson, Elizabeth d1972 *WhoHol 92*
Jackson, Ellen B. 1943- *SmATA 75 [port]*
Jackson, Ellen Swepson 1935- *WhoBlA 94*
Jackson, Elmer Carter, Jr. 1912- *WhoBlA 94*
Jackson, Elmer Joseph 1920- *WhoAm 94*
Jackson, Elmer Martin, Jr. 1906- *WhoAm 94*
Jackson, Emil A. 1911- *WhoBlA 94*
Jackson, Emory Napoleon 1937- *WhoBlA 94*
Jackson, Eric Scott 1964- *WhoBlA 94*
Jackson, Ernestine *WhoHol 92*
Jackson, Esther Cooper 1917- *WhoBlA 94*
Jackson, Ethel d1952 *WhoHol 92*
Jackson, Eugene 1916- *WhoHol 92*
Jackson, Eugene Bernard 1915- *WhoAm 94*
Jackson, Eugene D. 1943- *AfrAmAl 6, WhoBlA 94*
Jackson, Eugene L. 1939- *WhoBlA 94*
Jackson, Everatt 1942- *WrDr 94*
Jackson, Everett Gee 1900- *WhoAm 94, WhoAmA 93*
Jackson, Felix W. 1920- *WhoBlA 94*
Jackson, Fields Lee, Jr. 1957- *WhoMW 93*
Jackson, Fleda Brown *DrAPF 93*
Jackson, Francis Alan 1917- *IntWW 93, Who 94*
Jackson, Francis Charles 1917- *WhoAm 94*
Jackson, Francis Joseph 1932- *WhoAm 94*
Jackson, Frank Cameron 1943- *IntWW 93*
Jackson, Frank Donald 1951- *WhoBlA 94*
Jackson, Frank Thomas 1934- *WhoWest 94*
Jackson, Franklin D. B. 1934- *WhoBlA 94*
Jackson, Fred 1952- *WhoFI 94, WhoScEn 94*
Jackson, Fred H., Jr. 1933- *WhoBlA 94*
Jackson, Freda d1990 *WhoHol 92*
Jackson, Freddie 1958- *WhoBlA 94*
Jackson, Frederick 1928- *WhoBlA 94*
Jackson, Frederick George 1860-1938 *WhWE*
Jackson, Frederick Herbert 1919- *WhoAm 94*
Jackson, Frederick Hume 1918- *Who 94*
Jackson, Frederick Leon 1934- *WhoBlA 94*
Jackson, G. Mark 1952- *WrDr 94*
Jackson, Gabriel 1921- *WhoAm 94*
Jackson, Gail P. 1960- *WhoBlA 94*
Jackson, Gale P. *DrAPF 93*
Jackson, Gary E. 1951- *WhoAmP 93*
Jackson, Gary Monroe 1945- *WhoBlA 94*
Jackson, Gayle Pendleton White 1946- *WhoMW 93*
Jackson, George K. 1919- *WhoBlA 94*
Jackson, George Lyman 1923- *WhoAm 94*
Jackson, George W. 1924- *WhoAmP 93*
Jackson, George Winfield 1937- *WhoAmP 93*
Jackson, Georgina 1957- *WhoBlA 94*
Jackson, Gerald Breck 1916- *Who 94*
Jackson, Gerald E. 1949- *WhoBlA 94*
Jackson, Gerald Milton 1943- *WhoBlA 94*
Jackson, Geraldine 1934- *WhoFI 94*
Jackson, Giles B. 1924- *WhoBlA 94*
Jackson, Gina Marie 1959- *WhoFI 94*
Jackson, Glenda 1936- *IntMPA 94, IntWW 93, Who 94, WhoAm 94, WhoHol 92*
Jackson, Glenn T. 1960- *WhoIns 94*
Jackson, Gloria June 1940- *WhoAmP 93*
Jackson, Gordon d1990 *WhoHol 92*
Jackson, Gordon Alexander 1913- *WhoFI 94*
Jackson, Gordon Noel 1913- *Who 94, WrDr 94*
Jackson, Governor Eugene, Jr. 1951- *WhoBlA 94*
Jackson, Grandvel Andrew 1910- *WhoBlA 94*
Jackson, Grant Dwight 1942- *WhoBlA 94*
Jackson, Gregory Wayne 1950- *WhoMW 93*
Jackson, Guida *DrAPF 93*
Jackson, H. Clark 1944- *WhoIns 94*
Jackson, Hal 1915- *NewYTBS 93 [port], WhoBlA 94*
Jackson, Hall 1739-1797 *WhAmRev*
Jackson, Harold 1953- *WhoAm 94*
Jackson, Harold Baron, Jr. 1939- *WhoBlA 94*
Jackson, Harold Jerome 1953- *WhoBlA 94*
Jackson, Harold Leonard, Jr. 1955- *WhoBlA 94*
Jackson, Harry d1973 *WhoHol 92*
Jackson, Harry Andrew 1924- *WhoAm 94, WhoAmA 93, WhoWest 94*
Jackson, Haywood *DrAPF 93*
Jackson, Hazel Brill d1991 *WhAm 10, WhoAmA 93N*
Jackson, Helen Hunt 1830-1885 *HisWorL [port]*
Jackson, Helen Margaret 1939- *Who 94*
Jackson, Helen Maria Fiske Hunt 1830-1885 *AmSocL [port]*
Jackson, Helen Maria Hunt 1830-1885 *BlmGWL*
Jackson, Henry 1747-1809 *WhAmRev*
Jackson, Henry fl. 19th cent.- *EncNAR*
Jackson, Henry Alden d1952 *WhoAmA 93N*
Jackson, Henry Ralph 1915- *WhoBlA 94*
Jackson, Herb 1945- *WhoAm 94, WhoAmA 93*
Jackson, Hermoine Prestine 1945- *WhoAm 94, WhoBlA 94*
Jackson, Holly A. 1965- *WhoMW 93*
Jackson, Horace 1935- *WhoBlA 94*
Jackson, Horace Franklin 1934- *WhoFI 94*
Jackson, Humphrey 1717-1801 *DcNaB MP*
Jackson, Ian (Macgilchrist) 1914- *Who 94*
Jackson, Inigo *WhoHol 92*
Jackson, Innes *ConAu 142*
Jackson, Ira L. 1930- *WhoAmP 93*
Jackson, Isaiah 1945- *WhoAm 94, WhoMW 93*
Jackson, Isaiah Allen 1945- *WhoBlA 94*
Jackson, J. David 1949- *WhoAm 94, WhoAmL 94*
Jackson, J. Elvin 1938- *WhoAmP 93*
Jackson, J. Scott 1953- *WhoAmL 94*
Jackson, Jack C. *WhoAmP 93*
Jackson, Jacquelyne Johnson 1932- *WhoBlA 94*
Jackson, James 1757-1806 *AmRev, WhAmRev [port]*
Jackson, James Arthur 1970- *WhoBlA 94*
Jackson, James Conroy 1913- *WhoBlA 94*
Jackson, James F. 1939- *WhoAm 94*
Jackson, James Fraser 1919- *WhoMW 93*
Jackson, James Garfield 1933- *WhoBlA 94*
Jackson, James H. 1939- *WhoBlA 94*
Jackson, James Holmen 1949- *WhoBlA 94*
Jackson, James Jeffrey 1958- *WhoAmL 94*
Jackson, James Larry 1940- *WhoAm 94*
Jackson, James M. 1943- *WhoIns 94*
Jackson, James Oswald 1940- *WhoWest 94*
Jackson, James Sidney 1944- *WhoAm 94, WhoBlA 94*
Jackson, James Talmadge 1921- *WhoBlA 94*
Jackson, Jane Therese 1955- *Who 94*
Jackson, Jane W. 1944- *WhoWest 94*
Jackson, Janet 1966- *AfrAmAl 6, ConBlB 6 [port], WhoBlA 94*
Jackson, Janet Damita 1966- *WhoAm 94*
Jackson, Janet E. *WhoBlA 94*
Jackson, Janet Hosea 1933- *WhoMW 93*
Jackson, Jeanette Bucklin 1946- *WhoAmP 93*
Jackson, Jeffrey Chryst 1961- *WhoWest 94*
Jackson, Jenie d1976 *WhoHol 92*
Jackson, Jermaine 1954- *WhoHol 92*
Jackson, Jermaine Lajuane 1954- *WhoBlA 94*
Jackson, Jerry Donald 1944- *WhoFI 94*
Jackson, Jerry Dwayne 1941- *WhoAmP 93*
Jackson, Jesse 1941- *AfrAmAl 6*
Jackson, Jesse L., Jr. *WhoBlA 94*
Jackson, Jesse Louis 1941- *AmSocL, IntWW 93, WhoAm 94, WhoAmP 93, WhoBlA 94*
Jackson, Jewel 1942- *WhoWest 94*
Jackson, Jim d1937 *WhoHol 92*
Jackson, Jimmy Joe 1947- *WhoFI 94*
Jackson, Jimmy Lynn 1957- *WhoScEn 94*
Jackson, Joe *WhoAm 94*
Jackson, Joe d1942 *WhoHol 92*
Jackson, Joe, Jr. d1991 *WhoHol 92*
Jackson, John 1948- *WhoBlA 94*
Jackson, John Berrye 1919- *WhoBlA 94*
Jackson, John Brinckerhoff 1909- *WhoWest 94*
Jackson, John Charles 1939- *WhoMW 93*
Jackson, John David 1925- *WhoAm 94*
Jackson, John Earnest 1941- *WhoFI 94*
Jackson, John Edgar 1942- *WhoAm 94*
Jackson, John Edwin 1875- *WhoAmA 93N*
Jackson, John Ellett 1892-1989 *WhAm 10*
Jackson, John H. 1912- *WhoBlA 94*
Jackson, John H. 1943- *WhoBlA 94*
Jackson, John Henry 1916- *IntMPA 94*
Jackson, John Henry 1948- *Who 94*
Jackson, John Hollis, Jr. 1941- *WhoAmL 94*
Jackson, John Howard 1932- *WhoAm 94*
Jackson, John N. 1925- *WrDr 94*
Jackson, John Tillson 1921- *WhoAm 94*
Jackson, John Victor, II 1947- *WhoAmL 94*
Jackson, John Wingfield 1905- *WhoAmL 94*
Jackson, John Wyant 1944- *WhoAm 94*
Jackson, Johnny, Jr. *WhoAmP 93*
Jackson, Johnny, Jr. 1943- *WhoBlA 94*
Jackson, Jonathan 1743-1810 *WhAmRev*
Jackson, Joni Bradley 1932- *WhoAmP 93*
Jackson, Joseph Brian 1946- *WhoWest 94*
Jackson, Joseph Charles 1954- *WhoMW 93*
Jackson, Joseph Devonsher 1783-1857 *DcNaB MP*
Jackson, Joseph H. 1904-1990 *AfrAmAl 6 [port]*
Jackson, Joseph T. 1916- *WhoBlA 94*
Jackson, Julia Carolyn 1934- *WhoAmP 93*
Jackson, Julian Ellis 1913- *WhoAm 94*
Jackson, Julius Hamilton 1944- *WhoBlA 94*
Jackson, Karen Denice 1947- *WhoBlA 94*
Jackson, Karl Dion 1942- *WhoAm 94*
Jackson, Karl Don 1947- *WhoBlA 94*
Jackson, Kate 1948- *WhoHol 92*
Jackson, Kate 1949- *IntMPA 94*
Jackson, Keith Hunter 1953- *WhoBlA 94*
Jackson, Keith Jerome 1965- *WhoAm 94, WhoBlA 94*
Jackson, Keith M. 1948- *WhoBlA 94*
Jackson, Keith MacKenzie 1928- *WhoAm 94*
Jackson, Kendall *WhoHol 92*
Jackson, Kennell A., Jr. 1942- *WhoBlA 94*
Jackson, Kenneth Arthur 1930- *WhoAm 94, WhoScEn 94*
Jackson, Kenneth T(erry) 1939- *WrDr 94*
Jackson, Kenneth Terry 1939- *WhoAm 94*
Jackson, Kenneth William 1924- *WhoBlA 94*
Jackson, Kenny 1962- *WhoBlA 94*
Jackson, Kevin *WhoBlA 94*
Jackson, Kingsbury Temple 1917- *WhoAm 94*
Jackson, Kristine Claire 1956- *WhoWest 94*
Jackson, Laban Phelps 1914- *WhoAmP 93*
Jackson, Laird Gray 1930- *WhoAm 94*
Jackson, Larron Deonne 1949- *WhoBlA 94*
Jackson, Larry Artope 1925- *WhoAm 94*
Jackson, Larry Eugene 1943- *WhoBlA 94*
Jackson, Larry R. 1941- *WhoAm 94*
Jackson, LaToya 1956- *WhoBlA 94*
Jackson, Laura 1901-1991 *WhAm 10, WrDr 94N*
Jackson, Laurence Dean 1955- *WhoAm 94, WhoAmL 94*
Jackson, Lawrence 1926- *Who 94*
Jackson, Lawrence (Walter) 1913- *Who 94*
Jackson, Lee *WhoAm 94*
Jackson, Lee 1909- *WhoAmA 93*
Jackson, Lee Arthur 1950- *WhoBlA 94*
Jackson, Lee F. 1950- *WhoAmP 93*
Jackson, Lee Franklin 1950- *WhoAmL 94*
Jackson, Lenwood A. 1944- *WhoBlA 94*
Jackson, Leo A. 1920- *WhoBlA 94*
Jackson, Leo Edwin 1925- *WhoBlA 94*
Jackson, Leonard *WhoHol 92*
Jackson, Leroy Anthony, Jr. 1935- *WhoBlA 94*
Jackson, LeRoy Eugene 1933- *WhoAm 94*
Jackson, Lesley 1866-1958 *WhoAmA 93N*
Jackson, Leslie Elaine 1949- *WhoBlA 94*
Jackson, Lewis Albert 1912- *WhoAm 94*
Jackson, Lillian *WhoBlA 94*
Jackson, Lillian Ann 1956- *WhoAmL 94*
Jackson, Lloyd G., II 1952- *WhoAmP 93*
Jackson, Loretta Y. Blunt 1935- *WhoAmP 93*
Jackson, Lucious 1941- *BasBi*
Jackson, Luke 1919- *WhoBlA 94*
Jackson, Lurline Bradley 1937- *WhoBlA 94*
Jackson, Luther Porter, Jr. 1925- *WhoBlA 94*
Jackson, Lyman Hood 1961- *WhoFI 94*
Jackson, Lynda Kay 1949- *WhoFI 94*
Jackson, Lynn Robertson 1947- *WhoAmL 94*
Jackson, M. Dorothy 1945- *WhoMW 93*
Jackson, M. Kate 1938- *WhoAmP 93*
Jackson, Mabel I. 1907- *WhoBlA 94*
Jackson, Mae *DrAPF 93*
Jackson, Mahalia d1972 *WhoHol 92*
Jackson, Mahalia 1911-1972 *AmCulL, ConBlB 5 [port]*
Jackson, Mahalia 1912-1972 *AfrAmAl 6 [port]*
Jackson, Margaret Myfanwy Wood *Who 94*
Jackson, Maria Pilar 1949- *WhoHisp 94*
Jackson, Marian J. A. *ConAu 140*
Jackson, Marian Ruck 1922- *WhoAmP 93*
Jackson, Marion Elizabeth 1941- *WhoAmA 93*
Jackson, Marion Leroy 1914- *WhoAm 94, WhoMW 93*
Jackson, Mark 1965- *BasBi*
Jackson, Mark A. 1965- *WhoBlA 94*
Jackson, Martha d1969 *WhoAmA 93N*
Jackson, Marvin Alexander 1927- *WhoBlA 94*
Jackson, Mary 1909- *WhoHol 92*
Jackson, Mary 1910- *WhoAm 94*
Jackson, Mary 1932- *WhoBlA 94*
Jackson, Mary Ann 1923- *WhoHol 92*
Jackson, Mattie J. 1921- *WhoBlA 94*
Jackson, Mattie Lee 1924- *WhoBlA 94*
Jackson, Mattie Mashaw *WhoAm 94*
Jackson, Maxie C. 1939- *WhoBlA 94*
Jackson, Maynard 1938- *AfrAmAl 6, WhoAm 94*
Jackson, Maynard Holbrook 1938- *WhoAmP 93, WhoBlA 94*
Jackson, Melbourne Leslie 1915- *WhoAm 94*
Jackson, Melodee Sue 1947- *WhoAmP 93*
Jackson, Michael 1734-1801 *WhAmRev*
Jackson, Michael 1958- *AfrAmAl 6 [port], IntMPA 94, Who 94, WhoBlA 94, WhoHol 92*
Jackson, Michael (Derek) 1940- *WrDr 94*
Jackson, Michael (Roland) 1919- *Who 94*
Jackson, Michael David 1944- *Who 94*
Jackson, Michael John 1938- *WhoAm 94*
Jackson, Michael Joseph 1958- *IntWW 93, WhoAm 94*
Jackson, Michel Tah-Tung 1961- *WhoScEn 94*
Jackson, Mick *IntMPA 94*
Jackson, Mike d1945 *WhoHol 92*
Jackson, Mike 1953- *WhoAmP 93*
Jackson, Miles Merrill 1929- *WhoAm 94, WhoWest 94*
Jackson, Milton 1923- *WhoAm 94, WhoBlA 94*
Jackson, Milton Reed 1942- *WhoAmP 93*
Jackson, Muriel W. *Who 94*
Jackson, (Audrey) Muriel W. *Who 94*

Jackson, Murray Earl 1926- *WhoAmP 93, WhoBlA 94*
Jackson, Nathaniel G. 1942- *WhoBlA 94*
Jackson, Neal A. 1943- *WhoAm 94, WhoAmL 94*
Jackson, Neville 1923- *WrDr 94*
Jackson, Nicholas (Fane St. George) 1934- *Who 94*
Jackson, Norlishia A. 1942- *WhoBlA 94*
Jackson, Norman A. 1932- *WhoBlA 94*
Jackson, Ocie 1904- *WhoBlA 94*
Jackson, Oliver James V. *Who 94*
Jackson, Oliver Lee 1935- *WhoAmA 93*
Jackson, Oscar Jerome 1929- *WhoBlA 94*
Jackson, Pamela J. 1967- *WhoBlA 94*
Jackson, Patrick *Who 94*
Jackson, (John) Patrick 1940- *Who 94*
Jackson, (Walter) Patrick 1929- *Who 94*
Jackson, Patrick John 1932- *WhoAm 94*
Jackson, Paul *Who 94*
Jackson, (Kevin) Paul 1947- *IntWW 93, Who 94*
Jackson, Paul L. 1907- *WhoBlA 94*
Jackson, Paulina Ruth 1932- *WhoAmP 93*
Jackson, Pazel 1932- *WhoBlA 94*
Jackson, Peaches *WhoHol 92*
Jackson, Peter (Michael) 1928- *Who 94*
Jackson, Peter (William Russell) 1926- *WrDr 94*
Jackson, Peter Edward 1962- *WhoScEn 94*
Jackson, Peter John 1947- *IntWW 93*
Jackson, Peter John Edward 1944- *Who 94*
Jackson, Peter Vorious, III 1927- *WhoAm 94, WhoWest 94*
Jackson, Philip C. *WhoAmP 93*
Jackson, Philip Chilton, Jr. 1949- *WhoMW 93*
Jackson, Philip Douglas 1945- *WhoAm 94, WhoMW 93*
Jackson, Phillip 1953- *WhoAmL 94*
Jackson, Phillip Ellis 1952- *WhoAm 94*
Jackson, Price Arthur, Jr. 1952- *WhoAmP 93*
Jackson, Prince Albert, Jr. 1925- *WhoBlA 94*
Jackson, R. Graham 1913- *WhoAm 94*
Jackson, Ralph Ward 1806-1880 *DcNaB MP*
Jackson, Randall Calvin, Jr. 1957- *WhoAmL 94*
Jackson, Randall W. 1954- *WhoFI 94*
Jackson, Randolph 1943- *WhoBlA 94*
Jackson, Rashleigh Esmond 1929- *IntWW 93*
Jackson, Ray d1989 *WhoHol 92*
Jackson, Raymond Allen 1927- *Who 94*
Jackson, Raymond Carl 1928- *WhoAm 94, WhoScEn 94*
Jackson, Raymond Sidney, Jr. 1938- *WhoAm 94, WhoAmL 94*
Jackson, Raymond T. 1933- *WhoBlA 94*
Jackson, Raynard 1960- *WhoBlA 94*
Jackson, Rebecca R. 1942- *WhoAm 94, WhoAmL 94*
Jackson, Reggie 1946- *AfrAmAl 6 [port]*
Jackson, Reggie Martinez 1946- *WhoBlA 94*
Jackson, Reginald Leo 1945- *WhoBlA 94*
Jackson, Reginald Martinez 1946- *WhoAm 94*
Jackson, Reginald Sherman, Jr. 1946- *WhoAmL 94, WhoMW 93*
Jackson, Reginald W. 1955- *WhoAmL 94*
Jackson, Renard I. 1946- *WhoBlA 94*
Jackson, Richard *DrAPF 93*
Jackson, Richard d1787 *WhAmRev*
Jackson, Richard Brinkley 1929- *WhoFI 94*
Jackson, Richard Brooke 1947- *WhoAm 94, WhoAmL 94*
Jackson, Richard Delyn 1937- *WhoFI 94*
Jackson, Richard E., Jr. 1945- *WhoBlA 94*
Jackson, Richard Edward 1950- *WhoAmP 93*
Jackson, Richard George 1940- *WhoAm 94*
Jackson, Richard H. 1933- *WhoBlA 94*
Jackson, Richard H. 1941- *WhoWest 94*
Jackson, Richard Michael 1940- *Who 94*
Jackson, Richard Montgomery 1920- *WhoAm 94*
Jackson, Rickey Anderson 1958- *WhoBlA 94*
Jackson, Robert 1750-1827 *WhAmRev*
Jackson, Robert 1910- *Who 94*
Jackson, Robert, Jr. 1936- *WhoBlA 94*
Jackson, Robert Andrew 1959- *WhoBlA 94*
Jackson, Robert Bennett 1941- *WhoMW 93*
Jackson, Robert Benton, IV 1965- *WhoScEn 94*
Jackson, Robert D. 1943- *WhoWest 94*
Jackson, Robert E. 1937- *WhoBlA 94*
Jackson, Robert Henry 1922-1990 *WhAm 10*
Jackson, Robert J 1936- *WrDr 94*
Jackson, Robert John 1922- *WhoFI 94*
Jackson, Robert Keith 1943- *WhoFI 94*
Jackson, Robert L. 1962- *WhoFI 94*
Jackson, Robert Lee 1963- *WhoFI 94*
Jackson, Robert Lee, II 1942- *WhoAm 94*
Jackson, Robert Loring 1926- *WhoMW 93, WhoScEn 94*
Jackson, Robert R. 1945- *WhoAmL 94*
Jackson, Robert Toussaint, Jr. 1948- *WhoAmL 94*
Jackson, Robert Victor 1946- *Who 94*
Jackson, Robert W. 1936- *WhoIns 94*
Jackson, Robert Walter 1943- *WhoAmP 93*
Jackson, Robert William 1930- *WhoAm 94, WhoFI 94*
Jackson, Rodney *Who 94*
Jackson, (Michael) Rodney 1935- *Who 94*
Jackson, Ronald G. 1952- *WhoBlA 94*
Jackson, Ronald J. *WhoAm 94, WhoFI 94*
Jackson, Ronald Lee 1943- *WhoBlA 94*
Jackson, Rose Valdez 1953- *WhoHisp 94*
Jackson, Rosemary Elizabeth 1917- *WrDr 94*
Jackson, Roswell F. 1922- *WhoBlA 94*
Jackson, Roy Arthur 1928- *Who 94*
Jackson, Roy Gene 1939- *WhoMW 93*
Jackson, Roy Joseph, Jr. 1944- *WhoBlA 94*
Jackson, Roy Lee 1954- *WhoBlA 94*
Jackson, Rudolph Ellsworth 1935- *WhoAm 94, WhoBlA 94*
Jackson, Rupert Matthew 1948- *Who 94*
Jackson, Russell A. 1934- *WhoBlA 94*
Jackson, Rusty 1953- *WhoBlA 94*
Jackson, Ruth 1902- *WhoAm 94*
Jackson, Ruth Amelia *WhoAmA 93*
Jackson, Ruth Farrier 1923- *WhoAmP 93*
Jackson, Ruth Moore 1938- *WhoAm 94, WhoBlA 94*
Jackson, Sally Marie 1932- *WhoAmP 93*
Jackson, Sammy *WhoHol 92*
Jackson, Sampson, II *WhoAmP 93*
Jackson, Samuel L. 1949- *IntMPA 94*
Jackson, Samuel S., Jr. 1934- *WhoBlA 94*
Jackson, Sara 1954- *WrDr 94*
Jackson, Sarah 1924- *WhoAmA 93*
Jackson, Sarah Jeanette 1924- *WhoAm 94*
Jackson, Seaton J. 1914- *WhoBlA 94*
Jackson, Selmer d1971 *WhoHol 92*
Jackson, Seymour Scott 1897- *WhAm 10*
Jackson, Sharonjoy Alice 1945- *WhoMW 93*
Jackson, Sheila Cathryn *DrAPF 93*
Jackson, Sheldon 1834-1909 *DcAmReB 2, EncNAR*
Jackson, Sherry 1942- *WhoHol 92*
Jackson, Sherry Diane 1943- *WhoScEn 94*
Jackson, Shirley 1919-1965 *BlmGWL, EncSF 93*
Jackson, Shirley (Hardie) 1916-1965 *RfGShF*
Jackson, Shirley Ann 1946- *AfrAmAl 6, WhoBlA 94*
Jackson, Spoon *DrAPF 93*
Jackson, Steven Mark 1961- *WhoFI 94*
Jackson, Stoney *WhoHol 92*
Jackson, Stu *WhoAm 94*
Jackson, Stuart Wayne 1955- *WhoBlA 94*
Jackson, Suzanne Fitzallen 1944- *WhoAmA 93*
Jackson, Suzanne H. 1963- *WhoAmL 94*
Jackson, Terrance Sheldon 1964- *WhoScEn 94*
Jackson, Terrence Michael 1946- *WhoAmL 94, WhoWest 94*
Jackson, Tessa *Who 94*
Jackson, Thelma Conley 1934- *WhoBlA 94*
Jackson, Theodore Marshall 1928- *WhoAm 94*
Jackson, Theodore Roosevelt 1913- *WhoAmP 93*
Jackson, Thomas *Who 94*
Jackson, Thomas 1824-1863 *HisWorL [port]*
Jackson, Thomas 1925- *Who 94*
Jackson, (William) Thomas 1927- *Who 94*
Jackson, Thomas E. d1967 *WhoHol 92*
Jackson, Thomas F. 1927- *WhoAmP 93*
Jackson, Thomas Francis, III 1940- *WhoAmL 94*
Jackson, Thomas Gene 1949- *WhoAm 94, WhoAmL 94*
Jackson, Thomas Humphrey 1950- *WhoAm 94*
Jackson, Thomas Louis 1956- *WhoAmL 94*
Jackson, Thomas Micajah, Jr. 1957- *WhoAmP 93*
Jackson, Thomas Mitchell 1932- *WhoBlA 94*
Jackson, Thomas Penfield 1937- *CngDr 93, WhoAm 94, WhoAmL 94*
Jackson, Timothy James 1963- *WhoMW 93*
Jackson, Tom 1951- *WhoBlA 94*
Jackson, Tomi L. 1923- *WhoBlA 94*
Jackson, Tommy L. 1914- *WhoBlA 94*
Jackson, Toni Lee *WhoAmL 94*
Jackson, Tracy Camille 1966- *WhoBlA 94*
Jackson, Vaughn L. 1920- *WhoAmA 93*
Jackson, Velma Louise 1945- *WhoAmL 94*
Jackson, Velma Reece 1954- *WhoFI 94*
Jackson, Vera Ruth 1912- *WhoBlA 94*
Jackson, Victor Louis 1933- *WhoAm 94*
Jackson, Victoria 1959- *WhoHol 92*
Jackson, Vincent Edward 1962- *ConAu 141*
Jackson, Virginia Adams Knight 1951- *WhoWest 94*
Jackson, W. Bruce 1943- *WhoAm 94*
Jackson, W. Charles 1947- *WhoAmL 94*
Jackson, W. Sherman 1939- *WhoBlA 94*
Jackson, Walter K. 1914- *WhoBlA 94*
Jackson, Ward 1928- *WhoAm 94, WhoAmA 93*
Jackson, Warren d1950 *WhoHol 92*
Jackson, Warren Garrison *WhoBlA 94*
Jackson, Wendy S. Lewis 1965- *WhoMW 93*
Jackson, Wes 1936- *EnvEnc*
Jackson, William 1730-1803 *NewGrDO*
Jackson, William 1759-1828 *WhAmRev*
Jackson, William (Godfrey Fothergill) 1917- *Who 94, WrDr 94*
Jackson, William (Peter Uprichard) 1918- *WrDr 94*
Jackson, William Bruce 1926- *WhoMW 93*
Jackson, William David 1927- *WhoAm 94*
Jackson, William E. 1936- *WhoBlA 94*
Jackson, William Ed 1932- *WhoBlA 94*
Jackson, William Eldred 1919- *WhoAm 94*
Jackson, William Elmer, Jr. 1935- *WhoFI 94*
Jackson, William Frazier 1952- *WhoFI 94*
Jackson, William Gene 1946- *WhoMW 93*
Jackson, William Godfrey Fothergill 1917- *IntWW 93*
Jackson, William Gordon 1948- *Who 94*
Jackson, William Joseph 1943- *WhoMW 93*
Jackson, William Keith 1928- *WrDr 94*
Jackson, William MacLeod 1926- *WhoAm 94*
Jackson, William Paul, Jr. 1938- *WhoAm 94, WhoAmL 94*
Jackson, William Robert 1953- *WhoMW 93*
Jackson, William Theodore 1906- *Who 94*
Jackson, William Turrentine 1915- *WhoAm 94*
Jackson, William Unsworth 1926- *Who 94*
Jackson, William Vernon 1926- *WhoAm 94*
Jackson, William Ward 1913- *WhoAm 94*
Jackson, Willis Randell, II 1945- *WhoBlA 94*
Jackson, Wilma Littlejohn *WhoBlA 94*
Jackson, Yolanda Maria Cash 1958- *WhoAmL 94*
Jackson, Yvonne Brenda 1920- *Who 94*
Jackson-Brooks, Andrea *WhoAmP 93*
Jackson-Foy, Lucy Maye 1919- *WhoBlA 94*
Jackson Gougar, Helen 1843-1907 *WomPubS*
Jackson-Lipkin, Miles Henry *Who 94*
Jackson-Ransom, Bunnie 1940- *WhoBlA 94*
Jackson-Sirls, Mary Louise 1944- *WhoBlA 94*
Jackson-Smith, Princess Nadine 1946- *WhoWest 94*
Jackson-Stiritz, Marette McCauley 1931- *WhoAm 94*
Jackson-Stops, Gervase Frank Ashworth 1947- *Who 94*
Jackson-Stops, Timothy William Ashworth 1942- *Who 94*
Jackson-Teal, Rita F. 1949- *WhoBlA 94*
Jackson-Thompson, Marie O. 1947- *WhoBlA 94*
Jackvony, Bernard A. 1945- *WhoAmL 94*
Jackwood, Daral John 1956- *WhoMW 93*
Jaclot, Francois Charles 1949- *WhoAm 94*
Jaco, E(gbert) Gartly 1923- *WrDr 94*
Jaco, William H. 1940- *WhoAm 94, WhoScEn 94*
Jacob, Bernard Michel 1930- *WhoAm 94*
Jacob, Bernard Victor d1992 *Who 94N*
Jacob, Betty Muther 1910- *WhoWest 94*
Jacob, Bruce Robert 1935- *WhoAm 94, WhoAmL 94*
Jacob, Catherine *WhoHol 92*
Jacob, Charles Elmer 1931- *WhoAm 94*
Jacob, Charles Waldemar 1943- *WhAm 10*
Jacob, Cynthia Maxwell 1941- *WhoAmL 94*
Jacob, David Oliver Ll. *Who 94*
Jacob, Edward Ian Claud d1993 *IntWW 93N*
Jacob, Edward Ian Claud 1899- *IntWW 93*
Jacob, Edwin J. 1927- *WhoAm 94, WhoAmL 94*
Jacob, Elizabeth Ann 1950- *WhoMW 93*
Jacob, Ellis 1953- *WhoAm 94*
Jacob, Francois 1920- *IntWW 93, Who 94, WhoAm 94, WhoScEn 94, WorScD*
Jacob, Frederick Henry 1915- *Who 94*
Jacob, George Prasad 1950- *WhoScEn 94*
Jacob, Harry Myles 1913- *WhoAm 94*
Jacob, Herbert 1933- *WhoAm 94, WhoMW 93*
Jacob, (Edward) Ian (Claud) d1993 *Who 94N*
Jacob, Irene *WhoHol 92*
Jacob, Irene 1966?- *ConTFT 11*
Jacob, Isaac Hai 1908- *Who 94*
Jacob, James R. 1940- *WrDr 94*
Jacob, Jerry Rowland 1933- *WhoAm 94*
Jacob, John *DrAPF 93*
Jacob, John E. 1934- *AfrAmAl 6 [port]*
Jacob, John Edward 1934- *WhoAm 94, WhoBlA 94*
Jacob, Ken 1949- *WhoAmP 93*
Jacob, Leonard 1894- *WhAm 10*
Jacob, Marvin Eugene 1935- *WhoAm 94, WhoAmL 94*
Jacob, Mary Jane 1952- *WhoAmA 93*
Jacob, Nancy Louise 1943- *WhoAm 94*
Jacob, Naomi d1964 *WhoHol 92*
Jacob, Ned 1938- *WhoAmA 93*
Jacob, Ninni Sarah 1951- *WhoScEn 94*
Jacob, P. Walter d1977 *WhoHol 92*
Jacob, Paul Bernard, Jr. 1922- *WhoAm 94*
Jacob, Robert Allen 1941- *WhoScEn 94*
Jacob, Robert Edward 1954- *WhoMW 93*
Jacob, Robert Raphael Hayim 1941- *Who 94*
Jacob, Shalom 1962- *WhoAmL 94*
Jacob, Stanley Wallace 1924- *WhoAm 94, WhoScEn 94, WhoWest 94*
Jacob, Ted *WhoAmP 93*
Jacob, William Mungo 1944- *Who 94*
Jacob, Willis Harvey 1943- *WhoBlA 94*
Jacobacci, Vincenzo *NewGrDO*
Jacobetti, Dominic J. 1920- *WhoAmP 93*
Jacobey, John Arthur, III 1929- *WhoAm 94*
Jacobi, Carl (Richard) 1908- *EncSF 93*
Jacobi, Derek d1938 *WhoHol 92*
Jacobi, Derek 1938- *IntMPA 94*
Jacobi, Derek George 1938- *IntWW 93, Who 94, WhoAm 94*
Jacobi, Frederick 1891-1952 *NewGrDO*
Jacobi, Georg 1840-1906 *NewGrDO*
Jacobi, James (Edward) 1925- *Who 94*
Jacobi, Jan de Greeff 1944- *WhoMW 93*
Jacobi, Joe *WhoAm 94*
Jacobi, Johann Georg 1740-1814 *NewGrDO*
Jacobi, Joseph William, Jr. 1950- *WhoMW 93*
Jacobi, Lou 1913- *WhoHol 92*
Jacobi, Peter Paul 1930- *WhoAm 94*
Jacobi, Ronald N. 1947- *WhoAm 94*
Jacobi, William Mallett 1930- *WhoAm 94*
Jacobik, Gray *DrAPF 93*
Jacobini, Maria d1944 *WhoHol 92*
Jacobo, Esperanza Delao 1944- *WhoHisp 94*
Jacobo, John Rodriguez 1942- *WhoHisp 94*
Jacobovits de Szeged, Adriaan 1935- *IntWW 93*
Jacobowitz, Ellen Sue 1948- *WhoAm 94, WhoAmA 93, WhoScEn 94*
Jacobowitz, Gerald Norman 1934- *WhoAmL 94*
Jacobowitz, Harold Saul 1950- *WhoAmL 94*
Jacobowitz, Judah *DrAPF 93*
Jacobowitz, Ruth Scherr *WhoMW 93*
Jacobs, Abigail Conway 1942- *WhoAm 94*
Jacobs, Adrianus Gerardus 1936- *IntWW 93*
Jacobs, Alan 1947- *WhoAm 94, WhoAmL 94*
Jacobs, Alan Martin 1932- *WhoAm 94*
Jacobs, Albert James 1950- *WhoFI 94*
Jacobs, Albert Lionel, Jr. 1939- *WhoAm 94*
Jacobs, Alfred Jack 1925- *WhoMW 93*
Jacobs, Alicia Melvina 1955- *WhoFI 94*
Jacobs, Allan 1948- *WhoFI 94*
Jacobs, Alma Rau 1924- *WhoAmP 93*
Jacobs, Amos *WhAm 10*
Jacobs, Andrew, Jr. 1932- *CngDr 93, WhoAm 94, WhoAmP 93, WhoMW 93*
Jacobs, Angela d1951 *WhoHol 92*
Jacobs, Anita *DrAPF 93*
Jacobs, Ann Elizabeth 1950- *WhoAmL 94*

Jacobs, Anthony *Who 94*
Jacobs, (David) Anthony 1931- *Who 94*
Jacobs, Arnold Stephen 1940- *WhoAm 94*
Jacobs, Arthur (David) 1922- *NewGrDO*
Jacobs, Arthur David 1922- *Who 94, WrDr 94*
Jacobs, Arthur Dietrich 1933- *WhoFI 94, WhoWest 94*
Jacobs, Augusta Adelle 1925- *WhoMW 93*
Jacobs, Barbara Frank 1942- *WhoFI 94*
Jacobs, Barry 1924- *IntMPA 94*
Jacobs, Bernard B. 1916- *WhoAm 94*
Jacobs, Bradford McElderry 1920- *WhoAm 94*
Jacobs, Bruce Marrin 1926- *WhoWest 94*
Jacobs, Burleigh Edmund 1920- *WhoAm 94*
Jacobs, C. Bernard 1918- *WhoAm 94*
Jacobs, Carl Eugene 1942- *WhoMW 93*
Jacobs, Carl Nicholas 1895- *WhAm 10*
Jacobs, Carol Ann 1962- *WhoFI 94*
Jacobs, Charles P. 1950- *WhoAm 94, WhoAmL 94*
Jacobs, Christopher Harry 1948- *WhoFI 94*
Jacobs, Clifton W., Jr. 1937- *WhoIns 94*
Jacobs, Clyde (Edward) 1925- *WrDr 94*
Jacobs, Dan 1955- *WhoScEn 94*
Jacobs, Dan(iel) N(orman) 1924- *WrDr 94*
Jacobs, Daniel Wesley, Sr. 1933- *WhoBlA 94*
Jacobs, David (Theodore) 1932- *WhoAmA 93*
Jacobs, David H *WhoAm 94*
Jacobs, David Lewis 1926- *Who 94*
Jacobs, Dennis G. 1944- *WhoAm 94, WhoAmL 94, WhoAmP 93*
Jacobs, Denny 1937- *WhoAmP 93*
Jacobs, Donald P. 1927- *WhoMW 93*
Jacobs, Donald Paul 1942- *WhoAm 94*
Jacobs, Donald Phillip 1924- *WhoMW 93*
Jacobs, Donald Trent 1946- *WhoWest 94*
Jacobs, Donald Warren 1932- *WhoScEn 94*
Jacobs, Douglas George 1939- *WhoAmP 93*
Jacobs, Edwin Max 1925- *WhoAm 94*
Jacobs, Eleanor Alice 1923- *WhoAm 94*
Jacobs, Eli S. *WhoAm 94*
Jacobs, Emma *WhoHol 92*
Jacobs, Ernest Christopher 1957- *WhoMW 93*
Jacobs, Ferne K. 1942- *WhoAmA 93*
Jacobs, Francis Albin 1918- *WhoAm 94*
Jacobs, Francis G(eoffrey) 1939- *WrDr 94*
Jacobs, Francis Geoffrey 1939- *IntWW 93, Who 94*
Jacobs, Frank Charles 1967- *WhoFI 94*
Jacobs, Geoffrey Lane 1948- *WhoWest 94*
Jacobs, George 1924- *WhoAm 94*
Jacobs, Harold 1932- *WhoAmA 93*
Jacobs, Harold Robert 1936- *WhoAm 94*
Jacobs, Harriet Ann 1813-1897 *BlmGWL*
Jacobs, Harry Milburn, Jr. 1928- *WhoAm 94*
Jacobs, Harvey 1930- *EncSF 93*
Jacobs, Harvey Collins 1915- *WhoAm 94, WhoMW 93*
Jacobs, Hazel A. 1948- *WhoBlA 94*
Jacobs, Helen 1908- *BuCMET [port]*
Jacobs, Helen Hull 1908- *WhoAm 94, WrDr 94*
Jacobs, Helen Nichols 1924- *WhoAmA 93*
Jacobs, Hyde Spencer 1926- *WhoMW 93*
Jacobs, Ilene B. 1947- *WhoAm 94, WhoFI 94*
Jacobs, Ira 1931- *WhoAm 94*
Jacobs, Irving 1938- *Who 94*
Jacobs, Jack Bernard 1942- *WhoAmL 94*
Jacobs, Jack L. 1953- *ConAu 142*
Jacobs, James A. 1947- *WhoFI 94*
Jacobs, James John 1940- *WhoFI 94*
Jacobs, James P. 1952- *WhoFI 94*
Jacobs, James Paul 1930- *WhoFI 94*
Jacobs, Jan L. 1933- *WhoIns 94*
Jacobs, Jane *NewYTBS 93 [port]*
Jacobs, Jane 1916- *WrDr 94*
Jacobs, Jane Brand 1940- *WhoAm 94, WhoAmL 94*
Jacobs, Jeffrey Lee 1951- *WhoAmL 94*
Jacobs, Jeffrey P. *WhoAmP 93*
Jacobs, Jeffrey Paul 1963- *WhoMW 93*
Jacobs, Jeremy M. *WhoAm 94*
Jacobs, Jim 1942- *WhoAm 94*
Jacobs, Jim 1945- *WhoAmA 93*
Jacobs, Jo Ellen 1952- *WhoMW 93*
Jacobs, Jocelyn 1956- *WhoMW 93*
Jacobs, Joe c. 1945- *News 94-1 [port]*
Jacobs, Joel *WhoAmP 93*
Jacobs, John *IntMPA 94*
Jacobs, John (Arthur) 1916- *WrDr 94*
Jacobs, John Arthur 1916- *Who 94*
Jacobs, John Edward 1920- *WhoAm 94*
Jacobs, John Howard 1925- *WhoAm 94, WhoWest 94*
Jacobs, John Joseph 1955- *WhoFI 94*
Jacobs, John Patrick 1945- *WhoAm 94, WhoAmL 94*
Jacobs, John Robert Maurice 1925- *Who 94*
Jacobs, Jonathan Lewis 1954- *WhoScEn 94*
Jacobs, Joseph 1854-1916 *DcLB 141 [port]*
Jacobs, Joseph Donovan 1908- *WhoAm 94*
Jacobs, Joseph James 1925- *WhoAmL 94*
Jacobs, Joseph John 1916- *WhoAm 94, WhoFI 94*
Jacobs, Joseph Mark 1959- *WhoAmL 94*
Jacobs, Julian I. 1937- *CngDr 93, WhoAm 94, WhoAmL 94*
Jacobs, Karoniaktatie Alex *DrAPF 93*
Jacobs, Kenneth (Sydney) 1917- *Who 94*
Jacobs, Kenneth A. 1948- *WhoAm 94*
Jacobs, Kent Frederick 1938- *WhoAm 94, WhoWest 94*
Jacobs, Larry Ben 1959- *WhoBlA 94*
Jacobs, Laurence Stanton 1940- *WhoAm 94*
Jacobs, Lawrence-Hilton 1954- *WhoHol 92*
Jacobs, Leah 1927- *WrDr 94*
Jacobs, Leon 1915- *WhoAm 94*
Jacobs, Leonard S. *WhoAmP 93*
Jacobs, Leslie William 1944- *WhoAm 94, WhoAmL 94*
Jacobs, Lloydstone Leonard Fitzmorgan 1937- *IntWW 93*
Jacobs, Louis 1920- *Who 94, WrDr 94*
Jacobs, Lucky *DrAPF 93*
Jacobs, Manny *WhoHol 92*
Jacobs, Marc 1964- *WhoAm 94*
Jacobs, Marilyn Susan 1952- *WhoAm 94*
Jacobs, Marion Kramer *WhoAm 94*
Jacobs, Mark Elliott 1940- *WhoScEn 94*
Jacobs, Mark Neil 1946- *WhoAm 94*
Jacobs, Melvin d1993 *NewYTBS 93*
Jacobs, Michael Anthony 1961- *WhoMW 93*
Jacobs, Michael Joseph 1941- *WhoAm 94, WhoAmL 94*
Jacobs, Michael Robert 1946- *WhoMW 93*
Jacobs, Michel 1877-1958 *WhoAmA 93N*
Jacobs, Nicholas Joseph 1933- *WhoScEn 94*
Jacobs, Norma Morris 1949- *WhoBlA 94*
Jacobs, Norman Allan 1937- *WhoFI 94*
Jacobs, Norman Gabriel 1924- *WhoAm 94*
Jacobs, Norman Joseph 1932- *WhoAm 94*
Jacobs, Patricia Ann 1934- *Who 94*
Jacobs, Patricia Dianne 1950- *WhoBlA 94*
Jacobs, Paul 1946- *WhoAmL 94*
Jacobs, Paul Alan 1940- *WhoAm 94, WhoAmL 94, WhoWest 94*
Jacobs, Paula *WhoHol 92*
Jacobs, Peter c. 1807-1890 *EncNAR*
Jacobs, Peter Alan 1939- *WhoAmA 93*
Jacobs, Peter Alan 1943- *IntWW 93, Who 94*
Jacobs, Peter Daniel Alexander 1939- *WhoAm 94*
Jacobs, Peter James 1950- *WhoMW 93*
Jacobs, Peter Lanam 1960- *WhoFI 94*
Jacobs, Piers 1933- *IntWW 93, Who 94*
Jacobs, Ralph, Jr. 1940- *WhoAmA 93, WhoWest 94*
Jacobs, Ralph A. 1952- *WhoAmL 94*
Jacobs, Ralph Raymond 1942- *WhoScEn 94, WhoWest 94*
Jacobs, Randall Brian 1951- *WhoAmL 94, WhoWest 94*
Jacobs, Randall Charles 1947- *WhoMW 93*
Jacobs, Raymond d1993 *NewYTBS 93 [port]*
Jacobs, Rene 1946- *NewGrDO*
Jacobs, Rhoda S. *WhoAmP 93*
Jacobs, Richard Alan 1934- *WhoAm 94*
Jacobs, Richard Allen 1936- *WhoAm 94*
Jacobs, Richard B. 1945- *WhoAmL 94*
Jacobs, Richard Dearborn 1920- *WhoMW 93, WhoScEn 94*
Jacobs, Richard E. *WhoAm 94, WhoFI 94, WhoMW 93*
Jacobs, Richard James 1941- *WhoAm 94*
Jacobs, Richard Lewis 1950- *WhoAmP 93*
Jacobs, Richard Louis 1953- *WhoAmL 94*
Jacobs, Richard Matthew 1924- *WhoAm 94*
Jacobs, Rita Goldman 1927- *WhoAm 94*
Jacobs, Robert 1913- *WhoAm 94*
Jacobs, Robert Alan 1937- *WhoAm 94*
Jacobs, Robert Allan d1993 *NewYTBS 93*
Jacobs, Robert Allan 1905- *IntWW 93*
Jacobs, Robert C. 1951- *WhoAmL 94*
Jacobs, Robert Cooper 1939- *WhoAm 94, WhoWest 94*
Jacobs, Robert Edwin 1952- *WhoWest 94*
Jacobs, Robert Mark 1949- *WhoFI 94*
Jacobs, Rolly Warren 1946- *WhoAmL 94*
Jacobs, Rosetta 1932- *WhoAm 94*
Jacobs, Rusty 1967- *WhoHol 92*
Jacobs, Ruth Harriet 1924- *WhoAm 94*
Jacobs, Sanford Gregg 1963- *WhoAmL 94*
Jacobs, Seth Alan 1956- *WhoAmL 94*
Jacobs, Shannon K. 1947- *SmATA 77 [port]*
Jacobs, Sherry Raphael 1943- *WhoAm 94*
Jacobs, Sophia Yarnall d1993 *NewYTBS 93*
Jacobs, Sophia Yarnall 1902-1993 *ConAu 141*
Jacobs, Stephen Benjamin 1939- *WhoAm 94*
Jacobs, Stephen T. 1948- *WhoAmL 94*
Jacobs, Steven *WhoHol 92*
Jacobs, Steven Robin 1949- *WhoFI 94*
Jacobs, Suzanne 1936- *WhoAmP 93*
Jacobs, Sylvia Marie 1946- *WhoBlA 94*
Jacobs, Talmadge Jeffries *AfrAmG [port]*
Jacobs, Thomas Frank 1965- *WhoAmL 94*
Jacobs, Thomas Linwood 1933- *WhoBlA 94*
Jacobs, Timothy R. 1941- *WhoAmL 94*
Jacobs, Travis Beal 1936- *WhoAm 94*
Jacobs, Vernon K(enneth) 1936- *ConAu 41NR*
Jacobs, Vernon Kenneth 1936- *WhoFI 94*
Jacobs, Virginia Elizabeth 1922- *WhoMW 93*
Jacobs, W. W. 1863-1943 *DcLB 135 [port]*
Jacobs, W(illiam) W(ymark) 1863-1943 *RfGShF*
Jacobs, Walter Darnell 1922- *WrDr 94*
Jacobs, Wendell Early, Jr. 1945- *WhoAmL 94*
Jacobs, Wilbur R(ipley) *WrDr 94*
Jacobs, Wilbur Ripley *WhoAm 94, WhoWest 94*
Jacobs, Wilfred (Ebenezer) 1919- *Who 94*
Jacobs, Wilfred Ebenezer 1919- *IntWW 93*
Jacobs, William Russell, II 1927- *WhoAmL 94*
Jacobs, Woodrow Cooper 1908-1990 *WhAm 10*
Jacobs-Davis, Marie 1929- *WhoAmL 94*
Jacobsen, Adolf M.B. 1926- *WhoAm 94*
Jacobsen, Arthur 1921- *WhoAm 94*
Jacobsen, Darlene Elizabeth 1943- *WhoFI 94*
Jacobsen, Dean *WhoHol 92*
Jacobsen, Donald Weldon 1939- *WhoMW 93*
Jacobsen, Douglas G. 1951- *ConAu 141*
Jacobsen, Edward 1953- *WhoAmP 93*
Jacobsen, Edward Hastings 1926- *WhoScEn 94*
Jacobsen, Eric Kasner 1932- *WhoFI 94, WhoMW 93*
Jacobsen, Frithjof Halfdan 1914- *Who 94*
Jacobsen, Gerald Bernhardt 1939- *WhoScEn 94, WhoWest 94*
Jacobsen, Glenn Eugene 1928- *WhoAmP 93*
Jacobsen, Grete Krag 1943- *WhoScEn 94*
Jacobsen, Hazel Catherine 1909- *WhoMW 93*
Jacobsen, Hugh Newell 1929- *WhoAm 94*
Jacobsen, Josephine *DrAPF 93*
Jacobsen, Josephine 1908- *ConAu 18AS [port], WrDr 94*
Jacobsen, Josephine Winder Boylan 1908- *WhoAm 94*
Jacobsen, Judith Eva 1952- *WhoWest 94*
Jacobsen, Julia Mills 1923- *WhoFI 94*
Jacobsen, K(enneth) C. 1939- *WrDr 94*
Jacobsen, Ken *WhoAmP 93*
Jacobsen, Kim Andrew 1952- *WhoWest 94*
Jacobsen, Laren 1937- *WhoWest 94*
Jacobsen, Lawrence E. 1921- *WhoAmP 93*
Jacobsen, Lee Kay 1932- *WhoFI 94*
Jacobsen, Mark Lee 1965- *WhoWest 94*
Jacobsen, Michael A. 1942- *WhoAmA 93*
Jacobsen, Olivia Villa-Real 1948- *WhoAsA 94*
Jacobsen, Oscar Thorklid 1895- *WhAm 10*
Jacobsen, Raymond Alfred, Jr. 1949- *WhoAm 94, WhoAmL 94*
Jacobsen, Rebecca Hanson 1949- *WhoWest 94*
Jacobsen, Richard T. 1941- *WhoAm 94, WhoScEn 94, WhoWest 94*
Jacobsen, Robert 1912-1993 *NewYTBS 93*
Jacobsen, Rolf 1907- *ConWorW 93*
Jacobsen, Stephen Charles *WhoScEn 94*
Jacobsen, Theodore H. 1933- *WhoFI 94*
Jacobsen, Thomas Herbert 1939- *WhoAm 94, WhoFI 94, WhoMW 93*
Jacobsen, Thomas Warren 1935- *WhoAm 94*
Jacobsen, Thorkild d1993 *NewYTBS 93*
Jacobsen, William L., Jr. 1936- *WhoAmP 93*
Jacobshagen, N. Keith, II 1941- *WhoAmA 93*
Jacobsmeyer, Jay Michael 1959- *WhoScEn 94, WhoWest 94*
Jacobson, Alan Leonard 1949- *WhoScEn 94*
Jacobson, Alan P. 1953- *WhoAmL 94*
Jacobson, Alexander Donald 1933- *WhoScEn 94*
Jacobson, Alf Edgar 1924- *WhoAmP 93*
Jacobson, Alfred Thurl 1919- *WhoAm 94*
Jacobson, Allen Frank 1926- *WhoAm 94, WhoFI 94*
Jacobson, Allen H. 1939- *WhoFI 94*
Jacobson, Alma Frank 1905-1990 *WhAm 10*
Jacobson, Anna Sue 1940- *WhoFI 94, WhoMW 93*
Jacobson, Antone Gardner 1929- *WhoAm 94*
Jacobson, Arthur 1924- *WhoAmA 93, WhoWest 94*
Jacobson, Arthur Eli 1928- *WhoScEn 94*
Jacobson, Arthur John 1948- *WhoAmL 94*
Jacobson, Barry Stephen 1955- *WhoAmL 94, WhoFI 94*
Jacobson, Bonnie *DrAPF 93*
Jacobson, Bruce John 1949- *WhoMW 93*
Jacobson, Charles May 1941- *WhoFI 94*
Jacobson, Craig Louis 1947- *WhoFI 94*
Jacobson, Craig Lowell 1955- *WhoWest 94*
Jacobson, Dale *DrAPF 93*
Jacobson, Dale Richard 1949- *WhoMW 93*
Jacobson, Dan 1929- *BlmGEL [port], EncSF 93, IntWW 93, RfGShF, WrDr 94*
Jacobson, Daniel Delos 1954- *WhoAm 94*
Jacobson, Daniel P. 1961- *WhoAmP 93*
Jacobson, David 1909- *WhoAm 94*
Jacobson, David A. 1948- *WhoAmL 94*
Jacobson, David Cary 1951- *WhoAm 94, WhoAmL 94*
Jacobson, David Edward 1949- *WhoAm 94*
Jacobson, David Nisson 1939- *WhoFI 94*
Jacobson, Dawn Adele 1956- *WhoWest 94*
Jacobson, Donald Thomas 1932- *WhoWest 94*
Jacobson, Edward 1922- *WhoAm 94*
Jacobson, Eric Scott 1952- *WhoAmL 94, WhoWest 94*
Jacobson, Eugene Donald 1930- *WhoAm 94*
Jacobson, Frank 1948- *WhoAmA 93*
Jacobson, Frank Joel 1948- *WhoAm 94, WhoWest 94*
Jacobson, Fruman 1948- *WhoAmL 94*
Jacobson, Gary Ronald 1947- *WhoScEn 94*
Jacobson, Gary Steven 1951- *WhoAm 94*
Jacobson, Gaynor I. 1912- *WhoAm 94*
Jacobson, Gilbert H. 1956- *WhoAmL 94*
Jacobson, Gunnard Kenneth 1947- *WhoMW 93*
Jacobson, Hans d1993 *NewYTBS 93*
Jacobson, Harold Gordon 1912- *WhoAm 94*
Jacobson, Harold Karan 1929- *WhoAm 94*
Jacobson, Harold LeLand 1926- *WhoAm 94*
Jacobson, Henning *WhoAmP 93*
Jacobson, Henrietta d1988 *WhoHol 92*
Jacobson, Herbert Laurence 1915- *WhoAm 94*
Jacobson, Herbert Leonard 1940- *WhoAm 94*
Jacobson, Howard 1940- *WhoAm 94*
Jacobson, Howard Christian 1935- *WhoAmP 93*
Jacobson, Howard Newman 1923- *WhoScEn 94*
Jacobson, Ira David 1942- *WhoScEn 94*
Jacobson, Irving d1978 *WhoHol 92*
Jacobson, Ishier 1922- *WhoAm 94*
Jacobson, Ivar Hjalmar 1939- *WhoScEn 94*
Jacobson, J. Paul 1947- *WhoAmL 94*
Jacobson, James Bassett 1922- *WhoAm 94*
Jacobson, James Edmund 1934- *WhoAm 94*
Jacobson, James Lamma, Jr. 1946- *WhoFI 94*
Jacobson, Jeff *WhoAmP 93*
Jacobson, Jeffrey Eli 1956- *WhoAmL 94*
Jacobson, Jerold Dennis 1940- *WhoAm 94*
Jacobson, Joan 1924- *WhoMW 93*
Jacobson, Joel Ross 1918-1989 *WhAm 10*
Jacobson, John Howard, Jr. 1933- *WhoAm 94, WhoMW 93*
Jacobson, Jon Stanley 1938- *WhoWest 94*
Jacobson, Jonathan G. 1953- *WhoAmP 93*
Jacobson, Judith Helen 1939- *WhoAmP 93, WhoWest 94, WhoWomW 91*
Jacobson, Lawrence Seymour *WhoFI 94*
Jacobson, Leon Orris d1992 *IntWW 93N*

Jacobson, Leon Orris 1911-1992 CurBio 93N, WhAm 10
Jacobson, Leonard I. 1940- WhoAm 94, WhoScEn 94
Jacobson, Leonid IntDcB
Jacobson, Leslie Sari 1933- WhoAm 94
Jacobson, Linda Sue 1962- WhoScEn 94
Jacobson, Lloyd Eldred 1923- WhoMW 93
Jacobson, Margaret Jamieson 1951- WhoAmL 94
Jacobson, Marian Slutz 1945- WhoAm 94, WhoAmL 94
Jacobson, Mark 1948- WrDr 94
Jacobson, Melvin Joseph 1928- WhoAm 94
Jacobson, Michael Faraday 1943- WhoAm 94
Jacobson, Murray M. 1915- WhoScEn 94
Jacobson, Nathan 1910- IntWW 93, WhoAm 94
Jacobson, Norman L. 1918- WhoAm 94
Jacobson, Olof Hildebrand 1955- WhoScEn 94
Jacobson, Patricia Anne Fitts 1946- WhoAmL 94, WhoMW 93
Jacobson, Phillip Lee 1928- WhoAm 94
Jacobson, Ralph Henry 1931- WhoAm 94, WhoScEn 94
Jacobson, Raymond Earl 1922- WhoFI 94, WhoWest 94
Jacobson, Richard Joseph 1943- WhoAm 94
Jacobson, Richard Lee 1942- WhoAm 94, WhoAmL 94
Jacobson, Richard Randolph 1949- WhoFI 94
Jacobson, Robert Andrew 1932- WhoAm 94
Jacobson, Saul P. 1916- WhoAm 94
Jacobson, Sidney 1929- WhoAm 94
Jacobson, Steve Evan 1955- WhoWest 94
Jacobson, Susan Dene 1949- WhoMW 93
Jacobson, Susan S. DrAPF 93
Jacobson, Sverre Theodore 1922- WhoAm 94
Jacobson, Thomas Ernest 1931- WhoWest 94
Jacobson, Willard James 1922- WhoScEn 94
Jacobson, Yolande 1921- WhoAmA 93
Jacobson-Barnes, Darryl Lynn 1957- WhoWest 94
Jacobson-Kram, David WhoScEn 94
Jacobson-Wolf, Joan Elizabeth 1949- WhoAm 94
Jacobsson, Sten Wilhelm John 1899-1983 WhoAmA 93N
Jacobsson, Ulla d1982 WhoHol 92
Jacobus, Charles Joseph 1947- WhoAmL 94
Jacobus, Cheri Christine 1947- WhoAmP 93
Jacobus, John M. 1927- WhoAmA 93
Jacobus, Mary 1944- BlmGWL, WrDr 94
Jacoby, A. James 1939- WhoAm 94
Jacoby, Billy 1969- WhoHol 92
Jacoby, Bobby WhoHol 92
Jacoby, Carolyn Phyllis 1951- WhoAmL 94
Jacoby, David 1947- WhoAmL 94
Jacoby, Erika 1928- WhoWest 94
Jacoby, Francine 1943- WhoFI 94
Jacoby, Frank David 1925- IntMPA 94
Jacoby, George Alonzo 1904-1991 WhAm 10
Jacoby, Henry Donnan 1935- WhoAm 94
Jacoby, Jacob 1940- WhoAm 94
Jacoby, John Freedley 1945- WhoWest 94
Jacoby, John Primm 1941- WhoAm 94, WhoAmL 94
Jacoby, Joseph 1942- IntMPA 94
Jacoby, M. Elaine 1941- WhoAm 94, WhoAmL 94
Jacoby, Margaret Mary 1930- WhoScEn 94
Jacoby, Peter Fredrickson 1947- WhoWest 94
Jacoby, Robert Harold 1942- WhoAm 94
Jacoby, Robert Ottinger 1939- WhoScEn 94
Jacoby, Russell 1945- ConAu 42NR
Jacoby, Sanford Mark 1953- WhoWest 94
Jacoby, Scott 1956- IntMPA 94, WhoHol 92
Jacoby, Sidney Bernhard 1908-1990 WhAm 10
Jacoby, Stanley Arthur 1927- WhoAm 94
Jacoby, Tamar 1954- WhoAm 94
Jacoby, Teresa Michelle 1956- WhoFI 94
Jacoby, William Jerome, Jr. 1925- WhoAm 94
Jacomb, Charles Ernest 1888- EncSF 93
Jacomb, Martin (Wakefield) 1929- Who 94
Jacomb, Martin Wakefield 1929- IntWW 93
Jacomet, Joseph Allen 1948- WhoMW 93
Jacon, Bernard IntMPA 94
Jacovacci, Vincenzo 1811-1881 NewGrDO
Jacover, Jerold Alan 1945- WhoAm 94, WhoAmL 94, WhoMW 93
Jacovich, Stephen William 1946- WhoScEn 94
Jacovides, Linos Jacovou 1940- WhoAm 94
Jacovini, Joseph Henry 1940- WhoAm 94
Jacox, Ada Kathryn WhoAm 94
Jacox, John William 1938- WhoFI 94, WhoMW 93
Jacq, Marie 1919- WhoWomW 91
Jacquaint, Huguette Germaine 1942- WhoWomW 91
Jacquard 1937- WhoAmA 93
Jacquard, Joseph-Marie 1752-1834 WorInv
Jacquard, Robert Brian 1958- WhoAmP 93
Jacquemard, Simonne 1924- IntWW 93
Jacquemin, Robert IntMPA 94
Jacquemon, Pierre 1935- WhoAmA 93
Jacqueney, Stephanie Alice WhoAmL 94
Jacques, Baron 1905- Who 94
Jacques, Andre Charles 1921- WhoAm 94
Jacques, Beau ConAu 142
Jacques, Brian 1939- TwCYAW
Jacques, Cheryl A. WhoAmP 93
Jacques, Cornell 1949- WhoBlA 94
Jacques, Emile J. 1925- WhoAmP 93
Jacques, Francois Michel Jean 1960- WhoFI 94
Jacques, Hattie d1980 WhoHol 92
Jacques, Joseph William 1953- WhoFI 94
Jacques, Michael Louis 1945- WhoAmA 93
Jacques, Paul F. WhoAmP 93
Jacques, Peter Roy Albert 1939- Who 94
Jacques, Robert C. 1919- IntMPA 94
Jacques, Robin 1920- Who 94
Jacques, Russell Kenneth 1943- WhoAmA 93
Jacques, Yves Henri 1929- IntWW 93
Jacquet, Jean-Baptiste 1933- AfrAmAl 6
Jacquet, Jean Baptiste Illinois 1922- WhoBlA 94
Jacquet, Jeffrey 1966- WhoHol 92
Jacquet, Michel Antoine Paul Marie 1936- IntWW 93
Jacquet de la Guerre, Elisabeth-Claude 1666?-1729 NewGrDO
Jacquette, Yvonne Helene 1934- WhoAm 94, WhoAmA 93
Jacquez, Albert S. WhoHisp 94
Jacquez, Josephine 1930- WhoWest 94
Jacquinot, Charles-Hector 1796-1879 WhWE
Jacquinot, Pierre 1910- IntWW 93
Jacquot, David Charles 1962- WhoAmL 94
Jaczkowski, Frank Stanislaus 1935- WhoMW 93
Jade, Claude 1949- WhoHol 92
Jade, Symon EncSF 93
Jadhav Khedker, Chitresh Rao Vasant Rao 1936- WhoFI 94
Jadid, Salah d1993 NewYTBS 93 [port]
Jadiker, Mary D. 1937- WhoAmP 93
Jadin, Louis-Emmanuel 1768-1853 NewGrDO
Jadlow, Joseph Martin 1942- WhoAm 94
Jadlowiec, Kenneth M. 1951- WhoAmP 93
Jadlowker, Hermann 1877-1953 NewGrDO
Jadot, Jean Lambert Octave 1909- WhoAm 94
Jadra, Ramon WhoHisp 94
Jadvar, Hossein 1961- WhoAm 94, WhoMW 93, WhoScEn 94
Jadwin, Ted Richard 1948- WhoAmL 94
Jae 1947- WhoAmA 93
Jaech, Daniel Winfred 1943- WhoFI 94
Jaeckel, Richard 1926- IntMPA 94
Jaeckle, Edwin F. 1894- WhAm 10
Jaeger, Alvin A. 1943- WhoAm 94, WhoAmP 93, WhoMW 93
Jaeger, Boi Jon 1936- WhoAm 94
Jaeger, Brenda Kay 1950- WhoAmA 93
Jaeger, Charles Arthur 1949- WhoFI 94
Jaeger, David Arnold 1938- WhoAm 94, WhoFI 94
Jaeger, Frederick 1928- WhoHol 92
Jaeger, Jeff Todd 1964- WhoAm 94, WhoWest 94
Jaeger, Leonard Henry 1905- WhoAm 94
Jaeger, Leslie Gordon 1926- Who 94
Jaeger, Lowell DrAPF 93
Jaeger, Marc Julius 1929- WhoScEn 94
Jaeger, Muriel c. 1893- EncSF 93
Jaeger, Richard 1913- IntWW 93
Jaeger, Richard Charles 1944- WhoAm 94, WhoScEn 94
Jaeger, Richard L. 1933- WhAm 10
Jaeger, Robert Joseph 1932- WhoMW 93
Jaeger, Sharon Ann DrAPF 93
Jaeger, Sharon Ann 1945- WhoWest 94
Jaekle, Robert George 1951- WhoAmP 93
Jaenicke, Lothar 1923- IntWW 93
Jaenisch, Holger Marcel 1963- WhoScEn 94
Jaenzon, Julius 1885-1961 IntDcF 2-4 [port]
Jafari, Bahram Amir 1940- WhoScEn 94
Jafek, Bev DrAPF 93
Jafek, Bruce William 1941- WhoAm 94
Jaffa, George 1916- WrDr 94
Jaffe, Alan Steven 1939- WhoAm 94
Jaffe, Allen d1989 WhoHol 92
Jaffe, Andrew Mark 1938- WhoFI 94
Jaffe, Andrew Michael 1923- IntWW 93
Jaffe, Arthur Michael 1937- WhoAm 94, WhoScEn 94
Jaffe, Austin Jay 1952- WhoAm 94
Jaffe, Bernard Michael WhoAm 94
Jaffe, Betsy 1935- WrDr 94
Jaffe, Carl d1974 WhoHol 92
Jaffe, Dan DrAPF 93
Jaffe, David 1911-1990 WhAm 10
Jaffe, David Henry 1942- WhoScEn 94
Jaffe, Edward A. 1945- WhoAmL 94
Jaffe, Edward Ephraim 1928- WhoAm 94
Jaffe, Ernst Richard 1925- WhoAm 94
Jaffe, F. Filmore 1918- WhoAm 94, WhoAmL 94
Jaffe, Hans H. 1919-1989 WhAm 10
Jaffe, Harold DrAPF 93
Jaffe, Harold 1940- WhoAm 94
Jaffe, Harold W. 1946- IntWW 93
Jaffe, Howard Allen 1953- WhoMW 93
Jaffe, Ira S. 1943- WhoAmA 93
Jaffe, Irma B. WhoAmA 93
Jaffe, Irving 1913- WhoAmP 93
Jaffe, Jeffrey Martin 1954- WhoAm 94
Jaffe, Leo 1909- IntMPA 94, WhoAm 94
Jaffe, Leonard Sigmund 1916- WhoAm 94
Jaffe, Louise DrAPF 93
Jaffe, Maggie DrAPF 93
Jaffe, Mark M. 1941- WhoAmL 94
Jaffe, Marvin Eugene 1936- WhoAm 94
Jaffe, Melvin 1919- WhoAm 94
Jaffe, Michael 1940- WhoAm 94
Jaffe, (Andrew) Michael 1923- Who 94, WrDr 94
Jaffe, Morris Edward 1947- WhoFI 94
Jaffe, Murray Sherwood 1926- WhoAm 94
Jaffe, Nora 1928- WhoAm 94, WhoAmA 93
Jaffe, Norman d1993 NewYTBS 93 [port]
Jaffe, Paul Lawrence 1928- WhoAm 94, WhoAmL 94
Jaffe, Peter Edward 1962- WhoAmL 94
Jaffe, Richard P. 1944- WhoAmL 94
Jaffe, Richard Paul 1946- WhoAmL 94
Jaffe, Robert Benton 1933- WhoScEn 94
Jaffe, Robert S. 1946- WhoAmL 94
Jaffe, Rona WrDr 94
Jaffe, Rona 1932- WhoAm 94
Jaffe, Russell Merritt 1947- WhoScEn 94
Jaffe, Sam d1984 WhoHol 92
Jaffe, Seth WhoHol 92
Jaffe, Sheldon Eugene 1946- WhoAm 94
Jaffe, Sigmund 1921- WhoAm 94
Jaffe, Stanley R. 1940- IntMPA 94
Jaffe, Stanley Richard 1940- WhoAm 94, WhoFI 94
Jaffe, Steven-Charles 1954- IntMPA 94
Jaffe, Susan DrAPF 93, WhoAm 94
Jaffe, Susan 1962- IntDcB
Jaffe, Susan Lynn WhoFI 94
Jaffe, Theresa Ann 1948- WhoMW 93
Jaffe, William B. d1972 WhoAmA 93N
Jaffe, William Julian 1910- WhoScEn 94
Jaffee, Al(lan) 1921- WrDr 94
Jaffee, Annette Williams DrAPF 93
Jaffee, Annette Williams 1945- WrDr 94
Jaffee, Michael 1938- WhoAm 94
Jaffee, Sandra Schuyler 1943- WhoAm 94
Jaffe-Notier, Peter Andrew 1947- WhoMW 93
Jaffer, Adrian Michael 1943- WhoWest 94
Jaffer, Frances DrAPF 93
Jaffer, Melissa WhoHol 92
Jaffer, Rashida Amin WhoAmL 94
Jaffery, Sheldon (R.) EncSF 93
Jaffin, Charles Leonard 1928- WhoAm 94
Jaffin, David 1937- WrDr 94
Jaffray, Alistair Robert Morton 1925- Who 94
Jaffray, William Otho 1951- Who 94
Jaffrey, Ira 1939- WhoScEn 94
Jaffrey, Madhur 1933- WhoHol 92
Jaffrey, Saeed WhoHol 92
Jaffrey, Sakeena 1962- WhoHol 92
Jagacinski, Carolyn Mary 1949- WhoMW 93, WhoScEn 94
Jagadeesh, G. 1949- WhoAsA 94
Jagan, Cheddi 1918- IntWW 93, Who 94
Jagan, Janet 1920- IntWW 93
Jagel, Frederick 1897-1982 NewGrDO
Jagendorf, Andre Tridon 1926- IntWW 93, WhoAm 94, WhoScEn 94
Jager, Elizabeth Anne 1934- WhoFI 94, WhoMW 93
Jager, Ferdinand 1839-1902 NewGrDO
Jager, Fred Gerrit 1938- WhoFI 94, WhoWest 94
Jager, Martin Otto 1925- WrDr 94
Jager, Melvin Francis 1937- WhoAm 94, WhoAmL 94
Jager, Merle LeRoy 1942- WhoWest 94
Jager, Tammy S. 1963- WhoAmL 94, WhoWest 94
Jager, Tom WhoAm 94
Jagerman, David Lewis 1923- WhoScEn 94
Jager-Waldau, Arnulf Albert 1962- WhoScEn 94
Jaggard, Dwight Lincoln 1948- WhoScEn 94
Jaggard, William c. 1568-1623 DcNaB MP
Jagger, Bianca 1943- WhoHol 92
Jagger, Dean d1991 WhoHol 92
Jagger, Dean 1903?-1991 ConTFT 11
Jagger, Dean 1905-1991 WhAm 10
Jagger, Gillian 1930- WhoAmA 93
Jagger, Julia Bennett 1955- WhoAmL 94
Jagger, Mick 1943- IntMPA 94, IntWW 93, WhoAm 94, WhoHol 92
Jagger, Peter (John) 1938- WrDr 94
Jagger, Robert Edwin 1927- WhoAmL 94
Jaggers, George Henry, Jr. 1926- WhoBlA 94
Jaggi, Narendra K. 1954- WhoScEn 94
Jaggi, Yvette 1941- WhoWomW 91
Jaggs, Steve 1946- IntMPA 94
Jagiella, Diana Mary 1959- WhoAmL 94
Jagiello, Georgiana M. 1927- WhoScEn 94
Jaglan, Prem S. 1929- WhoAsA 94
Jaglom, Andre Richard 1953- WhoAmL 94
Jaglom, Henry 1941- WhoHol 92
Jaglom, Henry 1943- IntMPA 94
Jagnandan, Wilfred Lilpersaud 1920- WhoBlA 94
Jagner, Ronald Paul 1942- WhoMW 93
Jago, David Edgar John 1937- Who 94
Jago, June WhoHol 92
Jagoda, Barry Lionel 1944- WhoAm 94
Jagoda, Donald Robert 1929- WhoAm 94
Jagoda, Jerzy Antoni 1937- WhoScEn 94
Jagoda, Robert DrAPF 93
Jagodzinski, Ronald Edward 1957- WhoMW 93
Jagow, Charles Herman 1910- WhoFI 94
Jagow, Elmer 1922- WhoAm 94
Jahan, Marine 1959- WhoHol 92
Jahan, Muhammad Shah 1943- WhoScEn 94
Jahangir 1569-1627 HisWorL [port]
Jahde, Judy Ann 1949- WhoMW 93
Jahn, Billie Jane 1921- WhoScEn 94
Jahn, Gary Robert 1943- WhoMW 93
Jahn, Gerhard 1927- IntWW 93
Jahn, Gertrude 1940- NewGrDO
Jahn, Helmut 1940- WhoAm 94, WhoMW 93
Jahn, Laurence Roy 1926- WhoAm 94
Jahn, Mike 1943- EncSF 93
Jahn, Robert F. WhoAmP 93
Jahn, Robert George 1930- WhoAm 94
Jahn, Wolfgang 1918- Who 94
Jahns, Adam A. 1929- WhoAm 94, WhoFI 94
Jahns, Arthur William 1929- WhoMW 93
Jahns, James Douglas 1968- WhoMW 93
Jahns, Jeffrey 1946- WhoAm 94, WhoAmL 94
Jahns, T. R. DrAPF 93
Jahnsson, Evald Ferdinand EncSF 93
Jahoda, Gustav 1920- Who 94, WrDr 94
Jahoda, Marie 1907- Who 94
Jaicks, Frederick G. 1918- EncABHB 9
Jaicks, Frederick Gillies 1918- WhoAm 94
Jaicomo, Ronald James 1932- WhoAm 94, WhoMW 93
Jaid, Ildiko 1954- WhoHol 92
Jaidah, Ali Mohammed 1941- WhoFI 94
Jaidev d1980 WhoHol 92
Jaidinger, Judith C. 1941- WhoAmA 93
Jaime, Francisco 1960- WhoHisp 94
Jaime, Gerardo Martin 1967- WhoHisp 94
Jaime, Kalani 1961- WhoHisp 94
Jaime, Louis-Adolphe 1824-1901 NewGrDO
Jaime-Mena, Susana Griselda 1952- WhoHisp 94
Jaimes, Judit 1939- WhoHisp 94
Jain, Anil Kumar 1949- WhoMW 93
Jain, Arun K. 1952- WhoAsA 94
Jain, Ashit 1960- WhoAsA 94
Jain, Bimla Agarwal 1933- WhoAsA 94
Jain, Chandra Prabha 1948- WhoWest 94
Jain, Dipak Chand 1957- WhoMW 93
Jain, Girilal d1993 NewYTBS 93
Jain, Girilal 1923- IntWW 93
Jain, Girilal 1923-1993 ConAu 142
Jain, Himanshu 1955- WhoAsA 94, WhoScEn 94

Jain, Jitender K. 1947- *WhoAsA 94*
Jain, Lalit K. 1944- *WhoAmL 94*
Jain, Mahendra K. 1938- *WhoAsA 94*
Jain, Mukesh K. 1948- *WhoWest 94*
Jain, Naresh C. 1932- *WhoAsA 94*
Jain, Nemi Chand 1951- *WhoMW 93*
Jain, Piyare Lal 1921- *WhoAm 94, WhoAsA 94*
Jain, Raj 1951- *WrDr 94*
Jain, Raj Kumar 1949- *WhoScEn 94*
Jain, Rajeev K. 1957- *WhoAsA 94*
Jain, Rakesh 1956- *WhoAsA 94*
Jain, Sagar Chand 1930- *WhoAm 94*
Jain, Savitri 1930- *WhoAsA 94*
Jain, Sulekh Chand 1937- *WhoAsA 94*
Jain, Sunil 1963- *WhoScEn 94*
Jain, Surender K. 1938- *WhoAsA 94*
Jain, Surender Kumar 1938- *WhoMW 93*
Jain, Surinder Mohan 1945- *WhoScEn 94*
Jain, Sushil C. 1939- *WhoAsA 94*
Jain, Sushil Chand 1954- *WhoMW 93*
Jain, Sushil Chandra 1939- *WhoFI 94*
Jaine, Tom William Mahony 1943- *Who 94*
Jais, Meyer 1907-1993 *NewYTBS 93*
Jaisinghani, Rajan A. 1945- *WhoAsA 94*
Jaiswal, Gopaljee 1937- *WhoAsA 94*
Ja Ja of Opobo c. 1820-1891 *HisWorL [port]*
Jajuga, James P. *WhoAmP 93*
Jak *Who 94*
Jakab, Irene *WhoAm 94, WhoScEn 94*
Jakab, Robertne *WhoWomW 91*
Jakalunus fl. 1700-1800 *EncNAR*
Jakary, Ronald David 1944- *WhoMW 93*
Jakeman, Eric 1939- *Who 94*
Jakes, John 1932- *WhoAm 94, WrDr 94*
Jakes, John (William) 1932- *ConAu 43NR, EncSF 93*
Jakes, Peter H. 1946- *WhoAm 94, WhoAmL 94*
Jakes, William Chester 1922- *WhoAm 94*
Jakeway, (Francis) Derek 1915- *Who 94*
Jakhar, Bal Ram 1923- *IntWW 93*
Jaki, Stanley L. 1924- *IntWW 93*
Jaklitsch, Donald John 1947- *WhoScEn 94*
Jako, Geza Julius 1930- *WhoAmP 93*
Jakober, Marie 1941- *EncSF 93*
Jakobovits, Baron 1921- *Who 94*
Jakobovits, Immanuel 1921- *IntWW 93*
Jakobs, Kai 1957- *WhoScEn 94*
Jakobsdottir, Svava 1930- *BlmGWL, ConWorW 93*
Jakobsen, Carolyn Anne 1947- *WhoWomW 91*
Jakobsen, Carolyn Edith 1947- *WhoMW 93*
Jakobsen, Frode 1906- *IntWW 93*
Jakobsen, Jakob Knudsen 1912- *WhoAm 94, WhoScEn 94, WhoWest 94*
Jakobsen, Johan J. 1937- *IntWW 93*
Jakobsen, Mimi 1948- *IntWW 93*
Jakobson, Maggie *WhoHol 92*
Jakobson, Mark John 1923- *WhoAm 94*
Jakobson, Max 1923- *IntWW 93*
Jakobson, Roman 1896-1982 *BlmGEL*
Jakobsson, Ejler 1911-1986 *EncSF 93*
Jakobsson, Eric Gunnar 1938- *WhoScEn 94*
Jakova, Prenke 1917-1969 *NewGrDO*
Jakovac, John Paul 1948- *WhoScEn 94*
Jakowicka-Friderici, Teodozja *NewGrDO*
Jaksa, Thomas Michael 1948- *WhoMW 93*
Jakschik, Barbara A. 1931- *WhoScEn 94*
Jaksic, Ivan (Andrades) 1954- *ConAu 141*
Jaksic, Ivan A. 1954- *WhoMW 93*
Jakstas, Alfred John 1916- *WhoAm 94, WhoAmA 93*
Jakubauskas, Edward Benedict 1930- *WhoAm 94, WhoMW 93*
Jakubek, Helen Majerczyk 1931- *WhoMW 93*
Jakubik, Jerome W. 1945- *WhoAm 94*
Jakubowicz, Robert F. 1932- *WhoAmP 93*
Jakubowski, Maxim 1944- *EncSF 93*
Jakus, Stephanie 1926- *WhoMW 93*
Jalajas, Emil Walter Peter 1960- *WhoWest 94*
Jalal, Mahsoun B. 1936- *IntWW 93*
Jalaleddine, Sateh Mohamad Salim 1962- *WhoMW 93*
Jalan, Bimal *IntWW 93*
Jalan, Edi Lee *ConAu 141*
Jalandoni, Magdalena 1891-1978 *BlmGWL*
Jalapeeno, Jimmy *WhoAmA 93*
Jalbert, Joe Jay *IntMPA 94*
Jalbert, John 1925- *WhoAmP 93*
Jalbuena, Arnel Babiera 1961- *WhoAmL 94*
Jales, Mark *EncSF 93*
Jalil, Mazhar 1938- *WhoAsA 94*
Jalili, Mahir 1944- *WhoAm 94*
Jalkut, Richard Alan 1944- *WhoFI 94*
Jalkut, Thomas P. 1950- *WhoAmL 94*
Jalland, Pat(ricia) 1941- *WrDr 94*
Jalland, William Herbert Wainwright 1922- *Who 94*
Jaller, Michael M. 1924- *WhoScEn 94*
Jallins, Richard David 1957- *WhoAmL 94, WhoWest 94*
Jalloud, Abdul Salam Ahmed 1944- *IntWW 93*
Jaluria, Yogesh 1949- *WhoAsA 94*
Jalving, Clarence Louis 1895- *WhAm 10*
Jam, Jimmy *WhoBlA 94*
Jamail, Joseph Dahr, Jr. 1925- *WhoAmL 94*
Jamal, Ahmad 1930- *WhoBlA 94*
Jamal, Amir Habib 1922- *IntWW 93*
Jamal, Moez Ahamed 1955- *WhoFI 94*
Jamaludeen, Abdul Hamid 1945- *WhoBlA 94*
Jamar, Peter Norton 1957- *WhoWest 94*
Jamar, Steven Dwight 1953- *WhoAmL 94*
Jamba, Sousa 1966- *WrDr 94*
Jambois, Beverly Ann 1954- *WhoAmL 94*
Jambor, Agi 1909- *IntWW 93*
Jambor, Louise Irma *WhoAmP 93*
Jambor, Robert Vernon 1936- *WhoAm 94*
Jambrisak, Marija 1847-1937 *BlmGWL*
Jamero, Peter M. 1930- *WhoAsA 94*
Jamerson, Doug 1947- *WhoAmP 93*
Jamerson, Jerome Donnell 1950- *WhoBlA 94*
Jamerson, John William, Jr. 1910- *WhoBlA 94*
James *Who 94*
James, I *BlmGEL*
James, I 1406-1437 *BlmGEL*
James, I 1566-1625 *HisWorL [port]*
James, II fl. 1685-1688 *BlmGEL*
James, A. Everette, Jr. 1938- *WhoAmA 93*
James, Advergus Dell, Jr. 1944- *WhoBlA 94*
James, Alan 1943- *WrDr 94*
James, Albert Law, III 1943- *WhoAmL 94*
James, Alexander 1902-1953 *WorESoc [port]*
James, Alexander, Jr. 1933- *WhoBlA 94*
James, Alfred P. d1946 *WhoHol 92*
James, Alice 1848-1892 *BlmGWL*
James, Allix Bledsoe 1922- *WhoAm 94, WhoBlA 94*
James, Andrew *See* Midnight Oil *ConMus 11*
James, Anne Eleanor S. *Who 94*
James, Anthony *WhoHol 92*
James, Anthony Trafford 1922- *Who 94*
James, Arlo D. 1931- *WhoAmP 93*
James, Arlo Dee 1931- *WhoWest 94*
James, Arminta Susan 1924- *WhoBlA 94*
James, Art d1972 *WhoHol 92*
James, Aubrey Graham Wallen 1918- *Who 94*
James, Avon C. 1930- *AfrAmG [port]*
James, Barry Ray 1956- *WhoFI 94*
James, Basil 1918- *Who 94*
James, Ben d1966 *WhoHol 92*
James, Betty Harris 1932- *WhoBlA 94*
James, Betty L. 1921- *WhoMW 93*
James, Betty Nowlin 1936- *WhoBlA 94*
James, Bill 1929- *WrDr 94*
James, Bill 1943- *WhoAmA 93*
James, Bill 1949- *WrDr 94*
James, Bobby Charles 1946- *WhoBlA 94*
James, Brian 1920- *WhoHol 92*
James, Brian Robert 1936- *WhoAm 94*
James, Brion *WhoHol 92*
James, Brion 1945- *IntMPA 94*
James, Bruce David 1942- *WhoAm 94, WhoScEn 94*
James, Bruce Lowell 1961- *WhoAmL 94*
James, C(yril) L(ionel) R(obert) 1901-1989 *BlkWr 2*
James, Carlos Adrian 1946- *WhoBlA 94*
James, Carol Lee 1947- *WhoFI 94*
James, Carolyne Faye 1945- *WhoAm 94*
James, Carrie Houser 1949- *WhoBlA 94*
James, Catti 1940- *WhoAmA 93*
James, Cecil *Who 94*
James, (Thomas) Cecil (Garside) 1918- *Who 94*
James, Charles Alexander 1922- *WhoBlA 94*
James, Charles E., Jr. 1948- *WhoAm 94, WhoAmL 94*
James, Charles Edwin Frederic 1943- *Who 94*
James, Charles Ford 1935- *WhoBlA 94*
James, Charles Franklin, Jr. 1931- *WhoAm 94, WhoFI 94, WhoMW 93*
James, Charles H., III *WhoBlA 94*
James, Charles Howell, II 1930- *WhoBlA 94*
James, Charles L. 1934- *WhoBlA 94*
James, Cheryl *WhoBlA 94*
James, Christopher John 1932- *Who 94*
James, Christopher P. 1947- *WhoAmA 93*
James, Christopher Philip 1934- *Who 94*
James, Claire d1986 *WhoHol 92*
James, Clarence L., Jr. 1933- *WhoBlA 94*
James, Clifton d1963 *WhoHol 92*
James, Clifton 1921- *WhoHol 92*
James, Clifton 1925- *IntMPA 94*
James, Clive (Vivian Leopold) 1939- *WrDr 94*
James, Clive Vivian Leopold 1939- *IntWW 93, Who 94*
James, Colin Clement Walter *Who 94*
James, Colin Clement Walter 1926- *IntWW 93*
James, Craig T. 1941- *WhoAmP 93*
James, Cynlais Morgan 1926- *Who 94*
James, Cynlais (Kenneth) Morgan 1926- *IntWW 93*
James, Dakota 1922- *EncSF 93*
James, Daniel, Jr. 1920-1978 *AfrAmG, AfrAmAl 6 [port]*
James, Daniel J. 1920- *WhoAm 94*
James, Darryl Farrar 1954- *WhoBlA 94*
James, Dava Paulette *WhoBlA 94*
James, David *DrAPF 93*
James, David Edward 1937- *Who 94, WrDr 94*
James, David Geraint 1922- *WrDr 94*
James, David Gregg, Sr. 1965- *WhoMW 93*
James, David Gwynfor 1925- *Who 94*
James, David Lee 1933- *WhoWest 94*
James, David N. 1952- *ConAu 140*
James, David Phillip 1940- *WhoBlA 94*
James, David Randolph, Jr. 1924- *WhoFI 94*
James, David William Francis 1929- *Who 94*
James, Dennis 1917- *IntMPA 94, WhoHol 92*
James, Derek Claude 1929- *Who 94*
James, Dion 1962- *WhoBlA 94*
James, Don *WhoAm 94, WhoWest 94*
James, Dorothy Louise King 1952- *WhoMW 93*
James, Dorothy Marie 1936- *WhoBlA 94*
James, Dorris Clayton 1931- *WhoAm 94*
James, E. Pendleton 1929- *WhoAmP 93*
James, Earl Dennis 1952- *WhoWest 94*
James, Earl Eugene, Jr. 1923- *WhoAm 94, WhoFI 94, WhoScEn 94*
James, Eddie d1944 *WhoHol 92*
James, Edgar 1915- *Who 94*
James, Edward (Frederick) 1947- *EncSF 93*
James, Edward Foster 1917- *Who 94*
James, Edwin *EncSF 93*
James, Edwin 1923- *WrDr 94*
James, Edwin Clark 1932- *WhoAm 94*
James, Edwin Kenneth George 1916- *Who 94*
James, Eirian 1952- *NewGrDO*
James, Eleanor Mary 1935- *Who 94*
James, Elinor fl. 1681-1715 *BlmGWL*
James, Elizabeth 1945- *WrDr 94*
James, Elridge M. 1942- *WhoBlA 94*
James, Emrys d1989 *WhoHol 92*
James, Eric A. 1948- *WhoAmL 94*
James, Eric Arthur 1925- *Who 94*
James, Ernest Wilbur 1931- *WhoMW 93*
James, Etta 1938- *WhoBlA 94*
James, Evan Maitland 1911- *Who 94*
James, Felix 1937- *WhoBlA 94*
James, Forrest Hood, Jr. 1934- *IntWW 93*
James, Francis Crews 1930- *WhoScEn 94*
James, Francis Edward, Jr. 1931- *WhoAm 94*
James, Frank Munger 1939- *WhoFI 94*
James, Frank Samuel, III 1945- *WhoBlA 94*
James, Frederick *ConAu 140*
James, Frederick C. 1922- *WhoBlA 94*
James, Frederick Calhoun 1922- *WhoAm 94*
James, Frederick John 1938- *WhoBlA 94*
James, Gardner d1953 *WhoHol 92*
James, Gary Douglas 1954- *WhoScEn 94*
James, Gene Albert 1932- *WhoAm 94, WhoFI 94*
James, Geneva Behrens 1942- *WhoMW 93*
James, George Barker, II 1937- *WhoAm 94, WhoFI 94, WhoWest 94*
James, Geraint *Who 94*
James, (David) Geraint 1922- *Who 94*
James, Gerald d1917 *WhoHol 92*
James, Geraldine *WhoHol 92*
James, Geraldine 1950- *IntWW 93, Who 94*
James, Gerard Luz A., II 1953- *WhoAmP 93*
James, Gethin *Who 94*
James, (Ernest) Gethin 1925- *Who 94*
James, Gillette Oriel 1935- *WhoBlA 94*
James, Gladden d1948 *WhoHol 92*
James, Godfrey *WhoHol 92*
James, Gordon 1878- *WhoHol 92*
James, Gordon, III 1947- *WhoAmL 94*
James, Graham *WhoHol 92*
James, Graham Richard *Who 94*
James, Gregory Creed 1956- *WhoBlA 94*
James, Gus John, II 1938- *WhoAmL 94*
James, H. Rhett 1928- *WhoBlA 94*
James, H. Wynne, III 1944- *WhoAmL 94*
James, Hamice R., Jr. 1929- *WhoBlA 94*
James, Hamilton Evans 1951- *WhoAm 94*
James, Harold 1942- *WhoAmP 93*
James, Harold 1956- *IntWW 93*
James, Harold Arthur 1903- *WhoAm 94*
James, Harold L. 1912- *IntWW 93*
James, Harold Lee 1939- *WhoScEn 94*
James, Harry d1983 *WhoHol 92*
James, Harry 1916-1983 *ConMus 11 [port]*
James, Harry 1931- *WhoAmP 93*
James, Hawthorne *WhoBlA 94, WhoHol 92*
James, Henry 1843-1916 *BlmGEL, NewGrDO, RfGShF*
James, Henry, Jr. 1843-1916 *AmCulL [port]*
James, Henry David 1937- *WhoFI 94*
James, Henry Grady, III 1945- *WhoBlA 94*
James, Henry Gray *DrAPF 93*
James, Henry Leonard 1919- *Who 94*
James, Henry Nathaniel 1908- *WhoBlA 94*
James, Henry Thomas 1915- *WhoAm 94*
James, Herb Mark 1936- *WhoWest 94*
James, Herbert I. 1933- *WhoBlA 94*
James, Herman Delano 1943- *WhoAm 94, WhoBlA 94*
James, Horace D. d1925 *WhoHol 92*
James, Howell Malcolm Plowden 1954- *Who 94*
James, Hytolia Roberts 1929- *WhoBlA 94*
James, Ian Keith *WhoFI 94*
James, Ioan Mackenzie 1928- *IntWW 93, Who 94*
James, Isaac 1914- *WhoBlA 94*
James, Jacob *WhAmRev*
James, Jean Middleton 1930- *WhoMW 93*
James, Jeannette 1929- *WhoAmP 93*
James, Jefferson Ann 1943- *WhoMW 93*
James, Jennifer Austin 1943- *WhoFI 94*
James, Jesse, Jr. d1951 *WhoHol 92*
James, Jessica d1990 *WhoHol 92*
James, Jim Webb, III 1954- *WhoAmP 93*
James, Joe Paul 1967- *WhoFI 94*
James, John *WhoBlA 94*
James, John d1960 *WhoHol 92*
James, John 1906- *Who 94*
James, (David) John *ConAu 43NR*
James, John A. *Who 94*
James, John Alan 1927- *WhoAm 94, WhoFI 94*
James, John Christopher Urmston 1937- *Who 94*
James, John Delmar 1944- *WhoAm 94*
James, John Douglas 1949- *Who 94*
James, John Henry 1944- *Who 94*
James, John Ivor Pulsford 1913- *Who 94, WrDr 94*
James, John Jocelyn S. *Who 94*
James, John Nigel Courtenay 1935- *Who 94*
James, John V. 1918-1989 *WhAm 10*
James, Jonathan Elwyn Rayner 1950- *Who 94*
James, Joyce L. 1950- *WhoBlA 94*
James, Juanita T. 1952- *WhoBlA 94*
James, Kay C. 1949- *WhoBlA 94*
James, Keith 1937- *WhoHol 92*
James, Keith Alan 1957- *WhoAmL 94*
James, Kelvin Christopher *DrAPF 93*
James, Ken *WhoHol 92*
James, Kenneth *Who 94*
James, Kevin Porter 1964- *WhoBlA 94*
James, Kristin *ConAu 42NR*
James, Kyle *WhoHol 92*
James, Laurence 1942- *EncSF 93*
James, Lawrence Hoy 1956- *WhoScEn 94*
James, Lionel Frederic Edward 1912- *Who 94*
James, Lisa *WhoHol 92*
James, Livia 1957- *WrDr 94*
James, Lois Bradshaw 1939- *WhoMW 93*
James, (William) Louis (Gabriel) 1933- *WrDr 94*
James, Louis Meredith 1941- *WhoFI 94*
James, Luther 1928- *BlkWr 2, WhoBlA 94*
James, Lynmore 1937- *WhoAmP 93*
James, M(ontague) R(hodes) 1862-1936 *RfGShF*
James, Marie Moody 1928- *WhoMW 93*
James, Marie Ruppert 1942- *WhoFI 94*
James, Marilyn Shaw 1926- *WhoMW 93*
James, Marion Ray 1940- *WhoAm 94, WhoFI 94, WhoWest 94*
James, Mark A. 1959- *WhoAmP 93*
James, Marquita L. 1932- *WhoBlA 94*
James, Martin *DrAPF 93*
James, Mary *TwCYAW*
James, Mary 1927- *WrDr 94*
James, Mary Denny 1948- *WhoAmP 93*
James, Mary F. 1915- *WhoAmP 93*
James, Matthew 1923- *WrDr 94*
James, Michael *Who 94*
James, (Robert) Michael 1934- *Who 94*
James, Michael Andrew 1953- *WhoAmL 94*

Janku, Hana 1940- *NewGrDO*
Jankun, Jerzy Witold 1948- *WhoScEn 94*
Jankura, Donald Eugene 1929- *WhoAm 94, WhoWest 94*
Janman, Timothy Simon 1956- *Who 94*
Janneh, Bocar Ousman S. *Who 94*
Janner, Lady *Who 94*
Janner, Greville Ewan 1928- *Who 94*
Jannett, Thomas Cottongim 1958- *WhoScEn 94*
Jannetti, Tony 1947- *WhoAmA 93*
Janney, Christopher Draper 1950- *WhoAmA 93*
Janney, Donald Wayne 1952- *WhoAm 94, WhoAmL 94*
Janney, Leon d1980 *WhoHol 92*
Janney, Stuart Symington, III 1948- *WhoAm 94, WhoFI 94*
Janney, William 1908- *WhoHol 92*
Janning, John Louis 1928- *WhoMW 93*
Janning, Mary Bernadette 1917- *WhoAm 94*
Jannings, Emil d1950 *WhoHol 92*
Jannotti, Harry Peter 1924- *WhoAmP 93*
Jannucci, Robert *WhoHol 92*
Jannuzi, F. Tomasson 1934- *WhoAm 94*
Jannuzzo, Jeffrey Anthony 1949- *WhoAmL 94*
Janny, Amelia 1838-1914 *BlmGWL*
Janoff, Charles Joseph 1953- *WhoAmL 94*
Janoff, Ronald Wiley *DrAPF 93*
Janofsky, Julie Chapin 1959- *WhoAmL 94*
Janofsky, Leonard S. 1909- *WhoAm 94*
Janosik, Edward Gabriel 1918- *WhoAm 94*
Janoski, Henry Valentine 1933- *WhoAm 94, WhoFI 94*
Janot, Raymond Marcel Louis 1917- *IntWW 93*
Janousek, Arnold Lee 1930- *WhoWest 94*
Janov, Gwenellen P. 1948- *WhoAm 94*
Janover, Robert H. 1930- *WhoAmL 94, WhoMW 93*
Janovy, John, Jr. 1937- *ConAu 41NR*
Janowiak, Robert Michael 1935- *WhoAm 94*
Janowich, Ronald 1948- *WhoAmA 93*
Janowitz, Gerald Saul 1943- *WhoScEn 94*
Janowitz, Gundula 1937- *IntWW 93, NewGrDO*
Janowitz, James Arnold 1946- *WhoAmL 94*
Janowitz, Joel 1945- *WhoAmA 93*
Janowitz, Phyllis *DrAPF 93*
Janowitz, Robert J. 1943- *WhoAmL 94*
Janowitz, Tama *DrAPF 93*
Janowitz, Tama 1957- *WrDr 94*
Janowski, Gabriel 1947- *IntWW 93*
Janowski, Jan Stanislaw 1928- *IntWW 93*
Janowski, Marek *IntWW 93*
Janowski, Marek 1939- *NewGrDO*
Janowski, Thaddeus Marian 1923- *WhoAm 94, WrDr 94*
Janowsky, Oscar I. d1993 *NewYTBS 93 [port]*
Janowsky, Oscar I(saiah) 1900- *WrDr 94*
Janoy, Ellen d1976 *WhoHol 92*
Janquart, Laurence Francis 1928- *WhoMW 93*
Jans, Candace 1952- *WhoAmA 93*
Jans, Harry d1962 *WhoHol 92*
Jans, James Patrick 1927- *WhoAm 94*
Janschka, Fritz 1919- *WhoAmA 93*
Jansen, Allan W. 1948- *WhoAmL 94*
Jansen, Angela Bing 1929- *WhoAm 94, WhoAmA 93*
Jansen, Catherine Sandra 1950- *WhoAmA 93*
Jansen, Donald Orville 1939- *WhoAm 94*
Jansen, Donald William 1948- *WhoAmL 94*
Jansen, Elly 1929- *Who 94*
Jansen, G. Thomas 1926- *WhoAm 94*
Jansen, Gustav Richard 1930- *WhoWest 94*
Jansen, Jacques 1913- *NewGrDO*
Jansen, Jan Kristian Schoning 1931- *IntWW 93*
Jansen, Jared 1937- *WrDr 94*
Jansen, Kathryn Lynn 1957- *WhoScEn 94*
Jansen, Marius B(erthus) 1922- *WrDr 94*
Jansen, Michael E(lin) 1940- *WrDr 94*
Jansen, Peter Johan 1940- *IntWW 93, Who 94*
Jansen, Robert Bruce 1922- *WhoAm 94*
Jansen, Roger Edward 1968- *WhoMW 93*
Jansen, Ross (Malcolm) 1932- *Who 94*
Jansen, Sharon L. 1951- *ConAu 140*
Janse Van Vuuren, Cas 1930- *IntWW 93*
Jansky, Karl 1905-1950 *WorScD*
Janson, Agnes *WhoAmA 93*
Janson, Anthony Frederick 1943- *WhoAm 94*
Janson, Anthony Fredrick 1943- *WhoAmA 93*
Janson, Barbara Jean 1942- *WhoFI 94*
Janson, Hank *EncSF 93*
Janson, Horst *WhoHol 92*
Janson, Horst Woldemar 1913-1982 *WhoAmA 93N*
Janson, Joseph Bror, II 1928- *WhoAm 94*
Janson, Patrick 1967- *WhoAm 94*
Janson, Richard Wilford 1926- *WhoScEn 94*
Janson, Victor d1960 *WhoHol 92*
Jansonius, John V. 1955- *WhoAmL 94*
Jansons, Maris 1943- *IntWW 93*
Jansons, Mariss 1943- *Who 94*
Janss, Glenn Cooper 1932- *WhoAmA 93*
Janss, William Cluff 1918- *WhoAm 94*
Janssen, Andrew Gerard 1967- *WhoScEn 94*
Janssen, Baron Daniel 1936- *IntWW 93*
Janssen, Baron Paul-Emmanuel 1931- *IntWW 93*
Janssen, Dani *WhoHol 92*
Janssen, David d1980 *WhoHol 92*
Janssen, Erwin T. 1936- *WhoAm 94*
Janssen, Gail Edwin 1930- *WhoAm 94, WhoScEn 94*
Janssen, Hans *WhoAmA 93N*
Janssen, Herbert 1892-1965 *NewGrDO*
Janssen, Howard A. 1943- *WhoAmL 94*
Janssen, Laurence F. 1943- *WhoAmL 94*
Janssen, Leslie Lynn 1967- *WhoMW 93*
Janssen, Paul Adriaan Jan 1926- *WhoAm 94, WhoScEn 94*
Janssen, Peter Anton 1936- *WhoAm 94*
Janssen, Ramon E. 1937- *WhoAmP 93*
Janssen, Walter d1976 *WhoHol 92*
Janssen, Werner d1990 *WhoHol 92*
Janssen, Werner 1900-1990 *WhAm 10*
Janssens, Joseph William, Jr. 1935- *WhoAm 94*
Janssens, Robert Victor 1951- *WhoMW 93*
Janssen van Raay, James Leonard 1932- *IntWW 93*
Jansson, Jan-Magnus 1922- *IntWW 93*
Jansson, John Phillip 1918- *WhoScEn 94*
Jansson, Peter N. 1944- *WhoAmP 93*
Jansson, Tove 1914- *BlmGWL*
Jansson, Tove (Marika) 1914- *ConWorW 93, RfGShF*
Jans-Thomas, Susie 1955- *WhoMW 93*
Jansz, Hendrik Simon 1927- *IntWW 93*
Jansz, Willem fl. 160-?- *WhWE*
Janszky, Andrew Bela 1951- *WhoAm 94*
Jantsch, John J. 1960- *WhoMW 93*
Jantz, Jonathan Paul 1954- *WhoMW 93*
Jantz, Willfred D. 1931- *WhoFI 94*
Jantzen, Jens Carsten 1948- *WhoWest 94*
Jantzen, John Marc 1908- *WhoAm 94, WhoWest 94*
Janu, Ivana 1946- *WhoWomW 91*
January, Daniel Bruce 1953- *WhoMW 93, WhoScEn 94*
January, Lewis Edward 1910- *WhoAm 94*
January, Lois *WhoHol 92*
Janulaitis, M. Victor 1945- *WhoAm 94*
Janura, Jan Arol 1949- *WhoFI 94*
Janus, Julie *WhoAm 94*
Janus, Mark David 1953- *WhoMW 93, WhoScEn 94*
Janus, Sam (Shep) 1930- *WrDr 94*
Janvey, Richard Isaac *WhoAmL 94*
Janvier, Ivan *EncSF 93*
Janvier, Rosemary Farley 1939- *WhoAm 94*
Janvier, Thomas A(llibone) 1849-1913 *EncSF 93*
Janvrin, (Hugh) Richard Benest d1993 *Who 94N*
Janvrin, Robin Berry 1946- *Who 94*
Janzen, Betty Lou 1922- *WhoAmP 93*
Janzen, Daniel Hunt 1939- *IntWW 93, WhoAm 94*
Janzen, Jacob John 1919- *WhoAmP 93*
Janzen, Jean *DrAPF 93*
Janzen, Lee *WhoAm 94*
Janzen, Norine Madelyn Quinlan 1943- *WhoMW 93, WhoScEn 94*
Janzhong Zhaxi Doje 1925- *WhoPRCh 91*
Janzon, Bengt, Mrs. *Who 94*
Janzow, Walter Theophilus 1918- *WhoAm 94*
Jao, Radmar Agana 1966- *WhoAsA 94*
Japan, Emperor of *IntWW 93, Who 94*
Japikse, David *WhoScEn 94*
Japp, Nyla F. 1948- *WhoMW 93*
Japra, Romesh K. 1950- *WhoAsA 94*
Jaqua, Frederick William 1921- *WhoAmL 94, WhoFI 94*
Jaqua, Richard Allen 1938- *WhoAm 94*
Jaque, Louis 1919- *WhoAmA 93*
Jaque-Catelain d1965 *WhoHol 92*
Jaques, Carlos Eduardo 1946- *WhoHisp 94*
Jaques, Elliott 1917- *Who 94, WrDr 94*
Jaques, James Alfred, III 1940- *WhoScEn 94*
Jaques, Louis Barker 1911- *WhoAm 94, WrDr 94*
Jaques-Dalcroze, Emile 1865-1950 *NewGrDO*
Jaquet, Frank d1958 *WhoHol 92*
Jaquett, Peter d1834 *WhAmRev*
Jaquette, Peter Barnes 1952- *WhoFI 94*
Jaquish, Gail Ann 1955- *WhoAmL 94*
Jaquith, George Oakes 1916- *WhoAm 94, WhoScEn 94, WhoWest 94*
Jaquith, Richard Herbert 1919- *WhoAm 94*
Jara, Daniel *WhoHisp 94*
Jarabak, Andrew J. 1948- *WhoFI 94*
Jarabo Alvarez, José R. 1944- *WhoHisp 94*
Jara Diaz, Sergio R. 1951- *WhoScEn 94*
Jaraiz, Eladio Maldonado 1952- *WhoScEn 94*
Jaramillo, Ann *WhoHisp 94*
Jaramillo, Annabelle E. 1940- *WhoHisp 94*
Jaramillo, Anthony B. 1959- *WhoHisp 94*
Jaramillo, Arthur Lewis 1949- *WhoAm 94*
Jaramillo, Carlos Alberto 1952- *WhoMW 93*
Jaramillo, Debbie *WhoHisp 94*
Jaramillo, Delio Arturo, Jr. 1965- *WhoHisp 94*
Jaramillo, Ellen M. 1952- *WhoHisp 94*
Jaramillo, Ernesto 1963- *WhoHisp 94*
Jaramillo, George *WhoHisp 94*
Jaramillo, Henry, Jr. 1928- *WhoHisp 94*
Jaramillo, Jeannine D. 1960- *WhoHisp 94*
Jaramillo, M. Linda 1947- *WhoHisp 94*
Jaramillo, Mari-Luci 1928- *WhoHisp 94, WhoWest 94*
Jaramillo, María Mercedes 1949- *WhoHisp 94*
Jaramillo, Rudy *WhoHisp 94*
Jaramillo, Virginia 1939- *WhoAmA 93*
Jaramillo de Estrada, Cleopatra Marie 1951- *WhoHisp 94*
Jarashow, Richard L. 1946- *WhoAmL 94*
Jarausch, Konrad H(ugo) 1941- *WrDr 94*
Jaray, Hans d1990 *WhoHol 92*
Jaray, Tess 1937- *IntWW 93*
Jarblum, William 1945- *WhoAm 94*
Jarboe, John A. 1933- *WhoIns 94*
Jarboe, John Bruce 1940- *WhoAmL 94*
Jarboe, Mark Alan 1951- *WhoAm 94, WhoAmL 94*
Jarboro, Caterina 1903-1986 *NewGrDO*
Jarc, Frank Robert 1942- *WhoAm 94, WhoFI 94*
Jarcho, Leonard W. 1916- *WhoWest 94*
Jarcho, Saul Wallenstein 1906- *WhoAm 94*
Jarchow, Charles Christian 1894- *WhAm 10*
Jarchow, Homer E. *WhoAmP 93*
Jarcik, Edward Harold 1941- *WhoFI 94*
Jarda, Tudor 1922- *NewGrDO*
Jardetzky, Oleg 1929- *WhoAm 94, WhoScEn 94*
Jardin, Stephen Charles 1947- *WhoScEn 94*
Jardine, Alice A. 1951- *BlmGWL*
Jardine, Andrew (Colin Douglas) 1955- *Who 94*
Jardine, Betty d1945 *WhoHol 92*
Jardine, Donald Leroy 1926- *WhoAmA 93*
Jardine, Douglas Joseph 1954- *WhoScEn 94*
Jardine, James Christopher Macnaughton 1930- *Who 94*
Jardine, James Stuart 1946- *WhoAmL 94*
Jardine, Leslie James 1945- *WhoWest 94*
Jardine, Nicholas 1943- *Who 94*
Jardine, Ronald Charles C. *Who 94*
Jardine, Rupert Buchanan- *Who 94*
Jardine, (Andrew) Rupert (John) Buchanan- 1923- *Who 94*
Jardine, William 1784-1843 *DcNaB MP*
Jardine of Applegirth, Alexander Maule 1947- *Who 94*
Jardine Paterson, John (Valentine) 1920- *Who 94*
Jarecki, Henry George 1933- *WhoAm 94, WhoFI 94*
Jarecki, Henryk 1846-1918 *NewGrDO*
Jareckie, Stephen Barlow 1929- *WhoAm 94*
Jared, Jerry A. *WhoAmP 93*
Jares, Joe 1937- *WrDr 94*
Jaress, Jill *WhoHol 92*
Jargon, Jerry Robert 1939- *WhoScEn 94*
Jaric, Marko Vukobrat 1952- *WhoScEn 94*
Jarin, Kenneth M. 1951- *WhoAmL 94*
Jariwala, Sharad Lallubhai 1940- *WhoAsA 94*
Jarjura, Michael J. *WhoAmP 93*
Jarke, Frank Henry 1946- *WhoMW 93*
Jarman, A(lfred) O(wen) H(ughes) 1911- *WrDr 94*
Jarman, Claude, Jr. 1934- *IntMPA 94, WhoHol 92*
Jarman, Derek 1942- *IntWW 93, Who 94*
Jarman, Donald Ray 1928- *WhoWest 94*
Jarman, Douglas 1942- *WrDr 94*
Jarman, Franklin Maxey 1931- *IntWW 93*
Jarman, Joseph 1937- *WhoAm 94*
Jarman, Mark *DrAPF 93*
Jarman, Nicholas Francis Barnaby 1938- *Who 94*
Jarman, Roger Whitney 1935- *Who 94*
Jarman, Rosemary (Josephine) Hawley (Smith) 1935- *WrDr 94*
Jarman, Scott Allen 1963- *WhoScEn 94*
Jarman, Walton Maxey 1904-1980 *WhoAmA 93N*
Jarmer, Gary Edward 1941- *WhoMW 93*
Jarmie, Nelson 1928- *WhoAm 94*
Jarmin, Jill *WhoHol 92*
Jarmoc, Stephen M. *WhoAmP 93*
Jarmon, James Henry, Jr. 1942- *WhoBlA 94*
Jarmon, Lawrence 1946- *WhoWest 94*
Jarmus, Stephan Onysym 1925- *WhoAm 94*
Jarmusch, Jim 1953- *IntMPA 94, IntWW 93, WrDr 94*
Jarnagan, Harry William, Jr. 1953- *WhoFI 94*
Jarnefelt, (Edvard) Armas 1869-1958 *NewGrDO*
Jarnevic, Dragolja 1812-1875 *BlmGWL*
Jaroch, Timothy D. 1942- *WhoAm 94, WhoAmL 94*
Jarocki, Jerzy 1929- *IntWW 93*
Jaroff, Leon Morton 1927- *WhoAm 94, WrDr 94*
Jarolin, Stanley J. 1933- *WhoAmP 93*
Jaron, Dov 1935- *WhoAm 94, WhoScEn 94*
Jaron, Stephen Michael 1963- *WhoFI 94*
Jaros, Dean 1938- *WhoAm 94, WhoWest 94*
Jaros, Mike 1944- *WhoAmP 93*
Jaros, Robert James 1939- *WhoFI 94*
Jaroska, Faythe Ann 1945- *WhoAmP 93*
Jaroski, Edward L. 1946- *WhoIns 94*
Jaroslovsky, Alan 1948- *WhoAm 94, WhoAmL 94, WhoWest 94*
Jaroslow, Ruth *WhoHol 92*
Jarosova, Marie 1920- *WhoWomW 91*
Jarosu Urszula, Wanda *WhoWomW 91*
Jarosz, Boleslaw Francis 1953- *WhoScEn 94*
Jaroszewicz, Piotr 1909-1992 *AnObit 1992*
Jaroszewski, Jerzy W. 1950- *WhoScEn 94*
Jaroudi, Saeb 1929- *IntWW 93*
Jarrard, Leonard Everett 1930- *WhoAm 94*
Jarrard-Dimond, Terry 1945- *WhoAmA 93*
Jarrat, Henri Aaron 1938- *WhoAm 94*
Jarratt, Alexander Anthony 1924- *IntWW 93, Who 94*
Jarratt, Devereux 1733-1801 *DcAmReB 2*
Jarratt, John *WhoHol 92*
Jarratt, Peter 1935- *Who 94*
Jarre, Jean Michel Andre 1948- *IntWW 93*
Jarre, Maurice 1924- *IntDcF 2-4, IntMPA 94*
Jarre, Maurice Alexis 1924- *IntWW 93*
Jarreau, Al 1940- *WhoBlA 94*
Jarreau, Alwyn Lopez 1940- *WhoAm 94*
Jarred, Mary 1899- *NewGrDO*
Jarrel, Stig 1910- *WhoHol 92*
Jarrell, F. Fincher 1944- *WhoAmL 94*
Jarrell, John W. *WhoFI 94*
Jarrell, Mack 1926- *WhoAmP 93*
Jarrell, Mary Long 1929- *WhoAmP 93*
Jarrell, Randall 1914-1965 *AmCulL, WhoAmA 93N*
Jarrell, Tommy d1985 *WhoHol 92*
Jarrell, Wesley Michael 1948- *WhoScEn 94, WhoWest 94*
Jarret, Gabe *WhoHol 92*
Jarrett, Alexis 1948- *WhoFI 94, WhoMW 93*
Jarrett, Anthony 1930- *WhoAm 94*
Jarrett, Art d1987 *WhoHol 92*
Jarrett, Arthur d1960 *WhoHol 92*
Jarrett, Catherine *WhoHol 92*
Jarrett, Clifford (George) 1909- *Who 94*
Jarrett, Dan d1938 *WhoHol 92*
Jarrett, Derek 1928- *WrDr 94*
Jarrett, Emmett *DrAPF 93*
Jarrett, Eugene Lawrence 1942- *WhoAm 94*
Jarrett, Hobart Sidney 1915- *WhoBlA 94*
Jarrett, Keith 1945- *IntWW 93, WhoAm 94*
Jarrett, Martyn William *Who 94*
Jarrett, Noel 1921- *WhoAm 94*
Jarrett, Ronald Douglas 1952- *WhoWest 94*
Jarrett, Ruth 1942- *WhoFI 94*
Jarrett, Thomas D. 1912- *WhoBlA 94*
Jarrett, Valerie B. 1956- *WhoBlA 94*
Jarrett, Vernon D. 1921- *WhoBlA 94*
Jarrett, William Fleming Hoggan 1928- *IntWW 93, Who 94*
Jarrico, Paul 1915- *IntMPA 94*
Jarriel, Thomas Edwin 1934- *WhoAm 94*
Jarrin, Jaime 1935- *WhoHisp 94*

Jeffe, Douglas Ivan 1943- *WhoWest 94*
Jeffe, Huldah C. *WhoAmA 93*
Jeffe, Huldah Cherry *WhoAm 94*
Jeffe, Sidney David 1927- *WhoAm 94*
Jeffee, Saul 1918-1991 *WhAm 10*
Jeffer, Bruce P. 1942- *WhoAmL 94*
Jefferds, Vincent Harris 1916-1992 *WhAm 10*
Jefferies, Charlotte S. 1944- *WhoBlA 94*
Jefferies, David George 1933- *Who 94*
Jefferies, Douglas d1959 *WhoHol 92*
Jefferies, Gregory Scott 1967- *WhoAm 94, WhoMW 93*
Jefferies, Jack P. 1928- *WhoAm 94, WhoAmL 94*
Jefferies, John 1745-1819 *WhAmRev*
Jefferies, John D. 1928- *WhoAmP 93*
Jefferies, John Trevor 1925- *WhoAm 94, WhoScEn 94, WhoWest 94*
Jefferies, Michael John 1941- *WhoAm 94*
Jefferies, Richard 1848-1887 *BlmGEL, DcLB 141 [port]*
Jefferies, (John) Richard 1848-1887 *EncSF 93*
Jefferies, Robert Aaron, Jr. 1941- *WhoAm 94, WhoAmL 94*
Jefferies, Roger David 1939- *Who 94*
Jefferies, Sheelagh 1926- *Who 94*
Jefferies, Stephen 1951- *IntDcB, Who 94*
Jefferis, D. Allen 1937- *WhoAmP 93*
Jeffers, Arnold P. 1929- *WhoAmP 93*
Jeffers, Ben L. 1944- *WhoBlA 94*
Jeffers, Clifton R. 1934- *WhoBlA 94*
Jeffers, Crystal Lee 1938- *WhoAmP 93*
Jeffers, Dale Welborn 1952- *WhoScEn 94*
Jeffers, Donald E. 1925- *WhoAm 94*
Jeffers, E. L. *DrAPF 93*
Jeffers, George d1979 *WhoHol 92*
Jeffers, Grady Rommel 1943- *WhoBlA 94*
Jeffers, H. Paul *WrDr 94*
Jeffers, Jack 1928- *WhoBlA 94*
Jeffers, John Norman Richard 1926- *Who 94*
Jeffers, Leslie Joy 1961- *WhoWest 94*
Jeffers, Mary L. *WhoAmP 93*
Jeffers, Michael Bogue 1940- *WhoAm 94, WhoAmL 94*
Jeffers, Susan 1942- *ChlLR 30 [port]*
Jeffers, Thomas Lee 1956- *WhoMW 93*
Jeffers, Wendy Jane 1948- *WhoAmA 93*
Jeffers, William d1959 *WhoHol 92*
Jefferson, Alan 1921- *WrDr 94*
Jefferson, Alphine Wade 1950- *WhoBlA 94*
Jefferson, Andrew L., Jr. 1934- *WhoBlA 94*
Jefferson, Arthur 1938- *WhoBlA 94*
Jefferson, Arthur Stanley 1890-1965 *DcNaB MP*
Jefferson, Austin, Jr. *WhoBlA 94*
Jefferson, B. J. *WhoHol 92*
Jefferson, Bryan *Who 94*
Jefferson, (John) Bryan 1928- *Who 94*
Jefferson, Clifton 1928- *WhoBlA 94*
Jefferson, Daisy d1967 *WhoHol 92*
Jefferson, Doris Vernice 1924- *WhoAmP 93, WhoMW 93*
Jefferson, Fredrick Carl, Jr. 1934- *WhoBlA 94*
Jefferson, Galen 1950- *WhoWest 94*
Jefferson, Gary Scott 1945- *WhoBlA 94*
Jefferson, George Rowland 1921- *IntWW 93, Who 94*
Jefferson, Herb, Jr. 1946- *WhoHol 92*
Jefferson, Hilda Hutchinson 1920- *WhoBlA 94*
Jefferson, Hilton d1968 *WhoHol 92*
Jefferson, Horace Lee 1924- *WhoBlA 94*
Jefferson, Ian *EncSF 93*
Jefferson, James, Jr. 1951- *WhoAmL 94*
Jefferson, James E. 1922- *WhoBlA 94*
Jefferson, James Walter 1937- *WhoAm 94, WhoScEn 94*
Jefferson, Joan Ena 1946- *Who 94*
Jefferson, John Daniel 1948- *WhoWest 94*
Jefferson, Joseph d1905 *WhoHol 92*
Jefferson, Joseph L. 1940- *WhoBlA 94*
Jefferson, June L., Jr. 1924- *WhoBlA 94*
Jefferson, Karen L. 1952- *WhoBlA 94*
Jefferson, M. Ivory 1924- *WhoBlA 94*
Jefferson, Marcia D. 1935- *WhoBlA 94*
Jefferson, Melvin Dorsey 1922- *WhoAm 94, WhoMW 93*
Jefferson, Mervyn Stewart D. *Who 94*
Jefferson, Michael L 1949- *WhoScEn 94*
Jefferson, Myra LaVerne Tull *WhoWest 94*
Jefferson, Nancy B. 1923-1992 *WhoBlA 94N*
Jefferson, Overton C. *WhoBlA 94*
Jefferson, Paris *WhoHol 92*
Jefferson, Patricia Ann 1951- *WhoBlA 94*
Jefferson, Peter Augustus 1928- *WhoAm 94*
Jefferson, Reginald Jirod 1968- *WhoBlA 94*
Jefferson, Richard 1931- *WhoAmP 93*
Jefferson, Robert R. 1932- *WhoBlA 94*
Jefferson, Robert Wayne 1939- *WhoFI 94*
Jefferson, Roland S(pratlin) 1939- *BlkWr 2*
Jefferson, Roland Spratlin 1939- *WhoBlA 94*
Jefferson, Roy Lee, Jr. 1943- *WhoBlA 94*
Jefferson, Shirley Almira 1929- *WhoAmP 93*
Jefferson, Thomas d1932 *WhoHol 92*
Jefferson, Thomas 1743-1826 *AmCulL, DcAmReB 2, EncEth, HisWorL [port], WhAmRev [port], WorInv*
Jefferson, Wayne 1948- *WhoMW 93*
Jefferson, William J. 1947- *CngDr 93, WhoAm 94, WhoAmP 93, WhoBlA 94*
Jefferson, William Winter d1946 *WhoHol 92*
Jefferson-Ford, Charmain 1963- *WhoBlA 94*
Jefferson-Moss, Carolyn 1945- *WhoBlA 94*
Jefferson Smith, Peter 1939- *Who 94*
Jeffery, David John 1936- *Who 94*
Jeffery, Geoffrey Marron 1919- *WhoAm 94*
Jeffery, James Nels 1944- *WhoWest 94*
Jeffery, John Edward 1915- *WhoWest 94*
Jeffery, Lawrence 1953- *WrDr 94*
Jeffery, Maria Aoling Chea 1962- *WhoFI 94*
Jeffery, Michael Ives 1944- *WhoAmL 94*
Jeffery, Peter Grant 1953- *WhoAm 94*
Jeffery, Robert Martin Colquhoun 1935- *Who 94*
Jeffery, William 1943- *WrDr 94*
Jeffery, William Richard 1944- *WhoAm 94*
Jefferys, Charles William 1869-1951 *WhoAmA 93N*
Jefferys, William Hamilton, III 1940- *WhoAm 94*
Jeffett, Frank Asbury 1927- *WhoAm 94*
Jeffires, Haywood Franklin 1964- *WhoAm 94*
Jefford, Barbara 1930- *WhoHol 92*
Jefford, Barbara Mary 1930- *Who 94*
Jefford, Bat *ConAu 42NR*
Jeffords, Edward Alan 1945- *WhoAmL 94*
Jeffords, James M. 1934- *CngDr 93*
Jeffords, James Merrill 1934- *IntWW 93, WhoAm 94, WhoAmP 93*
Jeffords, Walter M., Jr. 1915-1990 *WhAm 10*
Jeffredo, John Victor 1927- *WhoFI 94, WhoWest 94*
Jeffrey, Charles James, Jr. 1925- *WhoBlA 94*
Jeffrey, Francis 1773-1850 *BlmGEL*
Jeffrey, Francis 1950- *WrDr 94*
Jeffrey, Graham 1935- *WrDr 94*
Jeffrey, Howard d1988 *WhoHol 92*
Jeffrey, John E. 1938- *WhoAmP 93*
Jeffrey, John Orval 1963- *WhoWest 94*
Jeffrey, Marcus Fannin 1934- *WhoScEn 94*
Jeffrey, Michael d1960 *WhoHol 92*
Jeffrey, Mildred M. *DrAPF 93*
Jeffrey, Peter 1929- *WhoHol 92*
Jeffrey, Renwick Byron 1935- *WhoWest 94*
Jeffrey, Richard Carl 1926- *IntWW 93*
Jeffrey, Robert Asahel, Jr. 1922- *WhoScEn 94*
Jeffrey, Robert Campbell 1927- *WhoAm 94*
Jeffrey, Robert George, Jr. 1933- *WhoAm 94*
Jeffrey, Robin Campbell 1939- *Who 94*
Jeffrey, Ronald James 1949- *WhoWest 94*
Jeffrey, Ronnald James 1949- *WhoBlA 94*
Jeffrey, Thomas E. 1947- *WrDr 94*
Jeffrey, Walter Leslie 1908- *WhoAm 94*
Jeffrey, William Alexander 1948- *Who 94*
Jeffreys, Baron 1957- *Who 94*
Jeffreys, Judge *BlmGEL*
Jeffreys, Alec *WorInv*
Jeffreys, Alec John 1950- *IntWW 93, Who 94*
Jeffreys, Anne 1923- *IntMPA 94, WhoHol 92*
Jeffreys, David Alfred 1934- *Who 94*
Jeffreys, Ellis d1943 *WhoHol 92*
Jeffreys, Elystan Geoffrey 1926- *WhoAm 94, WhoFI 94*
Jeffreys, J. G. 1908- *WrDr 94*
Jeffreys, John H. 1940- *WhoBlA 94*
Jeffreys, Judith Diana 1927- *Who 94*
Jeffreys, Margaret Villar 1953- *WhoFI 94*
Jeffreys, Stephen 1950- *ConDr 93*
Jeffreys, William Armistead 1936- *WhoFI 94*
Jeffries, Carson Dunning 1922- *IntWW 93, WhoAm 94*
Jeffries, Charles Dean 1929- *WhoAm 94*
Jeffries, Fran 1939- *WhoHol 92*
Jeffries, Freddie L. 1939- *WhoBlA 94*
Jeffries, Haywood Franklin 1964- *WhoBlA 94*
Jeffries, Herb 1914- *WhoHol 92*
Jeffries, James E. 1925- *WhoAmP 93*
Jeffries, James J. d1953 *WhoHol 92*
Jeffries, John (Francis) 1929- *Who 94*
Jeffries, Lang d1987 *WhoHol 92*
Jeffries, Leonard *WhoBlA 94*
Jeffries, Lionel 1926- *IntMPA 94, IntWW 93, WhoHol 92*
Jeffries, Lionel Charles 1926- *Who 94*
Jeffries, McChesney Hill 1922- *WhoAm 94*
Jeffries, McChesney Hill, Jr. 1954- *WhoAmL 94*
Jeffries, Mina d1978 *WhoHol 92*
Jeffries, Robert Alan 1933- *WhoAm 94, WhoScEn 94*
Jeffries, Robert Joseph 1923- *WhoAm 94*
Jeffries, Roderic 1926- *WrDr 94*
Jeffries, Rosalind R. 1936- *WhoBlA 94*
Jeffries, Russell Morden 1935- *WhoWest 94*
Jeffries, Thomas William 1947- *WhoMW 93*
Jeffries, William Patrick 1945- *IntWW 93*
Jeffries, William Worthington 1914-1989 *WhAm 10*
Jeffs, (George) James (Horatio) 1900- *Who 94*
Jeffs, Julian 1931- *Who 94, WrDr 94*
Jeffs, Kenneth Peter 1931- *Who 94*
Jeffs, M. Dayle 1930- *WhoAmL 94*
Jeffs, Rae 1921- *WrDr 94*
Jeffs, Thomas Hamilton, II 1938- *WhoAm 94, WhoFI 94*
Jeffs, Wallace E. 1926- *WhoIns 94*
Jeffus, Maggie 1934- *WhoAmP 93*
Jeftic, Ljubomir Mile 1936- *WhoScEn 94*
Jegasothy, Brian Vasanthakumar 1943- *WhoAm 94*
Jegen, Lawrence A., III 1934- *WhoAm 94*
Jeger, Baroness 1915- *Who 94, WhoWomW 91*
Jegham, Samir 1960- *WhoScEn 94*
Jeghelli, Federico *NewGrDO*
Jegla, Dorothy Eldredge 1939- *WhoMW 93*
Jegley, Dawn Catherine 1961- *WhoScEn 94*
Jehangir, Hirji 1915- *Who 94*
Jehle, Michael Edward 1954- *WhoAm 94*
Jehlen, Patricia D. 1943- *WhoAmP 93*
Jehn, Betty L. 1921- *WhoMW 93*
Jehn, Lawrence Andrew 1921- *WhoMW 93*
Jehnsen, David Charles 1943- *WhoAmP 93*
Jeitschko, Wolfgang Karl 1936- *WhoScEn 94*
Jejeebhoy, Jamsetjee 1913- *Who 94*
Jekel, James Franklin 1934- *WhoAm 94*
Jekel, Joseph Frank 1958- *WhoMW 93*
Jekel, Pam *DrAPF 93*
Jekel, Pamela Lee 1948- *WrDr 94*
Jeker, Robert A. 1935- *IntWW 93*
Jekyll, Gertrude 1843-1932 *DcNaB MP*
Jelalian, Albert V. 1933- *WhoScEn 94*
Jelavich, Barbara 1923- *WhoAm 94*
Jelen, Denise Marie 1964- *WhoMW 93*
Jelen, Jaroslaw Andrzej 1943- *WhoWest 94*
Jelensperger, Francis J. 1943- *WhoAm 94*
Jelf, Richard William 1904- *Who 94*
Jelinek, Elfriede 1946- *BlmGWL*
Jelinek, Frederick 1932- *WhoAm 94*
Jelinek, Hans d1992 *WhoAmA 93N*
Jelinek, Hans 1910-1992 *WhAm 10*
Jelinek, John Joseph 1955- *WhoAm 94*
Jelinek, Josef Emil 1928- *WhoAm 94*
Jelinek, Otto John 1940- *IntWW 93*
Jelinek, Robert 1929- *WhoAm 94*
Jeljaszewicz, Janusz 1930- *IntWW 93*
Jelks, Edward Baker 1922- *WhoAm 94*
Jellema, Jon 1943- *WhoMW 93*
Jellema, Rod *DrAPF 93*
Jellett, James Morgan 1940- *WhoAm 94*
Jelley, Scott Allen 1960- *WhoScEn 94*
Jellico, John Anthony 1914- *WhoAmA 93, WhoWest 94*
Jellico, Nancy R. 1939- *WhoAmA 93*
Jellico, Nancy Rose 1939- *WhoWest 94*
Jellicoe, Earl 1918- *IntWW 93, Who 94*
Jellicoe, Ann *Who 94*
Jellicoe, Ann 1927- *BlmGEL, BlmGWL, WrDr 94*
Jellicoe, (Patricia) Ann 1927- *ConDr 93, IntDcT 2, Who 94*
Jellicoe, Geoffrey (Alan) 1900- *IntWW 93, Who 94*
Jellicoe, Geoffrey (Alan) 1900-1993 *WrDr 94N*
Jellicorse, John Lee 1937- *WhoAm 94*
Jelliffe, Charles Gordon 1914- *WhoAm 94*
Jelliffe, Roger Woodham 1929- *WhoAm 94, WhoScEn 94*
Jellinek, George 1919- *WhoAm 94*
Jellinek, Miles Andrew 1947- *WhoAm 94, WhoAmL 94*
Jellinek, Paul s. 1951- *WhoAm 94*
Jellinek, Roger 1938- *WhoAm 94, WhoWest 94*
Jellinek, Tristram *WhoHol 92*
Jellison, James Logan, II 1922- *WhoMW 93*
Jelmoli, Hans 1877-1936 *NewGrDO*
Jelstrom, Evelyn Maja 1955- *WhoAm 94*
Jelyotte, Pierre de 1713-1797 *NewGrDO*
Jemelian, John Nazar 1933- *WhoAm 94*
Jemison, Anna *WhoHol 92*
Jemison, Mae C. 1956- *AfrAmAl 6 [port], CurBio 93 [port], WhoBlA 94*
Jemison, Theodore Judson 1918- *WhoAm 94, WhoBlA 94*
Jemmott, Hensley B. 1947- *WhoBlA 94*
Jen, Calvin Chi-en 1954- *WhoMW 93*
Jen, Chih Kung 1906- *WhoAsA 94*
Jen, Frank Chifeng 1931- *WhoAm 94*
Jen, Gish 1955- *WhoAsA 94, WrDr 94*
Jen, Horatio H. 1936- *WhoAsA 94*
Jen, James A. 1944- *WhoAsA 94*
Jen, Joseph Jwu-Shan 1939- *WhoAsA 94*
Jen, Lillian C. 1955- *WhoAsA 94*
Jen, Philip HungSun 1944- *WhoAsA 94*
Jen, Serena *WhoAsA 94*
Jen, Tien-Chien 1959- *WhoScEn 94*
Jena, Purusottam 1943- *WhoAsA 94*
Jenab, S. Abe 1936- *WhoScEn 94*
Jenbach, Bela 1871-1943 *NewGrDO*
Jenckes, Thomas Allen 1939- *WhoWest 94*
Jencks, Charles (Alexander) 1939- *WrDr 94*
Jencks, Charles Alexander 1939- *Who 94*
Jencks, Christopher Sandys 1936- *WhoAm 94*
Jencks, William Platt 1927- *IntWW 93, WhoAm 94, WhoScEn 94*
Jenden, Donald James 1926- *WhoAm 94, WhoScEn 94*
Jendly, Roger *WhoHol 92*
Jendrzejewski, Andrew John 1946- *WhoAmA 93*
Jenefsky, Jack 1919- *WhoFI 94, WhoMW 93*
Jenekhe, Samson Ally 1951- *WhoScEn 94*
Jenes, Theodore George, Jr. 1930- *WhoAm 94, WhoWest 94*
Jenesky, George *WhoHol 92*
Jeney, Peggy Jean 1934- *WhoAmP 93*
Jeng, Tzyy-Wen 1947- *WhoMW 93, WhoScEn 94*
Jenifer, Daniel of St. Thomas 1723-1790 *WhAmRev*
Jenifer, Franklin G. 1939- *AfrAmAl 6*
Jenifer, Franklyn Green 1939- *WhoBlA 94*
Jeniker, Charles J. 1924- *WhoAmP 93*
Jenke, Dennis Roger 1954- *WhoMW 93*
Jenkens, Garlan F. 1949- *WhoAmA 93*
Jenkin *Who 94*
Jenkin, Bernard Christison 1959- *Who 94*
Jenkin, Conrad *Who 94*
Jenkin, (David) Conrad 1928- *Who 94*
Jenkin, Ian (Evers) Tregarthen 1920- *Who 94*
Jenkin, Len 1941- *ConDr 93, WrDr 94*
Jenkin, Simon William Geoffrey 1943- *Who 94*
Jenkin Of Roding, Baron 1926- *IntWW 93, Who 94*
Jenkins *Who 94*
Jenkins, Adam, Jr. 1942- *WhoBlA 94*
Jenkins, Adelbert Howard 1934- *WhoBlA 94*
Jenkins, Alan 1914-1993 *WrDr 94N*
Jenkins, Alan Deloss 1949- *WhoScEn 94*
Jenkins, Alan Roberts 1926- *Who 94*
Jenkins, Albert Felton, Jr. 1941- *WhoAm 94*
Jenkins, Alexander, III 1934- *WhoAm 94*
Jenkins, Allen d1974 *WhoHol 92*
Jenkins, Althea H. 1941- *WhoBlA 94*
Jenkins, Andrew 1936- *WhoBlA 94*
Jenkins, Andrew 1941- *WhoAmP 93*
Jenkins, Andrew James 1941- *WhoBlA 94*
Jenkins, Anthony Curtis 1958- *WhoMW 93*
Jenkins, Aubrey Dennis 1927- *Who 94*
Jenkins, Augustus G., Jr. 1943- *WhoBlA 94*
Jenkins, Barbara Williams 1934- *WhoBlA 94*
Jenkins, Benjamin Larry 1938- *WhoAm 94, WhoIns 94*
Jenkins, Betty Jean 1940- *WhoWest 94*
Jenkins, Bobby G. 1939- *WhoBlA 94*
Jenkins, Brian (Garton) 1935- *Who 94*
Jenkins, Bruce 1948- *WhoAm 94*
Jenkins, Bruce Armand 1933- *WhoFI 94*
Jenkins, Bruce Sterling 1927- *WhoAm 94, WhoAmL 94, WhoWest 94*
Jenkins, Burris 1897-1966 *WhoAmA 93N*
Jenkins, Caren 1958- *WhoWest 94*
Jenkins, Carl Scarborough 1916- *WhoBlA 94*
Jenkins, Carol Ann 1944- *WhoBlA 94*
Jenkins, Cecil R., Jr. *WhoAmP 93*
Jenkins, Charla R. 1947- *WhoMW 93*

Jenkins, Charles 1941- *IntMPA 94*
Jenkins, Charles E., Sr. 1928- *WhoBlA 94*
Jenkins, Charles H., Jr. 1916- *WhoAm 94*
Jenkins, Charles Peter de Brisay 1923- *Who 94*
Jenkins, Chester L. *WhoAmP 93*
Jenkins, Chip *WhoBlA 94*
Jenkins, Christopher *Who 94*
Jenkins, (James) Christopher 1939- *Who 94*
Jenkins, Christopher Dennis Alexander M. *Who 94*
Jenkins, Clara Barnes *WhoBlA 94*
Jenkins, Clara Barnes 1943- *WhoAm 94, WhoFI 94*
Jenkins, Claude 1877-1959 *DcNaB MP*
Jenkins, Clay Lewis 1964- *WhoAmL 94*
Jenkins, Clive *Who 94*
Jenkins, (David) Clive 1926- *IntWW 93, Who 94*
Jenkins, Curtis S. *WhoAmP 93*
Jenkins, Cynthia 1924- *WhoBlA 94*
Jenkins, Cynthia Ann Latiolais 1952- *WhoAmP 93*
Jenkins, Dan 1916- *IntMPA 94*
Jenkins, Daniel Edwards, Jr. 1916- *WhoAm 94*
Jenkins, Daniel H. *WhoHol 92*
Jenkins, David 1912- *Who 94*
Jenkins, David A. *WhoAmL 94, WhoFI 94*
Jenkins, David Alan 1952- *WhoMW 93*
Jenkins, David B. *WhoFI 94*
Jenkins, David Edward *Who 94*
Jenkins, David Edward 1925- *IntWW 93*
Jenkins, David Edward Stewart 1949- *Who 94*
Jenkins, David Graham 1933- *IntWW 93*
Jenkins, David John 1948- *Who 94*
Jenkins, David L. 1931- *WrDr 94*
Jenkins, Donald John 1931- *WhoAm 94, WhoAmA 93*
Jenkins, Drewie Gutrimez 1915- *WhoBlA 94*
Jenkins, E. Cynthia 1921- *WhoAmP 93*
Jenkins, Edgar Lanier 1933- *WhoAmP 93*
Jenkins, Edmond Thomas 1930- *WhoBlA 94*
Jenkins, Elaine B. 1916- *WhoBlA 94*
Jenkins, Elizabeth *IntWW 93, Who 94, WrDr 94*
Jenkins, Elizabeth d1965 *WhoHol 92*
Jenkins, Elizabeth Ameta 1929- *WhoBlA 94*
Jenkins, Ella Louise 1924- *WhoBlA 94*
Jenkins, Emmanuel Lee 1934- *WhoBlA 94*
Jenkins, Everett Wilbur, Jr. 1953- *WhoAmL 94, WhoWest 94*
Jenkins, Ferguson 1943- *NewYTBS 93 [port], WhoBlA 94*
Jenkins, Ferguson Arthur, Jr. 1943- *WhoAm 94*
Jenkins, Frank Graham 1923- *Who 94*
Jenkins, Frank Shockley 1925- *WhoBlA 94*
Jenkins, Garth John 1933- *Who 94*
Jenkins, Gary 1928- *WrDr 94*
Jenkins, Gayle Expose 1927- *WhoBlA 94*
Jenkins, George 1908- *IntMPA 94, WhoAm 94*
Jenkins, George 1911- *IntDcF 2-4*
Jenkins, George Arthur, Jr. 1955- *WhoBlA 94*
Jenkins, George Charles 1927- *Who 94*
Jenkins, George E., III 1957- *WhoBlA 94*
Jenkins, George Henry 1929- *WhoMW 93*
Jenkins, George L. 1940- *WhoAm 94*
Jenkins, Gilbert Kenneth 1918- *Who 94*
Jenkins, Graeme (James Ewers) 1958- *NewGrDO*
Jenkins, Harold 1909- *IntWW 93, Who 94, WrDr 94*
Jenkins, Harold Richard 1918-1989 *WhAm 10*
Jenkins, Harry Lancaster 1932- *WhoBlA 94*
Jenkins, Henry Alfred 1925- *Who 94*
Jenkins, Herman Lee 1940- *WhoBlA 94*
Jenkins, Howard, Jr. 1915- *WhoBlA 94*
Jenkins, Howard M. 1951- *WhoAm 94, WhoFI 94*
Jenkins, Hugh Royston 1933- *Who 94*
Jenkins, Ivor 1913- *Who 94*
Jenkins, Jackie 1938- *WhoHol 92*
Jenkins, James Allister 1923- *WhoAm 94*
Jenkins, James E. 1939- *WhoBlA 94*
Jenkins, James Robert 1945- *WhoAmL 94*
Jenkins, James Stanley 1935- *WhoWest 94*
Jenkins, James Thomas 1942- *WhoScEn 94*
Jenkins, James William 1953- *WhoMW 93, WhoScEn 94*
Jenkins, Janet Ann 1950- *WhoAmP 93*
Jenkins, Janet E. 1941- *WhoWest 94*
Jenkins, Janet Elaine 1941- *WhoAmP 93*
Jenkins, Jean Alice 1938- *WhoWomW 91*
Jenkins, Jeffrey M. 1963- *WhoWest 94*
Jenkins, Jennifer *Who 94*
Jenkins, (Mary) Jennifer 1921- *IntWW 93, Who 94*
Jenkins, Jerry Ray 1944- *WhoAmL 94*
Jenkins, Jimmy Raymond 1943- *WhoBlA 94*
Jenkins, John Anthony 1926- *WhoAm 94*
Jenkins, John George 1919- *Who 94*
Jenkins, John Geraint 1929- *WrDr 94*
Jenkins, John Henry 1898- *WhAm 10*
Jenkins, John J. 1937- *WrDr 94*
Jenkins, John Owen 1922- *Who 94*
Jenkins, John Reese 1952- *WhoAm 94*
Jenkins, John Robin 1912- *Who 94*
Jenkins, John Smith 1932- *WhoAm 94*
Jenkins, Joryn *WhoAmL 94*
Jenkins, Joseph A. *WhoAmP 93*
Jenkins, Joseph Walter, Jr. 1941- *WhoBlA 94*
Jenkins, Julius *WhoBlA 94*
Jenkins, Katharine Mary 1945- *Who 94*
Jenkins, Kenneth Vincent *WhoAm 94, WhoBlA 94*
Jenkins, Kevin J. *WhoAm 94*
Jenkins, Larry Flash *WhoHol 92*
Jenkins, Lawrence Eugene 1933- *WhoAm 94*
Jenkins, Leo Donald 1932- *WhoAmP 93*
Jenkins, Leroy 1932- *WhoAm 94*
Jenkins, Loren 1941- *WhoAmP 93*
Jenkins, Louis *DrAPF 93*
Jenkins, Louis 1947- *WhoAmP 93*
Jenkins, Louis E. 1931- *WhoBlA 94*
Jenkins, Lozelle DeLuz *WhoBlA 94*
Jenkins, Luther Neal *WhoBlA 94*
Jenkins, M. T. Pepper 1917- *WhoAm 94*
Jenkins, Margaret Aikens 1925- *WhoWest 94*
Jenkins, Margaret Bunting 1935- *WhoAm 94*
Jenkins, Marilyn Joyce 1943- *WhoBlA 94*
Jenkins, Martha 1961- *WhoAmP 93*
Jenkins, Mary 1939- *WhoAmP 93*
Jenkins, Mary Anne Keel 1929- *WhoAmA 93*
Jenkins, Matthew Grady 1950- *WhoFI 94, WhoMW 93*
Jenkins, Megs 1917- *WhoHol 92*
Jenkins, Melvin 1962- *WhoBlA 94*
Jenkins, Melvin E., Jr. 1923- *WhoBlA 94*
Jenkins, Melvin L. 1947- *WhoBlA 94*
Jenkins, Michael (Romilly Heald) 1936- *Who 94, WrDr 94*
Jenkins, Michael Nicholas Howard 1932- *Who 94*
Jenkins, Michael Romilly Heald 1936- *IntWW 93*
Jenkins, Mirtlean Jackson *WhoMW 93*
Jenkins, Mona Pendergrass 1937- *WhoFI 94*
Jenkins, Monica 1961- *WhoBlA 94*
Jenkins, Neil 1945- *NewGrDO*
Jenkins, Neil Edmund 1949- *WhoFI 94*
Jenkins, Neil Martin James 1945- *Who 94*
Jenkins, Newell (Owen) 1915- *NewGrDO*
Jenkins, Orville Wesley 1913- *WhoAm 94*
Jenkins, Owain (Trevor) 1907- *Who 94*
Jenkins, Ozella 1945- *WhoBlA 94*
Jenkins, Pamela Gardner 1950- *WhoAmP 93*
Jenkins, Paul *DrAPF 93*
Jenkins, Paul 1923- *WhoAm 94, WhoAmA 93*
Jenkins, Paul R. 1942- *WhoAm 94*
Jenkins, Paul Ripley 1904-1974 *WhoAmA 93N*
Jenkins, Peter 1934-1992 *AnObit 1992*
Jenkins, Peter White 1937- *Who 94*
Jenkins, Phillip Lane 1923- *WhoFI 94*
Jenkins, Ray(mond Leonard) 1935- *WrDr 94*
Jenkins, Rebecca *WhoHol 92*
Jenkins, Rex Warren 1962- *WhoFI 94*
Jenkins, Richard *WhoHol 92*
Jenkins, Richard Lee 1931- *WhoAm 94, WhoFI 94*
Jenkins, Richard Peter Vellacott 1943- *Who 94*
Jenkins, Robert Berryman 1950- *WhoFI 94*
Jenkins, Robert Kenneth, Jr. 1947- *WhoBlA 94*
Jenkins, Robert Lee 1932- *WhoAm 94, WhoWest 94*
Jenkins, Robert Nesbit 1951- *WhoAm 94*
Jenkins, Robert Rowe 1933- *WhoAmL 94*
Jenkins, Robert Spurgeon 1921-1992 *WhAm 10*
Jenkins, Robin *Who 94*
Jenkins, (John) Robin 1912- *WrDr 94*
Jenkins, Roger J. 1939- *WhoBlA 94*
Jenkins, Ronald Patrick 1960- *WhoWest 94*
Jenkins, Roy (Harris) 1920- *WrDr 94*
Jenkins, Royal Gregory 1936- *WhoAm 94, WhoFI 94, WhoWest 94*
Jenkins, Ruben Lee 1929- *WhoAm 94*
Jenkins, Samuel Leroy 1928- *WhoWest 94*
Jenkins, Shirley Lymons 1936- *WhoBlA 94*
Jenkins, Simon 1943- *WrDr 94*
Jenkins, Simon David 1943- *IntWW 93, Who 94*
Jenkins, Speight 1937- *NewGrDO, WhoAm 94, WhoWest 94*
Jenkins, Stanley Kenneth 1920- *Who 94*
Jenkins, Stanley Michael 1940- *WhoFI 94*
Jenkins, Stephen Charles 1967- *WhoFI 94*
Jenkins, Stephen Robert 1952- *WhoMW 93*
Jenkins, Susan Leigh 1963- *WhoFI 94*
Jenkins, Thomas Edward 1902- *Who 94*
Jenkins, Thomas Harris 1920- *Who 94*
Jenkins, Thomas K. *WhoAmP 93*
Jenkins, Thomas Llewellyn 1927- *WhoAm 94*
Jenkins, Thomas M. *WhoBlA 94*
Jenkins, Thomas O. 1926- *WhoBlA 94*
Jenkins, Van 1911- *WhoBlA 94*
Jenkins, Vivian Evan 1918- *Who 94*
Jenkins, Walter Donald *WhoMW 93*
Jenkins, Warren d1989 *WhoHol 92*
Jenkins, Will F. *EncSF 93*
Jenkins, William Atwell 1922- *WhoAm 94*
Jenkins, William Ivy 1940- *WhoAm 94, WhoMW 93*
Jenkins, William Kenneth 1947- *WhoAm 94, WhoScEn 94*
Jenkins, William Maxwell 1919- *WhoAm 94*
Jenkins, William Robert *WhAm 10*
Jenkins, William Walter 1943- *WhoWest 94*
Jenkins, Woodie R., Jr. 1940- *WhoBlA 94*
Jenkins, Yolanda L. 1945- *WhoBlA 94*
Jenkins Miller, Janet 1937- *WhoWomW 91*
Jenkins Of Hillhead, Baron 1920- *IntWW 93, Who 94*
Jenkins Of Hillhead, Lady *Who 94*
Jenkins Of Putney, Baron 1908- *Who 94*
Jenkinson, Anthony d1611 *WhWE*
Jenkinson, Biddy 1929- *BlmGWL*
Jenkinson, David Stewart 1928- *Who 94*
Jenkinson, Jeffrey Charles 1939- *Who 94*
Jenkinson, John (Banks) 1945- *Who 94*
Jenkinson, Marion Anne 1937- *WhoMW 93*
Jenkins-Scott, Jackie 1949- *WhoBlA 94*
Jenko, Davorin 1835-1914 *NewGrDO*
Jenks, Cindy Steel 1961- *WhoAmL 94*
Jenks, Downing Bland 1915- *IntWW 93, WhoAm 94*
Jenks, Frank d1962 *WhoHol 92*
Jenks, Gerald Erwin 1945- *WhoScEn 94*
Jenks, Homer Simeon 1914- *WhoAm 94*
Jenks, Michael Ronald 1945- *WhoAmL 94*
Jenks, Richard Atherley 1906- *Who 94*
Jenks, Sarah Isabel 1913- *WhoMW 93*
Jenks, Si d1970 *WhoHol 92*
Jenks, Thomas Edward 1929- *WhoAm 94*
Jenks, (Clarence) Wilfred 1909-1973 *DcNaB MP*
Jenkyns, Henry Leigh 1917- *Who 94*
Jenne, Kenneth C. 1946- *WhoAmP 93*
Jenner, Ann Maureen 1944- *Who 94*
Jenner, Bruce 1949- *WhoAm 94, WhoHol 92*
Jenner, Edward 1749-1823 *WorScD*
Jenner, George d1946 *WhoHol 92*
Jenner, Jesse Jacob 1947- *WhoAmL 94*
Jenner, William Alexander 1915- *WhoAm 94, WhoMW 93, WhoScEn 94*
Jennerich, Edward John 1945- *WhoAm 94, WhoWest 94*
Jennerjahn, W. P. 1922- *WhoAmA 93*
Jeness, Phyllis 1922- *WhoAm 94*
Jennett, (William) Bryan 1926- *Who 94*
Jennett, Frederick Stuart 1924- *Who 94*
Jennett, Joseph Charles 1940- *WhoAm 94*
Jennett, Shirley Shimmick 1937- *WhoWest 94*
Jennette, Noble Stevenson, III 1953- *WhoAmL 94*
Jennewein, C. Paul 1890-1978 *WhoAmA 93N*
Jennewein, James Joseph 1929- *WhoAm 94*
Jenney, Judith Ann 1964- *WhoMW 93*
Jenney, Lucinda *WhoHol 92*
Jenney, Neil 1945- *WhoAmA 93*
Jenney, Neil Franklin, Jr. 1945- *WhoAm 94*
Jenney, William 1832-1907 *WorInv*
Jenney-West, Roxanne Elizabeth 1960- *WhoFI 94*
Jenni, Donald Alison 1932- *WhoAm 94, WhoWest 94*
Jennifer, Susan 1933- *WrDr 94*
Jennings, A. Drue *WhoFI 94*
Jennings, Al d1961 *WhoHol 92*
Jennings, Albert Victor d1993 *Who 94N*
Jennings, Alston 1917- *WhoAm 94*
Jennings, Alston, Jr. 1947- *WhoAmL 94*
Jennings, Alvin R. 1905-1990 *WhAm 10*
Jennings, Arnold Harry 1915- *Who 94*
Jennings, Audrey Mary 1928- *Who 94*
Jennings, Bennie Alfred 1933- *WhoBlA 94*
Jennings, Bernard Waylon-Handel 1968- *WhoBlA 94*
Jennings, Brent *WhoHol 92*
Jennings, Burgess Hill 1903- *WhoAm 94*
Jennings, Charles Richard 1941- *WhoFI 94*
Jennings, Charles Wayne 1944- *WhoWest 94*
Jennings, Claudia d1979 *WhoHol 92*
Jennings, Coleman Alonzo 1933- *WhoAm 94*
Jennings, Dana Andrew *DrAPF 93*
Jennings, David Thomas, III 1949- *WhoScEn 94*
Jennings, David Willfred Michael 1944- *Who 94*
Jennings, De Witt d1937 *WhoHol 92*
Jennings, Dean 1909- *WrDr 94*
Jennings, Deborah E. 1949- *WhoAmL 94*
Jennings, Douglas, Jr. *WhoAmP 93*
Jennings, Edward Harrington 1937- *WhoAm 94*
Jennings, Elizabeth 1926- *BlmGEL, BlmGWL, IntWW 93*
Jennings, Elizabeth (Joan) 1926- *Who 94, WrDr 94*
Jennings, Emmit M. 1922- *WhoWest 94*
Jennings, Emmit Martin 1922- *WhoAmP 93*
Jennings, Everett Joseph 1938- *WhoBlA 94*
Jennings, Francis 1910- *WhoAmA 93*
Jennings, Frank Gerard 1915- *WhoAm 94*
Jennings, Frank Louis *WhoAm 94*
Jennings, Frederic Beach, Jr. 1945- *WhoScEn 94*
Jennings, Gray 1945- *WhoAmL 94*
Jennings, Grover Cullen 1939- *WhoAmP 93*
Jennings, Harry 1917- *WhoAmP 93*
Jennings, (Frank) Humphrey (Sinkler) 1907-1950 *DcNaB MP*
Jennings, James 1925- *Who 94*
Jennings, James 1949- *WhoHisp 94*
Jennings, James Burnett 1940- *WhoFI 94*
Jennings, James Walsh 1937- *WhoAm 94*
Jennings, James Wilson, Jr. 1943- *WhoAmL 94*
Jennings, Jan 1943- *WhoAmA 93*
Jennings, Jay Bradford 1957- *WhoWest 94*
Jennings, Jeanette 1945- *WhoBlA 94*
Jennings, Jerry D. 1940- *WhoAm 94*
Jennings, Jerry L. 1955- *WhoScEn 94*
Jennings, Jesse David 1909- *WhoAm 94*
Jennings, John R. R. 1937- *IntWW 93*
Jennings, John Southwood 1937- *IntWW 93, Who 94*
Jennings, Joseph Ashby 1920- *WhoAm 94*
Jennings, Joseph Leslie, Jr. 1937- *WhoAm 94, WhoFI 94*
Jennings, Judith Madrone 1949- *WhoWest 94*
Jennings, Karla (Mari) 1956- *WrDr 94*
Jennings, Kate *DrAPF 93*
Jennings, Kenneth Neal 1930- *Who 94*
Jennings, Lane *DrAPF 93*
Jennings, Lee Byron 1927- *WhoAm 94*
Jennings, Lee Newlin 1932- *WhoWest 94*
Jennings, Lillian Pegues *WhoBlA 94*
Jennings, Loren G. 1951- *WhoAmP 93*
Jennings, Madelyn Pulver 1934- *WhoAm 94*
Jennings, Marcella Grady 1920- *WhoFI 94, WhoScEn 94, WhoWest 94*
Jennings, Margaret Elaine 1943- *WhoBlA 94*
Jennings, Marianne Moody 1953- *ConAu 42NR*
Jennings, Mark Edward 1962- *WhoFI 94*
Jennings, Matthew 1970- *WhoMW 93*
Jennings, Michael Eugene 1945- *WhoAm 94*
Jennings, Nancy Ann 1932- *WhoMW 93*
Jennings, Pat 1945- *WorESoc*
Jennings, Paul Christian 1936- *WhoAm 94, WhoWest 94*
Jennings, Percival Henry 1903- *Who 94*
Jennings, Peter 1937- *Who 94*
Jennings, Peter 1938- *IntMPA 94*
Jennings, Peter Charles 1938- *WhoAm 94*
Jennings, Peter Navile Wake 1934- *Who 94*
Jennings, Phillip C. 1946- *EncSF 93*
Jennings, Raymond (Winter) 1897- *Who 94*
Jennings, Renz D. 1941- *WhoAmP 93*
Jennings, Richard Vernon 1930- *WhoFI 94*
Jennings, Robert (Yewdall) 1913- *Who 94*
Jennings, Robert Burgess 1926- *WhoAm 94, WhoScEn 94*
Jennings, Robert Lee 1942- *WhoMW 93*

Jessel, Oliver Richard 1929- *Who 94*
Jessel, Patricia d1968 *WhoHol 92*
Jessel, Penelope 1920- *Who 94*
Jessel, Toby Francis Henry 1934- *Who 94*
Jesselson, Ludwig d1993 *NewYTBS 93*
Jessen, Borge 1907- *IntWW 93*
Jessen, David Wayne 1950- *WhoAm 94*
Jessen, Diane Marie 1962- *WhoFI 94*
Jessen, Shirley Agnes 1921- *WhoAmA 93*
Jesser, Benn Wainwright 1915- *WhoAm 94*
Jesser, Harold L. 1954- *WhoMW 93*
Jesser, Roger Franklyn 1926- *WhoAm 94*
Jesseramsing, Chitmansing 1933- *WhoAm 94*
Jesserer, Henry L., III 1946- *WhoAmL 94*
Jessie, Dewayne *WhoHol 92*
Jessie, Waymon Thomas 1945- *WhoBlA 94*
Jessing, Theodore Charles 1949- *WhoWest 94*
Jessner, Irene 1901- *NewGrDO*
Jessop, Alexander Smethurst 1943- *Who 94*
Jessop, William 1603-1675 *DcNaB MP*
Jessop, William 1745-1814 *DcNaB MP*
Jessup, Deborah Hitchcock 1934- *ConAu 141*
Jessup, Gayle Louise 1957- *WhoBlA 94*
Jessup, Harley 1954- *WhoAm 94*
Jessup, Joe Lee 1913- *WhoAm 94, WhoFI 94*
Jessup, John Baker 1921- *WhoAm 94*
Jessup, Marsha Edwina 1944- *WhoBlA 94*
Jessup, Paul Frederick 1939- *WhoAm 94*
Jessup, Philip C. 1897-1986 *HisDcKW*
Jessup, Philip Caryl, Jr. 1926- *WhoAm 94*
Jessup, Robert 1952- *WhoAmA 93*
Jessup, Roger L. 1929- *WhoAmP 93*
Jessup, Stanley d1945 *WhoHol 92*
Jessup, Stewart E. 1924- *WhoAm 94, WhoFI 94*
Jessup, W. Edgar, Jr. 1922- *WhoAmL 94, WhoWest 94*
Jessup, Warren T. 1916- *WhoAm 94, WhoWest 94*
Jessup, William Eugene 1952- *WhoAmL 94*
Jessup, William Walker 1938- *WhoFI 94*
Jessye, Eva d1992 *WhoBlA 94N*
Jessye, Eva 1895-1992 *AfrAmAl 6, NewGrDO*
Jeste, Dilip Vishwanath 1944- *WhoWest 94*
Jester, Carroll Gladstone 1957- *WhoAmL 94*
Jester, Jack D. 1946- *WhoAmL 94*
Jester, Katharine M. 1928- *WhoAmP 93*
Jester, Roberts Charles, Jr. 1917- *WhoAm 94*
Jester, Royston, III 1913- *WhoAmP 93*
Jestin, Heimwarth B. 1918- *WhoAm 94*
Jesty, Benjamin 1736-1816 *DcNaB MP*
Jesurun, Harold Mendez 1915- *WhoAm 94*
Jesus, Carolina Maria de 1914-1977 *BlmGWL*
Jesus and Mary Chain, The *ConMus 10 [port]*
Jesus of Nazareth c. 6BC-c. 27AD *HisWorL [port]*
Jesus of Nazareth c. 4BC-27AD *EncEth*
Jeswald, Joseph 1927- *WhoAmA 93*
Jeszenszky, Geza 1941- *IntWW 93*
Jeter, Clifton B., Jr. 1944- *WhoBlA 94*
Jeter, Delores DeAnn 1949- *WhoBlA 94*
Jeter, Felicia Rene 1948- *WhoBlA 94*
Jeter, Frank Hamilton, Jr. 1918- *WhoAmP 93*
Jeter, Howard *WhoAmP 93*
Jeter, Howard F. *WhoAm 94*
Jeter, James *WhoHol 92*
Jeter, Joseph C., Jr. 1961- *WhoBlA 94*
Jeter, Juanita Dolores 1946- *WhoBlA 94*
Jeter, K.W. 1950- *EncSF 93, WrDr 94*
Jeter, Katherine Leslie Brash 1921- *WhoAmL 94, WhoFI 94*
Jeter, Michael 1952- *ConTFT 11, IntMPA 94, WhoAm 94, WhoHol 92*
Jeter, Randy Joe 1937-1987 *WhoAmA 93N*
Jeter, Sheila Ann 1952- *WhoBlA 94*
Jeter, Thomas Elliott 1929- *WhoBlA 94*
Jeter, Velma Marjorie Dreyfus 1906- *WhoBlA 94*
Jeter, Wayburn Stewart 1926- *WhoScEn 94*
Jethanandani, Ashok 1958- *WhoAsA 94*
Jethwani, Mohan 1938- *WhoScEn 94*
Jetson, Raymond 1956- *WhoAmP 93*
Jett, Arthur Victor, Sr. 1906- *WhoBlA 94*
Jett, Charles Cranston 1941- *WhoAm 94, WhoMW 93*
Jett, Dennis *WhoAm 94, WhoAmP 93*
Jett, James *WhoBlA 94*
Jett, Joan 1960- *CurBio 93 [port], WhoHol 92*
Jett, Kevin *NewYTBS 93 [port]*
Jett, Sheldon d1960 *WhoHol 92*
Jett, Stephen Clinton 1938- *WhoAm 94, WrDr 94*
Jette, Ernest Arthur 1945- *WhoAmL 94*
Jette, Lorraine Doris 1942- *WhoMW 93*
Jetter, Arthur Carl, Jr. 1947- *WhoMW 93*
Jettke, Harry Jerome 1925- *WhoMW 93*
Jetton, C. Loring, Jr. 1943- *WhoAm 94, WhoAmL 94*
Jetton, Clyde Thomas 1918- *WhAm 10*
Jetton, Girard Reuel, Jr. 1924- *WhoAm 94*
Jeub, Michael Leonard 1943- *WhoAm 94*
Jeung, In-Seuck 1952- *WhoScEn 94*
Jevicky, John E. 1954- *WhoAmL 94*
Jevon, Thomas 1652-1688 *BlmGEL*
Jevons, Frederic Raphael 1929- *Who 94*
Jevorn, Thomas 1652-1688 *BlmGEL*
Jewel, Izetta d1978 *WhoHol 92*
Jewel, Jimmy 1912- *WhoHol 92*
Jewel, Julie S. 1953- *WhoAmP 93*
Jewelewicz, Raphael 1932- *WhoScEn 94*
Jewell, Ann Lynette 1959- *WhoMW 93*
Jewell, Austin *WhoHol 92*
Jewell, Byron Frank 1946- *WhoAm 94*
Jewell, David John 1934- *Who 94*
Jewell, David R. 1947- *WhoAmL 94*
Jewell, Edmund Francis 1896- *WhAm 10*
Jewell, Edward Dunbar 1928- *WhoFI 94*
Jewell, George Benson 1944- *WhoAmL 94, WhoFI 94*
Jewell, George Hiram 1922- *WhoAm 94, WhoAmL 94*
Jewell, Isabel d1972 *WhoHol 92*
Jewell, Jerry D. 1930- *WhoAmP 93*
Jewell, Jerry Donal 1930- *WhoBlA 94*
Jewell, Joyce 1945- *WhoAmA 93*
Jewell, Karen Donohoe 1953- *WhoAmL 94*
Jewell, Paula L. 1943- *WhoBlA 94*
Jewell, Peter Arundel 1925- *Who 94*
Jewell, Robert V. 1954- *WhoAmL 94*
Jewell, Terri L. *DrAPF 93*
Jewell, Thomas Keith 1946- *WhoScEn 94*
Jewell, Tommy Edward, III 1954- *WhoBlA 94*
Jewell, William M. 1905-1990 *WhoAmA 93N*
Jewell, William Sylvester 1932- *WhoAm 94, WhoScEn 94*
Jewers, William George 1921- *Who 94*
Jewett, Carol H. 1949- *WhoAmL 94*
Jewett, Charlie Ruth 1936- *WhoBlA 94*
Jewett, David Stuart 1941- *WhoScEn 94*
Jewett, George Frederick, Jr. 1927- *WhoAm 94*
Jewett, Henry d1930 *WhoHol 92*
Jewett, Hugh Judge 1903-1990 *WhAm 10*
Jewett, Jack B. 1946- *WhoAmP 93*
Jewett, James Michael 1948- *WhoAmL 94*
Jewett, John Persinger 1943- *WhoAm 94*
Jewett, John Rhodes 1922- *WhoAm 94*
Jewett, Jonathan 1943- *WhoAmL 94*
Jewett, Lucille McIntyre 1929- *WhoWest 94*
Jewett, Sarah Orne 1849-1909 *BlmGWL*
Jewett, (Theodora) Sarah Orne 1849-1909 *RfGShF*
Jewett, Stephen Carl 1947- *WhoScEn 94*
Jewett, Theodora Sarah Orne 1849-1909 *AmCulL*
Jewison, Norman Frederick 1926- *IntWW 93, WhoAm 94*
Jewison, Norman P. 1926- *IntMPA 94*
Jewitt, David Willard Pennock 1921- *WhoAm 94*
Jewkes, Delos d1984 *WhoHol 92*
Jewkes, Gordon (Wesley) 1931- *Who 94*
Jewkes, Gordon Wesley 1931- *IntWW 93*
Jewsbury, Geraldine 1812-1880 *BlmGWL*
Jewsbury, Geraldine Endsor 1812-1880 *BlmGEL*
Jewsbury, Roger Alan 1947- *WhoScEn 94*
Jewson, Richard Wilson 1944- *Who 94*
Jex, Michael William 1957- *WhoWest 94*
Jeyaraman, Ramasubbu 1944- *WhoScEn 94*
Jeyaretnam, J. B. 1926- *IntWW 93*
Jeydel, Richard K. 1950- *WhoAm 94*
Jeye, Peter Austin 1959- *WhoFI 94*
Jeyendran, Rajasingam Sivaperagasam 1948- *WhoScEn 94*
Jeynes, Mary Kay 1941- *WhoAm 94*
Jeynes, Paul 1927- *WhoAmA 93*
Jezek, Kenneth C. *WhoAm 94*
Jezek, Kenneth Charles 1951- *WhoScEn 94*
Jezequel, Julie *WhoHol 92*
Jezuit, Leslie James 1945- *WhoAm 94*
Jha, Akhillshwar 1932- *WrDr 94*
Jha, Mahesh Chandra 1945- *WhoAsA 94*
Jha, Nand Kishore 1941- *WhoScEn 94*
Jhabvala, Ruth Prawar 1927- *BlmGEL [port]*
Jhabvala, Ruth Prawer *DrAPF 93*
Jhabvala, Ruth Prawer 1927- *BlmGWL, DcLB 139 [port], IntDcF 2-4, IntMPA 94, IntWW 93, Who 94, WhoAm 94, WrDr 94*
Jhaveri, Arunkumar Ganpatlal 1938- *WhoAsA 94*
Jhon, Myung S. 1944- *WhoAsA 94*
Ji, Chueng Ryong 1954- *WhoAsA 94*
Ji, Inhae 1938- *WhoAsA 94*
Ji, Taehwa 1941- *WhoAsA 94*
Ji, Xinhua 1948- *WhoScEn 94*
Jia, Hong 1960- *WhoScEn 94*
Jia, Quanxi 1957- *WhoScEn 94*
Jia Cai *WhoPRCh 91*
Jia Chunwang 1938- *IntWW 93, WhoPRCh 91 [port]*
Jia Di'e *WhoPRCh 91*
Jia Genzheng *WhoPRCh 91*
Jiagge, Annie Ruth 1918- *IntWW 93*
Jia Jun 1917- *WhoPRCh 91 [port]*
Jia Jun 1948- *WhoPRCh 91 [port]*
Jialanella, John James 1941- *WhoWest 94*
Jia Lanpo 1908- *IntWW 93*
Jiambalvo, John Richard 1947- *WhoMW 93*
Jiampietro, Joseph Richard 1941- *WhoAmP 93*
Jia-mu-xiang Luo-sang-jiu-mei Tu-dan Que-ji-ni-ma *WhoPRCh 91*
Jiamuyang Luosangjiumei Tudanquejinima *WhoPRCh 91*
Jian, Song 1931- *WhoScEn 94*
Jia-na-bu-er *WhoPRCh 91*
Jiang, Hongwen 1960- *WhoScEn 94*
Jiang, Li Jin 1919- *IntWW 93*
Jiang, Nai-Siang 1931- *WhoAsA 94*
Jiang, Renfang 1952- *WhoMW 93*
Jiang, Wenbin 1963- *WhoScEn 94*
Jiang, William Yuying 1955- *WhoAsA 94*
Jiang, Xixiang 1957- *WhoAsA 94*
Jiang, Zhenying 1949- *WhoAsA 94*
Jiang Baolin 1942- *IntWW 93*
Jiang Boju *WhoPRCh 91*
Jiang Boju 1937- *IntWW 93*
Jiang Chunyun 1930- *IntWW 93, WhoPRCh 91 [port]*
Jiang Chuping 1937- *WhoPRCh 91 [port]*
Jiangcun Luobu *WhoPRCh 91*
Jiang Cuo 1939- *WhoPRCh 91 [port]*
Jiang Dahai 1947- *WhoPRCh 91*
Jiang Daning 1919- *WhoPRCh 91*
Jiang Daning 1929- *IntWW 93*
Jiang Dian 1943- *WhoPRCh 91*
Jiang Dingxian *WhoPRCh 91*
Jiang Enzhu *WhoPRCh 91*
Jiang Futang 1941- *WhoPRCh 91 [port]*
Jiang Guanghua 1926- *WhoPRCh 91 [port]*
Jiang Guanzhuang *WhoPRCh 91*
Jiang Hongquan 1932- *WhoPRCh 91*
Jiang Hua 1907- *IntWW 93, WhoPRCh 91 [port]*
Jiang Jiafu 1938- *WhoPRCh 91 [port]*
Jiang Jialiang 1963- *WhoPRCh 91 [port]*
Jiang Jingbo *WhoPRCh 91*
Jiang Kang *WhoPRCh 91*
Jiang Kexu *WhoPRCh 91*
Jiang Kexuan 1931- *WhoPRCh 91*
Jiang Kongyang 1922- *WhoPRCh 91*
Jiang Lijin 1919- *WhoPRCh 91 [port]*
Jiang Ming 1931- *WhoPRCh 91 [port]*
Jiang Minkuan 1930- *IntWW 93, WhoPRCh 91 [port]*
Jiang Peilu 1921- *WhoPRCh 91 [port]*
Jiang Ping 1920- *WhoPRCh 91 [port]*
Jiang Qing 1913- *WhoPRCh 91 [port]*
Jiang Qing 1914-1991 *HisWorL [port]*
Jiang Qingxiang 1915- *WhoPRCh 91*
Jiang Qingxiang 1918- *IntWW 93*
Jiang Shengjie 1913- *WhoPRCh 91 [port]*
Jiang Shiqu *WhoPRCh 91*
Jiang Shunxue 1926- *WhoPRCh 91 [port]*
Jiang Siyi 1920- *WhoPRCh 91 [port]*
Jiang Tiefeng 1938- *WhoPRCh 91*
Jiang Weiqing 1907- *IntWW 93, WhoPRCh 91*
Jiang Wen 1952- *WhoPRCh 91 [port]*
Jiang Xi *WhoPRCh 91*
Jiang Xiang *WhoPRCh 91*
Jiang Xiesheng 1928- *IntWW 93, WhoPRCh 91 [port]*
Jiang Xinsong *WhoPRCh 91*
Jiang Xinxiong 1931- *IntWW 93, WhoPRCh 91 [port]*
Jiang Yahui *WhoPRCh 91*
Jiang Yiwei 1920- *IntWW 93, WhoPRCh 91*
Jiang Yizhen *WhoPRCh 91*
Jiang Yonghui 1916- *WhoPRCh 91*
Jiang Yun 1954- *WhoPRCh 91 [port]*
Jiang Yutian 1927- *WhoPRCh 91 [port]*
Jiang Zejia *WhoPRCh 91*
Jiang Zemin 1926- *IntWW 93, WhoPRCh 91 [port]*
Jiang Zhaohe 1904- *WhoPRCh 91 [port]*
Jiang Zhizeng 1930- *WhoPRCh 91*
Jiang Zhuping 1937- *IntWW 93*
Jiang Zilong 1941- *IntWW 93, WhoPRCh 91 [port]*
Jian Tiancong 1921- *WhoPRCh 91 [port]*
Jian Xian'ai 1906- *WhoPRCh 91 [port]*
Jiao, Jianzhong, Sr. 1955- *WhoMW 93, WhoScEn 94*
Jiao, Shou-shu 1945- *WhoMW 93*
Jiao Bin *WhoPRCh 91*
Jiao Linyi 1920- *IntWW 93*
Jiao Ruoyu 1916- *IntWW 93, WhoPRCh 91 [port]*
Jiao Shanmin *WhoPRCh 91*
Jiao Shizhai *WhoPRCh 91*
Jiao Shunfa 1945- *WhoPRCh 91 [port]*
Jiao Zhimin *WhoPRCh 91 [port]*
Jia Pingwa 1953- *IntWW 93, WhoPRCh 91 [port]*
Jia Qinglin 1940- *IntWW 93, WhoPRCh 91 [port]*
Jia-ya *WhoPRCh 91*
Jia Yibin 1912- *WhoPRCh 91 [port]*
Jia Youfu 1943- *WhoPRCh 91 [port]*
Jia Zhijie 1935- *IntWW 93, WhoPRCh 91 [port]*
Jia Zuoguang *WhoPRCh 91*
Jibaja, Gilbert 1935- *WhoFI 94*
Jibben, Laura Ann 1949- *WhoAm 94, WhoMW 93*
Ji Chaozhu 1929- *IntWW 93, Who 94, WhoPRCh 91*
Ji Chongwei 1933?- *WhoPRCh 91 [port]*
Jicinsky, Zdenek 1929- *IntWW 93*
Jickling, John Ward 1921- *WhoAm 94*
Jiggetts, Charles B. *AfrAmG [port]*
Jiggetts, Danny Marcellus 1954- *WhoBlA 94*
Ji Guobiao 1932- *WhoPRCh 91 [port]*
Ji Hanxing 1921- *WhoPRCh 91 [port]*
Ji Hua 1925- *WhoPRCh 91*
Jilani, Asaf 1934- *Who 94*
Jilek, Frantisek 1913- *NewGrDO*
Jilek, Ray R. 1933- *WhoAmP 93*
Jiler, William Laurence 1925- *WhoAm 94*
Jiles, Dwayne 1961- *WhoBlA 94*
Jiles, Paulette 1943- *BlmGWL*
Jilg, Michael Florian 1947- *WhoAmA 93*
Jilhewar, Ashok 1947- *WhoMW 93, WhoScEn 94*
Ji Lide *WhoPRCh 91*
Jillette, Penn 1955- *See* Penn and Teller *WhoCom*
Jillette, Penn 1955- *See* Penn and Teller *WhoHol 92*
Jillian, Ann 1950- *WhoAm 94*
Jillian, Ann 1951- *IntMPA 94, WhoHol 92*
Jillings, Godfrey Frank 1940- *Who 94*
Jills, The *See* Jivin' Jacks and Jills, The *WhoHol 92*
Jillson, Andrew E. 1954- *WhoAmL 94*
Jillson, Joyce 1947- *WhoHol 92*
Jiloty, Joseph Paul 1956- *WhoAmL 94*
Jim, Kam Fook 1953- *WhoScEn 94*
Jimenez, A. Jimmy *WhoHisp 94*
Jimenez, Andres Eugenio 1953- *WhoHisp 94*
Jimenez, Andres L. 1943- *WhoHisp 94*
Jimenez, Angel F. *WhoHisp 94*
Jimenez, Bettie Eileen 1932- *WhoMW 93*
Jimenez, Braulio Dueno 1950- *WhoScEn 94*
Jimenez, Christina Lee 1958- *WhoAsA 94*
Jimenez, Cristobal 1932- *WhoHisp 94*
Jimenez, Daniel 1936- *WhoHisp 94*
Jimenez, David 1961- *WhoHisp 94*
Jimenez, Donna 1961- *WhoHisp 94*
Jimenez, Eduardo 1959- *WhoHisp 94*
Jimenez, Elpidio D. 1956- *WhoHisp 94*
Jimenez, Eradio T. *WhoHisp 94*
Jimenez, Felix J. 1949- *WhoHisp 94*
Jimenez, Fernando R. 1947- *WhoHisp 94*
Jimenez, Francisco *DrAPF 93*
Jimenez, Francisco 1943- *WhoHisp 94, WhoWest 94*
Jimenez, Francisco J. 1940- *WhoHisp 94*
Jiménez, Iris C. 1951- *WhoHisp 94*
Jimenez, Ivonne Ruiz 1955- *WhoHisp 94*
Jimenez, Javier 1961- *WhoHisp 94*
Jimenez, Jeronimo *NewGrDO*
Jimenez, Joaquin Bernardo, II 1955- *WhoHisp 94*
Jimenez, Jose Olivio *WhoHisp 94*
Jimenez, Josephine Santos 1954- *WhoAsA 94, WhoFI 94*
Jimenez, Juan Carlos 1952- *WhoHisp 94*
Jimenez, Juan Ignacio 1958- *WhoScEn 94*
Jimenez, Juan Ramon 1881-1958 *DcLB 134 [port], HispLC [port], PoeCrit 7 [port]*
Jimenez, Luis A., Jr. 1940- *WhoHisp 94*
Jimenez, Luis Alexander 1954- *WhoHisp 94*
Jimenez, Luis Alfonso, Jr. 1940- *WhoAm 94, WhoAmA 93*
Jiménez, María C. 1932- *WhoHisp 94*
Jimenez, Maria De Los Angeles 1950- *WhoHisp 94*
Jimenez, Maria J. 1964- *WhoHisp 94*
Jiménez, Maria Margarita 1968- *WhoHisp 94*
Jimenez, Marie John 1932- *WhoHisp 94*

Johnson, Clarence Leonard 1910-1990 *WhAm 10*
Johnson, Clarissa 1913- *WhoBlA 94*
Johnson, Clark *WhoHol 92*
Johnson, Clark Eugene, Jr. 1930- *WhoAm 94, WhoFI 94*
Johnson, Clark Everette, Jr. 1923- *WhoAm 94*
Johnson, Clark Hughes 1935- *WhoFI 94*
Johnson, Clarke Courtney 1936- *WhoAm 94*
Johnson, Claude *WhoHol 92*
Johnson, Clayton Errold 1921-1992 *WhAm 10*
Johnson, Cleveland, Jr. 1934- *WhoBlA 94*
Johnson, Cleveland Thomas 1955- *WhoMW 93*
Johnson, Cliff 1951- *WhoAmP 93*
Johnson, Clifford d1976 *WhoHol 92*
Johnson, Clifford Andrew, III 1945- *WhoAm 94*
Johnson, Clifford R. 1923- *WhoAm 94*
Johnson, Clifton E. *WhoBlA 94*
Johnson, Clifton Herman 1921- *WhoAm 94*
Johnson, Clinisson Anthony 1947- *WhoBlA 94*
Johnson, Clint d1975 *WhoHol 92*
Johnson, Clinton Lamont 1953- *WhoAmP 93*
Johnson, Clinton Lee 1947- *WhoAmP 93*
Johnson, Clinton Lee, Sr. 1947- *WhoBlA 94*
Johnson, Colin 1938- *WrDr 94*
Johnson, Colin 1939- *WrDr 94*
Johnson, Collis, Jr. 1946- *WhoBlA 94*
Johnson, Conor Deane 1943- *WhoAm 94*
Johnson, Constance Ada 1934- *WhoAmP 93*
Johnson, Content d1949 *WhoAmA 93N*
Johnson, Corinthian (Kripp) d1990 *WhoHol 92*
Johnson, Corwin Waggoner 1917- *WhoAm 94*
Johnson, Craig N. 1954- *WhoIns 94*
Johnson, Craig Norman 1942- *WhoAm 94*
Johnson, Craig R. 1951- *WhoFI 94*
Johnson, Craig Theodore 1955- *WhoFI 94*
Johnson, Craig W. 1946- *WhoAmL 94*
Johnson, Crocket 1906-1976 *WhoAmA 93N*
Johnson, Curt *WhoAmP 93*
Johnson, Curtis Eduard 1941- *WhoAmP 93*
Johnson, Curtis Lee 1928- *WhoAm 94*
Johnson, Curtis Scott 1954- *WhoMW 93*
Johnson, Cynthia Elaine 1953- *WhoFI 94*
Johnson, Cynthia Le Mae 1952- *WhoAmL 94*
Johnson, Cyrus Edwin 1929- *WhoAm 94, WhoBlA 94*
Johnson, D(avid) Gale 1916- *WrDr 94*
Johnson, D. Mead d1993 *NewYTBS 93*
Johnson, Dale A. 1937- *WhoAm 94, WhoFI 94, WhoMW 93*
Johnson, Dale Gedge 1930- *WhoWest 94*
Johnson, Dale L(eonard) 1934- *WrDr 94*
Johnson, Dale Springer 1932- *WhoFI 94*
Johnson, Dan *DrAPF 93*
Johnson, Dan d1982 *WhoHol 92*
Johnson, Dan Myron 1944- *WhoScEn 94*
Johnson, Dana Ernest 1948- *WhoMW 93*
Johnson, Dana Lee 1956- *WhoScEn 94*
Johnson, Daniel, Jr. 1948- *WhoAm 94, WhoAmL 94*
Johnson, Daniel Arthur 1953- *WhoWest 94*
Johnson, Daniel Eugene 1952- *WhoFI 94*
Johnson, Daniel Fredrick 1953- *WhoWest 94*
Johnson, Daniel Lee, Sr. 1936- *WhoWest 94*
Johnson, Daniel Leroy 1951- *WhoAm 94*
Johnson, Daniel Lloyd 1953- *WhoScEn 94*
Johnson, Daniel McDonald 1953- *WhoAm 94*
Johnson, Daniel Robert 1938- *WhoAm 94*
Johnson, Danielle Verstaen 1950- *WhoWest 94*
Johnson, Darlene Ann 1949- *WhoMW 93*
Johnson, Darryl Norman 1938- *WhoAm 94, WhoAmP 93*
Johnson, Daryle G. 1936- *WhoIns 94*
Johnson, Dave *WhoAm 94*
Johnson, Dave 1970- *WhoBlA 94*
Johnson, Davey 1943- *WhoAm 94, WhoMW 93*
Johnson, David *DrAPF 93*
Johnson, David, III 1943- *WhoBlA 94*
Johnson, David (Charles) 1942- *NewGrDO*
Johnson, David Allen 1954- *WhoAm 94, WhoMW 93*
Johnson, David Burnham 1930- *Who 94*
Johnson, David Chester 1933- *WhoAm 94, WhoMW 93*
Johnson, David Elliot 1933- *WhoAm 94*
Johnson, David Freeman 1925- *WhoBlA 94*
Johnson, David Gale 1916- *IntWW 93, WhoAm 94*
Johnson, David Horace 1925- *WhoBlA 94*
Johnson, David Hugh Nevil 1920- *Who 94*
Johnson, David James 1953- *WhoMW 93*
Johnson, David John 1938- *Who 94*
Johnson, David L. 1929- *WhoIns 94*
Johnson, David Lee 1958- *WhoScEn 94*
Johnson, David Lincoln 1929- *WhoAm 94, WhoAmL 94*
Johnson, David Lynn 1934- *WhoAm 94, WhoMW 93*
Johnson, David Michael 1949- *WhoAmL 94*
Johnson, David Raymond 1946- *WhoAm 94, WhoAmL 94*
Johnson, David Robert W. *Who 94*
Johnson, David Sellie 1935- *WhoScEn 94, WhoWest 94*
Johnson, David Simonds 1924- *WhoAm 94, WhoScEn 94*
Johnson, David W. *WhoAmP 93*
Johnson, David W., Jr. 1942- *WhoAm 94, WhoScEn 94*
Johnson, David William 1959- *WhoMW 93*
Johnson, David Willis 1932- *WhoAm 94, WhoFI 94, WhoScEn 94*
Johnson, David Wolcott 1940- *WhoAm 94, WhoMW 93, WhoScEn 94*
Johnson, Davis 1934- *WhoBlA 94*
Johnson, Dean E. 1931- *WhoIns 94*
Johnson, Dean Elton 1947- *WhoAmP 93*
Johnson, Dean P. *WhoAmA 93*
Johnson, Deborah Crosland Wright 1951- *WhoScEn 94*
Johnson, Debra *WhoHol 92*
Johnson, D'Elaine A. Herard *WhoAmA 93*
Johnson, Delmas Wayne 1965- *WhoWest 94*
Johnson, Denis 1949- *EncSF 93, WrDr 94*
Johnson, Denise Doreen 1964- *WhoScEn 94*
Johnson, Denise R. 1947- *WhoAmP 93*
Johnson, Denise Reinke 1947- *WhoAmL 94*
Johnson, Dennis 1954- *BasBi, WhoBlA 94*
Johnson, Dennis Duane 1938- *WhoAm 94*
Johnson, Dennis E. *WhoAmP 93*
Johnson, Dennis Lester 1938- *WhoAm 94*
Johnson, Dennis Neal 1942- *WhoWest 94*
Johnson, Dewey Edward 1935- *WhoAm 94, WhoFI 94, WhoScEn 94*
Johnson, Diana L. 1940- *WhoAmA 93*
Johnson, Diana Lynn 1954- *WhoAmL 94*
Johnson, Diane *DrAPF 93*
Johnson, Diane 1929- *WhoBlA 94*
Johnson, Diane 1934- *WrDr 94*
Johnson, (L.) Diane *WhoAmA 93*
Johnson, Diane Chalmers 1943- *WhoAmA 93*
Johnson, Diane Harvey *WhoAmP 93*
Johnson, Diane Lain 1934- *WhoAm 94*
Johnson, Dick 1955- *WrDr 94*
Johnson, Dick Winslow *WhoHol 92*
Johnson, Dolores *WhoHol 92*
Johnson, Don 1948- *CngDr 93, WhoAm 94, WhoAmP 93*
Johnson, Don 1949- *IntMPA 94, WhoHol 92*
Johnson, Don Edwin 1939- *WhoAmL 94*
Johnson, Don Wayne 1949- *WhoAm 94*
Johnson, Donald Edward 1924- *WhoAmP 93*
Johnson, Donald Edwin 1920- *Who 94*
Johnson, Donald L. 1931- *WhoAmP 93*
Johnson, Donald Lee 1934- *WhoMW 93*
Johnson, Donald Lee 1935- *WhoAm 94, WhoScEn 94*
Johnson, Donald Ray 1942- *WhoAmA 93*
Johnson, Donald Rex 1938- *WhoAm 94, WhoAmP 93, WhoScEn 94*
Johnson, Donald Wallace, III 1959- *WhoWest 94*
Johnson, Donald Wayne 1950- *WhoAmL 94*
Johnson, Donn S. 1947- *WhoBlA 94*
Johnson, Donna Alligood 1956- *WhoBlA 94*
Johnson, Dora Myrtle Knudtson 1900- *WhoAm 94*
Johnson, Doris Ann 1950- *WhoWest 94*
Johnson, Doris Elayne 1954- *WhoBlA 94*
Johnson, Doris Miller 1909- *WhoAmA 93*
Johnson, Dorothy Gail 1942- *WhoAmP 93*
Johnson, Dorothy Phyllis 1925- *WhoMW 93*
Johnson, Dorothy Turner 1915- *WhoBlA 94*
Johnson, Dotts d1986 *WhoHol 92*
Johnson, Douglas H. 1943- *WhoBlA 94*
Johnson, Douglas J. 1942- *WhoAmP 93*
Johnson, Douglas Walter 1946- *WhoAmA 93, WhoWest 94*
Johnson, Douglas Wells 1949- *WhoAmL 94*
Johnson, Douglas William John 1925- *IntWW 93, Who 94*
Johnson, Durward Elton 1932- *WhoAmP 93*
Johnson, Dwight Alan 1945- *WhoAmL 94*
Johnson, E. Eric 1927- *WhoFI 94, WhoWest 94*
Johnson, E. Lamont d1984 *WhoHol 92*
Johnson, E. Perry 1943- *WhoAm 94, WhoAmL 94*
Johnson, E(mil) Richard 1937- *WrDr 94*
Johnson, Earl 1943- *WhoBlA 94*
Johnson, Earl, Jr. 1933- *WhoAm 94*
Johnson, Earl E. 1926- *WhoBlA 94*
Johnson, Earle Bertrand 1914- *WhoAm 94*
Johnson, Earvin 1959- *IntWW 93, WhoAm 94, WhoWest 94*
Johnson, Earvin, Jr. 1959- *AfrAmAl 6 [port], ConAu 141, WhoBlA 94*
Johnson, Ed F. 1937- *WhoBlA 94*
Johnson, Eddie A. 1959- *WhoBlA 94*
Johnson, Eddie Bernice 1935- *CngDr 93, WhoAm 94, WhoAmP 93, WhoBlA 94, WhoWomW 91*
Johnson, Eddie C. 1920- *WhoBlA 94*
Johnson, Edgar d1987 *WhoHol 92*
Johnson, Edgar (Raymond) 1912-1990 *TwCYAW*
Johnson, Edgar Frederick 1899-1991 *WhAm 10*
Johnson, Edith d1969 *WhoHol 92*
Johnson, Edmond R. 1937- *WhoBlA 94*
Johnson, Edna DeCoursey 1922- *WhoBlA 94*
Johnson, Edna Scott 1913- *WhoMW 93*
Johnson, Edward 1878-1959 *NewGrDO*
Johnson, Edward, Jr. 1955- *WhoBlA 94*
Johnson, Edward A. *WhoScEn 94*
Johnson, Edward A. 1917- *WhoAm 94*
Johnson, Edward A. 1940- *WhoBlA 94*
Johnson, Edward Crosby, II 1898- *WhAm 10*
Johnson, Edward Crosby, III 1930- *WhoAm 94, WhoFI 94*
Johnson, Edward Elemuel *WhoBlA 94*
Johnson, Edward Elemuel 1926- *WhoAm 94*
Johnson, Edward Lee 1931- *WhoWest 94*
Johnson, Edward M. 1943- *WhoBlA 94*
Johnson, Edward Michael 1944- *WhoAmL 94*
Johnson, Edward Roy 1940- *WhoAm 94*
Johnson, Edwin George 1922- *WhoAmP 93*
Johnson, Eileen Frances 1936- *WhoMW 93*
Johnson, Einar William 1955- *WhoAmL 94*
Johnson, Elaine Glenn 1943- *WhoMW 93*
Johnson, Elaine McDowell 1942- *WhoAm 94, WhoBlA 94*
Johnson, Eldon 1930- *WhoAmP 93*
Johnson, Elizabeth 1966- *WhoMW 93*
Johnson, Elizabeth Diane Long 1945- *WhoAmL 94*
Johnson, Elizabeth Hill 1913- *WhoWest 94*
Johnson, Elizabeth M. 1931- *WhoAmP 93*
Johnson, Ellen Christine 1948- *WhoFI 94, WhoMW 93*
Johnson, Ellen Hulda 1910-1992 *WhoAmA 93N*
Johnson, Ellen Schultz 1918- *WhoMW 93*
Johnson, Elmer Hubert 1917- *WrDr 94*
Johnson, Elmer Marshall 1930- *WhoAm 94, WhoScEn 94*
Johnson, Elmer William 1932- *WhoAm 94, WhoAmL 94*
Johnson, Elmore W. 1944- *WhoBlA 94*
Johnson, Emery Allen 1929- *WhoAm 94*
Johnson, Emily F. 1947- *WhoAmL 94*
Johnson, Emory d1960 *WhoHol 92*
Johnson, Enid C. 1931- *WhoBlA 94*
Johnson, Eric 1953- *WhoAmP 93*
Johnson, Eric Alfred George 1911- *Who 94*
Johnson, Eric Carl 1951- *WhoMW 93*
Johnson, Eric Elliott *WhoWest 94*
Johnson, Eric G. 1951- *WhoBlA 94*
Johnson, Eric Norman 1952- *WhoAmP 93*
Johnson, Eric W(arner) 1918- *WrDr 94*
Johnson, Eric Walter 1958- *WhoScEn 94*
Johnson, Erma Chansler 1942- *WhoBlA 94*
Johnson, Ernest (Melvin) 1924- *WhoAmA 93*
Johnson, Ernest Frederick, Jr. 1918- *WhoAm 94*
Johnson, Ernest Kaye, III 1950- *WhoBlA 94*
Johnson, Ernest L. 1950- *WhoBlA 94*
Johnson, Eugene Joseph 1937- *WhoAmA 93*
Johnson, Eugene Laurence 1936- *WhoAm 94*
Johnson, Eugene Walter 1939- *WhoAm 94, WhoMW 93, WhoScEn 94*
Johnson, Eunice Walker *WhoBlA 94*
Johnson, Eunita E. 1939- *WhoBlA 94*
Johnson, Evelyn F. 1925- *WhoBlA 94*
Johnson, Evelyn Marie *WhoAmP 93*
Johnson, Everett Ramon 1915- *WhoAm 94*
Johnson, Ewell Calvin 1926- *WhoAm 94*
Johnson, Ezra Ray 1955- *WhoBlA 94*
Johnson, F. Brent 1942- *WhoWest 94*
Johnson, F. J., Jr. 1930- *WhoBlA 94*
Johnson, F. Michael 1953- *WhoMW 93, WhoScEn 94*
Johnson, F. Raymond 1920- *WhoBlA 94*
Johnson, Falk S(immons) 1913- *WrDr 94*
Johnson, Faye *WhoAmP 93*
Johnson, Fenton *DrAPF 93*
Johnson, Ferd 1905- *WhoAm 94, WhoWest 94*
Johnson, Fern L. *WhoAm 94*
Johnson, Fletcher M., Jr. 1957- *WhoAmL 94*
Johnson, Frances d1933 *WhoHol 92*
Johnson, Francis Edward, Jr. 1948-1992 *WhoBlA 94N*
Johnson, Francis Rea 1921- *Who 94*
Johnson, Francis Severin 1918- *WhoAm 94*
Johnson, Frank 1958- *WhoBlA 94*
Johnson, Frank Anthony 1962- *WhoFI 94*
Johnson, Frank B., Jr. *WhoAmP 93*
Johnson, Frank Corliss 1927- *WhoAm 94*
Johnson, Frank Edward 1920- *WhoAm 94*
Johnson, Frank Harris 1908-1990 *WhAm 10*
Johnson, Frank J. 1939- *WhoBlA 94*
Johnson, Frank M., Jr. 1918- *WhoAmP 93*
Johnson, Frank Minis, Jr. 1918- *WhoAm 94, WhoAmL 94*
Johnson, Frank Robert 1943- *Who 94*
Johnson, Frank Scott 1956- *WhoBlA 94*
Johnson, Frank Sidney Roland 1917- *Who 94*
Johnson, Frank Stanley, Jr. 1930- *WhoAm 94*
Johnson, Frank William 1948- *WhoFI 94*
Johnson, Franklin Ridgway 1912- *WhoAm 94*
Johnson, Franklyn Arthur 1921- *WhoAm 94*
Johnson, Fred d1971 *WhoHol 92*
Johnson, Fred D. 1933- *WhoBlA 94*
Johnson, Fred Lee 1931- *WhoAmP 93*
Johnson, Freda S. 1947- *WhoAm 94*
Johnson, Frederick, Jr. 1940- *WhoBlA 94*
Johnson, Frederick Alistair 1928- *Who 94*
Johnson, Frederick Dean 1911- *WhoFI 94*
Johnson, Frederick Douglass 1946- *WhoBlA 94*
Johnson, Frederick E. 1941- *WhoBlA 94*
Johnson, Frederick Ross 1931- *IntWW 93*
Johnson, Fridolf Lester 1905-1988 *WhAm 10, WhoAmA 93N*
Johnson, G. Griffith 1912- *IntMPA 94*
Johnson, G. R. Hovey 1930- *WhoBlA 94*
Johnson, G. Roberts 1940- *WhoAmL 94*
Johnson, Gabriel Ampah 1930- *IntWW 93*
Johnson, Gage 1924- *WhoBlA 94*
Johnson, Gardiner 1905- *WhoAmP 93*
Johnson, Garey A. 1947- *WhoBlA 94*
Johnson, Garey Antony 1947- *WhoWest 94*
Johnson, Garrett Bruce 1946- *WhoAmL 94*
Johnson, Garry (Dene) 1937- *Who 94*
Johnson, Gary Charles 1946- *WhoAmP 93*
Johnson, Gary Harold 1943- *WhoFI 94, WhoMW 93*
Johnson, Gary Keith 1951- *WhoMW 93*
Johnson, Gary Kenneth 1939- *WhoAmP 93*
Johnson, Gary Kent 1936- *WhoWest 94*
Johnson, Gary Lee 1951- *WhoFI 94*
Johnson, Gary M. 1947- *WhoAm 94, WhoAmL 94*
Johnson, Gary Neil 1951- *WhoAmP 93*
Johnson, Gary R. 1956- *WhoAmP 93*
Johnson, Gary Ray 1949- *WhoAm 94*
Johnson, Gary Robert 1949- *WhoMW 93*
Johnson, Gary Thomas 1950- *WhoAm 94, WhoAmL 94, WhoFI 94*
Johnson, Gary Wayne 1950- *WhoScEn 94*
Johnson, Gary William 1957- *WhoScEn 94*
Johnson, Gene
See Diamond Rio *ConMus 11*
Johnson, Gene Allen 1960- *WhoFI 94*
Johnson, Gene C. 1941- *WhoBlA 94*
Johnson, Geneva B. *WhoBlA 94*
Johnson, Geneva Bolton *WhoAm 94*
Johnson, Geoffrey McClure 1951- *WhoAmL 94*
Johnson, Georgann *WhoHol 92*
Johnson, George 1920- *WhoAm 94, WhoMW 93*
Johnson, George, Jr. 1926- *WhoAm 94*

Johnson, George, Jr. 1934- *WhoBlA 94*
Johnson, George (Laclede) 1952- *WrDr 94*
Johnson, George Clayton 1929- *EncSF 93*
Johnson, George E. 1927- *AfrAmAl 6 [port]*
Johnson, George Edwin 1933- *WhoScEn 94*
Johnson, George Ellis 1927- *WhoBlA 94*
Johnson, George F. *WhoAmP 93*
Johnson, George M. 1900- *WhoBlA 94*
Johnson, George Patrick 1932- *WhoScEn 94*
Johnson, George Robert 1927- *WhoMW 93*
Johnson, George T. 1955- *BasBi*
Johnson, George Taylor 1930- *WhoMW 93*
Johnson, George William 1928- *WhoAm 94*
Johnson, George William 1949- *WhoMW 93*
Johnson, Georgia Anna 1930- *WhoBlA 94*
Johnson, Georgia Douglas c. 1880-1966 *BlmGWL*
Johnson, Georgia Douglas 1886-1966 *AfrAmAl 6*
Johnson, Georgianna 1930- *WhoBlA 94*
Johnson, Gerald, III 1945- *WhoScEn 94*
Johnson, Gerald Arlen 1941- *WhoAm 94*
Johnson, Gerald Lynn 1950- *WhoAmP 93*
Johnson, Geraldine Ross 1946- *WhoBlA 94*
Johnson, Gerard G. 1941- *WhoAm 94*
Johnson, Gertrude 1894-1973 *NewGrDO*
Johnson, Gifford Kenneth 1918- *WhoScEn 94*
Johnson, Gina Curry 1960- *WhoWest 94*
Johnson, Glen D., Jr. 1954- *WhoAmP 93*
Johnson, Glen Roger 1929- *WhoAm 94*
Johnson, Glendon E. 1924- *WhoIns 94*
Johnson, Glenn Edwin 1951- *WhoAmL 94*
Johnson, Glenn T. 1917- *WhoBlA 94*
Johnson, Glenn Thompson 1917- *WhoAm 94, WhoAmL 94*
Johnson, Gloria Dean 1948- *WhoBlA 94*
Johnson, Golden Elizabeth 1944- *WhoBlA 94*
Johnson, Gordon *Who 94*
Johnson, (Denis) Gordon 1911- *Who 94*
Johnson, Gordon Arthur 1938- *Who 94*
Johnson, Gordon Selby 1918- *WhoAm 94*
Johnson, Gordon V. 1938- *WhoAmL 94*
Johnson, Grace Manchester 1907- *WhoAmP 93*
Johnson, Graham Rhodes 1950- *Who 94*
Johnson, Grant Lester 1929- *WhoAm 94, WhoAmL 94, WhoFI 94*
Johnson, Greg *DrAPF 93*
Johnson, Greg 1953- *ConAu 140*
Johnson, Gregory L. *WhoAmL 94, WhoFI 94*
Johnson, Gregory Paul 1954- *WhoFI 94*
Johnson, Gregory Wayne 1953- *WhoBlA 94*
Johnson, Gus 1938- *BasBi*
Johnson, Gus LaRoy 1947- *WhoAm 94*
Johnson, Guy c. 1740-1788 *AmRev, WhAmRev*
Johnson, Guy 1927- *WhoAmA 93*
Johnson, Guy Benton 1901-1991 *WhAm 10*
Johnson, Guy Charles 1933- *WhoMW 93*
Johnson, Gwenavere Anelisa 1909- *WhoWest 94*
Johnson, H. Arvid 1936- *WhoAm 94, WhoAmL 94*
Johnson, H. T. 1936- *WhoIns 94*
Johnson, H(erbert) Webster 1906- *WrDr 94*
Johnson, Hal Harold Gustav 1915- *WhoAm 94*
Johnson, Hall d1970 *WhoHol 92*
Johnson, Halvard *DrAPF 93*
Johnson, Hansford Tillman 1936- *WhoAm 94*
Johnson, Hardwick Smith, Jr. 1958- *WhoAm 94*
Johnson, Harlan C. 1919- *WhoBlA 94*
Johnson, Harmer Frederik 1943- *WhoFI 94*
Johnson, Harold d1978 *WhoHol 92*
Johnson, Harold Earl 1939- *WhoAm 94*
Johnson, Harold Edward 1944- *WhoFI 94*
Johnson, Harold Gene 1934- *WhoAmL 94*
Johnson, Harold L. 1927- *WhoFI 94*
Johnson, Harold Leonard 1944- *WhoAm 94*
Johnson, Harold Ogden 1891-1962 See Olsen and Johnson *WhoCom*
Johnson, Harold R. 1926- *WhoAm 94, WhoBlA 94*
Johnson, Harris Tucker 1943- *WhoFI 94*
Johnson, Harry A. 1920- *WhoBlA 94*
Johnson, Harry A., III 1949- *WhoAm 94, WhoAmL 94*
Johnson, Harry J. d1993 *NewYTBS 93*
Johnson, Harvey William 1921- *WhoAmA 93*
Johnson, Hayman d1993 *Who 94N*
Johnson, Haynes Bonner 1931- *WhoAm 94*
Johnson, Hazel Lynn 1955- *WhoAmL 94*
Johnson, Hazel W. 1927- *AfrAmAl 6 [port]*
Johnson, Heidi Smith 1946- *WhoWest 94*
Johnson, Helen *WhoHol 92*
Johnson, Helen Chaffin 1905- *WhoAmP 93*
Johnson, Helen Jeannette 1951- *WhoAmP 93*
Johnson, Helen M. 1928- *WhoAmP 93*
Johnson, Henderson A., III 1929- *WhoBlA 94*
Johnson, Henry *DrAPF 93*
Johnson, Henry 1748-1835 *WhAmRev*
Johnson, Henry 1897-1929 *AfrAmAl 6*
Johnson, Henry 1937- *WhoBlA 94*
Johnson, Henry Clyde 1914- *WhoFI 94*
Johnson, Henry Wade 1947- *WhoBlA 94*
Johnson, Herbert Alan 1934- *WhoAm 94*
Johnson, Herbert Conrad 1909-1990 *WhAm 10*
Johnson, Herbert Fisk 1901-1980 *WhoAmA 93N*
Johnson, Herbert Frederick 1934- *WhoAm 94*
Johnson, Herbert M. 1941- *WhoBlA 94*
Johnson, Herbert Michael 1936- *WhoAm 94*
Johnson, Herman Leonall 1935- *WhoScEn 94, WhoWest 94*
Johnson, Hermon M., Sr. 1929- *WhoBlA 94*
Johnson, Herschel Lee 1948- *WhoBlA 94*
Johnson, Hester *WhoBlA 94*
Johnson, Hollis Eugene 1893- *WhAm 10*
Johnson, Hollis Eugene, III 1935- *WhoAm 94*
Johnson, Hollis Ralph 1928- *WhoAm 94*
Johnson, Homer 1925- *WhoAmA 93*
Johnson, Horace Richard 1926- *WhoAm 94*
Johnson, Horton Anton 1926- *WhoAm 94*
Johnson, Howard Arthur, Jr. 1952- *WhoFI 94*
Johnson, Howard Eugene 1915- *WhoFI 94*
Johnson, Howard George 1939- *WhoAmL 94*
Johnson, Howard Michael 1960- *WhoAm 94*
Johnson, Howard Paul 1923- *WhoScEn 94*
Johnson, Howard R. 1942- *WhoBlA 94*
Johnson, Howard Sydney 1911- *Who 94*
Johnson, Howard Wesley 1922- *IntWW 93, WhoAm 94*
Johnson, Hubert C. 1930- *WrDr 94*
Johnson, Hugh A. d1979 *WhoHol 92*
Johnson, Hugh Bailey 1904-1992 *WhAm 10*
Johnson, Hugh Eric Allan 1939- *IntWW 93, Who 94*
Johnson, Hugh Leon 1951- *WhoFI 94*
Johnson, I. S. Leevy 1942- *WhoAmP 93, WhoBlA 94*
Johnson, Ingolf Birger 1913- *WhoAm 94*
Johnson, Iola Vivian 1947- *WhoBlA 94*
Johnson, Irene L. 1918- *WhoAmP 93*
Johnson, Irma Maria Z. 1930- *WhoHisp 94*
Johnson, Irving Stanley 1925- *WhoAm 94*
Johnson, Ivan Earl 1911- *WhoAmA 93*
Johnson, Iver Christian 1928- *WhoFI 94*
Johnson, Ivory 1938- *WhoBlA 94*
Johnson, J. Bernard 1942- *WhoBlA 94*
Johnson, J. Bond 1926- *IntMPA 94*
Johnson, J. Chester 1944- *WhoAm 94*
Johnson, J. David 1947- *WhoMW 93*
Johnson, J. J. *WhoAm 94*
Johnson, J. J. 1924- *AfrAmAl 6*
Johnson, J. Louis d1954 *WhoHol 92*
Johnson, J. M. Hamlin 1925- *WhoAm 94*
Johnson, J. Michael, Sr. 1935- *WhoWest 94*
Johnson, J.R. *BlkWr 2*
Johnson, J. Rosamond d1954 *WhoHol 92*
Johnson, J. Seward, Jr. 1930- *WhoAmA 93*
Johnson, J. Stewart 1925- *WhoAmA 93*
Johnson, Jack d1946 *WhoHol 92*
Johnson, Jack 1878-1946 *AfrAmAl 6*
Johnson, Jack Leo 1933- *WhoIns 94*
Johnson, Jack Stoddard 1932- *WhoWest 94*
Johnson, Jack Thomas 1915- *WhoAm 94*
Johnson, Jackson Melvin 1940- *WhoFI 94, WhoMW 93*
Johnson, Jacob Edwards, III 1922- *WhoBlA 94*
Johnson, Jacqueline *DrAPF 93*
Johnson, James *WhoAmP 93*
Johnson, James 1908- *Who 94*
Johnson, James, Jr. 1933- *WhoBlA 94*
Johnson, James A. *WhoBlA 94*
Johnson, James A. 1943- *WhoAm 94, WhoFI 94*
Johnson, James Alan 1945- *WhoAmA 93*
Johnson, James Arnold 1939- *WhoAm 94*
Johnson, James B(lair) 1944- *EncSF 93*
Johnson, James Bass 1949- *WhoWest 94*
Johnson, James Bek, Jr. 1943- *WhoAm 94*
Johnson, James C., Jr. *WhoAmP 93*
Johnson, James Clyde 1957- *WhoAmP 93*
Johnson, James Daniel 1944- *WhoWest 94*
Johnson, James David 1948- *WhoWest 94*
Johnson, James Dow 1934- *WhoAm 94*
Johnson, James Edgar *Who 94*
Johnson, James Edward 1931- *WhoBlA 94*
Johnson, James Edwin 1942- *WhoAmA 93*
Johnson, James Erling 1942- *WhoFI 94*
Johnson, James F., IV 1941- *WhoAmL 94*
Johnson, James Gann, Jr. 1915- *WhoAm 94*
Johnson, James Gibb 1937- *WhoAm 94*
Johnson, James Gibson, Jr. 1938- *WhoFI 94, WhoWest 94*
Johnson, James H. 1932- *WhoBlA 94*
Johnson, James Harold 1944- *WhoAm 94, WhoAmL 94*
Johnson, James Henry 1930- *WrDr 94*
Johnson, James Hodge 1932- *WhoScEn 94*
Johnson, James J. *WhoAmL 94*
Johnson, James Kenneth 1942- *WhoBlA 94*
Johnson, James Lawrence 1953- *WhoScEn 94, WhoWest 94*
Johnson, James M. *WhoAm 94*
Johnson, James Myron 1927- *WhoAm 94*
Johnson, James Nathaniel 1932- *Who 94*
Johnson, James Norman 1939- *WhoScEn 94*
Johnson, James P. 1894-1955 *AfrAmAl 6*
Johnson, James P. 1930- *WhoAmP 93*
Johnson, James R. 1934- *WhoBlA 94*
Johnson, James Ralph 1922- *WhoAmA 93, WhoWest 94, WrDr 94*
Johnson, James Richards, Jr. 1915- *WhoAmP 93*
Johnson, James Robert 1923- *WhoAm 94*
Johnson, James Robert 1939- *WhoFI 94*
Johnson, James S. 1918- *WhoBlA 94*
Johnson, James Terence 1942- *WhoAm 94*
Johnson, James W., Jr. 1951- *WhoAmP 93*
Johnson, James Wallace 1951- *WhoMW 93*
Johnson, James Walter, Jr. 1941- *WhoBlA 94*
Johnson, James Wayne 1945- *WhoAm 94, WhoAmL 94*
Johnson, James Weldon 1871-1938 *AfrAmAl 6, ChlLR 32 [port], ConBlB 5 [port], HisWorL [port]*
Johnson, James William 1927- *WhoAm 94*
Johnson, James William, III 1938- *WhoWest 94*
Johnson, James Winston 1930- *WhoAm 94*
Johnson, Janet *WhoHol 92*
Johnson, Janet 1940- *WhoAmP 93*
Johnson, Janet A. 1940- *WhoAm 94*
Johnson, Janet B. 1940- *WhoMW 93*
Johnson, Janet Helen 1944- *WhoAm 94*
Johnson, Janet LeAnn Moe 1941- *WhoScEn 94*
Johnson, Janis 1946- *WhoWomW 91*
Johnson, Janis Tyler 1930- *ConAu 141*
Johnson, Jared Modell 1960- *WhoBlA 94, WhoMW 93*
Johnson, Jason d1977 *WhoHol 92*
Johnson, Jay d1954 *WhoHol 92*
Johnson, Jay 1947- *WhoBlA 94*
Johnson, Jay Sewell 1943- *WhoAmL 94*
Johnson, Jean DeWitt 1923- *WhoFI 94, WhoMW 93*
Johnson, Jean Elaine 1925- *WhoAm 94, WhoScEn 94*
Johnson, Jeanne Payne 1887-1958 *WhoAmA 93N*
Johnson, Jed, Jr. 1939- *WhoAmP 93*
Johnson, Jed Joseph, Jr. 1939- *WhoAm 94*
Johnson, Jeffrey Allan 1967- *WhoScEn 94*
Johnson, Jeffrey D. 1958- *WhoAmP 93*
Johnson, Jeffrey Parker 1944- *WhoMW 93*
Johnson, Jeffrey R. 1954- *WhoAmL 94*
Johnson, Jeh Vincent 1931- *WhoAm 94, WhoBlA 94*
Johnson, Jennifer J. 1962- *WhoWest 94*
Johnson, Jennifer Ursula 1946- *WhoWomW 91*
Johnson, Jeraldine I. 1947- *WhoMW 93*
Johnson, Jere W. 1942- *WhoAmP 93*
Johnson, Jerome L. *WhoAm 94*
Johnson, Jerome Linne 1929- *WhoFI 94, WhoScEn 94, WhoWest 94*
Johnson, Jerry *WhoAmP 93*
Johnson, Jerry A. 1931- *WhoAm 94*
Johnson, Jerry Calvin 1920- *WhoBlA 94*
Johnson, Jerry D. 1945- *WhoAmL 94*
Johnson, Jerry Douglas 1947- *WhoScEn 94*
Johnson, Jerry K. 1933- *WhoAmP 93*
Johnson, Jerry L. 1947- *WhoBlA 94*
Johnson, Jesse Charles 1894- *WhAm 10*
Johnson, Jesse J. 1914- *WhoBlA 94, WrDr 94*
Johnson, Jesse J. 1921- *WhoBlA 94*
Johnson, Jimmy 1943- *News 93-3 [port], WhoAm 94*
Johnson, Joan 1943- *WhoAmP 93, WhoWest 94*
Johnson, Joan B. 1929- *WhoAm 94, WhoBlA 94, WhoFI 94*
Johnson, Joan J 1942- *WrDr 94*
Johnson, Joan Kiff 1929- *WhoAmP 93*
Johnson, JoAnn Lee 1944- *WhoMW 93*
Johnson, Joanna *WhoHol 92*
Johnson, Joe *DrAPF 93, IntWW 93*
Johnson, Joe 1940- *WhoBlA 94*
Johnson, Joe Arley 1930- *WhoAmP 93*
Johnson, Joe C. 1926- *WhoHisp 94*
Johnson, Joe William 1908- *WhoAm 94*
Johnson, John *EncNAR*
Johnson, John 1742-1830 *AmRev, WhAmRev*
Johnson, John 1922- *WhoAmP 93*
Johnson, John 1947- *BasBi*
Johnson, John (Rodney) 1930- *Who 94*
Johnson, John A. 1915- *WhoAm 94*
Johnson, John Allen 1950- *WhoFI 94*
Johnson, John Andrew 1942- *WhoMW 93*
Johnson, John Arthur 1934- *WhoAmL 94*
Johnson, John Brayton 1916- *WhoAm 94*
Johnson, John C. *WhoFI 94*
Johnson, John C. 1944- *WhoAmP 93*
Johnson, John David 1938- *WhoWest 94*
Johnson, John Edlin, Jr. 1945- *WhoWest 94*
Johnson, John Edwin 1931- *WhoMW 93*
Johnson, John Frank 1942- *WhoAm 94, WhoFI 94*
Johnson, John Gray 1924- *WhoAm 94*
Johnson, John Griffith, Jr. 1950- *WhoAm 94*
Johnson, John H. 1918- *AfrAmAl 6 [port], DcLB 137 [port], IntWW 93, WhoAm 94, WhoBlA 94, WhoFI 94, WhoMW 93*
Johnson, John H(arold) 1918- *WrDr 94*
Johnson, John Henry *ProFbHF*
Johnson, John Irwin, Jr. 1931- *WhoAm 94, WhoScEn 94*
Johnson, John J. *WhoBlA 94*
Johnson, John J. 1912- *WhoAm 94*
Johnson, John Jay 1954- *WhoMW 93*
Johnson, John Philip 1949- *WhoWest 94*
Johnson, John Prescott 1921- *WhoAm 94*
Johnson, John Randall, Sr. 1945- *WhoAm 94*
Johnson, John Recter 1923- *WhoWest 94*
Johnson, John Robert 1936- *WhoScEn 94*
Johnson, John Robin 1927- *Who 94*
Johnson, John Rodney 1930- *IntWW 93*
Johnson, John Rosamond 1873-1954 *AfrAmAl 6*
Johnson, John T. 1945- *WhoAmL 94*
Johnson, John Thomas 1942- *WhoBlA 94*
Johnson, John W. 1934- *WhoBlA 94*
Johnson, John Walter, III 1947- *WhoAmL 94*
Johnson, John Warren 1929- *WhoAm 94*
Johnson, John William, Jr. 1932- *WhoAm 94*
Johnson, Johnnie *Who 94*
Johnson, Johnnie Dean 1938- *WhoFI 94*
Johnson, Johnnie L., Jr. 1946- *WhoBlA 94*
Johnson, Johnny 1938- *WhoScEn 94*
Johnson, Johnny B. 1920- *WhoBlA 94*
Johnson, Johnny Burl 1944- *WhoWest 94*
Johnson, Johnny Ray 1929- *WhoAm 94*
Johnson, Jon D. 1948- *WhoAmP 93, WhoBlA 94*
Johnson, Jon E. 1963- *WhoAm 94*
Johnson, Jonas Talmadge 1947- *WhoAm 94*
Johnson, Jonathan Edwin, II 1936- *WhoAm 94*
Johnson, Jondelle H. 1924- *WhoBlA 94*
Johnson, Joscelyn Andrea 1966- *WhoBlA 94*
Johnson, Joseph *WhoAmP 93*
Johnson, Joseph A. 1925- *WhoBlA 94*
Johnson, Joseph B. 1934- *WhoBlA 94*
Johnson, Joseph Benjamin 1934- *WhoAm 94*
Johnson, Joseph Bernard 1919- *WhoAm 94*
Johnson, Joseph Clayton, Jr. 1943- *WhoAmL 94*
Johnson, Joseph David 1945- *WhoBlA 94*
Johnson, Joseph E. *WhoAmP 93*
Johnson, Joseph Earl 1946- *WhoAmP 93*
Johnson, Joseph Edward 1934- *WhoBlA 94*
Johnson, Joseph Eggleston, III 1930- *IntWW 93, WhoAm 94*
Johnson, Joseph Erle 1951- *WhoScEn 94*
Johnson, Joseph Ernest 1942- *WhoIns 94*

Johnson, Joseph Esrey 1906-1990 *WhAm 10*
Johnson, Joseph H. 1922-1991 *WhAm 10*
Johnson, Joseph H., Jr. 1925- *WhoAm 94, WhoAmL 94*
Johnson, Joseph Harvey 1916- *WhoBlA 94*
Johnson, Joseph Kelly 1897- *WhAm 10*
Johnson, Joseph Pickett, Jr. 1931- *WhoAmP 93*
Johnson, Josephine Winslow 1910-1990 *WhAm 10*
Johnson, Joshua 1949- *WhoBlA 94*
Johnson, Joy J. 1921- *WhoBlA 94*
Johnson, Joy Joseph 1922- *WhoAmP 93*
Johnson, Joyce 1929- *WhoAmA 93*
Johnson, Joyce (Glassman) 1935- *WrDr 94*
Johnson, Joyce Colleen 1939- *WhoBlA 94*
Johnson, Joyce Marie 1952- *WhoScEn 94*
Johnson, Joyce May 1952- *WhoAmP 93*
Johnson, Joyce Sandeen *DrAPF 93*
Johnson, Judith *DrAPF 93*
Johnson, Judith Ekberg 1949- *WhoMW 93*
Johnson, Judith Kay 1939- *WhoAm 94, WhoAmL 94*
Johnson, Juel S. 1923- *WhoAmP 93*
Johnson, Juliana Cornish 1957- *WhoBlA 94*
Johnson, Julie Marie 1953- *WhoAm 94, WhoMW 93*
Johnson, Julius Frank 1940- *AfrAmG [port], WhoAm 94, WhoBlA 94*
Johnson, June d1987 *WhoHol 92*
Johnson, Justin Morris 1933- *WhoBlA 94*
Johnson, Karen 1943- *WhoAmP 93*
Johnson, Karen Ann 1941- *WhoAmP 93*
Johnson, Karen Ruble 1944- *WhoAmL 94*
Johnson, Karl Clinthorne, Jr. 1957- *WhoFI 94*
Johnson, Karl Richard 1907-1991 *WhAm 10*
Johnson, Kate Chamness *WhoAmA 93*
Johnson, Kate Knapp *DrAPF 93*
Johnson, Katherine d1978 *WhoHol 92*
Johnson, Katherine Anne 1947- *WhoAmL 94*
Johnson, Katherine Grace 1960- *WhoAm 94*
Johnson, Katherine King 1906- *WhoAmA 93N*
Johnson, Katie d1957 *WhoHol 92*
Johnson, Kay d1975 *WhoHol 92*
Johnson, Kay Durbahn 1937- *WhoMW 93*
Johnson, Kay E. 1945- *WhoAmL 94*
Johnson, Keith 1921- *IntWW 93*
Johnson, Keith Edward 1968- *WhoScEn 94*
Johnson, Keith Gilbert 1931- *WhoAm 94*
Johnson, Keith Ronald 1929- *WhoWest 94*
Johnson, Keith Windsor 1952- *WhoFI 94*
Johnson, Kelley Antonio 1962- *WhoBlA 94*
Johnson, Ken *EncSF 93*
Johnson, Kenneth 1942- *ConTFT 11*
Johnson, Kenneth, II d1974 *WhoHol 92*
Johnson, Kenneth Albert 1942- *WhoMW 93*
Johnson, Kenneth C. 1953- *WhoAmL 94*
Johnson, Kenneth F. 1938- *WhoAmL 94*
Johnson, Kenneth Harvey 1936- *WhoAm 94*
Johnson, Kenneth James 1926- *Who 94*
Johnson, Kenneth Lance 1963- *WhoBlA 94*
Johnson, Kenneth Langstreth 1925- *IntWW 93, Who 94, WhoScEn 94*
Johnson, Kenneth Lavon 1937- *WhoBlA 94*
Johnson, Kenneth Michael 1950- *WhoMW 93*
Johnson, Kenneth O. 1920- *WhoFI 94*
Johnson, Kenneth Odell 1922- *WhoAm 94, WhoFI 94, WhoMW 93*
Johnson, Kenneth Oscar 1920- *WhoAm 94*
Johnson, Kenneth Owen 1920- *WhoAm 94*
Johnson, Kenneth Peter 1930- *WhoBlA 94*
Johnson, Kenneth Peter 1932- *WhoScEn 94*
Johnson, Kenneth Peter, Sr. 1930- *WhoAmP 93*
Johnson, Kenneth Stuart 1928- *WhoFI 94, WhoMW 93*
Johnson, Kenneth T., Jr. 1947- *WhoAmL 94*
Johnson, Kenneth W. 1942- *WhoAmL 94*
Johnson, Kennett Conrad 1927- *WhoAm 94*
Johnson, Kent L. 1949- *WhoAmP 93*
Johnson, Kerry Gerard 1967- *WhoBlA 94*
Johnson, Kevin 1964- *WhoWest 94*
Johnson, Kevin Blaine 1956- *WhoAmL 94*
Johnson, Kevin Maurice 1966- *WhoBlA 94*
Johnson, Kevin R. 1958- *WhoHisp 94*
Johnson, Kevin Raymond 1958- *WhoAmL 94*
Johnson, Kim "Howard" 1955- *WrDr 94*
Johnson, Krista Ellen 1954- *WhoMW 93*
Johnson, Kristin Ann 1946- *WhoFI 94*
Johnson, Kristin Leigh 1965- *WhoAm 94*
Johnson, Kurt d1986 *WhoHol 92*
Johnson, Kyle *WhoHol 92*
Johnson, L. Neil 1940- *WhoMW 93*
Johnson, L(eroy) P(eter) V(ernon) 1905- *EncSF 93*
Johnson, L. Ronald 1938- *WhoMW 93, WhoScEn 94*
Johnson, Lady Bird *NewYTBS 93 [port]*
Johnson, Lady Bird 1912- *WhoAm 94*
Johnson, Lael Frederic 1938- *WhoAm 94, WhoAmL 94, WhoFI 94*
Johnson, Lamont 1920- *WhoHol 92*
Johnson, Lamont 1922- *IntMPA 94*
Johnson, Lance Franklin 1938- *WhoAmP 93*
Johnson, Laraine *WhoHol 92*
Johnson, Larry 1949- *AfrAmAl 6*
Johnson, Larry 1969- *News 93-3 [port]*
Johnson, Larry Alan 1935- *WhoAmP 93*
Johnson, Larry Dean 1953- *WhoWest 94*
Johnson, Larry Demetric 1969- *WhoAm 94, WhoBlA 94*
Johnson, Larry Robert 1943- *WhoMW 93*
Johnson, Larry Walter 1934- *WhoAm 94*
Johnson, Larry Wayne 1940- *WhoFI 94*
Johnson, Larry Wayne 1958- *WhoFI 94*
Johnson, Larry Wayne 1961- *WhoFI 94*
Johnson, Laura 1958- *WhoHol 92*
Johnson, Laurie 1927- *IntMPA 94*
Johnson, Lawrence Alan 1947- *WhoAm 94, WhoScEn 94*
Johnson, Lawrence E., Sr. 1948- *WhoBlA 94*
Johnson, Lawrence H. 1926- *WhoAmP 93*
Johnson, Lawrence M. 1940- *WhoAm 94, WhoFI 94, WhoWest 94*
Johnson, Lawrence Washington 1901- *WhoBlA 94*
Johnson, Lawrence Wilbur, Jr. 1955- *WhoAmL 94*
Johnson, Laymon, Jr. 1948- *WhoWest 94*
Johnson, Le Roy *WhoHol 92*
Johnson, Leardrew L. 1921- *WhoBlA 94*
Johnson, Leary J. 1934- *WhoAmP 93*
Johnson, Lectoy Tarlington 1931- *WhoBlA 94*
Johnson, Lee 1935- *WhoAmA 93*
Johnson, Lee Carroll 1933- *WhoWest 94*
Johnson, Lee Frederick 1946- *WhoScEn 94*
Johnson, Lee Harnie 1909- *WhoAm 94*
Johnson, Leigh Thornton 1943- *WhoWest 94*
Johnson, Lemuel A. 1941- *BlkWr 2, ConAu 43NR, WhoBlA 94*
Johnson, Lennart Ingemar 1924- *WhoMW 93, WhoScEn 94*
Johnson, Leon 1930- *WhoBlA 94*
Johnson, Leon, Jr. 1946- *WhoBlA 94*
Johnson, Leon Bernard *WhoAmA 93*
Johnson, Leon F. 1926- *WhoBlA 94*
Johnson, Leonard Hjalma 1957- *WhoAmL 94*
Johnson, Leonard James 1951- *WhoAmL 94*
Johnson, Leonidas Alexander 1959- *WhoWest 94*
Johnson, Leroy *WhoBlA 94*
Johnson, Leroy d1992 *WhoBlA 94N*
Johnson, Leroy Reginald *WhoBlA 94*
Johnson, Leroy Ronald 1944- *WhoBlA 94*
Johnson, Leslie Royston 1924- *IntWW 93*
Johnson, Leslie Whiting 1943- *WhoAmP 93*
Johnson, Lester 1947- *WhoBlA 94*
Johnson, Lester F. 1919- *WhoAmA 93*
Johnson, Lester Fredrick 1919- *WhoAm 94*
Johnson, Lester L. 1937- *AfrAmAl 6, WhoAmA 93*
Johnson, Linda *WhoHol 92*
Johnson, Linda Arlene 1946- *WhoMW 93*
Johnson, Linda C. 1945- *WhoBlA 94*
Johnson, Linda Louise 1951- *WhoMW 93*
Johnson, Linda Sue 1950- *WhoAmP 93, WhoWest 94*
Johnson, Linda Thelma 1954- *WhoScEn 94*
Johnson, Linn Valen 1942- *WhoWest 94*
Johnson, Linton Kwesi 1952- *BlmGEL, WrDr 94*
Johnson, Lionel Washington 1923- *WhoAmP 93*
Johnson, Lissa H(alls) 1955- *WrDr 94*
Johnson, Livingstone M. 1927- *WhoBlA 94*
Johnson, Lloyd A. 1932- *WhoBlA 94*
Johnson, Lloyd Peter 1930- *WhoAm 94, WhoMW 93*
Johnson, Lloyd Warren 1941- *WhoWest 94*
Johnson, Lockrem 1924-1977 *NewGrDO*
Johnson, Loering M. 1926- *WhoAm 94*
Johnson, Lois Eileen 1942- *WhoWest 94*
Johnson, Lois Jean 1950- *WhoWest 94*
Johnson, Lois Marlene 1942- *WhoAmA 93*
Johnson, Lonnie L. 1932- *WhoBlA 94*
Johnson, Loren Ray 1951- *WhoWest 94*
Johnson, Loretta Pearl 1947- *WhoMW 93*
Johnson, Lorna Karen 1958- *WhoBlA 94*
Johnson, Lorraine Jefferson 1918- *WhoBlA 94*
Johnson, Lorretta 1938- *WhoBlA 94*
Johnson, Louis 1937- *WhoAmP 93*
Johnson, Louis A. 1891-1966 *HisDcKW*
Johnson, Louis W. 1903- *WhoBlA 94*
Johnson, Louise Mason 1917- *WhoBlA 94*
Johnson, Louise Napier 1940- *Who 94*
Johnson, Lowell C. 1920- *WhoMW 93*
Johnson, Lowell Curtis 1920- *WhoAmP 93*
Johnson, Lowell Ferris 1912- *WhoAm 94*
Johnson, Lowell Rexford 1895- *WhAm 10*
Johnson, Lucien Love 1941- *WhoBlA 94*
Johnson, Lucille Lewis 1943- *WhoAm 94*
Johnson, Lucy Black 1924- *WhoAmP 93*
Johnson, Luther, Jr. 1939- *WhoHol 92*
Johnson, Luther Mason, Jr. 1930- *WhoBlA 94*
Johnson, Lydia d1979 *WhoHol 92*
Johnson, Lyndon Baines 1908-1973 *HisWorL [port]*
Johnson, Lynn-Holly 1959- *WhoHol 92*
Johnson, M. Scott 1944- *WhoAmL 94*
Johnson, Mable Jean 1920- *WhoAmP 93*
Johnson, Mack Evans 1942- *WhoAmP 93*
Johnson, Magic *ConAu 141*
Johnson, Magic 1959- *BasBi, WhoAm 94, WhoBlA 94, WhoWest 94*
Johnson, Mal 1924- *WhoBlA 94*
Johnson, Malcolm Clinton, Jr. 1925- *WhoAm 94*
Johnson, Malcolm Pratt 1941- *WhoScEn 94*
Johnson, Malvin Gray 1896-1934 *WhoAmA 93N*
Johnson, Manuel H., Jr. 1949- *IntWW 93*
Johnson, Marc 1943- *WhoWest 94*
Johnson, Margaret Douglas 1951- *WhoMW 93*
Johnson, Margaret H. 1933- *WhoMW 93*
Johnson, Margaret Helen 1933- *WhoFI 94*
Johnson, Margaret Kathleen 1920- *WhoAm 94*
Johnson, Margaret L. *WhoAmP 93*
Johnson, Margie N. 1938- *WhoBlA 94*
Johnson, Marguerite M. 1948- *WhoBlA 94*
Johnson, Marian Ilene 1929- *WhoAm 94, WhoWest 94*
Johnson, Marian Willard 1904- *WhoAmA 93N*
Johnson, Marie Elizabeth 1948- *WhoBlA 94*
Johnson, Marie Love 1925- *WhoBlA 94*
Johnson, Marilyn d1960 *WhoHol 92*
Johnson, Marion I. 1915- *WhoBlA 94*
Johnson, Marion Phillip 1931- *WhoAm 94*
Johnson, Marion T. 1948- *WhoBlA 94*
Johnson, Mark *IntMPA 94, WhoAmP 93*
Johnson, Mark 1945- *ConTFT 11*
Johnson, Mark 1949- *WhoAmP 93*
Johnson, Mark Alan 1958- *WhoFI 94*
Johnson, Mark Alan 1960- *WhoAm 94*
Johnson, Mark Allan 1966- *WhoScEn 94*
Johnson, Mark Daniel 1946- *WhoFI 94*
Johnson, Mark David 1953- *WhoScEn 94*
Johnson, Mark David 1956- *WhoAm 94*
Johnson, Mark David 1962- *WhoAmL 94*
Johnson, Mark Dee 1954- *WhoScEn 94*
Johnson, Mark Edwin 1943- *WhoAmL 94*
Johnson, Mark Eugene 1951- *WhoAm 94, WhoAmL 94*
Johnson, Mark Henry 1960- *WhoScEn 94*
Johnson, Mark Lee 1960- *WhoMW 93*
Johnson, Mark M. 1950- *WhoAmA 93*
Johnson, Mark P. 1955- *WhoAmL 94*
Johnson, Marlene 1946- *WhoAm 94, WhoAmP 93, WhoMW 93*
Johnson, Marlene E. 1936- *WhoBlA 94*
Johnson, Marlin Deon 1938- *WhoScEn 94*
Johnson, Marlys Dianne 1948- *WhoAm 94, WhoMW 93*
Johnson, Marques 1956- *BasBi*
Johnson, Marques Kevin 1956- *WhoBlA 94*
Johnson, Martha *WhoHol 92*
Johnson, Martha Ellen McArthur 1926- *WhoAmP 93*
Johnson, Martin d1937 *WhoHol 92*
Johnson, Martin Allen 1931- *WhoAm 94*
Johnson, Martin Brian 1951- *WhoAmA 93*
Johnson, Martin Chester 1954- *WhoWest 94*
Johnson, Martin Clyde-Vandivort 1959- *WhoFI 94*
Johnson, Martin Hume 1944- *Who 94*
Johnson, Martin Leroy 1941- *WhoBlA 94*
Johnson, Martin Marion 1951- *WhoAm 94*
Johnson, Martin Wayne 1946- *WhoAm 94*
Johnson, Martin Wigge 1893- *WhAm 10*
Johnson, Marv d1993 *NewYTBS 93*
Johnson, Marvin Donald 1928- *WhoAm 94*
Johnson, Marvin Melrose 1925- *WhoAm 94, WhoMW 93*
Johnson, Marvin Richard Alois 1916- *WhoAm 94*
Johnson, Mary *WhoAm 94*
Johnson, Mary Ann 1956- *WhoMW 93*
Johnson, Mary Anne 1954- *WhoAmP 93*
Johnson, Mary Beatrice 1952- *WhoBlA 94*
Johnson, Mary Blow 1925- *WhoAmP 93*
Johnson, Mary Elizabeth 1905- *WhoMW 93*
Johnson, Mary Elizabeth 1943- *WhoMW 93*
Johnson, Mary Elizabeth Susan 1947- *WhoAm 94*
Johnson, Mary Ignacia 1933- *WhoHisp 94*
Johnson, Mary Jane 1952- *WhoAmP 93*
Johnson, Mary Lee Alexander 1944- *WhoAmP 93*
Johnson, Mary Susan 1937- *WhoMW 93*
Johnson, Maryann *WhoAmP 93*
Johnson, Maryl Rae 1951- *WhoMW 93*
Johnson, Mattiedna 1918- *WhoBlA 94*
Johnson, Maurice Glen 1936- *WhoAm 94*
Johnson, Maurice Verner, Jr. 1925- *WhoScEn 94*
Johnson, Maynard *DrAPF 93*
Johnson, Mel 1939- *WrDr 94*
Johnson, Melinda 1936- *WhoWest 94*
Johnson, Melodie 1944- *WhoHol 92*
Johnson, Melvin Russell 1946- *WhoBlA 94*
Johnson, Mertha Ruth *WhoBlA 94*
Johnson, Mervil V. 1953- *WhoBlA 94*
Johnson, Merwyn *Who 94*
Johnson, (Willis) Merwyn 1923- *Who 94*
Johnson, Met 1941- *WhoAmP 93*
Johnson, Miani (Marianne) Guthrie 1948- *WhoAmA 93*
Johnson, Micah William 1963- *WhoAm 94, WhoFI 94*
Johnson, Michael *WhAmRev, WhoBlA 94*
Johnson, Michael 1959- *WhoBlA 94*
Johnson, Michael Anthony 1951- *WhoBlA 94*
Johnson, Michael Edward 1960- *WhoAmL 94*
Johnson, Michael Fleet 1956- *WhoAmL 94*
Johnson, Michael Howard 1930- *Who 94*
Johnson, Michael Kevin 1960- *WhoBlA 94*
Johnson, Michael L. *DrAPF 93*
Johnson, Michael P(aul) 1941- *WrDr 94*
Johnson, Michael Paul 1941- *WhoAm 94*
Johnson, Michael R. 1951- *WhoAmL 94*
Johnson, Michael Randy 1946- *WhoFI 94*
Johnson, Michael Russell 1948- *WhoAmL 94*
Johnson, Michael T. *WhoAmP 93*
Johnson, Michael York- *Who 94*
Johnson, Michele 1959- *WhoBlA 94*
Johnson, Michelle 1965- *WhoHol 92*
Johnson, Mickey 1952- *BasBi*
Johnson, Mijo d1988 *WhoHol 92*
Johnson, Mike *WhoHol 92*
See Also Dinosaur Jr. *ConMus 10*
Johnson, Mike 1931-1992 *WrDr 94N*
Johnson, Mildred D *WrDr 94*
Johnson, Mildred H. *WhoBlA 94*
Johnson, Millard Wallace, Jr. 1928- *WhoAm 94*
Johnson, Milton D. 1928- *WhoBlA 94*
Johnson, Milton H. 1923- *WhoWest 94*
Johnson, Minnie Redmond 1910- *WhoBlA 94*
Johnson, Miriam B. *WhoBlA 94*
Johnson, Miriam Massey 1928- *WhoWest 94*
Johnson, Mitchell A. 1942- *WhoBlA 94*
Johnson, Moffat d1935 *WhoHol 92*
Johnson, Monica *Who 94*
Johnson, Monna Lynn 1952- *WhoMW 93*
Johnson, Myron L. 1935- *WhoFI 94*
Johnson, Nancy Jill 1960- *WhoMW 93*
Johnson, Nancy L. 1935- *CngDr 93, WhoAmP 93, WhoWomW 91*
Johnson, Nancy Lee 1935- *WhoAm 94*
Johnson, Nancy M. 1947- *WhoIns 94*
Johnson, Nancy Marie 1947- *WhoMW 93*
Johnson, Narelle *WhoHol 92*
Johnson, Nathan 1944- *WhoBlA 94*
Johnson, Nathaniel J., Sr. 1940- *WhoBlA 94*
Johnson, Neal Sox 1933- *WhoAmP 93*
Johnson, Ned 1926- *WhoAm 94*
Johnson, Ned Keith 1932- *WhoScEn 94*
Johnson, Neil Anthony 1949- *Who 94*
Johnson, Nellie Stone *WhoAmP 93*

Johnson, Nelson Clarence 1948- *WhoAm 94*
Johnson, Nely Lupovici 1947- *WhoAmL 94*
Johnson, Neva Wiley Pemberton Maddox 1919- *WhoAmP 93*
Johnson, Nevil 1929- *Who 94*
Johnson, Neville Lawrence 1949- *WhoAmL 94*
Johnson, Newell Walter 1938- *Who 94*
Johnson, Nicholas 1934- *WhoAm 94, WrDr 94*
Johnson, Nick *DrAPF 93*
Johnson, Niel Melvin 1931- *WhoMW 93*
Johnson, Nina Sidler 1927- *WhoAmP 93*
Johnson, Noble d1978 *WhoHol 92*
Johnson, Noel *WhoHol 92*
Johnson, Noel Lars 1957- *WhoAm 94, WhoScEn 94, WhoWest 94*
Johnson, Nora *DrAPF 93*
Johnson, Norma Holloway *CngDr 93, WhoAm 94, WhoAmL 94, WhoBlA 94*
Johnson, Norma J. 1925- *WhoMW 93*
Johnson, Norman 1928- *WhoAm 94*
Johnson, Norman B. *WhoBlA 94*
Johnson, Norman J. 1919- *WhoBlA 94*
Johnson, Norman Kimball 1956- *WhoAmL 94*
Johnson, Norris Brock 1942- *WhoBlA 94*
Johnson, Nota 1923- *WhoAmA 93*
Johnson, Nunnally 1897-1977 *IntDcF 2-4*
Johnson, Odell 1936- *WhoAmP 93*
Johnson, Ogden Carl 1929-1988 *WhAm 10*
Johnson, Olendruff Lerey 1956- *WhoBlA 94*
Johnson, Oliver Thomas, Jr. 1946- *WhoAm 94, WhoAmL 94*
Johnson, Omotunde Evan George 1941- *WhoFI 94, WhoScEn 94*
Johnson, Onette E. *WhoBlA 94*
Johnson, Orrin d1943 *WhoHol 92*
Johnson, Orrin Wendell 1920- *WhoAm 94*
Johnson, Osa d1953 *WhoHol 92*
Johnson, Oscar d1970 *WhoHol 92*
Johnson, Otis Samuel 1942- *WhoAmP 93, WhoBlA 94*
Johnson, Owen H. 1929- *WhoAmP 93*
Johnson, Owen M(cMahon) 1878-1952 *EncSF 93*
Johnson, Page 1930- *WhoHol 92*
Johnson, Pam McAllister 1945- *WhoBlA 94*
Johnson, Pamela Hansford 1912-1981 *BlmGEL, BlmGWL*
Johnson, Parker Collins 1961- *WhoBlA 94*
Johnson, Pat *WhoHol 92*
Johnson, Patrice Doreen 1952- *WhoBlA 94*
Johnson, Patricia 1934- *NewGrDO*
Johnson, Patricia Altenbernd 1945- *WhoMW 93*
Johnson, Patricia Anita 1944- *WhoBlA 94*
Johnson, Patricia Dumas 1950- *WhoBlA 94*
Johnson, Patricia Duren 1943- *WhoBlA 94*
Johnson, Patricia Gayle 1947- *WhoWest 94*
Johnson, Patricia L. 1956- *WhoBlA 94*
Johnson, Patricia Lyn 1957- *WhoScEn 94*
Johnson, Patrick 1904- *Who 94*
Johnson, Patrick, Jr. 1955- *WhoAmL 94*
Johnson, Patrick D. 1955- *WhoFI 94*
Johnson, Patrick Eliot 1955- *Who 94*
Johnson, Patti Lynn 1958- *WhoMW 93*
Johnson, Paul 1959- *WhoAmP 93*
Johnson, Paul (Bede) 1928- *IntWW 93, Who 94, WrDr 94*
Johnson, Paul Christian 1928- *WhoAm 94*
Johnson, Paul E. *WhoAm 94, WhoWest 94*
Johnson, Paul Edwin 1933- *WhoBlA 94*
Johnson, Paul Edwin 1934- *WhoAmP 93*
Johnson, Paul L. 1943- *WhoBlA 94*
Johnson, Paul Lawrence 1931- *WhoBlA 94*
Johnson, Paul Michael 1960- *WhoMW 93*
Johnson, Paul Oren 1937- *WhoAm 94, WhoAmL 94*
Johnson, Paul Owen 1919- *WhoAmL 94, WhoMW 93*
Johnson, Paul Ronald 1955- *WhoWest 94*
Johnson, Paul W. 1941- *WhoAmP 93*
Johnson, Pauline d1948 *WhoHol 92*
Johnson, Pauline 1861-1913 *BlmGWL*
Johnson, Pauline Benge 1932- *WhoMW 93, WhoScEn 94*
Johnson, Pepper 1964- *WhoAm 94*
Johnson, Pete, Jr. *WhoAmP 93*
Johnson, Peter (Colpoys Paley) 1930- *Who 94*
Johnson, Peter (Colpoys Paley), Sir 1930- *WrDr 94*
Johnson, Peter Forbes 1934- *WhoFI 94*
Johnson, Peter Lars 1953- *WhoFI 94*
Johnson, Philip *NewYTBS 93 [port]*
Johnson, Philip 1947- *WhoFI 94*
Johnson, Philip Ashley 1949- *WhoAmP 93*
Johnson, Philip Cortelyou 1906- *AmCulL, IntWW 93, Who 94, WhoAm 94*
Johnson, Philip Martin 1940- *WhoAmL 94*
Johnson, Philip McBride 1938- *WhoAm 94*
Johnson, Philip Wayne 1944- *WhoAmL 94*
Johnson, Phillip E. 1940- *WrDr 94*
Johnson, Phillip Eugene 1937- *WhoAm 94*
Johnson, Phyllis Campbell 1954- *WhoBlA 94*
Johnson, Phyllis Jean 1937- *WhoWest 94*
Johnson, Phyllis Mercedes 1919- *WhoBlA 94*
Johnson, Pierre Marc 1946- *IntWW 93*
Johnson, Pompie Louis, Jr. 1926- *WhoAmP 93, WhoBlA 94*
Johnson, Porter Wear 1942- *WhoMW 93*
Johnson, Qulan Adrian 1942- *WhoFI 94, WhoScEn 94, WhoWest 94*
Johnson, R. Benjamin 1944- *WhoBlA 94*
Johnson, R. Erick, II 1951- *WhoAmL 94*
Johnson, R. J. 1961- *WhoAmP 93*
Johnson, R(obert) V(incent) 1927- *WrDr 94*
Johnson, Rachel Ramírez 1937- *WhoHisp 94*
Johnson, Rady Alan 1936- *WhoAm 94*
Johnson, Rafer 1935- *WhoHol 92*
Johnson, Raleigh West 1934- *WhoAmP 93*
Johnson, Ralph C. 1941- *WhoBlA 94*
Johnson, Ralph Edson 1919- *WhoAmP 93*
Johnson, Ralph H. 1923- *WhoAmP 93*
Johnson, Ralph Hudson d1993 *Who 94N*
Johnson, Ralph Raymond 1943- *WhoAm 94*
Johnson, Ralph Theodore, Jr. 1935- *WhoScEn 94*
Johnson, Randall David 1963- *WhoAm 94, WhoWest 94*
Johnson, Randall Morris 1936- *WhoBlA 94*
Johnson, Ray d1976 *WhoHol 92*
Johnson, Ray 1927- *WhoAmA 93*
Johnson, Ray 1935- *WhoBlA 94*
Johnson, Ray Clifford 1927- *WhoAm 94*
Johnson, Raymond A. 1942- *WhoWest 94*
Johnson, Raymond Allen Constan 1923- *WhoAmP 93*
Johnson, Raymond L. 1936- *WhoBlA 94*
Johnson, Raymond L., Sr. 1922- *WhoBlA 94*
Johnson, Raymond Lewis 1943- *WhoBlA 94*
Johnson, Raymond W. 1934- *WhoWest 94*
Johnson, Rebecca L. 1956- *WrDr 94*
Johnson, Rebecca M. 1905- *WhoBlA 94*
Johnson, Reggie *WhoAm 94*
Johnson, Renie 1925- *WhoMW 93*
Johnson, Reuben Botsford d1993 *NewYTBS 93*
Johnson, Reverdy 1937- *WhoAm 94*
Johnson, Rex 1921- *Who 94*
Johnson, Rheuben C. 1937- *WhoIns 94*
Johnson, Rhoda E. 1946- *WhoBlA 94*
Johnson, Richard *ConAu 140*
Johnson, Richard 1753-1827 *DcNaB MP*
Johnson, Richard 1927- *IntMPA 94, WhoHol 92*
Johnson, Richard 1963- *WhoBlA 94*
Johnson, Richard A. 1942- *WhoAmA 93*
Johnson, Richard Alan 1942- *WhoAm 94*
Johnson, Richard Allison 1956- *WhoFI 94*
Johnson, Richard Arlo 1952- *WhoAmL 94*
Johnson, Richard Arnold 1937- *WhoAm 94, WhoMW 93*
Johnson, Richard Arthur 1936- *WhoAm 94*
Johnson, Richard August 1937- *WhoAm 94*
Johnson, Richard Clark 1937- *WhoAm 94*
Johnson, Richard Clayton 1930- *WhoAm 94*
Johnson, Richard Craig 1937- *WhoAm 94*
Johnson, Richard D. 1935- *WhoAmP 93*
Johnson, Richard Damerau 1934- *WhoAm 94*
Johnson, Richard David 1927- *WhoAm 94*
Johnson, Richard Dean 1936- *WhoScEn 94*
Johnson, Richard Fred 1944- *WhoAm 94, WhoAmL 94*
Johnson, Richard H. 1930- *WhoAmP 93*
Johnson, Richard Howard 1931- *WhoBlA 94*
Johnson, Richard J. 1950- *WhoAmL 94*
Johnson, Richard James Vaughan 1930- *WhoAm 94*
Johnson, Richard Jerome 1932- *WhoMW 93*
Johnson, Richard Karl 1947- *WhoWest 94*
Johnson, Richard Keith 1927- *IntWW 93, Who 94*
Johnson, Richard Ned 1942- *WhoMW 93*
Johnson, Richard T. 1931- *WhoAm 94*
Johnson, Richard Tenney 1930- *WhoAm 94, WhoAmL 94, WhoAmP 93, WhoFI 94*
Johnson, Richard Thomas 1922- *WhoMW 93*
Johnson, Richard Walter 1928- *WhoFI 94, WhoMW 93*
Johnson, Richard Warren 1939- *WhoAm 94*
Johnson, Richard Warren 1947- *WhoScEn 94*
Johnson, Richard Winslow *WhAm 10*
Johnson, Rita *DrAPF 93*
Johnson, Rita d1965 *WhoHol 92*
Johnson, Rita Falkener *WhoBlA 94*
Johnson, Rita Nielsen *WhoAmP 93*
Johnson, Rob 1955- *WhoAmP 93*
Johnson, Rob Carl 1952- *WhoFI 94, WhoWest 94*
Johnson, Robert d1982 *WhoHol 92*
Johnson, Robert 1937- *WhoBlA 94*
Johnson, Robert (Lionel) 1933- *Who 94*
Johnson, Robert A. 1919- *WhoAmP 93*
Johnson, Robert Alan 1923- *WhoWest 94*
Johnson, Robert Alan 1933- *WhoScEn 94*
Johnson, Robert Alan 1944- *WhoAm 94, WhoAmL 94*
Johnson, Robert Allison 1928- *WhoAm 94*
Johnson, Robert Andrew 1954- *WhoScEn 94*
Johnson, Robert Arthur 1963- *WhoAmL 94*
Johnson, Robert Aylwin 1928- *WhoAmP 93*
Johnson, Robert B. 1928- *WhoBlA 94*
Johnson, Robert Bertram 1941- *WhoAm 94*
Johnson, Robert Britten 1924- *WhoAm 94, WhoScEn 94, WhoWest 94*
Johnson, Robert Bruce 1912- *WhoAm 94*
Johnson, Robert C. 1945- *WhoBlA 94*
Johnson, Robert C. 1948- *WhoAmL 94*
Johnson, Robert Clyde 1919- *WhoAm 94, WrDr 94*
Johnson, Robert Dale 1943- *WhoAmP 93*
Johnson, Robert Dale 1965- *WhoMW 93*
Johnson, Robert David 1957- *WhoFI 94*
Johnson, Robert E. 1936- *WhoAm 94*
Johnson, Robert E(rwin) 1923- *WrDr 94*
Johnson, Robert Edward 1922- *WhoBlA 94*
Johnson, Robert Elliott 1907-1989 *WhAm 10*
Johnson, Robert Eugene 1911- *WhoAm 94*
Johnson, Robert Flynn 1948- *WhoAmA 93*
Johnson, Robert G. 1944- *WhoAm 94, WhoAmL 94*
Johnson, Robert Gahagen, Jr. 1952- *WhoScEn 94*
Johnson, Robert Gerald 1928- *WhoAm 94*
Johnson, Robert Glenn 1922- *WhoMW 93, WhoScEn 94*
Johnson, Robert H. 1938- *WhoBlA 94*
Johnson, Robert Henry 1916- *WhoAmP 93*
Johnson, Robert Henry 1921- *WhoAm 94*
Johnson, Robert Hersel 1923- *WhoAm 94, WhoWest 94*
Johnson, Robert Jay 1951-1990 *WhoAmA 93N*
Johnson, Robert Joseph 1938- *WhoAm 94*
Johnson, Robert Junius 1929- *WhoBlA 94*
Johnson, Robert Kellogg 1913-1990 *WhAm 10*
Johnson, Robert L. *WhoBlA 94*
Johnson, Robert L. 1946- *AfrAmAl 6, WhoBlA 94*
Johnson, Robert L., III *WhoAmP 93*
Johnson, Robert Lawrence, Jr. 1945- *WhoAm 94*
Johnson, Robert Leonard 1930- *WhoAmP 93*
Johnson, Robert Leslie 1923- *WhoWest 94*
Johnson, Robert Lewis, Jr. 1935- *WhoAm 94, WhoFI 94*
Johnson, Robert Louis 1946- *WhoAm 94, WhoFI 94*
Johnson, Robert M. 1934- *WhoAmP 93*
Johnson, Robert Maurice 1945- *WhoAm 94*
Johnson, Robert Max 1942- *WhoAmL 94*
Johnson, Robert Merrill 1926- *WhoAm 94*
Johnson, Robert Milton 1962- *WhoMW 93*
Johnson, Robert Raymond 1917- *WhoAm 94*
Johnson, Robert T. *WhoAmL 94, WhoBlA 94*
Johnson, Robert Thane 1945- *WhoAmP 93*
Johnson, Robert Veiling, II 1939- *WhoAmL 94*
Johnson, Robert W. 1931- *WhoAmP 93*
Johnson, Robert W(illard) 1921- *WrDr 94*
Johnson, Robert Wayne 1951- *WhoWest 94*
Johnson, Robert White 1912- *Who 94*
Johnson, Robert Willard 1921- *WhoAm 94*
Johnson, Robin *DrAPF 93*
Johnson, Robin 1964- *WhoHol 92*
Johnson, Robin C. *WhoAmP 93*
Johnson, Rod 1953- *WhoAmP 93*
Johnson, Rod 1957- *WhoAmP 93*
Johnson, Rodell C. 1913- *WhoAmA 93*
Johnson, Rodney Dale 1944- *WhoWest 94*
Johnson, Rodney Marcum 1947- *WhoAmL 94*
Johnson, Rodney William 1955- *WhoScEn 94*
Johnson, Roger 1934- *WhoAm 94, WhoAmP 93*
Johnson, Roger Christie 1925- *WhoAmP 93*
Johnson, Roger Dean 1935- *WhoIns 94*
Johnson, Roger Iner 1940- *WhoMW 93*
Johnson, Roger J. 1936- *WhoIns 94*
Johnson, Roger Paul 1931- *Who 94*
Johnson, Roger Thornton 1938- *WhoMW 93*
Johnson, Roger W. 1935- *WhoAm 94, WhoFI 94, WhoWest 94*
Johnson, Roger Warren 1960- *WhoScEn 94*
Johnson, Rogers Bruce 1928- *WhoAm 94*
Johnson, Roland A. *WhoAm 94, WhoMW 93*
Johnson, Rolland Clair 1944- *WhoAm 94*
Johnson, Ron 1958- *WhoBlA 94*
Johnson, Ronald *DrAPF 93*
Johnson, Ronald 1935- *ConAu 42NR, WrDr 94*
Johnson, Ronald 1936- *WhoBlA 94*
Johnson, Ronald (Ernest Charles) 1913- *Who 94*
Johnson, Ronald Bryan 1948- *WhoFI 94*
Johnson, Ronald C. 1941- *WhoIns 94*
Johnson, Ronald Carl 1935- *WhoAm 94*
Johnson, Ronald Clyde 1949- *WhoAmP 93*
Johnson, Ronald Cornelius 1946- *WhoBlA 94*
Johnson, Ronald Douglas 1949- *WhoWest 94*
Johnson, Ronald G. 1943- *WhoAmP 93*
Johnson, Ronald Glenn 1949- *WhoWest 94*
Johnson, Ronald Henry 1936- *WhoMW 93*
Johnson, Ronald N. 1933- *WhoAmP 93*
Johnson, Ronald Sanders 1952- *WhoScEn 94*
Johnson, Ronald W. 1937- *WhoAmA 93*
Johnson, Ronald Wayne 1956- *WhoFI 94*
Johnson, Ronald Webster 1948- *WhoWest 94*
Johnson, Roosevelt, Jr. 1924- *WhoBlA 94*
Johnson, Roosevelt Young 1946- *WhoBlA 94*
Johnson, Rosemary Wrucke 1924- *WhoFI 94*
Johnson, Ross 1939- *WhoAmP 93*
Johnson, Ross Jeffrey 1955- *WhoScEn 94*
Johnson, Roy Edward 1959- *WhoBlA 94*
Johnson, Roy Lee 1955- *WhoBlA 94*
Johnson, Roy Lynn 1954- *WhoBlA 94*
Johnson, Roy Ragnar 1932- *WhoAm 94, WhoScEn 94*
Johnson, Roy Steven 1956- *WhoBlA 94*
Johnson, Roy W., Jr. *WhoAmP 93*
Johnson, Royal C. 1925- *WhoAmP 93*
Johnson, Rudolph *WhoAmP 93*
Johnson, Russell 1924- *IntMPA 94, WhoHol 92*
Johnson, Russell L. 1943- *WhoAmL 94*
Johnson, Ruth Ann Craig Goswick 1946- *WhoMW 93*
Johnson, Ruth Marie 1917- *WhoMW 93*
Johnson, Ruthie 1924- *WhoAmP 93*
Johnson, Sally A. 1953- *WhoAmL 94*
Johnson, Sally Stripling 1951- *WhoFI 94*
Johnson, Sam *WhoBlA 94*
Johnson, Sam 1930- *CngDr 93*
Johnson, Sam D. 1920- *WhoAm 94, WhoAmL 94, WhoAmP 93*
Johnson, Sam R. 1930- *WhoAmP 93*
Johnson, Samuel 1696-1772 *DcAmReB 2*
Johnson, Samuel 1709-1784 *BlmGEL [port], EncSF 93*
Johnson, Samuel 1930- *WhoAm 94*
Johnson, Samuel Curtis 1928- *WhoAm 94, WhoFI 94, WhoMW 93*
Johnson, Samuel Harrison 1916- *WhoBlA 94*
Johnson, Samuel Q., III 1939- *WhoAmP 93*
Johnson, Samuel Walter, II 1948- *WhoScEn 94*
Johnson, Sankey Anton 1940- *WhoAm 94*
Johnson, Sarah H. 1938- *WhoBlA 94*
Johnson, Sarah Yvonne 1950- *WhoBlA 94*

Johnson, Sargent 1888-1967 *AfrAmAl 6, WhoAmA 93N*
Johnson, Scott 1952- *SmATA 76 [port]*
Johnson, Scott Clarence 1955- *WhoFI 94*
Johnson, Scott J. 1949- *WhoAmL 94*
Johnson, Scott William 1940- *WhoAm 94, WhoAmL 94*
Johnson, Searcy Lee 1908-1991 *WhAm 10*
Johnson, Selina (Tetzlaff) *WhoAmA 93*
Johnson, Sharon Kay 1944- *WhoMW 93*
Johnson, Sharon Marie 1951- *WhoMW 93*
Johnson, Sharon Reed 1944- *WhoBlA 94*
Johnson, Sheila *DrAPF 93*
Johnson, Sheila Monroe 1957- *WhoBlA 94*
Johnson, Shelli Wright 1953- *WhoAmL 94*
Johnson, Sherman E(lbridge) 1908-1993 *ConAu 141*
Johnson, Shirley 1937- *WhoAmP 93*
Johnson, Shirley Elaine 1941- *WhoBlA 94*
Johnson, Shirley Elaine 1946- *WhoFI 94, WhoMW 93*
Johnson, Shorty d1978 *WhoHol 92*
Johnson, Sidney *WhoAmP 93*
Johnson, Sidney Malcolm 1924- *WhoScEn 94*
Johnson, Sondra Lea 1952- *WhoMW 93*
Johnson, Staci Sharp 1960- *WhoAmL 94*
Johnson, Stafford Quincy 1948- *WhoBlA 94*
Johnson, Stanford Leland 1924- *WhoAm 94*
Johnson, Stanley 1912- *Who 94*
Johnson, Stanley C. *WhoAmP 93*
Johnson, Stanley E. 1934- *WhoAmP 93*
Johnson, Stanley F. 1927- *WhoAmP 93*
Johnson, Stanley Patrick 1940- *Who 94*
Johnson, Stanley R. 1938- *WhoScEn 94*
Johnson, Stephanie 1961- *BlmGWL*
Johnson, Stephanye 1959- *WhoBlA 94*
Johnson, (John) Stephen 1947- *WrDr 94*
Johnson, Stephen Abbott 1961- *WhoMW 93*
Johnson, Stephen C. 1942- *WhoAmL 94*
Johnson, Stephen C. 1946- *WhoAmL 94*
Johnson, Stephen L. 1944- *WhoBlA 94*
Johnson, Stephen L. 1951- *WhoAm 94*
Johnson, Stephen M. *ConAu 141*
Johnson, Stephen Randall 1957- *WhoAm 94*
Johnson, Sterling 1934- *WhoBlA 94*
Johnson, Sterling, Jr. 1934- *WhoAm 94, WhoAmL 94*
Johnson, Steve 1957- *WhoBlA 94*
Johnson, Steve Kenneth 1942- *WhoAmP 93*
Johnson, Steven Douglas 1950- *WhoFI 94*
Johnson, Steven R. *WhoAmP 93*
Johnson, Steven William 1962- *WhoMW 93*
Johnson, Stewart Willard 1933- *WhoAm 94, WhoScEn 94, WhoWest 94*
Johnson, Stowers *WrDr 94*
Johnson, Stuart *Who 94*
Johnson, Stuart 1942- *WhoFI 94*
Johnson, (Reginald) Stuart 1933- *Who 94*
Johnson, Sue Beth 1953- *WhoFI 94*
Johnson, Sue Reiner 1955- *WhoIns 94*
Johnson, Suellen O. 1942- *WhoAmP 93*
Johnson, Sunny d1984 *WhoHol 92*
Johnson, Susan (M) 1939- *WrDr 94*
Johnson, Susanne Louise 1941- *WhoMW 93*
Johnson, Suzanne 1952- *WhoWest 94*
Johnson, Suzanne Curtis *WhoMW 93*
Johnson, Sylvia Sue 1940- *WhoWest 94*
Johnson, T. J. *WhoBlA 94*
Johnson, Tammy Adele 1965- *WhoBlA 94*
Johnson, Taylor Herbert 1933- *WhoBlA 94*
Johnson, Tefft d1956 *WhoHol 92*
Johnson, Terence Grant 1946- *WhoMW 93*
Johnson, Terry 1955- *ConDr 93, WrDr 94*
Johnson, Terry Charles 1936- *WhoAm 94, WhoScEn 94*
Johnson, Tesla Francis 1934- *WhoFI 94, WhoScEn 94*
Johnson, Theodore 1925- *WhoWest 94*
Johnson, Theodore, Sr. 1920- *WhoBlA 94*
Johnson, Theodore A. *WhoBlA 94*
Johnson, Theodore Armand 1924- *WhoAmP 93*
Johnson, Theodore L. 1929- *WhoBlA 94*
Johnson, Theodore Mebane 1934- *WhoFI 94*
Johnson, Theodore Oliver, Jr. 1929- *WhoAm 94*
Johnson, Theodore Thomas 1949- *WhoBlA 94*
Johnson, Therese Myers 1926- *WhoAmP 93*
Johnson, Thomas 1732-1819 *WhAmRev*
Johnson, Thomas 1802-1865 *EncNAR*
Johnson, Thomas 1964- *WhoBlA 94*
Johnson, Thomas Allibone Budd 1955- *WhoFI 94*
Johnson, Thomas E. *DrAPF 93, WhoAmP 93*
Johnson, Thomas Edward 1936- *WhoAm 94*
Johnson, Thomas Floyd 1943- *WhoAm 94*
Johnson, Thomas G., Jr. 1942- *WhoAmL 94*
Johnson, Thomas H. *WhoFI 94*
Johnson, Thomas H. 1932- *WhoBlA 94*
Johnson, Thomas L. 1945- *WhoAmL 94, WhoAmP 93*
Johnson, Thomas Quentin 1950- *WhoAmL 94*
Johnson, Thomas R. 1946- *WhoAm 94, WhoAmL 94*
Johnson, Thomas S. 1940- *IntWW 93*
Johnson, Thomas Stephen 1940- *WhoAm 94*
Johnson, Thomas Stuart 1942- *WhoAmL 94, WhoMW 93*
Johnson, Thomas Webber, Jr. 1941- *WhoAm 94, WhoAmL 94, WhoWest 94*
Johnson, Tim 1946- *CngDr 93*
Johnson, Timothy Augustin, Jr. 1945- *WhoAmL 94*
Johnson, Timothy Julius, Jr. 1935- *WhoBlA 94*
Johnson, Timothy P. 1946- *WhoAmP 93*
Johnson, Timothy Patrick 1954- *WhoMW 93*
Johnson, Timothy Peter 1946- *WhoAm 94, WhoMW 93*
Johnson, Timothy Vincent 1946- *WhoAmP 93*
Johnson, Tobe 1929- *WhoBlA 94*
Johnson, Tod Stuart 1944- *WhoAm 94*
Johnson, Tom *DrAPF 93*
Johnson, Tom 1939- *NewGrDO*
Johnson, Tom 1949- *WhoAmP 93*
Johnson, Tom Loftin 1854-1911 *AmSocL*
Johnson, Tom Milroy 1935- *WhoAm 94*
Johnson, Tommie Ulmer 1925- *WhoBlA 94*
Johnson, Tor d1971 *WhoHol 92*
Johnson, Torrence Vaino 1944- *WhoAm 94, WhoWest 94*
Johnson, Troy Dwan 1962- *WhoBlA 94*
Johnson, U. Alexis 1908- *HisDcKW, IntWW 93, WhoAm 94, WhoAmP 93*
Johnson, Ulysses Johann, Jr. 1929- *WhoBlA 94*
Johnson, Una E. *WhoAmA 93, WrDr 94*
Johnson, Urmia *WhoWomW 91*
Johnson, Vahe Duncan 1938- *WhoAm 94*
Johnson, Valrie E. *WhoBlA 94*
Johnson, Van 1916- *IntMPA 94, WhoHol 92*
Johnson, Vance Douglas 1948- *WhoBlA 94*
Johnson, Vance Edward 1963- *WhoBlA 94*
Johnson, Vannette William 1930- *WhoAmP 93, WhoBlA 94*
Johnson, Vard 1939- *WhoAmP 93*
Johnson, Vaughan 1962- *WhoAm 94*
Johnson, Vaughan Monroe 1962- *WhoBlA 94*
Johnson, Vaughn Arzah 1951- *WhoBlA 94*
Johnson, Verdia Earline 1950- *WhoBlA 94*
Johnson, Vermelle Jamison 1933- *WhoBlA 94*
Johnson, Verna Mae 1930- *WhoMW 93*
Johnson, Verner Carl 1943- *WhoWest 94*
Johnson, Vicki Kristine *WhoMW 93*
Johnson, Victor Lawrence 1928- *WhoAm 94*
Johnson, Victor Louis d1988 *WhoHol 92*
Johnson, Vincent L. 1931- *WhoBlA 94*
Johnson, Vinnie 1956- *WhoBlA 94*
Johnson, Violet Erosemond 1915- *WhoAmP 93*
Johnson, Virgil Allen 1921- *WhoAm 94*
Johnson, Virgil Joel 1932- *WhoAmP 93*
Johnson, Virginia 1925- *WrDr 94*
Johnson, Virginia 1937- *WhoAmP 93*
Johnson, Virginia 1950- *IntDcB [port]*
Johnson, Virginia Alma Fairfax 1950- *WhoAm 94, WhoBlA 94*
Johnson, Virginia Eshelman 1925- *See* Masters, William Howell 1915- *AmSocL*
Johnson, Virginia Gayle 1946- *WhoMW 93*
Johnson, Virginia McPherson 1943- *WhoMW 93*
Johnson, Viteria Copeland 1941- *WhoBlA 94*
Johnson, Vivian Wells 1896- *WhAm 10*
Johnson, Waine Cecil 1928- *WhoAm 94*
Johnson, Waldo Emerson, Jr. 1955- *WhoBlA 94*
Johnson, Walker Reed 1931- *WhoAm 94*
Johnson, Wallace Darnell 1956- *WhoBlA 94*
Johnson, Walter d1964 *WhoHol 92*
Johnson, Walter Curtis 1913- *WhoAm 94*
Johnson, Walter Curtis, Jr. 1939- *WhoWest 94*
Johnson, Walter Earl 1942- *WhoScEn 94, WhoWest 94*
Johnson, Walter Frank, Jr. 1945- *WhoAmL 94*
Johnson, Walter Frank, III 1939- *AfrAmG [port]*
Johnson, Walter Hamlet 1917- *Who 94*
Johnson, Walter J. 1957- *WhoBlA 94*
Johnson, Walter Kline 1923- *WhoAm 94*
Johnson, Walter L. 1927- *WhoAm 94*
Johnson, Walter Lee 1918- *WhoBlA 94*
Johnson, Walter Louis, Sr. 1949- *WhoBlA 94*
Johnson, Walter Thaniel, Jr. 1940- *WhoBlA 94*
Johnson, Walton Richard 1909- *WhoBlA 94*
Johnson, Warren 1922- *WhoAmP 93*
Johnson, Warren A 1937- *WrDr 94*
Johnson, Warren David, Jr. 1940- *WhoMW 93*
Johnson, Warren Donald 1922- *WhoAm 94*
Johnson, Warren Eliot 1961- *WhoScEn 94*
Johnson, Warren Lyle 1939- *WhoWest 94*
Johnson, Warren S. 1947- *WhoBlA 94*
Johnson, Warren T(hurston) 1925- *WrDr 94*
Johnson, Watts Carey 1925- *WhoAmL 94*
Johnson, Wayne 1956- *WrDr 94*
Johnson, Wayne Alan 1961- *WhoBlA 94*
Johnson, Wayne D. 1932- *WhoAm 94, WhoFI 94*
Johnson, Wayne Eaton 1930- *WhoAm 94, WhoWest 94*
Johnson, Wayne Harold 1942- *WhoAm 94, WhoAmP 93, WhoWest 94*
Johnson, Wayne Lee 1953- *WhoBlA 94*
Johnson, Wayne Leslie 1953- *WhoAmL 94*
Johnson, Wayne Wright, III 1953- *WhoBlA 94*
Johnson, Wendell L., Jr. 1922- *WhoBlA 94*
Johnson, Wendell Louis 1944- *WhoBlA 94*
Johnson, Wendell Norman *AfrAmG [port]*
Johnson, Wendell Norman, Sr. 1933- *WhoBlA 94*
Johnson, Wendy Robin 1956- *WhoBlA 94*
Johnson, Wentworth Paul 1897- *WhAm 10*
Johnson, Weyman Thompson, Jr. 1951- *WhoAmL 94*
Johnson, Wilbur Eugene 1954- *WhoBlA 94*
Johnson, Wilhelmina Lashaun 1950- *WhoBlA 94*
Johnson, Willard Raymond 1935- *WhoAm 94, WhoBlA 94*
Johnson, William 1715-1774 *AmRev, WhAmRev [port]*
Johnson, William 1805-1842 *EncNAR*
Johnson, William 1903- *Who 94*
Johnson, William 1922- *IntWW 93, Who 94*
Johnson, William A. 1917- *WhoBlA 94*
Johnson, William A., Jr. *WhoAmP 93*
Johnson, William A., Jr. 1942- *WhoBlA 94*
Johnson, William A., II 1952- *WhoBlA 94*
Johnson, William Alexander 1934- *WhoAm 94*
Johnson, William Arthur 1950- *WhoMW 93*
Johnson, William Arthur 1952- *WhoBlA 94*
Johnson, William Arvill 1924- *WhoAmP 93*
Johnson, William Bruce 1948- *WhoMW 93*
Johnson, William C. *WhoAmP 93*
Johnson, William C. 1930- *WhoBlA 94*
Johnson, William David 1924- *WhoAm 94*
Johnson, William Douglas, Jr. 1958- *WhoFI 94*
Johnson, William E. 1932- *WhoMW 93*
Johnson, William E. 1936- *WhoBlA 94*
Johnson, William E. 1941- *WhoAm 94, WhoFI 94*
Johnson, William Glenn 1946- *WhoAmL 94*
Johnson, William H. 1901-1970 *AfrAmAl 6*
Johnson, William Hall 1943- *WhoAm 94*
Johnson, William Harry 1941- *WhoFI 94, WhoWest 94*
Johnson, William Henry 1926- *WhoBlA 94*
Johnson, William Herbert 1928- *WhoMW 93, WhoScEn 94*
Johnson, William Howard 1922- *WhoAm 94, WhoScEn 94*
Johnson, William Hugh, Jr. 1935- *WhoAm 94, WhoWest 94*
Johnson, William J. *WhoAmP 93*
Johnson, William Jennings 1955- *WhoFI 94*
Johnson, William Joseph 1941- *WhoAm 94*
Johnson, William L. d1993 *NewYTBS 93*
Johnson, William L. 1932- *WhoBlA 94*
Johnson, William Lewis 1948- *WhoWest 94*
Johnson, William Paul, Jr. 1963- *WhoBlA 94*
Johnson, William Potter 1935- *WhoAm 94, WhoFI 94, WhoWest 94*
Johnson, William R. 1930- *WhoAm 94, WhoAmL 94, WhoAmP 93*
Johnson, William Randolph 1930- *WhoBlA 94*
Johnson, William Ray 1930- *WhoFI 94*
Johnson, William Richard 1947- *WhoAm 94*
Johnson, William Richard, Jr. 1942- *WhoAm 94*
Johnson, William Samuel 1727-1819 *WhAmRev*
Johnson, William Smith 1941- *WhoBlA 94*
Johnson, William Summer 1913- *IntWW 93, WhoAm 94, WhoScEn 94*
Johnson, William T. M. 1921- *WhoBlA 94*
Johnson, William Theolious 1943- *WhoBlA 94*
Johnson, William Thomas 1960- *WhoBlA 94*
Johnson, William Vincent 1940- *WhoAmL 94*
Johnson, William Weber 1909-1992 *WrDr 94N*
Johnson, William Winfred 1950- *WhoFI 94*
Johnson, Willie d1980 *WhoHol 92*
Johnson, Willie 1925- *WhoBlA 94*
Johnson, Willie F. 1939- *WhoBlA 94*
Johnson, Willie Roy 1947- *WhoMW 93, WhoScEn 94*
Johnson, Winston Conrad 1943- *WhoAm 94, WhoScEn 94*
Johnson, Wyatt Thomas, Jr. 1941- *WhoAm 94*
Johnson, Wyneva 1948- *WhoBlA 94*
Johnson, Zane Quentin 1924- *WhoAm 94*
Johnson, Zodie Anderson 1920- *WhoBlA 94*
Johnson-Blount, Theresa 1952- *WhoBlA 94*
Johnson-Brown, Hazel W. 1927- *AfrAmG [port]*
Johnson-Brown, Hazel Winfred 1927- *WhoBlA 94*
Johnson-Carson, Linda D. 1954- *WhoBlA 94*
Johnson-Champ, Debra Sue 1955- *WhoAmL 94*
Johnson Cook, Suzan Denise 1957- *WhoBlA 94*
Johnson-Crockett, Mary Alice 1937- *WhoBlA 94*
Johnson-Crosby, Deborah A. 1951- *WhoBlA 94*
Johnson-Dismukes, Karen 1947- *WhoBlA 94*
Johnson-Ferguson, Ian (Edward) 1932- *Who 94*
Johnson-Gilbert, Ronald Stuart 1925- *Who 94*
Johnson-Gilbert, Thomas Ian 1923- *Who 94*
Johnson-Granat, Judy Leé 1956- *WhoAmL 94*
Johnson-Laird, Philip Nicholas 1936- *IntWW 93, Who 94*
Johnson-Lesson, Charleen Ann 1949- *WhoMW 93*
Johnson-Marshall, Percy E(dwin) A(lan) 1915-1993 *ConAu 142*
Johnson-Marshall, Percy Edwin Alan d1993 *Who 94N*
Johnson-Masters, Virginia E. 1925- *WhoAm 94*
Johnson-McKenzie, Janis 1955- *WhoAmP 93*
Johnson-Odim, Cheryl 1948- *WhoBlA 94*
Johnson-Ross, Robyn 1946- *WhoAmA 93*
Johnson-Sadur, Kristina Joy 1953- *WhoAmP 93*
Johnson-Scott, Jerodene Patrice 1952- *WhoBlA 94*
Johnson Sirleaf, Ellen *IntWW 93*
Johnson Smith, Geoffrey 1924- *Who 94*
Johnsrud, Duwayne 1943- *WhoAmP 93*
Johnsrude, Junne Margarette 1920- *WhoAmP 93*
Johnsson, A. Lave K. *WhoMW 93*
Johnston *Who 94*
Johnston, Alan (William) 1942- *WrDr 94*
Johnston, Alan Charles Macpherson 1942- *Who 94*
Johnston, Alan Cope 1946- *WhoAm 94*
Johnston, Alan Rogers 1914- *WhoAm 94*

Johnston, Alexander 1905- *Who 94*
Johnston, Alexander Graham 1944- *Who 94*
Johnston, Alistair D. 1937- *WhoIns 94*
Johnston, Allan Hugh 1941- *WhoScEn 94*
Johnston, Allan James 1949- *WhoMW 93*
Johnston, Allen Howard 1912- *IntWW 93, Who 94*
Johnston, Amy *WhoHol 92*
Johnston, Andrew William 1932- *WhoAmP 93*
Johnston, Anthony Sudekum 1944- *WhoFI 94*
Johnston, Archibald 1865-1947 *EncABHB 9*
Johnston, Archibald Currie 1945- *WhoAm 94, WhoScEn 94*
Johnston, Augustus 1730-1790 *WhAmRev*
Johnston, Barry d1953 *WhoHol 92*
Johnston, Barry Woods *WhoAmA 93*
Johnston, Ben(jamin' Burwell, Jr.) 1926- *NewGrDO*
Johnston, Ben Earl 1938- *WhoAm 94*
Johnston, Betty Joan 1916- *Who 94*
Johnston, Bill 1894-1946 *BuCMET [port]*
Johnston, Brian (Alexander) 1912- *Who 94*
Johnston, Brian Howard 1949- *WhoScEn 94*
Johnston, Bruce Foster 1919- *WhoAm 94*
Johnston, Bruce Gilbert 1905- *WhAm 10*
Johnston, Cameron I. 1955- *WhoWest 94*
Johnston, Carol Arlene 1952- *WhoScEn 94*
Johnston, Carol Strickland 1957- *WhoWest 94*
Johnston, Caroline K. d1962 *WhoHol 92*
Johnston, Charles Bernie, Jr. 1931- *WhoAm 94*
Johnston, Charles Bruce 1951- *WhoMW 93*
Johnston, Charles F. 1933- *WhoIns 94*
Johnston, Charles Leland, III 1946- *WhoWest 94*
Johnston, Charles Vincent 1950- *WhoFI 94*
Johnston, Christina Jane 1952- *WhoFI 94*
Johnston, Clarence Dinsmore H. *Who 94*
Johnston, Clifford Thomas 1955- *WhoScEn 94*
Johnston, Colleen Kelly 1932- *WhoAmP 93*
Johnston, Craig Alan 1955- *WhoWest 94*
Johnston, Cyrus Conrad, Jr. 1929- *WhoAm 94*
Johnston, David 1936- *Who 94*
Johnston, David Alan H. *Who 94*
Johnston, David E. 1948- *WhoAmL 94*
Johnston, David Eric Lothian 1961- *Who 94*
Johnston, David Ian 1932- *WhoAm 94*
Johnston, David Lawrence 1936- *Who 94*
Johnston, David Lloyd 1941- *IntWW 93, Who 94, WhoAm 94*
Johnston, (William) Denis 1901-1984 *ConDr 93, IntDcT 2*
Johnston, Dennis Roy 1937- *WhoFI 94*
Johnston, Dennis W. 1942- *WhoAmP 93*
Johnston, Dick *WhoWest 94*
Johnston, Dolores Mae Mascik 1927- *WhoMW 93*
Johnston, Don 1927- *IntWW 93*
Johnston, Douglas Frederick 1930- *WhoAm 94, WhoFI 94*
Johnston, E. Russell, Jr. *WhoScEn 94*
Johnston, Edward Allan 1921- *WhoAm 94*
Johnston, Edward Elliott 1918- *WhoAm 94*
Johnston, Elizabeth Lichtenstein 1764-1848 *AmRev*
Johnston, Ellis Murray 1946- *WhoAmL 94*
Johnston, Ernest, Jr. 1938- *WhoBlA 94*
Johnston, Ernestine *WhoHol 92*
Johnston, Faber Laine, Jr. 1927- *WhoAmL 94*
Johnston, Francis Claiborne, Jr. 1943- *WhoAm 94*
Johnston, Frank C. 1955- *WhoScEn 94*
Johnston, Frederick Mervyn Kieran 1911- *Who 94*
Johnston, Frederick Patrick Mair 1935- *Who 94*
Johnston, Gary *DrAPF 93*
Johnston, Gary 1948- *WhoMW 93*
Johnston, George (Benson) 1913- *WrDr 94*
Johnston, George Gustin 1932- *WhoAm 94*
Johnston, George Sim 1924-1991 *WhAm 10*
Johnston, George Toshio 1961- *WhoAsA 94*
Johnston, George W. 1950- *WhoAm 94, WhoAmP 93*
Johnston, Gerald Andrew 1931- *WhoAm 94, WhoFI 94, WhoScEn 94*

Johnston, Gerald McArthur 1942- *WhoFI 94*
Johnston, Gladys Styles 1942- *WhoBlA 94*
Johnston, Gordon Innes 1953- *WhoScEn 94*
Johnston, Gordon MacKenzie 1941- *Who 94*
Johnston, Grace *WhoHol 92*
Johnston, Grace Eliette 1957- *WhoFI 94*
Johnston, Gwinavere Adams 1943- *WhoAm 94, WhoWest 94*
Johnston, Hampton L. 1948- *WhoAm 94, WhoFI 94*
Johnston, Harold S. 1920- *IntWW 93*
Johnston, Harold Sledge 1920- *WhoAm 94, WhoScEn 94*
Johnston, Harry A. 1931- *CngDr 93*
Johnston, Harry A., II 1931- *WhoAm 94, WhoAmP 93*
Johnston, Harry Hamilton 1858-1927 *WhWE*
Johnston, Harry Melville, III 1945- *WhoAmL 94*
Johnston, Helen Head *WhoAmA 93N*
Johnston, Henry Bruce 1927- *WhoBlA 94*
Johnston, Henry Butler M. *Who 94*
Johnston, Howard Andrews 1895- *WhAm 10*
Johnston, Hugh Philip 1927- *Who 94*
Johnston, Ian Alistair 1944- *Who 94*
Johnston, Ian Henderson 1925- *Who 94*
Johnston, J. Bennett 1932- *CngDr 93*
Johnston, J. Bennett, Jr. 1932- *WhoAmP 93*
Johnston, J(ohn) Bennett, Jr. 1932- *IntWW 93*
Johnston, J. J. *WhoHol 92*
Johnston, J. W. d1946 *WhoHol 92*
Johnston, Jacqueline Rose 1946- *WhoAmP 93*
Johnston, James 1903- *NewGrDO*
Johnston, James Bennett 1943- *WhoScEn 94*
Johnston, James Campbell 1912- *Who 94*
Johnston, James Frederick Junor 1939- *Who 94*
Johnston, James Monroe, III 1940- *WhoAm 94*
Johnston, James Wesley 1946- *WhoAm 94, WhoFI 94*
Johnston, Jeffrey A. 1958- *WhoFI 94*
Johnston, Jeffrey Martin 1951- *WhoAm 94*
Johnston, Jennifer 1930- *BlmGWL, Who 94, WrDr 94*
Johnston, Jill 1929- *GayLL, WrDr 94*
Johnston, Jocelyn Elaine 1954- *WhoAmL*
Johnston, John 1881-1950 *EncABHB 9 [port]*
Johnston, John (Baines) 1918- *IntWW 93, Who 94*
Johnston, John (Frederick Dame) 1922- *Who 94*
Johnston, John Bennett, Jr. 1932- *WhoAm 94*
Johnston, John Devereaux, Jr. 1932- *WhoAm 94*
Johnston, John Douglas Hartley 1935- *Who 94*
Johnston, John Joseph 1954- *WhoAmL 94*
Johnston, John MacLin 1898- *WhAm 10*
Johnston, John Philip 1935- *WhoAm 94*
Johnston, John Thomas 1930- *WhoScEn 94*
Johnston, John Wayne 1943- *WhoMW 93*
Johnston, Johnny d1931 *WhoHol 92*
Johnston, Johnny 1915- *WhoHol 92*
Johnston, Joshua c. 1765-1830 *AfrAmAl 6*
Johnston, Julanne d1988 *WhoHol 92*
Johnston, Julia Mayo 1926- *WhoBlA 94*
Johnston, Justine *WhoHol 92*
Johnston, Karen Lang 1949- *WhoAmP 93*
Johnston, Kenneth Robert Hope 1905- *Who 94*
Johnston, Kevin P. 1950- *WhoAmP 93*
Johnston, Kevin Richard 1955- *WhoMW 93*
Johnston, Lanny Ray 1941- *WhoMW 93*
Johnston, Larea Dennis 1935- *WhoScEn 94*
Johnston, Laurance Scott 1950- *WhoAm 94*
Johnston, Leland Mann, Jr. 1947- *WhoFI 94*
Johnston, Lionel 1954- *WhoHol 92*
Johnston, Lloyd Douglas 1940- *WhoAm 94*
Johnston, Logan T. 1900-1977 *EncABHB 9*
Johnston, Logan Truax, III 1947- *WhoAmL 94, WhoWest 94*
Johnston, Lorene Gayle 1952- *WhoAmP 93*
Johnston, Lorimer d1941 *WhoHol 92*
Johnston, Lynn 1947- *Au&Arts 12 [port]*
Johnston, Lynn H. 1931- *WhoIns 94*
Johnston, Mac d1977 *WhoHol 92*

Johnston, Malcolm Carlyle 1934- *WhoAm 94*
Johnston, Margaret *IntMPA 94, Who 94*
Johnston, Margaret 1917- *WhoHol 92*
Johnston, Marguerite 1917- *WhoAm 94*
Johnston, Marjorie Diane 1943- *WhoWest 94*
Johnston, Marshall William 1919- *WhoAm 94*
Johnston, Mary 1870-1936 *BlmGWL*
Johnston, Mary Hollis 1946- *WhoMW 93*
Johnston, Maurice (Robert) 1929- *Who 94*
Johnston, Means, Jr. 1916-1989 *WhAm 10*
Johnston, Michael Alexander Ninian C. *Who 94*
Johnston, Michael Francis 1947- *WhoMW 93*
Johnston, Michael L. 1945- *WhoAmP 93*
Johnston, Michael Richard 1946- *WhoAm 94*
Johnston, Murray Lloyd, Jr. 1940- *WhoAm 94*
Johnston, Nancy Dahl 1954- *WhoFI 94*
Johnston, Neil 1929-1978 *BasBi*
Johnston, Norma *Au&Arts 12 [port], WrDr 94*
Johnston, Norman John 1918- *WhoAm 94*
Johnston, Oliver d1966 *WhoHol 92*
Johnston, Patricia Kathleen 1936- *WhoWest 94*
Johnston, Patrick 1946- *WhoAmP 93*
Johnston, Paula P. 1945- *WhoAmP 93*
Johnston, Peter William 1943- *Who 94*
Johnston, Philip *WhoAm 94*
Johnston, Philip Crater 1943- *WhoAm 94, WhoAmL 94*
Johnston, Philip William 1944- *WhoAmP 93*
Johnston, Phillip M. 1944- *WhoAmA 93*
Johnston, Phillip Michael 1944- *WhoAm 94*
Johnston, R(onald) J(ohn) 1941- *WrDr 94*
Johnston, Ralph Kennedy, Sr. 1942- *WhoScEn 94*
Johnston, Ralph L. 1927- *WhoAmP 93*
Johnston, Ralph Thomas 1954- *WhoAm 94*
Johnston, Randy J(ames) *WhoAmA 93*
Johnston, Richard Alan 1950- *WhoAm 94, WhoAmL 94*
Johnston, Richard B. *WhoAmP 93*
Johnston, Richard Fourness 1925- *WhoAm 94*
Johnston, Richard M. 1942- *WhoAmA 93*
Johnston, Rita *WhoWomW 91*
Johnston, Rita Margaret 1935- *Who 94, WhoAm 94*
Johnston, Robert Alan 1924- *IntWW 93, Who 94*
Johnston, Robert Chapman 1930- *WhoAm 94*
Johnston, Robert Cossin 1913- *WhoAm 94*
Johnston, Robert Donaghy 1929- *WhoAm 94*
Johnston, Robert Fowler 1936- *WhoAm 94*
Johnston, Robert Gordon Scott 1933- *Who 94*
Johnston, Robert Graham 1957- *WhoMW 93*
Johnston, Robert Harold 1928- *WhoAmA 93*
Johnston, Robert Jake 1947- *WhoAm 94, WhoAmL 94*
Johnston, Robert Kent 1945- *WhoWest 94*
Johnston, Robert Lloyd, Jr. 1931- *WhoAm 94, WhoFI 94*
Johnston, Robert Morris 1930- *WhoMW 93*
Johnston, Robert Smith *Who 94*
Johnston, Roger Glenn 1954- *WhoWest 94*
Johnston, Ronald 1926- *WrDr 94*
Johnston, Ronald John 1941- *IntWW 93, Who 94*
Johnston, Ronald Vernon 1942- *WhoFI 94*
Johnston, Ross W. 1947- *WhoWest 94*
Johnston, Roy E. 1936- *WhoAmA 93*
Johnston, Roy G. 1914- *WhoAm 94*
Johnston, Ruby Charlotte 1918- *WhoMW 93*
Johnston, Russell *Who 94*
Johnston, (David) Russell 1932- *Who 94, WrDr 94*
Johnston, Samuel 1733-1816 *WhAmRev*
Johnston, Samuel Thomas 1924- *WhoAm 94*
Johnston, Sheryl L. 1944- *WhoMW 93*
Johnston, T. Miles G. 1957- *WhoScEn 94*
Johnston, Taylor Jimmie 1940- *WhoMW 93*
Johnston, Terry C(onrad) 1947- *WrDr 94*
Johnston, Terry D. 1947- *WhoAmP 93*

Johnston, Thomas Alexander 1956- *Who 94*
Johnston, Thomas Alix 1941- *WhoAmA 93*
Johnston, Thomas John 1922- *WhoAm 94, WhoFI 94*
Johnston, Thomas Lothian 1927- *IntWW 93, Who 94*
Johnston, Thomas M. 1948- *WhoAmL 94*
Johnston, Thomas McElree 1897- *WhAm 10*
Johnston, Thomas Patrick 1956- *WhoMW 93*
Johnston, Thomas Watts 1936- *WhoAm 94*
Johnston, Timothy Sidney 1966- *WhoMW 93*
Johnston, Velda *WrDr 94*
Johnston, Virginia Evelyn 1933- *WhoWest 94*
Johnston, Waldo Cory Melrose 1913- *WhoAm 94*
Johnston, Wallace O. 1929- *WhoBlA 94*
Johnston, Walt 1932- *WhoWest 94*
Johnston, Walter Eugene, III 1936- *WhoAmP 93*
Johnston, Walter Wesley 1946- *WhoWest 94*
Johnston, Warren E. 1933- *WhoAm 94*
Johnston, William 1925- *WrDr 94*
Johnston, William Bryce 1921- *IntWW 93, Who 94*
Johnston, William David 1944- *WhoAm 94, WhoMW 93*
Johnston, William Francis 1930- *Who 94*
Johnston, William James 1919- *Who 94*
Johnston, William James 1942- *WhoAmP 93*
Johnston, William Medford 1941- *WhoAmA 93*
Johnston, William Murray 1936- *WrDr 94*
Johnston, William Noel 1919- *WhoAm 94*
Johnston, William Norville 1922-1989 *WhAm 10*
Johnston, William Ralph 1936- *WhoAmA 93*
Johnston, William Robert Patrick K. *Who 94*
Johnston, William Webb 1933- *WhoAm 94*
Johnston, Ynez 1920- *WhoAm 94, WhoAmA 93*
Johnston-Calati, Kathleen Louise *WhoAmP 93*
Johnstone *Who 94*
Johnstone, Lord 1971- *Who 94*
Johnstone, Alexander Vallance Riddell 1916- *Who 94*
Johnstone, Belle Stoddard d1950 *WhoHol 92*
Johnstone, Beryl d1969 *WhoHol 92*
Johnstone, Chauncey Olcott 1943- *WhoAm 94, WhoFI 94*
Johnstone, Clint *WhoFI 94, WhoWest 94*
Johnstone, D. Bruce 1941- *IntWW 93, WhoAm 94*
Johnstone, D(avid) Lawson *EncSF 93*
Johnstone, David Kirkpatrick d1993 *Who 94N*
Johnstone, Deborah Blackmon 1953- *WhoAmL 94*
Johnstone, Douglas Inge 1941- *WhoAmP 93*
Johnstone, Edmund Frank 1909- *WhoAm 94*
Johnstone, Edward H. 1922- *WhoAm 94, WhoAmL 94*
Johnstone, Frederic (Allan George) 1906- *Who 94*
Johnstone, George 1730-1787 *WhAmRev*
Johnstone, George W. 1938- *WhoFI 94*
Johnstone, Henry Webb, Jr. 1920- *WhoAm 94*
Johnstone, Iain Gilmour 1943- *Who 94*
Johnstone, Irvine Blakeley, III 1948- *WhoAmL 94*
Johnstone, Isobel Theodora 1944- *Who 94*
Johnstone, James George 1920- *WhoAm 94*
Johnstone, John 1749-1828 *NewGrDO*
Johnstone, John W., Jr. 1932- *IntWW 93*
Johnstone, John Wallace Claire 1931- *WhoAm 94*
Johnstone, John William, Jr. 1932- *WhoAm 94, WhoFI 94, WhoScEn 94*
Johnstone, Justine d1982 *WhoHol 92*
Johnstone, Keith *ConDr 93, WrDr 94*
Johnstone, Kenneth Ernest 1929- *WhoWest 94*
Johnstone, L. Craig *WhoAmP 93*
Johnstone, Lamar d1919 *WhoHol 92*
Johnstone, Larry Anthony 1958- *WhoAmL 94*
Johnstone, Mark 1953- *WhoAmA 93*
Johnstone, Michael Anthony 1936- *Who 94*
Johnstone, Paula Sue 1947- *WhoMW 93*

Johnstone, Philip MacLaren 1961- *WhoAmL 94, WhoFI 94*
Johnstone, Quintin 1915- *WhoAm 94*
Johnstone, R(obert) Edgeworth 1900- *Who 94*
Johnstone, Raymond *Who 94*
Johnstone, (John) Raymond 1929- *Who 94*
Johnstone, Robert Milton 1944- *WhoAmL 94*
Johnstone, Robert Philip 1943- *WhoAm 94, WhoAmL 94*
Johnstone, Rose Mamelak 1928- *WhoAm 94*
Johnstone, Sally Mac 1949- *WhoWest 94*
Johnstone, William 1908- *WhoHol 92*
Johnstone, William 1915- *Who 94*
Johnstone, William 1936- *Who 94*
Johnstone, William A. 1944- *WhoAmL 94*
Johnstone, William Mervyn 1946- *WhoWest 94*
Johnstone, William W. 1938- *EncSF 93*
Johnstone, Vanden-Bempde- *Who 94*
Johnston Of Rockport, Baron 1915- *Who 94*
Johore, Mahmood Iskandar ibni Al-Marhum Ismail, H.H. Sultan of 1932- *IntWW 93*
Johsnon, Arte 1934- *WhoCom*
Joicey, Baron d1993 *Who 94N*
Joicey, Baron 1953- *Who 94*
Joijoi fl. 1870- *EncNAR*
Joiner, Burnett 1941- *WhoBlA 94*
Joiner, Charles, Jr. 1947- *WhoBlA 94*
Joiner, Charles Wycliffe 1916- *WhoAm 94, WhoAmL 94, WhoMW 93*
Joiner, Dennis Ashley 1953- *WhoWest 94*
Joiner, James E. 1942- *WhoAmL 94*
Joiner, Larry J. 1939- *WhoMW 93*
Joiner, Lorell Howard 1945- *WhoFI 94*
Joiner, Patricia d1978 *WhoHol 92*
Joiner, Webb Francis 1933- *WhoFI 94*
Joist, Johann Heinrich 1935- *WhoAm 94*
Jokai, Mor 1825-1904 *EncSF 93*
Jokipii, Liisa 1943- *IntWW 93*
Jokl, Alois Louis 1924- *WhoScEn 94*
Jokl, Ernst F. 1907- *WhoAm 94*
Jokl, Fritzi 1895-1974 *NewGrDO*
Joklik, Gunther Franz 1928- *WhoAm 94, WhoFI 94, WhoWest 94*
Joklik, Wolfgang Karl 1926- *IntWW 93, WhoAm 94*
Jolaoso 1930- *WrDr 94*
Jolas, Betsy 1926- *NewGrDO, WhoAm 94*
Jolicoeur, Paul 1945- *WhoAm 94*
Joliet, Rene 1938- *IntWW 93*
Jolif, Claude Emmanuel 1933- *IntWW 93*
Jolin, Peg 1952- *WhoAmP 93*
Joliot, Pierre Adrien 1932- *IntWW 93*
Joliot-Curie, Frederic 1900-1958 *WorScD [port]*
Joliot-Curie, Irene 1897-1956 *WorScD [port]*
Jolissaint, Mark Alan 1949- *WhoAmP 93*
Jolivet, Andre 1905-1974 *NewGrDO*
Jolivet, Linda Catherine 1950- *WhoBlA 94*
Jolivet, Pierre *WhoHol 92*
Jolivet, Rita 1894- *WhoHol 92*
Joll, James 1918- *WrDr 94*
Joll, James Bysse 1918- *Who 94*
Joll, Phillip 1954- *NewGrDO*
Jolles, Georges Edgar Rene 1929- *WhoScEn 94*
Jolles, Ira Hervey 1938- *WhoAm 94, WhoAmL 94, WhoFI 94*
Jolles, Pierre 1927- *WhoScEn 94*
Jolley, David 1942- *WhoAm 94*
Jolley, Donal Clark 1933- *WhoAmA 93, WhoWest 94*
Jolley, Elizabeth 1923- *BlmGWL [port]*
Jolley, (Monica) Elizabeth 1923- *RfGShF, WrDr 94*
Jolley, Geraldine H. 1911- *WhoAmA 93N*
Jolley, I. Stanford d1978 *WhoHol 92*
Jolley, Stan 1926- *IntMPA 94*
Jolli, Antonio c. 1700-1777 *NewGrDO*
Jollie, Mark d1993 *NewYTBS 93*
Jollie, Susan Barbara 1950- *WhoAmL 94*
Jolliet, Louis 1645-1700 *WhWE*
Jolliff, Carl R. 1926- *WhoAm 94*
Jolliff, Robert Allen 1943- *WhoFI 94*
Jolliffe *Who 94*
Jolliffe, Anthony (Stuart) 1938- *Who 94*
Jolliffe, Christopher 1912- *Who 94*
Jolliffe, John (Hedworth) 1935- *WrDr 94*
Jolliffe, William Orlando 1925- *Who 94*
Jollivette, Cyrus Martin 1946- *WhoAm 94*
Jolly, Bruce Dwight 1943- *WhoAm 94*
Jolly, Charles Nelson 1942- *WhoAmL 94, WhoFI 94*
Jolly, Daniel Ehs 1952- *WhoMW 93, WhoScEn 94*
Jolly, Don d1979 *WhoHol 92*
Jolly, E. Grady *WhoAmP 93*
Jolly, E. Grady 1937- *WhoAm 94, WhoAmL 94*
Jolly, Edward Lee 1939- *WhoScEn 94*
Jolly, Elton 1931- *WhoBlA 94*
Jolly, John Russell, Jr. 1942- *WhoAmL 94*
Jolly, Marva Lee 1937- *WhoBlA 94*
Jolly, Mary B. 1940- *WhoBlA 94*
Jolly, Michael John 1960- *WhoWest 94*
Jolly, Mike *WhoHol 92*
Jolly, Richard *Who 94*
Jolly, (Arthur) Richard 1934- *Who 94*
Jolly, Robert Dudley 1930- *IntWW 93*
Jolly, Robert Malcolm 1920- *Who 94*
Jolly, Sylvie *WhoHol 92*
Jolly, Thomas R. 1943- *WhoAmL 94*
Jolly, W(illiam) P(ercy) 1922- *WrDr 94*
Jolly, Wayne Travis 1940- *WhoAm 94, WhoScEn 94*
Jolly, William Lee 1927- *WhoAm 94*
Jollymore, Nicholas John 1946- *WhoAmL 94*
Jolovitz, Herbert Allen 1930- *WhoAmP 93*
Jolowicz, J(ohn) A(nthony) 1926- *WrDr 94*
Jolowicz, John Anthony 1926- *Who 94*
Jolson, Al 1886-1950 *ConMus 10 [port]*
Jolson, Alfred James 1928- *WhoAm 94*
Joly, Alain 1938- *IntWW 93*
Joly, Cyril Matthew, Jr. 1925- *WhoAmP 93*
Joly, Jean-Gil 1940- *WhoAm 94, WhoScEn 94*
Joly, Jean Robert 1950- *WhoAm 94*
Joly de Lotbiniere, Edmond 1903- *Who 94*
Jommelli, Niccolo 1714-1774 *NewGrDO*
Jo-Mo, Dr. *DrAPF 93*
Jonah, Dolly d1983 *WhoHol 92*
Jonaitis, Aldona 1948- *WhoAmA 93*
Jonas, Ann *DrAPF 93*
Jonas, Ann 1932- *WrDr 94*
Jonas, Christopher William 1941- *Who 94*
Jonas, Ernesto A. 1939- *WhoBlA 94*
Jonas, Gary Fred 1945- *WhoAm 94*
Jonas, George *DrAPF 93*
Jonas, George 1935- *WrDr 94*
Jonas, Gerald *DrAPF 93*
Jonas, Gilbert 1930- *WhoFI 94*
Jonas, Hans d1993 *NewYTBS 93 [port]*
Jonas, Hans 1903-1993 *ConAu 140*
Jonas, Harry S. 1926- *WhoAm 94*
Jonas, Jiri 1932- *WhoAm 94, WhoMW 93, WhoScEn 94*
Jonas, Joan 1936- *WhoAm 94, WhoAmA 93, WhoWest 94*
Jonas, John Francis 1950- *WhoAm 94*
Jonas, John Joseph 1932- *WhoAm 94*
Jonas, Manfred 1927- *WrDr 94*
Jonas, Peter 1946- *IntWW 93, NewGrDO, Who 94*
Jonas, Ruth Haber 1935- *WhoScEn 94*
Jonas, Saran 1931- *WhoAm 94, WhoScEn 94*
Jonas, Steven 1936- *WhoAm 94*
Jonassen, James O. 1940- *WhoAm 94*
Jonassohn, Kurt 1920- *WhoAm 94*
Jonatansson, Halldor 1932- *WhoFI 94*
Jonay, Roberta d1976 *WhoHol 92*
Joncas, Grace Lucille 1923- *WhoAmP 93*
Joncich, David Michael 1946- *WhoScEn 94*
Joncieres, Victorin (de) 1839-1903 *NewGrDO*
Jonckheere, Alan Mathew 1947- *WhoAm 94*
Jonckowski, Lynn 1954- *WhoWest 94*
Jondahl, H. Lynn *WhoAmP 93*
Jondle, Douglas John 1956- *WhoMW 93*
Jones *Who 94*
Jones, Mrs. *NewGrDO*
Jones, A. Timothy 1942- *WhoAmL 94*
Jones, Aaron Delmas, II 1966- *WhoBlA 94*
Jones, Abbott C. 1934- *WhoAm 94*
Jones, Adrianne Shirley 1938- *Who 94*
Jones, Adrienne 1915- *WrDr 94*
Jones, Agnes Elizabeth 1832-1868 *DcNaB MP*
Jones, Aidan Drexel 1945- *WhoAm 94*
Jones, Alan C. 1942- *WhoFI 94*
Jones, Alan Griffith 1943- *WrDr 94*
Jones, Alan Payan P. *Who 94*
Jones, Alan Porter, Jr. 1925- *WhoFI 94, WhoMW 93*
Jones, Alan Robert 1945- *WhoAmP 93*
Jones, Alan Stanley 1946- *IntWW 93*
Jones, Alan Wingate 1939- *Who 94*
Jones, Albert 1929- *WhoAmP 93*
Jones, Albert Allen 1913- *WhoBlA 94*
Jones, Albert J. 1928- *WhoBlA 94*
Jones, Albert L. 1945- *WhoBlA 94*
Jones, Albert Pearson 1907- *WhAm 10*
Jones, Albert Stanley 1925- *Who 94*
Jones, Alberta Camphor 1934- *WhoMW 93*
Jones, Albertus Eugene 1882-1957 *WhoAmA 93N*
Jones, Alex S. 1946- *WhoAm 94, WrDr 94*
Jones, Alexander Elvin 1920- *WhoAm 94*
Jones, Alexander R. 1952- *WhoBlA 94*
Jones, Alexandra *WhoHol 92*
Jones, Alfred d1981 *WhoHol 92*
Jones, Alfredean 1940- *WhoBlA 94*
Jones, Alice *DrAPF 93*
Jones, Alice J. 1953- *WhoAm 94*
Jones, Allan 1905- *WhoHol 92*
Jones, Allan 1907-1992 *ConTFT 11*
Jones, Allan Frewin 1954- *TwCYAW*
Jones, Allan W. 1929- *WhoIns 94*
Jones, Allen 1739-1798 *WhAmRev*
Jones, Allen 1937- *IntWW 93, Who 94*
Jones, Allen, Jr. 1930- *WhoAmL 94*
Jones, Allen E. 1938- *WhoMW 93*
Jones, Allen N. *WhoAm 94, WhoFI 94*
Jones, Alphonzo James 1946- *WhoBlA 94*
Jones, Alun *Who 94*
Jones, (Robert) Alun 1949- *Who 94*
Jones, Alun Denry Wynn 1939- *Who 94*
Jones, Alwyn Rice *Who 94*
Jones, Ammia W. 1910- *WhoBlA 94*
Jones, Amy Holden 1953- *IntMPA 94*
Jones, Andras *WhoHol 92*
Jones, Andrew Nolan 1943- *WhoAm 94*
Jones, Angela *Who 94*
Jones, (Sybil) Angela (Margaret) 1940- *Who 94*
Jones, Anissa d1976 *WhoHol 92*
Jones, Ann *Who 94*
Jones, Ann Haydon 1938- *BuCMET*
Jones, Ann R. 1921- *WhoBlA 94*
Jones, Annabel *ConAu 43NR*
Jones, Anne 1935- *Who 94*
Jones, Anne Hudson 1944- *WrDr 94*
Jones, Anne P. 1935- *WhoAmP 93*
Jones, Anne Patricia 1935- *WhoAm 94*
Jones, Annette *WhoAmP 93*
Jones, Annette 1944- *WhoFI 94*
Jones, Annette Merritt 1946- *WhoBlA 94*
Jones, Anthony, Jr. 1933- *WhoBlA 94*
Jones, Anthony Edward 1944- *Who 94*
Jones, Anthony George Clifford 1923- *Who 94*
Jones, Anthony Graham Hume 1942- *Who 94*
Jones, Anthony W. *Who 94*
Jones, Anthony Ward 1947- *WhoBlA 94*
Jones, Arlender *WhoBlA 94*
Jones, Arnold Pearson *WhoBlA 94*
Jones, Arthur Carhart 1896- *WhAm 10*
Jones, Arthur Edwin, Jr. 1918- *WhoAm 94*
Jones, Arthur Francis 1946- *WhoWest 94*
Jones, Arthur L. 1922-1992 *WhoBlA 94N*
Jones, Arthur McDonald, Sr. 1947- *WhoAm 94, WhoFI 94*
Jones, Arthur Stanley 1932- *Who 94*
Jones, Arves E. 1925- *WhoAmP 93*
Jones, Asbury Paul 1914- *WhoBlA 94*
Jones, Aubrey 1911- *IntWW 93, Who 94, WrDr 94*
Jones, Aubrey Lee, Jr. 1953- *WhoAmP 93*
Jones, Audrey Boswell *WhoBlA 94*
Jones, B. Rees 1937- *WhoIns 94*
Jones, Barbara Ann Posey 1943- *WhoAm 94, WhoBlA 94*
Jones, Barbara Ewer 1942- *WhoMW 93, WhoScEn 94*
Jones, Barbara Loretta 1944- *WhoMW 93*
Jones, Barclay George 1931- *WhoMW 93*
Jones, Barclay Gibbs 1925- *WhoScEn 94*
Jones, Barclay Gibbs, III 1960- *WhoAm 94*
Jones, Barry *Who 94*
Jones, Barry d1981 *WhoHol 92*
Jones, Barry Owen 1932- *IntWW 93*
Jones, Barton T. 1946- *WhoAmL 94*
Jones, Bartow Ned 1944- *WhoAmP 93*
Jones, Basil Douglas d1992 *Who 94N*
Jones, Beatrice Eleanor 1904- *WhoAmP 93*
Jones, Beau *WhoAmP 93*
Jones, Belling, Jr. 1897- *WhAm 10*
Jones, Ben 1912- *WhoAm 94*
Jones, Ben 1941- *WhoAmP 93, WhoHol 92*
Jones, Ben 1942- *AfrAmAl 6, WhoAmA 93*
Jones, Ben F. 1942- *WhoBlA 94*
Jones, Ben Joseph 1924- *IntWW 93*
Jones, Benjamin Angus, Jr. 1926- *WhoMW 93, WhoScEn 94*
Jones, Benjamin E. 1935- *WhoBlA 94*
Jones, Bernard H., Sr. 1931- *WhoBlA 94*
Jones, Bernie 1952- *WhoBlA 94*
Jones, Bertha Diggs *WhoBlA 94*
Jones, Bertha H. 1918- *WhoBlA 94*
Jones, Beti 1919- *Who 94*
Jones, Betty Jean T. 1943- *WhoBlA 94*
Jones, Betty Jeanne 1946- *WhoMW 93*
Jones, Beverly Ann Miller 1927- *WhoScEn 94*
Jones, Bill T. 1952?- *CurBio 93 [port], WhoAm 94*
Jones, Billy d1940 *WhoHol 92*
Jones, Billy Emanuel 1938- *WhoBlA 94*
Jones, Billy Ernest 1933- *WhoAm 94*
Jones, Billy Mac 1925- *WhoMW 93, WrDr 94*
Jones, Bob, Jr. 1911- *WhoAm 94, WrDr 94*
Jones, Bob Gordon 1932- *WhoWest 94*
Jones, Bobby 1933- *WhoBlA 94*
Jones, Bobby 1951- *BasBi [port]*
Jones, Bobby Truesdell 1933- *WhoAmP 93*
Jones, Boisfeuillet, Jr. 1946- *WhoAm 94*
Jones, Bonnie Louise 1952- *WhoBlA 94*
Jones, Booker Tee, Sr. 1939- *WhoBlA 94*
Jones, Bradley Carl 1962- *WhoFI 94*
Jones, Bradley Mitchell 1952- *WhoAmL 94*
Jones, Brennon 1945- *WrDr 94*
Jones, Brent M. 1946- *WhoBlA 94*
Jones, Brereton C. 1939- *WhoAm 94, WhoAmP 93*
Jones, Brian d1969 *WhoHol 92*
Jones, Brian 1938- *WrDr 94*
Jones, Brian Leslie 1930- *Who 94*
Jones, Brian Matthew 1959- *WhoMW 93*
Jones, Bridget 1955- *ConAu 141*
Jones, Brinley *Who 94*
Jones, (Robert) Brinley 1929- *Who 94*
Jones, Bruce Hovey 1947- *WhoScEn 94*
Jones, Buck d1942 *WhoHol 92*
Jones, Butler Alfonso 1916- *WhoBlA 94*
Jones, C. Goodman *WhoIns 94*
Jones, C. Kevin 1963- *WhoFI 94*
Jones, C. Paul 1927- *WhoAm 94*
Jones, Caldwell 1950- *BasBi, WhoBlA 94*
Jones, Calvin B(ell) 1934- *WhoAmA 93*
Jones, Calvin Bell 1934- *WhoBlA 94*
Jones, Carl *WhoBlA 94*
Jones, Carl L. 1933- *WhoBlA 94*
Jones, Carleton Shaw 1942- *WhoAm 94*
Jones, Carol Ann 1950- *WhoAm 94*
Jones, Carol Joyce 1938- *WhoBlA 94*
Jones, Caroline Robinson 1942- *WhoBlA 94*
Jones, Carolyn d1983 *WhoHol 92*
Jones, Carolyn G. 1943- *WhoBlA 94*
Jones, Carter R(uthven), Jr. 1945- *WhoAmA 93*
Jones, Casey C. 1915- *WhoAmP 93, WhoBlA 94*
Jones, Catesby Brooke 1925- *WhoAm 94*
Jones, Catherine Ann 1936- *WhoAm 94*
Jones, Cedric Decorrus 1960- *WhoBlA 94*
Jones, Charisse Monsio 1965- *WhoBlA 94*
Jones, Charlene *WhoHol 92*
Jones, Charles 1962- *WhoBlA 94*
Jones, Charles, Jr. 1946- *WhoBlA 94*
Jones, Charles A. 1934- *WhoBlA 94*
Jones, Charles Beynon Lloyd 1932- *Who 94*
Jones, Charles Calhoun 1940- *WhoFI 94, WhoMW 93*
Jones, Charles Colcock d1863 *DcAmReB 2*
Jones, Charles D. 1950- *WhoAmP 93, WhoBlA 94*
Jones, Charles David 1943- *WhoMW 93*
Jones, Charles Davis 1917- *WhoFI 94*
Jones, Charles Edward 1918- *WhoAm 94*
Jones, Charles Edward 1920- *WhoAm 94*
Jones, Charles Eric, Jr. 1957- *WhoAmL 94*
Jones, Charles Franklin 1911-1991 *WhAm 10*
Jones, Charles Fred 1930- *WhoAmP 93*
Jones, Charles Hill, Jr. 1933- *WhoAm 94*
Jones, Charles Ian McMillan 1934- *Who 94*
Jones, Charles Irving 1943- *WhoAm 94, WhoWest 94*
Jones, Charles J. 1940- *WhoWest 94*
Jones, Charles Lee 1957- *WhoScEn 94*
Jones, Charles Leonard 1949- *WhoAm 94, WhoMW 93*
Jones, Charles R. 1944- *WhoAmP 93*
Jones, Charles Sam 1956- *WhoAmP 93*
Jones, Charles W. 1923- *WhoAm 94, WhoFI 94, WhoMW 93*
Jones, Charles Weldon 1953- *WhoScEn 94*
Jones, Charles William 1951- *WhoAmL 94*
Jones, Charles Williams 1905-1989 *WhAm 10*
Jones, Charlie *WhoAm 94*
Jones, Charlott Ann 1927- *WhoAm 94, WhoAmA 93*
Jones, Charlotte *WhoHol 92*
Jones, Charlotte Foltz 1945- *SmATA 77 [port]*
Jones, Cheri Lynn 1963- *WhoAmL 94*
Jones, Cherry *WhoHol 92*
Jones, Chester d1975 *WhoHol 92*
Jones, Chester Ray 1946- *WhoBlA 94*
Jones, Chet *WhoAmP 93*
Jones, Chet R. 1949- *WhoMW 93*
Jones, Christine Massey 1929- *WhoAm 94*
Jones, Christine Miller *WhoBlA 94*
Jones, Christine Miller 1929- *WhoAmP 93*
Jones, Christopher 1937- *WrDr 94*
Jones, Christopher 1941- *WhoHol 92*
Jones, Christopher L. *Who 94*
Jones, Christopher Vyn 1958- *WhoWest 94*
Jones, Christy D. 1952- *WhoAmL 94*

Jones, Chuck 1912- *IntDcF 2-4 [port], IntMPA 94*
Jones, Chuck 1943- *IntMPA 94*
Jones, Clara Stanton 1913- *WhoBlA 94*
Jones, Clarence B. 1931- *AfrAmAl 6*
Jones, Clarence J., Jr. 1933- *WhoBlA 94*
Jones, Claris Eugene, Jr. 1942- *WhoAm 94*
Jones, Claude Earl *WhoHol 92*
Jones, Clement *Who 94*
Jones, (John) Clement 1915- *Who 94*
Jones, Cleon Boyd 1961- *WhoWest 94*
Jones, Clifford 1939- *WhoAm 94, WhoFI 94*
Jones, Clifford Aaron 1912- *WhoAm 94, WhoAmL 94*
Jones, Clifford L. 1927- *WhoAmP 93*
Jones, Clifford M 1902- *WrDr 94*
Jones, Clifton Patrick 1927- *WhoBlA 94*
Jones, Clifton Ralph 1910- *WhoBlA 94*
Jones, Clive Lawson 1937- *Who 94*
Jones, Cloyzelle Karrelle *WhoBlA 94*
Jones, Clyde Eugene 1954- *WhoBlA 94*
Jones, Cobi N'Gai *WhoBlA 94*
Jones, Colin Elliott 1941- *WhoScEn 94*
Jones, Cornell 1923- *WhoBlA 94*
Jones, Craig Ward 1947- *WhoAm 94*
Jones, Cranston Edward 1918-1992 *WhAm 10*
Jones, Curley C. 1941- *WhoBlA 94*
Jones, Curtis H. *WhoAmP 93*
Jones, D(ennis) F(eltham) 1917-1981 *EncSF 93*
Jones, D(ouglas) G(ordon) 1929- *WrDr 94*
Jones, D. Michael 1942- *WhoAm 94, WhoWest 94*
Jones, D. Paul, Jr. 1942- *WhoAm 94, WhoFI 94*
Jones, D. S. 1922- *ConAu 141*
Jones, D. Terence 1946- *WhoAmL 94*
Jones, Dale Cherner 1948- *WhoMW 93*
Jones, Dale Edwin 1948- *WhoAmL 94*
Jones, Dale Leslie 1952- *WhoScEn 94*
Jones, Dale P. 1936- *WhoAm 94, WhoFI 94*
Jones, Daniel (Jenkyn) 1912- *NewGrDO*
Jones, Daniel Gruffydd 1933- *Who 94*
Jones, Daniel Hare 1949- *WhoAm 94*
Jones, Daniel Jenkyn 1912- *IntWW 93*
Jones, Daniel Lee 1954- *WhoWest 94*
Jones, Daniel Silas 1943- *WhoScEn 94*
Jones, Daniel W. 1830-1915 *EncNAR*
Jones, Danise Ann 1959- *WhoFI 94*
Jones, Danny 1950- *WhoAmP 93*
Jones, Darby d1986 *WhoHol 92*
Jones, Darryl Louis 1968- *WhoMW 93*
Jones, Daryl *DrAPF 93*
Jones, Daryl (Emrys) 1946- *WrDr 94*
Jones, Daryl Emrys 1946- *WhoWest 94*
Jones, Daryl L. 1955- *WhoAmP 93*
Jones, David *ProFbHF [port], WhoHol 92*
Jones, David 1736-1820 *WhAmRev [port]*
Jones, David 1934- *IntMPA 94*
Jones, David 1940- *Who 94*
Jones, David A. *Who 94*
Jones, David Allan 1942- *WhoScEn 94*
Jones, David Allen 1931- *WhoAm 94, WhoFI 94*
Jones, David Alwyn 1934- *WhoScEn 94*
Jones, David Anthony 1939- *WhoAmL 94*
Jones, David Charles 1921- *IntWW 93, WhoAm 94*
Jones, David Charles 1935- *WhoFI 94*
Jones, David Charles 1943- *Who 94*
Jones, David Edwin 1963- *WhoAmL 94*
Jones, David Eugene 1942- *WhoAm 94*
Jones, David Evan Alun 1925- *Who 94*
Jones, David G. *Who 94*
Jones, David George 1941- *Who 94*
Jones, David (Erik) Hay 1959- *WrDr 94*
Jones, David Hugh 1934- *Who 94, WhoAm 94*
Jones, David Huw 1934- *Who 94*
Jones, David Ian Stewart 1934- *Who 94*
Jones, David John 1933- *WhoIns 94*
Jones, David John 1934- *WhoAm 94, WhoWest 94*
Jones, David le Brun 1923- *Who 94*
Jones, David Lee 1948- *WhoAmA 93*
Jones, David Leroy 1947- *WhoAmL 94*
Jones, David Lewis 1945- *Who 94*
Jones, David M. *Who 94*
Jones, David M. 1951- *WhoAmP 93*
Jones, David Martin 1944- *Who 94*
Jones, David Michael 1895-1974 *BlmGEL*
Jones, David Milton 1938- *WhoAm 94*
Jones, David Morgan 1915- *Who 94*
Jones, David Norris 1948- *WhoAmP 93*
Jones, David R. 1937- *WhoFI 94*
Jones, David Rhodes 1932- *WhoAm 94*
Jones, David Robert 1941- *WhoAm 94, WhoScEn 94*
Jones, David Robert 1947- *WhoAm 94*
Jones, David Russell 1948- *WhoBlA 94*
Jones, David Thomas c. 1796-1844 *EncNAR*
Jones, David W(yn) 1950- *WrDr 94*
Jones, Davy 1945- *WhoHol 92*
Jones, Deacon 1934- *WhoBlA 94*
Jones, Dean 1931- *IntMPA 94, WhoHol 92*
Jones, Dean Carroll 1933- *WhoAm 94*
Jones, Dean Clarence 1932- *WhoWest 94*
Jones, Dean Mervyn 1963- *IntWW 93*
Jones, Debora Elaine 1959- *WhoBlA 94*
Jones, Deborah 1954- *WhoAm 94*
Jones, Della *Who 94*
Jones, Della 1946- *NewGrDO*
Jones, Delmos J. 1936- *WhoBlA 94*
Jones, Delna 1940- *WhoWomW 91*
Jones, Delna L. 1940- *WhoAmP 93*
Jones, Delores 1954- *WhoBlA 94*
Jones, Delwin 1924- *WhoAmP 93*
Jones, Dennis L. 1941- *WhoAmP 93*
Jones, Dennis Lee 1941- *WhoAmL 94*
Jones, Dennis Pierce 1940- *WhoWest 94*
Jones, Denzil Eugene 1910- *WhoAmP 93*
Jones, Derek A. *Who 94*
Jones, Derek John Claremont 1927- *Who 94*
Jones, Derek R. *Who 94*
Jones, Derwyn Dixon 1925- *Who 94*
Jones, DeVerges Booker 1950- *WhoBlA 94*
Jones, Dexter 1926- *WhoAmA 93N*
Jones, Diana Wynne 1934- *Au&Arts 12 [port], EncSF 93, TwCYAW, WhoAm 94, WrDr 94*
Jones, Dick(ie) 1927- *WhoHol 92*
Jones, Don *DrAPF 93*
Jones, Don E. 1949- *WhoAmP 93*
Jones, Donald Forsyth 1942- *WhoWest 94*
Jones, Donald L. *WhoAm 94, WhoWest 94*
Jones, Donald Ray 1947- *WhoFI 94, WhoWest 94*
Jones, Donald W. 1939- *WhoBlA 94*
Jones, Donna M. 1939- *WhoAmP 93*
Jones, Donna Marilyn 1939- *WhoAm 94, WhoFI 94, WhoWest 94*
Jones, Dorinda A. 1926- *WhoBlA 94*
Jones, Dorothy Cameron 1922-1989 *WhAm 10*
Jones, Dorothy Joanne *WhoWest 94*
Jones, Doug 1929- *WhoAmA 93*
Jones, Douglas 1949- *WhoHisp 94*
Jones, Douglas C 1924- *WrDr 94*
Jones, Douglas Clyde 1924- *WhoAm 94, WhoWest 94*
Jones, Douglas Epps 1930- *WhoAm 94*
Jones, Douglas R. *WhoAmP 93*
Jones, Douglas Rawlinson 1919- *Who 94*
Jones, Douglas Samuel 1922- *IntWW 93, Who 94*
Jones, Douglas W. 1948- *WhoAmL 94*
Jones, Duane d1988 *WhoHol 92*
Jones, Duane L. 1937- *WhoBlA 94*
Jones, Dudley 1914- *WhoHol 92*
Jones, Dylan 1960- *ConAu 142*
Jones, E. Bradley 1927- *IntWW 93*
Jones, E. Stewart, Jr. 1941- *WhoAmL 94, WhoFI 94*
Jones, E. Thomas 1950- *WhoAmL 94*
Jones, Earl Frederick 1949- *WhoBlA 94*
Jones, Eben Lee 1949- *WhoFI 94*
Jones, Ebon Richard 1944- *WhoAm 94, WhoWest 94*
Jones, Ed *WhoHol 92*
Jones, Ed 1912- *WhoAmP 93*
Jones, Eddie 1935- *EncSF 93*
Jones, Eddie J. *WhoAm 94*
Jones, Edgar Allan, Jr. 1921- *WhoAm 94*
Jones, Edith H. *WhoAmP 93*
Jones, Edith Hollan 1949- *WhoAm 94, WhoAmL 94*
Jones, Edith Irby 1927- *WhoBlA 94*
Jones, Edward *Who 94*
Jones, Edward 1935- *WhoAm 94*
Jones, (Charles) Edward (Webb) 1936- *Who 94*
Jones, (John) Edward 1914- *Who 94*
Jones, Edward David 1920- *WhoScEn 94*
Jones, Edward David Brynmor 1939- *Who 94*
Jones, Edward E. d1993 *NewYTBS 93*
Jones, Edward E(llsworth) 1926-1993 *ConAu 142*
Jones, Edward G. *Who 94*
Jones, Edward George 1939- *WhoAm 94*
Jones, Edward Lee 1951- *WhoBlA 94*
Jones, Edward Louis 1922- *WhoAm 94, WhoBlA 94, WhoWest 94*
Jones, Edward Magruder 1928- *WhoAm 94*
Jones, Edward Martin F. *Who 94*
Jones, Edward Norman 1914- *WhoBlA 94*
Jones, Edward P. 1950- *BlkWr 2, ConAu 142*
Jones, Edward P. 1951- *ConLC 76 [port]*
Jones, Edward Powis 1919- *WhoAm 94, WhoAmA 93*
Jones, Edward W. *Who 94*
Jones, Edward Warburton d1993 *Who 94N*
Jones, Edward White, II 1921- *WhoAm 94, WhoAmL 94*
Jones, Edward Witker 1929- *WhoMW 93*
Jones, Edwin Channing, Jr. 1934- *WhoAm 94*
Jones, Edwin Michael 1916- *WhoAm 94*
Jones, Effie Hall 1928- *WhoBlA 94*
Jones, Eifion 1912- *Who 94*
Jones, Elaine R. *NewYTBS 93 [port]*
Jones, Elaine R. 1944- *WhoBlA 94*
Jones, Elayne 1928- *AfrAmAl 6*
Jones, Eleri Wynne 1933- *Who 94*
Jones, Elizabeth *WhoHol 92*
Jones, Elizabeth 1898- *WhAm 10*
Jones, Elizabeth A. B. 1935- *WhoAmA 93*
Jones, Elizabeth Anne 1941- *WhoWest 94*
Jones, Elizabeth Nordwall 1934- *WhoAm 94*
Jones, Elnetta Griffin 1934- *WhoBlA 94*
Jones, Elvin 1927- *AfrAmAl 6*
Jones, Emil, Jr. 1935- *WhoAmP 93, WhoBlA 94, WhoMW 93*
Jones, Emlyn Bartley *Who 94*
Jones, Emma Pettway 1945- *WhoBlA 94*
Jones, Emrys *Who 94*
Jones, Emrys d1972 *WhoHol 92*
Jones, Emrys 1920- *Who 94, WrDr 94*
Jones, (William) Emrys 1915- *Who 94*
Jones, Emrys Lloyd 1931- *Who 94*
Jones, Enoch 1922- *WhoBlA 94*
Jones, Eric Lionel 1936- *WrDr 94*
Jones, Eric S. *Who 94*
Jones, Ernest 1923- *WhoBlA 94*
Jones, Ernest Edward 1931- *Who 94, WhoAm 94*
Jones, Ernest Edward 1944- *WhoBlA 94*
Jones, Ernest Paul 1952- *WhoMW 93*
Jones, Ervin Edward 1938- *WhoBlA 94*
Jones, Esther B. 1969- *WhoBlA 94*
Jones, Etta *WhoAm 94*
Jones, Eugene Gordon 1929- *WhoFI 94, WhoMW 93*
Jones, Euine Fay 1921- *WhoAm 94*
Jones, Eurfron Gwynne 1934- *Who 94*
Jones, Eva 1931- *WhoBlA 94*
Jones, Eva (Eleonore) 1913- *WrDr 94*
Jones, Evan *WhoAmP 93*
Jones, Evan 1788-1872 *EncNAR*
Jones, Evan (Lloyd) 1931- *WrDr 94*
Jones, Ewan Perrins W. *Who 94*
Jones, Ewart (Ray Herbert) 1911- *Who 94*
Jones, Ewart Ray Herbert 1911- *IntWW 93*
Jones, F(rank) Llewellyn- 1907- *Who 94*
Jones, Farrell 1926- *WhoBlA 94*
Jones, Fay 1922- *WhoAm 94, WhoScEn 94*
Jones, Ferdinand Taylor, Jr. 1932- *WhoBlA 94*
Jones, Fielding *Who 94*
Jones, (Norman) Fielding 1931- *Who 94*
Jones, Florence 1909- *EncNAR*
Jones, Floresta Deloris 1950- *WhoBlA 94*
Jones, Floyd Carl 1932- *WhoMW 93*
Jones, Frances Ann 1927- *WhoMW 93*
Jones, Francis *WhoBlA 94*
Jones, Francis 1908- *Who 94*
Jones, Francis A., III 1935- *WhoAmP 93*
Jones, Francis John 1928- *Who 94*
Jones, Frank 1937- *ConAu 43NR*
Jones, Frank 1950- *WhoBlA 94*
Jones, Frank, Jr. 1959- *WhoMW 93*
Jones, Frank Benson 1938- *WhoBlA 94*
Jones, Frank Cater 1925- *WhoAm 94, WhoAmL 94*
Jones, Frank Edward 1917- *WhoAm 94*
Jones, Frank Griffith 1941- *WhoAm 94*
Jones, Frank Joseph *WhoFI 94*
Jones, Frank Lancaster 1937- *WrDr 94*
Jones, Frank Ralph 1944- *WhoScEn 94*
Jones, Frank Ray 1945- *WhoAm 94*
Jones, Frank S. 1928- *WhoBlA 94*
Jones, Frank William 1915- *WhoAm 94*
Jones, Frank Wyman 1940- *WhoAm 94*
Jones, Franklin D. 1935- *WhoBlA 94*
Jones, Franklin D. 1939- *WhoBlA 94*
Jones, Franklin Reed 1921- *WhoAmA 93*
Jones, Franklin Ross 1920- *WhoAm 94*
Jones, Fred 1920- *Who 94*
Jones, Fred E. 1926- *WhoAm 94*
Jones, Fred Leslie 1944- *WhoMW 93*
Jones, Fred Reese 1935- *WhoAmP 93*
Jones, Fred Richard 1947- *WhoAm 94*
Jones, Freda M. d1976 *WhoHol 92*
Jones, Freddie 1927- *WhoHol 92*
Jones, Frederick 1940- *WhoAmA 93*
Jones, Frederick Douglass, Jr. 1955- *WhoBlA 94*
Jones, Frederick McKinley 1892-1961 *AfrAmAl 6*
Jones, Frederick McKinley 1893-1961 *WorInv*
Jones, Fredrick E. *WhoBlA 94*
Jones, Furman Madison, Jr. 1927- *WhoBlA 94*
Jones, G. Daniel *WhoBlA 94*
Jones, G. William d1993 *NewYTBS 93*
Jones, Galen Everts 1928- *WhoAm 94*
Jones, Galen Ray 1948- *WhoWest 94*
Jones, Gareth *Who 94*
Jones, Gareth (Elwyn) 1939- *ConAu 41NR*
Jones, Gareth (Hywel) 1930- *Who 94, WrDr 94*
Jones, (John) Gareth 1936- *Who 94*
Jones, Garth Nelson 1925- *WhoAm 94*
Jones, Gary 1942- *WhoBlA 94*
Jones, Gary DeWayne 1967- *WhoBlA 94*
Jones, Gary Leland 1944- *WhoAmP 93*
Jones, Gary Lendell 1951- *WhoFI 94*
Jones, Gayl 1949- *AfrAmAl 6, BlkWr 2, WhoBlA 94, WrDr 94*
Jones, Gayle 1949- *BlmGWL*
Jones, Gaynelle Griffin *WhoAmL 94*
Jones, Gemma 1942- *IntMPA 94, WhoHol 92*
Jones, Geoffrey *Who 94*
Jones, (John) Geoffrey 1928- *Who 94*
Jones, Geoffrey M. *Who 94*
Jones, Geoffrey Melvill 1923- *WhoAm 94, WhoScEn 94*
Jones, Geoffrey Rippon R. *Who 94*
Jones, George 1766-1838 *WhAmRev*
Jones, George 1931- *WhoAm 94*
Jones, George Bobby 1946- *WhoAmA 93*
Jones, George Briscoe 1929- *Who 94*
Jones, George E. 1893- *WhAm 10*
Jones, George Fleming 1935- *WhoAm 94, WhoAmP 93*
Jones, George H. 1856-1941 *EncABHB 9*
Jones, George H. 1942- *WhoBlA 94*
Jones, George Henry 1942- *WhoAm 94*
Jones, George Humphrey 1923- *WhoMW 93, WhoScEn 94*
Jones, George L. 1950- *WhoAm 94, WhoFI 94*
Jones, George Quentin 1945- *Who 94*
Jones, George Richard 1930- *WhoScEn 94*
Jones, George W. 1924-1980 *WhoBlA 94N*
Jones, George William 1938- *Who 94*
Jones, George Williams 1931- *WhoBlA 94*
Jones, George Wilson 1926- *WhoAmP 93*
Jones, Geraint Iwan 1917- *IntWW 93, Who 94*
Jones, Geraint Stanley 1936- *Who 94*
Jones, Gerald 1939- *Who 94*
Jones, Gerald E. 1937- *WhoBlA 94*
Jones, Gerald Joseph 1920- *WhoWest 94*
Jones, Gerald Winfield 1931- *WhoAm 94, WhoAmL 94, WhoBlA 94*
Jones, Geraldine J. 1939- *WhoBlA 94*
Jones, Geraldine W. 1929- *WhoAmP 93*
Jones, Gerallt *Who 94*
Jones, (Robert) Gerallt 1934- *Who 94*
Jones, Gerre Lyle 1926- *WhoFI 94, WhoWest 94*
Jones, Gillian *WhoHol 92*
Jones, Gladys Hurt 1920- *WhoScEn 94*
Jones, Glendell Asbury, Jr. 1939- *WhoAmP 93*
Jones, Glenn *WhoBlA 94*
Jones, Gloria Lee 1923- *WhoAmP 93*
Jones, Glower Whitehead 1936- *WhoAmL 94*
Jones, Glyn 1905- *WrDr 94*
Jones, (Morgan) Glyn 1905- *RfGShF*
Jones, Glyndwr 1935- *Who 94*
Jones, Glynn 1933- *Who 94*
Jones, (Thomas Frederick) Gonner *EncSF 93*
Jones, Gordon d1963 *WhoHol 92*
Jones, Gordon (Pearce) 1927- *Who 94*
Jones, Gordon Edwin 1921- *WhoAm 94*
Jones, Gordon Frederick 1929- *Who 94*
Jones, Gordon Kempton 1946- *WhoMW 93*
Jones, Gordon Merrill 1896- *WhAm 10*
Jones, Grace 1952- *IntMPA 94, IntWW 93, WhoHol 92*
Jones, Grace 1954- *WhoBlA 94*
Jones, Graham Edward 1944- *Who 94*
Jones, Graham Julian 1936- *Who 94*
Jones, Grant 1922- *WhoAmP 93*
Jones, Gregg H. 1950- *WhoAmL 94*
Jones, Gregory Gilman *WhoAm 94*
Jones, Gregory Knox 1961- *WhoMW 93*
Jones, Greta Waller 1939- *WhoAmP 93*
Jones, Grier Patterson 1942- *WhoAmL 94*
Jones, Griff Rhys 1953- *WhoHol 92*
Jones, Griffith 1910- *IntMPA 94, WhoHol 92*
Jones, Griffith R. *Who 94*
Jones, Griffith Winston Guthrie 1914- *Who 94*
Jones, Grover William, Jr. 1934- *WhoBlA 94*
Jones, Gwendolyn Beth 1955- *WhoMW 93*
Jones, Gwendolyn J. 1953- *WhoBlA 94*
Jones, Gwenyth Ellen 1952- *WhoAm 94*
Jones, Gwilym Haydn *Who 94*
Jones, Gwyn *Who 94*
Jones, Gwyn 1907- *DcLB 139 [port], Who 94, WrDr 94*
Jones, Gwyn Idris M. *Who 94*
Jones, Gwyn Owain 1917- *Who 94, WrDr 94*

Jones, Gwyneth 1936- *IntWW 93, NewGrDO, Who 94, WhoAm 94*
Jones, Gwyneth (Ann) 1952- *EncSF 93*
Jones, Gwyneth A. 1952- *WrDr 94*
Jones, Gwynoro Glyndwr 1942- *Who 94*
Jones, H. Thomas, II 1944- *WhoBlA 94*
Jones, H. W. Kasey 1942- *WhoMW 93*
Jones, Hank *WhoHol 92*
Jones, Hank 1918- *AfrAmAl 6*
Jones, Hannah *WhoHol 92*
Jones, Hardi Liddell 1942- *WhoBlA 94*
Jones, Harley M. 1936- *WhoBlA 94*
Jones, Harold Antony 1943- *WhoAm 94*
Jones, Harold Charles 1903- *WhoScEn 94*
Jones, Harold Gilbert, Jr. 1927- *WhoAm 94*
Jones, Harold Henry 1940- *WhoAmA 93*
Jones, Harold M. 1934- *WhoBlA 94*
Jones, Harold Roger 1947- *WhoWest 94*
Jones, Harry (Ernest) 1911- *Who 94*
Jones, Harry Willmer d1993 *NewYTBS 93 [port]*
Jones, Harvie Paul 1930- *WhoAm 94*
Jones, Haydn Harold 1920- *Who 94*
Jones, Hazel d1974 *WhoHol 92*
Jones, Hazel Lucile James 1915-1989 *WhAm 10*
Jones, Helen *WhoHol 92*
Jones, Helen 1903- *WrDr 94N*
Jones, Helen Hampton 1941- *WhoBlA 94*
Jones, Helen Hart 1921- *WhoAm 94*
Jones, Helen M. 1924- *WhoAmP 93*
Jones, Henrik 1960- *WhoWest 94*
Jones, Henry 1912- *IntMPA 94, WhoAm 94, WhoHol 92*
Jones, Henry Arthur 1851-1929 *BlmGEL, IntDcT 2*
Jones, Henry Arthur 1917- *Who 94*
Jones, Henry Earl 1940- *WhoAm 94*
Jones, Henry Wanton 1925- *WhoAmA 93*
Jones, Herb, Jr. 1923- *WhoAmA 93*
Jones, Herbert *WhoAmP 93*
Jones, Herbert, Jr. 1930- *WhoAmP 93*
Jones, Herbert C. 1936- *WhoBlA 94*
Jones, Herman Harvey, Jr. 1925- *WhoBlA 94*
Jones, Herman Otto, Jr. 1933- *WhoFI 94*
Jones, Hettie *DrAPF 93*
Jones, Hobert W 1957- *WhoScEn 94*
Jones, Horace Charles 1910- *WhoAm 94*
Jones, Hortense 1918- *WhoBlA 94*
Jones, Houston Gwynne 1924- *WhoAm 94*
Jones, Howard James 1944- *WhoBlA 94*
Jones, Howard Langworthy 1917- *WhoAm 94*
Jones, Howard St. Claire, Jr. 1921- *WhoAm 94, WhoScEn 94*
Jones, Howard W. 1895- *WhAm 10*
Jones, Howard Wilbur, Jr. 1910- *WhoAm 94*
Jones, Howard William 1922- *WhoAmA 93*
Jones, Hugh *Who 94*
Jones, (Robert William) Hugh 1911- *Who 94*
Jones, Hugh Alan 1950- *WhoAmP 93*
Jones, Hugh Duncan Hitchings 1937- *Who 94*
Jones, Hugh Edward 1955- *WhoMW 93*
Jones, Hugh (Hugo) Jarrett H. *Who 94*
Jones, Hugh M. 1944- *WhoAmL 94*
Jones, Hugh Richard 1914- *WhoAm 94*
Jones, Hugh Richard, Jr. 1938- *WhoAm 94*
Jones, Hughie *Who 94*
Jones, (Thomas) Hughie 1927- *Who 94*
Jones, Hywel Francis 1928- *Who 94*
Jones, Hywel Glyn 1948- *Who 94*
Jones, Hywel James 1918- *Who 94*
Jones, I. Gene *WhoBlA 94*
Jones, Ian C. *Who 94*
Jones, Ian E. *Who 94*
Jones, Ida Kilpatrick 1924- *WhoBlA 94*
Jones, Ida M. 1953- *WhoBlA 94*
Jones, Idus, Jr. 1927- *WhoBlA 94*
Jones, Ieuan Wyn 1949- *Who 94*
Jones, Ilston Percival Ll. *Who 94*
Jones, Ina *DrAPF 93*
Jones, Ingrid Saunders 1945- *WhoBlA 94*
Jones, Inigo 1573-1651 *BlmGEL*
Jones, Inigo 1573?-1652 *NewGrDO*
Jones, Isaac, Jr. 1933- *WhoBlA 94*
Jones, Isham d1956 *WhoHol 92*
Jones, Ivor R. *Who 94*
Jones, Ivy *WhoHol 92*
Jones, J. Barrie 1946- *WrDr 94*
Jones, J. Benton, Jr. 1930- *WhoAm 94*
Jones, J.E.M. *DrAPF 93*
Jones, J. Gilbert 1922- *WhoWest 94*
Jones, J. Kenley 1935- *WhoAm 94*
Jones, J. Kenneth 1945- *WhoAm 94*
Jones, J. Knox, Jr. 1929- *WhoAm 94*
Jones, J. L. 1962- *WhoMW 93*
Jones, J. Sorton 1941- *WhoAmL 94*
Jones, Jack 1938- *WhoHol 92*
Jones, Jack Allen 1935- *WhoScEn 94*
Jones, Jack Bristol 1931- *WhoWest 94*
Jones, Jack Dellis 1925- *WhoAm 94*
Jones, Jack Hugh 1944- *WhoScEn 94*
Jones, Jack L. *Who 94*
Jones, Jacobine *WhoAmA 93N*
Jones, Jacqueline 1948- *WrDr 94*
Jones, Jacqueline Yvonne 1928- *WhoAmP 93*
Jones, Jacqui *Who 94*
Jones, James *WhoBlA 94*
Jones, James (Duncan) 1914- *Who 94*
Jones, James A. 1932-1992 *WhoBlA 94N*
Jones, James A., III 1944- *WhoAmL 94*
Jones, James Arthur 1917- *WhoAm 94*
Jones, James Bennett 1931- *WhoBlA 94*
Jones, James Beverly 1923- *WhoScEn 94*
Jones, James C. 1913- *WhoBlA 94*
Jones, James E. 1931- *WhoAmP 93*
Jones, James Earl 1931- *AfrAmAl 6 [port], AmCulL, ConTFT 11, IntMPA 94, WhoAm 94, WhoBlA 94, WhoHol 92*
Jones, James Edward 1937- *WhoAmA 93*
Jones, James Edward 1939- *WhoMW 93*
Jones, James Edward, Jr. 1924- *WhoAm 94, WhoBlA 94*
Jones, James Eirug Thomas 1927- *Who 94*
Jones, James Fleming, Jr. 1947- *WhoAm 94*
Jones, James Francis, Jr. 1934- *WhoAmP 93*
Jones, James G. 1936- *WhoBlA 94*
Jones, James Gary 1950- *WhoAmP 93*
Jones, James Graham 1948- *WhoAm 94*
Jones, James Harold 1930- *WhoWest 94*
Jones, James L. 1949- *WhoAmL 94*
Jones, James Lamar 1958- *WhoMW 93, WhoScEn 94*
Jones, James Larkin 1913- *IntWW 93, Who 94*
Jones, James Leonard 1945- *WhoAm 94*
Jones, James McCoy 1941- *WhoBlA 94*
Jones, James Ogden 1935- *WhoScEn 94*
Jones, James P. 1914- *WhoBlA 94*
Jones, James Parker 1940- *WhoAm 94, WhoAmP 93*
Jones, James R. 1939- *WhoAm 94, WhoFI 94*
Jones, James R., III 1944- *WhoBlA 94*
Jones, James Ray 1958- *WhoScEn 94*
Jones, James Rees 1916- *WhoAm 94*
Jones, James Richard 1940- *WhoAm 94*
Jones, James Robert 1939- *WhoAmP 93*
Jones, James Roosevelt 1961- *WhoBlA 94*
Jones, James Thomas 1942- *WhoAmP 93*
Jones, James Thomas 1949- *WhoFI 94*
Jones, James Thomas, Jr. 1946- *WhoFI 94*
Jones, James V. 1942- *WhoBlA 94*
Jones, James W. 1945- *WhoAmL 94*
Jones, James Warren 1931-1978 *DcAmReB 2*
Jones, James Wesley 1935- *WhoBlA 94*
Jones, Jan Laverty *WhoAmP 93, WhoWest 94*
Jones, Janet 1962- *WhoHol 92*
Jones, Janet Benson J.B. *WhoWest 94*
Jones, Janet Lee 1957- *WhoScEn 94*
Jones, Janette Lee 1953- *WhoWest 94*
Jones, Jean *DrAPF 93*
Jones, Jeffery Lynn 1960- *WhoScEn 94*
Jones, Jeffrey *WhoHol 92*
Jones, Jeffrey 1947- *IntMPA 94*
Jones, Jeffrey Foster 1944- *WhoAm 94, WhoAmL 94*
Jones, Jeffrey J. 1952- *WhoAmL 94*
Jones, Jeffrey Richard 1921- *Who 94*
Jones, Jenk, Jr. 1936- *WhoAm 94*
Jones, Jenkin Lloyd 1843-1918 *DcAmReB 2*
Jones, Jenkin Lloyd 1911- *WhoAm 94*
Jones, Jennie Y. 1921- *WhoBlA 94*
Jones, Jennifer *Who 94, WhoBlA 94*
Jones, Jennifer 1919- *IntMPA 94, WhoHol 92*
Jones, Jennifer Lynn 1968- *WhoFI 94*
Jones, Jennifer Lynne 1966- *WhoAmL 94*
Jones, Jennings Hinch 1913- *WhoAm 94*
Jones, Jerald Elton 1932- *WhoAmL 94*
Jones, Jerome B. 1947- *WhoBlA 94*
Jones, Jerrauld Cory 1954- *WhoAmP 93*
Jones, Jerry *WhoHol 92*
Jones, Jerry 1942- *WhoAm 94*
Jones, Jerry Edward 1951- *WhoScEn 94*
Jones, Jerry Lee 1953- *WhoFI 94*
Jones, Jerry Lynn 1933- *WhoAm 94*
Jones, Jerry R. 1940- *WhoIns 94*
Jones, Jerve Maldwyn 1918- *WhoWest 94*
Jones, Jesse W. 1931- *WhoAmP 93, WhoBlA 94*
Jones, Jim Belton 1940- *WhoAmP 93*
Jones, Jimmie Dene 1939- *WhoBlA 94*
Jones, Jimmy 1945- *BasBi*
Jones, Jo d1985 *WhoHol 92*
Jones, Joanna 1922- *WrDr 94*
Jones, Joanna Patricia 1935- *WhoWest 94*
Jones, Jocelyn *WhoHol 92*
Jones, Joe d1993 *NewYTBS 93*
Jones, Joel Mackey 1937- *WhoAm 94, WhoWest 94*
Jones, John *Who 94*
Jones, John (Henry) 1942- *ConAu 140*
Jones, (Henry) John (Franklin) 1924- *Who 94, WrDr 94*
Jones, John (Lewis) 1923- *Who 94*
Jones, John Arthur 1921- *WhoAm 94, WhoAmL 94*
Jones, John Bailey 1927- *WhoAm 94, WhoAmL 94*
Jones, John Barclay, Jr. 1928- *WhoAm 94*
Jones, John Buttrick 1824-1876 *EncNAR*
Jones, John Charles 1921- *WhoAm 94*
Jones, John Earl 1934- *WhoAm 94, WhoFI 94*
Jones, John Elfed 1933- *Who 94*
Jones, John Ellis 1941- *WhoFI 94*
Jones, John Ernest A. *Who 94*
Jones, John Ernest P. *Who 94*
Jones, John Evan 1930- *WhoAm 94*
Jones, John F(inbar) 1929- *WrDr 94*
Jones, John Finbar 1929- *WhoWest 94*
Jones, John Frank 1922- *WhoAmL 94*
Jones, John Gornal 1938- *WhoAm 94*
Jones, John H. *Who 94*
Jones, John H., Jr. 1944- *WhoIns 94*
Jones, John Harris 1922- *WhoAm 94*
Jones, John Henry H. *Who 94*
Jones, John Hubert E. *Who 94*
Jones, John Knighton C. *Who 94*
Jones, John L. 1939- *WhoBlA 94*
Jones, John Lou 1929- *WhoAm 94*
Jones, John Martin, Jr. 1928- *WhoAm 94*
Jones, John Maurice 1931- *Who 94*
Jones, John Murray R. *Who 94*
Jones, John P. 1915- *WhoBlA 94*
Jones, John Paul 1747-1792 *AmRev, HisWorL [port], WhAmRev [port]*
Jones, John Paul 1924- *WhoAmA 93*
Jones, John Paul 1944- *WhoAmL 94*
Jones, John Philip 1930- *WrDr 94*
Jones, John Prichard *Who 94*
Jones, John R(obert) 1926- *SmATA 76 [port]*
Jones, John Stephen Langton d1992 *Who 94N*
Jones, John T. 1940- *WhoIns 94*
Jones, John Treasure d1993 *NewYTBS 93*
Jones, John Wesley 1942- *WhoFI 94, WhoWest 94*
Jones, Johnie H. 1929- *WhoAm 94, WhoFI 94*
Jones, Johnnie A., III 1953- *WhoAmL 94, WhoWest 94*
Jones, Johnnie Anderson 1919- *WhoBlA 94*
Jones, Johnny d1962 *WhoHol 92*
Jones, Johnny L. 1933- *WhoBlA 94*
Jones, Joie Pierce 1941- *WhoAm 94*
Jones, Jon Shayne 1959- *WhoMW 93*
Jones, Jonathan d1978 *WhoHol 92*
Jones, Jonathan Owen 1954- *Who 94*
Jones, Joni Lou 1932- *WhoBlA 94*
Jones, Joseph 1727-1805 *WhAmRev*
Jones, Joseph 1928- *WhoBlA 94*
Jones, Joseph John 1909-1963 *WhoAmA 93N*
Jones, Joseph Marion, Jr. 1908-1990 *WhAm 10*
Jones, Joseph Wayne 1936- *WhoAm 94*
Jones, Joy Vida 1950- *WhoAmL 94*
Jones, Judy Ann 1935- *WhoAmP 93*
Jones, Judy Voss 1949- *WhoAmA 93*
Jones, Julia 1923- *WrDr 94*
Jones, Julia Coleman 1919- *WhoAmP 93*
Jones, Julia Hughes 1939- *WhoAmP 93*
Jones, Julie 1935- *WhoAm 94*
Jones, K.C. 1932- *BasBi, WhoAm 94, WhoBlA 94*
Jones, K. Steven 1944- *WhoAmL 94*
Jones, Karen Mae 1938- *WhoMW 93*
Jones, Katharine Jean 1940- *WhoScEn 94*
Jones, Katherine Elizabeth Butler 1936- *WhoBlA 94*
Jones, Kathleen 1922- *Who 94*
Jones, Kathy 1949- *IntMPA 94*
Jones, Kaylie *DrAPF 93*
Jones, Kaylie (Ann) 1960- *WrDr 94*
Jones, Keith (Stephen) 1911- *Who 94*
Jones, Keith Alden 1941- *WhoAm 94*
Jones, Keith H. *Who 94*
Jones, Kelsey A. 1933- *WhoBlA 94*
Jones, Ken 1930- *WhoHol 92*
Jones, Ken 1938-1993 *WhoBlA 94N*
Jones, Kenneth *Who 94*
Jones, Kenneth (George Illtyd) 1921- *Who 94*
Jones, (John) Kenneth (Trevor) 1910- *Who 94*
Jones, Kenneth Leroy *WhoBlA 94*
Jones, Kenneth MacDonald 1947- *WhoMW 93*
Jones, Kenneth Merle 1937- *WhoWest 94*
Jones, Kenneth Sheldon, II 1968- *WhoAmP 93*
Jones, Kensinger 1919- *WhoAm 94*
Jones, Kenton Rush 1967- *WhoWest 94*
Jones, Kevin Raymond 1953- *WhoMW 93*
Jones, King Solomon *WhoBlA 94*
Jones, Kirkland C. 1938- *WhoBlA 94*
Jones, Kristin 1956- *WhoAmA 93*
Jones, L. Q. 1927- *WhoAm 94, WhoHol 92*
Jones, Lafayette Glenn 1944- *WhoBlA 94*
Jones, Landon Y., Jr. *WhoAm 94*
Jones, Landon Y(oung) 1943- *WrDr 94*
Jones, Langdon 1942- *EncSF 93*
Jones, Larry *DrAPF 93*
Jones, Larry 1941- *BasBi*
Jones, Larry Earl 1946- *WhoBlA 94*
Jones, Larry Mallory 1939- *WhoAmP 93*
Jones, Larry Wayne 1950- *WhoBlA 94*
Jones, Laura Ann 1968- *WhoMW 93*
Jones, Lauren *WhoHol 92*
Jones, Lauren Denise 1964- *WhoAmL 94*
Jones, Laurence (Alfred) 1933- *Who 94*
Jones, Lauretta Marie 1953- *WhoAm 94*
Jones, Laurie Ganong 1936- *WhoWest 94*
Jones, Laurie Lynn 1947- *WhoAm 94*
Jones, Lawrence Kelly 1953- *WhoAmL 94*
Jones, Lawrence Marion 1931- *WhoMW 93*
Jones, Lawrence McCeney, Jr. 1924- *WhoAm 94*
Jones, Lawrence N. 1921- *WhoBlA 94*
Jones, Lawrence Neale 1921- *WhoAm 94*
Jones, Lawrence Ryman 1921- *WhoScEn 94*
Jones, Lawrence Tunnicliffe 1950- *WhoAmL 94*
Jones, Lawrence W. 1942- *WhoBlA 94*
Jones, Lawrence William 1925- *WhoAm 94, WhoMW 93*
Jones, Le Roi *IntWW 93*
Jones, (Everett) Le Roi (Imamu Baraka) 1934- *IntWW 93*
Jones, Leander Corbin 1934- *WhoBlA 94, WhoMW 93*
Jones, Lee Bennett 1938- *WhoAm 94*
Jones, Leeland Newton, Jr. 1921- *WhoBlA 94*
Jones, Lemuel B. 1929- *WhoBlA 94*
Jones, Leon C. 1919- *WhoBlA 94*
Jones, Leon Herbert, Jr. 1923- *WhoAm 94*
Jones, Leonade Diane 1947- *WhoAm 94, WhoBlA 94*
Jones, Leonard Dale 1948- *WhoScEn 94*
Jones, Leonard Virgil 1921-1993 *WhoBlA 94N*
Jones, Leora 1960- *WhoBlA 94*
Jones, LeRoi *BlkWr 2, ConDr 93, DrAPF 93, IntDcT 2*
Jones, LeRoi 1934- *WhoAm 94, WhoBlA 94*
Jones, (Everett) LeRoi 1934- *WrDr 94*
Jones, Leslie 1917- *Who 94*
Jones, Lewis Bevel, III 1926- *WhoAm 94*
Jones, Lewis C. *Who 94*
Jones, Lilian Pauline N. *Who 94*
Jones, Lillie Agnes 1910- *WhoWest 94*
Jones, Lillie Mae 1929- *WhoAm 94*
Jones, Lincoln, III 1933- *WhoAm 94*
Jones, Linda Bebko 1946- *WhoAmP 93*
Jones, Linda Den Besten 1947- *WhoAm 94*
Jones, Lisa 1961- *WrDr 94*
Jones, Lisa Payne 1958- *WhoBlA 94*
Jones, Lloyd *WhoAmP 93*
Jones, Lloyd O. 1944- *WhoBlA 94*
Jones, Lois Mailou *WhoAm 94*
Jones, Lois Mailou 1905- *WhoAmA 93, WhoBlA 94*
Jones, Lois Swan 1927- *WhoAmA 93*
Jones, Lorean Electa 1938- *WhoBlA 94*
Jones, Loren Farquhar 1905- *WhoAm 94*
Jones, Lou *WhoAmA 93*
Jones, Louis B. *ConAu 141*
Jones, Louis C. 1908-1990 *WhoAmA 93N*
Jones, Louis Clayton 1935- *WhoBlA 94*
Jones, Lovana S. 1935- *WhoAmP 93*
Jones, Lucian Cox 1942- *WhoAm 94, WhoAmL 94*
Jones, Lucinda 1971- *WhoHol 92*
Jones, Lucius 1918- *WhoBlA 94*
Jones, Lyle Vincent 1924- *IntWW 93, WhoAm 94*
Jones, Lynn Harvard 1947- *WhoFI 94*
Jones, Lynne Mary 1951- *Who 94*
Jones, Mable Veneida 1950- *WhoBlA 94*
Jones, Madison (Percy, Jr.) 1925- *WrDr 94*
Jones, Madison Ralph, III 1938- *WhoAmL 94*
Jones, Maitland, Jr. 1937- *WhoScEn 94*
Jones, Malcolm V(ince) 1940- *WrDr 94*
Jones, Malinda Thiessen 1947- *WhoFI 94*
Jones, Marc Edmund 1888-1980 *AstEnc*
Jones, Marcia Mae 1924- *WhoHol 92*
Jones, Marcus Earl 1943- *WhoBlA 94*
Jones, Marcus Edmund 1960- *WhoBlA 94*
Jones, Margaret *EncSF 93*
Jones, Margaret Doris 1942- *WhoFI 94*
Jones, Margaret E. W 1938- *WrDr 94*
Jones, Margaret Eileen Zee 1936- *WhoAm 94*

Jones, Sherman Jarvis 1935- WhoAmP 93, WhoBlA 94
Jones, Shirley 1933- WhoHol 92
Jones, Shirley 1934- IntMPA 94, WhoAm 94
Jones, Shirley Ann Who 94
Jones, Shirley Joan 1931- WhoBlA 94
Jones, Shirley M. 1939- WhoAmP 93
Jones, Shirley Machocky 1937- WhoAmP 93
Jones, (James) Sidney 1861-1946 NewGrDO
Jones, Sidney A., Jr. 1909- WhoBlA 94
Jones, Sidney Alexander 1934- WhoBlA 94
Jones, Sidney Eugene 1936- WhoBlA 94
Jones, Sidney Lewis 1933- WhoAm 94
Jones, Sidney Pope, Jr. WhoAmP 93
Jones, Silas DrAPF 93
Jones, Simmons 1920- WrDr 94
Jones, Simon 1950- WhoHol 92
Jones, Simon (Warley Frederick) Benton 1941- Who 94
Jones, (Matilda) Sissieretta 1869-1933 NewGrDO
Jones, Sondra Michelle 1948- WhoBlA 94
Jones, Sonia Josephine 1945- WhoFI 94
Jones, Sonny d1990 WhoHol 92
Jones, Sophia Lorraine 1967- WhoMW 93
Jones, Spencer 1946- WhoBlA 94
Jones, Spike d1965 WhoHol 92
Jones, Spike 1911-1965 WhoCom
Jones, Stan ProFbHF
Jones, Stan d1963 WhoHol 92
Jones, Stanley Bernard 1961- WhoBlA 94
Jones, Stanley Boyd 1938- WhoAm 94
Jones, Stanley Conroy 1964- WhoMW 93
Jones, Stanley Seburn, Jr. 1949- WhoAmL 94
Jones, Stephan L. 1935- WhoIns 94
Jones, Stephanie Tubbs 1949- WhoBlA 94
Jones, Stephen Who 94
Jones, Stephen 1940- WhoAmL 94, WhoAmP 93
Jones, Stephen 1953- WrDr 94
Jones, (John) Stephen 1944- Who 94
Jones, Stephen Barry 1938- Who 94
Jones, Stephen James 1945- WhoIns 94
Jones, Stephen Morris 1948- Who 94
Jones, Stephen R. DrAPF 93
Jones, Stephen Roger Curtis 1944- Who 94
Jones, Stephen W. 1942- WhoAmL 94
Jones, Stephen Wallace 1953- WhoMW 93
Jones, Stephen Witsell 1947- WhoAmL 94
Jones, Stephen Yates 1958- WhoScEn 94
Jones, Steven Charles 1948- WhoMW 93
Jones, Steven Emrys 1957- WhoAmL 94
Jones, Sue WhoHol 92
Jones, Susan WhoHol 92
Jones, Susan Emily 1948- WhoAm 94
Jones, Susan Short 1953- WhoAmL 94
Jones, Susan Sutton WhoBlA 94
Jones, Suzanne Ellis 1953- WhoAmP 93
Jones, T. C. d1971 WhoHol 92
Jones, T. Lawrence WhoIns 94
Jones, Terence Leavesley 1926- Who 94
Jones, Terence Valentine 1939- Who 94
Jones, Terrence Dale 1948- WhoMW 93
Jones, Terry 1942- IntMPA 94, Who 94, WhoAm 94, WhoHol 92
See Also Monty Python's Flying Circus WhoCom
Jones, Thad 1923-1986 AfrAmAl 6
Jones, Thaddeus d1960 WhoHol 92
Jones, Theodore WhoAmP 93
Jones, Theodore 1923- WhoBlA 94
Jones, Theodore A. WhoBlA 94
Jones, Theodore Cornelius 1941- WhoBlA 94
Jones, Theodore Joseph 1938- WhoAmA 93
Jones, Theodore Lawrence 1920- WhoAm 94, WhoAmL 94, WhoFI 94
Jones, Theodore William 1924- WhoAm 94
Jones, Theresa C. WhoBlA 94
Jones, Theresa Diane 1953- WhoBlA 94
Jones, Theresa Mitchell 1917- WhoBlA 94
Jones, Thom 1945?- ConLC 81 [port]
Jones, Thomas 1731-1792 AmRev, WhAmRev
Jones, Thomas A. 1945- WhoAmP 93
Jones, Thomas C. 1946- WhoIns 94
Jones, Thomas Chester 1946- WhoAm 94
Jones, Thomas Curtis 1939- WhoAm 94
Jones, Thomas E. Who 94
Jones, Thomas Edward 1948- WhoFI 94
Jones, Thomas Glanville 1931- Who 94
Jones, Thomas Gordon 1951- WhoScEn 94
Jones, Thomas Gwynn 1871-1949 DcNaB MP
Jones, Thomas John, Jr. 1955- WhoAmL 94
Jones, Thomas L. 1941- WhoBlA 94
Jones, Thomas Leroy 1918- WhoAmP 93
Jones, Thomas M. 1947- WhoAm 94, WhoAmP 93
Jones, Thomas Nance 1950- WhoAmL 94
Jones, Thomas Neal 1930- WhoAm 94
Jones, Thomas Philip 1931- IntWW 93
Jones, Thomas Quentin 1949- WhoMW 93
Jones, Thomas R. 1945- WhoAmL 94
Jones, Thomas Robert 1950- WhoWest 94
Jones, Thomas Russell 1913- WhoBlA 94
Jones, Thomas Victor 1920- IntWW 93
Jones, Thomas W. WhoBlA 94
Jones, Thomas W. 1949- WhoIns 94
Jones, Thomas Walter 1945- WhoAm 94
Jones, Thomas Watson 1951- WhoFI 94
Jones, Thomas Wharton 1808-1891 DcNaB MP
Jones, Thomas William 1942- WhoAmA 93
Jones, Thornton Keith 1923- WhoWest 94
Jones, Timothy Fraser 1931- Who 94
Jones, Tiny d1952 WhoHol 92
Jones, Tom DrAPF 93
Jones, Tom 1940- ConMus 11 [port], IntWW 93, News 93 [port], WhoAm 94
Jones, Tommy Lee 1946- IntMPA 94, WhoAm 94, WhoHol 92
Jones, Tommy Lee c. 1947- News 94-2 [port]
Jones, Tony Armstrong ConAu 43NR
Jones, Tony Clyde 1955- WhoFI 94
Jones, Too Tall 1951- WhoBlA 94
Jones, Tracey Kirk, Jr. 1917- WhoAm 94
Jones, Trefor d1965 WhoHol 92
Jones, Trevor Who 94, WhoHol 92
Jones, Trevor 1950- Who 94
Jones, (Owen) Trevor 1927- Who 94
Jones, Trevor David K. Who 94
Jones, Trevor Morgan 1899- NewGrDO
Jones, Trevor Owen 1930- WhoAm 94, WhoMW 93
Jones, Trina Wood WhoMW 93
Jones, Tristan 1924- WrDr 94
Jones, Ulysses, Jr. 1951- WhoAmP 93
Jones, Valerie Kaye 1956- WhoMW 93
Jones, Vann Kinckle 1940- WhoBlA 94
Jones, Vaughan Frederick Randal 1952- Who 94
Jones, Veda Rae Boyd 1948- WhoMW 93
Jones, Velma Lois WhoBlA 94
Jones, Vera June Who 94
Jones, Vera Massey 1943- WhoBlA 94
Jones, Vernon 1960- WhoAmP 93
Jones, Vernon A., Jr. 1924- WhoBlA 94
Jones, Vernon Quentin 1930- WhoScEn 94, WhoWest 94
Jones, Vernon Thomas 1929- WhoFI 94
Jones, Victoria Gene 1948- WhoBlA 94
Jones, Vincent S. d1993 NewYTBS 93 [port]
Jones, Viola 1933- WhoBlA 94
Jones, Virgil 1949- WhoAmP 93
Jones, Virginia Jemison 1966- WhoAmL 94
Jones, Volcano 1932- WrDr 94
Jones, W. Louis 1943- WhoAmA 93
Jones, W. Robert 1937- WhoIns 94
Jones, W. Seaborn 1942- WhoAmL 94
Jones, W. Wilson 1945- WhoAmL 94
Jones, Wallace d1936 WhoHol 92
Jones, Wallace Sylvester 1917-1989 WhAm 10
Jones, Walter B., Jr. WhoAmP 93
Jones, Walter Beaman 1913-1992 AnObit 1992, WhAm 10
Jones, Walter Bryan 1895- WhAm 10
Jones, Walter Dean 1938- WhoMW 93
Jones, Walter Harrison 1922- WhoAm 94, WhoScEn 94
Jones, Walter Heath Who 94
Jones, Walter L. 1928- WhoBlA 94
Jones, Walter Minitre, III 1955- WhoAmL 94
Jones, Walton Linton 1918- WhoAm 94, WhoScEn 94
Jones, Wanda Carol 1956- WhoWest 94
Jones, Warren David 1914- WhoAm 94
Jones, Warren Thomas 1942- WhoAm 94
Jones, Wayne M. 1954- WhoAmP 93, WhoMW 93
Jones, Webb WrDr 94
Jones, Wendell Oren 1941- WhoWest 94
Jones, Wilbur Boardman, Jr. 1915- WhoAm 94
Jones, Wilbur Devereux 1916- WrDr 94
Jones, Wilfred 1926- Who 94
Jones, Wilfred Denton 1922- WhoAmP 93
Jones, William 1753-1822 WhAmRev
Jones, William 1760-1831 WhAmRev
Jones, William 1934- WhoBlA 94
Jones, William A., Jr. 1934- WhoBlA 94
Jones, William Allen 1941- WhoAm 94, WhoAmL 94, WhoBlA 94, WhoFI 94
Jones, William Armand Thomas Tristan G. Who 94
Jones, William Arnold 1924- WhoAm 94
Jones, William Augustus, Jr. 1927- WhoAm 94, WhoMW 93
Jones, William Benjamin, Jr. 1924- WhoAm 94
Jones, William Bowdoin 1928- WhoAm 94, WhoBlA 94
Jones, William C. 1933- WhoBlA 94
Jones, William Catron 1926- WhoAm 94
Jones, William Charles 1937- WhoWest 94
Jones, William Edward 1930- WhoBlA 94
Jones, William Edward 1942- WhoAm 94, WhoWest 94
Jones, William Ernest 1936- WhoAm 94
Jones, William George Tilston 1942- Who 94
Jones, William H. 1932- WhoAmP 93
Jones, William Harold 1952- WhoAmP 93
Jones, William Hawood 1927- WhoWest 94
Jones, William Houston 1932- WhoFI 94
Jones, William J. 1915- WhoBlA 94
Jones, William James 1933- WhoMW 93
Jones, William Jenipher 1912- WhoBlA 94
Jones, William Kenneth 1930- WhoAm 94
Jones, William Kinzy 1946- WhoScEn 94
Jones, William Lawless 1914- WhoBlA 94
Jones, William Leon 1949- WhoAmP 93
Jones, William McKendrey 1927- WhoAm 94
Jones, William O. WhoBlA 94
Jones, William Pearce A. Who 94
Jones, William Randall 1955- WhoAm 94
Jones, William Rex 1922- WhoAm 94, WhoAmL 94
Jones, William Ronald 1933- WhoBlA 94
Jones, William Vincent 1952- WhoScEn 94
Jones, William W. 1928- WhoBlA 94
Jones, Willie 1740-1801 WhAmRev
Jones, Willie 1932- WhoBlA 94
Jones, Willie C. 1941- WhoBlA 94
Jones, Winton Dennis, Jr. 1941- WhoBlA 94
Jones, Woodrow Harold 1913- WhoBlA 94
Jones, Wyn Who 94
Jones, (Graham) Wyn 1943- Who 94
Jones, (Gwilym) Wyn 1926- Who 94
Jones, Wynn Normington H. Who 94
Jones, Yvonne De Marr WhoBlA 94
Jones, Yvonne Harris WhoBlA 94
Jones, Yvonne Vivian 1946- WhoBlA 94
Jones, Zoia L. 1926- WhoBlA 94
Jones & Ginzel WhoAmA 93
Jonesco, Jane Riggs 1949- WhoMW 93
Jones-Davis, Georgia 1951- WhoWest 94
Jones-Grimes, Mable Christine 1943- WhoBlA 94
Jones Hammond, Katherine Ann 1953- WhoMW 93
Jones-Johnson, Gloria 1956- WhoMW 93
Jones-Lyons, Monika 1949- WhoFI 94
Jones-Moreland, Betsy WhoHol 92
Jones Parry, Emyr 1947- Who 94
Jones-Pugliese, Julia d1993 NewYTBS 93
Jones-Schenk, Janea 1952- WhoWest 94
Jones-Shoemaker, Cynthia Cavenaugh 1938- WhoAm 94
Jones-Smith, Jacqueline 1952- WhoAm 94, WhoAmP 93, WhoBlA 94, WhoFI 94
Jones-Steinberg, Lee Ann 1960- WhoFI 94
Jones-Trent, Bernice R. 1946- WhoBlA 94
Jones-Williams, Dafydd Wyn 1916- Who 94
Jones-Wilson, Faustine Clarisse 1927- WhoAm 94, WhoBlA 94
Jong, Dola de 1911- BlmGWL
Jong, Erica DrAPF 93
Jong, Erica 1942- BlmGWL
Jong, Erica (Mann) 1942- EncSF 93, WrDr 94
Jong, Erica Mann 1942- IntWW 93, WhoAm 94
Jong, Mark M. T. 1937- WhoAsA 94
Jong, Petrus J. S. de 1915- IntWW 93
Jong, Theresa Ann 1965- WhoFI 94
Jongen, Leon (Marie Victor Justin) 1884-1969 NewGrDO
Jongeward, George Ronald 1934- WhoScEn 94, WhoWest 94
Jonish, Arley Duane 1927- WhoAm 94
Jonish, James Edward 1941- WhoAm 94
Jonke, Erica Elizabeth 1969- WhoScEn 94
Jonker, Ingrid 1933-1965 BlmGWL
Jonker, Nate WhoAmP 93
Jonker, Peter Emile 1948- WhoWest 94
Jonkiert, Casimir S. 1928- WhoAmP 93
Jonkman, (Pieter Jan) Hans 1925- Who 94
Jonkouski, Jill Ellen WhoMW 93
Jonsen, Albert R. 1931- IntWW 93, WhoAm 94
Jonson, Ben 1572?-1637 DramC 4 [port], NewGrDO
Jonson, Ben(jamin) 1572-1637 IntDcT 2 [port]
Jonson, Benjamin 1572-1637 BlmGEL
Jonson, Dan L. 1943- WhoIns 94
Jonson, Jon M. 1893-1947 WhoAmA 93N
Jonson, Raymond 1891-1982 WhoAmA 93N
Jonsson, Eysteinn 1906- IntWW 93
Jonsson, Inge 1928- IntWW 93
Jonsson, Jens Johannes 1922- WhoAm 94
Jonsson, John Norman 1925- WhoAm 94
Jonsson, Kjartan A. 1940- WhoFI 94
Jonsson, Lars Olov 1952- WhoScEn 94
Jonsson, Reidar ConAu 140
Jonsson, Richard Eugene 1935- WhoWest 94
Jonsson, Ted 1933- WhoAmA 93
Jontiff, Scott Jeffrey 1962- WhoAmL 94
Jontz, Gale Prather 1955- WhoFI 94
Jontz, James 1951- WhoAmP 93
Jontz, Jeffry Robert 1944- WhoAm 94, WhoAmL 94
Jontz, Polly 1928- WhoAm 94
Jonzen, Karin 1914- Who 94
Joose, Barbara M(onnot) 1949- WrDr 94
Joost, Richard Elmer 1957- WhoMW 93
Jooste, Gerhardus Petrus 1904- HisDcKW
Joost-Gaugier, Christiane L. WhoAmA 93
Joost-Gaugier, Christiane Louise WhoWest 94
Jope, Edward Martyn 1915- IntWW 93, Who 94
Joplin, Albert Frederick 1919- WhoFI 94, WhoWest 94
Joplin, Graham Frank 1927- IntWW 93
Joplin, Janis d1970 WhoHol 92
Joplin, Janis Lyn 1943-1970 AmCulL
Joplin, Julian Mike 1936- WhoAm 94, WhoAmL 94
Joplin, Larry E. 1946- WhoAmL 94
Joplin, Scott 1868-1917 AfrAmAl 6 [port], AmCulL [port], ConBlB 6 [port], ConMus 10 [port], NewGrDO
Jopling, (Thomas) Michael 1930- IntWW 93, Who 94
Joppa, Robert Glenn 1922- WhoAm 94
Jorandby, Richard Leroy 1938- WhoAmL 94
Jorberg, Lennart 1927- IntWW 93
Jordahl, Geir Arild 1957- WhoWest 94
Jordan, Abbie H. WhoBlA 94
Jordan, Alexander Joseph, Jr. 1938- WhoAm 94, WhoAmL 94
Jordan, Alma Theodora 1929- WrDr 94
Jordan, Amos Azariah, Jr. 1922- WhoAm 94
Jordan, Angel Goni 1930- WhoAm 94
Jordan, Anne Devereaux 1943- WrDr 94
Jordan, Anne Harrison 1959- WhoAmL 94
Jordan, Anne Knight WhoBlA 94
Jordan, Arthur Kent 1932- WhoScEn 94
Jordan, Barbara DrAPF 93
Jordan, Barbara 1936- AfrAmAl 6 [port]
Jordan, Barbara 1957- BuCMET
Jordan, Barbara C. 1936- CurBio 93 [port], WhoAm 94
Jordan, Barbara Charline 1936- WhoBlA 94
Jordan, Barbara Schwinn WhoAm 94, WhoAmA 93
Jordan, Beth McAninch 1918- WhoAmA 93
Jordan, Bettye Davis 1946- WhoBlA 94
Jordan, Bobbi WhoHol 92
Jordan, Bobby d1965 WhoHol 92
Jordan, Bobby 1923-1965
See East Side Kids WhoCom
Jordan, Brian Lee 1964- WhoFI 94
Jordan, Brian O'Neil 1967- WhoBlA 94
Jordan, Bryce 1924- WhoAm 94
Jordan, Carl Rankin 1924- WhoBlA 94
Jordan, Carole 1941- Who 94
Jordan, Carolyn D. 1941- WhoBlA 94
Jordan, Carolyne Lamar WhoBlA 94
Jordan, Casper LeRoy 1924- WhoBlA 94
Jordan, Charles WhoHol 92
Jordan, Charles C. 1952- WhoAmL 94
Jordan, Charles F., Jr. 1943- WhoAmP 93
Jordan, Charles Milton 1949- WhoAm 94, WhoAmL 94
Jordan, Charles Morrell 1927- WhoAm 94, WhoFI 94
Jordan, Charles Wesley 1933- WhoAm 94, WhoBlA 94
Jordan, Charles William 1949- WhoMW 93
Jordan, Clarence L. 1930- WhoFI 94
Jordan, Clarence Lee 1897- WhAm 10
Jordan, Clifford d1993 NewYTBS 93 [port]
Jordan, Clifford Henry 1921- WhoAm 94
Jordan, Dan 1959- WhoAmP 93
Jordan, Daniel P(orter), Jr. 1938- WrDr 94
Jordan, Daniel R. E. 1960- WhoAmL 94
Jordan, Danny Joseph 1948- WhoWest 94
Jordan, Darin Godfrey 1964- WhoBlA 94

Jordan, Darrell Eddy 1938- *WhoAm 94*
Jordan, David *WhoAmP 93*
Jordan, David Crichton *WhoAmP 93*
Jordan, David Francis, Jr. 1928- *WhoAm 94, WhoAmL 94*
Jordan, David Harold 1924- *Who 94*
Jordan, David Lee 1933- *WhoBlA 94*
Jordan, David Lewis 1937- *WhoFI 94*
Jordan, David Loran 1933- *WhoAm 94*
Jordan, Don D. 1932- *WhoAm 94, WhoFI 94*
Jordan, Donald Lewis 1896- *WhAm 10*
Jordan, Doris *WhoHol 92*
Jordan, Dorothy d1988 *WhoHol 92*
Jordan, Douglas Arthur 1918- *Who 94*
Jordan, Eddie Jack, Sr. 1927- *WhoBlA 94*
Jordan, Edmond Rhodes 1955- *WhoAmP 93*
Jordan, Edward George 1929- *WhoAm 94*
Jordan, Edward Petrie, II 1959- *WhoAmL 94*
Jordan, Egon d1978 *WhoHol 92*
Jordan, Elke 1937- *WhoAm 94*
Jordan, Ellen Rausen 1943- *WhoWest 94*
Jordan, Emma Coleman 1946- *WhoBlA 94*
Jordan, Francis Leo 1930- *Who 94*
Jordan, Frank *WhoAmP 93*
Jordan, Frank George 1931- *WhoWest 94*
Jordan, Frank M. *WhoWest 94*
Jordan, Fred *WhoAm 94*
Jordan, Frederick Douglass 1901- *WhoBlA 94*
Jordan, Frederick E. 1937- *WhoBlA 94*
Jordan, Gary Patrick 1950- *WhoAmL 94*
Jordan, George E. 1957- *WhoBlA 94*
Jordan, George Edwin 1940- *WhoAmA 93*
Jordan, George Eugene 1953- *WhoScEn 94*
Jordan, George Lee, Jr. 1935- *WhoBlA 94*
Jordan, George Lyman, Jr. 1921- *WhoAm 94*
Jordan, George R., Jr. 1920- *WhoIns 94*
Jordan, George Washington, Jr. 1938- *WhoBlA 94, WhoFI 94, WhoScEn 94*
Jordan, Gerard Michael 1929- *Who 94*
Jordan, Glenn 1936- *IntMPA 94, WhoAm 94*
Jordan, Glenn Logan 1958- *WhoMW 93*
Jordan, Graham Harold Ben 1945- *Who 94*
Jordan, Gregory Wayne 1937- *WhoScEn 94*
Jordan, Hamilton *IntWW 93*
Jordan, (William) Hamilton (McWhorter) 1944- *IntWW 93*
Jordan, Hamilton McWhorter 1944- *WhoAm 94*
Jordan, Harold Willoughby 1937- *WhoBlA 94*
Jordan, Harvey Bryant 1895-1965 *EncABHB 9 [port]*
Jordan, Henrietta 1917- *IntMPA 94*
Jordan, Henry 1919- *Who 94*
Jordan, Henry Hellmut, Jr. 1921- *WhoFI 94*
Jordan, Henry Hunter, Jr. 1943- *WhoAmP 93*
Jordan, Hilary Peter 1952- *WhoAmL 94*
Jordan, Howard Emerson 1926- *WhoAm 94*
Jordan, Irene 1919- *NewGrDO*
Jordan, Irving King *WhoAm 94*
Jordan, J. St. Girard 1944- *WhoBlA 94*
Jordan, Jack 1927- *WhoAmA 93*
Jordan, Jack Terrell *WhoWest 94*
Jordan, James *WhoAm 94*
Jordan, James c. 1936-1993 *News 94-1*
Jordan, James Douglas, Jr. 1965- *WhoWest 94*
Jordan, Jeffrey Guy 1950- *WhoWest 94*
Jordan, Jennie R. *WhoAmP 93*
Jordan, Jerry Lee 1941- *WhoAm 94, WhoFI 94*
Jordan, Jerry Neville 1928- *WhoAm 94*
Jordan, Jim d1988 *WhoHol 92*
Jordan, Joan Kowalski 1941- *WhoFI 94*
Jordan, Joe J. 1923- *WhoAm 94*
Jordan, John Allen, Jr. 1935- *WhoAm 94*
Jordan, John Duffield d1984 *WhoHol 92*
Jordan, John E(mory) 1919- *WrDr 94*
Jordan, John Edward 1930- *WhoBlA 94*
Jordan, John Emory 1919- *WhoAm 94*
Jordan, John L. (Gaudeamus) 1944- *WhoAmA 93*
Jordan, John M. 1936- *WhoAmP 93*
Jordan, John Patrick 1934- *WhoAm 94*
Jordan, John Richard, Jr. 1921- *WhoAm 94, WhoAmP 93*
Jordan, John Wesley 1941- *WhoBlA 94*
Jordan, Joseph 1919-1992 *WhAm 10*
Jordan, Joseph Rembert 1947- *WhoAm 94*
Jordan, Josephine E. C. 1935- *WhoBlA 94*
Jordan, Judd L. 1950- *WhoAm 94*
Jordan, Juliet *WhoHol 92*
Jordan, June 1936- *AfrAmAl 6, BlkWr 2, BlmGWL, TwCYAW, WrDr 94*
Jordan, June M. 1936- *WhoAm 94, WhoBlA 94*
Jordan, Karen Leigh 1954- *WhoAm 94*
Jordan, Kathleen Marie 1951- *WhoAmP 93*
Jordan, Kathy 1959- *BuCMET*
Jordan, Keith *WhoAmP 93*
Jordan, Kenneth U. *AfrAmG [port]*
Jordan, Kenneth Ulys 1944- *WhoBlA 94*
Jordan, Larry M. *WhoAmP 93*
Jordan, Larry Reginald 1946- *AfrAmG [port]*
Jordan, Laura 1948- *WrDr 94*
Jordan, Lawrence William 1931- *WhoWest 94*
Jordan, Lee 1931- *WrDr 94*
Jordan, Lena E. *WhoAmA 93N*
Jordan, Leo Clayton 1943- *WhoAm 94*
Jordan, Leo John 1931- *WhoAm 94, WhoAmL 94*
Jordan, Leroy A. 1941- *WhoBlA 94*
Jordan, Lewis H. *WhoAm 94, WhoFI 94*
Jordan, Lillian *WhoAmP 93*
Jordan, Lois Heywood 1913- *WhoWest 94*
Jordan, Louis d1975 *WhoHol 92*
Jordan, Louis 1908-1975 *ConMus 11 [port]*
Jordan, Louis 1909-1975 *AfrAmAl 6 [port]*
Jordan, Louis Hampton 1922- *WhoAm 94*
Jordan, Luther H., Jr. 1950- *WhoAmP 93*
Jordan, Mabel B. 1912- *WhoBlA 94*
Jordan, Marian d1961 *WhoHol 92*
Jordan, Marilyn E. 1944- *WhoBlA 94*
Jordan, Marjorie W. 1924- *WhoBlA 94*
Jordan, Mark Henry 1915- *WhoAm 94, WhoScEn 94*
Jordan, Mary H. 1944- *WhoAmP 93*
Jordan, Mary Katharine 1963- *WhoMW 93*
Jordan, Max 1952- *WhoAmP 93*
Jordan, Michael *NewYTBS 93 [port]*
Jordan, Michael 1963- *AfrAmAl 6 [port], BasBi [port], ConBlB 6 [port], WhoBlA 94*
Jordan, Michael Anthony 1931- *Who 94*
Jordan, Michael B. 1949- *WhoAmL 94*
Jordan, Michael Hugh 1936- *WhoAm 94*
Jordan, Michael Jay 1954- *WhoAmL 94*
Jordan, Michael Jeffery 1963- *IntWW 93, WhoAm 94*
Jordan, Michelle Denise 1954- *WhoAm 94, WhoBlA 94*
Jordan, Michelle Henrietta 1948- *WhoAm 94*
Jordan, Milton C. *WhoBlA 94*
Jordan, Miriam 1908- *WhoHol 92*
Jordan, Neal Francis 1932- *WhoScEn 94*
Jordan, Neil 1950- *CurBio 93 [port], IntMPA 94, IntWW 93, News 93-3 [port], WrDr 94*
Jordan, Neil Patrick 1950- *WhoAm 94*
Jordan, Nora Margaret 1958- *WhoAmL 94*
Jordán, Octavio Manuel 1912- *WhoHisp 94*
Jordan, Orchid I. 1910- *WhoBlA 94*
Jordan, Orchid Irene 1910- *WhoAmP 93*
Jordan, (Zweledinga) Pallo 1942- *IntWW 93*
Jordan, Patricia Carter 1946- *WhoBlA 94*
Jordan, Patrick 1923- *WhoHol 92*
Jordan, Paul Howard, Jr. 1919- *WhoAm 94*
Jordan, Paul Scott (Ricky) 1965- *WhoBlA 94*
Jordan, Peggy *WhoHisp 94*
Jordan, Peter Albion 1930- *WhoMW 93*
Jordan, Peter Colin 1936- *WhoAm 94*
Jordan, Philip Harding, Jr. 1931- *WhoAm 94, WhoMW 93*
Jordan, Ralph 1926- *WhoBlA 94*
Jordan, Raymond A., Jr. 1943- *WhoAmP 93*
Jordan, Raymond Alan 1942- *WhoWest 94*
Jordan, Raymond Bruce 1912- *WhoWest 94*
Jordan, Rhoda d1962 *WhoHol 92*
Jordan, Richard d1993 *IntMPA 94N*
Jordan, Richard 1937- *IntMPA 94*
Jordan, Richard 1937-1993 *NewYTBS 93 [port]*
Jordan, Richard 1938- *WhoHol 92*
Jordan, Richard A. 1946- *WhoIns 94*
Jordan, Richard Bowen 1902- *Who 94*
Jordan, Richard Charles 1909- *WhoAm 94*
Jordan, Robert *ConAu 140, WhoBlA 94*
Jordan, Robert 1925- *WhoAmA 93*
Jordan, Robert 1940- *WhoAm 94*
Jordan, Robert A. 1932- *WhoBlA 94*
Jordan, Robert B. 1939- *ConAu 141*
Jordan, Robert B., III 1932- *WhoAmP 93*
Jordan, Robert Elijah, III 1936- *WhoAm 94*
Jordan, Robert Frederick 1950- *WhoAmL 94*
Jordan, Robert Howard, Jr. 1943- *WhoBlA 94*
Jordan, Robert K. 1948- *WhoAmL 94*
Jordan, Robert L. 1906- *WhoBlA 94*
Jordan, Robert Leon 1928- *WhoAm 94, WhoWest 94*
Jordan, Robert Leon 1934- *WhoAm 94, WhoAmL 94*
Jordan, Robert Maynard 1924- *WhoAm 94*
Jordan, Robert R. 1937- *WhoAm 94, WhoScEn 94*
Jordan, Robert Smith 1929- *WhoAm 94, WrDr 94*
Jordan, Robert Thomas 1937- *WhoFI 94*
Jordan, Robert W. 1945- *WhoAm 94, WhoAmL 94*
Jordan, Ruth 1926- *WrDr 94*
Jordan, Sally *WhoAmP 93*
Jordan, Sandra Dickerson 1951- *WhoAmL 94*
Jordan, Sharon Lee 1946- *WhoWest 94*
Jordan, Sharon Lee 1952- *WhoAmP 93*
Jordan, Sid d1970 *WhoHol 92*
Jordan, Sidney *EncSF 93*
Jordan, Stanley 1959- *WhoAm 94, WhoBlA 94*
Jordan, Steve Russell 1961- *WhoBlA 94*
Jordan, Steven Russell 1961- *WhoAm 94, WhoMW 93*
Jordan, Susan *DrAPF 93*
Jordan, Terry Gilbert 1938- *WhoAm 94*
Jordan, Terry L. 1948- *WhoAmP 93*
Jordan, Thomas Frederick 1936- *WhoAm 94*
Jordan, Thomas Hillman 1948- *WhoAm 94*
Jordan, Thomas L. d1993 *NewYTBS 93*
Jordan, Thomas Richard 1928- *WhoAm 94*
Jordan, Thurman 1936- *WhoBlA 94*
Jordan, V. Craig 1947- *WhoAm 94*
Jordan, Vance 1943- *WhoAmA 93*
Jordan, Vernon E., Jr. 1935- *AfrAmAl 6 [port], CurBio 93 [port], WhoBlA 94*
Jordan, Vernon Eulion, Jr. 1935- *WhoAm 94*
Jordan, Vincent Andre 1965- *WhoBlA 94*
Jordan, W. Carl 1949- *WhoAmL 94*
Jordan, Wayne Robert 1940- *WhoAm 94*
Jordan, Wesley Lee 1941- *WhoBlA 94*
Jordan, Wilbert Cornelious 1944- *WhoBlA 94*
Jordan, Will *WhoHol 92*
Jordan, Will 1929- *WhoCom*
Jordan, William *WhoHol 92*
Jordan, William Alfred, III 1934- *WhoBlA 94*
Jordan, William B. 1940- *WhoAmA 93*
Jordan, William Brian 1936- *Who 94*
Jordan, William Bryan, Jr. 1940- *WhoAm 94*
Jordan, William Chester 1948- *WhoAm 94*
Jordan, William Davis 1940- *WhoAm 94*
Jordan, William Reynier Van Evera, Sr. *WhoAm 94*
Jordan, William Spencer 1939- *WhoWest 94*
Jordan, Wilma Elizabeth Hacker 1948- *WhoAm 94*
Jordan, Winthrop Donaldson 1931- *WhoAm 94*
Jordan, Wrenza Lou 1929- *WhoAm 94*
Jordan-Dillon, Araceli 1954- *WhoHisp 94*
Jordan Haight, Mary Ellen 1927- *WrDr 94*
Jordan-Harris, Katherine 1927- *WhoBlA 94*
Jordan-Holmes, Clark 1946- *WhoAmL 94*
Jordania, Vakhtang 1942- *WhoWest 94*
Jordan-Moss, Norman 1920- *Who 94*
Jordano, Danny *WhoHol 92*
Jorden, Edwin William, Jr. 1947- *WhoAm 94*
Jorden, Eleanor Harz *WhoAm 94*
Jorden, James Roy 1934- *WhoAm 94, WhoScEn 94*
Jorden, William John 1923- *ConAu 140, WhoAm 94*
Jordon, Alexis Hill 1941- *WrDr 94*
Jordon, Harry d1945 *WhoHol 92*
Jordon, James T. 1925- *WhoAmP 93*
Jordon, Neil *HorFD*
Jordon, Robert Earl 1938- *WhoAm 94*
Jordy, William H 1917- *WrDr 94*
Jordy, William Henry 1917- *WhoAm 94*
Jorg *DrAPF 93*
Jorge, Antonio *WhoHisp 94*
Jorge, Edwin Santos 1940- *WhoHisp 94*
Jorge, Lidia 1946- *BlmGWL [port]*
Jorge, Nuno Maria Roque 1947- *WhoFI 94*
Jorge, Paul d1939 *WhoHol 92*
Jorge, Silvia 1945- *WhoHisp 94*
Jorgensen, Allison Mari-Dering 1961- *WhoMW 93*
Jorgensen, Anker 1922- *IntWW 93*
Jorgensen, Bo Barker 1946- *IntWW 93*
Jorgensen, Darrell L. 1953- *WhoAmP 93*
Jorgensen, Donald Allan 1952- *WhoWest 94*
Jorgensen, Emilius d1963 *WhoHol 92*
Jorgensen, Eric Edward 1961- *WhoScEn 94*
Jorgensen, Eric W. 1943- *WhoAmL 94*
Jorgensen, Erik 1921- *WhoAm 94*
Jorgensen, Erik Holger 1916- *WhoAmL 94, WhoWest 94*
Jorgensen, Flemming 1934- *WhoAmA 93*
Jorgensen, Gordon D. 1932- *WhoIns 94*
Jorgensen, Gordon David 1921- *WhoAm 94, WhoFI 94, WhoWest 94*
Jorgensen, Ivar *EncSF 93*
Jorgensen, Ivar 1935- *WrDr 94*
Jorgensen, James Douglas 1948- *WhoAm 94, WhoScEn 94*
Jorgensen, James H. 1946- *WhoScEn 94*
Jorgensen, John Marc 1961- *WhoFI 94*
Jorgensen, Joyce Orabelle 1928- *WhoWest 94*
Jorgensen, Judith Ann *WhoWest 94*
Jorgensen, Judy Hesler 1939- *WhoMW 93*
Jorgensen, Kay Susan 1951- *WhoAmP 93*
Jorgensen, Leland Howard 1924- *WhoScEn 94*
Jorgensen, Lou Ann Birkbeck 1931- *WhoWest 94*
Jorgensen, Mark Christopher 1951- *WhoWest 94*
Jorgensen, Palle Erik Tikob 1947- *WhoMW 93*
Jorgensen, Paul A(lfred) 1916- *WrDr 94*
Jorgensen, Paul Alfred 1916- *WhoAm 94, WhoWest 94*
Jorgensen, Paul J. 1930- *WhoAm 94*
Jorgensen, Ralph Gubler 1937- *WhoAmL 94*
Jorgensen, Richard E. *DrAPF 93*
Jorgensen, Roger M. 1919- *WhoAmA 93*
Jorgensen, Sandra 1934- *WhoAmA 93*
Jorgensen, Sven-Aage 1929- *IntWW 93*
Jorgensen, Thomas A. 1943- *WhoAmL 94*
Jorgensen, Tilton Dennis 1945- *WhoWest 94*
Jorgensen, William Ernest 1913- *WhoAm 94*
Jorgensen, William L. 1949- *WhoAm 94*
Jorgenson, Dale Alfred 1926- *WhoAmA 93*
Jorgenson, Dale W. 1933- *IntWW 93*
Jorgenson, Dale Weldeau 1933- *WhoAm 94*
Jorgenson, Gordon Victor 1933- *WhoMW 93*
Jorgenson, Ivar *EncSF 93*
Jorgenson, James Wallace 1952- *WhoScEn 94*
Jorgenson, Mary Ann 1941- *WhoAm 94, WhoAmL 94*
Jorisch, Gary Neal 1950- *WhoFI 94*
Jorn, Asger 1914-1973 *WhoAmA 93N*
Jorn, Karl 1873-1947 *NewGrDO*
Jorndt, Louis Daniel 1941- *WhoAm 94, WhoFI 94*
Jorne, Jacob 1941- *WhoAm 94*
Jorns, Byron Charles 1898-1958 *WhoAmA 93N*
Jorns, David Lee 1944- *WhoAm 94*
Joron, Andrew *DrAPF 93*
Jorre De St. Jorre, Danielle Marie-Madeleine 1941- *Who 94*
Jorritsma-Lebbink, Annemarie 1950- *WhoWomW 91*
Jorsater, Steven Bertil 1955- *WhoScEn 94*
Jorth, Bruce James 1959- *WhoFI 94*
Jortner, Joshua 1933- *IntWW 93, WhoScEn 94*
Jorve, Barry M. *WhoIns 94*
Jory, Edward John 1936- *IntWW 93*
Jory, Howard Roberts 1931- *WhoAm 94*
Jory, Victor d1982 *WhoHol 92*
Josbeno, Larry Joseph 1938- *WhoScEn 94*
Joscelyn, Kent Buckley 1936- *WhoAm 94, WhoAmL 94, WhoFI 94, WhoMW 93, WhoScEn 94*
Joscelyn, William Wilkie 1926- *WhoAmP 93*
Joscelyne, Richard Patrick 1934- *Who 94*
Jose, Edward d1930 *WhoHol 92*
Jose, Ernesto Y. 1938- *WhoHisp 94*
Jose, Felix 1965- *WhoHisp 94*
José, Jorge V. 1949- *WhoHisp 94*
Jose, Phyllis Ann 1949- *WhoMW 93*
Jose, Richard J. d1941 *WhoHol 92*
Joseff, Joan Castle 1922- *WhoFI 94*
Josefowits, Teri d1958 *WhoHol 92*
Josefowitz, Natasha *DrAPF 93*
Josefsen, Turi 1936- *WhoFI 94*
Jose-Kampfner, Christina 1950- *WhoHisp 94*
Joselow, Beth Baruch *DrAPF 93*
Joselyn, Jo Ann 1943- *WhoAm 94*
Joseph, Baron 1918- *IntWW 93, Who 94*

Joseph, II 1741-1790 HisWorL [port], NewGrDO
Joseph, Alfred S., III 1943- WhoAmL 94
Joseph, Allan Jay 1938- WhoAm 94
Joseph, Anita Davis 1948- WhoBlA 94
Joseph, Anthony Lee 1944- WhoAm 94
Joseph, Antoine L. 1923- WhoBlA 94
Joseph, Burton M. 1921- WhoAm 94
Joseph, Cedric Luckie 1933- IntWW 93
Joseph, Charles Homer, III 1948- WhoMW 93
Joseph, Daniel Donald 1929- WhoAm 94, WhoScEn 94
Joseph, Daniel Mordecai 1941- WhoAm 94, WhoAmL 94
Joseph, David DrAPF 93
Joseph, David J., Jr. 1916- WhoAm 94
Joseph, Donald Louis 1942- WhoFI 94
Joseph, Edward David 1919-1991 WhAm 10
Joseph, Eleanor Ann 1944- WhoMW 93
Joseph, Ellen R. WhoAmL 94
Joseph, Ezekiel 1938- WhoWest 94
Joseph, Frederick Harold 1937- WhoAm 94
Joseph, George Manley 1930- WhoWest 94
Joseph, Geraldine M. 1923- WhoAmP 93
Joseph, Geri Mack 1923- WhoAm 94
Joseph, Gregory Nelson 1946- WhoAm 94, WhoWest 94
Joseph, Gregory Paul 1951- WhoAm 94, WhoAmL 94
Joseph, Helen 1905-1992 AnObit 1992
Joseph, Helen (Beatrice May) 1905-1992 ConAu 140
Joseph, Jackie 1934- WhoHol 92
Joseph, James Alfred 1935- WhoAm 94, WhoBlA 94
Joseph, Jennifer Inez 1948- WhoBlA 94
Joseph, Jenny 1932- BlmGEL
Joseph, John 1923- WhoAm 94
Joseph, John Lawrence 1945- WhoAm 94
Joseph, Joseph Paul 1935- WhoAmP 93
Joseph, Judith R. 1948- WhoAm 94
Joseph, Jules K. 1927- WhoAm 94
Joseph, Kevin Mark 1954- WhoFI 94
Joseph, L. Anthony, Jr. 1940- WhoAm 94
Joseph, Lawrence DrAPF 93
Joseph, Leonard 1919- WhoAm 94
Joseph, Leslie 1925- Who 94
Joseph, Lloyd Leroi 1934- WhoBlA 94
Joseph, Lura Ellen 1947- WhoScEn 94
Joseph, M(ichael) K(ennedy) 1914-1981 EncSF 93
Joseph, Marjory L. 1917-1988 WhAm 10
Joseph, Maurice Franklin 1905- WhoAmP 93
Joseph, Metropolitan Bishop 1942- WhoAm 94
Joseph, Michael Anthony 1944- WhoAm 94
Joseph, Michael E. 1951- WhoAmL 94
Joseph, Michael Sarkies 1950- WhoAm 94
Joseph, Michael Thomas 1927- WhoAm 94
Joseph, Paul Gerard 1960- WhoScEn 94
Joseph, Paul R. 1951- WhoAmL 94
Joseph, Peter Maron 1939- WhoScEn 94
Joseph, Poet DrAPF 93
Joseph, Ramon Rafael 1930- WhoAm 94
Joseph, Raymond Alcide 1931- WhoBlA 94
Joseph, Rene Michele 1958- WhoMW 93
Joseph, Robert Edward 1935- WhoAm 94
Joseph, Robert George 1948- WhoAmL 94
Joseph, Robert Thomas 1946- WhoAm 94, WhoAmL 94
Joseph, Rodney Randy 1945- WhoFI 94
Joseph, Ronald G. WhoHol 92
Joseph, Ruth WhoAmP 93
Joseph, Stephen Laurence 1954- WhoAmL 94
Joseph, Stephen M. DrAPF 93
Joseph, Stephen M. 1938- WrDr 94
Joseph, Susan B. 1958- WhoAmL 94, WhoFI 94
Joseph, Todd M. 1950- WhoAmL 94
Joseph, Vivienne 1948- BlmGWL
Joseph, William A(llen) 1947- ConAu 41NR
Joseph, William R. 1946- WhoAmL 94
Joseph-McIntyre, Mary 1942- WhoBlA 94
Josephs, Babette 1940- WhoAmP 93
Josephs, Harold 1937- WhoFI 94
Josephs, Judith Belle 1956- WhoFI 94
Josephs, Laurence DrAPF 93
Josephs, Melvin Jay 1926- WhoAm 94, WhoScEn 94
Josephs, Naomi Malter 1929- WhoFI 94
Josephs, Ray 1912- WhoAm 94, WrDr 94
Josephs, Wilfred 1927- IntWW 93, NewGrDO, Who 94
Josephson, Brian D. WorInv
Josephson, Brian David 1940- IntWW 93, Who 94, WhoScEn 94, WorScD
Josephson, David Lane 1956- WhoWest 94
Josephson, Diana Hayward 1936- WhoAm 94, WhoWest 94
Josephson, Erland 1923- IntMPA 94, IntWW 93, WhoHol 92
Josephson, Harold Allan 1944- WhoWest 94
Josephson, Joe P. 1933- WhoAmP 93
Josephson, John Richard 1944- WhoMW 93
Josephson, Kenneth Bradley 1932- WhoAm 94, WhoAmA 93
Josephson, Linda Susan 1950- WhoWest 94
Josephson, Mark Eric 1943- WhoAm 94
Josephson, Marvin 1927- WhoAm 94
Josephson, Marvin A. 1927- IntMPA 94
Josephson, Richard Carl 1947- WhoAm 94
Josephson, Richard L. 1948- WhoAmL 94
Josephson, William Howard 1934- WhoAm 94, WhoAmL 94
Josephy, Alvin M., Jr. 1915- WrDr 94
Josephy, Robert S. 1903-1993 NewYTBS 93
Josey, Charles Conant 1893- WhAm 10
Josey, E. J. 1924- WhoBlA 94
Josey, E(lonnie) J(unius) 1924- BlkWr 2, ConAu 42NR
Josey, Elonnie Junius 1924- WhoAm 94
Josey, Leronia Arnetta WhoBlA 94
Joshi, Amol Prabhatchandra 1963- WhoScEn 94
Joshi, Bhairav D. 1939- WhoAsA 94
Joshi, Damayanti 1932- IntWW 93
Joshi, Harideo 1921- IntWW 93
Joshi, Jagmohan 1933- WhoAsA 94, WhoScEn 94
Joshi, Mukund Shankar 1947- WhoAsA 94
Joshi, Pravin d1979 WhoHol 92
Joshi, R. Malatesha 1946- WhoScEn 94
Joshi, S(unand) T(ryambak) 1958- WrDr 94
Joshi, Sada D. 1950- WhoAsA 94
Joshi, Satish Devdas 1950- WhoScEn 94, WhoWest 94
Joshi, Sewa Ram 1933- WhoAsA 94
Joshi, Sudha Vijay 1940- WhoWomW 91
Joshi, Suresh Meghashyam WhoAm 94
Joshi, Suresh Meghashyam 1946- WhoAsA 94
Joshua, Aaron 1957- WhoWest 94
Joshua, Larry WhoHol 92
Josi, Tim 1950- WhoAmP 93
Josiah, Walter J., Jr. 1933- IntMPA 94
Josif, Enriko 1924- NewGrDO
Josika, Miklos EncSF 93
Josimovich, George 1894- WhoAmA 93N
Josipovici, Gabriel 1940- BlmGEL
Josipovici, Gabriel (David) 1940- WrDr 94
Joskow, Jules WhoAm 94
Joskow, Paul Lewis 1947- WhoAm 94, WhoScEn 94
Joskow, Renee W. 1960- WhoScEn 94
Joslin, Alfred Hahn 1914-1991 WhAm 10
Joslin, Gary James 1943- WhoAmL 94
Joslin, Howard d1975 WhoHol 92
Joslin, Margaret d1956 WhoHol 92
Joslin, Margaret M. 1947- WhoAmL 94
Joslin, Norman E. 1925- WhoAmP 93
Joslin, Peter David 1933- Who 94
Joslin, Robert Scott 1929- WhoMW 93
Joslin, Rodney Dean 1944- WhoAm 94, WhoAmL 94
Joslin, Roger 1936- WhoIns 94
Joslin, Roger Scott 1936- WhoAm 94, WhoFI 94
Joslin, Sesyle 1929- WrDr 94
Josling, John Francis d1993 Who 94N
Joslyn, Allyn d1981 WhoHol 92
Joslyn, Jay Thomas 1923- WhoAm 94
Joslyn, Kristine B. 1948- WhoAmP 93
Joslyn, Wallace Danforth 1939- WhoMW 93
Joslyn Gage, Matilda 1826-1898 WomPubS
Josol, Sanny d1980 WhoHol 92
Jospin, Lionel Robert 1937- IntWW 93
Jospin, Walter Ehrenreich 1952- WhoAmL 94
Joss, Paul Christopher 1945- WhoAm 94
Joss, W. H. D. d1987 WhoHol 92
Joss, William Hay 1927- Who 94
Josselin, Ralph 1617-1683 DcNaB MP
Jossem, Jared H. 1942- WhoAmP 93
Jossem, Jared Haym 1942- WhoAmL 94
Josserand, Robert Warren 1896- WhoAmP 93
Josset, Lawrence 1910- Who 94
Josset, Raoul 1900-1957 WhoAmA 93N
Jost, H. Peter 1921- Who 94
Jost, Lawrence John 1944- WhoAm 94, WhoAmL 94
Jost, Lee Fred 1928- WhoMW 93
Jost, Peter Hafner 1949- WhoAm 94
Jost, Richard Frederic, III 1947- WhoAmL 94
Josten, Robert E. 1942- WhoAm 94, WhoAmL 94
Jostyn, Jay d1976 WhoHol 92
Joswick, David D. 1944- WhoAmL 94
Josz, Marcel 1899- WhoHol 92
Jotcham, Thomas Denis 1918- WhoAm 94, WhoFI 94
Joteyko, Tadeusz 1872-1932 NewGrDO
Jotikasthira, Tongchan 1933- Who 94
Jotischky, Andrew 1965- WrDr 94
Jotuni, Maria 1880-1943 BlmGWL
Jotwani, Chandru 1945- WhoAsA 94
Jouane, Patrick WhoHol 92
Joube, Romuald d1949 WhoHol 92
Joubert, Daniel Malan 1928- IntWW 93
Joubert, Elsa 1922- BlmGWL
Joubert, John (Pierre Herman) 1927- NewGrDO
Joubert, Linda BlmGWL
Joudry, Patricia 1921- BlmGWL
Jouett, Jack 1754-1822 AmRev
Joughin, Michael 1926- Who 94
Joukowsky, Artemis A. W. 1930- WhoAm 94
Joule, James Prescott 1818-1889 WorScD
Joulwan, George A. WhoAm 94
Jouppila, Riitta Marie Kaarina 1940- WhoWomW 91
Jourdain, Alice Marie 1923- WhoAm 94
Jourdain, John d1619 WhWE
Jourdain, (Emily) Margaret 1876-1951 DcNaB MP
Jourdain, Silvester d1650 WhWE
Jourdan, Albert M., Jr. 1935- WhoAmP 93
Jourdan, Catherine WhoHol 92
Jourdan, Louis 1920- IntMPA 94, WhoHol 92
Jourdan, Louis 1921- WhoAm 94
Jourdan, Raymond WhoHol 92
Jourdren, Marc Henri 1960- WhoAm 94, WhoFI 94
Jourgensen, Al 195-?- See Ministry ConMus 10
Jourjine, Alexander N. 1953- WhoScEn 94
Journet, Alan Robert Pierre 1945- WhoMW 93
Journet, Francoise d1720 NewGrDO
Journet, Marcel 1867-1933 NewGrDO [port]
Journey, Drexel Dahlke 1926- WhoAm 94, WhoAmL 94, WhoFI 94
Journey, Lula Mae 1934- WhoBlA 94
Journeycake, Charles 1817-1894 EncNAR
Jousset, Anne WhoHol 92
Joutel, Henri c. 1645-c. 1730 WhWE
Jouven, Pierre Jean Antoine 1908- IntWW 93
Jouvet, Louis d1951 WhoHol 92
Jouy, (Victor-Joseph-)Etienne de 1764-1846 NewGrDO
Jouzel, Jean 1947- WhoScEn 94
Jova, Henri Vatable 1919- WhoAm 94
Jova, Joseph J. d1993 NewYTBS 93
Jova, Joseph John 1916- IntWW 93, WhoAmP 93
Jova, Joseph John 1916-1993 WhoHisp 94N
Jovanovic, Miodrag 1936- WhoAm 94
Jovanovich, Peter William 1949- WhoAm 94
Jovanovich, William DrAPF 93
Jovanovich, William 1920- WrDr 94
Jovanovich, William Iliya 1920- IntWW 93
Jovanovski, Meto 1928- ConAu 142
Jove, Richard 1955- WhoMW 93, WhoScEn 94
jovel, jinni DrAPF 93
Jovene, Nicholas Angelo, Jr. 1938- WhoWest 94
Jover, Juan Manuel 1956- WhoFI 94
Jovick, Robert L. 1950- WhoWest 94
Jovine, Marcel 1921- WhoAmA 93
Jow, Pat WhoAmA 93
Jowell, Jeffrey Lionel 1938- Who 94
Jowell, Tessa Jane Helen Douglas 1947- Who 94
Jowers, Johnnie Edward, Sr. 1931- WhoBlA 94
Jowett, Alfred 1914- Who 94
Jowett, John Martin 1954- WhoScEn 94
Jowitt, Edwin (Frank) 1929- Who 94
Jowitt, Juliet Diana Margaret 1940- Who 94
Joxe, Pierre Daniel 1934- IntWW 93, Who 94
Joy, Brent Michael 1963- WhoWest 94
Joy, C. Turner 1895-1956 HisDcKW
Joy, Carla Marie 1945- WhoWest 94
Joy, Christipher WhoHol 92
Joy, Daniel Webster 1931- WhoBlA 94
Joy, David 1825-1903 DcNaB MP
Joy, David 1932- Who 94
Joy, David (Anthony Welton) 1942- WrDr 94
Joy, David Anthony 1957- WhoScEn 94
Joy, Donald Marvin 1928- WrDr 94
Joy, Edward Bennett 1941- WhoAm 94
Joy, Ernest d1924 WhoHol 92
Joy, Henry L. WhoAmP 93
Joy, James Bernard, Jr. 1937- WhoBlA 94
Joy, Leatrice d1985 WhoHol 92
Joy, Marilyn D. 1956- WhoMW 93
Joy, Michael Gerard Laurie d1993 Who 94N
Joy, Nicholas d1964 WhoHol 92
Joy, Peter 1926- Who 94
Joy, Robert 1948- WhoHol 92
Joy, Robert 1951- IntMPA 94
Joy, Robert John Thomas 1929- WhoAm 94
Joy, Thomas Alfred 1904- Who 94, WrDr 94
Joy, Timothy John 1956- WhoWest 94
Joy, William d1951 WhoHol 92
Joyal, Gary J. 1953- WhoIns 94
Joyaux, Alain Georges 1950- WhoAm 94, WhoAmA 93
Joyaux, Philippe ConWorW 93
Joyce, Alice d1955 WhoHol 92
Joyce, Anna d1986 WhoHol 92
Joyce, Bob Michael 1956- WhoMW 93
Joyce, Brenda 1917- WhoHol 92
Joyce, Brian WhoAmP 93
Joyce, Brian 1962- WhoAmL 94
Joyce, Burton Montgomery 1942- WhoFI 94
Joyce, Christopher 1950- ConAu 140
Joyce, Claude Clinton 1931- WhoFI 94
Joyce, Craig Douglas 1951- WhoAmL 94, WhoWest 94
Joyce, Donald Franklin 1938- BlkWr 2, WhoBlA 94
Joyce, Edward Rowen 1927- WhoScEn 94
Joyce, Eileen d1991 WhAm 10
Joyce, Elaine 1945- WhoHol 92
Joyce, Ella WhoBlA 94
Joyce, J. David 1946- WhoAmA 93
Joyce, James 1882-1941 BlmGEL [port], TwCLC 52 [port]
Joyce, James (Augustine Aloysius) 1882-1941 RfGShF
Joyce, James Daniel 1921- WhoAm 94
Joyce, James Edward, Sr. 1926- WhoIns 94
Joyce, James Joseph, Jr. 1947- WhoAmL 94
Joyce, Jane Wilson DrAPF 93
Joyce, Jeremiah E. 1943- WhoAmP 93
Joyce, Jerome J. 1939- WhoAmP 93
Joyce, Jimmy d1979 WhoHol 92
Joyce, John Michael 1908-1989 WhAm 10
Joyce, John T. 1935- WhoAm 94, WhoFI 94
Joyce, Joseph James 1943- WhoAm 94
Joyce, Joyce Ann 1949- WhoMW 93
Joyce, Julia ConAu 42NR
Joyce, Marshall Woodside 1912- WhoAmA 93
Joyce, Marty d1937 WhoHol 92
Joyce, Michael J. 1942- WhoAm 94
Joyce, Michael Patrick 1960- WhoAmL 94
Joyce, Michael Stewart 1942- WhoAm 94
Joyce, Natalie WhoHol 92
Joyce, Patricia Marie 1953- WhoAmP 93
Joyce, Peggy Hopkins d1957 WhoHol 92
Joyce, Philip Halton 1928- WhoAm 94
Joyce, Randolph Perkins d1977 WhoHol 92
Joyce, Raymond M. H. WhoAmP 93
Joyce, Robert Francis 1896-1990 WhAm 10
Joyce, Robert Hyland 1928- WhoAm 94
Joyce, Robert John H. Who 94
Joyce, Robert Joseph 1948- WhoAm 94
Joyce, Robin Hank 1960- WhoWest 94
Joyce, Rose Marie WhoHisp 94
Joyce, Rosemary A. 1956- ConAu 141
Joyce, Stephen WhoHol 92
Joyce, Stephen Francis 1941- WhoAm 94, WhoFI 94
Joyce, Stephen Michael 1945- WhoAmL 94, WhoWest 94
Joyce, Susan M. 1951- WhoAmP 93
Joyce, Terence Thomas 1946- WhoScEn 94
Joyce, Tim 1958- WhoAmP 93
Joyce, Todd Eric 1963- WhoMW 93
Joyce, Walter Joseph 1930- WhoFI 94
Joyce, William DrAPF 93
Joyce, William Brooke 1906-1946 DcNaB MP
Joyce, William H. 1935- WhoScEn 94
Joyce, William Leonard 1942- WhoAm 94
Joyce, William R., Jr. 1921- Who 94
Joyce, William Robert 1936- WhoFI 94
Joyce, Yootha d1980 WhoHol 92
Joyce-Brady, Martin Francis 1953- WhoScEn 94
Joye, Billy W., Jr. WhoAmP 93
Joye, Larry W. 1952- WhoAmL 94
Joyeux, Odette 1917- WhoHol 92
Joyner, Arthenia Lee 1943- WhoBlA 94

Jung, Andre 1939- *WhoScEn 94*
Jung, Audrey Moo Hing 1945-
 WhoAsA 94
Jung, Byung Il 1942- *WhoAsA 94*
Jung, Calvin *WhoHol 92*
Jung, Carl 1875- *AstEnc*
Jung, Carl 1875-1961 *BlmGEL*
Jung, Carl Gustav 1875-1961 *EncSPD*
Jung, Christopher Harold 1943-
 WhoMW 93
Jung, Donald T. 1953- *WhoWest 94*
Jung, Doris 1924- *NewGrDO, WhoAm 94*
Jung, Emma 1915- *WhoAsA 94*
Jung, Eugene 1957- *WhoWest 94*
Jung, Hans Gernot *IntWW 93N*
Jung, Hans-Joachim Gerhard 1954-
 WhoMW 93
Jung, Henry Hung 1957- *WhoWest 94*
Jung, John R. 1937- *WhoAsA 94*
Jung, Kwan Yee 1932- *WhoAmA 93,
 WhoAsA 94*
Jung, Lawrence Kwok Leung 1950-
 WhoAsA 94
Jung, Louise Rebecca 1949- *WhoAsA 94*
Jung, Manfred 1940- *NewGrDO*
Jung, Mankil 1950- *WhoAsA 94,
 WhoScEn 94*
Jung, Nawab Mir Nawaz 1904- *IntWW 93*
Jung, Peter Michael 1955- *WhoAmL 94*
Jung, Reinhard Paul 1946- *WhoFI 94,
 WhoScEn 94*
Jung, Rodney C. 1920- *WhoAm 94*
Jung, Soon J. 1941- *WhoAsA 94*
Jung, Timothy Tae Kun 1943-
 WhoWest 94
Jung, William Frederic 1958-
 WhoAmL 94
Jung, Yee Wah 1936- *WhoAmA 93,
 WhoAsA 94*
Jungalwala, Firoze Bamanshaw 1936-
 WhoAsA 94
Jungbluth, Connie Carlson 1955-
 WhoFI 94, WhoWest 94
Jungbluth, Kirk E. 1949- *WhoFI 94,
 WhoWest 94*
Junge, Alfred 1886-1964 *IntDcF 2-4 [port]*
Jungeberg, Thomas Donald 1950-
 WhoAmL 94
Jungels, Eleanor E. 1922- *WhoAmP 93*
Jungels, Pierre Jean Marie Henri 1944-
 Who 94
Junger, Ernst 1895- *EncSF 93, IntWW 93*
Junger, Miguel Chapero 1923-
 WhoAm 94, WhoScEn 94
Jungerius, Pieter Dirk 1933- *IntWW 93*
Jungerman, John Albert 1921- *WhoAm 94*
Jungers, Blaine Carroll 1944- *WhoAm 94,
 WhoFI 94*
Jungers, Francis 1926- *WhoAm 94*
Junghans, Paula Marie 1949- *WhoAm 94,
 WhoAmL 94*
Jungius, James (George) 1923- *Who 94*
Jungkenn, Friedrich Christian Arnold
 1732-1806 *WhAmRev*
Jungkind, Walter 1923- *WhoAm 94,
 WhoWest 94*
Jungkuntz, Richard Paul 1918-
 WhoAm 94
Jungren, Jon Erik 1927- *WhoScEn 94,
 WhoWest 94*
Jungwirth, Leonard D. 1903-1964
 WhoAmA 93N
Jungwirth, Manfred 1919- *NewGrDO*
Junid, Seri Sanusi bin 1943- *IntWW 93*
Junior, E. J., III 1959- *WhoBlA 94*
Junior, Ester James, Jr. 1932- *WhoBlA 94*
Junior, Gary R. 1940- *WhoAmP 93*
Junior, Samella E. 1931- *WhoBlA 94*
Junius *BlmGEL*
Junk, Virginia Wickstrom 1945-
 WhoWest 94
Junkel, Eric Franz 1959- *WhoMW 93*
Junker, Christine Rosetta 1953-
 WhoMW 93
Junker, Edward P., III *WhoAm 94,
 WhoFI 94*
Junker, Karin 1940- *WhoWomW 91*
Junker, Wilhelm Johann 1840-1892
 WhWE
Junkermann, Hans d1943 *WhoHol 92*
Junkin, John 1930- *WhoHol 92*
Junkin, John R., II *WhoAmP 93*
Junkin, Marion Montague 1905-1977
 WhoAmA 93N
Junkin, Trey Kirk 1961- *WhoBlA 94*
Junkins, Bobby Mac 1946- *WhoAmP 93*
Junkins, Donald *DrAPF 93*
Junkins, Donald (Arthur) 1931- *WrDr 94*
Junkins, Jerry R. 1937- *WhoAm 94,
 WhoFI 94, WhoScEn 94*
Junkins, Lowell Lee 1944- *WhoAmP 93*
Junor, John 1919- *Who 94*
Junor, John Donald Brown 1919-
 IntWW 93
Junquera, Mercedes 1930- *WhoHisp 94*
Juntereal, F. A., Jr. 1934- *WhoIns 94*
Junz, Helen B. *IntWW 93, WhoAm 94*

Juon, Lester Allen 1938- *WhoAm 94,
 WhoMW 93*
Jupe, George Percival 1930- *Who 94*
Jupina, Andrea Ann 1950- *WhoFI 94*
Jupiter, Clyde Peter 1928- *WhoBlA 94*
Jupp, Kenneth Graham 1917- *Who 94*
Juppe, Alain Marie 1945- *IntWW 93,
 Who 94*
Jura, James J. 1942- *WhoAm 94*
Jurado, Alicia 1915- *BlmGWL*
Jurado, Katy 1927- *IntMPA 94,
 WhoHol 92*
Jurado, Patrick R. 1941- *WhoHisp 94*
Jurado, Rosendo B. 1913- *WhoHisp 94*
Juran, Joseph Moses 1904- *WhoScEn 94*
Juranek, Alan Gary 1948- *WhoFI 94*
Jurasik, Peter *WhoHol 92*
Jurca, David F. 1946- *WhoAmL 94*
Jurcik, Alois Soban 1947- *WhoFI 94*
Jurcyk, John Joseph, Jr. 1930-
 WhoAmL 94
Jurczyk, Joanne Monica 1958-
 WhoScEn 94
Jurdana, Ernest J. 1944- *WhoAm 94*
Jurdem, Scott 1951- *WhoAmL 94*
Jurecka, Cyril 1884- *WhoAmA 93N*
Jurecki, Casimer John Joseph 1952-
 WhoWest 94
Juredine, David Graydon 1937-
 WhoFI 94
Jurek, Kenneth J. 1948- *WhoAm 94,
 WhoAmL 94*
Juren, Dennis Franklin 1935- *WhoFI 94*
Jurewicz, Benjamin R. 1942- *WhoIns 94*
Jurewicz, Benjamin Raymond 1942-
 WhoWest 94
Jurey, Wes *WhoAm 94, WhoFI 94*
Jurgens, Conrad R. 1947- *WhoIns 94*
Jurgens, Curt d1982 *WhoHol 92*
Jurgens, Deana *WhoHol 92*
Jurgens, George B., II 1953- *WhoAmL 94*
Jurgens, Leonard John 1933-
 WhoWest 94
Jurgens, Paul Eugene 1927- *WhoAmP 93*
Jurgensen, Sonny *ProFbHF [port]*
Jurgensen, Warren Peter 1921-
 WhoAm 94
Jurgenson, Candy A. Hunter 1946-
 WhoMW 93
Juric, Maria *BlmGWL*
Jurika, Stephen, Jr. d1993 *NewYTBS 93*
Jurinac, Sena 1921- *IntWW 93,
 NewGrDO [port]*
Jurinac, (Srebrenka) Sena 1921- *Who 94*
Jurinko, Andy 1939- *WhoAmA 93*
Jurisic, Melita *WhoHol 92*
Jurist, Ed d1993 *NewYTBS 93*
Jurith, Edward Howard 1951-
 WhoAmL 94
Jurjevskaya, Zinaida 1896?-1925
 NewGrDO
Jurkat, Martin Peter 1935- *WhoAm 94*
Jurkiewicz, Maurice John 1923-
 WhoAm 94
Jurkovic, Danica 1925- *WhoWomW 91*
Jurkowski, John *DrAPF 93*
Jurmain, Suzanne 1945- *WrDr 94*
Jurmu, Stephen Inghart 1951-
 WhoAmL 94
Jurney, Donald (Benson) 1945-
 WhoAmA 93
Jurney, Dorothy Misener 1909-
 WhoAm 94
Jurney, James Jasper 1927- *WhoMW 93*
Jurock, Oswald Erich 1944- *WhoAm 94*
Juron, Albert Aaron 1927- *WhoAmL 94*
Jurow, Martin 1911- *IntMPA 94*
Jurs, Peter Christian 1943- *WhoScEn 94*
Jursevskis, Zigfrids 1910- *WhoAmA 93*
Jurtshuk, Peter, Jr. 1929- *WhoAm 94*
Jury, Archibald George 1907- *Who 94*
Jury, David Earl 1964- *WhoFI 94*
Jury, Eliahu Ibraham 1923- *WhoAm 94*
Jury, Victor R., Jr. 1954- *WhoFI 94*
Jusinski, Leonard Edward 1955-
 WhoWest 94
Juskalian, Lee Jon 1947- *WhoAmP 93*
Jusseaume, Rene c. 1789-c. 1830 *WhWE*
Just, Ernest Everett 1883-1941 *AfrAmAl 6,
 WorScD*
Just, Jennie Martha 1936- *WhoMW 93*
Just, Johann August c. 1750-1791
 NewGrDO
Just, Richard Eugene 1948- *WhoAm 94*
Just, Ward Swift 1935- *WhoAm 94*
Juster, Norton 1929- *TwCYAW, WrDr 94*
Justesen, Don Robert 1930- *WhoAm 94*
Justice, Barry d1980 *WhoHol 92*
Justice, Blair 1927- *WhoAm 94,
 WhoScEn 94*
Justice, Bob Joe 1946- *WhoFI 94*
Justice, Brady Richmond, Jr. 1930-
 WhoAm 94, WhoMW 93
Justice, David Christopher 1966-
 WhoAm 94, WhoBlA 94
Justice, Donald *DrAPF 93*
Justice, Donald (Rodney) 1925- *WrDr 94*
Justice, Donald Rodney 1925- *WhoAm 94*

Justice, Franklin Pierce, Jr. 1938-
 WhoAm 94
Justice, Gary L. 1954- *WhoAmL 94*
Justice, Jack Burton 1931- *WhoAm 94*
Justice, Jack R. *DrAPF 93*
Justice, James Robertson d1975
 WhoHol 92
Justice, Katherine 1942- *WhoHol 92*
Justice, Max Edward 1945- *WhoAmL 94*
Justice, Norman E. 1925- *WhoAmP 93,
 WhoBlA 94*
Justice, Phillip Howard 1948- *WhoFI 94,
 WhoMW 93*
Justice, Phyllis C. 1915- *WhoMW 93*
Justice, William F. *WhoAmP 93*
Justice, William Wayne 1920-
 WhoAm 94, WhoAmL 94
Justin, John 1917- *WhoHol 92*
Justin, Joseph Eugene 1945- *WhoWest 94*
Justin, Morgan d1974 *WhoHol 92*
Justinger, Amy Lynn 1967- *WhoMW 93*
Justinian, I 483-565 *HisWorL [port]*
Justis, Gary (Allen) 1953- *WhoAmA 93*
Justus, Jack Glenn 1931- *WhoFI 94*
Justus, Larry T. 1932- *WhoAmP 93*
Justus, Michael Donald 1960- *WhoFI 94*
Justus, Roy Braxton 1901-1983
 WhoAmA 93N
Jusuf, Andi Mohamad 1929- *IntWW 93*
Juszczak, Nicholas Mauro 1955-
 WhoScEn 94
Juszczyk, James Joseph 1943-
 WhoAmA 93
Jutamulia, Suganda 1954- *WhoScEn 94*
Jute, Andre 1945- *WrDr 94*
Jutikkala, Eino Kaarlo Ilmari 1907-
 IntWW 93
Jutkowitz, Joel M. 1942- *WhoAmP 93*
Jutra, Claude d1987 *WhoHol 92*
Jutras, Larry Mark 1965- *WhoScEn 94*
Juttner, Christian *WhoHol 92*
Jutz, Jakob Johann 1942- *WhoScEn 94*
Juvarra, Filippo 1676-1736 *NewGrDO*
Juvelier, Jeanne d1981 *WhoHol 92*
Juvenal 60?-130? *BlmGEL*
Juves, Jose A. 1944- *WhoHisp 94*
Juvet, Richard Spalding, Jr. 1930-
 WhoAm 94, WhoWest 94
Juviler, Peter Henry 1926- *WhoAm 94*
Juvo, Nicola *NewGrDO*
Juvonen, Helvi 1919-1959 *BlmGWL*
Juxon, John *WrDr 94*
Juzeliunas, Julius 1916- *NewGrDO*
Juzwin, Kathryn Rossetto 1960-
 WhoMW 93
Jyranki, Antero 1933- *IntWW 93*

K

Kaa, Wi Kuki *WhoHol 92*
Kaaihue, Johnny d1971 *WhoHol 92*
Kaanta, Leonard Arthur 1948- *WhoAmL 94*
Kaapcke, Wallace Letcher 1916- *WhoAm 94*
Kaaren, Suzanne 1916- *WhoHol 92*
Kaarsted, Tage 1928- *IntWW 93*
Kaart, Hans (Johannes Jansen) 1920-1963 *NewGrDO*
Kaas, Jon H. *WhoAm 94*
Kaasa, Walter *WhoHol 92*
Kaatz, Ronald B. 1934- *WhoAm 94*
Kabachnik, Martin Izrailevich 1908- *IntWW 93*
Kabacik, Pawel 1963- *WhoScEn 94*
Kabadi, Balachandra Narayan 1933- *WhoAsA 94*
Kabaivanska, Raina 1934- *NewGrDO*
Kabak, Douglas Thomas 1957- *WhoAmL 94*
Kabala, Edward John 1942- *WhoAmL 94*
Kabalevsky, Dmitry Borisovich 1904-1987 *NewGrDO*
Kabanda, Celestin 1936- *IntWW 93*
Kabat, Elvin Abraham 1914- *IntWW 93, WhoAm 94, WhoScEn 94, WrDr 94*
Kabat, Linda Georgette 1951- *WhoMW 93*
Kabeiseman, Karl William 1927- *WhoAmL 94*
Kabel, Robert James 1946- *WhoAm 94*
Kabel, Robert Lynn 1932- *WhoAm 94*
Kaberry, Christopher Donald 1943- *Who 94*
Kabeya Wa Mukeba 1935- *IntWW 93*
Kabibble, Ish 1908- *WhoCom, WhoHol 92, WrDr 94*
Kabich, Vyacheslau Frantsavich (Vyacheslav Frantsevich) 1936- *IntWW 93*
Kabir, Abulfazal M. Fazle *WhoAsA 94*
Kable, Lawrence Philip 1926- *WhoIns 94*
Kabnick, Lisa D. 1955- *WhoAmL 94*
Kabrhelova, Marie 1925- *WhoWomW 91*
Kac, Victor G. 1943- *WhoAm 94*
Kacek, Don J. 1936- *WhoAm 94*
Kacere, John C. 1920- *WhoAmA 93*
Kach, Albert Wade 1947- *WhoAmP 93*
Kachadoorian, Zubel 1924- *WhoAm 94, WhoAmA 93*
Kachalov, Vassilli Ivanovich d1948 *WhoHol 92*
Kachel, Harold Stanley 1928- *WhoAmA 93*
Kachel, Wayne M. 1946- *WhoScEn 94*
Kachergis, George Joseph 1917-1974 *WhoAmA 93N*
Kachigian, Amerik A. 1933- *WhoAmL 94*
Kachinsky, Alexander 1888-1958 *WhoAmA 93N*
Kachiroubas, Leonard Dar 1953- *WhoAmP 93*
Kachiroubas, Christopher 1955- *WhoMW 93*
Kachlein, George Frederick, Jr. 1907-1989 *WhAm 10*
Kachmar, Jessie *DrAPF 93*
Kachornprasart, Sanan 1944- *IntWW 93*
Kachouei, Mahmoud H. *WhoWest 94*
Kachru, Braj B. 1932- *WhoAsA 94*
Kachru, Braj Behari 1932- *WhoAm 94*
Kachru, Yamuna 1933- *WhoAm 94*

Kachur, Betty Rae 1930- *WhoMW 93*
Kachur, Lewis *ConAu 142*
Kacir, Barbara Brattin 1941- *WhoAm 94, WhoAmL 94*
Kacker, Raghu Nath 1951- *WhoAsA 94*
Kaclik, Debi Louise 1953- *WhoFI 94*
Kacmarcik, Thomas 1925- *WhoFI 94*
Kacmarcik-Baker, Mary Elizabeth 1960- *WhoWest 94*
Kacsoh, Pongrac 1873-1923 *NewGrDO*
Kacur, Lois Marie 1915- *WhoMW 93*
Kaczanowski, Carl Henry 1948- *WhoScEn 94*
Kaczmarek, Jan 1920- *IntWW 93*
Kaczmarek, Jane *WhoHol 92*
Kaczmarek, Robert Brian 1957- *WhoMW 93*
Kaczmarek, Zdzislaw 1928- *IntWW 93*
Kaczmarski, Michael John 1953- *WhoAm 94*
Kaczorowski, Gregory John 1949- *WhoAm 94*
Kaczvinsky, Joseph Robert, Jr. 1957- *WhoMW 93*
Kaczynski, David A. 1939- *WhoAmP 93*
Kaczynski, Don 1948- *WhoScEn 94*
Kaczynski, Lech Aleksander 1949- *IntWW 93*
Kaczynski, William F. 1959- *WhoWest 94*
Kadaba, Prasanna Venkatarama 1931- *WhoAsA 94*
Kadagishvili, Amiran 1949- *LngBDD*
Kadane, David Kurzman 1914-1991 *WhAm 10*
Kadane, Joseph B. 1941- *WhoAm 94*
Kadannikov, Vladimir Vasilevich 1941- *LngBDD*
Kadannikov, Vladimir Vasilievich 1941- *IntWW 93*
Kadanoff, Leo Philip 1937- *IntWW 93, WhoAm 94, WhoScEn 94*
Kadar, Bela 1934- *IntWW 93*
Kadar, Janos 1912-1989 *HisWorL [port]*
Kadare, Elena 1943- *BlmGWL*
Kadare, Ismail *IntWW 93*
Kadas, Mike 1956- *WhoAmP 93*
Kaddori, Fakhri Yassin 1932- *IntWW 93*
Kaddu, John Baptist 1945- *WhoScEn 94*
Kadeg, Roger Dan 1951- *WhoWest 94*
Kadel, Kim Marie 1953- *WhoMW 93*
Kadel, William Howard 1913-1990 *WhAm 10*
Kademova, Litka d1979 *WhoHol 92*
Kaden, Ellen Oran *WhoAmL 94*
Kaden, Lewis B. 1942- *WhoAm 94*
Kader, Cheryl 1944- *WhoMW 93*
Kader, Nancy Stowe 1945- *WhoAmP 93*
Kader, Omar 1943- *WhoAmP 93*
Kaderli, Dan *DrAPF 93*
Kades, Charles Louis 1906- *WhoAm 94*
Kadet, Samuel 1949- *WhoAm 94, WhoAmL 94*
Kadhafi, Mu'ammar Muhammed al- *IntWW 93*
Kadin, Alan Mitchell 1952- *WhoScEn 94*
Kadin, Marshall Edward 1939- *WhoAm 94*
Kading, Kevin Henry 1957- *WhoFI 94*
Kading, Stanley Donald 1951- *WhoAmP 93*
Kadir, Djelal 1946- *WhoAm 94*
Kadish, Alon 1950- *WrDr 94*
Kadish, Mark J. 1943- *WhoAmL 94*

Kadish, Richard L. 1943- *WhoAm 94, WhoFI 94*
Kadish, Sanford Harold 1921- *WhoAm 94*
Kadison, Alexander 1895- *WhAm 10*
Kadison, Richard Vincent 1925- *WhoAm 94, WhoScEn 94*
Kadison, Stuart L. 1923- *WhoAm 94*
Kadler, Karen d1984 *WhoHol 92*
Kadner, Carl George 1911- *WhoWest 94*
Kadner, Robert Joseph 1942- *WhoAm 94*
Kado, Clarence Isao 1936- *WhoAm 94*
Kadochnikova, Larisa *WhoHol 92*
Kadohata, Cynthia 1956?- *ConAu 140*
Kadohata, Cynthia Lynn 1956- *WhoAsA 94*
Kadomoto, Thomas 1917- *WhoAsA 94*
Kadomtsev, Boris Borisovich 1928- *IntWW 93*
Kadoorie, Baron d1993 *Who 94N*
Kadoorie, Baron 1899- *IntWW 93, Who 94*
Kadoorie, Horace 1902- *IntWW 93, Who 94*
Kadoorie, Lawrence d1993 *NewYTBS 93 [port]*
Kadosa, Pal 1903-1983 *NewGrDO*
Kadota, Takashi Theodore 1930- *WhoAm 94*
Kadowaki, Joe George 1919- *WhoAsA 94*
Kadra, Nourredine 1943- *IntWW 93*
Kadrey, Richard 1957- *EncSF 93*
Kadri, Sibghatullah 1937- *Who 94*
Kaduk, Frank J. 1916- *WhoAmP 93*
Kaduk, James Albert 1952- *WhoMW 93*
Kaduma, Ibrahim Mohamed 1937- *IntWW 93*
Kadushin, Alfred 1916- *WrDr 94*
Kadushin, Karen D. 1943- *WhoAmL 94*
Kaebitzsch, Reinhold Johannes *DrAPF 93*
Kaechele, Diane J. 1952- *WhoFI 94*
Kaegel, Ray Martin 1925- *WhoFI 94*
Kaegel, Richard James 1939- *WhoAm 94*
Kael, Pauline 1919- *IntWW 93, WhoAm 94, WrDr 94*
Kaelin, Barney James 1951- *WhoScEn 94*
Kaelin, Eugene Francis 1926- *WhoAm 94*
Kaemmerer, Michael E. 1951- *WhoAmL 94*
Kaempf, Robert Francis 1953- *WhoFI 94*
Kaempfer, Engelbrecht 1651-1716 *WhWE*
Kaempfert, Wade *ConAu 141, EncSF 93, SmATA 76*
Kaenzig, Fritz Alexander 1952- *WhoMW 93*
Kaep, Louis Joseph 1903-1991 *WhAm 10, WhoAmA 93N*
Kaericher, John Conrad 1936- *WhoAmA 93*
Kaernbach, Christian 1960- *WhoScEn 94*
Kaesberg, Paul Joseph 1923- *WhoAm 94*
Kaeser, Clifford Richard 1936- *WhoAm 94, WhoFI 94*
Kaestle, Carl F. 1940- *IntWW 93*
Kaeutner, Helmut d1980 *WhoHol 92*
Kafaoglu, Adnan Baser 1926- *IntWW 93*
Kafarova, Elmira Mikail kyzy 1934- *WhoWomW 91*
Kafarski, Mitchell I. 1917- *WhoAm 94*
Kafele, Baruti Kwame 1960- *WhoBlA 94*
Kafes, William Owen 1935- *WhoAm 94*
Kaff, Albert Ernest 1920- *WhoAm 94*
Kaffel, Edward Anthony, Jr. 1967- *WhoMW 93*
Kaffer, Roger Louis 1927- *WhoAm 94*

Kaffka, Johann Christoph 1759-c. 1803 *NewGrDO*
Kaffka, Margit 1880-1918 *BlmGWL*
Kafi, Ali *IntWW 93*
Kafin, Robert Joseph 1942- *WhoAm 94, WhoAmL 94*
Kafity, Samir 1933- *Who 94*
Kafka, Alexandre 1917- *IntWW 93*
Kafka, Franz 1883-1924 *EncSF 93, RfGShF, TwCLC 53 [port]*
Kafka, Gerald Andrew 1951- *WhoAm 94*
Kafka, Louis L. 1945- *WhoAmP 93*
Kafka, Tomas 1936- *WhoScEn 94*
Kafoglis, Nicholas 1930- *WhoAmP 93*
Kafoury, Stephen 1941- *WhoAmP 93*
Kafrawy, Hasaballah El- 1930- *IntWW 93*
Kafu, Nagai 1879-1959 *TwCLC 51 [port]*
Kagalovsky, Konstantin Grigorevich 1957- *LngBDD*
Kagami, Hideo 1923- *IntWW 93*
Kagan, Baron 1915- *Who 94*
Kagan, Andrew Aaron 1947- *WhoAmA 93*
Kagan, Diane *WhoHol 92*
Kagan, Donald 1932- *WhoAm 94, WrDr 94*
Kagan, Irving 1936- *WhoFI 94*
Kagan, Janet 1945- *EncSF 93*
Kagan, Jeffrey Allen 1958- *WhoFI 94*
Kagan, Jeremy 1945- *IntMPA 94*
Kagan, Jeremy Paul 1945- *WhoAm 94*
Kagan, Jerome 1929- *WhoAm 94, WrDr 94*
Kagan, Julia Lee 1948- *WhoAm 94*
Kagan, Marvin Bernard 1944- *WhoScEn 94*
Kagan, Norman *EncSF 93*
Kagan, Robert Alexander 1924- *WhoAmL 94*
Kagan, Sioma 1907- *WhoAm 94, WhoMW 93, WhoScEn 94*
Kagan, Stephen Bruce 1944- *WhoAm 94, WhoFI 94*
Kagarlitski, Julius (Iosifovich) 1926- *EncSF 93*
Kagarlitsky, Boris 1958- *WrDr 94*
Kagawa, Kathleen Hatsuyo 1952- *WhoFI 94*
Kagel, Allen David 1945- *WhoAmP 93*
Kagel, John 1940- *WhoWest 94*
Kagel, Mauricio 1931- *WhoAm 94*
Kagel, Mauricio (Raul) 1931- *NewGrDO*
Kagel, Ronald Oliver 1936- *WhoMW 93*
Kagemoto, Haro 1952- *WhoAmA 93, WhoWest 94*
Kagemoto, Patricia Jow 1952- *WhoAmA 93*
Kagen, Sergius 1909-1964 *NewGrDO*
Kagetsu, Tadashi Jack 1931- *WhoAsA 94*
Kagey, F. Eileen 1925- *WhoMW 93*
Kageyama, David Kenji 1948- *WhoWest 94*
Kageyama, Rodney *WhoHol 92*
Kageyama, Yoshiro 1922- *WhoScEn 94*
Kaghazchi, Tahereh 1947- *WhoScEn 94*
Kagiwada, George 1931- *WhoAsA 94*
Kagiwada, Harriet H. Natsuyama 1937- *WhoAsA 94*
Kagiwada, Reynold Shigeru 1938- *WhoAm 94, WhoWest 94*
Kagle, Joseph L., Jr. 1932- *WhoAmA 93*
Kagle, Joseph Louis, Jr. 1932- *WhoAm 94*
Kagy, Sheffield Harold 1907-1989 *WhoAmA 93N*

Kalenscher, Alan Jay 1926- WhoWest 94
Kaler, Ellen Redding 1952- WhoMW 93
Kaler, Robert Joseph 1956- WhoAmL 94
Kaletsky, Anatole 1952- Who 94
Kaley, Arthur Warren 1921- WhoAm 94
Kaley, J. R. 1918- WhoAmP 93
Kalfatovic, Martin R. 1961- ConAu 141
Kalff, Jacob 1935- WhoScEn 94
Kalfon, Jean-Pierre WhoHol 92
Kalfus, Melvin 1931- WrDr 94
Kali WhoAmA 93
Kalib, David Leonard 1940- WhoIns 94
Kaliba, Layding DrAPF 93
Kalich, Bertha d1939 WhoHol 92
Kalich, Jacob d1975 WhoHol 92
Kalichstein, Joseph 1946- IntWW 93
Kalidasa c. 5th cent.- IntDcT 2
Kaliealoa, Luuiklaluana d1980 WhoHol 92
Kaliff, Joseph Alfred 1922-1992 WhAm 10
Kaliher, Michael Dennis 1947- WhoWest 94
Kalijarvi, Thorsten Valentine 1897- WhAm 10
Kalik, Barbara Faith 1936- WhoAmP 93, WhoWomW 91
Kalik, Vaclav 1891-1951 NewGrDO
Kalika, Dale Michele 1948- WhoFI 94
Kalikow, Peter Steven 1942- WhoAm 94
Kalikow, Richard R. 1949- WhoAmL 94
Kalikow, Theodora J. 1941- WhoAm 94
Kalil, Farris George 1938- WhoAm 94
Kalilombe, Patrick-Augustine 1933- IntWW 93
Kalimi, Mohammed Yahya 1939- WhoAsA 94
Kalimo, Esko Antero 1937- WhoScEn 94
Kalin, Robert 1921- WhoAm 94, WhoScEn 94
Kalina, Richard 1946- WhoAm 94, WhoAmA 93
Kalina, Robert Edward 1936- WhoAm 94
Kalinec, Lawrence 1943- WhoAmL 94
Kaliner, Michael Aron 1941- WhoScEn 94
Kalinger, Daniel Jay 1952- WhoAm 94
Kalinowsky, Lothar Bruno d1992 IntWW 93N
Kalionzes, Janet d1961 WhoHol 92
Kalipha, Stephan 1940- WhoHol 92
Kalis, Barbara Harriet 1943- WhoWest 94
Kalis, Henry J. 1937- WhoAmP 93
Kalis, Peter John 1950- WhoAmL 94
Kalisch, Alfred 1863-1933 NewGrDO
Kalisch, Beatrice Jean 1943- WhoAm 94
Kalisch, Paul 1855-1946 NewGrDO
Kalisch, Philip A. 1942- WhoAm 94
Kalish, Arthur 1930- WhoAm 94, WhoAmL 94
Kalish, Daniel Harold 1919- WhoFI 94
Kalish, Donald 1919- WhoAm 94
Kalish, Eddie 1939- IntMPA 94
Kalish, Katherine McAulay 1945- WhoAmL 94
Kalish, Myron 1919- WhoAm 94
Kalish, Paddy 1955- WhoFI 94, WhoMW 93
Kalisher, Michael David Lionel 1941- Who 94
Kalisher, Simpson 1926- WhoAmA 93
Kalishman, Reesa Joan 1959- WhoFI 94
Kaliski, Alan Edward 1947- WhoIns 94
Kaliski, Mary 1938- WhoScEn 94
Kaliski, Stephan Felix 1928- WhoAm 94
Kalisky, Avram 1927- WhoFI 94
Kaliz, Armand d1941 WhoHol 92
Kalkbrenner, Edward Joseph, Jr. 1942- WhoWest 94
Kalkhof, Thomas Corrigan 1919- WhoScEn 94
Kalkhoff, Ronald Kenneth 1933-1990 WhAm 10
Kalkhurst, Eric d1957 WhoHol 92
Kalkus, Stanley 1931- WhoAm 94
Kalkwarf, Leonard V. 1928- WhoAm 94
Kallaher, Michael Joseph 1940- WhoAm 94
Kalland, Lloyd Austin 1914- WhoAm 94
Kallay, Michael Frank, II 1944- WhoWest 94
Kallem, Henry 1912- WhoAmA 93N
Kallen, Horace Meyer 1882-1974 DcAmReB 2
Kallen, Jackie c. 1946- News 94-1 [port]
Kallen, Kitty WhoHol 92
Kallen, Lucille (Chernos) WrDr 94
Kallenberg, John Kenneth 1942- WhoAm 94, WhoWest 94
Kallenberg, Siegfried Garibaldi 1867-1944 NewGrDO
Kallenberger, Larry Brian 1948- WhoAmP 93
Kaller, Robert Jameson d1988 WhoAmA 93N
Kalleres, Michael Peter 1939- WhoAm 94
Kallet, Marilyn DrAPF 93
Kallfelz, Francis A. 1938- WhoAm 94
Kallfelz, Hans Carlo 1933- WhoScEn 94
Kallgren, Edward Eugene 1928- WhoAm 94, WhoAmL 94
Kallgren, Joyce Kislitzin 1930- WhoAm 94
Kallianiotes, Helena WhoHol 92
Kallianpur, Gopinath 1925- WhoScEn 94
Kallich, Martin (Irvin) 1918- WrDr 94
Kallifatides, Theodor 1938- ConAu 43NR
Kallina, Emanuel John, II 1948- WhoAmL 94
Kallio, Heikki Olavi 1937- IntWW 93
Kallipetis, Michel Louis 1941- Who 94
Kallir, Jane Katherine WhoAm 94
Kallir, Jane Katherine 1954- WhoAmA 93
Kallir, John 1923- WhoAm 94
Kallir, Otto 1894-1978 WhoAmA 93N
Kalliwoda, Johann Wenzel 1801-1866 NewGrDO
Kallman, Chester 1921-1975 NewGrDO
Kallman, Dick d1980 WhoHol 92
Kallman, Franz J. 1897-1965 EncSPD
Kallman, Ralph Arthur 1934- WhoMW 93
Kallman, Robert Friend 1922- WhoWest 94
Kallmann, Helmut Max 1922- WhoAm 94
Kallmann, Stanley Walter 1943- WhoAm 94, WhoAmL 94
Kallner, Norman Gust 1950- WhoMW 93
Kallok, Michael John 1948- WhoAm 94
Kallsen, T. J. DrAPF 93
Kallsen, Theodore John 1915- WhoAm 94
Kallstrom, Charles Clark 1943- WhoMW 93
Kalm, William Dean 1951- WhoWest 94
Kalman, Andrew 1919- WhoAm 94
Kalman, Arnold I. 1948- WhoAm 94, WhoAmL 94
Kalman, Calvin Shea 1944- WhoScEn 94
Kalman, Emmerich 1882-1953 NewGrDO
Kalman, Laura 1955- ConAu 140
Kalman, Maira 1949?- ChlLR 32 [port]
Kalman, Oszkar 1887-1971 NewGrDO
Kalman, Rudolf Emil 1930- WhoAm 94, WhoScEn 94
Kalmanoff, Martin 1920- NewGrDO, WhoAm 94
Kalmanowitz, Stuart Mark 1950- WhoFI 94
Kalmaz, Ekrem Errol 1940- WhoScEn 94
Kalmink, Jack O. 1947- WhoAmL 94
Kalms, Stanley 1931- Who 94
Kalmus, Allan Henry 1917- WhoAm 94
Kalmus, George Ernest 1935- Who 94
Kalmus, Morris A. DrAPF 93
Kalmus, Peter Ignaz Paul 1933- Who 94
Kalnay, Eugenia 1942- WhoHisp 94
Kalnins, Alfreds 1879-1951 NewGrDO
Kalnins, Haralds 1911- LngBDD
Kalnins, Imants 1941- NewGrDO
Kalnins, Janis 1904- NewGrDO
Kalo, Kwamala 1929- Who 94
Kalogredis, Vasilios J. 1949- WhoAmL 94
Kalomiris, Manolis 1883-1962 NewGrDO
Kaloogian, Howard James 1959- WhoWest 94
Kalousova, Eva 1941- WhoWomW 91
Kalow, Werner 1917- WhoAm 94
Kalpage, Stanley 1925- IntWW 93
Kalpakian, Laura DrAPF 93
Kalphat-Lopez, Henriet Michelle 1963- WhoScEn 94
Kalpokas, Donald IntWW 93
Kalra, Bhupinder Singh 1936- WhoAsA 94
Kalra, Rajiv 1952- WhoAsA 94, WhoFI 94
Kalra, Yash Pal 1940- WhoScEn 94
Kals, Stephen A. 1947- WhoAm 94, WhoAmL 94
Kalser, Erwin d1958 WhoHol 92
Kalsher, Michael John 1956- WhoScEn 94
Kalshoven, James Edward, Jr. 1948- WhoScEn 94
Kalsner, Stanley 1936- WhoAm 94
Kalson, Albert E(ugene) 1932- WrDr 94
Kalsow, Kathryn Ellen 1938- WhoMW 93
Kalt, Howard Michael 1943- WhoAm 94
Kalt, Marvin Robert 1945- WhoAm 94
Kaltenbach, Carl Colin 1939- WhoScEn 94, WhoWest 94
Kaltenbach, Hubert Leonard 1922- WhoAm 94
Kaltenborn, H. V. d1965 WhoHol 92
Kalter, Alan WhoAm 94
Kalter, Bella Briansky DrAPF 93
Kalter, Edmond Morey 1950- WhoAm 94
Kalter, Sabine 1890-1957 NewGrDO
Kalter, Seymour Sanford 1918- WhoAm 94
Kalthoff, Klaus Otto 1941- WhoAm 94, WhoScEn 94
Kaltinick, Paul R. 1932- WhoAm 94
Kalton, Graham 1936- WhoAm 94
Kalton, Robert Rankin 1920- WhoAm 94
Kaltsos, Angelo John 1930- WhoScEn 94
Kaludis, George 1938- WhoAm 94
Kalugin, Oleg Danilovich 1934- LngBDD
Kalule, Ayub 1953- IntWW 93
Kalur, Jerome S. 1944- WhoAmL 94
Kalus, Richard A. 1940- WhoMW 93
Kalustian, Lisa Ann 1963- WhoWest 94
Kalvanas, Jonas 1914- LngBDD
Kalver, Gail Ellen 1948- WhoAm 94
Kalvin, Douglas Mark 1954- WhoScEn 94
Kalvinskas, John Joseph 1927- WhoWest 94
Kalvoda, Jan 1953- IntWW 93
Kalwinsky, Charles Knowlton 1946- WhoAm 94
Kam, James T.-K. 1945- WhoAsA 94
Kam, Lit-Yan 1939- WhoAsA 94
Kam, Lydia B. 1952- WhoIns 94
Kam, Mei K. 1938- WhoAmA 93
Kam, Mei-Ki F. P. 1938- WhoAsA 94
Kam, Thomas K. Y. 1955- WhoAsA 94
Kam, Vernon T. 1933- WhoAsA 94
Kam, William 1923- WhoAsA 94
Kamaiko, Laurie Ann 1954- WhoAmL 94
Kamal, Aleph 1950- WrDr 94
Kamal, Musa Rasim 1934- WhoScEn 94
Kamali, Bahman 1951- WhoFI 94
Kamali, Norma 1945- IntWW 93, WhoAm 94
Kamalii, Kinau Boyd 1930- WhoAmP 93
Kaman, Charles Huron 1919- WhoAm 94, WhoFI 94
Kamana, Dunstan Weston 1937- IntWW 93
Kamanda Wa Kamanda 1940- IntWW 93
Kamanga, Reuben Chitandika 1929- IntWW 93
Kamarck, Andrew Martin 1914- IntWW 93
Kamarouskaja, Zinaida Mikalauna 1952- LngBDD
Kamaryt, Joseph d1977 WhoHol 92
Kamas, Lewis Melvin 1921- WhoAmP 93
Kamau, John Cauri 1923- IntWW 93
Kamau, Mosi 1955- WhoBlA 94
Kamb, Walter Barclay 1931- WhoAm 94
Kamba, Walter Joseph 1931- IntWW 93, Who 94
Kamback, Marvin Carl 1939- WhoMW 93
Kambara, George Kiyoshi 1916- WhoAm 94
Kambarhan 1922- WhoPRCh 91 [port]
Kambayashi, Chohei EncSF 93
Kamber, Bernard M. IntMPA 94
Kamber, Victor Samuel 1944- WhoAm 94, WhoFI 94
Kambic, Helen Elizabeth 1946- WhoMW 93
Kambour, Annaliese Spofford 1961- WhoAmL 94
Kambour, Roger Peabody 1932- WhoAm 94
Kamdem, Donatien Pascal 1955- WhoScEn 94
Kamei, Masao 1916- IntWW 93
Kamel, Ted A. 1960- WhoAmP 93
Kamel Ahmed, Kamal El-Din 1927- IntWW 93
Kamemoto, Fred Isamu 1928- WhoAm 94
Kamemoto, Garett Hiroshi 1966- WhoWest 94
Kamemoto, Haruyuki 1922- WhoAm 94, WhoScEn 94
Kamen, Betty 1925- ConAu 43NR
Kamen, Harry Paul 1933- WhoAm 94, WhoAmL 94, WhoFI 94
Kamen, Henry 1936- WrDr 94
Kamen, Martin D. 1913- IntWW 93
Kamen, Martin David 1913- WhoAm 94, WhoWest 94
Kamen, Milt d1977 WhoHol 92
Kamen, Rebecca 1950- WhoAmA 93
Kamenetz, Rodger DrAPF 93
Kamenka, Eugene 1928- IntWW 93, WrDr 94
Kamens, Harold 1917- WhoAmL 94
Kamens, Matthew Henry 1951- WhoAmL 94
Kamenske, Bernard Harold 1927- WhoAm 94
Kamensky, Marvin 1939- WhoAmL 94
Kamentsky, Louis Aaron 1930- WhoAm 94
Kameny, Franklin 1925- AmSocL
Kamer, Joel Victor 1942- WhoAm 94
Kamer, William 1951- WhoAmL 94
Kamerick, Eileen Ann 1958- WhoAmL 94
Kamerlingh Onnes, Heike 1853-1926 WorScD
Kamerman, Ken 1931- WhoAmP 93
Kamerman, Kenneth M. 1931- WhoWest 94
Kamerman, Sheila Brody 1928- WhoAm 94
Kamerow, Norman Warren 1927- WhoFI 94
Kamerschen, David Roy 1937- WhoAm 94
Kamerschen, Robert Jerome 1936- WhoAm 94, WhoFI 94
Kames, Kenneth F. 1935- WhoAm 94
Kamesar, Adam 1956- WhoMW 93
Kamey, Paul 1912- IntMPA 94
Kamhi, Samuel Vitali 1922- WhoFI 94
Kamholz, Stephan L. 1947- WhoAm 94
Kamien, Kalvin 1950- WhoAmL 94
Kamienecki, Ruth Rosa 1949- WhoMW 93
Kamienski, Maciej 1734-1821 NewGrDO
Kamihira, Ben 1925- WhoAmA 93
Kamijo, Fumihiko 1934- WhoScEn 94
Kamikawa, Alden Tanemitsu 1940- WhoFI 94
Kamil, Alan C(urtis) 1941- WrDr 94
Kamil, Geoffrey Harvey 1942- Who 94
Kamilli, Robert Joseph 1947- WhoScEn 94, WhoWest 94
Kamin, Amy Rose 1960- WhoFI 94
Kamin, Benjamin Alon 1953- WhoAm 94
Kamin, C. Richard 1944- WhoAmP 93
Kamin, Chester Thomas 1940- WhoAm 94
Kamin, Franz DrAPF 93
Kamin, Henry 1920-1988 WhAm 10
Kamin, Kay Hodes 1940- WhoAmL 94, WhoMW 93
Kamin, Lawrence O. 1950- WhoAm 94
Kamin, Lawrence Owen 1950- WhoAmL 94
Kamin, Nick 1939- EncSF 93
Kamin, Sherwin 1927- WhoAm 94
Kamine, Bernard Samuel 1943- WhoAmL 94, WhoWest 94
Kaminer, Peter H. 1915- WhoAm 94
Kaminow, Ivan Paul 1930- WhoAm 94
Kamins, Barry Michael 1943- WhoAmL 94
Kamins, David Stone 1959- WhoScEn 94
Kamins, John Mark 1947- WhoAm 94, WhoAmL 94
Kamins, Philip E. 1936- WhoAm 94, WhoWest 94
Kaminska, Ida d1980 WhoHol 92
Kaminski, Bruce David 1958- WhoWest 94
Kaminski, Charles Anthony WhoFI 94
Kaminski, Edward Jozef 1926- WhoMW 93
Kaminski, Ernest Joseph 1956- WhoMW 93
Kaminski, Heinrich 1886-1946 NewGrDO
Kaminski, John WhoAm 94
Kaminski, Joseph C. 1943- WhoIns 94
Kaminski, Joseph Casmir 1943- WhoAm 94
Kaminski, Jozef 1919- IntWW 93
Kaminski, Mark d1993 NewYTBS 93
Kaminski, Michael John 1963- WhoFI 94
Kaminsky, Alice R WrDr 94
Kaminsky, Alice Richkin WhoAm 94
Kaminsky, Daniel DrAPF 93
Kaminsky, Howard 1940- WhoAm 94
Kaminsky, Jack 1922- WrDr 94
Kaminsky, Jack Allan 1949- WhoAmA 93
Kaminsky, Judith Gerson 1942- WhoFI 94
Kaminsky, Larry Michael 1952- WhoAmL 94
Kaminsky, Manfred Stephan 1929- WhoAm 94
Kaminsky, Marc DrAPF 93
Kaminsky, Richard Alan 1951- WhoAmL 94
Kaminsky, Stuart 1934- WrDr 94
Kamionsky, Oscar 1869-1917 NewGrDO
Kamisar, Yale 1929- WhoAm 94, WhoMW 93
Kamiya, Noriaki 1948- WhoScEn 94
Kamiya, Yoshio 1930- WhoScEn 94
Kamiyama, Osamu 1947- WhoAsA 94
Kamiyama, Sojin d1954 WhoHol 92
Kamke, Paul Burton 1959- WhoFI 94
Kamke, Sarah L. 1943- WhoMW 93
Kamlang-Ek, Arthit IntWW 93
Kamleshwar ConWorW 93
Kamlesvar 1932- ConWorW 93
Kamlet, Adam Lawrence 1969- WhoMW 93
Kamlet, David Andrew 1964- WhoFI 94
Kamlot, Robert 1926- WhoAm 94
Kamm, Antony 1931- ConAu 41NR
Kamm, Dorinda 1952- WrDr 94
Kamm, Dorothy Lila 1957- WhoAmA 93
Kamm, Herbert 1917- WhoAm 94, WhoWest 94
Kamm, Jacob Oswald 1918- WhoAm 94, WhoFI 94, WrDr 94
Kamm, Josephine 1905-1989 TwCYAW
Kamm, Kris WhoHol 92
Kamm, Laurence Richard 1939- WhoAm 94
Kamm, Linda Heller 1939- WhoAm 94
Kamm, Robert B. 1919- WhoAm 94
Kamm, Thomas Allen 1925- WhoAm 94
Kamman, Alan Bertram 1931- WhoAm 94, WhoFI 94, WhoWest 94
Kamman, Curtis W. 1939- WhoAmP 93
Kamman, Curtis Warren 1939- WhoAm 94
Kamman, Madeleine NewYTBS 93 [port]
Kamman, William 1930- WhoAm 94
Kammen, Michael 1936- WhoAm 94, WrDr 94

Kammer, Kerry 1948- *WhoAmP 93*
Kammer, Klaus d1964 *WhoHol 92*
Kammer, Raymond Gerard, Jr. 1947- *WhoAm 94*
Kammer, Robert Arthur, Jr. 1945- *WhoAmL 94*
Kammer, William Nolan 1942- *WhoAm 94, WhoAmL 94*
Kammerer, Hans 1922- *IntWW 93*
Kammerer, Kelly Christian 1941- *WhoAm 94*
Kammerer, Marvin Julius 1937- *WhoAmP 93*
Kammerer, Ricky Joe 1953- *WhoMW 93*
Kammerer, William H. d1993 *NewYTBS 93*
Kammholz, Theophil Carl 1909- *WhAm 10*
Kammin, William Robert 1953- *WhoScEn 94*
Kammler, David William 1940- *WhoMW 93*
Kamo, Roy 1921- *WhoScEn 94*
Kamo, Yoshinori 1958- *WhoAsA 94*
Kamoche, Jidlaph Gitau 1942- *WhoBlA 94*
Kamon, David Anthony 1945- *WhoMW 93*
Kamougue, Wadal Abdelkader 1939- *IntWW 93*
Kamp, Arthur Joseph, Jr. 1945- *WhoAmL 94*
Kamp, Cynthia Lea 1956- *WhoMW 93*
Kamp, Margreet 1942- *WhoWomW 91*
Kamp, Norbert 1927- *IntWW 93*
Kamp, Ronald Carl 1934- *WhoAmL 94, WhoWest 94*
Kampelman, Max M. 1920- *IntWW 93, WhoAm 94, WhoAmL 94, WhoAmP 93*
Kampen, Emerson 1928- *WhoAm 94, WhoFI 94, WhoMW 93, WhoScEn 94*
Kamper, Robert Andrew 1933- *WhoScEn 94*
Kamper, William Douglas 1963- *WhoMW 93*
Kampers, Fritz d1950 *WhoHol 92*
Kamperschroer, George R. 1949- *WhoAmL 94*
Kampf, Avram S. 1920- *WhoAmA 93*
Kampf, Marilyn Jeanne 1940- *WhoMW 93*
Kampf, William Ira 1943- *WhoAm 94*
Kamphoefner, Henry Leveke 1907-1990 *WhAm 10*
Kampley, Linda *DrAPF 93*
Kampmann, Steve 1951- *WhoHol 92*
Kampmeier, Curtis Neil 1941- *WhoFI 94, WhoMW 93*
Kampmeier, Jack August 1935- *WhoAm 94*
Kampmeier, Rudolph Herman 1898- *WhAm 10*
Kampouris, Emmanuel Andrew 1934- *IntWW 93, WhoAm 94, WhoFI 94*
Kamps, Charles Q. 1932- *WhoAm 94*
Kamps, Lee Alan 1948- *WhoMW 93*
Kamrowski, Gerome 1914- *WhoAm 94, WhoAmA 93*
Kamsky, Leonard 1918- *WhoAm 94*
Kamu, Okko 1946- *IntWW 93*
Kamy, Hassan 1941- *NewGrDO*
Kamys, Walter 1917- *WhoAmA 93*
Kamysz, John Walter 1964- *WhoMW 93*
Kamyszew, Christopher D. 1958- *WhoAm 94*
Kan, Bill Yuet Him 1941- *WhoScEn 94*
Kan, Diana 1926- *WhoAmA 93, WhoAsA 94*
Kan, Diana Artemis Mann Shu 1926- *WhoAm 94*
Kan, Kenny Wai 1966- *WhoFI 94, WhoWest 94*
Kan, Kit-Keung 1943- *WhoAmA 93, WhoAsA 94*
Kan, Michael 1933- *WhoAmA 93, WhoAsA 94*
Kan, Paul Man-Lok 1947- *WhoFI 94*
Kan, Victor 1946- *WhoAsA 94*
Kan, Yue-Sai 1947- *WhoAsA 94*
Kan, Yuet Wai 1936- *IntWW 93, Who 94, WhoAm 94, WhoAsA 94, WhoScEn 94*
Kanaan, Taher Hamdi 1935- *IntWW 93*
Kanabus, Henry *DrAPF 93*
Kanaday, Thomas Parker, Jr. 1943- *WhoAmL 94*
Kanaga, Conseulo 1894-1978 *WhoAmA 93N*
Kanagy, Steven Albert 1956- *WhoFI 94*
Kanakaratne, Neville 1923- *IntWW 93*
Kanal, Emanuel 1957- *WhoScEn 94*
Kanaley, James Edward 1941- *WhoFI 94*
Kanaly, Steve 1946- *WhoHol 92*
Kanaly, Steven Francis 1946- *WhoAm 94*
Kanamori, Hiroo 1936- *WhoScEn 94*
Kanamori, Masao 1911- *IntWW 93*
Kanan, B. D. *WhoAmP 93*
Kanan, Gregory Brian 1949- *WhoAmL 94*
Kananack, Michael Jesse 1947- *WhoAmL 94*
Kananin, Roman Grigorevich 1935- *IntWW 93*
Kanao, Minoru 1914- *IntWW 93*
Kanapacki, Ibrahim Barysavic 1949- *LngBDD*
Kanarkowski, Edward Joseph 1947- *WhoAm 94, WhoFI 94*
Kanarowski, Stanley Martin 1912- *WhoAm 94, WhoScEn 94*
Kanasewich, Ernest Roman 1931- *WhoScEn 94*
Kanawa, Kiri te *NewGrDO*
Kanaya, Barbara J. 1946- *WhoAsA 94*
Kanazawa, Shuzo 1910- *IntWW 93*
Kanazir, Dusan 1921- *WhoScEn 94*
Kanbur, Ravi 1954- *IntWW 93*
Kancelbaum, Joshua Jacob 1936- *WhoAm 94*
Kancheli, Giya (Georgy) 1935- *IntWW 93*
Kancheli, Giya Alexandrovich 1935- *NewGrDO*
Kanchier, Carole *WrDr 94*
Kancler, Edward 1939- *WhoAm 94*
Kanda, Motohisa 1943- *WhoAm 94*
Kandaras, Homer Michael 1929- *WhoAmP 93*
Kandarian, Keith A. 1952- *WhoAmL 94*
Kandasamy, Sathasiva Balakrishna 1945- *WhoScEn 94*
Kandel, Aben d1993 *NewYTBS 93*
Kandel, Lenore *WrDr 94*
Kandel, Michael 1941- *EncSF 93*
Kandel, Nelson Robert 1929- *WhoAmL 94*
Kandel, Sue Ellen 1951- *WhoMW 93*
Kandel, William Lloyd 1939- *WhoAm 94, WhoAmL 94*
Kandell, Marshall Jay 1937- *WhoWest 94*
Kander, John Harold 1927- *WhoAm 94*
Kandetzki, Carl Arthur 1941- *WhoScEn 94*
Kandil, Abdel Hadi 1935- *IntWW 93*
Kandil, Osama Abd El Mohsin 1944- *WhoScEn 94*
Kandinsky, Alexey Ivanovich 1918- *NewGrDO*
Kandle, Todd Timothy 1954- *WhoMW 93*
Kandler, Joseph Rudolph 1921- *WhoWest 94*
Kandler, Paul Alfred 1939- *WhoWest 94*
Kandravy, John 1935- *WhoAm 94, WhoAmL 94*
Kandt, Ronald Kirk 1954- *WhoFI 94, WhoScEn 94*
Kandula, Max 1948- *WhoScEn 94*
Kane, Alan K. 1940- *WhoAm 94*
Kane, Alice T. 1948- *WhoIns 94*
Kane, Alice Theresa 1948- *WhoAm 94, WhoAmL 94, WhoFI 94*
Kane, Annette P. 1933- *WhoAm 94*
Kane, Bartholomew Aloysius 1945- *WhoAm 94, WhoWest 94*
Kane, Betty Ann 1941- *WhoAmP 93*
Kane, Bill 1951- *WhoAmA 93*
Kane, Bob Paul 1937- *WhoAmA 93*
Kane, Bradford Ross 1960- *WhoAmL 94*
Kane, Bryon d1984 *WhoHol 92*
Kane, Carol 1952- *IntMPA 94, WhoAm 94, WhoHol 92*
Kane, Caroline Marie 1949- *WhoWest 94*
Kane, Carolyn 1944- *WhoMW 93*
Kane, Cecelia D. 1915- *WhoAmP 93*
Kane, Christopher 1944- *WhoAm 94, WhoAmL 94*
Kane, Cynthia Sullivan 1958- *WhoMW 93*
Kane, Daniel A. 1942- *WhoAm 94*
Kane, Daniel Hipwell 1908- *WhoAm 94*
Kane, Daniel J. 1944- *WhoAmP 93*
Kane, David Michael 1947- *WhoMW 93*
Kane, David N. 1945- *WhoIns 94*
Kane, David Schilling 1907-1988 *WhAm 10*
Kane, David Sheridan 1940- *WhoFI 94*
Ka'ne, Dayton *WhoHol 92*
Kane, Diana d1977 *WhoHol 92*
Kane, Eddie d1969 *WhoHol 92*
Kane, Edward J. 1951- *WhoAmP 93*
Kane, Edward James 1935- *WhoAm 94*
Kane, Edward K. *WhoAmL 94*
Kane, Edward Leonard 1929- *WhoAm 94, WhoFI 94*
Kane, Edward R. 1918- *IntWW 93*
Kane, Edward Rynex 1918- *WhoAm 94*
Kane, Elisha Kent 1820-1857 *WhWE [port]*
Kane, Elizabeth 1942- *WrDr 94*
Kane, Falilou 1938- *IntWW 93*
Kane, Gail d1966 *WhoHol 92*
Kane, George 1916- *Who 94*
Kane, George Joseph 1916- *WhoAm 94*
Kane, Gloria J. 1951- *WhoAmP 93*
Kane, Gordon Leon 1937- *WhoMW 93*
Kane, Helen d1966 *WhoHol 92*
Kane, Herman William 1939- *WhoAm 94*
Kane, Howard Edward 1927- *WhoAm 94*
Kane, Irene *WhoHol 92*
Kane, Jack 1911- *Who 94*
Kane, Jack Allison 1921- *WhoFI 94*
Kane, Jackson D. *WhoHol 92*
Kane, Jacqueline Anne 1946- *WhoBlA 94*
Kane, James Golden 1926- *WhoAm 94*
Kane, James Harry 1848- *WhoScEn 94*
Kane, James Patrick 1946- *WhoWest 94*
Kane, James Robert 1959- *WhoFI 94*
Kane, Jay Brassler 1931- *WhoAm 94*
Kane, Joan S. 1928- *WhoAmP 93*
Kane, John *IntMPA 94*
Kane, John d1969 *WhoHol 92*
Kane, John C. 1939- *WhoFI 94*
Kane, John Dandridge Henley, Jr. 1921- *WhoAm 94*
Kane, John J. 1924- *WhoAmP 93*
Kane, John Lawrence, Jr. 1937- *WhoAm 94, WhoAmL 94, WhoWest 94*
Kane, John Michael 1950- *WhoFI 94*
Kane, John Vincent, Jr. 1928- *WhoScEn 94*
Kane, Jonathan 1945- *WhoAmL 94*
Kane, Jonathan A. 1945- *WhoAm 94*
Kane, Joseph Edward 1945- *WhoAmL 94*
Kane, Joseph Thomas 1934- *WhoAm 94*
Kane, Julie *DrAPF 93*
Kane, Karen Marie 1947- *WhoFI 94, WhoWest 94*
Kane, Katherine *DrAPF 93*
Kane, Katherine D. 1950- *WhoWest 94*
Kane, Kevin Thomas 1952- *WhoScEn 94*
Kane, Larry Joe 1945- *WhoMW 93*
Kane, Leslie 1945- *ConAu 140*
Kane, Lida d1955 *WhoHol 92*
Kane, Louis Isaac 1931- *WhoAm 94, WhoFI 94*
Kane, Lucile Marie 1920- *WhoAm 94*
Kane, Margaret Brassler 1909- *WhoAm 94, WhoAmA 93*
Kane, Marilyn Elizabeth 1941- *WhoAm 94, WhoFI 94*
Kane, Marion d1943 *WhoHol 92*
Kane, Marjorie 1909- *WhoHol 92*
Kane, Michael *WhoHol 92*
Kane, Michael Joel 1951- *WhoScEn 94*
Kane, Michael Joseph 1922- *WhoAm 94*
Kane, Pablo *EncSF 93*
Kane, Patricia Lanegran 1926- *WhoAm 94*
Kane, Patrick J. *WhoAmP 93*
Kane, Paul *DrAPF 93*
Kane, Paul 1810-1871 *WhWE*
Kane, Penny 1945- *WrDr 94*
Kane, Richard 1938- *WhoHol 92*
Kane, Richard F. 1943- *WhoAmL 94*
Kane, Richard Joseph 1941- *WhoAm 94*
Kane, Robert B. 1928- *WhoMW 93*
Kane, Robert Francis 1926- *WhoAm 94, WhoAmP 93*
Kane, Robert John 1958- *WhoAmL 94*
Kane, Robert Louis 1940- *WhoAm 94*
Kane, Robert M. 1942- *WhoAmP 93*
Kane, Ronald 1944- *WhoAm 94*
Kane, Sam 1919- *WhoFI 94*
Kane, Sid *WhoHol 92*
Kane, Siegrun Dinklage 1938- *WhoAmL 94*
Kane, Stanley Bruce 1920- *WhoAm 94*
Kane, Stanley D. 1907- *IntMPA 94*
Kane, Stanley Phillip 1930- *WhoAm 94*
Kane, Stratton J. 1938- *WhoIns 94*
Kane, Thomas Patrick 1942- *WhoAm 94, WhoAmL 94*
Kane, Thomas Reif 1924- *WhoAm 94, WhoWest 94*
Kane, Timothy Joseph 1946- *WhoFI 94*
Kane, Tommy Henry 1964- *WhoBlA 94*
Kane, Whitford d1956 *WhoHol 92*
Kane, Wilson *EncSF 93*
Kaneda, Hiromitsu 1934- *WhoAsA 94*
Kaneeda fl. 1800- *EncNAR*
Kanegai, Toy *WhoAsA 94*
Kanegis, Arthur L.D. 1947- *WhoFI 94, WhoWest 94*
Kanegis, Sidney S. 1922- *WhoAmA 93*
Kanehann, Joseph Anthony 1929- *WhoWest 94*
Kanehiro, Kenneth Kenji 1934- *WhoWest 94*
Kane Hittner, Marcia Susan 1959- *WhoFI 94*
Kaneko, Hisashi 1933- *WhoAm 94, WhoFI 94, WhoScEn 94*
Kaneko, Iwazo 1907- *IntWW 93*
Kaneko, Lonny *DrAPF 93*
Kaneko, Masao 1942- *WhoScEn 94*
Kaneko, Mitsuru *WhoAm 94*
Kaneko, Ryoji Lloyd 1951- *WhoAsA 94*
Kaneko, William Masami 1960- *WhoAsA 94*
Kaneko, Yoshihiro 1922- *WhoScEn 94*
Kanellos, Nicolás 1945- *WhoHisp 94*
Kanemaru, Shin 1915- *IntWW 93*
Kanemitsu, Matsumi 1922- *WhoAm 94*
Kanemitsu, Matsumi 1922-1992 *AnObit 1992, WhoAmA 93N, WhoAsA 94N*
Kanenaka, Rebecca Yae 1958- *WhoWest 94*
Kaner, H(yman) 1896-1973 *EncSF 93*
Kaner, Harvey Sheldon 1930- *WhoAm 94, WhoFI 94*
Kanerova, Mita Castle *ConAu 142*
Kanerva, Ilkka Armas Mikael 1948- *IntWW 93*
Kanes, Eveline L. 1929- *ConAu 141*
Kanes, Steven R. 1946- *WhoAmL 94*
Kanes, William Henry 1934- *WhoAm 94, WhoScEn 94*
Kaneshige, Harry Masato 1929- *WhoAsA 94*
Kaneshige, Melvin Yoshio 1948- *WhoAmL 94*
Kaneshina, Shoji 1942- *WhoScEn 94*
Kanesta, Nellie Rose 1939- *WhoWest 94*
Kanet, Roger Edward 1936- *WhoAm 94, WhoMW 93*
Kane-Vanni, Patricia Ruth 1954- *WhoAmL 94, WhoFI 94*
Kanew, Jeff *IntMPA 94*
Kanfer, Frederick Howard *WhoAm 94*
Kanfer, Julian Norman 1930- *WhoAm 94*
Kang, Bann C. 1939- *WhoScEn 94*
Kang, Benjamin Toyeong 1931- *WhoAm 94*
Kang, Bin Goo 1936- *WhoScEn 94*
Kang, Byung I. 1943- *WhoAsA 94*
Kang, Chang-Yuil 1954- *WhoAsA 94, WhoWest 94*
Kang, Dong-Suk 1954- *IntWW 93*
Kang, Eun Chul 1953- *WhoAsA 94*
Kang, Heesook Sophia 1958- *WhoAsA 94*
Kang, Hyungwon 1963- *WhoAsA 94*
Kang, James Jyh-Huei 1955- *WhoAsA 94*
Kang, Joonhee 1955- *WhoAsA 94*
Kang, Juan 1935- *WhoMW 93*
Kang, Juliana Haeng-Cha 1941- *WhoScEn 94*
Kang, Jun-Koo 1957- *WhoAsA 94*
Kang, Jung Il 1942- *WhoFI 94*
Kang, Keebom 1953- *WhoAsA 94*
Kang, Kyoung Sook 1942- *WhoMW 93*
Kang, Minho 1946- *WhoScEn 94*
Kang, Mohinder Singh 1945- *WhoMW 93*
Kang, Paul Sung-Uh 1961- *WhoFI 94*
Kang, Sang Joon 1940- *WhoScEn 94*
Kang, Shin Il 1955- *WhoScEn 94*
Kang, Shin T. *WhoAsA 94*
Kang, Sugwon 1936- *WhoAsA 94*
Kang, Sung Kyew 1941- *WhoScEn 94*
Kang, Sung-Mo 1945- *WhoAm 94*
Kang, Weng Poo 1953- *WhoAsA 94*
Kang, Wi Jo 1930- *WhoAsA 94*
Kang, Young Hoon 1922- *IntWW 93, Who 94*
Kang, Young Woo 1944- *WhoMW 93*
Kang, Yung C. 1955- *WhoAsA 94*
Kangas, Edward A. 1944- *WhoAm 94, WhoFI 94*
Kangas, Gene 1944- *WhoAmA 93*
Kang-ba-er-han *WhoPRCh 91*
Kang Beisheng 1941- *WhoPRCh 91 [port]*
Kanger, Stig Gustaf 1924-1988 *WhAm 10*
Kang-Huneke, Myung Hee 1966- *WhoAmL 94*
Kang Jimin *WhoPRCh 91*
Kang Keqing 1912- *WhoPRCh 91 [port]*
Kang Kon 1918-1950 *HisDcKW*
Kang Kyung-Shik 1936- *IntWW 93*
Kang Ling *WhoPRCh 91*
Kang Shi'en 1915- *IntWW 93, WhoPRCh 91 [port]*
Kang Shiyao 1921- *WhoPRCh 91 [port]*
Kan Guanqing 1916- *WhoPRCh 91 [port]*
Kang Xi c. 1654-1722 *HisWorL*
Kang Yonghe 1915- *WhoPRCh 91 [port]*
Kang Yuwei 1858-1927 *HisWorL [port]*
Kang Zhenhuang 1920- *WhoPRCh 91 [port]*
Kang Zhijie 1921- *WhoPRCh 91 [port]*
Kang Zhonglun 1932- *WhoPRCh 91 [port]*
Kang Zhuo 1920- *WhoPRCh 91*
Kani, John *IntWW 93*
Kania, Alan James 1949- *WhoWest 94*
Kanicki, Jerzy 1954- *WhoScEn 94*
Kanidinc, Salahattin 1927- *WhoAm 94, WhoAmA 93*
Kaniecki, Michael Joseph 1935- *WhoAm 94, WhoWest 94*
Kanig, Lavinia Ludlow 1916- *WhoAmP 93*
Kanigel, Robert 1946- *WrDr 94*
Kanin, Dennis Roy 1946- *WhoAm 94*
Kanin, Fay *IntMPA 94, WhoAm 94*
Kanin, Fay 1917- *WhoHol 92*
Kanin, Garson 1912- *ConDr 93, IntDcF 2-4, IntMPA 94, IntWW 93, WhoAm 94, WrDr 94*
Kanin, Michael d1993 *IntMPA 94N*
Kanin, Michael 1910-1993 *ConAu 140, ConTFT 11, NewYTBS 93 [port]*
Kanitz, Mary Helen 1957- *WhoMW 93*
Kanjorski, Paul E. 1937- *CngDr 93*
Kanjorski, Paul Edmund 1937- *WhoAm 94, WhoAmP 93*
Kankaanpaa, Matti 1927- *IntWW 93*
Kan-Mitchell, June 1949- *WhoAsA 94*

Kaplow, Robert David 1947- WhoAmL 94
Kaplowitz, Karen Jill 1946- WhoWest 94
Kaplowitz, Richard Allen 1940- WhoWest 94
Kaplowitz, Stan Allen 1945- WhoMW 93
Kapnick, Harvey Edward, Jr. 1925- IntWW 93, WhoAm 94, WhoFI 94
Kapnick, Richard Bradshaw 1955- WhoAm 94, WhoAmL 94, WhoFI 94
Kapnick, Stewart 1956- WhoFI 94
Kapoor, Anish 1954- IntWW 93, Who 94
Kapoor, Harish K. 1957- WhoAsA 94
Kapoor, Jagmohan 1940- WhoAsA 94
Kapoor, Jennifer WhoHol 92
Kapoor, Pincho WhoHol 92
Kapoor, Prithvi Raj d1972 WhoHol 92
Kapoor, Raj d1988 WhoHol 92
Kapoor, Sanjiv 1961- WhoAsA 94
Kapoor, Shashi 1938- IntMPA 94, IntWW 93
Kapoor, Shashi 1939- WhoHol 92
Kapoor, Shiv G. 1948- WhoAsA 94
Kapoor, Tarun 1955- WhoAsA 94
Kapor, Mitchell David 1950- WhoAm 94, WhoScEn 94
Kapp, C. Terrence 1944- WhoAmL 94
Kapp, Colin 1928- EncSF 93, WrDr 94
Kapp, Eleanor Jeanne 1933- WhoWest 94
Kapp, Eugen 1908- NewGrDO
Kapp, James W., Jr. 1944- WhoAmL 94
Kapp, Joe WhoHol 92
Kapp, John Paul 1938- WhoAm 94, WhoAmL 94
Kapp, Julius 1883-1962 NewGrDO
Kapp, M. Keith 1953- WhoAmP 93
Kapp, Michael Keith 1953- WhoAmL 94
Kapp, Nancy Gladys 1945- WhoMW 93
Kapp, Richard P. 1936- WhoAm 94
Kapp, Robert Harris 1934- WhoAm 94
Kapp, Ronald Ormond 1935-1990 WhAm 10
Kapp, Villem 1913-1964 NewGrDO
Kappas, Attallah 1926- WhoAm 94, WhoScEn 94
Kappe, David Syme 1935- WhoScEn 94
Kappel, Frederick R. 1902- IntWW 93, Who 94
Kappel, Gertrude 1884-1971 NewGrDO
Kappel, Philip 1901-1981 WhoAmA 93N
Kappeler, Alfred d1945 WhoHol 92
Kappen, Claudia Therese 1958- WhoWest 94
Kappes, Philip Spangler 1925- WhoFI 94, WhoMW 93
Kappmeyer, Keith K. WhoScEn 94
Kappner, Augusta Souza 1944- WhoAm 94, WhoBlA 94
Kapral, Frank Albert 1928- WhoAm 94, WhoScEn 94
Kaprelian, Edward K. 1913- WhoAm 94
Kaprielian, Walter 1934- WhoAm 94
Kaprio, Leo 1918- IntWW 93
Kapriskv, Valerie 1963- WhoHol 92
Kaprov, Susan 1946- WhoAmA 93
Kapsalis, John DrAPF 93
Kapsalis, Thomas Harry 1925- WhoAmA 93
Kapshtyk, Ivan Markovych 1939- LngBDD
Kapsis, Robert E. 1943- ConAu 141
Kapsomera, Celia Stavroula 1960- WhoFI 94
Kapsperger, Giovanni Girolamo c. 1580-1651 NewGrDO
Kapstein, Sherwin J. WhoAmP 93
Kaptain, Eudokia 1945- WhoIns 94
Kapteyn, Paul Joan George 1928- IntWW 93
Kaptur, Angela 1946- WhoWomW 91
Kaptur, Marcia Carolyn 1946- WhoAm 94, WhoMW 93
Kaptur, Marcy 1946- CngDr 93
Kaptur, Marcy C. 1946- WhoAmP 93
Kapur, Kailash Chander 1941- WhoAm 94
Kapur, Kamal K. 1948- WhoAsA 94
Kapur, Krishan Kishore 1930- WhoAm 94
Kapur, Rajiv A. 1951- WrDr 94
Kapur, Sanjiv K. 1961- WhoAmL 94
Kapur, Sudarshan 1940- ConAu 142
Kapuscinski, Ryszard 1932- IntWW 93
Kapusinski, Albert Thomas 1937- WhoFI 94, WhoScEn 94
Kapusta, Joseph Irving 1952- WhoMW 93
Kapusta, Paul ConAu 42NR
Kara, Paul Mark 1954- WhoAmL 94
Karaba, Frank Andrew 1927- WhoAm 94
Karabasz, Felix Francois 1939- WhoMW 93
Karabatsos, Elizabeth Ann 1932- WhoFI 94, WhoWest 94
Karabots, Joseph William 1956- WhoFI 94, WhoScEn 94
Karacan, Ismet 1927- WhoScEn 94
Karachi, Archbishop of 1918- Who 94
Karadjordjevic, Alexander IntWW 93
Karady, George Gyorgy 1930- WhoAm 94, WhoFI 94
Karadzic, Radovan IntWW 93
Karaev, Tamerlan Elmar Ogly 1952- LngBDD
Karaevli, Ahmet 1949- IntWW 93
Karafel, Lorraine 1956- WhoAmA 93
Karaganov, Sergei Aleksandrovich LngBDD
Karageorge, Michael EncSF 93
Karageorge, Yuri Vidov DrAPF 93
Karageorghis, Vassos 1929- IntWW 93
Karahalios, Sue WhoAmP 93
Karahalios, Sue M. Compton 1949- WhoWest 94
Karaim, Betty June 1936- WhoAm 94
Karajan, Herbert von 1908-1989 NewGrDO
Kara Juro 1940?- IntDcT 2
Karakas, Rita S. 1949- WhoAm 94
Karakash, John J. 1914- WhoAm 94
Karakawa, Walter W. d1993 NewYTBS 93
Karakey, Sherry JoAnne 1942- WhoWest 94
Karakozov, Sergei Dmitrievich 1956- WhoScEn 94
Karalash, Beverly Kay 1958- WhoWest 94
Karalekas, Anne 1946- WhoAm 94
Karalekas, George Steven 1939- WhoAm 94
Karales, James Harry 1930- WhoAm 94
Karalis, John Peter 1938- WhoAm 94
Karam, Elena WhoHol 92
Karaman, Aleksandr Akimovich 1956- LngBDD
Karamanlis, Konstantinos 1907- Who 94
Karamanlis, Konstantinos G. 1907- IntWW 93
Karamanos, Teresa S. 1956- WhoAmP 93
Karamanov, Uzakbai Karamanovich 1937- LngBDD
Karami, Omar IntWW 93
Karamouz, Mohammad 1954- WhoAm 94, WhoScEn 94
Karamustafa, Ahmet Targon 1956- WhoMW 93
Karamzin, Nikolay Mikhaylovich 1766-1826 NewGrDO
Karan, Donna 1948- IntWW 93, WhoAm 94
Karan, Paul Richard 1936- WhoAmL 94
Karanik, John Alexander 1944- WhoIns 94
Karanikas, Alexander 1916- WhoAm 94, WrDr 94
Karanja, Josphat Njuguna 1931- IntWW 93, Who 94
Karantokis, Nicolas Georgiou 1917- WhoFI 94
Karaosmanoglu, Attila 1932- IntWW 93
Karapostoles, Demetrios Aristides 1936- WhoFI 94, WhoScEn 94
Karas, Anton d1985 WhoHol 92
Karas, Meletios Speros 1955- WhoMW 93
Karas, Steven Lawrence 1951- WhoMW 93
Karasa, Norman Lukas 1951- WhoWest 94
Karasawa, Shunjiro 1930- IntWW 93
Karasick, Carol 1941- WhoAm 94
Karasov, Phyllis 1951- WhoAmL 94
Karasu, Toksoz Byram 1935- WhoAm 94
Karasz, Arthur 1907-1992 WrDr 94N
Karasz, Mariska 1898-1960 WhoAmA 93N
Karasz, Peter 1941- WhoAm 94
Karath, Kym 1959- WhoHol 92
Karato, Shun-ichiro 1949- WhoMW 93, WhoScEn 94
Karatsu, Osamu 1947- WhoFI 94, WhoScEn 94
Karatz, Bruce E. 1945- WhoWest 94
Karatz, William Warren 1926- WhoAm 94
Karatzas, Basil WhoFI 94
Karavite, Carlene Marie 1939- WhoMW 93
Karavolas, Harry John 1936- WhoAm 94
Karawina, Erica WhoAmA 93
Karawina, Erica 1904- WhoAm 94
Karayanis, Plato 1928- NewGrDO
Karayannis, Nicholas Marios 1931- WhoAm 94
Karayev, Kara (Abul'faz-ogli) 1918-1982 NewGrDO
Karayev, Tamerlan 1953- IntWW 93
Karayn, James, Jr. 1933- WhoAm 94
Karberg, Richard Elmer 1941- WhoMW 93
Karbo, Karen DrAPF 93
Karbo, Karen (Lee) 1956?- ConAu 141
Karch, Charles Phillip 1953- WhoFI 94
Karch, George Frederick, Jr. 1933- WhoAm 94
Karch, Robert E. 1933- WhoFI 94
Karch, Sargent 1936- WhoAm 94
Karcher, Alan J. 1943- WhoAmP 93
Karcher, Charles William 1920- WhoAm 94
Karcher, John Clarence 1894- WhAm 10
Karcher, John Drake 1939- WhoFI 94
Karchin, Louis Samuel 1951- WhoAm 94
Karchow, Ernest d1953 WhoHol 92
Karczewski, Witold Andrzej 1930- IntWW 93
Karczmar, Mieczyslaw 1923- WhoFI 94
Karczmarz, Kazimierz 1933- WhoScEn 94
Karczykowski, Ryszard 1942- NewGrDO
Kardas, Sigmund Joseph, Jr. 1940- WhoScEn 94
Kardes, Frank Robert 1958- WhoScEn 94
Kardish, Laurence 1945- IntMPA 94
Kardomateas, George Alexander 1958- WhoScEn 94
Kardon, Carol WhoAmA 93
Kardon, Janet WhoAm 94, WhoAmA 93
Kardon, Robert 1922- WhoAm 94
Kardos, Mel D. 1947- WhoAmL 94
Kardos, Paul James 1937- WhoFI 94
Kardously, George J. 1964- WhoScEn 94
Kare, Graciela Salinas 1957- WhoHisp 94
Kare, Morley Richard 1922-1990 WhAm 10
Karefa-Smart, John Musselman 1915- IntWW 93
Karegeannes, Peter C. 1947- WhoAmL 94
Kareh, Jorge 1960- WhoHisp 94
Karei, Hidekazu 1960- WhoFI 94
Kareken, Francis A. 1930- WhoAm 94
Karel, Frank, III 1935- WhoAm 94
Karel, Marcus 1928- WhoAm 94
Karel, Rudolf 1880-1945 NewGrDO
Karelis, Charles Howard 1945- WhoAm 94
Karelitz, Robert Nelson 1948- WhoAm 94
Karelli, Zoe 1901- BlmGWL
Karels, Harvey d1975 WhoHol 92
Karem, David Kevin 1943- WhoAmP 93
Karem, Michael G. 1946- WhoAmP 93
Karen, Anna WhoHol 92
Karen, Anna 1936- WhoHol 92
Karen, James 1922- WhoHol 92
Karetnikov, Nikolai Nikolayevich 1930- IntWW 93
Karetnikov, Nikolay 1930- NewGrDO
Karetzky, Stephen 1946- WhoAm 94
Karff, Samuel Egal 1931- WhoAm 94
Karfiol, Bernard 1886-1952 WhoAmA 93N
Kargbo, Tom Obakeh 1945- IntWW 93
Karge, Stewart W. 1953- WhoAm 94
Karger, Delmar William 1913- WrDr 94
Karhilo, Aarno 1927- IntWW 93
Kari, Donald G. 1946- WhoAmL 94
Kari, Hilda 1949- WhoWomW 91
Karian, Zaven Albert 1941- WhoMW 93
Kariel, Henry S 1924- WrDr 94
Karieva, Bernara 1936- IntWW 93
Karig, Walter 1898-1956 EncSF 93
Karigan, James Andrew 1927- WhoAm 94
Karigl, Gunther 1953- WhoScEn 94
Karim, Amin H. 1951- WhoScEn 94
Karim, Mustai 1919- IntWW 93
Karim-Lamrani, Mohammed 1919- IntWW 93
Karimo, Aarno EncSF 93
Karimov, Islam 1938- IntWW 93
Karimov, Islam Abduganievich 1938- LngBDD
Karin, Rita WhoHol 92
Karin, Rita 1919-1993 NewYTBS 93
Karin, Sidney 1943- WhoAm 94, WhoScEn 94
Karina, Anna 1940- IntMPA 94, IntWW 93, WhoHol 92
Karinska, Barbara 1886-1983 IntDcB
Karinthy, Ferenc d1992 IntWW 93N
Karinthy, Frigyes 1887-1938 EncSF 93
Karis, Thomas Edward 1954- WhoScEn 94
Karis, William George 1948- WhoFI 94
Karita, Teiko 1932- WhoWomW 91
Kariya, Hiroshi 1948- WhoAmA 93
Kariya, Paul WhoAsA 94
Kark, Austen Steven 1926- IntWW 93, Who 94
Kark, Evelyn Florence 1928- Who 94
Kark, Leslie Who 94
Kark, (Arthur) Leslie 1910- Who 94
Kark, Nina Mary Who 94
Kark, Raymond d1986 WhoHol 92
Kark, Robert M. 1911- WhoAm 94
Karker, Stephen John 1949- WhoFI 94
Karkheck, John Peter 1945- WhoScEn 94
Karkia, Mohammad Reza 1949- WhoScEn 94
Karklins, Rasma 1946- WhoMW 93
Karklins, Vija L. 1929- WhoAm 94
Karkut, Emil Joseph 1916- WhoAm 94
Karkut, Richard Theodore 1948- WhoMW 93, WhoScEn 94
Karkutt, Marilyn N. 1938- WhoAmP 93
Karl, Barry Dean 1927- WhoAm 94
Karl, Daniel William 1951- WhoScEn 94
Karl, Dennis (R.) 1954- WrDr 94
Karl, Elfriede 1933- IntWW 93, WhoWomW 91
Karl, Frederick (Robert) 1927- WrDr 94
Karl, Gabriel 1937- WhoAm 94, WhoScEn 94
Karl, George 1951- WhoAm 94, WhoWest 94
Karl, Mark William 1962- WhoMW 93
Karl, Max Henry 1910- WhoAm 94
Karl, Roger d1984 WhoHol 92
Karl, Theodor NewGrDO
Karlan, Mitchell A. 1955- WhoAmL 94
Karlan, Richard 1919- WhoHol 92
Karle, Hellmut (William Arthur) 1932- ConAu 142
Karle, Isabella 1921- IntWW 93, WhoAm 94, WhoScEn 94
Karle, Jean Marianne 1950- WhoScEn 94
Karle, Jerome 1918- IntWW 93, Who 94, WhoAm 94, WhoScEn 94
Karlen, Arno DrAPF 93
Karlen, Douglas Lawrence 1951- WhoAm 94, WhoMW 93
Karlen, John 1933- WhoHol 92
Karlen, Merrill, Jr. 1956- WhoAmP 93
Karlen, Neal Stuart 1959- WhoMW 93
Karlen, Peter H. WhoAmA 93
Karlen, Peter Hurd 1949- WhoAmL 94, WhoWest 94
Karleskint, Barry Michael 1941- WhoWest 94
Karl Eugen NewGrDO
Karlin, Bernie 1927- WrDr 94
Karlin, Bo-Peep d1969 WhoHol 92
Karlin, Edward J. 1952- WhoAmL 94
Karlin, Fred 1936- IntMPA 94
Karlin, Gary Lee 1934- WhoFI 94, WhoMW 93
Karlin, James Edward 1950- WhoMW 93
Karlin, Michael Jonathan Abraham 1952- WhoAm 94
Karlin, Miriam 1925- WhoHol 92
Karlin, Myron D. 1918- IntMPA 94, WhoAm 94
Karlin, Robert E. 1916- WhoAmP 93
Karlin, Samuel 1924- IntWW 93, WhoAm 94, WhoScEn 94, WhoWest 94
Karlin, Teri Lea 1963- WhoAm 94
Karlin, Wayne DrAPF 93
Karlin, Wayne (Stephen) 1945- WrDr 94
Karlinger, Angela C. 1903- WhoAmP 93
Karlins, Mark DrAPF 93
Karlins, Martin William 1932- WhoAm 94
Karlinsky, Simon 1924- WhoAm 94
Karll, Jo Ann 1948- WhoAmP 93, WhoMW 93
Karloff, Boris d1969 WhoHol 92
Karlove, Bettina Lee 1958- WhoMW 93
Karlovich, Robert Joseph 1964- WhoWest 94
Karlovitz, Les Andrew 1936-1990 WhAm 10
Karlow, Edwin Anthony 1942- WhoScEn 94
Karls, John B. 1931- WhoMW 93
Karls, John Spencer 1942- WhoAm 94, WhoAmL 94
Karlsefni, Thorfinn fl. 100-?- WhWE
Karlsen, John WhoHol 92
Karlson, Kevin Wade 1952- WhoScEn 94
Karlsson, Erik Lennart 1918- IntWW 93
Karlsson, Ingemar Harry 1944- WhoScEn 94
Karlsson, Irmtraut 1944- WhoWomW 91
Karlstadt, Liesl d1960 WhoHol 92
Karlstrom, Paul Johnson 1941- WhoAm 94, WhoAmA 93
Karlton, Lawrence K. 1935- WhoAm 94, WhoAmL 94, WhoWest 94
Karlweis, Oscar d1956 WhoHol 92
Karmal, Babrak d1992 IntWW 93N
Karman, Arthur Bennett 1936- WhoMW 93
Karman, James Anthony 1937- WhoFI 94
Karman, Kenneth Allen 1943- WhoFI 94
Karmeier, Delbert Fred 1935- WhoAm 94
Karmel, Alexander D. 1904- Who 94
Karmel, Peter Henry 1922- IntWW 93, Who 94, WrDr 94
Karmel, Roberta S. 1937- WhoAm 94, WhoAmL 94, WhoAmP 93
Karmen, Arthur 1930- WhoAm 94
Karmi, Ram 1931- IntWW 93
Karmiloff-Smith, Annette Dionne 1938- Who 94
Karmin, Monroe William 1929- WhoAm 94
Karmins'ky, Mark 1930- NewGrDO
Karmovkov, Khachim Mukhamedovich 1941- LngBDD
Karn, Gloria Stoll 1923- WhoAmA 93
Karn, Richard Wendall 1927- WhoAm 94
Karn, Valerie Ann 1939- Who 94
Karna, James Timothy 1951- WhoAmL 94
Karnad, Girish 1938- IntWW 93
Karnad, Girish (Raghunath) 1938- ConDr 93
Karnath, Joan Edna 1947- WhoMW 93
Karnaugh, Maurice 1924- WhoAm 94
Karnes, David K. 1948- WhoAmP 93
Karnes, Evan Burton, II WhoMW 93
Karnes, Jan Arla 1960- WhoMW 93

Karnes, Karen 1925- WhoAmA 93
Karnes, Robert d1979 WhoHol 92
Karnette, Betty WhoAmP 93
Karney, James Lynn 1941- WhoScEn 94
Karni, Edi 1944- WhoAm 94
Karni, Shlomo 1932- WhoAm 94
Karnik, Avinash Ramkrishna 1940- WhoWest 94
Karnik, Sadashiva 1954- WhoMW 93
Karnilova, Maria 1920- WhoHol 92
Karniol, Hilda 1910- WhoAmA 93
Karno, Fred 1866-1941 DcNaB MP
Karnofsky, Mollyne DrAPF 93
Karnos, David D. 1947- ConAu 141
Karnovsky, Manfred L. 1918- WhoAm 94
Karnovsky, Morris John 1926- WhoAm 94, WhoScEn 94
Karnow, Curtis Edward Andrew 1953- WhoAmL 94
Karnow, Stanley 1925- WhoAm 94, WrDr 94
Karns, Barry Wayne 1946- WhoAmL 94
Karns, Jeanne Ann 1951- WhoMW 93
Karns, Margaret Padelford 1943- WhoMW 93
Karns, Roscoe d1970 WhoHol 92
Karns, Todd WhoHol 92
Karns, Virginia d1990 WhoHol 92
Karodia, Farida 1942?- BlmGWL
Karol, Alexander 1925- WrDr 94
Karol, Frederick John 1933- WhoAm 94
Karol, John Jacob, Jr. 1935- WhoFI 94
Karol, Nathaniel H. 1929- WhoAm 94
Karol, Pamala DrAPF 93
Karol, Reuben Hirsh 1922- WhoAm 94, WhoScEn 94
Karol, Stephen John 1948- WhoAmP 93
Karolak, Dale Walter 1959- WhoFI 94
Karoli, Hermann 1906- IntWW 93
Karolin, Stella Helene 1922- WhoMW 93
Karon, Daniel Richard 1966- WhoAmL 94
Karotkin, Stephen K. 1951- WhoAm 94, WhoAmL 94
Karoui, Hamed 1927- IntWW 93
Karouna, Kir George 1929- WhoScEn 94
Karp, Aaron S. 1947- WhoAmA 93, WhoWest 94
Karp, Abraham J. 1921- WrDr 94
Karp, Abraham Joseph 1921- WhoAm 94
Karp, Allen 1940- WhoFI 94
Karp, Daniel Joseph 1928- WhoMW 93
Karp, David 1922- EncSF 93, IntWW 93, Who 94, WhoAm 94, WrDr 94
Karp, Donald Mathew 1937- WhoAm 94
Karp, Gary Edward 1969- WhoFI 94
Karp, Gene 1936- WhoAmP 93
Karp, Harvey Lawrence 1927- WhoAm 94, WhoFI 94
Karp, Herbert Rubin 1921- WhoAm 94
Karp, Leon d1951 WhoAmA 93N
Karp, Marshall Warren 1942- WhoAm 94
Karp, Martin Everett 1922- WhoAm 94
Karp, Michael Harris 1964- WhoMW 93
Karp, Nathan 1915- WhoAm 94, WhoAmP 93
Karp, Peter Simon 1935- WhoFI 94
Karp, Richard Alan 1944- WhoWest 94
Karp, Richard Gordon 1933- WhoAmA 93
Karp, Richard M. 1929- WhoAm 94, WhoFI 94
Karp, Richard Manning 1935- WhoAm 94
Karp, Robert 1934- WhoAm 94
Karp, Sherman 1935- WhoAm 94
Karp, Warren Bill 1944- WhoScEn 94
Karpan, Kathleen Marie 1942- WhoAm 94, WhoAmP 93, WhoWest 94, WhoWomW 91
Karpat, Kemal H. 1925- WrDr 94
Karpati, George 1934- WhoScEn 94
Karpatkin, Rhoda Hendrick 1930- WhoAm 94
Karpe, Brian Stanley 1960- WhoAmL 94
Karpe, Richard 1929- WhoAmL 94
Karpeh, Enid Juah Hildegard 1957- WhoBlA 94
Karpel, Craig S. 1944- WhoAm 94
Karpel, Eli 1916- WhoAmA 93
Karpel, Ian Sven 1964- WhoAmL 94
Karpeles, David 1936- WhoWest 94
Karpeles, Michael Dean 1958- WhoAmL 94
Karpen, Marian Joan 1944- WhoAm 94, WhoFI 94
Karpenko, Victor Nicholas 1922- WhoWest 94
Karpenko, Vitalii Opasnovych 1941- LngBDD
Karpick, John 1884-1960 WhoAmA 93N
Karpiel, Doris Catherine 1935- WhoAmP 93, WhoMW 93
Karpilow, Craig 1947- WhoWest 94
Karpinski, Helen Bernice WhoAmP 93
Karpinski, Jacek 1927- WhoScEn 94
Karpinski, John Stanley 1956- WhoAmL 94
Karpinski, Joseph Paul 1940- WhoFI 94
Karpinsky, Len Vyacheslavovich 1932- LngBDD
Karplus, Henry Berthold 1926- WhoScEn 94
Karplus, Martin 1930- IntWW 93, WhoAm 94, WhoScEn 94
Karplus, Walter J. 1927- WhoAm 94, WrDr 94
Karpman, Harold Lew 1927- WhoAm 94
Karpman, Robert Ronald 1952- WhoFI 94, WhoWest 94
Karpman, Scott 1958- WhoFI 94
Karpoff, Michael Steven 1950- WhoAmL 94
Karpov, Anatoliy Yevgenievich 1951- IntWW 93
Karpov, Anatoly Evgenevich 1951- LngBDD
Karpov, Viktor Pavlovich 1928- IntWW 93
Karpov, Vladimir Vasilyevich 1922- IntWW 93
Karpowicz, Terrence Edward 1948- WhoAmA 93
Karpowitz, Anthony Victor 1907- WhoMW 93
Karr, Alan Francis 1947- WhoAm 94
Karr, Bernard LeRoy 1947- WhoAmL 94
Karr, Cheryl Lofgreen 1954- WhoWest 94
Karr, Darwin d1945 WhoHol 92
Karr, David Dean 1953- WhoAmL 94
Karr, Gerald Lee 1936- WhoAmP 93, WhoMW 93
Karr, Herbert William 1925-1990 WhAm 10
Karr, James Barry 1945- WhoFI 94
Karr, James Richard 1943- WhoScEn 94
Karr, Jo WhoAmP 93
Karr, Joseph Peter 1925- WhoMW 93, WhoScEn 94
Karr, Lloyd 1912-1990 WhAm 10
Karr, Mary DrAPF 93
Karr, Norman 1927- WhoAm 94
Karr, William Hamilton, III 1946- WhoMW 93
Karraker, Naneen 1949- WhoWest 94
Karran, Graham 1939- Who 94
Karras, Alex 1935- IntMPA 94, WhoAm 94, WhoHol 92
Karras, Donald George 1953- WhoWest 94
Karras, John M. 1944- WhoAmP 93
Karras, Nolan E. 1944- WhoAmP 93
Karras, Nolan Eldon 1944- WhoWest 94
Karrer, Carol Converse 1940- WhoMW 93
Karrer, Kathleen Marie 1949- WhoMW 93
Karrh, Bruce Wakefield 1936- WhoAm 94
Karri, Surya B. Reddy 1959- WhoScEn 94
Karr i Alfonsetti, Carme 1865-1943 BlmGWL
Karriem, Jaleelah DrAPF 93
Karron, Richard WhoHol 92
Karros, Eric Peter 1967- WhoAm 94, WhoWest 94
Kar Roy, Arjun 1967- WhoScEn 94
Karrs, Stanley Richard 1949- WhoScEn 94
Karsavina, Jean DrAPF 93
Karsavina, Tamara 1885-1978 IntDcB [port]
Karsch, Anna Louisa 1722-1791 BlmGWL
Karsch, Jay Harris 1942- WhoAmL 94
Karsen, Sonja Petra 1919- WhoAm 94
Karsenti, Rene 1950- IntWW 93
Karsh, Yousuf 1908- IntWW 93, Who 94, WhoAm 94, WhoAmA 93
Karson, Allen Ronald 1947- WhoFI 94
Karson, Burton Lewis 1934- WhoAm 94
Karson, Catherine June 1956- WhoScEn 94
Karson, Emile 1921- WhoAm 94
Karson, Samuel 1924- WhoAm 94
Karson, Stanley WhoHisp 94
Karst, Kenneth L(eslie) 1929- WrDr 94
Karst, Kenneth Leslie 1929- WhoAm 94
Karstaedt, Arthur R. 1951- WhoAmL 94
Karsten, Christofer Christian 1756-1827 NewGrDO
Karsten, Ian George Francis 1944- Who 94
Kartalia, Mitchell P. 1913- WhoAm 94
Kartalian, Buck WhoHol 92
Kartell, Irving P. d1993 NewYTBS 93
Karten, Harvey Jules 1935- WhoAm 94
Karter, Jerome 1937- WhoIns 94
Kartha, Mukund K. 1936- WhoAsA 94
Kartiganer, Joseph 1935- WhoAm 94
Kartomi, Margaret Joy 1940- IntWW 93
Kartousch, Louise 1886-1964 NewGrDO
Kartozian, William F. 1938- IntMPA 94
Kartte, Wolfgang 1927- IntWW 93
Kartzev, Vladimir Petrovich 1938- IntWW 93
Kartzinel, Ronald 1945- WhoAm 94
Karu, Gilda Mall 1951- WhoMW 93
Karukubiro-Kamunanwire, Perezi 1937- IntWW 93
Karunakaran, Shri K. 1918- IntWW 93
Karunandhi, Muthuvel 1924- IntWW 93
Karunaratne, Nuwarapaksa Hewayalage Asoka Mahaname 1918- IntWW 93
Karusseit, Ursula 1939- IntWW 93
Karvan, Claudia 1973- WhoHol 92
Karvas, Peter 1920- IntDcT 2
Karvelas, Dennis E. 1958- WhoScEn 94
Karvelis, Leon J., Jr. 1942- WhoAm 94
Karwacki, Robert Lee 1933- WhoAmL 94
Karwatzki, Irmgard 1940- WhoWomW 91
Karwelis, Donald Charles 1934- WhoAmA 93
Karwoski, John P. 1940- WhoAmP 93
Karwoski, Richard Charles 1938- WhoAmA 93
Karwowski, Robert Allyn 1944- WhoFI 94
Karyakin, Yury Fedorovich 1930- LngBDD
Karyo, Tcheky 1953- WhoHol 92
Kasa, Pamela Dorothy 1943- WhoAm 94
Kasaback, Ronald Lawrence 1935- WhoScEn 94
Kasack, Hermann EncSF 93
Kasahara, Yukio 1925- IntWW 93
Kasai, Paul Haruo 1932- WhoScEn 94
Kasak, Nikolai WhoAmA 93
Kasama, Hideto Peter 1946- WhoFI 94, WhoWest 94
Kasanin, Mark Owen 1929- WhoAm 94
Kasaravalli, Girish 1950- IntWW 93
Kasarda, John Dale 1945- WhoAm 94
Kasari, Leonard Samuel 1924- WhoWest 94
Kasatkina, Natalya Dmitriyevna 1934- IntWW 93
Kasatonov, Igor Vladimirovich 1939- IntWW 93, LngBDD
Kasbeer, Stephen Frederick 1925- WhoAm 94
Kaschak, Lillian Anne WhoFI 94
Kaschmann, Giuseppe 1847-1925 NewGrDO
Kaschnitz, Marie Luise 1901-1974 BlmGWL [port]
Kaschovska, Felicie 1867-1951 NewGrDO
Kasdan, Lawrence 1949- IntMPA 94
Kasdan, Lawrence Edward 1949- IntWW 93, WhoAm 94
Kasdorf, Julia DrAPF 93
Kasdorf, Lenore 1948- WhoHol 92
Kase, Nathan Ginden 1930- WhoAm 94
Kasem, Casey 1932- WhoHol 92
Kasem, Casey 1933- WhoAm 94
Kasem, Jean 1956- WhoHol 92
Kaseman, A. Carl, III 1941- WhoAm 94, WhoAmL 94
Kasemeyer, Edward Johns 1945- WhoAmP 93
Kasen, Stewart Michael 1939- WhoAm 94, WhoFI 94
Kasenter, Robert Albert 1946- WhoAm 94, WhoFI 94
Kaser, David 1924- WhoAm 94
Kaser, Helmut Alfred 1912- IntWW 93
Kaser, Michael Charles 1926- IntWW 93, Who 94, WrDr 94
Kash, Don E 1934- WrDr 94
Kash, Don Eldon 1934- WhoAm 94
Kash, Jeffrey Alan 1953- WhoScEn 94
Kash, Marie 1960- WhoAmA 93
Kash, Marsha Elaine DrAPF 93
Kash, Murray WhoHol 92
Kasha, Kenneth John 1933- WhoAm 94
Kasha, Lawrence N. 1934-1990 WhAm 10
Kashani, Hamid Reza 1955- WhoAmL 94
Kashani, Javad Hassan-Nejad 1937- WhoAm 94
Kashanian, Shahriar 1960- WhoAmL 94
Kashar, Lawrence Joseph 1933- WhoScEn 94
Kashay, Abe d1965 WhoHol 92
Kashdan, David Stuart 1950- WhoScEn 94
Kashdin, Gladys Shafran 1921- WhoAmA 93
Kashevarov, Aleksandr Filippovich 1808-1866 WhWE
Kashfi, Anna 1934- WhoHol 92
Kashgarian, Michael 1933- WhoAm 94
Kashif, Ghayth Nur 1933- WhoBlA 94
Kashif, Lonnie 1933- WhoBlA 94
Kashin, Daniil Nikitich c. 1770-1841 NewGrDO
Kashio, Tadao d1993 NewYTBS 93
Kashiwa, Hank Charles 1949- WhoAsA 94
Kashiwagi, Brian Rio 1942- WhoAsA 94
Kashiwagi, Hiroshi DrAPF 93
Kashiwagi, Soji Charles 1962- WhoAsA 94
Kashiwagi, Yusuke 1917- IntWW 93
Kashlev, Yuriy Borisovich 1934- IntWW 93
Kashner, Dave d1985 WhoHol 92
Kashner, Samuel DrAPF 93
Kashperov, Vladimir Nikitich 1826-1894 NewGrDO
Kashulines, Juanita E. WhoAmP 93
Kashyap, Moti Lal 1939- WhoAsA 94
Kashyap, Pankaj Kumar 1962- WhoAsA 94
Kashyap, Rangasami Lakshmi Narayan 1938- WhoAm 94
Kasich, John R. 1952- CngDr 93, WhoAm 94, WhoAmP 93, WhoMW 93
Kasik, David Joseph 1949- WhoWest 94
Kasik, Maribeth Montgomery 1952- WhoMW 93
Kasimer, Solomon 1946- WhoAm 94
Kasimos, John Nicholas 1955- WhoMW 93, WhoScEn 94
Kasinec, Edward 1945- WhoAm 94
Kasinoff, Bernard Herman 1920- WhoAm 94
Kasischke, Laura DrAPF 93
Kasischke, Louis Walter 1942- WhoAm 94, WhoAmL 94
Kaske, Karlheinz 1928- IntWW 93
Kaske, Robert Earl 1921-1989 WhAm 10
Kaskel, Neal T. 1943- WhoWest 94
Kaskell, Peter Howard 1924- WhoAm 94
Kasket, Harold 1915- WhoHol 92
Kaskey, Raymond John 1943- WhoAmA 93
Kaskowitz, Edwin 1936- WhoAm 94
Kasle, Gertrude 1917- WhoAmA 93
Kasler, Richard Eugene Jeff 1925- WhAm 10
Kaslick, Ralph Sidney 1935- WhoAm 94
Kaslik, Vaclav 1917-1989 NewGrDO
Kasloff, Steve 1952- IntMPA 94
Kaslow, Florence (Whiteman) 1930- ConAu 41NR
Kaslow, Florence W. WhoAm 94
Kaslow, John Francis 1932- WhoAm 94
Kasmer, Joseph 1951- WhoWest 94
Kasmin, John 1934- IntWW 93, Who 94
Kasmir, Gail Alice 1958- WhoFI 94
Kasnowski, Chester N. 1944- WhoAmA 93
Kasnowski, Chester Nelson 1944- WhoAm 94
Kasowitz, Marc Elliot 1952- WhoAm 94, WhoAmL 94
Kasparek, Timothy G. 1948- WhoAmL 94
Kasparov (Vainshtein), Gary Kinovich 1963- LngBDD
Kasparov, Garri Kimovich 1963- IntWW 93
Kasper, Christine Eleana 1953- WhoWest 94
Kasper, Daniel M. 1945- WhoAmP 93
Kasper, Daniel Matthew 1945- WhoFI 94
Kasper, Horst Manfred 1939- WhoAmL 94, WhoFI 94, WhoScEn 94
Kasper, James Michael 1945- WhoAmP 93
Kasper, Larry John 1947- WhoFI 94
Kasper, Raymond Paul 1962- WhoMW 93
Kasper, Ronald Wayne 1944- WhoAm 94
Kasper, Walter Josef 1933- IntWW 93
Kasperbauer, Michael John 1929- WhoAm 94
Kasperczyk, Jurgen 1941- WhoFI 94
Kasperko, Jean Margaret 1949- WhoFI 94
Kaspers, William Freeman 1948- WhoAmL 94
Kasperson, Richard Willet 1927- WhoAm 94
Kasperson, Roger E 1938- WrDr 94
Kaspin, Jeffrey Marc 1948- WhoFI 94
Kasprick, Lyle Clinton 1932- WhoAm 94, WhoFI 94, WhoMW 93
Kasprowicz, Betty M. 1941- WhoIns 94
Kasprowicz, Daniel Ernest 1939- WhoFI 94
Kasprzak, Lucian Alexander 1943- WhoAm 94
Kaspszyk, Jacek 1952- IntWW 93
Kasputis, Edward 1961- WhoAmP 93
Kasputys, Joseph Edward 1936- WhoAm 94
Kasrashvili, Makvala 1948- IntWW 93
Kass, Arthur 1931- WhoAmP 93
Kass, Benny Lee 1936- WhoAm 94, WhoAmL 94
Kass, Deborah 1952- WhoAmA 93
Kass, Edward Harold 1917-1990 WhAm 10
Kass, Jacob James 1910- WhoAmA 93
Kass, Leon Richard 1939- WhoAm 94, WhoScEn 94
Kass, Ray 1944- WhoAmA 93
Kassam, Amirali Hassanali 1943- WhoScEn 94
Kassam, Jeanette Leboeuf BlmGWL
Kassan, Stuart S. 1946- WhoScEn 94, WhoWest 94
Kassander, Arno Richard, Jr. 1920- WhoAm 94
Kassar, Mario 1951- IntMPA 94
Kassar, Mario F. 1951- WhoAm 94
Kassas, Mohamed 1921- WhoScEn 94
Kasse, Rosa E. WhoHisp 94
Kassebaum, Donald Gene 1931- WhoAm 94

Kassebaum, John Philip 1932- *WhoAmL 94*
Kassebaum, Nancy 1932- *WhoWomW 91*
Kassebaum, Nancy Landon 1932- *CngDr 93, IntWW 93, WhoAm 94, WhoAmP 93, WhoMW 93*
Kassebohm, Walter 1898- *WhAm 10*
Kassel, Jeffrey Jan 1951- *WhoAmL 94*
Kassel, Michael Jon 1957- *WhoAmL 94*
Kassel, Tichi Wilkerson 1932- *WhoAm 94*
Kassel, Virginia Weltmer *WhoAm 94*
Kassell, Neal Frederic 1946- *WhoAm 94*
Kassem, Abdul-Rauf al- 1932- *IntWW 93*
Kasser, Ivan Michael 1940- *WhoWest 94*
Kassewitz, Ruth Eileen Blower 1928- *WhoFI 94*
Kassicieh, Suleiman Khalil 1952- *WhoWest 94*
Kassim bin Mohammed Hussein 1928- *Who 94*
Kassinger, Theodore William 1953- *WhoAmL 94*
Kassirer, Paul Lawrence 1952- *WhoAmL 94*
Kassis, Mose 1926- *WhoAmP 93*
Kassis, Noura I. 1943- *WhoWest 94*
Kassler, Haskell A. 1936- *WhoAmL 94*
Kassler, Jamie C(roy) 1938- *WrDr 94*
Kassman, Herbert Seymour 1924- *WhoAm 94*
Kassman, Shirley 1929- *WhoAmA 93*
Kassmeier, Frances C. 1929- *WhoAmP 93*
Kassner, Michael Ernest 1950- *WhoAm 94, WhoWest 94*
Kassof, Allen H. 1930- *WhoFI 94*
Kasson, James Matthews 1943- *WhoAm 94*
Kassoy, Bernard 1914- *WhoAmA 93*
Kassoy, Hortense 1917- *WhoAmA 93*
Kastantin, Joseph Thomas 1947- *WhoMW 93*
Kastel, Howard L. 1932- *WhoAm 94*
Kastel, Warren *EncSF 93*
Kastelic, Robert Frank 1934- *WhoAm 94*
Kasten, Betty Lou 1938- *WhoAmP 93*
Kasten, Karl Albert 1916- *WhoAm 94, WhoAmA 93*
Kasten, Mary Alice C. 1928- *WhoAmP 93*
Kasten, Melvin Charles 1924- *WhoMW 93*
Kasten, Paul Rudolph 1923- *WhoAm 94, WhoScEn 94*
Kasten, Richard John 1938- *WhoAm 94*
Kasten, Robert W., Jr. 1942- *IntWW 93, WhoAm 94, WhoAmP 93*
Kasten, Stanley Harvey 1952- *WhoAm 94*
Kasten, William Arthur 1956- *WhoAmP 93*
Kastenbaum, Marvin Aaron 1926- *WhoScEn 94*
Kastenholz, Mary Ellen Connelly 1958- *WhoMW 93*
Kastenmeier, Robert William 1924- *WhoAmP 93*
Kaster, Laura A. 1948- *WhoAm 94, WhoAmL 94*
Kaster, Lewis Ross 1932- *WhoAmL 94*
Kaster, Robert Andrew 1948- *WhoMW 93*
Kastin, Abba Jeremiah 1934- *WhoAm 94*
Kastl, Jorg 1922- *IntWW 93*
Kastl, Rose Marie 1942- *WhoMW 93*
Kastle, Herbert D(avid) 1924-1987 *EncSF 93*
Kastle, Leonard 1929- *NewGrDO*
Kastner, Barbara H. 1936- *WhoAmA 93*
Kastner, Bruno d1932 *WhoHol 92*
Kastner, Christine Kriha 1951- *WhoMW 93*
Kastner, Daphna *WhoHol 92*
Kastner, Elliott 1933- *IntMPA 94, IntWW 93*
Kastner, Elwood Curt 1905-1992 *WhAm 10*
Kastner, Jean-Georges 1810-1867 *NewGrDO*
Kastner, Joseph 1907- *WrDr 94*
Kastner, Leslie James 1911- *Who 94*
Kastner, Menachem Jacob 1951- *WhoAmL 94*
Kastner, Peter *WhoHol 92*
Kastor, Frank Sullivan 1933- *WhoAm 94*
Kastor, Hugo *WhoAmA 93N*
Kastor, John Alfred 1931- *WhoAm 94*
Kastorsky, Vladimir 1871-1948 *NewGrDO*
Kasuba, Aleksandra 1923- *WhoAmA 93*
Kasube, Herbert Emil 1949- *WhoMW 93*
Kasunic, Richard A. 1947- *WhoAmP 93*
Kasurinen, Anna-Liisa 1940- *WhoWomW 91*
Kasuya, Terumi 1924- *WhoWomW 91*
Kas'yanov, Alexander Alexandrovich 1891-1982 *NewGrDO*
Kaszak, Nancy *WhoAmP 93*
Kasznar, Kurt d1979 *WhoHol 92*
Kaszniak, Alfred Wayne 1949- *WhoAm 94, WhoWest 94*
Kaszuba, Kevin C. 1951- *WhoFI 94*
Kata, Edward John 1941- *WhoAm 94*
Katagiri, George 1926- *WhoAsA 94*
Katai, Andrew Andras 1937- *WhoAm 94, WhoFI 94*
Katakkar, Suresh Balaji 1944- *WhoScEn 94*
Katano, Marc 1952- *WhoAmA 93*
Katarincic, Joseph Anthony 1931- *WhoAm 94*
Katayama, Alyce Coyne 1950- *WhoAm 94, WhoAmL 94*
Katayama, Arthur Shoji 1927- *WhoAm 94*
Katayama, Robert Nobuichi 1924- *WhoAm 94, WhoAmL 94*
Katayama, Tetsuya 1953- *WhoScEn 94*
Katayama, Toshihiro 1928- *WhoAm 94, WhoAmA 93*
Katbi, Karl 1956- *WhoFI 94*
Katch, Kurt d1958 *WhoHol 92*
Katchadourian, Herant A(ram) 1933- *ConAu 42NR*
Katchalski-Katzir, Ephraim *Who 94*
Katchen, Carole Lee 1944- *WhoAmA 93*
Katcher, Aram *WhoHol 92*
Katcher, Avrum L. 1925- *WhoAm 94*
Katcher, Richard 1918- *WhoAm 94*
Katchmer, George Andrew 1916- *WrDr 94*
Katchur, Marlene Martha 1946- *WhoScEn 94, WhoWest 94*
Kateb, George Anthony 1931- *WhoAm 94*
Katell, Sidney 1915-1990 *WhAm 10*
Katenga-Kaunda, Reid Willie 1929- *Who 94*
Kates, Henry E. 1939- *WhoAm 94*
Kates, J. *DrAPF 93*
Kates, Morris 1923- *WhoAm 94*
Kates, Robert William 1929- *IntWW 93, WhoAm 94, WhoScEn 94*
Katgerman, Laurens 1945- *WhoScEn 94*
Kath, Camelia *WhoHol 92*
Kath, Katharine *WhoHol 92*
Kath, Ruth Robert 1948- *WhoMW 93*
Kathan, Ralph Herman 1929- *WhoMW 93*
Katharina von Gebweiler dc. 1340 *BlmGWL*
Kather, Gerhard 1939- *WhoWest 94*
Katherine, Robert Andrew 1941- *WhoAm 94*
Katherine of Sutton d1376 *BlmGWL*
Kathirgamanathan, Poopathy 1952- *WhoScEn 94*
Kathka, David Arlin *WhoAm 94, WhoWest 94*
Kathman, R. Deedee 1948- *WhoScEn 94*
Kathol, Anthony Louis 1964- *WhoWest 94*
Kathol, Roger Gerald 1948- *WhoMW 93*
Kathrada, Ahmed 1929- *IntWW 93*
Kathrein, Michael Lee 1953- *WhoMW 93*
Kathwari, M. Farooq 1944- *WhoAm 94, WhoFI 94*
Katic, Peter 1954- *WhoAmP 93*
Katims, Milton 1909- *WhoWest 94*
Katims, Robert *WhoHol 92*
Katin, Peter 1930- *IntWW 93*
Katin, Peter Roy 1930- *Who 94*
Katisch, Patricia Anne 1944- *WhoFI 94*
Katkin, Edward Samuel 1937- *WhoAm 94*
Katleman, Harris L. *WhoAm 94*
Katleman, Harris L. 1928- *IntMPA 94*
Katlic, John Edward 1928- *WhoAm 94*
Katner, Garth Todd 1962- *WhoMW 93*
Kato, Daisuke *WhoHol 92*
Kato, Daisuke 1942- *WhoScEn 94*
Kato, Dean M. 1965- *WhoAsA 94*
Kato, Eileen A. 1950- *WhoWest 94*
Kato, Goro 1948- *WhoAsA 94*
Kato, Ichiro 1922- *IntWW 93*
Kato, Kay *WhoAmA 93*
Kato, Koichi 1939- *IntWW 93*
Kato, Masanobu 1946- *WhoAm 94, WhoAmL 94*
Kato, Masatoshi 1945- *WhoAsA 94*
Kato, Michinobu 1926- *WhoScEn 94*
Kato, Mutsuki 1926- *IntWW 93*
Kato, Pamela Kiyomi 1964- *WhoAmL 94*
Kato, Shuichi 1919- *IntWW 93, WrDr 94*
Kato, Susumu 1928- *IntWW 93*
Kato, Tadao 1916- *IntWW 93, Who 94*
Kato, Takeshi *WhoHol 92*
Kato, Theodore Toshihiko 1936- *WhoAsA 94*
Kato, Tosio 1917- *WhoAsA 94*
Kato, Walter Y. 1924- *WhoAsA 94*
Kato, Walter Yoneo 1924- *WhoAm 94, WhoScEn 94*
Kato, Yoshi *WhoHol 92*
Katon, John Edward 1929- *WhoAm 94*
Katona, Jozsef 1791-1830 *IntDcT 2*
Katona, Peter Geza 1937- *WhoAm 94*
Katona, Tamas 1932- *IntWW 93*
Katope, Christopher George 1918- *WhoAm 94*
Katopes, Peter *DrAPF 93*
Katopodis, Gregory John 1947- *WhoAmP 93*
Katrakis, Manos d1984 *WhoHol 92*
Katrinak, Thomas Paul 1954- *WhoScEn 94*
Katritzky, Alan Roy 1928- *IntWW 93, Who 94, WhoAm 94*
Katsahnias, Thomas George 1928- *WhoAm 94*
Katsakiores, George Nicholas 1924- *WhoAmP 93*
Katsakiores, Phyllis Hemeon 1934- *WhoAmP 93*
Katsambas, Christakis Joannou 1925- *IntWW 93*
Katsampes, Theodore P. 1949- *WhoFI 94*
Katsav, Moshe 1945- *IntWW 93*
Katselas, Milton George 1933- *IntMPA 94*
Katsh, Abraham Isaac 1908- *WhoAm 94*
Katsh, M. Ethan 1945- *WhoAmL 94, WrDr 94*
Katsh, Salem Michael 1948- *WhoAm 94, WhoAmL 94*
Katsh, Seymour 1918- *WhoWest 94*
Katsianis, John Nick 1960- *WhoMW 93*
Katsifaras, Georgios 1935- *IntWW 93*
Katsiff, Bruce 1945- *WhoAm 94, WhoAmA 93*
Katsikadelis, John 1937- *WhoScEn 94*
Katsikas, Sokratis Konstantine 1960- *WhoScEn 94*
Katsikis, Miriam Polli *DrAPF 93*
Katsnelson, Esfir Z. 1933- *WhoMW 93*
Katsoris, Constantine Nicholas 1932- *WhoAmL 94*
Katsoulidis, Panagiotis 1933- *WhoAmA 93*
Katsu, Shintaro *WhoHol 92*
Katsuki, Hirohiko 1921- *WhoScEn 94*
Katsulas, Andreas *WhoHol 92*
Katt, William 1955- *IntMPA 94, WhoHol 92*
Kattakuzhy, George Chacko 1944- *WhoAsA 94*
Kattan, Naim 1928- *IntWW 93*
Kattas, Paula Louise 1959- *WhoMW 93*
Katten, Melvin L. 1936- *WhoAm 94*
Katten, Richard L. 1946- *WhoIns 94*
Katti, Shriniwas K. 1936- *WhoAsA 94*
Kattwinkel, John 1941- *WhoAm 94*
Katul'skaya, Yelena Kliment'yevna 1888-1966 *NewGrDO*
Katz, Abraham 1926- *IntWW 93, WhoAm 94*
Katz, Adrian Izhack 1932- *WhoAm 94*
Katz, Alan Stewart 1953- *WhoFI 94, WhoWest 94*
Katz, Alex 1927- *WhoAm 94, WhoAmA 93*
Katz, Allan *WhoHol 92*
Katz, Andy 1961- *WhoAmP 93*
Katz, Arnold 1930- *WhoAm 94*
Katz, Arnold Martin 1932- *WhoAm 94*
Katz, Arnold Martin 1940- *WhoFI 94*
Katz, Aya 1960- *WhoAmL 94*
Katz, Barbara 1956- *ConAu 142*
Katz, Bennett David 1918- *WhoAmP 93*
Katz, Bernard 1911- *IntWW 93, Who 94, WhoScEn 94, WorScD*
Katz, Bobbi 1933- *WrDr 94*
Katz, Burton 1942- *WhoFI 94*
Katz, Carlos 1934- *WhoAm 94*
Katz, Charles J., Jr. 1948- *WhoAmL 94*
Katz, Colleen *WhoAm 94*
Katz, David Allan 1933- *WhoAmL 94*
Katz, David Yale 1950- *WhoScEn 94*
Katz, Donald 1948- *WhoAmL 94*
Katz, Donald Laverne 1907-1989 *WhAm 10*
Katz, Edward Morris 1921- *WhoAm 94*
Katz, Edwin I. 1935- *WhoAm 94, WhoAmL 94*
Katz, Elias 1912- *WhoWest 94*
Katz, Ephraim 1932- *WrDr 94*
Katz, Eunice *WhoAmA 93*
Katz, Gerald 1939- *WhoAm 94, WhoIns 94*
Katz, Gloria *IntMPA 94*
Katz, Gregory 1950- *WhoAm 94*
Katz, Harold 1937- *WhoAm 94*
Katz, Harold A. 1921- *WhoAmP 93*
Katz, Harold Ambrose 1921- *WhoAm 94*
Katz, Henry 1937- *WhoAm 94*
Katz, Hilda 1909- *WhoAm 94, WhoAmA 93, WhoFI 94*
Katz, Hilliard Joel 1918- *WhoAm 94*
Katz, Howard Carl 1939- *WhoAm 94, WhoFI 94*
Katz, Irvin Ronald 1963- *WhoScEn 94*
Katz, Irwin 1942- *WhoFI 94*
Katz, Israel 1917- *WhoScEn 94*
Katz, Jack 1934- *WhoAm 94*
Katz, Jason Lawrence 1947- *WhoAm 94*
Katz, Jay 1922- *WhoAm 94*
Katz, Jeffrey Harvey 1947- *WhoAmL 94*
Katz, Jeri Beth 1964- *WhoAmL 94*
Katz, Jerome Charles 1950- *WhoAm 94, WhoAmL 94*
Katz, Jerry Paul 1944- *WhoFI 94, WhoWest 94*
Katz, Joel *WhoHol 92*
Katz, Joette *WhoAmP 93*
Katz, Joette 1953- *WhoAmL 94*
Katz, John 1938- *WhoAm 94*
Katz, John W. 1943- *WhoWest 94*
Katz, Jonathan (Ned) 1938- *GayLL*
Katz, Jonathan Garber 1950- *WhoAm 94, WhoFI 94*
Katz, Jose 1944- *WhoScEn 94*
Katz, Joseph Jacob 1912- *WhoAm 94, WhoScEn 94*
Katz, Joseph Louis 1938- *WhoAm 94*
Katz, Joseph M. 1913- *WhoAmA 93N*
Katz, Joseph Morris 1913-1991 *WhAm 10*
Katz, Julian 1937- *WhoAm 94, WhoScEn 94*
Katz, Lawrence Allen 1942- *WhoAm 94, WhoAmL 94*
Katz, Lawrence M. 1942- *WhoAmL 94*
Katz, Leandro *DrAPF 93*
Katz, Leandro 1938- *WhoAm 94, WhoAmA 93, WhoHisp 94*
Katz, Leon 1921- *WhoAm 94*
Katz, Lewis Robert 1938- *WhoAm 94*
Katz, Lori Susan 1965- *WhoScEn 94*
Katz, M. Marvin 1935- *WhoAm 94*
Katz, Marc Paul 1953- *WhoAmL 94*
Katz, Marcia 1950- *WhoAm 94*
Katz, Martha Lessman 1952- *WhoAmL 94*
Katz, Martin 1929- *WrDr 94*
Katz, Martin 1952- *WhoFI 94*
Katz, Martin Howard 1931- *WhoAm 94, WhoAmP 93*
Katz, Marty 1947- *IntMPA 94, WhoAm 94*
Katz, Marvin 1930- *WhoAm 94, WhoAmL 94*
Katz, Melvin Seymour 1915- *WhoAmL 94*
Katz, Menke 1906-1991 *WrDr 94N*
Katz, Michael 1928- *IntWW 93, WhoAm 94*
Katz, Michael Allan 1949- *WhoFI 94*
Katz, Michael J. *DrAPF 93*
Katz, Michael Jeffery 1950- *WhoAmL 94*
Katz, Michael Ray 1944- *WhoAm 94, WrDr 94*
Katz, Mickey d1985 *WhoHol 92*
Katz, Mickey 1909-1985 *WhoCom*
Katz, Milton 1907- *IntWW 93, Who 94, WhoAm 94*
Katz, Morris *WhoAmA 93*
Katz, Morton Norris 1919- *WhoAmL 94*
Katz, Norman 1925- *WhoAm 94, WhoFI 94*
Katz, Norman B. 1919- *IntMPA 94*
Katz, Paul 1907- *WhAm 10*
Katz, Perry Marc 1951- *WhoWest 94*
Katz, Peter 1947- *WhoAm 94*
Katz, Phyllis Pollak 1939- *WhoAm 94*
Katz, (Alexander) Raymond 1895-1974 *WhoAmA 93N*
Katz, Richard 1948- *WhoMW 93*
Katz, Richard 1950- *WhoAmP 93*
Katz, Richard William 1954- *WhoAmL 94*
Katz, Robert Langdon 1917- *WhoAm 94*
Katz, Robert Lawrence 1937- *WhoMW 93*
Katz, Robert Lee 1926- *WhoAm 94*
Katz, Robert S. 1936- *WhoAmP 93*
Katz, Robert S. 1942- *WhoAmL 94*
Katz, Robert Stephen 1944- *WhoMW 93*
Katz, Roberta R. 1947- *WhoAmL 94*
Katz, Roger Martin 1945- *WhoFI 94*
Katz, Ronald Lewis 1932- *WhoAm 94*
Katz, Ronald S. 1936- *WhoAmL 94*
Katz, Ronald S. 1946- *WhoAm 94, WhoAmL 94*
Katz, Ronald Stanley 1945- *WhoAm 94*
Katz, Samuel 1923- *WhoAm 94*
Katz, Samuel Lawrence 1927- *IntWW 93, WhoAm 94*
Katz, Sanford N 1933- *WrDr 94*
Katz, Sanford Noah 1933- *WhoAm 94*
Katz, Saul Milton 1915- *WhoAm 94*
Katz, Sherman E. 1943- *WhoAm 94, WhoAmL 94*
Katz, Sidney L. 1915-1978 *WhoAmA 93N*
Katz, Sol 1913- *WhoAm 94*
Katz, Stanley H. d1993 *NewYTBS 93 [port]*
Katz, Stanley Nider 1934- *WhoAm 94, WhoAmL 94*
Katz, Stephen Edward 1943- *WhoAmL 94*
Katz, Steve *DrAPF 93*
Katz, Steve 1935- *WrDr 94*
Katz, Steven Bernard 1962- *WhoAmL 94*
Katz, Steven Edward 1937- *WhoAm 94, WhoScEn 94*
Katz, Steven Martin 1941- *WhoAmL 94*
Katz, Steven T(heodore) 1944- *WrDr 94*
Katz, Steven Theodore 1944- *WhoAm 94*
Katz, Stuart Charles 1937- *WhoAm 94*
Katz, Stuart Z. 1942- *WhoAmL 94*
Katz, Susan A. *DrAPF 93*
Katz, Susan Audrey 1956- *WhoAm 94*
Katz, Susan Stanton 1951- *WhoAmL 94*
Katz, Ted 1937- *WhoAmA 93*
Katz, Thomas Owen 1958- *WhoAmL 94*
Katz, Tonnie *WhoAm 94*
Katz, Vera 1933- *WhoAm 94, WhoAmP 93, WhoWest 94, WhoWomW 91*

Kauzmann, Walter Joseph 1916- *IntWW 93, WhoAm 94, WhoScEn 94*
Kava, Caroline *WhoHol 92*
Kavadas-Pappas, Iphigenia Katherine 1958- *WhoMW 93*
Kavalek, Lubomir 1943- *WhoAm 94*
Kavaler, Rebecca *DrAPF 93*
Kavaler, Rebecca 1933- *WrDr 94*
Kavaler, Thomas J. 1948- *WhoAm 94, WhoAmL 94*
Kavalier, Franziska Helena Appolonia *NewGrDO*
Kavaloski, Vincent 1946- *WhoMW 93*
Kavan, Anna 1901-1968 *EncSF 93*
Kavanagh, Aidan Joseph 1929- *WhoAm 94*
Kavanagh, Cheryl Elizabeth 1949- *WhoFI 94*
Kavanagh, Dan 1946- *WrDr 94*
Kavanagh, Julia 1824-1877 *BlmGEL, BlmGWL*
Kavanagh, Kevin Patrick 1932- *WhoAm 94, WhoFI 94*
Kavanagh, P. J. 1931- *Who 94*
Kavanagh, P(atrick) J(oseph) 1931- *WrDr 94*
Kavanagh, Patrick *WhoHol 92*
Kavanagh, Patrick Bernard 1923- *Who 94*
Kavanagh, Peter 1916- *WrDr 94*
Kavanagh, Yvonne Marie 1964- *WhoScEn 94*
Kavanaugh, Cynthia 1915- *WrDr 94*
Kavanaugh, Dorrie d1983 *WhoHol 92*
Kavanaugh, Everett Edward, Jr. 1941- *WhoAm 94*
Kavanaugh, Howard Van Zant 1931- *WhoScEn 94*
Kavanaugh, Ian 1910- *WrDr 94*
Kavanaugh, James 1935- *WrDr 94*
Kavanaugh, James Francis, Jr. 1949- *WhoAmL 94*
Kavanaugh, James Joseph 1936- *WhoMW 93*
Kavanaugh, Robert 1947- *WhoAmL 94*
Kavanaugh, Walter J. 1933- *WhoAmP 93*
Kavanne, Risto *EncSF 93*
Kavasoglu, Abdulkadir Yekta 1952- *WhoScEn 94*
Kavee, Robert Charles 1934- *WhoAm 94*
Kaveney, Roz 1949- *EncSF 93*
Kavesh, Robert A. 1927- *WhoAm 94*
Kavesh, Sheldon 1933- *WhoScEn 94*
Kavetas, Harry L. 1937- *WhoAm 94, WhoFI 94*
Kaviany, Massoud 1948- *WhoScEn 94*
Kavic, Lorne John 1936- *WrDr 94*
Kaviraj *DrAPF 93*
Kavka, Gregory Stephen 1947- *WhoAm 94*
Kavli, Fred 1927- *WhoFI 94*
Kavner, Julie 1951- *IntMPA 94, WhoAm 94, WhoHol 92*
Kavner, Robert M. 1943- *WhoFI 94*
Kavoukjian, Michael Edward 1958- *WhoAmL 94*
Kavrakos, Dimitri 1946- *NewGrDO*
Kavulich, John Steven, II 1961- *WhoFI 94*
Kawa, Florence Kathryn 1912- *WhoAmA 93*
Kawa, Nancy Ann 1967- *WhoMW 93*
Kawabata, Minoru 1911- *WhoAmA 93*
Kawabata, Nariyoshi 1935- *WhoScEn 94*
Kawabata Yasunari 1899-1972 *RfGShF*
Kawachi, Michael Tateo 1955- *WhoAm 94*
Kawachika, James Akio 1947- *WhoAmL 94, WhoWest 94*
Kawafuchi, Glenn Misaki 1951- *WhoAsA 94*
Kawaguchi, Hiroshi *WhoHol 92*
Kawaguchi, Meredith Ferguson 1940- *WhoAmL 94*
Kawaguchi, Stanley Kenji 1940- *WhoAsA 94*
Kawahara, Fred Katsumi 1921- *WhoScEn 94*
Kawahara, Lindon Ken 1955- *WhoAsA 94*
Kawahara, Mutsuto 1942- *WhoScEn 94*
Kawahara, Ronald Akira 1943- *WhoWest 94*
Kawahara, William T. 1937- *WhoAsA 94*
Kawai, Ryoichi 1917- *IntWW 93*
Kawaichi, Ken M. 1941- *WhoAsA 94*
Kawaja, Kaleem U. 1941- *WhoAsA 94*
Kawakami, Bertha C. 1931- *WhoAmP 93*
Kawakami, Hiroshi 1942- *IntWW 93*
Kawakami, Yutaka 1956- *WhoScEn 94*
Kawakubo, Rej 1943- *IntWW 93*
Kawamata, Motoo 1936- *WhoScEn 94*
Kawamata, Tadashi 1953- *IntWW 93*
Kawamoto, Brian Michio 1953- *WhoAsA 94*
Kawamoto, Nobuhiko 1917- *IntWW 93*
Kawamura, Mitsunori 1939- *WhoScEn 94*
Kawano, Arnold H. 1948- *WhoAsA 94*
Kawano, Hiroshi 1925- *WhoScEn 94*
Kawano, James Conrad *WhoFI 94*
Kawano, Randall Toshio 1959- *WhoFI 94, WhoWest 94*
Kawara, Tsutomu 1937- *IntWW 93*
Kawari, Hamad Abdelaziz al- 1948- *IntWW 93*
Kawasaki, Lillian Y. 1950- *WhoAsA 94*
Kawasaki, Seiichi 1922- *IntWW 93*
Kawasaki, Teruo 1918- *IntWW 93*
Kawashima, Edith T. 1932- *WhoAsA 94*
Kawashima, Takeshi 1930- *WhoAmA 93*
Kawata, Paul Akio *WhoAsA 94*
Kawauchi, Hiroshi 1940- *WhoAm 94, WhoScEn 94*
Kawawa, Rashidi Mfaume 1929- *IntWW 93*
Kawazu, Seizaburo *WhoHol 92*
Kawecki, Jean Mary 1926- *WhoAmA 93*
Kawer, Dina Rochelle 1957- *WhoMW 93*
Kawharu, (Ian) Hugh 1927- *Who 94*
Kawin, Bruce F. *DrAPF 93*
Kawin, Bruce F 1945- *WrDr 94*
Kawusu Conteh, Sheku Bockari *IntWW 93N*
Kay, Alan 1940- *WhoScEn 94*
Kay, Alan Cooke *WhoAm 94, WhoAmL 94, WhoWest 94*
Kay, Albert Joseph 1920- *WhoFI 94, WhoMW 93*
Kay, Andrew Watt 1916- *Who 94*
Kay, Beatrice d1986 *WhoHol 92*
Kay, Bernard 1938- *WhoHol 92*
Kay, Bernard Hubert Gerard 1925- *Who 94*
Kay, Bernard Melvin 1932- *WhoAm 94*
Kay, Brian Wilfrid 1921- *Who 94*
Kay, Carol McGinnis 1941- *WhoAm 94*
Kay, Charles 1930- *WhoHol 92*
Kay, Charles R. 1927- *WhoAmP 93*
Kay, Cyril Eyton d1993 *Who 94N*
Kay, Cyril Max 1931- *WhoAm 94, WhoScEn 94*
Kay, Dennis Matthew 1936- *WhoMW 93*
Kay, Dianne 1954- *WhoHol 92*
Kay, Douglas *WhoAm 94*
Kay, Douglas Casey 1932- *WhoAm 94*
Kay, Elizabeth Alison 1928- *WhoScEn 94*
Kay, Ellen 1943- *WrDr 94*
Kay, Ernest 1915- *Who 94*
Kay, Fenton Ray 1942- *WhoWest 94*
Kay, Geoffrey 1938- *WrDr 94*
Kay, George 1936- *WrDr 94*
Kay, Gilbert Lee *IntMPA 94*
Kay, Gordon 1916- *IntMPA 94*
Kay, Guy Gavriel 1954- *WrDr 94*
Kay, Harry 1919- *Who 94*
Kay, Helen *WhoAsA 94*
Kay, Herbert 1924- *WhoAm 94*
Kay, Herma Hill 1934- *WhoWest 94*
Kay, Humphrey Edward Melville 1923- *Who 94*
Kay, Irene Pramisloff 1920- *WhoMW 93*
Kay, Jack 1951- *WhoMW 93*
Kay, Jack Garvin 1930- *WhoAm 94*
Kay, Jackie 1961- *BlmGWL*
Kay, James Fredrick 1922- *WhoAm 94*
Kay, Jerald 1945- *WhoMW 93*
Kay, Jerome 1920- *WhoAm 94*
Kay, Jerome Harold 1921- *WhoAm 94*
Kay, Joel Phillip 1936- *WhoAm 94*
Kay, John *DrAPF 93, WorInv*
Kay, John (William) 1943- *Who 94*
Kay, John Anderson 1948- *IntWW 93*
Kay, John Franklin, Jr. 1929- *WhoAm 94*
Kay, John Menzies 1920- *Who 94*
Kay, Jolyon Christopher 1930- *Who 94*
Kay, Kathleen A. 1934- *WhoAmP 93*
Kay, Kenneth Jeffrey 1955- *WhoAm 94*
Kay, Kenneth Robert 1951- *WhoAm 94*
Kay, Marjorie d1949 *WhoHol 92*
Kay, Marsha Helen 1961- *WhoMW 93*
Kay, Maurice Ralph 1942- *Who 94*
Kay, Neil Vincent 1936- *Who 94*
Kay, Patrick Richard 1921- *Who 94*
Kay, Paul de Young 1934- *WhoAm 94*
Kay, Peter 1924- *WhoAmP 93*
Kay, Peter Steven 1937- *WhoMW 93*
Kay, Reed 1925- *WhoAmA 93*
Kay, Richard 1937- *WhoHol 92*
Kay, Richard Allan 1945- *WhoAm 94, WhoAmL 94*
Kay, Richard M. 1958- *WhoMW 93*
Kay, Robert Lee 1928- *WhoAm 94*
Kay, Robert O. 1922- *WhoAmP 93*
Kay, Robin Langford 1919- *WrDr 94*
Kay, Samuel M. *EncSF 93*
Kay, Saul 1914- *WhoAm 94*
Kay, Stanley Lloyd 1942- *WhoAm 94*
Kay, Sylvia 1936- *WhoHol 92*
Kay, Thomas Oliver 1929- *WhoAm 94*
Kay, Ulysses 1917- *AfrAmAl 6 [port], WhoBlA 94*
Kay, Ulysses (Simpson) 1917- *NewGrDO*
Kay, Ulysses Simpson 1917- *WhoAm 94*
Kaya, Douglas Hifuto, Jr. 1939- *WhoAsA 94*
Kayal, Alawi Darweesh 1936- *IntWW 93*
Kayalar, Lutfullah 1952- *IntWW 93*
Kayama, Yuzo *WhoHol 92*
Kayashota 1725-c. 1795 *AmRev*
Kayatta, William J., Jr. 1953- *WhoAmL 94*
Kaye, A. P. d1946 *WhoHol 92*
Kaye, Andrew W. 1948- *WhoIns 94*
Kaye, Barrington 1924- *WrDr 94*
Kaye, Caren *WhoHol 92*
Kaye, Celia 1944- *WhoHol 92*
Kaye, Clarissa *WhoHol 92*
Kaye, Danny d1987 *WhoHol 92*
Kaye, Danny 1913-1987 *WhoCom [port]*
Kaye, Darwood 1929- *WhoHol 92*
Kaye, David Alexander Gordon 1919- *Who 94*
Kaye, David Haigh 1947- *WhoAmA 93*
Kaye, David Harris 1947- *WhoAmL 94*
Kaye, Davy *WhoHol 92*
Kaye, Donald 1931- *WhoAm 94*
Kaye, Douglas Robert Beaumont 1909- *Who 94*
Kaye, Elaine Hilda 1930- *Who 94*
Kaye, Emmanuel 1914- *Who 94*
Kaye, Evelyn d1990 *WhoHol 92*
Kaye, Evelyn Patricia 1937- *WhoAm 94*
Kaye, Gail Leslie 1955- *WhoMW 93*
Kaye, Geoffrey John 1935- *Who 94*
Kaye, George 1911- *WhoAmA 93*
Kaye, Geraldine 1925- *WrDr 94*
Kaye, Gordon Israel 1935- *WhoAm 94*
Kaye, Harvey Jordan 1949- *IntWW 93*
Kaye, Ivan Nathaniel 1932- *WhoWest 94*
Kaye, Jerome R. 1928- *WhoAm 94*
Kaye, Jhani 1949- *WhoWest 94*
Kaye, John Phillip Lister L. *Who 94*
Kaye, Judith S. 1938- *WhoAmP 93*
Kaye, Judith Smith *NewYTBS 93 [port]*
Kaye, Judith Smith 1938- *WhoAm 94, WhoAmL 94*
Kaye, Judy 1948- *WhoAm 94, WhoHol 92*
Kaye, Kenneth Marc 1960- *WhoScEn 94*
Kaye, Lila 1932- *WhoHol 92*
Kaye, Linda 1944- *WhoHol 92*
Kaye, Lindsey Joy *Who 94*
Kaye, Lori *WhoFI 94*
Kaye, M(ary) M(argaret) 1908- *WrDr 94*
Kaye, Marc Mendell 1959- *WhoAmL 94*
Kaye, Martin Barry 1949- *WhoAmL 94*
Kaye, Marvin *DrAPF 93*
Kaye, Marvin 1938- *WrDr 94*
Kaye, Marvin (Nathan) 1938- *ConAu 41NR, EncSF 93*
Kaye, Mary Margaret *Who 94*
Kaye, Melanie *ConAu 141*
Kaye, Michael 1925- *Who 94*
Kaye, Mildred Elaine 1929- *WhoAmA 93*
Kaye, Mitchell Adam, Sr. 1957- *WhoAmP 93*
Kaye, Neil S. *WhoScEn 94*
Kaye, Nora 1920-1987 *IntDcB [port]*
Kaye, Norman *WhoHol 92*
Kaye, Peter Frederic 1928- *WhoAm 94*
Kaye, Phil d1959 *WhoHol 92*
Kaye, Richard William 1939- *WhoMW 93*
Kaye, Robert 1917- *WhoAm 94*
Kaye, Roger Godfrey 1946- *Who 94*
Kaye, Rosalind Anne *Who 94*
Kaye, Sammy d1987 *WhoHol 92*
Kaye, Sparky d1971 *WhoHol 92*
Kaye, Stephen Rackow 1931- *WhoAm 94*
Kaye, Stuart Martin 1946- *WhoAmL 94*
Kaye, Stubby 1918- *WhoHol 92*
Kaye, Suzi *WhoHol 92*
Kaye, Sylvia Fine 1940-1991 *WhAm 10*
Kaye, Tom 1924- *WrDr 94*
Kaye, Walter 1927- *WhoAm 94*
Kaye, Wilbur Irving 1922- *WhoAm 94*
Kaye, William Samuel 1953- *WhoAm 94*
Kaye/Kantrowitz, Melanie *DrAPF 93*
Kaye/Kantrowitz, Melanie 1945- *ConAu 141*
Kayes, Dennis S. 1942- *WhoAmL 94*
Kaye-Smith, Sheila 1887-1956 *BlmGWL*
Kayfetz, Victor Joel 1945- *WhoWest 94*
Kay Gee c. 1970- *See* Naughty by Nature *ConMus 11*
Kayhart, Roger V. 1922- *WhoAmP 93*
Kayla, Ziya 1912- *IntWW 93*
Kaylan, Howard *WhoHol 92*
Kaylan, Howard Lawrence 1947- *WhoWest 94*
Kayll, Joseph Robert 1914- *Who 94*
Kaylor, Cynthia Anne 1950- *WhoAmL 94*
Kaylor, Jefferson Daniel, Jr. 1947- *WhoFI 94, WhoScEn 94*
Kaylor, Robert 1934- *IntMPA 94*
Kaylor-Rhoads, Suzanne Elizabeth 1956- *WhoMW 93*
Kayman, Philip M. 1941- *WhoAmL 94*
Kaymor, Patrice Maguilene *BlkWr 2*
Kayn, Hilde B. 1903-1950 *WhoAmA 93N*
Kaynak, Erdener 1947- *WhoAm 94*
Kayne, Jon Barry 1943- *WhoMW 93*
Kaynor, Sanford Bull 1926- *WhoAm 94*
Kays, Stanley J. 1945- *WhoScEn 94*
Kays, William Morrow 1920- *WhoAm 94*
Kaysen, Carl 1920- *IntWW 93, Who 94, WhoAm 94*
Kayser, Charles Willy d1942 *WhoHol 92*
Kayser, David William 1939- *WhoWest 94*
Kayser, Donald Robert 1930- *WhoAm 94*
Kayser, Elmer Louis 1896- *WhAm 10*
Kayser, Margaretha Susanna c. 1690-c. 1748 *NewGrDO*
Kayser, Paul William 1918-1990 *WhAm 10*
Kayser, Sophie Amalia 1711-1747 *NewGrDO*
Kayser, Thomas Arthur 1935- *WhoAm 94, WhoAmA 93*
Kayser, Thomas Charles, Sr. 1937- *WhoAm 94*
Kay-Shuttleworth *Who 94*
Kayssler, Christian d1944 *WhoHol 92*
Kayssler, Friedrich d1945 *WhoHol 92*
Kayton, Howard H. 1936- *WhoIns 94*
Kayton, Myron 1934- *WhoAm 94, WhoWest 94*
Kaz 1922- *WhoAmA 93*
Kaz, Joyce Zickerman 1936-1979 *WhoAmA 93N*
Kaz, Nathaniel 1917- *WhoAm 94, WhoAmA 93*
Kaza, Greg John 1960- *WhoMW 93*
Kaza, Gregory John 1960- *WhoAmP 93*
Kazakov, Iurii (Pavlovich) 1927-1982 *RfGShF*
Kazakov, Vasiliy Ivanovich 1927- *IntWW 93*
Kazan, Benjamin 1917- *WhoAm 94, WhoScEn 94, WhoWest 94*
Kazan, Elia 1909- *AmCulL, IntMPA 94, IntWW 93, Who 94, WhoAm 94, WhoHol 92, WrDr 94*
Kazan, Lainie 1940- *WhoHol 92*
Kazan, Lainie 1942- *IntMPA 94, WhoAm 94*
Kazan, Robert Peter 1947- *WhoMW 93, WhoScEn 94*
Kazanjian, Howard G. 1943- *IntMPA 94*
Kazanjian, John Harold 1949- *WhoAm 94, WhoAmL 94*
Kazankina, Tatyana 1951- *IntWW 93*
Kazannik, Aleksei Ivanovich 1941- *LngBDD*
Kazanova, Ulla d1985 *WhoHol 92*
Kazantzaki, Galateia 1886-1962 *BlmGWL*
Kazantzakis, Nikos 1883-1957 *IntDcT 2 [port]*
Kazantzis, Judith 1940- *BlmGWL, WrDr 94*
Kazarian, Paul 1955- *WhoAm 94*
Kazarinoff, Nicholas D. 1929-1991 *WhAm 10*
Kazarnovskaya, Lubov Yurievna 1956- *IntWW 93*
Kazarosian, Marsha Veron 1956- *WhoAmL 94*
Kazaryan, Yuri *NewGrDO*
Kazazis, Kostas 1934- *WhoAm 94*
Kazem, Ismail 1931- *WhoAm 94, WhoScEn 94*
Kazemi, Farhad 1943- *WhoAm 94*
Kazemi, Homayoun 1934- *WhoAm 94, WhoScEn 94*
Kazemi, Hossein 1938- *WhoAm 94*
Kazemzadeh, Firuz 1924- *WhoAm 94, WrDr 94*
Kazemzadeh, Monireh Margaret 1963- *WhoAmL 94*
Kazen, George Philip 1940- *WhoAm 94, WhoAmL 94*
Kazenas, Susan Jean 1956- *WhoMW 93*
Kazhdan, David 1946- *WhoAm 94*
Kazi, Aftab *WhoFI 94*
Kazi, Hyder Ali 1934- *IntWW 93*
Kazi-Ferrouillet, Kuumba 1951- *WhoBlA 94*
Kazik, John Stanley 1942- *WhoAm 94*
Kazim, Parvez *IntWW 93*
Kazimierczuk, Marian Kazimierz 1948- *WhoAm 94, WhoMW 93*
Kazimir, Donald Joseph 1934- *WhoScEn 94*
Kazin, Alfred 1915- *IntWW 93, WhoAm 94, WrDr 94*
Kazir, Yehudit 1963- *BlmGWL*
Kazlauskas, Edward John 1942- *WhoWest 94*
Kazle, Elynmarie 1958- *WhoFI 94, WhoWest 94*
Kazmann, Raphael Gabriel 1916- *WhoScEn 94*
Kazmayer, Robert Henderson 1908-1991 *WhAm 10*
Kazmerski, Lawrence Lee 1945- *WhoAm 94*
Kazor, Virginia Ernst 1940- *WhoAmA 93*
Kazor, Walter Robert 1922- *WhoScEn 94*
Kazragis, Gary Walter 1951- *WhoAmL 94*
Kazurinsky, Tim *WhoHol 92*
Kazurinsky, Tim 1950- *IntMPA 94*
Kchessinska, Mathilde *IntDcB*
Ke, Gang 1950- *WhoAsA 94*
Kea, Neville *EncSF 93*
Keable-Elliott, (Robert) Anthony 1924- *Who 94*
Keables, Michael John 1955- *WhoWest 94*
Keach, James 1948- *WhoHol 92*
Keach, John A., Jr. 1938- *WhoAmP 93*

Keach, Margaret Sally 1903- *WhoMW 93*
Keach, Stacy 1941- *WhoHol 92*
Keach, Stacy 1942- *IntMPA 94, IntWW 93*
Keach, Stacy, Sr. *WhoHol 92*
Keach, Stacy, Sr. 1914- *IntMPA 94, WhoAm 94*
Keach, Stacy, Jr. 1941- *WhoAm 94*
Keady, George Cregan, Jr. 1924- *WhoAm 94, WhoAmL 94*
Keady, William Colbert 1913-1989 *WhAm 10*
Keal, Edwin Ernest Frederick 1921- *Who 94*
Keala, Francis Ahloy 1930- *WhoAm 94*
Kealey, Edward J 1936- *WrDr 94*
Kealey, William Peter 1963- *WhoAmL 94*
Kealiinohomoku, Joann Wheeler 1930- *WhoWest 94*
Keally, Francis 1889-1978 *WhoAmA 93N*
Kealy, Robin Andrew 1944- *Who 94*
Kealy, William James 1940- *WhoAm 94, WhoFI 94*
Kean, Arnold Wilfred Geoffrey 1914- *Who 94*
Kean, Benjamin H. d1993 *NewYTBS 93 [port]*
Kean, Benjamin Harrison 1912- *WhoAm 94*
Kean, Benjamin Harrison 1912-1993 *ConAu 142*
Kean, Betty d1986 *WhoHol 92*
Kean, Charles Thomas 1941- *WhoAm 94*
Kean, Edmund 1787?-1833 *BlmGEL*
Kean, Hamilton Fish 1925- *WhoAm 94*
Kean, James Allen 1949- *WhoScEn 94*
Kean, James Campbell 1956- *WhoAmL 94*
Kean, Jane 1924- *WhoHol 92*
Kean, John 1756-1795 *WhAmRev*
Kean, John 1929- *WhoAm 94*
Kean, John Vaughan 1917- *WhoAmL 94, WhoFI 94*
Kean, Marie 1922- *WhoHol 92*
Kean, Mary Stewart *DrAPF 93*
Kean, Michael Henry 1945- *WhoWest 94*
Kean, Norman 1934- *WhAm 10*
Kean, Richard d1959 *WhoHol 92*
Kean, Ronald Allen 1949- *WhoMW 93*
Kean, Thomas H. 1935- *IntWW 93, WhoAm 94, WhoAmP 93*
Keanan, Staci *WhoHol 92*
Keane, Bil 1922- *WhoAm 94, WhoAmA 93*
Keane, Constance d1973 *WhoHol 92*
Keane, Cornelius J. 1921- *WhoAmP 93*
Keane, Daniel J. 1939- *WhoAm 94*
Keane, David Roger 1943- *NewGrDO*
Keane, Desmond St. John 1941- *Who 94*
Keane, Doris d1945 *WhoHol 92*
Keane, Edward d1959 *WhoHol 92*
Keane, Francis Joseph 1936- *Who 94*
Keane, George 1917- *WhoFI 94*
Keane, Gustave Robert 1914- *WhoAm 94*
Keane, Horace James Basil 1926- *WhoBlA 94*
Keane, James 1952- *WhoHol 92*
Keane, James Francis 1934- *WhoAmP 93*
Keane, James Patrick 1946- *WhoAmP 93*
Keane, John B(rendan) 1928- *ConAu 42NR, ConDr 93, IntDcT 2, WrDr 94*
Keane, John Brendan 1928- *IntWW 93*
Keane, John Joseph 1839-1918 *DcAmReB 2*
Keane, John Michael 1954- *WhoAmP 93*
Keane, Kerrie *WhoHol 92*
Keane, Mark Edward 1919- *WhoAm 94*
Keane, Mary Nesta 1904- *Who 94*
Keane, Mary Nesta 1905- *IntWW 93*
Keane, Michael J. 1953- *WhoAmL 94*
Keane, Molly 1904- *BlmGWL [port]*
Keane, Noel 1938- *WrDr 94*
Keane, Peter Leo 1917- *WhoAm 94*
Keane, Raymond d1973 *WhoHol 92*
Keane, Richard (Michael) 1909- *Who 94*
Keane, Richard J. 1933- *WhoAmP 93*
Keane, Robert Emmett d1981 *WhoHol 92*
Keane, Teri *WhoHol 92*
Keane, William Francis 1942- *WhoAm 94, WhoScEn 94*
Keane, William K. 1944- *WhoAm 94, WhoAmL 94*
Keaney, John Joseph 1932- *WhoAm 94*
Keaney, Mark Theodore 1947- *WhoAm 94, WhoAmL 94*
Keaney, William Regis 1937- *WhoAm 94, WhoMW 93*
Keans, Sandra Balomenos 1942- *WhoAmP 93*
Keany, Sutton 1943- *WhoAm 94, WhoAmL 94*
Kear, Bernard Henry 1931- *WhoAm 94, WhoScEn 94*
Kear, David 1923- *IntWW 93*
Kear, Graham Francis 1928- *Who 94*
Kear, Maria Martha Ruscitella 1954- *WhoAmL 94*
Kearfott, Joseph Conrad 1947- *WhoAm 94, WhoAmL 94*
Kearl, Bryant Eastham 1921- *WhoAm 94*
Kearl, Stanley Brandon 1913- *WhoAmA 93*
Kearley *Who 94*
Kearley, F. Furman 1932- *WhoAm 94*
Kearley, Richard Irven, III 1953- *WhoFI 94*
Kearney, Brian 1935- *Who 94*
Kearney, Carolyn 1939- *WhoHol 92*
Kearney, (Elfric Wells) Chalmers 1881-1966 *EncSF 93*
Kearney, Daniel Patrick 1939- *WhoAm 94, WhoFI 94*
Kearney, Douglas Charles 1945- *WhoAmL 94*
Kearney, Dyre d1791 *WhAmRev*
Kearney, Eric Henderson 1963- *WhoAmL 94*
Kearney, Gillian *WhoHol 92*
Kearney, Hugh (Francis) 1924- *WrDr 94*
Kearney, Hugh Francis 1924- *WhoAm 94*
Kearney, James V. 1948- *WhoAmL 94*
Kearney, Jesse L. 1950- *WhoBlA 94*
Kearney, John d1945 *WhoHol 92*
Kearney, John (W) 1924- *WhoAmA 93*
Kearney, John Francis, III 1947- *WhoAmL 94*
Kearney, John Joseph, Jr. 1924- *WhoAm 94*
Kearney, John Walter 1924- *WhoAm 94*
Kearney, Joseph Laurence 1927- *WhoAm 94, WhoWest 94*
Kearney, Joseph Matthew, Jr. 1956- *WhoAmP 93*
Kearney, Keith L. 1950- *WhoAm 94*
Kearney, Kerry A. 1949- *WhoAm 94, WhoAmL 94*
Kearney, Lester T., Jr. 1924-1988 *WhAm 10*
Kearney, Lynn Haigh 1927- *WhoAmA 93*
Kearney, Mary Patricia 1920- *WhoAmP 93*
Kearney, Michael *WhoHol 92*
Kearney, Michael John 1940- *WhoFI 94, WhoMW 93*
Kearney, Michelle 1945- *WhoHisp 94*
Kearney, Philip Charles 1932- *WhoScEn 94*
Kearney, Richard D. 1914- *IntWW 93*
Kearney, Richard James 1927- *WhoFI 94*
Kearney, Robert *WhoAm 94, WhoFI 94*
Kearney, Sheila Jane 1961- *WhoAmL 94*
Kearney, Stephen *WhoHol 92*
Kearney, Stephen Michael 1956- *WhoAm 94*
Kearney, Thomas B. 1956- *WhoIns 94*
Kearney, William (John Francis) 1935- *Who 94*
Kearns, Allen d1956 *WhoHol 92*
Kearns, David Richard 1935- *WhoScEn 94*
Kearns, David Todd 1930- *IntWW 93, Who 94, WhoScEn 94*
Kearns, Ellen C. 1945- *WhoAmL 94*
Kearns, Francis Emner 1905-1992 *WhAm 10*
Kearns, Homer H. *WhoWest 94*
Kearns, James Cannon 1944- *WhoAmL 94*
Kearns, James Joseph 1924- *WhoAm 94, WhoAmA 93*
Kearns, James T. 1938- *WhoIns 94*
Kearns, Janet Catherine 1940- *WhoAm 94*
Kearns, John J., III 1951- *WhoAm 94*
Kearns, Joseph d1962 *WhoHol 92*
Kearns, Joseph James 1942- *WhoAm 94*
Kearns, Lionel (John) 1937- *WrDr 94*
Kearns, Merle Grace *WhoAmP 93*
Kearns, Merle Grace 1938- *WhoMW 93*
Kearns, Peter Francis 1943- *WhoAmL 94*
Kearns, R. Jerome 1936- *WhoAmP 93*
Kearns, Terrance Brophy 1946- *WhoAm 94*
Kearns, Warren Kenneth 1929- *WhoAm 94*
Kearns, William Edward 1934- *Who 94*
Kearns, William Michael, Jr. 1935- *WhoAm 94, WhoFI 94*
Kearny, Stephen Watts 1794-1848 *WhWE*
Kearny, Thomas M. 1948- *WhoAm 94*
Kearse, Amalya 1937- *WhoAmP 93*
Kearse, Amalya Lyle 1937- *AfrAmAl 6, WhoAm 94, WhoAmL 94, WhoBlA 94*
Kearse, Barbara Stone 1936- *WhoBlA 94*
Kearse, David Grier 1937- *WhoWest 94*
Kearse, Gregory Sashi 1949- *WhoBlA 94*
Kearton, Baron d1992 *IntWW 93N*
Keary, Geraldine 1935- *WhoWest 94*
Keary, William J. 1897- *WhAm 10*
Keasley, Dawn Delayne 1967- *WhoWest 94*
Keatan, Harry d1966 *WhoHol 92*
Keathley, George *WhoMW 93*
Keating, Bern 1915- *WrDr 94*
Keating, Carole Joanna 1958- *WhoScEn 94*
Keating, Charles 1941- *WhoHol 92*
Keating, Charles H., III 1955- *WhoFI 94*
Keating, Cornelius Francis 1925- *WhoAm 94, WhoFI 94*
Keating, Daniel Bernard 1954- *WhoMW 93*
Keating, Donald Norman 1924- *Who 94*
Keating, E. Michael, III 1948- *WhoAmL 94*
Keating, Eugene Kneeland 1928- *WhoAm 94*
Keating, Francis Anthony, II 1944- *WhoAm 94, WhoAmP 93*
Keating, Frank 1937- *Who 94*
Keating, Fred d1961 *WhoHol 92*
Keating, Gladys Brown 1923- *WhoAmP 93*
Keating, H(enry) R(aymond) F(itzwalter) 1926- *EncSF 93*
Keating, H(enry) R(eymond) F(itzwalter) 1926- *WrDr 94*
Keating, Henry Reymond Fitzwalter 1926- *IntWW 93, Who 94*
Keating, John Richard 1934- *WhoAm 94*
Keating, Joy Marie 1944- *WhoWest 94*
Keating, Justin 1931- *IntWW 93*
Keating, Karen Rupert 1954- *WhoAm 94, WhoFI 94*
Keating, Kay Rosamond Blundell 1943- *Who 94*
Keating, L(ouis) Clark 1907- *WrDr 94*
Keating, Larry d1963 *WhoHol 92*
Keating, Larry Grant 1944- *WhoScEn 94, WhoWest 94*
Keating, Michael Burns 1940- *WhoAm 94*
Keating, Michael J. 1944- *WhoAmP 93*
Keating, Michael Stockton 1940- *Who 94*
Keating, Monica d1985 *WhoHol 92*
Keating, Paul John 1944- *IntWW 93, Who 94*
Keating, Peter J(ohn) 1939- *WrDr 94*
Keating, Richard Joseph *WhoFI 94*
Keating, Richard P. 1935- *WhoIns 94*
Keating, Robert B. 1924- *WhoAm 94, WhoAmP 93*
Keating, Terry Michael 1958- *WhoFI 94*
Keating, Thomas F. 1928- *WhoAmP 93*
Keating, Thomas Francis 1928- *WhoWest 94*
Keating, Thomas Patrick 1949- *WhoFI 94*
Keating, Tristan Jack 1917- *WhoScEn 94*
Keating, William John 1927- *WhoMW 93*
Keating, William John, Jr. 1953- *WhoAmL 94*
Keating, William R. *WhoAmP 93*
Keatinge, Cornelia Wyma 1952- *WhoAmL 94*
Keatinge, Edgar (Mayne) 1905- *Who 94*
Keatinge, Richard Harte 1919-1992 *WhAm 10*
Keatinge, William Richard 1931- *IntWW 93, Who 94*
Keatley, Charlotte 1960- *ConDr 93*
Keaton, Buster d1966 *WhoHol 92*
Keaton, Buster 1895-1966 *AmCulL [port], WhoCom [port]*
Keaton, Charles Howard 1937- *WhoAm 94*
Keaton, Diane *IntWW 93, NewYTBS 93*
Keaton, Diane 1946- *IntMPA 94, WhoAm 94, WhoCom, WhoHol 92*
Keaton, Harry d1966 *WhoHol 92*
Keaton, Joe d1946 *WhoHol 92*
Keaton, Lawrence Cluer 1924- *WhoScEn 94*
Keaton, Louise d1981 *WhoHol 92*
Keaton, Michael 1951- *IntMPA 94, IntWW 93, WhoAm 94, WhoHol 92*
Keaton, Myra d1955 *WhoHol 92*
Keaton, William Bruce 1945- *WhoAmL 94*
Keaton, William T. *WhoBlA 94*
Keator, Margaret Whitley 1945- *WhoAmP 93*
Keats, Donald Howard 1929- *WhoAm 94, WhoWest 94*
Keats, Eleanor *DrAPF 93*
Keats, Ezra Jack 1916-1983 *WhoAmA 93N*
Keats, Glenn Arthur 1920- *WhoMW 93*
Keats, Harold Alan 1913- *WhoAm 94*
Keats, John 1795-1821 *BlmGEL [port]*
Keats, Roger A. 1948- *WhoAmP 93*
Keats, Steven 1945- *WhoHol 92*
Keats, Theodore Eliot 1924- *WhoAm 94*
Keats, Viola 1911- *WhoHol 92*
Keaty, Robert Burke 1949- *WhoFI 94*
Keaveney, James R. *EncSF 93*
Keaveney, Raymond 1948- *IntWW 93*
Keaveney, Sydney Starr 1939- *WhoAmA 93*
Keay, John 1941- *WrDr 94*
Keay, Lou Carter 1927- *WhoWest 94*
Keay, Ronald William John 1920- *Who 94*
Keays-Byrne, Hugh *WhoHol 92*
Kebabian, Paul Blakeslee 1917- *WhoAm 94*
Kebblish, John Basil 1925- *WhoAm 94, WhoScEn 94*
Kebede, Ashenafi Amde 1938- *WhoBlA 94*
Kececioglu, Dimitri Basil 1922- *WhoAm 94, WhoScEn 94*
Ke Changtang 1940- *WhoPRCh 91*
Kechel, Daniel Clark 1925- *WhoMW 93*
Keck, Charles 1875-1951 *WhoAmA 93N*
Keck, Donald Bruce 1941- *WhoAm 94, WhoScEn 94*
Keck, Gary Kyle 1951- *WhoMW 93*
Keck, Hardu 1940- *WhoAmA 93*
Keck, James Collyer 1924- *WhoScEn 94*
Keck, James Moulton 1921- *WhoAm 94*
Keck, Jeanne Gentry 1938- *WhoAmA 93*
Keck, Leander Earl 1928- *WhoAm 94*
Keck, Merel Fogg 1928- *WhoAm 94*
Keck, Paul H. 1942- *WhoAmL 94*
Keck, Philip Walter 1947- *WhoFI 94*
Keck, Richard Joseph 1963- *WhoFI 94*
Keck, Richard Paul 1960- *WhoAmL 94*
Keck, Robert C., Jr. 1943- *WhoAm 94, WhoAmL 94*
Keck, Robert Clifton 1914- *WhoAm 94, WhoAmL 94, WhoFI 94, WhoMW 93*
Keck, Robert Michael 1963- *WhoFI 94*
Keck, Ronald Ward 1950- *WhoFI 94*
Keck, Sheldon d1993 *NewYTBS 93 [port]*
Keck, Sheldon Waugh 1910- *WhoAmA 93*
Keck, William 1908- *WhoAm 94*
Keckel, Peter J. 1942- *WhoFI 94*
Keckley, Elizabeth *WorInv*
Keckley, Jane d1963 *WhoHol 92*
Kedah, H.R.H. The Sultan of 1927- *IntWW 93*
Keddafi, Mu'ammar al- *IntWW 93*
Keddie, Roland Thomas 1928- *WhoAm 94*
Ke Deming *WhoPRCh 91*
Kedia, Ullas V. 1946- *WhoAsA 94*
Keding, Ann Maxwell 1944- *WhoFI 94, WhoWest 94*
Kedourie, Elie d1992 *IntWW 93N*
Kedourie, Elie 1926-1992 *WrDr 94N*
Kedrakas, Nassos d1981 *WhoHol 92*
Kedrof, Mikhail d1972 *WhoHol 92*
Kedrova, Lila 1918- *WhoHol 92*
Kedrowski, David Ray 1942- *WhoAmP 93*
Kedzie, Daniel P. 1930- *WhoIns 94*
Kee, Howard Clark 1920- *WhoAm 94*
Kee, James 1917-1989 *WhAm 10*
Kee, Marsha Goodwin 1942- *WhoBlA 94*
Kee, Norman Dean 1931- *WhoAmP 93*
Kee, Robert 1919- *EncSF 93, IntWW 93, Who 94, WrDr 94*
Kee, Sharon Phillips 1950- *WhoAm 94*
Kee, Shirley Ann 1935- *WhoMW 93*
Kee, Virginia Moshang 1932- *WhoAmP 93*
Kee, Walter Andrew 1914- *WhoAm 94*
Kee, William 1921- *Who 94*
Kee, Willie 1936- *WhoAsA 94*
Keeble, (Herbert Ben) Curtis 1922- *IntWW 93, Who 94*
Keeble, John *DrAPF 93*
Keeble, Neil H(oward) 1944- *WrDr 94*
Keeble, Robert 1911- *Who 94*
Keeble, Thomas Whitfield 1918- *Who 94*
Keech, John H. 1943- *WhoAmA 93*
Keedy, Christian D. 1945- *WhoAmL 94*
Keedy, Michael H. 1943- *WhoAmP 93*
Keefe, Cornelius d1972 *WhoHol 92*
Keefe, David Lawrence 1951- *WhoFI 94*
Keefe, Deborah Lynn 1950- *WhoScEn 94*
Keefe, Edmund M. 1908- *WhoAmP 93*
Keefe, F. Barry 1942- *WhoAmL 94*
Keefe, Francis Joseph 1949- *WhoScEn 94*
Keefe, John B. 1928- *WhoAmP 93*
Keefe, Kenneth M., Jr. 1941- *WhoAmL 94*
Keefe, Robert D. 1946- *WhoAmL 94*
Keefe, Robert Joseph 1934- *WhoAmP 93*
Keefe, Roger Manton 1919-1992 *WhAm 10*
Keefe, William Joseph 1925- *WhoAm 94, WhoAmP 93*
Keefe, William Robert 1965- *WhoScEn 94*
Keefe, Zena d1977 *WhoHol 92*
Keefer, Barbara Jo 1955- *WhoAmL 94*
Keefer, Don *WhoHol 92*
Keefer, James Michael 1947- *WhoAm 94*
Keefer, Scott King 1927- *WhoAmP 93*
Keeffe, Barrie 1945- *WrDr 94*
Keeffe, Barrie (Colin) 1945- *ConDr 93*
Keeffe, Barrie Colin 1945- *Who 94*
Keeffe, Bernard 1925- *IntWW 93*
Keeffe, Emmet Britton 1942- *WhoWest 94*
Keeffe, John Arthur 1930- *WhoAmL 94*
Keeffe, Mary Ann 1944- *WhoAmP 93*
Keegan, Barry d1977 *WhoHol 92*
Keegan, Danis Michael 1924- *Who 94*
Keegan, David Lloyd 1939- *WhoAm 94*
Keegan, Donna 1960- *WhoHol 92*
Keegan, George J., Jr. d1993 *NewYTBS 93 [port]*
Keegan, Gerard C. *WhoAm 94, WhoFI 94*
Keegan, Jane 1956- *WhoAm 94*
Keegan, Jane Ann 1950- *WhoFI 94*
Keegan, John *WhoAmP 93*
Keegan, John 1934- *IntWW 93*
Keegan, John (Desmond Patrick) 1934- *WrDr 94*
Keegan, John E. 1943- *WhoAmL 94*

Keegan, Kenneth Donald 1927- *WhoAm 94*
Keegan, (Joseph) Kevin 1951- *Who 94*
Keegan, Kevin Gerard 1962- *WhoFI 94*
Keegan, Linda *DrAPF 93*
Keegan, Phil 1942- *WhoAmP 93*
Keegan, Richard John 1924- *WhoAm 94*
Keegan, Robert d1988 *WhoHol 92*
Keegan, Thomas d1981 *WhoHol 92*
Keegan, Thomas G. 1939- *WhoAmP 93*
Keegan, William James Gregory 1938- *Who 94*
Keegan-Hutchinson, Karen 1946- *WhoAmP 93*
Keehn, Silas 1930- *WhoAm 94*
Keehner, Michael Arthur Miller 1943- *WhoAm 94, WhoFI 94*
Keehr, Royce Aaron 1965- *WhoMW 93*
Keel, Alton G., Jr. 1943- *IntWW 93, WhoAmP 93*
Keel, Alton Gold, Jr. 1943- *WhoAm 94*
Keel, Harold *WhoHol 92*
Keel, Howard 1917- *WhoHol 92*
Keel, Howard 1919- *IntMPA 94*
Keel, Michael Clarence 1940- *WhoFI 94*
Keele, Cindi Rae 1951- *WhoMW 93*
Keele, Elizabeth Rulon 1955- *WhoAmP 93*
Keele, Harold M. 1901-1991 *WhAm 10*
Keele, Lyndon Alan 1928- *WhoFI 94*
Keele, Mildred Marie Linch 1930- *WhoMW 93*
Keeler, Anna May d1935 *WhoHol 92*
Keeler, Clinton *DrAPF 93*
Keeler, David Boughton 1931- *WhoAmA 93*
Keeler, David Lee *WhoWest 94*
Keeler, James Leonard 1935- *WhoAm 94, WhoFI 94*
Keeler, Janet Bradford 1947- *WhoAm 94*
Keeler, Jill Rolf 1950- *WhoScEn 94*
Keeler, John S. 1949- *WhoAmP 93*
Keeler, Kathleen Howard 1947- *WhoMW 93*
Keeler, Lynne Livingston Mills 1934- *WhoMW 93, WhoScEn 94*
Keeler, Orville Alan 1938- *WhoWest 94*
Keeler, Roger Norris 1930- *WhoScEn 94*
Keeler, Ross Vincent 1948- *WhoFI 94*
Keeler, Ruby d1993 *IntMPA 94N*
Keeler, Ruby 1909- *WhoHol 92*
Keeler, Ruby 1909?-1993 *CurBio 93N*
Keeler, Ruby 1910-1993 *NewYTBS 93 [port], News 93*
Keeler, Theodore Edwin 1945- *WhoAm 94*
Keeler, Vernes *WhoBlA 94*
Keeler, Virginia Lee 1930- *WhoAmP 93*
Keeler, William Henry 1931- *WhoAm 94*
Keeler, Willie d1964 *WhoHol 92*
Keeley, Brian 1945- *WhoAm 94*
Keeley, Edmund *DrAPF 93*
Keeley, Edmund LeRoy 1928- *WhoAm 94, WrDr 94*
Keeley, Irene Patricia Murphy 1944- *WhoAm 94, WhoAmL 94*
Keeley, John Lemuel 1904-1992 *WhAm 10*
Keeley, Patrick J. 1948- *WhoAmL 94*
Keeley, Robert T., Jr. *WhoAmP 93*
Keeley, Robert V. 1929- *WhoAmP 93*
Keeley, Robert Vossler 1929- *IntWW 93, WhoAm 94*
Keeling, Charles David 1928- *WhoAm 94*
Keeling, Henry Cornelious 1923- *WhoAmA 93*
Keeling, Joe Keith 1936- *WhoAm 94*
Keeling, John 1921- *Who 94*
Keeling, John Henry 1895- *WhAm 10*
Keeling, John Michael 1947- *WhoAmP 93*
Keeling, Larry Dale 1947- *WhoAm 94*
Keeling, Laura C. 1949- *WhoBlA 94*
Keeling, Robert William Maynard 1917- *Who 94*
Keels, James Dewey 1930- *WhoBlA 94*
Keels, Paul C. *WhoBlA 94*
Keel-Williams, Mildred *DrAPF 93*
Keely, George Clayton 1926- *WhoAm 94, WhoAmL 94*
Keely, Stanley Jean 1953- *WhoFI 94*
Keemer, Edgar B. 1913- *WhoBlA 94*
Keemer, Peter John Charles 1932- *Who 94*
Keen, (David) Alan 1937- *Who 94*
Keen, Alan Robert 1941- *WhoScEn 94*
Keen, Benjamin 1913- *WrDr 94*
Keen, Charles L. 1922- *WhoAmP 93*
Keen, Charlotte Elizabeth 1943- *WhoAm 94*
Keen, Constantine 1925- *WhoAm 94*
Keen, Diane 1946- *WhoHol 92*
Keen, Ernest 1937- *WrDr 94*
Keen, Geoffrey 1918- *WhoHol 92*
Keen, Kenneth Roger 1946- *Who 94*
Keen, Malcolm d1970 *WhoHol 92*
Keen, Margaret Mary 1953- *WhoMW 93*
Keen, Maria Elizabeth 1918- *WhoMW 93*
Keen, Maurice Hugh 1933- *Who 94*
Keen, Noah 1924- *WhoHol 92*
Keen, Pat *WhoHol 92*
Keen, Richard Sanderson 1954- *Who 94*
Keen, Sam *DrAPF 93*
Keen, Thomas W. 1943- *WhoAmL 94*
Keena, Betty Karen 1942- *WhoWest 94*
Keena, Janet Laybourn 1928- *WhoAmA 93*
Keenan, Anthony Harold Brian 1940- *WhoAm 94, WhoFI 94*
Keenan, Barbara M. *WhoAmP 93*
Keenan, Barbara Milano *WhoAmL 94*
Keenan, C. Robert, III 1954- *WhoAmL 94*
Keenan, Deborah *DrAPF 93*
Keenan, Dennis Joseph 1946- *WhoAmL 94*
Keenan, Edward Joseph 1932- *WhoWest 94*
Keenan, Edward Louis 1935- *WhoAm 94*
Keenan, Frances d1950 *WhoHol 92*
Keenan, Francis Joyce 1924- *WhoAmP 93*
Keenan, Frank d1929 *WhoHol 92*
Keenan, James George 1944- *WhoAm 94*
Keenan, James Ignatius, Jr. 1932- *WhoAmL 94, WhoIns 94*
Keenan, James Richardson 1936- *WhoFI 94*
Keenan, John 1950- *WhoIns 94*
Keenan, John Fontaine 1929- *WhoAm 94, WhoAmL 94*
Keenan, Kathleen *WhoAmP 93*
Keenan, Mary Ann 1950- *WhoAm 94*
Keenan, Michael Edgar 1934- *WhoAm 94*
Keenan, Mike *NewYTBS 93 [port], WhoAm 94*
Keenan, Nancy A. 1952- *WhoAmP 93*
Keenan, Patrick John 1932- *IntWW 93*
Keenan, Patrick Joseph 1826-1894 *DcNaB MP*
Keenan, Paul d1986 *WhoHol 92*
Keenan, Paul John 1921- *WhoAmP 93*
Keenan, R. Mark 1948- *WhoAm 94*
Keenan, Richard 1952- *WhoAmL 94*
Keenan, Robert 1950- *WhoWest 94*
Keenan, Robert Anthony 1930- *WhoAm 94*
Keenan, Terrance *DrAPF 93*
Keenan, Terrance 1924- *WhoAm 94*
Keenan, William Francis, Jr. 1957- *WhoFI 94*
Keene, Barry 1938- *WhoAmP 93*
Keene, Burt *ConAu 42NR*
Keene, Carolyn *EncSF 93*
Keene, Carolyn 1905- *WrDr 94*
Keene, Carolyn 1936- *WrDr 94*
Keene, Carolyn 1949- *WrDr 94*
Keene, Christopher 1946- *IntWW 93, NewGrDO, WhoAm 94*
Keene, Clifford Henry 1910- *WhoAm 94, WhoScEn 94, WhoWest 94*
Keene, David Wolfe 1941- *Who 94*
Keene, Day d1969 *WhoHol 92*
Keene, Day 1904-1969 *EncSF 93*
Keene, Derek John 1942- *Who 94*
Keene, Donald 1922- *WrDr 94*
Keene, Douglas Ralph 1944- *WhoAm 94*
Keene, Elsie d1973 *WhoHol 92*
Keene, Gloria 1939- *WhoHisp 94*
Keene, James A(llen) 1932- *ConAu 43NR*
Keene, John Clark 1931- *WhoAm 94, WhoAmL 94*
Keene, John Robert R. *Who 94*
Keene, Mattie d1944 *WhoHol 92*
Keene, Michael Andrew 1956- *WhoWest 94*
Keene, Patricia d1981 *WhoHol 92*
Keene, Paul 1920- *WhoAmA 93*
Keene, Richard d1971 *WhoHol 92*
Keene, Richard Clinton 1938- *WhoAmL 94*
Keene, Sharon C. 1948- *WhoBlA 94*
Keene, Stephen Winslow 1938- *WhoIns 94*
Keene, Tom d1963 *WhoHol 92*
Keene, William Blair 1933- *WhoAm 94*
Keene Blakely, Nancy Alice 1958- *WhoWest 94*
Keene-Burgess, Ruth Frances 1948- *WhoWest 94*
Keener, Charles Richard 1939- *WhoAm 94*
Keener, Eliott *WhoHol 92*
Keener, Frederick M(ichael) 1937- *ConAu 43NR*
Keener, Hazel d1979 *WhoHol 92*
Keener, John Wesley 1927- *WhoWest 94*
Keener, Joyce *DrAPF 93*
Keener, LuAnn *DrAPF 93*
Keener, Mary Lou 1944- *WhoAm 94, WhoAmL 94*
Keener, Polly Leonard 1946- *WhoAmA 93, WhoMW 93*
Keener, Robert W. 1931- *WhoFI 94*
Keeney, Allen Lloyd 1933- *WhoAmA 93*
Keeney, Arthur Hail 1920- *WhoAm 94*
Keeney, Dale Steve, Jr. 1961- *WhoFI 94*
Keeney, Daniel Paul 1963- *WhoMW 93*
Keeney, Dennis Raymond 1937- *WhoAm 94, WhoMW 93, WhoScEn 94*
Keeney, E. Andrew 1951- *WhoAm 94*
Keeney, Edmund Ludlow 1908- *WhoAm 94*
Keeney, John Christopher 1922- *WhoAm 94, WhoAmL 94*
Keeney, John Christopher, Jr. 1951- *WhoAm 94, WhoAmL 94*
Keenleyside, Hugh L(lewellyn) 1898-1992 *WrDr 94N*
Keenleyside, Hugh Llewellyn 1898- *WhAm 10*
Keenleyside, Hugh Llewellyn d1992 *IntWW 93N, Who 94N*
Keenon, Una H. R. 1933- *WhoBlA 94*
Keens, William *DrAPF 93*
Keeny, Spurgeon Milton, Jr. 1924- *WhoAm 94, WhoAmP 93*
Keep, Charles Reuben 1932- *Who 94*
Keep, Judith N. 1944- *WhoAm 94, WhoAmL 94, WhoWest 94*
Keep, Michael *WhoHol 92*
Keep, Stephen *WhoHol 92*
Keepers, William L. 1938- *WhoFI 94*
Keepin, George Robert, Jr. 1923- *WhoAm 94, WhoScEn 94*
Keeping, Charles (William James) 1924-1988 *ConAu 43NR*
Keer, Leon Morris 1934- *WhoAm 94, WhoScEn 94*
Keerl, Bayat 1948- *WhoAmA 93*
Kees, Beverly 1941- *WhoAm 94*
Keese, John Stanley 1952- *WhoWest 94*
Keesee, Oscar d1968 *WhoHol 92*
Keesee, Thomas Woodfin, Jr. 1915- *WhoAm 94*
Keesey, Ulker Tulunay 1932- *WhoAm 94*
Keeshan, Bob 1927- *IntMPA 94, WhoAm 94, WrDr 94*
Keeshan, Lawrence W. 1945- *WhoAmL 94*
Keeshan, Michael *WhoAm 94, WhoFI 94*
Keeshan, William Francis, Jr. 1934- *WhoAm 94*
Keeshen, Kathleen Kearney 1937- *WhoFI 94*
Keeshing-Tobias, Lenore *BlmGWL*
Keesing, Nancy 1923- *BlmGWL*
Keesing, Nancy (Florence) 1923- *WrDr 94*
Keesing, Roger M(artin) 1935- *WrDr 94*
Keesler, Allen John, Jr. 1938- *WhoFI 94*
Keesley, William P. 1953- *WhoAmP 93*
Keesling, Francis Valentine, Jr. 1908- *WhoAm 94*
Keesling, Karen Ruth 1946- *WhoAm 94*
Keesling, Nina Katherine 1954- *WhoFI 94*
Keesling, Phyllis Jean 1949- *WhoMW 93*
Keet, Jim 1949- *WhoAmP 93*
Keeter, James Edwin, Sr. 1933- *WhoAm 94*
Keeton, Charles R. 1949- *WhoAmL 94*
Keeton, John T., Jr. *WhoAmP 93*
Keeton, Kathy 1939- *CurBio 93 [port], WhoHol 92*
Keeton, Morris Teuton 1917- *WhoAm 94, WrDr 94*
Keeton, Paul C. 1913- *WhoAmP 93*
Keeton, Robert Ernest 1919- *WhoAm 94, WhoAmL 94*
Keets, John David, Jr. 1948- *WhoMW 93*
Keevan, Kim 1950- *WhoAmA 93*
Keevert, Sandra Lynn 1955- *WhoMW 93*
Keevil, Norman Bell 1938- *WhoAm 94, WhoScEn 94*
Keevil, Philip Clement 1946- *WhoAm 94, WhoFI 94*
Keezer, Dexter Merriam 1895-1991 *WhAm 10*
Keezer, Philip Willard 1945- *WhoMW 93*
Kefala, Antigone 1935- *BlmGWL*
Kefauver, Nancy d1967 *WhoAmA 93N*
Kefauver, Weldon Addison 1927- *WhoAm 94*
Kefeli, Valentin Ilich 1937- *WhoScEn 94*
Keffala, Ann Lazopoulos 1923- *WhoAmP 93*
Keffer, Charles Joseph 1941- *WhoAm 94*
Kegel, Gerhard Theodor Otto 1912- *IntWW 93*
Kegel, William George 1922- *WhoAm 94*
Kegeles, Gerson 1917- *WhoAm 94*
Kegeles, S. Stephen 1925- *WhoScEn 94*
Kegerreis, Robert James 1921- *WhoAm 94*
Keglar, Shelvy Haywood 1947- *WhoBlA 94*
Kegley, James Allen 1943- *WhoAmL 94*
Kegley, Kermit 1918- *WhoHol 92*
Kehaya, Barbara M. 1921- *WhoAmP 93*
Kehaya, Ery W. 1923- *WhoAm 94, WhoFI 94*
Kehew, William James 1937- *WhoMW 93*
Kehl, Randall Herman 1954- *WhoAmL 94*
Kehler, Carolyn S. *WhoAmP 93*
Kehler, Dorothea Faith 1936- *WhoWest 94*
Kehlet, Niels 1938- *IntDcB [port]*
Kehlmann, Robert 1942- *WhoAmA 93, WhoWest 94*
Kehm, Walter Howard 1937- *WhoAm 94*
Kehoe, Jack 1938- *WhoHol 92*
Kehoe, James W. 1925- *WhoAm 94, WhoAmL 94*
Kehoe, Kathy B. 1959- *WhoAmP 93*
Kehoe, L. Paul 1938- *WhoAmP 93*
Kehoe, Marie-Louise 1928- *WhoAmP 93*
Kehoe, Patrice 1952- *WhoAmA 93*
Kehoe, Patricia D. 1951- *WrDr 94*
Kehoe, Robert E., Jr. 1947- *WhoAmL 94*
Kehoe, Steven Edward 1959- *WhoMW 93*
Kehoe, Vincent Jeffre-Roux 1921- *WhoWest 94*
Kehoe, William Francis 1933- *WhoAm 94*
Kehr, August Ernest 1914- *WhoScEn 94*
Kehrer, Daniel M. 1953- *WhoAm 94*
Kehret, Peg 1936- *WhoAm 94*
Ke Hua 1915- *IntWW 93, WhoPRCh 91 [port]*
Keicher, William Eugene 1947- *WhoScEn 94*
Keidel, Mark Alan 1961- *WhoFI 94*
Keiderling, Kyle R. 1942- *WhoAmP 93*
Keier, Richard Frederick 1939- *WhoAmP 93, WhoFI 94*
Keifer, Orion Paul 1951- *WhoScEn 94*
Keiffer, Edwin Gene 1929- *WhoAm 94, WhoFI 94*
Keighley, Michael Robert Burch 1943- *Who 94*
Keighley, Thomas Christopher 1951- *Who 94*
Keighley, William d1984 *WhoHol 92*
Keighly-Peach, Charles Lindsey 1902- *Who 94*
Keightley, Cyril d1929 *WhoHol 92*
Keightley, Richard Charles 1933- *Who 94*
Keigler, John E. 1929- *WhoScEn 94*
Keil, Alfred Adolf Heinrich 1913- *WhoAm 94*
Keil, Alfredo 1850-1907 *NewGrDO*
Keil, Arno d1974 *WhoHol 92*
Keil, Birgit 1944- *IntDcB [port]*
Keil, Charles 1939- *ConAu 140*
Keil, David J. 1946- *WhoAm 94*
Keil, John Mullan 1922- *WhoAm 94*
Keil, Klaus 1934- *WhoAm 94, WhoScEn 94*
Keil, M. David 1931- *WhoAm 94*
Keil, Norma Fern 1906- *WhoAmP 93*
Keilbar, Mona Hubbard *WhoAmP 93*
Keilberth, Joseph 1908-1968 *NewGrDO*
Keilhacker, Kurt Anthony 1963- *WhoFI 94*
Keilis-Borok, Vladimir Isaakovich 1921- *IntWW 93*
Keill, John Henry 1953- *WhoMW 93*
Keill, Stuart Langdon 1927- *WhoAm 94*
Keillor, Garrison *DrAPF 93*
Keillor, Garrison 1942- *WhoCom*
Keillor, Garrison (Edward) 1942- *WrDr 94*
Keillor, Garrison Edward 1942- *IntWW 93, WhoAm 94*
Keillor, Sharon Ann 1945- *WhoAm 94*
Keim, Barbara Howell 1946- *WhoMW 93*
Keim, Betty Adele T. 1935- *WhoMW 93*
Keim, Betty Lou 1938- *WhoHol 92*
Keim, Brian T. 1943- *WhoAmL 94*
Keim, Donald William 1942- *WhoAm 94, WhoAmL 94*
Keim, John Richard 1962- *WhoMW 93*
Keim, Michael Ray 1951- *WhoWest 94*
Keim, Robert Bruce 1946- *WhoAmL 94*
Keim, Robert Phillip 1920- *WhoAm 94*
Keim, Robert Thomas 1949- *WhoWest 94*
Keim, Terry 1958- *WhoWest 94*
Keim, Wayne Franklin 1923- *WhoAm 94*
Keiner, Jeffrey Douglas 1946- *WhoAmL 94*
Keiner, Robert Bruce, Jr. 1942- *WhoAm 94, WhoAmL 94*
Keiper, Marilyn Morrison 1930- *WhoWest 94*
Keir, Andrew 1926- *WhoHol 92*
Keir, David *WhoHol 92*
Keir, Gerald Janes 1943- *WhoAm 94, WhoWest 94*
Keir, James Dewar 1921- *Who 94*
Keirns, James Jeffrey 1947- *WhoAm 94*
Keiser, Bernhard Edward 1928- *WhoAm 94*
Keiser, Edmund Davis, Jr. 1934- *WhoAm 94*
Keiser, George *WhoAmP 93*
Keiser, Harry Robert 1933- *WhoAm 94*
Keiser, Henry Bruce 1927-1992 *WhAm 10*
Keiser, L. Thomas 1927- *WhoAmP 93*
Keiser, Paul Harold 1927- *WhoAm 94*
Keiser, Reinhard 1674-1739 *NewGrDO*
Keiser, Sophia (Dorothea Louisa) 1712?-1768 *NewGrDO*
Keiser, W. Jack 1944- *WhoAmL 94*
Keisler, Ben Lawrence 1957- *WhoAmL 94*
Keisler, Howard Jerome 1936- *WhoAm 94*
Keisling, Phil 1955- *WhoAmP 93*
Keisling, Phillip A. 1955- *WhoAm 94, WhoWest 94*
Keister, Jean Clare 1931- *WhoAmL 94, WhoWest 94*
Keister, Steve 1949- *WhoAmA 93*

Keistler, Betty Lou 1935- *WhoFI 94*
Keitel, Harvey 1939- *IntMPA 94, IntWW 93, WhoHol 92*
Keitel, Harvey 1941- *WhoAm 94*
Keith *Who 94*
Keith, Lord *WhAmRev*
Keith, A. M. *WhoAmP 93*
Keith, Alan George 1946- *WhoAm 94*
Keith, Alexander MacDonald 1928- *WhoAm 94, WhoAmL 94, WhoMW 93*
Keith, Allan Hoiles 1941- *WhoMW 93*
Keith, Bill 1919- *WhoAmP 93*
Keith, Brenda Elaine 1956- *WhoAmP 93*
Keith, Brian 1921- *IntMPA 94, WhoHol 92*
Keith, Brian Michael 1921- *WhoAm 94*
Keith, Brian Richard 1944- *Who 94*
Keith, Bruce Edgar 1918- *WhoWest 94*
Keith, Carlton 1914-1991 *WrDr 94N*
Keith, Dale Martin 1940- *WhoMW 93, WhoScEn 94*
Keith, Damon J. *WhoAmP 93*
Keith, Damon J. 1922- *AfrAmAl 6 [port]*
Keith, Damon Jerome 1922- *WhoAm 94, WhoAmL 94, WhoBlA 94*
Keith, David *DrAPF 93, Who 94*
Keith, David 1906- *WrDr 94*
Keith, David 1954- *IntMPA 94, WhoHol 92*
Keith, Donald d1969 *WhoHol 92*
Keith, Donald Malcolm 1932- *WhoWest 94*
Keith, Donald Merle 1928- *WhoAmP 93*
Keith, Donald Raymond 1927- *WhoAm 94*
Keith, Doris T. 1924- *WhoBlA 94*
Keith, Eugene d1955 *WhoHol 92*
Keith, Frederick W., Jr. 1921- *WhoScEn 94*
Keith, Garnett Lee, Jr. 1935- *WhoAm 94, WhoFI 94*
Keith, George 1638?-1716 *DcAmReB 2*
Keith, Harold (Verne) 1903- *SmATA 74 [port], TwCYAW, WrDr 94*
Keith, Herbert Ross 1946- *WhoMW 93*
Keith, Ian d1960 *WhoHol 92*
Keith, Isabelle d1979 *WhoHol 92*
Keith, Jane d1944 *WhoHol 92*
Keith, Jennie 1942- *WhoAm 94*
Keith, Jerry M. 1940- *WhoScEn 94*
Keith, John Ray 1948- *WhoAmP 93*
Keith, Karen C. 1957- *WhoBlA 94*
Keith, Kenneth (James) 1937- *Who 94*
Keith, Kent Marsteller 1948- *WhoAm 94, WhoWest 94*
Keith, Kevin Lawrence 1957- *WhoFI 94*
Keith, Leigh *EncSF 93*
Keith, Leroy 1939- *WhoBlA 94*
Keith, Leroy, Jr. 1939- *WhoAm 94*
Keith, M. Langhorne 1936- *WhoAmL 94*
Keith, Michael C(urtis) 1945- *WrDr 94*
Keith, Norman Thomas 1936- *WhoWest 94*
Keith, Paul 1944- *WhoHol 92*
Keith, Pauline Mary 1924- *WhoWest 94*
Keith, Penelope 1930- *WhoHol 92*
Keith, Penelope 1939- *IntMPA 94*
Keith, Penelope Anne Constance *Who 94*
Keith, Penelope Anne Constance 1940- *IntWW 93*
Keith, Phillip Edwin 1950- *WhoAmL 94*
Keith, Rhonda Cheryl 1947- *WhoMW 93*
Keith, Richard d1976 *WhoHol 92*
Keith, Robert d1966 *WhoHol 92*
Keith, Robert Allen 1924- *WhoWest 94*
Keith, Robert R. 1941- *WhoAm 94*
Keith, Roger Horn 1933- *WhoScEn 94*
Keith, Rosalind 1912- *WhoHol 92*
Keith, Sara Anne 1954- *WhoMW 93*
Keith, Sheila 1920- *WhoHol 92*
Keith, Sherwood d1972 *WhoHol 92*
Keith, Stephen C. 1942- *WhoAmP 93*
Keith, Stephen Ernest 1958- *WhoScEn 94*
Keith, Sydney d1982 *WhoHol 92*
Keith, Theo Gordon, Jr. 1939- *WhoScEn 94*
Keith, Thomas Joseph 1941- *WhoAmP 93*
Keith, Thomas Warren, Jr. 1951- *WhoMW 93*
Keith, Timothy Zook 1952- *WhoAm 94*
Keith, William Raymond 1929- *WhoAmP 93*
Keithcart, Kerry Edward 1954- *WhoWest 94*
Keith-Johnston, Colin d1980 *WhoHol 92*
Keithley, Bradford Gene 1951- *WhoAm 94, WhoAmL 94*
Keithley, George *DrAPF 93*
Keithley, George 1935- *WhoAm 94*
Keithley, Joseph Faber 1915- *WhoAm 94*
Keith-Lucas, Alan 1910- *ConAu 42NR*
Keith-Lucas, Bryan 1912- *Who 94, WrDr 94*
Keith-Lucas, David 1911- *Who 94, WhoScEn 94*
Keith Of Castleacre, Baron 1916- *IntWW 93, Who 94*
Keith Of Kinkel, Baron 1922- *Who 94*
Keitt, L. 1938- *WhoBlA 94*
Keizer, Joel Edward 1942- *WhoAm 94*
Kejr, Joe *WhoAmP 93*
Ke Jun *WhoPRCh 91*
Ke Juya *WhoPRCh 91 [port]*
Kekatos, Deppie-Tinny Z. 1960- *WhoScEn 94*
Kekedo, Mary (Angela) 1919- *Who 94*
Kekes, John 1936- *WhoAm 94*
Kekule von Stradonitz, (Friedrich) August 1829-1896 *WorScD [port]*
Kekwick, Ralph Ambrose 1908- *Who 94*
Kelada, Nabih Philobbos 1930- *WhoScEn 94*
Kelahan, John Anthony, Jr. 1952- *WhoFI 94*
Kelaher, James Peirce 1951- *WhoAmL 94*
Kelaiditis, Anestis 1948- *WhoFI 94*
Kelalis, Panayotis 1932- *WhoAm 94*
Ke Lan *WhoPRCh 91*
Kelbaugh, Douglas Stewart 1945- *WhoAm 94*
Kelberg, Howard S. 1946- *WhoAmL 94*
Kelbie, David 1945- *Who 94*
Kelbley, Stephen Paul 1942- *WhoAm 94*
Kelburn, Viscount of 1978- *Who 94*
Kelcey, Herbert d1917 *WhoHol 92*
Kelch, Robert Paul 1942- *WhoAm 94*
Kelcy, Michael C. 1945- *WhoAmL 94*
Kelder, Diane M. 1934- *WhoAmA 93*
Keldish, Yury Vsevolodovich 1907- *NewGrDO*
Keldysh, Leonid Veniaminovich 1931- *WhoScEn 94*
Keleher, James P. 1931- *WhoAm 94, WhoMW 93*
Keleher, Joseph Michael 1945- *WhoFI 94*
Keleher, Mary Patricia 1959- *WhoAmL 94*
Kelemen, Charles F. 1943- *WhoAm 94*
Kelemen, Denis George *WhoScEn 94*
Kelemen, Milko 1924- *NewGrDO*
Kelemen, Pal 1894- *WhoAmA 93*
Kelemen, Zoltan 1926-1979 *NewGrDO*
Kelen, Joyce Arlene 1949- *WhoWest 94*
Kelen, Julia Laura 1950- *WhoWest 94*
Kelen, Stephen 1912- *WrDr 94*
Keliher, John G. *WhoAmP 93*
Ke-li-mu Huo-jia *WhoPRCh 91*
Ke Lin 1901- *WhoPRCh 91*
Kelk, Jackie *WhoHol 92*
Kelker, Sally Lorraine 1942- *WhoAmP 93*
Kell, Christopher J. 1943- *WhoAmL 94*
Kell, Ernest Eugene, Jr. 1928- *WhoAm 94, WhoWest 94*
Kell, Ernie *WhoAmP 93*
Kell, James H. 1930- *WhAm 10*
Kell, Joseph *TwCYAW, Who 94*
Kell, Joseph 1917- *WrDr 94*
Kell, Richard (Alexander) 1927- *WrDr 94*
Kell, Scott K. 1928- *WhoAmL 94*
Kell, Vernon George Waldegrave 1873-1942 *DcNaB MP*
Kell, Vette Eugene 1915- *WhoAmL 94*
Kellam, Norma Dawn 1938- *WhoWest 94*
Kellam, Richard B. 1909- *WhoAm 94, WhoAmL 94*
Kellam, Robert T. 1922- *WhoAmP 93*
Kelland, Gilbert James 1924- *Who 94*
Kelland, John William 1929- *Who 94*
Kellar, Charles Lionel 1909- *WhoBlA 94*
Kellar, Jeff 1949- *WhoAmA 93*
Kellar, Marie Terese 1934- *WhoMW 93*
Kellar, Martha Robbins 1949- *WhoAmA 93*
Kellar, Von *EncSF 93*
Kellard, John E. d1929 *WhoHol 92*
Kellard, Ralph d1955 *WhoHol 92*
Kellard, Robert d1981 *WhoHol 92*
Kellas, Arthur Roy Handasyde 1915- *IntWW 93, Who 94*
Kellas, Elizabeth Ellen 1963- *WhoAmL 94*
Kellaway, Cecil d1973 *WhoHol 92*
Kellaway, Peter 1920- *WhoAm 94, WhoScEn 94*
Kellaway, (Charles) William 1926- *Who 94*
Kellberg, Love 1922- *IntWW 93*
Kelle, Jill Diane 1962- *WhoMW 93*
Kelleam, Joseph E(veridge) 1913-1975 *EncSF 93*
Kelleher, Bob 1913- *BuCMET*
Kelleher, Carolyn Virginia 1943- *WhoMW 93*
Kelleher, D. Ring 1927- *WhoAmL 94*
Kelleher, Herbert David 1931- *WhoAm 94, WhoFI 94*
Kelleher, James Francis 1930- *IntWW 93*
Kelleher, Joan 1915- *Who 94*
Kelleher, John M. *WhoAmL 94, WhoFI 94*
Kelleher, Kathleen 1951- *WhoFI 94*
Kelleher, Matthew Dennis 1939- *WhoWest 94*
Kelleher, Neil William 1923- *WhoAmP 93*
Kelleher, Patrick Joseph 1917-1985 *WhoAmA 93N*
Kelleher, Richard Cornelius 1949- *WhoFI 94, WhoWest 94*
Kelleher, Robert Joseph 1913- *WhoAm 94, WhoAmL 94, WhoWest 94*
Kelleher, Robert Joseph 1922- *WhoAmP 93*
Kelleher, Ronald Ray 1951- *WhoWest 94*
Kelleher, Sean Francis 1963- *WhoMW 93*
Kelleher, Thomas F. 1923- *WhoAmL 94, WhoAmP 93*
Kelleher, Thomas J., Jr. 1943- *WhoAmL 94*
Kelleher, Timothy John 1940- *WhoAm 94*
Kelleher, Victor (Michael Kitchener) 1939- *EncSF 93, SmATA 75, TwCYAW, WrDr 94*
Kelleher, William Eugene, Jr. 1953- *WhoAmL 94*
Kelleher, William Joseph 1929- *WhoScEn 94*
Kellen, Michael L. 1948- *WhoIns 94*
Kellen, Stephen Max 1914- *WhoFI 94*
Keller, Alex Stephen 1928- *WhoAm 94, WhoAmL 94*
Keller, Alfred d1989 *WhoHol 92*
Keller, Allison MacGregor 1960- *WhoMW 93*
Keller, Andrew 1925- *IntWW 93, Who 94*
Keller, Arthur Michael 1957- *WhoWest 94*
Keller, Ben Robert, Jr. 1936- *WhoScEn 94*
Keller, Billy 1947- *BasBi*
Keller, Bryan J. 1950- *WhoFI 94*
Keller, C. Graden, Jr. 1949- *WhoFI 94*
Keller, Charles 1942- *ConAu 43NR*
Keller, Charles Ray 1901-1990 *WhAm 10*
Keller, Christoph, Jr. 1915- *WhoAm 94*
Keller, Dale Arther 1951- *WhoFI 94*
Keller, Darla Lynn 1956- *WhoMW 93*
Keller, David *DrAPF 93*
Keller, David H(enry) 1880-1966 *EncSF 93*
Keller, David Lester 1919- *WhoAmP 93*
Keller, Dawn Susan 1962- *WhoMW 93*
Keller, Deane 1901-1992 *WhAm 10, WhoAmA 93N*
Keller, Dennis James 1941- *WhoMW 93*
Keller, Dennis John 1947- *WhoFI 94*
Keller, Diane Marie 1950- *WhoMW 93*
Keller, Donald R. 1949- *WhoAmL 94*
Keller, E. W. 1936- *WhoAmP 93*
Keller, Edmond Joseph 1942- *WhoBlA 94*
Keller, Edward Clarence, Jr. 1932- *WhoAm 94*
Keller, Edward Lowell 1939- *WhoAm 94*
Keller, Eliot Aaron 1947- *WhoAm 94, WhoMW 93*
Keller, Emily *DrAPF 93*
Keller, Frank S. 1951- *WhoAmA 93*
Keller, Gary D. 1943- *WhoHisp 94*
Keller, George Henrik 1931- *WhoAm 94*
Keller, George Henry 1950- *WhoScEn 94*
Keller, George M. 1923- *IntWW 93*
Keller, George Matthew 1923- *WhoAm 94, WhoWest 94*
Keller, George R. 1951- *WhoIns 94*
Keller, Gertrude d1951 *WhoHol 92*
Keller, Glen Elven, Jr. 1938- *WhoAm 94, WhoAmL 94*
Keller, Gottfried 1819-1890 *DcLB 129 [port], NewGrDO, RfGShF*
Keller, H. Michael 1951- *WhoAmL 94*
Keller, Hans Gustav 1902- *IntWW 93*
Keller, Harold William 1922- *WhoMW 93*
Keller, Helen d1968 *WhoHol 92*
Keller, Helen Adams 1880-1968 *AmSocL, EncDeaf*
Keller, Henry G. 1870-1949 *WhoAmA 93N*
Keller, Hiram 1944- *WhoHol 92*
Keller, Holly 1942- *SmATA 76 [port]*
Keller, Jack 1928- *WhoAm 94*
Keller, James Robert 1954- *WhoAmL 94*
Keller, James Wesley 1958- *WhoFI 94, WhoWest 94*
Keller, John Francis 1925- *WhoAm 94*
Keller, John Kistler 1950- *WhoAm 94, WhoAmL 94*
Keller, John Milton 1922- *WhoMW 93*
Keller, John Richard 1924- *WhoAm 94*
Keller, Joseph *WhoAmP 93*
Keller, Joseph Bishop 1923- *IntWW 93, WhoAm 94, WhoScEn 94*
Keller, Juan Dane 1943- *WhoAm 94, WhoAmL 94*
Keller, Kenneth Christen 1939- *WhoMW 93*
Keller, Kenneth Harrison 1934- *WhoAm 94*
Keller, Kent Eugene 1941- *WhoFI 94, WhoWest 94*
Keller, Kevin John 1957- *WhoFI 94*
Keller, Laurent 1961- *WhoScEn 94*
Keller, LeRoy 1905- *WhoAm 94*
Keller, Madeleine *DrAPF 93*
Keller, Margaret Marie 1944- *WhoAmL 94*
Keller, Mark 1907- *WhoScEn 94*
Keller, Martha *WhoAmA 93*
Keller, Marthe 1945- *WhoHol 92*
Keller, Marthe 1946- *IntMPA 94*
Keller, Mary Barnett 1938- *WhoBlA 94*
Keller, Mary Page 1961- *WhoHol 92*
Keller, Maryanne 1949- *WhoAmP 93*
Keller, Michael Crosley 1949- *WhoWest 94*
Keller, Millett Frederick 1915- *WhoAmP 93*
Keller, Myron Eugene 1923- *WhoAmP 93*
Keller, Nell Clark d1965 *WhoHol 92*
Keller, Paul 1921- *WhoAm 94*
Keller, Reed T. 1938- *WhAm 10*
Keller, Rene Jacques 1914- *Who 94*
Keller, Robert 1942- *WhoAm 94, WhoFI 94*
Keller, Robert Lee 1945- *WhoWest 94*
Keller, Robert Lee 1946- *WhoWest 94*
Keller, Robert Scott 1945- *WhoWest 94*
Keller, Ronald Charles 1932- *WhoFI 94*
Keller, Ronald E. 1936- *WhoIns 94*
Keller, Ronald L. 1937- *WhoAmP 93*
Keller, Rudolf Ernst 1920- *Who 94*
Keller, Samuel William 1930- *WhoAm 94*
Keller, Sharon R. *ConAu 142*
Keller, Shirley Irene 1938- *WhoAmP 93*
Keller, Stanley 1938- *WhoAm 94*
Keller, Stephen 1932- *WhoScEn 94*
Keller, Susan Agnes 1952- *WhoFI 94, WhoWest 94*
Keller, Thomas Clements 1938- *WhoAm 94, WhoAmL 94*
Keller, Thomas Franklin 1931- *WhoAm 94, WhoFI 94*
Keller, Thomas J. 1943- *WhoAmL 94*
Keller, Tsipi Edith *DrAPF 93*
Keller, Vernon V. 1926- *WhoAmP 93*
Keller, William D. 1934- *WhoAm 94, WhoAmL 94, WhoWest 94*
Keller, William F. 1951- *WhoAmP 93*
Keller, William Francis 1922- *WhoAm 94*
Keller, William L. 1923- *WhoAmL 94*
Kelleran, Rebecca Johnston 1943- *WhoWest 94*
Kellerman, Faye (Marder) 1952- *WrDr 94*
Kellerman, Faye Marder 1952- *WhoWest 94*
Kellerman, Jonathan 1949- *WrDr 94*
Kellerman, Jonathan Seth 1949- *WhoAm 94*
Kellerman, Sally 1936- *IntMPA 94, WhoHol 92*
Kellerman, Sally Claire 1937- *WhoAm 94*
Kellerman, Susan *WhoHol 92*
Kellermann, Annette d1975 *WhoHol 92*
Kellermann, Barbara *WhoHol 92*
Kellermann, Bernhard 1879-1951 *EncSF 93*
Kellermann, Hope Patricia Iversen 1924- *WhoMW 93*
Kellermann, Kenneth Irwin 1937- *WhoAm 94, WhoScEn 94*
Kellermeyer, Robert William 1929- *WhoAm 94*
Kellett, Alfred Henry 1904- *Who 94*
Kellett, Arnold 1926- *ConAu 41NR, WrDr 94*
Kellett, Brian (Smith) 1922- *Who 94*
Kellett, Brian Smith 1922- *IntWW 93*
Kellett, Howard Pearson d1993 *NewYTBS 93*
Kellett, Morris C. 1935- *WhoAm 94*
Kellett, Stanley Charles 1940- *Who 94*
Kellett, Timothy K. 1953- *WhoAmL 94*
Kellett, William Hiram, Jr. 1930- *WhoAm 94, WhoScEn 94*
Kellett-Bowman, Edward Thomas 1931- *Who 94*
Kellett-Bowman, Elaine 1924- *WhoWomW 91*
Kellett-Bowman, (Mary) Elaine 1924- *Who 94*
Kelley, Albert Benjamin 1936- *WhoAm 94*
Kelley, Albert Joseph 1924- *WhoAm 94, WhoFI 94, WhoScEn 94*
Kelley, Allen Charles 1937- *WhoAm 94*
Kelley, Aloysius Paul 1929- *WhoAm 94*
Kelley, Barry 1908-1991 *WhoHol 92*
Kelley, Bennett Wallace 1926- *WhoMW 93*
Kelley, Betty Marie 1955- *WhoFI 94*
Kelley, Bob d1966 *WhoHol 92*
Kelley, Bruce Allan 1947- *WhoFI 94*
Kelley, Bruce Dutton 1957- *WhoWest 94*
Kelley, Bruce Gunn 1954- *WhoFI 94, WhoIns 94*
Kelley, Charles Ray 1922- *WhoScEn 94*
Kelley, Christine Ruth 1951- *WhoMW 93*
Kelley, Clarence M. 1911- *IntWW 93*
Kelley, Clarence Marion 1911- *WhoAmL 94*
Kelley, Dale Edward 1927- *WhoMW 93*
Kelley, Dale Russell 1939- *WhoAmP 93*
Kelley, Dana F. 1920- *WhoAmP 93*
Kelley, Daniel, Jr. 1922- *WhoBlA 94*
Kelley, David G. 1928- *WhoAmP 93*
Kelley, David L. 1949- *WhoAmP 93*
Kelley, David Lee 1936- *WhoAm 94*
Kelley, David O'Hara 1946- *WhoMW 93*
Kelley, De Forest 1920- *WhoHol 92*

Kelley, Dean Maurice 1926- *WhoAm 94*
Kelley, Deborah Maverick 1953- *WhoAmA 93*
Kelley, DeForest 1920- *IntMPA 94*
Kelley, Delores G. 1936- *WhoAmP 93, WhoBlA 94*
Kelley, Donald Castell *WhoAmA 93*
Kelley, Donald E. 1908- *WhoAmP 93*
Kelley, Donald Edmund, Jr. 1948- *WhoAmL 94*
Kelley, Donald Reed 1931- *WhoAm 94*
Kelley, Donald William 1939- *WhoAmA 93*
Kelley, Duane Matthew 1947- *WhoAm 94*
Kelley, Edgar Alan 1940- *WhoMW 93*
Kelley, Edith Summers 1884-1956 *BlmGWL*
Kelley, Edward Allen 1927- *WhoAm 94*
Kelley, Edward Watson, Jr. 1932- *WhoAm 94, WhoFI 94*
Kelley, Eugene John 1922- *WhoAm 94*
Kelley, Everette Eugene 1938- *WhoAm 94*
Kelley, Florence 1859-1932 *AmSocL, WomPubS*
Kelley, Frank J. 1924- *WhoAmP 93*
Kelley, Frank Joseph 1924- *WhoAm 94, WhoAmL 94, WhoMW 93*
Kelley, Frank Nicholas 1935- *WhoMW 93, WhoScEn 94*
Kelley, G. Daniel, Jr. 1940- *WhoAmL 94*
Kelley, Gaynor Nathaniel 1931- *WhoAm 94, WhoFI 94, WhoScEn 94*
Kelley, George Gregory 1956- *WhoWest 94*
Kelley, Harold H. 1921- *IntWW 93*
Kelley, Harold Harding 1921- *WhoAm 94*
Kelley, Hoyt Frank 1923- *WhoAmP 93*
Kelley, Jack *WhoAmP 93*
Kelley, Jack Albert 1920- *WhoBlA 94*
Kelley, Jack H. 1932- *WhoIns 94*
Kelley, Jackson DeForest 1920- *WhoAm 94*
Kelley, Jacquelyn Larson 1945- *WhoWest 94*
Kelley, Jacquie A. *WhoAmP 93*
Kelley, James E. 1895- *WhAm 10*
Kelley, James Francis 1941- *WhoAm 94*
Kelley, James G. 1948- *WhoFI 94*
Kelley, James Lee 1947- *WhoWest 94*
Kelley, James Reeves *WhoAmP 93*
Kelley, James Terry 1953- *WhoWest 94*
Kelley, James Thayer 1938- *WhoFI 94*
Kelley, Janet Godsey 1953- *WhoAmL 94*
Kelley, Jeffrey Wendell 1949- *WhoAm 94, WhoAmL 94*
Kelley, Joan 1926- *Who 94*
Kelley, Joanna Elizabeth 1910- *Who 94*
Kelley, John Dennis 1900- *WhoAm 94*
Kelley, John Joseph, Jr. 1936- *WhoAm 94*
Kelley, John Landrum 1918- *WhoFI 94*
Kelley, John M. 1926- *WhoAmP 93*
Kelley, John Paul 1919- *WhoAm 94*
Kelley, Kevin Patrick 1954- *WhoWest 94*
Kelley, Larry Dale 1944- *WhoMW 93*
Kelley, Leo P(atrick) 1928- *EncSF 93, WrDr 94*
Kelley, Leona A. 1919- *WhoAmP 93*
Kelley, Lisa Stone 1947- *WhoWest 94*
Kelley, Lyle Ardell 1944- *WhoFI 94*
Kelley, Lyn Schraff 1956- *WhoFI 94, WhoMW 93*
Kelley, Mark *WhoAmP 93*
Kelley, Mark Alan 1951- *WhoFI 94, WhoWest 94*
Kelley, Maurice Leslie, Jr. 1924- *WhoAm 94, WhoScEn 94*
Kelley, Michael Cornell 1954- *WhoAmL 94*
Kelley, Michael James 1955- *WhoFI 94*
Kelley, Michael John 1942- *WhoAm 94, WhoMW 93*
Kelley, Mike 1954- *WhoAm 94, WhoAmA 93*
Kelley, Noble Henry 1901- *WhoAm 94*
Kelley, Pat 1948- *WhoMW 93*
Kelley, Patricia Colleen 1953- *WhoFI 94*
Kelley, Patrick *IntMPA 94*
Kelley, Patrick Michael 1948- *WhoAmP 93*
Kelley, Paul Xavier 1928- *WhoAm 94*
Kelley, Phillip Barry 1947- *WhoAmP 93*
Kelley, Ralph Houston 1928- *WhoAm 94, WhoAmL 94*
Kelley, Ramon 1939- *WhoAmA 93*
Kelley, Richard Alan 1952- *WhoAm 94*
Kelley, Richard Everett 1927- *WhoFI 94*
Kelley, Richard Roy 1933- *WhoAm 94, WhoWest 94*
Kelley, Robb Beardsley 1917- *WhoAm 94, WhoIns 94*
Kelley, Robert (Lloyd) 1925- *WrDr 94*
Kelley, Robert E. 1938- *WhoAm 94*
Kelley, Robert Franklin 1961- *WhoFI 94, WhoScEn 94, WhoWest 94*
Kelley, Robert Lloyd 1925- *WhoAm 94*
Kelley, Robert N. 1921- *WhoAmP 93*
Kelley, Robert Otis 1944- *WhoAm 94, WhoWest 94*
Kelley, Robert Paul, Jr. 1942- *WhoFI 94, WhoWest 94*
Kelley, Robert W. 1940- *WhoBlA 94*
Kelley, Robert William 1913- *WhoBlA 94*
Kelley, Sheila *WhoHol 92*
Kelley, Sheila Seymour *WhoAm 94*
Kelley, Steve 1953- *WhoAmP 93*
Kelley, Sylvia Johnson 1929- *WhoFI 94*
Kelley, Terry Wayne 1952- *WhoWest 94*
Kelley, Thomas Joseph 1936- *WhoAmL 94*
Kelley, Thomas P. 1905-1982 *EncSF 93*
Kelley, Timothy Edward 1954- *WhoAmL 94*
Kelley, Timothy M. 1947- *WhoAmP 93*
Kelley, Troy Xavier 1964- *WhoAmL 94*
Kelley, Vincent Charles 1916- *WhoAm 94*
Kelley, Walter *WhoHol 92*
Kelley, Wayne Plumbley, Jr. 1933- *WhoAm 94*
Kelley, Wendell J. 1926- *WhoAm 94*
Kelley, Wilbourne Anderson, III *WhoBlA 94*
Kelley, Wilbur Edrald 1908-1989 *WhAm 10*
Kelley, William E. 1939- *WhoBlA 94*
Kelley, William Joseph, II 1959- *WhoAmL 94*
Kelley, William Melvin *DrAPF 93*
Kelley, William Melvin 1937- *EncSF 93, WhoBlA 94, WrDr 94*
Kelley, William Nimmons 1939- *WhoAm 94, WhoScEn 94*
Kelley, William Thomas 1917- *WhoAm 94*
Kellgren, Johan Henrik 1751-1795 *NewGrDO*
Kellgren, Jonas Henrik 1911- *Who 94*
Kelliher, Peter Maurice 1912- *WhoAm 94*
Kellin, Mike d1983 *WhoHol 92*
Kelling, David Henry 1953- *WhoFI 94*
Kelling, Hans-Wilhelm 1932- *WrDr 94*
Kellino, Pamela 1916- *WhoHol 92*
Kellino, Roy d1956 *WhoHol 92*
Kellino, Will P. d1958 *WhoHol 92*
Kellis, Eugene F. 1937- *WhoAmP 93*
Kellis, Randal Anthony 1960- *WhoMW 93*
Kellison, Donna Louise George 1950- *WhoMW 93*
Kellison, James Bruce 1922- *WhoAm 94*
Kellison, Stephen George 1942- *WhoAm 94*
Kelljan, Robert d1982 *WhoHol 92*
Kellman, Anthony *DrAPF 93*
Kellman, Barnet Kramer 1947- *WhoAm 94*
Kellman, Denis Elliott 1948- *WhoBlA 94*
Kellman, Ian Arthur 1942- *WhoFI 94*
Kellman, Ira Stuart 1940- *WhoAm 94*
Kellman, Joel David 1942- *WhoAmL 94*
Kellman, Mark Alec 1953- *WhoAm 94*
Kellman, Steven G. 1947- *WhoAm 94*
Kellner, Bruce 1930- *WrDr 94*
Kellner, Ellen A. 1943- *WhoAmP 93*
Kellner, Irwin L. 1938- *WhoAm 94*
Kellner, Jamie *WhoAm 94, WhoFI 94, WhoWest 94*
Kellner, Leon B. 1945- *WhoAm 94*
Kellner, Richard George 1943- *WhoScEn 94, WhoWest 94*
Kellner, Robert C. 1952- *WhoAmL 94*
Kello, Esther *BlmGWL*
Kellock, Alan 1914-1992 *WhAm 10*
Kellock, Alan Converse 1942- *WhoAm 94*
Kellock, Jane Ursula 1925- *Who 94*
Kellock, Thomas Oslaf d1993 *Who 94N*
Kellog, Junius 1928- *BasBi*
Kellogg, Brent Nelson 1951- *WhoWest 94*
Kellogg, C. Burton, II 1934- *WhoFI 94*
Kellogg, Cal Stewart, II 1947- *WhoAm 94*
Kellogg, Carol Kay 1941- *WhoAm 94*
Kellogg, Charles Gary 1948- *WhoScEn 94*
Kellogg, Clara (Louise) 1842-1916 *NewGrDO*
Kellogg, Clark 1961- *WhoBlA 94*
Kellogg, Cornelia d1934 *WhoHol 92*
Kellogg, David 1950- *WhoAm 94*
Kellogg, Dennis Lee 1947- *WhoMW 93*
Kellogg, Dorothy M. 1920- *WhoAmP 93*
Kellogg, Edmund Halsey d1993 *NewYTBS 93*
Kellogg, Frederic Hartwell 1904- *WhoAm 94*
Kellogg, Frederic Rogers 1942- *WhoAm 94*
Kellogg, Frederick 1929- *WhoWest 94*
Kellogg, Gregg Barnum 1957- *WhoWest 94*
Kellogg, Herbert Humphrey 1920- *WhoAm 94*
Kellogg, Hilde *WhoAmP 93*
Kellogg, John *WhoHol 92*
Kellogg, John Harvey *WorInv*
Kellogg, John Harvey 1852-1943 *AmSocL [port]*
Kellogg, Karl Stuart 1943- *WhoScEn 94*
Kellogg, Kenyon P. 1946- *WhoAm 94, WhoAmL 94*
Kellogg, Lynn *WhoHol 92*
Kellogg, Marion Knight 1904-1989 *WhAm 10*
Kellogg, Marjorie Bradley 1946- *EncSF 93*
Kellogg, Maurice Dale 1919-1984 *WhoAmA 93N*
Kellogg, Paul Underwood 1879-1958 *AmSocL*
Kellogg, Peter R. 1942- *WhoAm 94, WhoFI 94*
Kellogg, Philip M. 1912- *IntMPA 94*
Kellogg, Ray d1981 *WhoHol 92*
Kellogg, Reginald J. 1933- *WhoBlA 94*
Kellogg, Robert Leland 1928- *WhoAm 94*
Kellogg, Robert LeRoy 1952- *WhoMW 93*
Kellogg, Steven 1941- *WhoAm 94, WrDr 94*
Kellogg, Thomas L. 1936- *WhoIns 94*
Kellogg, Tom N. 1936- *WhoIns 94*
Kellogg, Tommy Nason 1936- *WhoAm 94*
Kellogg, Will Keith *WorInv*
Kellogg, William Welch 1917- *WhoAm 94, WhoScEn 94*
Kellogg Wright Davis, Paulina 1813-1876 *WomPubS*
Kellor, Frances Alice 1873-1952 *AmSocL*
Kellou, Mohamed 1931- *IntWW 93*
Kellow, Kathleen *BlmGWL, ConAu 140, SmATA 74*
Kells, Albert J. 1935- *WhoFI 94*
Kells, J. A. *WhoScEn 94*
Kells, Richard B., Jr. 1953- *WhoAmL 94*
Kells, Robert T. 1944- *WhoAmP 93*
Kellshaw, Terence 1936- *WhoAm 94, WhoWest 94*
Kellstadt, Charles H. 1896- *WhAm 10*
Kellum, Carmen Kaye 1952- *WhoFI 94*
Kellum, James Earl 1936- *WhoAmP 93*
Kellum, Norman Bryant, Jr. 1937- *WhoAmL 94*
Kelly, A. David 1948- *WhoAm 94, WhoAmL 94*
Kelly, Al d1966 *WhoHol 92*
Kelly, Al 1896-1966 *WhoCom*
Kelly, Alexander Joseph 1941- *WhoScEn 94*
Kelly, Allan James 1951- *WhoScEn 94*
Kelly, Alonzo Hyatt, Jr. 1922- *WhoAm 94*
Kelly, Anne Catherine 1916- *WhoAmP 93*
Kelly, Anthony 1929- *IntWW 93, Who 94*
Kelly, Anthony Odrian 1935- *WhoAm 94*
Kelly, Arleen P. *WhoAmA 93*
Kelly, Arthur Lloyd 1937- *WhoAm 94, WhoFI 94, WhoMW 93*
Kelly, Arthur Paul 1938- *WhoAm 94*
Kelly, Asa, Jr. 1922- *WhoAmP 93*
Kelly, Aurel Maxey 1923- *WhoAm 94*
Kelly, Barbara 1923- *WhoHol 92*
Kelly, Barbara Mary 1940- *Who 94*
Kelly, Basil *Who 94*
Kelly, (John William) Basil 1920- *Who 94*
Kelly, Bernard V. 1917- *WhoAmP 93*
Kelly, Bernard Wayne 1918- *WhoFI 94*
Kelly, Brendan William 1934- *WhoFI 94*
Kelly, Brian *Who 94*
Kelly, Brian 1932- *WhoHol 92*
Kelly, (Herbert) Brian 1921- *Who 94*
Kelly, Brian Francis 1952- *WhoWest 94*
Kelly, Brian Matthew 1956- *WhoWest 94*
Kelly, Brian McLoughlin 1965- *WhoFI 94*
Kelly, Brigit Pegeen *DrAPF 93*
Kelly, Bruce d1993 *NewYTBS 93*
Kelly, Carol Johnson 1938- *WhoScEn 94*
Kelly, Carol White 1946- *WhoFI 94*
Kelly, Carolyn Sue 1952- *WhoAm 94, WhoWest 94*
Kelly, Charles Arthur 1932- *WhoAm 94*
Kelly, Charles Eugene, II 1958- *WhoWest 94*
Kelly, Charles Henry 1930- *Who 94*
Kelly, Charles J., Jr. 1929- *WhoAm 94*
Kelly, Chris *WhoBlA 94*
Kelly, Chris 1946- *WhoAmP 93*
Kelly, Christine Ann 1952- *WhoFI 94*
Kelly, Christopher William 1946- *Who 94*
Kelly, Claire *WhoHol 92*
Kelly, Clare *WhoHol 92*
Kelly, Cynthia Ference *WhoAmA 93*
Kelly, Dan 1950- *WhoAmP 93*
Kelly, Dan, III 1938- *WhoAmP 93*
Kelly, Daniel Grady, Jr. 1951- *WhoAm 94, WhoAmL 94*
Kelly, Daniel Hugh 1953- *WhoHol 92*
Kelly, Daniel John 1940- *WhoMW 93, WhoScEn 94*
Kelly, Danny C. 1950- *WhoAmL 94*
Kelly, Darlene Okamoto 1944- *WhoAsA 94*
Kelly, Dave *DrAPF 93*
Kelly, David 1930- *WhoHol 92*
Kelly, David A. 1938- *WhoBlA 94*
Kelly, David Austin 1938- *WhoAm 94, WhoFI 94*
Kelly, David Hoover 1944- *WhoAm 94*
Kelly, David Patrick *WhoHol 92*
Kelly, David Reid 1947- *WhoScEn 94*
Kelly, David Richard 1940- *WhoWest 94*
Kelly, David Robert Corbett 1936- *Who 94*
Kelly, David Stuart 1949- *WhoAmL 94*
Kelly, Dee J. 1929- *WhoAm 94, WhoAmL 94*
Kelly, DeeDee Helen 1941- *WhoAmP 93*
Kelly, Dennis John 1947- *WhoAm 94, WhoAmL 94*
Kelly, Dennis Joseph 1941- *WhoFI 94*
Kelly, Dennis Michael 1943- *WhoAm 94, WhoAmL 94*
Kelly, Dennis Ray 1948- *WhoWest 94*
Kelly, Dermot d1980 *WhoHol 92*
Kelly, Don d1966 *WhoHol 92*
Kelly, Donald 1941- *WhoAmP 93*
Kelly, Donald Ignatius *WhoWest 94*
Kelly, Donald P. 1922- *IntWW 93*
Kelly, Donald Philip 1922- *WhoAm 94, WhoFI 94, WhoMW 93*
Kelly, Donna C. 1943- *WhoAmP 93*
Kelly, Dorothy d1966 *WhoHol 92*
Kelly, Dorothy Ann 1929- *WhoAm 94*
Kelly, Dorothy Helen d1969 *WhoHol 92*
Kelly, Douglas 1934- *WhoAm 94*
Kelly, Douglas Barrack 1952- *WhoMW 93*
Kelly, Douglas Elliott 1932- *WhoScEn 94*
Kelly, Douglas Laird 1949- *WhoAmL 94*
Kelly, E. Michael 1947- *WhoAmL 94*
Kelly, Eamon Michael 1936- *WhoAm 94*
Kelly, Earl Lee 1956- *WhoBlA 94*
Kelly, Earl M. *WhoAmP 93*
Kelly, Edmund Joseph 1937- *WhoAm 94*
Kelly, Edna Flannery 1906- *WhoAmP 93*
Kelly, Edward James 1911-1986 *WhAm 10*
Kelly, Edward Ronald 1928- *Who 94*
Kelly, Edward W. 1935- *WhoAmP 93*
Kelly, Edwin Frost 1946- *WhoAmL 94*
Kelly, Eileen Patricia 1955- *WhoFI 94*
Kelly, Ellsworth 1923- *IntWW 93, WhoAm 94, WhoAmA 93*
Kelly, Emery Leonard 1960- *WhoScEn 94*
Kelly, Emmett d1979 *WhoHol 92*
Kelly, Eric Damian 1947- *WhoAmL 94, WhoMW 93*
Kelly, Ernece Beverly 1937- *WhoBlA 94*
Kelly, Eugene 1961- *WhoMW 93*
Kelly, Eugene Walter, Jr. 1936- *WhoAm 94*
Kelly, Everett A. 1926- *WhoAmP 93*
Kelly, Fanny d1925 *WhoHol 92*
Kelly, Fiona *ConAu 142, SmATA 75*
Kelly, Florence Ann 1948- *WhoWest 94*
Kelly, Florida L. 1920- *WhoBlA 94*
Kelly, Francis Daniel 1909- *WhoAm 94*
Kelly, Francis J., Jr. 1929- *WhoAm 94*
Kelly, Francis Joseph 1963- *WhoAm 94*
Kelly, Francis Patrick 1950- *Who 94*
Kelly, Frank K(ing) 1914- *EncSF 93*
Kelly, Frank King 1914- *WhoWest 94*
Kelly, Franklin Wood 1953- *WhoAm 94, WhoAmA 93*
Kelly, Gabrielle Mary 1953- *WhoWest 94*
Kelly, Gene 1912- *IntMPA 94, WhoHol 92*
Kelly, Gene Curran 1912- *IntWW 93, WhoAm 94*
Kelly, George (Edward) 1887-1974 *ConDr 93*
Kelly, George A(nthony) 1916- *ConAu 43NR*
Kelly, George Anthony 1916- *WhoAm 94*
Kelly, George T., Jr. 1930- *WhoAmP 93*
Kelly, George Whitthorne 1960- *WhoAmL 94*
Kelly, Gerald Wayne 1944- *WhoFI 94, WhoScEn 94*
Kelly, Glenda Marie 1944- *WhoAmP 93, WhoMW 93*
Kelly, Grace d1982 *WhoHol 92*
Kelly, Grace Dentino 1934- *WhoMW 93*
Kelly, Graham *Who 94*
Kelly, (Robert Henry) Graham 1945- *Who 94*
Kelly, Gregory d1927 *WhoHol 92*
Kelly, Gregory Maxwell 1930- *IntWW 93*
Kelly, Gwen 1922- *BlmGWL*
Kelly, Harley Lawrence 1937- *WhoFI 94*
Kelly, Harold d1941 *WhoHol 92*
Kelly, Harry d1936 *WhoHol 92*
Kelly, Henry Ansgar 1934- *WhoAm 94*
Kelly, Hugh *WhAmRev*
Kelly, Hugh Padraic 1931- *WhoAm 94*
Kelly, Hugh Rice 1942- *WhoAm 94, WhoAmL 94, WhoFI 94*
Kelly, Ida B. 1925- *WhoBlA 94*
Kelly, Isaac Perry 1925- *WhoAmA 93*
Kelly, Isabella c. 1759-1857 *DcNaB MP*
Kelly, J. Clinton 1949- *WhoAmL 94*
Kelly, J. Gordon d1939 *WhoHol 92*
Kelly, J. Michael 1943- *WhoAmL 94*
Kelly, J. Peter 1941- *WhoAm 94, WhoFI 94*
Kelly, Jack 1927- *WhoAmP 93, WhoHol 92*
Kelly, Jack Arthur 1916- *WhoBlA 94*
Kelly, James 1913- *WhoAm 94, WhoAmA 93*

Kelly, James Andrew 1936- *WhoAm 94*
Kelly, James Anthony, Jr. 1926- *WhoAmP 93*
Kelly, James Burton 1931- *WhoIns 94*
Kelly, James Clement 1928- *WhoBlA 94*
Kelly, James Johnson 1928- *WhoBlA 94*
Kelly, James Joseph 1941- *WhoMW 93*
Kelly, James McGirr *WhoAm 94, WhoAmL 94*
Kelly, James Michael 1947- *WhoAmL 94*
Kelly, James P. 1942- *WhoWest 94*
Kelly, James P. 1943- *WhoAmL 94*
Kelly, James Patrick 1946- *WhoAmL 94, WhoFI 94*
Kelly, James Patrick 1951- *EncSF 93, WrDr 94*
Kelly, James Patrick, Jr. 1933- *WhoAm 94*
Kelly, James T. d1933 *WhoHol 92*
Kelly, Jay Thomas 1950- *WhoAm 94, WhoMW 93*
Kelly, Jeffrey 1946- *WrDr 94*
Kelly, Jeffrey Jennings 1947- *WhoScEn 94*
Kelly, Jerome Bernard 1954- *WhoFI 94, WhoWest 94*
Kelly, Jerry Bob 1942- *WhoMW 93*
Kelly, Jim *IntMPA 94, WhoHol 92*
Kelly, Jim 1960- *WhoAm 94*
Kelly, Joe d1959 *WhoHol 92*
Kelly, John *WhoAm 94*
Kelly, John d1947 *WhoHol 92*
Kelly, John Barnes 1925- *WhoAmP 93*
Kelly, John F. 1938- *WhoIns 94*
Kelly, John Francis 1938- *WhoAmL 94*
Kelly, John Francis 1949- *WhoAmP 93*
Kelly, John G. 1927- *WhoIns 94*
Kelly, John H. *WhoAmP 93*
Kelly, John Hubert 1939- *IntWW 93, WhoAm 94*
Kelly, John James 1949- *WhoAmL 94*
Kelly, John Joseph, Jr. 1940- *WhoAm 94*
Kelly, John Love 1924- *WhoFI 94*
Kelly, John Michael 1939- *WhoAm 94, WhoAmL 94, WhoFI 94*
Kelly, John Norman Davidson 1909- *IntWW 93, Who 94*
Kelly, John Patrick, Jr. 1957- *WhoFI 94*
Kelly, John Paul, Jr. 1941- *WhoBlA 94*
Kelly, John Russell 1947- *WhoBlA 94*
Kelly, John Vincent 1926- *WhoAmP 93*
Kelly, Joseph Benjamin 1937- *WhoMW 93*
Kelly, Joseph Francis 1945- *WhoAm 94*
Kelly, Joseph Francis, Jr. 1938- *WhoAm 94*
Kelly, Joseph J. *DrAPF 93*
Kelly, Joseph Patrick 1940- *WhoAmL 94*
Kelly, Joseph Winston 1964- *WhoBlA 94*
Kelly, Josephine Kaye 1944- *WhoMW 93*
Kelly, Judy 1913- *WhoHol 92*
Kelly, Kevin 1934- *WhoAm 94, WhoFI 94, WrDr 94*
Kelly, Kevin 1953- *WhoAmP 93*
Kelly, Kevin Francis 1949- *WhoAmL 94*
Kelly, Kitty d1968 *WhoHol 92*
Kelly, Kristine Joan 1951- *WhoFI 94*
Kelly, L. Thomas 1945- *WhoAm 94*
Kelly, Laura J. 1956- *WhoAmL 94*
Kelly, Laurence Charles Kevin 1933- *Who 94*
Kelly, Lawrence James, Sr. 1935- *WhoAmP 93*
Kelly, Lawrence V. 1944- *WhoAmL 94*
Kelly, Leontine T. C. *WhoBlA 94, WhoWest 94*
Kelly, Leontine T. C. 1920- *AfrAmAl 6*
Kelly, Lew d1944 *WhoHol 92*
Kelly, Lew 1879-1944 *WhoCom*
Kelly, Linda 1936- *WrDr 94*
Kelly, Linna Schaffner 1956- *WhoMW 93*
Kelly, Louis Gerard 1935- *WrDr 94*
Kelly, Lucie Stirm Young 1925- *WhoAm 94*
Kelly, Luther Wrentmore, Jr. 1925- *WhoAm 94*
Kelly, Lynn C. 1947- *WhoFI 94*
Kelly, M(ilton) T(erry) 1947- *ConAu 43NR*
Kelly, Maeve 1930- *BlmGWL*
Kelly, Margaret Blake 1935- *WhoAmP 93*
Kelly, Margaret Boyer 1929- *WhoAmP 93*
Kelly, Margaret Elizabeth 1960- *WhoFI 94*
Kelly, Marie-Noële 1907- *WrDr 94*
Kelly, Marion Greenup 1947- *WhoBlA 94*
Kelly, Marjorie Helen 1953- *WhoMW 93*
Kelly, Mary d1941 *WhoHol 92*
Kelly, Mary 1941- *WhoAmA 93*
Kelly, Mary (Theresa) 1927- *WrDr 94*
Kelly, Mary Quella 1940- *WhoAm 94, WhoAmL 94*
Kelly, Matthew Arnold d1993 *NewYTBS 93 [port]*
Kelly, Matthew Edward 1928- *WhoAm 94*
Kelly, Maureen Ann 1965- *WhoFI 94*
Kelly, Maurice d1974 *WhoHol 92*
Kelly, Maurice 1919- *WrDr 94*
Kelly, Michael 1762-1826 *NewGrDO*
Kelly, Michael 1940- *Who 94*
Kelly, Michael 1948- *WhoAmP 93*
Kelly, Michael Joseph 1949- *Who 94*
Kelly, Moira 1951- *WhoAmA 93*
Kelly, Nan d1978 *WhoHol 92*
Kelly, Nancy 1921- *IntMPA 94, WhoHol 92*
Kelly, Nancy Folden 1951- *WhoAm 94*
Kelly, Nancy Karen 1935- *WhoWest 94*
Kelly, Nell d1939 *WhoHol 92*
Kelly, Nora Hickson 1910- *WrDr 94*
Kelly, Owen 1932- *Who 94*
Kelly, Pamela Davis 1947- *WhoAmL 94*
Kelly, Patricia 1932- *WhoAmP 93*
Kelly, Patrick d1993 *NewYTBS 93*
Kelly, Patrick A. *Who 94*
Kelly, Patrick Altham 1938- *IntWW 93*
Kelly, Patrick F. 1929- *WhoAm 94, WhoAmL 94, WhoMW 93*
Kelly, Patrick J. d1938 *WhoHol 92*
Kelly, Patrick J. 1926- *WhoAm 94*
Kelly, Patrick Lyle 1958- *WhoMW 93*
Kelly, Patrick M. 1943- *WhoAm 94, WhoAmL 94*
Kelly, Patsy d1981 *WhoHol 92*
Kelly, Paul d1956 *WhoHol 92*
Kelly, Paul Hamilton 1937- *WhoWest 94*
Kelly, Paul J., Jr. 1940- *WhoAmP 93*
Kelly, Paul Joseph, Jr. 1940- *WhoAm 94, WhoAmL 94, WhoWest 94*
Kelly, Paul Knox 1940- *WhoAm 94, WhoFI 94*
Kelly, Paul S. 1939- *WhoAmP 93*
Kelly, Paula *WhoHol 92*
Kelly, Paula 1944- *WhoHol 92*
Kelly, Peter (John) 1922- *Who 94*
Kelly, Peter Dillon 1948- *WhoAmP 93*
Kelly, Peter Galbraith 1937- *WhoAm 94, WhoAmL 94, WhoAmP 93, WhoFI 94*
Kelly, Peter M. 1922- *WhoFI 94*
Kelly, Petra 1947-1992 *AnObit 1992*
Kelly, Petra (Karin) 1947-1992 *CurBio 93N*
Kelly, Petra Karin d1992 *IntWW 93N*
Kelly, Petra Karin 1947-1992 *WhAm 10*
Kelly, Philip Charles 1948- *Who 94*
Kelly, Philip John 1946- *Who 94*
Kelly, Phyllis Matheis 1921- *WhoAmP 93*
Kelly, Prescott Vail 1943- *WhoAm 94*
Kelly, Randy C. 1950- *WhoAmP 93*
Kelly, Raymond Boone 1898- *WhAm 10*
Kelly, Raymond Case 1942- *WhoMW 93*
Kelly, Raymond Francis 1939- *WhoAm 94*
Kelly, Raymond M. 1939- *WhoIns 94*
Kelly, Raymond W. *NewYTBS 93 [port]*
Kelly, Regina Fogel 1943- *WhoAmL 94*
Kelly, Richard *DrAPF 93*
Kelly, Richard 1937- *WrDr 94*
Kelly, Richard F., Jr. 1936- *WhoAmP 93*
Kelly, Richard Lee Woods *WhoScEn 94*
Kelly, Richard Leo 1938- *WhoIns 94*
Kelly, Richard Michael 1955- *WhoScEn 94*
Kelly, Richard Smith 1925- *WhoAm 94*
Kelly, Rita 1953- *BlmGWL [port]*
Kelly, Robert *DrAPF 93*
Kelly, Robert d1949 *WhoHol 92*
Kelly, Robert 1935- *ConAu 19AS [port], DcLB 130 [port], EncSF 93, WhoAm 94, WrDr 94*
Kelly, Robert Donald 1929- *WhoAm 94*
Kelly, Robert Edward, Jr. 1950- *WhoAm 94, WhoAmL 94*
Kelly, Robert Emmett 1929- *WhoAm 94*
Kelly, Robert Emmett 1952- *WhoFI 94*
Kelly, Robert F. 1935- *WhoAm 94, WhoAmL 94*
Kelly, Robert J. 1942- *WhoAm 94, WhoFI 94*
Kelly, Robert J. 1952- *WhoAmL 94*
Kelly, Robert James 1958- *WhoAmA 93*
Kelly, Robert Lee 1948- *WhoAm 94, WhoAmL 94*
Kelly, Robert Lynn 1939- *WhoAm 94, WhoFI 94*
Kelly, Robert Thomas 1924- *WhoAm 94*
Kelly, Robert Vincent, Jr. 1938- *WhoAm 94, WhoFI 94, WhoMW 93*
Kelly, Robert Vincent, III 1962- *WhoFI 94*
Kelly, Roberto Conrado 1964- *WhoAm 94, WhoBlA 94, WhoHisp 94, WhoMW 93*
Kelly, Ronald Raymond 1951- *WhoFI 94*
Kelly, Ros 1948- *IntWW 93, WhoWomW 91*
Kelly, Rosaline 1922- *Who 94*
Kelly, Roz 1947- *WhoHol 92*
Kelly, Ryan Gene d1981 *WhoHol 92*
Kelly, Sam, Jr. 1926- *WhoAmP 93*
Kelly, Sarah Elizabeth 1959- *WhoScEn 94*
Kelly, Seamus d1979 *WhoHol 92*
Kelly, Sean *WhoHol 92*
Kelly, Sharon Marie 1951- *WhoAmL 94*
Kelly, Sharon Pratt 1944- *WhoAm 94, WhoAmP 93, WhoBlA 94*
Kelly, Shaun P. *WhoAmP 93*
Kelly, Stephen John 1940- *WhoAm 94*
Kelly, Susan *Who 94*
Kelly, Sylvia *DrAPF 93*
Kelly, Terry Lee 1953- *WhoScEn 94*
Kelly, Theo 1907- *IntWW 93, Who 94*
Kelly, Thomas 1909-1992 *WrDr 94N*
Kelly, Thomas, Jr. 1951- *WhoBlA 94*
Kelly, Thomas Brooke 1943- *WhoAm 94*
Kelly, Thomas Cajetan 1931- *WhoAm 94*
Kelly, Thomas H. 1942- *WhoIns 94*
Kelly, Thomas J. 1943- *WhoAm 94, WhoAmL 94*
Kelly, Thomas James 1931- *WhoFI 94*
Kelly, Thomas Jesse, Jr. 1941- *WhoAm 94*
Kelly, Thomas Joseph, III 1947- *WhoAm 94*
Kelly, Thomas Lloyd, II 1958- *WhoFI 94*
Kelly, Thomas Maurice, III 1950- *WhoBlA 94*
Kelly, Thomas Michael 1958- *WhoAmL 94*
Kelly, Thomas P., Jr. 1946- *WhoFI 94*
Kelly, Thomas Paine, Jr. 1912- *WhoAm 94, WhoAmL 94*
Kelly, Thomas Philip, Jr. 1936- *WhoAmL 94*
Kelly, Thomas Walter 1966- *WhoFI 94*
Kelly, Tim 1937- *WrDr 94*
Kelly, Tim 1944- *WhoAmP 93*
Kelly, Tim Donahue 1944- *WhoAm 94, WhoWest 94*
Kelly, Timothy Michael 1938- *WhoAm 94*
Kelly, Timothy Michael 1947- *WhoAm 94*
Kelly, Tish *WhoAmP 93*
Kelly, Tom 1950- *WhoAm 94, WhoMW 93*
Kelly, Tommy 1925- *WhoHol 92*
Kelly, Verna Margaret 1940- *WhoAmP 93*
Kelly, Victoria Kathryn 1948- *WhoMW 93*
Kelly, Vincent Michael, Jr. 1933- *WhoScEn 94*
Kelly, W. Michael 1948- *WhoAmL 94*
Kelly, Walter C. d1939 *WhoHol 92*
Kelly, Wanda Sue 1948- *WhoAmL 94*
Kelly, William 1811-1888 *WorInv*
Kelly, William Bret 1922- *WhoWest 94*
Kelly, William Charles, Jr. 1946- *WhoAm 94, WhoAmL 94*
Kelly, William Clark 1922- *WhoAm 94*
Kelly, William Crowley 1929- *WhoScEn 94*
Kelly, William E. 1914- *WhoAm 94*
Kelly, William Franklin, Jr. 1938- *WhoAm 94, WhoAmL 94*
Kelly, William Garrett 1947- *WhoAmL 94*
Kelly, William Grier, Jr. 1944- *WhoAmL 94*
Kelly, William Harold 1926- *WhoAm 94, WhoScEn 94*
Kelly, William J. d1949 *WhoHol 92*
Kelly, William J. 1942- *WhoIns 94*
Kelly, William J., Jr. 1951- *WhoAmL 94*
Kelly, William John 1927- *WhoAmL 94*
Kelly, William Joseph 1943- *WhoAmA 93*
Kelly, William Patrick 1848-1916 *EncSF 93*
Kelly, William Patrick 1939- *WhoMW 93*
Kelly, William R. 1905- *WhoAm 94, WhoFI 94*
Kelly, William States 1956- *WhoWest 94*
Kelly, William Theodore *Who 94*
Kelly, William Thomas 1919- *WhoAmP 93*
Kelly, William Watkins 1928- *WhoAm 94*
Kelly, Winfield M., Jr. 1935- *WhoAmP 93*
Kelly-Benjamin, Kathleen *ConAu 140*
Kelm, Bonnie G. 1947- *WhoAm 94, WhoAmA 93, WhoMW 93*
Kelm, Linda 1944- *WhoAm 94*
Kelm, Thomas Arthur 1930- *WhoAmP 93*
Kelman, Arthur 1918- *IntWW 93, WhoAm 94*
Kelman, Bruce Jerry 1947- *WhoScEn 94, WhoWest 94*
Kelman, Charles 1930- *WhoAm 94*
Kelman, Charles D. 1930- *IntWW 93, WhoScEn 94*
Kelman, Donald Brian 1942- *WhoMW 93, WhoScEn 94*
Kelman, Edward Michael 1943- *WhoAmL 94, WhoFI 94*
Kelman, Herbert Chanoch 1927- *WrDr 94*
Kelman, Maureen (S.) 1952- *WhoAmA 93*
Kelman, Paul *WhoHol 92*
Kelman, Rick 1951- *WhoHol 92*
Kelman, Robert Andrew 1945- *WhoAm 94, WhoAmL 94*
Kelman, Wolfe 1923-1990 *WhAm 10*
Kelmar, Steven B. 1953- *WhoAmP 93*
Kelmenson, Leo-Arthur 1927- *WhoAm 94, WhoFI 94*
Kelmenson, Lita 1932- *WhoAmA 93*
Kelne, Nathan 1918- *WhoAm 94*
Kelpe, Paul 1902-1985 *WhoAmA 93N*
Kelpe, Paul Robert 1948- *WhoMW 93*
Kels, James 1933- *WhoAm 94*
Kelsall, Charles 1782-1857 *DcNaB MP*
Kelsall, John Arthur Brooks 1943- *Who 94*
Kelsall, Moultrie d1980 *WhoHol 92*
Kelsall, William 1914- *Who 94*
Kelsay, David Roland 1955- *WhoAmP 93*
Kelsch, RaeAnn *WhoAmP 93*
Kelsch, Thomas Edward 1939- *WhoAm 94*
Kelsen, Iris Helene 1952- *WhoMW 93*
Kelsey, Clyde Eastman, Jr. 1924- *WhoAm 94*
Kelsey, Edith Jeanine 1937- *WhoWest 94*
Kelsey, Floyd Lamar, Jr. 1925- *WhoAm 94*
Kelsey, Fred d1961 *WhoHol 92*
Kelsey, Gary Matthew 1954- *WhoBlA 94*
Kelsey, Henry c. 1667-1729 *WhWE*
Kelsey, John 1920- *Who 94*
Kelsey, John T. 1921- *WhoAmP 93*
Kelsey, Josephine *WhoBlA 94*
Kelsey, Julian George 1922- *Who 94*
Kelsey, Linda 1946- *IntMPA 94, WhoHol 92*
Kelsey, Linda 1952- *Who 94*
Kelsey, Morton T(rippe) 1917- *WrDr 94*
Kelsey, Randy Jay 1963- *WhoFI 94*
Kelsey, Thomas R. 1944- *WhoAmL 94*
Kelsh, Jerome G. 1940- *WhoAmP 93*
Kelsick, Osmund Randolph 1922- *Who 94*
Kelso, Alec John 1930- *WhoAm 94*
Kelso, Becky 1948- *WhoAmP 93*
Kelso, David William 1948- *WhoAmA 93*
Kelso, Frank Benton, II 1933- *IntWW 93, WhoAm 94, WhoAmP 93*
Kelso, Gwendolyn Lee 1935- *WhoFI 94*
Kelso, Harold Glen 1929- *WhoAm 94*
Kelso, John d1978 *WhoHol 92*
Kelso, John Hodgson 1925- *WhoAm 94*
Kelso, John Morris 1922- *WhoAm 94*
Kelso, Linda Yayoi 1946- *WhoAmL 94*
Kelso, Lloyd Thomas 1950- *WhoAmL 94*
Kelso, Louis Orth 1913-1991 *WhAm 10*
Kelso, Mayme d1946 *WhoHol 92*
Kelson, Irwin S. 1932- *WhoIns 94*
Kelston, David Leo 1944- *WhoAmL 94*
Kelt, John d1935 *WhoHol 92*
Keltch, Peter Michael 1947- *WhoAmP 93*
Kelterborn, Rudolf 1931- *NewGrDO*
Keltner, David E. 1950- *WhoAm 94, WhoAmL 94*
Keltner, John William 1918- *WhoWest 94*
Keltner, Leila Hocking 1954- *WhoWest 94*
Keltner, Raymond Marion, Jr. 1929- *WhoAm 94*
Kelton, Arthur Marvin, Jr. 1939- *WhoFI 94, WhoWest 94*
Kelton, Elmer 1926- *WrDr 94*
Kelton, Frank d1938 *WhoHol 92*
Kelton, Kenneth Franklin 1954- *WhoScEn 94*
Kelton, Pert d1968 *WhoHol 92*
Kelton, Richard d1978 *WhoHol 92*
Kelton, William A. 1939- *WhoIns 94*
Kelts, Kerry R. 1947- *WhoMW 93*
Kelvin, Lord *WorInv*
Kem, Richard Samuel 1934- *WhoAm 94*
Kemal, Yasar 1922- *ConWorW 93*
Kemal, Yashar 1923- *IntWW 93*
Kemal Ataturk, Mustafa 1881-1938 *HisWorL [port]*
Ke Maosheng *WhoPRCh 91*
Kemball, Charles 1923- *IntWW 93, Who 94*
Kemball, Humphrey Gurdon 1919- *Who 94*
Kemball, (Richard) John 1939- *Who 94*
Kemball-Cook, Brian Hartley 1912- *Who 94*
Kember, Anthony Joseph 1931- *Who 94*
Kember, Harry, Jr. 1934- *WhoAmP 93*
Kember, William Percy 1932- *Who 94*
Kemble, Adelaide 1814-1879 *NewGrDO*
Kemble, Ernest Dell 1935- *WhoAm 94*
Kemble, Frances 1809-1893 *BlmGWL*
Kemble, John Haskell 1912-1990 *WhAm 10*
Kemble, John Philip 1757-1823 *BlmGEL*
Kemble, Peter 1704-1789 *WhAmRev*
Kemble, Richard 1932- *WhoAmA 93*
Kemble, Stephen c. 1730-1822 *WhAmRev*
Kemelman, Harry 1908- *WhoAm 94, WrDr 94*
Kemeny, John *IntMPA 94*
Kemeny, John 1926-1992 *AnObit 1992*
Kemeny, John G. d1992 *IntWW 93N*
Kemeny, John G. 1926- *WorInv*
Kemeny, John G(eorge) 1926- *WrDr 94*
Kemeny, John G(eorge) 1926-1992 *ConAu 140, CurBio 93N*
Kemenyffy, Steven 1943- *WhoAm 94, WhoAmA 93*
Kemenyffy, Susan B. Hale 1941- *WhoAmA 93*
Kemler, Robert Michael 1945- *WhoAmL 94*
Kemmer, Ed 1923- *WhoHol 92*
Kemmer, Frank Nelson 1917- *WhoMW 93*
Kemmer, Nicholas 1911- *IntWW 93, Who 94*
Kemmer, Richard Julius 1945- *WhoAm 94*

Kengo Wa Dondo 1935- *IntWW 93*
Kenig, Noe 1923- *WhoMW 93, WhoScEn 94*
Kenilorea, Peter 1943- *IntWW 93*
Kenilorea, Peter (Kauona Keninaraiso'ona) 1943- *Who 94*
Kenilworth, Baron 1954- *Who 94*
Kenin, Alexa d1985 *WhoHol 92*
Kenin, David S. 1934- *WhoAm 94*
Kenison, Linda B. 1943- *WhoAmP 93*
Kenison, Lynn T. 1943- *WhoWest 94*
Kenison, Raymond Robert 1932- *WhoMW 93*
Kenkel, James Edward 1934- *WhoAm 94*
Kenkel, James Lawrence 1944- *WhoFI 94, WhoScEn 94*
Kenkel, Joel Nicklas 1941- *WhoIns 94*
Kenkel, William (Francis) 1925- *WrDr 94*
Kenley, Elizabeth Sue 1945- *WhoFI 94*
Kenley, Howard 1945- *WhoAmP 93*
Kenlis, Lord 1989- *Who 94*
Kenly, Granger Farwell 1919- *WhoAm 94, WhoFI 94*
Kenna, E. Douglas *WhoAm 94*
Kenna, Edgar Douglas 1924- *WhoAm 94, WhoFI 94*
Kenna, James Joseph, Jr. 1932- *WhoFI 94*
Kenna, Lawrence Allan 1960- *WhoFI 94*
Kenna, Michael 1953- *WhoAmA 93*
Kenna, Peter d1987 *WhoHol 92*
Kenna, Peter (Joseph) 1930-1987 *ConDr 93, WrDr 94N*
Kennaby, Noel Martin 1905- *Who 94*
Kennamer, Lorrin Garfield, Jr. 1924- *WhoAm 94*
Kennamer, Stephen Money 1954- *WhoAmP 93*
Kennan, Christopher James 1949- *WhoFI 94*
Kennan, Elizabeth Topham 1938- *WhoAm 94*
Kennan, George (Frost) 1904- *WrDr 94*
Kennan, George F. 1904- *HisDcKW*
Kennan, George Frost 1904- *IntWW 93, Who 94, WhoAm 94*
Kennan, Kent Wheeler 1913- *WhoAm 94, WrDr 94*
Kennard, Donald Ray 1937- *WhoAmP 93*
Kennard, George (Arnold Ford) 1915- *WrDr 94*
Kennard, George Arnold Ford 1915- *Who 94*
Kennard, Joyce *WhoAm 94, WhoWest 94*
Kennard, Joyce F. *WhoAmL 94*
Kennard, Joyce L. *WhoAmP 93, WhoAsA 94*
Kennard, Olga 1924- *IntWW 93, Who 94*
Kennard, Patricia A. 1949- *WhoBlA 94*
Kennard, Robert Alexander 1920- *WhoBlA 94*
Kennaway, Alexander 1923- *Who 94*
Kennaway, James 1928-1968 *EncSF 93*
Kennaway, John (Lawrence) 1933- *Who 94*
Kenneally, Dennis Michael 1946- *WhoAm 94, WhoAmP 93*
Kenneally, Lynn Anne 1961- *WhoAmL 94*
Kenneally, Michael 1945- *WrDr 94*
Kenneally, Philip *WhoHol 92*
Kennealy, Jerry 1938- *ConAu 142*
Kennealy, Patricia 1946- *EncSF 93*
Kennedy *Who 94*
Kennedy, Mrs. *NewGrDO*
Kennedy, A(lfred) James 1921- *Who 94*
Kennedy, Adam *WhoHol 92*
Kennedy, Adrienne 1931- *BlmGWL, WrDr 94*
Kennedy, Adrienne (Lita) 1931- *BlkWr 2, ConDr 93, IntDcT 2*
Kennedy, Adrienne Lita 1931- *WhoAm 94, WhoBlA 94*
Kennedy, Alex 1933- *WhoIns 94*
Kennedy, Alfred Doby 1939- *WhoAm 94*
Kennedy, Alton Edward 1926- *WhoAmP 93*
Kennedy, Anne 1959- *BlmGWL*
Kennedy, Anne Gamble 1920- *WhoBlA 94*
Kennedy, Annie Brown *WhoAmA 93*
Kennedy, Anthony M. 1936- *CngDr 93, IntWW 93*
Kennedy, Anthony McLeod 1936- *Who 94, WhoAm 94, WhoAmL 94, WhoAmP 93*
Kennedy, Arthur d1990 *WhoHol 92*
Kennedy, Arthur Colville 1922- *Who 94*
Kennedy, Arthur Ralph 1935- *WhoAmP 93*
Kennedy, Barbara Ellen Perry 1937- *WhoMW 93*
Kennedy, Berenice Connor *WhoAm 94*
Kennedy, Bernard R. 1895- *WhAm 10*
Kennedy, Beth Blumenreich 1950- *WhoAm 94*
Kennedy, Betty *WhoHol 92*
Kennedy, Beverly Kleban Burris 1943- *WhoFI 94*
Kennedy, Bill 1912- *WhoHol 92*
Kennedy, Brenda Picola *WhoBlA 94*
Kennedy, Brian James 1941- *WhoAm 94, WhoFI 94*
Kennedy, Brian Melville 1948- *WhoAmL 94*
Kennedy, Brian Patrick 1961- *WhoAmP 93*
Kennedy, Brian T. 1934- *WhoAmP 93*
Kennedy, Burt 1922- *IntMPA 94*
Kennedy, Burt Raphael 1922- *WhoAm 94*
Kennedy, Byrl James 1921- *WhoAm 94*
Kennedy, Cain James 1937- *WhoAmP 93, WhoBlA 94*
Kennedy, Callas Faye 1954- *WhoBlA 94*
Kennedy, Caroline (Bouvier) 1957- *ConAu 140*
Kennedy, Charlene Farrington 1947- *WhoWest 94*
Kennedy, Charles d1950 *WhoHol 92*
Kennedy, Charles Allen 1940- *WhoAmL 94, WhoMW 93*
Kennedy, Charles G. 1954- *WhoAm 94*
Kennedy, Charles Peter 1959- *Who 94*
Kennedy, Cheryl 1947- *WhoHol 92*
Kennedy, Cheryl Lynn 1946- *WhoMW 93*
Kennedy, Chester Ralph, Jr. 1926- *WhoAm 94*
Kennedy, Christopher Robin 1948- *WhoAm 94*
Kennedy, Clyde (David Allen) 1912- *Who 94*
Kennedy, Cornelia G. *WhoAmP 93*
Kennedy, Cornelia Groefsema 1923- *WhoAm 94, WhoAmL 94, WhoMW 93*
Kennedy, Cornelius Bryant 1921- *WhoAm 94, WhoAmL 94*
Kennedy, Cortez 1968- *WhoAm 94, WhoBlA 94*
Kennedy, Craig Allen 1951- *WhoAmP 93*
Kennedy, Crystal Marie 1962- *WhoAmL 94*
Kennedy, D. J. Laurie *WhoScEn 94*
Kennedy, Dan F. 1957- *WhoWest 94*
Kennedy, Dana Forrest 1917- *SmATA 74 [port]*
Kennedy, Daniel James 1968- *WhoMW 93*
Kennedy, Daniel O'Connor 1964- *WhoAmL 94*
Kennedy, Daun d1958 *WhoHol 92*
Kennedy, David 1940- *Who 94*
Kennedy, David Boyd 1933- *WhoAm 94, WhoAmP 93*
Kennedy, David Matthew 1905- *Who 94*
Kennedy, David Michael 1941- *WhoAm 94, WrDr 94*
Kennedy, David Patrick 1954- *WhoAmP 93*
Kennedy, David Stewart 1944- *WhoAm 94, WhoAmL 94*
Kennedy, David Tinsley 1919- *WhoAmL 94*
Kennedy, Debra Joyce 1955- *WhoWest 94*
Kennedy, Dennis L. 1950- *WhoAmL 94*
Kennedy, Diane Elmore 1947- *WhoAmP 93*
Kennedy, Don McClurg 1945- *WhoAm 94*
Kennedy, Donald 1931- *IntWW 93, WhoAm 94, WhoAmP 93, WhoWest 94*
Kennedy, Donald J. 1944- *WhoAmL 94*
Kennedy, Douglas d1973 *WhoHol 92*
Kennedy, Douglas Wayne 1971- *WhoScEn 94*
Kennedy, Eamon 1921- *IntWW 93, Who 94*
Kennedy, Edgar d1948 *WhoHol 92*
Kennedy, Edgar 1890-1948 *WhoCom*
Kennedy, Edgar Rees *EncSF 93*
Kennedy, Edmund 1818-1848 *WhWE*
Kennedy, Edward Arthur Gilbert 1920- *Who 94*
Kennedy, Edward Eugene 1894- *WhAm 10*
Kennedy, Edward James 1951- *WhoAmP 93*
Kennedy, Edward M. 1932- *CngDr 93, NewYTBS 93 [port], WrDr 94*
Kennedy, Edward Moore 1932- *IntWW 93, Who 94, WhoAm 94, WhoAmP 93*
Kennedy, Edwin Lust 1904- *WhoAm 94*
Kennedy, Eugene Cullen 1928- *WhoAm 94*
Kennedy, Eugene Patrick 1919- *IntWW 93, WhoAm 94, WhoScEn 94*
Kennedy, Eugene Richard 1919- *WhoAm 94*
Kennedy, Florynce 1916- *WhoBlA 94*
Kennedy, Floyd C. 1925- *WhoBlA 94*
Kennedy, Francis 1926- *Who 94*
Kennedy, Frank Robert 1914- *WhoAm 94*
Kennedy, Fred d1958 *WhoHol 92*
Kennedy, G. Alfred 1940- *WhoAm 94*
Kennedy, Gavin 1940- *WrDr 94*
Kennedy, Gene 1946- *WhoAmA 93*
Kennedy, Gene Allen 1928- *WhoAmP 93*
Kennedy, Geoffrey Anketell Studdert 1883-1929 *DcNaB MP*
Kennedy, George 1925- *IntMPA 94, WhoHol 92*
Kennedy, George 1926- *WhoAm 94*
Kennedy, George Alexander 1928- *WhoAm 94*
Kennedy, George D. 1926- *WhoAm 94, WhoFI 94*
Kennedy, George Danner 1926- *IntWW 93*
Kennedy, George Hunt 1936- *WhoAm 94*
Kennedy, George Wendell 1945- *WhoAmL 94*
Kennedy, Gerard *WhoHol 92*
Kennedy, Goldie L. 1905- *WhoAmP 93*
Kennedy, Graham *WhoHol 92*
Kennedy, Harold Appleby 1923- *WhoAmL 94*
Kennedy, Harold Edward 1927- *WhoAm 94, WhoAmL 94, WhoFI 94*
Kennedy, Harold J. d1988 *WhoHol 92*
Kennedy, Harold Laverne 1962- *WhoWest 94*
Kennedy, Harriet Forte *WhoAmA 93*
Kennedy, Harvey Edward 1928- *WhoAm 94*
Kennedy, Helena Ann 1950- *Who 94*
Kennedy, Henry H., Jr. 1948- *WhoBlA 94*
Kennedy, Horas Tristram 1917- *Who 94*
Kennedy, Howard E. 1941- *WhoBlA 94*
Kennedy, Howard L. 1928- *WhoAmP 93*
Kennedy, Ian (Alexander) 1930- *Who 94*
Kennedy, Ian Glen 1945- *WhoAm 94*
Kennedy, Ian McColl 1941- *Who 94*
Kennedy, J. William 1903- *WhoAmA 93*
Kennedy, Jack d1964 *WhoHol 92*
Kennedy, Jack 1950- *WhoMW 93*
Kennedy, Jack, Jr. 1956- *WhoAmP 93*
Kennedy, Jack Edward 1945- *WhoAmL 94*
Kennedy, Jack Leland 1924- *WhoAm 94, WhoAmL 94*
Kennedy, Jack S. 1945- *WhoAmL 94*
Kennedy, Jacqueline Lee Bouvier *IntWW 93*
Kennedy, James *Who 94*
Kennedy, James Andrew 1937- *WhoAm 94, WhoFI 94*
Kennedy, James B. 1944- *WhoAmL 94*
Kennedy, James C. 1947- *WhoAm 94, WhoFI 94*
Kennedy, James E. 1933- *WhoBlA 94*
Kennedy, James E. 1938- *WhoBlA 94*
Kennedy, James Edward 1933- *WhoAmA 93*
Kennedy, James Harrington 1924- *WhoFI 94*
Kennedy, James J. 1941- *WhoAmL 94*
Kennedy, James L. 1937- *WhoAm 94*
Kennedy, James Patrick 1932- *WhoAm 94*
Kennedy, James Waite 1937- *WhoAm 94*
Kennedy, James William, Jr. 1940- *WhoWest 94*
Kennedy, Jane Elizabeth 1958- *Who 94*
Kennedy, Janet Robson 1902-1974 *WhoAmA 93N*
Kennedy, Jayne 1951- *WhoBlA 94*
Kennedy, Jayne 1954- *WhoHol 92*
Kennedy, Jerry Wayne 1947- *WhoAmL 94*
Kennedy, Jimhi *WhoHol 92*
Kennedy, Jimmie Vernon 1925- *WhoBlA 94*
Kennedy, Jo 1962- *WhoHol 92*
Kennedy, Joanna Alicia Gore 1950- *Who 94*
Kennedy, Joanne Patricia 1963- *WhoScEn 94*
Kennedy, Joe David, Jr. 1956- *WhoAm 94*
Kennedy, John 1930- *Who 94*
Kennedy, John 1938- *WhoAmP 93*
Kennedy, John, Jr. 1939- *WhoAmP 93*
Kennedy, John A. 1898- *WhAm 10*
Kennedy, John Edward 1930- *WhoWest 94*
Kennedy, John Edward 1947- *WhoAmL 94*
Kennedy, John F. d1960 *WhoHol 92*
Kennedy, John Fisher 1933-1991 *WhAm 10*
Kennedy, John Fitzgerald 1917-1963 *HisWorL [port]*
Kennedy, John Fitzgerald 1961- *WhoAmP 93*
Kennedy, John Foran 1924- *WhoAmL 94*
Kennedy, John H., Jr. 1954- *WhoAm 94, WhoAmP 93*
Kennedy, John Harvey 1933- *WhoWest 94*
Kennedy, John Joseph 1914- *WhoAm 94*
Kennedy, John Joseph 1948- *WhoFI 94*
Kennedy, John Maxwell 1934- *Who 94*
Kennedy, John Patrick 1943- *WhoFI 94*
Kennedy, John Paul 1941- *WhoAmP 93*
Kennedy, John Raymond 1930- *WhoAm 94, WhoFI 94*
Kennedy, John Stodart d1993 *IntWW 93N, Who 94N*
Kennedy, John William 1956- *WhoFI 94, WhoScEn 94*
Kennedy, John Wright 1963- *WhoAmL 94*
Kennedy, Jon 1950- *WhoWest 94*
Kennedy, Joseph 1923- *WrDr 94*
Kennedy, Joseph Everett 1930- *WhoAmP 93*
Kennedy, Joseph J., Jr. 1923- *WhoBlA 94*
Kennedy, Joseph P., II 1952- *CngDr 93, WhoAmP 93*
Kennedy, Joseph Patrick, II 1952- *WhoAm 94*
Kennedy, Joseph Paul 1928- *WhoAm 94*
Kennedy, Joseph Winston 1932- *WhoAmL 94*
Kennedy, Joyce d1943 *WhoHol 92*
Kennedy, Joyce S. 1943- *WhoBlA 94*
Kennedy, Kael Behan 1941- *WhoFI 94*
Kennedy, Karel R. 1946- *WhoBlA 94*
Kennedy, Kathleen *IntMPA 94, WhoAm 94*
Kennedy, Keith Furnival 1925-1992 *WhAm 10*
Kennedy, Keith Sanford 1945- *WhoFI 94, WhoMW 93*
Kennedy, Ken 1945- *WhoAm 94, WhoScEn 94*
Kennedy, Kenneth *WhoAmP 93*
Kennedy, Kenneth Adrian Raine 1930- *WhoAm 94*
Kennedy, Kevin 1937- *Who 94*
Kennedy, Kevin Curtis *WhoAm 94*
Kennedy, Kieran A. 1935- *WrDr 94*
Kennedy, King d1974 *WhoHol 92*
Kennedy, L. Thomas 1934- *WhoWest 94*
Kennedy, Laura Marie 1966- *WhoMW 93*
Kennedy, Lawrence Allan 1937- *WhoAm 94*
Kennedy, Lawrence W. 1952- *ConAu 141*
Kennedy, Leigh 1951- *EncSF 93, WrDr 94*
Kennedy, Leon Isaac 1949- *WhoHol 92*
Kennedy, Lillian Baker 1953- *WhoAmL 94*
Kennedy, Linda A. 1955- *WhoFI 94*
Kennedy, Liv 1934- *ConAu 140*
Kennedy, Ludovic (Henry Coverley) 1919- *WrDr 94*
Kennedy, Ludovic Henry Coverley 1919- *IntWW 93, Who 94*
Kennedy, Madge d1987 *WhoHol 92*
Kennedy, Manley d1977 *WhoHol 92*
Kennedy, Marc J. 1945- *WhoAm 94, WhoAmL 94, WhoFI 94*
Kennedy, Margaret 1896-1967 *BlmGWL*
Kennedy, Marjorie Ellen 1946- *WhoAm 94*
Kennedy, Mark 1952- *WhoAmL 94, WhoAmP 93*
Kennedy, Mark Raymond 1957- *WhoAm 94, WhoFI 94*
Kennedy, Martin P. 1931- *WhoAmP 93*
Kennedy, Marvin James 1931- *WhoBlA 94*
Kennedy, Mary Evelyn 1935- *WhoMW 93*
Kennedy, Mary Louise 1951- *WhoAmL 94*
Kennedy, Mary Madeline 1937- *WhoAmP 93*
Kennedy, Mary Virginia 1946- *WhoAm 94*
Kennedy, Matthew W. 1921- *WhoBlA 94*
Kennedy, Matthew Washington 1921- *WhoAm 94*
Kennedy, Merna d1944 *WhoHol 92*
Kennedy, Michael *Who 94*
Kennedy, Michael 1926- *IntWW 93, WrDr 94*
Kennedy, (George) Michael (Sinclair) 1926- *NewGrDO, Who 94*
Kennedy, Michael Denis 1937- *Who 94*
Kennedy, Michael Edward 1956- *Who 94*
Kennedy, Michael John 1937- *WhoAmL 94*
Kennedy, Michael Kevin 1950- *WhoAmL 94*
Kennedy, Mimi 1949- *WhoHol 92*
Kennedy, Moira *Who 94*
Kennedy, Moorhead 1930- *WhoAm 94, WrDr 94*
Kennedy, Nathelyne Archie 1938- *WhoBlA 94*
Kennedy, Nigel 1956- *IntWW 93*
Kennedy, Nigel (Paul) 1956- *ConAu 140*
Kennedy, Nigel Paul 1956- *Who 94*
Kennedy, Orin 1939- *WhoWest 94*
Kennedy, Pat 1908-1957 *BasBi*
Kennedy, Patricia 1917- *WhoHol 92*
Kennedy, Patrick J. *WhoAmP 93*
Kennedy, Patrick Michael 1947- *WhoMW 93, WhoScEn 94*
Kennedy, Paul 1945- *CurBio 93 [port]*
Kennedy, Paul (Joseph Morrow) 1935- *Who 94*
Kennedy, Paul Michael 1945- *IntWW 93, WhoAm 94, WrDr 94*
Kennedy, Peter (Elliott) 1943- *WrDr 94*
Kennedy, Peter Smithson 1934- *WhoWest 94*
Kennedy, Quentin J., Sr. 1933- *WhoAm 94, WhoAmL 94, WhoFI 94*
Kennedy, R.A. *EncSF 93*
Kennedy, Raoul Dion 1944- *WhoAm 94, WhoAmL 94*
Kennedy, Raymond *DrAPF 93*
Kennedy, Raymond McCormick, Jr. 1930- *WhoWest 94*
Kennedy, Richard (Jerome) 1932- *WrDr 94*
Kennedy, Richard E. 1933- *WhoAmP 93*

Kennedy, Richard Frederick 1933- WhoAm 94
Kennedy, Richard Jerome 1932- WhoAm 94, WhoWest 94
Kennedy, Richard L. 1933- WhoAmP 93
Kennedy, Richard Paul 1949- Who 94
Kennedy, Richard Robert 1947- WhoAmP 93
Kennedy, Richard Terrance 1953- WhoWest 94
Kennedy, Richard Thomas 1919- WhoAm 94, WhoAmP 93
Kennedy, Rick Alan 1958- WhoMW 93
Kennedy, Rita M. 1948- WhoHisp 94
Kennedy, Robert WhoAmP 93
Kennedy, Robert 1925-1968 HisWorL [port]
Kennedy, Robert B. WhoAmP 93
Kennedy, Robert Delmont 1932- WhoAm 94, WhoFI 94
Kennedy, Robert Dunn 1958- WhoAmL 94
Kennedy, Robert Emmet 1910- WhoAm 94
Kennedy, Robert Emmet, Jr. 1941- WhoAm 94, WrDr 94
Kennedy, Robert Eugene 1942- WhoAm 94
Kennedy, Robert Lanny 1938- WhoAmP 93
Kennedy, Robert Lee, Jr. 1946- WhoMW 93
Kennedy, Robert M. WhoAmL 94
Kennedy, Robert Samuel 1936- WhoScEn 94
Kennedy, Robert Spayde 1933- WhoAm 94
Kennedy, Roderick 1951- NewGrDO
Kennedy, Roger George 1926- WhoAm 94
Kennedy, Rosario 1945- WhoHisp 94
Kennedy, Rose Fitzgerald 1890- WhoAm 94
Kennedy, Samuel 1730-1778 AmRev
Kennedy, Sandra Denise 1957- WhoAmP 93, WhoBlA 94, WhoWest 94
Kennedy, Scott 1934- IntMPA 94
Kennedy, Sheila WhoHol 92
Kennedy, Sheila Grace 1949- WhoWest 94
Kennedy, Stephen Andrew 1962- WhoAmL 94
Kennedy, Stephen Dandridge 1942- WhoAm 94, WhoScEn 94
Kennedy, Stephen Joseph 1960- WhoAmL 94
Kennedy, Stephen William 1949- WhoAmP 93
Kennedy, Susan Estabrook 1942- ConAu 43NR
Kennedy, Susan P. WhoAmP 93
Kennedy, T. Richard 1935- WhoIns 94
Kennedy, Terry DrAPF 93
Kennedy, Theodore Clifford 1930- WhoAm 94, WhoFI 94
Kennedy, Theodore Reginald 1936- WhoBlA 94
Kennedy, Thomas WhoAm 94
Kennedy, Thomas (Lawrie) 1928- Who 94
Kennedy, Thomas Alexander 1920- Who 94
Kennedy, Thomas Crawford 1932- WhoWest 94
Kennedy, Thomas E. DrAPF 93
Kennedy, Thomas Edgar 1958- WhoFI 94
Kennedy, Thomas J. 1947- WhoAm 94, WhoAmL 94
Kennedy, Thomas Leo 1936- WhoAm 94
Kennedy, Thomas Patrick 1932- WhoAm 94, WhoFI 94
Kennedy, Thomas Patrick 1951- WhoAmP 93
Kennedy, Tom d1965 WhoHol 92
Kennedy, V. Wayne 1938- WhoWest 94
Kennedy, Walter 1912-1977 BasBi
Kennedy, Walter Jeff, Jr. 1928- WhoAmL 94
Kennedy, Walter Lawrence 1920- WhoAmP 93
Kennedy, Walter P. WhoAmP 93
Kennedy, Wilbert Keith, Sr. 1919- WhoAm 94
Kennedy, Wilbert Keith, Jr. 1943- WhoAm 94
Kennedy, William DrAPF 93
Kennedy, William d1988 WhAm 10
Kennedy, William (Joseph) 1928- WrDr 94
Kennedy, William Andrew 1948- Who 94
Kennedy, William Bean 1926- WhoAm 94
Kennedy, William Francis 1918- WhoAm 94
Kennedy, William J., III 1922- WhoBlA 94
Kennedy, William James 1944- WhoFI 94, WhoScEn 94
Kennedy, William Joseph 1928- IntWW 93, WhoAm 94
Kennedy, William Thomas 1952- WhoWest 94
Kennedy, William Thomas, Jr. 1928- WhoBlA 94
Kennedy, Willie B. 1923- WhoAmP 93, WhoBlA 94
Kennedy, X.J. DrAPF 93
Kennedy, X. J. 1929- WhoAm 94, WrDr 94
Kennedy, Yvonne 1945- WhoAmP 93, WhoBlA 94
Kennedy Franklin, Linda Cheryl 1950- WhoBlA 94
Kennedy-Good, John 1915- Who 94
Kennedy Martin, (Francis) Troy 1932- Who 94
Kennedy-Minott, Rodney WhoAm 94, WhoWest 94
Kennedy-Morgan, Juanita WhoWomW 91
Kennedy-Overton, Jayne 1951- WhoBlA 94
Kennel, Charles Frederick 1939- WhoAm 94, WhoScEn 94, WhoWest 94
Kennel, Elliot Byron 1957- WhoScEn 94
Kennelly, Barbara B. 1936- CngDr 93, WhoAm 94, WhoWomW 91
Kennelly, Barbara Bailey 1936- WhoAmP 93
Kennelly, (Timothy) Brendan 1936- WrDr 94
Kennelly, John Jerome 1918- WhoAmL 94
Kennelly, Karen Margaret 1933- WhoAm 94
Kennelly, Kevin Joseph 1934- WhoScEn 94
Kennelly, Laura Ballard DrAPF 93
Kennelly, Tamara DrAPF 93
Kennelly, William James 1948- WhoScEn 94
Kennemer, William 1946- WhoAmP 93
Kennemore, Tim 1957- WrDr 94
Kenner, Brian T. 1951- WhoAm 94, WhoAmL 94
Kenner, Carol J. 1950- WhoAm 94, WhoAmL 94
Kenner, Carole Ann 1953- WhoMW 93
Kenner, Doris 1941- See Shirelles, The ConMus 11
Kenner, (William) Hugh 1923- WrDr 94
Kenner, Laurel 1954- WhoWest 94
Kenner, Patricia E. WhoAmP 93
Kennerknecht, Richard Eugene 1961- WhoWest 94
Kennerley, (James) Anthony (Machell) 1933- Who 94
Kennerly, Roland Francis 1934- WhoAmP 93
Kennessey, Joseph d1951 WhoHol 92
Kennet 1923- IntWW 93
Kennet, Baron 1923- Who 94
Kenneth, Keith WhoHol 92
Kennett, Brackley c. 1713-1782 DcNaB MP
Kennett, James Peter 1940- WhoAm 94, WhoScEn 94
Kennett, Margaret Brett fl. 1723-1725 BlmGWL
Kennett, Robert L. WhoAm 94
Kennett, Ronald John 1935- Who 94
Kennett, William Alexander 1932- WhoAm 94
Kennett, William Eric 1914- WhoWest 94
Kennett Brown, David 1938- Who 94
Kennett-Charles, Ann Jean 1951- WhoMW 93
Kennevick, Jack C. WhoAmP 93
Kenney, Anthony 1942- Who 94
Kenney, Brigid E. 1951- WhoAmL 94
Kenney, Catherine (McGehee) 1948- WrDr 94
Kenney, Charles 1950- WrDr 94
Kenney, Donna Denise 1960- WhoFI 94
Kenney, Douglas 1962- WhoAmA 93
Kenney, Edward Beckham 1929- WhoAmP 93
Kenney, Edward John 1924- IntWW 93, Who 94
Kenney, Estelle Koval 1928- WhoAmA 93
Kenney, F. Donald 1918- WhoFI 94
Kenney, Frank Deming 1921- WhoAm 94
Kenney, George T., Jr. 1957- WhoAmP 93
Kenney, H. Wesley 1926- IntMPA 94
Kenney, Harry Wesley, Jr. 1926- WhoAm 94
Kenney, Horace d1955 WhoHol 92
Kenney, Howard Washington 1917- WhoAm 94
Kenney, James d1982 WhoHol 92
Kenney, James F. WhoAmP 93
Kenney, James Francis 1921- WhoAm 94, WhoAmL 94
Kenney, Jeffrey Jay 1956- WhoMW 93
Kenney, Jerome P. 1941- WhoAm 94, WhoFI 94
Kenney, John Arthur 1948- WhoAmL 94
Kenney, John Joseph 1943- WhoAm 94, WhoAmL 94
Kenney, John William, III 1950- WhoWest 94
Kenney, Louis Augustine 1917- WhoAm 94
Kenney, Marianne 1933- WhoWest 94
Kenney, Martin Steven 1960- WhoAmL 94
Kenney, Raymond Joseph, Jr. 1932- WhoAm 94
Kenney, Richard (L.) 1948- WrDr 94
Kenney, Richard Alec 1924- WhoAm 94
Kenney, Richard John 1941- WhoAm 94
Kenney, Richard L. DrAPF 93
Kenney, Richard Laurence 1948- WhoAm 94
Kenney, Robert James, Jr. 1948- WhoAm 94, WhoAmL 94
Kenney, Thomas Frederick 1941- WhoAm 94
Kenney, Timothy P. 1963- WhoScEn 94
Kenney, Virgil Cooper 1926- WhoBlA 94
Kenney, W. John 1904-1992 WhAm 10
Kenney, Walter T. 1930- WhoBlA 94
Kenney, Walter Thomas 1930- WhoAmP 93
Kenney, William Fitzgerald 1935- WhoAmL 94, WhoFI 94, WhoWest 94
Kenney, William John, Jr. 1949- WhoAm 94
Kenney-Wallace, Geraldine 1943- WhoScEn 94
Kennicott, James W. 1945- WhoAmL 94
Kennicutt, Maribeth Antoinette 1944- WhoMW 93
Kenniff, Patrick J. 1943- WhoAm 94
Kennison, Wayne A. 1925- WhoAmP 93
Kennon, Arthur Bruce 1933- WhoAmA 93
Kennon, Daniel, Jr. 1910- WhoBlA 94
Kennon, John David 1917- WhoIns 94
Kennon, Larry 1952- BasBi
Kennon, Rozmond H. 1935- WhoBlA 94
Kennon-Wilson, James d1984 WhoHol 92
Kenny, Adele DrAPF 93
Kenny, Alan Dennis 1963- WhoWest 94
Kenny, Alexander Donovan 1925- WhoAm 94
Kenny, Alfreida B. 1950- WhoBlA 94
Kenny, Anthony (John Patrick) 1931- Who 94, WrDr 94
Kenny, Anthony John Patrick 1931- IntWW 93
Kenny, Anthony Marriott 1939- Who 94
Kenny, Arthur William 1918- Who 94
Kenny, Bernard F., Jr. 1946- WhoAmP 93
Kenny, Bill d1978 WhoHol 92
Kenny, Brian (Leslie Graham) 1934- IntWW 93, Who 94
Kenny, Colin d1968 WhoHol 92
Kenny, David Culber 1945- WhoAm 94
Kenny, David John 1940- Who 94
Kenny, Douglas d1980 WhoHol 92
Kenny, Douglas T. 1923- IntWW 93
Kenny, Douglas Timothy 1923- Who 94, WhoAm 94, WhoScEn 94
Kenny, Edmund Joyce 1920- WhoAm 94
Kenny, Erin L. 1960- WhoAmP 93
Kenny, Herbert Cornelius d1992 WhoBlA 94N
Kenny, James Casey 1953- WhoMW 93
Kenny, John Edward 1945- WhoFI 94
Kenny, John Logan 1938- WhoIns 94
Kenny, Kathryn 1916- WrDr 94
Kenny, Leola d1956 WhoHol 92
Kenny, Maurice DrAPF 93
Kenny, Michael 1941- IntWW 93, Who 94
Kenny, Michael H. 1937- WhoAm 94, WhoWest 94
Kenny, Patricia d1983 WhoHol 92
Kenny, Patrick Edward 1948- WhoAm 94
Kenny, Peter J. 1941- WhoAmL 94
Kenny, R. Timothy WhoAm 94, WhoFI 94
Kenny, Raymond Patrick 1933- WhoMW 93
Kenny, Robert Martin WhoFI 94
Kenny, Roger Michael 1938- WhoAm 94, WhoFI 94
Kenny, Sean 1932-1973 NewGrDO
Kenny, Shirley Strum 1934- WhoAm 94
Kenny, Yvonne 1950- NewGrDO
Kenny-Wallace, G. A. WhoScEn 94
Kenoff, Jay Stewart 1946- WhoAmL 94, WhoWest 94
Kenojuak 1933- WhoAmA 93
Kenrich, John Lewis 1929- WhoAm 94, WhoAmL 94
Kenrick, Charles William 1946- WhoAm 94, WhoAmL 94
Kenrick, Francis Patrick 1796-1863 DcAmReB 2
Kenrick, John R. 1942- WhoAmL 94
Kenrick, Tony 1935- WrDr 94
Kensel, Neven Michael 1940- WhoAmL 94
Kensett, John Frederick 1816-1872 AmCulL [port]
Kenshalo, Daniel Ralph 1922- WhoAm 94
Kensinger, George 1922-1993 WrDr 94N
Kensinger, John William 1947- WhoFI 94
Kensinger, Loren L. 1942- WhoAmL 94
Kensington, Area Bishop of 1935- Who 94
Kensington, Baron 1933- Who 94
Kensington, Holland 1945- WhoFI 94
Kensit, Patsy IntWW 93
Kensit, Patsy 1968- IntMPA 94, WhoHol 92
Kenswood, Baron 1930- Who 94
Kent, Duke of 1935- Who 94R
Kent, H.R.H. the Duke of 1935- IntWW 93
Kent, Alan 1933- WrDr 94
Kent, Alan Heywood 1946- WhoAm 94
Kent, Alexander 1924- WrDr 94
Kent, Allegra 1938- IntDcB [port], WhoHol 92
Kent, Allen 1921- WhoAm 94
Kent, April WhoHol 92
Kent, Arnold d1928 WhoHol 92
Kent, Arthur (William Charles) 1925- WrDr 94
Kent, Arthur William 1913- Who 94
Kent, Barbara 1909- WhoHol 92
Kent, Bartis Milton 1925- WhoScEn 94
Kent, Bill WhoAm 94
Kent, Brad EncSF 93
Kent, Bruce 1929- IntWW 93, Who 94
Kent, Bruce Eric 1932- IntWW 93
Kent, Calvin Albert 1941- WhoAm 94
Kent, Charles d1923 WhoHol 92
Kent, Christopher WhoHol 92
Kent, Christopher Andrew 1940- WhoWest 94
Kent, Crauford d1953 WhoHol 92
Kent, D. Randall, Jr. WhoScEn 94
Kent, Dale Vivienne 1942- WrDr 94
Kent, Darrel Arthur 1954- WhoWest 94
Kent, David Charles 1953- WhoAm 94, WhoAmL 94
Kent, David W. WhoAmP 93
Kent, Dennis Vladimir 1946- WhoAm 94, WhoScEn 94
Kent, Donald Charles 1923- WhoAm 94
Kent, Dorothea d1990 WhoHol 92
Kent, Edgar Robert, Jr. 1941- WhoAm 94, WhoFI 94
Kent, Ernest 1955- WhoBlA 94
Kent, Ethel d1952 WhoHol 92
Kent, Francis William 1942- IntWW 93
Kent, Frank Ward 1912-1977 WhoAmA 93N
Kent, Frederick Heber 1905- WhoAm 94, WhoAmL 94
Kent, Gayle Steverson 1938- WhoAm 94
Kent, Geoffrey 1914- WhoAm 94
Kent, Geoffrey 1922-1992 AnObit 1992
Kent, Geoffrey Charles d1992 IntWW 93N
Kent, George Cantine, Jr. 1914- WhoAm 94
Kent, Gerald d1944 WhoHol 92
Kent, H. Latham 1930- WhoAmA 93
Kent, Harold Simcox 1903- Who 94
Kent, Harry Christison 1930-1991 WhAm 10
Kent, Helen 1938- WrDr 94
Kent, Homer Austin, Jr. 1926- WrDr 94
Kent, Howard Lees 1930- WhoScEn 94
Kent, Jack 1920-1985 WhoAmA 93N
Kent, James A. 1922- WhoAm 94
Kent, James Gardner 1952- WhoFI 94, WhoMW 93
Kent, James Guy 1952- WhoWest 94
Kent, James Richard 1952- WhoFI 94
Kent, Jan Georg 1942- WhoScEn 94
Kent, Jean 1921- IntMPA 94, WhoHol 92
Kent, Jeffrey Sark 1950- WhoMW 93
Kent, Jill Elspeth 1948- WhoAm 94
Kent, Joe 1938- WhoAmP 93
Kent, John B. 1939- IntMPA 94
Kent, John Philip Cozens 1928- IntWW 93, Who 94
Kent, Julie 1969- WhoHol 92
Kent, Kate d1934 WhoHol 92
Kent, Katie ConAu 41NR
Kent, Kelvin EncSF 93
Kent, Keneth d1963 WhoHol 92
Kent, Larry d1967 WhoHol 92
Kent, Lenita d1987 WhoHol 92
Kent, Lenny d1985 WhoHol 92
Kent, Leon d1943 WhoHol 92
Kent, Linda Gail 1946- WhoAm 94
Kent, M. Elizabeth 1943- WhoAmL 94
Kent, Mallory EncSF 93
Kent, Marjorie 1939- WhoHol 92
Kent, Marsha d1971 WhoHol 92
Kent, Marshall WhoHol 92
Kent, Melvin Floyd 1953- WhoBlA 94
Kent, Norman 1903-1972 WhoAmA 93N
Kent, Pamela WrDr 94
Kent, Paul Welberry 1923- Who 94
Kent, Paula WhoAm 94
Kent, Pendarell Hugh 1937- Who 94
Kent, Philip EncSF 93
Kent, Raymond d1948 WhoHol 92
Kent, Raymond Knezevich 1929- WhoAm 94
Kent, Robert d1955 WhoHol 92
Kent, Robert Brydon 1921- WhoAm 94

Kerouac, John GayLL
Kerpelman, Larry Cyril 1939- WhoAm 94
Kerpsack, Robert William, Jr. 1961- WhoAmL 94
Kerr Who 94
Kerr, A(rthur) Stewart 1915- WhAm 10
Kerr, Alan Grainger 1935- Who 94
Kerr, Alexander 1945- WhoAmL 94
Kerr, Alexander Duncan, Jr. 1943- WhoAmL 94
Kerr, Alexander McBride 1921- WrDr 94
Kerr, Allen 1926- Who 94
Kerr, Andrea Moore 1940- ConAu 141
Kerr, Andrew Mark 1940- Who 94
Kerr, Andrew Stevenson 1918- Who 94
Kerr, Annette WhoHol 92
Kerr, Anthony Robert 1941- WhoAm 94
Kerr, Arthur 1926-1979 WhoAmA 93N
Kerr, Baine Perkins 1919- WhoAm 94
Kerr, Bill 1922- WhoHol 92
Kerr, Bob d1960 WhoHol 92
Kerr, Brian Francis 1948- Who 94
Kerr, Carole 1935- WrDr 94
Kerr, Charles Randall 1933- WhoAm 94
Kerr, Chester Brooks 1913- IntWW 93
Kerr, Clarence Francis 1929- WhoMW 93
Kerr, Clarence William 1923- WhoAm 94
Kerr, Clark 1911- IntWW 93, Who 94, WhoAm 94, WrDr 94
Kerr, Dave 1945- WhoAmP 93
Kerr, David Leigh 1923- Who 94
Kerr, David Mills 1945- WhoMW 93
Kerr, David Nicol Sharp 1927- Who 94
Kerr, David Wylie 1943- WhoAm 94, WhoFI 94
Kerr, Deborah 1921- IntMPA 94, WhoHol 92
Kerr, Deborah Jane 1921- IntWW 93, Who 94
Kerr, Desmond Moore 1930- Who 94
Kerr, Donald d1977 WhoHol 92
Kerr, Donald Frederick 1915- Who 94
Kerr, Donald MacLean, Jr. 1939- WhoAm 94, WhoScEn 94
Kerr, Dorothy Marie Burmeister 1935- WhoAm 94
Kerr, E. Coe 1914-1973 WhoAmA 93N
Kerr, E. Katherine 1937- WhoHol 92
Kerr, Edmund Hugh 1924-1992 WhAm 10
Kerr, Edwin 1926- Who 94
Kerr, Elizabeth WhoHol 92
Kerr, Elizabeth M(argaret) 1905-1991 WrDr 94N
Kerr, Ewing Thomas 1900-1992 WhAm 10
Kerr, Frances Mills 1919- WhoBlA 94
Kerr, Francis Robert Newsam 1916- Who 94
Kerr, Frank Floyd 1924- WhoScEn 94
Kerr, Frank John 1918- WhoAm 94, WhoScEn 94
Kerr, Fraser 1931- IntMPA 94
Kerr, Fred A. WhoAmP 93
Kerr, Frederick d1933 WhoHol 92
Kerr, Frederick 1921- WrDr 94
Kerr, Frederick H. 1936- WhoAm 94
Kerr, Geoffrey 1895- WhoHol 92
Kerr, George J. 1954- WhoAmP 93
Kerr, Gib 1927- WhoWest 94
Kerr, Gordon Charles 1945- WhoAmP 93
Kerr, Graham 1934- WrDr 94
Kerr, Gregory Alan 1950- WhoFI 94, WhoWest 94
Kerr, Guy Hardie 1953- WhoAm 94, WhoAmL 94
Kerr, H. Sinclair, Jr. 1947- WhoAmL 94
Kerr, Harris Eastham 1951- WhoAmL 94
Kerr, Hortense R. 1926- WhoBlA 94
Kerr, Hugh Thomson 1909-1992 WhAm 10
Kerr, James 1928- Who 94
Kerr, James Joseph 1926- WhoAm 94
Kerr, James W. 1914- WhoAm 94, WhoWest 94
Kerr, James Wilfrid 1897- WhoAmA 93, WhoWest 94
Kerr, James Wilson 1921- WhoScEn 94
Kerr, Jane d1954 WhoHol 92
Kerr, Jean 1922- WrDr 94
Kerr, Jean 1923- IntWW 93, WhoAm 94
Kerr, Jimmie Barry 1934- WhoWest 94
Kerr, John 1931- IntMPA 94, WhoHol 92
Kerr, John (Beverley) 1937- Who 94
Kerr, John (Olav) 1942- Who 94
Kerr, John F. DrAPF 93
Kerr, John H., III 1936- WhoAmP 93
Kerr, John Olav 1942- IntWW 93
Kerr, Johnny 1932- BasBi
Kerr, (Anne) Judith 1923- WrDr 94
Kerr, Judy WhoHol 92
Kerr, K. Austin 1938- WrDr 94
Kerr, Kathryn DrAPF 93
Kerr, Kelle WhoHol 92
Kerr, Keron WhoAmP 93
Kerr, Kleon Harding 1911- WhoWest 94
Kerr, Larry d1968 WhoHol 92
Kerr, Louise A. 1938- WhoHisp 94
Kerr, M. D. 1934- WhoFI 94
Kerr, M. E. 1927- TwCYAW, WrDr 94
Kerr, Marilyn Marie 1943- WhoMW 93
Kerr, Michael EncSF 93
Kerr, Michael 1933- WrDr 94
Kerr, Michael (Robert Emanuel) 1921- Who 94
Kerr, Norbert Lee 1948- WhoScEn 94
Kerr, Patrick Corbitt 1950- WhoAm 94
Kerr, Peter Donald 1920- WhoScEn 94
Kerr, Philip 1956- WrDr 94
Kerr, Renee Rochelle 1952- WhoMW 93
Kerr, Robert D. 1893- WhAm 10
Kerr, Robert Mark 1932- WhoAmP 93
Kerr, Robert Reid 1914- Who 94
Kerr, Robert Samuel, III 1950- WhoAmP 93
Kerr, Robert Shaw 1917- WhoAm 94
Kerr, Rose 1953- Who 94
Kerr, Sandra Lee 1952- WhoScEn 94
Kerr, Sandria Neidus 1940- WhoAm 94
Kerr, Stanley B. 1928- WhoAm 94
Kerr, Thomas Adolphus 1923- WhoAm 94
Kerr, Thomas Andrew 1953- WhoScEn 94
Kerr, Thomas Henry 1924- Who 94
Kerr, Thomas Jefferson, IV 1933- WhoAm 94
Kerr, Thomas Robert 1950- WhoAmP 93
Kerr, Tim 1960- WhoAm 94
Kerr, Tom 1950- SmATA 77 [port]
Kerr, Vernon Norman 1928- WhoAmP 93
Kerr, Walter 1913- IntWW 93
Kerr, Walter (Francis) 1913- WrDr 94
Kerr, Walter F. 1913- WhoAm 94
Kerr, Walter L. 1928- WhoBlA 94
Kerr, Wayne Nelson 1961- WhoMW 93
Kerr, Wayne P. 1953- WhoFI 94
Kerr, William 1919- WhoAm 94
Kerr, William Andrew 1934- WhoAm 94
Kerr, William Francis Kennedy 1923- Who 94
Kerr, William G. 1945- WhoAmP 93
Kerr, William Gregg 1927- WhoAm 94
Kerr, William Sterling, III 1939- WhoFI 94
Kerr, William T. 1941- WhoAm 94
Kerrebrock, Jack Leo 1928- WhoAm 94
Kerrey, Bob 1943- IntWW 93, WhoAm 94, WhoMW 93
Kerrey, J. Robert 1943- CngDr 93
Kerrey, Joseph Robert 1943- WhoAmP 93
Kerr-Green, Gretchen Hodgson 1935- WhAm 10
Kerrick, David E. 1951- WhoAmP 93
Kerrick, David Ellsworth 1951- WhoAmL 94, WhoWest 94
Kerrick, Gray 1943- WhoFI 94
Kerrick, Thomas d1927 WhoHol 92
Kerridge, Linda 1959- WhoHol 92
Kerridge, Mary 1914- WhoHol 92
Kerrigan, Anthony 1918- WhoAm 94
Kerrigan, Edward J. 1931- WhoAmP 93
Kerrigan, Greer Sandra 1948- Who 94
Kerrigan, Herbert Aird 1945- Who 94
Kerrigan, J. M. d1964 WhoHol 92
Kerrigan, J. Warren d1947 WhoHol 92
Kerrigan, James P. 1927- WhoAmP 93
Kerrigan, John E. WhoMW 93
Kerrigan, Joseph Michael 1919- WhoAmL 94
Kerrigan, Kathleen d1957 WhoHol 92
Kerrigan, Maurie 1951- WhoAmA 93
Kerrigan, Patricia WhoHol 92
Kerrigan, T. S. DrAPF 93
Kerrigan, Timothy George 1954- WhoAmL 94
Kerrigan, Walter W., II 1953- WhoMW 93
Kerruish, (Henry) Charles 1917- IntWW 93, Who 94
Kerry, Knight of Who 94
Kerry, Cameron F. 1950- WhoAmL 94
Kerry, John F. 1943- CngDr 93
Kerry, John Forbes 1943- IntWW 93, WhoAm 94, WhoAmP 93
Kerry, John M. WhoAmP 93
Kerry, Juanita Ann Merideth 1951- WhoMW 93
Kerry, Lois SmATA 75, TwCYAW
Kerry, Lois 1934- WrDr 94
Kerry, Margaret 1929- WhoHol 92
Kerry, Michael (James) 1923- Who 94
Kerry, Norman d1956 WhoHol 92
Kerry, Pat X. d1962 WhoHol 92
Kerry, Reta Christina 1923- WhoAmP 93
Kerry, Richard John 1915- WhoAmP 93
Kerr y Baca, Stephen P. 1944- WhoHisp 94
Kersbergen, John Jay 1948- WhoFI 94
Kersbergen, Robert 1951- WhoIns 94
Kersch, Jennifer Lynn 1968- WhoWest 94
Kerschner, Edward WhoFI 94
Kerschner, Lee Ronald 1931- WhoAm 94, WhoWest 94
Kerse, Christopher Stephen 1946- Who 94
Kersey, B. Franklin, IV 1942- WhoBlA 94
Kersey, Bertha Brinnett 1954- WhoBlA 94
Kersey, Elizabeth T. 1956- WhoBlA 94
Kersey, Jerome 1962- WhoBlA 94
Kersey, Sharyn R. 1951- WhoAmP 93
Kersey, Tanya-Monique 1961- BlkWr 2
Kersey, Terry Lee 1947- WhoScEn 94, WhoWest 94
Kersh, Cyril d1993 Who 94N
Kersh, Cyril 1925- WrDr 94
Kersh, Cyril 1925-1993 ConAu 141
Kersh, DeWitte Talmadge, Jr. 1930- WhoAmL 94
Kersh, Gerald 1911-1968 EncSF 93
Kersh, Kathy 1942- WhoHol 92
Kershaw, Baron 1936- Who 94
Kershaw, Alister (Nasmyth) 1921- ConAu 41NR
Kershaw, Anthony Who 94
Kershaw, (John) Anthony 1915- Who 94
Kershaw, Carol Jean 1947- WhoScEn 94
Kershaw, Eleanor d1971 WhoHol 92
Kershaw, Henry Aidan 1927- Who 94
Kershaw, Ian 1943- Who 94
Kershaw, Joseph Alexander 1913-1989 WhAm 10
Kershaw, Joseph Anthony 1935- Who 94
Kershaw, Kenneth Andrew 1930- WhoAm 94
Kershaw, Michael Who 94
Kershaw, (Philip) Michael 1941- Who 94
Kershaw, Peter 1933- WrDr 94
Kershaw, Robert Alan 1947- WhoAm 94
Kershaw, Robert Barnsley 1952- WhoAmL 94
Kershaw, Thomas Abbott 1938- WhoFI 94
Kershaw, W.J.S., Mrs. Who 94
Kershaw, Willette d1960 WhoHol 92
Kershaw, William Edgar 1911- Who 94
Kershner, Gerald Anthony 1950- WhoMW 93
Kershner, Howard Eldred 1891-1990 WhAm 10
Kershner, Irvin WhoHol 92
Kershner, Irvin 1923- IntMPA 94
Kershner, Jerry Wayne 1950- WhoFI 94
Kershner, William Franklin 1939- WhoAm 94
Kerslake, John Francis 1898- WhAm 10
Kerslake, Kenneth Alvin 1930- WhoAm 94, WhoAmA 93
Kerslake, Susan 20th cent.- BlmGWL
Kersnowski, Frank Louis 1934- WhoAm 94
Kerson, Edward W. 1947- WhoAmL 94
Kerss, William 1931- Who 94
Kerst, Donald W(illiam) 1911-1993 CurBio 93N
Kerst, Donald William 1911- IntWW 93
Kerst, Donald William 1911-1993 NewYTBS 93 [port]
Kersten, James Burke 1960- WhoAmP 93, WhoMW 93
Kersten, Robert Donavon 1927- WhoScEn 94
Kersten, Timothy Wayne 1944- WhoWest 94
Kersters, Willem 1929- NewGrDO
Kerstetter, Michael James 1936- WhoAm 94
Kerstiens, Francis Lyle 1950- WhoWest 94
Kersting, Edwin Joseph 1919- WhoAm 94
Kersting, Henk d1993 NewYTBS 93
Kersting, Lisa Gayle WhoMW 93
Kerswill, J. W. Roy 1925- WhoAmA 93
Kert, Larry d1991 WhoHol 92
Kertesz, Istvan 1929-1973 NewGrDO
Kerth, Leroy T. 1928- WhoAm 94
Kertscher, Richard H. WhoAmP 93
Kerttula, Jalmar M. 1929- WhoAmP 93
Kertz, Hubert Leonard 1910- WhoAm 94
Kertz, Marsha Helene 1946- WhoWest 94
Kertzer, Anita Elizabeth WhoAmA 93
Kerver, Thomas Joseph 1934- WhoWest 94
Kervina-Thompson, Mimi 1945- WhoMW 93
Ker Wilson, Barbara 1929- SmATA 18AS [port]
Kerwin, Brian 1949- IntMPA 94, WhoHol 92
Kerwin, Carolyn Ann 1950- WhoMW 93
Kerwin, Courtney Michael 1944- WhoScEn 94
Kerwin, Joseph Peter 1932- WhoAm 94, WhoScEn 94
Kerwin, Kenneth Hills, II 1939- WhoWest 94
Kerwin, Lance 1960- WhoHol 92
Kerwin, Larkin 1924- IntWW 93, Who 94, WhoAm 94
Kerwin, Mary Ann Collins 1931- WhoAmL 94
Kerwin, Maureen WhoHol 92
Kerwin, William James 1922- WhoAm 94
Kerwood, Dick d1924 WhoHol 92
Kerxton, Alan Smith 1938- WhoAm 94
Keryczynskyj, Leo Ihor 1948- WhoAmL 94
Kerzelli, Frants fl. 1794- NewGrDO
Kerzelli, Ivan fl. 1773-1780 NewGrDO
Kerzelli Family NewGrDO
Kerzie, Ted L. 1943- WhoAmA 93
Kerzman, James A. WhoAmP 93
Keseru, Janos 1939- WhoFI 94
Kesey, Ken DrAPF 93
Kesey, Ken 1935- WhoAm 94, WhoWest 94
Kesey, Ken (Elton) 1935- TwCYAW, WrDr 94
Keshavan, Krishnaswamiengar 1929- WhoAsA 94
Keshian, Richard 1934- WhoAmL 94
Keshishian, John M. 1923- EncSF 93
Kesisoglu, Garbis 1936- WhoFI 94
Keska, Jerry Kazimierz 1945- WhoScEn 94, WhoWest 94
Keskiner, Ali 1929- WhoScEn 94
Kesler, Clyde Ervin 1922- WhoAm 94
Kesler, David Bruce 1946- WhoAmL 94
Kesler, Jay Lewis 1935- WhoAm 94
Kesler, John A. 1923- WhoAmL 94
Kesler, Ruth Evalyn 1925- WhoAmP 93
Kesler, Stephen Edward 1940- WhoAm 94
Kessar, Yisrael 1931- IntWW 93
Kessel, Brina 1925- WhoAm 94, WhoScEn 94, WhoWest 94
Kessel, Harlan Robert 1928- WhoWest 94
Kessel, John (Joseph Vincent) 1950- EncSF 93
Kessel, John Howard 1928- WhoAm 94, WrDr 94
Kessel, Laura Elizabeth 1969- WhoMW 93
Kessel, Mark 1941- WhoAm 94
Kessel, Nancy 1947- WhoAmP 93
Kessel, Richard Glen 1931- WhoAm 94
Kessel, William Ivor Neil 1925- Who 94
Kesselhaut, Arthur M. 1935- WhoIns 94
Kesselhaut, Arthur Melvyn 1935- WhoAm 94, WhoWest 94
Kesselhaut, Glenn David 1956- WhoAmL 94
Kessell, Steven Clarke 1961- WhoAmL 94
Kesselly, Edward Binyah IntWW 93
Kesselman, Bruce Alan 1951- WhoAm 94
Kesselman, Jonathan Rhys 1946- WhoAm 94
Kesselman, Theodore Leonard 1932- WhoAm 94
Kesselman, Wendy (Ann) ConDr 93, WrDr 94
Kesselring, Leo John 1933- WhoAmP 93
Kessen, William 1925- WhoAm 94, WrDr 94
Kessenich, Karl Otto 1963- WhoScEn 94
Kessinger, Tom G. 1941- WhoAm 94
Kessler, A. D. 1923- WhoFI 94, WhoWest 94
Kessler, Alan 1945- WhoAmA 93
Kessler, Alan Craig 1950- WhoAm 94, WhoAmL 94
Kessler, Bernard Milton 1927- WhoFI 94
Kessler, David 1951- WhoAmP 93
Kessler, David A. 1951- WhoAm 94, WhoScEn 94
Kessler, Dietrich 1936- WhoAm 94, WhoScEn 94
Kessler, Donna Kay Ens 1953- WhoMW 93, WhoScEn 94
Kessler, Edwin 1928- WhoAm 94
Kessler, F. James 1942- WhoMW 93
Kessler, Frederic S. 1953- WhoAmL 94
Kessler, Helen Joyce 1952- WhoMW 93
Kessler, Henry H. 1896- WhAm 10
Kessler, Herbert Leon 1941- WhoAm 94, WhoAmA 93
Kessler, Irving Isar 1931- WhoAm 94
Kessler, Irving K. d1993 NewYTBS 93 [port]
Kessler, Jacques Isaac 1929- WhoAm 94
Kessler, Jane Q. 1946- WhoAmA 93
Kessler, Jascha DrAPF 93
Kessler, Jascha (Frederick) 1929- WrDr 94
Kessler, Jeffrey L. 1954- WhoAm 94, WhoAmL 94
Kessler, Joan F. 1943- WhoAm 94
Kessler, John Otto 1928- WhoAm 94, WhoScEn 94
Kessler, John Paul, Jr. 1946- WhoFI 94
Kessler, John Whitaker 1936- WhoAm 94
Kessler, Jon A. 1957- WhoAmA 93
Kessler, Judd Lewis 1938- WhoAm 94, WhoAmL 94
Kessler, Karl Gunther 1919- WhoAm 94
Kessler, Lauren Jeanne 1950- WhoWest 94
Kessler, Leonard H. 1921- WhoAmA 93
Kessler, Lillian Ruth d1993 NewYTBS 93 [port]
Kessler, Lynn WhoAmP 93
Kessler, Lynn Elizabeth 1941- WhoWest 94
Kessler, Margaret Jennings 1944- WhoAmA 93
Kessler, Mark Keil 1936- WhoAm 94
Kessler, Mary Carolyn 1947- WhoAmP 93
Kessler, Melody Sheryl 1968- WhoWest 94

Kidwell, David Stephen 1940- WhoAm 94, WhoFI 94
Kidwell, Michael Eades 1950- WhoScEn 94
Kidwell, Raymond Incledon 1926- Who 94
Kidwell, Richard Patrick 1954- WhoAmL 94
Kidwell, William F. 1947- WhoFI 94
Kiebala, Susan Marie 1952- WhoMW 93
Kieber, Walter 1931- IntWW 93
Kiebert, Kermit V. WhoAmP 93
Kiebic, Viaceslau Francjevic 1936- LngBDD
Kiechlin, Robert Jerome 1919- WhoAm 94
Kiecker, Greg 1951- WhoAmP 93
Kieckhefer, Richard 1946- WhoMW 93
Kieda, David Basil 1960- WhoWest 94
Kief, Paul Allan 1934- WhoAm 94
Kiefer, Anselm 1945- IntWW 93
Kiefer, Gary WhoMW 93
Kiefer, Helen Chilton WhoMW 93
Kiefer, John Harold 1932- WhoScEn 94
Kiefer, John Robert 1951- WhoWest 94
Kiefer, Kit Annette 1958- WhoAm 94
Kiefer, Louis 1936- WrDr 94
Kiefer, Nat Gerard 1939- WhoAmP 93
Kiefer, Peter H. 1949- WhoAmL 94
Kiefer, Rita DrAPF 93
Kiefer, Robert John 1936- WhoWest 94
Kiefer, Timothy Edward 1968- WhoFI 94
Kiefer, Warren (David) 1930- WrDr 94
Kieferndorf, Frederick George 1921- WhoAmA 93
Kiefert, Alice Stockwell 1929- WhoFI 94
Kieff, Elliott Dan 1943- WhoAm 94
Kieffer, George David 1947- WhoAmL 94
Kieffer, James Marshall 1940- WhoAmL 94
Kieffer, James Milton 1921- WhoAm 94
Kieffer, Jarold A. 1923- WhoAmP 93
Kieffer, Jarold Alan 1923- WhoAm 94
Kieffer, Joyce Loretta 1940- WhoAm 94
Kieffer, Mary Jane WhoAmA 93
Kieffer, Phillip d1962 WhoHol 92
Kieffer, R. Leo WhoAmP 93
Kieffer, Ronald Joseph 1941- WhoMW 93
Kieffer, Ruth d1965 WhoHol 92
Kieffer, Stephen Aaron 1935- WhoAm 94
Kieffer, Susan Werner 1942- WhoAm 94, WhoScEn 94, WhoWest 94
Kieffer, William Franklinn 1915- WhoAm 94
Kiefl, Robert Frances 1953- WhoScEn 94
Kieft, Gerald Nelson 1946- WhoMW 93
Kieft, Thomas Lamar 1951- WhoScEn 94
Kiehn, Mogens Hans 1918- WhoWest 94
Kiehne, Anna Marie 1947- WhoWest 94
Kiehne, Lynn Sheree 1955- WhoAm 94, WhoFI 94
Kiekhofer, William Henry 1952- WhoAmL 94
Kiel, Edward Rowland 1944- WhoAmL 94
Kiel, Frederick Orin 1942- WhoAm 94, WhoAmL 94
Kiel, Ollie Mae 1931- WhoAmP 93
Kiel, Richard 1939- IntMPA 94, WhoHol 92
Kiel, William Frederick 1935- WhoScEn 94
Kielarowski, Henry Edward 1946- WhoFI 94, WhoWest 94
Kielb, Robert Evans 1949- WhoMW 93, WhoScEn 94
Kielhorn, Richard Werner 1931- WhoWest 94
Kielich, Christina Marie 1951- WhoAmP 93
Kieling, Wolfgang WhoHol 92
Kielkopf, James Robert 1939- WhoAmA 93
Kielmansegg, Johann Adolf 1906- IntWW 93
Kielsmeier, Catherine Jane WhoWest 94
Kielty, John Lawrence, III 1943- WhoAm 94
Kiely, Benedict 1919- WrDr 94
Kiely, Bruce Fraser 1944- WhoAmL 94
Kiely, Dan Ray 1944- WhoAm 94, WhoAmL 94, WhoFI 94
Kiely, David George 1925- Who 94
Kiely, Jerome 1925- WrDr 94
Kiely, Maureen d1977 WhoHol 92
Kiely, Patrick James 1951- WhoAmP 93
Kiely, Robert (James) 1931- WrDr 94
Kiemele, Laurie Ann WhoWest 94
Kienbaum, Thomas Gerd 1942- WhoAm 94, WhoAmL 94
Kienbusch, William Austin 1914-1979 WhoAmA 93N
Kienel, Frederick Edward 1938- WhoFI 94
Kienel, Paul A. 1933- WhoAm 94
Kiener, John Leslie 1940- WhoAmL 94
Kiengsiri, Kanha BlmGWL
Kienholz, Lyn WhoAmA 93
Kienholz, Lyn Shearer WhoWest 94
Kienlen, Johann Christoph 1783?-1829 NewGrDO
Kienol, Mark Steven 1955- WhoMW 93
Kienzl, Wilhelm 1857-1941 NewGrDO
Kienzle, William X(avier) 1928- WrDr 94
Kienzle, William Xavier 1928- WhoMW 93
Kiep, Walther Leisler 1926- IntWW 93
Kiepper, Alan Frederick 1928- WhoAm 94
Kiepper, James Julius 1933- WhoAm 94
Kiepura, Jan d1966 WhoHol 92
Kiepura, Jan 1902-1966 NewGrDO
Kiepura, Sally 1938- WhoMW 93
Kier, Porter Martin 1927- WhoAm 94
Kier, Raymond Edward 1942- WhoWest 94
Kier, Udo 1944- WhoHol 92
Kier, William McKee 1956- WhoScEn 94
Kierans, Eric William 1914- IntWW 93
Kieren, Thomas Henry 1941- WhoAm 94
Kierinaszek-Lamla, W. WhoWomW 91
Kierkegaard, Peder 1928- IntWW 93
Kierkegaard, Soren (Aabye) 1813-1855 EncEth
Kiernan, Brian 1937- WrDr 94
Kiernan, Christopher Charles 1936- Who 94
Kiernan, Edwin A., Jr. 1926- WhoAm 94
Kiernan, James d1975 WhoHol 92
Kiernan, Joan Julich 1943- WhoAmP 93
Kiernan, John d1981 WhoHol 92
Kiernan, Owen Burns 1914- WhoAm 94
Kiernan, Peter Delacy 1923-1989 WhAm 10
Kiernan, Richard Francis 1935- WhoAm 94
Kiernan, William Joseph, Jr. 1932- WhoAm 94
Kiernat, Bruce E. 1941- WhoAmL 94
Kieronska, Dorota Helena 1965- WhoScEn 94
Kiersch, George Alfred 1918- WhoAm 94, WhoScEn 94, WhoWest 94
Kierscht, Charles M. 1939- WhoAm 94, WhoFI 94
Kierstead, James Allan 1969- WhoScEn 94
Kierstine, Julie Annette 1960- WhoWest 94
Kies, Cosette Nell 1936- WhoAm 94
Kies, David M. 1944- WhoAm 94
Kies, Edward Joseph 1942- WhoMW 93
Kies, Kenneth J. 1952- WhoAm 94
Kieschnick, William F. 1923- IntWW 93
Kiesel, Stanley DrAPF 93
Kieselmann, Gerhard Maria 1956- WhoScEn 94
Kieser, John Frederick 1937- WhoFI 94
Kieser, Kenneth Lester 1953- WhoMW 93
Kieser, Randall John 1958- WhoMW 93
Kiesler, Charles Adolphus 1934- WhoAm 94
Kiesler, Dolores Ann 1953- WhoMW 93
Kiesler, Frederick J. 1892-1966 WhoAmA 93N
Kiesler, Hedy WhoHol 92
Kiesling, Ernst Willie 1934- WhoAm 94, WhoScEn 94
Kiesling, Gerald Kenneth 1933- WhoIns 94
Kiesling, Lynnwood Allen 1951- WhoMW 93
Kiesling, Walt d1962 ProFbHF
Kieslowski, Krzysztof 1941- ConTFT 11, IntWW 93
Kiessling, B. Robbins 1950- WhoAmL 94
Kiessling, Ronald Frederick 1934- WhoMW 93
Kiest, Alan Scott 1949- WhoWest 94
Kieswetter, James Kay 1942- WhoWest 94
Kiev, Ari 1933- WrDr 94
Kieve, Loren 1948- WhoAm 94, WhoAmL 94
Kiewel, Harold Dean 1951- WhoMW 93
Kifer, Alan Craig 1952- WhoFI 94
Kiffmeyer, Ralph R. WhoAmP 93
Kifner, John William 1941- WhoAm 94
Kiger, Angie Marie 1965- WhoMW 93
Kiger, Joseph Charles 1920- WhoAm 94
Kiger, Robby 1973- WhoHol 92
Kiger, Robert William 1940- WhoAm 94
Kight, Edward Hill 1935- WhoAm 94
Kigin, Thomas John 1948- WhoMW 93
Kigoshi, Kunihiko 1919- WhoAm 94, WhoScEn 94
Kihano, Daniel James 1933- WhoAmP 93
Kihira, Teiko 1928- WhoWomW 91
Kihle, Donald Arthur 1934- WhoAmL 94
Kihm, Kyung D. 1957- WhoScEn 94
Kihn, Harry 1912- WhoAm 94
Kihn, William Langdon 1898-1957 WhoAmA 93N
Kiilu, Raphael Muli 1938- IntWW 93
Kijanka, Stanley Joseph 1937-1981 WhoAmA 93N
Kijek, Nancy 1963- WhoFI 94
Kijewski, Michael Casimer 1949- WhoMW 93
Kijima, Torazo 1901- IntWW 93
Kikabidze, Vakhtang Konstantinovich 1938- IntWW 93
Kikel, Rudy John DrAPF 93
Kiker, Billy Frazier 1936- WhoAm 94
Kiker, Douglas 1930-1991 WhAm 10
Kiker, Evelyn Coalson 1932- WhoAmA 93
Kikhia, Mansur Rashid 1931- IntWW 93
Kiki, Albert Maori d1993 IntWW 93N
Kiki, (Albert) Maori d1993 Who 94N
Kiko, Philip George 1951- WhoAm 94
Kikoin, Konstantin 1945- IntWW 93
Kikoler, Stephen Philip 1945- WhoAmL 94
Kikuchi, Carl H. 1950- WhoAsA 94
Kikuchi, George Susumu WhoAsA 94
Kikuchi, Kiyoaki 1922- IntWW 93
Kikuchi, Ryoichi 1919- WhoWest 94
Kikuchi, Shinya 1943- WhoAsA 94, WhoScEn 94
Kikuchi, William Kenji 1935- WhoAsA 94
Kikuchi-Yngojo, Alan 1949- WhoAmA 93
Kikume, Al d1972 WhoHol 92
Kikumura, Akemi WhoAsA 94
Kikutake, Kiyonori 1928- IntWW 93
Kil, Bong-Seop 1938- WhoScEn 94
Kiland, Lance Edward 1947- WhoAmA 93
Kilander, Donald J. WhoAmP 93
Kilanowski, Michael Charles, Jr. 1948- WhoAm 94
Kilbane, Sally Conway 1942- WhoMW 93
Kilbane, Thomas M. 1953- WhoAmL 94
Kilbane, Thomas Stanton 1941- WhoAm 94
Kilberg, William Jeffrey 1946- WhoAmL 94, WhoAmP 93
Kilbert, Kenneth Keith 1955- WhoAmL 94
Kilborne, George Briggs 1930- WhoFI 94
Kilborne, William Skinner 1912- WhoAm 94
Kilbourn, Bernard Mason 1924- WhoAmP 93
Kilbourn, Matt 1928- WrDr 94
Kilbourn, William (Morley) 1926- WrDr 94
Kilbourn, William Douglas, Jr. 1924- WhoAmL 94
Kilbourne, Barbara Jean 1941- WhoFI 94, WhoMW 93
Kilbourne, Christopher N. 1956- WhoAmL 94
Kilbourne, Edwin Dennis 1920- WhoAm 94
Kilbourne, John Dwight 1926- WhoAm 94
Kilbourne, Lewis Buckner 1947- WhoAm 94, WhoFI 94
Kilbracken, Baron 1920- Who 94
Kilbracken, Lord 1920- WrDr 94
Kilbrick, Leonard 1924- WhoHol 92
Kilbrick, Sidney 1928- WhoHol 92
Kilbride, Dennis J. 1921- WhoAmP 93
Kilbride, James J. 1934- WhoIns 94
Kilbride, Percy d1964 WhoHol 92
Kilbride, Richard d1967 WhoHol 92
Kilburn, Edwin Allen 1933- WhoAm 94
Kilburn, Henry Thomas, Jr. 1931- WhoAm 94, WhoFI 94
Kilburn, Kaye Hatch 1931- WhoWest 94
Kilburn, Mary Helen 1945- WhoMW 93
Kilburn, Penelope White 1940- WhoFI 94, WhoScEn 94
Kilburn, Terry 1926- WhoHol 92
Kilburn, Tom 1921- IntWW 93, Who 94
Kilbury, Charles Debriel 1919- WhoAmP 93
Kilby, Craig McCoy 1959- WhoAmP 93
Kilby, Eric Christian 1949- WhoFI 94
Kilby, Gregory G. 1948- WhoFI 94
Kilby, Jack St. Clair 1923- WhoAm 94, WhoScEn 94, WorInv
Kilby, Michael Leopold 1924- Who 94
Kilby, Oscar Marchant 1897- WhAm 10
Kilcarr, Andrew Joseph 1932- WhoAm 94, WhoAmL 94
Kilcarr, J. Kenneth 1918- WhoAm 94
Kilcline, Thomas John 1925- WhoAm 94
Kilcrease, David Parker 1952- WhoWest 94
Kilcrease, Irvin Hugh, Jr. 1931- WhoBlA 94
Kildare, Marquess of 1948- Who 94
Kildare, Michel Walter Andre 1935- WhoBlA 94
Kildare And Leighlin, Bishop of 1931- Who 94
Kilde, Jeanne Halgren 1957- WhoMW 93
Kildee, Dale E. 1929- CngDr 93, WhoAmP 93
Kildee, Dale Edward 1929- WhoAm 94, WhoMW 93
Kildoo-Brown, Florence Ella 1918- WhoAmP 93
Kildsig, Nancy Evaline 1936- WhoMW 93
Kilduff, Helen d1959 WhoHol 92
Kile, Bradford E. 1943- WhoAmL 94
Kile, Carol Ann 1946- WhoAmL 94, WhoMW 93
Kile, Darryl Andrew 1968- WhoAm 94
Kile, Raymond Lawrence 1946- WhoWest 94
Kilenyi, Edward A. 1911- Who 94
Kilenyi, Julio 1886-1959 WhoAmA 93N
Kiley, Allan James 1946- WhoWest 94
Kiley, Dan (Edward) 1942- WrDr 94
Kiley, Daniel Urban 1912- WhoAm 94
Kiley, Edward A. 1941- WhoAmL 94
Kiley, James William 1944- WhoAm 94
Kiley, Richard 1922- IntMPA 94, WhoHol 92
Kiley, Richard B. WhoAmP 93
Kiley, Richard Paul 1922- WhoAm 94
Kiley, Robert Ralph 1948- WhoWest 94
Kiley, Roger J. 1937- WhoAm 94
Kiley, Thomas 1937- WhoWest 94
Kiley, Thomas James, Jr. 1949- WhoFI 94
Kiley, William Roger 1947- WhoMW 93
Kilfedder, James (Alexander) 1928- Who 94
Kilfoil, Geoffrey Everard 1939- Who 94
Kilfoyle, Peter 1946- Who 94
Kilgallen, Dorothy d1965 WhoHol 92
Kilgallen, Rob 1936- WhoHol 92
Kilgarin, Karen 1957- WhoAmP 93
Kilgarlin, William Wayne 1932- WhoAmP 93
Kilgore, Al 1927-1983 WhoAmA 93N
Kilgore, Donald Gibson, Jr. 1927- WhoAm 94, WhoFI 94, WhoScEn 94
Kilgore, Edwin Carroll 1923- WhoAm 94
Kilgore, Eugene Sterling, Jr. 1920- WhoAm 94
Kilgore, Glenn Kennedy 1946- WhoAmP 93
Kilgore, James Clifford, Jr. 1946- WhoFI 94
Kilgore, Joe Everett, Jr. 1954- WhoWest 94
Kilgore, Joe Madison 1918- WhoAm 94, WhoAmP 93
Kilgore, Joe Moffatt 1916- WhoMW 93
Kilgore, John Edward, Jr. 1921- WhoAm 94
Kilgore, Kathryn DrAPF 93
Kilgore, Rupert 1910-1971 WhoAmA 93N
Kilgore, Thomas, Jr. 1913- WhoBlA 94
Kilgore, Thomas M. 1935- WhoAmP 93
Kilgore, Tom D. 1944- WhoAm 94, WhoFI 94
Kilgore, Twanna Debbie 1954- WhoBlA 94
Kilgore, William Jackson 1917- WhoAm 94
Kilgour, Frederick Gridley 1914- WhoAm 94
Kilgour, John Lowell 1924- Who 94
Kilgour, Joseph d1933 WhoHol 92
Kilgour, Mary Cameron 1940- WhoAm 94
Kilham, Walter H. 1868-1948 WhoAmA 93N
Kilham, Walter H., Jr. 1904- WhoAm 94
Kilian, Austin Farland 1920- WhoAmA 93
Kilian, Crawford 1941- EncSF 93, WrDr 94
Kilian, Krzysztof 1958- IntWW 93
Kilian, Michael D. 1939- WhoAm 94
Kilian, Robert Joseph 1942- WhoScEn 94
Kilian, Thomas Randolph 1924- WhoMW 93
Kilian, Victor d1979 WhoHol 92
Kilian, Walter Daniel 1935- WhoAmP 93
Kilibarda, Vesna´ 1958- WhoMW 93
Kilichowski, Robert WhoAmP 93
Kilimanjaro, John Marshall 1930- WhoBlA 94
Kilina, Patricia GayLL
Kilkeary, John 1932- WhoIns 94
Kilkelly, Brian Holten 1943- WhoScEn 94
Kilkelly, Marjorie L. 1954- WhoAmP 93
Kilkenny, James H. 1923- WhoBlA 94
Kilkenny, John F. 1901- WhoAm 94, WhoAmL 94, WhoWest 94
Kilkenny, Timothy Rhodes 1957- WhoWest 94
Kilker, Clarence Christian 1905-1988 WhAm 10
Kilkson, Rein 1927- WhoScEn 94
Kill, Lawrence 1935- WhoAm 94
Killaloe, Bishop of 1922- Who 94
Killam, Anne Loretta 1928- WhoAmP 93
Killam, Eva King 1921- WhoAm 94
Killam, Jill Minervini 1954- WhoFI 94
Killam, Walt 1907-1979 WhoAmA 93N
Killanin, Baron 1914- IntWW 93, Who 94
Killday, K. Brian 1961- WhoScEn 94
Killdeer, John ConAu 42NR
Killdeer, John 1930- WrDr 94
Kille, Willard Bronson, III 1946- WhoFI 94
Killea, Lucy 1922- WhoHisp 94
Killea, Lucy Lytle 1922- WhoAmP 93
Killearn, Baron 1919- Who 94
Killebrew, Charles Joseph 1941- WhoScEn 94
Killebrew, Ellen Jane 1937- WhoScEn 94
Killebrew, Gwendolyn 1939- NewGrDO

Killebrew, James Robert 1918- *WhoAm 94*
Killebrew, Larry E. 1943- *WhoAmL 94*
Killebrew, Robert Sterling, Jr. 1939- *WhoAm 94, WhoFI 94*
Killeen, Henry Walter 1946- *WhoAm 94, WhoAmL 94*
Killeen, Melissa Helen 1955- *WhoAmA 93*
Killeen, Michael John 1949- *WhoAm 94, WhoAmL 94*
Killefer, Campbell 1950- *WhoAm 94*
Killefer, Tom 1917- *WhoAm 94*
Killen, Carroll Gorden 1919- *WhoAm 94, WhoFI 94*
Killen, (Denis) James 1925- *Who 94*
Killenberg, George Andrew 1917- *WhoAm 94*
Killens, John Oliver 1916-1987 *BlkWr 2*
Killen-Wolf, Anne 1959- *WhoFI 94*
Killey, Frances Ada 1911- *WhoAmP 93*
Killgore, Andrew Ivy 1919- *WhoAm 94*
Killgore, Mark William 1956- *WhoScEn 94*
Killhour, William Gherky 1925- *WhoFI 94*
Killiam, Paul 1916- *IntMPA 94*
Killian, Allan Joseph 1946- *WhoWest 94*
Killian, George Ernest 1924- *WhoAm 94, WhoWest 94*
Killian, Lewis Martin 1919- *WhoAm 94*
Killian, Mark W. 1955- *WhoAmP 93*
Killian, Patricia Dee 1942- *WhoAmP 93*
Killian, Richard M. 1942- *WhoWest 94*
Killian, Robert Kenneth 1919- *WhoAm 94, WhoAmP 93*
Killian, Robert Kenneth, Jr. 1947- *WhoAmL 94*
Killian, Ruth Selvey 1921- *WhoScEn 94*
Killian, William Paul 1935- *WhoAm 94*
Killick, Anthony John 1934- *Who 94*
Killick, John (Edward) 1919- *Who 94*
Killick, John Edward 1919- *IntWW 93*
Killick, Paul Victor St. John 1916- *Who 94*
Killick, Tony *Who 94*
Killigrew, Anne c. 1660-1685 *BlmGWL, DcLB 131 [port]*
Killigrew, Thomas 1612-1683 *BlmGEL*
Killin, Charles Clark 1923- *WhoAm 94*
Killingbeck, Maria A. 1943- *WhoMW 93*
Killinger, George Glenn 1908- *WhoAm 94*
Killinger, Kerry Kent 1949- *WhoAm 94, WhoFI 94, WhoWest 94*
Killingsworth, Charles Clinton 1917- *WhoAm 94*
Killingsworth, Colleen 1964- *WhoWest 94*
Killingsworth, James Woodrow, Jr. 1945- *WhoFI 94*
Killingsworth, Kathleen Nola 1952- *WhoWest 94*
Killingsworth, Thomas Ike 1948- *WhoAmP 93*
Killingsworth Finley, Sandra Jean 1950- *WhoBlA 94*
Killion, Frederick William, Jr. 1934- *WhoAmL 94*
Killion, Theo M. 1951- *WhoBlA 94*
Killion, William L. 1948- *WhoAmL 94*
Killip, Christopher David 1946- *IntWW 93*
Killmaster, John H. 1934- *WhoAmA 93*
Killmayer, Wilhelm 1927- *NewGrDO*
Killoran, Grant Colin 1964- *WhoAmL 94*
Killorin, Edward Wylly 1928- *WhoScEn 94*
Killorin, Robert Ware 1959- *WhoAmL 94*
Killory, Diane Silberstein 1954- *WhoAm 94*
Killough, Larry Neil 1932- *WhoAm 94*
Killough, (Karen) Lee 1942- *EncSF 93, WrDr 94*
Killpack, James Robert 1922- *WhoAm 94*
Killpack, Robert H. M. 1929- *WhoAmP 93*
Killum, Guy *WhoHol 92*
Killus, James Peter, Jr. 1950- *WhoWest 94*
Killy, Jean-Claude 1943- *IntWW 93, WhoHol 92*
Kilmaine, Baron 1948- *Who 94*
Kilman, James William 1931- *WhoAm 94*
Kilmann, Ralph Herman 1946- *WhoAm 94, WhoFI 94*
Kilmarnock, Baron 1927- *Who 94*
Kilmartin, Edward John 1923- *WhoAm 94*
Kilmartin, Joseph Francis, Jr. 1924- *WhoFI 94*
Kilmartin, Peter F. *WhoAmP 93*
Kilmartin, Sean Edward 1962- *WhoFI 94*
Kilmartin, Thomas John, III 1939- *WhoAm 94*
Kilmarx, Mary Neidlinger 1927- *WhoAmP 93*
Kilmer, James E. 1940- *WhoIns 94*
Kilmer, Karen Lynn 1951- *WhoMW 93*
Kilmer, Maurice Douglas 1928- *WhoWest 94*
Kilmer, Neal Harold 1943- *WhoScEn 94, WhoWest 94*
Kilmer, Patricia Marie 1959- *WhoWest 94*
Kilmer, Sally Jean 1936- *WhoMW 93*
Kilmer, Val 1959- *IntMPA 94, WhoAm 94, WhoHol 92*
Kilmister, (Claude Alaric) Anthony 1931- *Who 94*
Kilmister, Clive William 1924- *Who 94, WrDr 94*
Kilmore, Bishop of 1926- *Who 94*
Kilmore, Elphin And Ardagh, Bishop of 1941- *Who 94*
Kilmorey *Who 94*
Kilner, Suzanne Miiller 1951- *WhoMW 93*
Kilner Brown, Ralph *Who 94*
Kilpack, Bennett d1962 *WhoHol 92*
Kilpatric, Gary 1942- *WhoAmL 94*
Kilpatrick, Ada Arilla d1951 *WhoAmA 93N*
Kilpatrick, Andrew 1943- *ConAu 140*
Kilpatrick, Carolyn Cheeks 1945- *WhoAmP 93, WhoBlA 94, WhoMW 93*
Kilpatrick, Charles Otis 1922- *WhoAm 94*
Kilpatrick, Don 1939- *WhoAmP 93*
Kilpatrick, Ellen Perkins 1877-1951 *WhoAmA 93N*
Kilpatrick, Eric *WhoHol 92*
Kilpatrick, Francesca *Who 94*
Kilpatrick, George H. 1936- *WhoAm 94*
Kilpatrick, George Roosevelt 1938- *WhoBlA 94*
Kilpatrick, J. Thomas 1943- *WhoAmL 94*
Kilpatrick, James Jackson 1920- *WrDr 94*
Kilpatrick, James Jackson, Jr. 1920- *WhoAm 94*
Kilpatrick, Lincoln 1933- *WhoHol 92*
Kilpatrick, Mark Kevin 1955- *WhoAm 94*
Kilpatrick, Patrick *WhoHol 92*
Kilpatrick, Richardo Ivan 1952- *WhoBlA 94*
Kilpatrick, Robert 1924- *IntWW 93*
Kilpatrick, Robert 1926- *Who 94*
Kilpatrick, Robert Donald 1924- *WhoAm 94*
Kilpatrick, Robert Paul 1945- *WhoBlA 94*
Kilpatrick, Stewart *Who 94*
Kilpatrick, (George) Stewart 1925- *Who 94*
Kilpatrick, Thomas E. 1931- *WhoAmP 93*
Kilpi, Eeva 1928- *BlmGWL*
Kilpi, Volter *EncSF 93*
Kilroe, Patricia Anne 1955- *WhoMW 93*
Kilroy, Alix *Who 94*
Kilroy, James F(rancis) 1935- *WrDr 94*
Kilroy, John Muir 1918- *WhoAm 94*
Kilroy, Mary A. *WhoAmA 93*
Kilroy, Richard Ignatius 1927- *WhoAm 94*
Kilroy, Thomas 1934- *ConDr 93, IntDcT 2, WrDr 94*
Kilroy, William Terrence 1950- *WhoAm 94, WhoAmL 94*
Kilroy-Silk, Robert 1942- *Who 94*
Kilsheimer, Sidney Arthur 1930- *WhoMW 93*
Kilson, Marion D. de B. 1936- *WrDr 94*
Kilson, Martin Luther, Jr. 1931- *WhoAm 94, WhoBlA 94*
Kiltie, Richard Alan 1951- *WhoScEn 94*
Kilty, Jerome Timothy 1922- *WhoAm 94*
Kilty, William 1757-1821 *WhAmRev*
Kiltz, Sharon Saltzman 1937- *WhoAmP 93*
Kilvert, (Robert) Francis 1840-1879 *DcNaB MP*
Kilvert, Robert Francis 1840-1879 *BlmGEL*
Kilvington, Frank Ian 1924- *Who 94*
Kilworth, Garry 1941- *WrDr 94*
Kilworth, Garry (Douglas) 1941- *EncSF 93*
Kilzer, Louis Charles 1951- *WhoAm 94, WhoMW 93*
Kim, Alan Hyun-Oak 1932- *WhoAsA 94*
Kim, Anna Charr *WhoAsA 94*
Kim, Augustine H. 1965- *WhoAsA 94*
Kim, Bang Ja 1940- *WhoAsA 94*
Kim, Bong Hwan *WhoAsA 94*
Kim, Bong Yohl 1932- *WhoAsA 94*
Kim, Bonn-Oh 1956- *WhoAsA 94*
Kim, Byong-Kon 1929- *WhoAsA 94*
Kim, Byung-Dong 1943- *WhoScEn 94*
Kim, Byung Guk 1953- *WhoAsA 94*
Kim, Byung Kyu 1931- *WhoScEn 94*
Kim, Byung Suk 1942- *WhoAsA 94*
Kim, Chaesik 1949- *WhoAsA 94*
Kim, Chan-Hie 1935- *WhoAsA 94*
Kim, Chan-Wung 1958- *WhoAsA 94*
Kim, Chang Kyu 1949- *WhoAsA 94*
Kim, Changwook 1953- *WhoAsA 94*
Kim, Changyup Daniel 1921- *WhoAsA 94*
Kim, Charles Wesley 1926- *WhoAm 94*
Kim, Chin 1926- *WhoAsA 94*
Kim, Chin Hui 1956- *WhoAsA 94*
Kim, Chin-Woo 1936- *WhoAm 94*
Kim, Chong Lim 1937- *WhoAsA 94*
Kim, Choong Soon 1938- *WhoAsA 94*
Kim, Chulwan 1954- *WhoAsA 94*
Kim, Chung-Sook Charlotte 1940- *WhoAsA 94*
Kim, Chung Wook 1934- *WhoAm 94, WhoAsA 94*
Kim, David Doyung 1966- *WhoAsA 94*
Kim, David Ho-Sik 1935- *WhoAsA 94*
Kim, David Sang Chul 1915- *WhoAm 94, WhoAsA 94*
Kim, David U. 1932- *WhoAsA 94*
Kim, Diann Hyung 1958- *WhoAmL 94*
Kim, Donald Chang Won 1928- *WhoAsA 94*
Kim, Dongcheol 1955- *WhoAsA 94*
Kim, Donna A. 1952- *WhoAmP 93*
Kim, Donna Mercado *WhoAsA 94*
Kim, E. Han 1946- *WhoAm 94*
Kim, Earl 1920- *WhoAm 94*
Kim, Earnest Jae-Hyun 1938- *WhoFI 94*
Kim, Edward Ik Hwan 1919- *WhoAsA 94*
Kim, Edward J. 1934- *WhoAsA 94*
Kim, Edward Kui Nam, Jr. 1952- *WhoWest 94*
Kim, Edward William 1949- *WhoAm 94, WhoWest 94*
Kim, Elaine H(aikyung) 1942- *WrDr 94*
Kim, Eun Mee 1958- *WhoAsA 94*
Kim, Evan C. *WhoHol 92*
Kim, H. J. 1943- *WhoMW 93*
Kim, Haewon Chang 1943- *WhoAsA 94*
Kim, HakLin 1956- *WhoAsA 94*
Kim, Han-Seob 1934- *WhoAsA 94*
Kim, Hee-Jin 1927- *WhoAsA 94*
Kim, HeeMin 1958- *WhoAsA 94*
Kim, Heesook Park 1958- *WhoScEn 94*
Kim, Helen 1948- *WhoAsA 94*
Kim, Hesook Suzie 1939- *WhoAsA 94*
Kim, Hong Nack 1933- *WhoAsA 94*
Kim, Hong Yung 1939- *WhoAsA 94*
Kim, Hyong Sok 1962- *WhoAsA 94*
Kim, Hyun Kap 1934- *WhoAsA 94*
Kim, Hyun Wang 1945- *WhoAsA 94*
Kim, Hyung J. 1943- *WhoAsA 94*
Kim, Ih Chin 1925- *WhoScEn 94*
Kim, Il-Woon 1949- *WhoAsA 94*
Kim, Il Young 1947- *WhoAsA 94*
Kim, Ilpyong J. 1931- *WhoAsA 94*
Kim, Inn Seock 1954- *WhoScEn 94*
Kim, Irving Ilwoong 1940- *WhoFI 94, WhoWest 94*
Kim, Jae Hoon 1952- *WhoAsA 94*
Kim, Jae Nyoung 1960- *WhoScEn 94*
Kim, Jae Won 1947- *WhoAsA 94*
Kim, Jaegwon 1934- *WhoAm 94*
Kim, Jai Soo 1925- *WhoAm 94, WhoScEn 94*
Kim, James Hyung Jin *WhoWest 94*
Kim, James Joo-Jin 1936- *WhoAm 94, WhoAsA 94*
Kim, Jason Jungsun 1947- *WhoAsA 94*
Kim, Jay *WhoAmP 93*
Kim, Jay 1939- *CngDr 93, WhoAm 94, WhoWest 94*
Kim, Jay C. 1939- *WhoAsA 94*
Kim, Jay Chul 1936- *WhoAsA 94*
Kim, Jay S. 1958- *WhoAsA 94*
Kim, Jin-Keun 1952- *WhoScEn 94*
Kim, Jinchoon 1943- *WhoAsA 94*
Kim, Joanne Young 1940- *WhoAsA 94*
Kim, Jonathan Jang-Ho 1932- *WhoAsA 94*
Kim, Jonathan Yongchan 1963- *WhoMW 93*
Kim, Jong H. 1952- *WhoAsA 94*
Kim, Jong-Jin 1952- *WhoAsA 94*
Kim, Jong Koo 1933- *WhoAsA 94*
Kim, Jong Soo 1954- *WhoScEn 94*
Kim, Jong-Sung 1958- *WhoAsA 94*
Kim, Joochul 1948- *WhoAsA 94*
Kim, Joseph K. 1959- *WhoAsA 94*
Kim, Joung-Im 1947- *WhoWest 94*
Kim, Julie AngMi 1968- *WhoFI 94*
Kim, Jung Hwan 1955- *WhoAsA 94*
Kim, Jung Won 1948- *IntWW 93*
Kim, Jungnam Ego 1943- *WhoAsA 94*
Kim, Junguk Lawrence 1955- *WhoAsA 94*
Kim, Jwa Keun 1952- *WhoAsA 94*
Kim, Karl Eujung 1957- *WhoAsA 94*
Kim, Kathleen M. 1958- *WhoAsA 94*
Kim, Ke Chung 1934- *WhoAm 94*
Kim, Ken I. 1941- *WhoAsA 94*
Kim, Ki Hang 1936- *WhoAsA 94*
Kim, Ki Hoon 1933- *WhoAm 94, WhoAsA 94, WhoFI 94*
Kim, Ki Hwan 1946- *WhoAsA 94*
Kim, Kitai 1933- *WhoAsA 94*
Kim, Kunsoo 1943- *WhoAsA 94*
Kim, Kwan Hee 1952- *WhoAsA 94*
Kim, Kwang Ho 1946- *WhoScEn 94*
Kim, Kwang-Shin 1937- *WhoAsA 94*
Kim, Kyong-Min 1935- *WhoScEn 94*
Kim, Kyoo Hong 1948- *WhoAsA 94*
Kim, Kyuil 1952- *WhoFI 94*
Kim, Leo 1942- *WhoAsA 94*
Kim, Martha V. 1952- *WhoAmL 94*
Kim, Matthew Hidong 1958- *WhoWest 94*
Kim, Mi Ja 1940- *WhoAm 94*
Kim, Michael Charles 1950- *WhoAmL 94*
Kim, Michael Kyong-il 1940- *WhoAsA 94*
Kim, Michael Wooyung 1958- *WhoAsA 94*
Kim, Michael Yong 1962- *WhoAsA 94*
Kim, Moon G. 1941- *WhoAsA 94*
Kim, Moon H. 1934- *WhoAsA 94*
Kim, Moon Hyun 1934- *WhoAm 94*
Kim, Moon-Il 1929- *WhoScEn 94*
Kim, Moon Kyu 1943- *WhoAsA 94*
Kim, Myung-Hye 1953- *WhoAsA 94, WhoMW 93*
Kim, Myung Mi 1957- *WhoAsA 94*
Kim, Myung Soo 1948- *WhoScEn 94*
Kim, Myunghee 1932- *WhoScEn 94*
Kim, Nelli Vladimirovna 1957- *IntWW 93*
Kim, Neung Jip 1952- *WhoAsA 94*
Kim, Pan Soo 1947- *WhoFI 94*
Kim, Paul Chulhie 1963- *WhoFI 94*
Kim, Paul Myungchyun 1951- *WhoAsA 94, WhoWest 94*
Kim, Peter Sung-bai 1958- *WhoScEn 94*
Kim, Pilkyu 1940- *WhoAsA 94*
Kim, Po (Hyun) *WhoAmA 93*
Kim, Po Hyun *WhoAsA 94*
Kim, Poe *WhoAsA 94*
Kim, Quee-Young 1940- *WhoAsA 94*
Kim, Rhyn H. 1936- *WhoAsA 94*
Kim, Rhyn Hyun 1936- *WhoAm 94*
Kim, Richard E. *DrAPF 93*
Kim, Richard E. 1932- *WhoAsA 94, WrDr 94*
Kim, Robert 1930- *WhoAsA 94*
Kim, Robert Hyung-chan 1938- *WhoAsA 94*
Kim, Saeja Oh 1953- *WhoAsA 94*
Kim, Samuel Homer 1936- *WhoScEn 94*
Kim, Sang Phill 1954- *WhoAsA 94*
Kim, Sangtae 1958- *WhoScEn 94*
Kim, Sonja Chung 1941- *WhoMW 93*
Kim, Soon Jin 1927- *WhoAsA 94*
Kim, Soon-Kyu *WhoAsA 94*
Kim, Stephen Sou-hwan 1922- *IntWW 93*
Kim, Stephen Tae 1965- *WhoWest 94*
Kim, Sung Bok 1932- *WhoAsA 94*
Kim, Sung Chul 1945- *WhoScEn 94*
Kim, Sung-Hou 1937- *WhoAm 94, WhoScEn 94*
Kim, Sung Jin *WhoWest 94*
Kim, Sung Wan 1940- *WhoAsA 94, WhoScEn 94*
Kim, Suzy Linda 1961- *WhoAsA 94*
Kim, Synja P. *WhoAm 94, WhoFI 94*
Kim, Tae-Chul 1943- *WhoScEn 94*
Kim, Thomas Kunhyuk 1929- *WhoAm 94, WhoAsA 94*
Kim, Uichol 1958- *WhoAsA 94*
Kim, Vivian C. 1941- *WhoAsA 94*
Kim, Wan Hee 1926- *WhoAm 94*
Kim, Wan Joo 1942- *WhoScEn 94*
Kim, Wendell Kealohopauloe 1950?- *WhoAsA 94*
Kim, Willa *WhoAm 94*
Kim, Wun Jung 1950- *WhoAsA 94*
Kim, Yee S. 1928- *WhoAsA 94*
Kim, Yeong Ell 1933- *WhoMW 93*
Kim, Yong Bok 1940- *WhoAsA 94*
Kim, Yong Choon 1935- *WhoAm 94, WhoAsA 94*
Kim, Yong-Dal 1957- *WhoScEn 94*
Kim, Yong-Gwan 1957- *WhoAsA 94*
Kim, Yong Ik *WhoAsA 94*
Kim, Yong K. 1947- *WhoAsA 94*
Kim, Yong-Ki 1932- *WhoAsA 94*
Kim, Yongjeung 1898- *WhAm 10*
Kim, Yongmin 1953- *WhoScEn 94, WhoWest 94*
Kim, Yongshik 1925- *WhoAsA 94*
Kim, Yoon Berm 1929- *WhoAm 94, WhoScEn 94*
Kim, Yoonchung Park 1944- *WhoAsA 94*
Kim, Youdan 1960- *WhoScEn 94*
Kim, Youn-Suk 1934- *WhoAsA 94*
Kim, Young 1949- *WhoAmL 94*
Kim, Young (Hum) 1920- *WrDr 94*
Kim, Young-Bae 1936- *WhoAsA 94*
Kim, Young Chan 1956- *WhoAsA 94*
Kim, Young Choo 1923- *Who 94*
Kim, Young-Gurl 1956- *WhoAsA 94*
Kim, Young-Jin 1932- *WhoAsA 94*
Kim, Young Kil 1956- *WhoScEn 94*
Kim, Youngsoo Richard 1958- *WhoAsA 94*
Kim, Youngsuk 1954- *WhoAsA 94*
Kim, Yun 1934- *WhoAsA 94*
Kim, Yung Mo 1939- *WhoAsA 94*
Kim, Yunghi 1962- *WhoAsA 94*
Kim, Zaezeung 1929- *WhoMW 93, WhoScEn 94*
Kimack, Michael Allen 1942- *WhoAmP 93*
Kimak, George 1921-1972 *WhoAmA 93N*
Kimball, Baron 1928- *Who 94*
Kimball, Albert Boggess, Jr. 1940- *WhoAmL 94*
Kimball, Allyn Winthrop 1921- *WhoAm 94*
Kimball, Andrew 1858- *EncNAR*
Kimball, Bruce *WhoHol 92*
Kimball, Bruce Arnold 1941- *WhoAm 94*
Kimball, Catherine D. *WhoAmL 94*
Kimball, Charles Newton 1911- *WhoAm 94*

Kimball, Clyde Walker 1942- *WhoAmP 93*
Kimball, Clyde William 1928- *WhoAm 94*
Kimball, Curtis Rollin 1950- *WhoWest 94*
Kimball, Donald Robert 1938- *WhoMW 93*
Kimball, Donald W. 1947- *WhoWest 94*
Kimball, Edward Lawrence 1930- *WhoAm 94*
Kimball, Edward M. d1938 *WhoHol 92*
Kimball, Edward Martin 1946- *WhoMW 93*
Kimball, Elden Allen 1931- *WhoFI 94*
Kimball, Harry R. 1937- *WhoAm 94*
Kimball, John (Ward) 1931- *WrDr 94*
Kimball, K. Randall 1951- *WhoWest 94*
Kimball, Kerry E. *WhoAmP 93*
Kimball, Lindsley Fiske 1894-1992 *WhAm 10*
Kimball, Louis d1936 *WhoHol 92*
Kimball, Pauline Garrett d1919 *WhoHol 92*
Kimball, Raymond Alonzo 1918- *WhoAm 94*
Kimball, Raymond Joel 1948- *WhoAm 94, WhoAmL 94*
Kimball, Reid Roberts 1926- *WhoAm 94*
Kimball, Richard Allen, Jr. 1943- *WhoAmP 93*
Kimball, Richard Arthur, Jr. 1930- *WhoAm 94*
Kimball, Richard Nephi 1936- *WhoWest 94*
Kimball, Roger 1953- *WrDr 94*
Kimball, Spencer Wooley 1895-1985 *DcAmReB 2*
Kimball, Warren Forbes 1935- *IntWW 93*
Kimball, Wilford Wayne, Jr. 1943- *WhoAmA 93*
Kimball, Yeffe 1914-1978 *WhoAmA 93N*
Kimbell, Marion Joel 1923- *WhoWest 94*
Kimber, Charles Dixon 1912- *Who 94*
Kimber, Derek Barton 1917- *IntWW 93, Who 94*
Kimber, Herbert Frederick Sidney 1917- *Who 94*
Kimber, Lesly H. 1934- *WhoBlA 94*
Kimber, William 1872-1961 *DcNaB MP*
Kimberley, Earl of 1924- *Who 94*
Kimberley, A. G., Jr. 1939- *WhoWest 94*
Kimberley, Barry Paull *WhoScEn 94*
Kimberley, Berv 1929- *WhoAmP 93*
Kimberley, John A. *WhoScEn 94*
Kimberley, Maggie *WhoHol 92*
Kimberling, Charles Ronald 1950- *WhoAmP 93*
Kimberling, John Farrell 1926- *WhoAmL 94*
Kimberling, Paul Leroy 1953- *WhoMW 93*
Kimberly, Gail 1937- *EncSF 93*
Kimberly, John Robbins 1903-1992 *AnObit 1992*
Kimberly, John Robert 1942- *WhoAm 94*
Kimberly, William Essick 1933- *WhoAm 94, WhoFI 94*
Kimble, Bettye Dorris 1936- *WhoBlA 94*
Kimble, Bo (Greg) 1966- *WhoBlA 94*
Kimble, David (Bryant) 1921- *Who 94*
Kimble, David Wayne 1960- *WhoAmP 93*
Kimble, Fred R. 1949- *WhoAmP 93*
Kimble, George (Herbert Tinley) 1908- *Who 94, WrDr 94*
Kimble, Gregory Adams 1917- *WhoAm 94*
Kimble, James A. 1937- *WhoMW 93*
Kimble, James Alan 1960- *WhoMW 93*
Kimble, Mark Stephen 1952- *WhoWest 94*
Kimble, William Earl 1926- *WhoAm 94*
Kimbler, Delbert Lee, Jr. 1945- *WhoScEn 94*
Kimbler, Larry Bernard 1938- *WhoFI 94*
Kimbley, Dennis *IntMPA 94*
Kimbrell, Fuller Asbury *WhoAmP 93*
Kimbrell, Grady Ned 1933- *WhoWest 94*
Kimbrell, Jeffrey Andrew Drane 1956- *WhoFI 94, WhoMW 93*
Kimbrell, Leonard Buell 1922- *WhoAmA 93*
Kimbrell, Odell Culp, Jr. 1927- *WhoAm 94*
Kimbrell, Willard Duke 1924- *WhoAm 94*
Kimbrew, Joseph D. 1929- *WhoBlA 94*
Kimbriel, Katharine Eliska 1956- *EncSF 93*
Kimbro, Dennis Paul 1950- *WhoBlA 94*
Kimbro, Jean 1929- *WrDr 94*
Kimbro, John M. 1929- *WrDr 94*
Kimbrough, Allen Wayne 1953- *WhoAm 94, WhoAmL 94*
Kimbrough, Betty d1979 *WhoHol 92*
Kimbrough, Charles 1937-1989 *WhoHol 92*
Kimbrough, Charles Edward 1927- *WhoBlA 94*
Kimbrough, Clarence B. 1922- *WhoBlA 94*
Kimbrough, Clint 1936- *WhoHol 92*
Kimbrough, David Lester 1951- *WhoMW 93*
Kimbrough, Fred H. 1931- *WhoBlA 94*
Kimbrough, John 1920- *WhoHol 92*
Kimbrough, John Douglas 1959- *WhoAmL 94*
Kimbrough, Katheryn 1929- *WrDr 94*
Kimbrough, Marjorie L. 1937- *WhoBlA 94*
Kimbrough, Ralph Bradley, Sr. 1922- *WhoAm 94*
Kimbrough, Robert (Alexander, III) 1929- *WrDr 94*
Kimbrough, Robert Averyt 1933- *WhoAmL 94*
Kimbrough, Robert L. 1922- *WhoBlA 94*
Kimbrough, Roosevelt 1932-1991 *WhoBlA 94N*
Kimbrough, Sara Dodge d1990 *WhoAmA 93N*
Kimbrough, Ted D. *WhoBlA 94*
Kimbrough, Thomas J. 1934- *WhoBlA 94*
Kimbrough, Warren Oakley 1923- *WhoAmL 94*
Kimbrough, William Adams, Jr. 1935- *WhoAm 94, WhoAmL 94*
Kimbrough, William Duke 1896- *WhAm 10*
Kimbrough, William Walter, III 1928- *WhoAm 94, WhoMW 93*
Kimbrough-Johnson, Donna L. 1948- *WhoBlA 94*
Kim Ch'aek 1903-1951 *HisDcKW*
Kim Chong-Won 1922-1964 *HisDcKW*
Kim Dae Jung 1924- *IntWW 93*
Kim Dong-Jo 1918- *IntWW 93*
Kime, J. William *WhoAm 94*
Kime, John William 1934- *WhoAmP 93*
Kime, Loran Edward 1932- *WhoMW 93*
Kime, Thomas Stephen 1947- *WhoMW 93*
Kimel, William Robert 1922- *WhoScEn 94*
Kimelman, Donald Bruce 1947- *WhoAm 94*
Kimelman, Steven 1946- *WhoAmL 94*
Kimenye, Barbara *WrDr 94*
Kimenye, Barbara 1940- *BlmGWL*
Kimerer, Neil Banard, Sr. 1918- *WhoAm 94, WhoScEn 94*
Kimerer, Sandra Lynn 1951- *WhoFI 94*
Kimes, Bret David 1964- *WhoMW 93*
Kimes, Don 1950- *WhoAmA 93*
Kimes, Mark Edward 1965- *WhoScEn 94*
Kim Il Sung 1912- *HisDcKW*
Kim Il Sung, Grand Marshal 1912- *IntWW 93*
Kimitake, Hiraoka *GayLL*
Kim Jong Il, Marshal 1942- *IntWW 93*
Kim Jong Pil, Brig.-Gen. 1926- *IntWW 93*
Kim Joon-Sung *IntWW 93*
Kimm, Fiona 1952- *NewGrDO*
Kimm, Kevin Allen 1952- *WhoMW 93*
Kimm, Robert George 1943- *WhoMW 93*
Kim Mahn-Je 1934- *IntWW 93*
Kimmance, Peter Frederick 1922- *Who 94*
Kimme, Ernest Godfrey 1929- *WhoWest 94*
Kimme, William Brian 1962- *WhoAmL 94*
Kimmel, Bernard 1926- *WhoAmP 93*
Kimmel, Bruce 1948- *WhoHol 92*
Kimmel, Eric A. 1946- *WrDr 94*
Kimmel, Eugene Mark 1940- *WhoAmP 93*
Kimmel, George Stuart 1934- *WhoAm 94, WhoFI 94*
Kimmel, H. Steven 1946- *WhoAm 94*
Kimmel, Marek 1953- *WhoScEn 94*
Kimmel, Mark 1940- *WhoFI 94*
Kimmel, Melvin Joel 1944- *WhoScEn 94*
Kimmel, Morton Richard 1940- *WhoAmL 94*
Kimmel, Paul Robert 1947- *WhoFI 94*
Kimmel, Peter Scott 1947- *WhoFI 94*
Kimmel, Richard John 1942- *WhoScEn 94*
Kimmel, Robert Irving 1922- *WhoAm 94, WhoFI 94, WhoScEn 94*
Kimmel, Robert O. 1928- *WhoFI 94, WhoWest 94*
Kimmel-Cohn, Roberta 1937- *WhoAmA 93*
Kimmell, Curtis Vollmer 1915- *WhoAmP 93*
Kimmelman, Burt *DrAPF 93*
Kimmelman, Harold 1923- *WhoAmA 93*
Kimmelman, Leslie (Grodinsky) 1958- *WrDr 94*
Kimmelman, Michael Simon 1958- *WhoAm 94*
Kimmelman, William Charles 1958- *WhoAmL 94*
Kimmerling, Baruch 1939- *ConAu 141*
Kimmet, James L. 1948- *WhoMW 93*
Kimmey, James Richard, Jr. 1935- *WhoAm 94*
Kimmey, Michael Bryant 1953- *WhoWest 94*
Kimmich, Christoph Martin 1939- *WhoAm 94*
Kimmins, Anthony d1964 *WhoHol 92*
Kimmins, Kenneth *WhoHol 92*
Kimmins, Simon Edward Anthony 1930- *Who 94*
Kimmins, William John, Jr. 1952- *WhoMW 93*
Kimmis, Shanna Deneane *WhoMW 93*
Kimmitt, Robert Michael 1947- *WhoAm 94, WhoAmP 93*
Kimmle, Manfred 1942- *WhoAm 94*
Kimmons, Carl Eugene 1920- *WhoBlA 94*
Kimmons, Willie James 1944- *WhoBlA 94*
Kimnach, Myron William 1922- *WhoAm 94*
Kimpel, Benjamin Franklin 1905- *WhoAm 94, WrDr 94*
Kimple, Louis T. 1922-1988 *WhAm 10*
Kimport, David Lloyd 1945- *WhoAmL 94*
Kimpton, David Raymond 1942- *WhoWest 94*
Kim Sae-Sun 1901-1989 *HisDcKW*
Kim Sang-Hyup 1920- *IntWW 93*
Kimsey, Marty E. 1958- *WhoAmP 93*
Kimsey, Rustin Ray 1935- *WhoWest 94*
Kimsey, Shirley I. 1930- *WhoAmP 93*
Kimsey, Shirley Irene 1930- *WhoMW 93*
Kim Suk Won 1893-1978 *HisDcKW*
Kim Sung Soo 1891-1955 *HisDcKW*
Kim Tu-Bong 1889-1961? *HisDcKW*
Kim Ung 1928- *HisDcKW*
Kimura, Alton Mahner 1961- *WhoFI 94*
Kimura, Brian 1949- *WhoAsA 94*
Kimura, Donna Junko 1964- *WhoAsA 94*
Kimura, Doreen *WhoAm 94*
Kimura, Gwen C. 1955- *WhoAsA 94*
Kimura, Haruo 1925- *WhoScEn 94*
Kimura, Joan Alexandra 1934- *WhoAmA 93*
Kimura, Kolin M. 1950- *WhoAsA 94*
Kimura, Kongo 1919- *WhoAsA 94*
Kimura, Lillian C. 1929- *WhoAsA 94*
Kimura, Massa Kichi d1918 *WhoHol 92*
Kimura, Mineo 1946- *WhoAsA 94*
Kimura, Motoo 1924- *IntWW 93, WorScD*
Kimura, Riisaburo 1924- *WhoAmA 93*
Kimura, Risaburo 1924- *WhoAsA 94*
Kimura, Robert Shigetsugu 1920- *WhoScEn 94*
Kimura, Sueko M. *WhoAmA 93*
Kimura, William Yusaburo 1920- *WhoAmA 93*
Kimweli, David Mutua 1955- *WhoFI 94*
Kim Woun-Gie 1924- *IntWW 93*
Kim Yong Shik 1913- *IntWW 93*
Kim Young Sam 1927- *IntWW 93*
Kimzey, John Howard 1922- *WhoScEn 94*
Kinaga, Patricia Anne 1953- *WhoAsA 94*
Kinahan, Charles Henry Grierson 1915- *Who 94*
Kinahan, Oliver John 1923- *Who 94*
Kinahan, Robert (George Caldwell) 1916- *Who 94*
Kinaka, William Tatsuo 1940- *WhoAmL 94*
Kinard, Frank d1985 *ProFbHF*
Kinard, Hargett Yingling 1912- *WhoAm 94*
Kinard, Helen Madison Marie Pawne *WhoBlA 94*
Kinard, James Campsen 1895- *WhAm 10*
Kinard, James E., Jr. *WhoAmP 93*
Kinard, Mike 1939- *WhoAmP 93*
Kinard, William Robert 1946- *WhoAmP 93*
Kinariwala, Bharat 1926- *WhoAm 94*
Kinashi, Doreen Ann 1957- *WhoWest 94*
Kinberg, Judy 1948- *WhoAm 94*
Kincade, James 1925- *Who 94*
Kincaid, Aron 1943- *WhoHol 92*
Kincaid, D. Thomas 1930- *WhoFI 94*
Kincaid, Donald R. 1936- *WhoAmP 93*
Kincaid, Hugh Reid 1934- *WhoAm 94*
Kincaid, J. D. 1936- *WrDr 94*
Kincaid, Jamaica *DrAPF 93*
Kincaid, Jamaica 1949- *BlkWr 2, BlmGWL, TwCYAW, WhoBlA 94, WrDr 94*
Kincaid, Joan Payne *DrAPF 93*
Kincaid, Lloyd H. 1925- *WhoAmP 93*
Kincaid, Owings Wilson 1921- *WhoAm 94*
Kincaid, Robert M., Jr. 1952- *WhoAm 94*
Kincaid, William K. 1911- *WhoAmP 93*
Kincart, Robert Owen 1949- *WhoAm 94, WhoFI 94*
Kinch, Anthony Alec 1926- *Who 94*
Kinch, E. L. Lee 1939- *WhoAmL 94, WhoAmP 93*
Kinch, Henry S. *WhoAmP 93*
Kinch, Myra d1981 *WhoHol 92*
Kincheloe, Lawrence Ray 1941- *WhoWest 94*
Kincheloe, William Ladd 1925- *WhoScEn 94*
Kinchen, Dennis Ray 1946- *WhoBlA 94*
Kinchen, Richard 1948- *Who 94*
Kinchen, Robert Preston 1933- *WhAm 10*
Kinchin Smith, Michael 1921- *Who 94*
Kinchlow, Harvey Ben 1936- *WhoBlA 94*
Kincke, John Milton 1954- *WhoFI 94*
Kincl, Frantisek 1941- *IntWW 93*
Kincraig, Hon. Lord 1918- *Who 94*
Kincses, Robert Andrew 1947- *WhoMW 93*
Kincses, Veronika *IntWW 93*
Kincses, Veronika 1948- *NewGrDO*
Kind, Dieter Hans 1929- *IntWW 93*
Kind, Johann Friedrich 1768-1843 *NewGrDO*
Kind, Joshua B. 1933- *WhoAmA 93*
Kind, Kenneth Wayne 1948- *WhoAmL 94, WhoWest 94*
Kind, Marien *BlmGWL*
Kind, Phyllis *WhoAmA 93*
Kind, Richard *WhoHol 92*
Kind, Richard John 1941- *WhoAm 94*
Kind, Roslyn 1951- *WhoHol 92*
Kindahl, Connie *WhoAmA 93*
Kindall, Luther Martin 1942- *WhoBlA 94*
Kindel, James Horace, Jr. 1913- *WhoAm 94*
Kindel, Joseph Martin 1943- *WhoWest 94*
Kinden, Terance John 1952- *WhoFI 94*
Kinder, Eric 1927- *Who 94*
Kinder, Harold M. 1911- *WhAm 10*
Kinder, James Allen 1946- *WhoAm 94*
Kinder, Peter *WhoAmP 93*
Kinder, Randolph Samuel, Jr. 1944- *WhoBlA 94*
Kinder, Richard Dan 1944- *WhoAm 94, WhoFI 94*
Kinder, Tonja Valrie 1966- *WhoAmL 94*
Kindermann, August 1817-1891 *NewGrDO*
Kindermann, Hedwig Reicher- *NewGrDO*
Kindermann, Helmmo 1947- *WhoAmA 93*
Kindersley, Baron 1929- *Who 94*
Kindersley, Claude Richard Henry d1993 *Who 94N*
Kindersley, David Guy 1915- *Who 94*
Kindersley, Peter David 1941- *Who 94*
Kinderwater, Joseph C. 1922- *WhoAm 94*
Kindig, Fred Eugene 1920- *WhoAm 94*
Kindleberger, Charles P., II 1910- *WhoAm 94, WhoFI 94*
Kindleberger, Charles Poor 1910- *IntWW 93*
Kindley, Jeffrey (Bowman) 1945- *WrDr 94*
Kindness, Thomas Norman 1929- *WhoAm 94, WhoAmP 93*
Kindred, Wendy 1937- *WrDr 94*
Kindrick, Robert LeRoy 1942- *WhoAm 94, WhoWest 94*
Kinds, Herbert Eugene 1933- *WhoMW 93*
Kindschuh, Jeffery Alan 1956- *WhoFI 94*
Kindschy, Errol Roy 1938- *WhoAmP 93*
Kindt, John Warren, Sr. 1950- *WhoAm 94, WhoAmL 94*
Kindt, Lois Jeannette 1927- *WhoAmP 93*
Kindt, Thomas James 1939- *WhoAm 94, WhoScEn 94*
Kiner, Ralph 1922- *WhoAm 94*
Kiner, William Allen 1945- *WhoAmP 93*
King *Who 94*
King, Ada d1940 *WhoHol 92*
King, Adam Jeremy 1955- *WhoMW 93*
King, Adele Cockshoot 1932- *WhoMW 93*
King, Adrian R. 1943- *WhoAmL 94*
King, Adrienne *WhoHol 92*
King, Alan *NewYTBS 93 [port]*
King, Alan 1926- *WhoCom [port]*
King, Alan 1927- *IntMPA 94, WhoAm 94, WhoHol 92*
King, Albert *EncSF 93*
King, Albert 1905- *Who 94*
King, Albert 1923-1992 *AnObit 1992, WhoBlA 94N*
King, Albert 1959- *WhoBlA 94*
King, Albert I. 1934- *WhoScEn 94*
King, Albert Leslie 1911- *Who 94*
King, Alexander 1900-1965 *WhoCom*
King, Alexander 1909- *Who 94*
King, Alexander Hyatt 1911- *Who 94*
King, Alexander Louis 1914- *WhoWest 94*
King, Alfred Meehan 1933- *WhoFI 94*
King, Algin Braddy 1926- *WhoAm 94, WhoFI 94*
King, Alison Beth 1957- *WhoScEn 94*
King, Allen H. 1947- *WhoAmL,94*
King, Allyn d1930 *WhoHol 92*
King, Alvin M. 1935- *WhoAmP 93*
King, Amy C. 1947- *WhoAmP 93*
King, Andre Richardson 1931- *WhoAm 94*
King, Andrea 1915- *WhoHol 92*
King, Andrea 1919- *IntMPA 94*
King, Anita d1963 *WhoHol 92*
King, Anita 1931- *WhoBlA 94*
King, Anna Elizabeth 1897- *WhAm 10*
King, Annette Faye 1947- *WhoWomW 91*
King, Anthony 1934- *WrDr 94*
King, Anthony Gabriel 1953- *WhoAm 94*
King, Anthony Stephen 1934- *Who 94*
King, Arnold Kimsey 1901-1992 *WhAm 10*
King, Arthur Hood 1927- *WhoAm 94*
King, Arthur Thomas 1938- *WhoBlA 94*
King, August Allen 1910-1990 *WhAm 10*
King, B. B. 1925- *AfrAmAl 6 [port], IntWW 93, WhoAm 94, WhoHol 92*
King, B. B. (Riley) 1925- *WhoBlA 94*

King, Barbara Lewis 1930- *WhoBlA 94*
King, Barrington 1930- *WhoAmP 93*
King, Bernard 1946- *Who 94*
King, Bernard 1956- *BasBi, WhoBlA 94*
King, Bernard T. 1935- *WhoAmL 94*
King, Bernice Albertine *WhoBlA 94*
King, Betsy *WhoAm 94*
King, Betty 1932- *WhoAmP 93*
King, Betty (Alice) 1919- *WrDr 94*
King, Betty Marie 1937- *WhoAmP 93*
King, Billie Jean 1943- *BuCMET [port], IntWW 93, Who 94, WrDr 94*
King, Billie Jean Moffitt 1943- *WhoAm 94*
King, Billy d1972 *WhoHol 92*
King, Blondie Cherry 1933- *WhoAm 94*
King, Boyd d1940 *WhoHol 92*
King, Brian Edmund 1928- *Who 94*
King, Bruce *WhoAmP 93*
King, Bruce 1924- *WhoAm 94, WhoWest 94*
King, Bruce (Alvin) 1933- *WrDr 94*
King, Bruce A(lvin) 1933- *ConAu 41NR*
King, Bruce Allen 1952- *WhoAmL 94*
King, Burton d1944 *WhoHol 92*
King, Calvin 1951- *WhoWest 94*
King, Calvin E. 1928- *WhoBlA 94*
King, Cammie 1934- *WhoHol 92*
King, Carl B. 1942- *WhoAmL 94, WhoFI 94*
King, Carl Edward 1940- *WhoFI 94*
King, Carl Leander 1924- *WhoAmP 93*
King, Carlton d1932 *WhoHol 92*
King, Carol Ertel 1954- *WhoFI 94*
King, Carole 1941- *WhoHol 92*
King, Carole 1942- *WhoAm 94*
King, Carolyn Dineen *WhoAmP 93*
King, Carolyn Dineen 1938- *WhoAm 94, WhoAmL 94*
King, Cary Judson, III 1934- *WhoAm 94*
King, Cecilia D. 1950- *WhoBlA 94*
King, Celes, III 1923- *WhoBlA 94*
King, Ceola 1927- *WhoBlA 94*
King, Charles d1944 *WhoHol 92*
King, Charles d1957 *WhoHol 92*
King, Charles Abraham 1924- *WhoBlA 94*
King, Charles Andrew Buchanan 1915- *Who 94*
King, Charles E. 1911- *WhoBlA 94*
King, Charles E. 1920- *WhoBlA 94*
King, Charles G. 1944- *WhoAmL 94*
King, Charles Herbert, Jr. 1927- *WhoScEn 94*
King, Charles Homer 1938- *WhoMW 93*
King, Charles Larry 1950- *WhoAm 94*
King, Charles Martin M. *Who 94*
King, Charles McDonald, Jr. 1934- *WhoAm 94*
King, Charles Ross 1925- *WhoAm 94, WhoMW 93*
King, Charolette Elaine 1945- *WhoWest 94*
King, Chester Harding, Jr. 1913- *WhoAm 94*
King, Christine Ledesma 1945- *WhoAm 94*
King, Clarence 1842-1901 *WhWE [port]*
King, Clarence Maurice, Jr. 1934- *WhoBlA 94*
King, Clark Chapman, Jr. 1929- *WhoAm 94*
King, Claude d1941 *WhoHol 92*
King, Clinton Blair 1901-1979 *WhoAmA 93N*
King, (David) Clive 1924- *WrDr 94*
King, Clyde Richard 1924- *WhoAm 94*
King, Colbert I. 1939- *WhoBlA 94*
King, Colin 1943- *SmATA 76 [port]*
King, Colin Sainthill W. *Who 94*
King, Coretta Scott 1927- *AfrAmAl 6 [port], AmSocL, HisWorL [port], IntWW 93, WhoAm 94, WhoBlA 94*
King, Cristina Marta 1965- *WhoHisp 94*
King, Cynthia *DrAPF 93*
King, Cynthia 1925- *WrDr 94*
King, D. Brian 1963- *WhoAmL 94*
King, Damon D. 1934- *WhoAm 94*
King, Daniel Patrick 1942- *WhoFI 94*
King, Daniel Richard 1940- *WhoWest 94*
King, David 1929- *WhoHol 92*
King, David 1940- *WhoWest 94*
King, David 1968- *WhoMW 93*
King, David Anthony 1939- *IntWW 93, Who 94*
King, David Burnett 1930- *WhoWest 94*
King, David Carlton 1947- *WhoAmL 94*
King, David Edgar 1936- *WhoAm 94*
King, David Milton 1943- *WhoAmP 93*
King, David O. 1938- *WhoAmP 93*
King, David Roy 1950- *WhoAm 94, WhoAmL 94*
King, David Steven 1960- *WhoScEn 94*
King, David W. 1946- *WhoAm 94, WhoAmP 93, WhoWest 94*
King, Delutha Harold 1924- *WhoBlA 94*
King, Dennis d1971 *WhoHol 92*
King, Dennis, Jr. d1986 *WhoHol 92*
King, (William) Dennis 1941- *WrDr 94*
King, Diana *WhoHol 92*
King, Dominic Benson 1928- *WhoAm 94, WhoFI 94*
King, Dominique Desiree 1956- *WhoAmP 93*
King, Don 1931- *WhoBlA 94*
King, Don 1932- *WhoAm 94*
King, Don E. 1939- *WhoScEn 94*
King, Donald C. 1930- *WhoAm 94*
King, Donald E. 1934- *WhoBlA 94*
King, Donald Edward 1951- *WhoAm 94*
King, Dorothy E. *DrAPF 93*
King, Douglas Lohr 1941- *WhoAm 94*
King, Edgar Lee *WhoBlA 94*
King, Edith 1896- *WhoHol 92*
King, Edmund James 1914- *Who 94*
King, Edward J. 1925- *WhoAmP 93*
King, Edward Laurie 1920- *Who 94*
King, Edward Louis 1920- *WhoAm 94*
King, Edward William 1923- *WhoAm 94*
King, Elaine A. 1947- *WhoAm 94, WhoAmA 93*
King, Eleanor 1909- *WhoAmA 93*
King, Elizabeth *WhoAmP 93*
King, Ellen McGinty 1946- *WhoAmL 94*
King, Elmer Richard 1916-1992 *WhAm 10*
King, Emeline *AfrAmAl 6*
King, Emery C. 1948- *WhoBlA 94*
King, Emmett d1953 *WhoHol 92*
King, Eugene d1950 *WhoHol 92*
King, Evelyn Mansfield 1907- *Who 94*
King, Florence 1936- *ConAu 41NR*
King, Francis 1923- *DcLB 139 [port]*
King, Francis (Henry) 1923- *WrDr 94*
King, Francis Henry 1923- *IntWW 93, Who 94*
King, Francis P 1922- *WrDr 94*
King, Frank *WhoWest 94*
King, Frank (Douglas) 1919- *Who 94*
King, Frank Douglas 1919- *IntWW 93*
King, Frank O. 1883-1969 *WhoAmA 93N*
King, Frank P. 1921- *WhoAmP 93*
King, Frank William 1922- *WhoWest 94*
King, Franklin Weaver 1942- *WhoAmL 94*
King, Frederic 1937- *WhoWest 94*
King, Frederick Alexander 1925- *WhoAm 94, WhoScEn 94*
King, Frederick Ernest *Who 94*
King, Frederick J., Jr. 1945- *WhoAmP 93*
King, Frederick Jenks, Jr. 1945- *WhoAmL 94*
King, G. Roger 1946- *WhoAm 94, WhoAmL 94*
King, Garr Michael 1936- *WhoAmL 94*
King, Gary K. *WhoAmP 93*
King, George Gerard 1940- *WhoAm 94, WhoFI 94*
King, George Raleigh 1931- *WhoMW 93*
King, George Savage, Jr. 1941- *WhoAmL 94*
King, George W., Jr. 1936- *WhoBlA 94*
King, Gilbert 1898- *WhAm 10*
King, Glynda Bowman 1946- *WhoAmP 93*
King, Graham (Peter) 1930- *WrDr 94*
King, Gundar Julian 1926- *WhoAm 94, WhoWest 94*
King, Gwendolyn S. *WhoFI 94*
King, Gwendolyn Stewart *WhoBlA 94*
King, Gwendolyn Stewart 1940- *WhoAmP 93*
King, Hamilton 1871-1952 *WhoAmA 93N*
King, Harley *DrAPF 93*
King, Harold Lloyd 1926- *WhoAmP 93*
King, Harry Robert *WhoAm 94*
King, Hedley 1949- *ConAu 141*
King, Helen Eileen 1920- *WhoWest 94*
King, Henry d1974 *WhoHol 92*
King, Henry d1982 *WhoHol 92*
King, Henry 1592-1669 *BlmGEL*
King, Henry Lawrence 1928- *WhoAm 94*
King, Hetty d1972 *WhoHol 92*
King, Hilary William 1919- *Who 94*
King, Hodge 1914- *WhoBlA 94*
King, Howard O. 1925- *WhoBlA 94*
King, Hulas H. 1946- *WhoBlA 94*
King, Imogene M. 1923- *WhoAm 94*
King, Indle Gifford 1934- *WhoAm 94, WhoWest 94*
King, Isobel Wilson *Who 94*
King, Ivan R(obert) 1927- *IntWW 93*
King, Ivan Robert 1927- *WhoAm 94, WhoWest 94*
King, J. B. *WhoAmL 94*
King, Jack d1943 *WhoHol 92*
King, Jack A. 1936- *WhoAmL 94, WhoIns 94*
King, Jack L. 1939- *WhoFI 94*
King, Jacquelyn S. 1965- *WhoMW 93*
King, James 1750-1784 *WhWE*
King, James 1925- *NewGrDO*
King, James, Jr. 1933- *WhoBlA 94*
King, James B. 1935- *WhoAm 94*
King, James Barton 1935- *WhoAmP 93*
King, James Calvin 1945- *WhoAm 94, WhoMW 93*
King, James Cecil 1924- *WhoAm 94*
King, James Claude 1924- *WhoAm 94*
King, James E., Jr. 1939- *WhoAmP 93*
King, James Edward 1940- *WhoAm 94*
King, James Lawrence 1922- *Who 94*
King, James Lawrence 1927- *WhoAm 94, WhoAmL 94*
King, James Nedwed 1947- *WhoAm 94*
King, James P. *WhoAmP 93*
King, James Patrick 1946- *WhoFI 94*
King, James R. 1946- *WhoAm 94, WhoAmL 94*
King, Jane Cudlip Coblentz 1922- *WhoWest 94*
King, Jane Louise 1951- *WhoWest 94*
King, Janet Carlson 1941- *WhoWest 94*
King, Janey 1947- *WrDr 94*
King, Jean Ledwith 1924- *WhoAmP 93*
King, Jeanne Faith 1934- *WhoBlA 94*
King, Jeffrey William Hitchen 1906- *Who 94*
King, Jerry Daniel 1945- *WhoAmP 93*
King, Jerry Wayne 1942- *WhoMW 93, WhoScEn 94*
King, Jodie W. 1957- *WhoAmL 94*
King, John *EncSF 93*
King, John d1987 *WhoHol 92*
King, John 1937- *WhoAmP 93*
King, John (Christopher) 1933- *Who 94*
King, John (Edward) 1947- *WrDr 94*
King, John A. 1925- *WhoAmP 93*
King, John Arthur Charles 1933- *Who 94*
King, John Charles Peter 1949- *WhoAm 94*
King, John Earl 1946- *WhoIns 94*
King, John Edward 1922- *Who 94*
King, John Ethelbert, Jr. 1913- *WhoAm 94*
King, John Francis 1925- *WhoAm 94*
King, John G. 1925- *WhoBlA 94*
King, John J., Jr. 1945- *WhoAmL 94*
King, John Joseph 1924- *WhoFI 94, WhoMW 93*
King, John L. 1952- *WhoBlA 94*
King, John Lane 1924- *WhoAm 94*
King, John LaVerne, III 1946- *WhoScEn 94*
King, John Norman 1945- *WhoMW 93*
King, John Q. Taylor, Sr. 1921- *AfrAmG [port], WhoBlA 94*
King, John Quill Taylor 1921- *WhoAm 94*
King, John Reed d1979 *WhoHol 92*
King, John Robert 1948- *EncSF 93*
King, John Thomas 1935- *WhoBlA 94*
King, John W. 1918- *WhoAmP 93*
King, John William Beaufoy 1927- *Who 94*
King, Jonathan 1925- *WhoAm 94*
King, Jonathan Alan 1941- *WhoScEn 94*
King, Jonathan David 1958- *WhoWest 94*
King, Joseph d1951 *WhoHol 92*
King, Joseph d1989 *Who 94N*
King, Joseph Bertram 1924- *WhoAm 94*
King, Joseph E. 1941- *WhoIns 94*
King, Joseph E. 1945- *WhoAmP 93*
King, Joseph Michael 1953- *WhoAmL 94*
King, Joseph Paul 1941- *WhoAm 94*
King, Joseph Prather 1927- *WhoBlA 94*
King, Joseph Willet 1934- *WhoScEn 94*
King, Julian F. 1931- *WhoBlA 94*
King, Julius Wade 1922- *WhoAmP 93*
King, Kathryn Theresa 1960- *WhoMW 93*
King, Kay Sue 1948- *WhoMW 93*
King, Keith E. 1954- *WhoFI 94*
King, Kenneth *DrAPF 93*
King, Kenneth H., Jr. 1948- *WhoAmL 94*
King, Kenneth R. *WhoAmP 93*
King, Kenneth Vernon, Jr. 1950- *WhoScEn 94*
King, Kernan Francis 1944- *WhoAm 94, WhoAmL 94, WhoFI 94*
King, Kerry c. 1967- *See* Slayer *ConMus 10*
King, Kimberly Nelson 1953- *WhoScEn 94*
King, Kip 1934- *WhoHol 92*
King, L. Ellis 1939- *WhoAm 94*
King, Larry 1933- *IntMPA 94, WhoAm 94*
King, Larry 1934- *WhoHol 92*
King, Larry L. 1929- *WhoAm 94, WhoHol 92, WrDr 94*
King, Laura Jane 1947- *WhoMW 93*
King, Lauren Alfred 1904- *WhoMW 93*
King, Laurie R. 1952- *ConAu 140*
King, Lawrence C. *WhoBlA 94*
King, Lawrence P. 1940- *WhoBlA 94*
King, Lawrence Patrick 1940- *WhoBlA 94*
King, Lawrence Philip 1929- *WhoAm 94, WhoAmL 94*
King, Leland W. 1907- *WhoAm 94*
King, Leon 1921- *WhoAm 94*
King, Leonard James 1925- *IntWW 93, Who 94*
King, LeRoy J. 1920- *WhoBlA 94*
King, Leslie d1947 *WhoHol 92*
King, Leslie Darnell 1949- *WhoAmP 93*
King, Leslie John 1934- *WhoAm 94*
King, Lewis Henry *WhoBlA 94*
King, Lewis M. 1942- *WhoBlA 94*
King, Lionel Detlev Percival 1906- *WhoScEn 94, WhoWest 94*
King, Llewellyn Joseph, Jr. *WhoFI 94*
King, Lloyd 1936- *WhoBlA 94*
King, Louis d1962 *WhoHol 92*
King, Lowell Restell 1932- *WhoAm 94*
King, Lucille d1977 *WhoHol 92*
King, Lyndel Irene Saunders 1943- *WhoAm 94, WhoAmA 93*
King, Mabel *WhoHol 92*
King, Mabel Debra 1895-1950 *WhoAmA 93N*
King, MacLellan Edgar, Jr. 1937- *WhoWest 94*
King, Marcellus, Jr. 1943- *WhoBlA 94*
King, Marcia 1940- *WhoAm 94, WhoWest 94*
King, Margaret Ann 1936- *WhoFI 94, WhoMW 93*
King, Margaret Leah 1947- *WhoAm 94*
King, Marjorie Pitter 1921- *WhoAmP 93*
King, Mark Charles 1961- *WhoFI 94*
King, Martha *DrAPF 93*
King, Martin Luther, Sr. 1899-1984 *HisWorL*
King, Martin Luther, Jr. 1929-1968 *AfrAmAl 6 [port], AmSocL [port], BlkWr 2, DcAmReB 2, EncEth, HisWorL [port]*
King, Mary Booker 1937- *WhoBlA 94*
King, Mary-Claire 1946- *WhoScEn 94*
King, Mary Elizabeth 1940- *WhoAmP 93*
King, Mary Etta *WhoAmA 93*
King, Matthew Peter c. 1773-1823 *NewGrDO*
King, Mattie M. 1919- *WhoBlA 94*
King, Maurice Athelstan 1936- *IntWW 93*
King, Max 1959- *WhoFI 94*
King, Maxwell E. P. *WhoAm 94*
King, Mervyn Allister 1948- *IntWW 93, Who 94*
King, Michael *Who 94*
King, Michael 1934- *Who 94*
King, (Denys) Michael (Gwilym) 1929- *Who 94*
King, Michael B. 1952- *WhoAmP 93*
King, Michael Gardner 1920- *Who 94*
King, Michael Howard 1943- *WhoAm 94, WhoAmL 94*
King, Mollie d1982 *WhoHol 92*
King, Morgana 1930- *WhoAm 94, WhoHol 92*
King, Morris Kenton 1924- *WhoAm 94*
King, Myron Lyzon 1921- *WhoAmA 93*
King, Nancy Jane 1945- *WhoFI 94*
King, Ned *WhoAmP 93*
King, Nicolette Jane 1962- *WhoWest 94*
King, Nina Davis 1941- *WhoAm 94*
King, Norah M. 1949- *WhoAm 94, WhoAmL 94*
King, Norman (Ross Dutton) 1933- *Who 94*
King, Nosmo d1949 *WhoHol 92*
King, Olin B. 1934- *WhoAm 94, WhoFI 94*
King, Oliver *Who 94*
King, (John) Oliver (Letts) 1914- *Who 94*
King, Ordie Herbert, Jr. 1933- *WhoAm 94*
King, Oscar Lloyd 1922- *WhoWest 94*
King, Patricia 1941- *WhoAm 94*
King, Patricia Ann 1942- *WhoBlA 94, WhoScEn 94*
King, Patricia E. 1943- *WhoBlA 94*
King, Patricia Miller 1937- *WhoAm 94*
King, Patrick J. 1951- *WhoAmA 93*
King, Paul 1867-1947 *WhoAmA 93N*
King, Paul 1922- *WrDr 94*
King, Paul H. *WhoAmP 93*
King, Paul Louis 1934- *WhoIns 94*
King, Paula *EncSF 93*
King, Paula 1951- *WrDr 94*
King, Pee Wee 1914- *WhoHol 92*
King, Peggy 1931- *WhoHol 92*
King, Peggy Diane 1942- *WhoAmL 94*
King, Perry 1948- *IntMPA 94, WhoHol 92*
King, Peter 1928- *IntMPA 94*
King, Peter Cotterill 1930- *WhoAm 94*
King, Peter Francis 1922- *Who 94*
King, Peter J. 1938- *WhoAmL 94*
King, Peter Joseph, Jr. 1921- *WhoAm 94*
King, Peter T. *WhoAm 94*
King, Peter T. 1944- *CngDr 93*
King, Peter Thomas 1944- *WhoAmP 93*
King, Philip David 1935- *Who 94*
King, Philip Parker 1793-1856 *WhWE*
King, Phillip 1934- *IntWW 93, Who 94*
King, Ralph Malcolm MacDonald 1911- *Who 94*
King, Randall Kent 1950- *WhoScEn 94*
King, Ray 1950- *WhoAmA 93*
King, Ray John 1933- *WhoAm 94, WhoWest 94*
King, Raymond Lamprey 1929- *WhoAmP 93*
King, Reatha Clark 1938- *WhoBlA 94*
King, Reginald F. 1935- *WhoBlA 94*
King, Rex d1977 *WhoHol 92*
King, Rhonda Gail Sugarman 1960- *WhoFI 94*

Kinnamon, Donald Herbert 1937- *WhoAmP 93*
Kinnamon, Gregory H. 1958- *WhoAmP 93*
Kinnamon, Jay Brian 1959- *WhoIns 94*
Kinnamon, Keneth 1932- *WhoAm 94, WrDr 94*
Kinnamon, Kenneth Ellis 1934- *WhoAm 94*
Kinnan, Mary 1763-1848 *BlmGWL*
Kinnan, Roy Doug 1951- *WhoIns 94*
Kinnard, William James, Jr. 1932- *WhoAm 94*
Kinnard, William Noble, Jr. 1926- *WhoFI 94*
Kinne, Frances Bartlett *WhoAm 94*
Kinnear, Ian Albert Clark 1924- *Who 94*
Kinnear, James Wesley, III 1928- *IntWW 93, WhoAm 94, WhoFI 94*
Kinnear, Michael Steward Read 1937- *WrDr 94*
Kinnear, Nigel Alexander 1907- *Who 94*
Kinnear, Roy d1988 *WhoHol 92*
Kinnear, Timothy E. 1964- *WhoFI 94*
Kinneary, Joseph Peter 1905- *WhoAm 94, WhoAmL 94, WhoMW 93*
Kinneberg, Arthur Hempton 1921- *WhoAm 94*
Kinnebrew, Jackson Metcalfe 1941- *WhoAm 94, WhoAmL 94*
Kinnebrew, Larry D. 1960- *WhoBlA 94*
Kinnee, Sandy 1947- *WhoAmA 93, WhoWest 94*
Kinnell, Galway *DrAPF 93*
Kinnell, Galway 1927- *IntWW 93, WhoAm 94, WrDr 94*
Kinnell, Ian 1943- *Who 94*
Kinnell, Murray d1954 *WhoHol 92*
Kinnen, Edwin 1925- *WhoAm 94*
Kinnersley, David John 1926- *IntWW 93*
Kinney, Abbott Ford 1909- *WhoAm 94, WhoFI 94*
Kinney, Anthony John 1958- *WhoScEn 94*
Kinney, Arthur F. 1933- *WrDr 94*
Kinney, Arthur Frederick 1933- *WhoAm 94*
Kinney, Clyde d1962 *WhoHol 92*
Kinney, Donald Gregory 1957- *WhoScEn 94*
Kinney, Earl Robert 1917- *WhoAm 94*
Kinney, Edna M. 1905- *WhoBlA 94*
Kinney, Francis S. d1993 *NewYTBS 93*
Kinney, Francis S(herwood) 1915-1993 *ConAu 140*
Kinney, Gerald Richard 1950- *WhoAmP 93*
Kinney, Gilbert Hart 1931- *WhoAmA 93*
Kinney, Gregg Alan 1948- *WhoWest 94*
Kinney, Gregory Hoppes 1947- *WhoAmL 94*
Kinney, Harry Edwin 1924- *WhoAmP 93*
Kinney, James Howard 1937- *WhoAm 94*
Kinney, Jay MacNeal 1950- *WhoWest 94*
Kinney, John Francis 1937- *WhoAm 94, WhoMW 93*
Kinney, Kenneth Parrish 1921- *WhoAm 94*
Kinney, Lisa 1951- *WhoAmP 93*
Kinney, Lisa Frances 1951- *WhoWest 94*
Kinney, Mark Elliott 1956- *WhoFI 94*
Kinney, Martha Jane 1936- *WhoAmP 93*
Kinney, Paula J. 1929- *WhoAmP 93*
Kinney, Raleigh Earl 1938- *WhoWest 94*
Kinney, Ray d1972 *WhoHol 92*
Kinney, Richard Gordon 1939- *WhoAmL 94*
Kinney, Robert Bruce 1937- *WhoAm 94*
Kinney, Robert Edgar 1935- *WhoFI 94*
Kinney, Sean 1966- *See* Alice in Chains *ConMus 10*
Kinney, Stephen Hoyt, Jr. 1948- *WhoAm 94, WhoAmL 94*
Kinney, Terry *WhoHol 92*
Kinney, Theodore *WhoAmP 93*
Kinney, William Light, Jr. 1933- *WhoAm 94*
Kinney, William Rudolph, Jr. 1942- *WhoAm 94*
Kinnict, Kinni *DrAPF 93*
Kinnie, Kenneth Ivan 1923- *WhoAmP 93*
Kinnie, Robert H. *WhoAm 94, WhoFI 94, WhoWest 94*
Kinniebrew, Robert Lee 1942- *WhoBlA 94*
Kinnison, Harry Austin 1935- *WhoWest 94*
Kinnison, Robert Wheelock 1914- *WhoWest 94*
Kinnison, Tom 1947- *WhoAmP 93*
Kinnison, William Andrew 1932- *WhoAm 94, WhoMW 93*
Kinnock, Neil Gordon 1942- *IntWW 93, Who 94*
Kinnoin, Meyer D. *WhoAmP 93*
Kinnoull, Earl of 1935- *Who 94*
Kinnune, William P. 1939- *WhoFI 94*
Kino, Eusebio Francisco 1645-1711 *DcAmReB 2, EncNAR, WhWE [port]*
Kino, Gordon Stanley 1928- *WhoAm 94*
Kino, Lloyd *WhoHol 92*
Kino, Robert *WhoHol 92*
Kinoe, Yosuke 1961- *WhoScEn 94*
Kinon, Marion Hardy 1929- *WhoAmP 93*
Kinoshita, Gene 1935- *WhoAmA 93*
Kinoshita, Jin H. 1922- *WhoAsA 94*
Kinoshita, Keisuke 1912- *IntWW 93*
Kinoshita, Shigeru 1950- *WhoScEn 94*
Kinoshita, Toichiro 1925- *WhoAm 94, WhoAsA 94, WhoScEn 94*
Kinoshita, Tomio 1944- *WhoScEn 94*
Kinoshita Junji 1914- *IntDcT 2*
Kinosian, Janet Marie 1957- *WhoAm 94*
Kinosita, Riojun 1893- *WhAm 10*
Kinosz, Donald Lee 1940- *WhoScEn 94*
Kinoy, Ernest *IntMPA 94*
Kinra, Vikram Kumar 1946- *WhoAsA 94*
Kinross, Baron 1949- *Who 94*
Kinross, Albert 1870-1929 *EncSF 93*
Kins, Juris 1942- *WhoAm 94, WhoAmL 94*
Kinsbourne, Marcel 1931- *WhoScEn 94*
Kinsel, Michael Leslie 1947- *WhoAmA 93*
Kinsell, Jeffrey Clift 1951- *WhoWest 94*
Kinsella, Daniel John 1952- *WhoScEn 94*
Kinsella, Gary Robert 1939- *WhoMW 93*
Kinsella, John Degan 1941- *WhoAmL 94*
Kinsella, Kathleen d1961 *WhoHol 92*
Kinsella, Ralph Aloysius, Jr. 1919- *WhoAm 94*
Kinsella, Thomas *DrAPF 93*
Kinsella, Thomas 1928- *IntWW 93, Who 94, WrDr 94*
Kinsella, W. P. *DrAPF 93*
Kinsella, W(illiam) P(atrick) 1935- *RfGShF, WrDr 94*
Kinsella, Walter d1975 *WhoHol 92*
Kinsella, William Patrick 1935- *IntWW 93, WhoAm 94, WhoWest 94*
Kinser, Dianne Lee 1944- *WhoFI 94*
Kinser, Douglas M. 1947- *WhoAmP 93*
Kinser, Katherine Anne 1954- *WhoAmL 94*
Kinser, Patrick d1983 *WhoHol 92*
Kinser, Richard Edward 1936- *WhoFI 94*
Kinseth, Leslie Bernald 1955- *WhoMW 93*
Kinsey, Alfred Charles 1894-1956 *AmSocL*
Kinsey, Barbara Cutshall 1947- *WhoWest 94*
Kinsey, Bernard *WhoBlA 94*
Kinsey, Carlos M. 1943- *WhoHisp 94*
Kinsey, Charles John 1922- *WhoFI 94*
Kinsey, Elizabeth 1906- *WrDr 94*
Kinsey, James 1731-1805 *WhAmRev*
Kinsey, James Lloyd 1934- *WhoAm 94, WhoScEn 94*
Kinsey, John Scott 1949- *WhoMW 93, WhoScEn 94*
Kinsey, Lance *ConTFT 11, WhoHol 92*
Kinsey, Robert Everett 1927- *WhoAmP 93*
Kinsey, Robert Wayne 1943- *WhoAmP 93*
Kinsey, Thomas Richard Moseley 1929- *Who 94*
Kinsey, William Charles 1935- *WhoAm 94*
Kinsinger, Jack Burl 1925- *WhoAm 94*
Kinsinger, Robert Earl 1923- *WhoAm 94*
Kinskey, Leonid 1903- *WhoHol 92*
Kinski, Klaus 1925- *WhoHol 92*
Kinski, Klaus 1926-1991 *WhAm 10*
Kinski, Nastassja *WhoAm 94*
Kinski, Nastassja 1960- *IntMPA 94, WhoHol 92*
Kinski, Nastassja 1961- *IntWW 93*
Kinsler, Bruce Whitney 1947- *WhoWest 94*
Kinsley, Craig Howard 1954- *WhoScEn 94*
Kinsley, Homan Benjamin, Jr. 1940- *WhoScEn 94*
Kinsley, Michael E. 1951- *WhoAm 94, WhoAmP 93*
Kinsley, Robert *DrAPF 93*
Kinsley, Robert Lee 1953- *WhoMW 93*
Kinsley, William Benton 1934- *WhoAm 94*
Kinslow, Henry Cargile 1954- *WhoAmP 93*
Kinsman, Francis Michael 1925- *Who 94*
Kinsman, Frank Ellwood 1932- *WhoScEn 94*
Kinsman, Lawrence *DrAPF 93*
Kinsman, Robert Donald 1929- *WhoAm 94, WhoAmA 93*
Kinsman, Robert Preston 1949- *WhoFI 94, WhoScEn 94, WhoWest 94*
Kinsock, Thomas B. 1950- *WhoAmL 94*
Kinsolving, Augustus Blagden 1940- *WhoAm 94*
Kinsolving, Charles McIlvaine, Jr. 1927- *WhoAm 94, WhoAmP 93*
Kinsolving, Laurence Edwin 1941- *WhoAm 94, WhoAmL 94*
Kinsolving, Lee d1974 *WhoHol 92*
Kinsolving, Susan Baumann *DrAPF 93*
Kinstle, James Francis 1938- *WhoMW 93, WhoScEn 94*
Kinstler, Bradley Dean 1953- *WhoIns 94*
Kinstler, Everett Raymond 1926- *WhoAm 94, WhoAmA 93*
Kinstlinger, Jack 1931- *WhoAm 94*
Kintanar, Roman 1929- *IntWW 93*
Kintigh, Bob 1922- *WhoAmP 93*
Kintner, Earl Wilson 1912-1991 *WhAm 10*
Kintner, Elisabeth Turner 1957- *WhoScEn 94*
Kintner, William R. 1915- *IntWW 93*
Kintner, William Roscoe 1915- *WhoAm 94*
Kintore, Earl of 1939- *Who 94*
Kintup fl. 188-?- *WhWE*
Kintz, Richard L. 1944- *WhoAmL 94*
Kintzele, John Alfred 1936- *WhoAm 94, WhoAmL 94*
Kinvig, Clifford Arthur 1934- *Who 94*
Kinyon, Lawrence Clifford 1946- *WhoMW 93*
Kinyon, Mary L. *WhoFI 94*
Kinzel, Augustus Frederick 1937- *WhoMW 93*
Kinzelberg, Harvey 1945- *WhoAm 94, WhoMW 93*
Kinzelman, Brian Peter 1954- *WhoMW 93*
Kinzer, Allen Shawn 1963- *WhoAmL 94*
Kinzer, Debra Anne 1959- *WhoMW 93*
Kinzer, Donald Louis 1914- *WhoAm 94*
Kinzer, James Raymond 1928- *WhoAm 94*
Kinzer, Robert Lee 1941- *WhoScEn 94*
Kinzer, Stephen 1951- *ConAu 142*
Kinzer, William Luther 1929- *WhoAm 94*
Kinzey, Warren Glenford 1935- *WhoAm 94*
Kinzie, Daniel Joseph 1966- *WhoScEn 94*
Kinzie, Mark Alan 1964- *WhoAmL 94*
Kinzie, Mary 1944- *WrDr 94*
Kinzie, Raymond Wyant 1930- *WhoAm 94*
Kinzinger, Rhonda 1961- *WhoMW 93*
Kinzler, Peter 1943- *WhoAmL 94*
Kinzler, Stephen Boyd 1964- *WhoMW 93*
Kinzler, Thomas Benjamin 1950- *WhoAm 94*
Kinzly, Robert Edward 1939- *WhoAm 94*
Kionka, Edward James 1939- *WhoAm 94*
Kiousis, Linda Weber *WhoAmA 93*
Kip, Richard deR. 1913- *WhoIns 94*
Kiper, Ali Muhlis 1924- *WhoAm 94*
Kipfer, Barbara Ann 1954- *WrDr 94*
Kipkulei, Benjamin Kipkech 1946- *Who 94*
Kiple, Kenneth Franklin 1939- *WhoMW 93*
Kipling, Arthur Wellesley *EncSF 93*
Kipling, Richard d1965 *WhoHol 92*
Kipling, Rudyard 1865-1936 *BlmGEL, DcLB 141 [port]*
Kipling, (Joseph) Rudyard 1865-1936 *EncSF 93, RfGShF*
Kiplinger, Austin Huntington 1918- *WhoAm 94*
Kiplinger, Glenn Francis 1930- *WhoAm 94*
Kiplinger, Knight A. 1948- *WhoAm 94*
Kipnis, Alexander 1891-1978 *NewGrDO*
Kipnis, David Morris 1927- *WhoAm 94*
Kipnis, Igor 1930- *WhoAm 94*
Kipnis, Mark S. 1947- *WhoAm 94, WhoAmL 94*
Kipniss, Robert 1931- *WhoAm 94, WhoAmA 93*
Kipp, Carl Robert 1959- *WhoScEn 94*
Kipp, Georgiana Eugenia 1942- *WhoMW 93*
Kipp, June Carol 1932- *WhoWest 94*
Kipp, Lyman 1929- *WhoAmA 93*
Kipp, Orval 1904- *WhoAmA 93*
Kipp, Robert Almy 1932- *WhoAm 94*
Kippax, John 1915-1974 *EncSF 93*
Kippel, Gary M. *WhoAm 94*
Kippen, Manart d1947 *WhoHol 92*
Kippen, Richard Marlin 1932- *WhoFI 94*
Kippenberger, Martin 1953- *WhoAmA 93*
Kippenhahn, Rudolf 1926- *IntWW 93*
Kippenhan, Charles Jacob 1919- *WhoAm 94*
Kipper, Barbara Levy 1942- *WhoMW 93*
Kipperman, Lawrence I. 1941- *WhoAm 94*
Kipperman, Mark 1952- *WhoMW 93*
Kippert, Robert John, Jr. 1952- *WhoMW 93*
Kipphardt, Heinar 1922-1982 *IntDcT 2*
Kipping, Frederic Stanley *WorInv*
Kipping, Vernon Louis 1921- *WhoFI 94, WhoWest 94*
Kippley, Terry Loren 1964- *WhoFI 94, WhoMW 93*
Kippur, Merrie Margolin 1962- *WhoWest 94*
Kira, Gerald Glenn 1951- *WhoScEn 94*
Kira, Tatuo 1919- *IntWW 93*
Kiralfy, Albert Kenneth Roland 1915- *Who 94*
Kiraly, Izabella B. *WhoWomW 91*
Kiraly, Karch 1961- *WhoAm 94*
Kiran, Erdogan 1946- *WhoScEn 94*
Kirban, Lloyd 1931- *WhoAm 94*
Kirbens, Samuel Morris 1918- *WhoWest 94*
Kirby, Ada M. *WhoHisp 94*
Kirby, Albert 1875- *EncNAR*
Kirby, Allan Price, Jr. 1931- *WhoAm 94*
Kirby, Anthony John 1935- *IntWW 93, Who 94*
Kirby, Bruce *WhoHol 92*
Kirby, Bruno 1949- *WhoHol 92*
Kirby, Burno 1949- *IntMPA 94*
Kirby, Charles William, Jr. 1926- *WhoAm 94*
Kirby, Dan Laird 1946- *WhoAmL 94*
Kirby, David *DrAPF 93*
Kirby, David d1954 *WhoHol 92*
Kirby, David Donald 1933- *Who 94*
Kirby, David Peter 1936- *WrDr 94*
Kirby, Dean *WhoAmP 93*
Kirby, Dennis 1923- *Who 94*
Kirby, Dorothy Manville 1917- *WhoMW 93*
Kirby, Edward Paul 1928- *WhoAmP 93*
Kirby, Emily Baruch 1929- *WhoAm 94*
Kirby, Ephraim 1757-1804 *WhAmRev*
Kirby, Fred Morgan, II 1919- *WhoAm 94, WhoFI 94*
Kirby, Gary Neil 1935- *WhoScEn 94*
Kirby, George d1953 *WhoHol 92*
Kirby, George 1925- *WhoHol 92*
Kirby, George Albert, III 1944- *WhoAmP 93*
Kirby, Gilbert Walter 1914- *WrDr 94*
Kirby, Gordon William 1934- *Who 94*
Kirby, Gwendolen Maud 1911- *Who 94*
Kirby, Harmon E. 1934- *WhoAmP 93*
Kirby, Jack 1917- *EncSF 93*
Kirby, Jacqueline 1946- *WhoBlA 94*
Kirby, James Cordell, Jr. 1928-1989 *WhAm 10*
Kirby, James Thornton, Jr. 1952- *WhoScEn 94*
Kirby, James W. 1947- *WhoAmP 93*
Kirby, James Wallace 1947- *WhoAmL 94*
Kirby, Joe Patrick 1953- *WhoIns 94*
Kirby, John d1973 *WhoHol 92*
Kirby, John D. 1944- *WhoAm 94, WhoAmL 94*
Kirby, John Joseph, Jr. 1939- *WhoAm 94*
Kirby, Josh 1928- *EncSF 93*
Kirby, Kenneth Ralph 1957- *WhoAmL 94*
Kirby, Kent Bruce 1934- *WhoAm 94, WhoAmA 93*
Kirby, Kevin Andrew 1950- *WhoScEn 94*
Kirby, Le Grand Carney, III 1941- *WhoAmL 94*
Kirby, Louis 1928- *Who 94*
Kirby, Louis Albert Francis 1928- *IntWW 93*
Kirby, Matthew T. 1947- *WhoAmL 94*
Kirby, Max *WhoHol 92*
Kirby, Max Mitchell 1920- *WhoFI 94*
Kirby, Michael *WhoHol 92*
Kirby, Michael Donald 1939- *IntWW 93, Who 94*
Kirby, Money Alian 1914- *WhoBlA 94*
Kirby, Montanges 1953- *WhoBlA 94*
Kirby, Nancy J. 1940- *WhoBlA 94*
Kirby, Norman George 1926- *Who 94*
Kirby, Ollie d1964 *WhoHol 92*
Kirby, Richard (Clarence) 1904- *Who 94*
Kirby, Richard Melvin 1946- *WhoAmL 94*
Kirby, Ron Lemmie 1940- *WhoAmP 93*
Kirby, Ronald Hubert 1936- *IntWW 93*
Kirby, Shaun Keven 1967- *WhoScEn 94*
Kirby, Steve T. *WhoAmP 93*
Kirby, Steve T. 1952- *WhoMW 93*
Kirby, Thomas J. *WhoAmP 93*
Kirby, Thomas Wesley 1950- *WhoAm 94*
Kirby, Ward Nelson 1939- *WhoAm 94*
Kirby, Wayne Edward 1964- *WhoBlA 94*
Kirby, William Joseph 1937- *WhoAm 94*
Kirby, William Murray Maurice 1914- *WhoAm 94*
Kirby, William Thomas 1911-1990 *WhAm 10*
Kirby, William West c. 1826-1907 *EncNAR*
Kirch, Maria Winkelmann *WorScD*
Kirch, Max Samuel 1915- *WhoAm 94*
Kirch, Patrick Vinton 1950- *WhoWest 94*
Kirchenbauer, Bill *WhoHol 92*
Kirchenbauer, Diane *WhoAmP 93*
Kircher, Athanasius 1602-1680 *EncSF 93*
Kircher, John Joseph 1938- *WhoAmL 94, WhoMW 93*
Kircher, Marvin Larry 1950- *WhoWest 94*
Kircher, Philip G. 1950- *WhoAm 94, WhoAmL 94*
Kircheva, Elena Peikova 1949- *WhoWomW 91*
Kirchgasser, Werner 1937- *IntWW 93*
Kirchheimer, Arthur Edward 1931- *WhoAm 94*
Kirchheimer, Gloria L. *DrAPF 93*
Kirchhofer, Wilma Ardine Lyghtner 1940- *WhoBlA 94*
Kirchhoff, Fritz d1953 *WhoHol 92*

Kirchhoff, Gustav Robert *WorInv*
Kirchhoff, Gustav Robert 1824-1887 *WorScD*
Kirchhoff, Michael Kent 1963- *WhoMW 93*
Kirchhoff, Walter 1879-1951 *NewGrDO*
Kirchhoff, William Hayes 1936- *WhoScEn 94*
Kirchick, Calvin B. 1946- *WhoAm 94, WhoAmL 94*
Kirchick, Stuart David 1963- *WhoAmL 94*
Kirchick, William Dean 1950- *WhoAm 94, WhoAmL 94*
Kirchknopf, Erin Massie 1963- *WhoWest 94*
Kirchman, Charles Vincent 1935- *WhoAmL 94*
Kirchmayer, Leon Kenneth 1924- *WhoAm 94*
Kirchmayer-Hilprecht, Martin 1923- *WhoScEn 94*
Kirchner, Alfred 1937- *IntWW 93, NewGrDO*
Kirchner, Bharti *WhoAsA 94*
Kirchner, Bruce McHarg 1948- *WhoAm 94*
Kirchner, Claude d1993 *NewYTBS 93*
Kirchner, Emil J(oseph) 1942- *WrDr 94*
Kirchner, Ernst Karl 1937- *WhoWest 94*
Kirchner, James William 1920- *WhoAm 94, WhoMW 93, WhoScEn 94*
Kirchner, John Albert 1915- *WhoAm 94*
Kirchner, Leon 1919- *NewGrDO, WhoAm 94*
Kirchner, Peter James 1920- *Who 94*
Kirchner, Richard Jay 1930- *WhoMW 93*
Kirchner, William G. *WhoAmP 93*
Kirchschlager, Rudolf 1915- *IntWW 93*
Kirchwey, Deborah Wendell 1963- *WhoAmL 94*
Kirdar, Nemir A. *NewYTBS 93 [port]*
Kirdar, Nemir Amin 1936- *WhoAm 94*
Kirgis, Frederic L. 1907- *WhoAm 94*
Kirgis, Frederic Lee, Jr. 1934- *WhoAm 94*
Kirgo, George 1926- *WhoHol 92*
Kirick, Daniel John 1953- *WhoMW 93, WhoScEn 94*
Kirienko, Zinaida *WhoHol 92*
Kirila, Carol Elizabeth 1952- *WhoMW 93*
Kiriyama, Iku *WhoAsA 94*
Kirjas, Zoran Nikola 1942- *WhoMW 93*
Kirjassoff, Gordon Louis 1922- *WhoAm 94*
Kirk (Bush), Phyllis 1926- *IntMPA 94*
Kirk, Alan G. 1888-1963 *HisDcKW*
Kirk, Alexis Vemian 1938- *WhoAm 94*
Kirk, Andrew Charles 1947- *WhoFI 94*
Kirk, Andy 1898-1992 *AnObit 1992*
Kirk, Ballard Harry Thurston 1929- *WhoMW 93*
Kirk, Bertha d1928 *WhoHol 92*
Kirk, Betty Virginia 1923- *WhoAmP 93*
Kirk, Bradley Reed 1964- *WhoWest 94*
Kirk, Carmen Zetler 1941- *WhoFI 94, WhoWest 94*
Kirk, Cassius Lamb, Jr. 1929- *WhoFI 94, WhoWest 94*
Kirk, Colleen Jean 1918- *WhoAm 94*
Kirk, Daniel Lee 1919- *WhoAm 94*
Kirk, David Starr 1943- *WhoFI 94*
Kirk, Dennis Dean 1950- *WhoAmL 94*
Kirk, Donald 1938- *WhoAm 94, WrDr 94*
Kirk, Donald James 1932- *WhoAm 94, WhoFI 94*
Kirk, Earl, Jr. 1927- *WhoAm 94*
Kirk, Edgar Lee 1923- *WhoAm 94*
Kirk, Edward Norris 1802-1874 *DcAmReB 2*
Kirk, Flora Kay Stude 1944- *WhoMW 93*
Kirk, Frank C. 1889-1963 *WhoAmA 93N*
Kirk, Gary Vincent 1943- *WhoFI 94*
Kirk, Geoffrey Stephen 1921- *IntWW 93, Who 94, WrDr 94*
Kirk, Gerald Arthur 1940- *WhoAm 94*
Kirk, Grayson 1903- *IntWW 93*
Kirk, Grayson Louis 1903- *Who 94, WhoAm 94*
Kirk, Henry Port 1935- *WhoAm 94, WhoWest 94*
Kirk, Herbert Victor 1912- *Who 94*
Kirk, Hugh Adam 1916- *WhoAmL 94*
Kirk, Irina *DrAPF 93*
Kirk, Jack d1948 *WhoHol 92*
Kirk, James Albert 1929- *WhoWest 94*
Kirk, James Robert 1941- *WhoAm 94*
Kirk, James William 1930- *WhoWest 94*
Kirk, Janet Brown 1929- *WhoWest 94*
Kirk, Jennifer Joy 1955- *WhoFI 94*
Kirk, Jenny N. 1945- *WhoWomW 91*
Kirk, Jerome 1923- *WhoAmA 93*
Kirk, Joe d1975 *WhoHol 92*
Kirk, John Henry 1907- *Who 94*
Kirk, John Robert, Jr. 1935- *WhoAmL 94*
Kirk, Kent Sand 1948- *IntWW 93*
Kirk, Lee Crawley *DrAPF 93*
Kirk, Leroy W. 1924- *WhoBlA 94*
Kirk, Lynda Pounds 1946- *WhoAm 94*
Kirk, Mark Steven 1959- *WhoFI 94*
Kirk, Marshall (Kenneth) 1957- *WrDr 94*
Kirk, Maurice Blake 1921- *WhoAm 94*
Kirk, Michael 1928- *WrDr 94*
Kirk, Michael 1947- *WhoAmA 93*
Kirk, Michael C. 1974- *WhoAmL 94*
Kirk, Michael Thomas 1946- *WhoMW 93*
Kirk, Norman Andrew *DrAPF 93*
Kirk, Orville 1936- *WhoBlA 94*
Kirk, Patrick Laine 1948- *WhoAmL 94*
Kirk, Paul 1914- *WhoAm 94*
Kirk, Paul G., Jr. 1938- *WhoAmP 93*
Kirk, Paul Grattan, Jr. 1938- *IntWW 93, WhoAm 94*
Kirk, Phillip James, Jr. 1944- *WhoAmP 93*
Kirk, Phyllis 1926- *WhoHol 92*
Kirk, Phyllis O. 1943- *WhoBlA 94*
Kirk, Rahsaan Roland 1936-1977 *AfrAmAl 6*
Kirk, Raymond Maurice 1923- *Who 94*
Kirk, Rea Helene 1944- *WhoWest 94*
Kirk, Richard *EncSF 93*
Kirk, Richard Dillon 1953- *WhoAmL 94*
Kirk, Robert Leonard 1929- *WhoAm 94*
Kirk, Roger 1930- *WhoAmP 93*
Kirk, Rudolf 1898-1989 *WhAm 10*
Kirk, Russel Amos 1918- *WhoAm 94*
Kirk, Russell (Amos) 1918- *WrDr 94*
Kirk, Russell Amos 1918- *WhoMW 93*
Kirk, Ruth *Who 94*
Kirk, (Lucy) Ruth *Who 94*
Kirk, Ruth M. 1930- *WhoAmP 93*
Kirk, Samuel Alexander 1904- *WhoAm 94, WhoWest 94*
Kirk, Sarah Virgo 1934- *WhoBlA 94*
Kirk, Sherwood 1924- *WhoAm 94*
Kirk, Thomas Garrett, Jr. 1943- *WhoAm 94*
Kirk, Thomas Kent 1940- *WhoAm 94, WhoScEn 94*
Kirk, Tommy 1941- *WhoHol 92*
Kirk, Wiley Price, Jr. 1942- *WhoScEn 94*
Kirk, William L., Jr. 1943- *WhoAmL 94*
Kirk, Wyatt D. 1935- *WhoBlA 94*
Kirkbride, Chalmer Gatlin 1906- *WhoAm 94, WhoScEn 94*
Kirkbride, Earle R. 1891-1968 *WhoAmA 93N*
Kirkbride, Thomas Story 1809-1883 *EncSPD*
Kirkby, Emma 1949- *IntWW 93, Who 94*
Kirkby, (Carolyn) Emma 1949- *NewGrDO*
Kirkby, Maurice Anthony 1929- *WhoAm 94*
Kirkconnell, Clare *WhoHol 92*
Kirkconnell, Watson 1895- *WhAm 10*
Kirk-Duggan, Cheryl Ann 1951- *WhoBlA 94*
Kirk-Duggan, Michael Allan 1931- *WhoAm 94, WhoAmL 94*
Kirke, David Walter 1915- *Who 94*
Kirke, Donald d1971 *WhoHol 92*
Kirke, Gerald Michael 1943- *WhoAmP 93*
Kirkegaard, Knud E. 1942- *IntWW 93*
Kirkegaard, Raymond Lawrence, Jr. 1937- *WhoAm 94*
Kirkendall, Donald Eugene 1939- *WhoAm 94*
Kirkendall, Jeffrey Lawrence 1954- *WhoWest 94*
Kirkendall, John Neal 1938- *WhoAmL 94*
Kirkendall, Lester A. 1903-1991 *WrDr 94N*
Kirkendall, Richard Stewart 1928- *WhoAm 94*
Kirkendoll, Chester Arthur, II 1914- *WhoBlA 94*
Kirkenslager, Larry Keith 1944- *WhoAmP 93*
Kirker, Jack M. *WhoAm 94, WhoWest 94*
Kirkey, Jaclyn Hilliard 1951- *WhoMW 93*
Kirk-Greene, Anthony (Hamilton Millard) 1925- *WrDr 94*
Kirk-Greene, Christopher (Walter Edward) 1926- *WrDr 94*
Kirkham, Don 1908- *WhoAm 94*
Kirkham, Donald Herbert 1936- *Who 94*
Kirkham, E. Bruce 1938- *WrDr 94*
Kirkham, Francis Robison 1904- *WhoAm 94*
Kirkham, Ira Lloyd 1942- *WhoAmP 93*
Kirkham, James Alvin 1935- *WhoMW 93*
Kirkham, James Francis 1933- *WhoAm 94*
Kirkham, John Dudley Galtrey *Who 94*
Kirkham, John Spencer 1944- *WhoAmL 94*
Kirkham, Kathleen d1961 *WhoHol 92*
Kirkham, Keith Edwin 1929- *Who 94*
Kirkham, M. B. *WhoAm 94*
Kirkham, Nellie *EncSF 93*
Kirkhill, Baron 1930- *Who 94*
Kirkhope, Timothy John Robert 1945- *Who 94*
Kirkinen, Heikki 1927- *IntWW 93*
Kirking, Clayton Carroll 1949- *WhoWest 94*
Kirkland, Alexander 1908- *WhoHol 92*
Kirkland, Alfred Younges, Sr. 1917- *WhoAm 94, WhoAmL 94, WhoMW 93*
Kirkland, Bryant Mays 1914- *WhoAm 94*
Kirkland, Caroline Matilda Stansbury 1801-1864 *BlmGWL*
Kirkland, Cornell R. *WhoBlA 94*
Kirkland, David d1964 *WhoHol 92*
Kirkland, Gelsey 1952- *IntDcB [port]*
Kirkland, Gelsey 1953- *IntWW 93, WhoAm 94, WrDr 94*
Kirkland, Gerry Paul 1943- *WhoFI 94, WhoMW 93*
Kirkland, Hardee d1929 *WhoHol 92*
Kirkland, Jack A. 1931- *WhoBlA 94*
Kirkland, James Ian 1954- *WhoWest 94*
Kirkland, James M. 1947- *WhoAmP 93*
Kirkland, John Clarence 1963- *WhoAmL 94, WhoWest 94*
Kirkland, John David 1933- *WhoAm 94*
Kirkland, John Leonard 1926- *WhoAm 94*
Kirkland, Joseph J. 1925- *WhoAm 94*
Kirkland, Joseph Lane 1922- *Who 94, WhoAm 94, WhoAmP 93*
Kirkland, Kenny David 1955- *WhoBlA 94*
Kirkland, (Joseph) Lane 1922- *IntWW 93*
Kirkland, Leroy, Sr. 1932- *WhoAmP 93*
Kirkland, Matthew Carl 1959- *WhoScEn 94*
Kirkland, Moses *WhAmRev*
Kirkland, Moses d1787 *AmRev*
Kirkland, Muriel d1971 *WhoHol 92*
Kirkland, Ned Matthews 1953- *WhoScEn 94*
Kirkland, Randall Lee 1952- *WhoFI 94*
Kirkland, Reo, Jr. 1947- *WhoAmP 93*
Kirkland, Sally 1944- *IntMPA 94, WhoHol 92*
Kirkland, Samuel 1741-1808 *AmRev, EncNAR*
Kirkland, Shari Lynn 1961- *WhoScEn 94*
Kirkland, Thaddeus *WhoAmP 93*
Kirkland, Theodore 1934- *WhoBlA 94*
Kirkland, Vance Hall 1904-1981 *WhoAmA 93N*
Kirkland-Briscoe, Gail Alicia 1960- *WhoBlA 94*
Kirkland-Holmes, Gloria 1952- *WhoBlA 94*
Kirkle, Diane Luise 1944- *WhoMW 93*
Kirkley, Dorothy Yates 1946- *WhoAmL 94*
Kirkley, T. A. *WhoFI 94*
Kirkley-Bey, Marie Lopez *WhoAmP 93*
Kirklin, George Lincoln 1937- *WhoAm 94*
Kirklin, Perry William 1935- *WhoBlA 94*
Kirkman, Denis Allan 1935- *WhoMW 93*
Kirkman, Jay Urban, III 1954- *WhoAmP 93*
Kirkman, William Patrick 1932- *Who 94, WrDr 94*
Kirkness, Donald James 1919- *Who 94*
Kirkorian, Donald George 1938- *WhoWest 94*
Kirkpatrick, Andrew Booth, Jr. 1929- *WhoAm 94*
Kirkpatrick, Anne Saunders 1938- *WhoMW 93*
Kirkpatrick, Carl Kimmel 1936- *WhoAmL 94*
Kirkpatrick, Charles Harvey 1931- *WhoAm 94*
Kirkpatrick, Clayton 1915- *IntWW 93, WhoAm 94*
Kirkpatrick, Dennis Oerting 1946- *WhoFI 94*
Kirkpatrick, Diane 1933- *WhoAmA 93*
Kirkpatrick, Dow N. 1944- *WhoAmL 94*
Kirkpatrick, Edward Scott 1941- *WhoAm 94*
Kirkpatrick, Edward Thomson 1925- *WhoAm 94*
Kirkpatrick, Elwood *WhoFI 94*
Kirkpatrick, Forrest H. 1905- *EncABHB 9*
Kirkpatrick, Forrest Hunter 1905- *WhoAm 94*
Kirkpatrick, Francis Hubbard, Jr. 1943- *WhoAm 94*
Kirkpatrick, Garland Penn 1932- *WhoBlA 94*
Kirkpatrick, Gavin Alexander Yvone 1938- *Who 94*
Kirkpatrick, George Grier, Jr. 1938- *WhoAmP 93*
Kirkpatrick, Howard Delane 1935- *WhoAmP 93*
Kirkpatrick, Ivone Elliott 1942- *Who 94*
Kirkpatrick, Jeane 1926- *WhoAmP 93*
Kirkpatrick, Jeane (Duane Jordan) 1926- *WrDr 94*
Kirkpatrick, Jeane Duane Jordan 1926- *IntWW 93, WhoAm 94*
Kirkpatrick, Jeffery Roger 1963- *WhoAmP 93*
Kirkpatrick, Jess d1976 *WhoHol 92*
Kirkpatrick, John Elson 1908- *WhoAm 94*
Kirkpatrick, John Gildersleeve 1917- *WhoAm 94*
Kirkpatrick, John Lister 1927- *Who 94*
Kirkpatrick, Nancy Foster 1933- *WhoAm 94*
Kirkpatrick, Patricia *DrAPF 93*
Kirkpatrick, Richard Alan 1947- *WhoWest 94*
Kirkpatrick, Robert Hugh 1954- *WhoMW 93*
Kirkpatrick, Robert James 1946- *WhoAm 94*
Kirkpatrick, Samuel Alexander *WhoAm 94*
Kirkpatrick, Sidney D(ale) 1955- *WrDr 94*
Kirkpatrick, Smith *DrAPF 93*
Kirkpatrick, Susan Elizabeth *WhoAmP 93*
Kirkpatrick, Susan Elizabeth D. 1950- *WhoWest 94*
Kirkpatrick, Wendy Ann 1962- *WhoMW 93*
Kirkpatrick, William Brown 1934- *Who 94*
Kirks, James Harvey, Jr. 1937- *WhoWest 94*
Kirksey, Avanelle 1926- *WhoAm 94, WhoMW 93*
Kirksey, Henry 1915- *HisWorL*
Kirksey, Henry J. *WhoAmP 93*
Kirksey, Jack Edwin 1928- *WhoAmP 93*
Kirksey, M. Janette 1946- *WhoBlA 94*
Kirksey, Peter J. 1904-1991 *WhoBlA 94N*
Kirkup, James 1918- *IntWW 93*
Kirkup, James 1923- *Who 94*
Kirkup, James (Falconer) 1923- *WrDr 94*
Kirkwood, Baron 1931- *Who 94*
Kirkwood, Hon. Lord 1932- *Who 94*
Kirkwood, Andrew (Tristram Hammett) 1944- *Who 94*
Kirkwood, Archy 1946- *Who 94*
Kirkwood, Byron (Ray) 1946- *ConAu 141*
Kirkwood, David Herbert Waddington 1924- *WhoAm 94*
Kirkwood, Gene *IntMPA 94*
Kirkwood, Gene 1945- *WhoAm 94*
Kirkwood, Gertrude Robinson d1962 *WhoHol 92*
Kirkwood, Ian Candlish *Who 94*
Kirkwood, Jack d1964 *WhoHol 92*
Kirkwood, James d1963 *WhoHol 92*
Kirkwood, James 1930-1989 *WhAm 10*
Kirkwood, James, Jr. d1989 *WhoHol 92*
Kirkwood, Joe, Jr. 1920- *WhoHol 92*
Kirkwood, Kenneth 1919- *Who 94*
Kirkwood, Lawrence Robert 1941- *WhoAmP 93*
Kirkwood, Mary Burnette 1904- *WhoAmA 93*
Kirkwood, Maurice Richard 1920- *WhoAm 94*
Kirkwood, Pat 1921- *WhoHol 92*
Kirkwood, Richard Edwin 1927- *WhoAm 94*
Kirkwood, Robert Carter 1939- *WhoAmP 93*
Kirkwood, Robert H. 1746-1791 *WhAmRev*
Kirkwood, Robert Keith 1961- *WhoScEn 94*
Kirkwood-Hackett, Eva d1968 *WhoHol 92*
Kirloskar, Shantanu Laxman 1903- *IntWW 93*
Kirmaci, Ismail 1953- *WhoWest 94*
Kirman, Charles Gary 1949- *WhoAm 94*
Kirman, Lyle Edward 1946- *WhoScEn 94*
Kirmser, Philip George 1919- *WhoAm 94*
Kirn, Walter 1962- *ConAu 142*
Kirner, Joan *WhoWomW 91*
Kirner, Joan Elizabeth 1938- *IntWW 93, Who 94*
Kiron, Ravi 1959- *WhoAsA 94*
Kirpal, Prem Nath 1909- *IntWW 93*
Kirpalani, Maynard M. 1953- *WhoAmL 94*
Kirpichnikov, Yury Aleksandrovich 1939- *LngBDD*
Kirpishchikova, Anna Aleksandrovna 1848-1927 *BlmGWL*
Kirsch, Alan 1953- *WhoWest 94*
Kirsch, Anthony Thomas 1930- *WhoAm 94*
Kirsch, Arthur William 1941- *WhoAm 94*
Kirsch, Irving 1943- *WrDr 94*
Kirsch, Jack Frederick 1934- *WhoAm 94*
Kirsch, Jeffrey Scott 1947- *WhoMW 93*
Kirsch, Laurence Stephen 1957- *WhoAmL 94*
Kirsch, Robert 1952- *WhoScEn 94*
Kirsch, Sarah 1935- *BlmGWL, ConWorW 93*
Kirsch, Ted Michael 1950- *WhoScEn 94*
Kirsch, William Joseph 1956- *WhoAmL 94*
Kirschbaum, James Louis 1940- *WhoAm 94*
Kirschbaum, Myron 1949- *WhoAm 94, WhoAmL 94*
Kirschenbaum, Bernard Edwin 1924- *WhoAmA 93*
Kirschenbaum, David E. d1993 *NewYTBS 93*
Kirschenbaum, Jules 1930- *WhoAmA 93*

Kirschenbaum, William 1944- *WhoAm 94, WhoFI 94*
Kirschenmann, Frederick Ludwig 1935- *WhoMW 93*
Kirschenmann, Henry George, Jr. 1930- *WhoAm 94*
Kirschner, Barbara Starrels 1941- *WhoAm 94*
Kirschner, David *WhoAm 94*
Kirschner, Fritz *ConAu 42NR*
Kirschner, John Michael 1960- *WhoFI 94*
Kirschner, Karen Marie 1956- *WhoMW 93*
Kirschner, Kerry G. 1946- *WhoAmP 93*
Kirschner, Marc S. 1942- *WhoAm 94, WhoAmL 94*
Kirschner, Marc Wallace 1945- *WhoScEn 94*
Kirschner, Melvin Henry 1926- *WhoWest 94*
Kirschner, Richard Michael 1949- *WhoWest 94*
Kirschner, Ronald Allen 1942- *WhoScEn 94*
Kirschner, Ruth Brin 1924- *WhoMW 93*
Kirschner, Stanley 1927- *WhoAm 94*
Kirschstein, Ruth L. 1926- *IntWW 93*
Kirschstein, Ruth Lillian 1926- *WhoAm 94, WhoScEn 94*
Kirscht, Robert Leon 1942- *WhoAmP 93*
Kirsh, Herbert *WhoAmP 93*
Kirsh, Michael Alan 1952- *WhoFI 94*
Kirshbaum, Howard M. *WhoAmP 93*
Kirshbaum, Howard M. 1938- *WhoAm 94, WhoAmL 94, WhoWest 94*
Kirshbaum, Jack D. 1902- *WhoWest 94*
Kirshen, Paul Howard 1948- *WhoScEn 94*
Kirshenbaum, Binnie *DrAPF 93*
Kirshenbaum, Richard Irving 1933- *WhoScEn 94*
Kirshner, Alan I. 1935- *WhoIns 94*
Kirshner, Judith Russi 1942- *WhoAmA 93*
Kirshner, Norman 1923- *WhoAm 94*
Kirshner, Robert P. 1949- *WhoAm 94, WhoScEn 94*
Kirslis, Peter Andre Christopher 1954- *WhoWest 94*
Kirsner, Joseph Barnett 1909- *WhoAm 94*
Kirsner, Robert 1921- *WhoAm 94*
Kirsop, Arthur Michael Benjamin 1931- *IntWW 93, Who 94*
Kirsop, Douglas Lee 1960- *WhoMW 93*
Kirst, Bruce Joseph 1954- *WhoMW 93*
Kirst, Hans Hellmut 1914-1989 *EncSF 93*
Kirst, Michael 1939- *IntWW 93*
Kirstein, David Peter 1948- *WhoFI 94*
Kirstein, Lincoln 1907- *IntDcB [port], IntWW 93, WhoAm 94, WrDr 94*
Kirstein, Lincoln Edward 1907- *Who 94*
Kirstein, Natalie *DrAPF 93*
Kirsten, Dorothy 1910-1992 *AnObit 1992, CurBio 93N, WhAm 10*
Kirsten, Dorothy 1915 *NewGrDO*
Kirsten, Dorothy 1919- *WhoHol 92*
Kirsten, Hendrik Albertus 1942- *WhoScEn 94*
Kirsten, Nicholas 1947- *WhoAmA 93*
Kirsten-Daiensai, Richard Charles 1920- *WhoAmA 93*
Kirsteuer, Ernst Karl Eberhart 1933- *WhoAm 94*
Kir-Stimon, William *DrAPF 93*
Kir-Stimon, William 1910- *WhoMW 93*
Kirszenstein-Szewinska, Irena 1946- *IntWW 93*
Kirtland, G. B. 1929- *WrDr 94*
Kirtland, John C. 1939- *WhoAm 94*
Kirtland, Louise 1905- *WhoHol 92*
Kirtley, Hattie Mae 1934- *WhoMW 93*
Kirtley, Jane Elizabeth 1953- *WhoAmL 94*
Kirtley, Virginia d1956 *WhoHol 92*
Kirton, Hugh 1910- *Who 94*
Kirton, James 1909- *WrDr 94*
Kirts, Wayne Charles 1934- *WhoWest 94*
Kirtz, William Dennison 1945- *WhoFI 94*
Kirven, Gerald 1922- *WhoAm 94, WhoAmL 94*
Kirven, Mythe Yuvette 1956- *WhoBlA 94*
Kirven, Peyton Edward 1924- *WhoAm 94*
Kirven, Timothy J. *WhoAmP 93*
Kirwan, Betty-Jane 1947- *WhoAm 94, WhoAmL 94*
Kirwan, Gayle M. 1950- *WhoScEn 94*
Kirwan, Laurence *Who 94*
Kirwan, (Archibald) Laurence (Patrick) 1907- *Who 94*
Kirwan, Laurence Joseph 1941- *WhoAmP 93*
Kirwan, Ralph DeWitt 1942- *WhoAm 94, WhoAmL 94*
Kirwan, Roberta Claire *WhoBlA 94*
Kirwan, Thomas M. 1940-1992 *WhAm 10*
Kirwan, William E. 1938- *IntWW 93*
Kirwan, William English, II 1938- *WhoAm 94*
Kirwan-Taylor, Peter Robin 1930- *WhoFI 94*
Kirwin, Kenneth F. 1941- *WhoAm 94*
Kirya, George Barnabas 1939- *Who 94*
Kis, Danilo 1935-1989 *RfGShF*
Kisabeth, Tim Charles 1957- *WhoMW 93*
Kisak, Paul Francis 1956- *WhoScEn 94*
Kisber, Matthew Harris 1960- *WhoAmP 93*
Kisburg, Nicholas M. d1993 *NewYTBS 93 [port]*
Kiscaden, Sheila M. 1946- *WhoAmP 93*
Kisch, Gloria 1941- *WhoAmA 93*
Kisch, Raymond R. *WhoIns 94*
Kisch, Royalton *Who 94*
Kisch, (Alastair) Royalton 1919- *Who 94*
Kisch, Steven Gene 1948- *WhoFI 94*
Kischer, Clayton Ward 1930- *WhoScEn 94, WhoWest 94*
Kischuk, Richard Karl 1949- *WhoAm 94*
Kise, James Nelson 1937- *WhoAm 94*
Kisekka, Samson *IntWW 93*
Kiselev, Evgeny 1956- *LngBDD*
Kiselewski, Joseph 1901- *WhAm 10*
Kiselewski, Joseph 1901-1986 *WhoAmA 93N*
Kiselik, Paul Howard 1937- *WhoAm 94, WhoFI 94*
Kiser, Clyde Vernon 1904- *WhoAm 94, WhoScEn 94*
Kiser, Don Curtis 1953- *WhoScEn 94*
Kiser, Glenn Augustus 1917- *WhoFI 94, WhoScEn 94*
Kiser, Jackson L. 1929- *WhoAm 94, WhoAmL 94*
Kiser, James Webb 1934- *WhoAm 94*
Kiser, Karen Maureen 1951- *WhoMW 93, WhoScEn 94*
Kiser, Kenneth Maynard 1929- *WhoScEn 94*
Kiser, Lisa Jean 1949- *WhoMW 93*
Kiser, Mose, III 1956- *WhoFI 94*
Kiser, Nagiko Sato 1923- *WhoWest 94*
Kiser, Roberta Katherine 1938- *WhoWest 94*
Kiser, Samuel Curtis 1944- *WhoAmP 93*
Kiser, T. Keith 1962- *WhoFI 94*
Kiser, Terry *WhoHol 92*
Kiser, Thelma Kay 1944- *WhoScEn 94*
Kiser, Virginia *WhoHol 92*
Kiser, William Sites 1928- *WhoAm 94*
Kish, Carla Elene *WhoAmP 93*
Kish, George 1914-1989 *WhAm 10*
Kish, Joseph Laurence, Jr. 1933- *WhoAm 94*
Kish, Leslie 1910- *WhoAm 94, WrDr 94*
Kish, Marie de Alcuaz 1955- *WhoWest 94*
Kish, Michael Stephen 1961- *WhoScEn 94*
Kishan, K. T. 1950- *WhoMW 93*
Kishel, Gregory Francis 1951- *WhoAm 94, WhoAmL 94*
Kishen Singh d1921 *WhWE*
Kishi, Glen Yo 1958- *WhoWest 94*
Kishi, Keiko *WhoHol 92*
Kishida, Kyoko 1930- *WhoHol 92*
Kishida Kunio 1890-1954 *IntDcT 2*
Kishimoto, Kazuo 1952- *WhoScEn 94*
Kishimoto, Richard Noriyuki 1939- *WhoAsA 94*
Kishimoto, Uichiro 1922- *WhoAm 94, WhoScEn 94*
Kishimoto, Yasunobu 1919- *IntWW 93*
Kishimoto, Yasuo 1925- *WhoAsA 94*
Kishimoto, Yoriko 1955- *WhoAsA 94, WhoWest 94*
Kishlansky, Mark Alan 1948- *IntWW 93*
Kishtmand, Sultan Ali 1935- *IntWW 93*
Kisicki, Mary Kathleen 1959- *WhoMW 93*
Kisielowski, Eugene 1932- *WhoScEn 94*
Kisim, Marwan al- 1938- *IntWW 93*
Kiska, Timothy Olin 1952- *WhoAm 94*
Kiskadden, Robert Morgan 1918- *WhoAmA 93*
Kiskaddon, William V. 1929- *WhoAmP 93*
Kislik, Louis A. 1931- *WhoAm 94*
Kislik, Richard William 1927- *WhoAm 94, WhoFI 94*
Kisling, Stephen C. 1951- *WhoAmL 94*
Kislovski, Andre Serge 1933- *WhoScEn 94*
Kislyuk, Mikhail Borisovich 1951- *LngBDD*
Kismaric, Carole Lee 1942- *WhoAm 94*
Kisner, Ignatius 1925- *WhoAmP 93*
Kisner, Jacob 1926- *WhoAm 94*
Kisner, James Martin *DrAPF 93*
Kisner, Ned Bernard 1938- *WhoWest 94*
Kisner, Robert Garland 1940- *WhoBlA 94*
Kison, Carol *WhoMW 93*
Kisor, Henry Du Bois 1940- *WhoAm 94, WhoMW 93*
Kispert, Dorothy Lee 1928- *WhoBlA 94*
Kiss, Gyula 1954- *IntWW 93*
Kiss, Robert S. 1957- *WhoAmP 93*
Kiss, Vince Mihaly 1941- *WhoMW 93*
Kissa, Erik 1923- *WhoAm 94, WhoScEn 94*
Kissam, Ed *DrAPF 93*
Kissane, James Donald 1930- *WhoAm 94*
Kissane, Mary Elizabeth *WhoFI 94*
Kissane, Ray William 1894- *WhAm 10*
Kissane, Thomas *WhoAmL 94*
Kisseberth, Paul Barto 1932- *WhoAm 94*
Kissel, Howard William 1942- *WhoAm 94*
Kissel, John A. *WhoAmP 93*
Kissel, Peter Charles 1947- *WhoAmL 94*
Kissel, Richard John 1936- *WhoAm 94*
Kissel, William Thorn, Jr. 1920- *WhoAmA 93*
Kissell, Kenneth Eugene 1928- *WhoScEn 94*
Kissen, Murray d1958 *WhoHol 92*
Kissick, Gary *DrAPF 93*
Kissick, William Lee 1932- *WhoAm 94, WhoScEn 94*
Kissileff, Alfred 1908- *WhoScEn 94*
Kissiloff, William 1929- *WhoAm 94*
Kissin, Baron 1912- *Who 94*
Kissin, Harry 1912- *IntWW 93*
Kissin, Yevgeny Igorevich 1971- *IntWW 93*
Kissinger, Harold Arthur 1922- *WhoAm 94*
Kissinger, Henry 1923- *HisWorL [port]*
Kissinger, Henry (Alfred) 1923- *WrDr 94*
Kissinger, Henry Alfred 1923- *IntWW 93, Who 94, WhoAm 94, WhoAmP 93*
Kissinger, William David 1960- *WhoAmL 94*
Kissling, John Robert, Jr. 1945- *WhoMW 93*
Kisslinger, Carl 1926- *WhoScEn 94, WhoWest 94*
Kisslinger, Lawrence E. 1944- *WhoAmP 93*
Kisslinger, Leonard Sol 1930- *WhoAm 94*
Kist, A. Jack 1940- *WhoFI 94*
Kis-Tamas, Attila 1939- *WhoScEn 94*
Kister, Henry Z. *WhoScEn 94*
Kister, James Milton 1930- *WhoAm 94*
Kistiakowsky, Vera 1928- *WhoAm 94*
Kistler, Alan Lee 1928- *WhoAm 94*
Kistler, Alan Lewis 1943- *WhoScEn 94*
Kistler, Cyrill 1848-1907 *NewGrDO*
Kistler, Darci 1964- *IntDcB, IntWW 93*
Kistler, Darci Anna 1964- *WhoAm 94*
Kistler, Joy William 1898- *WhAm 10*
Kistler, Robert L. 1925- *WhoAmP 93*
Kistler, Vera *DrAPF 93*
Kistler, William *DrAPF 93*
Kistner, David Harold 1931- *WhoAm 94, WhoScEn 94, WhoWest 94*
Kistner, Diane *DrAPF 93*
Kistner, Melvin Carl 1947- *WhoAmP 93*
Kistner, Robert William 1917- *WrDr 94*
Kisvarsanyi, Eva Bognar 1935- *WhoMW 93*
Kit, Saul 1920- *WhoAm 94*
Kita, George Isao 1964- *WhoWest 94*
Kita, Sadao *WhoAsA 94*
Kita, Shuji *IntWW 93*
Kitada, Shinichi 1948- *WhoScEn 94, WhoWest 94*
Kitaen, Tawny 1961- *WhoHol 92*
Kitagawa, Audrey Emiko 1951- *WhoAmL 94*
Kitagawa, Ishimatsu *IntWW 93*
Kitagawa, Joseph 1915-1992 *AnObit 1992*
Kitagawa, Joseph Mitsuo 1915-1992 *WhAm 10, WhoAsA 94N*
Kitagawa, Takeshi 1916- *IntWW 93*
Kitagawa, Toshikazu 1958- *WhoScEn 94*
Kitahara, David James 1951- *WhoAsA 94*
Kitahara, Shizuo 1922- *WhoScEn 94*
Kitahata, Stacy Dee 1961- *WhoAsA 94*
Kitaj, R. B. 1932- *IntWW 93, Who 94, WhoAm 94, WhoAmA 93*
Kitamura, Hiroshi 1929- *IntWW 93, Who 94*
Kitamura, Kazuo *WhoHol 92*
Kitamura, So 1952- *IntWW 93*
Kitamura, Toshinori 1947- *WhoScEn 94*
Kitani, Osamu 1935- *WhoScEn 94*
Kitano, Harry H. L. 1926- *WrDr 94*
Kitano, Kazuaki 1939- *WhoScEn 94*
Kitao, T. Kaori 1933- *WhoAmA 93*
Kitasato, Shibasaburo 1852-1931 *WorScD [port]*
Kitayenko, Dmitriy Georgievich 1940- *IntWW 93*
Kitazawa, Koichi 1943- *WhoAm 94, WhoScEn 94*
Kitbunchu, Michael Michai 1929- *IntWW 93*
Kitcat, Mable Greenhow 1859-1922 *DcLB 135*
Kitcatt, Peter (Julian) 1927- *Who 94*
Kitch, Edmund Wells 1939- *WhoAm 94*
Kitch, Frederick David 1928- *WhoAm 94*
Kitch, James C. 1947- *WhoAmL 94*
Kitch, Richard Alfred 1930- *WhoAm 94, WhoAmL 94*
Kitch, Sally L. 1946- *ConAu 140*
Kitchak, Peter Ramon 1941- *WhoAm 94*
Kitchel, Denison 1908- *WhoAm 94*
Kitchel, Jan Kelly 1951- *WhoAm 94*
Kitchell, Shawn Ray 1962- *WhoFI 94, WhoScEn 94*
Kitchen, Charles William 1926- *WhoAmL 94*
Kitchen, Fred d1951 *WhoHol 92*
Kitchen, Frederick Bruford 1912- *Who 94*
Kitchen, Hyram 1932-1990 *WhAm 10*
Kitchen, John Howard 1957- *WhoFI 94*
Kitchen, John Martin 1936- *WhoAm 94, WhoWest 94*
Kitchen, John Milton 1912- *WhoAm 94*
Kitchen, Jonathan Saville 1948- *WhoAmL 94*
Kitchen, Judith *DrAPF 93*
Kitchen, Lawrence Oscar 1923- *IntWW 93, WhoAm 94*
Kitchen, Mark Scott 1953- *WhoWest 94*
Kitchen, Martin 1936- *WrDr 94*
Kitchen, Michael 1948- *Who 94, WhoHol 92*
Kitchen, Paddy 1934- *WrDr 94*
Kitchen, Paul Howard 1937- *WhoAm 94*
Kitchen, Stanley 1913- *Who 94*
Kitchen, Wayne Leroy 1948- *WhoBlA 94*
Kitchener, Horatio Herbert 1850-1916 *HisWorL [port]*
Kitchener, Ruth Mae 1907- *WhoAmP 93*
Kitchener Of Khartoum, Earl 1919- *Who 94*
Kitchens, Ashton C. 1902-1992 *WhoBlA 94N*
Kitchens, Clarence Wesley, Jr. 1943- *WhoAm 94*
Kitchens, Frederick Lynton, Jr. 1940- *WhoFI 94*
Kitchens, William H. 1948- *WhoAmL 94*
Kitcher, Philip Stuart 1947- *WhoAm 94*
Kitchin, James D., III 1931- *WhoAm 94*
Kitchin, John Joseph 1933- *WhoAmL 94*
Kitchin, Laurence 1913- *WhoHol 92*
Kitchin, Laurence Tyson 1913- *Who 94, WhoAm 94*
Kitchin, Thomas 1719-1784 *DcNaB MP*
Kitching, Christopher John 1945- *Who 94*
Kitching, George 1910- *Who 94*
Kitching, John Alwyne 1908- *IntWW 93, Who 94*
Kitching, Peter 1938- *WhoScEn 94*
Kite, Keith D. 1956- *WhoAm 94*
Kite, Marilyn S. 1947- *WhoAmL 94*
Kite, Pat *DrAPF 93*
Kite, Steven B. 1949- *WhoAm 94*
Kite, Thomas O. Tom, Jr. 1949- *WhoAm 94*
Kite, William McDougall 1923- *WhoAm 94, WhoAmL 94*
Kiteley, Brian 1956- *WrDr 94*
Kithcart, Larry E. 1939- *WhoBlA 94*
Kitner, David N. 1948- *WhoAmL 94*
Kitner, Harold 1921- *WhoAmA 93*
Kito, Teruo 1932- *WhoFI 94*
Kitovani, Tengiz *IntWW 93*
Kitson *Who 94*
Kitson, Alexander Harper 1921- *Who 94*
Kitson, Frank (Edward) 1926- *Who 94*
Kitson, George McCullough 1922- *Who 94*
Kitson, James 1807-1885 *DcNaB MP*
Kitson, Linda Frances 1945- *IntWW 93*
Kitson, Michael William Lely 1926- *Who 94*
Kitson, Timothy (Peter Geoffrey) 1931- *Who 94*
Kitsopoulos, Sotirios C. 1930- *WhoScEn 94*
Kitt, Eartha 1928- *IntMPA 94, WhoHol 92*
Kitt, Eartha Mae 1928- *IntWW 93, WhoAm 94, WhoBlA 94*
Kitt, Loren Wayne 1941- *WhoAm 94*
Kitt, Tamara 1914- *WrDr 94*
Kitt, Walter 1925- *WhoMW 93*
Kitta, John Noah 1951- *WhoAmL 94*
Kittaka, Atsushi 1959- *WhoScEn 94*
Kittani, Ismat 1930- *IntWW 93*
Kittel, Charles 1916- *IntWW 93, WhoAm 94*
Kittel, Donna 1959- *WhoMW 93*
Kittel, Hermine 1879-1948 *NewGrDO*
Kittel, Norman Griffith 1932- *WhoAmP 93*
Kittell, Donald D. 1937- *WhoFI 94*
Kittell, Ernest L. 1927- *WhoAmP 93*
Kittelsen, Rodney Olin 1917- *WhoAmL 94*
Kittelson, David James 1931-1989 *ConAu 142*
Kittikachorn, Thanom 1911- *IntWW 93*
Kittl, Jan Bedrich 1806-1868 *NewGrDO*
Kittle, Charles Frederick 1921- *WhoAm 94*
Kittle, Paul Edwin 1948- *WhoWest 94*
Kittleman, Robert H. 1926- *WhoAmP 93*
Kittleson, Henry Marshall 1929- *WhoAm 94, WhoAmL 94, WhoFI 94*
Kittlitz, Rudolf Gottlieb, Jr. 1935- *WhoAm 94*
Kittner, Edwin Henry 1925- *WhoFI 94*
Kitto, Frank (Walters) 1903- *Who 94*
Kitto, Franklin Curtis 1954- *WhoWest 94*
Kitto, John Buck, Jr. 1952- *WhoMW 93, WhoScEn 94*

Kittredge, John Kendall 1927- *WhoAm 94*
Kittredge, Nancy (Elizabeth) 1938- *WhoAmA 93*
Kittredge, Thomas M. 1940- *WhoAm 94, WhoAmL 94*
Kittredge, William *DrAPF 93*
Kittredge, William 1932- *WrDr 94*
Kittredge, William Alfred 1932- *WhoWest 94*
Kittrell, Benjamin Upchurch 1937- *WhoScEn 94*
Kittrell, Steven Dan 1953- *WhoAm 94*
Kittrie, Nicholas Norbert Nehemiah 1930- *WhoAm 94, WhoAmL 94*
Kittross, John Michael 1929- *WhoAm 94*
Kittson, Norman Wolfred 1814-1888 *WhWE*
Kituomba *BlkWr 2, ConAu 43NR*
Kitz, Richard John 1929- *WhoAm 94*
Kitzberger, Peter Joseph 1950- *WhoAmP 93*
Kitzes, William Fredric 1950- *WhoAmL 94*
Kitzhaber, John Albert 1947- *WhoAmP 93*
Kitzie, John, Jr. 1954- *WhoAm 94*
Kitzinger, Ernst 1912- *WhoAmA 93*
Kitzinger, Sheila 1929- *WrDr 94*
Kitzinger, Sheila Helena Elizabeth 1929- *IntWW 93, Who 94*
Kitzinger, Uwe 1928- *IntWW 93, Who 94, WrDr 94*
Kitzis, Gary David 1953- *WhoScEn 94*
Kitzke, Eugene David 1923- *WhoAm 94*
Kitzmiller, Greg Louis 1950- *WhoMW 93*
Kitzmiller, John d1965 *WhoHol 92*
Kitzmiller, Karen Bittermann 1947- *WhoAmP 93*
Kitzmiller, Karl William 1931- *WhoMW 93, WhoScEn 94*
Kitzmiller, William Michael 1931- *WhoAm 94*
Kiuchi, Takashi Tachi 1935- *WhoWest 94*
Kiurina, Berta 1882-1933 *NewGrDO*
Kiuttu, Ronald Neil 1957- *WhoHisp 94*
Kivelidi, Ivan Kharlampievich 1949- *LngBDD*
Kivelson, Margaret Galland 1928- *WhoAm 94, WhoScEn 94, WhoWest 94*
Kivengere, Festo 1920- *IntWW 93*
Kivenko, Kenneth *WhoAm 94*
Kiver, Eugene Paul 1937- *WhoWest 94*
Kivette, Ruth Montgomery 1926- *WhoAm 94*
Kiviat, Philip Jay 1937- *WhoAm 94*
Kivikas, Toivelemb 1937- *WhoScEn 94*
Kivinen, Seppo Tapio 1946- *WhoScEn 94*
Kivisto, Peter John 1948- *WhoMW 93*
Kiwala, Terrence E. 1945- *WhoAmL 94*
Kiwan, Abdul Mageed Metwally 1934- *WhoScEn 94*
Kiwitt, Sidney 1928- *WhoAm 94*
KixMiller, Richard Wood 1920- *WhoScEn 94*
Kiyabu, Ken S. 1937- *WhoAmP 93*
Kizer, Carolyn *DrAPF 93*
Kizer, Carolyn 1925- *ConLC 80 [port], WrDr 94*
Kizer, Carolyn Ashley 1925- *WhoAm 94*
Kizer, John Oscar 1913- *WhoAm 94*
Kizer, Kenneth Wayne 1951- *WhoAm 94*
Kizer, William M. 1925- *WhoIns 94*
Kizorek, William Leonard 1945- *WhoFI 94*
Kizziar, James H., Jr. 1951- *WhoAmL 94*
Kizziar, Janet Wright *WhoAm 94, WhoWest 94*
Kjar, Rolland William 1932- *WhoAmP 93*
Kjeldaas, Terje, Jr. 1924- *WhoAm 94*
Kjeldgaar, Richard H. 1952- *WhoAmL 94*
Kjelgaard, Jim *EncSF 93*
Kjellen, Bo 1933- *IntWW 93*
Kjellertz, Gosta d1984 *WhoHol 92*
Kjellin, Alf d1988 *WhoHol 92*
Kjellmark, Eric William, Jr. 1928- *WhoAm 94*
Kjetsaa, Geir 1937- *IntWW 93*
Kjome, David John 1936- *WhoMW 93*
Kjonstad, Asbjorn 1943- *IntWW 93*
Kjos, Victoria Ann 1953- *WhoAmL 94*
Klaar, Richard 1941- *WhoWest 94*
Klaas, Erwin Eugene 1935- *WhoMW 93*
Klaas, Nicholas Paul 1925- *WhoAm 94*
Klaas, Paul Barry 1952- *WhoAm 94, WhoAmL 94*
Klaas, Richard Lee 1945- *WhoAm 94*
Klaaste, Aggrey Zola 1940- *IntWW 93*
Klabosh, Charles Joseph 1920- *WhoFI 94*
Klabunde, Charles Spencer 1935- *WhoAmA 93*
Klacsmann, John Anthony 1921- *WhoAm 94*
Klaerner, Curtis Maurice 1920- *WhoAm 94*
Klafkowski, Alfons d1992 *IntWW 93N*
Klafsky, Katharina 1855-1896 *NewGrDO*
Klafter, Cary Ira 1948- *WhoAm 94, WhoAmL 94*
Klagsbrunn, Hans Alexander 1909- *WhoAm 94, WhoFI 94*
Klah, Hosteen 1867-1937 *EncNAR*
Klahr, Gary Peter 1942- *WhoAmL 94, WhoWest 94*
Klahr, Myra *DrAPF 93*
Klahr, Saulo 1935- *WhoAm 94*
Klain, Ronald Alan 1961- *WhoAm 94*
Klairmont, Larry Merton 1926- *WhoMW 93*
Klajbor, Dorothea M. 1915- *WhoAmL 94*
Klakeg, Clayton Harold 1920- *WhoWest 94*
Klamerus, Kenneth James 1954- *WhoMW 93*
Klamkin, Marian 1926- *WrDr 94*
Klammer, Joseph Francis 1925- *WhoFI 94, WhoWest 94*
Klamon, Lawrence Paine 1937- *WhoAm 94*
Klampe, Terry 1949- *WhoAmP 93*
Klane, Larry Allan 1960- *WhoFI 94*
Klang, Kathy Jo 1961- *WhoFI 94*
Klaniczay, Tibor d1992 *IntWW 93N*
Klann, Paul Gerhardt 1927- *WhoMW 93*
Klaper, Martin Jay 1947- *WhoAm 94, WhoAmL 94*
Klaperman, Gilbert 1921- *WhoAm 94*
Klaperman, Joel Simcha 1946- *WhoAm 94, WhoAmL 94*
Klapisch-Zuber, Christiane 1936- *IntWW 93*
Klapman, Jarvis Randolph 1916- *WhoAmP 93*
Klapoetke, Thomas Matthias 1961- *WhoScEn 94*
Klapp, Enrique H. *WhoHisp 94*
Klapper, Andrew David 1965- *WhoAmL 94*
Klapper, Byron D. 1938- *WhoFI 94*
Klapper, Carol Lorraine 1923- *WhoAm 94*
Klapper, Molly *WhoAmL 94*
Klapperich, Frank Lawrence, Jr. 1934- *WhoAm 94*
Klappert, Peter *DrAPF 93*
Klappert, Peter 1942- *WrDr 94*
Klaproth, Martin Heinrich 1743-1817 *WorScD*
Klar, Gary 1947- *WhoHol 92*
Klare, George Roger 1922- *WhoAm 94, WrDr 94*
Klare, Hugh J 1916- *WrDr 94*
Klare, Hugh John 1916- *Who 94*
Klare, Michael T(homas) 1942- *WrDr 94*
Klare, Michael Thomas 1942- *WhoAm 94*
Klarer, Fredrick 1948- *WhoAmL 94*
Klarfeld, Jonathan Michael 1937- *WhoAm 94*
Klarfeld, Peter James 1947- *WhoAmL 94*
Klarich, David J. 1963- *WhoAmP 93*
Klarich, David John 1963- *WhoMW 93*
Klarich, Janet Carlson 1931- *WhoAmP 93*
Klarich, Nina Marie *WhoAm 94*
Klarin, Winifred Erlick *WhoAmA 93*
Klaristenfeld, Harry I. 1950- *WhoIns 94*
Klaritch, Thomas Michael, Sr. 1957- *WhoWest 94*
Klarman, Herbert Elias 1916- *WhoAm 94*
Klarman, Karl Joseph 1922- *WhoScEn 94*
Klarmann, Dave *WhoAm 94*
Klarreich, Susan Rae 1942- *WhoScEn 94*
Klarwein, Franz 1914- *NewGrDO*
Klas, John Hall 1917- *WhoAmP 93*
Klasing, Susan Allen 1957- *WhoScEn 94*
Klasko, Herbert Ronald 1949- *WhoAm 94, WhoAmL 94*
Klass, Donald William 1928- *WhoMW 93*
Klass, Marvin Joseph 1913- *WhoAmL 94*
Klass, Morton 1927- *WhoAm 94*
Klass, Perri 1958- *WrDr 94*
Klass, Philip *EncSF 93*
Klass, Philip Julian 1919- *WhoAm 94*
Klass, Sheila Solomon *DrAPF 93*
Klass, Sheila Solomon 1927- *WrDr 94*
Klassek, Christine Paulette 1947- *WhoMW 93*
Klassen, Albert D(ale), Jr. 1931- *WrDr 94*
Klassen, Alvin Henry 1949- *WhoWest 94*
Klassen, Elmer Theodore 1908-1990 *WhAm 10*
Klassen, Jane Frances 1956- *WhoScEn 94*
Klassen, Lynell W. 1947- *WhoScEn 94*
Klassen, Peter James 1930- *WhoAm 94*
Klatchkin, Raphael d1987 *WhoHol 92*
Klatell, Jack 1918- *WhoAm 94*
Klatell, Robert Edward 1945- *WhoAm 94, WhoFI 94*
Klatsky, Bruce J. 1948- *WhoFI 94*
Klatt, David Frederick 1948- *WhoAm 94*
Klatt, Gordon Roy 1942- *WhoAm 94, WhoWest 94*
Klatt, John Harold 1956- *WhoMW 93*
Klatt, John Paul 1958- *WhoWest 94*
Klatt, Roger James 1938- *WhoFI 94*
Klatte, Diethard W. 1950- *WhoScEn 94*
Klauber, Gertan 1932- *WhoHol 92*
Klauber, James Shuler 1966- *WhoAmP 93*
Klauber, Rick 1950- *WhoAmA 93*
Klauberg, William Joseph 1926- *WhoAm 94*
Klaubert, Earl Christian 1930- *WhoScEn 94*
Klauck, Daniel L. *DrAPF 93*
Klauder, John Rider 1932- *WhoAm 94*
Klauder, N. Jeffrey 1952- *WhoAm 94*
Klaus, Carl Hanna 1932- *WhoAm 94*
Klaus, Charles 1935- *WhoAm 94*
Klaus, Elmer Erwin 1921- *WhoAm 94*
Klaus, Josef 1910- *IntWW 93*
Klaus, Suzanne Lynne 1956- *WhoMW 93*
Klaus, Vaclav 1941- *IntWW 93*
Klaus, William Robert *WhoAm 94*
Klause, Annette Curtis *TwCYAW*
Klause, Annette Curtis 1953- *WhoAm 94*
Klausen, Raymond 1939- *WhoAm 94*
Klauser, James Roland 1939- *WhoMW 93*
Klausler, Alfred Paul 1910-1991 *WhAm 10*
Klausmann, Walter Joseph 1937- *WhoFI 94*
Klausmeier, Herbert John 1915- *WhoAm 94*
Klausmeyer, David Michael 1934- *WhoFI 94, WhoScEn 94*
Klausner, Betty 1928- *WhoAmA 93*
Klausner, Jack Daniel 1945- *WhoAmL 94, WhoWest 94*
Klausner, Samuel Zundel 1923- *WhoAm 94*
Klausner, Willette Murphy 1939- *WhoBlA 94*
Klavan, Andrew *DrAPF 93*
Klavano, Paul Arthur 1919- *WhoScEn 94*
Klavans, Minnie 1915- *WhoAmA 93*
Klaven, Marvin L. 1931- *WhoAmA 93*
Klaver, Martin Arnold, Jr. 1932- *WhoScEn 94*
Klaviter, Helen Lothrop 1944- *WhoAm 94, WhoMW 93*
Klavun, Walter d1984 *WhoHol 92*
Klaw, Barbara Van Doren 1920- *WhoAm 94*
Klaw, Spencer 1920- *WhoAm 94*
Klawans, Harold L(eo) 1937- *WrDr 94*
Klawe, Maria Margaret 1951- *WhoWest 94*
Klawiter, Donald Casimir 1950- *WhoAm 94*
Klawitter, George Albert 1942- *WhoMW 93*
Klawitter, Robert Louis 1938- *WhoMW 93*
Klawonn, William Edward 1954- *WhoAmL 94*
Klayman, Barry Martin 1952- *WhoAm 94, WhoAmL 94*
Klearman, Margie 1933- *WhoAmP 93*
Kleban, Cheryl Christine 1955- *WhoFI 94*
Kleban, Edward Lawrence 1939-1987 *WhAm 10*
Kleban, Kenneth A. 1950- *WhoAm 94, WhoAmL 94*
Kleban, Morton Harold 1931- *WhoScEn 94*
Klebanoff, Howard Michael 1937- *WhoAmL 94, WhoAmP 93*
Klebanoff, Philip Samuel 1918- *WhAm 10*
Klebanoff, Seymour Joseph 1927- *WhoAm 94, WhoScEn 94, WhoWest 94*
Klebanoff, Stanley Milton 1926- *WhoAmL 94*
Klebba, Lorraine Marie 1969- *WhoMW 93*
Klebba, Raymond Allen 1934- *WhoMW 93*
Klebe, Donald Fred 1936- *WhoMW 93*
Klebe, Gene 1918- *WhoAmA 93N*
Klebe, Giselher 1925- *IntWW 93*
Klebe, Giselher (Wolfgang) 1925- *NewGrDO*
Kleberg, Jack Carl 1930- *WhoAm 94*
Klebesadel, Ray William 1932- *WhoMW 93*
Kleck, Gary 1951- *ConAu 140*
Kleck, Robert Eldon 1937- *WhoAm 94, WhoScEn 94*
Kleckner, Betty Ann 1922- *WhoAmP 93*
Kleckner, Dean Ralph 1932- *WhoAm 94, WhoMW 93, WhoScEn 94*
Kleckner, Marlin Dallas 1932- *WhoScEn 94*
Kleckner, Robert George, Jr. 1932- *WhoAmL 94*
Kleckner, Roger Eugene 1947- *WhoAmP 93*
Kleckner, Susan 1941- *WhoAmA 93*
Klecko, Joe *WhoHol 92*
Kleczek, David James 1955- *WhoMW 93*
Kleczka, Gerald D. 1943- *CngDr 93, WhoAm 94, WhoMW 93*
Kleczka, Gerald Daniel 1943- *WhoAmP 93*
Klee, Bernhard 1936- *NewGrDO*
Klee, Karl Heinz *WhoAmL 94, WhoFI 94*
Klee, Kenneth Nathan 1949- *WhoAm 94*
Klee, Miriam Louise Shatzer 1926- *WhoMW 93*
Klee, Victor La Rue 1925- *WhoAm 94, WhoScEn 94, WhoWest 94*
Kleeb, Helen *WhoHol 92*
Kleeman, Harry 1928- *Who 94*
Kleeman, Michael Jeffrey 1949- *WhoAm 94*
Kleeman, Walter Benton, Jr. 1918- *WhoAm 94*
Kleemann, Ron 1937- *WhoAmA 93*
Kleemann, Ronald Allen 1937- *WhoAm 94*
Kleen, Vernon Melvin 1942- *WhoMW 93*
Kleene, Stephen Cole 1909- *WhoAm 94, WhoScEn 94*
Klees, Robert E. 1927- *IntMPA 94*
Kleese, William Carl 1940- *WhoWest 94*
Kleespies, Mark Frederick 1959- *WhoMW 93*
Klegerman, Melvin Earl 1945- *WhoMW 93*
Klehr, Harvey 1945- *WrDr 94*
Klehr, Leonard M. 1950- *WhoAmL 94*
Klehs, Henry John Wilhelm 1910- *WhoWest 94*
Klehs, Johan 1952- *WhoAmP 93*
Kleiber, Carlos 1930- *NewGrDO*
Kleiber, Douglas Harold 1955- *WhoWest 94*
Kleiber, Erich 1890-1956 *NewGrDO*
Kleidon, Dennis Arthur 1942- *WhoAmA 93*
Kleiger, Robert Edward 1934- *WhoMW 93*
Kleihues, Josef Paul 1933- *IntWW 93*
Kleiman, Alan 1938- *WhoAmA 93*
Kleiman, Alan Boyd 1938- *WhoAm 94*
Kleiman, Ansel 1925- *WhoAm 94*
Kleiman, Bernard 1928- *EncABHB 9 [port], WhoAm 94, WhoAmL 94, WhoFI 94*
Kleiman, David Harold 1934- *WhoAm 94*
Kleiman, Devra Gail 1942- *WhoScEn 94*
Kleiman, Ed 1932- *WrDr 94*
Kleiman, Gary Howard 1952- *WhoAm 94, WhoFI 94*
Kleiman, Harlan Philip 1940- *WhoAm 94, WhoWest 94*
Kleiman, Joseph 1919- *WhoAm 94*
Kleiman, Norman Jay 1959- *WhoScEn 94*
Kleiman, Steven Lawrence 1942- *WhoAm 94*
Klein, Abraham 1927- *WhoAm 94*
Klein, Adelaide d1983 *WhoHol 92*
Klein, Al d1951 *WhoHol 92*
Klein, Alexander 1923- *WrDr 94*
Klein, Allan William 1942- *WhoMW 93*
Klein, Allen 1931- *IntMPA 94*
Klein, Allen 1938- *WrDr 94*
Klein, Andrew Manning 1941- *WhoAm 94*
Klein, Anne Sceia 1942- *WhoFI 94*
Klein, Arnold Meyer 1950- *WhoFI 94*
Klein, Arnold Spencer 1951- *WhoAm 94*
Klein, Arnold William 1945- *WhoScEn 94, WhoWest 94*
Klein, Arthur L. 1943- *WhoAm 94, WhoAmL 94*
Klein, Arthur Luce 1916- *WhoAm 94*
Klein, Barbara Diane 1963- *WhoMW 93*
Klein, Benjamin 1943- *WhoAm 94*
Klein, Bernard 1921- *WhoAm 94, WhoFI 94*
Klein, Bernard W. *WhoMW 93*
Klein, Bernat 1922- *Who 94*
Klein, Binnie *DrAPF 93*
Klein, Calvin Richard 1942- *IntWW 93, WhoAm 94*
Klein, Carol *DrAPF 93*
Klein, Cecelia F. 1938- *WhoAmA 93*
Klein, Charles Edward 1957- *WhoFI 94*
Klein, Charles Henle 1908- *WhoFI 94, WhoMW 93*
Klein, Christopher Carnahan 1953- *WhoFI 94, WhoScEn 94*
Klein, Clayton C., Jr. 1949- *WhoAmP 93*
Klein, Dale Edward 1947- *WhoScEn 94*
Klein, Dale Mathew 1934- *WhoFI 94*
Klein, David 1919- *IntWW 93, WhoAm 94, WhoWest 94*
Klein, David M. 1946- *WhoIns 94*
Klein, Dennis Franklin 1951- *WhoFI 94*
Klein, Diane Lehman 1964- *WhoAmL 94*
Klein, Donald Franklin 1928- *WhoAm 94*
Klein, Doris 1918- *WhoAmA 93*
Klein, Doris Elaine 1929- *WhoMW 93*
Klein, Edith Miller 1915- *WhoAmL 94, WhoAmP 93, WhoWest 94*
Klein, Edward Joel 1936- *WhoAm 94*
Klein, Edward Robert 1950- *WhoScEn 94*
Klein, Edward William, III 1950- *WhoAmP 93*
Klein, Elaine 1929- *WhoFI 94*
Klein, Eleanor 1919- *WhoWest 94*
Klein, Elizabeth *DrAPF 93*
Klein, Ellen Lee *WhoAmA 93*
Klein, Esther M. 1907- *WhoAmA 93*
Klein, Fred J. 1927- *WhoAmL 94*

Klein, Frederic William 1922- *WhoAm 94*
Klein, Gabriella Sonja 1938- *WhoAm 94, WhoFI 94, WhoMW 93*
Klein, Gary J. 1947- *WhoAmL 94*
Klein, Genevieve Sanchez d1993 *NewYTBS 93*
Klein, George 1925- *ConAu 140, IntWW 93*
Klein, George D. 1933- *WhoAm 94, WhoScEn 94*
Klein, Gerard *WhoHol 92*
Klein, Gerard 1937- *EncSF 93*
Klein, Gerhart Leopold 1948- *WhoFI 94*
Klein, Gwenda J. 1949- *WhoAmA 93*
Klein, Hans 1931- *IntWW 93*
Klein, Harold J. *IntMPA 94*
Klein, Harold Paul 1921- *WhoScEn 94*
Klein, Harriet Farber 1948- *WhoAmL 94*
Klein, Henry 1920- *WhoAm 94*
Klein, Henry 1949- *WhoAmL 94*
Klein, Herbert 1930- *WhoAmP 93*
Klein, Herbert C. 1930- *CngDr 93*
Klein, Herbert C. 1931- *WhoAm 94*
Klein, Herbert George 1918- *IntWW 93, WhoAm 94, WhoWest 94*
Klein, Howard Bruce 1950- *WhoAm 94, WhoAmL 94*
Klein, Irving d1986 *WhoHol 92*
Klein, Jacqueline K. *WhoAmP 93*
Klein, James Mikel 1953- *WhoWest 94*
Klein, Jeffrey S. 1953- *WhoAm 94*
Klein, Jeffrey Steven 1953- *WhoAmP 93*
Klein, Jerry Emanuel 1933- *WhoFI 94*
Klein, Jill Abrams 1958- *WhoFI 94*
Klein, Joan Dempsey 1924- *WhoAm 94*
Klein, John E. 1945- *WhoFI 94*
Klein, John Nicholas, III 1946- *WhoAmP 93*
Klein, Joseph Alan 1946- *WhoAmL 94*
Klein, Joseph Mark 1921- *WhoAm 94*
Klein, Joseph Michelman 1936- *WhoAm 94*
Klein, Josephine (F. H.) 1926- *WrDr 94*
Klein, Judah B. 1923- *WhoAmL 94*
Klein, Julia Meredith 1955- *WhoAm 94*
Klein, Julius d1966 *WhoHol 92*
Klein, Kathleen Gregory 1946- *WrDr 94*
Klein, Kay Janis 1942- *WhoFI 94*
Klein, Lawrence R(obert) 1920- *WrDr 94*
Klein, Lawrence Robert 1920- *IntWW 93, Who 94, WhoAm 94, WhoFI 94*
Klein, Leander Francis 1932- *WhoWest 94*
Klein, Leonard *WhoScEn 94*
Klein, Linda Ann 1959- *WhoAmL 94*
Klein, Louis Edward 1920- *WhoFI 94*
Klein, Lynn (Ellen) 1950- *WhoAmA 93*
Klein, Lynn E. 1950- *WhoAm 94*
Klein, Malcolm C. 1927- *IntMPA 94*
Klein, Marc S. 1949- *WhoAm 94*
Klein, Marcia Schneiderman 1940- *WhoScEn 94*
Klein, Marcus 1928- *WrDr 94*
Klein, Marilyn Weiland 1928- *WhoAm 94*
Klein, Marjorie Hanson 1933- *WhoMW 93*
Klein, Mark Samuel 1957- *WhoAmL 94*
Klein, Marshall S. 1926- *WhoScEn 94*
Klein, Martin *WhoScEn 94*
Klein, Martin I. 1947- *WhoAmL 94*
Klein, Martin Jesse 1924- *WhoAm 94, WhoScEn 94*
Klein, Matthew M. *WhoAmP 93*
Klein, Maurice J. 1908- *WhoAm 94*
Klein, Maxine Manther 1934- *WhoMW 93*
Klein, Michael *DrAPF 93*
Klein, Michael D. 1951- *WhoAm 94*
Klein, Michael Eugene 1940- *WhoAmA 93*
Klein, Michael Lawrence 1940- *WhoAm 94*
Klein, Michael Roger 1942- *WhoAm 94*
Klein, Michael Tully 1955- *WhoAm 94, WhoScEn 94*
Klein, Michael William 1931- *WhoAm 94*
Klein, Miles Vincent 1933- *WhoAm 94, WhoScEn 94*
Klein, Morton 1925- *WhoAm 94, WhoScEn 94*
Klein, Morton Joseph 1928- *WhoAm 94*
Klein, Norma 1938-1989 *TwCYAW, WhAm 10*
Klein, Otto G., III 1950- *WhoAmL 94*
Klein, Paul E. 1934- *WhoAm 94, WhoAmL 94*
Klein, Perry Fred 1959- *WhoMW 93*
Klein, Peter 1907- *NewGrDO*
Klein, Peter Martin 1934- *WhoAm 94, WhoAmL 94, WhoFI 94*
Klein, Peter William 1955- *WhoAmL 94, WhoFI 94*
Klein, Peter Wolfgang 1931- *IntWW 93*
Klein, Philip Alexander 1927- *WhoAm 94, WrDr 94*
Klein, Philip Alexandre 1966- *WhoWest 94*
Klein, Philip S. d1993 *NewYTBS 93 [port]*
Klein, Philip Shriver 1909-1993 *ConAu 140*
Klein, Philipp Hillel 1926- *WhoScEn 94*
Klein, R. Kent 1944- *WhoAmL 94*
Klein, Ralph *WhoAm 94, WhoWest 94*
Klein, Raymond Maurice 1938- *WhoAm 94, WhoAmL 94, WhoWest 94*
Klein, Richard Benson 1939- *WhoAmL 94*
Klein, Richard Dean 1932- *WhoAm 94*
Klein, Richard Lee 1933- *WhoFI 94*
Klein, Richard Lewis 1945- *WhoWest 94*
Klein, Richard Stephen 1938- *WhoAm 94*
Klein, Robert d1960 *WhoHol 92*
Klein, Robert 1924- *WhoAm 94*
Klein, Robert 1942- *IntMPA 94, WhoAm 94, WhoCom, WhoHol 92*
Klein, Robert Dale 1951- *WhoAmL 94*
Klein, Robert Edward 1926- *WhoFI 94, WhoMW 93*
Klein, Robert Emil 1955- *WhoMW 93*
Klein, Robert G. *WhoAmP 93*
Klein, Robert Gordon 1947- *WhoAmL 94, WhoWest 94*
Klein, Robert H. 1932- *WhoMW 93*
Klein, Robert J. 1927-1993 *NewYTBS 93*
Klein, Robert M. 1949- *WhoAmL 94*
Klein, Robert Majer 1940- *WhoFI 94*
Klein, Robert Marshall 1957- *WhoAmL 94*
Klein, Robin 1936- *BlmGWL, TwCYAW*
Klein, Robin (McMaugh) 1936- *WrDr 94*
Klein, Ron 1957- *WhoAmP 93*
Klein, Ronald Don 1948- *WhoScEn 94*
Klein, Ronald Lloyd 1939- *WhoAm 94*
Klein, Rudolf Ewald 1930- *Who 94*
Klein, Ruth B. 1908- *WhoMW 93*
Klein, Sami Weiner 1939- *WhoAm 94*
Klein, Samuel Edwin 1946- *WhoAm 94*
Klein, Sandor C. 1912- *WhoAmA 93*
Klein, Sheldon 1935- *WhoAm 94*
Klein, Snira Lubovsky *WhoWest 94*
Klein, Steven Douglas 1952- *WhoFI 94*
Klein, Stuart M(arc) 1932- *WrDr 94*
Klein, Theodore Eibon Donald 1947- *WhoAm 94*
Klein, Verle Wesley 1933- *WhoAm 94*
Klein, Wallis Cherniack Weil 1941- *WhoMW 93*
Klein, William, II 1919- *WhoAmL 94*
Klein, Zachary 1948- *WrDr 94*
Kleinau, Willy A. d1957 *WhoHol 92*
Kleinbach, Henry *WhoHol 92*
Kleinbard, Edward D. 1951- *WhoAm 94, WhoAmL 94*
Kleinbardt, Ernest 1875-1962 *WhoAmA 93N*
Kleinbauer, W. Eugene 1937- *WhoAmA 93, WhoMW 93*
Kleinbaum, Richard Nathan 1943- *WhoAmP 93*
Kleinberg, Aviad M. 1957- *ConAu 141*
Kleinberg, David Lewis 1943- *WhoAm 94*
Kleinberg, Howard J. 1932- *WhoAm 94*
Kleinberg, Israel 1930- *WhoAm 94*
Kleinberg, Jacob 1914- *WhoAm 94*
Kleinberg, James P. 1943- *WhoAmL 94*
Kleinberg, Judith G. 1946- *WhoAmL 94*
Kleinberg, Kenneth Allan 1942- *WhoWest 94*
Kleinberg, Lawrence H. 1943- *WhoAm 94*
Kleinberg, Marvin H. 1927- *WhoAm 94*
Kleinberg, Norman Charles 1946- *WhoAm 94, WhoAmL 94*
Kleinberg, Robert Irwin 1937- *WhoAm 94, WhoAmL 94, WhoFI 94*
Kleinberg, Susan *WhoAmA 93*
Kleindienst, Richard Gordon 1923- *IntWW 93, Who 94, WhoAm 94, WhoAmP 93*
Kleindl, James Nicholas 1930- *WhoMW 93*
Kleine, Herman 1920- *WhoAm 94*
Kleine, Thomas R. 1946- *WhoFI 94*
Kleine-Ahlbrandt, William Laird 1932- *WrDr 94*
Kleiner, Fred Scott 1948- *WhoAm 94*
Kleiner, Harry 1916- *IntMPA 94*
Kleiner, Richard Arthur 1921- *WhoAm 94*
Kleinert, Harold Earl 1922- *WhoAm 94*
Kleinfeld, Andrew J. *WhoAmP 93*
Kleinfeld, Andrew Jay 1945- *WhoAm 94, WhoAmL 94, WhoWest 94*
Kleinfeld, Erwin 1927- *WhoAm 94*
Kleinfeld, Margaret Ann 1938- *WhoMW 93*
Kleinfeld, Vincent A. d1993 *NewYTBS 93*
Kleingartner, Archie 1936- *WhoAm 94*
Kleinhandler, Neil C. 1942- *WhoAmL 94*
Kleinhenz, Christopher 1941- *WhoAm 94*
Kleinknecht, Christian Frederick 1924- *WhoAm 94*
Kleinknecht, Kenneth Samuel 1919- *WhoAm 94*
Kleinlein, Kathy Lynn 1950- *WhoFI 94*
Kleinman, Arthur 1941- *IntWW 93*
Kleinman, Arthur Michael 1941- *WhoAm 94*
Kleinman, Burton Howard 1923- *WhoMW 93*
Kleinman, George 1951- *WhoFI 94*
Kleinman, Joel B. 1949- *WhoAmL 94*
Kleinman, Paul Bennett 1961- *WhoAmL 94*
Kleinman, Philip (Julian) 1932- *WrDr 94*
Kleinman, Randall 1952- *WhoIns 94*
Kleinman, Robert W. 1946- *WhoAmL 94*
Kleinman, Sue *WhoAmA 93*
Kleinman, Susan Phyllis 1947- *WhoMW 93*
Kleinmichel, Richard 1846-1901 *NewGrDO*
Kleinoder, Jack d1993 *NewYTBS 93 [port]*
Kleinpeter, Joseph Andrew 1943- *WhoScEn 94*
Kleinpoppen, Hans Johann Willi 1928- *Who 94, WhoScEn 94*
Kleinrock, Leonard 1934- *WhoAm 94, WhoWest 94*
Kleinrock, Virginia Barry 1947- *WhoFI 94*
Klein-Rogge, Rudolf d1955 *WhoHol 92*
Kleinsasser, Leland P. *WhoAmP 93*
Kleinschmidt, Edward *DrAPF 93*
Kleinschrod, Walter Andrew 1928- *WhoAm 94*
Kleinschuster, Stephen John 1939- *WhoAm 94*
Kleinsmith, Bruce John *WhoAmA 93*
Kleinsmith, Bruce John 1942- *WhoAm 94, WhoWest 94*
Kleinsmith, Gene 1942- *WhoAmA 93, WhoWest 94*
Kleinsmith, Lewis Joel 1942- *WhoAm 94*
Kleinwald, Martin 1940- *WhoAm 94*
Kleinwort, Kenneth (Drake) 1935- *Who 94*
Kleinzahler, August *DrAPF 93*
Kleinzeller, Arnost 1914- *WhoAm 94*
Kleiser, John Randal 1946- *WhoAm 94*
Kleiser, Randal 1946- *IntMPA 94*
Kleisner, George Harry 1909-1987 *WhAm 10*
Kleist, (Bernd) Heinrich (Wilhelm) von 1777-1811 *IntDcT 2 [port], NewGrDO, RfGShF*
Klekoda-Baker, Antonia Marie 1939- *WhoMW 93*
Klem, Bruce Terrence 1948- *WhoMW 93*
Klem, Christopher A. 1952- *WhoAm 94*
Klema, Ernest Donald 1920- *WhoAm 94*
Klemann, Elizabeth Perkins 1943- *WhoAmP 93*
Klemann, Gilbert Lacy, II 1950- *WhoAmL 94*
Klemann, Lawrence Paul 1943- *WhoScEn 94*
Klemarczyk, Thaddeus E. 1920- *WhoAmP 93*
Klemens, Paul Gustav 1925- *WhoAm 94*
Klemens, Thomas Lloyd 1952- *WhoAm 94, WhoFI 94*
Klement, Frank L. 1908- *WrDr 94*
Klement, Haim 1935- *WhoScEn 94*
Klement, Vera 1929- *WhoAm 94, WhoAmA 93*
Klements, Joseph Michael 1953- *WhoAmL 94*
Klemic, George Gerard 1949- *WhoFI 94, WhoWest 94*
Klemm, Arthur Paul, Jr. 1948- *WhoAmP 93*
Klemm, LeRoy Henry 1919- *WhoWest 94*
Klemm, Richard Henry 1931- *WhoAm 94*
Klemm, Richard O. 1932- *WhoAmP 93*
Klemme, Carl William 1928- *WhoAm 94*
Klemme, Howard Charles 1930- *WhoAm 94*
Klemme, Ralph *WhoAmP 93*
Klempay, Mary Jane 1959- *WhoMW 93*
Klemperer, Otto 1885-1973 *NewGrDO*
Klemperer, Walter George 1947- *WhoScEn 94*
Klemperer, Werner 1920- *WhoHol 92*
Klemperer, William 1927- *IntWW 93, WhoAm 94*
Klempner, Larry Brian 1956- *WhoScEn 94*
Klenau, Paul (August) von 1883-1946 *NewGrDO*
Klenck, Margaret *WhoHol 92*
Klenk, James Andrew 1949- *WhoAm 94, WhoAmL 94*
Klenk, Timothy Carver 1939- *WhoAmL 94*
Klenke, Daniel Frederick 1955- *WhoAmL 94*
Klepac, Robert Karl 1943- *WhoAm 94*
Klepfisz, Irena *DrAPF 93*
Klepfisz, Irena 1941- *BlmGWL*
Klepinger, Brian Wiley 1937- *WhoWest 94*
Klepinger, John William 1945- *WhoWest 94*
Klepner, Jerry D. 1944- *WhoAm 94*
Kleponis, Jerome Albert 1955- *WhoScEn 94*
Kleppe, Johan 1928- *IntWW 93*
Kleppe, John Arthur 1939- *WhoAm 94*
Kleppe, Per 1923- *IntWW 93*
Kleppe, Thomas S. 1919- *IntWW 93*
Klepper, Elizabeth Lee 1936- *WhoAm 94, WhoScEn 94*
Klepper, Harry George 1907- *WhoWest 94*
Klepper, John Christian 1945- *WhoWest 94*
Klepper, John Richard 1947- *WhoScEn 94*
Klepper, Martin 1947- *WhoAm 94*
Kleppinger, Moselle Lee 1956- *WhoWest 94*
Kleppner, Daniel 1932- *WhoAm 94, WhoScEn 94*
Klepsch, Egon Alfred 1930- *IntWW 93, Who 94*
Klercker, George A. F. d1951 *WhoHol 92*
Klerman, Gerald Lawrence 1928-1992 *WhAm 10*
Kleschick, William Anthony, III 1950- *WhoMW 93*
Klesius, Phillip Harry 1938- *WhoAm 94*
Klestil, Thomas 1932- *IntWW 93*
Klett, Edwin Lee 1935- *WhoAm 94, WhoAmL 94*
Klett, Gordon A. 1925- *WhoAm 94*
Klett, Mark 1952- *WhoAmA 93*
Klett, Mark C. 1952- *WhoAm 94*
Klett, Walter Charles 1897-1966 *WhoAmA 93N*
Kletzel, Martin d1699 *NewGrDO*
Kletzkine, Philippe 1957- *WhoScEn 94*
Klevan, Rodney Conrad 1940- *Who 94*
Klevatt, Steve *WhoScEn 94*
Kleveland, Ase 1949- *WhoWomW 91*
Kleven, Elisa 1958- *SmATA 76 [port]*
Kleven, Leslie J. *WhoAmP 93*
Kleven, Thomas 1942- *WhoBlA 94*
Klevorick, Alvin K. 1943- *WhoFI 94*
Klewans, Samuel N. 1941- *WhoAmL 94*
Kleweno, Gilbert H. 1933- *WhoAm 94, WhoAmL 94, WhoWest 94*
Kley, Alfred Julius 1895-1957 *WhoAmA 93N*
Kley, John Arthur 1921- *WhoAm 94*
Kley, Stephen John 1951- *WhoMW 93*
Kleyman, Henry Semyon 1926- *WhoScEn 94*
Kliban, B(ernard) 1935-1990 *WhAm 10*
Klibanov, Alexander Maxim 1949- *WhoAm 94, WhoScEn 94*
Klibansky, Raymond 1905- *Who 94*
Klibi, Chedli 1925- *IntWW 93*
Klieback, Hy 1931- *WhoWest 94*
Kliebhan, Mary Camille 1923- *WhoAm 94*
Kliefoth, Arthur Bernhard, III 1942- *WhoAm 94, WhoScEn 94*
Kliegman, Edwin J. 1925- *WhoFI 94*
Kliem, Peter Otto 1938- *WhoAm 94*
Klieman, Charles 1940- *ConAu 140*
Klieman, Rikki Jo 1948- *WhoAmL 94*
Klien, Wolfgang Josef 1942- *WhoWest 94*
Klier, John Doyle 1944- *ConAu 141*
Kliesch, William Frank 1928- *WhoScEn 94*
Kliewer, Henry J. 1871-1943 *EncNAR*
Kliewer, Kenneth Lee 1935- *WhoAm 94*
Kliewer, Warren *DrAPF 93*
Kliger, Gary *WhoHol 92*
Kliger, Jack *WhoAm 94*
Kliger, Milton Richard 1922- *WhoAm 94*
Kligerman, Morton M. 1917- *WhoAm 94*
Kligfield, Paul David 1945- *WhoAm 94*
Klim, Michael Stephen 1955- *WhoAmL 94*
Klima, Ivan 1931- *ConWorW 93*
Klima, Jerry V. 1943- *WhoAmL 94*
Klima, Jon Edward 1939- *WhoScEn 94*
Klima, Martha Scanlan 1938- *WhoAmP 93*
Klima, Roger R. *WhoWest 94*
Klimack, William Klaeve 1957- *WhoFI 94*
Klimas, Antanas 1924- *WhoAm 94*
Klimaszewski, Mieczyslaw 1908- *IntWW 93*
Kliment, Robert Michael 1933- *WhoAm 94, WhoScEn 94*
Kliment, Stephen Alexander 1930- *WhoAm 94*
Klimentova, Maria Nikolayevna 1857-1946 *NewGrDO*
Klimerman, Edward 1942- *WhoAmL 94*
Klimesz, Henry Roman 1926- *WhoFI 94*
Klimisch, Richard Leo 1938- *WhoAm 94*
Klimko, Ronald James 1936- *WhoWest 94*
Klimkowski, Robert John 1930- *WhoScEn 94*
Klimm, John C. *WhoAmP 93*
Klimo, Jon *DrAPF 93*
Klimoski, David Bruce 1946- *WhoWest 94*
Klimov, Elem Germanovich 1933- *IntWW 93*
Klimov, Fedor Matveevich 1935- *LngBDD*
Klimov, Oleg Aleksandrovich 1936- *LngBDD*
Klimova, Rita d1993 *NewYTBS 93 [port]*
Klimow, Sergei Nicholas 1939- *WhoWest 94*
Klimowicz, Thomas F. 1955- *WhoScEn 94*

K. M. *GayLL*
Kmenta, Jan 1928- *WhoMW 93*
Kmentt, Waldemar 1929- *NewGrDO*
Kmet, Joseph Paul 1942- *WhoWest 94*
Kmet, Rebecca Eugenia Patterson 1948- *WhoWest 94*
Kmetz, Christopher Paul 1969- *WhoScEn 94*
Kmetz, Donald R. *WhoAm 94*
Kmiec, Bogumil Leon 1944- *WhoScEn 94*
Kmiec, Douglas William 1951- *WhoAm 94*
Kmiotek, Jacqueline J. 1959- *WhoAmL 94*
Knaak, Fritz 1953- *WhoAmP 93*
Knaapen, David Raymond 1958- *WhoAmL 94*
Knab, Donald Ralph 1922- *WhoAm 94*
Knabe, George William, Jr. 1924- *WhoAm 94*
Knabe, Otis Eugene 1951- *WhoMW 93*
Knabe, Steven William 1948- *WhoMW 93*
Knable, Bobbie Margaret Brown 1936- *WhoBlA 94*
Knabusch, Charles Thair 1939- *WhoAm 94, WhoFI 94*
Knachel, Philip Atherton 1926- *WhoAm 94*
Knack, Martha Carol 1948- *WhoWest 94*
Knack, Wallson George 1935- *WhoAmL 94*
Knackstedt, Gunter Whilhelm Karl 1929- *IntWW 93*
Knadle, Richard D. *WhoFI 94*
Knag, Paul Everett 1948- *WhoAm 94, WhoAmL 94*
Knaggs, Kenneth James 1920- *Who 94*
Knaggs, Nelson Stuart 1907-1992 *WhAm 10*
Knaggs, Skelton d1955 *WhoHol 92*
Knaive, Henry Louis 1902- *WhoBlA 94*
Knake, Ellery Louis 1927- *WhoAm 94*
Knapik, Michael R. *WhoAmP 93*
Knapik, Thomas Michael 1954- *WhoFI 94*
Knapman, Paul Anthony 1944- *Who 94*
Knapman, Roger Maurice 1944- *Who 94*
Knapowski, Jan Boleslaw 1933- *WhoScEn 94*
Knapp, Brian Francis 1959- *WhoAmL 94*
Knapp, Charles *WhoHol 92*
Knapp, Charles 1946- *IntWW 93*
Knapp, Charles B. 1946- *WhoAm 94*
Knapp, Cleon Talboys 1937- *WhoAm 94, WhoWest 94*
Knapp, Clifford J. *WhoIns 94*
Knapp, Daniel C. 1915-1988 *WhAm 10*
Knapp, David *Who 94, WhoHol 92*
Knapp, (John) David 1926- *Who 94*
Knapp, David Hebard 1938- *WhoAm 94*
Knapp, David Wayne 1936- *WhoFI 94*
Knapp, Dennis L. 1945- *WhoFI 94*
Knapp, Dennis Raymond 1912- *WhoAm 94, WhoAmL 94*
Knapp, Don 1932 *WhoAmP 93*
Knapp, Donald Roy 1919- *WhoAm 94*
Knapp, Dorothy Tester 1935- *WhoMW 93*
Knapp, Eber Guy 1916- *WhoWest 94*
Knapp, Edward 1937- *WrDr 94*
Knapp, Edward Alan 1932- *WhoAm 94, WhoScEn 94*
Knapp, Edward Ronald 1919- *Who 94*
Knapp, Evalyn d1981 *WhoHol 92*
Knapp, Frederick M., Jr. 1942- *WhoAmL 94*
Knapp, Frederick Whiton 1915- *WhoScEn 94*
Knapp, Gayle 1949- *WhoWest 94*
Knapp, George G. P. 1923- *WhoIns 94*
Knapp, George Griff Prather 1923- *WhoAm 94*
Knapp, George M. 1954- *WhoAm 94, WhoAmL 94*
Knapp, George Robert 1947- *WhoAm 94, WhoAmL 94*
Knapp, Halsey G., Jr. 1955- *WhoAmL 94*
Knapp, J. Merrill d1993 *NewYTBS 93 [port]*
Knapp, J(ohn) Merrill 1914-1993 *ConAu 140*
Knapp, James 1940- *Who 94*
Knapp, James Ian Keith 1943- *WhoAm 94, WhoAmP 93*
Knapp, Jeffrey *DrAPF 93*
Knapp, John J. 1934- *WhoAmP 93*
Knapp, John Williams 1932- *WhoAm 94*
Knapp, Joseph Burke 1913- *WhoFI 94*
Knapp, Kenneth J. 1946- *WhoWest 94*
Knapp, Lloyd W. 1931- *WhoFI 94*
Knapp, Mark Israel 1923- *WhoScEn 94*
Knapp, Max d1979 *WhoHol 92*
Knapp, Mildred Florence 1932- *WhoMW 93*
Knapp, N. Guy 1945- *WhoIns 94*
Knapp, Ole 1931- *IntWW 93*
Knapp, Paul Raymond 1945- *WhoMW 93*
Knapp, Peter 1947- *NewGrDO*
Knapp, Peter Hobart 1916-1992 *WhAm 10*
Knapp, Peter Osborn 1930- *WhoAm 94*
Knapp, Richard Bruce 1933- *WhoAm 94*
Knapp, Richard Maitland 1941- *WhoAm 94*
Knapp, Richard S. 1942- *WhoAm 94*
Knapp, Robert *WhoHol 92*
Knapp, Robert Charles 1927- *WhoAm 94*
Knapp, Robert Stanley 1940- *WhoWest 94*
Knapp, Roger 1943- *WhoAmP 93*
Knapp, Ronald R. 1925- *WhoAmP 93*
Knapp, Sadie Magnet 1909- *WhoAmA 93*
Knapp, Stefan 1921- *IntWW 93*
Knapp, Thomas Edwin 1925- *WhoAm 94, WhoWest 94*
Knapp, Tom 1925- *WhoAmA 93*
Knapp, Trevor Frederick William Beresford 1937- *Who 94*
Knapp, Whitman 1909- *WhoAm 94, WhoAmL 94*
Knapp, William Bernard 1921- *WhoMW 93, WhoScEn 94*
Knappenberger, Paul Henry, Jr. 1942- *WhoAm 94, WhoMW 93*
Knapper, David Lee 1961- *WhoAmL 94*
Knappertsbusch, Hans 1888-1965 *NewGrDO*
Knapp-Fisher, Edward George 1915- *Who 94, WrDr 94*
Knapple, Kevin Frederick 1954- *WhoAmP 93*
Knaresborough, Bishop Suffragan of 1932- *Who 94*
Knarr, Willard A., Jr. 1947- *WhoIns 94*
Knasel, Thomas Lowell 1959- *WhoScEn 94*
Knatchbull *Who 94*
Knaths, (Otto) Karl 1891-1971 *WhoAmA 93N*
Knatz, Geraldine 1951- *WhoWest 94*
Knatz, Nikita *WhoHol 92*
Knaub, Raymond L. 1940- *WhoAmA 93*
Knauer, Georg Nicolaus 1926- *WhoAm 94*
Knauer, James A. 1946- *WhoAmL 94*
Knauer, Nancy Burdge 1946- *WhoMW 93*
Knauer, Virginia Harrington 1915- *WhoAm 94, WhoAmP 93*
Knauerhase, Evelyn Charlotte 1956- *WhoAmL 94*
Knauf, Konrad Steve 1944- *WhoFI 94, WhoMW 93*
Knauft, Milford Roy, Jr. 1918- *WhoAmP 93*
Knaus, Susanne Marie 1949- *WhoMW 93*
Knauss, Anne Llewellyn 1947- *WhoFI 94*
Knauss, Earl L. 1933- *WhoFI 94*
Knauss, John Atkinson 1925- *WhoAm 94, WhoScEn 94*
Knauss, Robert Lynn 1931- *WhoAm 94*
Knauth, Stephen *DrAPF 93*
Knavish, Timothy Michael 1965- *WhoFI 94*
Knayfel', Alexander Aronovich 1943- *NewGrDO*
Knazko, Milan 1945- *IntWW 93*
Kneale, (Robert) Bryan (Charles) 1930- *IntWW 93, Who 94*
Kneale, George Victor Harris 1918- *Who 94*
Kneale, (Thomas) Nigel 1922- *EncSF 93, WrDr 94*
Knebel, Donald Earl 1946- *WhoAm 94, WhoAmL 94*
Knebel, Fletcher *DrAPF 93*
Knebel, Fletcher d1993 *NewYTBS 93 [port]*
Knebel, Fletcher 1911- *WhoWest 94*
Knebel, Fletcher 1911-1992? *EncSF 93*
Knebel, Fletcher 1911-1993 *ConAu 140, SmATA 75, WrDr 94N*
Knebel, Jack Gillen 1939- *WhoAm 94, WhoAmL 94, WhoWest 94*
Knebel, John Albert 1936- *WhoAm 94, WhoAmP 93*
Knebworth, Viscount 1989- *Who 94*
Knecht, Ben Harrold 1938- *WhoWest 94*
Knecht, Charles Daniel 1932- *WhoAm 94*
Knecht, James Herbert 1925- *WhoAm 94*
Knecht, John 1947- *WhoAmA 93*
Knecht, Justin Heinrich 1752-1817 *NewGrDO*
Knecht, Raymond Lawrence 1948- *WhoWest 94*
Knecht, Robert Jean 1926- *WrDr 94*
Knecht, William L. 1946- *WhoAmL 94*
Knechtges, David Richard 1942- *WhoAm 94*
Knee, Stephen H. 1940- *WhoAm 94, WhoAmL 94*
Kneebone, Alice Jeannette 1956- *WhoWest 94*
Kneebone, Todd Correll 1956- *WhoFI 94*
Kneece, Daniel Rufus, III 1956- *WhoWest 94*
Kneedler, Alvin Richard 1943- *WhoAm 94*
Kneeland, Douglas Eugene 1929- *WhoAm 94*
Kneeland, George Royal 1918- *WhoAmP 93*
Kneeland, Richard *WhoAmP 93*
Kneen, Geoffrey 1949- *WhoScEn 94*
Kneepkens, Thomas John 1951- *WhoFI 94*
Kneer, Tom Edwin 1932- *WhoMW 93*
Knef, Hildegard 1925- *IntWW 93, WhoHol 92*
Kneifel, Hans *EncSF 93*
Kneip, Frederick C. 1943- *WhoAmL 94*
Kneip, Frederick Evoy 1914-1990 *WhAm 10*
Kneipp, (Joseph Patrick) George 1922- *Who 94*
Kneipper, Richard Keith 1943- *WhoAm 94, WhoAmL 94*
Kneisel, Edmund M. 1946- *WhoAm 94, WhoAmL 94*
Kneiser, Richard John 1938- *WhoAm 94, WhoFI 94, WhoMW 93*
Kneissl, William Lee 1936- *WhoAm 94*
Kneitel, Thomas Stephen 1933- *WhoAm 94*
Knell, David *WhoHol 92*
Knell, Gary Evan 1954- *WhoAm 94*
Knell, Gary G. 1950- *WhoAmP 93*
Knell, Ronald Alan 1947- *WhoAmL 94*
Kneller, Alister Arthur 1927- *Who 94*
Kneller, Eckart Friedrich 1928- *IntWW 93, WhoScEn 94*
Kneller, John William 1916- *WhoAm 94*
Kneller, William Arthur 1929- *WhoAm 94*
Knepp, Christopher A. 1954- *WhoAmL 94*
Knepp, Gerald Everett 1934- *WhoAm 94*
Knepp, Lee Emerson 1952- *WhoAmP 93*
Knepp, Stanley Gerald 1948- *WhoFI 94*
Knepp, Virginia Lee Hahn 1946- *WhoMW 93*
Knepper, Andrew Charles 1968- *WhoMW 93*
Knepper, Dale Bender, Jr. 1956- *WhoFI 94*
Knepper, Eugene Arthur 1926- *WhoFI 94, WhoMW 93*
Knepper, George W. 1926- *WhoAm 94*
Knepper, Randolph Leroy 1950- *WhoAmP 93*
Knepper, Rob *WhoHol 92*
Knepper, Thomas M. 1945- *WhoAmL 94*
Knepper, William E. 1909- *WhoIns 94*
Knepper, William Edward 1909- *WhoAm 94*
Kner, Andrew Peter 1935- *WhoAm 94*
Knerly, Mary Johnson 1925- *WhoFI 94*
Knerly, Stephen John, Jr. 1949- *WhoAmL 94*
Knerr, Reinhard H. 1939- *WhoAm 94*
Knesek, Gerald Eugene 1951- *WhoMW 93*
Knesel, Ernest Arthur, Jr. 1945- *WhoAm 94*
Kness, Richard Maynard 1937- *WhoAm 94*
Knetter, Michael Mark 1960- *WhoFI 94*
Knevel, Adelbert Michael 1922- *WhoAm 94*
Knevitt, Charles (Philip Paul) 1952- *WrDr 94*
Knezevic, Stojan 1923- *IntWW 93*
Knezevich, Janice A. 1960- *WhoMW 93*
Knezovich, Jeffrey Paul 1957- *WhoMW 93*
Kniaseff, Boris 1900-1975 *IntDcB [port]*
Kniasev, Boris 1900-1975 *IntDcB [port]*
Knibb, Michael Anthony 1938- *Who 94*
Knibbs, David Ralph 1953- *WhoScEn 94*
Knickerbocker, Daniel Candee, Jr. 1919- *WhoAm 94*
Knickerbocker, Gerald 1943- *WhoAmP 93*
Knickerbocker, Helaine Joyce 1928- *WhoAmL 94*
Knickerbocker, Julia d1993 *NewYTBS 93*
Knickerbocker, Robert Platt, Jr. 1944- *WhoAm 94, WhoAmL 94*
Knickrehm, Donald E. 1945- *WhoAmL 94*
Knickrehm, Glenn Allen 1948- *WhoFI 94*
Knief, Helen Jeanette 1907- *WhoAmA 93*
Kniep, Susan G. 1943- *WhoAmP 93*
Knierim, Ann Wilson 1921- *WhoAmP 93*
Knierim, Kim Phillip 1945- *WhoWest 94*
Knierim, Paul J. 1965- *WhoAmP 93*
Knierim, Robert Valentine 1916- *WhoWest 94*
Knies, Paul Henry 1918- *WhoAm 94*
Kniesler, Frederick Cornelius 1930- *WhoAmP 93*
Knievel, Evel 1939- *WhoHol 92*
Kniewasser, Andrew Graham 1926- *WhoAm 94*
Kniffen, Jan Rogers 1948- *WhoAm 94, WhoMW 93*
Kniffin, Paula Sichel 1941- *WhoFI 94*
Kniffin, Ralph Gus 1946- *WhoAmA 93*
Knight, Al J. 1941- *WhoAmP 93*
Knight, Alan Edward Whitmarsh 1946- *WhoScEn 94*
Knight, Alan Sydney 1946- *Who 94*
Knight, Alanna (Cleet) *WrDr 94*
Knight, Alexander Francis 1939- *Who 94*
Knight, Alice Tirrell 1903- *WhoAmP 93*
Knight, Allan Walton 1910- *Who 94*
Knight, Andrew Stephen Bower 1939- *IntWW 93, Who 94*
Knight, Angela Ann 1950- *Who 94*
Knight, Arthur 1916-1991 *ConTFT 11*
Knight, Arthur (William) 1917- *Who 94*
Knight, Arthur Robert 1938- *WhoAm 94*
Knight, Arthur Winfield *DrAPF 93*
Knight, Arthur Winfield 1937- *ConAu 41NR*
Knight, Athelia Wilhelmenia 1950- *WhoAm 94, WhoBlA 94*
Knight, Barry R. 1953- *WhoAmL 94*
Knight, Bernard 1931- *WrDr 94*
Knight, Bernard Henry 1931- *Who 94*
Knight, Billy 1952- *BasBi*
Knight, Bob *WhoAmP 93*
Knight, Bobby 1940- *BasBi, WhoAm 94, WhoMW 93*
Knight, Brenda Lee 1958- *WhoMW 93*
Knight, Brian Joseph 1941- *Who 94*
Knight, Bubba *WhoBlA 94*
Knight, Burton Wilder, II 1955- *WhoAmP 93*
Knight, Charles d1979 *WhoHol 92*
Knight, Charles Field 1936- *WhoAm 94, WhoFI 94, WhoMW 93*
Knight, Charles Frasuer 1932- *WhoAm 94*
Knight, Charlott d1977 *WhoHol 92*
Knight, Christopher 1957- *WhoHol 92*
Knight, Christopher Allen 1950- *WhoAm 94, WhoAmA 93*
Knight, Christopher Nichols 1946- *WhoAm 94*
Knight, Connie Lynn 1964- *WhoMW 93*
Knight, Constance Bracken 1937- *WhoWest 94*
Knight, D(avid) M(arcus) *WrDr 94*
Knight, Damon (Francis) 1922- *EncSF 93*
Knight, David *WhoHol 92*
Knight, David 1921- *WrDr 94*
Knight, David 1927- *WhoHol 92*
Knight, Davis J. 1970- *WhoMW 93*
Knight, Debra Ann Mizer 1960- *WhoMW 93*
Knight, Dempsey *WhoHol 92*
Knight, Dennis Fred 1926- *WhoWest 94*
Knight, Dewey W., Jr. 1930- *WhoBlA 94*
Knight, Don *WhoHol 92*
Knight, Douglas Maitland 1921- *IntWW 93, WhoAm 94*
Knight, Dudley *WhoHol 92*
Knight, Edmund Alan 1919- *Who 94*
Knight, Edward Howden 1933- *WhoAm 94*
Knight, Edward Jim 1952- *WhoFI 94*
Knight, Edward R. 1917- *WhoAm 94, WhoAmL 94*
Knight, Edward Stanley 1951- *WhoHisp 94*
Knight, Esmond d1987 *WhoHol 92*
Knight, Felix *WhoHol 92*
Knight, Francis Grogan 1914- *WhoAmP 93*
Knight, Frank 1905- *WrDr 94*
Knight, Frank Bardsley 1933- *WhoAm 94*
Knight, Frank W., Jr. 1923- *WhoBlA 94*
Knight, Franklin W. 1942- *WhoBlA 94*
Knight, Fred Barrows 1925- *WhoAm 94*
Knight, Frederic Charles 1898-1979 *WhoAmA 93N*
Knight, Fuzzy d1976 *WhoHol 92*
Knight, Gareth *ConAu 41NR*
Knight, Gareth 1930- *WrDr 94*
Knight, Gary 1939- *WhoAm 94*
Knight, Gary Charles 1950- *WhoScEn 94*
Knight, Geoffrey Cureton 1906- *Who 94*
Knight, Geoffrey Egerton 1921- *Who 94*
Knight, Geoffrey Wilfred 1920- *Who 94*
Knight, George A(ngus) F(ulton) 1909- *ConAu 42NR, WrDr 94*
Knight, Gillian 1939- *NewGrDO*
Knight, Gladys 1944- *AfrAmAl 6 [port], WhoHol 92*
Knight, Gladys Maria 1944- *WhoAm 94, WhoBlA 94*
Knight, Gordon Raymond 1940- *WhoWest 94*
Knight, Gregory 1949- *Who 94*
Knight, Gretchen Schwab 1965- *WhoAmL 94*
Knight, H. Elvin, Jr. 1944- *WhoAmL 94*
Knight, H. Stuart 1921- *WhoAm 94*
Knight, Hank d1930 *WhoHol 92*
Knight, Hardwicke 1911- *WrDr 94*
Knight, Harold 1960- *WhoMW 93*
Knight, Harold (Murray) 1919- *Who 94*
Knight, Harold Edwin Holm, Jr. 1930- *WhoAm 94, WhoFI 94, WhoScEn 94*
Knight, Harold Murray 1919- *IntWW 93*
Knight, Harry Adam *EncSF 93*
Knight, Harry W. 1909- *WhoAm 94, WhoFI 94*
Knight, Henry Scarborough, Jr. 1944- *WhoAm 94, WhoAmL 94*
Knight, Herbert Borwell 1928- *WhoAm 94*
Knight, Howard Atwood 1942- *WhoFI 94*
Knight, Jack 1938- *WhoHol 92*

Knight, Jacob Jaskoviak 1938- *WhoAmA 93*
Knight, James c. 1640-c. 1721 *WhWE*
Knight, James A. 1927- *WhoAm 94*
Knight, James Allen 1918- *WhoAm 94, WrDr 94*
Knight, James Atwood 1954- *WhoFI 94*
Knight, James L. 1909-1991 *WhAm 10*
Knight, James Rodney, Jr. 1949- *WhoWest 94*
Knight, Jeffrey Lin 1959- *WhoAmL 94*
Knight, Jeffrey Richard 1962- *WhoWest 94*
Knight, Jeffrey Russell 1936- *IntWW 93, Who 94*
Knight, Jeffrey William 1949- *WhoAm 94*
Knight, Jill 1927- *WhoWomW 91*
Knight, Joan Christabel Jill *Who 94*
Knight, John dc. 1606 *WhWE*
Knight, John 1945- *WhoAmA 93*
Knight, John Allan 1931- *WhoAm 94*
Knight, John Allan, Jr. 1961- *WhoAmL 94*
Knight, John F., Jr. *WhoAmP 93*
Knight, John F., Jr. 1945- *WhoBlA 94*
Knight, John Francis 1919- *WhoAm 94*
Knight, Joseph Adams 1930- *WhoAm 94*
Knight, June d1987 *WhoHol 92*
Knight, Karl Frederick 1930- *WrDr 94*
Knight, Kenneth Vincent 1944- *WhoFI 94*
Knight, Kevin Kyle 1963- *WhoScEn 94*
Knight, Kit *DrAPF 93*
Knight, Lester Benjamin 1907-1989 *WhAm 10*
Knight, Lillian d1946 *WhoHol 92*
Knight, Lynnon Jacob 1920- *WhoBlA 94*
Knight, M. L. Mickey 1946- *WhoAmP 93*
Knight, Malcolm Donald 1944- *WhoFI 94*
Knight, Mallory T. *ConAu 43NR*
Knight, Margaret E. 1838-1914 *WorInv*
Knight, Margarett Lee 1923- *WhoAmL 94*
Knight, Margery Harlow 1943- *WhoAmP 93*
Knight, Maureen K. *Who 94*
Knight, Max d1993 *NewYTBS 93*
Knight, Max 1909-1993 *ConAu 142*
Knight, Michael (William Patrick) 1932- *Who 94*
Knight, Michael E. 1959- *WhoHol 92*
Knight, Muriel Bernice 1922- *WhoBlA 94*
Knight, Negele Oscar 1967 *WhoBlA 94*
Knight, Nellie d1977 *WhoHol 92*
Knight, Norman 1924- *WhoAm 94*
Knight, Norman L(ouis) 1895-1972 *EncSF 93*
Knight, Patricia 1918- *WhoHol 92*
Knight, Peggy Steed 1929- *WhoAmP 93*
Knight, Percival d1923 *WhoHol 92*
Knight, Peter Carter 1948- *WhoAm 94, WhoAmL 94*
Knight, Peter Clayton 1947- *Who 94*
Knight, Peter Leonard 1947- *Who 94*
Knight, Philip 1938- *News 94-1 [port]*
Knight, Philip Hampson 1938- *WhoAm 94, WhoFI 94, WhoWest 94*
Knight, Reo Lindsay 1931- *IntWW 93*
Knight, Richard, Jr. 1945- *WhoBlA 94*
Knight, Richard James 1915- *Who 94*
Knight, Robert *EncSF 93*
Knight, Robert Edward 1941- *WhoFI 94, WhoMW 93*
Knight, Robert G. 1941- *WhoAm 94, WhoMW 93*
Knight, Robert Gene 1927- *WhoMW 93*
Knight, Robert Huntington 1919- *WhoAm 94, WhoAmL 94*
Knight, Robert Milton 1940- *WhoMW 93*
Knight, Robert Patrick 1935-1992 *WhAm 10*
Knight, Robert S. 1929- *WhoBlA 94*
Knight, Robert Vernon 1935- *WhoMW 93*
Knight, Roger David Verdon 1946- *Who 94*
Knight, Roger John Beckett 1944- *Who 94*
Knight, Ronald *WhoHol 92*
Knight, Ronald Allen 1937- *WhoAm 94*
Knight, Rosalind *WhoHol 92*
Knight, Sandra *WhoHol 92*
Knight, Sarah Kemble 1666-1727 *BlmGWL*
Knight, Shirley 1936- *IntMPA 94*
Knight, Shirley 1937- *WhoHol 92*
Knight, Tack 1895-1976 *WhoAmA 93N*
Knight, Ted d1986 *WhoHol 92*
Knight, Ted 1923-1986 *WhoCom*
Knight, Theodore O. 1946- *SmATA 77 [port]*
Knight, Thomas A. 1933- *WhoAmP 93*
Knight, Thomas J., Jr. 1955- *WhoWest 94*
Knight, Thomas Joseph 1937- *WhoWest 94*
Knight, Thomas L. 1945- *WhoAmL 94*
Knight, Tom, Jr. 1925- *WhoAmA 93*
Knight, Townsend Jones 1928- *WhoAm 94*
Knight, Tuesday *WhoHol 92*
Knight, V. C. 1904- *WhoAm 94*
Knight, Vick, Jr. 1928- *WhoWest 94*
Knight, W. Donald, Jr. 1941- *WhoAmL 94*
Knight, W. H., Jr. 1954- *WhoBlA 94*
Knight, Walker Leigh 1924- *WhoAm 94*
Knight, Wallace E. *DrAPF 93*
Knight, Walter Early 1911- *WhoAm 94*
Knight, Walter R. 1933- *WhoBlA 94*
Knight, Warburton Richard 1932- *Who 94*
Knight, Wayne *WhoHol 92*
Knight, William Arnold 1915- *Who 94*
Knight, William Hubbard *WhoHol 92*
Knight, William J. 1929- *WhoAm 94, WhoAmP 93, WhoWest 94*
Knight, William Kender 1924- *WhoAmP 93*
Knight, William Rogers 1945- *WhoBlA 94*
Knight, Wm. David 1942- *WhoIns 94*
Knight, Wyatt 1955- *WhoHol 92*
Knighten, James M. 1938- *WhoIns 94*
Knighten, Robert Lee 1940- *WhoWest 94*
Knightley *Who 94*
Knightley, Phillip (George) 1929- *WrDr 94*
Knighton, Alton Lefleur, Jr. 1945- *WhoAmL 94*
Knighton, David Reed 1949- *WhoAm 94*
Knighton, Robert Syron 1914- *WhoWest 94*
Knighton, Walter Berkett, IV 1955- *WhoWest 94*
Knighton, William Myles 1931- *Who 94*
Knight-Pulliam, Keshia 1979- *WhoBlA 94*
Knights, Baron 1920- *Who 94*
Knights, Edwin Munroe 1924- *WhoAm 94*
Knights, L(ionel) C(harles) 1906- *ConAu 43NR, WrDr 94*
Knights, Lionel Charles 1906- *Who 94*
Knights, Rosemary Margaret 1945- *Who 94*
Knigin, Michael Jay 1942- *WhoAmA 93*
Knilans, Michael Jerome 1927- *WhoAm 94*
Knill, John Kenelm Stuart 1913- *Who 94*
Knill, John Lawrence 1934- *IntWW 93, Who 94*
Knipfer, Dennis Ray 1950- *WhoMW 93*
Knipling, Edward Fred 1909- *WhoScEn 94*
Kniplova, Nadezda 1932- *NewGrDO*
Knipp, Helmut 1943- *WhoAm 94*
Knippa, Gregory Duane 1954- *WhoAmP 93*
Knipper, Andrei Lvovich 1931- *WhoScEn 94*
Knipper, Lev Konstantinovich 1898-1974 *NewGrDO*
Knippers, Edward 1946- *WhoAmA 93*
Knippers, Ottis Jewell, Jr. 1944- *WhoAmP 93*
Knipper-Tschech, Olga d1959 *WhoHol 92*
Knipping Victoria, Eladio 1933- *IntWW 93*
Knipscheer, Joseph d1977 *WhoHol 92*
Knipscher, Gerard Allen 1935- *WhoAmA 93*
Knipschild, Robert 1927- *WhoAm 94, WhoAmA 93*
Knisbacher, Jeffrey Mark 1941- *WhoScEn 94*
Knisely, Beth Ann 1959- *WhoMW 93*
Knisely, Douglas Charles 1948- *WhoFI 94*
Knisely, Marc O. 1950- *WhoAmL 94*
Knisely, Ralph Franklin 1927- *WhoScEn 94*
Knisely, Robert August 1940- *WhoAm 94*
Kniska, George T. 1938- *WhoMW 93*
Kniskern, Joseph Warren 1951- *WhoAm 94, WhoAmL 94*
Kniskern, Maynard 1912- *WhoAm 94*
Knittle, Peter Joseph 1953- *WhoAmP 93*
Knittle, William Joseph, Jr. 1945- *WhoWest 94*
Knizak, Milan 1940- *IntWW 93*
Knize, Randall James 1953- *WhoScEn 94, WhoWest 94*
Knizeski, Justine Estelle 1954- *WhoMW 93*
Knobbe, Kyler Gene 1949- *WhoAmL 94*
Knobbe, Urban *WhoAm 94, WhoFI 94*
Knobel, Dale Thomas 1949- *WhoAm 94*
Knobel, Ralph J. 1933- *WhoAmP 93*
Knobelsdorf, Karl Robert 1956- *WhoFI 94*
Knobil, Ernst 1926- *WhoAm 94*
Knoblauch, Gregory Eugene 1958- *WhoMW 93*
Knoblauch, Mark George 1947- *WhoAm 94*
Knobler, Alfred Everett 1915- *WhoAm 94*
Knobler, Lois Jean 1929- *WhoAmA 93*
Knobler, Nathan 1926- *WhoAm 94, WhoAmA 93*
Knobler, Peter Stephen 1946- *WhoAm 94*
Knobloch, Carl William, Jr. 1930- *WhoAm 94*
Knobloch, Ferdinand J. 1916- *WhoAm 94*
Knock, Thomas J. 1950- *ConAu 141*
Knode, Marilu 1959- *WhoAmA 93*
Knodell, Robert James 1932- *WhoMW 93*
Knoebel, David Jon 1949- *WhoAmA 93*
Knoebel, Suzanne Buckner 1926- *WhoAm 94*
Knoedler, Andrew James 1968- *WhoScEn 94*
Knoedler, Elmer L. 1912- *WhoAm 94*
Knoepfle, John *DrAPF 93*
Knoepfle, John 1923- *WrDr 94*
Knoepfler, Nestor Beyer 1918- *WhoScEn 94*
Knoepfler, Peter Tamas 1929- *WhoAm 94, WhoWest 94*
Knoepflmacher, Ulrich Camillus 1931- *WhoAm 94*
Knoke, David Harmon 1947- *WhoAm 94*
Knoles, George Harmon 1907- *WhoAm 94*
Knoll, Andrew Herbert 1951- *WhoAm 94*
Knoll, Bruce Evans 1953- *WhoAm 94*
Knoll, Catherine Baker *WhoAmP 93*
Knoll, David E. 1944- *WhoFI 94*
Knoll, Erwin 1931- *WhoAm 94*
Knoll, Florence Schust 1917- *WhoAm 94, WhoScEn 94*
Knoll, Franklin Jude 1940- *WhoAmP 93*
Knoll, Glenn Frederick 1935- *WhoAm 94*
Knoll, Herman Joseph 1934- *WhoIns 94*
Knoll, Isabel A. Giampietro *WhoAmA 93*
Knoll, Jacqueline Sue 1932- *WhoMW 93*
Knoll, James L. 1942- *WhoAmL 94*
Knoll, Jerry 1924- *WhoAm 94*
Knoll, Jozsef 1925- *IntWW 93*
Knoll, Max *WorInv*
Knoll, Michael Allen 1943- *WhoFI 94*
Knoll, Michael Steven 1957- *WhoAmL 94*
Knoll, Robert R. 1940- *WhoMW 93*
Knollenberg, Joe 1933- *CngDr 93*
Knollenberg, Joseph 1933- *WhoAmP 93*
Knollenberg, Joseph 1934- *WhoAm 94, WhoMW 93*
Knollenberg, Mary Tarleton d1992 *NewYTBS 93*
Knoller, Guy David 1946- *WhoWest 94*
Knollys, Viscount 1931- *Who 94*
Knoop, Floyd C. 1944- *WhoMW 93*
Knoop, Vern Thomas 1932- *WhoScEn 94, WhoWest 94*
Knop, Charles Milton 1931- *WhoMW 93*
Knope, Alfred, Jr. 1918- *IntWW 93*
Knopf, Alfred, Jr. 1918- *WhoAm 94*
Knopf, Barry Abraham 1946- *WhoAmL 94*
Knopf, Donna Braverman *WhoAmA 93*
Knopf, Kent Ronald 1963- *WhoWest 94*
Knopf, Kenyon Alfred 1921- *WhoAm 94*
Knopf, Leigh Walter 1952- *WhoFI 94*
Knopf, Marcy 1969- *ConAu 142*
Knopf, Margaret *WhoHol 92*
Knopf, Paul Mark 1936- *WhoAm 94, WhoScEn 94*
Knopf, Terry Ann *WrDr 94*
Knopfler, Mark *IntWW 93*
Knopik, Christopher Scott 1959- *WhoAmL 94*
Knopman, David S. 1950- *WhoAm 94*
Knopoff, Leon 1925- *IntWW 93, WhoAm 94*
Knopow, Gary Alan 1947- *WhoFI 94*
Knopp, Albert J. 1924- *WhoAm 94*
Knopp, Alex Andrew 1947- *WhoAmP 93*
Knopp, Hans-Georg 1945- *WhoAmA 93*
Knopp, Joe *WhoAmP 93*
Knopp, Marvin Isadore 1933- *WhoAm 94*
Knopp, Timothy John 1958- *WhoAmL 94*
Knorek, Lee J. 1921- *WhoAmP 93*
Knorpel, Henry 1924- *Who 94*
Knorr, Fred William 1927- *WhoFI 94*
Knorr, Iwan (Otto Armand) 1853-1916 *NewGrDO*
Knorr, Jeanne Boardman *WhoAmA 93*
Knorr, John Christian 1921- *WhoMW 93*
Knorr, Klaus (Eugene) 1911- *WrDr 94*
Knorr, Klaus Eugene 1911-1990 *WhAm 10*
Knorre, Dmitri Georgievich 1926- *IntWW 93*
Knortz, Herbert Charles 1921- *WhoAm 94*
Knortz, Walter Robert 1919- *WhoAm 94*
Knospe, William Herbert 1929- *WhoAm 94, WhoScEn 94*
Knot, Alvan Paul 1949- *WhoAmL 94*
Knote, Heinrich 1870-1953 *NewGrDO*
Knotek, Robert Frank 1945- *WhoFI 94*
Knoth, Jess Franke 1957- *WhoMW 93*
Knoth, Russell Laine 1957- *WhoScEn 94*
Knott, Adelbert d1933 *WhoHol 92*
Knott, Albert Paul, Jr. 1935- *WhoBlA 94*
Knott, Bill 1940- *WrDr 94*
Knott, Cargill Gilston 1856-1922 *DcNaB MP*
Knott, Carol Rede 1930- *WhoMW 93*
Knott, Clara d1926 *WhoHol 92*
Knott, Dee D. 1943- *WhoAmA 93*
Knott, Douglas Ronald 1927- *WhoAm 94*
Knott, Else d1975 *WhoHol 92*
Knott, James Robert 1910- *WhoAm 94*
Knott, John Frederick 1938- *Who 94*
Knott, John Laurence 1910- *Who 94*
Knott, John Ray, Jr. 1937- *WhoAm 94*
Knott, John Robert 1937- *WhoMW 93, WhoScEn 94*
Knott, Lydia d1955 *WhoHol 92*
Knott, Mable Marguerite *WhoBlA 94*
Knott, Ronald George 1917- *Who 94*
Knott, Wiley Eugene 1938- *WhoFI 94, WhoWest 94*
Knott, William Alan 1942- *WhoWest 94*
Knott, William C(ecil) 1927- *WrDr 94*
Knottenbelt, Hans Jorgen 1934- *WhoScEn 94*
Knotts, Don 1924- *IntMPA 94, WhoAm 94, WhoCom, WhoHol 92*
Knotts, Joseph B. 1938- *WhoAm 94*
Knotts, Robert Lee 1942- *WhoFI 94*
Knous, Ted R. 1949- *WhoMW 93*
Knowelden, John 1919- *Who 94*
Knowland, Alice d1930 *WhoHol 92*
Knowland, Raymond Reginald 1930- *Who 94*
Knowland, William F. 1908-1974 *HisDcKW*
Knowles, Alison *DrAPF 93*
Knowles, Alison 1933- *WhoAm 94, WhoAmA 93*
Knowles, Ann *Who 94*
Knowles, (Patricia) Ann 1944- *Who 94*
Knowles, Asa Smallidge 1909-1990 *WhAm 10*
Knowles, Bill 1930- *WhoAmP 93*
Knowles, Carrie J. *DrAPF 93*
Knowles, Charles (Francis) 1951- *Who 94*
Knowles, Charles Timothy 1949- *WhoAmP 93*
Knowles, Christopher Allan 1949- *WhoFI 94, WhoScEn 94*
Knowles, Colin George 1939- *Who 94*
Knowles, David *WhoAmP 93*
Knowles, David A. 1949- *WhoAmP 93*
Knowles, David Eugene 1959- *WhoScEn 94*
Knowles, David L. *WhoAm 94*
Knowles, Dorothy 1906- *WrDr 94*
Knowles, Eddie (Adenola) 1946- *WhoBlA 94*
Knowles, Edward Frank 1929- *WhoAm 94*
Knowles, Elizabeth 1958- *WhoAmA 93*
Knowles, Elizabeth Pringle 1943- *WhoAm 94*
Knowles, Em Claire 1952- *WhoBlA 94*
Knowles, Emmitt Clifton 1951- *WhoAmL 94*
Knowles, Faye 1949- *WhoAmL 94*
Knowles, George Peter 1919- *Who 94*
Knowles, Graeme Paul 1951- *Who 94*
Knowles, Jack Oliver 1916- *WhoAm 94*
Knowles, James Kenyon 1931- *WhoAm 94, WhoWest 94*
Knowles, James Thomas 1831-1908 *DcNaB MP*
Knowles, Jeremy Randall 1935- *IntWW 93, Who 94, WhoAm 94, WhoScEn 94*
Knowles, John *DrAPF 93*
Knowles, John 1926- *TwCYAW, WhoAm 94, WrDr 94*
Knowles, Kevin G. *WhoAmP 93*
Knowles, Leo A. 1951- *WhoAmL 94*
Knowles, Leonard Joseph 1916- *Who 94*
Knowles, Malachi 1941- *WhoBlA 94*
Knowles, Malcolm Shepherd 1913- *WhoAm 94*
Knowles, Marjorie Fine 1939- *WhoAm 94*
Knowles, Michael 1942- *Who 94*
Knowles, Michael Ernest 1942- *Who 94*
Knowles, Patric 1911- *IntMPA 94, WhoHol 92*
Knowles, Peter Francis Arnold 1949- *Who 94*
Knowles, R. G. d1919 *WhoHol 92*
Knowles, Ralph Lewis 1928- *WhoWest 94*
Knowles, Randall Gene 1951- *WhoWest 94*
Knowles, Richard (Marchant) 1917- *Who 94*
Knowles, Richard Alan John 1935- *WhoAm 94*
Knowles, Richard H. 1934- *WhoAmA 93*
Knowles, Richard James Robert 1943- *WhoScEn 94*
Knowles, Richard John 1956- *WhoAmL 94*
Knowles, Richard Norris 1935- *WhoScEn 94*
Knowles, Richard T. 1916- *WhoAmP 93*
Knowles, Richard Thomas 1916- *WhoWest 94*
Knowles, Robert G. *WhoIns 94*
Knowles, Stanley Howard 1908- *IntWW 93*
Knowles, Stephen Howard 1940- *WhoScEn 94*
Knowles, Susan Christine 1951- *WhoWomW 91*
Knowles, Susan Williams 1952- *WhoAmA 93*
Knowles, Susanne 1911- *WrDr 94*
Knowles, Timothy 1938- *Who 94*
Knowles, Tony 1943- *WhoAmP 93*

Knowles, W(illiam) P(lenderleith) 1891- *EncSF 93*
Knowles, Warren P. d1993 *NewYTBS 93 [port]*
Knowles, Warren P. 1908- *WhoAmP 93*
Knowles, Warren Perley 1908- *WhoAm 94*
Knowles, William Leroy Bill 1935- *WhoAm 94*
Knowles, William W. 1941- *WhoBlA 94*
Knowles, Wyn 1923- *Who 94*
Knowlton, Austin E. *WhoAm 94, WhoMW 93*
Knowlton, Daniel Gibson 1922- *WhoAmA 93*
Knowlton, Derrick 1921- *WrDr 94*
Knowlton, E. Ute 1933- *WhoAmP 93*
Knowlton, Edgar Colby, Jr. 1921- *WhoAm 94*
Knowlton, Franklin W. 1922- *WhoAmP 93*
Knowlton, Grace Farrar 1932- *WhoAm 94, WhoAmA 93*
Knowlton, Jonathan 1937- *WhoAmA 93*
Knowlton, Kevin Charles 1957- *WhoAmL 94*
Knowlton, Maude Briggs 1876-1956 *WhoAmA 93N*
Knowlton, Nancy 1949- *WhoScEn 94*
Knowlton, Richard James 1928- *Who 94*
Knowlton, Richard L. 1932- *IntWW 93, WhoAm 94, WhoFI 94, WhoMW 93*
Knowlton, Thomas 1740-1776 *AmRev, WhAmRev*
Knowlton, Thomas A. 1946- *WhoAm 94*
Knowlton, William Allen 1920- *WhoAm 94, WhoFI 94*
Knox *Who 94*
Knox, Agnes Ruth 1911- *WhoAm 94*
Knox, Alexander 1907- *IntMPA 94, WhoHol 92*
Knox, Andrew Gibson 1923- *WhoAmP 93*
Knox, Ann B. *DrAPF 93*
Knox, Arthur Lloyd 1932- *WhoAmP 93, WhoMW 93*
Knox, Bernard MacGregor Walker 1914- *WhoAm 94, WrDr 94*
Knox, Bryce (Muir) 1916- *Who 94*
Knox, Bryce Harry 1929- *Who 94*
Knox, C. Neal 1935- *WhoAm 94*
Knox, Calvin M. *EncSF 93*
Knox, Calvin M. 1935- *WrDr 94*
Knox, Caroline *DrAPF 93*
Knox, Charles Graham 1948- *WhoAm 94, WhoAmL 94*
Knox, Charles Milton 1937- *WhoMW 93*
Knox, Charles Stuart 1922- *WhoMW 93*
Knox, Chuck 1932- *WhoAm 94, WhoWest 94*
Knox, Daniel F. 1948- *WhoAmL 94*
Knox, David *Who 94*
Knox, (Alexander) David 1925- *Who 94*
Knox, David Broughton 1916- *WrDr 94*
Knox, David Laidlaw 1933- *Who 94*
Knox, David LaLonde 1930- *WhoScEn 94*
Knox, Dick 1936- *WhoAmP 93*
Knox, (Alfred) Dillwyn 1884-1943 *DcNaB MP*
Knox, Elizabeth 1944- *WhoAmA 93*
Knox, Elizabeth 1959- *BlmGWL*
Knox, Elyse 1917- *WhoHol 92*
Knox, Eric *WhoScEn 94*
Knox, Ernest Rudder 1916- *WhoAm 94*
Knox, G.D. *EncSF 93*
Knox, Gary *WhoHol 92*
Knox, George 1922- *WhoAmA 93*
Knox, George F. 1943- *WhoBlA 94*
Knox, George L., III 1943- *WhoBlA 94*
Knox, George Levi, III 1943- *WhoAm 94*
Knox, Gordon *IntMPA 94*
Knox, Gordon, Jr. 1943- *WhoAmP 93*
Knox, Grannell Edward 1950- *WhoFI 94*
Knox, Henry 1750-1806 *AmRev, WhAmRev [port]*
Knox, Henry Macdonald 1916- *Who 94, WrDr 94*
Knox, James *DrAPF 93, SmATA 76*
Knox, James Edwin 1937- *WhoAm 94, WhoFI 94*
Knox, James Lester 1919- *WhoAm 94*
Knox, James Marshall 1944- *WhoAmL 94, WhoMW 93*
Knox, Jean M. *Who 94*
Knox, John 1505-1572 *BlmGEL*
Knox, John c. 1513-1572 *HisWorL [port]*
Knox, John c. 1514-1572 *DcLB 132 [port]*
Knox, John 1913- *Who 94*
Knox, John 1936- *Who 94*
Knox, John, Jr. 1932- *WhoAm 94*
Knox, John (Leonard) 1925- *Who 94*
Knox, John Andrew 1937- *Who 94*
Knox, John Henderson 1927- *Who 94*
Knox, John Marshall 1925-1987 *WhAm 10*
Knox, Jolyne 1937- *SmATA 76 [port]*
Knox, Lance Lethbridge 1944- *WhoAm 94*
Knox, Mickey *WhoHol 92*
Knox, Northrup Rand 1928- *WhoAm 94*
Knox, Pamela Naber *WhoMW 93*
Knox, Ralph David 1961- *WhoScEn 94*
Knox, Randall Shaw 1949- *WhoAmP 93*
Knox, Richard Marshall 1933- *WhoWest 94*
Knox, Robert 1904- *Who 94*
Knox, Robert Arthur 1943- *WhoScEn 94*
Knox, Robert Buick 1918- *WrDr 94*
Knox, Robert Seiple 1931- *WhoAm 94*
Knox, Ronald A(rbuthnott) 1888-1957 *EncSF 93*
Knox, Selby Albert Richard 1944- *IntWW 93*
Knox, Seymour H. 1898-1990 *WhAm 10*
Knox, Seymour Horace, III 1926-1990 *WhAm 10, WhoAm 94*
Knox, Stanley *WhoMW 93*
Knox, Stanley 1939- *WhoBlA 94*
Knox, Susan Hirsch 1940- *WhoWest 94*
Knox, Susan Marie 1941- *WhoAmL 94*
Knox, Teddy d1974 *WhoHol 92*
Knox, Terence 1951- *WhoHol 92*
Knox, W. David, II 1944- *WhoAmL 94*
Knox, Wayne D. P. 1947- *WhoBlA 94*
Knox, Wayne Harrison 1942- *WhoBlA 94*
Knox, Wayne N. 1927- *WhoAmP 93*
Knox, Wilbur Benjamin 1912- *WhoBlA 94*
Knox, William 1732-1810 *WhAmRev*
Knox, William 1928- *WrDr 94*
Knox, William David 1920- *WhoAm 94*
Knox, William Edward 1927- *Who 94*
Knox, William Jordan 1921- *WhoScEn 94*
Knox, William Robert 1951- *WhoBlA 94*
Knox, William T., IV 1943- *WhoAmL 94*
Knox-Benton, Shirley 1937- *WhoBlA 94*
Knox-Johnston, Robin 1939- *Who 94, WrDr 94*
Knox-Lecky, Samuel 1926- *Who 94*
Knox-Mawer, Ronald 1925- *Who 94*
Knox Rios, Delilah Jane 1954- *WhoAmL 94*
Knuckles, Kenneth J. *WhoBlA 94*
Knudeson, Jason 1963- *WhoWest 94*
Knudsen, Betty Ann 1926- *WhoAmP 93*
Knudsen, Christian 1945- *WhoAmA 93*
Knudsen, Conrad Calvert 1923- *IntWW 93, WhoAm 94*
Knudsen, Daniel Curtis 1955- *WhoMW 93*
Knudsen, Darrell G. *WhoAm 94, WhoFI 94, WhoMW 93*
Knudsen, James George 1920- *WhoAm 94*
Knudsen, Knud-Endre 1921- *WhoScEn 94*
Knudsen, Margrethe June 1934- *WrDr 94*
Knudsen, Peggy d1980 *WhoHol 92*
Knudsen, Raymond Barnett 1919- *WhoAm 94, WhoFI 94*
Knudsen, Rudolph Edgar, Jr. 1939- *WhoAm 94*
Knudsen, Semon Emil 1912- *IntWW 93, Who 94, WhoAm 94*
Knudsen, Terrence K. 1946- *WhoAmL 94*
Knudsen, William Claire 1925- *WhoAm 94*
Knudson, Albert Cornelius 1873-1953 *DcAmReB 2*
Knudson, Alfred George, Jr. 1922- *WhoAm 94, WhoScEn 94*
Knudson, Danny Alan 1940- *WrDr 94*
Knudson, David L. 1950- *WhoAmL 94*
Knudson, David Stewart 1941- *WhoAmP 93*
Knudson, Douglas Marvin 1936- *WhoAm 94*
Knudson, Harry Edward, Jr. 1921- *WhoAm 94*
Knudson, Kenneth 1927- *WhoAmP 93*
Knudson, Knute, Jr. 1949- *WhoAmP 93*
Knudson, Melvin Robert 1917- *WhoWest 94*
Knudson, R. R. 1932- *SmATA 18AS [port], TwCYAW*
Knudson, R(ozanne) R 1932- *WrDr 94*
Knudson, Scott Gregory 1953- *WhoAmL 94*
Knudson, Thomas Jeffery 1953- *WhoAm 94, WhoWest 94*
Knudson, Warren 1953- *WhoMW 93*
Knudtzon, Halvor, Jr. 1926- *WhoAm 94*
Knue, Paul Frederick 1947- *WhoAm 94, WhoMW 93*
Knuepfer, Robert Claude, Jr. 1952- *WhoAmL 94*
Knull, Erhard 1929- *WhoMW 93*
Knull, William H., III 1948- *WhoAm 94*
Knup, Stephen Charles 1942- *WhoAm 94*
Knupfer, Nancy Nelson 1950- *WhoMW 93, WhoScEn 94*
Knupfer, Paul 1866-1920 *NewGrDO*
Knupfer, Walter Richard 1949- *WhoMW 93*
Knupp, Larry Sheldon 1940- *WhoWest 94*
Knupp, Patrick Michael 1953- *WhoWest 94*
Knuppel, William Harold 1939- *WhoAmP 93*
Knussen, (Stuart) Oliver 1952- *IntWW 93, NewGrDO, Who 94*
Knussmann, Willard Theodore 1942- *WhoWest 94*
Knuteson, Harold Douglas 1953- *WhoWest 94*
Knuteson, Miles Gene 1952- *WhoMW 93*
Knuth, Daniel J. *WhoAmP 93*
Knuth, Donald Ervin 1938- *IntWW 93, WhoAm 94, WhoScEn 94*
Knuth, Eldon Luverne 1925- *WhoAm 94, WhoWest 94*
Knuth, Gustav d1987 *WhoHol 92*
Knuth, Mona May 1912- *WhoMW 93*
Knuti, Robert A. 1942- *WhoAm 94, WhoAmL 94*
Knutsen, Conrad Arthur 1940- *WhoMW 93*
Knutsford, Viscount 1926- *Who 94*
Knutson, Byron *WhoAmP 93*
Knutson, David Harry 1934- *WhoAm 94*
Knutson, David Lee 1959- *WhoAmP 93, WhoMW 93*
Knutson, Elliot Knut 1924- *WhoWest 94*
Knutson, Howard Arthur 1929- *WhoAmP 93*
Knutson, Jack Ross 1955- *WhoWest 94*
Knutson, John A. 1940- *WhoIns 94*
Knutson, John Franklin 1942- *WhoAm 94*
Knutson, Knute B. 1909- *WhoAmP 93*
Knutson, Lynn Douglas 1946- *WhoScEn 94*
Knutson, Nancy Roxbury *DrAPF 93*
Knutson, Orville Kenneth 1922- *WhoAmP 93*
Knutson, Ronald Dale 1940- *WhoAm 94, WhoAmP 93*
Knutson, Sidney R. 1915- *WhoAmP 93*
Knutsson, Anders 1937- *WhoAmA 93*
Knutton, Harry 1921- *Who 94*
Knutzen, Raymond Edward 1941- *WhoAm 94, WhoAmL 94*
Knyazhnin, Yakov Borisovich 1742?-1791 *NewGrDO*
Knycha, Josef 1953- *WhoWest 94*
Knye, Cassandra *EncSF 93*
Knye, Cassandra 1937- *WrDr 94*
Knye, Cassandra 1940- *WrDr 94*
Knyphausen, Wilhelm, Baron von 1716-1800 *WhAmRev*
Knyphausen, Wilhelm von 1716-1800 *AmRev*
Knyvet, Henry 1537?-1598 *DcNaB MP*
Ko, Ada 1956- *WhoAsA 94*
Ko, Anthony 1934- *WhoAmA 93N*
Ko, Bing H. 1955- *WhoAsA 94*
Ko, Cheng Chia Charles 1929- *WhoAsA 94*
Ko, Edmond Inq-Ming 1952- *WhoAsA 94*
Ko, Elaine Ikoma 1952- *WhoAsA 94*
Ko, Hon-Chung 1937- *WhoAsA 94*
Ko, Hsien Ching 1928- *WhoAm 94*
Ko, Kathleen Lim 1958- *WhoAsA 94*
Ko, Kei-Yu *WhoAsA 94*
Ko, Myoung-Sam 1930- *WhoScEn 94*
Ko, Seung Kyun 1936- *WhoWest 94*
Ko, Steven W. 1967- *WhoAsA 94*
Ko, Wen-Hsiung 1923- *WhoAm 94, WhoAsA 94*
Ko, Wen-hsiung 1939- *WhoAsA 94*
Ko, William Weng-Ping 1962- *WhoAsA 94*
Ko, Winston T. 1943- *WhoAsA 94*
Ko, Won *DrAPF 93*
Kobak, Alfred Julian, Jr. 1935- *WhoMW 93*
Kobak, Hope McEldowney 1922- *WhoAm 94*
Kobak, James Benedict 1921- *WhoAm 94*
Kobak, James Benedict, Jr. 1944- *WhoAm 94, WhoAmL 94*
Kobart, Ruth 1924- *WhoHol 92*
Kobashigawa, Ben 1944- *WhoAsA 94*
Kobayashi, Albert Satochi 1924- *WhoAsA 94*
Kobayashi, Albert Satoshi 1924- *WhoAm 94*
Kobayashi, Ann H. 1937- *WhoAmP 93*
Kobayashi, Bert Nobuo 1933- *WhoAsA 94*
Kobayashi, Bertrand 1944- *WhoAmP 93, WhoAsA 94*
Kobayashi, Chris *DrAPF 93*
Kobayashi, Deanna Hasuye 1941- *WhoAsA 94*
Kobayashi, Francis Masao 1925- *WhoAsA 94*
Kobayashi, Hideaki 1950- *WhoAsA 94*
Kobayashi, Hisako 1946- *WhoAmA 93*
Kobayashi, Hisashi 1938- *WhoAm 94*
Kobayashi, Jerry T. 1952- *WhoAsA 94*
Kobayashi, John M. 1948- *WhoAsA 94*
Kobayashi, Keiju *WhoHol 92*
Kobayashi, Key K. 1922?-1992 *WhoAsA 94N*
Kobayashi, Koichi 1945- *WhoAsA 94*
Kobayashi, Koji 1907- *IntWW 93*
Kobayashi, Mitsue 1933- *WhoScEn 94*
Kobayashi, Naomasa 1929- *WhoScEn 94*
Kobayashi, Nobuhisa 1950- *WhoAsA 94, WhoScEn 94*
Kobayashi, Riki 1924- *WhoAm 94*
Kobayashi, Shinji 1954- *WhoMW 93*
Kobayashi, Shiro 1924- *WhoAm 94*
Kobayashi, Susumu 1939- *WhoFI 94, WhoScEn 94*
Kobayashi, Taiyu 1912- *IntWW 93*
Kobayashi, Tom Toru *WhoAm 94*
Kobayashi, Toshiro 1939- *WhoScEn 94*
Kobayashi, William N., Jr. 1946- *WhoAsA 94*
Kobayashi, Yoshiko 1937- *WhoAsA 94*
Kobayashi, Yoshinari 1934- *WhoScEn 94*
Kobayashi, Yutaka 1924- *WhoAm 94, WhoAsA 94*
Kobbe, Gustav 1857-1918 *NewGrDO*
Kobben, Andre J. F. 1925- *IntWW 93*
Kobe, Gail 1929- *WhoHol 92*
Kobekin, Vladimir Alexandrovich 1947- *NewGrDO*
Kobelinski, Mitchell Peter 1928- *WhoAm 94*
Kobelius, Johann Augustin 1674-1731 *NewGrDO*
Kobelski, Robert John 1948- *WhoScEn 94*
Kober, Alfred John 1937- *WhoAmA 93*
Kober, Arletta Refshauge 1919- *WhoMW 93*
Kober, Carl Leopold 1913- *WhoAm 94*
Kober, Dieter 1920- *WhoMW 93*
Kober, Jane 1943- *WhoAm 94*
Kober, Jeff *WhoHol 92*
Kobert, Joel A. 1943- *WhoAmL 94*
Kobert, Norman 1929- *WhoFI 94*
Kobert, Roy Scott 1962- *WhoAmL 94*
Kobets, Konstantin Ivanovich 1939- *LngBDD*
Kobiakova, Aleksandra Petrovna 1823-1892 *BlmGWL*
Kobin, William H. 1929- *WhoWest 94*
Koblentz, Robert Alan 1946- *WhoAmL 94*
Koblenz, Michael Robert 1948- *WhoAmL 94, WhoFI 94*
Kobler, John 1910- *WhoAm 94*
Kobler, Raymond 1945- *WhoAm 94*
Koblick, Daniel Cecil 1922- *WhoMW 93*
Koblin, Donald Daryl 1949- *WhoWest 94*
Koblin, Ronald Lee 1946- *WhoWest 94*
Koblitz, Michael Jay 1949- *WhoFI 94*
Kobrin, Lawrence Alan 1933- *WhoAm 94*
Kobrine, Arthur 1943- *WhoAm 94*
Kobs, Ann Elizabeth Jane 1944- *WhoMW 93*
Kobs, James Fred 1938- *WhoAm 94*
Kobsa, Henry 1929- *WhoScEn 94*
Kobus, David Allan 1952- *WhoScEn 94*
Kobus, Kenneth 1959- *WhoFI 94*
Kobus, Richard Lawrence 1952- *WhoFI 94, WhoScEn 94*
Koby, Herman Louis 1933- *WhoMW 93*
Kobylarczyk, Marguerite 1940- *WhoAmP 93*
Kobza, Dennis Jerome 1933- *WhoWest 94*
Kobzarev, Yuriy Borisovich d1992 *IntWW 93N*
Koc, Vehbi 1901- *IntWW 93*
Kocan, Katherine Mautz 1946- *WhoScEn 94*
Kocaoglu, Dundar F. 1939- *WhoAm 94, WhoFI 94, WhoScEn 94, WhoWest 94*
Kocar, George Frederick 1948- *WhoAmA 93*
Kocarnik, Ivan 1944- *IntWW 93*
Kocen, Joel Evan 1936- *WhoAm 94*
Kocen, Lorraine Ayral 1956- *WhoWest 94*
Kocer, Albert J. 1930- *WhoAmP 93*
Kocevar, John Thomas 1934- *WhoMW 93*
Koch, Albert Acheson 1942- *WhoAm 94, WhoFI 94, WhoMW 93*
Koch, Albert William 1956- *WhoMW 93*
Koch, Alisa Erika 1956- *WhoScEn 94*
Koch, Arnold Theodore, Jr. 1930- *WhoAmP 93*
Koch, Arthur Robert 1934- *WhoAmA 93*
Koch, Augusta Down 1923- *WhoFI 94*
Koch, Bertha Couch 1899-1975 *WhoAmA 93N*
Koch, Bruce R. 1933- *WhoAm 94*
Koch, C(hristopher) J(ohn) 1932- *WrDr 94*
Koch, Carl Galland 1916-1986 *WhAm 10*
Koch, Carole Jackson 1951- *WhoMW 93*
Koch, Charles de Ganahl 1935- *WhoAm 94, WhoMW 93*
Koch, Charles John *WhoAm 94, WhoFI 94*
Koch, Charles Joseph 1919- *WhoAm 94*
Koch, Charles Stephen 1948- *WhoWest 94*
Koch, Claude *DrAPF 93*
Koch, Craig R. 1946- *WhoFI 94*
Koch, Donald LeRoy 1937- *WhoScEn 94*
Koch, Dorie Jo 1959- *WhoWest 94*
Koch, Edna Mae 1951- *WhoAmL 94*
Koch, Edward I. *WhoHol 92*
Koch, Edward I. 1924- *IntWW 93, WhoAm 94*
Koch, Edward I(rving) 1924- *WrDr 94*
Koch, Edward Irving 1924- *Who 94, WhoAmP 93*
Koch, Edward Richard 1953- *WhoAmL 94, WhoFI 94*
Koch, Edwin E. 1915- *WhoAmA 93*
Koch, Edwin Ernest 1915- *WhoAm 94*
Koch, Eric 1919- *EncSF 93*

Koch, Evamaria Wysk 1961- *WhoScEn 94*
Koch, Francis Andre 1964- *WhoAmL 94*
Koch, George William 1926- *WhoAm 94*
Koch, Gerald D. 1924- *WhoAmP 93*
Koch, Gerald Douglas 1943- *WhoWest 94*
Koch, Gerd (Herman) 1929- *WhoAmA 93*
Koch, Harold D. *WhoAmP 93*
Koch, Heinrich Hermann Robert 1843-1910 *WorScD*
Koch, Howard 1902- *IntDcF 2-4*, *IntMPA 94*
Koch, Howard W. 1916- *IntMPA 94*
Koch, Howard W., Jr. 1945- *IntMPA 94*, *WhoAm 94*
Koch, Howard Winchel 1916- *WhoAm 94*
Koch, Hugo B. d1926 *WhoHol 92*
Koch, James Arthur 1951- *WhoFI 94*
Koch, James Verch 1942- *WhoAm 94*
Koch, Jill Warnecke 1954- *WhoMW 93*
Koch, Joanne 1929- *IntMPA 94*
Koch, John 1909-1978 *WhoAmA 93N*
Koch, Karl Joseph 1960- *WhoAmL 94*
Koch, Kathleen Day 1948- *WhoAm 94*
Koch, Kenneth *DrAPF 93*
Koch, Kenneth 1925- *ConDr 93*, *WhoAm 94*, *WrDr 94*
Koch, Kevin Robert 1967- *WhoScEn 94*
Koch, Marianne 1930- *WhoHol 92*
Koch, Neal David 1954- *WhoWest 94*
Koch, Norman Edward 1934- *WhoWest 94*
Koch, Peter 1920- *WhoAm 94*
Koch, Peter F. 1933- *WhoAm 94*
Koch, Philip 1948- *WhoAmA 93*
Koch, Ralph Richard 1928- *WhoAm 94*
Koch, Richard 1921- *WhoAm 94*
Koch, Robert 1918- *WhoAmA 93*
Koch, Robert Kent 1943- *WhoFI 94*
Koch, Robert Louis, II 1939- *WhoAm 94*
Koch, Robert Michael 1964- *WhoScEn 94*
Koch, Ronald H. 1949- *WhoIns 94*
Koch, Sidney 1935- *WhoAm 94*, *WhoFI 94*
Koch, Stephen *DrAPF 93*
Koch, Tad Harbison 1943- *WhoAm 94*
Koch, Thomas F. 1942- *WhoAmP 93*
Koch, Virginia *WhoAmA 93*
Koch, Walter A. 1895-1970 *AstEnc*
Koch, Werner *IntWW 93N*
Koch, William Emery 1922-1987 *WhoAmA 93N*
Koch, William Joseph 1949- *WhoMW 93*
Kochak, Gregory Michael 1953- *WhoScEn 94*
Kochakian, Charles Daniel 1908- *WhoAm 94*
Kochan, Miriam (Louise) 1929- *WrDr 94*
Kochan, Robert Joseph 1950- *WhoMW 93*
Kochanowska, Anna *WhoWomW 91*
Kochar, Mahendr Singh 1943- *WhoAm 94*
Kochell, Howard Eugene 1958- *WhoAmL 94*
Kochems, Robert Gregory 1951- *WhoAmL 94*
Kocher, John Arthur 1945- *WhoAmP 93*
Kocher, Juanita Fay 1933- *WhoFI 94*, *WhoMW 93*
Kocher, Kurt Allen 1962- *WhoFI 94*
Kocher, Robert Lee 1929- *WhoAmA 93*
Kocher, Walter William 1934- *WhoAm 94*, *WhoAmL 94*, *WhoFI 94*
Kocherga, Anatoly Ivanovich 1947- *IntWW 93*
Kochergin, Edvard Stepanovich 1937- *IntWW 93*
Kocherlakota, Sreedhar 1965- *WhoScEn 94*
Kocherthaler, Mina *WhoAmA 93*
Kochetkov, Nikolay Konstantinovich 1915- *IntWW 93*
Kochevitsky, George A. d1993 *NewYTBS 93*
Kochhar, Devendra M. 1938- *WhoAsA 94*
Kochhar, Man Mohan 1932- *WhoAsA 94*
Kochheiser, Thomas H. 1956- *WhoAmA 93*
Kochi, Jay K. 1927- *IntWW 93*
Kochi, Jay Kazuo 1927- *WhoAm 94*, *WhoScEn 94*
Kochiyama, William 1921-1993 *WhoAsA 94N*
Kochka, Al 1928- *WhoAm 94*, *WhoAmA 93*, *WhoMW 93*
Kochman, Alexandra D. 1936- *WhoAmA 93*
Kochno, Boris 1904-1991 *IntDcB [port]*
Kochno, Boris Yevgen'yevich 1904-1990 *NewGrDO*
Koch-Riehl, Rudolf d1956 *WhoHol 92*
Kochs, Herbert William 1903- *WhoAm 94*
Kochta, Ruth Martha 1924- *WhoAm 94*, *WhoAmA 93*
Kochunas, Bradley Wayne 1950- *AstEnc*
Koci, Henry James 1952- *WhoFI 94*, *WhoScEn 94*
Koci, Ludvik Frank 1936- *WhoAm 94*
Kociolko, John S. 1949- *WhoAmP 93*
Kocisko, Stephen John 1915- *WhoAm 94*
Kociubes, Joseph Leib 1947- *WhoAm 94*, *WhoAmL 94*
Kocivar, Ben 1916- *WhoScEn 94*
Kock, Lars Anders Wolfram 1913- *WhoScEn 94*
Kock, Robert Marshall 1942- *WhoFI 94*
Kocka, Jan Vilem 1946- *WhoScEn 94*
Kocka, Juergen 1941- *WrDr 94*
Kocka, Thomas John 1957- *WhoScEn 94*
Kockelmans, Joseph J. 1923- *WhoAm 94*
Kockelmans, Joseph J(ohn) 1923- *ConAu 41NR*
Kock-Petersen, Elsebeth 1949- *IntWW 93*, *WhoWomW 91*
Kocman, Ali 1943- *IntWW 93*
Koco, Linda Gale 1945- *WhoMW 93*
Kocoras, Charles Petros 1938- *WhoAm 94*, *WhoAmL 94*
Kocsis, James Paul 1936- *WhoAm 94*, *WhoAmA 93*
Kocsis, John 1948- *WhoAmP 93*
Kocsis, Sandor 1929- *WorESoc*
Kocsis, Zoltan 1952- *IntWW 93*
Koczera, Robert Michael 1953- *WhoAmP 93*
Koda-Callan, Elizabeth 1944- *WrDr 94*
Kodaka, Kunio 1932- *WhoFI 94*
Kodali, Hari Prasad 1949- *WhoScEn 94*
Kodalli, Nevit 1924- *NewGrDO*
Kodaly, Zoltan 1882-1967 *NewGrDO*
Kodamanoglu, Nuri 1923- *IntWW 93*
Kodar, Oja *WhoHol 92*
Koder, David George 1962- *WhoMW 93*
Kodes, Jan 1945- *BuCMET*
Kodes, Jan 1946- *IntWW 93*
Kodis, Mary Caroline 1927- *WhoWest 94*
Kodish, Arline Betty 1934- *WhoMW 93*
Kodjo, Edem 1938- *IntWW 93*
Kodner, Martin 1934- *WhoAmA 93*, *WhoMW 93*
Kodosky, Thomas Michael 1942- *WhoFI 94*
Kodousek, Kim Robert 1951- *WhoAmL 94*
Kodym, Miloslav 1930- *WhoScEn 94*
Koea, Shonagh 1939- *BlmGWL*
Koechlin, Samuel 1925- *IntWW 93*
Koechlin-Smythe, Patricia Rosemary 1928- *Who 94*
Koechlin von Stein, Jorge Javier 1950- *WhoHisp 94*
Koedel, John Gilbert, Jr. 1937- *WhoAm 94*
Koedel, Robert Craig 1927- *WhoAm 94*
Koeffler, Deborah P. 1948- *WhoAmL 94*
Koefoed, Ingerlise 1922- *WhoWomW 91*
Koegel, William Fisher 1923- *WhoAm 94*, *WhoAmL 94*
Koegen, Roy Jerome 1949- *WhoAm 94*
Koehl, Camille Joan 1943- *WhoFI 94*, *WhoMW 93*
Koehl, Edward J., Jr. 1945- *WhoAmL 94*
Koehler, Agnes Theresa 1921- *WhoWest 94*
Koehler, Charlotte d1977 *WhoHol 92*
Koehler, Frederick *WhoHol 92*
Koehler, George Applegate 1921- *WhoAm 94*
Koehler, Gustav Adolphus 1944- *WhoWest 94*
Koehler, Harry George 1954- *WhoFI 94*
Koehler, Henry 1927- *WhoAmA 93*
Koehler, John Edget 1941- *WhoAm 94*, *WhoFI 94*
Koehler, John Theodore 1904-1989 *WhAm 10*
Koehler, Judy 1926- *WhoAmP 93*
Koehler, Phoebe 1955- *WrDr 94*
Koehler, Reginald Stafford, III 1932- *WhoAm 94*
Koehler, Ronald Gene 1950- *WhoAmA 93*
Koehler, Rudolph August 1934- *WhoAm 94*, *WhoFI 94*
Koehler, Stanley *DrAPF 93*
Koehler, Werner Ray 1929- *WhoFI 94*
Koehn, Emil Alvin 1916- *WhoAmP 93*
Koehn, George Waldemar 1943- *WhoAm 94*
Koehn, William James 1936- *WhoMW 93*
Koehnke, Francis 1918- *WhoAmP 93*
Koekoek, Roelof 1963- *WhoScEn 94*
Koelb, Clayton T. 1942- *WrDr 94*
Koelb, Clayton Talmadge 1920- *WhoAm 94*
Koelbl, Christian G., III 1945- *WhoAmL 94*
Koella, Carl O., Jr. 1933- *WhoAmP 93*
Koelle, George Brampton 1918- *IntWW 93*, *WhoAm 94*
Koeller, Robert Marion 1940- *WhoAmL 94*, *WhoMW 93*
Koelling, Herbert Lee 1932- *WhoAm 94*, *WhoFI 94*
Koelmel, Lorna Lee 1936- *WhoFI 94*, *WhoScEn 94*, *WhoWest 94*
Koelsch, M. Oliver 1912- *WhoWest 94*
Koeltl, John George 1945- *WhoAm 94*, *WhoAmL 94*
Koelzer, George Joseph 1938- *WhoAm 94*
Koelzer, Victor Alvin 1914- *WhoAm 94*
Koeman, Ronald 1963- *WorESoc*
Koen, Billy Vaughn 1938- *WhoAm 94*
Koen, Clifford Mock, Jr. 1949- *WhoAmL 94*
Koen, Robert G. 1946- *WhoAmL 94*
Koenegstein, Mildred Lorraine 1919- *WhoAmP 93*
Koenekamp, Fred J. 1922- *IntMPA 94*
Koenen, Ludwig 1931- *WhoMW 93*
Koenig, Aaron Joseph 1953- *WhoMW 93*
Koenig, Allen Edward 1939- *WhoAm 94*
Koenig, Bonnie 1957- *WhoAm 94*
Koenig, Carl Frederick, III 1952- *WhoAmL 94*
Koenig, Catherine Catanzaro 1921- *WhoAmA 93*
Koenig, David John 1960- *WhoMW 93*
Koenig, Elizabeth 1937- *WhoAmA 93*
Koenig, Gottlieb 1940- *WhoScEn 94*
Koenig, Harold Martin 1940- *WhoAm 94*
Koenig, Howard D. *DrAPF 93*
Koenig, Jack L. 1933- *WhoMW 93*, *WhoScEn 94*
Koenig, James Edward 1947- *WhoAm 94*
Koenig, Joan Foster 1930- *WhoAmP 93*
Koenig, John Franklin 1924- *WhoAmA 93*
Koenig, John L. 1938- *WhoFI 94*
Koenig, Josef d1938 *WhoHol 92*
Koenig, Mark 1904-1993 *NewYTBS 93 [port]*
Koenig, Mary Gonzalez 1936- *WhoHisp 94*
Koenig, Michael Edward Davison 1941- *WhoAm 94*
Koenig, Peter Edward 1956- *WhoAmL 94*
Koenig, Peter L. 1933- *WhoAmA 93*
Koenig, Pierre 1925- *IntWW 93*
Koenig, Robert J. 1935- *WhoAmA 93*
Koenig, Rodney Curtis 1940- *WhoAm 94*, *WhoAmL 94*
Koenig, Virgil 1913-1989 *WhAm 10*
Koenig, Walter *WhoHol 92*
Koenig, Walter 1936- *IntMPA 94*
Koenig, Wayne Lynn 1945- *WhoFI 94*
Koenigs, Deo A. 1935- *WhoAmP 93*, *WhoMW 93*
Koenigsberg, I. Fred 1947- *WhoAmL 94*
Koenigsberger, Gloria S. 1951- *WhoAm 94*
Koenigsberger, Helmut Georg 1918- *Who 94*, *WrDr 94*
Koenigsknecht, Roy A. 1942- *WhoAm 94*
Koeninger, Edward Calvin 1930- *WhoAm 94*
Koeninger, George R. *WhoMW 93*
Koep, Mary A. 1932- *WhoAmP 93*
Koepcke, F. Kristen 1935- *WhoAmL 94*
Koepf, Michael *DrAPF 93*
Koepf, Werner Karl 1942- *WhoFI 94*
Koepfer, Donald Julius 1936- *WhoFI 94*
Koepfinger, Joseph Leo 1925- *WhoAm 94*
Koepke, Christine Margaret 1964- *WhoMW 93*
Koepke, Donald Herbert 1923- *WhoFI 94*, *WhoMW 93*
Koepke, Jack Edward 1942- *WhoFI 94*, *WhoIns 94*
Koepke, John Arthur 1929- *WhoAm 94*
Koepke, Lonnie Dean 1956- *WhoMW 93*
Koepnick, Robert Charles 1907- *WhoAmA 93*
Koepp, Donald William 1929- *WhoAm 94*
Koepp, Donna Pauline Petersen 1941- *WhoMW 93*
Koepp, Jane Elizabeth 1947- *WhoWest 94*
Koeppe, Eugene Charles, Jr. 1955- *WhoMW 93*, *WhoScEn 94*
Koeppe, Patsy Poduska 1932- *WhoScEn 94*
Koeppel, Gary Merle 1938- *WhoWest 94*
Koeppel, John A. 1947- *WhoAm 94*, *WhoAmL 94*
Koeppel, Noel Immanuel 1930- *WhoFI 94*
Koeppel, William Edward 1951- *WhoAmP 93*
Koeppen, Raymond Bradley 1954- *WhoMW 93*
Koeppl, John 1941- *WhoAmL 94*
Koepsel, Wellington Wesley 1921- *WhoScEn 94*
Koerber, Hilde d1969 *WhoHol 92*
Koerber, John Robert 1955- *WhoWest 94*
Koering, Marilyn Jean 1938- *WhoAm 94*
Koerner, Henry 1915-1991 *WhAm 10*, *WhoAmA 93N*
Koerner, Hermine d1969 *WhoHol 92*
Koerner, James D. 1923- *WrDr 94*
Koerner, James David 1923- *WhoAm 94*
Koerner, Jane Goetze 1950- *WhoWest 94*
Koerner, Philip Donald 1946- *WhoIns 94*
Koertge, Ron 1940- *Au&Arts 12 [port]*
Koertge, Ron(ald) 1940- *TwCYAW*
Koertge, Ronald *DrAPF 93*
Koerv, Alan Ago *WhoFI 94*
Koessel, Donald Ray 1929- *WhoAm 94*
Koessler, Hans 1853-1926 *NewGrDO*
Koestel, Mark Alfred 1951- *WhoWest 94*
Koestenbaum, Phyllis *DrAPF 93*
Koestenbaum, Wayne *DrAPF 93*
Koestenbaum, Wayne 1958- *WrDr 94*
Koester, Berthold Karl 1931- *WhoWest 94*
Koester, Helmut Heinrich 1926- *WhoAm 94*
Koester, J. Anthony 1942- *WhoScEn 94*
Koester, Robert Gregg 1932- *WhoAm 94*
Koester, Rudolf 1936- *WhoWest 94*
Koesterer, Sandy Jean 1962- *WhoMW 93*
Koestler, Arthur 1905-1983 *BlmGEL*, *EncSF 93*
Koestler, Fred 1934- *WhoAm 94*
Koestler, Robert John 1950- *WhoScEn 94*
Koestner, Don 1923- *WhoAmA 93*
Koethe, John *DrAPF 93*
Koethke, Charles Richard 1945- *WhoWest 94*
Koetsch, Philip Wayne 1935- *WhoWest 94*
Koetser, David 1906- *WhoFI 94*, *WhoWest 94*
Koetsier, Johan Carel 1936- *WhoScEn 94*
Koetzle, Gil 1952- *WhoMW 93*
Koetzle, Gilbert 1952- *WhoAmP 93*
Koff, Andrew 1962- *WhoScEn 94*
Koff, Bernard L. 1927- *WhoAm 94*, *WhoScEn 94*
Koff, Howard Michael 1941- *WhoAmL 94*
Koff, Richard M 1926- *WrDr 94*
Koff, Robert Hess 1938- *WhoAm 94*, *WhoMW 93*
Koffel, William Barry 1948- *WhoAm 94*
Koffigoh, Joseph Kokou 1948- *IntWW 93*
Koffler, Stephen Alexander 1942- *WhoFI 94*
Koffler, Warren William 1938- *WhoAmL 94*
Kofford, Cree-L 1933- *WhoAmL 94*
Kofmehl, Kenneth Theodore 1920- *WhoMW 93*
Kofod-Svendsen, Flemming 1944- *IntWW 93*
Kofoed, Niels Anker 1929- *IntWW 93*
Koford, Helen *WhoHol 92*
Koford, Kenneth J. 1948- *ConAu 140*
Koford, Luella d1989 *WhoHol 92*
Koford, Stuart Keith 1953- *WhoMW 93*
Kofranek, Anton Miles 1921- *WhoAm 94*
Kofsky, Frank Joseph 1935- *WhoWest 94*
Kofstad, Per Kristen 1929- *IntWW 93*
Koga, Mary 1920- *WhoAm 94*, *WhoAmA 93*
Koga, Mary H. 1920- *WhoAsA 94*
Koga, Rokutaro 1942- *WhoAsA 94*, *WhoWest 94*
Koga, Tatsuzo 1935- *WhoScEn 94*
Koga, Toyoki 1912- *WhoAsA 94*
Koga, Yoshi Tanji 1924- *WhoAsA 94*
Kogan, Deborah 1940- *WhoAmA 93*
Kogan, Edward d1984 *WhoHol 92*
Kogan, Evgeny Vladimirovich 1954- *LngBDD*
Kogan, Gerald 1933- *WhoAm 94*, *WhoAmL 94*, *WhoAmP 93*
Kogan, Herman 1914-1989 *WhAm 10*
Kogan, Maurice 1930- *Who 94*
Kogan, Milt 1936- *WhoHol 92*
Kogan, Nathan *WhoHol 92*
Kogan, Norman 1919- *WrDr 94*
Kogan, Richard Jay 1941- *WhoAm 94*
Kogatko, Grigory Iosifovich 1944- *LngBDD*
Kogawa, Joy 1935- *BlmGWL*, *ConLC 78 [port]*
Kogawa, Joy Nozomi 1935- *WrDr 94*
Kogel, Marcus David 1903-1989 *WhAm 10*
Kogelnik, Herwig Werner 1932- *WhoAm 94*, *WhoScEn 94*
Koger, Frank Williams 1930- *WhoAm 94*, *WhoAmL 94*
Koger, Ira McKissick 1912- *WhoAmA 93*
Koger, Linwood Graves, III 1951- *WhoBlA 94*
Koger, Lisa (Jan) 1953- *WrDr 94*
Koger, Michael Pigott, Sr. 1953- *WhoBlA 94*
Koger, Mildred Emmelene Nichols 1928- *WhoScEn 94*
Koger, Ronny Stewart 1953- *WhoWest 94*
Koger, W. R. 1924- *WhoMW 93*
Kogge, Peter Michael 1946- *WhoAm 94*
Kogi, Hiroko 1955- *WhoFI 94*
Kogler, James Foley 1939-1987 *WhAm 10*
Koglin, Norman Alfred 1928- *WhoMW 93*
Kogoj, Marij 1895-1956 *NewGrDO*
Kogovsek, Daniel Charles 1951- *WhoAmL 94*
Kogovsek, John J. 1946- *WhoAmP 93*
Kogovsek, Ray P. 1941- *WhoAmP 93*
Kogure, Gohei 1924- *IntWW 93*
Kogut, John Anthony 1942- *WhoAm 94*
Kogut, Kenneth Joseph 1947- *WhoScEn 94*
Kogut, Maurice David 1930- *WhoAm 94*
Koh, Carolyn Ann 1965- *WhoScEn 94*
Koh, Eusebio Legarda 1931- *WhoWest 94*
Koh, Kilsan 1950- *WhoAsA 94*

Koh, Kwang K. *WhoAsA 94*
Koh, Peter TongBak 1943- *WhoMW 93*
Koh, Pun Kien 1914- *WhoFI 94, WhoScEn 94*
Koh, Severino Legarda 1927- *WhoAm 94*
Koh, Tommy Thong Bee 1937- *IntWW 93*
Kohan, (Alan) Buz 1933- *ConTFT 11*
Kohan, Dennis Lynn 1945- *WhoWest 94*
Kohara, David Noboru 1950- *WhoAsA 94*
Kohashi, Ethel Tsukiko 1910?-1993 *WhoAsA 94N*
Kohaut, (Wenzel) Josef (Thomas) 1738-1793? *NewGrDO*
Kohel, Russell James 1934- *WhoAm 94, WhoScEn 94*
Kohl, Barbara 1940- *WhoAmA 93*
Kohl, Benedict M. 1931- *WhoAm 94*
Kohl, David 1942- *WhoAm 94*
Kohl, Helmut 1930- *IntWW 93, News 94-1 [port], Who 94*
Kohl, Herb 1935- *CngDr 93*
Kohl, Herbert 1935- *WhoAm 94, WhoAmP 93, WhoMW 93*
Kohl, Jacquelyn Marie 1950- *WhoAmL 94*
Kohl, Jeanne *WhoAmP 93*
Kohl, John Preston 1942- *WhoWest 94*
Kohl, MaryAnn F. 1947- *SmATA 74*
Kohl, Robert L. 1944- *WhoAmL 94*
Kohla, Donald S. 1942- *WhoAmL 94*
Kohlberg, Jerome, Jr. 1925- *WhoAm 94, WhoFI 94*
Kohlenberg, Stanley 1932- *WhoFI 94*
Kohlenberger, Jim 1962- *WhoWest 94*
Kohler, Charlotte 1908- *WhoAm 94*
Kohler, Dolores Marie 1928- *WhoWest 94*
Kohler, Dylan Whitaker 1966- *WhoScEn 94*
Kohler, Eric Dave 1943- *WhoWest 94*
Kohler, Foy David 1908-1990 *WhAm 10*
Kohler, Fred, Sr. d1938 *WhoHol 92*
Kohler, Fred, Jr. *WhoHol 92*
Kohler, Fred Christopher 1946- *WhoFI 94*
Kohler, Georges J. F. 1946- *WhoScEn 94*
Kohler, Herbert Vollrath, Jr. 1939- *WhoMW 93*
Kohler, Irene *Who 94*
Kohler, Jeffrey Martin 1956- *WhoAm 94*
Kohler, John Michael 1949- *WhoWest 94*
Kohler, Kaufmann 1843-1926 *DcAmReB 2*
Kohler, Max Adam 1915- *WhoAm 94*
Kohler, Peter Ogden 1938- *WhoAm 94, WhoWest 94*
Kohler, Rose 1873-1947 *WhoAmA 93N*
Kohler, Ruth DeYoung 1941- *WhoAmA 93, WhoMW 93*
Kohler, Sandra *DrAPF 93*
Kohler, Steven Alan 1951- *WhoAmL 94*
Kohler, William Charles 1929- *WhoWest 94*
Kohles, David Allan 1952- *WhoAmL 94*
Kohlhaussen, Martin 1935- *Who 94*
Kohlhepp, Dorothy Irene d1964 *WhoAmA 93N*
Kohlhepp, Edward John 1943- *WhoFI 94*
Kohlhepp, Norman d1986 *WhoAmA 93N*
Kohlhoff, Hans-Peter 1948- *WhoAmP 93*
Kohlhorst, Gail Lewis 1946- *WhoAm 94*
Kohli, Tejbans Singh 1958- *WhoScEn 94*
Kohlman, David Leslie 1937- *WhoAm 94*
Kohlman, Louis Freddie d1990 *WhoHol 92*
Kohlmar, Lee d1946 *WhoHol 92*
Kohlmeier, Louis Martin, Jr. 1926- *WhoAm 94*
Kohlmeier, Ronald Harold 1936- *WhoMW 93*
Kohlmeier, Sharon Louise 1944- *WhoScEn 94*
Kohlmeister, Benjamin Gottlieb 1756-1844 *EncNAR*
Kohlmey, Gunther 1913- *IntWW 93*
Kohlmeyer, Ida (R.) 1912- *WhoAmA 93*
Kohlmeyer, Ida Rittenberg 1912- *WhoAm 94*
Kohloss, Frederick Henry 1922- *WhoAm 94*
Kohlstedt, James August 1949- *WhoAm 94*
Kohlstedt, Sally Gregory 1943- *WhoAm 94*
Kohn, A. Eugene 1930- *WhoAm 94*
Kohn, Alan Charles 1932- *WhoAmL 94*
Kohn, Alan J. 1931- *WhoWest 94*
Kohn, Barbara Ann 1954- *WhoScEn 94*
Kohn, Clyde Frederick 1911-1989 *WhAm 10*
Kohn, Gabriel 1910-1975 *WhoAmA 93N*
Kohn, George C(hilds) 1940- *ConAu 42NR*
Kohn, Gerhard 1921- *WhoWest 94*
Kohn, Harold Elias 1914- *WhoAm 94, WhoAmL 94*
Kohn, Henry 1917- *WhoAm 94*
Kohn, Howard Edward, II 1920- *IntMPA 94*
Kohn, Immanuel 1926- *WhoAm 94*
Kohn, James Paul 1924- *WhoAm 94*
Kohn, Janet Ann 1931- *WhoAmP 93*
Kohn, Jeffrey Ira 1959- *WhoAmL 94*
Kohn, Jerome Milton 1915- *WhoWest 94*
Kohn, John Peter, Jr. 1902- *WhoAm 94*
Kohn, Joseph John 1932- *WhoAm 94*
Kohn, Julieanne 1946- *WhoMW 93*
Kohn, Karen Josephine 1951- *WhoMW 93*
Kohn, Larry Michael 1953- *WhoMW 93*
Kohn, Martin Benne 1898- *WhAm 10*
Kohn, Mary Louise Beatrice 1920- *WhoMW 93*
Kohn, Melvin L. 1928- *WhoAm 94*
Kohn, Michael Bundy 1958- *WhoAmA 93, WhoWest 94*
Kohn, Michael Charles 1941- *WhoScEn 94*
Kohn, Misch 1916- *WhoAmA 93*
Kohn, Misch Harris 1916- *WhoWest 94*
Kohn, Richard E. 1946- *WhoFI 94*
Kohn, Richard H. 1940- *WhoAm 94*
Kohn, Robert Alfred 1944- *WhoAmP 93*
Kohn, Robert Samuel, Jr. 1949- *WhoFI 94, WhoWest 94*
Kohn, Roger Alan 1946- *WhoWest 94*
Kohn, Shalom L. 1949- *WhoAm 94, WhoAmL 94*
Kohn, Stephen Martin 1956- *WhoAmL 94*
Kohn, Timothy F. 1961- *WhoAmL 94*
Kohn, Walter 1923- *IntWW 93, WhoAm 94, WhoScEn 94*
Kohn, William Irwin 1951- *WhoAm 94, WhoAmL 94*
Kohn, William Roth 1931- *WhoAmA 93*
Kohne, Raymond Ernest 1962- *WhoWest 94*
Kohne, Richard Edward 1924- *WhoAm 94, WhoScEn 94, WhoWest 94*
Kohner, Pancho 1939- *IntMPA 94*
Kohner, Susan 1936- *IntMPA 94, WhoHol 92*
Kohnhorst, Earl Eugene 1947- *WhoScEn 94*
Kohnke, Edward F., IV 1946- *WhoAmL 94*
Kohnstam, George 1920- *Who 94*
Kohnstamm, Lee W. 1936- *WhoFI 94*
Kohnstamm, Max 1914- *Who 94*
Koho, Clarence Herbert 1931- *WhoWest 94*
Kohoban-Wickreme, Alfred Silva 1914- *Who 94*
Kohonen, Teuvo Kalevi 1934- *IntWW 93*
Kohout, Pavel 1928- *EncSF 93*
Kohoutek, Richard 1943- *WhoScEn 94*
Kohr, Roland Ellsworth 1931- *WhoAm 94, WhoFI 94, WhoMW 93, WhoScEn 94*
Kohring, Dagmar Luzia 1951- *WhoFI 94*
Kohrman, Arthur Fisher 1934- *WhoAm 94*
Kohrs, Diana Joyce 1929- *WhoMW 93*
Kohrt, Carl Fredrick 1943- *WhoAm 94*
Koht, Paul 1913- *Who 94*
Kohut, John Walter 1946- *WhoAm 94, WhoFI 94*
Kohut, Lorene 1929- *WhoAmA 93*
Kohut, Thomas A. 1950- *ConAu 142*
Koide, Frank Takayuki 1935- *WhoAm 94, WhoAsA 94*
Koide, Samuel Saburo 1923- *WhoAsA 94*
Koile, Earl 1917- *WhoAm 94*
Koinis, Steven W. 1956- *WhoFI 94*
Koirala, Ginja Prasad *IntWW 93*
Koirala, Matrika Prasad 1912- *IntWW 93*
Koiter, Warner Tjardus 1914- *IntWW 93*
Koivisto, Don *WhoAmP 93*
Koivisto, Mauno Henrik 1923- *IntWW 93*
Koivulehto, Jorma Juhani 1934- *IntWW 93*
Koizumi, Carl Jan 1943- *WhoWest 94*
Koizumi, Junichiro *IntWW 93*
Koizumi, Shunzo 1946- *WhoScEn 94*
Kojian, Varujan d1993 *NewYTBS 93*
Kojic-Prodic, Biserka 1938- *WhoScEn 94*
Kojima, Kenn N. *WhoAmL 94*
Kojima, Kiyoshi 1920- *IntWW 93*
Kojima, Ryuichi O. 1949- *WhoScEn 94*
Kojis, Don 1939- *BasBi*
Kok, Frans Johan 1943- *WhoFI 94*
Kok, Peter 1919- *WhoAmP 93*
Kok, Wim 1938- *IntWW 93*
Kokalj, James Edward 1933- *WhoWest 94*
Kokan, Ghiasuddin 1945- *WhoAsA 94*
Kokanovich, Jon Douglas 1951- *WhoFI 94*
Kokaska, Charles James 1937- *WhoAm 94*
Kokatnur, Mohan Gundo 1930- *WhoAsA 94*
Koke, Richard Joseph 1916- *WhoAm 94*
Koken, Bernd Krafft 1926- *WhoAm 94, WhoFI 94*
Kokes, Alois Harold 1955- *WhoAmL 94*
Kokhno, Boris Yevgen'yevich *NewGrDO*
Koki, Stan T. 1946- *WhoAmP 93*
Kokini, Klod 1954- *WhoScEn 94*
Kokkalis, Anastasios 1957- *WhoScEn 94*
Kokkinakis, Demetrius Michael 1950- *WhoScEn 94*
Kokko, Juha Pekka 1937- *WhoAm 94*
Kokkonen, Joonas 1921- *NewGrDO*
Koknat, Friedrich Wilhelm 1938- *WhoMW 93*
Koko 1928- *WhoBlA 94*
Kokopeli, Peter Heine 1954- *WhoScEn 94*
Kokoruda, Thomas G. 1947- *WhoAmL 94*
Kokoschka, Oskar 1886-1980 *IntDcT 2*
Kokoshin, Andrei Afanasevich 1945- *LngBDD*
Kokoshin, Andrei Afanasievich 1945- *IntWW 93*
Kokot, Franciszek Jozef 1929- *WhoScEn 94*
Kokov, Valery Mukhamedovich 1941- *LngBDD*
Kokubo, Christina 1950- *WhoHol 92*
Kokunko, Georgy Valentinovich 1961- *LngBDD*
Kola, Arthur Anthony 1939- *WhoAm 94*
Kola, Pamela *BlmGWL*
Kolakowski, Diana Jean 1943- *WhoMW 93*
Kolakowski, Leszek 1927- *IntWW 93, Who 94*
Kolakowski, Marilyn 1953- *WhoWest 94*
Koland, David Jerome 1942- *WhoAmP 93*
Kolane, John Teboho 1926- *Who 94*
Kolanoski, Thomas Edwin 1937- *WhoFI 94, WhoWest 94*
Kolansky, Harold 1924- *WhoAm 94*
Kolanz, John Andrew 1962- *WhoAmL 94*
Kolar, Barry R. 1951- *WhoAmP 93*
Kolar, Edward Louis 1909- *WhoAmP 93*
Kolar, Jiri 1914- *IntWW 93*
Kolar, Mary Jane 1941- *WhoAm 94*
Kolarcik, Kenneth Ernest 1946- *WhoAmL 94*
Kolarova, Daniela 1946- *WhoWomW 91*
Kolasa, Ann Cathryn 1960- *WhoMW 93*
Kolash, Ronald Brent 1964- *WhoFI 94*
Kolasky, William Joseph, Jr. 1946- *WhoAmL 94*
Kolatch, Alfred Jacob 1916- *WhoAm 94*
Kolatch, Myron 1929- *WhoAm 94*
Kolatkar, Arun (Balkrishna) 1932- *WrDr 94*
Kolattukudy, Pappachan Ettoop 1937- *WhoScEn 94*
Kolb, Annette 1870-1967 *BlmGWL*
Kolb, Bertha Mae 1925- *WhoFI 94*
Kolb, Charles Chester 1940- *WhoScEn 94*
Kolb, Charles Eugene 1945- *WhoAm 94*
Kolb, Clarence d1964 *WhoHol 92*
Kolb, Daniel Francis 1941- *WhoAm 94*
Kolb, David Allen 1939- *WhoAm 94*
Kolb, Gwin Jackson 1919- *WhoAm 94*
Kolb, Harold Hutchison, Jr. 1933- *WhoAm 94*
Kolb, Henry George 1950- *WhoMW 93*
Kolb, James A. 1947- *WhoScEn 94*
Kolb, Jerry Wilbert 1935- *WhoAm 94, WhoFI 94*
Kolb, Keith Robert 1922- *WhoAm 94*
Kolb, Kelly Haze 1961- *WhoAmL 94*
Kolb, Ken *DrAPF 93*
Kolb, Ken Lloyd 1926- *WhoAm 94, WhoWest 94*
Kolb, Lawrence Coleman 1911- *WhoAm 94*
Kolb, Mark Andrew 1962- *WhoScEn 94*
Kolb, Nancy Dwyer 1940- *WhoAm 94*
Kolb, Nathaniel Key, Jr. 1933- *WhoAm 94, WhoFI 94*
Kolb, Noel Joseph 1930- *WhoScEn 94*
Kolb, R. Frank, II 1946- *WhoAmP 93*
Kolb, Richard Eugene 1931- *WhoFI 94*
Kolb, Theodore Alexander 1920- *WhoAm 94*
Kolb, Therese d1935 *WhoHol 92*
Kolb, William Thomas 1956- *WhoMW 93*
Kolba, Stahanouch Tamara *WhoAmA 93*
Kolbas, Robert Michael 1953- *WhoScEn 94*
Kolbe, Adolf Wilhelm Hermann 1818-1884 *WorScD*
Kolbe, Hellmuth Walter 1926- *WhoScEn 94*
Kolbe, James Thomas 1942- *WhoAm 94, WhoAmP 93, WhoWest 94*
Kolbe, Jane Boegler 1944- *WhoAm 94*
Kolbe, Jim 1942- *CngDr 93*
Kolbe, John William 1940- *WhoAm 94, WhoWest 94*
Kolbe, Karl William, Jr. 1926- *WhoAm 94, WhoAmL 94*
Kolberg, William d1970 *WhoHol 92*
Kolbert, Colin Francis 1936- *Who 94*
Kolbo, Kevin P. *WhoAmP 93*
Kolbowski, Silvia 1953- *WhoAmA 93*
Kolbye, Albert Christian, Jr. 1935- *WhoAm 94*
Kolczynski, Phillip John 1947- *WhoAmL 94*
Kolda, Thomas Joseph 1939- *WhoMW 93*
Kolde, Bert *WhoAm 94, WhoWest 94*
Kolde, Frederick William 1870- *WhoAmA 93N*
Kolde, Richard Arthur 1944- *WhoFI 94*
Koldewey, Karl Christian 1837-1908 *WhWE*
Kolditz, Lothar 1929- *WhoScEn 94*
Koldorf, Irene Janet 1925- *WhoAmA 93*
Koldovsky, Otakar 1930- *WhoWest 94*
Koldunov, Aleksandr Ivanovich 1923- *IntWW 93*
Koldys, Mark Edward 1946- *WhoAmP 93*
Kole, Janet Stephanie 1946- *WhoAmL 94*
Kole, John William 1934- *WhoAm 94*
Kolehmainen, Jan Waldroy 1940- *WhoAm 94*
Kolek, Mary Eileen 1947- *WhoMW 93*
Kolek, Robert Edward 1943- *WhoAm 94, WhoAmL 94*
Kolesar, Peter John 1936- *WhoAm 94*
Kolesnikov, Mikhail Petrovich 1939- *IntWW 93, LngBDD*
Kolesnikov, Vladislav Grigoryevich 1925- *IntWW 93*
Koleson, Donald Ralph 1935- *WhoMW 93*
Kolf, James 1948- *WhoFI 94*
Kolff, Willem Johan 1911- *IntWW 93, WhoWest 94*
Koliatsos, Vassilis Eleftherios 1957- *WhoScEn 94*
Kolin, Alexander 1910- *WhoWest 94*
Kolin, Philip C(harles) 1945- *ConAu 43NR*
Kolin, Sacha 1911-1975 *WhoAmA 93N*
Kolingba, Andre *IntWW 93*
Kolinsky, Martin 1936- *WrDr 94*
Kolisevski, Lazar 1914- *IntWW 93*
Kolisnyk, Peter 1934- *WhoAmA 93*
Kolker, Adam 1959- *WhoAmL 94*
Kolker, Allan Erwin 1933- *WhoAm 94*
Kolker, Henry d1947 *WhoHol 92*
Kolker, Richard Lee 1939- *WhoAmP 93*
Kolker, Roger Russell 1929- *WhoAm 94*
Kolkey, Daniel Miles 1952- *WhoAm 94, WhoAmL 94, WhoWest 94*
Kolkey, Eric Samuel 1960- *WhoMW 93*
Kolkin, Mitchell 1950- *WhoAmL 94*
Kolkman, Paul F. 1946- *WhoIns 94*
Kolko, Gabriel 1932- *WhoAm 94*
Kolko, Joyce 1933- *WrDr 94*
Koll, Richard Leroy 1925- *WhoAm 94*
Kollaer, Jim C. 1943- *WhoAm 94, WhoFI 94*
Kollar, Sybil *DrAPF 93*
Kollat, David Truman 1938- *WhoAm 94*
Kollek, Amos *WhoHol 92*
Kollek, Teddy 1911- *CurBio 93 [port]*
Kollek, Theodore 1911- *IntWW 93*
Koller, Arnold 1933- *IntWW 93*
Koller, Charles William 1896- *WhAm 10*
Koller, Don 1942- *WhoAmP 93*
Koller, Duncan G. 1946- *WhoWest 94*
Koller, Elizabeth Rose 1965- *WhoAmL 94*
Koller, Herbert Josef 1911- *IntWW 93*
Koller, James *DrAPF 93*
Koller, James 1936- *WrDr 94*
Koller, Karen Kathryn 1949- *WhoMW 93*
Koller, Kathrine d1993 *NewYTBS 93*
Koller, Kevin 1924- *WrDr 94*
Koller, Lewis R. d1993 *NewYTBS 93*
Koller, Loren D. 1940- *WhoAm 94*
Koller, Marita A. 1955- *WhoMW 93*
Koller, Marvin Robert 1919- *WhoAm 94, WrDr 94*
Koller, William Carl 1945- *WhoMW 93*
Koller-Davies, Eva 1925- *WhoAmA 93*
Kollias, George Van, Jr. 1947- *WhoAm 94*
Kollias, Konstantinos V. 1901- *IntWW 93*
Kolliker, Rudolph Albert von 1817-1905 *WorScD*
Kolliker, William Augustin 1905- *WhoAmA 93*
Kollin, Gary 1953- *WhoAmL 94*
Kolling, Charles Joseph 1950- *WhoAmP 93*
Kollios, Paul *WhoAmP 93*
Kollmann, Hilda Hanna 1913- *WhoAm 94*
Kollmar, Richard d1971 *WhoHol 92*
Kollo, Rene 1937- *IntWW 93, NewGrDO*
Kollo, (Elimar) Walter 1878-1940 *NewGrDO*
Kollo, Willi d1988 *WhoHol 92*
Kollontai, Aleksandra 1872-1952 *BlmGWL*
Kollontai, Alexandra 1872-1952 *HisWorL [port]*
Kollros, Peter Richard 1953- *WhoScEn 94*
Kolluri, Arthur Noble 1940- *WhoFI 94*
Kollwitz, Kathe 1867-1945 *BlmGWL*
Kolm, Henry Herbert 1924- *WhoAm 94*
Kolm, Ron *DrAPF 93*
Kolman, Mark Herbert 1946- *WhoAm 94*
Kolmar, Gertrud 1894-1943? *BlmGWL*
Kolmogorov, Andrei Nikolaevich 1903- *WorScD*
Kolo, Sule 1926- *Who 94*
Kolodey, Fred James 1936- *WhoAm 94, WhoAmL 94*
Kolodinsky, Alison *DrAPF 93*
Kolodkin, Anatoliy Lazarevich 1928- *IntWW 93*
Kolodner, Ignace Izaak 1920- *WhoAm 94*
Kolodner, Nathan K. 1950- *WhoAmA 93N*
Kolodny, Edwin Hillel 1936- *WhoAm 94*
Kolodny, Nancy J. 1946- *SmATA 76 [port]*

Kolodny, Richard 1943- WhoAm 94
Kolodny, Stanley Charles 1923- WhoAm 94
Kolodny, Stephen Arthur 1940- WhoWest 94
Kolodziej, Edward Albert 1935- WhoAm 94
Kolodziej, Gloria WhoAmP 93
Kolodziej, Ryan Henry 1957- WhoAmP 93
Kolodziejski, Charles W. 1927- WhoAmP 93
Kolokolov, Boris Leonidovich 1924- IntWW 93
Kolombatovic, Vadja Vadim 1924- WhoAm 94
Kolonel, Laurence Norman 1942- WhoAm 94
Kolor, Michael Garrett 1934- WhoFI 94, WhoScEn 94
Kolotyrkin, Yakov Mikhailovich 1910- IntWW 93
Kolowich, Patricia Ann 1958- WhoMW 93
Kolozsvari-Grandpierre, Emil d1992 IntWW 93N
Kolpakova, Irina 1933- IntDcB [port], WhoAm 94
Kolpakova, Irina Aleksandrovna 1933- IntWW 93
Kolpas, Sidney J. 1947- WhoWest 94
Kolpin, Alexander 1965- IntDcB [port]
Kolsen, Helmut Max 1926- WrDr 94
Kolsky, Allan 1932- WhoFI 94
Kolsky, Herbert 1916-1992 WhAm 10
Kolsky, Thomas A. 1942- WrDr 94
Kolsrud, Henry Gerald 1923- WhoWest 94
Kolstad, Allen C. 1931- WhoAmP 93
Kolstad, Eva 1918- IntWW 93
Kolstad, George Andrew 1919- WhoScEn 94
Kolstad, James L. WhoAmP 93
Kolstad, Robert Bruce 1953- WhoWest 94
Koltai, Ralph 1924- IntWW 93, NewGrDO, Who 94
Koltai, Stephen Miklos 1922- WhoFI 94, WhoScEn 94, WhoWest 94
Kolter, Joseph Paul 1926- WhoAm 94, WhoAmP 93
Kolterjahn, Paul Henry 1924-1992 WhAm 10
Kolthoff, Carol Cottone 1954- WhoWest 94
Kolthoff, Izaak Maurits d1993 NewYTBS 93 [port]
Koltin, Allan David 1957- WhoAm 94
Koltnow, Peter Gregory 1929- WhoAm 94
Kolton, Paul 1923- WhoAm 94
Koltun, Frances Lang WhoAmA 93
Koltzow, Liv 1945- BlmGWL
Kolumban, Nicholas DrAPF 93
Kolupayev, Viktor (Dmitrievich) 1936- EncSF 93
Kolve, V. A. 1934- WhoAm 94
Kolvek, Janice Annas 1953- WhoMW 93
Kolvenbach, Peter-Hans 1928- IntWW 93
Kolvenbach, Walter 1922- IntWW 93
Kolyer, Steven Terry 1956- WhoAmL 94
Kolz, Beverly Anne 1946- WhoMW 93
Komack, Jimmie 1950- WhoHol 92
Komai, Michael Mikio WhoAsA 94
Komai, Tetsu d1970 WhoHol 92
Koman, Victor 1944- EncSF 93
Komando, Kimberly Ann 1964- WhoFI 94
Komar 1943- & Melamid 1945- WhoAmA 93
Komar, Arthur B. 1931- WhoAm 94
Komar, Mathias 1909- WhoAmA 93N
Komar, Paul 1938- WhoAm 94, WhoFI 94
Komar, Vitaliy 1943- IntWW 93
Komar, Vitaly WhoAmA 93
Komarcic, Lazar EncSF 93
Komarek, Thomas Charles WhoAm 94
Komarin, Gary 1951- WhoAmA 93
Komaroff, Stanley 1935- WhoAm 94
Komarov, Evgeny Borisovich 1942- LngBDD
Komarov, Igor Sergeyevich 1917- IntWW 93
Komarova, Varvara Dmitrievna 1862-1942 BlmGWL
Komarovsky, Mirra WhoAm 94
Komarovsky, Yury Vladimirovich 1952- LngBDD
Komatsu, Koh 1921- IntWW 93
Komatsu, S. Richard 1916- WhoAm 94, WhoWest 94
Komatsu, Sakyo 1931- EncSF 93
Komatz, David G. 1950- WhoFI 94
Komdat, John Raymond 1943- WhoFI 94, WhoScEn 94, WhoWest 94
Komen, Leonard 1943- WhoAmL 94, WhoMW 93
Komenda, Frank Joseph 1934- WhoAmP 93
Komendant, Grigory Ivanovich 1946- LngBDD
Komenich, Kim 1956- WhoAm 94, WhoWest 94
Komer, Robert William 1922- IntWW 93, WhoAm 94
Komidar, Joseph Stanley 1916- WhoAm 94
Komie, Stephen Mark 1949- WhoAmL 94
Kominek, Leo Aloysius 1937- WhoMW 93
Komisar, Arnold 1947- WhoAm 94, WhoScEn 94
Komisar, David Daniel 1917- WhoAm 94
Komisar, Jerome Bertram 1937- WhoAm 94, WhoWest 94
Komisar, Lucy 1942- WhoFI 94
Komissarzhevsky, Fyodor Petrovich 1838-1905 NewGrDO
Komives, Howard 1941- BasBi
Komiyama, Jushiro 1928- IntWW 93
Komkov, Vadim 1919- WhoAm 94
Komleva, Gabriela Trofimovna 1938- IntWW 93
Komlos, Peter 1935- IntWW 93
Komlossy, Erzsebet 1933- NewGrDO
Kommandeur, Jan 1929- IntWW 93
Kommedahl, Thor 1920- WhoAm 94, WhoMW 93, WhoScEn 94
Komodore, Bill 1932- WhoAmA 93
Komorita, Samuel Shozo 1927- WhoScEn 94
Komoroske, John Herman 1949- WhoAmP 93
Komorous, Rudolf 1931- NewGrDO
Komorzynski, Egon 1878-1963 NewGrDO
Komoto, Toshio 1911- IntWW 93
Komp, Diane Marilyn 1940- WhoAm 94
Kompala, Dhinakar S. 1958- WhoAsA 94
Kompala, Dhinakar Sathyanathan 1958- WhoWest 94
Kompass, Edward John 1926- WhoAm 94
Komplektov, Viktor Georgiyevich 1932- IntWW 93
Komunyakaa, Yusef DrAPF 93
Komvopoulos, Kyriakos 1955- WhoScEn 94
Komyo, Naoko 1952- WhoFI 94
Kona, Martha Mistina WhoMW 93
Konadu, Asare BlkWr 2
Konadu, S(amuel) A(sare) 1932- BlkWr 2
Konare, Alpha Omar 1946- IntWW 93
Konarski, Feliks (Ref-Ren) 1907-1991 WhAm 10
Koncel, James E. 1929- WhoScEn 94
Koncelik, Joseph Arthur 1940- WhoAm 94
Konchalovsky, Andrei 1937- IntMPA 94
Koncilja, Frances Ann 1948- WhoAmL 94
Kondapavulur, Venkateswara Rao Tirumala 1962- WhoWest 94
Kondas, Nicholas Frank 1929- WhoAm 94, WhoFI 94
Kondelik, Evelyn Marguerite 1937- WhoAmP 93
Kondo, C. Kimi WhoAsA 94
Kondo, Jiro 1917- IntWW 93
Kondo, Jun 1930- WhoScEn 94
Kondo, Masatoshi Stephan 1940- WhoAm 94
Kondo, Tetsuo 1929- IntWW 93
Kondoleon, Harry 1955- ConDr 93, WrDr 94
Kondonassis, Alexander John 1928- WhoAm 94
Kondorossy, Leslie 1915-1989 NewGrDO
Kondracki, Edward John 1932- WhoAmL 94
Kondrashin, Kirill (Petrovich) 1914-1981 NewGrDO
Kondrasuk, Jack N. 1942- WhoWest 94
Kondratas, Skirma Anna 1944- WhoAm 94
Kondratev, Aleksandr Andreevich 1947- LngBDD
Kondratev, Aleksei Aleksandrovich 1930- LngBDD
Kondratev, Georgy Grigorevich 1944- LngBDD
Kondratiyeva, Marina Viktorovna 1934- IntWW 93
Kondrich, Ted V. WhoAmP 93
Kondwani, Kofi Anum 1955- WhoBlA 94
Kone, Russell Joseph 1929- WhoAm 94
Koneck, John M. 1953- WhoAm 94
Konecky, Edith DrAPF 93
Konecky, Milton Stuart 1922- WhoScEn 94
Konecny, Theodora 1924- WhoWomW 91
Konecsni, John-Emery 1946- WhoFI 94
Koner, Pauline 1912- WhoAm 94
Koneski, Blaze 1921- ConWorW 93
Konetzni(-Wiedmann), Anny 1902-1968 NewGrDO
Konetzni, Hilde 1905-1980 NewGrDO
Konezny, Lorette M. Sobol 1948- WhoFI 94
Kong, Ana C. 1940- WhoAsA 94
Kong, Chhean 1945- WhoAsA 94
Kong, Corita Shuk Sinn WhoAsA 94
Kong, Dongsung 1957- WhoAsA 94
Kong, Eric Siu-Wai 1953- WhoAsA 94
Kong, Jin Au 1942- WhoAm 94
Kong, Laura S. L. 1961- WhoWest 94
Kong, Luis John 1956- WhoHisp 94
Kong, Ronald A. 1937- WhoAsA 94
Kong, Stanley Young 1957- WhoAsA 94
Kong, William T. 1929- WhoAsA 94
Kongabel, H. Fred 1929- WhoAm 94
Kong Boji 1932- WhoPRCh 91
Kong Chang'an 1953- WhoPRCh 91
Kong Fan WhoPRCh 91
Kong Fannong WhoPRCh 91
Kong Fei 1911- IntWW 93, WhoPRCh 91 [port]
Kong Jiesheng 1952- IntWW 93, WhoPRCh 91 [port]
Kong Lingren 1924- WhoPRCh 91 [port]
Kong Mai WhoPRCh 91
Kong Shiquan 1909- WhoPRCh 91 [port]
Kong Xiao WhoPRCh 91
Kong Zhongji 1934- WhoPRCh 91
Koni, Nicolaus 1911- WhoAmA 93
Koniecko, Edward Stanley 1913- WhoAm 94
Konieczny, James Michael 1960- WhoWest 94
Konieczny, Sharon Louise 1952- WhoMW 93
Konig, Alma Johanna 1887-1942? BlmGWL
Konig, Barbara 1925- IntWW 93
Konig, Franz 1905- IntWW 93
Konig, Friedrich 1774?-1833 WorInv
Konig, Heinz Johannes Erdmann 1929- WhoScEn 94
Konig, Herbert 1925- IntWW 93
Konig, Johann Ulrich von 1688-1744 NewGrDO
Konig, Karl 1902-1966 DcNaB MP
Konig, Klaus 1934- NewGrDO
Konig, Rene d1992 IntWW 93N
Konigsberg, Allen Stewart 1935- WhoAm 94
Konigsberg, Frank 1933- IntMPA 94
Konigsberg, Ira 1935- WhoAm 94
Konigsberg, William Henry 1930- WhoScEn 94
Konigsburg, E(laine) L. 1930- WrDr 94
Konigsburg, E(laine) L(obl) 1930- TwCYAW
Konigsburg, Elaine Lobl 1930- WhoAm 94
Konigsdorf, Helga 1938- BlmGWL
Koning, Hans DrAPF 93
Koning, Hans 1924- WhoAm 94, WrDr 94
Koningsberger, Hans DrAPF 93
Koningsberger, Hans 1924- WrDr 94
Konink, Servaas de 1654?-1701? NewGrDO
Konishi, Kenji 1929- WhoScEn 94
Konishi, Masakazu 1933- WhoAm 94, WhoAsA 94
Konisky, Jordan 1941- WhoAm 94
Konjovic, Petar 1883-1970 NewGrDO
Konkel, Richard Steven 1950- WhoScEn 94, WhoWest 94
Konkle, Janet Everest 1917- WrDr 94
Konkol, Peter Adam 1933- WhoWest 94
Konner, Joan Weiner 1931- WhoAm 94
Konner, Melvin (Joel) 1946- WrDr 94
Konney, Paul Edward 1944- WhoAmL 94
Konnick, Ronald John 1943- WhoWest 94
Konnyu, Ernest L. 1937- WhoAmP 93
Konnyu, Ernest Leslie 1937- WhoAm 94, WhoWest 94
Kono, Hideto 1922- WhoAsA 94
Kono, Kristo 1907-1991 NewGrDO
Kono, Tetsuro 1925- WhoAm 94, WhoAsA 94
Kono, Yohei IntWW 93
Kononov, Anatoly Leonidovich 1947- LngBDD
Kononov, Vitalii Mykolayovych 1956- LngBDD
Konop, Kenneth E. 1942- WhoAmL 94
Konopinski, Emil Jan 1911-1990 WhAm 10
Konopisos, Konstantine Andrew 1919- WhoAmL 94
Konopka, Gisela Peiper 1910- WhoAm 94
Konopka, Joseph 1932- WhoAmA 93
Konopnicka, Maria 1842-1910 BlmGWL
Konoshima, Joji 1920- WhoAsA 94
Kono Taeko 1926- BlmGWL
Konowalow, Daniel Dimitri 1929- WhoWest 94
Konowitz, Herbert Henry 1937- WhoAmP 93, WhoFI 94
Konrad, Adolf Ferdinand WhoAmA 93
Konrad, Adolf Ferdinand 1915- WhoAm 94
Konrad, Dorothy WhoHol 92
Konrad, Dusan 1935- WhoAm 94
Konrad, George ConWorW 93
Konrad, Gyorgy 1933- ConWorW 93, IntWW 93
Konrad, Peter Allen WhoAm 94
Konrad, William Lawrence 1921- WhoScEn 94
Konrad von Wurzburg c. 1230-1287 DcLB 138 [port]
Konsalik, Heinz G. 1921- IntWW 93
Konselman, Douglas Derek 1958- WhoAmL 94
Konsis, Kenneth Frank 1952- WhoMW 93
Konski, James Louis 1917- WhoAm 94
Konsowa, Mokhtar Hassan 1953- WhoScEn 94
Konstam, Phyllis d1976 WhoHol 92
Konstant, David Every Who 94
Konstantin, Leopoldine d1965 WhoHol 92
Konstantinidis, Aris 1913- IntWW 93
Konstantinis, Robert 1967- WhoFI 94
Konstantinova, Elka Georgeiva 1932- WhoWomW 91
Kont, Paul 1920- NewGrDO
Konta, Frederick P. 1942- WhoAmL 94
Kontis, Kris John 1954- WhoWest 94
Kontny, Vincent 1937- WhoAm 94, WhoFI 94, WhoScEn 94, WhoWest 94
Kontogeorgis, Georgios 1912- IntWW 93
Kontos, C. William 1922- WhoAmP 93
Kontos, Carol A. 1946- WhoAmP 93
Kontos, Constantine William 1922- IntWW 93
Kontos, Emmanuel George 1932- WhoScEn 94
Kontos, George John, Jr. 1958- WhoMW 93
Konuk, Nejat 1928- IntWW 93
Konuma, Michiji 1931- IntWW 93
Konuma, Mitsuharu 1950- WhoScEn 94
Konvitz, Jeffrey 1944- WrDr 94
Konvitz, Milton R 1908- WrDr 94
Konvitz, Milton Ridbaz 1908- WhoAm 94
Konwicki, Tadeusz 1926- ConWorW 93, IntDcF 2-4, IntWW 93
Konwin, Thor Warner 1943- WhoFI 94, WhoWest 94
Konwitschny, Franz 1901-1962 NewGrDO
Konya, Imrene WhoWomW 91
Konya, Sandor 1923- NewGrDO
Konz, Gerald Keith 1932- WhoAm 94
Konzal, Joseph 1905- WhoAmA 93
Konzal, Joseph Charles 1905- WhoAm 94
Konzett, Heribert 1912- IntWW 93
Koo, Anthony Ying Chang 1918- WhoAsA 94
Koo, Benjamin Hai-Chang 1920- WhoAsA 94
Koo, Delia 1921- WhoAsA 94
Koo, Delia Z. F. 1921- WhoMW 93
Koo, George P. 1938- WhoAsA 94
Koo, George Ping Shan 1938- WhoAm 94
Koo, Ja Hung 1938- WhoAsA 94
Koo, Michelle E. M. 1956- WhoAsA 94
Koob, Charles Edward 1944- WhoAm 94, WhoAmL 94
Koob, Kenneth Leroy 1945- WhoAmP 93
Koob, Robert Duane 1941- WhoWest 94
Koock, Guich 1944- WhoHol 92
Kooi, Mari Reeves 1954- WhoFI 94
Kooistra, Bill 1956- WhoMW 93
Kooistra, Paul G. 1952- ConAu 141
Kooistra, Scott Alan 1958- WhoMW 93
Kooistra, William Henry 1936- WhoMW 93
Kooken, John Frederick 1931- WhoAm 94
Kooker, David Merrill 1964- WhoWest 94
Koolish, Lynda DrAPF 93
Koomanoff, Frederick Alan 1926- WhoScEn 94
Koomey, Jonathan Garo 1962- WhoWest 94
Koomey, Richard Alan 1932- WhoAmL 94
Koon, Larry Labruce 1944- WhoAmP 93
Koon, Norman Carroll 1938- WhoAm 94
Koon, Ray Harold 1934- WhoWest 94
Koon, Robin Charles 1953- WhoFI 94, WhoWest 94
Koonce, Cal d1993 NewYTBS 93
Koonce, John Peter 1932- WhoFI 94, WhoWest 94
Koonce, Kenneth Terry 1938- WhoAm 94
Koonce, Mary Ann 1962- WhoMW 93
Koonce, Neil Wright 1947- WhoAm 94, WhoAmL 94
Koons, Carolyn WrDr 94
Koons, Darell J. 1924- WhoAmA 93
Koons, Donaldson 1917- WhoAm 94
Koons, Irvin Louis 1922- WhoAm 94
Koons, James L. 1915- WhoAmP 93
Koons, Lawrence Franklin 1927- WhoScEn 94
Koons, Michael Marion 1945- WhoAmP 93
Koons, Stephen Eugene 1951- WhoFI 94
Koons, Susan Ann 1949- WhoMW 93
Koonts, J. Calvin DrAPF 93
Koonts, Jones Calvin 1924- WhoAm 94
Koonts, Robert Henry 1927- WhoAm 94
Koontz, Alfred Joseph, Jr. 1942- WhoAm 94, WhoWest 94
Koontz, Carl Lennis, II 1942- WhoFI 94
Koontz, Dean R. 1945- ConLC 78 [port], TwCYAW
Koontz, Dean R(ay) 1945- EncSF 93, WrDr 94
Koontz, Dean Ray 1945- WhoAm 94
Koontz, Eldon Ray 1913- WhoFI 94

Koontz, Eva Isabelle 1935- *WhoMW 93*
Koontz, James L. 1934- *WhoScEn 94*
Koontz, Margaret Ann 1947- *WhoWest 94*
Koontz, Richard Harvey 1940- *WhoAm 94*
Koontz, Tom *DrAPF 93*
Koontz, Warren Woodson, Jr. 1932- *WhoAm 94*
Koonz, Claudia (Ann) *WrDr 94*
Koop, C. Everett 1916- *IntWW 93*
Koop, Charles Everett 1916- *AmSocL, WhoAm 94, WhoScEn 94*
Koopalethes, Olivia *WhoAmA 93*
Koopman, Antonius Gerhardus Michael 1944- *IntWW 93*
Koopman, John R. 1881-1949 *WhoAmA 93N*
Koopman, William James 1945- *WhoAm 94, WhoScEn 94*
Koopmann, Gary Hugo 1939- *WhoScEn 94*
Koopmann, Reta Collene 1944- *WhoFI 94*
Koopmans, Cheryl Bette 1950- *WhoFI 94, WhoMW 93*
Koopmans, Tjalling Charles 1910- *WhoAm 94, WhoFI 94*
Koops, Mary Claire *Who 94*
Koops, Matthias fl. 1789-1805 *DcNaB MP*
Koornhof, Pieter Gerhardus Jacobus 1925- *IntWW 93*
Kooser, Robert Galen 1941- *WhoScEn 94*
Kooser, Ted *DrAPF 93*
Kooser, Ted 1939- *WrDr 94*
Koot, Hank M. *WhoIns 94*
Kootenay, Bishop of 1937- *Who 94*
Kootz, Samuel M(elvin) 1898-1946 *WhAm 10*
Koovshinoff, Dimitri 1930- *WhoWest 94*
Kooy, Pete d1963 *WhoHol 92*
Kooyman, Richard E. 1956- *WhoAmA 93*
Kooyoomjian, K. Jack 1942- *WhoScEn 94*
Koozin-Door, Kristine Lynn 1950- *WhoMW 93*
Kop, Tim M. 1946- *WhoScEn 94, WhoWest 94*
Kopa, Raymond 1931- *WorESoc [port]*
Kopack, Pamela Lee 1951- *WhoMW 93*
Kopacz, Gregory M. 1949- *WhoAmL 94*
Kopal, Zdenek d1993 *NewYTBS 93, Who 94N*
Kopal, Zdenek 1914- *WrDr 94*
Kopal, Zdenek 1914-1993 *ConAu 141, CurBio 93N*
Kopala, Peter Steven 1946- *WhoScEn 94*
Kopchick, John Joseph 1950- *WhoMW 93*
Kopczak, Eugene Edward 1934- *WhoAmP 93*
Kopczynski, Frank Joseph 1947- *WhoFI 94*
Kopec, Frank John 1943- *WhoAm 94*
Kopecek, Jindrich 1940- *WhoWest 94*
Kopech, David Albert 1952- *WhoAmL 94*
Kopech, Robert Irving 1951- *WhoAm 94*
Kopecki, Alan F. 1945- *WhoAmL 94*
Kopecko, Dennis Jon 1947- *WhoScEn 94*
Kopecky, Jan 1919- *IntWW 93*
Kopecky, Kenneth John 1943- *WhoAm 94*
Kopeczi, Bela 1921- *IntWW 93*
Kopekov, Danatar 1933- *LngBDD*
Kopel, David 1910- *WhoAm 94*
Kopel, Gerald 1928- *WhoAmP 93*
Kopel, Robert Frank 1954- *WhoWest 94*
Kopell, Bernie 1933- *WhoHol 92*
Kopelman, Arie L. 1938- *WhoAm 94*
Kopelman, Arthur Harold 1952- *WhoScEn 94*
Kopelman, Ian Stuart 1949- *WhoAmL 94*
Kopelman, Kenneth P. 1952- *WhoAm 94*
Kopelman, Leonard 1940- *WhoAm 94, WhoAmL 94*
Kopelman, Richard Eric 1943- *WhoAm 94*
Kopelowitz, (Jacob) Lionel (Garstein) 1926- *Who 94*
Kopelson, Arnold 1935- *IntMPA 94*
Kopenhaver, Lillian Lodge 1941- *WhoFI 94*
Kopenhaver, Patricia Ellsworth *WhoAm 94*
Koper, Alex 1917- *WhoWest 94*
Kopera, John Joseph Christopher 1968- *WhoMW 93*
Koperwas, Sam *DrAPF 93*
Kopetski, Michael Joseph 1949- *WhoAmP 93*
Kopetski, Mike 1949- *CngDr 93, WhoAm 94, WhoWest 94*
Kopetz, Vinette Nadine 1935- *WhoMW 93*
Kopf, John Oscar 1938- *WhoWest 94*
Kopf, Richard G. 1946- *WhoAm 94, WhoAmL 94, WhoMW 93*
Kopf, Robert Y., Jr. 1944- *WhoAmL 94*
Kopf, Silas 1949- *WhoAmA 93*
Kopff, Gary Jo 1945- *WhoFI 94*
Kopicki, Benjamin F. 1960- *WhoWest 94*
Kopicki, John R. 1943- *WhoAm 94*
Kopiloff, George 1939- *WhoAm 94*
Kopins, Karen *WhoHol 92*
Kopis, F. Jan 1942- *WhoMW 93*
Kopis, William Floyd 1943- *WhoAm 94*
Kopit, Alan Stuart 1952- *WhoAmL 94*
Kopit, Arthur 1937- *WhoAm 94*
Kopit, Arthur (Lee) 1937- *ConDr 93, IntDcT 2, WrDr 94*
Kopke, Monte Ford 1949- *WhoScEn 94*
Koplan, Jeffrey Powell 1945- *WhoAm 94*
Koplaski, John 1964- *WhoScEn 94*
Koplewicz, Harold Samuel 1953- *WhoAm 94*
Koplin, Donald Leroy 1932- *WhoWest 94*
Koplovitz, Kay 1945- *WhoAm 94*
Koplow, Meyer G. 1951- *WhoAmL 94*
Koplowitz, Benjamin 1893- *WhoAmA 93N*
Kopman, Benjamin 1887-1965 *WhoAmA 93N*
Kopmeyer, David Louis 1950- *WhoMW 93*
Koponen, Niilo E. *WhoAmP 93*
Kopp, Bradford B. 1951- *WhoAm 94*
Kopp, Charles Gilbert 1933- *WhoAm 94, WhoAmL 94, WhoFI 94*
Kopp, David Charles 1945- *WhoAm 94*
Kopp, David Eugene 1951- *WhoWest 94*
Kopp, Debra Lynn 1964- *WhoScEn 94*
Kopp, Donald Lee 1935- *WhoAmP 93*
Kopp, Erwin d1928 *WhoHol 92*
Kopp, Eugene Howard 1929- *WhoAm 94*
Kopp, Eugene Paul 1934- *WhoAm 94*
Kopp, Harriet Green 1917- *WhoAm 94, WhoWest 94*
Kopp, Karl *DrAPF 93*
Kopp, Mila d1973 *WhoHol 92*
Kopp, Monica 1957- *WhoScEn 94*
Kopp, Nancy Kornblith 1943- *WhoAmP 93*
Kopp, Philip David 1950- *WhoAmL 94*
Kopp, Quentin L. *WhoWest 94*
Kopp, Quentin Lewis 1928- *WhoAmP 93*
Kopp, Richard Edgar 1931- *WhoAm 94*
Kopp, Richard L 1934- *WrDr 94*
Kopp, Robert Walter 1935- *WhoAm 94*
Kopp, Steven Eugene 1953- *WhoAmP 93*
Kopp, W. Brewster *WhoAm 94*
Kopp, Wendy *News 93-3 [port]*
Koppa, Rodger Joseph 1936- *WhoScEn 94*
Koppany, Charles Robert 1941- *WhoScEn 94*
Koppe, Richard 1916- *WhoAmA 93N*
Koppel, Donald Theodore 1925- *WhoAmP 93*
Koppel, Gary Allen 1943- *WhoAm 94*
Koppel, Herman D(avid) 1908- *NewGrDO*
Koppel, Lone 1938- *NewGrDO*
Koppel, Steven C. 1960- *WhoAmL 94*
Koppel, Ted *IntWW 93*
Koppel, Ted 1940- *WhoAm 94*
Koppel, Thomas Paul 1943- *WhoWest 94*
Koppell, G. Oliver 1940- *WhoAmP 93*
Koppelman, Chaim 1920- *WhoAm 94, WhoAmA 93*
Koppelman, Charles *WhoAm 94*
Koppelman, Dorothy 1920- *WhoAmA 93*
Koppelman, Dorothy Myers 1920- *WhoAm 94*
Koppen, Jerry Lynn 1945- *WhoIns 94*
Koppen, Marvin Charles 1952- *WhoAmP 93*
Koppenaal, Richard John 1930- *WhoAm 94*
Koppendrayer, Leroy J. 1941- *WhoAmP 93*
Koppenhoefer, Robert Mack 1909- *WhoFI 94*
Koppenhofer, Maria d1948 *WhoHol 92*
Kopper, Hilmar 1935- *IntWW 93*
Kopper, William D. 1948- *WhoAmL 94*
Koppes, Rebecca Ann 1952- *WhoAmL 94*
Koppes, Steven Nelson 1957- *WhoWest 94*
Koppes, Wayne Farland 1902- *WhAm 10*
Koppett, Leonard 1923- *WhoAm 94*
Koppinger, Thomas J. 1941- *WhoIns 94*
Kopple, Kenneth D. 1930- *WhoAm 94*
Koppman, Edward S. 1943- *WhoAmL 94*
Koppman, Steve *DrAPF 93*
Koppus, Betty Jane 1922- *WhoFI 94*
Kopriva, Sharon 1948- *WhoAmA 93*
Koprivica, Dorothy Mary 1921- *WhoMW 93*
Koproski, Alexander Robert 1934- *WhoFI 94*
Koprowski, Hilary *WhoAm 94, WhoScEn 94*
Koprowski, Kenneth M. *DrAPF 93*
Koprucki, Patricia Jane 1949- *WhoAmL 94*
Kops, Bernard 1926- *ConDr 93, WrDr 94*
Kopsa, Gregory Joe 1948- *WhoMW 93*
Kopsky, Raymond John, Jr. 1960- *WhoMW 93*
Kopson, Mark Stephen 1959- *WhoAmL 94*
Kopsov, Anatoly Yakovlevich 1942- *LngBDD*
Koptev, Yury Nikolaevich 1941- *LngBDD*
Koptis, William Harvey 1927- *WhoMW 93*
Koptyug, Valentin Afanasiyevich 1931- *IntWW 93*
Kopylova, Aleksandra Vasilevna *WhoWomW 91*
Kopysov, Viktor Andreevich 1940- *LngBDD*
Kopytman, Mark 1929- *NewGrDO*
Korab, Arnold Alva 1917- *WhoFI 94*
Koral, Alan M. 1941- *WhoAm 94*
Koral, Mark A. 1945- *WhoAmL 94*
Koralek, Paul George 1933- *IntWW 93, Who 94*
Koram, M. Jamal 1949- *WhoBlA 94*
Koran, Dennis *DrAPF 93*
Koran, Dennis Howard 1947- *WhoAm 94, WhoWest 94*
Koran, Janet M. 1949- *WhoAm 94*
Koranda, David Edward 1947- *WhoFI 94*
Korando, Donna Kay 1950- *WhoAm 94*
Korangteng, Daniel Agyei 1927- *WhoAm 94*
Koranyi, Adam 1932- *WhoAm 94*
Koras, George *WhoAmA 93*
Koras, William 1932- *WhoAm 94, WhoFI 94*
Korayem, Essam Ali 1941- *WhoScEn 94*
Korb, Donald Lee 1948- *WhoAm 94, WhoAmL 94*
Korb, Kenneth Allan 1932- *WhoAm 94, WhoAmL 94, WhoFI 94*
Korb, Lawrence John 1930- *WhoWest 94*
Korb, Philip B. 1948- *WhoAmL 94*
Korb, Robert William 1929- *WhoWest 94*
Korb, William Brown, Jr. 1940- *WhoAm 94*
Korban, Bernard 1923- *IntMPA 94*
Korban, Schuyler Safi 1954- *WhoScEn 94*
Korber, Mark F. 1947- *WhoAmL 94*
Korbin, Bernard d1993 *IntMPA 94N*
Korbitz, Bernard Carl 1935- *WhoAm 94, WhoMW 93, WhoScEn 94*
Korcak, Josef 1921- *IntWW 93*
Korchin, Judith Miriam 1949- *WhoAm 94, WhoAmL 94*
Korchmaros, Gabor Gabriele 1948- *WhoScEn 94*
Korchmaryov, Klimenty Arkad'yevich 1899-1958 *NewGrDO*
Korchynsky, Michael 1918- *WhoAm 94, WhoScEn 94*
Korczak, Edward Stanley 1945- *WhoMW 93*
Kord, Kazimierz 1930- *NewGrDO*
Kord, Victor George 1935- *WhoAmA 93*
Korda, Alexander 1893-1956 *IntDcF 2-4*
Korda, Maria *WhoHol 92*
Korda, Michael (Vincent) 1933- *WrDr 94*
Korda, Michael Vincent 1933- *IntWW 93, WhoAm 94*
Korda, Reva 1926- *WhoAm 94*
Korda, Vincent *WhoAmA 93N*
Korda, Vincent 1897-1979 *IntDcF 2-4*
Kordalski, Anthony Tadausz 1926- *WhoAm 94*
Kordenbrock, Douglas William 1964- *WhoScEn 94*
Kordes, Hagen 1942- *WhoScEn 94*
Kordesch, Martin Eric 1956- *WhoScEn 94*
Kordik, Daniel Joseph 1959- *WhoMW 93*
Kordons, Uldis 1941- *WhoAm 94*
Korducki, Barbara Joan 1956- *WhoWest 94*
Koree, Jean Ulyxes 1894- *WhAm 10*
Koreh, Endre 1906-1960 *NewGrDO*
Korelitz, Jean Hanff *DrAPF 93*
Korelitz, Jean Hanff 1961- *WrDr 94*
Koren, Edward B. 1935- *WhoAmA 93*
Koren, Edward Benjamin 1935- *WhoAm 94*
Koren, Edward Franz 1946- *WhoAm 94, WhoAmL 94*
Koren, Henry Joseph 1912- *WrDr 94*
Koren, Jerome Quentin 1947- *WhoMW 93*
Koren, Samuel M. 1941- *WhoIns 94*
Korenberg, Jacob 1930- *WhoScEn 94*
Korenic, Lynette Marie 1950- *WhoAmA 93*
Korenman, Stanley George *WhoAm 94*
Koresh, David 1959- *NewYTBS 93 [port]*
Koresh, David c. 1960-1993 *News 93*
Koretzky, I. Harold 1942- *WhoAmL 94*
Korey, Lois Balk 1933-1990 *WhAm 10*
Korey-Krzeczowski, George J. M. Kniaz 1921- *WhoAm 94*
Korf, Gene Robert 1952- *WhoAm 94*
Korf, Richard Earl 1956- *WhoWest 94*
Korff, Arnold d1944 *WhoHol 92*
Korff, Ira A. 1949- *WhoAm 94, WhoFI 94*
Korff, Serge Alexander 1906-1989 *WhAm 10*
Korfker, Dena 1908- *WrDr 94*
Korg, Jacob 1922- *WhoAm 94, WrDr 94*
Korhonen, Antti Samuli 1950- *WhoScEn 94*
Korhonen, Keijo Tero 1934- *IntWW 93*
Korinek, Miloslav 1925- *NewGrDO*
Korinkova, Kvetoslava *WhoWomW 91*
Korinkova, Kvetoslava 1940- *IntWW 93*
Korins, Leopold *WhoAm 94, WhoFI 94, WhoWest 94*
Koritarova, Rosa (Smirna) Vasileva 1921- *WhoWomW 91*
Koritz, Terence Christopher 1963- *WhoMW 93*
Korjus, Miliza d1980 *WhoHol 92*
Korkes, Jon *WhoHol 92*
Korlin, Boris *WhoHol 92*
Korman, Barbara 1938- *WhoAm 94, WhoAmA 93*
Korman, Edward R. 1942- *WhoAm 94, WhoAmL 94*
Korman, Gerd 1928- *WhoAm 94*
Korman, Harriet R. 1947- *WhoAmA 93*
Korman, Harvey 1927- *IntMPA 94, WhoCom, WhoHol 92*
Korman, Harvey Herschel 1927- *WhoAm 94*
Korman, James William 1943- *WhoAm 94*
Korman, Jeffrey R. *WhoAmP 93*
Korman, Jess J. 1933- *WhoAm 94*
Korman, Lewis J. 1945- *IntMPA 94, WhoAm 94*
Korman, Nathaniel Irving 1916- *WhoAm 94*
Korman, Timothy James 1952- *WhoFI 94*
Kormendi, Eugene 1889-1959 *WhoAmA 93N*
Kormendi, Roger Charles 1949- *WhoFI 94*
Kormes, John Winston 1935- *WhoAmL 94, WhoFI 94*
Kormilev, Nicholas Alexander 1901- *WhoScEn 94*
Kormoczi, Suzi 1924- *BuCMET*
Kormondy, Edward J(ohn) 1926- *WrDr 94*
Kormondy, Edward John 1926- *WhoAm 94, WhoWest 94*
Korn, Artur 1937- *NewGrDO*
Korn, Barry Paul 1944- *WhoFI 94*
Korn, Candy Lee 1942- *WhoMW 93*
Korn, David 1933- *WhoAm 94, WhoWest 94*
Korn, David 1934- *WhoAm 94, WhoAmP 93*
Korn, Edward David 1928- *WhoAm 94, WhoScEn 94*
Korn, Elizabeth P. 1900- *WhoAmA 93N*
Korn, Granino Arthur 1922- *WhoWest 94*
Korn, Henry *DrAPF 93*
Korn, Iris d1982 *WhoHol 92*
Korn, Jerry Arlen *WhoWest 94*
Korn, John Carsten 1897- *WhAm 10*
Korn, Lester Bernard 1936- *WhoAm 94*
Korn, Michael Jeffrey 1954- *WhoAmL 94*
Korn, Monte Marvin 1919- *WhoMW 93*
Korn, Peter A. 1939- *WhoAm 94*
Korn, Steven Eric 1944- *WhoFI 94*
Korn, Steven W. *WhoAmL 94*
Korn, Walter 1908- *WhoWest 94*
Kornadt, Hans-Joachim Kurt 1927- *WhoScEn 94*
Kornai, Janos 1928- *IntWW 93*
Kornberg, Alan William 1952- *WhoAm 94, WhoAmL 94*
Kornberg, Arthur 1918- *IntWW 93, Who 94, WhoAm 94, WhoScEn 94, WhoWest 94, WorScD*
Kornberg, Hans (Leo) 1928- *IntWW 93, Who 94*
Kornberg, Hans Leo 1928- *WhoScEn 94*
Kornberg, Roger David 1947- *WhoAm 94*
Kornberg, Warren Stanley 1927- *WhoAm 94*
Kornblatt, Barbara Rodbell 1931- *WhoAmA 93*
Kornblatt, Judith Deutsch 1955- *ConAu 141*
Kornblau, Gerald 1928- *WhoAmA 93*
Kornblet, Donald Ross 1943- *WhoAm 94*
Kornblith, John Howard 1924-1992 *WhAm 10*
Kornblith Kopp, Nancy 1943- *WhoWomW 91*
Kornbluh, Edward Calvin 1926- *WhoAmP 93*
Kornblum, Allan *DrAPF 93*
Kornblum, Barry A. *WhoFI 94*
Kornblum, Cinda *DrAPF 93*
Kornblum, James Andrew 1951- *WhoAmL 94*
Kornblum, John Christian 1943- *WhoAm 94*
Kornblum, Myrtle 1909- *WhoAmA 93*
Kornbluth, C(yril) M. 1923-1958 *EncSF 93*
Kornbluth, Frances 1920- *WhoAmA 93*
Kornbluth, Genevra Alisoun 1954- *WhoMW 93*
Kornbluth, Sandra Joan 1951- *WhoFI 94*
Kornbluth, Sheldon Edwin 1933- *WhoFI 94*
Kornbrath, Brian Joseph 1959- *WhoAmL 94*
Kornbrekke, Ralph Erik 1951- *WhoMW 93, WhoScEn 94*
Kornegay, Francis A. 1913- *WhoBlA 94*

Kostmayer, Peter Houston 1946- *WhoAm 94, WhoAmP 93*
Kostner, Jaclyn Patti 1945- *WhoWest 94*
Kostohryz, Richard Joseph 1930- *WhoAmP 93*
Kostopoulos, Thomas George 1961- *WhoMW 93*
Kostoulas, Ioannis Georgiou 1936- *WhoFI 94, WhoWest 94*
Kostov, Dimitar Tzvetkov 1932- *IntWW 93*
Kostrikin, Marybeth Elaine 1954- *WhoWest 94*
Kostrzewski, Jan Karol 1915- *IntWW 93*
Kostrzewski, Paul J. 1969- *WhoFI 94*
Kostuch, Dorothy Ann 1935- *WhoMW 93*
Kostuch, Mitchell John 1931- *WhoAm 94*
Kostyniak, Paul John 1947- *WhoScEn 94*
Kostyniuk, Ronald P. 1941- *WhoAmA 93*
Kostyo, Jack Lawrence 1931- *WhoAm 94*
Kostyo, John Francis 1955- *WhoAmL 94*
Kostyra, Richard Joseph 1940- *WhoAm 94, WhoFI 94*
Kostyuk, Platon Grigorevich 1924- *WhoScEn 94*
Kostyuk, Platon Grigorievich 1924- *IntWW 93*
Kosub, James Albert 1948- *WhoAmL 94*
Kosugi, Sho 1947- *WhoHol 92*
Kosut, Kenneth Paul 1949- *WhoAm 94, WhoAmL 94*
Kosuth, Joseph 1945- *IntWW 93, WhoAm 94, WhoAmA 93*
Kosygin, Alexei 1904-1980 *HisWorL [port]*
Kosygin, Yuriy Aleksandrovich 1911- *IntWW 93*
Koszarowski, Tadeusz Tomasz 1915- *IntWW 93*
Koszarski, Richard 1947- *WhoAm 94*
Koszewski, Bohdan Julius 1918- *WhoScEn 94*
Koszi, Louis A. 1944- *WhoScEn 94*
Koszut, Urszula 1940- *NewGrDO*
Kotaite, Assad 1924- *IntWW 93*
Kotala, Stanislaw Waclaw 1909- *WhoAmA 93*
Kotan, Richard Marvin 1949- *WhoFI 94*
Kotani, Eric 1933- *EncSF 93*
Kotani, Masao d1993 *NewYTBS 93*
Kotani, Shigeto 1945- *WhoAsA 94*
Kotani, Yuriko 1959- *WhoAmL 94*
Kotarek, Douglas James 1961- *WhoAmL 94*
Kotas, Robert Vincent 1938- *WhoAm 94*
Kotaska, Gary F. 1949- *WhoAm 94, WhoAmL 94*
Kotch, Alex 1926- *WhoAm 94*
Kotch, Laurie *Who 94*
Kotcheff, Ted 1931- *IntMPA 94, IntWW 93*
Kotcheff, William Theodore 1931- *WhoAm 94*
Kotcher, Ezra 1903-1990 *WhAm 10*
Kotcher, Raymond Lowell 1951- *WhoAm 94, WhoFI 94*
Kotcher, Shirley J. W. 1924- *WhoAmL 94, WhoFI 94*
Koteas, Elias 1961- *WhoHol 92*
Kotecha, Mahesh Kanjibhai 1947- *WhoAm 94*
Kotelly, George Vincent 1931- *WhoAm 94*
Kotelly, John T. 1938- *WhoAmL 94*
Kotelnikov, Vladimir Aleksandrovich 1908- *IntWW 93, LngBDD*
Koten, John A. 1929- *WhoAm 94*
Kotenkov, Aleksandr Alekseevich 1952- *LngBDD*
Kotero, Apollonia 1959- *WhoHol 92*
Koth, Erika 1927-1989 *NewGrDO*
Kotha, Subbaramaiah 1960- *WhoScEn 94*
Kothari, Ajay P. 1954- *WhoAsA 94*
Kothari, Bijay Singh 1928- *WhoFI 94*
Kothari, Kanti G. 1947- *WhoMW 93*
Kothe, Charles Aloysius 1912- *WhoAm 94*
Kothera, Lynne M. 1938- *WhoScEn 94*
Kothmann, Glenn Harold 1928- *WhoAmP 93*
Koths, Jay Sanford 1926- *WhoAm 94*
Kotiakan dc. 1890 *EncNAR*
Kotik, Charlotta 1940- *WhoAmA 93*
Kotin, Albert 1907-1980 *WhoAmA 93N*
Kotin, Armine Avakian *ConAu 41NR*
Kotite, Rich 1942- *WhoAm 94*
Kotker, Mary Zane *DrAPF 93*
Kotker, Norman *DrAPF 93*
Kotker, Norman R. 1931- *WrDr 94*
Kotker, Zane *DrAPF 93*
Kotker, Zane H. 1934- *WrDr 94*
Kotkin, David 1956- *WhoAm 94*
Kotkin, Edward S. *WhoHol 92*
Kotkov, Benjamin 1910- *WhoScEn 94*
Kotlan, C.M. *EncSF 93*
Kotlarz, Joseph S. 1956- *WhoAmP 93*
Kotler, Martin 1925- *WhoAm 94*
Kotler, Milton 1935- *WhoAm 94*
Kotler, Pamela Lee 1946- *WhoWest 94*
Kotler, Philip 1931- *WhoAm 94, WrDr 94*
Kotler, Richard Lee 1952- *WhoAmL 94, WhoWest 94*
Kotler, Steven 1947- *WhoAm 94, WhoFI 94*
Kotlowitz, Alex *WhoAm 94*
Kotlowitz, Robert *DrAPF 93*
Kotlowitz, Robert 1924- *WhoAm 94*
Kotlyakov, Vladimir Michailovich 1931- *WhoScEn 94*
Koto, Paul 1948- *WhoWest 94*
Kotoske, Roger Allen 1933- *WhoAm 94, WhoAmA 93*
Kotovsky, Kenneth 1939- *WhoScEn 94*
Kotsiuba, Oleksandr Pavlovych 1939- *LngBDD*
Kotsokoane, Joseph Riffat Larry 1922- *IntWW 93, Who 94*
Kotsonaros, George d1933 *WhoHol 92*
Kotsuki, Hiyoshizo 1951- *WhoScEn 94*
Kott, David Russell 1952- *WhoAm 94, WhoAmL 94*
Kott, Frantisek Bedrich 1808-1884 *NewGrDO*
Kott, Jan 1914- *IntWW 93*
Kott, Jan K. 1914- *WhoAm 94*
Kott, Pete 1949- *WhoAmP 93*
Kottamasu, Mohan Rao 1947- *WhoScEn 94*
Kottanner, Helene 1400-c. 1470 *BlmGWL*
Kottas, John Frederick 1940- *WhoAm 94*
Kottemann, George 1931- & Kottemann, Norma 1932- *WhoAmA 93*
Kottemann, Norma 1932- *See* Kottemann, George 1931- & Kottemann, Norma 1932- *WhoAmA 93*
Kottemann, Norma 1932- *WhoAmA 93*
Kottemann, Richard Allen, Jr. 1957- *WhoMW 93*
Kottenstette, Christopher Joseph 1962- *WhoWest 94*
Kotter, John Paul 1947- *WhoAm 94*
Kottick, Edward Leon 1930- *WhoAm 94*
Kottkamp, Jeffrey Dean 1960- *WhoAmL 94*
Kottkamp, John Harlan 1930- *WhoAm 94*
Kottke, Frederick Edward 1926- *WhoFI 94, WhoWest 94*
Kottke, John William 1946- *WhoMW 93*
Kottler, Howard William 1930- *WhoAmA 93N*
Kottler, Howard William 1930-1989 *WhAm 10*
Kottler, Jeffrey (A.) 1951- *WrDr 94*
Kottler, Raymond George Michael 1966- *WhoFI 94*
Kottlowski, Frank Edward 1921- *WhoAm 94, WhoScEn 94, WhoWest 94*
Kottman, Roy Milton 1916- *WhoAm 94*
Kottmyer, Diane M. 1945- *WhoAmL 94*
Kotto, Yaphet 1937- *IntMPA 94, WhoHol 92*
Kotto, Yaphet Fredrick 1944- *IntWW 93, WhoBlA 94*
Kotula, Karl Robert 1955- *WhoMW 93*
Kotulak, Ronald 1935- *WhoAm 94*
Kotulski, Rick 1945- *WhoAmP 93*
Kotun, Henry Paul 1931- *WhoAm 94, WhoAmA 93*
Kotvis, Jill Alison 1957- *WhoAmL 94*
Kotwal, Girish Jayant 1954- *WhoScEn 94*
Kotynek, George Roy 1938- *WhoScEn 94*
Kotz, David Michael 1943- *WhoAm 94*
Kotz, Nathan Kallison 1932- *WhoAm 94*
Kotz, Samuel 1930- *WhoAm 94*
Kotzabassis, Constantinos 1958- *WhoScEn 94*
Kotzebue, August von 1761-1819 *IntDcT 2 [port], NewGrDO*
Kotzebue, Otto Von 1787-1846 *WhWE*
Kotzee, Flores Petrus 1926- *IntWW 93*
Kotzen, Richie 1972- *See* Poison *ConMus 11*
Kotzky, Alex Sylvester 1923- *WhoAmA 93*
Kotzwinkle, William 1938- *EncSF 93, WhoAm 94, WrDr 94*
Kouandete, Maurice 1939- *IntWW 93*
Kouassi, Kwam *IntWW 93*
Kouba, Marilyn Jean 1929- *WhoMW 93*
Kouba, Richard *WhoAmP 93*
Kouba, Tony Ray 1930- *WhoAmP 93*
Kouchner, Bernard 1939- *CurBio 93 [port], IntWW 93*
Kouchoukos, Nicholas Thomas 1936- *WhoAm 94*
Koucky, Frank Louis Blair, III 1950- *WhoFI 94*
Koucky, John Richard 1934- *WhoAm 94*
Kouf, Jim *ConAu 141*
Kouf, M(arvin) James, Jr. 1951- *ConAu 141*
Kougl, Patricia Anne 1919- *WhoAmP 93*
Koukos, Periklis 1960- *NewGrDO*
Koul, Hira Lal 1943- *WhoAsA 94*
Koulhaas, Christina Louisa c. 1700-1735? *NewGrDO*
Kouloumbis, Evangelos 1929- *IntWW 93*
Koulourianos, Dimitri 1930- *IntWW 93*
Koumjian, Vaughn *DrAPF 93*
Koumoulides, John Thomas Anastasios 1938- *WhoMW 93*
Kounadis, Arghyris 1924- *NewGrDO*
Kounovsky, Nicholas d1993 *NewYTBS 93*
Kouns, Lawrence J. 1954- *WhoAmL 94*
Kountz, Charles Edward, Jr. 1946- *WhoAmP 93*
Kountz, Samuel L. 1930-1981 *WorInv*
Kountz, Samuel L. 1931-1981 *AfrAmAl 6*
Kountze, Mabray 1910- *WhoBlA 94*
Kountze, Vallery J. *WhoBlA 94*
Koupal, Carl Mathias, Jr. 1953- *WhoAmP 93*
Koupf, Gary I. 1950- *WhoIns 94*
Koupparis, Michael Andreas 1950- *WhoScEn 94*
Kourganoff, Vladimir 1912- *IntWW 93*
Kouri, Donald Jack 1938- *WhoAm 94*
Kouri, Gustavo Pedro 1936- *WhoScEn 94*
Kourides, Peter Theologos 1910- *WhoAm 94*
Kouros, Andreas Kyriakou 1918- *IntWW 93*
Kourouma, Ahmadou 1940- *BlkWr 2*
Kourpias, George J. 1932- *WhoAm 94, WhoFI 94*
Koursaros, Harry G. 1928-1986 *WhoAmA 93N*
Koury, Aleah George 1925- *WhoAm 94*
Koury, Ellis Glenn 1947- *WhoAmL 94*
Kousser, Joseph Morgan 1943- *WhoAm 94, WhoWest 94*
Koussevitzky, Serge Alexandrovich 1874-1951 *AmCulL*
Koussevitzky, Sergey (Alexandrovich) 1874-1951 *NewGrDO*
Koutecky, Josef 1930- *IntWW 93*
Koutoukas, H.M. 1947- *ConDr 93*
Koutras, Demetrios A. 1930- *WhoScEn 94*
Koutros, Stephen Anthony 1955- *WhoFI 94*
Koutrouvelis, Panos George 1928- *WhoScEn 94*
Kouts, Herbert John Cecil 1919- *WhoAm 94*
Koutsky, Dean Roger 1935- *WhoAm 94*
Koutsoheras, Ioannis *IntWW 93*
Kouvel, James Spyros 1926- *WhoAm 94*
Kouwenhoven, John A. 1909-1990 *WhoAmA 93N*
Kouwenhoven, John Atlee 1909-1990 *WhAm 10*
Kouymjian, Dickran 1934- *WhoAm 94, WhoWest 94*
Kouyoumjian, Aida Mardiros 1928- *WhoWest 94*
Kouyoumjian, Charles H. 1940- *WhoAm 94, WhoFI 94*
Kouza, Loujaya M. *BlmGWL*
Kouzi, Samir 1961- *WhoWest 94*
Kouzmanoff, Alexander 1915- *WhoAm 94*
Kouznetsov, Maria *NewGrDO*
Kovac, Frederick James 1930- *WhoAm 94*
Kovac, Jeffrey Dean 1948- *WhoScEn 94*
Kovac, Michal *IntWW 93*
Kovac, Richard *DrAPF 93*
Kovac, Steven 1954- *WhoAmP 93*
Kovacevich, Christopher 1928- *WhoMW 93*
Kovacevich, Richard M. *WhoAm 94, WhoFI 94, WhoMW 93*
Kovacevich, Stephen 1940- *Who 94*
Kovach, Andrew Louis 1948- *WhoFI 94*
Kovach, Barbara Ellen 1941- *WhoAm 94*
Kovach, Bill 1932- *WhoAm 94*
Kovach, David Joseph 1952- *WhoAmL 94*
Kovach, Doris Anne 1945- *WhoMW 93*
Kovach, Eugene George 1922- *WhoAm 94*
Kovach, James Michael 1955- *WhoScEn 94*
Kovach, John Stephen 1936- *WhoAm 94*
Kovach, Joseph William 1946- *WhoMW 93, WhoScEn 94*
Kovach, Ronald 1946- *WhoWest 94*
Kovachevich, Elizabeth Anne 1936- *WhoAm 94, WhoAmL 94*
Kovachy, Edward Miklos, Jr. 1946- *WhoWest 94*
Kovacic, Edward P. *WhoMW 93*
Kovacic, Ernst 1943- *IntWW 93*
Kovacic, Gary Anton 1951- *WhoAmL 94*
Kovacic, William Evan 1952- *WhoAmL 94*
Kovacik, Karen *DrAPF 93*
Kovacik, Neal Stephen 1952- *WhoFI 94, WhoMW 93*
Kovack, Nancy 1937- *WhoHol 92*
Kovacs, Andras 1925- *IntWW 93*
Kovacs, Austin 1938- *WhoScEn 94*
Kovacs, Charles Joseph Leslie Thomas 1945- *WhoFI 94*
Kovacs, Denes 1930- *IntWW 93*
Kovacs, Diane Kaye 1962- *WhoMW 93*
Kovacs, Elizabeth Ann 1944- *WhoAm 94, WhoFI 94*
Kovacs, Elizabeth J. 1957- *WhoScEn 94*
Kovacs, Ernie d1962 *WhoHol 92*
Kovacs, Ernie 1919-1962 *WhoCom [port]*
Kovacs, Joseph Anton, III 1950- *WhoMW 93*
Kovacs, Laszlo 1933- *IntDcF 2-4 [port], IntMPA 94, WhoAm 94*
Kovacs, Mary d1981 *WhoHol 92*
Kovacs, Mia d1982 *WhoHol 92*
Kovacs, Rosemary *WhoMW 93*
Kovacs, Steven 1946- *WrDr 94*
Kovacs, William Lawrence 1947- *WhoAmL 94*
Koval, Charles Francis 1938- *WhoAm 94*
Koval, Charles Terrance 1933- *WhoFI 94*
Koval, Don O. 1942- *WhoAm 94*
Koval, George Carl 1936- *WhoIns 94*
Koval', Marian Viktorovich 1907-1971 *NewGrDO*
Kovalcheck, Nancy Margaret 1954- *WhoMW 93*
Kovalcik, Kenneth John 1946- *WhoAm 94*
Kovalev, Aleksandr Yakovlevich 1942- *LngBDD*
Kovalev, Anatoliy Gavrilovich 1923- *IntWW 93*
Kovalev, Mikhail Vasilevich 1925- *IntWW 93*
Kovalev, Sergei Adamovich 1930- *LngBDD*
Kovalevskaia, Sof'ia Vasil'evna 1850-1891 *BlmGWL*
Kovalevsky, Jean 1929- *IntWW 93*
Kovalevsky, Sonya Valsilyevna 1850-1891 *WorScD*
Koval-Samborskiy, Ivan d1962 *WhoHol 92*
Kovaly, John Joseph 1928- *WhoAm 94*
Kovanda, Janet Louise 1946- *WhoFI 94*
Kovar, Dan Rada 1934- *WhoScEn 94*
Kovar, Margaret W. 1933- *WhoAmP 93*
Kovarik, Wenzel J. *WhoAmP 93*
Kovarovic, Karel 1862-1920 *NewGrDO*
Kovash, Jon Robert 1949- *WhoWest 94*
Kovatch, Jak 1929- *WhoAmA 93*
Kovatch, Jak Gene 1929- *WhoAm 94*
Kovatch, Ronald R. *WhoAmA 93*
Kove, Kenneth 1893- *WhoHol 92*
Kove, Martin 1947- *WhoHol 92*
Kovel, Joel 1936- *WrDr 94*
Kovel, Lee Ralph 1951- *WhoAm 94, WhoWest 94*
Kovel, Ralph M. *WhoAm 94*
Kovel, Ralph Mallory *WrDr 94*
Kovel, Terry Horvitz *WhoAm 94*
Kovel, Terry Horvitz 1928- *WrDr 94*
Koveleski, Kathryn Delane 1925- *WhoMW 93*
Koven, Howard Richard 1921- *WhoAm 94*
Koven, (Henry Louis) Reginald de *NewGrDO*
Koven, Steven Gerald 1946- *WhoMW 93*
Kovenklioglu, Suphan Remzi 1947- *WhoScEn 94*
Kovera, Robert Richard 1940- *WhoFI 94*
Koverman, Gerald Allen 1940- *WhoMW 93*
Kovinick, Philip Peter 1924- *WhoAmA 93*
Kovler, Allen *DrAPF 93*
Kovlyagin, Anatoly Fedorovich 1938- *LngBDD*
Kovnat, Karel Debra 1955- *WhoMW 93*
Kovolenko, Samuel 1957- *WhoAmP 93*
Kovrig, Bennett 1940- *WhoAm 94*
Kovtynovich, Dan 1952- *WhoScEn 94, WhoWest 94*
Kowal, Cal (Lee) 1944- *WhoAmA 93*
Kowal, Charles Thomas 1940- *WhoAm 94, WhoScEn 94*
Kowal, Dennis J. 1937- *WhoAmA 93*
Kowal, Mitchell d1971 *WhoHol 92*
Kowal, Robert Paul 1942- *WhoAm 94*
Kowal, Steven Martin 1949- *WhoAmL 94*
Kowalczewski, Doreen Mary Thurlow 1926- *WhoWest 94*
Kowalczyk, Ellen Marie 1955- *WhoAmP 93*
Kowalczyk, Maciej Stanislaw 1956- *WhoScEn 94*
Kowalczyk, Richard Leon 1935- *WhoAm 94*
Kowalek, Jon W. 1934- *WhoAmA 93N*
Kowalewich, Betty Jean 1930- *WhoAmP 93*
Kowalewski, Kim Marie 1956- *WhoMW 93*
Kowalewski, Michael (John) 1956- *ConAu 140*
Kowalke, Kim H. 1948- *WhoAm 94, WrDr 94*
Kowalke, Ronald Leroy 1936- *WhoAmA 93*
Kowalski, Dennis Allen 1938- *WhoAmA 93*
Kowalski, Gregor 1949- *Who 94*
Kowalski, Henri 1841-1916 *NewGrDO*
Kowalski, Jochen 1954- *NewGrDO*
Kowalski, Kathiann Meissner 1955- *WhoAmL 94*
Kowalski, Kazimierz 1946- *WhoWest 94*

Kowalski, Kenneth Lawrence 1932- *WhoAm 94, WhoMW 93*
Kowalski, Kenneth R. 1945- *WhoWest 94*
Kowalski, Libby R. 1940- *WhoAmA 93*
Kowalski, Lynn Mary 1955- *WhoScEn 94*
Kowalski, Neal Anthony 1945- *WhoFI 94*
Kowalski, Raymond Alois 1933- *WhoAmA 93*
Kowalski, Richard Sheldon 1944- *WhoAm 94*
Kowalski, Stephen Wesley 1931- *WhoAm 94*
Kowalsky, William Allen 1946- *WhoFI 94*
Kowanko, Pete *WhoHol 92*
Kowarski, Allen Avinoam 1927- *WhoAm 94*
Kowel, Stephen Thomas 1942- *WhoAm 94*
Kowit, Steve *DrAPF 93*
Kowitt, Arthur Jay 1933- *WhoAm 94*
Kowlessar, Muriel 1926- *WhoScEn 94*
Kox, Hans 1930- *NewGrDO*
Koxlien, Lisa Louise 1959- *WhoMW 93*
Koyama, Hachiro 1922- *WhoAm 94*
Koyano, Keiichirou 1953- *WhoFI 94*
Koyyalamudi, Sundarrao 1956- *WhoScEn 94*
Koza, Joan Lorraine 1941- *WhoMW 93*
Kozai, Yoshihide 1928- *WhoScEn 94*
Kozak, Ellen *EncSF 93*
Kozak, Ellen M. 1944- *WhoAmP 93*
Kozak, Harley Jane 1953- *WhoHol 92*
Kozak, Harley Jane 1957- *IntMPA 94*
Kozak, Jan 1921- *IntWW 93*
Kozak, John W. 1943- *WhoAmL 94, WhoMW 93*
Kozak, Robert William 1953- *WhoScEn 94*
Kozar, Martha Cecile 1963- *WhoFI 94*
Kozberg, Donna Walters *DrAPF 93*
Kozberg, Donna Walters 1952- *WhoFI 94*
Kozberg, Steven Freed 1953- *WhoMW 93*
Kozbial, Richard James 1933- *WhoMW 93*
Kozelka, Edward William 1912- *WhoMW 93*
Kozeluch, Johann Antonin 1738-1814 *NewGrDO*
Kozeluch, Leopold 1747-1818 *NewGrDO*
Kozer, Jose *DrAPF 93*
Kozer, José 1940 *WhoHisp 94*
Kozer, Stephen Louis 1951- *WhoMW 93*
Kozhevnikova, Irina N. 1959- *WhoScEn 94*
Kozhuharov, Christophor 1946- *WhoFI 94, WhoScEn 94*
Koziar, Stephen Francis, Jr. 1944- *WhoAmL 94*
Kozick, Richard James 1964- *WhoScEn 94*
Kozik, Patricia Jane 1931- *WhoMW 93*
Kozikowski, Mitchell 1935- *WhoAm 94, WhoFI 94*
Kozin, Frank 1930-1990 *WhAm 10*
Kozinski, Alex *WhoAmP 93*
Kozinski, Alex 1950- *WhoAm 94, WhoAmL 94, WhoWest 94*
Koziol, Dennis Leon 1946- *WhoMW 93*
Koziol, Michael John 1951- *WhoScEn 94*
Kozitka, Richard Eugene 1934- *WhoAm 94*
Koziura, Joseph F. 1946- *WhoAmP 93*
Kozlak, Rita Burke 1919- *WhoAmP 93*
Kozloff, Joyce 1942- *WhoAmA 93*
Kozloff, Lloyd M. 1923- *WhoAm 94*
Kozloff, Max 1933- *WhoAmA 93*
Kozloff, Theodore J. 1941- *WhoAmL 94*
Kozlov, Alexander Igor 1956- *WhoWest 94*
Kozlov, Leonid 1947- *WhoAm 94*
Kozlova, Valentina 1957- *WhoAm 94*
Kozlovsky, Alexey Fedorovich 1905-1977 *NewGrDO*
Kozlovsky, Ivan d1993 *NewYTBS 93*
Kozlovsky, Ivan Semyonovich 1900- *NewGrDO*
Kozlovsky, Pavel Pavlovich 1942- *IntWW 93*
Kozlow, Richard 1926- *WhoAmA 93*
Kozlowiski, L. Dennis 1947- *WhoAm 94, WhoFI 94*
Kozlowski, Edward C. 1927- *WhoAmA 93*
Kozlowski, James Michael 1949- *WhoMW 93*
Kozlowski, Janiece Rae 1959- *WhoFI 94*
Kozlowski, Joseph George 1938- *WhoFI 94*
Kozlowski, Karen Ann 1961- *WhoMW 93*
Kozlowski, L. Dennis 1946- *WhoAm 94*
Kozlowski, Linda 1956- *IntMPA 94*
Kozlowski, Linda 1958- *WhoHol 92*
Kozlowski, Ronald Stephan 1937- *WhoAm 94*
Kozlowski, Steve W.J. 1952- *WhoScEn 94*
Kozlowski, Theodore Thomas 1917- *WhoAm 94*
Kozlowski, Thomas Joseph, Jr. 1950- *WhoAm 94*
Kozma, Adam 1928- *WhoAm 94*
Kozma, Lynn *DrAPF 93*
Kozmetsky, George 1917- *WhoScEn 94*
Kozmon, George 1960- *WhoAmA 93*
Kozodoy, Neal 1942- *WhoAm 94*
Kozol, Jonathan 1936- *IntWW 93, WhoAm 94, WrDr 94*
Kozolchyk, Boris 1934- *WhoAmL 94, WhoHisp 94, WhoWest 94*
Kozubowski, Walter S. 1939- *WhoAmP 93*
Kozumi, Rei *EncSF 93*
Kozyrev, Andrei Vladimirovich 1952- *LngBDD*
Kozyrev, Andrey Vladimirovich 1951- *IntWW 93*
Kozyris, Phaedon John 1932- *WhoAm 94*
Kraai, Gerald Mark 1942- *WhoAm 94, WhoAmL 94*
Krabbe, Jeroen 1944- *ConTFT 11, IntMPA 94, IntWW 93, WhoHol 92*
Krabbe, Katrin 1970- *IntWW 93*
Krabbenhoft, Kenneth Lester 1923- *WhoAm 94*
Krabill, Robert Elmer 1934- *WhoMW 93*
Krach, Mitchell Peter 1924- *WhoAm 94, WhoFI 94*
Kracht, Richard William 1936- *WhoAmL 94*
Kracke, Robert Russell 1938- *WhoAmL 94*
Kracke, Waud Hocking 1939- *WhoMW 93*
Krackow, Jurgen 1923- *IntWW 93*
Kraczkowski, Phil 1916- *WhoAmA 93*
Kraehe, Enno Edward 1921- *WhoAm 94, WrDr 94*
Kraemer, James S. 1919- *WhoAmP 93*
Kraemer, Jay Roy 1948- *WhoAm 94*
Kraemer, Kenneth Leo 1936- *WhoAm 94*
Kraemer, Lillian Elizabeth 1940- *WhoAm 94, WhoAmL 94*
Kraemer, Michael Frederick 1947- *WhoAm 94*
Kraemer, (Thomas Whilhelm) Nicholas 1945- *Who 94*
Kraemer, Philipp 1931- *WhoFI 94*
Kraemer, Sandy Frederick 1937- *WhoAm 94*
Kraemer, Sue Ella 1943- *WhoFI 94*
Kraepelin, Emil 1856-1926 *EncSPD*
Kraessel, Alfred *WhoAm 94*
Kraeutler, Eric 1954- *WhoAmL 94*
Kraf, Elaine *DrAPF 93*
Krafft, Karl Ernst 1900-1945 *AstEnc*
Kraft, Arthur 1944- *WhoAm 94*
Kraft, Benjamin F. 1948- *WhoBlA 94*
Kraft, Burnell D. 1931- *WhoAm 94*
Kraft, C. William, Jr. 1903- *WhoAm 94, WhoAmL 94*
Kraft, C. William, III 1943- *WhoAmL 94, WhoWest 94*
Kraft, Christopher Columbus, Jr. 1924- *IntWW 93*
Kraft, Daniel Lee 1956- *WhoAmL 94*
Kraft, David Christian 1937- *WhoAm 94*
Kraft, Donald Bowman 1927- *WhoAm 94*
Kraft, Donald James 1936- *WhoMW 93*
Kraft, George Howard 1936- *WhoAm 94, WhoWest 94*
Kraft, Gerald 1935- *WhoAm 94, WhoFI 94*
Kraft, Henry R. 1946- *WhoAmL 94*
Kraft, Jill 1930- *WhoHol 92*
Kraft, Kenneth H. 1950- *WhoAmL 94*
Kraft, Kenneth Houston, Jr. 1934- *WhoFI 94*
Kraft, Leo Abraham 1922- *WhoAm 94*
Kraft, Peter George 1960- *WhoAm 94*
Kraft, Richard Austin *Who 94*
Kraft, Richard Joe 1944- *WhoWest 94*
Kraft, Robert *EncSF 93*
Kraft, Robert A(lan) 1934- *WrDr 94*
Kraft, Robert Alan 1934- *WhoAm 94*
Kraft, Robert Paul 1927- *IntWW 93, WhoAm 94, WhoScEn 94, WhoWest 94*
Kraft, Scott *WhoHol 92*
Kraft, Scott Corey 1955- *WhoWest 94*
Kraft, Sue Ann 1953- *WhoMW 93*
Kraft, Sumner Charles 1928- *WhoAm 94*
Kraft, Tanya Aline 1957- *WhoWest 94*
Kraft, William *WhoAm 94*
Kraft, William Armstrong 1926- *WhoWest 94*
Kraft, William F 1938- *WrDr 94*
Kraftson, Daniel J. 1951- *WhoAmL 94*
Kraftson, Raymond H. 1940- *WhoAm 94, WhoFI 94*
Krafve, Allen Horton 1937- *WhoFI 94, WhoMW 93*
Krag, Olga 1937- *WhoWest 94*
Krage, Terry Robert 1959- *WhoMW 93*
Kragerud, Alv 1932- *IntWW 93*
Krages, Bert Petty 1957- *WhoAmL 94*
Kraggerud, Egil 1939- *IntWW 93*
Krah, Marc d1973 *WhoHol 92*
Krahel, Thomas Stephen 1947- *WhoFI 94*
Krahl, Enzo 1924- *WhoAm 94*
Krahl, Hilde 1915- *WhoHol 92*
Krahling, John *WhoAmP 93*
Krahmer, Donald L., Jr. 1957- *WhoAmL 94, WhoFI 94, WhoWest 94*
Krahmer, Johannes Robert 1932- *WhoAmL 94*
Krahn, Maria d1977 *WhoHol 92*
Krahulik, Jon D. 1944- *WhoAmP 93*
Krahulik, Robert Emil 1965- *WhoAmL 94*
Kraigher, Sergej 1914- *IntWW 93*
Kraijenhoff, Jonkheer Gualtherus 1922- *IntWW 93*
Kraiko, Aleksandr Nikolaevich 1934- *LngBDD*
Krainer, Edward Frank 1939- *WhoScEn 94*
Kraines, Merrill M. 1955- *WhoAmL 94*
Krainev, Vladimir Vsevolodovich 1944- *IntWW 93*
Krainik, Ardis 1929- *WhoAm 94, WhoMW 93*
Krainik, Ardis Joan 1929- *NewGrDO*
Krainin, Julian Arthur 1941- *WhoAm 94*
Kraiss, Glenn S. 1933- *WhoFI 94*
Kraivichien, Thanin 1927- *IntWW 93*
Krajewski, Joan L. *WhoAmP 93*
Krajewski, Michal Dymitr *EncSF 93*
Krajewski-Jaime, Elvia Rosa 1938- *WhoMW 93*
Krajina, Borislav 1930- *IntWW 93*
Krakauer, Albert Alexander 1937- *WhoAm 94*
Krakauer, Daniel *DrAPF 93*
Krakauer, Henry 1947- *WhoScEn 94*
Krakauer, Thomas Henry 1942- *WhoAm 94*
Krakoff, Irwin Harold 1923- *WhoAm 94*
Krakoff, Robert Leonard 1935- *WhoAm 94, WhoFI 94*
Krakow, Amy Ginzig 1950- *WhoAm 94, WhoFI 94*
Krakow, Barbara L. 1936- *WhoAmA 93*
Krakow, Barbara Levy 1936- *WhoAm 94*
Krakower, Bernard Hyman 1935- *WhoFI 94*
Krakower, Cecil Alexander 1907-1989 *WhAm 10*
Krakowiak, Edward T. 1928- *WhoMW 93*
Krakowiecki, Marion J. 1941- *WhoIns 94*
Krakowski, Linda S. 1949- *WhoMW 93*
Krakowski, Richard John 1946- *WhoAmL 94, WhoMW 93*
Kral, Frank 1940- *WhoAm 94*
Kral, Ivan *WhoWest 94*
Kral, Richard F. *WhoAm 94*
Kral, William George 1946- *WhoAmL 94*
Kralewski, John Edward 1932- *WhoScEn 94*
Kralick, Richard Louis 1933- *WhoAmL 94*
Kralj, Gregory Franklin 1955- *WhoMW 93*
Krall, Hanna c. 1933- *BlmGWL*
Krallinger, Joseph Charles 1931- *WhoAm 94*
Kraly, Hanns 1885-1950 *IntDcF 2-4*
Kram, Guenther Reinhard 1957- *WhoMW 93*
Kram, Michael Arnold 1950- *WhoAm 94*
Kram, Shirley Wohl 1922- *WhoAm 94, WhoAmL 94*
Kraman, Cynthia *DrAPF 93*
Kraman, Steve Seth 1944- *WhoScEn 94*
Kramarsic, Roman Joseph 1926- *WhoWest 94*
Krambeck, Robert Harold 1943- *WhoAm 94*
Kramberg, Ross 1955- *WhoAm 94*
Kramer, Aaron *DrAPF 93*
Kramer, Aaron 1921- *WhoAm 94, WrDr 94*
Kramer, Aaron J. 1942- *WhoAmL 94*
Kramer, Alan Sharfsin 1934- *WhoAm 94*
Kramer, Albert H. 1940- *WhoAm 94, WhoAmL 94, WhoAmP 93*
Kramer, Alex John 1939- *WhoMW 93*
Kramer, Alexander Gottlieb 1964- *WhoWest 94*
Kramer, Andrea S. 1955- *WhoAmL 94*
Kramer, Andrew Michael 1944- *WhoAm 94, WhoAmL 94*
Kramer, Barry Alan 1948- *WhoWest 94*
Kramer, Bernard 1922- *WhoAm 94*
Kramer, Bert 1942- *WhoHol 92*
Kramer, Burton 1932- *WhoAm 94, WhoAmA 93*
Kramer, Carl Edward 1946- *WhoMW 93*
Kramer, Carol Gertrude 1939- *WhoMW 93*
Kramer, Cecile E. 1927- *WhoAm 94*
Kramer, Charles Henry 1922- *WhoAm 94*
Kramer, Dale 1936- *WrDr 94*
Kramer, Dale Vernon 1936- *WhoAm 94*
Kramer, David Alan 1962- *WhoScEn 94*
Kramer, Diana 1928- *WhoAm 94, WhoFI 94*
Kramer, Donald 1937- *WhoAm 94*
Kramer, Donald A. 1942- *WhoFI 94*
Kramer, Donald William 1938- *WhoAm 94*
Kramer, Donovan Mershon, Sr. 1925- *WhoWest 94*
Kramer, Edward George 1950- *WhoAmL 94*
Kramer, Edward John 1939- *WhoAm 94*
Kramer, Edwin J. 1934- *WhoAmP 93*
Kramer, Elliot Paul 1949- *WhoAmL 94*
Kramer, Eugene L. 1939- *WhoAm 94*
Kramer, Eugene Leo 1939- *WhoMW 93*
Kramer, Evan Nicholas 1963- *WhoAmL 94*
Kramer, Ferdinand 1901- *WhoAm 94*
Kramer, Frank Raymond 1908- *WhoAm 94*
Kramer, Franklin David 1945- *WhoAmL 94*
Kramer, Fred Russell 1942- *WhoAm 94*
Kramer, Geoffrey Philip 1953- *WhoMW 93, WhoScEn 94*
Kramer, George Nicholas 1896- *WhAm 10*
Kramer, George P. 1927- *WhoAm 94*
Kramer, Gerhardt Theodore 1909- *WhoAm 94*
Kramer, Gertrude M. *WhoAmA 93*
Kramer, Gordon 1937- *WhoScEn 94, WhoWest 94*
Kramer, Gordon Edward 1946- *WhoWest 94*
Kramer, Gunter 1940- *NewGrDO*
Kramer, Henry *WhoFI 94*
Kramer, Hilton 1928- *WhoAmA 93, WrDr 94*
Kramer, Horst Emil Adolf 1936- *WhoScEn 94*
Kramer, Hugh E. 1929- *WhoWest 94*
Kramer, Ida d1930 *WhoHol 92*
Kramer, Irvin Raymond 1912- *WhoAm 94*
Kramer, Ivor Robert Horton 1923- *Who 94*
Kramer, Jack 1921- *BuCMET [port]*
Kramer, Jack N. 1923-1984 *WhoAmA 93N*
Kramer, James 1927- *WhoAmA 93*
Kramer, James Joseph 1927- *WhoWest 94*
Kramer, Jane 1938- *WhoAm 94, WrDr 94*
Kramer, Jay Harlan 1952- *WhoScEn 94*
Kramer, Jeffrey *WhoHol 92*
Kramer, Jeffrey Warren 1951- *WhoAmL 94*
Kramer, JoAnn Mary 1956- *WhoWest 94*
Kramer, Joel Roy 1948- *WhoAm 94*
Kramer, John d1976 *WhoHol 92*
Krámer, John George *WhoMW 93*
Kramer, John Paul 1928- *WhoAm 94*
Kramer, John Robert, Jr. 1942- *WhoMW 93*
Kramer, Jonathan D. 1942- *WrDr 94*
Kramer, Joseph 1924- *WhoFI 94*
Kramer, Joyce L. *WhoAm 94, WhoFI 94*
Kramer, Kathryn Elizabeth 1933- *WhoMW 93*
Kramer, Ken 1942- *WhoAmP 93*
Kramer, Kenneth B. 1942- *CngDr 93*
Kramer, Kenneth Bentley 1942- *WhoAm 94, WhoAmL 94*
Kramer, Kenneth Scott 1957- *WhoAmL 94*
Kramer, Kenneth Stephen 1941- *WhoAm 94, WhoAmL 94*
Kramer, Kenneth Steven 1938- *WhoFI 94*
Kramer, Larry *DrAPF 93*
Kramer, Larry 1935- *GayLL, IntMPA 94, WhoAm 94*
Kramer, Lawrence John 1939- *WhoAm 94*
Kramer, Lawrence Stephen 1950- *WhoAm 94, WhoWest 94*
Kramer, Leonie (Judith) 1924- *Who 94, WrDr 94*
Kramer, Leonie Judith 1924- *IntWW 93*
Kramer, Leopold d1942 *WhoHol 92*
Kramer, Linda Lewis 1937- *WhoAmA 93*
Kramer, Lorne C. *WhoWest 94*
Kramer, Lotte (Karoline Wertheimer) 1923- *WrDr 94*
Kramer, Louise *WhoAmA 93*
Kramer, Magdalene E. 1898- *WhAm 10*
Kramer, Marc B. 1944- *WhoAm 94*
Kramer, Margia *WhoAmA 93*
Kramer, Maria d1980 *WhoHol 92*
Kramer, Mary E. 1935- *WhoAmP 93*
Kramer, Mary Ellen Forbes d1993 *NewYTBS 93*
Kramer, Mary Vincent 1957- *WhoFI 94*
Kramer, Meyer 1919- *WhoAm 94*
Kramer, Michael Jeffrey 1952- *WhoWest 94*
Kramer, Milt Louis 1937- *WhoMW 93*
Kramer, Milton 1929- *WhoMW 93*
Kramer, Mitchell Alvin 1933- *WhoAmL 94*
Kramer, Morris Joseph 1941- *WhoAm 94*
Kramer, Morton 1914- *WhoAm 94*
Kramer, Orin Stuart 1945- *WhoFI 94*
Kramer, Pamela Kostenko 1944- *WhoMW 93*
Kramer, Paul J(ackson) 1904- *WrDr 94*
Kramer, Paul Jackson 1904- *IntWW 93, WhoAm 94*

Kramer, Paul R. 1933- *WhoAmP 93*
Kramer, Paul R. 1936- *WhoAmL 94*
Kramer, Phil d1972 *WhoHol 92*
Kramer, Philip 1921- *WhoAm 94*
Kramer, Philip Joseph 1936- *WhoAmL 94*
Kramer, Reuben 1909- *WhoAmA 93*
Kramer, Reuben Robert 1909- *WhoAm 94*
Kramer, Rex W., Jr. 1934- *WhoScEn 94*
Kramer, Richard Harry, Jr. 1953- *WhoScEn 94*
Kramer, Robert *DrAPF 93*
Kramer, Robert 1913- *WhoAm 94*
Kramer, Robert Frank 1946- *WhoMW 93*
Kramer, Robert G. *WhoAmP 93*
Kramer, Robert Ivan 1933- *WhoAm 94*
Kramer, Ruth 1925- *WhoFI 94*
Kramer, Samual Noah 1897-1990 *WhAm 10*
Kramer, Sandra 1943- *WhoFI 94*
Kramer, Sidney 1911- *IntMPA 94*
Kramer, Sidney B. 1915- *WhoAm 94*
Kramer, Simon 1919- *WhoAm 94*
Kramer, Stanley 1913- *IntWW 93*
Kramer, Stanley E. 1913- *IntMPA 94, WhoAm 94*
Kramer, Ted *GayLL*
Kramer, Thomas Rollin 1943- *WhoScEn 94*
Kramer, Toni 1935- *NewGrDO*
Kramer, Victor Mark 1927- *WhoFI 94*
Kramer, Werner 1917- *IntWW 93*
Kramer, William David 1944- *WhoAm 94, WhoAmL 94*
Kramer, Wright d1941 *WhoHol 92*
Kramish, Arnold 1923- *WhoAm 94*
Kramish, Marc Eric 1958- *WhoAmL 94*
Kramm, Deborah Ann 1949- *WhoFI 94*
Kramm, Deborah Lucille *WhoAmL 94, WhoFI 94*
Kramnick, Isaac 1938- *WhoAm 94*
Kramolowsky, E. Vince *WhoMW 93*
Kramp, Richard William 1945- *WhoAm 94*
Krampf, John Edward 1947- *WhoAm 94, WhoAmL 94*
Krampf, Thomas *DrAPF 93*
Krampits, Mark William 1955- *WhoScEn 94*
Kramrisch, Stella *WhoAmA 93*
Kramrisch, Stella d1993 *Who 94N*
Kramrisch, Stella 1896?-1993 *ConAu 142, NewYTBS 93*
Kramvis, Andreas Constantinos 1952- *WhoFI 94*
Krance, Charles Andrew 1937- *WhoMW 93*
Krandievskaia (-Tolstaia), Nataliia Vasil'evna 1888-1965 *BlmGWL*
Krandievskaia, Anastasiia Romanovna 1865-1938 *BlmGWL*
Krane, Jonathan 1952- *IntMPA 94*
Krane, Robert Alan 1933- *WhoAm 94*
Krane, Stephen Martin 1927- *WhoAm 94*
Krane, Steven Charles 1957- *WhoAmL 94*
Krane, Susan 1954- *WhoAmA 93*
Kraner, Florian G. 1908- *WhoAmA 93N*
Kranes, David *DrAPF 93*
Kranich, Wilmer Leroy 1919-1992 *WhAm 10*
Kranidas, Kathleen Collins *DrAPF 93*
Kranidiotis, Nicos 1911- *IntWW 93*
Kranis, Michael David 1955- *WhoAmL 94*
Kranis, Richard 1937- *WhoAmL 94*
Kranitz, Theodore Mitchell 1922- *WhoAm 94, WhoAmL 94*
Kranking, Margaret Graham 1930- *WhoAmA 93*
Kranowitz, Alan Michael 1941- *WhoAmP 93*
Kranseler, Lawrence Michael 1958- *WhoAmL 94*
Krantz, Gerald William 1928- *WhoScEn 94*
Krantz, Hazel *WrDr 94*
Krantz, John Howell 1960- *WhoScEn 94*
Krantz, Judith *WrDr 94*
Krantz, Judith 1928- *BlmGWL [port], IntWW 93*
Krantz, Judith Tarcher 1927- *WhoAm 94*
Krantz, Kermit Edward 1923- *WhoAm 94*
Krantz, Les 1945- *WhoAmA 93*
Krantz, Melissa Marianne 1954- *WhoAm 94*
Krantz, Palmer Eric, III 1950- *WhoAm 94*
Krantz, Sanford Burton 1934- *WhoAm 94*
Krantz, Sheldon 1938- *WhoAm 94*
Krantz, Stephen Falk 1923- *WhoAm 94*
Krantz, Steve 1923- *ConTFT 11, IntMPA 94*
Krantz, William Bernard 1939- *WhoWest 94*
Kranwinkle, Conrad Douglas 1940- *WhoAm 94, WhoWest 94*
Kranz, Kenneth Louis, Jr. 1946- *WhoMW 93*
Kranz, Mary Rosaria 1914- *WhoMW 93*
Kranz, Norman 1924- *WhoAm 94*
Kranz, Robert James 1943- *WhoFI 94*
Kranzberg, Melvin 1917- *WhoAm 94, WrDr 94*
Kranzdorf, Jeffrey Paul 1955- *WhoAmL 94*
Kranzdorf, Norman M. *WhoFI 94*
Kranze, Clair Lorraine 1925- *WhoAmP 93*
Kranzow, Ronald Roy 1931- *WhoAm 94, WhoFI 94*
Krape, Paul Edward 1950- *WhoFI 94*
Krape, Philip Joseph 1948- *WhoScEn 94*
Krapf, Johann Ludwig 1810-1881 *WhWE*
Krapf, Norbert *DrAPF 93*
Krappe, Kirk Gary 1961- *WhoFI 94*
Krappinger, Herbert Ernst 1950- *WhoScEn 94*
Krar, Stephen Frank 1924- *ConAu 42NR*
Kraras, Gust C. 1921- *WhoFI 94*
Krasa, Hans 1899-1944 *NewGrDO*
Kraschneske, Margarethe Regina 1911- *WhoMW 93*
Krasean, Thomas Karl 1940- *WhoMW 93*
Krash, Abe 1927- *WhoAm 94*
Krashen, Stephen D. 1941- *WrDr 94*
Krasheninnikov, Stepan Petrovich 1711-1755 *WhWE*
Krashes, Barbara *WhoAmA 93*
Krasik, Carl 1944- *WhoAm 94, WhoAmL 94*
Krasikov, Anatoly Andreevich 1931- *LngBDD*
Krasilovsky, Alexis Rafael 1950- *WhoWest 94*
Krasilovsky, Phyllis 1926- *WrDr 94*
Krasinski, Zygmunt 1812-1859 *IntDcT 2*
Kraske, Karl Vincent 1935- *WhoAm 94*
Krasker, Elaine S. 1927- *WhoAmP 93*
Krasker, Robert 1913-1981 *IntDcF 2-4 [port]*
Kraslow, David 1926- *WhoAm 94*
Krasna, Alvin Isaac 1929- *WhoAm 94*
Krasna, Norman 1909-1984 *IntDcF 2-4*
Krasna, Suzanne 1946- *WhoFI 94*
Krasner, Daniel Walter 1941- *WhoAmL 94, WhoFI 94*
Krasner, Lee 1908-1984 *WhoAmA 93N*
Krasner, Louis 1903- *WhoAm 94*
Krasner, Milton 1901-1988 *IntDcF 2-4 [port]*
Krasner, Oscar Jay 1922- *WhoWest 94*
Krasner, Paul R. 1951- *WhoScEn 94*
Krasner, Robert Charles Jeffrey 1947- *WhoAm 94*
Krasner, Wendy L. 1953- *WhoAm 94*
Krasner, William *DrAPF 93*
Krasner, William 1917- *WrDr 94*
Krasney, Ethel Levin 1961- *WhoScEn 94*
Krasney, Samuel Joseph 1925- *WhoAm 94*
Krasniewski, Walter Jacob 1929- *WhoAm 94, WhoAmL 94*
Krasnoff, Abraham *WhoFI 94*
Krasnohorska, Eliska 1847-1926 *NewGrDO*
Krasnov, Vladislav Georgievich 1937- *WrDr 94*
Krasnow, Erwin Gilbert 1936- *WhoAm 94*
Krasnow, Frances H. 1953- *WhoAmL 94*
Krasnow, Jordan Philip 1944- *WhoAmL 94*
Krasnow, Maurice 1944- *WhoScEn 94*
Krasnow, Richard P. 1947- *WhoAmL 94*
Krasnow, Sheryl Edith 1934- *WhoMW 93*
Krasnoyarov, Evgeny Alekseevich 1939- *LngBDD*
Krasny, Harvey Charles 1945- *WhoScEn 94*
Krasny, Paul 1935- *ConTFT 11*
Krasnyansky, Anatole Lvovich 1930- *WhoAmA 93*
Krasova, Marta 1901-1970 *NewGrDO*
Krasovskaya, Vera Mikhailovna 1915- *IntWW 93*
Krasovskiy, Nikolay Nikolayevich 1924- *IntWW 93*
Krasser, Hans Wolfgang 1937- *WhoScEn 94*
Krassner, J. David *WhoHol 92*
Krasucki, Henri 1924- *IntWW 93*
Kraszewski, Andrzej Wojciech 1933- *WhoScEn 94*
Krathen, David Howard 1946- *WhoAmL 94*
Krathwohl, David Reading 1921- *WhoAm 94*
Kratina, K. George 1910- *WhoAmA 93*
Kratochvil, Byron George 1932- *WhoAm 94*
Kratochvil, Louis Glen 1922- *WhoAm 94*
Kratochvilova, Jarmila 1951- *IntWW 93*
Kratovil, Edward DeWolf 1944- *WhoAmP 93*
Kratt, Mary *DrAPF 93*
Kratt, Peter George 1940- *WhoAm 94*
Kratz, John E., Jr. 1946- *WhoAmL 94*
Kratz, Mildred Sands *WhoAmA 93*
Kratz, Ruediger 1943- *WhoScEn 94*
Kratz, Timothy Harold 1965- *WhoAmL 94*
Kratzel, Ekkehard 1935- *WhoScEn 94*
Kratzer, Guy Livingston 1911- *WhoAm 94, WhoScEn 94*
Kratzer, Guy Miller 1941- *WhoAmP 93*
Kratzert, Arthur William 1925- *WhoAmP 93*
Krauch, Carl Heinrich 1931- *IntWW 93*
Kraul, Edward Garcia 1930- *WhoHisp 94*
Kraus, Albert Andrew, Jr. 1948- *WhoFI 94, WhoMW 93*
Kraus, Alfredo 1924- *WhoAm 94*
Kraus, Alfredo 1927- *NewGrDO*
Kraus, Andreas 1922- *IntWW 93*
Kraus, Auguste *NewGrDO*
Kraus, Christine *DrAPF 93*
Kraus, Douglas M. 1949- *WhoAm 94, WhoAmL 94*
Kraus, Eileen S. *WhoAm 94*
Kraus, Ernst 1863-1941 *NewGrDO*
Kraus, Felix von 1870-1937 *NewGrDO*
Kraus, Gerald Anthony, Jr. 1956- *WhoMW 93*
Kraus, Henry 1923- *WhoMW 93*
Kraus, Herbert Myron 1921- *WhoAm 94*
Kraus, Jean Elizabeth Grau 1932- *WhoFI 94*
Kraus, Jeffrey Miles 1953- *WhoWest 94*
Kraus, Jim *DrAPF 93*
Kraus, Joanna Halpert 1937- *WrDr 94*
Kraus, John Delbert 1960- *WhoFI 94*
Kraus, John Walter 1918- *WhoWest 94*
Kraus, Joseph Martin 1756-1792 *NewGrDO*
Kraus, Michael John 1955- *WhoMW 93*
Kraus, Norma Jean 1931- *WhoAm 94, WhoFI 94*
Kraus, Otakar 1909-1980 *NewGrDO*
Kraus, Pansy Daegling 1916- *WhoFI 94, WhoWest 94*
Kraus, (Wolfgang Ernst) Richard 1902-1978 *NewGrDO*
Kraus, Richard Arnold 1937- *WhoAmP 93*
Kraus, Robert *WhoAmP 93*
Kraus, Robert 1925- *WrDr 94*
Kraus, Robert David 1957- *WhoAm 94*
Kraus, Sherry Stokes 1945- *WhoAmL 94*
Kraus, Ted Richard 1945- *WhoAm 94*
Kraus, (Ersilia) Zili *WhoAmA 93*
Krause, Bernard Leo 1938- *WhoAm 94*
Krause, Bonnie Jean 1942- *WhoAmA 93*
Krause, Carolyn H. *WhoAmP 93*
Krause, Charles Joseph 1937- *WhoAm 94*
Krause, Chester Lee 1923- *WhoAm 94, WhoMW 93*
Krause, David James 1953- *WhoAm 94*
Krause, David William 1967- *WhoMW 93*
Krause, Gary Ellsworth 1948- *WhoAmL 94*
Krause, George 1937- *WhoAmA 93*
Krause, Gunther 1953- *IntWW 93*
Krause, Harold Allen 1940- *WhoAmP 93*
Krause, Harry Dieter 1932- *WhoAm 94*
Krause, Heather Dawn 1956- *WhoMW 93*
Krause, Helen F. 1919- *WhoAmP 93*
Krause, James William 1930- *WhoFI 94*
Krause, Jerry 1939- *WhoAm 94, WhoMW 93*
Krause, John A. 1937- *WhoAmL 94*
Krause, Joseph Lee, Jr. 1958- *WhoScEn 94*
Krause, Karen Ratigan 1950- *WhoMW 93*
Krause, Kurt Lamont 1956- *WhoScEn 94*
Krause, Kurth Werner 1940- *WhoWest 94*
Krause, L. William 1942- *WhoFI 94, WhoWest 94*
Krause, LaVerne Erickson 1924- *WhoAmA 93*
Krause, Lawrence Allen 1939- *WhoAm 94*
Krause, Lois Ruth Breur 1946- *WhoFI 94, WhoScEn 94*
Krause, Manfred Otto 1931- *WhoAm 94*
Krause, Michael D. 1952- *WhoIns 94*
Krause, Richard Michael 1925- *WhoAm 94, WhoScEn 94*
Krause, Richard William 1936- *WhoAm 94*
Krause, Robert Stanley 1942- *WhoAm 94, WhoAmL 94*
Krause, Sonja 1933- *WhoAm 94, WhoScEn 94*
Krause, Thomas Evans 1951- *WhoWest 94*
Krause, Tom 1934- *NewGrDO*
Krause, Victor Carter 1935- *WhoAmP 93*
Krause, Walter 1919- *WhoAm 94*
Krause, Werner William 1937- *WhoFI 94*
Krause, William Austin 1930- *WhoAm 94*
Krausen, Anthony Sharnik 1944- *WhoMW 93*
Krauser, Jary J. 1962- *WhoWest 94*
Kraushaar, Antoinette M. *WhoAmA 93*
Kraushaar, John Florence 1932- *WhoAm 94*
Kraushaar, Otto Frederick 1901-1989 *WhAm 10*
Kraushaar, William L. 1920- *IntWW 93*
Kraushaar, William Lester 1920- *WhoAm 94, WhoMW 93*
Kraushar, Jonathan Pollack 1948- *WhoAm 94*
Kraushar, Peter Maximilian 1934- *WrDr 94*
Krauskopf, Charles Joseph 1931- *WhoMW 93*
Krauskopf, Konrad (Bates) 1910- *WrDr 94*
Krauskopf, Konrad Bates 1910- *IntWW 93, WhoAm 94*
Krausman, John Anthony 1948- *WhoScEn 94*
Kraus-Osborne, Adrienne von 1873-1951 *NewGrDO*
Krauss, Alan Robert 1943- *WhoAm 94*
Krauss, Alison c. 1971- *ConMus 10 [port]*
Krauss, Bruno 1914- *WrDr 94*
Krauss, Carl F. 1936- *WhoAm 94*
Krauss, Charles d1931 *WhoHol 92*
Krauss, Charles Anthony, Jr. 1931- *WhoAm 94*
Krauss, Clemens 1893-1954 *NewGrDO*
Krauss, Clifford 1953- *WrDr 94*
Krauss, (Marie) Gabrielle 1842-1906 *NewGrDO*
Krauss, George 1933- *WhoAm 94*
Krauss, George H. 1941- *WhoAmL 94*
Krauss, Hans Ludwig 1927- *WhoScEn 94*
Krauss, Harvey 1936- *WhoAmL 94*
Krauss, Herbert Harris 1940- *WhoAm 94*
Krauss, Janet *DrAPF 93*
Krauss, Jonathan Seth 1945- *WhoScEn 94*
Krauss, Judith Belliveau 1947- *WhoAm 94*
Krauss, Keith A. 1953- *WhoAmL 94*
Krauss, Matt 1950- *WhoAmP 93*
Krauss, Michael Edward 1934- *WhoAm 94, WhoWest 94*
Krauss, Michael Ian 1951- *WhoAm 94*
Krauss, Ray Herbert 1949- *WhoAm 94*
Krauss, Robert Wallfar 1921- *WhoScEn 94*
Krauss, Rosalind E. 1940- *WhoAmA 93*
Krauss, Ruth *DrAPF 93*
Krauss, Ruth d1993 *NewYTBS 93*
Krauss, Ruth 1911- *WrDr 94*
Krauss, Ruth (Ida) 1911- *ConDr 93*
Krauss, Ruth (Ida) 1911-1993 *ConAu 141, SmATA 75*
Krauss, Steven James 1942- *WhoAm 94*
Krauss, Sue Elizabeth 1951- *WhoScEn 94*
Krauss, Warren J. 1940- *WhoAmL 94*
Krauss, Werner d1959 *WhoHol 92*
Kraussneck, Arthur d1941 *WhoHol 92*
Kraus Trujillo, Alfredo 1924- *WhoAm 94*
Krausz, Ernest 1931- *WrDr 94*
Krausz, Laszlo 1903-1979 *WhoAmA 93N*
Krausz, Michael 1942- *WhoAm 94*
Kraut, Gerald Anthony 1951- *WhoAm 94*
Kraut, Joanne Lenora 1949- *WhoMW 93, WhoScEn 94*
Kraut, Joel Arthur 1937- *WhoScEn 94*
Kraut, Richard 1944- *WrDr 94*
Kraut, Rochelle *DrAPF 93*
Krauter, Aaron 1956- *WhoAmP 93*
Krauter, Aaron Joseph 1956- *WhoMW 93*
Krauter, Adam *WhoAmP 93*
Krauter, Stefan Christof Werner 1963- *WhoScEn 94*
Krauth, Charles Porterfield 1823-1883 *DcAmReB 2*
Krauth, Harald 1923- *WhoAmA 93*
Krauthamer, Nina 1951- *WhoAmL 94*
Krauthammer, Charles 1950- *IntWW 93, WhoAm 94*
Krautkramer, Raymond George 1908- *WhoAmP 93*
Krautkremer, James J. 1934- *WhoAmP 93*
Krautler, Bernhard 1946- *WhoScEn 94*
Krautschun, Harvey C. *WhoAmP 93*
Krauz, Stanislawa *WhoWomW 91*
Krauze, Tadeusz Karol 1934- *WhoScEn 94*
Krauze, Zygmunt 1938- *NewGrDO*
Krauzer, Steven M. *DrAPF 93*
Kravath, Richard Elliot 1935- *WhoScEn 94*
Kravchenko, Piotr Kuzmich 1930- *IntWW 93*
Kravchuk, Leonid M. 1934- *CurBio 93 [port]*
Kravchuk, Leonid Makarovich 1934- *IntWW 93*
Kravchuk, Leonid Makarovych 1934- *LngBDD*
Kravchuk, Robert Sacha 1955- *WhoFI 94*
Kravec, Cynthia Vallen 1951- *WhoScEn 94*
Kraver, Richard Matthew 1946- *WhoAmL 94*
Kravets, Barbara Zeitlin 1935- *WhoMW 93*
Kravetz, Walter J. d1993 *NewYTBS 93*
Kravis, Henry R. *WhoAm 94, WhoFI 94*
Kravis, Irving Bernard 1916-1992 *WhAm 10*
Kravis, Janis 1935- *WhoAmA 93*

Kravis, Raymond Field d1993 *NewYTBS 93*
Kravitch, Phyllis A. *WhoAmP 93*
Kravitch, Phyllis A. 1920- *WhoAm 94, WhoAmL 94*
Kravitt, Jason Harris Paperno 1948- *WhoAm 94*
Kravitz, Ellen King 1929- *WhoAm 94, WhoWest 94*
Kravitz, Hilard Leonard 1917- *WhoWest 94*
Kravitz, Jeffrey R. 1943- *WhoAmL 94*
Kravitz, Jeffrey Stephen 1950- *WhoAm 94*
Kravitz, Mark Richard 1950- *WhoAmL 94*
Kravitz, Rubin 1928- *WhoAm 94, WhoScEn 94*
Kravitz, Steven J. 1946- *WhoAmL 94*
Kravitz, Walter 1938- *WhoAmA 93*
Kravjansky, Mikulas 1928- *WhoAmA 93, WhoWest 94*
Kraw, George Martin 1949- *WhoAmL 94, WhoFI 94, WhoWest 94*
Krawczuk, Aleksander 1922- *IntWW 93*
Krawetz, Arthur Altshuler 1932- *WhoMW 93, WhoScEn 94*
Krawetz, Stephen Andrew 1955- *WhoMW 93, WhoScEn 94*
Krawiec, Richard *DrAPF 93*
Krawiec, Stanley J. *WhoAmP 93*
Krawiecki, Edward Charles, Jr. 1952- *WhoAmP 93*
Krawitz, Herman Everett 1925- *WhoAm 94*
Kray, Elaine Louise 1943- *WhoMW 93*
Kray, Walter d1989 *WhoHol 92*
Kraybill, Paul Nissley 1925- *WhoAm 94*
Kraysler, Stephen F. 1942- *WhoIns 94*
Krchma, Stephen Peter 1947- *WhoMW 93*
Kreager, Eileen Davis 1924- *WhoFI 94, WhoMW 93*
Kreager, Henry Dewayne 1912- *WhoAm 94*
Kreamer, Barbara Osborn 1948- *WhoAmP 93*
Krebill, Lorrie Leabo *WhoMW 93*
Krebs, Arno William, Jr. 1942- *WhoAm 94, WhoAmL 94*
Krebs, Carol Marie 1958- *WhoMW 93*
Krebs, Edward H. 1944- *WhoAmP 93*
Krebs, Edwin Gerhard 1918- *IntWW 93, Who 94, WhoAm 94, WhoScEn 94, WhoWest 94*
Krebs, Elizabeth Louise 1968- *WhoMW 93*
Krebs, Ernst Theodor, Jr. 1912- *WhoAm 94, WhoWest 94*
Krebs, Gene *WhoAmP 93*
Krebs, Hans Adolf 1900-1981 *WorScD [port]*
Krebs, Helmut 1913- *NewGrDO*
Krebs, Hope Paula 1961- *WhoAmL 94*
Krebs, James Norton 1924- *WhoScEn 94*
Krebs, John H. 1926- *WhoAm 94*
Krebs, John Hans 1926- *WhoAmP 93*
Krebs, John Richard 1945- *IntWW 93, Who 94*
Krebs, Karl August 1804-1880 *NewGrDO*
Krebs, Margaret Eloise 1927- *WhoFI 94*
Krebs, Max Vance 1916- *WhoAm 94*
Krebs, Nita d1991 *WhoHol 92*
Krebs, Patsy *WhoAmA 93*
Krebs, Robert Duncan 1942- *IntWW 93, WhoAm 94, WhoFI 94*
Krebs, Robert Preston 1948- *WhoAmP 93*
Krebs, Rockne 1938- *WhoAmA 93*
Krebs, Roger Donavon 1949- *WhoWest 94*
Krebs, Stephen Jeffrey 1950- *WhoWest 94*
Krebs, Thomas Gary 1948- *WhoAmL 94*
Krebsbach, Karen K. *WhoAmP 93, WhoMW 93*
Krebsbach, Scott Lee 1968- *WhoAmP 93*
Krech, Warren *WhoHol 92*
Krechel, Ursula 1947- *BlmGWL*
Krecke, Charles Francis 1926- *WhoAm 94*
Krecklow, Douglas Earl 1952- *WhoMW 93*
Kredel, Elmar Maria 1922- *IntWW 93*
Kredi, Olga Amary 1960- *WhoHisp 94*
Kreegar, Phillip Keith 1937- *WhoMW 93*
Kreeger, David Lloyd 1909-1990 *WhAm 10*
Kreek, Louis Francis, Jr. 1928- *WhoAmL 94*
Kreek, Mary Jeanne *WhoScEn 94*
Kreer, Irene Overman 1926- *WhoFI 94, WhoMW 93*
Kreer, John Belshaw 1927- *WhoAm 94*
Krefetz, Gerald Saul 1932- *WrDr 94*
Krefting, Carol Lee 1948- *WhoAm 94*
Krefting, Robert John 1944- *WhoAm 94*
Kregal, Ann *DrAPF 93*
Kregel, J. A 1944- *WrDr 94*
Kregel, James 1951- *WhoMW 93*
Kreger, James Merlin 1950- *WhoFI 94*
Kreger, Melvin Joseph 1937- *WhoAmL 94, WhoWest 94*
Kreh, Kent Q. 1935- *WhoAm 94*
Krehbiel, Darren David 1963- *WhoMW 93, WhoScEn 94*
Krehbiel, David Kent 1966- *WhoScEn 94*
Krehbiel, Frederick August, II 1941- *WhoAm 94, WhoFI 94*
Krehbiel, Harry 1897- *WhAm 10*
Krehbiel, Henry (Edward) 1854-1923 *NewGrDO*
Krehbiel, John H. 1906- *WhoAm 94, WhoFI 94*
Krehbiel, John H., Jr. 1937- *WhoAm 94, WhoFI 94*
Krehbiel, Robert *WhoAmP 93*
Krehbiel, Robert J. 1948- *WhoAmL 94*
Krehel, Roberta Mae 1927- *WhoFI 94*
Kreibich, Robin G. *WhoAmP 93*
Kreider, Anne Elizabeth 1958- *WhoMW 93*
Kreider, Jim 1955- *WhoAmP 93*
Kreider, Leonard Cale 1910- *WhoFI 94*
Kreider, Leonard Emil 1938- *WhoFI 94, WhoMW 93*
Kreidler, Mike 1943- *CngDr 93, WhoAm 94, WhoWest 94*
Kreidler, Myron Bradford 1943- *WhoAmP 93*
Kreidler, Robert Neil 1929-1992 *WhAm 10*
Kreidler, Terry James 1948- *WhoWest 94*
Kreighbaum, John Scott 1946- *WhoAm 94*
Kreil, Curtis Lee 1955- *WhoWest 94*
Kreil, Dale Donald 1955- *WhoMW 93*
Kreilick, Marjorie E. 1925- *WhoAmA 93*
Kreilick, Robert W. 1938- *WhoAm 94*
Kreiman, Keith *WhoAmP 93*
Kreiman, Robert T. 1924- *IntMPA 94*
Kreiman, Robert Theodore 1924- *WhoWest 94*
Krein, William A. 1940- *WhoAm 94*
Kreindler, Doris Barsky 1901-1974 *WhoAmA 93N*
Kreindler, Peter Michael 1945- *WhoAmL 94*
Kreinin, Mordechai 1930- *WrDr 94*
Kreinin, Mordechai Eliahu 1930- *WhoAm 94, WhoMW 93*
Kreipke, Merrill Vincent 1916- *WhoFI 94*
Kreis, Willi 1924- *WhoAm 94*
Kreisberg, Neil Ivan 1945- *WhoAm 94, WhoFI 94*
Kreisel, Georg 1923- *IntWW 93, Who 94*
Kreisel, Henry 1922- *WhAm 10, WrDr 94*
Kreisel, Henry 1922-1991 *ConAu 42NR*
Kreiser, Frank David 1930- *WhoMW 93*
Kreisky, Bruno 1911-1990 *WhAm 10*
Kreisman, Arthur 1918- *WhoAm 94*
Kreisman, Norman Richard 1943- *WhoScEn 94*
Kreismann, Ronald 1944- *WhoAmL 94*
Kreiter-Foronda, Carolyn *DrAPF 93*
Kreithen, Melvin Louis 1941- *WhoScEn 94*
Kreitler, John E. 1946- *WhoAmL 94*
Kreitler, Richard Rogers 1942- *WhoWest 94*
Kreitman, Benjamin Zvi 1920- *WhoAm 94*
Kreitner, John 1897- *WhAm 10*
Kreitzberg, Fred Charles 1934- *WhoAm 94, WhoScEn 94, WhoWest 94*
Kreitzer, David Martin 1942- *WhoAmA 93, WhoWest 94*
Kreitzer, Jack *DrAPF 93*
Kreitzer, Jerry D. 1949- *WhoAmP 93*
Kreitzer, Lois Helen 1933- *WhoFI 94*
Kreitzman, Ralph J. 1945- *WhoAm 94, WhoAmL 94*
Krejca, Otomar 1921- *IntWW 93*
Krejci, Isa 1904-1968 *NewGrDO*
Krejci, Jaroslav 1916- *WrDr 94*
Krejci, Miroslav 1891-1964 *NewGrDO*
Krejci, Robert Henry 1943- *WhoWest 94*
Krejci, Stanley Leon 1942- *WhoFI 94*
Krejcova, Zdenka 1942- *WhoWomW 91*
Krejcsi, Cynthia Ann 1948- *WhoMW 93*
Krekeler, Heinz L. 1906- *IntWW 93*
Krekorian, Michael H. *DrAPF 93*
Krekorian, Robert C. 1962- *WhoAmP 93*
Krell, George Frederick 1938- *WhoWest 94*
Krelle, Wilhelm Ernst 1916- *IntWW 93*
Kremen, Pete 1951- *WhoAmP 93*
Kremen, Richard M. 1945- *WhoAmL 94*
Krementz, Edward Thomas 1917- *WhoAm 94*
Krementz, Jill 1940- *WhoAm 94*
Kremer, Arthur J. 1935- *WhoAm 94*
Kremer, Arthur Jerome 1935- *WhoAmP 93*
Kremer, Eugene R. 1938- *WhoAm 94*
Kremer, Fred, Jr. 1926- *WhoAm 94*
Kremer, Gidon 1947- *IntWW 93*
Kremer, Honor Frances 1939- *WhoFI 94*
Kremer, Joseph M. 1921- *WhoAmP 93*
Kremer, Robert John 1950- *WhoMW 93*
Kremkoski, Joe E. 1949- *WhoAmP 93*
Kreml, Franklin Martin 1907- *WhoAm 94, WhoMW 93*
Kremnev, Roald Savvovich 1929- *IntWW 93*
Kremp, Herbert 1928- *IntWW 93*
Krempasky, Lisa D. 1965- *WhoAmL 94*
Krempel, Ralf 1935- *WhoAmA 93*
Krempel, Ralf Hugo Bernhard 1935- *WhoWest 94*
Krempel, Roger Ernest 1926- *WhoWest 94*
Krempl, Erhard 1934- *WhoAm 94*
Kren, Margo 1939- *WhoAmA 93*
Kren, Thomas John 1950- *WhoAm 94*
Krendel, Ezra Simon 1925- *WhoAm 94*
Kreneck, Lynwood 1936- *WhoAmA 93*
Krenek, Debbie *WhoAm 94*
Krenek, Ernst 1900-1991 *NewGrDO, WhAm 10*
Krenek, Ronald Richard 1929- *WhoMW 93*
Krenitsky, Michael V. 1915- *WhoAm 94*
Krenitsky, Thomas Anthony 1938- *WhoAm 94*
Krenitsyn, Pyotr Kuzmich d1770 *WhWE*
Krenke, Frederick William 1946- *WhoScEn 94*
Krenkel, Peter Ashton 1930- *WhoAm 94*
Krenkel, Roy G(erald, Jr.) 1918-1983 *EncSF 93*
Krenn, Fritz 1887-1964 *NewGrDO*
Krenn, Werner 1943- *NewGrDO*
Krens, Thomas *WhoAmA 93*
Krens, Thomas 1946- *IntWW 93, WhoAm 94*
Krensky, Harold 1912- *WhoAm 94*
Krents, Milton Ellis 1911- *WhoAm 94*
Krentz, Edgar Martin 1928- *WrDr 94*
Krentz, Eugene Leo 1932- *WhoAm 94*
Krentz, Jane 1952- *WhoAmP 93*
Krentz, Jayne Ann 1948- *WrDr 94*
Krentzin, Earl 1929- *WhoAmA 93*
Krenz, Dean Albert 1930- *WhoAm 94*
Krenz, Egon 1937- *IntWW 93*
Krenz, Jan 1926- *IntWW 93*
Krenzer, Sandi *WhoAmP 93*
Krenzler, Alvin Irving 1921- *WhoAm 94*
Krepinevich, Kevin W. 1954- *WhoAm 94*
Krepps, Ethel Constance 1937- *WhoAmL 94*
Kreps, David Marc 1950- *WhoAm 94, WhoFI 94, WhoWest 94*
Kreps, Juanita M(orris) 1921- *WrDr 94*
Kreps, Juanita Morris 1921- *IntWW 93, WhoAm 94*
Kreps, Robert Wilson 1946- *WhoAm 94*
Kresa, Kent 1938- *IntWW 93, WhoAm 94, WhoFI 94, WhoWest 94*
Krese, Michael Joseph 1956- *WhoMW 93*
Kresge, Alexander Jerry 1926- *WhoAm 94*
Kresge, Bruce Anderson 1931- *WhoAm 94*
Kresh, David *DrAPF 93*
Kresh, J. Yasha 1948- *WhoAm 94, WhoScEn 94*
Kresh, Michael D. 1954- *WhoFI 94*
Kresh, Paul 1919- *WhoAm 94, WrDr 94*
Kresina, Thomas Francis 1954- *WhoScEn 94*
Kreski, Connie *WhoHol 92*
Kresowik, Timothy Frank 1976- *WhoMW 93*
Kress, Albert Otto, Jr. 1950- *WhoScEn 94*
Kress, Andrew A. 1953- *WhoAmL 94*
Kress, George F. 1903- *WhoAm 94*
Kress, Gerard Clayton, Jr. 1934- *WhoScEn 94*
Kress, Gladys d1969 *WhoHol 92*
Kress, Gloria W. 1921- *WhoAmP 93*
Kress, Harold F. 1913- *IntMPA 94*
Kress, Heather Gabrielle 1944- *WhoAm 94*
Kress, Leonard *DrAPF 93*
Kress, Nancy *DrAPF 93*
Kress, Nancy (Anne) 1948- *EncSF 93*
Kress, Ralph Herman 1904- *WhoAm 94*
Kress, Viktor Melkhiorovich 1948- *LngBDD*
Kresse, Martin H. 1941- *WhoAmL 94*
Kresse, William Joseph 1958- *WhoAmL 94*
Kressel, Henry 1934- *WhoAm 94*
Kressel, Neil Jeffrey 1957- *WhoScEn 94*
Kressel, Robert J. 1947- *WhoAm 94, WhoAmL 94*
Kressler, James Phillip 1931- *WhoAm 94*
Kressyn, Miriam 1915?- *WhoHol 92*
Krestensen, Ann M. 1939- *WhoAmA 93*
Kreston, Martin Howard 1931- *WhoAm 94*
Krestovskaia, Mariia Vsevolodovna 1862-1910 *BlmGWL*
Krestovskii, V. *BlmGWL*
Kresy-Poree, R. Jean 1931- *WhoBlA 94*
Kretchmer, Kathy L. 1952- *WhoAmL 94*
Kretchmer, Norman 1923- *WhoAm 94*
Kretsch, Michael Gene 1959- *WhoScEn 94*
Kretschmar, William Edward 1933- *WhoAmP 93, WhoMW 93*
Kretschmer, Frank F., Jr. 1930- *WhoAm 94*
Kretschmer, Keith Hughes 1934- *WhoAm 94, WhoFI 94*
Kretschmer, Paul Robert 1929- *WhoAm 94*
Kretsinger, Mary Amelia 1915- *WhoAmA 93*
Kretzberg, Hermann d1951 *WhoHol 92*
Kretzenbacher, Leopold 1912- *IntWW 93*
Kretzer, William T. *WhoAm 94, WhoFI 94*
Kretzinger, Rik J. 1953- *WhoWest 94*
Kretzmer, Herbert 1925- *Who 94*
Kretzschmar, William Addison, Jr. 1953- *WhoAm 94*
Kreuger, Kurt 1916- *WhoHol 92*
Kreuger, Kurt 1917- *IntMPA 94*
Kreuger, Larry Willard 1945- *WhoMW 93*
Kreul, Carol Ann 1956- *WhoMW 93*
Kreul, Richard Theodore 1924- *WhoAmP 93*
Kreuscher, Wayne C. 1946- *WhoAm 94*
Kreuscher, Wayne Charles 1946- *WhoAmL 94*
Kreuter, Gretchen V. 1934- *WhoAm 94*
Kreuter, Konrad Franz 1939- *WhoScEn 94*
Kreutz, James Kirk 1940- *WhoAmP 93*
Kreutz, Martha Hill 1943- *WhoAmP 93*
Kreutz, Paul E. 1942- *WhoAmL 94*
Kreutzberg, David W. 1953- *WhoAm 94, WhoAmL 94*
Kreutzer, Conradin 1780-1849 *NewGrDO*
Kreutzer, Franklin David 1940- *WhoAm 94, WhoAmL 94*
Kreutzer, Leon Charles Francois 1817-1868 *NewGrDO*
Kreutzer, Louis G., Jr. 1929- *WhoAm 94*
Kreutzer, Robert Lee 1946- *WhoMW 93*
Kreutzer, Rodolphe 1766-1831 *NewGrDO*
Kreutzer, S. Stanley *WhoAm 94*
Kreutzer-Baraglia, Lynne *WhoMW 93*
Kreuz, Roger James 1961- *WhoScEn 94*
Kreuzer, June April 1944- *WhoAmP 93*
Kreuzer, Lisa *WhoHol 92*
Krevans, Julius Richard 1924- *WhoAm 94, WhoWest 94*
Krewson, Lorraine Wilma 1930- *WhoMW 93*
Krewson, Lyle Reid 1943- *WhoAmP 93*
Krey, Mary Ann Reynolds 1947- *WhoAm 94*
Krey, Robert Dean 1929- *WhoAm 94*
Kreyche, Gerald Francis 1927- *WhoAm 94*
Kreyling, Edward George, Jr. 1923- *WhoAm 94*
Kreznar, Richard J. 1940- *WhoAmA 93*
Kriak, John Michael 1947- *WhoAm 94*
Kriangsak Chomanan, Gen. 1917- *IntWW 93*
Kribel, Robert Edward 1937- *WhoAm 94*
Krichever, Mark 1941- *WhoScEn 94*
Krick, Irving Parkhurst 1906- *WhoAm 94, WhoScEn 94, WhoWest 94*
Kricka, Jaroslav 1882-1969 *NewGrDO*
Krickstein, Aron 1967- *WhoAm 94*
Kricorian, Nancy *DrAPF 93*
Kridel, James S. 1940- *WhoAm 94*
Kridel, William J., Jr. 1942- *WhoAmL 94*
Krider, E. Philip 1940- *WhoScEn 94*
Krider, Jaunita Faye 1933- *WhoAmP 93*
Krider, Patricia Ann 1956- *WhoMW 93*
Kriebel, Charles Hosey 1933- *WhoAm 94*
Krieg, Arthur Frederick 1930- *WhoAm 94*
Krieg, Dorothy Linden 1919- *WhoAm 94*
Krieg, Martha Fessler 1948- *WhoMW 93*
Kriegel, Alan 1947- *WhoAmL 94*
Kriegel, Leonard *DrAPF 93*
Kriegel, Leonard 1933- *WrDr 94*
Krieger, Abbott Joel 1939- *WhoAm 94*
Krieger, David Malcolm 1942- *WhoWest 94*
Krieger, Dolores Esther 1935- *WhoMW 93*
Krieger, Florence *WhoAmA 93*
Krieger, Gary Robert 1951- *WhoAm 94*
Krieger, Ian *DrAPF 93*
Krieger, Irvin Mitchell 1923- *WhoAm 94, WhoScEn 94*
Krieger, Johann 1652-1735 *NewGrDO*
Krieger, Johann Philipp 1649?-1725 *NewGrDO*
Krieger, Lee d1967 *WhoHol 92*
Krieger, Leonard 1918-1990 *WhAm 10*
Krieger, Martin Erwin 1923- *WhoFI 94*
Krieger, Michael Raymond 1954- *WhoWest 94*
Krieger, Michael Thomas 1950- *WhoAmL 94*
Krieger, Murray 1923- *WhoAm 94, WhoWest 94, WrDr 94*
Krieger, Paul Edward 1942- *WhoAm 94, WhoAmL 94, WhoFI 94*
Krieger, Robert Edward 1925- *WhoAm 94*
Krieger, Robert Lee, Jr. 1946- *WhoFI 94*
Krieger, Ruth M. 1922- *WhoAmA 93*
Krieger, Sanford 1943- *WhoAm 94, WhoAmL 94*
Krieger, Stanley Leonard 1942- *WhoFI 94*

Kronsnoble, Jeffrey Michael 1939- *WhoAmA 93*
Kronstad, Warren Ervind 1932- *WhoAm 94*
Kronstadt, Arnold Mayo 1919- *WhoAm 94*
Kronstam, Henning 1934- *IntDcB*
Kronstein, Max 1895-1992 *WhAm 10*
Kronstein, Werner J 1930- *WhoAm 94*
Kroo, Gyorgy 1926- *IntWW 93*
Krook, Margretha *WhoHol 92*
Kroon, Ciro Dominico 1916- *IntWW 93*
Kropf, Joan R. 1949- *WhoAmA 93*
Kropiwnicki, Jerzy Janusz 1945- *IntWW 93*
Kropla, Steven Mark 1955- *WhoWest 94*
Kropotkin, Peter 1842-1921 *WhWE*
Kropotoff, George Alex 1921- *WhoScEn 94, WhoWest 94*
Kropp, Arthur John 1957- *WhoAm 94*
Kropp, David Arthur 1933- *WhoAm 94*
Kropp, John J. 1946- *WhoAmL 94*
Kropp, Lloyd *WrDr 94*
Kropp, Richard P. 1940- *WhoIns 94*
Kropschot, Richard H. 1927- *WhoAm 94*
Krosin, Kenneth E. 1944- *WhoAmL 94*
Krosnick, Joel 1941- *WhoAm 94*
Krosnicki, Kathleen A. 1950- *WhoAmP 93*
Krossner, Rhonda Parrella 1951- *WhoMW 93*
Kroth, Jeannie Mae 1944- *WhoMW 93*
Krotinger, Myron Nathan 1914- *WhoAmL 94*
Krotki, Karol Jozef 1922- *WhoAm 94, WhoScEn 94, WhoWest 94*
Kroto, Harold Walter 1939- *Who 94, WhoScEn 94*
Krotz, Edward William 1925- *WhoMW 93*
Krotz, James E. *WhoMW 93*
Krouner, Leonard William 1947- *WhoAmL 94*
Krouse, Ann Wolk 1945- *WhoAm 94*
Krouse, George Raymond, Jr. 1945- *WhoAm 94, WhoAmL 94*
Krout, Boyd Merrill 1931- *WhoWest 94*
Krovatin, Gerald 1952- *WhoAmL 94*
Krovopuskov, Viktor Alekseevich 1948- *IntWW 93*
Krowe, Allen Julian 1932- *WhoAm 94, WhoFI 94*
Kroyer, Haraldur 1921- *IntWW 93*
Kroyer, Robert W. *WhoAm 94*
Krpata, Anne Marie 1933- *WhoAmL 94*
Krstic, Petar 1877-1957 *NewGrDO*
Krstic, Radivoj V(ase) 1935- *ConAu 142*
Krsul, John Aloysius, Jr. 1938- *WhoAmL 94*
Kruchkow, Diane *DrAPF 93*
Kruchten, Marcia H. *DrAPF 93*
Kruckeberg, Arthur Rice 1920- *WhoAm 94*
Kruckenberg, Homer Andrew 1935- *WhoAmP 93*
Kruckenberg, Joyce Lavon 1938- *WhoAmP 93*
Krucks, William 1918- *WhoAm 94, WhoFI 94*
Krucky, Anton Chalmers 1952- *WhoWest 94*
Krudener, Barbara Juliane von 1764-1824 *BlmGWL*
Krueger, Alan Douglas 1937- *WhoFI 94, WhoMW 93*
Krueger, Anne O. 1934- *IntWW 93*
Krueger, Artur W. G. 1940- *WhoFI 94*
Krueger, Betty Jane 1923- *WhoFI 94, WhoMW 93*
Krueger, Bonnie Lee 1950- *WhoAm 94, WhoMW 93*
Krueger, Bum d1971 *WhoHol 92*
Krueger, Daniel Carl 1946- *WhoMW 93*
Krueger, Darrell George 1948- *WhoScEn 94*
Krueger, Darrell William 1943- *WhoAm 94, WhoMW 93*
Krueger, Donald Marc 1952- *WhoFI 94*
Krueger, Eric Eugene 1958- *WhoFI 94*
Krueger, Eugene Rex 1935- *WhoAm 94*
Krueger, Hans-Joachim 1938- *IntWW 93*
Krueger, Harvey Mark 1929- *WhoAm 94*
Krueger, Herbert William 1948- *WhoAm 94*
Krueger, Howard W., Jr. 1940- *WhoMW 93*
Krueger, J. Frann 1947- *WhoWest 94*
Krueger, James A. 1943- *WhoAmL 94*
Krueger, John Charles 1951- *WhoFI 94*
Krueger, John William 1930- *WhoAmL 94*
Krueger, Katherine Kamp 1944- *WhoFI 94*
Krueger, Keith Roger 1957- *WhoAmP 93*
Krueger, Kenneth John 1946- *WhoAm 94*
Krueger, Kurt Donn 1952- *WhoAmL 94, WhoAmP 93*
Krueger, Kurt Edward 1952- *WhoFI 94, WhoScEn 94, WhoWest 94*
Krueger, Larry Eugene 1944- *WhoAmL 94, WhoFI 94, WhoWest 94*
Krueger, Lorraine *WhoHol 92*
Krueger, Lothar David 1919- *WhoAmA 93*
Krueger, Maynard C. 1906-1991 *WhAm 10*
Krueger, Phillip Eric 1955- *WhoMW 93*
Krueger, Ralph Ray 1927- *WhoAm 94*
Krueger, Richard Arnold 1949- *WhoAmP 93*
Krueger, Richard H. 1933- *WhoAmP 93*
Krueger, Robert *WhoAmP 93*
Krueger, Robert Blair 1928- *WhoAm 94, WhoAmL 94*
Krueger, Robert William 1916- *WhoAm 94, WhoAmP 93*
Krueger, Ronald 1958- *WhoScEn 94*
Krueger, Ronald P. 1940- *IntMPA 94*
Krueger, Tom *WhoAmP 93*
Krug, Edward Charles 1947- *WhoScEn 94*
Krug, Harry Elno 1930- *WhoAmA 93*
Krug, Karen-Ann 1951- *WhoFI 94*
Krug, Maurice F. 1929- *WhoScEn 94*
Krug, Michael Steven 1956- *WhoAmL 94*
Krug, Philip L. 1929- *WhoFI 94*
Krug, Shirley 1958- *WhoAmP 93*
Kruger, Alma d1960 *WhoHol 92*
Kruger, Arthur Martin 1932- *WhoAm 94*
Kruger, Arthur Newman 1916- *WhoAm 94*
Kruger, Barbara 1945- *WhoAmA 93*
Kruger, Charles Herman, Jr. 1934- *WhoAm 94, WhoWest 94*
Kruger, Fred d1961 *WhoHol 92*
Kruger, Gilbert Nelson 1941- *WhoAmL 94*
Kruger, Gustav Otto, Jr. 1916- *WhoAm 94*
Kruger, Hardy 1928- *IntMPA 94, IntWW 93, WhoHol 92*
Kruger, Horst 1919- *IntWW 93*
Kruger, Jeffrey S. 1931- *IntMPA 94*
Kruger, Jerome 1927- *WhoAm 94, WhoScEn 94*
Kruger, Johann *NewGrDO*
Kruger, Johann Philipp *NewGrDO*
Kruger, Kathleen M. 1942- *WhoMW 93*
Kruger, Kenneth Charles 1930- *WhoAm 94*
Kruger, Lawrence 1929- *WhoAm 94*
Kruger, Lewis 1935- *WhoAm 94*
Kruger, Manfred Paul 1938- *IntWW 93*
Kruger, Otto d1974 *WhoHol 92*
Kruger, Patricia Regina 1954- *WhoAmL 94*
Kruger, Paul d1960 *WhoHol 92*
Kruger, Paul 1825-1904 *HisWorL [port]*
Kruger, Paul 1925- *WhoScEn 94, WhoWest 94*
Kruger, Paul Robert 1957- *WhoFI 94, WhoWest 94*
Kruger, Prudence Margaret *Who 94*
Kruger, Richard Hunt 1953- *WhoMW 93*
Kruger, Rudolf 1916- *WhAm 10*
Kruger, Stubby d1965 *WhoHol 92*
Kruger, Thomas E. 1944- *WhoAmL 94*
Kruger, Weldon Dale 1931- *WhoAm 94*
Kruger, William Arnold 1937- *WhoAm 94, WhoMW 93, WhoScEn 94*
Kruger, Wolf *WrDr 94*
Kruglick, Burton S. 1925- *WhoAmP 93*
Kruglick, Lewis *DrAPF 93*
Kruglov, Anatoly Sergeevich 1951- *LngBDD*
Krugman, Lou 1914- *WhoHol 92*
Krugman, Morris d1993 *NewYTBS 93 [port]*
Krugman, Paul Robin 1953- *IntWW 93, WhoAm 94, WhoFI 94*
Krugman, Saul 1911- *WhoAm 94*
Krugman, Stanley Lee 1925- *WhoAm 94, WhoWest 94*
Krugman, Stanley Liebert 1932- *WhoScEn 94*
Kruguer, Ignacio 1939- *WhoFI 94*
Kruh, Janet Jackson 1926- *WhoMW 93*
Kruh, Robert F. 1925- *WhoAm 94*
Kruidenier, David 1921- *WhoAm 94, WhoMW 93*
Kruijtbosch, Egbert Diederik Jan 1925- *IntWW 93*
Kruizenga, Richard John 1930- *WhoFI 94*
Kruk, John Martin 1961- *WhoAm 94*
Krukowski, Lucian 1929- *WhoAm 94, WhoAmA 93*
Krul, Michael Henry 1948- *WhoAmL 94*
Krul, Michael Paul 1963- *WhoMW 93*
Krulak, Charles Chandler 1942- *WhoAm 94*
Krulak, Victor Harold 1913- *WhoAm 94, WhoWest 94*
Krulewich, Helen D. 1948- *WhoAmL 94*
Krulfeld, Ruth Marilyn 1931- *WhoAm 94*
Krulik, Barbara S. 1955- *WhoAm 94, WhoAmA 93*
Krulitz, Leo Morrion 1938- *WhoAm 94, WhoAmP 93*
Krull, Annie 1876-1947 *NewGrDO*
Krull, Charles Fred 1933- *WhoAm 94*
Krull, Dennis Keith 1963- *WhoMW 93*
Krull, Edward Alexander 1929- *WhoMW 93, WhoScEn 94*
Krull, Jeffrey Robert 1948- *WhoAm 94, WhoMW 93*
Krull, Kevin Charles 1952- *WhoAmL 94*
Krum, Charles Leo, Jr. 1939- *WhoAmP 93*
Krumbein, Charles Harvey 1944- *WhoAm 94*
Krumbhaar, George Douglas, Jr. 1936- *WhoAmP 93*
Krumboltz, John Dwight 1928- *WhoAm 94*
Krumgold, Joseph (Quincy) 1908-1980 *TwCYAW*
Krumhansl, Carol Lynne 1947- *WhoScEn 94*
Krumholt, Ann 1933- *WhoAmA 93*
Krumholz, Dennis Jonathan 1952- *WhoAm 94, WhoAmL 94*
Krumins, Girts 1932- *WhoAm 94*
Krumm, Charles Ferdinand 1941- *WhoAm 94*
Krumm, Daniel J. d1993 *NewYTBS 93*
Krumm, Daniel J. 1926- *IntWW 93*
Krumm, Daniel John 1926- *WhoAm 94, WhoFI 94*
Krumm, Gene William 1942- *WhoMW 93*
Krumm, John McGill 1913- *WhoAm 94, WhoWest 94*
Krumm, Paul Jesse 1940- *WhoMW 93*
Krumm, William Frederick 1923- *WhoAm 94*
Krummacher, Hans-Henrik 1931- *IntWW 93*
Krumme, George William 1922- *WhoAmP 93*
Krummel, Donald William 1929- *WhoAm 94*
Krummel, Richard Frank 1925- *WhoMW 93*
Krummenacher, Aimee Jeanne 1969- *WhoMW 93*
Krump, Gary Joseph 1946- *WhoAm 94*
Krumschmidt, Eberhard d1956 *WhoHol 92*
Krupa, Gene d1973 *WhoHol 92*
Krupansky, Blanche 1925- *WhoAm 94*
Krupansky, Robert B. *WhoAmP 93*
Krupansky, Robert Bazil 1921- *WhoAm 94, WhoAmL 94, WhoMW 93*
Krupat, Arnold 1941- *WhoAm 94*
Kruper, Paul D. 1949- *WhoAmL 94*
Krupinski, Elizabeth Anne 1960- *WhoWest 94*
Krupinski, Jerry W. 1941- *WhoAmP 93*
Krupka, Robert George 1949- *WhoAm 94, WhoAmL 94*
Krupkat, Ann Katherine 1926- *WhoMW 93*
Krupman, William Allan 1936- *WhoAm 94*
Krupnick, Elizabeth Rachel 1949- *WhoAm 94, WhoFI 94*
Krupnick, Jerold Barry 1943- *WhoFI 94*
Krupnick, Mark 1939- *WhoMW 93*
Krupnick, Mark L. 1939- *WrDr 94*
Krupnik, Vee M. *WhoAm 94, WhoFI 94*
Krupowicz, John Joseph 1946- *WhoScEn 94*
Krupp, Clarence William 1929- *WhoAm 94*
Krupp, Edwin Charles 1944- *WhoAm 94, WhoScEn 94, WhoWest 94*
Krupp, Fred 1954- *WhoAm 94*
Krupp, Georg 1936- *IntWW 93*
Krupp, Marcus Abraham 1913- *WhoAm 94*
Krupp, Robert Allen 1951- *WhoMW 93*
Krupp, Robin Rector 1946- *WrDr 94*
Krupp, Vera d1967 *WhoHol 92*
Krupsak, Mary Anne 1932- *WhoAmP 93*
Krupska, Danya 1921- *WhoAm 94*
Krus, David James 1940- *WhoAm 94*
Krusceniski, Salomea 1872-1952 *NewGrDO [port]*
Kruschen, Jack 1922- *WhoHol 92*
Kruse, Alvin L. 1943- *WhoAmL 94*
Kruse, David Louis, II 1944- *WhoAm 94, WhoFI 94*
Kruse, Dennis K. 1946- *WhoAmP 93*
Kruse, Douglas Charles 1951- *WhoFI 94*
Kruse, Edgar Christ 1912- *WhoAm 94*
Kruse, F. Michael *WhoAm 94, WhoAmL 94, WhoWest 94*
Kruse, Fred A. 1932- *WhoAmP 93*
Kruse, James Joseph 1932- *WhoAm 94*
Kruse, John Alphonse 1926- *WhoAm 94, WhoAmL 94*
Kruse, Layne E. 1951- *WhoAmL 94*
Kruse, Lise Fiaux 1947- *WhoFI 94*
Kruse, Martin 1929- *IntWW 93*
Kruse, Olan E. 1921- *WhoScEn 94*
Kruse, Pamela Jean 1950- *WhoAmL 94*
Kruse, Paul Walters, Jr. 1927- *WhoAm 94*
Kruse, Richard Kareth, Jr. 1938- *WhoAm 94*
Kruse, Scott August 1947- *WhoAm 94, WhoAmL 94*
Kruse, Wilbur Ferdinand 1922- *WhoMW 93*
Krusee, Michael 1959- *WhoAmP 93*
Krusen, Dave *See* Pearl Jam *News 94-2*
Krusen, Henry Stanley 1907- *WhoAm 94*
Krusenstern, Adam Ivan Ritter Von 1770-1846 *WhWE*
Krusenstjerna, Agnes Julie Fredrika von 1894-1940 *BlmGWL*
Krushat, William Mark 1949- *WhoScEn 94*
Krushenick, John 1927- *WhoAmA 93*
Krushenick, Nicholas 1929- *WhoAm 94, WhoAmA 93*
Krusick, Margaret Ann 1956- *WhoAmP 93, WhoMW 93*
Krusin, Stanley (Marks) 1908- *Who 94*
Kruskal, Martin David 1925- *WhoAm 94, WhoScEn 94*
Kruskal, William Henry 1919- *WhoAm 94*
Kruskamp, Janet 1934- *WhoAmA 93*
Krusoe, James *DrAPF 93*
Krusos, Denis Angelo 1927- *WhoAm 94*
Kruszenski, Donald Michael 1942- *WhoFI 94*
Kruszewski, George Henry 1952- *WhoFI 94*
Kruszewski, Kenneth E. 1945- *WhoAmP 93*
Kruszewski, Z. Anthony 1928- *WrDr 94*
Krutch, Joseph Wood 1893-1970 *EnvEnc*
Krutchkoff, Richard Gerald 1933- *WhoAm 94*
Kruteck, Laurence R. 1941- *WhoAmL 94, WhoFI 94*
Krutilek, Daniel Ray 1942- *WhoIns 94*
Krutter, Forrest Nathan 1954- *WhoAmL 94, WhoMW 93*
Krutz, Ronald L. 1938- *WhoScEn 94*
Krutzch, Gus *ConAu 41NR*
Kruus, Harri Kullervo 1950- *WhoScEn 94*
Kruvant, M. Charito 1945- *WhoHisp 94*
Kruyf, Ton de 1937- *NewGrDO*
Kruzan, Mark R. 1960- *WhoAmP 93*
Kryder, George M., III 1951- *WhoAmL 94*
Kryder, Mark Howard 1943- *WhoAm 94*
Kryeziu, Said Bey d1993 *NewYTBS 93*
Kryn, Randall Lee 1949- *WhoFI 94, WhoMW 93*
Krynicki, Beth Ann 1969- *WhoWest 94*
Krynski, Magnus Jan 1922-1989 *WhAm 10*
Krys, Alejandro J. 1967- *WhoHisp 94*
Krys, Sheldon J. 1934- *WhoAmP 93*
Krys, Sheldon Jack 1934- *WhoAm 94*
Kryshak, Gerald John 1933- *WhoMW 93*
Kryshak, Thaddeus Francis 1930- *WhoAm 94*
Kryshak, Thomas E. 1935- *WhoIns 94*
Krysiak, Carolyn *WhoAmP 93*
Krysiak, Joseph Francis 1915- *WhoFI 94*
Krysinski, Linda Ann 1957- *WhoAm 94*
Krysl, Marilyn *DrAPF 93*
Krystal, Andrew Darrell 1960- *WhoScEn 94*
Krysztoforski, Joseph Theodore 1953- *WhoFI 94*
Kryter, Karl David 1914- *WhoAm 94*
Kryuchenkova, Nadezhda Aleksandrovna *WhoWomW 91*
Kryuchkov, Vasiliy Dmitrevich 1928- *IntWW 93*
Kryuchkov, Vladimir Aleksandrovich 1924- *IntWW 93, LngBDD*
Kryukov, Vladimir Nikolayevich 1902-1960 *NewGrDO*
Kryza, Elmer Gregory 1922- *WhoAm 94, WhoAmP 93*
Kryzhanivskyi, Volodymyr Petrovych 1940- *LngBDD*
Krzanowski, Joseph John, Jr. 1940- *WhoAm 94*
Krzysztofowicz, Roman 1947- *WhoAm 94*
Krzyzan, Judy Lynn 1951- *WhoFI 94*
Krzyzanowska, Olga 1929- *WhoWomW 91*
Krzyzanowski, Eve 1951- *WhoAm 94*
Krzyzanowski, Richard Lucien 1932- *WhoAm 94, WhoAmL 94, WhoFI 94*
Krzyzewski, Mike *WhoAm 94*
Ksansnak, James E. 1940- *WhoAm 94, WhoFI 94*
Kschesinska, Matilda 1872-1971 *IntDcB [port]*
Kshepakaran, Kuzhilethu Krishnan 1935- *WhoMW 93*
Kshesinskaya, Matilda 1872-1971 *IntDcB [port]*
Kshirsagar, Anant M. 1931- *WhoAsA 94*
Ksienski, Aharon Arthur 1924- *WhoAm 94*
Ku, David Nelson 1956- *WhoAsA 94*
Ku, Jentung *WhoScEn 94*
Ku, Mei-Chin Hsiao 1937- *WhoAsA 94*
Ku, Peter 1938- *WhoAsA 94*

Ku, Thomas Hsiu-Heng 1948- WhoScEn 94
Ku, Wen-Chi 1942- WhoAsA 94
Ku, William H. 1950- WhoAsA 94
Ku, Y. H. 1902- WhoAm 94, WhoScEn 94
Kuan, David A. 1940- WhoAsA 94
Kuan, Jenny W. 1944- WhoAsA 94
Kuan, Kah-Jin 1957- WhoAsA 94
Kuan, Pui 1945- WhoScEn 94, WhoWest 94
Kuan, Shia Shiong 1933- WhoAsA 94
Kuan, Wei Eihn 1933- WhoAsA 94, WhoMW 93
Kuang, Yang 1965- WhoWest 94
Kuang Fuzhao 1914- WhoPRCh 91 [port]
Kuang Ji 1929- WhoPRCh 91 [port]
Kuang Jianlian 1929- WhoPRCh 91
Kuang Peizi WhoPRCh 91
Kuang Yaming WhoPRCh 91 [port]
Kuang Yaming 1906- IntWW 93
Kuang Yemei WhoPRCh 91
Kuan Han-ch'ing IntDcT 2
Kuba, Galen Masashi 1951- WhoWest 94
Kuba, John Albert 1940- WhoFI 94, WhoMW 93
Kubach, David DrAPF 93
Kubacki, Krzysztof Stefan 1953- WhoScEn 94
Kubacki, Robert Walter 1947- WhoAmL 94
Kubale, Bernard Stephen 1928- WhoAm 94
Kubale, Marek Edward 1946- WhoScEn 94
Kubanek, George R. 1937- WhoScEn 94
Kubar, Abd al-Majid IntWW 93
Kubarev, Eduard Alekseevich 1939- LngBDD
Kubas, Gregory Joseph 1945- WhoScEn 94
Kubat, Milan 1927- IntWW 93
Kube, Daniel Cornelius 1934- WhoWest 94
Kube, Harold Deming 1910- WhoFI 94
Kubek, Anthony Christopher 1935- WhoAm 94
Kubek, Ralph A. 1955- WhoAm 94
Kubelik, Rafael 1914- IntWW 93, Who 94
Kubelik, Rafael (Jeronym) 1914- NewGrDO
Kube-McDowell, Michael P. 1954- EncSF 93
Kubesh, Eugene Robert 1946- WhoMW 93
Kubesh, Nell 1924- WhoAmP 93
Kubetz, Bernard J. 1948- WhoAmL 94
Kubiak, Dan 1938- WhoAmP 93
Kubiak, Jon Stanley 1935- WhoAmL 94
Kubiak, L. B. 1945- WhoAmP 93
Kubiak, Teresa 1937- NewGrDO
Kubicek, J. L. DrAPF 93
Kubicek, Robert Vincent 1935- WhoAm 94
Kubida, Judith Ann 1948- WhoAm 94
Kubida, William Joseph 1949- WhoAmL 94, WhoFI 94, WhoScEn 94, WhoWest 94
Kubiet, Leo Lawrence 1924- WhoAm 94
Kubik, Jack L. 1955- WhoAmP 93
Kubilius, Janos 1921- IntWW 93
Kubilus, John Vito 1947- WhoFI 94
Kubilus, Norbert John 1948- WhoAm 94, WhoFI 94
Kubin, Alfred EncSF 93
Kubin, Michael Ernest 1951- WhoAm 94
Kubin, Patrick Ludwig 1959- WhoWest 94
Kubin, Rudolf 1909-1973 NewGrDO
Kubina, Gene 1948- WhoAmP 93
Kubisen, Steven Joseph, Jr. 1952- WhoAm 94
Kubista, Theodore Paul 1937- WhoMW 93, WhoScEn 94
Kubistal, Patricia Bernice 1938- WhoFI 94, WhoMW 93
Kublai Khan 1215-1294 HisWorL [port]
Kubler, George Alexander 1912- WhoAmA 93
Kubler-Ross, Elisabeth 1926- WhoAm 94, WhoScEn 94, WrDr 94
Kubly, Herbert DrAPF 93
Kubly, Herbert 1915- WhoAm 94
Kubly, Herbert (Oswald) 1915- WrDr 94
Kubo, Edward Hachiro, Jr. 1953- WhoWest 94
Kubo, Gary Michael 1952- WhoMW 93
Kubo, Isoroku 1942- WhoScEn 94
Kubo, Jacqueline Lea Hanako 1966- WhoWest 94
Kubo, Ryogo 1920- IntWW 93
Kubo Sakae 1900-1958 IntDcT 2
Kubota, Carole Ann 1946- WhoAsA 94
Kubota, Gerald K. WhoAsA 94
Kubota, Joe WhoAm 94
Kubota, Kenneth R. 1952- WhoAsA 94
Kubota, Manae 1924- WhoWomW 91
Kubota, Mitsuru 1932- WhoAsA 94, WhoWest 94
Kubota, Shigeko 1937- WhoAmA 93

Kubrick, Stanley 1928- EncSF 93, IntMPA 94, IntWW 93, Who 94, WhoAm 94, WrDr 94
Kuby, Barbara Eleanor 1944- WhoMW 93
Kuby, Edward R. 1938- WhoIns 94
Kuby, Edward Raymond 1938- WhoAm 94
Kuby, Lolette Beth DrAPF 93
Kubzansky, Philip Eugene 1928- WhoAm 94
Kucan, Milan 1941- IntWW 93
Kucan, Zeljko 1934- WhoScEn 94
Kuc Bozenna, Marianna WhoWomW 91
Kucera, Daniel Jerome 1939- WhoAm 94
Kucera, Daniel William 1923- WhoAm 94, WhoMW 93
Kucera, Henry 1925- WhoAm 94
Kucera, Jaroslav 1929- IntDcF 2-4
Kucera, Keith Edward 1960- WhoMW 93
Kuchak, JoAnn Marie 1949- WhoAm 94
Kuchar, Kathleen Ann 1942- WhoAmA 93, WhoMW 93
Kucharski, Daniel Thomas 1952- WhoWest 94
Kucharski, John Michael 1936- WhoAm 94, WhoFI 94
Kucharski, Robert Joseph 1932- WhoAm 94
Kucharz, Lawrence DrAPF 93
Kuchel, Konrad G. 1937- WhoAmA 93
Kuchel, Roland Karl WhoAm 94
Kuchel, Thomas Henry 1910- WhoAmP 93
Kucheman, Clark Arthur 1931- WhoAm 94, WhoWest 94
Kuchera, Michael Louis 1955- WhoMW 93
Kuchera, Thomas John 1929- WhoAmP 93
Kuchibhotla, Sudhakar 1964- WhoScEn 94
Kuchinski, Steve 1928- WhoAmP 93
Kuchinsky, Dori Anne 1959- WhoAmL 94
Kuchler, Sandra Rose 1948- WhoWest 94
Kuchma, Leonid Danylovych 1938- LngBDD
Kuchma, Leonid Maximovich 1938- IntWW 93
Kuchner, Eugene Frederick 1945- WhoScEn 94
Kuchta, Gladys 1923- NewGrDO
Kuchta, John Albert 1955- WhoMW 93
Kuchta, Ronald A. 1935- WhoAmA 93
Kuchta, Ronald Andrew 1935- WhoAm 94
Kuchta, Steven Jerry 1961- WhoScEn 94
Kuchta, Thomas Walter 1942- WhoAm 94
Kucic, Joseph 1964- WhoAm 94, WhoFI 94, WhoScEn 94
Kucic, Michael J. 1961- WhoMW 93
Kucich, John Richard 1952- WhoMW 93
Kucij, Timothy Michael 1954- WhoAm 94
Kuck, David Jerome 1937- WhoAm 94, WhoScEn 94
Kuck, Marie Elizabeth Bukovsky 1910- WhoScEn 94
Kuckreja, Vipin 1947- WhoFI 94
Kuczka, Peter 1923- EncSF 93
Kuczkir, Mary 1933- ConAu 42NR, WrDr 94
Kuczkowski, Joseph Edward 1939- WhoMW 93
Kuczmarski, Erin J. WhoAmP 93
Kuczmarski, Susan Smith 1951- WhoMW 93
Kuczun, Ann-Marie WhoAmA 93
Kuczun, Ann-Marie 1935- WhoWest 94
Kuczwara, Thomas Paul 1951- WhoAmL 94
Kuczynski, Pedro-Pablo 1938- WhoFI 94
Kudaka, Geraldine DrAPF 93
Kuddes, James Lee 1956- WhoMW 93
Kudelka, James 1955- IntDcB
Kudenholdt, Sharon Sue 1942- WhoMW 93
Kuderer, Elton Alois 1929- WhoAmL 94
Kudian, Mischa WrDr 94
Kudish, David J. 1943- WhoAm 94
Kudla, James Matthew 1950- WhoWest 94
Kudlow, Lawrence A. 1947- IntWW 93
Kudlow, Lawrence Alan 1947- WhoAmP 93
Kudo, Eigo H. 1933- WhoAsA 94
Kudo, Emiko Iwashita 1923- WhoWest 94
Kudo, Franklin Ty 1950- WhoWest 94
Kudravetz, David Waller 1948- WhoAmL 94
Kudrick, Catherine Alice 1928- WhoAmP 93, WhoMW 93
Kudrle, Judy Sanberg 1951- WhoAmP 93
Kudrle, Robert Thomas 1942- WhoAm 94
Kudrna, Frank Louis, Jr. 1943- WhoScEn 94
Kudrnac, Kristian Ivoj 1949- WhoAm 94
Kudryashov, Oleg 1932- IntWW 93
Kudryavtsev, Gennady Georgievich 1941- LngBDD
Kudryavtsev, Vladimir Nikolaevich 1923- IntWW 93

Kudryk, Oleg 1912- WhoAm 94
Kudsi, Nazem el 1906- IntWW 93
Kuebeler, Glenn Charles 1935- WhoFI 94, WhoScEn 94
Kuebler, David Wayne 1947- WhoFI 94
Kuebrich, David 1943- WrDr 94
Kuechle, John Merrill 1951- WhoAm 94
Kuechle, Richard Theodore 1930- WhoAm 94
Kuehl, Hans Henry 1933- WhoAm 94
Kuehl, LeRoy Robert 1931- WhoAm 94
Kuehler, Jack Dwyer 1932- WhoAm 94, WhoFI 94, WhoScEn 94
Kuehn, David Laurance 1940- WhoAm 94
Kuehn, Edmund Karl 1916- WhoAm 94, WhoAmA 93
Kuehn, Frances 1943- WhoAmA 93
Kuehn, Gary 1939- WhoAmA 93
Kuehn, George E. 1946- WhoAm 94, WhoAmL 94, WhoFI 94
Kuehn, Glenn Dean 1942- WhoWest 94
Kuehn, James Marshall 1926- WhoAm 94
Kuehn, Klaus Karl Albert 1938- WhoWest 94
Kuehn, Mariellen Laucht 1939- WhoMW 93
Kuehn, Patricia Susan 1945- WhoAmP 93
Kuehn, Richard Arthur 1939- WhoFI 94
Kuehn, Ronald L., Jr. 1935- WhoAm 94
Kuehne, Benedict P. 1954- WhoAmL 94
Kuehne, Edna d1922 WhoHol 92
Kuehnelt-Leddihn, Erik 1909- WrDr 94
Kuehneman, Adrienne Weissman WhoAmL 94
Kuehnert, Deborah Anne 1949- WhoFI 94, WhoScEn 94
Kuehnert, Robert Gerhardt 1916- WhoWest 94
Kuehnl, Claudia Ann 1948- WhoAmA 93
Kuehnle, Christopher Charles 1944- WhoFI 94
Kuehnle, Kenton Lee 1945- WhoAm 94, WhoAmL 94, WhoFI 94, WhoMW 93
Kuekelmann, Gertrud d1979 WhoHol 92
Kuekes, Edward D. 1901-1987 WhoAmA 93N
Kuelbs, John Thomas 1942- WhoAm 94, WhoAmL 94
Kueller, Julie Ann Toohill 1967- WhoMW 93
Kuemmel, Jospeh Kenneth 1945- WhoMW 93
Kuemmerlein, Janet 1932- WhoAmA 93
Kuempel, Edmund 1942- WhoAmP 93
Kuen, Paul 1910- NewGrDO
Kuendig, William Norman, II 1945- WhoMW 93
Kuenheim, Eberhard von 1928- IntWW 93
Kuenne, Robert Eugene 1924- WrDr 94
Kuenneke, Evelyn WhoHol 92
Kuennen, Thomas Gerard 1953- WhoAm 94
Kuenssberg, Ekkehard von 1913- Who 94
Kuenssberg, Nicholas Christopher Dwelly 1942- Who 94
Kuenster, John Joseph 1924- WhoAm 94
Kuenstler, Frank DrAPF 93
Kueny, Gregory Alan 1967- WhoMW 93
Kuenzel, Robert Varde 1949- WhoAmL 94
Kuenzel, Steven Paul 1952- WhoAmL 94
Kuenzel, Wayne John 1942- WhoScEn 94
Kuenzler, Edward Julian 1929- WhoAm 94, WhoScEn 94
Kuenzli, Gwen Lee 1936- WhoMW 93
Kuerti, Anton Emil 1938- WhoAm 94
Kues, Irvin William 1936- WhoFI 94
Kuesel, Thomas Robert 1926- WhoAm 94, WhoScEn 94
Kuester, Kristen 1953- WhoWest 94
Kuether, John Frederick 1943- WhoAmL 94
Kufeld, William Manuel 1922- WhoAm 94
Kufeldt, James 1938- WhoAm 94, WhoFI 94
Kuffel, Edmund 1924- WhoAm 94
Kufner, Sharon K. 1956- WhoMW 93
Kugblenu, George Ofoe WhoBlA 94
Kugelman, Irwin Jay 1937- WhoScEn 94
Kugler, Lawrence Dean 1941- WhoAm 94
Kuglitsch, Maureen Rose 1944- WhoMW 93
Kuh, Ernest Shiu-Jen 1928- WhoAm 94, WhoAsA 94, WhoWest 94
Kuh, Howard 1899- WhoAmA 93
Kuh, Katharine 1904- WhoAmA 93
Kuh, Richard H 1921- WrDr 94
Kuh, Richard Henry 1921- WhoAm 94, WhoAmL 94
Kuhajek, Eugene James 1934- WhoAm 94
Kuhar, June Carolynn 1935- WhoFI 94
Kuharic, Franjo 1919- IntWW 93
Kuhel, James Joseph 1934- WhoMW 93
Kuhi, Leonard Vello 1936- WhoAm 94, WhoScEn 94
Kuhl, David Edmund 1929- WhoAm 94, WhoScEn 94

Kuhl, Frederick William 1923- WhoWest 94
Kuhl, Henry Young 1930- WhoAmP 93
Kuhl, John H. 1949- WhoAmL 94
Kuhl, John R., Jr. 1943- WhoAmP 93
Kuhl, Margaret Helen Clayton WhoAm 94, WhoFI 94, WhoMW 93
Kuhl, Paul Beach 1935- WhoAm 94, WhoAmL 94
Kuhl, Ronald Webster 1938- WhoWest 94
Kuhl, Steven Allen 1951- WhoMW 93
Kuhl, Wayne Elliott 1947- WhoWest 94
Kuhlau, Friedrich (Daniel Rudolph) 1786-1832 NewGrDO
Kuhlenschmidt, Richard Edward 1951- WhoAmA 93
Kuhler, Deborah Gail 1952- WhoAmP 93
Kuhler, Otto August 1894-1977 WhoAmA 93N
Kuhlke, William Charles 1930- WhoScEn 94
Kuhlken, Ken DrAPF 93
Kuhlman, Kathryn 1907-1976 DcAmReB 2
Kuhlman, Kimberly Ann 1954- WhoMW 93
Kuhlman, Paul Wayne 1940- WhoAmL 94
Kuhlman, Richard Sherwin 1943- WhoAmL 94
Kuhlman, Robert E. 1932- WhoScEn 94
Kuhlman, Susan WhoMW 93
Kuhlman, Walter Egel 1918- WhoAm 94, WhoAmA 93, WhoWest 94
Kuhlmann, Fred L. 1916- WhoAm 94
Kuhlmann, Fred Mark 1948- WhoAmL 94, WhoFI 94
Kuhlmann, Kathleen 1950- NewGrDO
Kuhlmann, Kathleen Mary 1950- IntWW 93
Kuhlmann-Wilsdorf, Doris 1922- WhoAm 94
Kuhlmey, Walter Trowbridge 1918- WhoAm 94
Kuhlthau, John Suydam 1937- WhoAmL 94
Kuhn, Albert Joseph 1926- WhoAm 94
Kuhn, Audrey Grendahl 1929- WhoAmA 93
Kuhn, Bob 1920- WhoAmA 93
Kuhn, Charles Clayton 1942- WhoWest 94
Kuhn, Craig Cameron 1962- WhoWest 94
Kuhn, David Alan 1929- WhoAm 94
Kuhn, Donald Marshall 1922- WhoFI 94, WhoWest 94
Kuhn, Edgar Dean 1946- WhoMW 93
Kuhn, Evelyn d1976 WhoHol 92
Kuhn, Frank Stuart 1928- WhoFI 94, WhoWest 94
Kuhn, Gustav 1946- IntWW 93
Kuhn, Gustav 1947- NewGrDO
Kuhn, Heinrich Gerhard 1904 IntWW 93, Who 94
Kuhn, Howard Arthur 1940- WhoAm 94
Kuhn, Irvin Nelson 1928- WhoAm 94
Kuhn, James Paul 1937- WhoAm 94, WhoFI 94
Kuhn, Josephine M. Keller 1937- WhoMW 93
Kuhn, Jurgen 1929- IntWW 93
Kuhn, Karl Heinz 1919- Who 94
Kuhn, Kathleen Jo 1947- WhoFI 94, WhoMW 93
Kuhn, Leigh Ann 1967- WhoScEn 94
Kuhn, Lesley DrAPF 93
Kuhn, Margaret 1905- WhoAm 94
Kuhn, Mary Croughan 1914- WhoWest 94
Kuhn, Marylou 1923- WhoAmA 93
Kuhn, Matthew 1936- WhoAm 94, WhoScEn 94
Kuhn, Michael WhoAm 94
Kuhn, Paul Hubert, Jr. 1943- WhoAm 94
Kuhn, Peter Mouat 1920- WhoAm 94
Kuhn, Richard 1900-1967 WorScD
Kuhn, Robert Edward 1949- WhoAmP 93
Kuhn, Robert Herman 1946- WhoFI 94, WhoMW 93, WhoScEn 94
Kuhn, Ryan Anthony 1947- WhoMW 93
Kuhn, Sherman McAllister 1907-1991 WhAm 10
Kuhn, Thomas G. 1935- IntMPA 94
Kuhn, Thomas R. 1946- WhoAm 94
Kuhn, Thomas S. 1922- IntWW 93, WrDr 94
Kuhn, Walt 1880-1949 WhoAmA 93N
Kuhn, Willis E., II 1948- WhoAm 94
Kuhn, Willis Evan, II 1948- WhoAmL 94
Kuhnau, Johann 1660-1722 NewGrDO
Kuhne, Friedrich d1958 WhoHol 92
Kuhne, Gunther Albert Hermann 1939- IntWW 93
Kuhner, Herbert DrAPF 93
Kuhner, John d1984 WhoHol 92
Kuhnmuench, John Richard, Jr. 1944- WhoMW 93
Kuhns, Craig Shaffer 1928- WhoWest 94

Kuhns, David George 1956- *WhoWest 94*
Kuhns, James Howard 1953- *WhoScEn 94*
Kuhns, William *DrAPF 93*
Kuhns, William George 1922- *WhoAm 94*
Kuhn-Shepard, Rita d1980 *WhoHol 92*
Kuhr, James R. *WhoIns 94*
Kuhr, Ronald John 1939- *WhoScEn 94*
Kuhrau, Edward W. 1935- *WhoAm 94, WhoAmL 94, WhoWest 94*
Kuhrmeyer, Carl Albert 1928- *WhoAm 94*
Kuhrt, Gordon Wilfred 1941- *Who 94*
Kuhse, Hanne-Lore 1925- *NewGrDO*
Kuiper, Douglas Scott 1960- *WhoFI 94*
Kuiperi, Hans Cornelis 1939- *WhoScEn 94*
Kuipers, Carl Jacob 1905- *WhoAmP 93*
Kuipers, J. D. 1918- *IntWW 93*
Kuipers, John Melles 1918- *Who 94*
Kuipers, Judith L. *WhoMW 93*
Kuisle, William Edward 1958- *WhoMW 93*
Kuitert, John Herman 1908- *WhoAmP 93*
Kuivila, Henry Gabriel 1917- *WhoAm 94*
Kujala, Walfrid Eugene 1925- *WhoAm 94*
Kujawa, Jerome P. *WhoAmL 94*
Kujawa, Walter Andrew, II 1955- *WhoWest 94*
Kujawa, Warren Paul 1938- *WhoAmL 94*
Kujundzic, Zeljko D. 1920- *WhoAmA 93*
Kuka, King D. *DrAPF 93*
Kukan, Eduard 1939- *IntWW 93*
Kukharets, Volodymyr Oleksiiovych 1938- *LngBDD*
Kukkonen, Carl Allan 1945- *WhoWest 94*
Kukla, Richard David 1953- *WhoMW 93*
Kukla, Robert John 1932- *WhoAm 94*
Kukla, Walter Joseph 1933- *WhoFI 94*
Kuklin, Anthony Bennett 1929- *WhoAm 94, WhoAmL 94*
Kuklin, Jeffrey Peter 1935- *WhoAmL 94, WhoFI 94, WhoWest 94*
Kuklin, Susan 1941- *WrDr 94*
Kukovich, Allen G. 1947- *WhoAmP 93*
Kukuk, Alvin H. 1937- *WhoAmP 93*
Kukulinsky, Nancy Elaine 1950- *WhoMW 93*
Kukull, Walter Anthony 1945- *WhoScEn 94*
Kukushkin, Vladimir Ivanovich 1931- *WhoScEn 94*
Kula, Judith Christina 1958- *WhoFI 94*
Kulak, Dennis Michael 1948- *WhoFI 94*
Kulakov, Mikhail Petrovich 1927- *LngBDD*
Kulakowski, Lois Linder 1939- *WhoWest 94*
Kulander, Kenneth Charles 1943- *WhoScEn 94*
Kulas, Myron J. 1942- *WhoAmP 93*
Kulasiri, Gamalathge Don 1957- *WhoScEn 94*
Kulbin, Vello 1937- *WhoFI 94*
Kulcsar, Kalman 1928- *IntWW 93*
Kulesh, William Adam 1929- *WhoFI 94*
Kulesha, Kevin John 1956- *WhoFI 94*
Kulesher, Robert Roy 1952- *WhoAm 94*
Kulesz, David Terrell 1955- *WhoAmL 94*
KuLesza, Frank William 1920- *WhoScEn 94*
Kulewicz, John Joseph 1954- *WhoAmL 94*
Kulhavy, Raymond William 1940- *WhoWest 94*
Kulich, James 1957- *WhoMW 93*
Kulich, Roman Theodore 1953- *WhoMW 93*
Kulick, Richard John 1949- *WhoFI 94, WhoScEn 94*
Kulicke, Charles Scott 1949- *WhoAm 94*
Kulicke, Robert M. 1924- *WhoAmA 93*
Kulidzhanov, Lev Aleksandrovich 1924- *IntWW 93*
Kuliev, Avdy 1936- *IntWW 93, LngBDD*
Kulik, Boles 1942- *WrDr 94*
Kulik, Joseph Michael 1957- *WhoAmL 94*
Kulik, Rosalyn Franta 1951- *WhoAm 94*
Kulik, Seymour 1923- *IntMPA 94*
Kulikov, Viktor Georgiyevich 1921- *IntWW 93*
Kulikowski, Casimir A. 1944- *WhoScEn 94*
Kulikowski, M. Karl *DrAPF 93*
Kulinsky, Lois 1946- *WhoAmL 94*
Kuljeric, Igor 1938- *NewGrDO*
Kulka, Konstanty Andrzej 1947- *IntWW 93*
Kulka, Richard A. 1945- *WrDr 94*
Kulkarni, Anand K. 1946- *WhoAsA 94*
Kulkarni, Arun Digambar 1947- *WhoAsA 94*
Kulkarni, Arun P. 1941- *WhoAsA 94*
Kulkarni, Dilip 1950- *WhoAsA 94*
Kulkarni, Gopal S. 1927- *WhoAsA 94*
Kulkarni, Kishore G. 1953- *WhoAsA 94*
Kulkarni, Krishnaji Hanamant 1948- *WhoAsA 94*
Kulkarni, Ravi S. 1942- *WhoAsA 94*
Kulkarni, Ravi Shripad 1942- *WhoScEn 94*
Kulkarni, Sanjeev Ramesh 1963- *WhoScEn 94*
Kulkarni, Shrinivas R. *WhoScEn 94*
Kulkarni, Uday Ravindra 1954- *WhoAsA 94*
Kulkosky, Paul Joseph 1949- *WhoWest 94*
Kulky, Henry d1965 *WhoHol 92*
Kull, Lorenz A. 1937- *WhoFI 94*
Kull, William Franklin 1956- *WhoWest 94*
Kullas, Albert John 1917- *WhoAm 94*
Kullberg, Duane Reuben 1932- *WhoAm 94*
Kullberg, Gary Walter 1941- *WhoAm 94*
Kullberg, John Francis 1939- *WhoAm 94*
Kullberg, Rolf 1930- *IntWW 93*
Kulle, Jarl 1927- *WhoHol 92*
Kullenberg, Roger Dale 1930- *WhoAm 94*
Kuller, Henry M. 1946- *WhoAmL 94*
Kuller, Jonathan Mark 1951- *WhoAmL 94*
Kullers, John d1985 *WhoHol 92*
Kullerud, Gunnar 1921-1989 *WhAm 10*
Kullgren, Thomas Edward 1941- *WhoMW 93*
Kullman, Charles d1983 *WhoHol 92*
Kullman, Charles 1903-1983 *NewGrDO*
Kullmann Five, Kaci 1951- *WhoWomW 91*
Kulmala, Elmer Pete 1951- *WhoAmL 94*
Kul'man, Elisaveta Borisovna 1808-1825 *BlmGWL [port]*
Kulok, William Allan 1940- *WhoFI 94*
Kulongoski, Theodore R. 1940- *WhoAm 94, WhoAmL 94, WhoWest 94*
Kulongoski, Theodore Ralph 1940- *WhoAmP 93*
Kulp, J. Robert 1935- *WhoFI 94*
Kulp, Nancy d1991 *WhoHol 92*
Kulp, Nancy Jane 1921-1991 *WhAm 10*
Kulp, Philip Masterton 1929- *WhoAm 94*
Kulpa, John Edward 1929- *WhoAm 94*
Kulper, Perry Dean 1953- *WhoAm 94*
Kulseth, John Roger, Jr. 1963- *WhoAmL 94*
Kulsharipov, Marat Makhmutovich 1941- *LngBDD*
Kulski, Julian Eugeniusz 1929- *WhoAm 94*
Kulski, Wladyslaw Wszebor 1903-1989 *WhAm 10*
Kultermann, Udo 1927- *WhoAm 94, WhoAmA 93, WrDr 94*
Kulukundis, Eddie 1932- *Who 94*
Kuluris, Bradley Eugene 1957- *WhoWest 94*
Kuluva, Will d1990 *WhoHol 92*
Kulwicki, Alan *WhoAm 94*
Kulwicki, Alan d1993 *NewYTBS 93 [port]*
Kulyk Keefer, Janice 1952- *BlmGWL*
Kulzick, Kenneth Edmund 1927- *WhoAm 94*
Kumagai, James 1934- *WhoAmP 93*
Kumagai, Lynn Yasuko 1964- *WhoWest 94*
Kumagai, Takenobu 1937- *WhoFI 94*
Kumagai, Yoshifumi 1915- *IntWW 93*
Kumai, Motoi 1920- *WhoAsA 94*
Kumanyika, Makaza d1993 *NewYTBS 93 [port]*
Kumanyika, Shiriki K. 1945- *WhoBlA 94*
Kumar, Alok 1954- *ConAu 142*
Kumar, Anil 1952- *WhoScEn 94, WhoWest 94*
Kumar, Arvind 1956- *WhoAsA 94*
Kumar, Ashir 1945- *WhoAsA 94*
Kumar, Ashok 1949- *WhoAsA 94*
Kumar, Ashok 1956- *Who 94*
Kumar, Atul 1962- *WhoAsA 94*
Kumar, Bhagavatula Vijaya 1953- *WhoScEn 94*
Kumar, Binod 1946- *WhoScEn 94*
Kumar, Birendra 1954- *WhoFI 94*
Kumar, Devendra 1944- *WhoAsA 94*
Kumar, Jatinder 1940- *WhoAsA 94*
Kumar, Jothi V. *WhoAsA 94*
Kumar, Kamalesh 1957- *WhoAsA 94*
Kumar, Kaplesh 1947- *WhoFI 94*
Kumar, Kishore d1987 *WhoHol 92*
Kumar, Krishan 1944- *WhoFI 94*
Kumar, (Jagdish) Krishan 1942- *WrDr 94*
Kumar, Krishna 1936- *WhoScEn 94*
Kumar, Kusum 1949- *WhoAsA 94*
Kumar, Kusum Verma 1930- *WhoAsA 94*
Kumar, Manish 1963- *WhoScEn 94*
Kumar, Meera *WhoAsA 94*
Kumar, Mythili 1954- *WhoAsA 94*
Kumar, Narinder M. *WhoAsA 94*
Kumar, Panganamala Ramana 1952- *WhoAm 94, WhoAsA 94*
Kumar, Prasanna K. 1937- *WhoAsA 94*
Kumar, Prem 1945- *WhoAsA 94*
Kumar, Raj 1932- *WhoAsA 94*
Kumar, Rajendra 1948- *WhoScEn 94, WhoWest 94*
Kumar, Ram Sakthi 1959- *WhoAsA 94*
Kumar, Ramesh 1949- *WhoAsA 94*
Kumar, Ranganathan 1954- *WhoAsA 94*
Kumar, Romesh 1944- *WhoAm 94, WhoAsA 94*
Kumar, Sanjay 1961- *WhoScEn 94*
Kumar, Sanjeev d1985 *WhoHol 92*
Kumar, Saran Kandakuri 1953- *WhoAsA 94*
Kumar, Satyendra 1954- *WhoAsA 94*
Kumar, Shiv K(umar) 1921- *WrDr 94*
Kumar, Subodh 1953- *WhoFI 94*
Kumar, Sudhir 1933- *WhoAsA 94*
Kumar, Sudhir 1942- *WhoMW 93*
Kumar, Surendra Mohan 1956- *WhoAsA 94*
Kumar, Suresh A. 1953- *WhoAsA 94*
Kumar, Surinder 1944- *WhoFI 94, WhoScEn 94*
Kumar, Surinder 1945- *WhoAm 94*
Kumar, Sushil 1939- *WhoAsA 94*
Kumar, Udaya 1960- *ConAu 142*
Kumar, V. 1957- *WhoAsA 94*
Kumar, Verinder 1932- *WhoFI 94*
Kumar, Vijay A. 1940- *WhoAsA 94*
Kumar, Vipin 1956- *WhoAsA 94*
Kumaran, A. Krishna 1932- *WhoAsA 94*
Kumaranatunga, Chandrika B. *WhoWomW 91*
Kumari, Meena d1972 *WhoHol 92*
Kumaroo, K. 1931- *WhoAsA 94*
Kumata, Gerald Hiroshi 1943- *WhoAsA 94*
Kumbel *ConWorW 93*
Kumble, Steven Jay 1933- *WhoAm 94*
Kumbula, Tendayi Sengerwe 1947- *WhoBlA 94*
Kumbula, Tendayi Sengerwe John 1947- *WhoMW 93*
Kume, Tadashi 1932- *IntWW 93*
Kume, Yutaka 1921- *IntWW 93, Who 94*
Kumel, Harry 1940- *HorFD*
Kumin, Maxine 1925- *BlmGWL, WrDr 94*
Kumin, Maxine W. *DrAPF 93*
Kumin, Maxine Winokur 1925- *WhoAm 94*
Kumler, Kipton (Cornelius) 1940- *WhoAmA 93*
Kumler, Kipton Cornelius 1940- *WhoAm 94*
Kumler, Rose Marie 1935- *WhoWest 94*
Kumm, Doris 1929- *WhoAmP 93*
Kumm, Marguerite Elizabeth d1992 *WhoAmA 93N*
Kumm, William Howard 1931- *WhoFI 94*
Kummel, Eugene H. 1923- *WhoAm 94*
Kummel, Patricia E. 1952- *WhoAmL 94*
Kummer, Daniel William *WhoAm 94*
Kummer, Glenn F. 1933- *WhoAm 94, WhoFI 94, WhoWest 94*
Kummer, Richard Edward, Jr. 1948- *WhoAmL 94*
Kummer, Wolfgang 1935- *IntWW 93*
Kummerle, Herman Frederick 1936- *WhoMW 93*
Kummert, Richard Osborne 1932- *WhoAm 94*
Kummings, Donald D. *DrAPF 93*
Kummler, Ralph H. 1940- *WhoAm 94*
Kumorowski, Victoria McKay 1947- *WhoAmL 94*
Kump, Ernest Joseph 1911- *IntWW 93, WhoAm 94*
Kump, Kary Ronald 1952- *WhoAmL 94*
Kump, Michael Joseph 1952- *WhoAmL 94*
Kump, Michael Roy 1953- *WhoWest 94*
Kumpe, David Allen 1941- *WhoWest 94*
Kun, Joyce Anne 1946- *WhoMW 93*
Kun, Kenneth A. 1930- *WhoAm 94*
Kun, Magda d1945 *WhoHol 92*
Kun, Michael (Stuart) 1962- *WrDr 94*
Kun, Neila 1951- *WhoAmA 93*
Kun, Zsuzsa 1934- *IntDcB*
Kunad, Rainer 1936- *NewGrDO*
Kunadze, Georgy Fridrikhovich 1948- *IntWW 93*
Kunasek, Carl J. *WhoAmP 93*
Kunath, Bryan Eric 1966- *WhoMW 93*
Kunath, Hellmuth d1961 *WhoHol 92*
Kunayev, Dinmukhamed A. d1993 *NewYTBS 93 [port]*
Kunc, Joseph Anthony 1943- *WhoAm 94, WhoScEn 94*
Kunc, Karen 1952- *WhoAmA 93*
Kunc, Zinka *NewGrDO*
Kuncewicz, Eileen *Who 94*
Kunda, Gideon 1952- *ConAu 141*
Kunda, Ronald James 1963- *WhoMW 93*
Kundahl, George Gustavus 1940- *WhoAm 94, WhoAmP 93*
Kunde, Anne d1960 *WhoHol 92*
Kundel, Harold Louis 1933- *WhoAm 94, WhoScEn 94*
Kundera, Milan 1929- *ConWorW 93, IntDcT 2, IntWW 93, RfGShF, WhoAm 94*
Kundert, Alice E. 1920- *WhoAm 94, WhoAmP 93, WhoMW 93*
Kundert, Gust 1913- *WhoAmP 93*
Kundig, Ernst Peter 1946- *WhoScEn 94*
Kundla, John 1916- *BasBi*
Kundtz, John Andrew 1933- *WhoAm 94*
Kundu, Bejoy B. 1938- *WhoAsA 94*
Kundu, Debabrata 1957- *WhoScEn 94*
Kundu, Mukul Ranjan 1930- *WhoAsA 94*
Kundur, Prabha Shankar 1939- *WhoAm 94*
Kuneralp, Zeki 1914- *Who 94*
Kunert, Gunter 1929- *ConWorW 93, IntWW 93*
Kunes, Ken R. 1932- *WhoBlA 94*
Kunes, Steven Marshall 1951- *WhoMW 93*
Kunetka, James *EncSF 93*
Kung, Alice How Kuen 1956- *WhoAsA 94*
Kung, Frank F. C. *WhoAsA 94*
Kung, H. T. 1945- *WhoAsA 94, WhoScEn 94*
Kung, Hans 1928- *IntWW 93, Who 94*
Kung, Harold H. 1949- *WhoAsA 94*
Kung, Jeffrey 1939- *WhoAsA 94*
Kung, Lila Marie 1954- *WhoWest 94*
Kung, Ling-Yang 1944- *WhoScEn 94*
Kung, Pang-Jen 1959- *WhoScEn 94, WhoWest 94*
Kung, Patrick Chung-Shu 1947- *WhoAm 94, WhoAsA 94*
Kung, Shain-dow 1934- *WhoAsA 94*
Kung, Shain-dow 1935- *WhoScEn 94*
Kung, Steven Christopher 1955- *WhoMW 93*
Kunhardt, Edith 1937- *WrDr 94*
Kunhardt, Erich Enrique 1949- *WhoAm 94, WhoScEn 94*
Kunicki, Jan Ireneusz 1950- *WhoScEn 94*
Kunicki, Walter J. 1958- *WhoAm 94, WhoAmP 93, WhoMW 93*
Kuniczak, W(ieslaw) S(tanislaw) 1930- *ConAu 42NR*
Kunieda, Hironobu 1948- *WhoScEn 94*
Kuniji, Miyazaki 1930- *IntWW 93*
Kunimura, Tony T. 1923- *WhoAmP 93*
Kunin, Devra L. *DrAPF 93*
Kunin, Madeleine May 1933- *IntWW 93, NewYTBS 93 [port], WhoAm 94, WhoAmP 93, WhoWomW 91*
Kunisch, Robert Dietrich 1941- *WhoAm 94, WhoFI 94*
Kunitz, Stanley *DrAPF 93*
Kunitz, Stanley (Jasspon) 1905- *WrDr 94*
Kunitz, Stanley J. 1905- *IntWW 93*
Kunitz, Stanley Jasspon 1905- *WhoAm 94*
Kunitzsch, Paul Horst Robert 1930- *IntWW 93*
Kuniyoshi, Yasuo 1893-1953 *WhoAmA 93N*
Kunjufu, Jawanza 1953- *WhoBlA 94, WhoMW 93*
Kunjukunju, Pappy 1939- *WhoFI 94*
Kunkee, Ralph Edward 1927- *WhoAm 94, WhoWest 94*
Kunkel, Barbara 1945- *WhoAm 94*
Kunkel, David Nelson 1943- *WhoAm 94*
Kunkel, George d1937 *WhoHol 92*
Kunkel, Louis Martens 1949- *WhoAm 94, WhoScEn 94*
Kunkel, Richard *WhoAmP 93*
Kunkel, Richard Lester 1944- *WhoWest 94*
Kunkel, Russell Jeffrey 1942- *WhoAm 94*
Kunkel, Scott William 1945- *WhoWest 94*
Kunkle, Donald Edward 1928- *WhoScEn 94*
Kunkle, Sandra Lee 1960- *WhoAm 94*
Kunkle, William Joseph, Jr. 1941- *WhoAmL 94*
Kunkler, Arnold William 1921- *WhoAm 94*
Kunneke, Eduard 1885-1953 *NewGrDO*
Kuno, H. John 1938- *WhoAm 94*
Kunos, George 1942- *WhoAm 94*
Kunov, Hans 1938- *WhoAm 94, WhoScEn 94*
Kunsch, Louis 1937- *WhoAmA 93*
Kunst, Jennifer Lynne 1966- *WhoWest 94*
Kunstler, David B. 1934- *WhoFI 94*
Kunstler, Morton 1931- *WhoAmA 93*
Kunstler, William M. 1919- *WrDr 94*
Kunstler, William Moses *NewYTBS 93 [port]*
Kunstler, William Moses 1919- *WhoAm 94, WhoAmL 94*
Kuntsch, Margaretha Susanna von 1651-1716 *BlmGWL*
Kuntz, Charles Powers 1944- *WhoAmL 94*
Kuntz, Dieter Kurt 1951- *WhoMW 93*
Kuntz, Hal Goggan 1937- *WhoFI 94, WhoScEn 94*
Kuntz, Joel Dubois 1946- *WhoAm 94, WhoAmL 94*
Kuntz, John Kenneth 1934- *WrDr 94*
Kuntz, Lee Allan 1943- *WhoAm 94, WhoAmL 94, WhoFI 94*
Kuntz, Lila Elaine 1931- *WhoMW 93*
Kuntz, Louis Edward 1949- *WhoAm 94*
Kuntz, Marion Lucile Leathers 1924- *WhoAm 94*
Kuntz, Mary M. Kohls 1928- *WhoMW 93*
Kuntz, Paul Grimley 1915- *WhoAm 94*
Kuntz, Robert Roy 1937- *WhoMW 93*

Kusch, P(olykarp) 1911-1993 *CurBio 93N*
Kusch, Polykarp d1993 *IntWW 93N, Who 94N*
Kusch, Polykarp 1911-1993 *NewYTBS 93 [port]*
Kusche, Benno 1916- *NewGrDO*
Kuse, James Russell 1930- *WhoAm 94, WhoFI 94*
Kusek, Carol Joan 1955- *WhoMW 93*
Kusheloff, David Leon 1917- *WhoAm 94*
Kushen, Allan Stanford 1929- *WhoAm 94*
Kushi, Francis Xavier 1938- *WhoAm 94*
Kushida, Toshimoto 1920- *WhoAsA 94*
Kushla, John Dennis 1955- *WhoWest 94*
Kushlan, James A. 1947- *ConAu 142, WhoScEn 94*
Kushlan, Samuel Daniel 1912- *WhoAm 94*
Kushman, Frank Knight 1958- *WhoFI 94*
Kushner, Aleksandr (Semenovich) 1936- *ConWorW 93*
Kushner, Aleksandr Semyonovich 1936- *IntWW 93*
Kushner, Bill *DrAPF 93*
Kushner, Brian Harris 1951- *WhoScEn 94*
Kushner, Carol Scarvalone *DrAPF 93*
Kushner, David Zakeri 1935- *WhoAm 94*
Kushner, Donn 1927- *WrDr 94*
Kushner, Dorothy Browdy *WhoAmA 93*
Kushner, Eva 1929- *WhoAm 94*
Kushner, Harold Joseph 1933- *WhoAm 94*
Kushner, Harold S. 1935- *WrDr 94*
Kushner, Harvey David 1930- *WhoAm 94*
Kushner, James A(lan) 1945- *WrDr 94*
Kushner, Jeffrey L. 1948- *WhoAm 94*
Kushner, Lawrence Maurice 1924- *WhoAm 94*
Kushner, Linda 1939- *WhoWomW 91*
Kushner, Linda J. 1939- *WhoAmP 93*
Kushner, Lindsey Joy 1952- *Who 94*
Kushner, Malcolm 1952- *WrDr 94*
Kushner, Michael James 1951- *WhoScEn 94*
Kushner, Robert Arnold 1935- *WhoAmL 94*
Kushner, Robert Ellis 1949- *IntWW 93, WhoAm 94, WhoAmA 93*
Kushner, Rose 1929-1990 *WhAm 10*
Kushner, Tony *WhoAm 94*
Kushner, Tony 1956- *ConDr 93, GayLL*
Kushner, Tony 1957?- *ConLC 81 [port]*
Kushuwe, Jack fl. 19th cent.-20th cent. *EncNAR*
Kusiak, Andrew 1949- *WhoFI 94*
Kusin, Vladimir V 1929- *WrDr 94*
Kuska, John Joseph, Jr. 1953- *WhoFI 94*
Kuske, Edward Alan 1940- *WhoAm 94*
Kuskin, Karla 1932- *WhoAm 94, WrDr 94*
Kuskin, Karla (Seidman) 1932- *ConAu 41NR*
Kuskin, Lawrence d1993 *NewYTBS 93*
Kusko, Bruce Harris 1953- *WhoWest 94*
Kusler, Jim 1947- *WhoAmP 93*
Kusler, Mary-Margaret 1945- *WhoMW 93*
Kusma, Kyllikki 1943- *WhoAmL 94*
Kusmiak, Eugene 1959- *WhoWest 94*
Kusnerz, Peggy Ann F. 1947- *WhoAmA 93*
Kusnetz, Hyman 1939- *WhoFI 94*
Kusniewicz, Andrzej 1904- *IntWW 93*
Kusnitz, Adele L. *WhoAmP 93*
Kuspit, Donald Burton 1935- *WhoAm 94, WhoAmA 93*
Kuss, Henry John, Jr. 1922-1990 *WhAm 10*
Kuss, Rene 1913- *IntWW 93*
Kuss, Richard L. 1923- *WhoAm 94*
Kuss, Susan Lynn 1950- *WhoAmL 94*
Kussel, William Ferdinand, Jr. 1957- *WhoAmL 94*
Kusser, Johann Sigismund 1660?-1727 *NewGrDO*
Kusserow, Richard Phillip 1940- *WhoAm 94, WhoAmP 93*
Kust, Leonard Eugene 1917-1989 *WhAm 10*
Kust, Roger Nayland 1935- *WhoScEn 94*
Kuster, Robert Kenneth 1932- *WhoWest 94*
Kuster, Theodore R. 1943- *WhoAmP 93*
Kustin, Kenneth 1934- *WhoAm 94, WhoScEn 94*
Kustow, Michael (David) 1929- *WrDr 94*
Kustow, Michael David 1939- *Who 94*
Kustra, Bob 1943- *WhoAmP 93*
Kustra, Robert W. 1943- *WhoMW 93*
Kusumaatmadja, Mochtar 1929- *IntWW 93*
Kusumi, Akihiro 1952- *WhoMW 93, WhoScEn 94*
Kusumoto, Sadahei 1928- *WhoAsA 94*
Kuswa, Glenn Wesley 1940- *WhoWest 94*
Kusy, Robert Peter 1947- *WhoAm 94*
Kusz, Natalie 1962- *ConAu 141*
Kusz, Natalie Leigh 1962- *WhoMW 93*
Kuta, Jeffrey 1947- *WhoAm 94, WhoAmL 94*
Kutakov, Leonid Nikolayevich 1919- *IntWW 93*
Kutasi, Katalin Erzsebet 1956- *WhoFI 94*
Kutasi, Leslie, Jr. 1959- *WhoAmP 93*
Kutavicius, Bronislovas 1932- *NewGrDO*
Kutchins, Michael Joseph 1941- *WhoAm 94*
Kuter, Kay E. 1925- *WhoWest 94*
Kuter, Kaye E. *WhoHol 92*
Kuthy, Douglas E. 1956- *WhoAmL 94*
Kuti, Fela Anikulapo 1938- *IntWW 93*
Kutler, Laurence 1953- *ConAu 142*
Kutler, Marilyn Z. 1949- *WhoAmL 94*
Kutler, Stanley Ira 1934- *WhoAm 94, WhoMW 93*
Kutner, Janet 1937- *WhoAm 94, WhoAmA 93*
Kutner, Luis d1993 *NewYTBS 93*
Kutner, Luis 1908-1993 *ConAu 140*
Kutner, Martin *IntMPA 94*
Kutner, Maurice Jay 1940- *WhoAmL 94*
Kutney, James Peter 1932- *WhoAm 94*
Kutnick, Richard William 1954- *WhoMW 93*
Kutrzeba, Joseph Stanislaw 1927- *WhoAm 94*
Kutscher, Hans d1993 *Who 94N*
Kutscher, Hans 1911- *IntWW 93*
Kutschinski, Dorothy Irene 1922- *WhoMW 93*
Kutsunugi, Takeko 1922- *WhoWomW 91*
Kuttan, Appu 1941- *WhoAsA 94*
Kuttan, Roger 1973- *WhoAsA 94*
Kuttler, Carl Martin, Jr. 1940- *WhoAm 94*
Kuttner, Bernard A. 1934- *WhoAmL 94*
Kuttner, Henry 1914-1958 *EncSF 93*
Kuttner, Paul *DrAPF 93*
Kuttner, Stephan George 1907- *IntWW 93, WhoAmL 94*
Kuttner, Stephan George 1909- *WhoWest 94*
Kutun, Barry 1941- *WhoAmP 93*
Kutuzov, Mikhail 1745-1813 *HisWorL [port]*
Kutvirt, Duda Chytilova Ruzena 1919- *WhoWest 94*
Kutyna, Donald Joseph 1933- *WhoAm 94, WhoWest 94*
Kutz, Kenneth John 1926- *WhoAm 94*
Kuure, Bojan Marlena 1942- *WhoWest 94*
Kuusik, Tiyt (Ditrikh Yanovich) 1911- *NewGrDO*
Kuuskoski, Eeva Maija Kaarina 1946- *IntWW 93*
Kuuskoski-Vikatmaa, Eeva Maija Kaarina 1946- *WhoWomW 91*
Kuvin, Lawrence Philip 1933- *WhoAmL 94*
Kuvshinoff, Bertha Horne 1915- *WhoAmA 93*
Kuvshinoff, Nicolai 1910- *WhoAmA 93*
Kuwa, George K. d1931 *WhoHol 92*
Kuwabara, Dennis Matsuichi 1945- *WhoWest 94*
Kuwabara, Takeo 1904- *IntWW 93*
Kuwahara, Frank *WhoAsA 94*
Kuwahara, Mitsunori 1936- *WhoFI 94*
Kuwahara, Steven Sadao 1940- *WhoAsA 94*
Kuwait, H.H. The Ruler of *IntWW 93*
Kuwaiz, Abdullah Ibrahim el 1939- *IntWW 93*
Kuwana, Eric Alan 1966- *WhoAmL 94*
Kuwata, Kazuhiro 1942- *WhoScEn 94*
Kuwayama, George 1925- *WhoAm 94, WhoAmA 93, WhoAsA 94, WhoWest 94*
Kuwayama, Tadaaki 1932- *WhoAmA 93*
Kuwayri, Yusuf al- *EncSF 93*
Kux, Dennis 1931- *WhoAmP 93*
Kuyatt, Brian Lee 1952- *WhoScEn 94*
Kuyatt, Chris Ernie Earl 1930- *WhoAm 94*
Kuyk, Dirk (A.), Jr. 1934- *WrDr 94*
Kuyk, Willem 1934- *WhoScEn 94*
Kuykendal, Robert Lee 1945- *WhoMW 93*
Kuykendall, Crystal Arlene 1949- *WhoBlA 94*
Kuykendall, Gregory John 1961- *WhoAmL 94*
Kuykendall, John Wells 1938- *WhoAm 94*
Kuykendall, Terry Allen 1953- *WhoScEn 94*
Kuyper, Paul 1932- *WhoScEn 94*
Kuyper, Peter Walk 1942- *WhoWest 94*
Kuzel, Kenneth 1960- *WhoMW 93*
Kuzel, Victoria Nelson 1945- *WhoMW 93*
Kuzell, William Charles 1914- *WhoAm 94, WhoWest 94*
Kuzma, David Richard 1945- *WhoFI 94*
Kuzma, George Martin 1925- *WhoAm 94, WhoWest 94*
Kuzma, Greg *DrAPF 93*
Kuzmanovic, Bogdan Ognjan 1914- *WhoScEn 94*
Kuzmanovic, Tomislav Zlatan 1963- *WhoAmL 94*
Kuzmic, Petr 1955- *WhoScEn 94*
Kuzmin, Anatoly Alekseevich 1933- *LngBDD*
Kuzmin, Leonid Filoppovich 1930- *IntWW 93*
Kuzmin, Mikhail (Alexeyevich) 1872-1936 *GayLL*
Kuznets, Simon Smith 1901-1985 *AmSocL*
Kuznetsov, Boris Yurevich 1935- *LngBDD*
Kuznetsov, Evgeny Semenovich 1938- *LngBDD*
Kuznetsov, German Serapionovich 1948- *IntWW 93, LngBDD*
Kuznetsov, Vladimir Sergeevich 1954- *LngBDD*
Kuznetsova, Galina Nikolaevna 1902-1976 *BlmGWL*
Kuznetsova, Mariya Nikolayevna 1880-1966 *NewGrDO*
Kuznetzoff, Adia d1954 *WhoHol 92*
Kuzniar, Linda Southard 1949- *WhoMW 93*
Kuznik, Susan Marie 1956- *WhoMW 93*
Kuzwayo, Ellen 1914- *BlmGWL*
Kuzwayo, Ellen (Kate) 1914- *WrDr 94*
Kuzyk, Mimi *WhoHol 92*
Kvalheim, Kenneth Cecil 1957- *WhoAmP 93*
Kvalseth, Tarald Oddvar 1938- *WhoAm 94, WhoScEn 94*
Kvam, Adolph L. *WhoAmP 93*
Kvam, Wayne *DrAPF 93*
Kvamme, John Peder 1918- *WhoScEn 94*
Kvapil, Jaroslav 1868-1950 *NewGrDO*
Kvapil, Jaroslav 1892-1959 *NewGrDO*
Kvapil, Radoslav 1934- *IntWW 93*
Kvaran, Agust 1952- *WhoScEn 94*
Kvares, Donald d1993 *NewYTBS 93*
Kvasov, Vladimir Petrovich 1936- *LngBDD*
Kvenvolden, Keith Arthur 1930- *WhoWest 94*
Kverndal, Roald 1921- *WhoWest 94*
Kvidal, Mary 1943- *IntWW 93*
Kvint, Vladimir Lev 1949- *WhoAm 94, WhoFI 94, WhoScEn 94*
Kvitash, Vadim Issay 1936- *WhoAm 94*
Kvitsinsky, Youli Aleksandrovich 1936- *IntWW 93*
Kwa, Raymond Pain-Boon 1944- *WhoAm 94*
Kwaan, Hau Cheong 1931- *WhoMW 93*
Kwai, Athena Man-Ha 1960- *WhoFI 94*
Kwak, Hoon 1941- *WhoAmA 93*
Kwak, No Kyoon 1932- *WhoAsA 94*
Kwak, Nowhan 1928- *WhoScEn 94*
Kwak, Sung 1941- *WhoAm 94*
Kwak, Wikil 1956- *WhoAsA 94*
Kwakye, Emmanuel Bamfo d1993 *Who 94N*
Kwamena-Poh, M(ichael Albert) 1932- *WrDr 94*
Kwan, Catherine Ning 1938- *WhoAsA 94*
Kwan, Eddy 1959- *WhoWest 94*
Kwan, Elaine 1950- *WhoMW 93*
Kwan, Franco Chang-Hong 1950- *WhoAsA 94*
Kwan, Henry King-Hong 1950- *WhoScEn 94*
Kwan, Kian M. 1929- *WhoAsA 94*
Kwan, Michelle *NewYTBS 93 [port]*
Kwan, Nancy 1939- *WhoHol 92*
Kwan, Nancy Kashen 1939- *WhoAsA 94*
Kwan, Simon Hing-Man 1961- *WhoAsA 94*
Kwan, Yuen-yin Kathy 1959- *WhoAsA 94*
Kwan-Gett, Mei Lin 1967- *WhoAsA 94*
Kwapong, Alex. A. 1927- *IntWW 93*
Kwapong, Alexander Adum 1927- *Who 94*
Kwasnick, Paul Jack 1925- *WhoAm 94*
Kwasniewski, Aleksander 1954- *IntWW 93*
Kwass, Sidney J. 1908- *WhoAmL 94*
Kwei, Ti-Kang 1929- *WhoAsA 94*
Kwiat, Joseph J. *WhoAm 94*
Kwicien, John Martin 1950- *WhoIns 94*
Kwiecinski, Chester Martin 1924- *WhoAmA 93*
Kwietniewska, Anna Jolanta *WhoWomW 91*
Kwiker, Louis A. 1935- *WhoAm 94*
Kwilas, Anthony Robert 1962- *WhoAmL 94*
Kwiram, Alvin L. 1937- *WhoAm 94*
Kwit, Nathaniel Troy, Jr. 1941- *IntMPA 94*
Kwiterovich, Peter Oscar, Jr. 1940- *WhoScEn 94*
Kwoh, Stewart 1948- *WhoAsA 94*
Kwoh, Yik San *WorInv*
Kwok, Chuck Chun-yau 1956- *WhoAsA 94*
Kwok, Daniel W. Y. 1932- *WhoAsA 94*
Kwok, Daphne *WhoAsA 94*
Kwok, Hoi-Sing 1951- *WhoAsA 94*
Kwok, Joseph *WhoAsA 94*
Kwok, Lance Stephen 1954- *WhoScEn 94*
Kwok, Raymond Hung Fai 1963- *WhoScEn 94*
Kwok, Reginald Yin-Wang 1937- *WhoAsA 94*
Kwok, Russell Chi-Yan 1935- *WhoScEn 94*
Kwok, Si Ho 1962- *WhoMW 93*
Kwok, Sun 1949- *WhoScEn 94, WhoWest 94*
Kwok, Wo Kong 1936- *WhoAsA 94*
Kwon, Byoung Se 1947- *WhoMW 93, WhoScEn 94*
Kwon, Glenn S. 1963- *WhoScEn 94*
Kwon, Jeffrey Young 1956- *WhoAsA 94*
Kwon, Joon Taek 1935- *WhoScEn 94*
Kwon, Myoung-ja L. 1943- *WhoAsA 94*
Kwon, Ojoung 1955- *WhoMW 93*
Kwon, Ronald Chi-Oh 1947- *WhoAsA 94*
Kwon, Taek Mu 1956- *WhoMW 93*
Kwon, Young Ha 1962- *WhoAsA 94*
Kwon, Young Wuk 1959- *WhoAsA 94*
Kwon-Chung, Kyung Joo 1933- *WhoAsA 94*
Kwong, Bill Wai Lam 1958- *WhoAsA 94*
Kwong, Eva 1954- *WhoAmA 93, WhoAsA 94*
Kwong, James Kin-Ping 1954- *WhoScEn 94, WhoWest 94*
Kwong, Peter Kong Kit 1936- *WhoAm 94*
Kwouk, Burt 1930- *WhoHol 92*
Ky, Nguyen Cao *IntWW 93*
Kyasht, Lydia 1885-1959 *IntDcB [port]*
Kybett, Brian David 1938- *WhoScEn 94*
Kyburg, Henry Guy Ely, Jr. 1928- *WhoAm 94*
Kyd, Thomas 1558-1594 *BlmGEL, IntDcT 2, LitC 22*
Kydd, Sam d1982 *WhoHol 92*
Kyffin, Maurice c. 1560-1598 *DcLB 136*
Kyger, Joanne *DrAPF 93*
Kyger, Joanne 1934- *WrDr 94*
Kyhl, Robert Louis 1917- *WhoAm 94*
Kyhos, Thomas Flynn 1947- *WhoAmL 94*
Kyin, Saw William 1954- *WhoScEn 94*
Kyl, John Henry 1919- *WhoAm 94*
Kyl, Jon 1942- *CngDr 93, WhoAm 94, WhoWest 94*
Kyl, Jon Llewellyn 1942- *WhoAmP 93*
Kylander, Chester R. 1932- *WhoMW 93*
Kyle, Alan M. *WhoAmP 93*
Kyle, Austin C. d1916 *WhoHol 92*
Kyle, Barry Albert 1947- *Who 94*
Kyle, Benjamin Gayle 1927- *WhoMW 93, WhoScEn 94*
Kyle, Beverly Ann 1950- *WhoWest 94*
Kyle, Billy d1966 *WhoHol 92*
Kyle, Chester Richard 1927- *WhoScEn 94*
Kyle, Corinne Silverman 1930- *WhoFI 94*
Kyle, David A. c. 1912- *EncSF 93*
Kyle, Duncan *WrDr 94*
Kyle, Frank Ansley, Jr. 1948- *WhoMW 93*
Kyle, Gene Magerl 1919- *WhoMW 93*
Kyle, Genghis 1923- *WhoBlA 94*
Kyle, Henry Carper 1909- *WhoAmL 94*
Kyle, Howard d1950 *WhoHol 92*
Kyle, Jackson *WhoHol 92*
Kyle, James 1925- *Who 94*
Kyle, James F. 1950- *WhoAmP 93*
Kyle, Jeanne Ellen 1954- *WhoWest 94*
Kyle, John Emery 1926- *WhoAm 94*
Kyle, John Hamilton 1925- *WhoAm 94*
Kyle, Marcus Aurelius 1923- *WhoAmP 93*
Kyle, Mary J. *WhoBlA 94*
Kyle, Odes J., Jr. 1931- *WhoBlA 94*
Kyle, Penelope Ward 1947- *WhoAmL 94*
Kyle, Richard *WhoAmP 93*
Kyle, Richard H. 1937- *WhoAm 94, WhoAmL 94, WhoMW 93*
Kyle, Richard Henry 1943- *Who 94*
Kyle, Robert Arthur 1928- *WhoAm 94, WhoScEn 94*
Kyle, Robert Campbell, II 1935- *WhoAm 94, WhoFI 94*
Kyle, Robert Tourville 1910- *WhoWest 94*
Kyle, Stella Ortiz *WhoHisp 94*
Kyle, Susan (Spaeth) 1946- *ConAu 141*
Kyle, Susan S. *ConAu 141*
Kyle, Terrence Wayne 1950- *WhoAm 94*
Kyle, Thomas Marvin 1955- *WhoFI 94*
Kyles, Dwain Johann 1954- *WhoBlA 94*
Kyles, Josephine H. 1900- *WhoBlA 94*
Kyles, Sharron Faye 1950- *WhoBlA 94*
Kylian, Jiri 1947- *IntDcB [port], WhoAm 94*
Kylstra, Johannes Arnold 1925- *WhoAm 94*
Kyman, Alexander Leon 1929- *WhoAm 94*
Kyme, Anne *BlmGWL*
Kyme, Brian Robert 1935- *Who 94*
Kynaston, Edward 1643-1712 *BlmGEL*
Kynaston, Nicolas 1941- *IntWW 93, Who 94*
Kyncl, John Jaroslav 1936- *WhoMW 93*
Kyndrup, Morten 1952- *ConAu 140*
Kynoch, George Alexander Bryson 1946- *Who 94*
Kynoch, James Brent 1959- *WhoAm 94*
Kynsok, Anna Maria *WhoWomW 91*
Kyo, Machiko 1924- *IntWW 93, WhoHol 92*
Kyprianou, Demetrios 1931- *IntWW 93*
Kyprianou, Spyros 1932- *IntWW 93, Who 94*
Kyra 1947- *WhoAmA 93*

Kyreyko, Vitaly 1926- *NewGrDO*
Kyriacou, Demetrios 1922- *WhoScEn 94*
Kyriazides, Nikos Panayis 1927- *Who 94*
Kyriazidis, Nicolas 1927- *IntWW 93*
Kyriazis, Arthur John 1958- *WhoAmL 94*
Kyrillos, Joseph M., Jr. 1960-
    WhoAmP 93
Kyrle Pope, Michael Donald 1916-
    Who 94
Kyrouac, Scott M. 1960- *WhoAmL 94*
Kysar, Raymond L., Jr. 1951-
    WhoAmP 93
Kyser, Kay d1985 *WhoHol 92*
Kyte, Janet M. 1953- *WhoMW 93*
Kyte, Lydiane 1919- *WhoWest 94*
Kytle, Ray *DrAPF 93*
Kyung-Wha Chung *IntWW 93*
Kyurkchiiski, Krasimir 1936- *NewGrDO*
Kyveli, Mme. d1978 *WhoHol 92*

L

L., Marie-Sophie *WhoHol 92*
Laabs, Allison C. 1944- *WhoAm 94, WhoMW 93*
Laabs, Jeffery Arnold 1954- *WhoFI 94*
Laage, Barbara 1925- *WhoHol 92*
Laage, Gerhart 1925- *IntWW 93*
Laaly, Heshmat Ollah 1927- *WhoScEn 94, WhoWest 94*
Laananen, David Horton 1942- *WhoScEn 94*
Laano, Archie Bienvenido Maano 1939- *WhoAm 94, WhoScEn 94*
Laar, Mart 1960- *IntWW 93, LngBDD*
Laartz, Esther Elizabeth 1913- *WhoAm 94*
Laas, Virginia Jeans 1943- *WhoMW 93*
Laatsch, Audrey Frieda 1929- *WhoMW 93*
Laatsch, Gary 1956- *WhoAmA 93N*
Laatsch, James Fred 1940- *WhoAmP 93*
Laba, Marvin 1928- *WhoAm 94, WhoFI 94, WhoWest 94*
La Badie, Florence d1917 *WhoHol 92*
Labadie, George Sherman 1916- *WhoWest 94*
La Balme, Augustin Mottin *WhAmRev*
Labalme, Patricia Hochschild 1927- *WhoAm 94*
LaBan, Myron Miles 1936- *WhoAm 94*
Laban, Saad Lotfy 1960- *WhoScEn 94*
LaBant, Robert James 1945- *WhoAm 94, WhoFI 94*
LaBar, Tom *DrAPF 93*
LaBarbera, Andrew Richard 1948- *WhoMW 93*
LaBarbera, Nicole Alexandra 1966- *WhoAmL 94*
Labarca, Angela 1942- *WhoHisp 94*
Labardakis, Augoustinos 1938- *IntWW 93*
Labardi, Jillian Gay 1945- *WhoFI 94*
La Bare, M. *DrAPF 93*
Labaree, Leonard Woods 1897- *WhAm 10*
Labarge, John V. 1952- *WhoAmP 93*
LaBarge, Karin Peterson 1953- *WhoFI 94*
LaBarge, Richard Allen 1934- *WhoFI 94*
La Barge, William Joseph 1943- *WhoMW 93*
Labaria, Violeta T. 1934- *WhoWomW 91*
LaBarre, Carl Anthony 1918- *WhoAm 94*
LaBarre, Dennis W. 1942- *WhoAm 94*
LaBarre, James A. 1951- *WhoAmL 94*
La Barre, Michel de c. 1675-1745 *NewGrDO*
Labarre, Theodore(-Francois-Joseph) 1805-1870 *NewGrDO*
LaBarre, Weston 1911- *WrDr 94*
Labarrere-Paule, Andre 1928- *IntWW 93*
Labarthe Correa, Javier 1924- *IntWW 93*
Labasan, Alejandro B. 1935- *WhoAsA 94*
Labat, Eric Martin 1962- *WhoBlA 94*
Labat, Tony 1951- *WhoAmA 93*
Labat, Wendy L. 1957- *WhoBlA 94*
LaBath, Octave Aaron 1941- *WhoScEn 94*
Labatt, Weir *WhoAmP 93*
Labay, Eugene Benedict 1938- *WhoAmL 94*
Labayen, Louie Anthony Lopez 1960- *WhoMW 93*
Labbe, Armand Joseph 1944- *WhoFI 94, WhoWest 94*
L'abbe, Gerrit Karel 1940- *WhoAm 94, WhoScEn 94*
Labbe, Paul 1939- *WhoAm 94*

Labbett, John Edgar 1950- *WhoAm 94, WhoFI 94*
Labbette, Dora 1898-1984 *NewGrDO*
Labe, Louise Charlin Perrin 1520-1566 *BlmGWL*
Labedz, Bernice 1919- *WhoAmP 93*
Labedz, Leopold d1993 *NewYTBS 93*
Labelle, Eugene Jean-Marc 1941- *WhoAm 94*
LaBelle, Patti 1944- *WhoAm 94, WhoBlA 94, WhoHol 92*
LaBelle, Robert Michael 1954- *WhoAmL 94*
LaBelle, Thomas Jeffrey 1941- *WhoAm 94*
Laben, Dorothy Lobb 1914- *WhoScEn 94*
Laberge, Marie 1950- *IntDcT 2*
Labes, Leon Martin 1913-1989 *WhAm 10*
Labia, Maria 1880-1953 *NewGrDO*
La Bianca, Salvatore Tony 1910- *WhoMW 93*
Labiche, Eugene (Marin) 1815-1888 *IntDcT 2*
Labiche, Walter Anthony 1924-1979 *WhoAmA 93N*
La Billardiere, Jacques-Julien Houtou De 1755-1834 *WhWE*
Labingli *WhoPRCh 91*
Labinsky, Andrey 1871-1941 *NewGrDO*
Labis, Attilio 1936- *IntWW 93*
Labissoniere, Erin d1976 *WhoHol 92*
Lablache, Luigi 1794-1858 *NewGrDO*
La Blanc, Charles Wesley, Jr. 1925- *WhoAm 94, WhoFI 94*
La Blanc, Robert Edmund 1934- *WhoAm 94*
Lablanche, Jean-Marc Andre 1946- *WhoScEn 94*
Lable, Eliot 1937- *WhoAmA 93*
Labo, Flaviano (Mario) 1927-1991 *NewGrDO*
La Bobgah, Robert Gordon 1936- *WhoAmA 93*
Laboe, Norman J. 1940- *WhoAm 94*
Laboe, Ronald F. 1944- *WhoAmL 94*
La Boetie, Etienne de 1530-1563 *GuFrLit 2*
La Bombard, Joan *DrAPF 93*
La Bombarda, Michael *DrAPF 93*
Labombarde, Philip deGaspe 1921- *WhoAmP 93*
La Bonte, Clarence Joseph 1939- *WhoAm 94*
LaBonte, Jovite 1933- *WhoAm 94*
LaBoon, Lawrence Joseph 1938- *WhoFI 94*
LaBoon, Robert Bruce 1941- *WhoAm 94*
Laborde, Alden James 1915- *WhoAm 94*
Laborde, Ana Maria 1956- *WhoHisp 94*
LaBorde, Benjamin Franklin 1910- *WhoAmP 93*
LaBorde, Jean-Benjamin(-Francois) de 1734-1794 *NewGrDO*
Laborde, John Peter 1923- *WhoAm 94*
Laborde, Raymond J. 1927- *WhoAmP 93*
LaBorde, Ronald Garrett 1955- *WhoMW 93*
Laborteaux, Matthew 1965- *WhoHol 92*
Laborteaux, Patrick 1963- *WhoHol 92*
Labouchere, George (Peter) 1905- *Who 94*
Labouisse, H. R., Mrs. *Who 94*
Laboulaye, Francois Rene de 1917- *IntWW 93*

Labourier, Dominique *WhoHol 92*
Labovitch, Neville *Who 94*
Labovitz, John R. 1943- *WhoAmL 94*
Labowitz, Aaron Paul 1968- *WhoWest 94*
Laboy, Eduardo 1957- *WhoHisp 94*
Laboy, Elizabeth 1940- *WhoHisp 94*
LaBoy, Jose Antonio 1949- *WhoHisp 94*
La Brake, Harrison d1933 *WhoHol 92*
LaBrec, David John 1948- *WhoAm 94*
LaBreche, Anthony Wayne 1936- *WhoFI 94*
LaBrecque, Leon Charles 1955- *WhoFI 94*
Labrecque, Richard Joseph 1938- *WhoAm 94*
Labrecque, Theodore Joseph 1903- *WhoAm 94, WhoAmL 94*
Labrecque, Thomas G. 1938- *WhoAm 94, WhoFI 94*
LaBree, G. Anne 1931- *WhoMW 93*
Labrie, Christy 1943- *WhoAmA 93*
Labrie, Fernand 1937- *WhoAm 94*
Labrie, Harrington 1909- *WhoBlA 94*
LaBrie, Peter, Jr. 1940- *WhoBlA 94*
LaBrie, Rose 1916-1986 *WhoAmA 93N*
LaBrie, Teresa Kathleen 1960- *WhoScEn 94*
Labrie, Vida Yvonne 1946- *WhoBlA 94*
Labriola, Joseph Arthur 1949- *WhoScEn 94*
La Bruere, Charles-Antoine Le Clerc de 1714-1754 *NewGrDO*
La Bruno, Carmen Michael *DrAPF 93*
La Bruyere, Jean de 1645-1696 *GuFrLit 2*
Labsvirs, Janis 1907- *WhoMW 93*
LaBua, Paul Joseph 1941- *WhoFI 94*
Labuda, Barbara *WhoWomW 91*
Labuda, Gerard 1916- *IntWW 93*
La Budde, Kenneth James 1920- *WhoAm 94*
LaBudde, Roy Christian 1921- *WhoAm 94, WhoAmL 94, WhoFI 94, WhoMW 93*
Labunski, Stephen Bronislaw 1924- *WhoAm 94*
Labuz, Ronald Matthew 1953- *WhoScEn 94*
Labuza, Theodore Peter 1940- *WhoMW 93*
Lac, Ming Q. 1948- *WhoFI 94*
Lacagnina, Michael Anthony 1932- *WhoAm 94*
LaCaille, Rupert Andrew 1917-1989 *WhoBlA 94N*
Lacalle Herrera, Luis Alberto 1941- *IntWW 93*
La Calprenede, Gautier de Costes, sieur de 1610?-1663 *GuFrLit 2*
Lacan, Jacques *BlmGWL*
Lacan, Jacques 1901-1981 *BlmGEL*
Lacant, Jacques 1915- *IntWW 93*
LaCapra, Dominick Charles 1939- *WhoAm 94*
LaCasse, James Phillip 1948- *WhoAmL 94*
Lacatena, Victor Anthony 1924- *WhoAm 94*
La Cava, Donald Leon 1928- *WhoFI 94*
LaCava, Frederick William 1945- *WhoAm 94*
Lacayo, Carmela G. 1943- *WhoHisp 94*
Lacayo, Henry L. 1931- *WhoAmP 93*
Lacaze, Jeannou 1924- *IntWW 93*

Laccavole, Dennis Mark 1953- *WhoAmL 94*
La Celle, Paul Louis 1929- *WhoAm 94, WhoScEn 94*
Lacer, Alfred Antonio 1952- *WhoAmL 94*
Lacera, Jana L. 1952- *WhoMW 93*
Lacerda, Francisco De d1798 *WhWE*
Lacerna, Leocadio Valderrama 1958- *WhoScEn 94*
Lacerra, Ronald J. 1939- *WhoIns 94*
Lacey, A(lan) R(obert) 1926- *WrDr 94*
Lacey, Adele d1953 *WhoHol 92*
Lacey, Beatrice Cates 1919- *WhoAm 94*
Lacey, Catherine d1979 *WhoHol 92*
Lacey, Clifford George 1921- *Who 94*
Lacey, Cloyd Eugene 1918- *WhoAm 94*
Lacey, Daniel Damian 1950-1992 *WhAm 10*
Lacey, David Morgan 1950- *WhoAmL 94*
Lacey, Diane E. *WhoBlA 94*
Lacey, Edward Martin 1948- *WhoMW 93*
Lacey, Elizabeth A. 1954- *WrDr 94*
Lacey, Frank 1919- *Who 94*
Lacey, Frederick Bernard 1920- *WhoAm 94*
Lacey, Frederick Milburn, Jr. 1934- *WhoFI 94*
Lacey, Gary Eugene 1942- *WhoAmL 94*
Lacey, George William Brian 1926- *Who 94*
Lacey, Howard Raymond 1919- *WhoMW 93*
Lacey, Hugh Matthew 1939- *WhoAm 94*
Lacey, Jack *WhoAmP 93*
Lacey, John 1755-1814 *WhAmRev*
Lacey, John Irving 1915- *WhoAm 94*
Lacey, John William Charles 1930- *WhoAm 94*
Lacey, Marc Steven 1965- *WhoBlA 94*
Lacey, Margaret d1988 *WhoHol 92*
Lacey, Nicola 1958- *WrDr 94*
Lacey, Pamela Anne 1955- *WhoAmL 94*
Lacey, Richard Westgarth 1940- *IntWW 93, Who 94*
Lacey, Robert 1944- *ConAu 43NR, WrDr 94*
Lacey, Ronald d1991 *WhoHol 92*
Lacey, Ronald Edward 1958- *WhoWest 94*
Lacey, Sam 1948- *BasBi*
Lacey, Wilbert, Jr. 1936- *WhoBlA 94*
Lach, Alma Elizabeth *WhoAm 94, WhoMW 93*
Lach, Eileen Marie 1950- *WhoAm 94*
Lach, Joseph Theodore 1934- *WhoAm 94*
Lach, Phillip Edward 1957- *WhoMW 93*
Lachance, Douglas A. 1965- *WhoAmP 93*
LaChance, Murdock Henry 1920- *WhoWest 94*
Lachance, Paul Albert 1933- *WhoAm 94, WhoFI 94*
Lachance, Sherry *DrAPF 93*
Lachapelle, Cleo Edward 1925- *WhoFI 94*
LaChapelle, Joseph Robert 1943- *WhoAmA 93*
La Chapelle, Mary *DrAPF 93*
La Chapelle, Mary 1955- *WrDr 94*
Lacharriere, Guy Ladreit de 1919- *IntWW 93*
La Chaussee, Pierre-Claude Nivelle de *GuFrLit 2*
Lachel, Dennis John 1939- *WhoScEn 94*
Lachemann, Rene George 1945- *WhoAm 94*

Lachenbruch, Arthur Herold 1925- WhoAm 94
Lachenbruch, David 1921- WhoAm 94
Lachens, Catherine WhoHol 92
Lacher, Hans 1912- IntWW 93
Lacher, Taylor WhoHol 92
Laches, Robert Duane 1953- WhoMW 93
Lachey, James Michael 1963- WhoAm 94
Lachica, Edward Anthony 1960- WhoAsA 94
Lachman, Alan B. 1935- WhoWest 94
Lachman, Branton George 1952- WhoWest 94
Lachman, Ed 1948- IntMPA 94
Lachman, Lawrence 1916- WhoAm 94
Lachman, Marguerite Leanne 1943- WhoAm 94
Lachman, Morton 1918- WhoAm 94
Lachman, Ralph Steven 1935- WhoBlA 94
Lachmann, Hedwig 1865-1918 NewGrDO
Lachmann, Peter Julius 1931- IntWW 93, Who 94
Lachmet, Djanet 1953- BlmGWL
Lachner, Bernard Joseph 1927- WhoAm 94
Lachner, Franz Paul 1803-1890 NewGrDO
Lachner, Ignaz 1807-1895 NewGrDO
Lachner, Marshall Smith 1914-1991 WhAm 10
Lachnith, Ludwig Wenzel 1746-1820 NewGrDO
Lachs, Henry Lazarus 1927- Who 94
Lachs, John 1934- WhoAm 94, WrDr 94
Lachs, Manfred d1993 IntWW 93N, Who 94N
Lachs, Susanna E. 1952- WhoAmL 94
Lach-Szyrma, W(ladislaw) S(omerville) 1841-1915 EncSF 93
Lachut, Ervin R. 1924- WhoAmP 93
Lacina, Ferdinand 1942- IntWW 93
Lacitis, Erik 1949- WhoAm 94
Lack, James J. 1944- WhoAmP 93
Lack, John A. WhoFI 94
Lack, Larry Henry 1952- WhoWest 94
Lack, Leon 1922- WhoAm 94
Lack, Paul D. 1944- ConAu 140
Lack, Richard Frederick 1928- WhoAmA 93
Lack, Simon d1980 WhoHol 92
Lack, Stephen WhoHol 92
Lack, Stephen 1946- WhoAmA 93
Lackas, John Christopher 1904-1990 WhAm 10
Lackaye, Helen d1940 WhoHol 92
Lackaye, James d1919 WhoHol 92
Lackaye, Richard d1951 WhoHol 92
Lackaye, Wilton d1932 WhoHol 92
Lackenmier, James Richard 1938- WhoAm 94
Lackens, John Wendell, Jr. 1934- WhoAm 94
Lackey, Bernice Catherine 1917- WhoAmP 93
Lackey, Doug 1949- WhoAmL 94
Lackey, Edgar F. 1930- WhoBlA 94
Lackey, Edwin Keith Who 94
Lackey, Henry Grider 1947- WhoAmP 93
Lackey, Jack W., Jr. 1947- WhoMW 93
Lackey, James Franklin, Jr. 1932- WhoScEn 94
Lackey, Jane W. 1948- WhoAmA 93
Lackey, Kathleen Friend 1945- WhoAmL 94
Lackey, Larry Alton, Sr. 1940- WhoAmL 94, WhoFI 94
Lackey, Lawrence Bailis, Jr. 1914- WhoAm 94
Lackey, Mary Josephine 1925- Who 94
Lackey, Mary Michele 1955- WhoScEn 94
Lackey, Mercedes EncSF 93
Lackey, Mercedes R. 1950- TwCYAW
Lackey, Robert Thomas 1944- WhoWest 94
Lackey, Russell Wayne 1963- WhoFI 94
Lackey, S. Allen WhoAmL 94, WhoFI 94
Lackland, Ben d1959 WhoHol 92
Lackland, John 1939- WhoAm 94, WhoAmL 94
Lackland, Theodore Howard 1943- WhoAm 94
Lackner, James Robert 1940- WhoAm 94, WhoScEn 94
Lackoff, Martin Robert 1946- WhoScEn 94
Lackritz, Marc E. 1946- WhoAm 94, WhoFI 94
Lackteen, Frank d1968 WhoHol 92
Lacktman, Michael 1938- WhoAmA 93
Laclede, Pierre Ligueste 1724-1778 WhWE
Laclette, Fernando Javier 1942- WhoHisp 94
Laclos, Pierre-Ambroise-Francois, Choderlos de 1741-1803 GuFrLit 2
Laclotte, Michel Rene 1929- IntWW 93, Who 94
Lacom, Wayne Carl 1922- WhoAmA 93
Lacomba, Justo WhoHisp 94
Lacombe, Albert 1827-1916 EncNAR
Lacombe, Claire 1765- BlmGWL
Lacombe, Henri 1913- IntWW 93
Lacombe, Louis 1818-1884 NewGrDO
Lacombe, Rita Jeanne 1947- WhoWest 94
LaCombe, Ronald Dean 1962- WhoScEn 94
Lacome, Myer 1927- Who 94
Lacome, Paul(-Jean-Jacques) 1838-1920 NewGrDO
Lacon, Edmund (Vere) 1936- Who 94
La Condamine, Charles-Marie De 1701-1774 WhWE
Laconte, Pierre 1934- IntWW 93
La Cosa, Juan De WhWE
Lacoste, Louis de c. 1675-1753? NewGrDO
Lacoste, Paul 1923- IntWW 93, Who 94, WhoAm 94
Lacoste, Rene 1905- BuCMET [port]
La Coste, Warren 1941- ConAu 141
Lacotte, Pierre 1932- IntDcB
La Cour, Louis Bernard 1926- WhoAmL 94, WhoBlA 94, WhoMW 93
LaCour, Nathaniel Hawthorne 1938- WhoBlA 94
Lacour, Vanue B. 1915- WhoBlA 94
Lacourse, Ronald 1933- WhoAmP 93
Lacouture, Felipe Ernesto 1928- WhoAm 94
Lacouture, Jean Marie Gerard 1921- ConAu 43NR
Lacovara, Philip Allen 1943- WhoAm 94, WhoAmL 94
Lacroix, Christian Marie Marc 1951- IntWW 93, Who 94, WhoAm 94
La Croix, Frederic Skelton 1933- WhoMW 93
La Croix, I(sobyl) F. 1933- ConAu 142
La Croix, Sumner Jonathan 1954- WhoWest 94
Lacrosil, Michele 1915- BlmGWL
LaCuesta, Lloyd R. 1947- WhoAsA 94
LaCuesta, Wesley Ray, Sr. 1942- WhoAsA 94
Lacy, Alan Jasper 1953- WhoAm 94
Lacy, Alexander Shelton 1921- WhoAm 94
Lacy, Bill 1933- WhoAm 94
Lacy, Claud H. Sandberg 1947- WhoScEn 94
Lacy, Creighton Boutelle 1919- WrDr 94
Lacy, Edward, Jr. WhAmRev
Lacy, Edward J. 1922- WhoBlA 94
Lacy, Elizabeth B. WhoAmP 93
Lacy, Elizabeth Bermingham 1945- WhoAmL 94
Lacy, Elsie A. 1947- WhoAmP 93
Lacy, Fern 1920- WhoAmP 93
Lacy, Herman Edgar 1935- WhoAm 94, WhoFI 94, WhoMW 93
Lacy, Hugh Gale 1948- WhoBlA 94
Lacy, Hugh Maurice Pierce 1943- Who 94
Lacy, James Daniel 1947- WhoAm 94
Lacy, James Vincent 1952- WhoAmP 93
Lacy, Jerry 1936- WhoHol 92
Lacy, John 1615?-1681 BlmGEL
Lacy, John (Trend) 1928- Who 94
Lacy, John Ford 1944- WhoAm 94, WhoAmL 94
Lacy, John R. 1942- WhoAmL 94
Lacy, Joseph Newton 1905- WhoAm 94
Lacy, Lee Marva Lou 1942- WhoWest 94
Lacy, Margo d1987 WhoHol 92
Lacy, Mark Edward 1955- WhoScEn 94
Lacy, Michael Rophino 1795-1867 NewGrDO
Lacy, Norris Joiner 1940- WhoAm 94
Lacy, Paul Eston 1924- WhoAm 94
Lacy, Phillip W. 1943- WhoAmL 94
Lacy, Priti Sheila 1942- WhoMW 93
Lacy, Ralph E. 1915- WhoAmP 93
Lacy, Robinson Burrell 1952- WhoAm 94, WhoAmL 94
Lacy, Steve 1934- WhoAm 94
Lacy, Suzanne 1945- WhoAmA 93
Lacy, Terri 1953- WhoAmL 94
Lacy, Tom WhoHol 92
Lacy, Versia Lindsay 1929- WhoBlA 94
Lacy, Walter 1942- WhoBlA 94
Laczkowski, Pawel 1942- IntWW 93
Lada, Elizabeth A. WhoScEn 94
LaDage, Janet Lee 1949- WhoMW 93
Ladage, Linda Rolf 1960- WhoMW 93
Ladanyi, Branko 1922- WhoAm 94
Ladar, Jerrold Morton 1933- WhoAm 94, WhoAmL 94
Ladar, Samuel Abraham 1903- WhAm 10
Ladas, Diana Margaret 1913- Who 94
Ladas, Ioannis 1920- IntWW 93
Ladau, Robert Francis 1940- WhoAm 94
Laday, Kerney 1942- WhoBlA 94
Ladd, Alan d1964 WhoHol 92
Ladd, Alan, Jr. 1937- IntMPA 94
Ladd, Alan Walbridge, Jr. 1937- WhoAm 94, WhoFI 94, WhoWest 94
Ladd, Alana 1943- WhoHol 92
Ladd, Charles Barton 1957- WhoAmP 93
Ladd, Charles Cushing, III 1932- WhoAm 94, WhoScEn 94
Ladd, Cheryl 1951- IntMPA 94, WhoAm 94, WhoHol 92
Ladd, David 1947- WhoHol 92
Ladd, David Alan 1947- IntMPA 94
Ladd, David N. 1938- WhoIns 94
Ladd, Diane IntMPA 94
Ladd, Diane 1932- WhoHol 92
Ladd, Diane 1943- WhoAm 94
Ladd, Ernest Howard d1940 WhoHol 92
Ladd, Everett Carll 1937- WhoAm 94
Ladd, Florence Cawthorne 1932- WhoBlA 94
Ladd, Hank d1982 WhoHol 92
Ladd, James Roger 1943- WhoAm 94
Ladd, Jeffrey Raymond 1941- WhoAmL 94, WhoMW 93
Ladd, John Curran 1945- WhoAm 94
Ladd, Joseph Carroll 1927- WhoAm 94
Ladd, Louise Elizabeth 1950- WhoFI 94
Ladd, Marcia Lee 1950- WhoMW 93
Ladd, Margaret 1945- WhoHol 92
Ladd, Marion WhoHol 92
Ladd, Mason 1898- WhAm 10
Ladd, Richard Edward, Jr. 1960- WhoAmL 94
Ladd, Schuyler d1961 WhoHol 92
Laddaga, Lawrence Alexander 1957- WhoAmL 94
Laddie, Hugh Ian Lang 1946- Who 94
Laddon, Warren Milton 1933- WhoAm 94
Ladd-Powell, Roberta Kay 1953- WhoAm 94
Ladefoged, Peter Nielsen 1925- WhoAm 94
Ladehoff, Leo William 1932- WhoAm 94
Ladehoff, Robert Louis 1932- WhoAm 94, WhoWest 94
Laden, Ben Ellis 1942- WhoAm 94
Laden, Karl 1932- WhoAm 94
Ladenheim, Kala DrAPF 93
Ladenson, Mark Lawrence 1941- WhoMW 93
Lader, Lawrence 1919- WhoAm 94
Lader, Malcolm Harold 1936- IntWW 93
Lader, Melvin Paul 1947- WhoAmA 93
Laderach, Paul A. 1933- WhoIns 94
Laderman, Ezra 1924- NewGrDO, WhoAm 94
Laderman, Gabriel 1929- WhoAm 94, WhoAmA 93
Laderoute, Charles David 1948- WhoFI 94, WhoScEn 94
Ladgham, Bahi 1913- IntWW 93
Ladies of Llangollen, The BlmGWL
Ladin, Eugene 1927- WhoAm 94, WhoFI 94
Ladino, Cynthia Anne 1962- WhoScEn 94
Ladisch, Thomas Peter 1953- WhoScEn 94
Ladjevardi, Hamid 1948- WhoAm 94, WhoFI 94
Ladly, Frederick Bernard 1930- WhoAm 94, WhoFI 94
Ladman, Aaron Julius 1925- WhoAm 94
Ladman, Jerry R. 1935- WhoAm 94
Ladmiral, Nicole d1958 WhoHol 92
Ladmirault, Paul (Emile) 1877-1944 NewGrDO
Ladner, Heber Austin 1902- WhoAmP 93
Ladner, Joyce A(nn) 1943- BlkWr 2
Ladner, Kurt 1943- WrDr 94
Ladner, Mark P. 1953- WhoAmL 94
Ladner, Terria Roushun 1962- WhoBlA 94
Ladner, Thomas E. 1916- WhoAm 94
Ladouceur, Harold Abel 1927- WhoScEn 94
Ladouceur, Patricia Allaire 1955- WhoWest 94
LaDouceur, Philip Alan 1950- WhoAmA 93
LaDoux, Rita C. 1951- SmATA 74
LaDow, C. Stuart 1925- WhoAm 94
Ladreit De Lacharriere, Marc 1940- IntWW 93
Ladson, Louis Fitzgerald 1951- WhoBlA 94
La Du, Bert Nichols, Jr. 1920- WhoAm 94, WhoMW 93, WhoScEn 94
LaDue, Robin Annette 1954- WhoScEn 94
LaDuke, Nancie WhoFI 94
Ladurner, Ignace Antoine (Francois Xavier) 1766-1839 NewGrDO
Ladwig, Alan Michael 1948- WhoAm 94
Ladwig, Bonnie L. 1939- WhoAmP 93
Ladwig, E. James 1938- WhoAmP 93
Ladwig, Patti Heidler 1958- WhoAmL 94
Ladwig, Tina Marie 1965- WhoMW 93
Ladysz, Bernard 1922- NewGrDO
Laelia fl. 2nd cent.BC- BlmGWL
Laemmle, Carl 1867-1939 AmCulL
Laemmle, Carl, Sr. 1867-1939 IntDcF 2-4 [port]
Laemmle, Carl, Jr. 1908-1979 IntDcF 2-4 [port]
Laemmle, Cheryl 1947- WhoAmA 93
Laerkesen, Anna 1942- IntDcB
Laessig, Robert 1920- WhoAmA 93
Laessig, Robert H. 1913- WhoAm 94
Laessig, Ronald Harold 1940- WhoAm 94, WhoScEn 94
Laessig, Walter Bruce 1941- WhoAm 94
Laessoe, Jorgen 1924- IntWW 93
Laettner, Christian Donald 1969- WhoAm 94, WhoMW 93
Laeuchli, Ann Jordan 1927- WhoAmL 94
Laeyendecker, Leonardus 1930- IntWW 93
Lafair, Theodore 1927- WhoFI 94
LaFalce, John J. 1939- CngDr 93, WhoAmP 93
La Falce, John Joseph 1939- WhoAm 94
Lafarge, Catherine 1935- WhoAm 94
La Farge, John 1880-1963 DcAmReB 2
Lafarge, Louis Bancel 1900-1989 WhAm 10
La Farge, Timothy 1930- WhoScEn 94
Lafargue, James F. 1925- WhoAmL 94
Lafargue, Philip 1850-1939 EncSF 93
LaFauci, Horatio Michael 1917- WhoAm 94
Lafaurie, Jean 1914- IntWW 93
Lafave, Hugh Gordon John 1929- WhoAm 94
La Fave, John 1949- WhoAmP 93
LaFave, LeAnn Larson 1953- WhoAmL 94
Lafaye, Nell Murray 1937-1990 WhoAmA 93N
Lafayette, Comtesse de 1634-1693 BlmGWL
Lafayette, Marquis de 1757-1834 HisWorL [port]
Lafayette, Bernard, Jr. 1940- WhoBlA 94
Lafayette, Ivan C. WhoAmP 93
Lafayette, James Armistead WhAmRev
Lafayette, James Armistead 17th cent.- AfrAmAl 6 [port]
LaFayette, Kate Bulls 1935- WhoBlA 94
Lafayette, Marie Joseph de Motier, Marquis de 1757-1834 WhAmRev [port]
Lafayette, Marie-Joseph-Paul-Yves-Roch-Gilbert du Motier 1757-1834 AmRev
Lafayette, Marie-Madeleine Pioche de la Vergne, comtesse de 1634-1693 GuFrLit 2
Lafayette, Rene EncSF 93
Lafayette, Rene 1961- WhoWomW 91
Lafayette, Rene M. 1961- WhoAmP 93
Lafayette, Ruby d1935 WhoHol 92
LaFeber, Walter Frederick 1933- WhoAm 94, WrDr 94
Lafee, Alfredo 1921- IntWW 93
Lafer, Fred Seymour 1929- WhoAm 94
Laferriere, Dany 1953- ConAu 142
La Ferte, Denis Pierre Jean Papillon de NewGrDO
Lafever, Howard Nelson 1938- WhoAm 94
Laffan, Brigid 1955- IntWW 93
Laffan, Kevin (Barry) 1922- ConDr 93, WrDr 94
Laffan, Patricia 1919- WhoHol 92
Laffer, Arthur IntWW 93, WhoAm 94
Lafferty, James Martin 1916- WhoAm 94
Lafferty, Nancy Ann 1936- WhoMW 93
Lafferty, Perry 1920- IntMPA 94
Lafferty, R(aphael) A(loysius) 1914- EncSF 93, WrDr 94
Lafferty, Richard Thomas 1932- WhoAm 94
Laffin, Dominique d1985 WhoHol 92
Laffin, John 1922- WrDr 94
Laffitte, Hector M. 1934- WhoHisp 94
Laffitte, Hector Manuel 1934- WhoAm 94, WhoAmL 94
Laffitte, Pierre Paul 1925- IntWW 93
Laffont, Robert Raoul 1916- IntWW 93
Laffoon, Carthrae Merrette 1920- WhoAm 94
Lafi, Noa WhoAmP 93
Lafitau, Joseph Francois 1681-1746 EncNAR
Lafite, Marie-Elisabeth Bouee de 1750?-1794 BlmGWL
Lafitte, Francois 1913- Who 94
Lafitte, Leon 1875-1938 NewGrDO
Lafitte y Perez del Pulgar, Maria de los Reyes 1902- BlmGWL
LaFlam, Robert J. 1931- WhoAmP 93
La Flesche, Francis 1857-1932 HisWorL
La Flesche, Susan 1865-1915 HisWorL [port]
La Flesche, Susette 1854-1903 HisWorL
La Fleur, Art WhoHol 92
Lafleur, Guy 1951- WhoAm 94
La Fleur, Joy d1957 WhoHol 92
LaFleur, Larry F. 1945- WhoFI 94
Lafley, Alan Frederick 1922- WhoAm 94
La Follette, Bronson Cutting 1936- WhoAmP 93
LaFollette, Charles Sanborn 1929- WhoAm 94

La Follette, Douglas J. 1940- WhoAm 94, WhoAmP 93, WhoMW 93
LaFollette, Ernest Carlton 1934- WhoAmL 94
La Follette, Robert M., Sr. 1855-1925 HisWorL [port]
La Follette, Robert M., Jr. 1895-1953 HisWorL
Lafon, Dee J. 1929- WhoAmA 93
La Fon, Julia Anna 1919-1981 WhoAmA 93N
LaFon, Richard Harland 1948- WhoWest 94
LaFond, Stephen Dennis 1947- WhoAmL 94
Lafont, Bernadette IntMPA 94
Lafont, Bernadette 1938- WhoHol 92
Lafont, Jean-Philippe 1951- NewGrDO
La Font, Joseph de 1686-1725 NewGrDO
Lafont, Pauline d1988 WhoHol 92
La Fontaine, Mademoiselle c. 1655-1738 IntDcB
La Fontaine, Mlle de 1655-1738 NewGrDO
Lafontaine, Hernán 1934- WhoHisp 94
La Fontaine, Jean de 1621-1695 GuFrLit 2
Lafontaine, Oskar 1943- IntWW 93
Lafontaine, Pat 1965- WhoAm 94
LaFontaine, Thomas E. 1952- WhoScEn 94
Lafontant, Jewel 1922- WhoAmP 93
Lafontant, Julien J. WhoBlA 94
Lafontant-Mankarious, Jewel 1922- WhoAm 94, WhoBlA 94
Lafontsee, Dane 1946- WhoMW 93
La Force, Charlotte Rose Caumont de 1650-1724 BlmGWL
La Force, James Clayburn, Jr. 1928- WhoAm 94, WhoFI 94, WhoWest 94
LaForce, William Leonard, Jr. 1940- WhoAm 94
LaFore, E. T. WhoHisp 94
Lafore, John A., Jr. d1993 NewYTBS 93
LaForest, Gerard V. (J.) 1926- WrDr 94
La Forest, Gerard Vincent 1926- WhoAm 94
LaForest, James John 1927- WhoAm 94
Laforet (Diaz), Carmen 1921- ConWorW 93
Laforet, Carmen 1921- BlmGWL
Laforet, Marie WhoHol 92
LaForge, Elwood Lincoln, Jr. 1944- WhoAm 94
LaForge, Mary Cecile 1945- WhoFI 94
Laforte, Conrad 1921- IntWW 93
LaForte, Michael J., Jr. 1949- WhoAm 94, WhoFI 94
La Fortune, Knolly Stephen 1920- WrDr 94
LaFosse, Guy 1950- WhoAmL 94
La Fosse, Robert WhoAm 94
LaFosse, Robert 1959- ConTFT 11
La Fountaine, George 1934- ConAu 41NR
LaFourest, Judith Ellen WhoMW 93
LaFrance, Joan 1957- WhoIns 94
LaFrance, Joseph Percy 1931- WhoMW 93
LaFrance, Leo James 1942- WhoWest 94
La Frange, Joseph William, III 1940- WhoFI 94
Lafratta, Charles Anthony 1925- WhoIns 94
La Frenais, Ian 1937- Who 94
La Freniere, (B. Marie) Celine 1950- WrDr 94
LaFuze, William L. 1946- WhoAmL 94
Lafving, Brian Douglas 1953- WhoAm 94, WhoAmL 94
Lag, Jul 1915- IntWW 93
Lagacos, Eustace P. 1921- Who 94
Lagally, Max Gunter 1942- WhoAm 94, WhoMW 93, WhoScEn 94
Lagana, Antonio 1944- WhoScEn 94
LaGanga, Donna Brandeis 1950- WhoFI 94
LaGarde, Frederick H. 1928- WhoBlA 94
Lagarde, Jocelyn d1979 WhoHol 92
Lagarde, Paul 1934- IntWW 93
La Garde, Pierre de 1717-c. 1792 NewGrDO
Lagardere, Jean-Luc 1928- CurBio 93 [port], IntWW 93
Lagarias, John Samuel 1921- WhoAm 94
Lagarias, Peter C. 1951- WhoAmL 94
LaGasse, Alfred Bazil, III 1954- WhoAm 94
Lagasse, Bruce Kenneth 1940- WhoWest 94
Lagasse, Raphael 1927- IntWW 93
Lagatta, John 1894-1976 WhoAmA 93N
LaGattuta, Margo DrAPF 93
Lage de Volude, Marquise de 1764-1842 BlmGWL
Lagendries, Raymond 1943- IntWW 93
Lager, Claude SmATA 74
Lager, Douglas Roy 1947- WhoWest 94
Lager, Fannie 1911- WhoAmA 93
Lager, Robert John 1934- WhoAm 94
Lagercrantz, Olof 1911- IntWW 93
Lagerfeld, Karl 1938- IntWW 93
Lagerfeld, Karl Otto 1938- WhoAm 94
Lagerfelt, Caroline WhoHol 92
Lagergren, Gunnar Karl Andreas 1912- IntWW 93
Lagerkvist, Par 1891-1974 ShSCr 12 [port]
Lagerkvist, Par (Fabian) 1891-1974 IntDcT 2, RfGShF
Lagerlof, Ronald Stephen 1956- WhoScEn 94, WhoWest 94
Lagerlof, Selma Ottilia Lovisa 1858-1940 BlmGWL
Lagerlund, Terrence Daniel 1953- WhoMW 93
Lagerstrom, Paco Axel 1914-1989 WhAm 10
Lageschulte, Ray 1922- WhoAmP 93
Lagesen, Philip (Jacobus) 1923- Who 94
Laghzaoui, Mohammed 1906- Who 94
Lagier, Jennifer DrAPF 93
Lagin, Neil 1942- WhoFI 94
Lagina, James Joseph 1958- WhoAmP 93
Lagle, John Franklin 1938- WhoAmL 94
Lago, Armando M. 1939- WhoHisp 94
Lago, John Kent 1964- WhoMW 93
Lago, Mary McClelland 1919- WhoAm 94
Lago, Rafael A. WhoHisp 94
Lagomarsino, Carlos 1964- WhoHisp 94
Lagomarsino, Nancy DrAPF 93
Lagomarsino, Robert John 1926- WhoAmP 93
Lagoria, Georgianna Marie 1953- WhoAm 94, WhoAmA 93
Lagorio, Gina 1930- BlmGWL
Lagorio, Irene R. 1921- WhoAmA 93
Lagorio, Irene Rose 1921- WhoWest 94
Lagos, Archbishop of 1936- Who 94
Lagos, Bishop of Who 94
Lagos, Dickens M. 1936- WhoHisp 94
Lagos, George Peter 1954- WhoAm 94
Lagos, James Harry 1951- WhoAmL 94
Lagos, Poppy d1982 WhoHol 92
Lagos, Ramona C. 1942- WhoHisp 94
Lagos, Rene Guzman 1942- WhoHisp 94
Lagos Escobar, Ricardo 1938- IntWW 93
Lagova, Hana WhoWomW 91
Lagowski, Barbara Jean 1955- WhoAm 94
Lagowski, Joseph John 1930- WhoAm 94
LaGrand, Louis E. 1935- WrDr 94
Lagrange, Joseph Louis 1736-1813 WorScD
Lagrange, Louise d1979 WhoHol 92
Lagrange, Valerie WhoHol 92
Lagrange-Chancel, Francois-Joseph de 1677-1758 NewGrDO
Lagrave, Comtesse de fl. 18th cent.- BlmGWL
La Greca, Annette M(arie) 1950- ConAu 142
LaGreca, John S. 1941- WhoFI 94
LaGreca, T. R. DrAPF 93
Lagree, Ernest-Marc-Louis De Gonzague Doudartde WhWE
LaGreen, Alan Lennart 1951- WhoWest 94
Lagrenee, Maurice d1953 WhoHol 92
LaGrone, Alfred Hall 1912- WhoAm 94
LaGrone, Roy E. d1993 NewYTBS 93
LaGrone, Troy Howard 1934- WhoAm 94
Lagrotta, Frank 1958- WhoAmP 93
La Grua, Tom WhoHol 92
Lagu, Joseph 1931- IntWW 93
LaGuardia, Julie Anne 1967- WhoMW 93
Laguardia, Louis Manuel 1948- WhoHisp 94
Laguatan, Karen A. 1967- WhoFI 94
LaGuerre, Eduardo 1948- WhoHisp 94
La Guerre, Irma-Estel WhoHisp 94
Laguerre, John d1748 NewGrDO
Laguerre, Marie-Josephine 1755-1783 NewGrDO
Laguerre, Michel S. 1943- WhoBlA 94
Lagueruela, Earline 1952- WhoHisp 94
Lagueux, Ronald Rene 1931- WhoAm 94, WhoAmL 94
Laguiller, Arlette 1940- BlmGWL
Laguna, Asela Rodriguez 1946- WhoHisp 94
Laguna, Frederica de 1906- IntWW 93
Laguna, Mariella WhoAmA 93
Laguna, Miguel A., Jr. 1935- WhoHisp 94
Laguna, Richard B. 1940- WhoHisp 94
Lagunoff, David 1932- WhoAm 94, WhoMW 93
Lagura, Franklin Sasutana 1937- WhoAsA 94
Lahaderne, Paul B. 1947- WhoAmL 94
Laham, Sandra Lee 1950- WhoMW 93
La Harpe, Bernard De WhWE
LaHay, David George Michael 1949- WhoAm 94
La Hayne, David WhoHol 92
Lahey, Christine DrAPF 93
Lahey, Edward Vincent, Jr. 1939- WhoAm 94, WhoAmL 94
Lahey, John H. 1946- WhoAm 94
Lahey, Joseph Patrick 1947- WhoAm 94
Lahey, Marguerite Duprez 1880-1958 WhoAmA 93N
Lahey, Richard (Francis) 1893-1979 WhoAmA 93N
Lahiri, Debomoy Kumar 1955- WhoScEn 94
Lahman, Larry D. 1943- WhoAmP 93
Lahmers, David Earl, Sr. 1950- WhoMW 93
Lahn, Jacquelyn Jo 1952- WhoAmP 93
Lahn, Mervyn Lloyd 1933- WhoAm 94
Lahnstein, Manfred 1937- IntWW 93, Who 94
Lahontan, Louis-Armand De Lom D'Arce, Baron De c. 1666-1716 WhWE
LaHood, Marvin J(ohn) 1933- WrDr 94
LaHood, Ray H. 1945- WhoAmP 93
La Hotan, Robert L. 1927- WhoAmA 93
Lahourcade, John Brosius 1924- WhoAm 94
Lahr, Bert d1967 WhoHol 92
Lahr, Bert 1895-1967 WhoCom
Lahr, Brian Scott 1961- WhoScEn 94
Lahr, Charles Dwight 1945- WhoBlA 94
Lahr, Charles Homer 1929- WhoMW 93
Lahr, J(ohn) Stephen 1943- WhoAmA 93
Lahr, Jack Leroy 1934- WhoAm 94
Lahr, John DrAPF 93
Lahr, John 1941- WhoAm 94
Lahr, John (Henry) 1941- WrDr 94
Lahr, John William 1950- WhoMW 93
Lahti, Christine 1950- ConTFT 11, IntMPA 94, WhoAm 94, WhoHol 92
Lahti, Kenneth R. 1934- WhoMW 93
Lahti, Richard 1943- WhoAmP 93, WhoMW 93
Lai, Albert Wenben 1952- WhoAsA 94
Lai, Amy 1966- WhoAsA 94
Lai, Ching-San 1946- WhoAsA 94
Lai, Dennis Fu-hsiung 1939- WhoAsA 94
Lai, Francis 1932- IntDcF 2-4, IntMPA 94
Lai, George Ying-Dean 1940- WhoScEn 94
Lai, Him Mark 1925- WhoWest 94
Lai, Jai-Lue Leon 1940- WhoAsA 94
Lai, Kai Sun 1937- WhoAsA 94
Lai, Kuo-Yann 1946- WhoAsA 94
Lai, Michael Ming-Chiao 1942- WhoAsA 94
Lai, Ming-Chia 1957- WhoScEn 94
Lai, Ming-Yee 1952- WhoAsA 94
Lai, Ngai Chin 1956- WhoWest 94
Lai, Patrick Kinglun 1944- WhoAsA 94
Lai, Ralph Wei-meen 1936- WhoAsA 94
Lai, Richard Jean 1940- WhoScEn 94
Lai, Richard Thomas 1953- WhoAsA 94
Lai, Richard Tseng-yu 1937- WhoAsA 94
Lai, Shu Tim 1938- WhoScEn 94
Lai, Tsong-Yue 1947- WhoAsA 94
Lai, Tze Leung 1945- WhoAsA 94
Lai, Waihang 1939- WhoAmA 93, WhoAsA 94, WhoWest 94
Lai, Wei Michael 1930- WhoAm 94
Lai, Ying-San 1937- WhoAsA 94
Laible, Jon Morse 1937- WhoAm 94
Laibson, Peter Robert 1933- WhoAm 94
Laico, Colette WhoAmA 93
Laidi, Ahmed 1934- Who 94
Laidig, Eldon Lindley 1932- WhoFI 94, WhoWest 94
Laidig, Gary Wayne 1948- WhoAmP 93
Laidig, William Rupert 1927- IntWW 93, WhoAm 94
Laidlaw, Andrew R. 1946- WhoAmL 94
Laidlaw, Brett DrAPF 93
Laidlaw, Bruce W. 1948- WhoAmL 94
Laidlaw, Christopher (Charles Fraser) 1922- Who 94
Laidlaw, Christophor Charles Fraser 1922- IntWW 93
Laidlaw, David Hales 1961- WhoWest 94
Laidlaw, Douglas McNeill, Jr. 1954- WhoWest 94
Laidlaw, Ethan d1963 WhoHol 92
Laidlaw, Harry Hyde, Jr. 1907- WhoAm 94, WhoScEn 94, WhoWest 94
Laidlaw, Marc 1960- EncSF 93
Laidlaw, (Henry) Renton 1939- Who 94
Laidlaw, Robert Richard 1923- WhoAm 94
Laidlaw, Roy d1936 WhoHol 92
Laidlaw, William Samuel Hugh 1956- WhoAm 94
Laidler, David Ernest William 1938- IntWW 93, WhoAm 94
Laidler, (Gavin) Graham 1908-1940 DcNaB MP
Laidler, Keith James 1916- WrDr 94
Laight, Barry Pemberton Who 94
Laigo, Valeriano Emerciano Montante 1930-1992 WhoAsA 94N
Lai Hanxuan WhoPRCh 91
Lai Jinlie WhoPRCh 91
Laikin, George Joseph 1910- WhoAm 94
Lail, Doris Leonhardt 1937- WhoAmP 93
Laila, Abduhameed Abdelrahman 1943- WhoScEn 94
Laimbeer, Bill 1957- WhoAm 94
Laimbeer, William 1934- WhoFI 94
Lain, Allen Warren 1953- WhoScEn 94
Lain, David Cornelius 1955- WhoScEn 94
Laina, Maria 1947- BlmGWL
Lainati, Carlo Ambrogio NewGrDO
Laine, Cleo 1927- ConMus 10 [port], IntWW 93, Who 94, WhoAm 94, WhoBlA 94, WhoHol 92
Laine, Edward M. 1948- WhoAmL 94
Laine, Frankie 1913- WhoHol 92
Laine, Jermu Tapani 1931- IntWW 93
Laine, Katie Myers 1947- WhoAm 94
Laine, Richard R. 1940- WhoAm 94, WhoFI 94
Laine, Roberta Sue 1953- WhoMW 93
Laine, Steven Elliott 1967- WhoFI 94
Laing Who 94
Laing, Alastair Stuart 1920- Who 94
Laing, Alexander (Kinnan) 1903-1976 EncSF 93
Laing, Alexander Gordon 1793-1826 WhWE
Laing, Alfred Benson d1976 WhoHol 92
Laing, Dona Martin 1949- WhoMW 93
Laing, Douglas Rees 1936- Who 94
Laing, Edward A. 1942- WhoBlA 94
Laing, Gerald IntWW 93
Laing, Gerald O. Who 94
Laing, Hugh d1988 WhoHol 92
Laing, Hugh 1911-1988 IntDcB [port]
Laing, James Findlay 1933- Who 94
Laing, Jennifer 1947- IntWW 93
Laing, John d1979 WhoHol 92
Laing, John Archibald 1919- Who 94
Laing, Karel Ann 1939- WhoAm 94
Laing, Kirby Who 94
Laing, (William) Kirby 1916- Who 94
Laing, Malcolm Brian 1955- WhoScEn 94
Laing, Martin Who 94
Laing, (John) Martin (Kirby) 1942- Who 94
Laing, Maurice Who 94
Laing, (John) Maurice 1918- IntWW 93, Who 94
Laing, Michael Andrew 1961- WhoAmL 94
Laing, Nora d1982 WhoHol 92
Laing, Peter Anthony Neville Pennethorne 1922- Who 94
Laing, R(obert) Stanley 1918- IntWW 93
Laing, Richard Harlow 1932- WhoAmA 93
Laing, Ronald David 1927-1989 EncSPD
Laing, (William James) Scott 1914- Who 94
Laing, Stanley IntWW 93
Laing, Stuart Who 94
Laing, (John) Stuart 1948- Who 94
Laing, Susan Ann 1967- WhoMW 93
Laingen, Lowell Bruce 1922- WhoAm 94
Laing Of Dunphail, Baron 1923- IntWW 93, Who 94
Lainoff, Kerry Wayne 1945- WhoMW 93
Lainson, Ralph 1927- IntWW 93, Who 94
Laiou, Angeliki E. 1941- WhoAm 94, WhoAmA 93
Lair, Clara 1895- BlmGWL
Lair, Grace d1955 WhoHol 92
Lair, Helen May 1918- WhoMW 93
Lair, Robert Louis 1921- WhoAm 94
Laird, Alan Douglas Kenneth 1914- WhoAm 94
Laird, Andrew Kenneth 1943- WhoWest 94
Laird, Charles David 1939- WhoAm 94
Laird, Charles F. 1941- WhoAmP 93
Laird, David 1927- WhoAm 94
Laird, David Logan 1937- Who 94
Laird, Donald Anderson 1897- WhAm 10
Laird, Douglas S. 1952- WhoAmL 94
Laird, E. Ruth 1921- WhoAmA 93
Laird, Edward DeHart, Jr. 1952- WhoAmL 94
Laird, Effie d1986 WhoHol 92
Laird, Elizabeth 1943- SmATA 77 [port]
Laird, Endell Johnston Who 94
Laird, Evalyn Walsh 1902- WhoAm 94, WhoAmL 94
Laird, Frank N. 1952- WhoWest 94
Laird, Gavin Harry 1933- IntWW 93, Who 94
Laird, Jack 1923- WhoHol 92
Laird, Jean Elouise Rydeski 1930- WhoMW 93
Laird, Jenny 1915- WhoHol 92
Laird, Jere Don 1933- WhoWest 94
Laird, Margaret Heather 1933- Who 94
Laird, Mary WhoAm 94, WhoFI 94, WhoWest 94
Laird, Melvin R. 1922- Who 94
Laird, Melvin Robert 1922- IntWW 93, WhoAm 94, WhoAmP 93
Laird, Michael S. 1951- WhoAmL 94
Laird, Naomi Affholder WhoAmP 93
Laird, Pamela Sue 1955- WhoWest 94
Laird, Paul Craig 1923- WhoAmP 93
Laird, Richard Joel 1939- WhoAmP 93
Laird, Robert Winslow 1936- WhoAm 94

Laird, Rodney Alan 1961- WhoWest 94
Laird, Roy Dean 1925- WhoAm 94
Laird, Trevor WhoHol 92
Laird, Walter Jones, Jr. 1926- WhoAm 94
Laird, Wesley L. 1962- WhoAmL 94
Laird, Wilbur David, Jr. 1937- WhoAm 94
Laird, William Everette, Jr. 1934- WhoAm 94
Laire, Howard George 1938- WhoScEn 94
Laire, Judson d1979 WhoHol 92
Laires, Fernando 1925- WhoAm 94
Lairet, Dolores Person 1935- WhoBlA 94
Lais, Francois NewGrDO
Lai Shaoqi 1915- IntWW 93, WhoPRCh 91
Lai Shenru 1929- WhoPRCh 91 [port]
Laishes, Brian Anthony 1947- WhoFI 94
Laisse, Madame de fl. 18th cent.- BlmGWL
Laister, Peter 1929- IntWW 93, Who 94
Laisure, Sharon Emily Goode 1954- WhoBlA 94
Lait, Jacqui 1947- Who 94
Lait, Leonard Hugh Cecil 1930- Who 94
Lait, Robert 1921- WrDr 94
Laithwaite, Eric Roberts 1921- IntWW 93, Who 94, WrDr 94
Laithwaite, John 1920- Who 94
Laitin, David Dennis 1945- WhoAm 94
Laitin, Howard 1931- WhoWest 94
Laitin, Joseph 1914- WhoAm 94, WhoAmP 93
Laitone, Edmund Victor 1915- WhoScEn 94, WhoWest 94
Laiwala, Sadrudin 1955- WhoWest 94
Lajarte, Theodore (Edouard Dufaure de) 1826-1890 NewGrDO
Lajeunesse, Marcel 1942- WhoAm 94
Lajeunesse, Michael A. 1944- WhoAmP 93
LaJeunesse, Robert Paul 1950- WhoScEn 94
Lajoie, Roland 1936- WhoAm 94
Lajoinie, Andre 1929- IntWW 93
La Jone, Jay Allen 1953- WhoAm 94
Lajtha, Abel 1922- WhoScEn 94
Lajtha, Laszlo George 1920- Who 94
Lakas Bahas, Demetrio Basilio 1925- IntWW 93
Lakatos, Jozsefne WhoWomW 91
Lakdawala, Vishnu Keshavlal 1951- WhoScEn 94
Lake, Alan d1984 WhoHol 92
Lake, Alfreeda Elizabeth 1923- WhoBlA 94
Lake, Alice d1967 WhoHol 92
Lake, Ann Winslow 1919- WhoAm 94
Lake, Anthony WhoAm 94
Lake, Anthony 1939- IntWW 93
Lake, Arthur d1987 WhoHol 92
Lake, Brian James 1946- WhoAm 94
Lake, Carnell Augustino 1967- WhoBlA 94
Lake, Charles William, Jr. 1918- WhoMW 93
Lake, Christopher Robert 1952- WhoFI 94
Lake, Claude BlmGWL
Lake, David (John) 1929- WrDr 94
Lake, David J. 1929- ConAu 41NR
Lake, David J(ohn) 1929- EncSF 93
Lake, David S. 1938- WhoAm 94, WhoWest 94
Lake, Edwin S. WhoAmP 93
Lake, F. David, Jr. 1943- WhoAmL 94
Lake, Finley Edward 1934- WhoAm 94, WhoWest 94
Lake, Florence d1980 WhoHol 92
Lake, Frank d1936 WhoHol 92
Lake, Frederic WhoAmA 93N
Lake, George, Jr. 1920- WhoMW 93
Lake, (Atwell) Graham 1923- Who 94
Lake, Harriet WhoHol 92
Lake, Isaac Beverly, Jr. 1934- WhoAmP 93
Lake, James Howard 1937- WhoAmP 93
Lake, Janet WhoHol 92
Lake, Jerry Lee 1941- WhoAmA 93
Lake, Joseph Edward 1941- WhoAm 94, WhoAmP 93
Lake, Kathleen C. 1955- WhoAmL 94
Lake, Kevin Bruce 1937- WhoWest 94
Lake, Larry Wayne 1946- WhoScEn 94
Lake, Lew d1939 WhoHol 92
Lake, Mack Clayton 1890-1954 EncABHB 9
Lake, Michael WhoHol 92
Lake, Oliver DrAPF 93
Lake, Paul DrAPF 93
Lake, Peter Stevenson 1960- WhoAmL 94
Lake, Randall 1947- WhoAmA 93, WhoWest 94
Lake, Richard Arthur 1946- WhoIns 94
Lake, Ricki NewYTBS 93 [port]
Lake, Ricki 1968- IntMPA 94, WhoHol 92
Lake, Robert Charles 1941- WhoAm 94
Lake, Simeon Timothy, III 1944- WhoAm 94, WhoAmL 94
Lake, Stanley James 1926- WhoWest 94
Lake, Veronica d1973 WhoHol 92
Lake, W. Anthony NewYTBS 93 [port]
Lake, W. Anthony 1939- WhoAmP 93
Lake, Walter L. 1921- WhoAmP 93
Lake, William Thomas 1910- WhoAm 94
Lake, William Truman 1943- WhoAm 94
Lakeman, Enid 1903- Who 94, WrDr 94
Laken, B. 1936- WrDr 94
Laken, Neoma Ann 1934- WhoMW 93
Lake Poets BlmGEL
Laker, Freddie 1922- Who 94
Laker, Frederick Alfred 1922- IntWW 93
Laker, Rosalind WrDr 94
Lakes, Gary 1950- NewGrDO
Lakes, Gordon Harry 1928- Who 94
Lakes, Roderic Stephen 1948- WhoMW 93
Lakes, Stephen Charles 1951- WhoScEn 94
Lakey, Arnold Neil 1937- WhoFI 94
Lakey, John Richard Angwin 1929- Who 94
Lakhani, Dilawar 1943- WhoFI 94
Lakhani, Kamlesh Who 94
Lakhova, Ekaterina Filippovna 1948- LngBDD
Laki, Krisztina 1944- NewGrDO
Lakin, Charles Dean 1936- WhoMW 93
Lakin, Deborah Anne 1947- WhoFI 94
Lakin, James Dennis 1945- WhoAm 94, WhoMW 93
Lakin, John Francis 1960- WhoAmL 94
Lakin, Michael 1934- Who 94
Lakin, R. D. DrAPF 93
Lakin, Scott 1957- WhoAmP 93
Lakin, Scott Bradley 1957- WhoMW 93
Laking, George (Robert) 1912- IntWW 93, Who 94
Lakkaraju, Harinarayana Sarma 1946- WhoAsA 94, WhoScEn 94
Lakly, Daniel Joseph 1942- WhoAmP 93
Lako, Charles Michael, Jr. 1947- WhoAmL 94
Lakoff, Evelyn 1932- WhoWest 94
Lakoff, Sanford 1931- WhoAm 94
Lakritz, Isaac 1952- WhoAm 94
Lakshman, Govind 1948- WhoAsA 94
Lakshmanan, Chithra 1933- WhoAsA 94
Lakshmanan, Mark Chandrakant 1953- WhoMW 93, WhoScEn 94
Lakshmikantham, Vangipuram 1926- WhoAm 94
Lakshminarayana, Budugur 1935- WhoAm 94, WhoScEn 94
Lakshminarayanan, Vasudevan 1957- WhoWest 94
Lal, Bansi 1927- IntWW 93
Lal, Bipen Behari 1917- IntWW 93
Lal, Deepak Kumar 1940- IntWW 93
Lal, Devendra 1929- IntWW 93, Who 94, WhoAm 94
Lal, Devi 1914- IntWW 93
Lal, Dhyan 1948- WhoAsA 94
Lal, Rattan 1944- WhoAm 94, WhoAsA 94
Lala, Dominick J. 1928- WhoAm 94
Lala, Peeyush Kanti 1934- WhoAm 94
Lala, Tapan Kanti WhoWest 94
Lalande, Gilles 1927-1988 WhAm 10
Lalande, Maria d1968 WhoHol 92
Lalande, Michel-Richard de 1657-1726 NewGrDO
Lalandi-Emery, Lina Who 94
Lalanne, Bernard Michel L. Who 94
LaLanne, Laurel C. 1951- WhoAmL 94
Lalbhai, Arvind N. 1918- IntWW 93
Lalemant, Gabriel 1610-1649 WhWE
Lalemant, Jerome 1593-1673 EncNAR
LaLena, John Charles 1931- WhoAm 94
La Liberte, Ann Gillis 1942- WhoMW 93
Laliberte-Bourque, Andree WhoAm 94
Lalic, Ivan V. 1931- ConWorW 93
Lalive d'Epinay, Pierre 1923- IntWW 93
Lalka Dart, Judith C. 1947- WhoAmL 94
Lall, Arthur Samuel 1911- IntWW 93
Lall, B. Kent 1939- WhoScEn 94
Lalla, Diallo WhoWomW 91
Lalla Aicha, H.R.H. Princess IntWW 93
Lallement, Jacques Georges Paulin 1922- IntWW 93
Lalley, Frank Edward 1944- WhoAm 94
Lalli, Cele G. EncSF 93
Lalli, (Benedetto) Domenico 1679-1741 NewGrDO
Lalli, Michael Anthony 1955- WhoAmL 94
Lalliam, Nafissa WhoWomW 91
L'Allier, James Joseph 1945- WhoFI 94
L'Allier, Jean-Paul WhoAm 94
Lallinger, E. Michael 1915- WhoAm 94
Lallo, M. J. DrAPF 93
Lallouette, Jean Francois 1651-1728 NewGrDO
Lally, Donald J., Jr. 1955- WhoAmP 93
Lally, James WhoHol 92
Lally, James Joseph 1945- WhoAmA 93
Lally, John Anthony 1962- WhoAmL 94
Lally, Margaret DrAPF 93
Lally, Michael DrAPF 93
Lally, Michael d1985 WhoHol 92
Lally, Michael David 1942- WhoAm 94
Lally, Mick WhoHol 92
Lally, Richard Francis 1925- WhoAm 94
Lally, Thomas Joseph 1965- WhoMW 93
Lally, William Joseph 1937- WhoFI 94
Lally-Green, Maureen Ellen 1949- WhoAmL 94
Lalo, Edouard(-Victoire-Antoine) 1823-1892 NewGrDO
La Loca DrAPF 93
LaLoggia, Frank 1955- HorFD
Lalonde, Brice 1946- IntWW 93
Lalonde, John Stephen, Sr. 1948- WhoMW 93
LaLonde, Larry c. 1969- See Primus ConMus 11
LaLonde, Leo Francis 1942- WhoAmP 93
Lalonde, Leo R. WhoAmP 93
Lalonde, Marc 1929- IntWW 93, Who 94, WhoAm 94
Lalonde, Martha d1944 WhoHol 92
Lalonde, Raymond 1940- WhoAmP 93
LaLonde, Robert Frederick 1922- WhoAmP 93, WhoWest 94
LaLonde, Robert Thomas 1931- WhoScEn 94
Lalor, Frank d1932 WhoHol 92
Lalor, Patrick Joseph 1926- IntWW 93
Lalouette, Marie Joseph Gerard d1992 Who 94N
Laloy, Jean Leonard 1912- IntWW 93
Laloy, Louis 1874-1944 NewGrDO
Laluah, Aquah BlkWr 2
La Lumia, Frank 1948- WhoAmA 93
La Lumia, Frank Munzueto 1948- WhoWest 94
Lalumiere, Catherine 1935- Who 94
Lalumiere, Catherine 1936- IntWW 93
La Luz, José A. 1950- WhoHisp 94
La Luz, Wilfredo Azul 1946- WhoMW 93
Laly, Amy 1947- WhoAsA 94
Lam, Alex W. WhoAsA 94
Lam, An Ngoc 1964- WhoAsA 94
Lam, Bing Kit 1957- WhoScEn 94
Lam, Chow-Shing 1947- WhoAsA 94
Lam, Chun H. WhoAsA 94
Lam, Daniel Haw 1961- WhoScEn 94
Lam, David WhoAm 94
Lam, Dick 1939- WhoAsA 94
Lam, Eppie C. F. 1941- WhoAsA 94
Lam, Fat C. 1946- WhoAsA 94
Lam, Gerald N.Y.C. 1951- WhoFI 94
Lam, Gilbert Nim-Car 1951- WhoAsA 94
Lam, James Chi-Chiu 1961- WhoFI 94
Lam, Jennette (Brinsmade) 1911-1985 WhoAmA 93N
Lam, Leo Kongsui 1946- WhoAsA 94
Lam, Lui 1944- WhoAsA 94, WhoWest 94
Lam, Martin Philip 1920- Who 94
Lam, Nelson Jen-Wei 1960- WhoAsA 94
Lam, Peggy 1928- WhoWomW 91
Lam, Robert Marcus 1925- WhoFI 94
Lam, Sau-Hai 1930- WhoAm 94, WhoAsA 94
Lam, Simon Shin-Sing 1947- WhoAm 94, WhoAsA 94, WhoScEn 94
Lam, Thomas Manpan 1957- WhoAsA 94
Lam, Toan Hoang 1951- WhoAsA 94
Lam, Tony 1936- WhoAsA 94
Lam, Truong Buu 1933- WrDr 94
Lama, Alberto De WhoAmA 93
Lama, Juan-Carlos 1960- WhoFI 94
Lama, Luciano 1921- IntWW 93
Lamac, Karl d1952 WhoHol 92
Lamadrid, Enrique R. 1948- WhoHisp 94
LaMagna, John Thomas 1961- WhoScEn 94
Lamagra, Anthony James 1935- WhoAm 94
Lamal, Christopher Thomas 1951- WhoAmL 94
Lamale, Ellen Z. 1953- WhoIns 94
La Malfa, James Thomas 1937- WhoAmA 93
LaMalfa, Joachim Jack 1915- WhoMW 93
Lamalie, Robert Eugene 1931- WhoAm 94, WhoFI 94
Laman, Jerry Thomas 1947- WhoScEn 94
Lamanec, Tracy 1941- WhoAm 94
Lamanna, Carmen 1927-1991 WhoAmA 93N
LaManna, Joseph Charles 1949- WhoMW 93
La Mantia, Charles Robert 1939- WhoAm 94, WhoFI 94, WhoScEn 94
Lamantia, James 1923- WhoAmA 93
Lamantia, Paul (Christopher) Zombek 1938- WhoAmA 93
Lamantia, Philip DrAPF 93
Lamantia, Philip 1927- WrDr 94
Lamar, Cleveland James 1924- WhoBlA 94
Lamar, Donovan Eugene 1956- WhoWest 94
Lamar, Dwight 1951- BasBi
Lamar, Hilary L. 1948- WhoAmL 94
Lamar, Howard Roberts 1923- WhoAm 94, WrDr 94
Lamar, Jake 1961- WhoBlA 94
Lamar, James Lewis, Jr. 1959- WhoScEn 94
Lamar, Mario Anselmo 1946- WhoHisp 94
Lamar, William, Jr. 1952- WhoBlA 94
LaMarca, Anthony 1944- WhoMW 93
LaMarca, Howard J. 1934- WhoAmA 93
Lamarck, Jean Baptiste 1744-1829 WorScD
Lamare, Nappy d1988 WhoHol 92
Lamarque, Maurice Patrick Jean 1948- WhoScEn 94
La Marr, Barbara d1926 WhoHol 92
LaMarr, Catherine Elizabeth 1960- WhoBlA 94
Lamarr, Hedy 1913- WhoHol 92
Lamarr, Hedy 1915- IntMPA 94
La Marr, Richard d1975 WhoHol 92
Lamarre, Bernard 1931- WhoAm 94, WhoScEn 94
LaMarre, John H. d1993 NewYTBS 93
Lamarre, Paul WhoAmA 93
Lamas, Fernando d1982 WhoHol 92
Lamas, José Francisco 1940- WhoHisp 94
Lamas, Lorenzo 1958- IntMPA 94, WhoAm 94, WhoHisp 94, WhoHol 92
Lamas, Maria 1893-1983 BlmGWL
La Master, Slater 1890- EncSF 93
Lamaute, Denise 1952- WhoBlA 94
Lamb Who 94
Lamb, Adrian S. d1989 WhoAmA 93N
Lamb, Albert Who 94
Lamb, Albert Thomas 1921- Who 94
Lamb, Alberta Carmella WhoAmA 93
Lamb, Allan Joseph 1954- IntWW 93
Lamb, Andrew (Martin) 1942- NewGrDO
Lamb, Angela K. 1944- WhoAmP 93
Lamb, Berton Lee, II 1945- WhoWest 94
Lamb, Caroline 1785-1828 BlmGEL, BlmGWL
Lamb, Charles d1989 WhoHol 92
Lamb, Charles 1775-1834 BlmGEL
Lamb, Charlotte 1937- WrDr 94
Lamb, Christina 1965- ConAu 140
Lamb, Darlis Carol WhoAmA 93, WhoWest 94
Lamb, Denis 1937- IntWW 93
Lamb, Don Carroll 1965- WhoMW 93
Lamb, Edward Allen, Jr. 1957- WhoScEn 94
Lamb, Elizabeth Searle DrAPF 93
Lamb, Elizabeth Searle 1917- WrDr 94
Lamb, F(rank) Bruce 1913-1992 WrDr 94N
Lamb, Florence d1966 WhoHol 92
Lamb, Frederic Davis 1931- WhoAm 94
Lamb, G(eoffrey) F(rederick) ConAu 41NR
Lamb, Geoffrey Frederick WrDr 94
Lamb, George C., III 1953- WhoAmL 94
Lamb, George Colin 1923- Who 94
Lamb, George Richard 1928- WhoAm 94
Lamb, Gil 1906- WhoHol 92
Lamb, Gordon Howard 1934- WhoAm 94, WhoMW 93
Lamb, Harold Norman 1922- Who 94
Lamb, Henry Grodon 1906- WhoScEn 94
Lamb, Howard Allen 1924- WhoAmP 93
Lamb, Hubert Horace 1913- WrDr 94
Lamb, James B(arrett) 1919- WrDr 94
Lamb, James L. 1924- WhoAmP 93
Lamb, Jamie Parker, Jr. 1933- WhoAm 94
Lamb, Jane Marie, Sister 1936- WhoMW 93
Lamb, Joan Eugenia 1939- WhoAmP 93
Lamb, John 1735-1800 AmRev, WhAmRev [port]
Lamb, John Michael 1926- WhoMW 93
Lamb, Joseph Fairweather 1928- Who 94
Lamb, Karl A(llen) 1933- WrDr 94
Lamb, Kenneth Henry Lowry 1923- Who 94
Lamb, Kenneth Robert 1960- WhoAmL 94
Lamb, Kevin Thomas 1956- WhoAmL 94
Lamb, Larry WhoHol 92
Lamb, Larry 1929- Who 94
Lamb, Lester Lewis 1932- WhoAm 94
Lamb, Lowell David 1955- WhoScEn 94
Lamb, Margaret Weldon 1935- WhoScEn 94
Lamb, Mary Ann 1764-1847 BlmGEL
Lamb, Michael Edward 1963- WhoAmP 93
Lamb, Mildred Shimonishi 1913- WhoWest 94
Lamb, Norman 1935- WhoAmP 93
Lamb, Patricia Clare DrAPF 93
Lamb, Peter James 1947- WhoAm 94, WhoScEn 94
Lamb, Rebecca Ann 1948- WhoMW 93
Lamb, Rex McNaughton, III 1949- WhoAmL 94
Lamb, Richard Compton 1933- WhoMW 93

Lamb, Robert E. 1936- *WhoAmP 93*
Lamb, Robert Edward 1936- *WhoAm 94*
Lamb, Robert Lee 1930- *WhoAm 94* .
Lamb, Robert Lewis 1932- *WhoAm 94*
Lamb, Roger 1756-1830 *AmRev, WhAmRev*
Lamb, Stephen P. 1949- *WhoAmL 94*
Lamb, Sydney MacDonald 1929- *WhoAm 94*
Lamb, Thomas A. 1927- *WhoAmP 93*
Lamb, Trevor David 1948- *Who 94*
Lamb, Ursula Schaefer 1914- *WhoAm 94*
Lamb, Wally *DrAPF 93*
Lamb, Wally 1950- *ConAu 140*
Lamb, Walter *ConAu 140*
Lamb, William *EncSF 93*
Lamb, William Augustus 1953- *WhoFI 94*
Lamb, William John d1993 *Who 94N*
Lamb, Willis E(ugene), Jr. 1913- *Who 94*
Lamb, Willis Eugene, Jr. 1913- *IntWW 93, WhoAm 94, WhoScEn 94, WhoWest 94*
Lambardi, Mario fl. 1895-1915 *NewGrDO*
Lambart *Who 94*
Lambart, Ernest d1945 *WhoHol 92*
Lamb-Brassington, Kathryn Evelyn 1935- *WhoWest 94*
Lambdin, Dewey (W.) 1945- *ConAu 140*
Lambe, Catherine van de Velde 1950- *WhoAmL 94*
Lambe, Dean R. *EncSF 93*
Lambe, Thomas William 1920- *WhoAm 94*
Lambe, Walter fl. 1476-1499 *DcNaB MP*
Lambeau, Earl d1965 *ProFbHF [port]*
Lambeck, Kurt 1941- *IntWW 93*
Lambelet, Edouardos 1820?-1903 *NewGrDO*
Lambelet, Napoleon 1864-1932? *NewGrDO*
Lamberg, Joan Bernice 1935- *WhoMW 93*
Lamberg, Lynne Friedman 1942- *WhoScEn 94*
Lamberg, Stanley Lawrence 1933- *WhoAm 94*
Lamberg-Karlovsky, Clifford Charles 1937- *WhoAm 94, WhoScEn 94*
Lamberson, C. Allen 1932- *WhoMW 93*
Lamberson, Harry P. 1942- *WhoAmL 94*
Lamberson, John Roger 1933- *WhoAm 94*
Lambert, Marquise de 1647-1733 *BlmGWL*
Lambert, Viscount 1912- *Who 94*
Lambert, Anne Louise *WhoHol 92*
Lambert, Anthony (Edward) 1911- *Who 94*
Lambert, Benjamin Franklin 1933- *WhoBlA 94*
Lambert, Benjamin J., III 1937- *WhoBlA 94*
Lambert, Benjamin Joseph, III 1937- *WhoAmP 93*
Lambert, Betty 1933-1983 *BlmGWL*
Lambert, Blanche M. 1960- *CngDr 93, WhoAm 94*
Lambert, Blanche Meyers 1960- *WhoAmP 93*
Lambert, Carol A. 1941- *WhoMW 93*
Lambert, Charles Frederic 1896- *WhAm 10*
Lambert, Charles H. 1948- *WhoBlA 94*
Lambert, Christopher 1957- *IntMPA 94, IntWW 93, WhoHol 92*
Lambert, Constant d1951 *WhoHol 92*
Lambert, Constant 1905-1951 *IntDcB*
Lambert, Dale John 1946- *WhoAmL 94, WhoAmP 93*
Lambert, Daniel Michael 1941- *WhoAm 94*
Lambert, Darwin 1916- *WrDr 94*
Lambert, David 1952- *WhoMW 93*
Lambert, David Arthur Charles 1933- *Who 94*
Lambert, David George 1940- *Who 94*
Lambert, David L. *WhoScEn 94*
Lambert, Dennis Edson 1941- *WhoAmP 93*
Lambert, Dennis Michael 1947- *WhoScEn 94*
Lambert, Derek (William) 1929- *WrDr 94*
Lambert, Douglas d1986 *WhoHol 92*
Lambert, Ed 1949- *WhoAmA 93*
Lambert, Edward (Thomas) 1901- *Who 94*
Lambert, Edward M., Jr. 1958- *WhoAmP 93*
Lambert, Eleanor *WhoAm 94*
Lambert, Eric Thomas Drummond 1909- *Who 94*
Lambert, Eugene Isaak 1935- *WhoAm 94*
Lambert, Eugene Kent 1944- *WhoMW 93*
Lambert, Frederick William 1943- *WhoAm 94*
Lambert, Gavin 1924- *WrDr 94*
Lambert, George Robert 1933- *WhoAm 94, WhoAmL 94*
Lambert, Harold George 1910- *Who 94*
Lambert, Henry Uvedale Antrobus 1925- *IntWW 93, Who 94*
Lambert, Jack *ProFbHF [port]*

Lambert, Jack d1976 *WhoHol 92*
Lambert, Jack 1920- *WhoHol 92*
Lambert, Jack Robert 1946- *WhoMW 93*
Lambert, James Allen 1956- *WhoScEn 94*
Lambert, James LeBeau 1934- *WhoScEn 94*
Lambert, James Michael 1959- *WhoScEn 94*
Lambert, James Morrison 1928- *WhoScEn 94*
Lambert, Jane *WhoHol 92*
Lambert, Jay J. 1943- *WhoAmL 94*
Lambert, Jean Denise 1950- *Who 94*
Lambert, Jeanette H. 1949- *WhoBlA 94*
Lambert, Jeremiah Daniel 1934- *WhoAm 94*
Lambert, Jimmy 1970- *WhoHol 92*
Lambert, Joan 1946- *WhoAmP 93*
Lambert, John (Henry) 1921- *Who 94*
Lambert, John Boyd 1929- *WhoAm 94, WhoScEn 94*
Lambert, John Paul 1964- *WhoWest 94*
Lambert, John Phillip 1944- *WhoAm 94*
Lambert, John Sinclair 1948- *Who 94*
Lambert, John T., Jr. 1955- *WhoAmP 93*
Lambert, Jon Kelly 1954- *WhoScEn 94*
Lambert, Joseph Buckley 1940- *WhoAm 94, WhoScEn 94*
Lambert, Joseph C. 1936- *WhoBlA 94*
Lambert, Joseph E. 1948- *WhoAmP 93*
Lambert, Joseph Earl 1948- *WhoAmL 94*
Lambert, Keith Harwood 1914- *WhoAmP 93*
Lambert, L. Gary 1937- *WhoWest 94*
Lambert, Latham d1781 *WhAmRev*
Lambert, Lawrence Arthur 1921- *WhoAmP 93*
Lambert, LeClair Grier *WhoBlA 94, WhoMW 93*
Lambert, Leonard W. 1938- *WhoBlA 94*
Lambert, Lloyd Tupper 1901- *WhoFI 94*
Lambert, Lyn Dee 1954- *WhoAmL 94*
Lambert, Margaret (Barbara) 1906- *Who 94*
Lambert, Margaret Kidd 1940- *WhoAmP 93*
Lambert, Mark *WhoHol 92*
Lambert, Martha Lowery 1937- *WhoAmP 93, WhoWest 94*
Lambert, Mary *IntMPA 94*
Lambert, Mary Pulliam 1944- *WhoMW 93*
Lambert, Michael Gerard 1952- *WhoFI 94*
Lambert, Michael Irving 1958- *WhoScEn 94*
Lambert, Michael Malet 1930- *WhoAm 94*
Lambert, Mikal Stewart 1957- *WhoAmL 94*
Lambert, Nadine Murphy *WhoAm 94*
Lambert, Olaf Cecil 1920- *WhoAm 94*
Lambert, Olaf Francis d1993 *Who 94N*
Lambert, Pamela Susann 1945- *WhoMW 93*
Lambert, Patricia 1926- *Who 94*
Lambert, Paul *WhoHol 92*
Lambert, Paul C. 1928- *WhoAmP 93*
Lambert, Paul Christopher 1928- *WhoAm 94*
Lambert, Paul Richard 1952- *WhoAmP 93*
Lambert, Peggy Lynne Bailey 1948- *WhoAmL 94*
Lambert, Peter John Biddulph 1952- *Who 94*
Lambert, Philip 1925- *WhoAm 94*
Lambert, Phyllis 1927- *IntWW 93*
Lambert, Piggy 1888-1958 *BasBi*
Lambert, Ralph William 1946- *WhoScEn 94*
Lambert, Raymond Edward 1945- *WhoAmP 93*
Lambert, Richard Bowles, Jr. 1939- *WhoScEn 94*
Lambert, Richard Dale, Jr. 1952- *WhoScEn 94*
Lambert, Richard Peter 1944- *IntWW 93, Who 94*
Lambert, Richard William 1928- *WhoScEn 94, WhoWest 94*
Lambert, Robert 1960- *ConTFT 11*
Lambert, Robert Frank 1924- *WhoAm 94*
Lambert, Robert Joe 1921- *WhAm 10*
Lambert, Robert Lowell 1923- *WhoAm 94*
Lambert, Rollins Edward 1922- *WhoBlA 94*
Lambert, Roy D. 1946- *WhoAmL 94*
Lambert, S.H. *EncSF 93*
Lambert, Samuel Fredrick 1928- *WhoBlA 94*
Lambert, Samuel Waldron, III 1938- *WhoAm 94, WhoAmL 94*
Lambert, Steve *WhoHol 92*
Lambert, Steven Charles 1947- *WhoAm 94*
Lambert, Steven Judson 1948- *WhoWest 94*
Lambert, Tex d1976 *WhoHol 92*
Lambert, Thomas Howard 1926- *Who 94*
Lambert, Thomas P. 1946- *WhoAmL 94*

Lambert, Toby Joseph d1972 *WhoHol 92*
Lambert, Verity *IntMPA 94*
Lambert, Verity Ann *Who 94*
Lambert, Victor d1940 *WhoHol 92*
Lambert, William G. 1920- *WhoAm 94*
Lambert, William Wilson 1919- *WhoAm 94*
Lambert, Yves Maurice 1936- *IntWW 93*
Lambert Barton, Nelda Ann 1929- *WhoWomW 91*
Lamberth, Royce C. 1943- *CngDr 93, WhoAm 94, WhoAmL 94*
Lamberti, Gary Anthony 1953- *WhoMW 93*
Lamberti, Giorgio (Casellato-) 1938- *NewGrDO*
Lamberti, Marjorie 1937- *WhoAm 94*
Lamberti, Michael Joseph 1958- *WhoFI 94*
Lamberton, Donald McLean 1927- *WrDr 94*
Lamberton, William John 1948- *WhoAmP 93*
Lambertsen, Christian James 1917- *WhoAm 94*
Lambertson, David F. *WhoAmP 93*
Lambertson, David Floyd 1940- *WhoAm 94*
Lamberty, Patricia Ann 1942- *WhoAmP 93*
Lamberty, Sharlene Louise 1936- *WhoMW 93*
Lambeth, Archdeacon of *Who 94*
Lambeth, James Erwin 1916- *WhoAmP 93*
Lambeth, Thomas Willis 1935- *WhoAmP 93*
Lambeth, Victor Neal 1920- *WhoAm 94*
Lambetti, Ellie d1983 *WhoHol 92*
Lambi, Ivo Nikolai 1931- *WrDr 94*
Lambie, David 1925- *Who 94*
Lambie, Margaret McClements *WhoWest 94*
Lambie-Nairn, Martin John 1945- *Who 94*
Lambird, Mona Salyer 1938- *WhoAm 94*
Lambird, Perry Albert 1939- *WhoAmP 93*
Lambirth, Thomas Thurman 1949- *WhoScEn 94*
Lamble, Lloyd 1914- *WhoHol 92*
Lambo, (Thomas) Adeoye 1923- *IntWW 93*
Lambo, Thomas Adeoye 1923- *Who 94*
Lamboll, Alan Seymour 1923- *Who 94*
Lamborghini, Ferruccio d1993 *NewYTBS 93 [port]*
Lamborghini, Ferruccio 1916-1993 *News 93-3*
Lamborn, LeRoy Leslie 1937- *WhoAm 94*
Lambos, William Andrew 1956- *WhoScEn 94*
Lambot, Isobel Mary 1926- *WrDr 94*
Lambourne, John 1893- *EncSF 93*
Lambowitz, Sheila 1947- *WhoMW 93*
Lambrakis, Christos 1934- *IntWW 93*
Lambrecht, Carol Ann 1958- *WhoFI 94*
Lambrechts, Marc 1955- *WhoAmA 93*
Lambrechts, Robert John 1959- *WhoAmL 94*
Lambremont, Edward Nelson, Jr. 1928- *WhoAm 94, WhoScEn 94*
Lambright, Stephen Kirk 1942- *WhoAm 94*
Lambrinos, Jorge J. 1944- *WhoHisp 94*
Lambrinos, Vassili *WhoHol 92*
Lambro, Donald Joseph 1940- *WhoAm 94*
Lambro, Phillip 1935- *WhoAm 94*
Lambron, Helen Katherine 1950- *WhoMW 93*
Lambropoulos, Vassilios Dionysios 1953- *WhoMW 93*
Lambros, Lambros John 1935- *WhoAm 94*
Lambros, Thomas Demetrios 1930- *WhoAm 94, WhoAmL 94, WhoMW 93*
Lambsdorff, Otto Friedrich Wilhelm von der Wenge 1926- *IntWW 93*
Lambton *Who 94*
Lambton, Viscount 1922- *Who 94*
Lambton, Ann Katharine Swynford 1912- *Who 94*
Lambton, Anne *DrAPF 93*
Lambton, Antony (Claud Frederick) 1922- *WrDr 94*
Lamburn, Patricia *Who 94*
Lamby, Werner 1924- *IntWW 93*
Lame Bill dc. 1900 *EncNAR*
Lame Deer, John c. 1900-1976 *EncNAR*
Lameiro, Gerard Francis 1949- *WhoFI 94, WhoScEn 94, WhoWest 94*
Lameiro, Paul Ambrose 1957- *WhoWest 94*
Lamel, Linda H. 1943- *WhoIns 94*
Lamel, Linda Helen 1943- *WhoAm 94*
Lamela, Luis 1950- *WhoHisp 94*
LaMell, Philip Alan 1946- *WhoWest 94*
Lamell, Robert (C.) 1913- *WhoAmA 93*
LaMendola, Walter F. *WhoAm 94*

Lamer, Antonio 1933- *Who 94, WhoAm 94*
La Mere, Oliver fl. 20th cent.- *EncNAR*
Lamere, Robert Kent 1926- *WhoAmL 94*
Lamerle, Paul Jacques de 1688-1751 *DcNaB MP*
Lamerton, Leonard Frederick 1915- *Who 94*
Lamfalussy, Alexandre 1929- *IntWW 93*
Lamford, (Thomas) Gerald 1928- *Who 94*
Lamia, Thomas Roger 1938- *WhoAm 94*
Laming, (William) Herbert 1936- *Who 94*
Lamirande, Arthur Gordon 1936- *WhoScEn 94*
Lamirande, Carole Ann 1940- *WhoAmP 93*
Lamirande, Emilien 1926- *WhoAm 94, WrDr 94*
Lamis, Leroy 1925- *WhoAm 94, WhoAmA 93*
Lamizana, Aboubakar Sangoule 1916- *IntWW 93*
Lamjav, Banzraghiin 1920- *IntWW 93*
Lamka, Bruce 1951- *WhoAmL 94*
Lamka, Nancy Carolyn 1944- *WhoWest 94*
Lamkin, Bill Dan 1929- *WhoAm 94*
Lamkin, Gerald I. 1936- *WhoMW 93*
Lamkin, Martha Dampf 1942- *WhoMW 93*
Lamkin, William Pierce 1919- *WhoAm 94*
Lamle, Hugh Roy 1945- *WhoFI 94*
Lamley, Karla Christine 1965- *WhoMW 93*
Lamm, Carolyn Beth 1948- *WhoAm 94, WhoAmL 94*
Lamm, Donald Lee 1943- *WhoScEn 94*
Lamm, Donald Stephen 1931- *IntWW 93, WhoAm 94*
Lamm, Harvey H. 1935- *WhoFI 94*
Lamm, Karen *WhoHol 92*
Lamm, Lester Paul 1934- *WhoAm 94*
Lamm, Michael Emanuel 1934- *WhoAm 94*
Lamm, Norman 1927- *WhoAm 94*
Lamm, Richard D. 1935- *IntWW 93, WhoAmP 93*
Lammers, Ann Conrad 1945- *WhoWest 94*
Lammers, Gerda 1915- *NewGrDO*
Lammers, Jerome Bryce 1937- *WhoAmP 93*
Lammers, John Charles 1944- *WhoWest 94*
Lammers, Lennis Larry 1937- *WhoFI 94*
Lammers, Michael Gerrard 1961- *WhoFI 94*
Lammers, Nancy Alice 1940- *WhoMW 93*
Lammers, Nitzia I. 1947- *WhoMW 93*
Lammers, Thomas Gerard 1955- *WhoScEn 94*
Lammers, Wayne P. 1951- *ConAu 140*
Lammert, Richard Alan 1949- *WhoAmL 94*
Lammert, Thomas Edward 1947- *WhoAmL 94*
Lammertsma, Koop 1949- *WhoScEn 94*
Lammiman, David Askey 1932- *Who 94*
Lamming, George *DrAPF 93*
Lamming, George 1927- *BlmGEL*
Lamming, George (Eric) 1927- *WrDr 94*
Lamming, George (William) 1927- *BlkWr 2*
Lamming, Robert Love 1910- *WhoScEn 94*
Lamneck, David Arthur 1952- *WhoIns 94*
Lamo De Espinosa y Michels De Champourcin, Jaime 1941- *IntWW 93*
Lamon, Harry Vincent, Jr. 1932- *WhoAm 94, WhoAmL 94, WhoFI 94*
Lamona, Thomas Adrian 1925- *WhoFI 94*
LaMonaca, Joseph Salvador 1918- *WhoAmP 93*
Lamond, James Alexander 1928- *Who 94*
Lamone, Rudolph Philip 1931- *WhoAm 94, WhoFI 94*
Lamonica, John 1954- *WhoWest 94*
Lamonica, Paul Raymond 1944- *WhoAm 94, WhoAmL 94*
Lamonica, Roberto de 1933- *IntWW 93*
LaMont, Andre 1957- *WhoAm 94*
Lamont, Barbara 1939- *WhoBlA 94*
LaMont, Barbara Gibson 1951- *WhoAm 94*
Lamont, Corliss 1902- *WrDr 94*
Lamont, Donal 1911- *IntWW 93*
Lamont, Donald Alexander 1947- *Who 94*
LaMont, Duane Richard 1965- *WhoWest 94*
Lamont, Duncan 1918- *WhoHol 92*
Lamont, Frances K. d1975 *WhoAmA 93N*
Lamont, Frances Stiles 1914- *WhoAmP 93*
Lamont, Gene 1946- *WhoAm 94, WhoMW 93*
Lamont, Harry d1957 *WhoHol 92*
Lamont, Jack d1936 *WhoHol 92*
Lamont, Johann von *WorScD*
Lamont, Lansing 1930- *WhoAm 94*

Lamont, Lee WhoAm 94
Lamont, Molly 1910- WhoHol 92
Lamont, Norman Stewart Hughson 1942- IntWW 93, Who 94
Lamont, Rosette Clementine WhoAm 94
LaMont, Sanders Hickey 1940- WhoAm 94
Lamont, Syl d1982 WhoHol 92
La Mont, Tawana Faye 1948- WhoFI 94, WhoWest 94
Lamont, Thomas William 1870-1948 EncABHB 9
LaMontagne, Armand M. 1938- WhoAmA 93
Lamontagne, (J.) Gilles 1919- Who 94
La Montaine, John 1920- NewGrDO
Lamont-Brown, Raymond 1939- WrDr 94
La Monte, Angela Mae 1944- WhoAmA 93
Lamont-Havers, Ronald William 1920- WhoAm 94
LaMon-Thornton, April Yvonnie 1961- WhoHisp 94
La More, Chet Harmon 1908-1980 WhoAmA 93N
LaMore, Eugene P. 1940- WhoAmL 94
Lamore, George L. 1926- WhoFI 94
Lamoreaux, Calvin Gene 1938- WhoMW 93
LaMoreaux, David Albert 1924- WhoMW 93
Lamoreaux, Joyce 1938- WhoWest 94
LaMoreaux, Philip Elmer 1920- WhoAm 94, WhoScEn 94
Lamoree, Charles O'Neil 1945- WhoAmL 94
Lamoree, Paul R. 1942- WhoAmL 94
Lamorena, Alberto C., III 1949- WhoAm 94, WhoAmL 94, WhoWest 94
Lamorena, Alberto Cristobal, III 1949- WhoAmP 93
Lamoreux, Frederick Holmes 1941- WhoAm 94
Lamoriello, Louis Anthony 1942- WhoAm 94
Lamos, Mark 1946- WhoAm 94
Lamothe, Isidore J., Jr. 1924- WhoBlA 94
La Mothe, Louise Ann 1946- WhoAmL 94
Lamothe, William E. 1926- IntWW 93
LaMott, Paul I. 1917- WhoAmP 93
La Motta, Jake 1922- WhoHol 92
La Motta, John WhoHol 92
la Motte GuFrLit 2
Lamotte, Antoine Houdar de 1672-1731 NewGrDO
LaMotte, Jean Moore 1938- WhoBlA 94
LaMotte, Lawrence Alan 1949- WhoAmP 93
LaMotte, William Mitchell 1938- WhoFI 94
LaMountain, Joseph R. 1941- WhoAmP 93
Lamour, Dorothy 1914- ConTFT 11, IntMPA 94, WhoHol 92, WrDr 94
Lamour, Philippe d1992 IntWW 93N
LaMoure, Martin Scott 1954- WhoWest 94
Lamouret, Robert d1959 WhoHol 92
Lamoureux, Charles 1834-1899 NewGrDO
Lamoureux, Charles Harrington 1933- WhoWest 94
Lamoureux, Kimberly Ann 1963- WhoWest 94
Lamoureux, Robert 1920- WhoHol 92
Lamp, Benson J. 1925- WhoScEn 94
Lamp, John Ernest 1943- WhoAm 94
Lampard, Martin Robert 1926- Who 94
Lamparter, William C. 1929- WhoAm 94
Lampe, Mrs. NewGrDO
Lampe, Annacarol 1951- WhoAm 94
Lampe, Frederick Walter 1927- WhoAm 94
Lampe, Henry Oscar 1927- WhoAmP 93, WhoFI 94
Lampe, Johann Friedrich 1744-c. 1788 NewGrDO
Lampe, John Frederick 1702?-1751 NewGrDO
Lampe, Joseph Heydon 1955- WhoAmL 94
Lampel, Ronald B. 1943- WhoFI 94
Lampen, Richard Jay 1953- WhoAm 94
Lampert, Catherine Emily 1946- Who 94
Lampert, Eleanor Verna WhoFI 94, WhoMW 93
Lampert, James B. 1938- WhoAm 94
Lampert, Joseph A. 1941- WhoIns 94
Lampert, Leonard Franklin 1919- WhoMW 93, WhoScEn 94
Lampert, Steven A. 1944- WhoAmL 94
Lampert, Wayne Morris 1941- WhoFI 94
Lampert, Zohra 1936- WhoHol 92
Lamperti, John Williams 1932- WhoAm 94
Lamphier, Fay d1959 WhoHol 92
Lampin, Georges d1979 WhoHol 92
Lampinen, John A. 1951- WhoMW 93
Lampitoc, Rol Ponce WhoAmA 93
Lampitt, Dinah 1937- WrDr 94
Lampkin, Charles d1989 WhoHol 92
Lampkin, Cheryl Lyvette 1961- WhoBlA 94
Lampkin, Stephen Bradley 1952- WhoAm 94
Lampkins, Lillian Ernestine 1920- WhoBlA 94
Lampl, Annie Wagner 1917- WhoWest 94
Lampl, Frank (William) 1926- Who 94
Lampl, Jack Willard, Jr. 1921- WhoAm 94
Lampl, Peggy Ann 1930- WhoAm 94
Lampley, Calvin D. WhoBlA 94
Lampley, Edward Charles 1931- WhoBlA 94
Lampley, Paul Clarence 1945- WhoBlA 94
Lamplugh, Lois 1921- EncSF 93, WrDr 94
Lamport, Anthony Matthew 1935- WhoAm 94
Lamport, Felicia 1916- WhoAm 94
Lamport, Leslie B. 1941- WhoAm 94
Lamppa, William R. 1928- WrDr 94
Lamprecht, Gunter WhoHol 92
Lamprey, George S. WhoAmP 93
Lampros, George L. 1957- WhoMW 93
Lampson Who 94
Lampson, Butler Wright 1943- WhoScEn 94
Lampson, Francis Keith 1924- WhoWest 94
Lamptey, Jonathan Charles 1950- WhoMW 93
Lampton, Chris 1950- EncSF 93
Lampton, Dee d1919 WhoHol 92
Lampton, Mason Houghland 1947- WhoAm 94
Lampton, Nancy 1942- WhoIns 94
Lampugnani, Giovanni Battista 1708-1788 NewGrDO
Lamrani, Mohammed Karim IntWW 93
Lams, Edmond George 1941- WhoMW 93
Lamson, David Hinkley 1939- WhoAmL 94
Lamson, Evonne Viola 1946- WhoFI 94, WhoScEn 94
Lamson, George Herbert 1940- WhoAm 94
LaMunyon, Craig Willis 1960- WhoScEn 94
La Mura, Mark WhoHol 92
Lamy, Jean Baptiste 1814-1888 DcAmReB 2
Lamy, Pascal Lucien Fernand 1947- IntWW 93
Lamy, Peter Paul 1925- WhoAm 94
Lan, Chuan-Tau Edward 1935- WhoAsA 94
Lan, David 1952- ConDr 93, WrDr 94
Lan, Donald Paul 1930- WhoAmP 93
Lan, Donald Paul, Jr. 1952- WhoAm 94
Lan, Dong Ping 1947- WhoAsA 94
Lan, Tsong-Long 1965- WhoFI 94
Lana, Philip K. WhoScEn 94
Lanahan, Daniel J. 1940- WhoAmL 94
Lanahan, John Stevenson 1922- WhoAm 94
Lanam, Linda L. 1948- WhoIns 94
Lanam, Linda Lee 1948- WhoAmL 94
Lanari, Alessandro 1790-1862 NewGrDO
Lanc, Erwin 1930- IntWW 93
Lancaster, Archdeacon of Who 94
Lancaster, Bishop of 1929- Who 94
Lancaster, Bishop Suffragan of 1943- Who 94
Lancaster, Ann d1970 WhoHol 92
Lancaster, Barbara Mae 1930- WhoFI 94
Lancaster, Ben c. 1880-1953 EncNAR
Lancaster, Bill 1931- WhoAmP 93
Lancaster, Billy Douglas 1933- WhoAmP 93
Lancaster, Burt 1913- IntMPA 94, WhoHol 92
Lancaster, Burt(on) Stephen 1913- IntWW 93
Lancaster, Burton 1913- WhoAm 94
Lancaster, Carroll Townes, Jr. 1929- WhoAm 94, WhoFI 94
Lancaster, Charles Doerr, Jr. 1943- WhoAmP 93
Lancaster, David 1944- WrDr 94
Lancaster, David Lynn 1942- WhoFI 94
Lancaster, Edwin Beattie 1916- WhoAm 94
Lancaster, F(rederick) Wilfrid 1933- ConAu 42NR
Lancaster, Francine Elaine 1947- WhoScEn 94
Lancaster, Frederick Wilfrid 1933- WhoAm 94
Lancaster, G. B. BlmGWL
Lancaster, Gary Lee 1949- WhoBlA 94
Lancaster, H. Martin 1943- CngDr 93, WhoAmP 93
Lancaster, Harold Martin 1943- WhoAm 94
Lancaster, Henry Oliver 1913- IntWW 93, WrDr 94
Lancaster, Herman Burtram 1942- WhoBlA 94
Lancaster, James c. 1554-1618 WhWE
Lancaster, Jean 1909- Who 94
Lancaster, John d1935 WhoHol 92
Lancaster, John Graham 1918- WhoBlA 94
Lancaster, John Howard 1917- WhoScEn 94
Lancaster, John Lynch, III 1936- WhoAm 94
Lancaster, Kelvin John 1924- WhoAm 94
Lancaster, Lucie WhoHol 92
Lancaster, Mark 1938- WhoAmA 93
Lancaster, (Christopher Ronald) Mark 1938- IntWW 93
Lancaster, Nicholas 1948- WhoWest 94
Lancaster, Patricia Margaret 1929- Who 94
Lancaster, Peter 1929- WhoAm 94
Lancaster, Ralph Ivan, Jr. 1930- WhoAm 94, WhoAmL 94
Lancaster, Rita Funderburk 1943- WhoAmP 93
Lancaster, Robert Samuel 1909- WhoAm 94
Lancaster, Sally Rhodus 1938- WhoAm 94
Lancaster, Sheila 1937- WrDr 94
Lancaster, Stuart WhoHol 92
Lancaster, Tom d1947 WhoHol 92
Lancaster Brown, Peter 1927- WrDr 94
Lancaster Lewis, Joan Cadogan d1992 Who 94N
Lance, Alan G. 1949- WhoAmP 93
Lance, Alan George 1949- WhoAmL 94
Lance, Albert 1925- NewGrDO
Lance, Betty Rita Gomez DrAPF 93
Lance, George Milward 1928- WhoAm 94
Lance, Gina Juliett d1977 WhoHol 92
Lance, James Waldo 1926- IntWW 93, WhoScEn 94, WrDr 94
Lance, Jeanne DrAPF 93
Lance, Kathryn 1943- EncSF 93, SmATA 76 [port]
Lance, Larry K. 1941- WhoIns 94
Lance, Larry Kent 1941- WhoFI 94
Lance, Leonard WhoAmP 93
Lance, Peggy Ann 1936- WhoWest 94
Lance, Thomas Bertram 1931- WhoAm 94, WhoAmP 93
Lance, Wesley L. 1908- WhoAmP 93
Lancellotta, John J. 1953- WhoAmP 93
Lancel McElhinney, James 1952- WhoAmA 93
Lancelot, James Bennett 1952- Who 94
Lancelot, Sir WhoHol 92
Lancetti, Lucia fl. 1722-1737 NewGrDO
Lanchbery, John Arthur 1923- IntWW 93, Who 94
Lanchester, Elsa d1986 WhoHol 92
Lanchin, Gerald 1922- Who 94
Lanchner, Bertrand Martin 1929- WhoAm 94
Lanciani, Flavio Carlo 1661-1706 NewGrDO
Lancione, Bernard Gabe 1939- WhoAmL 94, WhoAmP 93, WhoMW 93
Lancione, Nelson 1921- WhoAmP 93
Lancour, Gene 1947- EncSF 93
Lancour, Karen Louise 1946- WhoMW 93
Lanctin, Charles-Francois-Honore NewGrDO
Lanctot, Micheline WhoHol 92
Land, Chester LaSalle 1938- WhoBlA 94
Land, David Benjamin 1950- WhoWest 94
Land, David Potts 1944- WhoAm 94
Land, Edwin Herbert 1909-1991 WhAm 10, WorInv
Land, Ernest Albert 1918- WhoAmA 93
Land, Geoffrey Allison 1942- WhoScEn 94
Land, Gillian Who 94
Land, Jane 1916- WrDr 94
Land, John Calhoun, III 1941- WhoAmP 93
Land, John W. 1944- WhoAmL 94
Land, Judith Broten 1951- WhoFI 94
Land, Kenneth Carl 1942- WhoAm 94
Land, Kenneth Dean 1931- WhoWest 94
Land, Michael Francis 1942- IntWW 93, Who 94
Land, Ming Huey 1940- WhoAsA 94
Land, Nicholas Charles Edward 1948- Who 94
Land, Paul WhoHol 92
Land, Reginald Brian 1927- WhoAm 94
Land, Richard Dale 1946- WhoAm 94
Land, Ross 1916- WrDr 94
Land, Sarah Agnes Riley WhoAmA 93
Land, Steven Jack 1946- WhoAm 94
Land, Susan DrAPF 93
Land, Ted J. 1936- WhoAmP 93
Land, Thornton Reddoch 1941- WhoIns 94
Landa, Abram 1902- Who 94
Landa, Alfredo WhoHol 92
Landa, Howard Martin 1943- WhoAm 94
Landa, Louis A. 1901-1989 WhAm 10
Landa, Lynda Who 94
Landa, Max d1933 WhoHol 92
Landa, William Robert 1919- WhoAm 94
Landaburu Illarramendi, Eneko 1948- IntWW 93
Landacre, Paul 1893-1963 WhoAmA 93N
Landahl, Herbert Daniel 1913- WhoAm 94
Landais, Hubert Leon 1921- IntWW 93
Landais, Pierre c. 1731-1820 WhAmRev
Landale, David (William Neil) 1934- Who 94
Landan, Henry Sinclair 1943- WhoAm 94, WhoAmL 94, WhoFI 94
Landar, Herbert Jay 1927- WhoWest 94
Landau, Annette Henkin DrAPF 93
Landau, Bernard Robert 1926- WhoAm 94
Landau, Charles Robert 1950- WhoWest 94
Landau, Davis d1935 WhoHol 92
Landau, Dennis (Marcus) 1927- Who 94
Landau, Ellis 1944- WhoAm 94, WhoFI 94
Landau, Ely 1920- WhoAm 94
Landau, Ely A. d1993 NewYTBS 93 [port]
Landau, Ely A. 1920- IntMPA 94
Landau, Felix 1947- WhoAmL 94
Landau, Genevieve Millet d1993 NewYTBS 93
Landau, Genevieve Millet 1927-1993 ConAu 141
Landau, George W. 1920- WhoAmP 93
Landau, George Walter 1920- WhoAm 94
Landau, Henry Groh 1943- WhoWest 94
Landau, Irwin WhoAm 94
Landau, Jack L. 1953- WhoAmL 94
Landau, Jacob 1917- WhoAm 94, WhoAmA 93
Landau, Jean-Pierre 1946- IntWW 93
Landau, Kenneth Jeffrey 1955- WhoAmL 94
Landau, Lauri Beth 1952- WhoFI 94
Landau, Lucy WhoHol 92
Landau, Mark Steven 1957- WhoFI 94
Landau, Martin 1921- WhoAm 94
Landau, Martin 1929- WhoHol 92
Landau, Martin 1931- IntMPA 94
Landau, Martin 1934- WhoAm 94
Landau, Mason Stephen 1948- WhoMW 93
Landau, Michael B. 1953- WhoAmL 94
Landau, Michael Roy 1946- WhoAm 94
Landau, Mitzi 1925- WhoAmA 93
Landau, Moshe 1912- IntWW 93
Landau, Myra WhoAmA 93
Landau, Peter 1935- IntWW 93
Landau, Peter Edward 1933- WhoAm 94, WhoFI 94
Landau, Ralph 1916- WhoAm 94
Landau, Richard H. 1914- IntMPA 94
Landau, Richard L. 1916- WhoAm 94
Landau, Robert Irwin 1933- WhoAm 94
Landau, Saul 1936- WhoAm 94
Landau, Saul (I.) 1936- WrDr 94
Landau, Sidney I. 1933- WhoAm 94
Landau, Walter Loeber 1931- WhoAm 94, WhoAmL 94
Landau, William Milton 1924- WhoAm 94, WhoScEn 94
Landauer, Jay Paul 1935- WhoAm 94
Landauer, Jeramy Lanigan 1939- WhoAm 94
Landauer, Rolf William 1927- WhoAm 94, WhoScEn 94
Landauer, Thomas Andrew 1958- WhoFI 94
Landauro, Sergio Antonio 1953- WhoHisp 94
Landavazo, George WhoHisp 94
Landaw, Stephen Arthur 1936- WhoAm 94
Landay, Andrew Herbert 1920- WhoAmL 94
Landay, David Mark 1957- WhoAmL 94
Landazuri Ricketts, Juan 1913- IntWW 93
Landberg, Kevin William 1956- WhoAmL 94
Lande, Alexander 1936- WhoScEn 94
Lande, C. Charles 1940- WhoAmP 93
Lande, David S. 1944- WhoAmP 93
Lande, James Avra 1930- WhoAm 94
Lande, Lawrence Montague 1906- WrDr 94
Landeck, Armin 1905- WhoAmA 93N
Landeck, Robin Elaine 1966- WhoScEn 94
Landefeld, Charles Willis 1923- WhoAm 94
Landefeld, Edward Kent 1933- WhoIns 94
Landefeld, Stewart M. 1954- WhoAmL 94
Landeira, Ricardo 1944- WhoHisp 94
Landel, Robert Franklin 1925- WhoAm 94
Landels, William 1928- Who 94
Landen, Dinsdale 1932- WhoHol 92
Landen, Dinsdale (James) 1932- Who 94
Landen, Ernest William 1908- WhoMW 93

Landen, Robert Geran 1930- *WhoAm 94*
Lander, C. Victor 1954- *WhoBlA 94*
Lander, Cresswort Caleb 1925- *WhoBlA 94*
Lander, David Allan 1944- *WhoAm 94, WhoAmL 94*
Lander, David L. 1947- *WhoHol 92*
Lander, Deborah Rosemary 1962- *WhoScEn 94*
Lander, Donald H. 1925- *WhoAm 94*
Lander, Ernest McPherson, Jr. 1915- *WrDr 94*
Lander, Fred Leonard, III 1927- *WhoBlA 94*
Lander, George 1943- *WhoAmL 94*
Lander, Harald 1905-1971 *IntDcB*
Lander, Howard 1950- *WhoAm 94*
Lander, Jack Robert 1921- *WrDr 94*
Lander, James Albert 1930- *WhoAmP 93*
Lander, James French 1931- *WhoWest 94*
Lander, Margot 1910-1961 *IntDcB [port]*
Lander, Richard Lemon 1804-1834 *WhWE*
Lander, Richard Leon 1928- *WhoAm 94*
Lander, Richard N. d1993 *NewYTBS 93 [port]*
Lander, Toni 1931-1985 *IntDcB [port]*
Landero, Reynaldo Rivera, II 1941- *WhoAsA 94*
Landeros, Robert 1951- *WhoHisp 94*
Landers, Ann *NewYTBS 93 [port]*
Landers, Ann 1918- *WhoAm 94*
Landers, Audrey 1958- *WhoHol 92*
Landers, Bertha *WhoAmA 93*
Landers, Billy N., Jr. 1949- *WhoWest 94*
Landers, David Scott 1962- *WhoAmL 94*
Landers, H. Lacy 1927- *WhoAmP 93*
Landers, Hal 1928- *IntMPA 94*
Landers, Hal 1928-1991 *ConTFT 11*
Landers, Harry 1921- *WhoHol 92*
Landers, James Michael 1951- *WhoAm 94*
Landers, Judy 1959- *WhoHol 92*
Landers, Mary Kenny 1905-1990 *WhAm 10*
Landers, Muriel d1977 *WhoHol 92*
Landers, Naaman Garnett 1938- *WhoBlA 94*
Landers, Patrick F., III 1959- *WhoAmP 93*
Landers, Paul E., Jr. 1939- *WhoAm 94*
Landers, Steven E. 1947- *WhoAm 94, WhoAmL 94*
Landers, Thomas Patrick 1959- *WhoMW 93*
Landers, Vernette Trosper 1912- *WhoAm 94, WhoFI 94, WhoWest 94*
Landers, William Lytle 1926- *WhoAmP 93*
Landersman, Stuart David 1930- *WhoScEn 94, WhoWest 94*
Landes, David S. 1924- *IntWW 93*
Landes, George Miller 1928- *WhoAm 94*
Landes, Michael 1939- *IntMPA 94*
Landes, Robert Nathan 1930- *WhoAm 94, WhoAmL 94*
Landes, Ruth 1908-1991 *WhAm 10*
Landes, William M. 1939- *WhoAm 94*
Landesberg, Steve *WhoHol 92*
Landesberg, Steve 1945- *WhoCom*
Landesman, Fredric Rocco 1947- *WhoAm 94*
Landesman, Heidi *WhoAm 94*
Landess, Fred S. 1933- *WhoAm 94*
Landfair, Stanley W. 1954- *WhoAm 94*
Landfield, Richard 1941- *WhoAmL 94*
Landfield, Ronnie 1947- *WhoAmA 93*
Landgard, Janet *WhoHol 92*
Landgraf, Susan *DrAPF 93*
Landgraf, Vernon H. 1924- *WhoAmP 93*
Landgrebe, David Allen 1934- *WhoAm 94, WhoMW 93*
Landgrebe, John Allan 1937- *WhoAm 94*
Landgrebe, Ludwig 1902- *ConAu 142*
Landgren, Craig Randall 1947- *WhoAm 94*
Landgren, George Lawrence 1919- *WhoAm 94*
Landguth, Daniel P. 1946- *WhoMW 93*
Landham, Sonny 1941- *WhoHol 92*
Landi, Dale Michael 1938- *WhoAm 94*
Landi, Elissa d1948 *WhoHol 92*
Landi, Lamberto 1882-1950 *NewGrDO*
Landi, Marco *NewGrDO*
Landi, Marla 1937- *WhoHol 92*
Landi, Stefano 1587?-1639 *NewGrDO*
Landin, David Craig 1946- *WhoAm 94*
Landin, Felix, Jr. 1941- *WhoHisp 94*
Landin, Hope d1973 *WhoHol 92*
Landin, Thomas Milton 1937- *WhoAm 94*
Landing, Benjamin Harrison 1920- *WhoAm 94, WhoWest 94*
Landini, Richard George 1929- *WhoAm 94, WhoMW 93*
Landis, Arhtur H(arold) 1917-1986 *EncSF 93*
Landis, Benson Young 1897-1966 *DcAmReB 2*
Landis, Brent William 1947- *WhoMW 93*
Landis, Carole d1948 *WhoHol 92*
Landis, Cullen d1975 *WhoHol 92*
Landis, David M. 1948- *WhoAmP 93*
Landis, David Morrison 1948- *WhoMW 93*
Landis, Edgar David 1932- *WhoAm 94, WhoFI 94*
Landis, Ellen Jamie 1941- *WhoAmA 93, WhoWest 94*
Landis, Elwood Winton 1928- *WhoAm 94*
Landis, Fred 1923- *WhoAm 94, WhoScEn 94*
Landis, Fred Simon 1943- *WhoFI 94, WhoWest 94*
Landis, Frederick 1912-1990 *WhAm 10*
Landis, Geoffrey Alan 1955- *WhoMW 93*
Landis, George Arthur 1940- *WhoAm 94*
Landis, George Harvey 1918- *WhoMW 93*
Landis, Harvey B. 1953- *WhoAmP 93*
Landis, J(ames) D(avid) 1942- *WrDr 94*
Landis, James David 1942- *WhoAm 94*
Landis, James M. 1945- *WhoAmL 94*
Landis, Jessie Royce d1972 *WhoHol 92*
Landis, John 1950- *IntMPA 94*
Landis, John David 1950- *WhoAm 94*
Landis, John Michael 1950- *WhoAmL 94*
Landis, John William 1917- *WhoAm 94*
Landis, Kenneth K. *WhoAmP 93*
Landis, Larry Seabrook 1945- *WhoMW 93*
Landis, Margaret d1981 *WhoHol 92*
Landis, Marie *EncSF 93*
Landis, Monty *WhoHol 92*
Landis, Nina *WhoHol 92*
Landis, Pamela Ann Youngman 1941- *WhoScEn 94*
Landis, Paul Groff 1932- *WhoAm 94*
Landis, Richard Gordon 1920- *WhoWest 94*
Landis, Robert M. 1920- *WhoAmL 94*
Landis, Wayne G. 1952- *WhoScEn 94*
Landman, Bette Emeline 1937- *WhoAm 94*
Landmesser, Harold Leon 1917- *WhoMW 93*
Lando, Jerome Burton 1932- *WhoAm 94*
Landolfi, Tommaso 1908-1979 *EncSF 93*
Landolfi, Tony *WhoHol 92*
Landolt, Arlo Udell 1935- *WhoAm 94*
Landolt, Robert George 1939- *WhoAm 94*
Landon, Avice d1976 *WhoHol 92*
Landon, David H. 1953- *WhoAmP 93*
Landon, David Neil 1936- *Who 94*
Landon, Donald Dean 1930- *WhoMW 93*
Landon, Edward August 1911-1984 *WhoAmA 93N*
Landon, Forrest M. 1933- *WhoAm 94*
Landon, H(oward) C(handler) Robbins 1926- *NewGrDO, WrDr 94*
Landon, Harry Raymond 1935- *WhoFI 94*
Landon, Howard Chandler Robbins 1926- *IntWW 93, Who 94*
Landon, James Henry 1945- *WhoAmL 94*
Landon, John Campbell 1937- *WhoAm 94*
Landon, John William 1937- *WhoAm 94*
Landon, Kenneth P. d1993 *NewYTBS 93*
Landon, Laurene 1958- *WhoHol 92*
Landon, Letitia 1802-1838 *BlmGWL*
Landon, Lucinda 1950- *WrDr 94*
Landon, Margaret 1903-1993 *NewYTBS 93 [port]*
Landon, Marshall Scott 1951- *WhoAmP 93*
Landon, Michael 1936-1991 *WhAm 10, WhoHol 92*
Landon, Robert Gray 1928- *WhoAm 94, WhoMW 93*
Landon, Robert Kirkwood 1929- *WhoAm 94, WhoIns 94*
Landon, Ruth Christoff 1931- *WhoMW 93*
Landon, Sealand Whitney 1896- *WhoAm 94*
Landon, Susan Melinda 1950- *WhoScEn 94*
Landon, Wayne Edward 1953- *WhoFI 94*
Landor, (Arnold) Henry (Savage) 1867-1924 *DcNaB MP*
Landor, Walter Savage 1775-1864 *BlmGEL*
Landovsky, John 1935- *WhoWest 94*
Landovsky, Pavel *WhoHol 92*
Landovsky, Rosemary Reid 1933- *WhoMW 93*
Landow, George P(aul) 1940- *ConAu 41NR*
Landow, George Paul 1940- *WhoAm 94*
Landow, Nathan *WhoAmP 93*
Landow-Esser, Janine Marise 1951- *WhoAm 94, WhoAmL 94*
Landowski, Marcel 1915- *NewGrDO*
Landrau, Marge 1939- *WhoHisp 94*
Landre, Debra Ann 1955- *WhoWest 94*
Landre, Guillaume 1905-1968 *NewGrDO*
Landreau, Anthony Norman 1930- *WhoAmA 93*
Landreaux, Kenneth Francis 1954- *WhoBlA 94*
Landreneau, Rodney Edmund, Jr. 1929- *WhoScEn 94*
Landres, Morris M. *WhAm 10*
Landres, Paul 1912- *IntMPA 94*
Landreth, Derek 1920- *Who 94*
Landreth, Gertrude Griffith d1969 *WhoHol 92*
Landreth, Kathryn E. *WhoAmL 94*
Landreth, Libbie 1952- *WhoWest 94*
Landreth, Marsha Ann 1947- *ConAu 140*
Landrey, David Ryan 1944- *WhoAmL 94*
Landriault, Jacques Emile 1921- *WhoAm 94*
Landrieu, Mary 1955- *WhoAmP 93*
Landrieu, Mitch 1960- *WhoAmP 93*
Landrieu, Moon 1930- *IntWW 93*
Landrigan, Philip John 1942- *WhoAm 94*
Landron, Michel John 1946- *WhoAmL 94*
Landrum, Hugh Linson, Jr. 1963- *WhoScEn 94*
Landrum, Larry James 1943- *WhoFI 94, WhoScEn 94, WhoWest 94*
Landrum, Peter Franklin 1947- *WhoMW 93*
Landrum, Philip Mitchell 1907-1990 *WhAm 10*
Landrum, Teri 1960- *WhoHol 92*
Landrum, Thomas Lowell 1935- *WhoMW 93*
Landrum, Tito Lee 1954- *WhoBlA 94*
Landry, Albert 1919- *WhoAmA 93*
Landry, Alfred Ronald 1936- *WhoAmL 94*
Landry, Dolores Branche 1928- *WhoBlA 94*
Landry, Donald Paul 1940- *WhoAmP 93*
Landry, G. Yves *WhoAm 94, WhoFI 94*
Landry, Jane Lorenz 1936- *WhoAm 94*
Landry, John *WhoHol 92*
Landry, Karen *WhoHol 92*
Landry, L. Bartholomew 1936- *WhoBlA 94*
Landry, Lawrence Aloysius 1935- *WhoBlA 94*
Landry, Mark Edward 1950- *WhoMW 93*
Landry, Michael Gerard 1946- *WhoFI 94*
Landry, Monique 1937- *IntWW 93, WhoAm 94, WhoWomW 91*
Landry, Paul L. 1950- *WhoAm 94*
Landry, Richard Miles 1938- *WhoAmA 93*
Landry, Robert Edward 1929- *WhoAm 94*
Landry, Roger D. 1934- *WhoAm 94*
Landry, Ron 1943- *WhoAmP 93*
Landry, Thomas Henry 1946- *WhoAm 94*
Landry, Tom *ProFbHF [port]*
Landry, Tom 1924- *ConAu 141, WhoAm 94*
Landry, Walter J. 1931- *WhoAmP 93*
Landsberg, David *WhoHol 92*
Landsberg, Dennis Robert 1948- *WhoScEn 94*
Landsberg, Jerry 1933- *WhoAm 94*
Landsberg, Lewis 1938- *WhoScEn 94*
Landsberg, Melvin 1926- *ConAu 142*
Landsberg, Michele 1939- *WhoAm 94*
Landsberger, Henry A. 1926- *WhoAm 94*
Landsbergis, Vytautas 1932- *IntWW 93, LngBDD*
Landsborough, Ron James 1955- *WhoWest 94*
Landsburg, Alan 1933- *IntMPA 94*
Landsburg, Steven Elliot 1954- *WhoWest 94*
Landsburg, Valerie 1959- *WhoHol 92*
Landsdowne, Marquis of *WhAmRev*
Landske, Dorothy Suzanne 1937- *WhoAmP 93, WhoMW 93*
Landsman, Myril 1921- *WhoAm 94*
Landsman, R. Broh 1954- *WhoAmL 94*
Landsman, Sandy *DrAPF 93*
Landsman, Sheldon I. 1942- *WhoAmL 94*
Landsman, Stanley 1930- *WhoAmA 93N*
Landsman, Stephen A. 1942- *WhoAm 94, WhoAmL 94*
Landsmann, Leanna 1946- *WhoAm 94*
Landsmark, Theodore Carlisle 1946- *WhoBlA 94*
Landsteiner, Karl 1868-1943 *WorScD*
Landt, Dan B. 1937- *WhoMW 93*
Landuyt, Bernard Francis 1907- *WhoAm 94, WhoMW 93*
Land-Weber, Ellen 1943- *WhoAm 94, WhoWest 94*
Land-Weber, Ellen E. 1943- *WhoAmA 93*
Landwehr, Arthur John 1934- *WhoMW 93*
Landwehr, William Charles 1941- *WhoAm 94, WhoAmA 93, WhoMW 93*
Landy, Burton Aaron 1929- *WhoAm 94, WhoAmL 94*
Landy, Carol Lynn 1944- *WhoMW 93*
Landy, Hanna *WhoHol 92*
Landy, James Joseph 1954- *WhoFI 94*
Landy, Joseph P. 1932- *WhoAm 94*
Landy, Matthew A. 1937- *WhoFI 94*
Landy, Richard Allen 1931- *WhoAm 94*
Lane *Who 94*
Lane, Baron 1918- *IntWW 93, Who 94*
Lane, A. B. d1968 *WhoHol 92*
Lane, Abbe 1932- *WhoHol 92*
Lane, Abbe 1935- *ConAu 140*
Lane, Adelaide Irene 1939- *WhoScEn 94*
Lane, Adele d1957 *WhoHol 92*
Lane, Al *WhoAmP 93*
Lane, Allan d1973 *WhoHol 92*
Lane, Allan C. 1948- *WhoBlA 94*
Lane, Alvin Huey, Jr. 1942- *WhoAm 94*
Lane, Alvin S. 1918- *WhoAm 94, WhoAmA 93*
Lane, Anthony John 1926- *Who 94*
Lane, Anthony John 1939- *Who 94*
Lane, Anthony Milner 1928- *IntWW 93, Who 94*
Lane, Arthur Alan 1945- *WhoAm 94, WhoAmL 94*
Lane, Barbara Miller 1934- *WhoAm 94*
Lane, Barry Michael 1932- *Who 94*
Lane, Bradley David 1962- *WhoMW 93*
Lane, Brian M. 1951- *WhoMW 93*
Lane, Bruce Stuart 1932- *WhoAm 94, WhoAmL 94*
Lane, Burton 1912- *WhoAm 94*
Lane, Carol Elaine 1935- *WhoMW 93*
Lane, Carolyn 1926- *WrDr 94*
Lane, Charles d1945 *WhoHol 92*
Lane, Charles 1899- *WhoHol 92*
Lane, Charles 1953- *WhoBlA 94*
Lane, Charles 1954- *WhoHol 92*
Lane, Charles Stuart 1924- *WhoFI 94*
Lane, Charlotte R. 1948- *WhoAmP 93*
Lane, Christopher M. *WhoAmP 93*
Lane, Clarence D. 1922- *WhoAmP 93*
Lane, David (William Stennis Stuart) 1922- *Who 94*
Lane, David G. 1948- *WhoAmL 94*
Lane, David Goodwin 1945- *Who 94*
Lane, David John 1935- *Who 94*
Lane, David Judson 1927- *WhoAmP 93*
Lane, David Neil 1928- *Who 94*
Lane, David Oliver 1931- *WhoAm 94*
Lane, David Pulaski, Sr. 1912- *WhoBlA 94*
Lane, David S. 1938- *WhoAmL 94*
Lane, David Stuart 1933- *Who 94*
Lane, Dewey Hobson, Jr. 1934- *WhoAmP 93*
Lane, Diane 1965- *IntMPA 94, WhoHol 92*
Lane, Dick *ProFbHF [port]*
Lane, Dick 1927- *WhoAmP 93*
Lane, Dina Hunter 1945- *WhoHisp 94*
Lane, Donald Steven 1956- *WhoAmP 93*
Lane, Douglas Calder 1945- *WhoFI 94*
Lane, Eddie Burgyone 1939- *WhoBlA 94*
Lane, Edward Alphonso Richard 1953- *WhoFI 94*
Lane, Edward Wood, Jr. 1911- *WhoAm 94*
Lane, Eleanor Tyson 1938- *WhoBlA 94*
Lane, Eugene Numa 1936- *WhoAm 94*
Lane, Fielding H. 1926- *WhoAm 94*
Lane, Francis Bliss 1937- *WhoFI 94*
Lane, Frank Joseph, Jr. 1934- *WhoAmL 94*
Lane, Frank Laurence d1993 *Who 94N*
Lane, Frederic S. *WhoAm 94*
Lane, Frederick Carpenter 1949- *WhoAm 94*
Lane, Frederick E. d1993 *NewYTBS 93 [port]*
Lane, Frederick Stanley 1915- *WhoAm 94*
Lane, Gary (Martin) 1943- *WrDr 94*
Lane, George Alphonsus 1934- *WhoMW 93*
Lane, George M. 1928- *WhoAmP 93*
Lane, George S., Jr. 1932- *WhoBlA 94*
Lane, Gloria 1930- *NewGrDO*
Lane, Gloria Julian 1932- *WhoAm 94, WhoWest 94*
Lane, Grace d1956 *WhoHol 92*
Lane, Hana Umlauf 1946- *WhoAm 94*
Lane, Harlan 1936- *WrDr 94*
Lane, Harold Edwin 1913- *WhoAm 94*
Lane, Harry d1943 *WhoHol 92*
Lane, Harry d1960 *WhoHol 92*
Lane, Howard Raymond 1922-1988 *WhAm 10*
Lane, Isaac 1834-1937 *AfrAmAl 6*
Lane, James F. 1953- *WhoWest 94*
Lane, James Franklin 1931- *WhoAm 94, WhoAmL 94*
Lane, James Garland, Jr. 1934- *WhoAm 94*
Lane, James McConkey 1929- *WhoAm 94, WhoMW 93*
Lane, James Vernon 1944- *WhoAmL 94*
Lane, Jane d1978 *WhoHol 92*
Lane, Jane 1905-1978 *EncSF 93*
Lane, Janis Olene *WhoBlA 94*
Lane, Jay
See Primus *ConMus 11*
Lane, Jeffrey Bruce 1942- *WhoAm 94, WhoFI 94*
Lane, Jeffrey H. 1949- *WhoAmL 94*
Lane, Jerome 1966- *WhoBlA 94*
Lane, Joan Lorine 1938- *WhoAmP 93*
Lane, Jocelyn 1940- *WhoHol 92*
Lane, John *DrAPF 93, EncSF 93*

Lappert, Michael Franz 1928- Who 94
Lappi, Santo NewGrDO
Lappin, Albert Abraham 1897- WhAm 10
Lappin, Joan E. 1943- WhoFI 94
Lappin, Richard C. 1944- WhoAm 94, WhoFI 94
Lapping, Anne Shirley Lucas 1941- Who 94
Lapping, Brian (Michael) 1937- WrDr 94
Lapping, Edward C. d1993 NewYTBS 93
Lapping, Peter Herbert 1941- Who 94
Lappo-Danilevskaia, Nadezhda Aleksandrova 1875?-1951 BlmGWL
LaPrade, Carter 1942- WhoAmL 94
Lapsley, James Norvell, Jr. 1930- WhoAm 94
Lapsley, John (Hugh) 1916- Who 94
Lapsley, William Winston 1910- WhoAm 94
Laptev, Adolf Fedorovich LngBDD
Laptev, Ivan Dmitrievich 1934- LngBDD
Laptev, Ivan Dmitrievich 1936- IntWW 93
Laptev, Vladimir Viktorovich 1924- IntWW 93
La Puma, John Joseph WhoMW 93
La Puma, Salvatore DrAPF 93
La Puma, Salvatore 1929- WrDr 94
Lapun, Paul 1923- Who 94
Lapworth, Arthur 1872-1941 DcNaB MP
Lapworth, Charles 1842-1920 DcNaB MP
LaQuaglia, Michael Patrick 1950- WhoScEn 94
Laqueur, Walter 1921- ConAu 19AS [port], IntWW 93, Who 94, WhoAm 94, WrDr 94
Laquinta, Fred John 1949- WhoFI 94
Lara, Contessa 1849-1896 BlmGWL
Lara, Adam R. 1959- WhoHisp 94
Lara, Edison R., Sr. WhoBlA 94
Lara, Gloria E. 1953- WhoHisp 94
Lara, Henry 1960- WhoHisp 94
Lara, Isidore de NewGrDO
Lara, Jim S. 1944- WhoHisp 94
Lara, Juan Francisco 1943- WhoHisp 94
Lara, Linda O. 1939- WhoHisp 94
Lara, Marc 1944- WhoHisp 94
Lara, Myrella Gonzalez WhoHisp 94
Lara, Tony Richard 1947- WhoFI 94
Larabee, Louise WhoHol 92
Lara Bustamante, Fernando 1911- IntWW 93
Laracuente-Ast, María Elisa 1933- WhoHisp 94
Laragh, John Henry 1924- WhoScEn 94
Laraki, Azeddine 1929- IntWW 93
Laraki, Moulay Ahmed 1931- IntWW 93
Laramee, Eva Andree 1956- WhoAmA 93
Laramore, Don Nelson 1906-1989 WhAm 10
Laramore, Robert Dwayne 1952- WhoMW 93
Larance, Charles Larry 1938- WhoIns 94
Larason, Linda H. 1947- WhoAmP 93
Larason, Timothy Manuel 1939- WhoAmL 94
Laraway, Kenneth Harold 1953- WhoFI 94
Laraway, Steven Allan 1954- WhoFI 94
Larcada, Richard Kenneth 1935- WhoAmA 93N
Larch, John 1922- WhoHol 92
L'Archeveque, Andre Robert 1923- WhoAmA 93
Larco Cox, Guillermo 1932- IntWW 93
Larcom, (Charles) Christopher (Royde) 1926- Who 94
Larcom, Lucy 1824-1893 BlmGWL
Lardas, Konstantinos DrAPF 93
Larde, Enrique Roberto 1934- WhoIns 94
Lardizabal, Alfred C. WhoAmP 93
Lardner, George, Jr. 1934- WhoAm 94
Lardner, Henry Petersen 1932- WhoAm 94
Lardner, Peter 1932- WhoIns 94
Lardner, Ring DrAPF 93
Lardner, Ring d1933 WhoHol 92
Lardner, Ring, Jr. 1915- IntDcF 2-4
Lardner, Ring(gold Wilmer) 1885-1933 RfGShF
Lardner, Ring W., Jr. 1915- IntMPA 94
Lardner, Ring Wilmer, Jr. 1915- WhoAm 94
Lardner, Ringgold Wilmer 1885-1933 AmCulL [port]
Lardy, Henry Arnold 1917- IntWW 93, WhoAm 94
Lardy, Nicholas R. 1946- ConAu 140
Lardy, Nicholas Richard 1946- WhoWest 94
Lardy, Susan Marie, Sister 1937- WhoMW 93
Lardy, William J. WhoAmP 93
Lareau, N. Peter 1943- WhoAmL 94
Lareau, Richard George 1928- WhoAm 94
Laredo, David Cary 1950- WhoAmL 94, WhoWest 94
Laredo, Julio Richard 1952- WhoHisp 94
Laren, Kuno 1924- WhoAm 94
La Reno, Dick d1945 WhoHol 92
Larenz, Karl 1903- IntWW 93
Lares, Linda WhoHisp 94
Larese, Edward John 1935- WhoAm 94, WhoFI 94
Larew, Hiram Gordon, III 1953- WhoScEn 94
Largay, Raymond d1974 WhoHol 92
Largay, Roy J. WhoHol 92
Largay, Timothy L. 1943- WhoAmL 94
Large, Andrew Mcleod Brooks 1942- IntWW 93, Who 94
Large, Brian 1939- NewGrDO
Large, David C. ConAu 140
Large, David Clay 1945- ConAu 140, IntWW 93, WrDr 94
Large, Donald 1937- WhoAmP 93
Large, E(rnest) C(harles) d1976 EncSF 93
Large, G. Gordon M. 1940- WhoAm 94
Large, James Mifflin, Jr. 1932- WhoAm 94, WhoFI 94
Large, Jerry D. 1954- WhoBlA 94
Large, John Andrew 1947- WhoAm 94
Large, John Barry 1930- Who 94
Large, Peter 1931- Who 94
Largen, Cheryl Renee 1957- WhoFI 94
Largen, Joseph 1940- WhoAm 94
Largent, Steve 1954- WhoAm 94, WhoWest 94
Largey, Kathleen Kiernan 1958- WhoAmL 94
Largman, Kenneth 1949- WhoScEn 94
Laria, Maria 1959- WhoHisp 94
Larible, David NewYTBS 93 [port]
Laric, Michael Victor 1945- WhoAm 94
LaRico, Benje WhoAmA 93
Larimer, David George 1944- WhoAm 94, WhoAmL 94
Larimer, Janet McMaster 1942- WhoAmP 93, WhoWomW 91
Larimer, Thornton Michael, Jr. 1964- WhoWest 94
Larimore, Earle d1947 WhoHol 92
Larimore, Mary Nold 1956- WhoAmL 94
Larín, Alfredo 1925- WhoHisp 94
Larionov, Mikhail 1881-1964 IntDcB
La Riviere, Jan Willem Maurits 1923- IntWW 93, WhoScEn 94
Larizadeh, Mohammed Reza 1947- WhoAm 94, WhoWest 94
Lark, David Lee 1947- WhoWest 94
Lark, M. Ann 1952- WhoWest 94
Lark, Raymond 1939- WhoAm 94, WhoAmA 93, WhoBlA 94
Lark, Ronald Edwin 1934- WhoScEn 94
Lark, Sylvia 1947- WhoAmA 93N
Larkam, Peter Howard 1962- WhoFI 94
Larke, Katherine Mary 1967- WhoMW 93
Larken, Anthea 1938- Who 94
Larken, (Edmund Shackleton) Jeremy 1939- Who 94
Larkey, Sanford V(incent) 1898- WhAm 10
Larkin, Alfred Sinnott, Jr. 1947- WhoAm 94
Larkin, Amy ConAu 41NR
Larkin, Barry Louis 1964- WhoAm 94, WhoBlA 94, WhoMW 93
Larkin, Bruce F. WhoAmP 93
Larkin, (John) Cuthbert 1906- Who 94
Larkin, Edward Colby 1951- WhoFI 94
Larkin, Emmet 1927- WhoAm 94
Larkin, Eugene 1921- WhoAmA 93
Larkin, Eugene David 1921- WhoAm 94
Larkin, Felix Edward 1909-1991 WhAm 10
Larkin, George d1946 WhoHol 92
Larkin, J. Donald 1948- WhoFI 94
Larkin, James WhoHol 92
Larkin, James 1876-1947 DcNaB MP
Larkin, James J. 1925- IntMPA 94
Larkin, James Thomas 1931- WhoAm 94, WhoFI 94
Larkin, Jay Robert 1946- WhoAm 94, WhoAmL 94
Larkin, Joan DrAPF 93
Larkin, Joan 1939- WhoAm 94
Larkin, John d1936 WhoHol 92
Larkin, John d1965 WhoHol 92
Larkin, John E., Jr. 1930- WhoAmA 93
Larkin, John Montague 1936- WhoAm 94
Larkin, John Paul, II 1969- WhoAmP 93
Larkin, June Noble 1922- WhoAm 94
Larkin, Lee Roy 1928- WhoAm 94
Larkin, Leo Paul, Jr. 1925- WhoAm 94, WhoAmL 94
Larkin, Maia ConAu 41NR
Larkin, Mary WhoHol 92
Larkin, Mary Ann DrAPF 93
Larkin, Maurice (John Milner) 1932- WrDr 94
Larkin, Michael John 1950- WhoAm 94
Larkin, Michael Joseph 1941- WhoAm 94, WhoFI 94
Larkin, Michael Todd 1963- WhoBlA 94
Larkin, Moscelyne 1925- WhoAm 94
Larkin, Nelle Jean 1925- WhoWest 94
Larkin, Oliver 1896-1970 WhoAmA 93N
Larkin, Peter Anthony 1924- WhoAm 94, WhoScEn 94
Larkin, Peter J. 1953- WhoAmP 93
Larkin, Philip 1922-1985 BlmGEL [port]
Larkin, Robert W. d1993 NewYTBS 93
Larkin, Rochelle 1935- WrDr 94
Larkin, Terence Alphonsus 1924- IntWW 93
Larkin, Terrence B. 1954- WhoAmL 94
Larkin, William c. 1580-1619 DcNaB MP
Larkin, William 1902-1969 WhoAmA 93N
Larkin, William J., Jr. 1928- WhoAmP 93
Larkins, Brian Allen 1946- WhoScEn 94
Larkins, E. Pat WhoBlA 94
Larkins, Gary Thomas 1956- WhoAm 94
Larkins, Howard Lee 1941- WhoFI 94, WhoMW 93
Larkins, John Davis, Jr. 1909-1990 WhAm 10
Larkins, John Rodman 1913- WhoBlA 94
Larkins, William Conyers 1934- WhoBlA 94
Larkridge, Theodore Kenneth 1960- WhoMW 93
Larky, Steven Philip 1962- WhoScEn 94
Larmer, Oscar Vance 1924- WhoAmA 93
Larmeu, Paul Gordon 1952- WhoMW 93
Larminie, (Ferdinand) Geoffrey 1929- Who 94
Larmore, Thomas R. 1944- WhoAmL 94
Larmour, Edward Noel 1916- Who 94
Larned, Bill 1872-1926 BuCMET
Larned, William Edmund, Jr. 1919- WhoAm 94
Larner, Henry A. 1945- WhoAmL 94
Larner, Jeremy DrAPF 93
Laro, David 1942- CngDr 93, WhoAmL 94, WhoAmP 93
La Rocca, Aldo Vittorio 1926- WhoScEn 94
LaRocca, Francis P., Jr. 1952- WhoAmL 94
Larocca, James Lawrence 1943- WhoAm 94
LaRocca, Patricia Darlene McAleer 1951- WhoMW 93, WhoScEn 94
La Rocca, Renato V. 1957- WhoScEn 94
LaRocco, Larry 1946- CngDr 93, WhoAm 94, WhoAmP 93, WhoWest 94
Laroche, Gerard A. 1927- WhoBlA 94
LaRoche, Guilhem 1644-1710 BlmGWL
LaRoche, Lynda L. 1947- WhoAmA 93
La Roche, Marie-Elaine 1949- WhoAm 94
La Roche, Mary WhoHol 92
LaRoche, Sophie 1730-1807 BlmGWL
Laroche Daillon, Joseph de d1656 EncNAR
La Rochefoucauld, Francois, VI, duc de 1613-1680 GuFrLit 2
Larochelle, Denis Alphonse 1961- WhoWest 94
LaRochelle, Dennis Omer 1948- WhoAmL 94
LaRochelle, Diane Racine 1945- WhoAm 94
La Rochelle, Pierre-Louis 1928- WhoAm 94
Larochelle, Roger B. 1924- WhoAmP 93
Larock, Bruce Edward 1940- WhoWest 94
La Rocque, Eugene Philippe 1927- WhoAm 94
La Rocque, Gene Robert 1918- WhoAm 94
LaRocque, Judith Anne 1956- Who 94, WhoAm 94
Larocque, Leigh B. 1934- WhoAmP 93
LaRocque, Marilyn Ross Onderdonk 1934- WhoFI 94, WhoWest 94
La Rocque, Rod d1969 WhoHol 92
Laroon, Marcellus 1679-1772 NewGrDO
La Roque, Sieur de NewGrDO
Laroque, Dale Charles 1937- WhoAmP 93
Laroque, Francois G. 1948- ConAu 140
La Rosa, Fernando 1943- WhoHisp 94
LaRosa, John Charles 1941- WhoScEn 94
La Rosa, Julius 1930- WhoHol 92
Larosa, Paul A. WhoAmP 93
Larose, Lawrence Alfred 1958- WhoAmL 94
LaRose, Michael H. 1953- WhoMW 93
Larose, Roger 1910- WhoAm 94
La Rose, Rose d1972 WhoHol 92
Larosiere de Champfeu, Jacques Martin Henri Marie de Who 94
Larosiere De Champfeu, Jacques Martin Henri Marie de 1929- IntWW 93
Larosiliere, Jean Darly Martin 1963- WhoAmL 94, WhoBlA 94
La Rossa, James Michael 1931- WhoAm 94, WhoAmL 94
LaRossa, Richard J. 1946- WhoAmP 93
LaRouche, Lyndon H., Jr. 1922- WhoAm 94, WhoAmP 93
Larounis, George Philip 1928- WhoAm 94
Laroussi, Mounir 1955- WhoScEn 94
LaRow, DeChantal 1926- WhoAm 94
La Roy, Rita 1907- WhoHol 92
Larpent, Anna Margaretta fl. 1815-1830 BlmGWL
Larpenteur, Charles 1807-1872 WhWE
Larpenteur, James Albert, Jr. 1935- WhoAm 94
Larquey, Pierre d1962 WhoHol 92
Larquie, Andre Olivier 1938- IntWW 93
Larr, Peter 1939- WhoAm 94
Larrabee, Donald Richard 1923- WhoAm 94
Larrabee, Eric 1922-1990 WhAm 10
Larrabee, Martin Glover 1910- IntWW 93, WhoAm 94
Larrabee, Matthew L. 1955- WhoAmL 94
Larrabee, Peter Norman 1946- WhoAmL 94
Larragoite, Patricio C. 1950- WhoHisp 94
Larrain, Michael 1945- WhoHol 92
Larramendi Blakely, Lara WhoHisp 94
Larraz, Julio F. 1944- WhoAmA 93
Larrazabal Antezana, Erik 1958- WhoScEn 94
Larre, Rene J. 1915- IntWW 93
Larrea, Milton Fernandez 1955- WhoHisp 94
Larreta de Gandara, Carmen Rodriguez BlmGWL
Larrick, Nancy 1910- WrDr 94
Larrie, Reginald Reese 1928- WhoBlA 94
Larrimore, David Roberts 1952- WhoWest 94
Larrimore, Francine d1975 WhoHol 92
Larrimore, Randall Walter 1947- WhoAm 94
Larrison, Evelyn Hubbard 1938- WhoMW 93
Larrison, Kathleen Ann 1962- WhoFI 94
Larrivee, Anne M. 1943- WhoAmP 93
Larrivee, Henri 1737-1802 NewGrDO
Larroca, Raymond G. 1930- WhoAm 94, WhoAmL 94
Larrocha, Alicia de 1923- IntWW 93
Larroquette, John 1947- IntMPA 94, WhoHol 92
Larroquette, John Bernard 1947- WhoAm 94
Larrouilh, Michel 1935- WhoAm 94
Larrowe, Charles Patrick 1916- WhoAm 94
Larrowe, Vernon Lodge 1921- WhoMW 93
Larry, Charles Edward 1944- WhoBlA 94
Larry, David Heath 1941- WhoAm 94
Larry, Jerald Henry 1944- WhoAmP 93, WhoBlA 94
Larry, R. Heath 1914- EncABHB 9 [port], WhoAm 94
Lars, Claudia BlmGWL
Larsen, Alan Scott WhoAm 94
Larsen, Allan F. 1919- WhoAmP 93
Larsen, Alvin Henry 1939- WhoScEn 94
Larsen, Art 1925- BuCMET
Larsen, Ashby Brooks 1940- WhoWest 94
Larsen, B. Neil 1954- WhoWest 94
Larsen, Carl Erik 1911- WhoAmA 93
Larsen, Charles Martin 1948- WhoWest 94
Larsen, Cyril Anthony d1993 Who 94N
Larsen, D. Dane 1950- WhoAmA 93
Larsen, Dale Leverne 1950- WhoWest 94
Larsen, Dana Allan 1960- WhoMW 93
Larsen, Darrell R., Jr. 1951- WhoAmL 94
Larsen, David C. 1946- WhoAmL 94
Larsen, David Carl 1948- WhoAmP 93
Larsen, David Coburn 1944- WhoAmL 94
Larsen, Donna Kay WhoWest 94
Larsen, Edwin Merritt 1915- WhoAm 94
Larsen, Eric 1941- WrDr 94
Larsen, Erik 1911- WhoAm 94
Larsen, Ernest Albert 1932- WhoAmP 93
Larsen, Ester WhoWomW 91
Larsen, Gary Loy 1945- WhoAm 94
Larsen, Helge 1915- IntWW 93
Larsen, Ib Hyldstrup 1919- WhoScEn 94
Larsen, Jack Lenor 1927- WhoAmA 93
Larsen, Jack Lucas 1924- WhoAmP 93
Larsen, Janice Casey 1954- WhoFI 94
Larsen, Janine Louise 1959- WhoScEn 94
Larsen, Jeanne DrAPF 93
Larsen, Jeanne (Louise) 1950- WrDr 94
Larsen, Jesper Kampmann 1950- WhoScEn 94
Larsen, John Christian WhoAmA 93
Larsen, John Walter 1914-1990 WhAm 10
Larsen, Jonathan Zerbe 1940- WhoAm 94
Larsen, Joseph Reuben 1927-1989 WhAm 10
Larsen, Kai 1926- IntWW 93
Larsen, Karen Beth 1946- WhoMW 93
Larsen, Kathleen Mary 1956- WhoMW 93
Larsen, Keith 1926- WhoHol 92
Larsen, Kenneth David 1947- WhoWest 94
Larsen, Kent Sheldon 1935- WhoAmP 93
Larsen, L. Vernon 1918- WhoMW 93
Larsen, Larry Joseph 1955- WhoFI 94
Larsen, Libby (Brown) 1950- NewGrDO
Larsen, Lotte WhoHol 92

Larsen, Lynn Beck 1945- *WhoAmL 94*
Larsen, Mark Leif 1956- *WhoMW 93*
Larsen, Mary Ann Indovina 1929- *WhoMW 93*
Larsen, Mernet Ruth 1940- *WhoAmA 93*
Larsen, Nella 1891-1964 *AfrAmAl 6, BlmGWL*
Larsen, Niels Bjorn 1913- *IntDcB*
Larsen, Ole d1984 *WhoAmA 93N*
Larsen, Oscar N., Jr. 1929- *WhoAmP 93*
Larsen, Patrick Heffner 1945- *WhoAmA 93*
Larsen, Paul Emanuel 1933- *WhoAm 94*
Larsen, Peder Olesen 1934- *IntWW 93*
Larsen, Phillip Nelson 1929- *WhoAm 94*
Larsen, Ralph Irving 1928- *WhoAm 94, WhoScEn 94*
Larsen, Ralph Stanley 1938- *IntWW 93, WhoAm 94, WhoFI 94*
Larsen, Randy John 1954- *WhoMW 93*
Larsen, Richard Gary 1948- *WhoAm 94*
Larsen, Richard Lee 1934- *WhoAm 94, WhoAmP 93, WhoWest 94*
Larsen, Robert Dhu 1922- *WhoAm 94*
Larsen, Robert Emmett 1946- *WhoAm 94, WhoAmL 94*
Larsen, Robert LeRoy 1934- *WhoAm 94*
Larsen, Robert Wesley 1923- *WhoAmA 93*
Larsen, Rolf 1934- *WhoAmL 94, WhoAmP 93*
Larsen, Samuel Harry 1947- *WhoWest 94*
Larsen, Steven 1951- *WhoMW 93*
Larsen, Susan C. 1946- *WhoAmA 93*
Larsen, Terrance A. *WhoAm 94, WhoFI 94*
Larsen, Thomas A. 1949- *WhoAmL 94*
Larsen, Thomas Everett 1947- *WhoWest 94*
Larsen, Viggo d1957 *WhoHol 92*
Larsen, Wendy Wilder *DrAPF 93*
Larsen, William Lawrence 1926- *WhoAm 94*
Larsen-Todsen, Nanny 1884-1982 *NewGrDO*
Larsh, Howard William 1914- *WhoAm 94*
Larson, Alan P. *WhoAmP 93*
Larson, Alan Philip 1949- *WhoAm 94*
Larson, Allan Louis 1932- *WhoAm 94*
Larson, Arthur 1910- *IntWW 93*
Larson, (Lewis) Arthur 1910-1993 *ConAu 141, CurBio 93N*
Larson, Bennett Charles 1941- *WhoAm 94, WhoScEn 94*
Larson, Betty Jean 1949- *WhoScEn 94*
Larson, Blaine (Gledhill) 1937- *WhoAmA 93*
Larson, Bob *IntMPA 94*
Larson, Brendan Lane 1967- *WhoMW 93*
Larson, Brent T. 1942- *WhoAm 94, WhoWest 94*
Larson, Bryce J. 1952- *WhoMW 93*
Larson, Cal 1930- *WhoAmP 93*
Larson, Carl Shipley 1934- *WhoMW 93, WhoScEn 94*
Larson, Catherine *WhoHol 92*
Larson, Charles 1922- *WrDr 94*
Larson, Charles Fred 1936- *WhoAm 94, WhoFI 94*
Larson, Charles Lester 1922- *WhoAm 94, WhoWest 94*
Larson, Charles R. *DrAPF 93*
Larson, Charles Robert 1936- *WhoAm 94, WhoWest 94*
Larson, Charles W., Jr. *WhoAmP 93*
Larson, Cherie Kay 1963- *WhoWest 94*
Larson, Christine d1973 *WhoHol 92*
Larson, Christopher Brace 1952- *WhoWest 94*
Larson, Clarence Edward 1909- *WhoAm 94, WhoAmP 93*
Larson, Dale Irving 1937- *WhoAm 94, WhoMW 93*
Larson, Daniel Norris 1954- *WhoWest 94*
Larson, Darrell 1951- *WhoHol 92*
Larson, David Allen 1954- *WhoMW 93*
Larson, David Bruce 1947- *WhoAm 94*
Larson, David E. 1953- *WhoAmL 94*
Larson, Deanna Kay 1948- *WhoMW 93*
Larson, Delray Lyle 1947- *WhoAmP 93*
Larson, Diane Kay 1949- *WhoAmP 93*
Larson, Diane LaVerne Kusler 1942- *WhoMW 93*
Larson, Dick 1953- *WhoWest 94*
Larson, Don 1946- *WhoAmP 93*
Larson, Donald Clayton 1934- *WhoAm 94*
Larson, Donald Dumford 1951- *WhoIns 94*
Larson, Donald Edward 1946- *WhoWest 94*
Larson, Donald Harold 1959- *WhoMW 93*
Larson, Donald R. 1930- *WhoMW 93*
Larson, Dorothy Ann 1934- *WhoWest 94*
Larson, Doyle Eugene 1930- *WhoAm 94*
Larson, Earl Richard 1911- *WhoAm 94*
Larson, Edward Duane 1946- *WhoWest 94*
Larson, Elizabeth Ann 1958- *WhoMW 93*
Larson, Emilie Gustava 1919- *WhoMW 93*
Larson, Eric *WhoHol 92*
Larson, Eric Heath 1950- *WhoScEn 94*
Larson, Eric Victor 1957- *WhoWest 94*
Larson, Frederick H. 1913- *Who 94*
Larson, Gary 1950- *ConAu 41NR, IntWW 93, WhoAm 94, WrDr 94*
Larson, Gaylen Nevoy 1940- *WhoAm 94, WhoFI 94*
Larson, George Charles 1942- *WhoAm 94*
Larson, George L. 1943- *WhoFI 94*
Larson, Gerald Lee 1937- *WhoWest 94*
Larson, Glen A. 1937- *EncSF 93*
Larson, Harry Robert 1945- *WhoFI 94*
Larson, Harry Thomas 1921- *WhoAm 94*
Larson, Harvey Casper 1922- *WhoAmP 93*
Larson, Jack 1933- *WhoHol 92*
Larson, James Lee 1931- *WhoWest 94*
Larson, Jane (Warren) 1922- *WhoAmA 93*
Larson, Jean Ann 1959- *WhoMW 93*
Larson, Jean McLaughlin 1925- *WhoAmP 93*
Larson, Jerry L. 1936- *WhoAm 94, WhoAmL 94, WhoAmP 93, WhoMW 93*
Larson, John B. 1948- *WhoAmP 93*
Larson, John Barry 1948- *WhoAm 94*
Larson, John David 1941- *WhoAm 94, WhoIns 94*
Larson, John Hyde 1930- *WhoAm 94*
Larson, John Wallace 1927- *WhoAmL 94*
Larson, John William 1935- *WhoAm 94*
Larson, Joseph Stanley 1933- *WhoAm 94*
Larson, Judy L. 1952- *WhoAmA 93*
Larson, Julia Louise Fink 1950- *WhoFI 94*
Larson, Karen Elaine 1947- *WhoAm 94, WhoFI 94*
Larson, Kay L. 1946- *WhoAmA 93*
Larson, Keith Donald 1964- *WhoMW 93*
Larson, Keith Wayne 1952- *WhoMW 93*
Larson, Kermit Dean 1939- *WhoAm 94*
Larson, Kim Marvine 1954- *WhoMW 93*
Larson, Kris *DrAPF 93*
Larson, L. Arthur d1993 *NewYTBS 93*
Larson, Larry 1940- *WhoAm 94*
Larson, Lawrence John 1904-1992 *WhAm 10*
Larson, Leonard Louis 1936- *WhoAm 94*
Larson, Lyle T. *WhoAmP 93*
Larson, Marian Gertrude 1927- *WhoMW 93*
Larson, Mark Allan 1948- *WhoAm 94*
Larson, Mark Edward, Jr. 1947- *WhoAmL 94, WhoFI 94*
Larson, Mark Stuart 1951- *WhoAmL 94*
Larson, Marlene Louise 1952- *WhoMW 93*
Larson, Martin Alfred 1897- *WhoAm 94*
Larson, Mary Corinne 1959- *WhoMW 93*
Larson, Mary Hartl 1940- *WhoMW 93*
Larson, Maureen Inez 1955- *WhoWest 94*
Larson, Maurice Allen 1927- *WhoAm 94*
Larson, Mel Leon 1929- *WhoAm 94, WhoFI 94*
Larson, Melinda Sue 1954- *WhoMW 93*
Larson, Meria Ellena 1942- *WhoAmL 94, WhoMW 93*
Larson, Michael Len 1944- *WhoFI 94, WhoMW 93*
Larson, Muriel Koller 1924- *WrDr 94*
Larson, Nancy Celeste 1951- *WhoMW 93, WhoScEn 94*
Larson, Neil Edwin 1954- *WhoWest 94*
Larson, Nils H., Jr. 1934- *WhoAmP 93*
Larson, Patricia B. *WhoAmP 93*
Larson, Patricia Bryan 1954- *WhoAmP 93*
Larson, Paul d1989 *WhoHol 92*
Larson, Paul Edward 1952- *WhoAm 94*
Larson, Philip C. 1946- *WhoAmL 94*
Larson, Philip Seely 1944- *WhoAmA 93*
Larson, R. A. *DrAPF 93*
Larson, Ray Reed 1951- *WhoWest 94*
Larson, Reed Eugene 1922- *WhoAm 94*
Larson, Reed William 1950- *WhoScEn 94*
Larson, Richard 1928- *WhoAmP 93*
Larson, Richard Bondo 1941- *WhoAm 94*
Larson, Richard Carl 1942- *WhoWest 94*
Larson, Richard Charles 1943- *WhoAm 94*
Larson, Richard Gustaf 1942- *WhoAm 94*
Larson, Richard James 1954- *WhoMW 93*
Larson, Robert Eric 1943- *WhoMW 93*
Larson, Robert Frederick 1930- *WhoAm 94, WhoMW 93*
Larson, Robert J. 1932- *WhoAmP 93*
Larson, Robert P. 1944- *WhoAmL 94*
Larson, Robert Walter 1927- *WhoWest 94*
Larson, Roberta M. 1960- *WhoMW 93*
Larson, Rodney Allen 1952- *WhoAmP 93*
Larson, Ronald Gary 1953- *WhoScEn 94*
Larson, Ronald Gordon 1949- *WhoFI 94*
Larson, Ronald L. 1934- *WhoAmP 93*
Larson, Roy 1929- *WhoAm 94*
Larson, Russell Edward 1917- *WhoAm 94*
Larson, Russell George 1942- *WhoAm 94*
Larson, Ryan 1950- *WhoIns 94*
Larson, Shelley Beth 1966- *WhoMW 93*
Larson, Sidney 1923- *WhoAm 94, WhoAmA 93*
Larson, Stephen P. 1944- *WhoAmL 94*
Larson, Taft Alfred 1910- *WhoAmP 93*
Larson, Thomas A. 1942- *WhoAmL 94*
Larson, Thomas D. *WhoAmP 93*
Larson, Vernon Leroy 1948- *WhoAmP 93*
Larson, Ward Jerome 1924- *WhoAm 94*
Larson, Wilfred Joseph 1927- *WhoAm 94*
Larson, William G. 1942- *WhoAmA 93*
Larson, Wolf *WhoHol 92*
Larsson, Anders Lars 1952- *WhoScEn 94*
Larsson, Eric Verner 1954- *WhoMW 93*
Larsson, Hans Lennart 1942- *WhoFI 94*
Larsson, John 1938- *Who 94*
Larsson, Lars-Erik 1908- *IntWW 93*
Larter, Leslie Harold 1956- *WhoMW 93*
Lartigue, Roland E. 1951- *WhoBlA 94*
LaRubio, Daniel Paul, Jr. 1959- *WhoFI 94, WhoScEn 94*
La Rue, Carl Forman 1929- *WhoAm 94*
La Rue, Frank d1960 *WhoHol 92*
La Rue, Grace d1956 *WhoHol 92*
La Rue, Henry Aldred 1927- *WhoAm 94*
La Rue, Jack d1984 *WhoHol 92*
La Rue, Jan Pieters 1918- *WhoAm 94*
La Rue, Jean d1956 *WhoHol 92*
LaRue, L. H. 1938- *WrDr 94*
La Rue, Lash 1917- *WhoHol 92*
LaRue, Paul Hubert 1922- *WhoAm 94, WhoAmL 94*
LaRue, Paul Hubert, Jr. 1950- *WhoAm 94, WhoAmL 94*
Laruette, Jean-Louis 1731-1792 *NewGrDO*
Larush, M. Sirilla 1892-1976 *EncNAR*
La Russa, Adrienne *WhoHol 92*
LaRussa, Joseph Anthony 1925- *WhoAm 94*
La Russa, Tony, Jr. 1944- *WhoAm 94, WhoWest 94*
LaRusso, Anthony Carl 1949- *WhoFI 94*
LaRusso, Nicholas F. *WhoScEn 94*
LaRusso, Rudy 1937- *BasBi*
Larusso-Reis, Michael 1956- *WhoHisp 94*
Larvadain, Edward, Jr. 1941- *WhoBlA 94*
Larwood, Charles (Homer) 1895- *WhAm 10*
Lary, Banning Kent 1949- *WhoFI 94*
Lary, Peter Paul 1950- *WhoMW 93*
Lary, Yale *ProFbHF*
Larzelere, H. T., Jr. 1943- *WhoAmL 94*
Larzelere, Harry J. 1941- *WhoIns 94*
Larzelere, Judith Ann 1944- *WhoAmA 93*
Lasaga, Antonio C. 1949- *WhoAm 94*
Lasaga, Manuel 1952- *WhoHisp 94*
Lasagna, Louis Cesare 1923- *WhoAm 94*
Lasak, John Joseph 1944- *WhoAmL 94*
La Sala, Joseph P. 1948- *WhoAmL 94*
La Salle, Arthur Edward 1930- *WhoAm 94*
La Salle, Eriq *WhoHol 92*
La Salle, John Randall *WhoHisp 94*
LaSalle, Jon George 1948- *WhoAmP 93*
La Salle, Peter 1947- *WrDr 94*
La Salle, Rene-Robert Cavelier, Sieur De 1643-1687 *WhWE [port]*
La Salle, Victor *EncSF 93*
Lasalle, Victor 1935- *WrDr 94*
Lasana, Oronde *DrAPF 93*
LaSane, Joanna Emma 1935- *WhoBlA 94*
Lasansky, Leonardo 1946- *WhoAmA 93*
Lasansky, Mauricio L. 1914- *WhoAmA 93*
Lasarow, William Julius 1922- *WhoAm 94, WhoAmL 94, WhoWest 94*
Lasater, Donna Kathleen 1948- *WhoAmP 93*
Lasater, John Robert 1966- *WhoMW 93*
Lasater, William Robert, Jr. 1944- *WhoAmL 94*
Lascara, Vincent Alfred 1919- *WhoAm 94*
Las Casas, Bartolome de 1474-1566 *DcAmReB 2*
Lascelles *Who 94*
Lascelles, Viscount 1950- *Who 94*
Lascelles, Henry Anthony 1912- *Who 94*
Lascelles, Mary Madge 1900- *Who 94*
Lasch, Christopher 1932- *WhoAm 94, WrDr 94*
Lasch, Pat 1944- *WhoAmA 93*
Lasch, Robert 1907- *WhoAm 94, WhoWest 94*
Lascher, Alan Alfred 1941- *WhoAm 94, WhoAmL 94*
Laschi, Anna Maria Querzoli *NewGrDO*
Laschi, Filippo fl. 1739-1789 *NewGrDO*
Laschi, Luisa 176-?-1789 *NewGrDO*
Laschuk, Roy Bogdan 1932- *WhoAm 94*
Lascoe, Henry d1964 *WhoHol 92*
Lasdon, Stanley S. d1993 *NewYTBS 93*
Lasdun, Denys (Louis) 1914- *IntWW 93, Who 94*
Lasecki, Robert Richard 1943- *WhoMW 93*
Lasee, Alan J. 1937- *WhoAmP 93*
Lasegue, Ernest Charles 1816-1883 *EncSPD*
La Selva, Vincent 1929- *WhoAm 94*
Lasenby, Jack 1931- *WrDr 94*
Laser, Bradley Harlan 1965- *WhoFI 94*
Laserna, Blas de 1751?-1816 *NewGrDO*
La Serre *NewGrDO*
La Serre, Jean-Louis-Ignace de 1662-1756 *NewGrDO*
Lash, Donald R. 1912- *WhoAmP 93*
Lash, Fredda P. 1929- *WhoMW 93*
Lash, Jeffrey N. 1949- *WrDr 94*
Lash, Jennifer (Anne Mary) 1938- *WrDr 94*
Lash, Kenneth 1918-1985 *WhoAmA 93N*
Lash, Myles Perry 1946- *WhoAm 94*
Lash, N(icholas) L(angrishe) A(lleyne) 1934- *WrDr 94*
Lash, Nicholas Langrishe Alleyne 1934- *Who 94*
Lash, Richard Anthony 1961- *WhoAmL 94*
Lash, Stephen Sycle 1940- *WhoAm 94*
Lash, Timothy David 1953- *WhoMW 93*
Lashbrooke, Elvin Carroll, Jr. 1939- *WhoAm 94*
LaShelle, Charles Stanton 1947- *WhoAm 94, WhoFI 94*
La Shelle, Joseph c. 1905-1989 *IntDcF 2-4*
Lasher, Donald R. 1929- *WhoIns 94*
Lasher, Donald Rex 1929- *WhoAm 94*
Lasher, Donna Maria 1948- *WhoAmL 94*
Lasher, Howard Louis 1944- *WhoAmP 93*
Lasher, Steven Howe 1944- *WhoFI 94*
Lashinger, Joseph A., Jr. 1953- *WhoAmP 93*
Lashkowitz, Herschel *WhoAmP 93*
Lashlee, Jolynne Van Marsdon 1948- *WhoScEn 94*
Lashlee, Jon David 1962- *WhoScEn 94*
Lashley, Curtis Dale 1956- *WhoAmL 94, WhoFI 94, WhoMW 93*
Lashley, Virginia Stephenson Hughes 1924- *WhoScEn 94, WhoWest 94*
Lashman, Shelley Bortin 1917- *WhoAmL 94*
Lashuay, Kenneth Edward 1955- *WhoAmP 93*
Lashutka, Gregory S. *WhoAmP 93*
Lashutka, Gregory S. 1944- *WhoAm 94, WhoAmL 94, WhoMW 93*
Lashway, Joseph William 1927- *WhoAmP 93*
Lasiter, Jack Brinkley 1930- *WhoFI 94*
Lask, Berta 1878-1967 *BlmGWL*
Laska, David 1920- *WhoAmA 93*
Laskar, Devi Sen 1966- *WhoAsA 94*
Laske, Lyle F. 1937- *WhoAmA 93*
Lasker, Gabriel Ward 1912- *WhoAm 94*
Lasker, Joe 1919- *SmATA 17AS [port], WhoAmA 93*
Lasker, Jonathan 1948- *WhoAmA 93*
Lasker, Jonathan Lewis 1948- *WhoAm 94*
Lasker, Joseph L. 1919- *WhoAm 94*
Lasker, Judith N. 1947- *WrDr 94*
Lasker, Lawrence 1949- *ConTFT 11*
Lasker, Mary *WhoAm 94*
Lasker, Morris E. *WhoAm 94, WhoAmL 94*
Lasker, Richard S. 1947- *WhoAmL 94*
Lasker-Schuler, Else 1869-1945 *BlmGWL*
Laskey, Kathleen *WhoHol 92*
Laskey, Richard Anthony 1936- *WhoAm 94*
Laskey, Ronald Alfred 1945- *Who 94*
Laskey, Thomas Penrose 1931- *WhoAmP 93*
Laski, James J., Jr. *WhoAmP 93*
Laski, Marghanita 1915-1988 *EncSF 93*
Laskier, Michael M. 1949- *ConAu 142*
Laskin, Barbara Virginia 1939- *WhoAmL 94, WhoWest 94*
Laskin, Daniel M. 1924- *WhoAm 94*
Laskin, Lee B. 1936- *WhoAmP 93*
Laskin, Michael *WhoHol 92*
Laskin, Myron, Jr. 1930- *WhoAmA 93*
Laskin, Pam *DrAPF 93*
Laskin, Pamela L. 1954- *ConAu 142, SmATA 75 [port]*
Lasko, Allen Howard 1941- *WhoWest 94*
Lasko, Peter Erik 1924- *IntWW 93, Who 94*
Lasko, Warren Anthony 1940- *WhoAm 94*
Laskowski, Ernst d1935 *WhoHol 92*
Laskowski, Janusz Stanislaw 1936- *WhoAm 94*
Laskowski, Leonard Francis, Jr. 1919- *WhoAm 94*
Laskowski, Michael, Jr. 1930- *WhoAm 94*
Laskowski, Robert Anthony 1951- *WhoAm 94*
Lasky, David 1932- *WhoAm 94, WhoAmL 94*
Lasky, Jesse L. 1880-1958 *IntDcF 2-4 [port]*
Lasky, Kathryn 1944- *TwCYAW*
Lasky, Kenneth Jordan 1959- *WhoAmL 94*
Lasky, Laurence D. 1940- *WhoAm 94*
Lasky, Melvin Jonah 1920- *Who 94*

Lasky, Michael B. 1952- WhoAmL 94
Lasky, Moses 1907- WhoAm 94
Lasky, Victor 1918-1990 WhAm 10
Laslett, Peter 1915- IntWW 93
Laslett, (Thomas) Peter (Ruffell) 1915- Who 94
Lasley, Harold F. 1948- WhoAmP 93
Lasley, Phelbert Quincy, III 1940- WhoBlA 94
Lasley, Thomas J. 1947- WhoMW 93
Laslie, Berry 1947- WhoAmP 93
Lasmanis, Raymond 1938- WhoWest 94
Lasnick, Julius 1929- WhoFI 94
Lasoen, Patricia 1948- BlmGWL
Lasoff, Mark WhoAm 94
Lasok, Dominik 1921- Who 94
Lasorda, Thomas Charles 1927- WhoAm 94, WhoWest 94
La Sorrentina d1973 WhoHol 92
La Sorsa, William George 1945- WhoAmL 94
Lasry, Jean-Michel 1947- WhoAm 94, WhoScEn 94
Lass, Ernest Donald 1938- WhoAm 94
Lass, Roger 1937- WrDr 94
Lassalle, Ferdinand 1825-1864 DcLB 129 [port]
Lassalle, Jacques Louis Bernard 1936- IntWW 93
Lassalle, Jean 1847-1909 NewGrDO
Lassally, Walter 1926- IntDcF 2-4 [port], IntMPA 94
Lassander, Dagmar WhoHol 92
Lassar, Scott R. 1950- WhoAm 94, WhoAmL 94
Lassart, James A. 1943- WhoAmL 94
Lassaw, Ibram 1913- WhoAm 94, WhoAmA 93
Lassell, Michael DrAPF 93
Lassen, Ben d1968 WhoAmA 93N
Lassen, Charles William 1929- WhoFI 94
Lassen, Eduard 1830-1904 NewGrDO
Lassen, John Kai 1942- WhoFI 94
Lassen, John R. 1922- WhoFI 94
Lassen, Sandra Lake DrAPF 93
Lasser, Howard Gilbert 1926- WhoScEn 94
Lasser, Johann Baptist 1751-1805 NewGrDO
Lasser, Joseph Robert 1923- WhoAm 94, WhoFI 94
Lasser, Louise 1939- IntMPA 94, WhoAm 94, WhoCom, WhoHol 92
Lasserre, Bruno Marie Andre 1954- IntWW 93
Lassers, Willard J. 1919- WhoAm 94, WhoAmL 94
Lasseter, Dillard Brown 1894- WhAm 10
Lasseter, Earle Forrest 1933- WhoAmL 94
Lasseter, Kenneth Carlyle 1942- WhoAm 94
Lassettre, Edwin Nichols 1911-1990 WhAm 10
Lassettre, Edwin Richie 1934- WhoWest 94
Lassick, Sydney 1922- WhoHol 92
Lassila, Jaakko Sakari 1928- IntWW 93
Lassiter, Barbara Ann 1960- WhoFI 94
Lassiter, Charles Gregory, II 1961- WhoFI 94
Lassiter, Charles Keeling DrAPF 93
Lassiter, Christo 1957- WhoAmL 94
Lassiter, James Edward, Jr. 1934- WhoBlA 94
Lassiter, James Hugh 1945- WhoAmP 93
Lassiter, John 1937- WhoBlA 94
Lassiter, John 1941- WhoAmP 93
Lassiter, Kenneth T. 1935- WhoAm 94
Lassiter, Mary 1945- WrDr 94
Lassiter, Phillip B. WhoAm 94, WhoFI 94
Lassiter, Wright Lowenstein, Jr. 1934- WhoBlA 94
Lasslo, Andrew 1922- WhoAm 94, WhoScEn 94
Lassman, Donald Ralph 1958- WhoAmL 94
Lassman, Iro Richard 1946- WhoAmL 94
Lassman, Malcolm 1938- WhoAm 94
Lassner, Franz George 1926- WhoAm 94
Lassner, Jacob 1935- ConAu 42NR
Lassner, Keith Michael 1949- WhoAm 94
Lasson, Kenneth 1943- WrDr 94
Lasswell, Marcia 1927- WrDr 94
Lasswell, Marcia Lee 1927- WhoAm 94
Lasswell, Thomas Ely 1919- WhoAm 94
Lasswitz, Kurd 1848-1910 EncSF 93
Last, Christopher Neville 1935- Who 94
Last, Jerold Alan 1940- WhoWest 94
Last, Joan 1908- WrDr 94
Last, John William 1940- Who 94
Last, Michael P. 1946- WhoAm 94, WhoAmL 94
Last, Raymond Jack d1993 Who 94N
Last, Robert Louis 1958- WhoScEn 94
Last, Robin James 1956- WhoFI 94
La Starza, Roland 1927- WhoHol 92
Laster, Atlas, Jr. 1948- WhoMW 93
Laster, Brenda Hope 1941- WhoScEn 94
Laster, Leonard 1928- WhoAm 94
Laster, Paul 1951- WhoAmA 93
Laster, Ralph William, Jr. 1951- WhoAm 94
Laster, Richard 1923- WhoAm 94, WhoScEn 94
Lastinger, Allen Lane, Jr. 1942- WhoAm 94, WhoFI 94
Lastman, Melvin D. 1933- WhoAm 94
Lastowka, James Anthony 1951- WhoAm 94, WhoAmP 93
Lastra, Cesar R. 1939- WhoHisp 94
Lastra, Jose Ramon 1939- WhoScEn 94
Lastra, Pedro M. DrAPF 93
Lastra, William A. 1956- WhoWest 94
Lastrapes, William Dud WhoAmP 93
Lasuchin, Michael 1923- WhoAmA 93
Lasuen, Leanna 1955- WhoAmP 93
La Susa, Lawrence R. 1960- WhoAmL 94
Laszlo, Andrew 1926- IntMPA 94
Laszlo, Ernest 1896?-1984 IntDcF 2-4
Laszlo, Ervin 1932- WrDr 94
Laszlo, Magda 1919- NewGrDO
Laszlo, Paul d1993 NewYTBS 93
Lataif, Lawrence P. 1943- WhoAm 94, WhoAmL 94
La Taille, Jean de 1533?-c. 1607 GuFrLit 2
Latane, Bibb 1937- WhoAm 94
Latanision, Ronald Michael 1942- WhoAm 94, WhoScEn 94
Latanzio, P. NewGrDO
Latarjet, Raymond 1911- IntWW 93
Latasi, Naama WhoWomW 91
Latch, Edward Gardiner d1993 NewYTBS 93 [port]
Latcham, Franklin Chester 1922- WhoAm 94
Latchaw, Paul d1985 WhoHol 92
Latcholia, Kenneth Edward 1922- WhoBlA 94
Latchum, James Levin 1918- WhoAm 94, WhoAmL 94
Lateef, Abdul Bari 1939- WhoAsA 94
Lateef, Yusef 1920- WhoAm 94, WhoBlA 94
Latef, Javed Anver 1943- WhoFI 94
Lateiner, Donald 1944- WhoMW 93, WrDr 94
Latell, Anthony, Jr. WhoAmP 93
Latell, Lyle d1967 WhoHol 92
Latella, Robert Natale 1942- WhoAm 94
Later, Michael Monte 1950- WhoAmL 94
Laterza, Vito 1926- IntWW 93
Latevola, Ronald Albert 1953- WhoFI 94
Latey, John (Brinsmead) 1914- Who 94
Latham, Baron 1954- Who 94
Latham, Allen, Jr. 1908- WhoAm 94
Latham, Arthur Charles 1930- Who 94
Latham, Cecil Thomas 1924- Who 94
Latham, Christopher George Arnot 1933- Who 94
Latham, David (Nicholas Ramsay) 1942- Who 94
Latham, Dudley Eugene, III 1943- WhoMW 93
Latham, Eleanor Ruth Earthrowl 1924- WhoScEn 94
Latham, James David 1942- WhoAm 94
Latham, Jean Lee 1902- TwCYAW, WhoAm 94, WrDr 94
Latham, Joseph Al, Jr. 1951- WhoAm 94
Latham, Larry Lee 1945- WhoAm 94
Latham, Louise WhoHol 92
Latham, Mavis SmATA 74
Latham, Mavis 1909- WrDr 94
Latham, Michael (Anthony) 1942- Who 94
Latham, Patricia Horan 1941- WhoAmL 94
Latham, Paul Walker, II 1957- WhoScEn 94
Latham, Peter Anthony 1925- Who 94
Latham, Peter Samuel 1940- WhoAmL 94
Latham, Philip WhoHol 92
Latham, Philip 1902-1981 EncSF 93
Latham, R. James 1942- WhoAmP 93
Latham, Raymond R., Jr. 1945- WhoFI 94
Latham, Richard Brunton 1947- Who 94
Latham, Richard Thomas Paul 1934- Who 94
Latham, Robert Clifford 1912- Who 94
Latham, Roger Alan 1950- Who 94
Latham, Steve Howard 1948- WhoMW 93
Latham, Stuart WhoHol 92
Latham, Weldon Hurd 1947- WhoAm 94, WhoAmL 94, WhoBlA 94
Latham, William Peters 1917- WhoAm 94
Lathbury, Stanley 1873- WhoHol 92
Lathe, Grant Henry 1913- Who 94
Lathe, Robert Edward 1945- WhoFI 94
Lathem, Edward Connery 1926- WhoAm 94
Lathen, Calvin Wesley 1940- WhoWest 94
Lathen, Deborah Ann 1953- WhoBlA 94
Lathen, Emma WrDr 94
Lathen, John William 1916- WhoBlA 94
Latherow, Clifford Brandon 1915- WhoAmP 93
Lathi, Bhagawandas Pannalal 1933- WhoScEn 94, WhoWest 94
Lathlaen, Robert Frank 1925- WhoAm 94
Lathon, Lamar Lavantha 1967- WhoBlA 94
Lathram, Thomas W. 1945- WhoAmL 94
Lathrop, Ann 1935- WhoAm 94
Lathrop, Gertrude Adams 1921- WhoAm 94
Lathrop, Gertrude K. 1896-1986 WhoAmA 93N
Lathrop, Gertrude Katherine 1896- WhAm 10
Lathrop, Irvin Tunis 1927- WhoAm 94, WhoWest 94
Lathrop, Julia Clifford 1858-1932 AmSocL [port]
Lathrop, Kaye Don 1932- WhoScEn 94
Lathrop, Lawrence Erwin, Jr. 1942- WhoWest 94
Lathrop, Lester Wayne 1935- WhoScEn 94
Lathrop, Mack d1985 WhoHol 92
Lathrop, Mitchell Lee 1937- WhoAm 94, WhoAmL 94, WhoWest 94
Lathrop, Philip 1916- IntMPA 94
Lathrop, Rose Hawthorne 1851-1926 DcAmReB 2
Lathrop, Trayton LeMoine 1923- WhoAmL 94
Laties, Victor Gregory 1926- WhoAm 94
Latiff-Bolet, Ligia 1953- WhoScEn 94
Latilla, Gaetano 1711-1788 NewGrDO
Latimer, Allie B. WhoAm 94, WhoBlA 94
Latimer, Cheri WhoHol 92
Latimer, Douglas Hamilton 1937- WhoAm 94
Latimer, Frank Edward 1947- WhoBlA 94
Latimer, Frank Edward, Jr. 1947- WhoFI 94
Latimer, George 1935- WhoAm 94, WhoAmP 93
Latimer, George Webster, Jr. WhoScEn 94
Latimer, Graham (Stanley) 1926- Who 94
Latimer, Henry d1963 WhoHol 92
Latimer, Hugh 1490?-1555 BlmGEL
Latimer, Hugh 1492?-1555 DcLB 136 [port]
Latimer, Hugh 1913- WhoHol 92
Latimer, Ina Pearl 1934- WhoBlA 94
Latimer, James Hearn 1941- WhoScEn 94
Latimer, Jennifer Ann 1953- WhoBlA 94
Latimer, John Francis 1903-1991 WhAm 10
Latimer, John H. 1941- WhoAmP 93
Latimer, John Leslie 1897- WhAm 10
Latimer, Kenneth Alan 1943- WhoAm 94, WhoAmL 94
Latimer, Lewis Howard 1848-1928 AfrAmAl 6, WorInv
Latimer, Linda Gay 1943- WhoWest 94
Latimer, Michael WhoHol 92
Latimer, Paul Jerry 1943- WhoScEn 94
Latimer, Robert Who 94
Latimer, (Courtenay) Robert 1911- Who 94
Latimer, Roy Truett 1928- WhoAm 94
Latimer, Sheila 1907- WrDr 94
Latimer, Stephen Paul 1957- WhoFI 94
Latimer, Steve B. 1927- WhoBlA 94
Latimer, Thomas Hugh 1932- WhoAm 94
Latimore, Frank 1925- WhoHol 92
Latini, Anthony A. 1942- WhoAm 94
Latini, Henry Peter WhoFI 94, WhoWest 94
Latinovits, Zoltan d1976 WhoHol 92
Latiolais, Rene Louis 1942- WhoFI 94
Latis, Mary J. WrDr 94
Latner, Albert Louis d1992 Who 94N
Latner, Barry P. 1957- WhoWest 94
Latney, Harvey, Jr. 1944- WhoBlA 94
Latno, Arthur Clement, Jr. 1929- WhoAm 94
Latore, Daniel J. 1939- WhoIns 94
LaTores, Santo Joseph 1949- WhoAm 94
La Torre, Charles d1990 WhoHol 92
LaTorre, L. Donald 1937- WhoAm 94, WhoFI 94
LaTorre, Marion Joseph 1933- WhoFI 94
Latorre, Robert G. 1949- WhoHisp 94
Latorre, Robert George 1949- WhoAm 94, WhoScEn 94
LaTorre, Ruben WhoHisp 94
Latorre, Victor Robert 1931- WhoWest 94
Latos-Valier, Paula 1946- WhoAmA 93
Latour, Jose E. 1961- WhoAmL 94
Latour-Adrien, (Jean Francois) Maurice 1915- IntWW 93, Who 94
La Tour du Pin, Henrietta Lucy Dillon de 1770-1853 BlmGWL
La Tourelle, Alyce WhoHol 92
Latourelle, Rene 1918- WrDr 94
La Tourette, Aileen 1946- EncSF 93
LaTourette, Brainerd William, Jr. 1930- WhoMW 93
La Tourette, John Ernest 1932- IntWW 93, WhoAm 94, WhoMW 93
Latourette, Kenneth Scott 1884-1968 DcAmReB 2
La Tourneaux, Robert d1986 WhoHol 92
La Tourrette, Jacqueline 1926- WrDr 94
LaTourrette, James Thomas 1931- WhoAm 94
Latovick, Paula Rae 1954- WhoAmL 94
Latowski, Carol Jean 1955- WhoMW 93
Latrobe, Benjamin Henry 1764-1820 AmCulL
La Trobe-Bateman, Richard George Saumarez 1938- Who 94
Latshaw, John 1921- WhoAm 94
Latshaw, Patricia Joan Herget 1930- WhoMW 93
Latshaw, Paula Alexander 1940- WhoAmL 94
Latsis, Otto Rudolfovich 1934- IntWW 93, LngBDD
Latsis, Peter C. 1919- IntMPA 94
Latt, Samuel Arch 1938-1988 WhAm 10
Latta, Delbert L. 1920- WhoAmP 93
Latta, Gregory Edwin 1952- WhoBlA 94
Latta, Richard 1946- ConAu 41NR
Latta, Richard J. 1946- WrDr 94
Latta, Robert P. 1954- WhoAmL 94
Latta, William Atherton 1941- WhoWest 94
Lattal, Kennon Andy 1943- WhoScEn 94
Lattanzi, Matt IntMPA 94
Lattanzi, Matt 1959- WhoHol 92
Lattanzio, Frances 1949- WhoAmA 93
Lattanzio, Stephen Paul 1949- WhoAm 94, WhoWest 94
Lattanzio, Vito 1926- IntWW 93
Lattauzio, John 1938- WhoAmP 93
Latter, Daniel Stuart 1956- WhoWest 94
Latter, Leslie William 1921- Who 94
Lattes, Armand 1934- WhoScEn 94
Lattes, Raffaele 1910- WhoAm 94
Lattes, Robert 1927- IntWW 93
Latteur, Jean Pierre 1936- IntWW 93
Lattimer, Agnes Dolores 1928- WhoBlA 94
Lattimer, Gary Lee 1939- WhoAm 94
Lattimer, John Kingsley 1914- WhoAm 94
Lattimore, Caroline Louise 1945- WhoBlA 94
Lattimore, Jessie 1931- WrDr 94
Lattimore, Jessie 1940- WrDr 94
Lattimore, Joy Powell 1954- WhoMW 93
Lattimore, Owen 1900-1989 WhAm 10
Lattimore, Stella d1961 WhoHol 92
Lattin, Albert Floyd 1950- WhoAm 94
Lattin, Vernon E. 1938- WhoHisp 94
Lattis, Richard Lynn 1945- WhoAm 94, WhoScEn 94
Lattman, Laurence Harold 1923- WhoAm 94, WhoWest 94
Latto, Douglas 1913- Who 94
Latto, Lewis M., Jr. 1940- WhoAm 94
Lattre, Andre Marie Joseph de 1923- IntWW 93
Latts, Leatrice Lynne 1938- WhoAmL 94
Lattuada, Alberto 1914- IntMPA 94
Lattuada, Felice 1882-1962 NewGrDO
Lattuca, Joseph J. 1947- WhoMW 93
Latus, Gerald M. 1938- WhoAm 94, WhoAmL 94
Latymer, Baron 1926- Who 94
Latymer, Lord NewGrDO
Latymer, William 1498-1583 DcLB 132
Latz, G. Irving, II 1920- WhoAm 94
Latz, John Paul 1969- WhoScEn 94
Latz, William John 1943- WhoFI 94
Latza, Beverly Ann 1960- WhoMW 93
Latzen, Ellen Hamilton WhoHol 92
Latzer, Richard N. 1937- WhoIns 94
Latzer, Richard Neal 1937- WhoAm 94
Lau, Alan Chong DrAPF 93
Lau, Albert Kai-Fay 1949- WhoAsA 94
Lau, B. Peck 1932- WhoWest 94
Lau, Bennett M. K. 1930- WhoAsA 94
Lau, Bobby Wai-Man 1944- WhoWest 94
Lau, Carolyn DrAPF 93
Lau, Cheryl WhoAm 94, WhoWest 94
Lau, Cheryl Ann 1944- WhoAmP 93, WhoAsA 94
Lau, Daniel B. T. 1919- WhoIns 94
Lau, David T. 1939- WhoAsA 94
Lau, Edward C. Y. 1942- WhoAsA 94
Lau, Emily S. 1965- WhoAmL 94
Lau, Estelle Pau On WhoAsA 94
Lau, Eugene Wing Iu 1931- WhoAmL 94, WhoWest 94
Lau, Fred H. 1949- WhoAsA 94
Lau, Frederick C. 1957- WhoAsA 94
Lau, Gilbert Minjun 1927- WhoAsA 94
Lau, Gloria J. 1954- WhoAsA 94
Lau, Harry Hung-Kwan 1939- WhoScEn 94
Lau, Helen Hai-Chu 1951- WhoMW 93
Lau, Hon-Shiang 1947- WhoAsA 94
Lau, Ian Van 1950- WhoAm 94
Lau, Jark C. 1935- WhoAsA 94
Lau, Jeffrey Daniel 1948- WhoAmL 94

Lause, Michael Francis 1948- *WhoAm 94, WhoAmL 94*
Lauson, James Garfield, II 1943- *WhoMW 93*
Laustsen, Agnete 1935- *IntWW 93, WhoWomW 91*
Laut, Harold William 1933- *WhoIns 94*
Lauten, Nancy Ann 1951- *WhoAmL 94*
Lautenbach, Esther Luann 1941- *WhoMW 93*
Lautenbach, Terry 1938- *WhoBlA 94*
Lautenbach, Terry Robert 1938- *WhoFI 94*
Lautenbacher, Conrad Charles, Jr. 1942- *WhoAm 94*
Lautenberg, Frank R. 1924- *CngDr 93, IntWW 93, WhoAm 94, WhoAmP 93*
Lautenschlager, Hans Werner 1927- *IntWW 93*
Lautenschlager, Peggy A. 1955- *WhoAmP 93*
Lautenschlager, Peggy Ann 1955- *WhoAmL 94*
Lautenschlager, Thomas J. *WhoAmP 93*
Lautenslager, Alfred John 1956- *WhoMW 93*
Lauter, Ed 1936- *WhoHol 92*
Lauter, Ed 1940- *IntMPA 94*
Lauter, Harry d1990 *WhoHol 92*
Lauter, James Donald 1931- *WhoAm 94, WhoFI 94*
Lauter, Ken *DrAPF 93*
Lauterbach, Ann *DrAPF 93*
Lauterbach, Hans 1934- *WhoScEn 94*
Lauterbach, Robert Alan 1921-1988 *WhAm 10*
Lauterbach, Robert Emil 1918- *WhoAm 94*
Lauterborn, Robert F. 1936- *WhoAm 94*
Lauterbur, Paul Christian 1929- *WhoAm 94, WhoScEn 94*
Lauterer, Arch 1904- *WhoAmA 93N*
Lauterpacht, Elihu 1928- *Who 94*
Lauters, Pauline *NewGrDO*
Lauterstein, Ingeborg 1933- *WrDr 94*
Lauterstein, Joseph 1934- *WhoScEn 94*
Lauth, Harold Vincent 1933- *WhoWest 94*
Lauth, Robert Edward 1927- *WhoFI 94, WhoScEn 94, WhoWest 94*
Lauti, Toaripi 1928- *IntWW 93, Who 94*
Lautmann, Rudiger 1935- *IntWW 93*
Lautner, Georges Charles 1926- *IntWW 93*
Lautreamont, Comte de 1846-1870 *BlmGEL, ShSCr 14 [port]*
Lauture, Denize *DrAPF 93*
Lautz, Lindsay Allan 1947- *WhoAm 94*
Lautzenheiser, Barbara J. 1938- *WhoIns 94*
Lautzenheiser, Marvin Wendell 1929- *WhoWest 94*
Lauven, Peter Michael 1948- *WhoScEn 94*
Lauvergeon, Anne Alice Marie 1959- *IntWW 93*
Laux, David Charles 1945- *WhoScEn 94*
Laux, Dorianne *DrAPF 93*
Laux, James Michael 1927- *WhoAm 94*
Laux, Russell Frederick 1918- *WhoAmL 94, WhoFI 94*
Lauzanne, Bernard 1916- *IntWW 93*
Lauzen, Chris *WhoAmP 93*
Lauzon, Marc C. 1948- *WhoAmP 93*
Lauzun, Armand Louis de Gontaut-Biron 1747-1793 *AmRev*
Lauzun, Armand-Louis de Gontaut-Biron, Duc de 1747-1793 *WhAmRev [port]*
Lauzun-Stoney, Virginia 1911- *WhoMW 93*
Lavadour, James 1949- *WhoAmA 93*
LaVail, Jennifer Hart 1943- *WhoAm 94*
Laval, Carl Gustaf de 1849-1913 *WorInv*
Laval, Michel-Jean 1725-1777 *NewGrDO*
Laval, Pierre 1883-1945 *HisWorL [port]*
Lavalle, Cleo d1925 *WhoHol 92*
LaValle, Gerald J. 1932- *WhoAmP 93*
LaValle, Irving Howard 1939- *WhoAm 94*
LaValle, Kenneth P. 1939- *WhoAmP 93*
Lavallee, Barbara 1941- *SmATA 74 [port]*
Lavallee, Calixa 1842-1891 *NewGrDO*
Lavallee, H.-Claude 1938- *WhoScEn 94*
LaValley, Frederick J. M. 1947- *WhoAm 94*
Lavalli, Kari Lee 1960- *WhoScEn 94*
Lavan, Alton 1946- *WhoBlA 94*
Lavan, John Martin 1911- *Who 94*
Lavanant, Dominique *WhoHol 92*
Lavanoux, Maurice d1974 *WhoAmA 93N*
Lavant, Christine 1915-1973 *BlmGWL*
La Vaque, Theodore Joseph 1940- *WhoMW 93*
La Varre, Myrtland d1959 *WhoHol 92*
La Varre, William 1898- *WhAm 10*
Lavatelli, Carla 1928- *WhoAmA 93*
Lavatelli, Leo Silvio 1917- *WhoScEn 94*
Lavater-Sloman, Mary 1891-1980 *BlmGWL*
La Vay, Richard Alan 1953- *WhoAmP 93*
Lave, Charles Arthur 1938- *WhoAm 94*
Lave, Judith Rice *WhoAm 94*
Lave, Lester B. 1939- *IntWW 93*
Lave, Lester Bernard 1939- *WhoAm 94*
Lave, Roy Ellis 1935- *WhoWest 94*
LaVean, Michael Gilbert 1954- *WhoMW 93*
LaVeck, Gerald DeLoss 1927- *WhoAm 94*
LaVeist, Thomas Alexis 1961- *WhoBlA 94*
LaVella, Barbara Ward 1947- *WhoMW 93*
LaVelle, Arthur 1921- *WhoAm 94*
LaVelle, Avis 1954- *WhoAm 94*
LaVelle, Betty Sullivan Dougherty 1941- *WhoAmL 94*
Lavelle, Brian Francis David 1941- *WhoAmL 94, WhoFI 94*
Lavelle, Charles Joseph 1950- *WhoAmL 94*
La Velle, Kay d1965 *WhoHol 92*
Lavelle, Kenneth E. 1956- *WhoFI 94*
Lavelle, Kenneth John 1957- *WhoMW 93*
Lavelle, Michael Joseph 1934- *WhoAm 94, WhoMW 93*
Lavelle, Paul Michael 1956- *WhoAm 94*
Lavelle, Robert R. 1915- *WhoBlA 94*
Lavelle, Roger Garnett 1932- *IntWW 93, Who 94*
Lavelle, Sean Marius 1928- *WhoScEn 94*
LaVelle-Nichols, Robin Ann 1959- *WhoFI 94*
Lavelli, Dante *ProFbHF [port]*
Lavelli, Jorge 1931- *NewGrDO*
Laven, Arnold 1922- *IntMPA 94*
Laven, David Lawrence 1953- *WhoScEn 94*
Lavenant, Rene Paul, Jr. 1925- *WhoAm 94*
Lavenas, Suzanne 1942- *WhoFI 94*
Lavenda, Bernard Howard 1945- *WhoScEn 94*
Lavenda, Nathan 1918- *WhoScEn 94*
Lavendel, Giuliana Avanzini *WhoAm 94*
Lavender, Gerard 1943- *Who 94*
Lavender, Ian 1946- *WhoHol 92*
Lavender, Larry Lynn 1947- *WhoFI 94*
Lavender, Peter d1988 *WhoHol 92*
Lavender, Robert Eugene 1926- *WhoAm 94, WhoAmL 94, WhoAmP 93*
Lavengood, Lawrence Gene 1924- *WhoAm 94*
Lavenson, James H. 1919- *WhoAm 94*
Lavenson, Susan Barker 1936- *WhoAm 94, WhoFI 94*
Laventhol, David 1933- *IntWW 93*
Laventhol, David Abram 1933- *WhoAm 94, WhoWest 94*
Laventhol, Hank 1927- *WhoAmA 93*
Laventhol, Henry Lee 1927- *WhoAm 94*
Laver, Frederick John Murray 1915- *Who 94*
Laver, John David Michael Henry 1938- *Who 94*
Laver, Murray Lane 1932- *WhoScEn 94, WhoWest 94*
Laver, Patrick Martin 1932- *Who 94*
Laver, Rod 1938- *BuCMET [port]*
Laver, Rod(ney) George 1938- *IntWW 93*
Laver, Steven G. 1941- *WhoAmL 94*
Laver, William Graeme 1929- *Who 94*
LaVerdiere, Bruno E. 1937- *WhoAmA 93*
La Vere, Earl d1962 *WhoHol 92*
Lavere, June d1991 *WhoHol 92*
La Verendrye, Louis-Joseph Gaultier De *WhWE*
La Verendrye, Pierre Gaultier De Varennes Et De *WhWE*
Laverge, Jan 1909- *WhoAm 94*
LaVergne, Luke Aldon 1938- *WhoBlA 94*
Lavergneau, Rene L. 1933- *WhoBlA 94*
Laverick, Elizabeth 1925- *Who 94*
Laverick, June 1932- *WhoHol 92*
Laverne, Dorothy d1940 *WhoHol 92*
Laverne, Henry d1953 *WhoHol 92*
La Verne, Lucille d1945 *WhoHol 92*
Laverne, Michel Marie-Jacques 1928- *WhoAm 94*
Lavernia, Enrique Jose 1960- *WhoScEn 94*
Lavernia, Milton 1935- *WhoHisp 94*
La Vernie, Laura d1939 *WhoHol 92*
Laveroni, Paul J. 1943- *WhoAmL 94*
Laverov, Nikolai Pavlovitch 1930- *WhoScEn 94*
Lavers, Betty Jean Young 1935- *WhoAmL 94*
Lavers, Norman *DrAPF 93*
Lavers, Norman 1935- *EncSF 93*
Lavers, Patricia Mae 1919- *Who 94*
Lavers, Richard Marshall 1947- *WhoAm 94, WhoAmL 94*
Laverty, Donald *EncSF 93*
Laverty, Maura 1907-1966 *BlmGWL*
Lavery, Bryony 1947- *ConDr 93, WrDr 94*
Lavery, Daniel P. 1932- *WhoAm 94*
Lavery, Vincent Joseph 1936- *WhoWest 94*
Laves, Alan L. 1960- *WhoAmL 94*
Laves, Benjamin Samuel 1946- *WhoAmL 94*
La Vey, Anton 1930- *WhoHol 92*
Lavey, Gerald Michael 1945- *WhoFI 94*
Lavey, Kenneth Henry 1923- *WhoAm 94*
Lavey, Kevin J. *DrAPF 93*
Lavey, Stewart Evan 1945- *WhoAm 94, WhoAmL 94*
Lavezzi, John Charles 1940- *WhoMW 93*
Lavi, Daliah 1942- *WhoHol 92*
La Via, Mariano Francis 1926- *WhoAm 94*
Lavidge, Robert James 1921- *WhoAm 94*
Lavier, Bertrand 1949- *IntWW 93, WhoAmA 93*
Laviera, Tato 1951- *WhoHisp 94*
LaVigna, Michael Paul 1940- *WhoAm 94*
Lavigna, Vincenzo 1776-1836 *NewGrDO*
Lavigne, Denise Marie 1956- *WhoMW 93*
Lavigne, James R. 1951- *WhoAmL 94*
Lavigne, Lawrence Neil 1957- *WhoAmL 94*
La Villa, Ronald Albert 1935- *WhoHisp 94*
LaVilla-Havelin, James S. *DrAPF 93*
Lavin, Bernice E. 1925- *WhoAm 94*
Lavin, Charles Blaise, Jr. 1940- *WhoAm 94*
Lavin, Deborah Margaret 1939- *Who 94*
Lavin, Irving 1927- *WhoAmA 93*
Lavin, John Halley 1932- *WhoAm 94*
Lavin, Laurence Michael 1940- *WhoWest 94*
Lavin, Leonard H. 1919- *WhoAm 94, WhoFI 94*
Lavin, Linda 1937- *IntMPA 94, WhoAm 94, WhoCom, WhoHol 92*
Lavin, Marilyn Aronberg 1925- *WhoAmA 93*
Lavin, Mary 1912- *BlmGWL, IntWW 93, RfGShF, Who 94, WrDr 94*
Lavin, Maud 1954- *ConAu 142*
Lavin, Rafael *WhoHisp 94*
Lavin, S. R. *DrAPF 93*
Lavin, Sylvia 1960- *ConAu 142*
Lavin, William Kane 1944- *WhoAm 94, WhoFI 94*
La Vinder, Gracille d1973 *WhoHol 92*
Lavine, Clifford I. 1953- *WhoFI 94*
Lavine, David 1929- *WhoAmP 93*
Lavine, Gary J. *WhoFI 94*
Lavine, Henry Wolfe 1936- *WhoAm 94*
Lavine, Jim E. 1949- *WhoAmL 94*
Lavine, John M. 1941 *WhoAm 94*
Lavine, Lawrence Neal 1951- *WhoAm 94, WhoFI 94*
Lavine, Leroy Stanley 1918- *WhoScEn 94*
La Vine, Ronald Scott 1957- *WhoWest 94*
Lavine, Sigmund Arnold 1908- *ConAu 41NR, WrDr 94*
Lavine, Steven David 1947- *WhoAm 94, WhoWest 94*
Lavine, Thelma Zeno *WhoAm 94*
Lavington, Michael Richard 1943- *WhoAm 94*
Lavinsky, Larry Monroe 1929- *WhoAm 94*
Lavinson, Joseph *ConAu 41NR*
Laviolette, Bruce Edward 1949- *WhoFI 94*
LaViolette, Catherine Patricia 1935- *WhoMW 93*
Lavirgen, Pedro 1930- *NewGrDO*
Lavit, Theodore Howard 1939- *WhoAmP 93*
La Vita, Roberto 1950- *WhoFI 94*
Lavitt, Mel S. 1937- *WhoAm 94*
Lavizzo-Mourey, Risa Juanita 1954- *WhoBlA 94*
Lavkulich, Leslie Michael 1939- *WhoScEn 94*
Lavoe, Hector d1993 *NewYTBS 93, WhoHisp 94N*
Lavoie, John Gerard 1965- *WhoAmL 94*
Lavoie, Judith Anne *Who 94*
Lavoie, Lionel A. 1937- *WhoAm 94*
La Voie, Roger Michael 1947- *WhoWest 94*
Lavoie, Serge 1963- *WhoAm 94*
LaVoie, Steven Paul *DrAPF 93*
Lavoie-Roux, Therese 1928- *WhoWomW 91*
Lavoisier, Antoine-Laurent 1743-1794 *WorScD [port]*
Lavond, Paul Dennis *EncSF 93*
Lavorando, Joseph, Jr. 1953- *WhoAmP 93*
Lavorato, Louis A. *WhoAmL 94, WhoMW 93*
Lavorato, Louis A. 1934- *WhoAmP 93*
Lavrangas, Dionyssios 1860?-1941 *NewGrDO*
Lavrov, Sergey Viktorovich 1950- *IntWW 93*
Lavrov, Vladimir Sergeyevich 1919- *IntWW 93*
Lavrovskaya, Yelizaveta Andreyevna 1845-1919 *NewGrDO*
Lavrovsky, Leonid 1905-1967 *IntDcB*
Lavrovsky, Mikhail 1941- *IntDcB [port]*
Lavrushin, Vladimir Fedorovich 1912- *IntWW 93*
Lavry, Marc 1903-1967 *NewGrDO*
Law *Who 94*
Law, Andrew 1749-1821 *WhAmRev*
Law, Bernard F. 1931- *IntWW 93*
Law, Bernard Francis Cardinal 1931- *WhoAm 94*
Law, Betty d1955 *WhoHol 92*
Law, Bob 1934- *IntWW 93*
Law, Burton d1963 *WhoHol 92*
Law, C. Anthony 1916- *WhoAmA 93*
Law, Chung King 1947- *WhoScEn 94*
Law, Clarene 1933- *WhoAmP 93*
Law, Colin Nigel 1932- *Who 94*
Law, David Holbrook 1946- *WhoAm 94*
Law, Davis Joseph 1923- *WhoAm 94*
Law, Denis 1940- *WorESoc*
Law, Don d1959 *WhoHol 92*
Law, Ellen Marie 1960- *WhoAmL 94*
Law, Ellen T. 1918- *WhoBlA 94*
Law, Flora Elizabeth 1935- *WhoWest 94*
Law, Francis Stephen 1916- *Who 94*
Law, Frederick Masom 1934- *WhoAm 94*
Law, George Llewellyn 1929- *Who 94*
Law, Gerald H. 1944- *WhoAmP 93*
Law, H. David 1949- *WhoAsA 94*
Law, Horace (Rochfort) 1911- *Who 94*
Law, Horace Rochfort 1911- *IntWW 93*
Law, James 1926- *Who 94*
Law, James George 1944- *WhoFI 94, WhoWest 94*
Law, James L. 1926- *WhoAmP 93*
Law, James N. 1947- *WhoAmP 93*
Law, John Harold 1931- *WhoAm 94*
Law, John Manning 1927- *WhoAm 94, WhoAmL 94*
Law, John Phillip 1937- *IntMPA 94, WhoHol 92*
Law, Lindsay *IntMPA 94*
Law, Lloyd William 1910- *WhoAm 94*
Law, M. Eprevel 1943- *WhoAmP 93, WhoBlA 94*
Law, Margaret *WhoAmA 93N*
Law, Michael R. 1947- *WhoAm 94, WhoAmL 94*
Law, Patricia Anne 1958- *WhoAmL 94*
Law, Phillip Garth 1912- *IntWW 93, Who 94*
Law, Richard 1733-1806 *WhAmRev*
Law, Robert 1930- *WhoAm 94*
Law, Roger 1941- *Who 94*
Law, Roger Alan 1933- *WhoAmL 94*
Law, Scott Alan 1963- *WhoAmL 94*
Law, Stephen J. *WhoAmP 93*
Law, Sylvia 1931- *Who 94*
Law, Thomas Melvin 1926- *WhoBlA 94*
Law, Walter d1940 *WhoHol 92*
Law, William Ronald 1957- *WhoMW 93*
Lawaetz, Bent 1939- *WhoAmP 93*
Lawaetz, Frits 1907- *WhoAmP 93*
Lawall, David Barnard 1935- *WhoAmA 93*
LaWare, John Patrick 1928- *WhoAm 94, WhoFI 94*
Lawatsch, Frank Emil, Jr. 1944- *WhoAm 94, WhoAmL 94*
Lawden, Derek Frank 1919- *WrDr 94*
Lawder, Donald *DrAPF 93*
Lawder, Douglas W. *DrAPF 93*
Lawes, Verna 1927- *WhoBlA 94*
Lawfer, I. Ronald *WhoAmP 93*
Lawford, Betty d1960 *WhoHol 92*
Lawford, Christopher 1955- *WhoHol 92*
Lawford, Ernest d1940 *WhoHol 92*
Lawford, G. Ross 1941- *WhoAm 94, WhoScEn 94*
Lawford, Herb 1851-1925 *BuCMET*
Lawford, Lady May d1972 *WhoHol 92*
Lawford, Peter d1984 *WhoHol 92*
Lawford, Sydney d1953 *WhoHol 92*
Lawhead, Stephen R. 1950- *EncSF 93*
Lawhon, John E., III 1934- *WhoAm 94*
Lawhon, William Griffith 1942- *WhoAm 94, WhoAmL 94*
Lawhorn, Jess Sherman 1933- *WhoFI 94*
Lawhorn, John B. 1925- *WhoBlA 94*
Lawhorn, Robert Martin 1943- *WhoBlA 94*
Lawhorne, Thomas W., Sr. 1924- *WhoAmP 93*
Lawi, David Steven 1935- *WhoAm 94*
Lawing, Jack L. 1938- *WhoAmL 94*
Lawing, Raymond Quinton 1910- *WhoBlA 94*
Lawit, John Walter 1950- *WhoAmL 94*
Lawlah, Gloria Gary 1939- *WhoAmP 93, WhoBlA 94*
Lawler, Edmund Oliver 1953- *WhoMW 93*
Lawler, Edward James 1908- *WhoAmL 94*
Lawler, Geoffrey John 1954- *Who 94*
Lawler, George S. 1950- *WhoAmL 94*
Lawler, James Edward 1951- *WhoScEn 94*
Lawler, James F. *WhoAmP 93*
Lawler, James F. 1935- *WhoMW 93*
Lawler, James Ronald 1929- *IntWW 93, WhoAm 94*
Lawler, John Mark 1952- *WhoMW 93*
Lawler, Larry 1939- *WhoAmP 93*

Lawler, Lawrence Thomas, Jr. 1949- *WhoFI 94*
Lawler, Lucille 1908- *WrDr 94*
Lawler, Mary G. 1943- *WhoAmL 94*
Lawler, Michael B. 1942- *WhoAmL 94*
Lawler, Patrick *DrAPF 93*
Lawler, Patrick 1948- *WrDr 94*
Lawler, Peter (James) 1921- *Who 94*
Lawler, Ray(mond Evenor) 1921- *ConDr 93, IntDcT 2, WrDr 94*
Lawler, Richard Francis 1945- *WhoAm 94*
Lawler, Rick M. 1949- *WhoWest 94*
Lawler, Simon William 1949- *Who 94*
Lawless, Emily 1845-1913 *BlmGWL*
Lawless, Gary *DrAPF 93*
Lawless, John A. 1957- *WhoAmP 93*
Lawless, John Joseph 1908- *WhoScEn 94*
Lawless, Joseph Francis, III 1945- *WhoAmP 93*
Lawless, Kirby Gordon, Jr. 1924- *WhoAmP 93*
Lawless, Michael William 1948- *WhoWest 94*
Lawless, Robert C. 1957- *WhoAmP 93*
Lawless, Robert William 1937- *WhoAm 94*
Lawless, William Burns 1922- *WhoAmL 94*
Lawley, Alan 1933- *WhoAm 94*
Lawley, Leonard Edward 1922- *Who 94*
Lawley, Susan 1946- *Who 94*
Lawley, Susan Marc 1951- *WhoFI 94*
Lawlor, Bruce Michael 1948- *WhoAmP 93*
Lawlor, John J. 1951- *WhoAmL 94*
Lawlor, John James 1918- *Who 94, WrDr 94*
Lawlor, Mary 1911- *WhoHol 92*
Lawlor, Michael P. *WhoAmP 93*
Lawlor, Richard Patrick 1946- *WhoAmP 93*
Lawn, Beverly *DrAPF 93*
Lawn, Ian David 1947- *WhoScEn 94*
Lawn, John C. 1935- *WhoAm 94, WhoAmP 93*
Lawn, Tony *WhoHol 92*
Lawner, Lynne *DrAPF 93*
Lawner, Mordecai *WhoHol 92*
Lawniczak, James Michael 1951- *WhoAm 94, WhoAmL 94*
Lawrance, Charles H. 1920- *WhoScEn 94*
Lawrance, Charles Holway 1920- *WhoAm 94*
Lawrance, John Ernest 1928- *Who 94*
Lawrance, June Cynthia 1933- *Who 94*
Lawrance, Keith Cantwell 1923- *Who 94*
Lawrence *EncSF 93, Who 94*
Lawrence fl. 1706-1718 *NewGrDO*
Lawrence, Baron 1937- *Who 94*
Lawrence, Albert James 1947- *WhoAm 94*
Lawrence, Albert Weaver 1928- *WhoAm 94, WhoFI 94, WhoIns 94*
Lawrence, Annie L. 1926- *WhoBlA 94*
Lawrence, Archie 1947- *WhoBlA 94*
Lawrence, Azar Malcolm 1952- *WhoBlA 94*
Lawrence, Barbara *WhoAmP 93*
Lawrence, Barbara 1930- *IntMPA 94, WhoHol 92*
Lawrence, Barbara 1944- *WhoAm 94*
Lawrence, Barry Howard 1942- *WhoAm 94, WhoAmL 94*
Lawrence, Berta *WrDr 94*
Lawrence, Betty Jean 1934- *WhoMW 93*
Lawrence, Brian Denton 1961- *WhoMW 93*
Lawrence, Bruno 1940- *WhoHol 92*
Lawrence, Bryan d1983 *WhoHol 92*
Lawrence, Bryan Hunt 1942- *WhoFI 94*
Lawrence, C(lifford) H(ugh) 1921- *WrDr 94*
Lawrence, Caleb James *Who 94*
Lawrence, Carmen Mary 1948- *IntWW 93, Who 94*
Lawrence, Carol 1934- *WhoHol 92*
Lawrence, Carolyn Marie 1963- *WhoScEn 94*
Lawrence, Charles B. 1920- *WhoBlA 94*
Lawrence, Charles Edmund 1927- *WhoAm 94*
Lawrence, Charles Joseph 1959- *WhoFI 94, WhoMW 93*
Lawrence, Charles Stephen 1948- *WhoWest 94*
Lawrence, Christopher Nigel 1936- *Who 94*
Lawrence, Christopher Rueckert 1953- *WhoAm 94*
Lawrence, Clifford Hugh 1921- *Who 94*
Lawrence, D. H. 1885-1930 *BlmGEL [port]*
Lawrence, D(avid) H(erbert) 1885-1930 *IntDcT 2, RfGShF*
Lawrence, D(avid) H(erbert Richards) 1885-1930 *GayLL*
Lawrence, Daniel Eugene 1950- *WhoMW 93*
Lawrence, David, Jr. 1942- *WhoAm 94*
Lawrence, David (Roland Walter) 1929- *Who 94*
Lawrence, David Bruce 1929- *WhoFI 94*
Lawrence, David Michael 1943- *WhoAm 94*
Lawrence, Dean Grayson 1901- *WhoWest 94*
Lawrence, Deborah Anne 1963- *WhoAmL 94*
Lawrence, Del d1965 *WhoHol 92*
Lawrence, Delphi 1926- *WhoHol 92*
Lawrence, Denis 1940- *WhoAmP 93*
Lawrence, Dennis George Charles 1918- *Who 94*
Lawrence, Doug *WhoAmP 93*
Lawrence, Douglass Ray 1957- *WhoMW 93*
Lawrence, Eddie 1921- *WhoCom, WhoHol 92*
Lawrence, Edward d1931 *WhoHol 92*
Lawrence, Edward 1935- *WhoBlA 94*
Lawrence, Edward J. 1931- *WhoAmP 93*
Lawrence, Edward Peabody 1941- *WhoAm 94, WhoAmL 94*
Lawrence, Eileen B. 1919- *WhoBlA 94*
Lawrence, Elizabeth *WhoHol 92*
Lawrence, Erma Jean 1926- *WhoBlA 94*
Lawrence, Ernest Orlando 1901-1958 *WorInv*
Lawrence, Estelene Yvonne 1933- *WhoMW 93*
Lawrence, Eva M. 1930- *WhoAmP 93*
Lawrence, Florence d1938 *WhoHol 92*
Lawrence, Frances Elizabeth 1925- *WhoWest 94*
Lawrence, Francis Warren d1993 *NewYTBS 93*
Lawrence, Frederic Cunningham 1899-1989 *WhAm 10*
Lawrence, Gary George 1938- *WhoAm 94*
Lawrence, Gary Michael 1951- *WhoAmL 94*
Lawrence, Geoffrey 1880-1971 *DcNaB MP*
Lawrence, Geoffrey Charles 1915- *Who 94*
Lawrence, George Calvin 1918- *WhoBlA 94*
Lawrence, George Durwood, Jr. 1950- *WhoAm 94*
Lawrence, George Hubbard Clapp 1937- *WhoFI 94*
Lawrence, Gerald d1957 *WhoHol 92*
Lawrence, Gerald Graham 1947- *WhoAm 94, WhoFI 94*
Lawrence, Gertrude d1952 *WhoHol 92*
Lawrence, Glenn Robert 1930- *WhoAm 94, WhoAmL 94*
Lawrence, Gloria Edith *WhoAmP 93*
Lawrence, Gloria Jean 1954- *WhoMW 93*
Lawrence, Guy Kempton 1914- *Who 94*
Lawrence, Happy James 1944- *WhoWest 94*
Lawrence, Helen Humphreys 1878- *WhoAmA 93N*
Lawrence, Henry 1951- *WhoBlA 94*
Lawrence, Henry L(ionel) 1908- *EncSF 93*
Lawrence, Henry Sherwood 1916- *IntWW 93, WhoAm 94*
Lawrence, Howard Ray 1936- *WhoAmA 93*
Lawrence, Ivan (John) 1936- *Who 94*
Lawrence, J(udith) A(nn) *EncSF 93*
Lawrence, Jacob 1917- *AfrAmAl 6 [port], WhoAm 94, WhoAmA 93, WhoWest 94*
Lawrence, Jacob A. 1917- *WhoBlA 94*
Lawrence, James A. 1910- *WhoAmA 93*
Lawrence, James Albert 1910- *WhoWest 94*
Lawrence, James Bland 1947- *WhoAm 94*
Lawrence, James Franklin 1949- *WhoBlA 94*
Lawrence, James Kaufman Lebensburger 1940- *WhoAm 94*
Lawrence, James Paul 1950- *WhoMW 93*
Lawrence, James T. 1921- *WhoBlA 94*
Lawrence, Janice 1962- *BasBi*
Lawrence, Jay d1987 *WhoHol 92*
Lawrence, Jaye A. 1939- *WhoAmA 93*
Lawrence, Jeanne d1945 *WhoHol 92*
Lawrence, Jerome 1915- *ConDr 93, WhoAm 94, WhoWest 94, WrDr 94*
Lawrence, Jim 1918- *EncSF 93*
Lawrence, Joan W. *WhoAmP 93*
Lawrence, Jody d1986 *WhoHol 92*
Lawrence, John d1974 *WhoHol 92*
Lawrence, John 1933- *Who 94*
Lawrence, John (Waldemar) 1907- *Who 94*
Lawrence, John Alan 1949- *WhoAmP 93*
Lawrence, John E. 1941- *WhoBlA 94*
Lawrence, John Hundale 1904-1991 *WhAm 10*
Lawrence, John Kidder 1949- *WhoAm 94, WhoAmL 94, WhoFI 94, WhoMW 93*
Lawrence, John Thornett 1920- *Who 94*
Lawrence, John Warren 1928- *WhoMW 93*
Lawrence, John Wilfred 1933- *Who 94*
Lawrence, Jordan 1929- *WhoScEn 94*
Lawrence, Justus Baldwin 1903-1987 *WhAm 10*
Lawrence, Kathleen Ann 1946- *WhoAmP 93*
Lawrence, Kathleen Rockwell *DrAPF 93*
Lawrence, Kathleen Rockwell 1945- *WrDr 94*
Lawrence, Kathleen Wilson 1940- *WhoAmP 93*
Lawrence, L. David d1981 *WhoHol 92*
Lawrence, Larry *WhoHol 92*
Lawrence, Larry James 1944- *WhoFI 94*
Lawrence, Leonard E. 1937- *WhoBlA 94*
Lawrence, Les 1940- *WhoAm 94, WhoAmA 93*
Lawrence, Lesley 1909- *WrDr 94*
Lawrence, Lillian d1926 *WhoHol 92*
Lawrence, Lonnie R. 1946- *WhoBlA 94*
Lawrence, Louise 1943- *EncSF 93, TwCYAW, WrDr 94*
Lawrence, Marc 1909- *WhoHol 92*
Lawrence, Marc 1914- *IntMPA 94*
Lawrence, Margaret *WhoHol 92*
Lawrence, Margaret Morgan 1914- *WhoBlA 94*
Lawrence, Margery Hulings 1934- *WhoFI 94, WhoScEn 94*
Lawrence, Margot *WrDr 94*
Lawrence, Marjie *WhoHol 92*
Lawrence, Marjorie (Florence) 1909-1979 *NewGrDO*
Lawrence, Mark W. 1958- *WhoAmP 93*
Lawrence, Martin *WhoBlA 94*
Lawrence, Martin 1965- *ConBlB 6 [port]*
Lawrence, Martin c. 1966- *News 93 [port]*
Lawrence, Martin William 1943- *WhoScEn 94*
Lawrence, Mary *WhoHol 92*
Lawrence, Merle 1915- *WhoAm 94*
Lawrence, Merlisa Evelyn 1965- *WhoBlA 94*
Lawrence, Merloyd Ludington 1932- *WhoAm 94*
Lawrence, Michael *WhoAmA 93*
Lawrence, Michael Hugh 1920- *Who 94*
Lawrence, Michelle 1948- *WhoAmP 93*
Lawrence, Montague Schiele 1923- *WhoBlA 94*
Lawrence, Murray *Who 94*
Lawrence, (Walter Nicholas) Murray 1935- *Who 94*
Lawrence, Nancy Ann 1959- *WhoFI 94, WhoMW 93*
Lawrence, Nancy Morrison 1952- *WhoAmL 94*
Lawrence, Norman B. 1928- *WhoAmP 93*
Lawrence, Ollie, Jr. 1951- *WhoBlA 94*
Lawrence, P. 1919- *WrDr 94*
Lawrence, Patricia Ann Loving 1958- *WhoFI 94*
Lawrence, Patrick *Who 94*
Lawrence, (John) Patrick (Grosvenor) 1928- *Who 94*
Lawrence, Paul Frederic *WhoBlA 94*
Lawrence, Paul Frederic 1912- *BlkWr 2, WhoWest 94*
Lawrence, Paul Roger 1922- *WhoAm 94*
Lawrence, Paula Denise 1959- *WhoWest 94*
Lawrence, Peter Anthony 1941- *IntWW 93, Who 94*
Lawrence, Philip d1987 *WhoHol 92*
Lawrence, Philip Martin 1950- *WhoBlA 94, WhoMW 93*
Lawrence, Prestonia D. 1957- *WhoBlA 94*
Lawrence, Ralph Waldo 1941- *WhoMW 93*
Lawrence, Raymond d1976 *WhoHol 92*
Lawrence, Raymond Jeffery 1939- *WhoScEn 94*
Lawrence, Richard *Who 94*
Lawrence, (Henry) Richard (George) 1946- *Who 94*
Lawrence, Richard T. 1954- *WhoAmL 94*
Lawrence, Richard Wesley, Jr. 1909- *WhoAm 94*
Lawrence, Robert Allen 1935- *WhoAm 94, WhoAmL 94*
Lawrence, Robert Don 1941- *WhoWest 94*
Lawrence, Robert Edward 1946- *WhoScEn 94*
Lawrence, Robert G. 1932- *WhoIns 94*
Lawrence, Robert H., Jr. 1935-1967 *AfrAmAl 6 [port]*
Lawrence, Robert Michael 1961- *WhoScEn 94*
Lawrence, Robert Swan 1938- *IntWW 93, WhoAm 94*
Lawrence, Rodell 1946- *WhoBlA 94*
Lawrence, Roderick John 1949- *WhoScEn 94*
Lawrence, Rodney Steven 1951- *WhoAmA 93*
Lawrence, Rosina 1914- *WhoHol 92*
Lawrence, Ruddick Carpenter 1912- *WhoAm 94*
Lawrence, Sally Clark 1930- *WhoAm 94, WhoWest 94*
Lawrence, Sandra 1938- *WhoBlA 94*
Lawrence, Sanford Hull 1919- *WhoWest 94*
Lawrence, Seymour 1926- *WhoAm 94*
Lawrence, Sidney S. 1948- *WhoAmA 93*
Lawrence, Spencer 1949- *WhoAmA 93*
Lawrence, Stanton Townley, III 1945- *WhoAmL 94*
Lawrence, Stephanie *WhoHol 92*
Lawrence, Stephen *EncSF 93*
Lawrence, Steve 1935- *ConTFT 11, IntMPA 94, WhoAm 94, WhoHol 92*
Lawrence, Steven C. 1924- *WrDr 94*
Lawrence, Susan 1939- *WhoAmA 93*
Lawrence, T. E. 1888-1935 *HisWorL [port]*
Lawrence, T(homas) E(dward) 1888-1935 *GayLL*
Lawrence, Theresa A. B. 1953- *WhoBlA 94*
Lawrence, Thomas Edward 1888-1935 *WhWE*
Lawrence, Thomas Edwin, Jr. 1941- *WhoAmP 93*
Lawrence, Thomas Patterson 1946- *WhoAm 94, WhoFI 94*
Lawrence, Thomas R., Jr. 1929- *WhoBlA 94*
Lawrence, Timothy 1942- *Who 94*
Lawrence, Tracy 1968- *ConMus 11 [port]*
Lawrence, Trudy d1978 *WhoHol 92*
Lawrence, Vicki 1949- *IntMPA 94, WhoHol 92*
Lawrence, Vicki Schultz 1949- *WhoAm 94*
Lawrence, Viola Poe 1926- *WhoBlA 94*
Lawrence, Virgil Edward, Jr. 1933- *WhoFI 94*
Lawrence, W. Vernon 1898- *WhAm 10*
Lawrence, Walter d1961 *WhoHol 92*
Lawrence, Walter, Jr. 1925- *WhoAm 94*
Lawrence, Walter Nicholas Murray 1935- *IntWW 93*
Lawrence, Wayne Allen 1938- *WhoAm 94*
Lawrence, Willard Earl 1917- *WhoAm 94*
Lawrence, William d1947 *WhoHol 92*
Lawrence, William (Fettiplace) 1954- *Who 94*
Lawrence, William F. *WhoAmP 93*
Lawrence, William Joseph, Jr. 1918- *WhoAm 94*
Lawrence, William Porter 1930- *WhoAm 94*
Lawrence, William Robert 1942- *Who 94*
Lawrence, William Wesley 1939- *WhoBlA 94*
Lawrence, Zan 1945- *WhoWest 94*
Lawrence-Jones, Christopher 1940- *Who 94*
Lawrence of Arabia *GayLL*
Lawrenson, Peter John 1933- *IntWW 93, Who 94*
Lawrenz, Donald R. 1923 *WhoIns 94*
Lawrey, Keith 1940- *Who 94*
Lawrie, Duncan H. 1943- *WhoAm 94*
Lawrie, Gerald Murray 1945- *WhoAm 94*
Lawrie, Henry DeVos, Jr. 1942- *WhoAmL 94*
Lawrie, Lee 1877-1963 *WhoAmA 93N*
Lawrie, Peter 1945- *WhoIns 94*
Lawrie, Robert George 1945- *WhoFI 94*
Lawrimore, Eugene Salmon Napier 1947- *WhoAmL 94, WhoAmP 93*
Lawritson, Jon Lorry 1941- *WhoAmL 94*
Lawroski, Harry 1928- *WhoAm 94*
Lawry, Roger Harlow 1956- *WhoWest 94*
Lawry, Sylvia *WhoAm 94*
Laws, Barry *WhoHol 92*
Laws, Clarence A. 1911- *WhoBlA 94*
Laws, Courtney Alexander 1934- *Who 94*
Laws, Edward Ernest, III 1945- *WhoWest 94*
Laws, Edward Raymond 1938- *WhoAm 94*
Laws, Frederick Geoffrey 1928- *Who 94*
Laws, John (Grant McKenzie) 1945- *Who 94*
Laws, John William 1921- *Who 94*
Laws, Richard Maitland 1926- *IntWW 93, Who 94*
Laws, Robert E. 1927- *WhoFI 94*
Laws, Robert Franklin 1914-1991 *WhAm 10*
Laws, Ruth M. 1912- *WhoBlA 94*
Laws, Sam d1990 *WhoHol 92*
Laws, Stephen Charles 1950- *Who 94*
Lawser, John Jutten 1941- *WhoScEn 94*
Law-Smith, David John 1940- *WhoFI 94*
Law-Smith, (Richard) Robert d1992 *Who 94N*
Law-Smith, (Richard) Robert 1914- *IntWW 93*
Lawson *Who 94*
Lawson, Abram Venable 1922- *WhoAm 94*
Lawson, Al 1948- *WhoAmP 93*
Lawson, Albert Thomas 1898-1963 *EncABHB 9 [port]*

Lazarus, Jonathan Doniel 1951- *WhoFI 94*
Lazarus, Kenneth Anthony 1942- *WhoAm 94*
Lazarus, Marvin P. 1918-1982 *WhoAmA 93N*
Lazarus, Maurice 1915- *WhoAm 94*
Lazarus, Mell *WhoAm 94*
Lazarus, Pat 1935- *WrDr 94*
Lazarus, Paul N. 1913- *IntMPA 94*
Lazarus, Paul N., III 1938- *IntMPA 94*
Lazarus, Peter (Esmond) 1926- *Who 94*
Lazarus, Richard S. 1922- *WrDr 94*
Lazarus, Richard Stanley 1922- *WhoAm 94, WhoWest 94*
Lazarus, Rochelle Braff 1947- *WhoAm 94, WhoFI 94*
Lazarus, Simon, III 1941- *WhoAmL 94, WhoAmP 93*
Lazarus, Steven S. 1943- *WhoScEn 94*
Lazarus, Theodore R. 1919- *IntMPA 94*
Lazear, Bruce Charles 1959- *WhoAmL 94*
Lazear, Edward Paul 1948- *WhoAm 94*
Lazechko, Molly 1926- *WhoAmP 93*
Lazenby, Alec 1927- *IntWW 93, Who 94*
Lazenby, Dexter 1955- *WhoAmA 93*
Lazenby, Fred Wiehl 1932- *WhoAm 94, WhoIns 94*
Lazenby, George 1939- *WhoHol 92*
Lazenby, Norman (Austin) 1914- *WrDr 94*
Lazenby, Norman A(ustin) 1914- *EncSF 93*
Lazer, Hank *DrAPF 93*
Lazer, Joan *WhoHol 92*
Lazer, Peter 1946- *WhoHol 92*
Lazer, William 1924- *WrDr 94*
Lazerson, Earl Edwin 1930- *WhoAm 94, WhoMW 93*
Lazerson, Jack 1936- *WhoAm 94*
Lazich, Daniel 1941- *WhoScEn 94*
Lazich, Mary A. 1952- *WhoAmP 93*
Lazier, Gil 1939- *WhoAm 94*
Lazinsky, Craig Barry 1951- *WhoFI 94*
Lazio, Rick A. 1958- *CngDr 93, WhoAm 94*
Lazio, Rick A. 1968- *WhoAmP 93*
Lazo, Douglas T. 1942- *WhoAsA 94*
Lazo, Jacqui Fiske 1951- *WhoAmL 94*
Lazo, Jorge Frank *WhoHisp 94*
Lazo, Nelson 1957- *WhoHisp 94*
Lazor, Theodosius 1933- *WhoAm 94*
Lazorchak, James Michael 1947- *WhoMW 93*
Lazorko, Anthony, Jr. 1935- *WhoMW 93*
Lazorko, Jack *NewYTBS 93 [port]*
Lazowska, Edward Delano 1950- *WhoWest 94*
Lazrus, Benjamin 1894- *WhAm 10*
Lazure, Gabrielle *WhoHol 92*
Lazzara, Bernadette 1948- *WhoAm 94*
Lazzara, Dennis Joseph 1948- *WhoMW 93*
Lazzari, Pietro 1898-1979 *WhoAmA 93N*
Lazzari, (Joseph) Sylvio 1857-1944 *NewGrDO*
Lazzari, Virgilio 1887-1953 *NewGrDO*
Lazzaro, Anthony Derek 1921- *WhoAm 94*
Lazzaro, Clifford Emanuel 1959- *WhoAmL 94*
Lazzell, Blanche 1878-1956 *WhoAmA 93N*
Lazzuri, Michael Joseph 1944- *WhoFI 94*
Le, Binh P. 1959- *WhoAsA 94*
Le, Christine Dung 1958- *WhoAsA 94*
Le, Hy Xuan 1957- *WhoAsA 94*
Le, Khanh Tuong 1936- *WhoScEn 94, WhoWest 94*
Le, Quang Nam 1953- *WhoScEn 94*
Le, Tieng Quang 1944- *WhoAsA 94*
Le, Vy Phuong 1960- *WhoAsA 94*
Le, Xuan Khoa *WhoAsA 94*
Lea, Christopher Gerald 1917- *Who 94*
Lea, David Edward 1937- *Who 94*
Lea, Eleanor Lucille 1916- *WhoMW 93*
Lea, Homer 1876-1912 *EncSF 93*
Lea, James F(ranklin) 1945- *WrDr 94*
Lea, Jeanne Evans 1931- *WhoBlA 94*
Lea, John (Stuart Crosbie) 1923- *Who 94*
Lea, Laurie Jane 1948- *WhoAmA 93*
Lea, Lola Stendig 1934- *WhoAm 94*
Lea, Lorenzo Bates 1925- *WhoAm 94*
Lea, Pat 1928- *WhoAmP 93*
Lea, Robert Norman 1939- *WhoWest 94*
Lea, Scott Carter 1931- *WhoAm 94*
Lea, Stanley E. 1930- *WhoAm 94, WhoAmA 93*
Lea, Sydney *DrAPF 93*
Lea, Thomas (William) 1973- *Who 94*
Lea, Timothy *ConAu 43NR*
Lea, Tom 1907- *WhoAmA 93, WrDr 94*
Lea, Wendy Smith 1954- *WhoFI 94*
Leab, Daniel Josef 1936- *WrDr 94*
Leabhart, Thomas Glenn 1944- *WhoWest 94*
Leace, Donal Richard 1939- *WhoBlA 94*
Leach, Alan Ross 1952- *WhoFI 94*
Leach, Allan William 1931- *Who 94*
Leach, Anthony Raymond 1939- *WhoFI 94*
Leach, Barbara Mary Enright 1945- *WhoAmP 93*
Leach, Barbara Wills 1925- *WhoBlA 94*
Leach, Britt *WhoHol 92*
Leach, Cheryll Jean 1947- *WhoMW 93*
Leach, Christiana fl. 1765-1796 *BlmGWL*
Leach, Claude *WhoAmP 93*
Leach, Clive William 1934- *Who 94*
Leach, Cynthia Diane 1958- *WhoMW 93*
Leach, Dave Francis 1945- *WhoMW 93*
Leach, David Andrew 1911- *Who 94*
Leach, David Warren 1958- *WhoFI 94*
Leach, Donald Frederick 1931- *Who 94*
Leach, Donald Paul 1945- *WhoFI 94*
Leach, Douglas Edward 1920- *WrDr 94*
Leach, Eleanor Winsor 1937- *WhoMW 93*
Leach, Elizabeth Anne 1957- *WhoAmA 93*
Leach, Franklin Rollin 1933- *WhoAm 94*
Leach, Henry (Conyers) 1923- *IntWW 93, Who 94*
Leach, James A. 1942- *CngDr 93*
Leach, James Albert Smith 1942- *WhoAm 94, WhoMW 93*
Leach, James Francis 1953- *WhoFI 94*
Leach, Jeffrey Dale 1954- *WhoMW 93*
Leach, Jim 1942- *WhoAmP 93*
Leach, John d1918 *WhoHol 92*
Leach, John Frank 1921- *WhoFI 94*
Leach, John Leonard 1946- *WhoFI 94*
Leach, Joseph Lee 1921- *WhoAm 94*
Leach, Julian Gilbert 1894- *WhAm 10*
Leach, Lois D. 1941- *WhoMW 93*
Leach, Louis Lawrence 1885-1957 *WhoAmA 93N*
Leach, Mada 1939- *WhoAmA 93*
Leach, Margarette R. *WhoAmP 93*
Leach, Marjorie S. 1911- *ConAu 142*
Leach, Maurice Derby, Jr. 1923- *WhoAm 94*
Leach, Michael Glen 1940- *WhoAm 94*
Leach, Norman 1912- *Who 94*
Leach, Norman Stewart 1963- *WhoAm 94*
Leach, Paul Arthur 1915- *Who 94*
Leach, Penelope 1937- *WrDr 94*
Leach, Ralph F. 1917- *WhoAm 94*
Leach, Richard Heald 1922- *WhoAm 94*
Leach, Richard Maxwell, Jr. 1934- *WhoFI 94, WhoWest 94*
Leach, Robert Ellis 1931- *WhoAm 94, WhoScEn 94*
Leach, Robin 1939- *WhoAmP 93*
Leach, Robin 1941- *WhoAm 94*
Leach, Rodney *Who 94*
Leach, Rodney 1932- *Who 94*
Leach, (Charles Guy) Rodney 1934- *Who 94*
Leach, Ronald (George) 1907- *Who 94*
Leach, Ronald George 1907- *IntWW 93*
Leach, Ronald George 1938- *WhoAm 94*
Leach, Ronald W. 1944- *WhoIns 94*
Leach, Rosemary 1925- *WhoHol 92*
Leach, Russell 1922- *WhoAm 94, WhoAmL 94, WhoAmP 93*
Leach, Suzanne d1945 *WhoHol 92*
Leach, Thomas J. 1946- *WhoAmL 94*
Leach-Clark, Mary A. 1931- *WhoMW 93*
Leachman, Cloris 1930- *IntMPA 94, WhoAm 94, WhoCom, WhoHol 92*
Leachman, Roger Mack 1942- *WhoAm 94*
Leacock, Ferdinand S. 1934- *WhoBlA 94*
Leacock, Stephen (Butler) 1869-1944 *ConAu 141, EncSF 93, RfGShF*
Leacock, Stephen Jerome 1943- *WhoAmL 94, WhoBlA 94*
Lead, Jane 1624-1704 *BlmGWL*
Lead, Jane Ward 1623-1704 *DcLB 131*
Leadabrand, Ray L. 1927- *WhoAm 94*
Leadbeater, Howell 1919- *Who 94*
Leadbetter, Alan James 1934- *Who 94*
Leadbetter, David Hulse 1908- *Who 94*
Leadbetter, Mark Renton, Jr. 1944- *WhoScEn 94*
Leadbitter, Edward 1919- *Who 94*
Leader, Garnet Rosamonde *WhoAmA 93*
Leader, James L. 1945- *WhoAmL 94*
Leader, Jeffery James 1963- *WhoWest 94*
Leader, Jeremy 1961- *WhoWest 94*
Leader, Robert John 1933- *WhoAmL 94*
Leader, Robert Wardell 1919- *WhoAm 94*
Leadford, John Austin, Jr. 1946- *WhoFI 94*
Leadon, Denise Lynn 1959- *WhoWest 94*
Leaf, Alexander 1920- *IntWW 93, WhoAm 94, WhoScEn 94*
Leaf, David Allen 1952- *WhoWest 94*
Leaf, Douglass, Jr. 1927- *WhoFI 94*
Leaf, Hayim d1993 *NewYTBS 93*
Leaf, Howard Westley 1923- *WhoAm 94*
Leaf, June 1929- *WhoAmA 93*
Leaf, Munro 1906-1977 *WhoAmA 93N*
Leaf, Paul 1929- *WhoAm 94, WrDr 94*
Leaf, Robert Jay 1944- *WhoFI 94*
Leaf, Robert Stephen 1931- *WhoAm 94*
Leaf, Roger Warren 1946- *WhoAm 94*
Leaf, Ruth *WhoAmA 93*
Leafe, Joseph A. *WhoAmP 93*
League, Cheryl Perry 1945- *WhoBlA 94*
Leaheey, J. Bradford 1946- *WhoAmL 94*
Leahey, Miles Cary 1952- *WhoFI 94*
Leahigh, Alan Kent 1944- *WhoAm 94*
Leahy, Bernard Ryder 1938- *WhoMW 93*
Leahy, Charles Farrington 1935- *WhoAmL 94*
Leahy, Daniel P. *WhoAmP 93*
Leahy, Edward J. 1951- *WhoAmL 94*
Leahy, Edward James 1953- *WhoFI 94*
Leahy, Elizabeth Clare 1911- *WhoAmP 93*
Leahy, Eugene d1967 *WhoHol 92*
Leahy, Gerald Philip 1936- *WhoAm 94*
Leahy, J. Michael 1946- *WhoWest 94*
Leahy, John (Henry Gladstone) 1928- *Who 94*
Leahy, John H. G. 1928- *IntWW 93*
Leahy, John Martin 1886-1967 *EncSF 93*
Leahy, Lourdes C. 1962- *WhoHisp 94*
Leahy, Margaret d1967 *WhoHol 92*
Leahy, Michael H. 1945- *WhoAmL 94*
Leahy, Michael J. 1951- *WhoAmL 94*
Leahy, Michael Joseph 1939- *WhoAm 94*
Leahy, Osmund A. 1915-1989 *WhAm 10*
Leahy, Patrick *DrAPF 93*
Leahy, Patrick J. 1940- *CngDr 93, WhoAmP 93*
Leahy, Patrick Joseph 1940- *IntWW 93, WhoAm 94*
Leahy, T. Liam 1952- *WhoAm 94, WhoWest 94*
Leahy, William *DrAPF 93*
Leahy, William B. 1943- *WhoAmL 94*
Leahy, William F. 1913- *WhoAm 94*
Leak, Alberta Hedgley 1936- *WhoMW 93*
Leak, Elizabeth 1776?-1808? *NewGrDO*
Leak, Jennifer *WhoHol 92*
Leak, Lee Virn 1932- *WhoBlA 94*
Leak, Lorie Kay 1953- *WhoMW 93*
Leak, Margaret Elizabeth 1946- *WhoAm 94, WhoFI 94*
Leak, Robert E. 1934- *WhoAm 94*
Leake, Barbara *WhoHol 92*
Leake, Bernard Elgey 1932- *Who 94*
Leake, Cynthia *WhoHol 92*
Leake, David *Who 94*
Leake, Donald Lewis 1931- *WhoAm 94, WhoScEn 94*
Leake, Eugene W. 1911- *WhoAmA 93*
Leake, Gerald 1885-1975 *WhoAmA 93N*
Leake, Larry B. 1950- *WhoAmP 93*
Leake, Larry Bruce 1950- *WhoAmL 94*
Leake, Mildred Breland 1916- *WhoAmP 93*
Leake, Nolan C. 1945- *WhoAmL 94*
Leake, Philip Gregory 1958- *WhoWest 94*
Leake, Preston Hildebrand 1929- *WhoAm 94*
Leake, Richard Scott 1948- *WhoMW 93*
Leake, Rosemary Dobson 1937- *WhoWest 94*
Leake, Sam D. 1945- *WhoAmP 93*
Leake, Velmalene Stevens 1930- *WhoAmP 93*
Leake, William D. 1929- *WhoAm 94*
Leake, Willie Mae James 1932- *WhoBlA 94*
Leakey, Arundell Rea 1915- *Who 94*
Leakey, Caroline Woolmer 1827-1881 *BlmGWL*
Leakey, David Martin 1932- *Who 94*
Leakey, Felix William 1922- *Who 94*
Leakey, Mary (Douglas) 1913- *WrDr 94*
Leakey, Mary Douglas 1913- *IntWW 93, Who 94, WhoScEn 94*
Leakey, Richard 1944- *News 94-2 [port]*
Leakey, Richard (Erskine Frere) 1944- *WrDr 94*
Leakey, Richard Erskine 1944- *WhoScEn 94*
Leakey, Richard Erskine Frere 1944- *IntWW 93, Who 94*
Leal, Alfred G. *WhoHisp 94*
Leal, Antonio, Jr. 1946- *WhoHisp 94*
Leal, Francisco Rene 1961- *WhoMW 93*
Leal, George D. 1934- *WhoScEn 94*
Leal, Gumersindo R. 1928- *WhoHisp 94*
Leal, Herbert Allan Borden 1917- *WhoAm 94*
Leal, J. Gilbert 1946- *WhoHisp 94*
Leal, Joe Luis 1960- *WhoFI 94*
Leal, John Erwin 1957- *WhoWest 94*
Leal, Joseph Rogers 1918- *WhoScEn 94*
Leal, Leslie Gary 1943- *WhoAm 94*
Leal, Luis 1907- *WhoHisp 94*
Leal, Manuel D. *WhoHisp 94*
Leal, Martin Gary 1962- *WhoHisp 94*
Leal, Milagros d1975 *WhoHol 92*
Leal, Raymond Robert 1946- *WhoHisp 94*
Leal, Robert L. 1945- *WhoHisp 94*
Leal, Rosie B. 1933- *WhoHisp 94*
Leal, Steve *WhoHisp 94*
Leal, Susan *WhoHisp 94*
Leal, Widad 1959- *WhoHisp 94*
Leale, B(arry) C(avendish) 1930- *WrDr 94*
Leale, Olivia Mason 1944- *WhoWest 94*
Leal Moreira, Antonio *NewGrDO*
Lealofi, IV 1922- *IntWW 93*
Leaman, David Martin 1935- *WhoAm 94*
Leaman, Gordon James, Jr. 1951- *WhoScEn 94*
Leaman, Jack Ervin 1932- *WhoAm 94, WhoWest 94*
Leaming, Marj Patricia *WhoWest 94*
Leaming, Thomas 1748-1797 *WhAmRev*
Leamon, Tom B. 1940- *WhoScEn 94*
Leamy, Cameron J. D. 1932- *WhoIns 94*
Lean, Cecil d1935 *WhoHol 92*
Lean, David 1908-1991 *WhAm 10*
Leander, Nils *WhoHol 92*
Leander, Zarah d1981 *WhoHol 92*
Leane, Patrick Daniel d1953 *WhoHol 92*
Leaney, Alfred Robert Clare 1909- *WrDr 94*
Leaning, David 1936- *Who 94*
Leaning, Jennifer 1945- *WrDr 94*
Leap, Darrell Ivan 1937- *WhoScEn 94*
Leapaldt, David Alvin 1957- *WhoMW 93*
Leaper, Robert Anthony Bernard 1921- *Who 94*
Leaphart, Eldridge 1927- *WhoBlA 94*
Leapman, Michael (Henry) 1938- *ConAu 41NR*
Leapor, Mary 1722-1746 *BlmGWL*
Lear, Clyde Graves 1944- *WhoMW 93*
Lear, Edward 1812-1888 *BlmGEL*
Lear, Erwin 1924- *WhoAm 94, WhoScEn 94*
Lear, Evelyn *IntWW 93, WhoHol 92*
Lear, Evelyn 1926- *NewGrDO*
Lear, Evelyn 1930- *WhoAm 94*
Lear, Floyd Raymond, III 1942- *WhoFI 94*
Lear, Floyd Seyward 1895- *WhAm 10*
Lear, George 1879-1956 *WhoAmA 93N*
Lear, Gerard Robert 1939- *WhoAmL 94*
Lear, John 1909- *WhoAm 94, WrDr 94*
Lear, Jonathan *WrDr 94*
Lear, Joyce *Who 94*
Lear, Norman 1922- *IntMPA 94*
Lear, Norman Milton 1922- *WhoAm 94, WhoWest 94*
Lear, Peter 1936- *WrDr 94*
Lear, Phillip William 1945- *WhoAmL 94*
Lear, Robert William 1917- *WhoAm 94*
Lear, William M., Jr. 1950- *WhoAmL 94, WhoAmP 93*
Leard, David Carl 1958- *WhoAmL 94*
Learey, Fred Don 1906- *WhoAm 94*
Learmont, John (Hartley) 1934- *Who 94*
Learmonth, Andrew (Thomas Amos) 1916- *WrDr 94*
Learn, Bessie d1987 *WhoHol 92*
Learn, Doris Lynn 1949- *WhoFI 94*
Learn, Elmer Warner 1929- *WhoAm 94*
Learnard, William Ewing 1935- *WhoAm 94*
Learned, Ebenezer 1728-1801 *AmRev, WhAmRev*
Learned, Henry Dexter 1893- *WhAm 10*
Learned, Michael 1939- *IntMPA 94, WhoHol 92*
Learner, Howard Alan 1955- *WhoAmL 94*
Learning, Walter J. 1938- *WrDr 94*
Learoyd, Roderick Alastair Brook 1913- *Who 94*
Leary, Brian Leonard 1929- *Who 94*
Leary, Daniel 1955- *WhoAmA 93*
Leary, Denis 1958- *News 93-3 [port], WhoAm 94*
Leary, Edward A 1913- *WrDr 94*
Leary, James E. 1935- *WhoBlA 94*
Leary, Jay Francis 1938- *WhoAm 94*
Leary, Leo William 1919- *WhoAm 94*
Leary, Lewis 1906-1990 *WhAm 10*
Leary, Lois M. d1988 *WhoHol 92*
Leary, Michael Warren 1949- *WhoAm 94*
Leary, Nancy Jane 1952- *WhoFI 94*
Leary, Nolan d1987 *WhoHol 92*
Leary, Patrick Thomas 1946- *WhoMW 93*
Leary, Richard Lee 1936- *WhoMW 93*
Leary, Robin Janell 1954- *WhoMW 93*
Leary, Shelby Jean 1936- *WhoAmP 93*
Leary, Thomas Barrett 1931- *WhoAm 94, WhoAmL 94*
Leary, Timothy 1920- *WhoAm 94, WhoHol 92*
Leary, William James 1931- *WhoAm 94*
Leas, Philip Joseph 1949- *WhoAmL 94*
Lease, Jane Etta 1924- *WhoWest 94*
Lease, Joseph *DrAPF 93*
Lease, M. Harry, Jr. 1927- *WhoAmP 93*
Lease, Martin Harry, Jr. 1927- *WhoAm 94*
Lease, Mary Elizabeth 1853-1933 *HisWorL [port]*
Lease, Mary Elizabeth Clyens 1853-1933 *AmSocL*
Lease, Rex d1966 *WhoHol 92*
Lease, Richard Jay 1914- *WhoWest 94*
Lease, Robert K. 1948- *WhoAm 94, WhoAmL 94*
Lease, Ronald Charles 1940- *WhoAm 94*
Leaseburge, Bud d1987 *WhoHol 92*
Leask, Henry (Lowther Ewart Clark) 1913- *Who 94*

Leask, John Edward, Jr. 1957- *WhoMW 93*
Leasor, (Thomas) James 1923- *Who 94, WrDr 94*
Leates, Margaret *Who 94*
Leath, Charles Alexander, Jr. 1944- *WhoFI 94*
Leath, Kenneth Thomas 1931- *WhoScEn 94*
Leath, Marvin 1931- *WhoAmP 93*
Leath, William Jefferson, Jr. 1945- *WhoAmL 94*
Leatham, Aubrey (Gerald) 1920- *Who 94*
Leatham, John Tonkin 1936- *WhoAm 94*
Leatham, Mary Ellen Jeppesen 1928- *WhoAmP 93*
Leathart, James Anthony 1915- *Who 94*
Leather, Edwin (Hartley Cameron) 1919- *Who 94*
Leather, Edwin Hartley Cameron 1919- *IntWW 93*
Leather, George 1921- *WrDr 94*
Leather, Richard Brenk 1932- *WhoFI 94*
Leather, Ted *Who 94*
Leatherberry, Anne Knox Clark 1953- *WhoMW 93*
Leatherdale, Douglas West 1936- *WhoAm 94, WhoFI 94*
Leatherdale, Marcus Andrew 1952- *WhoAmA 93*
Leatherland, Baron d1992 *Who 94N*
Leatherman, Allen H. 1935- *WhoIns 94*
Leatherman, Hugh Kenneth, Sr. 1931- *WhoAmP 93*
Leatherman, Janie Lee 1959- *WhoMW 93*
Leatherman, Omar S., Jr. *WhoBlA 94*
Leathers, Viscount 1908- *Who 94*
Leathers, Frederick Alan 1908- *IntWW 93*
Leathers, John R. 1945- *WhoAmL 94*
Leathers, L. Hudson d1993 *NewYTBS 93*
Leathers, Winston Lyle 1932- *WhoAmA 93*
Leatherwood, Larry Lee 1939- *WhoBlA 94*
Leatherwood, Richard L. *WhoAm 94*
Leatherwood, Robert P. 1920- *WhoBlA 94*
Leatherwood, Tom *WhoAmP 93*
Leathwood, Barry 1941- *Who 94*
Leaton, Anne *DrAPF 93*
Leaton, Anne 1932- *WrDr 94*
Leaton, Marcella Kay 1952- *WhoFI 94*
Leaud, Jean-Pierre 1944- *IntMPA 94, IntWW 93, WhoHol 92*
Leavel, Willard Hayden 1927- *WhoAmP 93*
Leavell, Allen 1957- *WhoBlA 94*
Leavell, Dorothy R. 1944- *WhoBlA 94*
Leavell, Landrum Pinson, II 1926- *WhoAm 94*
Leavell, Michael Ray 1955- *WhoScEn 94*
Leavell, Walter F. 1934- *WhoBlA 94*
Leavengood, Victor Price 1924- *WhoAm 94*
Leavens, Thomas R. 1948- *WhoAmL 94*
Leavenworth, Frances Wilson 1934- *WhoAmP 93*
Leavenworth, Henry 1783-1834 *WhWE*
Leaver, Christopher 1937- *IntWW 93, Who 94*
Leaver, Christopher John 1942- *IntWW 93, Who 94*
Leaver, Peter Lawrence Oppenheim 1944- *Who 94*
Leaver, Phillip 1904- *WhoHol 92*
Leaver, Ruth *WrDr 94*
Leavett, Alan 1924- *Who 94*
Leavey, John Anthony 1915- *Who 94*
Leavis, Frank Raymond 1895-1978 *BlmGEL*
Leavis, Q. D. 1906-1981 *BlmGWL*
Leavitt, Audrey Faye Cox 1932- *WhoAm 94*
Leavitt, Caroline *DrAPF 93*
Leavitt, Charles Loyal 1921- *WhoAm 94*
Leavitt, Dana Gibson 1925- *WhoAm 94, WhoFI 94*
Leavitt, David 1961- *DcLB 130 [port], GayLL, WrDr 94*
Leavitt, David Adam 1961- *WhoAm 94*
Leavitt, Dixie L. 1929- *WhoAmP 93*
Leavitt, Douglas d1960 *WhoHol 92*
Leavitt, Harold Jack 1922- *WhoAm 94*
Leavitt, Henrietta Swan 1868-1921 *WorScD*
Leavitt, Jeffrey Stuart 1946- *WhoAm 94, WhoAmL 94, WhoMW 93*
Leavitt, Jerome Edward 1916- *WhoAm 94*
Leavitt, Joan Kazanjian 1926- *WhoAm 94*
Leavitt, Joseph d1990 *WhAm 10*
Leavitt, Judith Walzer 1940- *WhoMW 93*
Leavitt, Julian *WhoAm 94*
Leavitt, Lois Hutcheon 1920- *WhoWest 94*
Leavitt, Mark Aaron 1958- *WhoAm 94, WhoFI 94*
Leavitt, Martin Jack 1940- *WhoAmL 94, WhoMW 93*
Leavitt, Michael Okerlund 1951- *WhoAm 94, WhoWest 94*
Leavitt, Mike *WhoAmP 93*
Leavitt, Norman *WhoHol 92*
Leavitt, Thomas Whittlesey 1930- *WhoAm 94, WhoAmA 93*
Leavitt, William 1941- *WhoAmA 93*
Leavy, Edward 1929- *WhoAm 94, WhoAmL 94, WhoAmP 93, WhoWest 94*
Leavy, Elizabeth G. 1941- *WhoAmL 94*
Leavy, Herbert Theodore 1927- *WhoAm 94*
Leax, John *DrAPF 93*
Leb, Arthur S. 1930- *WhoAm 94*
Le Bailly, Louis (Edward Stewart Holland) 1915- *Who 94*
Lebamoff, Ivan A. 1932- *WhoAmP 93*
Lebamoff, Ivan Argire 1932- *WhoAm 94, WhoAmL 94, WhoMW 93*
Leban, William Victor, Jr. 1946- *WhoMW 93*
Lebar, John *EncSF 93*
Le Bargy, Charles d1936 *WhoHol 92*
LeBaron, Anthony *EncSF 93*
Le Baron, Bert d1956 *WhoHol 92*
LeBaron, Charles Frederick, Jr. 1949- *WhoAmL 94*
LeBaron, Donald Ralph 1926- *WhoAmP 93*
LeBaron, Edward Wayne, Jr. 1930- *WhoAm 94*
Le Baron, Joseph 1947- *WhoAm 94*
LeBaron, Melvin Jay 1930- *WhoWest 94*
LeBarron, Suzanne Jane 1945- *WhoWest 94*
Lebas, Philippe *WhoHol 92*
Lebbad, John A. 1955- *WhoAm 94*
Lebeau, Bernard Pierre 1932- *WhoMW 93*
Le Beau, Bettine 1938- *WhoHol 92*
LeBeau, Carol Lynn 1962- *WhoFI 94*
LeBeau, Charles Paul 1944- *WhoAm 94*
LeBeau, Charles Ray 1938- *WhoWest 94*
LeBeau, Christopher John 1959- *WhoWest 94*
LeBeau, Edward Charles 1929- *WhoAm 94*
Lebeau, Gary D. *WhoAmP 93*
LeBeau, Hector Alton, Jr. 1931- *WhoAm 94*
Le Beau, Madeline *WhoHol 92*
LeBeau, Paul Andrew 1950- *WhoFI 94*
LeBeau, Roy 1935- *WrDr 94*
Lebec, Alain 1950- *WhoAm 94*
Lebeck, Carol E. 1931- *WhoAmA 93*
Lebeck, Steven Wade 1953- *WhoMW 93*
Lebeck, Warren Wells 1921- *WhoAm 94*
Lebed, Aleksandr Ivanovich 1950- *LngBDD*
Lebed, Hartzel Zangwill 1928- *WhoAm 94*
Lebedeff, Ivan d1953 *WhoHol 92*
Lebedev, Yevgeniy Alekseyevich 1917- *IntWW 93*
Lebedoff, David M. 1938- *WhoAm 94*
Lebedoff, David Michael 1938- *WhoAmP 93*
Lebedoff, Jonathan Galanter 1938- *WhoAm 94, WhoAmL 94*
Lebedoff, Randy Miller 1949- *WhoAm 94, WhoAmL 94*
Lebedow, Aaron Louis 1935- *WhoAm 94*
Lebegern, Howard Fisher, Jr. 1927- *WhoAmP 93*
Lebegue, Daniel Simon Georges 1943- *IntWW 93*
Lebel, Irenee Remi 1926- *WhoAmP 93*
Lebel, Robert Roger 1945- *WhoMW 93*
Le Bel, Roger *WhoHol 92*
Lebensfeld, Harry 1904- *WhoAm 94, WhoFI 94*
Lebentritt, Julia *DrAPF 93*
Le Beque de Presle *WhAmRev*
Leber, Georg 1920- *IntWW 93*
Leber, Lester 1913- *WhoAm 94*
Leber, Mariann C. 1921- *WhoBlA 94*
Leber, Steven Edward 1941- *WhoAm 94*
Leberman, Joseph d1990 *WhoHol 92*
Le Berthon, Adam 1962- *WhoWest 94*
Lebesgue, Henri Leon 1875-1941 *WorScD*
Lebey, Barbara 1939- *WhoAmA 93*
Lebius, Aenderly d1921 *WhoHol 92*
Lebl, Michal 1951- *WhoScEn 94*
Leblanc 1750?-1827 *NewGrDO*
Le Blanc, Bart 1946- *IntWW 93*
LeBlanc, Bertrand, II 1948- *WhoAmL 94*
LeBlanc, Camille (Andre) 1898- *WhAm 10*
Leblanc, Camille Andre 1898- *Who 94*
LeBlanc, Frank von Phul, III 1957- *WhoAmL 94*
Leblanc, Georgette d1941 *WhoHol 92*
Leblanc, Georgette 1875-1941 *NewGrDO*
LeBlanc, Hugh Linus 1927- *WhoAm 94*
Leblanc, Hugues 1924- *WhoAm 94*
LeBlanc, James E. 1942- *WhoFI 94, WhoMW 93*
Leblanc, Jerry 1956- *WhoAmP 93*
LeBlanc, Laurie Alison 1964- *WhoFI 94*
Leblanc, Maurice 1864-1941 *TwCLC 49 [port]*
LeBlanc, Michael J. 1950- *WhoBlA 94*
LeBlanc, Michael Stephen 1952- *WhoMW 93*
Leblanc, Nicolas 1742-1806 *WorInv*
LeBlanc, Richard Philip 1946- *WhoAmL 94*
Leblanc, Roger Maurice 1942- *WhoAm 94, WhoScEn 94*
LeBlanc, Rufus Joseph, Sr. 1917- *WhoAm 94*
LeBlanc, Sam A., III 1938- *WhoAmP 93*
LeBlanc, Steven Randel 1957- *WhoFI 94*
LeBlanc, Tina *WhoAm 94*
LeBlang, Skip Alan 1953- *WhoAmL 94*
Lebleu, Conway 1918- *WhoAmP 93*
Leblon, Jean Marcel 1928- *WhoWest 94*
Leblond, C(harles) P(hilippe) 1910- *Who 94*
Leblond, Charles Philippe 1910- *IntWW 93, WhoAm 94*
LeBlond, Christy Benton 1948- *WhoWest 94*
Le Blond, Patricia Morrison 1933- *WhoMW 93*
LeBlond, Paul Henri 1938- *WhoAm 94*
LeBlond, Richard Knight, II 1920- *IntWW 93, WhoAm 94*
Lebo, William C., Jr. *WhoFI 94*
Leboeuf, Marcel *WhoHol 92*
LeBoeuf, Michael 1942- *WrDr 94*
LeBoeuf, Raymond Walter 1946- *WhoFI 94*
LeBoff, Gail F. 1950- *WhoAmA 93*
Le Bon, Douglas Kent 1953- *WhoFI 94*
Lebon, Philippe 1767-1804 *WorInv*
Lebor, John Francis 1906- *WhoAm 94*
LeBorg, Reginald 1902-1989 *HorFD [port]*
Leborne, Aime (Ambroise Simon) 1797-1866 *NewGrDO*
Lebotsa, Mohamane Masimole 1927- *IntWW 93*
Lebouder, Jean-Pierre 1944- *IntWW 93*
Lebouitz, Martin Frederick 1946- *WhoAm 94*
LeBourgeois, Cynthia Carrie 1962- *WhoAmL 94*
LeBoutillier, John *WhoFI 94*
LeBoutillier, John 1953- *WhoAmP 93*
Le Bovier de Fontenelle, Bernard *NewGrDO*
Lebovits, Moses 1951- *WhoAmL 94*
Lebovits, N'siah Chana 1965- *WhoMW 93*
Lebovitz, Harold Paul 1916- *WhoAm 94*
Lebovitz, Joan Mond 1933- *WhoAmL 94*
LeBow, Bennett S. 1938- *WhoAm 94, WhoFI 94*
Lebow, Eileen F. 1925- *WrDr 94*
Lebow, Irwin Leon 1926- *WhoAm 94*
Lebow, Jeanne *DrAPF 93*
Lebow, Jeanne 1951- *WrDr 94*
Lebow, Jeffrey Albert 1958- *WhoFI 94*
Lebow, Laurel Mary Lavin 1956- *WhoFI 94*
Lebow, Mark Denis 1940- *WhoAm 94*
Lebowitz, Albert 1922- *WhoAm 94, WrDr 94*
Lebowitz, Catharine Koch 1915- *WhoAmP 93*
Lebowitz, Harvey M. 1929- *WhoAm 94*
Lebowitz, Joel L. 1930- *IntWW 93*
Lebowitz, Joel Louis 1930- *WhoAm 94, WhoScEn 94*
Lebowitz, Marshall 1923- *WhoAm 94*
Lebowitz, Michael David 1939- *WhoAm 94*
Lebowsky, Stanley d1986 *WhoHol 92*
Lebra, Takie Sugiyama 1930- *WhoWest 94*
Le Brandt, Gertrude d1955 *WhoHol 92*
Lebrat, Jean Marcel Hubert 1933- *IntWW 93*
Lebrato, Mary Theresa 1950- *WhoAmL 94*
Le Breton, Auguste *ConAu 41NR*
Le Breton, Binka 1942- *ConAu 142*
Le Breton, David Francis Battye 1931- *IntWW 93, Who 94*
Le Breton, Flora 1898- *WhoHol 92*
Le Brock, Kelly 1960- *WhoHol 92*
Le Brocquy, Louis 1916- *IntWW 93, Who 94*
Lebron, Luisa *WhoAmP 93*
Lebron, Michael A. *NewYTBS 93 [port]*
Lebron, Michael A. 1954- *WhoAmA 93*
Lebron, Michael A., III 1954- *WhoHisp 94*
LeBron, Victor 1950- *WhoHisp 94*
Lebron Lamboy, Julio *WhoAmP 93*
Le Brun, Carol 1942- *WhoAmA 93*
Le Brun, Christopher Mark 1951- *IntWW 93, Who 94*
Lebrun, Daniele *WhoHol 92*
Lebrun, Francoise *WhoHol 92*
Lebrun, Franziska (Dorothea) *NewGrDO*
Lebrun, Franziska (Dorothea) 1756-1791 *See* Danzi Family *NewGrDO*
Lebrun, Louis-Sebastien 1764-1829 *NewGrDO*
Le Brun, Mignon d1941 *WhoHol 92*
Lebrun, Patricia Ann Olson 1941- *WhoFI 94*
Lebrun, Rico 1900-1964 *WhoAmA 93N*
Lebrun Moratinos, Jose Ali 1919- *IntWW 93*
Lebsack, Phyllis Jean 1921- *WhoMW 93*
Le Buhn, Robert 1932- *WhoAm 94*
Leburton, Edmond Jules Isidore 1915- *IntWW 93*
Le Cain, Errol (John) 1941-1989 *ConAu 42NR*
LeCale, Errol *EncSF 93*
Le Cam, Lucien Marie 1924- *WhoAm 94*
Le Camus, Madame fl. 17th cent.- *BlmGWL*
Lecanuet, Jean Adrien Francois d1993 *IntWW 93N, NewYTBS 93 [port]*
Lecaron, Joseph c. 1586-1632 *EncNAR*
Le Carre, John *IntWW 93, Who 94*
le Carre, John 1931- *WhoAm 94, WrDr 94*
Lecat, Jean-Philippe 1935- *IntWW 93*
Lecca, Pedro J. *WhoHisp 94*
Lecceadone, Thomas Patrick 1966- *WhoFI 94*
Lecerf, Olivier Maurice Marie 1929- *IntWW 93, WhoAm 94*
Le Cerf de la Vieville, Jean Laurent 1674-1707 *NewGrDO*
LeCesne, Terrel M. 1939- *WhoBlA 94*
Le Chatelier, Henry Louis 1850-1936 *WorInv, WorScD*
Lechay, James 1907- *WhoAm 94, WhoAmA 93*
Lechebo, Semie 1935- *WhoBlA 94*
Lechelt, Eugene Carl 1942- *WhoAm 94*
Le Cheminant, Peter 1926- *Who 94*
Le Cheminant, Peter (de Lacey) 1920- *Who 94*
Lechevalier, Hubert Arthur 1926- *WhoAm 94*
Lechevalier, Mary Pfeil 1928- *WhoScEn 94*
LeChevallier, Mark William 1955- *WhoMW 93*
Lechin Oquendo, Juan 1915- *IntWW 93*
Lechin Suarez, Juan 1921- *IntWW 93, Who 94*
Lechlitner, Thane Mark *WhoMW 93*
Lechmere, Berwick (Hungerford) 1917- *Who 94*
Lechner, Alfred James, Jr. 1948 *WhoAm 94, WhoAmL 94*
Lechner, Bernard Joseph 1932- *WhoAm 94*
Lechner, George William 1931- *WhoMW 93*
Lechner, Ira Mark 1934- *WhoAmP 93*
Lechner, Jane Ann 1949- *WhoMW 93*
Lechner, Joseph Hadrian 1951- *WhoMW 93*
Lechner, Robert 1918- *WrDr 94*
Lechón, J. Daniel 1929- *WhoHisp 94*
Lechowicz, Lisa Marie 1954- *WhoFI 94*
Lechowicz, Thaddeus Stanley 1938- *WhoAmP 93*
Lecht, Leonard A 1920- *WrDr 94*
Lechtzin, Stanley 1936- *WhoAmA 93*
Lecker, Abraham 1916- *WhoAm 94*
Lecker, Jonathan Mitchell 1961- *WhoFI 94*
Leckerling, Jon Peter 1948- *WhoAmL 94*
Leckey, Andrew A. 1949- *WhoAm 94, WhoMW 93*
Leckie, Frederick Alexander 1929- *WhoAm 94*
Leckie, Gavin Frederick 1958- *WhoAmL 94*
Leckie, Keith (Ross) 1952- *WrDr 94*
Leckie, Robert Bedford 1947- *WhoAm 94*
Leckman, James Frederick 1947- *WhoScEn 94*
Lecky, Arthur Terence 1919- *Who 94*
Lecky, Samuel K. *Who 94*
Lecky, Susan 1940- *WhoAmA 93*
LeClair, Brian A. 1962- *WhoAmL 94*
Le Clair, Charles 1914- *WhoAmA 93*
Le Clair, Charles George 1914- *WhoAm 94*
LeClair, D'Arcy Harrison 1947- *WhoAm 94*
Le Clair, Douglas Marvin 1955- *WhoAmL 94, WhoWest 94*
LeClair, J. Maurice 1927- *IntWW 93*
Leclair, Jean-Marie 1697-1764 *NewGrDO*
Le Clair, Lucille Blackton d1984 *WhoHol 92*
Le Clair, Michael *WhoHol 92*
LeClair, Thomas 1944- *ConAu 43NR*
LeClair, Tom *ConAu 43NR*
LeClaire, Cynthia *DrAPF 93*
Le Claire, Harry Walter 1914-1991 *WhAm 10*
Leclant, Jean 1920- *IntWW 93*
Leclerc, Annie 1940- *BlmGWL*
Leclerc, Charles J. 1912- *WhoAmP 93*
Leclerc, Edouard 1926- *IntWW 93*
Leclerc, Ginette *WhoHol 92*
Leclerc, Ivor 1915- *WrDr 94*

Lee, Robert 1929- *WhoAm 94, WhoAsA 94*
Lee, Robert 1948- *WhoFI 94*
Lee, Robert Andrew 1923- *WhoWest 94*
Lee, Robert C. 1945- *WhoWest 94*
Lee, Robert E. d1993 *NewYTBS 93 [port]*
Lee, Robert E. 1807-1870 *HisWorL [port]*
Lee, Robert E. 1924- *WhoBlA 94*
Lee, Robert E(dwin) 1918- *ConDr 93, WrDr 94*
Lee, Robert E(mmet) 1912-1993 *CurBio 93N*
Lee, Robert Earl 1928- *WhoAm 94*
Lee, Robert Edward, Jr. 1941- *WhoAmL 94*
Lee, Robert Edward, III 1942- *WhoMW 93*
Lee, Robert Edwin 1918- *WhoAm 94*
Lee, Robert Ellsworth, Sr. 1938- *WhoFI 94*
Lee, Robert Emile 1948- *WhoBlA 94*
Lee, Robert Erich 1955- *WhoFI 94*
Lee, Robert Eugene 1958- *WhoMW 93*
Lee, Robert Gum Hong 1924- *WhoScEn 94*
Lee, Robert Hugh 1950- *WhoFI 94*
Lee, Robert J. 1921- *WhoAmA 93*
Lee, Robert Jeffrey 1955- *WhoScEn 94*
Lee, Robert John 1929- *WhoAm 94*
Lee, Robert Justin 1945- *WhoFI 94*
Lee, Robert M. 1933- *WhoAmA 93*
Lee, Robert Sanford 1924- *WhoAm 94*
Lee, Robert Terry 1957- *WhoAsA 94*
Lee, Robert Wah d1988 *WhoHol 92*
Lee, Rodger Alan 1956- *WhoMW 93*
Lee, Roger 1942- *WhoAmA 93*
Lee, Roger Edwin Mark 1940- *WhoWest 94*
Lee, Rolf Elmer 1913- *WhoWest 94*
Lee, Ronald B. 1932- *WhoBlA 94*
Lee, Ronald Barry 1932- *WhoAm 94*
Lee, Ronald Demos 1941- *WhoAm 94*
Lee, Ronald Derek 1959- *WhoAmL 94, WhoWest 94*
Lee, Ronald Eugene 1960- *WhoFI 94*
Lee, Rosealee Marie 1951- *WhoMW 93*
Lee, Rotan 1906- *WhoBlA 94*
Lee, Rowland Thomas Lovell 1920- *Who 94*
Lee, Rowland V. d1975 *WhoHol 92*
Lee, Roy Noble 1915- *WhoAmP 93*
Lee, Ruben 1955- *WhoHisp 94*
Lee, Russell Harold 1949- *WhoMW 93*
Lee, Russell W. 1903-1986 *WhoAmA 93N*
Lee, Ruta 1936- *WhoHol 92*
Lee, Ruth d1975 *WhoHol 92*
Lee, S. Whitfield 1944- *WhoFI 94*
Lee, Sally 1943- *WrDr 94*
Lee, Sam d1980 *WhoHol 92*
Lee, Sammy d1968 *WhoHol 92*
Lee, Sammy 1920- *WhoAm 94, WhoWest 94*
Lee, Samuel S. II. 1930- *WhoAmP 93*
Lee, Sanboh 1948- *WhoScEn 94*
Lee, Sang-Gak 1948- *WhoScEn 94*
Lee, Sang Moon 1939- *WhoAm 94, WhoAsA 94*
Lee, Sarah Tomerlin *WhoAm 94*
Lee, Seung Jai 1947- *WhoAmL 94*
Lee, Sharon *EncSF 93*
Lee, Sheila Jackson *WhoAmP 93*
Lee, Sheila Jackson 1950- *WhoBlA 94*
Lee, Shelton Jackson 1957- *BlkWr 2, ConAu 42NR*
Lee, Sheng Yen 1924- *WhoAsA 94*
Lee, Sherman Emery 1918- *WhoAm 94, WhoAmA 93, WrDr 94*
Lee, Sheryl 1966- *WhoHol 92*
Lee, Shih-Ying 1918- *WhoAm 94, WhoAsA 94*
Lee, Shirley Freeman 1928- *WhoBlA 94*
Lee, Shirley Williams 1924- *WhoAmP 93*
Lee, Shuishih Sage 1948- *WhoAm 94, WhoAsA 94*
Lee, Shyan Jer 1961- *WhoScEn 94*
Lee, Shyu-tu 1940- *WhoAsA 94*
Lee, Si Young 1951- *WhoAsA 94*
Lee, Siani 1962- *WhoAsA 94*
Lee, Sidney Phillip 1920- *WhoAmP 93*
Lee, Sidney Phillip 1926- *WhoAm 94*
Lee, Sidney Seymour 1921-1992 *WhAm 10*
Lee, Silas, III 1954- *WhoBlA 94*
Lee, Siu-Lam 1941- *WhoAsA 94*
Lee, Sondra 1930- *WhoHol 92*
Lee, Soo See 1966- *WhoAsA 94*
Lee, Soo-Young 1955- *WhoAsA 94*
Lee, Sooncha A. *WhoAsA 94*
Lee, Sophia 1750-1824 *BlmGWL*
Lee, Spike *BlkWr 2, ConAu 42NR*
Lee, Spike 1957- *AfrAmAl 6 [port], ConBlB 5 [port], IntMPA 94, IntWW 93, WhoAm 94, WhoBlA 94, WhoHol 92, WrDr 94*
Lee, Stan 1922- *CurBio 93 [port], EncSF 93, WhoAm 94*
Lee, Stanley *Who 94*
Lee, Stanley 1919- *WhoAm 94*
Lee, (Edward) Stanley 1907- *Who 94*
Lee, Stephen *WhoScEn 94*
Lee, Stephen E. 1938- *WhoAm 94*
Lee, Stephen Sheng-hao 1945- *WhoMW 93*
Lee, Stephen W. 1949- *WhoAm 94, WhoAmL 94*
Lee, Steven Gregory 1952- *WhoWest 94*
Lee, Stratton Creighton 1920- *WhoBlA 94*
Lee, Sue Ying 1940- *WhoAsA 94*
Lee, Suk Hun 1957- *WhoAsA 94*
Lee, Sul Hi 1936- *WhoAm 94*
Lee, Sun Bok 1953- *WhoScEn 94*
Lee, Sun-Young Won 1943- *WhoAsA 94*
Lee, Sung Jai 1955- *WhoScEn 94*
Lee, Sung Mook 1933- *WhoAsA 94*
Lee, Sung Taick 1957- *WhoScEn 94*
Lee, Sunggyu 1952- *WhoAsA 94*
Lee, Susan *WrDr 94*
Lee, Susan H. *WhoAsA 94*
Lee, Sylvan d1962 *WhoHol 92*
Lee, T. Jerry 1937- *WhoIns 94*
Lee, Taehee 1952- *WhoAsA 94*
Lee, Tanith 1947- *EncSF 93, TwCYAW, WrDr 94*
Lee, Terry *DrAPF 93*
Lee, Terry James 1947- *WhoScEn 94*
Lee, Theodore Robert 1923- *WhoAmP 93*
Lee, Thomas *EncSF 93*
Lee, Thomas Dongho 1940- *WhoAmL 94*
Lee, Thomas F. 1925- *WhoBlA 94*
Lee, Thomas Henry 1923- *WhoAm 94, WhoScEn 94*
Lee, Thomas J. 1935- *WhoScEn 94*
Lee, Thomas Joseph, Jr. 1921- *WhoAm 94, WhoFI 94*
Lee, Thomas Ludwell 1730-1777 *WhAmRev*
Lee, Thomas Sim 1745-1819 *WhAmRev*
Lee, Tien-Chang 1943- *WhoAsA 94*
Lee, Tien Pei 1933- *WhoAm 94*
Lee, Timothy Earl 1947- *WhoMW 93*
Lee, Ting David, Jr. 1933- *WhoWest 94*
Lee, Tom Stewart 1941- *WhoAm 94, WhoAmL 94*
Lee, Tommy d1976 *WhoHol 92*
Lee, Tong Hun 1931- *WhoAm 94*
Lee, Tony J. F. 1942- *WhoAsA 94*
Lee, Tsaifeng Mazie 1936- *WhoAsA 94*
Lee, Tsoung-Chao 1935- *WhoAsA 94*
Lee, Tsu Tian 1949- *WhoScEn 94*
Lee, Tsung-Dao 1926- *Who 94, WhoAm 94, WhoAsA 94, WhoScEn 94*
Lee, Tung-Kwang 1934- *WhoAsA 94*
Lee, Tyre Douglas, Jr. 1946- *WhoAmP 93*
Lee, Tyronne T. 1949- *WhoBlA 94*
Lee, Tzesan David 1947- *WhoAsA 94*
Lee, Usik 1956- *WhoScEn 94*
Lee, Van Spencer 1942- *WhoBlA 94*
Lee, Vanessa 1920- *WhoHol 92*
Lee, Vernon 1856-1935 *BlmGWL, GayLL*
Lee, Vernon Roy 1952- *WhoAm 94*
Lee, Vic Ling 1946- *WhoAsA 94*
Lee, Victor Ho 1960- *WhoAmL 94*
Lee, Vin Jang Thomas 1937- *WhoWest 94*
Lee, Ving J. 1951- *WhoAsA 94*
Lee, Virginia Ann 1930- *WhoAmP 93*
Lee, Vivian Booker 1938- *WhoBlA 94*
Lee, Vivian Wai-fun 1959- *WhoAsA 94*
Lee, W. David 1944- *WhoWest 94*
Lee, W(illiam) Storrs, III 1906- *WrDr 94*
Lee, Wallace Williams, Jr. 1915- *WhoAm 94*
Lee, Walt(er William) 1931- *EncSF 93*
Lee, Walter William, Jr. 1931- *WhoAm 94*
Lee, Wayne C. 1917- *ConAu 41NR, WrDr 94*
Lee, Wea Hwa 1948- *WhoAsA 94*
Lee, Wei-chin 1956- *WhoAsA 94*
Lee, Wei-Kuo 1943- *WhoAsA 94*
Lee, Wei-Na 1957- *WhoAsA 94*
Lee, Wei-ping Andrew 1957- *WhoAsA 94*
Lee, Wei William 1958- *WhoWest 94*
Lee, Weiming 1953- *WhoFI 94*
Lee, Wendy d1968 *WhoHol 92*
Lee, Will d1982 *WhoHol 92*
Lee, William *EncSF 93, GayLL, WorInv*
Lee, William 1739-1795 *WhAmRev*
Lee, William 1744- *AmRev*
Lee, William 1914- *WrDr 94*
Lee, William (Allison) 1907- *Who 94*
Lee, William Charles 1938- *WhoAm 94, WhoAmL 94, WhoMW 93*
Lee, William Chien-Yeh 1932- *WhoAm 94*
Lee, William Franklin, III 1929- *WhoAm 94*
Lee, William Gentry 1944- *WhoAmL 94*
Lee, William H. 1936- *WhoBlA 94*
Lee, William J. 1925- *WhoAmP 93*
Lee, William J. 1936-1992 *WhoBlA 94N*
Lee, William James Edwards, III 1928- *WhoBlA 94*
Lee, William John 1936- *WhoAm 94, WhoScEn 94*
Lee, William Johnson 1924- *WhoAmL 94, WhoMW 93*
Lee, William Kendall, Jr. 1949- *WhoFI 94*
Lee, William Marshall 1922- *WhoAm 94, WhoAmL 94*
Lee, William R(owland) 1911- *ConAu 42NR*
Lee, William Richard 1953- *WhoAmP 93*
Lee, William Rowland *WrDr 94*
Lee, William Saul 1938- *WhoAm 94*
Lee, William States 1929- *WhoAm 94, WhoFI 94, WhoScEn 94*
Lee, William Swain 1935- *WhoAmL 94, WhoAmP 93*
Lee, William Thomas 1942- *WhoBlA 94*
Lee, William Wai-Lim 1948- *WhoAsA 94*
Lee, Willy *GayLL*
Lee, Wol Sue 1938- *WhoAsA 94*
Lee, Won Jay 1938- *WhoScEn 94*
Lee, Wonyong 1930- *WhoAsA 94*
Lee, Wooyoung 1938- *WhoAsA 94*
Lee, Yeh Kwong Charles 1936- *IntWW 93*
Lee, Yeu-Tsu Margaret 1936- *WhoAsA 94*
Lee, Ying K. 1932- *WhoAsA 94*
Lee, Young Jack 1942- *WhoAm 94*
Lee, Young Ki 1946- *WhoScEn 94*
Lee, Young Moo 1954- *WhoScEn 94*
Lee, Yow-Min R. 1924- *WhoAsA 94*
Lee, Yuan Tseh 1936- *IntWW 93, Who 94, WhoAm 94, WhoAsA 94, WhoScEn 94, WhoWest 94*
Lee, Yue-Wei 1946- *WhoAsA 94*
Lee, Yuen Fung 1940- *WhoScEn 94*
Lee, Yul W. 1951- *WhoAsA 94*
Lee, Yung-Keun 1929- *WhoAm 94, WhoScEn 94*
Lee, Yung-Ming 1957- *WhoScEn 94*
Lee, Yur-Bok 1934- *WhoAsA 94, WhoMW 93*
Lee, Yvonne Alberta 1933- *WhoAm 94*
Lee, Zuk-Nae 1940- *WhoScEn 94*
Leean, Joseph 1942- *WhoAmP 93, WhoMW 93*
Leeb, Charles Samuel 1945- *WhoScEn 94, WhoWest 94*
Lee-Barber, John 1905- *Who 94*
Leeber, Sharon Corgan 1940- *WhoAmA 93*
Lee Bum Suk *HisDcKW*
Leece, Gifford Vannin 1898- *WhAm 10*
Leech, Charles Russell, Jr. 1930- *WhoAm 94*
Leech, David Bruce 1934- *Who 94*
Leech, Geoffrey Neil 1936- *Who 94, WrDr 94*
Leech, Hilton 1906-1969 *WhoAmA 93N*
Leech, James William 1947- *WhoAm 94, WhoFI 94*
Leech, Jeffrey James 1946- *WhoAmL 94*
Leech, John 1925- *Who 94*
Leech, John Dale 1939- *WhoAm 94*
Leech, Kenneth 1939- *Who 94, WrDr 94*
Leech, Margaret Kernochan 1893- *WhAm 10*
Leech, Michael John 1951- *WhoAm 94*
Leech, Noyes Elwood 1921- *WhoAm 94*
Leech, Richard 1922- *WhoHol 92*
Leech, Robert Radcliffe 1919- *Who 94*
Leech, Sally 1940- *WhoScEn 94*
Lee Chong Ch'an 1916-1983 *HisDcKW*
Lee Chu-Ming, Martin 1938- *Who 94*
Leed, Jacob *DrAPF 93*
Leed, Jacob 1924- *WrDr 94*
Leeder, Louis I. 1964- *WhoAmL 94*
Leeder, Stuart L. 1943- *WhoAm 94*
Leedom, E. Paul 1925- *WhoFI 94*
Leedom, John Nesbett *WhoAmP 93*
Leedom-Ackerman, Joanne *DrAPF 93*
Leeds, Archdeacon of *Who 94*
Leeds, Bishop of 1930- *Who 94*
Leeds, Andrea d1984 *WhoHol 92*
Leeds, Annette *WhoAmA 93*
Leeds, Anthony 1925-1989 *WhAm 10*
Leeds, Barry H 1940- *WrDr 94*
Leeds, Charles Alan 1951- *WhoAm 94*
Leeds, Christopher (Anthony) 1935- *Who 94, WrDr 94*
Leeds, David Emerson 1958- *WhoAmP 93*
Leeds, Douglas Brecker 1947- *WhoAm 94*
Leeds, Eileen Marie 1952- *WhoAmL 94*
Leeds, Frederic Gordon 1960- *WhoAmL 94*
Leeds, Lila 1928- *WhoHol 92*
Leeds, Lilo J. 1928- *WhoAm 94*
Leeds, Marian d1961 *WhoHol 92*
Leeds, Martin N. 1916- *IntMPA 94*
Leeds, Morton Harold 1921- *WrDr 94*
Leeds, Peter *WhoHol 92*
Leeds, Phil *WhoHol 92*
Leeds, Robert Lewis, Jr. 1930- *WhoAm 94*
Leeds, Robin Leigh 1942- *WhoFI 94*
Leeds-Horwitz, Susan Beth 1950- *WhoWest 94*
Leedy, Daniel Loney 1912- *WhoAm 94*
Leedy, Emily L. Foster 1921- *WhoMW 93*
Leedy, Jim 1929- *WhoAmA 93*
Leedy, Paul D 1908- *WrDr 94*
Leedy, R. Allan, Jr. 1942- *WhoAm 94, WhoAmL 94*
Leedy, Robert Allan 1909- *WhoAm 94*
Leefe, James Morrison 1921- *WhoAm 94*
Leege, David Calhoun 1937- *WhoAm 94*
Lee Hak-ku 1920-1953 *HisDcKW*
Leehey, Patrick 1921- *WhoAm 94*
Leehey, Paul Wade 1954- *WhoAmL 94*
Lee Hsien Loong, Brig.-Gen. 1952- *IntWW 93*
Lee Huan 1917- *IntWW 93*
Lee Hyung Keun 1920- *HisDcKW*
Leek, Everett Paul 1929- *WhoBlA 94*
Leek, Jay Wilbur 1928- *WhoFI 94*
Leek, Sandra D. 1954- *WhoBlA 94*
Leek, Sandra Donnette 1954- *WhoAmL 94*
Leeke, John F. 1939- *WhoBlA 94*
Lee Kim Sai, Datuk 1937- *IntWW 93*
Leekley, John Robert 1943- *WhoAm 94, WhoAmL 94*
Leekley, Marie Valpoon 1941- *WhoMW 93*
Leekpai, Chuan 1938- *IntWW 93*
Lee Kuan Yew 1923- *IntWW 93, Who 94*
Lee Kwon Mu 1910- *HisDcKW*
Leeland, Steven Brian 1951- *WhoFI 94, WhoScEn 94, WhoWest 94*
Leeman, Cavin Philip 1932- *WhoAm 94*
Leeman, Susan Epstein 1930- *WhoScEn 94*
Leemann, Ursula 1936- *WhoWomW 91*
Leemans, Alphonse d1979 *ProFbHF*
Leemans, Wim Pieter 1963- *WhoScEn 94*
Leeming, Cheryl Elise Kendall *Who 94*
Leeming, Geraldine Margaret *Who 94*
Leeming, Ian 1948- *Who 94*
Leeming, John Coates 1927- *Who 94*
Leen, Todd Kevin 1955- *WhoWest 94*
Leener, Jack Joseph 1926- *WhoAm 94*
Leeney, Robert Joseph 1916- *WhoAm 94*
Leepa, Allen 1919- *WhoAm 94, WhoAmA 93*
Lee Peng-Fei, Allen 1940- *Who 94*
Leeper, Doris Marie 1929- *WhoAmA 93*
Leeper, Harold Harris 1916- *WhoAmL 94*
Leeper, John Palmer 1921- *WhoAm 94, WhoAmA 93*
Leeper, Lemuel Cleveland 1927- *WhoBlA 94*
Leeper, Lucius Walter 1922- *WhoBlA 94*
Leeper, Michael Edward 1917- *WhoAm 94*
Leeper, Robert J. 1958- *WhoAmP 93*
Leeper, Ronald James 1944- *WhoBlA 94*
Leeper, Roy V. 1941- *WhoMW 93*
Leeper, Zane H. 1922- *WhoFI 94*
Lee-Potter, Jeremy Patrick 1934- *Who 94*
Leerburger, Benedict A 1932- *WrDr 94*
Lees, Allan Milne 1959- *WhoWest 94*
Lees, Anthony David d1992 *IntWW 93N, Who 94N*
Lees, Anthony Philip 1930- *WhoFI 94*
Lees, Antoinette *WhoHol 92*
Lees, Antony *Who 94*
Lees, (William) Antony Clare 1935- *Who 94*
Lees, Benjamin 1924- *NewGrDO, WhoAm 94*
Lees, Brian P. 1953- *WhoAmP 93*
Lees, C(harles) Norman 1929- *Who 94*
Lees, David (Bryan) 1936- *IntWW 93, Who 94*
Lees, Dennis Samuel 1924- *Who 94*
Lees, Florence Sarah 1840-1922 *DcNaB MP*
Lees, Francis Anthony 1931- *WhoAm 94*
Lees, Geoffrey William 1920- *Who 94*
Lees, Harry Hanson *WhoAmA 93N*
Lees, James Edward 1939- *WhoAm 94, WhoMW 93*
Lees, Marjorie Berman 1923- *WhoAm 94*
Lees, Martin Henry 1929- *WhoAm 94*
Lees, Meg Heather 1948- *WhoWomW 91*
Lees, Michael 1927- *WhoHol 92*
Lees, Nicholas Ernest Samuel 1939- *Who 94*
Lees, Norman *Who 94*
Lees, Ray 1931- *WrDr 94*
Lees, Robert Ferguson 1938- *Who 94*
Lees, Robin Lowther 1931- *Who 94*
Lees, Ron Milne 1939- *WhoScEn 94*
Lees, Sidney 1917- *WhoAm 94*
Lees, Thomas (Edward) 1925- *Who 94*
Lees, Thomas Harcourt Ivor 1941- *Who 94*
Lees, William 1924- *Who 94*
Lees, William Glenwood 1916- *WhoFI 94*
Lee Sang Cho 1915- *HisDcKW*
Lee Sang-Ok *IntWW 93*
Leese, John Henry Vernon 1901- *Who 94*
Leeser, David O. 1917- *WhoScEn 94*
Leeser, Isaac 1806-1868 *DcAmReB 2*
Lee-Sissom, E. 1934- *WhoAmA 93*
Lee Six, Abigail (Etta) 1960- *WrDr 94*
Lees-Milne, James 1908- *IntWW 93, Who 94, WrDr 94*
Lee-Smith, Hughie 1915- *AfrAmAl 6, ConBlB 5 [port], WhoAm 94, WhoAmA 93, WhoBlA 94*
Leeson, David Brent 1937- *WhoAm 94*

Leeson, Janet Caroline Tollefson 1933- *WhoMW 93*
Leeson, R.A. *SmATA 76*
Leeson, Robert (Arthur) 1928- *EncSF 93, SmATA 76 [port], TwCYAW, WrDr 94*
Leeson, Tom 1945- *WhoAmA 93*
Lees-Spalding, Ian Jaffery 1920- *Who 94*
Lee-Steere, Ernest (Henry) 1912- *Who 94*
Leet, James Jay 1947- *WhoAmP 93*
Leet, James Lawrence 1951- *WhoAmL 94*
Leet, Judith *DrAPF 93*
Leet, Mildred Robbins 1922- *WhoAm 94*
Leet, Richard *WhoAmA 93*
Leet, Richard Eugene 1936- *WhoAmA 93*
Leet, Richard Hale 1926- *WhoAm 94*
Lee Ta-Hai 1919- *IntWW 93*
Leetaru, Ilse 1915- *WhoAmA 93*
Leetch, Brian 1968- *WhoAm 94*
Leete, Edward 1928-1992 *WhAm 10*
Leete, William White 1929- *WhoAm 94, WhoAmA 93*
Lee Teng-Hui 1923- *IntWW 93*
Lee Tsung-Dao 1926- *IntWW 93*
Lee Tung *EncSF 93*
Leetz, John Richard 1933- *WhoFI 94, WhoMW 93*
Lee Tzu Pheng 1946- *BlmGWL*
Leeuw, Gene R. 1944- *WhoAmP 93*
Leeuw, Ton de 1926- *NewGrDO*
Leeuwenhoek, Antoni van 1632-1723 *WorScD [port]*
Leever, Harold 1914- *WhoAm 94*
Leevy, Carroll M. 1920- *WhoBlA 94*
Leevy, Carroll Moton 1920- *WhoAm 94*
Lee Won Kyung 1922- *IntWW 93*
Leewood, Jack 1913- *IntMPA 94*
Lee Yock Suan 1946- *IntWW 93*
Lee Yong Leng 1930- *IntWW 93, Who 94*
Lee Yuan-Tseh 1936- *IntWW 93*
Le Faber, Eleanor d1978 *WhoHol 92*
LeFante, Joseph A. 1928- *WhoAmP 93*
Le Fante, Michael 1954- *WhoIns 94*
LeFanu, Elizabeth *Who 94*
Le Fanu, J. S. 1814-1873 *BlmGEL*
Le Fanu, Joseph Sheridan 1814-1873 *ShSCr 14 [port]*
Le Fanu, Mark 1946- *Who 94*
LeFanu, Nicola (Frances) 1947- *NewGrDO*
LeFanu, Nicola Frances 1947- *Who 94*
Lefanu, Sarah 1953- *EncSF 93*
Le Fanu, (Joseph Thomas) Sheridan 1814-1873 *RfGShF*
Le Fanu, Victor *Who 94*
Le Fanu, (George) Victor (Sheridan) 1925- *Who 94*
Lefaur, Andre d1952 *WhoHol 92*
Le Fave, Gene Marion 1924- *WhoFI 94, WhoScEn 94, WhoWest 94*
Lefco, Kathy Nan 1949- *WhoAmL 94*
Lefcoe, Vann H. 1943- *WhoAm 94*
Lefcort, Hugh George 1962- *WhoScEn 94*
Lefcourt, Irwin 1910- *WhoAmA 93*
Lefcourt, Peter 1941- *ConAu 140*
Lefcowitz, Barbara F. *DrAPF 93*
Lefeaux, Charles 1909- *WhoHol 92*
Lefebre, John 1905-1986 *WhoAmA 93N*
Lefebure, Alain Paul 1946- *WhoScEn 94*
Lefebure, Molly *WrDr 94*
Lefebvre, Albert Paul Conrad 1930- *WhoAmL 94*
Lefebvre, Arthur Henry 1923- *Who 94, WhoAm 94*
Lefebvre, Charles Edouard 1843-1917 *NewGrDO*
Lefebvre, Gabriel Felicien 1932- *WhoAm 94*
Lefebvre, Gren Gordon 1943- *WhoMW 93*
Lefebvre, Jean *WhoHol 92*
Lefebvre, Jim 1943- *WhoAm 94, WhoMW 93*
Lefebvre, Joseph 1761-c. 1822 *NewGrDO*
Lefebvre, Louise-Rosalie *NewGrDO*
Lefebvre, Rolf d1974 *WhoHol 92*
Lefebvre, Ronald J. 1923- *WhoAmP 93*
Lefebvre, Yves *WhoHol 92*
Lefebvre D'Argence, Rene-Yvon 1928- *WhoAmA 93*
Lefer, Allan Mark 1936- *WhoAm 94, WhoScEn 94*
Lefer, Diane *DrAPF 93*
Lefert, Gerald W. 1940- *WhoAm 94*
Le Feuvre, Guy d1950 *WhoHol 92*
Le Feuvre, Ned d1966 *WhoHol 92*
Lefever, Ernest W. 1919- *WhoAm 94*
Lefever, Kenneth Ernest 1915- *Who 94*
Le Fever, Kit *WhoHol 92*
LeFever, Michael Grant 1947- *WhoAm 94*
Lefevers, Pearl Ray 1937- *WhoAmP 93*
LeFevre, Adam *DrAPF 93*
Le Fevre, Adam 1950- *WhoHol 92*
LeFevre, David E. 1944- *WhoAm 94, WhoAmL 94*
Lefevre, Donald Keith 1956- *WhoFI 94, WhoMW 93*
LeFevre, Elbert Walter, Jr. 1932- *WhoAm 94, WhoScEn 94*
Lefevre, Greg Louis 1947- *WhoWest 94*
Lefevre, Gui *ConAu 42NR*
Lefevre, Lawrence E. 1904-1960 *WhoAmA 93N*
LeFevre, Perry Deyo 1921- *WhoAm 94*
Lefevre, Rene 1898- *WhoHol 92*
Le Fevre, Richard John 1931- *WhoAmA 93*
Lefevre, Thomas Vernon 1918- *WhoAm 94*
Lefevre d'Etaples, Jacques c. 1460-1536 *GuFrLit 2*
Leff, Alan Richard 1945- *WhoAm 94*
Leff, Arthur 1908- *WhoAm 94*
Leff, Carl 1897- *WhoAm 94*
Leff, David 1933- *WhoAmL 94*
Leff, Gordon 1926- *Who 94, WrDr 94*
Leff, Harvey Sherwin 1937- *WhoWest 94*
Leff, Joseph Norman 1923- *WhoAm 94*
Leff, Julian Paul 1938- *Who 94*
Leff, Sandra H. 1939- *WhoAm 94*
Leffall, LaSalle Doheny, Jr. 1930- *WhoBlA 94*
Leffek, Kenneth Thomas 1934- *WhoAm 94*
Leffel, Russell C. 1948- *WhoAmP 93*
Leffel, Russell Calvin 1948- *WhoAmL 94*
Lefferdink, John S. 1951- *WhoAmP 93*
Lefferts, George *IntMPA 94, WhoAm 94*
Lefferts, Gillet, Jr. 1923- *WhoAm 94*
Lefferts, John M. 1957- *WhoFI 94*
Lefferts, William Geoffrey 1943- *WhoAm 94*
Leffland, Ella 1931- *WrDr 94*
Leffler, Adrienne Karel 1934- *WhoWest 94*
Leffler, Anne Charlotte *BlmGWL*
Leffler, Carole Elizabeth 1942- *WhoMW 93*
Leffler, Hermann d1929 *WhoHol 92*
Leffler, Melvyn P. 1945- *WhoAm 94*
Leffler, Robert d1940 *WhoHol 92*
Leffler, Ross Lillie 1886-1964 *EncABHB 9 [port]*
Leffler, Sheldon S. 1942- *WhoAmP 93*
Leffler-Burckhardt, Martha 1865-1954 *NewGrDO*
Lefiti, Fa'afetai *WhoAmP 93*
Lefko, Jeffrey Jay 1945- *WhoFI 94*
Lefko, Morris E. 1907- *IntMPA 94*
Lefko, Orville Bradford 1922- *WhoFI 94*
Lefkoff, Merle Schlesinger 1938- *WhoAmP 93*
Lefkovitz, Lori Hope 1956- *WhoMW 93*
Lefkowith, Edwin Frank 1931- *WhoFI 94*
Lefkowitz, Alan Zoel 1932- *WhoAmL 94*
Lefkowitz, Howard N. 1936- *WhoAm 94*
Lefkowitz, Hugh Walter 1930- *WhoFI 94*
Lefkowitz, Irving 1921- *WhoAm 94*
Lefkowitz, Ivan Martin 1952- *WhoAmL 94*
Lefkowitz, Jerome 1931- *WhoAmL 94*
Lefkowitz, Jerry 1945- *WhoAmL 94, WhoFI 94*
Lefkowitz, Lawrence 1938- *WhoAm 94*
Lefkowitz, Louis J. 1904- *WhoAmP 93*
Lefkowitz, Mary (Rosenthal) 1935- *WrDr 94*
Lefkowitz, Mary Rosenthal 1935- *ConAu 41NR*
Lefkowitz, Paul Safford 1949- *WhoAmL 94*
Lefkowitz, Robert Joseph 1943- *WhoAm 94*
Le Flem, Paul 1881-1984 *NewGrDO*
le Fleming, Morris John 1932- *Who 94*
Le Fleming, Peter Henry John 1923- *Who 94*
le Fleming, Quentin (John) 1949- *Who 94*
Lefler, John N. *WhoAmL 94*
Lefler, Lawrence Glenn 1926- *WhoAmP 93*
Leflerova, Helena 1921- *WhoWomW 91*
Le Floch-Prigent, Loik 1943- *IntWW 93*
LeFlore, Larry 1949- *WhoBlA 94*
LeFlore, Obie Laurence, Jr. 1951- *WhoBlA 94*
Leflore, Robert, Jr. 1931- *WhoAmP 93*
LeFlore, William B. 1930- *WhoBlA 94*
Leflores, George O., Jr. 1921- *WhoBlA 94*
Lefond, Anne May 1917- *WhoWest 94*
LeForge, P. V. *DrAPF 93*
Lefort, Claude 1924- *IntWW 93*
Le Fort, Gertrud von 1876-1971 *BlmGWL*
LeFrak, Francine *WhoAm 94*
Lefrak, Joseph Saul 1930- *WhoAm 94*
LeFrak, Richard Stone 1945- *WhoAm 94, WhoFI 94*
LeFrak, Samuel J. 1918- *WhoAm 94, WhoFI 94*
Lefranc, Margaret *WhoAmA 93*
Lefrancois, Jacques Roger 1929- *IntWW 93*
Le Froid de Mereaux, Nicolas-Jean *NewGrDO*
Lefstein, Norman 1937- *WhoAm 94*
Lefter, J. Baird 1946- *WhoAmL 94*
Lefton, Al Paul, Jr. 1928- *WhoAm 94*
Lefton, David Edward 1960- *WhoAmL 94*
Leftwich, Alexander d1947 *WhoHol 92*
Leftwich, Bill James 1923- *WhoAmP 93*
Leftwich, Hal West 1955- *WhoAm 94*
Leftwich, James Stephen 1956- *WhoFI 94, WhoWest 94*
Leftwich, Keith C. 1954- *WhoAmP 93*
Leftwich, Norma Bogues 1948- *WhoBlA 94*
Leftwich, Richard Henry 1920- *WhoAm 94*
Leftwich, William 1770-1843 *DcNaB MP*
Leftwich, Willie L. 1937- *WhoBlA 94*
Legal, Ernst d1955 *WhoHol 92*
LeGall, Terrence George 1954- *WhoBlA 94*
Le Gallienne, Eva 1899- *AmCulL*
Le Gallienne, Eva 1899-1991 *WhAm 10, WhoHol 92*
Legan, Gregory Mark 1957- *WhoMW 93*
Legan, Kenneth Dale 1946- *WhoAmP 93*
Legan, Thomas L. 1933- *WhoFI 94*
Legard, Charles Thomas *Who 94*
Legard, John *NewGrDO*
Legare, Henri Francis 1918- *WhoWest 94*
Legare, Ovila d1978 *WhoHol 92*
Le Garrec, Evelyne *BlmGWL*
Legat, Michael (Ronald) 1923- *WrDr 94*
Legat, Nikolai 1869-1937 *IntDcB [port]*
LeGates, John Crews Boulton 1940- *WhoAm 94, WhoFI 94, WhoScEn 94*
Le Gault, Lance *WhoHol 92*
Legazpi, Miguel Lopez De c. 1510-1572 *WhWE*
Legenc, Stanley Martin 1943- *WhoMW 93*
Legendre, Adrien-Marie 1752-1833 *WorScD*
Legendre, Andre 1918- *IntWW 93*
LeGendre, Henri A. 1924- *WhoBlA 94*
Legendre, Louis 1945- *WhoAm 94*
Leger, Alexis *ConAu 43NR*
Leger, (Marie-Rene Auguste) Alexis Saint-Leger 1887-1975 *ConAu 43NR*
Leger, Paul-Emile 1904-1991 *WhAm 10*
Leger, Raymond *EncSF 93*
Leger, Richard Roubine 1935- *WhoWest 94*
Leger, Saintleger *ConAu 43NR*
Leger, Teresa Isabel 1954- *WhoHisp 94*
Leger, Walter John, Jr. 1951- *WhoAmL 94*
Legere, Laurence Joseph 1919- *WhoAm 94*
Legerton, Clarence William, Jr. 1922- *WhoAm 94*
Legg, Allan Aubrey R. *Who 94*
Legg, Barry Charles 1949- *Who 94*
Legg, Benson Everett 1947- *WhoAm 94, WhoAmL 94*
Legg, Brian James 1945- *Who 94*
Legg, Cyrus Julian Edmund 1946- *Who 94*
Legg, David E. 1955- *WhoWest 94*
Legg, Keith (Leonard Charles) 1924- *Who 94*
Legg, Michael William 1952- *WhoAmL 94*
Legg, Reagan Houston 1924- *WhoAmL 94*
Legg, Robert Henry 1917-1992 *WhAm 10*
Legg, Ronald Otis 1945- *WhoMW 93*
Legg, Thomas (Stuart) 1935- *Who 94*
Legg, William Jefferson 1925- *WhoAm 94, WhoAmL 94*
Leggans, Thomas Edward 1963- *WhoAmL 94*
Leggat, Lois Burnett 1917- *WhoAmP 93*
Leggate, Robin 1946- *NewGrDO*
Leggatt, Alexander 1940- *WrDr 94*
Leggatt, Alison d1990 *WhoHol 92*
Leggatt, Andrew (Peter) 1930- *Who 94*
Leggatt, Hugh (Frank John) 1925- *Who 94*
Legge *Who 94*
Legge, Charles Alexander 1930- *WhoAm 94, WhoAmL 94, WhoWest 94*
Legge, Francis 1719-1783 *WhAmRev*
Legge, John Christopher 1964- *WhoMW 93*
Legge, John David 1921- *WrDr 94*
Legge, (John) Michael 1944- *Who 94*
Legge, Walter 1906-1979 *NewGrDO*
Legge, William *WhAmRev*
Legge, William Gordon 1913- *Who 94*
Legge Kemp, Diane 1949- *WhoAm 94, WhoMW 93*
Legge-Schwarzkopf, Elisabeth *Who 94*
Legget, Robert Ferguson 1904- *WhoAm 94*
Leggett, Clarence (Arthur Campbell) 1911- *Who 94*
Leggett, Donald Yates 1935- *WhoAm 94*
Leggett, Douglas Malcolm Aufrere 1912- *Who 94*
Leggett, Glenn 1918- *WhoAm 94*
Leggett, John *DrAPF 93*
Leggett, John Carl 1930- *WhoAm 94*
Leggett, Malcolm H. 1937- *WhoIns 94*
Leggett, Otis A. 1919- *WhoAmP 93*
Leggett, Renee 1949- *WhoBlA 94*
Leggett, Roberta Jean 1926- *WhoAm 94*
Leggett, Sonyia Elizabeth 1936- *WhoFI 94*
Leggett, Stephen *DrAPF 93*
Leggett, Thomas Parrish 1945- *WhoAmL 94*
Leggett, Vincent Omar 1953- *WhoBlA 94*
Leggett, William C. 1939- *WhoAm 94, WhoScEn 94*
Leggette, Lemire 1949- *WhoBlA 94*
Leggette, Violet Olevia Brown *WhoAmP 93, WhoBlA 94*
Leggo, Christopher 1897- *WhAm 10*
Leggon, Cheryl Bernadette 1948- *WhoScEn 94*
Leggon, Herman W. 1930- *WhoBlA 94*
Leggott, Michele 1956- *BlmGWL*
Legh *Who 94*
Legh-Jones, Piers Nicholas 1943- *Who 94*
Legiardi-Laura, Roland *DrAPF 93*
Leginska, Ethel 1886-1970 *NewGrDO*
LeGlvre de Richebourg, Madame fl. 18th cent.- *BlmGWL*
Legler, Donald Wayne 1931- *WhoAm 94*
Legler, Mitchell Wooten 1942- *WhoAm 94, WhoAmL 94*
Legley, Vic(tor) 1915- *NewGrDO*
Legnani, Pierina 1863-1923 *IntDcB [port]*
Legneur, Charles d1956 *WhoHol 92*
Lego, Paul Edward 1930- *IntWW 93, WhoAm 94, WhoFI 94*
Le Goc, Michel Jean-Louis 1921- *WhoFI 94*
Le Goff, Jacques Louis 1924- *IntWW 93*
Le Goff, Rene Jean 1944- *WhoFI 94*
LeGoffic, Francois 1936- *WhoScEn 94*
Legorreta Vilchis, Ricardo 1931- *IntWW 93*
Legouix, (Isidore) Edouard 1834-1916 *NewGrDO*
Legowski, Claire Elise 1951- *WhoMW 93*
Legowsky, Robert Alan 1952- *WhoFI 94*
Le Goy, Raymond Edgar Michel 1919- *IntWW 93, Who 94*
LeGrand, Bob 1943- *WhoBlA 94*
Le Grand, Clay 1911- *WhoAm 94*
LeGrand, Etienne Randall 1956- *WhoBlA 94*
Legrand, Michel 1932- *IntDcF 2-4 [port], WhoHol 92*
Legrand, Michel Jean 1932- *IntMPA 94*
Legrand, Ronald Lyn 1952- *WhoScEn 94*
Legrand, Shawn Pierre 1960- *WhoWest 94*
LeGrand, Yvette Marie 1950- *WhoBlA 94*
LeGrande, William Hunt *WhoMW 93*
LeGrand-Vargas, Jean Ann 1962- *WhoHisp 94*
Legras, Guy 1938- *IntWW 93*
Legrenzi, Giovanni 1626-1690 *NewGrDO*
Legrid, Gloria Jean 1929- *WhoAmP 93*
Le Gros, James *WhoHol 92*
LeGros, John Edward 1923- *WhoAm 94*
Legros, Joseph 1739-1793 *NewGrDO*
LeGros, Susan Packard 1948- *WhoAm 94, WhoAmL 94*
Legters, Lyman Howard 1928- *WhoAm 94*
Le Guere, George d1947 *WhoHol 92*
Leguey-Feilleux, Jean-Robert 1928- *WhoMW 93*
LeGuin, Ursula 1929- *BlmGWL*
Le Guin, Ursula K. *DrAPF 93*
Le Guin, Ursula K. 1929- *ShSCr 12 [port]*
Le Guin, Ursula K(roeber) 1929- *EncSF 93, GayLL, TwCYAW, WrDr 94*
Le Guin, Ursula Kroeber 1929- *IntWW 93, WhoAm 94*
Leguire, Lawrence Edward 1951- *WhoMW 93*
Leguizamo, John *WhoHisp 94*
Leguizamo, John 1965- *ConTFT 11, IntMPA 94*
Leguizamon, Edgard 1945- *WhoHisp 94*
Legum, Colin 1919- *WrDr 94*
Legum, Jeffrey Alfred 1941- *WhoAm 94, WhoFI 94*
Legwaila, Legwaila Joseph 1937- *IntWW 93*
Leh, Christopher Marshall 1962- *WhoAmL 94*
Leh, Dennis Edward 1946- *WhoAmP 93*
Lehan, Jonathan Michael 1947- *WhoAmL 94*
Lehan, Richard D'Aubin 1930- *WhoAm 94*
LeHane, Louis James 1930- *WhoFI 94*
Lehane, Maureen *Who 94*
Lehane, Maureen 1932- *NewGrDO*
Lehar, Franz (Christian) 1870-1948 *NewGrDO*
Lehberger, Charles Wayne 1944- *WhoScEn 94*
Lehe, Jean Robert 1946- *WhoScEn 94*
Lehfeldt, Hans M. d1993 *NewYTBS 93*
Lehikoinen, Urho Albert 1922- *WhoMW 93*
Lehinger, Mark Evan 1958- *WhoAmL 94*
Lehiste, Ilse 1922- *WhoAm 94*
Lehma, Alfred Baker 1931- *WhoScEn 94*

Leighton, Joseph 1921- *WhoAm 94*
Leighton, Larry J. 1941- *WhoMW 93*
Leighton, Lawrence Ward 1934- *WhoAm 94*
Leighton, Lee 1906- *WrDr 94*
Leighton, Leonard Horace 1920- *Who 94*
Leighton, Lillian d1956 *WhoHol 92*
Leighton, Loren Frederick 1926- *WhoAmP 93*
Leighton, Margaret d1976 *WhoHol 92*
Leighton, Michael (John Bryan) 1935- *Who 94*
Leighton, Patricia MacInnes 1950- *WhoAmA 93*
Leighton, Paul Joe 1953- *WhoAm 94, WhoFI 94*
Leighton, Porter D. 1932- *WhoAmP 93*
Leighton, Queenie d1943 *WhoHol 92*
Leighton, Robert Benjamin 1919- *IntWW 93*
Leighton, Robert Lyman 1917- *WhoWest 94*
Leighton, Ronald 1930- *Who 94*
Leighton, Ronald B. 1951- *WhoAmL 94*
Leighton, Thomas Charles 1913-1976 *WhoAmA 93N*
Leighton, Veronica V. 1940- *WhoAsA 94*
Leighton Of St. Mellons, Baron 1922- *Who 94*
Leighton Williams, John *Who 94*
Leija, Joseph G. 1957- *WhoHisp 94*
Leija, Salomon *WhoAmP 93, WhoHisp 94*
Lei Jieqiong 1905- *IntWW 93*
Lei Jieqiong 1906- *WhoPRCh 91 [port]*
Leijon, Anna-Greta 1939- *IntWW 93*
Leijonhufvud, Axel Stig Bengt 1933- *IntWW 93, WhoAm 94*
Leiken, Earl Murray 1942- *WhoAm 94, WhoAmL 94*
Leikin, Jerrold Blair 1954- *WhoMW 93*
Leikin, Sergey L. 1961- *WhoScEn 94*
Leiman, Sid Zalman 1941- *WhoAm 94*
Leimbach, Martha 1963- *WrDr 94*
Leimback, Harry *WhoAmP 93*
Leimer, Phyllis Hancock 1936- *WhoFI 94*
Lei Ming *WhoPRCh 91*
Lei Mingqiu *WhoPRCh 91*
Leimkuehler, Suellen Renee 1964- *WhoMW 93*
Leimkuhler, Ferdinand Francis 1928- *WhoAm 94*
Leimkuhler, Gerard Joseph, Jr. 1948- *WhoAm 94*
Lein, Allen 1913- *WhoWest 94*
Lein, Malcolm Emil 1913- *WhoAm 94, WhoAmA 93*
Leinard, Philip Eric 1962- *WhoMW 93*
Leinbach, Frederick Swavely 1910-1990 *WhAm 10*
Leinbach, Philip Eaton 1935- *WhoAm 94*
Leinberger, Christopher Brown 1951- *WhoWest 94*
Leinen, Margaret Sandra 1946- *WhoScEn 94*
Leinenweber, Harry D. 1937- *WhoAm 94, WhoAmL 94, WhoMW 93*
Leinenweber, Harry Daniel 1937- *WhoAmP 93*
Leiner, Katherine 1949- *WrDr 94*
Leinieks, Valdis 1932- *WhoAm 94, WhoMW 93*
Leininger, Lester Norman 1925- *WhoMW 93*
Leininger, Madeleine Monica 1925- *WhoAm 94, WhoMW 93*
Leininger, Robert Farnes 1946- *WhoWest 94*
Leininger, Steven J. 1948- *WhoMW 93*
Leino, Deanna Rose 1937- *WhoWest 94*
Leinonen, Tatu Einari 1938- *IntWW 93*
Leinsdorf, Erich d1993 *Who 94N*
Leinsdorf, Erich 1912- *IntWW 93, NewGrDO, WhoAm 94*
Leinsdorf, Erich 1912-1993 *ConAu 142, CurBio 93N, NewYTBS 93 [port]*
Leinster, Duke of 1914- *Who 94*
Leinster, Murray 1896-1975 *EncSF 93*
Leinwand, Harris Donald 1944- *WhoAmL 94*
Leiper, Esther M. *DrAPF 93*
Leiper, Thomas 1745-1825 *WhAmRev*
Lei Pingyi *WhoPRCh 91*
Leipper, Dale Frederick 1914- *WhoAm 94*
Leipzig, Arthur 1918- *WhoAm 94, WhoAmA 93*
Leiran, Keith Murray 1961- *WhoMW 93*
Leird, Donna Smithers 1959- *WhoFI 94*
Lei Renmin 1909- *IntWW 93*
Lei Renmin 1910- *WhoPRCh 91 [port]*
Leirner, Sheila 1948- *IntWW 93*
Leis, Colin Philip 1961- *WhoAmL 94*
Leis, Marietta Patricia *WhoAmA 93*
Leis, Philip Edward 1931- *WhoAm 94*
Leiseca, Sergio A. Jr. 1946- *WhoAm 94*
Leiseca, Sergio Alfredo 1946- *WhoHisp 94*
Leisen, Mitchell d1972 *WhoHol 92*
Leiser, Burton M. 1930- *ConAu 42NR*
Leiser, Burton Myron 1930- *WhoAm 94*
Leiser, Eric J. 1960- *WhoWest 94*
Leiser, Ernest Stern 1921- *WhoAm 94*
Leisey, April Louise Snyder 1955- *WhoScEn 94*
Leish, Kenneth William 1936- *WhoAm 94*
Leishman, Frederick John 1919- *Who 94*
Lei Shuyan 1942- *WhoPRCh 91 [port]*
Leising, Jean *WhoMW 93*
Leising, Jean 1949- *WhoAmP 93*
Leisner, Anthony Baker 1941- *WhoFI 94*
Leisner, Emmi 1885-1958 *NewGrDO*
Leisner, James Keith 1956- *WhoFI 94*
Leisner, James Winge 1924- *WhoWest 94*
Leissa, Arthur William 1931- *WhoAm 94, WhoMW 93, WhoScEn 94*
Leist, Elisabeth Pasek 1927- *WhoFI 94, WhoMW 93*
Leist, M. C. 1940- *WhoAmP 93*
Leisten, Arthur Gaynor 1941- *WhoAm 94, WhoAmL 94, WhoFI 94*
Leister, Frederick d1970 *WhoHol 92*
Leistico, Charles William, Jr. 1927- *WhoMW 93*
Leistner, Mary Edna 1929- *WhoMW 93*
Leisure, David 1951- *WhoHol 92*
Leisure, George Stanley, Jr. 1924- *WhoAm 94*
Leisure, Peter Keeton 1929- *WhoAm 94, WhoAmL 94*
Leisure, Robert Glenn 1938- *WhoWest 94*
Leisy, Douglas Jerald 1954- *WhoWest 94*
Leisy, James Franklin 1927-1989 *WhAm 10*
Leitch, Alma May 1924- *WhoAm 94*
Leitch, Craig H. B. *WhoScEn 94*
Leitch, David Alexander 1931- *Who 94*
Leitch, David Bruce 1940- *WrDr 94*
Leitch, David R. 1948- *WhoAmP 93*
Leitch, Donovan *IntMPA 94*
Leitch, Donovan 1967- *WhoHol 92*
Leitch, George 1915- *Who 94*
Leitch, Gordon James 1937- *WhoAm 94*
Leitch, John Daniel 1921- *WhoAm 94*
Leitch, Maurice *WrDr 94*
Leitch, Monty S. *DrAPF 93*
Leitch, Vincent Barry 1944- *WhoAm 94, WhoMW 93*
Leitch, William Andrew 1915- *Who 94*
Leite, Carlos Alberto 1939- *WhoScEn 94*
Leiter, Donald Eugene 1932- *WhoAm 94*
Leiter, Elliot 1933- *WhoAm 94*
Leiter, Jonathan *DrAPF 93*
Leiter, Richard Allen 1952- *WhoAmL 94*
Leiter, Robert Allen 1949- *WhoAm 94*
Leiter, William 1928- *WhoAmL 94*
Leiter, William C. 1939- *WhoAm 94*
Leith *Who 94*
Leith, Andrew George F. *Who 94*
Leith, Cecil Eldon, Jr. 1923- *WhoAm 94*
Leith, Emmett Norman 1927- *WhoAm 94*
Leith, James Clark 1937- *WhoAm 94*
Leith, John Haddon 1919- *WhoAm 94*
Leith, Linda 1949- *WrDr 94*
Leith, Prudence Margaret 1940- *IntWW 93, Who 94*
Leith, Prue 1940- *WrDr 94*
Leith, Roderick Gordon 1928- *WhoAm 94*
Leith, Susan *WhoHol 92*
Leith, Virginia 1932- *WhoHol 92*
Leithart, Paul Walter 1921- *WhoMW 93*
Leithauser, Brad *DrAPF 93*
Leithauser, Brad 1953- *EncSF 93, WrDr 94*
Leithauser, Mark Alan 1950- *WhoAmA 93*
Leith-Buchanan, Charles (Alexander James) 1939- *Who 94*
Leithead, James Douglas 1911- *Who 94*
Leithead, R. James 1930- *WhoAmL 94*
Leitheiser, James Victor 1962- *WhoScEn 94*
Leithman, John Kenneth 1930- *WhoAmP 93*
Leith-Ross, Harry 1886- *WhoAmA 93N*
Leith-Ross, Prudence 1922- *WrDr 94*
Lei Tianjue 1913- *WhoPRCh 91 [port]*
Leitman, Samuel 1908-1981 *WhoAmA 93N*
Leitmann, George 1925- *WhoAm 94, WhoWest 94*
Leitner, Alfred 1921- *WhoAm 94*
Leitner, David Larry 1956- *WhoAmL 94, WhoMW 93*
Leitner, Elliot 1930- *WhoIns 94*
Leitner, Ferdinand 1912- *NewGrDO*
Leitner, Gregory Marc 1957- *WhoAmL 94*
Leitner, Kay Syms 1938- *WhoAmP 93*
Leitner, Mark Matthew 1958- *WhoAmL 94*
Leitner, Paul R. 1928- *WhoAm 94, WhoAmL 94*
Leito, Ben M. 1923- *IntWW 93*
Leitz, Robert C(harles), III 1944- *WrDr 94*
Leitze, Annette Emily Ricks 1951- *WhoMW 93*
Leitzell, Terry Lee 1942- *WhoAm 94*
Leitzke, Jacque Herbert 1929- *WhoFI 94, WhoMW 93*
Leiweke, Timothy 1957- *WhoAm 94, WhoWest 94*
Leiwig, Judith Ann 1944- *WhoMW 93*
Lei Yang 1920- *IntWW 93*
Lei Yu 1934- *WhoPRCh 91*
Leizear, Charles William 1922- *WhoAm 94*
Lei Zuhua *WhoPRCh 91*
LeJambre, Susan E. 1942- *WhoAmP 93*
Lejeune, Anthony 1928- *WrDr 94*
LeJeune, Dennis Edward 1942- *WhoAm 94*
Le Jeune, Francis Ernest, Jr. 1929- *WhoAm 94*
Lejeune, Jerome Jean Louis Marie 1926- *IntWW 93*
LeJeune, Joseph Guillaume 1914- *WhoFI 94*
Lejeune, Michael L. 1918- *IntWW 93*
Lejeune, Michel 1907- *IntWW 93*
Lejeune, Paul 1591-1664 *EncNAR*
Lejins, Peter Pierre 1909- *WhoAm 94*
Lekai, Louis J 1916- *WrDr 94*
Lekan, Briana Marker 1955- *WhoMW 93*
Lekatsas, Barbara *DrAPF 93*
Lekberg, Barbara Hult 1925- *WhoAmA 93*
Lekberg, Robert David 1920- *WhoMW 93, WhoScEn 94*
Lekhanya, Justin *IntWW 93*
Lekim, Dac 1936- *WhoScEn 94*
Lekota, Mosiuoa Patrick (Terror) 1948- *IntWW 93*
L.E.L. *BlmGWL*
Lelacheur, Edward A. *WhoAmP 93*
Leland, Billy d1976 *WhoHol 92*
Leland, Burton 1948- *WhoAmP 93*
Leland, Christopher Towne *DrAPF 93*
Leland, David d1987 *WhoHol 92*
Leland, David 1947- *IntMPA 94*
Leland, David D. 1935- *WhoAm 94, WhoWest 94*
Leland, Dawn Carolyn 1920- *WhoAmP 93*
Leland, George Thomas 1944-1989 *AfrAmAl 6 [port]*
Leland, Harold Robert 1931- *WhoScEn 94*
Leland, Jeremy Francis David 1932- *WrDr 94*
Leland, John 1503?-1552 *DcLB 136*
Leland, John 1754-1841 *DcAmReB 2*
Leland, Joy Hanson 1927- *WhoAm 94, WhoWest 94*
Leland, Joyce F. 1941- *WhoBlA 94*
Leland, Lawrence 1915- *WhoAm 94*
Leland, Marc Ernest 1938- *WhoAm 94, WhoAmP 93*
Leland, Mary *BlmGWL*
Leland, Mickey 1944-1989 *WhAm 10*
Leland, Paula Susan 1953- *WhoAm 94*
Leland, Richard G. 1949- *WhoAm 94, WhoAmL 94*
Leland, Sara 1941- *WhoAm 94*
Leland, Simeon Elbridge 1897- *WhAm 10*
Leland, Timothy 1937- *WhoAm 94*
Leland, Warren Hanan 1915- *WhoAm 94*
Leland, Whitney Edward 1945- *WhoAmA 93*
Le Lannou, Maurice d1992 *IntWW 93N*
Lelchuk, Alan *DrAPF 93*
Lelchuk, Alan 1938- *WhoAm 94, WrDr 94*
Lele, Padmakar Pratap 1927- *WhoAm 94*
Lelewer, David Kann 1940- *WhoAm 94*
Lelewer, Debra Ann 1951- *WhoWest 94*
le Lievre, Audrey 1923- *WrDr 94*
Lelio, Umberto di *NewGrDO*
Lell, Eberhard 1927- *WhoScEn 94*
Lello, Walter Barrington 1931- *Who 94*
Leloir, Luis F. d1987 *NobelP 91N*
Lelong, Pierre Alexandre 1931- *IntWW 93*
Lelong, Pierre Jacques 1912- *IntWW 93*
Lelouch, Claude 1937- *IntMPA 94, IntWW 93, WhoHol 92*
LeLoup, Lance Theodore 1949- *WhoMW 93*
Lely, Durward d1944 *WhoHol 92*
Lelyveld, Arthur Joseph 1913- *WhoAm 94*
Lelyveld, Joseph Salem 1937- *WhoAm 94*
Lem, Betty d1986 *WhoHol 92*
Lem, Kwok Wai 1952- *WhoAsA 94, WhoScEn 94*
Lem, Nora Wan 1953- *WhoWest 94*
Lem, Richard Douglas 1933- *WhoAmA 93, WhoWest 94*
Lem, Stanislaw 1921- *ConWorW 93, EncSF 93, IntWW 93*
LeMahieu, James Joseph 1936- *WhoFI 94*
LeMaire, Charles 1897-1985 *IntDcF 2-4*
Lemaire, Ferdinand fl. 1860-1870 *NewGrDO*
Le Maire, George d1930 *WhoHol 92*
Lemaire, Jacques 1945- *WhoAm 94*
Le Maire, Jakob c. 1565-1616 *WhWE*
Lemaire, Paul Joseph 1953- *WhoScEn 94*
Lemaire, Philippe *WhoHol 92*
Le Maire, William d1933 *WhoHol 92*
Le Maistre, Charles Aubrey 1924- *WhoAm 94*
Lemaitre, Georges Henri 1894-1966 *WorScD*
Lemaldi, Eleanora Yolanda Renna 1920- *WhoAmP 93*
Lema-Moya, Jose *WhoAmP 93*
Leman, Alexander B. 1926- *IntWW 93*
Leman, Eugene D. 1942- *WhoFI 94*
Leman, Gary Edward 1943- *WhoFI 94*
Leman, Loren D. 1950- *WhoAmP 93*
Leman, Loren Dwight 1950- *WhoWest 94*
Lemann, Nancy 1956- *WrDr 94*
Lemann, Thomas Berthelot 1926- *WhoAm 94, WhoAmL 94*
Lemanski, Kenneth Michael 1954- *WhoAmP 93*
Lemanski, Larry Fredrick 1943- *WhoAm 94*
LeMarbe, Edward Stanley 1952- *WhoFI 94, WhoScEn 94*
Lemarchand, Elizabeth (Wharton) 1906- *WrDr 94*
Le Marchant, Francis (Arthur) 1939- *Who 94*
Le Marechal, Robert Norford 1939- *Who 94*
LeMassena, William d1993 *NewYTBS 93*
Le Massena, William 1916- *WhoHol 92*
Le Master, Brenda Joyce 1952- *WhoMW 93*
Lemaster, David 1949- *WhoAmP 93*
Le Master, Dennis Clyde 1939- *WhoAm 94*
Lemaster, J. R. *DrAPF 93*
LeMaster, J. R. 1934- *WrDr 94*
Lemaster, James Gary 1946- *WhoAmP 93*
Le Master, Joyce Brown 1936- *WhoAmP 93*
LeMaster, Robert Allen 1953- *WhoScEn 94*
Lemasters, John N. *WhoAm 94*
LeMasters, Kim *IntMPA 94*
Lemasters, Steven Craig *WhoIns 94*
Le Masurier, Robert (Hugh) 1913- *Who 94*
LeMasurier, Wesley Ernest 1934- *WhoWest 94*
Le Mat, Paul *WhoHol 92*
Le Mat, Paul 1945- *IntMPA 94*
Lemaure, Catherine-Nicole 1704-1786 *NewGrDO*
Lemay, Curtis E. 1906-1990 *WhAm 10*
Lemay, Frank M. d1993 *NewYTBS 93 [port]*
Le May, G(odfrey) H(ugh) L(ancelot) 1920- *WrDr 94*
Lemay, Gerald J. 1949- *WhoScEn 94*
LeMay, Jacques 1940- *WhoAm 94*
LeMay, Marjorie Jeannette 1917- *WhoScEn 94*
LeMay, Peter John 1943- *WhoMW 93*
Lemay, Raymond 1927- *WhoFI 94*
Lembeck, Harvey d1982 *WhoHol 92*
Lembeck, Harvey 1923-1982 *WhoCom*
Lembeck, Michael 1948- *WhoHol 92*
Lemberg, Howard Lee 1949- *WhoScEn 94*
Lemberg, Jonathan Henry 1959- *WhoAmL 94*
Lemberg, Louis 1916- *WhoAm 94*
Lemberg, Steven Floyd 1953- *WhoMW 93*
Lemberger, August Paul 1926- *WhoAm 94*
Lemberger, Louis 1937- *WhoAm 94*
Lemberger, Norma 1944- *WhoFI 94*
Lembersky, Mark Raphael 1945- *WhoWest 94*
Lembitz, Edward Lawrence 1926- *WhoAm 94*
Lembke, Janet *DrAPF 93*
Lembo, Mark Anthony 1961- *WhoFI 94*
Lembong, Johannes Tarcicius 1930- *WhoScEn 94*
Lemcoe, M. Marshall 1921- *WhoAm 94*
Leme, Hugo de Almeida 1917- *IntWW 93*
Lemeh, Dorotha Hill *WhoBlA 94*
Le Mehaute, Bernard Jean 1927- *WhoAm 94*
Lemein, Gregg D. 1950- *WhoAm 94*
Lemelin, Roger 1919-1992 *WhAm 10*
Le Melle, Gerald Anthony 1962- *WhoAmL 94*
LeMelle, Tilden J. 1929- *WhoBlA 94*
LeMelle, Tilden John 1929- *WhoAm 94*
LeMelle, Wilbert John 1931- *WhoBlA 94*
Lemelson, Jerome *WhoAm 94*
Lemelson, Jerome 1923- *WorInv*
Lemelson, Jerome H. 1923- *WhoScEn 94*
Lemen, Deborah Jean 1959- *WhoMW 93*
Lemen, Richard Alan 1943- *WhoAm 94*
Lemen, Robert Norton 1943- *WhoAmP 93*
Lemenager, Beverly Marie 1961- *WhoMW 93*
Le Menager, Lois M. 1934- *WhoMW 93*
Lemene, Francesco de 1634-1704 *NewGrDO*
Lemens, William Vernon, Jr. 1935- *WhoFI 94*
LeMense, Fay Ann 1965- *WhoMW 93*
Lementowski, Michal 1943- *WhoScEn 94*
Lemer, Andrew Charles 1944- *WhoAm 94*

Lemer, Ellen Terry 1943- *WhoAmA 93*
Lemerle, Paul 1927- *IntWW 93*
Lemert, James Bolton 1935- *WhoAm 94, WhoWest 94*
Lemesh, Nicholas Thomas 1946- *WhoAm 94*
Lemeshev, Sergei d1977 *WhoHol 92*
Lemeshev, Sergey (Yakovlevich) 1902-1977 *NewGrDO*
LeMessurier, William James 1926- *WhoScEn 94*
Le Mesurier, John d1983 *WhoHol 92*
Lemiere, Marie-Jeanne 1733-1786 *NewGrDO*
Lemiere de Corvey, Jean Frederic Auguste 1770-1832 *NewGrDO*
Lemieux, Annette Rose 1957- *WhoAmA 93*
Lemieux, Bonne A. 1921- *WhoAmA 93*
Lemieux, Carrie d1925 *WhoHol 92*
Lemieux, Irenee 1931- *WhoAmA 93*
Lemieux, Jean Paul 1904- *WhoAmA 93N*
Lemieux, (M.) Joseph 1902- *Who 94*
Lemieux, Joseph Henry 1931- *IntWW 93, WhoAm 94, WhoFI 94*
LeMieux, Linda Dailey 1953- *WhoWest 94*
Lemieux, Mario 1965- *WhoAm 94*
Lemieux, Raymond Urgel 1920- *IntWW 93, Who 94, WhoAm 94, WhoScEn 94*
Leming, William Vaughn 1945- *WhoScEn 94*
Lemire, Andre 1943- *WhoFI 94*
Lemire, Beverly 1950- *ConAu 141*
Lemire, David Stephen 1949- *WhoWest 94*
Lemire, George 1929- *WhoAmP 93*
Lemire, Robert Rolland 1937- *WhoFI 94*
Lemire, Roland A. *WhoAmP 93*
Lemke, Cindy Ann 1963- *WhoMW 93, WhoScEn 94*
Lemke, Heinz Ulrich 1941- *WhoScEn 94*
Lemke, James Underwood 1929- *WhoAm 94*
Lemke, Judith A. 1952- *WhoAm 94*
Lemke, Kurt Thomas 1963- *WhoMW 93*
Lemke, Nancy Lee 1942- *WhoFI 94*
Lemke, Paul Arenz 1937- *WhoAm 94, WhoScEn 94*
Lemke, William *WhoAmP 93*
Lemke-Schulte, Eva-Maria 1948- *WhoWomW 91*
Lemkin, James Anthony 1926- *Who 94*
Lemkow, Tutte *WhoHol 92*
Lemle, Robert Spencer 1953- *WhoAm 94, WhoAmL 94, WhoFI 94*
Lemley, Barbara Wink 1930- *WhoAm 94*
Lemley, Jack Kenneth 1935- *Who 94*
Lemley, Steven Smith 1945- *WhoAm 94*
Lemly, Thomas Adger 1943- *WhoAm 94, WhoAmL 94*
Lemmer, Corinne M., Sister 1951- *WhoMW 93*
Lemmer, Jan Theresa 1954- *WhoMW 93*
Lemmerhirt, Wayne Alan 1951- *WhoFI 94*
Lemmerman, Marc David 1950- *WhoFI 94*
Lemmon, Chris(topher) 1954- *WhoHol 92*
Lemmon, Cyril Whitefield 1901- *Who 94*
Lemmon, Dave *WhoAmP 93*
Lemmon, David (Hector) 1931- *WrDr 94*
Lemmon, David Bryon 1957- *WhoMW 93*
Lemmon, David Hector 1931- *Who 94*
Lemmon, George Colborne *Who 94*
Lemmon, Hal Elmont 1932- *WhoScEn 94*
Lemmon, Harry T. 1930- *WhoAmP 93*
Lemmon, Harry Thomas 1930- *WhoAmL 94*
Lemmon, Jack *NewYTBS 93 [port]*
Lemmon, Jack 1925- *IntMPA 94, IntWW 93, WhoAm 94, WhoCom, WhoHol 92*
LemMon, Jean Marie 1932- *WhoAm 94*
Lemmon, John Uhler, II d1961 *WhoHol 92*
Lemmon, Marilyn Sue 1939- *WhoFI 94*
Lemmon, Willard Lincoln 1924- *WhoAmP 93, WhoFI 94*
Lemmond, Charles D., Jr. 1929- *WhoAmP 93*
Lemmond, J. Shawn *WhoAmP 93*
Lemmons, Herbert Michael 1952- *WhoBlA 94*
Lemmons, Patricia Katherine 1957- *WhoMW 93*
Lemmons, Thom 1955- *WrDr 94*
Lemmy 1945- *See* Motorhead *ConMus 10*
Lemnios, Andrew Zachery 1931- *WhoAm 94*
Lemnitz, Tiana (Luise) 1897- *NewGrDO*
Lemnitzer, Lyman L. 1899-1988 *HisDcKW*
Le Moal, Henri-Jean Alain 1912- *IntWW 93*
Lemoine, Danny 1951- *WhoAmP 93*
Lemoine-Luccioni, Eugenie 1912- *BlmGWL*
Lemole, Gerald Michael 1936- *WhoAm 94*
Lemon, Chester Earl 1955- *WhoBlA 94*
Lemon, (Richard) Dawnay 1912- *Who 94*
Lemon, Douglas Karl 1950- *WhoScEn 94*
Lemon, Eric V. 1942- *WhoAm 94, WhoAmL 94*
Lemon, Genevieve *WhoHol 92*
Lemon, Henry Martyn 1915- *WhoAm 94*
Lemon, Lee Thomas 1931- *WrDr 94*
Lemon, Leslie Gene 1940- *WhoAm 94*
Lemon, Meadowlark 1932- *WhoBlA 94*
Lemon, Meadowlark 1936- *BasBi*
Lemon, Michael Wayne, Sr. 1953- *WhoBlA 94*
Lemon, Robert S., Jr. 1938- *WhoAmA 93*
Lemon, Sharon Kay 1949- *WhoMW 93*
Lemon, Stephen Weldon 1962- *WhoAmL 94*
Lemon, William Jacob 1932- *WhoAmL 94*
LeMond, Gregory James 1961- *WhoAm 94*
Lemond, Joseph Michael 1965- *WhoAmL 94*
Lemonick, Aaron 1923- *WhoAm 94, WhoScEn 94*
LeMonnier, Daniel Brian 1955- *WhoMW 93*
Lemonnier, Louis-Augustin 1793-1875 *NewGrDO*
Lemons, Charles Fred 1926- *WhoAmP 93*
Lemons, Clifton Dale 1931- *WhoMW 93*
Lemons, James Stanley 1938- *WrDr 94*
Lemons, Keith David 1954- *WhoAmL 94*
Lemont, Kenneth 1951- *WhoAmP 93*
Lemos, Alberto Santos 1921- *WhoWest 94*
Lemos, Carlos d1988 *WhoHol 92*
Lemos, Noah Marcelino 1956- *WhoHisp 94*
Lemos, Ramon Marcelino 1927- *WhoAm 94, WhoHisp 94, WrDr 94*
Lemos Simmonds, Carlos *IntWW 93*
Le Moyne, Charles d1956 *WhoHol 92*
LeMoyne, Irve Charles 1939- *WhoAm 94*
Le Moyne, Jacques De Morgues d1588 *WhWE*
Le Moyne, Jean-Baptiste *WhWE*
Lemoyne, Jean-Baptiste 1751-1796 *NewGrDO*
Le Moyne, Pierre *WhWE*
Lemoyne, Simon 1604-1665 *EncNAR, WhWE*
Lemp, James Frederick 1939- *WhoFI 94*
Lemp, John, Jr. 1936- *WhoFI 94*
Lemper, Ute 1963- *IntWW 93*
Lempert, Edward T. 1961- *WhoAmP 93*
Lempert, Lawrence Steven 1950- *WhoAmL 94*
Lempert, Richard Owen 1942- *WhoAm 94*
Lemr, James Charles 1951- *WhoMW 93*
Lemr, Sandra J. 1951- *WhoMW 93*
Lemsine, Aicha 1942- *BlmGWL [port]*
Lemsky, William Joseph 1952- *WhoFI 94*
Lemuels, William d1953 *WhoHol 92*
Lemus, Fraterno 1948- *WhoHisp 94*
Lemus, Jose Maria d1993 *IntWW 93N*
Lemus, Jose Maria 1911- *IntWW 93*
Lemus, Ron Elroy d1976 *WhoHol 92*
Lemus Lopez, Jose d1993 *NewYTBS 93*
Lena, Dan 1955- *WrDr 94*
Lena, Marie H(oward) 1956- *WrDr 94*
Lenaert, Henri 1915- *IntWW 93*
Lenahan, Peter d1987 *WhoHol 92*
Lenahan, Walter Clair 1934- *WhoAm 94*
Lenail, Laura 1946- *WrDr 94*
Lenard, Eric Scott 1962- *WhoWest 94*
Lenard, Grace d1987 *WhoHol 92*
Lenard, James David 1948- *WhoMW 93*
Lenard, Lloyd Edgar 1922- *WhoAmP 93, WhoFI 94*
Lenard, Mark 1927- *WhoHol 92*
Lenard, Michael Barry 1955- *WhoWest 94*
Lenard, Philipp Eduard Anton 1862-1947 *WorScD*
Lenardic, Kenneth Ralph 1945- *WhoMW 93*
Lenardon, Robert Joseph 1928- *WhoAm 94*
Lenauer, Jean H. d1983 *WhoHol 92*
Lence, Emil d1993 *NewYTBS 93*
Lence, Julio G. *WhoHisp 94*
Lencek, Rado L. 1921- *WhoAm 94*
Lenclos, Anne (Ninon) de 1620?-1704? *BlmGWL*
Lenczycki, Wayne Alan 1946- *WhoAmL 94*
Lendall, Jim Everett 1947- *WhoAmP 93*
Lendaris, George Gregory 1935- *WhoAm 94*
Lender, Adam 1921- *WhoAm 94*
Lender, Herman Joseph 1923- *WhoAm 94*
Lender, Mary Lou *WhoHol 92*
Lendl, Ivan 1960- *BuCMET [port], IntWW 93, WhoAm 94*
Lendorff, Gertrud 1900-1986 *BlmGWL*
Lendrum, Alan Chalmers 1906- *Who 94*
Lendrum, James Thoburn 1907- *WhoAm 94*
Lends His Horse Long, Madonna Marie 1963- *WhoMW 93*
Lendt, Harold Hanford 1922- *WhoMW 93*
Lendvai, Paul 1929- *WrDr 94*
LeNeau, Thomas Ervin 1950- *WhoWest 94*
Lenehan, Michael Daniel 1949- *WhoMW 93*
Lenehan, Nancy *WhoHol 92*
Lenehan, William Thurman 1930- *WhoAm 94*
Lenepveu, Charles Ferdinand 1840-1910 *NewGrDO*
Leness, George Crawford 1936- *WhoAm 94*
Leney, George Willard 1927- *WhoScEn 94*
Lenfant, Claude Jean-Marie 1928- *WhoAm 94, WhoScEn 94*
L'Enfant, Pierre Charles 1754-1825 *AmRev, WhAmRev*
Lenfest, Harold Fitz Gerald 1930- *WhoAm 94*
Leng, Gerard Siew-Bing 1963- *WhoScEn 94*
Leng, Marguerite Lambert 1926- *WhoScEn 94*
Leng, Peter (John Hall) 1925- *Who 94*
Leng, Shao Chuan 1921- *WhoAm 94*
Leng, Virginia Helen Antoinette 1955- *Who 94*
Leng, Xin-Fu 1927- *WhoScEn 94*
Lenga, J. Thomas 1942- *WhoAm 94, WhoAmL 94*
Lengbach, Georg d1952 *WhoHol 92*
Lengel, James Hanjo 1949- *WhoAmL 94*
Lengemann, Frederick William 1925- *WhoAm 94*
Lengieza, Kenneth John 1951- *WhoMW 93*
L'Engle, Madeleine 1918- *BlmGWL, EncSF 93, TwCYAW, WhoAm 94, WrDr 94*
L'Engle, Madeleine (Camp Franklin) 1918- *SmATA 75 [port]*
L'Engle, William Johnson 1884-1957 *WhoAmA 93N*
Lenglen, Suzanne d1938 *WhoHol 92*
Lenglen, Suzanne 1899-1938 *BuCMET [port]*
Lengomin, Juan Alberto 1953- *WhoHisp 94*
Lengyel, Alfonz 1921- *WhoAm 94, WhoAmA 93*
Lengyel, Cornel (Adam) 1915- *WrDr 94*
Lengyel, Cornel Adam *DrAPF 93*
Lengyel, Cornel Adam 1915- *WhoAm 94, WhoWest 94*
Lengyel, Joseph William 1941- *WhoScEn 94*
Lengyel, Jozsef 1896-1975 *RfGShF*
Lengyel, Peter *EncSF 93*
Lenhardt, Alfonso Emanual 1943- *AfrAmG [port]*
Lenhardt, Alfonso Emanuel 1943- *WhoBlA 94*
Lenhardt, Shirley M. 1934- *WhoAmA 93*
Lenhart, Gary *DrAPF 93*
Lenhart, James Robert 1952- *WhoWest 94*
Lenhart, James Thomas 1946- *WhoAm 94*
Lenher, Irene K. 1907-1986 *WhAm 10*
Lenherr, Donald William 1940- *WhoIns 94*
Lenherr, Frederick Keith 1943- *WhoAm 94*
Lenhoff, Howard Maer 1929- *WhoAm 94, WhoWest 94*
Leniado-Chira, Joseph 1934- *WhoAm 94*
Lenica, Jan 1928- *IntDcF 2-4, IntWW 93*
Lenihan, Brian Joseph 1930- *IntWW 93, Who 94*
Lenihan, Deidre *WhoHol 92*
Lenihan, J. Michael 1943- *WhoAmP 93*
Lenihan, Winifred d1964 *WhoHol 92*
Lenin, V. I. 1870-1924 *HisWorL [port]*
Lenisa, Cheryl Jeanne 1960- *WhoFI 94*
Lenix-Hooker, Catherine Jeanette 1947- *WhoBlA 94*
Lenk, Hans Albert Paul 1935- *IntWW 93*
Lenk, Thomas 1933- *IntWW 93*
Lenke, Joanne Marie 1938- *WhoAm 94*
Lenker, Floyd William 1933- *WhoMW 93*
Lenker, Marlene N. 1932- *WhoAmA 93*
Lenker, William Fred 1923- *WhoAmP 93*
Lenkoski, Leo Douglas 1925- *WhoAm 94*
Lenkov, Jeffrey Myles 1965- *WhoAmL 94*
Lenman, Bruce Philip 1938- *WhoAm 94*
Lenman, Tomas Stig 1945- *WhoMW 93*
Lenn, Stephen Andrew 1946- *WhoAm 94*
Lennard, Arthur d1954 *WhoHol 92*
Lennard, Hugh Dacre B. *Who 94*
Lennart, Isobel 1915-1971 *IntDcF 2-4*
Lennarz, William Joseph 1934- *WhoAm 94*
Lennep, Jonkheer Emile van 1915- *IntWW 93*
Lennes, Gregory 1947- *WhoAm 94*
Lennette, Edwin Herman 1908- *WhoAm 94*
Lenney, Annie 1910- *WhoAmA 93N*
Lenney, James F. 1918- *WhoWest 94*
Lennie, Angus 1930- *WhoHol 92*
Lennie, Douglas 1910- *Who 94*
Lennings, Manfred 1934- *IntWW 93*
Lennkh, Georg 1939- *IntWW 93*
Lennon, A. Max 1940- *WhoAm 94*
Lennon, Frank M. 1938- *WhoFI 94*
Lennon, Gerard Patrick 1951- *WhoScEn 94*
Lennon, (George) Gordon 1911- *Who 94*
Lennon, Jarrett *WhoHol 92*
Lennon, John d1980 *WhoHol 92*
Lennon, Joseph Luke 1919- *WhoAm 94*
Lennon, Marilyn Ellen 1954- *WhoAm 94*
Lennon, Patricia Lavin 1961- *WhoFI 94*
Lennon, Peter Dean 1949- *WhoAmP 93*
Lennon, Thomas Michael 1942- *WhoAm 94*
Lennon, Timothy 1938- *WhoAmA 93*
Lennox *Who 94*
Lennox, Annie 1954- *WhoAm 94, WhoHol 92*
Lennox, Carol 1938- *WhoWest 94*
Lennox, Charlotte 1727?-1804 *BlmGEL*
Lennox, Charlotte (Ramsay) 1729?-1804 *BlmGWL*
Lennox, Donald Duane 1918- *WhoAm 94*
Lennox, Edward Newman 1925- *WhoFI 94*
Lennox, Gloria 1931- *WhoWest 94*
Lennox, Lionel Patrick Madill 1949- *Who 94*
Lennox, Lottie d1947 *WhoHol 92*
Lennox, Robert Smith 1909- *Who 94*
Lennox, Susan Lee 1948- *WhoAmL 94*
Lennox, Vera d1985 *WhoHol 92*
Lennox-Boyd *Who 94*
Lennox-Boyd, Mark Alexander 1943- *Who 94*
Lennox-Boyd, Simon Ronald Rupert *IntWW 93*
Lennox Buchthal, Margaret Agnes 1913- *WhoScEn 94, WhoWest 94*
Lennox-Smith, Judith (Elizabeth) 1953- *WrDr 94*
Leno, Catherine d1993 *NewYTBS 93*
Leno, Charles d1972 *WhoHol 92*
Leno, Dan d1904 *WhoHol 92*
Leno, Dan, Jr. d1962 *WhoHol 92*
Leno, Jay 1950- *IntMPA 94, WhoAm 94, WhoCom [port], WhoHol 92*
Leno, M. John 1944- *WhoAmP 93*
Lenoff, Michele Malka 1961- *WhoAmL 94*
Lenoir, Gloria Cisneros 1951- *WhoFI 94*
Lenoir, Gloria Taylor 1928- *WhoFI 94*
Lenoir, Henry 1912- *WhoBlA 94*
Lenoir, Jack d1981 *WhoHol 92*
Lenoir, Jean-Joseph-Etienne 1822-1900 *WorInv*
Lenoir, Kip 1943- *WhoBlA 94*
Lenoir, William Benjamin 1939- *WhoScEn 94*
LeNoire, Rosetta 1911- *WhoBlA 94, WhoHol 92*
Lenon, Richard Allen 1920- *WhoAm 94*
Lenowitz, Harris *DrAPF 93*
Lenox, Charles Newton, Jr. 1938- *WhoAm 94*
Lenox, James 1800-1880 *DcLB 140 [port]*
Lenox, Mary Frances 1944- *WhoAm 94, WhoMW 93*
Lenrow, Bernie d1963 *WhoHol 92*
Lenschau, Hermann d1977 *WhoHol 92*
Lense, Edward *DrAPF 93*
Lensink, Everett R. *WhoAmP 93*
Lenska, Rula 1947- *WhoHol 92*
Lenski, Lois 1893- *WhoAmA 93N*
Lenski, Lois 1893-1974 *BlmGWL, ConAu 41NR*
Lensky, Leib d1991 *WhoHol 92*
Lenson, Michael 1903-1971 *WhoAmA 93N*
Lenssen, Heidi *WhoAmA 93*
Lent, Berkeley 1921- *WhoAm 94, WhoAmP 93*
Lent, Blair 1930- *WhoAmA 93, WrDr 94*
Lent, John A 1936- *WrDr 94*
Lent, John Anthony 1936- *WhoAm 94*
Lent, Norman F. 1931- *WhoAmP 93*
Lent, Norman Frederick, Jr. 1931- *WhoAm 94*
Lentelli, Leo 1882-1962 *WhoAmA 93N*
Lentes, David Eugene 1951- *WhoFI 94, WhoWest 94*
Lenthall, Franklyn 1919- *WhoAm 94, WhoHol 92*
Lentine, John *WhoAmA 93N*
Lentol, Joseph Roland 1943- *WhoAmP 93*
Lenton, Aylmer Ingram 1927- *IntWW 93*
Lenton, (Aylmer) Ingram 1927- *Who 94*
Lents, Don Glaude 1949- *WhoAm 94, WhoAmL 94*
Lents, Thomas Alan 1946- *WhoScEn 94*
Lentz, Harold James 1947- *WhoAmL 94*

Lentz, Irene d1962 WhoHol 92
Lentz, Linda Kay 1936- WhoMW 93
Lentz, Mark Steven 1949- WhoMW 93
Lentz, Richard David 1942- WhoMW 93, WhoScEn 94
Lentz, Thomas Lawrence 1939- WhoScEn 94
Lenya, Lotte d1981 WhoHol 92
Lenya, Lotte 1898-1981 NewGrDO [port]
Lenz, Charles Eldon 1926- WhoScEn 94
Lenz, Edward Arnold 1942- WhoAm 94
Lenz, Henry Paul 1925- WhoAm 94, WhoFI 94
Lenz, Jakob Michael Reinhold 1751-1792 IntDcT 2, NewGrDO
Lenz, Kay 1953- IntMPA 94, WhoAm 94, WhoHol 92
Lenz, Marlene 1932- WhoWomW 91
Lenz, Oskar 1848-1925 WhWE
Lenz, Philip Joseph 1940- WhoWest 94
Lenz, Randolph W. 1947- WhoAm 94, WhoFI 94
Lenz, Rick 1939- WhoHol 92
Lenz, Siegfried 1926- ConWorW 93, IntWW 93, RfGShF
Lenz, Widukind 1919- IntWW 93
Lenzi, Margot Gendreau 1952- WhoMW 93
Lenzi, Mark WhoAm 94
Lenzie, Charles Albert 1937- WhoFI 94
Lenzo, Thomas John 1949- WhoWest 94
Leo, Alan 1860-1917 AstEnc
Leo, Andre 1824-1900 BlmGWL
Leo, Domenic A. 1960- WhoAmL 94
Leo, Jacqueline WhoAm 94
Leo, Kathleen Ripley DrAPF 93
Leo, Leonardo (Ortensio Salvatore de) 1694-1744 NewGrDO
Leo, Louis J. WhoWest 94
Leo, Malcolm 1944- WhoAm 94
Leo, Mary d1989 Who 94N
Leo, Mary Gaye 1951- WhoWest 94
Leo, Melissa WhoHol 92
Leo, Robert Joseph 1939- WhoWest 94
Leo Africanus c. 1485-c. 1554 WhWE
Leoba d779 BlmGWL
Leobgyth d779 BlmGWL
Leodore, Richard Anthony 1954- WhoScEn 94
Leofsky, Joan Carole 1938- WhoWest 94
LeoGrande, William Mark 1949- WhoAm 94
Leon 1962- WhoHol 92
Leon, A. Cynthia 1947- WhoHisp 94
Leon, Abilio WhoHisp 94
Leon, Alonso De c. 1640-c. 1710 WhWE
Leon, Anne WhoHol 92
Leon, Arthur Sol 1931- WhoAm 94
Leon, Benjamin Joseph 1932- WhoAm 94
Leon, Bruno 1924- WhoAm 94
Leon, Connie d1955 WhoHol 92
Leon, Dennis 1933- WhoAm 94, WhoAmA 93
Leon, Donald Francis 1932- WhoAm 94
Leon, Edward 1925- WhoFI 94
Leon, Fernando 1932- WhoHisp 94
León, Fernando Luis 1916- WhoHisp 94
León, Heriberto 1956- WhoHisp 94
Leon, Jerry d1987 WhoHol 92
Leon, John (Ronald) 1934- Who 94
Leon, John Philip 1956- WhoAmL 94
Leon, Joseph WhoHol 92
Leon, Juan Ponce De WhWE
Leon, Julio WhoHisp 94
Leon, Luis Manuel, Jr. 1955- WhoHisp 94
Leon, Maria Teresa de 1904- BlmGWL
León, Nancy WhoHisp 94
Leon, Pauline 1769- BlmGWL
Leon, Pedro d1931 WhoHol 92
Leon, Pierre R. 1926- ConAu 43NR
Leon, Ralph 1929- WhoHisp 94
Leon, Ralph Bernard 1932- WhoAmA 93
Leon, Raymond J. 1949- WhoHisp 94
León, Reinaldo, Jr. 1957- WhoHisp 94
Leon, Richard J. 1949- WhoAm 94
Leon, Robert Leonard 1925- WhoAm 94
Leon, Robert S. 1947- WhoHisp 94
Leon, Rolando Luis 1952- WhoAmL 94
Leon, Sol 1913- IntMPA 94
Leon, Tania J. 1943- WhoBlA 94, WhoHisp 94
Leon, Tania Justina 1943- WhoAm 94
Leon, Tania Justina 1944- AfrAmAl 6
Leon, Valerie WhoHol 92
Leon, Vicki 1942- WrDr 94
Leon, Victor 1858-1940 NewGrDO
Leon, Wilmer J., Jr. 1920- WhoBlA 94
Leonard, Archie d1959 WhoHol 92
Leonard, Arlene Athena 1917- WhoAmP 93
Leonard, Barbara M. WhoAm 94, WhoAmP 93
Leonard, Benny d1947 WhoHol 92
Leonard, Billy d1974 WhoHol 92
Leonard, Bradley Charles 1959- WhoMW 93
Leonard, Brian E. 1936- IntWW 93
Leonard, Byrdie A. Larkin WhoBlA 94
Leonard, Carol 1945- WhoAmP 93
Leonard, Carolyn Marie 1943- WhoBlA 94
Leonard, Catherine W. 1909- WhoBlA 94
Leonard, Constance 1923- WrDr 94
Leonard, Constance Joanne 1963- WhoScEn 94
Leonard, Daniel 1740-1829 WhAmRev
Leonard, David d1967 WhoHol 92
Leonard, David Arthur 1928- WhoAm 94
Leonard, David Morse 1949- WhoAm 94, WhoAmL 94
Leonard, David William 1945- WhoAm 94
Leonard, Dick Who 94
Leonard, Dorothy Louise 1932- WhoFI 94
Leonard, Douglas WhoHol 92
Leonard, Eddie d1941 WhoHol 92
Leonard, Edward F. 1932- WhoAm 94
Leonard, Edward Paul 1935- WhoAm 94
Leonard, Edward R. 1953- WhoAmL 94
Leonard, Edwin Deane 1929- WhoAm 94
Leonard, Elizabeth Adney 1917- WhoWest 94
Leonard, Elizabeth Ann 1950- WhoMW 93, WhoScEn 94
Leonard, Elmore 1925- IntWW 93, WrDr 94
Leonard, Elmore John 1925- WhoAm 94
Leonard, Emilio Manuel, Jr. 1945- WhoHisp 94
Leonard, Eugene Albert 1935- WhoAm 94
Leonard, Frances 1939- ConAu 141
Leonard, Francois EncSF 93
Leonard, George 1742-1826 WhAmRev
Leonard, George Edmund 1940- WhoAm 94, WhoFI 94
Leonard, George H. 1921- EncSF 93
Leonard, George Jay 1946- WhoAm 94
Leonard, Gerald E. 1924- WhoAmP 93
Leonard, Gerald Thomas 1954- WhoAmP 93
Leonard, Gilbert Stanley 1941- WhoFI 94, WhoScEn 94
Leonard, Glen M. 1938- WhoAm 94, WhoWest 94
Leonard, Gloria Jean 1947- WhoBlA 94
Leonard, Graham Douglas 1921- IntWW 93, Who 94
Leonard, Gus d1939 WhoHol 92
Leonard, H. Jeffrey 1954- WhoFI 94
Leonard, Harry d1917 WhoHol 92
Leonard, Herman Beukema 1952- WhoAm 94
Leonard, Hugh 1926- ConDr 93, IntDcT 2, IntWW 93, Who 94, WhoAm 94, WrDr 94
Leonard, Irvin Alan 1944- WhoAm 94, WhoAmL 94
Leonard, Irving A(lbert) 1896- WhAm 10
Leonard, J. S. ConAu 142
Leonard, Jack d1921 WhoHol 92
Leonard, Jack d1988 WhoHol 92
Leonard, Jack E. d1973 WhoHol 92
Leonard, Jack E. 1911-1973 WhoCom
Leonard, Jack E. 1943- WhoMW 93
Leonard, James d1930 WhoHol 92
Leonard, James Charles Beresford Whyte 1905- Who 94
Leonard, James Joseph 1924- WhoAm 94
Leonard, James R., Sr. d1993 NewYTBS 93
Leonard, James S. 1947- ConAu 142
Leonard, Jeff 1955- WhoBlA 94
Leonard, Jerris 1931- WhoAmP 93
Leonard, Joanne 1940- WhoAm 94, WhoAmA 93
Leonard, Joel I. 1939- WhoScEn 94
Leonard, John DrAPF 93, Who 94
Leonard, (Hamilton) John 1926- Who 94
Leonard, John Dunbar, Jr. 1933- WhoFI 94
Leonard, John Harry 1922- WhoAm 94
Leonard, John P. WhoAmP 93
Leonard, John Peter 1940- WhoAm 94
Leonard, John William, Jr. 1925- WhoAm 94
Leonard, Joseph B. 1943- WhoAm 94
Leonard, June 1926- WhoAmP 93
Leonard, Kathleen Mary 1954- WhoScEn 94
Leonard, Kurt John 1939- WhoMW 93, WhoScEn 94
Leonard, Laura 1923- ConAu 142, SmATA 75
Leonard, Leon Lank, Sr. 1922- WhoBlA 94
Leonard, Lorraine 1954- WhoFI 94
Leonard, Lu WhoHol 92
Leonard, Margaret J. WhoAmP 93
Leonard, Marion d1956 WhoHol 92
Leonard, Mary Christine 1947- WhoWest 94
Leonard, Maurice 1939- WrDr 94
Leonard, Michael 1941- WhoAm 94
Leonard, Michael A. 1937- WhoFI 94, WhoMW 93
Leonard, Michael Steven 1947- WhoAm 94
Leonard, Michael William 1916- Who 94
Leonard, Minnie d1940 WhoHol 92
Leonard, Molly Ann 1932- WhoAmP 93
Leonard, Murray d1970 WhoHol 92
Leonard, Nelson Jordan 1916- IntWW 93, WhoAm 94, WhoScEn 94
Leonard, Paul Haralson 1925- WhoAm 94
Leonard, Paul Roger 1943- WhoAmP 93
Leonard, Queenie 1905- WhoHol 92
Leonard, R. Michael 1953- WhoAm 94
Leonard, Ray Charles 1956- IntWW 93
Leonard, Raymond Wesley 1909- WhoFI 94
Leonard, Rex Dean 1931- WhoMW 93
Leonard, Richard 1954- ConAu 141
Leonard, Richard D., Jr. 1931- WhoIns 94
Leonard, Richard Graydon 1939- WhoFI 94
Leonard, Richard Hart 1921- WhoAm 94
Leonard, Richard Lawrence 1930- Who 94
Leonard, Richard Manning 1908- WhoAm 94
Leonard, Rita d1981 WhoHol 92
Leonard, Robert d1948 WhoHol 92
Leonard, Robert Dougherty 1942- WhoFI 94, WhoMW 93
Leonard, Robert Sean 1968- WhoHol 92
Leonard, Robert Sean 1969- IntMPA 94, WhoAm 94
Leonard, Robert Warren 1926- WhoAm 94
Leonard, Robert Z. d1968 WhoHol 92
Leonard, Roy Junior 1929- WhoAm 94
Leonard, Samuel Atchison 1947- WhoMW 93
Leonard, Sheldon 1907- IntMPA 94, WhoAm 94, WhoHol 92
Leonard, Stanley Strenger 1931- WhoAm 94
Leonard, Sugar Ray 1956- WhoAm 94
Leonard, Sugar Ray 1957- WhoBlA 94
Leonard, Thomas A. 1946- WhoAmP 93
Leonard, Thomas Allen 1941- WhoScEn 94
Leonard, Thomas Aloysius 1946- WhoAm 94, WhoAmL 94
Leonard, Tim 1940- WhoAmP 93
Leonard, Timothy Dwight 1940- WhoAm 94, WhoAmL 94
Leonard, Tom 1944- WrDr 94
Leonard, Walter Fenner 1907- WhoBlA 94
Leonard, Walter J. 1929- WhoBlA 94
Leonard, Walter Raymond 1923- WhoAm 94
Leonard, Warren Grant 1918- WhoFI 94
Leonard, Will Ernest, Jr. 1935- WhoAm 94
Leonard, William Carson 1934- WhoWest 94
Leonard, William R. 1947- WhoAmP 93
Leonard, William Robert 1935- WhoFI 94
Leonard, Zenas 1809-1857 WhWE
Leonardi, Hector 1930- WhoAmA 93
Leonardi, Susan J. 1946- WrDr 94
Leonardo da Vinci 1452-1519 WorInv [port]
Leonardos, Gregory 1935- WhoScEn 94
Leonardos, Stela 1923- BlmGWL
Leonard-Williams, Harold Guy 1911- Who 94
Leonati, Carlo Ambrogio NewGrDO
Leonberger, Frederick John 1947- WhoAm 94
Leoncavallo, Ruggero 1857-1919 NewGrDO
"Leonce" d1935 WhoHol 92
Leon Dub, Marcelo 1946- WhoScEn 94
Leone, Anthony Joseph, Jr. 1950- WhoMW 93
Leone, Francesco Bartolomeo de NewGrDO
Leone, George Frank 1926- WhoAm 94
Leone, Giovanni 1908- IntWW 93
Leone, Henri d1922 WhoHol 92
Leone, John J. 1946- WhoAmP 93
Leone, Johnny d1986 WhoHol 92
Leone, L. Ruthe 1924- WhoAmP 93
Leone, Lyn 1950- WhoAmP 93
Leone, Lynn DrAPF 93
Leone, Maude d1930 WhoHol 92
Leone, Peter R. 1940- WhoAm 94
Leone, Stephan Robert 1939- WhoAmL 94
Leone, Stephen Robert 1948- WhoAm 94
Leone, William Charles 1924- WhoAm 94, WhoWest 94
Leonelli, Elisa WhoHol 92
Leonett, Anthony Arthur 1929- WhoAm 94
Leonetti, Matthew Frank WhoAm 94
Leonetti, Michael Edward 1955- WhoFI 94, WhoMW 93
Leonetti, Tommy d1979 WhoHol 92
Leoney, Antoinette E. M. 1950- WhoBlA 94
Leong, Al WhoHol 92
Leong, Carol Jean 1942- WhoFI 94, WhoWest 94
Leong, G. Keong 1950- WhoMW 93
Leong, George H. DrAPF 93
Leong, Jack Y. H. 1925- WhoAsA 94
Leong, James B. d1963 WhoHol 92
Leong, Joseph P. 1915- WhoAmP 93
Leong, Kirby Hung-Loy 1945- WhoWest 94
Leong, Mang Su 1960- WhoScEn 94
Leong, Robin Yee 1971- WhoAsA 94
Leong, Russell (C.) 1950- ConAu 142
Leong, Russell C. DrAPF 93
Leong, Russell C. 1950- WhoAsA 94
Leong, Sue 1930- WhoMW 93
Leon Guerrero, Juan Duenas 1935- WhoHisp 94
Leon Guerrero, Wilfred Pacelli 1942- WhoWest 94
Leonhard, Ernest Rudolph 1896- WhAm 10
Leonhard, Kurt Albert Ernst 1910- IntWW 93
Leonhardt, Clifton Andrew 1947- WhoAmP 93
Leonhardt, Frederick Wayne 1949- WhoAm 94, WhoAmL 94
Leonhardt, Kenneth DrAPF 93
Leonhardt, Robert 1877-1923 NewGrDO
Leonhardt, Rudolf Walter 1921- IntWW 93
Leonhardt, Thomas Wilburn 1943- WhoAm 94
Leonhart, William 1919- IntWW 93
Leoni, Franco 1864-1949 NewGrDO
Leoni, Kirk Benson 1954- WhoFI 94
Leoni, Michael 1760?-1796 NewGrDO
Leonid 1896-1976 WhoAmA 93N
Leonidas 1913- WorESoc
Leonidas, I d480BC HisWorL [port]
Leonidov, Leonid d1941 WhoHol 92
Leoning, John d1977 WhoHol 92
Leonis, John Michael 1933- WhoFI 94
Leonor, Queen of Portugal 1458-1525 BlmGWL
Leonov, Aleksey Arkhipovich 1934- IntWW 93
Leonov, Leon Ivanovich c. 1813-1872 NewGrDO
Leonov, Yury Yurevich 1963- LngBDD
Leonova, Dar'ya Mikhaylovna 1829-1896 NewGrDO
Leon Portilla, Miguel 1926- IntWW 93
Leon-Sanz, Miguel 1957- WhoScEn 94
Leonsis, Theodore John 1956- WhoAm 94
Leontie, Roger Eugene 1937- WhoWest 94
Leontief, Estelle DrAPF 93
Leontief, Wassily 1906- AmSocL, IntWW 93, Who 94, WhoAm 94, WhoFI 94
Leontief, Wassily (W.) 1906- WrDr 94
Leontieff, Alexandre 1948- IntWW 93
Leontium fl. 2nd cent.- BlmGWL
Leontovich, Eugenie 1894- WhoHol 92
Leontovich, Eugenie 1900-1993 NewYTBS 93 [port]
Leontovych, Mykola Dmytrovych 1877-1921 NewGrDO
Leontsinis, George John 1937- WhoAmL 94
Leonty, Metropolitan of Kherson 1928- LngBDD
Leonty, Metropolitan of Orenburg 1913- LngBDD
Leopardi, Giacomo EncSF 93
Leopold, I 1640-1705 NewGrDO
Leopold, II 1747-1792 NewGrDO
Leopold, II 1835-1909 HisWorL [port]
Leopold, Aldo 1886-1948 ConAu 141
Leopold, Aldo 1887-1948 EnvEnc [port]
Leopold, Christopher ConAu 142
Leopold, Ethelreda 1917- WhoHol 92
Leopold, Irving H. d1993 NewYTBS 93
Leopold, Joan Silverberg 1947- WhoWest 94
Leopold, Louis Emanuel 1922- WhoAmP 93
Leopold, Luna Bergere 1915- IntWW 93, WhoAm 94, WhoScEn 94, WhoWest 94
Leopold, Lynn Merryl 1961- WhoAmL 94
Leopold, M. Edwin 1934- WhoIns 94
Leopold, Robert Livingston 1922- WhoAm 94
Leopold, Susan 1960- WhoAmA 93
Leopold, Warren Edward 1953- WhoIns 94
Leoro-Franco, Galo Who 94
Leotard, Francois Gerard Marie 1942- IntWW 93, Who 94
Leotard, Philippe 1941- WhoHol 92
Leourier, Christian 1948- EncSF 93
Lepa, Robert Arthur 1958- WhoFI 94
Le Page, Francois 1709-1780? NewGrDO
LePage, Gerald Alvin 1917- WhoWest 94
Le Page, Rand EncSF 93
Lepage, Robert IntWW 93, WhoHol 92
LePage, Wilbur Reed 1911- WhoAm 94, WhoScEn 94
Lepak, David John 1959- WhoAmP 93

LePan, Douglas (Valentine) 1914- *WrDr 94*
Lepape, Harry Leonard 1930- *WhoFI 94, WhoWest 94*
Le Parmentier, Richard *WhoHol 92*
Le Paul, Paul d1958 *WhoHol 92*
Lepawsky, Albert 1908-1992 *WhAm 10*
Lepe d1967 *WhoHol 92*
Lepelstat, Martin L. 1947- *WhoAmL 94*
Le Pen, Jean-Marie 1928- *IntWW 93*
Lepene, Alan R. 1946- *WhoAmL 94*
Le Pensec, Louis 1937- *IntWW 93*
Le Pere, Paul d1965 *WhoHol 92*
Le Person, Paul *WhoHol 92*
Lepeshinskaya, Olga 1916- *IntDcB [port]*
Lepic, Charles 1744?-c. 1806 *IntDcB*
Le Pichon, Xavier 1937- *IntWW 93*
Lepico, Charles 1744?-c. 1806 *IntDcB*
Le Picq, Charles 1744?-c. 1806 *IntDcB, NewGrDO*
L'Epine d1782 *WhAmRev*
L'Epine, (Francesca) Margherita c. 1680-1746 *NewGrDO*
Lepkowski, Francis Joseph 1955- *WhoMW 93*
Lepkowski, Wil 1934- *WhoAm 94*
Lepley, John R. 1950- *WhoIns 94*
Lepley, William *WhoAm 94*
Le Poer, Baron 1987- *Who 94*
Le Poer Trench *Who 94*
Le Poer Trench, Brinsley *Who 94*
Lepore, Albert Ralph 1920-1989 *WhAm 10*
Lepore, Amato V. 1918- *WhoAmP 93*
Lepore, Dominick *DrAPF 93*
Lepore, Michael Joseph 1910- *WhoAm 94*
Lepore, Ralph Thomas, III 1954- *WhoAmL 94*
Le Pore, Richard *WhoHol 92*
Leporiere, Ralph Dennis 1932- *WhoWest 94*
Le Pors, Anicet 1931- *IntWW 93*
Le Portz, Yves 1920- *IntWW 93, Who 94*
Le Poulain, Jean d1988 *WhoHol 92*
Lepovitz, Helena Waddy 1945- *WrDr 94*
Lepow, Leslie Hugh 1949- *WhoAmL 94*
Lepp, Tara Marie 1958- *WhoWest 94*
Leppanen, Urpo Olavi 1944- *IntWW 93*
Leppard, Keith Andre 1924- *Who 94*
Leppard, Raymond (John) 1927- *NewGrDO*
Leppard, Raymond John 1927- *IntWW 93, Who 94, WhoAm 94, WhoMW 93*
Lepper, Mark Roger 1944- *WhoAm 94, WhoWest 94*
Leppert, Charles, Jr. 1932- *WhoAmP 93*
Leppert, Richard David 1943- *WhoAm 94*
Leppik, Margaret White 1943- *WhoAmP 93*
Lepping, George (Geria Dennis) 1947- *Who 94*
Leppla, David Charles 1953- *WhoScEn 94*
Leprette, Jacques 1920- *IntWW 93*
Le Prince, Gabriella d1953 *WhoAmA 93N*
Le Prince de Beaumont, Marie *BlmGWL*
Leprince-Ringuet, Louis 1901- *IntWW 93*
Leprohon, Rosanna 1832-1879 *BlmGWL*
Leps, Thomas MacMaster 1914- *WhoAm 94*
Lepschy, Giulio Ciro 1935- *Who 94*
L'Epy, Heliogenes de fl. 17th cent.- *EncSF 93*
Lequesne, Bruno Patrice Bernard 1956- *WhoMW 93*
Le Quesne, (John) Godfray 1924- *IntWW 93, Who 94*
LeQuesne, James Richard 1957- *WhoWest 94*
Le Quesne, Leslie Philip 1919- *Who 94*
Le Quesne, Martin *IntWW 93, Who 94*
Le Quesne, (Charles) Martin 1917- *IntWW 93, Who 94*
Le Quesne, Philip William 1939- *WhoAm 94*
Le Queux, William (Tufnell) 1864-1927 *EncSF 93*
Le Queux, William Tufnell 1864-1927 *DcNaB MP*
Leraaen, Allen Keith 1951- *WhoFI 94, WhoWest 94*
Lerach, William S. *NewYTBS 93 [port]*
Lerach, William S. 1946- *WhoAmL 94*
Lerangis, Peter *EncSF 93*
Leray, Jean 1906- *IntWW 93*
Lerch, Jerome N. 1944- *WhoAmL 94*
Lerch, John Albert 1950- *WhoAm 94*
Lerch, Keith Walter 1946- *WhoAmL 94*
Lerch, Kimberly Ann 1960- *WhoFI 94, WhoMW 93*
Lerch, Richard Heaphy 1924- *WhoAm 94*
Lerch, Sharon *DrAPF 93*
Lerche, Peter Fritz Franz 1928- *IntWW 93*
Lerda, Patti Collins 1960- *WhoAmL 94*
Lere, Mark Allen 1950- *WhoAmA 93*
Lerer, Neal M. 1954- *WhoAmL 94*
Lerer, Robert Jan 1946- *WhoMW 93*
Lerer, Seth 1955- *WrDr 94*
Lerescu, Emil 1921- *NewGrDO*
Lerew, Parker David 1948- *WhoAmP 93*
Le Riche, William Harding 1916- *WrDr 94*
Leritz, Lawrence 1952- *WhoAm 94*
Le Riverend, Julio 1916- *IntWW 93*
Le Riverend, Pablo 1907- *WhoHisp 94N*
Lerksamran, Lalita *WhoWomW 91*
Lerman, Cary B. 1948- *WhoAmL 94*
Lerman, Doris (Harriet) *WhoAmA 93*
Lerman, Eileen R. 1947- *WhoAmL 94, WhoWest 94*
Lerman, Eleanor *DrAPF 93*
Lerman, Gerald Steven 1951- *WhoFI 94, WhoScEn 94*
Lerman, Israel Cesar 1940- *WhoScEn 94*
Lerman, Jeanette Paula 1948- *WhoAm 94*
Lerman, Jeffrey R. 1945- *WhoAmL 94*
Lerman, Kenneth Barry 1947- *WhoFI 94*
Lerman, Leo 1914- *WhoAmA 93*
Lerman, Leonard Solomon 1925- *WhoAm 94*
Lerman, Ora 1938- *WhoAmA 93*
Lerman, Rhoda *DrAPF 93*
Lerman, Rhoda 1936- *WrDr 94*
Lerman, Steven A. 1948- *NewYTBS 93 [port]*
Lermontov, Mikhail Yurevich 1814-1841 *IntDcT 2*
Lermontov, Mikhail Yur'yevich 1814-1841 *NewGrDO*
Lerner, Abe 1908- *WhoAmA 93*
Lerner, Abram 1913- *WhoAm 94, WhoAmA 93*
Lerner, Alan Burton 1930- *WhoAm 94, WhoFI 94*
Lerner, Alexander Robert 1946- *WhoFI 94*
Lerner, Alexandria Sandra *WhoAmA 93*
Lerner, Alfred 1933- *WhoAm 94, WhoFI 94*
Lerner, Andrea 1954- *WrDr 94*
Lerner, Armand 1932- *WhoScEn 94*
Lerner, Arnold Stanley 1930- *WhoAm 94*
Lerner, Arthur *DrAPF 93*
Lerner, Frederic Howard 1957- *WhoFI 94*
Lerner, Harriet Goldhor *WhoAm 94*
Lerner, Harry 1939- *WhoAm 94, WhoAmL 94*
Lerner, Harry Jonas 1932- *WhoAm 94*
Lerner, Henry Hyam 1940- *WhoScEn 94*
Lerner, Herbert J. 1938- *WhoAm 94, WhoFI 94*
Lerner, Ina Roslyn 1938- *WhoAm 94*
Lerner, Irving d1976 *WhoHol 92*
Lerner, Irwin *WhoFI 94*
Lerner, James Peter 1956- *WhoScEn 94*
Lerner, Jane H. 1947- *WhoAmL 94*
Lerner, Jonathan J. 1948- *WhoAmL 94*
Lerner, Joseph *IntMPA 94*
Lerner, Joseph 1942- *WhoScEn 94*
Lerner, Laurence (David) 1925- *WrDr 94*
Lerner, Linda *DrAPF 93*
Lerner, Loren Ruth 1948- *WhoAmA 93*
Lerner, Marilyn 1942- *WhoAmA 93*
Lerner, Marshall L. 1947- *WhoAmL 94*
Lerner, Martin 1936- *ConAu 141, WhoAm 94, WhoAmA 93*
Lerner, Max d1992 *IntWW 93N*
Lerner, Max 1902-1992 *AnObit 1992, WhAm 10, WrDr 94N*
Lerner, Max Kasner 1916- *WhoAmL 94*
Lerner, Michael *NewYTBS 93 [port]*
Lerner, Michael 1941?- *ConTFT 11, IntMPA 94*
Lerner, Michael 1943- *News 94-2 [port], WhoHol 92*
Lerner, Michael Albers 1943- *WhoAm 94*
Lerner, Nathan Bernard 1913- *WhoAm 94, WhoAmA 93*
Lerner, Peter M. *WhoAmP 93*
Lerner, Preston 1956- *WhoWest 94*
Lerner, Ralph 1949- *WhoAm 94*
Lerner, Ralph E. 1943- *WhoAm 94, WhoAmL 94*
Lerner, Richard Alan 1938- *WhoScEn 94*
Lerner, Richard J. 1929-1982 *WhoAmA 93N*
Lerner, Robert E(arl) 1940- *WrDr 94*
Lerner, Samuel d1993 *NewYTBS 93*
Lerner, Sandra *WhoAm 94, WhoAmA 93*
Lerner, Sandy R. 1918- *WhoAmA 93*
Lerner, Sandy Richard *WhoAm 94*
Lerner, Sheldon 1939- *WhoScEn 94, WhoWest 94*
Lerner, Stephen Alexander 1938- *WhoAm 94, WhoMW 93*
Lerner, Stuart L. 1930- *WhoIns 94*
Lerner, Warren 1929- *WhoAm 94*
Le Rochois, Marie c. 1658-1728 *NewGrDO*
Le Roux, Carmen d1942 *WhoHol 92*
LeRoux, David Bain 1951- *WhoIns 94*
Leroux, Gaston 1868-1927 *EncSF 93*
Leroux, Maxime *WhoHol 92*
Leroux, Xavier (Henry Napoleon) 1863-1919 *NewGrDO*
Le Roy, Bruce Murdock 1920- *WhoAm 94*
Leroy, Claude 1947- *WhoAm 94, WhoScEn 94*
Leroy, David Henry 1947- *WhoAm 94, WhoAmL 94, WhoAmP 93, WhoWest 94*
Le Roy, Eddie *WhoHol 92*
LeRoy, Edward Carwile 1933- *WhoAm 94, WhoScEn 94*
LeRoy, G. Palmer 1929- *WhoAm 94*
LeRoy, Gen *WrDr 94*
Le Roy, Gloria *WhoHol 92*
Le Roy, Hal d1985 *WhoHol 92*
Le Roy, Harold M. 1905- *WhoAmA 93N*
Leroy, Hugh Alexander 1939- *WhoAmA 93*
Le Roy, Ken 1927- *WhoHol 92*
Le Roy, L. David 1920- *WhoAm 94*
Leroy, Louis 1941- *WhoAmA 93*
Le Roy, Mervyn d1987 *WhoHol 92*
Leroy, Philippe 1930- *WhoHol 92*
Leroy, Pierre Elie 1948- *WhoAm 94, WhoFI 94*
Le Roy, Victor d1920 *WhoHol 92*
Leroy-Beaulieu, Philippine *WhoHol 92*
Le Roy Ladurie, Emmanuel 1929- *IntWW 93*
Le Roy Ladurie, Emmanuel Bernard 1929- *Who 94*
LeRoy-Lewis, David Henry 1918- *Who 94*
Lerrigo, Edith Mary 1910-1989 *WhAm 10*
Lerssen, Mary Kay 1946- *WhoMW 93*
Lerteth, Oben *EncSF 93*
Lerud, Joanne Van Ornum 1949- *WhoAm 94*
Lerud-Chubb, DiAnne Kay 1942- *WhoMW 93*
Lerude, Warren Leslie 1937- *WhoWest 94*
Lervik, Ase Hiorth 1933- *IntWW 93*
Le Sache, Bernadette *WhoHol 92*
Lesage, Alain-Rene 1668-1747 *GuFrLit 2, IntDcT 2*
Le Sage, Bernard E. 1949- *WhoAmL 94*
LeSage, Carolyn Lee Bailey 1936- *WhoMW 93*
LeSage, Janet Billings 1947- *WhoMW 93*
Le Sage, William Alexander 1949- *WhoAm 94*
Le Saint, Edward d1940 *WhoHol 92*
Le Saint, Stella Razetto d1948 *WhoHol 92*
Lesar, Hiram Henry 1912- *WhoAm 94, WhoAmL 94*
LeSatz, Stephen, Jr. 1937- *WhoAmL 94*
Lescano, Javier A. 1935- *WhoHisp 94*
Lescaze, Lee Adrien 1938- *WhoAm 94*
Lescaze, William 1896- *WhAm 10*
Lesch, Alma Wallace 1917- *WhoAmA 93*
Lesch, Barry M. 1945- *WhoAmL 94*
Lesch, George Henry 1909- *WhoAm 94*
Lesch, John E(mmett) 1945- *WrDr 94*
Lesch, Michael 1939- *WhoAm 94*
Lesch, Michael Oscar 1938- *WhoAm 94*
Leschetizky, Theodor 1830-1915 *NewGrDO*
Lescoe, John J. *WhoAmP 93*
Lescot, C. Francois c. 1720-c. 1801 *NewGrDO*
Lescoulie, Jack d1987 *WhoHol 92*
Lescovitz, Victor John 1953- *WhoAmP 93*
Lescroart, John T. 1948- *WrDr 94*
Lese, Elliot Richard 1934- *WhoFI 94*
Leseman, Robert G. 1940- *WhoIns 94*
Le Senechal de Kerkado, Mlle. *NewGrDO*
Leser, Bernard H. *WhoAm 94*
Leser, Lawrence A. 1935- *WhoFI 94*
Lesesne, Joab Mauldin, Jr. 1937- *WhoAm 94*
Lesesne, Robert Harleston 1963- *WhoAmL 94*
Lesewski, Arlene J. 1936- *WhoAmP 93*
Lesh, James Richard 1944- *WhoScEn 94*
Lesh, Philip Chapman 1940- *WhoAm 94*
Lesh, Richard D. 1927- *WhoAmA 93*
LeShan, Eda J 1922- *WrDr 94*
Le Shana, David Charles 1932- *WhoAm 94*
Lesher, Dean d1993 *NewYTBS 93 [port]*
Lesher, Dean Stanley 1902- *WhoAm 94*
Lesher, Donald Miles 1915- *WhoAm 94*
Lesher, John Lee, Jr. 1934- *WhoAm 94, WhoFI 94*
Lesher, Marie Palmisano 1919- *WhoAmA 93*
Lesher, Richard Lee 1933- *WhoAm 94, WhoFI 94*
Lesher, Robert Overton 1921- *WhoAm 94*
Lesher, William Richard 1924- *WhoAm 94*
Leshikar, Steven William 1963- *WhoFI 94*
Leshko, Brian Joseph 1962- *WhoScEn 94*
Leshnower, Alan Lee 1938- *WhoScEn 94*
Leshoai, Benjamin Letholoa 1920- *BlkWr 2*
Leshy, John 1913- *WhoAmP 93*
Leshy, John D. 1944- *WhoAm 94, WhoAmL 94*
Leshyk, Tonie 1950- *WhoAmA 93*
Lesiak, Lucille Ann 1946- *WhoMW 93*
Lesiak, Michael Donald 1957- *WhoMW 93*
LeSieg, Theo. *SmATA 75*
Le Sieg, Theo 1904-1991 *WrDr 94N*
Lesikar, James Daniel, II 1954- *WhoScEn 94*
Lesikar, Raymond Vincent 1922- *WhoAm 94, WrDr 94*
Lesiter, Malcolm Leslie 1937- *Who 94*
Lesjak, Lisa Mary 1963- *WhoMW 93*
Leskien, Hermann 1939- *IntWW 93*
Leskinen, Steve Peter 1953- *WhoAmL 94*
Lesko, Diane *WhoAmA 93*
Lesko, Harry Joseph 1920- *WhoAm 94*
Lesko, John Nicholas, Jr. 1957- *WhoScEn 94*
Lesko, Leonard Henry 1938- *WhoAm 94*
Lesko, Ronald Michael 1948- *WhoWest 94*
Lesko, Wendy 1950- *WrDr 94*
Leskow, Olive 1919- *WhoMW 93*
Lesley, Carole d1974 *WhoHol 92*
Lesley, Lorna *WhoHol 92*
Lesley, Serena Sinclair 1926- *WhoWest 94*
Leslie *Who 94*
Leslie, Lord 1958- *Who 94*
Leslie, Alan *Who 94*
Leslie, (Colin) Alan (Bettridge) 1922- *Who 94*
Leslie, Aleen 1908- *IntMPA 94*
Leslie, Alexander 1731-1794 *AmRev*
Leslie, Alexander c. 1740-1794 *WhAmRev*
Leslie, Ann Elizabeth Mary *Who 94*
Leslie, Arthur d1970 *WhoHol 92*
Leslie, Bethel 1927- *WhoHol 92*
Leslie, Bob d1991 *WhoHol 92*
Leslie, Charlotte Lesley 1949- *WhoMW 93*
Leslie, David Clement d1993 *Who 94N*
Leslie, Desmond 1921- *WrDr 94*
Leslie, Desmond (Peter Arthur) 1921- *EncSF 93*
Leslie, Donald Wilmot 1942- *WhoAm 94*
Leslie, Edith d1973 *WhoHol 92*
Leslie, Elinor d1929 *WhoHol 92*
Leslie, Fred d1945 *WhoHol 92*
Leslie, Gene d1953 *WhoHol 92*
Leslie, Gerrie Allen 1941- *WhoAm 94*
Leslie, Gilbert Frank 1909- *Who 94*
Leslie, Gladys d1976 *WhoHol 92*
Leslie, Gordon A. 1946- *WhoIns 94*
Leslie, Henry Arthur 1921- *WhoAm 94, WhoFI 94*
Leslie, Henry David 1822-1896 *DcNaB MP*
Leslie, J. Hubert d1953 *WhoHol 92*
Leslie, Jack d1945 *WhoHol 92*
Leslie, Jacques Robert, Jr. 1947- *WhoAm 94*
Leslie, James Bolton 1922- *Who 94*
Leslie, James Hill 1930- *WhoFI 94*
Leslie, Joan 1925- *IntMPA 94, WhoHol 92*
Leslie, John 1923- *WhoAmA 93*
Leslie, John (Norman Ide) 1916- *Who 94*
Leslie, John Ethelbert 1910-1991 *WhAm 10*
Leslie, John Hampton 1914- *WhoAm 94*
Leslie, John Walter 1929- *WhoAm 94*
Leslie, John Webster, Jr. 1954- *WhoAm 94*
Leslie, John William 1923- *WhoAm 94, WhoFI 94*
Leslie, Kenneth *Who 94*
Leslie, (Ernest) Kenneth 1911- *Who 94*
Leslie, Larry Lee 1938- *WhoWest 94*
Leslie, Larry M. 1949- *WhoAmP 93*
Leslie, Lily d1940 *WhoHol 92*
Leslie, Linda Brown 1949- *WhoFI 94*
Leslie, Marcia Louise 1952- *WhoBlA 94*
Leslie, Marlene Marie *WhoWest 94*
Leslie, Maxine *WhoHol 92*
Leslie, Nan *WhoHol 92*
Leslie, Noel d1974 *WhoHol 92*
Leslie, O.H. *EncSF 93*
Leslie, O. L. 1927- *WrDr 94*
Leslie, Peter 1922- *EncSF 93*
Leslie, Peter (Evelyn) 1931- *Who 94*
Leslie, Peter Evelyn 1931- *IntWW 93*
Leslie, Richard *ConAu 42NR*
Leslie, Robert Anthony 1942- *IntWW 93*
Leslie, Robert B. 1939- *WhoAmP 93*
Leslie, Robert Fremont 1952- *WhoScEn 94*
Leslie, Robert Lorne 1947- *WhoAmL 94, WhoWest 94*
Leslie, Rochelle *DrAPF 93*
Leslie, Seaver 1946- *WhoAmA 93*
Leslie, Seymour Marvin 1922- *WhoAm 94*
Leslie, Stephen Windsor 1947- *Who 94*
Leslie, Sylvia 1900- *WhoHol 92*
Leslie, Theodore *Who 94*
Leslie, (Percy) Theodore 1915- *Who 94*
Leslie, Tim 1942- *WhoAmP 93, WhoWest 94*
Leslie, Ward S. 1926- *WrDr 94*
Leslie, William 1924- *WhoHol 92*
Leslie, William, Jr. 1918-1990 *WhAm 10*

Leslie, William Cairns 1920- *WhoAm 94*
Leslie, William Houghton 1932- *WhoAm 94*
Leslie Melville *Who 94*
Lesly, Philip 1918- *WhoAm 94, WhoFI 94, WrDr 94*
Lesman, Michael Steven 1953- *WhoAmL 94*
Lesnevich, Gus d1964 *WhoHol 92*
Lesniak, Raymond J. 1946- *WhoAmP 93*
Lesnick, Stephen William 1931- *WhoAmA 93*
Lesok, Eddie Monroe 1948- *WhoFI 94*
Lesonsky, Rieva 1952- *WhoAm 94*
Lesotho, King of *IntWW 93*
LeSourd, Leonard (E.) 1919- *WrDr 94*
LeSourd, Nancy Susan Oliver 1953- *WhoAmL 94*
Lesourne, Jacques 1928- *ConAu 142*
Lesourne, Jacques Francois 1928- *IntWW 93, Who 94*
Lesowitz, Mikki Lynn 1962- *WhoWest 94*
Lespinasse, Julie-Jeanne-Eleonore de 1732-1776 *BlmGWL*
Le Squyer, Scipio 1579-1659 *DcNaB MP*
Lessard, Charles Stephen 1936- *WhoHisp 94*
Lessard, Claude 1949- *IntWW 93*
Lessard, Michel M. 1939- *WhoAm 94*
Lessard, Raymond W. 1930- *WhoAm 94*
Lessard, Robert Bernard 1931- *WhoAmP 93*
Lessard, Roger A. 1944- *WhoScEn 94*
Lessard, Rudy 1944- *WhoAmP 93*
Lessel, John C. 1948- *WhoAmL 94*
Lessel, Wincenty Ferdynand c. 1750-c. 1825 *NewGrDO*
Lessels, Norman 1938- *IntWW 93, Who 94*
Lessen, Larry Lee 1939- *WhoAm 94, WhoAmL 94*
Lessen, Martin 1920- *WhoAm 94*
Lessenco, Gilbert Barry 1929- *WhoAm 94*
Lesseps, Jean-Baptiste-Barthelemy, Baron De 1766-1834 *WhWE*
Lesseps, Tauni De 1920- *WhoAmA 93*
Lesser, Bruce R. 1947- *WhoAmL 94*
Lesser, Derwin *EncSF 93*
Lesser, Edward Arnold 1934- *WhoAm 94, WhoFI 94*
Lesser, Eugene *DrAPF 93*
Lesser, Frederick Alan 1934- *WhoWest 94*
Lesser, Harvey Lloyd 1951- *WhoWest 94*
Lesser, Henry 1947- *WhoAmL 94*
Lesser, Joan L. *WhoAm 94, WhoAmL 94*
Lesser, Joseph M. 1928- *WhoAm 94*
Lesser, Laurence 1938- *WhoAm 94*
Lesser, Lawrence J. 1939- *WhoAm 94, WhoFI 94*
Lesser, Len *WhoHol 92*
Lesser, Margo Rogers 1950- *WhoAmL 94*
Lesser, Milton 1928- *EncSF 93, WrDr 94*
Lesser, Rika *DrAPF 93*
Lesser, Robert *WhoHol 92*
Lesser, Ronald Peter 1946- *WhoScEn 94*
Lesser, Seth Richard 1960- *WhoAmL 94*
Lesser, Sidney Lewis 1912- *Who 94*
Lesser, Wendy 1952- *ConAu 140, WhoAm 94, WhoWest 94*
Lesser, William Melville 1927- *WhoAmL 94*
Lesses, Maurice Falcon 1932- *WhoAm 94*
Lessey, George d1947 *WhoHol 92*
Lessick, Mira Lee 1949- *WhoMW 93*
Lessig, John d1958 *WhoHol 92*
Lessin, Andrew Richard 1942- *WhoAm 94*
Lessin, Lawrence Stephen 1937- *WhoAm 94*
Lessing, Charlotte *Who 94*
Lessing, Doris *DrAPF 93*
Lessing, Doris 1919- *BlmGEL, BlmGWL, DcLB 139 [port], EncSF 93, RfGShF, WhoAm 94*
Lessing, Doris (May) 1919- *ConDr 93, Who 94, WrDr 94*
Lessing, Doris May 1919- *IntWW 93*
Lessing, Gotthold Ephraim 1729-1781 *IntDcT 2 [port]*
Lessis, Gary Paul 1960- *WhoWest 94*
Lessiter, Frank Donald 1939- *WhoAm 94*
Lessiter, Mike (J.) 1969- *WrDr 94*
Lessler, Richard Sigmund 1924- *WhoAm 94*
Lesslie, Colin d1974 *WhoHol 92*
Lessman, Harry *WhoHol 92*
Lessman, Robert Edward 1947- *WhoAmL 94*
Lessner, Erwin (Christian) 1898-1959 *EncSF 93*
Lessof, Maurice Hart 1924- *Who 94*
Lesson, Rene-Primevere 1794-1849 *WhWE*
Lessore, Helen 1907- *Who 94*
Lessy, Ben *WhoHol 92*
Lessy, Roy Paul, Jr. 1944- *WhoAm 94, WhoAmL 94*
Lestage, Daniel Barfield 1939- *WhoAm 94*
Lester *Who 94*
Lester, Andrew *EncSF 93*
Lester, Andrew William 1956- *WhoAm 94, WhoAmL 94*
Lester, Anthony Paul 1936- *IntWW 93*
Lester, Barnett Benjamin 1912- *WhoAm 94*
Lester, Betty J. 1945- *WhoBlA 94*
Lester, Bruce 1912- *WhoHol 92*
Lester, Buddy *WhoHol 92*
Lester, Charles Turner, Jr. 1942- *WhoAm 94*
Lester, Charles Willard 1892- *WhAm 10*
Lester, David 1942- *WrDr 94*
Lester, Donald 1944- *WhoBlA 94*
Lester, Edward 1831-1905 *EncSF 93*
Lester, Elton J. 1944- *WhoBlA 94*
Lester, G(odfrey) A(llen) 1943- *WrDr 94*
Lester, Garner McConnico 1897- *WhAm 10*
Lester, Henry Bernard 1956- *WhoWest 94*
Lester, Irvin *EncSF 93*
Lester, Jacqueline 1949- *WhoBlA 94*
Lester, James Dudley 1935- *WhoAm 94*
Lester, James George 1897- *WhAm 10*
Lester, James Luther 1932- *WhoAmP 93*
Lester, James Theodore 1932- *Who 94*
Lester, Jeff *WhoHol 92*
Lester, Jerry 1910- *WhoCom*
Lester, Jerry 1911- *WhoHol 92*
Lester, John Clayton 1940- *WhoWest 94*
Lester, John James Nathaniel, II 1952- *WhoWest 94*
Lester, Julius 1939- *Au&Arts 12 [port], WhoBlA 94, WrDr 94*
Lester, Julius (Bernard) 1939- *BlkWr 2, ConAu 43NR, SmATA 74 [port], TwCYAW*
Lester, Julius B. 1939- *WhoAm 94*
Lester, Kalman J. 1929- *WhoFI 94*
Lester, Kate d1924 *WhoHol 92*
Lester, Keith 1904- *IntDcB*
Lester, Ketty 1934- *WhoHol 92*
Lester, Louise d1952 *WhoHol 92*
Lester, Malcolm 1924- *WhoAm 94*
Lester, Mark 1876- *WhoHol 92*
Lester, Mark 1934- *WrDr 94*
Lester, Mark 1958- *IntMPA 94, WhoHol 92*
Lester, Mark Leslie 1946- *IntMPA 94*
Lester, Michelle 1942- *WhoAmA 93*
Lester, Nina Mack *WhoBlA 94*
Lester, R. C. 1922- *WhoAmP 93*
Lester, Richard 1932- *IntMPA 94, IntWW 93, Who 94, WhoAm 94*
Lester, Richard Allen 1908- *WhoAm 94*
Lester, Richard Garrison 1925- *WhoAm 94*
Lester, Robert Carlton 1933- *WhoAm 94*
Lester, Robin Dale 1939- *WhoMW 93*
Lester, Roy David 1949- *WhoAmL 94*
Lester, Tom 1938- *WhoHol 92*
Lester, Virginia Laudano 1931- *WhoAm 94*
Lester, William *WhoHol 92*
Lester, William Alexander, Jr. 1937- *WhoAm 94, WhoBlA 94*
Lester, William L. G. 1943- *WhoAm 94*
Lester Of Herne Hill, Baron 1936- *Who 94*
Lester Smith, Ernest *Who 94*
Lestocq, Humphrey d1984 *WhoHol 92*
Leston, Patrick John 1948- *WhoAm 94, WhoAmL 94*
Lestor, Joan *Who 94*
Lestor, Joan 1931- *WhoWomW 91*
L'Estrange, Anna *WrDr 94*
Le Strange, Dick d1963 *WhoHol 92*
L'Estrange, Julian d1918 *WhoHol 92*
L'Estrange, Miles fl. 19th cent.- *EncSF 93*
Le Strange, Norme d1936 *WhoHol 92*
Lestz, Earl 1938- *IntMPA 94*
Le Suer, Meridel 1900- *WrDr 94*
Lesueur, Charles-Alexandre 1778-1857 *WhWE*
Lesueur, Daniel *BlmGWL*
Le Sueur, Hal d1963 *WhoHol 92*
Le Sueur, Jean-Francois 1760-1837 *NewGrDO*
LeSueur, Meridel 1900- *BlmGWL*
Le Sueur, Pierre-Charles c. 1657-c. 1705 *WhWE*
LeSueur, Stephen C. 1952- *WrDr 94*
LeSueur, Susan M. 1952- *WhoAmP 93*
Lesur, Daniel *NewGrDO*
Leta, David E. 1951- *WhoAmL 94*
L'Etang, Hugh Joseph Charles James 1917- *Who 94*
L'Etang, Leo Lawrence 1965- *WhoFI 94*
Letarte, Richard Homer 1943- *WhoFI 94*
Letaw, Harry, Jr. 1926- *WhoFI 94*
Letchford, Stanley 1924- *WrDr 94*
Letellier, Roy *WhoAmP 93*
Letendre, Rita 1928- *WhoAmA 93*
Leterrier, Eugene 1843-1884 *NewGrDO*
Leterrier, Francois 1929- *WhoHol 92*
Letessier, Dorothee 1953- *BlmGWL*
Letey, John Joseph, Jr. 1933- *WhoAm 94*
Lethbridge, Francis Donald 1920- *WhoAm 94*
Lethbridge, Robert (David) 1947- *WrDr 94*
Lethbridge, Thomas (Periam Hector Noel) 1950- *Who 94*
Lethin, Lori *WhoHol 92*
Letiche, John Marion 1918- *WhoAm 94*
Letko, Ken *DrAPF 93*
Letley, Emma 1949- *WrDr 94*
Letnanova, Elena 1942- *ConAu 140*
Leto, Sam S., Jr. 1938- *WhoHisp 94*
Le Tocq, Eric George 1918- *Who 94*
Letokhov, Vladilen Stepanovich 1939- *IntWW 93, WhoScEn 94*
Letondal, Henri d1955 *WhoHol 92*
Letourneau, Anne *WhoHol 92*
LeTourneau, Duane John 1926- *WhoAm 94*
Letourneau, Jean-Paul 1930- *WhoAm 94*
LeTourneau, Richard Howard 1925- *WhoAm 94*
Letowska, Ewa Anna 1940- *IntWW 93*
Letowski, Tomasz Rajmund 1942- *WhoScEn 94*
Letsie, Joshua Sekhobe 1947- *IntWW 93*
Letsie, Thaabe 1940- *IntWW 93*
Letsinger, Robert Lewis 1921- *WhoAm 94, WhoMW 93, WhoScEn 94*
Letson, Michael Lee 1942- *WhoWest 94*
Letson, S. R. 1940- *WhoAmP 93*
Letsou, George Vasilios 1958- *WhoScEn 94*
Lett, Cynthia Ellen Wein 1957- *WhoFI 94*
Lett, Gerald William 1926- *WhoBlA 94*
Lett, John David 1952- *WhoAmL 94*
Lett, Mack Edward 1929- *WhoAmP 93*
Lett, Philip Wood, Jr. 1922- *WhoAm 94, WhoMW 93*
Lett, Phillip David 1952- *WhoWest 94*
Lett, Raymond D. 1934- *WhoAmP 93*
Lett, Sherri J. 1949- *WhoMW 93*
Lett, Thomas Patrick 1948- *WhoFI 94*
Lett, Winston Tatum 1947- *WhoAmP 93*
Letta, Vin Sini' d1921 *WhoHol 92*
Lettch, Raymond d1946 *WhoHol 92*
Lette, Kathy 1958- *WrDr 94*
Letteer, Ray Allen 1954- *WhoMW 93*
Lettenstrom, Dean Roger 1941- *WhoAmA 93*
Letter, Louis N. 1937- *IntMPA 94*
Letterman, David 1947- *IntMPA 94, IntWW 93, WhoAm 94, WhoCom [port]*
Letterman, Ernest Eugene 1950- *WhoFI 94*
Letterman, Ira Spencer 1915- *WhoAmP 93*
Lettes, Arthur Eli 1928- *WhoFI 94*
Lettieri, Al d1975 *WhoHol 92*
Lettieri, Richard Joseph 1947- *WhoAm 94, WhoAmL 94*
Lettinger, Rudolf d1937 *WhoHol 92*
Letton, Alva Hamblin 1916- *WhoAm 94*
Lettow, Charles Frederick 1941- *WhoAm 94, WhoAmL 94, WhoFI 94*
Letts, Anthony Ashworth 1935- *Who 94*
Letts, Charles Trevor 1905- *Who 94*
Letts, J. Spencer 1934- *WhoAm 94, WhoAmL 94, WhoWest 94*
Letts, Lindsay Gordon 1948- *WhoScEn 94*
Letts, Melinda Jane Frances 1956- *Who 94*
Letts, Pauline 1917- *WhoHol 92*
Lettvin, Theodore 1926- *WhoAm 94*
Letuli, Olo *WhoAmP 93*
Letuli, Olo Uluao Misilagi 1919- *WhoAm 94*
Letumu, Talauega F. *WhoAmP 93*
Letwin, Jeffrey William 1953- *WhoAmL 94*
Letwin, Leon 1929- *WhoAm 94*
Letwin, Shirley Robin 1924-1993 *ConAu 141*
Letwin, William 1922- *Who 94*
Letz, George *WhoHol 92*
Letzring, Tracy John 1962- *WhoScEn 94*
Leu, Dennis Thomas 1953- *WhoAsA 94*
Leu, Donald A., Jr. 1951- *WhoAmP 93*
Leu, Ming C. 1951- *WhoAsA 94*
Leu, Rong-Jin 1956- *WhoAsA 94*
Leubas, Louis d1932 *WhoHol 92*
Leube, Kurt Rudolph 1943- *WhoWest 94*
Leubert, Alfred Otto Paul 1922- *WhoAm 94, WhoFI 94*
Leubsdorf, Carl Philipp 1938- *WhoAm 94, WhoFI 94*
Leuchars, Peter Raymond 1921- *Who 94*
Leuchars, William Douglas d1991 *Who 94N*
Leuchtmann, Mark R. 1946- *WhoAmL 94*
Leuci, Mary Simon 1955- *WhoMW 93*
Leucippus *WorScD*
Leuck, Claire M. *WhoAmP 93*
Leuckert, Jean Elizabeth *Who 94*
Leudesdorff, Ernst d1954 *WhoHol 92*
Leukart, Barbara J. 1948- *WhoAmL 94*
Leukart, Richard Henry, II 1942- *WhoAm 94, WhoAmL 94*
Leumann, Hans Erminio 1928- *WhoFI 94*
Leung, Benjamin Shuet-Kin 1938- *WhoAsA 94*
Leung, Charles Cheung-Wan 1946- *WhoAsA 94, WhoScEn 94, WhoWest 94*
Leung, Chi Kin 1958- *WhoAsA 94*
Leung, Christopher Chung-Kit 1939- *WhoAsA 94*
Leung, Chung-Ngoc 1956- *WhoAsA 94*
Leung, Dennis B. 1945- *WhoAsA 94*
Leung, Edwin Pak-Wah 1950- *WhoAsA 94*
Leung, Firman 1957- *WhoFI 94*
Leung, Frankie Fook-Lun 1949- *WhoAm 94*
Leung, Ida M. 1951- *WhoAsA 94*
Leung, Joseph Y. 1950- *WhoMW 93*
Leung, Joseph Yuk-Tong 1950- *WhoAsA 94*
Leung, Ka-Wing 1952- *WhoAsA 94*
Leung, Kai-Cheong 1936- *WhoAsA 94*
Leung, Kam-Ching 1935- *WhoMW 93*
Leung, Kam H. 1951- *WhoScEn 94*
Leung, Kason Kai Ching 1962- *WhoWest 94*
Leung, Kenneth Ch'uan-k'ai 1944- *WhoAsA 94*
Leung, Kok Ming 1951- *WhoAsA 94*
Leung, Louis W. 1954- *WhoAsA 94*
Leung, Margaret W. 1964- *WhoAsA 94*
Leung, Pak Sang 1935- *WhoAsA 94*
Leung, Peter 1955- *WhoAsA 94*
Leung, PingSun 1952- *WhoAsA 94*
Leung, Pui-Tak 1953- *WhoAsA 94*
Leung, Som-Lok 1965- *WhoAsA 94*
Leung, Ted Tit-Hung 1941- *WhoAm 94*
Leung, Wai-Tung 1946- *WhoWomW 91*
Leung, Wing Hai 1937- *WhoAsA 94*
Leung, Woon-Fong 1954- *WhoAsA 94, WhoScEn 94*
Leung, Yuen-Sang 1949- *WhoAsA 94*
Leupena, Tupua 1922- *Who 94*
Leusch, Mark Steven 1961- *WhoScEn 94*
Leuschen, James Walter 1940- *WhoMW 93*
Leuschen, Mary Patricia 1943- *WhoMW 93*
Leushkin, Sergei Gennadevich 1950- *LngBDD*
Leus McFarlen, Patricia Cheryl 1954- *WhoScEn 94, WhoWest 94*
Leussing, Joanne Gilbert 1932- *WhoMW 93*
Leussink, Hans 1912- *IntWW 93*
Leutenegger, Gertrud 1948- *BlmGWL*
Leutenegger-Oberholzer, Susanne *WhoWomW 91*
Leutermann, John Gerard 1955- *WhoAmP 93*
Leutheuser, Sylvia Mae 1924- *WhoAmP 93*
Leuthold, Raymond Martin 1940- *WhoAm 94*
Leutwiler, Fritz 1924- *IntWW 93, Who 94*
Leuty, Gerald Johnston 1919- *WhoWest 94*
Leutze, James Richard 1935- *WhoAm 94*
Leuven, Adolphe de 1800-1884 *NewGrDO*
Leuver, Robert Joseph 1927- *WhoAm 94*
Leuwerik, Ruth 1926- *WhoHol 92*
Lev, Alexander Shulim 1945- *WhoScEn 94*
Lev, Allen P. 1947- *WhoAm 94, WhoAmL 94*
Lev, Baruch Itamar 1938- *WhoAm 94*
Lev, Donald *DrAPF 93*
Le Va, Barry 1941- *WhoAmA 93*
Leva, James Robert 1932- *WhoAm 94, WhoFI 94*
Leva, Marx 1915- *WhoAm 94*
Levack, Arthur Paul 1909- *WhoAm 94*
Levack, Daniel J.H. *EncSF 93*
Levada, William Joseph 1936- *WhoAm 94, WhoWest 94*
Levade, Charles(-Gaston) 1869-1948 *NewGrDO*
Leval, Pierre Nelson 1936- *WhoAm 94, WhoAmL 94*
Leval, Susana Torruella *WhoHisp 94*
Levalier, Dotian 1943- *WhoAm 94*
Levall, G. E. d1922 *WhoHol 92*
Le Valle, Cleo d1925 *WhoHol 92*
Le Van, Daniel Hayden 1924- *WhoAm 94, WhoFI 94*
LeVan, Marijo O'Connor 1936- *WhoAm 94*
Le-Van, Ngo 1949- *WhoScEn 94*
Le Vander, Harold 1910-1992 *WhAm 10*
Levandowski, Barbara Sue 1948- *WhoMW 93*
Levandowski, Donald William 1927- *WhoAm 94*
Levane, Fuzzy 1920- *BasBi*
Levant, Oscar d1972 *WhoHol 92*
Levao, Richard A. 1948- *WhoAm 94*
Levar, Patrick *WhoAmP 93*
Levasseur, Nicolas (Prosper) 1791-1871 *NewGrDO*
Levasseur, Rosalie 1749-1826 *NewGrDO*

Levasseur, William Ryan 1935- *WhoAm 94, WhoAmL 94*
Le Vay, David 1915- *WrDr 94*
LeVay, Simon 1943- *ConAu 142*
Levdansky, David K. 1954- *WhoAmP 93*
Leve, Alan Donald 1927- *WhoAm 94*
Levee, John H. 1924- *WhoAmA 93*
Levee, John Harrison 1924- *WhoAm 94*
Leveille, Gilbert Antonio 1934- *WhoAm 94*
Level, Allison Vickers *WhoScEn 94*
Levell, Edward, Jr. 1931- *WhoBlA 94*
Levels, Calvin 1954- *WhoHol 92*
Levelt, Willem J. M. 1938- *IntWW 93*
Levelt, Willem J(ohannes) M(aria) 1938- *WrDr 94*
Levelt Sengers, Johanna Maria Henrica 1929- *WhoAm 94*
Leven, Earl of 1924- *Who 94*
Leven, Ann R. 1940- *WhoAmA 93*
Leven, Ann Ruth 1940- *WhoAm 94*
Leven, Boris 1912-1986 *IntDcF 2-4*
Leven, Charles Louis 1928- *WhoAm 94*
Leven, Jeremy 1941- *EncSF 93*
Levenberg, Charles M. 1946- *WhoAmL 94*
Levenberg, Diane *DrAPF 93*
Levendosky, Charles *DrAPF 93*
Levendusky, Philip George 1946- *WhoAm 94*
Levene, Ben 1938- *IntWW 93, Who 94*
Levene, Malcolm 1937- *EncSF 93*
Levene, Malcolm Irvin 1951- *Who 94*
Levene, Mark 1953- *ConAu 142*
Levene, Peter (Keith) 1941- *Who 94*
Levene, Peter Keith 1941- *IntWW 93*
Levene, Philip *EncSF 93*
Levene, Phoebus Aaron Theodor 1869-1940 *WorScD*
Levene, Sam d1980 *WhoHol 92*
Levenfeld, Milton Arthur 1927- *WhoAm 94*
Levengood, William C. 1925- *WhoAm 94*
Levenkron, Steven 1941- *TwCYAW*
Levenson, Alan Bradley 1935- *WhoAm 94, WhoAmL 94*
Levenson, Alan Ira 1935- *WhoAm 94, WhoWest 94*
Levenson, Carl 1905-1990 *WhAm 10*
Levenson, Christopher 1934- *WrDr 94*
Levenson, Corey Howard 1954- *WhoWest 94*
Levenson, Harvey Stuart 1940- *WhoAm 94, WhoFI 94*
Levenson, Jacob Clavner 1922- *WhoAm 94*
Levenson, Marc David 1945- *WhoAm 94*
Levenson, Maria Nijole 1940- *WhoScEn 94*
Levenson, Milton 1923- *WhoAm 94*
Levenson, Rustin S. 1947- *WhoAmA 93*
Levenson, Sam 1911-1980 *WhoCom*
Levenson, Stanley Richard 1933- *WhoAm 94*
Levenstein, Alan Peter 1936- *WhoAm 94*
Levenstein, Gary I. 1951- *WhoAmL 94*
Levenstein, Roslyn M. 1920- *WhoWest 94*
Levental, Valery Yakovlevich 1942- *IntWW 93*
Leventhal, Ann Z. *DrAPF 93*
Leventhal, Bennett (L.) 1949- *WrDr 94*
Leventhal, Carl M. 1933- *WhoAm 94, WhoScEn 94*
Leventhal, Colin David 1946- *Who 94*
Leventhal, Ellen Iris 1949- *WhoFI 94*
Leventhal, Nathan 1943- *WhoAm 94*
Leventhal, Robert Stanley 1927- *WhoAm 94, WhoFI 94, WhoWest 94*
Leventhal, Ruth Lee 1923-1989 *WhoAmA 93N*
Leventis, Nicholas 1957- *WhoScEn 94*
Leventis, Phil Peter 1945- *WhoAmP 93*
Leventon, Annabel 1942- *WhoHol 92*
Leveque, Eddie d1989 *WhoHol 92*
Leveque, Jean Andre Eugene 1929- *IntWW 93*
Leveque, Jean Maxime 1923- *IntWW 93*
Le Veque, Matthew Kurt 1958- *WhoWest 94*
Lever *Who 94*
Lever, Charles James 1806-1872 *BlmGEL*
Lever, Christopher *Who 94*
Lever, (Tresham) Christopher (Arthur Lindsay) 1932- *Who 94, WrDr 94*
Lever, Jack Q., Jr. 1948- *WhoAmL 94*
Lever, Jeremy Frederick 1933- *IntWW 93, Who 94*
Lever, John Darcy 1952- *Who 94*
Lever, Lafayette 1960- *BasBi, WhoBlA 94*
Lever, (John) Michael 1928- *Who 94*
Lever, Paul 1944- *Who 94*
Lever, R. Hayley 1876-1968 *WhoAmA 93N*
Levere, James Gordon 1957- *WhoScEn 94*
Levere, Richard David 1931- *WhoAm 94, WhoScEn 94*
Leverence, John 1946- *WrDr 94*
Leverenz, Humboldt Walter 1909- *WhoScEn 94*
Leverenz, Winifred 1913- *WhoWest 94*
Leverett, Miles Corrington 1910- *WhoAm 94*
Leverhulme, Viscount 1915- *IntWW 93, Who 94*
Leverich, Kathleen *DrAPF 93*
Leveridge, Richard 1670?-1758 *NewGrDO*
Levering, Frank (Graham) 1952- *ConAu 43NR*
Levering, Kathryn H. 1950- *WhoAmL 94*
Levering, Robert K. 1919- *WhoAmA 93*
Levermore, Claudette Madge 1939- *WhoBlA 94*
LeVernois, Earle Mose 1934- *WhoWest 94*
Leverock, Robert Elmo, Jr. 1964- *WhoFI 94*
Lever Of Manchester, Baron 1914- *IntWW 93, Who 94*
Leversedge, Leslie Frank 1904- *Who 94*
Leversee, Loretta *WhoHol 92*
Leverson, Ada Esther 1862-1933 *DcNaB MP*
LeVert, Eddie *WhoBlA 94*
LeVert, Francis E. 1940- *WhoBlA 94*
LeVert, Francis Edward 1940- *WhoAm 94*
LeVert, Gerald *WhoBlA 94*
LeVert, Gregory Allen 1946- *WhoMW 93*
Levert, John Bertels, Jr. 1931- *WhoAm 94*
Leverton, Colin Allen H. *Who 94*
Leverton, Roger Frank 1939- *Who 94*
Levertov, Denise *DrAPF 93*
Levertov, Denise 1923- *BlmGEL, BlmGWL, ConAu 19AS [port], WhoAm 94, WrDr 94*
Leveson, Lord 1959- *Who 94*
Leveson, Brian Henry 1949- *Who 94*
Leveson, Irving Frederick 1939- *WhoAm 94*
Leveson Gower *Who 94*
Levesque, Charles J. 1954- *WhoAmP 93*
Levesque, Georges Henri 1903- *IntWW 93*
Levesque, J. Michael 1953- *WhoAmP 93*
Levesque, Louis 1908- *Who 94, WhoAm 94*
Levesque, Louise Cavelier 1703-1743 *BlmGWL*
Levesque, Marcel d1962 *WhoHol 92*
Levesque, Mary E. 1952- *WhoAmP 93*
Levesque, Maurice J. 1925- *WhoAmP 93*
Levesque, Rene Jules Albert 1926- *WhoAm 94, WhoScEn 94*
Levet, Richard Harrington 1894- *WhAm 10*
Levetan, Liane 1936- *WhoAmP 93*
Levetown, Robert Alexander 1935- *WhoAm 94, WhoAmL 94, WhoFI 94*
Levett, James Michael 1949- *WhoMW 93*
Levett, Michael John 1939- *IntWW 93*
Levett, Oswald *EncSF 93*
Levey, Allan C. 1935- *WhoAmP 93*
Levey, Barry *WhoAmP 93*
Levey, Barry 1930- *WhoMW 93*
Levey, Ethel d1955 *WhoHol 92*
Levey, Gerald Saul 1937- *WhoAm 94*
Levey, Michael (Vincent) 1927- *IntWW 93, Who 94, WrDr 94*
Levey, Richard Michael 1959- *WhoMW 93*
Levey, Robert Frank 1945- *WhoAm 94*
Levey, Samuel 1932- *WhoAm 94*
Levey, Sandra Collins 1944- *WhoScEn 94*
Levi, Albert William 1911-1988 *WhAm 10*
Levi, Anthony H. T 1929- *WrDr 94*
Levi, Arlo Dane 1933- *WhoAm 94*
Levi, Arrigo 1926- *IntWW 93*
Levi, Carlo 1902-1975 *WhoAmA 93N*
Levi, Connie 1939- *WhoAmP 93*
Levi, Darrell E(rville) 1940- *WrDr 94*
Levi, David F. 1951- *WhoAm 94, WhoAmL 94, WhoWest 94*
Levi, Edward H(irsch) 1911- *WrDr 94*
Levi, Edward Hirsch 1911- *IntWW 93, Who 94, WhoAm 94, WhoAmL 94, WhoAmP 93, WhoMW 93*
Levi, Herbert A. 1931- *WhoWest 94*
Levi, Herbert Walter 1921- *WhoAm 94*
Levi, Hermann 1839-1900 *NewGrDO*
Levi, Ilan Mosche 1943- *WhoAm 94*
Levi, Isaac 1930- *IntWW 93*
Levi, James Harry 1939- *WhoAm 94*
Levi, Jan Heller *DrAPF 93*
Levi, John G. 1948- *WhoAm 94, WhoAmL 94*
Levi, Jonathan *ConLC 76 [port]*
Levi, Josef 1938- *WhoAmA 93*
Levi, Josef Alan 1938- *WhoAm 94*
Levi, Judith Naomi 1944- *WhoMW 93*
Levi, Julian (E.) 1900-1982 *WhoAmA 93N*
Levi, Julian Hirsch 1909- *WhoAm 94*
Levi, Kurt 1910- *WhoAm 94*
Levi, Maurice (David) 1945- *ConAu 43NR*
Levi, Maurice David 1945- *WhoAm 94*
Levi, Peter (Chad Tigar) 1931- *WrDr 94*
Levi, Peter Chad Tigar 1931- *Who 94*
Levi, Primo 1919-1987 *EncSF 93, ShSCr 12 [port]*
Levi, Renato 1926- *Who 94*
Levi, Robert Hofeller 1948- *WhoAm 94*
Levi, Samuele 1813-1883 *NewGrDO*
Levi, Steven Channing 1948- *WhoWest 94*
Levi, Toni Mergentime *DrAPF 93*
Levi, Yoel 1950- *WhoAm 94*
Leviant, Curt *DrAPF 93*
Leviatin, David 1961- *WrDr 94*
Levi Baldini, Natalia 1916- *WhoWomW 91*
Levich, Robert Alan 1941- *WhoScEn 94*
Levick, Irving, Mrs. *WhoAmA 93*
Levick, Mark Douglas 1963- *WhoAmL 94*
Levick, William Russell 1931- *IntWW 93, Who 94*
Le Vie, Donn, Jr. 1951- *WrDr 94*
Levie, Howard Sidney 1907- *WhoAm 94*
Levie, Joseph Henry *WhoAm 94*
Levie, Rex Dean 1937?- *EncSF 93*
Levie, Simon Hijman 1925- *IntWW 93*
Le Vien, Jack 1918- *IntMPA 94*
Le Vien, John Douglas 1918- *WhoAm 94*
Levien, Joy *WhoAm 94, WhoFI 94*
Levien, Sonya 1888-1960 *IntDcF 2-4 [port]*
Leviero, Anthony 1905-1956 *HisDcKW*
Le Vigan, Robert d1972 *WhoHol 92*
Levi-Montalcini, Rita 1909- *IntWW 93, Who 94, WhoAm 94, WhoScEn 94, WorScD*
Levin, A. Leo 1919- *WhoAm 94, WhoAmP 93*
Levin, Aaron Reuben 1929- *WhoAm 94*
Levin, Alan M. 1926- *WhoAm 94*
Levin, Alan Scott 1938- *WhoWest 94*
Levin, Alvin Irving 1921- *WhoWest 94*
Levin, Andrew C. 1946- *WhoAmP 93*
Levin, Barbara Ann 1968- *WhoFI 94*
Levin, Barry S. 1954- *WhoAmL 94*
Levin, Barton John 1944- *WhoAm 94*
Levin, Benjamin 1899- *WhAm 10*
Levin, Bernard 1928- *WrDr 94*
Levin, Bernard 1942- *WhoAm 94*
Levin, (Henry) Bernard 1928- *IntWW 93, Who 94*
Levin, Bernard H. 1942- *WhoScEn 94*
Levin, Betsy 1935- *WhoAm 94, WhoAmL 94*
Levin, Betty (Lowenthal) 1927- *WrDr 94*
Levin, Bob *DrAPF 93*
Levin, Bruce Alan 1939- *WhoAm 94*
Levin, Burton *WhoAmP 93*
Levin, Burton 1930- *WhoAm 94*
Levin, Carl *WhoAm 94*
Levin, Carl 1934- *IntWW 93, WhoAm 94, WhoAmP 93, WhoMW 93*
Levin, Carl M. 1934- *CngDr 93*
Levin, Charles *WhoHol 92*
Levin, Charles Edward 1946- *WhoAm 94, WhoMW 93*
Levin, Charles Leonard 1926- *WhoAmL 94, WhoAmP 93*
Levin, Clifford Ellis 1947- *WhoWest 94*
Levin, David A. 1947- *WhoAmL 94*
Levin, David Harold 1928- *WhoAmL 94*
Levin, David P. 1944- *WhoAmL 94*
Levin, Debbe Ann 1954- *WhoAmL 94, WhoMW 93*
Levin, Donald Robert 1947- *WhoFI 94*
Levin, Donna 1954- *WrDr 94*
Levin, Doron P. 1950- *WrDr 94*
Levin, E. Theodore 1944- *WhoAmP 93*
Levin, Edward Jesse 1951- *WhoAm 94, WhoAmL 94*
Levin, Edward M. 1934- *WhoAmL 94*
Levin, Ellis B. 1945- *WhoAmP 93*
Levin, Ezra Gurion 1934- *WhoAm 94*
Levin, Fredric Gerson 1937- *WhoAmL 94*
Levin, Gail 1948- *WhoAmA 93*
Levin, Geoffrey Arthur 1955- *WhoAm 94*
Levin, Gerald 1929- *WrDr 94*
Levin, Gerald M. 1939- *ConTFT 11, IntMPA 94*
Levin, Gerald Manuel 1939- *IntWW 93, WhoAm 94, WhoFI 94*
Levin, Harry d1993 *NewYTBS 93*
Levin, Harry 1912- *WrDr 94*
Levin, Harry (Tuchman) 1912- *IntWW 93*
Levin, Harry Tuchman 1912- *WhoAm 94*
Levin, Herman 1907-1990 *WhAm 10*
Levin, Hervey Phillip 1942- *WhoAmL 94*
Levin, Howard Alan 1954- *WhoWest 94*
Levin, Howard Jay 1945- *WhoFI 94*
Levin, Hugh Lauter 1951- *WhoAmA 93*
Levin, Ira 1929- *EncSF 93, IntWW 93, WhoAm 94, WrDr 94*
Levin, Irving H. 1915- *WhoAmP 93*
Levin, Jack 1932- *WhoAm 94*
Levin, Jack 1941- *ConAu 41NR*
Levin, Jack S. 1936- *WhoAm 94*
Levin, Jacob Joseph 1926- *WhoAm 94*
Levin, Jay B. 1951- *WhoAmP 93*
Levin, Jay J. 1949- *WhoAmL 94*
Levin, Jerry Wayne 1944- *WhoAm 94, WhoFI 94*
Levin, Joseph W. 1939- *WhoIns 94*
Levin, Jules Fred 1940- *WhoAm 94*
Levin, Ken 1951- *WhoScEn 94*
Levin, Kenneth I. 1949- *WhoAmL 94*
Levin, Kenneth Sherman 1937- *WhoAm 94*
Levin, Kim *WhoAmA 93*
Levin, Lawrence Adam 1953- *WhoWest 94*
Levin, Lawrence Leigh 1935- *WhoAm 94, WhoAmL 94*
Levin, Mario 1953- *WhoWest 94*
Levin, Mark J. 1949- *WhoAmL 94*
Levin, Marshall Abbott 1920- *WhoAm 94, WhoAmL 94*
Levin, Martin P. 1918- *WhoAm 94*
Levin, Marvin Edgar 1924- *WhoAm 94*
Levin, Michael (Graubart) 1958- *WrDr 94*
Levin, Michael David 1942- *WhoAm 94, WhoAmL 94*
Levin, Michael Eric 1943- *WrDr 94*
Levin, Michael Henry 1942- *WhoAmL 94*
Levin, Michael Joseph 1943- *WhoAmL 94*
Levin, Morton D. 1923- *WhoAmA 93*
Levin, Morton David 1923- *WhoAm 94*
Levin, Murray Simon 1943- *WhoAm 94, WhoAmL 94*
Levin, Myles Jeffrey 1966- *WhoMW 93*
Levin, Myrtilla Fones 1938- *WhoAmP 93*
Levin, Peter J. 1939- *WhoAm 94*
Levin, Peter Jay 1942- *WhoAmL 94*
Levin, Peter Lawrence 1961- *WhoScEn 94*
Levin, Phillis *DrAPF 93*
Levin, Rachel *WhoHol 92*
Levin, Richard 1910- *Who 94*
Levin, Richard C. 1945- *WhoAm 94, WhoAmL 94*
Levin, Richard Charles 1947- *NewYTBS 93 [port], WhoAm 94*
Levin, Richard Louis 1922- *WhoAm 94, WrDr 94*
Levin, Robert Alan 1957- *WhoFI 94, WhoWest 94*
Levin, Robert B. *IntMPA 94*
Levin, Robert Bruce 1918- *WhoScEn 94*
Levin, Robert Daniel 1930- *WhoAm 94, WhoAmL 94*
Levin, Robert Joseph 1928- *WhoAm 94*
Levin, Roger Michael 1942- *WhoAmL 94*
Levin, Ronald Mark 1950- *WhoAmL 94*
Levin, S. Michael 1944- *WhoAmL 94*
Levin, Sander M. 1931- *CngDr 93, WhoAm 94, WhoAmP 93, WhoMW 93*
Levin, Simon 1942- *WhoAm 94, WhoAmL 94*
Levin, Susan Bass 1952- *WhoAmP 93*
Levin, Tereska *DrAPF 93*
Levin, William Cohn 1917- *WhoAm 94*
Levin, William Edward 1954- *WhoAmL 94, WhoWest 94*
Levin, Zel 1913- *WhoAmP 93*
Levinas, Emmanuel 1906- *EncEth*
Levine, Aaron 1917- *WhoAm 94*
Levine, Alan 1948- *WhoAmL 94*
Levine, Alan J. 1947- *WhoAm 94, WhoFI 94, WhoWest 94*
Levine, Allan 1956- *WrDr 94*
Levine, Allen 1929- *WhoAm 94*
Levine, Anna *WhoHol 92*
Levine, Anne-Marie *DrAPF 93*
Levine, Arnold Jay 1939- *WhoAm 94, WhoScEn 94*
Levine, Arnold Milton 1916- *WhoScEn 94, WhoWest 94*
Levine, Arthur Elliott 1948- *WhoAm 94*
Levine, Arthur Samuel 1936- *WhoAm 94, WhoScEn 94*
Levine, Barry Wm. 1942- *WhoAmL 94*
Levine, Bernard d1993 *NewYTBS 93*
Levine, Beryl J. 1935- *WhoAmP 93*
Levine, Beryl Joyce 1935- *WhoAmL 94*
Levine, Bradley Scott 1958- *WhoAmL 94*
Levine, Brian D. 1958- *WhoFI 94*
Levine, Bruce Carlan 1949- *WhoMW 93*
Levine, C. Bruce 1945- *WhoAmL 94*
Levine, Carl Morton 1931- *WhoAm 94*
Levine, Charles Howard 1939-1988 *WhAm 10*
Levine, Charles Michael 1942- *WhoAm 94*
Levine, Daniel 1934- *WhoAm 94*
Levine, Daniel 1950- *WhoFI 94*
Levine, David 1926- *IntWW 93, WhoAm 94, WhoAmA 93*
Levine, David Ethan 1955- *WhoAmL 94*
Levine, David Lawrence 1919- *WhoAm 94*
Levine, David M. 1949- *WhoAm 94*
LeVine, Donald Jay 1921- *WhoFI 94, WhoScEn 94*
Levine, Donald Nathan 1931- *WhoAm 94*
Levine, Donald Paul 1945- *WhoMW 93*
Le Vine, Duane Gilbert 1933- *WhoAm 94*
Levine, Edward 1928- *WhoAmA 93*
Levine, Edward Leslie 1927- *WhoAm 94, WhoAmL 94*
Levine, Edwin Burton 1920- *WhoAm 94*
Levine, Ellen *DrAPF 93*
Levine, Erik 1960- *WhoAmA 93*
Levine, Evan 1962- *SmATA 74, -77 [port]*
Levine, Gail Janice 1947- *WhoMW 93*
Levine, Gene Norman 1930- *WhoWest 94*
Levine, George 1931- *ConAu 42NR*
Levine, George Lewis 1931- *WhoAm 94*
Levine, George Richard 1929- *WhoAm 94*
Levine, Gerald Richard 1936- *WhoAm 94*

Levine, Harold 1931- *WhoAm 94, WhoAmL 94, WhoFI 94*
Levine, Harry d1947 *WhoHol 92*
Levine, Harry 1922- *WhoAm 94*
Levine, Helen Saxon d1989 *WhAm 10*
Levine, Henry David 1951- *WhoAm 94*
Levine, Herbert Samuel 1928- *WhoAm 94*
Levine, Howard Arnold 1932- *WhoAmL 94, WhoAmP 93*
Levine, Howard Harris 1949- *WhoAm 94*
Levine, I. Stanley 1928- *WhoAm 94*
Levine, Irving Raskin *WhoAm 94, WhoFI 94*
Levine, Israel E. 1923- *WhoAm 94, WrDr 94*
Levine, Jack 1915- *IntWW 93, WhoAm 94, WhoAmA 93*
Levine, Jack A. 1946- *WhoAm 94*
Levine, Jack Anton 1946- *WhoAmL 94*
Levine, James 1943- *IntWW 93, NewGrDO, WhoAm 94*
Levine, Jerome Lester 1940- *WhoAmL 94, WhoWest 94*
Levine, Jerry *WhoHol 92*
Levine, Joel Seth 1947- *WhoWest 94*
Levine, John David 1936- *WhoAm 94*
Levine, Joseph 1912- *WhoAm 94*
Levine, Joseph E. 1905-1987 *IntDcF 2-4*
Levine, Joseph Manney 1948- *WhoAmL 94*
Levine, Keith Farrel 1955- *WhoFI 94*
Levine, Kenneth Mark 1946- *WhoWest 94*
Levine, Lainie 1942- *WhoAm 94*
Levine, Larry 1928- *WhoWest 94*
Levine, Laurence Brandt 1941- *WhoAm 94, WhoFI 94*
Levine, Laurence Harvey 1946- *WhoAm 94, WhoAmL 94*
Levine, Laurence William 1931- *WhoAm 94*
Levine, Lawrence Steven 1934- *WhoAm 94*
Levine, Lawrence William 1933- *WhoAm 94*
Levine, Leon 1937- *WhoFI 94*
Levine, Leon 1946- *WhoScEn 94*
Levine, Les 1935- *WhoAmA 93*
Levine, Louis David 1940- *WhoAm 94, WhoScEn 94*
Levine, Lowell J. 1937- *WhoAm 94*
Levine, Lucy d1939 *WhoHol 92*
Levine, Madeline Geltman 1942- *WhoAm 94*
Levine, Maita Faye 1930- *WhoMW 93*
Levine, Marilyn Anne 1935- *WhoAmA 93*
Levine, Marilyn Markovich 1930- *WhoAmL 94*
Levine, Marion Lerner 1931- *WhoAmA 93*
Levine, Mark Lee 1943- *WhoAmL 94*
Levine, Mark Leonard 1945- *WhoAm 94*
Levine, Martin 1945- *WhoAmA 93*
Levine, Martin David 1938- *WhoAm 94, WhoScEn 94*
Levine, Martin P. d1993 *NewYTBS 93*
Levine, Marvin 1928- *WhoScEn 94*
Levine, Meldon E. 1943- *WhoAmP 93*
Levine, Meldon Edises 1943- *WhoWest 94*
Levine, Melinda (Esther) 1947- *WhoAmA 93*
Levine, Melvin Charles 1930- *WhoAmL 94, WhoFI 94*
Levine, Michael 1939- *WrDr 94*
Levine, Michael 1954- *WhoAm 94, WhoWest 94*
Levine, Michael Joseph 1945- *WhoWest 94*
Levine, Michael Lawrence 1947- *WhoFI 94*
Levine, Michael William 1943- *WhoScEn 94*
Levine, Milton I. d1993 *NewYTBS 93 [port]*
Levine, Miriam *DrAPF 93*
Levine, Montague (Bernard) 1922- *Who 94*
Levine, Mortimer 1922- *WrDr 94*
Levine, Naomi Bronheim 1923- *WhoAm 94*
Levine, Norman 1924- *WrDr 94*
Levine, Norman Dion 1912- *WhoAm 94*
Levine, Norman G. *WhoIns 94*
Levine, Norman Gene 1926- *WhoAm 94, WhoWest 94*
Levine, Norman H. 1949- *WhoAmL 94*
Levine, Paul Allan 1944- *WhoScEn 94*
Levine, Paul Michael 1934- *WhoAm 94*
Levine, Peter Hughes 1938- *WhoAm 94*
Levine, Philip *DrAPF 93*
Levine, Philip 1922- *WhoAm 94*
Levine, Philip 1928- *WhoAm 94, WrDr 94*
LeVine, Philip Robert 1940- *WhoWest 94*
Levine, Rachmiel 1910- *WhoAm 94*
Levine, Raphael David 1938- *WhoAm 94, WhoScEn 94*
Levine, Rhea Joy Cottler 1939- *WhoAm 94*
Levine, Richard A. *WhoAmL 94*
Levine, Richard E. 1950- *WhoAm 94, WhoAmL 94*
Levine, Richard James 1942- *WhoAm 94*
Levine, Richard Neil 1937- *WhoWest 94*
LeVine, Robert Alan 1932- *WhoAm 94*
Levine, Robert Arthur 1930- *WhoAm 94*
Levine, Robert Jay 1950- *WhoAm 94, WhoAmL 94*
Levine, Robert John 1934- *WhoAm 94*
Levine, Robert Sidney 1921- *WhoAm 94*
Levine, Ronald H. 1935- *WhoAm 94*
Levine, Ronald Jay 1953- *WhoAm 94, WhoAmL 94*
Levine, Ruth Rothenberg *WhoAm 94*
Levine, Samuel Milton 1929- *WhoAmL 94*
Levine, Sanford Harold 1938- *WhoAmL 94*
Levine, Seymour 1924- *WhoAmL 94*
Levine, Seymour 1925- *IntWW 93, WhoScEn 94*
Levine, Shepard 1922- *WhoAmA 93*
Levine, Sol 1922- *IntWW 93, WhoAm 94*
Levine, Solomon Bernard 1920- *WhoAm 94*
Levine, Stanley A. 1936- *WhoAm 94*
Levine, Stanley Walter 1929- *WhoFI 94*
LeVine, Stephen Mark 1965- *WhoWest 94*
Levine, Steven Alan 1951- *WhoFI 94, WhoMW 93*
Levine, Steven Jon 1942- *WhoAmL 94*
Levine, Steven Marc 1964- *WhoAmL 94*
Levine, Stuart George 1932- *WhoAm 94, WrDr 94*
Levine, Sumner Norton 1923- *WhoAm 94*
Levine, Suzanne Braun 1941- *WhoAm 94*
Levine, Sydney 1923- *Who 94*
Levine, Ted *WhoHol 92*
Levine, Theodore A. 1944- *WhoAmL 94*
Levine, Thomas Jeffrey Pello 1952- *WhoAmL 94*
Levine, Tom 1945- *WhoAmA 93*
Levine, Tomar 1945- *WhoAmA 93*
Le Vine, Victor Theodore 1928- *WhoAm 94, WhoMW 93*
LeVine, Walter Daniel 1941- *WhoAmL 94*
Levine, Walter Martin 1946- *WhoFI 94*
Levine, William Silver 1941- *WhoAm 94*
Levine, Zachary Howard 1955- *WhoScEn 94*
Levine-Battista, Sandra 1935- *WhoFI 94*
Le Viness, Carl d1964 *WhoHol 92*
Leving, Jeffery Mark 1951- *WhoAmL 94*
Levinge, Richard (George Robin) 1946- *Who 94*
Levinger, Beryl Beth 1947- *WhoAm 94*
Levinger, Joseph Solomon 1921- *WhoAm 94*
Levings, Charles Sandford, III 1930- *WhoAm 94*
Levings, Theresa Lawrence 1952- *WhoAmL 94*
Levingston, Clifford Eugene 1961- *WhoBlA 94*
Levingston, Ernest Lee 1921- *WhoFI 94, WhoScEn 94*
Levingston, John Colville Bowring 1929- *WhoFI 94, WhoWest 94*
Levingston, Roberto Marcelo 1920- *IntWW 93*
Levin-Rice, Patricia Oppenheim 1932- *WhoMW 93*
Levins, Ilyssa 1958- *WhoAm 94, WhoFI 94*
Levins, James George 1953- *WhoAmL 94*
Levins, John Raymond 1944- *WhoAm 94, WhoFI 94*
Levinsky, Frieda L. *DrAPF 93*
Levinsky, Norman George 1929- *WhoAm 94, WhoScEn 94*
Levins-Morales, Aurora *DrAPF 93*
Levins Morales, Ricardo Manuel 1956- *WhoHisp 94*
Levinsohn, Florence H(amlish) 1926- *WrDr 94*
Levinson, Art *IntMPA 94*
Levinson, Arthur David 1950- *WhoAm 94, WhoScEn 94, WhoWest 94*
Levinson, Barry 1932- *WrDr 94*
Levinson, Barry 1942- *ConTFT 11, IntMPA 94, IntWW 93*
Levinson, Barry L. 1942- *WhoAm 94*
Levinson, Burton S. *WhoAm 94*
Levinson, Cary S. 1943- *WhoAmL 94*
Levinson, Charles Bernard 1912- *WhoMW 93*
Levinson, Daniel Ronald 1949- *WhoAm 94, WhoAmP 93*
Levinson, David N. *WhoAmP 93*
Levinson, Deirdre *DrAPF 93*
Levinson, Harry 1922- *WhoAm 94, WrDr 94*
Levinson, Irving Bert 1947- *WhoAm 94, WhoAmL 94*
Levinson, Joel D. 1953- *WhoAmA 93*
Levinson, John Milton 1927- *WhoAm 94*
Levinson, Kenneth Lee 1953- *WhoAmL 94, WhoFI 94, WhoWest 94*
Levinson, Kenneth S. 1947- *WhoAmL 94*
Levinson, Lawrence Edward 1930- *WhoAm 94*
Levinson, Leslie Harold 1929- *WhoAm 94*
Levinson, Luisa Mercedes 1914- *BlmGWL*
Levinson, Marc A. 1948- *WhoAmL 94*
Levinson, Michael R. 1954- *WhoAmL 94*
Levinson, Milton Richard 1915- *WhoMW 93*
Levinson, Mimi 1940- *WhoAmA 93*
Levinson, Mon 1926- *WhoAmA 93*
Levinson, Morris L. d1993 *NewYTBS 93 [port]*
Levinson, Norm *IntMPA 94*
Levinson, Olga May *WrDr 94*
Levinson, Paul Howard 1952- *WhoAmL 94*
Levinson, Peter Joseph 1943- *WhoAmL 94*
Levinson, Philip Z. 1929- *WhoAmL 94*
Levinson, Richard (Leighton) 1934-1987 *ConAu 41NR*
Levinson, Robert Alan 1925- *WhoAm 94*
Levinson, Robert E. 1925- *WrDr 94*
Levinson, Sanford Victor 1941- *WhoAm 94*
Levinson, Stephen Curtis 1947- *Who 94*
Levinson, Stephen Eliot 1944- *WhoAm 94*
Levinson, Steven H. *WhoAmP 93*
Levinson, Steven H. 1946- *WhoAmL 94*
Levinthal, David Lawrence 1949- *WhoAmA 93*
Levinthal, Elliott Charles 1922- *WhoAm 94*
Levintoff, Carina 1951- *WhoAmL 94*
Levinton, Jeffrey S. 1946- *WhoAm 94*
Levinton, Michael Jay 1957- *WhoScEn 94*
Levintow, Leon 1921- *WhoAm 94*
Levion, Leon L. *WhoAmP 93*
Levis, Allen 1917- *WhoAm 94*
Levis, Derek George d1993 *Who 94N*
Levis, Donald James 1936- *WhoAm 94, WhoScEn 94*
Levis, Larry *DrAPF 93*
Levis, Larry (Patrick) 1946- *WrDr 94*
Levi-Sandri, Lionello d1991 *IntWW 93N*
Levi-Setti, Riccardo *WhoAm 94*
Levison, Charles *WhoHol 92*
Levison, Harold George 1947- *WhoAm 94*
Levison, Mary Irene 1923- *Who 94*
Levister, Ernest Clayton, Jr. 1936- *WhoBlA 94*
Levister, Robert L. 1918-1992 *WhoBlA 94N*
Levister, Wendell P. 1928- *WhoBlA 94*
Levi-Strauss, Claude 1908- *IntWW 93, Who 94*
Levit, Edithe Judith 1926- *WhoAm 94*
Levit, Herschel 1912-1986 *WhoAmA 93N*
Levit, Jay Joseph 1934- *WhoAmL 94*
Levit, Lawrence A. 1945- *WhoAmL 94*
Levit, Louis W. 1923- *WhoAm 94*
Levit, Milton 1924- *WhoAm 94*
Levit, Saul 1945- *WhoAmL 94*
Levit, Victor B. 1930- *WhoIns 94*
Levit, Victor Bert 1930- *WhoAm 94, WhoAmL 94, WhoWest 94*
Levit, William Harold, Jr. 1938- *WhoAm 94, WhoAmL 94*
Levitan, Aida Tomas 1948- *WhoHisp 94*
Levitan, Dan 1957- *WhoAm 94, WhoFI 94*
Levitan, David Eric 1961- *WhoFI 94*
Levitan, David Maurice 1915- *WhoAm 94, WhoAmL 94*
Levitan, Howard Jay 1945- *WhoAm 94, WhoAmL 94*
Levitan, James A. 1925- *WhoAm 94*
Levitan, Katherine D. 1933- *WhoAmL 94*
Levitan, Laurence 1933- *WhoAm 94, WhoAmL 94, WhoAmP 93*
Levitan, Roger Stanley 1933- *WhoAmL 94, WhoWest 94*
Levitas, Elliott Harris 1930- *WhoAmP 93*
Levitas, Mitchel Ramsey 1929- *WhoAm 94*
Levithan, Allen B. 1946- *WhoAmL 94*
Levitin, Sonia 1934- *TwCYAW*
Levitin, Sonia (Wolff) 1934- *WrDr 94*
Levitine, George 1916- *WhoAmA 93N*
Levitine, George 1916-1989 *WhAm 10*
Leviton, Alan Edward 1930- *WhoAm 94*
Levitsky, Melvyn 1938- *WhoAm 94, WhoAmP 93*
Levitt, Alfred 1894- *WhoAmA 93*
Levitt, Annabel Wood *DrAPF 93*
Levitt, Arthur, Jr. 1931- *WhoAm 94, WhoAmP 93, WhoFI 94*
Levitt, Brian Michael 1947- *IntWW 93, WhoAm 94, WhoFI 94*
Levitt, Daniel Philip 1936- *WhoAm 94, WhoAmL 94*
Levitt, Edward J. 1944- *WhoAmL 94*
Levitt, George 1925- *WhoScEn 94*
Levitt, Gerald Steven 1944- *WhoAm 94*
Levitt, Helen 1918- *WhoAmA 93*
Levitt, Irving Francis 1915- *WhoAm 94*
Levitt, Israel Monroe 1908- *WhoAm 94, WhoScEn 94*
Levitt, Lawrence David 1944- *WhoFI 94*
Levitt, LeRoy Paul 1918- *WhoAm 94*
Levitt, Mitchell 1944- *WhoAm 94*
Levitt, Morton P(aul) 1936- *ConAu 43NR*
Levitt, Peter *DrAPF 93*
Levitt, Robert Elwood 1926- *WhoAmL 94, WhoAmP 93, WhoMW 93*
Levitt, Ruby R. 1907-1992 *ConTFT 11*
Levitt, Seymour Herbert 1928- *WhoAm 94*
Levitt, Steve *WhoHol 92*
Levitz, John Blaşe 1956- *WhoFI 94*
Levitz, Paul Elliot 1956- *WhoAm 94*
Levitzki, Mischa d1941 *WhoHol 92*
Levka, Uta *WhoHol 92*
Lev-Landau 1895-1979 *WhoAmA 93N*
Levorson, Kathryn Grace 1931- *WhoMW 93*
Levovitz, Pesach Zechariah 1922- *WhoAm 94*
Levoy, Myron 1930- *TwCYAW, WhoAm 94, WrDr 94*
Levulis, Raymond John 1933- *WhoMW 93*
Levy, Aaron 1742-1815 *WhAmRev*
Levy, Alain 1946- *IntWW 93*
Levy, Alain M. 1946- *WhoAm 94*
Levy, Alan 1932- *WrDr 94*
Levy, Alan Bruce 1953- *WhoMW 93*
Levy, Alan David 1938- *WhoWest 94*
Levy, Alan Joel 1937- *WhoAm 94*
Levy, Alan Joseph 1932- *WhoAm 94*
Levy, Alan M. 1940- *WhoAmL 94*
Levy, Allan Edward 1942- *Who 94*
Levy, Amy 1861-1889 *BlmGWL*
Levy, Andrew David 1956- *WhoAmL 94*
Levy, Arnold Stuart 1941- *WhoAm 94, WhoFI 94, WhoMW 93*
Levy, Arthur James 1947- *WhoAm 94*
Levy, Avner M. *WhoWest 94*
Levy, Barbara Susan 1953- *WhoWest 94*
Levy, Beatrice S. 1892-1974 *WhoAmA 93N*
Levy, Benjamin 1937- *WhoFI 94*
Levy, Benjamin 1940- *WhoAm 94*
Levy, Benjamin Hirsch 1912-1988 *WhAm 10*
Levy, Benn W(olfe) 1900-1973 *ConDr 93*
Levy, Bernard *IntMPA 94*
Levy, Bernard 1917- *WhoAmA 93*
Levy, Bernard-Henri 1948- *CurBio 93 [port], IntWW 93*
Levy, Bertram Louis 1947- *WhoAmL 94*
Levy, Boris 1927- *WhoScEn 94*
Levy, Bud 1928- *IntMPA 94*
Levy, Burton 1912- *WhoAm 94*
Levy, Charles M. 1939- *WhoAm 94*
Levy, Dale Penneys 1940- *WhoAm 94, WhoAmL 94*
Levy, Daniel 1957- *WhoFI 94, WhoScEn 94*
Levy, Daniel H. 1943- *WhoAm 94, WhoFI 94*
Levy, David *IntMPA 94, WhoAm 94, WhoWest 94*
Levy, David 1913- *EncSF 93*
Levy, David 1932- *WhoAmL 94, WhoWest 94*
Levy, David 1937- *WhoAmL 94*
Levy, David 1938- *IntWW 93*
Levy, David 1953- *WhoAmP 93*
Levy, David A. 1953- *CngDr 93*
Levy, David A. 1955- *WhoAm 94*
Levy, David Alfred 1930- *WhoAm 94*
Levy, David Corcos 1938- *WhoAm 94, WhoAmA 93*
Levy, David Matthew 1954- *WhoAmL 94*
Levy, David Steven 1955- *WhoWest 94*
Levy, Deborah 1959- *ConDr 93*
Levy, Delores Jane 1928- *WhoWest 94*
Levy, Dennis Martyn 1936- *Who 94*
Levy, Donald 1935- *WhoMW 93*
Levy, Donald Harris 1939- *WhoAm 94, WhoScEn 94*
Levy, Dorothea Yvette 1948- *WhoWest 94*
Levy, Edward Charles, Jr. 1931- *WhoAm 94*
Levy, Edward K. *WhoScEn 94*
Levy, Elizabeth 1942- *SmATA 18AS [port]*
Levy, Emanuel 1918- *WhoIns 94*
Levy, Etienne Paul Louis 1922- *WhoScEn 94*
Levy, Eugene *WhoHol 92*
Levy, Eugene 1946- *IntMPA 94*
Levy, Eugene Howard 1944- *WhoAm 94, WhoScEn 94, WhoWest 94*
Levy, Eugene Pfeifer 1936- *WhoAm 94*
Levy, Ewart Maurice 1897- *Who 94*
Levy, Florence N. 1870-1947 *WhoAmA 93N*
Levy, Franklin I. 1944- *WhoFI 94*
Levy, George Charles 1944- *WhoAm 94*
Levy, George Joseph 1927- *Who 94*
Levy, George Michael 1948- *WhoAmL 94*
Levy, Gerhard 1928- *WhoAm 94*
Levy, Gilbert Joseph 1893- *WhAm 10*
Levy, Harold David 1938- *WhoScEn 94*
Levy, Harold James 1925- *WhoScEn 94*
Levy, Helen Fiddyment 1937- *ConAu 142*
Levy, Herbert Monte 1923- *WhoAmL 94*

Lewis, Paul Martin 1943- *WhoScEn 94*
Lewis, Paul Thomas 1960- *WhoWest 94*
Lewis, Peggy Sue 1957- *WhoMW 93*
Lewis, Peirce Fee 1927- *WhoAm 94*
Lewis, Percy Lee 1937- *WhoBlA 94*
Lewis, Percy Wyndham 1882-1957 *BlmGEL*
Lewis, Perry Joshua 1938- *WhoAm 94*
Lewis, Peter 1937- *Who 94*
Lewis, Peter (Elvet) 1937- *WrDr 94*
Lewis, Peter B. 1933- *WhoIns 94*
Lewis, Peter Benjamin 1933- *WhoAm 94, WhoFI 94*
Lewis, Peter Ronald 1926- *Who 94*
Lewis, Peter Tyndale 1929- *Who 94*
Lewis, Philip 1913- *WhoAm 94*
Lewis, Philip M. 1931- *WhoAm 94*
Lewis, Philip Patrick 1952- *WhoAm 94*
Lewis, Phillip Harold 1922- *WhoAm 94, WhoAmA 93*
Lewis, Phillip Vernon 1942- *WhoWest 94*
Lewis, Polly Meriwether 1949- *WhoBlA 94*
Lewis, Preston W(ilhelm) 1896- *WhAm 10*
Lewis, Prinic Herbert, Sr. 1930- *WhoBlA 94*
Lewis, R(obert) Donald 1897- *WhAm 10*
Lewis, Ralph d1937 *WhoHol 92*
Lewis, Ralph Jay, III 1942- *WhoFI 94, WhoWest 94*
Lewis, Ralph Milton 1919- *WhoAm 94*
Lewis, Ramsey Emanuel, Jr. 1935- *WhoAm 94, WhoBlA 94*
Lewis, Randall DeWayne 1964- *WhoMW 93*
Lewis, Reggie 1965-1993 *WhoBlA 94*
Lewis, Reggie c. 1966-1993 *News 94-1*
Lewis, Regina Marie 1954- *WhoAmL 94*
Lewis, Reginald 1942-1993 *News 93-3*
Lewis, Reginald F. 1942-1993 *AfrAmAl 6 [port], ConBlB 6 [port], NewYTBS 93 [port], WhoBlA 94N*
Lewis, Richard *DrAPF 93, Who 94*
Lewis, Richard d1935 *WhoHol 92*
Lewis, Richard 1914-1990 *NewGrDO*
Lewis, Richard 1935- *Who 94*
Lewis, Richard 1947?- *CurBio 93 [port], WhoCom*
Lewis, Richard 1948- *WhoAm 94*
Lewis, Richard 1949- *WhoHol 92*
Lewis, (John Hubert) Richard *Who 94*
Lewis, Richard Allan 1952- *WhoAm 94*
Lewis, Richard Eugene 1950- *WhoAmL 94*
Lewis, Richard H. 1937- *WhoAmP 93*
Lewis, Richard Jay 1933- *WhoAm 94, WhoFI 94*
Lewis, Richard John, Sr. 1936- *WhoBlA 94*
Lewis, Richard Phelps 1936- *WhoAm 94*
Lewis, Richard Stanley 1916- *WhoAm 94*
Lewis, Richard U. 1926- *WhoBlA 94*
Lewis, Richard Van 1951- *WhoScEn 94*
Lewis, Richard Warren 1951- *WhoAm 94*
Lewis, Rita Hoffman 1947- *WhoAm 94, WhoFI 94*
Lewis, Robert Alan 1933- *WhoAm 94*
Lewis, Robert Alvin, Jr. 1945- *WhoBlA 94*
Lewis, Robert C., Jr. d1993 *NewYTBS 93*
Lewis, Robert Charles 1943- *WhoAm 94*
Lewis, Robert David 1953- *WhoAmL 94*
Lewis, Robert Earl 1929- *WhoMW 93*
Lewis, Robert Edward 1903- *WhoBlA 94*
Lewis, Robert Edwin, Jr. 1947- *WhoAm 94*
Lewis, Robert Enzer 1934- *WhoAm 94*
Lewis, Robert Hugh Cecil 1925- *Who 94*
Lewis, Robert James 1945- *WhoFI 94*
Lewis, Robert Lawrence 1919- *WhoAm 94*
Lewis, Robert Lee, III 1949- *WhoWest 94*
Lewis, Robert Louis 1936- *WhoBlA 94*
Lewis, Robert Michael 1934- *ConTFT 11*
Lewis, Robert Q. 1921- *WhoHol 92*
Lewis, Robert Steve 1946- *WhoWest 94*
Lewis, Robert Turner 1923- *WhoWest 94*
Lewis, Rodney E., Jr. 1949- *WhoAmL 94*
Lewis, Roger Allen 1941- *WhoWest 94*
Lewis, Roger Charles 1944- *WhoAmP 93*
Lewis, Roger Curzon 1909- *Who 94*
Lewis, Roger Kutnow 1941- *WhoAm 94*
Lewis, Roland Swaine 1908- *Who 94*
Lewis, Rolland Wilton 1930- *WhoMW 93*
Lewis, Ron E. 1953- *WhoAmP 93*
Lewis, Ronald d1982 *WhoHol 92*
Lewis, Ronald Alexander 1968- *WhoBlA 94*
Lewis, Ronald C. 1934- *WhoBlA 94*
Lewis, Ronald Stephen 1950- *WhoBlA 94*
Lewis, Ronald Walter 1945- *WhoAmA 93*
Lewis, Ronald Wayne 1943- *WhoAmL 94*
Lewis, Roy 1913- *WrDr 94*
Lewis, Roy 1933- *WrDr 94*
Lewis, (Ernest Michael) Roy 1913- *EncSF 93*
Lewis, Roy Roosevelt 1935- *WhoScEn 94*
Lewis, Ruby Anne 1941- *WhoWest 94*
Lewis, Rupert 1947- *ConAu 142*
Lewis, Russell T. *WhoAm 94, WhoFI 94*
Lewis, Sam d1963 *WhoHol 92*
Lewis, Samella 1924- *WhoBlA 94*
Lewis, Samella Sanders 1924- *WhoAm 94, WhoAmA 93*
Lewis, Samuel, Jr. 1953- *WhoBlA 94*
Lewis, Samuel Winfield 1930- *IntWW 93, WhoAm 94, WhoAmP 93*
Lewis, Scott P. 1950- *WhoAmL 94*
Lewis, Sean D. *Who 94*
Lewis, Shannon 1937- *WrDr 94*
Lewis, Shari 1934- *WhoAm 94*
Lewis, Sheldon d1958 *WhoHol 92*
Lewis, Sheldon Noah 1934- *WhoAm 94*
Lewis, Sherman 1942- *WhoBlA 94*
Lewis, Sherman Richard, Jr. 1936- *WhoAm 94, WhoFI 94*
Lewis, Shirley Jeane 1937- *WhoWest 94*
Lewis, Sidney Allison 1945- *WhoFI 94*
Lewis, (Harry) Sinclair 1885-1951 *EncSF 93*
Lewis, Stanley 1930- *WhoAmA 93*
Lewis, Stephen *WhoHol 92*
Lewis, Stephen 1937- *IntWW 93*
Lewis, Stephen C. 1943- *WhoAmP 93*
Lewis, Stephen C. 1950- *WhoAmL 94*
Lewis, Stephen Christopher 1950- *WhoBlA 94*
Lewis, Stephen Richmond, Jr. 1939- *WhoAm 94, WhoMW 93*
Lewis, Sterling Thomas, Jr. 1951- *WhoAmP 93*
Lewis, Steve *WhoAm 94*
Lewis, Steve Earl 1969- *WhoBlA 94*
Lewis, Steven C. *WhoAmL 94*
Lewis, Stuart Weslie 1938- *WhoScEn 94*
Lewis, Sydney 1919- *WhoAm 94, WhoFI 94*
Lewis, Sylvia Austin 1921- *WhoBlA 94*
Lewis, Sylvia Gail 1945- *WhoAm 94*
Lewis, Ted d1971 *WhoHol 92*
Lewis, Ted 1894-1970 *DcNaB MP*
Lewis, Ted Adam 1960- *WhoAmP 93*
Lewis, Ted D. 1949- *WhoAmP 93*
Lewis, Terence 1935- *Who 94*
Lewis, Terence (Murray) 1928- *Who 94*
Lewis, Terry *WhoBlA 94*
Lewis, Terry 1956- *See* Jimmy Jam 1959- *ConMus 11*
Lewis, Terry Lee 1948- *WhoAmL 94*
Lewis, Theodore E. 1926- *WhoIns 94*
Lewis, Theodore Edgar 1926- *WhoFI 94*
Lewis, Theodore Radford, Jr. 1946- *WhoBlA 94*
Lewis, Therthenia W. 1947- *WhoBlA 94*
Lewis, Thomas B. *WhoAm 94*
Lewis, Thomas Bradford 1962- *WhoAmL 94*
Lewis, Thomas E. 1947- *WhoAmP 93*
Lewis, Thomas F. 1924- *WhoAmP 93*
Lewis, Thomas F., Jr. 1924- *WhoAm 94*
Lewis, Thomas H. 1919- *ConAu 141*
Lewis, Thomas L. T 1918- *WrDr 94*
Lewis, Thomas Loftus Townshend 1918- *Who 94*
Lewis, Thomas P. 1936- *WhoBlA 94*
Lewis, Thomas P(arker) 1936- *WrDr 94*
Lewis, Thomas Proctor 1930- *WhoAm 94*
Lewis, Thomas Robert, III 1961- *WhoFI 94*
Lewis, Timothy K. 1954- *WhoAm 94, WhoAmL 94*
Lewis, Timothy Richards 1841-1886 *DcNaB MP*
Lewis, Todd Jay 1954- *WhoWest 94*
Lewis, Tola Ethridge, Jr. 1945- *WhoAm 94*
Lewis, Tom d1927 *WhoHol 92*
Lewis, Tom 1924- *CngDr 93*
Lewis, Tommy *WhoHol 92*
Lewis, Tony *Who 94*
Lewis, Tony 1967- *WhoHisp 94*
Lewis, Trevor *Who 94*
Lewis, Trevor 1933- *IntWW 93, Who 94*
Lewis, (Derek) Trevor 1936- *Who 94*
Lewis, Trevor Oswin 1935- *Who 94*
Lewis, Vera d1956 *WhoHol 92*
Lewis, Vera Margaret *Who 94*
Lewis, Vernita Ann Wickliffe 1955- *WhoMW 93*
Lewis, Vincent V. 1938- *WhoBlA 94*
Lewis, Viola Gambrill 1939- *WhoBlA 94*
Lewis, Virginia Elnora 1907- *WhoAmA 93*
Lewis, Virginia Hill 1948- *WhoBlA 94*
Lewis, Vivian M. *WhoBlA 94*
Lewis, W. Arthur d1991 *NobelP 91N*
Lewis, W. Arthur 1930- *WhoBlA 94*
Lewis, W(alter) David 1931- *WrDr 94*
Lewis, W. Walker 1944- *WhoAm 94, WhoFI 94*
Lewis, Walter d1981 *WhoHol 92*
Lewis, Walter David 1931- *WhoAm 94*
Lewis, Walter P. d1932 *WhoHol 92*
Lewis, Walton A. 1910- *WhoBlA 94*
Lewis, Welbourne Walker, Jr. 1915- *WhoAm 94*
Lewis, Wendell J. 1949- *WhoBlA 94*
Lewis, Wilbur Curtis 1930- *WhoAm 94*
Lewis, Wilbur H. 1930- *WhoAm 94*
Lewis, William 1935- *NewGrDO*
Lewis, William A., Jr. 1946- *WhoBlA 94*
Lewis, William Arthur 1915-1991 *WhAm 10, WhoBlA 94N*
Lewis, William Arthur 1918- *WhoAmA 93*
Lewis, William Arthur, Jr. 1946- *WhoAmP 93*
Lewis, William Bryant 1931- *WhoAm 94*
Lewis, William Frederick 1949- *WhoFI 94*
Lewis, William Headley, Jr. 1934- *WhoFI 94*
Lewis, William Henry, Jr. 1942- *WhoAm 94*
Lewis, William Leonard 1946- *WhoAm 94*
Lewis, William M., Jr. *WhoBlA 94*
Lewis, William R. 1920- *WhoAmA 93*
Lewis, William Russell 1926- *WrDr 94*
Lewis, William Scheer 1927- *WhoAm 94, WhoFI 94, WhoScEn 94*
Lewis, William Sylvester 1952- *WhoBlA 94*
Lewis, William V., Jr. 1959- *WhoFI 94*
Lewis, William W. *WhoAmP 93*
Lewis, William Walker 1942- *WhoAm 94*
Lewis, Wilmarth Sheldon 1895-1979 *DcLB 140 [port]*
Lewis, Woodrow *WhoAmP 93, WhoBlA 94*
Lewis, (Percy) Wyndham 1884-1957 *EncSF 93*
Lewis-Bowen, Thomas Edward Ifor 1933- *Who 94*
Lewisham, Archdeacon of *Who 94*
Lewisham, Viscount 1949- *Who 94*
Lewis-Jones, (Robert) Gwilym 1922- *Who 94*
Lewis-Kolbus, Melinda Anne 1958- *WhoFI 94*
Lewis Of Newnham, Baron 1928- *Who 94*
Lewisohn, Anthony Clive Leopold 1925- *Who 94*
Lewisohn, James *DrAPF 93*
Lewisohn, Mark 1958- *WrDr 94*
Lewisohn, Neville Joseph 1922- *Who 94*
Lewisohn, Victor M. d1934 *WhoHol 92*
Lewison, Kim Martin Jordan 1952- *Who 94*
Lewison, Peter George Hornby d1992 *Who 94N*
Lewis-Smith, Anne 1925- *WrDr 94*
Lewis-Williams, J(ames) David 1934- *ConAu 41NR*
Lewitas, Laurence Tod 1963- *WhoAmL 94*
Lewitin, Landes d1966 *WhoAmA 93N*
Lewitt, Miles Martin 1952- *WhoFI 94, WhoScEn 94, WhoWest 94*
Lewitt, S.N. 1954- *EncSF 93*
Lewitt, Sol 1928- *IntWW 93, WhoAm 94, WhoAmA 93*
Lewitter, Lucian Ryszard 1922- *Who 94*
Lewitzky, Bella 1916- *WhoAm 94, WhoWest 94*
Lewkow, Victor I. 1949- *WhoAmL 94*
Lewman, Highe d1976 *WhoHol 92*
Lewnes, Peter A. 1929- *WhoFI 94*
Lewontin, Timothy (Andrew) 1955- *WrDr 94*
Lewris, Basil J. 1949- *WhoAmL 94*
Lewry, Thomas Arthur 1957- *WhoAmL 94*
Lewter, Andy C., Sr. 1929- *WhoBlA 94*
Lewter, Andy C., Jr. 1954- *WhoBlA 94*
Lewthwaite, Gordon Rowland 1925- *WhoWest 94*
Lewthwaite, Rainald Gilfrid 1913- *Who 94*
Lewthwaite, William Anthony 1912- *Who 94*
Lewton, Val 1904-1951 *IntDcF 2-4*
Lewton, Val Edwin 1937- *WhoAmA 93*
Lewty, Marjorie 1906- *WrDr 94*
Lewy, Alfred Jones 1945- *WhoWest 94*
Lewy, John Edwin 1935- *WhoAm 94*
Lewy, Ralph I. 1931- *WhoAm 94*
Lewyn, John fl. 1364-1398 *DcNaB MP*
Lewyn, Thomas Mark 1930- *WhoAm 94*
Lex, Barbara Wendy 1941- *WhoScEn 94*
Lexa, Jake d1973 *WhoHol 92*
Lexau, Henry 1928- *WhoAm 94*
Lexau, Joan M. *WrDr 94*
Lexy, Edward 1897- *WhoHol 92*
Ley, Alice Chetwynd 1913- *WrDr 94*
Ley, Andrew James 1945- *WhoAm 94, WhoAmL 94*
Ley, Arthur Harris 1903- *Who 94*
Ley, Beth Marie 1964- *WhoWest 94*
Ley, Francis (Douglas) 1907- *Who 94*
Ley, Herbert Leonard, Jr. 1923- *WhoAm 94*
Ley, John *WhoHol 92*
Ley, Linda Sue 1949- *WhoMW 93*
Ley, Ronald 1929- *WhoAm 94*
Ley, Steven Victor 1945- *Who 94*
Ley, Timothy James 1953- *WhoMW 93*
Ley, Wesley Jon 1960- *WhoFI 94*
Ley, Willy 1906-1969 *EncSF 93*
Leybourne, Douglas Marwood, Jr. 1948- *WhoFI 94*
Leybovich, Alexander Yevgeny 1948- *WhoScEn 94*
Leyda, Margaret Larue 1923- *WhoMW 93*
Leyden, Dennis Roger 1933- *WhoAm 94*
Leyden, Donald Elliott 1938- *WhoAm 94*
Leyden, Michael Joseph, II 1950- *WhoFI 94, WhoWest 94*
Leyden, Norman *WhoWest 94*
Leyden, Peter Vail 1959- *WhoMW 93*
Leydenfrost, A(lexander) 1889-1961 *EncSF 93*
Leydenfrost, Alexander 1889-1961 *WhoAmA 93N*
Leydet, Francois Guillaume 1927- *WhoWest 94*
Leydorf, Frederick Leroy 1930- *WhoAm 94*
Leyendecker, Joseph C. 1874-1951 *WhoAmA 93N*
Leygue, Louis Georges d1992 *IntWW 93N*
Leyh, George Francis 1931- *WhoAm 94, WhoScEn 94*
Leyh, Richard Edmund, Sr. 1930- *WhoAm 94*
Leyland, James Richard 1944- *WhoAm 94*
Leyland, Philip Vyvian N. *Who 94*
Leyland, Ronald Arthur 1940- *Who 94*
Leylek, James H. *WhoScEn 94*
Leymaster, Glen R. 1915- *WhoAm 94*
Leys, Dale Daniel 1952- *WhoAmA 93*
Leysen, Anna 1942- *WhoWomW 91*
Leyser, Karl (Joseph) 1920- *WrDr 94*
Leyser, Karl Joseph d1992 *IntWW 93N*
Leyshon, Emrys 1922- *WhoHol 92*
Leyssac, Paul d1946 *WhoHol 92*
Leyton, George d1948 *WhoHol 92*
Leyton, Israel 1927- *WhoHisp 94*
Leyton, John 1939- *WhoHol 92*
Leyton, Sophie 1928- *WrDr 94*
Leyva, Frank d1981 *WhoHol 92*
Leyva, Nick Tom 1953- *WhoHisp 94*
Lezak, Muriel Deutsch 1927- *WhoScEn 94*
Lezak, Sidney Irving 1924- *WhoAmL 94*
Lezama, Jose Luis 1946- *WhoHisp 94*
Lezama Lima, Jose 1910-1976 *GayLL*
Lezardiere, Marie Charlotte Pauline 1754-1835 *BlmGWL*
Lezay Marnezia, Marquise de d1785 *BlmGWL*
Lezcano, Ismael, IV 1951- *WhoHisp 94*
Lezdey, John 1931- *WhoAmL 94*
Lezell, Mark L. 1947- *WhoAmL 94*
Lhalu Cewang Doje *WhoPRCh 91*
Lherie, Leon *NewGrDO*
Lherie, Paul 1844-1937 *NewGrDO*
Lheriter de Villandon, Marie-Jeanne 1664-1734 *BlmGWL*
L'Hermite, Tristan *GuFrLit 2*
Lhermitte, Francois Augustin 1921- *IntWW 93*
Lhermitte, Thierry *WhoHol 92*
L'Heureux, John *DrAPF 93*
L'Heureux, John (Clarke) 1934- *WrDr 94*
L'Heureux, John Clarke 1934- *WhoAm 94*
L'Heureux, Richard B. 1936- *WhoWest 94*
L'Heureux, Robert J. 1940- *WhoAmP 93*
L'Heureux, Willard John 1947- *WhoAm 94*
L'Heureux-Dube, Claire 1927- *WhoAm 94*
Lhevine, Dave Bernard 1922- *WhoAm 94*
L'Homme, Robert Arthur 1941- *WhoMW 93*
L'Hommedieu, Ezra 1734-1811 *WhAmRev*
Lho Shin-Yong 1930- *IntWW 93*
Lhost, John H. 1949- *WhoAmL 94*
Lhotka, Bonny Pierce 1942- *WhoAmA 93*
Lhotka-Kalinski, Ivo 1913-1987 *NewGrDO*
L'Huillier, Peter 1926- *WhoAm 94*
Lhunzhub Tabkyai 1906- *WhoPRCh 91 [port]*
Li, Albert P. 1951- *WhoMW 93*
Li, Bichuan 1951- *WhoAsA 94*
Li, Bing An 1941- *WhoAsA 94*
Li, Bob Cheng-Liang 1936- *WhoAsA 94*
Li, Bruce *WhoHol 92*
Li, C. C. 1912- *WhoAsA 94*
Li, Charles N. 1940- *WhoAsA 94, WhoWest 94*
Li, Che-Yu 1934- *WhoAsA 94*
Li, Cheng 1956- *WhoAsA 94*
Li, Chia-Chuan 1946- *WhoAsA 94*
Li, Chia-yu 1941- *WhoAsA 94*
Li, Ching-Chung 1932- *WhoAm 94, WhoAsA 94*
Li, Ching James 1957- *WhoAsA 94*
Li, Choh Hai 1913-1987 *WorScD*
Li, Christian Francis 1963- *WhoFI 94*
Li, Chu-Tsing 1920- *WhoAm 94, WhoAmA 93, WhoAsA 94*
Li, Conan K. N. 1951- *WhoAsA 94*
Li, David Wen-Chung 1929- *WhoWest 94*
Li, Dening 1947- *WhoAsA 94*
Li, Diane Dai 1962- *WhoAsA 94*
Li, Eldon Y. 1952- *WhoWest 94*
Li, Florence Tim Oi 1907-1992 *AnObit 1992*

Li, Fook Kow 1922- Who 94
Li, George S. 1943- WhoAsA 94
Li, Gerald 1942- WhoAm 94
Li, Guodong 1958- WhoAsA 94
Li, Hanna Wu 1934- WhoAsA 94
Li, Hong 1962- WhoScEn 94
Li, Ivan C. 1955- WhoAsA 94
Li, James C. M. 1925- WhoAsA 94
Li, James Chen Min 1925- WhoAm 94, WhoScEn 94
Li, Jennifer L. H. 1954- WhoAsA 94
Li, Jia 1945- WhoAsA 94
Li, Jianming 1956- WhoScEn 94
Li, Joseph Kwok-Kwong 1940- WhoWest 94
Li, Kai 1954- WhoAsA 94
Li, Kam Wu 1934- WhoScEn 94
Li, Ke Wen 1933- WhoAsA 94
Li, Kuiyuan 1955- WhoAsA 94
Li, Lillian M. WhoAsA 94
Li, Lily Elizabeth 1962- WhoAsA 94
Li, Ling-Fong 1944- WhoAsA 94
Li, Linxi 1956- WhoScEn 94
Li, Liqiang 1963- WhoScEn 94
Li, Marjorie H. 1942- WhoAsA 94
Li, Ming 1959- WhoAsA 94
Li, Norman N. 1933- WhoAm 94, WhoAsA 94
Li, Paul Michael 1938- WhoAmL 94, WhoWest 94
Li, Pearl Nei-Chien Chu 1946- WhoFI 94
Li, Peter Ta 1938- WhoAsA 94
Li, Peter Wai-Kwong 1952- WhoAsA 94, WhoWest 94
Li, Qiang 1953- WhoAsA 94
Li, San-pao 1942- WhoAsA 94
Li, Sheng S. 1938- WhoAsA 94
Li, Shin-Hwa 1958- WhoAsA 94
Li, Shing Ted 1938- WhoAsA 94
Li, Shuhe 1961- WhoAsA 94
Li, Simon Fook Sean 1922- Who 94
Li, Steven Shoei-lung 1938- WhoAsA 94
Li, Ta Mei 1948- WhoWest 94
Li, Tien-yi 1915- WrDr 94
Li, Tien-Yien 1945- WhoAsA 94
Li, Tingye 1931- WhoAm 94, WhoAsA 94
Li, Tze-chung 1927- WhoAm 94
Li, Victor C. 1954- WhoAsA 94
Li, Victor On-Kwok 1954- WhoAsA 94
Li, Vivien 1954- WhoAsA 94
Li, Wen-Hsiung 1918- WhoAsA 94
Li, William Wei-Lin 1962- WhoAsA 94
Li, Wu 1958- WhoAsA 94
Li, Xiao-Bing 1954- WhoAsA 94
Li, Ya 1960- WhoAsA 94
Li, Yao 1958- WhoScEn 94
Li, Yao-En 1958- WhoMW 93
Li, Yao Tzu 1914- WhoAsA 94
Li, Yiping Y.P. 1943- WhoScEn 94
Li, Yonghong 1966- WhoScEn 94
Li, Yongji 1933- WhoAsA 94
Li, Yu-ku 1939- WhoAsA 94
Li, Yuzhuo 1958- WhoAsA 94
Li, Zili 1956- WhoScEn 94
Lia, Gary Peter 1941- WhoIns 94
Li'a, Tufele WhoAmP 93
Liacos, Paul Julian 1929- WhoAm 94, WhoAmL 94, WhoAmP 93
Li Aisun WhoPRCh 91
Liakishev, Nikolai Pavlovich 1929- WhoScEn 94
Lian, Eric Chun-Yet 1938- WhoAsA 94
Lian, Maria Z. N. 1939- WhoAsA 94
Li Ang 1952- BlmGWL
Liang, Bruce T. 1956- WhoAsA 94
Liang, Chang-seng 1941- WhoAsA 94
Liang, Diana F. WhoAsA 94
Liang, Edison Park-tak 1947- WhoAsA 94
Liang, George Hsueh-Lee 1934- WhoAsA 94, WhoMW 93
Liang, Jason Chia 1935- WhoScEn 94, WhoWest 94
Liang, Jeffrey Der-Shing 1915- WhoScEn 94, WhoWest 94
Liang, Junxiang 1932- WhoScEn 94
Liang, Matthew H. 1944- WhoAsA 94
Liang, Nong 1958- WhoScEn 94
Liang, Steven Yuehsan 1958- WhoAsA 94
Liang, Tehming 1945- WhoAsA 94, WhoMW 93
Liang, Ting-Peng 1953- WhoMW 93
Liang, Vera Beh-Yuin Tsai 1946- WhoScEn 94
Liang Bin 1914- WhoPRCh 91
Liang Biye 1916- WhoPRCh 91 [port]
Liang Buting 1921- IntWW 93, WhoPRCh 91 [port]
Liang Chengye 1924- IntWW 93
Liang Dong-Cai 1932- IntWW 93, WhoPRCh 91
Liang Feng WhoPRCh 91
Liang Guangda WhoPRCh 91 [port]
Liang Guangdi WhoPRCh 91
Liang Guanglie WhoPRCh 91
Liang Guoqing 1938- WhoPRCh 91 [port]
Liang Heng 1954- ConAu 142
Liang Jia 1921- WhoPRCh 91 [port]
Liang Jinguang ConWorW 93
Liang Keyong WhoPRCh 91
Liang Lingguang 1916- IntWW 93, WhoPRCh 91 [port]
Liang Nan 1927- WhoPRCh 91
Liang Ning 1958- WhoPRCh 91 [port]
Liang Shangli 1920- WhoPRCh 91 [port]
Liang Shoupan WhoPRCh 91
Liang Shoupan 1916- IntWW 93
Liang Shufen 1934- WhoPRCh 91 [port]
Liang Taiping WhoPRCh 91
Liang Taosheng WhoPRCh 91
Liang Wanggui 1930- WhoPRCh 91 [port]
Liang Xiang 1919- IntWW 93
Liang Xiaosheng 1949- IntWW 93, WhoPRCh 91 [port]
Liang Yeping WhoPRCh 91
Liang Yujin WhoPRCh 91 [port]
Liang Yuning 1939- WhoPRCh 91 [port]
Lianis, Georgios 1926- IntWW 93
Lian Yin 1929- WhoPRCh 91 [port]
Lian Zhong WhoPRCh 91
Liao 1936- WhoAmA 93
Liao, Chung Min 1957- WhoScEn 94
Liao, Eric Nan-Kang 1938- WhoWest 94
Liao, Hsiang Peng 1924- WhoAm 94, WhoScEn 94
Liao, Kevin Chii Wen 1937- WhoScEn 94
Liao, Mei-June WhoAm 94
Liao, Mei-June 1951- WhoAsA 94
Liao, Ming 1950- WhoAsA 94
Liao, Paul Foo-Hung 1944- WhoAm 94, WhoAsA 94
Liao, Shiou-Ping 1936- WhoAm 94
Liao, Shun-Kwung 1937- WhoAsA 94
Liao, Shutsung 1931- WhoAm 94, WhoAsA 94
Liao, T. Warren 1957- WhoAsA 94
Liao, Wayne M. 1950- WhoAmL 94
Liao, Woody M. 1942- WhoAsA 94
Liao Bingxiong 1915- IntWW 93
Liao Bokang 1924- WhoPRCh 91 [port]
Liao Canhui 1923- WhoPRCh 91 [port]
Liao Gailong WhoPRCh 91
Liao Hansheng 1911- WhoPRCh 91 [port]
Liao Hansheng, Lieut.-Gen. 1911- IntWW 93
Liao Hui 1941- IntWW 93, WhoPRCh 91 [port]
Liao Jingdan 1916- WhoPRCh 91 [port]
Liao Jingwen WhoPRCh 91 [port]
Liao Mosha 1907- WhoPRCh 91 [port]
Liao Poon-Huai, Donald 1929- Who 94
Liao Qiuzhong WhoPRCh 91
Liao Shantao 1920- IntWW 93
Liao Wenhai WhoPRCh 91 [port], WhoWomW 91
Liao Xilong 1940- WhoPRCh 91 [port]
Liao Yanxiong 1922- WhoPRCh 91 [port]
Liao Zhigao 1908- WhoPRCh 91
Liapakis, Pamela Anagnos 1947- WhoAmL 94
Liard, Jean-Francois 1943- WhoMW 93
Liardet, Guy Francis 1934- Who 94
Liardet, Henry Maughan 1906- Who 94
Lias, Thomas R. WhoAmA 93N
Liaskos, George DrAPF 93
Liautaud, Loretta Torres 1942- WhoHisp 94
Liaw, Hang Ming 1936- WhoWest 94
Liaw, Haw-Ming 1942- WhoScEn 94
Liba, Peter Michael 1940- WhoAm 94
Libai, David 1934- IntWW 93
Libanio Christo, Carlos Alberto 1944- IntWW 93
Li Baocheng WhoPRCh 91
Li Baoguo WhoPRCh 91
Li Baoheng 1931- WhoPRCh 91
Li Baohua 1908- IntWW 93, WhoPRCh 91 [port]
Li Baolian 1963- WhoPRCh 91 [port]
Libassi, Frank Peter 1930- WhoAm 94, WhoAmP 93
Libbey, I. Aldrich d1925 WhoHol 92
Libbin, Anne Edna 1950- WhoAm 94
Libbin, James David 1950- WhoWest 94
Libbrecht, Kenneth WhoScEn 94
Libby, Donald Gerald 1934- Who 94
Libby, Fred WhoHol 92
Libby, Gary Russell 1944- WhoAm 94, WhoAmA 93
Libby, Gerold Willis 1942- WhoAmL 94
Libby, Jack L. WhoAmP 93
Libby, James D. WhoAmP 93
Libby, John Kelway 1926- WhoAm 94
Libby, Lauren Dean 1951- WhoFI 94, WhoWest 94
Libby, Peter 1947- WhoAm 94
Libby, Richard Allan 1958- WhoWest 94
Libby, Ronald T(heodore) 1941- WrDr 94
Libby, Ronald Theodore 1941- WhoAm 94, WhoFI 94
Libby, Willard Frank 1908-1980 WorScD
Libby, William C. 1919- WhoAmA 93N
Libchaber, Albert Joseph 1934- WhoAm 94, WhoScEn 94
Libcke, John Hanson 1935- WhoMW 93
Libeau, Gustave d1957 WhoHol 92
Liben, Michael Paul 1954- WhoAm 94
Liber, John Douglas 1938- WhoAmL 94
Liber, Nevin Jerome 1965- WhoWest 94
Libera, Sharon DrAPF 93
Liberace d1987 WhoHol 92
Liberace, George d1983 WhoHol 92
Liberaki, Margarita 1919- IntWW 93
Liberatore, Anthony Francis 1947- WhoFI 94
Liberatore, Joseph Michael 1952- WhoFI 94
Liberatore, Nicholas Alfred 1916- WhoAm 94
Liberi, Dante 1919- WhoAmA 93
Liberia-Peters, Maria IntWW 93
Liberman, Alexander 1912- IntWW 93, WhoAm 94, WhoAmA 93
Liberman, Alvin Meyer 1917- WhoAm 94
Liberman, Frank P. 1917- IntMPA 94
Liberman, Howard M. 1946- WhoAmL 94
Liberman, Ira L. 1926- WhoAm 94
Liberman, Irving 1937- WhoScEn 94
Liberman, Keith Gordon 1956- WhoAmL 94
Liberman, Lee Marvin 1921- WhoAm 94, WhoMW 93
Liberman, Lee Sarah 1956- WhoAm 94
Liberman, Michael 1938- WhoScEn 94
Liberman, Robert Barton 1948- WhoFI 94
Liberman, Robert Paul 1937- WhoAm 94, WhoScEn 94
Liberson, Sanford 1936- IntMPA 94
Libert, Donald Joseph 1928- WhoAm 94, WhoAmL 94
Liberte, Jean 1896- WhAm 10
Liberte, Jean 1896-1965 WhoAmA 93N
Liberti, Paul A. 1936- WhoAm 94
Liberti, Ray 1946- WhoAmP 93
Libertini, Richard IntMPA 94, WhoHol 92
Libertiny, George Zoltan 1934- WhoAm 94
Libertiny, Thomas Gabor 1966- WhoFI 94
Liberto, Joseph Salvatore 1929- WhoAm 94
Liberts, Ludolfs 1895-1959 WhoAmA 93N
Liberty, Marcus 1968- WhoBlA 94
Libet, Benjamin 1916- WhoWest 94
Libhart, Myles Laroy 1931-1990 WhoAmA 93N
Libin, Jerome B. 1936- WhoAm 94, WhoAmL 94
Libin, Paul 1930- WhoAm 94
Li Bing WhoPRCh 91 [port]
Li Binghe WhoPRCh 91
Li Binkui 1947- WhoPRCh 91
Liblang, Dani Kathleen 1955- WhoAmL 94
Libnoch, Joseph Anthony 1934- WhoMW 93, WhoScEn 94
Libo, Kenneth (Harold) 1937- WrDr 94
Libo, Lester Martin 1923- WhoWest 94
Liboff, Richard Lawrence 1931- WhoAm 94
Libonati, Michael Ernest 1944- WhoAm 94
Li Boning WhoPRCh 91
Libous, Alfred Joseph 1928- WhoAmP 93
Libous, Thomas W. 1953- WhoAmP 93
Libove, Charles 1923- WhoAm 94
Li Boyong 1932- IntWW 93, WhoPRCh 91 [port]
Librett, Jeffrey Scott 1958- WhoMW 93
LiBrizzi, Rose Marie Meola 1940- WhoAm 94
Libro, Antoinette DrAPF 93
Libshitz, Herman I. 1939- WhoScEn 94
Liburd, Almando 1953- WhoAmP 93
Licata, Arthur Frank 1947- WhoAmL 94
Licata, Jack Joseph 1961- WhoFI 94
Licata, Steven Karl 1956- WhoMW 93
LiCausi, Paul Anthony 1949- WhoIns 94
Liccardi, Vincent G. IntMPA 94
Liccione, Alexander 1948- WhoAmA 93
Liccione, Maureen T. 1953- WhoAmL 94
Licea, Carlos J. 1948- WhoHisp 94
Licea, Rafael V. 1943- WhoHisp 94
Liceaga, Carlos Arturo 1958- WhoScEn 94
Licens, Lila Louise 1949- WhoWest 94
Licette, Miriam 1892-1969 NewGrDO
Lich, Glen Ernst 1948- WhoAm 94, WhoFI 94
Lichacz, Sheila Enit 1942- WhoAmA 93
Li Chang 1914- IntWW 93, WhoPRCh 91 [port]
Li Chang'an 1935- IntWW 93, WhoPRCh 91
Li Changchun 1944- IntWW 93, WhoPRCh 91 [port]
Li Changxing 1931- WhoPRCh 91 [port]
Lichaw, Pessia WhoAmA 93
Li Chen 1916- WhoPRCh 91 [port]
Li Chengren 1938- WhoPRCh 91 [port]
Li Chengrui 1921- WhoPRCh 91
Li Chengyu 1946- WhoPRCh 91 [port]
Lichfield, Archdeacon of Who 94
Lichfield, Bishop of 1934- Who 94
Lichfield, Dean of Who 94
Lichfield, Earl of 1939- IntWW 93, Who 94
Lichfield, Nathaniel 1916- Who 94
Lichine, David d1972 WhoHol 92
Lichine, David 1910-1972 IntDcB [port]
Lichine, David, Mme. Who 94
Li Ch'ing-chao BlmGWL
Lichnerowicz, Andre 1915- IntWW 93
Lichnowsky, Mechthilde 1879-1958 BlmGWL
Licho, Edgar d1944 WhoHol 92
Li Chonghuai 1916- WhoPRCh 91 [port]
Lichstein, Edgar 1936- WhoScEn 94
Lichstein, Henry Alan 1943- WhoFI 94
Lichstein, Herman Carlton 1918- WhoAm 94, WhoScEn 94
Lichstein, Jacob 1908- WhAm 10
Lichstein, Toni C. 1947- WhoAmL 94
Licht, Alice Vess 1937- WhoWest 94
Licht, Charles A. 1924- WhoFI 94, WhoMW 93
Licht, Evelyn M. 1905- WhoAmA 93
Licht, Jeremy 1971- WhoHol 92
Licht, Paul 1938- WhoAm 94
Licht, Richard A. 1948- WhoAm 94, WhoAmL 94, WhoAmP 93
Lichtblau, John H. 1921- WhoAm 94
Lichtblau, Myron I 1925- WrDr 94
Lichtblau, Myron Ivor 1925- WhoAm 94
Lichte, DeAnn 1951- WhoMW 93
Lichten, Frances 1889-1961 WhoAmA 93N
Lichten, Nancy G. 1960- WhoFI 94, WhoMW 93
Lichtenberg, Byron K. 1948- WhoAm 94, WhoScEn 94
Lichtenberg, Don Bernett 1928- WhoMW 93
Lichtenberg, Jacqueline 1942- EncSF 93, WrDr 94
Lichtenberg, Larry Ray 1938- WhoWest 94
Lichtenberg, Manes WhoAmA 93
Lichtenberg, Margaret Klee 1941- WhoAm 94
Lichtenberg, Paul 1911- IntWW 93
Lichtenberg, Philip 1926- WrDr 94
Lichtenberger, Frank H. 1937- WhoIns 94
Lichtenberger, Horst William 1935- WhoFI 94
Lichtenberger, Lee S. 1952- WhoAmP 93
Lichtenberger, William Robert 1925- WhoIns 94
Lichtenheld, Frank Robert 1923- WhoScEn 94
Lichtenstein, Adam Van 1965- WhoAmL 94
Lichtenstein, Donald Ray 1956- WhoWest 94
Lichtenstein, Elissa Charlene 1954- WhoAm 94
Lichtenstein, Gary 1953- WhoAmA 93
Lichtenstein, Harvey 1929- WhoAm 94
Lichtenstein, Karl August, Freiherr von 1767-1845 NewGrDO
Lichtenstein, Lawrence Jay 1929- WhoAm 94
Lichtenstein, Lawrence Mark 1934- WhoAm 94
Lichtenstein, Mitchell 1956- WhoHol 92
Lichtenstein, Natalie G. 1953- WhoAmL 94
Lichtenstein, Robert Jay 1948- WhoAm 94, WhoAmL 94
Lichtenstein, Roy 1923- AmCulL, IntWW 93, News 94-1 [port], Who 94, WhoAm 94, WhoAmA 93
Lichtenstein, Sara 1929- WhoAmA 93N
Lichtenstein, Sarah Carol 1953- WhoAmL 94
Lichtenthaler, Frieder Wilhelm 1932- WhoScEn 94
Lichtenwalner, Owen C. 1937- WhoScEn 94
Lichtenwalter, James Philip 1937- WhoMW 93
Lichter, Edward Arthur 1928- WhoAm 94
Lichter, Paul Richard 1939- WhoAm 94, WhoScEn 94
Lichter, Robert Louis 1941- WhoScEn 94
Lichter-Heath, Laurie Jean 1951- WhoAmL 94
Lichterman, Harvey S. 1940- WhoAm 94
Lichterman, Martin 1918- WhoAm 94
Lichterman, Marvin WhoHol 92
Lichti, Barbara Jean 1942- WhoMW 93
Lichti, Reuben Boyd 1923- WhoAmP 93
Lichtig, Leo Kenneth 1953- WhoFI 94, WhoScEn 94
Lichtin, J. Leon 1924- WhoAm 94
Lichtin, Norman Nahum 1922- WhoAm 94
Lichtman, David Michael 1942- WhoAm 94
Lichtmann, Samuel Arthur 1898- WhAm 10
Lichtner, Schomer Frank 1905- WhoAmA 93

Li Gang 1926- IntWW 93, WhoPRCh 91 [port]
Li Gang 1951- WhoPRCh 91
Li Gangzhong WhoPRCh 91 [port]
Li Ganliu 1933- WhoPRCh 91 [port]
Ligare, Kathleen Meredith 1950- WhoAm 94
Ligendza, Catarina 1937- NewGrDO
Li Genshen 1930- WhoPRCh 91 [port]
Li Genshen 1931- IntWW 93
Ligero, Miguel d1989 WhoHol 92
Ligeti, Gyorgy (Sandor) 1923- NewGrDO
Ligeti, Gyorgy Sandor 1923- IntWW 93, Who 94
Ligett, Waldo Buford 1916- WhoAm 94
Liggero, John (Gerold) 1921- WrDr 94
Liggett, Hiram Shaw, Jr. 1932- WhoAm 94
Liggett, Lawrence Melvin 1917- WhoAm 94
Liggett, Louis d1928 WhoHol 92
Liggett, Mark William 1957- WhoScEn 94
Liggett, Ronald D. WhoAmP 93
Liggett, Thomas 1918- WrDr 94
Liggett, Thomas Jackson 1919- WhoAm 94
Liggett, Thomas Milton 1944- WhoWest 94
Liggett, Twila Marie Christensen 1944- WhoAm 94, WhoFI 94
Liggins, George Lawson 1937- WhoWest 94
Liggins, Graham (Collingwood) Who 94
Liggins, Graham Collingwood 1926- IntWW 93
Liggio, Carl Donald 1943- WhoAm 94, WhoAmL 94, WhoFI 94
Light, Albert 1927- WhoAm 94
Light, Alfred Robert 1949- WhoAmL 94
Light, Arthur Heath WhoAm 94
Light, Betty Jensen Pritchett 1924- WhoAm 94
Light, Christopher Upjohn 1937- WhoAm 94, WhoMW 93
Light, (Sidney) David 1919- Who 94
Light, Dorothy Kaplan 1937- WhoAm 94, WhoFI 94
Light, Douglas Bruce 1956- WhoMW 93
Light, Francis 1740-1794 DcNaB MP
Light, Harold L. 1929- WhoAm 94
Light, Ivan I. 1943- WhoAmL 94
Light, James Forest 1921- WhoAm 94
Light, Jo Knight 1936- WhoFI 94
Light, John EncSF 93
Light, John Caldwell 1934- WhoAm 94
Light, John Ralph 1955- WhoIns 94
Light, John Robert 1941- WhoAm 94, WhoAmL 94
Light, Judith 1949- IntMPA 94
Light, Ken 1951- WhoAmA 93, WhoWest 94
Light, Kenneth B. 1932- WhoAm 94
Light, Kenneth Freeman 1922- WhoAm 94
Light, Lawrence 1941- WhoAm 94
Light, Murray Benjamin 1926- WhoAm 94
Light, Richard Jay 1942- WhoAm 94
Light, Robert WhoHol 92
Light, Robert M. 1911- WhoAm 94
Light, Robert S. WhoAmP 93
Light, Robley Jasper 1935- WhoAm 94
Light, Russell Jeffers 1949- WhoAmL 94
Light, Timothy 1938- WhoAm 94
Light, Walter Frederick 1923- WhoAm 94
Light, William Allan 1950- WhoScEn 94
Light, William Randall 1958- WhoAmL 94
Lightbody, Ian (Macdonald) 1921- Who 94
Lightbody, Roden S. 1943- WhoAmP 93
Lightbown, David Lincoln 1932- Who 94
Lightbown, Ronald William 1932- Who 94
Lighter, Eric Aaron 1950- WhoFI 94
Lightfoot, Alexander d1972 WhoHol 92
Lightfoot, Claude M. 1910-1991 WhoBlA 94N
Lightfoot, Connie Dae 1952- WhoMW 93
Lightfoot, David William 1945- WhoAm 94
Lightfoot, Gary Duane 1940- WhoFI 94
Lightfoot, George Michael 1936- Who 94
Lightfoot, Gordon Meredith 1938- WhoAm 94
Lightfoot, James Ross 1938- WhoAm 94, WhoMW 93
Lightfoot, Jean Drew WhoBlA 94
Lightfoot, Jean Harvey 1935- WhoBlA 94
Lightfoot, Jim 1938- CngDr 93
Lightfoot, Jim Ross 1938- WhoAmP 93
Lightfoot, Joe Dean 1961- WhoMW 93
Lightfoot, Mark Raleigh 1965- WhoAmL 94
Lightfoot, Sara Lawrence BlkWr 2, ConAu 142, WhoBlA 94
Lightfoot, Warren Bricken 1938- WhoAmL 94
Lightfoot, William P. 1920- WhoBlA 94
Lightfoot, William P., Jr. WhoAmP 93
Lightfoote, Marilyn Madry WhoScEn 94
Lightfoote, William Edward, II 1942- WhoBlA 94
Light-Harris, Donald 1944- WhoWest 94
Lighthill, James 1924- IntWW 93
Lighthill, (Michael) James 1924- Who 94
Lighthizer, Robert E. 1947- WhoAm 94, WhoAmL 94
Lightman, Alan 1948- ConLC 81 [port]
Lightman, Alan P. 1948- ConAu 141
Lightman, Alan Paige 1948- WhoAm 94
Lightman, Gavin Anthony 1939- Who 94
Lightman, Harold 1906- Who 94
Lightman, Ivor Harry 1928- Who 94
Lightman, Lionel 1928- Who 94
Lightman, M. A. 1915- IntMPA 94
Lightner, A. LeRoy, Jr. 1921- WhoFI 94
Lightner, A(lice) M(artha) 1904-1988 EncSF 93
Lightner, Candy Lynne 1946- WhoAm 94
Lightner, Clarence WhoAmP 93
Lightner, Clarence E. 1921- WhoBlA 94
Lightner, Drew Warren 1948- WhoMW 93
Lightner, E. Allan 1907- HisDcKW
Lightner, Edwin Allan, Jr. 1907-1990 WhAm 10
Lightner, Michael R. 1950- WhoWest 94
Lightner, Winnie d1971 WhoHol 92
Lighton, Christopher Robert d1993 Who 94N
Lighton, Linda 1948- WhoAmA 93
Lighton, Thomas (Hamilton) 1954- Who 94
Lights, Rikki DrAPF 93
Lightsey, Deborah A. WhoAmP 93
Lightstone, Ronald 1938- WhoAm 94, WhoAmL 94, WhoWest 94
Lightwood, Carol Wilson 1941- WhoFI 94, WhoWest 94
Ligi, Barbara Jean 1959- WhoScEn 94
Ligi, Elio Emiliano DrAPF 93
Ligman, James Edmund 1950- WhoAmL 94
Lignarolo, Fini 1950- WhoHisp 94
Lignell, Kathleen DrAPF 93
Ligomenides, Panos Aristides 1928- WhoAm 94
Ligon, Bradford V. 1922- WhoAmP 93
Ligon, Claude M. 1935- WhoBlA 94
Ligon, Daisy Matutina 1947- WhoScEn 94
Ligon, Doris Hillian 1936- WhoBlA 94
Ligon, Grover d1965 WhoHol 92
Ligon, Tom 1945- WhoHol 92
Ligon, William Austin 1951- WhoFI 94
Ligotti, Eugene Ferdinand 1936- WhoScEn 94
Ligrani, Phillip Meredith 1952- WhoWest 94
Li Guangsheng WhoPRCh 91
Li Gui 1915- WhoPRCh 91 [port]
Li Guibin WhoPRCh 91
Li Guilian 1946- WhoPRCh 91 [port]
Li Guixian 1937- IntWW 93, WhoPRCh 91 [port]
Li Guiying 1927- WhoPRCh 91 [port]
Li Guohao 1913- IntWW 93, WhoPRCh 91 [port]
Liguori, Frank Nickolas 1946- WhoFI 94
Liguori, Patrick A. 1940- WhoAmL 94
Liguori, Robert E. 1939- WhoAmL 94
Li Guowen 1930- WhoPRCh 91 [port]
Li Guoxin WhoPRCh 91
Li Haifeng 1949- WhoPRCh 91 [port]
Li Haitao 1932- WhoPRCh 91 [port]
Li Haizhong 1929- WhoPRCh 91 [port]
Li Hangyu 1957- WhoPRCh 91 [port]
Li Hao 1927- IntWW 93, WhoPRCh 91 [port]
Li Haopei WhoPRCh 91
Li Hemin 1921- WhoPRCh 91
Li Honglin 1926- WhoPRCh 91
Li Hou 1923- IntWW 93, WhoPRCh 91 [port]
Li Hua 1907- WhoPRCh 91 [port]
Li Huahua 1962- WhoPRCh 91 [port]
Li Huaji 1931- IntWW 93, WhoPRCh 91 [port]
Li Huamei WhoPRCh 91
Li Huamin WhoPRCh 91
Li Huanzheng 1936- WhoPRCh 91 [port]
Li Huanzhi WhoPRCh 91 [port]
Li Huifen 1940- IntWW 93, WhoPRCh 91 [port]
Li Huifen 1941- WhoWomW 91
Li Huixin 1937- BlmGWL
Liikanen, Erkki Antero 1950- IntWW 93
Lijertwood, Lucita 1921- WhoHol 92
Li Ji WhoPRCh 91
Li Jiahao 1924- WhoPRCh 91 [port]
Li Jian'an 1922- WhoPRCh 91 [port]
Li Jianbai 1918- WhoPRCh 91 [port]
Li Jiansheng 1908- WhoPRCh 91 [port]
Li Jianzhen 1906- WhoPRCh 91 [port]
Li Jiaquan WhoPRCh 91 [port]
Li Jiasong WhoPRCh 91
Li Jiayu 1923- WhoPRCh 91 [port]
Li Jifeng 1923- WhoPRCh 91 [port]
Li Jijun 1934- WhoPRCh 91 [port]
Li Jijun, Lieut.-Gen. 1934- IntWW 93
Li Ji'nai WhoPRCh 91
Li Jing 1930- WhoPRCh 91 [port]
Li Jing, Vice-Adm. 1930- IntWW 93
Li Jingwen WhoPRCh 91
Li Jinhua WhoPRCh 91
Li Jinhua 1943- WhoPRCh 91 [port]
Li Jinmin WhoPRCh 91
Lijinsky, William 1928- WhoAm 94
Li Jinyan 1968- WhoPRCh 91 [port]
Li Jinyun WhoPRCh 91
Li Jiulong 1929- WhoPRCh 91 [port]
Li Jiulong, Lieut.-Gen. 1929- IntWW 93
Li Jiuru WhoPRCh 91
Li Jiwu 1931- WhoPRCh 91 [port]
Lijn, Liliane DrAPF 93
Lijn, Liliane 1939- WhoAmA 93
Lijoi, Peter Bruno 1953- WhoAmL 94, WhoFI 94
Li Jun 1929- WhoPRCh 91 [port]
Li Kaixin WhoPRCh 91
Likaku, Victor Timothy 1934- Who 94
Li-Kam-Wa, Patrick 1958- WhoScEn 94
Likan, Gustav 1912- WhoAmA 93
Li Ka-Shing 1928- IntWW 93
Likavec, Thomas John 1950- WhoFI 94
Li Ke 1920- WhoPRCh 91 [port]
Li Kechun WhoPRCh 91 [port]
Likens, Gene E. 1935- IntWW 93
Likens, Gene Elden 1935- WhoAm 94
Likens, James Dean 1937- WhoAm 94, WhoFI 94, WhoWest 94
Likens, Suzanne Alicia 1945- WhoWest 94
Li K'e-nung 1898-1962 HisDcKW
Li Keqiang 1955- WhoPRCh 91 [port]
Liker, Jack 1926- WhoFI 94
Li Keyu 1929- IntWW 93
Likhachev, Dmitriy Sergeyevich 1906- IntWW 93
Likhachev, Dmitry Sergeevich 1906- LngBDD
Likierman, (John) Andrew 1943- Who 94
Likimani, Muthoni BlmGWL [port]
Liking, Werewere BlmGWL
Likins, Peter William 1936- WhoAm 94
Likoff, Bruce L. 1950- WhoAmL 94
Li Kongzheng 1959- WhoPRCh 91 [port]
Likouris, Mary Ruth 1957- WhoMW 93
Liksom, Rosa 1958- BlmGWL
Li Kwoh-Ting 1910- IntWW 93
Li Laizhu 1932- WhoPRCh 91 [port]
Li Laizhu, Lieut.-Gen. 1932- IntWW 93
Li Lan 1943- WhoAmA 93, WhoAsA 94
Li Lanqing 1932- IntWW 93, WhoPRCh 91 [port], WhoWomW 91
Lilar, Francoise ConWorW 93
Lilburn, Monte Wayne 1965- WhoMW 93
Lile, Bill 1946- WhoAmP 93
Liles, Catharine (Burns) 1944- WhoAmA 93
Liles, Malcolm Henry 1950- WhoFI 94
Liles, Mike James 1945- WhoAmP 93
Liles, Raeford Bailey 1923- WhoAmA 93
Liles, Rutledge Richardson 1942- WhoAmL 94
Liley, Peter Edward 1927- WhoAm 94
Lilford, Baron 1931- Who 94
Li Li WhoPRCh 91
Li Li'an 1920- IntWW 93, WhoPRCh 91 [port]
Liliana, Lili WhoHol 92
Li Lianghui 1939- WhoPRCh 91
Lilien, Mark Ira 1953- WhoAm 94
Lilien, Robert S. 1947- WhoAmL 94
Lilienfield, Karl d1966 WhoAmA 93N
Lilienfield, Lawrence Spencer 1927- WhoAm 94
Lilienstern, O. Clayton 1943- WhoAm 94
Lilienthal, Alfred Morton 1915- WhoAm 94
Lilienthal, Otto 1848-1896 WorInv [port]
Li Ligong 1925- IntWW 93, WhoPRCh 91 [port]
Li Lin 1923- IntWW 93, WhoPRCh 91 [port]
Li Ling WhoPRCh 91
Li Ling 1913- IntWW 93
Li Ling 1956- WhoPRCh 91 [port]
Li Lingwei 1964- IntWW 93, WhoPRCh 91 [port]
Li Lishi WhoPRCh 91
Liljedahl, Maria WhoHol 92
Liljegren, Dorothy WhoAmP 93
Liljegren, Frank 1930- WhoAmA 93
Liljegren, Frank Sigfrid 1930- WhoAm 94
Liljestrand, Bengt Tson 1919- IntWW 93
Liljestrand, Howard Michael 1953- WhoScEn 94
Liljestrand, James Stratton 1941- WhoFI 94
Lilker, Dan
See Anthrax ConMus 11
Lill, John Richard 1944- IntWW 93, Who 94
Lillard, Charlotte d1946 WhoHol 92
Lillard, John Franklin, III 1947- WhoAm 94, WhoAmL 94
Lillard, Leo, II 1939- WhoBlA 94
Lillard, Mark Hill, III 1943- WhoAm 94
Lillard, Robert Emmitt 1907- WhoBlA 94
Lillard, W. Lovell 1936- WhoBlA 94
Lillee, Dennis K. 1949- IntWW 93
Lillegraven, Jason Arthur 1938- WhoWest 94
Lillehaug, David Lee 1954- WhoAmL 94
Lillehei, Clarence Walton 1918- WhoAm 94
Liller, Karen DeSafey 1956- WhoScEn 94
Lillestol, Jane Marie 1936- WhoAm 94
Lillevang, Omar Johansen 1914- WhoAm 94
Lilley, Albert Frederick 1932- WhoAm 94
Lilley, Daniel T. 1920- WhoAmP 93
Lilley, Geoffrey Michael 1919- Who 94
Lilley, James Roderick 1928- IntWW 93, WhoAm 94, WhoAmP 93
Lilley, John fl. 19th cent.- EncNAR
Lilley, John Mark 1939- WhoAm 94
Lilley, John Robert, II 1929- WhoAm 94
Lilley, Mili Della WhoFI 94
Lilley, Peter Bruce 1943- IntWW 93, Who 94
Lilley, Sandra 1963- WhoHisp 94
Lilley, Theodore Robert 1923- WhoAm 94
Lilley, William, III 1938- WhoAm 94
Lillibridge, John Lee 1924- WhoAm 94
Lillich, Alice Louise 1940- WhoMW 93
Lillicrap, Harry George 1913- Who 94
Lillie, Beatrice d1989 WhoHol 92
Lillie, Beatrice 1894-1989 WhoCom
Lillie, Charisse Ranielle 1952- WhoAm 94
Lillie, James Woodruff, Jr. 1931- WhoAm 94
Lillie, John Mitchell 1937- WhoAm 94, WhoFI 94, WhoWest 94
Lillie, Mildred Loree 1915- WhoAmL 94, WhoWest 94
Lillie, Vernell A. 1931- WhoBlA 94
Lilliehook, Johan Bjorn Olof 1945- WhoScEn 94
Lillingston, George David I. I. Who 94
Lillingston, Sandie WhoHol 92
Lillington, John WhAmRev
Lillington, John Alexander c. 1725-1786 WhAmRev
Lillington, Kenneth (James) 1916- TwCYAW, WrDr 94
Lillis, Joan Frances 1936- WhoAmP 93
Lillo, George 1691-1739 IntDcT 2
Lillo, George 1693-1739 BlmGEL
Lillo, Giuseppe 1814-1863 NewGrDO
Lilly, Bob ProFbHF [port]
Lilly, Doris 1921-1991 WhAm 10
Lilly, Edward Guerrant, Jr. 1925- WhoAm 94
Lilly, Frank 1930- IntWW 93, WhoAm 94
Lilly, J. K., Jr. 1893-1966 DcLB 140 [port]
Lilly, Jane Anne Feeley 1947- WhoWest 94
Lilly, John Cunningham 1915- WhoAm 94
Lilly, John Russell 1929- WhoAm 94
Lilly, John Thomas 1960- WhoAmL 94
Lilly, Les J. 1950- WhoScEn 94
Lilly, Malcolm Douglas 1936- IntWW 93, Who 94
Lilly, Mark 1950- WrDr 94
Lilly, Martin Stephen 1944- WhoAm 94
Lilly, Michael Alexander 1946- WhoAm 94, WhoAmL 94, WhoWest 94
Lilly, Peter Byron 1948- WhoAm 94
Lilly, Raymond Lindsay, Jr. 1949- WhoWest 94
Lilly, Shannon Jeanne 1966- WhoAm 94
Lilly, Sharon Louise 1957- WhoWest 94
Lilly, Thelma Maxine 1925- WhoMW 93
Lilly, Thomas Gerald 1933- WhoAm 94, WhoAmL 94
Lilly, Thomas Joseph 1931- WhoAmL 94
Lilly, Thomas Joseph, Jr. 1959- WhoAmL 94
Lilly, Thomas More 1942- WhoFI 94
Lilly, Walt William 1954- WhoMW 93
Lilly, William 1602-1681 AstEnc
Lilly, William Eldridge 1921- WhoAm 94
Lillya, Clifford Peter 1910- WhoAm 94
Lillyman, William John 1937- WhoAm 94
Lilov, Alexander Vassilev 1933- IntWW 93
Li Lun 1927- WhoPRCh 91 [port]
Lily, William 1468?-1522 BlmGEL, DcLB 132 [port]
Lilyquist, Christine 1940- WhoAmA 93
Lim, Alexander Rufasta 1942- WhoScEn 94
Lim, Antonio Lao 1935- WhoAsA 94
Lim, Billy Bee Lee 1962- WhoMW 93
Lim, Billy Lee 1962- WhoAsA 94
Lim, Catherine 1942- BlmGWL [port]
Lim, Chhorn E. 1945- WhoAsA 94
Lim, Chong C. 1946- WhoAsA 94
Lim, Daniel V. 1948- WhoAsA 94

Lim, David J. 1935- *WhoAsA 94*
Lim, David Jong Jai 1935- *WhoAm 94*
Lim, Edward Hong 1956- *WhoAsA 94*
Lim, Genny *DrAPF 93*
Lim, Henry Chol 1935- *WhoWest 94*
Lim, John K. 1935- *WhoAmP 93, WhoAsA 94*
Lim, Joo Kun 1956- *WhoAsA 94*
Lim, Josefina Paje 1941- *WhoAsA 94*
Lim, Joseph Dy 1948- *WhoScEn 94*
Lim, Kam Ming 1964- *WhoAsA 94*
Lim, Kap Chul 1947- *WhoAsA 94*
Lim, Kieran Fergus 1962- *WhoScEn 94*
Lim, Kim 1936- *IntWW 93*
Lim, Kwee-Eng Lyn 1945- *WhoAsA 94*
Lim, Larry Kay 1948- *WhoWest 94*
Lim, Nancy Wong 1948- *WhoAsA 94*
Lim, Narzalina *WhoWomW 91*
Lim, Paul Stephen 1944- *WhoAsA 94*
Lim, Paulino Marquez, Jr. 1935- *WhoAsA 94*
Lim, Poh C. 1957- *WhoAsA 94*
Lim, Ralph Wei Hsiong 1953- *WhoAsA 94*
Lim, Ramon Khe-Siong 1933- *WhoAsA 94, WhoMW 93, WhoScEn 94*
Lim, Richard 1963- *WhoAsA 94*
Lim, Robert Cheong, Jr. 1933- *WhoAm 94*
Lim, Robert Kho-Seng 1897- *WhAm 10*
Lim, Rodney Gene 1963- *WhoAsA 94*
Lim, Sally-Jane *WhoWest 94*
Lim, Shirley Geok-lin 1944- *BlmGWL, ConAu 140, WhoAsA 94*
Lim, Shun Ping 1947- *WhoMW 93, WhoScEn 94*
Lim, Sonia Yii 1924- *WhoAm 94*
Lim, Soon-Sik 1944- *WhoAsA 94*
Lim, Teck-Kah 1942- *WhoAsA 94*
Lim, Toh-Bin 1934- *WhoWest 94*
Lim, Yong Keun 1935- *WhoAsA 94*
Lim, Youngil 1932- *WhoScEn 94*
Lima, Charlene 1953- *WhoAmP 93*
Lima, Donald Allan 1953- *WhoWest 94*
Lima, Frank *DrAPF 93*
Lima, George Charles 1921- *WhoAmP 93*
Lima, George Silva 1919- *WhoAmP 93, WhoBlA 94*
Lima, Gustavo Raul *WhoHisp 94*
Lima, Jacqueline (Dutton) 1949- *WhoAmA 93*
Lima, Jeronimo Francisco de 1741-1822 *NewGrDO*
Lima, Luis 1948- *NewGrDO*
Lima, Luis Eduardo 1950- *WhoAm 94*
Lima, Margaret Mary Pawlowicz 1949- *WhoMW 93*
Lima, Robert *DrAPF 93*
Lima, Robert 1935- *WhoAm 94*
Lima, Robert (F., Jr.) 1935- *WrDr 94*
Lima, Robert F., Jr. 1935- *WhoHisp 94*
Liman, Arthur L. 1932- *WhoAm 94, WhoAmL 94*
LiMandri, Charles Salvatore 1955- *WhoAmL 94, WhoWest 94*
Limann, Hilla 1934- *IntWW 93, Who 94*
Limardo, Felix R. 1952- *WhoHisp 94*
Li Marzi, Joseph *WhoAmA 93*
LiMarzi, Joseph 1907- *WhoAm 94*
Limato, Edward Frank 1936- *WhoAm 94*
Limauro, Stephen L. *WhoIns 94*
Limb, Ben C. 1893-1976 *HisDcKW*
Limb, Ben Quincy 1936- *WhoAsA 94*
Limbach, Walter F. 1924- *WhoAm 94*
Limbacher, James L 1926- *WrDr 94*
Limbaugh, Ronald Hadley 1938- *WhoAm 94, WhoWest 94*
Limbaugh, Rush *NewYTBS 93 [port]*
Limbaugh, Rush 1951- *CurBio 93 [port]*
Limbaugh, Rush H., III 1951?- *ConAu 142*
Limbaugh, Rush Hudson 1951- *WhoAm 94*
Limbaugh, Stephen N., Jr. 1952- *WhoAmP 93*
Limbaugh, Stephen Nathaniel 1927- *WhoAm 94, WhoAmL 94, WhoMW 93*
Limbaugh, Stephen Nathaniel, Jr. 1952- *WhoAmL 94*
Limbeck, Randal M. 1954- *WhoAmL 94*
Limbu *Who 94*
Limburg, Peter R 1929- *WrDr 94*
Lim Chong Eu 1919- *IntWW 93*
Lime, Yvonne *WhoHol 92*
Li Meisu 1959- *WhoPRCh 91 [port]*
Li Menghua 1922- *WhoPRCh 91 [port]*
Limerick, Countess of 1935- *Who 94*
Limerick, Earl of 1930- *IntWW 93, Who 94*
Limerick And Killaloe, Bishop of 1933- *Who 94*
Lim Fat, (Maxime) Edouard (Lim Man) *Who 94*
Li Ming 1927- *IntWW 93, WhoPRCh 91 [port]*
Li Mingyu *WhoPRCh 91*
Li Minhua 1917- *WhoPRCh 91 [port]*
Li Min Hua 1936- *WhoAm 94*
Limkeman, Darrell Roger 1950- *WhoAmP 93*
Lim Keng Yaik, Dato' Dr. 1939- *IntWW 93*
Lim Kim San 1916- *IntWW 93*
Limmer, Warren E. *WhoAmP 93*
Limon, Donald William 1932- *Who 94*
Limón, Graciela 1938- *WhoHisp 94*
Limon, Jose d1972 *WhoHol 92*
Limone, Frank 1938- *WhoAmA 93*
Limón-Galvin, Yvette 1969- *WhoHisp 94*
Limonov, Eduard 1952- *IntWW 93*
Limont, Naomi Charles *WhoAmA 93*
Li Moran *WhoPRCh 91*
Limpert, John Arthur 1934- *WhoAm 94*
Lim Pin 1936- *IntWW 93, Who 94*
Limpitlaw, John Donald 1935- *WhoAm 94*
Limpy, Josephine Head Swift 1900-1980 *EncNAR*
Lim Yunchun 1938- *WhoPRCh 91 [port]*
Lin, Alice Lee Lan 1937- *WhoFI 94, WhoScEn 94*
Lin, Binshan 1953- *WhoAsA 94*
Lin, Cen-Tsong 1952- *WhoAsA 94*
Lin, Chaote 1930- *WhoAsA 94*
Lin, Charles Fley-Fung 1942- *WhoAsA 94*
Lin, Chengmin Michael 1955- *WhoAsA 94*
Lin, Chhiu-Tsu 1943- *WhoAsA 94*
Lin, Chi-Hung 1943- *WhoScEn 94*
Lin, Chi Yung 1938- *WhoAsA 94*
Lin, Chia-Chiao 1916- *IntWW 93, WhoAsA 94*
Lin, Chien-Chang 1937- *WhoAsA 94*
Lin, Chin-Chu 1935- *WhoAm 94, WhoAsA 94*
Lin, Chin-Ti 1944- *WhoMW 93*
Lin, Ching-Fang 1954- *WhoScEn 94*
Lin, Chinlon 1945- *WhoAsA 94*
Lin, Chiu-Hong 1934- *WhoAsA 94*
Lin, Cho-Liang 1960- *IntWW 93*
Lin, Dennis Kon-Jin 1959- *WhoAsA 94*
Lin, Diane Chang 1944- *WhoAsA 94*
Lin, Elizabeth 1950- *WhoAsA 94*
Lin, Eva I. 1964- *WhoAsA 94*
Lin, Fei-Jann 1934- *WhoScEn 94*
Lin, Felix 1963- *WhoAsA 94*
Lin, Feng-Bao 1954- *WhoAsA 94*
Lin, Forest 1938- *WhoAsA 94*
Lin, Fred Reggie 1965- *WhoAsA 94*
Lin, Fred Z. 1963- *WhoFI 94*
Lin, George H. Y. 1938- *WhoAsA 94*
Lin, Guang Hai 1942- *WhoScEn 94*
Lin, Hsiu-San 1935- *WhoAsA 94*
Lin, Hun-Chi 1953- *WhoWest 94*
Lin, Hung Chang 1919- *WhoAsA 94*
Lin, I-Huei 1941- *WhoMW 93*
Lin, Ilan S. 1949- *WhoAsA 94*
Lin, James C. 1932- *WhoAsA 94*
Lin, James Chih-I 1942- *WhoAm 94, WhoAsA 94*
Lin, James Chow 1954- *WhoAsA 94*
Lin, James P. 1917- *WhoAsA 94*
Lin, James Peicheng 1949- *WhoAsA 94, WhoWest 94*
Lin, James Y. 1958- *WhoAsA 94*
Lin, Jason Jia-Yuan 1955- *WhoAsA 94*
Lin, Jason Zse-Cherng 1955- *WhoWest 94*
Lin, Jennifer Jen-Huey 1964- *WhoAsA 94*
Lin, Jian *WhoAsA 94*
Lin, Jiann-Tsyh 1940- *WhoAsA 94*
Lin, Joseph Pen-Tze 1932- *WhoAm 94, WhoAsA 94*
Lin, Josh Chia Hsin 1954- *WhoWest 94*
Lin, Juiyuan William 1937- *WhoAsA 94*
Lin, Julia C. 1928- *WhoAsA 94*
Lin, Jung-Chung 1939- *WhoScEn 94*
Lin, Justin Yifu 1952- *WhoScEn 94*
Lin, Kai-Ching 1955- *WhoAsA 94*
Lin, Kuan-Pin 1948- *WhoAsA 94*
Lin, L. Yu 1957- *WhoAsA 94*
Lin, Lawrence I-Kuei 1948- *WhoAsA 94*
Lin, Lawrence Shuh Liang 1938- *WhoWest 94*
Lin, Lei 1944- *WhoWest 94*
Lin, Li-Min 1944- *WhoScEn 94*
Lin, Liang-Shiou 1953- *WhoAsA 94*
Lin, Maria C. H. 1942- *WhoAmL 94*
Lin, Maya 1959- *CurBio 93 [port], WhoAm 94*
Lin, Maya Y. *WhoAmA 93*
Lin, Maya Ying *WhoAsA 94*
Lin, Ming-Chang 1936- *WhoAsA 94*
Lin, Ming Shek 1937- *WhoScEn 94*
Lin, Nina S. F. 1946- *WhoAsA 94*
Lin, Nora *BlmGWL*
Lin, Otto Chui Chau 1938- *WhoScEn 94*
Lin, Patricia Yu 1969- *WhoAsA 94*
Lin, Paul Kuang-Hsien 1946- *WhoAsA 94*
Lin, Pen-Min 1928- *WhoAm 94, WhoAsA 94*
Lin, Pi-Erh 1938- *WhoAsA 94*
Lin, Ping-Wha 1925- *WhoAsA 94, WhoMW 93, WhoScEn 94*
Lin, Poping 1954- *WhoAsA 94*
Lin, Robert Peichung 1942- *WhoAsA 94*
Lin, Roxanne Veronica 1957- *WhoAsA 94*
Lin, See-Yan 1939- *IntWW 93*
Lin, Shield B. 1953- *WhoAsA 94*
Lin, Shin 1945- *WhoAm 94, WhoAsA 94*
Lin, Shu 1936- *WhoAm 94*
Lin, Shundar *WhoScEn 94*
Lin, Sin-Shong 1933- *WhoAsA 94*
Lin, Stephen Yaw-rui 1939- *WhoAsA 94*
Lin, Su-Chen Jonathon 1953- *WhoAsA 94*
Lin, Sung P. 1937- *WhoAsA 94*
Lin, Tao 1958- *WhoScEn 94, WhoWest 94*
Lin, Thomas Wen-shyoung 1944- *WhoFI 94, WhoWest 94*
Lin, Ting-Ting Yao 1958- *WhoAsA 94*
Lin, Tom Tung-Hoa 1950- *WhoFI 94*
Lin, Tu 1941- *WhoScEn 94*
Lin, Tung Hua 1911- *WhoAm 94*
Lin, Tung Yen 1911- *WhoAm 94, WhoAsA 94, WhoScEn 94*
Lin, Wallace *ConAu 142, DrAPF 93*
Lin, Wen Chun 1926- *WhoAsA 94, WhoWest 94*
Lin, William Wen-Rong 1942- *WhoAm 94*
Lin, Wunan 1942- *WhoAsA 94*
Lin, Wuu-Long 1939- *WhoAm 94*
Lin, Xiao-Song 1957- *WhoAsA 94*
Lin, Y. K. 1923- *WhoAm 94, WhoScEn 94*
Lin, Yeong-Jer 1936- *WhoAsA 94*
Lin, Yeou-Lin 1957- *WhoScEn 94*
Lin, Yi-Hua 1953- *WhoScEn 94*
Lin, Ying 1944- *WhoWest 94*
Lin, Ying-Chih 1949- *WhoScEn 94*
Lin, You-An Robert 1950- *WhoAsA 94*
Lin, You Ju 1942- *WhoScEn 94*
Lin, Yu-Chong 1935- *WhoAsA 94, WhoWest 94*
Lin, Yu-sheng 1934- *WhoAsA 94*
Lin, Yuet-Chang Joseph 1951- *WhoAsA 94*
Lin, Yuh-Lang 1949- *WhoAsA 94*
Lin, Yuh Meei 1941- *WhoMW 93*
Lin, Yuyi 1952- *WhoAsA 94*
Lin, Zhen-Biao 1938- *WhoScEn 94*
Linacre, (John) Gordon (Seymour) 1920- *IntWW 93, Who 94*
Linacre, Thomas 1460?-1524 *BlmGEL*
Linahon, James Joseph 1951- *WhoWest 94*
Lin Aili *WhoPRCh 91*
Linaker, Kay *WhoHol 92*
Linaker, Lawrence Edward 1934- *IntWW 93, Who 94*
Liñan, Francisco S. 1948- *WhoHisp 94*
Linander, Nils Otto 1925- *WhoAm 94*
Linane, William Edward 1928- *WhoAm 94, WhoFI 94*
Li Nanzheng *WhoPRCh 91*
Linares, Guillermo *WhoAmP 93*
Linares, Guillermo 1950- *WhoHisp 94*
Linares, Henry Amaya 1941- *WhoHisp 94*
Linares, Marcelo Lopez d1986 *WhoHol 92*
Linares, Nora *WhoHisp 94*
Linares, Nora Alice 1954- *WhoAmP 93*
Linaweaver, Brad 1952- *EncSF 93*
Lin Biao 1907-1971 *HisWorL [port]*
Lin Botang 1931- *WhoPRCh 91 [port]*
Lince, John Alan 1940- *WhoMW 93*
Linch, Claude Eldon 1933- *WhoAmP 93*
Linch, Larry A. 1948- *WhoAmP 93*
Lin Ching-Hsia 1955- *IntWW 93*
Lin Chin-Sheng 1916- *IntWW 93*
Linchitz, Richard Michael 1947- *WhoAm 94*
Lincicome, David Richard 1914- *WhoScEn 94*
Lincke, (Carl Emil) Paul 1866-1946 *NewGrDO*
Linclau, Denise Marie 1951- *WhoMW 93*
Lincoln, Aaron of d1186 *DcNaB MP*
Lincoln, Archdeacon of *Who 94*
Lincoln, Bishop of 1936- *Who 94*
Lincoln, Dean of *Who 94*
Lincoln, Earl of 1913- *Who 94*
Lincoln, Abbey *WhoBlA 94*
Lincoln, Abbey 1930- *WhoAm 94, WhoHol 92*
Lincoln, Abbey 1940- *AfrAmAl 6*
Lincoln, Abraham 1809-1865 *DcAmReB 2, HisWorL [port], WorInv*
Lincoln, Alexander, III 1943- *WhoWest 94*
Lincoln, Anthony (Handley) 1911- *Who 94*
Lincoln, Benjamin 1733-1810 *AmRev, WhAmRev [port]*
Lincoln, Bruck Kenneth 1948- *WhoMW 93*
Lincoln, C. Eric 1924- *WhoBlA 94*
Lincoln, C(harles) Eric 1924- *BlkWr 2, WrDr 94*
Lincoln, Caryl d1983 *WhoHol 92*
Lincoln, Catherine Ruth 1941- *WhoAmP 93*
Lincoln, Charles Eric 1924- *WhoAm 94*
Lincoln, Dennis William 1939- *Who 94*
Lincoln, E. K. d1958 *WhoHol 92*
Lincoln, Edmond Lynch 1949- *WhoAm 94, WhoFI 94*
Lincoln, Elizabeth *DrAPF 93*
Lincoln, Elmo d1952 *WhoHol 92*
Lincoln, Emma Ethel 1914- *WhoAmP 93*
Lincoln, F(redman) Ashe *Who 94*
Lincoln, Franklin Benjamin, Jr. d1993 *NewYTBS 93*
Lincoln, Franklin Benjamin, Jr. 1908- *WhoAm 94, WhoAmL 94*
Lincoln, Geoffrey 1923- *WrDr 94*
Lincoln, Georgianna 1943- *WhoAmP 93*
Lincoln, J. William 1940- *WhoAmP 93*
Lincoln, Janet Elizabeth 1945- *WhoScEn 94*
Lincoln, Jeannine Marguerite 1935- *WhoAmP 93*
Lincoln, Joseph L. 1948- *WhoAmL 94*
Lincoln, Lar Park *WhoHol 92*
Lincoln, Lucian Abraham 1926- *WhoAm 94, WhoMW 93*
Lincoln, Mary Lynda Eagle 1942- *WhoMW 93*
Lincoln, Maurice 1887?- *EncSF 93*
Lincoln, Raynard C., Jr. 1934- *WhoFI 94*
Lincoln, Richard Lee 1946- *WhoWest 94*
Lincoln, Richard Mather 1929- *WhoAmA 93*
Lincoln, Sandra Eleanor 1939- *WhoWest 94*
Lincoln, Steve *WhoHol 92*
Lincoln, Thomas R. d1993 *NewYTBS 93*
Lincoln, Victor D. 1941- *WhoIns 94*
Lincoln, Walter Butler, Jr. 1941- *WhoScEn 94*
Lind, Carl Bradley 1929- *WhoAm 94*
Lind, Cynthia M. 1964- *WhoFI 94, WhoMW 93*
Lind, Della *WhoHol 92*
Lind, Dennis Barry 1940- *WhoWest 94*
Lind, Elizabeth Sue 1947- *WhoFI 94*
Lind, Emil d1948 *WhoHol 92*
Lind, Gillian d1983 *WhoHol 92*
Lind, Gus A. d1951 *WhoHol 92*
Lind, Ilse d1955 *WhoHol 92*
Lind, James Forest 1925- *WhoAm 94*
Lind, Jenny 1820-1887 *NewGrDO [port]*
Lind, Jim 1955- *WhoAmP 93*
Lind, Jon Robert 1935- *WhoAm 94, WhoAmL 94, WhoMW 93*
Lind, José 1964- *WhoHisp 94*
Lind, Karen *DrAPF 93*
Lind, Levi Robert 1906- *WrDr 94*
Lind, Marilyn Marlene 1934- *WhoAmP 93*
Lind, Marshall L. *WhoWest 94*
Lind, Maurice David 1934- *WhoWest 94*
Lind, Niels Christian 1930- *WhoAm 94*
Lind, Per 1916- *Who 94*
Lind, Rebecca Ann 1955- *WhoMW 93*
Lind, Terrie Lee 1948- *WhoWest 94*
Lind, Thomas A. 1918- *WhoAmP 93*
Lind, Thomas Otto 1937- *WhoAm 94*
Lind, Traci *WhoHol 92*
Linda, Gerald 1946- *WhoAm 94*
Lindaas, Elroy *WhoAmP 93*
Lindahl, David *WhoAmP 93*
Lindahl, Leon Kenneth 1897- *WhAm 10*
Lindahl, Thomas Jefferson 1937- *WhoMW 93*
Lindahl, Tomas Robert 1938- *Who 94*
Lin Daiyu *WhoPRCh 91 [port]*
Lindall, Robert Josefson 1944- *WhoAmL 94*
Lindamood, John B. 1941- *WhoAmL 94*
Lindars, Frederick C(hevallier) 1923- *WrDr 94*
Lindars, Laurence Edward 1922- *WhoAm 94*
Lindau, James H. 1933- *WhoFI 94, WhoMW 93*
Lindau, James Harold 1933- *WhoAmP 93*
Lindau, Joan *DrAPF 93*
Lindauer, John Howard, II 1937- *WhoAm 94, WhoWest 94*
Lindauer, Martin 1918- *IntWW 93*
Lindbeck, Assar 1930- *IntWW 93*
Lindbeck, (K.) Assar (E.) 1930- *WrDr 94*
Lindberg, Armas *NewGrDO*
Lindberg, Charles David 1928- *WhoAm 94, WhoAmL 94, WhoMW 93*
Lindberg, Donald Allan Bror 1933- *WhoAm 94, WhoScEn 94*
Lindberg, Garry Martin 1941- *WhoAm 94*
Lindberg, George W. 1932- *WhoAm 94, WhoAmL 94*
Lindberg, Helge 1926- *WhoFI 94*
Lindberg, Janice Bethany 1936- *WhoMW 93*
Lindberg, John Edward 1955- *WhoMW 93*
Lindberg, Lawrence V. 1947- *WhoAm 94, WhoAmL 94*
Lindberg, Michael Charles 1951- *WhoAmL 94*
Lindberg, Pamela Jan 1963- *WhoMW 93*
Lindberg, Richard Carl 1953- *WhoMW 93*
Lindberg, Robert E., Jr. 1953- *WhoScEn 94*
Lindberg, Stanley William 1939- *WhoAm 94*
Lindbergh, Anne Morrow 1906- *WrDr 94*
Lindbergh, Anne Spencer d1993 *NewYTBS 93 [port]*

Lindbergh, Anne Spencer Morrow 1906- *Who 94, WhoAm 94*
Lindbergh, Charles Augustus, Jr. 1902-1974 *AmSocL [port]*
Lindblad, Richard Arthur 1937- *WhoAm 94*
Lindblad, William John 1954- *WhoMW 93*
Lindblade, Eric N. 1916- *WhoAmP 93*
Lindblom, Gunnel 1931- *IntMPA 94*
Lindblom, Gunnel 1935- *WhoHol 92*
Lindblom, Marjorie Press 1950- *WhoAm 94*
Lindblom, Seppo Olavi 1935- *IntWW 93*
Lindbohm, Denis *EncSF 93*
Lindburg, Lela Almeta 1906- *WhoAmP 93*
Linde, Hans Arthur 1924- *WhoAm 94, WhoAmP 93, WhoWest 94*
Linde, Harold George 1945- *WhoScEn 94*
Linde, Karl von 1842-1934 *WorInv*
Linde, Kenneth J. *WhoIns 94*
Linde, Lucille Mae Jacobson 1919- *WhoWest 94*
Linde, Maxine Helen 1939- *WhoAm 94, WhoMW 93*
Linde, Nancy *DrAPF 93*
Linde, Robert Hermann 1944- *WhoAm 94, WhoScEn 94*
Linde, Ronald Keith 1940- *WhoAm 94*
Linde, Shirley Motter *WrDr 94*
Linde, William Walker 1932- *WhoAmP 93*
Lindegren, Jack Kenneth 1931- *WhoWest 94*
Lindelheim, Joanna Maria d1724 *NewGrDO*
Lindell, Edward Albert 1928- *WhoAm 94*
Lindell, James Thorsten 1958- *WhoFI 94*
Lindell, Michael Keith 1946- *WhoScEn 94*
Lindeman, Anne *WhoAmP 93*
Lindeman, Fredrik Otto 1936- *IntWW 93*
Lindeman, George Jens 1927- *WhoAmL 94*
Lindeman, Jack *DrAPF 93*
Lindeman, Philip James 1937- *WhoMW 93*
Lindemann, Donald Lee 1936- *WhoAm 94, WhoMW 93*
Lindemann, Edna M. *WhoAmA 93*
Lindemer, Lawrence Boyd 1921- *WhoAm 94*
Lindemulder, Carol Ann 1936- *WhoWest 94*
Lindemulder, Paul 1960- *WhoMW 93*
Linden, Anya 1933- *Who 94*
Linden, Barnard Jay 1943- *WhoScEn 94*
Linden, Eric 1909- *WhoHol 92*
Linden, Hal 1931- *IntMPA 94, WhoAm 94, WhoHol 92*
Linden, Henry Robert 1922- *WhoAm 94, WhoMW 93, WhoScEn 94*
Linden, Jennie 1939- *WhoHol 92*
Linden, Lynette Lois 1951- *WhoScEn 94*
Linden, Marta d1990 *WhoHol 92*
Linden, Robert d1980 *WhoHol 92*
Linden, Theodore Anthony 1938- *WhoWest 94*
Linden, William M. 1932- *WhoAmL 94*
Lindenau, Judith Wood *DrAPF 93*
Lindenau, Judith Wood 1941- *WhoMW 93*
Lindenbaum, Pija 1955- *SmATA 77 [port]*
Lindenbaum, Sandford Richard 1948- *WhoAm 94*
Lindenbaum, Seymour Joseph 1925- *WhoScEn 94*
Lindenberg, Kaethe d1980 *WhoHol 92*
Lindenberg, Mary Jean 1952- *WhoAmL 94*
Lindenberg, Mary K. 1921- *WhoAmA 93*
Lindenberger, Herbert Samuel 1929- *WhoAm 94, WhoWest 94*
Lindenblad, Nils E. 1895- *WhAm 10*
Lindenfeld, Peter 1925- *WhoAm 94*
Lindenstrand, Sylvia 1942- *NewGrDO*
Lindenstrauss, Joram 1936- *IntWW 93*
Linder, Alfred d1957 *WhoHol 92*
Linder, Cec *WhoHol 92*
Linder, Christa *WhoHol 92*
Linder, Don *DrAPF 93*
Linder, Donald Ernst 1938- *WhoAmP 93*
Linder, Forrest Edward 1906-1988 *WhAm 10*
Linder, Harvey Ronald 1949- *WhoAmL 94*
Linder, James Benjamin 1925- *WhoAm 94*
Linder, Jeffrey Mark 1950- *WhoAmP 93, WhoMW 93*
Linder, John 1942- *CngDr 93*
Linder, John E. 1942- *WhoAm 94, WhoAmP 93*
Linder, Lionel d1992 *NewYTBS 93*
Linder, Marc 1946- *ConAu 142*
Linder, Max d1925 *WhoHol 92*
Linder, Max 1883-1925 *WhoCom*
Linder, Rex Kenneth 1948- *WhoAmL 94*
Linder, Robert D 1934- *WrDr 94*
Linder, Robert David 1920- *WhoIns 94*
Linder, Ronald Jay 1934- *WhoWest 94*
Linderberg, Jan Erik 1934- *IntWW 93*
Linderman, Albert Lee 1955- *WhoMW 93*
Linderman, Charles L. *WhoAmP 93*
Linderman, Dean 1943- *WhoFI 94*
Linderman, Earl William 1931- *WhoAmA 93*
Linderoth, Karl-Axel 1927- *IntWW 93*
Lindesay-Bethune *Who 94*
Lindesmith, Larry Alan 1938- *WhoMW 93, WhoScEn 94*
Lindfors, Viveca *WhoAm 94*
Lindfors, Viveca 1920- *IntMPA 94, WhoHol 92*
Lindgreen, Jorgen *EncSF 93*
Lindgren, Arne Sigfrid 1932- *WhoAm 94, WhoAmL 94*
Lindgren, Astrid 1907- *BlmGWL*
Lindgren, Astrid (Anna Emilia) 1907- *ConWorW 93*
Lindgren, Charlotte 1931- *WhoAmA 93*
Lindgren, Derbin Kenneth, Jr. 1932- *WhoAm 94*
Lindgren, Henry Clay 1914- *WrDr 94*
Lindgren, Jay Randolph 1961- *WhoAmP 93*
Lindgren, John Ralph 1933- *WhoAm 94*
Lindgren, Jon 1938- *WhoAmP 93*
Lindgren, Karin Johanna 1960- *WhoAmL 94, WhoWest 94*
Lindgren, Peter *WhoHol 92*
Lindgren, Richard Dan 1931- *WhoFI 94*
Lindgren, Robert Donald, Jr. 1950- *WhoFI 94*
Lindgren, Robert Kemper 1939- *WhoFI 94, WhoWest 94*
Lindgren, Steven Obed 1949- *WhoAmP 93*
Lindgren, Theodore F. 1923- *WhoAmP 93*
Lindgren, Timothy Joseph 1937- *WhoAm 94*
Lindgren, William Dale 1936- *WhoAm 94*
Lindh, Allan Goddard 1943- *WhoScEn 94, WhoWest 94*
Lindh, Patricia Sullivan 1928- *WhoAm 94, WhoAmP 93*
Lindh, Sten 1922- *IntWW 93*
Lindh, Ylva Anna Maria 1957- *IntWW 93*
Lindhard, Jens 1922- *IntWW 93*
Lindheim, Richard David 1939- *WhoAm 94*
Lindholm, Berit 1934- *NewGrDO*
Lindholm, Charles T. 1946- *WrDr 94*
Lindholm, Clifford F., II 1930- *WhoAmP 93*
Lindholm, Clifford Falstrom, II 1930- *WhoScEn 94*
Lindholm, Dwight Henry 1930- *WhoAm 94, WhoWest 94*
Lindholm, Frances Marion 1918- *WhoAmP 93*
Lindholm, Fredrik Arthur 1936- *WhoAm 94*
Lindholm, John Victor 1934- *WhoAm 94*
Lindholm, Richard Theodore 1960- *WhoWest 94*
Lindholm, Richard W(adsworth) 1913- *WrDr 94*
Lindholm, Ulric Svante 1931- *WhoAm 94*
Lindisfarne, Archdeacon of *Who 94*
Lindland, Frances Kay 1954- *WhoWest 94*
Lindler, Keith William 1954- *WhoScEn 94*
Lindley, Arnold (Lewis George) 1902- *Who 94*
Lindley, Arnold Lewis George 1902- *IntWW 93*
Lindley, Audra 1923- *WhoHol 92*
Lindley, Bert d1953 *WhoHol 92*
Lindley, Bryan Charles 1932- *Who 94*
Lindley, David Morrison 1949- *WhoAm 94, WhoAmL 94*
Lindley, Dennis Victor 1923- *Who 94*
Lindley, James Gunn 1931- *WhoAm 94, WhoFI 94*
Lindley, John Lambert 1954- *WhoFI 94*
Lindley, John M., III 1945- *WhoAmP 93*
Lindley, John William 1920- *WhoAmP 93*
Lindley, Norman Dale 1937- *WhoWest 94*
Lindley, Simon Geoffrey 1948- *Who 94*
Lindley, Thomas Ernest 1948- *WhoAm 94*
Lindman, Dale Bruce 1944- *WhoAmL 94*
Lindmark, Arne 1929- *WhoAmA 93*
Lindner, Albert Michael 1952- *WhoScEn 94*
Lindner, Arlon 1935- *WhoAmP 93*
Lindner, Carl *DrAPF 93*
Lindner, Carl H. 1919- *WhoIns 94*
Lindner, Carl H., III 1953- *WhoIns 94*
Lindner, Carl Henry 1919- *IntWW 93, WhoAm 94, WhoFI 94*
Lindner, Duane Lee 1950- *WhoScEn 94*
Lindner, Elizabeth M. 1951- *WhoIns 94*
Lindner, Gerhard 1930- *IntWW 93, Who 94*
Lindner, Joseph, Jr. 1929- *WhoAm 94*
Lindner, K. David 1939- *WhoAmL 94*
Lindner, Keith E. *WhoAm 94*
Lindner, Kenneth Edward 1922- *WhoAm 94*
Lindner, Kurt Julius 1922- *WhoAm 94*
Lindner, Patricia Reid *WhoAmP 93, WhoMW 93*
Lindner, Richard 1901-1978 *WhoAmA 93N*
Lindner, Robert (Mitchell) 1914-1956 *EncSF 93*
Lindner, Robert David 1920- *WhoAm 94, WhoFI 94*
Lindner, Ronald John 1934- *WhoAm 94*
Lindner, Scott-Eric 1965- *WhoMW 93*
Lindner, Vicki *DrAPF 93*
Lindo, Delroy *WhoHol 92*
Lindo, J. Trevor 1925- *WhoBlA 94*
Lindo, Olga d1968 *WhoHol 92*
Lindo, Stephen T. 1947- *WhoAmL 94*
Lindo-Fuentes, Héctor 1952- *WhoHisp 94*
Lindon, Jerome 1925- *IntWW 93*
Lindon, Vincent *WhoHol 92*
Lindop, Norman 1921- *Who 94*
Lindop, Patricia Joyce 1930- *Who 94*
Lindow, Donald August 1916- *WhoAm 94*
Lindow, John Wesley 1910- *WhoAm 94*
Lindow, Louisa Rose 1922- *WhoWest 94*
Lindpaintner, Peter Joseph von 1791-1856 *NewGrDO*
Lindquist, Anders Gunnar 1942- *WhoScEn 94*
Lindquist, Barbara Louise 1930- *WhoMW 93*
Lindquist, Claude S. 1940- *WhoAm 94*
Lindquist, Dana Rae 1963- *WhoScEn 94*
Lindquist, Edward Lee 1942- *WhoScEn 94*
Lindquist, Emory Kempton 1908-1992 *WhAm 10*
Lindquist, Evan 1936- *WhoAm 94, WhoAmA 93*
Lindquist, Everett Carlton 1912- *WhoMW 93*
Lindquist, Frej *WhoHol 92*
Lindquist, John Robert 1921-1989 *WhAm 10*
Lindquist, Louis William 1944- *WhoScEn 94, WhoWest 94*
Lindquist, Mark 1949- *WhoAmA 93*
Lindquist, Mark 1959- *WrDr 94*
Lindquist, Mark Alvin 1949- *WhoAm 94*
Lindquist, Ray *DrAPF 93*
Lindquist, Raymond Irving 1907- *WhoAm 94*
Lindquist, Richard James 1960- *WhoFI 94*
Lindquist, Robert Arvid 1929- *WhoAmP 93*
Lindquist, Stanley Elmer 1917- *WhoWest 94*
Lindquist, Susan Pratzner 1940- *WhoAm 94*
Lindquist, Victor Robert 1929- *WhoMW 93*
Lindquist, Wallace Lawrence, Jr. 1934- *WhoAmP 93*
Lindqvist, Bengt 1936- *IntWW 93*
Lindqvist, Gunnar Jan 1950- *WhoFI 94*
Lindqvist, Jens Harry 1967- *WhoScEn 94*
Lindroos, Peter 1944- *NewGrDO*
Lindros, Eric *NewYTBS 93 [port]*
Lindros, Eric Bryan 1973- *WhoAm 94*
Lindroth, Helen d1956 *WhoHol 92*
Lindroth, Linda 1946- *WhoAmA 93*
Lindroth, Linda Hammer 1946- *WhoAm 94*
Lindsay *Who 94*
Lindsay, Earl of 1955- *Who 94*
Lindsay, Master of 1991- *Who 94*
Lindsay, Alexander *WhAmRev*
Lindsay, Arturo 1946- *WhoAmA 93*
Lindsay, Beverly 1948- *WhoBlA 94*
Lindsay, Bruce William 1949- *WhoFI 94*
Lindsay, Bryan Eugene *DrAPF 93*
Lindsay, Bryan Eugene 1931- *WhoAm 94*
Lindsay, Charles Joseph 1922- *WhoAm 94*
Lindsay, Courtenay Traice David 1910- *Who 94*
Lindsay, Crawford B. 1905- *WhoBlA 94*
Lindsay, Crawford Callum Douglas 1939- *Who 94*
Lindsay, Dale Richard 1913- *WhoAm 94*
Lindsay, David c. 1485-1555 *DcLB 132*
Lindsay, David c. 1490-1555 *BlmGEL*
Lindsay, David 1878-1945 *EncSF 93*
Lindsay, David Breed, Jr. 1922- *WhoAm 94*
Lindsay, Della *WhoHol 92*
Lindsay, Donald Dunrod 1910- *Who 94*
Lindsay, Donald J. 1941- *WhoAm 94*
Lindsay, Donald Parker 1915- *WhoAm 94*
Lindsay, Douglas Allan 1951- *WhoAmL 94*
Lindsay, Eddie H. S. 1931- *WhoBlA 94*
Lindsay, Franklin Anthony 1916- *WhoAm 94*
Lindsay, George Carroll 1928- *WhoAm 94*
Lindsay, George Edmund 1916- *WhoAm 94*
Lindsay, George Nelson 1919- *WhoAm 94*
Lindsay, George Peter 1948- *WhoAm 94, WhoAmL 94*
Lindsay, Gross C. 1930- *WhoAmP 93*
Lindsay, Gwendolyn Ann Burns 1947- *WhoBlA 94*
Lindsay, Horace Augustin 1938- *WhoBlA 94*
Lindsay, Howard d1968 *WhoHol 92*
Lindsay, Hugh 1927- *Who 94*
Lindsay, James d1928 *WhoHol 92*
Lindsay, James Harvey Kincaid Stewart 1915- *Who 94*
Lindsay, James Louis 1906- *Who 94*
Lindsay, James Wiley 1934- *WhoAm 94*
Lindsay, John (Edmund Fredric) 1935- *Who 94*
Lindsay, John (Vliet) 1921- *WrDr 94*
Lindsay, John C. 1959- *WhoAmP 93*
Lindsay, John V. 1921- *WhoHol 92*
Lindsay, John Vliet 1921- *IntWW 93, Who 94, WhoAm 94, WhoAmP 93*
Lindsay, Kenneth C. 1919- *WhoAmA 93*
Lindsay, Kevin d1975 *WhoHol 92*
Lindsay, Lara *WhoHol 92*
Lindsay, Lex d1971 *WhoHol 92*
Lindsay, Loelia (Mary) 1902- *WrDr 94*
Lindsay, Lois d1982 *WhoHol 92*
Lindsay, Margaret d1981 *WhoHol 92*
Lindsay, Mark 1955- *WhoHol 92*
Lindsay, Maurice *Who 94*
Lindsay, Maurice 1918- *WrDr 94*
Lindsay, (John) Maurice 1918- *Who 94*
Lindsay, Michael Anthony 1958- *WhoAmL 94*
Lindsay, Nathan James 1936- *WhoAm 94, WhoWest 94*
Lindsay, Norman Roy 1936- *WhoWest 94*
Lindsay, Orland Ugham *Who 94*
Lindsay, Phillip d1988 *WhoHol 92*
Lindsay, Rachel *WrDr 94*
Lindsay, Reginald C. 1945- *WhoBlA 94*
Lindsay, Reginald Carl 1945- *WhoAmL 94*
Lindsay, Richard *EncSF 93*
Lindsay, Richard Clark 1905-1990 *WhAm 10*
Lindsay, Richard Paul 1945- *WhoWest 94*
Lindsay, Robert 1924- *WhoAm 94, WhoScEn 94*
Lindsay, Robert 1949- *IntMPA 94, WhoHol 92*
Lindsay, Robert 1951- *ConTFT 11, IntWW 93*
Lindsay, Robert V. 1926- *IntWW 93*
Lindsay, Robert Van Cleef 1926- *WhoAm 94*
Lindsay, Roger Alexander 1941- *WhoAm 94*
Lindsay, S. Brian 1961- *WhoWest 94*
Lindsay, Stephen Prout 1944- *WhoAm 94, WhoAmL 94*
Lindsay, (Nicholas) Vachel 1879-1931 *EncSF 93*
Lindsay, William Kerr 1920- *WhoAm 94*
Lindsay, William Neish, III 1947- *WhoWest 94*
Lindsay-Hogg, Edward William 1910- *Who 94*
Lindsay Of Birker, Baron 1909- *Who 94*
Lindsay of Dowhill, Ronald Alexander 1933- *Who 94*
Lindsay-Smith, Iain-Mor 1934- *Who 94*
Lindsell, Harold 1913- *WhoAm 94*
Lindseth, Alfred A. 1944- *WhoAmL 94*
Lindseth, Paul Douglas 1952- *WhoMW 93*
Lindseth, Richard Emil 1935- *WhoAm 94, WhoMW 93, WhoScEn 94*
Lindseth, Roy Oliver 1925- *WhoAm 94*
Lindsey, Archdeacon of *Who 94*
Lindsey, Earl of 1931- *Who 94*
Lindsey, Alfred Walter 1942- *WhoScEn 94*
Lindsey, Alton A(nthony) 1907- *WrDr 94*
Lindsey, Anne West 1914- *WhoMW 93*
Lindsey, Benjamin Barr 1869-1943 *AmSocL*
Lindsey, Casimir Charles 1923- *WhoAm 94*
Lindsey, David (L.) *WrDr 94*
Lindsey, David Hosford 1950- *WhoAm 94*
Lindsey, Douglas 1919- *WhoScEn 94*
Lindsey, Douglas Lee 1946- *WhoMW 93*
Lindsey, George 1935- *WhoHol 92*
Lindsey, Hal *WrDr 94*
Lindsey, Henry Carlton 1918- *WhAm 10*
Lindsey, Jefferson Franklin, III 1942- *WhoMW 93*
Lindsey, Jerome W. 1932- *WhoBlA 94*
Lindsey, Jim *DrAPF 93*
Lindsey, Johanna 1952- *WrDr 94*
Lindsey, John Cunningham 1953- *WhoFI 94, WhoWest 94*
Lindsey, John Hall, Jr. 1938- *WhoWest 94*
Lindsey, John Horace 1922- *WhoAm 94*
Lindsey, Jonathan Asmel 1937- *WhoAm 94*
Lindsey, Julie Miller Ward 1960- *WhoFI 94*

Lindsey, Karen DrAPF 93
Lindsey, Lawrence Benjamin 1954- WhoAm 94, WhoAmP 93, WhoFI 94
Lindsey, Lowell L. WhoAm 94
Lindsey, Mark Kelly 1955- WhoFI 94
Lindsey, Mary fl. 1697-1712 NewGrDO
Lindsey, Melvin Wesley 1955-1992 WhoBlA 94N
Lindsey, Ouida 1927- WhoBlA 94
Lindsey, Richard J. 1956- WhoAmP 93
Lindsey, Robert G., Jr. 1921- WhoAmP 93
Lindsey, S. L. 1909- WhoBlA 94
Lindsey, Sanford Chapdu 1914- WhoMW 93
Lindsey, Stephen Wilson 1958- WhoFI 94
Lindsey, Terry Lamar 1950- WhoBlA 94
Lindsey, Thomas Kenneth 1959- WhoAmL 94
Lindsey, W. H. WhoAmP 93
Lindskog, David Richard 1936- WhoAm 94
Lindskog, Norbert F. 1932- WhoMW 93
Lindsley, Donald Benjamin 1907- IntWW 93, WhoAm 94
Lindsley, James Bruce 1941- WhoMW 93
Lindsley, Jerry Charles 1956- WhoAmP 93
Lindsley, Michelle LaBrosse 1962- WhoWest 94
Lindsley-Griffin, Nancy 1943- WhoMW 93
Lindstedt, Carl-Gustaf WhoHol 92
Lindstedt-Siva, June 1941- WhoAm 94
Lindsten, Jan Eric 1935- IntWW 93
Lindstrom, Allan d1981 WhoHol 92
Lindstrom, Barry Lee 1952- WhoWest 94
Lindstrom, Beth 1961- WhoWomW 91
Lindstrom, Eric Everett 1936- WhoScEn 94
Lindstrom, Eugene Shipman 1923- WhoAm 94
Lindstrom, Gaell 1919- WhoAmA 93
Lindstrom, Gregory P. 1953- WhoAmL 94
Lindstrom, John Russell 1956- WhoAmL 94
Lindstrom, Jorgen WhoHol 92
Lindstrom, Kris Peter 1948- WhoScEn 94
Lindstrom, Larry Wayne 1958- WhoMW 93
Lindstrom, Pia 1938- WhoHol 92
Lindstrom, Rune 1916- WhoHol 92
Lindstrom, Timothy Rhea 1952- WhoScEn 94
Lindstrom, Torsten L. 1921- IntWW 93
Lindstrom, Ulla 1909- IntWW 93
Lindstrom, Wendell Don 1927- WhoMW 93
Lindt, Auguste Rudolph 1905- IntWW 93, Who 94
Lindt, Karl Ludwig d1971 WhoHol 92
Linduska, Joseph Paul 1913- WhoAm 94
Lindvall, Frederick Charles 1903-1989 WhAm 10
Lindwall, Raymond Russell 1921- IntWW 93
Lindzen, Richard Siegmund 1940- WhoAm 94, WhoScEn 94
Lindzey, Gardner 1920- WhoWest 94
Line, David ConAu 43NR
Line, David 1922- WrDr 94
Line, Frances Mary 1940- Who 94
Line, Maurice Bernard 1928- Who 94, WrDr 94
Line, Millard Filmore, Jr. 1940- WhoFI 94
Lineback, Charles David 1948- WhoIns 94
Linebarger, Jim DrAPF 93
Linebarger, Libby 1947- WhoAmP 93
Lineberger, Larry Watson 1943- WhoWest 94
Lineberger, William Carl 1939- WhoAm 94, WhoScEn 94
Lineberry, Albert S., Sr. 1918- WhoAmP 93
Lineberry, Gene Thomas 1955- WhoScEn 94
Linehan, Anthony John 1931- Who 94
Linehan, John Andrew 1924- WhoAmP 93
Linehan, Joseph Richard 1961- WhoIns 94
Linehan, Patrick Francis, Jr. 1945- WhoFI 94
Linehan, Stephen 1947- Who 94
Lineiro, Jorge Xavier WhoHisp 94
Lineker, Gary 1960- WorESoc
Lineker, Gary Winston 1960- IntWW 93
Linemeyer, David Lee 1949- WhoAm 94
Linen, James Alexander, IV 1938-1989 WhAm 10
Liner, Richard Mark 1953- WhoWest 94
Linero, Jeannie WhoHol 92
Linert, Susan Marie 1949- WhoFI 94
Lines, Michael Sherrod 1958- WhoFI 94
Lines, (Walter) Moray 1922- Who 94
Linett, Deena DrAPF 93
Linevsky, Milton Joshua 1928- WhoScEn 94
Lin Fengmian 1900- WhoPRCh 91 [port]
Linfoot Shannon, Marylin 1941- WhoWomW 91
Linford, Alan C. Who 94
Linford, Golden C. 1927- WhoAmP 93
Linford, Laurance Dee 1951- WhoWest 94
Linford, Rulon Kesler 1943- WhoScEn 94, WhoWest 94
Ling, Alan Campbell 1940- WhoWest 94
Ling, Alexander 1922- WhoAsA 94
Ling, Amy 1939- WhoAsA 94
Ling, Arthur George 1913- Who 94
Ling, Christine N. 1926- WhoAsA 94
Ling, Daniel 1926- WhoAm 94
Ling, Dwight L. 1923- WhoAm 94
Ling, Edward Hugo 1933- WhoScEn 94
Ling, Fergus Alan Humphrey 1914- Who 94
Ling, Hao 1959- WhoAsA 94
Ling, Hsin Yi 1930- WhoAsA 94
Ling, Hubert 1942- WhoAsA 94
Ling, Hung Chi 1950- WhoAsA 94
Ling, Jack Chieh-Sheng 1930- WhoAsA 94
Ling, Jahja Wang-Chieh 1951- WhoAm 94
Ling, James J. 1922- IntWW 93
Ling, Jeffrey 1939- Who 94
Ling, John de Courcy Who 94
Ling, Joseph Tso-Ti 1919- WhoAm 94, WhoScEn 94
Ling, Kathryn Wrolstad 1943- WhoMW 93
Ling, Matthew S. 1963- WhoAsA 94
Ling, Moses D.F. 1952- WhoFI 94
Ling, Paul 1949- WhoAsA 94
Ling, Paul Kimberley 1953- WhoAsA 94
Ling, Peter J(ohn) 1956- WrDr 94
Ling, Richie d1937 WhoHol 92
Ling, Robert Malcolm 1931- WhoWest 94
Ling, Roger (John) 1942- ConAu 41NR, WrDr 94
Ling, Rung Tai 1943- WhoScEn 94
Ling, Suilin 1930- WhoAm 94, WhoFI 94
Ling, Ta-Yung 1943- WhoAsA 94
Ling, Victor 1943- WhoScEn 94
Ling, Yu-long 1938- WhoAsA 94
Ling, Zhi-Kui 1961- WhoAsA 94
Lingafelter, Edward Clay, Jr. 1914- WhoAm 94
Lingamneni, Jaganmohan Rao 1942- WhoAm 94
Lingappa, Banadakoppa Thimmappa 1927- WhoAsA 94
Lingappa, Yamuna 1929- WhoAsA 94
Lingard, (Peter) Anthony 1916- Who 94
Lingard, Joan 1932- SmATA 74 [port]
Lingard, Joan (Amelia) WrDr 94
Lingard, Joan (Amelia) 1932- TwCYAW
Lingard, Robin Anthony 1941- Who 94
Lingelbach, Albert Lane 1940- WhoAmL 94
Lingelbach, Doris 1928- WhoAmP 93
Lingeman, Richard 1931- WrDr 94
Lingeman, Richard Roberts 1931- WhoAm 94
Lingen, Theo d1978 WhoHol 92
Lingenfelter, Barbara Sue 1962- WhoMW 93
Lingenfelter, Richard Emery 1934- WrDr 94
Lingenfelter, Sherwood Galen 1941- WhoAm 94
Lingham, Thomas d1950 WhoHol 92
Ling Huan WhoPRCh 91
Lingl, Friedrich Albert 1927- WhoAm 94
Lingle, Kathleen McCall 1944- WhoFI 94
Lingle, Marilyn Felkel 1932- WhoMW 93
Lingle, Muriel Ellen WhoMW 93
Lingle, Sarah Elizabeth 1955- WhoAm 94
Ling Liong Sik, Dato' 1943- IntWW 93
Ling Qihan 1906- WhoPRCh 91 [port]
Ling Qihong 1933- WhoPRCh 91 [port]
Lings, Martin 1909- Who 94
Ling Shuhua 1904- BlmGWL
Linguiti, Francis Michael 1950- WhoAmL 94
Lingwood, Tom 1927- NewGrDO
Ling Yaozhong 1954- WhoPRCh 91 [port]
Ling Zeti WhoPRCh 91
Ling Zhi WhoPRCh 91
Ling Zifeng 1917- WhoPRCh 91 [port]
Lin Haiyin 1919- BlmGWL
Lin Hanxiong 1929- IntWW 93, WhoPRCh 91 [port]
Linhardt, Margarita Agcaoili 1947- WhoWest 94
Linhares, Claudette Jeanne 1937- WhoAmP 93
Linhares, Judith 1940- WhoAmA 93
Linhares, Philip E. 1939- WhoAmA 93
Lin Hengyuan 1909- WhoPRCh 91 [port]
Linhoff, William P., Jr. 1946- WhoAmL 94
Lin Hu 1927- WhoPRCh 91 [port]
Lin Hua WhoPRCh 91
Lin Huaxuan WhoPRCh 91
Lin Hujia 1916- WhoPRCh 91 [port]
Lini, Walter Hadye 1942- IntWW 93
Linihan, Martin G. 1940- WhoAmL 94
Li Ning 1963- WhoPRCh 91 [port]
Linington, Victor A. 1908- WhoAmP 93
Lin Jiamei WhoPRCh 91 [port]
Lin Jianqing 1921- IntWW 93, WhoPRCh 91 [port]
Lin Jigui 1930- WhoPRCh 91 [port]
Lin Jizhou WhoPRCh 91
Link, Adolph d1933 WhoHol 92
Link, Ann McCormick 1947- WhoWest 94
Link, Antony Cole 1947- WhoAmL 94
Link, Arthur A. 1914- WhoAmP 93
Link, Arthur S(tanley) 1920- WrDr 94
Link, Arthur Stanley 1920- WhoAm 94
Link, Carl Dean 1934- WhoMW 93
Link, Charles Dale 1939- WhoAm 94
Link, Charles Edward 1927- WhoWest 94
Link, Christoph 1933- IntWW 93
Link, David M. 1930- WhoAm 94
Link, Deborah Ann 1954- WhoMW 93
Link, E. G. 1952- WhoFI 94, WhoMW 93
Link, Frank Albert 1930- WhoAm 94, WhoMW 93
Link, Fred Motter 1904- WhoAm 94
Link, Frederick Charles 1948- WhoScEn 94
Link, Frederick M(artin) 1930- WrDr 94
Link, Gary Steven 1949- WhoAmL 94
Link, George Hamilton 1939- WhoAm 94, WhoAmL 94
Link, Harriet Mae 1934- WhoAmP 93
Link, Howard Anthony 1934- WhoAmA 93
Link, Jay Earl 1969- WhoMW 93
Link, Joyce Battle 1956- WhoBlA 94
Link, Lawrence John 1942- WhoAmA 93
Link, Mae Mills 1915- WhoAm 94
Link, Mark J(oseph) 1924- ConAu 42NR
Link, Mary Catherine 1934- WhoWest 94
Link, Michael Paul 1949- WhoWest 94
Link, Nina Beth 1943- WhoAm 94
Link, Peter Karl 1930- WhoAm 94, WhoWest 94
Link, Phyllida K. 1940- WhoAmA 93
Link, Robert Allen 1932- WhoAm 94, WhoFI 94
Link, Steven Otto 1953- WhoScEn 94
Link, Val James 1940- WhoAmA 93
Link, William d1937 WhoHol 92
Link, William 1933- ConAu 41NR, IntMPA 94
Link, William E. d1949 WhoHol 92
Link, William Theodore 1933- WhoAm 94
Lin Kai 1924- WhoPRCh 91 [port]
Lin Kaiqin 1934- WhoPRCh 91 [port]
Linke, Paul 1948- WhoHol 92
Linken, Dennis C. 1947- WhoAmL 94
Linke-Poot ConAu 141
Linker, Jonathan Steven 1949- WhoAm 94
Linker, Kerrie Lynn 1966- WhoScEn 94
Linker, Lewis Craig 1956- WhoScEn 94
Linker, Paul J. 1950- WhoAmL 94
Linkevich, Michael Paul 1948- WhoFI 94
Linkie, William Sinclair 1931- Who 94
Linkkila, Leslie Elizabeth 1959- WhoFI 94, WhoWest 94
Linklater, Eric (Robert Russell) 1899-1974 EncSF 93, RfGShF
Linklater, Isabelle Stanislawa Yarosh-Galazka 1939- WhoMW 93
Linklater, Magnus (Duncan) 1942- WrDr 94
Linklater, Magnus Duncan 1942- Who 94
Linklater, Nelson Valdemar 1918- Who 94
Linklater, William Joseph 1942- WhoAm 94, WhoAmL 94
Linkletter, Art 1912- IntMPA 94, WhoHol 92
Linkletter, Art(hur Gordon) 1912- WrDr 94
Linkletter, Arthur Gordon 1912- WhoAm 94
Linkmann, Ludwig d1963 WhoHol 92
Linkner, Monica Farris 1947- WhoAmL 94
Linkous, T. Cecil 1920- WhoAmP 93
Linkous, William Joseph, Jr. 1929- WhoAm 94
Links, Mary Who 94
Lin Lanying 1917- IntWW 93, WhoPRCh 91 [port]
Linley, Viscount 1961- Who 94
Linley, Betty d1951 WhoHol 92
Linley, George 1798-1865 NewGrDO
Linley, Thomas 1733-1795 NewGrDO
Linley, Thomas 1756-1778 NewGrDO
Lin Lin 1910- IntWW 93, WhoPRCh 91 [port]
Linlithgow, Marquess of 1946- Who 94
Lin Liyun 1933- IntWW 93, WhoPRCh 91 [port], WhoWomW 91
Linman, Beverly Kay 1959- WhoMW 93
Linman, James William 1924- WhoAm 94
Lin Mingyu WhoPRCh 91
Lin Mohan 1913- WhoPRCh 91 [port]
Linn, Bambi 1926- WhoHol 92
Linn, Brian James 1947- WhoAmL 94, WhoWest 94
Linn, Bud d1968 WhoHol 92
Linn, Carole Anne 1945- WhoScEn 94, WhoWest 94
Linn, Edward Allen 1922- WhoAm 94
Linn, Eldon R. 1934- WhoIns 94
Linn, James 1749-1821 WhAmRev
Linn, James Eldon, II 1943- WhoFI 94
Linn, James Herbert 1925- WhoAm 94
Linn, John 1763-1821 WhAmRev
Linn, John J. 1935- WhoIns 94
Linn, John William 1936- WhoAmA 93
Linn, Judy 1947- WhoAmA 93
Linn, Leonard Jess 1917- WhoAmP 93
Linn, Margaret d1973 WhoHol 92
Linn, Paul Anthony 1958- WhoScEn 94
Linn, Richard 1944- WhoAmL 94
Linn, Robert Allen 1932- WhoAmL 94
Linn, Robert Bruce 1943- WhoIns 94
Linn, Roberta WhoHol 92
Linn, Steven Allen 1943- WhoAmA 93
Linn, Stuart Michael 1940- WhoAm 94
Linn, Thomas W. 1948- WhoAmL 94
Linna, Timo Juhani 1937- WhoAm 94
Linnabary, Steven Ralph 1954- WhoAmP 93
Linnaeus, Carl 1707-1778 WorScD
Linnane, Anthony William 1930- IntWW 93, Who 94
Linnane, Joe d1981 WhoHol 92
Linnansalo, Vera 1950- WhoMW 93
Linnartz, Lawrence R. 1944- WhoAmL 94
Linn-Baker, Mark 1952- WhoHol 92
Linn-Baker, Mark 1954- IntMPA 94
Linnehan, Joseph Arthur, Jr. 1953- WhoAmL 94
Linnell, David George Thomas 1930- Who 94
Linnell, Robert Hartley 1922- WhoAm 94
Linneman, Dale Lee 1963- WhoAmL 94
Linnemann, Hans 1931- IntWW 93
Linnemeier, Thomas Jay 1936- WhoFI 94, WhoMW 93
Linnen, Thomas Francis 1925- WhoFI 94
Linner, Carl Sture 1917- IntWW 93
Linnerud, Mark Alan 1950- WhoMW 93
Linnett, Michael Joseph 1926- Who 94
Linney, Beverly 1923- WhoAm 94
Linney, Romulus 1930- ConDr 93, WhoAm 94, WrDr 94
Linnville, Steven Emory 1956- WhoScEn 94
Lino, Marisa Rose WhoAm 94
Linoff, Alan Lee 1934- WhoFI 94
Linow, Ivan 1888- WhoHol 92
Linowes, David Francis 1917- WhoAm 94, WhoFI 94, WhoMW 93, WhoScEn 94, WrDr 94
Linowes, Harry Michael 1928- WhoAm 94
Linowitz, Sol Myron 1913- IntWW 93, WhoAm 94, WhoAmL 94, WhoAmP 93, WhoFI 94
Lin Piao 1907-1971 HisDcKW
Lin Ping 1920- IntWW 93
Lin Ping 1923- WhoPRCh 91 [port]
Lin Qishui 1937- WhoPRCh 91
Lin Ran 1947- WhoPRCh 91
Lin Ruilian WhoPRCh 91
Lin Ruo 1924- IntWW 93, WhoPRCh 91 [port]
Lins, Mark Francis 1955- WhoMW 93
Linscheid, Gustav A. 1875-1942 EncNAR
Linschoten, Jan Huyghen Van 1563-1611 WhWE
Linscott, J. Curtis 1965- WhoAmL 94
Linscott, Jerry R. 1941- WhoAm 94
Linscott, Walt Addison 1960- WhoAmL 94
Linsenmann, William Michael 1919- WhoAm 94
Linsenmeyer, John Michael 1940- WhoAm 94
Linsey, Nathaniel L. WhoBlA 94
Lin Sheng 1931- IntWW 93, WhoPRCh 91 [port]
Lin Shengzhong 1942- IntWW 93, WhoPRCh 91 [port]
Lin Shuilong 1931- IntWW 93, WhoPRCh 91 [port]
Linsk, Michael Stephen 1940- WhoAm 94
Linskens, Hansferdinand 1921- IntWW 93
Linsky, Leonard 1922- WrDr 94
Linsley, Ray Keyes 1917-1990 WhAm 10
Linsley, Robert Martin 1930- WhoAm 94
Linson, Art 1942- IntMPA 94
Linson, Robert Edward 1922- WhoMW 93
Linstead, Stephen Guy 1941- Who 94
Linstedt, Walter Griffiths 1933- WhoAmL 94
Linstone, Harold Adrian 1924- WhoWest 94
Linstroth, Paul J. 1953- WhoAmL 94
Linstroth, Tod B. 1947- WhoAmL 94
Linstrum, Derek 1925- WrDr 94
Lintault, Roger Paul 1938- WhoAmA 93
Linthicum, John DrAPF 93

Linthicum, Leslie Jean 1958- *WhoWest 94*
Lintner, Matthew Frank 1964- *WhoAmL 94*
Linton, Alan Henry Spencer 1919- *Who 94*
Linton, Barbara J. 1952- *WhoAmP 93, WhoMW 93*
Linton, Eliza Lynn 1822-1898 *BlmGEL, BlmGWL, NinCLC 41 [port]*
Linton, Frederick M. 1932- *WhoAm 94*
Linton, Gladys Morris 1930- *WhoAmP 93*
Linton, Gordon J. 1948- *WhoAmP 93, WhoBlA 94*
Linton, Jack Arthur 1936- *WhoAmL 94*
Linton, Marigold L. *WhoWest 94*
Linton, Robert D. 1954- *WhoIns 94*
Linton, Robert David 1954- *WhoAm 94, WhoFI 94*
Linton, Ron M. 1929- *WhoAmP 93*
Linton, Roy Nathan 1918- *WhoAm 94*
Linton, Ruth Coleman 1955- *WhoWest 94*
Linton, Samuel C. 1923- *WhoAmP 93*
Linton, Sheila Lorraine 1950- *WhoBlA 94*
Linton, William Carl 1929- *WhoAmP 93, WhoMW 93*
Linton, William Henry 1925- *WhoWest 94*
Linton, William Sidney 1950- *WhoScEn 94*
Lin Tongji *WhoPRCh 91*
Lintott, Edward Barnard 1875-1951 *WhoAmA 93N*
Lintott, Henry 1908- *Who 94*
Lintott, Henry (John Bevis) 1908- *IntWW 93*
Lintott, Robert Edward 1932- *Who 94*
Lintz, Frank D. E. 1951- *WhoBlA 94*
Lintz, Paul Rodgers 1941- *WhoScEn 94*
Lintz, Robert Carroll 1933- *WhoAm 94*
Linvill, John Grimes 1919- *WhoAm 94*
Linville, Albert d1985 *WhoHol 92*
Linville, Joanne 1928- *WhoHol 92*
Linville, Judith Ann 1943- *WhoMW 93*
Linville, Kelli *WhoAmP 93*
Linville, Larry 1939- *WhoHol 92*
Linville, Ronald G. 1954- *WhoAmL 94*
Lin Xiao 1920- *WhoPRCh 91 [port]*
Lin Ximing 1925- *WhoPRCh 91 [port]*
Linxwiler, James David 1949- *WhoAmL 94, WhoWest 94*
Linxwiler, Louis Major, Jr. 1931- *WhoFI 94, WhoWest 94*
Lin Yamin *WhoPRCh 91*
Lin Yang-Kang 1927- *IntWW 93*
Linyard, Richard 1930- *WhoBlA 94*
Linyard, Samuel Edward Goldsmith 1937- *WhoScEn 94*
Lin Yincai 1930- *IntWW 93, WhoPRCh 91 [port]*
Lin Ying 1914- *WhoPRCh 91 [port]*
Lin Yinghai 1932- *WhoPRCh 91 [port]*
Lin Yong 1942- *WhoPRCh 91 [port]*
Lin Yongsan 1939- *WhoPRCh 91 [port]*
Lin Yuanchun *WhoPRCh 91*
Lin Yueqin 1914- *WhoPRCh 91 [port]*
Lin Yutang 1895-1976 *EncSF 93*
Linz, Anthony James 1948- *WhoMW 93, WhoScEn 94*
Linz, Michael Frederick 1943- *WhoAmL 94*
Linz, Werner Mark 1935- *WhoAm 94*
Lin Zexu c. 1785-1850 *HisWorL*
Linzey, Bobby Lee 1938- *WhoAmP 93*
Lin Zhaohua 1936- *IntWW 93, WhoPRCh 91*
Lin Zhen *WhoPRCh 91*
Lin Zhongjie *WhoPRCh 91*
Lin Zhun 1927- *IntWW 93, WhoPRCh 91*
Linzin-Vanderspeeten, Anna-Marie 1949- *WhoWomW 91*
Linzmeyer, Peter C. 1942- *WhoAmL 94*
Linzner, Charles 1948- *WhoAmL 94, WhoFI 94*
Linzner, Joel 1952- *WhoAmL 94*
Lin Zongtang 1926- *WhoPRCh 91 [port]*
Lin Zuyi 1931- *WhoPRCh 91 [port]*
Lio *WhoHol 92*
Lion, Jacques Kenneth 1922- *Who 94*
Lion, Leon M. d1947 *WhoHol 92*
Lion, Margo d1989 *WhoHol 92*
Lion, Paul Michel, III 1934- *WhoAm 94*
Lionaes, Aase 1907- *IntWW 93*
Lionakis, George 1924- *WhoAm 94, WhoWest 94*
Lionberger, Erle Talbot Lund 1933- *WhoAmP 93*
Lione, Henry Vincent 1928-1988 *WhAm 10*
Lionel, Robert *EncSF 93*
Lionel, Robert 1935- *WrDr 94*
Lionello, Alberto *WhoHol 92*
Lionett, David J. 1943- *WhoAmP 93*
Lionni, Leo 1910- *WhoAm 94, WhoAmA 93, WrDr 94*
Lions, Jacques L. 1928- *IntWW 93*
Lions, Jacques Louis 1928- *WhoScEn 94*
Liotta, Joseph Anthony 1955- *WhoFI 94*
Liotta, Lance A. 1947- *WhoScEn 94*
Liotta, P. H. *DrAPF 93*
Liotta, P. H. 1956- *WrDr 94*
Liotta, Ray 1954- *WhoHol 92*
Liotta, Ray 1955- *IntMPA 94, WhoAm 94*
Liotta, William Anthony 1957- *WhoMW 93*
Liotta-Stolzenberger, Arlene Louise 1948- *WhoFI 94*
Liou, Fue-Wen 1957- *WhoAsA 94*
Liou, Jenn-Chorng 1956- *WhoScEn 94*
Liou, K. T. 1956- *WhoAsA 94*
Liou, Kuo-Nan 1943- *WhoAsA 94*
Liou, Ming Jaw 1956- *WhoAsA 94*
Liou, Ming-Lei 1935- *WhoAm 94*
Liou, Shy-Sheng P. 1959- *WhoAsA 94*
Liou, Sy-Hwang 1951- *WhoAsA 94*
Liou, Yihwa Irene 1958- *WhoAsA 94*
Lioz, Lawrence Stephen 1945- *WhoAm 94*
Lipari, Joseph 1954- *WhoAmL 94*
Lipchik, Harold 1928- *WhoWest 94*
Lipchitz, Jacques 1891-1973 *WhoAmA 93N*
Lipcon, Charles Roy 1946- *WhoAmL 94*
Lipe, Linda Bon 1948- *WhoFI 94*
Li Peichuan *WhoPRCh 91*
Li Peiji *WhoPRCh 91*
Li Peiyao 1933- *WhoPRCh 91 [port]*
Lipel, Michael Earl 1957- *WhoMW 93*
Lipeles, Maxine Ina 1953- *WhoAm 94, WhoAmL 94*
Li Peng 1921- *WhoPRCh 91*
Li Peng 1928- *IntWW 93, WhoPRCh 91 [port]*
Lipford, Rocque Edward 1938- *WhoAm 94, WhoAmL 94*
Lipford-Sullivan, Lisa Mary-Francesca 1967- *WhoMW 93*
Lipfriend, Alan 1916- *Who 94*
Liphard, Arthur Francis 1939- *WhoMW 93*
Lipin, Alfred Jerome 1920- *WhoAmP 93*
Li Ping 1932- *WhoPRCh 91*
Li Pingxiang 1923- *WhoPRCh 91 [port]*
Li Pingyi 1956- *WhoPRCh 91 [port]*
Lipinski, Ann Marie *WhoAm 94, WhoMW 93*
Lipinski, Eugene *WhoHol 92*
Lipinski, Robert Henry 1939- *WhoWest 94*
Lipinski, William O. 1937- *CngDr 93, WhoAmP 93*
Lipinski, William Oliver 1937- *WhoAm 94, WhoMW 93*
Lipinsky, Edward Solomon 1929- *WhoAm 94*
Lipinsky de Orlov, Lino S. 1958- *WhoWest 94*
Lipinsky de Orlov, Lucian Christopher 1962- *WhoFI 94*
Lipitsky, Vasily Semenovich 1947- *LngBDD*
Lipka, James Joseph 1954- *WhoMW 93*
Lipkin, Bernice Sacks 1927- *WhoScEn 94*
Lipkin, David 1913- *WhoAm 94*
Lipkin, Edward B. 1945- *WhoAm 94, WhoFI 94*
Lipkin, George 1930- *WhoScEn 94*
Lipkin, Jean 1926- *BlmGWL*
Lipkin, Mack, Jr. 1943- *WhoAm 94*
Lipkin, Martin 1926- *WhoAm 94, WhoScEn 94*
Lipkin, Mary Castleman Davis 1907- *WhoScEn 94, WhoWest 94*
Lipkin, Miles Henry J. *Who 94*
Lipkin, Richard Martin 1961- *WhoScEn 94*
Lipkin, Semen Izrailevich 1911- *IntWW 93*
Lipkin, Seymour 1927- *WhoAm 94*
Lipking, Lawrence 1934- *WrDr 94*
Lipkowska, Lydia (Yakovlevna) 1882-1958 *NewGrDO*
Lipkowski, Jean-Noel de 1920- *IntWW 93*
Lipman, Allan M., Jr. 1934- *WhoFI 94*
Lipman, Bernard 1920- *WhoAm 94*
Lipman, Daniel Gordon 1912- *WhoScEn 94*
Lipman, David 1931- *WhoAm 94, WhoMW 93, WrDr 94*
Lipman, Elinor *DrAPF 93*
Lipman, Elinor 1950- *WrDr 94*
Lipman, Eugene Jay 1919- *WhoAm 94*
Lipman, Frederick D. 1935- *WhoAm 94, WhoAmL 94*
Lipman, Howard W. 1905-1992 *WhoAmA 93N*
Lipman, Ira Ackerman 1940- *WhoAm 94, WhoFI 94*
Lipman, Joel *DrAPF 93*
Lipman, Jonathan Bram 1953- *WhoMW 93*
Lipman, Marilyn Lee 1938- *WhoMW 93*
Lipman, Matthew 1923- *WrDr 94*
Lipman, Maureen 1946- *WhoHol 92*
Lipman, Maureen (Diane) 1946- *ConAu 141*
Lipman, Maureen Diane 1946- *Who 94*
Lipman, Noah 1959- *WhoAmL 94*
Lipman, Richard Paul 1935- *WhoScEn 94*
Lipman, Ross 1957- *WhoAmL 94*
Lipman, Samuel 1934- *WhoAm 94*
Lipman, Sumner H. 1941- *WhoAmP 93*
Lipman, Wynona M. *WhoAmP 93*
Lipmann, Fritz Albert 1899-1986 *WorScD*
Lipman-Wulf, Peter d1993 *NewYTBS 93 [port]*
Lipman-Wulf, Peter 1905- *WhoAm 94, WhoAmA 93*
Lipner, Harry 1922- *WhoAm 94*
Lipnick, Dale Keats 1964- *WhoAmL 94*
Lipoff, Lawrence Marc 1960- *WhoFI 94*
Lipofsky, Marvin B. 1938- *WhoAmA 93*
Lipomi, Michael Joseph 1953- *WhoScEn 94, WhoWest 94*
Lipovsek, Marjana 1946- *IntWW 93, NewGrDO*
Lipowitz, Jonathan 1937- *WhoScEn 94*
Lipowski, Zbigniew Jerzy 1924- *WhoAm 94*
Lipp, Robert I. 1938- *WhoAm 94, WhoFI 94*
Lipp, Wilma 1925- *NewGrDO*
Lippai, Steven Edward *WhoIns 94*
Lippard, Lucy R. *DrAPF 93*
Lippard, Lucy Rowland 1937- *WhoAmA 93*
Lippard, Stephen James 1940- *WhoAm 94, WhoScEn 94*
Lippard, Thomas Eugene 1943- *WhoAmL 94*
Lippe, Melvin Karl 1933- *WhoAm 94*
Lippe, Philipp Maria 1929- *WhoAm 94, WhoScEn 94, WhoWest 94*
Lippelman, Carl E. 1965- *WhoAmL 94*
Lipperini, Guendalina *BlmGWL*
Lipperman, Robert L. 1954- *WhoIns 94*
Lippert, Anne *WhoAmP 93*
Lippert, Jack Kissane 1902-1989 *WhAm 10*
Lippert, Leon *WhoAmA 93N*
Lippert, Nels T. 1943- *WhoAmL 94*
Lippert, Patrick d1993 *NewYTBS 93*
Lippert, Robert J., Jr. 1928- *IntMPA 94*
Lippert, Wayne Arthur 1946- *WhoMW 93*
Lippes, Gerald Sanford 1940- *WhoAm 94, WhoAmL 94, WhoFI 94*
Lippes, Richard James 1944- *WhoAmL 94*
Lippett, Ronnie Leon 1960- *WhoBlA 94*
Lippetz, Gregory Louis 1965- *WhoAmL 94*
Lippin, Renee *WhoHol 92*
Lippincott, David (McCord) 1925- *EncSF 93*
Lippincott, James Andrew 1930- *WhoAm 94*
Lippincott, Janet 1918- *WhoAmA 93*
Lippincott, Jonathan Ramsay 1946- *WhoMW 93*
Lippincott, Kenny Ray 1950- *WhoFI 94*
Lippincott, Philip Edward 1935- *WhoAm 94, WhoFI 94*
Lippincott, Richard 1745-1826 *WhAmRev*
Lippincott, Robert, III 1947- *WhoIns 94*
Lippincott, Sara Jane 1823-1904 *BlmGWL*
Lippincott, Sarah Lee 1920- *WhoAm 94*
Lippincott, Walter Heulings, Jr. 1939- *WhoAm 94*
Lippitt, Elizabeth Charlotte *WhoWest 94*
Lippitt, Frederick 1916- *WhoAmP 93*
Lippitt, John A. 1951- *WhoAmP 93*
Lippitt, Louis 1924- *WhoWest 94*
Lippman, Barry 1949- *WhoAm 94*
Lippman, Frederick 1935- *WhoAmP 93*
Lippman, Judith 1929- *WhoAmA 93*
Lippman, Kyle David 1954- *WhoAmL 94*
Lippman, Lois H. 1925- *WhoBlA 94*
Lippman, Louis Grombacher 1941- *WhoScEn 94*
Lippman, Marc Estes 1945- *WhoScEn 94*
Lippman, Muriel Marianne 1930- *WhoScEn 94*
Lippman, William Jennings 1925- *WhoAm 94*
Lippmann, Bruce Allan 1950- *WhoFI 94, WhoWest 94*
Lippmann, Friedrich 1932- *NewGrDO*
Lippmann, Gabriel Jonas 1845-1921 *WorInv*
Lippmann, Janet Gurian 1936- *WhoAmA 93*
Lippmann, Walter 1889-1974 *AmSocL [port]*
Lippold, Richard 1915- *IntWW 93, WhoAm 94, WhoAmA 93*
Lippold, Roland Will 1916- *WhoWest 94*
Lipps, Douglas Jay 1954- *WhoWest 94*
Lipps, Jere Henry 1939- *WhoWest 94*
Lipps, Louis Adam 1962- *WhoBlA 94*
Lipps, Patricia E. 1952- *WhoIns 94*
Liprandi, Nicolo *NewGrDO*
Lips, Evan E. 1918- *WhoMW 93*
Lips, Evan Edwin 1918- *WhoAmP 93*
Lips, J. Alan 1938- *WhoAmL 94*
Lipschultz, Geri *DrAPF 93*
Lipschultz, Howard Elliott 1947- *WhoFI 94*
Lipschultz, Jeremy Harris 1958- *WhoMW 93*
Lipschultz, Maurice A. 1912- *WhoAmA 93*
Lipschutz, Ilse Hempel 1923- *WhoAm 94*
Lipschutz, Michael Elazar 1937- *WhoAm 94*
Lipscomb, Al 1925- *WhoAmP 93*
Lipscomb, Albert 1951- *WhoAmP 93*
Lipscomb, Anna Rose Feeny 1945- *WhoFI 94, WhoWest 94*
Lipscomb, Darryl L. 1953- *WhoBlA 94*
Lipscomb, David 1831-1917 *DcAmReB 2*
Lipscomb, David Milton 1935- *WhoScEn 94*
Lipscomb, Dennis *WhoHol 92*
Lipscomb, Guy Fleming, Jr. 1917- *WhoAmA 93*
Lipscomb, Oscar Hugh 1931- *WhoAm 94*
Lipscomb, Paul Rogers 1914- *WhoAm 94*
Lipscomb, Scott David 1959- *WhoWest 94*
Lipscomb, Thomas Heber, Jr. 1912- *WhoScEn 94*
Lipscomb, Thomas Joseph 1946- *WhoAmL 94*
Lipscomb, Wanda Dean 1953- *WhoBlA 94*
Lipscomb, Wendell R. 1920- *WhoBlA 94*
Lipscomb, William Nunn 1919- *Who 94, WrDr 94*
Lipscomb, William Nunn, Jr. 1919- *IntWW 93, WhoAm 94, WhoScEn 94*
Lipscomb-Brown, Edra Evadean 1919- *WhoAm 94*
Lipscombe, Margaret Ann 1939- *WhoBlA 94*
Lipscombe, Trevor Charles Edmund 1962- *WhoScEn 94*
Lipset, Robert 1949- *WhoMW 93*
Lipset, Seymour Martin 1922- *IntWW 93, WhoAm 94, WhoWest 94, WrDr 94*
Lipsey, Alexander Columbus 1950- *WhoMW 93*
Lipsey, Charles E. 1950- *WhoAmL 94*
Lipsey, David (Lawrence) 1948- *WrDr 94*
Lipsey, David Lawrence 1948- *Who 94*
Lipsey, Freda Culwell 1926- *WhoAmP 93*
Lipsey, Howard Irwin 1936- *WhoAmL 94*
Lipsey, John C. 1930- *WhoAm 94*
Lipsey, Joseph, Jr. 1934- *WhoFI 94*
Lipsey, Richard George 1928- *Who 94, WhoAm 94*
Lipsey, Robert Edward 1926- *WhoAm 94*
Lipsey, Stanford 1927- *WhoAm 94*
Lipshie, Joseph 1911- *WhoAm 94*
Lipshitz, Howard David 1955- *WhoWest 94*
Lipshutz, Robert Jay 1955- *WhoWest 94*
Lipshutz, Robert Jerome 1921- *WhoAm 94, WhoAmP 93*
Lipsig, Ethan 1948- *WhoAm 94, WhoAmL 94*
Lipsit, Estie Michele 1952- *WhoAmL 94*
Lipsitt, Lewis Paeff 1929- *WhoAm 94*
Lipsitt, Martin Frederic 1934- *WhoAm 94*
Lipsitz, Lou *DrAPF 93*
Lipsitz, Lou 1938- *WrDr 94*
Lipska, Ewa 1945- *WrDr 94*
Lipska, Ewa (Aleksandra) 1945- *ConWorW 93*
Lipski, Donald G. 1947- *WhoAmA 93*
Lipsky, Burton G. 1937- *WhoAmL 94*
Lipsky, Eleazar d1993 *NewYTBS 93 [port]*
Lipsky, Eleazar 1911-1993 *CurBio 93N*
Lipsky, Ian David 1957- *WhoWest 94*
Lipsky, Joan 1919- *WhoAmP 93*
Lipsky, John Phillip 1947- *WhoFI 94*
Lipsky, Linda Ethel 1939- *WhoFI 94*
Lipsky, Stephen Edward 1932- *WhoAm 94*
Lipsman, Paulee 1947- *WhoAmP 93*
Lipsman, Richard Marc 1946- *WhoAmL 94*
Lipsmeyer, Jerome Dale 1956- *WhoAmL 94*
Lipson, Barry J. 1938- *WhoAmL 94*
Lipson, Charles Barry 1946- *WhoFI 94*
Lipson, Charles Henry 1948- *WhoMW 93*
Lipson, David 1951- *WhoWest 94*
Lipson, David Randall 1965- *WhoMW 93*
Lipson, Goldie 1905- *WhoAmA 93*
Lipson, Jack d1947 *WhoHol 92*
Lipson, Lawrence J. 1947- *WhoAmL 94*
Lipson, Leslie Michael 1912- *WhoAm 94*
Lipson, Melba d1953 *WhoHol 92*
Lipson, Melvin Alan 1936- *WhoAm 94*
Lipson, Paul S. 1915- *WhoAm 94*
Lipstein, Kurt 1909- *Who 94, WrDr 94*
Lipstein, Robert A. 1954- *WhoAm 94*
Lipstone, Howard H. 1928- *IntMPA 94*
Lipstone, Howard Harold 1928- *WhoAm 94, WhoWest 94*
Lipsyte, Robert (Michael) 1938- *TwCYAW, WrDr 94*
Liptak, Dennis George 1951- *WhoWest 94*
Liptak, Irene Frances 1926- *WhoAm 94, WhoFI 94*
Liptak, Michelle Ann 1954- *WhoMW 93*
Lipton, Allan 1938- *WhoAm 94*
Lipton, Alvin Elliot 1945- *WhoAm 94*
Lipton, Barbara B. *WhoAmA 93*
Lipton, Bronna Jane 1951- *WhoAm 94*

Lipton, Celia WhoHol 92
Lipton, Charles 1928- WhoAm 94, WhoFI 94
Lipton, Charles Jules 1931- WhoAmL 94
Lipton, Daniel Bernard WhoAm 94
Lipton, David A. d1993 IntMPA 94N
Lipton, Dean 1919-1992 WrDr 94N
Lipton, Eunice ConAu 140
Lipton, Jack Philip 1952- WhoAmL 94
Lipton, James Abbott 1946- WhoScEn 94
Lipton, Joan Elaine WhoAm 94
Lipton, John M. 1936- WhoAmP 93
Lipton, Lawrence d1975 WhoHol 92
Lipton, Leah WhoAmA 93
Lipton, Lenny 1940- WrDr 94
Lipton, Lester 1936- WhoFI 94, WhoScEn 94
Lipton, Martha 1916- NewGrDO
Lipton, Martin 1931- WhoAm 94
Lipton, Morris Abraham 1915-1989 WhAm 10
Lipton, Peggy 1947- IntMPA 94
Lipton, Peggy 1948- WhoHol 92
Lipton, Richard M. 1952- WhoAm 94
Lipton, Robert 1944- WhoHol 92
Lipton, Robert Stephen 1942- WhoAmL 94
Lipton, Robert Steven 1946- WhoAm 94, WhoAmL 94
Lipton, Sondra Sahlman WhoAmA 93
Lipton, Stanley C. 1935- WhoAmL 94
Lipton, Stuart 1942- IntWW 93
Lipton, Stuart Anthony 1942- Who 94
Lipton, Stuart Arthur 1950- WhoAm 94
Lipton, Thomas d1931 WhoHol 92
Lipton, Zelda 1923- WhoMW 93
Liptzin, Benjamin 1945- WhoAm 94
Liptzin, Sol 1901- WrDr 94
Li Pu WhoPRCh 91 [port]
Lipworth, Stephen Francis 1939- WhoFI 94
Lipworth, (Maurice) Sydney 1931- IntWW 93, Who 94
Lipzin, Janis Crystal 1945- WhoAmA 93
Li Qi 1918- WhoPRCh 91 [port]
Li Qi 1956- WhoPRCh 91 [port]
Li Qiang 1905- WhoPRCh 91 [port]
Li Qianyuan WhoPRCh 91
Li Qiaoyun WhoPRCh 91
Li Qimin WhoPRCh 91
Li Qiming 1908- WhoPRCh 91
Li Qing 1920- WhoPRCh 91 [port]
Li Qing 1971- WhoPRCh 91 [port]
Li Qingkui 1912- IntWW 93, WhoPRCh 91 [port]
Li Qingwei 1920- IntWW 93, WhoPRCh 91 [port]
Li Qingzhao 1084?-1151? BlmGWL
Li Qiyan 1938- IntWW 93, WhoPRCh 91 [port]
Liquido, Nicanor Javier 1953- WhoWest 94
Liquori, Martin William, Jr. 1949- WhoAm 94, WrDr 94
Lira, José Arturo 1950- WhoHisp 94
Lira, Ricardo 1957- WhoHisp 94, WhoMW 93
Lira-Powell, Julianne Hortensia 1945- WhoHisp 94
Li Renchen 1941- WhoPRCh 91 [port]
Li Renjun 1914- WhoPRCh 91 [port]
Li Renlin 1918- WhoPRCh 91 [port]
Li Renshen 1934- WhoPRCh 91 [port]
Liriano, Nelson Arturo 1964- WhoHisp 94
Li Rongguang 1930- WhoPRCh 91 [port]
Li Rongxi WhoPRCh 91
Li Rosi, Angelo C. 1941- WhoIns 94
Li Rui WhoPRCh 91
Li Rui 1917- IntWW 93
Li Ruihuan 1934- IntWW 93, WhoPRCh 91 [port]
Li Ruishan 1920- IntWW 93, WhoPRCh 91 [port]
Li Ruyun 1916- WhoPRCh 91 [port]
Lis, Anthony Stanley 1918- WhoAm 94
Lis, Daniel T. 1940- WhoAmL 94
Lis, Edward Francis 1918- WhoAm 94
Lis, Janet 1943- WhoAmA 93
Lisa, Joseph F. 1937- WhoAmP 93
Lisa, Manuel 1772-1820 WhWE
Lisack, John, Jr. 1945- WhoScEn 94
Lisak, Robert Philip 1941- WhoMW 93
Lisalda, Sylvia Ann 1949- WhoWest 94
Lisanby, James Walker 1928- WhoAm 94
Lisardi, Andrew H. 1947- WhoHisp 94
Lisbakken, James Robert 1945- WhoAm 94, WhoAmL 94
Lisboa, Henriqueta 1904-1985 BlmGWL
Lisboa, Irene do Ceu Viera 1892-1958 BlmGWL
Lisburne, Earl of 1918- Who 94
Lisch, Howard 1950- WhoAmL 94
Lischer, Ludwig Frederick 1915- WhoAm 94
Lisenbee, Alvis Lee 1940- WhoAm 94
Li Senmao 1929- IntWW 93, WhoPRCh 91 [port]
Lisette, Gabriel 1919- IntWW 93
Lish, Gordon DrAPF 93
Lish, Gordon 1934- DcLB 130 [port], WhoAm 94
Li Shan 1944- WhoPRCh 91 [port]
Li Shanqing WhoPRCh 91
Li Shaowen 1942- WhoPRCh 91 [port]
Li Shaoyan WhoPRCh 91 [port]
Li Shenglin WhoPRCh 91
Li Shenzhi 1923- WhoPRCh 91 [port]
Lisher, James Richard 1947- WhoAmL 94, WhoMW 93
Lisher, John Leonard 1950- WhoAmL 94, WhoMW 93
Li Shichun WhoPRCh 91
Li Shihan 1919- WhoPRCh 91
Li Shiji 1933- WhoPRCh 91 [port]
Li Shitian 1927- WhoPRCh 91
Li Shizhong 1933- WhoPRCh 91 [port]
Lishka, Edward Joseph 1949- WhoMW 93
Lishman, William Alwyn 1931- Who 94
Li Shoubao WhoPRCh 91 [port]
Li Shoushan 1929- IntWW 93, WhoPRCh 91 [port]
Li Shuben WhoPRCh 91
Li Shude WhoPRCh 91
Li Shuiqing 1917- WhoPRCh 91 [port]
Li Shuiqing, Maj.-Gen. 1917- IntWW 93
Li Shuji 1935- WhoPRCh 91 [port]
Li Shutian WhoPRCh 91
Li Shuzheng 1929- IntWW 93, WhoPRCh 91 [port]
Li Shuzheng 1930- WhoWomW 91
Lishwailait 182-?-c. 189-? EncNAR
Lisi, Virna 1937- IntMPA 94, WhoHol 92
Lisiansky, Yury Fyodorovich 1773-1839 WhWE
Lisicky, Paul Alexander DrAPF 93
Li Side 1906- WhoPRCh 91 [port]
Lisimachio, Jean Louis 1946- WhoAm 94
Lisinski, Vatroslav 1819?-1854 NewGrDO
Lisio, Donald John 1934- WhoAm 94
Lisitsyan, Pavel Gerasim 1911- NewGrDO
Lisitsyn, Anatoly Ivanovich 1947- LngBDD
Lisk, Barbara WhoAmP 93
Lisk, Jill (Rosina Ann) 1938- WrDr 94
Lisk, Penelope E. Tsaltas 1959- WhoAmA 93
Liska, George 1922- WhoAm 94
Liska, John J. WhoAmP 93
Liskamm, William Hugo 1931- WhoAm 94
Lisker, Sara 1918- WhoAmA 93
Liskov, Barbara Huberman 1939- WhoScEn 94
Lisle Who 94
Lisle, Baron 1903- Who 94
Lisle, Honor Grenville Basset c. 1495-1566 BlmGWL
Lisle, Laurie 1942- WrDr 94
Lisle, Martha Oglesby 1934- WhoScEn 94
Lisle, Robert Walton 1927- WhoAm 94
Lisle, Seward D. EncSF 93
Lisnek, Paul Michael 1958- WhoAmL 94
Lisnianskaia, Inna L'vovna 1928- BlmGWL
Lisnik, John 1946- WhoAmP 93
Lisnyanskaya, Inna L'vovna 1928- IntWW 93
Lisowski, Anthony Francis 1952- WhoAmP 93
Lisowski, Joseph DrAPF 93
Lispector, Clarice 1925-1977 BlmGWL [port], RfGShF
Liss, Herbert Myron 1931- WhoAm 94, WhoFI 94, WhoMW 93
Liss, Jeffrey F. 1951- WhoAm 94, WhoAmL 94
Liss, Norman 1932- WhoAmL 94
Liss, Norman Richard 1947- WhoFI 94
Liss, Peter Simon 1942- Who 94
Liss, Sheldon B 1936- WrDr 94
Lissack, Michael Robert 1958- WhoAm 94
Lissakers, Karin 1944- ConAu 141
Lissauer, Jack Jonathan 1957- WhoScEn 94
Lissek, Leon WhoHol 92
Lissim, Simon 1900-1981 WhoAmA 93N
Lissitz, Robert Wooster 1941- WhoAm 94
Liss-Katz, Julie 1955- WhoMW 93
Lissman, Barry Alan 1952- WhoAm 94
Lissmann, Hans Werner 1909- IntWW 93, Who 94
Lissner, Stephane Michel 1953- IntWW 93
Lissouba, Pascal 1931- IntWW 93
List, Charles Edward 1941- WhoMW 93
List, Clair Zamoiski 1953- WhoAmA 93
List, David Patton 1920- WhoAm 94
List, Diane Ruth 1948- WhoMW 93
List, Emanuel d1967 WhoHol 92
List, Emanuel 1888-1967 NewGrDO
List, Eugene d1985 WhoHol 92
List, Hans C. 1896- WhoScEn 94
List, Henry Clay WhoAmP 93
List, Irwin Norman 1932- WhoMW 93
List, John DeWitt 1935- WhoAm 94
List, Raymond Edward 1944- WhoAm 94, WhoFI 94, WhoWest 94
List, Robert Frank 1936- IntWW 93, WhoAmP 93
List, Roland 1929- IntWW 93, WhoAm 94
List, Shelley DrAPF 93
List, Vera G. 1908- WhoAmA 93
Listach, Pat Alan 1967- WhoAm 94, WhoMW 93
Listau, Thor 1938- IntWW 93
Lister Who 94
Lister, Alton Lavelle 1958- WhoBlA 94
Lister, Anne 1791-1840 BlmGWL, DcNaB MP
Lister, Ardele Diane 1950- WhoAmA 93
Lister, (Robert) Ashton 1845-1929 DcNaB MP
Lister, Bruce Alcott 1922- WhoScEn 94
Lister, Charles Allan 1918- WhoScEn 94
Lister, David Alfred 1939- WhoBlA 94
Lister, E. Edward 1934- WhoScEn 94
Lister, Francis d1951 WhoHol 92
Lister, Geoffrey Richard 1937- Who 94
Lister, Harry Joseph 1936- WhoAm 94, WhoFI 94
Lister, James 1923- Who 94
Lister, Joe U. 1927- WhoAmP 93
Lister, John Field 1916- Who 94
Lister, Joseph 1827-1912 WorScD [port]
Lister, Keith Fenimore 1917- WhoWest 94
Lister, Moira 1923- IntMPA 94, WhoHol 92
Lister, Patrick Who 94
Lister, (Robert) Patrick 1922- Who 94
Lister, Perri 1959- WhoHol 92
Lister, R(ichard) P(ercival) 1914- WrDr 94
Lister, Raymond (George) 1919- Who 94
Lister, Raymond George 1919- WrDr 94
Lister, Robert Hill 1915-1990 WhAm 10
Lister, Ruth Who 94
Lister, (Margot) Ruth (Aline) 1949- Who 94
Lister, Stephen Anthony 1942- WhoFI 94
Lister, Suzanne Marie 1963- WhoMW 93
Lister, Terry Lee 1948- WhoAmL 94
Lister, Thomas Mosie 1921- WhoAm 94
Lister, Tom 1924- Who 94
Lister, Toney J. WhoAmP 93
Lister, Unity (Viola) 1913- Who 94
Lister, Willa M. 1940- WhoBlA 94
Lister-Kaye, John (Phillip Lister) 1946- Who 94
Listerud, Brian 1951- WhoWest 94
Listerud, Mark Boyd 1924- WhoScEn 94, WhoWest 94
Listgarten, Max Albert 1935- WhoAm 94
Listick, Michael M. 1940- WhoAmL 94
Liston, Aaron Irving 1959- WhoScEn 94
Liston, Alan A. 1946- WhoAm 94
Liston, Albert Morris 1940- WhoWest 94
Liston, Florence Cary d1964 WhoAmA 93N
Liston, Hardy, Jr. WhoBlA 94
Liston, Hugh H. 1917- WhoBlA 94
Liston, James Malcolm 1909- Who 94
Liston, Mary Frances 1920- WhoAm 94
Liston, Melba 1926- AfrAmAl 6
Liston, Robert Todd Lapsley 1898- WhAm 10
Liston, Sonny d1970 WhoHol 92
Listowel, Earl of 1906- IntWW 93, Who 94
Listowski, Richard Francis 1941- WhoAmP 93
Listrom, Anthony Peter 1959- WhoAmL 94
Listrom, Elsie L. 1951- WhoMW 93
Listrom, Linda L. 1952- WhoAm 94, WhoAmL 94
Listvan, Marilyn Ann 1953- WhoMW 93
Li Sujie 1966- WhoPRCh 91 [port]
Lisulo, Daniel Muchiwa 1930- IntWW 93
Liszcz, Teresa 1944- WhoWomW 91
Liszczak, Theodore Michael 1942- WhoScEn 94
Liszka, James J. 1950- WhoWest 94
Liszt, Franz 1811-1886 NewGrDO
Litaker, Thomas (Franklin) 1904-1976 WhoAmA 93N
Litan, Robert E(li) 1950- WrDr 94
Litan, Robert Eli 1950- WhoAm 94
Li Tao WhoPRCh 91 [port]
Li Tao 1913- WhoPRCh 91 [port]
Litchfield, Jack Watson 1909- Who 94
Litchfield, Jean Anne 1942- WhoMW 93
Litchfield, John Shirley Sandys d1993 Who 94N
Litchfield, Richard 1944- WhoIns 94
Litchfield, Robert Latta, Jr. 1949- WhoAmL 94
Litchfield, Ruby (Beatrice) 1912- Who 94
Litel, John d1972 WhoHol 92
Literes, Antonio de 1673-1747 NewGrDO
Lites, James WhoAm 94
Litfin, Richard Albert 1918- WhoAm 94
Litherland, Albert Edward 1928- IntWW 93, Who 94, WhoAm 94
Litherland, Robert Kenneth 1930- Who 94
Lithgow, John 1945- ConTFT 11, IntMPA 94, WhoHol 92
Lithgow, John Arthur 1945- WhoAm 94
Lithgow, William (James) 1934- Who 94
Lithiby, John Grant 1930- Who 94
Lithman, Yngve Georg 1943- WrDr 94
Lithwick, Norman Harvey 1938- WhoAm 94
Li Tiangeng 1924- WhoPRCh 91 [port]
Li Tianxiang WhoPRCh 91
Li Tieying 1936- IntWW 93, WhoPRCh 91 [port]
Li Tingdong 1932- WhoPRCh 91
Litke, Arthur Ludwig 1922- WhoAm 94
Litke, Donald Paul 1934- WhoAm 94
Litke, Fyodor Petrovich 1797-1882 WhWE
Litke, John David 1944- WhoScEn 94
Litman, Bernard 1920- WhoAm 94
Litman, Brian David 1954- WhoWest 94
Litman, Diane Judith 1958- WhoScEn 94
Litman, Harry Peter 1958- WhoAm 94, WhoAmL 94
Litman, Raymond Stephen 1936- WhoAm 94
Litman, Robert Barry 1947- WhoAm 94
Litman, Ruth Ann 1959- WhoMW 93
Litman, Stephen Roger 1946- WhoAmL 94
Litolff, Henry (Charles) 1818-1891 NewGrDO
Litow, Merrill 1927- WhoAm 94
Litowinsky, Olga DrAPF 93
Litrownik, Alan Jay 1945- WhoAm 94, WhoWest 94
Litscher, Karen Kay 1951- WhoMW 93
Litschgi, A. Byrne 1920- WhoAm 94
Litschgi, Richard John 1937- WhoAm 94
Litsey, Roy Thomas WhoWest 94
Litsky, Alan S. 1952- WhoMW 93
Litsky, Warren 1924- WhoAm 94
Litster, James David 1938- WhoAm 94, WhoScEn 94
Li Tsusung WhoPRCh 91 [port]
Litt, Iris DrAPF 93
Litt, Larry DrAPF 93
Litt, Mitchell 1932- WhoAm 94
Litt, Morton Herbert 1926- WhoAm 94
Litt, Nahum 1935- WhoAm 94, WhoAmL 94
Littell, Franklin H(amlin) 1917- WrDr 94
Littell, Franklin Hamlin 1917- WhoAm 94
Littell, Jonathan 1969?- EncSF 93
Littell, Robert 1935- WrDr 94
Littell, Robert E. 1936- WhoAmP 93
Littell, Virginia Newman WhoAmP 93
Litten, Harold 1940- WrDr 94
Litten, Julian (William Sebastian) 1947- WrDr 94
Littig, Lawrence William 1927- WhoAm 94
Littky, Dennis S. 1944- WhoAmP 93
Little(-Augustithis), Vera (Pearl) 1928- NewGrDO
Little, Alan Brian 1925- WhoAm 94
Little, Ann d1984 WhoHol 92
Little, Arthur Dehon 1944- WhoAm 94
Little, Barbara Charon 1931- WhoAmP 93
Little, Billy Lee 1935- WhoMW 93
Little, Brian F. 1943- WhoAm 94
Little, Brian Keith 1959- WhoBlA 94
Little, Bryan (Desmond Greenway) 1913- WrDr 94
Little, Carl DrAPF 93
Little, Carl Maurice 1924- WhoAm 94
Little, Charles E 1931- WrDr 94
Little, Charles Gordon 1924- WhoAm 94, WhoScEn 94, WhoWest 94
Little, Charles Lawson 1946- WhoAm 94
Little, Chester H. 1907- WhoBlA 94
Little, Christopher Mark 1941- WhoAm 94
Little, Cleavon d1992 IntMPA 94N
Little, Cleavon 1939- WhoHol 92
Little, Cleavon 1939-1992 AnObit 1992
Little, Cleavon Jake 1939-1992 WhAm 10, WhoBlA 94N
Little, Deborah A. 1960- WhoAmL 94
Little, Dennis Gage 1935- WhoAm 94, WhoFI 94
Little, Dorothy Marion Sheila 1939- WhoScEn 94
Little, Douglas S. 1945- WhoAmL 94
Little, Duane Ewing 1937- WhoAmP 93
Little, Elbert Luther, Jr. 1907- WhoAm 94
Little, F. A., Jr. 1936- WhoAm 94, WhoAmL 94
Little, General T. 1946- WhoBlA 94
Little, George 1754-1809 WhAmRev
Little, George Daniel 1929- WhoAm 94
Little, George E., Jr. 1921- WhoAmP 93
Little, Geraldine C. DrAPF 93
Little, Helen R. 1962- WhoBlA 94

Little, Herman Kernel 1951- *WhoBlA 94*
Little, Hubert E. 1934- *WhoAmP 93*
Little, Ian (Malcolm David) 1918- *WrDr 94*
Little, Ian Malcolm David 1918- *IntWW 93, Who 94*
Little, J. Anderson 1945- *WhoAmP 93*
Little, Jack Edward 1938- *WhoAm 94, WhoFI 94, WhoScEn 94*
Little, Jack Merville 1934- *WhoAm 94*
Little, James d1969 *WhoHol 92*
Little, James 1952- *WhoAmA 93*
Little, James Arthur 1933- *WhoMW 93*
Little, James David 1940- *WhoAmL 94*
Little, James Morris 1952- *WhoAm 94*
Little, James Stuart 1941- *WhoAm 94*
Little, Jan Nielsen 1958- *WhoAmL 94*
Little, Janet 1759-1813 *BlmGWL*
Little, Jean 1932- *BlmGWL, SmATA 17AS [port]*
Little, (Flora) Jean 1932- *ConAu 42NR, TwCYAW, WrDr 94*
Little, Jeffrey Lee 1961- *WhoAmL 94*
Little, John 1907- *WhoAmA 93N*
Little, John Bertram 1929- *WhoAm 94, WhoScEn 94*
Little, John Dutton Conant 1928- *WhoAm 94*
Little, John Eric Russell 1913- *Who 94*
Little, John Philip Brooke B. *Who 94*
Little, John Wesley 1935- *WhoFI 94*
Little, John William 1944- *WhoAm 94*
Little, Joseph Clyde 1895- *WhAm 10*
Little, Julia Elizabeth 1932- *WhoWest 94*
Little, Ken Dawson 1947- *WhoAmA 93*
Little, Larry Chatmon 1945- *WhoAm 94, WhoBlA 94*
Little, Leone Bryson 1924- *WhoBlA 94*
Little, Lester Knox 1935- *WhoAm 94*
Little, Lewis Auburn 1933- *WhoAm 94*
Little, Little Jack d1956 *WhoHol 92*
Little, Loren Everton 1941- *WhoWest 94*
Little, Loyd Harry, Jr. 1940- *WhoAm 94*
Little, Mark *WhoHol 92*
Little, Mark McKenna 1957- *WhoFI 94*
Little, Meredith 1934- *WhoAmL 94*
Little, Michelle *WhoHol 92*
Little, Monroe Henry 1950- *WhoBlA 94*
Little, Moses 1724-1798 *AmRev*
Little, N. Clayton 1933- *WhoAmP 93*
Little, Nelson 1924- *WhoAmP 93*
Little, Noel Charlton 1895- *WhAm 10*
Little, Patricia *WhoAmP 93*
Little, Polly A. 1954- *WhoAmA 93*
Little, Reuben R. 1933- *WhoBlA 94*
Little, Rich 1938- *IntMPA 94, WhoHol 92*
Little, Rich 1939- *WhoCom*
Little, Richard 1898- *WhAm 10*
Little, Richard Allen 1939- *WhoScEn 94*
Little, Richard Caruthers 1938- *WhoAm 94*
Little, Richard Le Roy 1944- *WhoAm 94*
Little, Robert Andrews 1915- *WhoAm 94*
Little, Robert Benjamin 1955- *WhoBlA 94*
Little, Robert Clement 1925- *Who 94*
Little, Robert Colby 1920- *WhoAm 94*
Little, Robert David 1937- *WhoAm 94*
Little, Robert Eugene 1933- *WhoAm 94*
Little, Robert John, Jr. 1946- *WhoScEn 94*
Little, Ronald Eugene 1937- *WhoBlA 94*
Little, Stephen Abbot 1942- *WhoAmP 93*
Little, Suzanne 1957- *WhoAmP 93*
Little, T. D. 1942- *WhoAmP 93*
Little, Thomas A. 1954- *WhoAmP 93*
Little, Thomas Francis *Who 94*
Little, Thomas Mayer 1935- *WhoAm 94*
Little, Thomas Warren 1939- *WhoWest 94*
Little, Thomas William Anthony 1940- *Who 94*
Little, Travis L. *WhoAmP 93*
Little, W. Ken, Jr. 1959- *WhoScEn 94*
Little, W. Matthew 1922- *WhoAmP 93*
Little, Wayne Albert 1932- *WhoMW 93*
Little, William Arthur 1930- *WhoAm 94*
Little, William Henry 1948- *WhoWest 94*
Little, William John 1810-1894 *DcNaB MP*
Little, Willie Howard 1949- *WhoBlA 94*
Little Billy d1967 *WhoHol 92*
Little Bozo d1952 *WhoHol 92*
Little Chief, Barthell 1941- *WhoAmA 93*
Littlechild, Stephen Charles 1943- *IntWW 93, Who 94*
Little Coyote, Joe c. 1940- *EncNAR*
Littledale, Freya (Lota) *WrDr 94*
Littledale, Freya (Lota Brown) 1929-1992 *SmATA 74 [port]*
Littledale, Richard d1951 *WhoHol 92*
Littlefeather, Sacheen *WhoHol 92*
Littlefield, Carl D. 1948- *WhoAmP 93*
Littlefield, Catherine 1905?-1951 *IntDcB [port]*
Littlefield, Daniel Curtis 1941- *WhoMW 93*
Littlefield, Edmund Wattis 1914- *WhoAm 94*
Littlefield, John Walley 1925- *WhoAm 94, WhoScEn 94*
Littlefield, Lucien d1960 *WhoHol 92*
Littlefield, Martin 1940- *WhoAm 94*
Littlefield, Nick 1942- *WhoAmL 94*
Littlefield, Paul Damon 1920- *WhoAm 94*
Littlefield, Rick M. 1952- *WhoAmP 93*
Littlefield, Robert Stephen 1952- *WhoMW 93*
Littlefield, Roy Everett, III 1952- *WhoAmL 94, WhoFI 94*
Littlefield, Sue Brooks 1955- *WhoAmL 94*
Littlefield, Vivian Moore 1938- *WhoAm 94*
Littlefield, Wayne B. 1946- *WhoAmL 94*
Littlejohn, Alan Morrison 1925- *Who 94*
Littlejohn, Bill C. 1944- *WhoBlA 94*
Littlejohn, Cameron Bruce 1913- *WhoAmP 93*
Littlejohn, David 1937- *WhoAm 94*
Littlejohn, Doris 1935- *Who 94*
Littlejohn, Edward J. 1935- *WhoBlA 94*
Littlejohn, Gary *WhoHol 92*
Littlejohn, John B., Jr. 1942- *WhoBlA 94*
Littlejohn, Joseph Phillip 1937- *WhoBlA 94*
Littlejohn, Kent Oscar 1945- *WhoAmL 94*
Littlejohn, Lanny F. 1942- *WhoAmP 93*
Littlejohn, Marvin Leroy 1923- *WhoAmP 93*
Littlejohn, Samuel Gleason 1921- *WhoBlA 94*
Littlejohn, Walter L. 1932- *WhoBlA 94*
Littlejohn, William Hunter 1929- *Who 94*
Littlejohn Cook, George Steveni 1919- *Who 94*
Littlepage, Diane Martin 1956- *WhoAmL 94*
Littlepage, Samuel D. 1947- *WhoAm 94*
Littlepage, Samuel Dickinson 1947- *WhoAmL 94*
Littler, Charles Armstrong *WhoAmA 93*
Littler, Craig *WhoHol 92*
Littler, Gene Alec 1930- *WhoAm 94*
Littler, (James) Geoffrey 1930- *Who 94*
Littler, Shirley 1932- *Who 94*
Littler, Susan d1982 *WhoHol 92*
Littler, William Brian 1908- *Who 94*
Little Rascals, The *WhoCom*
Little Richard 1932- *AfrAmAl 6 [port], WhoAm 94, WhoBlA 94*
Little Richard 1935- *WhoHol 92*
Little Sky, Eddie *WhoHol 92*
Littleton *Who 94*
Littleton, Arthur C. 1942- *WhoBlA 94*
Littleton, Harvey K. 1922- *WhoAmA 93*
Littleton, Harvey Kline 1922- *WhoAm 94*
Littleton, Isaac Thomas, III 1921- *WhoAm 94*
Littleton, Jesse Talbot, III 1917- *WhoAm 94*
Littleton, Ralph Douglass 1908- *WhoBlA 94*
Littleton, Rupert, Jr. 1950- *WhoBlA 94*
Littleton, Taylor Dowe 1930- *WhoAm 94*
Littlewood, (Barbara) 1909- *Who 94*
Littlewood, Douglas Burden 1922- *WhoAm 94*
Littlewood, James 1922- *Who 94*
Littlewood, Joan 1914- *BlmGEL*
Littlewood, Joan (Maud) *IntWW 93, Who 94*
Littlewood, Thomas Benjamin 1928- *WhoAm 94*
Littleworth, Dennis Kent 1942- *WhoMW 93*
Littman, Earl 1927- *WhoAm 94*
Littman, Harold 1922- *WhoFI 94*
Littman, Howard 1927- *WhoAm 94*
Littman, Irving 1940- *WhoAm 94*
Littman, Lynne *IntMPA 94*
Littman, Mark 1920- *IntWW 93, Who 94*
Littman, Richard Anton 1919- *WhoAm 94, WhoWest 94*
Littman, Susan Joy 1957- *WhoScEn 94*
Littner, Ner 1915- *WhoAm 94*
Litto, George *IntMPA 94*
Litton, Andrew 1959- *IntWW 93*
Litton, Peter Stafford 1921- *Who 94*
Litton, Ted C. 1942- *WhoAmL 94*
Littrell, Doris Marie 1928- *WhoAmA 93*
Littrell, George H., Jr. 1934- *WhoAmP 93*
Litts, Stephen Douglas 1943- *WhoAmP 93*
Lituchy, Todd Stuart 1968- *WhoFI 94*
Li Tung *EncSF 93*
Litvack, Sanford Martin 1936- *WhoAm 94, WhoAmL 94*
Litvajova, Elena 1924- *WhoWomW 91*
Litvak, Lawrence 1929- *WhoAmL 94*
Litvak, Ronald 1938- *WhoMW 93*
Litvak King, Jaime 1933- *IntWW 93*
Litvin, Martin Jay 1928- *WhoMW 93*
Litvinchev, Igor Semionovich 1956- *WhoScEn 94*
Litvinne, Felia (Vasil'yevna) 1860-1936 *NewGrDO*
Litvinoff, Emanuel 1915- *WrDr 94*
Litvinoff, Si 1929- *IntMPA 94*
Litvinov, Pavel Mikhailovich 1940- *IntWW 93*
Litwack, Gerald 1929- *WhoAm 94*
Litwack, Leon 1929- *WrDr 94*
Litwack, Leon Frank 1929- *WhoAm 94*
Litwack, Susan *DrAPF 93*
Litwak, Leo *DrAPF 93*
Litweiler, John (Berkey) 1940- *ConAu 142*
Litweiler, John Berkey 1940- *WhoAm 94*
Litwin, Burton Howard 1944- *WhoAm 94, WhoAmL 94*
Litwin, Burton Lawrence 1931- *WhoAmL 94*
Litwin, Martin Stanley 1930- *WhoAm 94*
Litwin, Michael Joseph 1947- *WhoAm 94*
Litwin, Ruth Forbes 1933- *WhoAmA 93*
Litz, Arthur Walton, Jr. 1929- *WhoAm 94*
Litz, James C. 1948- *WhoAmA 93*
Litz, Jo Ellen 1951- *WhoAmP 93*
Litzke, Jennifer Leah 1966- *WhoMW 93*
Litzky, Eric Neal 1961- *WhoAmL 94*
Litzsinger, Orville Jack 1936- *WhoFI 94, WhoScEn 94*
Litzsinger, Paul Richard 1932- *WhoAm 94*
Liu, Alan Fong-Ching 1933- *WhoAsA 94, WhoScEn 94, WhoWest 94*
Liu, Alfred H. 1942- *WhoAsA 94*
Liu, Anne W. 1950- *WhoAsA 94*
Liu, Bai-Xin 1935- *WhoScEn 94*
Liu, Ben-chieh 1938- *WhoAm 94, WhoAsA 94*
Liu, Ben Shaw-Ching 1955- *WhoAsA 94*
Liu, Benjamin Y. H. 1934- *WhoAsA 94*
Liu, Benjamin Young-hwai 1934- *WhoAm 94, WhoMW 93*
Liu, Binyan 1925- *WrDr 94*
Liu, Chang Yu 1935- *WhoScEn 94*
Liu, Chao-Han 1939- *WhoAm 94*
Liu, Chao-Nan 1940- *WhoAsA 94*
Liu, Chaoqun 1945- *WhoScEn 94*
Liu, Charles Chung-Cha 1953- *WhoScEn 94*
Liu, Chen-Ching 1954- *WhoAsA 94*
Liu, Chian 1945- *WhoMW 93*
Liu, Ching-Tong 1931- *WhoAsA 94*
Liu, Chuan Sheng 1939- *WhoAsA 94*
Liu, Chung-Chiun 1936- *WhoAm 94, WhoAsA 94*
Liu, David Ta-ching 1936- *WhoAsA 94*
Liu, Donald Jiann-Tyng 1953- *WhoAsA 94*
Liu, Dwight Davidson 1958- *WhoAsA 94*
Liu, Edmund K. 1951- *WhoAsA 94*
Liu, Edward Chang-Kai 1946- *WhoScEn 94*
Liu, Edwin Chiap Henn 1942- *WhoWest 94*
Liu, Edwin H. 1942- *WhoAsA 94*
Liu, Edwin K. S. 1941- *WhoWest 94*
Liu, Eric P. 1968- *WhoAsA 94*
Liu, Ernest K. H. 1950- *WhoAm 94*
Liu, Frank Yining 1943- *WhoAsA 94*
Liu, Gerald Hanmin 1944- *WhoAsA 94*
Liu, Guosong 1956- *WhoScEn 94*
Liu, Han-Shou 1930- *WhoScEn 94*
Liu, Hanjun 1964- *WhoAsA 94*
Liu, Henry 1936- *WhoAsA 94*
Liu, Ho 1917- *WhoAmA 93*
Liu, Hong 1957- *WhoAsA 94*
Liu, Hong-Ting 1932- *WhoAsA 94*
Liu, Hsien-Tung 1935- *WhoAsA 94*
Liu, Hsun Kao 1945- *WhoAsA 94*
Liu, Hung 1948- *WhoAmA 93*
Liu, James *WhoHol 92*
Liu, James P. 1936- *WhoAsA 94*
Liu, Jia-ming 1953- *WhoWest 94*
Liu, Jiang Bo 1952- *WhoAsA 94*
Liu, Jianguo 1963- *WhoScEn 94*
Liu, Jianying 1953- *WhoFI 94*
Liu, Jie 1962- *WhoAsA 94*
Liu, John J. 1951- *WhoAsA 94*
Liu, Joseph T. C. 1934- *WhoAm 94*
Liu, Juanita Ching 1947- *WhoAsA 94*
Liu, Jun S. 1965- *WhoAsA 94*
Liu, Jyh-Charn Steve 1956- *WhoAsA 94*
Liu, Karen Chia-Yu 1949- *WhoAsA 94*
Liu, Katherine Chang *WhoAmA 93, WhoWest 94*
Liu, Keh-Fei Frank 1947- *WhoAsA 94*
Liu, Lee 1933- *WhoFI 94, WhoMW 93*
Liu, Leighton Kam Fat 1944- *WhoAsA 94*
Liu, LiLi 1971- *WhoAsA 94*
Liu, Lily Pao-Ih 1941- *WhoAsA 94*
Liu, Lin Chun 1963- *WhoAsA 94*
Liu, Louis F. 1931- *WhoAsA 94*
Liu, Maw-Shung 1940- *WhoAsA 94, WhoMW 93*
Liu, Mengxiong 1946- *WhoAsA 94*
Liu, Michael M. 1953- *WhoAmP 93*
Liu, Michael Minoru Fawn 1953- *WhoAmL 94*
Liu, Min 1959- *WhoAsA 94*
Liu, Ming Cheng 1951- *WhoAsA 94*
Liu, Mini 1949- *WhoAsA 94*
Liu, Nancy Shao-Lan 1932- *WhoAsA 94*
Liu, Nora M. 1956- *WhoAsA 94*
Liu, Peter Chi-Wah 1957- *WhoAsA 94*
Liu, Ping 1959- *WhoAsA 94*
Liu, Pinghui Victor 1924- *WhoAsA 94*
Liu, Pingyu 1941- *WhoScEn 94*
Liu, Qing-Huo 1963- *WhoAsA 94*
Liu, Ray H. 1942- *WhoAsA 94*
Liu, Ray Ho 1942- *WhoAm 94*
Liu, Richard Chung-Wen 1970- *WhoAsA 94*
Liu, Ruey-Wen 1930- *WhoAm 94*
Liu, Samuel Hsi-Peh 1934- *WhoAsA 94*
Liu, Samuel Tzung-Chee 1968- *WhoWest 94*
Liu, Shi Jesse 1953- *WhoScEn 94*
Liu, Shi-Yi 1960- *WhoWest 94*
Liu, Shia-Ling 1922- *WhoAsA 94*
Liu, Shin-Tse 1932- *WhoWest 94*
Liu, Shing Kin Francis 1953- *WhoFI 94*
Liu, Si-kwang *WhoAsA 94, WhoScEn 94*
Liu, Siakisone *WhoAmP 93*
Liu, Stephen Shu Ning *DrAPF 93*
Liu, Stephen Shu-Ning 1930- *WhoAsA 94*
Liu, Su-Feng 1934- *WhoAsA 94*
Liu, Susana Juh-mei 1942- *WhoAsA 94*
Liu, Suyi 1955- *WhoScEn 94*
Liu, Tally C. 1950- *WhoAsA 94*
Liu, Te-Hua 1924- *WhoAsA 94*
Liu, Thomas 1944- *WhoAsA 94*
Liu, Thomas Jyhcheng 1956- *WhoAsA 94*
Liu, Ti Lang 1932- *WhoScEn 94*
Liu, Timothy *DrAPF 93*
Liu, Tsu-huei 1943- *WhoAsA 94*
Liu, Ts'un-Yan 1917- *IntWW 93*
Liu, Tsz-Ming, Benjamin 1931- *Who 94*
Liu, Tze Shiu 1947- *WhoWest 94*
Liu, Vi-Cheng 1917- *WhoAm 94*
Liu, Warren Kuo-Tung 1952- *WhoAsA 94*
Liu, Wei-Min 1945- *WhoAsA 94*
Liu, Wei-Ying *WhoAsA 94*
Liu, Wing Kam 1952- *WhoAsA 94*
Liu, Wingyuen Timothy 1946- *WhoWest 94*
Liu, Wu-chi 1907- *WrDr 94*
Liu, Xingwu 1942- *WhoAsA 94*
Liu, Xu 1961- *WhoWest 94*
Liu, Yick Wah Edmund 1953- *WhoFI 94*
Liu, Yilu 1959- *WhoAsA 94*
Liu, Ying 1961- *WhoAsA 94*
Liu, Yinshi 1960- *WhoScEn 94*
Liu, Yong-Biao 1960- *WhoScEn 94*
Liu, Young King 1934- *WhoAm 94, WhoScEn 94*
Liu, Yu-Jih 1948- *WhoScEn 94*
Liu, Yuan Hsiung 1938- *WhoAsA 94, WhoMW 93, WhoScEn 94*
Liu, Yuanfang 1931- *WhoScEn 94*
Liu, Yung Sheng 1944- *WhoAsA 94*
Liu, Yung-Way 1955- *WhoAsA 94*
Liu, Yung Y. 1950- *WhoAsA 94*
Liu, Zhuang 1932- *WhoAsA 94*
Liu, Zhuangyi 1954- *WhoAsA 94*
Liu, Zi-Chao 1933- *WhoScEn 94*
Liu Anyuan 1927- *WhoPRCh 91 [port]*
Liu Anyuan, Lieut.-Gen. 1927- *IntWW 93*
Liu Bai *WhoPRCh 91*
Liu Bainian *WhoPRCh 91*
Liu Baiyu 1916- *WhoPRCh 91 [port]*
Liu Bin 1937- *WhoPRCh 91 [port]*
Liu Bing *WhoPRCh 91*
Liu Bingjiang 1937- *WhoPRCh 91*
Liu Bingyan 1915- *WhoPRCh 91*
Liu Bingyan, Maj.-Gen. 1915- *IntWW 93*
Liu Binyan 1925- *ConWorW 93, IntWW 93, WhoPRCh 91 [port]*
Liu Boran *WhoPRCh 91*
Liu Caipin *WhoPRCh 91*
Liu Changjie 1933- *WhoPRCh 91 [port]*
Liu Chaoming *WhoPRCh 91*
Liu Chu *WhoPRCh 91*
Liu Chun *WhoPRCh 91*
Liu Chun 1918- *IntWW 93*
Liu Chunfu 1925- *WhoPRCh 91 [port]*
Liu Chunlin *WhoPRCh 91*
Liu Cunxin 1926- *WhoPRCh 91 [port]*
Liu Cunzhi 1924- *WhoPRCh 91 [port]*
Liu Da 1913- *WhoPRCh 91 [port]*
Liu Danian 1915- *IntWW 93, WhoPRCh 91 [port]*
Liu Danzhai 1931- *IntWW 93, WhoPRCh 91 [port]*
Liu Daosheng *WhoPRCh 91*
Liu Daosheng 1915- *WhoPRCh 91 [port]*
Liu Daoyu 1933- *WhoPRCh 91 [port]*
Liu Deyou 1931- *WhoPRCh 91 [port]*
Liu Dongfan *WhoPRCh 91*
Liu Dongsheng 1917- *WhoPRCh 91 [port]*
Liu Fangren 1936- *IntWW 93, WhoPRCh 91 [port]*
Liu Feng *WhoPRCh 91 [port]*
Liu Feng 1937- *WhoPRCh 91 [port]*
Liu Fonian 1913- *WhoPRCh 91*
Liu Fusheng 1931- *WhoPRCh 91 [port]*
Liu Fuzhi 1917- *IntWW 93, WhoPRCh 91 [port]*
Liu Gao *WhoPRCh 91 [port]*
Liu Gengling *WhoPRCh 91*
Liu Gengyin 1926- *WhoPRCh 91 [port]*
Liu Guangfu *WhoPRCh 91*
Liu Guangyun 1932- *WhoPRCh 91 [port]*
Liu Guangzhi *WhoPRCh 91*

Liu Guangzhong *WhoPRCh 91*
Liu Guinan *WhoPRCh 91*
Liu Guofan 1929- *IntWW 93, WhoPRCh 91 [port]*
Liu Guoguang 1923- *IntWW 93, WhoPRCh 91 [port]*
Liu Guoxiong *WhoPRCh 91*
Liu Haiqing 1921- *IntWW 93, WhoPRCh 91 [port]*
Liu Haiquan 1922- *WhoPRCh 91 [port]*
Liu Haisu 1896- *WhoPRCh 91 [port]*
Liu Haisu (Pan Jifang) 1896- *IntWW 93*
Liu Hanzhen 1926- *WhoPRCh 91 [port]*
Liu Heqiao 1931- *WhoPRCh 91 [port]*
Liu Hongren *WhoPRCh 91*
Liu Hongru 1930- *IntWW 93, WhoPRCh 91 [port]*
Liu Housheng *WhoPRCh 91*
Liu Hsin-Wu *ConWorW 93*
Liu Hua *WhoPRCh 91*
Liu Huanzhang 1929- *WhoPRCh 91 [port]*
Liu Huanzhang 1930- *IntWW 93*
Liu Huaqing 1917- *WhoPRCh 91 [port]*
Liu Huaqing, Gen. 1916- *IntWW 93*
Liu Huaqiu *WhoPRCh 91*
Liu Huixian 1912- *WhoPRCh 91 [port]*
Liu Jialin 1959- *WhoPRCh 91*
Liu Jian *WhoPRCh 91*
Liu Jianfeng 1936- *IntWW 93, WhoPRCh 91 [port]*
Liu Jiang *NewYTBS 93 [port]*
Liu Jiang 1940- *WhoPRCh 91 [port]*
Liu Jianqing 1928- *WhoPRCh 91 [port]*
Liu Jianzhang *WhoPRCh 91*
Liu Jibin 1938- *WhoPRCh 91 [port]*
Liu Jie *WhoPRCh 91 [port]*
Liu Jinfeng 1926- *WhoPRCh 91 [port]*
Liu Jingfan *WhoPRCh 91 [port]*
Liu Jinghe 1926- *WhoPRCh 91*
Liu Jingji 1902- *WhoPRCh 91 [port]*
Liu Jingsong 1933- *WhoPRCh 91 [port]*
Liu Jingsong, Lieut.-Gen. 1933- *IntWW 93*
Liu Jirong 1931- *WhoPRCh 91*
Liu Jiyou 1918- *WhoPRCh 91 [port]*
Liu Jiyuan 1933- *WhoPRCh 91 [port]*
Liu Junchen *WhoPRCh 91*
Liu Junjie 1923- *WhoPRCh 91 [port]*
Liu Kai 1922- *WhoPRCh 91 [port]*
Liu Kaiqu 1904- *IntWW 93, WhoPRCh 91 [port]*
Liu Kaiyu *WhoPRCh 91*
Liu Kan 1926- *WhoPRCh 91 [port]*
Liu Kang *WhoPRCh 91*
Liu Keming 1919- *IntWW 93*
Liu Lantao 1910- *IntWW 93, WhoPRCh 91 [port]*
Liu Lide *WhoPRCh 91*
Liu Lifeng 1918- *WhoPRCh 91 [port]*
Liu Lifeng, Lieut.-Gen. 1918- *IntWW 93*
Liu Lin 1918- *WhoPRCh 91 [port]*
Liu Lingcang 1907- *WhoPRCh 91 [port]*
Liu Linji *WhoPRCh 91*
Liu Liying 1932- *WhoPRCh 91 [port]*
Liu Lizhen 1929- *WhoPRCh 91 [port]*
Liu Lunxian 1943- *WhoPRCh 91 [port]*
Lium, Elder Leonard 1896- *WhAm 10*
Liu Meijin *WhoPRCh 91*
Liu Minghui 1915- *WhoPRCh 91*
Liu Mingpu *WhoPRCh 91*
Liu Mingpu 1930- *WhoPRCh 91 [port]*
Liu Mingzu 1936- *WhoPRCh 91 [port]*
Liu Minxue *WhoPRCh 91*
Liu Nengyuan 1962- *WhoPRCh 91*
Liu Nianqu 1945- *IntWW 93*
Liu Nianzhi 1912- *WhoPRCh 91 [port]*
Liu Nienling 1934- *BlmGWL*
Liu Pin-Yen *ConWorW 93*
Liu Qibao 1953- *WhoPRCh 91 [port]*
Liu Qingyou *WhoPRCh 91*
Liu Ronghui 1939- *WhoPRCh 91*
Liu Shahe 1931- *IntWW 93, WhoPRCh 91 [port]*
Liu Shan *WhoPRCh 91*
Liu Shanxiang *WhoPRCh 91*
Liu Shaohui 1940- *IntWW 93, WhoPRCh 91*
Liu Shaoshan *WhoPRCh 91 [port]*
Liu Shaotang 1936- *IntWW 93, WhoPRCh 91 [port]*
Liu Shenggang *WhoPRCh 91*
Liu Shibai *WhoPRCh 91*
Liu Shikun *WhoPRCh 91 [port]*
Liu Shilan 1962- *WhoPRCh 91 [port]*
Liu Shirong *WhoPRCh 91*
Liu Shu 1935- *WhoPRCh 91 [port]*
Liu Shuangquan *WhoPRCh 91*
Liu Shulin *WhoPRCh 91*
Liu Shuqing 1925- *IntWW 93, WhoPRCh 91 [port]*
Liu Shusen *WhoPRCh 91*
Liu Shusheng 1926- *IntWW 93, WhoPRCh 91 [port]*
Liu Songhao *WhoPRCh 91*
Liu Suinian 1929- *WhoPRCh 91 [port]*
Liu Suola 1955- *BlmGWL*
Liu Tianfu 1926- *WhoPRCh 91*
Liu Tianrui *WhoPRCh 91 [port]*
Liu Tianwei 1954- *WhoPRCh 91*
Liu Wei 1916- *WhoPRCh 91 [port]*
Liu Weiming 1938- *IntWW 93, WhoPRCh 91 [port]*
Liu Wen *WhoPRCh 91*
Liu Wenxi 1933- *WhoPRCh 91 [port]*
Liu Wenzhi *WhoPRCh 91 [port]*
Liu Xian 1915- *IntWW 93, WhoPRCh 91 [port]*
Liu Xiangsan 1910- *WhoPRCh 91 [port]*
Liu Xiaocheng *WhoPRCh 91*
Liu Xiaodi 1954- *WhoPRCh 91*
Liu Xiaoqing 1952- *IntWW 93, WhoPRCh 91 [port]*
Liu Xihong 1961- *WhoPRCh 91 [port]*
Liu Xilin 1911- *WhoPRCh 91 [port]*
Liu Xing *WhoPRCh 91*
Liu Xingwen *WhoPRCh 91*
Liu Xinwu 1942- *ConWorW 93, IntWW 93, WhoPRCh 91 [port]*
Liu Xinzeng 1929- *WhoPRCh 91 [port]*
Liu Xiuhua *WhoPRCh 91*
Liu Xiwen 1916- *WhoPRCh 91 [port]*
Liu Xiyao 1916- *WhoPRCh 91 [port]*
Liu Xizhong 1930- *WhoPRCh 91 [port]*
Liu Xueji *WhoPRCh 91*
Liu Yan *WhoPRCh 91*
Liu Yandong 1944- *WhoPRCh 91 [port]*
Liu Yanhuan *WhoPRCh 91*
Liu Yanqing 1923- *WhoPRCh 91 [port]*
Liu Yi 1930- *IntWW 93, WhoPRCh 91 [port]*
Liu Yili *WhoPRCh 91*
Liu Ying *WhoPRCh 91*
Liu Ying 1924- *WhoPRCh 91 [port]*
Liu Yongye 1909- *WhoPRCh 91 [port]*
Liu Youfa 1922- *WhoPRCh 91 [port]*
Liu Youfa, Vice-Adm. 1922- *IntWW 93*
Liu Youfang 1926- *WhoPRCh 91 [port]*
Liu Youguang 1914- *WhoPRCh 91 [port]*
Liu Yuan 1951- *WhoPRCh 91 [port]*
Liu Yuanxuan 1911- *WhoPRCh 91 [port]*
Liu Yuanzhang *WhoPRCh 91*
Liu Yu'e 1935- *WhoPRCh 91 [port]*
Liu Yuhan *WhoPRCh 91*
Liu Yujie *WhoPRCh 91, WhoWomW 91*
Liu Yulin 1931- *WhoPRCh 91 [port]*
Liu Yuling 1947- *WhoPRCh 91 [port]*
Liu Yunbo 1905- *WhoPRCh 91*
Liu Yunzhao 1926- *WhoPRCh 91 [port]*
Liu Yuping *WhoPRCh 91*
Liu Yuren *WhoPRCh 91*
Liu Yuti 1923- *WhoPRCh 91 [port]*
Liu Zaifu 1941- *WhoPRCh 91 [port]*
Liu Zengkun 1923- *WhoPRCh 91 [port]*
Liu Zepeng 1946- *WhoPRCh 91 [port]*
Liu Zhanqiu 1935- *WhoPRCh 91 [port]*
Liu Zhao *WhoPRCh 91*
Liu Zhen 1915- *WhoPRCh 91 [port]*
Liu Zhen 1930- *BlmGWL, WhoPRCh 91 [port]*
Liu Zhen, Col.-Gen. 1915- *IntWW 93*
Liu Zheng 1929- *IntWW 93, WhoPRCh 91*
Liu Zheng 1930- *WhoPRCh 91 [port]*
Liu Zhengwei 1930- *IntWW 93, WhoPRCh 91 [port]*
Liu Zhenhua *WhoPRCh 91*
Liu Zhenhua 1921- *WhoPRCh 91 [port]*
Liu Zhenhua, Gen. 1921- *IntWW 93*
Liu Zhenqun *WhoPRCh 91*
Liu Zhenyi 1921- *WhoPRCh 91 [port]*
Liu Zhenyuan 1935- *WhoPRCh 91 [port]*
Liu Zhicheng *WhoPRCh 91*
Liu Zhiguang *WhoPRCh 91*
Liu Zhijian 1905- *WhoPRCh 91 [port]*
Liu Zhitian 1928- *WhoPRCh 91 [port]*
Liu Zhiwei *WhoPRCh 91*
Liu Zhizhi *WhoPRCh 91*
Liu Zhongde 1933- *IntWW 93, WhoPRCh 91 [port]*
Liu Zhongli 1934- *IntWW 93, WhoPRCh 91 [port]*
Liu Zhongyi 1930- *IntWW 93, WhoPRCh 91 [port]*
Liu Zhuanlian *WhoPRCh 91 [port]*
Liu Zhujin *WhoPRCh 91*
Liu Ziming 1927- *WhoPRCh 91*
Liu Zuci 1939- *WhoPRCh 91*
Liu Zunqi 1911- *WhoPRCh 91 [port]*
Liu Zuohui 1930- *WhoPRCh 91 [port]*
Liu Zuyu *WhoPRCh 91*
Liuzzi, Robert C. 1944- *WhoMW 93*
Liuzzi, Robert Carmen 1944- *WhoAm 94, WhoFI 94*
Liuzzo, Joseph Anthony 1926- *WhoAm 94*
Livadas, Dennis James 1914- *WhoAmP 93*
Livanos, Peter E., Jr. 1937- *WhoAmP 93*
Livanov, Boris d1972 *WhoHol 92*
Livaudais, Marcel, Jr. 1925- *WhoAm 94, WhoAmL 94*
Live, Israel 1907- *WhoAm 94*
Lively, Carol A. 1935- *WhoAm 94*
Lively, Diane Marie Compton 1941- *WhoFI 94*
Lively, Edwin Lester 1930- *WhoAm 94*
Lively, Edwin Lowe 1920- *WhoAm 94*
Lively, Elizabeth Anne 1953- *WhoMW 93*
Lively, Howard Randolph, Jr. 1934- *WhoFI 94*
Lively, Ira J. 1926- *WhoBlA 94*
Lively, John Pound 1945- *WhoAm 94*
Lively, Paul T. 1948- *WhoAmL 94*
Lively, Penelope 1933- *BlmGWL [port], WrDr 94*
Lively, Penelope Margaret 1933- *IntWW 93, Who 94*
Lively, Pierce 1921- *WhoAm 94, WhoAmL 94*
Lively, Robyn *WhoHol 92*
Lively, Roderick Lavern 1917- *WhoAmP 93*
Livengood, Henry *WhoAmP 93*
Livengood, John B. 1947- *WhoAmP 93*
Livengood, John Bryant 1947- *WhoMW 93*
Livengood, Richard Vaughn 1934- *WhoAm 94*
Livengood, Thomas Claude 1955- *WhoFI 94*
Livengood, Timothy Austin 1962- *WhoScEn 94*
Livengood, Victoria Ann 1959- *WhoAm 94*
Liverati, Giovanni 1772-1846 *NewGrDO*
Livergant, Harold Leonard 1924- *WhoAm 94*
Liverman, John Gordon 1920- *Who 94*
Livermore, Donald Raymond 1947- *WhoWest 94*
Livermore, Fern Chrisman 1921- *WhoWest 94*
Livermore, Joseph McMaster 1937- *WhoAm 94*
Livermore, Mary Ashton 1821-1905 *DcAmReB 2*
Livermore, Mary Ashton Rice 1820-1905 *AmSocL*
Livermore, Putnam 1922- *WhoAmP 93*
Livermore, Samuel 1732-1803 *WhAmRev*
Liverpool, Archbishop of 1920- *Who 94*
Liverpool, Archdeacon of *Who 94*
Liverpool, Auxiliary Bishop of *Who 94*
Liverpool, Bishop of 1929- *Who 94*
Liverpool, Dean of *Who 94*
Liverpool, Earl of 1944- *Who 94*
Liverpool, Charles Eric 1946- *WhoBlA 94*
Liverpool, Herman Oswald 1925- *WhoBlA 94*
Liversage, Richard Albert 1925- *WhoAm 94*
Liversidge, Henry Douglas 1913- *WrDr 94*
Livesay, Ann Louise 1951- *WhoAmP 93*
Livesay, Dorothy 1909- *BlmGWL, ConLC 79 [port], WrDr 94*
Livesay, Michael (Howard) 1936- *Who 94*
Livesay, Thomas Andrew 1945- *WhoAm 94, WhoAmA 93, WhoWest 94*
Livesey, Barrie 1904- *WhoHol 92*
Livesey, Bernard Joseph Edward 1944- *Who 94*
Livesey, Cassie 187-?- *WhoHol 92*
Livesey, Jack d1961 *WhoHol 92*
Livesey, Roger d1976 *WhoHol 92*
Livesey, Ronald John Dearden 1935- *Who 94*
Livesey, Sam d1936 *WhoHol 92*
Livet, Anne Hodge 1941- *WhoAmA 93*
Livi, Yvo *WhAm 10*
Livia 58BC-29AD *HisWorL [port]*
Livia, Anna *EncSF 93*
Livick, Malcolm Harris 1929- *WhoAm 94*
Livick, Stephen 1945- *WhoAm 94, WhoAmA 93*
Livigni, Filippo fl. 1773-1786 *NewGrDO*
Livigni, Russell A. 1934- *WhoScEn 94*
Living Color *AfrAmAl 6*
Living Colour *News 93-3 [port]*
Livingood, Clarence S. 1911- *WhoAm 94*
Livingood, James Weston 1910- *WrDr 94*
Livingood, Marvin Duane 1918- *WhoScEn 94*
Livings, Henry 1929- *ConDr 93, Who 94, WrDr 94*
Livingston, Abraham *WhAmRev*
Livingston, Alida Schuyler van Rensselaer 1656-1727 *BlmGWL*
Livingston, Ann Chambliss 1952- *WhoAmL 94*
Livingston, Anne (Nancy) Shippen 1763-1841 *BlmGWL*
Livingston, Barry 1953- *WhoHol 92*
Livingston, Berkeley 1908- *EncSF 93*
Livingston, Bernard *DrAPF 93*
Livingston, Bob 1943- *CngDr 93*
Livingston, Dana Alan 1957- *WhoWest 94*
Livingston, David Morse 1941- *WhoAm 94*
Livingston, Donald Earl 1924- *WhoAmP 93*
Livingston, Donald Ray 1952- *WhoAmL 94*
Livingston, Edward Michael 1948- *WhoAmL 94*
Livingston, Elizabeth Ann 1964- *WhoMW 93*
Livingston, F. L. *WhoAm 94*
Livingston, Graham 1928- *Who 94*
Livingston, Gretchen M. 1963- *WhoAmL 94*
Livingston, Harold 1924- *EncSF 93*
Livingston, Henry Beekman 1750-1831 *WhAmRev*
Livingston, Henry Brockholst 1757-1823 *WhAmRev*
Livingston, Homer J., Jr. 1935- *WhoAm 94*
Livingston, J. A. 1905-1989 *WhAm 10*
Livingston, James 1747-1832 *WhAmRev*
Livingston, James Thomas 1931- *WhoMW 93*
Livingston, Jane S. 1944- *WhoAmA 93*
Livingston, Jay 1915- *IntMPA 94*
Livingston, Jay Harold 1915- *WhoAm 94*
Livingston, Jayson 1965- *WrDr 94*
Livingston, John Henry 1746-1825 *DcAmReB 2*
Livingston, Johnston R. 1923- *WhoAm 94*
Livingston, Jon Jerald 1935- *WhoWest 94*
Livingston, Joyce *WhoBlA 94*
Livingston, L. Benjamin 1931- *WhoBlA 94*
Livingston, Louis Bayer 1941- *WhoAm 94, WhoAmL 94*
Livingston, Margaret d1984 *WhoHol 92*
Livingston, Margaret Gresham 1924- *WhoAmA 93*
Livingston, Marie Leigh 1955- *WhoWest 94*
Livingston, Mary M. 1948- *WhoScEn 94*
Livingston, Mollie Parnis d1992 *WhAm 10*
Livingston, Myra Cohn *DrAPF 93*
Livingston, Myra Cohn 1926- *WhoAm 94, WhoWest 94, WrDr 94*
Livingston, Nancy 1935- *WrDr 94*
Livingston, Paisley 1951- *WrDr 94*
Livingston, Patricia Ann 1954- *WhoWest 94*
Livingston, Peter Van Burgh 1710-1792 *WhAmRev*
Livingston, Philip 1716-1778 *WhAmRev*
Livingston, Princess d1976 *WhoHol 92*
Livingston, Richard d1786 *WhAmRev*
Livingston, Richard Lee 1940- *WhoAmP 93*
Livingston, Robert d1988 *WhoHol 92*
Livingston, Robert Burr 1918- *WhoAm 94, WhoScEn 94*
Livingston, Robert Henry 1934- *WrDr 94*
Livingston, Robert L., Jr. 1943- *WhoAmP 93*
Livingston, Robert Linlithgow, Jr. 1943- *WhoAm 94*
Livingston, Robert R. (the Elder) 1718-1775 *WhAmRev*
Livingston, Robert R. (the Younger) 1746-1813 *WhAmRev [port]*
Livingston, Rudolph 1928- *WhoBlA 94*
Livingston, Sidnee *WhoAmA 93*
Livingston, Stanley 1950- *WhoHol 92*
Livingston, Theodore A., Jr. 1946- *WhoAm 94*
Livingston, Thomas Eugene 1948- *WhoAm 94*
Livingston, Walter 1740-1797 *WhAmRev*
Livingston, William 1723-1790 *AmRev, WhAmRev [port]*
Livingston Booth, John Dick 1918- *Who 94*
Livingstone, Biganess *WhoAmA 93*
Livingstone, Charleen Thompson 1929- *WhoFI 94*
Livingstone, Daniel Archibald 1927- *WhoAm 94, WhoScEn 94*
Livingstone, David 1813-1873 *WhWE*
Livingstone, Douglas (James) 1932- *WrDr 94*
Livingstone, Elaine Biganess *WhoMW 93*
Livingstone, Frank d1932 *WhoHol 92*
Livingstone, Frank Brown 1928- *WhoAm 94*
Livingstone, Harrison Edward *DrAPF 93*
Livingstone, Joan 1948- *WhoAmA 93*
Livingstone, John Leslie 1932- *WhoAm 94*
Livingstone, Ken 1945- *Who 94*
Livingstone, Ken(neth) Robert 1945- *IntWW 93*
Livingstone, Mary d1983 *WhoHol 92*
Livingstone, Mary Moffat 1821-1862 *WhWE*
Livingstone, Michael Edwin 1953- *WhoWest 94*
Livingstone, Susan Morrisey 1946- *WhoAm 94*
Livingstone, William Edwin, III 1935- *WhoAm 94*
Livingston-White, Deborah J. H. 1947- *WhoBlA 94*
Livius, Peter 1729-1795 *WhAmRev*
Livo, Norma J. 1929- *SmATA 76 [port]*
Livolsi, Frank William, Jr. 1938- *WhoAmL 94*

Lloyd, Thomas Reese 1920- WhoAmP 93
Lloyd, Timothy Andrew Wigram 1946- Who 94
Lloyd, Timothy Charles 1951- WhoAm 94
Lloyd, Trevor Who 94
Lloyd, (Bertram) Trevor 1938- Who 94
Lloyd, Wanda 1949- WhoBlA 94
Lloyd, William F. 1947- WhoAm 94
Lloyd, William Robert, Jr. 1947- WhoAmP 93
Lloyd Davies, John Robert Who 94
Lloyd Davies, Trevor Arthur 1909- Who 94
Lloyd-Edwards, Norman 1933- Who 94
Lloyd-Eley, John 1923- Who 94
Lloyd George Who 94
Lloyd George, David 1863-1945 HisWorL [port]
Lloyd George Of Dwyfor, Earl 1924- Who 94
Lloyd-Hughes, Trevor Denby 1922- Who 94
Lloyd-Jacob, David Oliver 1938- Who 94
Lloyd Jones, Charles Beynon Who 94
Lloyd-Jones, David (Mathias) 1934- NewGrDO
Lloyd-Jones, David Mathias 1934- IntWW 93, Who 94
Lloyd-Jones, David Trevor 1917- Who 94
Lloyd-Jones, Donald J. 1931- WhoAm 94
Lloyd-Jones, (Peter) Hugh (Jefferd) 1922- IntWW 93, Who 94, WrDr 94
Lloyd-Jones, Jean 1929- WhoAmP 93, WhoWomW 91
Lloyd Jones, Richard (Anthony) 1933- Who 94
Lloyd-Jones, Robert 1931- Who 94
Lloyd-Mostyn Who 94
Lloyd Of Berwick, Baron 1929- Who 94
Lloyd of Hampstead, Baron d1992 Who 94N
Lloyd Owen, David Lanyon 1917- Who 94
Lloyd-Pack, Charles 1905- WhoHol 92
Lloyd-Pack, Roger 1944- WhoHol 92
Lloyd Webber, Andrew 1948- IntWW 93, NewGrDO, Who 94, WhoAm 94
Lloyd Webber, Julian 1951- IntWW 93, Who 94
Llubien, Jose H. DrAPF 93
Lluch, Myrna 1950- WhoHisp 94
Lluch Martin, Ernest 1937- IntWW 93
Llull, Ramon c. 1235-1316 ClMLC 12
Lluria, Eduardo P. 1955- WhoFI 94
Llwyd, Elfyn 1951- Who 94
Llywelyn, Morgan 1937- WrDr 94
Lo, Chi-Yuan 1952- WhoAsA 94
Lo, Chien-kuo 1946- WhoAsA 94
Lo, Chun-Lau John 1954- WhoScEn 94
Lo, Howard H. 1937- WhoAsA 94
Lo, Kenneth Hsiao Chien 1913- Who 94
Lo, Kwok-Yung 1947- WhoAsA 94, WhoScEn 94
Lo, Ronald Ping Wong 1936- WhoAm 94
Lo, Samuel E. 1931- WhoAsA 94
Lo, Sansom Chi-Kwong 1965- WhoWest 94
Lo, Shui-yin 1941- WhoScEn 94
Lo, Steven C. 1949- WrDr 94
Lo, Suzanne J. 1950- WhoAsA 94
Lo, Tou Ger 1947- WhoAsA 94
Lo, Vincent IntWW 93
Lo, Waituck 1919- WhoWest 94
Lo, Winston W. 1938- WrDr 94
Lo, Yao 1950- WhoAsA 94
Lo, Yuen-Tze 1920- WhoAsA 94
Loach, Kenneth 1936- IntWW 93, Who 94
Loader, Jay Gordon 1923- WhoAm 94
Loader, Jayne DrAPF 93
Loader, Leslie (Thomas) 1923- Who 94
Loades, Ann Lomas 1938- Who 94
Loades, David Henry 1937- Who 94
Loades, David Michael 1934- WrDr 94
Loadholt, Miles 1943- WhoAmL 94
Loane, Marcus Lawrence 1911- IntWW 93, Who 94
Loar, Peggy A. 1948- WhoAmA 93
Loarie, Thomas Merritt 1946- WhoWest 94
Loback, Marvin d1938 WhoHol 92
Lobanov, Vasily 1947- NewGrDO
Lobanov-Rostovsky, Oleg 1934- WhoAm 94
Lobao, Linda Mary 1952- WhoMW 93
Lobashev, Vladimir Mikhailovich 1934- IntWW 93, WhoScEn 94
Lobatchevsky, Nicholai Ivanovich WorScD
Lobato, Francesca WhoHisp 94
Lobato, Monteiro EncSF 93
Lobato, Toribio Q. 1954- WhoHisp 94
LoBaugh, Leslie E., Jr. WhoAmL 94, WhoFI 94
Lobay, Ivan 1911- WhoScEn 94
Lobb, Eric d1993 NewYTBS 93
Lobb, Howard Leslie Vicars d1992 Who 94N
Lobb, John Cunningham 1913-1990 WhAm 10
Lobb, Michael Louis 1942- WhoScEn 94
Lobb, William Atkinson 1951- WhoAm 94, WhoFI 94
Lobbia, John E. 1941- WhoAm 94, WhoFI 94
Lobdell, Frank 1921- WhoAm 94, WhoAmA 93, WhoWest 94
Lobdell, Henry Raymond 1961- WhoAmL 94
Lobdell, Robert Charles 1926- WhoAm 94
Lobe, Johann Christian 1797-1881 NewGrDO
Lobeck, Charles Champlin, Jr. 1926- WhoAm 94
Lobeck, Daniel John 1951- WhoAmL 94
Lobeck, Linda Marie 1960- WhoMW 93
Lobel, Adrianne ConTFT 11
Lobel, Anita 1934- WrDr 94
Lobel, Charles Irving 1921- WhoWest 94
Lobel, Irving 1917- WhoFI 94
Lobel, Martin 1941- WhoAmL 94
Lobel, Steven Alan 1952- WhoScEn 94
Lobell, Michael 1941- IntMPA 94
Lobello, Christopher Michael 1967- WhoMW 93
Lo Bello, Joseph David 1940- WhoAm 94
Lo Bello, Nino 1921- WhoAm 94
Lobello, Peter 1935- WhoAmA 93
Lobenfeld, Eric Jay 1950- WhoAmL 94
Lobengula c. 1836-1894 HisWorL [port]
Lobenherz, William Ernest 1949- WhoAmL 94
Lober, Georg J. 1892-1961 WhoAmA 93N
Loberg, Peter Eric 1943- WhoFI 94
Loberg, Robert Warren 1927- WhoAmA 93
Lobert fl. 1870- EncNAR
LoBianco, Tony 1936- ConTFT 11, IntMPA 94
Lo Bianco, Tony 1938- WhoHol 92
LoBiondo, Frank A. 1946- WhoAmP 93
Lobitz, W. Charles, III 1943- WhoWest 94
Lobitz, Walter Charles, Jr. 1911- WhoAm 94
Lobkowicz, Nicholas 1931- IntWW 93
Lobkowitz, Ferdinand Joseph Johann 1797-1868 NewGrDO
Lobkowitz, Ferdinand Philipp Joseph 1724-1784 NewGrDO
Lobkowitz, Joseph Franz Maximilian 1772-1816 NewGrDO
Lobkowitz, Philipp Hyacinth 1680-1734 NewGrDO
Lobkowitz Family NewGrDO
Lobl, Herbert Max 1932- WhoAm 94, WhoAmL 94
Lobley, Alan Haigh 1927- WhoAm 94
Lobo, Baltasar 1910-1993 NewYTBS 93
Lobo, Elias Alvares 1834-1901 NewGrDO
Lobo, Jennifer Helena 1954- WhoFI 94
Lobo, Jeronimo 1593-1678 WhWE
Lobo, Jose Carlos 1942- IntWW 93
Lobo, Mara BlmGWL
Lobo, Richard M. 1936- WhoHisp 94
Lobo, Rogerio Hyndman 1923- Who 94
Lobo, Roy Francis 1963- WhoScEn 94
Loboda, Mark J. 1962- WhoMW 93
Lo Bosco, Michael, Jr. 1960- WhoFI 94
Lobov, Oleg Ivanovich 1937- IntWW 93, LngBDD
Lobov, Vladimir Nikolaevich 1935- LngBDD
Lobregat, Ma. Clara L. 1921- WhoWomW 91
Lobron, Barbara L. 1944- WhoAm 94
Lobsenz, Amelia d1992 WhAm 10
Lobsenz, Herbert Munter 1932- WhoAm 94
Lobsinger, Thomas 1927- WhoWest 94
LoBue, Robert P. 1954- WhoAmL 94
LoBue, Vincent Edward 1941- WhoWest 94
Lo Buglio, Rudecinda Ann 1934- WhoHisp 94
Localio, S. Arthur 1911- WhoAm 94
Locane, Amy WhoHol 92
Locante, Sam WhoHol 92
Lo Cascio, Guy John 1952- WhoFI 94
LoCascio, Paul S. 1956- WhoIns 94
Locascio, Salvadore Joseph 1933- WhoAm 94
Locatelli, Giovanni Battista c. 1713-1790 NewGrDO
Locatelli, Paul Leo 1938- WhoAm 94, WhoWest 94
Loch, John Robert 1940- WhoMW 93
Loch, Patricia Ann 1944- WhoWest 94
Lochary, David d1977 WhoHol 92
Lochbiler, Marshall Leo 1895- WhAm 10
Loche, Lee Edward 1926- WhoBlA 94
Lochen, Yngvar Formo 1931- IntWW 93
Locher, Charles WhoHol 92
Locher, Duane 1947- WhoMW 93
Locher, Felix d1969 WhoHol 92
Locher, Ralph S. 1915- WhoAmP 93
Locher, Richard Earl 1929- WhoAm 94, WhoMW 93
Lochhaas, Thomas John DrAPF 93
Lochhead, Douglas (Grant) 1922- WrDr 94
Lochhead, Kenneth Campbell 1926- IntWW 93
Lochhead, Liz 1947- BlmGWL, ConDr 93, ConTFT 11, WrDr 94
Lochhead, Robert Bruce 1952- WhoAmL 94
Lochman, Jan Milic 1922- WrDr 94
Lochmiller, Kurtis L. 1952- WhoWest 94
Lochnan, Katharine A. 1946- WhoAmA 93
Lochner, Jim Warren 1940- WhoWest 94
Lochner, Philip Raymond, Jr. 1943- WhoAm 94, WhoFI 94
Lochovsky, Frederick Horst 1949- WhoScEn 94
Lochran, Peter WhoHol 92
Lochridge, Lloyd Pampell, Jr. 1918- WhoAmL 94
Lochridge, Patton G. 1949- WhoAmL 94
Lochridge, Thomas Newton, Jr. 1925- WhoFI 94
Lochrie, Elizabeth Davey 1890-1981 WhoAmA 93N
Lochry, Archibald WhAmRev
Lochte, Dick 1944- WrDr 94
Lochtenberg, Bernard Hendrik 1931- WhoAm 94, WhoFI 94
LoCicero, Joseph Lawrence 1947- WhoMW 93
Lock, Albert Larry, Jr. 1947- WhoFI 94, WhoMW 93
Lock, Chuck Choi 1930- WhoAsA 94
Lock, (George) David 1929- Who 94
Lock, Duncan Who 94
Lock, (John) Duncan 1918- Who 94
Lock, George C. 1948- WhoAmL 94
Lock, Gerald Seymour Hunter 1935- WhoAm 94
Lock, Graham Who 94
Lock, (Thomas) Graham 1931- Who 94
Lock, Joan 1933- WrDr 94
Lock, John Arthur 1922- Who 94
Lock, Richard William 1931- WhoAm 94
Lock, Robert Joseph 1955- WhoMW 93
Lock, Stephen Penford 1929- Who 94
Lock, Teri Lyn 1964- WhoMW 93
Lock, Thomas Graham 1931- IntWW 93
Lockard, Isabel 1915- ConAu 141
Lockard, John Allen 1944- WhoAm 94
Lockard, Jon Onye 1932- WhoBlA 94
Lockard, Walter Junior 1926- WhoScEn 94
Lockart, Barbetta 1947- WhoWest 94
Locke (Dering Prowse), Anne Vaughan fl. 1556-1590 BlmGWL
Locke, Alain 1886-1954 AfrAmAl 6 [port]
Locke, Arthur James 1915- WhoAmP 93
Locke, Bernadette 1958- WhoBlA 94
Locke, Burt 1948- WhoAmP 93
Locke, Carl Edwin, Jr. 1936- WhoAm 94
Locke, Charles Stanley 1929- WhoAm 94, WhoFI 94
Locke, David Henry 1927- WhoAmP 93
Locke, Dick 1947- WhoAmP 93
Locke, Don C. 1943- WhoBlA 94
Locke, Donald 1930- WhoBlA 94
Locke, Duane DrAPF 93
Locke, Edward DrAPF 93
Locke, Edwin Allen, Jr. 1910- IntWW 93, WhoAm 94
Locke, Edwin Allen, III 1938- WhoAm 94
Locke, Elsie (Violet) 1912- WrDr 94
Locke, Elsie Violet 1912- BlmGWL
Locke, Francis WhAmRev
Locke, Francis Philbrick 1912- WhoWest 94
Locke, Gary F. WhoAmP 93
Locke, Gary F. 1951- WhoAsA 94
Locke, George (Walter) 1936- EncSF 93
Locke, Harry d1987 WhoHol 92
Locke, Henry Daniel, Jr. 1936- WhoBlA 94
Locke, Hubert G. 1934- WhoBlA 94, WrDr 94
Locke, Hubert Gaylord 1934- WhoWest 94
Locke, James A. 1949- WhoAmL 94
Locke, John 1632-1704 BlmGEL, EncEth
Locke, John Christopher 1947- Who 94
Locke, John Erwin 1939- WhoFI 94
Locke, John Gardner 1926- WhoWest 94
Locke, John Howard 1920- WhoAmL 94
Locke, John Howard 1923- Who 94
Locke, John Whiteman, III 1936- WhoAm 94
Locke, Katherine 1916- WhoHol 92
Locke, Louis Noah 1928- WhoMW 93
Locke, Mamie Evelyn 1954- WhoBlA 94
Locke, Matthew c. 1622-1677 NewGrDO
Locke, Matthew 1730-1801 WhAmRev
Locke, Matthew J. 1957- WhoAmP 93
Locke, Michael 1929- WhoAm 94
Locke, Michelle Wilson 1947- WhoAmA 93
Locke, Mona M. DrAPF 93
Locke, Nancy WhoHol 92
Locke, Norton 1927- WhoAm 94
Locke, Patrick 1934- Who 94
Locke, Peter Fredrick, Jr. 1937- WhoAmP 93
Locke, Philip 1928- WhoHol 92
Locke, Richard Adams 1800-1871 EncSF 93
Locke, Sondra 1947- IntMPA 94, WhoHol 92
Locke, Steven Elliot 1945- WhoAm 94
Locke, Terrence d1982 WhoHol 92
Locke, W. Timothy 1955- WhoAm 94
Locke, William Henry 1947- WhoAmL 94
Locke, William John 1956- WhoFI 94
Locke, William Wesley 1935- WhoAm 94
Lockemy, James E. 1949- WhoAmP 93
Locker, Dale Le Roy 1929- WhoAmP 93
Locker, J. Gary 1937- WhoAm 94
Lockerbee, Beth d1968 WhoHol 92
Lockerbie, D(onald) Bruce 1935- WrDr 94
Lockerman, Geneva Lorene Reuben 1928- WhoBlA 94
Locket, Arnold, Jr. 1929- WhoBlA 94
Lockett, Barbara Ann 1936- WhoAm 94
Lockett, Bradford R. 1945- WhoBlA 94
Lockett, Harold James 1924- WhoBlA 94
Lockett, James D. WhoBlA 94
Lockett, Jane A. 1947- WhoMW 93
Lockett, Mary F. 1872- BlmGWL
Lockett, Peter Paul 1932- WhoWest 94
Lockett, Pierre WhoAm 94
Lockett, Reginald 1933- Who 94
Lockett, Reginald (Franklin) 1947- BlkWr 2
Lockett, Sandra Bokamba 1946- WhoBlA 94
Lockett, Stephen John 1961- WhoScEn 94
Lockett, Tyler C. 1932- WhoAmP 93
Lockett, Tyler Charles 1932- WhoAmL 94
Lockette, Agnes Louise 1927- WhoBlA 94
Lockette, Alice Faye 1944- WhoBlA 94
Lockey, Richard Funk 1940- WhoAm 94
Lockhard, Leonard EncSF 93
Lockhart, Aileene Simpson 1911- WhoAm 94
Lockhart, Andrew Glen 1961- WhoWest 94
Lockhart, Anne 1953- WhoHol 92
Lockhart, Anne Ivey 1943- WhoAmA 93
Lockhart, Barbara H. 1948- WhoBlA 94
Lockhart, Brian Alexander 1942- Who 94
Lockhart, Brooks Javins 1920- WhoAm 94
Lockhart, Calvin WhoHol 92
Lockhart, Eugene, Jr. 1961- WhoBlA 94
Lockhart, Frank David 1944- WhoScEn 94
Lockhart, Frank Roper 1931- Who 94
Lockhart, Gemma 1956- WhoMW 93
Lockhart, Gene d1957 WhoHol 92
Lockhart, Harry Eugene 1949- Who 94
Lockhart, James 1930- IntWW 93
Lockhart, James (Lawrence) 1930- NewGrDO
Lockhart, James B. 1936- WhoBlA 94
Lockhart, James Bicknell, III 1946- WhoAm 94
Lockhart, James Blakely 1936- WhoAm 94
Lockhart, James Lawrence 1930- Who 94
Lockhart, John Campbell 1963- WhoScEn 94
Lockhart, John Mallery 1911- WhoAm 94
Lockhart, June 1925- IntMPA 94, WhoHol 92
Lockhart, Kathleen d1978 WhoHol 92
Lockhart, Kenneth Burton 1916- WhoWest 94
Lockhart, Michael D. 1949- WhoAm 94
Lockhart, Raymond d1993 NewYTBS 93
Lockhart, Richard Spence 1927- WhoAmP 93
Lockhart, Robert W. 1941- WhoBlA 94
Lockhart, Simon John Edward Francis S. Who 94
Lockhart, Verdree 1924- WhoBlA 94
Lockhart, Wilfred Cornett 1906- WhAm 10
Lockhart-Moss, Eunice Jean 1942- WhoBlA 94
Lockhart-Mummery, Christopher John 1947- Who 94
Lockhead, Gregory Roger 1931- WhoAm 94, WhoScEn 94
Lockin, Daniel d1977 WhoHol 92
Locklear, Heather 1961- WhoHol 92
Locklear, Horace 1942- WhoAmP 93
Locklear, Lieutenant d1920 WhoHol 92
Lockley, Andrew John Harold 1951- Who 94
Lockley, Clyde William 1938- WhoBlA 94
Lockley, Harold 1916- Who 94
Lockley, Ronald M(athias) 1903- WrDr 94
Lockley, Ronald Mathias 1903- Who 94
Lockley, Stephen Randolph 1943- Who 94
Locklin, Francis Gerald, Jr. 1935- WhoFI 94
Locklin, Gerald DrAPF 93
Locklin, Gerald Ivan 1941- WrDr 94

Lomita, Solomon 1937- *IntMPA 94*
Lommel, Ulli *WhoHol 92*
Lommel, Ulli 1945- *HorFD*
Lomnicki, Tadeusz *IntWW 93N*
Lomon, Earle Leonard 1930- *WhoAm 94*
Lomonosoff, James Marc 1951- *WhoAm 94*
Lomosia, Andrew 1929- *WrDr 94*
Lompa, Susan Joyce 1941- *WhoAm 94*
Lomurro, Donald Michael 1950- *WhoAmL 94*
Lonardo, Joseph D. 1947- *WhoAmL 94*
Lonati, Carlo Ambrogio c. 1645-c. 1710 *NewGrDO*
Lonborg, James Reynold 1942- *WhoAm 94*
Loncar, Beba 1944- *WhoHol 92*
Loncar, Budimir *IntWW 93*
Londa, Jeffrey C. 1952- *WhoAmL 94*
Londen, Doris May 1930- *WhoAmP 93*
Londen, Jack W. 1953- *WhoAmL 94*
Londen, Jack Winston 1929- *WhoAmP 93*
Londesborough, Baron 1959- *Who 94*
Londin, Barbara *WhoAmA 93*
Londin, Jerome J. d1993 *NewYTBS 93 [port]*
London, Archdeacon of *Who 94*
London, Bishop in *Who 94*
London, Bishop of 1940- *Who 94*
London, Alan E. 1945- *WhoAm 94, WhoAmL 94*
London, Alexander *WhoAmA 93*
London, Anna 1913- *WhoAmA 93*
London, Babe d1980 *WhoHol 92*
London, Barbara *WhoHol 92*
London, Barbara 1946- *WhoAmA 93*
London, Barry *IntMPA 94*
London, Barry Joseph 1946- *WhoAm 94, WhoAmL 94*
London, Clement B. G. 1928- *WhoBlA 94*
London, Damian *WhoHol 92*
London, Eddie 1934- *WhoBlA 94*
London, Edward Charles 1944- *WhoBlA 94*
London, Elca 1930-1991 *WhoAmA 93N*
London, Fritz Wolfgang *WorScD*
London, Gary M. 1953- *WhoAmL 94*
London, George d1714 *DcNaB MP*
London, George 1920-1985 *NewGrDO*
London, Gloria D. 1949- *WhoBlA 94*
London, Heinz *WorScD*
London, Herbert I 1939- *WrDr 94*
London, Herbert Ira 1939- *WhoAm 94*
London, Irving Myer 1918- *IntWW 93*
London, J. Phillip 1937- *WhoAm 94, WhoScEn 94*
London, Jack d1966 *WhoHol 92*
London, Jack 1876-1916 *AmCulL, EncSF 93, RfGShF, TwCYAW*
London, Jack 1915-1988 *WhAm 10*
London, James Albert 1956- *WhoBlA 94*
London, James Harry 1949- *WhoAmL 94*
London, Jerry 1937- *IntMPA 94*
London, Jonathan *DrAPF 93*
London, Jonathan (Paul) 1947- *SmATA 74 [port]*
London, Julie 1926- *IntMPA 94, WhoHol 92*
London, Laura 1951- *WrDr 94*
London, Laura 1952- *WrDr 94*
London, Martin 1934- *WhoAm 94*
London, Milton H. 1916- *IntMPA 94*
London, Perry 1931-1992 *AnObit 1992*
London, Peter 1939- *WhoAmA 93*
London, Ray William 1943- *WhoAm 94, WhoFI 94, WhoScEn 94*
London, Roberta Levy *WhoBlA 94*
London, Roy *WhoHol 92*
London, Roy d1993 *NewYTBS 93*
London, Roy (Laird) 1943-1993 *ConAu 142*
London, Steve *WhoHol 92*
London, Terry 1940- *WhoAmP 93*
London, Tom d1963 *WhoHol 92*
London, William Thomas 1932- *WhoScEn 94*
Londonderry, Marchioness of *Who 94*
Londonderry, Marquess of 1937- *Who 94*
Londoner, David Jay 1937- *WhoAm 94, WhoFI 94*
Londono Paredes, Julio 1938- *IntWW 93*
Londrigan, Paul James 1942- *WhoMW 93*
Londrigan, Thomas Foster 1937- *WhoAmL 94*
Londynsky, Samuel 1921- *WhoFI 94*
Lone, John *IntMPA 94*
Lone, John 1961- *WhoHol 92*
Lone, Rita Joan 1938- *WhoMW 93*
Lone Bear, Sam 1879-1937 *EncNAR*
Lonegan, Thomas Lee 1932- *WhoFI 94*
Lonergan, Brian Joseph 1951- *WhoScEn 94*
Lonergan, Jeanette Nancy 1943- *WhoAm 94*
Lonergan, Joyce 1934- *WhoAmP 93*
Lonergan, Kevin 1954- *WhoAmL 94*
Lonergan, Lenore d1987 *WhoHol 92*
Lonergan, Lester d1931 *WhoHol 92*
Lonergan, Lester, Jr. d1959 *WhoHol 92*
Lonergan, Michael Henry 1949- *WhoWest 94*
Lonergan, Thomas Francis, III 1941- *WhoScEn 94, WhoWest 94*
Lonergan, Wallace Gunn 1928- *WhoWest 94*
Lonewolf, Delos Knowles 1870-1945 *EncNAR*
Loney, Carolyn Patricia 1944- *WhoBlA 94*
Loney, David Allen 1945- *WhoIns 94*
Loney, Glenn Meredith 1928- *WhoAm 94, WrDr 94*
Loney, Joanne Marie 1950- *WhoAmP 93*
Loney, Joy C. 1938- *WhoAmP 93*
Loney, Martin 1944- *WrDr 94*
Long, Viscount 1929- *Who 94*
Long, A(nthony) A(rthur) 1937- *WrDr 94*
Long, Alfred B. 1909- *WhoAm 94, WhoFI 94, WhoScEn 94*
Long, Alvin William 1923- *WhoAm 94*
Long, Amelia Rose 1944- *WhoMW 93*
Long, Andre Edwin 1957- *WhoAmL 94*
Long, Andu Trisa 1958- *WhoBlA 94*
Long, Anthony Arthur 1937- *WhoAm 94*
Long, Athelstan Charles Ethelwulf 1919- *Who 94*
Long, Audrey 1924- *WhoHol 92*
Long, Austin 1936- *WhoAm 94, WhoScEn 94, WhoWest 94*
Long, Austin Richard 1949- *WhoWest 94*
Long, Avon d1984 *WhoHol 92*
Long, Barbara Collier 1943- *WhoBlA 94*
Long, Bert L., Jr. 1940- *WhoAmA 93*
Long, Beth 1948- *WhoAmP 93*
Long, Beverly Glenn 1923- *WhoAm 94*
Long, Bobby *WhoAmP 93*
Long, Bruce J. 1951- *WhoAmP 93*
Long, Bruce Ronald 1964- *WhoAmL 94*
Long, Bruce William 1941- *WhoAmL 94*
Long, C. Chee 1942- *WhoAmA 93N*
Long, Carl Ferdinand 1928- *WhoAm 94, WhoScEn 94*
Long, Cathleen *DrAPF 93*
Long, Cathy 1924- *WhoAmP 93*
Long, Cedric William 1937- *WhoScEn 94*
Long, Charles Franklin 1938- *WhoAm 94*
Long, Charles H. 1926- *WhoBlA 94*
Long, Charles Houston 1926- *WhoAm 94*
Long, Charles R(ussell) 1904-1978 *EncSF 93*
Long, Charles Thomas 1942- *WhoAm 94, WhoAmL 94*
Long, Charlie Renn 1936- *WhoAmP 93*
Long, Christopher 1949- *WhoMW 93, WhoScEn 94*
Long, Christopher William 1938- *Who 94*
Long, Clarence Dickinson, Jr. *WhoAmP 93*
Long, Clarence Dickinson, III 1943- *WhoAmL 94*
Long, Clarence William 1917- *WhoAm 94*
Long, Clyde Clement d1942 *WhoHol 92*
Long, Crawford *WorScD*
Long, Darrell Don Earl 1962- *WhoWest 94*
Long, David *DrAPF 93*
Long, David Alexander 1963- *WhoWest 94*
Long, David W. 1942- *WhoAmL 94*
Long, Deborah Joyce 1953- *WhoIns 94*
Long, Dee 1939- *WhoMW 93*
Long, Devona Anderson 1939- *WhoAmP 93*
Long, Doc *DrAPF 93*
Long, Donald Eugene 1934- *WhoWest 94*
Long, Donald Gregory 1937- *WhoFI 94*
Long, Donlin Martin 1934- *WhoAm 94*
Long, Doughtry *DrAPF 93*
Long, Douglas Clark 1932- *WhoAm 94*
Long, Duncan 1949- *EncSF 93*
Long, Earnesteen 1939- *WhoBlA 94*
Long, Ed 1934- *WhoAmP 93*
Long, Edward Arlo 1927- *WhoAm 94*
Long, Edward Leroy, Jr. 1924- *WrDr 94*
Long, Edward W. 1946- *WhoAmL 94*
Long, Edwin Tutt 1925- *WhoAm 94, WhoMW 93*
Long, Electra 1943- *WhoAmA 93*
Long, Elgen Marion 1927- *WhoWest 94*
Long, Elliot 1928- *WrDr 94*
Long, Emily Green d1980 *WhoHol 92*
Long, Emmett Thaddeus 1923- *WhoWest 94*
Long, Enid Hammerman 1930- *WhoMW 93*
Long, Eric Charles 1962- *WhoMW 93, WhoScEn 94*
Long, Eugene Thomas 1935- *WrDr 94*
Long, Eugene Thomas, III 1935- *WhoAm 94*
Long, Forrest Edwin 1895-1988 *WhAm 10*
Long, Francis Mark 1929- *WhoAm 94*
Long, Frank Belknap 1903- *EncSF 93*
Long, Frank Weathers 1906- *WhoAmA 93*
Long, Franklin Asbury 1910- *WhoAm 94, WhoScEn 94*
Long, Frederic d1941 *WhoHol 92*
Long, G. Thomas 1945- *WhoAmP 93*
Long, Gary R. 1951- *WhoAmL 94*
Long, George Washington De *WhWE*
Long, Gerald 1923- *IntWW 93, Who 94*
Long, Gerald Bernard 1956- *WhoBlA 94*
Long, Gilbert Morris 1947- *WhoScEn 94*
Long, Grace Fan 1953- *WhoAsA 94*
Long, Grant Andrew 1966- *WhoBlA 94*
Long, Gregory Alan 1948- *WhoAm 94, WhoAmL 94*
Long, Harry 1932- *WhoScEn 94*
Long, Helen Halter *WhoAm 94*
Long, Henry Andrew 1910- *WhoBlA 94*
Long, Henry Arlington 1937- *WhoFI 94*
Long, Herbert Strainge 1919- *WhoAm 94*
Long, Hilda Sheets 1903- *WhoAmP 93*
Long, Howard Charles 1918- *WhoAm 94*
Long, Howard M. 1960- *WhoBlA 94*
Long, Hubert 1907-1992 *WhoAmA 93N*
Long, Hubert Arthur 1912- *Who 94*
Long, I. A. *WhoAm 94*
Long, Irene *WhoBlA 94*
Long, Isaac Adelbert 1899- *WhoMW 93*
Long, J. C. 1959- *WhoAmP 93*
Long, Jack d1938 *WhoHol 92*
Long, Jack A. *WhoAmP 93*
Long, James, Jr. 1931- *WhoBlA 94*
Long, James Alexander 1926- *WhoBlA 94*
Long, James Alvin 1917- *WhoScEn 94*
Long, James E. 1938- *WhoAmP 93*
Long, James Eugene *WhoAmP 93*
Long, James Harvey, Jr. 1944- *WhoWest 94*
Long, James L. 1937- *WhoBlA 94*
Long, James M. 1937- *WhoAmL 94*
Long, Jan Michael 1952- *WhoAmP 93, WhoMW 93*
Long, Jeanine Hundley 1928- *WhoAmP 93, WhoWest 94*
Long, Jefferson Marion, Jr. 1927- *WhoAmP 93*
Long, Jenny 1955- *WhoAmA 93*
Long, Jerry Wayne 1951- *WhoBlA 94*
Long, Jill 1952- *WhoAmP 93, WhoWomW 91*
Long, Jill L. 1952- *CngDr 93*
Long, Jill Lynette 1952- *WhoAm 94, WhoMW 93*
Long, Jim *WhoAmP 93*
Long, Jimmy Dale 1931- *WhoAmP 93*
Long, Joan Dorothy *IntWW 93*
Long, Jodi 1958- *WhoHol 92*
Long, John 1946- *WhoAmP 93*
Long, John 1956- *BasBi*
Long, John Bennie 1923- *WhoBlA 94*
Long, John Broaddus, Jr. 1944- *WhoAm 94*
Long, John D. 1920- *WhoAm 94*
Long, John D., III 1930- *WhoAmP 93*
Long, John Douglas 1920- *WhoIns 94*
Long, John Edward 1941- *WhoBlA 94*
Long, John Frederick 1924- *WhoMW 93*
Long, John Hamilton 1937- *WhoMW 93*
Long, John Kelley 1921- *WhoScEn 94*
Long, John Luther 1861-1927 *NewGrDO*
Long, John Michael 1941- *WhoMW 93*
Long, John Michael 1953- *WhoAmP 93*
Long, John Paul 1926- *WhoAm 94*
Long, John Richard 1931- *Who 94*
Long, John Sanderson 1913- *Who 94*
Long, John Vanderford 1920- *WhoAmL 94*
Long, Johnny d1972 *WhoHol 92*
Long, Joseph J., Sr. 1921- *WhoAmP 93*
Long, Joseph M. 1912-1990 *WhAm 10*
Long, Juanita Outlaw *WhoBlA 94*
Long, June 1926- *WhoMW 93*
Long, Kenneth Robert 1940- *WhoAm 94, WhoAmL 94*
Long, Kevin Jay 1961- *WhoAmL 94, WhoMW 93, WhoScEn 94*
Long, Lawland William 1954- *WhoWest 94*
Long, Lewis, Jr. 1936- *WhoAmP 93*
Long, Linda D. 1954- *WhoAmP 93*
Long, Linda Landeck 1943- *WhoAmL 94*
Long, Lorna Erickson 1944- *WhoAm 94*
Long, Lotus *WhoHol 92*
Long, Luray d1919 *WhoHol 92*
Long, Lyda Belknap *EncSF 93*
Long, Lydia D. 1953- *WhoAmP 93*
Long, Madeleine J. *WhoAm 94*
Long, Marceau 1926- *IntWW 93*
Long, Marshall 1936- *WhoAmP 93*
Long, Mary Kathryn Tobias 1936- *WhoMW 93*
Long, Matthew *WhoHol 92*
Long, Maurice Wayne 1925- *WhoAm 94*
Long, Maxine Master 1943- *WhoAmL 94*
Long, Melvin Durward 1931- *WhoAm 94*
Long, Melvyn Harry d1940 *WhoHol 92*
Long, Meredith J. 1928- *WhoAm 94, WhoAmA 93*
Long, Michael G. 1944- *WhoAmL 94*
Long, Michael Scott 1953- *WhoAmP 93*
Long, Michael Thomas 1942- *WhoAm 94, WhoAmP 93*
Long, Michael William 1946- *WhoScEn 94*
Long, Michelle L. Zimmer 1964- *WhoFI 94*
Long, Monti M. 1957- *WhoBlA 94*
Long, Nancy Hankins 1951- *WhoAmL 94*
Long, Naomi Cornelia *BlkWr 2*
Long, Nate 1930- *WhoBlA 94*
Long, Nia *WhoBlA 94*
Long, Nick, Jr. d1949 *WhoHol 92*
Long, Norman d1951 *WhoHol 92*
Long, Norton Enneking 1910- *WhoAm 94*
Long, Olivier 1915- *IntWW 93, Who 94*
Long, Ophelia 1940- *WhoBlA 94*
Long, Pamela Marjorie 1930- *Who 94*
Long, Patrick Brien 1943- *WhoAm 94*
Long, Phillip Clifford 1942- *WhoAm 94*
Long, Pierse 1739-1789 *WhAmRev*
Long, Randall Craig 1958- *WhoWest 94*
Long, Ray 1878-1935 *DcLB 137 [port]*
Long, Raymond Bruce 1946- *WhoAmP 93*
Long, Richard d1974 *WhoHol 92*
Long, Richard 1945- *IntWW 93*
Long, Richard A. 1927- *WhoBlA 94*
Long, Richard A(lexander) 1927- *BlkWr 2, ConAu 42NR*
Long, Richard Paul 1934- *WhoAm 94*
Long, Rick Jay 1947- *WhoMW 93*
Long, Rickie Steeb 1955- *WhoMW 93*
Long, Robert *DrAPF 93*
Long, Robert d1972 *WhoHol 92*
Long, Robert A. 1945- *WhoAmL 94*
Long, Robert Albert, Jr. 1934- *WhoFI 94*
Long, Robert C. Biggy 1919- *WhoAmP 93*
Long, Robert Douglas *WhoFI 94*
Long, Robert E. 1934- *WhoMW 93*
Long, Robert Emmet *DrAPF 93*
Long, Robert Emmet 1934- *WhoAm 94*
Long, Robert Eugene 1931- *WhoAm 94*
Long, Robert Hill *DrAPF 93*
Long, Robert Leroy 1936- *WhoFI 94*
Long, Robert Livingston 1937- *WhoFI 94*
Long, Robert Lyman John 1920- *WhoAm 94*
Long, Robert Merrill 1938- *WhoAm 94, WhoWest 94*
Long, Robert Nahum 1937- *WhoMW 93*
Long, Robert Radcliffe 1919- *WhoAm 94*
Long, Roger Arthur 1957- *WhoMW 93*
Long, Ronald d1986 *WhoHol 92*
Long, Ronald Alex 1948- *WhoAm 94, WhoFI 94*
Long, Rosalee Madeline 1931- *WhoAmL 94*
Long, Rose-Carol Washton 1938- *WhoAmA 93*
Long, Russell B. 1918- *IntWW 93, WhoAmP 93*
Long, Sally d1987 *WhoHol 92*
Long, Sam c. 1912- *EncNAR*
Long, Samuel Anthony 1944- *WhoAmP 93*
Long, Sarah d1987 *WhoHol 92*
Long, Sarah Ann 1943- *WhoAm 94*
Long, Scott 1917-1991 *WhoAmA 93N*
Long, Sharon Rugel 1951- *WhoAm 94, WhoScEn 94*
Long, Sheila Ann 1955- *WhoMW 93*
Long, Shelley 1949- *IntMPA 94, WhoAm 94, WhoHol 92*
Long, Speedy O. 1928- *WhoAmP 93*
Long, Stanley M. 1892-1972 *WhoAmA 93N*
Long, Steffan 1929- *WhoBlA 94*
Long, Stephen Carrel Mike 1951- *WhoAmL 94*
Long, Stephen Harriman 1784-1864 *WhWE*
Long, Stephen Ingalls 1946- *WhoWest 94*
Long, Stephen Michael 1954- *WhoAmL 94*
Long, Thad Gladden 1938- *WhoAm 94, WhoAmL 94*
Long, Thelma 1918- *BuCMET*
Long, Thomas E. 1944- *WhoIns 94*
Long, Thomas J. d1993 *NewYTBS 93*
Long, Thomas J., Jr. 1941- *WhoMW 93*
Long, Thomas Leslie 1951- *WhoAm 94*
Long, Thomas Michael 1943- *WhoFI 94*
Long, Thomas R. 1930- *WhoAmL 94*
Long, Timothy Scott 1937- *WhoScEn 94*
Long, Verne Everett 1925- *WhoAmP 93*
Long, Walter d1952 *WhoHol 92*
Long, Walter Edward 1935- *WhoAm 94*
Long, Walter Kinscella 1904-1986 *WhoAmA 93N*
Long, Wesley *EncSF 93*
Long, Will West 1875-1947 *EncNAR*
Long, William Allan 1928- *WhoAm 94*
Long, William D. 1937- *WhoWest 94*
Long, William Everett 1919- *WhoAm 94*
Long, William H., Jr. 1947- *WhoBlA 94*
Long, William Joseph 1922- *Who 94*
Long, William Joseph 1956- *WhoWest 94*
Long, William L. 1927- *WhoAmP 93*
Long, William McMurray 1948- *WhoMW 93, WhoScEn 94*
Long, William Robert 1961- *WhoFI 94*
Long, William W. *WhoHol 92*
Long, Willis Franklin 1934- *WhoAm 94*

Longacre, Lydia E. 1870-1951 *WhoAmA 93N*
Longacre, Margaret Gruen 1910-1976 *WhoAmA 93N*
Longacre, William Atlas 1937- *WhoWest 94*
Longair, Malcolm (Sim) 1941- *WrDr 94*
Longair, Malcolm Sim 1941- *Who 94*
Longaker, Jon Dasu 1920- *WhoAmA 93*
Longaker, Richard Pancoast 1924- *WhoAm 94*
Longan, George Baker, III 1934- *WhoFI 94, WhoMW 93*
Longanecker, Edwin Snyder, Jr. 1944- *WhoMW 93*
Longardner, Craig Theodor 1955- *WhoMW 93*
Longas, Maria Oliva *WhoMW 93*
Longbaugh, Harry 1931- *WrDr 94*
Longbeard, Frederick *EncSF 93*
Longbottom, Charles Brooke 1930- *Who 94*
Longbrake, William Arthur 1943- *WhoAm 94*
Longchampt, Michel 1934- *WhoFI 94*
Long Chuan *WhoPRCh 91*
Long-Coleman, Victoria Lynn 1956- *WhoMW 93*
Longcroft, James George Stoddart 1929- *Who 94*
Longden, Gilbert (James Morley) 1902- *Who 94*
Longden, Henry Alfred 1909- *Who 94*
Longden, John d1971 *WhoHol 92*
Longden, Wilson 1936- *Who 94*
Longdon, Terence 1922- *WhoHol 92*
Longenecker, Herbert Eugene 1912- *WhoAm 94*
Longenecker, Mark Hershey, Jr. 1951- *WhoAm 94, WhoAmL 94*
Longer, Verla Madonna 1932- *WhoMW 93*
Longespee, Roger c. 1215-1295 *DcNaB MP*
Longest, Beaufort Brown 1942- *WhoAm 94*
Longet, Claudine 1942- *WhoHol 92*
Longfellow, Don 1898- *WhAm 10*
Longfellow, Henry Wadsworth 1807-1882 *AmCulL [port]*
Longfellow, Layne 1937- *WhoScEn 94*
Longfield, Michael David 1928- *Who 94*
Longfield, William Herman 1938- *WhoAm 94, WhoFI 94*
Longford, Countess of 1906- *IntWW 93, Who 94, WrDr 94*
Longford, Earl of 1905- *IntWW 93, Who 94, WrDr 94*
Longford, Elizabeth *Who 94*
Longford, Raymond d1959 *WhoHol 92*
Longhi Lopresti, Lucia *BlmGWL*
Longhofer, Ronald Stephen 1946- *WhoAm 94, WhoAmL 94, WhoMW 93*
Longhurst, Andrew Henry 1939- *Who 94*
Longhurst, Robert E. 1949- *WhoAmA 93*
Longin, Thomas Charles 1939- *WhoAm 94*
Longinus, Dionysius Cassius fl. 1st cent.- *BlmGEL*
Longland, Jack 1905- *Who 94*
Longland, John Laurence *Who 94*
Longley, Ann Rosamund 1942- *Who 94*
Longley, Bernique *WhoAmA 93*
Longley, Bernique 1923- *WhoAm 94*
Longley, Christopher Quentin Mori 1961- *WhoMW 93*
Longley, Evelyn Louise 1921-1959 *WhoAmA 93N*
Longley, Glenn 1942- *WhoScEn 94*
Longley, Jack Winston 1941- *WhoFI 94*
Longley, Lawrence Douglas 1939- *WhoAmP 93*
Longley, Marjorie Watters 1925- *WhoAm 94*
Longley, Michael 1939- *WrDr 94*
Longley, Norman 1900- *Who 94*
Longley, Victoria *WhoHol 92*
Longley, W. B. 1951- *WrDr 94*
Long Lian *WhoPRCh 91*
Longman, Anne Strickland 1924- *WhoWest 94*
Longman, Edward G. d1969 *WhoHol 92*
Longman, Gary Lee 1948- *WhoAm 94*
Longman, Michael Douglas 1963- *WhoMW 93*
Longman, Peter Martin 1946- *Who 94*
Longman, Richard Winston 1943- *WhoAm 94*
Longman, Robert Albert *WhoAm 94*
Longmate, Norman Richard 1925- *WrDr 94*
Longmire, Adele c. 1917- *WhoHol 92*
Longmire, George 1915- *WhoAmP 93*
Longmire, William Polk, Jr. 1913- *WhoAm 94*
Longmore, Andrew Centlivres 1944- *Who 94*
Longmuir, Alan Gordon 1941- *WhoScEn 94*
Longnaker, John Leonard 1926- *WhoAm 94*
Longnecker, David E. 1939- *WhoAm 94*
Long Nian 1933- *WhoPRCh 91 [port]*
Longo, Billy 1933- *WhoHol 92*
Longo, Joseph Thomas 1942- *WhoScEn 94*
Longo, Lawrence Daniel 1926- *WhoAm 94, WhoScEn 94, WhoWest 94*
Longo, Leonard Frank 1926- *WhoFI 94*
Longo, Pietro 1935- *IntWW 93*
Longo, Robert 1953- *WhoAmA 93*
Longo, Ronald Anthony 1952- *WhoAmL 94*
Longo, Thomas J. 1942- *WhoAmP 93*
Longo, Tony 1962- *WhoHol 92*
Longo, Vincent 1923- *WhoAmA 93*
Longobardi, Joseph J. *WhoAm 94, WhoAmL 94*
Longobardi, Pam 1958- *WhoAmA 93*
Longobardo, Anna Kazanjian *WhoAm 94*
Longo-Muth, Linda L. 1948- *WhoAmA 93*
Longone, Daniel Thomas 1932- *WhoAm 94*
Longoria, Frank A. 1935- *WhoHisp 94*
Longoria, John A. *WhoHisp 94*
Longoria, John Amos 1945- *WhoAmP 93*
Longoria, Jose Francisco, Jr. 1944- *WhoHisp 94*
Longoria, José L. 1947- *WhoHisp 94*
Longoria, Leovaldo Carol 1927- *WhoHisp 94*
Longoria, Raul L. *WhoHisp 94*
Longoria, Roberto 1963- *WhoHisp 94*
Longoria, Salvador Gonzalez, Jr. 1958- *WhoHisp 94*
Longpre, Donald Joseph 1951- *WhoFI 94*
Longrigg, Anthony James 1944- *Who 94*
Longrigg, John Stephen 1923- *Who 94*
Longrigg, Roger 1929- *WrDr 94*
Longrigg, Roger Erskine 1929- *Who 94*
Longshore, Diane 1944- *WhoAmP 93*
Longson, Donald E. 1941- *WhoIns 94*
Longstaff, Ronald E. 1941- *WhoAm 94, WhoAmL 94, WhoMW 93*
Longstaffe, John Ronald 1934- *WhoAmA 93*
Longstreet, David Harmon 1960- *WhoMW 93*
Longstreet, Harry Stephen 1940- *WhoAm 94*
Longstreet, Stephen 1907- *IntMPA 94, WhoAm 94, WhoAmA 93, WhoWest 94, WrDr 94*
Longstreet, Victor Mendell 1907- *WhoAm 94, WhoAmP 93*
Longstreth, Bevis 1934- *WhoAm 94*
Longstreth, Emily *WhoHol 92*
Longstreth, Richard 1946- *WrDr 94*
Longstreth, Robert Christy 1956- *WhoAmL 94*
Longstreth, W. Thacher 1920- *WhoAmP 93*
Longstreth, W(illiam) Thacher 1920- *WrDr 94*
Longstreth Thompson, Francis Michael *Who 94*
Longsworth, Charles R. 1929- *WhoAm 94*
Longsworth, Ellen Louise 1949- *WhoFI 94*
Longsworth, Paul Morgan 1962- *WhoAmP 93*
Longuet, Gerard Edmond Jacques 1946- *IntWW 93*
Longuet, Gregory Arthur 1945- *WhoFI 94, WhoScEn 94*
Longuet-Higgins, Hugh Christopher 1923- *IntWW 93, Who 94*
Longuet-Higgins, Michael Selwyn 1925- *IntWW 93, Who 94*
Longval, Gloria 1931- *WhoAmA 93, WhoHisp 94*
Longway, A. Hugh *EncSF 93*
Longway, Cynthia Pominville 1953- *WhoMW 93*
Longwell, John Ploeger 1918- *WhoAm 94*
Longworth, Edward d1927 *WhoHol 92*
Longworth, Ian Heaps 1935- *Who 94*
Longworth, Peter 1942- *Who 94*
Longworth, Philip 1933- *WrDr 94*
Longworth, Richard Cole 1935- *WhoAm 94*
Longworth, Wilfred Roy 1923- *Who 94*
Longyear, Barry B. 1942- *WrDr 94*
Longyear, Barry B(rookes) 1942- *EncSF 93*
Longyear, Russell Hammond 1935- *WhoAm 94*
Long Zehui 1910- *WhoPRCh 91 [port]*
Long Zhiyi 1929- *WhoPRCh 91 [port]*
Lonidier, Fred Spencer 1942- *WhoAmA 93*
Lonks, John Richard 1960- *WhoScEn 94*
Lonneke, Michael Dean 1943- *WhoAm 94*
Lonnerstrand, Sture *EncSF 93*
Lonngren, Karl Erik 1938- *WhoAm 94*
Lonning, Inge Johan 1938- *IntWW 93*
Lonnquist, George Eric 1946- *WhoAm 94*
Lonnquist, Judith Alice 1940- *WhoAmL 94*
Lono, James d1954 *WhoHol 92*
Lonowski, Daniel Michael 1955- *WhoMW 93*
Lonquist, Bert Arthur 1926- *WhoAm 94*
Lonsdale, Earl of 1922- *Who 94*
Lonsdale, Errol Henry Gerrard 1913- *Who 94*
Lonsdale, H. G. d1923 *WhoHol 92*
Lonsdale, Harold Kenneth 1932- *WhoWest 94*
Lonsdale, Michel 1931- *WhoHol 92*
Lonsdale, Nancy Roberts 1954- *WhoAmL 94*
Lonsdale, Pamela *IntMPA 94*
Lonsdale, Robert Henry H. *Who 94*
Lonsdale, Roger Harrison 1934- *Who 94*
Lonsway, Thomas Joseph 1944- *WhoAmP 93*
Lontere, Jolene d1983 *WhoHol 92*
Lontoc, Leon d1974 *WhoHol 92*
Loo, Bessie *WhoHol 92*
Loo, Beverly Jane *WhoAm 94*
Loo, Cyrus W. 1918- *WhoAsA 94*
Loo, Jeffrey *DrAPF 93*
Loo, Richard d1983 *WhoHol 92*
Loo, Thomas S. 1943- *WhoAm 94, WhoAmL 94*
Loo, Ti Li 1918- *WhoAsA 94*
Loo, Walter Wei-To 1946- *WhoWest 94*
Loo, Wilson M. N. 1954- *WhoAmL 94*
Looby, Anne *WhoHol 92*
Looby, Joseph Lawrence 1917- *WhoAmP 93*
Looby, Michael John 1950- *WhoAmL 94*
Looby, Thomas Patrick 1950- *WhoWest 94*
Look, Dona 1948- *WhoAmA 93*
Look, Dwight Chester, Jr. 1938- *WhoScEn 94*
Look, Theone Priscilla Fish 1924- *WhoAmP 93*
Look, Vivian Ann *WhoFI 94*
Lookabill, Pamela P. 1957- *WhoFI 94*
Looker, Patricia *DrAPF 93*
Looker, Roger fl. 1660-1685 *DcNaB MP*
Looking Horse, Arval 1954- *EncNAR*
Lookinland, Mike 1960- *WhoHol 92*
Lookinland, Todd 1964- *WhoHol 92*
Looman, James R. 1952- *WhoAm 94*
Loomans, Leslie Louis 1943- *WhoFI 94*
Loome, James Lawrence Michael 1956- *WhoMW 93*
Loomes, Brian 1938- *WrDr 94*
Loomes, Harry d1946 *WhoHol 92*
Loomie, Albert Joseph 1922- *WrDr 94*
Loomis, Christopher Knapp 1947- *WhoWest 94*
Loomis, Clarence 1889-1965 *NewGrDO*
Loomis, Dawn Marie 1952- *WhoWest 94*
Loomis, Earl Alfred, Jr. 1921- *WhoScEn 94*
Loomis, Edward (Warren) 1924- *WrDr 94*
Loomis, Henry 1919- *IntWW 93, WhoAm 94*
Loomis, Howard Krey 1927- *WhoAm 94, WhoFI 94, WhoMW 93*
Loomis, James Prentice 1934- *WhoMW 93*
Loomis, Judi E. 1953- *WhoMW 93*
Loomis, Lee Rodger 1951- *WhoFI 94*
Loomis, Mary Ellen 1929- *WhoMW 93*
Loomis, Nancy *WhoHol 92*
Loomis, Noel (Miller) 1905-1969 *EncSF 93*
Loomis, Philip Clark 1926- *WhoAm 94*
Loomis, Richard Frank 1947- *WhoWest 94*
Loomis, Robert Arthur 1936- *WhoMW 93*
Loomis, Robert Duane 1926- *WhoAm 94*
Loomis, Rod *WhoHol 92*
Loomis, Ronald Earl 1954- *WhoScEn 94*
Loomis, Sabra *DrAPF 93*
Loomis, Susan Herrmann 1955- *ConAu 140*
Loomis, Walter Earl 1898- *WhAm 10*
Loomis, Wendell Sylvester 1926- *WhoAmL 94*
Loomis, Wesley Horace, III 1913- *WhoAm 94*
Loomis, Worth 1923- *WhoAm 94*
Loone, Eero 1935- *IntWW 93*
Looney, Claudia Arlene 1946- *WhoFI 94, WhoWest 94*
Looney, Cullen Rogers 1946- *WhoAmP 93*
Looney, Dennis Joseph, Jr. 1934- *WhoIns 94*
Looney, Dennis Matthew 1954- *WhoAm 94*
Looney, H. Ray 1935- *WhoFI 94*
Looney, James Alan 1952- *WhoFI 94*
Looney, Joseph Michael 1896- *WhAm 10*
Looney, Joseph W. 1948- *WhoAmL 94*
Looney, Martin Michael 1948- *WhoAmP 93*
Looney, Norman 1942- *WhoAmA 93*
Looney, Norman Earl 1938- *WhoAm 94, WhoScEn 94*
Looney, Ralph Edwin 1924- *WhoAm 94, WhoWest 94*
Looney, Robert Dudley 1919- *WhoAmL 94*
Looney, Robert Fain 1925- *WhoAmA 93*
Looney, Ronald Lee 1956- *WhoFI 94*
Looney, Thomas Albert 1947- *WhoScEn 94*
Looney, William Francis, Jr. 1931- *WhoAm 94, WhoAmL 94*
Loop, Bernadine P. *Who 94*
Looper, Donald Ray 1952- *WhoAmL 94*
Loor, Rueyming 1948- *WhoAsA 94, WhoWest 94*
Loory, Stuart Hugh 1932- *WhoAm 94*
Loos, A(mandus) William 1908- *WhAm 10*
Loos, Anita 1888-1981 *IntDcF 2-4 [port]*
Loos, Anne d1986 *WhoHol 92*
Loos, Cecile Ines 1883-1959 *BlmGWL*
Loos, Charles Delbert 1925- *WhoAmP 93*
Loos, Karel c. 1723-1772 *NewGrDO*
Loos, Mary 1914- *IntMPA 94*
Loos, Mary Anita *WhoHol 92*
Loos, Randolph Meade 1954- *WhoFI 94*
Loos, Robert T. 1946- *WhoAmL 94*
Loos, Theodor d1954 *WhoHol 92*
Loose, Emmy 1914-1987 *NewGrDO*
Loosen, Ann Marita 1923- *WhoAm 94*
Loosley, Brian 1948- *Who 94*
Loosley, William Robert *EncSF 93*
Loosli, S. Lynn 1935- *WhoAmP 93*
Loots, Barbara *DrAPF 93*
Loow, Maj-Lis 1936- *WhoWomW 91*
Looye, Johanna Wilhelmina 1956- *WhoMW 93*
Lopach, James J. 1942- *WrDr 94*
Lopach, James Joseph 1942- *WhoAm 94, WhoWest 94*
Lopacki, Edward Joseph, Jr. 1947- *WhoAmL 94*
Lopat, Eddie 1913-1992 *AnObit 1992*
Lopata, Edward J. 1941- *WhoAmL 94*
Lopata, Helena Znaniecka 1925- *WhoAm 94*
Lopata, Martin Barry 1939- *WhoWest 94*
Lopata, Melvin 1941- *WhoMW 93*
Lopata, Stanley Stephan 1936- *WhoAmL 94*
Lopate, Phillip *DrAPF 93*
Lopatin, Alan G. 1956- *WhoAmL 94*
Lopatin, Dennis Edward 1948- *WhoMW 93*
Lopatin, George 1929- *WhoScEn 94*
Lopatin, Judy *DrAPF 93*
Lopatin, Vladimir Nikolaevich 1960- *LngBDD*
Lopatkiewicz, Stefan M. 1948- *WhoAmL 94*
Lope de Vega (Carpio), Felix 1562-1635 *NewGrDO*
Lope de Vega Carpio *IntDcT 2*
Loper, Candice Kay 1953- *WhoMW 93*
Loper, Carl Richard, Jr. 1932- *WhoAm 94, WhoScEn 94*
Loper, Charlene Marie 1958- *WhoMW 93*
Loper, Don d1972 *WhoHol 92*
Loper, James Leaders 1931- *WhoAm 94, WhoWest 94*
Loper, John Carey 1931- *WhoMW 93*
Loper, John Robert 1951- *WhoFI 94*
Loper, Merle William 1940- *WhoAm 94*
Loper, Robert Bruce 1925- *WhoAm 94*
Loper, Warren Edward 1929- *WhoScEn 94, WhoWest 94*
Loperena, Ernesto 1942- *WhoHisp 94*
Lopert, Tanya *WhoHol 92*
Lopes *Who 94*
Lopes, Antonio Simoes 1934- *IntWW 93*
Lopes, Davey 1945- *WhoBlA 94*
Lopes, Francisco Caetano, Jr. 1959- *WhoHisp 94*
Lopes, Henri 1937- *IntWW 93*
Lopes, Henri (Marie-Joseph) 1937- *BlkWr 2*
Lopes, James L. 1947- *WhoAmL 94*
Lopes, John Alex 1937- *WhoMW 93*
Lopes, Joseph Alonzo 1949- *WhoAmP 93*
Lopes, Lola Lynn 1941- *WhoAm 94, WhoMW 93*
Lopes, Maria J. *WhoAmP 93*
Lopes, Michael *DrAPF 93*
Lopes, William H. 1946- *WhoBlA 94*
Lopes de Janeiro Almeida, Julia Valentina *BlmGWL*
Lopes-Graca, Fernando 1906- *IntWW 93*
Lopez, Aaron Galicia 1933- *WhoHisp 94*
Lopez, Abe *WhoHisp 94*
López, Adalberto 1943- *WhoHisp 94*
Lopez, Al 1908- *WhoHisp 94*
López, Alberto Muñoz 1960- *WhoHisp 94*
Lopez, Alfonso J. 1946- *WhoHisp 94*
López, Amalia Rebecca 1963- *WhoHisp 94*
Lopez, Ana M. 1956- *WhoHisp 94*
Lopez, Andy *WhoAm 94, WhoWest 94*
Lopez, Angel Andres 1943- *WhoHisp 94*

López, Ann Aurelia 1945- *WhoHisp 94*
López, Anna B. 1962- *WhoHisp 94*
Lopez, Anthony Gene, Jr. 1953- *WhoHisp 94*
Lopez, Antonio 1934- *WhoHisp 94*
Lopez, Antonio Manuel, Jr. 1949- *WhoHisp 94*
Lopez, Armando X. 1958- *WhoHisp 94*
Lopez, Arthur Larry 1943- *WhoHisp 94*
Lopez, Augustin V. 1931- *WhoHisp 94*
López, Aura A. 1933- *WhoHisp 94*
López, Aurelio 1948-1992 *WhoHisp 94N*
Lopez, Barry *DrAPF 93*
Lopez, Barry Holstun 1945- *WhoAm 94, WhoWest 94*
Lopez, Benito Moleiro, Jr. 1933- *WhoAm 94*
Lopez, Beverly Susan 1957- *WhoAmP 93*
Lopez, Carlos Celerino 1952- *WhoWest 94*
Lopez, Carlos Jose 1949- *WhoHisp 94*
Lopez, Carlos Urrutia 1932- *WhoHisp 94*
Lopez, Carmelita d1980 *WhoHol 92*
Lopez, Carmen Luisa 1951- *WhoHisp 94*
Lopez, Carol Robertson 1951- *WhoAmP 93*
Lopez, Carolyn Catherine 1951- *WhoMW 93, WhoScEn 94*
Lopez, Daniel *WhoHisp 94*
Lopez, David 1942- *WhoAmL 94*
Lopez, David 1951- *WhoHisp 94*
Lopez, David Ruben 1951- *WhoHisp 94*
Lopez, David Tiburcio 1939- *WhoAmL 94*
López, David W. 1951- *WhoHisp 94*
Lopez, Delia Olivia 1943- *WhoHisp 94*
López, Diana L. 1948- *WhoHisp 94*
Lopez, Diana Montes De Oca 1937- *WhoHisp 94*
Lopez, Diosdado *WhoHisp 94*
Lopez, Douglas Mark 1955- *WhoHisp 94*
López, Eddie *WhoHisp 94*
Lopez, Eddie 1929- *WhoHisp 94*
Lopez, Edgar *WhoAmP 93*
Lopez, Eduard A. 1953- *WhoHisp 94*
Lopez, Edward A. 1943- *WhoHisp 94*
Lopez, Edward Alexander 1954- *WhoHisp 94*
Lopez, Edward J. *WhoAmP 93*
López, Elias L. 1950- *WhoHisp 94*
Lopez, Elizabeth Marie *WhoHisp 94*
Lopez, Emilio M. D., Jr. 1964- *WhoHisp 94*
Lopez, Enrique Angel 1940- *WhoHisp 94*
Lopez, Eric 1954- *WhoHisp 94*
López, Ernie Manuel 1951- *WhoHisp 94*
Lopez, Felix C. 1957- *WhoHisp 94*
Lopez, Felix Caridad *WhoHisp 94*
Lopez, Fidencio Leal, Jr. 1951- *WhoHisp 94*
Lopez, Floyd William 1952- *WhoAmL 94*
Lopez, Francis P. *WhoHisp 94*
Lopez, Francisco Solano 1826-1870 *HisWorL [port]*
Lopez, Franklin A. 1942- *WhoHisp 94*
Lopez, Gabriel Reyes 1950- *WhoHisp 94*
López, Genaro 1947- *WhoHisp 94*
Lopez, George M., Sr. 1942- *WhoHisp 94*
Lopez, Gerard F. *WhoHisp 94*
Lopez, Gina Paula 1944- *WhoHisp 94*
López, Gloria Berta-Cruz 1937- *WhoHisp 94*
Lopez, Gloria E. 1951- *WhoHisp 94*
Lopez, Gloria Margarita 1948- *WhoHisp 94*
Lopez, Guillermo 1919- *WhoAm 94, WhoHisp 94*
Lopez, Hector 1947- *WhoHisp 94*
Lopez, Hugo Roberto 1930- *WhoHisp 94*
Lopez, Humberto S. *WhoHisp 94*
Lopez, Humberto Salazar 1944- *WhoHisp 94*
Lopez, Ignacio Alberto 1953- *WhoWest 94*
Lopez, Ignacio Javier 1956- *WhoHisp 94*
Lopez, Irene F. *WhoHisp 94*
Lopez, Isabel O. *WhoHisp 94*
Lopez, Israel 1922- *WhoHisp 94*
Lopez, J. Victor d1986 *WhoHol 92*
López, Javier *WhoHisp 94*
López, Javier Ortiz 1967- *WhoHisp 94*
Lopez, Jesus Luis 1951- *WhoHisp 94*
Lopez, Joanne Carol 1952- *WhoHisp 94*
Lopez, Joe Eddie 1939- *WhoAmP 93*
Lopez, Joe Eddy 1939- *WhoHisp 94*
Lopez, John C. *WhoHisp 94*
Lopez, John F. 1949- *WhoHisp 94*
Lopez, John J. 1947- *WhoHisp 94*
Lopez, John William 1957- *WhoHisp 94*
Lopez, Jorge Alberto 1955- *WhoHisp 94*
Lopez, Jorge Bernardo 1966- *WhoHisp 94*
Lopez, Jorge Washington 1948- *WhoScEn 94*
Lopez, Jose Eldad, Jr. 1957- *WhoWest 94*
Lopez, Jose Ignacio, Sr. 1932- *WhoHisp 94*
Lopez, Jose Luis 1955- *WhoHisp 94*
Lopez, Jose M., Jr. 1949- *WhoHisp 94*
Lopez, Jose R. 1940- *WhoHisp 94*
Lopez, Jose R. 1945- *WhoHisp 94*
Lopez, Jose Rafael 1957- *WhoHisp 94*
Lopez, Jose Tomas 1949- *WhoHisp 94*
López, Josefina 1969- *WhoHisp 94*
Lopez, Joseph 1952- *WhoHisp 94*
Lopez, Joseph Anthony 1951- *WhoHisp 94*
Lopez, Joseph Jack 1932- *WhoFI 94, WhoScEn 94*
Lopez, Joseph K. 1952- *WhoAmL 94*
Lopez, Kamala M. 1964- *WhoHisp 94*
Lopez, Kay Strickland 1946- *WhoFI 94*
Lopez, Lawrence Anthony 1939- *WhoHisp 94*
Lopez, Leonardo V. 1946- *WhoHisp 94*
Lopez, Lillian L. *WhoHisp 94*
Lopez, Louis 1954- *WhoHisp 94*
Lopez, Louis Rey 1946- *WhoHisp 94*
Lopez, Lourdes 1958- *WhoAm 94, WhoHisp 94*
López, Luz E. *WhoHisp 94*
López, Lynda Y. *WhoHisp 94*
Lopez, Manuel d1976 *WhoHol 92*
Lopez, Manuel 1927- *WhoHisp 94*
Lopez, Manuel, Sr. 1950- *WhoHisp 94*
Lopez, Marciano 1934- *WhoHisp 94*
Lopez, Marco Antonio 1957- *WhoHisp 94*
López, Marcus 1934- *WhoHisp 94*
Lopez, Maria De Jesus 1955- *WhoHisp 94*
Lopez, Mario 1942- *WhoHisp 94*
Lopez, Marisela 1956- *WhoHisp 94*
Lopez, Martha Louise 1947- *WhoHisp 94*
Lopez, Marvin J. 1937- *WhoHisp 94*
Lopez, Mary Gardner 1920- *WhoBlA 94*
Lopez, Michael F. 1952- *WhoHisp 94*
Lopez, Michael John 1937- *WhoAmA 93, WhoHisp 94*
Lopez, Miguel E. 1941- *WhoHisp 94*
Lopez, Miriam *WhoHisp 94*
Lopez, Nancy 1957- *WhoAm 94, WhoHisp 94*
Lopez, Noemi *WhoHisp 94*
Lopez, Norberto H. 1938- *WhoHisp 94*
López, Omar S. 1955- *WhoHisp 94*
Lopez, Oscar *WhoHisp 94*
Lopez, Oscar 1938- *WhoHisp 94*
Lopez, Oscar D. 1954- *WhoHisp 94*
Lopez, Pablo Vincent 1964- *WhoHisp 94*
López, Pedro E. 1962- *WhoHisp 94*
Lopez, Pedro Ramon *WhoHisp 94*
Lopez, Perry 1931- *WhoHol 92*
Lopez, Priscilla *WhoHol 92*
Lopez, Priscilla 1948- *WhoHisp 94*
Lopez, Rafael 1929- *WhoHisp 94, WhoScEn 94*
Lopez, Rafael C. 1931- *WhoHisp 94*
López, Ramón José 1951- *WhoHisp 94*
Lopez, Raul Jose 1959- *WhoHisp 94*
Lopez, Ray 1949- *WhoHisp 94*
Lopez, Raymond Henry 1940- *WhoHisp 94*
Lopez, Rhoda Le Blanc 1912- *WhoAmA 93*
Lopez, Ricardo *WhoHisp 94*
López, Ricardo Rafael 1957- *WhoHisp 94*
Lopez, Richard d1981 *WhoHol 92*
Lopez, Richard 1943- *WhoHisp 94*
Lopez, Richard Clarence 1949- *WhoHisp 94*
Lopez, Richard E. 1945- *WhoHisp 94*
Lopez, Richard G. 1934- *WhoHisp 94*
López, Richard V. *WhoHisp 94*
Lopez, Rigoberto Adolfo 1957- *WhoHisp 94*
López, Robert 1940- *WhoHisp 94*
Lopez, Robert 1950- *WhoHisp 94*
Lopez, Roberto J. 1968- *WhoHisp 94*
López, Roberto Monte Carlo 1932- *WhoHisp 94*
Lopez, Rose Mary 1938- *WhoAmP 93*
Lopez, Rosemary 1963- *WhoHisp 94*
Lopez, Roy Charles 1948- *WhoWest 94*
Lopez, Rubin R. 1947- *WhoHisp 94*
Lopez, Salvador P. d1993 *NewYTBS 93*
Lopez, Salvador P. 1911- *IntWW 93*
Lopez, Steven Regeser 1953- *WhoHisp 94*
Lopez, Steven Richard 1944- *WhoFI 94, WhoWest 94*
Lopez, Sylvia d1959 *WhoHol 92*
Lopez, Thomas *WhoHisp 94*
Lopez, Thomas Louis 1945- *WhoHisp 94*
Lopez, Thomas Marsh 1943- *WhoWest 94*
Lopez, Thomas R. *WhoHisp 94*
Lopez, Tina L. *WhoHisp 94*
Lopez, Tomas 1967- *WhoHisp 94*
Lopez, Tony *WhoHisp 94*
López, Trini 1937- *WhoHisp 94, WhoHol 92*
Lopez, Vicky E. 1952- *WhoHisp 94*
Lopez, Victor F. 1929- *WhoHisp 94*
Lopez, Vidal Noel 1968- *WhoHisp 94*
Lopez, Vince *WhoHisp 94*
Lopez, Vincent d1975 *WhoHol 92*
Lopez, Vito J. 1941- *WhoAmP 93, WhoHisp 94*
Lopez, Waldo E. 1930- *WhoHisp 94*
Lopez, Welquis Raimundo 1954- *WhoHisp 94*
Lopez, William, Sr. 1950- *WhoHisp 94*
Lopez, Yolanda Elva 1951- *WhoHisp 94*
López Adorno, Pedro J. 1954- *WhoHisp 94*
Lopez-Alegria, Michael Eladio 1958- *WhoHisp 94*
Lopez-Alves, Fernando 1950- *WhoHisp 94*
Lopez Arellano, Oswaldo 1921- *IntWW 93*
López-Bayrón, Juan L. 1955- *WhoHisp 94*
Lopez Buchardo, Carlos 1881-1948 *NewGrDO*
López-Calderón, José Luis 1948- *WhoHisp 94*
Lopez-Cambil, Rafael *WhoHisp 94*
Lopez-Candales, Angel 1960- *WhoMW 93, WhoScEn 94*
Lopez-Castro, Amadeo, Jr. *WhoHisp 94*
Lopez-Cepero, Robert Michael 1943- *WhoHisp 94*
Lopez-Cobos, Jesus 1940- *IntWW 93, NewGrDO, WhoAm 94, WhoMW 93*
Lopez de Arriortua, Jose Ignacio 1941- *News 93 [port]*
Lopez de Cordoba, Leonor c. 1362-1412 *BlmGWL*
Lopez de Gamero, Iliana Veronica 1963- *WhoHisp 94*
Lopez de Lacarra, Amalia 1956- *WhoHisp 94*
Lopez De Letona y Nunez Del Pino, Jose Maria 1922- *IntWW 93*
Lopez de Mantaras, Ramon 1952- *WhoScEn 94*
Lopez de Mendoza, Victor *WhoHisp 94*
Lopez De Vinaspre Urquiola, Teodoro 1939- *WhoScEn 94*
López-Enriquez, Alberto T. 1954- *WhoHisp 94*
Lopez Galarza, Hector 1940- *WhoHisp 94*
Lopez-Garcia, Antonio 1936- *IntWW 93*
López-González, Margarita María 1947- *WhoHisp 94*
Lopez-Gordienko, Mercedes *WhoWomW 91*
Lopez-Heredia, Jose 1922- *WhoHisp 94*
Lopez Hernandez, Juan 1928- *WhoAmP 93*
Lopez-Ibor, Juan Jose 1941- *IntWW 93*
Lopez-Isa, Jose *WhoHisp 94*
Lopez-Lee, David *WhoHisp 94*
López-López, Fernando José *WhoHisp 94*
López-Maltéz, Nicolás A. 1940- *WhoHisp 94*
López-Marrón, José M. 1947- *WhoHisp 94*
Lopez-Mayhew, Barbara D. 1959- *WhoHisp 94*
López-McKnight, Gloria 1937- *WhoHisp 94*
Lopez Michelsen, Alfonso 1913- *IntWW 93*
Lopez-Morillas, Juan 1913- *WhoAm 94, WhoHisp 94*
Lopez-Nakazono, Benito 1946- *WhoScEn 94*
Lopez-Nieves, Carlos Juan 1948- *WhoAmP 93, WhoHisp 94*
Lopez-Ortiz, Manuel 1939- *WhoHisp 94*
Lopez-Otin, Maria E. 1950- *WhoHisp 94*
López-Permouth, Sergio Roberto 1957- *WhoHisp 94*
Lopez-Portillo, Jose Ramon 1954- *WhoScEn 94*
Lopez-Portillo y Pacheco, Jose 1920- *IntWW 93*
Lopez Rodo, Laureano 1920- *IntWW 93*
Lopez Rodriguez, Nicolas de Jesus Cardinal 1936- *WhoAm 94*
López-Sanabria, Sixto 1928- *WhoHisp 94*
Lopez Sanchez, Maria del Pilar 1949- *WhoHisp 94*
López-Sanz, Mariano 1931- *WhoHisp 94*
Lopez Torres, Juan E. 1932- *WhoHisp 94*
Lopez Trujillo, Alfonso 1935- *IntWW 93*
Lopez-Trujillo, Virginia M. *WhoHisp 94*
Lopez-Vasquez, Alfonso 1950- *WhoHisp 94*
Lopez-Videla G., Ana Doris 1934- *WhoHisp 94*
Lopez-Woodward, Dina 1956- *WhoHisp 94*
LoPiccolo, Joseph 1943- *WhoAm 94*
Lopina, Lawrence Thomas 1930- *WhoAm 94*
Lopina, Louise Carol 1936- *WhoAmA 93*
Lopina, Robert Ferguson 1936- *WhoWest 94*
LoPinto, Charles Adam 1952- *WhoScEn 94*
LoPinto, Robert Anthony 1946- *WhoScEn 94*
Lopker, Anita Mae 1955- *WhoScEn 94*
Lopokova, Lydia 1891-1981 *IntDcB [port]*
Loppert, Max Jeremy 1946- *Who 94*
Loppnow, Harald 1954- *WhoScEn 94*
Loppnow, Milo Alvin 1914- *WhoAm 94*
Lopreato, Joseph 1928- *WhoAm 94, WhoScEn 94, WrDr 94*
LoPresti, Joseph J. 1947- *WhoAmL 94*
LoPresti, Michael, Jr. 1947- *WhoAmP 93*
Lopresti, Philip Vincent 1932- *WhoAm 94*
Lopresto, John George 1940- *WhoAmP 93*
LoPrete, James Hugh 1929- *WhoAm 94*
Lopshire, Jim N. 1950- *WhoMW 93*
Lopukhin, Vladimir Mikhailovich 1952- *LngBDD*
Lopukhov, Fedor 1886-1973 *IntDcB [port]*
Lopukhova, Ludmila A. *WhoAm 94*
Lopuszynski, Ted 1938- *WhoAmP 93*
Loquasto, Klaus Wolfgang 1946- *WhoMW 93*
Loquasto, Santo *WhoAm 94*
Loraine, Philip *WrDr 94*
Loraine, Robert d1935 *WhoHol 92*
Loraine, Violet d1956 *WhoHol 92*
Loram, David (Anning) 1924- *Who 94*
Loran, Erle 1905- *WhoAm 94, WhoAmA 93*
Loran, Martin *EncSF 93*
Lorance, Elmer Donald 1940- *WhoScEn 94, WhoWest 94*
Lorand, Colette 1923- *NewGrDO*
Lorand, Laszlo 1923- *WhoAm 94*
Lorans, Gilles 1944- *WhoFI 94*
Lorant, Stefan 1901- *IntWW 93, Who 94, WhoAm 94, WrDr 94*
Lorber, D. Martin H. B. 1943- *WhoAmA 93*
Lorber, Daniel Louis 1946- *WhoScEn 94*
Lorber, Lawrence Zel 1947- *WhoAm 94*
Lorber, Mortimer 1926- *WhoScEn 94*
Lorber, Richard 1946- *WhoAmA 93*
Lorber, Stephen Neil 1943- *WhoAmA 93*
Lorberbaum, Ralph Richard 1948- *WhoAmL 94*
Lorca, Federico Garcia *IntDcT 2, NewGrDO*
Lorca, Federico Garcia 1898-1936 *HispLC [port]*
Lorca, Isabel *WhoHol 92*
Lorca Di Corcia, Philip *WhoAmA 93*
Lorch, Edgar Raymond 1907-1990 *WhAm 10*
Lorch, Ernest Henry 1932- *WhoAm 94, WhoFI 94*
Lorch, Fred W. 1893- *WhAm 10*
Lorch, George A. 1941- *WhoFI 94*
Lorch, Kenneth F. 1951- *WhoAm 94, WhoAmL 94*
Lorch, Maristella De Panizza 1919- *WhoAm 94*
Lorch, Theodore d1947 *WhoHol 92*
Lorcini, Gino 1923- *WhoAmA 93*
Lord, Alan 1929- *IntWW 93, Who 94*
Lord, Albert Bates 1912-1991 *WhAm 10*
Lord, Alison *ConAu 142*
Lord, Alison 1933- *WrDr 94*
Lord, Anthony 1900- *WhoAm 94*
Lord, Barbara Joanni 1939- *WhoAmL 94*
Lord, Basil d1979 *WhoHol 92*
Lord, Bette Bao 1938- *ConAu 41NR, News 94-1 [port], WhoAsA 94*
Lord, Betty Bao 1938- *WrDr 94*
Lord, Carolyn Marie 1956- *WhoAmA 93*
Lord, Clyde Ormond 1937- *WhoBlA 94*
Lord, Del d1970 *WhoHol 92*
Lord, Evelyn Marlin *WhoAmP 93*
Lord, Evelyn Marlin 1926- *WhoAm 94*
Lord, Fonchen Usher 1926- *WhoAm 94*
Lord, Gabrielle 1946- *EncSF 93*
Lord, Geoffrey 1928- *Who 94*
Lord, George deForest 1919- *WhoAm 94*
Lord, Graham John 1943- *WrDr 94*
Lord, Guy Russell, Jr. 1943- *WhoScEn 94*
Lord, Harold Wilbur 1905- *WhoAm 94, WhoWest 94*
Lord, Harriet 1879-1958 *WhoAmA 93N*
Lord, Henry Robbins 1939- *WhoAm 94*
Lord, Herbert Mathew 1917- *WhoAm 94*
Lord, Jack 1920- *WhoHol 92*
Lord, Jack 1930- *IntMPA 94, WhoWest 94*
Lord, Jacklynn Jean 1940- *WhoWest 94*
Lord, Jacqueline Ward 1936- *WhoFI 94*
Lord, James Gregory 1947- *WhoMW 93*
Lord, Jean-Claude 1943- *ConTFT 11*
Lord, Jeffrey *ConAu 142, EncSF 93*
Lord, Jeffrey 1931- *WrDr 94*
Lord, Jeffrey 1933- *WrDr 94*
Lord, Jere Johns 1922- *WhoAm 94*
Lord, Jerome Edmund 1935- *WhoAm 94*
Lord, Jimmy *WhoAmP 93*
Lord, John 1941- *See* Deep Purple *ConMus 11*
Lord, John Herent 1928- *Who 94*
Lord, John Robert 1954- *WhoWest 94*
Lord, John Vernon 1939- *WrDr 94*
Lord, John Wesley 1902-1989 *WhAm 10*
Lord, Joseph Simon, III 1912-1991 *WhAm 10*
Lord, Keith Edward 1958- *WhoFI 94*
Lord, M. G. 1955- *WhoAm 94*
Lord, Marion d1942 *WhoHol 92*
Lord, Marjorie 1918- *WhoHol 92*
Lord, Marvin 1937- *WhoAm 94*
Lord, Mia W. 1920- *WhoWest 94*
Lord, Michael Harry 1954- *WhoAmA 93*
Lord, Michael Nicholson 1938- *Who 94*

Lord, Nancy *DrAPF 93*
Lord, Nancy 1922- *WrDr 94*
Lord, Norman William 1925- *WhoScEn 94*
Lord, Pauline d1950 *WhoHol 92*
Lord, Peter Herent 1925- *Who 94*
Lord, Philip d1968 *WhoHol 92*
Lord, Phillips H. d1975 *WhoHol 92*
Lord, Richard Collins 1910-1989 *WhAm 10*
Lord, Robert 1945- *WrDr 94*
Lord, Robert 1945-1992 *ConDr 93*
Lord, Roy Alvin 1918- *WhoAm 94*
Lord, Suzanne Molinet 1961- *WhoMW 93*
Lord, Thomas 1755-1832 *DcNaB MP*
Lord, Thomas Reeves 1943- *WhoScEn 94*
Lord, Walter 1917- *WhoAm 94, WrDr 94*
Lord, Wesley Webb 1936- *WhoAmP 93*
Lord, William Burton Housley 1919- *Who 94*
Lord, William Grogan 1914- *WhoAm 94*
Lord, Willis A. 1918- *WhoAmP 93*
Lord, Winston 1937- *IntWW 93, WhoAm 94, WhoAmP 93*
Lordahl, Jo Ann *DrAPF 93*
Lordan, Beth *DrAPF 93*
Lordan, (Ellenora) Beth 1948- *WrDr 94*
Lord Dunmore *AmRev*
Lorde, Athena d1973 *WhoHol 92*
Lorde, Audre *DrAPF 93*
Lorde, Audre 1934- *BlmGWL [port]*
Lorde, Audre 1934-1992 *AnObit 1992, ConBlB 6 [port]*
Lorde, Audre 1934-1993 *AfrAmAl 6*
Lorde, Audre (Geraldin) 1934-1992 *WrDr 94N*
Lorde, Audre (Geraldine) 1934-1992 *ConAu 142, GayLL*
Lorde, Audre Geraldine 1934-1992 *WhoBlA 94N*
Lordeman, James Engelbert 1923- *WhoFI 94*
Lordo, Phillip James 1959- *WhoMW 93*
Lords, Steven D. 1953- *WhoFI 94*
Lords, Traci 1968- *WhoHol 92*
Lore, Kenneth G. 1948- *WhoAmL 94*
Lore, Martin Maxwell 1914- *WhoAm 94*
Lorea, Frank A. 1944- *WhoHisp 94*
Loredo, Roberto F. 1952- *WhoHisp 94*
Lorell, Jeffrey W. 1947- *WhoAmL 94*
Lorelli (Svoboda), Elvira Mae 1927- *WhoAmA 93*
Lorelli, Charles A. 1953- *WhoFI 94*
Lorelli, Michael Kevin 1950- *WhoAm 94, WhoFI 94*
Loren, Donna 1947- *WhoHol 92*
Loren, Sophia 1934- *IntMPA 94, IntWW 93, Who 94, WhoAm 94, WhoHol 92*
Loren, Sophia 1936- *ConAu 142*
Lorengar, Pilar 1928- *NewGrDO*
Lorente, Carol Wiley 1951- *WhoMW 93*
Lorente De No, Rafael 1902-1990 *WhAm 10*
Lorentson, Holly Jean 1956- *WhoWest 94*
Lorentz, Francis 1942- *IntWW 93*
Lorentz, Hendrik Antoon 1853-1928 *WorScD*
Lorentz, Pare 1905-1992 *AnObit 1992*
Lorentz, Pauline *WhoAmA 93*
Lorentz, William Beall 1937- *WhoAm 94*
Lorentzen, Bent 1935- *NewGrDO*
Lorentzen, Carl Warren 1929- *WhoFI 94*
Lorenz, Alfred (Ottokar) 1868-1939 *NewGrDO*
Lorenz, Beth June 1961- *WhoScEn 94*
Lorenz, Carl Edward 1933- *WhoAm 94*
Lorenz, Edward Norton 1917- *WhoAm 94, WhoScEn 94*
Lorenz, Hans-Walter 1951- *IntWW 93*
Lorenz, Hugo Albert 1926- *WhoAm 94*
Lorenz, John d1972 *WhoHol 92*
Lorenz, John Douglas 1942- *WhoAm 94*
Lorenz, John George 1915- *WhoAm 94*
Lorenz, Konrad d1989 *NobelP 91N*
Lorenz, Laurie A. 1966- *WhoMW 93*
Lorenz, Lee Sharp 1932- *WhoAm 94*
Lorenz, Margo c. 1930- *WhoHol 92*
Lorenz, Mary Lou 1954- *WhoWest 94*
Lorenz, Max 1901-1975 *NewGrDO*
Lorenz, Richard Carl 1954- *WhoMW 93*
Lorenz, Richard Theodore, Jr. 1931- *WhoAm 94*
Lorenz, Ronald Theodore 1936- *WhoMW 93*
Lorenz, Ruediger 1932- *WhoScEn 94*
Lorenz, Sarah E. 1912- *WrDr 94*
Lorenz, Timothy Carl 1947- *WhoWest 94*
Lorenz, (Hermann Clemens) Werner 1921- *IntWW 93*
Lorenzani, Arthur Emanuele 1886-1986 *WhoAmA 93N*
Lorenzen, Coby 1905- *WhoScEn 94*
Lorenzen, Kenneth Dean 1942- *WhoWest 94*
Lorenzen, Paul Peter Wilhelm 1915- *IntWW 93*
Lorenzen, Robert Frederick 1924- *WhoAm 94, WhoScEn 94, WhoWest 94*
Lorenzetti, Ole John 1936- *WhoAm 94*
Lorenzetti, Richard Joseph 1950- *WhoMW 93*
Lorenzi, Armandina 1947- *WhoHisp 94*
Lorenzi, Giambattista 1719-1805 *NewGrDO*
Lorenzini, Phillip August 1951- *WhoFI 94*
Lorenzino, Gerardo Augusto 1959- *WhoScEn 94*
Lorenz-Meyer, Wolfgang 1935- *WhoScEn 94*
Lorenzo, Albert L. *WhoMW 93*
Lorenzo, Ariel 1956- *WhoWest 94*
Lorenzo, F. 1947- *WhoIns 94*
Lorenzo, Francisco A. 1940- *IntWW 93, WhoAm 94, WhoFI 94*
Lorenzo, Frank A. 1940- *WhoHisp 94*
Lorenzo, Laura 1957- *WhoHisp 94*
Lorenzo, Lynn Robin 1966- *WhoHisp 94*
Lorenzo, Marcos F. 1945- *WhoHisp 94*
Lorenzo, Michael 1920- *WhoAm 94*
Lorenzo, Nicholas Francis, Jr. 1942- *WhoAmL 94*
Lorenzo Fernandez, Oscar *NewGrDO*
Lorenzon, Livio d1971 *WhoHol 92*
Loret De Range, Aura *WhoWomW 91*
Lorey, Rachel Kathryn 1964- *WhoAmL 94*
Lorge, Charn Teresa Maria 1963- *WhoMW 93*
Lorge, Mary Jo *WhoAmP 93*
Lorge, Robert Gerald Augustine 1959- *WhoAmL 94*
Lorge, William D. 1960- *WhoAmP 93, WhoMW 93*
Loria, Christopher Joseph 1960- *WhoWest 94*
Loria, James Francis 1955- *WhoMW 93*
Loria, Martin A. 1951- *WhoAmL 94*
Loria, Robert Claude 1962- *WhoHisp 94*
Loria, Serafina Teresa 1953- *WhoWest 94*
Loriaux, Maurice Lucien 1909- *WhoAm 94*
Lorie, James Hirsch 1922- *WhoAm 94*
Lorient, Lisa *WhoHol 92*
Lorijn, Johannes Albertus 1925- *WhoScEn 94*
Lorimer, Amy McClellan *WhoAmA 93N*
Lorimer, (Thomas) Desmond 1925- *IntWW 93, Who 94*
Lorimer, Enid d1982 *WhoHol 92*
Lorimer, Frank 1894- *WhAm 10*
Lorimer, George Huntly 1942- *IntWW 93, Who 94*
Lorimer, Glennis 1913- *WhoHol 92*
Lorimer, Hew Martin d1993 *Who 94N*
Lorimer, John Douglass 1953- *WhoWest 94*
Lorimer, Linda Koch *WhoAm 94*
Lorimer, Louise *WhoHol 92*
Lorimor, Brent Gibson 1966- *WhoMW 93*
Lorin, Amii *WrDr 94*
Lorincz, Albert Bela 1922- *WhoAm 94*
Lorincz, Allan Levente 1924- *WhoAm 94*
Lorincz, Laszlo L. *EncSF 93*
Lorinczi, George Gabriel 1929- *WhoAm 94*
Lorincz-Nagy, Janos 1931- *Who 94*
Loring, Ann *WhoHol 92*
Loring, Arthur 1947- *WhoAm 94, WhoAmL 94*
Loring, Caleb, Jr. 1921- *WhoAm 94*
Loring, David William 1956- *WhoScEn 94*
Loring, Eugene d1982 *WhoHol 92*
Loring, Eugene 1911-1982 *IntDcB*
Loring, Gloria Jean 1946- *WhoAm 94*
Loring, John 1939- *WhoAmA 93*
Loring, John Hayes 1926- *WhoAmP 93*
Loring, John Robbins 1939- *IntWW 93, WhoAm 94*
Loring, Joshua, Jr. 1744-1789 *WhAmRev*
Loring, Lisa 1958- *WhoHol 92*
Loring, Lynn 1944- *WhoHol 92*
Loring, Steve Mark 1956- *WhoWest 94*
Loring, Teala c. 1927- *WhoHol 92*
Loring, Thomas Joseph 1921- *WhoScEn 94, WhoWest 94*
Loring, Val d1978 *WhoHol 92*
Lorinsky, Larry 1944- *WhoFI 94, WhoWest 94*
Lorio, Philip Donatien, III 1948- *WhoAmL 94*
Loriod, Yvonne 1924- *IntWW 93*
Loris, Fabien d1979 *WhoHol 92*
Lorman, Barbara K. 1932- *WhoAmP 93, WhoMW 93*
Lorman, William Rudolph 1910-1992 *WhAm 10*
Lorme, Anna *ConAu 142*
Lormer, Jon d1986 *WhoHol 92*
Lorne, Marquess of 1966- *Who 94*
Lorne, Constance d1969 *WhoHol 92*
Lorne, Marion d1968 *WhoHol 92*
Lorne, Simon Michael 1946- *WhoAmL 94, WhoFI 94*
Lorona, John H. *WhoHisp 94*
Loróna, Marie A. 1938- *WhoHisp 94*
Lorr, Kathy Auchincloss *DrAPF 93*
Lorrah, Jean *ConAu 41NR*
Lorrah, Jean c. 1942- *EncSF 93*
Lorrain, Charles d1933 *WhoHol 92*
Lorraine, Alden *EncSF 93*
Lorraine, Betty d1944 *WhoHol 92*
Lorraine, Emily d1944 *WhoHol 92*
Lorraine, Guido 1912- *WhoHol 92*
Lorraine, Harry d1934 *WhoHol 92*
Lorraine, Jean d1958 *WhoHol 92*
Lorraine, Leota d1974 *WhoHol 92*
Lorraine, Lilith *EncSF 93*
Lorraine, Lillian d1955 *WhoHol 92*
Lorraine, Louise d1981 *WhoHol 92*
Lorraine, Marie d1982 *WhoHol 92*
Lorraine, Oscar d1955 *WhoHol 92*
Lorraine, Paul *EncSF 93*
Lorraine, Victor d1973 *WhoHol 92*
Lorre, Peter d1964 *WhoHol 92*
Lorrimer, Claire 1921- *ConAu 42NR, WrDr 94*
Lorring, Joan 1926- *WhoHol 92*
Lorrnell, Marlise d1978 *WhoHol 92*
Lorsch, Jay William 1932- *WhoFI 94*
Lorscheider, Aloisio 1924- *IntWW 93*
Lorson, William Rex 1950- *WhoAmL 94*
Lorsung, Thomas Nicholas 1938- *WhoAm 94*
Lorsy, Pierre Augustus 1935- *WhoAmL 94*
Lortel, Lucille c. 1900- *WhoHol 92*
Lortel, Lucille 1905- *WhoAm 94*
Lorthridge, James E. *WhoBlA 94*
Lortie, Gary A. 1959- *WhoFI 94*
Lortkipanidze, Grigory Davidovich 1927- *LngBDD*
Lorton, Lewis 1939- *WhoAm 94*
Lorts, Jack E. *DrAPF 93*
Lortzing, (Gustav) Albert 1801-1851 *NewGrDO*
Lo Russo, Eddie *WhoHol 92*
Lorusso, Edward N. S. 1949- *WrDr 94*
LoRusso, Terri L. 1961- *WhoMW 93*
Lory, Earl C. 1906- *WhoAmP 93*
Lory, Jacques d1947 *WhoHol 92*
Lory, Loran Steven 1961- *WhoAmL 94*
Lory, Marc H. 1948- *WhoAm 94*
Lory, Robert (Edward) 1936- *EncSF 93*
Lorys, Denise d1930 *WhoHol 92*
Lorys, Diana *WhoHol 92*
Los, Marinus 1933- *WhoScEn 94*
Losada, Jorge *WhoHisp 94*
Losada, Marcial Francisco 1939- *WhoScEn 94*
Losang Dagwa *WhoPRCh 91*
Los Angeles, Victoria de 1923- *NewGrDO [port]*
Losavio, Samuel 1952- *WhoAmA 93*
Loscalzo, Anthony Joseph 1946- *WhoAmL 94*
Losch, Tilly d1975 *WhoHol 92*
Losch, Tilly 1904-1975 *WhoAmA 93N*
Loscheider, Paul Henry 1954- *WhoMW 93*
Lo Schiavo, John Joseph 1925- *WhoAm 94*
LoSchiavo, Linda Bosco 1950- *WhoAm 94*
Loschnak, Franz 1940- *IntWW 93*
Loscutoff, "Jungle Jim" 1930- *BasBi*
Loseau, Cary John 1953- *WhoIns 94*
Losee, Frank d1937 *WhoHol 92*
Losee, John Frederick, Jr. 1951- *WhoMW 93*
Losee, Thomas Penny, Jr. 1940- *WhoAm 94*
Loser, Randy Dennis 1955- *WhoAmL 94*
Losey, Ralph Colby 1951- *WhoAmL 94*
Losh, James 1763-1833 *DcNaB MP*
Loshuertos, Robert Herman 1937- *WhoAm 94*
Losi, Maxim John 1939- *WhoFI 94*
Losinska, Kathleen Mary 1924- *Who 94*
Loskarn, Franz d1978 *WhoHol 92*
Losleben, James Paul 1940- *WhoMW 93*
Losowsky, Monty Seymour 1931- *Who 94*
Losoya, Jack *WhoHisp 94*
Losoya, Raul C. *WhoHisp 94*
Loss, Ira Saul 1945- *WhoFI 94*
Loss, John C. 1931- *WhoAm 94, WhoFI 94, WhoScEn 94*
Loss, Louis 1914- *WhoAm 94, WrDr 94*
Loss, Margaret Ruth 1946- *WhoAm 94*
Loss, Stuart Harold 1946- *WhoAm 94*
Lossberg, Friedrich Wilhelm von c. 1720- *WhAmRev*
Losse, Arlyle Mansfield 1917- *WhoMW 93*
Losse, John William, Jr. 1916- *WhoAm 94*
Lossing, Frederick Pettit 1915- *WhoAm 94*
Lossy, Rella *DrAPF 93*
Losten, Basil Harry 1930- *WhoAm 94*
Losty, Howard Harold Walter 1926- *Who 94*
Lo Surdo, Antonio 1943- *WhoAm 94*
Lotas, Judith Patton 1942- *WhoAm 94*
LoTempio, Julia Matild 1934- *WhoFI 94*
Loten, Alexander William 1925- *Who 94*
Lothar, Hans d1967 *WhoHol 92*
Lothar, Mark 1902-1985 *NewGrDO*
Lothe, Jens 1931- *IntWW 93*
Lothian, Marquess of 1922- *Who 94*
Lothian, (Thomas Robert) Noel 1915- *WrDr 94*
Lothringer, Lori Dee 1962- *WhoMW 93*
Lothrop, Amy *BlmGWL*
Lothrop, Gloria Ricci 1934- *WhoWest 94*
Lothrop, Harriet Mulford Stone 1844-1924 *BlmGWL*
Lothrop, Kristin Curtis 1930- *WhoAm 94, WhoAmA 93*
Loti, Pierre 1850-1923 *NewGrDO*
Lotinga, Ernest d1951 *WhoHol 92*
Lotis, Dennis 1931- *WhoHol 92*
Lotito, Michael Joseph 1948- *WhoAm 94, WhoAmL 94*
Lotito, Nicholas Anthony 1949- *WhoAmL 94*
Lotman, Yuriy Mikhailovich 1922- *IntWW 93*
Lotocky, Innocent H. 1915- *WhoAm 94, WhoMW 93*
Loton, Brian Thorley 1929- *IntWW 93, Who 94*
Lotrick, Joseph *WhoScEn 94*
Lotringer, Sylvere 1938- *WhoAm 94, WhoAmA 93*
Lotruglio, Anthony F. 1938- *WhoFI 94*
Lotstein, James I. 1944- *WhoAm 94, WhoAmL 94*
Lott, Abraham 1726-1794 *WhAmRev*
Lott, Arnold S 1912- *WrDr 94*
Lott, Bernard Maurice 1922- *Who 94*
Lott, Brad *WhoAmP 93*
Lott, Brenda Louise 1955- *WhoFI 94*
Lott, Bret *DrAPF 93*
Lott, David Stuart 1943- *WhoAm 94*
Lott, Davis Newton 1913- *WhoWest 94*
Lott, Felicity 1947- *NewGrDO*
Lott, Felicity Ann 1947- *IntWW 93*
Lott, Felicity Ann Emwhyla 1947- *Who 94*
Lott, Gay Lloyd 1937- *WhoBlA 94*
Lott, George 1906-1991 *BuCMET*
Lott, Ira Totz 1941- *WhoScEn 94*
Lott, James *DrAPF 93*
Lott, Joyce Greenberg *DrAPF 93*
Lott, Judy Wright 1953- *WhoMW 93*
Lott, Kench Lee, Jr. 1920- *WhoAm 94*
Lott, Lawrence d1991 *WhoHol 92*
Lott, Marley 1947- *WhoAmL 94*
Lott, Milton 1919- *WrDr 94*
Lott, Ronnie 1959- *WhoAm 94, WhoBlA 94*
Lott, S. Makepeace *EncSF 93*
Lott, Thomas Luther 1946- *WhoFI 94*
Lott, Trent 1941- *CngDr 93, IntWW 93, WhoAm 94, WhoAmP 93*
Lott, Yancey Davis, Jr. 1939- *WhoAmP 93*
Lotter, Charles Robert 1937- *WhoAmL 94, WhoFI 94*
Lotter, Donald Willard 1952- *WhoScEn 94*
Lotterhos, Frederick Jacob, III 1954- *WhoAmL 94*
Lotterman, Hal 1920- *WhoAm 94, WhoAmA 93*
Lottes, John William 1934- *WhoAmA 93*
Lottes, Patricia Joette Hicks 1955- *WhoMW 93*
Lotti, Antonio c. 1667-1740 *NewGrDO*
Lotti, Santa *NewGrDO*
Lottimer, Eb *WhoHol 92*
Lottinger, Morris Albert, Jr. 1937- *WhoAmL 94*
Lottini, Antonio fl. 1717-1765 *NewGrDO*
Lottman, Eileen 1927- *EncSF 93*
Lottman, Herbert 1927- *WrDr 94*
Lotto, Claire d1952 *WhoHol 92*
Lotto, Fred d1937 *WhoHol 92*
Lotuaco, Luisa Go 1938- *WhoMW 93*
Lotven, Howard Lee 1959- *WhoAmL 94, WhoMW 93*
Lotwin, Stanford Gerald 1930- *WhoAm 94, WhoAmL 94*
Loty, Maud d1976 *WhoHol 92*
Lotz, Arthur William 1927- *WhoAm 94*
Lotz, Beverly Ruth 1959- *WhoMW 93*
Lotz, Denton 1939- *WhoAm 94*
Lotz, Joan Theresa 1948- *WhoFI 94*
Lotz, Kurt 1912- *Who 94*
Lotz, Louis E. 1949- *WhoAm 94*
Lotz, Steven Darryl 1938- *WhoAmA 93*
Lotz, William Allen 1932- *WhoScEn 94*
Lotz, Wolfgang d1993 *NewYTBS 93*
Lotze, Evie Daniel 1943- *WhoScEn 94*
Lotzer, Gerald Balthazar 1951- *WhoAmL 94*
Lotzova, Eva *WhoScEn 94*
Lou, Zheng David 1959- *WhoScEn 94*
Louanne 1972- *WhoHol 92*
Louard, Agnes A. 1922- *WhoBlA 94*
Louargand, Marc Andrew 1945- *WhoFI 94*
Loube, Samuel Dennis 1921- *WhoAm 94*

Lovejoy, George Montgomery, Jr. 1930- *WhoFI 94*
Lovejoy, Jack 1937- *EncSF 93, WhoMW 93*
Lovejoy, Lee Harold 1936- *WhoFI 94*
Lovejoy, Margot R. 1930- *WhoAmA 93*
Lovejoy, Marian E. 1931- *WhoAmP 93*
Lovejoy, Thomas Eugene 1941- *WhoAm 94, WhoScEn 94*
Lovejoy, Virginia K. 1927- *WhoAmP 93*
Lovejoy, William Joseph 1940- *WhoAm 94*
Lovekamp, Carl Lorenz 1932- *WhoAmP 93*
Lovelace, Countess of 1815-1852 *DcNaB MP*
Lovelace, Earl of 1951- *Who 94*
Lovelace, Alan Mathieson 1929- *WhoScEn 94*
Lovelace, Augusta Ada King, Countess of 1815-1852 *WorInv [port]*
Lovelace, Byron Keith 1935- *WhoAm 94, WhoFI 94*
Lovelace, Dean Alan 1946- *WhoBlA 94*
Lovelace, Earl 1935- *BlkWr 2, ConAu 41NR, WrDr 94*
Lovelace, Eldridge Hirst 1913- *WhoAm 94*
Lovelace, Eugene Arthur 1939- *WhoScEn 94*
Lovelace, Gloria Elaine 1945- *WhoBlA 94*
Lovelace, Jerry Lynn 1962- *WhoAmL 94*
Lovelace, John C. 1926- *WhoBlA 94*
Lovelace, Jon B. 1927- *WhoAm 94*
Lovelace, Linda Diane 1948- *WhoMW 93*
Lovelace, Onzalo Robert 1940- *WhoBlA 94*
Lovelace, Richard 1618-1657 *DcLB 131 [port], LitC 24 [port]*
Lovelace, Richard 1618-1658 *BlmGEL*
Lovelace, Robert Frank 1950- *WhoAm 94*
Lovelady, Carolyn Moore 1952- *WhoFI 94*
Lovelady, Rueben Leon 1958- *WhoBlA 94*
Lovelady, Steven M. 1943- *WhoAm 94*
Loveland, Curtis A. 1946- *WhoAmL 94*
Loveland, Don C. 1916- *WhoAmP 93*
Loveland, Donald William 1934- *WhoAm 94*
Loveland, Eugene Franklin 1920- *WhoAm 94*
Loveland, Holly Standish 1947- *WhoFI 94, WhoMW 93*
Loveland, L. Joseph, Jr. 1951- *WhoAmL 94*
Loveland, Laurie Jean 1958- *WhoAmL 94*
Loveland, Michael Glenn 1954- *WhoMW 93*
Loveland, Patricia Marie 1941- *WhoWest 94*
Loveland, Valoria *WhoAmP 93*
Loveland, Walter David 1939- *WhoWest 94*
Loveless, Edna Maye 1929- *WhoWest 94*
Loveless, Edward Eugene 1919- *WhoAm 94*
Loveless, George 1797-1874 *DcNaB MP*
Loveless, George Group 1940- *WhoAm 94*
Loveless, Herschel Cellel 1911-1989 *WhAm 10*
Loveless, Jim 1935- *WhoAmA 93*
Loveless, Patty 1957- *WhoAm 94*
Loveless, Ralph Peyton 1936- *WhoAmL 94*
Loveling, Virginie 1836-1923 *BlmGWL*
Lovell, Allan *WhoHol 92*
Lovell, Ann 1933- *ConAu 41NR*
Lovell, (Alfred Charles) Bernard 1913- *IntWW 93, Who 94, WrDr 94*
Lovell, Brian Noel 1965- *WhoAmL 94*
Lovell, Carl Erwin, Jr. 1945- *WhoAmL 94*
Lovell, Charles C. 1929- *WhoAm 94, WhoAmL 94, WhoWest 94*
Lovell, Charles Rickey 1957- *WhoScEn 94*
Lovell, Edward George 1939- *WhoAm 94*
Lovell, Francis Joseph, III 1949- *WhoFI 94*
Lovell, James 1737-1814 *WhAmRev*
Lovell, James, Jr. 1758-1850 *WhAmRev*
Lovell, James A., Jr. 1928- *WhoAm 94, WhoScEn 94*
Lovell, James Frederick 1934- *WhoAm 94*
Lovell, Jeffrey Dale 1952- *WhoWest 94*
Lovell, John 1710-1778 *WhAmRev*
Lovell, Kenneth Ernest Walter 1919- *Who 94*
Lovell, Leigh d1935 *WhoHol 92*
Lovell, Malcolm R., Jr. *WhoAmP 93*
Lovell, Malcolm Read, Jr. 1921- *WhoAm 94*
Lovell, Marc 1929- *WrDr 94*
Lovell, Margaretta Markle 1944- *WhoAmA 93*
Lovell, Mary Ann 1943- *WhoMW 93*
Lovell, Mary S(ybilla) 1941- *ConAu 140*
Lovell, Michael C. 1930- *WhoAm 94*
Lovell, Nancy Grace 1942- *WhoMW 93*
Lovell, Raymond d1953 *WhoHol 92*
Lovell, Robert Gibson 1920- *WhoAm 94*
Lovell, Robert Marlow, Jr. 1930- *WhoFI 94, WhoIns 94*
Lovell, Robert Roland 1937- *WhoScEn 94*
Lovell, Solomon d1801 *WhAmRev*
Lovell, Theodore 1928- *WhoFI 94, WhoScEn 94*
Lovell, Tom 1909- *WhoAmA 93, WhoWest 94*
Lovell, Walter Carl 1934- *WhoAm 94, WhoFI 94, WhoScEn 94*
Lovell-Davis, Baron 1924- *Who 94*
Lovellette, Clyde 1929- *BasBi [port]*
Lovell-Pank, Dorian Christopher 1946- *Who 94*
Lovelock, Douglas (Arthur) 1923- *Who 94*
Lovelock, James (Ephraim) *EncSF 93*
Lovelock, James Ephraim 1919- *EnvEnc [port], Who 94*
Lovelock, Raymond *WhoHol 92*
Lovely, F. Beirne, Jr. 1946- *WhoAmL 94*
Lovely, Louise d1980 *WhoHol 92*
Lovely, Robert Allyn 1948- *WhoMW 93*
Lovely, Thomas Dixon 1930- *WhoAm 94*
Loveman, E. Barry 1942- *WhoAmP 93*
Loveman, Stephen Charles Gardner 1943- *Who 94*
Loven, Andrew Witherspoon 1935- *WhoAm 94*
Loven, Charles John 1937- *WhoWest 94*
Loven, Mary Jean 1950- *WhoFI 94*
Lovenberg, Walter M. 1934- *WhoAm 94, WhoMW 93*
Lovenheim, David A. 1942- *WhoAmP 93*
Lovenheim, David Alan 1942- *WhoAm 94, WhoAmL 94*
Loventhal, Milton 1923- *WhoWest 94*
Loverde, James M. *DrAPF 93*
Loveridge, John (Henry) 1912- *Who 94*
Loveridge, John (Warren) 1925- *Who 94*
Loveridge, Marguerite d1925 *WhoHol 92*
Lovering, John Francis 1930- *Who 94*
Lovering, Richard S. 1954- *WhoAmL 94*
Loverseed, Amanda (Jane) 1965- *ConAu 142, SmATA 75 [port]*
Lovesey, Peter (Harmer) 1936- *WrDr 94*
Lovestone, Jay d1990 *WhAm 10*
Lovet-Lorski, Boris 1894-1973 *WhoAmA 93N*
Lovetot, John de c. 1236-1294 *DcNaB MP*
Lovett, Clara Maria 1939- *WhoAm 94*
Lovett, Dorothy 1917- *WhoHol 92*
Lovett, Edward P. 1902- *WhoBlA 94*
Lovett, Eva Gruber 1940- *WhoMW 93*
Lovett, John Robert 1931- *WhoAm 94*
Lovett, John Thomas 1954- *WhoAmL 94*
Lovett, Leonard 1939- *WhoBlA 94*
Lovett, Lyle *WhoAm 94*
Lovett, Lyle c. 1958- *News 94-1 [port]*
Lovett, Mack, Jr. 1931- *WhoBlA 94*
Lovett, Robert A. 1895-1986 *HisDcKW*
Lovett, Robert G. 1944- *WhoAm 94, WhoAmL 94*
Lovett, Thomas G., IV 1950 *WhoAmL 94*
Lovett, Wendell Harper 1922- *WhoAm 94*
Lovett, William Anthony 1934- *WhoAm 94, WhoAmL 94*
Lovett, Willie Clinton 1939- *WhoAmP 93*
Lovette, Blake Duane 1942- *WhoFI 94*
Loveys, Ralph A. 1929- *WhoAmP 93*
Lovi, George d1993 *NewYTBS 93*
Lovick, Albert Ernest Fred 1912- *Who 94*
Lovick, Norman 1942- *WhoFI 94*
Lovig, Lawrence, III 1942- *WhoFI 94*
Lovill, John (Roger) 1929- *Who 94*
Lovin, Hugh Taylor 1928- *WhoWest 94*
Lovin, Keith Harold 1943- *WhoAm 94*
Lovin, Roger *EncSF 93*
Loving, Al 1935- *WhoAmA 93*
Loving, Albert A., Jr. 1920- *WhoBlA 94*
Loving, Alvin Demar, Jr. 1935- *WhoAm 94*
Loving, George Gilmer, Jr. 1923- *WhoAm 94*
Loving, James Leslie, Jr. 1944- *WhoBlA 94*
Loving, Jean Franklin 1925- *WhoWest 94*
Loving, Oyoko *DrAPF 93*
Loving, Pamela Yvonne 1943- *WhoBlA 94*
Loving, Richard Maris 1924- *WhoAmA 93*
Loving, Rose 1927- *WhoBlA 94*
Loving, Susan B. *WhoAm 94, WhoAmL 94*
Loving, Susan Brimer 1950- *WhoAmP 93*
Lovinger, Warren Conrad 1915- *WhoAm 94*
Lovings, L. Edward 1932- *WhoAmP 93*
Lovini, Domenico *NewGrDO*
Lovins, Amory B. 1947- *EnvEnc [port]*
Lovins, Amory Bloch 1947- *WhoAm 94, WhoWest 94*
Lovins, L. Hunter 1950- *WhoWest 94*
Lovitt, Craig Edward 1932- *WhoAmP 93*
Lovitt, George Harold 1922- *WhoAm 94*
Lovitz, Jon 1957- *IntMPA 94, WhoAm 94, WhoHol 92*
Lovro, Istvan 1944- *WhoScEn 94*
Lovsky, Celia d1979 *WhoHol 92*
Lovvik, Daryl Vaughn 1941- *WhoWest 94*
Lovy, Andrew 1935- *WhoMW 93*
Low *Who 94*
Low, A(rchibald) M(ontgomery) 1888-1956 *EncSF 93*
Low, Alan (Roberts) 1916- *Who 94*
Low, Alfred D 1913- *WrDr 94*
Low, Alice 1926- *SmATA 76 [port]*
Low, Andrew M. 1952- *WhoAm 94, WhoAmL 94*
Low, Anthony 1935- *WhoAm 94, WrDr 94*
Low, Barbara Wharton 1920- *WhoAm 94*
Low, Boon Chye 1946- *WhoAm 94, WhoAsA 94, WhoScEn 94*
Low, Brian Buik 1937- *Who 94*
Low, Carl d1988 *WhoHol 92*
Low, Charles *WhoHol 92*
Low, Chow-Eng 1938- *WhoScEn 94*
Low, Daniel Abraham 1959- *WhoMW 93*
Low, David *DrAPF 93*
Low, Denise *DrAPF 93*
Low, Donald Anthony 1927- *Who 94*
Low, Donald Gottlob 1925- *WhoAm 94*
Low, Dorothy Mackie 1916- *WrDr 94*
Low, Emmet Francis, Jr. 1922- *WhoAm 94, WhoScEn 94*
Low, Ethelbert Herrick d1990 *WhAm 10*
Low, Francis Eugene 1921- *IntWW 93, WhoAm 94*
Low, Frank Norman 1911- *WhoAm 94, WhoScEn 94*
Low, (George) Graeme (Erick) 1928- *Who 94*
Low, Harold William 1949- *WhoAm 94, WhoAmL 94*
Low, Harry William 1931- *WhoAm 94, WhoAsA 94*
Low, Isaac 1735-1791 *WhAmRev*
Low, Jack d1958 *WhoHol 92*
Low, James A. 1925- *WhoAm 94*
Low, James (Richard) Morrison- 1925- *Who 94*
Low, James Patterson 1927- *WhoAm 94*
Low, John Henry 1954- *WhoFI 94*
Low, John L., IV 1946- *WhoAmL 94*
Low, John Wayland 1923- *WhoAm 94*
Low, Joseph 1911- *WhoAm 94*
Low, Leone Yarborough 1935- *WhoMW 93*
Low, Loh-Lee 1948- *WhoAsA 94*
Low, Louise Anderson 1944- *WhoMW 93*
Low, Merry Cook 1925- *WhoWest 94*
Low, Morton David 1935- *WhoAm 94*
Low, Norman C., Jr. 1925- *WhoAmP 93*
Low, Patricia Enid Rose 1932- *WhoBlA 94*
Low, Paul M. 1930- *WhoAm 94*
Low, Paul Revere 1933- *WhoFI 94*
Low, Philip Funk 1921- *WhoAm 94*
Low, Randall 1949- *WhoAsA 94*
Low, Richard H. 1927- *WhoAm 94*
Low, Robert A. 1919- *WhoAmP 93*
Low, Robert B. 1940- *WhoScEn 94*
Low, Sanford 1905-1964 *WhoAmA 93N*
Low, Stephen 1927- *IntWW 93, WhoAm 94, WhoAmP 93*
Low, Susan A. 1946- *WhoAmL 94, WhoMW 93*
Low, Warren d1989 *WhoHol 92*
Low, Wye Ming *WhoAmL 94*
Lowbury, Edward (Joseph Lister) 1913- *WrDr 94*
Lowd, Judson Dean 1918- *WhoAm 94*
Lowden, Desmond Scott 1937- *WrDr 94*
Lowden, Gordon Stuart 1927- *Who 94*
Lowden, John L. 1921- *WhoAm 94*
Lowden, Scott Richard 1940- *WhoAm 94*
Lowden, Suzanne 1952- *WhoAmP 93*
Lowder, James Daniel 1963- *WhoMW 93*
Lowder, Robert Jackson 1927- *WhoFI 94*
Lowdermilk, Dale 1948- *WhoWest 94*
Lowe, A. Lynn *WhoAmP 93*
Lowe, Al 1946- *WhoWest 94*
Lowe, Allen *WhoAmP 93*
Lowe, Angela Maria 1963- *WhoScEn 94*
Lowe, Arthur d1982 *WhoHol 92*
Lowe, Aubrey F. 1940- *WhoBlA 94*
Lowe, Bruce J. L. 1949- *WhoAmL 94*
Lowe, Cameron Anderson 1932- *WhoScEn 94*
Lowe, Chad 1968- *IntMPA 94, WhoAm 94, WhoHol 92*
Lowe, Clarence 1946- *WhoAmP 93*
Lowe, Cortnie A. *DrAPF 93*
Lowe, Craig Wesley 1952- *WhoAmL 94*
Lowe, Cynthia Lynn 1954- *WhoFI 94*
Lowe, David Alexander 1942- *Who 94*
Lowe, David Bruce Douglas 1935- *Who 94*
Lowe, David Nicoll 1909- *Who 94*
Lowe, Donald Cameron 1932- *WhoAm 94, WhoFI 94*
Lowe, Douglas (Charles) 1922- *Who 94*
Lowe, Douglas Ackley 1942- *IntWW 93, Who 94*
Lowe, Douglas George 1940- *WhoScEn 94*
Lowe, Edmund d1971 *WhoHol 92*
Lowe, Edwin Nobles 1912- *WhoAm 94, WhoAmL 94*
Lowe, Emily d1966 *WhoAmA 93N*
Lowe, Eugene Yerby, Jr. 1949- *WhoBlA 94*
Lowe, Felix Caleb 1933- *WhoAm 94*
Lowe, Florence Segal *WhoFI 94*
Lowe, Forrest Gilbert 1927- *WhoMW 93*
Lowe, Frank Budge 1941- *IntWW 93, Who 94, WhoAm 94, WhoFI 94*
Lowe, Frank C. 1885-1968 *HisDcKW*
Lowe, Geoffrey Colin 1920- *Who 94*
Lowe, George Henry 1939- *WhoAm 94*
Lowe, Gordon 1933- *Who 94*
Lowe, Harry d1963 *WhoHol 92*
Lowe, Harry 1922- *WhoAm 94, WhoAmA 93*
Lowe, Hazel Marie 1936- *WhoBlA 94*
Lowe, Hugh S. 1942- *WhoAmL 94*
Lowe, Ida Brandwayn 1946- *WhoFI 94*
Lowe, J. Michael 1942- *WhoAmA 93*
Lowe, Jackie *WhoBlA 94*
Lowe, James B. d1963 *WhoHol 92*
Lowe, James Edward, Jr. 1950- *WhoBlA 94*
Lowe, John 1922- *Who 94*
Lowe, John, III 1916- *WhoAm 94*
Lowe, John Burton 1953- *WhoMW 93, WhoScEn 94*
Lowe, John Eric Charles 1907- *Who 94*
Lowe, John Evelyn 1928- *Who 94*
Lowe, John Paul, Jr. 1951- *WhoAmL 94*
Lowe, John Raymond, Jr. 1922- *WhoScEn 94*
Lowe, John Stanley 1941- *WhoAmL 94*
Lowe, Jonathan F. *DrAPF 93*
Lowe, Jonathan Wayne 1947- *WhoAm 94, WhoAmL 94*
Lowe, Judah 1949- *WrDr 94*
Lowe, K. Elmo d1971 *WhoHol 92*
Lowe, Kathlene Winn 1949- *WhoAm 94*
Lowe, Kenneth Gordon 1917- *Who 94*
Lowe, Kenneth Stephen 1921- *WhoAm 94*
Lowe, Louis Robert, Jr. 1937- *WhoAmL 94*
Lowe, Marvin 1922- *WhoAm 94*
Lowe, Marvin 1927- *WhoAmA 93*
Lowe, Mary Frances 1952- *WhoAm 94*
Lowe, Mary Johnson 1924- *WhoAm 94*
Lowe, Michael G. 1945- *WhoAmL 94*
Lowe, Oariona 1948- *WhoWest 94*
Lowe, Philip L. 1917- *IntMPA 94*
Lowe, Philip Martin 1947- *Who 94*
Lowe, Ralph Edward 1931- *WhoAmL 94, WhoMW 93*
Lowe, Randall Brian 1948- *WhoAm 94*
Lowe, Richard Bryant, III 1941- *WhoBlA 94*
Lowe, Richard Gerald, Jr. 1960- *WhoFI 94, WhoWest 94*
Lowe, Rob 1964- *WhoAm 94, WhoHol 92*
Lowe, Robert Augustus 1952- *WhoWest 94*
Lowe, Robert B. 1946- *WhoAmP 93*
Lowe, Robert Charles 1927- *WhoAm 94*
Lowe, Robert Charles 1949- *WhoAm 94*
Lowe, Robert David 1930- *Who 94*
Lowe, Robert Stanley 1923- *WhoAm 94, WhoAmL 94, WhoWest 94*
Lowe, Robson 1905- *Who 94*
Lowe, Rolland Choy 1932- *WhoAsA 94*
Lowe, Ronald Dean 1961- *WhoScEn 94*
Lowe, Ronda Leigh 1957- *WhoAmL 94*
Lowe, Roy Goins 1926- *WhoAmL 94, WhoMW 93*
Lowe, Sam Jack 1950- *WrDr 94*
Lowe, Samuel M. 1918- *WhoBlA 94*
Lowe, Scott Miller 1942- *WhoBlA 94*
Lowe, Sheldon 1926- *WhoAm 94*
Lowe, Sidney 1961- *WhoAm 94, WhoMW 93*
Lowe, Sidney Rochell 1960- *WhoBlA 94*
Lowe, Stephen 1947- *ConDr 93, WrDr 94*
Lowe, Stephen Richard 1944- *Who 94*
Lowe, Steve *DrAPF 93*
Lowe, Sue Esther 1954- *WhoWest 94*
Lowe, Sylvia Oneice 1946- *WhoBlA 94*
Lowe, Teddy R. 1936- *WhoIns 94*
Lowe, Thomas d1783 *NewGrDO*
Lowe, Thomas (William Gordon) 1963- *Who 94*
Lowe, Todd Parker 1959- *WhoFI 94*
Lowe, Veronica Ann 1951- *Who 94*
Lowe, Walter Edward, Jr. 1951- *WhoBlA 94*
Lowe, William C. *WhoAm 94, WhoFI 94*
Lowe, William Curtis 1947- *WhoMW 93*
Lowe, William Daniel 1949- *WhoMW 93*
Lowell, Amy 1874-1925 *BlmGWL [port], DcLB 140 [port]*
Lowell, Amy (Lawrence) 1874-1925 *GayLL*
Lowell, Carey 1961- *WhoHol 92*
Lowell, Cym Hawksworth 1946- *WhoAm 94*
Lowell, Elizabeth 1944- *WrDr 94*
Lowell, Frederick K. 1948- *WhoAmL 94*
Lowell, H. Bret 1953- *WhoAmL 94*
Lowell, Helen d1937 *WhoHol 92*
Lowell, Howard Parsons 1945- *WhoAm 94*
Lowell, Jacqueline Peters *WhoAm 94*
Lowell, James Russell 1819-1891 *AmCulL*
Lowell, Joan d1967 *WhoHol 92*

Lowell, John d1937 *WhoHol 92*
Lowell, John 1743-1802 *WhAmRev*
Lowell, Josephine Shaw 1843-1905 *AmSocL*
Lowell, Juliet 1901- *WhoAm 94*
Lowell, Meredith P. 1950- *WhoAm 94*
Lowell, Orson Byron 1871-1956 *WhoAmA 93N*
Lowell, Robert (Traill Spence, Jr.) 1917-1977 *ConDr 93*
Lowell, Robert Traill Spence, Jr. 1917-1977 *AmCulL [port]*
Lowell, Stanley Herbert 1919- *WhoAmL 94*
Lowell, Wayne Brian 1955- *WhoFI 94*
Lowen, Alexander 1910- *WrDr 94*
Lowen, Gerard Gunther 1921- *WhoAm 94*
Lowen, Marilyn *DrAPF 93*
Lowen, Walter 1921- *WhoAm 94*
Lowenadler, Holger d1977 *WhoHol 92*
Lowenbaum, R. Michael 1952- *WhoAmL 94*
Lowenberg, Michael 1943- *WhoAm 94*
Lowenberg, Miriam Elizabeth 1897- *WhAm 10*
Lowenfeld, Andreas Frank 1930- *WhoAm 94*
Lowenfeld, Viktor 1903-1960 *WhoAmA 93N*
Lowenfels, Fred M. 1944- *WhoAm 94*
Lowenfels, Lewis David 1935- *WhoAmL 94*
Lowenfels, Manna *DrAPF 93*
Lowengrund, Margaret 1905-1957 *WhoAmA 93N*
Lowenhaupt, Charles Abraham 1947- *WhoAmL 94*
Lowenkamp, William Charles, Jr. 1941- *WhoScEn 94*
Lowens, Curt *WhoHol 92*
Lowenstam, Steven 1945- *WhoWest 94*
Lowenstein, Alan Victor 1913- *WhoAm 94*
Lowenstein, Alfred Samuel 1931- *WhoScEn 94*
Lowenstein, Derek Irving 1943- *WhoAm 94, WhoScEn 94*
Lowenstein, Harold Louis 1939- *WhoAmP 93*
Lowenstein, James Gordon 1927- *WhoAm 94, WhoAmP 93*
Lowenstein, Louis 1925- *WhoAm 94*
Lowenstein, Michele Sacks 1950- *WhoAmL 94*
Lowenstein, Otto Egon 1906- *Who 94*
Lowenstein, Peter David 1935- *WhoAm 94*
Lowenstein, Ralph Lynn 1930- *WhoAm 94*
Lowenstein, Roger Alan 1943- *WhoAmL 94*
Lowenstein, Tom *DrAPF 93*
Lowenstine, James R. 1923- *WhoFI 94*
Lowenstine, Maurice Richard, Jr. 1910- *WhoAm 94*
Lowenthal, Abraham Frederic 1941- *WhoAm 94*
Lowenthal, Constance 1945- *WhoAm 94, WhoAmA 93*
Lowenthal, David 1923- *ConAu 41NR*
Lowenthal, Henry 1931- *WhoAm 94*
Lowenthal, Jack *WhoIns 94*
Lowenthal, Jacob 1938- *WhoFI 94*
Lowenthal, Leo 1900- *WrDr 94*
Lowenthal, Leo 1900-1993 *ConAu 140*
Lowenthal, Margaret 1929- *WhoAmP 93*
Lowenthal, Susan 1946- *WhoFI 94*
Lowenthal, Tina Marie 1961- *WhoWest 94*
Lower, Joyce Q. 1943- *WhoAm 94, WhoAmL 94*
Lower, Louis Gordon, II 1945- *WhoAm 94, WhoFI 94*
Lower, Michael W. 1949- *WhoAmL 94*
Lower, Philip Edward 1949- *WhoAmL 94*
Lower, Richard Lawrence 1935- *WhoAm 94*
Lower, Robert Cassel 1947- *WhoAm 94, WhoAmL 94*
Lowerre, Susan (K.) 1962- *WrDr 94*
Lowery, Birl 1950- *WhoBlA 94*
Lowery, Bobby G. 1932- *WhoBlA 94*
Lowery, Bruce *DrAPF 93*
Lowery, Carolyn T. 1940- *WhoBlA 94*
Lowery, Charles Douglas 1937- *WhoAm 94*
Lowery, Clinton Hershey 1929- *WhoAm 94*
Lowery, David J. 1953- *WhoAmL 94*
Lowery, Donald Elliott 1956- *WhoBlA 94*
Lowery, Edna Mozell 1940- *WhoAmL 94*
Lowery, James William, Jr. 1963- *WhoFI 94*
Lowery, John David 1945- *WhoAmL 94*
Lowery, Joseph E. *WhoAm 94*
Lowery, Joseph E. 1924- *AfrAmAl 6 [port], WhoBlA 94*
Lowery, Lee Leon, Jr. 1938- *WhoAm 94, WhoScEn 94*
Lowery, Linda 1949- *ConAu 141, SmATA 74 [port]*
Lowery, Mike *DrAPF 93*
Lowery, Robert d1971 *WhoHol 92*
Lowery, Robert 1924- *WhoFI 94*
Lowery, Robert Chuck 1932- *WhoMW 93*
Lowery, Robert G. 1941- *WrDr 94*
Lowery, Robert O. 1916- *WhoBlA 94*
Lowery, Sarah 1925- *WhoAmP 93*
Lowery, Sharon A. 1943- *WhoFI 94*
Lowery, William D. 1947- *WhoAmP 93*
Lowery, William E. d1941 *WhoHol 92*
Lowery, William Herbert 1925- *WhoAm 94, WhoAmL 94*
Lowes, Albert Charles 1932- *WhoAmL 94*
Lowes, Mark E. 1955- *WhoAmL 94*
Lowes, Peter Donald 1926- *Who 94*
Lowet, Henry A. 1932- *WhoAm 94*
Lowey, Hans d1993 *NewYTBS 93 [port]*
Lowey, Nita 1937- *WhoWomW 91*
Lowey, Nita M. 1937- *CngDr 93, WhoAm 94, WhoAmP 93*
Lowi, Alvin, Jr. 1929- *WhoScEn 94, WhoWest 94*
Lowi, Theodore Jay 1931- *WhoAm 94*
Lowig, Henry Francis Joseph 1904- *WhoWest 94*
Lowing, Anne 1930- *WrDr 94*
Lowinger, Paul Ludwig 1923- *WhoWest 94*
Lowitsch, Klaus 1936- *WhoHol 92*
Lowitt, Richard 1922- *WhoAm 94*
Lowke, George E. 1939- *WhoScEn 94*
Lowman, George Frederick 1916- *WhoAm 94*
Lowman, Isom 1946- *WhoBlA 94*
Lowman, Larry Loyd *WhoWest 94*
Lowman, Sarah Ann 1962- *WhoAmL 94*
Lowman, Zelvin Don 1921- *WhoAmP 93*
Lown, Bernard 1921- *WhoScEn 94*
Lown, Elizabeth D. 1932- *WhoAmP 93*
Lowndes, David Alan 1947- *WhoWest 94*
Lowndes, John Foy 1931- *WhoAmL 94*
Lowndes, Rawlins 1721-1800 *WhAmRev*
Lowndes, Robert A(ugustine) W(ard) 1916- *EncSF 93, WrDr 94*
Lowne, C. M. d1941 *WhoHol 92*
Lowney, Bruce Stark 1937- *WhoAm 94, WhoAmA 93, WhoWest 94*
Lownie, Ralph Hamilton 1924- *Who 94*
Lownsdale, Gary Richard 1946- *WhoMW 93*
Lowrey, Alice 1905- *Who 94*
Lowrey, Charles Boyce 1941- *WhoFI 94*
Lowrey, D'Orvey Preston, III 1952- *WhoScEn 94*
Lowrey, E. James 1928- *WhoAm 94, WhoFI 94*
Lowrey, George Minter 1943- *WhoAmP 93*
Lowrey, Richard William 1938- *WhoFI 94*
Lowrie, Allen 1937- *WhoScEn 94*
Lowrie, James Stewart 1944- *WhoAmL 94*
Lowrie, Jean Elizabeth 1918- *WhoAm 94*
Lowrie, Walter Olin 1924- *WhoAm 94*
Lowrie, William G. 1943- *WhoAm 94, WhoFI 94, WhoMW 93*
Lowry, Baron 1919- *IntWW 93, Who 94*
Lowry, A. Leon, Sr. *WhoBlA 94*
Lowry, A. Robert 1919- *WhoAm 94*
Lowry, Bates 1923- *IntWW 93, WhoAm 94, WhoAmA 93*
Lowry, Betty *DrAPF 93*
Lowry, Beverly *DrAPF 93*
Lowry, Beverly (Fey) 1938- *WrDr 94*
Lowry, Bruce Roy 1952- *WhoAm 94*
Lowry, Candace Elizabeth 1950- *WhoWest 94*
Lowry, Charles W 1905- *WrDr 94*
Lowry, Charles Wesley 1905- *WhoAm 94*
Lowry, Damon *WhoHol 92*
Lowry, Daniel L. 1951- *WhoAmL 94*
Lowry, Dick *IntMPA 94*
Lowry, Dick M. *ConTFT 11*
Lowry, Donald Michael 1929- *WhoAmL 94*
Lowry, Donna Shirlynn 1957- *WhoBlA 94*
Lowry, Eddie Rountree, Jr. 1945- *WhoMW 93*
Lowry, Edward Francis, Jr. 1930- *WhoAm 94, WhoAmL 94, WhoWest 94*
Lowry, Edwin R. 1928- *WhoFI 94*
Lowry, Elizabeth Grace 1966- *WhoAmL 94*
Lowry, Ethel Joyce 1933- *WhoMW 93*
Lowry, Glenn David *WhoAm 94*
Lowry, Henry H. d1935 *EncNAR*
Lowry, Houston Putnam 1955- *WhoAmL 94*
Lowry, Hunt 1954- *IntMPA 94*
Lowry, James David 1942- *WhoAm 94*
Lowry, James E. 1942- *WhoBlA 94*
Lowry, James Hamilton 1939- *WhoAm 94, WhoBlA 94, WhoFI 94*
Lowry, Jane 1937- *WhoHol 92*
Lowry, Joan Marie Dondrea 1935- *WhoMW 93*
Lowry, Judith d1976 *WhoHol 92*
Lowry, Larry Kenneth 1949- *WhoWest 94*
Lowry, Larry Lorn 1947- *WhoAm 94, WhoWest 94*
Lowry, Lois 1937- *ConAu 43NR, TwCYAW*
Lowry, Lois (Hammersberg) 1937- *WrDr 94*
Lowry, Lois Hammersberg 1937- *WhoAm 94*
Lowry, Lynn *WhoHol 92*
Lowry, Malcolm 1909-1957 *BlmGEL*
Lowry, Michael Blair 1945- *WhoFI 94*
Lowry, Michael Edward 1939- *WhoAmP 93*
Lowry, Mike 1939- *WhoAm 94, WhoWest 94*
Lowry, Morton 1908- *WhoHol 92*
Lowry, Noreen Margaret 1925- *Who 94*
Lowry, Pat *Who 94*
Lowry, Patricia Lynn Otto 1947- *WhoAmL 94*
Lowry, (John) Patrick 1920- *IntWW 93, Who 94*
Lowry, Richard John 1924- *Who 94*
Lowry, Ritchie Peter 1926- *WrDr 94*
Lowry, Robert (James) 1919- *WrDr 94*
Lowry, Robert Dudley 1949- *WhoAmL 94*
Lowry, Robert Ronald 1932- *WhoWest 94*
Lowry, Robin Pearce 1947- *WhoScEn 94*
Lowry, Rudd d1965 *WhoHol 92*
Lowry, Sheldon Gaylon 1924- *WhoAm 94*
Lowry, W. McNeil 1913-1993 *NewYTBS 93 [port]*
Lowry, William E., Jr. 1935- *WhoBlA 94*
Lowry, William Ketchin, Jr. 1951- *WhoAm 94, WhoFI 94*
Lowry, William R. 1953- *ConAu 142*
Lowry, William Randall 1947- *WhoFI 94*
Lowry-Corry *Who 94*
Lowson, Ian (Patrick) 1944- *Who 94*
Lowson, Martin Vincent 1938- *Who 94*
Lowther *Who 94*
Lowther, Viscount 1949- *Who 94*
Lowther, Charles (Douglas) 1946- *Who 94*
Lowther, Frederick M. 1943- *WhoAmL 94*
Lowther, Gerald Halbert 1924- *WhoAm 94*
Lowther, James 1673-1755 *DcNaB MP*
Lowther, James E. *WhoAmP 93*
Lowther, John 1582-1637 *DcNaB MP*
Lowther, John 1643-1706 *DcNaB MP*
Lowther, John Luke 1923- *Who 94*
Lowther, Patricia Louise 1935-1975 *BlmGWL*
Lowther, William (Anthony) 1942- *WrDr 94*
Lowthian, Petrena 1931- *WhoMW 93*
Lowy, Frederick Hans 1933- *WhoAm 94*
Lowy, George Theodore 1931- *WhoAm 94*
Lowy, Israel 1957- *WhoScEn 94*
Lowy, Jay Stanton 1935- *WhoAm 94*
Lowy, Louis 1920-1991 *WhAm 10*
Loxam, John Gordon 1927- *Who 94*
Loxley, John 1942- *WhoAm 94*
Loxmith, John *EncSF 93*
Loxmith, John 1934- *WrDr 94*
Loy, Dennis K. 1951- *WhoAmL 94*
Loy, Francis David Lindley 1927- *Who 94*
Loy, Frank Ernest 1928- *WhoAm 94*
Loy, John Sheridan 1930- *WhoAmA 93*
Loy, Mina 1882-1966 *BlmGWL*
Loy, Myrna 1905- *IntMPA 94, WhoAm 94, WhoCom, WhoHol 92*
Loy, Myrna 1905-1993 *NewYTBS 93 [port], News 94-2*
Loy, Richard Franklin 1950- *WhoMW 93, WhoScEn 94*
Loy, Richard Nelson 1945- *WhoFI 94*
Loy, Rosetta 1931- *BlmGWL*
Loya, Ofelia Olivares 1929- *WhoHisp 94*
Loya, Ralph R. 1943- *WhoHisp 94*
Loya, Richard *WhoHisp 94*
Loyd, Alison d1935 *WhoHol 92*
Loyd, Christopher Lewis 1923- *Who 94*
Loyd, Francis Alfred 1916- *Who 94*
Loyd, Jan Brooks 1950- *WhoAmA 93*
Loyd, John Anthony Thomas 1933- *Who 94*
Loyd, Julian (St. John) 1926- *Who 94*
Loyd, Marianne *DrAPF 93*
Loyd, Walter, Jr. 1951- *WhoBlA 94*
Loyden, Edward 1923- *Who 94*
Loyfman, Alexander M. 1970- *WhoMW 93*
Loyn, H(enry) R(oyston) 1922- *ConAu 41NR*
Loyn, Henry *ConAu 41NR*
Loyn, Henry R. *ConAu 41NR*
Loyn, Henry Royston 1922- *IntWW 93, Who 94*
Loynaz, Dulce Maria 1903- *BlmGWL*
Loynd, Richard B. *WhoFI 94*
Loynd, Richard Birkett 1927- *WhoAm 94, WhoMW 93*
Loynes, Antoinette fl. 16th cent.- *BlmGWL*
Loynes, Camille de fl. 16th cent.- *BlmGWL*
Loynes, John Hamilton 1933- *WhoFI 94*
Loyola, Ignatius c. 1491-1556 *HisWorL [port]*
Loyonnet, Georges-Claude 1924- *WhoScEn 94*
Lozada, Claribel *WhoHisp 94*
Lozada-Rossy, Joyce 1952- *WhoHisp 94*
Lozano, Adrián 1921- *WhoHisp 94*
Lozano, Antonio, Jr. 1914- *WhoHisp 94*
Lozano, Conrad Russell *WhoHisp 94*
Lozano, Denise M. 1951- *WhoHisp 94*
Lozano, Frank Philip 1924- *WhoHisp 94*
Lozano, Fred C. 1949- *WhoHisp 94*
Lozano, Ignacio Eugenio, Jr. 1927- *WhoHisp 94, WhoWest 94*
Lozano, J. Alexandro 1948- *WhoHisp 94*
Lozano, John Manuel 1930- *WhoAm 94, WhoHisp 94*
Lozano, Jorge Anthony 1962- *WhoHisp 94*
Lozano, Jose 1941- *WhoHisp 94*
Lozano, Jose Carlos 1958- *WhoHisp 94*
Lozano, Leonard J. 1935- *WhoHisp 94*
Lozano, Margarita *WhoHol 92*
Lozano, Minerva D. *WhoHisp 94*
Lozano, Monica Cecilia 1956- *WhoHisp 94*
Lozano, Robert 1918- *WhoHisp 94*
Lozano, Rudolf J. *WhoHisp 94*
Lozano, Rudolpho 1942- *WhoAmL 94*
Lozano, Rudy 1942- *WhoAm 94, WhoHisp 94*
Lozano, Wilfredo 1946- *WhoHisp 94*
Lozansky, Edward Dmitry 1941- *WhoScEn 94*
Lozeau, Donnalee M. 1960- *WhoAmP 93*
Lozier, Allan G. 1933- *WhoMW 93*
Lozier, Clarence Eugene 1938- *WhoFI 94*
Lozier, W. Wallace d1993 *NewYTBS 93*
Lozong 1948- *WhoPRCh 91 [port]*
Lozoraitis, Stasis 1924- *IntWW 93*
Lozovatsky, Mikhail 1949- *WhoScEn 94*
Lozowick, Louis 1892-1973 *WhoAmA 93N*
Lozowicki, Edward B. 1944- *WhoAmL 94*
Lozoya-Solis, Jesus 1910- *IntWW 93*
Lozoya-Thalmann, Emilio 1947- *WhoAm 94*
Lozyniak, Andrew 1931- *WhoAm 94*
Lu, Catherine Mean Hoa 1963- *WhoScEn 94*
Lu, Cheng-yi 1954- *WhoScEn 94*
Lu, David John 1928- *WhoAm 94*
Lu, David Yun-Chen 1954- *WhoAsA 94*
Lu, Donghao Robert 1956- *WhoAsA 94*
Lu, Frank Kerping 1954- *WhoAsA 94*
Lu, Hsiao-ming 1956- *WhoScEn 94*
Lu, I-Tai 1953- *WhoAsA 94*
Lu, Janet C. 1938- *WhoAsA 94*
Lu, Janet Y. H. *WhoAsA 94*
Lu, John Y. 1933- *WhoAsA 94*
Lu, Jye-Chyi 1957- *WhoAsA 94*
Lu, Kau U. 1939- *WhoAsA 94*
Lu, Kwang-Tzu 1942- *WhoScEn 94*
Lu, Le-Wu 1933- *WhoAsA 94*
Lu, Liang-Ju 1949- *WhoMW 93*
Lu, Lina 1950- *WhoAsA 94*
Lu, Linyu Laura 1957- *WhoAsA 94*
Lu, Lisa *WhoHol 92*
Lu, Luo 1952- *WhoAsA 94*
Lu, Mi *WhoAsA 94*
Lu, Michael Y. 1955- *WhoAsA 94*
Lu, Min Zhan 1946- *WhoAsA 94*
Lu, Paul Haihsing 1921- *WhoScEn 94, WhoWest 94*
Lu, Pengzhe 1957- *WhoWest 94*
Lu, Ponzy 1942- *WhoAm 94, WhoAsA 94*
Lu, Ruth 1961- *WhoScEn 94*
Lu, Steven Zhiyun 1941- *WhoAsA 94*
Lu, Tian-Huey 1939- *WhoScEn 94*
Lu, Wuan-Tsun 1939- *WhoScEn 94, WhoWest 94*
Lu, Wudu 1947- *WhoScEn 94*
Lu, Yingzhong 1926- *WhoScEn 94*
Lualdi, Adriano 1885-1971 *NewGrDO*
Lualdi, Antonella 1931- *WhoHol 92*
Luallen, Donna Jean 1964- *WhoMW 93*
Luan Enjie *WhoPRCh 91*
Luan Jujie 1958- *IntWW 93, WhoPRCh 91 [port]*
Luanto, Regina di 1862?-1914 *BlmGWL*
Luard, Nicholas 1937- *WrDr 94*
Luart, Emma 1892-1968 *NewGrDO*
Lubachivsky, Myroslav Ivan 1914- *IntWW 93*
Lubalin, Peter *WhoAm 94*
Luban, Marshall 1936- *WhoScEn 94*
Lu Bangzheng 1937- *WhoPRCh 91 [port]*
Lu Baowei 1916- *WhoPRCh 91*
Lu Baoyun *WhoPRCh 91*
Lubar, Jeffrey Stuart 1947- *WhoAm 94*
Lubar, Joel F 1938- *WrDr 94*
Lubar, Sheldon Bernard 1929- *WhoMW 93*
Lubaroff, David Martin 1938- *WhoMW 93*
Lubaroff, Martin 1941- *WhoAmL 94*
Lubatti, Henry Joseph 1937- *WhoAm 94*
Lubben, David J. 1951- *WhoAm 94, WhoAmL 94*

Lubbers, Arend Donselaar 1931- WhoMW 93
Lubbers, Leland Eugene 1928- WhoAmA 93
Lubbers, Ruud Frans Marie 1939- IntWW 93
Lubbers, Teresa S. 1951- WhoMW 93
Lubbers, Teresa Smith 1951- WhoAmP 93
Lubbock Who 94
Lubbock, Christopher William Stuart 1920- Who 94
Lubbock, James Edward 1924- WhoFI 94, WhoMW 93
Lubchenco, Jane 1947- WhoScEn 94
Lubcke, Harry R. 1905- IntMPA 94
Lubeck, Marvin Jay 1929- WhoAm 94, WhoScEn 94, WhoWest 94
Lubeckis, Jean Marie 1951- WhoMW 93
Lubel, Alan E. 1950- WhoAmL 94
Lubell, Ellen 1950- WhoAmA 93
Lubell, Harold 1925- WhoAm 94
Lubenchenko, Konstantin Dmitrievich 1945- LngBDD
Lubenow, Josef Karl 1945- WhoMW 93
Luber, Thomas Julian 1949- WhoAm 94, WhoAmL 94
Luberda, George Joseph 1930- WhoAmL 94
Lubert, Mlle de 1710?-1779? BlmGWL
Lubetsky, Elsen DrAPF 93
Lubewaka, Teresa WhoWomW 91
Lubic, Robert Bennett 1929- WhoAmL 94
Lubic, Ruth Watson 1927- WhoAm 94
Lubich Silvia, Chiara 1920- IntWW 93
Lubick, Donald C. 1926- WhoAmP 93
Lubick, Donald Cyril 1926- WhoAm 94, WhoAmL 94
Lubin, Arthur 1901- IntMPA 94, WhoHol 92
Lubin, Bernard 1923- WhoAm 94, WrDr 94
Lubin, Donald G. 1934- WhoAm 94, WhoAmL 94
Lubin, Germaine (Leontine Angelique) 1890-1979 NewGrDO [port]
Lubin, Jack 1931- WhoAm 94
Lubin, Martin 1923- WhoAm 94
Lubin, Michael Frederick 1947- WhoAm 94
Lubin, Stanley 1941- WhoAmL 94, WhoWest 94
Lubin, Steven 1942- IntWW 93, WhoAm 94
Lubinsky, Anthony Richard 1946- WhoScEn 94
Lubis, Mochtar 1922- IntWW 93
Lu Bisong WhoPRCh 91 [port]
Lubitsch, Ernst d1947 WhoHol 92
Lubitsch, Ernst 1892-1947 AmCulL
Lubitz, A. Peter 1945- WhoAmL 94
Lubitz, Edward J. 1944- WhoAmL 94
Lubitz, Lester Marc 1948- WhoMW 93
Lubkin, Gloria Becker 1933- WhoAm 94
Lubkin, Virginia Leila 1914- WhoScEn 94
Lublin, Edward Louis WhoAm 94
Lublin, Mark Aaron 1942- WhoAmL 94
Lublinski, Michael 1951- WhoAm 94
Lubman, David 1934- WhoWest 94
Lubman, Stanley Bernard 1934- WhoAm 94
Lubnau, Thomas Edwin, II 1958- WhoAmL 94
Luborsky, Fred Everett 1923- WhoAm 94
Lubotsky, Mark Davidovich 1931- IntWW 93
Lubovitch, Lar WhoAm 94
Lubow, Arthur 1952- ConAu 140
Lubow, Nathan Myron 1929- WhoFI 94
Lubowsky, Jack 1940- WhoScEn 94
Lubowsky, Susan 1949- WhoAmA 93
Lubrani, Uri IntWW 93
Luby, Dallas W. 1940- WhoIns 94
Luby, Edna d1928 WhoHol 92
Luby, Ellen L. 1949- WhoAmL 94
Luby, Elliot Donald 1924- WhoAm 94
Luby, Jason 1929- WhoAmP 93
Luby, Thomas S. WhoAmP 93
Luc, Helene 1932- WhoWomW 91
Luca, Giuseppe de NewGrDO
Luca, Mark 1918- WhoAmA 93
Luca, Severo de NewGrDO
Lucak, Gerald Edward 1950- WhoFI 94
Lucal, Martha Jane 1938- WhoMW 93
Luca-Moretti, Maurizio 1945- WhoScEn 94
Lucan 39-65 BlmGEL
Lucan, Earl of 1934- Who 94
Lucan, Arthur d1954 WhoHol 92
Lucander, Henry 1940- WhoFI 94
Lucarelli, Jack WhoHol 92
Lucas Who 94
Lucas, Alexander Ralph 1931- WhoAm 94
Lucas, April C. 1950- WhoAmL 94
Lucas, Arthur Maurice 1941- Who 94
Lucas, Artie WhoAmP 93
Lucas, Aubrey Keith 1934- WhoAm 94
Lucas, Barbara DrAPF 93
Lucas, Barbara 1911- WrDr 94
Lucas, Barbara B. 1945- WhoAm 94
Lucas, Bert Albert 1933- WhoMW 93
Lucas, Billy Joe 1942- WhoAm 94, WhoScEn 94
Lucas, Bonnie Lynn 1950- WhoAmA 93
Lucas, Brian Humphrey 1940- Who 94
Lucas, C. Payne 1933- WhoBlA 94
Lucas, Carol Lee 1940- WhoAm 94
Lucas, Catherine E. WhoAm 94
Lucas, Celia 1938- WrDr 94
Lucas, Charles C. 1927-1983 WhoBlA 94N
Lucas, Christopher 1958- WhoAmA 93
Lucas, Christopher Charles 1920- Who 94
Lucas, Christopher John 1940- WrDr 94
Lucas, Clarence 1866-1947 NewGrDO
Lucas, Colin Renshaw 1940- Who 94
Lucas, Cornel 1923- IntWW 93
Lucas, Craig 1951- ConDr 93, IntWW 93, WhoAm 94
Lucas, Craig John 1962- WhoAmL 94
Lucas, Curt d1960 WhoHol 92
Lucas, Cyril (Edward) 1909- IntWW 93, Who 94
Lucas, David E., Sr. 1950- WhoAmP 93
Lucas, David Eugene 1950- WhoBlA 94
Lucas, Dennis DrAPF 93
Lucas, Donald 1951- WhoScEn 94
Lucas, Donald Leo 1930- WhoAm 94, WhoWest 94
Lucas, Dorothy J. 1949- WhoBlA 94
Lucas, E(dward) V(errall) 1868-1938 EncSF 93
Lucas, Earl S. 1938- WhoBlA 94
Lucas, Edward C. 1941- WhoAmP 93
Lucas, Eileen 1956- SmATA 76 [port]
Lucas, Elizabeth Mary 1954- WhoMW 93
Lucas, F(rank) L(aurence) 1894-1967 EncSF 93
Lucas, Frank D. 1960- WhoAmP 93
Lucas, Frank Edward 1934- WhoAm 94
Lucas, Fred Vance 1922- WhoAm 94
Lucas, G. Robert, II 1943- WhoAmL 94
Lucas, Gail d1990 WhoHol 92
Lucas, George 1944- ConTFT 11, EncSF 93, IntMPA 94, IntWW 93, Who 94
Lucas, George Ramsdell, Jr. 1949- WhoAm 94
Lucas, George W., Jr. 1944- WhoAm 94, WhoWest 94
Lucas, Georges 1915- IntWW 93
Lucas, Georgetta Marie Snell 1920- WhoMW 93
Lucas, Georgetta Snell 1920- WhoAmA 93
Lucas, Gerald Robert 1942- WhoBlA 94
Lucas, Henry Cameron, Jr. 1944- WhoAm 94
Lucas, Hugh Hampton 1937- WhoAm 94
Lucas, Ian Albert McKenzie 1926- Who 94
Lucas, Irvin R., III 1959- WhoMW 93
Lucas, Ivor Thomas Mark 1927- Who 94
Lucas, J(ames) R(aymond) 1950- ConAu 42NR
Lucas, J. Richard 1929- WhoAm 94
Lucas, James Evans 1933- WhoAm 94
Lucas, James Howard 1927- WhoIns 94
Lucas, James L. 1923- WhoBlA 94
Lucas, James R. 1922- WhoAmP 93
Lucas, James Raymond 1950- WhoFI 94
Lucas, James Walter 1940- WhoAm 94
Lucas, Jerry 1940- BasBi
Lucas, Jimmy d1949 WhoHol 92
Lucas, John NewYTBS 93 [port]
Lucas, John 1937- WrDr 94
Lucas, John 1953- BasBi, WhoBlA 94
Lucas, John Allen 1943- WhoAm 94, WhoAmL 94
Lucas, John H(arold) 1894- WhAm 10
Lucas, John Harding 1920- WhoBlA 94
Lucas, John Harding, Jr. 1953- WhoAm 94
Lucas, John Kenneth 1946- WhoAm 94, WhoAmL 94
Lucas, John Randolph 1929- Who 94, WrDr 94
Lucas, John Stewart 1940- WhoScEn 94
Lucas, Joseph Edward 1905- WhoAmL 94
Lucas, Juanita F. WhoMW 93
Lucas, June H. WhoAmP 93
Lucas, Keith Stephen 1924- Who 94
Lucas, L. Louise 1944- WhoAmP 93
Lucas, Larry WhoAmP 93
Lucas, Lawrence Newton 1906- WhoAm 94
Lucas, Leo Alexander 1912- WhoBlA 94
Lucas, Linda Gail 1947- WhoBlA 94
Lucas, Lisa 1961- WhoHol 92
Lucas, Malcolm Millar 1927- WhoAm 94, WhoAmL 94, WhoAmP 93, WhoWest 94
Lucas, Maurice 1952- BasBi, WhoBlA 94
Lucas, Maurice F. 1944- WhoBlA 94
Lucas, Melinda Ann 1953- WhoScEn 94
Lucas, Michael P. 1953- WhoAmL 94
Lucas, Nick d1982 WhoHol 92
Lucas, Patricia Lynn 1962- WhoMW 93
Lucas, Patricia Mary 1954- WhoAmL 94
Lucas, Percy Belgrave 1915- Who 94
Lucas, Peter Charles 1934- IntWW 93
Lucas, Peter Michael 1954- WhoWest 94
Lucas, Raleigh Barclay 1914- Who 94
Lucas, Rendella 1910- WhoBlA 94
Lucas, Rhett Roy 1941- WhoAm 94, WhoAmL 94, WhoWest 94
Lucas, Robert Anthony 1939- WhoWest 94
Lucas, Robert Elmer 1916- WhoAm 94
Lucas, Robert Frank 1935- WhoAmL 94
Lucas, Roy Edward, Jr. 1955- WhoAm 94
Lucas, Sam d1916 WhoHol 92
Lucas, Shirley Agnes Hoyt 1921- WhoFI 94, WhoMW 93
Lucas, Stanley Jerome 1929- WhoAm 94
Lucas, Stephen Edwin 1946- WhoMW 93
Lucas, Stephen Leonard 1948- WhoAmL 94
Lucas, Steven Mitchell 1948- WhoAmL 94
Lucas, Suzanne 1939- WhoWest 94
Lucas, Thomas (Edward) 1930- Who 94
Lucas, Timothy Alan 1959- WhoFI 94
Lucas, Victoria TwCYAW, WhoBlA 94
Lucas, Vivian Who 94
Lucas, (Charles) Vivian 1914- Who 94
Lucas, Wilfred d1940 WhoHol 92
Lucas, William 1925- WhoHol 92
Lucas, William 1928- WhoBlA 94
Lucas, William Jasper 1926- WhoFI 94
Lucas, William Max, Jr. 1934- WhoAm 94
Lucas, William Ray 1922- WhoAm 94
Lucas, William S. 1917- WhoBlA 94
Lucas, Willie Lee 1924- WhoBlA 94
Lucas, Wilmer Francis, Jr. 1927- WhoBlA 94
Lucas Garcia, Fernando Romeo IntWW 93
Lucas Of Chilworth, Baron 1926- Who 94
Lucas Of Crudwell, Baron 1951- Who 94
Lucas-Tooth, (Hugh) John 1932- Who 94
Lucca, Carmen D. DrAPF 93
Lucca, Don Anthony 1954- WhoScEn 94
Lucca, Francesco 1802-1872 NewGrDO
Lucca, John James 1921- WhoAm 94
Lucca, Pauline 1841-1908 NewGrDO [port]
Lucchesi, Andrea 1741-1801 NewGrDO
Lucchesi, Arsete Joseph 1933- WhoScEn 94
Lucchesi, Bruno 1926- WhoAm 94, WhoAmA 93
Lucchesi, Donald Albert 1950- WhoAm 94
Lucchesi, Gary 1955- IntMPA 94
Lucchesi, John C. WhoAm 94, WhoScEn 94
Lucchesi, Lionel Louis 1939- WhoAmL 94, WhoMW 93, WhoScEn 94
Lucchesina, La NewGrDO
Lucchesino, Il NewGrDO
Lucchi, Leonard Louis 1958- WhoAmP 93
Lucchini, Antonio Maria fl. 1716-1730 NewGrDO
Lucchino, Frank Joseph 1939- WhoAmP 93
Lucchino, Lawrence 1945- WhoAm 94, WhoAmL 94
Lucci, Susan 1946- WhoAm 94
Lucci, Susan 1948- IntMPA 94, WhoHol 92
Luccio, Francesco NewGrDO
Luce, C(harles Beardsley) 1947- WhoAmA 93
Luce, Charles F. 1917- IntWW 93
Luce, Charles Franklin 1917- WhoAm 94
Luce, Claire d1989 WhoHol 92
Luce, Connie P. 1941- WhoMW 93
Luce, Gay (Gaer) 1930- WrDr 94
Luce, Gregory DrAPF 93
Luce, Gregory M. WhoAm 94, WhoAmL 94
Luce, Henry, III 1925- IntWW 93, WhoAm 94
Luce, Henry Robinson 1898-1967 AmSocL [port]
Luce, James W. 1947- WhoIns 94
Luce, Jo Ann 1950- WhoMW 93
Luce, Michael Leigh 1952- WhoAmL 94
Luce, Polly d1973 WhoHol 92
Luce, Priscilla Mark 1947- WhoMW 93
Luce, R(obert) Duncan 1925- IntWW 93
Luce, Richard (Napier) 1936- Who 94
Luce, Richard Napier 1936- IntWW 93
Luce, Robert Duncan 1925- WhoAm 94, WhoWest 94
Luce, Stewart Edward 1938- WhoFI 94
Luce, Thomas Richard Harman 1939- Who 94
Luce, Thomas Warren, III 1940- WhoAm 94
Luce, Timothy Charles 1960- WhoScEn 94
Lucebert 1924- ConWorW 93, IntWW 93
Lucenay, Harry d1944 WhoHol 92
Luceno, James EncSF 93
Lucente, Rosemary Dolores 1935- WhoWest 94
Lucero, Alvin K. WhoHisp 94
Lucero, Amarante L., Jr. 1947- WhoHisp 94
Lucero, C. Steven 1967- WhoHisp 94
Lucero, Enrique d1989 WhoHol 92
Lucero, Gene A. 1947- WhoAm 94
Lucero, Helen R. 1943- WhoHisp 94
Lucero, Juan M. 1947- WhoHisp 94
Lucero, Leonard L. 1946- WhoHisp 94
Lucero, Leonor Jon 1966- WhoHisp 94
Lucero, Marcela DrAPF 93
Lucero, Michael (Lewis) 1953- WhoAmA 93
Lucero, Michael L. 1953- WhoHisp 94
Lucero, Ricardo 1940- WhoHisp 94
Lucero, Richard L. 1935- WhoHisp 94
Lucero, Rosalba 1964- WhoHisp 94
Lucero, Rose M. 1954- WhoHisp 94
Lucero, Scott Alan 1968- WhoWest 94
Lucero, Stephanie Denise 1957- WhoHisp 94
Lucero, Stephen Paul 1955- WhoHisp 94
Lucero-Schayes, Wendy 1964- WhoHisp 94
Lucey, Charles Timothy 1905- WhoAm 94
Lucey, Jack 1929- WhoAmA 93, WhoWest 94
Lucey, James D. 1923- WrDr 94
Lucey, Jerold Francis 1926- WhoAm 94
Lucey, John David, Jr. 1930- WhoAm 94
Lucey, John Edward 1941- WhoAmP 93
Lucey, Lawrence Haydn 1947- WhoMW 93
Lucey, Patrick Joseph 1918- WhoAmP 93
Lucey, Paula Ann 1954- WhoMW 93
Luchaire, Corinne d1950 WhoHol 92
Luchak, Frank Alexander 1950- WhoAm 94, WhoAmL 94
Lu Chaoqi 1925- WhoPRCh 91 [port]
Luche, Thomas Clifford 1934- WhoAm 94
Luchetti, Veriano 1939- NewGrDO
Luchin, Viktor Osipovich 1939- LngBDD
Luchini, Fabrice WhoHol 92
Luchins, Daniel Jonathan 1948- WhoMW 93
Luchinsky, Petre 1940- IntWW 93
Luchko, Katya WhoHol 92
Luchko, Klara Stepanovna 1925- IntWW 93
Luchs, Alison 1948- WhoAmA 93
Lucht, Albert F. 1919- WhoAmP 93
Lucht, John Charles 1933- WhoAm 94, WhoFI 94
Lucht, Sondra Moore 1942- WhoAmP 93
Luchterhand, Ralph Edward 1952- WhoFI 94, WhoWest 94
Lu Chuanzan 1932- WhoPRCh 91 [port]
Lucia, Ellis (Joel) 1922- WrDr 94
Lucia, Fernando de NewGrDO
Lucian EncSF 93
Lucian fl. 2nd cent.- BlmGEL
Lucian c. 120-c. 180 EncSF 93
Luciano, Felipe DrAPF 93
Luciano, Mark Joseph 1959- WhoWest 94
Luciano, Mark R. WhoIns 94
Luciano, Robert Peter 1933- WhoAm 94, WhoFI 94
Lucid, Robert Francis 1930- WhoAm 94
Lucid, Shannon W. 1943- WhoScEn 94
Lucido, Chester Charles, Jr. 1939- WhoAm 94
Lucido, Louis Charles 1948- WhoAm 94
Lucie, Doug 1953- ConDr 93, WrDr 94
Lucier, Gregory Thomas 1964- WhoWest 94
Lucier, Mary 1944- WhoAmA 93
Lucier, P. Jeffrey 1941- WhoAm 94
Lucier, Richard Leland 1943- WhoFI 94
Lucier, Ted 1947- WhoAmP 93
Lucie-Smith, Edward EncSF 93
Lucie-Smith, (John) Edward (McKenzie) 1933- Who 94, WrDr 94
Lucina, Mary DrAPF 93
Lucinschii, Petru Chiril 1940- LngBDD
Lucio, Benito, Jr. 1955- WhoHisp 94
Lucio, Eduardo, Jr. 1946- WhoAmP 93
Lucio, Eduardo A. 1946- WhoHisp 94
Lucio, Francesco c. 1628-1658 NewGrDO
Lucio, Ricardo, Jr. 1951- WhoHisp 94
Lucio Paredes, Antonio Jose 1923- IntWW 93
Luciuk, Juliusz 1927- NewGrDO
Luciuk, Lubomyr Y(aroslav) 1953- WrDr 94
Lucius, Wulf D. von 1938- IntWW 93
Luck, Clyde Alexander, Jr. 1929- WhoBlA 94
Luck, David Jonathan Lewis 1929- WhoAm 94
Luck, Dennis Noel 1939- WhoMW 93
Luck, Edward Carmichael 1948- WhoAm 94
Luck, Georg Hans Bhawani 1926- WhoAm 94
Luck, J. Murray 1899-1993 NewYTBS 93
Luck, James I. 1945- WhoAm 94
Luck, Robert d1977 WhoHol 92
Luck, Robert 1921- WhoAmA 93
Lucke, John Edward 1963- WhoScEn 94

Lundin, David Erik 1949- *WhoAm 94, WhoAmL 94*
Lundin, John E. 1940- *WhoAmL 94*
Lundin, Judith *DrAPF 93*
Lundin, Norman K. 1938- *WhoAmA 93*
Lundin, Ralph Lester 1941- *WhoFI 94*
Lundine, Stan 1939- *WhoAmP 93*
Lundine, Stanley Nelson 1939- *WhoAm 94*
Lunding, Christopher Hanna 1946- *WhoAm 94*
Lundman, Richard Jack 1944- *WhoAm 94*
Lundmark, William T. d1987 *WhoHol 92*
Lundquist, Carl Harold 1916-1991 *WhAm 10*
Lundquist, Charles Arthur 1928- *WhoAm 94, WhoScEn 94*
Lundquist, Dana R. 1941- *WhoAm 94*
Lundquist, Gene Alan 1943- *WhoAm 94*
Lundquist, Homer *WhoAmP 93*
Lundquist, James Harold 1931- *WhoAm 94*
Lundquist, John B. 1949- *WhoAmL 94*
Lundquist, Linda Ann Johnson 1945- *WhoMW 93*
Lundquist, Per Birger 1945- *WhoScEn 94*
Lundquist, Steve *WhoHol 92*
Lundquist, Virginia Areta 1949- *WhoMW 93*
Lundquist, Weyman Ivan 1930- *WhoAm 94*
Lundring, Lynn Karsten 1942- *WhoWest 94*
Lundsgaarde, Henry Peder 1938- *WhoAm 94*
Lundstedt, Sven Bertil 1926- *WhoAm 94*
Lundsten, E. Hans 1946- *WhoAmL 94*
Lundstrom, Gilbert Gene 1941- *WhoAmL 94*
Lundstrom, Hans Olof 1927- *IntWW 93*
Lundstrom, Mark Steven 1951- *WhoMW 93*
Lundstrom, Mary Meyer 1948- *WhoWest 94*
Lundstrom, Thomas John 1954- *WhoAmL 94*
Lundwall, Sam J(errie) 1941- *EncSF 93, WrDr 94*
Lundy, Benjamin 1789-1839 *AmSocL*
Lundy, Dale Allen 1950- *WhoMW 93*
Lundy, Daniel Francis 1930- *WhoFI 94*
Lundy, Gerald *WhoBlA 94*
Lundy, Gilbert Moulton, Jr. 1954- *WhoWest 94*
Lundy, Harold W. *WhoBlA 94*
Lundy, Jessica *WhoHol 92*
Lundy, John Kent 1946- *WhoWest 94*
Lundy, Joseph E. 1942- *WhoAm 94, WhoAmL 94*
Lundy, Joseph Edward 1915- *WhoAm 94, WhoMW 93*
Lundy, Joseph R. 1940- *WhoAm 94, WhoAmL 94*
Lundy, Ray 1916- *WhoAmP 93*
Lundy, Richard Alan 1934- *WhoAm 94*
Lundy, Richard Bruce 1941- *WhoMW 93*
Lundy, Roland 1950- *WhoAm 94*
Lundy, Sadie Allen 1918- *WhoFI 94, WhoMW 93*
Lundy, Ted Sadler 1933- *WhoAmP 93*
Lundy, Victor Alfred 1923- *IntWW 93, WhoAm 94*
Lundy, Walker *WhoAm 94, WhoMW 93*
Luneau, Claude 1935- *WhoAmA 93*
Lunenfeld, Bruno 1927- *IntWW 93*
Lung, Chang *ConAu 140*
Lung, Charles d1974 *WhoHol 92*
Lung, Clarence *WhoHol 92*
Lunger, Charles William 1927- *WhoAm 94*
Lunger, Irvin Eugene 1912- *WhoAm 94*
Lunghi, Cherie 1953- *WhoHol 92*
Lungren, Daniel Edward 1946- *WhoAm 94, WhoAmL 94, WhoAmP 93, WhoWest 94*
Lungren, John Howard 1925- *WhoAmL 94, WhoMW 93*
Lungren, Richard Willhelm 1910- *WhoWest 94*
Lungstrum, John W. 1945- *WhoAm 94, WhoAmL 94, WhoMW 93*
Luniewski, Allen William 1952- *WhoWest 94*
Lunin, Jesse 1918- *WhoScEn 94*
Lunin, Joseph 1940- *WhoAm 94*
Luning, Thomas P. 1942- *WhoAmL 94*
Lunkov, Nikolai Mitrofanovich 1919- *Who 94*
Lunn, Carolyn (Kowalczyk) 1960- *WrDr 94*
Lunn, David Ramsay *Who 94*
Lunn, Hugh Kingsmill 1889-1949 *DcNaB MP*
Lunn, Janet (Louise Swoboda) 1928- *WrDr 94*
Lunn, Janet Louise 1928- *BlmGWL*
Lunn, Jean *DrAPF 93*
Lunn, John Aleck 1894- *WhAm 10*
Lunn, (Louise) Kirkby 1873-1930 *NewGrDO*
Lunn, Peter Northcote 1914- *Who 94*
Lunney, Robert F. *WhoAm 94*
Lunny, William Francis 1938- *Who 94*
Luns, Joseph Marie Antoine Hubert 1911- *IntWW 93, Who 94*
Lunseth, John B., II 1949- *WhoAmL 94*
Lunsford, Beverly 1945- *WhoHol 92*
Lunsford, John (Crawford) 1933- *WhoAmA 93*
Lunsford, Julius Rodgers, Jr. 1915- *WhoAm 94, WhoAmL 94*
Lunsford, Lisa Michelle 1966- *WhoMW 93*
Lunsford, Lloyd Mitchell, Sr. 1922- *WhoAmL 94*
Lunsford, M. Rosser *DrAPF 93*
Lunsford, Marvin Carl 1947- *WhoFI 94*
Lunson, Lian *WhoHol 92*
Lunt, Alfred d1977 *WhoHol 92*
Lunt, Alfred David, Jr. 1893-1977 *AmCulL*
Lunt, Elizabeth Anne 1951- *WhoAmL 94*
Lunt, George (Gordon) 1943- *WrDr 94*
Lunt, Horace G(ray) 1918- *WrDr 94*
Lunt, Horace Gray 1918- *WhoAm 94*
Lunt, Jack 1944- *WhoAm 94*
Lunt, James Doiran 1917- *WrDr 94*
Lunt, James Dorian 1917- *Who 94*
Lunt, John C. 1939- *WhoFI 94*
Lunt, Larry Vernon 1943- *WhoAmP 93*
Lunt, Owen Raynal 1921- *WhoScEn 94*
Lunt, Ronald Geoffrey 1913- *Who 94*
Luntz, Irving 1929- *WhoAmA 93*
Luo, Hong Yue 1958- *WhoScEn 94*
Luo, Shen-Yi 1949- *WhoAsA 94*
Luo Anren *WhoPRCh 91*
Luo Bin Ji 1917- *IntWW 93, WhoPRCh 91*
Luo Busang *WhoPRCh 91*
Luo Daiyun *WhoPRCh 91*
Luo Dengyi 1906- *WhoPRCh 91 [port]*
Luo Gan 1935- *IntWW 93, WhoPRCh 91 [port]*
Luo Guanzong 1920- *WhoPRCh 91 [port]*
Luo Guibo 1908- *IntWW 93*
Luo Guibo 1911- *WhoPRCh 91*
Luo Hanxian 1922- *WhoPRCh 91 [port]*
Luo Haocai *WhoPRCh 91*
Luo-jia *WhoPRCh 91*
Luo Jibin *WhoPRCh 91*
Luo Jinghui *WhoPRCh 91*
Luo Jinxin 1930- *WhoPRCh 91 [port]*
Luo Kang *WhoPRCh 91*
Luo Keming 1920- *WhoPRCh 91 [port]*
Luo Lijia *WhoPRCh 91*
Luo Lipeng *WhoPRCh 91*
Luong, Son N. 1961- *WhoAsA 94*
Luongo, C. Paul 1930- *WhoAm 94*
Luongo, Stephen Earle 1947- *WhoAmL 94*
Luo Peilin *WhoPRCh 91*
Luo Pingan 1945- *IntWW 93*
Luo Qingchang 1918- *WhoPRCh 91 [port]*
Luo Qingquan *WhoPRCh 91*
Luo Qiong 1911- *WhoPRCh 91 [port]*
Luo Qiuyue 1921- *WhoPRCh 91 [port]*
Luo Sang *WhoPRCh 91*
Luo Shangcai 1929- *IntWW 93, WhoPRCh 91 [port]*
Luo Sheng'an *WhoPRCh 91*
Luo Shu 1903-1938 *BlmGWL*
Luo Shuzhen *WhoPRCh 91*
Luo Tian 1920- *IntWW 93, WhoPRCh 91 [port]*
Luo Tongda 1933- *WhoPRCh 91 [port]*
Luo Weilong *WhoPRCh 91*
Luo Xiaoge 1951- *WhoPRCh 91 [port]*
Luo Yang *WhoPRCh 91*
Luo Yuanzheng *WhoPRCh 91*
Luo Yuanzheng 1924- *IntWW 93*
Luo Yuntong *WhoPRCh 91*
Luo Yusheng *WhoPRCh 91*
Luo Zhengqi *WhoPRCh 91 [port]*
Luo Zhongli 1950- *WhoPRCh 91*
Lupack, Alan *DrAPF 93*
Lupash, Lawrence Ovidiu 1942- *WhoWest 94*
Lupberger, Edwin Adolph 1936- *WhoAm 94, WhoFI 94*
Lupe, John Edward, Jr. 1939- *WhoFI 94*
Lupe, Ronnie 1930- *WhoWest 94*
Lu Peijian 1928- *IntWW 93, WhoPRCh 91 [port]*
Lu Peixin *WhoPRCh 91*
Lupel, Warren 1942- *WhoAmL 94*
Luper, Clara M. 1923- *WhoBlA 94*
Luper, Frederick Morris 1940- *WhoAmL 94*
Lupert, Leslie Allan 1946- *WhoAmL 94*
Lupertz, Markus 1941- *IntWW 93*
Lupi, Roberto 1908-1971 *NewGrDO*
Lupi, Roldano d1989 *WhoHol 92*
Lupia, David Thomas 1950- *WhoFI 94*
Lupiani, Donald Anthony 1946- *WhoScEn 94*
Lupica, Michael Thomas *ConAu 142*
Lupica, Mike 1952- *ConAu 142*
Lupin, Ellis Ralph 1931- *WhoAm 94*
Lu Ping 1914- *WhoPRCh 91 [port]*
Lu Ping 1927- *IntWW 93*
Lu Ping 1929- *WhoPRCh 91 [port]*
Lu Ping 1948- *WhoPRCh 91*
Lupino, Barry d1962 *WhoHol 92*
Lupino, Constance d1959 *WhoHol 92*
Lupino, Ida 1914- *WhoHol 92*
Lupino, Ida 1918- *IntMPA 94*
Lupino, Mark d1930 *WhoHol 92*
Lupino, Richard *WhoHol 92*
Lupino, Rita *WhoHol 92*
Lupino, Stanley d1942 *WhoHol 92*
Lupino, Wallace d1961 *WhoHol 92*
Lupke, Duane Eugene 1930- *WhoMW 93*
Lupkin, Stanley Neil 1941- *WhoAmL 94*
Lupo, Alberto d1984 *WhoHol 92*
Lupo, Barbara Jane 1953- *WhoMW 93*
Lupo, George d1973 *WhoHol 92*
Lupo, Michael Vincent 1952- *WhoScEn 94*
Lupo, Raphael V. 1941- *WhoAmL 94*
Lupo, Robert Edward Smith 1953- *WhoFI 94*
Lupo, Samuel E. *WhoAmP 93*
Lupoff, Richard A(llen) 1935- *EncSF 93, WrDr 94*
Lupone, Patti 1949- *IntMPA 94, WhoAm 94, WhoHol 92*
Lu Pone, Robert *WhoHol 92*
Lupori, Peter John 1918- *WhoAmA 93*
Lupovitz, Sally 1930- *WhoAmP 93*
Lupp, Joerg Stefan 1955- *WhoAmL 94*
Lupper, Edward 1936- *WhoAmA 93*
Luppes, Steven John 1951- *WhoMW 93*
Luppi, Howard L. *WhoAmP 93*
Luppold, Chris Allen 1950- *WhoFI 94*
Lupro, Charles *WhoAmP 93*
Lupton, Ellen 1963- *WhoAm 94*
Lupton, John 1926- *WhoHol 92*
Lupton, John Mather, III 1947- *WhoAmP 93*
Lupton, Thomas 1918- *Who 94*
Lupu, Radu 1945- *IntWW 93, Who 94, WhoAm 94*
Lupulescu, Aurel Peter 1923- *WhoMW 93, WhoScEn 94*
Lupus, Peter 1937- *WhoHol 92*
Lu Qi *WhoPRCh 91*
Lu Qigang *WhoPRCh 91*
Lu Qihui 1936- *IntWW 93*
Lu Qikeng 1927- *IntWW 93*
Lu Qiutian *WhoPRCh 91*
Luquiens, Huc-Mazelet 1882-1961 *WhoAmA 93N*
Luquis, Glenda Karen 1965- *WhoAmL 94*
Luquis, Lavonne 1959- *WhoHisp 94*
Lura, Mick 1948- *WhoAmP 93*
Luraghi, Giuseppe 1905- *IntWW 93*
Luraschi, Luigi G. 1906- *IntMPA 94*
Luray, J. 1939- *WhoAmA 93*
Lurey, Alfred Saul 1942- *WhoAm 94, WhoAmL 94*
Lurey, Michael S. 1946- *WhoAmL 94*
Lurgan, Lester 1875-1949 *EncSF 93*
Luria, Gloria *WhoAmA 93*
Luria, Juan 1862-1943 *NewGrDO*
Luria, Mary Mercer 1942- *WhoAm 94*
Luria, Salvador (Edward) 1912-1991 *WrDr 94N*
Luria, Salvador Edward 1912-1991 *WhAm 10, WorScD [port]*
Luria, Zella Hurwitz 1924- *WhoAm 94*
Luria-Sukenick, Lynn *DrAPF 93*
Lurie, Alison *DrAPF 93*
Lurie, Alison 1926- *BlmGWL, IntWW 93, Who 94, WhoAm 94, WrDr 94*
Lurie, Alvin David 1923- *WhoAm 94*
Lurie, Boris 1924- *WhoAmA 93*
Lurie, Gerald B. 1944- *WhoAmL 94*
Lurie, Harold 1919- *WhoAm 94*
Lurie, John *WhoHol 92*
Lurie, Jonathan 1939- *WrDr 94*
Lurie, Jonathan Adam 1956- *WhoMW 93*
Lurie, Morris 1938- *WrDr 94*
Lurie, Paul Michael 1941- *WhoAm 94*
Lurie, Ranan Raymond 1932- *IntWW 93, WhoAm 94*
Lurie, Sheldon M. 1942- *WhoAmA 93*
Lurie, Toby *DrAPF 93*
Lurie, William L. 1931- *WhoAm 94*
Lurix, Paul Leslie, Jr. 1949- *WhoFI 94, WhoScEn 94*
Lu Rongjing 1933- *IntWW 93, WhoPRCh 91 [port]*
Lu Rongshu 1919- *WhoPRCh 91 [port]*
Lurton, H. William 1929- *WhoAm 94, WhoFI 94, WhoMW 93*
Lurton, Horace VanDeventer 1941- *WhoAm 94*
Lu Ruihua *WhoPRCh 91 [port]*
Lurvey, Ira Harold 1935- *WhoAmL 94, WhoWest 94*
Lurvey, Mildred Edwina 1927- *WhoAmP 93*
Lusaka, Paul John Firmino 1935- *IntWW 93*
Lusarreta, Pilar de 1914-1967 *BlmGWL*
Lusas, Edmund William 1931- *WhoScEn 94*
Lusby, John Martin 1943- *Who 94*
Lusch, Charles Jack 1936- *WhoScEn 94*
Luschei, Glenna *DrAPF 93*
Luscinski, Steven Michael 1951- *WhoAm 94*
Luscombe, David Edward 1938- *IntWW 93, Who 94*
Luscombe, George A., II 1944- *WhoAm 94*
Luscombe, Herbert Alfred 1916- *WhoAm 94*
Luscombe, Lawrence Edward 1924- *Who 94*
Luse, Keith *WhoAmP 93*
Lush, Christopher Duncan 1928- *Who 94*
Lush, George (Hermann) 1912- *Who 94*
Lush, George Hermann 1912- *IntWW 93*
Lush, Gerson Harrison 1912-1989 *WhAm 10*
Lush, Pamela Grace 1961- *WhoWest 94*
Lu Shaotang *WhoPRCh 91*
Lu Shaozeng *WhoPRCh 91*
Lu Shengdao 1936- *WhoPRCh 91 [port]*
Lu Shengzhong 1952- *IntWW 93*
Lushington, John (Richard Castleman) 1938- *Who 94*
Lu Shuiguang *WhoPRCh 91*
Lu Shuxiang 1904- *IntWW 93, WhoPRCh 91 [port]*
Lusic, Ronald R. 1947- *WhoFI 94*
Lusinchi, Jaime 1924- *IntWW 93*
Lusk, Daniel *DrAPF 93*
Lusk, Freeman d1970 *WhoHol 92*
Lusk, Harlan Gilbert 1943- *WhoAm 94*
Lusk, Harold F. 1893- *WhAm 10*
Lusk, Lisa Marie 1957- *WhoAmL 94*
Lusk, Nancy Lloyd 1946- *WhoMW 93*
Lusk, Patricia A. 1945- *WhoAmA 93*
Lusk, Robert Edward 1929- *WhoMW 93*
Lusk, Robert Neil 1958- *WhoMW 93*
Lusk, William Edward 1916- *WhoAm 94*
Lusker, Ron 1937- *WhoAmA 93*
Luskin, Bert L. 1911- *WhoAm 94*
Luskin, Robert David 1950- *WhoAmL 94*
Lusky, John A. 1951- *WhoAmL 94*
Lusky, Louis 1915- *WhoAm 94*
Luss, Dan 1938- *WhoAm 94*
Lussan, Marguerite de 1682-1758 *BlmGWL*
Lussan, Zelie de *NewGrDO*
Lussen, John Frederick 1942- *WhoAm 94*
Lusser, Markus 1931- *IntWW 93*
Lussi, Gustave d1993 *NewYTBS 93*
Lussier, Gaetan 1941- *WhoAm 94*
Lussier, Jacques 1941- *WhoAm 94*
Lussier, Jean-Paul 1917- *WhoAm 94*
Lussier, Martin P. 1920- *WhoAmP 93*
Lussier, Robert *WhoHol 92*
Lussu, Joyce Salvadori 1912- *BlmGWL*
Lust, Herbert Cohnfeldt, II 1926- *WhoFI 94*
Lust, Peter, Jr. 1960- *WhoWest 94*
Lust, Reimar 1923- *IntWW 93, Who 94*
Lust, Robert Maurice, Jr. 1955- *WhoScEn 94*
Lustbader, Eric *EncSF 93*
Lustbader, Eric Van 1946- *ConAu 42NR*
Lustbader, Monroe Jay *WhoAmP 93*
Lustbader, Philip Lawrence 1949- *WhoAm 94, WhoAmL 94*
Luste, Joseph Francis, Jr. 1940- *WhoFI 94*
Lusted, Lee Browning 1922- *WhoAm 94*
Lustenader, Barbara Diane 1953- *WhoMW 93*
Lustenberger, Louis Charles, Jr. 1936- *WhoAm 94*
Luster, George Orchard 1921- *WhoAm 94*
Luster, Jory *WhoBlA 94*
Luster, Martin A. 1942- *WhoAmP 93*
Lustgarten, Celia S. *DrAPF 93*
Lustgarten, Ira Howard 1929- *WhoAm 94*
Lustica, Katherine Grace 1958- *WhoWest 94*
Lustig, Arnost 1926- *ConWorW 93, IntWW 93*
Lustig, Edith Perkins 1929- *WhoMW 93*
Lustig, Harry 1925- *WhoAm 94*
Lustig, Joel Warren 1950- *WhoFI 94*
Lustig, Margaret Gallagher 1956- *WhoAmL 94*
Lustig, Stanley 1933- *WhoFI 94*
Lustiger, Jean-Marie 1926- *IntWW 93, Who 94*
Lusty, David 1961- *WhoFI 94*
Lusvardi, Anthony Amedeo 1958- *WhoAmL 94*
Lusztig, George 1946- *IntWW 93, Who 94*
Lusztig, Peter Alfred 1930- *WhoAm 94*
Lutali, A. P. 1919- *WhoAmP 93, WhoWest 94*
Lutcher, Nellie 1915- *WhoBlA 94*
Lute, Jack Anton 1935- *WhoWest 94*
Luten, Thomas Dee 1950- *WhoBlA 94*
Lutenski, Richard P. *WhoIns 94*
Luter, John 1919- *WhoAm 94, WhoWest 94*

Luter, Joseph Williamson, III 1940- *WhoAm 94, WhoFI 94*
Luter, Novella Marie 1939- *WhoMW 93*
Lutes, Dennis L. 1947- *WhoAmL 94*
Lutes, Donald Henry 1926- *WhoAm 94*
Lutes, Jim (James) 1955- *WhoAmA 93*
Lutes, Joseph Wycoff 1950- *WhoAm 94*
Lutfi, Aly *IntWW 93*
Lutgens, Harry Gerardus *WhoAm 94, WhoFI 94*
Luth, James Curtis 1961- *WhoFI 94*
Luther, Anna d1960 *WhoHol 92*
Luther, Arthur William 1919- *Who 94*
Luther, Darlene 1947- *WhoAmP 93*
Luther, David Byron 1936- *WhoAm 94*
Luther, David Gaston, Jr. 1951- *WhoAm 94, WhoAmL 94*
Luther, Frank d1980 *WhoHol 92*
Luther, George Aubrey 1933- *WhoAm 94, WhoMW 93*
Luther, James Howard 1928- *WhoAm 94*
Luther, Johnny d1960 *WhoHol 92*
Luther, Lester d1962 *WhoHol 92*
Luther, Lucius Calvin 1929- *WhoBlA 94*
Luther, M. Ida *WhoAmP 93*
Luther, Martin 1483-1546 *BlmGEL, EncEth, HisWorL [port]*
Luther, Nancy J. 1945- *WhoAmP 93*
Luther, Ray *EncSF 93*
Luther, Richard F. 1951- *WhoAmL 94*
Luther, Richard Wayne 1945- *WhoAmP 93*
Luther, Stephen O. 1949- *WhoAmP 93*
Luther, Susan Militzer *DrAPF 93*
Luther, William Lee 1952- *WhoFI 94*
Luther, William Paul 1945- *WhoAmP 93*
Luthey, Graydon Dean, Jr. 1955- *WhoAm 94, WhoAmL 94*
Luthi, Bruno *WhoScEn 94*
Luthringshauser, Daniel Rene 1935- *WhoAm 94*
Luthuli, Albert John 1898?-1967 *BlkWr 2*
Luthy, Chella *WhoHisp 94*
Luthy, Richard Godfrey 1945- *WhoAm 94, WhoScEn 94*
Luti, William Joseph 1953- *WhoWest 94*
Lutin, David Louis 1919- *WhoWest 94*
Lutin, Jerome Michael 1942- *WhoFI 94*
Lutins, Harvey Sidney 1928- *WhoAmL 94*
Lutjeharms, Joseph Earl 1933- *WhoAm 94*
Lutken, Hulda 1896-1947 *BlmGWL*
Lutkowski, Noel J. 1944- *WhoIns 94*
Lutkus, Gerald Francis 1952- *WhoAmL 94*
Lutley, John H. 1935- *WhoAm 94*
Lutnicki, Victor A. 1914-1988 *WhAm 10*
Luton, Jean-Marie 1942- *IntWW 93, WhoScEn 94*
Luton, John D. 1922- *WhoAmP 93*
Lutoslawski, Witold 1913- *IntWW 93, Who 94*
Lutringer, Richard Emil 1943- *WhoAm 94, WhoAmL 94*
Lutsep, Helmut 1927- *WhoMW 93*
Lutsk, Bruce Martin 1942- *WhoAmL 94*
Lutsky, Sheldon Jay 1943- *WhoFI 94*
Lutter, Alfred 1962- *WhoHol 92*
Lutter, Charles William, Jr. 1944- *WhoAmL 94*
Lutter, Marcus Michael 1930- *IntWW 93*
Lutter, Paul Allen 1946- *WhoAm 94, WhoAmL 94*
Lutterbach, Rogerio Alves 1958- *WhoScEn 94*
Luttier, Mark T. 1955- *WhoAmL 94*
Luttig, J. Michael *WhoAmP 93*
Luttig, J. Michael 1954- *WhoAm 94, WhoAmL 94*
Luttinen, Vilho Matti 1936- *IntWW 93*
Luttman, Horace Charles 1908- *WhoScEn 94*
Luttner, Edward F. 1942- *WhoMW 93*
Lutton, Robert Denton 1945- *WhoFI 94*
Luttrell, Allen William 1949- *WhoMW 93*
Luttrell, Dan Curtis 1952- *WhoWest 94*
Luttrell, Geoffrey Walter Fownes 1919- *Who 94*
Luttringer, Al d1953 *WhoHol 92*
Luttrull, Shirley JoAnn 1937- *WhoMW 93*
Luttwak, Edward (Nicolae) 1942- *WrDr 94*
Luttwak, Edward Nicolae 1942- *IntWW 93, WhoAm 94*
Lutu, Afoa Moega 1947- *WhoAmP 93*
Lutu, Fa'asuka S. *WhoAmP 93*
Lutvak, Mark Allen 1939- *WhoFI 94, WhoWest 94*
Lutwak, Leo 1928- *WhoAm 94*
Lutyens, (Agnes) Elisabeth 1906-1983 *NewGrDO*
Lutyens, Mary 1908- *Who 94, WrDr 94*
Lutz, Carl Freiheit 1934- *WhoAm 94*
Lutz, Carlene 1946- *WhoMW 93*
Lutz, Carol Lombard 1931- *WhoAmP 93*
Lutz, Christopher T. 1949- *WhoAmL 94*
Lutz, Dan S. 1906-1978 *WhoAmA 93N*
Lutz, Dennis Joseph 1947- *WhoMW 93*
Lutz, Edith Ledford 1914- *WhoAmP 93*
Lutz, Francis Charles 1944- *WhoAm 94*
Lutz, Hartwell Borden 1932- *WhoAm 94*
Lutz, Iri Karist 1934- *WhoAmP 93*
Lutz, James Gurney 1933- *WhoAmL 94*
Lutz, John (Thomas) 1939- *WrDr 94*
Lutz, John Shafroth 1943- *WhoAmL 94, WhoWest 94*
Lutz, Karl Evan 1949- *WhoAm 94, WhoAmL 94*
Lutz, L. Jack 1945- *WhoAmP 93*
Lutz, Larry Edward 1938- *WhoAmP 93*
Lutz, Marianne Christine 1922- *Who 94*
Lutz, Marjorie Brunhoff 1933- *WhoAmA 93*
Lutz, Matthew Charles 1934- *WhoAm 94*
Lutz, Michael Andrew 1948- *WhoMW 93*
Lutz, Oscar Joseph 1940- *WhoMW 93*
Lutz, Raymond Price 1935- *WhoAm 94*
Lutz, Robert A. 1932- *IntWW 93*
Lutz, Robert Anthony 1932- *WhoAm 94, WhoFI 94*
Lutz, Robert Brady, Jr. 1944- *WhoScEn 94*
Lutz, Thomas Philip 1947- *WhoAm 94, WhoAmL 94*
Lutz, William Andrew 1944- *WhoAm 94, WhoFI 94*
Lutz, William Lan 1944- *WhoAm 94*
Lutz, William Ralph 1963- *WhoWest 94*
Lutz, Winifred Ann 1942- *WhoAmA 93*
Lutze, Peter Michael 1944- *WhoFI 94*
Lutze, Ruth Louise 1917- *WhoFI 94*
Lutze, Tamara Jean 1969- *WhoMW 93*
Lutzer, David John 1943- *WhoAm 94*
Lutzke, Arthur Saul 1945- *WhoAm 94, WhoFI 94*
Lutzker, Arnold Paul 1947- *WhoAm 94, WhoAmL 94*
Lutzker, Elliot Howard 1953- *WhoAmL 94*
Luu, Jane *WhoScEn 94*
Luu, Lang Van 1935- *WhoAsA 94*
Luus, George Aarne 1937- *WhoMW 93*
Luvaas, William *DrAPF 93*
Luvisi, Lee 1937- *WhoAm 94*
Luvsangombo, Sonomyn 1924- *IntWW 93*
Lu Wei 1966- *WhoPRCh 91 [port]*
Lu Wenfu 1928- *IntWW 93, WhoPRCh 91 [port]*
Lu Wenxiong *WhoPRCh 91*
Lux, Gene 1926- *WhoAmP 93*
Lux, Gladys M. 1899- *WhoAmA 93*
Lux, Guillermo 1938- *WhoHisp 94*
Lux, Jimmy 1952- *WrDr 94*
Lux, John H. 1918- *WhoAm 94, WhoFI 94*
Lux, Josef 1956- *IntWW 93*
Lux, Kathleen Mary 1953- *WhoMW 93*
Lux, Lawrence Rowe 1959- *WhoMW 93*
Lux, Thomas *DrAPF 93*
Luxembourg, Grand Duke of *IntWW 93*
Luxemburg, Jack Alan 1949- *WhoAm 94*
Luxemburg, Rosa 1870-1919 *BlmGWL*
Luxemburg, Rosa 1871-1919 *HisWorL [port]*
Luxemburg, Wilhelmus Anthonius Josephus 1929- *WhoAm 94*
Luxen, Andre Jules Marie 1954- *WhoScEn 94*
Luxenberg, Malcolm Neuwahl 1935- *WhoAm 94*
Luxenberg, Michael Don 1945- *WhoWest 94*
Luxford, Nola *WhoHol 92*
Lu Xianlin *WhoPRCh 91*
LuXin'er 1949- *BlmGWL*
Lu Xinhua 1953- *WhoPRCh 91 [port]*
Luxmoore, Christopher Charles 1926- *Who 94*
Luxmoore, Robert John 1940- *WhoAm 94*
Luxon, Benjamin 1937- *NewGrDO*
Luxon, Benjamin Matthew 1937- *IntWW 93, Who 94*
Luxon, Norval Nell 1899-1989 *WhAm 10*
Lu Xuejian 1928- *WhoPRCh 91 [port]*
Lu Xueyi *WhoPRCh 91*
Lu Xun 1881-1936 *RfGShF*
Lu Xusheng 1931- *WhoPRCh 91 [port]*
Lu Xuzhang 1911- *WhoPRCh 91 [port]*
Lu Yanhao 1913- *WhoPRCh 91 [port]*
Lu Yanshao 1909- *IntWW 93, WhoPRCh 91 [port]*
Lu Yansun *WhoPRCh 91*
Lu Yanzhou 1928- *WhoPRCh 91 [port]*
Lu Yao 1949- *WhoPRCh 91 [port]*
Luye, Li *WhoAm 94*
Luyendyk, Bruce Peter 1943- *WhoAm 94, WhoScEn 94*
Lu Yin 1899-1934 *BlmGWL*
Lu Yongji 1951- *WhoPRCh 91 [port]*
Lu Yongsheng *WhoPRCh 91*
Lu Yongxiang 1942- *IntWW 93, WhoPRCh 91 [port]*
Lu Youmei 1934- *WhoPRCh 91 [port]*
Luyt, Richard (Edmonds) 1915- *Who 94*
Luyt, Richard Edmonds 1915- *IntWW 93*
Lu Yuan 1922- *WhoPRCh 91 [port]*
Lu Yuanjiu *WhoPRCh 91*
Lu Yucheng 1939- *WhoPRCh 91 [port]*
Lu Yuyi *WhoPRCh 91*
Luz, Franc *WhoHol 92*
Luz, Virginia 1911- *WhoAmA 93*
Luza, Radomir, Jr. *DrAPF 93*
Luza, Radomir Vaclav 1922- *WhoAm 94*
Luzbetak, Louis J(oseph) 1918- *WrDr 94*
Luzerne, Anne-Cesar 1741-1791 *AmRev*
Luzerne, Anne-Cesar de la c. 1743- *WhAmRev*
Lu Zhenfan 1919- *WhoPRCh 91 [port]*
Lu Zhichao 1933- *WhoPRCh 91 [port]*
Lu Zhijun *WhoPRCh 91*
Lu Zhixian *WhoPRCh 91*
Luzhkov, Yuri Mikhailovich 1936- *IntWW 93*
Luzhkov, Yury Mikhailovich 1936- *LngBDD*
Lu Zhonghe 1940- *WhoPRCh 91 [port]*
Luzi, Mario 1914- *ConWorW 93*
Luzkow, Jack Lawrence 1941- *WhoMW 93*
Lu Zongqing *WhoPRCh 91*
Luzovich, Steven Albert 1960- *WhoWest 94*
Luzzatto, Edgar 1914- *WhoAmL 94*
Luzzatto, Lucio 1936- *Who 94*
Luzzo, Francesco *NewGrDO*
L'vov, Alexey Fyodorovich 1798-1870 *NewGrDO*
L'vov, Nikolay Alexandrovich 1751-1803? *NewGrDO*
Lwin, U. 1912- *IntWW 93*
Lwoff, Andre Michael *WorScD*
Lwoff, Andre Michael 1902- *Who 94*
Lwoff, Andre Michel 1902- *IntWW 93, WhoAm 94, WhoScEn 94*
Ly, Kieu Kim 1965- *WhoAsA 94*
Ly, Tam Minh 1961- *WhoAsA 94*
Lyakhov, Vladimir Afanasyevich 1941- *IntWW 93*
Lyall, Andrew Gardiner 1929- *Who 94*
Lyall, Edna 1857-1903 *BlmGWL*
Lyall, Gavin (Tudor) 1932- *WrDr 94*
Lyall, Gavin Tudor 1932- *Who 94*
Lyall, Katharine Culbert 1941- *WhoAm 94, WhoMW 93*
Lyall, Katharine Elizabeth *Who 94*
Lyall, Michael Rodney 1945- *WhoFI 94*
Lyall, Tony Allen 1949- *WhoIns 94*
Lyall, William Chalmers 1921- *Who 94*
Lyall Grant, Ian Hallam 1915- *Who 94*
Lyandres, Yulian Semenovich 1931-1993 *ConAu 142*
Lyashenko, Vladimir Efimovich 1937- *LngBDD*
Lyatoshyns'ky, Borys Mykolayovych 1894?-1968 *NewGrDO*
Lybarger, John Steven 1956- *WhoWest 94*
Lybarger, Marjorie Kathryn 1956- *WhoWest 94*
Lybeck, Ray 1926- *WhoAmP 93*
Lybecker, Martin Earl 1945- *WhoAm 94, WhoAmL 94*
Lyberopoulos, Athanasios Nikolaos 1959- *WhoScEn 94*
Lybyer, Michael J. 1947- *WhoAmP 93*
Lycan, Gilbert L(ester) 1909- *WrDr 94*
Lycos, Tom *WhoHol 92*
Lycurgus fl. 9th cent.?BC- *BlmGEL*
Lyda, Wesley John 1914- *WhoBlA 94*
Lyday, John Russell 1954- *WhoMW 93*
Lyddon, (William) Derek (Collier) 1925- *Who 94*
Lydecken, Arvid *EncSF 93*
Lydecker, John *EncSF 93*
Lyden, Fremont James 1926- *WhoAm 94, WrDr 94*
Lyden, Pierce *WhoHol 92*
Lyder, Courtney Harvey 1966- *WhoMW 93*
Lydgate c. 1370-1449? *BlmGEL [port]*
Lydick, Lawrence Tupper 1916- *WhoAm 94, WhoAmL 94, WhoWest 94*
Lyding, Joseph William 1954- *WhoScEn 94*
Lydolph, Paul Edward 1924- *WhoAm 94, WrDr 94*
Lydon, James 1923- *IntMPA 94*
Lydon, Jimmy 1923- *WhoHol 92*
Lydon, John *WhoHol 92*
Lydon, Maria-Liisa 1943- *WhoAmL 94*
Lydon, Thomas J. 1927- *CngDr 93, WhoAmL 94*
Lye, Len 1901-1980 *IntDcF 2-4*
Lye, Len 1901-1981 *WhoAmA 93N*
Lye, Reg *WhoHol 92*
Lye, William Frank 1930- *WhoWest 94*
Lyel, Viola d1972 *WhoHol 92*
Lyell, Baron 1939- *Who 94*
Lyell, Charles 1797-1875 *BlmGEL, WorScD*
Lyell, Lottie d1925 *WhoHol 92*
Lyell, Nicholas (Walter) 1938- *IntWW 93, Who 94*
Lyells, Ruby E. Stutts *WhoBlA 94*
Lyerla, Bradford Peter 1954- *WhoAmL 94*
Lyford, Cabot 1925- *WhoAm 94, WhoAmA 93*
Lyford, Frederic E(ugene) 1895- *WhAm 10*
Lyford, Joseph Philip 1918-1992 *ConAu 140, WhAm 10*
Lygo, Raymond (Derek) 1924- *Who 94*
Lygo, Raymond Derek 1924- *IntWW 93*
Lyke, James P. 1939-1992 *WhoBlA 94N*
Lykes, Joseph T., III 1948- *WhoAm 94*
Lykiard, Alexis 1940- *WrDr 94*
Lykins, Gary D. 1961- *WhoAmL 94*
Lykins, Jay Arnold 1947- *WhoFI 94, WhoWest 94*
Lykins, Marshall Herbert 1944- *WhoAm 94*
Lykos, Peter George 1927- *WhoAm 94*
Lykoudis, Paul S. 1926- *WhoAm 94*
Lyle, Alexander Walter Barr 1958- *Who 94*
Lyle, Charles Thomas 1946- *WhoAm 94, WhoAmA 93*
Lyle, Clinton d1950 *WhoHol 92*
Lyle, Freddrenna M. 1951- *WhoBlA 94*
Lyle, Gavin Archibald 1941- *Who 94*
Lyle, Glenda Swanson *WhoAmP 93*
Lyle, James Arthur 1945- *WhoFI 94*
Lyle, John Tillman 1934- *WhoAm 94*
Lyle, John William, Jr. 1950- *WhoAmP 93*
Lyle, K. Curtis *DrAPF 93*
Lyle, Katie Letcher *DrAPF 93*
Lyle, Katie Letcher 1938- *TwCYAW*
Lyle, Leon Richards 1941- *WhoMW 93*
Lyle, Lyston d1920 *WhoHol 92*
Lyle, Mary Kay 1943- *WhoMW 93*
Lyle, Mary Stewart 1897- *WhAm 10*
Lyle, Michael *Who 94*
Lyle, (Archibald) Michael 1919- *Who 94*
Lyle, Percy H., Jr. 1937- *WhoBlA 94*
Lyle, Robert Edward 1926- *WhoAm 94, WhoScEn 94*
Lyle, Roberta Branche Blacke 1929- *WhoBlA 94*
Lyle, Ron 1943- *WhoBlA 94*
Lyle, Sandy *Who 94*
Lyles, A. C. 1918- *IntMPA 94*
Lyles, Anna Marie 1961- *WhoScEn 94*
Lyles, Aubrey d1932 *WhoHol 92*
Lyles, Aubrey 1884-1932 *See* Miller and Lyles *WhoCom*
Lyles, Carol Yvette 1954- *WhoMW 93*
Lyles, Dewayne 1947- *WhoBlA 94*
Lyles, Jean Elizabeth Caffey 1942- *WhoMW 93*
Lyles, John 1929- *Who 94*
Lyles, Leonard E. 1936- *WhoBlA 94*
Lyles, Lester Everett 1962- *WhoBlA 94*
Lyles, Lester L. 1946- *AfrAmG [port]*
Lyles, Lester Lawrence 1946- *WhoBlA 94*
Lyles, Madeline Lolita 1953- *WhoBlA 94*
Lyles, Marie Clark 1952- *WhoBlA 94*
Lyles, Roy E. 1923- *WhoAmP 93*
Lyles, Tracee *WhoHol 92*
Lyles, William K. *WhoBlA 94*
Lyly, John 1554-1606 *BlmGEL, IntDcT 2*
Lyman, Abe d1957 *WhoHol 92*
Lyman, Arthur Joseph 1953- *WhoAm 94, WhoMW 93*
Lyman, Beverly Ann 1956- *WhoScEn 94*
Lyman, Charles Edson 1946- *WhoScEn 94*
Lyman, Charles Peirson 1912- *WhoAm 94*
Lyman, Curtis Lee, Jr. 1952- *WhoAmL 94*
Lyman, David 1936- *WhoAm 94, WhoFI 94*
Lyman, Frederic A. 1934- *WhoAm 94*
Lyman, Henry 1915- *WhoAm 94*
Lyman, Howard Burbeck 1920- *WhoMW 93, WhoScEn 94*
Lyman, John d1967 *WhoAmA 93N*
Lyman, John 1921- *WhoAm 94*
Lyman, John Root 1939- *WhoAm 94*
Lyman, L. *WhoAmP 93*
Lyman, Mary Redington Ely 1887-1975 *DcAmReB 2*
Lyman, Nathan Marquis 1955- *WhoAmL 94*
Lyman, Peggy 1950- *WhoAm 94*
Lyman, Princeton Nathan 1935- *WhoAm 94, WhoAmP 93*
Lyman, Richard R. 1954- *WhoAm 94*
Lyman, Richard Wall 1923- *WhoAm 94*
Lyman, Ronald Theodore, Jr. 1905-1990 *WhAm 10*
Lyman, Thomas William 1926- *WhoAmA 93*
Lyman, Webster S. 1922- *WhoBlA 94*
Lyman, William *WhoHol 92*
Lyman, William Chester, Jr. 1921- *WhoFI 94*
Lyman, William Roy d1972 *ProFbHF*
Lyman, William W., Jr. 1916- *WhoAm 94*
Lymberaki, Margarita 1910- *BlmGWL*
Lymberis, Costas Triantafillos 1944- *WhoScEn 94*
Lymbery, Robert Davison 1920- *Who 94*
Lymington, Viscount 1981- *Who 94*
Lymington, John 1911-1983 *EncSF 93*
Lymon, Frankie d1968 *WhoHol 92*

Lyon, Keith Anthony 1952- *WhoFI 94*
Lyon, Lyman R. *EncSF 93*
Lyon, Mark Andrew 1953- *WhoWest 94*
Lyon, Mark Christopher 1961- *WhoFI 94*
Lyon, Mary 1797-1849 *AmSocL [port], HisWorL [port]*
Lyon, Mary Frances 1925- *IntWW 93, Who 94*
Lyon, Matthew 1750-1822 *WhAmRev*
Lyon, Maud Margaret 1954- *WhoAm 94, WhoMW 93*
Lyon, Maurice Cleverly 1926- *WhoWest 94*
Lyon, Nancy S. 1951- *WhoAmP 93*
Lyon, Philip Kirkland 1944- *WhoAm 94, WhoAmL 94, WhoFI 94*
Lyon, Phyllis Ann 1924- *GayLL*
Lyon, Priscilla d1980 *WhoHol 92*
Lyon, Quinter M(arcellus) 1898- *WhAm 10*
Lyon, Richard 1923- *WhoAm 94, WhoWest 94*
Lyon, Richard 1934- *WhoHol 92*
Lyon, Richard E., Jr. 1943- *WhoAmL 94*
Lyon, Richard Harold 1929- *WhoAm 94, WhoScEn 94*
Lyon, Richard K. *EncSF 93*
Lyon, Rick *DrAPF 93*
Lyon, Robert 1923- *Who 94*
Lyon, Robert Charles 1953- *WhoAmL 94*
Lyon, Robert F. 1952- *WhoAmA 94*
Lyon, Roger Wayne 1958- *WhoScEn 94*
Lyon, Ronald Edward 1936- *WhoFI 94*
Lyon, Sherman Orwig 1939- *WhoAm 94*
Lyon, Sterling Rufus 1927- *WhoAm 94*
Lyon, Sterling Rufus Webster 1927- *IntWW 93, Who 94*
Lyon, Steve 1961- *WhoHol 92*
Lyon, Stewart *Who 94*
Lyon, (Colin) Stewart (Sinclair) 1926- *Who 94*
Lyon, Sue 1946- *IntMPA 94, WhoHol 92*
Lyon, Ted B., Jr. 1948- *WhoAmP 93*
Lyon, Therese d1975 *WhoHol 92*
Lyon, Waldo Kampmeier 1914- *WhoAm 94*
Lyon, Wayne Barton 1932- *WhoAm 94, WhoFI 94, WhoMW 93*
Lyon, Wilford Charles, Jr. 1935- *WhoAm 94, WhoFI 94*
Lyon, William Carl 1938- *WhoAm 94*
Lyon-Dalberg-Acton *Who 94*
Lyons, A. Bates 1944- *WhoBlA 94*
Lyons, Arthur 1946- *WrDr 94*
Lyons, Arthur Edward 1931- *WhoWest 94*
Lyons, Beauvais 1958- *WhoAmA 93*
Lyons, Bernard 1913- *IntWW 93, Who 94*
Lyons, Brian Wesley 1950- *WhoMW 93*
Lyons, Bruce *WhoHol 92*
Lyons, Bruce M. *WhoAmL 94*
Lyons, Candy d1966 *WhoHol 92*
Lyons, Champ, Jr. 1940- *WhoAm 94*
Lyons, Charles A., Jr. 1926- *WhoBlA 94*
Lyons, Charles Albert 1929- *Who 94*
Lyons, Charles H. S., Jr. 1917- *WhoBlA 94*
Lyons, Charles Michael 1943- *WhoAmP 93*
Lyons, Charles R. 1933- *WhoAm 94*
Lyons, Chopeta C. *DrAPF 93*
Lyons, Christine 1943- *WrDr 94*
Lyons, Cliff d1974 *WhoHol 92*
Lyons, Clifford Pierson 1904-1992 *WhAm 10*
Lyons, Collette d1986 *WhoHol 92*
Lyons, David (Barry) 1935- *WrDr 94*
Lyons, David Barry 1935- *WhoAm 94*
Lyons, Delphine C. *EncSF 93*
Lyons, Dennis Gerald 1931- *WhoAm 94*
Lyons, Dennis John 1916- *Who 94*
Lyons, Donald Wallace 1945- *WhoBlA 94*
Lyons, Dorothy Marawee 1907- *WrDr 94*
Lyons, Earle Vaughan, Jr. 1917- *WhoAm 94*
Lyons, Eddie d1926 *WhoHol 92*
Lyons, Edward 1926- *Who 94*
Lyons, Edward Houghton *Who 94*
Lyons, Edward P. *WhoAmP 93*
Lyons, Elena 1928- *WrDr 94*
Lyons, Ellis 1915- *WhoAm 94*
Lyons, Francis E., Jr. 1943- *WhoAmA 93*
Lyons, Fred d1921 *WhoHol 92*
Lyons, Gene d1974 *WhoHol 92*
Lyons, Gene Martin 1924- *WhoAm 94*
Lyons, George Harris 1947- *WhoAmL 94*
Lyons, George Sage 1936- *WhoAm 94, WhoAmL 94*
Lyons, George W. C., Sr. 1923- *WhoBlA 94*
Lyons, Grant *DrAPF 93*
Lyons, H. Agar 1878- *WhoHol 92*
Lyons, Harry d1919 *WhoHol 92*
Lyons, (Isidore) Jack 1916- *Who 94*
Lyons, James (Reginald) 1910- *Who 94*
Lyons, James E., Sr. *WhoBlA 94*
Lyons, James Edward 1952- *WhoAm 94*
Lyons, James Elliott 1951- *WhoAm 94*
Lyons, James M. 1947- *WhoAmL 94*
Lyons, James Robert *WhoAm 94*

Lyons, Jeffrey *WhoAm 94*
Lyons, Jerry Lee 1939- *WhoAm 94, WhoMW 93, WhoScEn 94*
Lyons, Joan 1937- *WhoAmA 93*
Lyons, John 1926- *Who 94*
Lyons, John 1932- *IntWW 93, Who 94, WrDr 94*
Lyons, John David 1946- *WhoAm 94*
Lyons, John F. 1944- *WhoAmL 94*
Lyons, John Francis 1960- *WhoAmL 94*
Lyons, John Hempstead 1944- *WhoFI 94*
Lyons, John J. 1951- *WhoAmL 94*
Lyons, John Matthew 1948- *WhoFI 94*
Lyons, John Ormsby 1927- *WhoAm 94*
Lyons, John Rolland 1909- *WhoAm 94, WhoMW 93, WhoScEn 94*
Lyons, John Winship 1930- *WhoAm 94, WhoAmP 93*
Lyons, Joseph Chisholm 1927- *WhoAm 94*
Lyons, Joseph Nathaniel 1847-1917 *DcNaB MP*
Lyons, Kevin W. 1956- *WhoAmL 94*
Lyons, Laura Brown 1942- *WhoBlA 94*
Lyons, Laurence 1911- *WhoAm 94*
Lyons, Lawrence Ernest 1922- *IntWW 93*
Lyons, Lisa 1950- *WhoAmA 93*
Lyons, Lloyd Carson 1942- *WhoBlA 94*
Lyons, Malcolm Cameron 1929- *Who 94*
Lyons, Malcolm L. 1941- *WhoAmL 94*
Lyons, Michael Thomas 1949- *Who 94*
Lyons, Moira K. *WhoAmP 93*
Lyons, Nance 1943- *WhoAmL 94*
Lyons, Nick 1932- *WrDr 94*
Lyons, Patrice Ann 1942- *WhoAmL 94*
Lyons, Patricia M. 1947- *WhoAmP 93*
Lyons, Patrick H. *WhoAmP 93*
Lyons, Patrick Joseph 1943- *WhoScEn 94*
Lyons, Paul Michael 1932- *WhoAm 94*
Lyons, Paul Vincent 1939- *WhoAm 94, WhoAmL 94*
Lyons, Phillip Michael, Sr. 1941- *WhoFI 94*
Lyons, Richard *DrAPF 93*
Lyons, Richard Chapman 1919- *WhoAm 94*
Lyons, Richard Joseph 1923-1989 *WhAm 10*
Lyons, Robert F. 1940- *WhoHol 92*
Lyons, Robert John 1954- *WhoIns 94*
Lyons, Robert P. 1912- *WhoBlA 94*
Lyons, Roger Alan 1942- *Who 94*
Lyons, Sara Marion 1932- *WhoAmP 93*
Lyons, Shaun 1942- *Who 94*
Lyons, Stuart 1928- *IntMPA 94*
Lyons, Stuart Randolph 1943- *Who 94*
Lyons, Susan *WhoHol 92*
Lyons, Tex *WhoHol 92*
Lyons, Thomas G. 1931- *WhoAmP 93*
Lyons, Thomas Nicholas 1949- *WhoAm 94*
Lyons, Thomas Tolman 1934- *WrDr 94*
Lyons, Tommy Joe 1952 *WhoFI 94*
Lyons, Virginia 1932- *WhoAmP 93*
Lyons, W. T 1919- *WrDr 94*
Lyons, William Harry 1947- *WhoAmL 94*
Lyons Terhes, Joyce 1940- *WhoWomW 91*
Lyra, Carmen 1888-1951 *BlmGWL*
Lys, Lya d1986 *WhoHol 92*
Lysaght *Who 94*
Lysaught, Jerome P 1930- *WrDr 94*
Lysaught, Patrick 1949- *WhoAm 94*
Lysaught, Thomas Francis 1936- *WhoFI 94*
Lysen, King *WhoAmP 93*
Lysenko, Mykola Vitaliyovych 1842-1912 *NewGrDO*
Lysenko, Romelle Holmgren 1961- *WhoFI 94*
Lysenko, Vera 1910-1975 *BlmGWL*
Lyson, Hal Curtis 1953- *WhoFI 94, WhoMW 93*
Lysons, Sam d1953 *WhoHol 92*
Lyssarides, Vassos 1920- *IntWW 93*
Lyssiotis, Tes *ConDr 93*
Lystad, Mary Hanemann 1928- *WhoAm 94*
Lystad, Robert Arthur Lunde 1920- *WhoAm 94*
Lyster, W(illiam) S(aurin) 1827-1880 *NewGrDO*
Lysun, Gregory 1924- *WhoAmA 93*
Lysyk, Kenneth Martin 1934- *IntWW 93, WhoAm 94*
Lytel, Elaine G. 1923- *WhoAmP 93*
Lytell, Bert d1954 *WhoHol 92*
Lytell, Jimmy d1972 *WhoHol 92*
Lytell, Wilfred d1954 *WhoHol 92*
Lyter, John Bowman 1953- *WhoMW 93*
Lytess, Natasha *WhoHol 92*
Lythall, Basil Wilfrid 1920- *Who 94*
Lythcott, Janice Logue 1950- *WhoBlA 94*
Lythe, Robert fl. 1556-1574 *DcNaB MP*
Lythgo, Wilbur Reginald 1920- *Who 94*
Lythgoe, Basil 1913- *IntWW 93, Who 94*
Lythgoe, Ian Gordon 1914- *Who 94*
Lytle, Alice A. *WhoBlA 94*

Lytle, Andrew *DrAPF 93*
Lytle, Andrew (Nelson) 1902- *WrDr 94*
Lytle, Andrew Nelson 1902- *WhoAm 94*
Lytle, John Arden 1949- *WhoScEn 94*
Lytle, Marilyn Mercedes 1948- *WhoBlA 94*
Lytle, Markt L. *WhoAmP 93*
Lytle, Richard 1935- *WhoAmA 93*
Lytle, Richard Harold 1937- *WhoAm 94*
Lytle, Simon William St. John 1940- *Who 94*
Lytle, Victoria Elizabeth 1951- *WhoAm 94*
Lytle, William F. 1932- *WhoAmP 93*
Lyttelton *Who 94*
Lyttelton, George 1709-1773 *BlmGEL*
Lyttelton, Humphrey Richard Adeane 1921- *IntWW 93, Who 94*
Lyttle, Douglas Alfred 1919- *WhoAm 94*
Lyttle, James Brian Chambers 1932- *Who 94*
Lyttle, Ross Orville 1932- *WhoWest 94*
Lyttleton, Edith 1874-1945 *BlmGWL*
Lyttleton, Raymond Arthur 1911- *IntWW 93, Who 94*
Lytton, Baron 1803-1873 *EncSF 93*
Lytton, Earl of 1950- *Who 94*
Lytton, Lady d1947 *WhoHol 92*
Lytton, Bart d1969 *WhoAmA 93N*
Lytton, Constance B. *WhoAmA 93*
Lytton, Constance Georgina 1869-1923 *DcNaB MP*
Lytton, Doris d1953 *WhoHol 92*
Lytton, Edward George Earle Lytton Bulwer- 1803-1873 *BlmGEL*
Lytton, H(enry) A(lbert) 1865-1936 *NewGrDO*
Lytton, Herbert d1981 *WhoHol 92*
Lytton, Robert Leonard 1937- *WhoAm 94, WhoScEn 94*
Lytton, Rogers d1924 *WhoHol 92*
Lytton Cobbold *Who 94*
Lytvynenko-Vol'hemut, Mariya (Ivanovna) 1892-1966 *NewGrDO*
Lyubavina, Olga Samuilovna 1945- *WhoScEn 94*
Lyubimov, Yuriy Petrovich 1917- *IntWW 93*
Lyubimov, Yury (Petrovich) 1917- *NewGrDO*
Lyublinskaya, Irina E. 1963- *WhoScEn 94*
Lyubshin, Stanislav Andreyevich 1933- *IntWW 93*
Lyveden, Baron 1915- *Who 94*
Lyvenden, Lord d1926 *WhoHol 92*

M

Ma, Alan King-Yan 1966- *WhoAsA 94*
Ma, Chen-Lung Ringo 1952- *WhoAsA 94*
Ma, Ching-To Albert 1960- *WhoAsA 94*
Ma, Chueng-Shyang 1922- *WhoScEn 94*
Ma, Cindy Waisze 1962- *WhoFI 94*
Ma, David I 1952- *WhoScEn 94*
Ma, Fai 1954- *WhoAsA 94*
Ma, Fengchow Clarence 1919- *WhoFI 94,
  WhoScEn 94, WhoWest 94*
Ma, Jeanetta Ping Chan 1952-
  WhoScEn 94
Ma, Laurence J. C. 1937- *WhoAsA 94*
Ma, Li-Chen 1941- *WhoAsA 94*
Ma, Mark T. 1933- *WhoAsA 94*
Ma, Mark Tsu-han 1933- *WhoAm 94*
Ma, Michael 1955- *WhoAsA 94*
Ma, Shau Ping Alice 1947- *WhoMW 93*
Ma, Sheng-mei 1958- *WhoAsA 94*
Ma, Stephen K. 1945- *WhoAsA 94*
Ma, Tai-Loi 1945- *WhoAsA 94*
Ma, Tony Yong 1955- *WhoScEn 94*
Ma, Tso-Ping 1945- *WhoAsA 94*
Ma, Tsu Sheng 1911- *WhoAsA 94,
  WhoScEn 94*
Ma, Wen 1961- *WhoMW 93*
Ma, Wenhai 1954- *WhoAsA 94*
Ma, Xiaoyun 1945- *WhoAsA 94*
Ma, Yan 1957- *WhoAsA 94*
Ma, Yi Hua 1936- *WhoAsA 94*
Ma, Yinfa 1955- *WhoMW 93*
Ma, Yo Yo *WhoAm 94*
Ma, Yo Yo 1955- *IntWW 93, WhoAsA 94*
Ma, Yuan Yuan 1952- *WhoFI 94*
Ma, Yuzhen 1934- *Who 94*
Ma, Zuguang 1928- *WhoScEn 94*
Maack, Robert Donald 1939-
  WhoAmL 94
Maag, Peter 1919- *IntWW 93*
Maag, (Ernst) Peter (Johannes) 1919-
  NewGrDO
Maag, Urs Richard 1938- *WhoAm 94*
Maahs, Kenneth Henry, Sr. 1940-
  WhoAm 94
Maan 1934- *WrDr 94*
Maan, Bashir Ahmed 1926- *Who 94*
Maarbjerg, Mary Penzold 1943-
  WhoAm 94
Maas, Duane Harris 1927- *WhoAm 94*
Maas, Ernest H. 1956- *WhoMW 93*
Maas, Gloria Theresa 1953- *WhoMW 93*
Maas, Ivan G. 1959- *WhoMW 93*
Maas, James Beryl 1938- *WhoAm 94*
Maas, James Weldon 1929- *WhoAm 94*
Maas, Jane Brown *WhoAm 94*
Maas, Joe *WhoAm 94*
Maas, Joseph 1847-1886 *NewGrDO*
Maas, Marion Elizabeth 1930-
  WhoAmA 93
Maas, Peter 1929- *WhoAm 94, WrDr 94*
Maas, Werner Karl 1921- *WhoAm 94*
Maasoumi, Esfandiar 1950- *WhoScEn 94*
Maass, Arthur 1917- *WhoAm 94*
Maass, Brenda Joyce 1939- *WhoMW 93*
Maass, R. Andrew 1946- *WhoAm 94*
Maass, Richard Andrew 1946-
  WhoAmA 93
Maassen, Johannes Antonie 1945-
  WhoScEn 94
Maass-Moreno, Roberto 1952-
  WhoMW 93
Maat, Benjamin 1947- *WhoScEn 94*
Maathai, Wangari *IntWW 93*
Maathai, Wangari 1940- *CurBio 93 [port]*

Maatman, Gerald L. 1930- *WhoIns 94*
Maatman, Gerald Leonard 1930-
  WhoAm 94, WhoFI 94
Maazel, Lorin 1930- *IntWW 93, Who 94,
  WhoAm 94*
Maazel, Lorin (Varencove) 1930-
  NewGrDO
Mabbett, Ian William 1939- *WrDr 94*
Mabbott, Gilbert c. 1622-1670 *DcNaB MP*
Mabbs, Alfred Walter 1921- *WhoAm 94*
Mabbs, Edward Carl 1921- *WhoAm 94*
Mabe, Hugh Prescott, III 1945-
  WhoAmL 94
Mabe, Manabu 1924- *IntWW 93*
Mabee, Carleton 1914- *WhoAm 94,
  WrDr 94*
Mabee, Sandra Ivonne 1955- *WhoWest 94*
Mabellini, Teodulo 1817-1897 *NewGrDO*
Maben, Hayward C., Jr. 1922- *WhoBlA 94*
Mabey, Judith *WhoHol 92*
Mabey, Ralph R. 1944- *WhoAm 94,
  WhoAmL 94*
Mabey, Richard Thomas 1941- *Who 94,
  WrDr 94*
Mabin, Joseph E. *WhoBlA 94*
Ma Bingchen 1928- *WhoPRCh 91 [port]*
Mabley, Jack 1915- *WhoAm 94*
Mabley, Jackie d1975 *WhoHol 92*
Mabley, Jackie 1897-1975 *AfrAmAl 6*
Mabley, John D. 1947- *WhoAmL 94*
Mabley, Moms 1894-1975 *WhoCom*
Mabli, Charles E. 1941- *WhoIns 94*
Mabon, (Jesse) Dickson 1925- *Who 94*
Mabrey, Harold Leon 1933- *WhoBlA 94*
Mabrey, Leanne Clasby 1958- *WhoFI 94*
Mabrey, Marsha Eve 1949- *WhoBlA 94*
Mabrie, Herman James, III 1948-
  WhoBlA 94
Mabrouk, Ezzidin Ali 1932- *IntWW 93*
Mabry, Anna d1981 *WhoHol 92*
Mabry, Edward L. 1936- *WhoBlA 94*
Mabry, George Lafayette, Jr. 1917-1990
  WhAm 10
Mabry, Guy O. 1926- *WhoAm 94*
Mabry, Herbert H. *WhoAmP 93*
Mabry, Malcolm H., Jr. 1933-
  WhoAmP 93
Mabry, Samuel Stewart 1925-
  WhoScEn 94
Mabus, Catherine Adam 1948-
  WhoMW 93
Mabus, Ray *WhoAmP 93*
Mabus, Raymond Edwin, Jr. 1948-
  IntWW 93, WhoAmP 93
Maby, (Alfred) Cedric 1915- *Who 94*
Mac, Jennie d1984 *WhoHol 92*
Macadam, Peter 1921- *IntWW 93,
  Who 94*
MacAdam, Preston *GayLL*
MacAdam, Walter Kavanagh 1913-
  WhoAm 94
MacAdams, Lewis (Perry, Jr.) 1944-
  WrDr 94
MacAdams, Rhea d1982 *WhoHol 92*
MacAfee, James Jonathan 1954-
  WhoAmL 94
MacAfee, Norman *DrAPF 93*
Macagno, Eduardo *WhoHisp 94*
Macagy, Douglas Guernsey 1913-1973
  WhoAmA 93N
Macagy, Jermayne *WhoAmA 93N*
Macainsh, Noel Leslie 1926- *WrDr 94*

Macal, Zdenek 1936- *WhoAm 94,
  WhoMW 93*
Macala, Gerald Stephen 1968-
  WhoWest 94
Macalister, Kim Porter 1954- *WhoAm 94*
Macalister, Paul Ritter 1901-1990
  WhoAmA 93N
MacAlister, Robert Stuart 1924-
  WhoWest 94
MacAllan, Andrew *Who 94*
MacAllen, Andrew 1923- *WrDr 94*
Macallister, Robert David 1946-
  WhoFI 94
Macaluso, Frank Augustus 1931-
  WhoFI 94
Macaluso, James 1943- *WhoFI 94*
Macaluso, Mary Christelle, Sister 1931-
  WhoMW 93
Macaluso, Ralph Terry 1963-
  WhoWest 94
Macan, Thomas Townley 1946- *Who 94*
Macan, William Alexander, IV 1942-
  WhoAm 94
Mac An Airchinnigh, Micheal 1950-
  WhoScEn 94
MacAndrew, Baron 1945- *Who 94*
MacAnnan, George Burr d1970
  WhoHol 92
Macapagal, Diosdado 1910- *IntWW 93*
MacApp, C.C. 1917?-1971 *EncSF 93*
Macara, Alexander Wiseman 1932-
  Who 94
Macara, Hugh Kenneth 1913- *Who 94*
Macaranas, Howard I. 1955- *WhoAmP 93*
Macaray, Lawrence Richard 1921-
  WhoAmA 93
Macarell, John D. 1933- *WhoIns 94*
Macari, Emir Jose 1957- *WhoScEn 94*
Macario, Alberto Juan Lorenzo 1935-
  WhoAm 94
Macario, Erminio d1980 *WhoHol 92*
Macarón, Mark Andrew *WhoHisp 94*
Macarron Jaime, Ricardo 1926-
  IntWW 93
Macarthur, Arthur Leitch 1913- *Who 94*
MacArthur, Brian 1940- *Who 94*
MacArthur, Charles d1956 *WhoHol 92*
MacArthur, Charles 1895-1956
  IntDcF 2-4
Macarthur, Charles Ramsay *Who 94*
MacArthur, Donald 1901-1990 *WhAm 10*
Mac Arthur, Donald Malcolm 1931-1988
  WhAm 10
MacArthur, Douglas 1880-1964
  HisWorL [port], HisDcKW
MacArthur, Douglas, II 1909- *IntWW 93*
MacArthur, Ian 1925- *Who 94*
MacArthur, James 1937- *IntMPA 94,
  WhoAm 94, WhoHol 92, WhoWest 94*
MacArthur, John R. 1956- *ConAu 140*
MacArthur, John Roderick C. G. 1956-
  WhoAm 94
MacArthur, John Stewart 1856-1920
  DcNaB MP
MacArthur, Roy *WhoHol 92*
MacArthur, Sandra Lea 1946- *WhoFI 94*
Macartney, John Barrington 1917-
  Who 94
Macaskill, Brian Kenneth 1957-
  WhoMW 93
MacAskill, Kenneth M. 1928-
  WhoAmP 93

Macaulay, Alexander S. 1942-
  WhoAmP 93
Macaulay, Catharine 1731-1791 *AmRev,
  BlmGWL*
Macaulay, Christopher Todd 1959-
  WhoAmL 94
Macaulay, Colin Alexander 1931-
  WhoAm 94
MacAulay, David (Alexander) 1946-
  EncSF 93, WrDr 94
Macaulay, David Alexander 1946-
  WhoAmA 93
Macaulay, Hugh L. *WhoAm 94, WhoFI 94*
Macaulay, Janet Stewart Alison 1909-
  Who 94
Macaulay, John Clinton *WhoFI 94*
Macaulay, Joseph d1967 *WhoHol 92*
Macaulay, Robert Erwin 1930-
  WhoMW 93
Macaulay, Ronald Kerr Steven 1927-
  WhoAm 94
Macaulay, Rose 1881-1958 *BlmGWL*
Macaulay, (Emilie) Rose 1881-1958
  EncSF 93
Macaulay, Thomas Babington 1800-1859
  BlmGEL, NinCLC 42 [port]
Macaulay, Thomas S. 1946- *WhoAmA 93*
Macaulay, Tom 1951- *WhoAmP 93*
Macaulay, William Edward 1945-
  WhoAm 94
Macaulay of Bragar, Baron *Who 94*
Macauley, Charles Cameron 1923-
  WhoWest 94
Macauley, Ed 1928- *BasBi*
Macauley, Robie *DrAPF 93*
MacAuley, Robie (Mayhew) 1919-
  EncSF 93, TwCYAW
Macauley, Robie Mayhew 1919-
  WhoAm 94
Macauley, William Francis 1943-
  WhoAmL 94
MacAvoy, Paul Webster 1934-
  WhoAm 94, WhoFI 94
MacAvoy, R(oberta) A(nn) 1949-
  EncSF 93, TwCYAW
Mac Avoy, Roberta Ann 1949- *WrDr 94*
Mac Avoy, Thomas Coleman 1928-
  WhoAm 94
Macaya, Roman Federico 1966-
  WhoScEn 94
MacBain, Richard Norman 1897-
  WhAm 10
MacBain, William Halley 1916-
  WhoAm 94
Macbeath, Alexander Murray 1923-
  Who 94
Macbeath, Innis (Stewart) 1928- *WrDr 94*
MacBeth c. 1005-1057 *HisWorL [port]*
MacBeth, Angus 1942- *WhoAm 94,
  WhoAmL 94*
Macbeth, George 1932-1992 *AnObit 1992*
MacBeth, George (Mann) 1932- *WrDr 94*
MacBird, Rosemary (Simpson) 1921-
  WhoAmA 93
MacBride, Donald d1957 *WhoHol 92*
MacBride, John 1868-1916 *DcNaB MP*
MacBride, Lilyan *WhoHol 92*
MacBride, Mary H. *WhoAmP 93*
MacBride, Roger Lea 1929- *WhoAmP 93*
MacBride, Sean d1988 *NobelP 91N*
MacBride, Sean 1904- *HisWorL*

MacBride, Thomas Jamison 1914-
WhoAm 94, WhoAmL 94, WhoWest 94
MacBurney, Edward Harding 1927-
WhoAm 94, WhoMW 93
MacCabe, Brian Farmer d1992 *Who 94N*
MacCabe, Colin Myles Joseph 1949-
Who 94
MacCaffrey, Wallace T(revethic) 1920-
WrDr 94
MacCaig, Norman 1910- *BlmGEL*
MacCaig, Norman (Alexander) 1910-
Who 94, WrDr 94
MacCalien, Aubrey 1882- *WhoHol 92*
MacCallum, James Martin 1940-
WhoAm 94
MacCallum, Lorene 1928- *WhoScEn 94,
WhoWest 94*
Mac Cana, Proinsias 1926- *Who 94*
Maccanico, Antonio 1924- *IntWW 93*
Maccari, Giacomo c. 1700-1744?
NewGrDO
MacCarthy, Douglas Edward 1945-
WhoWest 94
MacCarthy, Fiona 1940- *WrDr 94*
MacCarthy, John Peters 1933- *WhoAm 94*
MacCarthy, Talbot Leland 1936-
WhoAm 94
MacCarthy, Terence 1934- *WhoAm 94,
WhoAmL 94*
MacCauley, Hugh Bournonville 1922-
WhoFI 94, WhoWest 94
MacChesney, John Burnette 1929-
WhoAm 94, WhoScEn 94
Macchi, Egisto 1928- *NewGrDO*
Macchi, Maria de 1870-1909 *NewGrDO*
Macchia, John d1967 *WhoHol 92*
Macchia, Joseph D. 1935- *WhoIns 94*
Macchia, Vincent Michael 1933-
WhoAmL 94
Macchiarola, Frank Joseph 1941-
WhoAm 94
Macchio, Ralph 1961- *WhoHol 92*
Macchio, Ralph 1962- *IntMPA 94*
Maccione, Aldo *WhoHol 92*
Maccioni, Giovanni Battista dc. 1678
NewGrDO
MacClane, Edward James 1907-1992
WhoBlA 94N
MacCleery, Douglas Watson 1942-
WhoAmP 93
Macclesfield, Archdeacon of *Who 94*
Macclesfield, Earl of d1992 *Who 94N*
Macclesfield, Earl of 1943- *Who 94*
MacClinchie, Robert Clanahan 1910-
WhoWest 94
MacClintock, Dorcas 1932- *WhoAmA 93*
MacCloskey, Ysabel d1981 *WhoHol 92*
MacCloud, Malcolm *EncSF 93*
MacCluggage, Reid 1938- *WhoAm 94*
MacClure, Victor (Thom MacWalter)
1887-1963 *EncSF 93*
Maccoby, Eleanor Emmons 1917-
WhoAm 94
MacCoby, Michael 1933- *WrDr 94*
MacColl, Catriona *WhoHol 92*
MacColl, Hugh *EncSF 93*
MacColl, J. A. 1948- *WhoAmL 94*
MacColl, James d1956 *WhoHol 92*
MacColl, Ray Edward 1956- *WhoFI 94*
MacCombie, Bruce Franklin 1943-
WhoAm 94
Maccone, Ron *WhoHol 92*
MacConkey, Dorothy I. *WhoAm 94*
MacConnell, Gary Scott 1958-
WhoScEn 94
MacConochie, John Angus 1908- *Who 94*
Mac Corkindale, Simon 1952- *IntMPA 94,
WhoHol 92*
MacCorkle, Emmett Wallace, III 1942-
WhoWest 94
MacCormac, Richard Cornelius 1938-
IntWW 93, Who 94
MacCormac, Vincent Peter 1936-
WhoIns 94
MacCormack, Frank d1941 *WhoHol 92*
MacCormack, Franklyn d1971
WhoHol 92
MacCormick, Iain Somerled MacDonald
1939- *Who 94*
MacCormick, Neil *Who 94*
MacCormick, (Donald) Neil 1941-
IntWW 93, Who 94, WrDr 94
MacCoun, Catherine 1953- *WrDr 94*
MacCracken, Mary 1926- *WrDr 94*
MacCracken, Mary Jo 1943- *WhoMW 93,
WhoScEn 94*
MacCrate, Robert 1921- *WhoAm 94*
Mac Cready, Paul Beattie 1925-
WhoAm 94
MacCreigh, James *EncSF 93*
MacCrimmon, Kenneth Robert 1937-
WhoAm 94
MacCrindle, Robert Alexander 1928-
Who 94, WhoAm 94
MacCulloch, Malcolm John 1936-
Who 94
MacCulloch, Patrick C. *WhoScEn 94*

MacCunn, Hamish (James) 1868-1916
NewGrDO
MacCurdy, Raymond Ralph, Jr. 1916-
WhoAm 94
MacDermot, Brian (Charles) 1914-
Who 94
Macdermot, Niall 1916- *IntWW 93,
Who 94*
MacDermott, Edmond Geoffrey *Who 94*
MacDermott, John Clarke 1927-
IntWW 93, Who 94
Macdermott, Kathleen 1964- *WhoAmL 94*
MacDermott, Marc d1929 *WhoHol 92*
MacDermott, Thomas Jerome 1960-
WhoFI 94
MacDiarmid, Alan Graham 1927-
WhoScEn 94
MacDiarmid, Hugh 1892-1978 *BlmGEL*
Mac Diarmid, William Donald 1926-
WhoAm 94
Macdona, Charles T. d1964 *WhoHol 92*
MacDonagh, Oliver Ormond Gerard
1924- *Who 94*
Macdonald *Who 94*
Macdonald, Baron 1947- *Who 94*
Macdonald, A. Ewan *WhoAm 94,
WhoFI 94, WhoWest 94*
Mac Donald, Alan Douglas 1939-
WhoAm 94, WhoAmL 94
Macdonald, Alan Hugh 1943- *WhoAm 94*
Macdonald, Alastair (A.) 1920- *WrDr 94*
Macdonald, Alastair John Peter 1940-
Who 94
MacDonald, Alexander Daniel 1923-
WhoScEn 94
Macdonald, Alexander Plath 1929-
WhoMW 93
MacDonald, Alistair Archibald 1927-
Who 94
Macdonald, Alistair H. 1925- *Who 94*
MacDonald, Amy 1951- *SmATA 76 [port],
WrDr 94*
MacDonald, Andrew Stephen 1953-
WhoAm 94
Macdonald, Angus Cameron 1931-
Who 94
Macdonald, Angus John 1940- *Who 94*
Macdonald, Angus Stewart 1935- *Who 94*
Macdonald, Anne L. 1920- *WrDr 94*
MacDonald, Anne Thompson d1993
NewYTBS 93 [port]
MacDonald, Anson *EncSF 93*
MacDonald, Arthur (Leslie) 1919- *Who 94*
MacDonald, Betty Ann 1936-
WhoAmA 93
Macdonald, Brian 1928- *IntDcB*
Macdonald, Brian Scott 1939- *WhoAm 94*
Macdonald, Bruce K. *WhoAmA 93*
Macdonald, Calum Alasdair 1956-
Who 94
Macdonald, Carol *WhoAmP 93*
Macdonald, Caroline 1948- *BlmGWL,
WrDr 94*
Macdonald, Catherine R. D. d1929
WhoHol 92
Macdonald, Charles *WhoAmP 93*
Macdonald, Charles Adam 1949- *Who 94*
Macdonald, Clifford Palmer 1919-
WhoAm 94
MacDonald, Clyde, Jr. 1929- *WhoAmP 93*
MacDonald, Colin Cameron 1943-
Who 94
MacDonald, Colin Somerled 1925-
WhoAmA 93
Macdonald, Cynthia *DrAPF 93*
MacDonald, Daniel H. d1993
NewYTBS 93
Macdonald, David Cameron 1936-
Who 94
MacDonald, David Richard 1953-
WhoMW 93, WhoScEn 94
Macdonald, David Robert 1930-
WhoAm 94, WhoAmL 94
Macdonald, Digby Donald 1943-
WhoScEn 94
MacDonald, Donald d1959 *WhoHol 92*
Macdonald, Donald (Stovel) 1932-
Who 94
MacDonald, Donald Farquhar Macleod
1915- *Who 94*
Macdonald, Donald Ian 1931-
WhoAm 94, WhoAmP 93
MacDonald, Donald Paul 1931-
WhoAmP 93
Macdonald, Donald S. d1993
NewYTBS 93
Macdonald, Donald Stovel 1932-
IntWW 93, WhoAm 94
MacDonald, Donald William 1935-
WhoAm 94
Macdonald, Dwight 1906-1982 *AmSocL*
MacDonald, Edmund d1951 *WhoHol 92*
MacDonald, Elaine 1943- *IntDcB*
Macdonald, Fergus 1936- *IntWW 93*
MacDonald, Finlay J. 1925- *WrDr 94*
MacDonald, Flora 1722-1790 *AmRev*
MacDonald, Flora Isabel 1926- *IntWW 93,
Who 94*

MacDonald, Gary Bruce 1950- *WhoFI 94*
MacDonald, George 1824-1905 *EncSF 93*
MacDonald, George Frederick 1938-
WhoAm 94
Macdonald, George Grant 1921- *Who 94*
Macdonald, George W. 1936-
WhoAmL 94
MacDonald, Gerald V. 1938- *WhoAm 94,
WhoFI 94, WhoMW 93*
MacDonald, Gordon Chalmers 1928-
WhoAm 94
Macdonald, Gordon James Fraser 1929-
IntWW 93, WhoAm 94, WhoWest 94
Macdonald, Grant 1909-1987
WhoAmA 93N
Macdonald, Gus *Who 94*
MacDonald, Harry d1943 *WhoHol 92*
Macdonald, Herbert 1898-1972
WhoAmA 93N
MacDonald, Hope 1928- *WrDr 94*
MacDonald, Howard *Who 94*
Macdonald, (John) Howard 1928- *Who 94*
MacDonald, Hubert Clarence 1941-
WhoScEn 94
Macdonald, Hugh (John) 1940- *NewGrDO*
MacDonald, Hugh Ian 1929- *WhoAm 94*
MacDonald, Hugh John 1940- *Who 94*
MacDonald, Iain Smith 1927- *Who 94*
MacDonald, Ian *Who 94*
Macdonald, (Hugh) Ian 1929- *Who 94*
MacDonald, Ian Alexander 1939- *Who 94*
MacDonald, Ian David 1932- *WrDr 94*
MacDonald, Ian Duncan 1944-
WhoAm 94
Macdonald, Ian Grant 1928- *IntWW 93,
Who 94*
MacDonald, Isabel Lillias *Who 94*
MacDonald, J. Farrell d1952 *WhoHol 92*
MacDonald, J. Fred(erick) 1941- *WrDr 94*
MacDonald, James d1991 *WhoHol 92*
Macdonald, James Alexander 1908-
Who 94
Macdonald, James Ellis 1950-
WhoAmL 94, WhoWest 94
Macdonald, James Kennedy, Jr. 1956-
WhoFI 94
Macdonald, James Ross 1923-
WhoAm 94, WhoScEn 94
MacDonald, James Samuel 1949-
WhoAmL 94
Macdonald, James W. A. 1824-1908
WhoAmA 93N
MacDonald, Jeanette d1965 *WhoHol 92*
MacDonald, Jerome Edward 1925-
WhoScEn 94
Mac Donald, John (Haskell) 1896-
WhAm 10
Macdonald, John A. 1815-1891
HisWorL [port]
Macdonald, John B(arfoot) 1918- *Who 94*
Macdonald, John Barfoot 1918-
WhoAm 94
MacDonald, John Charles 1910- *Who 94*
Macdonald, John Coury 1966-
WhoAmL 94
MacDonald, John D(ann) 1916-1986
EncSF 93
MacDonald, John Donald 1938- *Who 94*
MacDonald, John Grant 1932- *Who 94*
Macdonald, John M(arshall) 1920-
WrDr 94
MacDonald, John Reginald 1931- *Who 94*
MacDonald, John Thomas 1932-
WhoAm 94
MacDonald, John William 1938- *Who 94*
MacDonald, Joseph A. 1910- *WhoAmP 93*
Macdonald, Joseph Albert Friel 1942-
WhoAm 94
Macdonald, June Elizabeth Gostwycke
1864-1922 *BlmGWL*
Macdonald, Karen Ann 1963-
WhoMW 93
MacDonald, Katherine d1956 *WhoHol 92*
MacDonald, Kenneth d1972 *WhoHol 92*
Macdonald, Kenneth 1905- *WhoAm 94*
Macdonald, Kenneth (Carmichael) 1930-
Who 94
MacDonald, Kenneth J. 1926-
WhoAmP 93
MacDonald, Kenneth Richard 1912-
WhoWest 94
MacDonald, Kevin John 1946-
WhoAmA 93
Macdonald, Lenna Ruth 1962-
WhoAmL 94
MacDonald, Lynn Merle 1942-
WhoAmP 93
Macdonald, Malcolm 1932- *WrDr 94*
Mac Donald, Malcolm Murdoch 1935-
WhoAm 94
Macdonald, Margaret *Who 94*
Macdonald, Margaret d1993
NewYTBS 93
MacDonald, Margo 1943- *Who 94*
Macdonald, Mark A. 1942- *WhoAmP 93*
Macdonald, Mary Elizabeth 1910-
WhAm 10

MacDonald, Gary Bruce 1950- *WhoFI 94*
Mac Donald, Matthew Anita, Sr. 1938-
WhoAm 94
MacDonald, Maurice B. 1931-
WhoAmP 93
MacDonald, Mhairi Graham 1945-
WhoScEn 94
Macdonald, Morag 1947- *Who 94*
MacDonald, Nestor Joseph 1895-1991
WhAm 10
Macdonald, Nigel Colin Lock 1945-
Who 94
Macdonald, Norman Malcolm 1927-
WrDr 94
MacDonald, Norval Woodrow 1913-
WhoScEn 94, WhoWest 94
MacDonald, Pauline d1976 *WhoHol 92*
Mac Donald, Philip *IntMPA 94*
MacDonald, Philip 1899-1980 *EncSF 93*
Macdonald, R. Fulton 1940- *WhoFI 94*
MacDonald, Ralph 1944- *WhoBlA 94*
MacDonald, Ramsay 1866-1937
HisWorL [port]
MacDonald, Randal Stuart 1959-
WhoWest 94
MacDonald, Reynold C. 1918-
EncABHB 9
MacDonald, Richard Annis 1928-
WhoAm 94
MacDonald, Robert Bruce 1930-
WhoAm 94
MacDonald, Robert R. 1942-
WhoAmA 93
Macdonald, Robert Rigg, Jr. 1942-
WhoAm 94
MacDonald, Robert Taylor 1930-
WhoAm 94
Macdonald, Robert W. 1943- *WhoIns 94*
Macdonald, Roderick 1931- *WhoAm 94*
Macdonald, Roderick (Douglas) 1921-
Who 94
Macdonald, Roderick Francis 1951-
Who 94
MacDonald, Ronald Angus Neil 1935-
WhoAm 94
MacDonald, Ronald Clarence 1911-
Who 94
MacDonald, Ronald Francis 1946-
WhoFI 94
Macdonald, Ronald John 1919- *Who 94*
MacDonald, Scott 1942- *WhoAmA 93*
Macdonald, Sharman 1951- *ConDr 93*
MacDonald, Simon Gavin George 1923-
Who 94, WrDr 94
Macdonald, Stephen R. 1949-
WhoAmL 94
Macdonald, Stewart Dixon *WhoScEn 94*
Macdonald, Susan *DrAPF 93, WhoHol 92*
Macdonald, Thomas Brian 1911- *Who 94*
Macdonald, Thomas Conchar 1909-
Who 94
MacDonald, Thomas Cook, Jr. 1929-
WhoAm 94, WhoAmL 94
MacDonald, Thomas Joseph, Jr. 1940-
WhoFI 94
Macdonald, Thomas Reid 1908-
WhoAmA 93N
MacDonald, Timothy Lee 1948-
WhoScEn 94
Macdonald, Virginia B. 1920-
WhoAmP 93
Macdonald, Virginia Brooks 1918-
WhoWest 94
MacDonald, W. Cullen 1940-
WhoAmL 94
MacDonald, Wallace d1978 *WhoHol 92*
MacDonald, Walter E. d1993
NewYTBS 93
Macdonald, Wayne Douglas 1940-
WhoAm 94, WhoMW 93
MacDonald, Wayne Douglas 1954-
WhoAmP 93
MacDonald, Wesley Angus Reginald
1932- *WhoAm 94*
MacDonald, William L. 1921-
WhoAmA 93
Macdonald, William L(loyd) 1921-
WrDr 94
MacDonald, William Lloyd 1921-
WhoAm 94
MacDonald, William Weir 1927- *Who 94*
Macdonald-Buchanan, John 1925-
Who 94
Macdonald of Clanranald, Ranald
Alexander 1934- *Who 94*
Macdonald of Gwaenysgor, Baron 1915-
Who 94
Macdonald of Sleat *Who 94*
MacDonald Scott, Mary *Who 94*
Macdonald-Smith, Hugh 1923- *Who 94*
Macdonald-Smith, Sydney 1908- *Who 94*
Macdonald-Wright, Stanton 1890-1973
WhoAmA 93N
Macdonell, A(rchibald) G(ordon)
1895-1941 *EncSF 93*
Macdonell, Archibald Gordon 1895-1941
DcNaB MP
Macdonell, Cameron 1938- *WhoAmA 93*

MacDonell of Glengarry, Aeneas Ranald
  Donald 1913- *Who 94*
MacDonnell, Philip J. 1948- *WhoAmL 94*
Macdonnell, Thomas M. 1923-
  WhoAmP 93
MacDonogh, Giles 1955- *WrDr 94*
MacDonough, Robert Howard 1941-
  WhoWest 94
MacDougal, Gary Edward 1936-
  WhoAm 94, WhoFI 94
MacDougal, John *EncSF 93*
MacDougall, Allan Ross d1956
  WhoHol 92
MacDougall, Anne 1944- *WhoAmA 93*
MacDougall, (George) Donald (Alastair)
  1912- *IntWW 93, Who 94*
MacDougall, Hartland Molson 1931-
  WhoAm 94, WhoFI 94
Macdougall, Iver Cameron 1926-
  WhoAm 94
MacDougall, James D. d1932 *WhoHol 92*
MacDougall, John Douglas 1944-
  WhoAm 94
MacDougall, Laura Margaret *Who 94*
MacDougall, Malcolm Edward 1938-
  WhoAmL 94
Macdougall, Neil 1932- *Who 94*
Macdougall, Patrick Lorn 1939-
  IntWW 93, Who 94
MacDougall, Peter 1937- *WhoAm 94*
MacDougall, Peter Steven 1951-
  WhoAmA 93
MacDougall, Priscilla Ruth 1944-
  WhoAmL 94
MacDougall, Roger d1993
  NewYTBS 93 [port]
MacDougall, Roger 1910- *ConDr 93*
MacDougall, Ruth Doan *DrAPF 93*
Mac Dougall, William Lowell 1931-
  WhoAm 94
MacDowall, David William 1930- *Who 94*
MacDowell, Andie 1958- *IntMPA 94,
  News 93 [port], WhoAm 94, WhoHol 92*
MacDowell, Douglas Maurice 1931-
  Who 94, WrDr 94
MacDowell, Edward Alexander
  1860-1908 *AmCulL*
Macdowell, John 1954- *WrDr 94*
MacDowell, Melbourne d1941
  WhoHol 92
MacDuff, Alistair Geoffrey 1945- *Who 94*
Macduff, Nancy 1942- *WhoFI 94*
MacDuffee, Robert Colton 1923-
  WhoScEn 94
Mace, Barbara Jean 1945- *WhoAmP 93*
Mace, Brian Anthony 1948- *Who 94*
Mace, David 1951- *EncSF 93*
Mace, David Robert 1907-1990 *WhAm 10*
Mace, Fred d1917 *WhoHol 92*
Mace, John (Airth) 1932- *Who 94*
Mace, John Weldon 1938- *WhoAm 94,
  WhoScEn 94, WhoWest 94*
Mace, Paul d1983 *WhoHol 92*
Mace, Wynn d1955 *WhoHol 92*
MacEachen, Allan J. 1921- *IntWW 93*
MacEachen, Allan Joseph 1921- *Who 94,
  WhoAm 94*
MacEachern, Diane 1952- *WrDr 94*
MacEachern, Malcolm d1945 *WhoHol 92*
Macedo, Helder Malta 1935- *Who 94*
Macedo, Joelmir Campos de Araripe
  IntWW 93
Macedo, Richard Stanley 1941-
  WhoAm 94
Macek, Josef 1922- *IntWW 93*
Macek, Karel 1928- *WhoScEn 94*
Macel, Stanley Charles, III 1938-
  WhoAmL 94
MacEntee, Maire *BlmGWL*
MacEoin, Denis 1949- *ConAu 141,
  WrDr 94*
MacEoin, Gary 1909- *WrDr 94*
Macer, Dan Johnstone 1917- *WhoAm 94*
Macer, George Armen, Jr. 1948-
  WhoWest 94
Macer, Richard Charles Franklin 1928-
  Who 94
Macera, Salvatore 1931- *WhoAm 94*
Macero, Teo 1925- *WhoAm 94*
Macesic, Nedeljko 1956- *WhoScEn 94*
Macesich, George 1927- *WhoAm 94,
  WrDr 94*
MacEwan, Gwendolyn 1941-1987
  BlmGWL
MacEwan, Nigel Savage 1933- *WhoAm 94*
MacEwen, Ann Maitland 1918- *Who 94*
MacEwen, Edward Carter 1938-
  WhoAm 94
Mac Ewen, George Dean 1927-
  WhoAm 94
MacEwen, Malcolm 1911- *Who 94*
Macey, Carn 1928- *WrDr 94*
Macey, David Edward 1929- *Who 94*
Macey, Eric Harold 1936- *Who 94*
Macey, Morris William 1922- *WhoAm 94,
  WrDr 94*
Macey, Peter *EncSF 93*

Macey, William Blackmore 1920-
  WhoAm 94
Macfadden, Bernarr 1868-1955 *EncSF 93*
MacFadden, Gertrude d1967 *WhoHol 92*
MacFadden, Hamilton 1901- *WhoHol 92*
MacFadden, Howard 1946- *WhoAmP 93*
MacFadden, Kenneth Orville 1945-
  WhoScEn 94
MacFadden, William Semple 1895-
  WhAm 10
Macfadyen, Amyan 1920- *WrDr 94*
Macfadyen, Donald James Dobbie 1945-
  Who 94
Macfadyen, Ian David 1942- *Who 94*
MacFadyen, John Archibald, III 1948-
  WhoAmL 94
MacFarland, Craig George 1943-
  WhoAm 94
MacFarland, Dorothea d1988 *WhoHol 92*
MacFarland, Richard B. 1946-
  WhoAmL 94
Macfarlane *Who 94*
Macfarlane, Alan Donald James 1941-
  IntWW 93, Who 94
Macfarlane, Alastair Iain Robert 1940-
  WhoAm 94
MacFarlane, Alistair George James 1931-
  IntWW 93, Who 94
Macfarlane, Alwyn James Cecil 1922-
  Who 94
MacFarlane, Andrew Walker 1928-
  WhoAm 94
Macfarlane, Anne Bridget 1930- *Who 94*
MacFarlane, Bruce d1967 *WhoHol 92*
MacFarlane, David B. *WhoScEn 94*
Macfarlane, David Gordon 1947-
  WhoMW 93
MacFarlane, George d1932 *WhoHol 92*
MacFarlane, George (Gray) 1916- *Who 94*
MacFarlane, Gordon Frederick 1925-
  WhoAm 94, WhoWest 94
MacFarlane, James Douglas 1916-
  WrDr 94
Macfarlane, James Wright d1992
  Who 94N
MacFarlane, John Alexander 1916-
  WhoAm 94
Macfarlane, John Granger 1929-
  WhoAmP 93
MacFarlane, Laura d1983 *WhoHol 92*
Macfarlane, Leslie John 1924- *WrDr 94*
Macfarlane, M. James 1921- *WhoAmP 93*
Macfarlane, Malcolm Harris 1933-
  WhoMW 93
MacFarlane, Maureen Anne 1965-
  WhoAmL 94
Macfarlane, Neil *Who 94*
Macfarlane, (David) Neil 1936- *Who 94*
Macfarlane, Robert Bruce 1896-
  WhoAmL 94
MacFarlane, Robert Goudie 1917-
  Who 94
MacFarlane, Stephen *EncSF 93*
Macfarlane, William Noble, Jr. 1962-
  WhoMW 93
Macfarlane, William Thomson 1925-
  Who 94
Macfarlane Of Bearsden *IntWW 93*
Macfarlane of Bearsden, Baron 1926-
  Who 94
MacFarquhar, Roderick Lemonde 1930-
  Who 94
Macfarren, George Alexander 1813-1887
  NewGrDO
Macfarren, Natalia 1827-1916 *NewGrDO*
MacGaffey, Wyatt 1932- *WhoAm 94*
MacGarrahan, John Golden 1937-
  WhoAm 94
MacGaw, Wendy 1955- *WhoAmA 93*
MacGibbon, Barbara Haig 1928- *Who 94*
MacGibbon, Harriet d1987 *WhoHol 92*
MacGibbon, Jean 1913- *WrDr 94*
MacGill, George Roy Buchanan 1905-
  Who 94
MacGill, Moyna d1975 *WhoHol 92*
MacGillis, Robert Donald 1936-
  WhoAmA 93
MacGillivray, Barron Bruce 1927-
  Who 94
MacGillivray, Ian 1920- *Who 94*
MacGillivray, Lois Ann 1937- *WhoAm 94*
Macgilvary, Norwood 1874-1949
  WhoAmA 93N
MacGinitie, Laura Anne 1958-
  WhoScEn 94
MacGinitie, Walter Harold 1928-
  WhoAm 94, WhoWest 94
MacGinnis, Francis R. d1993
  NewYTBS 93
MacGinnis, Francis Robert d1993
  Who 94N
MacGinnis, Niall 1913- *WhoHol 92*
MacGlashan, Maureen Elizabeth 1938-
  Who 94
Macgougan, John 1913- *Who 94*
MacGowan, Charles Frederic 1918-
  WhoAm 94

MacGowan, Christopher (John) 1948-
  WrDr 94
Macgowan, Jonathan 1932- *WrDr 94*
MacGowan, Kenneth 1888-1963
  IntDcF 2-4
Mac Gowan, Mary Eugenia 1928-
  WhoAm 94, WhoAmL 94, WhoWest 94
MacGowran, Jack d1973 *WhoHol 92*
MacGowran, Tara *WhoHol 92*
Macgoye, Marjorie Olhude 1928-
  BlmGWL
MacGrath, C. Richard 1921- *WhoAm 94*
MacGrath, Leueen 1919- *WhoHol 92*
MacGraw, Ali 1938- *WhoHol 92*
Mac Graw, Ali 1939- *IntMPA 94,
  WhoAm 94*
MacGregor, Charles *WhoHol 92*
MacGregor, David Bruce 1953-
  WhoAm 94
MacGregor, David Lee 1932- *WhoAm 94*
MacGregor, Dorothea M. 1925-
  WhoAmP 93
Macgregor, Edwin (Robert) 1931- *Who 94*
MacGregor, Geddes *Who 94*
MacGregor, Geddes 1909- *WhoAm 94*
MacGregor, (John) Geddes 1909- *Who 94,
  WrDr 94*
MacGregor, George Lescher, Jr. 1936-
  WhoAm 94
MacGregor, Gregory Allen 1941-
  WhoAmA 93
MacGregor, Ian (Kinloch) 1912- *Who 94*
MacGregor, Ian Kinloch 1912- *IntWW 93*
MacGregor, James Grierson 1934-
  WhoAm 94
Macgregor, James Murdoch 1925-
  WrDr 94
MacGregor, James Thomas 1944-
  WhoScEn 94
MacGregor, John (Roddick Russell)
  1937- *Who 94*
MacGregor, John M. 1941- *WrDr 94*
Macgregor, John Malcolm 1946- *Who 94*
MacGregor, John Murdoch 1897-
  WhAm 10
MacGregor, John Roddick Russell 1937-
  IntWW 93
Macgregor, John Roy 1913- *Who 94*
MacGregor, Katherine c. 1925-
  WhoHol 92
MacGregor, Kenneth Robert 1906-
  WhoAm 94
MacGregor, Lee d1961 *WhoHol 92*
MacGregor, Loren J. 1950- *EncSF 93*
MacGregor, Mary Esther 1876-1961
  BlmGWL
MacGregor, Neil *Who 94*
MacGregor, (Robert) Neil 1946-
  IntWW 93, Who 94
MacGregor, Parke d1962 *WhoHol 92*
MacGregor, Richard *EncSF 93*
MacGregor, Susan Katriona 1941-
  Who 94
MacGregor, Thomas Gregor 1943-
  WhoAmL 94
Macgregor, Wallace 1917- *WhoAm 94*
MacGregor of MacGregor, Gregor 1925-
  Who 94
MacGuigan, Mark R. 1931- *IntWW 93,
  WhoAm 94, WrDr 94*
MacGuigan, Mark Rudolph 1931-
  Who 94
MacGuire, James 1952- *ConAu 142*
MacGunnigle, Bruce Campbell 1947-
  WhoFI 94
Mach, David 1956- *WhoAm 94*
Mach, Elyse (Janet) 1941- *WrDr 94*
Mach, Ernst 1838-1916 *WorScD*
Mach, Martin Henry 1940- *WhoWest 94*
Mach, Patricia Joan 1955- *WhoMW 93*
Macha, Barry Louis 1954- *WhoAmL 94*
Macha, Otmar 1922- *NewGrDO*
Machado, Adelio Alcino Sampaio Castro
  1942- *WhoScEn 94*
Machado, Alfredo C. 1922-1991
  WhAm 10
Machado, Augusto (de Oliveira)
  1845-1924 *NewGrDO*
Machado, Christian E. 1961- *WhoHisp 94*
Machado, Clarence P. 1930- *WhoHisp 94*
Machado, Eduardo 1953- *ConDr 93,
  WhoHisp 94*
Machado, Edward A. 1949- *WhoHisp 94*
Machado, Gilka 1893-1980 *BlmGWL*
Machado, Gus *WhoHisp 94*
Machado, Hector Antonio 1960-
  WhoHisp 94
Machado, Joao Somane 1946- *WhoAm 94*
Machado, John Louis 1968- *WhoHisp 94*
Machado, Jose Luis 1951- *WhoHisp 94*
Machado, Lois N. 1946- *WhoHisp 94*
Machado, Luz 1916- *BlmGWL*
Machado, Manuel Antonio, Jr. 1939-
  WhoHisp 94
Machado, Melinda 1961- *WhoHisp 94*
Machado, Mike M. *WhoHisp 94*
Machado, Rodolfo 1942- *WhoHisp 94*
Machado de Arnao, Luz *BlmGWL*

Machado de Assis, Joaquim Maria
  1839-1908 *RfGShF*
MacHale, Joseph P. 1951- *WhoAm 94,
  WhoFI 94*
Machalinski, Richard 1955- *WhoIns 94*
Machamer, Jefferson 1900-1960
  WhoAmA 93N
Machan, Katharyn Howd *DrAPF 93*
Machanic, Roger *WhoFI 94*
Machann, Clinton (John) 1947- *WrDr 94*
Machar, Agnes Maule 1837-1927
  BlmGWL
MacHarg, William *EncSF 93*
Macharski, Franciszek 1927- *IntWW 93*
Machaskee, Alex *WhoAm 94, WhoMW 93*
Machaty, Gustav d1963 *WhoHol 92*
Machatzke, Heinz Wilhelm 1932-
  WhoAm 94
Machaut, Guillaume de c. 1330-1377
  BlmGEL
Machavariani, Alexey Davidovich 1913-
  NewGrDO
Mache, Francois-Bernard 1935-
  IntWW 93
Machell, Arthur R. *WhoScEn 94*
Machemer, Robert 1933- *WhoAm 94*
Machen, Arthur 1863-1947 *EncSF 93*
Machen, Arthur Llewelyn Jones
  1863-1947 *DcNaB MP*
Machen, Arthur Webster, Jr. 1920-
  WhoAm 94
Machen, John Gresham 1881-1937
  DcAmReB 2
Machen, John P. 1951- *WhoAmL 94*
Macher, Janet Marie 1950- *WhoScEn 94*
Machetanz, Fred 1908- *WhoAmA 93*
Machi, Sueo 1934- *IntWW 93*
Machiavelli, Niccolo 1469-1527 *EncEth*
Machiavelli, Niccoletta *WhoHol 92*
Machiavelli, Nicolo di Bernardo dei
  1469-1527 *BlmGEL*
Ma Chi-Chuang 1912- *IntWW 93*
Machida, Gerald Kiyoyuku 1937-
  WhoAmP 93
Machida, Naoshi *WhoFI 94*
Machin, Arnold 1911- *Who 94*
Machin, David 1934- *Who 94*
Machin, Edward Anthony 1925- *Who 94*
Machin, Kenneth Arthur 1936- *Who 94*
Machin, Roger 1955- *WhoAmA 93*
Machinis, Peter Alexander 1912-
  WhoAm 94, WhoMW 93, WhoScEn 94
Machinski, Richard Henry 1952-
  WhoMW 93
Machiorlete, Patricia Anne *WhoAmA 93*
Machiz, Leon 1924- *WhoAm 94,
  WhoFI 94*
Machlachlan, Julia Bronwyn 1969-
  WhoScEn 94
Machlin, Eugene Solomon 1920-
  WhoAm 94
Machlin, Lawrence J. 1927- *WhoAm 94*
Machlin, Marc David 1957- *WhoAmL 94*
Machlin, Milton Robert 1924- *WhoAm 94*
Machlin, Sheldon M. 1918-1975
  WhoAmA 93N
Machlis, Joseph 1906- *NewGrDO*
Machlup, Stefan 1927- *WhoMW 93*
Machold, Roland Morris 1936-
  WhoAm 94
Machor, James L(awrence) 1950-
  ConAu 140
Machotka, Pavel 1936- *WhoScEn 94*
Machover, Carl 1927- *WhoScEn 94*
Machover, Tod 1953- *NewGrDO*
Macht, Stephen 1942- *WhoHol 92*
Macht, Stuart Martin 1930-1990
  WhAm 10
Machtley, Ronald K. 1948- *CngDr 93,
  WhoAmP 93*
Machtley, Ronald Keith 1948-
  WhoAm 94
Machtlinger, Otto d1985 *WhoHol 92*
Machuca-Carriel, Alejandro 1953-
  WhoHisp 94
Machulak, Edward Leon 1926-
  WhoAm 94, WhoFI 94, WhoMW 93
Machung, Anne 1947- *WrDr 94*
Ma Chung-Ch'en *IntWW 93*
Ma Chunwa *WhoPRCh 91*
Maciag, Gregory A. 1947- *WhoIns 94*
Macias, Albert M. 1932- *WhoHisp 94*
Macias, Edward S. 1944- *WhoAm 94*
Macias, Fernando R. *WhoAmP 93*
Macias, Fernando R. 1952- *WhoHisp 94*
Macias, Jesus Diego 1933- *WhoHisp 94*
Macias, Jose Miguel *WhoHisp 94*
Macías, Kenneth S. 1956- *WhoFI 94*
Macías, Manuel Jato 1929- *WhoHisp 94*
Macías, Maria-Solange 1949- *WhoHisp 94*
Macias, Norma A. 1953- *WhoHisp 94*
Macías, Reynaldo Flores *WhoHisp 94*
Macias, Salvador, III 1953- *WhoHisp 94*
Macías Brown, Marta 1944- *WhoHisp 94*
Macías N., Felipe E. *WhoHisp 94*

Maciej, James Valentine 1950- *WhoMW 93*
Maciejewski, Jeffrey John 1960- *WhoMW 93*
Maciel, René 1958- *WhoHisp 94*
MacIlroy, John Whittington 1946- *WhoAmL 94*
MacIlvaine, Chalmers Acheson 1921- *WhoAm 94*
Macinghi Strozzi, Alessandra 1407-1471 *BlmGWL*
MacInnes, Angus *WhoHol 92*
MacInnes, Archibald 1919- *Who 94*
MacInnes, Hamish 1930- *Who 94*
MacInnes, Keith Gordon 1935- *Who 94*
MacInnes, Mairi *DrAPF 93*
MacInnes, Mairi 1925- *ConAu 141*
Macinnis, Joseph Beverley 1937- *IntWW 93*
MacIntosh, Alexander John 1921- *WhoAm 94, WhoFI 94*
Macintosh, Charles 1766-1843 *WorInv*
Macintosh, Douglas Clyde 1877-1948 *DcAmReB 2*
Macintosh, Farquhar 1923- *Who 94*
MacIntosh, Frank Campbell d1992 *Who 94N*
MacIntosh, Frank Campbell 1909-1992 *WhAm 10*
Macintosh, Joan 1919- *Who 94*
Macintosh, Joan 1924- *WrDr 94*
MacIntosh, Robert Mallory 1923- *WhoAm 94*
MacIntosh, Susan Caryl 1953- *WhoWest 94*
MacIntosh, William James 1901-1989 *WhAm 10*
MacIntyre, Alasdair 1929- *WhoAm 94, WrDr 94*
MacIntyre, Alasdair C. 1926- *EncEth*
MacIntyre, Alasdair Chalmers 1929- *Who 94*
Macintyre, Angus Donald 1935- *Who 94*
Macintyre, Barbara Ann 1945- *WhoAmP 93*
Mac Intyre, Donald John 1939- *WhoAm 94*
MacIntyre, Duncan d1973 *WhoHol 92*
MacIntyre, Duncan 1915- *IntWW 93, Who 94*
MacIntyre, Elisabeth 1916- *WrDr 94*
MacIntyre, Iain 1924- *IntWW 93, Who 94*
MacIntyre, John Alexander 1937- *WhoFI 94*
MacIntyre, Malcolm Ames 1908-1992 *WhAm 10*
Macintyre, Margaret 1865-1943 *NewGrDO*
MacIntyre, Michael 1939- *WrDr 94*
MacIntyre, Norman Law 1940- *WhoWest 94*
MacIntyre, R. Douglas 1951- *WhoAm 94*
MacIntyre, Rod(erick Peter) 1947- *WrDr 94*
Macintyre, Stuart (Forbes) 1947- *WrDr 94*
MacIntyre, W(illiam) Ralph 1897- *WhAm 10*
Macintyre, William Ian 1943- *Who 94*
Macioce, Frank Michael, Jr. 1945- *WhoAm 94, WhoAmL 94*
Macioce, Thomas Matthew 1919-1990 *WhAm 10*
Macioci, R. Nikolas *DrAPF 93*
Macionski, Lawrence Edward 1949- *WhoScEn 94*
Maciorowski, Anthony Francis 1948- *WhoScEn 94*
MacIsaac, Fred(erick John) 1886-1940 *EncSF 93*
Maciste d1947 *WhoHol 92*
Maciulis, Linda S. 1949- *WhoScEn 94*
Maciunas, George 1931-1978 *WhoAmA 93N*
Maciuszko, Kathleen Lynn 1947- *WhoAm 94*
MacIver, Dale 1923- *WhoAmP 93*
Mac Iver, Douglas Yaney 1930- *WhoScEn 94*
MacIver, John Kenneth 1931- *WhoAm 94*
MacIver, Linda B. 1946- *WhoFI 94*
MacIver, Loren 1909- *WhoAm 94, WhoAmA 93*
Mack, Alan Osborne 1918- *Who 94*
Mack, Alan Wayne 1947- *WhoMW 93*
Mack, Ally Faye 1943- *WhoBlA 94*
Mack, Andrew d1931 *WhoHol 92*
Mack, Arien 1931- *ConAu 141*
Mack, Arthur d1942 *WhoHol 92*
Mack, Astrid Karona 1935- *WhoBlA 94*
Mack, Austin d1980 *WhoHol 92*
Mack, Betty d1980 *WhoHol 92*
Mack, Billy d1961 *WhoHol 92*
Mack, Brenda Lee 1940- *WhoWest 94*
Mack, Brian John 1949- *Who 94*
Mack, Buck d1959 *WhoHol 92*
Mack, Cactus d1962 *WhoHol 92*
Mack, Carol K *WrDr 94*
Mack, Cedric Manuel 1960- *WhoBlA 94*
Mack, Charles d1956 *WhoHol 92*
Mack, Charles Daniel, III 1942- *WhoWest 94*
Mack, Charles E. d1934 *WhoHol 92*
Mack, Charles Emmett d1927 *WhoHol 92*
Mack, Charles Randall 1940- *WhoAmA 93*
Mack, Charles Richard 1942- *WhoBlA 94*
Mack, Cleveland J., Sr. 1912- *WhoBlA 94*
Mack, Clifford Glenn 1927- *WhoAm 94*
Mack, Connie 1940- *CngDr 93, WhoAmP 93*
Mack, Connie, III 1940- *IntWW 93, WhoAm 94*
Mack, Daniel J. *WhoBlA 94*
Mack, Daniel R. 1947- *WhoAmA 93*
Mack, Daniel Richard 1947- *WhoAm 94*
Mack, David L. 1940- *WhoAm 94, WhoAmP 93*
Mack, Dennis Wayne 1943- *WhoAm 94, WhoAmL 94*
Mack, Donald J. 1937- *WhoBlA 94*
Mack, Donna *DrAPF 93*
Mack, Earle Irving 1939- *WhoAm 94, WhoFI 94*
Mack, Eddie d1944 *WhoHol 92*
Mack, Edward Gibson 1917- *WhoAm 94*
Mack, Faite 1919- *WhoBlA 94*
Mack, Frances d1967 *WhoHol 92*
Mack, Francis Marion 1949- *WhoAmL 94*
Mack, Fred Clarence 1940- *WhoBlA 94*
Mack, George E. d1948 *WhoHol 92*
Mack, Gertrude d1967 *WhoHol 92*
Mack, Gladys Walker 1934- *WhoBlA 94*
Mack, Gordon H. 1927- *WhoBlA 94*
Mack, Grace Hayward d1993 *NewYTBS 93*
Mack, Gregory Ambrose 1949- *WhoMW 93*
Mack, Gregory John 1954- *WhoFI 94*
Mack, Hayward d1921 *WhoHol 92*
Mack, Helen d1986 *WhoHol 92*
Mack, Hughie d1927 *WhoHol 92*
Mack, Hughie d1952 *WhoHol 92*
Mack, J. Curtis, II 1944- *WhoAm 94*
Mack, James Carl 1948- *WhoWest 94*
Mack, James E. 1941- *WhoBlA 94*
Mack, James Edgar 1934- *WhoMW 93*
Mack, James T. d1948 *WhoHol 92*
Mack, Jeffrey G. 1952- *WhoAmP 93*
Mack, Joan 1943- *WhoBlA 94*
Mack, Joe d1946 *WhoHol 92*
Mack, John Edward, III 1934- *WhoAm 94*
Mack, John L. 1942- *WhoBlA 94*
Mack, John W. 1937- *WhoBlA 94*
Mack, Joseph P. 1939- *WhoAm 94, WhoFI 94*
Mack, Joseph S. *WhoAmP 93*
Mack, Julia Cooper *WhoBlA 94*
Mack, Julia Cooper 1920- *WhoAm 94*
Mack, Julie Cooper 1920- *WhoAmP 93*
Mack, Keith Robert 1933- *Who 94*
Mack, Kerry *WhoHol 92*
Mack, Kevin 1962- *WhoBlA 94*
Mack, Lester d1972 *WhoHol 92*
Mack, Linda 1946- *WhoAmL 94*
Mack, Louie 1923- *WhoAmP 93*
Mack, Louise 1874-1935 *BlmGWL*
Mack, Lurene Kirkland 1948- *WhoBlA 94*
Mack, Marion d1989 *WhoHol 92*
Mack, Marion 1902-1989 *WhAm 10*
Mack, Mark Philip 1950- *WhoFI 94*
Mack, Mary Louise 1941- *WhoMW 93*
Mack, Max d1973 *WhoHol 92*
Mack, Maynard 1909- *WrDr 94*
Mack, Nate 1956- *WhoBlA 94*
Mack, Nila d1953 *WhoHol 92*
Mack, Pearl Willie 1941- *WhoBlA 94*
Mack, Peter G. 1945- *WhoAmL 94*
Mack, Phyllis Green 1941- *WhoBlA 94*
Mack, Raymond Francis 1912- *WhoAm 94*
Mack, Raymond Wright 1927- *WhoAm 94*
Mack, Robert d1949 *WhoHol 92*
Mack, Robert Emmet 1924- *WhoAm 94*
Mack, Roderick O'Neal 1955- *WhoBlA 94*
Mack, Rodger Allen 1938- *WhoAmA 93*
Mack, Ronald J. 1952- *WhoMW 93*
Mack, Rudy Eugene, Sr. 1941- *WhoBlA 94*
Mack, Russell Herbert 1897- *WhAm 10*
Mack, Shaen Case Hosie 1964- *WhoWest 94*
Mack, Shane Lee 1963- *WhoAm 94, WhoBlA 94, WhoMW 93*
Mack, Stephen W. 1954- *WhoFI 94, WhoMW 93*
Mack, Sylvia Jenkins 1931- *WhoBlA 94*
Mack, Theodore 1936- *WhoAmL 94*
Mack, Voyce J. 1921- *WhoBlA 94*
Mack, Walter Staunton 1895-1990 *WhAm 10*
Mack, Warren E. 1944- *WhoAmL 94*
Mack, Wilbur d1964 *WhoHol 92*
Mack, Wilbur Ollio 1919- *WhoBlA 94*
Mack, Wilhelmena 1951- *WhoBlA 94*
Mack, Willard d1934 *WhoHol 92*
Mack, William 1930- *WhoFI 94*
Mack, William B. d1955 *WhoHol 92*
Mack, William Joseph 1943- *WhoMW 93*
Mackaill, Dorothy d1990 *WhoHol 92*
Mackall, Laidler Bowie 1916- *WhoAm 94*
Mackall, Leonard L. 1879-1937 *DcLB 140 [port]*
Mackaness, George Bellamy 1922- *Who 94, WhoAm 94*
Mackay *Who 94*
Mackay, A(rthur) Stewart 1909- *Who 94*
Mackay, Alan Lindsay 1926- *Who 94*
Mackay, Alastair 1911- *Who 94*
MacKay, Alex d1985 *WhoHol 92*
Mackay, Alexander Russell 1911- *WhoScEn 94, WhoWest 94*
MacKay, Andrew Dougal 1946- *WhoFI 94*
MacKay, Andrew James 1949- *Who 94*
Mackay, Angus Iain Kenneth 1936- *Who 94*
Mackay, Barry 1906- *WhoHol 92*
Mackay, Buddy 1933- *WhoAmP 93*
Mackay, Charles d1935 *WhoHol 92*
Mackay, Charles 1927- *Who 94*
Mackay, Charles Dorsey 1940- *IntWW 93, Who 94*
Mackay, Claire (Bacchus) 1930- *WrDr 94*
Mackay, Colin Crichton 1943- *Who 94*
Mackay, David Ian 1945- *Who 94*
Mackay, Donald (Alexander) 1914- *WrDr 94*
MacKay, Donald (Iain) 1937- *WrDr 94*
Mackay, Donald Cameron 1906-1979 *WhoAmA 93N*
Mackay, Donald George 1929- *Who 94*
MacKay, Donald Iain 1937- *Who 94*
Mackay, Donald Sage 1946- *Who 94*
Mackay, Douglas Ian 1948- *Who 94*
Mackay, Edward 1936- *WhoMW 93, WhoScEn 94*
Mackay, Eileen Alison 1943- *Who 94*
Mackay, Elmer MacIntosh 1936- *IntWW 93*
Mackay, Eric Beattie 1922- *Who 94*
Mackay, Eric MacLachlan 1921- *Who 94*
Mackay, Fulton d1987 *WhoHol 92*
Mackay, Gordon *Who 94*
Mackay, (George Patrick) Gordon 1914- *Who 94*
MacKay, Harold Hugh 1940- *WhoAm 94*
Mackay, Harvey (B.) 1932- *WrDr 94*
Mackay, James Alexander 1936- *WrDr 94*
MacKay, James R. 1930- *WhoAmP 93*
Mackay, Jessie 1864-1938 *BlmGWL*
Mackay, Jock d1961 *WhoHol 92*
Mackay, John 1914- *Who 94, WhoScEn 94*
Mackay, John 1920- *WhoAm 94*
Mackay, John Alexander 1889-1983 *DcAmReB 2*
MacKay, John Norman 1946- *WhoAmL 94*
MacKay, John Robert, II 1934- *WhoAm 94*
Mackay, Kenneth 1917- *Who 94*
MacKay, (James Alexander) Kenneth 1859-1935 *EncSF 93*
Mackay, Kenneth Donald 1942- *WhoScEn 94*
MacKay, Kenneth Hood 1933- *WhoAm 94*
Mackay, Leonard d1929 *WhoHol 92*
MacKay, Malcolm 1940- *WhoAm 94*
Mackay, Mary *WhoHol 92*
MacKay, Neil Duncan 1931- *WhoFI 94*
MacKay, Norman 1936- *Who 94*
Mackay, Peter 1940- *Who 94*
Mac Kay, Pierre Antony 1933- *WhoAm 94*
Mackay, Raymond Arthur 1939- *WhoScEn 94*
Mackay, Shena 1945- *BlmGWL*
Mackay, Simon 1930- *WrDr 94*
MacKay, William Andrew 1929- *WhoAm 94*
Mackay-Dick, Iain Charles 1945- *Who 94*
Mackaye, Dorothy d1940 *WhoHol 92*
MacKaye, Dorothy Disney 1904-1992 *AnObit 1992*
Mackaye, Harold Steele 1866-1928 *EncSF 93*
MacKaye, Norman d1968 *WhoHol 92*
Mackaye, (James Morrison) Steele 1842-1894 *IntDcT 2*
MacKaye, William Ross 1934- *WhoAm 94*
Mackay of Ardbrecknish, Baron 1938- *Who 94*
Mackay Of Clashfern, Baron 1927- *IntWW 93, Who 94*
Mackay-Smith, Sandy 1941- *WhoAm 94*
Mack Bride, Johnny 1926- *WrDr 94*
Mack Daddy c. 1979- See Kris Kross *ConMus 11*
Macke, Donald LaVerne 1937- *WhoAm 94*
Macke, Gerald Fred 1939- *WhoMW 93*
Macke, Kenneth A. 1938- *WhoAm 94, WhoFI 94*
Macke, Richard Chester 1938- *WhoAm 94*
Mackechnie, Alistair (John) 1934- *Who 94*
MacKeigan, Ian Malcolm 1915- *Who 94, WhoAm 94*
Mackel, Audley Maurice 1904-1982 *WhoBlA 94N*
Mackel, Audley Maurice, III 1955- *WhoBlA 94*
Mackel, Marilyn Hortense 1945- *WhoAmL 94, WhoWest 94*
MacKellar, Michael John Randal 1938- *IntWW 93*
Mackel-Rice, Gwendolyn Rosetta 1941- *WhoMW 93*
MacKelvie, Charles George Franklin 1944- *WhoAm 94*
Mackelworth, R(onald) W(alter) 1930- *EncSF 93, WrDr 94*
Macken, Daniel Loos 1933- *WhoScEn 94*
Macken, Walter d1967 *WhoHol 92*
Mackendrick, Alexander d1993 *NewYTBS 93*
Mackendrick, Donald Anthony 1925- *WhoAmP 93*
MacKendrick, Paul Lachlan 1914- *WhoAm 94*
MacKenna, Kate d1957 *WhoHol 92*
MacKenna, Kenneth d1962 *WhoHol 92*
MacKenna, Robert Ogilvie 1913- *Who 94*
MacKenroth, Joyce Ellen 1946- *WhoWest 94*
Mackenzie *Who 94*
Mackenzie, Alex d1966 *WhoHol 92*
Mackenzie, Alexander 1764-1820 *WhWE*
Mackenzie, Alexander (Campbell) 1847-1935 *NewGrDO*
Mackenzie, Alexander Alwyne H. C. B. M. *Who 94*
Mackenzie, (Alexander George Anthony) Allan d1993 *Who 94N*
Mackenzie, Andrew Carr 1911- *WrDr 94*
MacKenzie, Andrew Ross 1934- *WhoAm 94, WhoFI 94*
MacKenzie, Anne 1949- *WhoAmP 93*
Mackenzie, Archibald Robert Kerr 1915- *Who 94*
Mackenzie, Cameron, Jr. d1993 *NewYTBS 93*
Mackenzie, Charles E. 1943- *WhoAmP 93*
Mackenzie, Charles Edward 1943- *WhoAm 94*
MacKenzie, Charles Sherrard 1924- *WhoAm 94*
Mackenzie, Charles Westlake, III 1946- *WhoAm 94*
Mackenzie, Colin Dalzell 1919- *Who 94*
Mackenzie, Colin Scott 1938- *Who 94*
Mackenzie, Compton d1972 *WhoHol 92*
Mackenzie, Compton 1883-1972 *BlmGEL*
Mackenzie, (Edward Montague) Compton 1883-1972 *EncSF 93*
MacKenzie, David 1927- *WrDr 94*
Mackenzie, David, IV 1942- *WhoAmA 93*
Mackenzie, David James Masterton 1905- *Who 94*
Mackenzie, David John 1929- *Who 94*
Mackenzie, Donald d1973 *WhoHol 92*
Mackenzie, Donald 1783-1851 *WhWE*
MacKenzie, Donald 1918- *WrDr 94*
Mackenzie, Donald 1918-1993 *ConAu 142*
MacKenzie, Donald Murray 1947- *WhoAm 94*
Mackenzie, Douglas George 1947- *WhoFI 94*
MacKenzie, Eric Francis 1893- *WhAm 10*
Mackenzie, Franklin Arthur 1965- *WhoMW 93*
Mackenzie, Frederick d1824 *WhAmRev*
MacKenzie, George d1975 *WhoHol 92*
MacKenzie, George 1949- *WhoFI 94*
MacKenzie, George Allan 1931- *WhoAm 94, WhoFI 94, WhoMW 93*
MacKenzie, Gillian Rachel *Who 94*
MacKenzie, Ginny *DrAPF 93*
Mackenzie, Guy *Who 94*
MacKenzie, Hector Uisdean 1940- *Who 94*
Mackenzie, Henry 1745-1831 *NinCLC 41 [port]*
MacKenzie, Hugh Seaforth 1928- *WhoAmA 93*
Mackenzie, Hugh Stirling 1913- *Who 94*
Mackenzie, Ian 1914- *IntWW 93*
Mackenzie, Ian Clayton 1909- *Who 94*
Mackenzie, James 1924- *Who 94*
MacKenzie, James Alexander Mackintosh 1928- *Who 94*
MacKenzie, James Sargent Porteous 1916- *Who 94*
Mackenzie, James Stuart 1719-1800 *DcNaB MP*
Mackenzie, James William Guy 1946- *Who 94*
Mackenzie, Jean West *DrAPF 93*

Mac Lean, Lloyd Douglas 1924- WhoAm 94
MacLean, Mary Elise 1963- WhoScEn 94
MacLean, Merrilee Ann 1952- WhoAmL 94
MacLean, Murdo 1943- Who 94
Maclean, Norman 1902-1990 ConLC 78 [port], ShSCr 13 [port]
MacLean, Norman 1932- Who 94
MacLean, Norman Fitzroy 1902-1990 WhAm 10
MacLean, Paul Donald 1913- WhoAm 94
MacLean, Peter WhoHol 92
MacLean, R. D. d1948 WhoHol 92
MacLean, Ranald Norman Munro Who 94
Maclean, Robert (Alexander) 1908- Who 94
MacLean, Sorley 1911- WrDr 94
Maclean, Stephanie Maria 1954- WhoWest 94
MacLean, William 1908- WhAm 10
MacLean, William Q., Jr. 1934- WhoAmP 93
Maclean of Dochgarroch, Allan Murray 1950- Who 94
Maclean of Dunconnel, Fitzroy 1911- IntWW 93
Maclean of Dunconnel, Fitzroy Hew 1911- Who 94
MacLeary, Alistair Ronald 1940- Who 94
Macleary, Donald 1937- IntDcB [port]
MacLeary, Donald Whyte 1937- Who 94
Macleay, Donald 1908- WhoAm 94
Macleay, John Henry James 1931- Who 94
Maclehose Who 94
MacLehose Of Beoch, Baron 1917- IntWW 93, Who 94
MacLeish, Archibald 1892-1982 AmCulL [port], ConDr 93
MacLeish, Archibald Bruce 1947- WhoAm 94
MacLeish, Roderick, Jr. 1952- WhoAmL 94
MacLellan, George Douglas Stephen 1922- Who 94
MacLellan, Patrick Who 94
MacLellan, (Andrew) Patrick (Withy) 1925- Who 94
MacLennan, Alastair 1912- Who 94
MacLennan, Beryce W. 1920- WhoAm 94
Mac Lennan, David Herman 1937- WhoAm 94, WhoScEn 94
MacLennan, David Ross 1945- Who 94
Maclennan, Duncan 1949- Who 94
MacLennan, Graeme Andrew Yule 1942- Who 94
Maclennan, Hugh 1907-1990 WhAm 10
MacLennan, (John) Hugh 1907-1990 ConAu 142, EncSF 93
Maclennan, Robert Adam Ross 1936- IntWW 93, Who 94
Macleod Who 94
Macleod, Alison 1920- WrDr 94
Macleod, Alistair 1936- RfGShF, WrDr 94
MacLeod, Angus 1906- EncSF 93
MacLeod, Aubrey Seymour H. Who 94
MacLeod, Bruce R. 1948- WhoAmL 94
MacLeod, Calum Alexander 1935- Who 94
MacLeod, Charlotte (Matilda) 1922- WrDr 94
MacLeod, Denis Frederick 1954- WhoMW 93
Macleod, Donald 1914- WhoAm 94
MacLeod, Donald Alexander 1938- Who 94
MacLeod, Donald Francis Graham d1993 Who 94N
MacLeod, Donald Martin 1929- WhoFI 94
MacLeod, Ellen Jane WrDr 94
Macleod, Gavin 1931- IntMPA 94, WhoHol 92
MacLeod, Gordon Albert 1926- WhoAm 94
Macleod, Hamish Who 94
Macleod, (Nathaniel William) Hamish 1940- IntWW 93, Who 94
Macleod, Hugh Angus Macintosh 1933- IntWW 93
Macleod, Hugh Angus McIntosh 1933- WhoWest 94
MacLeod, Iain Alasdair 1939- Who 94
Macleod, Ian Buchanan 1933- Who 94
MacLeod, Jack 1931- WhoAm 94
MacLeod, Jean S. 1908- WrDr 94
MacLeod, John 1937- BasBi, WhoAm 94
MacLeod, John 1939- Who 94
Macleod, John Amend 1942- WhoAm 94, WhoAmL 94, WhoFI 94
MacLeod, John Daniel, Jr. 1922- WhoAm 94
MacLeod, John Munroe 1937- WhoAm 94, WhoScEn 94
MacLeod, Kathleen Bromley 1953- WhoWest 94
MacLeod, Marylynn 1965- WhoMW 93
MacLeod, Maxwell Who 94
MacLeod, (John) Maxwell (Norman) 1952- Who 94
Macleod, Nigel Ronald Buchanan 1936- Who 94
MacLeod, Norman Donald 1932- Who 94
Macleod, Pegi Nichol WhoAmA 93N
MacLeod, Richard Patrick 1937- WhoScEn 94, WhoWest 94
MacLeod, Robert 1928- WrDr 94
MacLeod, Robert Angus 1921- WhoAm 94
MacLeod, Robert Fredric 1917- WhoAm 94, WhoWest 94
MacLeod, (Hugh) Roderick d1993 Who 94N
MacLeod, Sheila 1939- EncSF 93, WrDr 94
MacLeod, William B. 1951- WhoAm 94
MacLeod, William Cyrus 1952- WhoAmL 94
Macleod, Yan 1889-1978 WhoAmA 93N
Macleod-Ball, Michael Wesley 1953- WhoAmL 94
Macleod of Borve, Baroness 1915- Who 94, WhoWomW 91
MacLeod of MacLeod, John 1935- Who 94
Macleod-Smith, Alastair Macleod 1916- Who 94
MacLiammoir, Micheal d1978 WhoHol 92
Maclin, Alan Hall 1949- WhoAm 94, WhoAmL 94
Maclin, Ernest 1931- WhoAm 94
Mac Low, Jackson DrAPF 93
Mac Low, Jackson 1922- ConDr 93, WrDr 94
Mac Low, Mordecai-Mark 1963- WhoMW 93
Maclure, John (Robert Spencer) 1934- Who 94
Maclure, (John) Stuart 1926- Who 94
MacMahon, Aline 1899- WhoHol 92
MacMahon, Aline 1899-1991 ConTFT 11
Macmahon, Brian 1923- IntWW 93
MacMahon, Bryan Michael 1909- WrDr 94
MacMahon, Charles Hutchins, Jr. 1918- WhoAm 94
MacMahon, Gerald John 1909- Who 94
MacMahon, John G. d1968 WhoHol 92
MacMahon, Lloyd Francis 1912-1989 WhAm 10
MacMahon, Paul 1945- WhoAm 94
MacManus, Anna BlmGWL
MacManus, Bernard Ronald 1936- Who 94
MacManus, John Leslie Edward 1920- Who 94
MacManus, Susan Ann 1947- WhoAm 94, WhoFI 94
MacManus, Yvonne Cristina 1931- WhoAm 94
MacMaster, Daniel Miller 1913- WhoAm 94
MacMaster, Robert Ellsworth 1919- WhoAm 94, WrDr 94
Macmeeken, John Peebles 1924- WhoAm 94
Macmillan Who 94
Macmillan, Alexander Ross 1922- Who 94
MacMillan, Andrew 1928- Who 94
MacMillan, David Paul 1943- WhoFI 94
MacMillan, Douglas Clark 1912- WhoAm 94
Macmillan, Douglas Hathaway 1946- WhoAm 94
Macmillan, (John) Duncan 1939- ConAu 142
MacMillan, Gary Adams 1947- WhoAmL 94
Macmillan, Gilleasbuig Iain 1942- Who 94
Macmillan, Graham Who 94
Macmillan, (Alexander McGregor) Graham 1920- Who 94
Macmillan, Harold 1894-1986 HisWorL [port], WhAm 10
Macmillan, Iain Alexander 1923- Who 94
MacMillan, Jake Who 94
Macmillan, Jake 1924- IntWW 93
MacMillan, John 1924- Who 94
MacMillan, John Richard Alexander 1932- Who 94
MacMillan, Kenneth d1992 IntWW 93N, Who 94N
MacMillan, Kenneth 1929-1992 AnObit 1992, IntDcB [port], WhAm 10
MacMillan, Kip Van Metre 1937- WhoAm 94
Macmillan, Kirkpatrick 1812-1878 DcNaB MP
MacMillan, Logan T., Jr. 1949- WhoWest 94
Macmillan, Matthew 1926- Who 94
MacMillan, Patti 1947- WhoAmP 93
Macmillan, Robert Hugh 1921- Who 94
Macmillan, Robert Smith 1924- WhoAm 94, WhoFI 94, WhoScEn 94, WhoWest 94
MacMillan, Violet d1953 WhoHol 92
Macmillan, Wallace d1992 Who 94N
Macmillan, William Boyd Robertson 1927- Who 94
Macmillan, William Hooper 1923- WhoAm 94
MacMillan, William Leedom, Jr. 1913- WhoAm 94
Macmillan, William Miller 1885-1974 DcNaB MP
Macmillan of Ovenden, Viscount 1974- Who 94
MacMillen, Richard Edward 1932- WhoAm 94
MacMinn, Aleene Merle Barnes 1930- WhoAm 94
MacMinn, Pamela Lee 1951- WhoMW 93
MacMullen, Douglas Burgoyne 1919- WhoWest 94
MacMullen, Ramsay 1928- WhoAm 94
MacMurchy, Marjory BlmGWL
MacMurray, Fred 1907- WhoHol 92
MacMurray, Frederick Martin 1908-1991 WhAm 10
MacMurray, Mary Bell McMillan Who 94
MacMurray, Peter Joseph, Jr. 1949- WhoFI 94
MacMurren, Harold Henry, Jr. 1942- WhoScEn 94
MacNab, Charles H., Jr. 1946- WhoAmL 94
Macnab, Geoffrey (Alex Colin) 1899- Who 94
Macnab, P(eter) A(ngus) 1903- WrDr 94
Macnab, Roy (Martin) 1923- WrDr 94
MacNabb, Byron Gordon 1910- IntWW 93
Macnab of Macnab, James Charles 1926- Who 94
Macnaghten, Patrick (Alexander) 1927- Who 94
Macnaghten, Robin Donnelly 1927- Who 94
Macnair, Maurice John Peter 1919- Who 94
Mac Namara, Donal Eoin Joseph 1916- WhoAm 94
MacNamara, G. Allan 1894- WhAm 10
Macnamara, Thomas Edward 1929- WhoAm 94
Macnaughtan, Don 1939- WhoAmP 93
MacNaughton, Alan 1920- WhoHol 92
MacNaughton, Angus Athole 1931- IntWW 93, WhoAm 94, WhoFI 94, WhoWest 94
MacNaughton, Donald Sinclair 1917- IntWW 93, WhoAm 94, WhoFI 94
MacNaughton, John David Francis 1932- WhoAm 94
MacNaughton, John P. 1946- WhoAmL 94
Macnaughton, Malcolm (Campbell) 1925- Who 94
Macnaughton, Malcolm Campbell 1925- IntWW 93
Macnaughton, Robert WhoHol 92
Mac Naughton, Robert 1966- IntMPA 94
MacNaughton, Tom d1923 WhoHol 92
Macnee, Alan Breck 1920- WhoAm 94
Macnee, Patrick 1922- WhoAm 94, WhoHol 92
MacNeice, Louis 1907-1963 BlmGEL
MacNeil, Cornell 1922- NewGrDO
MacNeil, Cornell Hill 1922- IntWW 93
MacNeil, Duncan 1920- WrDr 94
Macneil, Ian Roderick 1929- WrDr 94
MacNeil, Joseph Neil Who 94
Mac Neil, Joseph Neil 1924- WhoAm 94, WhoWest 94
MacNeil, Robert Breckenridge Ware 1931- WhoAm 94
MacNeill, Alastair 1960- WrDr 94
MacNeill, Earl S(chworm) 1893- WhAm 10
MacNeill, Frederick Douglas 1929- WhoAmA 93
MacNeill, Hugh Gordon 1925- WhoFI 94
Mac Neill, James William 1928- WhoAm 94
MacNeill, John Sears, Jr. 1927- WhoFI 94
Macneil of Barra, Ian Roderick 1929- Who 94
Macneish, Richard Stockton 1918- IntWW 93, WhoAm 94, WhoScEn 94
Mac Nelly, Jeffrey Kenneth 1947- WhoAm 94, WhoAmA 93, WhoMW 93
MacNichol, Edward Ford, Jr. 1918- WhoAm 94
MacNicol, Peter 1957- WhoHol 92
MacNider, Jack 1927- WhoAm 94
Macnish, James Martin, Jr. 1935- WhoAmL 94
Mac-Noye, Shirley 1940- WhoWest 94
Macnutt, Evelyn L. 1915- WhoAmP 93
MacNutt, Glenn Gordon 1906-1987 WhAm 10, WhoAmA 93N
Maco, Paul Stephen, Jr. 1952- WhoAm 94
Maco, Teri Regan 1953- WhoFI 94
Macollum, Barry d1971 WhoHol 92
Macomb, John N. 1811-1889 WhWE
Macomber, Allison 1916-1979 WhoAmA 93N
Macomber, Harold M. WhoAmP 93
Macomber, John D. 1928- WhoAm 94
Macon, Irene Elizabeth 1935- WhoFI 94, WhoMW 93, WhoScEn 94
Macon, Jane Haun 1946- WhoAm 94, WhoAmL 94
Macon, Jerry Lyn 1941- WhoWest 94
Macon, John Edward 1938- WhoIns 94
Macon, Jorge 1924- WhoScEn 94
Macon, Mark L. 1969- WhoBlA 94
Macon, Nathaniel 1758-1837 WhAmRev
Macon, Richard Laurence 1944- WhoAm 94, WhoAmL 94
Macon, Seth Craven 1919- WhoAm 94
Macon, William Hartwell 1923- WhoAmP 93
Maconchy, Elizabeth 1907- NewGrDO, Who 94
Maconi, Richard Curtis 1922- WhoFI 94
Maconochie, Alexander 1787-1860 DcNaB MP
Macosko, Paul John, II 1952- WhoScEn 94
Macoun, Michael John 1914- Who 94
Macourek, Milos 1926- ConAu 140
Macovescu, George 1913- IntWW 93
Macovski, Albert 1929- WhoAm 94, WhoScEn 94, WhoWest 94
Macowan, Norman d1961 WhoHol 92
MacPatterson, F. EncSF 93
MacPhail, Andy WhoAm 94, WhoMW 93
MacPhail, Bruce (Dugald) 1939- Who 94
Macphail, Iain Duncan 1938- Who 94
Macphail, Moray St. John 1912- WhoAm 94
Macphearson, James 1937- WrDr 94
MacPhee, Craig Robert 1944- WhoAm 94
MacPhee, Donald Albert 1928- WhoAm 94
Macpherson Who 94
Macpherson, Aimee Semple d1944 WhoHol 92
Macpherson, Alexander Calderwood 1939- Who 94
Macpherson, Colin Robertson 1924- WhoAm 94
MacPherson, David Allan 1960- WhoFI 94
MacPherson, Donald EncSF 93
Macpherson, Elle WhoHol 92
Macpherson, Ewen Cameron Stewart 1942- Who 94
Macpherson, Ian 1936- Who 94
Macpherson, James 1736-1796 BlmGEL
Macpherson, James (Campbell) 1942- WrDr 94
MacPherson, James Gladstone d1932 WhoHol 92
Macpherson, (Jean) Jay 1918- BlmGWL
Macpherson, (Jean) Jay 1931- WrDr 94
Macpherson, Jeanie d1946 WhoHol 92
Macpherson, Jeanie 1884-1946 IntDcF 2-4 [port]
MacPherson, Jennifer B. DrAPF 93
Macpherson, John Stuart 1898-1971 DcNaB MP
Macpherson, Keith (Duncan) 1920- Who 94
MacPherson, Keith Duncan 1920- IntWW 93
Macpherson, Kevin 1956- WhoAmA 93
Macpherson, Margaret 1908- WrDr 94
MacPherson, Quinton d1940 WhoHol 92
MacPherson, Robert Duncan 1944- WhoAm 94, WhoScEn 94
Macpherson, Roderick Ewen 1916- Who 94
MacPherson, Stewart Myles 1908- Who 94
Macpherson, Thomas Who 94
Macpherson, (Ronald) Thomas (Stewart) 1920- Who 94
Macpherson of Cluny, William (Alan) 1926- Who 94
Macpherson of Drumochter, Baron 1924- Who 94
Macphie, Duncan Love 1930- Who 94
Macquaker, Donald Francis 1932- Who 94
MacQuarrie, Albert d1950 WhoHol 92
MacQuarrie, Frank d1950 WhoHol 92
MacQuarrie, Haven d1953 WhoHol 92
Macquarrie, Heath Nelson 1919- WhoAm 94
Macquarrie, John 1919- IntWW 93, Who 94, WrDr 94
MacQuarrie, Murdock d1942 WhoHol 92
Macqueen, Angus 1910- Who 94
MacQueen, John 1929- Who 94, WrDr 94

MacQueen, Robert Moffat 1938- *WhoAm 94, WhoScEn 94, WhoWest 94*
MacQueen, William Johnstone 1943- *WhoAmL 94*
MacQueen, Winifred (Wallace) 1928- *WrDr 94*
MacQuitty, James Lloyd 1912- *Who 94*
Mac Rae, Alfred Urquhart 1932- *WhoAm 94*
MacRae, Amy Frances 1958- *WhoMW 93*
Macrae, Arthur d1962 *WhoHol 92*
MacRae, Bette Jayne 1920- *WhoAmP 93*
MacRae, Cameron Farquhar, III 1942- *WhoAm 94*
MacRae, (Alastair) Christopher (Donald Summerhayes) 1937- *IntWW 93, Who 94*
MacRae, Donald Alexander 1916- *WhoAm 94*
MacRae, Donald Gunn 1921- *Who 94*
MacRae, Duncan d1967 *WhoHol 92*
MacRae, Duncan, Jr. 1921- *WhoAm 94*
MacRae, Elizabeth 1939- *WhoHol 92*
MacRae, Gordon d1986 *WhoHol 92*
MacRae, Heather 1947- *WhoHol 92*
Mac Rae, Herbert Farquhar 1926- *WhoAm 94*
Macrae, John Esmond Campbell 1932- *Who 94*
MacRae, Kenneth Charles 1944- *Who 94*
MacRae, Mary Jenkins 1954- *WhoFI 94*
MacRae, Meredith 1945- *WhoHol 92*
MacRae, Michael *WhoHol 92*
Macrae, Robert (Andrew Alexander Scarth) 1915- *Who 94*
MacRae, Sheila 1924- *WhoHol 92*
Macrakis, Kristie Irene 1958- *WhoMW 93*
Macreadie, John Lindsay 1946- *Who 94*
Macready, George d1973 *WhoHol 92*
Macready, Nevil (John Wilfrid) 1921- *Who 94*
Macri, Theodore William *WhoAm 94*
Macridis, Roy Constantine 1918-1991 *WhAm 10*
Macris, Michael 1949- *WhoAmL 94*
Macro, Lucia Ann 1959- *WhoAm 94*
MacRobbie, Enid Anne Campbell 1931- *Who 94*
MacRoberts, Paul Brooks 1938- *WhoFI 94*
Macroe-Wiegand, Viola Lucille 1920- *WhoScEn 94*
Macrorie, Alma d1970 *WhoHol 92*
Macrory, Patrick Arthur d1993 *Who 94N*
Macrory, Patrick Francis John 1941- *WhoAm 94*
Macrory, Richard Brabazon 1950- *Who 94*
MacRury, King 1915- *WhoAm 94*
Macsai, John 1926- *WhoAm 94*
Macsarin, Kenneth d1967 *WhoHol 92*
MacShane, Frank (Sutherland) 1927- *WrDr 94*
MacSharry, Ray 1938- *IntWW 93*
MacSharry, Raymond 1938- *Who 94*
MacSweeney, Barry 1948- *WrDr 94*
MacTaggart, Barry 1931- *WhoAm 94*
Mactaggart, Fiona 1953- *Who 94*
Mactaggart, John (Auld) 1951- *Who 94*
Mactaggart, Sandy A. 1928- *IntWW 93*
MacTaggart, Terrence Joseph 1946- *WhoAm 94, WhoMW 93*
Mactaggart, William Alexander 1906- *Who 94*
MacTaggart, William Keith 1929- *Who 94*
MacThòmais, Ruaraidh 1921- *WrDr 94*
MacThomas of Finegand, Andrew Patrick Clayhills 1942- *Who 94*
Mactier, Susie *BlmGWL*
MacTyre, Paul 1924- *EncSF 93*
Macumber, John Paul 1940- *WhoWest 94*
Macur, Patricia Alice *WhoFI 94*
Macurdy, John 1929- *NewGrDO*
Macurdy, John Edward 1929- *WhoAm 94*
MacVarish, Greg 1964- *WhoMW 93*
MacVean, Jean *WrDr 94*
MacVicar, Angus *EncSF 93*
Macvicar, Angus 1908- *WrDr 94*
MacVicar, Kenneth 1931- *Who 94*
Mac Vicar, Margaret Love Agnes 1943-1991 *WhAm 10*
MacVicar, Martha d1971 *WhoHol 92*
Macvicar, Neil 1920- *Who 94*
Mac Vicar, Robert William 1918- *WhoAm 94*
Mac Vittie, Robert William 1920- *WhoAm 94*
Mac Watters, Virginia Elizabeth *WhoAm 94*
MacWeeney, Alen Brazil 1939- *WhoAm 94*
Macwhinnie, Gordon (Menzies) 1922- *Who 94*
Mac Whinnie, John Vincent 1945- *WhoAm 94, WhoAmA 93*

MacWhorter, Robert Bruce 1930- *WhoAm 94*
MacWilliam, Alexander Gordon 1923- *Who 94*
MacWilliams, Bill *WhoHol 92*
MacWilliams, Kenneth Edward 1936- *WhoAm 94*
Macy, Anne Sullivan d1936 *WhoHol 92*
Macy, Bill 1922- *WhoHol 92*
Macy, Carleton d1946 *WhoHol 92*
Macy, Jack d1956 *WhoHol 92*
Macy, John Patrick 1955- *WhoAmL 94*
Macy, Jonathan Isaac 1950- *WhoWest 94*
Macy, Judith K. *WhoAmP 93*
Macy, Michael Gaylord 1957- *WhoWest 94*
Macy, Richard J. *WhoAmP 93*
Macy, Richard J. 1930- *WhoAm 94, WhoAmL 94, WhoWest 94*
Macy, W. H. *WhoHol 92*
Maczulski, Margaret Louise *WhoFI 94*
Madabhushi, Govindachari Venkata 1933- *WhoScEn 94, WhoWest 94*
Madach, Imre 1823-1864 *EncSF 93, IntDcT 2*
Madaio, Michael Peter *WhoScEn 94*
Ma Dajing 1947- *WhoPRCh 91 [port]*
Madakson, Peter Bitrus 1953- *WhoScEn 94*
Madalena, James Roger *WhoAmP 93*
Madalski, Wojtek 1956- *WhoMW 93*
Madan, Arun 1963- *WhoFI 94*
Madan, Bal Krishna 1911- *IntWW 93*
Madan, Dwarka Nath 1937- *WhoAsA 94*
Madan, Sudhir Yashpal 1961- *WhoScEn 94*
Madanat, Samer Michel 1963- *WhoScEn 94*
Madanayake, Lalith Prasanna 1965- *WhoScEn 94*
Madan-Shotkin, Rhoda *WhoAmA 93*
Madansky, Albert 1934- *WhoAm 94*
Madansky, Leon 1923- *WhoAm 94*
Madariaga (Y Rojo), Salvador de 1886-1978 *EncSF 93*
Madariaga, Isabel Margaret de 1919- *Who 94*
Ma Dayou 1915- *WhoPRCh 91 [port]*
Ma Dayou (Dah-You Maa) 1915- *IntWW 93*
Maddala, Gangadharrao Soundaryarao 1933- *WhoFI 94*
Maddalena, Frederick Louis 1947- *WhoScEn 94*
Maddalena, Lucille Ann 1948- *WhoAm 94*
Madden, Alice Donnelly 1958- *WhoAmL 94*
Madden, Arthur Allen 1960- *WhoScEn 94*
Madden, Bartley Joseph 1943- *WhoFI 94, WhoMW 93*
Madden, Bernard Patrick 1947- *WhoAmP 93*
Madden, Bill 1915- *IntMPA 94*
Madden, Bill 1945- *WrDr 94*
Madden, Catherine Rose 1943- *WhoFI 94*
Madden, Charles (Edward) 1906- *Who 94*
Madden, Cheryl Beth 1948- *WhoAmP 93*
Madden, Ciaran 1945- *WhoHol 92*
Madden, Colin Duncan 1915- *Who 94*
Madden, Dave *WhoHol 92*
Madden, David *DrAPF 93, IntMPA 94*
Madden, David 1933- *WhoAm 94, WrDr 94*
Madden, David Christopher Andrew McCulloch 1946- *Who 94*
Madden, Deirdre 1960- *WrDr 94*
Madden, Donald d1983 *WhoHol 92*
Madden, Donald Paul 1933- *WhoAm 94*
Madden, Eddie M. 1948- *WhoAmP 93*
Madden, Edward George, Jr. 1924- *WhoAmL 94*
Madden, Edward Harry 1925- *WhoAm 94*
Madden, Frederick *Who 94*
Madden, (Albert) Frederick (McCulloch) 1917- *IntWW 93, Who 94*
Madden, George Graham 1947- *WhoWest 94*
Madden, J. Patrick 1937- *WhoWest 94*
Madden, James Cooper, V 1961- *WhoFI 94*
Madden, James Desmond 1940- *WhoMW 93, WhoScEn 94*
Madden, Jeanne d1989 *WhoHol 92*
Madden, Jerome Anthony 1948- *WhoAmL 94*
Madden, Jerry Agnew 1943- *WhoAmP 93*
Madden, Joe *WhoHol 92*
Madden, John 1936- *WhoAm 94*
Madden, John Joseph 1946- *WhoAm 94*
Madden, John Kevin 1938- *WhoAm 94*
Madden, John T. 1896- *WhAm 10*
Madden, Joseph Daniel 1921- *WhoAm 94*
Madden, Keith Patrick 1953- *WhoMW 93*
Madden, Lance J. 1945- *WhoAmL 94*
Madden, Laurence Vincent 1953- *WhoScEn 94*
Madden, Marie Frances 1928- *WhoFI 94*

Madden, Martin Gerard 1949- *WhoAmP 93*
Madden, Max 1941- *Who 94*
Madden, Michael 1936- *Who 94*
Madden, Michael Daniel 1949- *WhoAm 94*
Madden, Murdaugh Stuart 1922- *WhoAm 94*
Madden, Nancy A. 1951- *WhoMW 93*
Madden, Neal D. 1946- *WhoAmL 94*
Madden, Palmer Brown 1945- *WhoAm 94, WhoAmL 94, WhoWest 94*
Madden, Patrick Thomas 1944- *WhoAmL 94*
Madden, Paul Daniel 1948- *WhoWest 94*
Madden, Paul Robert 1926- *WhoAm 94, WhoAmL 94, WhoWest 94*
Madden, Paul W. 1946- *WhoAmL 94*
Madden, Peter d1976 *WhoHol 92*
Madden, Peter E. 1942- *WhoAmP 93*
Madden, Richard Blaine 1929- *WhoAm 94, WhoFI 94, WhoWest 94*
Madden, Richard Lewis 1951- *WhoFI 94*
Madden, Robert E. 1943- *WhoAmL 94*
Madden, Robert George 1957- *WhoAmL 94*
Madden, Robert William 1927- *WhoScEn 94*
Madden, Stephan DuPont 1954- *WhoAmL 94*
Madden, Thomas James 1941- *WhoAmL 94*
Madden, Wales Hendrix, Jr. 1927- *WhoAm 94*
Madden, Wanda Lois 1929- *WhoWest 94*
Madden, William J., Jr. 1939- *WhoAm 94*
Madden-Work, Betty I. 1915- *WhoAmA 93, WhoFI 94*
Maddern, Victor d1993 *NewYTBS 93*
Maddern, Victor 1926- *WhoHol 92*
Maddex, Myron Brown 1924- *WhoAm 94*
Maddicott, John Robert Lewendon 1943- *Who 94*
Maddison, Angus 1926- *WrDr 94*
Maddison, David George 1947- *Who 94*
Maddison, Vincent Albert 1915- *Who 94*
Maddock, Diana Margaret 1945- *Who 94*
Maddock, Jerome Torrence 1940- *WhoScEn 94*
Maddock, Larry 1931- *EncSF 93*
Maddock, R(eginald) B(ertram) 1912- *WrDr 94*
Maddock, Thomas Smothers 1928- *WhoAm 94, WhoScEn 94*
Maddocks, Arthur Frederick 1922- *Who 94*
Maddocks, Bertram Catterall 1932- *Who 94*
Maddocks, Fiona Hamilton 1955- *Who 94*
Maddocks, Kenneth (Phipson) 1907- *Who 94*
Maddocks, Margaret (Kathleen Avern) 1906- *WrDr 94*
Maddocks, Morris Henry St. John 1928- *Who 94*
Maddocks, Robert Allen 1933- *WhoAm 94*
Maddocks, William Henry d1992 *Who 94N*
Maddow, Ben 1909-1992 *IntDcF 2-4*
Maddox, Alva Hugh 1930- *WhoAmP 93*
Maddox, Barbara Jean 1947- *WhoAmP 93*
Maddox, Carl *EncSF 93*
Maddox, Carl 1919- *WrDr 94*
Maddox, Charles J., Jr. 1949- *WhoAmL 94*
Maddox, David M. *WhoAm 94*
Maddox, E. Farrell 1931- *WhoAmP 93*
Maddox, Elton Preston, Jr. 1946- *WhoBlA 94*
Maddox, Garry Lee 1949- *WhoBlA 94*
Maddox, Hugh 1930- *WhoAm 94, WhoAmL 94*
Maddox, Jack H. 1927- *WhoBlA 94*
Maddox, Jerald Curtis 1933- *WhoAmA 93*
Maddox, Jerrold Warren 1932- *WhoAmA 93*
Maddox, Jim 1938- *WhoAmP 93*
Maddox, John (Royden) 1925- *Who 94*
Maddox, John D. 1940- *WhoAmL 94*
Maddox, Leland L. 1939- *WhoAmP 93*
Maddox, Luther Warren 1924- *WhoAmP 93*
Maddox, Lyndell Eugene 1955- *WhoFI 94*
Maddox, Margaret Johnnetta Simms 1952- *WhoBlA 94*
Maddox, O. Gene 1938- *WhoAmP 93*
Maddox, Ode L. 1912- *WhoAmP 93*
Maddox, Odinga Lawrence 1939- *WhoBlA 94*
Maddox, Robert A., Jr. 1960- *WhoAmP 93*
Maddox, Robert Alan 1944- *WhoAm 94, WhoScEn 94*
Maddox, Robert Allen 1953- *WhoWest 94*
Maddox, Robert James 1931- *WrDr 94*
Maddox, Robert Lytton 1924- *WhoAm 94*
Maddox, Robert Nott 1925- *WhoAm 94*

Maddox, Robin Lea 1963- *WhoMW 93*
Maddox, Ronald 1930- *Who 94*
Maddox, Timothy Dwain 1960- *WhoFI 94*
Maddox, Tom *EncSF 93*
Maddox, Yvonne Tarlton 1936- *WhoAm 94*
Maddrell, Beverly Jean 1943- *WhoAmP 93*
Maddrell, Geoffrey Keggen 1936- *Who 94*
Maddrell, Simon Hugh Piper 1937- *Who 94*
Maddrey, E. E., II *WhoAm 94, WhoFI 94*
Maddrey, Elizabeth Huntley 1942- *WhoAmP 93*
Maddrey, Willis Crocker 1939- *WhoAm 94*
Maddux, Elmer L. 1934- *WhoAmP 93*
Maddux, Greg 1966- *WhoAm 94*
Maddux, Parker Ahrens 1939- *WhoAm 94, WhoAmL 94*
Maddux, Rachel 1912-1983 *DcLB Y93 [port]*
Maddy, Donald Lee 1949- *WhoWest 94*
Maddy, Kenneth Leon 1934- *WhoAmP 93*
Maddy, Penelope Jo 1950- *IntWW 93, WhoWest 94*
Maddy, Y(ulisa) A(madu) 1936- *WrDr 94*
Maddy, Yulisa Amadu 1936- *ConDr 93*
Made Gowda, Netkal M. 1947- *WhoAsA 94*
Madeira, Crawford Clark 1894- *WhAm 10*
Madeira, Edward Walter, Jr. 1928- *WhoAm 94, WhoAmL 94*
Madeira, Francis King Carey 1917- *WhoAm 94*
Madeira, Humberto d1971 *WhoHol 92*
Madeira, Jean 1918-1972 *NewGrDO*
Madeira, Robert Lehman 1915- *WhoAm 94*
Madeja, Stanley Stephen 1934- *WhoMW 93*
Madel, (William) David 1938- *Who 94*
Madelin, Alain 1946- *IntWW 93*
Madelung, Wilfred Willy Ferdinand 1930- *Who 94*
Maden, Margaret 1940- *Who 94*
Madenski, Melissa (Ann) 1949- *SmATA 77 [port]*
Mader, Bryn John 1959- *WhoScEn 94*
Mader, Charles Lavern 1930- *WhoWest 94*
Mader, Dan 1955- *WhoAmP 93*
Mader, Douglas Paul 1963- *WhoScEn 94*
Mader, Friedrich W(ilhelm) 1866-1947 *EncSF 93*
Mader, Kelly F. 1952- *WhoAmP 93*
Mader, Kelly Forbes 1952- *WhoWest 94*
Mader, Thomas Edward 1949- *WhoMW 93*
Mader, William Steven 1943- *WhoMW 93*
Madera, Carmen Soria 1937- *WhoAmL 94*
Madera, Cornelius J., Jr. 1949- *WhoAmL 94*
Madera, Joseph J. 1927- *WhoAm 94*
Madera, Maria S. 1953- *WhoHisp 94*
Madera Fernandez, Jose E. 1936- *WhoHisp 94*
Madera-Orsini, Frank M. 1916- *WhoHisp 94*
Maderna, Bruno 1920-1973 *NewGrDO*
Ma Desheng 1952- *WhoPRCh 91*
Madeson, Marvin Louis 1925- *WhoAmP 93*
Madetoja, Leevi (Antti) 1887-1947 *NewGrDO*
Madey, John M. J. 1943- *WhoAm 94*
Madge, Charles (Henry) 1912- *WrDr 94*
Madge, Charles Henry 1912- *Who 94*
Madge, James Richard 1924- *Who 94*
Madge, Nicola 1949- *WrDr 94*
Madgett, Naomi Long *DrAPF 93*
Madgett, Naomi Long 1923- *BlkWr 2, WhoAm 94, WhoBlA 94, WrDr 94*
Madhanagopal, Thiruvengadathan 1955- *WhoScEn 94*
Madhavan, Ananthanarayanan 1933- *IntWW 93*
Madhoun, Fadi Salah 1962- *WhoScEn 94*
Madhubuti, Haki R. *DrAPF 93*
Madhubuti, Haki R. 1942- *AfrAmAl 6, BlkWr 2, WhoBlA 94, WrDr 94*
Madia, Chunilal Kalidas 1922- *IntWW 93*
Madia, William Juul 1947- *WhoAm 94*
Madich, Bernadine Marie Hoff 1934- *WhoMW 93*
Madigan, Amy 1951- *IntMPA 94, WhoHol 92*
Madigan, Debra Jean 1962- *WhoMW 93*
Madigan, Doris Mary 1925- *WhoMW 93*
Madigan, Edward 1936- *IntWW 93*
Madigan, Edward R. 1936- *WhoAm 94, WhoAmP 93*
Madigan, John William 1937- *WhoAm 94, WhoFI 94, WhoMW 93*

Madigan, Joseph Edward 1932- *WhoAm 94*
Madigan, Kimberly A. 1956- *WhoAm 94, WhoAmL 94, WhoFI 94*
Madigan, Martha *WhoAmA 93*
Madigan, Martha 1950- *WhoAm 94*
Madigan, Mary Jean Smith *WhoAmA 93*
Madigan, Michael J. 1942- *WhoAmP 93*
Madigan, Michael J. 1943- *WhoAm 94*
Madigan, Michael Joseph 1942- *WhoAm 94, WhoMW 93*
Madigan, Richard Allen 1937- *WhoAmA 93*
Madigan, Robert 1942- *WhoAmP 93*
Madigan, Roger A. 1930- *WhoAmP 93*
Madigan, Russel (Tullie) 1920- *Who 94*
Madigan, Russel Tullie 1920- *IntWW 93*
Mading, James E. 1936- *WhoMW 93*
Madison, Bernard L. 1941- *WhoAm 94*
Madison, C. J. d1975 *WhoHol 92*
Madison, Carol 1923- *WrDr 94*
Madison, Cleo d1964 *WhoHol 92*
Madison, Eddie L., Jr. 1930- *WhoBlA 94*
Madison, Ellen d1987 *WhoHol 92*
Madison, Frank 1939- *WrDr 94*
Madison, Gary (Brent) 1940- *WrDr 94*
Madison, George H. 1939- *WhoAmP 93*
Madison, Guy 1922- *IntMPA 94, WhoHol 92*
Madison, Harry d1936 *WhoHol 92*
Madison, Helene d1970 *WhoHol 92*
Madison, Jacqueline Edwina 1951- *WhoBlA 94*
Madison, James 1751-1836 *AmRev, HisWorL [port], WhAmRev [port]*
Madison, James 1933- *WhoAmP 93*
Madison, James Raymond 1931- *WhoAm 94*
Madison, Joseph Edward 1949- *WhoBlA 94*
Madison, Kenneth Edward 1957- *WhoWest 94*
Madison, Leatrice Branch 1922- *WhoBlA 94*
Madison, Mae *WhoHol 92*
Madison, Miles 1965- *WhoWest 94*
Madison, Noel d1975 *WhoHol 92*
Madison, Richard 1932- *WhoBlA 94*
Madison, Robert P. 1923- *WhoBlA 94*
Madison, Robert Prince 1923- *WhoAm 94*
Madison, Ronald L. 1942- *WhoBlA 94*
Madison, Shannon L. 1927- *WhoBlA 94*
Madison, Stanley D. 1932- *WhoBlA 94*
Madison, T. Jerome 1940- *WhoFI 94*
Madison, William L. 1933- *WhoBlA 94*
Madison, Willie Clarence 1942- *WhoAm 94*
Madix, Robert James 1938- *WhoWest 94*
Madjeckewiss c. 1735-c. 1805 *AmRev*
Madkour, Mary E. 1927- *WhoAmP 93*
Madl, Alfred William 1923- *WhoMW 93*
Madl, Ferenc 1931- *IntWW 93*
Madla, Frank 1937- *WhoAmP 93, WhoHisp 94*
Madlang, Rodolfo Mojica 1918- *WhoScEn 94*
Madlee, Dorothy *EncSF 93*
Madlock, Bill, Jr. 1951- *WhoBlA 94*
Madni, Asad Mohamed 1947- *WhoWest 94*
Madni, Azad M. 1945- *WhoFI 94*
Madoc, Philip 1934- *WhoHol 92*
Madoff, Bernard Lawrence 1938- *WhoFI 94*
Madoff, Michelle *WhoAmP 93*
Madole, Donald Wilson 1932- *WhoAmL 94, WhoFI 94*
Madonia, Ann C. *WhoAmA 93*
Madonia, Valerie *WhoAm 94*
Madonna 1958- *IntMPA 94, IntWW 93, WhoAm 94, WhoHol 92*
Madonna, Harry D. 1942- *WhoAmL 94*
Madonna, Jon C. *WhoAm 94, WhoFI 94*
Madore, Joyce Louise 1936- *WhoMW 93*
Madorsky, Bryan *WhoHol 92*
Madory, James Richard 1940- *WhoAm 94, WhoScEn 94*
Madory, Richard Eugene 1931- *WhoAmL 94*
Madow, Leo 1915- *WhoAm 94*
Madras, Bertha Kalifon 1942- *WhoScEn 94*
Madrid, Alyce Janine 1959- *WhoHisp 94*
Madrid, Arturo *WhoHisp 94*
Madrid, Carlos, Jr. *WhoHisp 94*
Madrid, Chilo L. 1945- *WhoHisp 94*
Madrid, Jay Joseph 1942- *WhoAm 94*
Madrid, Joe Hernandez 1944- *WhoHisp 94*
Madrid, John Mario 1953- *WhoFI 94*
Madrid, Jose Saul 1956- *WhoHisp 94*
Madrid, Leasher Dennis 1949- *WhoHisp 94, WhoWest 94*
Madrid, Tito O. 1950- *WhoHisp 94*
Madrid Hurtado, Miguel de la *IntWW 93*
Madrid-Mendenhall, Cassandra 1962- *WhoHisp 94*
Madrid-Mirabal, Henry Alexander 1943- *WhoHisp 94*
Madrigal, Ramón Anthony 1957- *WhoHisp 94*
Madrigal, Ray 1944- *WhoHisp 94*
Madriguera, Enric d1973 *WhoHol 92*
Madril, Lee Ann 1944- *WhoWest 94*
Madron, Thomas Wm 1937- *WhoAmP 93*
Madry, Randall H. H. 1949- *WhoFI 94*
Madrzyk, John S. 1939- *WhoAmP 93*
Madsen, Arch Leonard 1913- *WhoAm 94, WhoWest 94*
Madsen, Barbara A. *WhoAmL 94*
Madsen, Barbara A. 1952- *WhoAmP 93*
Madsen, Brigham Dwaine 1914- *WhoAm 94*
Madsen, Charles Clifford 1908- *WhAm 10*
Madsen, Donald Howard 1922- *WhoAm 94*
Madsen, Dorothy Louise *WhoMW 93*
Madsen, Egon 1942- *IntDcB [port]*
Madsen, Francis Armstrong, Jr. 1931- *WhoAmP 93*
Madsen, George Frank 1933- *WhoAmL 94*
Madsen, Harald d1949 *WhoHol 92*
Madsen, Henry Stephen 1924- *WhoAm 94*
Madsen, (Mark) Hunter 1955- *WrDr 94*
Madsen, Ib Henning 1942- *IntWW 93*
Madsen, Karl D. 1962- *WhoFI 94*
Madsen, Ken *WhoAmP 93*
Madsen, Loren Wakefield 1943- *WhoAm 94, WhoAmA 93*
Madsen, Mette 1924- *IntWW 93*
Madsen, Mette B. 1955- *WhoAmA 93*
Madsen, Michael 1947- *WhoHol 92*
Madsen, Michael 1958- *IntMPA 94*
Madsen, Natasha R. 1938- *WhoAmP 93*
Madsen, Peter Eric 1945- *WhoAm 94*
Madsen, Philip Dana 1954- *WhoMW 93*
Madsen, Roger B. 1947- *WhoAmP 93*
Madsen, Stephen A. 1950- *WhoAmL 94*
Madsen, Stephen Stewart 1951- *WhoAm 94, WhoAmL 94*
Madsen, Svend Age *EncSF 93*
Madsen, Viggo Holm 1925- *WhoAmA 93*
Madsen, Virginia 1961- *WhoHol 92*
Madsen, Virginia 1963- *IntMPA 94*
Madsen, William Wallace 1962- *WhoWest 94*
Madson, Arthur *DrAPF 93*
Madson, Jan Sue 1955- *WhoMW 93*
Madson, Paulette Kay 1957- *WhoMW 93*
Madson, Philip Ward 1948- *WhoScEn 94*
Madubuike, Ihechukwu 1944- *IntWW 93*
Madubuike, Ihechukwu (Chiedozie) 1943- *WrDr 94*
Madueme, Godswill C. 1943- *WhoScEn 94*
Maduit Du Plessis, Chevalier de *WhAmRev*
Madura, Jack Joseph 1941- *WhoAmA 93*
Madura, Jeffry David 1957- *WhoScEn 94*
Maduro, John Lawrence 1921- *WhoAmP 93*
Madva, Stephen Alan 1948- *WhoAm 94, WhoAmL 94*
Mae, Gloria *WhoHol 92*
Mae, Jimsey d1968 *WhoHol 92*
Maechling, Charles, Jr. 1920- *WhoAm 94*
Maeda, Hiroshi 1938- *WhoScEn 94*
Maeda, J. A. 1940- *WhoFI 94, WhoWest 94*
Maeda, Kazuo 1919- *IntWW 93*
Maeda, Robert J. 1932- *WhoAsA 94*
Maeda, Sharon 1945?- *WhoAsA 94*
Maeda, Toshihide Munenobu 1962- *WhoAm 94, WhoScEn 94*
Maeda, Yukio 1922- *WhoScEn 94*
Maeda, Yutaka 1955- *WhoAsA 94*
Maeder, Thomas 1951- *WrDr 94*
Maedjaja, Daniel 1931- *WhoAsA 94*
Maegaard, Jan Carl Christian 1926- *IntWW 93*
Maehata, Sachiko 1937- *WhoWomW 91*
Maehl, William Harvey 1915- *WhoAm 94, WhoWest 94*
Maehl, William Henry 1930- *WhoAm 94*
Maehler, Herwig Gustav Theodor 1935- *IntWW 93, Who 94*
Maehr, Martin Louis 1932- *WhoAm 94*
Maekawa, Mamoru 1942- *WhoScEn 94*
Maeno, John Y. 1908-1993 *WhoAsA 94N*
Maeno, Norikazu 1940- *WhoScEn 94*
Maenpaa, Pekka Heikki 1939- *WhoScEn 94*
Maepen, K.H. *EncSF 93*
Ma Erchi *WhoPRCh 91*
Maeroff, Gene I. 1939- *WhoAm 94*
Maersch, Nancy Kay 1942- *WhoMW 93*
Maertens, Willy d1967 *WhoHol 92*
Maerz, Florence Szerlag *DrAPF 93*
Maes, James Alfredo 1947- *WhoHisp 94*
Maes, Jeanette C. *DrAPF 93*
Maes, Lee William 1948- *WhoHisp 94*
Maes, Nelly 1941- *WhoWomW 91*
Maes, Petra Jimenez *WhoAm 94*
Maes, Petra Jimenez 1947- *WhoHisp 94*
Maes, Robert Adamson 1910-1991 *WhAm 10*
Maes, Roman M. *WhoAmP 93*
Maes, Román M. 1943- *WhoHisp 94*
Maes-Jelinek, Hena *WrDr 94*
Maestas, Billy D. 1951- *WhoHisp 94*
Maestas, Charles James 1951- *WhoHisp 94*
Maestas, Christopher 1944- *WhoHisp 94*
Maestas, Elizabeth 1935- *WhoAmP 93*
Maestas, Joseph Michael 1960- *WhoHisp 94*
Maestas, Ronald W. 1946- *WhoHisp 94*
Maestas, Samuel J. 1953- *WhoHisp 94*
Maestas, Sigfredo *WhoHisp 94*
Maestas-Flores, Margarita 1948- *WhoHisp 94*
Maestrini, Emilio 1939- *WhoWest 94*
Maestro, Giulio 1942- *WrDr 94*
Maestrone, Frank Eusebio 1922- *WhoAm 94*
Maeterlinck, Maurice 1862-1949 *BlmGEL, IntDcT 2 [port], NewGrDO*
Maeyama, Kikuko 1957- *WhoAsA 94*
Maez, Yvette Georgina 1965- *WhoHisp 94*
Mafatlal, Arvind N. 1923- *IntWW 93*
Ma Feng 1922- *WhoPRCh 91 [port]*
Ma Feng (Ma Shuming) 1922- *IntWW 93*
Maffei, Gregory B. 1960- *WhoFI 94*
Maffei, Rocco John 1949- *WhoAmL 94*
Maffei, Stephen Roger 1939- *WhoFI 94*
Maffei, Thomas Francis 1947- *WhoAm 94, WhoAmL 94*
Maffei, Wayne Lewis 1952- *WhoAmL 94*
Maffey *Who 94*
Maffie, Michael Otis 1948- *WhoFI 94*
Maffitt, James Strawbridge 1942- *WhoAm 94*
Maffly, Roy Herrick 1927- *WhoAm 94*
Maffoli, Vincenzo c. 1760-1794? *NewGrDO*
Maffre, Muriel 1966- *WhoAm 94*
Mafi, Mohammad 1954- *WhoScEn 94*
Mafico, Temba Levi Jackson 1943- *WhoAm 94*
Mafnas, Isabel Iglesias 1965- *WhoWest 94*
Mafnas, Jesus P. *WhoAmP 93*
Mafrice, Frank 1949- *WhoAmL 94*
Ma Furong *WhoPRCh 91*
Maga, Hubert Coutoucou 1916- *IntWW 93*
Maga, Joseph Andrew 1940- *WhoAm 94, WhoScEn 94*
Magad, Samuel 1932- *WhoAm 94*
Magadia, Farley Luna 1965- *WhoWest 94*
Magafan, Ethel *WhoAmA 93*
Magafan, Ethel d1993 *NewYTBS 93*
Magafan, Jennie 1916- *WhoAmA 93N*
Magafas, Diania Lee 1963- *WhoMW 93*
Magagnoli, Maria Ginevra fl. 1740-1752 *NewGrDO*
Magalhaes Pinto, Jose de 1909- *IntWW 93*
Magallanes, Nicholas d1977 *WhoHol 92*
Magallanes, Nicholas 1922-1977 *IntDcB [port]*
Magalnick, Elliott Ben 1945- *WhoWest 94*
Magaloff, Nikita d1992 *IntWW 93N, NewYTBS 93*
Magaloff, Nikita 1912-1992 *AnObit 1992*
Magalska, James M. 1942- *WhoIns 94*
Magan, Thomas Owen 1942- *WhoAmL 94*
Magana, Angel d1982 *WhoHol 92*
Magaña, Bertha *WhoHisp 94*
Magana, J. Raul 1949- *WhoHisp 94*
Magana, Manuel Rodelo 1931- *WhoHisp 94*
Magana, Maria de Lourdes *WhoWest 94*
Magaña, Raoul Daniel 1911- *WhoHisp 94*
Magana Borja, Alvaro 1926- *IntWW 93*
Magargee, William Scott, III 1940- *WhoAm 94*
Magarian, Robert Armen 1930- *WhoAm 94*
Magarill, Simon 1953- *WhoScEn 94*
Magarinos D., Victor 1924- *IntWW 93*
Magarity, Gregory T. 1947- *WhoAm 94*
Magarity, Russell Lynn 1946- *WhoAm 94*
Magaro, Polli *WhoHol 92*
Magasanik, Boris 1919- *WhoScEn 94*
Magaw, Jeffrey Donald *WhoScEn 94*
Magaw, John W. *WhoAm 94, WhoAmP 93*
Magaw, Robert d1789 *WhAmRev*
Magaw, Roger Wayne 1933- *WhoAm 94*
Magaz, Manuel Francisco 1958- *WhoHisp 94*
Magazine, Alan Harrison 1944- *WhoAm 94*
Magaziner, Elliot Albert 1921- *WhoAm 94*
Magaziner, Fred Thomas 1947- *WhoAm 94, WhoAmL 94*
Magaziner, Henry J. 1911- *IntWW 93*
Magaziner, Henry Jonas 1911- *WhoAm 94*
Magaziner, Ira C. 1947- *NewYTBS 93*
Magazzini, Gene 1914- *WhoAmA 93*
Magda, Margareta Tatiana 1936- *WhoScEn 94*
Magdamo, Patricia L. 1931- *WhoAsA 94*
Magdanz, Andrew R. 1951- *WhoAmA 93*
Magdol, Michael Orin 1937- *WhoAm 94*
Magee, A. Alan 1947- *WhoAm 94*
Magee, Alan 1947- *WhoAmA 93*
Magee, Alderson 1929- *WhoAmA 93*
Magee, Bryan 1930- *IntWW 93, Who 94, WrDr 94*
Magee, Douglas Macarthur 1942- *WhoAmP 93*
Magee, Forrest Craig 1943- *WhoAm 94*
Magee, Frank Lynn 1896- *WhAm 10*
Magee, Harriett d1954 *WhoHol 92*
Magee, James Allen 1940- *WhoAmL 94*
Magee, John Francis 1926- *WhoAm 94, WhoFI 94*
Magee, John Wilson 1956- *WhoMW 93*
Magee, Lloyd E. 1923- *WhoAmP 93*
Magee, Melissa Moore 1964- *WhoAmL 94*
Magee, Patrick d1982 *WhoHol 92*
Magee, Paul Terry 1937- *WhoAm 94*
Magee, Richard Stephen 1941- *WhoScEn 94*
Magee, Robert Paul 1947- *WhoAm 94*
Magee, Robert Walter 1951- *WhoBlA 94*
Magee, Sadie E. 1932- *WhoBlA 94*
Magee, Stephen Pat 1943- *WhoAm 94*
Magee, Thomas P. 1956- *WhoAm 94, WhoAmP 93*
Magee, Wayne Edward 1929- *WhoAm 94*
Magee, Wes 1939- *WrDr 94*
Magee, William *WhoAmP 93*
Magee, William Eugene 1952- *WhoAmL 94*
Magel, Catherine Anne 1956- *WhoAmA 93*
Magellan, Ferdinand c. 1480-1521 *WhWE [port]*
Magen, David 1945- *IntWW 93*
Magendie, Francois 1783-1855 *WorScD*
Magenta, Muriel 1932- *WhoAmA 93, WhoWest 94*
Mager, Artur 1919- *WhoAm 94*
Mager, Carol A. 1949- *WhoAmL 94*
Mager, Don *DrAPF 93*
Mager, Ezra Pascal 1941- *WhoAm 94*
Mager, Scott Alan 1962- *WhoAmL 94*
Magerman, William *WhoHol 92*
Magers, Howard Leo, Jr. 1928- *WhoMW 93*
Mages, Daniel John 1966- *WhoAmL 94*
Maggal, Moshe Morris 1908- *WhoWest 94, WrDr 94*
Maggard, Bill Neal 1939- *WhoScEn 94*
Maggard, Jim 1946- *WhoAmP 93*
Maggard, Woodrow Wilson, Jr. 1947- *WhoFI 94*
Maggart, Brandon *WhoHol 92*
Maggay, Isidore, III 1952- *WhoScEn 94*
Maggi, Carlo Maria 1630-1699 *NewGrDO*
Maggi, Luigi d1946 *WhoHol 92*
Maggio, Dante *WhoHol 92*
Maggio, Michael John 1951- *WhoAm 94, WhoMW 93*
Maggio, Mike *DrAPF 93*
Maggio, Pupella *WhoHol 92*
Maggio, Rosalie 1943- *WrDr 94*
Maggiolo, Allison Joseph 1943- *WhoAmL 94*
Maggiorani, Lamberto d1983 *WhoHol 92*
Maggiore, Francesco c. 1715-1782? *NewGrDO*
Maggiore, Richard Van 1955- *WhoMW 93*
Maggipinto, V. Anthony 1943- *WhoAmL 94*
Maggs, Arnaud (Cyril Benvenuti) 1926- *WhoAmA 93*
Maggs, Colin Gordon 1932- *WrDr 94*
Maggs, Peter Blount 1936- *WhoAm 94*
Maggs, William Jack 1914- *Who 94*
Maghrabi, Mahmoud Sulaiman 1935- *IntWW 93*
Maghut, Muhammad al- 1934- *ConWorW 93*
Magid, Creighton Reid 1961- *WhoAmL 94*
Magid, Gail Avrum 1934- *WhoAm 94, WhoWest 94*
Magida, Arthur Jay 1945- *WhoAm 94*
Magidoff, Robert 1905-1970 *EncSF 93*
Magidson, Peggy Adrienne 1951- *WhoHisp 94*
Magielnicki, Robert L. 1947- *WhoAm 94*
Magill, David W. 1955- *WhoWest 94*
Magill, Frank J. *WhoAmP 93*
Magill, Frank John 1927- *WhoAm 94, WhoAmL 94, WhoMW 93*
Magill, Frank N. *EncSF 93*
Magill, Graham Reese 1915- *Who 94*
Magill, James Marion 1921-1991 *WhAm 10*
Magill, Kathleen A. *DrAPF 93*
Magill, Samuel Hays 1928- *WhoAm 94*
Magilow, Mark G. 1943- *WhoAmL 94*

Magini-Coletti, Antonio 1855-1912 *NewGrDO*
Maginn, John Leo 1940- *WhoAm 94*
Maginn, M. Joseph 1938- *WhoFI 94*
Maginnis, John Edward 1919- *Who 94*
Maginnis, Ken 1938- *Who 94*
Magis, Thomas H. *WhoIns 94*
Magistretti, Vico 1920- *IntWW 93*
Magistro, Charles John 1941- *WhoAmA 93*
Maglaras, Arthur D. *WhoAmP 93*
Maglathlin, Leon Edward, Jr. 1926- *WhoFI 94*
Maglaty, Joseph Louis 1955- *WhoScEn 94*
Magleby, Frank 1928- *WhoAmA 93*
Magli, Giovanni Gualberto fl. 1604-1625 *NewGrDO*
Magliari, Marc Anthony 1957- *WhoMW 93*
Maglich, Bogdan C. 1928- *WhoAm 94*
Maglie, Sal(vatore Anthony) 1917-1992 *CurBio 93N*
Maglie, Salvatore Anthony 1917-1992 *AnObit 1992*
Magliery, Frank Thomas 1943- *WhoAm 94*
Magliocca, Larry Anthony 1943- *WhoMW 93*
Magloire, Paul 1907- *IntWW 93*
Magnaghi, Russell Mario 1943- *WhoMW 93*
Magnan, Oscar Gustav 1937- *WhoAmA 93*
Magnani, Anna d1973 *WhoHol 92*
Magnani, David P. 1944- *WhoAmP 93*
Magnano, Salvatore Paul 1934- *WhoFI 94*
Magnant, Lawrence C., Jr. 1949- *WhoIns 94*
Magnant, Suzanne Leonhard 1946- *WhoAmL 94*
Magnanti, Thomas L. 1945- *WhoScEn 94*
Magnard, (Lucien Denis Gabriel) Alberic 1865-1914 *NewGrDO*
Magnavita, Jeffrey Joseph 1953- *WhoScEn 94*
Magneli, Arne 1914- *IntWW 93, WhoScEn 94*
Magner, Fredric Michael 1950- *WhoAm 94*
Magner, James, Jr. *DrAPF 93*
Magner, Jerome Allen 1929- *WhoAm 94*
Magner, John Cruse 1921- *WhoAm 94*
Magner, Martin 1900- *WhoAm 94*
Magner, Philip Henry, Jr. 1927- *WhoAmL 94*
Magner, Rachel Harris *WhoFI 94*
Magnes, Harry Alan 1948- *WhoFI 94*
Magness, Bob John 1924- *WhoAm 94, WhoFI 94, WhoWest 94*
Magness, Michael Kenneth 1948- *WhoAmL 94*
Magness, Rhonda Ann 1946- *WhoWest 94*
Magni, Paolo c. 1650-1737 *NewGrDO*
Magniac, Hollingworth 1786-1867 *DcNaB MP*
Magniac, Vernon St. Clair Lane 1908- *Who 94*
Magnoli, Albert *IntMPA 94*
Magnotta, Vic d1987 *WhoHol 92*
Magnotti, Robert Andrew 1953- *WhoFI 94*
Magnus, Donald *WhoAmP 93*
Magnus, Erica 1946- *SmATA 77 [port]*
Magnus, Frederick Samuel 1932- *WhoAm 94*
Magnus, Laurence (Henry Philip) 1955- *Who 94*
Magnus, Philip Douglas *WhoScEn 94*
Magnus, Philip Douglas 1943- *Who 94*
Magnus, Samuel Woolf 1910- *WrDr 94*
Magnus, Wilhelm 1907-1990 *WhAm 10*
Magnusen, Olga C. 1949- *WhoHisp 94*
Magnus Erlendsson, Earl of Orkney c. 1080-1116 *DcNaB MP*
Magnuson, Alan Douglas 1942- *WhoWest 94*
Magnuson, Ann 1955- *WhoHol 92*
Magnuson, Ann 1956- *IntMPA 94*
Magnuson, Charles Emil 1939- *WhoScEn 94*
Magnuson, Donald Richard 1951- *WhoWest 94*
Magnuson, Harold Joseph 1913- *WhoAm 94*
Magnuson, Nancy 1944- *WhoAm 94*
Magnuson, Paul Arthur 1937- *WhoAm 94, WhoAmL 94, WhoMW 93*
Magnuson, Robert Martin 1927- *WhoAm 94*
Magnuson, Roger James 1945- *WhoAm 94, WhoAmL 94*
Magnuson, Warren Grant 1950-1989 *WhAm 10*
Magnussen, Einar 1931- *IntWW 93*
Magnussen, Max Gene 1927- *WhoWest 94*
Magnusson, Charles 1878-1948 *IntDcF 2-4*
Magnusson, Magnus 1929- *Who 94, WrDr 94*
Magnusson, Marylin Sue Shirey 1934- *WhoMW 93*
Magnusson, Thor Eyfeld 1937- *IntWW 93*
Magolske, Charles J. 1959- *WhoFI 94*
Magomedov, Magomed-Ali Magomedovich 1930- *LngBDD*
Magonet, Jonathan David 1942- *Who 94*
Magoon, Harold F. 1916- *WhoAmP 93*
Magor, Louis Roland 1945- *WhoAm 94*
Magor, (Edward) Walter (Moyle) 1911- *Who 94*
Magorian, James *DrAPF 93*
Magorian, Michelle 1947- *TwCYAW, WrDr 94*
Magowan, Peter Alden 1942- *IntWW 93, WhoAm 94, WhoFI 94, WhoWest 94*
Magowan, Robin *DrAPF 93*
Magrans, Ralph 1947- *WhoFI 94*
Magras, Clement 1949- *WhoAmP 93*
Magrath, Allan J. 1949- *ConAu 142*
Magrath, C. Peter 1933- *WhoAm 94*
Magre, Judith *WhoHol 92*
Magre, Steve Harvey 1948- *WhoAmP 93*
Magri, Charles George 1956- *IntWW 93*
Magrill, George d1952 *WhoHol 92*
Magrino, Peter Frank 1952- *WhoAmL 94*
Magris, Claudio 1939- *IntWW 93*
Magruder, Thomas Malone 1930- *WhoWest 94*
Magrutsch, Walter 1929- *Who 94*
Magry, Martha J. 1936- *WhoMW 93*
Magub, Timothy Arthur 1941- *WhoMW 93*
Maguenat, Alfred c. 1880-1928? *NewGrDO*
Maguire, Alan Edward 1954- *WhoWest 94*
Maguire, Albert Leo 1916- *WhoAm 94*
Maguire, Andrew 1939- *WhoAmP 93*
Maguire, Bassett 1904-1991 *WhAm 10*
Maguire, Charles David, Jr. 1958- *WhoAmL 94*
Maguire, Charlotte Edwards 1918- *WhoAm 94, WhoScEn 94*
Maguire, Dave 1949- *WhoMW 93*
Maguire, David Edward 1938- *WhoAm 94*
Maguire, Edward d1925 *WhoHol 92*
Maguire, Edward Francis 1944- *WhoAm 94*
Maguire, Frances d1962 *WhoHol 92*
Maguire, Gregory 1954- *WrDr 94*
Maguire, Harold John 1912- *Who 94*
Maguire, Henry Clinton, Jr. 1928- *WhoAm 94*
Maguire, Henry Pownall 1943- *WhoAmA 93*
Maguire, Hugh 1926- *Who 94*
Maguire, Jack 1945- *SmATA 74*
Maguire, James Henry 1944- *WhoWest 94*
Maguire, Jeff *NewYTBS 93 [port]*
Maguire, John Barry 1931- *WhoFI 94*
Maguire, John David 1932- *WhoAm 94, WhoWest 94*
Maguire, John Francis 1815-1872 *EncSF 93*
Maguire, John Joseph 1934- *Who 94*
Maguire, John Patrick 1917- *WhoAm 94*
Maguire, Johnny 1921- *WhoHol 92*
Maguire, Joseph F. 1919- *WhoAm 94*
Maguire, Kathleen d1989 *WhoHol 92*
Maguire, Kevin 1951- *WhoFI 94*
Maguire, Mairead C. *Who 94*
Maguire, Mary 1919- *WhoHol 92*
Maguire, Michael *Who 94*
Maguire, Michael 1945- *WrDr 94*
Maguire, (Albert) Michael 1922- *Who 94*
Maguire, Michael M. 1925- *WhoFI 94*
Maguire, Mildred May 1933- *WhoScEn 94*
Maguire, Robert Alan 1930- *WhoAm 94*
Maguire, Robert Edward 1928- *WhoFI 94*
Maguire, Robert Francis, III 1935- *WhoAm 94*
Maguire, Robert Kenneth 1923- *Who 94*
Maguire, Thomas Eldon 1952- *WhoWest 94*
Maguire, Tom d1934 *WhoHol 92*
Maguire, Waldo *Who 94*
Maguire, (Benjamin) Waldo 1920- *Who 94*
Maguire-Krupp, Marjorie Anne 1955- *WhoFI 94*
Ma Guorui *WhoPRCh 91 [port]*
Magurno, Richard Peter 1943- *WhoAm 94*
Magus, Carolus 1913- *WrDr 94*
Mah, Feng-hwa 1922- *WhoAm 94*
Mah, Richard Sze Hao 1934- *WhoAm 94, WhoAsA 94*
Maha, George Edward 1924- *WhoAm 94*
Mahabir, Valerie Indrani 1951- *WhoWest 94*
Mahachi, Moven Enock 1948- *IntWW 93*
Mahadev, Rajesh 1966- *WhoWest 94*
Mahadeva, Manoranjan 1955- *WhoFI 94*
Mahadeva, Wijeyaraj Anandakumar 1952- *WhoFI 94, WhoScEn 94*
Mahadevan, Dev 1944- *WhoAsA 94*
Mahadevan, Kumar 1948- *WhoAm 94, WhoAsA 94*
Mahaffey, Marcia Jeanne Hixson *WhoWest 94*
Mahaffey, Mary Ann *WhoAmP 93*
Mahaffey, Merrill Dean 1937- *WhoAmA 93*
Mahaffey, Michael Wayne 1948- *WhoAmP 93*
Mahaffey, Redge Allan 1949- *WhoAm 94*
Mahaffey, Richard Roberts 1950- *WhoScEn 94*
Mahaffey, Vicki 1952- *WrDr 94*
Mahajan, Anoop Kumar 1957- *WhoAsA 94*
Mahajan, Arvind 1951- *WhoAsA 94*
Mahajan, Harpreet 1953- *WhoAsA 94*
Mahajan, Jayashree *WhoAsA 94*
Mahajan, Roop L. 1943- *WhoAsA 94*
Mahajan, Satish Murlidhar 1955- *WhoAsA 94*
Mahajan, Vijay 1948- *WhoAsA 94*
Mahajan, Y. Lal 1938- *WhoAsA 94*
Mahak, Francine Timothy 1950- *WhoWest 94*
Mahal, Taj 1940- *WhoHol 92*
Mahal, Taj 1942- *WhoAm 94*
Mahalak, Edward E. 1921- *WhoAmP 93*
Mahalingam, R. *WhoAsA 94*
Mahallati, Narges Nancy 1964- *WhoAmL 94*
Maham, Hezekiah 1739-1789 *WhAmRev*
Mahan, Asa 1799-1889 *DcAmReB 2*
Mahan, Billy 1930- *WhoHol 92*
Mahan, Christopher Parker 1967- *WhoFI 94*
Mahan, Clarence 1939- *WhoAm 94, WhoScEn 94*
Mahan, David James 1934- *WhoAm 94, WhoMW 93*
Mahan, Eugene Robert 1933- *WhoAmP 93*
Mahan, Gerald Dennis 1937- *WhoAm 94*
Mahan, James Cameron 1943- *WhoAmL 94*
Mahan, Jeanne F. 1921- *WhoAmP 93*
Mahanaim, Anna *DrAPF 93*
Mahanes, David James, Jr. 1923- *WhoAm 94*
Mahaney, Calvin Merritt 1929- *WhoIns 94*
Mahaney, John Gage 1927- *WhoWest 94*
Mahaney, Patrick 1951- *WhoAmL 94*
Mahaney, Robert Timothy 1946- *WhoMW 93*
Mahan-Powell, Lena 1951- *WhoBlA 94*
Mahant, Vijay Kumar 1953- *WhoWest 94*
Mahanthappa, Kalyana T. 1934- *WhoAsA 94*
Mahanthappa, Kalyana Thipperudraiah 1934- *WhoAm 94*
Mahany, Carolyne T. *WhoAmP 93*
Mahar, William F., Sr. 1919- *WhoAmP 93*
Mahar, William F., Jr. 1947- *WhoAmP 93*
Maharidge, Dale Dimitro 1956- *WhoAm 94*
Maharis, George 1928- *IntMPA 94, WhoHol 92*
Mahasandana, Suli 1919- *IntWW 93*
Mahathir bin Mohamad 1925- *Who 94*
Mahathir Bin Mohamed 1925- *IntWW 93*
Mahboub, Kamyar Cyrus 1959- *WhoFI 94*
Mahbubani, Kishore 1948- *IntWW 93*
Mahbubuzzaman, Mohammad 1929- *IntWW 93*
Mahdavi, Rafael Sinclair 1946- *WhoAmA 93*
Mahdi, Sadiq Al 1936- *IntWW 93*
Mahdi Al Tajir, Mohamed 1931- *IntWW 93*
Mahe, Henry Edward, Jr. 1936- *WhoAmP 93*
Mahel, Tina L. 1962- *WhoMW 93*
Mahendra, Shobha d1980 *WhoHol 92*
Maher, Bill *WhoHol 92*
Maher, Brendan Arnold 1924- *WhoAm 94*
Maher, Daniel M. 1945- *WhoAmL 94*
Maher, David L. 1939- *WhoFI 94*
Maher, David Willard 1934- *WhoAm 94, WhoAmL 94, WhoMW 93*
Maher, Edward Joseph 1939- *WhoAmL 94*
Maher, Fran 1938- *WhoFI 94*
Maher, Francis Randolph *WhoScEn 94*
Maher, Frank Aloysius 1941- *WhoMW 93*
Maher, Jay Allison 1943- *WhoMW 93*
Maher, John Edward 1925- *WhoFI 94*
Maher, John Francis 1929- *WhoScEn 94*
Maher, John Francis 1943- *WhoFI 94, WhoWest 94*
Maher, Joseph 1933- *WhoHol 92*
Maher, Kim Leverton 1946- *WhoAm 94*
Maher, L. James, III 1960- *WhoMW 93*
Maher, Leo Thomas 1915-1991 *WhAm 10*
Maher, Louis James, Jr. 1933- *WhoAm 94, WhoScEn 94*
Maher, Mary 1940- *ConAu 140*
Maher, Mary Ann 1949- *WhoFI 94*
Maher, Patrick Joseph 1936- *WhoAm 94, WhoFI 94*
Maher, Peter Michael 1940- *WhoAm 94*
Maher, Philip Brooks 1894- *WhAm 10*
Maher, Robert Crawford 1962- *WhoScEn 94*
Maher, Stephen Albert 1944- *WhoAm 94, WhoFI 94*
Maher, Stephen Trivett 1949- *WhoAmL 94*
Maher, Terence 1941- *Who 94*
Maher, Terence Anthony 1935- *IntWW 93, Who 94*
Maher, Terry Marina 1955- *WhoMW 93*
Maher, Vincent F. 1955- *WhoAmL 94*
Maher, Wally d1951 *WhoHol 92*
Maher, William Alan 1929- *WhoAmP 93*
Maher, William Francis 1916- *Who 94*
Maher, William James 1937- *WhoFI 94*
Maherero, Samuel c. 1854-1923 *HisWorL*
Mahern, Louis J., Jr. *WhoAmP 93*
Mahesh, Mahadevappa Mysore 1963- *WhoScEn 94*
Mahesh, Virendra Bhushan 1932- *WhoAm 94, WhoAsA 94, WhoScEn 94*
Ma Hesheng 1954- *WhoPRCh 91*
Maheshwari, Arun K. 1944- *WhoAsA 94*
Maheshwari, Shriram 1931- *WrDr 94*
Maheswaran, Murugesapillai 1939- *WhoMW 93*
Maheu, Gilles *WhoHol 92*
Mahey, John A. 1932- *WhoAmA 93*
Mahey, John Andrew 1932- *WhoAm 94, WhoMW 93*
Mahfood, Stephen Michael 1949- *WhoMW 93*
Mahfouz, Naguib *ConWorW 93*
Mahfouz, Naguib 1911- *NobelP 91 [port], Who 94*
Mahfuz, Nagib 1911- *BlmGWL, IntWW 93*
Mahfuz, Nagib (Abdel Aziz al-Sabilgi) 1911- *ConWorW 93, RfGShF*
Mahgoub, Mohammed Ahmed 1908- *IntWW 93*
Mahilum, Benjamin C. 1931- *WhoAsA 94*
Mahin, George E. 1914- *WhoBlA 94*
Mahindra, Indira 1926- *WrDr 94*
Mahindra, Keshub 1923- *IntWW 93*
Mahishi, Sarojini 1927- *WhoWomW 91*
Mahjoub, Elisabeth Mueller 1937- *WhoScEn 94*
Mahl, George Franklin 1917- *WhoAm 94*
Mahl, George John, III 1944- *WhoScEn 94*
Mahle, Christoph Erhard 1938- *WhoAm 94*
Mahler, Barry *WhoAmL 94*
Mahler, Bruce *WhoHol 92*
Mahler, Carol *DrAPF 93*
Mahler, David 1911- *WhoFI 94, WhoScEn 94, WhoWest 94*
Mahler, Gustav 1860-1911 *NewGrDO*
Mahler, Halfdan 1923- *IntWW 93*
Mahler, Halfdan Theodor 1923- *Who 94*
Mahler, Harry Bez 1928- *WhoAm 94*
Mahler, Michael *WhoHol 92*
Mahler, Richard Mark 1951- *WhoWest 94*
Mahler, Richard T. 1943- *WhoAm 94*
Mahler, Robert Frederick 1924- *Who 94*
Mahler, Robert Louis 1954- *WhoWest 94*
Mahler, Stephanie Irene 1952- *WhoFI 94*
Mahler, Theodore Wesley 1942- *WhoIns 94*
Mahler-Kalkstein, Menahem *NewGrDO*
Mahler-Sussman, Leona *DrAPF 93*
Mahlke, Ernest D. 1930- *WhoAmA 93*
Mahlman, Henry Clayton 1930- *WhoAmL 94*
Mahlman, Jerry David 1940- *WhoAm 94, WhoScEn 94*
Mahlmann, John James 1942- *WhoAm 94, WhoAmA 93*
Mahmood, Ashfaq Baig 1944- *WhoMW 93*
Mahmoody, Betty 1945?- *ConAu 142*
Mahmoud, Adel A. F. 1941- *WhoAm 94*
Mahmoud, Aly Ahmed 1935- *WhoAm 94*
Mahmoud, Ben 1935- *WhoAmA 93*
Mahmoud, Eugene Leo 1951- *WhoWest 94*
Mahmoudi, Kooros Mohit 1945- *WhoWest 94*
Mahmud, Air Vice-Marshal Sultan *IntWW 93*
Mahmud, Anisul Islam 1947- *IntWW 93*
Mahmud, Mustafa 1927- *EncSF 93*
Mahmud, Syed Masud 1955- *WhoScEn 94*
Mahmud, Zahid 1951- *WhoFI 94*
Mahmud Husain, Syed Abul Basher 1916- *IntWW 93, Who 94*
Mahnic, Frank, Jr. 1946- *WhoAmP 93*
Mahnk, Karen 1956- *WhoAmL 94*
Mahnke, Hans d1978 *WhoHol 92*

Mallett, Conrad L. 1928- *WhoBlA 94*
Mallett, Conrad L., Jr. *WhoAmP 93*
Mallett, Conrad L., Jr. 1953- *WhoBlA 94*
Mallett, Conrad LeRoy, Jr. 1953- *WhoAm 94, WhoAmL 94, WhoMW 93*
Mallett, Conrad Richard 1919- *Who 94*
Mallett, Daryl F(urumi) 1969- *EncSF 93*
Mallett, Edmund Stansfield 1923- *Who 94*
Mallett, Francis Anthony 1924- *Who 94*
Mallett, Jane d1984 *WhoHol 92*
Mallett, Jerry J. 1939- *SmATA 76 [port]*
Mallett, Peter 1925- *Who 94*
Mallett, Rosa Elizabeth 1940- *WhoBlA 94*
Mallette, Alfred John 1938- *WhoAm 94*
Mallette, Allen Ray 1950- *WhoFI 94*
Mallette, Carol L. *WhoBlA 94*
Mallette, John M. 1932- *WhoBlA 94*
Mallette, Malcolm Francis 1922- *WhoAm 94*
Mallevialle, Joel Christian 1944- *WhoScEn 94*
Malley, James Henry Michael 1940- *WhoScEn 94*
Malley, John Wallace 1906-1988 *WhAm 10*
Malley, Robert Joseph 1923- *WhoAm 94*
Mallia, Michael Patrick 1946- *WhoAmL 94*
Mallick, Pankaj K. 1946- *WhoAsA 94*
Mallik, Provash *WrDr 94*
Mallik, Umesh 1916- *WrDr 94*
Mallin, Jay 1927- *WrDr 94*
Mallin, Judith Young *WhoAmA 93*
Mallin, Sanford Richard 1933- *WhoMW 93*
Mallin, Stewart Adam Thomson 1924- *Who 94*
Mallinckrodt, Georg Wilhelm von *Who 94*
Mallinckrodt, George W. 1930- *WhoAm 94*
Mallinger, Mathilde 1847-1920 *NewGrDO*
Mallinson, Anthony William 1923- *Who 94*
Mallinson, Dennis Hainsworth 1921- *Who 94*
Mallinson, Jeremy (John Crosby) *WrDr 94*
Mallinson, John Charles 1932- *WhoAm 94, WhoWest 94*
Mallinson, John Russell 1943- *Who 94*
Mallinson, Rory d1976 *WhoHol 92*
Mallinson, Sue *EncSF 93*
Mallinson, Vernon 1910- *WrDr 94*
Mallinson, William (John) 1942- *Who 94*
Mallinson, William Arthur 1922- *Who 94*
Mallipudi, Carmen D. C. 1950- *WhoHisp 94*
Mallisham, Joseph W. 1928- *WhoBlA 94*
Mallmann, Alexander James 1937- *WhoMW 93*
Malloch, David 1705?-1765 *BlmGEL*
Mallock, W. H. 1849-1923 *BlmGEL*
Mallo-Garrido, Josephine Ann 1955- *WhoAm 94*
Mallon, Catherine d1929 *WhoHol 92*
Mallon, David Joseph, Jr. 1946- *WhoAm 94, WhoAmL 94*
Mallon, Edward John 1944- *WhoIns 94*
Mallon, Florencia Elizabeth 1951- *WhoHisp 94, WhoMW 93*
Mallon, Joseph Laurence 1942- *Who 94*
Mallon, Joseph T. 1950- *WhoAmL 94*
Mallon, Loren J. 1945- *WhoAmL 94*
Mallon, Meg *WhoAm 94*
Mallon, Peter 1929- *WhoWest 94*
Mallon, Seamus 1936- *Who 94*
Mallon, Thomas 1951- *WrDr 94*
Mallonee, Richard L. 1950- *WhoMW 93*
Mallorie, Paul Richard 1923- *Who 94*
Mallory, Arthur Lee 1932- *WhoAm 94*
Mallory, Boots d1958 *WhoHol 92*
Mallory, Carole *WhoHol 92*
Mallory, Charles King, III 1936- *WhoAm 94*
Mallory, Charles Shannon *WhoAm 94*
Mallory, Charles William 1925- *WhoScEn 94*
Mallory, David Stanton 1958- *WhoScEn 94*
Mallory, Drew 1939- *WrDr 94*
Mallory, Drue *WhoHol 92*
Mallory, Edward *WhoHol 92*
Mallory, Frank Bryant 1933- *WhoAm 94*
Mallory, Frank Linus 1920- *WhoAm 94*
Mallory, George L., Jr. 1952- *WhoBlA 94*
Mallory, J(ames) P(atrick) 1945- *WrDr 94*
Mallory, John *WhoHol 92*
Mallory, Kathryn C. 1952- *WhoAmL 94*
Mallory, Lee *DrAPF 93*
Mallory, Margaret 1911- *WhoAmA 93*
Mallory, Marilyn May *WhoWest 94*
Mallory, Mark *EncSF 93*
Mallory, Mary Edith 1952- *WhoScEn 94*
Mallory, Molla 1884-1959 *BuCMET [port]*
Mallory, Nina Ayala *WhoAmA 93*
Mallory, Robert 1941- *WhoAmP 93*
Mallory, Robert Mark 1950- *WhoAm 94*
Mallory, Troy L. 1923- *WhoFI 94, WhoMW 93*
Mallory, Virgil Standish 1919- *WhoAm 94*
Mallory, William Barton, III 1944- *WhoAm 94, WhoFI 94*
Mallory, William Henry 1919- *WhoBlA 94*
Mallory, William L. *WhoAmP 93, WhoBlA 94*
Mallot, Yolande *WhoHol 92*
Malloum, Felix 1932- *IntWW 93*
Mallows, Harry Russell 1920- *Who 94*
Malloy, Dale R. 1945- *WhoAm 94*
Malloy, Edward Aloysius 1941- *WhoAm 94, WhoMW 93*
Malloy, Francetta d1978 *WhoHol 92*
Malloy, Grace Louise 1959- *WhoFI 94*
Malloy, H. Rembert 1913- *WhoBlA 94*
Malloy, James B. 1927- *WhoAm 94, WhoFI 94*
Malloy, James Joseph 1941- *WhoMW 93*
Malloy, James Matthew 1939- *WhoAm 94*
Malloy, John J. d1968 *WhoHol 92*
Malloy, John Richard 1932- *WhoAm 94, WhoFI 94*
Malloy, Kathleen Sharon 1948- *WhoAmL 94, WhoFI 94, WhoIns 94, WhoMW 93*
Malloy, Martin Gerard 1949- *WhoAmL 94*
Malloy, Michael Patrick 1951- *WhoAmL 94*
Malloy, Michael Terrence 1936- *WhoAm 94*
Malloy, William Manning 1922- *WhoFI 94*
Malloy, William Michael 1960- *WhoAm 94*
Mallozzi, Cos M. 1951- *WhoAm 94, WhoFI 94*
Mallozzi, Edward J. 1945- *WhoIns 94*
Malluche, Hartmut Horst 1943- *WhoScEn 94*
Mallum, Daniel William 1940- *WhoAm 94*
Malm, James Royal 1925- *WhoAm 94*
Malm, Mona *WhoHol 92*
Malm, Rita P. 1932- *WhoFI 94*
Malm, Roger Charles 1949- *WhoAmL 94*
Malman, Arthur B. 1942- *WhoAmL 94*
Malman, Bernard Deutsch 1936- *WhoMW 93*
Malman, Christina 1912-1958 *WhoAmA 93N*
Malmberg, Torsten 1923- *WhoScEn 94*
Malmberg, Virginia Ann 1939- *WhoMW 93*
Malmcrona-Friberg, Karin Elisabet 1959- *WhoScEn 94*
Malmedy, Francis, Marquis de *WhAmRev*
Malmen, Jeff L. 1967- *WhoAmP 93*
Malmesbury, Baron *WhAmRev*
Malmesbury, Bishop Suffragan of 1929- *Who 94*
Malmesbury, Earl of 1907- *Who 94*
Malmgren, Dallin 1949- *WrDr 94*
Malmgren, Harald Bernard 1935- *WhoAm 94*
Malmgren, Rene Louise 1938- *WhoWest 94*
Malmgren, Robert A. 1954- *WhoFI 94*
Malmquist, Carl Phillip 1934- *WhoMW 93*
Malmsjo, Jan *WhoHol 92*
Malmstedt, David Raymond 1955- *WhoMW 93*
Malmsten, Birger 1920- *WhoHol 92*
Malmuth, Bruce 1937- *IntMPA 94, WhoAm 94*
Malmuth, Norman David 1931- *WhoScEn 94, WhoWest 94*
Malnassy, Louis Sturges 1952- *WhoMW 93*
Malneck, Matty d1981 *WhoHol 92*
Malo, Alvaro *WhoHisp 94*
Malo, Douglas Dwane 1949- *WhoMW 93*
Malo, Gina d1963 *WhoHol 92*
Malo, Teri 1954- *WhoAmA 93*
Maloff, Saul *DrAPF 93*
Maloff, Stephen Martin 1941- *WhoWest 94*
Malohn, Donald A. 1928- *WhoWest 94*
Malone, Amanda Ella 1929- *WhoBlA 94*
Malone, Bennett 1944- *WhoAmP 93*
Malone, Charles A. *WhoBlA 94*
Malone, Charles Trescott 1966- *WhoScEn 94*
Malone, Claudine Berkeley *WhoBlA 94*
Malone, Cleo 1934- *WhoBlA 94*
Malone, Dan F. 1955- *WhoAm 94*
Malone, Daniel Lee 1949- *WhoFI 94, WhoMW 93*
Malone, Daniel Patrick 1953- *WhoAm 94, WhoAmL 94*
Malone, David Roy 1943- *WhoAmL 94, WhoAmP 93, WhoFI 94*
Malone, Deborah Frank 1964- *WhoWest 94*
Malone, Denis (Eustace Gilbert) 1922- *Who 94*
Malone, Dorothy 1925- *IntMPA 94, WhoHol 92*
Malone, Dudley Field d1950 *WhoHol 92*
Malone, E. T., Jr. *DrAPF 93*
Malone, Edmund 1741-1812 *BlmGEL*
Malone, Edward H. 1924- *WhoAm 94*
Malone, Edwin Scott, III 1938- *WhoAm 94*
Malone, Eugene William 1930- *WhoBlA 94*
Malone, Florence d1956 *WhoHol 92*
Malone, (Peter) Gerald 1950- *Who 94*
Malone, Gloria S. 1928- *WhoBlA 94*
Malone, Herman 1947- *WhoBlA 94*
Malone, J. Deotha 1932- *WhoBlA 94*
Malone, James F., III 1943- *WhoAmL 94*
Malone, James Hiram 1930- *WhoAmA 93, WhoBlA 94*
Malone, James L. *WhoAm 94*
Malone, James L. 1931- *WhoAmP 93*
Malone, James L. 1945- *WhoAmL 94*
Malone, James Laurence, III 1947- *WhoAm 94*
Malone, James Roland 1955- *WhoWest 94*
Malone, James William 1920- *WhoAm 94, WhoMW 93*
Malone, Jean Hambidge 1954- *WhoMW 93*
Malone, Jeff 1961- *BasBi*
Malone, Jeff Nigel 1961- *WhoBlA 94*
Malone, Joe L. *DrAPF 93*
Malone, John C. 1941- *WhoAm 94, WhoFI 94, WhoWest 94*
Malone, Joseph 1954- *WhoAm 94, WhoAmP 93*
Malone, Joseph James 1932- *WhoAm 94*
Malone, Joseph Lawrence 1937- *WhoAm 94*
Malone, Julia Louise 1947- *WhoAm 94*
Malone, Karl 1963- *BasBi, CurBio 93 [port], WhoAm 94, WhoBlA 94, WhoWest 94*
Malone, Laurence Adams 1911- *WhoMW 93*
Malone, Laurence Joseph 1957- *WhoFI 94*
Malone, Lee H. B. 1913-1989 *WhoAmA 93N*
Malone, Lisa Ann Qualls 1966- *WhoFI 94*
Malone, Mark *WhoHol 92*
Malone, Mark A. *WhoAmP 93*
Malone, Marvin *DrAPF 93*
Malone, Marvin Herbert 1930- *WhoWest 94*
Malone, Michael *DrAPF 93*
Malone, Michael 1942- *WrDr 94*
Malone, Michael Glen 1943- *WhoAmL 94*
Malone, Michael Gregory 1942- *WhoBlA 94*
Malone, Michael Patrick *DrAPF 93*
Malone, Michael Patrick 1951- *WhoMW 93*
Malone, Michael Peter 1940- *WhoWest 94*
Malone, Michael William 1956- *WhoWest 94*
Malone, Mike 1932- *WhoAmP 93, WhoWest 94*
Malone, Molly d1952 *WhoHol 92*
Malone, Moses 1955- *BasBi [port], WhoAm 94*
Malone, Moses Eugene 1955- *WhoBlA 94*
Malone, Nancy 1935- *WhoHol 92*
Malone, Nola Langner 1930- *ConAu 41NR, WhoAmA 93*
Malone, Pamela Altfeld *DrAPF 93*
Malone, Patricia Lynn 1930- *WhoAmA 93*
Malone, Pick d1962 *WhoHol 92*
Malone, Ray d1970 *WhoHol 92*
Malone, Richard Wayne 1951- *WhoFI 94*
Malone, Robert Joseph 1944- *WhoAm 94, WhoWest 94*
Malone, Robert R. 1933- *WhoAmA 93*
Malone, Robert Roy 1933- *WhoAm 94*
Malone, Sandra Dorsey *WhoBlA 94*
Malone, Stanley R. 1924- *WhoBlA 94*
Malone, Stephen Robert 1960- *WhoScEn 94*
Malone, Thomas Ellis 1926- *WhoBlA 94*
Malone, Thomas Francis 1917- *IntWW 93, WhoAm 94, WhoFI 94*
Malone, Thomas Patrick 1947- *WhoAmL 94*
Malone, Thomas William 1946- *WhoAmL 94*
Malone, Vincent 1931- *Who 94*
Malone, Wallace D., Jr. 1936- *WhoAm 94, WhoFI 94*
Malone, William Grady 1915- *WhoAm 94, WhoAmL 94*
Malone, Winfred Francis 1935- *WhoScEn 94*
Malone-Lee, Michael Charles 1941- *Who 94*
Maloney, Andrew J. *WhoAm 94*
Maloney, Carolyn B. 1948- *CngDr 93*
Maloney, Carolyn Bosher 1948- *WhoAm 94, WhoAmP 93*
Maloney, Carolyn Scott 1950- *WhoFI 94, WhoMW 93*
Maloney, Charles Calvin 1930- *WhoBlA 94*
Maloney, Cheryl Ann 1949- *WhoMW 93*
Maloney, David William 1938- *WhoMW 93*
Maloney, Dennis *DrAPF 93*
Maloney, Diane Marie 1951- *WhoMW 93*
Maloney, Douglas James 1933- *WhoAmL 94, WhoWest 94*
Maloney, Francis Patrick 1936- *WhoScEn 94*
Maloney, Frank 1927- *WhoAmL 94*
Maloney, George Thomas 1932- *WhoAm 94, WhoFI 94*
Maloney, Gerald P. 1933- *WhoAm 94, WhoFI 94*
Maloney, James d1978 *WhoHol 92*
Maloney, James 1939- *WhoAmP 93*
Maloney, James Edward 1951- *WhoAm 94, WhoAmL 94*
Maloney, James H. 1948- *WhoAmP 93*
Maloney, James John 1949- *WhoWest 94*
Maloney, Jerome, Sister 1926- *WhoMW 93*
Maloney, John *DrAPF 93*
Maloney, John Alexander 1927- *WhoAm 94*
Maloney, John Frederick 1913- *WhoAm 94*
Maloney, John Peter 1951- *WhoAm 94*
Maloney, Joseph Anthony, Jr. 1942- *WhoMW 93*
Maloney, Joseph Francis 1930- *WhoAmP 93*
Maloney, Leo d1929 *WhoHol 92*
Maloney, Mack *EncSF 93*
Maloney, Marilyn Clifford 1950- *WhoAmL 94*
Maloney, Marilyn Logelin 1931- *WhoMW 93*
Maloney, Mark A. 1957- *WhoIns 94*
Maloney, Mary Agnes 1947- *WhoAmP 93*
Maloney, Mary Patricia 1955- *WhoAmP 93*
Maloney, Marynell 1955- *WhoAmL 94*
Maloney, Michael 1957- *WhoHol 92*
Maloney, Michael James 1942- *WhoAm 94*
Maloney, Michael John 1932- *Who 94*
Maloney, Michael Joseph, Jr. 1929- *WhoAmP 93*
Maloney, Michael Patrick 1944- *WhoAm 94*
Maloney, Milford Charles 1927- *WhoAm 94, WhoScEn 94*
Maloney, Patrick E. 1945- *WhoAmL 94*
Maloney, Patsy Loretta 1952- *WhoWest 94*
Maloney, Paul Joseph 1954- *WhoAmL 94*
Maloney, Ray 1951- *WrDr 94*
Maloney, Robert B. 1933- *WhoAm 94, WhoAmL 94*
Maloney, Robert E., Jr. 1942- *WhoAm 94, WhoAmL 94*
Maloney, Simone 1936- *WhoFI 94*
Maloney, Stacey *WhoHol 92*
Maloney, Therese A. 1929- *WhoIns 94*
Maloney, Therese Adele 1929- *WhoAm 94, WhoFI 94*
Maloney, Thomas E. 1939- *WhoAmL 94*
Maloney, Thomas J. 1922- *WhoWest 94*
Maloney, Thomas M. 1931- *WhoAmP 93*
Maloney, Thomas Martin 1931- *WhoWest 94*
Maloney, Timothy Francis 1956- *WhoAmP 93*
Maloney, Vincent John 1949- *WhoAmL 94*
Maloney, William Gerard 1917- *WhoAm 94*
Maloof, Farahe Paul 1950- *WhoAmL 94*
Maloof, Giles Wilson 1932- *WhoWest 94*
Maloof, James Aloysius 1919- *WhoAmP 93*
Malooley, David Joseph 1951- *WhoFI 94, WhoMW 93, WhoScEn 94*
Maloon, James Harold 1926- *WhoAm 94*
Maloon, Jeffrey Lee 1958- *WhoAmL 94*
Maloon, Jerry L. 1938- *WhoAmL 94, WhoMW 93*
Malory, Thomas *BlmGEL*
Malotke, Mary Elizabeth 1946- *WhoMW 93*
Malott, Adele Renee 1935- *WhoAm 94, WhoWest 94*
Malott, Deane Waldo 1898- *IntWW 93, Who 94*
Malott, Dwight Ralph 1947- *WhoWest 94*
Malott, Harry C. 1921- *WhoAmP 93*
Malott, James Raymond, Jr. 1917- *WhoAm 94*
Malott, James Spencer 1940- *WhoWest 94*
Malott, John Raymond 1946- *WhoAm 94*
Malott, Mary *WhoAmA 93*

Malott, Robert H. 1926- IntWW 93
Malott, Robert Harvey 1926- WhoAm 94, WhoMW 93
Malott, Thomas J. 1937- WhoFI 94
Malouf, David 1934- WrDr 94
Malouf, David George Joseph 1934- IntWW 93
Malouf, Frederick LeRoy 1954- WhoWest 94
Malouff, Frank Joseph 1947- WhoAm 94
Malouin, Jean-Louis 1943- WhoAm 94
Malovance, Gregory J. 1954- WhoAm 94
Malovos, Kenneth M. 1944- WhoAmL 94
Maloy, Elmer J. 1896-1970 EncABHB 9
Maloy, Robert 1935- IntWW 93
Malozemoff, Plato 1909- WhoAm 94
Malpas, James Spencer 1931- Who 94
Malpas, Robert 1927- IntWW 93, Who 94, WhoAm 94
Malpass, Brian William 1937- Who 94
Malpass, Eric (Lawson) 1910- WrDr 94
Malpass, Leslie Frederick 1922- WhoAm 94
Malpass, Michael Allen 1946- WhoAmA 93
Malpass, Roy Southwell 1937- WhoScEn 94
Malpede, John 1945- WhoAmA 93
Malphurs, Roger Edward 1933- WhoFI 94, WhoWest 94
Malpighi, Marcello 1628-1694 WorScD
Malqinhu 1930- IntWW 93, WhoPRCh 91 [port]
Malraux, Andre 1901-1976 WhoAmA 93N
Malraux, Clara 1900- BlmGWL
Malry, Lenton 1931- WhoBlA 94
Malsack, James Thomas 1921- WhoAm 94
Malsch, Ellen L. d1988 WhoAmA 93N
Malsky, Stanley Joseph 1925-1992 WhoFI 94
Malsom, Marilyn Faye 1934- WhoAmP 93
Malson, Rex Richard 1931- WhoWest 94
Malstrom, Robert A. 1946- WhoAm 94
Malt, Ronald Bradford 1954- WhoFI 94
Malta, Archbishop of 1928- Who 94
Malta, Alexander 1942- NewGrDO
Malta, Victor Guillermo 1928- WhoHisp 94
Malta, Vincent 1922- WhoAmA 93
Maltagliati, Evi d1986 WhoHol 92
Maltby, Antony John 1928- Who 94
Maltby, Florence Helen 1933- WhoMW 93
Maltby, H. F. d1963 WhoHol 92
Maltby, John Newcombe 1928- IntWW 93, Who 94
Maltby, Per Eugen 1933- IntWW 93
Maltby, Richard, Jr. 1937- ConTFT 11
Maltby, Richard Eldridge, Jr. 1937- WhoAm 94
Malten, Therese 1853-1930 NewGrDO
Malter, Arnold Sheldon 1934- WhoAmL 94
Maltese, George John 1931- WhoAm 94
Maltese, Michael 1908-1981 IntDcF 2-4
Maltese, Serphin R. 1932- WhoAmP 93
Malthus, Thomas Robert 1766-1834 BlmGEL, EnvEnc
Maltin, Freda 1923- WhoWest 94
Maltin, Leonard 1950- ConTFT 11, WhoAm 94, WhoWest 94
Maltravers, Lord 1987- Who 94
Maltz, Albert 1908-1985 ConDr 93
Maltz, Andrew Hal 1960- WhoWest 94
Maltz, J. Herbert 1920- WhoAm 94
Maltz, Jerome Paul 1935- WhoWest 94
Maltz, Michael David 1938- WhoAm 94
Maltz, Robert 1935- WhoMW 93
Maltzman, Irving Myron 1924- WhoAm 94
Maltzman, Stanley 1921- WhoAmA 93
Malugen, Louise DeCarl 1945- WhoAm 94, WhoWest 94
Malula, Joseph 1917-1989 WhAm 10
Malveaux, Floyd WhoBlA 94
Malveaux, Julianne Marie 1953- WhoAm 94
Malvern, Viscount 1949- Who 94
Malvern, Corinne d1956 WhoAmA 93N
Malvern, Donald 1921- WhoAm 94
Malvern, Lawrence Earl 1916- WhoAm 94
Malvern, Paul d1993 NewYTBS 93
Malvestiti, Abel Orlando 1913-1992 WhoHisp 94N
Malwitz, Nelson Edward 1946- WhoScEn 94
Maly, George Joseph, Jr. 1933- WhoAm 94
Maly, Kurt John 1944- WhoAm 94
Malyon, Eily d1961 WhoHol 92
Malyshev, Nikolai Grigorevich 1945- LngBDD
Malzahn, Ray Andrew 1929- WhoAm 94
Malzbender, Thomas 1959- WhoWest 94
Malzberg, Barry (Nathaniel) 1939- WrDr 94
Malzberg, Barry N(orman) 1939- EncSF 93
Mamakos, Peter WhoHol 92
Mamalakis, Markos John 1932- WhoFI 94
Mamaloni, Solomon 1943- Who 94
Mamaloni, Solomon Sunaone 1943- IntWW 93
Ma Man Kee WhoPRCh 91
Mamantov, Gleb 1931- WhoAm 94
Mamat, Frank Trustick 1949- WhoAm 94, WhoAmL 94, WhoFI 94, WhoMW 93
Mamatey, Victor Samuel 1917- WhoAm 94
Mamba, George Mbikwakhe 1932- IntWW 93, Who 94
Mamduh, Aliya BlmGWL
Mamedov, Georgy Enverovich 1947- IntWW 93
Mamedova, Shevket (Hassan-kizi) 1897- NewGrDO
Mamelock, Emil d1954 WhoHol 92
Mamer, Stuart Mies 1921- WhoAm 94
Mamert, Jean Albert 1928- IntWW 93
Mamet, David WhoHol 92
Mamet, David 1947- AmCulL, DramC 4 [port], IntMPA 94, WrDr 94
Mamet, David (Alan) 1947- ConAu 41NR, ConDr 93, IntDcT 2 [port]
Mamet, David Alan 1947- IntWW 93, Who 94, WhoAm 94
Mamiaka, Raphael 1936- IntWW 93
Mamidala, Ramulu 1949- WhoAsA 94
Ma Mingliang 1920- WhoPRCh 91 [port]
Mamiya, Michio 1929- NewGrDO
Mamiya, Ron 1947- WhoAsA 94
Mamleyev, Yuri DrAPF 93
Mamlin, Gennadiy Semenovich 1925- IntWW 93
Mamlok, Ursula 1928- WhoAm 94
Mammel, Russell Norman 1926- WhoAm 94, WhoFI 94, WhoMW 93
Mammen, Abraham 1952- WhoAsA 94
Mammen, Thomas WhoAsA 94
Mammenga, Gene WhoAm 94
Mammi, Mario 1932- WhoScEn 94
Mammi, Oscar 1926- IntWW 93
Mammolite, Anthony 1950- WhoFI 94
Mammone, Richard James 1953- WhoScEn 94
Mammone, Robert WhoHol 92
Mammone Grossi, Natia 1954- WhoWomW 91
Mamo WhoHol 92
Mamo, Anthony (Joseph) 1909- Who 94
Mamo, Anthony Joseph 1909- IntWW 93
Mamo, John WhoHol 92
Mamon, Gary Allan 1958- WhoScEn 94
Mamontov, Savva Ivanovich 1841-1918 NewGrDO
Mamorsky, Jeffrey Dean 1946- WhoAm 94
Mamrak, Sandra Ann 1944- WhoMW 93
Mamula, Branko 1921- IntWW 93
Mamula, Mark 1953- WhoScEn 94
Mamut, Mary Catherine 1923- WhoMW 93
Mamutov Kurban 1922- WhoPRCh 91 [port]
Man, Archdeacon of Who 94
Man, Chi-Sing 1947- WhoAsA 94, WhoScEn 94
Man, Eugene Herbert 1923- WhoAm 94
Man, Kin Fung 1957- WhoScEn 94
Man, Xiuting Cheng 1965- WhoScEn 94
Manabe, Shunji 1930- WhoScEn 94
Manabe, Syukuro 1931- IntWW 93, WhoAm 94, WhoAsA 94, WhoScEn 94
Manabu, Mabe WhoAmA 93
Manac'h, Etienne Manoel d1992 IntWW 93N
Manafort, Paul John, Sr. 1923- WhoAmP 93
Manafort, Paul John, Jr. 1949- WhoAmP 93
Managadze, Nodar Shotayevich 1943- IntWW 93
Managan, Robert Alan 1955- WhoWest 94
Managan-Edwards, Mary Jean 1942- WhoMW 93
Manager, Vada O'Hara 1961- WhoBlA 94
Manahan, Larry W. WhoAmP 93
Manahan, Mark Steven 1955- WhoWest 94
Manahan, Sheila d1988 WhoHol 92
Manaka, Matsemela 1956- BlkWr 2, ConAu 140, ConDr 93
Manaker, Arnold Martin 1947- WhoFI 94, WhoScEn 94
Manakos, Froso 1931- WhoAmP 93
Manalich, Ramiro 1958- WhoAmL 94
Manalpuy WhoHol 92
Manankil, Norma Ronas WhoAsA 94
Manara, James Anthony 1945- WhoWest 94
Manaray, Thelma Alberta 1913- WhoAmA 93N
Manard, Biff WhoHol 92
Manard, Robert Lynn, III 1947- WhoAm 94, WhoAmL 94
Manary, Richard Deane 1944- WhoFI 94, WhoWest 94
Manasrah, Mustafa Moh'd 1940- WhoFI 94
Manasreh, Omar M. 1952- WhoScEn 94
Manassah, Jamal Tewfek 1945- WhoFI 94
Manasse, George 1938- IntMPA 94
Manasse, Henri Richard, Jr. 1945- WhoAm 94
Manasse, Roger 1930- WhoWest 94
Manasseh, Leonard Sulla 1916- IntWW 93, Who 94
Manassero, Henri J. P. 1932- WhoAm 94
Manatos, Andrew E. 1944- WhoAmP 93
Manatos, Andrew Emanuel 1944- WhoAm 94
Manatt, Charles Taylor 1936- IntWW 93
Manatt, Richard 1931- WhoAm 94
Manbeck, Harry Frederick, Jr. 1926- WhoAm 94, WhoAmP 93
Manbeck, Harvey B. 1942- WhoScEn 94
Manby, C. Robert d1993 NewYTBS 93
Manby, Mervyn Colet 1915- Who 94
Mancall, Elliott Lee 1927- WhoAm 94, WhoScEn 94
Mance, Andrew Mark 1952- WhoScEn 94
Mance, John J. 1926- WhoBlA 94
Mance, Jonathan Hugh 1943- Who 94
Mance, Mary Howarth Who 94
Mancel, Claude Paul 1942- WhoAm 94
Mancewicz, Jerome Frederick 1926- WhoMW 93
Mancha, Guillermo 1943- WhoHisp 94
Mancha, Lupe WhoHisp 94
Mancham, James Richard Marie 1939- IntWW 93, Who 94
Manchel, Frank 1935- WrDr 94
Mancher, Rhoda Ross 1935- WhoAm 94
Mancheski, Frederick John 1926- WhoAm 94, WhoFI 94
Manchester, Archdeacon of Who 94
Manchester, Bishop of 1935- Who 94
Manchester, Dean of Who 94
Manchester, Duke of 1938- Who 94
Manchester, Carol Ann Freshwater 1942- WhoMW 93, WhoScEn 94
Manchester, Diana 1955- WhoMW 93
Manchester, Hugh Wallace 1905-1988 WhAm 10
Manchester, Kenneth Edward 1925- WhoAm 94
Manchester, Paul Brunson 1942- WhoFI 94
Manchester, R. Henry 1915- WhoAmP 93
Manchester, Robert D. 1942- WhoAm 94
Manchester, William 1922- IntWW 93, Who 94, WhoAm 94, WrDr 94
Manchester, William (Maxwell) 1913- Who 94
Manchin, A. James 1927- WhoAmP 93
Manchin, Joe, III 1947- WhoAmP 93
Manchin, Mark Anthony 1952- WhoAmP 93
Mancia, Adrienne IntMPA 94
Mancia, Luigi c. 1665-1708? NewGrDO
Mancias, Fernando G. WhoHisp 94
Manciet, Lorraine Hanna 1950- WhoScEn 94
Mancinelli, Cristiana 1959- WhoHol 92
Mancinelli, Luigi 1848-1921 NewGrDO
Mancini, Albert Nicholas 1929- WhoMW 93
Mancini, Ernest Anthony 1947- WhoAm 94, WhoScEn 94
Mancini, Francesco 1672-1737 NewGrDO
Mancini, Giovanni Battista 1714-1800 NewGrDO
Mancini, Giuseppe Federico 1927- IntWW 93
Mancini, Henry 1924- IntDcF 2-4, IntMPA 94, IntWW 93, WhoAm 94
Mancini, Hortense 1646-1699 BlmGWL
Mancini, John 1925- WhoAmA 93
Mancini, Joseph A. 1918- WhoAmP 93
Mancini, Louis Joseph 1950- WhoMW 93
Mancini, Marie de 1640-1715 BlmGWL
Mancini, Marisa Angela 1962- WhoAmL 94
Mancini, Mary Catherine 1953- WhoScEn 94
Mancini, Nicholas Angelo 1944- WhoScEn 94
Mancini, Ray 1961- WhoHol 92
Mancini, Ric WhoHol 92
Mancini, Robert Karl 1954- WhoScEn 94, WhoWest 94
Mancini, Rocco Anthony 1931- WhoScEn 94
Mancini, Salvatore WhoAmP 93
Mancini, William F. 1959- WhoWest 94
Mancino, Douglas Michael 1949- WhoAm 94
Mancino, Nicola 1931- IntWW 93
Mancke, Richard Bell 1943- WhoAm 94
Manco, Hugo R. 1930- WhoHisp 94
Mancoff, Neal Alan 1939- WhoAm 94, WhoAmL 94
Mancroft, Baron 1957- Who 94
Mancuso, Carolina DrAPF 93
Mancuso, Frank 1922- WhoAmP 93
Mancuso, Frank, Jr. 1958- IntMPA 94
Mancuso, Frank G. IntWW 93
Mancuso, Frank G. 1933- ConTFT 11, IntMPA 94, WhoAm 94
Mancuso, Frank O. 1918- WhoAmP 93
Mancuso, James Vincent 1916- WhoAm 94, WhoFI 94
Mancuso, Joseph Edward 1955- WhoMW 93
Mancuso, Leni WhoAmA 93
Mancuso, Martin Joseph 1943- WhoFI 94
Mancuso, Mary Katherine Teall 1964- WhoMW 93
Mancuso, Nick WhoHol 92
Mancuso, Ted EncSF 93
Mand, Martin G. 1936- WhoAm 94, WhoFI 94
Mand, Ranjit Singh 1956- WhoScEn 94, WhoWest 94
Manda, Joseph Alexander, III 1952- WhoFI 94
Mandac, Evelyn 1945- NewGrDO
Mandal, Krishna Pada 1937- WhoScEn 94
Mandan, Robert 1932- WhoHol 92
Mandanici, Placido 1798-1852 NewGrDO
Mandavilli, Satya Narayana 1932- WhoScEn 94
Mandecki, Wlodek 1951- WhoMW 93
Mandel, Babaloo WhoAm 94
Mandel, Babaloo 1949?- ConTFT 11, IntMPA 94
Mandel, Barry Jay 1946- WhoAmL 94
Mandel, Charlotte DrAPF 93
Mandel, Charlotte 1925- ConAu 140
Mandel, David Michael 1951- WhoAm 94, WhoAmL 94
Mandel, David Scott 1959- WhoAmL 94
Mandel, Dominic Robert 1956- WhoWest 94
Mandel, Dorothy WhoAmA 93
Mandel, Eli(as Wolf) 1922- ConAu 43NR, WrDr 94N
Mandel, Elliott David 1961- WhoScEn 94
Mandel, Ernest 1923- WrDr 94
Mandel, Frances Wakefield d1943 WhoHol 92
Mandel, Harold George 1924- WhoAm 94
Mandel, Herbert Maurice 1924- WhoAm 94, WhoFI 94, WhoScEn 94
Mandel, Howard 1917- WhoAmA 93
Mandel, Howie 1956- WhoHol 92
Mandel, Howie 1957- WhoCom
Mandel, Irwin Daniel 1922- WhoAm 94
Mandel, Jack N. 1911- WhoAm 94
Mandel, Jeff 1952- WhoWest 94
Mandel, John 1941- WhoAmA 93
Mandel, Joseph David 1940- WhoAm 94, WhoAmL 94
Mandel, Karyl Lynn 1935- WhoFI 94, WhoMW 93
Mandel, Leon, III 1928- WhoAm 94
Mandel, Leonard WhoAm 94
Mandel, Leslie Ann 1945- WhoFI 94
Mandel, Loring 1928- IntMPA 94
Mandel, Martin Louis 1944- WhoAmL 94, WhoWest 94
Mandel, Marvin 1920- IntWW 93
Mandel, Maurice, II WhoAmL 94
Mandel, Mike 1950- WhoAmA 93
Mandel, Miriam 1930-1982 BlmGWL
Mandel, Morton 1924- WhoScEn 94
Mandel, Morton Leon 1921- WhoAm 94, WhoFI 94
Mandel, Newton W. 1926- WhoAmL 94
Mandel, Oscar DrAPF 93
Mandel, Oscar 1926- WhoWest 94, WrDr 94
Mandel, Richard Lloyd 1927- WhoAmL 94
Mandel, Robert IntMPA 94
Mandel, Robert Michael WhoWest 94
Mandel, Ronald James 1957- WhoScEn 94
Mandel, Ruth Blumenstock 1938- WhoWomW 91
Mandel, Siegfried 1922- WhoAm 94, WhoWest 94
Mandel, Stephen Barry 1943- WhoFI 94
Mandel, Steven Jay 1955- WhoAmL 94
Mandel, William Kurt 1948- WhoAm 94
Mandela, Nelson 1918- WrDr 94
Mandela, Nelson R(olihlahla) 1918- BlkWr 2, ConAu 43NR
Mandela, Nelson Rolihlahia 1918- IntWW 93, Who 94
Mandela, (Nomzano) Winnie 1934- IntWW 93, WhoWomW 91
Mandelbaum, Allen DrAPF 93
Mandelbaum, Barry Richard 1936- WhoAmL 94
Mandelbaum, Bernard 1922- WrDr 94

Mankiewicz, Joseph L(eo) 1909-1993 *ConAu 140*
Mankiewicz, Joseph Leo d1993 *IntWW 93N, Who 94N*
Mankiewicz, Joseph Leo 1909- *IntWW 93*
Mankiewicz, Tom 1942- *IntMPA 94*
Mankiller, Wilma *NewYTBS 93 [port]*
Mankin, Charles John 1932- *WhoAm 94, WhoScEn 94*
Mankin, Hart T. 1933- *CngDr 93*
Mankin, Hart Tiller 1933- *WhoAm 94, WhoAmL 94*
Mankin, Henry Jay 1928- *WhoAm 94*
Mankin, Robert Stephen 1939- *WhoAm 94, WhoFI 94*
Mankiw, Nicholas Gregory 1958- *WhoFI 94*
Manko, Joseph Martin, Sr. 1939- *WhoAm 94, WhoAmL 94*
Manko, Wesley Daniel 1957- *WhoMW 93*
Mankoff, Albert William 1926- *WhoWest 94*
Mankoff, Ronald Morton 1931- *WhoAm 94*
Mankowitz, Wolf 1924- *ConTFT 11, IntDcF 2-4, IntMPA 94, IntWW 93, Who 94, WrDr 94*
Mankowitz, (Cyril) Wolf 1924- *ConDr 93*
Mankowski, Bruno 1902-1990 *WhoAmA 93N*
Manktelow, Michael Richard John 1927- *Who 94*
Manley, Albert 1908- *WhoBlA 94*
Manley, Albert Edward 1908- *WhoAm 94*
Manley, Albert Leslie 1945- *IntWW 93*
Manley, Audrey Forbes 1934- *WhoAm 94, WhoBlA 94*
Manley, Bill 1943- *WhoBlA 94*
Manley, Charles d1916 *WhoHol 92*
Manley, Dave d1943 *WhoHol 92*
Manley, David Thomas 1938- *WhoFI 94, WhoMW 93*
Manley, Delarivier 1663-1724 *BlmGWL*
Manley, Delariviere 1663?-1724 *BlmGEL*
Manley, Dexter 1959- *WhoBlA 94*
Manley, Frank 1930- *WhoAm 94, WrDr 94*
Manley, Ivor Thomas 1931- *Who 94*
Manley, Jeffrey A. 1941- *WhoAmL 94*
Manley, Joan Adele Daniels 1932- *WhoAm 94, WhoWest 94*
Manley, John c. 1734-1793 *WhAmRev*
Manley, John Frederick 1939- *WhoAm 94*
Manley, John H. 1907-1990 *WhAm 10*
Manley, John Hugo 1932- *WhoAm 94*
Manley, John Ruffin 1925- *WhoBlA 94*
Manley, Lance Filson 1945- *WhoFI 94, WhoScEn 94*
Manley, Michael Norman 1924- *IntWW 93, Who 94*
Manley, Nancy Jane 1951- *WhoFI 94*
Manley, Richard Shannon 1932- *WhoAmP 93*
Manley, Richard Walter 1934- *WhoFI 94, WhoWest 94*
Manley, Robert Edward 1935- *WhoAm 94*
Manley, Stephen 1965- *WhoHol 92*
Manley, William Tanner 1929- *WhoAm 94*
Manlove, Benson 1943- *WhoBlA 94*
Manlove, C(olin) N(icholas) 1942- *EncSF 93*
Manlove, Colin (Nicholas) 1942- *WrDr 94*
Manlove, Robert Fletcher 1937- *WhoWest 94*
Manlowe, James Stewart 1963- *WhoWest 94*
Manly, Carol Ann 1947- *WhoScEn 94*
Manly, Charles M., III 1950- *WhoAmP 93*
Manly, Louis J. d1959 *WhoHol 92*
Manly, Marc Edward 1952- *WhoAm 94*
Manly, Samuel 1945- *WhoAmL 94*
Manly, Sarah G. 1927- *WhoAmP 93*
Manly, William Donald 1923- *WhoAm 94, WhoScEn 94*
Manmiller, Joseph C. 1925- *WhoAmP 93*
Mann *Who 94*
Mann, A. T. 1943- *AstEnc*
Mann, Abby 1927- *IntMPA 94*
Mann, Alfred 1917- *WhoAm 94*
Mann, Anthony *Who 94*
Mann, Arthur d1993 *NewYTBS 93*
Mann, Arthur 1922-1993 *ConAu 140*
Mann, Benjamin F. 1951- *WhoAmL 94*
Mann, Benjamin Howard 1958- *WhoFI 94, WhoMW 93*
Mann, Bernie *WhoAm 94*
Mann, Bertha d1967 *WhoHol 92*
Mann, Bill Wayne *WhoFI 94*
Mann, Billy d1974 *WhoHol 92*
Mann, Bruce Alan 1934- *WhoAm 94, WhoAmL 94*
Mann, Cato d1977 *WhoHol 92*
Mann, Cedric Robert 1926- *WhoAm 94*
Mann, Charles 1961- *WhoAm 94, WhoBlA 94*
Mann, Charles Edward *DrAPF 93*
Mann, Charles W. 1935- *WhoAmP 93*
Mann, Chris(topher Michael Zithulele) 1948- *WrDr 94*
Mann, Clarence Charles 1929- *WhoFI 94*
Mann, Claud Prentiss, Jr. 1925- *WhoWest 94*
Mann, Curtis J. 1950- *WhoAmL 94*
Mann, Daniel 1912-1991 *ConTFT 11, WhAm 10*
Mann, David 1939- *CngDr 93*
Mann, David Emerson 1924- *WhoAmP 93*
Mann, David Mark 1943- *WhoScEn 94*
Mann, David S. 1939- *WhoAmP 93*
Mann, David Scott 1939- *WhoAm 94, WhoMW 93*
Mann, David William 1947- *WhoAm 94, WhoMW 93*
Mann, Delbert 1920- *IntMPA 94, WhoAm 94*
Mann, Donald Cameron 1949- *WhoFI 94*
Mann, Donald J. 1949- *WhoAmL 94*
Mann, Donald Robert 1930- *WhoWest 94*
Mann, Donegan 1922- *WhoAmL 94*
Mann, Edward Beverly 1902-1989 *WhAm 10*
Mann, Emily 1952- *ConDr 93, WrDr 94*
Mann, Emily Betsy 1952- *WhoAm 94*
Mann, Eric John 1921- *Who 94*
Mann, Erika d1969 *WhoHol 92*
Mann, Felix Bernard 1931- *Who 94*
Mann, Frank 1953- *WhoAmA 93*
Mann, Frank E. 1920- *WhoAmP 93*
Mann, Franklin Balch 1941- *WhoAmP 93*
Mann, Fritz Alan 1953- *WhoWest 94*
Mann, George *Who 94*
Mann, (Francis) George 1917- *Who 94*
Mann, George Anthony 1951- *Who 94*
Mann, George K. d1977 *WhoHol 92*
Mann, George Levier 1901- *WhoBlA 94*
Mann, George Stanley 1932- *WhoAm 94*
Mann, Gerald C. 1907-1990 *WhAm 10*
Mann, Gloria d1961 *WhoHol 92*
Mann, Golo 1909- *IntWW 93*
Mann, H. George 1937- *WhoAm 94*
Mann, Hank d1971 *WhoHol 92*
Mann, Harold 1931- *WhoAmP 93*
Mann, Harvey Blount 1930- *WhoFI 94*
Mann, Helen d1947 *WhoHol 92*
Mann, Helen Louise 1943- *WhoAmP 93*
Mann, Henry Dean 1943- *WhoFI 94*
Mann, Herbie 1930- *WhoAm 94*
Mann, Horace 1796-1859 *AmSocL, DcAmReB 2*
Mann, Howard *WhoHol 92*
Mann, Jack *EncSF 93*
Mann, James 1938- *WrDr 94*
Mann, James Darwin 1936- *WhoScEn 94*
Mann, James E. 1943- *WhoAmL 94*
Mann, James E. 1948- *WhoAmL 94*
Mann, James Robert 1920- *WhoAm 94, WhoAmP 93*
Mann, Jean (Adah) 1927- *WhoAmA 93*
Mann, Jeff *WhoAm 94*
Mann, Jeffrey R. 1942- *WhoAmL 94*
Mann, Jerry d1987 *WhoHol 92*
Mann, Jessica *WrDr 94*
Mann, Jill 1943- *Who 94*
Mann, Jim 1919- *WhoAm 94*
Mann, John Frederick 1930- *Who 94*
Mann, John Kevin 1956- *WhoWest 94*
Mann, Jonathan Max 1947- *WhoAm 94*
Mann, Jonnie Yvonne 1939- *WhoFI 94*
Mann, Joseph B. 1939- *WhoBlA 94*
Mann, Josephine *ConAu 43NR, WrDr 94*
Mann, Katinka 1925- *WhoAmA 93*
Mann, Kenneth Gerard 1941- *WhoScEn 94*
Mann, Kenneth Henry 1923- *WhoAm 94*
Mann, Kenneth Walker 1914- *WhoAm 94*
Mann, Larry D. 1922- *WhoHol 92*
Mann, Laura Joy 1966- *WhoWest 94*
Mann, Laura Susan 1958- *WhoScEn 94*
Mann, Leonard *WhoHol 92*
Mann, Lester Perry 1921- *WhoScEn 94*
Mann, Louis d1931 *WhoHol 92*
Mann, Lowell Kimsey 1917- *WhoAm 94*
Mann, Margaret d1941 *WhoHol 92*
Mann, Margery 1919-1977 *WhoAmA 93N*
Mann, Marion 1920- *AfrAmG [port], WhoAm 94, WhoBlA 94*
Mann, Mark L. 1952- *WhoAmL 94*
Mann, Martin Edward 1943- *Who 94*
Mann, Maybelle 1915- *WhoAmA 93*
Mann, Merton L., Jr. *WhoAmP 93*
Mann, Michael 1930- *Who 94*
Mann, Michael 1943- *CurBio 93 [port], IntMPA 94*
Mann, Michael Ashley 1924- *Who 94*
Mann, Michael K. *WhoAm 94*
Mann, Michael K. 1943- *WrDr 94*
Mann, Michael Martin 1939- *WhoAm 94, WhoFI 94, WhoScEn 94, WhoWest 94*
Mann, Murray G. *Who 94*
Mann, Nancy Louise 1925- *WhoWest 94*
Mann, Ned H. d1967 *WhoHol 92*
Mann, Nicholas *Who 94*
Mann, (Colin) Nicholas (Jocelyn) 1942- *Who 94*
Mann, Oscar 1934- *WhoAm 94, WhoScEn 94*
Mann, Patricia Kathleen Randall 1937- *Who 94*
Mann, Paul 1915- *WhoHol 92*
Mann, Pauline *Who 94*
Mann, Peggy *DrAPF 93, WrDr 94*
Mann, Peggy d1990 *WhAm 10*
Mann, Perry E. 1921- *WhoAmP 93*
Mann, Peter 1939- *WhoHol 92*
Mann, Peter Woodley 1924- *Who 94*
Mann, Philip Melvin 1940- *WhoBlA 94*
Mann, Philip Roy 1948- *WhoAmL 94*
Mann, (Anthony) Phillip 1942- *EncSF 93, WrDr 94*
Mann, Phillip Lynn 1944- *WhoMW 93*
Mann, Richard *WhoBlA 94*
Mann, Richard E. 1931- *WhoMW 93*
Mann, Robert 1958- *ConAu 140*
Mann, Robert E. 1937- *WhoAmL 94*
Mann, Robert Nathaniel 1920- *WhoAm 94*
Mann, Robert Samuel 1936- *WhoWest 94*
Mann, Robert Wellesley 1924- *IntWW 93, WhoAm 94, WhoScEn 94*
Mann, Rupert (Edward) 1946- *Who 94*
Mann, Russell Duane 1922- *WhoAmL 94*
Mann, Sally 1951- *WhoAmA 93*
Mann, Sam Henry, Jr. 1925- *WhoAmL 94*
Mann, Seymour 1923-1989 *WhAm 10*
Mann, Seymour Zalmon 1921- *WhoAm 94*
Mann, Stanley *ConTFT 11*
Mann, Stanley d1953 *WhoHol 92*
Mann, Stephen Ashby 1947- *WhoFI 94*
Mann, Steven Gerald 1944- *WhoFI 94*
Mann, Terrence *WhoHol 92*
Mann, Terry Lawrence 1948- *WhoAmP 93*
Mann, Thaddeus Robert Rudolph 1908- *IntWW 93, Who 94*
Mann, Theodore 1924- *WhoAm 94*
Mann, Theodore R. 1928- *WhoAm 94*
Mann, Thomas 1875-1955 *NewGrDO*
Mann, Thomas, Jr. 1949- *WhoAmP 93*
Mann, (Paul) Thomas 1875-1955 *GayLL, RfGShF*
Mann, Thomas Edward 1944- *WhoAm 94*
Mann, Thomas J., Jr. 1949- *WhoBlA 94*
Mann, Thomas William, Jr. 1949- *WhoWest 94*
Mann, Timothy 1942- *WhoAm 94*
Mann, Tracey *WhoHol 92*
Mann, Ulrich 1952- *WhoScEn 94*
Mann, Ward Palmer *WhoAmA 93*
Mann, Wesley *WhoHol 92*
Mann, William A. 1944- *WhoAmL 94*
Mann, William D'Alton 1839-1920 *DcLB 137 [port]*
Mann, William J. *WhoMW 93*
Mann, William Jaggard 1942- *WhoFI 94*
Mann, William Neville 1911- *Who 94*
Mann, William S(omervell) 1924-1989 *NewGrDO*
Mann, Yuri Vladimirovich 1929- *IntWW 93*
Manna, Charlie d1971 *WhoHol 92*
Manna, Charlie 1925-1971 *WhoCom*
Manna, Gennaro 1715-1779 *NewGrDO*
Manna, Guy d1987 *WhoHol 92*
Manne, Alan S. 1925- *WhoAm 94, WhoWest 94*
Manne, Henry G 1928- *WrDr 94*
Manne, Henry Girard 1928- *WhoAm 94, WhoAmL 94*
Manne, S. Anthony 1940- *IntMPA 94*
Manne, Shelly d1984 *WhoHol 92*
Manne, Veeraswamy 1952- *WhoAsA 94*
Mannelli, Francesco *NewGrDO*
Manner, Eeva-Liisa 1921- *BlmGWL*
Mannerheim, Karl Gustaf 1867-1951 *HisWorL [port]*
Mannering, Jerry Vincent 1929- *WhoAm 94*
Mannering, Lewin d1932 *WhoHol 92*
Mannering, Vincent G. 1951- *WhoAmP 93*
Manners *Who 94*
Manners, Baron 1923- *Who 94*
Manners, Charles 1857-1935 *NewGrDO*
Manners, David 1900- *WhoHol 92*
Manners, Diana d1986 *WhoHol 92*
Manners, Dorothy d1949 *WhoHol 92*
Manners, Elizabeth Maude 1917- *Who 94*
Manners, George Emanuel 1910- *WhoAm 94*
Manners, Gerald 1932- *Who 94, WrDr 94*
Manners, Gloria d1982 *WhoHol 92*
Manners, Miss 1938- *WrDr 94*
Manners, Nancy *WhoWest 94*
Manners, Robert Alan 1913- *WhoAm 94, WrDr 94*
Manners, Thomas (Jasper) 1929- *Who 94*
Manners, Tyler Paul 1960- *WhoWest 94*
Mannes, Elena Sabin 1943- *WhoAm 94*
Mannes, Marya 1904-1990 *EncSF 93, WhAm 10*
Mannes, Paul 1933- *WhoAm 94, WhoAmL 94*
Manney, Bridget *DrAPF 93*
Manney, William A. 1931- *WhoBlA 94*
Mannheim, Karl *EncSF 93*
Mannheim, Lucie d1976 *WhoHol 92*
Mannheim, Walter 1930- *WhoScEn 94*
Manni, Ettore d1979 *WhoHol 92*
Manni, Victor Macedonio 1940- *WhoHisp 94*
Mannick, John Anthony 1928- *WhoAm 94, WhoScEn 94*
Mannie, William Edward 1931- *WhoBlA 94*
Manniello, John Baptiste Louis 1923- *WhoAm 94*
Mannin, Ethel 1900-1984 *BlmGWL*
Manning, Aileen d1946 *WhoHol 92*
Manning, Ambrose d1940 *WhoHol 92*
Manning, Arthur Brewster 1913- *WhoAm 94*
Manning, Aubrey William George 1930- *Who 94*
Manning, Blanche M. 1934- *WhoAmP 93*
Manning, Blanche Marie 1934- *WhoBlA 94*
Manning, Brent V. 1950- *WhoAm 94, WhoAmL 94*
Manning, Burt 1931- *WhoAm 94, WhoFI 94*
Manning, Charles Terrill 1925- *WhoAm 94*
Manning, Christopher Ashley 1945- *WhoFI 94*
Manning, D. James, Jr. 1942- *WhoAmL 94*
Manning, Daniel Ricardo 1966- *WhoBlA 94*
Manning, Danny 1966- *WhoAm 94*
Manning, Darrell V. 1932- *WhoWest 94*
Manning, David (John) 1938- *WrDr 94*
Manning, David Geoffrey 1949- *Who 94*
Manning, Donald J. 1929- *WhoAmP 93*
Manning, Donald O. *WhoAm 94, WhoWest 94*
Manning, Eddie James 1952- *WhoBlA 94*
Manning, Ellis E. 1933- *WhoAm 94*
Manning, Eric 1940- *WhoAm 94, WhoWest 94*
Manning, Ernest Charles 1908- *IntWW 93*
Manning, Eugene Baines 1940- *WhoAm 94*
Manning, Evelyn 1945- *WhoBlA 94*
Manning, Farley 1909- *WhoAm 94*
Manning, Francis Joseph 1933- *WhoAmP 93*
Manning, Frank Thomas 1931- *WhoWest 94*
Manning, Frederick Allan d1991 *Who 94N*
Manning, Frederick J. 1947- *WhoIns 94*
Manning, Frederick William 1924- *WhoAm 94*
Manning, Geoffrey 1929- *Who 94*
Manning, George Taylor 1948- *WhoAm 94*
Manning, Gerald Stephen 1948- *WhoAmL 94*
Manning, Glenn M. 1935- *WhoBlA 94*
Manning, Hilda Scudder d1988 *WhoAmA 93N*
Manning, Hope *WhoHol 92*
Manning, Howard Nick, Jr. 1943- *WhoBlA 94*
Manning, Hubert Vernon 1918- *WhoBlA 94*
Manning, Hugh 1920- *WhoHol 92*
Manning, Irene 1916- *WhoHol 92*
Manning, Jack 1916- *WhoHol 92*
Manning, Jack 1920- *WhoAm 94*
Manning, James 1735-1791 *WhAmRev*
Manning, James 1738-1791 *DcAmReB 2*
Manning, James Hamington, Jr. 1938- *WhoAmL 94*
Manning, Jane 1938- *IntWW 93*
Manning, Jane A. 1947- *WhoBlA 94*
Manning, Jane Marian 1938- *Who 94*
Manning, Jean Bell 1937- *WhoBlA 94*
Manning, Jerome Alan 1929- *WhoAm 94*
Manning, Jo 1923- *WhoAmA 93*
Manning, John Joseph 1930- *WhoFI 94*
Manning, John Lawrence 1943- *WhoAmL 94*
Manning, John Willard 1950- *WhoAm 94*
Manning, Joseph d1946 *WhoHol 92*
Manning, Joseph A. 1946- *WhoAm 94*
Manning, Joseph P. 1926- *WhoAmP 93*
Manning, Katy *WhoHol 92*
Manning, Kenneth Alan 1951- *WhoAm 94, WhoAmL 94*
Manning, Kenneth Paul 1942- *WhoAm 94, WhoFI 94*
Manning, Kirk R. 1946- *WhoAmL 94*
Manning, Knox d1980 *WhoHol 92*
Manning, Laura Jean 1960- *WhoMW 93*
Manning, Laurence (Edward) 1899-1972 *EncSF 93*

Manning, Lillian O'Neal 1956-
WhoMW 94
Manning, Lynn *DrAPF 93*
Manning, M. Joseph 1924- *WhoAmP 93*
Manning, Marbene d1942 *WhoHol 92*
Manning, Marjorie d1922 *WhoHol 92*
Manning, Marsha d1986 *WrDr 94N*
Manning, Martin *ConAu 140*
Manning, Matthew Nickerson 1962-
WhoFI 94
Manning, Mervyn H. 1932- *WhoFI 94*
Manning, Michael J. 1944- *WhoAmL 94*
Manning, Mitchell Wayne 1947-
WhoFI 94
Manning, Ned *WhoHol 92*
Manning, Noel Thomas 1939- *WhoAm 94*
Manning, Olivia 1908-1980 *BlmGWL*
Manning, Olivia 1915-1980 *BlmGEL*
Manning, Patricia Kamaras 1953-
WhoWest 94
Manning, Patrick Augustus Mervyn
1946- *IntWW 93, Who 94*
Manning, Peter J. *WhoAmP 93*
Manning, Peter Kirby 1940- *WhoAm 94,
WhoMW 93*
Manning, Phillip d1951 *WhoHol 92*
Manning, Preston 1942- *ConAu 141*
Manning, Ralph Fabian 1945- *WhoAm 94*
Manning, Randolph H. 1947- *WhoBlA 94*
Manning, Reg 1905-1986 *WhoAmA 93N*
Manning, Reuben D. 1931- *WhoBlA 94*
Manning, Richard 1943-1989 *WhAm 10*
Manning, Richard L. 1957- *WhoFI 94*
Manning, Robert *WhoHol 92*
Manning, Robert Hendrick 1941-
WhoMW 93
Manning, Robert Joseph 1919-
IntWW 93, WhoAm 94
Manning, Robert Thomas 1927-
WhoAm 94
Manning, Roberta Thompson 1940-
WrDr 94
Manning, Ronald Lee 1951- *WhoMW 93*
Manning, Rosemary 1911- *WrDr 94*
Manning, Sam P. *WhoAmP 93*
Manning, Sandra Kay 1951- *WhoFI 94,
WhoMW 93*
Manning, Susan Harriet Hinman 1943-
WhoMW 93
Manning, Sylvia 1943- *WhoAm 94*
Manning, Thomas 1772-1840 *WhWE*
Manning, Thomas Henry 1911- *Who 94*
Manning, Thomas Joseph 1955-
WhoMW 93
Manning, Timothy 1909-1989 *WhAm 10*
Manning, Timothy 1958- *WhoFI 94*
Manning, Tom d1936 *WhoHol 92*
Manning, V. C. *WhoAmP 93*
Manning, Victor Patrick, Jr. 1945-
WhoFI 94
Manning, W. H. d1933 *WhoHol 92*
Manning, Walter Scott 1912- *WhoAm 94,
WhoFI 94*
Manning, William Beckwith, III 1943-
WhoAm 94
Manning, William Dudley, Jr. 1934-
WhoAm 94, WhoFI 94
Manning, William Frederick 1920-
WhoAm 94
Manning, William George 1923-
WhoFI 94
Manning, William Henry 1951-
WhoAm 94, WhoAmL 94
Manning, William Joseph 1926-
WhoAm 94, WhoAmL 94
Manning, William Raymond 1920-
WhoAm 94
Manning, Winton Howard 1930-
WhoAm 94
Manningham-Buller *Who 94*
Manning-Sanders, Ruth 1895?-1988
ConAu 41NR
Mannino, Calogero 1939- *IntWW 93*
Mannino, Edward Francis 1941-
WhoAm 94, WhoAmL 94
Mannino, Franco 1924- *NewGrDO*
Mannino, J. Davis 1949- *WhoScEn 94,
WhoWest 94*
Mannino, James A. 1942- *WhoAmL 94*
Mannion, James Michael 1945-
WhoAmP 93
Mannion, John F. X. 1932- *WhoIns 94*
Mannion, John Francis Xavier 1932-
WhoAm 94
Mannis, Valerie Sklar 1939- *WhoMW 93*
Mannix, Brian F. 1951- *WhoFI 94*
Mannix, David K. 1952- *IntMPA 94*
Mannix, Kevin Leese 1949- *WhoAmP 93,
WhoWest 94*
Mannle, Ursula 1944- *WhoWomW 91*
Mannoni, Raymond 1921- *WhoAm 94*
Mannors, Sheila *WhoHol 92*
Mannoury d'Ectot, Madame de fl. 19th
cent.- *BlmGWL*
Manns, Roy Lokumal 1937- *WhoScEn 94*
Mannschreck, Stephen Lester 1945-

Mannweiler, Paul Steven 1949-
WhoAmP 93
Manny, Carter Hugh, Jr. 1918-
WhoAm 94
Mannyng, Robert fl. 1288-1338 *BlmGEL*
Mano, D. Keith *DrAPF 93*
Mano, D. Keith 1943- *EncSF 93*
Mano, Toru 1945- *WhoAmA 93*
Manocchi, James Charles 1953- *WhoFI 94*
Manoff, Dinah 1958- *IntMPA 94,
WhoHol 92*
Manoff, Dinah Beth *WhoAm 94*
Manoff, Marc D. 1963- *WhoAmL 94*
Manoff, Richard Kalman 1916-
WhoAm 94
Manoharan, Ramasamy 1962-
WhoScEn 94
Manolakas, Stanton Peter 1946-
WhoAmA 93, WhoWest 94
Manolescu, Florin *EncSF 93*
Manolov, Emanuil 1860-1902 *NewGrDO*
Manon, Gloria *WhoHol 92*
Manon, Marcia d1973 *WhoHol 92*
Manone, Wingy d1982 *WhoHol 92*
Manon Margarita d1981 *WhoHol 92*
Manoogian, Alex 1901- *WhoAm 94*
Manoogian, David E. 1944- *WhoAmL 94*
Manoogian, Richard Alexander 1936-
WhoAm 94, WhoFI 94, WhoMW 93
Manor, Jason 1920- *WrDr 94*
Manor, Timothy J. 1949- *WhoAmL 94*
Manos, Christopher Alexander 1956-
WhoWest 94
Manos, Christopher Lawrence 1952-
WhoAmL 94
Manos, John M. 1922- *WhoAm 94*
Manos, Pete Lazaros 1936- *WhoAm 94,
WhoFI 94*
Manos, Peter Nicholas, II 1958-
WhoWest 94
Manosevitz, Martin 1938- *WhoAm 94*
Manougian, Edward 1929- *WhoWest 94*
Manoukian, Noel Edwin 1938-
WhoAm 94, WhoAmP 93
Manoukian, Rita Chake 1964-
WhoWest 94
Manousos, James William 1919-
WhoAm 94
Manov, Gregory A. 1942- *WhoMW 93*
Manov, Leslie Joan Boyle 1948-
WhoAm 94, WhoMW 93
Manowarda, Josef von 1890-1942
NewGrDO
Manqour, Nasir Hamad al- 1927-
IntWW 93
Manray 1890-1976 *WhoAmA 93N*
Manrique, Carlos A. 1959- *WhoAmP 93*
Manrique, Jaime *DrAPF 93*
Manrique, Jaime 1949- *WhoHisp 94*
Manrique, Julius C. 1932- *WhoHisp 94*
Manross, Carl Arthur 1939- *WhoMW 93*
Mans, Keith Douglas Rowland 1946-
Who 94
Mans, Rowland Spencer Noel 1921-
Who 94
Mansager, Felix Norman 1911-
IntWW 93, Who 94
Mansaram *WhoAmA 93*
Mansard, Claude *WhoHol 92*
Mansbach, Robert Earl, Jr. 1957-
WhoAmL 94
Mansberg, Ruth 1924- *WrDr 94*
Mansberger, Arlie Roland, Jr. 1922-
WhoAm 94
Mansbridge, Francis 1943- *WrDr 94*
Mansbridge, Jane Jebb 1939- *WhoMW 93*
Mansel, James Seymour Denis 1907-
Who 94
Mansel, Philip 1943- *Who 94*
Mansel, Robert Edward 1948- *Who 94*
Mansel, Thomas 1667-1723 *DcNaB MP*
Mansel-Jones, David 1926- *Who 94*
Mansell, Buford H. L. 1938- *WhoBlA 94*
Mansell, Darrel 1934- *WrDr 94*
Mansell, Darrel Lee, Jr. 1934- *WhoAm 94*
Mansell, Gerard (Evelyn Herbert) 1921-
WrDr 94
Mansell, Gerard Evelyn Herbert 1921-
Who 94
Mansell, Nigel 1954- *IntWW 93*
Mansell, Nigel Ernest James 1953-
Who 94
Mansel Lewis, David Courtenay 1927-
Who 94
Mansell-Jones, Richard 1940- *Who 94*
Mansen, Steven Robert 1955- *WhoFI 94*
Manser, John *Who 94*
Manser, (Peter) John 1939- *Who 94*
Manser, Martin H(ugh) 1952-
ConAu 42NR
Manser, Michael John 1929- *IntWW 93,
Who 94*
Mansfield *Who 94*
Mansfield, Andrew K. 1931- *WhoBlA 94*
Mansfield, Anthony R. 1943-
WhoAmL 94
Mansfield, Bruce Edgar 1926- *WrDr 94*

Mansfield, Carl Major 1928- *WhoAm 94,
WhoBlA 94*
Mansfield, Christopher Charles 1950-
WhoAm 94, WhoAmL 94, WhoFI 94
Mansfield, Claudine Trotter 1921-
WhoAmP 93
Mansfield, David Parks 1912- *Who 94*
Mansfield, Duncan d1971 *WhoHol 92*
Mansfield, Edward Patrick, Jr. 1947-
WhoAm 94
Mansfield, Edwin 1930- *WhoAm 94*
Mansfield, Elizabeth *ConAu 41NR*
Mansfield, Eric Harold 1923- *IntWW 93,
Who 94*
Mansfield, Georganna Lynn 1961-
WhoMW 93
Mansfield, Gerard *Who 94*
Mansfield, (Edward) Gerard (Napier)
1921- *Who 94*
Mansfield, J(ohn) Kenneth 1921-
IntWW 93
Mansfield, James Norman, III 1951-
WhoAmL 94
Mansfield, Jayne d1967 *WhoHol 92*
Mansfield, Jayne Marie 1950- *WhoHol 92*
Mansfield, Jerry Leonard 1947-
WhoAmP 93
Mansfield, John d1956 *WhoHol 92*
Mansfield, Karen Lee 1942- *WhoAmL 94,
WhoMW 93*
Mansfield, Katherine 1888-1923
*BlmGEL [port], BlmGWL, GayLL,
RfGShF*
Mansfield, Libby *ConAu 41NR*
Mansfield, Lois Edna 1941- *WhoAm 94,
WhoScEn 94*
Mansfield, Marc Lewis 1955- *WhoAm 94*
Mansfield, Marian d1988 *WhoHol 92*
Mansfield, Martha d1923 *WhoHol 92*
Mansfield, Maynard Joseph 1930-
WhoAm 94
Mansfield, Michael 1941- *Who 94*
Mansfield, Michael J. 1903- *WhoAmP 93*
Mansfield, Michael Joseph 1903-
IntWW 93, WhoAm 94
Mansfield, Michele R. 1961- *WhoAmL 94*
Mansfield, Peter 1933- *IntWW 93,
Who 94*
Mansfield, Philip (Robert Aked) 1926-
Who 94
Mansfield, Philip Robert Aked 1926-
IntWW 93
Mansfield, Rankin d1969 *WhoHol 92*
Mansfield, Richard 1723-1820 *WhAmRev*
Mansfield, Robert Adams 1942-
WhoAmA 93
Mansfield, Roger Leo 1944- *WhoWest 94*
Mansfield, Ruth Stiles 1917- *WhoAmP 93*
Mansfield, Terence Arthur 1937-
IntWW 93, Who 94
Mansfield, Terence Gordon 1938- *Who 94*
Mansfield, W. Ed 1937- *WhoBlA 94*
Mansfield, William Amos 1929-
WhoAmL 94, WhoWest 94
Mansfield and Mansfield, Earl of 1930-
Who 94
Mansfield Cooper, William d1992
Who 94N
Manshard, Walther 1923- *IntWW 93*
Mansheim, David John 1945-
WhoAmP 93
Manshel, Warren Demian 1924-1990
WhAm 10
Manship, Charles Phelps, Jr. 1908-
WhoAm 94, WhoFI 94
Manship, Douglas 1918- *WhoAm 94*
Manship, John Paul 1927- *WhoAmA 93*
Manship, Patrick Jay 1958- *WhoMW 93*
Manship, Paul 1885-1966 *WhoAmA 93N*
Mansholt, Sicco Leendert 1908-
IntWW 93
Mansi, Joseph Anneillo 1935- *WhoAm 94,
WhoFI 94*
Mansi, Nicholas Anthony 1930-
WhoAmP 93
Mansilla, Daniel Garcia *BlmGWL*
Mansilla de Garcia, Eduarda 1838-1892
BlmGWL
Mansinghka, Surendra Kumar 1944-
WhoWest 94
Mansion, Gracie 1946- *WhoAmA 93*
Manske, John Thomas 1952-
WhoAmP 93
Manske, Lynn Darlene 1955- *WhoMW 93*
Manske, Paul Robert 1938- *WhoAm 94*
Mansker, Robert Thomas 1941-
WhoAmP 93
Manski, Wladyslaw Julian 1915-
WhoAm 94
Mansky, Arthur William 1956-
WhoScEn 94
Mansmann, Carol Los *WhoAmP 93*
Mansmann, Carol Los 1942- *WhoAm 94,
WhoAmL 94*
Mansmann, Herbert C., Jr. 1924-
WhoAm 94
Mansmann, J. Jerome 1942- *WhoAm 94,
WhoAmL 94*

Manso, Leo d1993 *NewYTBS 93 [port]*
Manso, Leo 1914- *WhoAmA 93*
Manson, Alan *WhoHol 92*
Manson, Arthur 1928- *IntMPA 94*
Manson, Bruce Malcolm 1944-
WhoAm 94
Manson, Eddy Lawrence *WhoAm 94*
Manson, Gordon 1922- *WhoMW 93*
Manson, Helena *WhoHol 92*
Manson, Ian Stuart 1929- *Who 94*
Manson, Joseph Lloyd, III 1949-
WhoAm 94, WhoAmL 94
Manson, Malcolm Hood 1938-
WhoWest 94
Manson, Maurice *WhoHol 92*
Manson, Michael Irving 1951- *WhoAm 94*
Manson, Pamela 1928- *WhoHol 92*
Manson, Paul David 1934- *WhoAm 94*
Manson-Hing, Lincoln Roy 1927-
WhoAm 94
Mansoor, Lutfi Gabrie, Jr. 1941-
WhoHisp 94
Mansoor, Menahem 1911- *WrDr 94*
Mansour, Awad Rasheed 1951-
WhoScEn 94
Mansour, Farid Fam 1942- *WhoScEn 94*
Mansour, George P. 1939- *WhoAm 94*
Mansour, Joyce 1928-1987 *BlmGWL*
Mansour, Tag Eldin 1924- *WhoAm 94*
Mansouri, Lotfi 1929- *NewGrDO*
Mansouri, Lotfollah 1929- *WhoAm 94,
WhoWest 94*
Manspeizer, Susan R. *WhoAmA 93*
Mansur, Iqbal 1955- *WhoAsA 94*
Mansur, Mallikarjun 1910- *IntWW 93*
Mansure, Edmund F. 1901-1992
WhAm 10
Mant, Arthur Keith 1919- *IntWW 93*
Mant, Keith *Who 94*
Mant, (Arthur) Keith 1919- *Who 94*
Mantas, John 1954- *WhoScEn 94*
Mantee, Paul *WhoHol 92*
Mantegazza, Paolo *EncSF 93*
Mantegna, Joe 1947- *IntMPA 94,
WhoHol 92*
Mantegna, Joe Anthony 1947- *WhoAm 94*
Manteiga, Roland Marcello 1920-
WhoHisp 94
Mantel, Hilary (Mary) 1952- *WrDr 94*
Mantel, Kenneth Haskell 1927- *WhoFI 94*
Mantel, Samuel J(oseph), Jr. 1921-
WrDr 94
Mantel, Samuel Joseph, Jr. 1921-
WhoAm 94
Mantell, Bruce d1933 *WhoHol 92*
Mantell, Charles (Barrie Knight) 1937-
Who 94
Mantell, Charles L. 1897- *WhAm 10*
Mantell, Joe *WhoHol 92*
Mantell, Lester J. 1937- *WhoAm 94*
Mantell, Michael *WhoHol 92*
Mantell, Robert B. d1928 *WhoHol 92*
Mantell, Suzanne 1944- *WhoAm 94*
Mantelli, Eugenia 1860-1926 ·*NewGrDO*
Manter, Debra Sue 1956- *WhoFI 94*
Manter, Margaret C. 1923- *WhoAmA 93*
Mantes, George 1937- *WhoAmP 93*
Manthe, Cora De Munck 1928- *WhoFI 94*
Manthei, Richard Dale 1935- *WhoAm 94,
WhoAmL 94, WhoFI 94*
Manthei, Robin Dickey 1956-
WhoMW 93
Manthey, Frank Anthony 1933-
WhoScEn 94
Manthey, Thomas Richard 1942-
WhoAm 94, WhoAmL 94
Manthorp, Brian Robert 1934- *Who 94*
Manthorpe, John Jeremy 1936- *Who 94*
Manthorpe, Rolf 1942- *WhoScEn 94*
Mantil, Joseph Chacko 1937- *WhoAsA 94,
WhoScEn 94*
Mantilla, Felix 1955- *WhoHisp 94*
Mantilla, Mercedes 1936- *WhoHisp 94*
Mantinband, Gerda (B.) 1917-
SmATA 74 [port]
Mantius, Eduard 1806-1874 *NewGrDO*
Mantle, C. Lee 1911- *WhoAmP 93*
Mantle, John Edward 1940- *WhoAm 94*
Mantle, Larry Edward 1959- *WhoWest 94*
Mantle, Mickey 1931- *WhoHol 92*
Mantle, Mickey Charles 1931- *WhoAm 94*
Mantle, Raymond Allan 1937-
WhoAm 94
Mantley, John (Truman) 1920- *EncSF 93*
Manto, Sadat Hasan 1912-1955 *RfGShF*
Manton, Baron 1924- *Who 94*
Manton, Edwin Alfred Grenville 1909-
WhoAm 94, WhoIns 94
Manton, Thomas J. 1932- *CngDr 93,
WhoAmP 93*
Manton, Thomas Joseph 1932-
WhoAm 94
Mantonya, John Butcher 1922-
WhoAm 94
Mantooth, John Albert 1947-
WhoAmL 94
Mantovani d1980 *WhoHol 92*

Mantovanina, La *NewGrDO*
Mantsch, Henry Horst 1935- *WhoAm 94*
Mantulin, William W. 1946- *WhoMW 93*
Manturuk, Robert Stanley 1946- *WhoFI 94*
Mantyla, Karen 1944- *WhoFI 94*
Mantz, Paul d1965 *WhoHol 92*
Mantzaros, Nikolaos 1795-1872 *NewGrDO*
Mantzell, Betty Lou 1938- *WhoMW 93*
Manuel, Charles B., Jr. 1949- *WhoAmL 94*
Manuel, Dale *WhoHisp 94*
Manuel, Dale 1949- *WhoAmP 93*
Manuel, Dennis Lee 1945- *WhoMW 93*
Manuel, Edward 1949- *WhoBlA 94*
Manuel, Jenny Lynn 1964- *WhoMW 93*
Manuel, John N. 1921- *WhoBlA 94*
Manuel, Kathryn Lee *WhoAmA 93*
Manuel, Lionel, Jr. 1962- *WhoBlA 94*
Manuel, Louis Calvin 1937- *WhoBlA 94*
Manuel, Oliver K. 1936- *WhoHisp 94*
Manuel, Phillip Earnest 1966- *WhoScEn 94*
Manuel, Ralph Nixon 1936- *WhoAm 94*
Manuel, Rex 1930- *WhoAmP 93*
Manuel, Richard d1986 *WhoHol 92*
Manuel, Robert *WhoHol 92*
Manuel, Robert 1916- *IntWW 93*
Manuel, Vivian 1941- *WhoFI 94*
Manuelidis, Laura 1942- *WhoScEn 94*
Manuella, Frank R. *WhoAmA 93*
Manuguerra, Matteo 1924- *NewGrDO*
Manukovsky, Andrei Borisovich 1960- *LngBDD*
Manulis, Martin 1915- *IntMPA 94, WhoAm 94*
Manus, Connie Sandage *WhoAmA 93*
Manus, Jane Elizabeth 1951- *WhoAmA 93*
Manus, Rex Leo 1950- *WhoWest 94*
Manvel, Allen Dailey 1912- *WhoAm 94*
Manvell, (Arnold) Roger 1909-1987 *EncSF 93*
Manville, Alfred R. 1917-1989 *WhAm 10*
Manville, Ella Viola Grainger 1889-1979 *WhoAmA 93N*
Manville, Elsie 1922- *WhoAmA 93*
Manville, Lesley *WhoHol 92*
Manwaring, Randle (Gilbert) 1912- *Who 94*
Manwell, Reginald Dickinson 1897- *WhAm 10*
Manx, Kate d1964 *WhoHol 92*
Many, Robert Todd 1958- *WhoFI 94*
Manygoats, Joanne Austin 1953- *WhoWest 94*
Manz, Linda 1961- *WhoHol 92*
Manz, Wolfgang 1960- *IntWW 93*
Manza, Luigi *NewGrDO*
Manzanares, Juan Manuel 1953- *WhoHisp 94*
Manzano, Sonia *WhoHisp 94*
Manzano, Virginia d1958 *WhoHol 92*
Manza Ralph 1922- *WhoHol 92*
Manzari, Laura Lynn 1959- *WhoAmL 94*
Manzella, Peter Franics 1962- *WhoFI 94*
Manzi, Jacki 1929- *WhoAmP 93*
Manzi, Jim Paul 1951- *WhoAm 94, WhoFI 94*
Manzi, Joseph Edward 1945- *WhoMW 93, WhoScEn 94*
Manzie, (Andrew) Gordon 1930- *Who 94*
Manzini, Aldo 1964- *WhoWest 94*
Manzini, Gianna 1896-1974 *BlmGWL*
Manzini, Italia Almirante d1941 *WhoHol 92*
Manzini, Raimondo 1913- *Who 94*
Manzo, Anthony Joseph *WhoAmA 93*
Manzo, Anthony Joseph 1928- *WhoWest 94*
Manzo, Carlo d1955 *WhoHol 92*
Manzo, Edward David 1950- *WhoAmL 94*
Manzo, Michael J. 1948- *WhoAmL 94*
Manzoni, Alessandro 1785-1873 *NewGrDO*
Manzoni, Giacomo 1932- *IntWW 93, NewGrDO*
Manzullo, Donald 1944- *CngDr 93*
Manzullo, Donald A 1944- *WhoAm 94, WhoAmP 93, WhoMW 93*
Manzuoli, Giovanni c. 1720-1782 *NewGrDO*
Manzuolino, Il *NewGrDO*
Mao, Boryeu 1949- *WhoMW 93*
Mao, Chung-Ling 1936- *WhoAsA 94*
Mao, Ho-kwang 1941- *WhoAm 94, WhoAsA 94, WhoScEn 94*
Mao, James Chieh-Hsia 1928- *WhoAsA 94*
Mao, Kent Keqiang 1956- *WhoScEn 94, WhoWest 94*
Ma'o, Leo'o Va'a 1945- *WhoAmP 93*
Mao, Nai-hsien 1934- *WhoWest 94*
Mao, Xiaoping 1958- *WhoScEn 94*
Mao, Yu-shi 1929- *WhoScEn 94*
Mao Dehua 1935- *WhoPRCh 91 [port]*
Mao Dun 1896-1981 *RfGShF*
Mao Jingquan 1930- *WhoPRCh 91 [port]*
Mao Junnian *WhoPRCh 91*
Mao Lirui 1905- *IntWW 93*
Mao Rubo 1938- *WhoPRCh 91 [port]*
Mao Shengxian 1929- *WhoPRCh 91 [port]*
Mao Tse-Tung 1893-1976 *HisDcKW*
Mao Zedong 1893-1976 *HisWorL [port]*
Mao Zhiyong 1929- *IntWW 93, WhoPRCh 91 [port]*
Mapa, Alec *WhoHol 92*
Mapa, Placido 1932- *IntWW 93*
Mapanje, Jack *WrDr 94*
Mapel, Patricia Jolene 1933- *WhoMW 93*
Mapel, William Marlen Raines 1931- *WhoAm 94*
Mapelli, Roland Lawrence 1922- *WhoAm 94, WhoFI 94, WhoWest 94*
Mapes, Doris Williamson 1920- *WhoAmA 93*
Mapes, Glynn Dempsey 1939- *WhoAm 94*
Mapes, Lynn Calvin 1928- *WhoAm 94*
Mapes, Mary A. 1910- *WrDr 94*
Mapes, Ted d1984 *WhoHol 92*
Maphis, Sam Wellington, IV 1954- *WhoWest 94*
Maple, Audrey d1971 *WhoHol 92*
Maple, Eric William 1915- *WrDr 94*
Maple, Goldie M. 1937- *WhoBlA 94*
Maple, Graham John 1947- *Who 94*
Maple, Mary Alice 1953- *WhoAmL 94*
Maple, Opal Lucille 1935- *WhoMW 93*
Maple, Vetrelle 1915- *WhoBlA 94*
Maples, Evelyn Palmer 1919- *WrDr 94*
Maples, Jeffrey Stanley 1916- *Who 94*
Maples, John Cradock 1943- *Who 94*
Maples, Percy L. 1938- *WhoAmP 93*
Maples, R. Benton 1946- *WhoFI 94*
Maples, Virginia *WhoHol 92*
Maples, William Ross 1937- *WhoScEn 94*
Maplesden, Lawrence Taylor 1960- *WhoFI 94*
Maples Earle, E. E. *Who 94*
Mapleson, James Henry 1830-1901 *NewGrDO*
Ma Po 1951- *WhoPRCh 91 [port]*
Maponya, Maishe 1951- *ConDr 93*
Maponya, Richard John 1926- *IntWW 93*
Mapother, Dillon Edward 1921- *WhoAm 94*
Mapother, Tom Cruise, IV 1962- *WhoAm 94*
Mapp, Alf Johnson, Jr. 1925- *WhoAm 94, WrDr 94*
Mapp, Calvin R. 1924- *WhoBlA 94*
Mapp, David Kenneth, Jr. 1951- *WhoBlA 94*
Mapp, Edward 1929- *WrDr 94*
Mapp, Edward C. 1929- *WhoBlA 94*
Mapp, Frederick Everett 1910- *WhoBlA 94*
Mapp, Jim *WhoHol 92*
Mapp, John Robert 1950- *WhoBlA 94*
Mapp, Kenneth E. 1955- *WhoAmP 93*
Mapp, Mitchell Jerome 1947- *WhoWest 94*
Mapp, Norman d1988 *WhoHol 92*
Mapp, Yolanda I. 1930- *WhoBlA 94*
Mapplethorpe, Robert 1946-1989 *AmCulL, WhAm 10, WhoAmA 93N*
Mappus, Theodore Tobias, Jr. 1926- *WhoAmP 93*
Mapula, Olga 1938- *WhoHisp 94*
Ma Qianqing 1926- *WhoPRCh 91 [port]*
Ma Qibin *WhoPRCh 91*
Ma Qide 1944- *WhoPRCh 91 [port]*
Ma Qingxiong 1917- *WhoPRCh 91 [port]*
Ma Qixin 1931- *WhoPRCh 91 [port]*
Maquet, Jacques Jerome Pierre 1919- *WhoAm 94*
Maquipour, Iraj 1942- *WhoWest 94*
Mar, Countess of 1940- *Who 94*
Mar, Earl of 1921- *Who 94*
Mar, Mistress of 1963- *Who 94*
Mar, Anna 1887-1917 *BlmGWL*
Mar, Dan K. 1925- *WhoAsA 94*
Mar, Fien De La d1965 *WhoHol 92*
Mar, Florentina del *ConWorW 93*
Mar, Laureen D. *DrAPF 93*
Mar, Margaret, Countess of 1940- *WhoWomW 91*
Mar, Maria *WhoHisp 94*
Mar, William David 1954- *WhoAsA 94*
Mara, Adele 1923- *IntMPA 94, WhoHol 92*
Mara, Barney *ConAu 140, SmATA 75*
Mara, Francis Gerard 1950- *WhoAmP 93*
Mara, George Edward 1921- *WhoFI 94*
Mara, Gertrud Elisabeth 1749-1833 *NewGrDO*
Mara, Kamisese Kapaiwai Tuimacilai *IntWW 93*
Mara, Ratu Sir Kamisese Kapaiwai Tuimacilai 1920- *Who 94*
Mara, Thomas E. 1964- *WhoWest 94*
Mara, Tim d1959 *ProFbHF [port]*
Mara, Timothy Gerald 1949- *WhoAmL 94*
Mara, Timothy Nicholas 1948- *Who 94*
Mara, Vincent Joseph 1930- *WhoAm 94*
Mara, Wellington T. 1916- *WhoAm 94*
Marable, Herman, Jr. 1962- *WhoAmL 94, WhoBlA 94*
Marable, June Morehead 1924- *WhoBlA 94*
Marable, Richard O. 1949- *WhoAmP 93*
Marachuk, Steve *WhoHol 92*
Maracle, Lee 1950- *BlmGWL*
Maradiaga, Ralph 1934-1985 *WhoAmA 93N*
Maradona, Diego Armando *WhoAm 94*
Maradona, Diego Armando 1960- *IntWW 93, WorESoc [port]*
Marafino, Vincent Norman 1930- *IntWW 93, WhoAm 94, WhoFI 94, WhoWest 94*
Maragliotti, Vincent 1888-1978 *WhoAmA 93N*
Maragni, Donald Peter 1930- *WhoFI 94*
Maragos, Andrew George 1945- *WhoMW 93*
Maragos, Andy *WhoAmP 93*
Maragos, Angelo 1964- *WhoAmL 94*
Maragos, Samuel C. 1922- *WhoAmP 93*
Maraini, Dacia 1936- *BlmGWL [port], ConWorW 93, IntWW 93*
Maraini, Fosco 1912- *IntWW 93*
Marais *WhoAmA 93*
Marais, Georg 1931- *IntWW 93*
Marais, Jean 1913- *IntMPA 94, IntWW 93, WhoHol 92*
Marais, Marin 1656-1728 *NewGrDO*
Marais, Pieter Gabriel 1932- *IntWW 93*
Maraj, James Ajodhya 1930- *Who 94*
Marak, Louis Bernard 1942- *WhoAmA 93*
Marak, Otakar 1872-1939 *NewGrDO*
Marakutsa, Grigory 1942- *LngBDD*
Maraldo, Pamela J. c. 1948- *News 93 [port]*
Maraldo, Pamela Jean 1947- *WhoAm 94*
Maraldo, Ushanna *WhoWest 94*
Maraldo, Ushanna F. *WhoAmA 93*
Maram, Barry S. 1946- *WhoAm 94*
Maraman, William Joseph 1923- *WhoScEn 94*
Maramarco, Anthony Martin 1949- *WhoFI 94*
Maramis, Johan Boudewijn Paul 1922- *IntWW 93*
Maramorosch, Karl 1915- *WhoAm 94*
Maramzin, Vladimir Rafailovich 1934- *IntWW 93*
Maran, Arnold George Dominic 1936- *Who 94*
Maran, David 1958- *WhoAmL 94*
Maran, Stephen Paul 1938- *WhoAm 94, WhoScEn 94*
Maranda, Guy 1936- *WhoAm 94*
Maranda, Pierre 1930- *WrDr 94*
Maranda, Pierre Jean 1930- *IntWW 93, WhoAm 94*
Marandas, Susan Margaret 1942- *WhoWest 94*
Marander, Carol Jean 1950- *WhoAmA 93*
Marane, Andre *WhoHol 92*
Maranhao, Heloisa 1925- *BlmGWL [port]*
Maraniss, David 1950- *WhoAm 94*
Marano, Anthony Joseph 1934- *WhoAm 94*
Marano, Lizbeth *WhoAmA 93*
Marano, Richard Michael 1960- *WhoAmL 94, WhoAmP 93*
Marano, Russell *DrAPF 93*
Marans, J. Eugene 1940- *WhoAm 94*
Marans, Mardi *IntMPA 94*
Marans, Moissaye 1902-1977 *WhoAmA 93N*
Marantz, Irving 1912-1972 *WhoAmA 93N*
Marantz, Kenneth A. 1927- *ConAu 142*
Marantz, Sylvia S. 1929- *ConAu 142*
Maranzano, Miguel Franscisco 1941- *WhoScEn 94*
Maras, Karl *EncSF 93*
Marasch, Milton R. 1937- *WhoWest 94*
Marasco, Rose 1948- *WhoAmA 93*
Marash, Alan Scott 1965- *WhoFI 94*
Marash, David 1942- *WhoAm 94*
Marash, Randy J. 1955- *WhoIns 94*
Marash, Stanley Albert 1938- *WhoAm 94, WhoFI 94*
Marasigan, Rogelio U. 1934- *WhoAsA 94*
Maratita, Edward Ulloa *WhoAmP 93*
Maratita, Mametto Ulloa 1951- *WhoAmP 93*
Maratti Zappi, Faustina c. 1680-1745 *BlmGWL*
Maravall Herrero, Jose Maria 1942- *IntWW 93*
Maravelias, Peter 1949- *WhoScEn 94*
Maravich, Mary Louise 1951- *WhoWest 94*
Maravich, Melissa Ann 1957- *WhoAmL 94*
Maravich, Pete 1948-1988 *BasBi*
Maraynes, Allan Lawrence 1950- *WhoAm 94*
Marazita, Eleanor Marie Harmon 1933- *WhoMW 93*
Maraziti, Joseph J. 1912-1991 *WhAm 10*
Marazzi, William 1947- *WhoAmA 93*
Marazzo, Joseph John 1958- *WhoScEn 94*
Marazzoli, Marco 1602?-1662 *NewGrDO*
Marba, Joseph d1938 *WhoHol 92*
Marbach, Ethel *SmATA 76*
Marbach, John O. 1958- *WhoFI 94*
Marberger, A. Aldar 1947-1988 *WhoAmA 93N*
Marble, Alice d1990 *WhoHol 92*
Marble, Alice 1913-1990 *BuCMET [port]*
Marble, Donald Raymond 1938- *WhoAmP 93*
Marble, Duane Francis 1931- *WhoAm 94*
Marble, John d1919 *WhoHol 92*
Marble, Samuel Davey 1915-1990 *WhAm 10*
Marbois, Barbe, Marquis de *WhAmRev*
Marburger, John Allen 1956- *WhoFI 94*
Marburger, John Harmen, III 1941- *WhoAm 94*
Marburg-Goodman, Jeffrey Emil 1957- *WhoAmL 94*
Marburgh, Bertram d1956 *WhoHol 92*
Marbury, Benjamin Edward 1914- *WhoAm 94*
Marbury, Carl Harris 1935- *WhoBlA 94*
Marbury, Donald Lee 1949- *WhoBlA 94*
Marbury, Howard W. 1924- *WhoBlA 94*
Marbury, Martha G. 1946- *WhoBlA 94*
Marbury, Sandra Nation 1950- *WhoFI 94*
Marbut, Robert Gordon 1935- *WhoAm 94, WhoFI 94*
Marc, David 1951- *WhoWest 94*
Marc, Peter *WhoHol 92*
Marcali, Jean Gregory 1926- *WhoScEn 94*
Marcano, Antonio G. 1960- *WhoHisp 94*
Marcano, Ray 1959- *WhoHisp 94*
Marcantel, Bernard Norman 1923- *WhoAmL 94*
Marcantonio, Arthur 1936- *WhoMW 93*
Marca-Relli, Conrad 1913- *WhoAm 94, WhoAmA 93*
Marcasiano, Mary Jane 1955- *WhoAm 94*
Marceau, Felicien 1913- *IntWW 93*
Marceau, Marcel *NewYTBS 93 [port]*
Marceau, Marcel 1923- *IntWW 93, Who 94, WhoAm 94, WhoCom, WhoHol 92*
Marceau, Sophie 1967- *WhoHol 92*
Marceau, Yvonne *WhoAm 94*
Marcel, Lucille 1877-1921 *NewGrDO*
Marceleno, Troy 1937- *WhoHisp 94*
Marceline d1927 *WhoHol 92*
Marceline 1873-1927 *WhoCom*
Marcelino, James d1986 *WhoHol 92*
Marcell, David Wyburn 1937- *WhoAm 94*
Marcell, Joseph *WhoHol 92*
Marcellas, Thomas Wilson 1937- *WhoFI 94, WhoScEn 94*
Marcellin, Raymond 1914- *IntWW 93*
Marcellino, Fred 1939- *WhoAm 94*
Marcellino, James J. 1943- *WhoAm 94, WhoAmL 94*
Marcellino, Stephen Michael 1950- *WhoAm 94*
Marcello, Anthony James 1967- *WhoFI 94*
Marcello, Benedetto 1686-1739 *NewGrDO*
Marcello, Carlos 1910-1993 *NewYTBS 93 [port]*
Marcello, Leo Luke *DrAPF 93*
Marcello, Matthew T., III 1946- *WhoAmL 94*
Marcello da Capua *NewGrDO*
Marcellus, John Robert, III 1939- *WhoAm 94*
Marcellus, Manley Clark, Jr. 1921- *WhoScEn 94*
Marcelo, Hugo *WhoHisp 94*
Marcelynas, Richard Chadwick 1937- *WhoWest 94*
Marcere, Norma Snipes 1908- *WhoBlA 94*
March, Anthony 1951- *WhoBlA 94*
March, Beryl Elizabeth 1920- *WhoAm 94*
March, Della d1973 *WhoHol 92*
March, Donald 1942- *IntMPA 94*
March, Elspeth *WhoHol 92*
March, Eve d1974 *WhoHol 92*
March, Fredric d1975 *WhoHol 92*
March, George Patrick 1924- *WhoWest 94*
March, Hal d1970 *WhoHol 92*
March, Hillary 1925- *WrDr 94*
March, Iris d1966 *WhoHol 92*
March, Jacqueline Front *WhoScEn 94*
March, James Gardner 1928- *WhoAm 94, WhoWest 94*
March, John William 1923- *WhoAm 94*
March, Jon G. 1944- *WhoAmL 94*
March, Josie 1941- *WrDr 94*
March, Kathleen Patricia 1949- *WhoAm 94, WhoAmL 94, WhoWest 94*
March, Kenneth Alfred 1956- *WhoWest 94*
March, Lee Anthony 1967- *WhoMW 93*
March, Linda d1933 *WhoHol 92*
March, Lionel John 1934- *Who 94*

March, Lori *WhoHol 92*
March, Marion D. 1923- *AstEnc*
March, N(orman) H(enry) 1927- *WrDr 94*
March, Nadine d1944 *WhoHol 92*
March, Norman Henry 1927- *Who 94*
March, Philippe d1980 *WhoHol 92*
March, Ralph Burton 1919- *WhoAm 94*
March, Richard S. 1941- *WhoIns 94*
March, Susana 1918- *BlmGWL*
March, Valerie *Who 94*
Marchais, Georges 1920- *IntWW 93*
Marchal, Arlette d1984 *WhoHol 92*
Marchal, Georges 1920- *WhoHol 92*
Marchal, Jean 1905- *IntWW 93*
Marchalonis, John Jacob 1940- *WhoAm 94, WhoScEn 94*
Marcham, Frederick George 1898-1992 *ConAu 140*
Marchamley, Baron 1922- *Who 94*
Marchand, Colette *WhoHol 92*
Marchand, Corinne 1937- *WhoHol 92*
Marchand, Guy *WhoHol 92*
Marchand, Henri d1959 *WhoHol 92*
Marchand, J. C. de Montigny 1936- *WhoAm 94*
Marchand, Jean-Baptiste 1863-1934 *WhWE*
Marchand, Leslie A(lexis) 1900- *WrDr 94*
Marchand, Leslie Alexis 1900- *WhoAm 94*
Marchand, Melanie Annette 1962- *WhoBlA 94*
Marchand, Nancy 1928- *IntMPA 94, WhoHol 92*
Marchand, Nathan 1916- *WhoAm 94*
Marchand, Philip (Edward) 1946- *WrDr 94*
Marchand, Philippe 1939- *IntWW 93*
Marchand, Theobald Hilarius 1741-1800 *NewGrDO*
Marchandise-Franquet, Jacques 1918- *IntWW 93*
March and Kinrara, Earl of 1955- *Who 94*
Marchant, Catherine *BlmGWL, Who 94*
Marchant, Catherine 1906- *WrDr 94*
Marchant, David J. 1939- *WhoAm 94, WhoAmL 94*
Marchant, Edgar Vernon 1915- *Who 94*
Marchant, Gary Elvin 1958- *WhoAmL 94*
Marchant, George John Charles 1916- *Who 94*
Marchant, Graham Leslie 1945- *Who 94*
Marchant, Henry 1741-1796 *WhAmRev*
Marchant, Ken 1951- *WhoAmP 93*
Marchant, Larry Conrad, Jr. 1962- *WhoAmP 93*
Marchant, Maurice Peterson 1927- *WhoAm 94*
Marchant, Omar *WhoHisp 94*
Marchant, T. Eston 1921- *WhoAmP 93*
Marchant, Thomas Mood, III 1940- *WhoAmP 93*
Marchant, Tony 1959- *ConDr 93, WrDr 94*
Marchant, Trelawney Eston 1921- *WhoAm 94*
Marchat, Jean d1966 *WhoHol 92*
Marchbanks, Claude V. 1923- *WhoAmP 93*
Marchbanks, Samuel *ConAu 42NR*
Marchbanks, Vance H. 1905-1973 *WorInv*
Marche, Gary Eldon 1953- *WhoFI 94*
Marchello, Joseph Maurice 1933- *WhoAm 94*
Marchenko, Anastasiia Iakovlevna 1830-1880 *BlmGWL*
Marchesano, John Edward 1927- *WhoScEn 94*
Marcheschi, (Louis) Cork 1945- *WhoAmA 93*
Marchese, Anthony John 1967- *WhoScEn 94*
Marchese, Lamar Vincent 1943- *WhoWest 94*
Marchese, Ronald Thomas 1947- *WhoAm 94, WhoMW 93*
Marchese Di Barsento *WhAm 10*
Marchesi, Blanche 1863-1940 *NewGrDO*
Marchesi, Gian Franco 1940- *WhoScEn 94*
Marchesi, Luigi 1755-1829 *NewGrDO*
Marchesi, Mathilde (de Castrone) 1821-1913 *NewGrDO*
Marchesi, Salvatore 1822-1908 *NewGrDO*
Marchesi Family *NewGrDO*
Marchesini, Maria Antonia *NewGrDO*
Marchesini, Nino d1961 *WhoHol 92*
Marchesini, Santa fl. 1706-1739 *NewGrDO*
Marchessault, Robert H. *WhoScEn 94*
Biorchetta, Anthony Joseph 1948- *WhoAm 94, WhoAmL 94*
Marchetti, Donald Merrill 1932- *WhoAm 94*
Marchetti, Filippo 1831-1902 *NewGrDO*
Marchetti, Gino *ProFbHF [port]*
Marchetti, Karen J. 1958- *WhoFI 94*
Marchetti, Marilyn H. 1947- *WhoAmL 94*

Marchetti, Peter Louis 1937- *WhoFI 94*
Marchetti Fantozzi, Maria (Vincenza) 1760?-1800? *NewGrDO*
Marchi, Antonio fl. 1692-1725 *NewGrDO*
Marchi, Emilio de *NewGrDO*
Marchi, John Joseph 1921- *WhoAmL 94, WhoAmP 93*
Marchi, Jon 1946- *WhoWest 94*
Marchibroda, Ted 1931- *WhoAm 94, WhoMW 93*
Marchick, Richard 1934- *WhoWest 94*
Marchione, Sharyn Lee 1947- *WhoScEn 94*
Marchioni, Allen *WhoAm 94*
Marchioro, Karen Louise 1933- *WhoAmP 93, WhoWomW 91*
Marchiselli, Vincent Andrew 1928- *WhoAmP 93*
Marchisio Family *NewGrDO*
Marchisotto, Robert 1929- *WhoScEn 94*
Marchlewicz, Margaret Ann 1950- *WhoMW 93*
Marchman, Fred A. *DrAPF 93*
Marchman, Robert Anthony 1958- *WhoBlA 94*
Marchman, Robert L., III 1925- *WhoAm 94, WhoAmL 94*
Marchuk, Evhen Kyrylovych 1941- *LngBDD*
Marchuk, Guriy Ivanovich 1925- *IntWW 93*
Marchuk, Gury Ivanovich 1925- *LngBDD*
Marchut, Stan 1943- *WhoIns 94*
Marchwood, Viscount 1936- *Who 94*
Marcial, David 1955- *WhoHisp 94*
Marcial, Edwin 1940- *WhoHisp 94*
Marcial, Victor A. 1924- *WhoHisp 94*
Marciano, Anthony R. 1942- *WhoAmP 93*
Marciano, Richard Alfred 1934- *WhoAm 94*
Marciano, Rocky d1969 *WhoHol 92*
Marcil, William Christ, Sr. 1936- *WhoAm 94, WhoMW 93*
Marcillo, Carlos E. 1939- *WhoHisp 94*
Marci-Mariani, Anita 1960- *WhoAm 94*
Marcincavage, Thomas Alan 1954- *WhoMW 93*
Marciniak, Thaddeus J. 1950- *WhoAm 94*
Marcinkevicius, Iustinas Moteiaus 1930- *IntWW 93*
Marcinkowski, Marion John 1931- *WhoAm 94*
Marcinkowski, Myron Anthony 1959- *WhoFI 94*
Marcinkus, Paul Casimir 1922- *IntWW 93*
Marcis, Richard G. 1940- *WhoAm 94*
Marck, Jan Van Der 1929- *WhoAmA 93*
Marcker, Kjeld Adrian 1932- *IntWW 93*
Marckus, Melvyn 1944- *Who 94*
Marckwardt, Harold Thomas 1920- *WhoWest 94*
Marco, Anton Nicholas 1943- *WhoWest 94*
Marco, David Duane 1951- *WhoWest 94*
Marco, Frank J. 1947- *WhoAmL 94*
Marco, Guy Anthony 1927- *WhoAm 94, WhoMW 93*
Marco, Raoul d1971 *WhoHol 92*
Marcoccia, Louis Gary 1946- *WhoAm 94*
Marcolini, Marietta c. 1780-1814? *NewGrDO*
Marcon, Andre *WhoHol 92*
Marcon, Fred R. 1937- *WhoIns 94*
Marconi, Guglielmo 1874-1937 *DcNaB MP, WorInv [port]*
Marconi, Jean d1972 *WhoHol 92*
Marconi, Saverio *WhoHol 92*
Marco Polo *WhWE*
Marcopoulos, Christos 1925- *IntWW 93*
Marcos, Ferdinand E. 1917-1989 *WhAm 10*
Marcos, Imelda Romualdez 1930- *IntWW 93*
Marcos, Luis Rojas 1943- *WhoHisp 94*
Marcos de Niza *WhWE*
Marcosson, Thomas I. 1936- *WhoAm 94*
Marcotte, Frank Basil 1923- *WhoAm 94*
Marcotte, Michael Vincent 1956- *WhoWest 94*
Marcotte, Michel Claude 1955- *WhoScEn 94*
Marcotte, Vincent Charles 1932- *WhoScEn 94*
Marcou, Constantin George 1954- *WhoWest 94*
Marcoux, Carl Henry 1927- *WhoAm 94*
Marcoux, Elizabeth Louise 1952- *WhoWest 94*
Marcoux, John W. 1922- *WhoAmA 93*
Marcoux, Jules Edouard 1924- *WhoAm 94*
Marcoux, Vanni *NewGrDO*
Marcoux, Vanni d1962 *WhoHol 92*
Marcoux, William C. 1956- *WhoAmP 93*
Marcoux, William Joseph 1927- *WhoAm 94*

Marcoux, Yvon 1941- *WhoAm 94, WhoFI 94*
Marcovici, Andrea 1948- *IntMPA 94, WhoHol 92*
Marcovitz, Leonard Edward 1934- *WhoAm 94, WhoFI 94, WhoWest 94*
Marcu, Speranta Mihaela 1969- *WhoMW 93*
Marcucci, Nicholas John 1956- *WhoMW 93*
Marcuccio, Phyllis Rose 1933- *WhoAm 94*
Marculescu, Petru 1943- *IntWW 93*
Marcum, Deanna Bowling 1946- *WhoAm 94*
Marcum, Gordon George, II 1942- *WhoAmL 94*
Marcum, Jack Arbuthnott 1947- *WhoFI 94*
Marcum, James Arthur 1951- *WhoScEn 94*
Marcum, James Benton 1938- *WhoAm 94*
Marcum, Joseph L. 1923- *WhoIns 94*
Marcum, Joseph LaRue 1923- *WhoAm 94, WhoFI 94, WhoMW 93*
Marcus, Adrianne *DrAPF 93*
Marcus, Alfred A(llen) 1950- *ConAu 43NR*
Marcus, Angelo P. *WhoAmA 93*
Marcus, Barry Philip 1953- *WhoAm 94, WhoAmL 94*
Marcus, Ben 1911- *WhoAm 94*
Marcus, Bernard 1924- *WhoAm 94*
Marcus, Bernard 1929- *WhoAm 94, WhoFI 94*
Marcus, Bernie d1971 *WhoHol 92*
Marcus, Claude 1924- *IntWW 93, WhoAm 94, WhoFI 94*
Marcus, Craig Brian 1939- *WhoAmL 94*
Marcus, David 1926- *WrDr 94*
Marcus, David 1939- *WhoAm 94, WhoFI 94*
Marcus, David Alan 1958- *WhoScEn 94*
Marcus, Donald (Edwin) 1946- *WrDr 94*
Marcus, Donald Howard 1916- *WhoAm 94, WhoMW 93*
Marcus, Donald Martin 1930- *WhoScEn 94*
Marcus, Edward 1918- *WhoAm 94, WhoFI 94*
Marcus, Edward Leonard 1927- *WhoAmL 94, WhoAmP 93*
Marcus, Edward S. 1910-1972 *WhoAmA 93N*
Marcus, Eric Peter 1950- *WhoAm 94, WhoAmL 94*
Marcus, Eric Robert 1944- *WhoScEn 94*
Marcus, Frank 1928- *WrDr 94*
Marcus, Frank 1933- *WhoAm 94*
Marcus, Frank (Ulrich) 1928- *ConDr 93*
Marcus, Frank Isadore 1928- *WhoAm 94, WhoWest 94*
Marcus, Frank Ulrich 1928- *Who 94*
Marcus, G. Robert 1942- *WhoAmL 94*
Marcus, George J. 1951- *WhoAmL 94*
Marcus, George Mathew 1941- *WhoFI 94*
Marcus, Gerald R. 1946- *WhoAmA 93*
Marcus, Greil Gerstley 1945- *WhoAm 94*
Marcus, Harold G. 1936- *WrDr 94*
Marcus, Harris Leon 1931- *WhoAm 94, WhoScEn 94*
Marcus, Hyman 1914- *WhoAm 94*
Marcus, Ira B. 1949- *WhoAmL 94*
Marcus, Irving E. 1929- *WhoAmA 93*
Marcus, Jacob Rader 1896- *WhoAm 94, WhoMW 93*
Marcus, James d1937 *WhoHol 92*
Marcus, James Elbert 1949- *WhoFI 94*
Marcus, James Stewart 1929- *WhoAm 94*
Marcus, Jeffrey Howard 1950- *WhoWest 94*
Marcus, Jeffrey Howard 1956- *WhoAmL 94*
Marcus, Joanna 1919- *WrDr 94*
Marcus, Joseph 1928- *WhoAm 94*
Marcus, Joy John 1951- *WhoScEn 94*
Marcus, Jules Alexander 1919- *WhoScEn 94*
Marcus, Larry 1925- *WrDr 94*
Marcus, Larry David 1949- *WhoMW 93*
Marcus, Laurence R. 1947- *WrDr 94*
Marcus, Lee Evan 1953- *WhoFI 94*
Marcus, Leon Charles 1936- *WhoAm 94, WhoAmL 94*
Marcus, Leonard *WhoAm 94, WhoFI 94*
Marcus, Leonard S. 1950- *WrDr 94*
Marcus, Louis 1936- *IntMPA 94*
Marcus, M. Boyd, Jr. 1952- *WhoAmP 93*
Marcus, Marcia 1928- *WhoAmA 93*
Marcus, Mark Jay 1941- *WhoAmP 93*
Marcus, Marshall Matthew 1933- *WhoFI 94*
Marcus, Marvin 1927- *WhoAm 94*
Marcus, Melvin Gerald 1929- *WhoWest 94*
Marcus, Mordecai *DrAPF 93*
Marcus, Morton *DrAPF 93*
Marcus, Norman 1932- *WhoAm 94, WhoAmL 94*

Marcus, Paul 1946- *WhoAm 94*
Marcus, Philip Irving 1927- *WhoAm 94*
Marcus, Philip Selmar 1936- *WhoMW 93*
Marcus, Phillip L. 1941- *WrDr 94*
Marcus, Richard *WhoHol 92*
Marcus, Richard Alan 1933- *WhoAm 94*
Marcus, Richard Greenwald 1947- *WhoAm 94*
Marcus, Richard S. 1932- *WhoAm 94*
Marcus, Richard Steven 1950- *WhoAmL 94*
Marcus, Robert 1925- *WhoAm 94, WhoWest 94*
Marcus, Robert Boris 1934- *WhoScEn 94*
Marcus, Robert Bruce 1942- *WhoAmL 94*
Marcus, Robert D. 1936- *WhoAm 94*
Marcus, Robert P., Mrs. 1923- *WhoAmA 93*
Marcus, Robert S. 1947- *WhoAmP 93*
Marcus, Rudolph Arthur 1923- *IntWW 93, Who 94, WhoAm 94, WhoScEn 94, WhoWest 94*
Marcus, Ruth Barcan *WhoAm 94*
Marcus, Ruth Barcan 1921- *IntWW 93*
Marcus, Sheldon 1937- *WhoAm 94*
Marcus, Sparky 1967- *WhoHol 92*
Marcus, Stanley *DrAPF 93*
Marcus, Stanley 1905- *IntWW 93, WhoAm 94, WhoAmA 93, WrDr 94*
Marcus, Stanley 1946- *WhoAm 94, WhoAmL 94*
Marcus, Stephen A. 1943- *WhoAm 94, WhoAmL 94*
Marcus, Stephen Cecil 1932- *WhoFI 94*
Marcus, Stephen D. 1941- *WhoAmL 94*
Marcus, Stephen Howard 1935- *WhoAm 94, WhoFI 94*
Marcus, Steven 1928- *WhoAm 94*
Marcus, Steven Irl 1949- *WhoAm 94, WhoScEn 94*
Marcus, Valerie Rae 1962- *WhoAmL 94*
Marcus, Walter F., Jr. 1927- *WhoAm 94, WhoAmL 94, WhoAmP 93*
Marcus, William Michael 1938- *WhoAm 94*
Marcus, Yizhak 1931- *WhoScEn 94*
Marcusa, Fred Haye 1946- *WhoAm 94, WhoAmL 94*
Marcus-Alterman, Rachel d1985 *WhoHol 92*
Marcus Aurelius 121-180 *HisWorL [port]*
Marcus Aurelius Antoninus, Emperor of Rome 121-180 *EncEth*
Marcuse, Adrian Gregory 1922- *WhoAm 94*
Marcuse, Dietrich 1929- *WhoAm 94*
Marcuse, Frederick Lawrence 1916- *WrDr 94*
Marcuse, Herbert 1898-1979 *AmSocL*
Marcuse, Manfred Joachim 1927- *WhoMW 93*
Marcuse, Theodore d1967 *WhoHol 92*
Marcuse, William 1924- *WhoFI 94*
Marcuss, Stanley Joseph 1942- *WhoAm 94, WhoAmL 94*
Marcuvitz, Nathan 1913- *WhoAm 94*
Marcy, Carl Milton 1913-1990 *WhAm 10*
Marcy, Randolph Barnes 1812-1887 *WhWE*
Marcy, Willard 1916- *WhoScEn 94, WhoWest 94*
Mardall, Cyril Leonard 1909- *IntWW 93*
Mardar, Dianna 1948- *WhoAm 94*
Mardell, Fred Robert 1934- *WhoAm 94*
Mardell, Peggy Joyce 1927- *Who 94*
Marden, Adrienne d1978 *WhoHol 92*
Marden, Brice 1938- *WhoAm 94, WhoAmA 93*
Marden, Donald Harlow 1936- *WhoAmP 93*
Marden, Harold D. *WhoAmP 93*
Marden, Janet J. 1948- *WhoMW 93*
Marden, John Louis 1919- *Who 94*
Marden, John Newcomb 1935- *WhoAm 94*
Marden, Kenneth Allen 1928- *WhoAm 94*
Marden, Orison Swett 1850-1924 *DcLB 137 [port]*
Marden, Philip Ayer 1911- *WhoAm 94*
Mardenborough, Leslie A. *WhoAm 94*
Mardenborough, Leslie A. 1948- *WhoBlA 94*
Marder, Bernard Arthur 1928- *Who 94*
Marder, Curtis Charles 1949- *WhoMW 93*
Marder, Dorie *WhoAmA 93*
Marder, John G. 1926- *WhoAm 94*
Marder, Michael Zachary 1938- *WhoAm 94*
Marder, William Zev 1947- *WhoScEn 94*
Mardh, Per-Anders 1941- *IntWW 93*
Mardian, Daniel 1917- *WhoFI 94, WhoWest 94*
Mardian, Robert Charles, Jr. 1947- *WhoFI 94, WhoWest 94*
Mardie 1933- *WhoFI 94*
Mardis, Hal Kennedy 1934- *WhoMW 93, WhoScEn 94*

Mardon, (John) Kenric La Touche d1993 *Who 94N*
Mardones, Jose 1869-1932 *NewGrDO*
Mare, Rolf de *IntDcB*
Mare, William Harold 1918- *WhoMW 93*
Maready, William Frank 1932- *WhoAmL 94*
Marean, Browning E. 1942- *WhoAmL 94*
Marechal, Adolphe (Alphonse) 1867-1935 *NewGrDO*
Marechal, Ambrose 1764-1828 *DcAmReB 2*
Marechal, (Charles) Henri 1842-1924 *NewGrDO*
Maree, John B. 1924- *IntWW 93*
Maree, Wendy 1938- *WhoWest 94*
Maree, Wendy P. 1938- *WhoAmA 93*
Marei, Ibrahim 1939- *WhoWest 94*
Marei, Sayed Ahmed 1913- *IntWW 93*
Marek, Dana 1952- *WhoWest 94*
Marek, Jiri *EncSF 93*
Marek, John 1940- *Who 94*
Marek, Vladimir 1928- *WhoAm 94*
Marella, Philip Daniel 1929- *WhoAm 94*
Marello, Laura *DrAPF 93*
Maremont, Arnold H. 1904-1978 *WhoAmA 93N*
Maren, Jerry *WhoHol 92*
Marenbon, John (Alexander) 1955- *WrDr 94*
Marenghi, John Henry 1952- *WhoFI 94*
Marens, Susan Joyce 1950- *WhoFI 94*
Marenstein, Harold 1916- *IntMPA 94*
Mares, Bill 1940- *WhoAmP 93*
Mares, Donald J. *WhoHisp 94*
Mares, Donald J. 1957- *WhoAmP 93*
Mares, Ernest Anthony *DrAPF 93*
Mares, Jan W. *WhoAmP 93*
Mares, Joseph Thomas 1960- *WhoScEn 94*
Mares, Michael Allen 1945- *WhoAm 94, WhoHisp 94*
Mares, Pablo 1913- *WhoHisp 94*
Maresca, Daniel G. 1952- *WhoFI 94*
Maresca, Louis M. *WhoScEn 94*
Marescalchi, Luigi 1745-1805? *NewGrDO*
Mareschi, Jean Pierre 1937- *WhoScEn 94*
Maresco, Stephen Peter 1928- *WhoFI 94*
Marescotti, Ivano *WhoHol 92*
Marese, Janie d1931 *WhoHol 92*
Maresh, Richard 1917- *WhoAmP 93*
Mareth, John William 1964- *WhoMW 93*
Mareth, Paul 1945- *WhoFI 94*
Maretskaya, Vera d1978 *WhoHol 92*
Maretzek, Max 1821-1897 *NewGrDO*
Mareuil, Simone d1954 *WhoHol 92*
Marey, Etienne-Jules 1830-1904 *WorInv [port]*
Marez, Jesus M. 1963- *WhoHisp 94*
Marfield, Dwight d1978 *WhoHol 92*
Margadale, Baron 1906- *Who 94*
Margain, Hugo B. 1913- *Who 94*
Margalef, Ramon 1919- *IntWW 93*
Margalith, Ethan Harold 1955- *WhoWest 94*
Margallo, Lucio N., II *WhoAsA 94*
Margalus, William T. *WhoAmP 93*
Margaret, Duchess of Argyll d1993 *NewYTBS 93*
Margaret, Duchess of Burgundy 1446-1503 *BlmGWL [port]*
Margaret, Princess 1930- *Who 94R*
Margaretha, Herbert Moriz Paul Maria 1911- *WhoScEn 94*
Margaret of Anjou 1430-1482 *BlmGEL, BlmGWL*
Margaret of Denmark 1353-1412 *HisWorL [port]*
Margaret of York 1446-1503 *BlmGWL [port]*
Margaret Rose, H.R.H. The Princess 1930- *IntWW 93*
Margaritis, John Paul 1949- *WhoAm 94, WhoFI 94*
Margaritoff, Dimitri Andrej 1947- *WhoFI 94*
Margaritov, Athanas 1912- *NewGrDO*
Margason, Geoffrey 1933- *Who 94*
Marge, Michael 1928- *WhoAm 94*
Margeot, Jean 1916- *IntWW 93*
Marger, Edwin 1928- *WhoAmL 94*
Margerison, Richard Wayne 1948- *WhoAm 94*
Margerison, Thomas Alan 1923- *Who 94*
Margerum, Dale William 1929- *WhoAm 94, WhoScEn 94*
Margerum, John David 1929- *WhoAm 94*
Margerum, Sonya L. 1930- *WhoAmP 93*
Margesson, Viscount 1922- *Who 94*
Margeton, Stephen George 1945- *WhoAm 94, WhoFI 94*
Margetson, Arthur d1951 *WhoHol 92*
Margetson, John (W. D.) 1927- *IntWW 93*
Margetson, John (William Denys) 1927- *Who 94*
Margetts, W. Thomas 1936- *WhoAm 94*
Margevich, Douglas Edward 1964- *WhoScEn 94*

Marghieri, Clotilde Betocchi 1897-1981 *BlmGWL*
Margileth, Andrew Menges 1920- *WhoAm 94*
Margiotta, Mary-Lou Ann 1956- *WhoScEn 94*
Margliss, Frances d1990 *WhoHol 92*
Margo d1985 *WhoHol 92*
Margo, Boris 1902- *WhoAmA 93*
Margo, George *WhoHol 92*
Margol, Irving 1930- *WhoAm 94, WhoFI 94, WhoWest 94*
Margoliash, Emanuel 1920- *IntWW 93, WhoAm 94*
Margolies, Ethel Polacheck 1907- *WhoAmA 93*
Margolies, George Howard 1948- *WhoAmL 94*
Margolies, Raymond 1920- *WhoAm 94, WhoMW 93*
Margolies-Mezvinsky, Marjorie 1942- *CngDr 93, WhoAm 94, WhoAmP 93*
Margolin, Burt M. 1950- *WhoAmP 93*
Margolin, Elias Leopold 1921- *WhoWest 94*
Margolin, Harold 1922- *WhoAm 94, WhoScEn 94*
Margolin, Janet d1993 *NewYTBS 93 [port]*
Margolin, Janet 1943- *IntMPA 94, WhoHol 92*
Margolin, Michael *DrAPF 93*
Margolin, Solomon Begelfor 1920 *WhoScEn 94*
Margolin, Stephen Joseph 1945- *WhoAmL 94*
Margolin, Stuart *WhoHol 92*
Margolin, Stuart 1940- *IntMPA 94*
Margolin, Victor 1941- *WrDr 94*
Margolin, William 1959- *WhoWest 94*
Margolis, Bernard Allen 1948- *WhoAm 94, WhoWest 94*
Margolis, Charles d1926 *WhoHol 92*
Margolis, Daniel Herbert 1926- *WhoAm 94*
Margolis, David 1911- *WhoAmA 93*
Margolis, David Israel 1930- *WhoAm 94, WhoFI 94*
Margolis, Diane Rothbard 1933- *WhoAmP 93*
Margolis, Donald L. 1945- *WhoWest 94*
Margolis, Edwin d1993 *NewYTBS 93*
Margolis, Emanuel 1926- *WhoAmL 94*
Margolis, Eugene 1935- *WhoAm 94, WhoAmL 94*
Margolis, Gary *DrAPF 93*
Margolis, George 1914- *WhoAm 94*
Margolis, Gerald Joseph 1935- *WhoAm 94*
Margolis, Gwen 1934- *WhoAmP 93, WhoWomW 91*
Margolis, Howard 1932- *WrDr 94*
Margolis, James David 1955- *WhoAmP 93*
Margolis, James Mark 1930- *WhoScEn 94*
Margolis, Jay M. 1949- *WhoFI 94*
Margolis, Jeff *ConTFT 11*
Margolis, Jeffrey Robert 1957- *WhoFI 94*
Margolis, Jeremy *WhoAm 94, WhoAmL 94*
Margolis, John D(avid) 1941- *WrDr 94*
Margolis, Joseph 1924- *WrDr 94*
Margolis, Julius 1920- *WhoAm 94*
Margolis, Karl L. *WhoFI 94*
Margolis, Lawrence S. 1935- *CngDr 93*
Margolis, Lawrence Stanley 1935- *WhoAm 94, WhoAmL 94*
Margolis, Leo 1927- *WhoAm 94*
Margolis, Louis Irving 1944- *WhoAm 94, WhoFI 94*
Margolis, Margo 1947- *WhoAmA 93*
Margolis, Milton Joseph 1925- *WhoAm 94*
Margolis, Nadia 1949- *ConAu 140*
Margolis, Philip Marcus 1925- *WhoAm 94*
Margolis, Richard M. 1943- *WhoAmA 93*
Margolis, Richard Martin 1943- *WhoAm 94*
Margolis, Sidney O. 1925- *WhoAm 94, WhoFI 94*
Margolis, Theodore 1941- *WhoAm 94*
Margolis, William J. *DrAPF 93*
Margolius, Harry Stephen 1938- *WhoAm 94, WhoScEn 94*
Margolyes, Miriam 1941- *WhoHol 92*
Margon, Bruce Henry 1948- *WhoAm 94*
Margoshes, Marvin 1925- *WhoScEn 94*
Margrave, John 1934- *IntWW 93*
Margrave, John Lee 1924- *WhoAm 94, WhoScEn 94*
Margrethe, II, H.M. 1940- *IntWW 93*
Margrethe, II, H.M. The Queen 1940- *WhoWomW 91*
Margrie, Victor Robert 1929- *Who 94*
Margroff, Robert E. 1930- *WrDr 94*
Margroff, Robert E(rvien) 1930- *EncSF 93*

Margron, Frederick Joseph 1963- *WhoScEn 94*
Marguerite d'Angouleme 1492-1549 *GuFrLit 2*
Marguerite d'Autriche 1480-1530 *BlmGWL*
Marguerite de Navarre *GuFrLit 2*
Marguerite de Navarre (d'Angouleme) 1492-1549 *BlmGWL*
Marguerite de Valois 1553-1615 *BlmGWL*
Marguerite d'Oingt 1286-1310 *BlmGWL*
Margueritte *DrAPF 93*
Margueritte, Jean-Victor d1942 *WhoHol 92*
Margules, Dehirsh 1899-1965 *WhoAmA 93N*
Margules, Gabriele Ella 1927- *WhoAmA 93*
Margulies, Andrew Michael *WhoScEn 94*
Margulies, Beth Zeldes 1954- *WhoAmL 94*
Margulies, David 1937- *WhoHol 92*
Margulies, Donald *ConLC 76 [port]*
Margulies, Herman 1922- *WhoAm 94*
Margulies, Isidore 1921- *WhoAmA 93*
Margulies, James Howard 1951- *WhoAm 94*
Margulies, Jeffrey J. 1946- *WhoAm 94, WhoAmL 94*
Margulies, Jimmy 1951- *WrDr 94*
Margulies, Joseph 1896- *WhAm 10*
Margulies, Joseph 1896-1986 *WhoAmA 93N*
Margulies, Leo 1900-1975 *EncSF 93*
Margulies, Martin B. 1940- *WhoAm 94, WhoAmL 94*
Margulies, Michael S. 1953- *WhoAmL 94*
Margulies, Robert Allan 1942- *WhoScEn 94*
Margulies, Stan 1920- *IntMPA 94*
Margulies, Virginia d1969 *WhoHol 92*
Margulis, Alexander Rafailo 1921- *WhoAm 94*
Margulis, Charlie d1967 *WhoHol 92*
Margulis, Howard Lee 1961- *WhoAmL 94*
Margulis, Lynn 1938- *IntWW 93, WhoAm 94*
Margulis, Martha (Boyer) 1928- *WhoAmA 93*
Margulis, Michael Howard 1952- *WhoWest 94*
Margulois, David 1912- *WhoAm 94*
Margus, Paul E. 1948- *WhoIns 94*
Marguth, Gilbert R., Jr. 1934- *WhoAmP 93*
Marhic, Michel Edmond 1945- *WhoAm 94*
Marhoefer, Gordon Joseph 1932- *WhoFI 94, WhoWest 94*
Mari *WhoAmA 93*
Mari, Febo d1949 *WhoHol 92*
Mari, Maria Del Carmen 1959- *WhoHisp 94*
Maria Antonio Walpurgis 1724-1780 *NewGrDO*
Mariacher, Marcia 1952- *WhoFI 94*
Maria del Occidente *BlmGWL*
Maria de Portugal 1521-1577 *BlmGWL*
Mariah, Paul *DrAPF 93*
Mariah, Paul 1937- *WrDr 94*
Mariam, Mengistu Haile 1937- *IntWW 93*
Mariama, Maillele *WhoWomW 91*
Marian, Ferdinand d1946 *WhoHol 92*
Mariani, Albert Joseph 1949- *WhoWest 94*
Mariani, Angelo (Maurizio Gaspare) 1821-1873 *NewGrDO*
Mariani, Carlo Maria 1935- *IntWW 93*
Mariani, Carlos 1957- *WhoAmP 93, WhoHisp 94*
Mariani, John Francis 1945- *ConAu 41NR*
Mariani, Luciano 1801-1859 *NewGrDO*
Mariani, Marcella d1956 *WhoHol 92*
Mariani, Paul *DrAPF 93*
Mariani, Ralph A. 1948- *WhoAmL 94*
Mariani, Tommaso fl. 1728-1739 *NewGrDO*
Marianne 1941- *WhoAmA 93*
Mariano, Luis d1970 *WhoHol 92*
Mariano, Roberto d1990 *WhoHol 92*
Mariano, Ronald *WhoAmP 93*
Maria of the West *BlmGWL*
Mariategui, Sandro 1922- *IntWW 93*
Maria the Jewess *WorInv*
Maria Theresa 1717-1780 *HisWorL [port]*
Marichal, Juan 1938- *WhoHisp 94*
Marick, Michael Miron 1957- *WhoAmL 94*
Maricle, Leona d1988 *WhoHol 92*
Maricle, Marijane *WhoHol 92*
Maricle, Russell Cletus 1943- *WhoAmP 93*
Marics, Monica Ann 1962- *WhoWest 94*
Marie fl. 13th cent.- *BlmGWL*
Marie, Aurelius John Baptiste Lamothe 1904- *IntWW 93*
Marie, Constance 1965- *WhoHol 92*

Marie, Lisa *WhoHol 92*
Marie-Antoinette 1755-1793 *HisWorL, NewGrDO*
Marie de France fl. 12th cent.- *BlmGWL*
Marie de France fl. c. 1180- *BlmGEL*
Marie de l'Incarnation 1599-1672 *BlmGWL*
Marie de l'Isle, (Claude Marie) Mecene 1811-1882 *NewGrDO*
Mariel, Serafin *WhoBlA 94, WhoHisp 94*
Mariella, Raymond P. 1919- *WhoAm 94*
Marielle, Jean-Pierre *WhoHol 92*
Marien, Marcel 1920-1993 *NewYTBS 93*
Marienchild, Eva 1957- *WhoFI 94*
Marienthal, George 1938- *WhoAm 94*
Marieta, Beth 1950- *WhoWomW 91*
Marietta, Beth 1950- *WhoAmP 93*
Marievsky, Joseph d1971 *WhoHol 92*
Mariger, Craig R. 1952- *WhoAmL 94*
Marihart, Donald Joseph 1926- *WhoAm 94*
Marihugh, Tammy 1953- *WhoHol 92*
Marik, Jan 1920- *WhoAm 94*
Marik, Karen L. 1967- *WhoMW 93*
Maril, Herman 1908-1986 *WhoAmA 93N*
Marill, Alvin H. 1934- *IntMPA 94*
Marimow, William Kalmon 1947- *WhoAm 94*
Marin, Alfred 1921- *WrDr 94*
Marin, Cheech 1946- *WhoHisp 94*
Marin, Connie Flores 1939- *WhoHisp 94*
Marin, Frank 1940- *WhoHisp 94*
Marin, Gerardo 1947- *WhoHisp 94*
Marin, Jack 1945- *BasBi*
Marin, Jacques 1919- *WhoHol 92*
Marin, Jaime G. 1961- *WhoHisp 94*
Marin, Jean 1909- *IntWW 93*
Marin, John 1870-1953 *WhoAmA 93N*
Marin, John Currey 1870-1953 *AmCulL*
Marin, Myra 1964- *WhoHisp 94*
Marin, Orlando 1963- *WhoHisp 94*
Marin, Patricia Woods 1939- *WhoAmL 94*
Marin, Paul *WhoHol 92*
Marin, Richard 1946- *IntMPA 94, WhoHol 92*
   See Also Cheech and Chong *WhoCom*
   See Also Cheech & Chong *WhoHol 92*
Marin, Richard Anthony 1946- *WhoAm 94*
Marin, Salvador *WhoHisp 94*
Marin, Vincent Arul 1959- *WhoMW 93*
Marina, Jeanne *DrAPF 93*
Marinaccio, Charles L. 1933- *WhoAmP 93*
Marinaccio, Charles Lindbergh 1933- *WhoAm 94*
Marinace, Kenneth Anthony 1944- *WhoFI 94*
Marinak, Jeanne LeeAnn 1951- *WhoWest 94*
Marinakos, Plato Anthony 1935- *WhoAm 94*
Marinari, Gaetano fl. 1764-1844 *NewGrDO*
Marinaro, Ed 1950- *WhoHol 92*
Marinaro, Edward Francis 1950- *WhoAm 94*
Marinaro, Gary *WhoAmP 93*
Marinaro, Michael Peter 1955- *WhoMW 93*
Marinas, Manuel Guillermo, Jr. 1954- *WhoScEn 94*
Marincic, Gary Lee 1949- *WhoFI 94*
Marin del Solar, Mercedes 1804-1866 *BlmGWL*
Marine, Clyde Lockwood 1936- *WhoAm 94, WhoFI 94*
Marine, Jeanne *WhoHol 92*
Marineau, Philip Albert 1946- *WhoAm 94, WhoFI 94*
Marinelli, Francis Ernest 1937- *WhoMW 93*
Marinelli, Gaetano 1754-1820? *NewGrDO*
Marinelli Vacca, Lucrezia 1571-1653 *BlmGWL*
Marinello, Robet Maggio 1945- *WhoIns 94*
Marinello, Salvatore John 1946- *WhoAmL 94*
Marinenko, George 1935- *WhoScEn 94*
Mariner, David *EncSF 93*
Mariner, Donna M. 1934- *WhoAmA 93*
Mariner, Scott *EncSF 93*
Mariner, William Martin 1949- *WhoWest 94*
Marines, Louis Lawrence 1942- *WhoAm 94*
Marinescu, Bogdan *IntWW 93*
Marinetti, F(ilippo) T(ommaso) 1876-1944 *IntDcT 2*
Marinez, Guadalupe *WhoHisp 94*
Marinez, Juan 1946- *WhoHisp 94*
Maring, Norma Ann 1933- *WhoMW 93*
Marin Gonzalez, Manuel 1949- *IntWW 93, Who 94*
Marini, Frank Nicholas 1935- *WhoAm 94*
Marini, Ignazio 1811-1873 *NewGrDO*

Markovich-Treece, Patricia 1941- *WhoFI 94, WhoScEn 94, WhoWest 94*
Markovits, Ronald D. *WhoIns 94*
Markovitz, Alvin 1929- *WhoAm 94*
Markow, Jack 1905-1983 *WhoAmA 93N*
Markowa, Nina Alexandrovna 1925- *ConAu 142*
Markowitsch, Helga 1944- *WhoWomW 91*
Markowitz, Alan Larry 1943- *WhoAm 94*
Markowitz, Diane *WhoAmP 93*
Markowitz, Harry M. 1927- *IntWW 93, NobelP 91 [port], Who 94, WhoAm 94, WhoFI 94, WrDr 94*
Markowitz, Lewis Harrison 1933- *WhoAmL 94*
Markowitz, Marilyn *WhoAmA 93*
Markowitz, Martin 1945- *WhoAmP 93*
Markowitz, Robert 1935- *IntMPA 94*
Markowitz, Samuel Solomon 1931- *WhoWest 94*
Markowska, Alicja Lidia 1948- *WhoScEn 94*
Markowski, Eugene David 1931- *WhoAmA 93*
Markowski, Roberta Jean 1967- *WhoScEn 94*
Marks *Who 94*
Marks, Alan 1957- *SmATA 77 [port]*
Marks, Alfred 1921- *IntMPA 94, WhoHol 92*
Marks, Andrew H. 1951- *WhoAm 94, WhoAmL 94*
Marks, Andrew Robert 1955- *WhoScEn 94*
Marks, Anthony Michael 1937- *WhoFI 94*
Marks, Arnold 1912- *WhoAm 94, WhoWest 94*
Marks, Arthur 1927- *IntMPA 94*
Marks, B. Mayes, Jr. 1959- *WhoAmP 93*
Marks, Bernard Bailin 1917- *WhoAm 94*
Marks, Bernard Montague 1923- *Who 94*
Marks, Bruce 1937- *WhoAm 94*
Marks, Cedric H., Mrs. *WhoAmA 93*
Marks, Charles Caldwell 1921- *WhoAm 94*
Marks, Charles Hardaway 1921- *WhoAmP 93*
Marks, Charles L. 1936- *WhoIns 94*
Marks, Claude 1915-1991 *WhoAmA 93N*
Marks, Craig 1929- *WhoAm 94*
Marks, Dale 1948- *WhoAmP 93*
Marks, David (Francis) 1945- *WrDr 94*
Marks, David Hunter 1939- *WhoAm 94, WhoScEn 94*
Marks, Dennis A. 1946- *WhoAm 94, WhoAmL 94*
Marks, Dennis Michael 1948- *IntWW 93, Who 94*
Marks, E. Matthew 1942- *WhoIns 94*
Marks, Edward B. 1911- *WhoAm 94*
Marks, Edwin S. 1926- *WhoAm 94*
Marks, Elaine 1930- *WhoAm 94*
Marks, Ernest E. 1950- *WhoScEn 94*
Marks, Esther L. 1927- *WhoMW 93*
Marks, Florence C. Elliott 1921- *WhoMW 93*
Marks, George B. 1923-1983 *WhoAmA 93N*
Marks, George Croydon 1858-1938 *DcNaB MP*
Marks, Guy d1987 *WhoHol 92*
Marks, Hannah K. 1926- *WrDr 94*
Marks, Henry Thomas 1908-1991 *WhAm 10*
Marks, Herbert Edward 1935- *WhoAm 94*
Marks, Herman H. *WhoAmP 93*
Marks, J. *DrAPF 93*
Marks, James Frederic 1928- *WhoScEn 94*
Marks, Janet *DrAPF 93*
Marks, Jean C. 1934- *WhoAmP 93*
Marks, Jerome 1931- *WhoAm 94*
Marks, Joe A. Cisneros *WhoHisp 94*
Marks, Joe E. d1973 *WhoHol 92*
Marks, John Barrett 1946- *WhoAmL 94*
Marks, John Boyd 1928- *WhoAmP 93*
Marks, John Emile *Who 94*
Marks, John Henry 1923- *WhoAm 94*
Marks, John Henry 1925- *Who 94*
Marks, Julie Ann 1960- *WhoAmL 94*
Marks, Laurence Michael 1947- *WhoAm 94*
Marks, Laurie J. 1957- *WrDr 94*
Marks, Lawrence Irwin 1925-1989 *WhAm 10*
Marks, Lee Otis 1944- *WhoBlA 94*
Marks, Leonard, Jr. 1921- *WhoAm 94*
Marks, Leonard Harold 1916- *IntWW 93, WhoAm 94*
Marks, Lou d1987 *WhoHol 92*
Marks, Marc Lincoln 1927- *WhoAmP 93*
Marks, Marie Schulz 1957- *WhoMW 93*
Marks, Martha Alford 1946- *WhoMW 93*
Marks, Matthew Stuart 1962- *WhoAmA 93*
Marks, Merle Byron 1925- *WhoWest 94*
Marks, Merton Eleazer 1932- *WhoAm 94, WhoAmL 94, WhoWest 94*
Marks, Meyer Benjamin 1907-1991 *WhAm 10*
Marks, Michael J. 1938- *WhoAm 94, WhoAmL 94*
Marks, Michael John Paul 1941- *Who 94*
Marks, Michael Joseph 1956- *WhoAmL 94*
Marks, Milton 1920- *WhoWest 94*
Marks, Milton, Jr. 1920- *WhoAmP 93*
Marks, Murry Aaron 1933- *WhoAmL 94*
Marks, Nehemiah d1799 *WhAmRev*
Marks, Paul Alan 1926- *IntWW 93, WhoAm 94, WhoScEn 94*
Marks, Paula Mitchell 1951- *WrDr 94*
Marks, Peter *ConAu 42NR, SmATA 77*
Marks, Peter Amasa 1948- *WhoWest 94*
Marks, Raymond H. 1922- *WhoAm 94*
Marks, Richard Charles 1945- *Who 94*
Marks, Richard Daniel 1944- *WhoAm 94, WhoAmL 94*
Marks, Richard E. *IntMPA 94*
Marks, Richard Henry Lee 1943- *WhoScEn 94*
Marks, Richard Lee 1923?- *ConAu 140*
Marks, Robert A. 1952- *WhoAmP 93*
Marks, Robert Arthur 1952- *WhoAmL 94, WhoWest 94*
Marks, Robert Herman, Jr. 1922- *WhoAmP 93*
Marks, Robert L. *WhoAm 94*
Marks, Robert W. d1993 *NewYTBS 93*
Marks, Robert William 1952- *WhoWest 94*
Marks, Roberta Barbara *WhoAmA 93*
Marks, Rose M. 1938- *WhoBlA 94*
Marks, Royal S. 1927-1987 *WhoAmA 93N*
Marks, Russell Edward, Jr. 1932- *WhoAm 94*
Marks, Ruth A. 1940- *WhoIns 94*
Marks, Sharon Lea 1942- *WhoWest 94*
Marks, Shula Eta 1936- *Who 94*
Marks, Sidney d1974 *WhoHol 92*
Marks, Stan(ley) 1929- *WrDr 94*
Marks, Stephen Paul 1943- *WhoAmL 94*
Marks, Theodore Lee 1935- *WhoAm 94, WhoAmL 94*
Marks, Tobin Jay 1944- *WhoAm 94, WhoScEn 94*
Marks, Walter *WhoMW 93*
Marks, William J. 1944- *WhoWest 94*
Marks, Willis d1952 *WhoHol 92*
Marksman, Peter c. 1815-1892 *EncNAR*
Marks of Broughton, Baron 1920- *Who 94*
Markson, Daniel Ben 1959- *WhoFI 94*
Markson, David *DrAPF 93*
Markson, David M 1927- *WrDr 94*
Markson, Eileen 1939- *WhoAmA 93*
Marktukanitz, Richard Peter 1953- *WhoScEn 94*
Markun, Frank O. 1947- *WhoFI 94*
Markus, Frank H. 1898-1992 *WhAm 10*
Markus, Fred H. 1927- *WhoAm 94*
Markus, Henry A. *WhoAmA 93N*
Markus, Julia *DrAPF 93*
Markus, Julia 1939- *WrDr 94*
Markus, Lawrence 1922- *WhoAm 94, WhoMW 93*
Markus, Richard M. 1930- *WhoAm 94*
Markus, Robert Austin 1924- *Who 94*
Markus, Robert D. 1940- *WhoAmL 94*
Markus, Robert M. 1930- *WhoFI 94*
Markus, Robert Michael 1934- *WhoAm 94*
Markus, Stephen Allan 1954- *WhoAmL 94*
Markusen, Ann Roell 1946- *ConAu 142*
Markusen, Thomas Roy 1940- *WhoAmA 93*
Markuson, Steven Dale 1952- *WhoMW 93*
Markussen, Joanne Marie 1956- *WhoScEn 94*
Markussen, Stuart 1959- *WhoFI 94*
Markuszka, Nancy Ann 1951- *WhoMW 93*
Markvart, Tomas 1950- *WhoScEn 94*
Markwardt, Kenneth Marvin 1928- *WhoAm 94*
Markwardt, L(orraine) J(oseph) 1889- *WhAm 10*
Markwell, Terry *WhoHol 92*
Markwick, Edward *EncSF 93*
Markwood, James S. 1954- *WhoAmP 93*
Markwood, Lewis Ardra 1932- *WhoAm 94*
Markyate, Christina of c. 1096- *DcNaB MP*
Marky Mark 1971- *News 93-3 [port]*
Marland, Alkis Joseph 1943- *WhoAm 94, WhoFI 94, WhoScEn 94*
Marland, Douglas d1993 *NewYTBS 93 [port]*
Marland, Melissa Kaye 1955- *WhoAmL 94*
Marland, Michael 1934- *Who 94, WrDr 94*
Marland, Paul 1940- *Who 94*
Marland, Sidney P., Jr. d1992 *IntWW 93N*
Marland, Sidney Percy, Jr. 1914-1992 *WhAm 10*
Marlane, Judith 1937- *WhoFI 94*
Marlantes, Leo 1916- *WhoWest 94*
Marlar, Robin Geoffrey 1931- *Who 94*
Marlas, James Constantine 1937- *WhoAm 94, WhoFI 94*
Marlatt, Daphne 1942- *BlmGWL*
Marlatt, Daphne (Buckle) 1942- *WrDr 94*
Marlatt, Jerry Ronald 1942- *WhoAm 94, WhoAmL 94*
Marlaud, Philippe d1981 *WhoHol 92*
Marlay, Robert Charles 1946- *WhoScEn 94*
Marlborough, Duke of 1926- *Who 94*
Marlborough, John Churchill, Duke of 1650-1722 *BlmGEL*
Marlborough, Leah d1954 *WhoHol 92*
Marle, Arnold d1970 *WhoHol 92*
Marle, Otto d1943 *WhoHol 92*
Marleau, Louise *WhoHol 92*
Marleau, Robert 1948- *WhoAm 94*
Marlen, James S. 1941- *WhoAm 94*
Marlenee, Ronald Charles 1935- *WhoAmP 93*
Marler, David Steele 1941- *Who 94*
Marler, Dennis Ralph Greville 1927- *Who 94*
Marler, Larry John 1940- *WhoWest 94*
Marler, Lawrence Arel 1935- *WhoMW 93*
Marler, Linda Susan 1951- *WhoMW 93*
Marler, Peter Robert 1928- *IntWW 93*
Marlesford, Baron 1931- *Who 94*
Marlett, De Otis Loring 1911- *WhoAm 94, WhoFI 94, WhoWest 94*
Marlette, Douglas Nigel 1949- *WhoAm 94*
Marley, Ben *WhoHol 92*
Marley, Bob d1981 *WhoHol 92*
Marley, Bob 1945-1981 *ConBlB 5 [port]*
Marley, Everett Armistead, Jr. 1933- *WhoAm 94*
Marley, James Earl 1935- *WhoAm 94, WhoFI 94*
Marley, John d1984 *WhoHol 92*
Marley, Rita 1947- *ConMus 10 [port]*
Marliani, Marco Aurelio 1805-1849 *NewGrDO*
Marlin, Donnell Charles 1930- *WhoScEn 94*
Marlin, James P. 1945- *WhoAmL 94*
Marlin, John Tepper 1942- *WhoFI 94, WhoScEn 94*
Marlin, Paul d1983 *WhoHol 92*
Marlin, Richard 1933- *WhoAm 94*
Marlin, William 1947- *WhoAmL 94*
Marling, Charles (William Somerset) 1951- *Who 94*
Marling, Lynwood Bradley 1944- *WhoAmL 94*
Marlis, Stefanie *DrAPF 93*
Marlitt, E. 1825-1887 *DcLB 129 [port]*
Marlitt, Eugenie 1825-1887 *BlmGWL*
Marlo, Mary d1960 *WhoHol 92*
Marlo, Steven *WhoHol 92*
Marlo, Timothy Louis 1964- *WhoFI 94*
Marlon, Ged *WhoHol 92*
Marlor, Clark Strang 1922- *WhoAmA 93, WrDr 94*
Marlow, Antony Rivers 1940- *Who 94*
Marlow, Audrey Swanson *WhoAmA 93*
Marlow, Bruce Wendell 1949- *WhoIns 94*
Marlow, David Ellis 1935- *Who 94*
Marlow, James Allen 1955- *WhoAmL 94*
Marlow, James R. 1941- *WhoAmL 94*
Marlow, James Richard Foster 1947- *WhoFI 94*
Marlow, Joseph 1939- *WhoScEn 94*
Marlow, Joyce 1929- *WrDr 94*
Marlow, Louis 1881-1966 *EncSF 93*
Marlow, Lucy 1932- *WhoHol 92*
Marlow, Max 1930- *WrDr 94*
Marlow, Orval Lee, II 1956- *WhoAmL 94*
Marlow, Tony d1962 *WhoHol 92*
Marlow, William J. 1926- *WhoAm 94*
Marlowe, Anthony d1975 *WhoHol 92*
Marlowe, Christopher 1564-1593 *BlmGEL, IntDcT 2, LitC 22 [port]*
Marlowe, Derek 1938- *WrDr 94*
Marlowe, Edward 1935- *WhoAm 94*
Marlowe, Faye 1926- *WhoHol 92*
Marlowe, Frank d1964 *WhoHol 92*
Marlowe, Howard David 1943- *WhoAm 94*
Marlowe, Hugh *Who 94*
Marlowe, Hugh d1982 *WhoHol 92*
Marlowe, Hugh 1939- *WrDr 94*
Marlowe, Jo Ann d1991 *WhoHol 92*
Marlowe, June d1984 *WhoHol 92*
Marlowe, Katherine 1941- *WrDr 94*
Marlowe, Marilyn d1975 *WhoHol 92*
Marlowe, Mary Louise 1957- *WhoAmL 94*
Marlowe, Mercedes d1987 *WhoHol 92*
Marlowe, Nora d1977 *WhoHol 92*
Marlowe, Rex d1979 *WhoHol 92*
Marlowe, Scott *WhoHol 92*
Marlowe, Stephen *EncSF 93*
Marlowe, Stephen 1928- *WrDr 94*
Marlowe, Webb *EncSF 93*
Marlowe, William 1932- *WhoHol 92*
Marly, Florence d1978 *WhoHol 92*
Marmaduke, Arthur Sandford 1926- *WhoWest 94*
Marmann, Sigrid 1938- *WhoFI 94, WhoScEn 94*
Marmaro, Marc 1948- *WhoAmL 94*
Marmas, James Gust 1929- *WhoAm 94*
Marmer, Harvey Joel d1976 *WhoHol 92*
Marmer, Lea d1974 *WhoHol 92*
Marmer, Melvin E. 1933- *WhoAm 94*
Marmer, Ronald Louis 1952- *WhoAm 94*
Marmero, Franc Joseph Henry 1948- *WhoAmL 94*
Marmet, Gottlieb John 1946- *WhoAmL 94*
Marmet, Paul 1932- *WhoAm 94*
Marmillion, Valsin Albert 1950- *WhoAmP 93*
Marmion, Barrie P. 1920- *Who 94*
Marmion, Frank J., Jr. 1917- *WhoAmP 93*
Marmion, William Henry 1907- *WhoAm 94*
Marmolejo, Adela Villa 1957- *WhoHisp 94*
Marmolejo, Charles Samuel 1943- *WhoHisp 94*
Marmon, Owen Holloway 1923- *WhoAm 94*
Marmon-Halm, Richard 1948- *WhoFI 94*
Marmont, Patricia 1921- *WhoHol 92*
Marmont, Percy d1977 *WhoHol 92*
Marmontel, Jean Francois 1723-1799 *NewGrDO*
Marmor, Judd 1910- *WhoAm 94*
Marmor, Michael Franklin 1941- *WhoAm 94*
Marmor, Theodore Richard 1939- *WhoScEn 94*
Marnac, Jeanne d1976 *WhoHol 92*
Marnane, Joseph P. 1937- *WhoAm 94*
Marnell, Russell I. 1958- *WhoAmL 94*
Marner, Der 1230?-c. 1287 *DcLB 138*
Marner, Richard *WhoHol 92*
Marner, Robert *EncSF 93*
Marni, Jeanne 1854-1910 *BlmGWL*
Marnoch, Hon. Lord 1938- *Who 94*
Marockie, Henry R. *WhoAm 94*
Maroff, Robert d1991 *WhoHol 92*
Marohn, Richard Charles 1934- *WhoAm 94*
Marois, Jim *WhoScEn 94*
Marold, Allen D. 1940- *WhoFI 94*
Marold, Karen Anne 1949- *WhoMW 93*
Marolda, Anthony Joseph 1939- *WhoAm 94*
Maron, Alfred d1986 *WhoHol 92*
Maron, Jeffrey 1949- *WhoAmA 93*
Maron, Margaret *WrDr 94*
Maron, Melvin Earl 1924- *WhoAm 94*
Maron, Michael Brent 1949- *WhoScEn 94*
Maron, Monika 1941- *BlmGWL*
Maronde, Robert Francis 1920- *WhoAm 94, WhoScEn 94, WhoWest 94*
Maroney, Dalton 1947- *WhoAmA 93*
Maroney, James H., Jr. 1943- *WhoAmA 93*
Maroney, Jane P. 1923- *WhoAmP 93, WhoWomW 91*
Maroney, Kelli *WhoHol 92*
Maroney, Michael James 1954- *WhoScEn 94*
Marongiu, Giovanni 1929- *IntWW 93*
Maroni, Donna Farolino 1938- *WhoAm 94*
Maroni, Gustavo Primo 1941- *WhoScEn 94*
Maroni, Yves 1920- *WhoFI 94*
Maroon, Fred J. 1924- *WrDr 94*
Maropis, Nicholas 1923- *WhoScEn 94*
Maross, Joe *WhoHol 92*
Maroszek, Dwayne Scott 1958- *WhoMW 93*
Marot, Clement 1496-1544 *GuFrLit 2*
Marothy-Soltesova, Elena 1855-1939 *BlmGWL*
Marotta, Alphonse S. *WhoAmP 93*
Marotta, George Raymond 1926- *WhoWest 94*
Marotta, Joseph Thomas 1926- *WhoAm 94*
Marotta, Nicholas G(ene) 1929-1991 *WhAm 10*
Marotta, Sabath Fred 1929- *WhoScEn 94*
Marotti, Keith Richard 1952- *WhoScEn 94*
Marouf, Taha Muhyiddin 1924- *IntWW 93*
Marovich, George M. 1931- *WhoAm 94, WhoAmL 94*
Marovitz, Abraham Lincoln 1905- *WhoMW 93*
Marovitz, James Lee 1939- *WhoAm 94*
Marovitz, William A. 1944- *WhoAmP 93, WhoMW 93*

Marowitz, Charles 1934- *Who 94, WrDr 94*
Marozsan, John Robert 1941- *WhoAm 94*
Marozzi, Eli Raphael 1913- *WhoAmA 93*
Marphatia, Raj 1959- *WhoAmL 94*
Marple, Dorothy Jane 1926- *WhoAm 94*
Marple, Gary Andre 1937- *WhoAm 94*
Marple, Stanley Lawrence, Jr. 1947- *WhoAm 94*
Marples, Brian John 1907- *IntWW 93, Who 94*
Marprelate, Martin *BlmGEL*
Marquand, Christian 1927- *WhoHol 92*
Marquand, David (Ian) 1934- *Who 94*
Marquand, David Ian 1934- *IntWW 93*
Marquand, John P., Jr. *DrAPF 93*
Marquand, Nancy d1982 *WhoHol 92*
Marquand, Serge *WhoHol 92*
Marquand, Tina *WhoHol 92*
Marquard, Paul Joseph 1958- *WhoWest 94*
Marquard, William A. 1920- *IntWW 93*
Marquardt, Ann Marie 1964- *WhoFI 94*
Marquardt, Christel Elisabeth 1935- *WhoAm 94, WhoAmL 94*
Marquardt, Kathleen Patricia 1944- *WhoFI 94*
Marquardt, Klaus Max 1926- *IntWW 93*
Marquardt, Lloyd B. 1952- *WhoWest 94*
Marquardt, Meril E. 1926- *WhoIns 94*
Marquardt, Richard G. 1923- *WhoAmP 93*
Marquardt, Robert Richard 1943- *WhoAmL 94*
Marques, Luis G. 1932- *IntWW 93*
Marques, Maria Elena *WhoHol 92*
Marques, Rene d1979 *WhoHol 92*
Marques, Rene 1919-1979 *HispLC [port], IntDcT 2*
Marques, Sarah *WhoHisp 94*
Marques, Walter Waldemar Pego 1936- *WhoFI 94*
Marquess, Lawrence Wade 1950- *WhoAmL 94, WhoWest 94*
Marquet, Mary d1979 *WhoHol 92*
Marquets, Anne de d1588 *BlmGWL*
Marquette, I. Edward 1950- *WhoAmL 94*
Marquette, Jacques 1637-1675 *DcAmReB 2, EncNAR, WhWE [port]*
Marquez, Alfredo C. 1922- *WhoAm 94, WhoWest 94*
Marquez, Alfredo Chavez 1922- *WhoHisp 94*
Marquez, Anthony Philip 1950- *WhoWest 94*
Marquez, Camilo Raoul 1942- *WhoBlA 94*
Marquez, Dario O., Jr. *WhoHisp 94*
Márquez, Enrique 1952- *WhoHisp 94*
Marquez, Felix S. 1942- *WhoHisp 94*
Marquez, Francisco Javier 1947- *WhoHisp 94*
Marquez, Gabriel Garcia *ConWorW 93, IntWW 93*
Marquez, Gabriel Garcia 1928- *Who 94*
Marquez, Harold B. 1935- *WhoHisp 94*
Marquez, Jaime Franz 1947- *WhoHisp 94*
Marquez, Joaquin Alfredo 1942- *WhoAm 94*
Marquez, Jose D. L. *WhoHisp 94*
Marquez, Leo 1932- *WhoHisp 94*
Marquez, Lorenzo Antonio, Jr. 1940- *WhoHisp 94*
Marquez, Maria D. 1931- *WhoHisp 94*
Márquez, Martina Zenaida 1935- *WhoHisp 94, WhoWest 94*
Marquez, Maxine F. 1940- *WhoHisp 94*
Marquez, Nancy *WhoHisp 94*
Marquez, Pascual Gregory 1937- *WhoHisp 94*
Marquez, Raul 1971- *WhoHisp 94*
Márquez, Rosa Luisa 1947- *WhoHisp 94*
Marquez, Rosalinda C. *WhoHisp 94*
Marquez, Rosanna Alicia 1959- *WhoHisp 94*
Márquez, Tony Estevan, Jr. 1966- *WhoHisp 94*
Marquez De La Plata Irarrazaval, Alfonso 1933- *IntWW 93*
Marquez-Villanueva, Francisco 1931- *WhoHisp 94*
Marquina, Gerardo E. 1950- *WhoHisp 94*
Marquis *Who 94*
Marquis, James Douglas 1921- *Who 94*
Marquis, Max *WrDr 94*
Marquis, Richard 1945- *WhoAmA 93*
Marquis, Robert B. 1927- *WhoAm 94*
Marquis, Robert Stillwell 1943- *WhoAmL 94*
Marquis, Rollin Park 1925- *WhoAm 94*
Marquis, William Oscar 1944- *WhoAmL 94*
Marr, Alice d1990 *WhoHol 92*
Marr, Barry W. 1948- *WhoAmL 94*
Marr, Carmel Carrington *WhoAmP 93*
Marr, Carmel Carrington 1921- *AfrAmAl 6 [port], WhoAm 94, WhoBlA 94*
Marr, David Erskine 1939- *WhoAmL 94*
Marr, David Francis 1933- *WhoAm 94*
Marr, David G(eorge) 1937- *WrDr 94*
Marr, Edward d1987 *WhoHol 92*
Marr, Geoffrey Vickers 1930- *IntWW 93*
Marr, Hans d1949 *WhoHol 92*
Marr, Henry L. 1927- *WhoMW 93*
Marr, Joyce Michelle 1954- *WhoAmL 94*
Marr, Kathleen Mary 1954- *WhoMW 93, WhoScEn 94*
Marr, Leslie Lynn 1922- *Who 94*
Marr, Luther Reese 1925- *WhoAm 94*
Marr, Richard d1984 *WhoHol 92*
Marr, Robert Bruce 1932- *WhoAm 94*
Marr, Sally 1942- *WhoHol 92*
Marr, Warren, II 1916- *WhoBlA 94*
Marr, William d1960 *WhoHol 92*
Marr, William Wei-Yi 1936- *WhoAsA 94*
Marra, Kathy Shields 1954- *WhoMW 93*
Marra, Peter Gerald 1940- *WhoWest 94*
Marra, Samuel Patrick 1927- *WhoMW 93*
Marrack, Philip Reginald 1922- *Who 94*
Marraffino, Elizabeth *DrAPF 93*
Marraffino, Lawrence Joseph 1959- *WhoAmL 94*
Marrapese, Edward V. 1942- *WhoAmP 93*
Marrash, William B. 1939- *WhoFI 94*
Marre, Romola Mary 1920- *Who 94*
Marren, Howard Leslie 1946- *WhoAm 94*
Marrero, Dilka E. 1961- *WhoHisp 94*
Marrero, Karen Mason 1956- *WhoHisp 94*
Marrero, Manuel 1954- *WhoHisp 94*
Marrero, Minerva 1949- *WhoHisp 94*
Marrero, Thomas R. 1936- *WhoHisp 94*
Marrero, Victor *WhoAmP 93*
Marrero, Victor 1941- *WhoHisp 94*
Marrero-Favreau, Gloria 1948- *WhoHisp 94*
Marrero Hueca, Manuel *WhoHisp 94*
Marrero Perez, Anibal *WhoHisp 94*
Marrero Perez, Annibal *WhoAmP 93*
Marrett, Cora B. 1942- *WhoBlA 94*
Marrett, Louis J. 1947- *WhoAmL 94*
Marric, J. J. 1927- *WrDr 94*
Marriner, Brian 1937- *ConAu 141*
Marriner, David Richard 1934- *WhoAm 94, WhoFI 94*
Marriner, Neville 1924- *IntWW 93, Who 94, WhoAm 94*
Marriner, William *WhAmRev*
Marringa, Jacques Louis 1928- *WhoAm 94*
Marrington, Bernard Harvey 1928- *WhoWest 94*
Marriott, Alice Sheets 1907- *WhoAm 94*
Marriott, Anne 1913- *BlmGWL*
Marriott, B. Gladys 1922- *WhoAmP 93*
Marriott, Bryant Hayes 1936- *Who 94*
Marriott, Charles d1917 *WhoHol 92*
Marriott, David *WhoHol 92*
Marriott, David Daniel 1939- *WhoAmP 93*
Marriott, Hugh Cavendish S. *Who 94*
Marriott, John d1977 *WhoHol 92*
Marriott, John Brook 1922- *Who 94*
Marriott, John Miles 1935- *Who 94*
Marriott, John Willard, Jr. 1932- *WhoAm 94, WhoFI 94*
Marriott, Martin Marriott 1932- *Who 94*
Marriott, Moore d1949 *WhoHol 92*
Marriott, Richard Edwin 1939- *WhoAm 94, WhoFI 94*
Marriott, Robert S. 1939- *WhoAmL 94*
Marriott, Salima Siler 1940- *WhoAmP 93, WhoBlA 94*
Marriott, Sandee d1962 *WhoHol 92*
Marriott, Sylvia *WhoHol 92*
Marriott, William Allen 1942- *WhoAmA 93*
Marriott-Watson, H(enry) B(rereton) 1863-1921 *EncSF 93*
Marriott-Watson, Henry Crocker 1835- *EncSF 93*
Marris, James Hugh Spencer 1937- *Who 94*
Marris, Robin Lapthorn 1924- *Who 94*
Marris, Stephen Nicholson 1930- *IntWW 93, Who 94*
Marrison, Geoffrey Edward 1923- *Who 94*
Marr-Johnson, Frederick James Maugham 1936- *Who 94*
Marro, Anthony James 1942- *WhoAm 94*
Marro, George Matthew 1927- *WhoAmA 93*
Marron, Bill Henry 1946- *WhoMW 93*
Marron, Darlene Lorraine 1946- *WhoFI 94*
Marron, Donald B. 1934- *WhoAmA 93*
Marron, Donald Baird 1934- *WhoAm 94, WhoFI 94*
Marron, Joan 1934- *WhoAmA 93*
Marron, Marie Anne Carrelet de 1725-1778 *BlmGWL*
Marrone, Daniel Scott 1950- *WhoFI 94, WhoScEn 94*
Marrone, Jose d1990 *WhoHol 92*
Marrone, Steven P(hillip) 1947- *WrDr 94*
Marroquin, Arturo 1939- *WhoHisp 94*
Marroquin, Manuel A. 1947- *WhoHisp 94*
Marroquin, Mario 1955- *WhoHisp 94*
Marroquin, Mauricio 1945- *WhoHisp 94*
Marroquin, Patricia 1957- *WhoHisp 94*
Marroquin, Samuel Najar 1932- *WhoHisp 94*
Marrou, Andre Verne 1938- *WhoAmP 93*
Marrow, James Henry 1941- *WhoAmA 93*
Marrow, Marva Jan 1948- *WhoWest 94*
Marrow, Steven Paul 1961- *WhoFI 94*
Marrow, Tracy *WhoAm 94*
Marrow-Mooring, Barbara A. 1945- *WhoBlA 94*
Marrs, Leo Richard, Jr. 1949- *WhoWest 94*
Marrs, Raphael Hildan 1966- *WhoBlA 94*
Marrs, Stella 1932- *WhoBlA 94*
Marrujo, Ralph 1934- *WhoHisp 94*
Marryat, Florence 1838-1899 *BlmGWL*
Marryat, Frederick 1792-1848 *BlmGEL*
Mars, Forrest E., Jr. *WhoAm 94, WhoFI 94*
Mars, Gerald 1933- *WrDr 94*
Mars, John F. 1935- *WhoAm 94, WhoFI 94*
Mars, Kenneth 1935- *WhoHol 92*
Mars, Kenneth 1936- *IntMPA 94*
Mars, Marjorie *WhoHol 92*
Mars, Robert 1955- *WhoWest 94*
Marsac, Laure *WhoHol 92*
Marsac, Maurice 1920- *WhoHol 92*
Marsalis, Branford 1960- *AfrAmAl 6, ConMus 10 [port], WhoAm 94, WhoBlA 94, WhoHol 92*
Marsalis, Wynton 1961- *AfrAmAl 6 [port], IntWW 93, WhoAm 94, WhoBlA 94*
Marsan, Jean-Claude 1938- *WhoAm 94*
Marsano, Francis C. *WhoAmP 93*
Marschalk, William John 1944-1991 *WhAm 10*
Marschall, Marlene Elizabeth 1936- *WhoAm 94*
Marscher, William Donnelly 1948- *WhoScEn 94*
Marsching, Ronald Lionel 1927- *WhoAm 94*
Marschner, Heinrich August 1795-1861 *NewGrDO*
Marschner, Walter Arthur 1940- *WhoAmP 93*
Marsden, Arthur Whitcombe 1911- *Who 94*
Marsden, Betty 1919- *WhoHol 92*
Marsden, Brian Geoffrey 1937- *WhoAm 94, WhoScEn 94*
Marsden, Charles Joseph 1940- *WhoAm 94*
Marsden, (Charles) David 1938- *Who 94*
Marsden, Edmund Murray 1946- *Who 94*
Marsden, Frank 1923- *Who 94*
Marsden, Jerrold Eldon 1942- *WhoScEn 94*
Marsden, John 1950- *TwCYAW, WrDr 94*
Marsden, John Christopher 1937- *Who 94*
Marsden, K. C. *WhoAmP 93*
Marsden, Lawrence Albert 1919- *WhoAm 94*
Marsden, Lorna R. 1942- *WhoWomW 91*
Marsden, Michael H. E. 1904- *WhoAmA 93*
Marsden, Nigel (John Denton) 1940- *Who 94*
Marsden, Peter Nicholas 1932- *Who 94*
Marsden, Roy 1941- *WhoHol 92*
Marsden, Samuel 1765-1838 *WhWE*
Marsden, Susan 1931- *Who 94*
Marsden, William 1940- *Who 94*
Marsden-Smedley, Philip 1961- *WrDr 94*
Marsee, Dewey Robert 1932- *WhoScEn 94*
Marsee, Stuart Earl 1917- *WhoAm 94*
Marsee, Susanne Irene 1941- *WhoAm 94*
Marseglia, Everard A. 1945- *WhoAmL 94*
Marseille d'Althouvitis fl. 16th cent.- *BlmGWL*
Marsella, Anthony Samuel 1947- *WhoAmP 93*
Marsh, Baron 1928- *IntWW 93, Who 94*
Marsh, Alphonso Howard 1938- *WhoBlA 94*
Marsh, Anne Steele 1901- *WhoAmA 93*
Marsh, B. J. 1940- *WhoAmP 93*
Marsh, Barrie *Who 94*
Marsh, (Graham) Barrie 1935- *Who 94*
Marsh, Bazil Roland 1921- *Who 94*
Marsh, Beaton 1914- *WhoAmP 93*
Marsh, Ben Franklin 1940- *WhoBlA 94*
Marsh, Benjamin Franklin 1927- *WhoAm 94, WhoAmP 93*
Marsh, Berridge R. 1951- *WhoAmL 94*
Marsh, Brice Felix 1938- *WhoAmP 93*
Marsh, Bryan Bell, III 1959- *WhoFI 94*
Marsh, Carol 1929- *WhoHol 92*
Marsh, Carole 1946- *WhoAm 94*
Marsh, Caryl Amsterdam 1923- *WhoAm 94*
Marsh, Caryl Glenn 1939- *WhoAm 94*
Marsh, Charles d1953 *WhoHol 92*
Marsh, Clare Teitgen 1934- *WhoMW 93*
Marsh, Clayton Edward 1942- *WhoMW 93*
Marsh, Daniel G. 1937- *WhoAmP 93*
Marsh, Dave 1950- *ConAu 41NR*
Marsh, Dave Rodney 1950- *WhoAm 94*
Marsh, David 1945- *WhoFI 94*
Marsh, David Foster 1926- *WhoAmA 93*
Marsh, David O. 1927- *WhoAm 94*
Marsh, Della d1973 *WhoHol 92*
Marsh, Derick Rupert Clement 1928- *IntWW 93, WrDr 94*
Marsh, Don Ermal 1938- *WhoFI 94*
Marsh, Don Seagle 1927- *WhoAm 94*
Marsh, Donald Gene 1936- *WhoBlA 94*
Marsh, Dorothy Marie *WhAm 10*
Marsh, Doug 1958- *WhoBlA 94*
Marsh, Edward Frank *Who 94*
Marsh, Frank I. 1924- *WhoAmP 93*
Marsh, Frank Irving 1924- *WhoAm 94, WhoMW 93*
Marsh, Frank Raymond 1938- *WhoWest 94*
Marsh, Fred Dana 1872-1961 *WhoAmA 93N*
Marsh, Fred William, Jr. 1943- *WhoAmL 94*
Marsh, Frederick William 1946- *WhoFI 94*
Marsh, Garry d1981 *WhoHol 92*
Marsh, Geoffrey *EncSF 93*
Marsh, Geoffrey Gordon Ward *Who 94*
Marsh, George Perkins 1801-1882 *EnvEnc*
Marsh, Georgia *WhoAmA 93*
Marsh, Gordon David 1967- *WhoFI 94*
Marsh, Gordon Victor 1929- *Who 94*
Marsh, Harry Dean 1928- *WhoAm 94*
Marsh, Helen Unger 1925- *WhoMW 93*
Marsh, Henry Hooper 1898- *Who 94*
Marsh, Henry L., III *WhoAmP 93*
Marsh, Henry L., III 1933- *WhoBlA 94*
Marsh, Herbert Rhea, Jr. 1957- *WhoScEn 94*
Marsh, Hugh Leroy, Jr. 1929- *WhoFI 94*
Marsh, James 1794-1842 *DcAmReB 2*
Marsh, James Robert 1947- *WhoWest 94*
Marsh, Jayne Elizabeth 1954- *WhoMW 93*
Marsh, Jean 1934- *ConTFT 11, IntMPA 94, WhoHol 92*
Marsh, Jean Lyndsey Torren 1934- *Who 94, WhoAm 94*
Marsh, Jeanne Cay 1948- *WhoAm 94*
Marsh, Jeremiah 1933- *WhoAm 94*
Marsh, Joan 1913- *WhoHol 92*
Marsh, Joan Knight 1934- *WhoMW 93*
Marsh, John 1904- *Who 94, WrDr 94*
Marsh, John F. *WhoAmP 93*
Marsh, John Harrison 1954- *WhoWest 94*
Marsh, John O., Jr. 1926- *WhoAmP 93*
Marsh, John Otho, Jr. 1926- *WhoAm 94*
Marsh, John S. d1993 *NewYTBS 93*
Marsh, Joseph Franklin, Jr. 1925- *WhoAm 94*
Marsh, Joseph Virgil 1952- *WhoFI 94*
Marsh, Judy Darlene 1948- *WhoMW 93*
Marsh, Keith *WhoHol 92*
Marsh, Kenneth Lee 1952- *WhoWest 94*
Marsh, Leonard George 1930- *Who 94*
Marsh, Linda 1940- *WhoHol 92*
Marsh, Mae d1968 *WhoHol 92*
Marsh, Malcolm F. 1928- *WhoAm 94, WhoAmL 94, WhoWest 94*
Marsh, Marcus M. 1949- *WhoAmP 93*
Marsh, Marguerite d1925 *WhoHol 92*
Marsh, Marian 1913- *WhoHol 92*
Marsh, Matthew *WhoHol 92*
Marsh, McAfee 1939- *WhoBlA 94*
Marsh, Michael *WhoAm 94*
Marsh, Michael Lawrence 1967- *WhoBlA 94*
Marsh, Michael Raymond 1957- *WhoFI 94*
Marsh, Miles L. *WhoAm 94, WhoFI 94*
Marsh, Myra d1964 *WhoHol 92*
Marsh, Nevill Francis 1907- *Who 94*
Marsh, Ngaio 1895-1982 *BlmGWL*
Marsh, Noel R 1931- *WhoWest 94*
Marsh, Norman Stayner 1913- *Who 94, WrDr 94*
Marsh, Paul Rodney 1947- *Who 94*
Marsh, Pearl-Alice 1946- *WhoBlA 94*
Marsh, Peter T 1935- *WrDr 94*
Marsh, Quinton Neely 1915- *WhoAm 94*
Marsh, R. Bruce 1929-1992 *WhAm 10*
Marsh, Reginald 1898-1954 *WhoAmA 93N*
Marsh, Reginald 1926- *WhoHol 92*
Marsh, Richard Alan 1952- *WhoWest 94*
Marsh, Richard C. 1943- *WhoAmL 94*
Marsh, Richard J. 1933- *WhoAm 94*
Marsh, Robert Charles 1924- *WhoAm 94, WhoMW 93*
Marsh, Robert Harry 1946- *WhoScEn 94*
Marsh, Robert Houston 1959- *WhoAmP 93*

Marsh, Robert Mortimer 1931-
WhoAm 94, WrDr 94
Marsh, Robert Thomas 1925- *WhoAm 94*
Marsh, Ronald Keith 1951- *WhoMW 93*
Marsh, Rosalind J(udith) 1950- *WrDr 94*
Marsh, Sandra M. 1943- *WhoBlA 94*
Marsh, Scott Clyde 1953- *WhoWest 94*
Marsh, Shirley Mac 1925- *WhoAmP 93*
Marsh, Stephen Hale c. 1805-c. 1888
NewGrDO
Marsh, Stuart Emmet 1951- *WhoWest 94*
Marsh, Susan 1958- *WhoFI 94*
Marsh, Tamra Gwendolyn 1946-
WhoBlA 94
Marsh, Terence *ConTFT 11*
Marsh, (Edwin) Thomas 1934-1991
WhoAmA 93N
Marsh, Thomas A. 1951- *WhoAmA 93*
Marsh, Thomas Archie 1951-
WhoWest 94
Marsh, Tiger Joe d1989 *WhoHol 92*
Marsh, Timothy John 1948- *WhoWest 94*
Marsh, William A., Jr. 1927- *WhoBlA 94*
Marsh, William Andrew, III 1958-
WhoBlA 94
Marsh, William Douglas 1947-
WhoAmL 94
Marsh, William Harrison 1931-
WhoAm 94
Marsh, William Laurence 1926-
WhoAm 94
Marsh, William Robert 1945- *WhoAm 94,
WhoAmL 94*
Marshak, Alan Howard 1938- *WhoAm 94*
Marshak, Marvin Lloyd 1946-
WhoAm 94, WhoScEn 94
Marshak, Robert E. 1916- *IntWW 93*
Marshak, Robert E(ugene) 1916-1992
CurBio 93N
Marshak, Robert Eugene 1916- *WrDr 94*
Marshak, Robert Eugene 1916-1992
AnObit 1992, ConAu 140
Marshak, Robert Reuben 1923-
WhoAm 94
Marshak, Sondra *EncSF 93*
Marshal, Alan d1961 *WhoHol 92*
Marshal, Kit *WhoWest 94*
Marshalek, Eugene Richard 1936-
WhoAm 94, WhoMW 93
Marshall *Who 94*
Marshall, Alan 1938- *IntMPA 94*
Marshall, Alan George 1944-
WhoScEn 94
Marshall, Alan R., Mrs. *Who 94*
Marshall, Alan Ralph *Who 94*
Marshall, Albert Prince 1914- *WhoBlA 94*
Marshall, Alexander Badenoch 1924-
IntWW 93, Who 94
Marshall, Alton Garwood 1921-
WhoAm 94
Marshall, Anita 1938- *WhoBlA 94*
Marshall, Ann Kelsey 1951- *WhoAmP 93*
Marshall, Archibald 1866-1934 *EncSF 93*
Marshall, Arthur Gregory George 1903-
Who 94
Marshall, Arthur Harold 1931-
WhoScEn 94
Marshall, Arthur Hedley 1904- *Who 94*
Marshall, Arthur K. 1911- *WhoAm 94,
WhoAmL 94, WhoWest 94*
Marshall, Arthur Stirling-Maxwell 1929-
Who 94
Marshall, Betty J. 1950- *WhoBlA 94*
Marshall, Bill *WhoWest 94*
Marshall, Boyd d1950 *WhoHol 92*
Marshall, Brenda 1915- *WhoHol 92*
Marshall, Bruce 1929- *WhoAmA 93*
Marshall, Bryan 1938- *WhoHol 92*
Marshall, Bryan Edward 1935-
WhoAm 94
Marshall, Burke 1922- *WhoAm 94*
Marshall, Byrd F., Jr. 1953- *WhoAmL 94*
Marshall, C. Travis 1926- *WhoAm 94,
WhoFI 94*
Marshall, Calvin Bromley, III 1932-
WhoBlA 94
Marshall, Cameron Lee 1964-
WhoAmL 94
Marshall, Carl Leroy 1914- *WhoBlA 94*
Marshall, Carol Joyce 1967- *WhoScEn 94*
Marshall, Carolyn Ann M. 1935-
WhoAm 94, WhoMW 93
Marshall, Carter Lee 1936- *WhoBlA 94*
Marshall, Cedric Russell 1936- *IntWW 93*
Marshall, Charlene Jennings 1933-
WhoBlA 94
Marshall, Charles d1975 *WhoHol 92*
Marshall, Charles 1929- *WhoAm 94*
Marshall, Charles Bowker 1936-
WhoWest 94
Marshall, Charles Burton 1908-
WhoAm 94
Marshall, Charles Donald, Jr. 1945-
WhoAmL 94
Marshall, Charles Francis 1943-
WhoScEn 94
Marshall, Charles Louis 1912- *WhoAm 94*

Marshall, Charles Noble 1942-
WhoAm 94, WhoFI 94
Marshall, Chet d1974 *WhoHol 92*
Marshall, Christopher 1709-1797
WhAmRev
Marshall, Cliff 1939- *WhoAmP 93*
Marshall, Clifford Wallace 1928-
WhoAm 94
Marshall, Colin (Marsh) 1933-
IntWW 93, Who 94
Marshall, Conrad Joseph 1934-
WhoWest 94
Marshall, Consuelo B. 1936- *WhoBlA 94*
Marshall, Consuelo Bland 1936-
WhoAm 94, WhoAmL 94, WhoWest 94
Marshall, Craig Douglas 1961-
WhoMW 93
Marshall, Dale Livingston 1944-
WhoFI 94
Marshall, Daniel 1706-1784 *DcAmReB 2*
Marshall, Daniel Alfred 1937-
WhoAmP 93
Marshall, Daniel Stuart 1930- *WhoAm 94*
Marshall, David 1914- *WhoScEn 94*
Marshall, David 1941- *Who 94*
Marshall, David Anthony *WhoHol 92*
Marshall, David Lawrence 1939-
WhoFI 94, WhoWest 94
Marshall, David Saul 1908- *IntWW 93*
Marshall, David Scott 1950- *WhoAmP 93*
Marshall, David Vance 1950- *WhoAm 94*
Marshall, Denis (Alfred) 1916- *Who 94*
Marshall, Diana E. 1948- *WhoAmL 94*
Marshall, Dodie *WhoHol 92*
Marshall, Don 1936- *WhoHol 92*
Marshall, Don A., Sr. 1929- *WhoBlA 94*
Marshall, Donald Glenn 1943-
WhoAm 94
Marshall, Donald James 1934-
WhoBlA 94
Marshall, Donald Stewart 1938-
WhoAm 94
Marshall, Donald Tompkins 1933-
WhoAm 94, WhoFI 94
Marshall, E. G. 1910- *IntMPA 94,
WhoAm 94*
Marshall, E. G. 1919- *WhoHol 92*
Marshall, Edison (Tesla) 1894-1967
EncSF 93
Marshall, Edmund 1938-1979
WhoAmA 93N
Marshall, Edmund Ian 1940- *Who 94*
Marshall, Edward *SmATA 75*
Marshall, Edward 1942- *WrDr 94*
Marshall, Edwin Cochran 1946-
WhoBlA 94
Marshall, Elaine *WhoAmP 93*
Marshall, Elizabeth Margaret 1926-
WrDr 94
Marshall, Ellen Ruth 1949- *WhoAmL 94*
Marshall, Eric C. 1958- *WhoAm 94*
Marshall, Etta Marie-Imes 1932-
WhoBlA 94
Marshall, F. Ray *WhoAm 94*
Marshall, Francis Joseph 1923-
WhoAm 94
Marshall, Frank *IntMPA 94*
Marshall, Frank Britt, III 1943-
WhoBlA 94
Marshall, Frank Graham 1942- *Who 94*
Marshall, Frank W. *WhoAm 94*
Marshall, Franklin Nick 1933-
WhoAm 94
Marshall, Fredda *Who 94*
Marshall, Frederick Joseph 1920-
WhoScEn 94
Marshall, Garland Ross 1940- *WhoAm 94*
Marshall, Garry 1934- *IntMPA 94,
WhoAm 94*
Marshall, Gary *WhoHol 92*
Marshall, Gary Lee 1955- *WhoMW 93*
Marshall, Gary Scott 1957- *WhoScEn 94*
Marshall, Geoffrey 1929- *IntWW 93,
Who 94, WrDr 94*
Marshall, Geoffrey 1938- *WhoAm 94*
Marshall, George d1975 *WhoHol 92*
Marshall, George C. 1880-1959
HisWorL [port], HisDcKW
Marshall, George Dwire 1940-
WhoAm 94
Marshall, George N. d1993 *NewYTBS 93*
Marshall, George N(ichols) 1920-1993
ConAu 140
Marshall, George Preston d1969
ProFbHF [port]
Marshall, Gerald Francis 1929-
WhoAm 94
Marshall, Gerald Robert 1934-
WhoAm 94
Marshall, Gloria A. 1938- *WhoBlA 94*
Marshall, Gordon Bruce 1943-
WhoAm 94, WhoMW 93
Marshall, Grayson William, Jr. 1943-
WhoWest 94
Marshall, Harold D. 1936- *WhoAm 94,
WhoFI 94*
Marshall, Hazel Eleanor *Who 94*
Marshall, Helen M. *WhoAmP 93*

Marshall, Henry H. 1954- *WhoBlA 94*
Marshall, Herbert d1966 *WhoHol 92*
Marshall, Herbert A. 1916- *WhoBlA 94*
Marshall, Herbert A. 1917- *WhoAm 94*
Marshall, Howard Lowen 1931-
WhoAm 94
Marshall, Howard Wright 1923- *Who 94*
Marshall, Hugh Phillips 1934- *Who 94*
Marshall, I. N. 1931- *WrDr 94*
Marshall, Irl Houston, Jr. 1929-
WhoMW 93
Marshall, J. Howard, II 1905- *IntWW 93,
WhoAm 94*
Marshall, Jack *DrAPF 93*
Marshall, Jack 1937- *WrDr 94*
Marshall, Jacqueline Wearstler 1960-
WhoFI 94
Marshall, James 1941- *Who 94*
Marshall, James 1942-1992 *AnObit 1992*
Marshall, James 1966- *WhoHol 92*
Marshall, James (Edward) 1942- *WrDr 94*
Marshall, James (Edward) 1942-1992
SmATA 75 [port], WhAm 10
Marshall, James Duard 1914-
WhoAmA 93
Marshall, James Frederick 1949-
WhoWest 94
Marshall, James Kenneth 1952-
WhoWest 94
Marshall, James Vance 1924- *WrDr 94*
Marshall, Janice 1946- *WhoIns 94*
Marshall, Jean McElroy 1922- *WhoAm 94*
Marshall, Jeff *ConAu 41NR*
Marshall, Jeffrey Scott 1961-
WhoScEn 94
Marshall, Jeremy *Who 94*
Marshall, (John) Jeremy (Seymour)
1938- *WrDr 94*
Marshall, John *Who 94, WhoAm 94,
WhoAmP 93*
Marshall, John c. 1659-1723 *DcNaB MP*
Marshall, John 1755-1835
HisWorL [port], WhAmRev
Marshall, John 1765-1845 *DcNaB MP*
Marshall, John 1915- *Who 94*
Marshall, John 1917- *WhoScEn 94*
Marshall, John 1922- *ConAu 43NR,
Who 94, WrDr 94*
Marshall, John 1957- *WhoAmA 93*
Marshall, John, Jr. 1894- *WhAm 10*
Marshall, John Alexander 1922- *Who 94*
Marshall, John Aloysius 1928-
WhoAm 94
Marshall, John Carl 1936- *WhoAmA 93*
Marshall, John David 1928- *ConAu 41NR*
Marshall, John David 1940- *WhoAm 94*
Marshall, John David 1956- *WhoScEn 94*
Marshall, John Dent 1946- *WhoBlA 94*
Marshall, John Donald 1921- *WhoBlA 94*
Marshall, John Elbert, III 1942-
WhoAm 94
Marshall, John Harris, Jr. 1924-
WhoScEn 94
Marshall, John Henry 1949- *WhoAmL 94*
Marshall, John Leslie 1940- *Who 94*
Marshall, John Murray 1930-
WhoWest 94
Marshall, John Patrick 1950- *WhoAm 94,
WhoAmL 94*
Marshall, John Paul 1941- *WhoFI 94*
Marshall, John Roger 1944- *Who 94*
Marshall, John Spenceley 1957-
WhoAmL 94
Marshall, John Treutlen 1934-
WhoAm 94
Marshall, Jonnie Clanton 1932-
WhoBlA 94
Marshall, Joseph C., III 1952-
WhoAmL 94
Marshall, Joseph Frank 1917-
WhoScEn 94
Marshall, Joseph L. 1949- *WhoAmL 94*
Marshall, Joyce 1913- *BlmGWL*
Marshall, Julian Howard, Jr. 1922-
WhoAm 94
Marshall, Kay Valerie 1960- *WhoFI 94*
Marshall, Kelvin A. A. 1947- *WhoAm 94*
Marshall, Ken 1951- *WhoHol 92*
Marshall, Kerry James 1955-
WhoAmA 93
Marshall, L. B. 1928- *WhoWest 94*
Marshall, Larry 1946- *WhoHol 92*
Marshall, Larry L. 1942- *WhoAmL 94*
Marshall, Larry Ronald 1962-
WhoScEn 94
Marshall, Laurence Arthur 1931- *Who 94*
Marshall, Lee D. 1956- *WhoMW 93*
Marshall, Leonard 1961- *WhoBlA 94*
Marshall, Leonard Allen 1961-
WhoAm 94
Marshall, Lewis West, Jr. 1958-
WhoBlA 94
Marshall, Linda Rae 1940- *WhoMW 93*
Marshall, Lois (Catherine) 1924-
NewGrDO
Marshall, Luther Gerald 1931-
WhoScEn 94

Marshall, Malcolm Denzil 1958-
IntWW 93
Marshall, Mara 1926- *WhoAmA 93*
Marshall, Margaret 1949- *NewGrDO*
Marshall, Margaret Anne 1949-
IntWW 93, Who 94
Marshall, Margaret Hilary 1944-
WhoAm 94, WhoAmL 94
Marshall, Marilyn Josephine 1945-
WhoAmL 94
Marshall, Marion 1930- *WhoHol 92*
Marshall, Mark Anthony 1937- *Who 94*
Marshall, Martin John 1914- *Who 94*
Marshall, Martin Vivan 1922- *WhoAm 94*
Marshall, Marvin Giffin 1937-
WhoAm 94, WhoFI 94
Marshall, Mary Aydelotte 1921-
WhoWomW 91
Marshall, Mary Margaret 1959-
WhoMW 93
Marshall, Maryann Chorba 1952-
WhoFI 94
Marshall, Max S(kidmore) 1897-
WhAm 10
Marshall, Michael *Who 94*
Marshall, (Robert) Michael 1930- *Who 94*
Marshall, Michael Eric 1936- *Who 94*
Marshall, Michael John 1932- *Who 94*
Marshall, Mike *WhoHol 92*
Marshall, Mort d1979 *WhoHol 92*
Marshall, Nancy Haig 1932- *WhoAm 94*
Marshall, Natalie Junemann 1929-
WhoAm 94
Marshall, Nathaniel d1989 *WhoHol 92*
Marshall, Noel Hedley 1934- *Who 94*
Marshall, Norman Bertram 1915- *Who 94*
Marshall, Norman Sturgeon 1934-
WhoAmL 94
Marshall, Owen 1941- *RfGShF*
Marshall, P(eter) J(ames) 1933- *WrDr 94*
Marshall, Patricia *WhoHol 92*
Marshall, Patricia Mary 1930-
WhoAmP 93
Marshall, Patricia Prescott 1933-
WhoBlA 94
Marshall, Paul 1949- *WhoWest 94*
Marshall, Paul M. 1947- *WhoBlA 94*
Marshall, Paul Macklin 1923-
WhoAm 94, WhoFI 94
Marshall, Paule *DrAPF 93*
Marshall, Paule 1929- *BlkWr 2,
BlmGWL, WrDr 94*
Marshall, Paule Burke 1929- *WhoBlA 94*
Marshall, Penny 1942- *WhoCom,
WhoHol 92*
Marshall, Penny 1943- *IntMPA 94,
WhoAm 94*
Marshall, (C.) Penny 1943- *IntWW 93*
Marshall, Peter *IntMPA 94*
Marshall, Peter 1924- *IntWW 93*
Marshall, Peter 1930- *Who 94,
WhoHol 92*
Marshall, Peter (H.) 1946- *ConAu 140*
Marshall, Peter (Harold Reginald) 1924-
Who 94
Marshall, Peter Izod 1927- *Who 94*
Marshall, Peter James 1933- *Who 94*
Marshall, Peter W. 1947- *WhoAm 94*
Marshall, Philippa Frances 1920- *Who 94*
Marshall, Philips Williamson 1935-
WhoAm 94
Marshall, Pluria W., Sr. 1937- *WhoBlA 94*
Marshall, Pluria William, Jr. 1962-
WhoBlA 94
Marshall, Prentice H., Jr. 1952-
WhoAm 94, WhoAmL 94
Marshall, Prentice Henry 1926-
WhoAmL 94
Marshall, Ralph 1923-1984
WhoAmA 93N
Marshall, Ray d1986 *WhoHol 92*
Marshall, Ray 1928- *IntWW 93*
Marshall, Reese 1942- *WhoBlA 94*
Marshall, Rex d1983 *WhoHol 92*
Marshall, Richard 1947- *WhoAm 94*
Marshall, Richard Dale 1934-
WhoScEn 94
Marshall, Richard Donald 1947-
WhoAmA 93
Marshall, Richard Henry Lee 1945-
WhoAmL 94
Marshall, Richard Lee 1950- *WhoWest 94*
Marshall, Richard Paul, Jr. 1949-
WhoAmL 94
Marshall, Richard Treeger 1925-
WhoAmL 94
Marshall, Robert (Braithwaite) 1920-
Who 94
Marshall, Robert Charles 1931-
WhoAm 94, WhoFI 94
Marshall, Robert G. 1944- *WhoAmP 93*
Marshall, Robert Gerald 1919-
WhoAm 94
Marshall, Robert Herman 1929-
WhoAm 94, WhoWest 94
Marshall, Robert I. 1946- *WhoAmP 93*
Marshall, Robert Leckie 1913- *Who 94*

Marshall, Robert Leroy 1944- *WhoAmA 93*
Marshall, Robert Lewis 1939- *WhoAm 94*
Marshall, Robert William 1933- *WhoAmL 94*
Marshall, Roger Sydenham 1913- *Who 94*
Marshall, Rosalind Kay *ConAu 41NR, WrDr 94*
Marshall, Roy *Who 94*
Marshall, Roy 1920- *WrDr 94*
Marshall, (Oshley) Roy 1920- *Who 94*
Marshall, Russell *Who 94*
Marshall, (Cedric) Russell 1936- *Who 94*
Marshall, Russell Frank 1941- *WhoFI 94*
Marshall, Sally *DrAPF 93*
Marshall, Sarah 1933- *WhoHol 92*
Marshall, Schuyler Bailer, IV 1945- *WhoAm 94*
Marshall, Scott *WhoAm 94*
Marshall, Scott Mark 1958- *WhoMW 93*
Marshall, Sean 1954- *WhoHol 92*
Marshall, Sheila Hermes 1934- *WhoAm 94*
Marshall, Sherrie Patrice 1953- *WhoAm 94, WhoFI 94*
Marshall, Stanley 1923- *WhoAm 94*
Marshall, Stephanie Dee 1949- *WhoMW 93*
Marshall, Stephen Arnold 1944- *WhoAmL 94*
Marshall, Terrell 1908- *WhoAm 94*
Marshall, Thomas 1929- *WhoFI 94*
Marshall, Thomas Carlisle 1935- *WhoAm 94*
Marshall, Thomas Daniel 1929- *Who 94*
Marshall, Thomas David 1939- *WhoWest 94*
Marshall, Thomas E. 1941- *WhoAmA 93*
Marshall, Thomas O. 1920- *WhoAmP 93*
Marshall, Thomas Oliver, Jr. 1920- *WhoAm 94, WhoAmL 94*
Marshall, Thomas W. 1940- *WhoAmP 93*
Marshall, Thurgood *AfrAmAl 6 [port]*
Marshall, Thurgood d1993 *IntWW 93N, Who 94N*
Marshall, Thurgood 1908-1993 *AfrAmAl 6 [port], CurBio 93N, HisWorL [port], NewYTBS 93 [port], News 93-3, WhoBlA 94N*
Marshall, Thurgood, Jr. 1956- *WhoAmP 93, WhoAsA 94, WhoBlA 94*
Marshall, Timothy H. 1949- *WhoBlA 94*
Marshall, Tina d1980 *WhoHol 92*
Marshall, Tom 1938- *WrDr 94*
Marshall, Tom, Sr. 1927- *WhoBlA 94*
Marshall, Tonie *WhoHol 92*
Marshall, Trudy 1922- *WhoHol 92*
Marshall, Tully d1943 *WhoHol 92*
Marshall, Valerie Margaret 1945- *Who 94*
Marshall, Victor Fray 1913- *WhoAm 94*
Marshall, Victor R. 1947- *WhoAmP 93*
Marshall, Vincent de Paul 1943- *WhoAm 94*
Marshall, Warren 1922- *WhoBlA 94*
Marshall, Wayne Keith 1948- *WhoScEn 94*
Marshall, Wilber Buddyhia 1962- *WhoBlA 94*
Marshall, Wilfred L. 1935- *WhoBlA 94*
Marshall, William 1672?-1792 *DcNaB MP*
Marshall, William 1912- *Who 94*
Marshall, William 1915- *WhoHol 92*
Marshall, William 1924- *WhoHol 92*
Marshall, William, Jr. 1925- *WhoAm 94*
Marshall, William (Leonard) 1944- *WrDr 94*
Marshall, William A. 1943- *WhoAmL 94*
Marshall, William C. *WhoAmP 93*
Marshall, William Edward 1925- *WhoAm 94*
Marshall, William Emmett 1935- *WhoAm 94*
Marshall, William Eugene 1932- *WhoWest 94*
Marshall, William G. 1942- *WhoAmP 93*
Marshall, William Horace 1924- *WhoBlA 94*
Marshall, William Huston 1926- *WhoAmP 93*
Marshall, William Leitch 1925- *WhoScEn 94*
Marshall, William Stuart 1963- *WhoWest 94*
Marshall, Willis Henry *WhoScEn 94*
Marshall, Zena 1926- *IntMPA 94, WhoHol 92*
Marshall-Andrews, Robert Graham 1944- *Who 94*
Marshall Evans, David *Who 94*
Marshall-Goodell, Beverly Sue 1953- *WhoMW 93*
Marshall-Hall, George W(illiam) L(ouis) 1862-1915 *NewGrDO*
Marshall-Nadel, Nathalie 1932- *WhoAmA 93*
Marshall Of Goring, Baron 1932- *IntWW 93, Who 94*
Marshall-Reed, Diane 1950- *WhoMW 93*
Marshall-Walker, Denise Elizabeth 1952- *WhoBlA 94*
Marsham *Who 94*
Marshburn, Everett Lee 1948- *WhoBlA 94*
Marshburn, Sandra *DrAPF 93*
Marshe, Vera d1984 *WhoHol 92*
Marshella, Thomas Joseph 1957- *WhoFI 94*
Marshman, Homer Henry 1898- *WhAm 10*
Marsick, Armand (Louis Joseph) 1877-1959 *NewGrDO*
Marsico, Ronald S. 1947- *WhoAmP 93*
Marsigli, Giuseppe fl. 1677-1727 *NewGrDO*
Marsiglia, Stephen C. 1953- *WhoIns 94*
Marsiglio, Lorrie 1948- *WhoMW 93*
Marsik, Frederic John 1943- *WhoScEn 94*
Mars-Jones, Adam 1954- *GayLL, Who 94*
Mars-Jones, William (Lloyd) 1915- *Who 94*
Marsland, Edward Abson 1923- *Who 94*
Marsnik, Bernard J. 1934- *WhoAmP 93*
Marsolais, Barry Joseph 1955- *WhoFI 94*
Marsolais, Harold Raymond 1942- *WhoAm 94*
Marsollier des Vivetieres, Benoit-Joseph 1750-1817 *NewGrDO*
Marson, Aileen d1939 *WhoHol 92*
Marson, Anthony 1938- *Who 94*
Marson, Una 1905-1965 *BlmGWL*
Marsteller, William A. 1914-1987 *WhoAmA 93N*
Marsten, Richard *EncSF 93*
Marsten, Richard 1926- *WrDr 94*
Marstiller, Phyllis C. 1947- *WhoAm 94, WhoFI 94*
Marstini, Rosita d1948 *WhoHol 92*
Marston, Ann d1971 *WhoHol 92*
Marston, Bertram *WhoAmP 93*
Marston, Charles *WhoAm 94*
Marston, David W. 1942- *WhoAmL 94*
Marston, Edgar Jean, III 1939- *WhoAm 94*
Marston, Elizabeth Holloway d1993 *NewYTBS 93*
Marston, Jeff *WhoAmP 93*
Marston, Joel 1922- *WhoHol 92*
Marston, John d1962 *WhoHol 92*
Marston, John 1575?-1634 *BlmGEL*
Marston, John 1576?-1634 *IntDcT 2*
Marston, Merlin d1990 *WhoHol 92*
Marston, Michael 1936- *WhoAm 94, WhoFI 94, WhoWest 94*
Marston, Robert Andrew 1937- *WhoAm 94*
Marston, Robert E. 1922- *WhoAmP 93*
Marston, Robert Quarles 1923- *IntWW 93, WhoAm 94*
Marston, Ronald Clyde 1942- *WhoAm 94*
Marston, William Emmett 1928- *WhoAmL 94*
Marston-Scott, Mary Vesta 1924- *WhoAm 94*
Marszalek, Jeanne A. 1942- *WhoAmP 93*
Marszalek, John F 1939- *WrDr 94*
Marta, Ferenc 1929- *IntWW 93*
Martan, Joseph Rudolf 1949- *WhoAmL 94, WhoFI 94*
Martegani, Enzo 1950- *WhoScEn 94*
Marteka, Vincent James, Jr. 1936- *WhoAm 94*
Martel, Bonnie Gillespie 1940- *WhoFI 94*
Martel, Charles c. 690-741 *HisWorL [port]*
Martel, Eugene Harvey 1934- *WhoFI 94*
Martel, Eva Leona 1945- *WhoFI 94*
Martel, Gene 1906- *IntMPA 94*
Martel, June d1978 *WhoHol 92*
Martel, Laura *WhoHol 92*
Martel, Richard 1950- *WhoAmA 93*
Martel, William *WhoHol 92*
Martel, William 1927- *WhoAm 94*
Martell, Alphonse d1976 *WhoHol 92*
Martell, Arthur Earl 1916- *WhoAm 94*
Martell, Barbara Bentley *WhoAmA 93*
Martell, Donna 1927- *WhoHol 92*
Martell, Hugh (Colenso) 1912- *Who 94*
Martell, James *ConAu 42NR*
Martell, Karl d1966 *WhoHol 92*
Martell, Marty d1979 *WhoHol 92*
Martell, Ralph G. *DrAPF 93*
Martell, Saundra Adkins 1946- *WhoAmL 94*
Martellaro, Joseph Alexander 1924- *WrDr 94*
Martelli, Claudio 1944- *IntWW 93*
Martelli, George Ansley 1903- *WrDr 94*
Martelli, Linda M. d1993 *NewYTBS 93*
Martelli, Lisa Marie *WhoFI 94*
Martelli, Vincent A., Jr. 1964- *WhoFI 94*
Martello, Pier Jacopo 1665-1727 *NewGrDO*
Marten, Francis William 1916- *Who 94*
Marten, Gordon Cornelius 1935- *WhoAm 94*
Marten, Jacqueline (Lee) 1923- *ConAu 141*
Marten, Lu 1879-1970 *BlmGWL*
Marten, Michael 1947- *WrDr 94*
Martenet, May D. H. d1993 *NewYTBS 93*
Martens, Barbara Lynne 1953- *WhoMW 93*
Martens, Craig Colwell 1958- *WhoWest 94*
Martens, Don Walter 1934- *WhoAmL 94*
Martens, Donald Mathias 1925- *WhoMW 93*
Martens, Frederick Herman 1874-1932 *NewGrDO*
Martens, Frederick Hilbert 1921- *WhoScEn 94*
Martens, John Dale 1943- *WhoFI 94*
Martens, John George 1945- *WhoAmP 93*
Martens, Keith Otto 1939- *WhoAm 94*
Martens, Patricia Margaret 1962- *WhoMW 93*
Martens, Paul *EncSF 93*
Martens, Pauline *WhoAmP 93*
Martens, Ralph R. 1943- *IntMPA 94*
Martens, Roy Michael 1950- *WhoFI 94, WhoMW 93*
Martens, Waldo Gerald 1921- *WhoAmP 93*
Martens, Wilfried 1936- *IntWW 93*
Martenson, David Louis 1934- *WhoAmP 93*
Martenson, Edward Allen 1949- *WhoAm 94, WhoMW 93*
Martenson, Jan 1933- *IntWW 93*
Martensson, Arne 1951- *IntWW 93*
Martensson, Ingela Birgitta 1939- *WhoWomW 91*
Martenstein, Thomas Ewing 1949- *WhoAm 94, WhoFI 94*
Marteny, Perry 1954- *WhoMW 93*
Marter, Joan 1946- *WhoAmA 93*
Marth, Edward C. *WhoAmP 93*
Marth, Elmer Herman 1927- *WhoAm 94*
Marth, Frank *WhoHol 92*
Marthers, John James 1931- *WhoAmP 93*
Marti, Jose 1853-1895 *HispLC [port], HisWorL [port]*
Marti, Kurt 1936- *WhoAm 94*
Marti, Oscar R. 1942- *WhoWest 94*
Martic, Peter Ante 1938- *WhoScEn 94*
Marticelli, Joseph John 1921- *WhoAm 94, WhoAmL 94*
Marticorena, Ernesto Jesus 1941- *WhoScEn 94*
Marticorena, William M. 1952- *WhoAmL 94*
Marti de Cid, Dolores 1916- *WhoHisp 94*
Martika 1969- *WhoHisp 94*
Martin *Who 94*
Martin, A. W. 1926- *WhoAmP 93*
Martin, Abraham Nguyen 1946- *WhoAsA 94*
Martin, Agnes 1912- *IntWW 93, WhoAm 94*
Martin, Agnes Bernice 1912- *WhoAmA 93*
Martin, Alan Edward 1965- *WhoFI 94*
Martin, Alastair 1915- *BuCMET*
Martin, Albert Carey 1913- *WhoAm 94*
Martin, Albert Charles 1928- *WhoAm 94*
Martin, Albertus 1913- *WhAm 10*
Martin, Alexander 1740-1807 *WhAmRev*
Martin, Alexander Toedt 1931- *WhoAmA 93*
Martin, Alfred 1919- *WhoAm 94*
Martin, Allan A. 1945- *WhoAmL 94*
Martin, Allen 1937- *WhoAm 94, WhoAmP 93*
Martin, Allen William 1962- *WhoMW 93*
Martin, Alson Robert 1946- *WhoAm 94, WhoAmL 94*
Martin, Alvin Charles 1933- *WhoAm 94*
Martin, Amon Achilles, Jr. 1940- *WhoBlA 94*
Martin, Andra 1935- *WhoHol 92*
Martin, Andrea *WhoHol 92*
Martin, Andrea 1947- *WhoAm 94*
Martin, Andrew *Who 94*
Martin, (Robert) Andrew (St. George) 1914- *Who 94*
Martin, Andrew Douglas 1960- *WhoFI 94*
Martin, Angela M. Coker 1953- *WhoBlA 94*
Martin, Ann M(atthews) 1955- *ChILR 32 [port]*
Martin, Ann Matthews 1955- *WhoAm 94*
Martin, Anne-Marie *WhoHol 92*
Martin, Annie B. 1925- *WhoBlA 94*
Martin, Anthony D. 1944- *WhoAmL 94*
Martin, Anthony G. 1945- *WhoHisp 94*
Martin, Archer J. P. *WorInv*
Martin, Archer John Porter 1910- *IntWW 93, Who 94, WhoScEn 94*
Martin, Arnold Lee, Jr. 1939- *WhoBlA 94*
Martin, Arthur Bryan 1928- *Who 94*
Martin, Arthur Mead 1942- *WhoAm 94*
Martin, Asa d1979 *WhoHol 92*
Martin, Augustus Christian 1944- *WhoAmL 94*
Martin, Barbara Ann 1955- *WhoBlA 94*
Martin, Barbara Clare 1939- *WhoMW 93*
Martin, Barbara Fern 1948- *WhoAmP 93*
Martin, Barbara Lee 1941- *WhoMW 93*
Martin, Barney *WhoHol 92*
Martin, Barney 1925- *WhoWest 94*
Martin, Baron H. 1926- *WhoBlA 94*
Martin, Basil Douglas 1941- *WhoBlA 94*
Martin, Bernard Lee 1923- *WhoAm 94*
Martin, Bernard Murray 1935- *WhoAmA 93*
Martin, Bertha M. 1928- *WhoBlA 94*
Martin, Bill 1906- *BuCMET*
Martin, Bill 1943- *WhoAm 94, WhoAmA 93*
Martin, Bill, Jr. 1916- *WrDr 94*
Martin, Billy 1928-1989 *WhAm 10*
Martin, Blanche 1937- *WhoBlA 94*
Martin, Bobby L. 1948- *WhoFI 94*
Martin, Boe Willis 1940- *WhoAm 94*
Martin, Boyce Ficklen, Jr. 1935- *WhoAm 94, WhoAmL 94, WhoAmP 93*
Martin, Boyd A 1911- *WrDr 94*
Martin, Boyd Archer 1911- *WhoAm 94, WhoWest 94*
Martin, Bradford Neal 1952- *WhoAmL 94*
Martin, Bruce *Who 94*
Martin, (Robert) Bruce 1938- *Who 94*
Martin, Bruce Douglas 1934- *WhoAm 94*
Martin, Bryan Leslie 1954- *WhoWest 94*
Martin, Burchard V. 1933- *WhoAmL 94*
Martin, C. D. 1943- *WhoAmL 94*
Martin, Carl *EncSF 93*
Martin, Carl E. 1931- *WhoBlA 94*
Martin, Carl Nigel 1949- *WhoScEn 94*
Martin, Carol 1948- *WhoBlA 94*
Martin, Carol Lahaman 1926- *WhoAmP 93*
Martin, Carolyn Ann 1943- *WhoBlA 94*
Martin, Catherine 1847-1937 *BlmGWL*
Martin, Catherine Carol 1920- *WhoAmP 93*
Martin, Celia Lopez 1946- *WhoHisp 94*
Martin, Charles *DrAPF 93, WhoHol 92*
Martin, Charles Bee 1931- *WhoAmP 93*
Martin, Charles E. 1910- *WhoAmA 93*
Martin, Charles Edmund 1939- *Who 94*
Martin, Charles Edward, Sr. 1943- *WhoBlA 94*
Martin, Charles Raymond 1953- *WhoScEn 94*
Martin, Charles Wallace 1916- *WhoAm 94*
Martin, Charlie *Who 94*
Martin, Cheri Christian 1956- *WhoMW 93*
Martin, Chester Y. 1934- *WhoAm 94*
Martin, Chris 1954- *WhoAmA 93*
Martin, Chris King *WhoHol 92*
Martin, Chris-Pin d1953 *WhoHol 92*
Martin, Christine Kaler 1958- *WhoScEn 94*
Martin, Christopher *WhoBlA 94*
Martin, Christopher 1942- *WhoHol 92*
Martin, Christopher George 1938- *Who 94*
Martin, Christopher Sanford 1938- *Who 94*
Martin, Chrys Anne 1953- *WhoAmL 94*
Martin, Claire 1914- *BlmGWL*
Martin, Claire 1933- *SmATA 76 [port]*
Martin, Clarence F. *WhoAmP 93*
Martin, Clarence L. *WhoBlA 94*
Martin, Claude Raymond, Jr. 1932- *WhoAm 94, WhoMW 93*
Martin, Claudia *WhoHol 92*
Martin, Clyde Verne 1933- *WhoAm 94, WhoScEn 94, WhoWest 94*
Martin, Connie Ruth 1955- *WhoAmL 94, WhoWest 94*
Martin, Cornelius A. *WhoBlA 94*
Martin, Cortez Hezekiah *WhoBlA 94*
Martin, Crystal Ann 1963- *WhoFI 94*
Martin, Curtis Jerome 1949- *WhoBlA 94*
Martin, Cye d1972 *WhoHol 92*
Martin, Damon *WhoHol 92*
Martin, Dana 1946- *WhoAmP 93*
Martin, Daniel *WhoHol 92*
Martin, Daniel E. 1932- *WhoBlA 94*
Martin, Daniel E., Sr. 1932- *WhoAmP 93*
Martin, Daniel Ezekiel, Jr. 1963- *WhoBlA 94*
Martin, Daniel Tunnie 1953- *WhoWest 94*
Martin, Daniel William 1918- *WhoAm 94*
Martin, Darris Lee 1950- *WhoFI 94*
Martin, David *DrAPF 93*
Martin, David 1915- *WrDr 94*
Martin, David Alfred 1929- *Who 94, WrDr 94*
Martin, David Briton Hadden, Jr. 1946- *WhoAm 94, WhoAmL 94*
Martin, David Charles 1961- *WhoScEn 94*
Martin, David Edward 1939- *WhoAm 94*
Martin, David Eric 1965- *WhoMW 93*
Martin, David George 1945- *WhoAmL 94*
Martin, David H. 1947- *WhoIns 94*
Martin, David J. 1937- *WhoAmL 94*

Martin, David John Pattison 1945- *Who 94*
Martin, David L. 1947- *WhoAmL 94*
Martin, David Louis 1950- *WhoFI 94, WhoWest 94*
Martin, David Nathan 1930- *WhoAm 94*
Martin, David O'Brien 1944- *WhoAmP 93*
Martin, David R. 1931- *WhoFI 94*
Martin, David Robert 1960- *WhoMW 93*
Martin, David S. 1937- *ConAu 142*
Martin, David Stone 1913-1992 *AnObit 1992, WhAm 10*
Martin, David Weir 1954- *Who 94*
Martin, David William, Jr. 1941- *WhoAm 94*
Martin, Dean 1917- *IntMPA 94, IntWW 93, WhoAm 94, WhoHol 92*
See Also Martin and Lewis *WhoCom*
Martin, Dean Paul d1987 *WhoHol 92*
Martin, Deana *WhoHol 92*
Martin, Del 1921- *GayLL*
Martin, Dennis Charles 1960- *WhoMW 93, WhoScEn 94*
Martin, Denny Ross 1952- *WhoAmL 94*
Martin, Derek 1923- *WhoAm 94*
Martin, Derek H. 1929- *Who 94*
Martin, Deric Kriston 1959- *WhoFI 94, WhoWest 94*
Martin, Derrel Leroy 1952- *WhoMW 93*
Martin, Dewey 1923- *IntMPA 94, WhoHol 92*
Martin, Dianne L. 1940- *WhoAmA 93*
Martin, Dick 1923- *WhoHol 92*
See Also Rowan and Martin *WhoCom*
Martin, Dom 1950- *WhoWest 94*
Martin, Don P. 1949- *WhoAm 94, WhoAmL 94*
Martin, Donald Creagh 1937- *WhoMW 93*
Martin, Donald E. 1937- *WhoIns 94*
Martin, Donald Leon 1920- *WhoAmL 94*
Martin, Donald Ray 1915- *WhoAm 94*
Martin, Donald Walter 1934- *WhoWest 94*
Martin, Donald William 1921- *WhoAm 94*
Martin, Donna Lee 1935- *WhoAm 94, WhoMW 93*
Martin, Dorcas Eglestone fl. 16th cent.- *BlmGWL*
Martin, Doris Ellen 1927- *WhoWest 94*
Martin, Doris-Marie Constable 1941- *WhoAmA 93*
Martin, Dorothy Regina 1943- *WhoMW 93*
Martin, Doug 1947- *WhoAmA 93*
Martin, Doug 1957- *WhoBlA 94*
Martin, Douglas Grant 1950- *WhoFI 94*
Martin, Douglas Jon 1959- *WhoMW 93*
Martin, Douglas K. *WhoAmP 93*
Martin, Duane C. 1949- *WhoAmL 94*
Martin, D'Urville d1984 *WhoHol 92*
Martin, D'Urville 1939- *WhoBlA 94*
Martin, Dwight Dee 1961- *WhoMW 93*
Martin, Edgar Thomas 1918- *WhoAm 94*
Martin, Edie d1964 *WhoHol 92*
Martin, Edith Waisbrot 1945- *WhoAm 94*
Martin, Edmund F. d1993 *NewYTBS 93*
Martin, Edmund F(ible) 1902-1993 *CurBio 93N*
Martin, Edmund Fible d1993 *IntWW 93N*
Martin, Edmund Fible 1902-1993 *EncABHB 9*
Martin, Edward 1936- *WhoBlA 94*
Martin, Edward Anthony 1935- *WhoBlA 94*
Martin, Edward Brian 1936- *WhoMW 93*
Martin, Edward Curtis, Jr. 1928- *WhoAm 94*
Martin, Edward Fontaine 1942- *WhoAm 94, WhoAmL 94*
Martin, Edward J., Jr. 1934- *WhoIns 94*
Martin, Edward Lee 1954- *WhoFI 94*
Martin, Edward Williford 1929- *WhoBlA 94*
Martin, Edwin Dennis 1920- *IntMPA 94*
Martin, Edwin John 1934- *WhoAm 94*
Martin, Edwin McCammon 1908- *WhoAmP 93*
Martin, Edwin McCammon, Jr. 1942- *WhoAm 94*
Martin, Edwin Pruitt 1938- *WhoAmL 94*
Martin, Edwin Webb 1917-1991 *WhAm 10*
Martin, Elaine M. 1942- *WhoAmL 94*
Martin, Elisa S. 1931- *WhoAmP 93*
Martin, Elizabeth A(nn) 1945- *WrDr 94*
Martin, Elizabeth Mason 1934- *WhoAmP 93*
Martin, Ellen M. 1947- *WhoAmL 94*
Martin, Elliot Edwards 1924- *WhoAm 94*
Martin, Elmer P. 1946- *WhoBlA 94*
Martin, Eric Lewis 1953- *WhoAmL 94*
Martin, Ernest D. 1921- *WhoAmP 93*
Martin, Ernest Douglass 1928- *WhoBlA 94*
Martin, Ernest George Buckley 1948- *WhoAmP 93*
Martin, Ernest H. 1919- *WhoAm 94*
Martin, Ernest Lionel 1937- *WhoFI 94*
Martin, Ernest Walter *WrDr 94*
Martin, Estrella Martinez 1945- *WhoHisp 94*
Martin, Evelyn B. 1908- *WhoBlA 94*
Martin, Evelyn Fairfax 1926- *Who 94*
Martin, F. David 1920- *WrDr 94*
Martin, F(rancis) X(avier) 1922- *WrDr 94*
Martin, Fletcher 1904-1979 *WhoAmA 93N*
Martin, Frances 1948- *WhoBlA 94*
Martin, Frank 1890-1974 *NewGrDO*
Martin, Frank 1946- *Who 94*
Martin, Frank C., II 1954- *WhoBlA 94*
Martin, Frank E(dward) 1895- *WhAm 10*
Martin, Frank Kieffer 1938- *WhoAm 94, WhoAmL 94, WhoAmP 93*
Martin, Frank Lee, III 1947- *WhoMW 93*
Martin, Frank Scott 1960- *WhoScEn 94*
Martin, Frank T. 1950- *WhoBlA 94*
Martin, Frank Vernon 1921- *Who 94*
Martin, Franklin Farnarwance 1950- *WhoBlA 94*
Martin, Fred 1925- *WhoAm 94*
Martin, Fred 1926- *WhoBlA 94*
Martin, Fred 1927- *WhoAm 94*
Martin, Fred Thomas 1927- *WhoAmA 93*
Martin, Freddie Anthony 1945- *WhoScEn 94*
Martin, Freddy d1983 *WhoHol 92*
Martin, Frederick Noel 1931- *WhoAm 94*
Martin, Frederick Royal 1919- *Who 94*
Martin, Fredric 1917- *WrDr 94*
Martin, Gary DeWayne 1954- *WhoWest 94*
Martin, Gary J. 1957- *WhoMW 93*
Martin, Gary O. 1944- *WhoAm 94*
Martin, Gary Wayne 1946- *WhoAm 94, WhoAmL 94*
Martin, Geoffrey *Who 94*
Martin, (Thomas) Geoffrey 1940- *Who 94*
Martin, Geoffrey Haward 1928- *Who 94, WrDr 94*
Martin, Geoffrey John 1934- *WrDr 94*
Martin, Geoffrey Thorndike 1934- *Who 94*
Martin, George *WhoHol 92*
Martin, George 1940- *WhoWest 94*
Martin, George Alexander, Jr. 1943- *WhoBlA 94*
Martin, George Coleman 1910- *WhoAm 94*
Martin, George Conner 1933- *WhoAm 94*
Martin, George Dwight 1953- *WhoBlA 94*
Martin, George Elwood 1946- *WhoAmL 94*
Martin, George Francis 1944- *WhoAm 94*
Martin, George G. 1943- *WhoAmL 94*
Martin, George Gilmore 1944- *WhoAmL 94*
Martin, George Henry 1926- *Who 94*
Martin, George J., Jr. 1942- *WhoAm 94, WhoAmL 94*
Martin, George Joseph 1932- *WhoFI 94*
Martin, George M. 1927- *WhoAm 94, WhoScEn 94, WhoWest 94*
Martin, George R(aymond) R(ichard) 1948- *EncSF 93, WrDr 94*
Martin, George Raymond Richard 1948- *WhoAm 94, WhoWest 94*
Martin, George Reilly 1933- *WhoScEn 94*
Martin, George Whitney 1926- *WhoAm 94, WrDr 94*
Martin, George Wilbur 1930- *WhoAm 94*
Martin, Gerard P. 1944- *WhoAmL 94*
Martin, Gertrude S. *WhoBlA 94*
Martin, Gladys Irene 1929- *WhoAmP 93*
Martin, Gordon Eugene 1925- *WhoWest 94*
Martin, Gordon Mather 1915- *WhoAm 94*
Martin, Grace B. *DrAPF 93*
Martin, Graham Anderson 1912-1990 *WhAm 10*
Martin, Graham Dunstan 1932- *EncSF 93*
Martin, Greg D. 1954- *WhoAmP 93*
Martin, Gregory Keith 1956- *WhoAmL 94*
Martin, Guillermo Joaquin 1942- *WhoHisp 94*
Martin, Guy 1911- *WhoAm 94*
Martin, Guy Richard 1942- *WhoAm 94, WhoAmL 94*
Martin, Gwendolyn Rose 1926- *WhoAmP 93, WhoBlA 94*
Martin, H. Gary 1938- *WhoMW 93*
Martin, Harold 1918- *WhoAmP 93*
Martin, Harold B. 1928- *WhoBlA 94*
Martin, Harold Clark 1917- *WhoAm 94*
Martin, Harold Eugene 1923- *WhoAm 94*
Martin, Harry Corpening 1920- *WhoAm 94, WhoAmL 94, WhoAmP 93*
Martin, Harry Lee 1956- *WhoScEn 94*
Martin, Helen 1916- *WhoHol 92*
Martin, Helen Dorothy *WhoBlA 94*
Martin, Henri-Jean 1924- *IntWW 93*
Martin, Henry Alan 1949- *WhoAmL 94*
Martin, Henry James 1910- *Who 94*
Martin, Herbert J. 1940- *WhoAmL 94*
Martin, Herbert Woodward *DrAPF 93*
Martin, Herman Henry, Jr. 1961- *WhoBlA 94*
Martin, Hilda C. 1934- *WhoAmP 93*
Martin, Horace Feleciano 1931- *WhoScEn 94*
Martin, Hosea L. 1937- *WhoBlA 94*
Martin, Hoyle Henry 1921- *WhoBlA 94*
Martin, Hugh Davie 1909- *WrDr 94*
Martin, I. Maximillian *WhoBlA 94*
Martin, Ian d1981 *WhoHol 92*
Martin, Ian 1946- *Who 94*
Martin, Ian Alexander 1935- *Who 94, WhoAm 94*
Martin, Ignacio 1928- *WhoHisp 94*
Martin, Ionis Bracy 1936- *AfrAmAl 6, WhoBlA 94*
Martin, Irene d1973 *WhoHol 92*
Martin, Ivy Ruth 1956- *WhoAmL 94*
Martin, J. Landis 1946- *WhoAm 94, WhoFI 94*
Martin, J. Lockard *WhoHol 92*
Martin, J. Patrick 1938- *WhoAm 94*
Martin, Jack Lee 1952- *WhoFI 94*
Martin, Jacques d1992 *IntWW 93N*
Martin, James *WhoAmP 93*
Martin, James (Thomas) 1933- *WrDr 94*
Martin, James Addison, Jr. 1945- *WhoAmL 94*
Martin, James Alfred, Jr. 1917- *WhoAm 94*
Martin, James Arthur 1944- *WhAm 10, WhoScEn 94*
Martin, James Brown 1953- *Who 94*
Martin, James C. 1938- *WhoBlA 94*
Martin, James Cullen 1928- *WhoAm 94, WhoScEn 94*
Martin, James Eugene 1953- *WhoIns 94*
Martin, James Francis 1945- *WhoAmP 93*
Martin, James Franklin 1929- *WhoWest 94*
Martin, James Gilbert 1926- *WhoAm 94*
Martin, James Glasgow, III 1947- *WhoAmL 94*
Martin, James Grubbs 1935- *IntWW 93, WhoAm 94, WhoAmP 93*
Martin, James Hanley 1960- *WhoAmL 94*
Martin, James John, Jr. 1936- *WhoAm 94*
Martin, James Kirby 1943- *WhoAm 94*
Martin, James Larence 1940- *WhoBlA 94*
Martin, James Lee 1948- *WhoAmP 93*
Martin, James M. 1946- *WhoAmL 94*
Martin, James Patrick 1946- *WhoWest 94*
Martin, James Paul 1929- *WhoAmP 93*
Martin, James R. 1937- *WhoAmL 94*
Martin, James R. 1941- *WhoHisp 94*
Martin, James Robert 1943- *WhoAm 94*
Martin, James Russell 1947- *WhoAm 94, WhoAmL 94*
Martin, James S. 1936- *WhoIns 94*
Martin, James Smith 1936 *WhoAm 94, WhoFI 94*
Martin, James Tyrone 1942- *WhoBlA 94*
Martin, James W. 1932- *WhoBlA 94*
Martin, James W(alter) 1893- *WhAm 10*
Martin, James Walter 1927- *WhoScEn 94*
Martin, James William 1949- *WhoAmL 94*
Martin, Jane 1943- *WhoAmA 93*
Martin, Jane Roland 1929- *ConAu 43NR*
Martin, Janet 1927- *Who 94*
Martin, Janette G. *DrAPF 93*
Martin, Janice R. *WhoBlA 94*
Martin, Janis 1939- *NewGrDO*
Martin, Jared 1940- *WhoHol 92*
Martin, Jay Herbert 1935- *WhoAm 94*
Martin, Jean *WhoHol 92*
Martin, Jean Baptiste fl. 1748-1757 *NewGrDO*
Martin, (Nicolas-)Jean-Blaise 1768-1837 *NewGrDO*
Martin, Jean Claude 1929- *WhoAm 94*
Martin, Jeffery Allen 1967- *WhoBlA 94*
Martin, Jeffery Willie 1961- *WhoFI 94*
Martin, Jeffrey Alan 1953- *WhoFI 94, WhoScEn 94*
Martin, Jeffrey Edward 1956- *WhoAmL 94*
Martin, Jeffry Ray 1954- *WhoWest 94*
Martin, Jerald Lynn 1953- *WhoHisp 94*
Martin, Jerry *WhoAm 94*
Martin, Jerry C. 1932- *WhoAm 94*
Martin, Jim *DrAPF 93*
Martin, Joan Callaham 1930- *WhoAm 94*
Martin, Joan M. *DrAPF 93*
Martin, Joanne 1956- *WhoMW 93*
Martin, Joanne Diodato 1959- *WhoScEn 94*
Martin, Joanne Lea 1954- *WhoScEn 94*
Martin, Joanne Mitchell 1947- *WhoBlA 94*
Martin, Joe 1948- *WhoAmP 93*
Martin, Joel Jerome 1939- *WhoScEn 94*
Martin, John *WhoHol 92*
Martin, John d1933 *WhoHol 92*
Martin, John (Edward Ludgate) 1918- *Who 94*
Martin, John Alfred 1921- *WhoAmP 93*
Martin, John Allen 1947- *WhoAmP 93*
Martin, John Brand 1937- *WhoScEn 94*
Martin, John Bruce 1922- *WhoAm 94*
Martin, John Charles 1943- *WhoAmL 94*
Martin, John Charles 1951- *WhoFI 94*
Martin, John Christopher 1926- *Who 94*
Martin, John David 1945- *WhoFI 94*
Martin, John E. 1945- *WhoWest 94*
Martin, John Edward 1916- *WhoAm 94, WhoWest 94*
Martin, John Edward 1937- *WhoMW 93*
Martin, John Francis 1943- *WhoAmL 94*
Martin, John Francis Ryde 1943- *Who 94*
Martin, John Gerard 1949- *WhoMW 93*
Martin, John Gustin 1928- *WhoAm 94, WhoFI 94*
Martin, John H.E. 1928- *WhoFI 94*
Martin, John Holland d1993 *NewYTBS 93*
Martin, John Hugh 1918- *WhoAm 94*
Martin, John J. 1934- *WhoAm 94*
Martin, John J. 1940- *WhoIns 94*
Martin, John Joseph 1922- *WhoAmP 93*
Martin, John Joseph 1938- *WhoAm 94*
Martin, John Joseph Charles 1940- *IntWW 93*
Martin, John L. 1941- *WhoAm 94, WhoAmP 93*
Martin, John M. 1950- *WhoAmL 94*
Martin, John Powell 1925- *Who 94*
Martin, John Richard 1951- *WhoMW 93, WhoScEn 94*
Martin, John Rupert 1916- *WhoAmA 93*
Martin, John S., Jr. 1935- *WhoAm 94, WhoAmL 94*
Martin, John Sharp Buchanan 1946- *Who 94*
Martin, John Sinclair 1931- *Who 94*
Martin, John Thomas 1920- *WhoBlA 94*
Martin, John Thomas 1924- *WhoMW 93*
Martin, John Vandeleur 1948- *Who 94*
Martin, John W. 1924- *WhoBlA 94*
Martin, John William 1946- *WhoMW 93*
Martin, John William, Jr. 1936- *WhoAm 94, WhoAmL 94, WhoFI 94*
Martin, John William Prior 1934- *Who 94*
Martin, Johnny Benjamin 1947- *WhoFI 94*
Martin, Jonathan Arthur 1942- *Who 94*
Martín, Jorge Luis 1953- *WhoHisp 94*
Martin, Jose Ginoris 1941- *WhoScEn 94*
Martin, Joseph, Jr. 1915- *WhoAm 94, WhoAmL 94, WhoFI 94, WhoWest 94*
Martin, Joseph Boyd 1938- *WhoAm 94, WhoWest 94*
Martin, Joseph F. 1943- *WhoAmL 94*
Martin, Joseph Plumb c. 1760-1850 *WhAmRev*
Martin, Joseph Ramsey 1930- *WhoAm 94*
Martin, Joseph Robert 1947- *WhoFI 94*
Martin, Joseph W. 1884-1968 *HisDcKW*
Martin, Joshua Wesley, III 1944- *WhoBlA 94*
Martin, Josiah 1737-1786 *WhAmRev*
Martin, Judith 1938- *WrDr 94*
Martin, Judith Sylvia 1938- *WhoAm 94*
Martin, Judson Phillips 1921- *WhoAm 94*
Martin, Julia M. 1924- *WhoBlA 94*
Martin, Julie (Breyer) 1938- *WrDr 94*
Martin, June Johnson Caldwell *WhoWest 94*
Martin, Kate Abbott 1952- *WhoAmL 94*
Martin, Kathleen Minder 1957- *WhoAmL 94*
Martin, Kathleen Suzanne 1950- *WhoAmL 94*
Martin, Kathryn Lee 1935- *WhoWest 94*
Martin, Keith 1953- *WhoAm 94*
Martin, Keith Morrow 1911-1983 *WhoAmA 93N*
Martin, Kenneth David 1952- *WhoWest 94*
Martin, Kenneth Douglas 1940- *WhoAm 94*
Martin, Kenneth Frank 1948- *WhoFI 94*
Martin, Kenneth Peter, Mrs. *Who 94*
Martin, Kevin Paul 1954- *WhoScEn 94*
Martin, Kiel d1990 *WhAm 10, WhoHol 92*
Martin, Knox 1923- *WhoAmA 93*
Martin, L. Morgan *WhoAmP 93*
Martin, Larry A. 1957- *WhoAmP 93*
Martin, Larry J. 1952- *WhoScEn 94*
Martin, Larry Jay 1943- *WhoAmL 94*
Martin, Larry Kenneth 1939- *WhoAmA 93*
Martin, Laura Belle 1915- *WhoMW 93*
Martin, Laurence (Woodward) 1928- *WrDr 94*
Martin, Laurence Woodward 1928- *IntWW 93, Who 94*
Martin, Lawrence Raymond 1935- *WhoBlA 94*
Martin, Lee *DrAPF 93*

Martin, Lee 1920- *WhoAm 94, WhoMW 93*
Martin, Lee 1938- *WhoBlA 94*
Martin, Lenore Marie 1963- *WhoScEn 94*
Martin, Leonard Austin, II 1949- *WhoWest 94*
Martin, Leonard Gilman 1937- *WhoWest 94*
Martin, Leonard Louis 1952- *WhoScEn 94*
Martin, Lequita Jerelene Alexander 1933- *WhoAmP 93*
Martin, LeRoy 1929- *WhoBlA 94*
Martin, Leslie *IntWW 93, Who 94*
Martin, (John) Leslie 1908- *IntWW 93, Who 94*
Martin, Leslie Vaughan 1919- *Who 94*
Martin, Lewis d1969 *WhoHol 92*
Martin, Lock d1959 *WhoHol 92*
Martin, Loretta Marsh 1933- *WhoAmA 93*
Martin, Lori 1947- *WhoHol 92*
Martin, Louis E. 1912- *WhoBlA 94*
Martin, Louis Edward 1928- *WhoAm 94*
Martin, Louis Frank 1951- *WhoScEn 94*
Martin, Lucille Caiar 1918- *WhoAmA 93*
Martin, Lucy Z. 1941- *WhoAm 94*
Martin, Ludwig Markus 1909- *IntWW 93*
Martín, Luis 1927- *WhoHisp 94*
Martin, Luther 1744-1826 *WhAmRev*
Martin, Lynn *DrAPF 93*
Martin, Lynn 1939- *IntWW 93*
Martin, Lynn Morley 1939- *WhoAmP 93, WhoWomW 91*
Martin, Lys 1957- *WhoAmA 93*
Martin, Malcolm Elliot 1935- *WhoAm 94, WhoAmL 94*
Martin, Manuel, Jr. 1934- *WhoHisp 94*
Martin, Marcella *WhoHol 92*
Martin, Margaret F. 1932- *WhoAmP 93*
Martin, Margaret M. 1940- *WhoAmA 93*
Martin, Maria Sonia 1951- *WhoHisp 94*
Martin, Marion d1985 *WhoHol 92*
Martin, Marjorie 1942- *WrDr 94*
Martin, Mark 1914- *WhoAm 94*
Martin, Mark William 1969- *WhoWest 94*
Martin, Marsha Ann 1952- *WhoAm 94*
Martin, Marshall Allen 1943- *WhoMW 93*
Martin, Mary d1990 *WhoHol 92*
Martin, Mary 1913?-1990 *ConTFT 11, WhAm 10*
Martin, Mary Agnes 1925- *WhoAmP 93*
Martin, Mary-Anne 1943- *WhoAm 94*
Martin, Mary E. Howell 1941- *WhoBlA 94*
Martin, Mary Ellen *WhoAmP 93*
Martin, Mary Finch 1916- *WhoAmA 93*
Martin, Mary Lenore 1925- *WhoMW 93*
Martin, Mary Priest 1933- *WhoMW 93*
Martin, Maurice John 1929- *WhoAm 94*
Martin, Maxine Smith 1944- *WhoBlA 94*
Martin, McKinley C. 1936- *WhoBlA 94*
Martin, Melissa Carol 1951- *WhoWest 94*
Martin, Melissa Diana 1967- *WhoMW 93*
Martin, Michael David 1946- *WhoWest 94*
Martin, Michael Dennis 1945- *WhoAm 94, WhoAmL 94*
Martin, Michael Eugene 1947- *WhoFI 94*
Martin, Michael John 1945- *Who 94*
Martin, Michael Ray 1952- *WhoScEn 94*
Martin, Michael Rex 1952- *WhoAmL 94*
Martin, Michael Robert Akers 1964- *WhoWest 94*
Martin, Michael Townsend 1941- *WhoFI 94*
Martín, Miguel D. 1949- *WhoHisp 94*
Martin, Miguel Lazaro 1952- *WhoHisp 94*
Martin, Mike 1960- *WhoAmP 93*
Martin, Millicent 1934- *IntMPA 94, WhoHol 92*
Martin, Milton T., Jr. 1939- *WhoAm 94*
Martin, Mona *WhoAmP 93*
Martin, Montez Cornelius, Jr. 1940- *WhoBlA 94*
Martin, Murray Simpson 1928- *WhoAm 94*
Martin, Nan *WhoHol 92*
Martin, Nancy L. 1931- *WhoWest 94*
Martin, Nathaniel Frizell Grafton 1928- *WhoAm 94*
Martin, Ned Harold 1945- *WhoAm 94*
Martin, Neil 1942- *WhoAm 94, WhoAmL 94*
Martin, Noel 1922- *WhoAm 94*
Martin, Oliver *ConAu 140*
Martin, Oliver Samuel 1919- *Who 94*
Martin, Oscar Thaddeus 1908- *WhoAm 94*
Martin, Osvaldo Jose 1952- *WhoScEn 94*
Martin, Owen d1960 *WhoHol 92*
Martin, Paige Arlene 1951- *WhoAmL 94*
Martin, Pamela Sue 1953- *IntMPA 94, WhoHol 92*
Martin, Patricia *DrAPF 93*
Martin, Patricia Elizabeth 1951- *WhoBlA 94*
Martin, Patrick 1941- *WhoAm 94*
Martin, Patrick William 1916- *Who 94*
Martin, Patsy C. 1938- *WhoFI 94*
Martin, Paul *DrAPF 93*
Martin, Paul 1903-1992 *AnObit 1992*
Martin, Paul 1938- *WhoFI 94*
Martin, Paul 1950- *WhoMW 93*
Martin, Paul Cecil 1931- *WhoAm 94, WhoScEn 94*
Martin, Paul Edward 1914- *WhoAm 94*
Martin, Paul Edward 1928- *WhoAmL 94, WhoFI 94*
Martin, Paul Elliott 1897- *WhAm 10*
Martin, Paul Joseph 1936- *WhoAm 94*
Martin, Paul Joseph James d1992 *IntWW 93N*
Martin, Paul W. 1940- *WhoBlA 94*
Martin, Pedro A. 1949- *WhoAmL 94*
Martin, Peggy 1947- *WhoAmP 93*
Martin, Pepper *WhoHol 92*
Martin, Peppy 1946- *WhoAmP 93*
Martin, Perry Clyde 1950- *WhoWest 94*
Martin, Pete *WhoHisp 94*
Martin, Peter *Who 94*
Martin, Peter 1890- *EncSF 93*
Martin, (Roy) Peter 1931- *Who 94, WrDr 94*
Martin, Peter Anthony 1946- *Who 94*
Martin, Peter C. 1928- *WhoAmP 93*
Martin, Peter Lawrence de Carteret 1920- *Who 94*
Martin, Peter Lewis 1918- *Who 94*
Martin, Peter William 1939- *WhoAm 94*
Martin, Phil *WhoAmP 93*
Martin, Phillip Dwight 1943- *WhoMW 93*
Martin, Phillip Hammond 1940- *WhoAm 94*
Martin, Phyllis R(odgers) *WrDr 94*
Martin, Pierre-Emile 1824-1915 *WorInv*
Martin, Preston 1923- *WhoAm 94, WhoFI 94, WhoWest 94*
Martin, Quinn William 1948- *WhoAm 94, WhoAmL 94*
Martin, R. Brad *WhoAmP 93*
Martin, R(obert) Bruce 1929- *IntWW 93*
Martin, R. Eden 1940- *WhoAm 94, WhoAmL 94*
Martin, R. Keith 1933- *WhoAm 94*
Martin, Rafael *WhoHisp 94*
Martin, Ralph (Guy) 1920- *WrDr 94*
Martin, Ralph C., II *WhoBlA 94*
Martin, Ralph Drury 1947- *WhoAmL 94*
Martin, Ralph Guy 1920- *WhoAm 94*
Martin, Ralph Harres 1926- *WhoFI 94*
Martin, Ray 1936- *WhoAm 94, WhoFI 94, WhoWest 94*
Martin, Rayfus 1930- *WhoBlA 94*
Martin, Raymond Bruce 1934- *WhoMW 93*
Martin, Raymond Charles 1938- *WhoMW 93*
Martin, Raymond Edward 1957- *WhoFI 94*
Martin, Raymond Leslie 1926- *Who 94*
Martin, Raymond Walter 1952- *WhoAmL 94*
Martin, Rebecca Reist 1952- *WhoAm 94*
Martin, Reddrick Linwood 1934- *WhoBlA 94*
Martin, Reginald 1956- *BlkWr 2*
Martin, Remi *WhoHol 92*
Martin, Renee Cohen 1928- *WhoFI 94*
Martin, Rhona 1922- *WrDr 94*
Martin, Riccardo 1874-1952 *NewGrDO*
Martin, Richard 1917- *WhoHol 92*
Martin, Richard (Harrison) 1946- *WhoAmA 93*
Martin, Richard Cornish 1936- *WhoBlA 94*
Martin, Richard Douglas 1959- *WhoScEn 94*
Martin, Richard Graham 1932- *Who 94*
Martin, Richard Harrison 1946- *WhoAm 94*
Martin, Richard Henry 1947- *WhoAmL 94*
Martin, Richard J. *DrAPF 93*
Martin, Richard Jay 1946- *WhoAm 94*
Martin, Richard Kelley 1952- *WhoAm 94, WhoAmL 94*
Martin, Richard L. 1932- *WhoAm 94*
Martin, Richard Warren 1933- *WhoMW 93*
Martin, Robert A. *WhoFI 94*
Martin, Robert Anthony 1960- *WhoScEn 94*
Martin, Robert Bernard 1918- *WrDr 94*
Martin, Robert Bruce 1929- *WhoAm 94, WhoScEn 94*
Martin, Robert Burton 1935- *WhoWest 94*
Martin, Robert C. 1926- *WhoIns 94*
Martin, Robert David 1944- *WhoAm 94, WhoAmL 94*
Martin, Robert Edward 1928- *WhoMW 93*
Martin, Robert Edward 1948- *WhoBlA 94*
Martin, Robert Edward, Jr. 1931- *WhoAm 94*
Martin, Robert Finlay, Jr. 1925- *WhoAm 94*
Martin, Robert Francis 1942- *WhoFI 94*
Martin, Robert Frederick, Sr. 1942- *WhoMW 93*
Martin, Robert Gregory 1959- *WhoWest 94*
Martin, Robert J. 1947- *WhoAmP 93*
Martin, Robert L. 1912- *WhoAmP 93*
Martin, Robert Logan 1950- *Who 94*
Martin, Robert Michael 1922- *WhoWest 94*
Martin, Robert Michael, Jr. 1921- *WhoAmL 94*
Martin, Robert R. *WhoAmP 93*
Martin, Robert Richard 1910- *WhoAm 94*
Martin, Robert Roy 1927- *WhoAm 94*
Martin, Robert William 1936- *WhoAm 94*
Martin, Robin Geoffrey 1921- *Who 94*
Martin, Roblee Boettcher 1922- *WhoAm 94*
Martin, Rod *EncSF 93*
Martin, Rod 1954- *WhoBlA 94*
Martin, Roderick 1940- *WrDr 94*
Martin, Roderick Harry 1961- *WhoScEn 94*
Martin, Rodger C. *DrAPF 93*
Martin, Rodney, Jr. 1952- *WhoIns 94*
Martin, Roger *WhoHisp 94*
Martin, Roger 1925- *WhoAmA 93*
Martin, Roger Allen 1934- *WhoAmP 93*
Martin, Roger Bond 1936- *WhoAm 94*
Martin, Roger H(arry) 1943- *WrDr 94*
Martin, Roger Harry 1943- *WhoAm 94*
Martin, Roger John Adam 1941- *Who 94*
Martin, Roger Lawrence 1958- *WhoAm 94*
Martin, Roger Leon Rene 1915- *IntWW 93*
Martin, Roland M. 1949- *WhoAmP 93*
Martin, Ronald 1919- *Who 94*
Martin, Ronald Lavern 1922- *WhoAm 94*
Martin, Ronald Michael 1948- *WhoAmL 94*
Martin, Rose Kocsis 1928- *WhoAmL 94*
Martin, Rosemary *WhoHol 92*
Martin, Rosetta P. 1930- *WhoBlA 94*
Martin, Ross d1981 *WhoHol 92*
Martin, Roy *Who 94*
Martin, Roy Butler, Jr. 1921- *WhoAm 94*
Martin, Roy Erik 1949- *WhoScEn 94*
Martin, Ruby Julene Wheeler 1931- *WhoBlA 94*
Martin, Rudolph G. 1916- *WhoBlA 94*
Martin, Rudy 1951- *WhoWest 94*
Martin, Russell *DrAPF 93*
Martin, Russell F. 1929- *WhoBlA 94*
Martin, Russell Lee 1947- *WhoMW 93*
Martin, Sallie d1988 *WhoHol 92*
Martin, Sally 1936- *WhoAmP 93*
Martin, Sam 1920- *WhoAm 94*
Martin, Samuel 1918- *WhoBlA 94*
Martin, Samuel Frederick Radcliffe 1918- *Who 94*
Martin, Sara d1955 *WhoHol 92*
Martin, Scott Graddy 1947- *WhoWest 94*
Martin, Scott Lawrence 1960- *WhoScEn 94*
Martin, Shedrick M., Jr. 1927- *WhoBlA 94*
Martin, Shirley *WhoWomW 91*
Martin, Sidney, Sr. 1919- *WhoAmP 93*
Martin, Simone 1943- *WhoWomW 91*
Martin, Siva 1925- *WhoAmL 94*
Martin, Skip *WhoHol 92*
Martin, Slater 1925- *BasBi*
Martin, Stanley A. 1955- *WhoAmL 94*
Martin, Stanley William Frederick 1934- *Who 94*
Martin, Stefan 1936- *WhoAmA 93*
Martin, Stephen David 1947- *WhoAmL 94*
Martin, Stephen Harcourt 1952- *Who 94*
Martin, Stephen Holliday 1956- *WhoAmP 93*
Martin, Stephen James 1930- *WhoAm 94*
Martin, Stephen John 1948- *WhoMW 93*
Martin, Stephen Paul 1948- *Who 94*
Martin, Steve *IntWW 93*
Martin, Steve 1945- *IntMPA 94, WhoAm 94, WhoHol 92*
Martin, Steven S. 1956- *WhoMW 93*
Martin, Strother d1980 *WhoHol 92*
Martin, Sunny 1913- *WhoWest 94*
Martin, Susan Fry 1952- *WhoAmL 94, WhoWest 94*
Martin, Susan Katherine 1942- *WhoAm 94*
Martin, Susan Melinda 1954- *WhoWest 94*
Martin, Susan Taylor 1949- *WhoAm 94*
Martin, Sylvia Cooke 1938- *WhoBlA 94*
Martin, Talmage McKinley, Jr. 1923- *WhoAmP 93*
Martin, Terrence H. 1936- *WhoAmP 93*
Martin, Theodore Krinn 1915- *WhoAm 94*
Martin, Theresa Marie 1965- *WhoMW 93*
Martin, Thomas *EncSF 93*
Martin, Thomas 1943- *WhoAmA 93*
Martin, Thomas (Philipp) 1909-1984 *NewGrDO*
Martin, Thomas Baldwin 1893- *WhAm 10*
Martin, Thomas Ballantyne 1901- *Who 94*
Martin, Thomas E. 1942- *WhoAm 94*
Martin, Thomas Gary 1949- *WhoAmL 94*
Martin, Thomas Lyle, Jr. 1921- *WhoAm 94*
Martin, Thomas Stephen 1946- *WhoAm 94*
Martin, Timothy W. 1947- *WhoAmL 94*
Martin, Todd *WhoHol 92*
Martin, Tom Francis 1951- *WhoFI 94*
Martin, Tony 1913- *IntMPA 94, WhoHol 92*
Martin, Tony 1942- *BlkWr 2, WhoBlA 94*
Martin, Townsend d1951 *WhoHol 92*
Martin, Tripp 1950- *WhoMW 93*
Martin, (Francis) Troy K. *Who 94*
Martin, Valentina Kuchynka 1925- *WhoMW 93*
Martin, Valerie 1948- *WrDr 94*
Martin, Valerie M. *DrAPF 93*
Martin, Victor Cecil 1915- *Who 94*
Martin, Victor Rous 1949- *WhoFI 94*
Martin, Victoria Carolyn 1945- *WrDr 94*
Martin, Vince *WhoHol 92*
Martin, Vincent Francis, Jr. 1941- *WhoWest 94*
Martin, Vincent George 1922- *WhoAm 94*
Martin, Vincent Lionel 1939- *WhoAm 94*
Martin, Violet Florence *BlmGWL*
Martin, Virginia d1971 *WhoHol 92*
Martin, Vivian d1987 *WhoHol 92*
Martin, Vivienne 1936- *WhoHol 92*
Martin, W. Terry 1948- *WhoAm 94*
Martin, Wallace A. *WhoAmP 93*
Martin, Walter 1912- *WhoAmL 94*
Martin, Walter Edwin 1908- *WhoAm 94*
Martin, Walter L. 1951- *WhoBlA 94*
Martin, Walter Lee 1921- *WhoIns 94*
Martin, Warren Howard 1964- *WhoWest 94*
Martin, Wayne 1949- *WhoBlA 94*
Martin, Wayne 1965- *WhoBlA 94*
Martin, Wayne David 1949- *WhoMW 93*
Martin, Wayne Mallott 1950- *WhoFI 94*
Martin, Webber *EncSF 93*
Martin, Wendy 1930- *WrDr 94*
Martin, Wesley Davis, Jr. 1956- *WhoScEn 94*
Martin, Wilfred Wesley 1917- *WhoWest 94*
Martin, William 1950- *ConAu 140*
Martin, William A. 1941- *WhoFI 94*
Martin, William Aubert 1931- *WhoAmL 94*
Martin, William Blain 1953- *WhoWest 94*
Martin, William C. 1893- *WhAm 10*
Martin, William C. 1937- *ConAu 41NR*
Martin, William C., III 1942- *WhoAmL 94*
Martin, William Charles 1923- *WhoAmL 94*
Martin, William F. *WhoAm 94, WhoAmL 94*
Martin, William George 1947- *WhoFI 94, WhoMW 93*
Martin, William Giese 1934- *WhoAm 94*
Martin, William H. *WhoAmP 93*
Martin, William Joseph 1953- *WhoAmP 93*
Martin, William Joseph, III 1953- *WhoAmL 94*
Martin, William L., Jr. 1946- *WhoAmL 94*
Martin, William McChesney 1906- *Who 94*
Martin, William N. 1945- *WhoAmP 93*
Martin, William Oliver 1919- *WhoIns 94*
Martin, William Patrick 1943- *WhoFI 94*
Martin, William R. 1926- *WhoBlA 94*
Martin, William Raymond 1939- *WhoFI 94*
Martin, William Robert 1927- *WhoFI 94*
Martin, William Royall, Jr. 1926- *WhoAm 94, WhoScEn 94*
Martin, William Scott 1965- *WhoMW 93*
Martin, William Truett 1924- *WhoAmP 93*
Martina, Dominico (Don) F. *IntWW 93*
Martinac, Paula *DrAPF 93*
Martinac, Paula 1954- *GayLL*
Martin and Lewis *WhoCom*
Martinazzoli, Mino Fermo 1931- *IntWW 93*
Martin-Bates, James Patrick 1912- *Who 94*
Martin-Bird, Richard Dawnay d1992 *Who 94N*
Martin-Bowen, Lindsey 1949- *WhoAm 94, WhoMW 93*
Martindale, Alan Rawes 1930- *Who 94*
Martindale, Andrew (Henry Robert) 1932- *WrDr 94*
Martindale, Catherine Ann 1946- *WhoAm 94*

Martindale, Donald Patrick 1955- *WhoMW 93*
Martindale, Larry Richard 1938- *WhoMW 93*
Martindale, Lowell C., Jr. 1940- *WhoAmL 94*
Martindale, Patrick Victor *ConAu 43NR*
Martin de Agar, Pilar Maria 1956- *WhoScEn 94*
Martin de Beauce, Thierry 1943- *IntWW 93*
Martindel, Edward d1955 *WhoHol 92*
Martin del Campo, Diego Ramiro 1929- *WhoFI 94*
Martin Delgado, Jose Maria 1947- *IntWW 93*
Martindell, Anne Clark *WhoAmP 93*
Martineau, Charles Herman 1908- *Who 94*
Martineau, Florence Baker d1993 *NewYTBS 93*
Martineau, Gerard M. 1958- *WhoAmP 93*
Martineau, Harriet 1802-1876 *BlmGEL, BlmGWL, EncDeaf*
Martineau, Paul 1921- *IntWW 93*
Martineau, Reed Lynn 1932- *WhoAm 94, WhoAmL 94*
Martineau, Robert Arnold Schurhoff 1913- *Who 94*
Martineau, Robert John 1934- *WhoAmL 94*
Martineau, Robert John, Jr. 1958- *WhoAmL 94*
Martineau, Thomas Richard 1946- *WhoFI 94*
Martineau-Walker, Roger Antony *Who 94*
Martinek, Frank Joseph 1921- *WhoScEn 94*
Martinelli, Angelo R. 1927- *WhoAmP 93*
Martinelli, Caterina 1589?-1608 *NewGrDO*
Martinelli, Elsa 1933- *WhoHol 92*
Martinelli, Ezio 1913- *WhoAmA 93N*
Martinelli, Gaetano fl. 1764-1795 *NewGrDO*
Martinelli, Giovanni d1969 *WhoHol 92*
Martinelli, Giovanni 1885-1969 *NewGrDO [port]*
Martinelli, Jean d1983 *WhoHol 92*
Martinelli, Kenneth Dean 1946- *WhoIns 94*
Martinelli, Rosemary 1957- *WhoFI 94*
Martinen, John A. 1938- *WhoAm 94*
Martinenghi, Antonio Francesco fl. 1677-1705 *NewGrDO*
Martines, Karen Louise 1952- *WhoWest 94*
Martines, Lauro 1927- *WhoAm 94*
Martines, Steven L. 1938- *WhoHisp 94*
Martinet, Gilles 1916- *IntWW 93*
Martinet, Marjoried 1886-1981 *WhoAmA 93N*
Martinette, Janice R. 1938- *WhoAmP 93*
Martinetti, Ronald Anthony 1945- *WhoWest 94*
Martínez, A *WhoHisp 94*
Martinez, A. 1949- *WhoHol 92*
Martínez, Adele Virginia Hansen 1920- *WhoHisp 94*
Martinez, Al 1929- *WhoAm 94, WhoHisp 94*
Martinez, Albert 1941- *WhoHisp 94*
Martinez, Albert 1960- *WhoHisp 94*
Martinez, Alejandro *WhoHisp 94*
Martínez, Alejandro Macias 1951- *WhoHisp 94*
Martinez, Alex G. *WhoHisp 94*
Martinez, Alex J. 1950- *WhoHisp 94*
Martinez, Alex J. 1951- *WhoHisp 94*
Martinez, Alfred 1944- *WhoAmA 93*
Martinez, Alfred P. 1939- *WhoHisp 94*
Martinez, Alicia 1956- *WhoHisp 94*
Martinez, Alma 1953- *WhoHisp 94*
Martinez, Alvaro A. 1944- *WhoHisp 94*
Martínez, Andrew Arthur 1941- *WhoHisp 94*
Martinez, Andrew Tredway 1930- *WhoAmL 94*
Martínez, Anna Louise 1952- *WhoHisp 94*
Martinez, Antonio F. *WhoHisp 94*
Martinez, Arabella 1937- *WhoHisp 94*
Martinez, Aristides 1937- *WhoHisp 94*
Martinez, Armando 1938- *WhoHisp 94*
Martinez, Arthur *WhoHisp 94*
Martinez, Arthur C. 1939- *WhoAm 94, WhoFI 94*
Martinez, Arthur D. *WhoHisp 94*
Martinez, Arturo David 1966- *WhoWest 94*
Martinez, Augusto Julio 1930- *WhoHisp 94*
Martinez, Avelino 1940- *WhoHisp 94*
Martínez, Azalía Veronica 1950- *WhoHisp 94*
Martinez, Ben *WhoAmP 93, WhoHisp 94*
Martinez, Benjamin 1943- *WhoHisp 94*
Martinez, Blas M. 1935- *WhoHisp 94*
Martinez, Bob 1934- *WhoHisp 94*
Martinez, Bobby R. *WhoHisp 94*
Martinez, Camilla Maria 1954- *WhoAmL 94, WhoWest 94*
Martínez, Camilo Amado, Jr. 1935- *WhoHisp 94*
Martinez, Cari-Anne J. 1958- *WhoHisp 94*
Martinez, Carlos Alberto 1965- *WhoBlA 94, WhoHisp 94*
Martinez, Carmelo 1960- *WhoHisp 94*
Martinez, Carmen L. *WhoHisp 94*
Martínez, Cecilia González 1958- *WhoHisp 94*
Martinez, Celestino 1945- *WhoHisp 94*
Martinez, Cervando, Jr. 1941- *WhoHisp 94*
Martínez, César Augusto 1944- *WhoHisp 94*
Martinez, Charles 1953- *WhoHisp 94*
Martinez, Charles A. 1938- *WhoHisp 94*
Martínez, Cleopatria 1948- *WhoHisp 94*
Martinez, D. M. 1918- *WhoAmP 93*
Martinez, Dagoberto M. 1945- *WhoHisp 94*
Martinez, Daniel Agustin 1954- *WhoHisp 94*
Martinez, Daniel Alan 1949- *WhoHisp 94*
Martinez, Daniel J. 1957- *WhoAmA 93*
Martinez, Daniel Lee 1948- *WhoAmP 93*
Martinez, Danny 1948- *WhoHisp 94*
Martinez, Dave 1964- *WhoHisp 94*
Martinez, David *WhoAmP 93*
Martínez, David 1963- *WhoHisp 94*
Martinez, David Anthony 1953- *WhoHisp 94*
Martinez, David G. *WhoHisp 94*
Martinez, David Herrera 1937- *WhoHisp 94*
Martinez, David Steven 1946- *WhoHisp 94*
Martinez, Demetria 1960- *WhoHisp 94*
Martinez, Dennis 1955- *WhoHisp 94*
Martinez, Dennis 1965- *WhoHisp 94*
Martinez, Diane *WhoAmP 93, WhoHisp 94*
Martinez, Diego Gutierrez 1948- *WhoHisp 94*
Martínez, Dionisio D. 1956- *WhoHisp 94*
Martinez, Edgar 1963- *WhoAm 94, WhoHisp 94, WhoWest 94*
Martinez, Edgardo Ruben 1943- *WhoHisp 94*
Martinez, Eduardo Vidal 1955- *WhoAmL 94*
Martinez, Edward Ernest 1954- *WhoHisp 94*
Martinez, Edwin A. *WhoHisp 94*
Martinez, Efren 1949- *WhoHisp 94*
Martinez, Elizabeth *WhoWest 94*
Martinez, Elizabeth 1943- *WhoHisp 94*
Martinez, Elmer 1933- *WhoHisp 94*
Martinez, Eloise Fontanet 1929- *WhoHisp 94*
Martinez, Eluid Levi 1944- *WhoHisp 94*
Martinez, Elvin L. 1934- *WhoAmP 93, WhoHisp 94*
Martinez, Elvira 1936- *WhoHisp 94*
Martinez, Enid *WhoAmP 93*
Martinez, Enid Margarita 1951- *WhoHisp 94*
Martinez, Erminio E. 1943- *WhoHisp 94*
Martinez, Ernest Alcario 1941- *WhoHisp 94*
Martinez, Ernesto, Jr. 1941- *WhoHisp 94*
Martinez, Ernesto Pedregon 1926- *WhoAmA 93, WhoHisp 94*
Martinez, Esteban Conde 1932- *WhoHisp 94*
Martinez, Estela M. *WhoHisp 94*
Martinez, Evelyn Romero 1944- *WhoHisp 94*
Martínez, Felix Leonardo 1967- *WhoHisp 94*
Martínez, Florian 1927- *WhoHisp 94*
Martinez, Francisco 1918- *WhoMW 93*
Martinez, Frank 1955- *WhoHisp 94*
Martinez, Gabriel Guerrero, Jr. 1951- *WhoHisp 94*
Martinez, George 1955- *WhoHisp 94*
Martinez, George R. 1920- *WhoAmP 93*
Martinez, Gerald Lafayette 1939- *WhoHisp 94*
Martinez, Gina Amelia 1960- *WhoHisp 94*
Martinez, Giovanna *WhoHol 92*
Martinez, Guillermo *WhoHisp 94*
Martinez, Gustave *WhoAm 94*
Martinez, Harold H. *WhoHisp 94*
Martinez, Harold Joseph 1959- *WhoHisp 94*
Martinez, Henry Emilio 1929- *WhoHisp 94*
Martinez, Henry J. *WhoHisp 94*
Martinez, Humberto L. 1944- *WhoHisp 94*
Martinez, Ignacio E. 1931- *WhoHisp 94*
Martinez, Irene B. 1944- *WhoHisp 94*
Martinez, Ivonne *WhoHisp 94*
Martinez, Jaime 1954- *WhoHisp 94*
Martínez, James José 1955- *WhoHisp 94*
Martínez, Jeordano Severo *WhoHisp 94*
Martinez, Jerry 1947- *WhoHisp 94*
Martinez, Jerry C. 1967- *WhoHisp 94*
Martinez, Jesus M. *WhoHisp 94*
Martinez, Jesus M. Valle *WhoAmP 93*
Martinez, Joaquin *WhoHol 92*
Martinez, Joaquin A. *WhoHisp 94*
Martínez, Joe L. 1944- *WhoHisp 94*
Martinez, John L. *WhoHisp 94*
Martinez, John Lee 1934- *WhoHisp 94*
Martinez, John Stanley 1930- *WhoHisp 94, WhoWest 94*
Martinez, John Z. 1946- *WhoHisp 94*
Martínez, Jorge 1940- *WhoHisp 94*
Martinez, Jose 1942- *WhoHisp 94*
Martinez, Jose 1950- *WhoHisp 94*
Martinez, Jose Angel 1946- *WhoHisp 94*
Martinez, Jose Benito, Jr. 1964- *WhoWest 94*
Martinez, Jose Eleazar 1954- *WhoHisp 94*
Martinez, Jose M., Jr. 1933- *WhoHisp 94*
Martinez, Jose Martin 1954- *WhoHisp 94*
Martinez, Joseph 1941- *WhoHisp 94*
Martinez, Joseph Phillip 1948- *WhoHisp 94*
Martinez, Joseph V. *WhoHisp 94*
Martinez, Josie 1955- *WhoHisp 94*
Martinez, Juan Angel d1984 *WhoHol 92*
Martinez, Juan David 1962- *WhoHisp 94*
Martínez, Judith 1955- *WhoHisp 94*
Martinez, Julia Jaramillo 1926- *WhoHisp 94*
Martinez, Julio Enrique, Jr. 1943- *WhoHisp 94*
Martinez, Julio J. 1943- *WhoAmP 93, WhoHisp 94*
Martinez, Julio J. 1965- *WhoAm 94*
Martinez, Kenneth A. 1935- *WhoHisp 94*
Martinez, Laudelina *WhoHisp 94*
Martinez, Lavern E. 1941- *WhoHisp 94*
Martinez, Lee William 1953- *WhoHisp 94*
Martinez, Leodoro, Jr. 1949- *WhoHisp 94*
Martinez, Lissa Ann 1954- *WhoHisp 94*
Martinez, Luis Enrique, Jr. 1969- *WhoScEn 94*
Martinez, Luis Osvaldo 1927- *WhoAm 94*
Martinez, Lupe 1945- *WhoHisp 94*
Martínez, Luz Alvarez *WhoHisp 94*
Martinez, M. A. Laura 1960- *WhoHisp 94*
Martínez, M. Salomé 1947- *WhoHisp 94*
Martinez, Manuel C. 1945- *WhoHisp 94*
Martinez, Manuel S. *WhoHisp 94*
Martinez, Marciano 1939- *WhoHisp 94*
Martínez, Marcos L. 1955- *WhoHisp 94*
Martinez, Maria J. 1951- *WhoHisp 94*
Martinez, Mario Antonio 1965- *WhoScEn 94*
Martinez, Mario G., Jr. 1924- *WhoHisp 94*
Martinez, Mario Xavier 1952- *WhoHisp 94*
Martínez, Marlo R. 1957- *WhoHisp 94*
Martinez, Marlo Ray 1957- *WhoWest 94*
Martinez, Martin *WhoHisp 94*
Martinez, Marvin Gerald 1947- *WhoHisp 94*
Martinez, Mary Jane 1953- *WhoHisp 94*
Martinez, Matt C. *WhoHisp 94*
Martinez, Matt G., Sr. 1917- *WhoHisp 94*
Martinez, Matthew G. 1929- *WhoAmP 93, WhoHisp 94*
Martinez, Matthew G., Jr. 1929- *CngDr 93*
Martinez, Matthew Gilbert 1929- *WhoAm 94, WhoWest 94*
Martinez, Maurice Edwin 1930- *WhoHisp 94*
Martinez, Melquiades R. 1946- *WhoAmL 94*
Martinez, Melvin H. *WhoHisp 94*
Martinez, Mercurio, Jr. 1937- *WhoHisp 94*
Martinez, Michael C. 1954- *WhoHisp 94*
Martinez, Michael E. *WhoHisp 94*
Martinez, Michael J. *WhoHisp 94*
Martinez, Michael N. *WhoAmL 94*
Martinez, Michael N. 1949- *WhoAmP 93, WhoHisp 94*
Martinez, Miguel A. 1930- *WhoHisp 94*
Martinez, Miguel Acevedo 1953- *WhoScEn 94*
Martinez, Miguel Agustín 1937- *WhoHisp 94*
Martinez, Miguel Angel 1930- *WhoMW 93*
Martinez, Miguel Carlos 1951- *WhoHisp 94*
Martinez, Milli M. 1949- *WhoHisp 94*
Martinez, Nabar Enrique 1946- *WhoHisp 94*
Martínez, Narciso 1911- *WhoHisp 94*
Martinez, Octavio Nestor, Jr. 1961- *WhoHisp 94*
Martinez, Octavio Vincent 1947- *WhoHisp 94*
Martinez, Orlando 1957- *WhoHisp 94*
Martinez, Oscar J. 1943- *WhoHisp 94*
Martinez, Oscar Luis 1952- *WhoHisp 94*
Martinez, Paco d1956 *WhoHol 92*
Martinez, Patricia Hincapie 1959- *WhoHisp 94*
Martinez, Paul Edward 1952- *WhoHisp 94*
Martinez, Pedro d1978 *WhoHol 92*
Martinez, Pedro 1924- *WhoHisp 94*
Martinez, Pedro Jaime 1971- *WhoHisp 94*
Martinez, Pedro L. 1951- *WhoHisp 94*
Martinez, Pete *WhoHisp 94*
Martinez, Pete 1941- *WhoHisp 94*
Martinez, Pete, Jr. 1943- *WhoHisp 94*
Martinez, Pete R. 1937- *WhoHisp 94*
Martinez, Polo J., Jr. 1945- *WhoHisp 94*
Martinez, R. Diane 1955- *WhoHisp 94*
Martinez, Ralph *WhoBlA 94*
Martinez, Ralph T., Jr. 1925- *WhoHisp 94*
Martinez, Ramon Jaime 1968- *WhoBlA 94, WhoHisp 94*
Martinez, Ramona Elizabeth 1943- *WhoHisp 94*
Martinez, Raul 1953- *WhoHisp 94*
Martinez, Raul Andres 1946- *WhoHisp 94*
Martinez, Raul Cisneros 1942- *WhoHisp 94*
Martinez, Raul L. 1949- *WhoAmP 93*
Martinez, Raul O. *WhoHisp 94*
Martinez, Raymond 1953- *WhoHisp 94*
Martinez, Ricardo 1955- *WhoHisp 94*
Martinez, Ricardo Pedro 1945- *WhoHisp 94*
Martinez, Ricardo Salazar 1951- *WhoHisp 94*
Martinez, Rich 1950- *WhoHisp 94*
Martinez, Richard *WhoHisp 94*
Martinez, Richard 1952- *WhoHisp 94*
Martinez, Richard 1955- *WhoHisp 94*
Martinez, Richard Isaac 1944- *WhoHisp 94*
Martinez, Richard Leon 1961- *WhoMW 93*
Martinez, Robert 1934- *IntWW 93, WhoAmP 93*
Martinez, Robert 1943- *WhoAmP 93, WhoHisp 94*
Martinez, Robert 1949- *WhoHisp 94*
Martinez, Robert A. *WhoHisp 94*
Martinez, Robert A. 1943- *WhoHisp 94*
Martinez, Robert E. *WhoHisp 94*
Martínez, Robert Lee 1944- *WhoHisp 94*
Martinez, Robert M. *WhoHisp 94*
Martinez, Robert Orlando 1944- *WhoHisp 94*
Martinez, Robert P. *WhoHisp 94*
Martinez, Roman, IV 1947- *WhoAm 94, WhoFI 94*
Martinez, Roman Octaviano 1958- *WhoAmP 93, WhoHisp 94*
Martinez, Ronald J. *WhoHisp 94*
Martinez, Rosa Borrero 1956- *WhoHisp 94*
Martinez, Roy *WhoHisp 94*
Martinez, Ruben Martin 1948- *WhoWest 94*
Martinez, Ruben O. 1952- *WhoHisp 94*
Martinez, Ruben Orlando 1952- *WhoWest 94*
Martinez, Sally Verdugo 1934- *WhoHisp 94*
Martinez, Salutario 1935- *WhoHisp 94*
Martinez, Salvador 1942- *WhoScEn 94*
Martínez, Sara 1958- *WhoHisp 94*
Martinez, Seledon C., Sr. 1921- *WhoHisp 94*
Martinez, Serge Anthony 1942- *WhoHisp 94*
Martinez, Sergio E. 1919- *WhoHisp 94*
Martinez, Steven F. *WhoHisp 94*
Martinez, Sylvia Ann 1951- *WhoHisp 94*
Martinez, Timothy J. 1961- *WhoHisp 94*
Martinez, Tino 1967- *WhoHisp 94*
Martinez, Tomas Eugene 1949- *WhoHisp 94*
Martinez, Tony, Jr. *WhoHisp 94*
Martinez, Tony F. *WhoHisp 94*
Martinez, Tony Ramon 1958- *WhoHisp 94*
Martinez, Vern 1941- *WhoHisp 94*
Martinez, Vicente Montaner 1940- *WhoHisp 94*
Martinez, Victor Hipolito 1924- *IntWW 93*
Martinez, Vilma S. 1943- *WhoHisp 94*
Martinez, Vilma Socorro 1943- *WhoAm 94, WhoAmL 94*
Martinez, Vince *WhoAmP 93*
Martínez, Virginia 1949- *WhoHisp 94*
Martinez, Virginia A. 1947- *WhoHisp 94*
Martinez, Walter 1951- *WhoAmP 93, WhoHisp 94*
Martinez, Walter Baldomero 1937- *WhoAm 94*
Martínez, Walter Kenneth, Jr. 1959- *WhoHisp 94*
Martinez, William Eliu 1959- *WhoHisp 94*
Martínez, William G. 1938- *WhoHisp 94*

Martinez, Yvette 1954- *WhoHisp 94*
Martínez, Zarela 1947- *WhoHisp 94*
Martinez, Zilliam *WhoHisp 94*
Martinez-Alvarez, Francisco J. 1960- *WhoHisp 94*
Martinez Benitez, Candida 1923- *WhoAmP 93*
Martinez-Bonati, Felix *WhoHisp 94*
Martinez-Borchard, Richard *WhoHisp 94*
Martinez-Brawley, Emilia E. *WhoHisp 94*
Martinez-Burgoyne, Toni 1943- *WhoHisp 94*
Martinez-Canas, Maria 1960- *WhoAmA 93*
Martinez-Carrion, Marino 1936- *WhoAm 94*
Martinez-Chavez, Diana 1955- *WhoHisp 94*
Martinez Cruz, Americo 1938- *WhoAmP 93, WhoHisp 94*
Martinez De Peron, Maria Estela (Isabelita) 1931- *IntWW 93*
Martinez de Pinillos, Joaquin Victor 1941- *WhoHisp 94*
Martínez-Díaz, Jorge L. 1956- *WhoHisp 94*
Martinez-Fonts, Alberto, Jr. 1943- *WhoHisp 94*
Martinez-Fonts, Pedro A. 1945- *WhoHisp 94*
Martinez-Frontanilla, Luis Alberto 1946- *WhoHisp 94*
Martinez-Galarce, Dennis Stanley 1961- *WhoScEn 94*
Martinez Gándara, Julio Antonio 1931- *WhoHisp 94*
Martinez-Garduño, Beatriz 1940- *WhoHisp 94*
Martinez-Lopez, Jorge Ignacio 1926- *WhoHisp 94*
Martinez-Lopez, Norman P. *WhoHisp 94*
Martinez-Luengo, Antonio T. 1957- *WhoHisp 94*
Martinez-Maldonado, Manuel 1937- *WhoAm 94, WhoHisp 94*
Martínez-Miranda, Luz Josefina 1956- *WhoHisp 94*
Martínez-Nazario, Ronaldo 1958- *WhoHisp 94*
Martinez Ordonez, Jose Roberto 1922- *IntWW 93*
Martínez-Ortiz, Daniel Louis 1954- *WhoHisp 94*
Martinez-Paula, Emilio *WhoHisp 94*
Martinez-Pino, Sandy *WhoHisp 94*
Martinez-Poblanno, Irene Elizabeth 1954- *WhoHisp 94*
Martínez-Purson, Rita 1955- *WhoHisp 94*
Martínez-Ramírez, José Roberto 1954- *WhoHisp 94*
Martinez-Reyes, Guillermo Alberto 1941- *WhoHisp 94*
Martinez-Roach, N. Patricia 1949- *WhoHisp 94*
Martinez-Romero, Sergio 1936- *WhoHisp 94*
Martinez Sanz, Antonio F. 1950- *WhoScEn 94*
Martinez Sierra, Maria de la O. 1874-1974 *BlmGWL*
Martinez Smith, Elizabeth *WhoAm 94, WhoWest 94*
Martinez Somalo, Eduardo 1927- *IntWW 93*
Martinez-Tejeda, Juan J. 1908- *WhoAm 94*
Martinez Toro, Vilma 1959- *WhoHisp 94*
Martinez Valls, Rafael 1887?-1946 *NewGrDO*
Martinez Zuviria, Gustavo 1915- *Who 94*
Martin Fernandez, Miguel 1943- *IntWW 93*
Marting, Michael G. 1948- *WhoAm 94, WhoAmL 94*
Martin Gaite, Carmen 1925- *BlmGWL, ConWorW 93*
Martin Garcia, Fernando *WhoAmP 93*
Martin-Harvey, John d1944 *WhoHol 92*
Martin-Harvey, Michael d1975 *WhoHol 92*
Martin-Harvey, Muriel d1988 *WhoHol 92*
Martini, Anita d1993 *NewYTBS 93*
Martini, Arthur Pete 1943- *WhoWest 94*
Martini, Carlo Maria 1927- *IntWW 93, Who 94*
Martini, Charles C. 1940- *WhoIns 94*
Martini, Fritz d1991 *IntWW 93N*
Martini, Galen *DrAPF 93*
Martini, Giovanni Battista 1706-1784 *NewGrDO*
Martini, Jean-Paul-Egide 1741-1816 *NewGrDO*
Martini, Maria Eletta 1922- *WhoWomW 91*
Martini, Nino d1976 *WhoHol 92*
Martini, Steve(n Paul) 1946- *ConAu 140*
Martini, Teri 1930- *WrDr 94*
Martinis, John Anthony 1930- *WhoAmP 93*
Martini-Urdaneta, Alberto 1930- *IntWW 93*
Martin-Jenkins, Christopher Dennis Alexander 1945- *Who 94*
Martin-Lof, Per Erik Rutger 1942- *IntWW 93*
Martin Mateo, Ramon 1928- *IntWW 93*
Martino, Al 1927- *WhoHol 92*
Martino, Antonio P. 1902-1988 *WhAm 10*
Martino, Babette *WhoAmA 93*
Martino, Dianne Marie 1954- *WhoWest 94*
Martino, Donald James 1931- *WhoAm 94*
Martino, Eva E. *WhoAmA 93*
Martino, Frank Dominic 1919- *WhoMW 93*
Martino, Giovanni 1908- *WhoAmA 93*
Martino, Joseph Paul 1931- *WhoAm 94*
Martino, Michael Charles 1950- *WhoAm 94*
Martino, Nina F. *WhoAmA 93*
Martino, Peter Dominic 1963- *WhoFI 94, WhoScEn 94*
Martino, Robert Salvatore 1931- *WhoAm 94*
Martino, Rocco Leonard 1929- *WhoFI 94*
Martinoff, I. d1928 *WhoHol 92*
Martinoty, Jean-Louis 1946- *NewGrDO*
Martins, Ana Paula 1960- *WhoScEn 94*
Martins, Antonio Gentil da Silva 1930- *IntWW 93*
Martins, Evelyn Mae 1929- *WhoWest 94*
Martins, Heitor Miranda 1933- *WhoAm 94*
Martins, Nilas 1967- *WhoAm 94*
Martins, Orlando 1899- *WhoHol 92*
Martins, Paul G. 1956- *WhoFI 94*
Martins, Peter 1946- *IntDcB [port], IntWW 93, WhoAm 94, WhoHol 92*
Martins, Rudolf 1915- *IntWW 93*
Martinsen, Ivar Richard 1922- *WhoAmA 93*
Martinsen, Martin *EncSF 93*
Martins-Green, Manuela 1947- *WhoWest 94*
Martinson, Constance Frye 1932- *WhoWest 94*
Martinson, David *DrAPF 93*
Martinson, Denise *DrAPF 93*
Martinson, Genevieve L. 1923- *WhoMW 93*
Martinson, Harry (Edmund) 1904-1978 *EncSF 93*
Martinson, Ida Marie 1936- *IntWW 93, WhoAm 94*
Martinson, Jacob Christian, Jr. 1933- *WhoAm 94*
Martinson, John Robert 1935- *WhoWest 94*
Martinson, Julia Ellenor 1951- *WhoWest 94*
Martinson, Moa 1890-1964 *BlmGWL*
Martinson, Rita R. 1937- *WhoAmP 93*
Martinson, Robert William 1946- *WhoAmP 93*
Martinson, Stanley E. 1935- *WhoAmL 94*
Martinu, Bohuslav (Jan) 1890-1959 *NewGrDO*
Martinucci, Nicola 1941- *NewGrDO*
Martinuzzi, Leo Sergio, Jr. 1928- *WhoAm 94*
Martin Villa, Rodolfo 1934- *IntWW 93*
Martin y Soler, (Atanasio Martin Ignacio) Vicente 1754-1806 *NewGrDO*
Martius, Carl Friedrich Phillipp Von 1794-1869 *WhWE*
Martlew, Eric Anthony 1949- *Who 94*
Martlew, Mary d1989 *WhoHol 92*
Martling, W. Kent 1924- *WhoAmP 93*
Martmer, William Philip 1939-1992 *WhoAmA 93N*
Marto, Paul James 1938- *WhoWest 94*
Martocci, Anthony Philip 1934- *WhoFI 94*
Marton, Eva 1943- *NewGrDO, WhoAm 94*
Marton, John P. 1926- *WhoAmP 93*
Marton, Joseph 1919- *WhoScEn 94*
Marton, Kati (Ilona) 1949- *ConAu 140*
Marton, Laurence Jay 1944- *WhoAm 94*
Marton, Marie Ducie 1959- *WhoAmL 94*
Marton, Pier 1950- *WhoAmA 93*
Marton, Tutzi 1936- *WhoAmA 93*
Martone, Frederick *WhoAmP 93*
Martone, Fredrick J. 1943- *WhoAmL 94, WhoWest 94*
Martone, Joanne 1951- *WhoFI 94*
Martone, Joseph Patrick 1953- *WhoAmL 94*
Martone, Michael *DrAPF 93*
Martone, Michael 1941- *WhoAmA 93*
Martone, Patricia Ann 1947- *WhoAm 94, WhoAmL 94*
Martone, William Robert 1945- *WhoAmA 93*
Martonmere, Baron 1963- *Who 94*
Martono 1925- *IntWW 93*
Martonosi, Anthony Nicholas 1928- *WhoAm 94*
Martorana, Sebastian Vincent 1919- *WhoAm 94*
Martorell, Joseph Anthony 1939- *WhoHisp 94*
Martori, Joseph Peter 1941- *WhoAm 94, WhoAmL 94*
Martre, Jean Francois Henri 1928- *IntWW 93*
Marts, Kenneth Patrick 1956- *WhoScEn 94*
Martschink, Sherry Shealy 1949- *WhoAmP 93*
Martson, William Frederick, Jr. 1947- *WhoAmL 94*
Marttinen, Tauno 1912- *NewGrDO*
Martucci, William Christopher 1952- *WhoAmL 94*
Marty, Francois 1904- *IntWW 93, Who 94*
Marty, Frederick S. 1945- *WhoAmL 94*
Marty, John J. *WhoAmP 93*
Marty, Julio E. *WhoHisp 94*
Marty, Lawrence A. 1926- *WhoAm 94, WhoAmL 94, WhoAmP 93, WhoWest 94*
Marty, Martin E. 1928- *IntWW 93, WrDr 94*
Marty, Martin Emil 1928- *WhoAm 94, WhoMW 93*
Marty, Sid 1944- *WrDr 94*
Martyak, Joseph J. *WhoAm 94*
Martyl 1918- *WhoAm 94, WhoAmA 93*
Martyn, Charles Roger Nicholas 1925- *Who 94*
Martyn, Daniel E., Jr. 1952- *WhoAmL 94*
Martyn, David William 1949- *WhoFI 94*
Martyn, Edward (Joseph) 1859-1923 *IntDcT 2*
Martyn, Jack d1953 *WhoHol 92*
Martyn, John c. 1618-1680 *DcNaB MP*
Martyn, Marty d1964 *WhoHol 92*
Martyn, Peter d1955 *WhoHol 92*
Martyn, Wyndham 1875- *EncSF 93*
Martyn-Hemphill *Who 94*
Martynov, Aleksandr Gavrilovich 1945- *LngBDD*
Martynov, Andrei Vladimirovich 1964- *LngBDD*
Martynov, Vladlen Arkadevich 1929- *IntWW 93*
Martynyuk, Anatoly Andreevich 1941- *WhoScEn 94*
Martyr, Margaret d1807 *NewGrDO*
Martz, Alfred George 1926- *WhoFI 94*
Martz, Clyde Ollen 1920- *WhoAm 94*
Martz, John Roger 1937- *WhoWest 94*
Martz, Karl 1912- *WhoAmA 93*
Martz, Linda 1939- *WrDr 94*
Martz, Louis (Lohr) 1913- *WrDr 94*
Martz, Louis Lohr 1913- *WhoAm 94*
Martz, Sandra Kay 1944- *WhoWest 94*
Martzett, Carol Marie Preston 1948- *WhoMW 93*
Marum, Andrew *DrAPF 93*
Marumoto, Barbara Chizuko 1939- *WhoWest 94*
Marumoto, Barbara D. 1939- *WhoAmP 93*
Marumoto, William Hideo 1934- *WhoAm 94, WhoAsA 94*
Maruoka Hideko 1903-1990 *BlmGWL*
Marur, Hanuman 1939- *WhoAsA 94*
Marusiak, Ronald John 1948- *WhoScEn 94*
Marusin, Yury 1947- *NewGrDO*
Maruska, Edward Joseph 1934- *WhoAm 94, WhoMW 93*
Maruvada, Pereswara Sarma 1938- *WhoAm 94*
Maruyama, Kiyoshi 1945- *WhoAsA 94*
Maruyama, Koshi 1932- *WhoScEn 94*
Maruyama, Masao 1914- *IntWW 93*
Maruyama, Takashi 1950- *WhoAsA 94*
Maruyama, Wendy 1952- *WhoAmA 93*
Maruyama, Yosh 1930- *WhoAm 94, WhoScEn 94*
Marvanova, Hana 1962- *WhoWomW 91*
Marve, Eugene Raymond 1960- *WhoBlA 94*
Marvel, Billy Bryan 1913- *WhoAmP 93*
Marvel, John Thomas 1938- *WhoScEn 94*
Marvel, John W. 1926- *WhoAmP 93*
Marvel, Kenneth Robert 1952- *WhoAmL 94*
Marvel, L. Paige 1949- *WhoAmL 94*
Marvel, Thomas Stahl 1935- *WhoAm 94*
Marvel, Wanda Faye 1951- *WhoMW 93*
Marvel, William 1909-1991 *WhAm 10*
Marvel Jova, Thomas S. 1935- *WhoHisp 94*
Marvell, Andrew 1621-1678 *BlmGEL, DcLB 131 [port]*
Marvell, Andrew 1896-1985 *EncSF 93*
Marvick, Elizabeth Wirth 1925- *ConAu 41NR*
Marvil, Patricia De L. *WhoHisp 94*
Marvin, Charles Arthur 1942- *WhoAmL 94*
Marvin, David Edward Shreve 1950- *WhoAmL 94, WhoMW 93*
Marvin, David Keith 1921- *WhoAm 94*
Marvin, Douglas Raymond 1947- *WhoAm 94*
Marvin, Harold Myers 1893- *WhAm 10*
Marvin, Helen Rhyne 1917- *WhoAmP 93*
Marvin, Jack d1956 *WhoHol 92*
Marvin, Jack Conway 1956- *WhoAmL 94*
Marvin, James Conway 1927- *WhoAm 94, WhoMW 93*
Marvin, Johnny d1944 *WhoHol 92*
Marvin, Julie *ConAu 142*
Marvin, Julie 1933- *WrDr 94*
Marvin, Lee d1987 *WhoHol 92*
Marvin, Oscar McDowell 1924- *WhoAm 94*
Marvin, Philip 1916- *WrDr 94*
Marvin, Robert Earle 1920- *WhoAm 94*
Marvin, Roy Mack 1931- *WhoAm 94*
Marvin, Susan *ConAu 142*
Marvin, Susan 1933- *WrDr 94*
Marvin, Warren Leete d1938 *WhoHol 92*
Marvin, William Glenn, Jr. 1920- *WhoAm 94*
Marvine, Brigitte *WhoHol 92*
Marvit, Robert Charles 1938- *WhoAm 94*
Marwedel, Warren John 1944- *WhoAm 94, WhoAmL 94*
Marwell, Gerald 1937- *WhoAm 94*
Marwick, Arthur 1936- *WrDr 94*
Marwick, Arthur John Brereton 1936- *Who 94*
Marwick, Ewan d1993 *Who 94N*
Marwick, Max(well) Gay 1916- *WrDr 94*
Marwill, Robert Douglas 1945- *WhoScEn 94*
Marwitz, Michael *WhoHol 92*
Marwood, William 1938- *WrDr 94*
Marx, Adam Neal 1961- *WhoWest 94*
Marx, Alan Lee 1943- *WhoAmL 94*
Marx, Anne *DrAPF 93, WhoAm 94*
Marx, Arthur 1921- *WhoAm 94, WrDr 94*
Marx, Brett *WhoHol 92*
Marx, Brian 1960- *WhoScEn 94*
Marx, Chico d1961 *WhoHol 92*
Marx, Chico 1887-1961
See Marx Brothers, The *WhoCom*
Marx, Chico 1891-1961
See Marx Brothers *AmCulL*
Marx, David, Jr. 1950- *WhoAm 94*
Marx, Enid Crystal Dorothy 1902- *Who 94*
Marx, Evelyn *WhoAmA 93*
Marx, Gary T 1938- *WrDr 94*
Marx, Gertie Florentine 1912- *WhoAm 94*
Marx, Groucho d1977 *WhoHol 92*
Marx, Groucho 1890-1977
See Marx Brothers *AmCulL*
Marx, Groucho 1890-1977
See Marx Brothers, The *WhoCom*
Marx, Groucho 1895- *WhAm 10*
Marx, Gummo 1892-1977
See Marx Brothers, The *WhoCom*
Marx, Gummo 1894-1977
See Marx Brothers *AmCulL*
Marx, Gyorgy 1927- *IntWW 93*
Marx, Harpo d1964 *WhoHol 92*
Marx, Harpo 1888-1964
See Marx Brothers, The *WhoCom*
Marx, Harpo 1893-1964
See Marx Brothers *AmCulL*
Marx, James John 1944- *WhoScEn 94*
Marx, Joseph Jacob 1956- *WhoWest 94*
Marx, Karl 1818-1883 *BlmGEL [port], DcLB 129 [port], HisWorL [port]*
Marx, Karl (Heinrich) 1818-1883 *EncEth*
Marx, Leo 1919- *WhoAm 94*
Marx, Marie-Luise 1959- *WhoMW 93*
Marx, Max d1925 *WhoHol 92*
Marx, Oscar Bruno, III 1939- *WhoAm 94, WhoFI 94*
Marx, Otto, Jr. 1909-1991 *WhAm 10*
Marx, Owen Cox 1947- *WhoAm 94*
Marx, Paul I. 1955- *WhoAmL 94*
Marx, Richard Brian 1968- *WhoScEn 94*
Marx, Robert (Frank) 1936- *WrDr 94*
Marx, Robert Ernst 1925- *WhoAmA 93*
Marx, Samuel d1933 *WhoHol 92*
Marx, Suzanne *WhoWest 94*
Marx, Thomas George 1943- *WhoAm 94*
Marx, William B., Jr. 1939- *WhoFI 94*
Marx, Zeppo d1979 *WhoHol 92*
Marx, Zeppo 1901-1979
See Marx Brothers *AmCulL*
Marx, Zeppo 1901-1979
See Marx Brothers, The *WhoCom*
Marx Brothers *AmCulL [port]*
Marx Brothers, The *WhoCom [port]*
Marxer, John A. 1943- *WhoAm 94, WhoAmL 94*
Marxman, Gerald Albert 1933- *WhoWest 94*
Marxuach, Rafael 1939- *WhoHisp 94*
Mary, Countess of Boulogne d1181 *BlmGWL*
Mary, Miss 1944- *WhoAmA 93*

Mary, Nun of Amesbury 1278-1332 BlmGWL
Mary, Queen of Scots 1542-1587 HisWorL [port]
Mary, I fl. 1553-1558 BlmGEL
Mary, II fl. 1689-1694 BlmGEL
Maryan BlmGWL
Maryan, Maryan S. 1927-1977 WhoAmA 93N
Marychurch, Peter (Harvey) 1927- Who 94
Marye, Madison Ellis 1925- WhoAmP 93
Mary Gilbert 1919- WrDr 94
Mary Jeremy, Sister 1907- WrDr 94
Maryland, Mary Angela 1953- WhoBlA 94
Marylander, Stuart Jerome 1931- WhoAm 94
Maryon Davis, Alan Roger 1943- Who 94
Mary Queen of Scots 1542-1567 BlmGEL
Mary Stuart, Queen of Scots 1542-1587 BlmGWL
Mary Tudor 1516-1558 BlmGWL [port]
Mary Tudor, I 1516-1558 HisWorL [port]
Marz, Loren Carl 1951- WhoScEn 94
Marzan, Julio DrAPF 93
Marzán, Julio 1946- WhoHisp 94
Marzani, Carl 1912- WrDr 94
Marzano, Albert 1919- WhoAmA 93
Marzano, Angelo Mario 1929- WhoAm 94, WhoFI 94
Marzec, Marcia Smith 1948- WhoMW 93
Marzec, Suzan Lynn 1954- WhoMW 93
Marzetti, Loretta A. 1943- WhoAm 94
Marzetti, Philip J. 1950- WhoAmL 94
Marzi, Franca d1989 WhoHol 92
Marziale, Antonio 1959- WhoFI 94
Marziano, Fredric G. WhoFI 94
Marzich, William Alan 1960- WhoFI 94
Marzilli, Jim 1958- WhoAmP 93
Marzinski, Lynn Rose 1951- WhoMW 93
Marzio, Peter Cort 1943- WhoAmA 93
Marzke, Mary Walpole 1937- WhoWest 94
Marzluf, George Austin 1935- WhoAm 94
Marzola, Joe d1976 WhoHol 92
Marzollo, Claudio 1938- WhoAmA 93
Marzollo, Jean 1942- SmATA 77 [port]
Marzulla, Roger Joseph 1947- WhoAm 94
Marzulli, John Anthony, Jr. 1953- WhoAm 94
Mas, Luis Pablo 1924- WhoHisp 94
Masagatani, Ernesta 1937- WhoWest 94
Masai, Mitsuo 1932- WhoAm 94, WhoScEn 94
Masak, Ron 1936- WhoHol 92
Masaki, Hideo Dennis 1948- WhoMW 93
Masako, Crown Princess 1963- News 93 [port]
Masamoto, Junzo 1937- WhoScEn 94
Masamune, Satoru 1928- WhoAm 94, WhoAsA 94
Masani, Minoo 1905- IntWW 93
Masani, Pesi Rustom 1919- WhoAm 94
Masao, Maruyama 1914- WrDr 94
Masaoka, Miya Joan 1958- WhoAsA 94
Masarsky, Mark Konstantinovich 1947- IntWW 93
Masaryk, Jan 1886-1948 HisWorL [port]
Masaryk, Thomas G. 1850-1937 HisWorL [port]
Masatova, Milada 1945- WhoWomW 91
Masback, Dennis WhoAmA 93
Mascagni, Pietro 1863-1945 NewGrDO
Mascall, Eric Lionel d1993 Who 94N
Mascall, Eric Lionel 1905- IntWW 93, WrDr 94
Mas-Canosa, Jorge L. 1939- WhoHisp 94
Mascarenas, Mark Scott 1962- WhoHisp 94
Mascarenhas, Joseph Peter 1929- WhoScEn 94
Mascavage, Joseph Peter 1956- WhoFI 94
Mascheroni, Edoardo 1852-1941 NewGrDO
Mascheroni, Eleanor Earle 1955- WhoFI 94
Maschler, Fay 1945- Who 94
Maschler, Thomas Michael 1933- IntWW 93, Who 94
Mascho, George Leroy 1925- WhoAm 94
Masci, Anthony John 1948- WhoMW 93
Mascia, Joseph Serafino 1939- WhoFI 94
Mascia, Tony WhoHol 92
Masciale, Diane Marie 1956- WhoWest 94
Masciarelli-Kisch, Leslie R. 1962- WhoMW 93
Masco, Dorothy Beryl 1918- WhoAmP 93
Mascoe, Michael Thomas 1956- WhoMW 93
Mascolo, Joe WhoHol 92
Mascotte, John Pierre 1939- WhoAm 94, WhoFI 94
Masdea, Jim
See Boston ConMus 11
Masdeu, Frida C. 1953- WhoHisp 94
Masdit, Supatra WhoWomW 91
Mase, Marino WhoHol 92
Masefield, Geoffrey (Bussell) 1911- WrDr 94
Masefield, John 1878-1967 BlmGEL
Masefield, John Thorold 1939- IntWW 93
Masefield, Joseph R. 1933- IntMPA 94
Masefield, Peter (Gordon) 1914- Who 94
Masefield, Peter Gordon 1914- IntWW 93
Masefield, Thorold Who 94
Masefield, (John) Thorold 1939- Who 94
Masek, Barry Michael 1955- WhoMW 93
Masek, Mark Joseph 1957- WhoMW 93
Masekela, Hugh 1939- CurBio 93 [port], IntWW 93
Masel, Richard Isaac 1951- WhoMW 93
Masella, Joseph 1950- WhoIns 94
Maselli, Giorgio 1947- WhoFI 94
Maselli, John Anthony 1929- WhoAm 94
Maselli, John Anthony 1954- WhoFI 94
Maser, Chris 1938- WrDr 94
Maser, Clark Walton 1925- WhoWest 94
Maser, Edward Andrew 1923-1988 WhoAmA 93N
Maser, Frederick Ernest 1908- WhoAm 94
Maser, Karl A. 1937- WhoIns 94
Masera, Rainer Stefano 1944- IntWW 93
Maseri, Attilio 1935- IntWW 93, Who 94
Masey, Jack 1924- WhoAm 94
Mash, Carolyn Beth 1963- WhoFI 94
Mash, Donald J. 1942- WhoAm 94
Mash, Jerry L. 1937- WhoAmL 94
Mashack, Barbara Jean 1953- WhoMW 93
Masham Of Ilton, Baroness 1935- Who 94, WhoWomW 91
Mashat, Muhammad Sadiq al- 1930- IntWW 93
Mashberg, Gregg M. 1951- WhoAm 94
Mashburn, Guerry Leonard 1952- WhoFI 94
Mashburn, Jamal WhoBlA 94
Mashburn, John Walter 1945- WhoScEn 94
Mashburn, Thomas Matthew 1960- WhoAmL 94
Masheck, Joseph Daniel 1942- WhoAm 94
Masheck, Joseph Daniel Cahill 1942- WhoAmA 93
Masheke, Malimba IntWW 93
Ma Shijiang 1924- WhoPRCh 91 [port]
Ma Shijun 1915- WhoPRCh 91 [port]
Mashits, Vladimir Mikhailovich 1953- LngBDD
Ma Shitu WhoPRCh 91
Mashologu, Mothusi Thamsanga 1939- IntWW 93
Mashunkashay, Ben c. 1879- EncNAR
Masi, Dale A. WhoAm 94
Masi, Edward A. 1947- WhoAm 94, WhoFI 94, WhoWest 94
Masi, Giovanni c. 1730-1776? NewGrDO
Masi, J. Roger 1954- WhoAmL 94
Masi, James Vincent 1938- WhoScEn 94
Masi, Jane Virginia 1947- WhoFI 94
Masi, Philip d1922 WhoHol 92
Masiello, Anthony M. 1947- WhoAmP 93
Masiello, Rocco Joseph 1922- WhoAm 94
Masiero, Ronald J. 1942- WhoIns 94
Masin, Michael Terry 1945- WhoAm 94
Masina, Giulietta 1920- WhoHol 92
Masina, Giulietta 1921- IntMPA 94, IntWW 93
Masina, Melchior 1941- WhoMW 93
Masini, Angelo 1844-1926 NewGrDO
Masini, Donna DrAPF 93
Masini, Eleonora Barbieri 1928- WrDr 94
Masini, Galliano 1896-1986 NewGrDO
Masini, Nadia 1949- WhoWomW 91
Masinissa c. 240BC-148BC HisWorL [port]
Masinter, Edgar Martin 1931- WhoAm 94
Masire, Quett 1925- ConBlB 5 [port]
Masire, Quett Ketumile Joni 1925- IntWW 93, Who 94
Ma Sizhong 1930- WhoPRCh 91 [port]
Ma Sizhong 1931- IntWW 93
Mask, Ace WhoHol 92
Maskaleris, Stephen Nicholas 1927- WhoAmL 94
Maskell, Daniel 1908-1992 BuCMET
Maskell, Donald Andrew 1963- WhoScEn 94, WhoWest 94
Maskell, Virginia d1968 WhoHol 92
Maskelyne, John Nevil 1839-1917 DcNaB MP
Masket, Edward Seymour 1923- WhoAm 94
Maskin, Arvin 1954- WhoAm 94
Maslach, Christina 1946- WhoAm 94
Maslach, George James 1920- WhoAm 94
Masland, Al WhoAmP 93
Masland, Charles Henry, IV 1955- WhoFI 94
Masland, Lynne S. 1940- WhoWest 94
Maslansky, Carol Jeanne 1949- WhoScEn 94
Maslansky, Paul 1933- IntMPA 94
Maslarova, Emiliya WhoWomW 91
Maslen, David Peter 1948- WhoAmL 94
Maslen, Stephen Harold 1926- WhoAm 94
Maslennikov, Arkady Afrikanovich 1931- LngBDD
Masler, Stuart d1978 WhoHol 92
Maslin, David Michael E. Who 94
Maslin, Harry 1948- WhoWest 94
Maslin, Harvey Lawrence 1939- WhoWest 94
Masling, Joseph Melvin 1923- WhoScEn 94
Maslo, William Ralph 1946- WhoFI 94
Masloff, Sophie 1917- WhoAm 94, WhoAmP 93, WhoWomW 91
Maslov, Viktor Pavlovich 1930- IntWW 93, WhoScEn 94
Maslow, Jonathan E(vans) 1948- WrDr 94
Maslow, Phyllis F. 1927- WhoWest 94
Maslow, Richard Emanuel 1929- WhoWest 94
Maslow, Walter WhoHol 92
Maslow, Will 1907- WhoAm 94
Maslowski, Edward M. 1947- WhoMW 93
Maslowski, Michael Joseph 1955- WhoFI 94
Maslyk, Cheri Ann 1949- WhoFI 94
Masnada, Dante A. 1953- WhoFI 94
Masnari, Nino Antonio 1935- WhoAm 94
Maso, Carole DrAPF 93
Masol, Vitaliy Andreyevich 1928- IntWW 93
Mason Who 94
Mason, Alastair Michael Stuart 1944- Who 94
Mason, Alden C. 1919- WhoAmA 93
Mason, Alice Frances 1895- WhoAmA 93N
Mason, Alice Trumball 1904-1971 WhoAmA 93N
Mason, Alpheus Thomas 1899-1989 WhAm 10
Mason, Anita 1942- EncSF 93
Mason, Ann d1948 WhoHol 92
Mason, Anthony (Frank) 1925- Who 94
Mason, Anthony Frank 1925- IntWW 93
Mason, Anthony Halstead 1938- WhoAmL 94, WhoWest 94
Mason, Arthur Malcolm 1915- Who 94
Mason, B. J. 1945- WhoBlA 94
Mason, Barry Jean 1930- WhoAm 94
Mason, Bertha d1950 WhoHol 92
Mason, Beryl 1921- WhoHol 92
Mason, Billy d1941 WhoHol 92
Mason, Billy Josephine 1918- WhoBlA 94
Mason, Bobbie Ann DrAPF 93
Mason, Bobbie Ann 1940- BlmGWL, TwCYAW, WhoAm 94, WrDr 94
Mason, Brenda Diane 1947- WhoBlA 94
Mason, Brewster d1987 WhoHol 92
Mason, Brian Harold 1917- WhoAm 94
Mason, Brian Wayne 1959- WhoAmP 93
Mason, Bruce 1939- WhoAm 94, WhoFI 94
Mason, Bruce (Edward George) 1921-1982 ConDr 93, IntDcT 2
Mason, Bruce Bonner 1923- WhoAmP 93
Mason, Buddy d1975 WhoHol 92
Mason, Catherine Emily Who 94
Mason, Charles d1976 WhoHol 92
Mason, Charles Ellis, III 1938- WhoAm 94
Mason, Charles H. 1866-1961 AfrAmAl 6
Mason, Charles Harrison 1866-1961 DcAmReB 2
Mason, Charles Perry 1932- WhoMW 93
Mason, Charlotte Maria Shaw 1842-1923 DcNaB MP
Mason, Cheryl Annette 1954- WhoBlA 94
Mason, Cheryl White 1952- WhoAm 94, WhoAmL 94
Mason, Clifford L. 1932- WhoBlA 94
Mason, Craig Watson 1954- WhoFI 94
Mason, DaCosta V. 1916- WhoBlA 94
Mason, Dan d1929 WhoHol 92
Mason, David DrAPF 93
Mason, David 1924-1974 EncSF 93
Mason, David Arthur 1946- Who 94
Mason, David Dickenson 1917- WhoAm 94
Mason, David Ernest 1928- WhoFI 94
Mason, David James 1954- WhoMW 93
Mason, David Kean 1928- Who 94
Mason, David Marion 1958- WhoAmP 93
Mason, David Stewart 1947- WhoMW 93
Mason, Dean Towle 1932- WhoAm 94, WhoScEn 94, WhoWest 94
Mason, Dennis Howard 1916- Who 94
Mason, Donald Roger 1942- WhoMW 93
Mason, Doris Ann 1943- WhoMW 93
Mason, Douglas Michael 1950- WhoMW 93
Mason, Douglas R(ankine) 1918- EncSF 93
Mason, Douglas Rankine 1918- WrDr 94
Mason, Earl James, Jr. 1923- WhoMW 93
Mason, Earl Leonard 1947- WhoFI 94
Mason, Edith (Barnes) 1893-1973 NewGrDO
Mason, Edmund (John) 1911-1993 WrDr 94N
Mason, Edward Allen 1926- WhoAm 94
Mason, Edward Eaton 1920- WhoAm 94
Mason, Edward James 1923- WhoBlA 94
Mason, Edward Sagendorph 1899-1992 WhAm 10
Mason, Eliza d1925 WhoHol 92
Mason, Elizabeth 1919- WhoAm 94
Mason, Elliott d1949 WhoHol 92
Mason, Ellsworth Goodwin 1917- WhoAm 94
Mason, Ernst EncSF 93
Mason, Evelyn d1926 WhoHol 92
Mason, Frances Jane Who 94
Mason, Francis K(enneth) 1928- WrDr 94
Mason, Francis Scarlett, Jr. 1921- WhoAmA 93
Mason, Frank Earl 1893- WhAm 10
Mason, Frank Henry, III 1936- WhoAm 94, WhoFI 94
Mason, Frank Herbert 1921- WhoAmA 93
Mason, Franklin Rogers 1936- WhoAm 94, WhoFI 94
Mason, Frederick (Cecil) 1913- Who 94
Mason, Frederick Cecil 1913- IntWW 93
Mason, Gary D. 1939- WhoAmP 93
Mason, George 1725-1792 WhAmRev
Mason, George H. 1929- WhoFI 94
Mason, George Robert 1932- WhoAm 94
Mason, Gilbert Rutledge 1928- WhoBlA 94
Mason, Gordon (Charles) 1921- Who 94
Mason, Gregory 1889-1968 EncSF 93
Mason, Haddon d1966 WhoHol 92
Mason, Harold 1937- WhoAmA 93
Mason, Harold Jesse 1926- WhAm 10
Mason, Haydn Trevor 1929- WrDr 94
Mason, Henry Lloyd 1921- WhoAm 94
Mason, Henry Lowell, III 1941- WhoAm 94, WhoAmL 94
Mason, Herbert (Molloy) 1927- WrDr 94
Mason, Herbert Warren, Jr. 1932- WhoAm 94
Mason, Herman, Jr. 1962- WhoBlA 94
Mason, Hilary 1917- WhoHol 92
Mason, Hilda Howland M. WhoBlA 94
Mason, Hilda Howland Mae 1916- WhoAmP 93
Mason, Homer B. d1959 WhoHol 92
Mason, Homer Livingston 1938- WhoAmP 93
Mason, Howard Francis 1910- WhoAmP 93
Mason, Howard Keith 1949- WhoBlA 94
Mason, J(ohn) Alden 1885- WhAm 10
Mason, J. William L. 1940- WhoAmL 94
Mason, Jackie 1930- WhoCom [port]
Mason, Jackie 1934- IntMPA 94, WhoAm 94, WhoHol 92
Mason, James d1959 WhoHol 92
Mason, James d1984 WhoHol 92
Mason, James Albert 1929- WhoAm 94, WhoWest 94
Mason, James Michael 1943- WhoScEn 94
Mason, James Michael 1950- WhoFI 94
Mason, James Osterman 1930- WhoAmP 93
Mason, James Ostermann 1930- WhoAm 94, WhoScEn 94
Mason, James Stephen 1935- Who 94
Mason, James Tate 1913- WhoAm 94
Mason, James W. 1948- WhoAmP 93
Mason, Jane Who 94
Mason, (Tania) Jane 1936- Who 94
Mason, Jeffrey Lynn 1944- WhoAmL 94
Mason, Jerry 1913-1991 WhAm 10
Mason, Joe Ben 1910- WhoWest 94
Mason, John IntWW 93, Who 94
Mason, John d1781 WhAmRev
Mason, John d1919 WhoHol 92
Mason, John 1927- WhoAmA 93
Mason, (Basil) John 1923- IntWW 93, Who 94
Mason, John (Charles Moir) 1927- IntWW 93, Who 94
Mason, John Dudley 1949- IntMPA 94, WhoFI 94
Mason, John Edwin 1914- WhoBlA 94
Mason, John Homans 1945- WhoAmL 94
Mason, John Joseph, III 1947- WhoMW 93
Mason, John Kenyon French 1919- Who 94
Mason, John Latimer 1923- WhoAm 94
Mason, John Milton 1938- WhoAm 94
Mason, John Peter Who 94
Mason, John Thomas, III 1938- WhoScEn 94
Mason, Jonathan Aaron 1947- WhoAmL 94
Mason, Joseph 1932- WhoAm 94
Mason, Joseph Wayne 1949- WhoWest 94
Mason, Ken Donald 1955- WhoWest 94
Mason, Kenneth Bruce 1928- Who 94

Mason, Kenneth M. 1917- IntMPA 94
Mason, Kenneth Staveley 1931- Who 94
Mason, Larry WhoHol 92
Mason, Larry Paul 1945- WhoHisp 94
Mason, Le Roy d1947 WhoHol 92
Mason, Lee W. 1939- WrDr 94
Mason, Leon Verne 1933- WhoAm 94, WhoFI 94
Mason, Linda 1946- WhoMW 93
Mason, Lisa 1953- EncSF 93
Mason, Lori Jean 1962- WhoFI 94
Mason, Lorna Cogswell 1937- WhoWest 94
Mason, Louis d1959 WhoHol 92
Mason, Luther Roscoe 1927- WhoBlA 94
Mason, Major Albert, III 1940- WhoBlA 94
Mason, Margaret Pendleton Pearson 1944- WhoAmL 94
Mason, Margery WhoHol 92
Mason, Marilyn Gell 1944- WhoAm 94, WhoMW 93
Mason, Marjorie d1968 WhoHol 92
Mason, Marlyn 1940- WhoHol 92
Mason, Marsha WhoAm 94
Mason, Marsha 1942- IntMPA 94, WhoHol 92
Mason, Marshall W. 1940- WhoAm 94
Mason, Mary EncSF 93
Mason, Mary d1980 WhoHol 92
Mason, Mary Martin 1946- WhoMW 93
Mason, Maude M. 1867-1956 WhoAmA 93N
Mason, Michael Edward 1951- WhoScEn 94
Mason, Molly Ann 1953- WhoAmA 93
Mason, Monica 1941- Who 94
Mason, Morgan 1956- WhoHol 92
Mason, Muriel d1988 WhoHol 92
Mason, Myron F. d1979 WhoHol 92
Mason, Nicholas 1938- WrDr 94
Mason, Norman Pierce 1896- WhAm 10
Mason, Novem M. 1942- WhoAmA 93
Mason, Orenthia Delois 1952- WhoBlA 94
Mason, Pamela WhoHol 92
Mason, Pamela 1918- IntMPA 94
Mason, Pamela Georgina Walsh Who 94
Mason, Pamela Helen 1922- WhoAm 94
Mason, Paul 1935- WhoAmP 93
Mason, Perry Carter 1939- WhoAm 94
Mason, Peter Who 94
Mason, (George Frederick) Peter 1921- Who 94
Mason, Peter Geoffrey 1914- Who 94
Mason, Peter H. 1951- WhoAmL 94
Mason, Peter Leonard WhoFI 94
Mason, Peter Ralph Who 94
Mason, Philip 1906- IntWW 93, Who 94, WrDr 94
Mason, Phillip Howard 1932- WhoAm 94
Mason, Portland 1948- WhoHol 92
Mason, Rachel Anne Who 94
Mason, Ralph Schweizer 1913-1988 WhAm 10
Mason, Raymond Adams 1936- WhoAm 94, WhoFI 94
Mason, Reginald d1962 WhoHol 92
Mason, Richard 1919- Who 94
Mason, Richard Anthony 1932- Who 94
Mason, Richard Gary 1960- WhoAmL 94
Mason, Richard J. 1951- WhoAmL 94
Mason, Richard John 1929- Who 94
Mason, Richard Randolph 1930- WhoScEn 94
Mason, Robert 1948- WhoAmL 94
Mason, Robert C(averly) 1942- EncSF 93, WrDr 94
Mason, Robert Joseph 1918- WhoAm 94
Mason, Robert P., Jr. 1918- WhoAmP 93
Mason, Robert Thomas 1959- WhoScEn 94
Mason, Ronald 1930- IntWW 93, Who 94
Mason, Ronald Charles 1912- WrDr 94
Mason, Ronald Edward 1948- WhoBlA 94
Mason, Ronald Lee 1951- WhoAmL 94
Mason, Roy WhoHol 92
Mason, Roy Martell 1886-1972 WhoAmA 93N
Mason, Sally W. 1930- WhoMW 93
Mason, Scott Aiken 1951- WhoAm 94
Mason, Scott Jeffrey 1958- WhoFI 94
Mason, Scott MacGregor 1923- WhoFI 94, WhoScEn 94
Mason, Sharon Michelle 1958- WhoMW 93
Mason, Shirley d1979 WhoHol 92
Mason, Sidney d1923 WhoHol 92
Mason, Sonja Kay 1939- WhoAmP 93
Mason, Sophia Thomas 1822-1861 EncNAR
Mason, Stanley George 1914-1987 WhAm 10
Mason, Stephen F(inney) 1923- ConAu 141
Mason, Stephen Finney 1923- IntWW 93, Who 94, WhoScEn 94
Mason, Stephen Olin 1952- WhoAm 94, WhoMW 93
Mason, Steven Charles 1936- WhoAm 94, WhoFI 94, WhoMW 93
Mason, Steven Gerald 1963- WhoAmL 94
Mason, Sully d1970 WhoHol 92
Mason, Suzanne G. 1948- WhoAmL 94
Mason, Sydney d1976 WhoHol 92
Mason, Sydney 1920- IntWW 93, Who 94
Mason, Tally EncSF 93
Mason, Theodore W. 1943- WhoAm 94, WhoAmL 94
Mason, Thomas A. WhoHisp 94
Mason, Thomas Albert 1936- WhoAm 94
Mason, Thomas Boyd WhoHol 92
Mason, Thomas Owen 1963- WhoAmL 94
Mason, Thomson 1733-1785 WhAmRev
Mason, Timothy Ian Godson 1945- Who 94
Mason, Tom WhoHol 92
Mason, Tom Lee 1944- WhoAmP 93
Mason, Vivian 1930- WhoHol 92
Mason, William d1941 WhoHol 92
Mason, William fl. 19th cent.- EncNAR
Mason, William Alvin 1926- WhoAm 94
Mason, William E. 1934- WhoBlA 94
Mason, William Ernest 1929- Who 94
Mason, William G. WhoAmP 93
Mason, William Randy 1944- WhoFI 94
Mason, William Thomas, Jr. 1926- WhoBlA 94
Masoner, Paul Henry 1908- WhoAm 94
Mason-Feilder, Clive Lee 1938- WhoWest 94
Mason Of Barnsley, Baron 1924- IntWW 93, Who 94
Masoro, Edward Joseph, Jr. 1924- WhoAm 94
Masotti, Louis Henry 1934- WhoAm 94
Masouredis, Serafeim Panagiotis 1922- WhoWest 94
Masover, Gerald Kenneth 1935- WhoScEn 94
Masri, Ahmad Fathi Al- 1932- IntWW 93
Masri, Merle Sid 1927- WhoScEn 94, WhoWest 94
Masri, Sami Faiz 1939- WhoAm 94
Masri, Taher Nashat 1942- IntWW 93, Who 94
Mass, Edna Elaine 1954- WhoBlA 94
Mass, Michael D. 1951- WhoAmP 93
Mass, William ConAu 42NR
Massa, Conrad Harry 1927- WhoAm 94
Massa, David J. 1955- WhoAmL 94
Massa, Edward Clement 1907- WhoAm 94
Massa, Paul Peter 1940- WhoAm 94
Massa, Roland 1933- WhoHisp 94
Massa, Salvatore Peter 1955- WhoAm 94
Massachi, Albert WhoFI 94
Massad, Stephen Albert 1950- WhoAm 94, WhoAmL 94
Massagee, Deanie Herman 1947- WhoFI 94
Massalitinova, Valvara O. d1945 WhoHol 92
Massalski, Thaddeus Bronislaw 1926- WhoAm 94
Massaquoi, Hans J. 1926- WhoBlA 94
Massarani, Renzo 1898-1975 NewGrDO
Massard, Robert 1925- NewGrDO
Massari, Kerry Michael 1943- WhoAmL 94
Massari, Lea 1933- WhoHol 92
Massaro, Edward Joseph 1933- WhoScEn 94
Massaro, Karen Thuesen 1944- WhoAmA 93
Massaro, Lorraine 1950- WhoAm 94
Massaro, Sheryl DrAPF 93
Massary, Fritzi d1969 WhoHol 92
Massary, Fritzi 1882-1969 NewGrDO
Masse, Donald D. 1934- WhoBlA 94
Masse, Laurence Raymond 1926- WhoFI 94
Masse, Marcel 1936- IntWW 93, Who 94
Masse, Marcel 1940- IntWW 93, WhoAm 94
Masse, Victor 1822-1884 NewGrDO
Masse, Yvon H. 1935- WhoAm 94, WhoFI 94
Massee, David Lurton, Jr. 1936- WhoAm 94
Massen, Osa 1916- IntMPA 94, WhoHol 92
Massenburg, Tony Arnel 1967- WhoBlA 94
Massenet, Jules (Emile Frederic) 1842-1912 NewGrDO
Massengale, Frank Eugene 1950- WhoAmL 94
Massengale, Jimmy Edgar 1942- WhoIns 94
Massengale, John Edward, III 1921-1988 WhAm 10
Massengale, Joseph d1983 WhoHol 92
Massengale, Martin Andrew 1933- IntWW 93, WhoAm 94, WhoMW 93
Massengill, David E. 1953- WhoAmL 94
Massereene, Viscount d1992 Who 94N
Massereene, Viscount 1940- Who 94
Masserman, Jules Homan 1905- WhoAm 94
Massevitch, Alla Genrikhovna 1918- IntWW 93, Who 94
Massey, Albert P. 1940- WhoAmP 93
Massey, Albert Paul 1940- WhoAmL 94
Massey, Andrew John 1946- WhoAm 94, WhoMW 93
Massey, Ann James 1951- WhoAmA 93
Massey, Anna 1937- IntMPA 94, WhoHol 92
Massey, Anna (Raymond) 1937- Who 94
Massey, Ardrey Yvonne 1951- WhoBlA 94
Massey, Carolyn Shavers 1941- WhoScEn 94
Massey, Carrie Lee 1922- WhoBlA 94
Massey, Charles Knox, Jr. 1936- WhoAm 94
Massey, Charles L. 1922- WhoAm 94
Massey, Charles Wesley, Jr. 1942- WhoAmA 93
Massey, Daniel 1933- IntMPA 94, WhoHol 92
Massey, Daniel (Raymond) 1933- Who 94
Massey, Desmond 1939- WhoAmL 94
Massey, Donald Wayne 1938- WhoFI 94
Massey, Doreen Elizabeth 1938- Who 94
Massey, Douglas Gordon 1926- WhoWest 94
Massey, Edith d1984 WhoHol 92
Massey, Ellen Gray 1921- ConAu 42NR
Massey, Eugene Aloysius 1942- WhoAm 94, WhoAmL 94
Massey, Eyre 1719-1804 AmRev
Massey, Gina WhoHol 92
Massey, (Robert) Graham 1943- Who 94
Massey, Hamilton W. WhoBlA 94
Massey, Henry P., Jr. 1939- WhoAmL 94
Massey, Ike WhoAm 94
Massey, Ilona d1974 WhoHol 92
Massey, Jack T. 1927- WhoIns 94
Massey, Jacquelene Sharp 1947- WhoBlA 94
Massey, James D. WhoAm 94
Massey, James Earl 1930- WhoBlA 94, WhoMW 93, WrDr 94
Massey, James L. 1943- WhoAm 94, WhoFI 94
Massey, L. Edward 1949- WhoScEn 94
Massey, Lawrence Jeremiah WhoScEn 94
Massey, Leon R. 1930- WhoAm 94
Massey, Marilyn Chapin WhoAm 94, WhoWest 94
Massey, Michael G. 1946- WhoAmP 93
Massey, Raymond d1983 WhoHol 92
Massey, Raymond Lee 1948- WhoAm 94, WhoAmL 94
Massey, Reginald Harold 1946- WhoBlA 94
Massey, Richard Sargent 1936- WhoFI 94
Massey, Richard Walter, Jr. 1917- WhoAm 94
Massey, Robert Joseph 1921- WhoAmA 93
Massey, Robert Unruh 1922- WhoAm 94
Massey, Roy Cyril 1934- Who 94
Massey, Ruth Braselton 1919- WhoAmP 93
Massey, Stephen Charles 1946- WhoAm 94
Massey, Stewart Richard 1957- WhoFI 94
Massey, Thomas Benjamin 1926- WhoAm 94
Massey, Tom C. 1931- WhoAmP 93
Massey, Vincent 1926- IntWW 93, Who 94, WhoMW 93
Massey, Walter E. 1938- ConBlB 5 [port]
Massey, Walter Eugene 1938- WhoAm 94, WhoBlA 94
Massey, William S. 1920- WhoAm 94
Massialas, Byron G 1929- WrDr 94
Massick, James William 1932- WhoWest 94
Massie, Allan 1938- WrDr 94
Massie, Allan Johnstone 1938- Who 94
Massie, Edward Lindsey, Jr. 1929- WhoAm 94, WhoFI 94
Massie, Harold Otha 1913- WhoAmP 93
Massie, Herbert William 1949- Who 94
Massie, Joseph Logan 1921- WrDr 94
Massie, Lorna 1938- WhoAmA 93
Massie, Michael Earl 1947- WhoAmL 94
Massie, Noel David 1949- WhoAm 94
Massie, Paul 1932- WhoHol 92
Massie, Robert Joseph 1949- WhoAm 94
Massie, Robert Kinloch 1929- WhoAm 94
Massie, Samuel Proctor 1919- WhoBlA 94
Massie, Samuel Proctor Trei, III 1958- WhoMW 93
Massie, Suzanne 1931- ConAu 142
Massieu, Jean 1772-1846 EncDeaf
Massimini, Joseph Nicholas 1959- WhoScEn 94
Massimino, Elisa Christine 1960- WhoAmL 94
Massimino, Roland V. 1934- WhoAm 94, WhoWest 94
Massin, Eugene Max 1920- WhoAmA 93
Massine, Leonide d1979 WhoHol 92
Massine, Leonide 1895-1979 IntDcB [port]
Massinger, Philip 1583-1640 BlmGEL, IntDcT 2 [port]
Massingham, Harold (William) 1932- WrDr 94
Massingham, John Dudley 1930- Who 94
Massingham, Richard d1953 WhoHol 92
Massler, Howard Arnold 1946- WhoAm 94, WhoAmL 94
Massman, Brian Vincent 1958- WhoWest 94
Massman, Patti 1945- ConAu 41NR
Massman, Richard Allan 1943- WhoAm 94
Massman, Virgil Frank WhoAm 94
Massol, Jean-Etienne August 1802-1887 NewGrDO
Massoletti, Dexter James, Sr. 1941- WhoWest 94
Massolo, Arthur James 1942- WhoAm 94
Massom, Margaret M. 1944- WhoAmP 93
Masson, Charles 1800-1853 DcNaB MP
Masson, David I(rvine) 1915- EncSF 93, WrDr 94
Masson, Diego 1935- NewGrDO
Masson, Jacques 1924- IntWW 93
Masson, Jeffrey Moussaieff 1941- WrDr 94
Masson, Paul-Marie 1882-1954 NewGrDO
Masson, Paul R(obert) 1946- ConAu 142
Masson, Pierre 1928- WhoAm 94, WhoFI 94
Masson, Robert Henry 1935- WhoAm 94
Massopust, Richard H. 1947- WhoAmL 94
Massoud, Ahmed Shah 1953- IntWW 93
Massoud, Hisham Zakaria 1949- WhoScEn 94
Massu, Jacques 1908- IntWW 93
Massura, Edward Anthony 1938- WhoAm 94
Massura, Eileen Kathleen 1925- WhoAm 94, WhoMW 93
Massy, Baron 1921- Who 94
Massy, William Francis 1934- WhoAm 94, WhoWest 94
Massy-Greene, (John) Brian 1916- IntWW 93, Who 94
Mast, Charles David 1961- WhoAmL 94
Mast, Frederick William 1910- WhoAm 94, WhoFI 94
Mast, Gerald 1908-1971 WhoAmA 93N
Mast, Gregory Lewis 1954- WhoAmL 94
Mast, Larry L. 1948- WhoIns 94
Mast, Mae Jerene 1922- WhoMW 93
Mast, Robert Edward 1953- WhoFI 94
Mast, Stewart Dale 1924- WhoAm 94
Mastaglio, Peter James 1941- WhoAmL 94
Mastaler, Richard Michael 1946- WhoAm 94
Mastandrea, Frank J. WhoAmP 93
Mastel, Royston John 1917- Who 94
Masteller, Barry 1945- WhoAmA 93
Masteller, Bruce Allen 1961- WhoMW 93
Masteller, Rand Alex 1951- WhoAmP 93
Masten, Charles C. 1943- WhoAm 94, WhoFI 94
Masten, Jeffrey Paul 1948- WhoAmL 94, WhoAmP 93
Master, Simon Harcourt 1944- IntWW 93, Who 94
Masterfield, Maxine 1933- WhoAmA 93
Master-Karnik, Paul 1948- WhoAmA 93
Master-Karnik, Paul Joseph 1948- WhoAm 94
Masterman, Jack Verner 1930- WhoAm 94, WhoFI 94
Master of Life, The BlkWr 2
Masters, Barbara J. 1933- WhoAmL 94
Masters, Ben 1947- IntMPA 94, WhoHol 92
Masters, Bettie Sue Siler 1937- WhoAm 94, WhoScEn 94
Masters, Brian 1939- ConAu 43NR
Masters, Brian Geoffrey John 1939- Who 94
Masters, Brian John Who 94
Masters, Charles Day 1929- WhoAm 94
Masters, Christopher 1947- Who 94
Masters, Daryl d1961 WhoHol 92
Masters, Dexter 1908-1989 EncSF 93
Masters, Edward E. 1924- WhoAm 94, WhoFI 94
Masters, Eugene Richard 1939- WhoScEn 94
Masters, Gary WhoAm 94
Masters, George Mallary 1936- WhoAm 94
Masters, George William 1940- WhoFI 94
Masters, Greg DrAPF 93
Masters, Harry d1974 WhoHol 92

Masters, Hilary *DrAPF 93*
Masters, J.D. *EncSF 93*
Masters, Jack Gerald 1931- *WhoMW 93*
Masters, John Christopher 1941- *WhoAm 94*
Masters, Jon Joseph 1937- *WhoAm 94*
Masters, Kenneth Halls 1943- *WhoAmP 93*
Masters, Larry William 1941- *WhoScEn 94*
Masters, Laurance E. 1932- *WhoIns 94*
Masters, Melvin Leroy, Jr. 1958- *WhoFI 94*
Masters, Natalie d1986 *WhoHol 92*
Masters, Olga 1919-1986 *BlmGWL*
Masters, Rick David 1950- *WhoWest 94*
Masters, Robert Edward Lee 1927- *WhoScEn 94*
Masters, Roger D. 1933- *WrDr 94*
Masters, Roger Davis 1933- *WhoAm 94*
Masters, Ron Anthony 1961- *WhoScEn 94*
Masters, Ruth d1969 *WhoHol 92*
Masters, Sheila Valerie *Who 94*
Masters, Sibilla c. 1670-1720 *WorInv*
Masters, William H 1915- *WrDr 94*
Masters, William Howell 1915- *AmSocL [port], WhoAm 94*
Masterson, Adrienne C. 1926- *WhoFI 94*
Masterson, Alexandra 1963- *WhoHol 92*
Masterson, Carlin 1940- *WhoAm 94*
Masterson, Charles Francis 1917- *WhoAm 94*
Masterson, Dan *DrAPF 93*
Masterson, J. B. 1922- *WrDr 94*
Masterson, James Francis 1926- *WhoAm 94*
Masterson, Joe A. 1943- *WhoAm 94*
Masterson, John Patrick 1925- *WhoAm 94*
Masterson, John Thomas, Jr. 1951- *WhoAmL 94*
Masterson, Joseph D. 1953- *WhoAm 94*
Masterson, Kenneth Rhodes 1944- *WhoAmL 94*
Masterson, Kleber Sandlin 1908- *WhoAm 94*
Masterson, Kleber Sanlin, Jr. 1932- *WhoAm 94*
Masterson, Linda Histen 1951- *WhoScEn 94*
Masterson, Mary Stewart 1966- *WhoAm 94*
Masterson, Mary Stuart 1966- *IntMPA 94, WhoHol 92*
Masterson, Michael Jon 1946- *WhoAmP 93*
Masterson, Michael Rue 1946- *WhoAm 94*
Masterson, Norton Edward 1902- *WhoIns 94*
Masterson, Patrick 1936- *IntWW 93*
Masterson, Peter 1934- *IntMPA 94, WhoAm 94, WhoHol 92*
Masterson, Roann Dee 1953- *WhoMW 93*
Masterson, Terry Ray 1956- *WhoMW 93*
Masterson, Thomas A. 1927- *WhoAm 94*
Masterson, Valerie *IntWW 93, Who 94*
Masterson, (Margaret) Valerie 1937- *NewGrDO*
Masterson, Whit 1920- *WrDr 94*
Masterton, Graham 1946- *WrDr 94*
Masterton, Nancy N. 1930- *WhoAmP 93*
Masthay, Carl (David) 1941- *ConAu 142*
Mastilovic, Danica 1933- *NewGrDO*
Mastin, Dave *WhoAmP 93*
Mastin, Gary Arthur 1954- *WhoWest 94*
Mastin, John 1865-1932 *EncSF 93*
Mastin, Timothy Jay 1965- *WhoMW 93*
Mastini, Giovanni Battista c. 1700-1771 *NewGrDO*
Mastny, Vojtech 1936- *WrDr 94*
Maston, Thomas Bufford 1897-1988 *WhAm 10*
Mastor, John Constantine *DrAPF 93*
Mastoraki, Jenny 1949- *BlmGWL*
Mastorakis, Nico 1941- *IntMPA 94*
Mastos, Louis T., Jr. 1921- *WhoIns 94*
Mastrangelo, Bobbi 1937- *WhoAmA 93*
Mastrangelo, Evelino William 1923- *WhoAmP 93*
Mastrangelo, Regina Mary 1938- *WhoAm 94*
Mastrangelo, Richard Edward 1938- *WhoAmP 93*
Mastrantonio, Mary Elizabeth 1958- *ConTFT 11, IntMPA 94, WhoAm 94, WhoHol 92*
Mastren, Carmen d1981 *WhoHol 92*
Mastriana, Robert Alan 1949- *WhoMW 93, WhoScEn 94*
Mastrini, Jane Reed 1948- *WhoWest 94*
Mastro, A. F. 1939- *WhoFI 94*
Mastro, Victor John 1948- *WhoScEn 94*
Mastrodonato, George Carl 1950- *WhoAm 94*
Mastroianni, Armand *HorFD*
Mastroianni, Luigi, Jr. 1925- *WhoAm 94, WhoScEn 94*
Mastroianni, Marcello 1923- *WhoHol 92*
Mastroianni, Marcello 1924- *IntMPA 94, IntWW 93, WhoAm 94*
Mastromarco, Dan Ralph 1958- *WhoAmL 94*
Mastromei, Giampietro 1932- *NewGrDO*
Mastromonaco, Ellen G. *WhoAm 94*
Mastropietro, John *WhoAmP 93*
Mastroserio, Joe 1935- *WhoAm 94*
Mastrosimone, William 1947- *ConDr 93, WrDr 94*
Masuda, Gohta 1940- *WhoAm 94, WhoScEn 94*
Masuda, Yoshinori 1953- *WhoWest 94*
Masudi, Abu Al-Hasan Ali Ibn Al-Husayn Al- d956? *WhWE*
Masuhara, Hiroshi 1944- *WhoScEn 94*
Masui, Yoshio 1931- *WhoScEn 94*
Masuo, Ryuichi 1928- *WhoAm 94, WhoScEn 94*
Masuoka, Hiroyuki 1923- *IntWW 93*
Masur, Dorothea E. 1923- *WhoAmP 93*
Masur, Harold Q 1909- *WrDr 94*
Masur, Kurt *NewYTBS 93 [port]*
Masur, Kurt 1927- *ConMus 11 [port], IntWW 93, NewGrDO, News 93 [port], WhoAm 94*
Masur, Richard *WhoHol 92*
Masur, Richard 1948- *IntMPA 94*
Masurel, Jean-Louis Antoine Nicolas 1940- *IntWW 93, WhoAm 94*
Masurok, Yuri Antonovich 1931- *IntWW 93*
Masurovsky, Gregory 1929- *WhoAmA 93*
Masursky, Harold 1923-1990 *WhAm 10*
Masyk, Konstiantyn Ivanovych 1932- *LngBDD*
Masyr, Caryl Lynn 1946- *WhoAm 94*
Ma Szu-Chung *IntWW 93*
Mata, David Joseph 1956- *WhoHisp 94, WhoWest 94*
Mata, Eduardo 1942- *IntWW 93, WhoAm 94, WhoHisp 94*
Mata, Edward *WhoHisp 94*
Mata, Guillermo Gonzalo 1949- *WhoHisp 94*
Mata, Marina Martha 1966- *WhoHisp 94*
Mata, Pedro F. 1944- *WhoHisp 94*
Mata, Pedro Francisco 1944- *WhoFI 94*
Mata, Zelma D. 1954- *WhoHisp 94*
Mata, Zoila 1937- *WhoScEn 94*
Matabane, Sebiletso Mokone 1945- *WhoBlA 94*
Mataca, Petero *Who 94*
Matacic, Lovro von 1899-1985 *NewGrDO*
Mataga, Noboru 1927- *WhoScEn 94*
Mataira, Katarina Te Heikoko 1932- *BlmGWL*
Matakovic, Boris 1969- *WhoMW 93*
Matalin, Mary *WhoAm 94*
Matalon, Moshe 1949- *WhoScEn 94*
Matalon, Norma 1949- *WhoAm 94, WhoFI 94*
Matalon, Vivian 1929- *WhoAm 94, WhoHol 92*
Matamoros, Lourdes M. 1963- *WhoHisp 94*
Matamoros, Mercedes 1851-1906 *BlmGWL*
Matane, Paulias (Nguna) 1932- *Who 94*
Matane, Paulias Nguna 1931- *IntWW 93*
Matanky, Arnie 1930- *WhoMW 93*
Matanky, Robert William 1955- *WhoAmL 94, WhoMW 93*
Matano, Robert Stanley 1925- *IntWW 93*
Matanzima, Kaiser 1915- *IntWW 93*
Mata-Pistokache, Theresa 1959- *WhoHisp 94*
Matarazzo, Joseph Dominic 1925- *WhoAm 94, WhoWest 94*
Matarazzo, Nicholas J. 1957- *WhoAm 94*
Matarazzo, Ruth Gadbois 1926- *WhoAm 94*
Matare, Herbert F. 1912- *WhoWest 94*
Matarrese, Armand Ray 1944- *WhoMW 93*
Matas, Julio 1931- *WhoHisp 94*
Matas, Myra Dorothea 1938- *WhoWest 94*
Matas, Raquel M. 1956- *WhoHisp 94*
Matasar, Ann B. 1940- *WhoAm 94*
Matasovic, Marilyn Estelle 1946- *WhoFI 94, WhoMW 93*
Matassa, John P. 1945- *WhoAmA 93*
Mata-Toledo, Ramon A. 1949- *WhoHisp 94*
Mata'utia, Tuiafono 1929- *WhoAmP 93*
Mataxis, Theodore Christopher 1917- *WhoAm 94*
Matayoshi, Coralie Chun 1956- *WhoAmL 94*
Matayoshi, Herbert Tatsuo 1928- *WhoAmP 93*
Match, Robert Kreis 1926- *WhoAm 94*
Matcha, Jack *DrAPF 93*
Matcham, Francis 1854-1920 *DcNaB MP*
Matchekewis c. 1735-c. 1805 *AmRev*
Matchett, Andrew James 1950- *WhoMW 93*
Matchett, Christine 1957- *WhoHol 92*
Matchett, Johnson, Jr. 1942- *WhoBlA 94*
Matchett, William H. *DrAPF 93*
Matchett, William H(enry) 1923- *WrDr 94*
Matchett, William Henry 1923- *WhoAm 94*
Matchette, Phyllis Lee 1921- *WhoMW 93*
Matchie, Thomas F. 1933- *WhoAmP 93*
Matchless Orinda *BlmGWL*
Mate, Martin 1929- *Who 94*
Mate, Rudolph 1898-1964 *IntDcF 2-4*
Mateas, Kenneth Edward 1949- *WhoAmL 94*
Mateen, Malik Abdul 1949- *WhoBlA 94*
Mateer, Charles Quentin 1922- *WhoAmP 93*
Mateju, Joseph Frank 1927- *WhoAm 94*
Mateker, Emil Joseph, Jr. 1931- *WhoScEn 94*
Mateles, Richard Isaac 1935- *WhoAm 94*
Ma Teng'ai 1921- *WhoPRCh 91 [port]*
Mateo, Fernando 1958- *WhoHisp 94*
Mateo, Juan A., Jr. 1956- *WhoHisp 94*
Mateo, Julio 1951- *WhoAmA 93*
Mateo, Julio, Jr. 1959- *WhoAmL 94, WhoWest 94*
Mater, Gene P. 1926- *WhoAm 94*
Mater, Maud E. *WhoAmL 94*
Matera, Richard Ernest 1925- *WhoAm 94*
Matern, Stephen Edgar 1943- *WhoWest 94*
Materna(-Friedrich), Amalie 1844-1918 *NewGrDO*
Materna, Thomas Walter 1944- *WhoFI 94, WhoScEn 94*
Materne, David 1956- *WhoMW 93*
Maternus, Julius fl. 50- *WhWE*
Materson, Richard Stephen 1941- *WhoScEn 94*
Mates, C. George 1933- *WhoFI 94*
Mates, Lawrence A., II 1954- *WhoFI 94*
Mates, Michael John 1934- *Who 94*
Mateus, Lois *WhoAm 94, WhoFI 94*
Math, John *WhoBlA 94*
Mathabane, Mark 1960- *BlkWr 2, ConBlB 5 [port], TwCYAW, WrDr 94*
Mathabane, Mark Johannes 1960- *WhoBlA 94*
Mathai, Anish 1949- *WhoAsA 94*
Mathai, Chirathalakal Varughese 1945- *WhoFI 94*
Mathai-Davis, Prema 1950- *WhoAsA 94*
Mathamel, Martin Steven 1949- *WhoFI 94*
Mathaudhu, Sukhdev Singh 1946- *WhoScEn 94, WhoWest 94*
Mathavan, Sudershan Kumar 1945- *WhoScEn 94*
Mathay, John Preston 1942- *WhoMW 93*
Mathe, Edouard d1934 *WhoHol 92*
Mathe, Georges 1922- *IntWW 93*
Matheny, Adam Pence, Jr. 1932- *WhoScEn 94*
Matheny, Bill Gene 1945- *WhoFI 94*
Matheny, Edward Taylor, Jr. 1923- *WhoAm 94*
Matheny, James Harnly 1924- *WhoWest 94*
Matheny, Jeffrey Robert 1958- *WhoFI 94*
Matheny, Rita M. 1922- *WhoAmP 93*
Matheny, Robert Lavesco 1933- *WhoAm 94, WhoWest 94*
Matheny, Ruth Ann 1918- *WhoAm 94*
Matheny, Tom Harrell *WhoAm 94, WhoAmL 94*
Mather, Allen Frederick 1922- *WhoAm 94*
Mather, Anne *WrDr 94*
Mather, Anthony Charles McClure 1942- *Who 94*
Mather, Aubrey d1958 *WhoHol 92*
Mather, Barbara W. 1944- *WhoAm 94, WhoAmL 94*
Mather, Berkely *WrDr 94*
Mather, Betty Bang 1927- *WhoAm 94*
Mather, Bryant 1916- *WhoAm 94*
Mather, Carol *Who 94*
Mather, (David) Carol (Macdonell) 1919- *Who 94*
Mather, Charles E., Jr. 1948- *WhoWest 94*
Mather, Charles E., III 1934- *WhoIns 94*
Mather, Cotton 1663-1728 *AmSocL, DcAmReB 2, DcLB 140 [port], HisWorL*
Mather, Dennis Bryan 1949- *WhoFI 94*
Mather, E. Cotton 1918- *WhoWest 94*
Mather, Elizabeth Vivian 1941- *WhoScEn 94*
Mather, Graham Christopher Spencer 1954- *IntWW 93, Who 94*
Mather, Increase 1639-1723 *AmSocL, DcAmReB 2, HisWorL [port]*
Mather, Jack d1966 *WhoHol 92*
Mather, John *WhoHol 92*
Mather, John Cromwell 1946- *WhoAm 94, WhoScEn 94*
Mather, John Douglas 1936- *Who 94*
Mather, John Norman 1942- *WhoAm 94*
Mather, John Russell 1923- *WhoAm 94*
Mather, Katharine 1916-1991 *WhAm 10*
Mather, Leonard (Charles) 1909- *WrDr 94*
Mather, Mildred Eunice 1922- *WhoAm 94*
Mather, Norman Wells 1914-1990 *WhAm 10*
Mather, Philip R. 1894- *WhAm 10*
Mather, Richard Burroughs 1913- *WhoAm 94*
Mather, Robert Laurance 1921- *WhoWest 94*
Mather, Roger Frederick 1917- *WhoAm 94, WhoMW 93*
Mather, Sydney d1925 *WhoHol 92*
Mather, William (Loris) 1913- *Who 94*
Matherlee, Thomas Ray 1934- *WhoAm 94*
Mathern, Dennis Charles 1951- *WhoFI 94*
Mathern, Tim 1950- *WhoAmP 93, WhoMW 93*
Matheron, Marie *WhoHol 92*
Matheron, Michael Earl 1947- *WhoWest 94*
Mathers, Daniel Eugene 1962- *WhoMW 93*
Mathers, Jerry 1948- *WhoHol 92*
Mathers, Peter 1931- *WrDr 94*
Mathers, Robert (William) 1928- *Who 94*
Mathers, Thomas Nesbit 1914- *WhoAm 94*
Mathers, William Harris 1914- *WhoAm 94*
Mathes, Caryn G. 1955- *WhoAm 94, WhoMW 93*
Mathes, Charles (Elliott) 1949- *ConAu 141*
Mathes, James R. *WhoBlA 94*
Mathes, John Charles 1931- *WhoAm 94*
Mathes, Rachel 1941- *NewGrDO*
Mathes, Sorrell Mark 1936- *WhoAm 94, WhoFI 94*
Mathes, Stephen Jon 1945- *WhoAm 94, WhoAmL 94*
Mathesius, Walter Emil Ludwig 1886-1966 *EncABHB 9 [port]*
Matheson, Alan Adams 1932- *WhoAm 94*
Matheson, Alastair Taylor 1929- *WhoAm 94*
Matheson, Ann 1940- *WrDr 94*
Matheson, Daniel Nicholas, III 1949- *WhoAm 94*
Matheson, Don *WhoHol 92*
Matheson, Duncan *Who 94*
Matheson, Ivan M. 1926- *WhoAmP 93*
Matheson, (Nicholas) James (Sutherland) 1796-1878 *DcNaB MP*
Matheson, James Gunn 1912- *Who 94*
Matheson, Jane A. 1949- *WhoAmL 94*
Matheson, (Henry) John (Parke) 1928- *NewGrDO*
Matheson, John Mackenzie 1912- *Who 94*
Matheson, Louis *Who 94*
Matheson, (James Adam) Louis 1912- *IntWW 93, Who 94*
Matheson, Max Smith 1913- *WhoMW 93*
Matheson, Murray d1985 *WhoHol 92*
Matheson, Richard (Burton) 1926- *EncSF 93, WrDr 94*
Matheson, Richard Christian 1953- *EncSF 93*
Matheson, Scott Milne 1929-1990 *WhAm 10*
Matheson, Stephen Charles Taylor 1939- *Who 94*
Matheson, Sylvia A. 1918- *WrDr 94*
Matheson, Tim 1947- *IntMPA 94, WhoHol 92*
Matheson, William Angus, Jr. 1919- *WhoMW 93*
Matheson, William Lyon 1924- *WhoAm 94*
Matheson of Matheson, Fergus (John) 1927- *Who 94*
Matheson of Matheson, Torquhil Alexander d1993 *Who 94N*
Matheu, Federico M. *WhoHisp 94*
Matheu, Federico Manuel 1941- *WhoAm 94*
Matheussen, John J. 1953- *WhoAmP 93*
Mathew, Ann d1976 *WhoHol 92*
Mathew, Edward 1729-1805 *WhAmRev*
Mathew, John Charles 1927- *Who 94*
Mathew, Ray(mond Frank) 1929- *ConDr 93, WrDr 94*
Mathew, Robert Knox 1945- *Who 94*
Mathew, Saramma T. 1938- *WhoAsA 94*
Mathew, Theobald David 1942- *Who 94*
Mathew, Valsa 1947- *WhoAsA 94*
Mathews, Arthur Francis 1938- *WhoAm 94*
Mathews, Arthur Kenneth d1992 *Who 94N*
Mathews, Barbara Edith 1946- *WhoScEn 94, WhoWest 94*

Mathews, Byron B., Jr. 1948- *WhoAm 94, WhoAmL 94*
Mathews, Carl d1959 *WhoHol 92*
Mathews, Carmen 1914- *WhoHol 92*
Mathews, Carmen Sylva 1918- *WhoAm 94*
Mathews, Carole 1920- *IntMPA 94, WhoHol 92*
Mathews, Christopher King 1937- *WhoAm 94*
Mathews, David 1935- *WhoAm 94, WhoScEn 94*
Mathews, (Forrest) David 1935- *IntWW 93*
Mathews, Donald G. 1932- *WhoAm 94*
Mathews, Duke *WhoHol 92*
Mathews, F. X. *DrAPF 93*
Mathews, Frances Amelia 1932- *WhoAmP 93*
Mathews, Francis T. d1947 *WhoHol 92*
Mathews, George *WhoBlA 94*
Mathews, George d1984 *WhoHol 92*
Mathews, George 1739-1812 *WhAmRev*
Mathews, George H. d1952 *WhoHol 92*
Mathews, George Meprathu 1960- *WhoFI 94*
Mathews, George W., Jr. 1927- *WhoFI 94*
Mathews, Harlan *WhoAm 94*
Mathews, Harlan 1927- *CngDr 93, WhoAmP 93*
Mathews, Harry *DrAPF 93*
Mathews, Harry Burchell 1930- *WhoAm 94*
Mathews, Ian Richard 1933- *IntWW 93*
Mathews, Jack Wayne 1939- *WhoAm 94*
Mathews, Jean H. 1941- *WhoAmP 93*
Mathews, Jeremy Fell 1941- *Who 94*
Mathews, Jessica Tuchman 1946- *WhoAm 94*
Mathews, John 1744-1802 *WhAmRev*
Mathews, John A. 1872-1935 *EncABHB 9 [port]*
Mathews, John David 1947- *WhoAm 94, WhoScEn 94*
Mathews, John Joseph 1895-1979 *ConAu 142*
Mathews, Joyce 1919- *WhoHol 92*
Mathews, Keith E. 1944- *WhoBlA 94*
Mathews, Kenneth Pine 1921- *WhoAm 94, WhoWest 94*
Mathews, Kerwin 1926- *WhoHol 92*
Mathews, Lawrence Talbert 1947- *WhoBlA 94*
Mathews, Linda McVeigh 1946- *WhoAm 94*
Mathews, Louise A. 1945- *WhoAmL 94*
Mathews, Louise Robison 1917- *WhoFI 94*
Mathews, Marina Sarah Dewe *Who 94*
Mathews, Marshall *NewYTBS 93 [port]*
Mathews, Michael Stone 1940- *WhoFI 94*
Mathews, Nancy Ellen 1958- *WhoScEn 94*
Mathews, Nancy Mowll 1947- *WhoAmA 93*
Mathews, Paul Joseph 1944- *WhoMW 93*
Mathews, Peter 1951- *WhoAsA 94*
Mathews, Richard *DrAPF 93*
Mathews, Robert Earl, II 1932- *WhoMW 93*
Mathews, Robert Edward 1909- *WhoAm 94*
Mathews, Roderick Bell 1941- *WhoAm 94, WhoAmL 94, WhoFI 94*
Mathews, Russell Lloyd 1921- *WrDr 94*
Mathews, Shailer 1863-1941 *DcAmReB 2*
Mathews, Sharon Walker 1947- *WhoAm 94*
Mathews, Susan McKiernan 1946- *WhoFI 94*
Mathews, Thom *WhoHol 92*
Mathews, Thomas John 1956- *WhoWest 94*
Mathews, Tomas Goodwin 1960- *WhoFI 94*
Mathews, Walter David 1949- *WhoMW 93*
Mathews, William Edward 1934- *WhoWest 94*
Mathews, William Henry 1919- *WhoAm 94, WhoScEn 94*
Mathews-Graham, Carla 1952- *WhoMW 93*
Mathewson, Charles Norman 1928- *WhoAm 94, WhoWest 94*
Mathewson, Christopher Colville 1941- *WhoAm 94, WhoScEn 94*
Mathewson, Christy d1925 *WhoHol 92*
Mathewson, George Atterbury 1935- *WhoAmL 94*
Mathewson, George Otis 1949- *WhoAmL 94*
Mathewson, George Ross 1940- *Who 94*
Mathewson, Hugh Spalding 1921- *WhoAm 94, WhoScEn 94*
Mathewson, James L. 1938- *WhoAmP 93*
Mathias, Alice Irene 1949- *WhoFI 94, WhoScEn 94*

Mathias, Anita *DrAPF 93*
Mathias, Baptiste 1876- *EncNAR*
Mathias, Betty Jane 1923- *WhoWest 94*
Mathias, Bob 1930- *WhoHol 92*
Mathias, Charles McC. 1922- *IntWW 93*
Mathias, Charles McC., Jr. 1922- *WhoAmP 93*
Mathias, Charles McCurdy 1922- *WhoAm 94, WhoAmL 94*
Mathias, Edward Charles 1959- *WhoScEn 94*
Mathias, Edward Joseph 1941- *WhoAm 94*
Mathias, Frank Russell Bentley 1927- *Who 94*
Mathias, Harry Michael 1945- *WhoWest 94*
Mathias, John Joseph 1929- *WhoAmL 94*
Mathias, Joseph Marshall 1914- *WhoAmL 94*
Mathias, Joseph Simon 1925- *WhoAm 94*
Mathias, Kimberly Jo 1963- *WhoMW 93*
Mathias, Leslie Michael 1935- *WhoFI 94, WhoWest 94*
Mathias, Margaret Grossman 1928- *WhoFI 94, WhoMW 94*
Mathias, Melba *WhoHol 92*
Mathias, Mildred Esther 1906- *WhoAm 94, WhoScEn 94*
Mathias, Pauline Mary 1928- *Who 94*
Mathias, Peter 1928- *IntWW 93, Who 94, WrDr 94*
Mathias, Reuben Victor 1926- *WhoAm 94*
Mathias, Robert Bruce 1930- *WhoAmP 93*
Mathias, Robert Joseph 1955- *WhoAmL 94*
Mathias, Roland (Glyn) 1915- *ConAu 41NR, WrDr 94*
Mathias, William (James) d1992 *IntWW 93N*
Mathias, William (James) 1934-1992 *NewGrDO*
Mathias, William J. 1934-1992 *WhAm 10*
Mathiasen, Lissa 1948- *WhoWomW 91*
Mathiason, Garry George 1946- *WhoAm 94, WhoAmL 94*
Mathies, Allen Wray, Jr. 1930- *WhoAm 94, WhoWest 94*
Mathies, Charlene *WhoHol 92*
Mathiesen, Matthias (Arnason) 1931- *IntWW 93*
Mathiesen, Thomas James 1947- *WhoMW 93*
Mathieson, Andrew Wray 1928- *WhoAm 94*
Mathieson, Carol Ann Fisher 1948- *WhoMW 93*
Mathieson, Donald Lindsay 1936- *WrDr 94*
Mathieson, Janet Hilary *Who 94*
Mathieson, Muir d1975 *WhoHol 92*
Mathieson, Muir 1911-1975 *IntDcF 2-4*
Mathieson, William Allan Cunningham 1916- *Who 94*
Mathieu, Emile (Louis Victor) 1844-1932 *NewGrDO*
Mathieu, Georges Victor Adolphe 1921- *IntWW 93*
Mathieu, Helen M. 1940- *WhoAmP 93*
Mathieu, Michael Ellis 1964- *WhoAmL 94*
Mathieu, Mireille *WhoHol 92*
Mathieu, Peter Francis 1963- *WhoAmL 94*
Mathieu, Simone Passemard 1908-1980 *BuCMET*
Mathieu, Thomas C. 1936- *WhoAmP 93*
Mathieu-Harris, Michele Suzanne 1950- *WhoMW 93*
Mathioudakis, Michael Robert 1963- *WhoFI 94, WhoMW 93*
Mathiprakasam, Balakrishnan 1942- *WhoAsA 94*
Mathis, Benton J., Jr. 1959- *WhoAmL 94*
Mathis, Billie F. 1936- *WhoAmA 93*
Mathis, Brian John 1945- *WhoFI 94*
Mathis, Byron Claude 1927-1989 *WhAm 10*
Mathis, Cleopatra *DrAPF 93*
Mathis, David 1947- *WhoBlA 94*
Mathis, David B. *WhoAm 94, WhoFI 94, WhoMW 93*
Mathis, Edith 1938- *IntWW 93, NewGrDO*
Mathis, Emile Henry, II 1946- *WhoAmA 93*
Mathis, Frank 1937- *WhoBlA 94*
Mathis, Jack David 1931- *WhoFI 94, WhoMW 93*
Mathis, James Forrest 1925- *WhoAm 94, WhoFI 94, WhoScEn 94*
Mathis, John Prentiss 1944- *WhoAmL 94*
Mathis, Johnny 1935- *CurBio 93 [port], WhoAm 94, WhoBlA 94, WhoMW 93*
Mathis, June d1927 *WhoHol 92*
Mathis, June 1892-1927 *IntDcF 2-4 [port]*
Mathis, June Green 1941- *WhoAm 94*
Mathis, Larry Lee 1943- *WhoAm 94*

Mathis, Lois Reno 1915- *WhoMW 93*
Mathis, Luster Doyle 1936- *WhoAm 94*
Mathis, Mark Jay 1947- *WhoAm 94*
Mathis, Marsha Debra 1953- *WhoFI 94*
Mathis, Milly d1965 *WhoHol 92*
Mathis, Nathan *WhoAmP 93*
Mathis, Robert Lee 1934- *WhoBlA 94*
Mathis, Sallye Brooks *WhoBlA 94*
Mathis, Samantha *WhoHol 92*
Mathis, Sharon Bell *DrAPF 93*
Mathis, Sharon Bell 1937- *Au&Arts 12 [port], BlkWr 2, TwCYAW, WhoAm 94, WhoBlA 94, WrDr 94*
Mathis, Sherry 1949- *WhoHol 92*
Mathis, Thaddeus P. 1942- *WhoBlA 94*
Mathis, Walter Lee, Sr. 1940- *WhoBlA 94*
Mathis, William Lawrence 1964- *WhoBlA 94*
Mathis, William Lowrey 1926- *WhoAm 94*
Mathis-Eddy, Darlene 1937- *IntWW 93*
Mathisen, Chris *WhoAmP 93*
Mathisen, Harold Clifford 1924- *WhoFI 94*
Mathisen-Reid, Rhoda Sharon 1942- *WhoMW 93*
Mathison, Ian William 1938- *WhoAm 94*
Mathison, Richard d1980 *WhoHol 92*
Mathison, Thomas Richard 1951- *WhoMW 93*
Mathlouthi, Mohamed 1940- *WhoScEn 94*
Mathna, Woodrow Wilson 1913- *WhoAmP 93*
Matho, Jean-Baptiste c. 1660-1746 *NewGrDO*
Mathog, Robert Henry 1939- *WhoAm 94*
Mathot, Leon d1968 *WhoHol 92*
Mathre, Sewell Jerome 1922- *WhoMW 93*
Mathues, Thomas Oliver 1923- *WhoAm 94*
Mathur, Achint P. 1945- *WhoAsA 94*
Mathur, Aditya P. 1948- *WhoAsA 94*
Mathur, Aditya Prasad 1948- *WhoMW 93*
Mathur, Ashok *WhoWest 94*
Mathur, Balbir Singh 1936- *WhoAsA 94, WhoMW 93*
Mathur, Harbans B. 1938- *WhoAsA 94*
Mathur, Ike 1943- *WhoAsA 94, WhoFI 94*
Mathur, Kailash V. 1934- *WhoAsA 94*
Mathur, Krishan 1928- *WhoBlA 94*
Mathur, Krishan D. 1928- *WhoAsA 94*
Mathur, Murari Lal 1931- *IntWW 93*
Mathur, Radhey Mohan 1936- *WhoScEn 94*
Mathur, Raghu P. 1948- *WhoAsA 94*
Mathur, Veerendra Kumar 1935- *WhoScEn 94*
Matia, Paul Ramon 1937- *WhoAm 94, WhoAmL 94, WhoAmP 93, WhoMW 93*
Matias-Rivera, Jenice C. 1952- *WhoHisp 94*
Matiba, Kenneth *IntWW 93*
Ma Tiejun *WhoPRCh 91*
Matiella, Ana Consuelo 1951- *WhoHisp 94*
Matienzo, Rafael Antonio 1956- *WhoScEn 94*
Matiesen, Otto d1932 *WhoHol 92*
Matigan, Robert 1961- *WhoScEn 94*
Matijevic, Egon 1922- *WhoAm 94, WhoScEn 94*
Matijevich, John S. 1927- *WhoAmP 93*
Matilainen, Riitta Marja 1948- *WhoScEn 94*
Matilal, B(imal) K(rishna) 1935-1991 *WrDr 94N*
Matilda, Countess of Winchester d1252 *BlmGWL*
Matilda, Empress 1102-1167 *BlmGWL*
Matilda of Tuscany 1046-1115 *HisWorL [port]*
Matilla, Alfredo 1937- *WhoHisp 94*
Matin, Abdul 1932- *IntWW 93*
Matin, Abdul 1941- *WhoScEn 94, WhoWest 94*
Matin, M. A. 1937- *IntWW 93*
Matis, Bonnie Leah *WhoMW 93*
Matis, Nina B. 1947- *WhoAm 94, WhoAmL 94*
Matisse, Henri 1869-1954 *IntDcB*
Matisse, Pierre 1900-1989 *WhAm 10, WhoAmA 93N*
Matjukhin, Georgii G. 1934- *IntWW 93*
Matkowsky, Bernard Judah 1939- *WhoAm 94, WhoScEn 94*
Matlack, Ardena Lavonne 1930- *WhoAmP 93*
Matlack, Don 1929- *WhoAmP 93*
Matlack, George Miller 1921- *WhoAm 94*
Matlack, Timothy 1730-1829 *WhAmRev*
Matley, Benvenuto Gilbert 1930- *WhoWest 94*
Matlhabaphiri, Gaotlhaetse Utlwang Sankoloba 1949- *Who 94*
Matlick, Gerald Allen 1947-1988 *WhoAmA 93N*

Matlin, David *DrAPF 93*
Matlin, David 1944- *ConAu 141*
Matlin, Marlee 1965- *IntMPA 94, WhoAm 94, WhoHol 92*
Matlin, Robin Beth 1952- *WhoAm 94*
Matlins, Stuart M. 1940- *WhoFI 94*
Matlock, Charles d1976 *WhoHol 92*
Matlock, Clifford Charles 1909- *WhoAm 94*
Matlock, Hudson 1919- *WhoAm 94*
Matlock, Jack F., Jr. 1929- *WhoAmP 93*
Matlock, Jack Foust 1929- *Who 94*
Matlock, Jack Foust, Jr. 1929- *IntWW 93, WhoAm 94*
Matlock, Kenneth Jerome 1928- *WhoAm 94, WhoFI 94*
Matlock, Kent *WhoBlA 94*
Matlock, Matty d1978 *WhoHol 92*
Matlock, Norman *WhoHol 92*
Matlock, Stephen J. 1949- *WhoWest 94*
Matlock, Terry Joe 1962- *WhoAmP 93*
Matloff, Maurice 1915- *WhoAm 94*
Matloff, Maurice 1915-1993 *ConAu 141*
Matlow, Linda Monique 1955- *WhoMW 93*
Matney, Rhonda Marie 1962- *WhoMW 93*
Matney, William Brooks, VII 1935- *WhoScEn 94*
Matney, William C., Jr. 1924- *WhoBlA 94*
Matochkin, Yury Semenovich 1931- *LngBDD*
Matoka, Peter Wilfred 1930- *IntWW 93, Who 94*
Matola, Sharon 1954- *CurBio 93 [port]*
Matolengwe, Patrick Monwabisi 1937- *Who 94*
Matomaki, Tauno 1937- *IntWW 93*
Matonabbee c. 1736-1782 *WhWE*
Matonovich, John S. 1959- *WhoAmP 93*
Matory, Deborah Love 1929- *WhoBlA 94*
Matory, William Earle, Jr. 1950- *WhoBlA 94*
Matory, Yvedt L. 1956- *WhoBlA 94*
Matos, German Esteban 1947- *WhoHisp 94*
Matos, Israel 1954- *WhoHisp 94*
Matos, John *WhoAm 94*
Matos, Jose Gilvomar Rocha 1944- *WhoScEn 94*
Matos, Mari d1952 *WhoHol 92*
Matos, Maria M. 1950- *WhoHisp 94*
Matos, Rafael Enrique 1967- *WhoHisp 94*
Matos, Wilfredo 1940- *WhoHisp 94*
Matos Ortiz, Vilma Esther 1960- *WhoHisp 94*
Matos Paoli, Francisco 1915- *WhoHisp 94*
Matosse, Jackie 1931- *WhoAmA 93*
Matossian, Jesse Nerses 1952- *WhoScEn 94, WhoWest 94*
Matovich, Mitchel Joseph, Jr. 1927- *WhoWest 94*
Matoy, Elizabeth Anne 1946- *WhoAm 94*
Matras, Christian 1903-1977 *IntDcF 2-4*
Matras, James Allen 1954- *WhoAm 94*
Matray, Ernst d1978 *WhoHol 92*
Matray, Gabor 1797-1875 *NewGrDO*
Matray, James I(rving) 1948- *WrDr 94*
Matrunich, Karen M. 1957- *WhoIns 94*
Matsch, Lee Allan 1935- *WhoWest 94*
Matsch, Richard P. 1930- *WhoAm 94, WhoAmL 94, WhoWest 94*
Matschinsky, Franz Maximilian 1931- *WhoAm 94*
Matschulat, Natel Kypriotou 1944- *WhoAm 94*
Matschullat, Dale Lewis 1945- *WhoAmL 94*
Matsebula, Mhlangano Stephen 1925- *IntWW 93*
Matsen, John Martin 1933- *WhoFI 94, WhoScEn 94, WhoWest 94*
Matsen, John Morris 1936- *WhoScEn 94*
Matsko, John G. *WhoAmP 93*
Matsler, Franklin Giles 1922- *WhoAm 94*
Matson, Audrey *WhoHol 92*
Matson, Clive *DrAPF 93*
Matson, Greta *WhoAmA 93*
Matson, Jim *WhoAmP 93*
Matson, John Jacob Leonard 1944- *WhoAmL 94*
Matson, Merwyn Dean 1937- *WhoWest 94*
Matson, Norman (Haghejm) 1893-1965 *EncSF 93*
Matson, Ollie *ProFbHF*
Matson, Ollie Genoa 1930- *WhoBlA 94*
Matson, Robert Arthur 1959- *WhoFI 94*
Matson, Robert Edward 1930- *WhoAm 94*
Matson, Suzanne *DrAPF 93*
Matson, Thomas d1978 *WhoHol 92*
Matson, Virginia Mae Freeberg 1914- *WhoMW 93*
Matson, Wallace I 1921- *WrDr 94*
Matson, Wesley Jennings 1924- *WhoAm 94, WhoMW 93*
Matson, William Robert 1927- *WhoAmP 93*

Matsubara, Naoko 1937- *WhoAmA 93*
Matsubara, Steve Yoshio 1951- *WhoMW 93*
Matsubara, Tomoo 1929- *WhoScEn 94*
Matsuda, Fay Chew 1949- *WhoAsA 94*
Matsuda, Fujio 1924- *WhoAm 94, WhoAsA 94, WhoWest 94*
Matsuda, Mari J. *ConAu 140*
Matsuda, Yasuhiro 1947- *WhoScEn 94*
Matsuda, Yusaku d1989 *WhoHol 92*
Matsugo, Seiichi 1952- *WhoScEn 94*
Matsui, Doris Kazue Okada 1944- *WhoAsA 94*
Matsui, Doris Okada 1944- *NewYTBS 93 [port]*
Matsui, Eiichi 1925- *WhoScEn 94*
Matsui, Iwao 1936- *WhoScEn 94*
Matsui, Jiro 1919- *WhoWest 94*
Matsui, Keiko 1961- *WhoAsA 94*
Matsui, Machiko 1950- *WhoAsA 94*
Matsui, Masanao 1917- *IntWW 93*
Matsui, Noriatsu 1945- *WhoAsA 94*
Matsui, Robert T. 1941- *CngDr 93*
Matsui, Robert Takeo 1941- *NewYTBS 93 [port], WhoAm 94, WhoAmP 93, WhoAsA 94, WhoWest 94*
Matsui, Suisei d1973 *WhoHol 92*
Matsukawa, Michiya 1924- *IntWW 93*
Matsumori, Douglas 1947- *WhoAmL 94*
Matsumoto, Donald Michiaki 1954- *WhoAsA 94*
Matsumoto, George 1922- *WhoAm 94, WhoAsA 94*
Matsumoto, Hiroshi 1948- *WhoScEn 94*
Matsumoto, Iku 1919- *WhoAsA 94*
Matsumoto, Juro *IntWW 93*
Matsumoto, Kazuko 1949- *WhoScEn 94*
Matsumoto, Keith Tadao 1957- *WhoFI 94, WhoWest 94*
Matsumoto, Ken 1935- *IntWW 93*
Matsumoto, Ken 1941- *WhoAsA 94*
Matsumoto, Mark R. 1955- *WhoAsA 94*
Matsumoto, Nancy K. *WhoAsA 94*
Matsumoto, Paul Tetsuo 1927- *WhoAmP 93*
Matsumoto, Randall Itsumi 1953- *WhoAsA 94*
Matsumoto, Ryujiro 1964- *WhoAsA 94*
Matsumoto, Takashi 1943- *WhoAsA 94*
Matsumoto, Teruo 1929- *WhoAm 94, WhoAsA 94*
Matsumura, Fumitake 1942- *WhoScEn 94*
Matsumura, Kenneth N. 1945- *WhoAm 94*
Matsumura, Takao 1942- *WrDr 94*
Matsunaga, Geoffrey Dean 1949- *WhoFI 94, WhoWest 94*
Matsunaga, Hikaru 1928- *IntWW 93*
Matsunaga, Masanao 1924- *IntWW 93*
Matsunaga, Matthew 1958- *WhoAmP 93*
Matsunaga, Matthew Masao 1958- *WhoWest 94*
Matsunaga, Spark Masayuki 1916-1990 *WhAm 10*
Matsuno, Koichiro 1940- *WhoScEn 94*
Matsuno, Raizo 1917- *IntWW 93*
Matsuo, Paul T. 1935- *WhoAsA 94*
Matsuoka, Eric Takao 1967- *WhoWest 94*
Matsuoka, James Toshio 1920- *WhoAsA 94*
Matsuoka, Matthew S. 1957- *WhoAsA 94*
Matsuoka, Shiro 1930- *WhoAsA 94*
Matsushige, Cary Shigeru 1953- *WhoAmL 94*
Matsushima, Charles Hiroshi 1939- *WhoAsA 94*
Matsushima, Janie Mitsuye 1944- *WhoAsA 94*
Matsushima, Keiji 1938- *WhoAm 94, WhoFI 94*
Matsushima, Mislyn Teruko 1958- *WhoWest 94*
Matsushita, Keiichiro 1953- *WhoScEn 94*
Matsushita, Masaharu 1912- *IntWW 93*
Matsuura, George A. 1960- *WhoWest 94*
Matsuura, Kumiko 1955- *ConAu 140*
Matsuura, Richard M. 1932- *WhoAmP 93*
Matsuura, Teruo 1925- *WhoScEn 94*
Matsuyama, Akira 1912- *IntWW 93*
Matsuyama, Yoshinori 1923- *IntWW 93*
Matsuzaki, Takao 1945- *WhoScEn 94*
Matsuzaki, Yuji 1939- *WhoScEn 94*
Matsuzawa, Takuji 1913- *IntWW 93*
Matt, Peter Kent 1947- *WhoAmL 94*
Matt, Walter J., Jr. 1938- *WhoAmL 94*
Matta, David Lyles 1945- *WhoHisp 94*
Matta, Frank B. 1945- *WhoHisp 94*
Matta, Ram Kumar 1946- *WhoAm 94*
Matta-Clark, Gordon 1945-1978 *WhoAmA 93N*
Mattan, Donald Emil 1942- *WhoMW 93*
Mattar, Ahmad 1939- *IntWW 93*
Mattar, Lawrence Joseph 1934- *WhoAmL 94*
Mattarella, Sergio 1941- *IntWW 93*
Mattathil, George Paul 1957- *WhoWest 94*
Mattauch, Robert Joseph 1940- *WhoAm 94, WhoScEn 94*
Mattausch, Thomas Edward 1944- *WhoAm 94*
Matte, Robert, Jr. *DrAPF 93*
Mattea, Kathy *WhoAm 94*
Mattei, C. A. *WhoFI 94*
Mattei, Colomba fl. 1743-1778 *NewGrDO*
Mattei, Ernest J. 1948- *WhoAmL 94*
Mattei, Saverio 1742-1795 *NewGrDO*
Mattel, Harvey Kenneth 1950- *WhoAmL 94*
Matten, Lawrence Charles 1938- *WhoMW 93*
Matteo, Sherri 1951- *ConAu 141*
Matteoli, Ralph, Jr. 1938- *WhoWest 94*
Matteotti, Giacomo 1885-1924 *HisWorL*
Matteotti, Gianmatteo 1921- *IntWW 93*
Matter, Raymond Wayne 1933- *WhoAmP 93*
Mattera, Connie J. 1951- *WhoMW 93*
Mattera, Gino d1960 *WhoHol 92*
Mattera, John 1953- *WrDr 94*
Mattera, Philip 1953- *WrDr 94*
Mattern, David Bruce 1952- *WhoMW 93*
Mattern, Donald Eugene 1930- *WhoAm 94*
Mattern, Douglas James 1933- *WhoScEn 94*
Mattern, Gerry A. 1935- *WhoScEn 94*
Mattern, James Michael 1962- *WhoScEn 94*
Mattern, Karl 1892-1969 *WhoAmA 93N*
Mattern, Patricia Ann 1950- *WhoAmL 94*
Matternes, Jay Howard 1933- *WhoAmA 93*
Matters, Arnold 1904-1990 *NewGrDO*
Matters, Clyde Burns 1924- *WhoAm 94*
Mattersdorff, Guenter Hans 1926- *WhoWest 94*
Matterstock, Albert d1960 *WhoHol 92*
Mattes, Eva 1955- *WhoHol 92*
Mattes, Hans George 1943- *WhoAm 94*
Mattes, Martin Anthony 1946- *WhoAm 94, WhoAmL 94*
Mattes, William M. 1963- *WhoAmL 94*
Matteson, E. David 1939- *WhoFI 94*
Matteson, Ira 1917- *WhoAmA 93*
Matteson, J. Harrold 1947- *WhoWest 94*
Matteson, Lawrence James 1939- *WhoFI 94*
Matteson, Robert Eliot 1914- *WhoAm 94*
Matteson, Sandra Anne 1956- *WhoWest 94*
Matteson, Thomas Dickens 1920- *WhoScEn 94*
Matteson, Thomas T. *WhoAm 94*
Matteson, William Bleecker 1928- *WhoAm 94, WhoAmL 94, WhoFI 94*
Mattessich, Richard Victor Alvarus 1922- *WhoAm 94*
Matteucci, Dominick Vincent 1924- *WhoFI 94, WhoWest 94*
Matteucci, Sherry Scheel 1947- *WhoAmL 94*
Matteuccio *NewGrDO*
Mattey, John Joseph 1927- *WhoAm 94, WhoFI 94*
Mattfield, Mary *DrAPF 93*
Matthaei, Gay Humphrey 1931- *WhoScEn 94*
Matthau, Charles 1964- *IntMPA 94*
Matthau, Charles Marcus 1964- *WhoWest 94*
Matthau, Walter 1920- *IntMPA 94, IntWW 93, WhoAm 94, WhoCom, WhoHol 92*
Matthaus, Lotthar 1961- *WorESoc*
Matthaus-Maier, Ingrid 1945- *IntWW 93, WhoWomW 91*
Matthee, Dalene 1938- *ConAu 141*
Matthei, Edward Hodge 1927- *WhoAm 94*
Matthei, Warren Douglas 1951- *WhoAm 94*
Matthei Aubel, Fernando 1925- *IntWW 93*
Matthes, Howard Kurt 1929- *WhoScEn 94*
Matthes, Ulrich 1959- *IntWW 93*
Mattheson, Johann 1681-1764 *NewGrDO*
Matthew, Chessor Lillie 1913- *Who 94*
Matthew, Christopher C. F. 1939- *WrDr 94*
Matthew, Clifton, Jr. 1943- *WhoBlA 94*
Matthew, (Henry) Colin Gray 1941- *IntWW 93, Who 94*
Matthew, Jean R. *DrAPF 93*
Matthew, Kathryn Kahrs *WhoAm 94, WhoWest 94*
Matthew, Lyn 1936- *WhoWest 94*
Matthew, Warren Body 1922- *WhoWest 94*
Matthewman, Keith 1936- *Who 94*
Matthews, Baron 1919- *IntWW 93, Who 94*
Matthews, A. Cynthia 1924- *WhoAmP 93*
Matthews, A. E. d1960 *WhoHol 92*
Matthews, Al *WhoHol 92*
Matthews, Albert D. 1923- *WhoBlA 94*
Matthews, Anne 1957- *ConAu 141*
Matthews, Aquilla E. *WhoBlA 94*
Matthews, Beatrice d1942 *WhoHol 92*
Matthews, Billie Watson 1930- *WhoBlA 94*
Matthews, Billy d1985 *WhoHol 92*
Matthews, Brad 1943- *WrDr 94*
Matthews, Brian 1953- *WhoHol 92*
Matthews, Brian W. 1938- *WhoAm 94*
Matthews, Bruce Rankin 1961- *WhoAm 94*
Matthews, Cari Pineiro 1942- *WhoAm 94*
Matthews, Carrie Leonda 1954- *WhoMW 93*
Matthews, Charles David 1946- *WhoMW 93*
Matthews, Charles Sedwick 1920- *WhoAm 94, WhoScEn 94*
Matthews, Christopher *WhoHol 92*
Matthews, Christopher John 1945- *WhoAmP 93*
Matthews, Clark Jio, II 1936- *WhoAm 94, WhoFI 94*
Matthews, Claude Lankford, Jr. 1941- *WhoBlA 94*
Matthews, Clay, Jr. 1956- *WhoBlA 94*
Matthews, Colin 1946- *Who 94*
Matthews, Craig Gerard 1943- *WhoAm 94, WhoFI 94*
Matthews, Cynthia Clark 1941- *WhoBlA 94*
Matthews, Dakin *WhoHol 92*
Matthews, Dale Samuel 1954- *WhoAm 94, WhoScEn 94*
Matthews, Dan Gus 1939- *WhoAm 94, WhoAmL 94*
Matthews, Daniel George 1932- *WhoAm 94*
Matthews, David *WhAmRev, Who 94*
Matthews, David 1920- *WhoAm 94, WhoBlA 94*
Matthews, David 1951- *WhoAmP 93*
Matthews, (William) David 1940- *Who 94*
Matthews, David John 1943- *Who 94*
Matthews, David Napier 1911- *Who 94*
Matthews, Davie Roe 1951- *WhoAmL 94*
Matthews, Dolores Evelyn 1938- *WhoBlA 94*
Matthews, Donald Rowe 1925- *WhoAm 94*
Matthews, Dorcas d1969 *WhoHol 92*
Matthews, Dorothy d1977 *WhoHol 92*
Matthews, Dorothy 1962- *WhoBlA 94*
Matthews, Douglas 1927- *Who 94*
Matthews, Douglas Eugene 1953- *WhoAmL 94*
Matthews, Drexel Gene 1952- *WhoFI 94, WhoScEn 94*
Matthews, Drummond Hoyle 1931- *Who 94*
Matthews, Duane Ellison 1929- *WhoAm 94*
Matthews, Edward E. 1931- *WhoAm 94, WhoFI 94*
Matthews, Edward Easton 1931- *WhoIns 94*
Matthews, Edwin James Thomas 1915- *Who 94*
Matthews, Edwin Spencer, Jr. 1934- *WhoAm 94*
Matthews, Elizabeth Woodfin 1927- *WhoAmL 94*
Matthews, Ernest 1904- *Who 94*
Matthews, Eugene Edward 1931- *WhoAm 94, WhoWest 94*
Matthews, Forrest d1951 *WhoHol 92*
Matthews, Francis 1927- *WhoHol 92*
Matthews, Francis P. 1887-1952 *HisDcKW*
Matthews, Francis Richard 1920- *WhoAm 94*
Matthews, Fred Lewis 1948- *WhoWest 94*
Matthews, Fritz *WhoHol 92*
Matthews, Gail Thunberg 1938- *WhoFI 94*
Matthews, Gareth B(lanc) 1929- *WrDr 94*
Matthews, Gary L. *WhoAmP 93*
Matthews, Gene 1931- *WhoAmA 93*
Matthews, Gene Leroy 1945- *WhoWest 94*
Matthews, Geoffrey 1917- *Who 94*
Matthews, Geoffrey Vernon Townsend 1923- *Who 94*
Matthews, George Lloyd 1917- *Who 94*
Matthews, George Tennyson 1917- *WhoAm 94*
Matthews, Gerald Eugene 1943- *WhoAm 94*
Matthews, Gertrude Ann Urch 1921- *WhoMW 93*
Matthews, Gilbert Elliott 1930- *WhoAm 94, WhoFI 94*
Matthews, Gloria *WhoHol 92*
Matthews, Gordon (Richards) 1908- *Who 94*
Matthews, Greg 1949- *WrDr 94*
Matthews, Gregory J. 1947- *WhoBlA 94*
Matthews, H. Freeman 1899-1986 *HisDcKW*
Matthews, Harriett 1940- *WhoAmA 93*
Matthews, Harry Bradshaw 1952- *WhoBlA 94*
Matthews, Henry Melvin 1926- *Who 94*
Matthews, Herbert Spencer 1921- *WhoAmP 93*
Matthews, Hewitt W. 1944- *WhoBlA 94*
Matthews, Horatio Keith 1917- *Who 94*
Matthews, Jack *DrAPF 93*
Matthews, Jack 1917- *WhoAm 94*
Matthews, Jack 1925- *WhoAm 94, WrDr 94*
Matthews, James Shadley 1951- *WhoAm 94*
Matthews, James Vernon, II 1948- *WhoBlA 94*
Matthews, Jean d1961 *WhoHol 92*
Matthews, Jeanne Pearson 1941- *WhoFI 94*
Matthews, Jeffery Edward 1928- *Who 94*
Matthews, Jessie d1981 *WhoHol 92*
Matthews, Jessie L. 1935- *WhoBlA 94*
Matthews, John 1930- *Who 94*
Matthews, John (Pengwerne) 1927- *ConAu 41NR*
Matthews, John Burr Lumley 1935- *Who 94*
Matthews, John Duncan 1921- *Who 94*
Matthews, John Floyd 1919- *WhoAm 94*
Matthews, John Frederick 1940- *Who 94*
Matthews, John G. 1917- *WhoAmP 93*
Matthews, John Louis 1932- *WhoAm 94, WhoWest 94*
Matthews, John Wesley, Jr. 1940- *WhoAmP 93*
Matthews, John William, III 1938- *WhoAmP 93*
Matthews, Junius d1978 *WhoHol 92*
Matthews, Kenneth L. *WhoAmP 93*
Matthews, L. White, III 1945- *WhoAm 94, WhoFI 94*
Matthews, Larryl Kent 1951- *WhoAm 94, WhoScEn 94*
Matthews, Lemuel Hatch 1909- *WhAm 10*
Matthews, Lena Dale *DrAPF 93*
Matthews, Leonard Louis 1930- *WhoBlA 94*
Matthews, Leonard Sarver 1922- *WhoAm 94*
Matthews, Lester d1975 *WhoHol 92*
Matthews, Linda Guerra 1949- *WhoHisp 94*
Matthews, Lloyd J. 1929- *ConAu 141*
Matthews, Lori 1947- *WhoFI 94, WhoMW 93*
Matthews, Mallory Louis 1953- *WhoBlA 94*
Matthews, Martin, Jr. 1926- *WhoAmP 93*
Matthews, Mary Alice 1926- *WhoMW 93*
Matthews, Mary Joan 1945- *WhoBlA 94*
Matthews, Merritt Stewart 1939- *WhoBlA 94*
Matthews, Michael d1993 *Who 94N*
Matthews, Michael Gough 1931- *Who 94*
Matthews, Michael Roland 1948- *WhoScEn 94*
Matthews, Miriam 1905- *WhoBlA 94*
Matthews, Nelson Ross, Jr. 1929- *WhoWest 94*
Matthews, Norman Sherwood, Jr. 1944- *WhoWest 94*
Matthews, Norman Stuart 1933- *WhoAm 94*
Matthews, Pamela Winifred 1914- *Who 94*
Matthews, Patricia 1927- *WrDr 94*
Matthews, Patrick John 1942- *WhoAm 94*
Matthews, Paul Deacon 1929- *WhoAm 94*
Matthews, Percy 1921- *Who 94*
Matthews, Peter, Mrs. *Who 94*
Matthews, Peter (Alec) 1922- *Who 94*
Matthews, Peter (Hugoe) 1934- *WrDr 94*
Matthews, Peter (Jack) 1917- *Who 94*
Matthews, Peter Alec 1922- *IntWW 93*
Matthews, Peter Bryan Conrad 1928- *IntWW 93, Who 94*
Matthews, Peter Hugoe 1934- *IntWW 93, Who 94*
Matthews, Philip Richard 1952- *WhoAmL 94*
Matthews, Rebecca Sue 1955- *WhoAmL 94*
Matthews, Richard Bonnar 1915- *Who 94*
Matthews, Richard Carroll 1926- *WhoAmP 93*
Matthews, Richard Ellis Ford 1921- *IntWW 93, Who 94*
Matthews, Richard J. 1927- *WhoScEn 94*
Matthews, Robert C(harles) O(liver) 1927- *WrDr 94*
Matthews, Robert Charles Oliver 1927- *IntWW 93*
Matthews, Robert Charles Oliver (Robin) 1927- *Who 94*
Matthews, Robert L. 1930- *WhoBlA 94*
Matthews, Robert L. 1947- *WhoBlA 94*

Matthews, Roderick Jon 1946-
WhoAmL 94, WhoFI 94
Matthews, Rodney 1945- EncSF 93
Matthews, Roger Hardin 1948-
WhoAm 94
Matthews, Ronald Sydney 1922- Who 94
Matthews, Saul WhAmRev
Matthews, Shaw Hall, III 1942-
WhoScEn 94, WhoWest 94
Matthews, Sondra WhoMW 93
Matthews, Stanley 1915- Who 94,
WorESoc [port]
Matthews, Steve Allen 1955- WhoAm 94
Matthews, Suzan Patricia 1947- Who 94
Matthews, T. Randall 1947- WhoAmL 94
Matthews, Thomas Stanley 1901-1991
WhAm 10
Matthews, Timothy John 1951- Who 94
Matthews, Tom WhoHol 93
Matthews, Tom 1956- WhoAmP 93
Matthews, Vincent 1947- WhoBlA 94
Matthews, Virgil E. 1928- WhoBlA 94
Matthews, Walter Bryan 1920- Who 94
Matthews, Wanda Miller 1930-
WhoAm 94, WhoAmA 93
Matthews, Warren W. 1939- WhoAmP 93
Matthews, Warren Wayne 1939-
WhoAmL 94, WhoWest 94
Matthews, Westina L. 1948- WhoAm 94,
WhoFI 94
Matthews, Westina Lomax 1948-
WhoBlA 94
Matthews, Wilbur Lee 1903- WhoAm 94,
WhoAmL 94
Matthews, William DrAPF 93
Matthews, William 1942-
ConAu 18AS [port], WrDr 94
Matthews, William Doty 1934-
WhoAm 94, WhoFI 94
Matthews, William Edmund 1930-
WhoMW 94
Matthews, William Elliott, IV 1929-
WhoFI 94
Matthews, William Procter 1942-
WhoAm 94
Matthews, Wyhomme S. 1948-
WhoMW 93
Matthews, Zachary E. 1956- WhoAmP 93
Matthews-Simonton, Stephanie 1947-
WrDr 94
Matthias, Franklin T. d1993
NewYTBS 93
Matthias, John DrAPF 93
Matthias, John (Edward) 1941- WrDr 94
Matthias, Judson Stillman 1931-
WhoWest 94
Matthias Johannessen ConWorW 93
Matthies, Frederick John 1925-
WhoAm 94
Matthies, Mary Constance T. 1948-
WhoAmL 94
Matthiesen, Leroy Theodore 1921-
WhoAm 94
Matthieson, Tim WhoHol 92
Matthiessen, Peter DrAPF 93
Matthiessen, Peter 1927- IntWW 93,
WhoAm 94, WrDr 94
Matthiessen, Poul Christian 1933-
IntWW 93
Matthis, James L., III 1955- WhoBlA 94
Matthison, Edith Wynne d1955
WhoHol 92
Matthofer, Hans 1925- IntWW 93,
Who 94
Matthus, Siegfried 1934- IntWW 93,
NewGrDO
Mattia, Ettore d1982 WhoHol 92
Mattice, Paul M. 1913- WhoIns 94
Mattielo, Brian E. WhoAmP 93
Mattila, John Peter 1943- WhoFI 94
Mattila, Karita (Marjatta) 1960-
NewGrDO
Mattila, Karita Marjatta 1960- IntWW 93
Mattingley, Christobel 1931-
SmATA 18AS [port]
Mattingley, Christobel (Rosemary) 1931-
WrDr 94
Mattingly, (James Thomas) 1934-
WhoAmA 93
Mattingly, Alan 1949- Who 94
Mattingly, Donald Arthur 1961-
WhoAm 94
Mattingly, George DrAPF 93
Mattingly, George A. 1948- WhoAmL 94
Mattingly, Hedley 1915- WhoHol 92
Mattingly, J. Virgil, Jr. 1944- WhoAmL 94
Mattingly, Mack F. 1931- WhoAm 94
Mattingly, Mack Francis 1931-
IntWW 93, WhoAmP 93
Mattingly, Paul R. 1950- WhoAm 94
Mattingly, Robert Kerker 1921-
WhoFI 94, WhoMW 93
Mattingly, Stephen 1922- Who 94
Mattingly, Thomas K. 1936- WhoAm 94,
WhoScEn 94
Mattingly, William Earl 1948- WhoAm 94
Mattioli, Andrea c. 1620-1679 NewGrDO
Mattioli, Luisa 1936- WhoHol 92

Mattioni, Thomas A. 1955- WhoWest 94
Mattis, Louis Price 1941- WhoAm 94,
WhoFI 94
Mattison, Alice DrAPF 93
Mattison, Donald Mangus 1905-1975
WhoAmA 93N
Mattison, Dorothy Love 1927-
WhoAmP 93
Mattison, Elisa Sheri 1952- WhoWest 94
Mattison, George Chester, Jr. 1940-
WhoScEn 94
Mattison, Harry D. 1936- WhoFI 94
Mattison, Jackie R. 1951- WhoAmP 93
Mattison, Richard 1946- WhoScEn 94
Mattison, Robert Myron 1954-
WhoMW 94
Mattlage, Karl P. 1940- WhoAmP 93
Mattlin, Sharon DrAPF 93
Matto, Sistro d1934 WhoHol 92
Mattoch, Ian L. WhoAmL 94
Mattocks, George 1734?-1804 NewGrDO
Mattocks, Isabella 1746-1826 NewGrDO
Matto de Turner, Clorinda 1909-
BlmGWL
Mattoli, Craig Leon 1952- WhoFI 94
Mattone, Vincent J. 1945- WhoAm 94,
WhoFI 94
Mattoon, Henry Amasa, Jr. 1914-
WhoAm 94
Mattoon, Peter Mills 1931- WhoAm 94
Mattoon, Sara Halsey 1947- WhoFI 94,
WhoWest 94
Mattos, James George 1932- WhoAmP 93
Mattotti, Lorenzo 1954- EncSF 93
Mattoussi, Hedi Mohamed 1959-
WhoScEn 94
Mattox, James Albon 1943- WhoAmP 93
Mattox, Kenneth Leon 1938- WhoAm 94
Mattox, Martha d1933 WhoHol 92
Mattox, Matt 1921- WhoHol 92
Mattran, Donald Albert 1934- WhoAm 94
Mattraw, Scott d1946 WhoHol 92
Matts, Frank d1990 WhoHol 92
Matts, Tom d1990 WhoHol 92
Mattson, Bradford Craig 1952-
WhoAm 94
Mattson, Brian Jay 1948- WhoFI 94
Mattson, Carol Linnette 1946-
WhoMW 93
Mattson, Catherine Marie 1935-
WhoAmP 93
Mattson, Clarence Russell 1924-
WhoScEn 94
Mattson, Doug Leif 1955- WhoAmP 93
Mattson, Edna O'Neill 1936- WhoAmP 93
Mattson, Francis Oscar 1931- WhoAm 94
Mattson, Geraldine Ellen 1932-
WhoAmP 93
Mattson, Henry (Elis) 1887-1971
WhoAmA 93N
Mattson, James Allen 1949- WhoWest 94
Mattson, James Stewart 1945-
WhoAmL 94
Mattson, Leroy Harry 1925- WhoAmL 94
Mattson, Lynn Paul 1947- WhoAmL 94
Mattson, Marcus 1904- WhoAm 94
Mattson, Michael Dane 1953-
WhoWest 94
Mattson, Robin 1956- WhoHol 92
Mattson, Roy Henry 1927- WhoAm 94,
WhoWest 94
Mattson, Stephen Joseph 1943-
WhoAm 94, WhoAmL 94
Mattson, Steven Roald 1955- WhoMW 93
Mattson, Walter Edward 1932-
WhoAm 94, WhoFI 94
Mattson, William Royce, Jr. 1946-
WhoAm 94
Mattsson, Ake 1929- WhoAm 94
Matula, Richard Allan 1939- WhoAm 94,
WhoScEn 94
Matulka, Jan 1890-1972 WhoAmA 93N
Matune, Frank Joseph 1948- WhoAmL 94
Matura, Mustapha 1939- BlmGEL,
ConDr 93, WrDr 94
Mature, Victor 1913- IntMPA 94
Mature, Victor 1915- WhoHol 92
Maturi, Raymond Rockne 1938-
WhoAm 94
Maturin, Charles R(obert) 1782-1824
EncSF 93
Maturin, Charles Robert 1782-1824
BlmGEL
Maturin, Eric d1957 WhoHol 92
Maturin, Sherry Sherwood 1961-
WhoFI 94
Matus, Wayne Charles 1950- WhoAmL 94
Matusiak, Romualda WhoWomW 91
Matusievic, Jan 1948- LngBDD
Matusinec, Sharon Bergold 1947-
WhoMW 93
Matuska, John E. 1945- WhoAm 94
Matusow, Allen J(oseph) 1937-
ConAu 142
Matusow, Allen Joseph 1937- WhoAm 94
Matusow, Naomi Caplan 1938-
WhoAmP 93
Matuszak, John d1989 WhoHol 92

Matuszak, John Daniel 1950-1989
WhAm 10
Matuszak, Marlys WhoAmP 93
Matuszczak, Bernadetta 1933?- NewGrDO
Matuszko, Anthony Joseph 1926-
WhoAm 94, WhoScEn 94
Matutani Miyoko 1926- BlmGWL
Matute (Ausejo), Ana Maria 1926-
ConWorW 93, RfGShF
Matute, Ana Maria 1926- BlmGWL
Matute Ausejo, Ana Maria 1925-
IntWW 93
Matutes Juan, Abel 1941- IntWW 93,
Who 94
Matveeva, Novella Nikolaevna 1934-
BlmGWL
Matveyev, Aleksey Nikolayevich 1922-
IntWW 93
Matveyeva, Novella Nikolaevna 1934-
IntWW 93
Matvienko, Anatolii Serhiiovych 1953-
LngBDD
Matway, Roy Joseph 1956- WhoScEn 94
Matyas, Diane C. 1961- WhoAmA 93
Matyas, Tom 1956- WhoAmP 93
Matyola, Daniel John 1941- WhoAmL 94
Matz, Jerry WhoHol 92
Matz, Johanna 1932- WhoHol 92
Matz, Kay Elaine 1946- WhoMW 93
Matz, Peter S. 1928- WhoAm 94
Matz, Robert 1931- WhoAm 94
Matzat, Gregory Mark 1967- WhoScEn 94
Matzdorff, James Arthur 1956- WhoFI 94,
WhoWest 94
Matzeder, Jean Marie Znidarsic 1948-
WhoAmL 94
Matzek, Peter Tucker 1958- WhoFI 94
Matzeliger, Jan 1852-1889 AfrAmAl 6
Matzeliger, Jan Ernst 1852-1889 WorInv
Matzen, Robert T. 1924- WhoIns 94
Matzenauer, Margaret d1963 WhoHol 92
Matzenauer, Margaret(e) 1881-1963
NewGrDO
Matzer, John Wayne 1945- WhoWest 94
Matzick, Kenneth John 1943- WhoAm 94,
WhoMW 93
Matziorinis, Kenneth N. 1954- WhoFI 94,
WhoScEn 94
Matzka, Michael Alan 1954- WhoAmL 94
Matzke, Frank J. 1922- WhoAm 94
Matzner, Bruce 1933- WhoWest 94
Matzner, Chester Michael WhoFI 94
Mauban, Maria WhoHol 92
Mauceri, Albert 1931- WhoIns 94
Mauceri, John 1945- NewGrDO
Mauceri, John Francis 1945- Who 94,
WhoAm 94
Mauch, Billy 1924- WhoHol 92
Mauch, Bobby 1924- WhoHol 92
Mauch, C. Alan 1950- WhoIns 94
Mauch, Hans 1919-1979
See Frick and Frack WhoCom
Mauch, Ursula 1935- WhoWomW 91
Maucher, Helmut 1927- IntWW 93
Mauchline, Lord 1942- Who 94
Mauchly, John 1907-1980 WorInv
Mauck, Elwyn Arthur 1910-1990
WhAm 10
Mauck, Henry Page, Jr. 1926- WhoAm 94
Mauck, William M., Jr. 1938- WhoFI 94
Maucker, Earl Robert 1947- WhoAm 94
Maud d1198 BlmGWL
Maud (Edith) 1079-1118 BlmGWL
Maud, Humphrey John Hamilton 1934-
IntWW 93, Who 94
Maude Who 94
Maude, Caitlin 1941-1982 BlmGWL
Maude, Charles d1943 WhoHol 92
Maude, Cyril d1951 WhoHol 92
Maude, Edward Joseph 1924- WhoAm 94
Maude, Francis Anthony Aylmer 1953-
Who 94
Maude, Joan 1908- WhoHol 92
Maude, Margery d1979 WhoHol 92
Maude Of Stratford-Upon-Avon, Baron
1912- IntWW 93, Who 94
Mauderli, Walter 1924- WhoAm 94
Mauderly, Joe Lloyd 1943- WhoAm 94
Maude-Roxby, Roddy 1930- WhoHol 92
Maudit, Israel 1708-1787 WhAmRev
Maudlin, C(ecil) V(earl) 1895- WhAm 10
Maudlin, Robert V. 1927- WhoFI 94,
WhoScEn 94
Maudslay, Henry 1771-1831 WorInv
Maudsley, Henry 1835-1918 DcNaB MP,
EncSPD
Mauer, Alvin Marx 1928- WhoAm 94,
WhoScEn 94
Mauer, Michael Leonard 1940-
WhoAm 94
Mauer, Richard David 1949-
WhoWest 94
Mauer, William F. 1930- WhoAmP 93
Mauerman, Mary Drake 1939-
WhoWest 94
Maugans, Edgar Hurley 1935-
WhoAm 94, WhoFI 94

Maugans, John Conrad 1938-
WhoAmL 94, WhoMW 93
Maugham, Frances 1944- WrDr 94
Maugham, Robin 1916-1981 GayLL
Maugham, W. Somerset d1965
WhoHol 92
Maugham, W(illiam) Somerset
1874-1965 IntDcT 2, RfGShF
Maugham, William Somerset 1874-1965
BlmGEL
Maughan, Anne Margery WrDr 94
Maughan, Charles Gilbert 1923- Who 94
Maughan, Deryck C. WhoAm 94,
WhoFI 94
Maughan, Kristen Kartchner 1962-
WhoMW 93
Maughan, Monica WhoHol 92
Maughan, Owen Eugene 1943-
WhoWest 94
Maughan, Willard Zinn 1944-
WhoWest 94
Maughelli, Mary L. 1935- WhoAmA 93
Maughmer, John Townsend 1954-
WhoAm 94, WhoAmL 94
Maughmer, Karrol June WhoAmP 93
Maughn, James David 1947- WhoIns 94
Mauk, Pamela Anne 1953- WhoWest 94
Mauk, Richard Kenneth 1953-
WhoAmP 93
Mauke, Otto Russell 1924- WhoAm 94
Maul, Mary Grace 1952- WhoMW 93
Maul, Stephen Bailey 1942- WhoFI 94
Maul, Terry Lee 1946- WhoWest 94
Maulde, Bruno Guy Andre Jean de 1934-
IntWW 93
Maulden, Jerry L. 1936- WhoFI 94
Mauldin, Bill 1921- WhoAmA 93,
WhoHol 92
Mauldin, Charles Robert 1938-
WhoScEn 94
Mauldin, David E. 1950- WhoAmL 94
Mauldin, Jean 1923- WhoAmP 93
Mauldin, Jean Humphries 1923-
WhoFI 94, WhoWest 94
Mauldin, John Inglis 1947- WhoAmL 94
Mauldin, Robert Ray 1935- WhoAm 94
Mauldin, William H. 1921- WhoAm 94,
WhoMW 93
Mauldin, William Henry 1921- AmSocL
Maule, Albert R. WhoBlA 94
Maule, Charles Gough 1929- WhoFI 94
Maule, Donovan d1982 WhoHol 92
Mauleverer, (Peter) Bruce 1946- Who 94
Maulik, Dev 1942- WhoAm 94
Maull, George Marriner 1947- WhoAm 94
Maulsby, Allen Farish 1922- WhoAm 94
Maulsby, Ruhl 1923- WhoAmP 93
Maultsby, Dorothy M. 1927- WhoBlA 94
Maultsby, Portia K. 1947- WhoBlA 94
Maultsby, Sylvester 1935- WhoBlA 94
Maulupe, Saofa'igaoalii WhoAmP 93
Maumenee, Irene Hussels 1940-
WhoScEn 94
Maun, Joseph Angus 1909- WhAm 10
Maun, Mary Ellen 1951- WhoFI 94
Maund, John Arthur Arrowsmith 1948-
Who 94
Maunder, Addison Bruce 1934-
WhoAm 94
Maunder, Annie Russell WorScD
Maunder, Leonard 1927- Who 94
Maunder, Wayne 1938- WhoHol 92
Maundrell, Michael Edward 1946-
WhoAmL 94
Maundrell, Wolseley David 1920- Who 94
Mauney, Donald Wallace, Jr. 1942-
WhoBlA 94
Maung Maung Gyee, U. 1921- IntWW 93
Maung Maung Kha, U. IntWW 93
Maung-Mercurio, Alice Marie 1949-
WhoMW 93
Maunoir, Peter Felix 1937- WhoFI 94
Maunsbach, George Eric 1890-
WhoAmA 93N
Maunsbach, Kay Benedicta 1933-
WhoAm 94
Maunsell, Charles d1968 WhoHol 92
Maunsell, Susan Pamela 1942- Who 94
Maupassant, Guy de 1850-1893
NinCLC 42 [port]
Maupassant, (Henri Rene Albert) Guy de
1850-1893 RfGShF
Maupi, Ernest d1949 WhoHol 92
Maupin 1670-1707 NewGrDO
Maupin, Armistead 1944- GayLL,
WrDr 94
Maupin, Armistead Jones 1914-
WhoAm 94
Maupin, Armistead Jones, Jr. 1944-
WhoAm 94
Maur, Meinhart d1964 WhoHol 92
Maura, Carmen 1945- IntMPA 94,
WhoHol 92
Maura, Carmen 1946- IntWW 93
Murath, Garry Caldwell 1952-
WhoScEn 94, WhoWest 94
Maureen, Mollie d1987 WhoHol 92

Maxwell, Vera d1950 WhoHol 92
Maxwell, Vernon 1965- WhoBlA 94
Maxwell, Vicky WrDr 94
Maxwell, Walter Henry 1935- WhoAmP 93
Maxwell, Wilbur Richard 1920- WhoAm 94
Maxwell, William DrAPF 93
Maxwell, William c. 1733-1796 AmRev, WhAmRev
Maxwell, William 1908- WhoAm 94, WrDr 94
Maxwell, William 1916- WrDr 94
Maxwell, William C. 1941- WhoAmA 93
Maxwell, William Jackson 1947- WhoAmA 93
Maxwell, William Laughlin 1934- WhoAm 94, WhoScEn 94
Maxwell, William Stirling 1922- WhoAm 94
Maxwell-Brogdon, Florence Morency 1929- WhoFI 94, WhoWest 94
Maxwell Davies, Peter IntWW 93
Maxwell-Hyslop, Kathleen Rachel 1914- Who 94
Maxwell-Hyslop, Robert John 1931- Who 94
Maxwell of Ardwell, Frederick Gordon 1905- Who 94
Maxwell Reid, Daphne Etta 1948- WhoBlA 94
Maxwell Scott, Dominic James 1976- Who 94
Maxwell-Scott, Jean (Mary Monica) 1923- Who 94
Maxwell-Willshire, Gerard d1947 WhoHol 92
Maxworthy, Tony 1933- WhoAm 94, WhoScEn 94, WhoWest 94
Maxx, Dave Frank 1955- WhoWest 94
May, Baron 1931- Who 94
May, Ada d1978 WhoHol 92
May, Addison Cushman 1933- WhoAm 94
May, Adolf Darlington 1927- WhoAm 94, WhoWest 94
May, Alan Alfred 1942- WhoAmL 94, WhoAmP 93, WhoMW 93
May, Alyce d1980 WhoHol 92
May, Ann d1985 WhoHol 92
May, Anthony WhoHol 92
May, Arthur W. 1937- WhoAm 94
May, Aviva Rabinowitz WhoMW 93
May, Bobby Lee 1958- WhoAmP 93
May, Brian Albert 1936- Who 94
May, Bruce Barnett 1948- WhoAm 94, WhoAmL 94
May, Charles Alan Maynard 1924- Who 94
May, Charles E(dward) 1941- ConAu 41NR
May, Charles Kent 1939- WhoAm 94, WhoAmL 94
May, Charles W. 1940- WhoBlA 94
May, Daniel Striger 1942- WhoAmA 93
May, Deborah WhoHol 92
May, Dennis James 1947- WhoAmP 93
May, Derwent (James) 1930- WrDr 94
May, Dickey R. 1950- WhoBlA 94
May, Donald 1928- WhoHol 92
May, Donald Francis 1946- WhoWest 94
May, Donald R. 1945- WhoAm 94
May, Doris d1984 WhoHol 92
May, Douglas Hutton 1941- WhoWest 94
May, Douglas James 1946- Who 94
May, Edgar 1929- WhoAm 94
May, Edna d1948 WhoHol 92
May, Edwin Hyland, Jr. 1924- WhoAmP 93
May, Elaine 1932- ConAu 142, ConDr 93, IntDcF 2-4 [port], IntMPA 94, IntWW 93, WhoAm 94, WhoHol 92, WrDr 94
See Also Nichols and May WhoCom
May, Ernest Max 1913- WhoAm 94
May, Ernest R(ichard) 1928- WrDr 94
May, Eva d1924 WhoHol 92
May, Everette Lee, Jr. 1914- WhoScEn 94
May, Felton Edwin 1935- WhoAm 94
May, Florissa ConAu 41NR
May, Floyd O'Lander 1946- WhoBlA 94
May, Francis Hart, Jr. 1917- WhoAm 94
May, Frank Brendan, Jr. 1945- WhoAmL 94
May, Fred O. 1919- WhoAmP 93
May, G. Lynwood 1927- WhoAm 94
May, Geoffrey Crampton 1930- Who 94
May, Georges 1920- IntWW 93
May, Gerald William 1941- IntWW 93, WhoAm 94, WhoWest 94
May, Gita 1929- WrDr 94
May, Gordon Leslie 1921- Who 94
May, Graham 1923- Who 94
May, Gregory Evers 1953- WhoAm 94
May, Harold Edward 1920- WhoAm 94
May, Harold R. d1973 WhoHol 92
May, Henry F(arnham) 1915- WrDr 94
May, Henry Stratford, Jr. 1947- WhoAmL 94
May, Hon. Sir Anthony (Tristram Kenneth) 1940- Who 94
May, Hugh 1621-1684 DcNaB MP
May, J. Joel 1935- WhoAm 94
May, J. Peter 1939- WhoAm 94
May, Jack 1922- WhoHol 92
May, James F. 1938- WhoBlA 94
May, James Nicholas Welby 1949- Who 94
May, James Shelby 1934- WhoBlA 94
May, James Warren, Jr. 1943- WhoAm 94
May, Jerry Russell 1942- WhoAm 94
May, Jodhi 1975- WhoHol 92
May, John 1912- Who 94
May, John (Douglas) 1923- Who 94
May, John Anthony Gerard 1941- Who 94
May, John H. 1922- WhoAmP 93
May, John Lawrence 1922- WhoAm 94, WhoMW 93
May, John Otto 1913- Who 94
May, Jonathan Z. 1964- WhoAmL 94
May, Joseph Leserman 1929- WhoAmL 94, WhoFI 94
May, Joy Elaine 1947- WhoFI 94
May, Julian 1931- EncSF 93, WrDr 94
May, Julie 1927- WhoHol 92
May, Karl 1842-1912 DcLB 129 [port]
May, Kenneth Myron 1949- WhoScEn 94
May, Kenneth Nathaniel 1930- WhoAm 94, WhoFI 94
May, Kenneth Spencer 1914- Who 94
May, Larry 1952- WhoMW 93
May, Lary L. 1944- WrDr 94
May, Laurence M. 1951- WhoAmL 94
May, Lawrence Edward 1947- WhoAmL 94
May, Lee Andrew 1943- WhoBlA 94
May, Mark 1959- WhoBlA 94
May, Marty d1975 WhoHol 92
May, Mary Louise 1946- WhoMW 93
May, Mathilde 1965- WhoHol 92
May, Melvin Arthur 1940- WhoAm 94
May, Mia d1980 WhoHol 92
May, Michael Joseph 1954- WhoMW 93
May, Michael Lee 1959- WhoAm 94, WhoScEn 94
May, Michael Wayne 1949- WhoWest 94
May, Nancy Kay 1940- WhoMW 93
May, Pamela 1917- IntDcB [port]
May, Paul 1907- Who 94
May, Paul Gerard 1961- WhoMW 93
May, Paul W., Jr. 1928- WhoAmP 93
May, Paula Joe 1947- WhoMW 93
May, Peter Barker Howard 1929- Who 94
May, Peter William 1942- WhoFI 94
May, Philip Raymond 1942- WhoAm 94
May, Phyllis Jean 1932- WhoFI 94, WhoMW 93
May, Randolph Joseph 1946- WhoAm 94, WhoAmL 94
May, Richard Edward 1946- WhoAm 94, WhoAmL 94
May, Richard George 1938- Who 94
May, Richard Lee 1943- WhoMW 93
May, Richard Paul 1946- WhoScEn 94, WhoWest 94
May, Ricky WhoHol 92
May, Robert A. 1911- WhoAm 94, WhoAmL 94
May, Robert George 1943- WhoAm 94
May, Robert McCredie 1936- IntWW 93, Who 94, WhoAm 94
May, Robin 1929- WrDr 94
May, Rollo 1909- WhoAm 94, WhoWest 94
May, Rollo (Reece) 1909- WrDr 94
May, Ronald Alan 1928- WhoAm 94
May, Ronny Joe 1934- WhoAmP 93, WhoWest 94
May, Stephen 1931- WhoAm 94, WhoAmP 93
May, Steven W. 1941- ConAu 141
May, Stuart Who 94
May, (William Herbert) Stuart 1937- Who 94
May, Stuart Lamphear 1920- WhoFI 94
May, Terrence Anthony 1956- WhoWest 94
May, Timothy James 1932- WhoAm 94, WhoAmP 93
May, Valentine Gilbert Delabere 1927- Who 94
May, Veronica Jean 1964- WhoAmL 94
May, Veronica Stewart 1920- WhoBlA 94
May, Walter Grant 1918- WhoAm 94
May, Walter Herbert, Jr. 1936- WhoMW 93
May, Walter Richard, Jr. 1945- WhoAmL 94
May, William Frederick 1915- WhoAm 94
May, William Hathaway WhoAmL 94
May, William John 1946- WhoFI 94
May, Woodford F. 1929- WhoAmP 93
May, Wynne WrDr 94
Maya, Dora Elssy 1955- WhoHisp 94
Maya, Gloria M. WhoHisp 94
Maya, Stephanie 1968- WhoHisp 94
Maya, Walter 1929- WhoWest 94
Mayakovsky, Vladimir d1930 WhoHol 92
Mayakovsky, Vladimir (Vladimirovich) 1893-1930 EncSF 93, IntDcT 2 [port]
Mayall, Herschel d1941 WhoHol 92
Mayall, John 1803-1876 DcNaB MP
Mayall, John 1933- WhoHol 92
Mayall, (Alexander) Lees d1992 Who 94N
Mayall, Nicholas U. d1993 NewYTBS 93
Mayall, Nicholas Ulrich d1993 IntWW 93N
Mayall, Rik WhoHol 92
Mayama, Miko WhoHol 92
Ma Yanli WhoPRCh 91
Mayans, Carlos WhoAmP 93
Ma Yaoji 1922- WhoPRCh 91 [port]
Maybach, Wilhelm 1846-1929 WorInv
Maybeck, Bernard Ralph 1862-1957 AmCulL
Mayberry, Alan Reed 1954- WhoAmL 94
Mayberry, Claude A., Jr. 1933- WhoBlA 94
Mayberry, Lee WhoBlA 94
Mayberry, Patricia Ann Tinthoff 1940- WhoWest 94
Mayberry, Patricia Marie 1951- WhoBlA 94
Mayberry, William Eugene 1929- WhoScEn 94
Mayberry-French, Ann G. 1960- WhoAmL 94
Mayboroda, Heorhy Ilarionovych 1913- NewGrDO
Maybury, Anne WrDr 94
Maybury, Greg J. 1951- WhoMW 93
Maybury, Richard Horace 1951- WhoFI 94
Maycock, Ernest Besley 1935- IntWW 93
Maycock, Ian David 1935- WhoAm 94, WhoFI 94
Maycock, Joseph Farwell, Jr. 1930- WhoAm 94
Maycock, William W. 1952- WhoAmL 94
Mayda, Jaro 1918- WhoAm 94
Maydak, Dawna M. DrAPF 93
Maydar, Damdinjavyn 1916- IntWW 93
Mayden, Barbara Mendel 1951- WhoAm 94, WhoAmL 94
Mayden, Ruth Wyatt 1946- WhoBlA 94
Maydew, Mary Jo 1949- WhoFI 94
Maye, Beatrice Carr Jones WhoBlA 94
Maye, Jimsy d1968 WhoHol 92
Maye, Richard 1933- WhoBlA 94
Maye-Bryan, Mamie Ellene 1954- WhoMW 93
Mayeda, Cynthia Joy Yoshiko 1949- WhoAmP 93
Mayehoff, Eddie 1914- WhoHol 92
Mayell, Jaspal Singh 1929- WhoAsA 94
Mayen, Paul 1918- WhoAmA 93
Mayence-Goossens, Jacqueline 1932- WhoWomW 91
Mayenkar, Krishna Vaman 1943- WhoWest 94
Mayenur 1929- WhoPRCh 91 [port]
Mayenzet, Maria WhoHol 92
Mayer, Adrian C 1922- WrDr 94
Mayer, Alan Eugene 1925- WhoAmP 93
Mayer, Alejandro Miguel 1950- WhoScEn 94
Mayer, Anthony Who 94
Mayer, (Ralph) Anthony (Jeffrey) 1946- Who 94
Mayer, Arno J(oseph) 1926- WrDr 94
Mayer, Arthur d1981 WhoHol 92
Mayer, Augustin 1911- IntWW 93
Mayer, Barbara 1939- SmATA 77
Mayer, Barbara J. DrAPF 93
Mayer, Bena Frank 1898-1991 WhoAmA 93N
Mayer, Bernadette DrAPF 93
Mayer, Bernadette 1945- WrDr 94
Mayer, Billy 1953- WhoAmA 93
Mayer, Carl 1894-1944 IntDcF 2-4
Mayer, Carl Joseph 1959- WhoAm 94, WhoAmL 94
Mayer, Charles WhoHol 92
Mayer, Charles Arthur 1949- WhoFI 94
Mayer, Chip WhoHol 92
Mayer, Christian 1922- IntWW 93
Mayer, Christopher 1946- WhoAmL 94
Mayer, Colin Peter 1953- Who 94
Mayer, Debby DrAPF 93
Mayer, Dennis Thomas 1901- WhoAm 94
Mayer, Edward Albert 1942- WhoAmA 93
Mayer, Erich Anton 1930- WhoFI 94
Mayer, Eugene Stephen 1938- WhoAm 94
Mayer, Foster Lee, Jr. 1942- WhoAm 94
Mayer, Frank Anthony 1942- WhoWest 94
Mayer, Frank D., Jr. 1933- WhoAm 94
Mayer, Frederick Miller 1898- WhoAm 94
Mayer, Frederick Rickard 1928- WhoAm 94
Mayer, Gene 1956- BuCMET
Mayer, George B(aker) 1895- WhAm 10
Mayer, Gerald IntMPA 94
Mayer, Gerda (Kamilla) 1927- WrDr 94
Mayer, Grace M. WhoAmA 93
Mayer, H. Robert 1941- CngDr 93, WhoAmP 93
Mayer, Haldane Robert 1941- WhoAm 94, WhoAmL 94
Mayer, Hans 1907- IntWW 93
Mayer, Harold Melvin 1916- WhoMW 93
Mayer, Henry Michael 1922- WhoAm 94
Mayer, Herbert Carleton, Jr. 1922- WhoWest 94
Mayer, J. Gerald 1908- WhoAm 94
Mayer, James Hock 1935- WhoAm 94
Mayer, James Joseph 1933- WhoAm 94, WhoAmL 94
Mayer, James Lamoine 1951- WhoMW 93
Mayer, James Walter 1930- WhoAm 94
Mayer, Jean 1920-1993 ConAu 140, CurBio 93N, NewYTBS 93 [port]
Mayer, Joe 1949- WhoAmP 93
Mayer, Joe H. 1929- WhoMW 93
Mayer, John 1948- WhoAm 94
Mayer, Josepha NewGrDO
Mayer, Julius Robert 1814-1878 WorScD
Mayer, Kay Magnor 1943- WhoMW 93
Mayer, Ken(neth) d1985 WhoHol 92
Mayer, Laurel Anthony 1937- WhoMW 93
Mayer, Lawrence Arnold 1918- WhoFI 94
Mayer, Lois Rae 1949- WhoMW 93
Mayer, Louis B. 1885-1957 AmCulL, IntDcF 2-4 [port]
Mayer, Margery Weil 1952- WhoAm 94
Mayer, Marilyn Gooder WhoFI 94
Mayer, Martin Prager 1928- WhoAm 94
Mayer, Michael F. 1917- IntMPA 94
Mayer, Morris Lehman 1925- WhoAm 94
Mayer, Musa 1943- WrDr 94
Mayer, Nancy WhoAm 94
Mayer, Nancy J. WhoAmP 93
Mayer, Patricia Jayne 1950- WhoFI 94, WhoWest 94
Mayer, Peter IntWW 93
Mayer, Peter 1936- WhoAm 94
Mayer, Peter Conrad 1938- WhoFI 94, WhoScEn 94
Mayer, Phillip Howard 1928- WhoMW 93
Mayer, Ralph 1895-1979 WhoAmA 93N
Mayer, Randolph John 1953- WhoAm 94
Mayer, Ray d1948 WhoHol 92
Mayer, Raymond (Richard) 1924- WrDr 94
Mayer, Raymond Richard 1924- WhoAm 94
Mayer, Richard Dean 1930- WhoAm 94
Mayer, Richard Edwin 1947- WhoAm 94
Mayer, Richard Thomas 1945- WhoScEn 94
Mayer, Robert 1939- WrDr 94
Mayer, Robert Anthony 1933- WhoAm 94, WhoAmA 93, WhoMW 93
Mayer, Robert Fabian 1946- WhoWest 94
Mayer, Robert Wallace 1909- WhoAm 94
Mayer, Roger Laurance 1926- IntMPA 94
Mayer, Ronald Franklin 1947- WhoFI 94
Mayer, Rosemary 1943- WhoAmA 93
Mayer, Sandy 1952- BuCMET
Mayer, Seymour R. 1912- IntMPA 94
Mayer, Sondra 1933- WhoAmA 93
Mayer, Stephen Edward 1954- WhoMW 93
Mayer, Stephen S. 1952- WhoAmL 94
Mayer, Steven L. 1949- WhoAmL 94
Mayer, Steven M. 1946- WhoFI 94
Mayer, Susan Martin 1931- WhoAmA 93
Mayer, Sylvie 1946- WhoWomW 91
Mayer, Theodore V.H. 1952- WhoAm 94, WhoAmL 94
Mayer, Thomas IntWW 93
Mayer, Thomas 1927- WhoWest 94
Mayer, Thomas 1928- Who 94
Mayer, Victor James 1933- WhoAm 94
Mayer, Wendy Wiviott 1962- WhoMW 93
Mayer, William (Robert) 1925- NewGrDO
Mayer, William Dixon 1928- WhoAm 94
Mayer, William Emilio 1940- WhoAm 94
Mayerhofer, James Thomas 1944- WhoAm 94
Mayeri, Beverly WhoAmA 93
Mayer-Kuckuk, Theo 1927- IntWW 93
Mayerle, Thomas Michael 1948- WhoAm 94, WhoAmL 94
Mayernik, David John 1952- WhoAmP 93
Mayeron, Carol Ann 1951- WhoAm 94
Mayeron, Janie S. 1951- WhoAmL 94
Mayers, Barbara W. 1940- WhoAm 94
Mayers, Daniel Kriegsman 1934- WhoAm 94
Mayers, David (Allan) 1951- WrDr 94
Mayers, Eugene David 1915- WhoAm 94
Mayers, Jean 1920- WhoAm 94
Mayers, Marvin K(eene) 1927- ConAu 43NR
Mayers, Roy WhoAm 94

Mayers, Stanley Penrose, Jr. 1926- *WhoAm 94*
Mayersohn, Nettie 1926- *WhoAmP 93*
Mayerson, Hy 1937- *WhoAmL 94*
Mayerson, Philip 1918- *WhoAm 94*
Mayerson, Sandra Elaine 1952- *WhoAm 94*
Mayes, Bill Edwin 1934- *WhoMW 93*
Mayes, Charlotte *WhoAmP 93*
Mayes, Cheryl Darlene 1948- *WhoMW 93*
Mayes, Clinton, Jr. *WhoBlA 94*
Mayes, David Lee 1947- *WhoWest 94*
Mayes, Doris Miriam 1928- *WhoBlA 94*
Mayes, Elaine 1938- *WhoAmA 93*
Mayes, Frances *DrAPF 93*
Mayes, Frank Gorr 1930- *WhoAm 94*
Mayes, Frederick Brian 1934- *Who 94*
Mayes, Gary 1945- *WhoAmL 94*
Mayes, Helen M. 1918- *WhoBlA 94*
Mayes, Herbert R. 1900-1987 *DcLB 137 [port]*
Mayes, Ian 1951- *Who 94*
Mayes, Jean Marie Keally 1942- *WhoMW 93*
Mayes, Jesse J. 1914- *WhoAmP 93*
Mayes, John Ernest 1950- *WhoFI 94*
Mayes, Mark Edward 1962- *WhoScEn 94*
Mayes, Maureen Davidica 1945- *WhoMW 93, WhoScEn 94*
Mayes, McKinley 1930- *WhoBlA 94*
Mayes, Michael Hugh Gunton *Who 94*
Mayes, Nathaniel H., Jr. 1941- *WhoBlA 94*
Mayes, Paul Eugene 1928- *WhoAm 94*
Mayes, Rueben 1963- *WhoBlA 94*
Mayes, Sharon Kay 1946- *WhoAmL 94*
Mayes, Shirley Ann *Who 94*
Mayes, Steven Lee 1939- *WhoAmA 93*
Mayes, Wendell 1919-1992 *AnObit 1992*
Mayes, Wendell Wise, Jr. 1924- *WhoAm 94*
Mayesh, Jay Philip 1947- *WhoAm 94, WhoAmL 94*
Mayeux, Jerry Vincent 1937- *WhoWest 94*
Mayfair, Mitzi d1976 *WhoHol 92*
Mayfield, Hon. Lord 1921- *Who 94*
Mayfield, Bruce Dewitt 1960- *WhoAmP 93*
Mayfield, Christopher John *Who 94*
Mayfield, Christopher John 1935- *IntWW 93*
Mayfield, Cleo d1954 *WhoHol 92*
Mayfield, Connie Elaine 1957- *WhoMW 93*
Mayfield, Curtis 1942- *AfrAmAl 6, WhoBlA 94, WhoHol 92*
Mayfield, Curtis Lee 1942- *WhoAm 94*
Mayfield, David Merkley 1942- *WhoAm 94*
Mayfield, Frank Henderson 1908-1991 *WhAm 10*
Mayfield, Harold Ford 1911- *WhoMW 93*
Mayfield, JoAnn H.O. 1932- *WhoBlA 94*
Mayfield, Julia 1904- *WrDr 94*
Mayfield, Julian d1984 *WhoHol 92*
Mayfield, Richard Dean 1944- *WhoIns 94*
Mayfield, Richard Heverin 1921- *WhoAm 94*
Mayfield, Robert Charles 1928- *WhoAm 94*
Mayfield, Signe S. *WhoAmA 93*
Mayfield, T. Brient, IV 1947- *WhoAm 94*
Mayfield, William Cary 1958- *WhoFI 94*
Mayfield, William S. 1919- *WhoBlA 94*
Mayfield, William Stephen 1919- *WhoAm 94*
Mayhall, Dorothy *WhoAmA 93*
Mayhall, Jane *DrAPF 93*
Mayhams, Norridge Bryant 1903- *WhoBlA 94*
Mayhar, Ardath 1930- *ConAu 42NR, EncSF 93*
Mayhar, Ardath (Hurst) 1930- *WrDr 94*
Mayhew, Baron 1915- *Who 94*
Mayhew, Christopher (Paget) 1915- *WrDr 94*
Mayhew, Christopher Paget 1915- *IntWW 93*
Mayhew, David Raymond 1937- *WhoAm 94, WrDr 94*
Mayhew, Edgar De Noailles 1913-1990 *WhoAmA 93N*
Mayhew, Elza *WhoAmA 93*
Mayhew, Eric George 1938- *WhoScEn 94*
Mayhew, Experience 1673-1758 *EncNAR*
Mayhew, Harry Eugene 1933- *WhoAm 94*
Mayhew, Jonathan 1720-1766 *DcAmReB 2*
Mayhew, Josephine 1924- *WhoAmP 93*
Mayhew, Kate d1944 *WhoHol 92*
Mayhew, Kenneth 1947- *Who 94*
Mayhew, Kenneth Edwin, Jr. 1934- *WhoAm 94, WhoFI 94*
Mayhew, Lawrence Lee 1933- *WhoAm 94*
Mayhew, Patrick Barnabas Burke 1929- *IntWW 93*
Mayhew, Peter 1944- *WhoHol 92*
Mayhew, Richard 1934- *WhoAmA 93*
Mayhew, Sir Patrick (Barnabas Burke) 1929- *Who 94*
Mayhew, Stella d1934 *WhoHol 92*
Mayhew, Thomas 1593-1682 *EncNAR*
Mayhew, Thomas c. 1621-1657 *EncNAR*
Mayhew, William A. 1940- *WhoAm 94*
Mayhew-Sanders, John (Reynolds) 1931- *Who 94*
Ma Yi 1922- *WhoPRCh 91 [port]*
Ma Yimin *WhoPRCh 91*
Ma-yi-nu-er *WhoPRCh 91*
Mayka, Stephen Paul 1946- *WhoAmL 94*
Mayland, Henry Fredrick 1935- *WhoWest 94*
Mayland, Kenneth Theodore 1951- *WhoAm 94*
Mayland, Ralph 1927- *Who 94*
Mayle, Robert Edward 1938- *WhoAm 94*
Maymi, Carmen 1938- *WhoHisp 94*
Maynard, Alan Keith 1944- *Who 94*
Maynard, Allegra 1897-1991 *WhAm 10*
Maynard, Arthur Homer 1915- *WhoWest 94*
Maynard, Bill 1928- *WhoHol 92*
Maynard, Brian Alfred 1917- *Who 94*
Maynard, Charles Douglas 1934- *WhoAm 94*
Maynard, Claire d1941 *WhoHol 92*
Maynard, Don *ProFbHF*
Maynard, Donald Nelson 1932- *WhoAm 94*
Maynard, Edward 1813-1891 *WorInv*
Maynard, Edward Samuel 1930- *WhoBlA 94*
Maynard, Edwin Francis George 1921- *Who 94*
Maynard, Geoffrey (Walter) 1921- *WrDr 94*
Maynard, Geoffrey Walter 1921- *Who 94*
Maynard, Harry d1976 *WhoHol 92*
Maynard, Harry Lee 1927- *WhoWest 94*
Maynard, Hugh M. 1949- *WhoAmL 94*
Maynard, Joan *Who 94*
Maynard, Joan 1932- *WhoMW 93*
Maynard, (Vera) Joan 1921- *Who 94*
Maynard, John 1940- *WhoAmL 94*
Maynard, John Howard, Jr. 1945- *WhoAmP 93*
Maynard, John M. 1929- *WhoAmP 93*
Maynard, John Ralph 1942- *WhoAm 94, WhoAmL 94, WhoFI 94*
Maynard, John Rogers 1941- *WhoAm 94*
Maynard, Ken d1973 *WhoHol 92*
Maynard, Kenneth Douglas 1931- *WhoAm 94*
Maynard, Kermit d1971 *WhoHol 92*
Maynard, Michael Anthony 1953- *WhoFI 94*
Maynard, Mimi *WhoHol 92*
Maynard, Nan(cy Kathleen Brazier) 1910- *WrDr 94*
Maynard, Nigel (Martin) 1921- *Who 94*
Maynard, Olivia Benedict 1936- *WhoAmP 93*
Maynard, Patricia 1942- *WhoHol 92*
Maynard, Richard (John) 1926- *EncSF 93*
Maynard, Richard Edwards 1933- *WhoAmP 93*
Maynard, Robert C. d1993 *NewYTBS 93 [port]*
Maynard, Robert C. 1937- *WhoBlA 94*
Maynard, Robert C(lyve) 1937-1993 *ConAu 142, CurBio 93N*
Maynard, Robert Clyve 1937- *WhoAm 94*
Maynard, Robert Edgerton *WhoIns 94*
Maynard, Robert Howell 1938- *WhoAm 94; WhoAmL 94*
Maynard, Roger Paul 1943- *Who 94*
Maynard, Ted *WhoHol 92*
Maynard, Tex *WhoHol 92*
Maynard, Valerie J. 1937- *WhoBlA 94*
Maynard, William 1921- *WhoAmA 93*
Maynard Smith, John 1920- *IntWW 93, Who 94*
Mayne, David Quinn 1930- *IntWW 93, Who 94*
Mayne, Diane 1934- *WhoAmL 94*
Mayne, Eric d1947 *WhoHol 92*
Mayne, Eric 1928- *Who 94*
Mayne, Ernie d1937 *WhoHol 92*
Mayne, Ferdy 1920- *WhoHol 92*
Mayne, John Fraser 1932- *Who 94*
Mayne, Lucille Stringer 1924- *WhoAm 94*
Mayne, Michael Clement Otway 1929- *Who 94*
Mayne, Richard 1926- *WrDr 94*
Mayne, Richard (John) 1926- *Who 94*
Mayne, Robert Blair 1915-1955 *DcNaB MP*
Mayne, Roger, Mrs. *Who 94*
Mayne, (David) Roger 1929- *IntWW 93*
Mayne, Seymour 1944- *WrDr 94*
Mayne, Thom 1944- *WhoAm 94*
Mayne, Wiley Edward 1917- *WhoAmL 94*
Mayne, Wiley Edward, Jr. 1945- *WhoAm 94, WhoAmL 94*
Mayne, William 1928- *Who 94, WhoAm 94*
Mayne, William 1929- *WrDr 94*
Mayne, William (James Carter) 1928- *EncSF 93, TwCYAW*
Maynen, James Donald 1937- *WhoMW 93*
Maynes, Charles William 1938- *WhoAm 94, WhoAmP 93*
Maynez, Bernice H. *WhoHisp 94*
Mayniel, Juliette *WhoHol 92*
Maynor, Asa *WhoHol 92*
Maynor, Dorothy 1910- *WhoBlA 94*
Maynor, Dorothy Leigh 1910- *AfrAmAl 6*
Maynor, Kevin Elliott 1954- *WhoBlA 94*
Maynor, Peggy Thompson 1929- *WhoAmP 93*
Maynor, Vernon Perry 1966- *WhoBlA 94*
Mayo, Earl of 1929- *Who 94*
Mayo, Alfredo d1985 *WhoHol 92*
Mayo, Barry Alan 1952- *WhoBlA 94*
Mayo, Blanche Irene 1946- *WhoBlA 94*
Mayo, Cathy *DrAPF 93*
Mayo, Clyde Calvin 1940- *WhoFI 94, WhoScEn 94*
Mayo, Edna d1970 *WhoHol 92*
Mayo, Eileen 1906- *Who 94*
Mayo, Eli 1933- *WhoFI 94*
Mayo, Elizabeth Broom 1948- *WhoAm 94, WhoAmL 94*
Mayo, Frank d1963 *WhoHol 92*
Mayo, Frank Rea 1933-1987 *WhAm 10*
Mayo, George d1950 *WhoHol 92*
Mayo, George Washington, Jr. 1946- *WhoAm 94*
Mayo, Gerald Edgar 1932- *WhoIns 94*
Mayo, Harry d1964 *WhoHol 92*
Mayo, Harry D., III 1939- *WhoBlA 94*
Mayo, J. Haskell, Jr. *WhoMW 93*
Mayo, James 1914- *WrDr 94*
Mayo, James Wellington 1930- *WhoBlA 94*
Mayo, Jerald Frank 1953- *WhoMW 93*
Mayo, Joan Bradley 1942- *WhoScEn 94*
Mayo, John *Who 94*
Mayo, (Edward) John 1931- *Who 94*
Mayo, John Sullivan 1930- *WhoAm 94, WhoFI 94, WhoScEn 94*
Mayo, Joseph Anthony d1966 *WhoHol 92*
Mayo, Joseph W. *WhoAmP 93*
Mayo, Julia A. 1926- *WhoBlA 94*
Mayo, Margaret Ellen 1944- *WhoAmA 93*
Mayo, Marti 1945- *WhoAmA 93*
Mayo, Noel 1937- *WhoFI 94*
Mayo, Oliver 1942- *WhoScEn 94*
Mayo, Pamela Elizabeth 1959- *WhoAmA 93*
Mayo, Patricia Elton 1915- *WrDr 94*
Mayo, Robert Bowers 1933- *WhoAmA 93*
Mayo, Robert Michael 1962- *WhoScEn 94*
Mayo, Robert Porter 1916- *WhoAm 94*
Mayo, Robert William 1909- *Who 94*
Mayo, Samuel Turberville 1921- *WhoMW 93*
Mayo, Simon Herbert 1937- *Who 94*
Mayo, Thomas O. 1930- *WhoAmP 93*
Mayo, Virginia *WhoHol 92*
Mayo, Virginia 1920- *IntMPA 94*
Mayo, Whitman *WhoHol 92*
Mayock, Robert Lee 1917- *WhoAm 94, WhoScEn 94*
Mayoh, Raymond Blanchflower 1925- *Who 94*
Mayol, Pedro Magdiel 1933- *WhoHisp 94*
Mayol, Richard Thomas 1949- *WhoWest 94*
Mayon, George d1982 *WhoHol 92*
Ma Yongwei 1942- *WhoPRCh 91*
Mayopoulos, Timothy J. 1959- *WhoAmL 94*
Mayor, A. Hyatt 1901-1980 *WhoAmA 93N*
Mayor, Archer H(untington) 1950- *WrDr 94*
Mayor, Augustin d1968 *WhoHol 92*
Mayor, Flora M. 1872-1931 *BlmGWL*
Mayor, Heather Donald 1930- *WhoAm 94*
Mayor, Hugh Robert 1941- *Who 94*
Mayor, Louis Enrique 1937- *WhoHisp 94*
Mayor, Richard Blair 1934- *WhoAm 94, WhoAmL 94*
Mayoral, Ernesto *WhoAmL 94*
Mayoral, Luis R. 1945- *WhoHisp 94*
Mayoral, Marina 1942- *BlmGWL*
Mayoras, Donald Eugene 1939- *WhoAm 94, WhoFI 94*
Mayorga, Dennis D. 1957- *WhoHisp 94*
Mayorga, Oscar Danilo 1949- *WhoHisp 94*
Mayorga, Rene N. 1956- *WhoHisp 94*
Mayor Zaragoza, Federico 1934- *IntWW 93, Who 94*
Mayotte, Tim 1960- *WhoAm 94*
Ma Youde *WhoPRCh 91*
Mayoux, Jacques Georges Maurice Sylvain 1924- *IntWW 93*
Mayow, John *WorScD*
Maypole, John Floyd 1939- *WhoAm 94*
Mayr, Ernst 1904- *IntWW 93, WhoAm 94, WhoScEn 94, WrDr 94*
Mayr, James Jerome 1942- *WhoMW 93*
Mayr, Richard 1877-1935 *NewGrDO [port]*
Mayr, (Johann) Simon 1763-1845 *NewGrDO*
Mayreder, Rosa 1858-1938 *BlmGWL*
Mayr-Harting, Henry Maria Robert Egmont 1936- *Who 94*
Mayrhofer, Manfred 1926- *IntWW 93*
Mayring, Lothar d1948 *WhoHol 92*
Mayrocker, Friederike 1924- *BlmGWL*
Mayron, Lewis Walter 1932- *WhoWest 94*
Mayron, Melanie 1952- *IntMPA 94, WhoAm 94, WhoHol 92*
Mayrose, Herman Everett 1893- *WhAm 10*
Mayrs, David Blair 1935- *WhoAmA 93*
Mays, Alfred Thomas 1947- *WhoBlA 94*
Mays, Benjamin E. 1894-1984 *AfrAmAl 6 [port]*
Mays, Benjamin Elijah 1895-1984 *DcAmReB 2*
Mays, Carol Jean 1933- *WhoAmP 93*
Mays, Carrie J. 1928- *WhoBlA 94*
Mays, Colin Garth 1931- *Who 94*
Mays, David 1949- *WhoBlA 94*
Mays, David Arthur 1929- *WhoScEn 94*
Mays, Dewey Orvric, Jr. 1929- *WhoBlA 94*
Mays, Edward Everett 1930- *WhoBlA 94*
Mays, Gerald Avery 1939- *WhoAm 94*
Mays, James A. 1939- *WhoBlA 94*
Mays, Janice Ann 1951- *WhoAmL 94*
Mays, Jeffrey 1952- *WhoAmP 93*
Mays, Joseph Barber, Jr. 1945- *WhoAm 94, WhoAmL 94*
Mays, L. Lowry 1935- *WhoAm 94*
Mays, M. Douglas 1950- *WhoAmP 93*
Mays, Paul Kirtland 1887-1961 *WhoAmA 93N*
Mays, Penny Sandra 1940- *WhoAm 94*
Mays, Tom *WhoAmP 93*
Mays, Travis Cortez 1968- *WhoBlA 94*
Mays, Vickie M. 1952- *WhoBlA 94*
Mays, Victor 1927- *WhoAmA 93*
Mays, W. Roy, III 1946- *WhoBlA 94*
Mays, William, Jr. 1929- *WhoBlA 94*
Mays, William Bernard 1957- *WhoWest 94*
Mays, William Fritz 1944- *WhoAm 94*
Mays, William J. 1939- *WhoAmL 94*
Mays, William O. 1934- *WhoBlA 94*
Mays, Willie 1931- *AfrAmAl 6 [port]*
Mays, Willie Howard, Jr. 1931- *WhoAm 94, WhoBlA 94, WhoWest 94*
Mayse, Thomas Matthew 1950- *WhoMW 93*
Maysent, Harold Wayne 1923- *WhoAm 94*
Maysles, Albert 1926- *IntMPA 94*
Maystadt, Philippe 1948- *IntWW 93*
Maystrick, David Paul 1951- *WhoScEn 94*
Maytham, Thomas Northrup 1931- *WhoAmA 93*
Maytum, Harry Rodell 1913- *WhoWest 94*
Ma Yuan 1923- *WhoPRCh 91 [port]*
Ma Yuan 1930- *IntWW 93*
Ma Yuanbiao 1934- *WhoPRCh 91 [port]*
Ma Yuhai *WhoPRCh 91*
Ma Yuhuai 1917- *IntWW 93, WhoPRCh 91 [port]*
Mayumura, Taku *EncSF 93*
Ma Yuzhen *WhoPRCh 91*
Ma Yuzhen 1934- *IntWW 93*
Mayuzumi, Toshiro 1929- *NewGrDO*
Maywhort, William Walter 1946- *WhoAmL 94*
Maywood, Augusta 1825-1876 *IntDcB [port]*
Mazadoorian, Harry Nicholas 1938- *WhoAmL 94*
Mazaev, Ivan Sergeevich 1933- *LngBDD*
Mazaev, Vladimir Aleksandrovich 1961- *LngBDD*
Mazakutemani, Paul c. 1806-1885 *EncNAR*
Mazalova, Gerta *WhoWomW 91*
Mazan, Walter Lawrence 1921- *WhAm 10*
Mazander, Charles A., Jr. 1927- *WhoAmP 93*
Mazanec, George L. 1936- *WhoFI 94*
Mazankowski, Donald Frank 1935- *IntWW 93, Who 94, WhoAm 94, WhoFI 94*
Mazar, Benjamin 1906- *IntWW 93*
Mazarakis, Michael Gerassimos *WhoScEn 94, WhoWest 94*
Mazarella, John Richard 1959- *WhoMW 93*
Mazarin, Jules 1602-1661 *HisWorL [port], NewGrDO*
Mazarrasa, Rafael 1948- *WhoHisp 94*
Mazeaud, Pierre 1929- *IntWW 93*

Mazek, Warren Felix 1938- WhoAm 94
Mazel, Joseph Lucas 1939- WhoFI 94
Mazelis, Mendel 1922- WhoWest 94
Mazenko, Donald Michael 1925-
WhoWest 94
Mazenko, Gene Francis 1945-
WhoScEn 94
Mazer, Anne 1953- WrDr 94
Mazer, Harry DrAPF 93
Mazer, Harry 1925- TwCYAW
Mazer, Lawrence 1937- WhoAmL 94
Mazer, Norma Fox DrAPF 93
Mazer, Norma Fox 1931- TwCYAW,
WhoAm 94, WrDr 94
Mazerolle, Alfred D. 1943- WhoAmP 93
Mazeski, Edward James, Jr. 1929-
WhoAm 94
Ma Zhongchen 1936- IntWW 93,
WhoPRCh 91 [port]
Maziarz, Lucille A. 1924- WhoAmP 93
Maziarz, Marysia DrAPF 93
Mazidah Binti Hj Zakaria WhoWomW 91
Mazie, Marvin Edward 1930- WhoAm 94
Mazilier, Joseph 1797-1868 IntDcB
Mazin, Ruth 1935- WhoFI 94
Mazique, Frances Margurite WhoBlA 94
Ma Zishu WhoPRCh 91
Mazlen, Roger Geoffrey 1937- WhoAm 94
Mazlish, Bruce 1923- WhoAm 94
Mazo, Mark Elliott 1950- WhoAm 94,
WhoAmL 94, WhoFI 94
Mazo, Robert Marc 1930- WhoAm 94,
WhoWest 94
Mazola, Ted WhoAmP 93
Mazon, Larri Wayne 1945- WhoBlA 94
Mazón, Manuel Reyes 1929- WhoHisp 94
Mazowiecki, Tadeusz 1927- IntWW 93
Mazrui, Ali A. 1933- IntWW 93, Who 94
Mazrui, Ali A(l'Amin) 1933- BlkWr 2,
WrDr 94
Mazrui, Ali Al'Amin 1933- WhoAm 94
Mazu, Michael John 1943- WhoMW 93
Mazuchelli, Elizabeth Sarah 1832-1914
WhWE
Mazumder, Jyotirmoy 1951- WhoScEn 94
Mazumder, Pinaki 1954- WhoMW 93
Mazur, Allan Carl 1939- WhoAm 94
Mazur, Bridget DrAPF 93
Mazur, D. Bennett 1924- WhoAmP 93
Mazur, Davia Odell 1958- WhoAmL 94
Mazur, Gail DrAPF 93
Mazur, James Andrew 1941- WhoAmP 93
Mazur, Jay J. WhoFI 94
Mazur, John 1920- WhoAmP 93
Mazur, John Mark DrAPF 93
Mazur, Meredith Margie Handley 1941-
WhoWest 94
Mazur, Michael 1935- WhoAm 94,
WhoAmA 93
Mazur, Rita Z. DrAPF 93
Mazur, Robert B. 1948- WhoAmL 94
Mazura, Adrianne C. 1951- WhoAm 94
Mazura, Franz 1924- NewGrDO
Mazur-Baker, Deborah Joan 1958-
WhoMW 93
Mazurek, Joseph P. 1948- WhoAm 94,
WhoAmL 94, WhoAmP 93, WhoWest 94
Mazurki, Mike d1990 WhoHol 92
Mazurkiewicz, John Anthony 1966-
WhoScEn 94
Mazurok, Yury (Antonovich) 1931-
NewGrDO
Mazursky, Paul 1930- IntMPA 94,
IntWW 93, WhoAm 94, WhoHol 92
Mazuski, John Edward 1951- WhoMW 93
Mazza, A. J. 1963- WhoScEn 94
Mazza, Cris DrAPF 93
Mazza, Cris 1956- WrDr 94
Mazza, Giuseppe 1806-1885 NewGrDO
Mazza, John Gamble 1945- WhoWest 94
Mazza, Larry Frank 1960- WhoFI 94
Mazza, Richard T. 1939- WhoAmP 93
Mazza, Roy Ross 1955- WhoFI 94
Mazza, Thomas Carmen 1940-
WhoAm 94
Mazza, Vito Michael 1935- WhoAmP 93
Mazzaferri, Ernest Louis 1936-
WhoAm 94
Mazzaferri, Katherine Aquino 1947-
WhoAmL 94
Mazzag, Istvan 1958- IntWW 93
Mazzanti, Ferdinando c. 1725-1805?
NewGrDO
Mazzanti, Geno M., Jr. 1929-
WhoAmP 93
Mazzanti, Rosaura fl. 1710- NewGrDO
Mazzaro, Jerome DrAPF 93
Mazzaro, Jerome 1934- WrDr 94
Mazzaropi, Amacio d1981 WhoHol 92
Mazze, Edward Mark 1941- WhoAm 94,
WhoFI 94
Mazze, Irving WhoAmA 93
Mazze, Roger Steven 1943- WhoAm 94
Mazzei, Anthony Thomas, Sr. 1955-
WhoFI 94
Mazzei, Augustine Anthony, Jr. 1936-
WhoAm 94
Mazzei, Philip 1730-1816 WhAmRev

Mazzi, Prospero fl. 1674-1689 NewGrDO
Mazzia, Valentino Don Bosco 1922-
WhoAm 94
Mazzilli, Paul John 1948- WhoAm 94
Mazzinghi, Joseph 1765-1844 NewGrDO
Mazzini, Giuseppe 1805-1872
HisWorL [port]
Mazzio, Joann 1926- SmATA 74 [port]
Mazzo, David Joseph 1956- WhoScEn 94
Mazzo, Kay 1946- IntDcB [port],
WhoAm 94
Mazzocca, Gus 1940- WhoAmA 93
Mazzocchi, Domenico 1592-1665
NewGrDO
Mazzocchi, Virgilio 1597-1646 NewGrDO
Mazzoccoli, Dominic WhoAmP 93
Mazzola, Alessandro 1942- WorESoc
Mazzola, Anthony Thomas 1923-
WhoAm 94
Mazzola, Caterino 1745-1806 NewGrDO
Mazzola, Claude Joseph 1936-
WhoScEn 94
Mazzola, John William 1928- WhoAm 94
Mazzola, Valentino 1919-1949
WorESoc [port]
Mazzoleni, Ester 1883-1982 NewGrDO
Mazzoleni, Ettore 1905-1968 NewGrDO
Mazzoli, Romano L. 1932- CngDr 93
Mazzoli, Romano Louis 1932-
WhoAm 94, WhoAmP 93
Mazzolla, D. Patrick 1947- WhoFI 94
Mazzone, A. David 1928- WhoAm 94,
WhoAmL 94
Mazzone, Domenico 1927- WhoAmA 93
Mazzoni, Antonio (Maria) 1717-1785
NewGrDO
Mazzoni Della Stella, Vittorio 1941-
IntWW 93
Mazzorin, Carlos E. WhoHisp 94
Mazzotta, Bruno Robert 1942-
WhoAm 94
Mazzotta, Vincent C. WhoAmP 93
Mazzotti, Richard Rene 1937-
WhoMW 93
Mazzuca, Robin Lynn 1958- WhoMW 93
Mazzucato, Alberto 1813-1877 NewGrDO
Mazzuconi, Daniela 1953-
WhoWomW 91
Mazzuki, Michael Robert 1960-
WhoFI 94
Mba, Lucie WhoWomW 91
Mba, Nina BlmGWL
Mbasogo, Teodoro Obiang Nguema
IntWW 93
Mbaya, Robert B. 1933- IntWW 93
M'baye, Keba 1924- IntWW 93
Mbekeani, Nyemba W. 1929- Who 94
Mbeki, Thabo 1942- IntWW 93
Mbere, Aggrey Mxolisi 1939- WhoBlA 94
M'bow, Amadou-Mahtar 1921-
IntWW 93, Who 94
Mboya, Tom 1930-1969 HisWorL [port]
McAbee, Jennings G. 1944- WhoAmP 93
McAboy, Thomas Hatfield 1930-
WhoAm 94
McAdam, Charles Vincent, Sr. 1892-1985
WhAm 10
McAdam, Ian (William James) 1917-
Who 94
McAdam, James 1930- Who 94
McAdam, John Loudon 1756-1836
WorInv
McAdam, Keith Paul William James
1945- Who 94
McAdam, Will 1921- WhoAm 94
McAdam Clark, James Who 94
McAdams, Brian 1942- WhoAm 94
McAdams, Dan P. 1954- ConAu 141
McAdams, David 1931- WhoBlA 94
McAdams, John P. 1949- WhoAm 94,
WhoAmL 94
McAdams, Linnie M. 1938- WhoBlA 94
McAdams, Robert, Jr. 1939- WhoAm 94
McAdams, Robert L. 1927- WhoBlA 94
Mc Adams, Ronald Earl 1910- WhoAm 94
McAdams, Stephen Edward 1953-
WhoScEn 94
McAdoo, Bob 1951- BasBi, WhoBlA 94
McAdoo, Carol Westbrook 1937-
WhoAmA 93
McAdoo, Donald Eldridge 1929-
WhoAmA 93N
Mc Adoo, Donald Eldridge 1929-1987
WhAm 10
McAdoo, Harriette P. 1940- WhoBlA 94
McAdoo, Henry Allen 1951- WhoBlA 94
McAdoo, Henry Robert 1916- Who 94
McAfee, Billy H. 1931- WhoAmP 93
McAfee, Carrie R. 1931- WhoBlA 94
McAfee, Charles Francis 1932-
WhoBlA 94
McAfee, David 1947- WhoAmP 93
McAfee, Deirdra DrAPF 93
McAfee, George ProFbHF
McAfee, Jerry 1916- IntWW 93,
WhoAm 94
McAfee, John Gilmour 1926- WhoAm 94
McAfee, John P. 1947- ConAu 141

McAfee, Joseph Ernest 1870-1947
DcAmReB 2
McAfee, Lawrance Wiley 1955-
WhoAm 94
McAfee, Leo C., Jr. 1945- WhoBlA 94
Mc Afee, Marilyn WhoAm 94,
WhoAmP 93
McAfee, Robert, Jr. 1937- WhoAm 94
McAfee, Robert William Montgomery
1944- Who 94
McAfee, Walter S. 1914- WhoBlA 94
Mc Afee, William 1910- WhoAm 94
McAfee, William Gage 1943-
WhoAmL 94, WhoFI 94
McAhren, Robert Willard 1935-
WhoAm 94
McAleavey, David DrAPF 93
McAlee, Richard G. 1951- WhoAmL 94
Mc Aleece, Donald John 1918-
WhoAm 94
McAleese, Mary Patricia 1951- Who 94
McAlenney, Paul F. 1942- WhoAmL 94
Mc Alester, Arcie Lee, Jr. 1933-
WhoAm 94
McAlevey, John Francis 1923- WhoAm 94
McAlexander, Thomas Victor 1939-
WhoScEn 94
McAley, David William 1949-
WhoMW 93
McAlindon, Mary Naomi 1935-
WhoMW 93
McAlindon, Thomas 1932- WrDr 94
McAlinney, Patrick WhoHol 92
McAliskey, (Josephine) Bernadette 1947-
Who 94
McAlister, Albert WhoAmP 93
McAlister, Joe Michael 1955- WhoBlA 94
McAlister, Maurice L. 1925- WhoAm 94,
WhoWest 94
McAlister, Michael Ian 1930- Who 94
McAlister, Robert Beaton 1932-
WhoAm 94, WhoAmP 93
McAlister, Ronald William Lorne 1923-
Who 94
McAlister, Susan Jane 1954- WhoMW 93
McAlister, William Harle Nelson 1940-
Who 94
McAllion, John 1948- Who 94
McAllister, Angus EncSF 93
McAllister, Archibald d1781 WhAmRev
McAllister, Bruce (Hugh) 1946-
EncSF 93, WrDr 94
McAllister, Byron Leon 1929-
WhoWest 94
McAllister, Chase Judson 1942-
WhoWest 94
McAllister, Chip WhoHol 92
McAllister, Claire DrAPF 93
McAllister, Dale Wayne 1956- WhoFI 94
McAllister, David Franklin 1941-
WhoScEn 94
McAllister, Donald d1993 NewYTBS 93
McAllister, Eric 1942- WhoFI 94
Mc Allister, Gerald Nicholas 1923-
WhoAm 94
McAllister, Geraldine E. 1925-
WhoAmA 93
McAllister, Ian Gerald 1943- Who 94
McAllister, John Brian 1941- Who 94
McAllister, Kenneth Wayne 1949-
WhoAmL 94
McAllister, LeRay L. 1930- WhoAmP 93
McAllister, Leroy Timothy, Sr. 1918-
WhoBlA 94
McAllister, Mary 1909- WhoHol 92
McAllister, Mary E. WhoAmP 93
McAllister, Patricia Anne 1951-
WhoFI 94
McAllister, Paul d1955 WhoHol 92
McAllister, Peter Michael 1938-
WhoWest 94
McAllister, Richard WhoAmP 93
McAllister, Robert Cowden 1940-
WhoAm 94, WhoFI 94
McAllister, Russell Benton 1958-
WhoScEn 94
McAllister, Singleton Beryl 1952-
WhoBlA 94
McAllister, William Howard, III 1941-
WhoAm 94
McAlmon, Robert 1896?-1956 GayLL
McAlmond, Russell Wayne 1952-
WhoFI 94
McAloon, Todd Richard 1962-
WhoScEn 94
McAlpin, David H(unter) 1897-1989
WhAm 10
McAlpin, Kirk Martin 1923- WhoAm 94,
WhoAmL 94
McAlpine Who 94
McAlpine, Christopher Who 94
McAlpine, Jane d1947 WhoHol 92
McAlpine, Kenneth Donald 1953-
WhoScEn 94
McAlpine, Rachel 1940- BlmGWL
McAlpine, Rachel (Taylor) 1940-
WrDr 94
McAlpine, Robert 1937- WhoBlA 94

McAlpine, Robert Douglas Christopher
1919- Who 94
McAlpine, Robert James 1932- Who 94
McAlpine, Robin d1993 Who 94N
McAlpine, Stephen A. 1949- WhoWest 94
McAlpine, Stephen Alan 1949-
WhoAmP 93
McAlpine, William 1922- NewGrDO
McAlpine, William (Hepburn) 1936-
Who 94
McAlpine of West Green, Baron 1942-
Who 94
McAmis, Edwin Earl 1934- WhoAm 94,
WhoAmL 94
McAnally, Mary DrAPF 93
McAnally, Ray d1989 WhoHol 92
McAnally-Knight, Mary DrAPF 93
McAnaw, Michael Francis 1952-
WhoFI 94
McAndrew, Anne E. Battle 1951-
WhoBlA 94
McAndrew, Elizabeth Peet 1953-
WhoWest 94
McAndrew, Francis Thomas 1953-
WhoMW 93
McAndrew, Gordon Leslie 1926-
WhAm 10
McAndrew, Marianne 1938- WhoHol 92
McAndrews, James Patrick 1929-
WhoAm 94
McAndrews, John GayLL
McAndrews, Mimi K. 1956- WhoAmP 93
McAndrews, Victoria Costa 1956-
WhoFI 94
McAndrews, William J. 1939-
WhoAmL 94
McAnespie, Robert Charles 1929-
WhoAmP 93
McAngus, W. Hugh 1950- WhoAmL 94
McAniff, Edward John 1934- WhoAm 94
McAninch, Harold D. 1933- WhoAm 94,
WhoMW 93
McAninch, Jack Herbert 1940-
WhoMW 93
Mc Aninch, Robert Danford 1942-
WhoScEn 94
McAnuff, Des 1952- WhoAm 94
McAnulty, Brenda Hart 1949- WhoBlA 94
Mc Anulty, Henry Joseph 1915-
WhoAm 94
McArdle, J. Patrick 1945- WhoMW 93
McArdle, Joan Terruso 1947-
WhoScEn 94
McArdle, John 1928- WhoAm 94
McArdle, John Edward 1928- WhoAm 94
McArdle, Paul Francis 1918- WhoAm 94
McArdle, Richard Joseph 1934-
WhoAm 94
McArdle, Stanley Lawrence 1922- Who 94
McArthur, Alex 1957- WhoHol 92
McArthur, Archibald WhAmRev
McArthur, Barbara Jean WhoBlA 94
McArthur, Eldon Durant 1941-
WhoScEn 94, WhoWest 94
Mc Arthur, George 1924- WhoAm 94
McArthur, Gregory Robert 1952-
WhoScEn 94
McArthur, Harvey King 1912- WrDr 94
McArthur, James Duncan 1937-
WhoWest 94
Mc Arthur, Janet Ward 1914- WhoAm 94
McArthur, John EncSF 93
McArthur, John Duncan 1938- Who 94
McArthur, John Hector 1934-
WhoAm 94, WhoFI 94
McArthur, John William, Jr. 1955-
WhoFI 94
McArthur, Kimberly WhoHol 92
McArthur, Mary DrAPF 93
McArthur, Thomas Burns 1938- Who 94
McAtee, Clyde d1947 WhoHol 92
McAtee, David Ray 1941- WhoAmL 94
McAtee, Miles F. 1934- WhoAmL 94
McAtee, Patricia Anne Rooney 1931-
WhoAm 94
McAtee, William J. 1947- WhoAmP 93
McAtee, Yolanda Martinez 1940-
WhoHisp 94
McAteer, James Francis 1931-
WhoAm 94, WhoWest 94
McAulay, Sara DrAPF 93
McAuley, James J. DrAPF 93
McAuley, James J. 1936- WrDr 94
McAuley, John P. 1952- WhoIns 94
McAuley, Paul J. 1955- EncSF 93
McAuley, Skeet 1951- WhoAmA 93
McAuley, Terry Francis 1947-
WhoMW 93
McAuley, Van Alfon 1926- WhoScEn 94
McAuliffe, Clayton Doyle 1918-
WhoAm 94
McAuliffe, Cornelius James 1949-
WhoAmP 93
McAuliffe, Daniel Joseph 1945-
WhoAm 94, WhoAmL 94, WhoFI 94
McAuliffe, Dennis Philip 1922-
WhoAm 94

McAuliffe, Gervais Ward, III 1960-
WhoAmL 94
McAuliffe, James Robert 1944-
WhoIns 94
McAuliffe, John F. *WhoAmP 93*
McAuliffe, John F. 1932- *WhoAm 94,*
WhoAmL 94
McAuliffe, Lawrence Francis 1952-
WhoAmL 94
McAuliffe, Leon d1988 *WhoHol 92*
Mc Auliffe, Michael F. 1920- *WhoAm 94,*
WhoMW 93
McAuliffe, Roger P. 1938- *WhoAmP 93*
McAuliffe, Rosemary *WhoAmP 93*
McAuliffe, Steven James 1948-
WhoAm 94, WhoAmL 94
McAvity, John Gillis 1950- *WhoAm 94*
McAvity, Thomas Adams, Jr. 1942-
WhoFI 94
McAvoy, Bruce Ronald 1933- *WhoAm 94*
McAvoy, Charles d1953 *WhoHol 92*
McAvoy, Gilbert Paul 1929- *WhoScEn 94*
McAvoy, Jean d1934 *WhoHol 92*
McAvoy, John Joseph 1933- *WhoAm 94,*
WhoAmL 94
McAvoy, John Joseph 1946- *WhoAmL 94*
McAvoy, (Francis) Joseph 1910- *Who 94*
McAvoy, Mai Lewerenz d1960
WhoHol 92
McAvoy, May d1984 *WhoHol 92*
McAvoy, Rita Cloutier 1917- *WhoAmP 93*
McAvoy, Rogers 1927- *WhoAm 94*
McAvoy, Thomas James *WhoAm 94,*
WhoAmL 94
McAvoy, Thomas McLaughlin 1943-
Who 94
McAward, Patrick Joseph, Jr. 1934-
WhoAm 94
McBain, Diane 1941- *WhoHol 92*
McBain, Diane Jean 1941- *WhoAm 94*
McBain, Ed *EncSF 93, IntWW 93,*
Who 94
Mc Bain, Ed 1926- *WhoAm 94, WrDr 94*
McBain, Gordon (Duncan, III)
1946-1992 *EncSF 93*
McBain, Laurie (Lee) 1949- *WrDr 94*
McBain, Malcolm *Who 94*
McBain, (David) Malcolm 1928- *Who 94*
McBain, Willie d1920 *WhoHol 92*
McBaine, John Neylan 1941- *WhoAm 94*
McBan, Mickey 1918- *WhoHol 92*
McBarnette, Bruce Olvin 1957-
WhoAmL 94
McBath, Donald Linus 1935-
WhoScEn 94
Mc Bath, James Harvey 1922- *WhAm 10*
McBay, Arthur John 1919- *WhoAm 94,*
WhoScEn 94
McBay, Henry Cecil *WhoBlA 94*
McBeath, Andrew Alan 1936- *WhoAm 94,*
WhoMW 93
McBeath, Gerald Alan 1942- *WhoWest 94*
McBee, Gary L. 1965- *WhoScEn 94*
McBee, Jerry Burton 1939- *WhoWest 94*
McBee, Louise 1924- *WhoAmP 93*
McBee, Vincent Clermont 1946-
WhoBlA 94
McBee, William K. 1932- *WhoAmP 93*
McBennett, Robert Joseph 1942-
WhoAm 94
McBeth, Kate *EncNAR*
McBeth, Susan Law 1830-1893 *EncNAR*
McBeth, Veronica Simmons 1947-
WhoBlA 94
McBeth-Reynolds, Sandra Kay 1950-
WhoBlA 94
McBey, James 1884-1959 *WhoAmA 93N*
McBirney, Bruce Henry 1954-
WhoAmL 94
McBlain, David Alexander 1940-
WhoAmP 93
McBlaine, Richard Michael 1956-
WhoMW 93
McBrain, Nicko
See Iron Maiden ConMus 10
McBratney, George 1927- *Who 94*
McBrayer, Annette Kerlin 1957-
WhoAmL 94
McBrayer, H. Eugene *WhoScEn 94*
McBrayer, Nathan Edward 1968-
WhoFI 94
McBreairty, James *WhoAmP 93*
McBrearty, Denise Dewenter 1952-
WhoAmP 93
McBrearty, Sally Ann 1949- *WhoScEn 94*
McBrearty, Tony 1946- *Who 94*
McBreen, Joan 1944- *BlmGWL*
McBreen, Maura Ann *WhoAm 94,*
WhoScEn 94
McBride, Abel Ernest 1933- *WhoAmP 93*
McBride, Angela Barron 1941-
WhoAmL 94
McBride, Barry Clarke 1940- *WhoAm 94*
McBride, Cris Don 1962- *WhoWest 94*
McBride, David B. 1942- *WhoAmP 93*
McBride, Duane Calvin 1946-
WhoMW 93
McBride, Frances E. *WhoBlA 94*

McBride, Francis DeSales, II 1962-
WhoWest 94
McBride, Frank E. 1943- *WhoAmP 93*
McBride, George Gustave 1968-
WhoScEn 94
Mc Bride, Guy Thornton, Jr. 1919-
WhoAm 94
McBride, Harlee *WhoHol 92*
McBride, Hazel 1949- *WhoHol 92*
McBride, Henry 1867-1962
WhoAmA 93N
McBride, J. Nevins d1993 *NewYTBS 93*
McBride, Jack J. 1936- *WhoFI 94*
McBride, James Francis 1946-
WhoAmL 94
McBride, Jerry E. 1939- *WhoAmP 93*
McBride, Jim 1941- *IntMPA 94*
McBride, Joan Greatrake 1962-
WhoWest 94
Mc Bride, John Alexander 1918-
WhoAm 94, WhoScEn 94, WhoWest 94
McBride, Jon Andrew 1943- *WhoScEn 94*
McBride, Jonathan Evans 1942-
WhoAm 94, WhoFI 94
McBride, Kathleen 1952- *WhoAmP 93*
McBride, Keith L. 1947- *WhoFI 94*
McBride, Keith Wesley 1944-
WhoAmL 94
McBride, Kenneth Eugene 1948-
WhoAmL 94
McBride, Laurie 1949- *WhoWest 94*
McBride, Lloyd 1916-1983
EncABHB 9 [port]
McBride, Loren Clare 1938- *WhoMW 93*
McBride, Mekeel *DrAPF 93*
McBride, Michael Flynn 1951-
WhoAm 94
McBride, Milford Lawrence, Jr. 1923-
WhoAmL 94, WhoFI 94
McBride, Monroe Clark 1954- *WhoFI 94*
McBride, Nancy Allyson 1952-
WhoAm 94
McBride, Patricia 1942- *IntDcB [port],*
WhoHol 92
McBride, Ralph D. 1946- *WhoAmL 94*
Mc Bride, Raymond Andrew 1927-
WhoAm 94, WhoScEn 94
McBride, Regina *DrAPF 93*
McBride, Robert 1941- *WrDr 94*
Mc Bride, Robert Dana 1927- *WhoAm 94*
McBride, Robert Terrence 1935-
WhoAm 94
McBride, Rodney Lester 1941-
WhoAm 94
McBride, Shelia Ann 1947- *WhoBlA 94*
McBride, Sherry Loueen 1937-
WhoWest 94
McBride, Teresa 1962- *WhoHisp 94*
McBride, Thomas Craig 1932-
WhoScEn 94
McBride, Thomas Francis 1935-
WhoFI 94
Mc Bride, Thomas Frederick 1929-
WhoAm 94
McBride, Timothy Dominic 1959-
WhoMW 93
McBride, Ullysses 1938- *WhoBlA 94*
McBride, Vonla *Who 94*
McBride, (Sara) Vonla (Adair) 1921-
Who 94
McBride, Warner F. *WhoAmP 93*
McBride, William 1928- *WhoWest 94*
McBride, William Bernard 1931-
WhoAm 94
McBride, William Griffith 1927-
IntWW 93, Who 94, WhoScEn 94
McBride, William Howard, Jr. 1945-
WhoAmL 94
McBride, William James 1940- *IntWW 93*
Mc Bride, William Leon 1938-
WhoAm 94
McBrien, Richard P(eter) 1936- *WrDr 94*
McBrien, Richard Peter 1936- *IntWW 93,*
WhoAm 94
McBrier, Vivian Flagg *WhoBlA 94*
McBroom, F. Pearl *WhoBlA 94*
McBroom, Thomas William 1963-
WhoScEn 94
Mc Bryde, Felix Webster 1908-
WhoAm 94, WhoScEn 94
McBryde, James Edward 1950-
WhoMW 93
McBryde, Jim *WhoAmP 93*
McBryde, John d1966 *WhoHol 92*
McBryde, John Henry 1931- *WhoAm 94,*
WhoAmL 94
McBryde, Neill Gregory 1944-
WhoAm 94, WhoAmL 94
McBryde, Sarah Elva 1942- *WhoAmA 93*
McBryde, Thomas Henry 1925-
WhoAmL 94
McBurnett, Robert Keith 1953-
WhoWest 94
Mc Burney, Andrew Marvell 1913-1991
WhAm 10
McBurney, Charles Walker, Jr. 1957-
WhoAmL 94

McBurney, George William 1926-
WhoAm 94, WhoAmL 94, WhoWest 94
McBurney, John Francis, III 1950-
WhoAmP 93
McBurney, Linda Lee 1942- *WhoAm 94*
McBurney, Margot B. *WhoAm 94*
McBurney, Mona 1862-1932 *NewGrDO*
McBurney, Ralph Edward 1906- *Who 94*
McBurnie, Tony 1929- *Who 94*
McCaa, John K. 1954- *WhoBlA 94*
McCabe, Beverly Jean 1942- *WhoAm 94*
McCabe, Cameron *ConAu 41NR*
McCabe, Charles Cardwell 1836-1906
DcAmReB 2
McCabe, Charles Kevin 1952-
WhoAmL 94
McCabe, Charles Law 1922- *WhoAm 94*
McCabe, Christopher John 1956-
WhoAmP 93
McCabe, Daniel Marie, Sr. 1924-
WhoAm 94
McCabe, David Allen 1940- *WhoAm 94,*
WhoAmL 94
McCabe, Dennis John 1951- *WhoFI 94*
McCabe, Dennis P. *WhoAm 94*
McCabe, Donald James 1932-
WhoMW 93
McCabe, Douglas Raymond 1964-
WhoScEn 94
McCabe, Eamon Patrick 1948- *IntWW 93*
McCabe, Eamonn Patrick 1948- *Who 94*
McCabe, Edward Aeneas 1917-
WhoAm 94, WhoAmL 94, WhoFI 94
McCabe, Eugene 1930- *ConDr 93,*
WrDr 94
McCabe, Eugene Louis 1937- *WhoBlA 94*
McCabe, Frank Lacey 1943- *WhoAm 94*
McCabe, Gary Franke 1945- *WhoMW 93*
McCabe, George d1917 *WhoHol 92*
Mc Cabe, Gerard Benedict 1930-
WhoAm 94
McCabe, Harry d1925 *WhoHol 92*
McCabe, James J. 1929- *WhoAm 94,*
WhoAmL 94
McCabe, James Walter, Sr. 1917-
WhoAmP 93
McCabe, Jewell Jackson 1945-
WhoBlA 94
McCabe, Joan Griffin *WhoAmP 93*
McCabe, Joe d1960 *WhoHol 92*
McCabe, John d1929 *WhoHol 92*
McCabe, John 1939- *IntWW 93,*
NewGrDO, Who 94
McCabe, John C(harles), III 1920-
WrDr 94
McCabe, John Cordell 1941- *WhoScEn 94*
McCabe, John L. 1941- *WhoAmL 94*
McCabe, John Lee 1923- *WhoMW 93,*
WhoScEn 94
McCabe, Lawrence James 1935-
WhoAmL 94
McCabe, Leo d1986 *WhoHol 92*
McCabe, Maureen M. *WhoAmA 93*
McCabe, May (North) d1949 *WhoHol 92*
McCabe, Michael 1938- *WhoAm 94*
McCabe, Monica Petraglia 1959-
WhoAmL 94
McCabe, Patrick 1955- *WrDr 94*
McCabe, Peter 1945- *ConAu 140*
McCabe, Richard Lee 1943- *WhoWest 94*
McCabe, Robert Albert 1914- *WhoAm 94*
McCabe, Robert James 1953- *WhoFI 94,*
WhoScEn 94
McCabe, Ruth *WhoHol 92*
McCabe, Sandra *WhoHol 92*
McCabe, Steven Lee 1950- *WhoMW 93,*
WhoScEn 94
McCabe, Thomas Edward 1955-
WhoAmL 94
McCabe, Tom I. 1948- *WhoAmP 93*
McCaffer, Ronald 1943- *Who 94*
McCafferty, E. L., III 1946- *WhoAmL 94*
McCafferty, Jane 1960- *ConAu 141*
McCafferty, Jay David 1948-
WhoAmA 93
McCafferty, John Martin 1956-
WhoMW 93
McCafferty, Marlyn Jeanette 1945-
WhoMW 93
McCafferty, Nell 1944- *BlmGWL*
McCafferty, Owen Edward 1952-
WhoMW 93
McCafferty, (Barbara) Taylor 1946-
WrDr 94
McCafferty, Timothy Mark 1958-
WhoFI 94
McCaffery, Margo 1938- *WrDr 94*
McCaffree, Benedict 1958- *WhoAm 94*
McCaffree, Burnham Clough, Jr. 1931-
WhoAm 94
McCaffree, Edward D. 1931- *WhoAmP 93*
McCaffrey, Anne 1926- *BlmGWL*
McCaffrey, Anne (Inez) 1926- *EncSF 93,*
TwCYAW, WrDr 94
McCaffrey, Anne Inez 1926- *WhoAm 94*
McCaffrey, Anthony Daniel 1937-
WhoFI 94

McCaffrey, Carlyn Sundberg 1942-
WhoAm 94, WhoAmL 94
McCaffrey, Edward Michael, Jr. 1958-
WhoFI 94
McCaffrey, Joann Wilkinson 1929-
WhoAmP 93
McCaffrey, Kevin John 1950- *WhoFI 94*
McCaffrey, Lawrence John 1925-
WhoMW 93
McCaffrey, Neil 1925- *WhoAm 94*
McCaffrey, Phillip *DrAPF 93*
McCaffrey, Rita Whalen 1937-
WhoAmP 93
McCaffrey, Robert Henry, Jr. 1927-
WhoAm 94, WhoFI 94
Mc Caffrey, Stanley Eugene 1917-
WhoWest 94
Mc Caffrey, Thomas R. *WhoAm 94*
McCaffrey, Thos Daniel 1922- *Who 94*
McCaffrey, Timothy T. 1939- *WhoIns 94*
McCaffrey, Walter 1949- *WhoAmP 93*
McCaffrey, William R. 1934-
WhoAmP 93
McCaffrey, William Thomas 1936-
WhoAm 94, WhoFI 94
McCaffry, Barbara Lesch 1947-
WhoWest 94
McCagg, William O., Jr. d1993
NewYTBS 93
McCaghren, Marty Don 1953- *WhoFI 94*
McCaghy, Charles Henry 1934-
WhoAm 94
McCahan, Joseph Bruce 1931-
WhoWest 94
McCahill, Barry Winslow 1947-
WhoAm 94
McCahill, Thomas Day 1918-
WhoScEn 94
McCaig, Jeffrey James 1951- *WhoAm 94,*
WhoFI 94
McCaig, John Robert 1929- *WhoAm 94,*
WhoFI 94
McCaig, Joseph J. 1944- *WhoAm 94,*
WhoFI 94
McCain, Arthur Williamson, Jr. 1934-
WhoFI 94
McCain, Audrey A. *WhoAmP 93*
McCain, Betty 1931- *WhoAmP 93*
McCain, Carter Braxton 1963-
WhoAmL 94
McCain, Charles Livingston 1955-
WhoFI 94
McCain, Claude, Jr. 1931- *WhoBlA 94*
McCain, Ella Byrd 1925- *WhoBlA 94*
McCain, Frances Lee *WhoHol 92*
McCain, George Wallace F. 1930-
WhoFI 94
McCain, H. Harrison 1927- *WhoFI 94*
McCain, John 1936- *CngDr 93*
McCain, John S. 1936- *WhoAmP 93*
McCain, John Sidney, III 1936-
IntWW 93, WhoAm 94, WhoWest 94
McCain, Martin George 1951- *WhoAm 94*
McCain, Thomas Charlie 1939-
WhoAmP 93
McCain, William Frederick 1931-
WhoAmP 93
McCain, William S. 1953- *WhoAmP 93*
McCairns, Regina Carfagno 1951-
WhoFI 94
McCaleb, Greg *WhoAmP 93*
McCaleb, Joe Wallace 1941- *WhoAmL 94*
McCaleb, Malcolm, Jr. 1945- *WhoAm 94,*
WhoAmL 94
McCalips, Merle Leroy, Jr. 1946-
WhoAmP 93
McCalister, Philip Vance 1953-
WhoAmL 94
Mc Call, Abner Vernon 1915- *WhoAm 94*
McCall, Ann 1941- *WhoAmA 93*
McCall, Anthony 1946- *WhoAmA 93*
McCall, Barbara Collins 1942-
WhoBlA 94
McCall, Billy Gene 1928- *WhoAm 94*
McCall, Brian 1958- *WhoAmP 93*
McCall, Brian Patrick 1959- *WhoFI 94*
McCall, Brooks Mitchell 1946- *WhoFI 94*
McCall, Carmen J. *WhoHol 92*
Mc Call, Charles Barnard 1928-
WhoAm 94
McCall, Christopher Hugh 1944- *Who 94*
McCall, Dan (Elliott) 1940- *WrDr 94*
McCall, Daniel Thompson, Jr. 1909-
WhoAm 94, WhoAmL 94
McCall, Daryl Lynn 1956- *WhoScEn 94*
McCall, David Bruce 1928- *WhoAm 94*
McCall, David Slesser 1934- *Who 94*
McCall, David W. 1928- *WhoAm 94,*
WhoScEn 94
McCall, Donn Jay 1949- *WhoAmL 94*
McCall, Dorothy Kay 1948- *WhoAm 94*
McCall, Duke Kimbrough 1914-
WhoAm 94
McCall, Edith 1911- *WrDr 94*
McCall, Edith (Sansom) 1911-
ConAu 43NR
McCall, Emmanuel Lemuel, Sr. 1936-
WhoBlA 94

McCall, Eugene 1921- *WhoAmP 93*
McCall, George Aloysius 1939- *WhoIns 94*
McCall, H. Carl *WhoAmP 93, WhoBlA 94*
McCall, Hugh 1767-1824 *AmRev*
McCall, James Andrew 1947- *WhoAm 94*
McCall, James Franklin 1934- *AfrAmG [port]*
Mc Call, Jerry Chalmers 1927- *WhoAm 94*
McCall, Joan *IntMPA 94*
McCall, John Anthony 1940- *WhoAm 94*
McCall, John Armstrong Grice 1913- *Who 94*
McCall, John Charles 1933- *WhoFI 94*
McCall, John Donald 1911- *Who 94*
McCall, John Patrick 1927- *WhoAm 94, WhoMW 93*
McCall, John Richard 1943- *WhoAm 94*
Mc Call, Julien Lachicotte 1921- *WhoAm 94*
McCall, June d1990 *WhoHol 92*
McCall, Keith R. 1959- *WhoAmP 93*
McCall, Linda Rae 1947- *WhoMW 93*
McCall, Marion G., Jr. 1930- *WhoBlA 94*
McCall, Marsh Howard, Jr. 1939- *WrDr 94*
McCall, Michael Allen 1945- *WhoMW 93*
McCall, Michael M. 1963- *WhoFI 94*
McCall, Nelda Dunn 1945- *WhoFI 94*
McCall, Patrick *Who 94*
McCall, (Charles) Patrick (Home) 1910- *Who 94*
McCall, Rex d1939 *WhoHol 92*
McCall, Richard Powell 1955- *WhoScEn 94*
McCall, Robert B. 1940- *WrDr 94*
Mc Call, Robert R. 1926- *WhoAm 94*
McCall, Robert Theodore 1919- *WhoAmA 93*
McCall, Ronald Leon 1941- *WhoAm 94*
McCall, Stephen Shawn 1950- *WhoWest 94*
McCall, Thomas J. *WhoAmP 93*
McCall, Wendell 1953- *WrDr 94*
McCall, William d1938 *WhoHol 92*
McCall, William 1929- *Who 94*
McCall, William Calder 1906- *WhoAm 94, WhoWest 94*
McCall, William David Hair *Who 94*
McCalla, Alexander Frederick 1937- *WhoAm 94*
McCalla, Erwin Stanley 1928- *WhoBlA 94*
McCalla, Irish 1929- *WhoHol 92*
McCalla, Jon P. 1947- *WhoAm 94, WhoAmL 94*
McCalla, Mary Elizabeth Hartson 1922- *WhoMW 93*
McCalley, William Carson 1952- *WhoAmL 94*
McCallie, Marshall F. *WhoAm 94, WhoAmP 93*
McCallin, Clement d1977 *WhoHol 92*
McCallion, Hazel *WhoAm 94*
McCallion, James 1918- *WhoHol 92*
McCallion, John James 1932- *WhoAm 94*
McCallion, Kenneth F. 1946- *WhoAmL 94*
McCallion, William Patrick 1951- *WhoFI 94*
McCallister, Lon 1923- *WhoHol 92*
McCallister, Richard Anthony 1937- *WhoFI 94*
McCallister, Todd Lee 1959- *WhoFI 94*
McCallister, Wren Vance 1969- *WhoWest 94*
McCallum, Alastair Grindlay 1947- *Who 94*
McCallum, Archibald Duncan Dugald 1914- *Who 94*
McCallum, Bennett Tarlton 1935- *WhoAm 94, WhoFI 94*
Mc Callum, Charles Alexander 1925- *WhoAm 94*
Mc Callum, Charles Edward 1939- *WhoAm 94, WhoAmL 94, WhoFI 94, WhoMW 93*
McCallum, Charles John, Jr. 1943- *WhoScEn 94*
McCallum, Corrie 1914- *WhoAmA 93*
McCallum, David 1933- *IntMPA 94, WhoAm 94, WhoHol 92*
McCallum, Donald (Murdo) 1922- *Who 94*
McCallum, Francis A. 1917- *WhoAm 94*
McCallum, George Walter 1919- *WhoAmP 93*
McCallum, Googie *Who 94*
McCallum, Ian *Who 94*
McCallum, Ian Stewart 1936- *Who 94*
BcCallum, James R. d1993 *NewYTBS 93*
McCallum, James Scott 1950- *WhoAm 94*
McCallum, Jay B. 1960- *WhoAmP 93*
McCallum, John 1917- *WhoHol 92*
McCallum, John 1918- *IntMPA 94*
McCallum, John (Ian) 1920- *Who 94*
McCallum, John A. d1923 *WhoHol 92*

McCallum, John Neil 1918- *Who 94*
McCallum, Kenneth James 1918- *WhoAm 94*
McCallum, Laurie Riach 1950- *WhoMW 93*
McCallum, Leo 1929- *WhoBlA 94*
McCallum, Mary Caroline 1929- *WhoAmP 93*
McCallum, Napoleon Ardel 1963- *WhoBlA 94*
McCallum, Neil d1976 *WhoHol 92*
McCallum, Ralph William 1947- *WhoMW 93*
McCallum, Richard Warwick 1945- *WhoAm 94*
McCallum, Robert Ian 1920- *Who 94*
McCallum, Scott *WhoMW 93*
McCallum, Scott 1950- *WhoAmP 93*
McCallum, Steven Douglas 1951- *WhoAmA 93*
McCallum, Taffy Gould 1942- *ConAu 141*
McCallum, Walter Edward 1936- *WhoBlA 94*
McCallum Koch, Phyllis 1911- *WrDr 94*
McCally, Charles Richard 1958- *WhoFI 94*
McCambridge, John James 1933- *WhoAm 94, WhoScEn 94*
McCambridge, Mercedes 1918- *IntMPA 94, WhoHol 92*
Mc Cameron, Fritz Allen 1929- *WhoAm 94*
McCamley, Graham (Edward) 1932- *Who 94*
McCamman, John William 1953- *WhoWest 94*
Mc Cammon, David Noel 1934- *WhoAm 94, WhoFI 94*
McCammon, Donald Lee 1955- *WhoScEn 94*
McCammon, James Andrew 1947- *WhoAm 94*
McCampbell, Ray Irvin 1959- *WhoBlA 94*
McCampbell, Wanda Mae Hennecke 1951- *WhoMW 93*
McCamus, Tom *WhoHol 92*
McCamy, Calvin Samuel 1924- *WhoScEn 94*
Mc Camy, James Lucian 1906- *WhoAm 94*
McCamy, Jean *DrAPF 93*
McCance, Robert Alexander d1993 *Who 94N*
McCance, Robert Alexander 1898- *IntWW 93*
McCance, Thomas Lawrence 1952- *WhoWest 94*
McCandless, Alfred A. 1927- *CngDr 93, WhoAm 94, WhoAmP 93, WhoFI 94, WhoWest 94*
McCandless, Barbara J. 1931- *WhoFI 94, WhoMW 93*
McCandless, Bruce, II 1937- *IntWW 93, WhoAm 94, WhoScEn 94*
McCandless, Carolyn Keller 1945- *WhoAm 94*
McCandless, David Wayne 1941- *WhoScEn 94*
McCandless, Jane Bardarah 1925- *WhoAm 94*
McCandless, John R. 1935- *WhoAmP 93*
McCandless, Sally 1939- *WhoAmP 93*
McCandless, Sandra Ravich 1948- *WhoAm 94, WhoAmL 94*
McCandless, Stephen Porter 1941- *WhoAm 94*
McCane, Charlotte Antoinette *WhoBlA 94*
McCanles, Michael Frederick 1936- *WhoAm 94*
McCanless, R. William 1957- *WhoAmL 94*
McCann, Anthony Francis 1940- *WhoFI 94*
McCann, Arthur *EncSF 93*
McCann, Bonnie Lou 1944- *WhoAmP 93*
Mc Cann, Cecile Nelken *WhoAm 94, WhoAmA 93*
McCann, Charles Andrew d1927 *WhoHol 92*
McCann, Chuck *WhoHol 92*
McCann, Clarence David, Jr. 1948- *WhoAm 94*
McCann, Darryl Lynn 1961- *WhoMW 93*
McCann, David DeWitt 1943- *WhoAm 94*
McCann, David R. *DrAPF 93*
McCann, Dean Merton 1927- *WhoAm 94, WhoAmL 94, WhoFI 94, WhoWest 94*
McCann, Donal 1944- *WhoHol 92*
McCann, Dorothy H. *WhoAmP 93*
McCann, Edson *ConAu 141, EncSF 93, SmATA 76*
McCann, Edson 1915- *WrDr 94*
McCann, Edward 1943- *WhoAm 94, WhoFI 94*
McCann, Elizabeth Ireland 1931- *WhoAm 94*
McCann, Frances d1963 *WhoHol 92*

Mc Cann, Frances Veronica 1927- *WhoAm 94*
McCann, Francis Daniel, Jr. 1938- *ConAu 43NR*
McCann, Francis X. *WhoAmP 93*
McCann, Frank D., Jr. *ConAu 43NR*
McCann, Gail Elizabeth 1953- *WhoAm 94, WhoAmL 94*
McCann, Graham 1961- *WrDr 94*
McCann, Helen 1948- *ConAu 142, SmATA 75 [port]*
McCann, Jack Arland 1926- *WhoWest 94*
McCann, James A. 1924- *WhoAmP 93*
McCann, James P. 1930- *WhoFI 94*
McCann, Janet *DrAPF 93*
McCann, John Francis 1937- *WhoAm 94, WhoFI 94*
Mc Cann, John Joseph 1937- *WhoAm 94, WhoAmL 94*
McCann, John W. 1923- *WhoAmP 93*
McCann, Joseph Leo 1948- *WhoAmL 94*
McCann, Louise Mary 1949- *WhoAmL 94*
McCann, Maurice Joseph 1950- *WhoAmL 94*
McCann, Michael John 1946- *WhoScEn 94*
McCann, Norman 1920- *IntWW 93*
McCann, Owen 1907- *IntWW 93, Who 94*
McCann, Peter Toland McAree 1924- *Who 94*
McCann, Raymond J. 1934- *WhoFI 94*
McCann, Richard *DrAPF 93*
McCann, Richard Eugene 1939- *WhoAm 94*
McCann, Robert *WhoAmP 93*
Mc Cann, Samuel McDonald 1925- *WhoAm 94*
McCann, Sean *WhoHol 92*
McCann, Sean 1929- *WrDr 94*
McCann, Sheila Kay 1963- *WhoMW 93*
McCann, Taylor Lee 1943- *WhoIns 94*
McCann, William H., Sr. 1929- *WhoAm 94*
McCann, William H., Jr. 1945- *WhoAmP 93*
McCann, William Vern, Jr. 1943- *WhoAm 94, WhoWest 94*
McCannel, Malcolm A., Mrs. 1915- *WhoAmA 93*
McCannon, Dindga Fatima 1947- *WhoBlA 94*
McCann-Vissepó, Patricia 1951- *WhoHisp 94*
McCants, Coolidge N. 1925- *WhoBlA 94*
McCants, Jesse Lee, Sr. 1936- *WhoBlA 94*
McCants, Keith 1968- *WhoBlA 94*
McCants, Louise Spears 1924- *WhoAm 94*
McCants, Malcolm Thomas 1917- *WhoScEn 94*
McCants, Odell 1942- *WhoBlA 94*
McCard, Harold Kenneth 1931- *WhoAm 94, WhoScEn 94*
McCardell, Claire 1905-1958 *AmCulL*
McCardell, Harriett Wynn 1922- *WhoWest 94*
McCardell, James Elton 1931- *WhoAm 94*
McCardell, John Malcolm, Jr. 1949- *WhoAm 94*
Mc Cardle, Randall Raymond 1931- *WhoWest 94*
McCarey, Leo d1969 *WhoHol 92*
McCargo, Marion *WhoHol 92*
McCarl, Henry N. 1941- *WhoFI 94, WhoScEn 94*
McCarragher, Bernard John 1927- *WhoAm 94*
McCarraher, David 1922- *Who 94*
McCarrell, Clark Gabriel, Jr. 1958- *WhoBlA 94*
McCarren, Fred *WhoHol 92*
Mc Carrick, Theodore Edgar 1930- *WhoAm 94*
McCarriston, Linda *DrAPF 93*
McCarroll, Dave *WhoAmP 93*
McCarroll, Frank d1954 *WhoHol 92*
McCarroll, Jeanne Louise 1946- *WhoFI 94*
McCarroll, Kathleen Ann 1948- *WhoMW 93, WhoScEn 94*
McCarroll, Richard T. 1943- *WhoAmL 94*
McCarron, John Francis 1949- *WhoAm 94*
McCarron, Paul *WhoAmP 93*
McCarron, Paul 1933- *WhoAmA 93*
McCarron, Robert Frederick, II 1952- *WhoScEn 94*
McCarry, Charles *DrAPF 93*
McCarry, Charles 1930- *ConAu 41NR, WrDr 94*
Mc Cartan, Patrick Francis 1934- *WhoAm 94*
McCarte, George W. C. 1949- *WhoAmL 94*
McCarten, Anthony (Peter Chanel Thomas Aquinas) 1961- *ConDr 93*
McCarten, William Weisel 1948- *WhoFI 94*

McCarter, Charles Chase 1926- *WhoAm 94*
Mc Carter, Francis E. P. 1917-1988 *WhAm 10*
Mc Carter, John Alexander 1918- *WhoAm 94*
Mc Carter, John Wilbur, Jr. 1938- *WhoAm 94*
McCarter, Mercedes Anita 1939- *WhoAmP 93*
McCarter, Neely D. *WhoAm 94*
McCarter, Pete Kyle, Jr. 1945- *WhoAm 94*
McCarter, Robert *WhoAm 94, WhoFI 94*
Mc Carter, Thomas N., III 1929- *WhoAm 94, WhoFI 94*
McCarter, W. Dudley 1950- *WhoAmL 94*
McCarther, Yvette d1993 *NewYTBS 93*
McCarther, Yvonne d1993 *NewYTBS 93*
McCarthy, Baron 1925- *Who 94*
McCarthy, Abigail Quigley 1915- *WhoAm 94*
McCarthy, Adolf Charles 1922- *Who 94*
McCarthy, Albert Henry 1944- *WhoFI 94*
McCarthy, Alice Ross 1924- *WhoMW 93*
McCarthy, Andrew 1962- *IntMPA 94, WhoHol 92*
McCarthy, Ann Price 1947- *WhoAmL 94*
McCarthy, Anne Marie 1958- *WhoMW 93*
McCarthy, Bea 1935- *WhoWest 94*
McCarthy, Beatrice C. 1935- *WhoAmP 93*
McCarthy, Bernard William 1941- *WhoAm 94, WhoAmL 94*
McCarthy, Betty Lynne Grue 1959- *WhoWest 94*
McCarthy, Beverly Fitch 1933- *WhoWest 94*
McCarthy, Brian Nelson 1945- *WhoWest 94*
McCarthy, Bridget d1986 *WhoHol 92*
McCarthy, Bryant 1939- *WhoAm 94, WhoFI 94*
McCarthy, Carol M. 1940- *WhoAm 94*
McCarthy, Catherine Frances 1921- *WhoAmL 94*
McCarthy, Charles, Jr. 1933- *ConAu 42NR*
McCarthy, Charles Francis, Jr. 1926- *WhoAmL 94*
Mc Carthy, Charles Joseph 1907- *WhoAm 94*
McCarthy, Charles Justin 1937- *WhoAm 94*
McCarthy, Charles Richard 1938- *WhoAmL 94*
McCarthy, Charlie *WhoHol 92*
McCarthy, Clem d1962 *WhoHol 92*
McCarthy, Colin (John) 1951- *SmATA 77 [port]*
McCarthy, Cormac *ConAu 42NR, DrAPF 93*
McCarthy, Cormac 1933- *WhoAm 94*
Mc Carthy, D. Justin *WhoAm 94*
Mc Carthy, Daniel Christopher, Jr. 1924- *WhoAm 94*
McCarthy, Daniel Fendrich 1895- *WhAm 10*
McCarthy, Daniel M. 1966- *WhoAmP 93*
McCarthy, David Edward 1960- *WhoScEn 94*
Mc Carthy, David Jerome, Jr. 1935- *WhoAm 94*
McCarthy, Denis 1935- *WhoAmA 93*
McCarthy, Dennis 1921- *WhoAmA 93*
McCarthy, Dennis 1935- *WhoAm 94*
McCarthy, Donal John 1922- *Who 94*
McCarthy, Doris Jean 1910- *WhoAmA 93*
McCarthy, Earl d1933 *WhoHol 92*
Mc Carthy, Edward, Jr. 1931- *WhoAmL 94*
McCarthy, Edward Anthony 1918- *WhoAm 94*
McCarthy, Edward David, Jr. 1955- *WhoFI 94*
Mc Carthy, Edward James 1914- *WhAm 10*
McCarthy, Edward Paul 1945- *WhoAmP 93*
McCarthy, Eugene d1943 *WhoHol 92*
McCarthy, Eugene (Joseph) 1916- *WrDr 94*
McCarthy, Eugene Joseph 1916- *IntWW 93, Who 94, WhoAm 94, WhoAmP 93*
McCarthy, Frank *WhoHol 92*
Mc Carthy, Frank Martin 1924- *WhoAm 94*
McCarthy, Fred 1924- *WhoBlA 94*
McCarthy, Frederick William 1941- *WhoFI 94*
McCarthy, G. Daniel 1949- *WhoAm 94, WhoAmL 94, WhoFI 94*
McCarthy, Gary 1943- *WrDr 94*
McCarthy, Gerald *DrAPF 93*
McCarthy, Gerald Michael 1941- *WhoAm 94, WhoMW 93*
McCarthy, Gerald Patrick 1943- *WhoFI 94*

McCarthy, Gerald T. 1909-1990
WhAm 10
McCarthy, Glen d1984 *WhoHol 92*
McCarthy, Harold C. 1926- *WhoIns 94*
Mc Carthy, Harold Charles 1926-
WhoAm 94
McCarthy, J. Donald 1942- *WhoAmL 94*
McCarthy, J. Howard, Jr. 1927-
WhoWest 94
McCarthy, J. Thomas 1937- *WhoAm 94,*
WhoAmL 94
McCarthy, James Joseph 1944-
WhoAm 94, WhoScEn 94
McCarthy, James P. 1935- *WhoAm 94*
McCarthy, James Patrick 1935-
WhoAmP 93
McCarthy, James Ray 1943- *WhoScEn 94*
McCarthy, Jeff *WhoHol 92*
McCarthy, Jeremiah Justin 1943-
WhoScEn 94
McCarthy, Joanne *DrAPF 93*
McCarthy, Joanne Haftle 1935-
WhoWest 94
McCarthy, John 1927- *WhoAm 94,*
WhoScEn 94
Mc Carthy, John Edward 1930-
WhoAm 94
Mc Carthy, John Francis, Jr. 1925-
WhAm 10
McCarthy, John J., Jr. 1930- *WhoAmP 93*
McCarthy, John J(oseph) 1909- *WrDr 94*
McCarthy, John P. d1962 *WhoHol 92*
McCarthy, John Russell 1931- *WhoFI 94*
McCarthy, John T. 1939- *WhoAmP 93*
McCarthy, John Thomas 1939-
WhoAm 94
McCarthy, Joseph 1908-1957
HisWorL [port]
McCarthy, Joseph D. 1955- *WhoAm 94*
McCarthy, Joseph Daniel 1893-
WhAm 10
McCarthy, Joseph Gerald 1938-
WhoAm 94, WhoScEn 94
McCarthy, Joseph Harold 1921-
WhoAm 94
Mc Carthy, Joseph Michael 1940-
WhoAm 94
McCarthy, Joseph W. *WhoAm 94,*
WhoFI 94
McCarthy, Judith Ann 1937- *WhoMW 93*
McCarthy, Juliana Marie 1958-
WhoMW 93
McCarthy, Justin 1892- *WhoAmA 93N*
McCarthy, Justin Huntly 1933-
WhoScEn 94
McCarthy, Justin Milton 1924- *WhoFI 94*
McCarthy, Karen 1947- *WhoAmP 93*
McCarthy, Karen P. 1947- *WhoMW 93*
McCarthy, Kate *DrAPF 93*
McCarthy, Kathleen *WhoAmA 93*
Mc Carthy, Kathryn A. 1924- *WhoAm 94*
McCarthy, Kerry Margaret 1964-
WhoMW 93
McCarthy, Kevin 1914- *IntMPA 94,*
WhoHol 92
McCarthy, Kevin Bart 1948-
WhoAmL 94, WhoMW 93
McCarthy, Kevin John 1941-
WhoAmL 94
McCarthy, Kevin Joseph 1938-
WhoAm 94
McCarthy, Kevin Patrick 1954-
WhoIns 94
McCarthy, Laurence James 1934-
WhoScEn 94, WhoWest 94
McCarthy, Leo T. 1930- *WhoAmP 93*
McCarthy, Leo Tarcisius 1930-
WhoAm 94, WhoWest 94
McCarthy, Leslie Anna 1957-
WhoAmL 94
McCarthy, Lillah d1960 *WhoHol 92*
McCarthy, Lin *WhoHol 92*
McCarthy, Mark 1964- *WhoMW 93*
McCarthy, Mark Francis 1951-
WhoAm 94, WhoAmL 94
McCarthy, Mark T. 1960- *WhoFI 94*
McCarthy, Martha May 1945-
WhoMW 93
McCarthy, Mary 1912- *BlmGWL*
Mc Carthy, Mary 1912-1989 *WhAm 10*
McCarthy, Mary Ann Bartley 1923-
WhoScEn 94, WhoWest 94
McCarthy, Mary Louise 1943- *WhoFI 94*
McCarthy, Mary Lynn 1950- *WhoAm 94*
McCarthy, Mary Therese 1912-1989
AmCulL [port]
McCarthy, Michael Joseph 1944-
WhoAmL 94
McCarthy, Michael S. 1950- *WhoAmL 94*
McCarthy, Molly *WhoHol 92*
McCarthy, Myles d1928 *WhoHol 92*
McCarthy, Neil 1935- *WhoHol 92*
McCarthy, Neil M. 1957- *WhoFI 94*
McCarthy, Nicholas Melvyn 1938-
Who 94
McCarthy, Nobu *WhoAsA 94*
McCarthy, Nobu 1938- *WhoHol 92*

McCarthy, Patricia Jean 1927-
WhoAmP 93
Mc Carthy, Patricia Margaret 1943-
WhoWest 94
McCarthy, Patrick A. 1945- *WhoAm 94*
Mc Carthy, Patrick Edward 1930-
WhoAm 94
McCarthy, Paul 1940- *WhoAm 94*
McCarthy, Paul Edward 1956-
WhoAmP 93
McCarthy, Paul Fenton 1934- *WhoAm 94*
McCarthy, Paul H. 1939- *WhoAm 94*
McCarthy, Paul Joseph 1928-
WhoMW 93
McCarthy, (Patrick) Peter 1919- *Who 94*
McCarthy, Peter Charles 1941-
WhoAmP 93
McCarthy, Raymond Malcolm
1927-1989 *WhAm 10*
McCarthy, Richard Dean 1927-
WhoAmP 93
McCarthy, Robert Emmett 1940-
WhoAmP 93
McCarthy, Robert Emmett 1951-
WhoAmL 94
McCarthy, Robert M. 1945- *WhoAmP 93*
McCarthy, Shaun 1928- *WrDr 94*
McCarthy, Shawna *EncSF 93*
McCarthy, Sheila 1956- *WhoHol 92*
Mc Carthy, Stephen Anthony 1908-1990
WhAm 10
McCarthy, Susan Stacy 1962- *WhoFI 94*
McCarthy, Thaddeus (Pearcey) 1907-
IntWW 93, Who 94
McCarthy, Thomas 1954- *WrDr 94*
McCarthy, Thomas J., Jr. 1932-
WhoIns 94
Mc Carthy, Thomas James 1941-
WhoAm 94
Mc Carthy, Thomas Patrick 1928-
WhoAm 94
McCarthy, Thomas William, II 1945-
WhoAmP 93, WhoMW 93
McCarthy, Tim *DrAPF 93*
McCarthy, Timothy Francis 1951-
WhoFI 94
McCarthy, Vincent Paul 1940-
WhoAm 94
Mc Carthy, Walter John, Jr. 1925-
WhoAm 94, WhoFI 94, WhoMW 93
McCarthy, Wilbert Alan 1945-
WhoScEn 94
McCarthy, William Daniel 1935-
WhoAm 94
McCarthy, William E(dward) J(ohn)
1925- *WrDr 94*
McCarthy, William Edward 1924-
WhoFI 94
McCarthy, William Francis 1944-
WhoAm 94, WhoAmL 94
McCarthy, William J. *WhoIns 94*
Mc Carthy, William J. 1919- *WhoAm 94*
McCarthy, Winnie d1986 *WhoHol 92*
McCartie, (Patrick) Leo *Who 94*
McCartin, James T. *DrAPF 93*
McCartin, William Francis 1905-
WhoAmA 93
McCartney, Allen Papin 1940- *WhoAm 94*
McCartney, Brian David 1950-
WhoMW 93
McCartney, Bruce Lloyd 1939-
WhoScEn 94
McCartney, Charles Edward, Jr. 1947-
WhoAmP 93
McCartney, Charles Price 1912-
WhoAm 94
McCartney, Dorothy *DrAPF 93*
McCartney, Gordon Arthur 1937- *Who 94*
McCartney, Hugh 1920- *Who 94*
McCartney, Ian 1951- *Who 94*
McCartney, James Harold 1925-
WhoFI 94
Mc Cartney, Kenneth Hall 1924-
WhoAm 94
McCartney, Linda 1941- *WhoHol 92*
McCartney, Louis Neil 1943-
WhoScEn 94
McCartney, Mike 1959- *WhoAmP 93*
McCartney, N. L. 1923- *WhoMW 93*
McCartney, Paul 1942- *IntMPA 94,*
WhoAm 94, WhoHol 92
McCartney, (James) Paul 1942-
IntWW 93, Who 94
Mc Cartney, Ralph Farnham 1924-
WhoAmL 94, WhoMW 93
Mc Cartney, Robert Charles 1934-
WhoAm 94, WhoAmL 94
Mc Carty, Bruce 1920- *WhoAm 94*
McCarty, Clifford 1929- *WrDr 94*
McCarty, Daryl John 1930- *WhoAmP 93*
McCarty, Dennis L. 1937- *WhoMW 93*
McCarty, Donald James 1921-
WhoAm 94
McCarty, Faith B. 1960- *WhoAsA 94*
McCarty, Frank William 1941-
WhoAmL 94
McCarty, Frederick Briggs 1926-
WhoAm 94

McCarty, Gil 1934- *WhoIns 94*
McCarty, Harry Downman 1946-
WhoAm 94
McCarty, James T. 1947- *WhoIns 94*
McCarty, Jim 1943-
See Yardbirds, The ConMus 10
McCarty, Judy *WhoAmP 93*
McCarty, Lorraine Chambers
WhoAmA 93
McCarty, Maclyn 1911- *IntWW 93,*
WhoAm 94, WhoScEn 94
McCarty, Marilyn Leona 1929-
WhoMW 93
McCarty, Mary d1980 *WhoHol 92*
McCarty, Michiel Cleve 1951- *WhoFI 94*
McCarty, Patti d1985 *WhoHol 92*
Mc Carty, Paul James, Jr. 1925-
WhoWest 94
Mc Carty, Perry Lee 1931- *WhoAm 94*
McCarty, Philip Norman 1938-
WhoAm 94
McCarty, Richard Charles 1947-
WhoAm 94, WhoScEn 94
McCarty, Richard Earl 1938- *WhoAm 94,*
WhoScEn 94
Mc Carty, Robert Lee 1920- *WhoAm 94*
McCarty, Roger Leland 1953- *WhoFI 94,*
WhoMW 93
McCarty, Ron *WhoAmP 93*
McCarty, Theodore Frederick 1937-
WhoAm 94
Mc Carty, Theodore Milson 1909-
WhoAm 94, WhoMW 93
McCarty, Thomas Joseph 1938-
WhoAm 94
McCarty, Virginia Dill 1924- *WhoAmP 93*
McCarty, Willard Duane 1930-
WhoWest 94
McCarty, William Bonner, Jr. 1921-
WhoAm 94, WhoFI 94
McCarty, William Britt 1953- *WhoFI 94,*
WhoScEn 94, WhoWest 94
McCarty, William Dennis 1943-
WhoAmP 93, WhoMW 93
McCarty, Winston H. 1928- *WhoAmP 93*
McCarus, Ernest Nasseph 1922-
WhoAm 94
McCarver, James Timothy 1941-
WhoAm 94
McCarville, Mark John 1946- *WhoAm 94*
McCary, Rod 1941- *WhoHol 92*
McCash, Thomas Mark 1961-
WhoMW 93
McCaskey, Daphne Theophilia 1912-
WhoBlA 94
McCaskey, Douglas William 1942-
WhoIns 94
McCaskey, Edward W. *WhoAm 94,*
WhoMW 93
McCaskey, Michael B. 1943- *WhoAm 94,*
WhoMW 93
McCaskill, Claire 1953- *WhoAmP 93*
McCaskill, Earle 1937-1992 *WhoBlA 94*
McCaskill, Eddie 1951- *WhoMW 93*
McCaskill, Patricia Lorenz 1948-
WhoMW 93
McCaslin, Bob 1926- *WhoAmP 93*
McCaslin, Bobby D. 1943- *WhoScEn 94*
McCaslin, Nellie 1914- *WrDr 94*
McCaslin, Teresa Eve 1949- *WhoWest 94*
McCaslin, Thomas Wilbert 1947-
WhoWest 94
McCaslin, Walter Wright 1924-
WhoAmA 93N
McCaughan, Charles *WhoHol 92*
McCaughan, Dennis Lee 1943-
WhoMW 93
McCaughan, John F. 1935- *WhoAm 94,*
WhoFI 94
McCaughey, Andrew Gilmour 1922-
WhoAm 94, WhoFI 94
McCaughey, Arnold Patrick 1943-
WhoAmA 93
McCaughey, (John) Davis 1914-
IntWW 93
McCaughey, John Davis 1914- *Who 94*
McCaughey, Patrick *WhoAm 94*
McCaughran, Geraldine 1951-
TwCYAW
McCaughren, Geraldine (Jones) 1951-
WrDr 94
McCaughren, Tom 1936- *ConAu 142,*
SmATA 75 [port], WrDr 94
McCaul, Joseph Patrick 1952-
WhoMW 93
McCauley, Barbara *DrAPF 93*
McCauley, Brian 1941- *WhoAmP 93*
McCauley, Bruce Gordon *WhoAm 94*
McCauley, Carole Spearin *DrAPF 93*
McCauley, Charles Irvin 1959-
WhoScEn 94
McCauley, Cleyburn Lycurgus 1929-
WhoAmL 94
McCauley, David W. 1958- *WhoAmL 94*
McCauley, Edna d1918 *WhoHol 92*
McCauley, Gardiner Rae 1933-
WhoAmA 93
McCauley, George 1945- *WhoWest 94*

McCauley, Hugh Wayne 1935-
WhoScEn 94
McCauley, Jack d1980 *WhoHol 92*
McCauley, James Weymann 1940-
WhoScEn 94
McCauley, John Corran, Jr. 1901-
WhAm 10
McCauley, John J., Jr. *WhoAmP 93*
McCauley, Martin 1934- *WrDr 94*
McCauley, Mary Ludwig Hays
1744?-1832 *AmRev*
McCauley, Michael S. 1947- *WhoAm 94*
McCauley, Michael Stephen 1947-
WhoAmL 94
Mc Cauley, R. Paul 1943- *WhoAm 94*
McCauley, Richard Gray 1940-
WhoAm 94, WhoAmL 94, WhoFI 94
McCauley, Robbie *DrAPF 93*
McCauley, Robert Jule 1949- *WhoMW 93*
McCauley, Robert William 1926-
WhoAm 94
McCauley, Stephen (D.) 1955- *ConAu 141*
McCauley, Sue *BlmGWL*
McCauley, Sue 1941- *ConAu 140*
McCauley, Thomas Matthew 1942-
WhoMW 93
McCaulley, James Alan, III 1948-
WhoBlA 94
McCausland, Benedict Maurice Perronet
T. *Who 94*
McCausland, Elizabeth 1899-1965
WhoAmA 93N
McCausland, Thomas James, Jr. 1934-
WhoAm 94, WhoFI 94
McCavanagh, James R. *WhoAmP 93*
McCave, Ian Nicholas 1941- *Who 94*
McCaw, Craig O. 1949- *WhoAm 94,*
WhoFI 94, WhoWest 94
McCaw, Robert Bruce 1943- *WhoAmL 94*
McCaw, Valerie Sue 1960- *WhoScEn 94*
McCawley, Austin 1925- *WhoAm 94*
McCay, Glenn *WhoHol 92*
McCay, Peggy *WhoHol 92*
McCay, (Zenas) Winsor 1871-1934 *IntDcF 2-4*
McCay, Winsor 1867-1934
EncSF 93
McChesney, Clifton 1929- *WhoAmA 93*
McChesney, James Dewey 1939-
WhoScEn 94
McChesney, Mary Fuller *WhoAmA 93*
Mc Chesney, Robert Pearson 1913-
WhoAm 94, WhoAmA 93
McChesney, S. Elaine 1954- *WhoAm 94*
McChesney, Samuel Parker, III 1945-
WhoMW 93
McChesney, William S. 1909-1990
WhAm 10
McChristy, Quentin L. 1921-
WhoAmA 93
McClafferty, Monica Harrison 1964-
WhoHisp 94
McClain, Andrew Bradley 1948-
WhoBlA 94
McClain, Billy d1950 *WhoHol 92*
McClain, Cady *WhoHol 92*
McClain, Charles James 1931-
WhoAm 94, WhoMW 93
McClain, Charles William, Jr. 1940-
WhoAm 94
McClain, David H. 1933- *WhoAmP 93*
McClain, Dorothy Mae 1931- *WhoBlA 94*
McClain, Earsalean J. 1910- *WhoBlA 94*
McClain, Edward B. *WhoAmP 93*
McClain, Gary Carl 1950- *WhoAmL 94*
McClain, James W. 1939- *WhoBlA 94*
McClain, Jerome Gerald 1939-
WhoBlA 94
McClain, Larry French 1937- *WhoFI 94*
McClain, Lee Bert 1943- *WhoAm 94*
McClain, Matthew 1956- *WhoAmA 93*
McClain, Michael F. 1947- *WhoAmP 93*
McClain, Paula Denice 1950- *WhoBlA 94*
McClain, Richard Douglas 1927-
WhoAmL 94
McClain, Richard Stan 1951-
WhoWest 94
McClain, Robert Lee 1953- *WhoAmA 93*
McClain, Ronald Theodore 1948-
WhoWest 94
McClain, Saundra *WhoHol 92*
McClain, Shirla R. 1935- *WhoBlA 94*
McClain, Thomas E. 1950- *WhoAm 94,*
WhoFI 94, WhoMW 93
McClain, William Andrew 1913-
WhoAmL 94, WhoBlA 94, WhoMW 93
Mc Clain, William Harold 1917-
WhoAm 94
McClain, William L. 1958- *WhoBlA 94*
McClain, William Ray 1927- *WhoBlA 94*
McClain, William Thomas 1926-
WhoAmL 94
McClammy, Thad C. 1942- *WhoBlA 94*
McClammy, Thad C., Jr. 1942-
WhoAmP 93
McClamroch, N. Harris 1942- *WhoAm 94*
McClanahan, Connie Dea 1948-
WhoMW 93
McClanahan, John D. *WhoAmA 93*

McClanahan, Larry Duncan 1938- *WhoFI 94, WhoScEn 94*
McClanahan, Marian 1926- *WhoAmP 93*
McClanahan, Mark C. 1930- *WhoAm 94*
McClanahan, Michael Nelson 1953- *WhoScEn 94*
McClanahan, Molly 1937- *WhoAmP 93, WhoWest 94*
McClanahan, Rue *IntMPA 94, WhoAm 94*
McClanahan, Rue 1935- *WhoHol 92*
McClanahan, Sally Louise 1960- *WhoMW 93*
McClanahan, Walter Val 1946- *WhoScEn 94*
McClanan, Glenn Brooks 1934- *WhoAmP 93*
McClane, Drayton, Jr. *WhoAm 94*
McClane, George Eddington 1958- *WhoWest 94*
McClane, Kenneth Anderson *DrAPF 93*
McClane, Kenneth Anderson, Jr. 1951- *WhoBlA 94*
McClane, Robert Sanford 1939- *WhoAm 94, WhoFI 94*
McClard, Jack Edward 1946- *WhoAm 94, WhoAmL 94*
Mc Clarren, Robert Royce 1921- *WhoAm 94*
McClary, Clyde d1939 *WhoHol 92*
McClary, James Daly 1917- *WhoAm 94*
McClary, Jane McIlvaine *DrAPF 93*
McClary, Jim Marston 1949- *WhoFI 94*
McClary, Stephen Rolfe 1948- *WhoMW 93*
McClary, Thomas Calvert 1909?-1972 *EncSF 93*
McClaskey, William H. 1912- *WhoBlA 94*
McClatchey, Frank Sandy 1956- *WhoAmP 93*
McClatchey, John Francis 1929- *WhoAm 94*
McClatchy, Charles Kenny 1927-1989 *WhAm 10*
McClatchy, J. D. *DrAPF 93*
McClatchy, J. D. 1945- *WhoAm 94*
McClatchy, J(oseph) D(onald) 1945- *WrDr 94*
McClatchy, James B. *WhoAm 94, WhoFI 94, WhoWest 94*
McClatchy, Richard A., Jr. 1929- *WhoAmP 93*
McClaugherty, Joe L. 1951- *WhoAmL 94*
McClaugherty, John L. 1931- *WhoAm 94*
McClaughry, John 1937- *WhoAmP 93*
McClaurin, Irma *DrAPF 93*
McClave, Donald Silsbee 1941- *WhoAm 94, WhoFI 94, WhoWest 94*
McClay, Harvey Curtis 1939- *WhoFI 94, WhoScEn 94*
McClean, (John) David 1939- *Who 94*
McClean, James Allen, Jr. 1953- *WhoAmL 94*
McClean, Kathleen *Who 94*
McClean, Vernon E. 1941- *WhoBlA 94*
McClear, Nicholas Willard 1948- *WhoAm 94*
McClear, Richard Vance 1946- *WhoWest 94*
McClearn, Billie 1937- *WhoBlA 94*
McCleary, Ann Heron *Who 94*
McCleary, Benjamin Ward 1944- *WhoAm 94*
McCleary, Elmer T. 1878-1930 *EncABHB 9 [port]*
McCleary, Henry Glen 1922- *WhoAm 94*
McCleary, Jane Marie 1969- *WhoMW 93*
McCleary, Lloyd Everald 1924- *WhoAm 94*
McCleary, Mary Fielding 1951- *WhoAmA 93*
McCleary, Michael L. 1944- *WhoAmP 93*
McCleary, Paul Frederick 1930- *WhoAm 94*
McCleary, Stephen Hill 1941- *WhoMW 93*
McCleary, William Robert 1939- *WhoMW 93*
McCleave, Mansel Philip 1926- *WhoBlA 94*
McCleave, Mildred Atwood Poston 1919- *WhoBlA 94*
McCleery, Gary *WhoHol 92*
McCleery, Nancy *DrAPF 93*
McCleery, Richard Grimes 1928- *WhoWest 94*
McClellan, Bennett E. 1952- *WhoWest 94*
McClellan, C. W. *WhoAm 94*
Mc Clellan, Catharine 1921- *WhoAm 94*
McClellan, Craig Rene 1947- *WhoAmL 94, WhoWest 94*
McClellan, David Lawrence 1930- *WhoFI 94, WhoScEn 94*
McClellan, Douglas Eugene 1921- *WhoAmA 93*
McClellan, Edward J. 1921- *WhoBlA 94*
McClellan, Frank Madison 1945- *WhoBlA 94*

McClellan, (Herbert) Gerard (Thomas) 1913- *Who 94*
McClellan, James E. 1926- *WhoAmP 93*
Mc Clellan, James Edward, Jr. 1922- *WhoAm 94*
McClellan, James Harold 1947- *WhoAm 94*
McClellan, James Michael 1958- *WhoMW 93*
McClellan, John Forrest 1932- *Who 94*
McClellan, Laurie Marie 1963- *WhoFI 94*
McClellan, Mark Howell 1957- *WhoWest 94*
McClellan, Richard Augustus 1930- *WhoFI 94*
McClellan, Roger Orville 1937- *WhoAm 94, WhoScEn 94*
McClellan, Stephen T. 1942- *WrDr 94*
Mc Clellan, William Monson 1934- *WhoAm 94*
McClelland, Alan 1955- *WhoScEn 94*
McClelland, Allan d1989 *WhoHol 92*
McClelland, Bramlette 1920- *WhoAm 94*
McClelland, Bruce *DrAPF 93*
McClelland, Charles Edgar 1940- *WrDr 94*
McClelland, Douglas *IntWW 93, Who 94*
McClelland, Emmy 1940- *WhoAmP 93*
McClelland, George Ewart 1927- *Who 94*
McClelland, (William) Grigor 1922- *Who 94*
McClelland, Ivy Lillian 1908- *WrDr 94*
Mc Clelland, James Craig 1901- *WhoAm 94*
McClelland, James Craig 1938- *WhoMW 93*
McClelland, James L. 1948- *WhoAm 94*
McClelland, James Morris 1943- *WhoFI 94*
McClelland, James Ray 1946- *WhoAmL 94*
McClelland, Jeanne C. *WhoAmA 93*
McClelland, John Morris 1915- *WhoWest 94*
McClelland, Marguerite Marie 1919- *WhoBlA 94*
McClelland, Maurice d1993 *NewYTBS 93*
McClelland, Michael 1947- *WhoAm 94, WhoFI 94*
McClelland, Nick *WhoHol 92*
McClelland, Raymond Cecil 1925- *WhoAmP 93*
McClelland, Rex Arnold 1936- *WhoAm 94, WhoFI 94*
Mc Clelland, Robert Nelson 1929- *WhoAm 94*
McClelland, Shearwood Junior 1947- *WhoScEn 94*
McClelland, Thomas Melville 1963- *WhoScEn 94*
McClelland, Vincent Alan 1933- *WrDr 94*
McClelland, W. Clark 1939- *WhoFI 94*
McClelland, W. Craig 1934- *IntWW 93*
McClellen, Burnell Homer 1955- *WhoMW 93*
McClements, Catherine *WhoHol 92*
McClenachan, Blair d1812 *WhAmRev*
McClenahan, Charles A. 1941- *WhoAmP 93*
McClenathen, William Richard 1915- *WhoAmL 94*
McClendon, Burwell Beeman, Jr. 1930- *WhoAmP 93*
McClendon, Carol A. 1942- *WhoBlA 94*
McClendon, Edwin James 1921- *WhoAm 94*
McClendon, Ernestine 1918- *WhoHol 92*
McClendon, Ernestine 1924- *WhoBlA 94*
McClendon, Ernestine Epps d1991 *WhAm 10*
McClendon, Fred Vernon *WhoFI 94*
McClendon, Irvin Lee, Sr. 1945- *WhoFI 94, WhoScEn 94, WhoWest 94*
McClendon, John Haddaway 1921- *WhoWest 94*
McClendon, Kellen 1944- *WhoBlA 94*
McClendon, Lloyd Glenn 1959- *WhoBlA 94*
McClendon, Maxine 1931- *WhoAmA 93*
McClendon, Moses C. 1934- *WhoBlA 94*
McClendon, Raymond *WhoBlA 94*
Mc Clendon, Sarah Newcomb 1910- *WhoAm 94*
McClendon, Sidney Smith, Jr. 1894- *WhAm 10*
Mc Clendon, William Hutchinson, III 1933- *WhoAm 94*
McClene, James 1730-1806 *WhAmRev*
McClenic, David A. 1926- *WhoBlA 94*
McClenic, Patricia Dickson 1947- *WhoBlA 94*
McClennand, Donald d1955 *WhoHol 92*
Mc Clennen, Louis 1912- *WhoAm 94*
McClennen, Miriam J. 1923- *WhoWest 94*
Mc Clenney, Byron Nelson 1939- *WhoAm 94*
McClenney, Cheryl Ilene 1948- *WhoAmA 93*

McClenney, Earl Hampton 1907- *WhoBlA 94*
McClenon, John Raymond 1937- *WhoAm 94*
McClernan, Henry *WhoAmP 93*
McCleverty, Jon Armistice 1937- *Who 94*
McClimon, Timothy John 1953- *WhoAm 94*
McCline, Richard L. 1944- *WhoBlA 94*
McClintic, Fred Frazier 1948- *WhoScEn 94*
McClintic, George Vance, III 1925- *WhoScEn 94*
McClintic, Howard Gresson 1951- *WhoAm 94*
Mc Clintock, Archie Glenn 1911- *WhoAm 94*
McClintock, Barbara d1992 *IntWW 93N*
McClintock, Barbara 1902-1992 *AnObit 1992, WhAm 10, WorScD [port]*
McClintock, Charles Michael 1949- *WhoAmP 93*
McClintock, Cyril Lawson Tait 1916- *Who 94*
McClintock, David 1913- *Who 94*
McClintock, Eric (Paul) 1918- *Who 94*
McClintock, Francis Leopold 1819-1907 *WhWE*
McClintock, George Dunlap 1920- *WhoAm 94*
McClintock, Harry d1957 *WhoHol 92*
McClintock, Jessica 1930- *WhoAm 94*
McClintock, Michael *DrAPF 93*
McClintock, Muriel Aymer 1909- *WhoAmP 93*
McClintock, Nicholas Cole 1916- *Who 94*
McClintock, Nivea Hernandez 1931- *WhoAmP 93*
McClintock, Poley d1980 *WhoHol 92*
McClintock, Samuel Alan 1957- *WhoScEn 94*
McClintock, Thomas Miller, II 1956- *WhoAmP 93*
McClintock, William Thomas 1934- *WhoAm 94, WhoScEn 94*
McClintock-Bunbury *Who 94*
McClintock-Hernandez, Kenneth 1957- *WhoAmP 93*
McClintock-Hernández, Kenneth Davison 1957- *WhoHisp 94*
McClinton, Curtis R., Jr. *WhoBlA 94*
Mc Clinton, Donald G. 1933- *WhoAm 94*
McClinton, Joann *WhoAmP 93*
McClinton, Katharine Morrison d1993 *NewYTBS 93*
McClinton, Katharine Morrison 1899-1993 *ConAu 140, CurBio 93N*
McClinton, Suzanne Y. 1955- *WhoBlA 94*
McClinton, Suzanne Yvette 1955- *WhoBlA 94*
McClomb, George E. 1940- *WhoBlA 94*
McClory, Daniel Kerr 1962- *WhoMW 93*
McClory, Michael Charles 1963- *WhoFI 94*
McClory, Michael Gerard 1963- *WhoAmL 94*
McClory, Sean 1923- *WhoHol 92*
McClory, Sean 1924- *IntMPA 94*
McCloskey, Bernard Mary 1924- *Who 94*
McCloskey, Frank 1939- *CngDr 93, WhoAm 94, WhoAmP 93, WhoMW 93*
McCloskey, Jack *WhoMW 93*
McCloskey, James Boswell 1945- *WhoAmL 94*
McCloskey, Jay P. *WhoAmL 94*
McCloskey, John Michael 1934- *WhoAm 94*
McCloskey, Leigh 1955- *WhoHol 92*
McCloskey, Mark *DrAPF 93*
McCloskey, Michael James 1932- *WhoAmP 93*
Mc Closkey, Paul N., Jr. 1927- *WhoAm 94, WhoAmP 93*
McCloskey, Peter Francis 1935- *WhoAm 94*
McCloskey, Richard John 1944- *WhoAm 94, WhoWest 94*
Mc Closkey, Robert 1914- *WhoAm 94, WrDr 94*
McCloskey, Robert James 1922- *IntWW 93, WhoAm 94, WhoAmP 93*
McCloskey, Thomas Henry 1946- *WhoScEn 94*
McCloskey, Thomas Warren 1964- *WhoScEn 94*
McCloskey, William Donald 1930- *WhoFI 94*
McClosky, Frank d1979 *WhoHol 92*
McCloud, Aaron C. 1933- *WhoBlA 94*
McCloud, Anece Faison 1937- *WhoBlA 94*
McCloud, George Aaron 1967- *WhoBlA 94*
McCloud, J. Oscar 1936- *WhoBlA 94*
McCloud, Laurie 1964- *WhoMW 93*
McCloud, Robert Olmsted, Jr. 1951- *WhoAmL 94*
McCloud, Roger Wayne 1952- *WhoFI 94*
McCloud, Ronald B. 1948- *WhoAmP 93*

McCloud, Ronnie 1947- *WhoBlA 94*
McCloud, Ruth 1921- *WhoAmP 93*
McCloud, Thomas H. 1948- *WhoAm 94*
McCloud, Thomas Henry 1948- *WhoBlA 94*
McClow, Roger James 1947- *WhoAmL 94*
McCloy, Carter James 1931- *WhoFI 94*
McCloy, Helen 1904- *WrDr 94*
Mc Cloy, John Jay 1895-1989 *WhAm 10*
McCloy, Shelby Thomas 1898- *WhAm 10*
McCluer, Franc Lewis 1896- *WhAm 10*
McClune, (William) James 1921- *Who 94*
McCluney, Ian 1937- *Who 94*
McCluney, Ross 1940- *WhoScEn 94*
McClung, Alexander Keith, Jr. 1934- *WhoFI 94*
McClung, Arthur J. 1912- *WhoAmP 93*
McClung, Clarence Erwin 1870-1946 *WorScD*
McClung, James Allen 1937- *WhoAm 94*
McClung, James David 1943- *WhoWest 94*
Mc Clung, Jim Hill 1936- *WhoAm 94, WhoFI 94*
McClung, John Arthur 1949- *WhoScEn 94*
McClung, John Robinson, Jr. 1914- *WhoAm 94*
McClung, Kenneth Austin, Jr. 1947- *WhoFI 94*
Mc Clung, Leland Swint 1910- *WhoAm 94*
McClung, Merle Steven 1943- *WhoAmL 94*
McClung, Nellie Letitia 1873-1951 *BlmGWL*
McClung, Richard Goehring 1913- *WhoAm 94*
McClung, Robert d1945 *WhoHol 92*
McClung, Robert Marshall 1916- *WrDr 94*
McClung, Willie David 1939- *WhoBlA 94*
McClure, Allan Howard 1925- *WhoScEn 94, WhoWest 94*
McClure, Alvin Bruce 1953- *WhoMW 93*
McClure, Anna Jo 1928- *WhoAmP 93*
McClure, Brooks 1919- *WhoAm 94*
McClure, Bryton Eric 1986- *WhoBlA 94*
McClure, Bud d1942 *WhoHol 92*
McClure, C. H. Barney 1941- *WhoAmP 93*
McClure, Constance 1934- *WhoAmA 93*
McClure, Daniel M. 1952- *WhoAm 94, WhoAmL 94*
McClure, David 1926- *Who 94*
McClure, David Robert 1963- *WhoWest 94*
McClure, David Woodard 1965- *WhoScEn 94*
McClure, Donald Edwin 1934- *WhoWest 94*
McClure, Donald Leon 1952- *WhoBlA 94*
McClure, Donald S. 1920- *IntWW 93*
Mc Clure, Donald Stuart 1920- *WhoAm 94, WhoScEn 94*
McClure, Doug 1935- *IntMPA 94, WhoHol 92*
McClure, Earie *WhoBlA 94*
McClure, Exal, Jr. 1941- *WhoBlA 94*
McClure, Frank d1960 *WhoHol 92*
McClure, Frederick Donald 1954- *WhoAm 94, WhoBlA 94*
McClure, Fredrick H. L. 1962- *WhoBlA 94*
McClure, Gillian Mary 1948- *WrDr 94*
McClure, Gladys d1933 *WhoHol 92*
McClure, Gordon 1922- *WhoFI 94*
McClure, Gregg 1918- *WhoHol 92*
McClure, Grover Benjamin 1918- *WhoAm 94*
McClure, Harold Monroe 1937- *WhoScEn 94*
McClure, Howe Elliott 1910- *WhoWest 94*
McClure, James 1939- *WrDr 94*
McClure, James A. 1924- *IntWW 93, WhoAmP 93, WhoWest 94*
McClure, James Focht, Jr. 1931- *WhoAm 94, WhoAmL 94*
Mc Clure, James J., Jr. 1920- *WhoAm 94, WhoAmP 93, WhoMW 93*
McClure, Janice *WhoAmP 93*
McClure, Janice Lee 1941- *WhoMW 93*
McClure, Jeffrey B. 1952- *WhoAmL 94*
McClure, John *WhoAmP 93*
McClure, John 1947- *Who 94*
McClure, John A. 1945- *WrDr 94*
McClure, John Casper 1944- *WhoScEn 94*
McClure, John Elmer 1893- *WhAm 10*
McClure, John Fletcher 1923- *WhoAmL 94*
McClure, John Quayle 1895- *WhAm 10*
McClure, Joseph Robert 1923- *Who 94*
McClure, Julie 1960- *WhoAmP 93*
McClure, Kenneth Allen 1947- *WhoIns 94*
McClure, Laura Lee *WhoAmP 93*
McClure, Marc 1957- *IntMPA 94, WhoHol 92*
McClure, Mary Anne 1939- *WhoAmP 93*

McClure, Mary Virginia 1954-
WhoMW 93
McClure, Michael *DrAPF 93*
McClure, Michael (Thomas) 1932-
ConDr 93
Mc Clure, Michael Thomas 1932-
WhoAm 94
McClure, Michal Clyde 1940- *WhoFI 94*
McClure, Molly *WhoHol 92*
McClure, Richard Bruce 1935-
WhoScEn 94
McClure, Richard Fowler 1927-
WhoAm 94
McClure, Robert A. 1897-1957 *HisDcKW*
McClure, Robert John Le Mesurier
1807-1873 *WhWE*
McClure, Roger J. 1943- *WhoAmP 93*
McClure, Roger John 1943- *WhoAmL 94*
McClure, Samuel Lee 1933- *WhoFI 94*
McClure, Samuel Sidney 1857-1949
AmSocL
McClure, Tane 1959- *WhoHol 92*
McClure, Thomas Edward 1954-
WhoAmL 94
McClure, Thomas F. 1920- *WhoAmA 93*
McClure, Thomas Fulton 1920-
WhoWest 94
McClure, Thomas James 1955-
WhoAmL 94
McClure, Wesley Cornelious *WhoBlA 94*
McCLure, William B., Jr. 1946-
WhoAm 94
McClure, William Earl 1946- *WhoFI 94*
McClure, William Owen 1937-
WhoScEn 94, WhoWest 94
McClure, William Pendleton 1925-
WhoAm 94
McClure-Bibby, Mary Anne 1939-
WhoAm 94
McClurg, E. Vane *WhoAmL 94*
McClurg, Edie 1951- *IntMPA 94,
WhoHol 92*
McClurg, James Edward 1945-
WhoAm 94
McClurkin, Johnson Thomas 1929-
WhoBlA 94
McCluskey, Baron 1929- *Who 94*
McCluskey, Dorothy Soest 1928-
WhoAmP 93
McCluskey, Edward Joseph 1929-
WhoAm 94, WhoScEn 94
McCluskey, Jack *WhoMW 93*
McCluskey, James Patrick 1953-
WhoFI 94
McCluskey, Jean Louise 1947-
WhoAm 94
McCluskey, John A., Jr. *DrAPF 93*
McCluskey, John A., Jr. 1944- *WhoBlA 94*
McCluskey, John Darrell 1950-
WhoMW 93
McCluskey, Kevin 1961- *WhoScEn 94*
McCluskey, Matthew Clair 1957-
WhoWest 94
McCluskey, Robert Timmons 1923-
WhoAm 94
McCluskey, Roger d1993
NewYTBS 93 [port]
McCluskie, John Cameron 1946- *Who 94*
McCluskie, Samuel Joseph 1932- *Who 94*
McClymonds, Jean Ellen *WhoFI 94*
McClymonds, Marita (Martha) P(etzoldt)
1935- *NewGrDO*
Mc Clymont, Hamilton 1944- *WhoAm 94*
McClymont, Kenneth Ross 1924-
WhoAm 94
McCobb, John Bradford, Jr. 1939-
WhoAmL 94
Mc Coin, John Mack 1931- *WhoFI 94,
WhoMW 93*
McColgan, John (Joseph) 1946- *WrDr 94*
McColl *Who 94*
McColl, Colin (Hugh Verel) 1932- *Who 94*
McColl, Hugh Francis 1938- *WhoFI 94*
McColl, Hugh Leon, Jr. 1935- *WhoAm 94,
WhoFI 94*
McColl, Ian 1915- *Who 94*
McColl, John Angus 1928- *WhoAmP 93*
McCollam, John Mason 1933-
WhoAmL 94
McCollam, William, Jr. 1925- *WhoAm 94*
McColley, Diane Kelsey 1934- *WrDr 94*
McColley, Robert McNair 1933-
WhoAm 94
McColley, Sutherland 1937- *WhoAmA 93*
Mc Collister, John Charles 1935-
WhoAm 94
McCollister, John Y. 1921- *WhoAmP 93*
McColloch, Murray Michael 1926-
WhoAmL 94, WhoIns 94
McColl Of Dulwich, Baron 1933-
IntWW 94, Who 94
McCollom, Jean Margaret *WhoScEn 94*
Mc Collom, Kenneth Allen 1922-
WhoAm 94
McCollough, Charles R(andolph) 1934-
ConAu 42NR
McCollough, Lucille Hanna 1905-
WhoAmP 93

McCollough, Michael Leon 1953-
WhoScEn 94
McCollough, Parker 1950- *WhoAmP 93*
McCollough, Patrick Hanna 1942-
WhoAmP 93
McCollough, Walter 1915-1991 *WhAm 10*
McCollow, Thomas James 1925-
WhoAm 94, WhoMW 93
McCollum, Alice Odessa 1947-
WhoBlA 94
McCollum, Allan 1944- *WhoAmA 93*
McCollum, Alvin August 1920-
WhoFI 94, WhoWest 94
McCollum, Anita LaVerne 1960-
WhoBlA 94
McCollum, Betty 1954- *WhoAmP 93*
McCollum, Bill 1944- *CngDr 93,
WhoAmP 93*
McCollum, Charles Edward 1942-
WhoBlA 94
McCollum, Clifford Glenn 1919-
WhoAm 94
McCollum, Dannel 1937- *WhoAmP 93*
McCollum, Elizabeth C. 1943-
WhoMW 93
McCollum, Elmer Verner 1879-1967
WorScD
Mc Collum, Ira William, Jr. 1944-
WhoAm 94
McCollum, James Fountain 1946-
WhoAmL 94
McCollum, Jean Hubble 1934-
WhoMW 93
McCollum, John Morris 1922- *WhoAm 94*
McCollum, Leonard F. d1993
NewYTBS 93 [port]
McCollum, Liam *Who 94*
McCollum, Michael A. 1946- *EncSF 93*
McCollum, Mike L. 1939- *WhoAmA 93*
McCollum, Robert Wayne 1925-
WhoAm 94
McCollum, Timothy David 1951-
WhoMW 93
McCollum, William (Paschal) 1933-
Who 94
McColough, Charles Peter 1922-
IntWW 93, WhoAmP 93
McColough, (Charles) Peter 1922- *Who 94*
McComas, Bruce James 1950-
WhoWest 94
McComas, Carroll d1962 *WhoHol 92*
McComas, Glenn d1959 *WhoHol 92*
McComas, J(esse) Francis 1911-1978
EncSF 93
McComas, James Douglas 1928-
WhoAm 94
McComas, Murray Knabb 1936-
WhoFI 94
McComas, Ralph d1924 *WhoHol 92*
McComb, Eleazer d1798 *WhAmRev*
McComb, Heather *WhoHol 92*
McComb, John Hess 1898- *WhAm 10*
McComb, Leonard William Joseph 1930-
Who 94
McCombe, Richard George Bramwell
1952- *Who 94*
McCombie, John Alexander Fergusson
1932- *Who 94*
McCombs, Billy J. *WhoAm 94*
McCombs, Eugene *WhoAmP 93*
Mc Combs, G. B. 1909- *WhoAm 94*
McCombs, Hugh R., Jr. 1946- *WhoAm 94,
WhoAmL 94*
McCombs, Jeanni d1981 *WhoHol 92*
McCombs, Jerome Lester 1951-
WhoScEn 94
McCombs, Judith *DrAPF 93*
McCombs, Shirley Ann 1937-
WhoAmP 93
Mc Comic, Robert Barry 1939-
WhoAm 94
McCommon, Hubert 1929- *WhoAm 94*
Mc Conagha, Glenn Lowery 1910-
WhoAm 94
McConahey, Stephen George 1943-
WhoFI 94
McConathy, Donald Reed, Jr. 1942-
WhoScEn 94
McConathy, James Leslie, Jr. 1956-
WhoAmP 93
McConchie, Irving H. 1923- *WhoAmP 93*
McCone, John A. 1902-1991 *WhAm 10*
McConeghey, Nelljean *DrAPF 93*
McConica, James Kelsey 1930- *WrDr 94*
McConkey, James *DrAPF 93*
McConkey, James (Rodney) 1921-
ConAu 41NR, WrDr 94
McConkey, James R. 1921- *WhoAm 94*
Mc Conkie, George Wilson 1937-
WhoAm 94
McConkie, James Wilson 1946-
WhoWest 94
McConkie, James Wilson, II 1946-
WhoAmP 93
McConkie, LaVonne May 1937-
WhoWest 94

McConkie, Oscar Walter 1926-
WhoAmL 94
McConkie, Sheldon Wayne 1934-
WhoFI 94
Mc Connaughey, George Carlton, Jr.
1925- *WhoAm 94, WhoAmL 94,
WhoFI 94*
McConnaughey, James Walter 1951-
WhoFI 94
Mc Connaughy, John Edward, Jr. 1929-
WhoAm 94
Mcconnel, Frances Ruhlen *DrAPF 93*
McConnel, Patricia *DrAPF 93*
McConnel, Patricia 1931- *WrDr 94*
McConnel, Richard Appleton 1933-
WhoScEn 94, WhoWest 94
McConnell, A. Mitchell, Jr. 1942-
WhoAmP 93
McConnell, Addison Mitchell, Jr. 1942-
WhoAm 94
McConnell, Albert Joseph d1993
Who 94N
McConnell, Albert Joseph 1903-
IntWW 93
McConnell, Anthony 1959- *WhoScEn 94*
McConnell, Barbara Wright 1936-
WhoAmP 93
McConnell, Calvin Dale 1928-
WhoAm 94, WhoWest 94
McConnell, Charles Goodloe 1943-
WhoAm 94, WhoFI 94
McConnell, Charles Warren 1939-
WhoAm 94
McConnell, Conrad (Peter) 1952-
WhoBlA 94
McConnell, David Graham 1926-
WhoAm 94
McConnell, David John 1944- *IntWW 93*
McConnell, David Kelso 1932-
WhoAmL 94
McConnell, David Moffatt 1912-
WhoAm 94
McConnell, David Stuart 1935-
WhoAm 94
McConnell, Dorothy Hughes *WhoBlA 94*
McConnell, E. Hoy, II 1941- *WhoAm 94,
WhoFI 94, WhoMW 93*
Mc Connell, Edward Bosworth 1920-
WhoAm 94, WhoAmL 94
McConnell, Elliott Bonnell, Jr. 1928-
WhoAm 94
McConnell, Francis John 1871-1953
DcAmReB 2
McConnell, Gladys d1979 *WhoHol 92*
McConnell, Glenn Fant 1947-
WhoAmP 93
McConnell, Grant 1915- *WrDr 94*
McConnell, Harden M. 1927- *IntWW 93*
McConnell, Harden Marsden 1927-
WhoAm 94, WhoScEn 94
McConnell, Harold Sanders 1928-
WhoFI 94
McConnell, James Desmond Caldwell
1930- *IntWW 93, Who 94*
McConnell, James Guy 1947- *WhoAm 94,
WhoAmL 94*
McConnell, James Hoge Tyler 1914-1989
WhAm 10
McConnell, James Joseph 1946-
WhoScEn 94
McConnell, James M. 1947- *WhoAm 94,
WhoFI 94*
Mc Connell, James Vernon 1925-1990
WhAm 10
McConnell, John 1939- *Who 94*
Mc Connell, John Douglas 1932-
WhoAm 94
McConnell, John Edward 1931-
WhoScEn 94
McConnell, John Henderson 1923-
WhoAm 94, WhoFI 94
McConnell, John Thomas 1945-
WhoAm 94, WhoMW 93
McConnell, John Wesley 1941-
WhoAm 94
Mc Connell, John Wilkinson 1907-
WhoAm 94
McConnell, John William, Jr. 1921-
WhoAm 94
McConnell, Joseph Fredrick 1939-
WhoMW 93
McConnell, Kathleen Ellen 1949-
WhoMW 93
McConnell, Kathryn J. 1948- *WhoFI 94*
McConnell, Keith d1987 *WhoHol 92*
McConnell, Lulu d1962 *WhoHol 92*
McConnell, Mary Patricia 1952-
WhoAmL 94
McConnell, Michael 1954- *WhoAm 94*
McConnell, Michael Arthur 1947-
WhoAm 94, WhoAmL 94
McConnell, Michael Patrick 1948-
WhoAmA 93
McConnell, Michael Theodore 1954-
WhoAm 94
McConnell, Mitch 1942- *CngDr 93*
McConnell, Mollie d1920 *WhoHol 92*

McConnell, Nicholas Stillwell 1946-
WhoAmL 94
McConnell, Patricia Ann 1935-
WhoFI 94, WhoMW 93, WhoScEn 94
McConnell, Randall Michael Scott 1945-
WhoWest 94
McConnell, Richard *WhoAmP 93*
McConnell, Richard Lynn 1950-
WhoMW 93
McConnell, Robert A. 1929- *WhoAmP 93*
McConnell, Robert Andrew 1949-
WhoAmL 94
Mc Connell, Robert Chalmers 1913-
WhoAm 94
Mc Connell, Robert Eastwood 1930-
WhoAm 94
McConnell, Robert Shean *Who 94*
McConnell, Robert William Brian 1922-
Who 94
McConnell, Roland C. 1910- *WhoBlA 94*
McConnell, Samuel Winfield, Jr. 1940-
WhoAmP 93
McConnell, Steven Charles 1962-
WhoWest 94
McConnell, Suzanne *DrAPF 93*
McConnell, William Thompson 1933-
WhoAm 94
McConnell Barrett, Barbara 1950-
WhoAmP 93
McConner, Dorothy 1929- *WhoBlA 94*
McConner, Stanley Jay, Sr. 1929-
WhoWest 94
McConnico, Stephen E. 1950-
WhoAmL 94
McConnochie, Rhys *WhoHol 92*
McConnon, James Charles 1926-
WhoAmP 93
McConomy, James Herbert 1937-
WhoAm 94, WhoAmL 94
McConomy, Thomas Arthur 1933-
WhoAm 94
McConville, Michael Anthony 1925-
Who 94
McConville, William *WhoAm 94*
McCoo, Marilyn *WhoBlA 94, WhoHol 92*
McCooe, Terry Alan 1950- *WhoMW 93*
McCook, John 1945- *WhoHol 92*
McCook, Kathleen de la Pena *WhoAm 94,
WhoHisp 94*
McCook, Richard Paul 1953- *WhoFI 94*
McCool, Douglas L. 1934- *WhoAmL 94*
McCool, Naomi Ellen 1922- *WhoAmP 93*
McCool, Richard Bunch 1925- *WhoFI 94,
WhoMW 93*
McCool, Stephen Ford 1943- *WhoWest 94*
McCoppin, Peter *WhoAm 94, WhoWest 94*
McCorcle, Marcus Duane 1951-
WhoMW 93
McCord, Alice Bird *WhoAm 94*
McCord, Guy *EncSF 93*
Mc Cord, Guyte Pierce, Jr. 1914-
WhoAmL 94
McCord, Howard *DrAPF 93*
Mc Cord, James Iley 1919-1990 *WhAm 10*
McCord, James Richard, III 1932-
WhoScEn 94
Mc Cord, John Harrison 1934-
WhoAm 94
Mc Cord, Kenneth Armstrong 1921-
WhoAm 94
McCord, Kent 1942- *WhoHol 92*
McCord, Lewis, Mrs. d1917 *WhoHol 92*
Mc Cord, Marshal 1917- *WhoAm 94*
Mc Cord, Mervyn Noel Samuel 1929-
Who 94
McCord, Michael Brian 1955-
WhoAmL 94
McCord, Ted 1898-1976 *IntDcF 2-4*
McCord, William Charles 1928-
WhoAm 94, WhoFI 94
Mc Corison, Marcus Allen 1926-
WhoAm 94, WhoAmA 93
McCorkell, Don L., Jr. 1947- *WhoAmP 93*
McCorkell, Michael William 1925-
Who 94
McCorkindale, Don *WhoHol 92*
McCorkindale, Douglas Hamilton 1939-
WhoAm 94, WhoAmL 94, WhoFI 94
Mc Corkle, Allan James 1931- *WhoFI 94*
McCorkle, George M. d1993
NewYTBS 93
McCorkle, Horace Jackson 1905-
WhoAm 94
McCorkle, Jill (Collins) 1958- *WrDr 94*
McCorkle, Michael 1944- *WhoFI 94*
McCorkle, Richard Anthony 1940-
WhoScEn 94
McCorkle, Robert Ellsworth 1938-
WhoAm 94, WhoWest 94
McCormac, Billy Murray 1920-
WhoAm 94
Mc Cormac, John Waverly 1926-
WhoAm 94
Mc Cormac, Weston Arthur 1911-
WhoWest 94
McCormack, Arthur Gerard d1992
Who 94N

McCracken, Shirley Ann Ross 1937-
WhoWest 94
McCracken, Steven Carl 1950-
WhoAm 94, WhoAmL 94
McCracken, Thomas James, Jr. 1952-
WhoAmP 93
McCrackin, Olympia F. 1950- *WhoBlA 94*
McCrady, James David 1930- *WhoAm 94*
McCrae, Alister Geddes 1909- *Who 94*
McCrae, Catherine Singleton 1952-
WhoMW 93
McCrae, David Anthony 1950-
WhoMW 93
McCrae, Georgiana Huntley 1804-1890
BlmGWL
McCrae, William 1934- *WhoIns 94*
McCraith, Patrick James Danvers 1916-
Who 94
Mc Craken, Robert Stanton 1924-1989
WhAm 10
McCrane, Paul 1961- *WhoHol 92*
McCrary, Darius *WhoHol 92*
McCrary, Douglas L. 1929- *WhoFI 94*
McCrary, Giles Connell 1919-
WhoAmP 93
McCrary, Jim *DrAPF 93*
McCrary, Larry Frank 1949- *WhoFI 94*
McCrary, Paul J. *WhoAmP 93*
McCrary, Thomas *WhoAmP 93*
McCrary-Simmons, Shirley Denise 1956-
WhoBlA 94
McCraven, Carl Clarke 1926- *WhoBlA 94,
WhoWest 94*
McCraven, Eva Stewart Mapes 1936-
WhoWest 94
McCraven, Gladys L. 1923- *WhoAmP 93*
McCraven, Marcus R. 1923- *WhoBlA 94*
McCraw, E. Dewitt *WhoAmP 93*
McCraw, John Randolph, Jr. 1942-
WhoAmP 93
McCraw, Les 1934- *WhoAm 94,
WhoFI 94, WhoWest 94*
McCraw, Thomas K. 1940- *WrDr 94*
McCraw, Thomas Kincaid 1940-
WhoAm 94
McCraw, Tom 1940- *WhoBlA 94*
McCray, Almator Felecia 1956-
WhoBlA 94
McCray, Billy Quincy 1927- *WhoAmP 93,
WhoMW 93*
McCray, Billy Quincy 1929- *WhoBlA 94*
McCray, Christopher Columbus 1925-
WhoBlA 94
McCray, Curtis Lee 1938- *WhoWest 94*
McCray, Harvey Lee 1931- *WhoMW 93*
McCray, Hubert Todd 1962- *WhoAmL 94*
McCray, Joe Richard 1928- *WhoBlA 94*
McCray, Kathleen S. 1959- *WhoMW 93*
McCray, Kevin Barney 1935-
WhoAmL 94
McCray, Maceo E. 1935- *WhoBlA 94*
McCray, Melvin 1946- *WhoBlA 94*
McCray, Mike *GayLL*
McCray, Richard Alan 1937-
WhoScEn 94
McCray, Rodney Earl 1961- *WhoBlA 94*
McCray, Ronald David 1957-
WhoAmL 94, WhoFI 94
McCray, Roy Howard 1946- *WhoBlA 94*
McCray, Thomas L. 1928- *WhoBlA 94*
McCrea, Ann *WhoHol 92*
McCrea, Charles Harold, Jr. 1949-
WhoAmL 94
McCrea, Jane c. 1754-1777 *WhAmRev*
McCrea, Jody 1934- *WhoHol 92*
McCrea, Joel d1990 *WhoHol 92*
McCrea, Peter 1939- *WhoAm 94,
WhoFI 94*
McCrea, Robert Thomas William 1948-
Who 94
McCrea, Russell James 1917-
WhoScEn 94
McCrea, Stephen Brian 1949-
WhoAmL 94, WhoWest 94
McCrea, William (Hunter) 1904- *Who 94,
WrDr 94*
McCrea, William Hunter 1904-
IntWW 94
McCreadie, Allan Robert 1951-
WhoScEn 94
McCready, Ed *WhoHol 92*
McCready, Eric Scott 1941- *WhoAmA 93*
McCready, Guy Michael 1960-
WhoAmL 94
McCready, Jack 1920- *WrDr 94*
McCready, Karen 1946- *WhoAmA 93*
McCready, Kenneth Frank 1939-
WhoAm 94, WhoFI 94, WhoWest 94
McCready, Mike 1966-
See Pearl Jam News 94-2
McCready, Robert d1976 *WhoHol 92*
McCready, Thomas d1976 *WhoHol 92*
McCready, William Floyd 1904-
WhoWest 94
McCreary, Bill 1933- *WhoBlA 94*
McCreary, Charles H. 1953- *WhoAmL 94*
McCreary, Dustin Campbell 1928-
WhoAm 94

McCreary, Frank E., III 1943-
WhoAmL 94
Mc Creary, James Franklin 1942-
WhoAm 94
McCreary, Robert Grosvenor, Jr. 1918-
WhoAm 94
McCreary, Terry Wade 1955-
WhoScEn 94
McCreary, W. Mark 1952- *WhoMW 93*
McCreath, Peter L. 1944- *WhoAm 94*
McCreath, Peter S. 1944- *WhoScEn 94*
McCredie, Andrew D(algarno) 1930-
NewGrDO
McCredie, Andrew Dalgarno 1930-
IntWW 94
McCree, Edward L. 1942- *WhoBlA 94*
McCree, Samuel W. *WhoBlA 94*
McCree, Wade Hampton, Jr. 1920-1987
AfrAmAl 6 [port]
McCreery, Bud 1925- *WhoHol 92*
McCreery, Charles Anthony Selby 1942-
WrDr 94
McCreery, Franc Root, Mrs. d1957
WhoAmA 93N
McCreery, Glenn Ernest 1943-
WhoWest 94
McCreery, James Allan 1933- *WhoFI 94*
McCreery, John Thomas 1948-
WhoMW 93
McCreery, (Henry Edwin) Lewis 1920-
Who 94
McCreery, William 1931- *WhoAm 94*
McCreevy, Charlie 1949- *IntWW 93*
McCreless, Thomas Griswold 1927-
WhoWest 94
McCrensky, Edward 1912- *WhoAm 94*
McCrery, James 1949- *WhoAm 94*
McCrery, Jim 1949- *CngDr 93,
WhoAmP 93*
McCrickard, Donald Cecil 1936- *Who 94*
Mc Crie, Robert Delbert 1938-
WhoAm 94
McCrillis, John Wilmarth 1897-
WhAm 10
McCrimmon, James McNab 1908-
WhoAm 94
McCrimon, Audrey L. 1954- *WhoBlA 94*
McCrindle, Alex d1990 *WhoHol 92*
McCrindle, Robert (Arthur) 1929-
Who 94
McCrirrick, (Thomas) Bryce 1927-
Who 94
McCrocklin, William Maurice, Jr. 1946-
WhoWest 94
McCrohon, Craig 1961- *WhoAmL 94*
McCron, Raymond Charles 1921-1990
WhAm 10
Mc Crone, Alistair William 1931-
WhoAm 94, WhoWest 94
McCrone, Kathleen E. 1941- *WrDr 94*
McCrone, Robert Gavin Loudon 1933-
Who 94
McCrone, Walter Cox 1916- *WhoAm 94,
WhoScEn 94*
McCroom, Eddie Winther 1932-
WhoBlA 94
McCrorey, H. Lawrence 1927- *WhoBlA 94*
McCrorie, Edward *DrAPF 93*
McCrorie, Linda Esther *Who 94*
McCrory, E. Cecil, Jr. 1951- *WhoAmP 93*
McCrory, John Brooks 1925- *WhoAm 94*
McCrory, Moy (Ellen) 1953- *WrDr 94*
McCrory, Robert Lee 1946- *WhoAm 94,
WhoScEn 94*
Mc Crory, Wallace Willard 1920-
WhoAm 94
McCroskey, William James 1937-
WhoAm 94
McCrum, Michael William 1924-
IntWW 93, Who 94
McCrumb, Sharyn *DrAPF 93, EncSF 93*
McCrystal, Thomas W. 1952-
WhoAmL 94
McCuan, William Patrick 1941-
WhoFI 94
McCubbin, Carrol J. 1920- *WhoAmP 93*
McCubbin, David 1929- *Who 94*
McCubbin, Hamilton I. 1941- *WhoAm 94*
McCubbin, Henry Bell 1942- *Who 94*
Mc Cue, Carolyn Moore 1916- *WhoAm 94*
McCue, Dennis Michael 1952- *WhoFI 94,
WhoWest 94*
McCue, Edward Patrick *DrAPF 93*
McCue, Gerald Mallon 1928- *WhoAm 94*
McCue, Harry 1944- *WhoAmA 93*
McCue, Howard McDowell, III 1946-
WhoAm 94, WhoAmL 94
McCue, James Joseph 1918- *WhoFI 94*
McCue, Judith W. 1948- *WhoAm 94,
WhoAmL 94*
McCue, Lillian Bueno 1902-1993
ConAu 142
McCue, Lisa (Emiline) 1959- *WrDr 94*
McCue, Matthew d1966 *WhoHol 92*
McCue, Stephen Patrick 1956-
WhoAmL 94
McCue, Steven J. 1957- *WhoAmP 93*

McCue, Thomas Albert 1950-
WhoWest 94
McCuen, John Francis, Jr. 1944-
WhoAm 94
McCuen, John Joachim 1926- *WhoFI 94,
WhoMW 93*
McCuen, W. J. 1943- *WhoAmP 93*
McCuen, William James 1943-
WhoAm 94
McCuistion, Peg Orem 1930- *WhoAm 94*
McCuistion, Robert Wiley 1927-
WhoAm 94
McCuiston, Frederick Douglass, Jr. 1940-
WhoBlA 94
McCuiston, Lloyd Carlisle, Jr. 1918-
WhoAmP 93
McCuiston, Pat M. 1917- *WhoAmP 93*
McCuiston, Stonewall, Jr. 1959-
WhoBlA 94
McCullagh, Grant Gibson 1951-
WhoMW 93
McCullagh, James Charles 1941-
WhoAm 94
McCullagh, Peter 1952- *WhoScEn 94*
McCullagh, Sheila K(athleen) 1920-
WrDr 94
McCullen, Allie Ray 1944- *WhoAmP 93*
McCullen, Joseph Thomas, Jr. 1935-
WhoAmP 93
McCuller, James 1940-1992 *WhoBlA 94N*
McCullers, Carson 1917-1967
BlmGWL [port], GayLL
McCullers, (Lula) Carson 1917-1967
RfGShF
McCullers, (Lula) Carson (Smith)
1917-1967 *TwCYAW*
McCullers, Eugene 1941- *WhoBlA 94*
McCullers, Lula Carson Smith 1917-1967
AmCulL
McCullin, Don(ald) 1935- *ConAu 141*
McCullin, Donald 1935- *IntWW 93,
Who 94*
McCulliss, Paul Leonard 1957-
WhoWest 94
McCulloch, Andrew *WhoHol 92*
McCulloch, Cathy Marie 1954- *WhoFI 94*
Mc Culloch, Ernest Armstrong 1926-
WhoAm 94, WhoScEn 94
McCulloch, Frank E. 1930- *WhoAmA 93*
Mc Culloch, Frank W. 1905- *WhoAm 94,
WhoAmP 93*
McCulloch, Frank Waugh 1905-
IntWW 93
McCulloch, Ian *WhoHol 92*
McCulloch, James Callahan 1947-
WhoAm 94
McCulloch, James Huston 1945-
WhoFI 94
McCulloch, John 1935- *WhoAmP 93*
McCulloch, John Cameron 1942-
WhoAmP 93
McCulloch, John Tyler *TwCYAW*
McCulloch, Linda Kay 1956- *WhoMW 93*
McCulloch, Nigel Simeon *Who 94*
McCulloch, Rachel 1942- *WhoAm 94,
WhoFI 94*
McCulloch, Robert Winslow 1910-
WhoAmP 93
Mc Culloch, Samuel Clyde 1916-
WhoAm 94
McCulloch, Sarah 1943- *WrDr 94*
McCulloch, Scott T. 1958- *WhoAmP 93*
McCulloch, William Henry 1941-
WhoWest 94
McCulloch, William Leonard 1921-
WhoAm 94
McCulloh, John Marshall 1943-
WhoAm 94
McCullough, Benjamin Franklin 1934-
WhoScEn 94
McCullough, Charles 1931- *Who 94*
McCullough, Colin David 1929-
WhoAm 94
McCullough, Colleen *WhoAm 94*
McCullough, Colleen 1937- *BlmGWL,
EncSF 93, IntWW 93, WrDr 94*
McCullough, David 1933-
CurBio 93 [port], WhoAm 94
McCullough, David William 1945-
WhoAmA 93
McCullough, Donald W. 1949- *WrDr 94*
McCullough, Edgar Joseph, Jr. 1931-
WhoAm 94
McCullough, Frances Louise 1941-
WhoBlA 94
McCullough, Frank Witcher, III 1945-
WhoAmL 94
McCullough, Gary William 1951-
WhoScEn 94
McCullough, George Bierce 1925-
WhoAm 94
McCullough, Geraldine 1928- *AfrAmAl 6*
Mc Cullough, Helen Craig 1918-
WhoAm 94
McCullough, Henry Glenn Luther 1939-
WhoMW 93, WhoScEn 94

McCullough, James Howard 1955-
WhoAmP 93
McCullough, James Richey 1949-
WhoAmP 93
McCullough, Jefferson Walker 1944-
WhoFI 94
McCullough, John A. 1932- *WhoAmP 93*
McCullough, John James, III 1959-
WhoFI 94, WhoScEn 94
McCullough, John Jeffrey 1938-
WhoAm 94
McCullough, John Martin 1940-
WhoWest 94
McCullough, John Norcott 1932-
WhoFI 94
Mc Cullough, John Phillip 1945-
WhoScEn 94
Mc Cullough, John Price 1925-
WhoAm 94
McCullough, Joseph 1922- *WhoAm 94,
WhoAmA 93*
McCullough, Julie 1965- *WhoHol 92*
McCullough, Kathryn T. Baker 1925-
WhoScEn 94
McCullough, Ken *DrAPF 93*
McCullough, Lauren Fink 1960-
WhoFI 94
McCullough, M. Bruce 1944- *WhoAm 94,
WhoAmL 94*
McCullough, Michael William, Jr. 1950-
WhoAm 94
McCullough, Paul d1936 *WhoHol 92*
McCullough, Paul 1883-1936
See Clark and McCullough WhoCom
McCullough, Philo d1981 *WhoHol 92*
McCullough, R. Michael 1938-
WhoAm 94, WhoFI 94
McCullough, Ralph d1943 *WhoHol 92*
Mc Cullough, Ralph Clayton, II 1941-
WhoAm 94, WhoAmL 94
McCullough, Ray Daniel, Jr. 1938-
WhoAm 94
McCullough, Richard Lawrence 1937-
WhoAm 94
McCullough, Robert Dale, II 1937-
WhoScEn 94
McCullough, Robert Frederick, Jr. 1950-
WhoFI 94
McCullough, Robert Willis 1920-
WhoAm 94
McCullough, Rohan *WhoHol 92*
McCullough, Roy Lynn 1934- *WhoAm 94,
WhoScEn 94*
McCullough, Samuel Alexander 1938-
WhoAm 94, WhoFI 94
McCullough-Wiggins, Lydia Statoria
1948- *WhoMW 93*
McCullum, Bartley d1916 *WhoHol 92*
McCullum, Donald Pitts 1928-
WhoBlA 94
McCullum, Gerald Edwin 1939-
WhoMW 93
McCully, Emily Arnold *DrAPF 93,
SmATA 76*
McCully, Emily Arnold 1939- *WhoAm 94*
McCully, Ruth Alida 1933- *WhoMW 93*
McCummings, LeVerne 1932- *WhoBlA 94*
Mc Cune, Barron Patterson 1915-
WhoAm 94, WhoAmL 94
McCune, David Franklin 1954-
WhoAm 94
McCune, Ellis E. 1921- *WhoAm 94,
WhoWest 94*
Mc Cune, Emmett Lee 1927- *WhAm 10*
McCune, Francis Kimber 1906-
IntWW 93
Mc Cune, George David 1924-1990
WhAm 10
Mc Cune, John Francis, III 1921-
WhoAm 94
McCune, John Robison 1926-
WhoAmP 93
McCune, Samuel Knox 1921- *WhoAm 94*
McCune, Shannon d1993
NewYTBS 93 [port]
McCune, Shannon 1913-1993 *ConAu 140*
McCune, William James, Jr. 1915-
IntWW 93, WhoScEn 94
McCune, William Minton 1922-
WhoAm 94
McCune-Davis, Debbie 1951-
WhoWomW 91
McCunn, Ruthanne Lum 1946-
ConAu 43NR
McCurdy, Brenda Wright 1946-
WhoBlA 94
McCurdy, Charles Gribbel 1955-
WhoAm 94
McCurdy, Dave 1950- *CngDr 93,
WhoAmP 93*
McCurdy, David B. 1946- *WhoMW 93*
McCurdy, David Keith 1950- *WhoAm 94*
Mc Curdy, Gilbert Geier 1922-
WhoAm 94
Mc Curdy, Harold Grier 1909- *WhoAm 94*
McCurdy, Harry Ward 1918- *WhoAm 94*

McCurdy, John Andrew, Jr. 1945-
WhoWest 94
McCurdy, Kurt Basquin 1952-
WhoMW 93
McCurdy, Larry Wayne 1935-
WhoAm 94, WhoFI 94
McCurdy, Michael Charles 1942-
WhoAmA 93
Mc Curdy, Patrick Pierre 1928-
WhoAm 94
McCurdy, Richard Clark 1909-
IntWW 93, WhoAm 94
McCurine, William, Jr. 1947-
WhoAmL 94
McCurley, Anna Anderson 1943- *Who 94*
McCurley, Carl Michael 1946-
WhoAmL 94
McCurley, Foster R., Jr. 1937- *WrDr 94*
Mc Curley, Robert Lee, Jr. 1941-
WhoAm 94
McCurn, Neal Peters 1926- *WhoAm 94,
WhoAmL 94*
McCurry, Harr Orr 1889-1964
WhoAmA 93N
McCurry, John d1989 *WhoHol 92*
McCurry, Margaret Irene 1942-
WhoAm 94, WhoMW 93
McCurry, Michael Demaree 1954-
WhoAm 94
Mc Curry, Paul D. 1903-1991 *WhAm 10*
McCurry, Virginia Marie 1928-
WhoMW 93
McCurry, William Jeffery 1947-
WhoFI 94
McCusker, Charles Frederick
WhoScEn 94
McCusker, J. Stephen 1946- *WhoAm 94*
McCusker, James (Alexander) 1913-
Who 94
McCusker, Mary Lauretta 1919-
WhoAm 94
McCusker, William LaValle 1918-
WhoAmL 94
McCuskey, Lowell 1930- *WhoAmP 93*
McCuskey, Michael Patrick 1948-
WhoMW 93
McCuskey, Robert Scott 1938-
WhoWest 94
McCutchan, Arad d1993 *NewYTBS 93*
McCutchan, Gordon E. 1935- *WhoIns 94*
McCutchan, Gordon Eugene 1935-
WhoAm 94, WhoAmL 94, WhoFI 94
McCutchan, Marcus Gene 1930-
WhoScEn 94
McCutchan, Philip 1920- *EncSF 93*
McCutchan, Philip (Donald) 1920-
WrDr 94
McCutchan, William Mark 1954-
WhoFI 94, WhoMW 93
McCutchen, Edna Elizabeth 1914-
WhoWest 94
McCutchen, Thomas English, Jr. 1919-
WhoAmL 94
McCutcheon, Andrew H., Jr. 1927-
WhoAmP 93
McCutcheon, Bill *WhoHol 92*
McCutcheon, Chester Myers 1907-
WhoFI 94
McCutcheon, Elsie (Mary Jackson) 1937-
WrDr 94
McCutcheon, Holly Marie 1950-
WhoMW 93
McCutcheon, Hugh Davie-Martin 1909-
WrDr 94
McCutcheon, James Miller 1932-
WhoWest 94
Mc Cutcheon, John Tinney, Jr. 1917-
WhoAm 94, WhoMW 93
McCutcheon, Lawrence 1950- *WhoBlA 94*
McCutcheon, Randall James 1949-
WhoWest 94
McCutcheon, Steven Clifton 1952-
WhoScEn 94
McCutcheon, Wallace d1928 *WhoHol 92*
McCutcheon, William Alan 1934-
Who 94, WrDr 94
McDade, Donald Alan 1959- *WhoFI 94*
McDade, James Russell 1925- *WhoFI 94*
McDade, Joe Billy *WhoBlA 94*
McDade, Joe Billy 1937- *WhoAm 94,
WhoAmL 94, WhoMW 93*
McDade, Joseph John 1930- *WhoScEn 94*
McDade, Joseph M. 1931- *CngDr 93*
McDade, Joseph Michael 1931-
WhoAm 94, WhoAmP 93
McDade, Linna Springer 1932-
WhoMW 93
McDade, Sandy S. 1947- *WhoAmP 93*
McDade, William Joseph 1937-
WhoAm 94
McDanel, Ralph Clipman 1893-
WhAm 10
McDaniel, Adam Theodore 1925-
WhoBlA 94
McDaniel, Barry 1930- *NewGrDO*
McDaniel, Billy Ray 1943- *WhoBlA 94*

McDaniel, Boyce Dawkins 1917-
IntWW 93, WhoAm 94
McDaniel, Bruce Alan 1946- *WhoWest 94*
McDaniel, Charles-Gene 1931-
WhoAm 94, WhoMW 93
McDaniel, Charles William 1927-
WhoBlA 94
McDaniel, Charlie Homer 1895-
WhAm 10
McDaniel, Charlotte Sue 1943-
WhoAmP 93, WhoWest 94
McDaniel, Craig Milton 1948-
WhoAmA 93
McDaniel, David 1939-1977 *EncSF 93*
McDaniel, David Allen 1959-
WhoAmL 94
McDaniel, Dolan Kenneth 1935-
WhoAm 94
McDaniel, Elizabeth 1952- *WhoBlA 94*
McDaniel, Etta d1946 *WhoHol 92*
McDaniel, Garvin William 1936-
WhoMW 93
McDaniel, George d1944 *WhoHol 92*
McDaniel, Hattie d1952 *WhoHol 92*
McDaniel, Hattie 1895-1952
ConBlB 5 [port]
McDaniel, Hattie 1898-1952
AfrAmAl 6 [port]
McDaniel, James Alan 1953- *WhoAm 94*
McDaniel, James Berkley, Jr. 1925-
WhoBlA 94
Mc Daniel, James Edwin 1931-
WhoAm 94, WhoAmL 94
McDaniel, Janella Kay 1956- *WhoMW 93*
McDaniel, Jarrel Dave 1930- *WhoAm 94,
WhoAmL 94*
McDaniel, John S., Jr. 1916-1992
WhAm 10
McDaniel, Joseph Chandler 1950-
WhoAmL 94, WhoWest 94
McDaniel, Judith *DrAPF 93*
McDaniel, K.C. 1952- *WhoAmL 94*
McDaniel, Kay Lynn 1960- *WhoAm 94*
McDaniel, Lauralyn 1963- *WhoMW 93*
McDaniel, Michael Conway Dixon 1929-
WhoAm 94
McDaniel, Myra A. 1932- *WhoAmP 93*
McDaniel, Myra Atwell 1932- *WhoAm 94,
WhoAmL 94, WhoBlA 94*
McDaniel, Paul Anderson 1930-
WhoBlA 94
McDaniel, Paul William 1916-
WhoWest 94
McDaniel, Randall Cornell 1964-
WhoAm 94, WhoMW 93
McDaniel, Reuben R. 1936- *WhoBlA 94*
McDaniel, Robert Anthony 1952-
WhoBlA 94
Mc Daniel, Roderick Rogers 1926-
WhoAm 94, WhoFI 94
McDaniel, Sam d1962 *WhoHol 92*
McDaniel, Sharon A. 1950- *WhoBlA 94*
McDaniel, Steve K. 1951- *WhoAmP 93*
McDaniel, Terrence Lee 1965-
WhoBlA 94
McDaniel, Tom *DrAPF 93*
McDaniel, Tom J. 1938- *WhoAmL 94*
McDaniel, Walter F. *WhoAmP 93*
McDaniel, Wayne Logan 1955- *WhoFI 94*
McDaniel, William Howard Taft, Jr.
1941- *WhoScEn 94*
McDaniel, William J. 1943- *WhoAm 94,
WhoWest 94*
McDaniel, William T., Jr. 1945-
WhoBlA 94
McDaniel, Xavier 1963- *BasBi*
McDaniel, Xavier Maurice 1963-
WhoBlA 94
McDaniels, Alfred F. 1940- *WhoBlA 94*
McDaniels, Jim 1948- *BasBi*
McDaniels, John Edward, Sr. 1921-
WhoBlA 94
McDaniels, John Francis 1935-
WhoAm 94
McDaniels, John Louis 1933- *WhoAm 94,
WhoScEn 94*
McDaniels, Warren E. *WhoBlA 94*
McDaniels, William E. 1941-
WhoAmL 94
Mc Dannald, Clyde Elliott, Jr. 1923-
WhoFI 94
McDarrah, Fred W. 1926- *WrDr 94*
McDarrah, Fred William 1926-
WhoAm 94, WhoAmA 93
McDarrah, Gloria Schoffel 1932-
WhoAm 94
McDavid, Douglas Warren 1947-
WhoWest 94
Mc David, George Eugene 1930-
WhoAm 94
McDavid, J. Gary 1947- *WhoAm 94,
WhoAmL 94*
McDavid, Janet Louise 1950- *WhoAm 94,
WhoAmL 94*
McDavid, John Sanford 1958-
WhoAmL 94
McDavid, Stephan Land 1960-
WhoAmL 94

McDavid, William Henry 1946-
WhoAm 94, WhoAmL 94, WhoFI 94
McDermid, Del d1941 *WhoHol 92*
McDermid, John Horton 1940-
WhoAm 94
McDermid, Norman George Lloyd Roberts
1927- *Who 94*
McDermid, Richard Thomas Wright
1929- *Who 94*
McDermid, Val *BlmGWL*
McDermit, Robert Edward 1932-
WhAm 10
McDermitt, Edward Vincent 1953-
WhoAmL 94
McDermot, Murtagh *EncSF 93*
McDermott, Agnes Charlene Senape
1937- *WhoAm 94*
Mc Dermott, Albert Leo 1923- *WhoAm 94*
McDermott, Alice *DrAPF 93*
McDermott, Aline L. d1951 *WhoHol 92*
McDermott, Catherine Ann 1953-
WhoMW 93
McDermott, David John 1958-
WhoWest 94
McDermott, Dennis *EncSF 93*
McDermott, Drew Vincent 1949-
WhoAm 94
McDermott, Dylan 1962- *WhoHol 92*
McDermott, Edward Aloysious 1920-
WhoAm 94, WhoAmP 93
McDermott, Emmet *Who 94*
McDermott, (Lawrence) Emmet 1911-
Who 94
McDermott, Francis A. 1943-
WhoAmL 94
McDermott, Francis Owen 1933-
WhoAm 94, WhoAmL 94
McDermott, Gerald (Edward) 1941-
SmATA 74 [port]
McDermott, Helena E. 1911- *WhoAmP 93*
McDermott, Hugh d1972 *WhoHol 92*
McDermott, James 1936- *WhoAmP 93*
McDermott, James A. 1936- *WhoAm 94,
WhoWest 94*
McDermott, James Alexander 1938-
WhoAm 94
McDermott, James Patrick 1939-
WhoAmP 93
McDermott, James T. 1926- *WhAm 10*
McDermott, Jim 1936- *CngDr 93*
McDermott, John d1946 *WhoHol 92*
McDermott, John Andrew 1926-
WhoMW 93
McDermott, John E. 1946- *WhoAmL 94*
Mc Dermott, John Francis, Jr. 1929-
WhoAm 94
McDermott, John Francis, IV 1926-
WhoScEn 94
McDermott, John Henry 1931-
WhoAm 94
McDermott, John J. 1951- *WhoAmL 94*
Mc Dermott, John Joseph 1932-
WhoAm 94
McDermott, Joseph d1923 *WhoHol 92*
McDermott, Katherine Buck 1937-
WhoAmP 93
McDermott, Keith *WhoHol 92*
McDermott, Kellie Marie 1958-
WhoWest 94
McDermott, Kevin Daniel 1954-
WhoFI 94
McDermott, Kevin J. 1935- *WhoAm 94,
WhoScEn 94*
McDermott, Michael 1962- *SmATA 76*
McDermott, Molly 1932- *WhoMW 93*
McDermott, Patricia L. *WhoAmP 93*
McDermott, Patrick *WhoHol 92*
McDermott, Patrick Anthony 1941-
Who 94
Mc Dermott, Philip Alan 1951-
WhoAm 94
McDermott, Renee Rassler 1950-
WhoAm 94, WhoAmL 94
McDermott, Richard T. 1940- *WhoAm 94,
WhoAmL 94*
McDermott, Robert B. 1927- *WhoAm 94*
Mc Dermott, Robert Francis 1920-
WhoAm 94, WhoFI 94
McDermott, Robert Francis, Jr. 1945-
WhoAm 94, WhoAmL 94
McDermott, Robert Hogan 1931-
WhoAmP 93
McDermott, Robert J. 1944- *WhoAmL 94*
McDermott, Robert James 1932-
WhoAmP 93
McDermott, Robert W. 1943- *WhoIns 94*
McDermott, Rory d1980 *WhoHol 92*
McDermott, Thomas Curtis 1936-
WhoFI 94
McDermott, Thomas John, Jr. 1931-
WhoAm 94
McDermott, Thomas M. 1948-
WhoAmP 93
McDermott, William Thomas 1945-
WhoFI 94
Mc Dermott, William Vincent, Jr. 1917-
WhoAm 94
McDevitt, Charles E. 1939- *WhoAmP 93*

McDevitt, Charles F. 1932- *WhoAmP 93*
McDevitt, Charles Francis 1932-
WhoAm 94, WhoAmL 94, WhoWest 94
McDevitt, Hugh O'Neill 1930-
WhoAm 94, WhoScEn 94
McDevitt, Jack 1935- *EncSF 93*
Mc Devitt, Joseph Bryan 1918-
WhoAm 94
McDevitt, Ray Edward 1943-
WhoAmL 94
McDevitt, Ruth d1976 *WhoHol 92*
McDevitt, Sheila Marie 1947-
WhoAmL 94
McDiarmid, Bruce W. 1947- *WhoAmL 94*
McDiarmid, Dorothy Shoemaker 1906-
WhoAmP 93
McDiarmid, Ian *WhoHol 92*
McDiarmid, Robert Campbell 1937-
WhoAmL 94
McDill, Thomas Allison 1926-
WhoAm 94
McDivitt, James Alton 1929-
WhoScEn 94
Mc Donagh, Edward Charles 1915-
WhoAm 94
Mcdonagh, Enda 1930- *IntWW 93*
Mcdonagh, Robert 1924- *IntWW 93*
McDonagh, Thomas Joseph 1932-
WhoAm 94, WhoFI 94
McDonald, Hon. Lord 1916- *Who 94*
McDonald, Alan Angus 1927- *WhoAm 94,
WhoAmL 94, WhoWest 94*
McDonald, Alan James 1946-
WhoAmL 94
McDonald, Albert 1930- *WhoAmP 93*
McDonald, Alden J., Jr. *WhoBlA 94*
McDonald, Alexander John 1919- *Who 94*
McDonald, Alice 1940- *WhoAmP 93*
McDonald, Alice Coig 1940- *WhoAm 94*
McDonald, Alistair 1925- *Who 94*
McDonald, Alistair Ian 1921- *Who 94*
McDonald, Allan *WhAmRev*
McDonald, Allan Stuart 1922- *Who 94*
McDonald, Alonzo Lowry, Jr. 1928-
WhoAm 94
Mc Donald, Andrew J. 1923- *WhoAm 94*
McDonald, Andrew Melvin, Jr. 1941-
WhoAm 94, WhoAmL 94
McDonald, Angus Wheeler 1927-
WhoFI 94
McDonald, Angus William, Jr. 1941-
WhoMW 93
McDonald, Anita Dunlop 1929-
WhoBlA 94
McDonald, Anne *WhoAmP 93*
McDonald, Arthur (William Baynes)
1903- *Who 94*
McDonald, Arthur Bruce 1943-
WhoAm 94
McDonald, B. J. 1933- *WhoAmP 93*
McDonald, Barbara Ann 1938-
WhoMW 93
McDonald, Bernard 1942-1991
WhoBlA 94N
McDonald, Bernard Robert 1940-
WhoScEn 94
McDonald, Bradley G. *WhoAmL 94*
McDonald, Brendan John 1930-
WhoAm 94
McDonald, Brian J. *WhoAmP 93*
McDonald, Brian M. 1947- *WhoAmL 94*
McDonald, Brian Robert 1952-
WhoAmP 93
McDonald, Bronce William 1949-
WhoMW 93
McDonald, Bruce L. 1941- *WhoAmL 94*
McDonald, Capers Walter 1951-
WhoAm 94
McDonald, Charles d1964 *WhoHol 92*
Mc Donald, Charles J. 1931- *WhoAm 94,
WhoBlA 94*
McDonald, Charles Raymond 1927-
WhoMW 93
McDonald, Charles William 1936-
WhoAmP 93
McDonald, Christopher *WhoHol 92*
McDonald, Curtis W. 1934- *WhoBlA 94*
McDonald, Daniel *WhoHol 92*
McDonald, Daniel Robert 1944-
WhoAmP 93, WhoWest 94
McDonald, Danny Lee *WhoAmP 93*
McDonald, David Arthur 1940- *Who 94*
McDonald, David J. 1902-1979
EncABHB 9 [port]
McDonald, David J. 1928- *WhoFI 94*
McDonald, David J. 1936- *WhoIns 94*
McDonald, David John 1959-
WhoAmL 94
McDonald, David P. 1938- *WhoAm 94,
WhoAmL 94*
Mc Donald, David William 1923-
WhoAm 94
McDonald, David Wylie 1927- *Who 94*
McDonald, Dennis A. 1938- *WhoAmP 93*
McDonald, Desmond P. 1927-
WhoAm 94, WhoFI 94
McDonald, Donald 1712- *WhAmRev*

McDonald, Dorothy Colette 1938-
WhoFI 94
McDonald, Duncan 1921- *IntWW 93,
Who 94*
McDonald, Edmund Morris 1917-
WhoBIA 94
McDonald, Edward Lawson 1918-
IntWW 93
McDonald, Elaine Maria 1943- *Who 94*
McDonald, Ella Seabrook *WhoBIA 94*
McDonald, Eva Rose 1909- *WrDr 94*
McDonald, F(rancis) James 1922- *Who 94*
McDonald, Flora 1722-1790 *WhAmRev*
McDonald, Forrest 1927- *IntWW 93,
WhoAm 94, WrDr 94*
McDonald, Francis d1968 *WhoHol 92*
McDonald, Frank d1980 *WhoHol 92*
Mc Donald, Frank Bethune 1925-
WhoAm 94
McDonald, Frank F., II *WhoAmP 93*
McDonald, G. Michael *WhoBIA 94*
McDonald, Gabrielle K. 1942- *WhoBIA 94*
McDonald, Gail C. *WhoAmP 93*
McDonald, Gail Clements 1944-
WhoAm 94, WhoAmL 94, WhoFI 94
McDonald, Gail Jacolev 1945-
WhoAm 94, WhoAmL 94
McDonald, Gail Margaret 1948-
WhoAm 94, WhoFI 94
McDonald, Garry *WhoHol 92*
McDonald, Glena June 1947- *WhoMW 93*
McDonald, Grace 1918- *WhoHol 92*
McDonald, Graeme Patrick Daniel 1930-
Who 94
McDonald, Gregory 1937- *WrDr 94*
Mcdonald, Gregory (Christopher) 1937-
ConAu 42NR
McDonald, Gregory Anthony 1956-
WhoMW 93
Mcdonald, Gregory Christopher 1937-
WhoAm 94
McDonald, Gregory James 1959-
WhoFI 94
McDonald, Guillermo Jurado *WhoHisp 94*
McDonald, Hal Mark 1956- *WhoMW 93*
McDonald, Helen Desmond 1953-
WhoAmL 94
Mc Donald, Henry Stanton 1927-
WhoAm 94
McDonald, Herbert G. 1929- *WhoBIA 94*
McDonald, Heyward Elliott 1925-
WhoAmP 93
McDonald, Hugh Joseph 1913-
WhoMW 93
McDonald, Ian *WhoHol 92*
McDonald, Ian 1960- *EncSF 93*
McDonald, Ian (A.) 1933- *WrDr 94*
McDonald, Ian MacLaren 1928-
WhoAm 94, WhoWest 94
McDonald, Iverach 1908- *Who 94*
McDonald, J. David 1942- *WhoIns 94*
McDonald, Jack 1880- *WhoHol 92*
McDonald, Jack H. 1932- *WhoAmP 93*
McDonald, James *Who 94*
McDonald, James Bott 1942- *WhoFI 94,
WhoWest 94*
McDonald, James Charles 1955-
WhoMW 93
McDonald, James Harold 1951-
WhoScEn 94
McDonald, James Joseph 1930-
WhoAmP 93
McDonald, James L. 1943- *WhoAm 94,
WhoFI 94*
Mc Donald, James Michael, Jr. 1924-
WhoAm 94
McDonald, Jamie 1919- *WrDr 94*
McDonald, Jay Briggs 1957- *WhoMW 93*
McDonald, Jean A. *WhoAmL 94*
McDonald, Jeanne Gray 1917-
WhoAm 94, WhoWest 94
McDonald, Jearl Shane 1953- *WhoMW 93*
McDonald, John C. 1936- *WhoAm 94*
McDonald, John Cecil 1924- *WhoAm 94,
WhoAmP 93*
McDonald, John Clifton 1930-
WhoAm 94
McDonald, John Cooper 1936-
WhoAmP 93
McDonald, John Corbett 1918- *Who 94*
McDonald, John Francis Patrick 1942-
WhoAm 94, WhoFI 94, WhoScEn 94
McDonald, John Freeman 1943-
WhoFI 94
McDonald, John Gregory 1937-
WhoAm 94, WhoFI 94
Mc Donald, John Joseph 1930-
WhoAm 94
Mc Donald, John Richard 1933-
WhoAm 94
McDonald, John Stanley 1943-1981
WhoAmA 93N
McDonald, John W. 1922- *IntWW 93*
Mc Donald, John Warlick 1922-
WhoAm 94
McDonald, Jon Franklin 1946-
WhoBIA 94

McDonald, Joseph Lee 1931-
WhoWest 94
McDonald, Joseph Paul 1914-
WhoAmP 93
Mc Donald, Joseph Valentine 1925-
WhoAm 94
McDonald, Joyce *DrAPF 93*
McDonald, Juanita *WhoAmP 93*
McDonald, Judith Louise 1939-
WhoMW 94
McDonald, Julian LeRoy, Jr. 1941-
WhoScEn 94
McDonald, Julie *DrAPF 93*
McDonald, Julie 1929- *ConAu 43NR*
McDonald, Julie Jensen *ConAu 43NR*
McDonald, Kean K. 1944- *WhoAm 94,
WhoAmL 94*
McDonald, Keith Leon 1923-
WhoWest 94
McDonald, Kenneth E. 1939- *WhoMW 93*
McDonald, Kenneth James 1930-
WhoAmP 93
McDonald, Kenneth William 1945-
WhoMW 93
McDonald, Larry Marvin 1952-
WhoBIA 94
McDonald, Larry William 1928-
WhoMW 93
McDonald, Lauren Wylie, Jr. 1938-
WhoAmP 93
McDonald, Lawson *Who 94*
McDonald, (Edward) Lawson 1918-
Who 94
McDonald, Leneen *Who 94*
McDonald, Lloyd Paul 1896- *WhAm 10*
McDonald, Lynn 1940- *WrDr 94*
McDonald, Malcolm Gideon 1932-
WhoWest 94
McDonald, Marianne 1937- *WhoAm 94,
WhoWest 94*
McDonald, Marie d1965 *WhoHol 92*
McDonald, Mark Douglas 1958-
WhoScEn 94
McDonald, Mark T. 1935- *WhoBIA 94*
McDonald, Mary Ann *WhoHol 92*
McDonald, Mary Ann Melody 1944-
WhoFI 94, WhoWest 94
McDonald, Mary M. 1944- *WhoAmL 94*
McDonald, Mavis 1944- *Who 94*
McDonald, Megan 1959- *WrDr 94*
McDonald, Michael Brian 1948-
WhoWest 94
McDonald, Michael Eugene 1956-
WhoAmL 94
McDonald, Michael Joseph 1954-
WhoAmL 94
McDonald, Michael Lee 1949- *WhoAm 94*
McDonald, Michael Shawn 1957-
WhoScEn 94
McDonald, Mike 1958- *WhoBIA 94*
Mc Donald, Miles Francis 1905-1991
WhAm 10
McDonald, Miller Baird 1920-
WhoAm 94, WhoAmP 93
McDonald, Nancy Hanks 1934-
WhoAmP 93
McDonald, Oonagh *Who 94*
McDonald, Parker Lee 1924- *WhoAm 94,
WhoAmL 94, WhoAmP 93*
Mc Donald, Patrick Allen 1936-
WhoAm 94
McDonald, Peggy Ann Stimmel 1931-
WhoFI 94
McDonald, Peyton Dean 1936- *WhoFI 94*
McDonald, R. Timothy 1940- *WhoBIA 94*
McDonald, Ray d1959 *WhoHol 92*
McDonald, Raymond *EncSF 93*
McDonald, Richard E. 1929- *WhoBIA 94*
McDonald, Robert 1933- *WhoWest 94*
McDonald, Robert Bond 1936-
WhoAm 94
McDonald, Robert Delos 1931-
WhoAm 94, WhoWest 94
Mc Donald, Robert Emmett 1915-
WhoAm 94
McDonald, Robert Garland 1942-
WhoWest 94
McDonald, Robert Herwick *WhoAmA 93*
McDonald, Robert Howat *Who 94*
McDonald, Robert Lendol 1924-
WhoAmP 93
McDonald, Roger 1941- *WrDr 94*
Mc Donald, Roy 1901-1990 *WhAm 10*
McDonald, Samson d1970 *WhoHol 92*
McDonald, Sloan Mebane 1952-
WhoWest 94
Mc Donald, Stephen Lee 1924-
WhoAm 94
McDonald, Stephen Paul 1939-
WhoAmL 94
McDonald, Steven E(dward) 1956-
EncSF 93
McDonald, Susan *WhoHol 92*
McDonald, Susan B. 1956- *WhoMW 93*
McDonald, Susan Strong 1943-
WhoAmA 93
McDonald, Terrence John 1949-
WhoAmP 93

McDonald, Thomas Alexander 1942-
WhoAm 94
McDonald, Thomas Edwin, Jr. 1939-
WhoScEn 94, WhoWest 94
McDonald, Thomas Muirhead 1952-
Who 94
McDonald, Tim 1965- *WhoAm 94,
WhoWest 94*
McDonald, Timothy, III 1954-
WhoBIA 94
McDonald, Tom 1923- *Who 94*
McDonald, W. R. 1929- *WhoFI 94,
WhoMW 94*
McDonald, Walter *DrAPF 93,
WhoAmP 93*
McDonald, Warren George 1939-
WhoAm 94, WhoFI 94
McDonald, William 1929- *Who 94*
McDonald, William (John Farquhar)
1911- *Who 94*
McDonald, William Andrew 1913-
WhoAm 94, WrDr 94
McDonald, William Brice 1945-
WhoMW 93
McDonald, William Crabtree 1927-
WhoMW 93
McDonald, William Emory 1924-
WhoBIA 94
McDonald, William Henry 1924-
WhoAm 94
McDonald, William Henry 1946-
WhoAmL 94
McDonald, William James Gilmour
1924- *Who 94*
McDonald, William Naylor, III 1913-
WhoFI 94
McDonald, Willie Ruth Davis 1931-
WhoBIA 94
McDonald, Willis, IV 1926- *WhoAm 94*
McDonall, Lois 1939- *NewGrDO*
McDonaugh, James 1912- *Who 94*
McDonell, Horace George, Jr. 1928-
WhoAm 94, WhoFI 94
McDonell, Robert Terry 1944- *WhoAm 94*
McDonell, William George 1952-
WhoWest 94
McDonnell *Who 94*
McDonnell, Archie Joseph 1936-
WhoScEn 94
McDonnell, Christopher Thomas 1931-
Who 94
McDonnell, David Croft 1943- *Who 94*
McDonnell, Denis Lane 1914- *Who 94*
McDonnell, Dennis J. 1942- *WhoAm 94,
WhoFI 94*
Mc Donnell, Edward Francis 1935-
WhoFI 94
McDonnell, Everett Nicholas 1893-
WhAm 10
McDonnell, John 1951- *Who 94*
McDonnell, John Beresford William
1940- *Who 94*
McDonnell, John Finney 1938-
WhoAm 94, WhoFI 94, WhoMW 93
McDonnell, John J. 1939- *WhoAmL 94*
McDonnell, John Patrick 1965-
WhoScEn 94
Mc Donnell, John Thomas 1926-
WhoAm 94
McDonnell, Joseph Anthony 1936-
WhoAmA 93
McDonnell, Kevin Lee 1932- *WrDr 94*
McDonnell, Kevin Paul 1958- *WhoFI 94*
McDonnell, Lois Eddy *WrDr 94*
Mc Donnell, Loretta Wade 1940-
WhoAmL 94
McDonnell, Mary *NewYTBS 93 [port]*
McDonnell, Mary 1952- *IntMPA 94,
WhoAm 94*
McDonnell, Mary 1953- *WhoHol 92*
McDonnell, Rex Graham, Jr. 1924-
WhoAmP 93
McDonnell, Robert F. 1954- *WhoAmP 93*
McDonnell, Sanford N. 1922- *IntWW 93*
McDonnell, Sanford Noyes 1922-
WhoAm 94
McDonnell, Sue Kartin 1948- *WhoAm 94,
WhoAmL 94*
McDonnell, Tom (Anthony) 1940-
NewGrDO
McDonnough, Paul Anthony 1966-
WhoAmP 93
McDonough, Alex *EncSF 93*
McDonough, Brian F. 1953- *WhoAmL 94*
McDonough, Dixie Jean 1935- *WhoFI 94*
McDonough, Edward Francis 1932-
WhoAmP 93
McDonough, Frank Kent 1951- *WhoFI 94*
Mc Donough, George Francis, Jr. 1928-
WhoAm 94
McDonough, James Francis 1939-
WhoAm 94
McDonough, John Edward 1953-
WhoAmP 93
McDonough, John Glennon 1960-
WhoScEn 94
McDonough, John Michael 1944-
WhoAm 94, WhoAmL 94

Mc Donough, John Richard 1919-
WhoAm 94
McDonough, Joseph d1944 *WhoHol 92*
McDonough, Joseph Corbett 1924-
WhoAm 94
McDonough, Joseph Richard 1950-
WhoAmL 94
McDonough, Kenneth Lee 1953-
WhoMW 93
McDonough, Mary 1961- *WhoHol 92*
McDonough, Mary Joan 1957-
WhoAmP 93
McDonough, Michael d1956 *WhoHol 92*
McDonough, Patrick Dennis 1942-
WhoAm 94, WhoMW 93
McDonough, Patrick Joseph 1943-
WhoAmL 94
McDonough, Patrick Joseph, Jr. 1941-
WhoAmL 94
McDonough, Patrick Kevin 1949-
WhoWest 94
McDonough, Paul F., Jr. 1944-
WhoAmL 94
McDonough, Reginald Milton 1936-
WhoAm 94
Mc Donough, Richard Doyle 1931-
WhoAm 94, WhoFI 94
McDonough, Robert d1945 *WhoHol 92*
McDonough, Robert E. *DrAPF 93*
McDonough, Russell 1924- *WhoAmP 93*
McDonough, Russell Charles 1924-
WhoAm 94, WhoAmL 94, WhoWest 94
McDonough, Susan Ellen 1949-
WhoAmL 94
McDonough, Thomas Joseph 1934-
WhoAmL 94
McDonough, Thomas R(edmond) 1945-
EncSF 93
McDonough, Travis Randall 1972-
WhoAmP 93
McDormand, Frances 1957- *WhoHol 92*
McDormand, Frances 1958- *IntMPA 94,
WhoAm 94*
McDougal, Alfred Leroy 1931-
WhoAm 94, WhoMW 93
McDougal, Dennis Edward 1947-
WhoWest 94
McDougal, Ivan Ellis 1927- *WhoAmA 93*
McDougal, Luther Love, III 1938-
WhoAm 94
McDougal, Marie Patricia 1946-
WhoMW 93
McDougal, Stuart Yeatman 1942-
WhoAm 94
McDougal, William Scott 1942-
WhoAm 94
McDougall, Alexander 1732-1786 *AmRev,
WhAmRev*
McDougall, Barbara Jean 1937-
*IntWW 93, Who 94, WhoAm 94,
WhoWomW 91*
McDougall, Dugald George 1942-
WhoAmP 93
Mc Dougall, Dugald Stewart 1916-
WhoAm 94
McDougall, George Millward 1821-1876
EncNAR
McDougall, I. Ross 1943- *WhoAm 94,
WhoWest 94*
McDougall, Ian 1930- *WhoFI 94*
McDougall, Jacquelyn Marie Horan
1924- *WhoWest 94*
McDougall, James Patrick 1965-
WhoFI 94
McDougall, John 1842-1917 *EncNAR*
McDougall, John Olin 1944- *WhoAmL 94*
McDougall, John Roland 1945-
WhoAm 94
McDougall, Ronald Alexander 1942-
WhoAm 94, WhoFI 94
McDougall, Sharon L. 1959- *WhoIns 94*
McDougall, Susan 1961- *WhoFI 94*
McDougall, Walter Allan 1946-
WhoAm 94
McDougle, Alan *WhoMW 93*
Mc Dow, John Jett 1925- *WhoAm 94*
McDow, Russell Edward, Jr. 1950-
WhoScEn 94
McDowall, Betty *IntMPA 94, WhoHol 92*
McDowall, Keith Desmond 1929- *Who 94*
McDowall, Roddy 1928- *IntMPA 94,
IntWW 93, WhoAm 94, WhoHol 92*
McDowall, Stuart 1926- *Who 94*
McDowall, Virginia 1927- *WhoHol 92*
McDowell, Angus 1946- *WhoAm 94*
McDowell, Aweda Loretta 1923-
WhoMW 93
McDowell, Benjamin A. 1939- *WhoBIA 94*
McDowell, Bobbie G. 1942- *WhoAmP 93*
McDowell, Bobby Allen 1958-
WhoAmP 93
McDowell, Carly Shaw 1957-
WhoWest 94
McDowell, Carter Nelson 1953-
WhoAmL 94
Mc Dowell, Charles Eager 1923-
WhoAm 94
McDowell, Claire d1966 *WhoHol 92*

McDowell, Cleve 1941- *WhoBlA 94*
McDowell, (Martin Rastall) Coulter d1993 *Who 94N*
McDowell, Daniel Quince, Jr. 1949- *WhoFI 94, WhoMW 93*
McDowell, David E. 1942- *WhoWest 94*
McDowell, David Keith 1937- *IntWW 93*
McDowell, Donald L. 1934- *WhoAm 94*
McDowell, Edward Homer, Jr. 1949- *WhoBlA 94*
McDowell, Edward R. H. 1932- *WhoAm 94*
McDowell, Edwin Stewart 1935- *WrDr 94*
McDowell, Elizabeth Mary 1940- *WhoAm 94*
McDowell, Eric (Wallace) 1925- *Who 94*
McDowell, Esther Arias 1948- *WhoHisp 94*
McDowell, Fletcher Hughes 1923- *WhoAm 94*
McDowell, Fred d1972 *WhoHol 92*
McDowell, Frederick P. W. 1915- *WrDr 94*
McDowell, George Edward 1944- *WhoMW 93*
McDowell, George Roy Colquhoun 1922- *Who 94*
McDowell, Harriette Fowlkes 1938- *WhoBlA 94*
McDowell, Harris B., III 1940- *WhoAmP 93*
McDowell, Henry (McLorinan) 1910- *Who 94*
McDowell, Jack Burns 1966- *WhoAm 94, WhoMW 93*
Mc Dowell, Jack Sherman 1914- *WhoAm 94*
McDowell, James E. 1924- *WhoAmP 93*
McDowell, James W., Jr. 1942- *WhoFI 94*
McDowell, Jay Hortenstine 1936- *WhoAm 94*
McDowell, Jeffrey Steven 1954- *WhoWest 94*
McDowell, Jennifer *DrAPF 93*
McDowell, Jennifer 1936- *WhoAm 94, WhoFI 94, WhoScEn 94, WhoWest 94*
McDowell, Jerry L. 1940- *WhoAm 94, WhoAmL 94*
McDowell, John (Henry) 1942- *WrDr 94*
Mc Dowell, John B. 1921- *WhoAm 94*
Mc Dowell, John Eugene 1927 *WhoAm 94*
McDowell, John Henry 1942- *IntWW 93, Who 94*
McDowell, John Henry 1957- *WhoAmL 94*
McDowell, Joseph 1756-1801 *WhAmRev*
McDowell, Karen Ann 1945- *WhoAmL 94*
McDowell, Malcolm 1943- *IntMPA 94, IntWW 93, Who 94, WhoAm 94, WhoHol 92*
McDowell, Mary Eliza 1854-1936 *AmSocL [port]*
McDowell, Michael 1950- *WrDr 94*
McDowell, Michael David 1948- *WhoAm 94, WhoAmL 94, WhoFI 94*
McDowell, Nelson d1947 *WhoHol 92*
McDowell, Paul *WhoHol 92*
McDowell, Peter Lee 1938- *WhoAmP 93*
McDowell, Robert *DrAPF 93*
McDowell, Robert 1924- *WhoFI 94*
McDowell, Robin Scott 1934- *WhoAm 94, WhoWest 94*
McDowell, Stanley 1941- *Who 94*
McDowell, Stirling 1931- *WhoAm 94*
McDowell, Susan *WhoAmP 93*
McDowell, Timothy Hill 1946- *WhoAmP 93*
McDowell, William D. 1927- *WhoAmP 93*
McDowell, William S. 1941- *WhoAm 94*
McDowell-Head, Lelia M. 1953- *WhoBlA 94*
McDuff, James d1937 *WhoHol 92*
McDuffie, David Wayne 1960- *WhoFI 94*
McDuffie, Deborah 1950- *WhoBlA 94*
McDuffie, Dwayne Glenn 1962- *WhoBlA 94*
McDuffie, Frederic Clement 1924- *WhoAm 94*
McDuffie, Hinfred 1949- *WhoBlA 94*
McDuffie, James Doyle 1929- *WhoAmP 93*
McDuffie, Joseph deLeon, Jr. 1950- *WhoBlA 94*
Mc Duffie, Malcolm 1915- *WhoAm 94*
McDunnough, Walter d1942 *WhoHol 92*
McEachen, James Allen 1925- *WhoWest 94*
McEachen, Richard Edward 1933- *WhoAm 94, WhoFI 94*
McEachern, Allan 1926- *Who 94, WhoAm 94, WhoWest 94*
McEachern, Bob 1927- *WhoAmP 93*
McEachern, D. Hector *WhoBlA 94*
McEachern, John Hugh 1940- *WhoAmL 94*
McEachern, Maceo R. 1946- *WhoBlA 94*
McEachern, William Archibald 1945- *WhoFI 94, WhoScEn 94*

McEachern, William Donald 1950- *WhoAmP 93*
McEachern-Ulmer, Sylvia L. 1934- *WhoBlA 94*
McEachin, Daniel Malloy, Jr. 1950- *WhoAmP 93*
McEachin, James 1930- *WhoBlA 94, WhoHol 92*
McEachran, Angus 1939- *WhoAm 94*
McEachran, Colin Neil 1940- *Who 94*
McEachron, Donald Lynn 1953- *WhoScEn 94*
McElaney, Andrew J., Jr. 1946- *WhoAmL 94*
McElderry, Betty *WhoAmP 93, WhoWomW 91*
McEldowney, Richard Dennis 1926- *WrDr 94*
McEldowney, Todd Richard 1955- *WhoAmL 94*
McElfresh, (Elizabeth) Adeline 1918- *WrDr 94*
McElgunn, James Douglas 1939- *WhoScEn 94*
McElhaney, James Harry 1933- *WhoAm 94*
Mc Elhaney, James Wilson 1937- *WhoAm 94*
Mc Elhaney, John Hess 1934- *WhoAm 94, WhoAmL 94*
McElhany, Thomas J. d1966 *WhoHol 92*
McElhatton, Daniel P. *WhoAmP 93*
McElhenny, Hugh *ProFbHF*
McElheny, Richard Lee 1936- *WhoAmP 93*
McElheran, John 1929- *Who 94*
McElhinney, Ian *WhoHol 92*
McElhinney, Robert Stanley 1933- *IntWW 93*
McElhinny, Wilson Dunbar 1929- *WhoAm 94*
McEligot, Donald Marinus *WhoWest 94*
McEllhiney, Robert Ross 1927- *WhoMW 93*
McElligott, Ann Theresa 1942- *WhoWest 94*
McElligott, Denise Nell 1963- *WhoMW 93*
McElligott, James Patrick, Jr. 1948- *WhoAm 94, WhoAmL 94*
McEllroy, William Swindler 1893- *WhAm 10*
McElmurray, Jeanne Frances 1921- *WhoAmP 93*
Mc Elrath, Gayle William 1915- *WhoAm 94*
Mc Elrath, Richard Elsworth 1932- *WhoAm 94*
McElrath, Wanda Faith 1959- *WhoBlA 94*
McElroy, Belinda Jewell 1961- *WhoFI 94*
McElroy, Benjamin Roland 1944- *WhoAmP 93*
McElroy, Bob d1976 *WhoHol 92*
McElroy, Charles Dwayne 1967- *WhoBlA 94*
McElroy, Charlotte Ann 1939- *WhoWest 94*
McElroy, Colleen J. *DrAPF 93*
McElroy, Colleen J. 1935- *WhoBlA 94, WrDr 94*
McElroy, Colleen J(ohnson) 1935- *BlkWr 2*
McElroy, David F., Jr. 1943- *WhoAmL 94*
McElroy, Frederick William 1939- *WhoAm 94*
McElroy, George A. 1922- *WhoBlA 94*
McElroy, Howard Chowning 1946- *WhoAmL 94*
McElroy, Jack d1959 *WhoHol 92*
McElroy, Jacquelyn Ann 1942- *WhoAmA 93*
McElroy, Jerome Lathrop 1937- *WhoFI 94*
Mc Elroy, John Harley 1936- *WhoAm 94*
McElroy, John Lee, Jr. 1931- *WhoFI 94*
McElroy, Joseph *DrAPF 93*
McElroy, Joseph 1930- *EncSF 93*
McElroy, Joseph (Prince) 1930- *WrDr 94*
McElroy, Laurince Dean 1962- *WhoMW 93*
McElroy, Lee 1926- *WrDr 94*
McElroy, Lee A., Jr. 1948- *WhoBlA 94*
McElroy, Leo Francis 1932- *WhoWest 94*
McElroy, Linda Ann 1942- *WhoMW 93*
McElroy, Michael 1939- *WhoAm 94, WhoScEn 94*
McElroy, Njoki *WhoBlA 94*
McElroy, Richard P. 1942- *WhoAm 94*
McElroy, Roy Granville 1907- *Who 94*
McElroy, Sam M. 1921- *WhoAmP 93*
McElroy, William David 1917- *IntWW 93, WhoAm 94, WhoAmP 93*
Mc Elroy, William Theodore 1925- *WhoAm 94*
McElvain, W. Lee 1939- *WhoAmP 93*
McElvane, Pamela Anne 1958- *WhoBlA 94*
McElveen, H. Donald 1935- *WhoAmP 93*

McElveen, Joseph T., Jr. 1946- *WhoAmP 93*
McElveen, Junius Carlisle, Jr. 1947- *WhoAm 94*
McElveen, William Powers, Jr. 1958- *WhoAmL 94*
McElvein, Thomas I., Jr. 1936- *WhoAmL 94*
McElwain, Edwina Jay 1936- *WhoMW 93*
Mc Elwain, Joseph Arthur 1919- *WhoAm 94, WhoWest 94*
McElwain, Joseph Mitchell 1941- *WhoAmP 93*
Mc Elwain, Lester Stafford 1910- *WhoAmL 94*
McElwaine, Guy 1936- *IntMPA 94*
McElwee, Dennis John 1947- *WhoScEn 94*
Mc Elwee, John Gerard 1921- *WhoAm 94*
McElwee, Richard Robert 1953- *WhoFI 94*
McElyea, David D. 1950- *WhoFI 94*
McElyea, James Michael 1948- *WhoAmL 94*
McElyea, Terry L. 1956- *WhoAmL 94*
McElyea, Ulysses, Jr. 1941- *WhoWest 94*
McEnelly, Minerva Perez 1955- *WhoHisp 94*
McEneny, John J. 1943- *WhoAmP 93*
McEnerney, Michael Thomas 1948- *WhoAmL 94*
McEnery, John 1945- *WhoHol 92*
McEnery, John H. 1925- *WrDr 94*
McEnery, John Hartnett 1925- *Who 94*
McEnery, Peter 1940- *Who 94, WhoHol 92*
McEnery, Thomas *WhoAmP 93*
McEnery, Thomas W. 1945- *WhoAm 94*
McEnery, Thomas 1945- *WhoAm 94*
McEniry, Robert Francis 1918- *WhoMW 93*
McEnnan, James Judd 1944- *WhoScEn 94*
McEnroe, Annie *WhoHol 92*
McEnroe, Caroline Ann 1935- *WhoScEn 94*
McEnroe, Harry A. 1931- *WhoAmP 93*
McEnroe, John 1959- *BuCMET [port]*
McEnroe, John Patrick 1935- *WhoAm 94*
McEnroe, John Patrick 1959- *IntWW 93*
Mc Enroe, John Patrick, Jr. 1959- *WhoAm 94*
McEnroe, Patrick 1966- *WhoAm 94*
McEnroe, Richard S. *EncSF 93*
McEntee, Michael J. 1952- *WhoAmP 93*
McEntee, Peter Donovan 1920- *IntWW 93, Who 94*
McEntee, Robert Edward 1932- *WhoAm 94*
McEntire, B. Joseph 1962- *WhoScEn 94*
McEntire, Maleta Mae 1957- *WhoWest 94*
McEntire, Reba 1954- *ConMus 11 [port], News 94-2 [port]*
McEntire, Reba 1955- *WhoHol 92*
McEntire, Reba N. 1955- *WhoAm 94*
Mc Entyre, Peter Michael 1917-1989 *WhAm 10*
McEnulty, Timothy Eugene 1959- *WhoMW 93*
McErlain, David Patrick 1947- *Who 94*
McErlane, Joseph James 1948- *WhoAm 94*
McEvedy, Colin (Peter) 1930- *WrDr 94*
McEveety, Bernard *IntMPA 94*
McEveety, Vincent *IntMPA 94*
McEvers, Duff Steven 1954- *WhoAmL 94*
McEvers, Joan *AstEnc*
Mc Evers, Robert Darwin 1930-1991 *WhAm 10*
McEvilley, Thomas 1939- *ConAu 140, WhoAmA 93*
McEvilly, James Lawrence 1926- *WhoAmP 93*
McEvilly, James Patrick, Jr. 1943- *WhoAmL 94*
Mc Evilly, Thomas Vincent 1934- *WhoAm 94, WhoWest 94*
McEvily, John Vincent, Jr. 1949- *WhoFI 94*
McEvoy, Anne-Marie 1975- *WhoHol 92*
McEvoy, Charles Lucien 1917- *WhoAm 94, WhoFI 94*
McEvoy, David Dand 1938- *Who 94*
McEvoy, Dorothea d1976 *WhoHol 92*
McEvoy, Gerald William 1948- *WhoAmL 94*
McEvoy, James F. 1931- *WhoAmL 94*
McEvoy, John Thomas 1937- *WhoAmP 93*
McEvoy, Marjorie 1909-1989 *WrDr 94N*
McEvoy, Mike *WhoAmP 93*
McEvoy, Richard Franklin 1946- *WhoWest 94*
McEvoy, Seth *EncSF 93*
McEwan, Angus David 1937- *IntWW 93*
McEwan, Bruce 1937- *WhoAmP 93*
McEwan, Geraldine 1932- *IntWW 93, Who 94, WhoHol 92*

McEwan, Ian 1948- *BlmGEL, CurBio 93 [port], IntWW 93, WrDr 94*
McEwan, Ian (Russell) 1948- *ConAu 41NR, EncSF 93*
McEwan, Ian Russell 1948- *Who 94*
Mc Ewan, Leonard 1925- *WhoAm 94*
McEwan, (John) Neil 1946- *WrDr 94*
McEwan, Robert Neal 1949- *WhoScEn 94*
McEwan, Robin Gilmour 1943- *Who 94*
McEwan, Willard Winfield, Jr. 1934- *WhoWest 94*
McEwen, Alexander Campbell 1926- *WhoAm 94*
McEwen, Bob 1950- *WhoAmP 93*
McEwen, James Stevenson d1993 *Who 94N*
McEwen, Jean 1923- *WhoAm 94, WhoAmA 93*
McEwen, John (Roderick Hugh) 1965- *Who 94*
McEwen, John L. *WhoAmP 93*
McEwen, Mark 1954- *ConBlB 5 [port], WhoBlA 94*
McEwen, Robert Cameron 1920- *WhoAmP 93*
McEwen, Robert Joseph 1916- *WhoFI 94*
McEwen, Willard Winfield, Jr. 1934- *WhoAm 94, WhoAmL 94*
McEwen, William Peter 1912-1990 *WhAm 10*
McEwing, Mitchell Dalton 1935- *WhoBlA 94*
McFadden, Arthur B. 1940- *WhoBlA 94*
McFadden, Bruce Alden 1930- *WhoWest 94*
McFadden, Cora C. 1945- *WhoBlA 94*
McFadden, Daniel Little 1937- *WhoAm 94*
McFadden, David 1940- *WrDr 94*
McFadden, David Revere *WhoAmA 93*
McFadden, David Revere 1947- *WhoAm 94*
McFadden, Dennis 1940- *WhoAm 94*
McFadden, Denyse Irene 1953- *WhoAmL 94*
McFadden, Douglas Bruce 1940- *WhoAmL 94*
McFadden, Frank Hampton 1925- *WhoAm 94, WhoAmL 94, WhoFI 94*
Mc Fadden, Frank William 1914-1990 *WhAm 10*
McFadden, Fred Lee 1942- *WhoFI 94*
McFadden, Frederick C., Jr. 1927- *WhoBlA 94*
Mc Fadden, G. Bruce 1934- *WhoAm 94*
McFadden, Gates *WhoHol 92*
Mc Fadden, George Linus 1927- *WhoAm 94*
McFadden, Gregory L. 1958- *WhoBlA 94*
McFadden, Ivor d1942 *WhoHol 92*
McFadden, James Frederick, Jr. 1920- *WhoAm 94, WhoMW 93, WhoScEn 94*
McFadden, James L. 1929- *WhoBlA 94*
Mc Fadden, James Patrick 1930- *WhoAm 94*
McFadden, Jean Alexandra 1941- *Who 94*
McFadden, Jo Beth 1938- *WhoWest 94*
McFadden, John Thomas 1954- *WhoFI 94*
Mc Fadden, John Volney 1931- *WhoAm 94, WhoFI 94*
Mc Fadden, Joseph Michael 1932- *WhoAm 94*
McFadden, Joseph Patrick 1939- *WhoAm 94, WhoIns 94*
McFadden, Leon Lambert 1920- *WhoAm 94, WhoWest 94*
McFadden, Mary 1938- *IntWW 93, WhoAmA 93*
Mc Fadden, Mary Josephine 1938- *WhoAm 94*
McFadden, Melton Ray 1962- *WhoMW 93*
McFadden, Nathaniel James 1946- *WhoAmP 93, WhoBlA 94*
McFadden, Pamela Ann 1950- *WhoScEn 94*
McFadden, Peter William 1932- *WhoAm 94*
McFadden, Robert Barker 1929- *WhoFI 94*
McFadden, Rosemary Theresa 1948- *WhoAm 94*
McFadden, Roy 1921- *WrDr 94*
McFadden, Samuel Wilton 1935- *WhoBlA 94*
McFadden, Terry Ted 1936- *WhoWest 94*
McFadden, Thomas 1935- *WhoAm 94, WhoWest 94*
McFadden, Tom *WhoHol 92*
McFadden, W. Clark, II 1946- *WhoAmL 94*
McFaddin, Theresa Garrison 1943- *WhoBlA 94*
McFadyean, Colin William 1943- *Who 94*
McFadyean, John 1853-1941 *DcNaB MP*
McFadzean d1992 *IntWW 93N*

McGehee, Thomas Rives 1924-
WhoAm 94, WhoFI 94
McGeoch, Ian (Lachlan Mackay) 1914-
Who 94
McGeorge, Ronald Kenneth 1944-
WhoAm 94
McGeough, Joseph Anthony 1940-
Who 94
McGeough, Michael Louis 1958-
WhoFI 94
McGeough, Robert Saunders 1930-
WhoAmL 94, WhoMW 93
McGeown, Mary Graham 1923- *Who 94*
McGervey, John Donald 1931-
WhoAm 94
McGervey, Paul John, III 1947- *WhoFI 94*
McGervey, Teresa Ann 1964-
WhoScEn 94
McGettigan, Charles Carroll, Jr. 1945-
WhoAm 94, WhoFI 94
McGhee, Brownie 1915- *WhoHol 92*
McGhee, George C. 1912- *IntWW 93*
McGhee, George Crews 1912- *Who 94,
WhoAm 94, WhoAmP 93*
McGhee, Georgia Mae 1934- *WhoBlA 94*
McGhee, Gloria d1964 *WhoHol 92*
McGhee, James Leon 1948- *WhoBlA 94*
McGhee, Johnny Ray *WhoHol 92*
McGhee, Nancy Bullock 1908-
WhoBlA 94
McGhee, Nelson 1931- *WhoAmP 93*
McGhee, Reginald D. 1927- *WhoBlA 94*
McGhee, Samuel T. 1940- *WhoBlA 94*
McGhee, Walter Brownie 1915-
WhoBlA 94
McGhie, James Marshall 1944- *Who 94*
McGibbon, Bill *WhoHol 92*
McGibbon, James R. 1946- *WhoAmL 94*
Mc Gibbon, Pauline Mills 1910-
WhoAm 94
McGiff, John Charles 1927- *WhoAm 94*
McGiffert, Arthur C., Jr. d1993
NewYTBS 93
McGiffert, Arthur Cushman 1861-1933
DcAmReB 2
Mc Giffert, David Eliot 1926- *WhoAm 94*
Mc Giffert, John Rutherford 1926-
WhoAm 94
McGiffert, Michael 1928- *WhoAm 94*
McGiffin, Robert Floyd, Jr. 1942-
WhoWest 94
McGilberry, Joe H. 1943- *WhoScEn 94*
McGilchrist, Iain 1953- *WrDr 94*
McGill, Angus *WrDr 94*
McGill, Angus 1927- *Who 94*
Mc Gill, Archie Joseph 1931- *WhoAm 94*
McGill, Archie Joseph, Jr. 1931-
IntWW 93
McGill, Bill 1939- *BasBi*
McGill, Bruce *WhoHol 92*
McGill, Charles Beatty 1922- *WhoIns 94*
McGill, Dan M(ays) 1919- *WrDr 94*
McGill, Dan Mays 1919- *WhoAm 94,
WhoIns 94*
McGill, Daniel W. 1950- *WhoAmL 94*
McGill, Esby Clifton 1914- *WhoAm 94*
McGill, Everett 1945- *WhoHol 92*
McGill, Forrest 1947- *WhoAmA 93*
McGill, Gilbert William 1947-
WhoAmL 94
McGill, Harold A. d1952 *WhoAmA 93N*
McGill, James T. 1940- *WhoIns 94*
McGill, Jennifer Houser 1957-
WhoAm 94
McGill, John Knox 1956- *WhoAmL 94*
McGill, John Y. 1952- *WhoAmP 93*
McGill, Karleen A. 1948- *WhoMW 93*
McGill, Lawrence David 1944-
WhoWest 94
McGill, Lovette Eunice 1953-
WhoAmP 93
McGill, Loy Barbre 1954- *WhoFI 94*
McGill, Mary Alice R. 1951- *WhoAmP 93*
McGill, Maurice Leon 1936- *WhoAm 94,
WhoFI 94*
McGill, Michael John *WhoMW 93*
McGill, Michele Nicole Johnson 1966-
WhoBlA 94
McGill, Nigel Harry Duncan 1916-
Who 94
McGill, Randall Earl 1952- *WhoMW 93*
Mc Gill, Robert Ernest, III 1931-
WhoAm 94
McGill, Stephen 1912- *Who 94*
McGill, Thomas Conley 1942-
WhoScEn 94
McGill, Thomas Emerson 1930-
WhoAm 94
McGill, Thomas L., Jr. 1946- *WhoBlA 94*
McGill, Warren Everett 1923- *WhoAm 94*
McGill, William James, Jr. 1936-
WhoAm 94
Mc Gillem, Clare Duane 1923-
WhoAm 94
McGilley, Mary Janet 1924- *WhoAm 94*
McGillicuddy, Joan Marie 1952-
WhoScEn 94, WhoWest 94

McGillicuddy, John Francis 1930-
IntWW 93, WhoAm 94, WhoFI 94
McGillicuddy, Lillian Grace 1893-
WhAm 10
McGilligan, Denis Brian 1921- *Who 94*
McGillis, Kelly *IntWW 93, WhoAm 94*
McGillis, Kelly 1957- *IntMPA 94,
WhoHol 92*
McGillivray, Alexander c. 1759-1793
AmRev, WhAmRev
McGillivray, David 1947- *WhoHol 92*
McGillivray, Donald Dean 1928-
WhoAm 94
McGillivray, Robert 1931- *Who 94*
McGilvery, Laurence 1932- *WhoAmA 93*
McGilvray, James William 1938- *Who 94*
Mc Gimpsey, Ronald Alan 1944-
WhoAm 94
Mc Gimsey, Charles Robert, III 1925-
WhoAm 94
McGinley, Donald F. 1920- *WhoAmP 93*
McGinley, Edward Stillman, II 1939-
WhoAm 94, WhoFI 94, WhoWest 94
McGinley, James D. 1948- *WhoAmL 94*
McGinley, John C. *WhoHol 92*
McGinley, John C. 1959- *IntMPA 94*
McGinley, Michael James 1949-
WhoIns 94
McGinley, Nancy Elizabeth 1952-
WhoAmL 94
McGinley, Ronald James 1950-
WhoAm 94
McGinley, Ted 1958- *WhoHol 92*
McGinn, Bernard John 1937- *WhoAm 94*
McGinn, Colin 1950- *IntWW 93*
McGinn, Connie 1947- *WhoMW 93*
McGinn, Max Daniel 1942- *WhoAmL 94*
McGinn, Patricia Ferris 1938-
WhoMW 93
McGinn, Susan Frances 1961-
WhoAm 94, WhoWest 94
McGinn, Walter d1977 *WhoHol 92*
Mc Ginnes, Edgar Allen, Jr. 1926-
WhoAm 94
McGinnes, Paul R. 1946- *WhoAm 94*
McGinness, Joseph M. 1947- *WhoAmP 93*
Mc Ginness, William George, III 1948-
WhoAm 94
McGinnies, Elliott Morse 1921-
WhoAm 94
McGinnis, Alfred Chester, Sr. 1930-
WhoAmP 93
Mc Ginnis, Arthur Joseph 1911-
WhoAm 94
McGinnis, Arthur Joseph, Jr. 1952-
WhoAm 94
McGinnis, Bob 1931- *WhoAmP 93*
McGinnis, Campbell 1948- *WhoAmL 94*
McGinnis, Charles Irving 1928-
WhoAm 94
McGinnis, Christine *WhoAmA 93*
McGinnis, Edgar John 1922- *WhoMW 93*
McGinnis, George 1950- *BasBi*
McGinnis, James Allan 1931-
WhoAmP 93
Mc Ginnis, James Michael 1944-
WhoAm 94, WhoAmP 93
McGinnis, James W. 1940- *WhoBlA 94*
McGinnis, John Oldham 1957-
WhoAm 94
McGinnis, Marcy Ann 1950- *WhoAm 94*
McGinnis, Michael Patrick 1950-
WhoWest 94
McGinnis, Michael Robert 1947-
WhoAmP 93
McGinnis, Robert Campbell 1918-
WhoAm 94
McGinnis, Robert E. 1931- *WhoAm 94*
McGinnis, Robert William 1936-
WhoFI 94, WhoWest 94
McGinnis, Scott 1958- *WhoHol 92*
McGinnis, W. Patrick *WhoFI 94*
Mc Ginniss, Joe 1942- *WhoAm 94,
WrDr 94*
McGinty, A. Edward 1942- *WhoAmL 94*
McGinty, Brian Donald 1937-
WhoAmL 94
McGinty, Doris Evans 1925- *WhoBlA 94*
McGinty, John 1911- *WhoAm 94*
McGinty, John B. 1930- *WhoAm 94*
McGinty, John Joseph 1935- *WhoAm 94*
Mc Ginty, John Milton 1935- *WhoAm 94*
McGinty, Michael Dennis 1942-
WhoAm 94
McGinty, Milton Bradford 1946-
WhoAm 94
McGinty, Thomas Edward 1929-
WhoAm 94
McGirk, Tim(othy Stephen) 1952-
WrDr 94
McGirr, David William John 1954-
WhoAm 94, WhoFI 94
McGirr, Edward McCombie 1916-
Who 94
McGirr, Jackelen Richardson 1941-
WhoFI 94
McGirt, James E(phraim) 1874-1930
BlkWr 2

McGirth, Daniel d1804 *AmRev*
McGiveney, Maura d1990 *WhoHol 92*
McGiveney, Owen d1967 *WhoHol 92*
McGiver, John d1975 *WhoHol 92*
McGivern, Arthur A. 1928- *WhoAm 94,
WhoAmL 94, WhoAmP 93, WhoMW 93*
McGiverin, Donald Scott 1924-
WhoAm 94, WhoFI 94
McGivern, Eugene 1938- *Who 94*
McGivern, Kevin 1954- *WhoFI 94*
McGivern, William P. *EncSF 93*
McGivney, John Joseph 1956-
WhoAmL 94
McGivney, Michael Joseph 1852-1890
DcAmReB 2
McGlade, Thomas Michael 1959-
WhoFI 94
McGlamery, Keith W. 1947- *WhoAmL 94*
Mc Glamery, Marshal Dean 1932-
WhoAm 94
McGlamry, Beverly 1932- *ConAu 43NR*
McGlamry, Max Reginald 1928-
WhoAmL 94
McGlashan, John Reid Curtis 1921-
Who 94
McGlashan, M(axwell) L(en) 1924-
WrDr 94
McGlashan, Maxwell Len 1924- *Who 94*
McGlasson, James Dean 1944-
WhoWest 94
McGlauchlin, Tom 1934- *WhoAm 94,
WhoAmA 93*
McGlaughlin, Daniel W. *WhoIns 94*
McGlaughlin, Thomas Howard 1928-
WhoWest 94
McGlaughlin, William *WhoAm 94*
McGlennon, John Joseph 1949-
WhoAmP 93
McGlinchey, Alex Herbert 1930-
WhoAmL 94
McGlinchey, Dermot Sheehan 1933-
WhoAm 94
McGlinchey, Joseph Dennis 1938-
WhoFI 94
McGlinchy, Judith Marie 1960-
WhoMW 93
McGlinn, Francis Michael 1945-
WhoIns 94
McGlinn, Frank C. P. 1914- *WhoAmP 93*
McGlinn, Frank Cresson Potts 1914-
WhoAm 94
McGlocklin, Jon 1943- *BasBi*
McGlone, John James 1955- *WhoScEn 94*
McGlone, Michael Anthony 1951-
WhoAmL 94
McGloshen, Thomas Hilton, Jr. 1938-
WhoMW 93
McGlothan, Ernest 1937- *WhoBlA 94*
McGlothen, Goree 1915- *WhoBlA 94*
McGlothlin, Donald Allen, Sr. 1926-
WhoAmP 93
McGlothlin, James Dwayne 1951-
WhoMW 93
Mc Glothlin, James Harrison 1910-
WhoAm 94
McGlotten, Robert Miller 1938-
WhoAm 94
McGlover, Stephen Ledell 1950-
WhoBlA 94
McGlynn, Betty Hoag 1914- *WhoWest 94*
McGlynn, Edward 1837-1900 *DcAmReB 2*
McGlynn, Elizabeth Joan 1930-
WhoMW 93
McGlynn, Frank d1951 *WhoHol 92*
McGlynn, Frank, Jr. d1939 *WhoHol 92*
McGlynn, John Francis 1941-
WhoAmL 94
McGlynn, Joseph Leo, Jr. 1925-
WhoAm 94, WhoAmL 94
McGlynn, Michael J. *WhoAmP 93*
McGlynn, Richard Bruce 1938-
WhoAm 94
Mc Glynn, Sean Patrick 1931- *WhoAm 94*
McGlynn, Thomas 1906- *WhoAmA 93N*
McGoldrick, James B. 1895- *WhAm 10*
Mc Goldrick, John Gardiner 1932-
WhoAm 94
McGoldrick, John Lewis 1941-
WhoAm 94, WhoAmL 94
McGolrick, J. Edward, Jr. 1932-
WhoAmL 94
McGonagle, Stephen 1914- *Who 94*
McGonegle, Timothy Joseph 1952-
WhoAmL 94
McGonigal, Edgar R. 1953- *WhoFI 94*
McGonigal, Pearl 1929- *WhoAm 94*
McGonigal, Richard M. 1940- *WhoAm 94*
McGonigle, George Lee 1927- *WhoFI 94*
McGonigle, James Gregory 1945-
WhoAm 94, WhoFI 94
McGonigle, John William 1938-
WhoAm 94
McGonigle, Thomas Patrick 1960-
WhoWest 94
McGoodwin, Jim 1953- *WhoAmP 93*
McGoodwin, Roland C. 1933- *WhoBlA 94*
McGoohan, Patrick 1928- *IntMPA 94,
WhoHol 92*

Mc Goon, Dwight Charles 1925-
WhoAm 94
McGorrill, Bruce Courtney 1931-
WhoAm 94
McGough, Charles E. 1927- *WhoAmA 93*
McGough, Duane Theodore 1932-
WhoAm 94
McGough, John Paul 1935- *WhoAm 94*
McGough, Roger 1937- *Who 94, WrDr 94*
McGough, Stephen C. 1949- *WhoAmA 93*
McGough, Walter Thomas 1919-
WhoAm 94, WhoAmL 94
McGough, Walter Thomas, Jr. 1953-
WhoAm 94, WhoAmL 94
McGourty, Glenn Thomas 1952-
WhoWest 94
McGovern, A. Lane 1924- *WhoAm 94*
McGovern, Ann 1930-
SmATA 17AS [port]
McGovern, Barry *WhoHol 92*
McGovern, Cynthia Ann 1948-
WhoAmP 93
McGovern, Deirdre Joan 1963- *WhoFI 94*
McGovern, Dianne 1948- *WhoAmL 94,
WhoMW 93*
McGovern, Elissa M. 1963- *WhoAmL 94*
McGovern, Elizabeth 1960- *WhoHol 92*
McGovern, Elizabeth 1961- *IntMPA 94*
McGovern, Eugene 1940- *WhoIns 94*
McGovern, Garry John 1946- *WhoMW 93*
McGovern, George 1922- *WhoAmP 93*
McGovern, George Stanley 1922-
IntWW 93, Who 94, WhoAm 94
McGovern, John Hugh 1924- *WhoAm 94,
WhoScEn 94*
McGovern, John James 1932- *WhoIns 94*
McGovern, John Joseph 1920- *WhoAm 94*
McGovern, John Phillip 1921-
WhoAm 94, WrDr 94
Mc Govern, Joseph W. 1909- *WhoAm 94*
McGovern, Maureen 1949- *WhoHol 92*
McGovern, Michael Barbot 1947-
WhoAm 94, WhoAmL 94
McGovern, Michael Patrick 1955-
WhoAmL 94
McGovern, Patricia *WhoAmP 93*
McGovern, Patricia Eileen 1954-
WhoAmP 93
McGovern, Richard Gordon 1926-
WhoAm 94
McGovern, Ricky James 1948-
WhoWest 94
McGovern, Robert *DrAPF 93*
McGovern, Robert F. 1933- *WhoAmA 93*
McGovern, Terence 1942- *WhoHol 92*
McGovern, Tim *WhoAm 94*
Mc Govern, Walter T. 1922- *WhoAm 94,
WhoAmL 94, WhoWest 94*
McGowan, Baron 1938- *Who 94*
McGowan, Alan Patrick 1928- *Who 94*
McGowan, Bruce Henry 1924- *Who 94*
McGowan, Charles *WhoHol 92*
McGowan, David Allen 1952-
WhoMW 93
McGowan, Diane Darby 1948-
WhoMW 93
McGowan, Edgar Leon 1920-
WhoAmP 93
McGowan, Elsie Henderson 1947-
WhoBlA 94
McGowan, George Vincent 1928-
WhoAm 94, WhoScEn 94
McGowan, Harold 1909- *WhoAm 94*
McGowan, Hugh Barry 1944- *WhoMW 93*
McGowan, Ian Duncan 1945- *Who 94*
McGowan, Inez *EncSF 93*
McGowan, J. P. d1952 *WhoHol 92*
McGowan, Jack d1977 *WhoHol 92*
McGowan, James *DrAPF 93, WhoAm 94*
Mc Gowan, James Atkinson 1914-
WhoAm 94
McGowan, Jeffrey Owen 1962-
WhoWest 94
McGowan, John 1944- *Who 94*
McGowan, John Edward, Jr. 1942-
WhoAm 94
McGowan, John Frank 1934-
WhoWest 94
McGowan, John Joseph 1950-
WhoScEn 94
McGowan, John P. 1953- *WrDr 94*
McGowan, Joseph Anthony, Jr. 1931-
WhoAm 94
McGowan, Joseph Augustine, III 1942-
WhoFI 94
McGowan, Margaret Mary 1931- *Who 94*
McGowan, Michael 1940- *Who 94*
McGowan, Michael B. 1950- *WhoFI 94*
McGowan, Michael Benedict 1941-
WhoAm 94
McGowan, Oliver d1971 *WhoHol 92*
McGowan, Patrick D. 1951- *WhoAmP 93*
McGowan, Patrick Francis 1940-
WhoAm 94, WhoAmP 93
McGowan, Patrick K. 1956- *WhoAmP 93*
McGowan, Sherry A. 1946- *WhoAmP 93*
McGowan, Thomas C. 1950- *WhoAmL 94*

McGowan, Thomas Randolph 1926-
WhoBlA 94
McGowan, William 1927-1992
AnObit 1992
McGowan, William Charles 1955-
WhoAmP 93
Mc Gowan, William George 1927-1992
WhAm 10
McGowan, William Kevin 1961-
WhoMW 93
McGowen, Courtenay C. 1945-
WhoAmP 93
McGowen, Ernest B., Sr. *WhoAmP 93*
McGowin, Ed 1938- *WhoAmA 94*
Mc Gowin, William Edward 1938-
WhoAm 94
McGown, Jill 1947- *WrDr 94*
McGown, John, Jr. 1949- *WhoAmL 94*
McGown, Richard Leon 1957-
WhoMW 93
McGrady, Eddie James 1928- *WhoBlA 94*
McGrady, Edward Kevin 1935- *Who 94*
McGrail, Jeane Kathryn 1947-
WhoAmA 93
McGrail, Michael Joseph 1954-
WhoMW 93
McGrail, Sean Francis 1928- *Who 94*
McGrail, Susan King 1952- *WhoMW 93*
McGrail, Walter d1970 *WhoHol 92*
McGranary, Al d1971 *WhoHol 92*
McGrane, Bernard 1947- *WrDr 94*
McGrane, Miles A., III 1947-
WhoAmL 94
McGrath, Alister E(dgar) 1953- *WrDr 94*
McGrath, Barry 1932- *WhoAmL 94*
McGrath, Brian Henry 1925- *Who 94*
McGrath, Campbell *DrAPF 93*
McGrath, Christopher Thomas 1958-
WhoAmL 94
McGrath, Clarice Hobgood 1951-
WhoBlA 94
McGrath, David Peter 1949- *WhoAmP 93*
McGrath, Dennis Britton 1937-
WhoAm 94
McGrath, Don John 1948- *WhoAm 94*
McGrath, Douglas *WhoHol 92*
McGrath, Earl James d1993
NewYTBS 93 [port]
McGrath, Earl James 1902-1993
ConAu 140, CurBio 93N
McGrath, Edward A. 1930- *WhoMW 93*
McGrath, Edward Joseph 1935-
WhoAm 94
McGrath, Eugene R. 1942- *WhoAm 94,
WhoFI 94*
Mc Grath, Francis Joseph 1908-
WhoAm 94
McGrath, Frank d1967 *WhoHol 92*
McGrath, Frank Joseph 1900-1989
WhAm 10
McGrath, Greg 1951- *WhoAmP 93*
McGrath, J. Brian 1942- *WhoAm 94*
McGrath, James A. 1932- *IntWW 93*
McGrath, James Aloysius 1932-
WhoAm 94
McGrath, James Charles, III 1942-
WhoAm 94
McGrath, James Thomas 1942-
WhoAm 94
McGrath, John 1935- *BlmGEL*
McGrath, John (Peter) 1935- *ConDr 93,
IntDcT 2, WrDr 94*
McGrath, John Christie 1949- *Who 94*
McGrath, John F. 1954- *WhoIns 94*
McGrath, John Francis 1925- *WhoAm 94*
McGrath, John Joseph 1949- *WhoMW 93*
McGrath, John Peter 1935- *Who 94*
McGrath, Joseph Edward 1927-
WhoAm 94
McGrath, Juliet Kaufmann *DrAPF 93*
McGrath, Kathryn Bradley 1944-
WhoAm 94, WhoFI 94
McGrath, Kenneth James 1953-
WhoScEn 94
McGrath, Kristina *DrAPF 93*
McGrath, Larry d1960 *WhoHol 92*
Mc Grath, Lee Parr *WhoAm 94*
McGrath, Lee Upton 1956- *WhoMW 93*
McGrath, Leonard Joseph 1945-
WhoAmP 93
McGrath, Marcos Gregorio 1924-
IntWW 93
McGrath, Mary F. 1954- *WhoFI 94*
McGrath, Michael d1976 *WhoHol 92*
McGrath, Michael Alan 1942-
*WhoAm 94, WhoAmP 93, WhoFI 94,
WhoMW 93*
McGrath, Michael William 1953-
WhoWest 94
McGrath, Patrick 1950- *WrDr 94*
McGrath, Patrick Gerard 1916- *Who 94*
McGrath, Patrick Joseph 1945-
WhoWest 94
McGrath, Patrick Michael 1952-
WhoFI 94
McGrath, Paul d1978 *WhoHol 92*
McGrath, Raymond J. 1942- *WhoAmP 93*
McGrath, Richard Paul 1929- *WhoAm 94*

McGrath, Richard William 1943-
WhoScEn 94
McGrath, Thomas *DrAPF 93*
McGrath, Thomas d1937 *WhoHol 92*
McGrath, Thomas Augustine 1919-1992
WhAm 10
McGrath, Thomas F., III 1947-
WhoIns 94
McGrath, Thomas J. 1932- *IntMPA 94,
WhoAm 94, WhoAmL 94*
McGrath, Tom 1940- *ConDr 93, WrDr 94*
McGrath, Viv 1916-1978 *BuCMET*
McGrath, William Joseph 1943-
WhoAm 94, WhoAmL 94
McGrath, William Loughney 1911-1988
WhAm 10
McGrath, William Lynn 1894- *WhAm 10*
Mc Grath, William Restore 1922-
WhoAm 94
McGrattan, Mary K. *WhoAmP 93*
McGraw, Charles d1980 *WhoHol 92*
Mc Graw, Darrell Vivian, Jr. 1936-
WhoAm 94, WhoAmL 94, WhoAmP 93
McGraw, Donald Jesse 1943- *WhoAm 94*
McGraw, Eloise Jarvis 1915- *TwCYAW,
WrDr 94*
McGraw, Harold Whittlesey, Jr. 1918-
WhoAm 94, WhoFI 94
McGraw, Harold Whittlesey, III 1948-
WhoFI 94
McGraw, Jack Wilson 1943- *WhoAm 94*
McGraw, James A. 1950- *WhoAmL 94*
McGraw, James L. 1917- *WhoAm 94*
McGraw, James Michael 1945-
WhoAm 94
McGraw, John J. d1934 *WhoHol 92*
McGraw, John O. 1945- *WhoFI 94*
McGraw, Katherine Annette 1943-
WhoScEn 94
McGraw, Lavinia Morgan 1924-
WhoFI 94
McGraw, Leslie G. *WhoFI 94*
McGraw, Mac 1952- *WhoAmP 93*
McGraw, Marcus P. 1942- *WhoAmL 94*
McGraw, Patrick John 1956- *WhoAmL 94*
McGraw, Robert Pierce 1954- *WhoAm 94*
McGraw, Vincent DePaul 1930-
WhoMW 93
McGraw, Walter John d1978 *WhoHol 92*
McGraw, Warren Randolph 1939-
WhoAmP 93
McGready, James 1758?-1817 *DcAmReB 2*
McGreal, Joseph A., Jr. 1935- *WhoAm 94*
McGreevey, James E. 1957- *WhoAmP 93*
McGreevey, Mark F. *WhoIns 94*
McGreevey, Michael *WhoHol 92*
McGreevy, Martin Kenneth 1931-
WhoIns 94
McGreevy, Mary 1935- *WhoScEn 94*
McGreevy, Terrence Gerard 1932-
WhoAm 94
McGreevy, William Joseph 1940-
WhoAmP 93
McGregor *Who 94*
McGregor, Alistair Gerald Crichton
1937- *Who 94*
McGregor, Angela Punch *WhoHol 92*
McGregor, Angus 1926- *Who 94*
McGregor, Cameron David 1953-
WhoFI 94
McGregor, Charles *WhoHol 92*
McGregor, Charles 1927- *IntMPA 94*
McGregor, Constance Leonard
WhoAmP 93
Mc Gregor, Donald Thornton 1924-
WhoAm 94
McGregor, Edna M. *WhoBlA 94*
McGregor, Frank Bobbitt, Jr. 1952-
WhoAmL 94
McGregor, Gordon Peter 1932- *Who 94*
McGregor, Gregor Ian 1944- *WhoAmL 94*
McGregor, Harmon d1948 *WhoHol 92*
McGregor, Harvey 1926- *IntWW 93,
Who 94*
McGregor, Ian (Alexander) 1922- *Who 94*
McGregor, Ian Alexander 1921- *Who 94*
McGregor, Ian Alexander 1922-
IntWW 93
McGregor, Iona 1929- *WrDr 94*
McGregor, Jack Edwin 1934- *WhoAm 94*
McGregor, James Stalker 1927- *Who 94*
McGregor, John d1928 *WhoHol 92*
McGregor, Malcolm d1945 *WhoHol 92*
Mc Gregor, Malcolm Francis 1910-1989
WhAm 10, WrDr 94N
McGregor, Martin Luther, Jr. 1940-
WhoAmL 94
Mc Gregor, Maurice 1920- *WhoAm 94*
McGregor, Michael H. 1936- *WhoAm 94,
WhoFI 94*
McGregor, Nancy Rohwer 1930-
WhoAmP 93
McGregor, Oran B. 1925- *WhoBlA 94*
McGregor, Peter 1926- *Who 94*
McGregor, Quentin John 1946-
WhoWest 94
McGregor, Scott Lee 1956- *WhoWest 94*

McGregor, Theodore Anthony 1944-
WhoFI 94, WhoScEn 94
McGregor, Walter 1937- *WhoAm 94,
WhoFI 94, WhoScEn 94*
McGregor Of Durris, Baron 1921-
IntWW 93, Who 94
McGrew, Bruce Elwin 1937- *WhoAmA 93*
McGrew, Elwin 1934- *WhoAmP 93*
McGrew, Melinda Louise 1960-
WhoWest 94
McGrew, R. Brownell 1916- *WhoAmA 93*
McGrew, Stephen Paul 1945-
WhoScEn 94
McGrew, Thomas James 1942-
WhoAm 94, WhoAmL 94
McGrier, Jerry, Sr. 1955- *WhoBlA 94*
McGriff, Deborah *WhoAm 94,
WhoMW 93*
McGriff, Deborah M. 1949- *WhoBlA 94*
McGriff, Fred 1963- *WhoAm 94*
McGriff, Frederick Stanley 1963-
WhoBlA 94
McGrigor, Charles Edward 1922- *Who 94*
Mc Groddy, James Cleary 1937-
WhoFI 94, WhoScEn 94
McGrogan, Michael Patrick 1947-
WhoWest 94
McGrory, John F. 1929- *WhoAmL 94*
McGrory, Joseph Bennett 1934-
WhoScEn 94
McGrory, Larry James 1957- *WhoAmL 94*
McGrory, Mary Kathleen 1933-
WhoAm 94
McGrouther, (Duncan) Angus 1946-
Who 94
McGruder, Charles E. 1925- *WhoBlA 94*
McGruder, Elaine 1949- *WhoAmP 93*
McGruder, James Patrick 1926-
WhoAmL 94, WhoWest 94
McGruder, Robert *WhoMW 93*
Mc Gruder, Stephen Jones 1943-
WhoAm 94
McGuane, Frank L., Jr. 1939-
WhoAmL 94
McGuane, Thomas *DrAPF 93*
McGuane, Thomas 1939- *WrDr 94*
McGuane, Thomas Fitzgerald 1950-
WhoAmL 94
Mc Guane, Thomas Francis, III 1939-
WhoAm 94, WhoWest 94
McGuane, Tom *WhoHol 92*
McGuckian, John Brendan 1939- *Who 94*
McGuckian, Medbh 1950- *BlmGWL*
McGuckian, Medbh (McCaughan) 1950-
WrDr 94
Mc Guckin, James Frederick 1930-
WhoAm 94
McGuckin, John H., Jr. 1946-
WhoAmL 94
McGuffee, George Orville 1908-
WhoAmP 93
McGuffey, Carroll Wade, Sr. 1922-
WhoAm 94
McGuffey, Kenneth Duane 1932-
WhoAmP 93
McGuffin, Dorothy Brown 1944-
WhoBlA 94
McGuffin, Mark 1947- *WrDr 94*
McGuffin, Peter 1949- *Who 94*
McGuigan, F. J(oseph) 1924- *WrDr 94*
Mc Guigan, Frank Joseph 1924-
WhoAm 94, WhoWest 94
Mc Guigan, James Edward 1931-
WhoAm 94
McGuigan, John Alexander 1931-
WhoFI 94
McGuigan, John V. 1949- *WhoAm 94,
WhoMW 93*
McGuigan, Thomas J. 1942- *WhoAm 94*
McGuigan Burns, Simon Hugh *Who 94*
McGuinn, Joe d1971 *WhoHol 92*
Mc Guinn, Martin Gregory 1942-
WhoAm 94, WhoAmL 94
McGuinness, Barbara Sue 1947-
WhoFI 94, WhoMW 93
McGuinness, Bradley Michael 1961-
WhoFI 94
McGuinness, Brendan Peter 1931-
Who 94
McGuinness, Frank 1953- *ConDr 93,
IntWW 93*
Mc Guinness, Frank Joseph 1928-
WhoAm 94
McGuinness, James Joseph *Who 94*
McGuinness, Joseph G. 1958-
WhoAmL 94
McGuinness, Seanne William 1955-
WhoFI 94
McGuire, Al 1928- *BasBi*
Mc Guire, Alfred James 1931- *WhoAm 94*
McGuire, Anthony Bartholomew 1945-
WhoMW 93
McGuire, Benjamin d1925 *WhoHol 92*
McGuire, Beryl Edward 1935-
WhoAm 94, WhoMW 93
McGuire, Biff 1926- *WhoHol 92*
McGuire, Blanche 1950- *WhoAm 94*
McGuire, Brian Lyle 1959- *WhoFI 94*

McGuire, Brian Robert 1958- *WhoFI 94*
McGuire, Carol Susann 1948-
WhoMW 93
McGuire, Charles Carroll, Jr. 1932-
WhoAm 94
McGuire, Chester C., Jr. 1936-
WhoBlA 94
McGuire, Cyril A. 1926- *WhoBlA 94*
McGuire, David Ottis 1942- *WhoAmP 93*
McGuire, Dick 1926- *BasBi*
McGuire, Don 1919- *IntMPA 94*
McGuire, Don Loye 1934- *WhoAmP 93*
McGuire, Dorothy 1918- *WhoHol 92*
McGuire, Dorothy 1919- *IntMPA 94*
Mc Guire, Dorothy Hackett 1916-
WhoAm 94
McGuire, E. James 1914- *WhoAmL 94*
McGuire, Edward David, Jr. 1948-
WhoAmL 94
McGuire, Eugene Guenard 1945-
WhoAmL 94
McGuire, Frank 1918- *BasBi*
McGuire, Frederick Clarence d1942
WhoHol 92
McGuire, Gary Herbert 1956- *WhoFI 94*
McGuire, Gerald 1918- *Who 94*
McGuire, Harp d1966 *WhoHol 92*
McGuire, Harvey Paul 1939- *WhoAmP 93*
McGuire, Ida d1987 *WhoHol 92*
McGuire, James Charles 1917-
WhoAm 94, WhoWest 94
McGuire, James Horton 1942-
WhoScEn 94
McGuire, Jean Mitchell 1931- *WhoBlA 94*
McGuire, Joanne *WhoFI 94*
McGuire, John d1980 *WhoHol 92*
McGuire, John Albert 1950- *WhoScEn 94*
McGuire, John C. *WhoAmP 93*
McGuire, John Francis, Jr. 1945-
WhoAmL 94
McGuire, John J(oseph) 1917-1981
EncSF 93
McGuire, John Lawrence 1942-
WhoAm 94, WhoScEn 94
McGuire, John Max, Jr. 1949-
WhoMW 93
McGuire, John Murray 1929- *WhoAm 94*
McGuire, John Patrick 1961- *WhoMW 93*
McGuire, Joseph Edward 1926-
WhoAmL 94
McGuire, Joseph Francis 1958- *WhoFI 94*
McGuire, Joseph James 1919-
WhoMW 93
McGuire, Joseph Smith 1931-
WhoWest 94
Mc Guire, Joseph William 1925-
WhoAm 94, WrDr 94
McGuire, Judith Marie 1944-
WhoAmP 93
McGuire, Julie Elizabeth 1958-
WhoAmL 94
McGuire, Kathryn d1978 *WhoHol 92*
McGuire, Kevin Robert 1957-
WhoWest 94
McGuire, Kim *WhoHol 92*
McGuire, Lisa Elizabeth 1955-
WhoMW 93
McGuire, Maeve 1937- *WhoHol 92*
McGuire, Marcy 1926- *WhoHol 92*
McGuire, Mark Alan 1968- *WhoMW 93*
McGuire, Mark William 1962-
WhoScEn 94
McGuire, Mary Jo 1956- *WhoAmP 93*
McGuire, Matthew Francis 1960-
WhoFI 94
McGuire, Maureen 1941- *WhoAmA 93*
McGuire, Maureen A. 1941- *WhoAm 94*
McGuire, Michael *DrAPF 93, WhoHol 92*
McGuire, Michael Francis 1946-
WhoAm 94
Mc Guire, Michael John 1947-
WhoWest 94
McGuire, Michael Thomas Francis 1926-
Who 94
McGuire, Michael William 1960-
WhoWest 94
McGuire, Mickey *WhoHol 92*
McGuire, Patricia A. 1952- *WhoAm 94,
WhoAmL 94*
McGuire, Patrick (Llewellyn) 1949-
EncSF 93
McGuire, Paul M., Jr. 1935- *WhoBlA 94*
McGuire, Raymond J. *WhoBlA 94*
McGuire, Raymond L. *WhoFI 94*
McGuire, Richard A. 1946- *WhoIns 94*
McGuire, Richard Allen 1946- *WhoFI 94*
McGuire, Robert Joseph 1933-
WhoAmL 94
McGuire, Roger Alan 1943- *WhoAm 94*
McGuire, Rosalie E. *WhoBlA 94*
McGuire, Stephanie Karl 1963-
WhoAmL 94
McGuire, Stephen A. 1949- *WhoFI 94*
McGuire, Timothy James 1949-
WhoAm 94, WhoMW 93

McGuire, Timothy William 1938-
WhoAm 94, WhoFI 94
McGuire, Tom d1954 *WhoHol 92*
McGuire, Tucker d1988 *WhoHol 92*
McGuire, William Benedict 1929-
WhoAmL 94
McGuire, William Dennis 1943-
WhoAm 94
Mc Guire, William James 1925-
WhoAm 94
Mc Guire, William Lawrence 1926-1992
WhAm 10
Mc Guire, William W. 1948- *WhoAm 94,
WhoFI 94*
McGuirk, Charles J. d1943 *WhoHol 92*
McGuirk, Harriet d1975 *WhoHol 92*
McGuirk, James R. 1946- *WhoAmL 94*
McGuirk, John F., Sr. *WhoAmP 93*
McGuirk, Paul A. 1939- *WhoAmP 93*
McGuirk, Ronald Charles 1938-
WhoAm 94, WhoFI 94
McGuirk, Terrence 1925- *WhoAm 94*
McGuirl, Marlene Dana Callis 1938-
WhoAmL 94
McGuirl, Robert Joseph 1952-
WhoAmL 94
McGuirt, Milford W. 1956- *WhoBlA 94*
Mc Guirt, Wayne Robert 1943-
WhoAm 94
McGulpin, Elizabeth Jane 1932-
WhoWest 94
McGunigle, Brian Edward 1947-
WhoAm 94
McGunnigle, George Francis, Jr. 1942-
WhoAmL 94
McGurk, Colin Thomas 1922- *Who 94*
McGurk, Harry 1936- *Who 94*
Mc Gurk, James Henry 1936- *WhoFI 94*
McGurk, Laureen Ellen 1961-
WhoAmL 94
McGurk, Robert d1959 *WhoHol 92*
McGurk, Slater *ConAu 140, SmATA 75*
McGurk-Kremkow, Heather 1966-
WhoMW 93
Mc Gurn, Barrett 1914- *WhoAm 94,
WrDr 94*
McGurn, George William 1914-
WhoAmL 94, WhoMW 93
McGurn, James (Edward) 1953- *WrDr 94*
McGurn, William Barrett, III 1943-
WhoAm 94
McGwire, Mark 1963- *WhoAm 94,
WhoWest 94*
McHale, Brian K. *WhoAmP 93*
McHale, Edward Robertson 1921-
WhoAm 94
McHale, James d1970 *WhoHol 92*
McHale, Keith Michael 1928- *Who 94*
McHale, Kevin 1957- *BasBi*
McHale, Kevin Edward 1957- *WhoAm 94*
McHale, Magda Cordell 1921-
WhoScEn 94
McHale, Maureen Bernadette Kenny
1955- *WhoFI 94*
McHale, Paul 1950- *CngDr 93,
WhoAm 94, WhoAmP 93*
McHale, Robert Michael 1932-
WhoAmL 94
McHale, Sheila A. 1940- *WhoAmP 93*
McHale, Thomas Anthony 1914-
WhoAm 94
McHale, Vincent Edward 1939-
WhoAm 94
McHam, Sarah Blake Wilk *WhoAmA 93*
M C Hammer 1962- *AfrAmAl 6*
McHardy, Louis William 1930-
WhoAm 94, WhoWest 94
McHardy, William Duff 1911-
IntWW 93, Who 94
McHarg, Ian Lennox 1920- *IntWW 93,
WhoAm 94*
McHarg, Robert Elwood 1923- *WhoFI 94*
Mc Hargue, Carl Jack 1926- *WhoScEn 94*
McHargue, Daniel Stephen, II 1945-
WhoAmP 93
McHargue, Georgess 1941-
SmATA 77 [port]
McHargue, Wayne Orval 1937- *WhoFI 94*
McHarris, William Charles 1937-
WhoAm 94
McHattie, Stephen *IntMPA 94,
WhoHol 92*
McHenry, Barnabas 1929- *WhoAm 94*
McHenry, Betty Lucille 1935- *WhoFI 94*
Mc Henry, Dean Eugene 1910-
WhoAm 94
McHenry, Donald F. 1936- *IntWW 93,
Who 94, WhoAm 94, WhoBlA 94*
McHenry, Douglas *WhoBlA 94*
McHenry, Douglas Bruce 1932-
WhoScEn 94
McHenry, Edward A. 1940- *WhoAmP 93*
McHenry, Emmit J. *WhoBlA 94*
McHenry, Gary Dwain 1946-
WhoAmL 94
McHenry, Henry Malcolm 1944-
WhoAm 94
McHenry, James 1753-1816 *WhAmRev*

McHenry, James O'Neal 1940-
WhoBlA 94
McHenry, Keith Welles, Jr. 1928-
WhoAm 94, WhoScEn 94
McHenry, Leemon B. 1956- *ConAu 140*
Mc Henry, Martin Christopher 1932-
WhoMW 93, WhoScEn 94
McHenry, Mary Williamson 1933-
WhoBlA 94
McHenry, Patricia Rose 1950-
WhoWest 94
Mc Henry, Powell 1926- *WhoAm 94,
WhoFI 94*
McHenry, Robert Dale 1945- *WhoAm 94*
McHugh, Adeliza Sorenson 1912-
WhoAmA 93
McHugh, Arona *DrAPF 93*
McHugh, Catherine d1954 *WhoHol 92*
McHugh, Charles d1931 *WhoHol 92*
McHugh, Connie 1938- *WhoAmP 93*
McHugh, Earl Stephen 1936-
WhoMW 93, WhoScEn 94
McHugh, Edward Francis, Jr. 1932-
WhoAm 94, WhoAmL 94
McHugh, Frank d1981 *WhoHol 92*
McHugh, Glenn 1894- *WhAm 10*
McHugh, Grace d1914 *WhoHol 92*
McHugh, H. Bart, III d1993 *NewYTBS 93*
McHugh, Heather *DrAPF 93*
McHugh, Heather 1948- *WrDr 94*
McHugh, Helen Frances 1931-
WhoScEn 94
McHugh, Jack d1983 *WhoHol 92*
McHugh, James 1915- *IntMPA 94*
McHugh, James 1930- *Who 94*
McHugh, James Francis d1968
WhoAmA 93N
McHugh, James Joseph 1930-
WhoAm 94, WhoWest 94
McHugh, James Lenahan, Jr. 1937-
WhoAm 94, WhoAmL 94
McHugh, James T. 1932- *WhoAm 94*
Mchugh, Jeannette 1934- *WhoWomW 91*
McHugh, Jimmy d1969 *WhoHol 92*
McHugh, John *WhoAm 94, WhoAmP 93,
WhoMW 93*
McHugh, John (Francis) 1927- *WrDr 94*
McHugh, John James 1931- *WhoAm 94*
Mc Hugh, John Laurence 1911-
WhoAm 94
McHugh, John M. 1948- *CngDr 93,
WhoAmP 93*
McHugh, John Michael 1948- *WhoAm 94*
McHugh, Kevin Paul 1948- *WhoAmL 94*
McHugh, Kitty d1954 *WhoHol 92*
McHugh, M. Colleen 1946- *WhoAmL 94*
Mc Hugh, Margaret Ann Gloe 1920-
WhoWest 94
McHugh, Mark James 1962- *WhoFI 94*
McHugh, Matt d1971 *WhoHol 92*
McHugh, Matthew Francis 1938-
WhoAmP 93
Mc Hugh, Paul R. 1931- *WhoAm 94,
WhoScEn 94*
Mc Hugh, Richard B. 1923- *WhoAm 94*
McHugh, Richard Walker 1952-
WhoAmL 94
Mc Hugh, Robert Clayton 1928-
WhoFI 94
McHugh, Simon Francis, Jr. 1938-
WhoAm 94
McHugh, Terence Patrick 1941-
WhoMW 93
McHugh, Thomas E. 1936- *WhoAmP 93*
McHugh, Thomas Edward 1936-
WhoAm 94, WhoAmL 94
McHugh, Tom Edward, II 1943-
WhoAmP 93
McHugh, Toni Walter 1946- *WhoMW 93*
McHugh, Vincent 1904-1983 *EncSF 93*
McHugh, William Dennis 1929-
WhoAm 94, WhoScEn 94
McHughes, Brian Andrew 1963-
WhoMW 93
McHughes, Larry Lynn 1941-
WhoMW 93
Mc Ilhenny, James Harrison 1927-
WhoAm 94, WhoAmL 94, WhoFI 94
McIlheran, Mark Lane 1961-
WhoScEn 94
McIllwain, William d1933 *WhoHol 92*
McIlraith, Frank *EncSF 93*
McIlrath, Donald Christner 1929-
WhoAm 94
McIlroy, Carol J. 1924- *WhoAmA 93*
McIlroy, Gary Thomas 1940-
WhoMW 93
McIlroy, Terry A. 1945- *WhoAmL 94*
McIlvain, Bill D. 1932- *WhoAmP 93*
McIlvain, Douglas Lee 1923- *WhoAmA 93*
McIlvain, Frances H. 1925- *WhoAmA 93*
McIlvain, Helen Graeme 1942-
WhoMW 93
McIlvain, Jess Hall 1933- *WhoScEn 94*
McIlvaine, Charles Pettit 1799-1873
DcAmReB 2
McIlvaine, Joseph Peter 1948- *WhoAm 94*

McIlvaine, Stephen Brownlee 1953-
WhoAmL 94
McIlvane, Edward James 1947-
WhoAm 94, WhoAmA 93
McIlvanney, William 1936- *WrDr 94*
McIlveen, Edward E. 1911- *WhoAm 94*
Mc Ilveen, Walter 1927- *WhoFI 94,
WhoScEn 94*
McIlvenna, John Antony 1919- *Who 94*
McIlvenna, Robert James 1950-
WhoFI 94
McIlwain, Albert Hood 1936-1989
WhoBlA 94N
McIlwain, Alexander Edward 1933-
Who 94
McIlwain, Carl Edwin 1931- *WhoAm 94*
McIlwain, Clara Evans 1919- *WhoFI 94*
McIlwain, Henry d1992 *IntWW 93N*
McIlwain, Henry 1912- *WrDr 94N*
McIlwain, Jeaneen J. 1960- *WhoBlA 94*
McIlwain, Nadine Williams 1943-
WhoBlA 94
McIlwain, Thomas David 1940-
WhoAm 94
McIlwain, William Clarence, Jr. 1926-
WhoIns 94
Mc Ilwain, William Franklin 1925-
WhoAm 94
McIlwain, William John 1953-
WhoAmL 94
McIlwaine, Deborah P. 1923-
WhoAmP 93
McIlwraith, Arthur Renwick 1914-
Who 94
McIlwraith, David *WhoHol 92*
McIlwraith, Jean Newton 1859-1938
BlmGWL
Mc Indoe, Darrell Winfred 1930-
WhoAm 94
McIndoe, William Ian 1929- *Who 94*
McIndoo, Walter Rolla 1934- *WhoMW 93*
McInerney, Bernie 1936- *WhoHol 92*
McInerney, Brian *DrAPF 93*
McInerney, Gary John 1948- *WhoAmP 93*
McInerney, Gene Joseph 1930-
WhoAmA 93
McInerney, James Eugene, Jr. 1930-
WhoAm 94
McInerney, Jay 1955- *WhoAm 94,
WrDr 94*
McInerney, John Gerard 1959-
WhoWest 94
McInerney, John Peter 1939- *Who 94*
McInerney, Joseph Aloysius 1939-
WhoAm 94
McInerney, Joseph John 1932-
WhoAm 94
McInerny, Ralph (Matthew) 1929-
WrDr 94
McInerny, Ralph Matthew 1929-
WhoAm 94, WhoMW 93
McIngvale, Wesley A. 1933- *WhoAmP 93*
Mc Ininch, Ralph Aubrey 1912-
WhoAm 94
McInnerny, Lizzy *WhoHol 92*
McInnerny, Tim *WhoHol 92*
McInnes, Graham (Campbell) 1912-1970
EncSF 93
McInnes, Harold A. 1927- *WhoAm 94,
WhoFI 94*
McInnes, John Colin 1938- *Who 94*
McInnes, John Duncan 1934- *WhoFI 94*
Mc Innes, Robert Malcolm 1930-
WhoAm 94
McInnes, Stewart D. 1937- *IntWW 93*
Mc Innes, William Charles 1923-
WhoAm 94
McInnis, David Fairley 1934-
WhoAmP 93
McInnis, Gerard Andrew 1964-
WhoAm 94
McInnis, Kenneth John 1948-
WhoAmP 93
McInnis, Mack *WhoAmP 93*
McInnis, Scott *CngDr 93*
McInnis, Scott Steve 1953- *WhoAm 94,
WhoAmP 93, WhoWest 94*
McInnis, Susan Muse 1955- *WhoFI 94,
WhoWest 94*
McInnis, William Donald 1932-
WhoAmP 93
McIntee, Dixie J. 1913- *WhoAmP 93*
McIntee, Gilbert George 1943-
WhoScEn 94
McIntire, C(arl) T(homas) 1939- *WrDr 94*
McIntire, Frank E. *WhoAmP 93*
McIntire, Jerald Gene 1938- *WhoAm 94*
McIntire, John d1991 *WhoHol 92*
McIntire, Lani d1951 *WhoHol 92*
McIntire, Larry Vern 1943- *WhoAm 94*
McIntire, Matilda Stewart 1920-
WhoScEn 94
Mc Intire, Richard Lee 1934- *WhoAm 94*
McIntire, Robert Allen 1947- *WhoAm 94,
WhoAmL 94*
McIntire, Tim d1986 *WhoHol 92*
McIntosh *Who 94*
McIntosh, Alice T. 1933- *WhoBlA 94*

McIntosh, Angus 1914- *Who 94*
McIntosh, Anne Caroline Ballingall 1954-
Who 94, WhoWomW 91
McIntosh, Burr d1942 *WhoHol 92*
McIntosh, Calvin Eugene 1926-
WhoMW 93
McIntosh, Christopher (Angus) 1943-
WrDr 94
McIntosh, Daniel G. 1944- *WhoAmL 94*
McIntosh, Dave *ConAu 142*
McIntosh, David Norman 1921-
ConAu 142
McIntosh, Don Leslie 1959- *WhoScEn 94*
McIntosh, Donald Harry 1919-
WhoAm 94, WhoScEn 94
McIntosh, Donald Waldron 1927-
WhoScEn 94
McIntosh, Douglas Lloyd 1947-
WhoWest 94
McIntosh, Frankie L. 1949- *WhoBlA 94*
McIntosh, Gary L. 1956- *WhoMW 93*
McIntosh, Genista Mary 1946-
IntWW 93, Who 94
McIntosh, Gregory Cecil 1949-
WhoScEn 94
McIntosh, Gregory Stephen 1946-
WhoAmA 93
McIntosh, Harold 1916-1986
WhoAmA 93N
McIntosh, Helen Horton *WhoScEn 94*
McIntosh, Hugh 1914- *Who 94*
McIntosh, Hugh Maurice 1945-
WhoAmL 94
McIntosh, Ian (Stewart) 1919- *Who 94*
McIntosh, J.T. 1925- *EncSF 93, WrDr 94*
McIntosh, James Albert 1933-
WhoAmL 94
McIntosh, James E. 1942- *WhoBlA 94*
Mc Intosh, James Eugene, Jr. 1938-
WhoAm 94
McIntosh, Joan *DrAPF 93*
McIntosh, John 1755-1826 *AmRev,
WhAmRev*
Mc Intosh, John Richard 1939-
WhoAm 94
McIntosh, Lachlan 1725- *AmRev*
McIntosh, Lachlan 1725-1806
WhAmRev [port]
McIntosh, Lorne William 1945-
WhoAm 94
McIntosh, Maggie *WhoAmP 93*
McIntosh, Malcolm Kenneth 1945-
IntWW 93, Who 94
McIntosh, Marc *WhoBlA 94*
McIntosh, Melinda Jane Frances *Who 94*
McIntosh, Naomi Ellen Sargant *Who 94*
McIntosh, Neil Scott Wishart 1947-
Who 94
McIntosh, Neil William David 1940-
Who 94
McIntosh, Peter C(hisholm) 1915-
WrDr 94
McIntosh, Rhodina Covington 1947-
WhoAm 94, WhoAmL 94, WhoBlA 94
McIntosh, Robert Alan 1943- *WhoAm 94*
McIntosh, Robert Edward, Jr. 1940-
WhoAm 94
McIntosh, Robert Gibbon 1962-
WhoAmL 94
McIntosh, Ronald (Robert Duncan)
1919- *Who 94*
McIntosh, Sandy *DrAPF 93*
McIntosh, Simeon Charles 1944-
WhoBlA 94
McIntosh, Walter Cordell 1927-
WhoBlA 94
McIntosh, William E., Jr. 1945-
WhoBlA 94
McIntosh, William M. 1918- *WhoAmP 93*
McIntosh of Haringey, Baron 1933-
Who 94
McIntosh Slaughter, Louise 1929-
WhoWomW 91
Mc Inturf, Faith Mary 1917- *WhoMW 93*
McInturff, Don A. 1939- *WhoIns 94*
McInturff, Floyd M. 1923- *WhoMW 93*
McInturff, Kim 1948- *WhoWest 94*
McIntyre, Adelbert 1929- *WhoWest 94*
McIntyre, Alasdair Duncan 1926- *Who 94*
McIntyre, Alister *Who 94*
McIntyre, (Meredith) Alister 1932-
Who 94
McIntyre, Bruce Herbert 1930-
WhoAm 94
McIntyre, Carl Henry, Jr. 1958-
WhoAmL 94
McIntyre, Carolyn 1939- *WhoWest 94*
McIntyre, Christine d1984 *WhoHol 92*
McIntyre, Clare *ConDr 93*
McIntyre, Colin 1944- *WhoAm 94*
McIntyre, Colin F. 1957- *WhoAm 94*
McIntyre, Deborah 1955- *WhoAm 94*
McIntyre, Dianne Ruth 1946- *WhoBlA 94*
McIntyre, Donald (Conroy) 1934-
NewGrDO, Who 94
McIntyre, Donald Conroy 1934-
IntWW 93, WhoAm 94

McIntyre, Douglas Alexander 1955-
WhoAm 94, WhoFI 94
McIntyre, Douglas Carmichael, II 1956-
WhoAmL 94
McIntyre, Edward J. 1941- *WhoAmL 94*
McIntyre, Edwina 1942- *WhoMW 93*
McIntyre, Frank d1949 *WhoHol 92*
McIntyre, Gary Allen 1938- *WhoWest 94*
McIntyre, Gary William 1953-
WhoMW 93
McIntyre, Gene Earl 1932- *WhoAmP 93*
McIntyre, Guy Maurice 1961-
WhoAm 94, WhoWest 94
Mc Intyre, Henry Langenberg 1912-
WhoAm 94
McIntyre, Hugh Baxter 1935-
WhoWest 94
McIntyre, Ian James 1931- *Who 94*
McIntyre, J. Lawrence 1942- *WhoAmL 94*
Mc Intyre, James A. 1932- *WhoAm 94,
WhoFI 94, WhoWest 94*
McIntyre, James Charles 1922- *WhAm 10*
McIntyre, James Francis Aloysius
1886-1979 *DcAmReB 2*
McIntyre, James Francis Cardinal d1979
WhoHol 92
McIntyre, James T., Jr. 1940- *IntWW 93,
WhoAmP 93*
McIntyre, Janice A. 1933- *WhoMW 93*
McIntyre, Jerry L. 1941- *WhoAmL 94*
McIntyre, Joel Franklyn 1938-
WhoAm 94
McIntyre, John 1916- *IntWW 93, Who 94*
McIntyre, John Armin 1928- *WhoAm 94*
McIntyre, John Duncan 1938- *WhoFI 94*
McIntyre, John George Wallace 1920-
WhoAm 94
McIntyre, John Henry, Sr. 1925-
WhoBlA 94
McIntyre, John Philip, Jr. 1949-
WhoScEn 94
McIntyre, Joseph B. 1957- *WhoAmP 93*
McIntyre, Kathryn Joan 1952-
WhoAm 94
McIntyre, Kenneth J. 1944- *WhoAm 94,
WhoAmL 94*
McIntyre, Leila d1953 *WhoHol 92*
McIntyre, Lucile *WhoHol 92*
McIntyre, Marion d1975 *WhoHol 92*
McIntyre, Michael Edgeworth 1941-
Who 94
McIntyre, Michael John 1942-
WhoAmL 94
McIntyre, Mildred J. *WhoBlA 94*
McIntyre, Molly d1952 *WhoHol 92*
McIntyre, Monty Alan 1955- *WhoAmL 94*
McIntyre, Nan McGowan 1947-
WhoMW 93
McIntyre, Neil 1934- *Who 94*
McIntyre, Norman F. 1945- *WhoAm 94,
WhoFI 94, WhoWest 94*
McIntyre, Oswald Ross 1932- *WhoAm 94*
McIntyre, Peter Mastin 1947-
WhoScEn 94
Mc Intyre, Robert Allen, Jr. 1940-
WhoAm 94
McIntyre, Robert Douglas 1913- *Who 94*
McIntyre, Robert Francis 1954-
WhoWest 94
McIntyre, Robert Malcolm 1923-
WhoAm 94, WhoWest 94
Mc Intyre, Robert Walter 1922-
WhoAm 94
McIntyre, Robert Wheeler 1936-
WhoWest 94
McIntyre, Ronald Llewellyn 1934-
WhoAm 94
McIntyre, Vonda N(eel) 1948- *EncSF 93,
TwCYAW, WrDr 94*
Mc Intyre, Vonda Neel 1948- *WhoAm 94*
McIntyre, W(illiam) David 1932-
WrDr 94
McIntyre, William Ian Mackay 1919-
Who 94
McIntyre-Ivy, Joan Carol 1939- *WhoFI 94*
Mc Isaac, George Scott 1930- *WhoAm 94*
McIsaac, Paul Rowley 1926- *WhoAm 94*
McIver, Claud L., III 1942- *WhoAmL 94*
McIver, G(eorge M.) *EncSF 93*
McIver, George d1957 *WhoHol 92*
McIver, John Douglas 1941- *WhoBlA 94*
McIver, Margaret Hill 1925- *WhoBlA 94*
McIver, Neil Frederick 1950-
WhoAmP 93
McIvor, Basil *Who 94*
McIvor, (William) Basil 1928- *Who 94*
McIvor, Donald Kenneth 1928- *Who 94,
WhoAm 94, WhoFI 94*
McIvor, (Frances) Jill 1930- *Who 94*
McIvor, John Wilfred 1931- *WhoAmA 93*
McIvor, Mary d1941 *WhoHol 92*
McJimsey, Robert Duncan 1936-
WhoWest 94
McJones, Robert Wayne 1922-
WhoWest 94
McJunkin, Louis M. 1931- *WhoAmP 93*
McK, Misha *WhoHol 92*
McKague, Thomas R. *DrAPF 93*

McKaig, Dianne L. 1930- *WhAm 10*
McKaig, (John) Rae 1922- *Who 94*
McKain, David *DrAPF 93*
McKain, Theodore F. 1946- *WhoScEn 94*
McKanders, Julius A., II 1941-
WhoBlA 94
McKanders, Kenneth Andre 1950-
WhoBlA 94
McKandes, Darnell Damon 1966-
WhoBlA 94
McKandes, Dorothy Dell 1937-
WhoBlA 94
McKane, David Bennett 1945-
WhoAm 94
McKane, Terry John 1941- *WhoAmP 93*
McKane, William 1921- *IntWW 93,
Who 94*
McKarns, James Stephen 1938-
WhoWest 94
McKaskle, Larry *WhoAmP 93*
McKasy, Bert J. *WhoAmP 93*
Mc Kaughan, Howard Paul 1922-
WhoWest 94
McKaughan, Larry (Scott) 1941-
ConAu 142, SmATA 75 [port]
McKay, Alexander Gordon 1924-
Who 94, WhoAm 94, WrDr 94
McKay, Alexander Matthew 1921-
Who 94
McKay, Alice Vitalich 1947- *WhoWest 94*
McKay, Allan George 1935- *Who 94*
McKay, Allen 1927- *Who 94*
McKay, Allison *WhoHol 92*
McKay, Anthony Norman *WhoHol 92*
McKay, Archibald Charles 1929- *Who 94*
McKay, Arthur Fortescue 1926-
WhoAmA 93
McKay, Brian 1945- *WhoAmP 93*
McKay, Carol Ruth 1948- *WhoAm 94*
Mc Kay, Charles Alan 1931- *WhAm 10*
McKay, Claude 1889-1948
ConBlB 6 [port]
McKay, Claude 1890-1948 *AfrAmAl 6*
McKay, Colin Bernard 1949-
WhoScEn 94
McKay, Colin Graham 1942- *Who 94*
McKay, Constance Gadow 1928-
WhoMW 93
McKay, D. Brian 1945- *WhoWest 94*
McKay, Daniel Joe 1949- *WhoMW 93*
McKay, David Oman 1873-1970
DcAmReB 2
Mc Kay, Dean Raymond 1921-
WhoAm 94
McKay, Donald A. 1945- *WhoAm 94,
WhoFI 94*
McKay, Donald Arthur 1931- *WhoFI 94,
WhoScEn 94*
Mc Kay, Emily Gantz 1945- *WhoAm 94*
McKay, Ernest d1981 *WhoHol 92*
McKay, Eugene Henry, Jr. 1929-
WhoMW 93
McKay, Floyd John 1935- *WhoWest 94*
McKay, Fred d1944 *WhoHol 92*
McKay, Frederick *Who 94*
McKay, (James) Frederick 1907- *Who 94*
McKay, Gardner 1932- *WhoHol 92*
McKay, George d1945 *WhoHol 92*
McKay, Glenda *WhoHol 92*
McKay, Ian Lloyd 1929- *Who 94*
McKay, Jack 1946- *WhoAmL 94*
McKay, Jack Alexander 1942- *WhoAm 94*
McKay, James Edgar 1939- *WhoFI 94*
McKay, Janet Holmgren 1948-
WhoWest 94
Mc Kay, Jim 1921- *WhoAm 94,
WhoHol 92*
McKay, John 1948- *WhoAmP 93*
McKay, John 1956- *WhoAmL 94,
WhoWest 94*
McKay, John (Andrew) 1912- *Who 94*
McKay, John A. 1933- *WhoFI 94*
McKay, John Douglas 1960- *WhoAmL 94*
McKay, John Henderson 1929- *Who 94*
McKay, John Judson, Jr. 1939-
WhoAmL 94
McKay, John Sangster 1921- *WhoAmA 93*
McKay, Karen Nimmons 1947-
WhoBlA 94
McKay, Kelsey Babcock 1924- *WhoFI 94*
McKay, Kenneth Gardiner 1917-
WhoAm 94
McKay, Koln Gunn 1925- *WhoAmP 93*
McKay, Margaret 1911- *Who 94*
McKay, Martha Clampitt 1920-
WhoAmP 93
McKay, Michael Dennis 1951-
WhoAm 94, WhoAmL 94
McKay, Monroe G. 1928- *WhoAmP 93*
McKay, Monroe Gunn 1928- *WhoAm 94,
WhoAmL 94, WhoWest 94*
McKay, Neil 1917- *WhoAm 94*
McKay, Raymond T. d1993 *NewYTBS 93*
McKay, Renee *WhoAmA 93*
Mc Kay, Robert Budge 1919-1990
WhAm 10
Mc Kay, Robert James, Jr. 1917-

McKay, Roy 1900- *Who 94*
McKay, Scott d1987 *WhoHol 92*
Mc Kay, Thomas, Jr. 1920- *WhoAm 94*
McKay, Timothy James 1954-
WhoAmL 94
McKay, Wanda 1919- *WhoHol 92*
McKay, William Robert 1939- *Who 94*
McKay, Woodrow M. 1941- *WhoAmP 93*
McKayle, Donald 1930- *WhoHol 92*
Mc Kayle, Donald Cohen 1930-
WhoAm 94, WhoBlA 94
McKeachie, Wilbert J 1921- *WrDr 94*
Mc Keachie, Wilbert James 1921-
WhoAm 94
McKeachnie, Gayle F. *WhoAmP 93*
McKeag, Ernest L(ionel) 1896-1976
EncSF 93
McKeag, John Keith 1940- *WhoAmL 94*
McKeage, Jonathan Fleming 1952-
WhoFI 94
McKeague, David William 1946-
WhoAm 94, WhoAmL 94, WhoMW 93
McKean, Andrew 1949- *WhoAmP 93*
McKean, Charles Alexander 1946-
Who 94
McKean, Dave 1963- *EncSF 93*
McKean, Douglas 1917- *Who 94*
McKean, Henry P. 1930- *WhoScEn 94*
Mc Kean, Hugh Ferguson 1908-
WhoAm 94, WhoAmA 93
McKean, J(ohn) M(aule) 1943- *WrDr 94*
McKean, James *DrAPF 93*
McKean, John F. d1993
NewYTBS 93 [port]
Mc Kean, John Rosseel Overton 1928-
WhoAm 94
Mc Kean, Keith Ferguson 1915-
WhoAm 94
McKean, Meryl Lin 1957- *WhoMW 93*
McKean, Michael *WhoAm 94*
McKean, Michael 1947- *IntMPA 94,
WhoHol 92*
McKean, Robert B. 1943- *WrDr 94*
McKean, Robert Jackson, Jr. 1925-
WhoAm 94
McKean, Ronald Alan 1956- *WhoMW 93*
McKean, Thomas 1734-1817 *WhAmRev*
McKean, Thomas Arthur 1941-
WhoWest 94
McKean, Thomas Wayne 1928-
WhoAm 94
McKearn, Thomas Joseph 1948-
WhoAm 94, WhoScEn 94
McKearney, Philip 1926- *Who 94*
McKechnie, Donna 1940- *WhoHol 92*
McKechnie, Ed 1963- *WhoAmP 93*
McKechnie, George 1946- *Who 94*
McKechnie, James d1964 *WhoHol 92*
McKechnie, John Charles 1935-
WhoScEn 94
McKechnie, Sheila Marshall 1948-
Who 94
McKechnie, William Elliott 1952-
WhoAmP 93
McKee, Adam E., Jr. 1932- *WhoBlA 94*
McKee, Alasdair 1963- *WrDr 94*
McKee, Alexander 1720-1799 *AmRev*
Mc Kee, Allen Page 1941- *WhoFI 94*
McKee, Bob 1938- *WhoAmP 93*
McKee, Buck d1944 *WhoHol 92*
McKee, Carol B. 1942- *WhoAmP 93*
McKee, Cecil *Who 94*
McKee, (William) Cecil 1905- *Who 94*
McKee, Christopher Fulton 1935-
WhoAm 94
McKee, Christopher Fulton 1942-
WhoAm 94
McKee, Clarence Vanzant 1942-
WhoBlA 94
McKee, Craig Lloyd 1960- *WhoAmL 94*
McKee, David (John) *WrDr 94*
McKee, David Lannen 1936- *WhoFI 94,
WhoScEn 94*
McKee, David Malcolm 1937-
WhoAmA 93
McKee, Donald d1968 *WhoHol 92*
McKee, Edith Merritt 1918- *WhoMW 93*
McKee, Edward Ray 1941- *WhoFI 94*
McKee, Edwin Dinwiddie 1906-1984
WhAm 10
Mc Kee, Fran 1926- *WhoAm 94*
McKee, Frances Barrett 1909-1975
WhoAmA 93N
McKee, Francis John 1943- *WhoAmL 94,
WhoFI 94, WhoWest 94*
McKee, Frederick A. 1945- *WhoWest 94*
Mc Kee, George Moffitt, Jr. 1924-
*WhoAm 94, WhoFI 94, WhoMW 93,
WhoScEn 94*
McKee, Harold Earl 1937-1992 *WhAm 10*
Mc Kee, James, Jr. 1918- *WhoAm 94*
McKee, James Stanley Colton
WhoScEn 94
McKee, James W., Jr. 1922- *IntWW 93*
McKee, John *WhoHol 92*
McKee, John d1953 *WhoHol 92*
McKee, John Angus 1935- *IntWW 93,
WhoFI 94*

McKee, John Carothers 1912- *WhoAm 94,
WhoFI 94, WhoWest 94*
McKee, Joseph Fulton 1921- *WhoAm 94*
McKee, Kathryn Dian Grant 1937-
WhoAm 94, WhoFI 94
McKee, Keith Earl 1928- *WhoAm 94,
WhoScEn 94*
Mc Kee, Kinnaird Rowe 1929-
WhoAm 94
McKee, Lafe d1959 *WhoHol 92*
McKee, Lonette 1954- *WhoHol 92*
McKee, Lonette 1959- *WhoBlA 94*
McKee, Louis *DrAPF 93*
McKee, M. Jean 1929- *WhoAmP 93*
McKee, Margaret Crile 1945-
WhoScEn 94
McKee, Margaret Jean 1929- *WhoAm 94,
WhoFI 94*
McKee, Maria c. 1965- *ConMus 11 [port]*
McKee, Mary Elizabeth 1949- *WhoAm 94*
McKee, Melissa Marie 1964- *WhoWest 94*
McKee, Pat d1950 *WhoHol 92*
McKee, Paul Vincent *WhoAm 94*
McKee, Penelope Melna 1938-
WhoAm 94, WhoWest 94
McKee, Ralph Dyer, Jr. 1925-
WhoAmL 94
McKee, Raymond d1984 *WhoHol 92*
Mc Kee, Raymond Walter 1899-
WhoFI 94, WhoWest 94
McKee, Robert Stanley 1943-
WhoAmP 93
McKee, Roger Curtis 1931- *WhoAm 94,
WhoAmL 94, WhoMW 93*
McKee, Scott d1945 *WhoHol 92*
McKee, Theodore A. *WhoBlA 94*
McKee, Thomas Frederick 1948-
WhoAm 94, WhoAmL 94
McKee, Thomas J. 1930- *WhoAm 94*
McKee, Timothy Carlton 1944- *WhoFI 94*
McKee, Tom d1960 *WhoHol 92*
McKee, William 1895- *WhAm 10*
McKee, William David 1926- *WhoAm 94*
McKee, William James Ernest 1929-
Who 94
McKee, William Lee 1946- *WhoFI 94*
McKee, William St. John 1944-
WhoAm 94
McKeeby, Byron Gordon 1936-1984
WhoAmA 93N
McKeegan, Pete P. 1915- *WhoAmP 93*
Mc Keel, Sam Stewart 1926- *WhoAm 94,
WhoMW 93*
McKeel, Thomas Burl 1944- *WhoBlA 94*
Mc Keen, Chester M., Jr. 1923-
WhoAm 94, WhoFI 94
McKeen, Elden *WhoAmP 93*
McKeen, Sunny d1933 *WhoHol 92*
McKeeth, Sylvia *WhoAmP 93*
McKee-Velasquez, Patrick 1953-
WhoHisp 94
Mc Keever, Brian Edward 1957- *WhoFI 94*
McKeever, Brian Evans 1949- *WhoAm 94,
WhoFI 94*
McKeever, John Eugene 1947-
WhoFI 94, WhoAmL 94
McKeever, Mike d1967 *WhoHol 92*
McKeever, Pamela Sue 1958-
WhoWest 94
McKeever, Porter 1915-1992 *WhAm 10*
McKeever, Sheila A. 1948- *WhoScEn 94*
McKeever, Thomas A. 1943- *WhoFI 94*
McKeever, Timothy A. 1950-
WhoAmP 93
McKeithen, John Julian 1918-
WhoAmP 93
McKeithen, Walter Fox 1946- *WhoAm 94,
WhoAmP 93*
McKeldin, Harry White, Jr. 1915-
WhoBlA 94
McKeldin, William Evans 1927-
WhoAm 94
McKell, Cyrus M. 1926- *WhoAm 94,
WhoWest 94*
McKell, Lynn J. 1943- *WhoWest 94*
McKellar, Andrew Robert 1945-
WhoAm 94
McKellar, C. H. 1937- *WhoFI 94*
McKellar, Stephen Alexander 1956-
WhoBlA 94
McKellen, Ian 1939- *ConTFT 11,
IntMPA 94, News 94-1 [port], WhoHol 92*
McKellen, Ian (Murray) 1939- *Who 94*
McKellen, Ian Murray 1939- *IntWW 93,
WhoAm 94*
McKeller, Thomas Lee 1940- *WhoBlA 94*
McKellips, David Allan 1943- *WhoFI 94*
McKellips, Gordon Wayne, Jr. 1941-
WhoAmL 94, WhoWest 94
McKellips, Roger D. *WhoAmP 93*
McKelpin, Joseph P. 1914- *WhoBlA 94*
McKelvey, Carole A. 1942- *WrDr 94*
McKelvey, Don Richard 1946- *WhoAm 94*
McKelvey, Edward Neil 1925- *IntWW 93*
McKelvey, Forrest L. *WhoAmP 93*
McKelvey, Gerald John *WhoAmP 93*
McKelvey, James Morgan 1925-
WhoAm 94

Mc Kelvey, Jean Trepp 1908- *WhoAm 94*
Mc Kelvey, John Clifford 1934-
WhoAm 94, WhoFI 94, WhoScEn 94
Mc Kelvey, John Jay, Jr. 1917- *WhoAm 94*
McKelvey, John Wesley 1914- *Who 94*
McKelvey, Judith Grant 1935-
WhoAm 94, WhoAmL 94
McKelvey, Louis William 1898-
WhAm 10
McKelvey, Robert John 1929- *Who 94*
McKelvey, Scott H. 1960- *WhoFI 94*
McKelvey, William 1934- *Who 94*
McKelvie, Peter 1932- *Who 94*
McKelvie, Roderick R. 1946- *WhoAm 94,
WhoAmL 94*
McKelvy, Natalie Ann 1950- *WhoMW 93*
McKemy, Wrenshall Vancel *WhoAmP 93*
McKendall, Robert Roland 1944-
WhoScEn 94
McKendree, William 1757-1835
DcAmReB 2
McKendry, John 1933-1975
WhoAmA 93N
McKendry, John H., Jr. 1950-
WhoAmL 94
Mc Kenna, Alex George 1914- *WhoAm 94*
McKenna, Alvin James 1943- *WhoAm 94*
McKenna, Andrew James 1929-
WhoAm 94, WhoMW 93
McKenna, Bernard James 1933-
WhoFI 94
McKenna, Charles Nicholas 1965-
WhoFI 94
McKenna, Colleen O'Shaughnessy 1948-
SmATA 76 [port]
McKenna, David 1911- *Who 94*
Mc Kenna, David Loren 1929-
WhoAm 94
McKenna, David William 1945-
WhoAmL 94
McKenna, Denis L. 1922- *WhoAmP 93*
McKenna, Fay Ann 1944- *WhoFI 94*
McKenna, Francis Joseph 1948- *Who 94*
McKenna, Frank Joseph 1948- *IntWW 93,
WhoAm 94*
McKenna, Frederick Gregory 1952-
WhoAmL 94
McKenna, George J., III 1940- *WhoBlA 94*
McKenna, George LaVerne 1924-
WhoAm 94, WhoAmA 93
McKenna, Hugh Francis 1921- *WhoIns 94*
McKenna, J. Frank, III 1948-
WhoAmL 94
McKenna, James *DrAPF 93*
Mc Kenna, James Aloysius 1918-
WhoAm 94
McKenna, James Emmet 1947-
WhoScEn 94
McKenna, James L. 1954- *WhoAmL 94*
McKenna, Janice Lynn 1949-
WhoAmP 93
McKenna, John Dennis 1940-
WhoScEn 94
McKenna, Kenneth F., Jr. 1943-
WhoAmP 93
McKenna, Keven A. 1945- *WhoAmP 93*
McKenna, Lawrence M. 1933-
WhoAm 94, WhoAmL 94
Mc Kenna, Malcolm Carnegie 1930-
WhoAm 94, WhoScEn 94
McKenna, Margaret Anne 1945-
WhoAm 94
Mc Kenna, Marian Cecilia 1926-
WhoAm 94, WhoWest 94, WrDr 94
McKenna, Mark Joseph 1962-
WhoScEn 94
McKenna, Mary Jane *WhoAmP 93*
McKenna, Matthew Morgan 1950-
WhoAm 94, WhoAmL 94
McKenna, Michael Francis 1951-
WhoAmL 94
McKenna, Michael Joseph 1935-
WhoFI 94
McKenna, Patrick James 1951- *WhoFI 94*
McKenna, Peter Dennis 1937-
WhoAmL 94
McKenna, Peter J. 1946- *WhoAmL 94*
McKenna, Quentin Carnegie 1926-
WhoAm 94, WhoFI 94
McKenna, Richard M(ilton) 1913-1964
EncSF 93
McKenna, Robert J. *WhoFI 94*
McKenna, Robert J. 1931- *WhoAmP 93*
Mc Kenna, Sidney F. 1922- *WhoAm 94*
McKenna, Siobhan d1986 *WhoHol 92*
McKenna, Stephen Francis 1939-
IntWW 93
McKenna, Stephen James 1940-
WhoAm 94, WhoAmL 94
McKenna, T. P. 1929- *WhoHol 92*
McKenna, Terence *News 93-3 [port]*
McKenna, Terence Patrick 1928-
WhoAm 94
McKenna, Thomas Edward 1962-
WhoScEn 94
Mc Kenna, Thomas Joseph 1929-
WhoAm 94

McKenna, Thomas Morrison, Jr. 1937-
WhoAm 94
McKenna, Thomas Patrick 1931-
IntWW 94
McKenna, Virginia 1931- *IntWW 93,
WhoHol 92*
McKenna, Willafay H. 1936- *WhoAmP 93*
Mc Kenna, William A., Jr. *WhoAm 94,
WhoFI 94*
Mc Kenna, William Edward 1919-
WhoAm 94
McKenna, William John 1926-
WhoAm 94, WhoFI 94, WhoMW 93
McKenna, William P. 1946- *WhoAmP 93*
McKenney, Frank Meath 1934-
WhoAmP 93
McKenney, Katherine 1932- *WhoAmP 93*
Mc Kenney, Walter Gibbs, Jr. 1913-
WhoFI 94
McKennon, Dallas *WhoHol 92*
McKennon, Elizabeth A. 1954-
WhoAmL 94
McKennon, Keith Robert 1933-
IntWW 93, WhoAm 94, WhoMW 93
McKennon, Richard Otey 1964-
WhoAmL 94
McKenny, Jere Wesley 1929- *WhoAm 94,
WhoFI 94*
McKenny, Stephen Richard 1959-
WhoFI 94
McKentry, Elizabeth d1920 *WhoHol 92*
McKenzie, Alexander 1896- *IntWW 93,
Who 94*
McKenzie, Allan Dean 1930-
WhoAmA 93, WhoWest 94
McKenzie, Arthur Leroy 1930-
WhoAmP 93
McKenzie, Barbara 1934- *WrDr 94*
McKenzie, Bob d1949 *WhoHol 92*
McKenzie, Dan Peter 1942- *IntWW 93,
Who 94*
McKenzie, Donald Francis 1931- *Who 94*
McKenzie, Edna B. 1923- *WhoBlA 94*
McKenzie, Eli, Jr. 1947- *WhoBlA 94*
McKenzie, Elizabeth McDaniel 1954-
WhoAmL 94
McKenzie, Ella d1987 *WhoHol 92*
McKenzie, Eva d1967 *WhoHol 92*
McKenzie, Fay 1920- *WhoHol 92*
McKenzie, Floretta D. 1935- *WhoBlA 94*
McKenzie, Gwendolyn Veron *WhoFI 94*
Mc Kenzie, Harold Cantrell, Jr. 1931-
WhoAm 94
Mc Kenzie, Harold Jackson 1904-1991
WhAm 10
Mc Kenzie, Hilton Eugene 1921-
WhoFI 94
McKenzie, Ida Mae d1986 *WhoHol 92*
McKenzie, James Franklin 1948-
WhoAmL 94
McKenzie, James Milton 1945-
WhoWest 94
McKenzie, Janet Stephens 1939-
WhoMW 93
Mc Kenzie, Jeremy Alec 1941- *WhoAm 94*
McKenzie, Jo 1931- *WhoAmP 93*
McKenzie, John Cormack 1927- *Who 94*
McKenzie, John Crawford 1937- *Who 94*
McKenzie, John F. 1947- *WhoAmL 94*
McKenzie, John Foster 1923- *Who 94*
Mc Kenzie, John Maxwell 1927-
WhoAm 94
McKenzie, John Michael 1954-
WhoAmP 93
McKenzie, Julia *WhoHol 92*
McKenzie, Julia 1941- *ConTFT 11*
McKenzie, Julia Kathleen 1941- *Who 94*
McKenzie, Kenneth *WhoFI 94*
McKenzie, Kenneth 1800-1861 *WhWE*
McKenzie, Kevin 1954- *IntDcB*
McKenzie, Kevin Patrick 1954-
WhoAm 94
McKenzie, Laura *WhoHol 92*
McKenzie, Lewis H. *WhoAmP 93*
Mc Kenzie, Lionel Wilfred 1919-
WhoAm 94
McKenzie, Louis *WhoHol 92*
McKenzie, Mary Beth *WhoAm 94*
McKenzie, Mary Beth 1946- *WhoAmA 93*
McKenzie, Mary Etna 1925- *WhoAmP 93*
McKenzie, Melinda *EncSF 93*
McKenzie, Michael 1943- *Who 94*
McKenzie, Michael K. *WhoAm 94,
WhoFI 94*
McKenzie, Miranda Mack 1955-
WhoBlA 94
McKenzie, Neil Robin 1961- *WhoWest 94*
McKenzie, Paul Ross 1953- *WhoFI 94*
Mc Kenzie, Ray 1927- *WhoAm 94*
McKenzie, Reginald 1950- *WhoBlA 94*
McKenzie, Richard 1930- *WhoHol 92*
McKenzie, Rita Lynn 1958- *WhoScEn 94*
McKenzie, Robert E. 1947- *WhoAmL 94*
McKenzie, Ronald Eugene 1949-
WhoAmP 93
McKenzie, Roy (Allan) 1922- *Who 94*
McKenzie, Ruth Bates Harris *WhoAmP 93*

McKenzie, Sally Freeman 1928-
WhoAmP 93
McKenzie, Therman, Sr. 1949-
WhoBlA 94
McKenzie, Tim *WhoHol 92*
McKenzie, Vinnorma Shaw 1890-1952
WhoAmA 93N
McKenzie, Wilford Clifton 1913-
WhoBlA 94
McKenzie, William P. 1954- *WrDr 94*
McKenzie Johnston, Henry Butler 1921-
Who 94
McKenzie Smith, Ian 1935- *Who 94*
McKeon, Doug 1966- *IntMPA 94,
WhoHol 92*
McKeon, Elizabeth Fairbanks 1931-
WhoFI 94
McKeon, George A. 1937- *WhoAmL 94,
WhoIns 94*
McKeon, Howard P. *WhoAm 94,
WhoAmP 93, WhoWest 94*
McKeon, Howard P. 1938- *CngDr 93*
McKeon, Nancy 1967- *WhoHol 92*
McKeon, Newton Felch 1904-1990
WhAm 10
McKeon, Philip 1964- *WhoHol 92*
McKeon, Robert B. 1954- *WhoFI 94*
McKeon, Stephen A. 1946- *WhoAmL 94*
McKeone, (Dixie) Lee *EncSF 93*
McKeough, William Darcy 1933-
WhoAm 94
McKeown, Elaine 1950- *WhoMW 93*
McKeown, Frank James 1931-
WhoAmL 94
McKeown, James Charles 1945-
WhoAm 94
McKeown, Martin 1943- *WhoFI 94*
McKeown, Mary Elizabeth *WhoMW 93*
McKeown, Mary Margaret 1951-
WhoAm 94, WhoAmL 94
McKeown, Patrick Arthur 1930- *Who 94*
McKeown, Tom *DrAPF 93*
McKeown, Tom 1937- *WrDr 94*
Mc Keown, William Taylor 1921-
WhoAm 94
McKercher, Robert Hamilton 1930-
IntWW 93
McKereghan, Peter Fleming 1960-
WhoScEn 94
McKern, Leo 1920- *IntMPA 94, Who 94,
WhoHol 92, WrDr 94*
McKern, Leo Reginald 1920- *IntWW 93*
McKernan, John *DrAPF 93*
McKernan, John Joseph 1942- *WhoAm 94*
McKernan, John R., Jr. 1948-
WhoAmP 93
McKernan, John Rettie 1948- *IntWW 93*
McKernan, John Rettie, Jr. 1948-
WhoAm 94
McKernan, Leo Joseph 1938- *WhoAm 94,
WhoFI 94, WhoMW 93*
McKernan, Llewellyn T. *DrAPF 93*
McKernan, Thomas Vincent, Jr. 1944-
WhoAm 94
McKernan, Victoria 1957- *ConAu 140*
McKerns, Charles Joseph 1935-
WhoAm 94
McKerracher, David Michael 1949-
WhoWest 94
McKerrow, Amanda *WhoAm 94*
McKerrow, June 1950- *Who 94*
McKerrow, Mary 1915- *WrDr 94*
McKerrow, R. B. 1872-1940 *BlmGEL*
McKerson, Effie M. 1924- *WhoBlA 94*
McKerson, Hayward *WhoAmP 93*
McKerson, Mazola 1921- *WhoBlA 94*
McKesson, Malcolm Forbes 1909-
WhoAmA 93
McKesson, Michael Alan 1950-
WhoMW 93
McKessy, Stephen W. 1937- *WhoAm 94,
WhoFI 94*
Mc Ketta, John J., Jr. 1915- *WhoAm 94,
WhoScEn 94*
McKetta, John J., III 1948- *WhoAmL 94*
McKevitt, Gerald Lawrence 1939-
WhoWest 94
McKewen, Jack Leard 1919- *WhoFI 94*
McKewon, Karen Lee 1952- *WhoWest 94*
McKey, Derrick Wayne 1966- *WhoBlA 94*
McKey, Thomas J. 1934- *WhoAm 94*
McKhann, Guy Mead 1932- *WhoAm 94*
McKibben, Bill 1960- *EnvEnc*
McKibben, Billy J. *WhoAmP 93*
McKibben, Eugene George 1895-
WhAm 10
McKibben, Gordon Charles 1930-
WhoAm 94
McKibben, Howard D. 1940- *WhoAm 94,
WhoAmL 94, WhoWest 94*
McKibben, Ryan Timothy 1958-
WhoAm 94
McKibben, William (Ernest) 1960-
WrDr 94
McKibbon, Columbia d1948 *WhoHol 92*
McKie, Angus 1951- *EncSF 93*
McKie, John David 1909- *Who 94*
McKie, Miles Lindsay 1949- *WhoMW 93*

McKie, Peter Halliday 1935- *Who 94*
Mc Kie, Todd Stoddard 1944- *WhoAm 94,
WhoAmA 93*
McKie, W. Gilmore 1927- *WhoFI 94*
McKiernan, Francis J. *Who 94*
McKiernan, John William 1923-
WhoAm 94
McKillip, Donna LuAnn Gage 1953-
WhoMW 93
McKillip, Patricia (Anne) 1948- *WrDr 94*
McKillip, Patricia A(nne) 1948-
EncSF 93, TwCYAW
McKillop, Daniel James 1948- *WhoAm 94*
McKillop, Malcolm C. *WhoAmP 93*
McKim, Adele W. 1914- *WhoAmP 93*
McKim, Charles Follen 1847-1909
AmCulL
McKim, Elizabeth *DrAPF 93*
McKim, Frank Hastings 1945- *WhoFI 94*
McKim, Harriet Megchelsen 1919-
WhoWest 94
McKim, Herbert Pope 1928- *WhoAmP 93*
McKim, Paul Arthur 1923- *WhoAm 94*
McKim, Robert d1927 *WhoHol 92*
McKim, Sammy 1924- *WhoHol 92*
McKim, Samuel John, III 1938-
*WhoAm 94, WhoAmL 94, WhoFI 94,
WhoMW 93*
McKim, William Wind 1916-
WhoAmA 93
McKimmy, Jerry Lee 1942- *WhoFI 94,
WhoMW 93*
McKimson, Robert 1910-1976 *IntDcF 2-4*
McKinin, Lawrence 1917- *WhoAmA 93N*
McKinlay, Brian John 1933- *WrDr 94*
McKinlay, Bruce 1936- *WhoFI 94*
McKinless, Kathy Jean 1954- *WhoAm 94,
WhoFI 94*
McKinley, Bernie 1928- *WhoAmP 93*
McKinley, Brunson 1943- *WhoAm 94,
WhoAmP 93*
McKinley, Camille Dombrowski 1922-
WhoMW 93
McKinley, Chuck 1941-1986 *BuCMET*
McKinley, David Bennett 1947-
WhoAmP 93
McKinley, David Cecil 1913- *Who 94*
McKinley, Deborah Kay 1955-
WhoMW 93
McKinley, J. Edward *WhoHol 92*
McKinley, James *DrAPF 93*
McKinley, James Frank, Jr. 1943-
WhoFI 94
McKinley, John K. 1920- *IntWW 93*
McKinley, John Key 1920- *Who 94,
WhoAm 94, WhoFI 94*
McKinley, John McKeen 1930-
WhoMW 93, WhoScEn 94
McKinley, Joseph Warner 1943-
WhoWest 94
McKinley, Loren Dhue 1920- *WhoAm 94*
McKinley, Ray E. 1925- *WhoBlA 94*
McKinley, Robert E. 1926- *WhoAmP 93*
McKinley, Robert Wilson 1944-
WhoAmL 94
McKinley, Robin 1952- *WhoAm 94*
McKinley, (Jennifer Carolyn) Robin
1952- *TwCYAW, WrDr 94*
McKinley, Ruth Gowdy 1931-1981
WhoAmA 93N
McKinley, William 1843-1901
HisWorL [port]
McKinley, William, Jr. 1924- *WhoBlA 94*
McKinley, William A. 1917- *WhoAm 94*
McKinley, William E. 1940- *WhoFI 94*
McKinley, William Frank 1961-
WhoFI 94
McKinley, William Thomas 1938-
WhoAm 94
McKinley-Haas, Mary *WhoAmA 93*
McKinly, John 1721-1796 *WhAmRev*
McKinnell, Norman d1932 *WhoHol 92*
Mc Kinnell, Robert Gilmore 1926-
WhoAm 94, WhoScEn 94
McKinnery, William Nelson, Jr. 1938-
WhoMW 93
Mc Kinney, Alexis 1907- *WhoAm 94*
McKinney, Alma Swilley 1930-
WhoBlA 94
McKinney, Betsy 1939- *WhoAmP 93*
McKinney, Betty Jo *WhoWest 94*
McKinney, Bill *WhoHol 92*
McKinney, Billy *WhoBlA 94*
McKinney, Bones 1919- *BasBi*
McKinney, Bryan Lee 1946- *WhoScEn 94*
McKinney, Carolyn Jean 1956-
WhoAmL 94
McKinney, Charles Cecil 1931-
WhoAm 94
McKinney, Collin Jo 1958- *WhoScEn 94*
McKinney, Cynthia 1955- *CngDr 93*
McKinney, Cynthia Ann *WhoAm 94*
McKinney, Cynthia Ann 1955-
WhoAmP 93, WhoBlA 94
McKinney, Cynthia Eileen 1949-
WhoScEn 94
McKinney, Cyrus Granger 1940-
WhoFI 94

McKinney, Daene Claude 1954- *WhoScEn 94*
Mc Kinney, David Ewing 1934- *WhoFI 94*
McKinney, (Sheila Mary) Deirdre 1928- *Who 94*
McKinney, Dennis *WhoAmP 93*
McKinney, Dennis Keith 1952- *WhoAmL 94*
McKinney, Donald 1931- *WhoAm 94, WhoAmA 93*
McKinney, Donald Lee 1923- *WhoAm 94*
McKinney, E. Kirk, Jr. 1923- *WhoAm 94*
McKinney, Eloise Vaughn *WhoBlA 94*
McKinney, Ernest Lee, Sr. 1923- *WhoBlA 94*
McKinney, Eva Doris 1921- *WhoBlA 94*
McKinney, Florine d1975 *WhoHol 92*
McKinney, Floyd L. *WhoMW 93*
Mc Kinney, Frank Edward, Jr. 1938-1992 *WhAm 10*
McKinney, George Dallas, Jr. 1932- *WhoBlA 94*
Mc Kinney, George Wesley, Jr. 1922- *WhoAm 94*
McKinney, Irene *DrAPF 93*
McKinney, J. E. 1927- *WhoAmP 93*
McKinney, Jack *EncSF 93*
McKinney, Jacob K. 1920- *WhoBlA 94*
Mc Kinney, James Carroll 1921- *WhoAm 94*
McKinney, James Clayton 1940- *WhoAm 94*
McKinney, James DeVaine, Jr. 1931- *WhoAmL 94*
McKinney, James Ray 1942- *WhoBlA 94*
McKinney, Janet Kay 1959- *WhoAmL 94, WhoMW 93*
McKinney, Jennifer *WhoHol 92*
McKinney, Jesse Doyle 1934- *WhoBlA 94*
McKinney, John Adams, Jr. 1948- *WhoAm 94*
McKinney, John Benjamin 1932- *WhoAm 94*
McKinney, Joseph Arthur 1943- *WhoFI 94*
McKinney, Judith *Who 94*
McKinney, Judson Thad 1941- *WhoAm 94*
McKinney, Kurt Robin *WhoHol 92*
McKinney, Larry J. 1944- *WhoAm 94, WhoAmL 94*
McKinney, Luther C. 1931- *WhoAmL 94*
McKinney, Mira d1978 *WhoHol 92*
Mc Kinney, Montgomery Nelson 1910- *WhoBlA 94*
McKinney, Nina Mae d1967 *WhoHol 92*
McKinney, Norma J. 1941- *WhoBlA 94*
McKinney, Olivia Davene Ross 1931- *WhoBlA 94*
McKinney, Paul 1923- *WhoBlA 94*
McKinney, Paul, Sr. *WhoAmP 93*
McKinney, Price c. 1863-1926
  *See Corrigan, James 1848-1908
  EncABHB 9*
McKinney, Richard Ishmael 1906- *WhoBlA 94*
McKinney, Robert Hurley 1925- *WhoAmP 93*
McKinney, Robert M. 1910- *WhoAmP 93*
McKinney, Robert Moody 1910- *IntWW 93, WhoAm 94, WhoWest 94*
Mc Kinney, Ross Erwin 1926- *WhoAm 94, WhoScEn 94*
McKinney, Rufus William 1930- *WhoBlA 94*
McKinney, Sally Brown 1933- *WhoMW 93*
McKinney, Samuel Berry 1926- *WhoBlA 94*
McKinney, Tatiana Ladygina *WhoAmA 93*
McKinney, Tina Lynn 1969- *WhoMW 93*
McKinney, Venora Ware 1937- *WhoAm 94, WhoBlA 94*
McKinney, Wade H., III 1925- *WhoBlA 94*
McKinney, Walter Byres 1894- *WhAm 10*
McKinney, Wayne 1950- *WhoAmP 93*
McKinney, Wayne Richard 1947- *WhoScEn 94*
McKinney, William Douthitt, Jr. 1955- *WhoFI 94*
McKinnickinnick, Margaret I. 1924- *WhoAmA 93*
McKinnis, Michael B. 1946- *WhoAm 94, WhoAmL 94*
McKinnon, Allan Bruce 1917-1990 *WhAm 10*
McKinnon, Arnold Borden 1927- *WhoAm 94, WhoFI 94*
Mc Kinnon, Clinton D. 1906- *WhoAm 94, WhoWest 94*
Mc Kinnon, Clinton Dan 1934- *WhoAm 94, WhoAmP 93*
McKinnon, Clinton Dotson 1906- *WhoAmP 93*
McKinnon, Daniel Wayne, Jr. 1934- *WhoAm 94*

McKinnon, Darlene Lorraine 1943- *WhoBlA 94*
McKinnon, Dennis Lewis 1961- *WhoBlA 94*
Mckinnon, Don *IntWW 93*
McKinnon, Donald Charles 1939- *Who 94*
McKinnon, Floyd Wingfield 1942- *WhoAm 94, WhoFI 94*
Mc Kinnon, Francis Arthur Richard 1933- *WhoAm 94*
McKinnon, James 1929- *IntWW 93, Who 94*
McKinnon, James Buckner 1916- *WhoFI 94, WhoWest 94*
McKinnon, John Kenneth 1936- *WhoAm 94, WhoWest 94*
McKinnon, Karen Quelle *DrAPF 93*
McKinnon, Kenneth Richard 1931- *Who 94*
McKinnon, Paul Damien 1961- *WhoWest 94*
McKinnon, Richard Anthony 1940- *WhoAm 94, WhoFI 94*
McKinnon, Robert Harold 1927- *WhoFI 94*
McKinnon, Ronald I(an) 1935- *WrDr 94*
McKinnon, Stuart (Neil) 1938- *Who 94*
McKinnon, Susan 1949- *WhoWest 94*
McKinnon, Walter Sneddon 1910- *Who 94*
McKinnon, William Beall 1954- *WhoMW 93*
McKinsey, Beverlee *WhoHol 92*
McKinstry, Robert Bruce, Jr. 1953- *WhoAmL 94*
McKinstry, Ronald Eugene 1926- *WhoAm 94, WhoAmL 94, WhoWest 94*
McKintosh, Ian 1938- *Who 94*
McKinzie, Carl Wayne 1939- *WhoAmL 94*
McKinzie, Howard Lee 1941- *WhoScEn 94*
McKinzie-Harper, Barbara A. 1954- *WhoBlA 94*
McKirahan, Richard Duncan, Jr. 1945- *WhoAm 94*
McKissack, Jimmie Don 1937- *WhoAmP 93*
McKissack, Leatrice Buchanan 1930- *WhoBlA 94*
McKissack, Patricia (L'Ann) C(arwell) 1944- *BlkWr 2*
McKissack, Perri 1965- *WhoBlA 94*
McKissack, William Deberry 1925- *WhoBlA 94*
McKissick, Evelyn Williams 1923- *WhoBlA 94*
McKissick, Floyd B. 1922-1981 *AfrAmAl 6*
McKissick, Floyd Bixler 1922-1991 *WhAm 10*
McKissick, Mabel F. Rice 1921- *WhoBlA 94*
McKissock, David Lee 1933- *WhoFI 94*
McKissock, Paul Kendrick 1925- *WhoAm 94*
McKissock, Wylie 1906- *Who 94*
McKitt, Willie, Jr. *WhoBlA 94*
McKitterick, Rosamond Deborah 1949- *Who 94*
McKittrick, D. Patrick 1941- *WhoAmL 94*
McKittrick, Daniel Patrick 1941- *WhoAmP 93*
McKittrick, Neil Alastair 1948- *Who 94*
McKittrick, Neil Vincent 1961- *WhoAmL 94*
McKittrick, Philip Thomas, Jr. 1964- *WhoScEn 94*
McKittrick, William Wood 1915- *WhoAm 94, WhoMW 93*
McKnew, Thomas Willson 1896-1990 *WhAm 10*
McKnight, Albert J. *WhoBlA 94*
McKnight, Anne d1930 *WhoHol 92*
McKnight, Charles Noel 1944- *WhoAmL 94*
McKnight, David *WhoHol 92*
McKnight, Frederick L. 1947- *WhoAm 94*
McKnight, Jennifer Lee Cowles 1952- *WhoScEn 94*
McKnight, Joe Nip 1933- *WhoAmP 93*
McKnight, John James 1948- *WhoIns 94*
Mc Knight, John Lacy 1931- *WhoAm 94*
McKnight, Joseph Webb 1925- *WhoAm 94*
McKnight, Joy Fowler 1947- *WhoFI 94*
McKnight, Lancess 1901- *WhoBlA 94*
McKnight, Lenore Ravin 1943- *WhoScEn 94, WhoWest 94*
McKnight, Michael Lance 1939- *WhoMW 93*
McKnight, Paul David 1948- *WhoFI 94*
McKnight, Reginald 1956- *WhoBlA 94*
McKnight, Robert Allen 1943- *WhoAmP 93*
Mc Knight, Robert Kellogg 1924- *WhAm 10*
McKnight, Robert Wayne 1944- *WhoAmP 93*

McKnight, Stephen Alen 1944- *WhoAmP 93*
McKnight, Steven Lanier 1949- *WhoAm 94, WhoScEn 94*
McKnight, Susan Coleman 1960- *WhoAmL 94*
McKnight, Thomas Frederick 1941- *WhoAmA 93*
McKnight, Tom Lee 1928- *WrDr 94*
McKnight, William Baldwin 1923- *WhoAm 94*
McKnight, William Hunter 1940- *IntWW 93, WhoAm 94*
Mc Knight, William Warren, Jr. 1913- *WhoAm 94, WhoWest 94*
McKone, Thomas Christopher 1917- *WhoAmL 94*
McKowen, Dorothy Keeton 1948- *WhoMW 93*
McKown, Delos B. 1930- *ConAu 141*
McKown, Jane Ann 1924- *WhoMW 93*
McKown, Janna Lyn 1955- *WhoWest 94*
McKown, Leslie Henry 1934- *WhoMW 93*
Mc Koy, Basil Vincent Charles 1938- *WhoAm 94*
McKoy, Clemencio Agustino 1928- *WhoBlA 94*
McKoy, Victor Grainger 1947- *WhoAmA 93*
McKuen, Rod 1933- *IntWW 93, Who 94, WhoAm 94, WhoHol 92, WrDr 94*
McKusick, Marshall Kirk 1954- *WhoWest 94*
Mc Kusick, Victor Almon 1921- *WhoAm 94*
McKusick, Vincent I. 1921- *WhoAmP 93*
McKusick, Vincent Lee 1921- *WhoAm 94, WhoAmL 94*
Mc Kwartin, Dan B. 1946- *WhoMW 93*
McLachlan, Andrew David 1935- *Who 94*
McLachlan, Angus Henry 1908- *Who 94*
McLachlan, C. Ian 1942- *WhoAmL 94*
McLachlan, Gordon 1918- *Who 94*
McLachlan, Ian Dougald 1911- *Who 94*
McLachlan, Peter John 1936- *Who 94*
McLachlin, Beverley 1943- *WhoAm 94*
McLafferty, Fred Warren 1923- *WhoAm 94, WhoScEn 94*
McLagan, Thomas Rodgie 1897- *WhAm 10*
McLaggan, Murray Adams 1929- *Who 94*
McLaglen, Andrew 1920- *WhoHol 92*
McLaglen, Andrew V. 1920- *IntMPA 94, IntWW 93*
McLaglen, Clifford d1978 *WhoHol 92*
McLaglen, Cyril 1900- *WhoHol 92*
McLaglen, John J. 1938- *WrDr 94*
McLaglen, Victor d1959 *WhoHol 92*
McLain, Christopher 1943- *WhoAmL 94*
McLain, John Lowell 1942- *WhoWest 94*
McLain, Roger Sette 1928- *WhoMW 93*
Mc Lanathan, Richard 1916- *WhoAm 94*
McLane, Allan 1746-1829 *WhAmRev*
McLane, Allen 1748-1829 *AmRev*
McLane, Betsy Ann *WhoWest 94*
McLane, David Glenn 1943- *WhoAm 94*
McLane, Frederick Berg 1941- *WhoAm 94, WhoAmL 94*
McLane, Harry H. 1925- *WhoAmP 93*
McLane, Henry Earl, Jr. 1932- *WhoAm 94*
McLane, James Woods 1939- *WhoAm 94, WhoFI 94*
McLane, Jean 1926- *WhoAmP 93*
Mc Lane, John Roy, Jr. 1916- *WhoAm 94*
McLane, Malcolm 1924- *WhoAmP 93*
McLane, Peter 1940- *WhoMW 93*
McLane, Peter J. 1941- *WhoAm 94*
McLane, Robert Drayton, Jr. 1936- *WhoAm 94*
McLane, Susan 1929- *WhoWomW 91*
McLane, Susan B. R. 1948- *WhoAmP 93*
McLane, Susan Neidlinger 1929- *WhoAmP 93*
McLaren *Who 94*
McLaren, Anne *IntWW 93*
McLaren, Anne (Laura) 1927- *Who 94*
McLaren, Archie Campbell, Jr. 1942- *WhoWest 94*
McLaren, Clare *Who 94*
McLaren, Conrad *WhoHol 92*
McLaren, Derryl 1949- *WhoAmP 93*
McLaren, Digby Johns 1919- *IntWW 93, Who 94, WhoAm 94, WhoScEn 94*
McLaren, Douglas Earl 1948- *WhoBlA 94*
McLaren, Hollis 1952- *WhoHol 92*
McLaren, Ian Alban Bryant 1940- *Who 94*
McLaren, Ian Francis 1912- *WrDr 94*
McLaren, James Clark 1925- *WhoAm 94*
McLaren, John 1932- *WrDr 94*
Mc Laren, John Alexander 1919- *WhoAm 94*
McLaren, John Paterson, Jr. 1952- *WhoScEn 94*
McLaren, Karen Lynn 1955- *WhoFI 94, WhoMW 93*
Mc Laren, Malcolm Grant, IV 1928- *WhoAm 94*
McLaren, Norman 1914- *IntDcF 2-4*

McLaren, Robin (John Taylor) 1934- *Who 94*
McLaren-Throckmorton, Clare *Who 94*
McLarnan, Donald Edward 1906- *WhoAm 94, WhoFI 94, WhoWest 94*
McLarney, Charles Patrick 1942- *WhoAm 94, WhoMW 93*
McLarty, James E. d1979 *WhoHol 92*
McLarty, Ron *WhoHol 92*
McLarty, Thomas F. *WhoAmP 93*
McLarty, Thomas F. 1946- *IntWW 93*
McLarty, Thomas F., III 1946- *NewYTBS 93 [port], WhoAm 94, WhoFI 94*
McLauchlan, D. C. Ramsay 1962- *WhoAmP 93*
McLauchlan, Derek John 1933- *Who 94*
McLauchlan, Keith Alan 1936- *Who 94*
McLauchlan, Madeline Margaret Nicholls 1922- *Who 94*
McLauchlan, Thomas Joseph 1917- *Who 94*
McLaughlan, Thomas Ford 1944- *WhoWest 94*
McLaughlan, Ian David 1919- *Who 94*
McLaughlan, Alexander C. J. 1925- *WhoFI 94*
McLaughlin, Andree Nicola 1948- *WhoBlA 94, WrDr 94*
McLaughlin, Ann 1941- *WhoAm 94*
McLaughlin, Ann Dore 1941- *IntWW 93*
McLaughlin, Ann L. 1928- *WrDr 94*
McLaughlin, Ann Landis *DrAPF 93*
McLaughlin, Audrey *IntWW 93*
McLaughlin, Audrey 1936- *WhoWomW 91*
McLaughlin, Barbara Connor 1931- *WhoAmP 93*
McLaughlin, Barbara Jeanette 1939- *WhoWest 94*
McLaughlin, Benjamin Wayne 1947- *WhoBlA 94*
McLaughlin, Betty *WhoHol 92*
McLaughlin, Bill *WhoHol 92*
Mclaughlin, Brett 1959- *WhoMW 93*
McLaughlin, Brian M. 1952- *WhoAmP 93*
McLaughlin, Brian P. 1949- *ConAu 141*
McLaughlin, Calvin Sturgis 1936- *WhoAm 94*
McLaughlin, Charles John 1950- *WhoMW 93*
McLaughlin, Charles P. 1937- *WhoAmP 93*
McLaughlin, David 1934- *WhoBlA 94*
McLaughlin, David J. 1936- *WhoAm 94*
McLaughlin, David Jordan 1940- *WhoAm 94*
Mc Laughlin, David Thomas 1932- *WhoAm 94*
McLaughlin, Dean (Benjamin, Jr.) 1931- *EncSF 93*
McLaughlin, Deborah Ann 1952- *WhoMW 93*
McLaughlin, Dolphy T. 1922- *WhoBlA 94*
McLaughlin, Donal 1875-1978 *WhoAmA 93N*
McLaughlin, Dorothy Claire *WhoWest 94*
McLaughlin, Edward 1928- *WhoAm 94*
McLaughlin, Edward David 1931- *WhoScEn 94*
McLaughlin, Eleanor Thomson 1938- *Who 94*
McLaughlin, Eurphan 1936- *WhoBlA 94*
McLaughlin, Frank 1895- *WhAm 10*
McLaughlin, Frank E. 1935- *WhoWest 94*
McLaughlin, George W. 1932- *WhoBlA 94*
McLaughlin, Gerald Lee 1949- *WhoMW 93, WhoScEn 94*
McLaughlin, Gibb d1960 *WhoHol 92*
McLaughlin, Glen 1934- *WhoAm 94, WhoFI 94*
McLaughlin, Harry d1920 *WhoHol 92*
Mc Laughlin, Harry Roll 1922- *WhoAm 94*
McLaughlin, Henry d1983 *WhoHol 92*
McLaughlin, Jacquelyn Snow 1943- *WhoBlA 94*
McLaughlin, James Daniel 1942- *WhoFI 94*
McLaughlin, James Daniel 1947- *WhoFI 94, WhoWest 94*
McLaughlin, James Hugh 1953- *WhoAmP 93*
McLaughlin, Jean Wallace 1950- *WhoAmA 93*
Mc Laughlin, Jerome Michael 1929- *WhoAm 94*
McLaughlin, John *WhoAm 94, WhoScEn 94*
McLaughlin, John 1898-1976 *WhoAmA 93N*
McLaughlin, John Bell 1925- *WhoAmP 93*
McLaughlin, John Belton 1903- *WhoBlA 94*
Mc Laughlin, John Francis 1927- *WhoAm 94, WhoScEn 94*

McLaughlin, John H. 1926- *WhoAmP 93*
McLaughlin, John Joseph 1927- *WhoAm 94*
McLaughlin, John Sherman 1932- *WhoAm 94*
McLaughlin, Joseph *DrAPF 93*
McLaughlin, Joseph M. 1933- *WhoAmP 93*
Mc Laughlin, Joseph Mailey 1928- *WhoAm 94*
McLaughlin, Joseph Michael 1933- *WhoAm 94, WhoAmL 94*
McLaughlin, Joseph Thomas 1944- *WhoAm 94, WhoAmL 94*
McLaughlin, Katye H. 1943- *WhoBlA 94*
McLaughlin, LaVerne Laney 1952- *WhoBlA 94*
Mc Laughlin, Leighton Bates, II 1930- *WhoAm 94*
McLaughlin, Linda Hodge 1942- *WhoAmL 94, WhoWest 94*
McLaughlin, Marguerite P. *WhoWest 94*
McLaughlin, Marguerite Pearl 1928- *WhoAmP 93*
McLaughlin, Marie 1954- *NewGrDO*
McLaughlin, Mary Rittling *WhoAm 94*
McLaughlin, Megan E. *WhoBlA 94*
McLaughlin, Michael 1949- *ConAu 141*
McLaughlin, Michael Angelo 1950- *WhoFI 94*
McLaughlin, Michael John 1944- *WhoAm 94, WhoFI 94*
McLaughlin, Michael John 1951- *WhoAm 94*
McLaughlin, Patricia *Who 94*
McLaughlin, (Florence) Patricia (Alice) 1916- *Who 94*
McLaughlin, Patrick Forrest 1947- *WhoMW 93*
McLaughlin, Patrick Michael 1946- *WhoAm 94*
McLaughlin, Peter 1949- *WhoAmP 93*
McLaughlin, Philip VanDoren, Jr. 1939- *WhoScEn 94*
McLaughlin, Richard Warren 1930- *WhoAm 94*
McLaughlin, Robert Leonard 1957- *WhoMW 93*
McLaughlin, Robert T. *DrAPF 93*
McLaughlin, Robert Toy 1939- *WhoFI 94*
McLaughlin, Robert William 1900-1989 *WhAm 10*
McLaughlin, Ruth *DrAPF 93*
McLaughlin, Sheila *WhoHol 92*
McLaughlin, Stanley A., Jr. 1943- *WhoMW 93*
McLaughlin, Susan 1952- *WhoAmL 94*
McLaughlin, T. Mark 1953- *WhoAm 94*
McLaughlin, Ted John 1921- *WhoAm 94*
McLaughlin, Thomas Daniel 1962- *WhoScEn 94*
McLaughlin, Thomas Ford 1944- *WhoWest 94*
McLaughlin, Thomas Jeffrey 1946- *WhoAm 94, WhoAmL 94*
McLaughlin, Thomas Orville 1940- *WhoAm 94*
McLaughlin, Thomas V. 1940- *WhoAmP 93*
McLaughlin, Walter Joseph 1931- *WhoFI 94*
McLaughlin, William *DrAPF 93*
McLaughlin, William Earle 1915- *IntWW 93*
Mc Laughlin, William Earle 1915-1991 *WhAm 10*
Mc Laughlin, William Gaylord 1936- *WhoFI 94*
McLaurin, Benjamin Philip 1947- *WhoBlA 94*
McLaurin, Daniel Washington 1940- *WhoBlA 94*
McLaurin, Eugene Bertram, II 1956- *WhoAmP 93*
McLaurin, Freddie Lewis, Jr. 1943- *WhoBlA 94*
McLaurin, Jasper Etienne 1927- *WhoBlA 94*
McLaurin, Ronald De 1944- *WhoAm 94*
McLaury, Ralph Leon 1942- *WhoScEn 94*
McLawhon, Ronald William 1957- *WhoScEn 94*
McLawhorn, Charles *WhoAmP 93*
McLawhorn, Daniel Francis 1948- *WhoAmL 94*
McLawhorn, James Thomas, Jr. 1947- *WhoBlA 94*
McLawhorn, Rebecca Lawrence 1949- *WhoScEn 94*
McLawhorn, William Benjamin 1960- *WhoFI 94*
McLay, James Kenneth *Who 94*
McLay, James Kenneth 1945- *IntWW 93*
McLeaish, Karen Thrash 1954- *WhoAmP 93*
McLeaish, Laurel Theresa 1960- *WhoAmP 93*
McLean, Alex *WhoAmP 93*

McLean, Allan c. 1725-1784 *WhAmRev*
McLean, Allan Campbell 1922- *WrDr 94*
McLean, Antonia (Maxwell) 1919- *WrDr 94*
McLean, Colin 1930- *IntWW 93, Who 94*
McLean, David *WhoHol 92*
McLean, Denis Bazeley Gordon 1930- *Who 94*
McLean, Dennis Ray 1951- *WhoBlA 94*
McLean, Don 1945- *IntWW 93, WhoAm 94*
Mc Lean, Donald Millis 1926- *WhoAm 94*
McLean, Doreen d1990 *WhoHol 92*
McLean, Edward Cochrane, Jr. 1935- *WhoAm 94*
McLean, Edward Peter 1941- *WhoAm 94*
McLean, Francis *WhAmRev*
McLean, Francis (Charles) 1904- *Who 94*
McLean, Gary Neil 1942- *WhoMW 93*
McLean, Geoffrey Daniel 1931- *Who 94*
Mc Lean, George Francis 1929- *WhoAm 94*
McLean, George Wallace, Jr. 1948- *WhoAmL 94*
McLean, Gordon Charles 1944- *WhoWest 94*
McLean, Hector John Finlayson 1934- *Who 94*
McLean, Helen Vincent 1894- *WhAm 10*
McLean, Helen Virginia 1933- *WhoBlA 94*
McLean, Hugh Angus 1925- *WhoWest 94*
McLean, Iain (S.) 1946- *WrDr 94*
McLean, Ian Graeme 1928- *Who 94*
McLean, Ian Small 1949- *WhoScEn 94, WhoWest 94*
McLean, J. Sloan 1914- *WrDr 94*
Mc Lean, Jackie 1932- *WhoAm 94*
McLean, Jacqueline *WhoAmP 93*
McLean, Jacqueline Fountain 1944- *WhoBlA 94*
McLean, James Albert 1928- *WhoAm 94, WhoAmA 93*
Mclean, John 1944- *WhoScEn 94*
McLean, John Alexander Lowry 1921- *Who 94*
McLean, John Alfred, Jr. 1926- *WhoBlA 94*
McLean, John F. 1943- *WhoAmL 94*
McLean, John Lenwood 1931- *WhoBlA 94*
Mc Lean, John William 1922- *WhoAm 94*
McLean, Kevin Andrew 1956- *WhoAmL 94*
McLean, Kirk 1966- *WhoAm 94, WhoWest 94*
McLean, Larry R. 1954- *WhoMW 93*
McLean, Mable Parker *WhoBlA 94*
McLean, Malcolm 1939- *Who 94, WhoScEn 94*
McLean, Marquita Sheila McLarty 1933- *WhoBlA 94*
McLean, Mary Cannon 1912- *WhoBlA 94*
McLean, Patricia Stanton d1993 *NewYTBS 93 [port]*
McLean, Peter Standley 1927- *Who 94*
McLean, Philip Alexander 1938- *Who 94*
McLean, R. Bruce 1946- *WhoAmL 94*
McLean, Rene 1946- *WhoBlA 94*
McLean, Richard Thorpe 1934- *WhoAmA 93*
McLean, Robert Alexander 1943- *WhoAmL 94*
McLean, Robert David 1945- *WhoAm 94, WhoAmL 94*
Mc Lean, Robert T. 1922- *WhoAm 94*
McLean, Robin Jennifer 1960- *WhoWest 94*
McLean, Ruari *Who 94*
McLean, (John David) Ruari 1917- *WrDr 94*
McLean, (John David) Ruari (McDowall Hardie) 1917- *Who 94*
McLean, Ryan John 1959- *WhoScEn 94*
McLean, Sammy 1929- *WrDr 94*
McLean, Sarah Pratt 1856-1935 *BlmGWL*
Mc Lean, Thomas Edwin 1925- *WhoAm 94*
McLean, Thomas Neil 1938- *WhoAm 94*
McLean, Thomas Pearson 1930- *Who 94*
McLean, Vincent Ronald 1931- *WhoAm 94*
McLean, Walter Franklin 1936- *IntWW 93, WhoAm 94*
McLean, William *WhoHol 92*
McLean, William F. 1916- *IntWW 93*
McLean, William George 1910- *WhoScEn 94*
Mc Lean, William L., III 1927- *WhoAm 94*
McLean, William Ronald 1921- *WhoFI 94, WhoScEn 94*
McLean, Zarah Gean 1942- *WhoBlA 94*
McLean-Wainwright, Pamela Lynne 1948- *WhoScEn 94*
McLearn, Michael Baylis 1936- *WhoAm 94, WhoAmL 94*
McLeay, Leo Boyce 1945- *Who 94*

McLeer, Laureen Dorothy 1955- *WhoFI 94*
McLees, Ainslie Armstrong 1947- *WrDr 94*
McLeish, David James Dow 1936- *WhoAm 94, WhoFI 94*
McLeish, Henry Baird 1948- *Who 94*
McLeish, Kenneth 1940- *WrDr 94*
McLellan, David 1940- *Who 94, WrDr 94*
McLellan, David S 1924- *WrDr 94*
McLellan, Edna M. 1929- *WhoAmP 93*
McLellan, Harold Linden 1937- *WhoFI 94*
McLellan, Hilary 1950- *WhoMW 93*
McLellan, Joseph Duncan 1929- *WhoAm 94*
McLellan, Katharine Esther 1963- *WhoScEn 94*
McLellan, Richard Douglas 1942- *WhoAm 94, WhoAmL 94*
McLellan, Robert N. 1924- *WhoAmP 93*
McLellan, Steven James 1957- *WhoWest 94*
McLelland, Charles James 1930- *Who 94*
McLelland, Joseph Cumming 1925- *WhoAm 94*
McLelland, Slaten Anthony 1962- *WhoScEn 94*
McLelland, Stan L. 1945- *WhoAmL 94, WhoFI 94*
McLellon, Richard Steven 1952- *WhoScEn 94*
McLemore, Andrew G. 1931- *WhoBlA 94*
McLemore, Donald Edward 1949- *WhoMW 93*
McLemore, Gary 1952- *WhoFI 94*
McLemore, Leslie Burl 1940- *WhoAmP 93, WhoBlA 94*
McLemore, Mark Tremell 1964- *WhoBlA 94*
McLemore, Nelson, Jr. 1934- *WhoBlA 94*
Mc Lemore, Robert Henry 1910- *WhoAm 94*
McLemore, Thomas 1970- *WhoBlA 94*
McLemore, Virginia Teresa 1955- *WhoWest 94*
McLendon, Christopher Martin 1961- *WhoFI 94*
McLendon, George Leland 1952- *WhoAm 94*
Mc Lendon, Heath Brian 1933 *WhoAm 94, WhoFI 94*
McLendon, James d1992 *WhoBlA 94N*
McLendon, Jesse Lawrence 1950- *WhoMW 93*
McLendon, John B., Jr. 1915- *WhoBlA 94*
McLendon, Mae Belle 1950- *WhoAmP 93*
McLendon, Robert J. *WhoAmP 93*
McLendon, Wallace Lamar 1940- *WhoAmP 93*
McLendon, William Woodard 1930- *WhoAm 94*
McLennan, Barbara Nancy 1940- *WhoAm 94*
McLennan, Bernice Claire 1936- *WhoFI 94*
McLennan, Donald Elmore 1919- *WhoScEn 94*
McLennan, Gordon 1924- *Who 94*
McLennan, Ian (Munro) 1909- *Who 94*
McLennan, Ian Munro 1909- *IntWW 93*
Mc Lennan, Kenneth Alan 1936- *WhoAm 94*
McLennan, Robert Gordon 1943- *WhoMW 93*
McLennan, Rod d1973 *WhoHol 92*
McLennan, Scott Mellin 1952- *WhoScEn 94*
McLennan, Will 1950- *WrDr 94*
McLennan, William Patrick 1942- *Who 94*
McLeod, Alan *WhoWest 94*
McLeod, Catherine 1921- *WhoHol 92*
McLeod, Charles Henry 1924- *Who 94*
McLeod, Christopher Kevin 1955- *WhoAm 94, WhoFI 94*
McLeod, Daniel R. 1913- *WhoAmP 93*
McLeod, Daniel R., Jr. 1946- *WhoAmL 94*
McLeod, Darwin Douglas 1935- *WhoMW 93*
McLeod, Dickson C. 1802-1840 *EncNAR*
McLeod, Douglas Powell 1965- *WhoAmL 94*
McLeod, Duncan *WhoHol 92*
McLeod, E. Douglas 1941- *WhoAm 94*
McLeod, Eugene Belton, Jr. 1949- *WhoAmP 93*
McLeod, Georgianna R. 1937- *WhoBlA 94*
McLeod, Gordon d1961 *WhoHol 92*
McLeod, Ian (George) 1926- *Who 94*
McLeod, James Francis 1946- *WhoAmL 94*
McLeod, James Graham 1932- *IntWW 93*
McLeod, James Richard 1942- *WhoWest 94*
McLeod, James S. 1939- *WhoBlA 94*
McLeod, Jenny (Helen) 1941- *NewGrDO*

McLeod, John 1925- *WhoWest 94*
McLeod, John 1926- *Who 94*
McLeod, John Arthur Sr. 1952- *WhoScEn 94*
McLeod, John Bryce 1929- *Who 94*
McLeod, John Hugh, Jr. 1911- *WhoWest 94*
McLeod, John William 1951- *WhoAmP 93*
McLeod, John Wishart 1908- *WhoAm 94*
McLeod, Keith Morrison 1920- *Who 94*
McLeod, Kenneth T. d1963 *WhoHol 92*
McLeod, Lionel E. 1927- *WhoAm 94*
McLeod, Malcolm Donald 1941- *Who 94*
McLeod, Malcolm Stewart 1941- *WhoFI 94*
McLeod, Michael Preston 1954- *WhoBlA 94*
McLeod, Peden Brown 1940- *WhoAmP 93*
McLeod, Philip R. 1943- *WhoAm 94, WhoMW 93*
McLeod, R. C. 1920- *WhoAmP 93*
McLeod, Rima L. 1945- *WhoMW 93*
McLeod, Robert Macfarlan 1925- *WhoAm 94*
McLeod, Robert Wesley 1949- *WhoFI 94*
McLeod, Rona *WhoHol 92*
McLeod, Stephen 1957- *WhoAmA 93*
McLeod, Tex d1973 *WhoHol 92*
McLeod, Wallace 1931- *WrDr 94*
McLeod, Walton James, Jr. 1906- *WhoAmL 94, WhoFI 94*
McLeod, William C. d1880 *WhWE*
McLeod, William James 1919- *WhoAmP 93*
McLeod, William Lasater, Jr. 1931- *WhoAmP 93*
McLeod, William Mullins 1942- *WhoAmP 93*
McLeod, Wilson Churchill 1938- *WhoAm 94*
McLeon, Nathaniel W. 1944- *WhoBlA 94*
Mc Leran, James Herbert 1931- *WhoAm 94*
McLerie, Allyn Ann 1926- *IntMPA 94, WhoHol 92*
McLernan, Kieran Anthony 1941- *Who 94*
McLeroy, Frederick Grayson 1951- *WhoAmL 94*
McLerran, Alice 1933- *WrDr 94*
McLeskey, Charles Hamilton 1946- *WhoWest 94*
McLester, Thelma Marie 1934- *WhoMW 93*
McLevie, John Gilwell 1929- *WhoWest 94*
McLewin, Philip James 1939- *WhoFI 94*
McLiam, John 1920- *WhoHol 92*
McLimans, Carol Ann 1936- *WhoMW 93*
McLin, James Curtis 1947- *WhoWest 94*
McLin, Lena Johnson 1928- *AfrAmAl 6, WhoBlA 94*
McLin, Nathaniel, Jr. 1928- *WhoMW 93*
McLin, Rhine L. *WhoAmP 93*
McLin, Rhine Lana 1948- *WhoMW 93*
McLin, Stephen T. 1946- *WhoAm 94*
McLin, William Merriman 1945- *WhoAm 94, WhoScEn 94*
McLinden, Dursley *WhoHol 92*
McLinden, James Hugh 1949- *WhoScEn 94*
McLindon, Gerald Joseph 1923- *WhoAm 94*
McLinn, Harry Marvin *WhoBlA 94*
McLintock, (Charles) Alan 1925- *Who 94*
McLintock, (George) Gordon 1903-1990 *WhAm 10*
McLintock, Michael (William) 1958- *Who 94*
McLish, Rachel Elizondo 1958- *WhoHisp 94*
McLoone, Michael E. 1945- *WhoIns 94*
McLorg, Terence Wyndham 1922- *WhoFI 94*
Mc Loughlin, Ellen Veronica d1989 *WhAm 10*
McLoughlin, George Leeke 1921- *Who 94*
McLoughlin, James *Who 94*
McLoughlin, John 1784-1857 *WhWE [port]*
McLoughlin, John C. 1949- *EncSF 93*
McLoughlin, Maurice 1890-1957 *BuCMET [port]*
McLoughlin, Patrick Allen 1957- *Who 94*
McLoughlin, Philip Robert 1946- *WhoFI 94*
McLoughlin, William G. d1993 *NewYTBS 94*
McLoughlin, William G. 1922-1993 *ConAu 140*
McLouth, Gary *DrAPF 93*
McLucas, John Luther 1920- *IntWW 93, WhoAm 94*
McLucas, William Robert 1950- *WhoAm 94, WhoFI 94*
McLuckey, John Alexander, Jr. 1940- *WhoScEn 94*
McLuckie, Steven J. 1956- *WhoAmP 93*

McLuhan, (Thomas) Eric (Marshall) 1942- *WrDr 94*
McLuhan, Marshall d1980 *WhoHol 92*
Mc Lure, Charles E., Jr. 1940- *WhoAm 94, WhoFI 94*
McLure, James *ConDr 93, WrDr 94*
McLurkin, Thomas Cornelius, Jr. 1954- *WhoAmL 94, WhoWest 94*
McLuskey, J(ames) Fraser 1914- *Who 94*
McMackin, F. Joseph, III 1946- *WhoAm 94*
McMackin, John Joseph 1908- *WhoFI 94*
McMackin, John William 1930- *WhoAm 94*
McMahan, Carl Austin 1953- *WhoAmL 94*
Mc Mahan, John William 1937- *WhoAm 94, WhoFI 94*
McMahan, Kent H. 1946- *WhoAmL 94*
McMahan, Oliver B. 1928- *WhoIns 94*
McMahan, Richard A. 1932- *WhoAmP 93*
McMahan, Susan Evon 1962- *WhoFI 94*
McMahand, Willie B. *WhoAmP 93*
McMahill, James Verne 1946- *WhoMW 93*
McMahon, A. Philip 1890- *WhoAmA 93N*
McMahon, Andrew 1920- *Who 94*
McMahon, Brian (Patrick) 1942- *Who 94*
McMahon, Brian J. 1952- *WhoAmL 94*
McMahon, Bryan T. *DrAPF 93*
McMahon, Christopher William 1927- *IntWW 93, Who 94*
McMahon, Colleen 1951- *WhoAm 94, WhoAmL 94*
McMahon, David d1972 *WhoHol 92*
McMahon, Denis J. d1993 *NewYTBS 93*
McMahon, Donald Aylward 1931- *WhoAm 94, WhoFI 94*
McMahon, Ed 1923- *IntMPA 94, WhoAm 94, WhoHol 92*
McMahon, Edward Francis 1930- *WhoAm 94, WhoFI 94*
McMahon, Edward Peter 1940- *WhoAm 94, WhoFI 94*
McMahon, Edward Richard 1949- *WhoAmL 94*
McMahon, Eleanor Marie 1929- *WhoAm 94*
McMahon, Ernest Edward 1910-1990 *WhAm 10*
McMahon, Fred 1920- *WhoWest 94*
Mc Mahon, George Joseph 1923- *WhoAm 94*
McMahon, Horace d1971 *WhoHol 92*
McMahon, Howard Oldford 1914-1990 *WhAm 10*
McMahon, Hugh Robertson 1938- *Who 94*
McMahon, James Charles 1951- *WhoAmL 94, WhoFI 94*
McMahon, James Edward 1937- *WhoAmA 93*
McMahon, James Francis 1942- *WhoScEn 94*
McMahon, James K. 1941- *WhoAmP 93*
McMahon, James Robert, Jr. 1929- *WhoAmP 93*
McMahon, Jim *WhoHol 92*
McMahon, Jim 1959- *WhoAm 94, WhoMW 93*
McMahon, John Alexander 1921- *IntWW 93, WhoAm 94*
McMahon, John J. 1932- *IntMPA 94*
McMahon, John Joseph 1949- *WhoAmL 94*
McMahon, John Joseph 1960- *WhoMW 93*
McMahon, John Patrick 1919- *WhoAm 94*
McMahon, John W. 1939- *WhoAmP 93*
McMahon, Joseph Einar 1940- *WhoAm 94*
McMahon, Joseph P., Jr. 1944- *WhoAmL 94*
McMahon, Judith Diane 1950- *WhoAmL 94*
McMahon, Kevin 1940- *WhoAmL 94*
McMahon, Kit *Who 94*
McMahon, Maribeth Lovette 1949- *WhoAm 94*
McMahon, Mary Frances 1955- *WhoAmP 93*
McMahon, Michael Edward 1955- *WhoFI 94*
McMahon, Michael P. 1950- *WhoAmL 94*
McMahon, Neil Michael 1953- *WhoFI 94*
McMahon, Pat *EncSF 93*
McMahon, Patricia Anne 1945- *WhoWest 94*
McMahon, Paul Francis 1945- *WhoAm 94*
McMahon, Robert Albert, Jr. 1950- *WhoAmL 94*
McMahon, Robert Lee, Jr. 1944- *WhoFI 94*
McMahon, Robert Matthew *WhoFI 94*
McMahon, Shannon *WhoHol 92*
McMahon, Thomas *Who 94*

McMahon, Thomas Arthur 1943- *WhoAm 94*
McMahon, Thomas Joseph 1956- *WhoAmL 94*
McMahon, Thomas Michael 1941- *WhoAm 94, WhoAmL 94*
McMahon, Thomas Patrick 1945- *WhoMW 93*
McMahon-Holden Kingsmore, Brandie Kathle 1970- *WhoWest 94*
McMains, F. Charles, Jr. 1948- *WhoAmP 93*
McMains, Melvin Lee 1941- *WhoAm 94*
McMakin, Joseph Hamilton 1946- *WhoFI 94*
McManama, Trudy E. 1945- *WhoMW 93*
McManaman, Kenneth Charles 1950- *WhoAmL 94, WhoMW 93*
McManamy, David Kenneth 1943- *WhoWest 94*
McManigal, Shirley Ann 1938- *WhoAm 94*
McManimon, Francis J. 1926- *WhoAmP 93*
McManis, Bruce Loren 1953- *WhoFI 94*
McManis, Kenneth Louis 1941- *WhoScEn 94*
McManners, (Joseph) Hugh 1952- *WrDr 94*
McManners, John 1916- *IntWW 93, Who 94*
Mc Manus, Charles Anthony, Jr. 1927- *WhoAm 94, WhoAmP 93*
McManus, Charles Edward 1926- *WhoAmP 93*
McManus, Daniel Albert 1954- *WhoWest 94*
McManus, Declan Patrick 1954- *WhoAm 94*
McManus, Edward Hubbard 1939- *WhoAm 94*
Mc Manus, Edward Joseph 1920- *WhoAm 94*
McManus, Francis Joseph 1942- *Who 94*
McManus, George d1954 *WhoHol 92*
McManus, George A., Jr. 1930- *WhoAmP 93*
McManus, James *DrAPF 93*
McManus, James 1882-1958 *WhoAmA 93N*
McManus, James F., Jr. 1945- *WhoAmP 93*
McManus, James William 1942- *WhoAmA 93*
McManus, James William 1944- *WhoScEn 94*
McManus, James William 1945- *WhoAm 94, WhoAmL 94*
McManus, Jason Donald 1934- *IntWW 93, WhoAm 94, WhoFI 94*
McManus, John Francis, III 1919- *WhoAm 94*
McManus, John Gerard 1960- *WhoScEn 94*
McManus, John J. 1931- *WhoIns 94*
McManus, Kay 1922- *WrDr 94*
McManus, Lowell Gene 1952- *WhoAmP 93*
McManus, Mark 1940- *WhoHol 92*
McManus, Martin Joseph 1919- *WhoAm 94, WhoAmL 94, WhoAmP 93*
McManus, Michael *WhoHol 92*
McManus, Michael Anderson 1955- *WhoAmL 94*
McManus, Michelle 1966- *WhoAmP 93*
McManus, Michelle Ann 1966- *WhoMW 93*
McManus, Mike 1933- *WhoAmP 93*
McManus, Paul Frederick, Jr. 1956- *WhoFI 94*
McManus, R. Louise d1993 *NewYTBS 93*
McManus, Rachel Elizabeth 1947- *WhoMW 93*
McManus, Richard Philip 1929- *WhoAm 94*
Mc Manus, Samuel Plyler 1938- *WhoAm 94*
McManus, Sharon 1937- *WhoHol 92*
McManus, Walter Leonard 1918- *WhoAm 94*
McManus, William J., II 1963- *WhoAmP 93*
McManus, William Jay 1900- *WhoAmP 93*
McManus, William Raymond, Jr. 1967- *WhoFI 94*
McMartin, Ian W. *WhoIns 94*
McMartin, John *IntMPA 94, WhoHol 92*
McMartin, Kenneth Esler 1951- *WhoScEn 94*
McMaster, Andrew d1962 *WhoHol 92*
McMaster, Brian (John) 1943- *NewGrDO*
McMaster, Brian John 1943- *IntWW 93, Who 94, WhoAm 94*
McMaster, Gordon James 1960- *Who 94*
McMaster, Grace Isabel 1923- *WhoWest 94*

McMaster, Henry *WhoAmP 93*
McMaster, Hughan James Michael 1927- *Who 94*
McMaster, Juliet (Sylvia) 1937- *WrDr 94*
McMaster, Juliet Sylvia 1937- *WhoWest 94*
McMaster, Niles *WhoHol 92*
McMaster, Peter 1931- *Who 94*
McMaster, Robert Raymond 1948- *WhoAm 94*
McMaster, Stanley Raymond d1992 *Who 94N*
McMasters, Barbara Jean 1944- *WhoMW 93*
McMath, Alexander S. 1945- *WhoBlA 94*
McMath, Carroll Barton, Jr. 1910- *WhoWest 94*
McMath, James Bruce 1949- *WhoAmL 94*
McMath, Phillip H. *DrAPF 93*
McMath, Virginia Katherine 1911- *WhoAm 94*
McMeekin, Bruce K. 1961- *WhoFI 94*
McMeekin, Dorothy 1932- *WhoAm 94*
Mc Meel, John Paul 1936- *WhoAm 94*
McMeen, Albert Ralph, III 1942- *WhoAm 94, WhoFI 94*
McMeen, Elmer Ellsworth, III 1947- *WhoAm 94, WhoAmL 94*
McMein, Neysa 1890- *WhoAmA 93N*
McMenamin, John Robert 1946- *WhoAm 94, WhoAmL 94*
McMenamin, Michael Terrence 1943- *WhoAmL 94*
McMenamin, Peter David 1948- *WhoFI 94*
McMenamin, Richard F. 1946- *WhoAm 94*
McMenamin, Thomas Paul 1954- *WhoAmL 94, WhoFI 94*
Mc Mennamin, George Barry 1922- *WhoAm 94*
McMichael, Andrew James 1943- *Who 94*
McMichael, Cathy A. 1955- *WhoIns 94*
McMichael, Donald Earl 1931- *WhoAmL 94*
McMichael, Earlene Clarisse 1963- *WhoBlA 94*
McMichael, Francis Clay 1937- *WhoAm 94*
McMichael, George E. d1989 *WhoHol 92*
McMichael, Jeane Casey 1938- *WhoMW 93*
McMichael, Joe d1944 *WhoHol 92*
McMichael, John d1993 *IntWW 93N, Who 94N*
McMichael, Joseph 1956- *WhoFI 94*
McMichael, Lawrence Grover 1953- *WhoAmL 94*
McMickens, Jacqueline Montgomery 1935- *WhoBlA 94*
McMicking, James Harvey 1929- *WhoMW 93*
McMillan, Alan Austen 1926- *Who 94*
McMillan, Alan D. 1945- *WhoDi 94*
Mc Millan, Brockway 1915- *WhoAm 94*
McMillan, C. Steven 1945- *WhoFI 94*
McMillan, Campbell White 1927- *WhoAm 94*
McMillan, Charles Frederick 1954- *WhoScEn 94*
McMillan, Charles William 1926- *WhoAm 94, WhoAmP 93*
McMillan, Colin R. 1935- *WhoAmP 93*
McMillan, Constance *WhoAmA 93*
McMillan, Donald 1906- *Who 94*
McMillan, Donald Edgar 1937- *WhoAm 94*
McMillan, Donald Ernest 1931- *WhoAm 94*
McMillan, Donald Neil, Monsignor 1925- *Who 94*
McMillan, Duncan d1993 *Who 94N*
McMillan, Edwin Mattison 1907-1991 *WhAm 10, WorInv, WorScD*
McMillan, Elridge W. *WhoBlA 94*
McMillan, Enolia Pettigen 1904- *WhoBlA 94*
McMillan, Florri *DrAPF 93*
McMillan, Francis Wetmore, II 1938- *WhoIns 94*
McMillan, Frew 1942- *BuCMET*
Mc Millan, George Duncan Hastie, Jr. 1943- *WhoAm 94, WhoAmP 93*
McMillan, Gilbert Edward *WhoAmP 93*
McMillan, Horace James 1919- *WhoBlA 94*
McMillan, Howard Lamar, Jr. 1939- *WhoAm 94, WhoFI 94*
McMillan, Hubert Stephen 1949- *WhoAmP 93*
McMillan, Ian 1956- *WrDr 94*
McMillan, J. Alex 1932- *CngDr 93, CngDr 93*
Mc Millan, James *WhoAm 94, WrDr 94*
McMillan, James 1929- *WhoMW 93*
McMillan, James Albert 1926- *WhoFI 94, WhoMW 93, WhoScEn 94*
McMillan, James Bates 1918- *WhoBlA 94*

McMillan, James Bryan 1916- *WhoAm 94, WhoAmL 94*
McMillan, James C. 1925- *WhoBlA 94*
McMillan, James Everett 1961- *WhoMW 93*
McMillan, John 1915- *Who 94*
McMillan, John A. 1931- *WhoAm 94, WhoFI 94, WhoWest 94*
McMillan, John Alexander, III 1932- *WhoAm 94*
McMillan, John-Douglas James 1947- *WhoBlA 94*
McMillan, Joseph H. 1929- *WhoBlA 94*
McMillan, Joseph T., Jr. *WhoBlA 94*
McMillan, Kenneth d1989 *WhoHol 92*
McMillan, Kenneth Gordon 1942- *WhoAmP 93, WhoMW 93*
McMillan, L. R. *WhoBlA 94*
McMillan, Lee Richards, II 1947- *WhoAm 94, WhoAmL 94, WhoFI 94*
McMillan, Lemmon Columbus 1917- *WhoBlA 94*
McMillan, M. Sean *WhoAm 94, WhoAmL 94*
McMillan, Mae F. 1936- *WhoBlA 94*
McMillan, Malcolm Cook 1910-1989 *WhAm 10*
McMillan, Mary 1895- *WhoAmA 93N*
McMillan, Mary Bigelow 1919- *WhoAm 94*
McMillan, Naomi 1950- *WhoBlA 94*
McMillan, Nathaniel 1964- *WhoBlA 94*
McMillan, Raymond V. 1933- *AfrAmG [port]*
McMillan, Regina Ellis 1964- *WhoBlA 94*
McMillan, Richard, Jr. 1944- *WhoAm 94, WhoAmL 94*
Mc Millan, Robert Bruce 1937- *WhoAm 94, WhoMW 93*
McMillan, Robert Frank, Jr. 1946- *WhoBlA 94*
McMillan, Robert John 1952- *WhoIns 94*
McMillan, Robert R. *NewYTBS 93 [port]*
McMillan, Robert Ralph 1932- *WhoAm 94, WhoAmL 94*
McMillan, Robert W. 1915-1991 *WhoAmA 93N*
McMillan, Robert Walker 1935- *WhoScEn 94*
McMillan, Roddy d1979 *WhoHol 92*
McMillan, Ronald Therow 1951- *WhoScEn 94*
McMillan, Samuel Sterling, III 1938- *WhoAm 94*
McMillan, Stephen A. 1941- *WhoAmP 93*
McMillan, Stephen Walker 1949- *WhoAmA 93*
McMillan, Terry *DrAPF 93*
McMillan, Terry 1951- *AfrAmAl 6, CurBio 93 [port], TwCYAW, WhoAm 94, WrDr 94*
McMillan, Terry (L.) 1951- *BlkWr 2, ConAu 140*
McMillan, Terry L. 1951- *WhoBlA 94*
McMillan, Thomas Michael 1945- *IntWW 93*
McMillan, William Asbury 1920- *WhoBlA 94*
McMillan-Scott, Edward 1949- *Who 94*
McMillen, Barbara *DrAPF 93*
McMillen, David L. 1941- *WhoScEn 94*
McMillen, Donald H. 1929- *WhoAmP 93*
McMillen, Howard *DrAPF 93*
McMillen, James Thomas 1942- *WhoAmL 94*
McMillen, John 1924- *WhoAmP 93*
McMillen, Larry *WhoAm 94*
McMillen, Louis Albert 1916- *WhoAm 94*
McMillen, Michael C(halmers) 1946- *WhoAmA 93*
McMillen, Neil Raymond 1939- *WrDr 94*
McMillen, Robert Stewart 1943- *WhoAmL 94*
McMillen, Sally G(regory) 1944- *WrDr 94*
McMillen, Thomas 1952- *WhoAm 94*
Mc Millen, Thomas Roberts 1916- *WhoAm 94, WhoAmL 94*
McMillen, Tom 1952- *CurBio 93 [port], WhoAmP 93*
Mc Millen, Wheeler 1893-1992 *WhAm 10*
McMillen, William *DrAPF 93*
McMiller, Anita Williams 1946- *WhoAm 94*
McMillian, Frank L. 1935- *WhoBlA 94*
McMillian, Jimmy, Jr. 1953- *WhoBlA 94*
McMillian, Josie 1940- *WhoBlA 94*
McMillian, Theodore 1919- *AfrAmAl 6, WhoAm 94, WhoAmL 94, WhoAmP 93, WhoBlA 94 [port]*
McMillin, David Robert 1948- *WhoAm 94*
McMillin, Glenn Reinhard 1930- *WhoAm 94, WhoFI 94*
McMillin, Jeanie Byrd 1939- *WhoAm 94*
McMillin, Larry H. 1951- *WhoAmL 94*
McMillin, Marilynn Patricia 1947- *WhoWest 94*

McMillion, John Macon 1929-
WhoAm 94, WhoWest 94
McMillon, R. L. 1921- *WhoIns 94*
McMindes, Roy James 1923- *WhoAm 94*
McMinn, B. C. 1921- *WhoAmP 93*
McMinn, Robert Matthew Hay 1923-
Who 94
McMinn, William A. *WhoAm 94,
WhoFI 94*
McMinn, William Gene 1931- *WhoAm 94*
McMinn, William Lowell, Jr. 1943-
WhoMW 93
McMinn, William Scott 1956- *WhoFI 94*
McMinnies, John Gordon 1919- *Who 94*
McMorris, Jacqueline Williams 1936-
WhoBlA 94
McMorris, Samuel Carter 1920-
WhoBlA 94
McMorris, William *WhoAm 94*
McMorrow, Mary Ann G. 1930-
WhoAmL 94, WhoAmP 93
McMorrow, Mary Ann Grohwin 1930-
WhoAmP 93
McMorrow, Rebecca Lynn 1951-
WhoMW 93
Mc Morrow, Richard Mark 1941-
WhoAm 94
McMulkin, Francis John 1915-
WhoAm 94
Mc Mullan, Dorothy 1911- *WhoAm 94*
McMullan, Gordon *Who 94*
McMullan, James Burroughs 1934-
WhoAmA 93
McMullan, James F., Jr. 1931-
WhoAmP 93
McMullan, James Franklin 1928-
WhoFI 94
McMullan, Jim 1938- *WhoHol 92*
McMullan, John J. *WhoAmP 93*
McMullan, Michael Brian 1926- *Who 94*
McMullan, William Patrick, Jr. 1925-
WhoAm 94
McMullan, William Patrick, III 1952-
WhoAm 94, WhoFI 94
McMullen, Daniel Robert 1948-
WhoMW 93
McMullen, David Lawrence 1939-
Who 94
McMullen, Dennis *WhoHol 92*
McMullen, E. Ormond 1888-
WhoAmA 93N
Mc Mullen, Edwin Wallace, Jr. 1915-
WhoAm 94
McMullen, Jeremy (John) 1948- *WrDr 94*
McMullen, John Henry, Jr. 1944-
WhoFI 94
McMullen, John J. *WhoAm 94*
McMullen, Kristi Kay 1962- *WhoMW 93*
McMullen, Lorraine 1926- *ConAu 41NR*
McMullen, Mary 1920- *WrDr 94*
McMullen, Patrick R. 1945- *WhoAmP 93*
McMullen, Richard E. *DrAPF 93*
McMullen, Sean (Christopher) 1948-
EncSF 94
Mc Mullen, Thomas Henry 1929-
WhoAm 94
Mc Mullian, Amos Ryals 1937-
WhoAm 94
McMullin, Carleton Eugene 1932-
WhoAm 94
McMullin, Craig Stephen 1957- *WhoFI 94*
McMullin, Dix Holt 1933- *WhoAmP 93*
McMullin, Duncan (Wallace) 1927-
Who 94
Mc Mullin, Ernan Vincent 1924-
WhoAm 94
McMullin, John Leonard, III 1946-
WhoAmL 94
McMullin, Kimball Ray 1945-
WhoAm 94, WhoAmL 94
McMullin, Ruth Roney 1942- *WhoAm 94,
WhoFI 94*
McMullins, Tommy 1942- *WhoBlA 94*
Mc Munn, Earl William 1910-
WhoAm 94, WhoAmP 93
McMurdo, C. Gregory 1946- *WhoAmP 93*
McMurdo, Mary-Jane 1924- *WhoAm 94,
WhoAmP 93*
McMurphy, Charles d1969 *WhoHol 92*
McMurphy, Michael Allen 1947-
WhoAm 94, WhoScEn 94
McMurray, Cecil Hugh 1942- *Who 94*
McMurray, David Bruce 1937- *Who 94*
McMurray, Jerry Lee 1956- *WhoFI 94*
McMurray, José Daniel 1949-
WhoHisp 94
McMurray, Joseph Patrick Brendan
1912- *IntWW 93, WhoAm 94*
McMurray, Kay 1918- *WhoAmP 93*
McMurray, Richard d1984 *WhoHol 92*
McMurray, Sam *WhoHol 92*
McMurray, William 1810-1894 *EncNAR*
McMurray, William 1929- *WhoAm 94*
McMurray-Schwarz, Paula 1961-
WhoMW 93
Mc Murrin, Lee Ray 1930- *WhoAm 94*
Mc Murrin, Sterling Moss 1914-

Mc Murry, Idanelle Sam 1924-
WhoAm 94
McMurry, Kermit Roosevelt, Jr. 1945-
WhoBlA 94
McMurry, Merley Lee 1949- *WhoBlA 94*
McMurry, Michael Baird 1941-
WhoAm 94, WhoAmL 94
McMurry, Richard M. 1939- *WrDr 94*
McMurry, Walter M., Jr. 1934-
WhoBlA 94
McMurry, William Scott 1921-
WhoMW 93
McMurtrey, James Edward, Jr. 1893-
WhAm 10
McMurtrie, Alexander B., Jr. *WhoAmP 93*
McMurtrie, Edith 1883- *WhoAmA 93N*
McMurtrie, Richard Angus 1909- *Who 94*
McMurtry, Donna 1967- *WhoMW 93*
McMurtry, James 1962- *ConMus 10 [port]*
McMurtry, Larry *DrAPF 93*
McMurtry, Larry 1936- *ConTFT 11,
IntWW 93, WhoAm 94*
McMurtry, Larry (Jeff) 1936-
ConAu 43NR, WrDr 94
McMurtry, Michael Ray 1961- *WhoFI 94*
McMurtry, R. Roy 1932- *WhoAm 94*
McMurtry, (Roland) Roy 1932- *Who 94*
McMyler, Pamela *WhoHol 92*
McNab, John Stanley 1937- *Who 94*
McNabb, Dianne Leigh 1956- *WhoFI 94*
McNabb, Frank William 1936-
WhoAm 94, WhoFI 94
McNabb, Leland Monte 1943-
WhoAmL 94
McNab Jones, Robin Francis 1922-
Who 94
McNail, Stanley *DrAPF 93*
McNair, Baron 1947- *Who 94*
McNair, Archie 1919- *Who 94*
McNair, Barbara 1934- *WhoHol 92*
McNair, Barbara J. 1939- *WhoBlA 94*
McNair, Carl Herbert, Jr. 1933-
WhoAm 94
McNair, Chris *WhoAmP 93, WhoBlA 94*
McNair, Dennis Michael 1945-
WhoScEn 94
McNair, Frances Ellen Firner 1950-
WhoMW 93
McNair, John Caldwell 1923-
WhoAmL 94
McNair, John Franklin, III 1927-
WhoAm 94, WhoFI 94
McNair, Joseph *DrAPF 93*
McNair, Robert Evander 1923-
WhoAmP 93
McNair, Ronald E. 1950-1986
AfrAmA 6 [port]
McNair, Russell Arthur, Jr. 1934-
WhoAm 94
McNair, Sylvia 1924- *SmATA 74*
McNair, Thomas Jaffrey 1927- *Who 94*
McNair, Wesley *DrAPF 93*
McNair-Wilson, (Robert) Michael (Conal)
d1993 *Who 94N*
McNair-Wilson, Patrick (Michael Ernest
David) 1929- *Who 94*
McNairy, Francine G. 1946- *WhoBlA 94*
McNairy, Sidney A. 1937- *WhoMW 93*
McNall, Bruce *WhoAm 94, WhoWest 94*
McNall, Lester Ray 1927- *WhoWest 94*
McNall, Orange d1963 *WhoHol 92*
Mc Nallen, James Berl 1930- *WhoAm 94*
McNally, Andrew, III 1909- *WhoAm 94*
McNally, Andrew, IV 1939- *WhoAm 94,
WhoFI 94, WhoMW 93*
McNally, Chris 1960- *WhoAmP 93*
McNally, Derek 1934- *IntWW 93*
McNally, Ed *WhoHol 92*
McNally, Edward Michael 1947-
WhoAmL 94
McNally, Frank Thomas 1936-
WhoAm 94
McNally, Harry John, Jr. 1938-
WhoScEn 94
McNally, James Henry 1936-
WhoWest 94
McNally, James Rand, III 1944-
WhoAmP 93
McNally, John d1985 *ProFbHF*
McNally, John Joseph 1927- *WhoAm 94*
McNally, Kevin *WhoHol 92*
McNally, Mark Matthew 1958-
WhoScEn 94
McNally, Nancy E. 1955- *WhoAm 94*
McNally, Patrick Joseph 1958-
WhoScEn 94
McNally, Shaun M. 1957- *WhoAmP 93*
McNally, Sheila John 1932- *WhoAmA 93*
McNally, Stephen 1913- *IntMPA 94*
McNally, Stephen (Horace) 1913-
WhoHol 92
McNally, Terrence *WhoHol 92*
McNally, Terrence 1939- *ConDr 93,
GayLL, WhoAm 94, WrDr 94*
McNally, Thomas Charles, III 1938-
WhoAm 94

McNally, Timothy John 1954-
WhoAmP 93
McNally, Tom 1943- *Who 94*
McNally, William Joseph 1948-
WhoAm 94
Mc Namar, Richard Timothy 1939-
WhoFI 94
McNamara, A. J. 1936- *WhoAm 94,
WhoAmL 94*
McNamara, Anne H. 1947- *WhoAm 94,
WhoAmL 94, WhoFI 94*
McNamara, Barry Thomas 1944-
WhoAmL 94
McNamara, Brian *WhoHol 92*
McNamara, David Joseph 1951-
WhoMW 93
McNamara, David Rea 1962-
WhoAmL 94
McNamara, Dennis L. 1945- *WrDr 94*
McNamara, Ed d1986 *WhoHol 92*
McNamara, Edward d1944 *WhoHol 92*
McNamara, Edward Howard 1926-
WhoAmP 93
McNamara, Ellen Marie 1950-
WhoAmL 94
McNamara, Eugene *DrAPF 93*
McNamara, Eugene Joseph 1930-
WrDr 94
McNamara, Francis John 1915-
WhoAm 94
Mc Namara, Francis Joseph, Jr. 1927-
WhoAm 94
McNamara, Francis T. *WhoAmP 93*
McNamara, Francis T. 1927- *WhoAm 94*
McNamara, George d1959 *WhoHol 92*
McNamara, Henry P. 1934- *WhoAmP 93*
McNamara, J. Patrick *WhoHol 92*
McNamara, John *WhoFI 94*
McNamara, John d1968 *WhoHol 92*
McNamara, John 1939- *WhoAmP 93*
McNamara, John 1950- *WhoAmA 93*
Mc Namara, John Donald 1924-
WhoAm 94
McNamara, John F. *WhoAmP 93*
McNamara, John F. 1935- *WhoAm 94,
WhoFI 94*
Mc Namara, John Joseph 1934-
WhoAm 94
McNamara, John Stephen 1950-
WhoAm 94
Mc Namara, Joseph Donald 1934-
WhoAm 94, WhoWest 94
McNamara, Keith 1928- *WhoAmP 93,
WhoMW 93*
McNamara, (Joseph) Kevin 1934-
Who 94
Mc Namara, Lawrence J. 1928-
WhoAm 94, WhoMW 93
McNamara, Lawrence John 1950-
WhoAm 94
McNamara, Maggie d1978 *WhoHol 92*
McNamara, Major James H. d1946
WhoHol 92
McNamara, Martin Burr 1947-
WhoAm 94
McNamara, Mary Jo 1950- *WhoAmA 93*
McNamara, Maureen Ann 1923-
WhoAmP 93
McNamara, Michael John 1948-
WhoAmL 94
McNamara, Neville (Patrick) 1923-
Who 94
Mc Namara, Rieman, Jr. 1928-
WhoAm 94
McNamara, Robert *DrAPF 93*
McNamara, Robert (Strange) 1916-
WrDr 94
McNamara, Robert James 1950-
WhoWest 94
McNamara, Robert Strange 1916-
IntWW 93, Who 94, WhoAm 94
McNamara, Ted d1928 *WhoHol 92*
McNamara, Thomas E. 1940- *IntWW 93*
McNamara, Thomas Edmund 1940-
WhoAmP 93
McNamara, Thomas Neal 1930-
WhoAm 94
McNamara, Timothy Kevin 1955-
WhoAmL 94
McNamara, Wanda G. 1944-
WhoAmP 93
McNamara, William 1965- *IntMPA 94,
WhoHol 92*
McNamara, William Patrick, Jr. 1946-
WhoAmA 93
McNamee, Bernard Joseph 1935-
WhoAmL 94
McNamee, Catherine 1931- *WhoAm 94*
McNamee, Daniel Vincent, III 1944-
WhoAm 94
McNamee, Dennis Patrick 1952-
WhoAmL 94
McNamee, Donald d1940 *WhoHol 92*
McNamee, Evelyn Haynes 1947-
WhoWest 94
McNamee, Graham d1942 *WhoHol 92*
McNamee, Gregory *DrAPF 93*
McNamee, Louise *WhoAm 94, WhoFI 94*

McNamee, Stafford F. 1942- *WhoAmL 94*
McNamee, Stephen M. 1942-
WhoAmL 94
McNamee, Stephen N. *WhoAm 94,
WhoWest 94*
McNamee, Thomas *DrAPF 93*
McNamee, William Lawrence 1931-
WhoScEn 94
McNames, Dennis W. 1947- *WhoAmL 94*
McNaney, Robert Trainor 1934-
WhoAmL 94
McNary, Oscar L. 1944- *WhoAmA 93*
McNary, Oscar Lee 1944- *WhoBlA 94*
McNatt, Isaac G. 1916- *WhoBlA 94*
McNaught, Harry F. 1954- *WhoAmL 94*
McNaught, John Graeme 1941- *Who 94*
McNaught, Judith 1944- *WrDr 94*
McNaught, William 1813-1881
DcNaB MP
McNaughton, Anne Elizabeth 1952-
WhoAmP 93
McNaughton, Charles d1955 *WhoHol 92*
McNaughton, Gus d1969 *WhoHol 92*
McNaughton, H(oward) D(ouglas) 1945-
WrDr 94
McNaughton, Harry d1969 *WhoHol 92*
McNaughton, Ian Kenneth Arnold 1920-
Who 94
McNaughton, Jack d1990 *WhoHol 92*
McNaughton, John 1950- *IntMPA 94*
McNaughton, John D. *WhoAm 94*
McNaughton, Michael Walford 1943-
WhoScEn 94
McNaughton, Robert Forbes, Jr. 1924-
WhoAm 94
McNaughton, Samuel Joseph 1939-
WhoAm 94
McNaughton, Stanley O. 1921-
WhoIns 94
McNeal, Clark E. 1942- *WhoAmP 93*
McNeal, Dale William, Jr. 1939-
WhoAm 94
McNeal, Don 1958- *WhoBlA 94*
McNeal, Harriet 1928- *WhoMW 93*
McNeal, John Alex, Jr. 1932- *WhoBlA 94*
McNeal, Julia *WhoHol 92*
McNeal, Palmer Craig 1950- *WhoAmP 93*
McNeal, Ralph Leroy, Sr. 1935-
WhoFI 94
McNeal, Shay 1946- *WhoAm 94*
McNeal, Sylvia Ann 1947- *WhoBlA 94*
McNeal, Travis S. 1967- *WhoBlA 94*
McNeal, William Clark 1930-
WhoAmP 93
McNealey, J. Jeffrey 1944- *WhoAm 94,
WhoAmL 94*
McNealy, Robert *WhoAmA 93*
Mc Nealy, Scott 1954- *WhoAm 94,
WhoFI 94, WhoWest 94*
McNear, Barbara Baxter 1939-
WhoAm 94, WhoFI 94
McNear, Everett C. 1904-1984.
WhoAmA 93N
McNear, Howard d1969 *WhoHol 92*
McNearney, John Patrick 1956-
WhoAmL 94
McNeary, Joseph Allen 1948- *WhoAm 94,
WhoFI 94*
McNee, David (Blackstock) 1925- *Who 94*
McNee, David Blackstock 1925-
IntWW 94
Mc Nee, Robert Bruce 1922-1992
WhAm 10
McNeece, John B., III 1950- *WhoAmL 94*
McNeel, Synott Lance 1923- *WhoIns 94*
McNeeley, Donald Robert 1954-
WhoAm 94
McNeely, Carol J. 1954- *WhoBlA 94*
McNeely, Charles E. 1951- *WhoBlA 94*
McNeely, D. Dean 1944- *WhoAm 94*
Mc Neely, E. L. 1918-1991 *WhAm 10*
McNeely, John J. 1931- *WhoAm 94,
WhoAmL 94*
McNeely, June *WhoAsA 94*
McNeely, Mark Hall 1950- *WhoAm 94*
McNeely, Matthew 1920- *WhoBlA 94*
McNeely, Michael Dale 1955- *WhoIns 94*
McNeely, Stephen Allen 1948-
WhoMW 93
McNeely-Johnson, Kathy Ann 1957-
WhoFI 94
McNees, Caryl 1938- *WhoWest 94*
Mc Neese, Aylmer Green, Jr. 1911-
WhAm 10
McNeese, Jack Marvin 1929- *WhoAm 94*
McNeice, Ian *WhoHol 92*
Mc Neice, John Ambrose, Jr. 1932-
WhoAm 94
McNeice, (Thomas) Percy (Fergus) 1901-
Who 94
McNeil, Allyson 1962- *WhoWest 94*
McNeil, Alvin J. 1920- *WhoBlA 94*
McNeil, Barbara Joyce 1941- *WhoAm 94*
McNeil, Barry 1944- *WhoAmL 94*
McNeil, Bill 1924- *WrDr 94*
McNeil, Claudia d1993
NewYTBS 93 [port]
McNeil, Claudia 1917- *WhoHol 92*

McNeil, Claudia Mae 1917- *WhoBlA 94*
McNeil, David James 1958- *WhoFI 94*
McNeil, Dean S. 1957- *WhoAmA 93*
McNeil, DeeDee *WhoBlA 94*
McNeil, Ernest Duke 1936- *WhoBlA 94*
McNeil, Florence 1937- *BlmGWL*
McNeil, Florence 1940- *WrDr 94*
McNeil, Frank 1937- *WhoBlA 94*
McNeil, Frank William 1948- *WhoBlA 94*
McNeil, Freeman 1959- *WhoBlA 94*
McNeil, George J. 1908- *WhoAmA 93*
McNeil, George Joseph 1908- *WhoAm 94*
McNeil, Heidi Loretta 1959- *WhoAmL 94*
McNeil, Ian Robert 1932- *Who 94*
McNeil, James H. 1937- *WhoAmL 94*
McNeil, John *Who 94*
McNeil, John 1939- *WrDr 94*
McNeil, (David) John 1937- *Who 94*
McNeil, John C. *WhoAmP 93*
McNeil, John D. 1934- *WhoAm 94, WhoFI 94, WhoIns 94*
McNeil, John Struthers 1907- *Who 94*
McNeil, John Stuart 1935- *WhoWest 94*
McNeil, John W. 1942- *WhoAmL 94*
McNeil, Kate 1959- *WhoHol 92*
McNeil, Kathy *WhoHol 92*
McNeil, Lori Michelle 1963- *WhoBlA 94*
McNeil, Marianne McFarland *DrAPF 93*
McNeil, Mark Sanford 1950- *WhoAmL 94*
McNeil, Mary *WrDr 94*
McNeil, Nellie Miller 1937- *WhoAmP 93*
McNeil, Norman d1938 *WhoHol 92*
McNeil, Ogretta V. 1932- *WhoBlA 94*
McNeil, Robert Duell 1935- *WhoWest 94*
McNeil, Steven Arthur 1942- *WhoAm 94*
McNeil, William C. d1993 *NewYTBS 93*
McNeill, Alfred Thomas, Jr. 1936- *WhoAm 94, WhoFI 94*
McNeill, Anthony *DrAPF 93*
McNeill, Anthony 1941- *BlkWr 2, WrDr 94*
Mc Neill, Carmen Mary *WhoFI 94, WhoIns 94*
Mc Neill, Charles James 1912- *WhoAm 94*
McNeill, Corbin Asahel, Jr. 1939- *WhoAm 94, WhoFI 94*
McNeill, Daniel 1947- *ConAu 141*
McNeill, Don 1918- *BuCMET*
McNeill, Douglas Arthur 1942- *WhoWest 94*
McNeill, Elisabeth 1931- *WrDr 94*
McNeill, Frederick Wallace 1932- *WhoAmL 94, WhoFI 94*
McNeill, G. David 1931- *WhoAm 94*
McNeill, Ian 1947- *WhoIns 94*
McNeill, James Walker 1952- *Who 94*
McNeill, Janet 1907- *BlmGWL, WrDr 94*
McNeill, John 1933- *Who 94, WhoAm 94*
McNeill, John Henderson 1941- *WhoAm 94, WhoAmL 94*
McNeill, John Hugh 1938- *WhoAm 94*
McNeill, John Malcolm 1909- *Who 94*
McNeill, Keith *Who 94*
McNeill, (Gordon) Keith 1953- *Who 94*
McNeill, Kenneth Gordon 1926- *WhoAm 94*
McNeill, Kevin Michael 1956- *WhoWest 94*
McNeill, Larry Parker 1950- *WhoAmL 94*
McNeill, Nolan G. 1934- *WhoAmP 93*
McNeill, Peter Grant Brass 1929- *Who 94*
Mc Neill, Robert Eugene 1921- *WhoAm 94*
McNeill, Robert Patrick 1941- *WhoAm 94, WhoFI 94*
McNeill, Susan Patricia 1947- *WhoBlA 94*
McNeill, Thomas B. 1934- *WhoAm 94*
McNeill, Thomas Ray 1952- *WhoAm 94, WhoAmL 94*
McNeill, Wehton R. 1917- *WhoAmP 93*
McNeill, William 1930- *WhoScEn 94*
Mc Neill, William Hardy 1917- *WhoAm 94, WrDr 94*
McNeill-Huntley, Esther Mae 1921- *WhoBlA 94*
McNeilly, Wilfred Glassford 1921-1983 *EncSF 93*
McNeish, Alexander Stewart 1938- *Who 94*
McNeish, James 1931- *WrDr 94*
McNellie, Elizabeth Anne 1964- *WhoAmL 94, WhoMW 93*
Mc Nelly, Frederick Wright, Jr. 1947- *WhoMW 93*
McNelly, John Taylor 1923- *WhoAm 94*
McNelly, Theodore Hart 1919- *WrDr 94*
McNelly, Walter C. 1898- *WhAm 10*
McNelly, Willis E(verett) 1920- *EncSF 93*
McNelty, Harry *WhoBlA 94*
McNenny, Kenneth G. *WhoAmP 93*
McNerney, Daniel P. 1920- *WhoAmP 93*
McNerney, Joan *DrAPF 93*
McNerney, Walter J. 1925- *IntWW 93*
Mc Nerney, Walter James 1925- *WhoAm 94*
McNett, Glenn Scott 1960- *WhoMW 93*
McNett, William Brown 1896-1968 *WhoAmA 93N*
Mc New, Bennie Banks 1931- *WhoAm 94*
McNew, Charles Sanders 1958- *WhoAmL 94*
McNew, Frances Wilkins 1930- *WhoMW 93*
McNew, Patrick Leon 1945- *WhoMW 93*
McNichol, Edward 1897- *BasBi*
McNichol, Jimmy 1961- *WhoHol 92*
McNichol, Kristy 1962- *IntMPA 94, WhoHol 92*
McNichol, Michele Leneve 1965- *WhoAmL 94*
McNicholas, David Paul 1941- *WhoAm 94, WhoFI 94*
McNicholas, John Patrick 1936- *WhoAmL 94*
McNichols, Gerald Robert 1943- *WhoFI 94*
McNichols, William H., Jr. 1910- *WhoAmP 93*
McNickle, Michael M. *WhoAm 94*
McNickle, Thomas Glen 1944- *WhoAmA 93*
McNickle, William D'Arcy 1904-1977 *AmSocL*
McNickle, William Edward 1949- *WhoFI 94*
McNicol, David Leon 1944- *WhoAm 94*
McNicol, David Williamson 1913- *Who 94*
McNicol, Donald 1939- *IntWW 93, Who 94*
Mc Nicol, Donald Edward 1921- *WhoAm 94*
McNicol, George Paul 1929- *IntWW 93, Who 94*
McNider, James Small, III 1956- *WhoAmL 94*
McNiel, D. Ferguson 1955- *WhoAmL 94*
McNish, Althea Marjorie *Who 94*
McNish, Frank L. d1924 *WhoHol 92*
McNitt, Joseph Edward 1929- *WhoAm 94*
Mc Nitt, Willard Charles 1920- *WhoAm 94*
McNorriell, Mozell M. 1922- *WhoBlA 94*
McNorton, Bruce Edward 1959- *WhoBlA 94*
McNown, John Stephenson 1916- *WhoAm 94, WhoScEn 94*
McNown, Mildred Louise 1922- *WhoMW 93*
McNulty, Anthony d1992 *IntWW 93N*
McNulty, Carrell Stewart, Jr. 1924- *WhoAm 94*
McNulty, Chester Howard 1935- *WhoAm 94*
McNulty, Dermot 1949- *WhoFI 94*
McNulty, Dorothy *WhoHol 92*
McNulty, Faith 1918- *WrDr 94*
McNulty, Frank John 1923- *WhoScEn 94*
McNulty, Harold d1978 *WhoHol 92*
McNulty, Henry Bryant 1947- *WhoAm 94*
McNulty, Jack Allison 1945- *WhoAmL 94*
McNulty, James F., Jr. 1925- *WhoAmP 93*
McNulty, James F. M. *WhoIns 94*
McNulty, John Alexander 1946- *WhoScEn 94*
McNulty, John Kent 1934- *WhoAm 94*
McNulty, John William 1927- *WhoAm 94*
McNulty, June d1984 *WhoHol 92*
Mc Nulty, Kneeland 1921- *WhAm 10*
McNulty, Kneeland 1921-1991 *WhoAmA 93N*
McNulty, Matthew Francis, Jr. 1914- *WhoAm 94, WhoFI 94, WhoScEn 94*
McNulty, Michael Francis 1951- *WhoAm 94, WhoAmL 94*
McNulty, Michael R. 1947- *CngDr 93*
McNulty, Michael Robert 1947- *WhoAm 94, WhoAmP 93*
McNulty, Peter J. 1941- *WhoScEn 94*
McNulty, Peter J. 1951- *WhoAm 94, WhoAmL 94*
McNulty, Richard Paul 1946- *WhoScEn 94*
McNulty, Robert Holmes 1940- *WhoAm 94*
McNulty, (Robert William) Roy 1937- *Who 94*
McNulty, Thomas Francis 1944- *WhoFI 94*
McNulty, William Charles 1884-1963 *WhoAmA 93N*
McNutt, Darrell Landes 1945- *WhoFI 94*
McNutt, Douglas Page 1935- *WhoWest 94*
McNutt, Jack Wray 1934- *WhoAm 94*
McNutt, James 1935- *WhoAmP 93*
McNutt, Kristen Wallwork 1941- *WhoAm 94*
McNutt, Philip J. 1948- *WhoAmL 94*
McNutt, R. H. 1937- *WhoScEn 94*
McNutt, Stephen Russell 1954- *WhoWest 94*
McNutt, Suzzanne Marie 1962- *WhoAm 94, WhoAmL 94*
McNutt, William James 1927- *WhoAm 94*
McOwen, C. Lynn 1953- *WhoAmA 93*
McOwen, Carol M. 1927- *WhoAmA 93*
McPartland, Jimmy d1991 *WhoHol 92*
McPartlin, Dennis William 1951- *WhoAmL 94, WhoAmP 93*
McPartlin, Noel 1939- *Who 94*
McPartlon, James Peter, III 1959- *WhoFI 94*
McPeak, Allan 1938- *WhoAmL 94*
McPeak, Merrill A. *WhoAmP 93*
McPeak, Merrill Anthony 1936- *IntWW 93, WhoAm 94*
McPeak, Sandy *WhoHol 92*
McPeters, Curtis *WhoHol 92*
McPhail, Addie *WhoHol 92*
Mc Phail, Andrew Tennent 1937- *WhoAm 94*
McPhail, Douglas d1942 *WhoHol 92*
McPhail, Evelyn 1930- *WhoWomW 91*
McPhail, Evelyn W. 1930- *WhoAmP 93*
McPhail, Irving P. 1949- *WhoBlA 94*
McPhail, Sharon M. 1948- *WhoBlA 94*
McPhail, Sharon Mae 1948- *WhoAmL 94*
McPhail, Weldon 1944- *WhoBlA 94*
McPharlin, Paul 1903-1948 *WhoAmA 93N*
McPhatter, Thomas H. 1923- *WhoBlA 94*
McPhearson, Geraldine June 1938- *WhoMW 93*
McPhedran, Norman Tait 1924- *WhoAm 94*
Mc Phee, Henry Roemer 1925- *WhoAm 94*
McPhee, James *EncSF 93*
McPhee, John (Angus) 1931- *WrDr 94*
Mc Phee, John Angus 1931- *WhoAm 94*
McPhee, Jonathan *WhoAm 94*
McPhee, Jonathan Trumbull 1946- *WhoAmL 94*
McPhee, Paula Ann 1951- *WhoMW 93*
McPhee, Roderick Fulton 1929- *WhoWest 94*
McPhee, Ronald P. 1933- *WhoIns 94*
McPhee, Susan Louise 1953- *WhoAmP 93*
McPheeters, Annie Lou 1908- *WhoBlA 94*
Mc Pheeters, Edwin Keith 1924- *WhoAm 94*
McPheeters, Jean McNiff 1951- *WhoAmP 93*
McPheron, Alan Beaumont 1914- *WhoAmL 94*
McPherson, Aimee Semple 1890-1944 *DcAmReB 2, HisWorL*
Mc Pherson, Alice Ruth 1926- *WhoAm 94*
McPherson, Andrew Francis 1942- *Who 94*
McPherson, Bruce Rice 1951- *WhoAmA 93*
McPherson, Christopher Geoffrey 1959- *WhoWest 94*
McPherson, David E. 1942- *WhoIns 94*
McPherson, Donald J. *WhoAm 94*
McPherson, Donald Paxton, III 1941- *WhoAm 94*
McPherson, Eric Scott 1951- *WhoAmP 93*
Mc Pherson, Frank Alfred 1933- *WhoAm 94, WhoFI 94*
McPherson, Gail *WhoFI 94*
McPherson, Gary Lee 1962- *WhoAmL 94*
McPherson, Gertrude d1987 *WhoHol 92*
McPherson, Harriet A. *WhoAmP 93*
McPherson, Harry Cummings, Jr. 1929- *IntWW 93, WhoAm 94*
McPherson, Heather 1942- *BlmGWL*
McPherson, James A(lan) 1943- *RfGShF, WrDr 94*
McPherson, James Alan *DrAPF 93*
McPherson, James Alan 1943- *AfrAmAl 6, ConLC 77 [port], WhoAm 94, WhoBlA 94, WhoMW 93*
McPherson, James Alexander Strachan 1927- *Who 94*
McPherson, James M. 1936- *IntWW 93*
Mc Pherson, James Munro 1936- *WhoAm 94, WrDr 94*
McPherson, James R. 1953- *WhoBlA 94*
McPherson, James Willis, III 1956- *WhoWest 94*
Mc Pherson, John Barkley 1917- *WhoAm 94*
McPherson, John Michael 1964- *WhoFI 94*
McPherson, Larry E. 1943- *WhoAmA 93*
McPherson, Larry Eugene 1943- *WhoAm 94*
McPherson, M. Peter 1940- *WhoAmP 93*
McPherson, Mary Patterson 1935- *WhoAm 94*
McPherson, Melville Peter 1940- *IntWW 93, WhoAm 94*
McPherson, Michael C. 1949- *WhoWest 94*
McPherson, Michael Dale 1952- *WhoWest 94*
McPherson, Orland Gordon 1930- *WhoAmP 93*
Mc Pherson, Paul Francis 1931- *WhoAm 94*
Mc Pherson, Robert Donald 1936- *WhoAm 94*
Mc Pherson, Rolf Kennedy *WhoAm 94*
McPherson, Ronald P. *WhoScEn 94*
McPherson, Roosevelt 1948- *WhoBlA 94*
McPherson, Sandra *DrAPF 93*
McPherson, Sandra 1943- *WrDr 94*
McPherson, Sandra Jean 1943- *WhoAm 94*
McPherson, Thomas Allen 1935- *WhoAmP 93*
McPherson, Tommy Eugene 1938- *WhoAmL 94*
McPherson, Vanzetta Penn 1947- *WhoAm 94, WhoAmL 94, WhoBlA 94*
McPherson, William Dean 1947- *WhoWest 94*
McPherson, William H. 1927- *WhoBlA 94*
McPherson, William Hauhuth 1922- *WhoAmP 93*
McPherson, William Joseph, Jr. 1950- *WhoAmP 93*
McPhie, Gaye Turnbow 1935- *WhoAmP 93*
McPhie, Neil Anthony Gordon 1945- *WhoAmL 94*
McPhillips, Elizabeth Nell 1958- *WhoMW 93*
McPhillips, Hugh d1990 *WhoHol 92*
McPhillips, Julian Lenwood, Jr. 1946- *WhoAmP 93*
McPhillips, Mary Margaret 1945- *WhoAmP 93*
McPike, Jim 1943- *WhoAmP 93*
McPike, Martin John, Jr. 1946- *WhoFI 94*
Mc Quade, Henry Ford 1915- *WhoAm 94*
McQuade, J. Stanley 1932- *WhoAmP 93*
McQuade, John d1979 *WhoHol 92*
McQuade, Kris *WhoHol 92*
Mc Quade, Lawrence Carroll 1927- *WhoAm 94, WhoAmL 94, WhoFI 94*
Mc Quade, Walter 1922- *WhoAm 94*
McQuaid, Bernard John 1823-1909 *DcAmReB 2*
McQuaid, J. Dennis 1939- *WhoAm 94, WhoAmL 94*
McQuaid, James 1939- *Who 94*
McQuaid, John G. 1918- *WhoAmL 94*
McQuaid, Joseph Woodbury 1949- *WhoAm 94*
McQuaid, Maureen 1952- *WhoAmL 94*
McQuaid, Phyllis W. 1928- *WhoAmP 93*
McQuaid, Salli Lou 1943- *WhoWest 94*
McQuail, Paul Christopher 1934- *Who 94*
McQuarrie, Albert 1918- *Who 94*
McQuarrie, Bruce Cale 1929- *WhoAm 94*
McQuarrie, Claude Monroe, III 1950- *WhoAm 94, WhoAmL 94*
McQuarrie, Donald Gray 1931- *WhoAm 94*
McQuarrie, Terry Scott 1942- *WhoScEn 94, WhoWest 94*
McQuater, Patricia A. 1951- *WhoBlA 94*
McQuay, James Phillip 1924- *WhoBlA 94*
McQuay, Mike 1949- *EncSF 93, WrDr 94*
McQuay, Sandra Sue 1944- *WhoAmL 94*
McQueen, Anjetta 1966- *WhoBlA 94*
McQueen, Armelia *WhoHol 92*
McQueen, Butterfly 1911- *AfrAmAl 6 [port], ConBlB 6 [port], WhoBlA 94, WhoHol 92*
McQueen, Chad 1960- *WhoHol 92*
McQueen, Cilla 1949- *BlmGWL, WrDr 94*
McQueen, Cyrus B. 1951- *WrDr 94*
McQueen, Daniel Bruce 1926- *WhoFI 94*
McQueen, Frederick Lee 1963- *WhoFI 94*
McQueen, George W. 1932- *WhoIns 94*
McQueen, John 1943- *WhoAmA 93*
McQueen, John R. 1948- *WhoAmL 94*
McQueen, Justice Ellis 1927- *WhoAm 94*
McQueen, Justus E. *WhoHol 92*
McQueen, Kevin Paige 1958- *WhoBlA 94*
McQueen, Michael Anthony 1956- *WhoBlA 94*
McQueen, Neile Adams *WhoHol 92*
McQueen, Rebecca Hodges 1954- *WhoScEn 94*
Mc Queen, Robert Charles 1921- *WhoAm 94*
McQueen, Ronald d1981 *WhoHol 92*
McQueen, Ronald A. *EncSF 93*
McQueen, Scott Robert 1946- *WhoAm 94*
McQueen, Simon *WhoHol 92*
McQueen, Stanley Eugene 1946- *WhoWest 94*
McQueen, Steve d1980 *WhoHol 92*
McQueen, Thomas K. 1949- *WhoAm 94, WhoAmL 94*
Mc Queeney, Henry Martin, Sr. 1938- *WhoAm 94*
McQueney, Patricia Ann 1966- *WhoScEn 94*
McQuern, Marcia Alice 1942- *WhoAm 94, WhoFI 94, WhoWest 94*
McQuerry, Wayne Harrison 1922- *WhoWest 94*
McQuiddy, David Newton, Jr. 1938- *WhoAm 94*

McQuigg, John Dolph 1931- *WhoAmL 94*
McQuiggan, John 1922- *Who 94*
McQuilkin, Frank *DrAPF 93*
McQuilkin, John Robertson 1927- *WhoAm 94*
McQuilkin, Rennie *DrAPF 93*
McQuilkin, Robert Rennie *DrAPF 93*
Mc Quilkin, William Winter 1907-1992 *WhAm 10*
McQuillan, Frances *WhoAmA 93*
McQuillan, James Brennan 1929- *WhoAmL 94*
Mc Quillan, Joseph Michael 1931- *WhoAm 94, WhoFI 94*
McQuillan, Karin 1950- *WrDr 94*
Mc Quillan, Margaret Mary *WhoFI 94*
McQuillan, Terry *WhoHol 92*
McQuillan, William Hugh 1935- *WhoAm 94*
McQuillan, William Rodger 1930- *Who 94*
McQuillen, Albert Lawrence, Jr. 1925- *WhoAm 94*
McQuillen, Harry A. *WhoAm 94, WhoFI 94*
McQuillen, Jeremiah Joseph 1941- *WhoFI 94*
McQuillen, Mary Theresa 1932- *WhoAmP 93*
Mc Quillen, Michael Paul 1932- *WhoAm 94*
McQuillen-Shelton, Pamela Jean 1959- *WhoWest 94*
McQuillin, Cynthia Ann 1953- *WhoWest 94*
McQuillin, Richard Ross 1956- *WhoFI 94, WhoWest 94*
McQuinn, Donald E. 1930- *EncSF 93*
Mc Quinn, William P. 1936- *WhoAm 94*
McQuiston, John Ward, II 1943- *WhoAmL 94*
McQuiston, Robert Earl 1936- *WhoAm 94*
McQuoid, Edwin d1950 *WhoHol 92*
McQuoid, Rose Lee d1962 *WhoHol 92*
McQuown, Eloise *WhoAmP 93*
McQuown, Judith H 1941- *WrDr 94*
McQuown, Judith Hershkowitz 1941- *WhoFI 94*
McRae, Alan *WhoHol 92*
McRae, Barry (Donald) 1935- *WrDr 94*
McRae, Brian Wesley 1967- *WhoBlA 94*
McRae, Bruce d1927 *WhoHol 92*
McRae, Carmen *WhoAm 94*
McRae, Carmen 1922- *AfrAmAl 6, WhoBlA 94, WhoHol 92*
McRae, Charles R. *WhoAmL 94*
McRae, Chuck 1939- *WhoAmP 93*
McRae, Daniel 1947- *WhoAmL 94*
McRae, David Carroll 1946- *WhoAm 94*
McRae, Duncan d1931 *WhoHol 92*
McRae, Ellen *WhoHol 92*
McRae, Emmett N. 1943- *WhoBlA 94*
McRae, Frances Anne *Who 94*
McRae, Frank 1952- *WhoHol 92*
McRae, Hal 1945- *WhoAm 94, WhoBlA 94, WhoMW 93*
McRae, Hamilton Eugene, Jr. 1905-1991 *WhAm 10*
McRae, Hamilton Eugene, III 1937- *WhoAm 94, WhoAmL 94, WhoWest 94*
McRae, Hamish Malcolm Donald 1943- *Who 94*
McRae, Helene Williams *WhoBlA 94*
McRae, Jack Ardon 1953- *WhoWest 94*
McRae, John Finley 1896- *WhAm 10*
McRae, John Leonidas 1917- *WhoScEn 94*
McRae, John Malcolm 1942- *WhoAm 94*
McRae, Karen K. 1944- *WhoAmP 93*
Mc Rae, Kenneth Douglas 1925- *WhoAm 94, WrDr 94*
McRae, Paul Anthony 1945- *WhoMW 93*
McRae, Robert Malcolm, Jr. 1921- *WhoAm 94, WhoAmL 94*
McRae, Ronald Edward 1955- *WhoBlA 94*
McRae, Thomas Kenneth 1906- *WhoAm 94*
McRae, Thomas W. 1924- *WhoBlA 94*
McRaith, John Jeremiah 1934- *WhoAm 94*
McRaney, Gerald 1947- *WhoHol 92*
McRaney, Gerald 1948- *IntMPA 94*
McRary, John Walter, III 1939- *WhoFI 94*
McRay, Paul *DrAPF 93*
Mc Ree, Edward Barxdale 1931- *WhoAm 94*
McRee, John Browning, Jr. 1950- *WhoScEn 94*
McReynolds, Allen, Jr. 1909- *WhoFI 94, WhoMW 93*
McReynolds, Barbara 1956- *WhoWest 94*
McReynolds, David Hobert 1953- *WhoFI 94*
McReynolds, Elaine A. 1948- *WhoBlA 94*

McReynolds, Glenna Jean 1953- *WhoWest 94*
McReynolds, Kirk *WhoAmA 93*
McReynolds, Mary Armilda 1946- *WhoAmL 94*
McReynolds, Neil Lawrence 1934- *WhoAm 94, WhoFI 94*
McReynolds, Paul Wyatt 1919- *WhoWest 94*
McReynolds, Ronald W. *DrAPF 93*
McReynolds, Stephen Paul 1938- *WhoAmL 94*
McRickard, Edmund J. d1993 *NewYTBS 93*
McRipley, G. Whitney 1957- *WhoBlA 94*
McRitchie, Bruce Dean 1938- *WhoAm 94, WhoFI 94, WhoWest 94*
McRobert, Gussie 1933- *WhoAmP 93*
McRobert, Marc Kelly 1954- *WhoWest 94*
McRobert, Rosemary Dawn Teresa 1927- *Who 94*
McRoberts, B. Joyce 1941- *WhoAmP 93*
McRoberts, Briony *WhoHol 92*
McRoberts, Darrel Sherman 1938- *WhoAmP 93*
McRoberts, Joyce 1941- *WhoWest 94*
McRoberts, Robert *DrAPF 93*
McRoberts, Robert M. 1895- *WhAm 10*
McRorie, William Edward 1940- *WhoAm 94, WhoIns 94*
Mc Rostie, Clair Neil 1930- *WhoAm 94*
McRoy, Paul Furgeson 1912-1988 *WhAm 10*
McRoy, Ruth Gail 1947- *WhoBlA 94*
MC Serch c. 1967- *ConMus 10 [port]*
McShain, John 1898-1989 *WhAm 10*
McShane, Edward James 1904-1989 *WhAm 10*
McShane, Eugene Mac 1950- *WhoScEn 94*
McShane, Ian 1942- *IntMPA 94, WhoHol 92*
McShane, John Q. 1946- *WhoAmL 94*
McShane, Kitty d1964 *WhoHol 92*
McShane, Mark 1929- *WrDr 94*
McSharry, Deirdre 1932- *Who 94*
McSharry, Deirdre Mary 1932- *IntWW 93*
McShea, Joseph 1907-1991 *WhAm 10*
McSheehy, Cornelia Marie 1947- *WhoAmA 93*
McShefferty, John 1929- *WhoAm 94, WhoFI 94*
Mc Sheffrey, Gerald Rainey 1931- *WhoAm 94*
McSherry, Frank David, Jr. 1927- *WhoScEn 94*
McSherry, G. X. *WhoAmP 93*
McSherry, James Francis 1953- *WhoFI 94*
McSherry, Walter Clinton 1929- *WhoAmP 93*
McSherry, William John, Jr. 1947- *WhoAmL 94*
McShine, Arthur Hugh *Who 94N*
McShine, Kynaston Leigh 1935- *WhoAmA 93, WrDr 94*
McSmith, Blanche Preston 1920- *WhoBlA 94*
McSoley, Patrick Shannon 1954- *WhoAmA 94*
McSorley, Cisco 1950- *WhoAmP 93, WhoWest 94*
McSorley, Jean Sarah 1958- *WrDr 94*
McSorley, John E. 1947- *WhoAmL 94*
McSpadden, Clem Rogers 1925- *WhoAmP 93*
McSpadden, Donna Casity 1934- *WhoAmP 93*
Mc Spadden, Peter Ford 1930- *WhoAm 94*
McSparran, Robert B. *WhoFI 94*
McStallworth, Paul 1910- *WhoBlA 94*
McStay, James P. 1945- *WhoAmP 93*
McSteen, Martha Abernathy 1923- *WhoAm 94*
McSwain, Berah D. 1935- *WhoBlA 94*
McSwain, David L. 1928- *WhoBlA 94*
McSwain, Eldridge Tracy 1898- *WhAm 10*
McSwain, Marc Daniell 1965- *WhoWest 94*
McSwain, Richard Horace 1949- *WhoAm 94, WhoScEn 94*
McSwain, Rodney 1962- *WhoBlA 94*
Mc Swain, William Adney 1904-1989 *WhAm 10*
McSween, Cirilo A. 1929- *WhoBlA 94*
McSween, Harold B. *DrAPF 93*
McSweeney, Austin John 1946- *WhoScEn 94*
McSweeney, E. Douglas, Jr. *WhoAmP 93*
McSweeney, Frances Kaye 1948- *WhoAm 94*
McSweeney, John *WhoAmP 93*
McSweeney, Maurice J. 1938- *WhoAm 94*
McSweeney, Michael Terrence 1937- *WhoAm 94*
McSweeney, Patrick *WhoAmP 93*

McSweeney, William Lincoln, Jr. 1930- *WhoAm 94*
McSweeny, Paul Edward 1942- *WhoScEn 94*
McSweeny, William Francis 1929- *WhoAm 94, WhoFI 94*
McSwiney, Charles Ronald 1943- *WhoAm 94, WhoAmL 94*
McSwiney, James Wilmer 1915- *IntWW 93, WhoAm 94*
McSwiney, Owen *NewGrDO*
McTaggart, Malcolm d1949 *WhoHol 92*
McTaggart-Cowan, Ian 1910- *WhoAm 94*
McTague, John Paul 1938- *WhoAm 94, WhoFI 94*
McTarnaghan, Roy E. *WhoAm 94*
McTeague, Bertrand Luke 1935- *WhoFI 94*
McTeague, David 1952- *WhoAmP 93*
McTeer, Douglas E., Jr. 1951- *WhoAmP 93*
McTeer, George Calvin 1938- *WhoBlA 94*
McTeer, Janet *WhoHol 92*
McTernan, Maureen E. 1955- *WhoIns 94*
McTernan, Myles James 1948- *WhoWest 94*
McTier, Roselyn Jones 1916- *WhoBlA 94*
McTiernan, John 1951- *ConTFT 11, IntMPA 94, WhoAm 94*
McTiernan, Miriam 1952- *WhoWest 94*
McTigue, Bernard Francis 1946- *WhoAm 94*
McTigue, Teresa Ann 1962- *WhoScEn 94*
McTurk, Joe d1961 *WhoHol 92*
McTurnan, Lee Bowes 1937- *WhoAmL 94*
McTwigan, Michael 1948- *WhoAmA 93*
McTyre, Robert Earl, Sr. 1955- *WhoBlA 94*
McVay, Barbara Chaves 1950- *WhoScEn 94*
McVay, Glen A. *WhoAmP 93*
McVay, John Edward 1931- *WhoAm 94, WhoWest 94*
McVeagh, Eve *WhoHol 92*
McVean, James 1937- *WrDr 94*
McVeery, Maureen *WhoHol 92*
McVeigh, Byron Joseph 1956- *WhoWest 94*
McVeigh, (Robert) Desmond 1939- *Who 94*
McVeigh, John Stephen 1955- *WhoAmL 94*
McVeigh, Miriam Lenig *WhoAmA 93*
McVeigh, Norman Shaw, III 1951- *WhoAmP 93*
McVeigh, Roger Hugh 1960- *WhoFI 94*
McVeigh-Pettigrew, Sharon Christine 1949- *WhoWest 94*
McVerry, Terrence F. 1943- *WhoAmP 93*
McVerry, Thomas Leo 1938- *WhoAm 94*
McVety, James Robert 1941- *WhoAmL 94*
McVey, Diane Elaine 1953- *WhoFI 94*
McVey, Eugene Steven 1927- *WhoAm 94*
McVey, Henry Hanna, III 1935- *WhoAm 94*
McVey, James William 1931- *WhoAm 94, WhoFI 94*
McVey, Jeanne Howard 1935- *WhoAmP 93*
McVey, Lane Leroy 1947- *WhoAmL 94*
McVey, Leza 1907-1984 *WhoAmA 93N*
McVey, Patrick d1973 *WhoHol 92*
McVey, Tyler *WhoHol 92*
McVey, Walter Lewis, Jr. 1922- *WhoAmP 93*
McVey, William M. 1905- *WhoAmA 93*
McVey, William Mozart 1905- *WhoAm 94*
McVicar, Mark Albert 1961- *WhoWest 94*
McVicar, Robert William, Jr. 1944- *WhoScEn 94*
McVicker, Charles Taggart 1930- *WhoAmA 93*
McVicker, H. Keith 1943- *WhoIns 94*
McVicker, J. Jay 1911- *WhoAmA 93*
McVicker, Jesse Jay 1911- *WhoAm 94*
McVicker, Julius d1940 *WhoHol 92*
McVicker, Mary Ellen Harshbarger 1951- *WhoMW 93*
Mc Vie, Christine Perfect 1943- *WhoAm 94, WhoWest 94*
McVisk, William Kilburn 1953- *WhoAm 94*
McVittie, George Cunliffe 1904-1988 *WhAm 10*
McVoy, Kirk Warren 1928- *WhoMW 93*
McVoy, Ross A. 1941- *WhoAmL 94*
McWade, Charles P. 1944- *WhoAm 94*
McWade, Edward d1943 *WhoHol 92*
McWade, Margaret d1956 *WhoHol 92*
McWade, Robert d1913 *WhoHol 92*
McWade, Robert d1938 *WhoHol 92*
McWalters, Peter 1946- *WhoAm 94*
McWard, Richard Alan 1938- *WhoMW 93*
McWaters, Thomas David 1942- *WhoScEn 94*

McWatters, George Edward 1922- *Who 94*
McWatters, Stephen John 1921- *Who 94*
McWeeny, Roy 1924- *Who 94*
McWethy, John Bertrand 1917- *WhoMW 93*
McWethy, Patricia Joan 1946- *WhoAm 94*
McWhan, Denis Bayman 1935- *WhoAm 94, WhoScEn 94*
McWherter, Ned R. 1930- *IntWW 93, WhoAmP 93*
McWherter, Ned Ray 1930- *WhoAm 94*
McWhiney, Grady 1928- *WhoAm 94*
Mc Whinney, Edward Watson 1924- *WhoAm 94*
McWhinney, Ian Renwick 1926- *WhoAm 94*
McWhinney, Madeline H. 1922- *WhoAm 94*
McWhinnie, Harold James 1929- *WhoAmA 93*
McWhirter, Bruce J. 1931- *WhoAm 94*
McWhirter, George 1939- *WrDr 94*
McWhirter, Glenna Suzanne 1929- *WhoAm 94*
McWhirter, James Herman 1924- *WhoAm 94*
McWhirter, James Jeffries 1938- *WhoWest 94*
McWhirter, Jillian *WhoHol 92*
McWhirter, Joan Brighton 1954- *WhoScEn 94*
McWhirter, Kent *WhoHol 92*
McWhirter, Norris Dewar 1925- *IntWW 93, Who 94*
McWhirter, Robert 1904- *Who 94*
McWhirter, William Buford 1918- *WhoAm 94*
McWhorter, Alan Louis 1930- *WhoAm 94*
McWhorter, Donald L. 1935- *WhoAm 94, WhoFI 94*
McWhorter, Elsie Jean 1932- *WhoAmA 93*
McWhorter, Grace Agee 1948- *WhoBlA 94*
Mc Whorter, Hezzie Boyd 1923- *WhoAm 94*
McWhorter, Hobart Amory, Jr. 1931- *WhoAm 94*
McWhorter, John Francis 1941 *WhoFI 94, WhoMW 93*
McWhorter, Kathleen 1953- *WhoAm 94, WhoScEn 94*
McWhorter, Millard Henry, III 1954- *WhoBlA 94*
McWhorter, Ralph Clayton 1933- *WhoAm 94, WhoFI 94*
McWhorter, Rosalynd D. 1960- *WhoBlA 94*
McWiggan, Thomas Johnstone 1918- *Who 94*
McWilliam, Candia 1955- *WrDr 94*
McWilliam, John David 1941- *Who 94*
McWilliam, Joss *WhoHol 92*
McWilliam, Michael Douglas 1933- *Who 94*
McWilliams, Alden S. d1993 *NewYTBS 93*
McWilliams, Alfred E., Jr. 1938- *WhoBlA 94*
McWilliams, Alfred Edeard 1911- *WhoBlA 94*
McWilliams, Arthur Thomas 1927- *WhoAmP 93*
McWilliams, Betty Jane *WhoAm 94*
McWilliams, Bruce Wayne 1932- *WhoAm 94*
McWilliams, C. Paul, Jr. 1931- *WhoScEn 94*
McWilliams, Carey 1905-1980 *DcLB 137 [port]*
McWilliams, Caroline *WhoHol 92*
McWilliams, Dennis Michael 1941- *WhoAmL 94*
McWilliams, Edwin Joseph 1919- *WhoAm 94*
McWilliams, Francis 1926- *Who 94*
McWilliams, James D. 1932- *WhoBlA 94*
McWilliams, Jim 1938- *WhoAmP 93*
McWilliams, John Lawrence, III 1943- *WhoAm 94*
McWilliams, John Michael 1939- *WhoAm 94, WhoAmL 94*
McWilliams, Karen 1943- *WrDr 94*
McWilliams, Margaret (Ann Edgar) 1929- *WrDr 94*
McWilliams, Margaret Ann 1929- *WhoAm 94*
McWilliams, Michael G. 1952- *WhoAm 94*
McWilliams, Mike C. 1948- *WhoAm 94, WhoAmL 94*
McWilliams, Pattie S. 1953- *WhoIns 94*
McWilliams, Richard *WhoHol 92*
McWilliams, Robert E. 1948- *WhoAmL 94*
McWilliams, Robert Hugh 1916- *WhoAm 94, WhoAmL 94, WhoWest 94*

McWilliams, Roger Dean 1954- *WhoWest 94*
McWorter, Gerald A. 1942- *WhoBlA 94*
McWright, Carter C. 1950- *WhoBlA 94*
McZeal, Alfred, Sr. 1931- *WhoBlA 94*
McZier, Arthur 1935- *WhoBlA 94*
Mdlalose, Frank Themba 1931- *IntWW 93*
Meacham, Anne 1925- *WhoHol 92*
Meacham, Beth 1951- *EncSF 93*
Meacham, Charles Harding 1925- *WhoAm 94*
Meacham, Charles P. 1947- *WhoWest 94*
Meacham, Christopher Lee 1943- *WhoAmP 93*
Meacham, Ellis K. *DrAPF 93*
Meacham, Ellis K(irby) 1913- *WrDr 94*
Meacham, Henry W. 1924- *WhoBlA 94*
Meacham, Margaret *DrAPF 93*
Meacham, Margaret 1952- *ConAu 42NR*
Meacham, Michael Robert 1953- *WhoAmP 93*
Meacham, Rebecca D. 1943- *WhoAmP 93*
Meacham, Robert B. 1933- *WhoBlA 94*
Meacham, Standish, Jr. 1932- *WhoAm 94, WrDr 94*
Meacham, William Feland 1913- *WhoAm 94*
Meacher, Michael Hugh 1939- *IntWW 93, Who 94*
Meachin, David James Percy 1941- *WhoAm 94, WhoFI 94*
Meachum, Paul 1939- *WhoHol 92*
Mead, Beverley Tupper 1923- *WhoAm 94*
Mead, Bob *WhoAmP 93*
Mead, Carver Andress 1934- *WhoAm 94*
Mead, Charles Philip 1887-1958 *DcNaB MP*
Mead, Chris 1959- *ConAu 142*
Mead, Christopher Curtis 1953- *ConAu 140*
Mead, Dana George 1936- *WhoAm 94, WhoFI 94*
Mead, David Edmund 1950- *WhoAm 94*
Mead, Edward Mathews 1926- *WhoAm 94*
Mead, Frank Waldreth 1922- *WhoScEn 94*
Mead, Franklin Braidwood, Jr. 1938- *WhoScEn 94*
Mead, George Wilson, II 1927- *WhoAm 94, WhoFI 94*
Mead, Gilbert Dunbar 1930- *WhoAm 94*
Mead, Glenn Arthur 1952- *WhoAmP 93*
Mead, Harold (Charles Hugh) 1910- *EncSF 93*
Mead, Hyrum Anderson, Jr. 1947- *WhoFI 94*
Mead, James *NewYTBS 93 [port]*
Mead, Jimmy Dwane 1947- *WhoMW 93*
Mead, John Milton 1924- *WhoAm 94*
Mead, Katherine Harper 1929- *WhoAmA 93N*
Mead, Kathryn Nadia 1959- *WhoScEn 94*
Mead, Larry Edward 1938- *WhoAmP 93*
Mead, Lawrence Myers, Jr. 1918- *WhoAm 94*
Mead, Margaret 1901-1978 *AmSocL [port]*
Mead, Matthew 1924- *WrDr 94*
Mead, Philip Bartlett 1937- *WhoAm 94*
Mead, Priscilla *WhoAmP 93*
Mead, Robert 1948- *WhoAmP 93*
Mead, Robert E. 1938- *WhoAm 94*
Mead, Robert W., Jr. 1945- *WhoAmL 94*
Mead, Sean Michael 1966- *WhoScEn 94*
Mead, Sedgwick 1911- *WhoWest 94*
Mead, Shepherd 1914- *EncSF 93*
Mead, (Edward) Shepherd 1914- *WrDr 94*
Mead, Sidney (Hirini) Moko 1927- *WrDr 94*
Mead, Stanton Witter 1900-1988 *WhAm 10*
Mead, Susan 1948- *WhoAmL 94*
Mead, Taylor *DrAPF 93, WhoHol 92*
Mead, Terry Eileen 1950- *WhoWest 94*
Mead, Wayland McCon 1931- *WhoAmL 94, WhoIns 94*
Mead, William Richard 1915- *Who 94*
Mead, William Rutherford 1846-1928 *AmCulL*
Meade *Who 94*
Meade, Alston B. 1930- *WhoBlA 94*
Meade, Claire d1968 *WhoHol 92*
Meade, Eric Cubitt 1923- *Who 94*
Meade, Erica Helm *DrAPF 93*
Meade, Everard Kidder, Jr. 1919- *WhoAm 94*
Meade, (Richard) Geoffrey (Austin) d1992 *Who 94N*
Meade, James (Edward) 1907- *WrDr 94*
Meade, James Edward 1907- *IntWW 93, Who 94, WhoAm 94*
Meade, Jodeen Vonne 1962- *WhoWest 94*
Meade, Julia 1928- *WhoHol 92*
Meade, Kenneth John 1925- *WhoWest 94*
Meade, Kevin R. 1956- *WhoAmP 93*
Meade, L. T. 1844-1914 *DcLB 141 [port]*
Meade, Melvin C. 1929- *WhoBlA 94*
Meade, Patricia Sue 1960- *WhoMW 93*
Meade, Patrick John 1913- *Who 94*
Meade, Richard Hardaway 1897- *WhAm 10*
Meade, Richard John Hannay 1938- *Who 94*
Meade, Robert Dale 1927- *WhoWest 94*
Meade, Russell Arthur 1946- *WhoAmL 94*
Meade, Thomas Wilson 1936- *Who 94*
Meade, William F. 1925- *WhoBlA 94*
Meade-King, Charles Martin 1913- *Who 94*
Meader, George d1963 *WhoHol 92*
Meader, George 1888-1963 *NewGrDO*
Meader, George 1907- *WhoAmP 93*
Meader, John Daniel 1931- *WhoAmL 94, WhoFI 94*
Meader, John Leon 1956- *WhoScEn 94*
Meader, Jonathan Grant *WhoAmA 93*
Meader, Paul G. *WhoAmP 93*
Meader, Ralph Gibson 1904- *WhoAm 94*
Meader, Vaughn 1936- *WhoCom*
Meader, Willard L. 1933- *WhoWest 94*
Meader, William d1979 *WhoHol 92*
Meaders, Donald W. 1947- *WhoAmL 94*
Meaders, Paul Le Sourd 1930- *WhoAm 94, WhoAmL 94*
Meades, Jonathan (Turner) 1947- *WrDr 94*
Meade-Tollin, Linda C. *WhoBlA 94*
Meade-Tollin, Linda Celida 1944- *WhoWest 94*
Meadlock, James W. 1933- *WhoAm 94, WhoFI 94*
Meadlock, Nancy B. 1938- *WhoFI 94*
Meadmore, Clement L. 1929- *WhoAmA 93*
Meador, Anna Marie 1932- *WhoFI 94*
Meador, Charles Lawrence 1946- *WhoScEn 94*
Meador, Daniel John 1926- *WhoAm 94, WhoAmL 94, WhoAmP 93*
Meador, John Milward, Jr. 1946- *WhoAm 94*
Meador, Richard Lewis 1934- *WhoAmP 93*
Meador, Ron 1952- *WhoAm 94*
Meadors, Allen Coats 1947- *WhoAm 94*
Meadors, Gayle Marleen 1946- *WhoAmL 94*
Meadors, Howard Clarence, Jr. 1938- *WhoAm 94*
Meadow, Lynne 1946- *WhoAm 94*
Meadow, Robin 1947- *WhoAmL 94*
Meadow, (Samuel) Roy 1933- *Who 94*
Meadowcroft, Michael James 1942- *Who 94*
Meadowcroft, Robert Stanley 1937- *WhoAm 94*
Meadowcroft, William Howarth 1929- *WhoAmP 93*
Meadows, Algur H. 1899-1980 *WhoAmA 93N*
Meadows, Arthur Jack 1934- *Who 94*
Meadows, Audrey *NewYTBS 93 [port], WhoAm 94*
Meadows, Audrey 1919- *WhoHol 92*
Meadows, Audrey 1924- *WhoCom*
Meadows, Audrey 1926- *IntMPA 94*
Meadows, Bernard William 1915- *IntWW 93, Who 94*
Meadows, Cheryl R. 1948- *WhoBlA 94*
Meadows, Denny d1964 *WhoHol 92*
Meadows, Donald Frederick 1937- *WhoAm 94*
Meadows, Ferguson Booker, Jr. 1942- *WhoBlA 94*
Meadows, Gary Glenn 1945- *WhoWest 94*
Meadows, Graham David 1941- *Who 94*
Meadows, James Dártlin 1957- *WhoAmL 94*
Meadows, Jayne 1920- *WhoHol 92*
Meadows, Jayne 1923- *WhoCom*
Meadows, Jayne 1924- *IntMPA 94*
Meadows, Jennifer Elizabeth 1947- *WhoAm 94*
Meadows, Jimmy R. 1947- *WhoFI 94*
Meadows, John Frederick 1926- *WhoAmL 94*
Meadows, Kristen *WhoHol 92*
Meadows, Leonard R. 1926- *WhoAmP 93*
Meadows, Lucile Smallwood 1918- *WhoAmP 93, WhoBlA 94*
Meadows, Matthew J. 1938- *WhoAmP 93*
Meadows, Michael Bruce 1956- *WhoAmP 93*
Meadows, P. B. 1938- *WhoAmA 93*
Meadows, Pamela Catherine 1949- *Who 94*
Meadows, Richard H. 1928- *WhoBlA 94*
Meadows, Robert d1986 *WhoHol 92*
Meadows, Robert 1902- *Who 94*
Meadows, Sharon Marie 1950- *WhoAm 94, WhoFI 94*
Meadows, Stanley *WhoHol 92*
Meadows, Stanley Howard 1945- *WhoAmL 94*
Meadows, Stephen *WhoHol 92*
Meadows, Swithin Pinder d1993 *Who 94N*
Meads, Donald Edward 1920- *WhoAm 94*
Meads, Kat *DrAPF 93*
Meads, Walter Frederick 1923- *WhoAm 94*
Meadway, (Richard) John 1944- *Who 94*
Meager, Michael Anthony 1931- *Who 94*
Meagher, Cynthia Nash 1947- *WhoAm 94, WhoWest 94*
Meagher, George Vincent 1919- *WhoAm 94*
Meagher, Mark Joseph 1932- *WhoAm 94*
Meagher, Michael 1942- *WhoWest 94*
Meagher, Ray *WhoHol 92*
Meakem, Carolyn Soliday 1936- *WhoFI 94*
Meaker, M. J. *TwCYAW*
Meaker, Marijane Agnes 1927- *WhoAm 94*
Meakin, Charles d1961 *WhoHol 92*
Meakin, John David 1934- *WhoScEn 94*
Meakin, Wilfred 1925- *Who 94*
Meal, Larie 1939- *WhoMW 93, WhoScEn 94*
Meale, (Joseph) Alan 1949- *Who 94*
Meale, Richard (Graham) 1932- *NewGrDO*
Mealey, George Allan 1933- *WhoAm 94, WhoFI 94*
Mealman, Glenn 1934- *WhoMW 93*
Mealman, Glenn Edward 1934- *WhoAm 94, WhoFI 94*
Mealor, William Theodore, Jr. 1940- *WhoAm 94*
Mealy, Dennis C. 1952- *WhoIns 94*
Mealy, Mark Williams 1957- *WhoFI 94*
Mealy, Rosemari *DrAPF 93*
Meana, Mitchell A. 1958- *WhoHisp 94*
Meaney, Donald V. *IntMPA 94*
Meaney, Michael Joseph 1952- *WhoAm 94, WhoAmL 94*
Meaney, Patrick Michael d1992 *IntWW 93N*
Meaney, Patrick Michael 1925- *WhAm 10*
Meaney, Thomas Francis 1927- *WhoScEn 94*
Meanor, H. Curtis 1929- *WhoAmL 94*
Means, Bertha E. 1920- *WhoBlA 94*
Means, Craig R. 1922- *WhoBlA 94*
Means, Cyril Chesnut, Jr. 1918-1992 *WhAm 10*
Means, David Hammond 1928- *WhoAm 94*
Means, Donald Bruce 1941- *WhoScEn 94*
Means, Donald Fitzgerald 1966- *WhoBlA 94*
Means, Elbert Lee 1945- *WhoBlA 94*
Means, Elizabeth Rose Thayer 1960- *WhoAmL 94, WhoFI 94*
Means, Elliott 1905-1962 *WhoAmA 93N*
Means, Florence Crannell 1891-1980 *TwCYAW*
Means, Fred E. *WhoBlA 94*
Means, George Robert 1907- *WhoAm 94, WhoMW 93*
Means, Gordon Paul 1927- *WrDr 94*
Means, Howard 1944- *ConAu 141*
Means, James Andrew 1937- *WhoWest 94*
Means, Jerry Taft, III 1956- *WhoFI 94*
Means, John Barkley 1939- *WhoAm 94*
Means, Kevin Michael 1955- *WhoBlA 94*
Means, L. L. *WhoAmP 93*
Means, LeRoy Dale 1931- *WhoMW 93*
Means, Marianne 1934- *WhoAm 94*
Means, Michael David 1950- *WhoAm 94*
Means, Paul Banwell 1894- *WhAm 10*
Means, Paul Richard 1943- *WhoWest 94*
Means, Raymond B. 1930- *WhoAm 94*
Means, Richard Dennis 1947- *WhoFI 94*
Means, Stephen Arden 1946- *WhoAmP 93*
Means, Terry Robert 1948- *WhoAm 94, WhoAmL 94*
Means, Thomas Cornell 1947- *WhoAm 94*
Meanwell, Doc 1884-1953 *BasBi*
Meany, George 1894-1980 *AmSocL*
Meany, John J. 1939- *WhoAm 94*
Meara, Anne *WhoAm 94*
Meara, Anne 1929- *IntMPA 94, WhoHol 92*
See Also Stiller and Meara *WhoCom*
Meares, Paula G. Allen 1948- *WhoBlA 94*
Meares, Paula Gwendolyn *WhoMW 93*
Mearns, Barbara (Crawford) 1955- *WrDr 94*
Mearns, Richard (James) 1950- *WrDr 94*
Mears, Adrian Leonard 1944- *Who 94*
Mears, Charlotte *DrAPF 93*
Mears, Edgar H. 1943- *WhoAmP 93*
Mears, Elizabeth d1988 *WhoHol 92*
Mears, Gary H. 1936- *WhoAm 94*
Mears, John Cledan 1922- *Who 94*
Mears, Martha d1986 *WhoHol 92*
Mears, Michael *WhoHol 92*
Mears, Orum Glenn, III 1958- *WhoMW 93*
Mears, Patrick Edward 1951- *WhoAm 94, WhoAmL 94, WhoMW 93*
Mears, Richard Riley 1951- *WhoWest 94*
Mears, Rick Ravon 1951- *WhoAm 94, WhoWest 94*
Mears, Roger Clifton, Jr. 1925- *WhoAmP 93*
Mears, Rona Robbins 1938- *WhoAmL 94*
Mears, Sandra A. 1954- *WhoAmL 94, WhoMW 93*
Mears, Walter Robert 1935- *WhoAm 94*
Mease, Quentin R. 1917- *WhoBlA 94*
Measelle, Richard L. 1938- *WhoAm 94, WhoFI 94*
Measham, Donald Charles 1932- *WrDr 94*
Measor, Adela d1933 *WhoHol 92*
Measor, Beryl d1965 *WhoHol 92*
Measure, Bruce 1951- *WhoAmP 93*
Meath, Bishop of 1940- *Who 94*
Meath, Earl of 1910- *Who 94*
Meath, Michael *WrDr 94*
Meath And Kildare, Bishop of 1934- *Who 94*
Meatloaf 1947- *WhoHol 92*
Meaton, Jeffrey Carl 1957- *WhoAmL 94*
Meats, Stephen *DrAPF 93*
Meaux, Alan Douglas 1951- *WhoScEn 94, WhoWest 94*
Meaux, Ronald 1942- *WhoBlA 94*
Meaux, Thomas W. 1954- *WhoAmP 93*
Meazza, Giuseppe 1910-1979 *WorESoc*
Mebane, Barbara Margot 1947- *WhoFI 94*
Mebane, David Cummins 1933- *WhoAm 94*
Mebane, George Allen 1929- *WhoAm 94, WhoFI 94*
Mebane, John Harrison 1909- *WrDr 94*
Mebane, William Black 1927- *WhoAm 94*
Mebane, William deBerniere 1949- *WhoAm 94*
Mebiame, Leon 1934- *IntWW 93*
Mebrak-Zaidi, Nora 1965- *WhoWomW 91*
Mebus, Charles Albert 1932- *WhoAm 94*
Mebus, Robert Gwynne 1940- *WhoAm 94, WhoAmL 94*
Mebust, Winston Keith 1933- *WhoAm 94*
Mecabe, Edwin Joseph 1956- *WhoFI 94*
Mecca, Joseph A. 1956- *WhoAmP 93*
Mech, George Joseph 1952- *WhoMW 93*
Mech, L(ucyan) David 1937- *WrDr 94*
Mech, Lucyan David 1937- *WhoScEn 94*
Mechakra, Yamina 1953- *BlmGWL*
Mecham, Evan 1924- *WhoAmP 93*
Mecham, Glenn Jefferson 1935- *WhoAmL 94, WhoWest 94*
Mecham, Paul F. 1937- *WhoAmP 93*
Mecham, Steven James 1953- *WhoWest 94*
Mechanic, Bill *IntMPA 94*
Mechanic, David 1936- *IntWW 93, WhoAm 94*
Mechanic, Jonathan L. 1952- *WhoAmL 94*
Mechem, Charles Stanley, Jr. 1930- *WhoAm 94*
Mechem, Edwin Leard 1912- *WhoAmL 94, WhoWest 94*
Mechem, Kirke 1925- *NewGrDO*
Mechigian, Nancy Lee 1941- *WhoMW 93*
Mechlin, George Francis 1923- *WhoAm 94*
Mechlin, Leila 1874-1949 *WhoAmA 93N*
Mechling, Curtis C. 1950- *WhoAm 94, WhoAmL 94*
Mechling, Paul Parks 1919- *WhoAmP 93*
Mechnikov, Ilya *WorScD*
Mechoso, Carlos Roberto 1942- *WhoHisp 94*
Mechtel, Angelika 1943- *BlmGWL*
Mechthild von Hackeborn 1241-1299 *BlmGWL*
Mechthild von Magdeburg c. 1207-c. 1282 *DcLB 138*
Mechthild von Magdeburg c. 1212-1294 *BlmGWL*
Mechura, Leopold Eugen 1804-1870 *NewGrDO*
Meciar, Vladimir 1942- *IntWW 93*
Mecimore, Charles Douglas 1934- *WhoAm 94*
Mecke, Theodore Hart McCalla, Jr. 1923- *WhoAm 94*
Meckel, Peter Timothy 1941- *WhoWest 94*
Meckel, Richard A(lan) 1948- *WrDr 94*
Mecklem, Austin Merrill 1894-1951 *WhoAmA 93N*
Mecklenburg, Gary Alan *WhoAm 94, WhoMW 93*
Mecklenburg, Karl Bernard 1960- *WhoAm 94, WhoWest 94*
Mecklenburg, Virginia McCord 1946- *WhoAmA 93*
Meckler, Alan Marshall 1945- *WhoAm 94*
Meckler, Michael Louis 1965- *WhoMW 93*
Meckler, Milton 1932- *WhoWest 94*
Meckseper, Friedrich 1936- *IntWW 93*

Mecom, Jane Franklin 1712-1794 *BlmGWL*
Meconi, Vincent P. 1951- *WhoAmP 93*
Medagli, M. Elizabeth 1947- *WhoAmL 94*
Medaglia, Mary-Elizabeth 1947- *WhoAmL 94*
Medairy, Mark Curtis, Jr. 1953- *WhoAmP 93*
Medak, Peter *IntWW 93*
Medak, Peter 1940- *IntMPA 94*
Medal, Eduardo Antonio 1950- *WhoHisp 94*
Medalie, Richard James 1929- *WhoAm 94*
Medani, Charles Richard 1949- *WhoAm 94*
Medaris, Florence Isabel *WhoMW 93*
Medavoy, Mike 1941- *IntMPA 94, WhoAm 94, WhoHisp 94*
Medawar, Jean 1913- *WrDr 94*
Medawar, Nicholas Antoine Macbeth 1933- *Who 94*
Medawar, P. B. d1987 *NobelP 91N*
Medawar, Peter Brian 1915- *WorScD*
Medcalf, Robert Randolph, Jr. *DrAPF 93*
Medd, David Leslie 1917- *Who 94*
Medd, Mary Beaumont 1907- *Who 94*
Medd, Patrick William 1919- *Who 94*
Medders, Clarence E. *WhoAm 94, WhoAmP 93*
Medders, Marion Wardner 1925- *WhoAmP 93*
Medders, Vernon S. 1919- *WhoAmP 93*
Meddin, Jeffrey Dean 1946- *WhoScEn 94*
Meddleton, Daniel J. 1936- *WhoAm 94*
Medearis, Donald Norman, Jr. 1927- *IntWW 93, WhoAm 94*
Medearis, Kenneth Gordon 1930- *WhoWest 94*
Medearis, Robert Park 1930- *WhoAmP 93*
Medearis, Roger 1920- *WhoAmA 93*
Medearis, Roger Norman 1920- *WhoAm 94*
Medearis, Victor L. 1921- *WhoBlA 94*
Medeiros, John J. 1929- *WhoAmP 93*
Medeiros, Matthew Francis 1945- *WhoAmL 94*
Medeiros, Russell Francis 1952- *WhoWest 94*
Medeiros, Teresa 1962- *ConAu 142*
Medek, Tilo 1940- *NewGrDO*
Medel, Felix d1951 *WhoHol 92*
Medel, Rebecca Rosalie 1947- *WhoAmA 93, WhoHisp 94*
Medelci, Mourad 1943- *IntWW 93*
Medellin, Jose H. 1941- *WhoHisp 94*
Medellin, Octavio 1907- *WhoHisp 94*
Meder, Johann Valentin c. 1649-1719 *NewGrDO*
Mederitsch(-Gallus), Johann (Georg Anton) c. 1752-1835 *NewGrDO*
Mederos, Carolina Luisa 1947- *WhoAm 94*
Mederos, Julio *WhoHisp 94*
Medford, Don 1917- *IntMPA 94*
Medford, Isabel *WhoBlA 94*
Medford, James A. 1945- *WhoAmL 94*
Medford, Kay d1980 *WhoHol 92*
Medhi, Deepankar 1962- *WhoMW 93*
Medhin, Tsegaye Gabre *BlkWr 2*
Medhurst, Brian 1935- *Who 94*
Mediano, Adolfo, Jr. 1955- *WhoHisp 94*
Medici, Catherine de' 1519-1589 *HisWorL [port]*
Medici, Giuseppe 1907- *IntWW 93*
Medici, Lorenzo de' 1449-1492 *HisWorL [port]*
Medici Family *NewGrDO*
Medicine-Eagle, Brooke 1943- *ConAu 140*
Medicine Elk, James 1907-1974 *EncNAR*
Medico, Frank 1924- *WhoAmP 93*
Medicraft, Rodney Horace 1931- *WhoFI 94*
Medicus, Heinrich Adolf 1918- *WhoAm 94*
Medin, A. Louis 1925- *WhoAm 94, WhoFI 94*
Medin, Lowell Ansgard 1932- *WhoFI 94, WhoMW 93*
Medin, Myron James, Jr. 1931- *WhoAm 94*
Medina, Earl of *Who 94*
Medina, Ada 1948- *WhoAmA 93*
Medina, Agustin 1950- *WhoHisp 94*
Medina, Agustin, Jr. 1946- *WhoHisp 94*
Medina, Andino, Jr. 1950- *WhoHisp 94*
Medina, Angel 1932- *WhoHisp 94*
Medina, Benny *WhoBlA 94*
Medina, Cesar Hjalmar 1963- *WhoHisp 94*
Medina, Cristobal Luis 1951- *WhoHisp 94*
Medina, Daniel Andrew 1957- *WhoWest 94*
Medina, David Albert 1935- *WhoHisp 94*
Medina, David Jonathan 1951- *WhoHisp 94*
Medina, Emma 1955- *WhoHisp 94*
Medina, Enrique 1953- *WhoHisp 94*
Medina, Evelio *WhoHisp 94*
Medina, George O. *WhoHisp 94*
Medina, Gilbert M. *WhoHisp 94*
Medina, Harold R. 1888-1990 *WhAm 10*
Medina, Isabel 1932- *WhoHisp 94*
Medina, J. Michael 1950- *WhoAmL 94*
Medina, James *WhoHol 92*
Medina, Jim 1940- *WhoHisp 94*
Medina, John A. 1942- *WhoHisp 94*
Medina, Jorge 1951- *WhoHisp 94*
Medina, Jose Enrique 1926- *WhoAm 94, WhoHisp 94*
Medina, José H. 1948- *WhoHisp 94*
Medina, Jose T. 1926- *WhoHisp 94*
Medina, Joseph A. *WhoWest 94*
Medina, Julian Phillip 1949- *WhoHisp 94*
Medina, Kathryn Bach *WhoAm 94*
Medina, Manuel *WhoHisp 94*
Medina, Manuel 1940- *WhoHisp 94*
Medina, Manuel, Jr. 1952- *WhoHisp 94*
Medina, Manuel Fernando 1961- *WhoMW 93*
Medina, Mel *WhoHisp 94*
Medina, Miguel A., Jr. 1946- *WhoHisp 94*
Medina, Ofelia *WhoHol 92*
Medina, Pablo *DrAPF 93*
Medina, Pablo 1948- *WhoHisp 94*
Medina, Patricia 1919- *WhoHol 92*
Medina, Patricia 1921- *IntMPA 94*
Medina, Rey S. 1934- *WhoHisp 94*
Medina, Robert C. 1924- *WhoHisp 94*
Medina, Rubens *WhoHisp 94*
Medina, Ruth M. 1957- *WhoHisp 94*
Medina, Sandra Sellman 1947- *WhoWest 94*
Medina, Sandrale Olivia 1942- *WhoHisp 94*
Medina, Solomon c. 1650-1730 *DcNaB MP*
Medina, Standish Forde, Jr. 1940- *WhoAm 94*
Medina, Thomas Julian 1928- *WhoWest 94*
Medina, Tina Marie 1965- *WhoHisp 94*
Medina, Vicente 1955- *WhoHisp 94*
Medina-Juarbe, Arturo 1951- *WhoHisp 94*
Medina-Lichtenstein, Betty *WhoHisp 94*
Medina-Puerta, Antonio 1956- *WhoWest 94*
Medina-Ruiz, Arturo 1941- *WhoHisp 94*
Medinger, John Donald 1948- *WhoAmP 93*
Medins, Janis 1890-1966 *NewGrDO*
Medins, Jazeps 1877-1947 *NewGrDO*
Medio, Dolores 1914- *BlmGWL*
Meditch, James Stephen 1934- *WhoAm 94, WhoWest 94*
Meditz, Walter Joseph 1917- *WhoAm 94*
Medland, Timothy Joseph 1948- *WhoMW 93*
Medland, William James 1944- *WhoAm 94*
Medler, John Francis, Jr. 1962- *WhoAmL 94*
Medley, Charles Robert Owen 1905- *IntWW 93*
Medley, Donald Matthias 1917- *WhoAm 94*
Medley, Edgar d1959 *WhoHol 92*
Medley, George Julius 1930- *Who 94*
Medley, James Robert 1940- *WhoAmP 93*
Medley, Landon Daryle 1949- *WhoAmP 93*
Medley, Michael Raymond 1946- *WhoWest 94*
Medley, (Charles) Robert (Owen) 1905- *Who 94*
Medley, Sherrilyn 1946- *WhoFI 94*
Medley, Steven Paul 1949- *WhoWest 94*
Medlicott, Michael Geoffrey 1943- *Who 94*
Medlin, Charles McCall 1960- *WhoAmL 94*
Medlin, Dennis B. 1942- *WhoIns 94*
Medlin, Donna Jane 1955- *WhoMW 93*
Medlin, John Grimes, Jr. 1933- *WhoAm 94, WhoFI 94*
Medlin, King Everett 1964- *WhoWest 94*
Medlin, Mark Stephen 1961- *WhoAmL 94*
Medlin, Victoria d1978 *WhoHol 92*
Medlock, Ann 1933- *WhoAm 94, WhoWest 94*
Medlock, Donald Larson 1927- *WhoAm 94*
Medlock, Eugene Shields 1954- *WhoWest 94*
Medlock, T. Travis 1934- *WhoBlA 94*
Medlock, Thomas Travis 1934- *WhoAm 94, WhoAmL 94, WhoAmP 93*
Medlycott, Mervyn (Tregonwell) 1947- *Who 94*
Medman, Edward A. 1937- *IntMPA 94*
Mednick, Murray *DrAPF 93*
Mednick, Murray 1939- *ConDr 93, WhoAm 94*
Mednick, Richard 1933- *WhoAmL 94*
Mednick, Robert 1940- *WhoAm 94, WhoFI 94*
Medof, Sandra Gwyn 1955- *WhoAmP 93*
Medoff, Eve *WhoAmA 93*
Medoff, James Lawrence 1947- *WhoAm 94*
Medoff, Mark *IntMPA 94, WhoHol 92*
Medoff, Mark (Howard) 1940- *ConDr 93, WrDr 94*
Medoff, Mark Howard 1940- *WhoAm 94, WhoWest 94*
Medoff, Marshall Hilary 1945- *WhoFI 94*
Medonis, Robert Xavier 1931- *WhoAmL 94*
Medow, Arnold 1930- *WhoMW 93*
Medow, Herman Marvin 1930- *WhoMW 93*
Medow, Jerry 1935- *WhoMW 93*
Medrano, Ambrosia *WhoAmP 93*
Medrano, Ambrosio 1953- *WhoHisp 94*
Medrano, Bill N. 1939- *WhoHisp 94*
Medrano, Evangeline M. 1944- *WhoHisp 94*
Medrano, Francisco 1920- *WhoAmP 93*
Medrano, Hugo *WhoHisp 94*
Medrano, Manuel F., Jr. 1949- *WhoHisp 94*
Medrano, Pauline 1955- *WhoAmP 93*
Medrea, Daniel Allan 1944- *WhoAmL 94*
Medrich, Libby E. *WhoAmA 93*
Meduna, Ladislas Joseph 1896- *WhAm 10*
Meduna, Ladislas Joseph von 1896-1964 *EncSPD*
Meduski, Jerzy Wincenty 1918- *WhoWest 94*
Medvecky, Robert Stephen 1931- *WhoAm 94*
Medvecky, Thomas Edward 1937- *WhoAmL 94*
Medved', Aleksandr Vasilyevich 1937- *IntWW 93*
Medved, Daniel Thomas 1962- *WhoAmL 94*
Medved, Diane 1951- *WrDr 94*
Medved, Eva 1922- *WhoWest 94*
Medved, Michael 1948- *WhoAm 94*
Medved, Robert Allen 1945- *WhoAm 94, WhoAmL 94*
Medvedev, Grigori 1933- *ConAu 141*
Medvedev, Nikolai Pavlovich 1952- *LngBDD*
Medvedev, Roi Aleksandrovich 1925- *LngBDD*
Medvedev, Roy (Alexandrovich) 1925- *WrDr 94*
Medvedev, Roy Aleksandrovich 1925- *IntWW 93*
Medvedev, Zhores (Alexandrovich) 1925- *WrDr 94*
Medvedev, Zhores Aleksandrovich 1925- *IntWW 93*
Medvedow, Jill 1954- *WhoAmA 93*
Medvei, Victor Cornelius 1905- *WrDr 94*
Medvin, Harvey N. 1936- *WhoIns 94*
Medvin, Harvey Norman 1936- *WhoAm 94, WhoFI 94*
Medvitz, James Thomas 1936- *WhoWest 94*
Medwadowski, Stefan J. 1924- *WhoAm 94*
Medway, Lord 1968- *Who 94*
Medwed, Mameve S. *DrAPF 93*
Medwick, Craig Steven 1953- *WhoAm 94*
Medwick, Joe d1975 *WhoHol 92*
Medwin, Michael 1923- *IntMPA 94, WhoHol 92*
Medwin, Robert Joseph G. *Who 94*
Medzihradsky, Fedor 1932- *WhoAm 94, WhoMW 93, WhoScEn 94*
Mee, Charles L., Jr. 1938- *WhoAm 94*
Mee, Herb, Jr. 1928- *WhoAm 94*
Mee, John Lawrence 1950- *WhoFI 94*
Mee, Susie *DrAPF 93*
Meece, Clyde B., Jr. 1958- *WhoFI 94*
Meech, Karen Jean 1959- *WhoScEn 94*
Meech, Norma M. 1936- *WhoAmP 93*
Meech, Richard Campbell 1921- *WhoAm 94*
Meech, Sonja Rosemary 1950- *WhoWest 94*
Meecham, William Coryell *WhoAm 94, WhoWest 94*
Meecham, William James 1958- *WhoWest 94*
Meechie, Helen Guild 1938- *Who 94*
Meeder, James L. 1946- *WhoAmL 94*
Meeds, Edwin Lloyd 1927- *WhoAm 94*
Meeds, Lloyd 1927- *WhoAmP 93*
Meehan, Barry d1974 *WhoHol 92*
Meehan, Danny d1978 *WhoHol 92*
Meehan, Elizabeth d1967 *WhoHol 92*
Meehan, Gerry *WhoAm 94*
Meehan, John *WhoAm 94, WhoMW 93*
Meehan, John Joseph 1945- *WhoAm 94*
Meehan, John Joseph, Jr. 1946- *WhoAm 94*
Meehan, John P. 1922- *WhoFI 94*
Meehan, Joseph 1941- *WhoAmL 94*
Meehan, Joseph Gerard 1931- *WhoAm 94*
Meehan, Kandy Lee 1951- *WhoMW 93*
Meehan, Lew d1951 *WhoHol 92*
Meehan, Martin T. 1956- *CngDr 93*
Meehan, Martin Thomas 1956- *WhoAm 94, WhoAmP 93*
Meehan, Maude *DrAPF 93*
Meehan, Michael Joseph 1942- *WhoAmL 94*
Meehan, Paula 1955- *BlmGWL*
Meehan, Paula Kent 1931- *WhoAm 94*
Meehan, Richard Thomas 1949- *WhoWest 94*
Meehan, Robert Henry 1946- *WhoFI 94, WhoScEn 94*
Meehan, Sharon Lynn 1954- *WhoFI 94*
Meehan, Thomas Joseph 1943- *WhoFI 94*
Meehan, William Dale 1930- *WhoAmA 93*
Meehan, William E. d1920 *WhoHol 92*
Meehl, Gerald Allen 1951- *WhoScEn 94*
Meehl, Paul Everett 1920- *WhoAm 94*
Meek, A. J. 1941- *WhoAmA 93*
Meek, Barbara Susan 1951- *WhoMW 93*
Meek, Brian Alexander 1939- *Who 94*
Meek, Carrie 1926- *ConBlB 6 [port]*
Meek, Carrie P. *WhoBlA 94*
Meek, Carrie P. 1926- *CngDr 93, WhoAm 94, WhoAmP 93*
Meek, Charles Innes 1920- *Who 94*
Meek, Donald d1946 *WhoHol 92*
Meek, Forrest Burns 1928- *WhoMW 93*
Meek, Gerry *WhoWest 94*
Meek, J. William, III 1950- *WhoAmA 93*
Meek, Jay *DrAPF 93*
Meek, Jeffrey *WhoHol 92*
Meek, John E. 1950- *WhoAmP 93*
Meek, John Martin 1929- *WhoFI 94*
Meek, John Millar 1912- *Who 94*
Meek, Joseph 1951- *WrDr 94*
Meek, Joseph L. 1810-1875 *WhWE*
Meek, Kate d1925 *WhoHol 92*
Meek, M(argaret) R(eid) D(uncan) 1918- *ConAu 142, WrDr 94*
Meek, Marshall 1925- *Who 94*
Meek, Paul Derald 1930- *IntWW 93, WhoAm 94, WhoFI 94*
Meek, Peter Gray 1911-1992 *WhAm 10*
Meek, Phillip Joseph 1937- *WhoAm 94, WhoFI 94*
Meek, Russell Charles 1937- *WhoBlA 94*
Meek, S(terner St.) P(aul) 1894-1972 *EncSF 93*
Meek, Susan Bieber 1951- *WhoAmL 94*
Meek, Violet Imhof 1939- *WhoMW 93*
Meek, William Donald 1948- *WhoMW 93*
Meeker, Anthony 1939- *WhoAmP 93*
Meeker, Arlene Dorothy Hallin 1935- *WhoFI 94*
Meeker, Barbara Miller 1930- *WhoAmA 93*
Meeker, Charles C. 1950- *WhoAmL 94*
Meeker, Charles R. *IntMPA 94*
Meeker, David Anthony 1939- *WhoAmP 93*
Meeker, Dean Jackson 1920- *WhoAmA 93*
Meeker, George d1963 *WhoHol 92*
Meeker, Guy Bentley 1945- *WhoAm 94, WhoFI 94*
Meeker, John G. 1946- *WhoWest 94*
Meeker, Jotham 1804-1855 *EncNAR*
Meeker, Larry K. 1938- *WhoAm 94, WhoAmL 94*
Meeker, Lawrence Edwin 1959- *WhoScEn 94*
Meeker, Milton Shy 1933- *WhoFI 94*
Meeker, Murray M. 1946- *WhoAmL 94*
Meeker, Ralph d1988 *WhoHol 92*
Meeker, Robert Bruce 1946- *WhoMW 93*
Meeker, Robert Eldon 1930- *WhoAm 94*
Meeker, Robert L. 1935- *WhoIns 94*
Meekins, Russ, Jr. *WhoAmP 93*
Meekison, MaryFran 1919- *WhoMW 93*
Meeks, Cordell David, Jr. 1942- *WhoBlA 94*
Meeks, Crawford Russell, Jr. 1931- *WhoScEn 94*
Meeks, Esther MacBain 1921- *WrDr 94*
Meeks, Gregory Weldon 1953- *WhoAmP 93*
Meeks, John Neal 1931- *WhoAmP 93*
Meeks, Joni Marsh 1931- *WhoAmP 93*
Meeks, Larry Gillette 1944- *WhoBlA 94*
Meeks, Linda Mae 1952- *WhoMW 93*
Meeks, Lisa Kaye 1965- *WhoScEn 94*
Meeks, Perker L., Jr. 1943- *WhoBlA 94*
Meeks, Reginald Kline 1954- *WhoAmP 93, WhoBlA 94*
Meeks, Robert James 1958- *WhoFI 94*
Meeks, Robert L. 1934- *WhoAmP 93*
Meeks, Wayne A 1932- *WrDr 94*
Meeks, Willis Gene 1938- *WhoBlA 94*
Meelheim, Richard Allen 1954- *WhoAmL 94*
Meelia, Richard J. *WhoAm 94, WhoFI 94*
Meem, James Lawrence, Jr. 1915- *WhoAm 94*
Meenakshi Sundaram, Kandasamy 1949- *WhoScEn 94*
Meenan, Patrick Henry 1927- *WhoAm 94, WhoAmP 93*

Meendsen, Fred Charles 1933- *WhoAm 94, WhoFI 94*
Meer, Fatima 1929- *WrDr 94*
Meer, Simon van der 1925- *WorScD*
Meer, Y. S. 1929- *WrDr 94*
Meeres, Norman Victor 1913- *Who 94*
Meerhoff, George Ellsworth 1931- *WhoAm 94*
Meers, Henry W. 1908- *WhoAm 94*
Meerson, Lazare 1900-1938 *IntDcF 2-4*
Meese, Celia Edwards *WhoFI 94*
Meese, Daniel Urban 1947- *WhoFI 94*
Meese, Edwin 1931- *IntWW 93, Who 94*
Meese, Edwin, III 1931- *WhoAmP 93*
Meese, Ernest Harold 1929- *WhoMW 93, WhoScEn 94*
Meese, Robert Allen 1956- *WhoMW 93*
Meeske, William J. 1947- *WhoAmL 94*
Meester, Louis de 1904-1987 *NewGrDO*
Meetz, Gerald David 1937- *WhoScEn 94*
Meetze, George Elias 1909- *WhoAmP 93*
Meezan, Elias 1942- *WhoAm 94*
Meffert, Chris 1943- *WhoAmP 93*
Meffre, Armand *WhoHol 92*
Mega, Christopher John 1930- *WhoAmP 93*
Megahan, Walter Franklin 1935- *WhoWest 94*
Megahey, Leslie 1944- *Who 94*
Megahy, Thomas 1929- *Who 94*
Megalostrata fl. 6th cent.?BC- *BlmGWL*
Megan, Thomas Ignatius 1913- *WhoAm 94*
Megapolensis, Johannes 1603-1670 *DcAmReB 2, EncNAR*
Megargel, Burton Jonathan 1954- *WhoAm 94*
Megaridis, Constantine Michael 1959- *WhoScEn 94*
Megarry, Robert (Edgar) 1910- *IntWW 93, Who 94*
Megasthenes fl. 29-?BC- *WhWE*
Megaw, Arthur Hubert Stanley 1910- *Who 94*
Megaw, John 1909- *Who 94*
Megaw, Neill *DrAPF 93*
Megaw, Robert Neill Ellison 1920- *WhoAm 94*
Megeath, Joe D. 1939- *WhoWest 94*
Megee, Vernon Edgar 1900-1992 *WhAm 10*
Megged, Aharon 1920- *WrDr 94*
Meggers, Betty J. 1921- *WrDr 94*
Meggers, Betty Jane 1921- *WhoAm 94*
Meggeson, Michael 1930- *Who 94*
Meggitt, Mervyn John 1924- *WrDr 94*
Meggs, Betty Sugg 1934- *WhoAmP 93*
Meggs, Brown (Moore) 1930- *WrDr 94*
Meggs, C. Lawrence 1935- *WhoMW 93*
Meggs, Philip B. 1942- *WhoAmA 93*
Meghelli, Fethi M. 1945- *WhoAmA 93*
Megherbi, Dalila 1957- *WhoScEn 94*
Meghreblian, Robert Vartan 1922- *WhoAm 94*
Megley, Sheila 1938- *WhoAm 94*
Megna, John 1952- *WhoHol 92*
Megowan, Don d1981 *WhoHol 92*
Megown, John William 1931-1992 *WhAm 10*
Megrath, Kimberley Lewis 1953- *WhoWest 94*
Megson, Claude Walter 1936- *IntWW 93*
Mehaffey, Blanche d1968 *WhoHol 92*
Mehaffey, Harry d1963 *WhoHol 92*
Mehaffey, James *Who 94*
Mehaffey, John Allen *WhoFI 94*
Mehaffey, Karen Rae 1959- *ConAu 140*
Mehaffy, Thomas N. 1932- *WhoAm 94*
Mehaignerie, Pierre 1939- *IntWW 93*
Mehalchin, John Joseph 1937- *WhoFI 94*
Mehalic, Mark Andrew 1958- *WhoScEn 94*
Meharry, Ronald Lee 1950- *WhoMW 93*
Mehdizadeh, Mostafa 1949- *WhoFI 94*
Mehdizadeh, Parviz 1934- *WhoWest 94*
Mehew, Peter 1931- *Who 94*
Mehl, Douglas Wayne 1948- *WhoWest 94*
Mehlburger, Donald Lee, Sr. 1937- *WhoAmP 93*
Mehle, David J. 1952- *WhoIns 94*
Mehlenbacher, Dohn Harlow 1931- *WhoFI 94, WhoScEn 94*
Mehler, Barry Alan 1947- *WhoMW 93*
Mehlig, Donald Homer 1935- *WhoIns 94, WhoWest 94*
Mehlinger, Howard Dean 1931- *WhoAm 94, WhoMW 93*
Mehlinger, Kermit Thorpe 1918- *WhoBlA 94*
Mehlman, Edwin Stephen 1935- *WhoAm 94, WhoScEn 94*
Mehlman, Lon Douglas 1959- *WhoFI 94, WhoScEn 94, WhoWest 94*
Mehlman, Mark Franklin 1947- *WhoAm 94, WhoAmL 94*
Mehlman, Myron A. 1934- *WhoScEn 94*
Mehlschau, Robert Eugene 1960- *WhoWest 94*
Mehlum, David L. 1950- *WhoWest 94*
Mehlum, Johan Arnt 1928- *WhoFI 94*
Mehmed the Conqueror, II 1432-1481 *HisWorL [port]*
Mehn, Jan (Von Der Golz) 1953- *WhoAmA 93*
Mehn, W. Harrison 1918- *WhoAm 94*
Mehne, Paul Herbert 1924- *WhoScEn 94*
Mehnert, Eric Martin 1960- *WhoAmL 94*
Mehnert, Lothar d1926 *WhoHol 92*
Mehnert, Thomas P. 1942- *WhoAmL 94*
Mehr, Rochelle Hope *DrAPF 93*
Mehra, Jagdish 1937- *WhoScEn 94*
Mehra, Lal Chand *WhoHol 92*
Mehra, Rajnish 1950- *WhoAm 94, WhoWest 94*
Mehra, Raman Kumar 1943- *WhoAm 94, WhoFI 94, WhoScEn 94*
Mehra, Ravinder C. 1942- *WhoAsA 94*
Mehrabi, M. Reza 1964- *WhoScEn 94*
Mehrabian, Albert 1939- *WhoWest 94, WrDr 94*
Mehrabian, Robert *WhoAm 94, WhoScEn 94*
Mehren, George Louis 1913- *WhAm 10*
Mehren, Lawrence Lindsay 1944- *WhoFI 94*
Mehreteab, Ghebre-Selassie 1941- *WhoBlA 94*
Mehring, Clinton Warren 1924- *WhoAm 94, WhoWest 94*
Mehring, Howard William 1931-1978 *WhoAmA 93N*
Mehring, James Warren 1950- *WhoScEn 94*
Mehrkens, Lyle 1937- *WhoAmP 93*
Mehrmann, Helen d1934 *WhoHol 92*
Mehrotra, Arvind Krishna 1947- *WrDr 94*
Mehrotra, Kishan Gopal 1941- *WhoAsA 94*
Mehrotra, Prakash Chandra 1925- *Who 94*
Mehrotra, Prem N. 1938- *WhoAsA 94*
Mehrotra, Ram Charan 1922- *IntWW 93, Who 94*
Mehrotra, Sriram 1931- *WrDr 94*
Mehrotra, Subhash Chandra 1940- *WhoScEn 94*
Mehrotra, Sudhir Chandra 1945- *WhoAsA 94*
Mehrotra, Vivek 1965- *WhoScEn 94*
Mehrpore, Abdul Rauf 1948- *WhoFI 94*
Mehrtens, Kit *WhoAmP 93*
Mehrtens, Sharon R. 1941- *WhoAmP 93*
Mehta, A. D. 1943- *IntWW 93*
Mehta, A. S. 1943- *WhoAm 94*
Mehta, Ajai Singh 1943- *WhoAsA 94*
Mehta, Amarjit 1941- *WhoAsA 94*
Mehta, Ashok V. 1951- *WhoAsA 94*
Mehta, Bharat V. 1930- *WhoAsA 94*
Mehta, Eileen Rose 1953- *WhoAmL 94*
Mehta, Gita *BlmGWL*
Mehta, Gurmukh Dass 1945- *WhoAsA 94*
Mehta, Jagjivan Ram 1951- *WhoScEn 94*
Mehta, Jawahar L. 1946- *WhoAsA 94*
Mehta, Jay 1943- *WhoFI 94*
Mehta, Kailash 1948- *WhoAsA 94*
Mehta, Kamlesh T. 1959- *WhoAsA 94*
Mehta, Kirtilal M. d1993 *NewYTBS 93*
Mehta, Kishor Singh 1941- *WhoAsA 94*
Mehta, Krishnakant Hiralal 1931- *WhoAsA 94*
Mehta, M. Paul 1936- *WhoAmP 93*
Mehta, Mahendra 1952- *WhoAsA 94*
Mehta, Mahesh 1935- *WhoAsA 94*
Mehta, Mehul Mansukh 1958- *WhoAsA 94*
Mehta, Mohinder Paul 1937- *WhoAsA 94*
Mehta, Narinder Kumar 1938- *WhoAm 94, WhoFI 94*
Mehta, Prakash V. 1946- *WhoAsA 94*
Mehta, Rahul 1949- *WhoAsA 94*
Mehta, Rahul Chandrakant 1959- *WhoWest 94*
Mehta, Raj B. 1962- *WhoAsA 94*
Mehta, Rajendra 1955- *WhoMW 93, WhoScEn 94*
Mehta, Rajendra G. 1947- *WhoAsA 94*
Mehta, Rakesh Kumar 1952- *WhoScEn 94*
Mehta, Sandeep 1966- *WhoFI 94*
Mehta, Shailesh J. 1949- *WhoAm 94*
Mehta, Sonny 1943- *WhoAsA 94*
Mehta, Sunil Kumar 1939- *WhoAsA 94*
Mehta, Ujjwal J. 1944- *WhoAsA 94*
Mehta, Ved 1934- *WhoAsA 94*
Mehta, Ved (Parkash) 1934- *Who 94, WrDr 94*
Mehta, Ved Parkash *DrAPF 93*
Mehta, Ved Parkash 1934- *WhoAm 94*
Mehta, Zarin 1938- *WhoAm 94*
Mehta, Zubin 1936- *ConMus 11 [port], IntWW 93, NewGrDO, Who 94, WhoAm 94, WhoAsA 94*
Mehta Malani, Hina 1958- *WhoScEn 94, WhoWest 94*
Mehul, Etienne-Nicolas 1763-1817 *NewGrDO*
Mehuron, William Otto 1937- *WhoAm 94, WhoFI 94*
Mei, Alexis Itale 1898- *WhAm 10*
Mei, Chiang Chung 1935- *WhoAsA 94*
Mei, June Y. *WhoAsA 94*
Mei, Kenneth K. 1932- *WhoAsA 94*
Mei, Wai-Ning 1949- *WhoAsA 94*
Meibeyer, Shirley Ann 1932- *WhoAmP 93*
Meiburg, Charles Owen 1931- *WhoAm 94*
Meider, Elmer Charles, Jr. 1946- *WhoAm 94*
Meidl, Kevin 1960- *WhoMW 93*
Meier, August 1923- *WhoAm 94, WhoBlA 94*
Meier, Ben 1918- *WhoAmP 93*
Meier, Bradley Kevin 1960- *WhoMW 93*
Meier, David Benjamin 1938- *Who 94*
Meier, David Timothy 1968- *WhoMW 93*
Meier, Derek I. 1943- *WhoAmL 94*
Meier, Dwight D. 1948- *WhoAmL 94*
Meier, George Karl, III 1944- *WhoAm 94*
Meier, Gregory Guilbert 1948- *WhoAmL 94, WhoAmP 93*
Meier, Gustav *WhoAm 94, WhoMW 93*
Meier, Harold Ellswith 1932- *WhoAmP 93*
Meier, Henry George 1929- *WhoAm 94*
Meier, Jeannette Patricia 1947- *WhoAmL 94*
Meier, Johanna 1938- *NewGrDO*
Meier, John George 1943- *WhoAm 94*
Meier, Josi J. *WhoWomW 91*
Meier, Jost 1939- *NewGrDO*
Meier, Kurt Frederick 1965- *WhoFI 94*
Meier, Louis Leonard, Jr. 1918- *WhoAm 94*
Meier, Margaret Kitchen 1931- *WhoAmP 93*
Meier, Mark F. 1925- *WhoAm 94, WhoScEn 94*
Meier, Matt S(ebastian) 1917- *ConAu 43NR*
Meier, Matthias Sebastian 1917- *WhoAm 94*
Meier, Michael Linahan 1932- *WhoMW 93*
Meier, Pamela Jean 1956- *WhoMW 93*
Meier, Paul 1924- *WhoAm 94, WhoScEn 94*
Meier, Paul D. *WrDr 94*
Meier, Richard Alan 1934- *AmCulL, IntWW 93, WhoAm 94, WhoAmA 93*
Meier, Richard Louis 1920- *WhoAm 94*
Meier, Robert Frank 1944- *WhoMW 93*
Meier, Robert Henry, III 1940- *WhoAm 94*
Meier, Robert Joseph, Jr. 1959- *WhoMW 93*
Meier, Roger Theodore 1954- *WhoMW 93*
Meier, Shirley *EncSF 93*
Meier, Thomas Joseph 1948- *WhoWest 94*
Meier, Thomas Keith 1940- *WhoAm 94*
Meier, Thomas Russell 1948- *WhoFI 94*
Meier, Waltraud 1956- *NewGrDO*
Meier, Wilbur Leroy, Jr. 1939- *WhoScEn 94*
Meier, William Henry 1904- *WhoAmP 93*
Meieran, Eugene Stuart 1937- *WhoWest 94*
Meierding, Loren E. 1946- *WhoWest 94*
Meiere, Hildreth d1961 *WhoAmA 93N*
Meierhenry, Mark V. 1944- *WhoAmP 93*
Meiering, Mark C. 1944- *WhoAmL 94*
Meiers, Steven Alan 1942- *WhoAmL 94*
Mei-Figner, Medea 1859-1952 *NewGrDO*
Meigel, David Walter 1957- *WhoWest 94*
Meighan, James, Jr. d1970 *WhoHol 92*
Meighan, Margaret d1961 *WhoHol 92*
Meighan, Stuart Spence 1923- *WhoWest 94*
Meighan, Thomas d1936 *WhoHol 92*
Meigher, S. Christopher, III 1946- *WhoAm 94*
Meigs, Cornelia Lynde 1884-1973 *TwCYAW*
Meigs, John Forsyth 1941- *WhoAm 94, WhoAmL 94*
Meigs, John Liggett 1916- *WhoAmA 93*
Meigs, Mary 1917- *WrDr 94*
Meigs, Return Jonathan 1740-1823 *AmRev, WhAmRev*
Meigs, Walter 1918-1988 *WhoAmA 93N*
Meigs, Walter Ralph 1948- *WhoAmL 94*
Meijer, Barbara Elizabeth 1964- *WhoFI 94*
Meijer, Douglas 1954- *WhoAm 94, WhoFI 94, WhoMW 93*
Meijer, Hendrik 1952- *WhoAm 94, WhoFI 94*
Meijer, Paul Herman Ernst 1921- *WhoAm 94*
Meijler, Frits Louis 1925- *IntWW 93*
Meijs, Gordon Francis 1956- *WhoScEn 94*
Meijsing, Doeschka (Maria Johanna) 1947- *BlmGWL*
Meikle, Dora Quinn Arney 1929- *WhoMW 93*
Meikle, Philip G. 1937- *WhoAm 94, WhoScEn 94*
Meikle, Thomas Harry, Jr. 1929- *WhoAm 94*
Meiklejohn, Al 1923- *WhoAmP 93*
Meiklejohn, Alvin J., Jr. 1923- *WhoWest 94*
Meiklejohn, David Shirra 1908-1989 *WhAm 10*
Meiklejohn, Donald 1909- *WhoAm 94*
Meiklejohn, Donald Stuart 1950- *WhoAmL 94*
Meiklejohn, Linda *WhoHol 92*
Meiklejohn, Lorraine J. 1929- *WhoAmP 93*
Meiklejohn, William Henry 1917- *WhoScEn 94*
Meiksin, Zvi H. 1926- *WhoAm 94*
Meilan, Celia 1920- *WhoAm 94*
Meilgaard, Morten Christian 1928- *WhoAm 94, WhoScEn 94*
Meilhac, Henri 1831-1897 *NewGrDO*
Meiling, Dean S. 1948- *WhoIns 94*
Meiling, George Robert Lucas 1942- *WhoAm 94, WhoFI 94, WhoMW 93*
Meiling, Gerald Stewart 1936- *WhoAm 94*
Meilinger, Peter Martin 1952- *WhoScEn 94*
Meillon, Alfonso 1926- *WhoHisp 94*
Meillon, John d1989 *WhoHol 92*
Meilman, Edward 1915- *WhoAm 94*
Meilman, Roy K. 1946- *WhoAmL 94*
Meilman, Stephanie Kallet 1949- *WhoAmL 94*
Meily, Pamela Jeanne 1965- *WhoWest 94*
Meima, Ralph Chester, Jr. 1927- *WhoAm 94*
Meindl, James Donald 1933- *WhoAm 94*
Meindl, John M. 1944- *WhoAmL 94*
Meindl, Robert James 1936- *WhoAm 94, WhoWest 94*
Meineke, Don 1930- *BasBi*
Meinel, Aden Baker 1922- *WhoAm 94, WhoScEn 94*
Meinel, Ernest d1977 *WhoHol 92*
Meinel, Marjorie Pettit 1922- *WhoWest 94*
Meiner, Richard 1918- *IntWW 93*
Meiner, Sue Ellen Thompson 1943- *WhoMW 93*
Meiners, John Alfred 1950- *WhoAmP 93*
Meiners, Phyllis A. 1940- *WhoFI 94, WhoMW 93*
Meiners, Roger Keith 1932- *WhoMW 93*
Meinert, John Raymond 1927- *WhoAm 94*
Meinert, Lynley Sheryl 1964- *WhoWest 94*
Meinertz, Jeffery Robert 1962- *WhoScEn 94*
Meinertzhagen, Peter 1920- *Who 94*
Meinertzhagen, Peter Richard 1946- *Who 94*
Meinertzhagen, Richard 1878-1967 *DcNaB MP*
Meinhard, Karl d1949 *WhoHol 92*
Meinhardt, Carolyn Loris 1949- *WhoMW 93*
Meinhardt, Peter 1903- *WrDr 94*
Meinhart, Robert David 1954- *WhoScEn 94*
Meinig, Donald William 1924- *WhoAm 94*
Meinke, James David 1949- *WhoMW 93*
Meinke, Peter *DrAPF 93*
Meinke, Peter 1932- *WhoAm 94, WrDr 94*
Meinke, Roy Walter 1929- *WhoAm 94*
Meinkema, Hannes 1943- *BlmGWL*
Meintjes, Victor A. *WhoIns 94*
Meinwald, Jerrold 1927- *IntWW 93, WhoAm 94, WhoScEn 94*
Meinzer, Richard A. *WhoScEn 94*
Meir, Golda 1898-1978 *HisWorL [port]*
Meireles, Cecilia 1901-1964 *BlmGWL*
Meirion-Jones, Gwyn Idris 1933- *Who 94*
Meirovitch, Leonard 1928- *WhoAm 94*
Meirovitz, Michael Brian 1957- *WhoMW 93*
Meirowitz, Claire Cecile 1934- *WhoAm 94*
Meisburg, Steve *WhoAmP 93*
Meisel, Alan 1946- *WhoAm 94*
Meisel, George Ira 1920- *WhoAm 94*
Meisel, George Vincent 1933- *WhoAm 94*
Meisel, Jerome 1934- *WhoAm 94*
Meisel, John 1923- *WhoAm 94, WhoScEn 94*
Meisel, Louis Koenig 1942- *WhoAm 94, WhoAmA 93*
Meisel, Martin 1931- *WhoAm 94*
Meisel, Perry 1949- *WhoAm 94*
Meisel, Steven 1954- *WhoAm 94*
Meisel, Susan Pear 1947- *WhoAmA 93*
Meisel, Werner Paul Ernst 1933- *WhoScEn 94*
Meiselas, Susan Clay 1948- *WhoAm 94*

Mellish, Vera Fuller d1950 WhoHol 92
Mellitt, Brian 1940- Who 94
Mellizo (Cuadrado), Carlos 1942- WrDr 94
Mellizo, Carlos 1942- WhoHisp 94
Mellman, Leonard 1924- WhoFI 94
Mello, Donald R. 1934- WhoWest 94
Mello, H. Joseph 1941- WhoAm 94, WhoAmL 94
Mello, Henry J. 1924- WhoAmP 93
Mello, Renee Lorraine 1964- WhoFI 94, WhoWest 94
Melloan, Erma Jean 1937- WhoAmP 93
Mellon, Agnes 1958- NewGrDO
Mellon, Alfred 1820-1867 NewGrDO
Mellon, Eleanor Mary 1894- WhAm 10
Mellon, James 1929- IntWW 93, Who 94
Mellon, John 1940- WhoAm 94
Mellon, Paul 1907- IntWW 93, Who 94, WhoAm 94, WhoAmA 93
Mellon, Richard Prosser 1939- WhoAm 94
Mellon, Seward Prosser 1942- WhoAm 94
Mellon, William Daniel 1951- WhoWest 94
Mellon, William Knox 1925- WhoWest 94
Mellon, William Robert 1957- WhoFI 94
Mellor, Arthur MCleod 1942- WhoScEn 94
Mellor, David 1930- Who 94
Mellor, David 1949- IntWW 93
Mellor, David Hugh 1938- IntWW 93, Who 94
Mellor, David John 1940- Who 94
Mellor, David John 1949- Who 94
Mellor, Derrick 1926- Who 94
Mellor, George Edward 1928-1987 WhoAmA 93N
Mellor, Hugh Wright 1920- Who 94
Mellor, James WhoHol 92
Mellor, James Frederick McLean 1912- Who 94
Mellor, James Robb 1930- WhoAm 94, WhoFI 94
Mellor, John W(illiams) 1928- WrDr 94
Mellor, John Walter 1927- Who 94
Mellor, John Williams 1928- WhoAm 94
Mellor, Kenneth Wilson Who 94
Mellor, Mark Adams 1951- WhoAmA 93
Mellor, Michael Lawton 1922- WhoAm 94
Mellor, Robert E. 1943- WhoAmL 94, WhoFI 94
Mellor, Ronald William 1930- Who 94
Mellors, Robert Charles 1916- WhoAm 94
Mellott, Cloyd Rowe 1923- WhoAm 94, WhoAmL 94
Mellott, Robert Vernon 1928- WhoAm 94, WhoFI 94, WhoMW 93
Mellow, Robert James 1942- WhoAmP 93
Mellows, Anthony (Roger) 1936- WrDr 94
Mellows, Anthony Roger 1936- Who 94
Melloy, Michael J. 1948- WhoAmL 94, WhoMW 93
Mellstedt, Hakan Soren Thure 1942- WhoScEn 94
Mellum, Gale Robert 1942- WhoAm 94, WhoAmL 94
Melly, Andree 1932- WhoHol 92
Melly, Diana 1937- WrDr 94
Melly, (Alan) George (Heywood) 1926- Who 94, WrDr 94
Mellyn, John Edward, Jr. 1945- WhoAmL 94
Melman, Joy 1927- WhoMW 93
Melman, Richard WhoMW 93
Melman, Yossi (Bili) 1950- ConAu 140
Melmon, Kenneth 1934- IntWW 93
Melmon, Kenneth Lloyd 1934- WhoAm 94, WhoScEn 94
Melmoth, Christopher George Frederick Frampton 1912- Who 94
Melnati, Umberto d1979 WhoHol 92
Melner, Sinclair Lewis 1928- WhoAm 94
Melngailis, Ivars 1933- WhoAm 94
Melnick, Daniel 1932- WhoAm 94
Melnick, Daniel 1934- IntMPA 94
Melnick, David DrAPF 93
Melnick, Edward Lawrence 1938- WhoFI 94
Melnick, Gilbert Stanley 1930- WhoAm 94
Melnick, Jane Fisher 1939- WhoMW 93
Melnick, John Latane 1935- WhoAmP 93
Melnick, Joseph L. 1914- WhoAm 94
Melnick, Lloyd Stuart 1965- WhoFI 94
Melnick, Michael B. 1948- WhoWest 94
Melnick, Myron J. 1959- WhoAmA 93
Melnick, Robert Russell 1956- WhoAmL 94
Melnick, Rowell Shep 1951- WhoAmP 93
Melnick, Roy E. 1954- WhoAmP 93
Melnick, Saul IntMPA 94
Melnicove, Mark DrAPF 93
Melnik, Robert Edward 1933- WhoAm 94
Melnik, Selinda A. 1951- WhoAmL 94
Melniker, Benjamin IntMPA 94
Melnikoff, Sarah Ann 1936- WhoMW 93
Melnikov, Igor Ivanovich 1949- LngBDD
Mel'nikov, Ivan Alexandrovich 1832-1906 NewGrDO
Melnikov, Paul 1951- WhoMW 93, WhoScEn 94
Melnikov, Vitaly Vyacheslavovich 1928- IntWW 93
Melnitzke, Gerald Joseph 1941- WhoFI 94
Melnizky, Walter 1928- IntWW 93
Melnyk, Dean Lynn 1950- WhoMW 93
Melnyk, Steven A. 1953- ConAu 142
Melnykovych, Andrew O. 1952- WhoAm 94
Melo, Thomas M. 1952- WhoAm 94, WhoAmL 94
Meloan, Rosann Marie 1953- WhoMW 93
Meloan, Taylor Wells 1919- WhoAm 94, WhoWest 94
Melody, Michael Edward 1943- WhoAm 94, WhoFI 94
Melone, Joseph James 1931- WhoAm 94, WhoFI 94
Melo Neto, Joao Cabral de 1920- ConWorW 93
Melookaran, Joseph 1955- WhoAsA 94
Meloon, Robert A. 1928- WhoAm 94, WhoMW 93
Melosh, Barbara 1950- WrDr 94
Melosio, Francesco 1609?-1670 NewGrDO
Melott, Ronald K. 1939- WhoWest 94
Meloy, Linda Sue 1949- WhoMW 93
Meloy, Peter Michael 1942- WhoAmP 93
Meloy, Sue England 1959- WhoFI 94
Meloy, Sybil Piskur 1939- WhoAm 94
Melrose, Barry James 1956- WhoAm 94, WhoWest 94
Melrose, Denis Graham 1921- Who 94
Melrose, Donald Blair 1940- IntWW 93
Melrose, Kendrick Bascom 1940- WhoAm 94, WhoFI 94
Melrose, Thomas S. 1922- WhoBlA 94
Melsa, James Louis 1938- WhoAm 94
Melsheimer, Friedrich Valentin 1749-1814 WhAmRev
Melsheimer, Harold 1927- WhoWest 94
Melsheimer, Mel Powell 1939- WhoAm 94
Melsher, Gary W. 1939- WhoAm 94
Melson, Robert Frank 1937- WhoMW 93
Melter, Robert Alan 1935- WhoScEn 94
Melton, Augustus Allen, Jr. 1942- WhoAm 94
Melton, Barry 1947- WhoAmL 94
Melton, Bob 1943- WhoAmP 93
Melton, Bryant 1940- WhoAmP 93, WhoBlA 94
Melton, Buckner Franklin 1923- WhoAmP 93
Melton, Charles Estel 1924- WhoAm 94
Melton, Charles Robert 1947- WhoAmL 94
Melton, Cheryl Ann 1949- WhoWest 94
Melton, David R. 1944- WhoAmL 94
Melton, David Reuben 1952- WhoAm 94
Melton, Edward Joseph 1957- WhoMW 93
Melton, Emory L. 1923- WhoAmP 93
Melton, Emory Leon 1923- WhoMW 93
Melton, Frank d1951 WhoHol 92
Melton, Frank E. WhoBlA 94
Melton, Frank LeRoy 1921- WhoBlA 94
Melton, Gary Bentley 1952- WhoAm 94
Melton, Grant Kemp 1929- WhoAmP 93
Melton, Harry d1965 WhoHol 92
Melton, Harry S. 1915- WhoBlA 94
Melton, Howell Webster, Sr. 1923- WhoAm 94, WhoAmL 94
Melton, James d1961 WhoHol 92
Melton, James 1904-1961 NewGrDO
Melton, Margaret Belle 1925- WhoAmP 93
Melton, Michael Eric 1958- WhoAmL 94, WhoFI 94
Melton, Owen B., Jr. 1946- WhoAm 94
Melton, Richard H. WhoAmP 93
Melton, Richard H. 1935- WhoAm 94
Melton, Richard Huntington 1935- IntWW 93
Melton, Samuel M. d1993 NewYTBS 93 [port]
Melton, Saundra Lou 1939- WhoMW 93
Melton, Sid 1920- WhoHol 92
Melton, William Allen, Sr. 1939- WhoFI 94
Meltzer, Allan H. 1928- WhoAm 94, WhoFI 94
Meltzer, Bernard David 1914- WhoAm 94, WhoMW 93
Meltzer, Bernard Nathan 1916- WhoAm 94
Meltzer, Brian 1944- WhoAm 94, WhoAmL 94
Meltzer, Charles Henry 1852-1936 NewGrDO
Meltzer, Daniel DrAPF 93
Meltzer, David DrAPF 93
Meltzer, David 1937- EncSF 93, WhoAm 94, WrDr 94
Meltzer, David Brian 1929- WhoAm 94
Meltzer, Donald Richard 1932- WhoAm 94
Meltzer, Herbert Yale 1937- WhoAm 94
Meltzer, Jack 1921- WhoAm 94
Meltzer, Jay H. 1944- WhoAm 94, WhoAmL 94
Meltzer, Milton 1915- TwCYAW, WhoAm 94
Meltzer, Peter Edward 1958- WhoAmL 94
Meltzer, Roger 1951- WhoAm 94
Meltzer, Sharon Bittenson 1940- WhoMW 93
Meltzer, Steve 1945- WhoWest 94
Meltzer, Steven Lee 1946- WhoAm 94, WhoAmL 94
Meltzer, Yale Leon 1931- WhoFI 94, WhoScEn 94
Meltzoff, Andrew N. 1950- WhoWest 94
Meltzoff, Julian 1921- WhoWest 94
Meluch, R(ebecca) M. 1956- EncSF 93, WrDr 94
Melum, Mara Minerva 1951- WhoMW 93
Melville Who 94
Melville, Viscount 1937- Who 94
Melville, Allan Scott 1964- WhoFI 94
Melville, Anne 1926- WrDr 94
Melville, Anthony Edwin 1929- Who 94
Melville, Arabella 1948- WrDr 94
Melville, David 1944- Who 94
Melville, Emilie d1932 WhoHol 92
Melville, Fred d1938 WhoHol 92
Melville, Grevis Whitaker 1904- WhoAmA 93
Melville, Harry (Work) 1908- IntWW 93, Who 94
Melville, Herman 1819-1891 AmCulL [port], EncSF 93, NewGrDO, RfGShF
Melville, James Who 94
Melville, James 1931- WrDr 94
Melville, Jenny 1922- WrDr 94
Melville, Leslie Galfreid 1902- IntWW 93, Who 94
Melville, Margarita WhoHisp 94
Melville, Nina d1966 WhoHol 92
Melville, Pauline 1948- BlmGWL
Melville, Robert Seaman 1913- WhoAm 94
Melville, Ronald (Henry) 1912- Who 94
Melville, Rose d1946 WhoHol 92
Melville, Sam d1989 WhoHol 92
Melville, Winifred d1950 WhoHol 92
Melville-Ross, Timothy David 1944- Who 94
Melvill Jones, Geoffrey 1923- IntWW 93, Who 94, WhoAm 94
Melvin, Ben Watson, Jr. 1926- WhoAm 94
Melvin, Billy Alfred 1929- WhoAm 94, WhoMW 93
Melvin, Charles Alfred, III 1950 WhoMW 93
Melvin, Charles Edward, Jr. 1929- WhoAm 94
Melvin, G. S. d1946 WhoHol 92
Melvin, Grace Wilson d1977 WhoAmA 93N
Melvin, Gregory Mark 1956- WhoFI 94
Melvin, Harold James 1941- WhoBlA 94
Melvin, John A. 1944- WhoIns 94
Melvin, John Lewis 1935- WhoAm 94
Melvin, John Turcan 1916- Who 94
Melvin, Joseph M. 1950- WhoFI 94
Melvin, Kenneth Ronald 1952- WhoAmP 93
Melvin, Murray 1932- WhoHol 92
Melvin, Norman Cecil 1916- WhoAm 94
Melvin, Orvis Alnie, Jr. 1947- WhoFI 94
Melvin, Ronald McKnight 1927- WhoAmA 93
Melvin, Russell Johnston 1925- WhoAm 94
Melvin, T. Stephen 1938- WhoAm 94
Melvin, Theresa J. WhoAmP 93
Melvyn Howe, George Who 94
Melwood, (Eileen) Mary WrDr 94
Melzack, Ronald 1929- WhoAm 94, WrDr 94
Melzacki, Krzysztof 1932- WhoScEn 94
Melzar, Frederic Preston 1920- WhAm 10
Melzer, Shephard W. 1942- WhoAmL 94
Membertou d1611 EncNAR
Membiela, Roymi Victoria 1957- WhoHisp 94
Membrives, Lola d1969 WhoHol 92
Memel, Sherwin Leonard 1930- WhoAm 94, WhoAmL 94
Meminger, Dean 1948- BasBi
Memmi, Albert 1920- ConWorW 93, IntWW 93
Memmoli, George d1985 WhoHol 92
Memmott, David DrAPF 93
Memoli, Michael Anthony 1950- WhoScEn 94
Memory, Jasper Durham 1936- WhoAm 94
Memory, Jasper Livingston 1901-1991 WhAm 10
Memphis, Ricky WhoHol 92
Memphis, Slim 1915- WhAm 10
Mena, David L. 1945- WhoHisp 94
Mena, Manuel Alfred 1941- WhoHisp 94
Mena, Xavier WhoHisp 94
Menack, Steven Boyd 1959- WhoAmL 94
Mena De Quevedo, Margarita IntWW 93
Menage, Gilles Marie Marcel 1943- IntWW 93
Menageot, Francois-Guillaume 1744-1816 NewGrDO
Menaghan, Elizabeth Grace 1949- WhoMW 93
Menahan, Jeanne d1963 WhoHol 92
Menahan, William Thomas 1935- WhoAmP 93
Menahem, Elijah c. 1232-1284 DcNaB MP
Menaker, Edward Goward 1919- WhoAmP 93
Menaker, Frank H., Jr. 1940- WhoAm 94, WhoAmL 94, WhoFI 94
Menaker, Michael 1934- WhoAm 94
Menaker, Ronald Herbert 1944- WhoFI 94
Menaker, Shirley Ann Lasch 1935- WhoAm 94
Menander 342BC-293BC BlmGEL, IntDcT 2 [port]
Menant, Paul d1934 WhoHol 92
Menard, Albert Louis 1937- WhoFI 94
Menard, Curt 1944- WhoAmP 93
Menard, Jayne Bush 1946- WhoFI 94
Menard, Joan M. 1935- WhoAmP 93
Menard, Orville D. 1933- WrDr 94
Menard, Pierre 1766-1844 WhWE
Menard, Rene R. 1957- WhoAmP 93
Menasco, Norman EncSF 93
Menashe, Samuel DrAPF 93
Mencer, Ernest James 1945- WhoBlA 94
Mencer, Glenn Everell 1925- WhoAm 94, WhoAmL 94
Mencer, Jetta 1959- WhoAmP 93
Mencer, Nellie T. 1924- WhoAmP 93
Mench, John William 1943- WhoAm 94
Menchaca, Richard P. WhoHisp 94
Menchel, Donald 1932- WhoAm 94
Mencher, Bruce Stephan 1935- WhoAm 94
Mencher, Melvin 1927- WhoAm 94
Mencher, Stuart Alan 1939- WhoAm 94
Menchhofer, Donald L. 1937- WhoMW 93
Menchhofer, Robert Henry 1948- WhoMW 93
Menchin, Robert Stanley 1923- WhoAm 94
Menchu, Rigoberta IntWW 93
Menchu, Rigoberta 1959- CurBio 93 [port], WhoAm 94
Mencin, Alan Jay 1957- WhoWest 94
Mencius 4th cent.BC- EncEth
Mencken, H. L. 1880-1956 DcLB 137 [port]
Mencken, Henry Louis 1880-1956 AmSocL, DcAmReB 2
Menco, Bernard 1946- WhoMW 93
Menconi, Ralph Joseph 1915-1972 WhoAmA 93N
Mendal, Geoffrey Owen 1961- WhoWest 94
Mendana, Alvaro De c. 1541-1595 WhWE
Mende, Erich 1916- IntWW 93, Who 94
Mende, Robert Graham 1926- WhoAm 94
Mendel, Gregor Johann 1822-1884 EncSPD
Mendel, Jerry Marc 1938- WhoAm 94
Mendel, Johann Gregor 1822-1884 WorScD [port]
Mendel, Lafayette Benedict WorScD
Mendel, Mark DrAPF 93
Mendel, Maurice 1942- WhoScEn 94
Mendel, Paul David 1930- Who 94
Mendel, Perry 1922- WhoFI 94
Mendel, Roberta DrAPF 93
Mendel, Verne Edward 1923- WhoAm 94
Mendel, Werner Max 1927-1990 WhAm 10
Mendeleev, Dmitry Ivanovich 1834-1907 WorScD
Mendell, Oliver M. 1925- WhoAm 94
Mendell, Phyllis 1949- WhoAm 94
Mendelowitz, Allan Irwin 1943- WhoFI 94
Mendelowitz, Daniel Marcus 1905-1980 WhoAmA 93N
Mendels, Joseph 1937- WhoAm 94
Mendels, Josepha (Judica) 1902- BlmGWL
Mendelsberg, Joanna Ajzenberg 1934- WhoMW 93
Mendelsohn, Alfred 1910-1966 NewGrDO
Mendelsohn, Avrum Joseph 1940- WhoScEn 94
Mendelsohn, Ben WhoHol 92
Mendelsohn, Dennis 1927- WhoScEn 94

Mendelsohn, Everett Irwin 1931-
 WhoAm 94, WhoScEn 94
Mendelsohn, Ezra 1940- *WrDr 94*
Mendelsohn, Felix, Jr. 1906- *EncSF 93*
Mendelsohn, Harold 1923- *WhoAm 94*
Mendelsohn, John 1936- *WhoAm 94,
 WhoScEn 94*
Mendelsohn, John 1949- *WhoAmA 93*
Mendelsohn, Louis Benjamin 1948-
 WhoFI 94
Mendelsohn, Martin 1935- *WrDr 94*
Mendelsohn, Martin 1942- *WhoAmL 94*
Mendelsohn, Ray Langer 1947-
 WhoScEn 94
Mendelsohn, Robert Victor 1946-
 WhoAm 94, WhoFI 94
Mendelsohn, Stuart 1952- *WhoAmL 94*
Mendelsohn, Walter 1897- *WhoAm 94*
Mendelsohn, Zehavah Whitney 1956-
 WhoMW 93
Mendelson (Prokof'yeva), Mira
 Alexandrovna 1914?-1968 *NewGrDO*
Mendelson, Alan Charles 1948-
 WhoAm 94, WhoAmL 94
Mendelson, David Frey 1925-
 WhoMW 93
Mendelson, Drew *EncSF 93*
Mendelson, Edward James 1946-
 WhoAm 94
Mendelson, Elliott 1931- *WhoAm 94*
Mendelson, Haim 1923- *WhoAm 94,
 WhoAmA 93*
Mendelson, Lee M. 1933- *WhoAm 94*
Mendelson, Leonard M. 1923-
 WhoAmL 94, WhoFI 94
Mendelson, Mary Adelaide 1917-
 WhoMW 93
Mendelson, Maurice Harvey 1943-
 Who 94
Mendelson, Morris 1922- *WrDr 94*
Mendelson, Ralph Richard 1917-
 WhoMW 93
Mendelson, Richard Donald 1933-
 WhoAm 94
Mendelson, Richard Paul 1953-
 WhoWest 94
Mendelson, Robert Allen 1930-
 WhoAm 94
Mendelson, Sol 1926- *WhoScEn 94*
Mendelson, Steven Earle 1948-
 WhoAmL 94
Mendelson, Tobias Matthew 1957-
 WhoAmL 94
Mendelssohn(-Bartholdy), (Jakob Ludwig)
 Felix 1809-1847 *NewGrDO*
Mendelssohn, Arnold (Ludwig)
 1855-1933 *NewGrDO*
Mendelssohn, Eleanora d1951 *WhoHol 92*
Mendenhall, Corwin (Guy), Jr. 1916-
 WrDr 94
Mendenhall, David *WhoHol 92*
Mendenhall, Donna Rae 1944- *WhoFI 94*
Mendenhall, George Emery 1916-
 WrDr 94
Mendenhall, Jack 1937- *WhoAmA 93*
Mendenhall, John Rufus 1948-
 WhoBlA 94
Mendenhall, John Ryan 1928- *WhoAm 94*
Mendenhall, Robert Lee 1954-
 WhoAmL 94
Mendenhall, Robert Vernon 1920-
 WhoAm 94
Mender, Mona (Siegler) 1926- *ConAu 141*
Mendes, Barbara 1948- *WhoAmA 93*
Mendes, Chico 1944-1988 *EnvEnc [port]*
Mendes, Donna M. 1951- *WhoBlA 94*
Mendes, Helen Althia 1935- *WhoBlA 94*
Mendes, Henry Pereira *EncSF 93*
Mendes, Henry Pereira 1852-1937
 DcAmReB 2
Mendes, John P. d1955 *WhoHol 92*
Mendes, Lothar d1974 *WhoHol 92*
Mendes, Robert Laurence 1947-
 WhoIns 94
Mendes, Sam *IntWW 93*
Mendes France, Pierre 1907-1982
 ConAu 43NR
Mendez, Albert Orlando 1935-
 WhoAm 94, WhoFI 94
Mendez, Alfred *WhoHisp 94*
Mendez, C. Beatriz 1952- *WhoScEn 94*
Mendez, C. Teresa 1960- *WhoHisp 94*
Mendez, Celestino Galo 1944-
 WhoScEn 94, WhoWest 94
Mendez, Charlotte *DrAPF 93*
Mendez, David B. 1960- *WhoHisp 94*
Mendez, Elena 1956- *WhoHisp 94*
Mendez, Francisco d1986 *WhoHol 92*
Mendez, George 1956- *WhoHisp 94*
Mendez, Giner E. d1993 *NewYTBS 93*
Mendez, Hector *WhoHisp 94*
Mendez, Hermann 1949- *WhoHisp 94*
Mendez, Hermann Armando 1949-
 WhoHisp 94
Mendez, Hugh B. 1933- *WhoBlA 94*
Mendez, Hugo Saul 1954- *WhoHisp 94*
Méndez, Ileana Maria 1952- *WhoHisp 94*
Mendez, Jana 1944- *WhoAmP 93*

Mendez, Jana Wells 1944- *WhoWest 94*
Mendez, Jesus 1951- *WhoHisp 94*
Mendez, Jorge H. Acevedo *WhoAmP 93*
Mendez, Julio Enrique 1948- *WhoHisp 94*
Méndez, Julio F. 1960- *WhoHisp 94*
Mendez, Maria 1954- *WhoHisp 94*
Mendez, Mauricio David 1944-
 WhoHisp 94
Mendez, Miguel A. *WhoHisp 94*
Méndez, Miguel Morales 1930-
 WhoHisp 94
Mendez, Olga A. *WhoAmP 93,
 WhoHisp 94*
Mendez, Rafael *WhoHisp 94*
Mendez, Rafael d1981 *WhoHol 92*
Mendez, Raul H. *WhoHisp 94*
Méndez, Robert G. *WhoHisp 94*
Mendez, Rogelio Francisco, Jr. 1948-
 WhoHisp 94
Mendez, Ruben Homero 1957-
 WhoHisp 94
Mendez, Veronica 1942- *WhoHisp 94*
Mendez, Victor 1945- *WhoHisp 94*
Mendez, Victor Manuel 1944-
 WhoHisp 94
Mendez, William, Jr. 1948- *WhoHisp 94*
Mendez, Yasmine M. 1960- *WhoHisp 94*
Mendez Montenegro, Julio Cesar 1915-
 IntWW 93
Méndez-Polo, Ceferino Anastasio 1913-
 WhoHisp 94
Mendez Santiago, Edwin 1954-
 WhoHisp 94
Mendez-Smith, Freda Ann 1939-
 WhoHisp 94
Mendham, Robert William, Jr. 1956-
 WhoMW 93
Mendicino, Jane A. 1934- *WhoAmP 93*
Mendicino, V. Frank 1939- *WhoAm 94*
Mendillo, Stephen 1943- *WhoHol 92*
Mendini, Douglas A. *DrAPF 93*
Mendiola-McLain, Emma Lilia 1956-
 WhoHisp 94
Mendis, Vernon Lorraine Benjamin
 1925- *IntWW 93, Who 94*
Mendius, Patricia Dodd Winter 1924-
 WhoWest 94
Mendivil, Fernando Quihuiz 1937-
 WhoHisp 94
Mendizabal, Maritza S. 1941-
 WhoHisp 94
Mendl, James Henry Embleton 1927-
 Who 94
Mendler, Edward Charles 1926-
 WhoAm 94
Mendler, Joel A. 1944- *WhoAmL 94*
Mendlowski, Bronislaw 1914-
 WhoScEn 94
Mendoliera, Salvatore 1952- *WhoScEn 94*
Mendonca, Maria Luisa 1962-
 WhoWest 94
Mendonsa, Arthur Adonel 1928-
 WhoAm 94
Mendosa, Rick 1935- *WhoHisp 94*
Mendoza, Agapito 1946- *WhoHisp 94*
Mendoza, Al, Jr. 1943- *WhoHisp 94*
Mendoza, Antonio De c. 1490-1552
 WhWE
Mendoza, Antonio G. 1941- *WhoAmA 93*
Mendoza, Candelario José 1919-
 WhoHisp 94
Mendoza, Conchita Maria 1948-
 WhoHisp 94
Mendoza, Corine 1952- *WhoHisp 94*
Mendoza, David Vasquez 1948-
 WhoHisp 94
Mendoza, Elia R. *WhoHisp 94*
Mendoza, Ernest A. *WhoHisp 94*
Mendoza, Eva 1950- *WhoHisp 94*
Mendoza, Fernando Sanchez 1948-
 WhoHisp 94
Mendoza, Genaro Tumamak 1943-
 WhoScEn 94
Mendoza, George 1934- *WhoAm 94,
 WhoHisp 94*
Mendoza, George 1955- *WhoHisp 94*
Mendoza, George John 1955-
 WhoWest 94
Mendoza, Gilbert Reyes 1939-
 WhoHisp 94
Mendoza, Harry R. 1953- *WhoHisp 94*
Mendoza, Henry C. *WhoHisp 94*
Mendoza, Henry Trevino, III 1947-
 WhoHisp 94
Mendoza, Jean *WhoHol 92*
Mendoza, John *WhoHisp 94*
Mendoza, Juan A. 1955- *WhoHisp 94*
Mendoza, Juan Andres 1961- *WhoHisp 94*
Mendoza, Julian Nava 1934- *WhoHisp 94*
Mendoza, June *WhoHisp 94*
Mendoza, June Yvonne *Who 94*
Mendoza, Lisa 1958- *WhoHisp 94*
Mendoza, Lydia 1916- *WhoHisp 94*
Mendoza, Manuel Osmundo 1933-
 WhoHisp 94
Mendoza, Maurice 1921- *Who 94*

Mendoza, Michael Dennis 1944-
 WhoHisp 94
Mendoza, Nicolas *WhoHisp 94*
Mendoza, Pablo, Jr. *WhoHisp 94*
Mendoza, Pedro De 1487-1537 *WhWE*
Mendoza, Ralph 1953- *WhoHisp 94*
Mendoza, Ricardo 1954- *WhoHisp 94*
Mendoza, Stanley Atran 1940- *WhoAm 94*
Mendoza, Stella Altamirano 1948-
 WhoHisp 94
Mendoza, Tony C. 1950- *WhoWest 94*
Mendoza, Vivian P. *Who 94*
Mendoza-Acosta, Felix 1929- *Who 94*
Mendrelyuk, Dmitry Evgenevich 1965-
 LngBDD
Mendrzycki, Edward C. 1937-
 WhoAmL 94
Mendyk, Stan A. E. 1953- *WrDr 94*
Menebhi, Saida 1952-1977 *BlmGWL*
Menebroker, Ann *DrAPF 93*
Meneeley, Edward 1927- *WhoAmA 93*
Meneeley, Edward Sterling 1927-
 WhoAm 94
Menefee, Frederick Lewis 1932-
 WhoMW 93
Menefee, Juan F. 1961- *WhoBlA 94*
Menefee, Samuel Pyeatt 1950-
 WhoAmL 94, WhoFI 94
Menegaz, Renee Marie 1927- *WhoMW 93*
Menelik, II 1844-1913 *HisWorL [port]*
Menell, Peter Seth 1958- *WhoWest 94*
Menem, Carlos Saul 1935- *IntWW 93*
Menemencioglu, Turgut 1914- *IntWW 93,
 Who 94*
Menendez, Albert J. 1942- *WrDr 94*
Menendez, Albert John 1942-
 WhoHisp 94
Menéndez, Ana Maria 1970- *WhoHisp 94*
Menendez, Antonio R. 1946- *WhoAmL 94*
Menendez, Carlos 1938- *WhoAm 94,
 WhoHisp 94*
Menendez, Catherine A. 1959- *WhoIns 94*
Menéndez, Jose 1957- *WhoHisp 94,
 WhoWest 94*
Menendez, Louis Joseph, Jr. 1961-
 WhoHisp 94
Menendez, Manuel, Jr. 1947- *WhoAm 94,
 WhoAmL 94, WhoHisp 94*
Menendez, Manuel E. *WhoHisp 94*
Menéndez, María de los Angeles 1950-
 WhoHisp 94
Menendez, Michael Joseph 1949-
 WhoHisp 94
Menendez, Nilo d1987 *WhoHol 92*
Menendez, Robert 1954- *CngDr 93,
 WhoAm 94, WhoAmP 93, WhoHisp 94*
Menendez De Aviles, Pedro 1519-1574
 WhWE [port]
Menendez-Monroig, Jose M. 1917-
 WhoAmP 93
Meneres, Maria Alberta 1930- *BlmGWL*
Menes, Pauline H. 1924- *WhoAmP 93*
Meneses, Adalberto 1926- *WhoHisp 94*
Meneses, Juana Josefa de 1651-1709
 BlmGWL
Meneses, Rubén Luis 1934- *WhoHisp 94*
Meneses, Walter Eduardo 1953-
 WhoHisp 94
Menevia, Bishop of 1929- *Who 94*
Meneweather, Earl W. 1917- *WhoBlA 94*
Menez, Bernard *WhoHol 92*
Meng, James Cheng-Sun 1943-
 WhoAsA 94
Meng, Jimmy Z. *WhoAsA 94*
Meng, Qing-Min 1954- *WhoAsA 94*
Meng, Wen Jin 1962- *WhoScEn 94*
Meng, Xiannong 1957- *WhoAsA 94*
Mengal, Martin-Joseph 1784-1851
 NewGrDO
Mengatti, John *WhoHol 92*
Mengden, Joseph Michael 1924-
 WhoAm 94
Menge, Richard Cramer 1935- *WhoAm 94*
Mengedoth, Donald Roy 1944-
 WhoAm 94
Mengel, Charles Edmund 1931-
 WhoAmL 94
Mengel, Christopher Emile 1952-
 WhoAmL 94
Mengel, David Bruce 1948- *WhoAm 94*
Mengel, Lynn Irene Sheets 1955-
 WhoFI 94, WhoScEn 94
Mengel, Philip Richard 1944- *WhoAm 94*
Mengel, Raymond Louis 1950-
 WhoWest 94
Mengel, Robert Morrow 1921-1990
 WhAm 10
Mengeling, William Lloyd 1933-
 WhoAm 94
Menger, Harold Charles, Jr. 1952-
 WhoMW 93
Menges, Carl Braun 1930- *WhoAm 94,
 WhoFI 94*
Menges, Chris *IntWW 93*
Menges, Chris 1940- *IntDcF 2-4,
 IntMPA 94, WhoAm 94*

Menges, Eugene Clifford 1952-
 WhoAmL 94
Menges, John Kenneth, Jr. 1957-
 WhoAmL 94
Menges, Joyce 1948- *WhoHol 92*
Meng Fulin 1933- *WhoPRCh 91 [port]*
Mengistu Haile Mariam *IntWW 93*
Meng Jiqing *WhoPRCh 91 [port]*
Mengle, Tobi Dara 1960- *WhoFI 94*
Menglet, Alex *WhoHol 92*
Meng Liankun 1925- *WhoPRCh 91 [port]*
Mengozzi, Bernardo 1758-1800 *NewGrDO*
Meng Qingping 1937- *WhoPRCh 91 [port]*
Menguy, Rene 1926- *WhoAm 94*
Meng Weizai 1933- *WhoPRCh 91 [port]*
Meng Ying *WhoPRCh 91*
Meng Ying 1913- *IntWW 93*
Meng Zhiyuan 1930- *WhoPRCh 91 [port]*
Menhall, Dalton Winn 1939- *WhoAm 94*
Menhennet, David 1928- *Who 94*
Men Huifeng 1937- *IntWW 93*
Menhusen, Monty Jay 1948- *WhoMW 93*
Menicucci, Bruno P. 1937- *WhoAmP 93*
Menicuccio *NewGrDO*
Menig, Beatrice Quay 1923- *WhoAmP 93*
Menihan, John Conway 1908-
 WhoAmA 93
Menihan, John Conway 1908-1992
 WhAm 10
Menikoff, Barry 1939- *WhoWest 94*
Menil, Georges de & Menil, Lois de
 WhoAmA 93
Menil, Lois de
 See Menil, Georges de & Menil, Lois de
 WhoAmA 93
Menil, Lois de *WhoAmA 93*
Menin, Malcolm James *Who 94*
Meninno, Frank Thomas 1958- *WhoFI 94*
Menino, Thomas M. *WhoAmP 93*
Menino, Thomas M. 1942- *WhoAm 94*
Menius, Arthur Clayton, Jr. 1916-
 WhoAm 94
Menius, Espie Flynn, Jr. 1923-
 WhoScEn 94
Menjo, Hiroshi 1954- *WhoWest 94*
Menjou, Adolphe d1963 *WhoHol 92*
Menjou, Henri d1956 *WhoHol 92*
Menk, Bruce A. 1948- *WhoAmL 94*
Menk, Carl William 1921- *WhoAm 94,
 WhoFI 94*
Menk, Louis W. 1918- *IntWW 93*
Menk, Louis Wilson 1918- *WhoAm 94*
Menk, Nancy Lee 1955- *WhoMW 93*
Menkart, John 1922- *WhoAm 94*
Menke, Allen Carl 1922- *WhoAm 94*
Menke, Catherine Christine Hudson
 1961- *WhoMW 93*
Menke, James Michael 1951-
 WhoScEn 94
Menke, Lester D. 1918- *WhoAmP 93*
Menke, Regis B. 1949- *WhoIns 94*
Menke, William Charles 1939-
 WhoAmL 94, WhoFI 94
Menkello, Frederick Vincent 1942-
 WhoAm 94
Menken, Alan 1949- *ConMus 10 [port],
 ConTFT 11*
Menken, Alan 1950- *IntMPA 94,
 WhoAm 94*
Menken, Helen d1966 *WhoHol 92*
Menken, Shepard *WhoHol 92*
Menkes, David 1922- *WhoFI 94*
Menkes, John Hans 1928- *WhoAm 94*
Menkes, Sigmund J. 1896-1986
 WhoAmA 93N
Menkes, Sigmund Josef 1896- *WhAm 10*
Menkes, Suzy Peta 1943- *Who 94*
Menkin, Christopher 1942- *WhoFI 94,
 WhoWest 94*
Menkin, Harlan Lee 1948- *WhoWest 94*
Menkiti, Ifeanyi *DrAPF 93*
Menn, Julius Joel 1929- *WhoAm 94*
Menne, Thomas Joseph 1934-
 WhoMW 93
Menneer, Stephen Snow 1910- *Who 94*
Mennella, Vincent Alfred 1922-
 WhoWest 94
Mennenga, Gordon W. *DrAPF 93*
Menning, Barbara Susan 1954-
 WhoMW 93
Menning, Marion 1945- *WhoAmP 93*
Menninger, Edward Joseph 1931-
 WhoAm 94
Menninger, John Robert 1935-
 WhoMW 93
Menninger, Karl Augustus 1893-1990
 WhAm 10
Menninger, Rosemary Jeanetta 1948-
 WhoMW 93
Menninger, Roy Wright 1926-
 WhoAm 94, WhoMW 93
Menninger, William Walter 1931-
 WhoAm 94, WhoScEn 94
Mennini, Louis (Alfred) 1920- *NewGrDO*
Mennis, Edmund Addi 1919- *WhoAm 94,
 WhoWest 94*
Meno, Lionel R. *WhoAm 94*
Menocal, Armando M., III *WhoHisp 94*

Menocal, Narciso Garcia 1936- *WhoMW 93*
Menoher, Paul Edwin, Jr. 1939- *WhoAm 94, WhoWest 94*
Menold, Ernest John 1960- *WhoFI 94*
Menon, Beryl Emmer d1993 *NewYTBS 93*
Menon, Gopinath K. 1943- *WhoAsA 94*
Menon, K. P. S. 1898-1982 *HisDcKW*
Menon, Mambillikalathil Govind Kumar 1928- *IntWW 93, Who 94, WhoScEn 94*
Menon, Mani *WhoAm 94*
Menon, Padmanabhan 1951- *WhoScEn 94*
Menon, Premachandran Rama 1931- *WhoAm 94*
Menon, V. K. Krishna 1896-1974 *HisDcKW*
Menon, Vatakke Kurupath Narayana 1911- *IntWW 93*
Menon, Vijaya Bhaskar 1934- *WhoAm 94*
Menor, Ron Christopher 1955- *WhoAmP 93*
Menotti, Carlo Lifavi d1993 *NewYTBS 93*
Menotti, Gian Carlo 1911- *AmCulL, IntWW 93, NewGrDO, Who 94, WhoAm 94*
Menoyo, Eric Felix 1944- *WhoAm 94, WhoAmL 94*
Mensah, E. Kwaku 1945- *WhoBlA 94*
Mensah, Joseph Henry 1928- *IntWW 93*
Menscer, Darrell V. 1934- *WhoFI 94*
Menschel, Robert Benjamin 1929- *WhoAm 94*
Menscher, Barnet Gary 1940- *WhoFI 94*
Mensching, Horst Georg 1921- *IntWW 93*
Mense, Allan Tate 1945- *WhoAm 94*
Menses, Jan 1933- *WhoAm 94, WhoAmA 93*
Mensforth, Eric 1906- *Who 94*
Mensh, Ivan Norman 1915- *WhoWest 94*
Menshov, Vladimir Valentinovich 1939- *IntWW 93*
Mensik, Vladimir *WhoHol 92*
Mensing, Stephen Gustav 1946- *WhoAm 94*
Mensinger, Peggy 1923- *WhoAmP 93*
Mensinger, Peggy Boothe 1923- *WhoAm 94*
Menson, Richard L. 1943- *WhoAmL 94*
Mentel, Michael Christopher 1961- *WhoAmL 94*
Menter, James (Woodham) 1921- *Who 94*
Menter, James Woodham 1921- *IntWW 93*
Menter, Martin Alan 1941- *WhoScEn 94*
Mentes, Cevdet 1915- *IntWW 93*
Menteth, James (Wallace) Stuart- 1922- *Who 94*
Menthe, Melissa 1948- *WhoAmA 93*
Mentley, Lee C. 1948- *WhoWest 94*
Mentlikowski, Donald Richard 1932- *WhoMW 93*
Menton, Francis James, Jr. 1950- *WhoAm 94, WhoAmL 94*
Menton, William Joseph *WhoAmP 93*
Mentre, Paul 1935- *IntWW 93*
Mentz, Donald 1933- *Who 94*
Mentz, Henry Alvan, Jr. 1920- *WhoAm 94*
Mentz, J. Roger 1942- *WhoAmP 93*
Mentz, Lawrence 1946- *WhoAmL 94, WhoFI 94*
Mentzer, John Raymond 1916- *WhoAm 94*
Mentzer, Merleen Mae 1920- *WhoMW 93*
Menuci, Tomasso *NewGrDO*
Menudin, Ibrahim 1948- *IntWW 93*
Menuhin, Baron 1916- *Who 94*
Menuhin, Yehudi 1916- *ConMus 11 [port], IntWW 93, WhoAm 94, WhoHol 92, WrDr 94*
Menville, Douglas (Alver) 1935- *EncSF 93*
Menyhert, Stephan 1937- *WhoMW 93*
Menyuk, Paula 1929- *WhoAm 94*
Menz, Fredric Carl 1943- *WhoFI 94*
Menze, Clemens 1928- *IntWW 93*
Menzel, Daniel Bruce 1934- *WhoWest 94*
Menzel, David L. 1948- *WhoAmL 94*
Menzel, David Washington 1928- *WhoScEn 94*
Menzel, Edward Barry 1951- *WhoFI 94*
Menzel, Jiri 1938- *IntWW 93, WhoHol 92*
Menzel, John 1957- *WhoAmL 94*
Menzer, Robert Everett 1938- *WhoAm 94*
Menzie, Donald E. 1922- *WhoAm 94, WhoScEn 94*
Menzie, Edward G. 1945- *WhoAmL 94*
Menzies, Carl Stephen 1932- *WhoScEn 94*
Menzies, Duncan Adam Young 1953- *Who 94*
Menzies, Heather 1949- *WhoHol 92*
Menzies, Ian Stuart 1920- *WhoAm 94*
Menzies, John Maxwell 1926- *Who 94*
Menzies, Leila Kay 1947- *WhoWest 94*
Menzies, Pattie (Maie) 1899- *Who 94*
Menzies, Paul Stewart 1948- *WhoIns 94*
Menzies, Peter (Thomson) 1912- *Who 94*
Menzies, Robert *WhoHol 92*
Menzies, Robert G. 1894-1978 *HisDcKW*
Menzies, Robert Gordon 1894-1978 *HisWorL [port]*
Menzies, Stephen Malcom 1941- *WhoFI 94*
Menzies, Trixie Te Arama (Tainui) 1936- *BlmGWL*
Menzies, William Cameron 1896-1957 *IntDcF 2-4*
Menzies-Wilson, William Napier 1926- *Who 94*
Menzinsky, Modeste 1875-1935 *NewGrDO*
Meo, Jean Alfred Emile Edouard 1927- *IntWW 93*
Meo, Michael 1947- *WhoWest 94*
Meo, Roxanne Marie 1959- *WhoMW 93*
Meola, John Thomas 1947- *WhoMW 93*
Meosky, Paul David 1964- *WhoAmL 94*
Meotti, Michael Patrick 1953- *WhoAmP 93*
M. E. R. 1875-1975 *BlmGWL*
Mer, Francis Paul 1939- *IntWW 93*
Mera, Edith d1935 *WhoHol 92*
Merak, A.J. *EncSF 93*
Meral, Gerald Harvey 1944- *WhoScEn 94*
Merande, Doro d1975 *WhoHol 92*
Merante, Louis 1828-1887 *IntDcB [port]*
Merante, Louis (Francois) 1828-1887 *NewGrDO*
Meranus, Arthur Richard 1934- *WhoAm 94, WhoFI 94*
Meranus, Leonard Stanley 1928- *WhoAm 94*
Merard de Saint-Just, Anne-Jeanne-Felicite d'Ormoy 1765-1830 *BlmGWL*
Merasty, Billy *WhoHol 92*
Meraz, Micheal J. 1954- *WhoHisp 94*
Merbach, Carol Lynn 1955- *WhoMW 93*
Merbah, Kasdi (Abdallah Khalef) 1938- *IntWW 93*
Merbaum, Michael 1933- *WhoAm 94*
Mercadante, (Giuseppe) Saverio (Raffaele) 1795-1870 *NewGrDO*
Mercado, Albert William 1961- *WhoHisp 94*
Mercado, Camelia 1928- *WhoHisp 94*
Mercado, Carlos 1949- *WhoHisp 94*
Mercado, Edward 1937- *WhoHisp 94*
Mercado, Hector 1949- *WhoHol 92*
Mercado, Ralph 1941- *WhoHisp 94*
Mercado, Rich 1945- *WhoHisp 94*
Mercado, Roger 1967- *WhoHisp 94*
Mercado, Romelia 1962- *WhoHisp 94*
Mercado Irizarry, Aurelio, Jr. 1948- *WhoHisp 94*
Mercado Jarrin, Luis Edgardo 1919- *IntWW 93*
Mercado-Valdes, Frank Marcelino 1962- *WhoBlA 94*
Mercado-Vargas, Ruben Luis 1950- *WhoHisp 94*
Mercant, Anthony John 1921- *WhoAmL 94*
Mercant, Jon Jeffry 1950- *WhoWest 94*
Mercanton, Jean d1947 *WhoHol 92*
Mercanton, Louis d1932 *WhoHol 92*
Mercator, Gerardus *WorInv*
Mercator, Gerardus 1512-1594 *WhWE [port]*
Mercator, Nicolaus c. 1620-1687 *DcNaB MP*
Merced, Nelson 1948- *WhoAmP 93, WhoHisp 94*
Merced, Orlando Luis 1966- *WhoHisp 94*
Merced, Victor 1956- *WhoHisp 94, WhoWest 94*
Merced-Reyes, Josue 1950- *WhoHisp 94*
Mercer, Alan 1931- *Who 94*
Mercer, Arthur, Sr. 1921- *WhoBlA 94*
Mercer, Bernard 1912- *WhoIns 94*
Mercer, Beryl d1939 *WhoHol 92*
Mercer, Charles Wayne *WhoAm 94*
Mercer, David 1928-1980 *BlmGEL, ConDr 93, IntDcT 2*
Mercer, David Robinson 1938- *WhoAm 94, WhoMW 93*
Mercer, Derrik 1944- *WrDr 94*
Mercer, Douglas 1918- *WhoAm 94*
Mercer, Edwin Wayne 1940- *WhoAm 94, WhoAmL 94*
Mercer, Elwyn Jarvis 1911- *WhAm 10*
Mercer, Eric Arthur John 1917- *Who 94*
Mercer, Frances 1917- *WhoHol 92*
Mercer, Geoffrey Dallas 1935- *Who 94*
Mercer, H. Dwight 1939- *WhoAm 94*
Mercer, Harry D. 1942- *WhoAmL 94*
Mercer, Henry Dickson 1893- *WhAm 10*
Mercer, Hugh 1725-1777 *AmRev, WhAmRev [port]*
Mercer, Ian Dews 1933- *Who 94*
Mercer, Jack d1984 *WhoHol 92*
Mercer, James 1736-1793 *WhAmRev*
Mercer, John 1791-1886 *WorInv*
Mercer, John A. 1957- *WhoAmP 93*
Mercer, John Charles Kenneth 1917- *Who 94*
Mercer, John Edward 1946- *WhoAmP 93*
Mercer, John Francis 1759-1821 *WhAmRev*
Mercer, John Whitty 1942- *WhoMW 93*
Mercer, Johnny d1976 *WhoHol 92*
Mercer, Johnny 1909-1976 *IntDcF 2-4*
Mercer, Joseph Henry 1937- *WhoAmL 94, WhoAmP 93, WhoWest 94*
Mercer, Lee William 1943- *WhoAm 94*
Mercer, Leo *WhoAmP 93*
Mercer, Leonard Preston, II 1941- *WhoAm 94*
Mercer, Linwood E. *WhoAmP 93*
Mercer, Mae *WhoHol 92*
Mercer, Marian 1935- *WhoAm 94, WhoHol 92*
Mercer, Mary Kathryn 1953- *WhoMW 93*
Mercer, Melvin Ray 1946- *WhoAm 94*
Mercer, Richard Eugene 1951- *WhoMW 93*
Mercer, Richard Joseph 1924- *WhoAm 94*
Mercer, Robert B. *WhoFI 94*
Mercer, Robert Edward 1924- *IntWW 93*
Mercer, Robert Giles Graham 1949- *Who 94*
Mercer, Robert Lee 1926- *WhoAm 94*
Mercer, Robert S. 1925- *WhoAmP 93*
Mercer, Robert William Stanley 1935- *Who 94*
Mercer, Roger James 1944- *Who 94*
Mercer, Ronald L. 1934- *WhoAm 94, WhoFI 94*
Mercer, Tony d1973 *WhoHol 92*
Mercer, Valerie June 1947- *WhoBlA 94*
Mercer, William 1765-1839 *EncDeaf*
Mercer, William Edward, II 1956- *WhoScEn 94*
Mercer Nairne Petty-Fitzmaurice *Who 94*
Merceron, Joseph c. 1764-1839 *DcNaB MP*
Mercer-Pryor, Diana 1950- *WhoBlA 94*
Merchak, Sally Hook 1951- *WhoAmL 94*
Merchand, Hernando 1942- *WhoHisp 94*
Merchant, Carl William, II 1949- *WhoFI 94*
Merchant, Diane Allene 1956- *WhoMW 93*
Merchant, Donald Joseph 1921- *WhoAm 94*
Merchant, Donna Rae 1948- *WhoFI 94*
Merchant, Ismail *WhoHol 92*
Merchant, Ismail 1936- *CurBio 93 [port], IntMPA 94, IntWW 93, Who 94*
Merchant, Ismail Noormohamed 1936- *WhoAm 94, WhoAsA 94*
Merchant, James S., Jr. 1954- *WhoBlA 94*
Merchant, John F. 1933- *WhoBlA 94*
Merchant, John Richard 1945- *Who 94*
Merchant, Livingston T. 1903-1976 *HisDcKW*
Merchant, Mylon Eugene 1913- *WhoAm 94, WhoFI 94*
Merchant, Natalie 1964- *WhoAm 94*
Merchant, Paul *EncSF 93*
Merchant, Piers Rolf Garfield 1951- *Who 94*
Merchant, Roland Samuel, Sr. 1929- *WhoAm 94, WhoFI 94, WhoScEn 94, WhoWest 94*
Merchant, Sharon J. 1963- *WhoAmP 93*
Merchant, Vasant V. 1933- *WhoAsA 94*
Merchant, Vivien d1982 *WhoHol 92*
Merchant, William Moelwyn 1913- *Who 94*
Merchenthaler, Istvan Jozsef 1949- *WhoScEn 94*
Mercieca, Joseph *Who 94*
Mercieca, Joseph 1928- *IntWW 93*
Mercier, Daniel Edmond 1950- *WhoScEn 94*
Mercier, Eileen Ann 1947- *WhoFI 94*
Mercier, Francois 1923- *WhoAm 94*
Mercier, Jacques Louis 1933- *WhoFI 94*
Mercier, Jean Claude 1940- *WhoAm 94*
Mercier, Jean-Louis 1934- *WhoAm 94, WhoFI 94*
Mercier, John Rene 1961- *WhoScEn 94*
Mercier, Louis 1901- *WhoHol 92*
Mercier, Louis-Sebastien 1740-1814 *EncSF 93*
Mercier, Michael Anthony 1959- *WhoWest 94*
Mercier, Michele 1939- *WhoHol 92*
Mercier, Richard Louis 1947- *WhoAmP 93*
Mercier, Robert Allan 1940- *WhoMW 93*
Mercoeur, Elisa 1809-1835 *BlmGWL*
Mercolino, Veronica Florence *WhoAmA 93*
Mercorella, Anthony J. 1927- *WhoAm 94*
Mercouri, Melina 1923- *WhoHol 92*
Mercouri, Melina 1925- *IntMPA 94, IntWW 93*
Mercure, Jean *WhoHol 92*
Mercure, Jean 1909- *IntWW 93*
Mercure, Monique *WhoHol 92*
Mercure, Monique 1930- *ConTFT 11*
Mercurio, Antonino Marco 1930- *WhoScEn 94*
Mercurio, Edward Peter 1944- *WhoWest 94*
Mercurio, Joseph Francis 1961- *WhoFI 94*
Mercurio, Renard Michael 1947- *WhoAm 94*
Mercy, Leland, Jr. 1942- *WhoBlA 94*
Merdek, Andrew Austin 1950- *WhoAm 94*
Merdinger, Charles (John) 1918- *WrDr 94*
Merdinger, Charles John 1918- *WhoAm 94*
Merdinger, Steven Marc 1954- *WhoFI 94*
Merdinger, Susan 1943- *WhoFI 94*
Mereau-Brentano, Sophie 1770-1806 *BlmGWL*
Mereaux, Nicolas-Jean Le Froid de 1745-1797 *NewGrDO*
Mereday, Richard F. 1929- *WhoBlA 94*
Meredith, Allen Kent 1949- *WhoAm 94, WhoFI 94, WhoWest 94*
Meredith, Amituana'i 1912- *WhoAmP 93*
Meredith, Bevan *Who 94*
Meredith, Burgess 1908- *WhoHol 92*
Meredith, Burgess 1909- *IntMPA 94, WhoAm 94*
Meredith, Charles d1964 *WhoHol 92*
Meredith, Cheerio d1964 *WhoHol 92*
Meredith, Dale Dean 1940- *WhoAm 94*
Meredith, Darris Roscoe 1937- *WhoWest 94*
Meredith, David Robert 1940- *WhoAm 94, WhoFI 94*
Meredith, Don *DrAPF 93*
Meredith, Dorothy Laverne 1906-1986 *WhoAmA 93N*
Meredith, Edwin Thomas, III 1933- *WhoAm 94*
Meredith, Ellis Edson 1927- *WhoAm 94*
Meredith, George 1828-1909 *BlmGEL*
Meredith, George Davis 1940- *WhoAm 94*
Meredith, George Marlor 1923- *WhoAm 94, WhoFI 94*
Meredith, Gwen 1907- *BlmGWL*
Meredith, Iris d1980 *WhoHol 92*
Meredith, James Creed 1875-1942 *EncSF 93*
Meredith, James H. 1933- *HisWorL*
Meredith, James Harris 1947- *WhoAmP 93*
Meredith, James Howard 1933- *AmSocL, WhoAm 94, WhoBlA 94*
Meredith, Jo Anne *WhoHol 92*
Meredith, Joan d1980 *WhoHol 92*
Meredith, Jody Berry 1946- *WhoAmP 93*
Meredith, John 1933- *WhoAmA 93*
Meredith, John Lacey 1962- *WhoAmL 94*
Meredith, John Michael 1934- *Who 94*
Meredith, Judi 1936- *WhoHol 92*
Meredith, Julia Alice 1943- *WhoScEn 94*
Meredith, Lee 1947- *WhoHol 92*
Meredith, Lewis Douglas 1905- *WhoAm 94*
Meredith, Louisa 1812-1895 *BlmGWL*
Meredith, Lu Anne *WhoHol 92*
Meredith, Lynnette Ann Logan 1966- *WhoMW 93*
Meredith, Mark Richard 1947- *WhoFI 94*
Meredith, Melba Melsing d1967 *WhoHol 92*
Meredith, Nicholas d1963 *WhoHol 92*
Meredith, Owen Nichols 1924- *WhoFI 94*
Meredith, Richard Alban Creed 1935- *Who 94*
Meredith, Richard C(arlton) 1937-1979 *EncSF 93*
Meredith, Richard Eugene 1934- *WhoAmP 93*
Meredith, Roger Louis *WhoAmL 94*
Meredith, Ronald Edward 1946- *WhoAm 94, WhoAmL 94*
Meredith, Samuel 1741-1817 *WhAmRev*
Meredith, Scott 1923- *WrDr 94*
Meredith, Scott 1923-1993 *ConAu 140, NewYTBS 93 [port]*
Meredith, Thomas C. *WhoAm 94*
Meredith, Timothy E. 1952- *WhoAmL 94*
Meredith, Wanda Marie 1936- *WhoAmP 93*
Meredith, William *DrAPF 93*
Meredith, William 1874-1958 *WorESoc [port]*
Meredith, William 1919- *IntWW 93, WhoAm 94*
Meredith, William (Morris, Jr.) 1919- *WrDr 94*
Meredith, Willis Carr 1949- *WhoAmL 94*
Meredith Davies, (James) Brian *Who 94*
Meredyth, Bess d1969 *WhoHol 92*
Meredyth, Bess 1890?-1969 *IntDcF 2-4 [port]*
Merelli, Bartolomeo 1794-1879 *NewGrDO*
Merenbloom, Robert Barry 1947- *WhoFI 94, WhoScEn 94*
Merenda, Luc *WhoHol 92*
Merendino, K. Alvin 1914- *WhoAm 94*
Merenivitch, Jarrow 1942- *WhoBlA 94*
Meres, Francis 1565-1647 *BlmGEL*

Merfeld, Gerald Lydon 1936- *WhoAmA 93*
Mergen, Dorothy Ann 1932- *WhoAmP 93*
Mergen, Francois 1925-1989 *WhAm 10*
Mergenovich, Shirley Ann 1938- *WhoMW 93*
Mergenthaler, Ottmar 1854-1899 *WorInv*
Mergler, H. Kent 1940- *WhoAm 94, WhoFI 94*
Mergler, Harry Winston 1924- *WhoAm 94*
Mergner, Hans Konrad 1917- *WhoScEn 94*
Merhaut, Josef 1917- *WhoScEn 94*
Merhige, Robert Reynold, Jr. 1919- *WhoAm 94, WhoAmL 94*
Meri, Lennart 1929- *IntWW 93*
Meri, Lennart Georg 1929- *LngBDD*
Meriam, Harold Austin, Jr. 1920- *WhoAm 94, WhoAmL 94*
Meriam, Thomas C. 1951- *WhoAmL 94*
Merian, Maria Sibylla 1647-1717 *BlmGWL*
Merian, Svende 1955- *BlmGWL*
Meric, Josephine de *NewGrDO*
Merickel, Michael Gene 1952- *WhoMW 93*
Meric-Lalande, Henriette (Clementine) 1799-1867 *NewGrDO*
Mericle, James Robert 1962- *WhoWest 94*
Mericle, Mark 1946- *WhoWest 94*
Mericle, Robert Bruce 1938- *WhoMW 93*
Merida, Frederick A. 1936- *WhoAmA 93*
Meriden, Terry 1946- *WhoAm 94, WhoMW 93*
Merideth, Charles Waymond 1940- *WhoBlA 94*
Merideth, Frank E., Jr. 1944- *WhoAm 94, WhoAmL 94*
Merideth, H. L., Jr. 1930- *WhoAmP 93*
Meridith, Denise P. 1952- *WhoBlA 94*
Meridith, Lynne Ann 1946- *WhoWest 94*
Meridor, Dan 1947- *IntWW 93*
Merifield, Anthony James 1934- *Who 94*
Merifield, Paul M. 1932- *WhoWest 94*
Merigan, Thomas Charles, Jr. 1934- *WhoAm 94, WhoWest 94*
Merighi, Antonia Margherita d1764 *NewGrDO*
Merighi, Giorgio 1939- *NewGrDO*
Merikanto, Aarre 1893-1958 *NewGrDO*
Merikanto, (Frans) Oskar 1868-1924 *NewGrDO*
Merikas, George 1911- *IntWW 93*
Merikoski, Jorma Kaarlo 1942- *WhoScEn 94*
Meril, Macha 1940- *WhoHol 92*
Merilan, Charles Preston 1926- *WhoScEn 94*
Merilan, Jean Elizabeth 1962- *WhoMW 93, WhoScEn 94*
Merilan, Michael Preston 1956- *WhoScEn 94*
Merillon, Jean-Marie 1926- *IntWW 93*
Merimee, Prosper 1803-1870 *NewGrDO, RfGShF*
Merimee, Thomas Joseph 1931- *WhoAm 94*
Merin, Robert Gillespie 1933- *WhoScEn 94*
Merin, Robert Lynn 1946- *WhoScEn 94, WhoWest 94*
Mering, Donald R. 1946- *WhoAmL 94*
Merino, Alfredo 1931- *WhoHisp 94*
Merino, Armando *WhoHisp 94*
Merino Castro, Jose Toribio 1915- *IntWW 93*
Meritt, Dennis Andrew 1940- *WhoAm 94*
Meritt, Eldon Ray 1938- *WhoAmP 93*
Merivale, John d1990 *WhoHol 92*
Merivale, Philip d1946 *WhoHol 92*
Meriweather, Melvin, Jr. 1937- *WhoBlA 94*
Meriwether, Heath J. 1944- *WhoAm 94, WhoMW 93*
Meriwether, James Babcock 1928- *WhoAm 94*
Meriwether, Lee 1935- *WhoHol 92*
Meriwether, Louise *BlmGWL, DrAPF 93*
Meriwether, Louise 1923- *WhoBlA 94*
Meriwether, Roy Dennis 1943- *WhoBlA 94*
Merjan, Stanley 1928- *WhoScEn 94*
Merk, Charles Adrian 1946- *WhoFI 94*
Merkel, Angela 1954- *IntWW 93*
Merkel, Jayne (Silverstein) 1942- *WhoAmA 93*
Merkel, Judi Kay 1946- *WhoMW 93*
Merkel, Una d1986 *WhoHol 92*
Merkelbach, Reinhold 1918- *IntWW 93*
Merkelo, Henri 1939- *WhoAm 94*
Merken, Lucretia Wilhelmina van 1721-1789 *BlmGWL*
Merker, Frank Ferdinand 1909- *WhoAm 94*
Merker, Steven Joseph 1947- *WhoAm 94, WhoAmL 94*
Merkert, George *WhoAm 94*
Merkin, Albert Charles 1924- *WhoWest 94*
Merkin, Daphne *DrAPF 93*
Merkin, Michael J. d1993 *NewYTBS 93 [port]*
Merkin, Richard Marshall 1938- *WhoAmA 93*
Merkin, William Leslie 1929- *WhoAm 94*
Merkl, Neil Matthew 1931- *WhoAm 94*
Merkle, Alan Ray 1947- *WhoAmL 94*
Merkle, Barbara Ramos 1954- *WhoHisp 94*
Merkle, John Hallock 1949- *WhoAm 94*
Merkle, Mark K., Jr. 1944- *WhoAmL 94*
Merkle, Ralph Charles 1952- *WhoWest 94*
Merklin, Sharon Renee 1960- *WhoAmL 94*
Merkouri, Melina *WhoWomW 91*
Merkt, John L. 1946- *WhoAmP 93*
Merku, Pavle 1927- *NewGrDO*
Merkuriev, Stanislav 1945- *IntWW 93*
Merkuriev, Vasili d1978 *WhoHol 92*
Merkyl, John *WhoHol 92*
Merkyl, Wilmuth d1954 *WhoHol 92*
Merle, H. Etienne 1944- *WhoFI 94*
Merle, John Howard 1948- *WhoFI 94*
Merle, Robert 1908- *EncSF 93, Who 94*
Merleno, Toni Autumn 1954- *WhoMW 93*
Merli, Francesco 1887-1976 *NewGrDO*
Merli, Maurizio d1989 *WhoHol 92*
Merlin, Christina 1911- *WrDr 94*
Merlin, David 1927- *WrDr 94*
Merlin, Jan *WhoHol 92*
Merlin, Joanna 1931- *WhoHol 92*
Merlin, Peter Helmuth 1928- *WhoAm 94, WhoAmL 94*
Merlin, Roberto Daniel 1950- *WhoMW 93*
Merlini, Cesare 1933- *IntWW 93*
Merlini, Elsa d1983 *WhoHol 92*
Merlini, Marisa *WhoHol 92*
Merlino, Anthony Frank 1930- *WhoScEn 94*
Merlino, Frank Gabriele 1959- *WhoAmL 94*
Merlino, Joseph Piedmont 1922- *WhoAmP 93*
Merlis, Anthony Logan 1943- *WhoMW 93*
Merlis, George 1940- *WhoAm 94*
Merlo, Andrew Eugene 1942- *WhoFI 94*
Merlo, Anthony d1976 *WhoHol 92*
Merlo, David 1931- *Who 94*
Merlo, Harry Angelo 1925- *WhoAm 94, WhoFI 94, WhoWest 94*
Merlo, Ismael d1984 *WhoHol 92*
Merloni, Vittorio 1933- *IntWW 93*
Merlyn, Arthur *EncSF 93*
Merlyn-Rees, Baron 1920- *IntWW 93, Who 94*
Mermagen, Herbert Waldemar 1912- *Who 94*
Merman, Ethel d1984 *WhoHol 92*
Merman, Ethel Agnes 1908-1984 *AmCulL*
Mermaz, Louis 1931- *IntWW 93*
Mermelstein, Jules Joshua 1955- *WhoAmL 94*
Mermet, Auguste 1810-1889 *NewGrDO*
Mermin, Mildred (Shire) d1985 *WhoAmA 93N*
Mermin, N. David 1935- *WhoAm 94, WhoScEn 94*
MernaLyn *WhoMW 93*
Merne, Oscar James 1943- *WrDr 94*
Mernissi, Fatima 1940- *BlmGWL*
Mernit, Susan *DrAPF 93*
Mero, Judith C. 1941- *WhoAmL 94*
Mero, Marjorie Anne 1940- *WhoFI 94*
Merola, Gaetano 1881-1953 *NewGrDO*
Merola, Mario 1931- *WhoAmA 93*
Merola, Raymond Anthony 1958- *WhoScEn 94*
Merolla, Michele Edward 1940- *WhoScEn 94*
Meron, Theodor 1930- *WhoAm 94*
Meroney, Fern Allen *WhAm 10*
Meroney, Robert Nelson 1937- *WhoAm 94*
Merow, Florence Lombardi 1932- *WhoAmP 93*
Merow, James F. 1932- *CngDr 93, WhoAm 94, WhoAmL 94*
Merow, John Edward 1929- *WhoAm 94*
Merrall, Mary d1973 *WhoHol 92*
Merran, Harold 1931- *WhoAmL 94*
Merrell, Elinor d1993 *NewYTBS 93*
Merrell, James Lee 1930- *WhoAm 94*
Merrell, Norman L. 1924- *WhoAmP 93*
Merrell, Richard G. 1937- *WhoMW 93*
Merrell, Robert Bruce 1945- *WhoWest 94*
Merrell, Victor Dallas 1936- *WhoWest 94*
Merrell, William John, Jr. 1943- *WhoAm 94*
Merrem-Nikisch, Grete 1887-1970 *NewGrDO*
Merrett, Charles Edwin 1923- *Who 94*
Merriam, Charlotte d1972 *WhoHol 92*
Merriam, Daniel Francis 1927- *WhoScEn 94*
Merriam, Dwight Haines 1946- *WhoAm 94, WhoAmL 94*
Merriam, Eleanor d1981 *WhoHol 92*
Merriam, Eve d1992 *WhAm 10*
Merriam, Eve 1916-1992 *AnObit 1992, TwCYAW, WrDr 94N*
Merriam, Gene 1944- *WhoAmP 93*
Merriam, Harry d1937 *WhoHol 92*
Merriam, J. Alec 1935- *WhoAm 94*
Merriam, John Goodwin 1933- *WhoMW 93*
Merriam, Mary-Linda Sorber 1943- *WhoAm 94*
Merriam, Sharan B. 1943- *WrDr 94*
Merrick, David 1912- *IntMPA 94, IntWW 93, WhoAm 94*
Merrick, George Boesch 1928- *WhoAm 94*
Merrick, Glenn Warren 1954- *WhoAmL 94*
Merrick, James Kirk 1905-1985 *WhoAmA 93N*
Merrick, Joseph Carey 1862-1890 *DcNaB MP*
Merrick, Keith Leon 1923- *WhoAmL 94*
Merrick, Lynn 1920- *WhoHol 92*
Merrick, Roswell Davenport 1922- *WhoAm 94*
Merrick, Terry Allen 1950- *WhoWest 94*
Merrick, Thomas William 1939- *WhoAm 94*
Merrick, Tom d1927 *WhoHol 92*
Merrick-Fairweather, Norma 1928- *WhoBlA 94*
Merricks, Walter Hugh 1945- *Who 94*
Merrier, Helen 1932- *WhoMW 93*
Merrifield, (Robert) Bruce 1921- *IntWW 93*
Merrifield, Donald Paul 1928- *WhoAm 94*
Merrifield, Dudley Bruce 1921- *WhoAm 94*
Merrifield, Robert Bruce 1921- *Who 94, WhoAm 94, WhoScEn 94*
Merrigan, Mary Ellen 1951- *WhoWest 94*
Merrigan, William Joseph 1934- *WhoAmL 94*
Merril, Judith 1923- *BlmGWL, EncSF 93*
Merril, (Josephine) Judith (Grossman) 1923- *WrDr 94*
Merrill, Abel Jay 1938- *WhoAmL 94*
Merrill, Albert Adams *EncSF 93*
Merrill, Alvin Seymour 1930- *WhoAmP 93*
Merrill, Amanda A. 1951- *WhoAmP 93*
Merrill, Ambrose Pond, Jr. 1909-1991 *WhAm 10*
Merrill, Arthur Alexander 1906- *WhoAm 94*
Merrill, Aubrey James 1948- *WhoScEn 94*
Merrill, Charles Eugene 1952- *WhoAm 94*
Merrill, Charles Merton 1907- *WhoAm 94, WhoAmL 94, WhoWest 94*
Merrill, Christopher *DrAPF 93*
Merrill, Christopher (Lyall) 1957- *WrDr 94*
Merrill, Corinne Swanberg 1961- *WhoMW 93*
Merrill, Dale Marie 1954- *WhoFI 94*
Merrill, Dana Noyes 1934- *WhoFI 94*
Merrill, David Kenneth 1935- *WhoAmA 93*
Merrill, Dick d1982 *WhoHol 92*
Merrill, Dina 1925- *WhoHol 92*
Merrill, Dina 1928- *IntMPA 94*
Merrill, E. Chouteau 1954- *WhoAmL 94*
Merrill, Edward Clifton, Jr. 1920- *WhoAm 94*
Merrill, Edward Wilson 1923- *WhoScEn 94*
Merrill, Fiona Claire *Who 94*
Merrill, Frances Hatch 1939- *WhoAmP 93*
Merrill, Frank d1966 *WhoHol 92*
Merrill, Frank Harrison 1953- *WhoWest 94*
Merrill, Gary d1990 *WhoHol 92*
Merrill, George Vanderneth 1947- *WhoAm 94, WhoAmL 94, WhoFI 94*
Merrill, Gerald P. 1926- *WhoAmP 93*
Merrill, Harvie Martin 1921- *WhoAm 94*
Merrill, Hugh Davis 1913- *WhoAmP 93*
Merrill, Jacob Micheal 1963- *WhoFI 94*
Merrill, James 1926- *IntWW 93, WhoAm 94*
Merrill, James (Ingram) 1926- *WrDr 94*
Merrill, James Allen 1925- *WhoAm 94*
Merrill, James I. *DrAPF 93*
Merrill, James Ingram 1926- *GayLL*
Merrill, James Mercer 1920- *WhoAm 94*
Merrill, James Walter 1948- *WhoFI 94*
Merrill, Jean (Fairbanks) 1923- *WrDr 94*
Merrill, Jean Fairbanks 1923- *WhoAm 94*
Merrill, John Calhoun 1924- *WhoAm 94*
Merrill, John Ogden 1896-1975 *AmCulL*
Merrill, John Russell 1931- *WhoWest 94*
Merrill, Kathryn D. *WhoAmP 93*
Merrill, Kenneth Coleman 1930- *WhoAm 94, WhoFI 94, WhoMW 93*
Merrill, Lee *DrAPF 93*
Merrill, Leland Gilbert, Jr. 1920- *WhoAm 94*
Merrill, Lindsey 1925- *WhoAm 94*
Merrill, Louis d1963 *WhoHol 92*
Merrill, Lynn Leslie 1951- *WhoWest 94*
Merrill, Martha 1946- *WhoAm 94*
Merrill, Maruice Hitchcock 1897- *WhAm 10*
Merrill, Mary Ann 1950- *WhoMW 93*
Merrill, Michael 1922- *WhoAmP 93*
Merrill, Nathaniel 1927- *NewGrDO*
Merrill, Perry H. d1993 *NewYTBS 93*
Merrill, Philip *WhoAm 94*
Merrill, Philip L. 1945- *WhoAmP 93*
Merrill, Richard James 1931- *WhoAm 94*
Merrill, Robert 1917- *NewGrDO*
Merrill, Robert 1919- *IntWW 93, WhoAm 94, WhoHol 92*
Merrill, Robert Alexander 1958- *WrDr 94*
Merrill, Robert Edward 1933- *WhoFI 94, WhoWest 94*
Merrill, Robert Hull 1922- *WhoWest 94*
Merrill, Ronald Thomas 1938- *WhoAm 94, WhoScEn 94, WhoWest 94*
Merrill, Ross M. 1943- *WhoAmA 93*
Merrill, Roy Richard 1946- *WhoWest 94*
Merrill, Stephen *WhoAm 94*
Merrill, Steven 1946- *WhoAmP 93*
Merrill, Steven William 1944- *WhoFI 94, WhoScEn 94, WhoWest 94*
Merrill, Susan *DrAPF 93*
Merrill, Thomas F. *WrDr 94*
Merrill, Thomas St. John 1946- *WhoWest 94*
Merrill, Vincent Nichols 1912- *WhoAm 94*
Merrill, William Dean 1915- *WhoAm 94*
Merrill, William Dickey 1909- *WhoAm 94*
Merrill, William H., Jr. 1942- *WhoAm 94*
Merriman, Alan *Who 94*
Merriman, (Henry) Alan 1929- *Who 94*
Merriman, Alex *EncSF 93*
Merriman, Basil Mandeville 1911- *Who 94*
Merriman, Catherine 1949- *ConAu 140*
Merriman, Ilah Coffee 1935- *WhoFI 94*
Merriman, James Henry Herbert 1915- *Who 94*
Merriman, Joe Jack 1926- *WhoAm 94*
Merriman, John A. 1942- *WhoAmP 93*
Merriman, John Allen 1942- *WhoAmL 94*
Merriman, Marion 1909- *WrDr 94*
Merriman, Nan 1920- *NewGrDO*
Merriman, Robert Douglas 1954- *WhoAmL 94*
Merriman, Robert E. 1929- *WhoIns 94*
Merrin, Alfred Mitchell, Jr. 1946- *WhoAm 94*
Merrin, Edward H. 1928- *WhoAmA 93*
Merrin, Seymour 1931- *WhoAm 94*
Merrion, James Michael 1944- *WhoAm 94*
Merriss, Dick d1974 *WhoHol 92*
Merriss, Philip Ramsay, Jr. 1948- *WhoAm 94, WhoFI 94*
Merrithew, Gerald S. 1931- *IntWW 93*
Merritt, A(braham) 1884-1943 *EncSF 93*
Merritt, Annette M. 1943- *WhoMW 93*
Merritt, Anthony Lewis 1940- *WhoBlA 94*
Merritt, Bishetta Dionne 1947- *WhoBlA 94*
Merritt, Bruce Gordon 1946- *WhoAm 94, WhoAmL 94, WhoWest 94*
Merritt, Cathy Lyn 1952- *WhoWest 94*
Merritt, Chris (Allan) 1952- *NewGrDO*
Merritt, Dawana Denean 1966- *WhoBlA 94*
Merritt, Deborah Foote 1961- *WhoAmP 93*
Merritt, Doris Honig 1923- *WhoAm 94, WhoMW 93, WhoScEn 94*
Merritt, Evelyn Caroline 1932- *WhoAm 94*
Merritt, Francis Sumner 1913- *WhoAmA 93*
Merritt, George d1977 *WhoHol 92*
Merritt, Gilbert S. *WhoAmP 93*
Merritt, Gilbert Stroud 1936- *WhoAm 94, WhoAmL 94*
Merritt, Harley Alfred 1943- *WhoAmL 94*
Merritt, Helen Henry 1920- *WhoMW 93*
Merritt, Howard Sutermeister 1915- *WhoAm 94*
Merritt, Jack Neil 1930- *WhoAm 94*
Merritt, James A., Jr. 1956- *WhoAmL 94*
Merritt, James Edward 1938- *WhoAm 94*
Merritt, James Francis 1944- *WhoScEn 94*
Merritt, James W. 1959- *WhoMW 93*
Merritt, James W., Jr. 1959- *WhoAmP 93*
Merritt, Joe Frank 1947- *WhoFI 94*
Merritt, John 1930- *WhoAmP 93*
Merritt, John C. 1940- *WhoAm 94, WhoFI 94*
Merritt, John Edward 1926- *Who 94*

Merritt, Joseph, Jr. 1934- *WhoAmP 93, WhoBlA 94*
Merritt, Joshua Levering, Jr. 1931- *WhoAm 94*
Merritt, Joy Ellen 1943- *WhoScEn 94*
Merritt, Katharine 1938- *WhoMW 93*
Merritt, Kenni Barrett 1950- *WhoAmL 94*
Merritt, LaVere Barrus 1936- *WhoAm 94*
Merritt, Lynn G. 1930- *WhoIns 94*
Merritt, Lynn Garnard 1930- *WhoAm 94*
Merritt, Nancy-Jo 1942- *WhoAm 94*
Merritt, Neil 1939- *Who 94*
Merritt, Paul Burwell 1924- *WhoAmP 93*
Merritt, Raymond Walter 1938- *WhoAm 94*
Merritt, Robert Edward 1941- *WhoAm 94, WhoAmL 94*
Merritt, Theresa 1929- *WhoHol 92*
Merritt, Thomas Butler 1939- *WhoAm 94, WhoAmL 94*
Merritt, Thomas Mack 1949- *WhoBlA 94*
Merritt, Willette T. *WhoBlA 94*
Merritt, William Alfred, Jr. 1936- *WhoAm 94*
Merritt, William E. 1935- *WhoIns 94*
Merritt, William E. 1945- *WrDr 94*
Merritt, William T. *WhoBlA 94*
Merritt-Cummings, Annette 1946- *WhoBlA 94*
Merrivale, Baron 1917- *Who 94*
Merriweather, Barbara Christine 1948- *WhoBlA 94*
Merriweather, Michael Lamar 1960- *WhoBlA 94*
Merriweather, Robert Eugene 1948- *WhoBlA 94*
Merriweather, Thomas L. 1932- *WhoBlA 94*
Merrow, George W. 1928- *WhoAmP 93*
Merrow, Jane 1941- *WhoHol 92*
Merry, Anthony 1756-1835 *DcNaB MP*
Merry, James Ralph 1927- *WhoAmP 93*
Merry, Mildred R. 1905- *WhoAmP 93*
Merry, Patricia Lynn 1952- *WhoMW 93*
Merryday, Stephen D. 1950- *WhoAm 94, WhoAmL 94*
Merryman, Michael Burdet 1942- *WhoFI 94*
Mersch, Carol Linda 1938- *WhoFI 94, WhoScEn 94*
Mersel, Marjorie Kathryn Pedersen 1923- *WhoWest 94*
Merser, Cheryl 1951- *ConAu 141*
Merser, Francis Gerard 1930- *WhoAm 94*
Mersereau, Hiram Stipe 1917- *WhoAm 94*
Mersereau, John, Jr. 1925- *WhoAm 94*
Mersereau, John (the Elder) *WhAmRev*
Mersereau, John LaGrange (the Younger) *WhAmRev*
Mersereau, Joshua *WhAmRev*
Mersereau, Lori Michelle 1963- *WhoAmL 94*
Mersereau, Russell Manning 1946- *WhoAm 94*
Mersereau, Stephen Crocker 1950- *WhoFI 94*
Mersereau, Susan 1946- *WhoAm 94*
Mersey, Viscount 1934- *Who 94*
Mershart, Eileen DeGrand 1944- *WhoAmP 93*
Mershart, Ronald Valere 1932- *WhoMW 93*
Mershimer, Robert John 1950- *WhoScEn 94*
Mershon, Jeffrey Bruce 1940- *WhoFI 94*
Mershon, John Hays 1946- *WhoAmL 94*
Mershon, Julia A. 1955- *WhoMW 93*
Mershon, Melissa A. 1953- *WhoAmP 93*
Mersky, Roy Martin 1925- *WhoAm 94, WhoAmL 94*
Merson, Billy d1947 *WhoHol 92*
Merson, Marc 1931- *IntMPA 94*
Merson, Michael 1945- *IntWW 93*
Merta, Paul James 1939- *WhoWest 94*
Merta De Velehrad, Jan 1944- *WhoScEn 94*
Merten, Alan Gilbert 1941- *WhoAm 94, WhoFI 94*
Merten, Utz Peter 1942- *WhoScEn 94*
Mertens, Charles Franklin 1933- *WhoAmP 93*
Mertens, Glen Henry 1956- *WhoAmL 94*
Mertens, James Arthur 1947- *WhoMW 93*
Mertens, Joan R. 1946- *WhoAm 94*
Mertens, Josef Wilhelm 1946- *WhoScEn 94*
Mertens, Karl Heinrich 1796-1830 *WhWE*
Mertens, Thomas Robert 1930- *WhoAm 94, WhoScEn 94*
Mertens De Wilmars, Josse (Marie Honore Charles) 1912- *Who 94*
Mertens De Wilmars, Josse Marie Honore Charles 1912- *IntWW 93*
Mertes, Christopher Patrick 1963- *WhoMW 93*
Mertes, Sharon Colleen 1958- *WhoMW 93*
Merthyr, Baron of *Who 94*
Mertin, Klaus 1922- *IntWW 93*
Mertin, Roger 1942- *WhoAm 94, WhoAmA 93*
Merting, John Webster 1943- *WhoAmL 94*
Mertins, James Walter 1943- *WhoMW 93*
Merton, Viscount 1971- *Who 94*
Merton, Colette d1968 *WhoHol 92*
Merton, Egon Stephen 1912- *WhoWest 94*
Merton, John d1959 *WhoHol 92*
Merton, John Ralph 1913- *IntWW 93, Who 94*
Merton, Joseph Lee 1923- *WhoBlA 94*
Merton, Patrick Anthony 1920- *IntWW 93, Who 94*
Merton, Robert C. 1944- *WhoAm 94*
Merton, Robert K. 1910- *IntWW 93, WhoAm 94*
Merton, Robert K(ing) 1910- *WrDr 94*
Merton, Thomas 1915-1968 *DcAmReB 2*
Mertz, Barbara (Louise) G(ross) 1927- *WrDr 94*
Mertz, Dolores M. 1928- *WhoAmP 93*
Mertz, Dolores Mary 1928- *WhoMW 93*
Mertz, Douglas Kemp 1949- *WhoAmL 94*
Mertz, Edwin Theodore 1909- *IntWW 93, WhoAm 94, WhoScEn 94*
Mertz, Elizabeth Ellen 1955- *WhoMW 93*
Mertz, Francis James 1937- *WhoAm 94*
Mertz, Fred J. 1938- *WhoMW 93*
Mertz, Patricia Mann 1939- *WhoScEn 94*
Mertz, Stuart Moulton 1915- *WhoAm 94*
Mertz, Susan Jeanne 1953- *WhoWest 94*
Mertz, Walter 1923- *WhoAm 94, WhoScEn 94*
Meruelo, Alex 1962- *WhoHisp 94*
Meruelo, Raul Pablo 1955- *WhoAmL 94*
Merullo, Roland 1953- *WrDr 94*
Merva, George Ellis *WhoAm 94*
Mervielle, Edgardo Jorge 1955- *WhoHisp 94*
Mervyn, Leonard 1930- *WhoScEn 94*
Mervyn, William d1976 *WhoHol 92*
Mervyn Davies, David Herbert *Who 94*
Merwin, Davis Underwood 1928- *WhoAm 94*
Merwin, Edwin Preston 1927- *WhoWest 94*
Merwin, Harmon Turner 1920- *WhoMW 93*
Merwin, Jack Clifford 1925- *WhoAm 94*
Merwin, John David 1921- *WhoAm 94*
Merwin, June Rae 1943- *WhoScEn 94*
Merwin, Robert Freeman 1913- *WhoAm 94*
Merwin, Sam, Jr. 1910- *EncSF 93*
Merwin, Sam(uel Kimball), Jr. 1910- *WrDr 94*
Merwin, W. S. *DrAPF 93*
Merwin, W(illiam) S(tanley) 1927- *WrDr 94*
Merwin, William Stanley 1927- *WhoAm 94*
Mery, (Francois-)Joseph(-Pierre-Andre) 1797-1865 *NewGrDO*
Meryhew, Nancy Lee 1948- *WhoMW 93*
Meryman, Hope d1975 *WhoAmA 93N*
Merz, Antony Willits 1932- *WhoScEn 94*
Merz, Carl Allen 1949- *WhoFI 94*
Merz, James Logan 1936- *WhoAm 94, WhoScEn 94, WhoWest 94*
Merz, Michael 1945- *WhoAm 94, WhoAmL 94*
Merz, Rollande *DrAPF 93*
Merzbach, Ralph Kenneth 1952- *WhoAmL 94*
Merzbacher, Eugen 1921- *WhoScEn 94*
Merzban, Mohammed Abdullah 1918- *IntWW 93*
Mesa, Dennis 1954- *WhoHisp 94*
Mesa, James Patrick 1943- *WhoHisp 94*
Mesa, Jose Ramon 1966- *WhoHisp 94*
Mesa, Mayra L. 1949- *WhoBlA 94*
Mesa, Raquel Chavez 1942- *WhoHisp 94*
Mesa, Reynaldo René 1959- *WhoHisp 94*
Mesa, Richard *WhoHisp 94, WhoWest 94*
Mesa-Bains, Amalia *WhoAmA 93*
Mesa-Bains, Amalia 1943- *WhoHisp 94*
Mesa-Lago, Carmelo 1934- *WhoAm 94, WhoHisp 94, WrDr 94*
Mesaros, Kenneth 1950- *WhoAmP 93*
Mesch, Barry 1943- *WhoAm 94*
Meschan, Isadore 1914- *WhoScEn 94*
Meschan, Isadore, Mrs. 1915- *WhoScEn 94*
Mescher, Anthony Louis 1949- *WhoMW 93*
Mescher, William Clarence 1927- *WhoAmP 93*
Meschery, Tom 1938- *BasBi*
Mesches, Arnold 1923- *WhoAmA 93*
Meschke, Herbert L. 1928- *WhoAmP 93*
Meschke, Herbert Leonard 1928- *WhoAm 94, WhoAmL 94, WhoMW 93*
Meschke, Paul F. 1962- *WhoMW 93*
Mescon, Richard A. 1945- *WhoAm 94*
Mescon, Richard Alan 1945- *WhoAmL 94*
Mesec, Donald Francis 1936- *WhoWest 94*
Meseke, Marguerite Arvis *WhoAmP 93*
Meselson, Matthew Stanley 1930- *IntWW 93, WhoAm 94, WhoScEn 94, WorScD*
Meserole, Vera Stromsted 1927- *WhoAmA 93*
Meserve, Bruce Elwyn 1917- *WhoWest 94*
Meserve, Christina Ann 1953- *WhoAmL 94*
Meserve, John H. 1947- *WhoAmP 93*
Meserve, Richard Andrew 1944- *WhoAm 94, WhoAmL 94*
Meserve, Robert William 1909- *WhoAm 94*
Meserve, Walter Joseph 1923- *WhoAm 94*
Meserve, Walter Joseph, Jr. 1923- *WrDr 94*
Meserve, William George 1940- *WhoAm 94*
Mesh, Daniel Evan 1964- *WhoMW 93*
Meshack, Lula M. *WhoBlA 94*
Meshack, Sheryl Hodges 1944- *WhoBlA 94*
Meshberg, Lev 1933- *IntWW 93*
Meshbesher, Ronald I. 1933- *WhoAmL 94, WhoMW 93*
Meshcheryakov, Sergei Alekseevich 1953- *LngBDD*
Meshel, Harry *WhoAmP 93*
Meshel, Harry 1924- *WhoMW 93*
Mesher, Barry Neal 1951- *WhoAm 94*
Meshew, Patricia Weber 1953- *WhoWest 94*
Meshii, Masahiro 1931- *WhoAsA 94, WhoMW 93, WhoScEn 94*
Meshke, George Lewis 1930- *WhoWest 94*
Meshowski, Frank Robert 1930- *WhoFI 94*
Mesiah, Raymond N. 1932- *WhoBlA 94*
Mesibov, Hugh 1916- *WhoAmA 93*
Mesic, Michael *DrAPF 93*
Mesiha, Mounir Sobhy 1945- *WhoScEn 94*
Mesirov, Leon Isaac 1912- *WhoAm 94*
Meskill, Katherine d1979 *WhoHol 92*
Meskill, Thomas J. 1928- *WhoAm 94, WhoAmL 94, WhoAmP 93*
Meskill, Thomas Joseph 1928- *IntWW 93*
Meskill, Victor Peter 1935- *WhoAm 94*
Mesler, Corey J. *DrAPF 93*
Mesler, Russell Bernard 1927- *WhoMW 93*
Mesloh, Warren Henry 1949- *WhoScEn 94, WhoWest 94*
Mesnard, Darrell Dean, Sr. 1923- *WhoFI 94*
Mesnikoff, Alvin Murray 1925- *WhoAm 94*
Mesogianes, Nicholas C. 1944- *WhoIns 94*
Mesolella, Vincent James, Jr. 1949- *WhoAmP 93*
Mesple, Mady 1931- *NewGrDO*
Mesquita, Henrique Alves de 1830-1906 *NewGrDO*
Mesquita, Rosalyn Esther 1935- *WhoWest 94*
Mesrobian, Arpena Sachaklian *WhoAm 94*
Mess, George Jo 1898-1962 *WhoAmA 93N*
Mess, Gordon Benjamin 1900-1959 *WhoAmA 93N*
Mess, Michael A. 1951- *WhoAmL 94*
Messac, Regis *EncSF 93*
Messager, Andre (Charles Prosper) 1853-1929 *NewGrDO*
Messager, Annette 1943- *IntWW 93*
Messagier, Jean 1920- *IntWW 93*
Messeguer, Villoro Benito 1930-1982 *WhoAmA 93N*
Messel, Harry 1922- *Who 94, WrDr 94*
Messel, Oliver 1904-1978 *NewGrDO*
Messel, Oliver 1905-1978 *IntDcB*
Messel, Rudolph 1848-1920 *DcNaB MP*
Messemer, Glenn Matthew 1947- *WhoAm 94, WhoAmL 94*
Messemer, Hannes 1924- *WhoHol 92*
Messengale, Frank Eugene 1950- *WhoAmL 94*
Messenger, Christian K(arl) 1943- *WrDr 94*
Messenger, Donald B. W. 1935- *WhoAmL 94*
Messenger, Donald Burdett White 1935- *WhoAmP 93*
Messenger, George Clement 1930- *WhoAm 94, WhoScEn 94, WhoWest 94*
Messenger, Michael Scott 1945- *WhoAmP 93*
Messenger, Phyllis (E.) Mauch 1950- *WrDr 94*
Messenkopf, Eugene John 1928- *WhoAm 94*
Messenlehner, Joanne Stofko 1939- *WhoAmP 93*
Messer, Allen 1949- *WhoMW 93*
Messer, Cholmeley Joseph 1929- *Who 94*
Messer, David James 1942- *WhoAmA 93*
Messer, Donald Edward 1941- *WhoAm 94, WhoAmP 93, WhoWest 94*
Messer, Mary E. 1933- *WhoMW 93*
Messer, Michael L. 1949- *WhoAmL 94*
Messer, Thomas M. 1920- *IntWW 93, WhoAmA 93, WrDr 94*
Messer, Thomas Maria 1920- *WhoAm 94*
Messer, William Alexander, III 1951- *WhoAmP 93*
Messerer, Asaf 1903-1992 *AnObit 1992, IntDcB [port]*
Messeri, Marco *WhoHol 92*
Messerle, Judith Rose 1943- *WhoAm 94*
Messerli, Douglas *DrAPF 93*
Messerli, Franz Hannes 1942- *WhoAm 94*
Messer-Rehak, Dabney Lee 1951- *WhoMW 93*
Messerschmidt, Daniel Gottlieb 1685-1735 *WhWE*
Messerschmidt, Gerald Leigh 1950- *WhoFI 94*
Messerschmitt, David Gavin 1945- *WhoAm 94*
Messersmith, Fred Lawrence 1924- *WhoAmA 93*
Messersmith, Harry Lee 1958- *WhoAmA 93*
Messersmith, Lanny Dee 1942- *WhoAmL 94*
Messervy, (Roney) Godfrey (Collumbell) 1924- *Who 94*
Messiaen, Olivier 1908-1992 *AnObit 1992, WhAm 10*
Messiaen, Olivier (Eugene Prosper Charles) 1908-1992 *NewGrDO*
Messick, Ben (Newton) 1901- *WhoAmA 93N*
Messick, Dale 1906- *WhoAmA 93*
Messick, Don 1926- *IntMPA 94, WhoAm 94*
Messick, John Decatur 1897- *WhAm 10*
Messick, Neil Tilden 1949- *WhoAmP 93*
Messick, Wiley Sanders 1929- *WhoAmL 94*
Messics, Mark Craig 1960- *WhoScEn 94*
Messier, Donald R. 1956- *WhoAmP 93*
Messier, Irene M. 1923- *WhoAmP 93*
Messier, Mark 1961- *WhoAm 94*
Messier, Pierre 1945- *WhoAm 94*
Messiha, Fathy S. 1936- *WhoMW 93, WhoScEn 94*
Messina, Cedric d1993 *NewYTBS 93*
Messina, Jerome Anthony 1941- *WhoAm 94*
Messina, Joseph R. 1904- *WhoAmA 93*
Messina, Louis Michael 1943- *WhoAmL 94*
Messing, Arnold Philip 1941- *WhoAm 94*
Messing, Carol *WhoHol 92*
Messing, Carol Sue *WhoMW 93*
Messing, Charles Garrett 1948- *WhoScEn 94*
Messing, Ellen Jean *WhoAmL 94*
Messing, Frank J. 1929- *WhoIns 94*
Messing, Frank John 1929- *WhoFI 94*
Messing, Fred M. 1947- *WhoAm 94*
Messing, Frederick Andrew, Jr. 1946- *WhoAm 94*
Messing, Harold d1993 *NewYTBS 93*
Messing, Janet Agnes Kapelsohn 1918- *WhoAm 94*
Messing, Jeffrey 1956- *WhoAmL 94*
Messing, Joachim Wilhelm 1946- *WhoAm 94, WhoScEn 94*
Messing, Mark P. 1948- *WhoAm 94*
Messing, Robin *DrAPF 93*
Messing, Shelley *DrAPF 93*
Messinger, Buddy d1965 *WhoHol 92*
Messinger, Cora R. 1930- *WhoFI 94*
Messinger, Donald Hathaway 1943- *WhoAm 94, WhoAmL 94, WhoFI 94*
Messinger, Gertrude 1911- *WhoHol 92*
Messinger, J. Henry 1944- *WhoAmL 94*
Messinger, James Peter 1953- *WhoIns 94*
Messinger, Josephine d1968 *WhoHol 92*
Messinger, Marie d1987 *WhoHol 92*
Messinger, Paul Raymond 1929- *WhoAmP 93*
Messinger, Ruth W. 1940- *WhoAmP 93*
Messinger, Scott James 1952- *WhoAm 94*
Messiter, Eric d1960 *WhoHol 92*
Messiter, Herbert Lindsell *Who 94*
Messiter, Malcolm 1949- *Who 94*
Messitte, Peter Jo 1941- *WhoAmL 94, WhoAmP 93*
Messlein, John d1920 *WhoHol 92*
Messman, Jack L. 1940- *WhoFI 94*
Messmann, Jon *EncSF 93*
Messmer, Donald Joseph 1936- *WhoAm 94*
Messmer, Otto 1892-1983 *IntDcF 2-4*
Messmer, Pierre Auguste Joseph 1916- *IntWW 93, Who 94*
Messmore, Charlotte K. 1948- *WhoAmP 93*
Messmore, David William *WhoAm 94*

Meyer, Conrad Ferdinand 1825-1898 *DcLB 129 [port]*
Meyer, Conrad John Eustace 1922- *Who 94*
Meyer, Cynthia Kay 1952- *WhoMW 93*
Meyer, Cynthia Louise 1958- *WhoMW 93*
Meyer, Dale Thomas 1948- *WhoWest 94*
Meyer, Daniel J. 1936- *WhoAmP 93*
Meyer, Daniel Joseph 1936- *WhoAm 94, WhoFI 94*
Meyer, Daniel Kramer 1957- *WhoWest 94*
Meyer, Daniel P. 1954- *WhoAmP 93*
Meyer, Daniel Patrick 1927- *WhoFI 94*
Meyer, Danny K. 1948- *WhoMW 93*
Meyer, Dean J. *WhoAmP 93*
Meyer, Dean Lewis 1951- *WhoMW 93*
Meyer, Delbert Henry 1926- *WhoScEn 94*
Meyer, Dennis Irwin 1935- *WhoAm 94*
Meyer, Donald Gordon 1934- *WhoAm 94*
Meyer, Donald Ray 1924- *WhoAm 94*
Meyer, Donald Robert 1942- *WhoAm 94, WhoAmL 94*
Meyer, Donna Maria 1950- *WhoAm 94*
Meyer, Dorothy d1987 *WhoHol 92*
Meyer, Duane Russell 1948- *WhoScEn 94*
Meyer, Edmond Gerald 1919- *WhoAm 94, WhoScEn 94*
Meyer, Edward C. 1928- *IntWW 93*
Meyer, Edward Henry 1927- *WhoAm 94, WhoFI 94*
Meyer, Edward N. 1939- *WhoAm 94*
Meyer, Edward Paul 1949- *WhoFI 94*
Meyer, Edwin Dale, Sr. 1943- *WhoMW 93*
Meyer, El(mer Frederick) 1910- *WhoAmA 93*
Meyer, Emile d1987 *WhoHol 92*
Meyer, Ernst Hermann 1905-1988 *NewGrDO*
Meyer, Eugene Carlton 1923- *WhoAm 94*
Meyer, Eugene L. 1942- *WrDr 94*
Meyer, Eugene Thomas 1949- *WhoMW 93*
Meyer, Eve d1977 *WhoHol 92*
Meyer, F. Weller 1942- *WhoAm 94*
Meyer, Ferd. Charles, Jr. 1939- *WhoAmL 94*
Meyer, Frank Henry 1915- *WhoScEn 94*
Meyer, Frank Hildbridge 1923- *WhoAmA 93*
Meyer, Franz Oswald 1945- *WhoFI 94*
Meyer, Fred (Robert) d1986 *WhoAmA 93N*
Meyer, Fred Albert, Jr. 1942- *WhoMW 93*
Meyer, Fred Josef 1931- *WhoAm 94, WhoFI 94*
Meyer, Fred William, Jr. 1924- *WhoFI 94, WhoMW 93*
Meyer, Frederic d1973 *WhoHol 92*
Meyer, Frederick G. 1945- *WhoAmL 94*
Meyer, Frederick H. 1873-1961 *WhoAmA 93N*
Meyer, Frederick Ray 1927- *WhoAmP 93*
Meyer, Frederick Richard 1938- *WhoMW 93*
Meyer, Frederick William 1943- *WhoIns 94*
Meyer, G. Christopher 1948- *WhoAm 94, WhoAmL 94*
Meyer, George Gotthold 1931- *WhoAm 94*
Meyer, George Herbert 1928- *WhoAm 94, WhoAmL 94*
Meyer, Gerald A. 1946- *WhoMW 93*
Meyer, Gerald Justin 1940- *WhoAm 94*
Meyer, Geraldine L. 1927- *WhoAmP 93*
Meyer, Gerard P. d1993 *NewYTBS 93*
Meyer, Grace Tomanelli 1935- *WhoAmL 94*
Meyer, Greg Charles 1935- *WhoFI 94*
Meyer, Gregory Joseph 1955- *WhoScEn 94*
Meyer, Greta d1965 *WhoHol 92*
Meyer, Hank 1920- *WhoAm 94*
Meyer, Hans *WhoHol 92*
Meyer, Hans 1858-1929 *WhWE*
Meyer, Hans Paul 1928- *WhoFI 94*
Meyer, Harold Louis 1916- *WhoAm 94, WhoFI 94, WhoMW 93, WhoScEn 94*
Meyer, Harry G. 1945- *WhoAmL 94*
Meyer, Harry Martin, Jr. 1928- *WhoAm 94*
Meyer, Harvey Kessler, II 1914- *WhoAm 94*
Meyer, Helen 1907- *WhoAm 94*
Meyer, Herbert 1882-1960 *WhoAmA 93N*
Meyer, Horst 1926- *WhoAm 94, WhoScEn 94*
Meyer, Howard H. 1957- *WhoMW 93*
Meyer, Hyman d1945 *WhoHol 92*
Meyer, Irwin Stephan 1941- *WhoAm 94, WhoAmL 94, WhoFI 94*
Meyer, Ivah Gene 1935- *WhoWest 94*
Meyer, J. Theodore 1936- *WhoAmL 94, WhoAmP 93, WhoFI 94, WhoMW 93*
Meyer, James A. *WhoAmP 93*
Meyer, James Christian 1956- *WhoFI 94*
Meyer, James H. *WhoAmP 93*
Meyer, James Henry 1928- *WhoScEn 94*
Meyer, James Henry 1943- *WhoMW 93*
Meyer, Jarold Alan 1938- *WhoAm 94, WhoScEn 94*
Meyer, Jean 1934- *WhoAm 94*
Meyer, Jean Leon Andre 1914- *IntWW 93*
Meyer, Jean-Pierre 1949- *WhoScEn 94*
Meyer, Jean-Pierre Gustave 1929- *WhoAm 94*
Meyer, Jeff Frank 1949- *WhoIns 94*
Meyer, Jeffory Edwin 1960- *WhoMW 93*
Meyer, Jeffrey A. 1963- *WhoAmL 94*
Meyer, Jerome J. 1938- *WhoAm 94, WhoFI 94, WhoWest 94*
Meyer, Jerry Don 1939- *WhoAmA 93*
Meyer, Johannes d1976 *WhoHol 92*
Meyer, John 1953- *WhoAm 94*
Meyer, John Andrew 1964- *WhoMW 93*
Meyer, John Edward 1931- *WhoAm 94*
Meyer, John Frederick 1934- *WhoAm 94*
Meyer, John Michael 1947- *WhoAmL 94*
Meyer, John R(obert) 1927- *WrDr 94*
Meyer, John Robert 1927- *WhoAm 94*
Meyer, John Stirling 1924- *WhoScEn 94*
Meyer, Jon Keith 1938- *WhoMW 93*
Meyer, Joseph B. 1941- *WhoAm 94, WhoAmL 94, WhoAmP 93, WhoWest 94*
Meyer, Joseph Urban 1948- *WhoAmP 93*
Meyer, Judith Louise 1933- *WhoMW 93*
Meyer, Julius Lothar *WorScD*
Meyer, June *BlkWr 2*
Meyer, June 1936- *WrDr 94*
Meyer, Karl 1899- *WhAm 10*
Meyer, Karl Ernest 1928- *WhoAm 94*
Meyer, Karl V. 1926- *WhoScEn 94*
Meyer, Karl William 1925- *WhoAm 94*
Meyer, Kathleen Anne 1951- *WhoScEn 94*
Meyer, Kendall Ray 1943- *WhoAmL 94*
Meyer, Kenneth J. 1959- *WhoAmP 93*
Meyer, Kenneth Marven 1932- *WhoAm 94*
Meyer, Kerstin 1928- *WhoAm 94*
Meyer, Kerstin (Margareta) 1928- *NewGrDO*
Meyer, Klaus 1928- *IntWW 93*
Meyer, Kraig Randolph 1966- *WhoWest 94*
Meyer, Krzysztof 1943- *NewGrDO*
Meyer, L. Donald 1933- *WhoScEn 94*
Meyer, Lasker Marcel 1926- *WhoAm 94*
Meyer, Lawrence 1941- *WrDr 94*
Meyer, Lawrence George 1940- *WhoAm 94, WhoAmL 94, WhoFI 94*
Meyer, Lee Gordon 1943- *WhoAmL 94, WhoWest 94*
Meyer, Leonard B. 1918- *WhoAm 94, WrDr 94*
Meyer, Linda S. 1950- *WhoAm 94*
Meyer, Louis B. 1933- *WhoAm 94, WhoAmL 94*
Meyer, Louis B., Jr. 1933- *WhoAmP 93*
Meyer, Lynda Joyce 1955- *WhoFI 94*
Meyer, Lynn *ConAu 41NR*
Meyer, M. E. Joseph, III *WhoFI 94, WhoWest 94*
Meyer, Malcolm Andrew 1946- *WhoAmL 94*
Meyer, Margaret Eleanor 1923- *WhoAm 94*
Meyer, Marilyn Louise 1951- *WhoFI 94*
Meyer, Mark 1963- *WhoAmP 93*
Meyer, Mark J. 1959- *WhoAmL 94*
Meyer, Marshall T. d1993 *NewYTBS 93 [port]*
Meyer, Marshall Theodore 1930- *WhoAm 94*
Meyer, Martin Jay 1932- *WhoAmL 94*
Meyer, Mary Jean 1947- *WhoAmP 93*
Meyer, Maurice Wesley 1925- *WhoAm 94*
Meyer, Max Earl 1918- *WhoAm 94, WhoAmL 94, WhoWest 94*
Meyer, Melvin A. 1933- *WhoMW 93*
Meyer, Michael (Leverson) 1921- *WrDr 94*
Meyer, Michael C. 1956- *WhoFI 94*
Meyer, Michael Edwin 1942- *WhoAm 94, WhoAmL 94, WhoWest 94*
Meyer, Michael Leverson 1921- *Who 94*
Meyer, Michael Louis 1940- *WhoAm 94*
Meyer, Michael Siegfried 1950- *Who 94*
Meyer, Milton E., Jr. 1922- *WhoAmA 93*
Meyer, Milton Edward, Jr. 1922- *WhoAm 94*
Meyer, Nancy Jo 1942- *WhoAmL 94*
Meyer, Nancy Reiter 1947- *WhoMW 93*
Meyer, Natalie 1930- *WhoAm 94, WhoAmP 93, WhoWest 94, WhoWomW 91*
Meyer, Nicholas *EncSF 93*
Meyer, Nicholas 1945- *IntMPA 94, WrDr 94*
Meyer, Olga 1889-1972 *BlmGWL*
Meyer, Patricia Morgan 1934- *WhoAm 94*
Meyer, Paul I. 1944- *WhoAmL 94*
Meyer, Paul James 1928- *WhoFI 94*
Meyer, Paul Joseph 1942- *WhoAm 94, WhoAmL 94*
Meyer, Paul Reims, Jr. *WhoAm 94, WhoMW 93, WhoScEn 94*
Meyer, Paul S. 1940- *WhoMW 93*
Meyer, Paul William 1924- *WhoAm 94*
Meyer, Paul William 1952- *WhoAm 94*
Meyer, Pauline Marie 1928- *WhoMW 93*
Meyer, Pearl *WhoAm 94*
Meyer, Peter 1920- *WhoAm 94, WhoScEn 94*
Meyer, Peter (Barrett) 1950- *ConAu 141*
Meyer, Peter Bert 1943- *WhoFI 94*
Meyer, Philip Edward 1930- *WhoAm 94*
Meyer, Philip Gilbert 1945- *WhoAmL 94*
Meyer, Pucci 1944- *WhoAm 94*
Meyer, Randall 1923- *WhoAm 94*
Meyer, Ray 1916- *BasBi*
Meyer, Raymond George, II 1947- *WhoAmL 94*
Meyer, Raymond Joseph 1913- *WhoAm 94*
Meyer, Raymond W. 1939- *WhoAmP 93*
Meyer, Richard 1942- *WhoScEn 94*
Meyer, Richard Carroll 1934- *WhoMW 93*
Meyer, Richard Charles 1930- *WhoAm 94*
Meyer, Richard David 1943- *WhoAm 94*
Meyer, Richard E(dward) 1939- *WhAm 10*
Meyer, Richard Erwin 1939- *WhoWest 94*
Meyer, Richard Jonah 1933- *WhoAm 94*
Meyer, Richard Schlomer 1945- *WhoAm 94*
Meyer, Richard Steven 1944- *WhoAmL 94*
Meyer, Richard Townsend 1925- *WhoAm 94*
Meyer, Robert A. 1950- *WhoAmL 94*
Meyer, Robert Alan 1946- *WhoFI 94*
Meyer, Robert Allen 1943- *WhoWest 94*
Meyer, Robert Anthony 1939- *WhoMW 93*
Meyer, Robert Dean 1934- *WhoIns 94*
Meyer, Robert Kenneth 1932- *IntWW 93*
Meyer, Robert Paul 1945- *WhoFI 94*
Meyer, Robert Verner 1954- *WhoScEn 94*
Meyer, Roelof Petrus 1947- *IntWW 93, Who 94*
Meyer, Roger Dennis 1941- *WhoWest 94*
Meyer, Roger Jess Christian 1928- *WhoWest 94*
Meyer, Roger Paul 1950- *WhoWest 94*
Meyer, Ron 1944- *WhoAm 94*
Meyer, Ronald 1952- *WrDr 94*
Meyer, Ronald Paul 1955- *WhoMW 93*
Meyer, Ross E. 1934- *WhoFI 94*
Meyer, Russ 1922- *IntMPA 94*
Meyer, Russel William, Jr. 1932- *WhoAm 94, WhoFI 94, WhoMW 93*
Meyer, Ruth Krueger 1940- *WhoAm 94, WhoAmA 93, WhoMW 93*
Meyer, Sally Cave 1937- *WhoWest 94*
Meyer, Samuel James 1896-1992 *WhAm 10*
Meyer, Sandra Lea 1945- *WhoAmL 94*
Meyer, Sandra Wasserstein 1937- *WhoAm 94*
Meyer, Scott D. 1949- *WhoAm 94*
Meyer, Seymour W. *WhoAmA 93*
Meyer, Sheldon 1926- *WhoAm 94*
Meyer, Stephen Leonard 1948- *WhoAmP 93*
Meyer, Steven John 1961- *WhoScEn 94, WhoWest 94*
Meyer, Steven Russell 1946- *WhoMW 93*
Meyer, Susan E. 1940- *WhoAm 94, WhoAmA 93*
Meyer, Sylvan Hugh 1921- *WhoAm 94*
Meyer, Theodore James 1948- *WhoAmL 94*
Meyer, Thomas *DrAPF 93*
Meyer, Thomas J. *WhoAmL 94*
Meyer, Thomas J. 1941- *WhoAm 94*
Meyer, Thomas J. 1949- *WhoMW 93*
Meyer, Thomas James 1955- *WhoAm 94*
Meyer, Thomas Robert 1936- *WhoFI 94, WhoScEn 94, WhoWest 94*
Meyer, Torben d1975 *WhoHol 92*
Meyer, Ursula *WhoAmA 93*
Meyer, Ursula 1927- *WhoWest 94*
Meyer, Vern *WhoAmP 93*
Meyer, Walter *WhoAmP 93*
Meyer, Walter 1932-1992 *WhAm 10*
Meyer, Walter George 1939- *WhoAmL 94*
Meyer, William Danielson 1923- *WhoAm 94*
Meyer, William Lorne 1946- *WhoAmL 94*
Meyer, William Michael 1940- *WhoFI 94*
Meyer, William Trenholm 1937- *WhoAm 94, WhoFI 94*
Meyer-Bahlburg, Heino F. L. 1940- *WhoAm 94*
Meyerbeer, Giacomo 1791-1864 *NewGrDO*
Meyercord, Andrew N. 1949- *WhoAmL 94*
Meyercord, David K. 1947- *WhoAmL 94*
Meyer-Cording, Ulrich 1911- *IntWW 93*
Meyerhof, Otto 1884-1951 *WorScD*
Meyerhoff, Arthur Augustus 1928- *WhoScEn 94*
Meyerhoff, Erich 1919- *WhoAm 94*
Meyerhoff, Jack Fulton 1926- *WhoAm 94*
Meyerink, Victoria Paige 1961- *WhoHol 92*
Meyerkhold, Vsevolod d1942 *WhoHol 92*
Meyer-Landrut, Andreas 1929- *IntWW 93*
Meyerowitz, Jan 1913- *NewGrDO*
Meyerowitz, Joel 1938- *IntWW 93, WhoAmA 93*
Meyerowitz, Patricia 1933- *WrDr 94*
Meyerowitz, William 1886-1981 *WhoAmA 93N*
Meyers, Abbey S. 1944- *WhoFI 94*
Meyers, Al *WhoAmP 93*
Meyers, Albert Irving 1932- *WhoAm 94, WhoWest 94*
Meyers, Ann 1956- *BasBi*
Meyers, Ann Elizabeth 1955- *WhoAm 94*
Meyers, Annette (Brafman) 1934- *WrDr 94*
Meyers, Ari 1969- *WhoHisp 94*
Meyers, Ari 1970- *WhoHol 92*
Meyers, Charles D. 1937- *WhoWest 94*
Meyers, Charles Richard 1930- *WhoAmP 93*
Meyers, Christine Laine 1946- *WhoAm 94*
Meyers, Dale *WhoAm 94, WhoAmA 93*
Meyers, Edward 1934- *WhoAm 94*
Meyers, Edward Alexander 1959- *WhoFI 94*
Meyers, Emil, Jr. 1927- *WhoAmP 93*
Meyers, Francis Joseph 1921- *WhoAmA 93*
Meyers, Frederick M. *WhoAm 94*
Meyers, George d1962 *WhoHol 92*
Meyers, George Edward 1928- *WhoFI 94*
Meyers, Gerald Carl 1928- *IntWW 93, WhoAm 94*
Meyers, Gregory William 1954- *WhoAmL 94*
Meyers, Hannes, Jr. 1932- *WhoAmP 93*
Meyers, Herbert 1931- *WhoWest 94*
Meyers, Howard Craig 1951- *WhoWest 94*
Meyers, Howard L. 1948- *WhoAm 94*
Meyers, Ishmael Alexander 1939- *WhoBlA 94*
Meyers, James William 1942- *WhoAm 94, WhoAmL 94, WhoWest 94*
Meyers, Jan 1928- *CngDr 93, WhoAm 94, WhoAmP 93, WhoMW 93, WhoWomW 91*
Meyers, Jean Brewer 1939- *WhoAmP 93*
Meyers, Jeanne F. 1944- *WhoAmA 93*
Meyers, Jeffrey 1939- *WrDr 94*
Meyers, Jennifer Lea 1965- *WhoAmL 94*
Meyers, Jerry Ivan 1946- *WhoAmL 94*
Meyers, JoAnne 1959- *WhoAmL 94*
Meyers, John Allen 1929- *WhoAm 94*
Meyers, John Charles 1950- *WhoFI 94*
Meyers, Karen Diane 1956- *WhoAmL 94, WhoFI 94*
Meyers, Karen Hopkins 1948- *WhoMW 93*
Meyers, Katherine May 1916- *WhoAmP 93*
Meyers, Kenneth E. *WhoIns 94*
Meyers, Leonard H. 1932-1979 *WhoAmA 93N*
Meyers, Linda Curtis *DrAPF 93*
Meyers, Lynn Betty 1952- *WhoMW 93*
Meyers, Mary Ann 1937- *WhoAm 94*
Meyers, Maurice 1932- *WhoAmP 93*
Meyers, Michael 1946- *WhoHol 92*
Meyers, Michael 1950- *WhoBlA 94*
Meyers, Michael K. 1939- *WhoAmA 93*
Meyers, Michael Neal 1945- *WhoMW 93*
Meyers, Morton Allen 1933- *WhoAm 94*
Meyers, Nancy Jane 1949- *WhoAm 94*
Meyers, Otto d1921 *WhoHol 92*
Meyers, Pamela Sue 1951- *WhoMW 93*
Meyers, Paul Allan 1958- *WhoScEn 94*
Meyers, Peter L. 1939- *WhoAm 94*
Meyers, Pieter, Jr. 1941- *WhoWest 94*
Meyers, Reid 1949- *WhoIns 94*
Meyers, Ric *EncSF 93*
Meyers, Richard *DrAPF 93*
Meyers, Richard J. 1947- *WhoAmL 94*
Meyers, Richard James 1940- *WhoAm 94*
Meyers, Richard S. 1953- *EncSF 93*
Meyers, Richard Stuart 1938- *WhoAm 94, WhoWest 94*
Meyers, Robert 1934- *IntMPA 94*
Meyers, Robert David 1956- *WhoAmL 94*
Meyers, Robert William 1919-1970 *WhoAmA 93N*
Meyers, Roger Joseph 1955- *WhoWest 94*
Meyers, Ron *WhoAmP 93*
Meyers, Ronald G. 1934- *WhoAmA 93*
Meyers, Rose M. 1945- *WhoBlA 94*
Meyers, Roy (Lethbridge) 1910-1974 *EncSF 93*
Meyers, Sheldon 1929- *WhoAm 94*
Meyers, Susan 1942- *WrDr 94*
Meyers, Tedson Jay 1928- *WhoAm 94*

Meyers, Theda Maria *WhoFI 94, WhoWest 94*
Meyers, Timothy d1989 *WhoHol 92*
Meyers, Walter E(arl) 1939- *EncSF 93*
Meyers, Wayne Marvin 1924- *WhoAm 94, WhoScEn 94*
Meyersick, Sharon Kay 1945- *WhoMW 93*
Meyers-Jouan, Michael Stuart 1948- *WhoScEn 94*
Meyerson, Adam 1953- *WhoAm 94*
Meyerson, Bruce Elliot 1947- *WhoAmL 94*
Meyerson, Ivan D. *WhoAmL 94*
Meyerson, Martin 1922- *IntWW 93, WhoAm 94*
Meyerson, Seymour 1916- *WhoScEn 94*
Meyerson, Stanley Phillip 1916- *WhoAmL 94*
Meyer von Schauensee, Franz Joseph Leonti 1720-1789 *NewGrDO*
Meyjes, Richard (Anthony) 1918- *Who 94*
Meyn, Niels *EncSF 93*
Meyn, Robert d1972 *WhoHol 92*
Meynardie, Jane Wallace 1960- *WhoAmL 94*
Meynell, Alice 1847-1922 *BlmGWL*
Meynell, Alix (Hester Marie) 1903- *Who 94*
Meynell, Benedict William 1930- *Who 94*
Meynell, Hugo A(nthony) 1936- *WrDr 94*
Meyner, Helen Stevenson 1929- *WhoAmP 93*
Meyner, Robert Baumle 1908-1990 *WhAm 10*
Meyr, Shari Louise 1951- *WhoScEn 94*
Meyrick, David (John Charlton) 1926- *Who 94*
Meyrick, George (Christopher Cadafael Tapps Gervis) 1941- *Who 94*
Meyrink, Gustav 1868-1932 *EncSF 93*
Meyrink, Michelle *WhoHol 92*
Meysenbug, Malvida von 1816-1903 *BlmGWL*
Meysey-Thompson, (Humphrey) Simon 1935- *Who 94*
Meystrik, Joseph Michael 1961- *WhoMW 93*
Meytus, Yuly Sergeyevich 1903- *NewGrDO*
Meyyappan, A. 1949- *WhoWest 94*
Meza, Beatrice 1953- *WhoHisp 94*
Meza, Carlos J. 1958- *WhoHisp 94*
Meza, James, Jr. 1948- *WhoHisp 94*
Meza, Roberto 1937- *IntWW 93*
Meza-Overstreet, Mark Lee 1950- *WhoHisp 94*
Mezentseva, Galina 1952- *IntDcB [port]*
Mezey, Robert *DrAPF 93*
Mezey, Robert 1935- *WhoAm 94, WhoWest 94, WrDr 94*
Mezhelaitis, Eduardas Beniamino 1919- *IntWW 93*
Mezhirov, Aleksandr Petrovich 1923- *IntWW 93*
Mezic, Richard Joseph 1968- *WhoScEn 94*
Mezo, Francine (Marie) *EncSF 93*
Mezvinsky, Edward M. 1937- *WhoAmP 93*
Mezzanotte, Paolo Alessandro 1943- *WhoScEn 94*
Mezzatesta, Jerry L. 1946- *WhoAmP 93*
Mezzatesta, Michael Philip *WhoAm 94*
Mezzich, Juan Enrique 1945- *WhoHisp 94*
Mezzogiorno, Vittorio *WhoHol 92*
Mezzullo, Louis Albert 1944- *WhoAmL 94*
Mfume, Kweisi *WhoBlA 94*
Mfume, Kweisi 1948- *AfrAmAl 6 [port], CngDr 93, ConBlB 6 [port], WhoAm 94, WhoAmP 93*
Mhac An tSaoi, Maire 1922- *BlmGWL*
Mhire, Herman P. 1947- *WhoAmA 93*
Mhlophe, Gcina 1958- *BlmGWL*
Mi, Yongli 1961- *WhoScEn 94*
Miah, Abdul J. 1937- *WhoAsA 94*
Miakwe, Akepa 1934- *Who 94*
Miall, (Rowland) Leonard 1914- *Who 94*
Miall, Robert *EncSF 93*
Miamis, James D. 1927- *WhoFI 94*
Mian, Athar S. 1962- *WhoAsA 94*
Mian, Farouk Aslam 1944- *WhoScEn 94*
Mian, Guo 1957- *WhoScEn 94*
Mian, Waqar Saeed 1958- *WhoAsA 94*
Miandad, Javed 1957- *IntWW 93*
Miank, David Charles 1946- *WhoWest 94*
Miano, Louis Stephen 1934- *WhoAm 94, WhoFI 94*
Miano, Marcia Rose 1968- *WhoMW 93*
Miano, Robert *WhoHol 92*
Miao, Shili 1950- *WhoScEn 94*
Miao Chunting 1919- *WhoPRCh 91 [port]*
Miasek, Stan 1922- *BasBi*
Mica, Daniel Andrew 1944- *WhoAmP 93*
Mica, Frantisek Adam 1746-1811 *NewGrDO*
Mica, Frantisek Antonin (Vaclav) 1694-1744 *NewGrDO*
Mica, John L. 1943- *CngDr 93, WhoAm 94, WhoAmP 93*
Mica, Robert Leonard 1936- *WhoAmP 93*
Micale, Albert *WhoAmA 93*
Micale, Frank Jude 1949- *WhoAmL 94*
Micci, Eugene D. 1945- *WhoAm 94*
Micciche, Salvatore Joseph 1928- *WhoAm 94*
Miccio, Joseph V. 1915- *WhoAm 94*
Miccoli, Arnaldo *WhoAmA 93*
Miccoli, Peter Albert, Jr. 1951- *WhoFI 94*
Miceika, Gene 1947- *WhoIns 94*
Miceli, James R. 1935- *WhoAmP 93*
Micha, David Allan 1939- *WhoScEn 94*
Michael, H.M. King 1921- *IntWW 93*
Michael, Alfred Frederick, Jr. *WhoAm 94, WhoScEn 94*
Michael, Alun Edward 1943- *Who 94*
Michael, Ann E. *DrAPF 93*
Michael, Bernard J. 1959- *WhoAmL 94*
Michael, Charlene Belton *WhoBlA 94*
Michael, Charles Joseph 1939- *WhoAmL 94*
Michael, Connie Elizabeth Trexler 1945- *WhoFI 94*
Michael, Dale R. 1942- *WhoBlA 94*
Michael, Donald F. 1929- *WhoAmP 93*
Michael, Donald Nelson 1923- *WhoAm 94*
Michael, Douglas Charles 1957- *WhoAmL 94*
Michael, Duncan 1937- *Who 94*
Michael, Ernest Arthur 1925- *WhoAm 94, WhoWest 94*
Michael, Frederick William 1943- *WhoMW 93*
Michael, Gary 1937- *WhoAmA 93*
Michael, Gary G. 1940- *WhoAm 94, WhoFI 94, WhoWest 94*
Michael, Gary Linn 1934- *WhoAm 94*
Michael, George 1963- *IntWW 93, WhoAm 94*
Michael, Gertrude d1964 *WhoHol 92*
Michael, Harold K. 1943- *WhoAmP 93*
Michael, Harold Louis 1920- *WhoAm 94*
Michael, Helen Katherine 1959- *WhoAmL 94*
Michael, Henry N. 1913- *WhoAm 94*
Michael, I(an) D(avid) L(ewis) 1936- *WrDr 94*
Michael, Ian (Lockie) 1915- *Who 94*
Michael, Ian David Lewis 1936- *Who 94*
Michael, James Daniel 1957- *WhoWest 94*
Michael, James Harry, Jr. 1918- *WhoAm 94, WhoAmL 94*
Michael, James Henry 1920- *IntWW 93*
Michael, Janet d1974 *WhoHol 92*
Michael, Jerrold Mark 1927- *WhoAm 94*
Michael, Joe Victor 1935- *WhoMW 93*
Michael, John A(rthur) 1921- *WrDr 94*
Michael, John M. 1950- *WhoAmP 93*
Michael, Julia Warner 1879- *BlmGWL*
Michael, Larry Perry 1956- *WhoAm 94*
Michael, M. Blane 1943- *WhoAmL 94*
Michael, Mary d1980 *WhoHol 92*
Michael, Michael L. 1949- *WhoFI 94*
Michael, Mickie d1973 *WhoHol 92*
Michael, Nicholas George 1960- *WhoAmL 94*
Michael, Patricia Ann 1953- *WhoAm 94*
Michael, Patricia Gordon 1940- *WhoAmA 93*
Michael, Patrick Doyle 1952- *WhoWest 94*
Michael, Peter (Colin) 1938- *Who 94*
Michael, Pierre *WhoHol 92*
Michael, Ralph 1907- *WhoHol 92*
Michael, Robert Roy 1946- *WhoAmL 94*
Michael, Thomas P. 1943- *WhoAmL 94*
Michael, Toby *WhoAmP 93, WhoHisp 94*
Michael, William Burton 1922- *WhoAm 94*
Michaelides, Constantine Evangelos 1930- *WhoAm 94*
Michaelides, Doros Nikita 1936- *WhoScEn 94*
Michaelides, George d1985 *WhoHol 92*
Michaelis, Arthur Frederick 1941- *WhoAm 94*
Michaelis, Elias K. 1944- *WhoScEn 94*
Michaelis, Hanny 1922- *BlmGWL*
Michaelis, Johann Benjamin 1746-1772 *NewGrDO*
Michaelis, Karin 1872-1950 *BlmGWL*
Michaelis, Lynn Otto 1944- *WhoAm 94*
Michaelis, Michael 1919- *WhoAm 94*
Michaelis, Paul Charles 1935- *WhoAm 94*
Michael-Kenney, Shari Ann 1957- *WhoFI 94*
Michael of Canterbury fl. 1275-1321 *DcNaB MP*
Michael of Kent, Prince 1942- *Who 94R*
Michaels, Alan Richard 1944- *WhoAm 94*
Michaels, Andrice 1950- *WhoAmP 93*
Michaels, Anthony Bruce 1948- *WhoMW 93*
Michaels, Barbara 1927- *WrDr 94*
Michaels, Beverly *WhoHol 92*
Michaels, Beverly 1929- *WhoHol 92*
Michaels, Brenda Hillman *DrAPF 93*
Michaels, Bret 1963- *See* Poison *ConMus 11*
Michaels, Brigitte Gisele 1959- *WhoMW 93*
Michaels, Claire *DrAPF 93*
Michaels, Dale 1918- *WrDr 94*
Michaels, Dolores 1930- *WhoHol 92*
Michaels, Fern *ConAu 42NR*
Michaels, Fern 1933- *WrDr 94*
Michaels, Fern 1942- *WrDr 94*
Michaels, Gary David 1955- *WhoAmL 94*
Michaels, George 1923- *WhoAmL 94*
Michaels, Glen 1927- *WhoAmA 93*
Michaels, Gordon Joseph 1930- *WhoScEn 94*
Michaels, James Walker 1921- *WhoAm 94, WhoFI 94*
Michaels, Jane 1947- *WhoAmL 94*
Michaels, Jennifer Alman 1948- *WhoAmL 94*
Michaels, Joanne 1950- *WhoAm 94*
Michaels, Joel B. 1938- *IntMPA 94*
Michaels, John Patrick, Jr. 1944- *WhoFI 94*
Michaels, Joseph Eugene 1951- *WhoAm 94*
Michaels, Judith Ann 1945- *WhoFI 94*
Michaels, Julie *WhoHol 92*
Michaels, Kristin 1930- *WrDr 94*
Michaels, Larry *DrAPF 93*
Michaels, Leonard *DrAPF 93*
Michaels, Leonard 1933- *DcLB 130 [port], WhoAm 94, WrDr 94*
Michaels, Leslie 1925- *Who 94*
Michaels, Loretta Ann 1950- *WhoMW 93*
Michaels, Loretta R. d1983 *WhoHol 92*
Michaels, Lorne *WhoAm 94*
Michaels, Lorne 1944- *Au&Arts 12 [port], ConAu 142, IntMPA 94*
Michaels, Marion Cecelia *WhoMW 93*
Michaels, Martha A. 1930- *WhoAmL 94*
Michaels, Mary Beth 1949- *WhoWest 94*
Michaels, Melisa C. *EncSF 93*
Michaels, Michael Israel d1992 *Who 94N*
Michaels, Patrick Francis 1925- *WhoWest 94*
Michaels, Patrick G. 1946- *WhoAmL 94*
Michaels, Richard 1936- *IntMPA 94*
Michaels, Richard Edward 1952- *WhoAmL 94*
Michaels, Steve 1924- *WrDr 94*
Michaels, Sully d1966 *WhoHol 92*
Michaels, Tanis d1987 *WhoHol 92*
Michaels, Theodore Peter, Jr. 1957- *WhoAmL 94*
Michaels, Willard A. 1917- *WhoAm 94*
Michaels, William M. 1917- *SmATA 77*
Michaelsen, Howard Kenneth 1927- *WhoAmL 94*
Michaelsen, Kari 1962- *WhoHol 92*
Michaelson, Arthur M. 1927- *WhoAm 94*
Michaelson, Benjamin, Jr. 1936- *WhoAmL 94, WhoFI 94*
Michaelson, Glenn Patrick 1955- *WhoFI 94*
Michaelson, Herbert Bernard 1916- *WhoScEn 94*
Michaelson, John Charles 1953- *WhoFI 94*
Michaelson, Julius Cooley 1922- *WhoAmP 93*
Michaelson, Martin 1943- *WhoAm 94, WhoAmL 94*
Michaelson, Steven W. 1959- *WhoFI 94*
Michaels-Paque, J. *WhoAmA 93*
Michaeu, Janine 1914-1976 *NewGrDO*
Michailova, Maria *NewGrDO*
Michak, Helen Barbara 1926- *WhoMW 93*
Michal, Philip Quentin 1940- *WhoMW 93*
Michalak, Craig Lance 1947- *WhoFI 94*
Michalak, Edward Francis 1937- *WhoAm 94*
Michalczyk, Mildred Joan 1959- *WhoAmL 94*
Michalesco, Michael d1957 *WhoHol 92*
Michalesi, Aloyse *NewGrDO*
Michalik, Edward Francis 1946- *WhoAm 94, WhoWest 94*
Michalik, John James 1945- *WhoAm 94, WhoAmL 94, WhoWest 94*
Michalko, James Paul 1950- *WhoAm 94*
Michalofsky, Michael A. 1944- *WhoFI 94*
Michalove, Sharon Deborah 1951- *WhoMW 93*
Michalowski, Jerzy 1909- *Who 94*
Michals, Duane 1932- *WhoAm 94, WhoAmA 93*
Michals, George Francis 1935- *WhoAm 94*
Michalske, Mike d1930 *ProFbHF*
Michalski, Paul Peter 1961- *WhoAmL 94*
Michalski, Thomas Joseph 1933- *WhoAm 94*
Michalski, Waclaw 1913- *WhoMW 93*
Micham, Nancy Sue 1956- *WhoMW 93*
Michas, Athanassios N. 1944- *WhoAm 94, WhoFI 94*
Michaud, David L. *WhoWest 94*
Michaud, Frederick Gilbert 1941- *WhoAmL 94*
Michaud, Georges Joseph 1940- *WhoScEn 94*
Michaud, Gerald Fredrick 1949- *WhoWest 94*
Michaud, Howard Henry 1902- *WhoAm 94*
Michaud, Jean-Claude Georges 1933- *IntWW 93*
Michaud, Michael Alan George 1938- *WhoAm 94*
Michaud, Michael Herman 1955- *WhoAmP 93*
Michaud, Norma Alice Palmer 1946- *WhoFI 94*
Michaud, Richard Omer 1941- *WhoScEn 94*
Michaux, Eric Coates 1941- *WhoBlA 94*
Michaux, Henry G. 1934- *WhoBlA 94*
Michaux, Henry Gaston 1934- *WhoAmA 93*
Michaux, Henry M., Jr. 1930- *WhoAmP 93, WhoBlA 94*
Michaux, Ronald Robert 1944- *WhoAmA 93*
Michaux-Chevry, Lucette Adrien 1929- *WhoWomW 91*
Micheaels, John Allan 1952- *WhoAmL 94*
Micheaux, Oscar Deveraux 1884-1951 *AfrAmAl 6*
Micheels, Peter A. 1945- *WrDr 94*
Michel, Albert *WhoHol 92*
Michel, Anthony Nikolaus 1935- *WhoAm 94*
Michel, Athenia Marie 1942- *WhoAmP 93*
Michel, Benoit 1940- *WhoAm 94, WhoFI 94*
Michel, C. Randall 1949- *WhoAmL 94*
Michel, Clifford Lloyd 1939- *WhoAm 94, WhoAmL 94*
Michel, Daniel Parker 1952- *WhoFI 94*
Michel, Diane Carol 1958- *WhoWest 94*
Michel, Donald Charles 1935- *WhoAm 94*
Michel, Francois Claude 1928- *IntWW 93*
Michel, Gary Q. 1951- *WhoAmL 94*
Michel, Gaston d1921 *WhoHol 92*
Michel, Harriet Richardson 1942- *WhoBlA 94*
Michel, Hartmut 1948- *NobelP 91 [port], Who 94, WhoScEn 94*
Michel, Henri Marie 1931- *WhoScEn 94*
Michel, Henry Ludwig 1924- *WhoAm 94*
Michel, James H. *WhoAmP 93*
Michel, James H. 1939- *WhoAm 94*
Michel, Joseph 1925- *IntWW 93*
Michel, Louis 1923- *IntWW 93*
Michel, Louise 1803-1905 *BlmGWL*
Michel, Lynn Francine 1956- *WhoMW 93*
Michel, Mary Ann Kedzuf 1939- *WhoAm 94, WhoWest 94*
Michel, Micheline *WhoHol 92*
Michel, Milton Scott 1916- *WrDr 94*
Michel, Patricia Owen 1955- *WhoFI 94*
Michel, Paul R. *WhoAmP 93*
Michel, Paul R. 1941- *CngDr 93*
Michel, Paul Redmond 1941- *WhoAm 94, WhoAmL 94*
Michel, Philip Martin 1939- *WhoFI 94*
Michel, Robert Charles 1927- *WhoAm 94*
Michel, Robert H. 1923- *CngDr 93*
Michel, Robert Henry 1923- *IntWW 93, WhoAm 94, WhoAmP 93, WhoMW 93*
Michel, Victor James, Jr. 1927- *WhoWest 94*
Michel, Virgil George 1890-1938 *DcAmReB 2*
Michel, Werner *IntMPA 94*
Michelangeli 1920- *IntWW 93*
Michelberger, Pal 1930- *IntWW 93*
Michele, Robert Charles 1959- *WhoFI 94*
Michelena, Beatriz d1942 *WhoHol 92*
Michelena, Juan A. 1939- *WhoHisp 94*
Michelena, Vera d1961 *WhoHol 92*
Michelet, Michel 1899- *IntMPA 94*
Micheletti, Gaston 1892-1959 *NewGrDO*
Micheletto, Joe Raymond 1936- *WhoAm 94*
Micheli, Benedetto c. 1700-1784? *NewGrDO*
Micheli, Frank James 1930- *WhoAm 94*
Micheli, Joseph Ronald 1948- *WhoAmP 93*
Micheli, Maurizio *WhoHol 92*
Michelin, Francois 1926- *IntWW 93*
Michelin, Reginald Townend 1903- *Who 94*
Micheline, Jack *DrAPF 93*
Michelini, Sylvia Hamilton 1946- *WhoFI 94*

Michelis, Jay 1937- *WhAm 10*
Michell, Allan Henry 1930- *IntWW 93*
Michell, Helena *WhoHol 92*
Michell, John *WorInv*
Michell, John 1724-1793 *WorScD*
Michell, John Charles 1946- *WhoFI 94*
Michell, Keith *Who 94*
Michell, Keith 1926- *IntMPA 94, WhoHol 92*
Michell, Keith 1928- *IntWW 93*
Michell, Michael John 1942- *Who 94*
Michell, Robert H. 1941- *IntWW 93*
Michell, Robert Hall 1941- *Who 94*
Michelle, Anne 1952- *WhoHol 92*
Michelle, Donna *WhoHol 92*
Michelle, Janee *WhoHol 92*
Michelle, Vicki 1950- *WhoHol 92*
Michelman, Henry D. *WhoAm 94*
Michelman, Kate *WhoWomW 91*
Michelman, Ken *WhoHol 92*
Michelmore, Clifford Arthur 1919- *Who 94*
Michelmore, Laurence 1909- *IntWW 93*
Michelotti, Robert Jock Giacomo, Jr. 1951- *WhoFI 94*
Michels, Alan 1950- *WhoFI 94, WhoWest 94*
Michels, Daniel Lester 1941- *WhoAm 94*
Michels, Eileen Manning 1926- *WhoAmA 93*
Michels, Elizabeth Frances 1959- *WhoWest 94*
Michels, Eugene 1926- *WhoAm 94*
Michels, John Rudolf 1944- *WhoAmP 93*
Michels, Joseph Howard 1964- *WhoMW 93*
Michels, Oren William 1963- *WhoFI 94*
Michels, Richard Steven 1951- *WhoScEn 94*
Michels, Robert 1936- *WhoAm 94*
Michels, Roy Samuel 1932- *WhoFI 94*
Michels, Stanley E. 1933- *WhoAmP 93*
Michelsen, Axel 1940- *IntWW 93*
Michelsen, Hans Gunter 1920- *IntWW 93*
Michelsen, John Ernest 1946- *WhoFI 94, WhoMW 93*
Michelsen, Neil Franklin 1931- *AstEnc*
Michelsen, Niall Guy 1955- *WhoMW 93*
Michelsen, Wolfgang Jost 1935- *WhoAm 94, WhoScEn 94*
Michelsohn, Marie-Louise 1941- *WhoScEn 94*
Michelson, Alan David 1950- *WhoScEn 94*
Michelson, Albert *WorInv*
Michelson, Albert Abraham 1852-1931 *WorScD*
Michelson, Edward J. 1915- *WhoAm 94*
Michelson, Gary Bryan 1958- *WhoMW 93*
Michelson, Gertrude Geraldine 1925- *WhoAm 94, WhoFI 94*
Michelson, Guy P. 1951- *WhoAmL 94*
Michelson, Harold 1920- *WhoWest 94*
Michelson, Irving 1922- *WhoAm 94*
Michelson, Joan *DrAPF 93*
Michelson, Lillian 1928- *WhoAm 94*
Michelson, Max, Jr. 1921- *WhAm 10*
Michelson, Peter *DrAPF 93*
Michelson, Philip L. 1948- *WhoAmA 93*
Michelson, Richard *DrAPF 93*
Michelson, Robert 1944- *WhoAmP 93*
Michelson, Sonia 1928- *WhoWest 94*
Michelson, William Michael 1940- *WrDr 94*
Michelstetter, Stanley Hubert 1946- *WhoAmL 94*
Michenaud, Gerald *WhoHol 92*
Michener, Charles Duncan 1918- *IntWW 93, WhoAm 94, WhoScEn 94*
Michener, Daniel Roland 1900-1991 *WhAm 10*
Michener, James *DrAPF 93*
Michener, James A(lbert) 1907- *EncSF 93, WhoAm 94*
Michener, James Albert 1907- *IntWW 93, Who 94, WhoAm 94*
Michenfelder, John Donahue 1931- *WhoAm 94*
Michenfelder, Joseph Francis 1929- *WhoAm 94*
Michero, William Henderson 1925- *WhoAm 94*
Michetti, Susan Jane 1948- *WhoFI 94, WhoMW 93*
Michi, Maria *WhoHol 92*
Michich, Velizar *WhoAmA 93*
Michie, Daniel Boorse, Jr. 1922- *WhoAmL 94*
Michie, David Alan Redpath 1928- *IntWW 93, Who 94*
Michie, Donald 1923- *IntWW 93, Who 94*
Michie, James 1927- *WrDr 94*
Michie, Jonathan 1957- *WrDr 94*
Michie, Mary 1922- *WhoAmA 93*
Michie, (Janet) Ray 1934- *Who 94, WhoWomW 91*

Michie, Thomas Johnson, Jr. 1931- *WhoAmP 93*
Michie, William 1935- *Who 94*
Michl, Josef 1939- *WhAm 10*
Michl, Joseph (Christian) Willibald 1745-1816 *NewGrDO*
Michles, Stewart d1978 *WhoHol 92*
Michlin, Arnold Sidney 1920- *WhoMW 93*
Michlovic, Michael George 1949- *WhoMW 93*
Michlovic, Thomas A. 1946- *WhoAmP 93*
Michnovicz, Jon Joseph 1953- *WhoScEn 94*
Michod, Susan A. 1945- *WhoAmA 93*
Michon, John Albertus 1935- *IntWW 93*
Michtom, Rose d1986 *WhoHol 92*
Micich, Paul *SmATA 74*
Mick, David Lee 1937- *WhoMW 93*
Mick, Elizabeth Ellen 1962- *WhoScEn 94*
Mick, Howard Harold 1934- *WhoAm 94*
Micka, Thomas Frederick 1949- *WhoMW 93*
Mickal, Abe 1913- *WhoAm 94*
Mickel, Emanuel J., Jr. 1937- *WrDr 94*
Mickel, Joseph Thomas 1951- *WhoAmL 94*
Mickelsen, Einer Bjegaard 1922- *WhoAmL 94*
Mickelson, Arlene Jo 1938- *WhoWest 94*
Mickelson, Arnold Rust 1922- *WhoAm 94*
Mickelson, Bob J. 1921- *WhoAmP 93*
Mickelson, Elliot Spencer 1934- *WhoScEn 94*
Mickelson, George S. d1993 *IntWW 93N, NewYTBS 93 [port]*
Mickelson, George S. 1941- *IntWW 93*
Mickelson, Gordon M. *WhoAmP 93*
Mickelson, Herald Fred 1938- *WhoWest 94*
Mickelson, Monty (Phillip) 1956- *ConAu 141*
Mickelson, Sig 1913- *WhoAm 94, WhoWest 94*
Mickelwait, Lowell Pitzer 1905- *WhoAm 94*
Micken, Ralph Arlington 1907-1989 *WhAm 10*
Mickenberg, David 1954- *WhoAmA 93*
Mickens, Maxine 1948- *WhoBlA 94*
Mickens, Ronald Elbert 1943- *WhoBlA 94*
Mickes, Thomas Aylward 1946- *WhoAmL 94*
Mickey, Gordon Eugene *WhoBlA 94*
Mickey, John Wesley 1942- *WhoAmP 93*
Mickey, Paul Fogle, Jr. 1949- *WhoAm 94, WhoAmL 94*
Mickey, Rosie Cheatham *WhoBlA 94*
Mickiewicz, Adam *EncSF 93*
Mickiewicz, Ellen Propper 1938- *WhoAm 94*
Mickins, Andel W. 1924- *WhoBlA 94*
Mickish, Verle L. 1928- *WhoAm 94*
Mickle, Andrea Denise 1952- *WhoBlA 94*
Mickle, Billy A. 1945- *WhoAmP 93*
Mickle, Elva L. 1949- *WhoBlA 94*
Mickle, Shelley Fraser 1944- *WrDr 94*
Micklewood, Eric 1911- *WhoHol 92*
Micklon, Stephanie 1947- *WhoAmP 93*
Micklow, Craig Woodward 1947- *WhoFI 94*
Micko, Alexander S. 1947- *WhoAm 94*
Mickolus, Edward (Francis) 1950- *WrDr 94*
Micks, Deitra R. H. 1945- *WhoBlA 94*
Micks, Don Wilfred 1918- *WhoAm 94*
Micolo, Anthony Michael 1949- *WhoAm 94*
Micou, Paul 1959- *ConAu 140*
Micozzi, Marc Stephen 1953- *WhoAm 94*
Micozzie, Nicholas Anthony 1930- *WhoAmP 93*
Miczek, Klaus Alexander 1944- *WhoAm 94*
Miczuga, Mark N. 1962- *WhoFI 94, WhoMW 93*
Midanek, Deborah Hicks 1954- *WhoFI 94*
Miday, Stephen Paul 1952- *WhoScEn 94*
Midda, Sara 1951- *WrDr 94*
Middaugh, Jack Kendall, II 1949- *WhoFI 94*
Middaugh, James 1946- *WhoAmP 93*
Middaugh, Robert Burton 1935- *WhoAm 94, WhoAmA 93*
Middeke, Richard Joseph 1960- *WhoMW 93*
Middelkamp, John Neal 1925- *WhoAm 94*
Midden, William Robert 1952- *WhoScEn 94*
Middendorf, Christelle Marie 1963- *WhoMW 93*
Middendorf, Henry Stump, Jr. 1923- *WhoAmP 93*
Middendorf, J. William, II 1924- *IntWW 93*
Middendorf, John Harlan 1922- *WhoAm 94*

Middendorf, John William, II 1924- *WhoAmP 93*
Middendorf, Max Harold 1941- *WhoAmP 93*
Middendorf, William Henry 1921- *WhoAm 94*
Middlebrook, David A. 1944- *WhoAmA 93*
Middlebrook, Grace Irene 1927- *WhoWest 94*
Middlebrook, Martin 1932- *WrDr 94*
Middlebrook, R. David *WhoWest 94*
Middlebrook, Robert David 1929- *WhoScEn 94*
Middlebrook, Stephen Beach *WhoAm 94, WhoAmL 94, WhoFI 94*
Middlebrook, Stephen Beach 1937- *WhoIns 94*
Middlebrooks, Arthur Gordon 1962- *WhoFI 94*
Middlebrooks, Donald M. 1946- *WhoAmL 94*
Middlebrooks, Eddie Joe 1932- *WhoAm 94, WhoFI 94*
Middlebrooks, Felicia 1957- *WhoBlA 94*
Middlebusher, Mark Alan 1966- *WhoScEn 94*
Middleditch, Brian Stanley 1945- *WhoScEn 94*
Middleditch, Edward *IntWW 93N*
Middleditch, Leigh Benjamin, Jr. 1929- *WhoAm 94, WhoAmL 94*
Middlekauff, Robert (Lawrence) 1929- *WrDr 94*
Middlekauff, Robert Lawrence 1929- *WhoAm 94*
Middlekauff, Roger David 1935- *WhoAm 94*
Middleman, Raoul F. 1935- *WhoAmA 93*
Middlemas, (Robert) Keith 1935- *WrDr 94*
Middlemas, Robert Keith 1935- *IntWW 93, Who 94*
Middlemass, Frank 1919- *WhoHol 92*
Middlemass, Robert d1949 *WhoHol 92*
Middlemiss, Robert William *DrAPF 93*
Middlesbrough, Auxiliary Bishop of *Who 94*
Middlesbrough, Bishop of 1941- *Who 94*
Middlesex, Archdeacon of *Who 94*
Middlesex, Earl of 1711-1769 *NewGrDO*
Middleswart, James Ira 1912- *WhoAmP 93*
Middleswart, Jeffery Brent 1969- *WhoFI 94*
Middleton, Baron 1921- *Who 94*
Middleton, Bishop Suffragan of *Who 94*
Middleton, Bishop Suffragan of d1992 *Who 94N*
Middleton, Anthony Wayne, Jr. 1939- *WhoScEn 94, WhoWest 94*
Middleton, Arthur 1742-1787 *WhAmRev*
Middleton, Bernice Bryant 1922- *WhoBlA 94*
Middleton, Beth Ann 1955- *WhoMW 93*
Middleton, Blackford 1957- *WhoWest 94*
Middleton, Charles d1949 *WhoHol 92*
Middleton, Charles 1726- *AmRev*
Middleton, Charles G., III 1947- *WhoAmP 93*
Middleton, Charles Gibson, III 1947- *WhoAmL 94*
Middleton, Charles Ronald 1944- *WhoWest 94*
Middleton, Christopher *DrAPF 93*
Middleton, Christopher c. 1700-1770 *WhWE*
Middleton, Christopher 1926- *BlmGEL, IntWW 93, WhoAm 94*
Middleton, (John) Christopher 1926- *WrDr 94*
Middleton, Clyde William 1928- *WhoAmP 93*
Middleton, David 1920- *WhoAm 94, WhoScEn 94*
Middleton, Donald Earl 1930- *WhoAm 94*
Middleton, Donald King 1922- *Who 94*
Middleton, Drew 1913-1990 *WhAm 10*
Middleton, Earl Matthew *WhoAmP 93*
Middleton, Edward Bernard 1948- *Who 94*
Middleton, Elliott, Jr. 1925- *WhoAm 94*
Middleton, Ernest J. 1937- *WhoBlA 94*
Middleton, Finley Norman, II 1945- *WhoIns 94*
Middleton, Francis 1913- *Who 94*
Middleton, Frank Walters, Jr. 1919- *WhoAm 94, WhoAmL 94*
Middleton, Frank Walters, III 1945- *WhoAmL 94*
Middleton, George (Humphrey) 1910- *Who 94*
Middleton, Gerard Viner 1931- *WhoAm 94, WhoScEn 94*
Middleton, Guy d1973 *WhoHol 92*
Middleton, Harry Joseph 1921- *WhoAm 94*
Middleton, Haydn 1955- *WrDr 94*

Middleton, Henry 1717-1784 *WhAmRev*
Middleton, Herman David, Sr. 1925- *WhoAm 94*
Middleton, J. Howard, Jr. 1939- *WhoAm 94*
Middleton, Jack Baer 1929- *WhoAm 94*
Middleton, James Arthur 1936- *WhoAm 94*
Middleton, James Boland 1934- *WhoAmL 94*
Middleton, James G. 1932- *WhoMW 93*
Middleton, John A. 1915- *WhoAmP 93*
Middleton, John Allen 1945- *WhoBlA 94*
Middleton, John Patrick Windsor 1938- *Who 94*
Middleton, John Ross, Jr. 1940- *WhoFI 94*
Middleton, Josephine d1971 *WhoHol 92*
Middleton, Kenneth William Bruce 1905- *Who 94*
Middleton, Lawrence (Monck) 1912- *Who 94*
Middleton, Lawrence John 1930- *Who 94*
Middleton, Linda Jean Greathouse 1950- *WhoAm 94*
Middleton, Linley Eric *Who 94*
Middleton, Lois Jean 1930- *WhoMW 93*
Middleton, Marc Stephen 1950- *WhoFI 94, WhoMW 93*
Middleton, Michael Humfrey 1917- *Who 94*
Middleton, Michael John 1940- *Who 94*
Middleton, Michael John 1953- *WhoScEn 94, WhoWest 94*
Middleton, Noelle *WhoHol 92*
Middleton, O(sman) E(dward) 1925- *WrDr 94*
Middleton, O(sman) E(dward Gordon) 1925- *RfGShF*
Middleton, Peter *NewYTBS 93 [port]*
Middleton, Peter d1781 *AmRev*
Middleton, Peter 1940- *IntWW 93*
Middleton, Peter (Edward) 1934- *Who 94*
Middleton, Peter Edward 1934- *IntWW 93*
Middleton, Peter James 1940- *Who 94*
Middleton, Ray d1984 *WhoHol 92*
Middleton, Richard LeRoy 1939- *WhoMW 93*
Middleton, Richard Temple, III 1942- *WhoBlA 94*
Middleton, Robert d1977 *WhoHol 92*
Middleton, Robert Allan, Jr. 1948- *WhoWest 94*
Middleton, Ronald George 1913- *Who 94*
Middleton, Rose Nixon 1932- *WhoBlA 94*
Middleton, S. Guy 1935- *WhoAmP 93*
Middleton, Stanley 1919- *Who 94, WrDr 94*
Middleton, Stephen Hugh d1993 *Who 94N*
Middleton, Thomas 1580-1627 *BlmGEL [port], IntDcT ?*
Middleton, Thomas F. 1945- *WhoAmP 93*
Middleton, Todd L. 1961- *WhoMW 93*
Middleton, Vertelle Delores 1942- *WhoBlA 94*
Middleton, Vincent Francis 1951- *WhoFI 94, WhoWest 94*
Middlewood, Martin Eugene 1947- *WhoWest 94*
Midei, Richard Allen 1947- *WhoMW 93*
Midener, Walter 1912- *WhoAmA 93*
Midgett, John Thomas 1952- *WhoAmL 94*
Midgette, Willard Franklin 1937-1978 *WhoAmA 93N*
Midgley, Alvin Rees, Jr. 1933- *WhoAm 94, WhoScEn 94*
Midgley, Dick d1956 *WhoHol 92*
Midgley, Douglas Merritt 1940- *WhoAmL 94*
Midgley, Eric Atkinson 1913- *Who 94*
Midgley, Fanny d1932 *WhoHol 92*
Midgley, Florence d1949 *WhoHol 92*
Midgley, Mary 1919- *ConAu 43NR*
Midkiff, Dale 1959- *WhoHol 92*
Midkiff, Donald Wayne 1940- *WhoWest 94*
Midkiff, John L., Jr. 1932- *WhoAm 94*
Midkiff, Kimberly Ann 1958- *WhoAmL 94*
Midkiff, Robert Richards 1920- *WhoAm 94*
Midlarsky, Manus Issachar 1937- *WhoAm 94*
Midler, Bette 1945- *ConTFT 11, IntMPA 94, IntWW 93, WhoAm 94, WhoCom, WhoHol 92*
Midleton, Viscount 1949- *Who 94*
Midnight Oil *ConMus 11 [port]*
Midori 1971- *IntWW 93, WhoAm 94, WhoAsA 94*
Midwig, William Carroll, Jr. 1951- *WhoFI 94*
Midwinter, Eric (Clare) 1932- *WrDr 94*
Midwinter, Eric Clare 1932- *Who 94*

Midwinter, John Edwin 1938- *IntWW 93, Who 94*
Midwinter, Stanley Walter 1922- *Who 94*
Midwood, Bart A. *DrAPF 93*
Midzic, Fatima 1929- *WhoWomW 91*
Miech, Allen C. 1939- *WhoAm 94, WhoFI 94, WhoWest 94*
Mieczkowski, Edwin 1929- *WhoAmA 93*
Mieczkowski, Rondo *DrAPF 93*
Miedel, Russell J. 1895- *WhAm 10*
Miedema, Douglas Jae 1961- *WhoMW 93*
Miedusiewski, American Joe 1949- *WhoAmP 93*
Miegel, Agnes 1879-1964 *BlmGWL*
Miel, Alice Marie 1906- *WrDr 94*
Miel, Vicky Ann 1951- *WhoWest 94*
Mielcuszny, Albert John 1941- *WhoAm 94*
Miele, Alfonse Ralph 1922- *WhoAm 94*
Miele, Angelo 1922- *WhoAm 94, WhoScEn 94, WrDr 94*
Miele, Anthony William 1926- *WhoAm 94*
Miele, Arthur Robert 1941- *WhoAm 94*
Miele, Eileen Cecelia *WhoAm 94*
Miele, Joel Arthur, Sr. 1934- *WhoScEn 94*
Mielke, Clarence Harold, Jr. 1936- *WhoAm 94, WhoWest 94*
Mielke, Erich 1907- *IntWW 93*
Mielke, Frederick William, Jr. 1921- *IntWW 93, WhoAm 94, WhoWest 94*
Mielke, Paul William, Jr. 1931- *WhoScEn 94*
Mielke, Sally Jean 1935- *WhoMW 93*
Mielke, Thomas R.P. *EncSF 93*
Mielke, Todd W. *WhoAmP 93*
Mielke, William John 1947- *WhoFI 94*
Mielziner, Jo 1901-1976 *WhoAmA 93N*
Mieno, Yasushi 1924- *IntWW 93*
Miera, Rick *WhoAmP 93, WhoHisp 94*
Miercort, Clifford Roy 1940- *WhoAm 94*
Miernyk, William Henry 1918- *WrDr 94*
Miers, David 1937- *IntWW 93*
Miers, (Henry) David (Alastair Capel) 1937- *Who 94*
Mierzwa, Joseph William 1951- *WhoAmL 94*
Mierzwinski, Wladyslaw 1850-1909 *NewGrDO*
Mies, John Charles 1946- *WhoFI 94*
Miescher, Johann Friedrich *WorScD*
Miesel, Sandra (Louise) 1941- *EncSF 93*
Miesen, Dale Lewis 1953- *WhoFI 94*
Miesen, Jonathan C. 1963- *WhoAmL 94*
Mies van der Rohe, Ludwig 1886-1969 *AmCulL, WhoAmA 93N*
Miettinen, Mauri Kalevi 1941- *IntWW 93*
Mieza, Carmen 1931-1976 *BlmGWL*
Miezajs, Dainis 1929- *WhoAmA 93*
Mifflin, Michael Jeffrey 1954- *WhoMW 93*
Mifflin, Richard Thomas 1959- *WhoScEn 94*
Mifflin, Thomas 1744-1800 *AmRev, WhAmRev [port]*
Mifsud, Lewis 1932- *WhoScEn 94*
Mifsud Bonnici, Carmelo 1933- *IntWW 93, Who 94*
Mifsud Bonnici, Ugo 1932- *IntWW 93*
Mifune, Toshiro 1920- *IntMPA 94, IntWW 93, WhoHol 92*
Migaki, James M. 1931- *WhoWest 94*
Migala, George Wesly 1948- *WhoMW 93*
Migala, Joseph 1913- *WhoMW 93*
Migala, Lucyna Jozefa 1944- *WhoMW 93*
Migdal, Sheldon Paul 1936- *WhoAm 94*
Migden, Chester L. 1921- *ConTFT 11, IntMPA 94, WhoAm 94*
Migdol, Marvin Jacob 1937- *WhoFI 94*
Migel, Christopher James 1951- *WhoIns 94*
Migenes, Julia 1945- *NewGrDO, WhoHisp 94*
Migenes, Julia 1947- *WhoHol 92*
Migenes-Johnson, Julia 1947- *See* Migenes, Julia 1947- *WhoHol 92*
Migeon, Claude Jean 1923- *WhoAm 94*
Mighell, Kenneth John 1931- *WhoAm 94, WhoAmL 94*
Mighetto, Lisa 1955- *ConAu 141*
Might, Thomas Owen 1951- *WhoAm 94*
Migl, Donald Raymond 1947- *WhoAm 94*
Migliari, Armando d1976 *WhoHol 92*
Migliaro, Eugene Alphonse, Jr. 1925- *WhoAmP 93*
Migliaro, Marco William 1948- *WhoAm 94*
Migliasso, Teresa 1942- *WhoWomW 91*
Migliavacca, Giovanni Ambrogio c. 1718-1787? *NewGrDO*
Miglio, Daniel Joseph 1940- *WhoFI 94*
Migliore, Leonard Robert 1944- *WhoFI 94*
Mignacca, Egidio Carmen 1931- *WhoMW 93*
Mignanelli, James Robert 1932- *WhoFI 94*
Mignani, Roberto 1946- *WhoScEn 94*
Mignatti, La *NewGrDO*
Mignella, Amy Tighe 1964- *WhoScEn 94*
Mignon, Helene 1934- *WhoWomW 91*
Mignone, Francisco (Paulo) 1897-1986 *NewGrDO*
Mignone, Mario B. 1940- *WhoAm 94*
Mignosa, Santo 1934- *WhoAmA 93*
Migot, Georges 1891-1976 *NewGrDO*
Migoya, James Angel 1932- *WhoHisp 94*
Migranyan, Andranik Movsevovich 1949- *LngBDD*
Migue, Jean Luc 1933- *WhoAm 94*
Miguez, Leopoldo (Americo) 1850-1902 *NewGrDO*
Miguez-Bonino, Jose 1924- *IntWW 93*
Migulin, Vladimir Vasiliyevich 1911- *IntWW 93*
Mihaesco, Eugene 1937- *WhoAmA 93*
Mihail, Alexandra d1975 *WhoHol 92*
Mihaileanu, Andrei Calin 1923- *WhoScEn 94*
Mihajlov, Mihajlo 1934- *IntWW 93, WrDr 94*
Mihalas, Dimitri Manuel 1939- *WhoAm 94, WhoMW 93*
Mihalcik, Eleanor 1929- *WhoAmP 93*
Mihalic, David Anthony 1946- *WhoAm 94*
Mihalic, Slavko 1928- *ConWorW 93*
Mihalich, Herman 1930- *WhoAmP 93*
Mihalik, Phyllis Ann 1952- *WhoFI 94, WhoMW 93*
Mihalik, Vojtech 1926- *IntWW 93*
Mihalov, John Donald 1937- *WhoScEn 94*
Mihalovich, Odon (Peter Jozsef de) 1842-1929 *NewGrDO*
Mihalovici, Marcel 1898-1985 *NewGrDO*
Mihaly, Andras 1917- *IntWW 93*
Mihaly, Eugene Bramer 1934- *WhoAm 94, WhoWest 94*
Mihan, Ralph George 1941- *WhoAmL 94*
Mihan, Richard 1925- *WhoWest 94*
Mihanovich, Clement Simon 1913- *WrDr 94*
Mihara, Asao 1909- *IntWW 93*
Mihara, Nathan 1950?- *WhoAsA 94*
Mihashi, Tatsua *WhoHol 92*
Mihelich, Janet Adele 1948- *WhoMW 93*
Mihich, Enrico 1928- *WhoAm 94, WhoScEn 94*
Mihlbaugh, Robert Holleran *WhoAmP 93*
Mihlbaugh, Robert Holleran 1932- *WhoAmL 94*
Mihm, John Clifford 1942- *WhoScEn 94*
Mihm, Martin Charles, Jr. *WhoAm 94*
Mihm, Michael Martin 1943- *WhoAm 94, WhoAmL 94, WhoMW 93*
Mihnea, Tatiana 1951- *WhoScEn 94, WhoWest 94*
Mihopoulos, Effie *DrAPF 93*
Mihos, Robert Stephen 1954- *WhoMW 93*
Mihran, Theodore Gregory 1924- *WhoAm 94*
Mihri Khatun *BlmGWL*
Mii, Nobuo 1934- *WhoFI 94*
Mijalis, Gus Sam 1934- *WhoAmP 93*
Mijares, Manny *WhoHisp 94*
Mijatovic, Cvijetin 1913- *IntWW 93*
Mi Jiashan 1948- *WhoPRCh 91 [port]*
Mijuskovic, Ben Lazare 1937- *WrDr 94*
Mika, Joseph John 1948- *WhoAm 94*
Mikael, Ludmilla *WhoHol 92*
Mikaelian, Harry V. 1943- *WhoFI 94*
Mikalow, Alfred Alexander, II 1921- *WhoScEn 94, WhoWest 94*
Mikals, John Joseph 1947- *WhoAm 94, WhoAmL 94*
Mikalson, Jon D. 1943- *ConAu 140*
Mikalson, Jon Dennis 1943- *WhoAm 94*
Mikan, Baron 1922- *WrDr 94*
Mikan, George 1924- *BasBi*
Mikardo, Ian d1993 *NewYTBS 93, Who 94N*
Mikeal, Patricia Ann 1960- *WhoWest 94*
Mikel, Thomas Kelly, Jr. 1946- *WhoWest 94*
Mikelberg, Arnold 1937- *WhoAm 94, WhoFI 94*
Mikell, Charles Donald 1934- *WhoBlA 94*
Mikell, George *IntMPA 94, WhoHol 92*
Mikell, Mike *WhoAmP 93*
Mikelonis, David Alan 1948- *WhoFI 94*
Mikels, James Ronald 1937- *WhoFI 94*
Mikels, Richard Eliot 1947- *WhoAm 94, WhoAmL 94*
Mikels, Ted V. *HorFD*
Mike-Nard, Beverly Jean 1957- *WhoMW 93*
Mikesell, Arthur David 1937- *WhoAm 94*
Mikesell, Janice H. *DrAPF 93*
Mikesell, Jason Lee 1970- *WhoMW 93*
Mikesell, Marvin Wray 1929- *WhoAm 94*
Mikesell, Raymond F(rech) 1913- *ConAu 41NR*
Mikesell, Raymond Frech 1913- *WhoAm 94*
Mikesell, Richard Lyon 1941- *WhoAmL 94, WhoFI 94*
Mikesell, Walter R., Jr. *WhoScEn 94*
Mikesic, David Paul 1944- *WhoAmP 93*
Mikhail, Edward H 1928- *WrDr 94*
Mikhail, Mary Attalla 1945- *WhoWest 94*
Mikhailov, Alexander *WhoHol 92*
Mikhailov, Viktor Grigorevich *LngBDD*
Mikhailov, Viktor Nikitovich 1934- *LngBDD*
Mikhalchenko, Alla Anatolyevna 1957- *IntWW 93*
Mikhalevich, Vladimir Sergeyevich 1930- *IntWW 93*
Mikhalkov, Nikita *WhoHol 92*
Mikhalkov, Nikita Sergeyevich 1945- *IntWW 93*
Mikhalkov, Sergey Vladimirovich 1913- *IntWW 93*
Mikhalkov-Konchalovsky, Andrey Sergeyevich 1937- *IntWW 93*
Mikhashoff, Yvar 1941-1993 *NewYTBS 93*
Mikhaylov, Maxim Dormidontovich 1893-1971 *NewGrDO*
Mikhaylova, Mariya (Alexandrovna) 1866-1943 *NewGrDO*
Mikhaylov-Stoyan, Konstantin Ivanovich 1853-1914 *NewGrDO*
Mikheev, Vladimir Andreyevich 1942- *IntWW 93*
Mikhoels, Salomon d1948 *WhoHol 92*
Miki, Akira 1921- *IntWW 93*
Miki, Minoru 1930- *NewGrDO*
Mikiewicz, Anna Daniella 1960- *WhoFI 94*
Mikita, Joseph Karl 1918- *WhoAm 94*
Mikitka, Gerald Peter 1943- *WhoAm 94*
Mikkelsen, Charles Roy 1954- *WhoAmL 94, WhoFI 94*
Mikkelsen, Richard 1920- *IntWW 93*
Mikkelsen, Vern 1928- *BasBi*
Mikkelson, Raymond Charles 1937- *WhoMW 93*
Miklave, Matthew Thaddeus 1959- *WhoAmL 94*
Mikley-Kemp, Barbara *NewGrDO*
Miklosko, Jozef 1939- *IntWW 93*
Miklowitz, Gloria D. 1927- *SmATA 17AS [port], TwCYAW, WrDr 94*
Miko, Andras 1922- *IntWW 93*
Mikol, Irene R. *WhoAmA 93*
Mikolaycak, Charles d1993 *NewYTBS 93*
Mikolaycak, Charles 1937-1993 *ConAu 141, SmATA 75*
Mikolji, Boris Hrvoje 1926- *WhoAm 94*
Mikolowski, Ken *DrAPF 93*
Mikropoulos, Anastassios 1961- *WhoScEn 94*
Mikrut, John Joseph, Jr. 1944- *WhoMW 93*
Miksch, Eileen Evans 1926- *WhoAmP 93*
Mikula, Kenneth Richard 1950- *WhoIns 94*
Mikulak, Stephen A. 1948- *WhoAmP 93*
Mikulas, Joseph Frank 1926- *WhoAm 94*
Mikulecky, Thomas J. 1938- *WhoMW 93*
Mikulic, Branko 1928- *IntWW 93*
Mikulich, V. *BlmGWL*
Mikulka, Ronald Troy 1962- *WhoWest 94*
Mikulski, Barbara A. 1936- *CngDr 93*
Mikulski, Barbara Ann 1936- *IntWW 93, WhoAm 94, WhoAmP 93, WhoWomW 91*
Mikulski, James Joseph 1934- *WhoAm 94*
Mikulski, Mark *WhoHol 92*
Mikulski, Piotr Witold 1925- *WhoAm 94*
Mikuni, Rentaro *WhoHol 92*
Mikus, Eleanore 1927- *WhoAmA 93*
Mikus, Eleanore Ann 1927- *WhoAm 94*
Mikutel, Steven *WhoAmP 93*
Mikva, Abner 1926- *CngDr 93*
Mikva, Abner J. 1926- *WhoAmP 93*
Mikva, Abner Joseph 1926- *WhoAm 94, WhoAmL 94*
Mila, Massimo 1910-1988 *NewGrDO*
Mila, Pablo Jose 1938- *WhoHisp 94*
Milad, Moheb Fawzy 1945- *WhoScEn 94*
Milam, David Kelton, Sr. 1932- *WhoHisp 94*
Milam, John Daniel 1933- *WhoScEn 94*
Milam, Joseph Walton, Jr. 1956- *WhoAmL 94*
Milam, June Matthews 1931- *WhoFI 94*
Milam, Pauline d1965 *WhoHol 92*
Milam, Susan Storey 1947- *WhoAmP 93*
Milam, Wade 1918- *WhoAmP 93*
Milam, William B. *WhoAmP 93*
Milam, William Bryant 1936- *WhoAm 94*
Milan, Archbishop of *Who 94*
Milan, Edgar J. 1934- *WhoHisp 94*
Milán, Edwin Ramón 1950- *WhoHisp 94*
Milan, Frank d1977 *WhoHol 92*
Milan, Thomas Lawrence 1941- *WhoAm 94*
Milan, Victor (Woodward) 1954- *EncSF 93*
Milander, Henry Martin 1939- *WhoAm 94, WhoWest 94*
Milanés, Juan Ever 1965- *WhoHisp 94*
Milani, Chef d1965 *WhoHol 92*
Milani, Milena 1922- *BlmGWL*
Milanich, Jerald Thomas 1945- *WhoAm 94*
Milani-Comparetti, Marco Severo 1926- *WhoScEn 94*
Milano, Alyssa 1972- *WhoHol 92*
Milano, Antonio 1931- *WhoScEn 94*
Milano, Charles Thomas 1951- *WhoScEn 94*
Milano, James Edward 1909- *WhoAmP 93*
Milano, John, Jr. 1957- *WhoAmL 94*
Milano, Mario *WhoHol 92*
Milanov, Zinka d1989 *WhAm 10*
Milanov, Zinka 1906-1989 *NewGrDO*
Milanovich, Fred Paul 1944- *WhoScEn 94*
Milant, Jean Robert 1943- *WhoAmA 93*
Milar, Adolph d1950 *WhoHol 92*
Milas, Robert Wayne 1944- *WhoScEn 94*
Milash, Robert d1954 *WhoHol 92*
Milashkina, Tamara (Andreyevna) 1934- *NewGrDO*
Milaski, John Joseph 1959- *WhoFI 94*
Milavsky, Harold Phillip 1931- *WhoFI 94, WhoWest 94*
Milazzo, Richard *WhoAmA 93*
Milbank, Anthony (Frederick) 1939- *Who 94*
Milbank, Jeremiah 1920- *WhoAm 94*
Milbanks, Patti d1977 *WhoHol 92*
Milberg, Melinda Sharon 1953- *WhoAmL 94*
Milberg, Morton Edwin 1926- *WhoScEn 94*
Milbert, Robert P. 1949- *WhoAmP 93*
Milbert, Roger P. 1940- *WhoIns 94*
Milborne-Swinnerton-Pilkington, T. H. *Who 94*
Milbourn, Graham Maurice 1930- *Who 94*
Milbourne, Larry William 1951- *WhoBlA 94*
Milbourne, Robert John 1941- *WhoFI 94*
Milbourne, Walter Robertson 1933- *WhoAm 94, WhoAmL 94*
Milbrath, Earlon L. 1941- *WhoIns 94*
Milbrath, Mary Merrill Lemke 1940- *WhoFI 94*
Milbrath, Robert Henry *WhoAm 94*
Milbrodt, Walter Frederick 1920- *WhoAmP 93*
Milburn, Alan 1958- *Who 94*
Milburn, Anthony (Rupert) 1947- *Who 94*
Milburn, Corinne M. 1930- *WhoBlA 94*
Milburn, Darrell Edward 1959- *WhoScEn 94*
Milburn, Donald B. *Who 94*
Milburn, Herbert Theodore 1931- *WhoAm 94, WhoAmL 94, WhoAmP 93*
Milburn, Richard Henry 1928- *WhoAm 94*
Milburn, Robert (Leslie Pollington) 1907- *WrDr 94*
Milburn, Robert Leslie Pollington 1907- *Who 94*
Milbury, Thomas Giberson 1951- *WhoScEn 94*
Milcarek, William Francis 1947- *WhoScEn 94*
Milch, Harold Carlton 1908- *WhoAmA 93N*
Milchan, Arnon 1944- *IntMPA 94, WhoAm 94*
Milcheva, Alexandrina 1936- *NewGrDO*
Milcinski, Janez 1913- *IntWW 93*
Milcrest, Howard d1920 *WhoHol 92*
Milczanowski, Andrzej Stanislaw 1939- *IntWW 93*
Mild, Edward Eugene 1943- *WhoWest 94*
Milde, Hans (Feodor) von 1821-1899 *NewGrDO*
Milde-Agthe, Rosa von 1825-1906 *NewGrDO*
Mildenburg, Anna *NewGrDO*
Milder, Jay 1934- *WhoAmA 93*
Milder-Hauptmann, (Pauline) Anna 1785-1838 *NewGrDO*
Mildmay, (Grace) Audrey (Louise St. John) 1900-1953 *NewGrDO*
Mildmay, Grace Sherrington 1552-1620 *BlmGWL*
Mildon, Arthur Leonard 1923- *Who 94*
Mildon, Marie Roberta 1935- *WhoAmL 94*
Mildren, Jack 1949- *WhoAm 94, WhoAmP 93*
Mildvan, Donna 1942- *WhoAm 94*
Miledi, Ricardo 1927- *IntWW 93, Who 94, WhoAm 94*

Mileikovsky, Abram Gerasimovich 1911- *IntWW 93*
Mileikowsky, Curt 1923- *IntWW 93*
Milelzcik, Gregory Francis 1957- *WhoFI 94*
Milenski, Paul *DrAPF 93*
Miles *EncSF 93*
Miles, Albert Edward William 1912- *Who 94*
Miles, Alfred Lee 1913- *WhoFI 94, WhoMW 93*
Miles, Anthony John 1930- *Who 94*
Miles, Anthony Lawrence 1932- *WhoAmP 93*
Miles, Art d1955 *WhoHol 92*
Miles, Arthur J. 1920- *WhoAm 94*
Miles, Barry 1943- *WrDr 94*
Miles, Bernard d1991 *WhoHol 92*
Miles, Bernard 1907- *WhAm 10, WrDr 94*
Miles, Betty *DrAPF 93*
Miles, Betty 1928- *TwCYAW, WrDr 94*
Miles, Brian 1937- *Who 94*
Miles, Carlotta G. 1937- *WhoBlA 94*
Miles, Caroline Mary 1929- *Who 94*
Miles, Charlene 1928- *WhoFI 94, WhoMW 93*
Miles, Charles Gentry 1950- *WhoAmP 93, WhoFI 94*
Miles, Charles William Noel 1915- *Who 94*
Miles, Christine M. 1951- *WhoAmA 93*
Miles, Christine Marie 1951- *WhoAm 94*
Miles, Christopher 1939- *IntMPA 94*
Miles, Christopher John 1939- *Who 94*
Miles, Cyril 1918- *WhoAmA 93*
Miles, David d1915 *WhoHol 92*
Miles, Dillwyn 1916- *Who 94*
Miles, Donald F. 1949- *WhoAmL 94*
Miles, Donald Geoffrey 1952- *WhoScEn 94, WhoWest 94*
Miles, Dorothy Marie 1950- *WhoBlA 94*
Miles, Douglas Everard 1951- *WhoFI 94*
Miles, Dudley (Robert Alexander) 1947- *WrDr 94*
Miles, E. W. 1934- *WhoBlA 94*
Miles, Eddie 1940- *BasBi*
Miles, Edward Lancelot 1939- *WhoBlA 94, WhoScEn 94*
Miles, Ellen Gross 1941- *WhoAm 94, WhoAmA 93*
Miles, Elton 1917- *WrDr 94*
Miles, Frank Charles 1926- *WhoAm 94*
Miles, Frank Edward 1930- *WhoAmP 93*
Miles, Frank J. W. 1944- *WhoBlA 94*
Miles, Frederick Augustus 1928- *WhoBlA 94*
Miles, Geoffrey 1922- *Who 94*
Miles, Gordon H. 1940- *WhoFI 94*
Miles, Gwyn 1947- *Who 94*
Miles, Hamish Alexander Drummond 1925- *Who 94*
Miles, Jack 1942- *WhoAm 94*
Miles, Jackie d1968 *WhoHol 92*
Miles, Jackie Dwain 1932- *WhoFI 94*
Miles, Janice Ann 1949- *WhoAm 94*
Miles, Jeanne Patterson *WhoAm 94*
Miles, Jeanne Patterson 1908- *WhoAmA 93*
Miles, Jenefer Mary *Who 94*
Miles, Jesse Mc Lane 1932- *WhoAm 94, WhoFI 94*
Miles, Jim *WhoAm 94, WhoAmP 93*
Miles, Jim 1935- *WhoAmP 93*
Miles, Joann Joyce 1934- *WhoAmP 93*
Miles, Joanna 1940- *WhoAm 94, WhoHol 92*
Miles, John Arthur Reginald 1913- *IntWW 93*
Miles, John Bill 1931- *WhoFI 94*
Miles, John E. *WhoAmP 93*
Miles, John Edwin Alfred 1919- *Who 94*
Miles, John Frederick 1926- *WhoAm 94*
Miles, John Gregory 1949- *WhoMW 93*
Miles, John Karl 1937- *WhoAm 94*
Miles, John Richard 1944- *Who 94*
Miles, John Seeley 1931- *Who 94*
Miles, John Wilder 1920- *IntWW 93*
Miles, Keith *EncSF 93*
Miles, Kenneth L. 1937- *WhoBlA 94*
Miles, Leland 1924- *WrDr 94*
Miles, Leland Weber 1924- *WhoAm 94*
Miles, Leo Fidelis 1931- *WhoBlA 94*
Miles, Lillian 1912- *WhoHol 92*
Miles, Linda Hudson 1956- *WhoAmL 94*
Miles, Lotta d1937 *WhoHol 92*
Miles, Luther d1946 *WhoHol 92*
Miles, M. Marianne *WhoAmA 93*
Miles, MarCine Miller 1942- *WhoAmL 94, WhoWest 94*
Miles, Margaret 1911- *Who 94, WrDr 94*
Miles, Margaret Ruth 1937- *WhoAm 94*
Miles, Marjorie Mae 1922- *WhoAmP 93*
Miles, Mary Alice 1948- *WhoBlA 94*
Miles, Michael *Who 94*
Miles, (Henry) Michael (Pearson) 1936- *Who 94*
Miles, Michael Arnold 1939- *WhoAm 94, WhoFI 94*
Miles, Michael Wade 1945- *WrDr 94*
Miles, Norman Kenneth 1946- *WhoBlA 94*
Miles, Oliver *Who 94*
Miles, (Richard) Oliver 1936- *Who 94*
Miles, Paula Effette 1960- *WhoScEn 94*
Miles, Peter 1939- *WhoHol 92*
Miles, Peter (Tremayne) 1924- *Who 94*
Miles, Peter Charles H. *Who 94*
Miles, Philip Napier 1865-1935 *NewGrDO*
Miles, Rachel Jean 1945- *WhoBlA 94*
Miles, Ralph Fraley, Jr. 1933- *WhoWest 94*
Miles, Raymond Edward 1932- *WhoAm 94*
Miles, Richard 1937- *WhoAm 94*
Miles, Robert Henry 1944- *WhoAm 94*
Miles, Robert Maple 1953- *WhoAmL 94*
Miles, Roger Steele 1937- *Who 94*
Miles, Rosalind *WhoHol 92*
Miles, Roy Brian Edward 1935- *IntWW 93*
Miles, Ruby A. Branch 1941- *WhoBlA 94*
Miles, Sally d1986 *WhoHol 92*
Miles, Samuel 1740-1805 *WhAmRev*
Miles, Samuel Israel 1949- *WhoAm 94, WhoWest 94*
Miles, Sara *DrAPF 93*
Miles, Sarah 1941- *IntMPA 94, IntWW 93, WhoHol 92*
Miles, Sheila Lee 1952- *WhoAmA 93, WhoWest 94*
Miles, Sherry *WhoHol 92*
Miles, Steen 1946- *WhoBlA 94*
Miles, Stephen *Who 94*
Miles, (Frank) Stephen 1920- *Who 94*
Miles, Steven Haverstock 1950- *WhoMW 93*
Miles, Sylvia 1932- *WhoHol 92*
Miles, Sylvia 1934- *IntMPA 94*
Miles, Thomas Caswell 1952- *WhoScEn 94*
Miles, Thomas James *WhoAmP 93*
Miles, Travis Anthony 1937- *WhoAmP 93*
Miles, Vera 1929- *IntMPA 94, WhoHol 92*
Miles, Vera 1930- *WhoAm 94*
Miles, Vera M. 1932- *WhoBlA 94*
Miles, Vic 1931- *WhoBlA 94*
Miles, Virginia 1916- *WhoAm 94*
Miles, Wendell A. 1916- *WhoAm 94, WhoAmL 94, WhoMW 93*
Miles, Wendy Ann *Who 94*
Miles, William 1933- *Who 94*
Miles, William (Napier Maurice) 1913- *Who 94*
Miles, William Henry 1828-1892 *AfrAmAl 6*
Miles, William Robert 1951- *WhoScEn 94*
Miles, Willie Leanna *WhoBlA 94*
Miles-Cumbo, Kattie M. *DrAPF 93*
Miles-LaGrange, Vicki 1953 *WhoAmL 94, WhoAmP 93, WhoWomW 91*
Miles Mulvihill, Cecilia Marie 1947- *WhoHisp 94*
Milestone, Lewis d1981 *WhoHol 92*
Miletich, Ivo 1936- *WhoMW 93*
Miletti, Kathryn Louise 1951- *WhoMW 93*
Miletus, Hecataeus of *WhWE*
Miletus, Rex *ConAu 42NR*
Milewski, Barbara Anne 1934- *WhoHol 92*
Milewski, Paul Ian 1951- *WhoMW 93*
Milewski, Stanislaw Antoni 1930- *WhoScEn 94*
Miley, Chuck (Charles) E. 1943- *WhoAmA 93*
Miley, Debra Charlet 1963- *WhoBlA 94*
Miley, George Hunter 1933- *WhoAm 94, WhoScEn 94*
Miley, George Kildare 1942- *WhoScEn 94*
Miley, Hugh Howard 1902- *WhoMW 93, WhoScEn 94*
Miley, Les 1934- *WhoAmA 93*
Miley, Mimi Conneen 1946- *WhoAmA 93*
Miley, Samuel A. 1957- *WhoAm 94, WhoAmL 94*
Miley, William Maynadler 1897- *WhAm 10*
Milford, Baron 1902- *Who 94*
Milford, Frederick John 1926- *WhoAm 94*
Milford, Gene 1903-1992 *ConTFT 11*
Milford, John *WhoHol 92*
Milford, John Tillman 1946- *Who 94*
Milford, John Wharton 1950- *WhoAmP 93*
Milford, John Windsor 1945- *WhoWest 94*
Milford, Kim d1988 *WhoHol 92*
Milford, Murray Hudson 1934- *WhoAm 94*
Milford, Penelope 1949- *WhoHol 92*
Milford Haven, Marquess of 1961- *Who 94*
Milgram, Gail Gleason 1942- *WrDr 94*
Milgram, Hank 1926- *IntMPA 94*
Milgram, Jerome H. 1938- *WhoAm 94*
Milgram, Morris 1916- *WhoFI 94*
Milgrim, Darrow A. 1945- *WhoWest 94*
Milgrim, Franklin Marshall 1925- *WhoAm 94*
Milgrim, Lynn 1940- *WhoHol 92*
Milgrim, Roger M. 1937- *WhoAm 94*
Milgrom, Felix 1919- *WhoAm 94, WhoScEn 94*
Milguelito c. 1865-1936 *EncNAR*
Milhaud, Darius 1892-1974 *IntDcB, IntDcF 2-4, NewGrDO*
Milhaus, Michael F.X. *EncSF 93*
Milhaven, John Giles 1927- *WhoAm 94, WrDr 94*
Milhoan, Bessie Lucille Atzenhoefer 1916- *WhoMW 93*
Milhoan, Randall Bell 1944- *WhoAmA 93*
Milhollan, David L. *WhoAm 94*
Milhorat, Thomas Herrick 1936- *WhoAm 94, WhoScEn 94*
Milhous, Katherine 1894-1977 *WhoAmA 93N*
Milhous, Robert E. 1937- *WhoFI 94*
Milhous, Robert Thurlow 1936- *WhoScEn 94*
Milhouse, Paul William 1910- *WhoAm 94, WrDr 94*
Mili, Mohamed Ezzedine 1917- *IntWW 93*
Milián, Arsenio 1945- *WhoHisp 94*
Milian, Evarist, Jr. 1958- *WhoHisp 94*
Milian, Tomas 1938- *WhoHol 92*
Milic, Louis Tonko 1922- *WhoAm 94*
Milic-Emili, Joseph 1931- *WhoAm 94, WhoScEn 94*
Mililotti, Pasquale fl. 1755-1782 *NewGrDO*
Miliman, David Jay 1957- *WhoAmL 94*
Milingo, Emanuel 1930- *Who 94*
Milingo, Emmanuel 1930- *IntWW 93*
Milinkovic, Georgine von 1913-1986 *NewGrDO*
Miliora, Maria Teresa 1938- *WhoAm 94*
Milios, Rita 1949- *WhoMW 93*
Military, Frank *WhoHol 92*
Militello, Samuel Philip 1947- *WhoAmL 94*
Militsyna, Elizaveta Mitrofanovna 1869-1930 *BlmGWL*
Milius, John 1944- *IntMPA 94*
Milius, John Frederick 1944- *IntWW 93, WhoAm 94*
Milius, Richard A. 1950- *WhoAm 94*
Milivojevicm, Dienisije 1898- *WhAm 10*
Miljan, John d1960 *WhoHol 92*
Miljevic, Vujo Ilija 1931- *WhoScEn 94*
Milk, Harvey Bernard 1930-1978 *AmSocL [port]*
Milken, Michael R. *NewYTBS 93 [port]*
Milkey, Virginia *WhoAmP 93*
Milkina, Nina 1919- *Who 94*
Milkis, Edward 1931- *IntMPA 94*
Milkman, Marianne Friedenthal 1931- *WhoMW 93*
Milkman, Martin Irving 1960- *WhoFI 94*
Milkman, Roger Dawson 1930- *WhoAm 94, WhoMW 93, WhoScEn 94*
Milko, Jean Ann 1934- *WhoAmP 93*
Milkomane, G. A. M. *Who 94*
Milks, Michael Millard 1954- *WhoMW 93*
Mill, Arnold van 1921- *NewGrDO*
Mill, James 1773-1836 *EncEth*
Mill, John Stuart 1806-1873 *BlmGEL, EncEth*
Mill, Robert Duguid Forrest P. *Who 94*
Millage, David A. 1953- *WhoAmP 93*
Millage, Mark Richard 1963- *WhoMW 93*
Milla Gravalos, Emilio 1944- *WhoScEn 94*
Millais, Geoffroy Richard Everett 1941- *Who 94*
Millais, Raoul 1901- *SmATA 77*
Millais-Scott, Imogen *WhoHol 92*
Millán, Angel, Jr. 1945- *WhoHisp 94*
Millan, Bruce 1927- *IntWW 93, Who 94*
Millan, Bruce E. *WhoMW 93*
Millán, Natacha 1936- *WhoHisp 94*
Millan, Pauline Perry d1985 *WhoHol 92*
Millan, Rafael 1893-1938 *NewGrDO*
Millan, Victor 1925- *WhoHol 92*
Milland, Ray d1986 *WhoHol 92*
Millane, John Vaughan, Jr. 1926- *WhoAmL 94*
Millane, Lynn 1928- *WhoAm 94*
Millar *Who 94*
Millar, Adelqui d1956 *WhoHol 92*
Millar, Anthony Bruce 1941- *Who 94*
Millar, Betty Phyllis Joy 1929- *Who 94*
Millar, Douglas George 1946- *Who 94*
Millar, Fergus Graham Burtholme 1935- *IntWW 93, Who 94*
Millar, George 1910- *WrDr 94*
Millar, George Reid 1910- *Who 94*
Millar, Gordon Halstead 1923- *WhoAm 94*
Millar, Ian Alastair D. *Who 94*
Millar, James Robert 1936- *WhoAm 94*
Millar, Jeffery Lynn 1942- *WhoAm 94*
Millar, John Donald 1934- *WhoAm 94*
Millar, John Francis 1936- *WhoAm 94, WhoFI 94*
Millar, John Stanley 1925- *Who 94*
Millar, Kenneth Irwin 1947- *WhoAm 94*
Millar, Lee d1941 *WhoHol 92*
Millar, Lee d1980 *WhoHol 92*
Millar, Margaret (Ellis) 1915- *WrDr 94*
Millar, Margaret Ellis 1915- *WhoAm 94*
Millar, Marjie d1966 *WhoHol 92*
Millar, Oliver (Nicholas) 1923- *ConAu 142, WrDr 94*
Millar, Oliver Nicholas 1923- *IntWW 93, Who 94*
Millar, Peter Carmichael 1927- *Who 94*
Millar, Raymond Irving 1930- *WhoAmP 93*
Millar, Richard William 1899-1990 *WhAm 10*
Millar, Richard William, Jr. 1938- *WhoAm 94, WhoAmL 94, WhoWest 94*
Millar, Robert 1958- *WhoAmA 93*
Millar, Ronald (Graeme) 1919- *ConDr 93, Who 94, WrDr 94*
Millar, Sally Gray 1946- *WhoAm 94*
Millar, Stuart 1929- *IntMPA 94*
Millar, Victor E. 1935- *WhoAm 94, WhoFI 94*
Millar, William Malcolm 1913- *Who 94*
Millard, Alan Ralph 1937- *WrDr 94*
Millard, Andre 1947- *WrDr 94*
Millard, Charles 1957- *WhoAmP 93*
Millard, Charles E., Jr. 1945- *WhoAmP 93*
Millard, Charles Phillip 1948- *WhoMW 93*
Millard, Charles Warren, III 1932- *WhoAm 94, WhoAmA 93*
Millard, David Ralph, Jr. 1919- *WhoAm 94*
Millard, Edward d1963 *WhoHol 92*
Millard, Elizabeth Sanborn 1944- *WhoAmP 93*
Millard, Esther Lound 1909- *WhoFI 94, WhoWest 94*
Millard, Evelyn d1941 *WhoHol 92*
Millard, George Richard 1914- *WhoWest 94*
Millard, Guy (Elwin) 1917- *Who 94*
Millard, Guy Elwin 1917- *IntWW 93*
Millard, Harry d1969 *WhoHol 92*
Millard, Helene 1906- *WhoHol 92*
Millard, Herbert Charles 1938- *WhoAmP 93*
Millard, James Kemper 1948- *WhoFI 94*
Millard, John Alden 1940- *WhoAm 94, WhoAmL 94*
Millard, Joseph (John) 1908- *EncSF 93*
Millard, Malcolm Stuart 1914- *WhoWest 94*
Millard, Naomi Adeline Helen 1914- *IntWW 93*
Millard, Neal Steven 1947- *WhoAm 94, WhoAmL 94, WhoWest 94*
Millard, Peter Tudor 1932- *WhoAm 94*
Millard, Raymond Spencer 1920- *Who 94*
Millard, Richard Steven 1952- *WhoAm 94*
Millard, Ronald Wesley 1941- *WhoMW 93*
Millard, Thomas Lewis 1927- *WhoBlA 94*
Millarde, Harry d1931 *WhoHol 92*
Millay, E. Vincent *GayLL*
Millay, Edna St. Vincent 1892-1950 *AmCulL, GayLL, TwCLC 49 [port]*
Millay, Edna St Vincent 1892-1950 *BlmGWL*
Millberg, John C. 1956- *WhoAmL 94*
Mille, Agnes de *IntDcB*
Mille, Herve d1993 *IntWW 93N*
Millea, Tom 1944- *WhoAmA 93*
Milledge, Luetta Upshur *WhoBlA 94*
Millen, Anthony Tristram Patrick 1928- *Who 94*
Millen, Frank d1931 *WhoHol 92*
Millen, Matt G. 1958- *WhoBlA 94*
Millen, Olive *WhoHol 92*
Millender, Dharathula H. 1920- *WhoBlA 94*
Millender, Mallory Kimerling 1942- *WhoBlA 94*
Millenson, Roy Handen 1921- *WhoAmP 93*
Miller *Who 94*
Miller, A. Edward 1918-1991 *WhAm 10*
Miller, A. McA. *DrAPF 93*
Miller, Abraham (H.) 1940- *WrDr 94*
Miller, Adam David *DrAPF 93*
Miller, Alan 1954- *WhoFI 94, WhoScEn 94*
Miller, Alan B. 1937- *WhoAm 94, WhoFI 94*
Miller, Alan Gershon 1931- *WhoAm 94*
Miller, Alan Jay 1936- *WhoAm 94*
Miller, Alan John McCulloch 1914- *Who 94*

Miller, Alan Robert 1939- *WhoAm 94, WhoAmL 94*
Miller, Alan Scott 1942- *WhoMW 93*
Miller, Alan Stanley 1949- *WhoAmL 94*
Miller, Alan Stuart 1956- *WhoAmL 94*
Miller, Alastair Cheape 1912- *Who 94*
Miller, Albert Jay 1927- *WhoAm 94*
Miller, Alexander Ronald 1915- *Who 94*
Miller, Alexandra Cecile 1959- *WhoScEn 94*
Miller, Alfred Jacob 1810-1874 *WhWE*
Miller, Alice *ConAu 142*
Miller, Alice Duer d1942 *WhoHol 92*
Miller, Alice M. *WhoAmP 93*
Miller, Alice Ruth 1939- *WhoMW 93*
Miller, Alison W. 1952- *WhoAmL 94*
Miller, Allan *WhoHol 92*
Miller, Allan John 1921- *WhoAm 94*
Miller, Allen Richard *WhoScEn 94*
Miller, Allen Terry, Jr. 1954- *WhoAmL 94*
Miller, Amelia *Who 94*
Miller, Andrea Lewis 1954- *WhoBlA 94*
Miller, Andrew 1936- *IntWW 93*
Miller, Andrew Lawrence 1956- *WhoAmL 94*
Miller, Andrew Peter 1949- *Who 94*
Miller, Andrew Pickens 1932- *WhoAm 94, WhoAmP 93*
Miller, Angela L. 1953- *WhoMW 93*
Miller, Angela Perez 1936- *WhoHisp 94*
Miller, Anita 1931- *WhoAmP 93*
Miller, Anita Hadassah 1938- *WhoWest 94*
Miller, Anita P. *WhoAmL 94*
Miller, Ann *WhoAm 94*
Miller, Ann 1919- *IntMPA 94*
Miller, Ann 1923- *WhoHol 92*
Miller, Ann G. 1944- *WhoAmL 94*
Miller, Anna M. 1923- *WhoBlA 94*
Miller, Anne 1741-1781 *BlmGWL*
Miller, Anne Kathleen 1942- *WhoWest 94*
Miller, Annmarie *WhoHisp 94*
Miller, Anthony 1942- *WhoAm 94, WhoFI 94*
Miller, Anthony 1965- *WhoBlA 94*
Miller, Anthony Bernard 1931- *WhoAm 94*
Miller, Arjay 1916- *IntWW 93, Who 94, WhoAm 94, WhoWest 94*
Miller, Arlyn James 1940- *WhoAm 94*
Miller, Arnold 1928- *WhoAm 94*
Miller, Arnold 1931- *WhoMW 93*
Miller, Arnold Joseph, Jr. 1957- *WhoWest 94*
Miller, Arthur *DrAPF 93*
Miller, Arthur 1915- *AmCulL, ConDr 93, ConLC 78 [port], ConTFT 11, IntDcT 2 [port], IntMPA 94, IntWW 93, NewGrDO, Who 94, WhoAm 94, WrDr 94*
Miller, Arthur C. 1895-1970 *IntDcF 2-4*
Miller, Arthur Dusty 1952- *WhoWest 94*
Miller, Arthur Green 1942- *WhoAmA 93*
Miller, Arthur Hawks, Jr. 1943- *WhoAm 94, WhoMW 93*
Miller, Arthur Herbert 1942- *WhoMW 93*
Miller, Arthur J. 1934- *WhoBlA 94*
Miller, Arthur J., Jr. 1946- *WhoAmP 93*
Miller, Arthur Leonard 1907- *WhoAm 94*
Miller, Arthur Raphael 1934- *WhoAm 94, WhoAmL 94*
Miller, Arthur Robert 1950- *WhoAm 94, WhoAmL 94, WhoMW 93*
Miller, Ashley d1948 *WhoHol 92*
Miller, Baila Hannah 1940- *WhoMW 93*
Miller, Barbara d1990 *WhoHol 92*
Miller, Barbara Darlene *WhoAmA 93, WhoWest 94*
Miller, Barbara Rogalle 1939- *WhoAmP 93*
Miller, Barbara S(toler) 1940-1993 *ConAu 141*
Miller, Barbara Stallcup 1919- *WhoWest 94*
Miller, Barbara Stoler *WhoAm 94*
Miller, Barry 1942- *Who 94, WhoAm 94*
Miller, Barry 1958- *IntMPA 94, WhoHol 92*
Miller, Barry Alan 1955- *WhoScEn 94*
Miller, Barry Rixmann 1945- *WhoAm 94*
Miller, Barse 1924-1973 *WhoAmA 93N*
Miller, Becky Lynn 1958- *WhoMW 93*
Miller, Ben Neely 1910- *WhoAm 94*
Miller, Benjamin *EncSF 93*
Miller, Benjamin K. 1936- *WhoAm 94, WhoAmL 94, WhoAmP 93, WhoMW 93*
Miller, Benjamin T. 1934- *WhoBlA 94*
Miller, Bennett 1938- *WhoAm 94*
Miller, Bernard *Who 94*
Miller, (Oswald) Bernard 1904- *Who 94*
Miller, Bernard Joseph, Jr. 1925- *WhoAm 94*
Miller, Bernice Johnson *WhoBlA 94*
Miller, Berns 1946- *WhoAmP 93*
Miller, Bertin 1936- *WhoMW 93*
Miller, Bertram Jack 1945- *WhoAm 94*
Miller, Beth 1941- *WhoAm 94, WrDr 94*
Miller, Betty *WhoHol 92*
Miller, Betty 1928- *WhoAmP 93*
Miller, Betty G. 1918- *WhoAmP 93*
Miller, Betty Jean 1958- *WhoAm 94*
Miller, Beverly G. 1951- *WhoAmL 94*
Miller, Beverly White *WhoAm 94*
Miller, Bill *DrAPF 93*
Miller, Bill 1933- *WhoWest 94*
Miller, Blair D. 1926- *WhoMW 93*
Miller, Bob H. 1953- *WhoMW 93*
Miller, Bonnie Sewell 1932- *WhoFI 94*
Miller, Brad Steven 1953- *WhoWest 94*
Miller, Bradley Lee 1937- *WhoWest 94*
Miller, Brenda *WhoAmA 93*
Miller, Brenda Kay 1965- *WhoMW 93*
Miller, Brown *DrAPF 93*
Miller, Bruce *Who 94*
Miller, Bruce A. 1927- *WhoAmP 93*
Miller, Bruce Abraham 1927- *WhoAmL 94*
Miller, Bruce Douglas 1958- *WhoMW 93*
Miller, Bruce Neil 1941- *WhoScEn 94*
Miller, Bruce Paul 1959- *WhoFI 94*
Miller, Burr 1904-1958 *WhoAmA 93N*
Miller, Burton Leibsle 1944- *WhoWest 94*
Miller, Buzz 1928- *WhoHol 92*
Miller, Byron Edward 1944- *WhoFI 94*
Miller, C. Arden 1924- *IntWW 93, WhoAm 94*
Miller, C. Conrad, Jr. 1950- *WhoBlA 94*
Miller, Callix Edwin 1924- *WhoMW 93*
Miller, Cameron *Who 94*
Miller, (Alan) Cameron 1913- *Who 94*
Miller, Carl d1979 *WhoHol 92*
Miller, Carl Duane 1941- *WhoWest 94*
Miller, Carl George 1942- *WhoAm 94*
Miller, Carl Jeffrey 1950- *WhoFI 94*
Miller, Carl Patterson, Sr. 1897- *WhAm 10*
Miller, Carlos Oakley 1923- *WhoAm 94*
Miller, Carole Ann 1942- *WhoAmP 93*
Miller, Carole Ann Lyons *WhoWest 94*
Miller, Caroll S. 1926- *WhoAmP 93*
Miller, Carroll Gerard, Jr. 1944- *WhoAmL 94*
Miller, Carroll Lee 1909- *WhoBlA 94*
Miller, Carroll Lee Liverpool 1909- *WhoAm 94*
Miller, Cary W. 1948- *WhoAmL 94*
Miller, Cate 1964- *WhoScEn 94*
Miller, Charles d1955 *WhoHol 92*
Miller, Charles 1959- *WhoMW 93*
Miller, Charles A 1937- *WrDr 94*
Miller, Charles Daly 1928- *WhoAm 94, WhoFI 94, WhoWest 94*
Miller, Charles E. 1944- *WhoAmL 94*
Miller, Charles Edmond 1938- *WhoAm 94*
Miller, Charles Edward, Jr. 1950- *WhoAm 94*
Miller, Charles Eldon 1953- *WhoMW 93*
Miller, Charles Erich 1941- *WhoAmL 94*
Miller, Charles Gregory 1960- *WhoScEn 94*
Miller, Charles Hampton 1928- *WhoAm 94*
Miller, Charles Leo, Jr. 1959- *WhoAmL 94*
Miller, Charles Leslie 1929- *WhoAm 94*
Miller, Charles Maurice 1948- *WhoAmL 94*
Miller, Charles P. 1918- *WhoAmP 93*
Miller, Charles T. 1948- *WhoAmL 94*
Miller, Charles William 1922- *WhoAm 94*
Miller, Cheryl 1943- *IntMPA 94, WhoHol 92*
Miller, Cheryl 1964- *BasBi [port]*
Miller, Cheryl De Ann 1964- *WhoBlA 94*
Miller, Cheryl Denise 1958- *WhoBlA 94*
Miller, Christopher James 1965- *WhoAm 94*
Miller, Chuck *DrAPF 93, EncSF 93*
Miller, Clara Burr 1912- *WhoWest 94*
Miller, Clarence 1922- *WhoHol 92*
Miller, Clarence E. 1917- *WhoAmP 93*
Miller, Clarence Terrell 1959- *WhoAmL 94*
Miller, Clark Alvin 1934- *WhoFI 94*
Miller, Cleaveland 1938- *WhoAm 94*
Miller, Cliff 1958- *WhoScEn 94*
Miller, Clifford Albert 1928- *WhoAm 94, WhoFI 94, WhoWest 94*
Miller, Clifford Joel 1947- *WhoAmL 94, WhoWest 94*
Miller, Clinton 1939- *WhoAmP 93*
Miller, Colin Brown 1946- *Who 94*
Miller, Colleen 1932- *WhoHol 92*
Miller, Constance Joan 1945- *WhoBlA 94*
Miller, Corbin Russell 1948- *WhoFI 94*
Miller, Court d1986 *WhoHol 92*
Miller, Craig *WhoAm 94*
Miller, Craig A. 1944- *WhoAmL 94*
Miller, Craig Johnson 1950- *WhoAm 94*
Miller, Curtis Herman 1947- *WhoMW 93*
Miller, D. Michael 1947- *WhoAmL 94*
Miller, Dale Andrew 1949- *WhoAmP 93*
Miller, Dan *WhoAmP 93*
Miller, Dan 1942- *CngDr 93*
Miller, Dan 1943- *WhoAm 94*
Miller, Daniel Dawson 1928- *WhoAmA 93*
Miller, Daniel Harlan 1960- *WhoAmL 94*
Miller, Daniel James 1958- *WhoWest 94*
Miller, Daniel Newton, Jr. 1924- *WhoAm 94, WhoScEn 94*
Miller, Dave 1966- *WhoMW 93*
Miller, David d1933 *WhoHol 92*
Miller, David 1906- *WhoAm 94*
Miller, David (Leslie) 1946- *WrDr 94*
Miller, David Andrew Barclay 1954- *WhoAm 94*
Miller, David Anthony 1946- *WhoAmL 94*
Miller, David B. 1953- *WhoAmL 94*
Miller, David Benedict 1909- *WhoAmP 93*
Miller, David E. 1945- *WhoAmP 93*
Miller, David Edmond 1930- *WhoScEn 94*
Miller, David Edwin 1931- *Who 94*
Miller, David Emanuel 1943- *WhoAm 94*
Miller, David Eugene 1926- *WhoAm 94*
Miller, David Foster 1940- *WhoWest 94*
Miller, David G. 1949- *WhoAmP 93*
Miller, David Harry 1939- *WhoMW 93*
Miller, David Hewitt 1918- *WhoAm 94*
Miller, David Jergen 1933- *WhoAm 94*
Miller, David Keith 1935- *WhoMW 93*
Miller, David Kent 1963- *WhoMW 93*
Miller, David L. 1941- *WhoAmL 94*
Miller, David L. 1947- *WhoIns 94*
Miller, David Louis 1930- *Who 94*
Miller, David Philip 1921- *WhAm 10*
Miller, David Powell 1942- *WhoAmL 94*
Miller, David Quentin 1936- *Who 94*
Miller, David R. 1954- *WhoAmP 93*
Miller, David Sigsbee 1957- *WhoAmL 94*
Miller, David W. 1950- *WhoAm 94*
Miller, David W. 1956- *WhoWest 94*
Miller, David Wayne 1949- *WhoWest 94*
Miller, David William 1940- *WhoAm 94*
Miller, David William 1959- *WhoScEn 94*
Miller, Dawn Marie 1963- *WhoFI 94, WhoScEn 94*
Miller, Dean 1927- *WhoHol 92*
Miller, Dean Arthur 1931- *WhoAm 94*
Miller, Dean R. *WhoHol 92*
Miller, Deane Guynes 1927- *WhoFI 94*
Miller, Debbie (S.) 1951- *WrDr 94*
Miller, Deborah *DrAPF 93*
Miller, Deborah Ann 1949- *WhoFI 94*
Miller, Deborah Jean 1951- *WhoFI 94, WhoMW 93*
Miller, Deborah Rogers 1954- *WhoMW 93*
Miller, Decatur Howard 1932- *WhoAm 94*
Miller, Delbert Dwight 1943- *WhoAm 94*
Miller, Dennis *WhoHol 92*
Miller, Dennis 1953- *WhoAm 94, WhoCom*
Miller, Dennis Dixon 1950- *WhoFI 94, WhoMW 93, WhoScEn 94*
Miller, Dennis Edward 1951- *WhoAm 94*
Miller, Dennis Weldon 1949- *WhoBlA 94*
Miller, Denny 1934- *WhoHol 92*
Miller, Denny Marvin 1939- *WhoAmP 93*
Miller, Dexter J., Jr. 1934- *WhoBlA 94*
Miller, Diana d1927 *WhoHol 92*
Miller, Diane Wilmarth 1940- *WhoWest 94*
Miller, Dick 1928- *IntMPA 94, WhoHol 92*
Miller, Dixon Fullerton 1948- *WhoAm 94*
Miller, Dodd *WhoAm 94*
Miller, Dolly (Ethel B.) 1927- *WhoAmA 93*
Miller, Don J. 1937- *WhoAmP 93*
Miller, Don K. 1935- *WhoIns 94*
Miller, Don Robert 1925- *WhoAm 94*
Miller, Don Wilson 1942- *WhoAm 94, WhoScEn 94*
Miller, Donald 1934- *WhoAmA 93*
Miller, Donald (John) 1927- *Who 94*
Miller, Donald B. 1946- *WhoAmL 94*
Miller, Donald Baldwin 1926- *WhoAm 94*
Miller, Donald C. *Who 94*
Miller, Donald Edward 1940- *WhoMW 93*
Miller, Donald Edward 1945- *WhoFI 94*
Miller, Donald Eugene 1947- *WhoAm 94*
Miller, Donald Frederick 1961- *WhoMW 93*
Miller, Donald George 1909- *WrDr 94*
Miller, Donald Keith 1932- *WhoAm 94, WhoFI 94*
Miller, Donald Kenneth 1925- *WhoScEn 94*
Miller, Donald LeSessne 1932- *WhoAm 94, WhoBlA 94*
Miller, Donald Lloyd d1993 *NewYTBS 93*
Miller, Donald Lloyd 1923- *WhoAmA 93*
Miller, Donald Morton 1930- *WhoAm 94*
Miller, Donald Muxlow 1924- *WhoMW 93*
Miller, Donald Richard 1925-1989 *WhAm 10, WhoAmA 93N*
Miller, Donald Ross 1927- *WhoAm 94, WhoFI 94*
Miller, Donald Sidney 1908-1989 *WhAm 10*
Miller, Donald Spencer 1932- *WhoAm 94, WhoScEn 94*
Miller, Donn Biddle 1929- *WhoAm 94*
Miller, Dorie 1919-1943 *AfrAmAl 6 [port]*
Miller, Doris Jean 1933- *WhoBlA 94*
Miller, Dorsey Columbus, Jr. 1943- *WhoBlA 94*
Miller, Douglas *Who 94*
Miller, (Ian) Douglas 1900- *Who 94*
Miller, Douglas (Sinclair) 1906- *Who 94*
Miller, Douglas Alan 1961- *WhoScEn 94*
Miller, Douglas L. 1950- *WhoAmL 94*
Miller, Douglas Lee 1942- *WhoAmP 93*
Miller, Douglas T 1937- *WrDr 94*
Miller, Duane King 1931- *WhoAm 94*
Miller, Duane L. 1937- *WhoIns 94*
Miller, Duane Leon 1937- *WhoAm 94*
Miller, Dusty Campbell 1920- *WhoFI 94, WhoWest 94*
Miller, Dwight Richard 1943- *WhoAm 94, WhoFI 94, WhoMW 93*
Miller, E. Ethelbert *DrAPF 93*
Miller, E. Ethelbert 1950- *WhoBlA 94*
Miller, E(ugene) Ethelbert 1950- *BlkWr 2, WrDr 94*
Miller, E. Willard 1915- *WhoAm 94*
Miller, Earl Lewis 1925- *WhoAmP 93*
Miller, Earl Vonnidore 1923- *WhoBlA 94*
Miller, Eddie *WhoHol 92*
Miller, Eddie d1971 *WhoHol 92*
Miller, Eddie LeRoy 1937- *WhoWest 94*
Miller, Edith *WhoBlA 94*
Miller, Edith Joan 1923- *WhoMW 93*
Miller, Edmond Trowbridge 1933- *WhoAm 94*
Miller, Edmund *DrAPF 93*
Miller, Edmund Kenneth 1935- *WhoAm 94, WhoWest 94*
Miller, Edward 1915- *Who 94*
Miller, Edward 1930- *Who 94*
Miller, Edward Albert 1931- *WhoAm 94*
Miller, Edward B. 1922- *WhoAm 94*
Miller, Edward Boone 1922- *WhoAmP 93*
Miller, Edward Daniel 1940- *WhoAm 94, WhoFI 94*
Miller, Edward David 1934- *WhoAm 94*
Miller, Edward Doring, Jr. 1943- *WhoAm 94*
Miller, Edward Lyle 1928- *WhoAmP 93*
Miller, Edward Percival 1924- *WhoAm 94*
Miller, Edward William 1897- *WhAm 10*
Miller, Edwin d1980 *WhoHol 92*
Miller, Edwin Louis 1955- *WhoFI 94*
Miller, Elaine Sandra *WhoAmA 93*
Miller, Eldon Earl 1919- *WhoAm 94*
Miller, Eleanora *DrAPF 93*
Miller, Eleanora Genevieve 1916- *WhoMW 93*
Miller, Elizabeth Rodriguez 1954- *WhoHisp 94*
Miller, Elliott Cairns 1934- *WhoAm 94*
Miller, Elmon A., Jr. *WhoAmP 93*
Miller, Emanuel 1917- *WhoAm 94, WhoAmL 94*
Miller, Emerson Waldo 1920- *WhoFI 94*
Miller, Emilie Feiza 1936- *WhoAmP 93*
Miller, Emmett Emmanuel *WhoWest 94*
Miller, Erenest Eugene 1948- *WhoBlA 94*
Miller, Eric Raymond 1943- *WhoAm 94, WhoAmL 94*
Miller, Erica A. 1963- *WhoMW 93*
Miller, Ernest Charles 1925- *WhoAm 94*
Miller, Ervin Dean 1939- *WhoAmP 93*
Miller, Esther Scobie Powers 1929- *WhoMW 93*
Miller, Ethel Jackson 1916- *WhoBlA 94*
Miller, Eugene 1925- *WhoAm 94, WhoFI 94, WhoMW 93*
Miller, Eugene 1928- *WhoAmP 93*
Miller, Eugene Albert *WhoAm 94, WhoMW 93*
Miller, Eugene E. 1930- *WrDr 94*
Miller, Eugene Ernest 1930- *WhoMW 93*
Miller, Eugene H. 1947- *WhoAmL 94*
Miller, Eugene Milo 1937- *WhoMW 93*
Miller, Evan 1956- *WhoAmL 94*
Miller, Evelyn B. *WhoBlA 94*
Miller, Everett George, Sr. 1921- *WhoAm 94*
Miller, Ewing Harry 1923- *WhoAm 94*
Miller, F. John 1929- *WhoAmA 93*
Miller, Florence Fenwick 1854-1935 *DcNaB MP*
Miller, Flournoy d1971 *WhoHol 92*
Miller, Flournoy E. 1887-1971 *See* Miller and Lyles *WhoCom*
Miller, Frances A. 1937- *TwCYAW, WrDr 94*
Miller, Frank *WhoAmP 93*
Miller, Frank d1933 *WhoHol 92*
Miller, Frank 1927- *IntWW 93*
Miller, Frank 1957- *EncSF 93*
Miller, Frank L., Jr. 1944- *WhoAm 94*

Miller, Frank Lee, Jr. 1944- *AfrAmG [port], WhoBlA 94*
Miller, Frank Levi 1910- *WhoAmP 93*
Miller, Frank Robert 1908- *Who 94*
Miller, Frank William 1921- *WhoAm 94*
Miller, Frank William 1953- *WhoAmL 94*
Miller, Franklin Emrick 1946- *WhoWest 94*
Miller, Franklin Rush 1902- *WhoMW 93*
Miller, Fred *WhoHol 92*
Miller, Frederick 1937- *WhoAm 94*
Miller, Frederick A. 1946- *WhoBlA 94*
Miller, Frederick E. 1931- *WhoBlA 94*
Miller, Frederick G. *WhoAmL 94*
Miller, Frederick Powell 1936- *WhoAm 94*
Miller, Frederick Robeson 1927- *WhoAm 94*
Miller, Frederick Staten 1930- *WhoAm 94*
Miller, Frederick Walter Gascoyne 1904- *WrDr 94*
Miller, Frederick William 1912- *WhoAm 94, WhoMW 93*
Miller, G. Kent 1951- *WhoIns 94*
Miller, G. William 1925- *IntWW 93*
Miller, G(eorge) William 1925- *Who 94*
Miller, Gabriel Lorimer 1928- *WhoAm 94*
Miller, Gale Timothy 1946- *WhoAm 94, WhoAmL 94*
Miller, Garfield Lankard, III 1950- *WhoAm 94*
Miller, Gary Allen 1960- *WhoMW 93*
Miller, Gary David 1960- *WhoFI 94*
Miller, Gary Evan 1935- *WhoAm 94*
Miller, Gary J. 1949- *WhoAm 94*
Miller, Gary W. 1940- *WhoIns 94*
Miller, Gavin 1926- *WhoAm 94, WhoAmL 94*
Miller, Gay Davis 1947- *WhoAmL 94*
Miller, Gene Edward 1928- *WhoAm 94*
Miller, Genevieve 1914- *WhoAm 94, WhoMW 93*
Miller, George *WhoAm 94, WhoAmP 93, WhoWest 94*
Miller, George 1945- *CngDr 93, IntMPA 94, IntWW 93, WhoAm 94, WhoAmP 93, WhoWest 94*
Miller, George 1948- *EncSF 93*
Miller, George A. 1920- *IntWW 93*
Miller, George Armitage 1920- *WhoAm 94, WhoScEn 94*
Miller, George Carroll, Jr. 1949- *WhoBlA 94*
Miller, George David 1930- *WhoAm 94*
Miller, George DeWitt, Jr. 1928- *WhoAmL 94*
Miller, George H. 1919- *WhoAm 94*
Miller, George McCord 1919- *WhoScEn 94*
Miller, George N., Jr. 1951- *WhoBlA 94*
Miller, George Roland 1894- *WhAm 10*
Miller, George W., Jr. 1930- *WhoAmP 93*
Miller, George William 1925- *WhoAm 94, WhoFI 94*
Miller, Gerald Foster 1941- *WhoAmL 94*
Miller, Gerald H. 1941- *WhoIns 94*
Miller, Gerald Raymond 1931- *WhoAm 94*
Miller, Gerri 1954- *WhoAm 94*
Miller, Gifford Hubbs 1946- *WhoAm 94*
Miller, Gilbert Neal 1941- *WhoFI 94*
Miller, Gladys 1896- *WhAm 10*
Miller, Glenn d1944 *WhoHol 92*
Miller, Glenn 1937- *WhoAm 94*
Miller, Gloria Jean 1943- *WhoMW 93*
Miller, Gordon d1962 *WhoHol 92*
Miller, Gordon Holman 1916- *WhoWest 94*
Miller, Gordon K. 1949- *WhoAmL 94*
Miller, Gray H. 1948- *WhoAmL 94*
Miller, Gregory Keith 1957- *WhoAmL 94*
Miller, Gregory M. 1961- *WhoWest 94*
Miller, Gregory R. *WhoAmL 94*
Miller, (Richard) Guy *WhoAmA 93*
Miller, H. Keith 1940- *WhoAmL 94*
Miller, H. Todd 1947- *WhoAm 94, WhoAmL 94*
Miller, Hainon A. 1930- *WhoAmP 93*
Miller, Hallie Joan 1965- *WhoAmL 94*
Miller, Harbaugh 1902- *WhoAm 94*
Miller, Harold d1972 *WhoHol 92*
Miller, Harold Arthur 1922- *WhoAmL 94*
Miller, Harold Edward 1926- *WhoAm 94*
Miller, Harold F. 1897- *WhAm 10*
Miller, Harold Joseph 1923- *WhoAm 94*
Miller, Harold Joseph, Jr. 1938- *WhoAmP 93*
Miller, Harold T. 1923- *IntWW 93*
Miller, Harold William 1920- *WhoScEn 94, WhoWest 94*
Miller, Harriet Evelyn 1919- *WhoWest 94*
Miller, Harris N. 1951- *WhoAmP 93*
Miller, Harry Benjamin 1924- *WhoAmL 94*
Miller, Harry Charles, Jr. 1928- *WhoAm 94*
Miller, Harry George 1941- *WhoAm 94*
Miller, Harry Johnson 1926- *WhoMW 93*
Miller, Hartman Cyril, Jr. 1948- *WhoScEn 94*
Miller, Harvey Alan *WhoHol 92*
Miller, Harvey Alfred 1928- *WhoAm 94, WhoScEn 94*
Miller, Harvey R. 1933- *WhoAm 94*
Miller, Harvey S. Shipley 1948- *WhoAm 94*
Miller, Hasbrouck Bailey 1923- *WhoAm 94*
Miller, Heather Ross *DrAPF 93*
Miller, Helen Hill 1899- *WrDr 94*
Miller, Helen Marie Dillen *WhoMW 93*
Miller, Helen Pendleton 1888-1957 *WhoAmA 93N*
Miller, Helen S. 1917- *WhoBlA 94*
Miller, Henry d1980 *WhoHol 92*
Miller, Henry B., Jr. 1940- *WhoBlA 94*
Miller, Henry Forster 1916- *WhoAm 94*
Miller, Henry Franklin 1938- *WhoAm 94, WhoAmL 94*
Miller, Henry George 1913-1976 *DcNaB MP*
Miller, Henry Valentine 1891-1980 *AmCulL*
Miller, Herbert Dell 1919- *WhoFI 94, WhoScEn 94*
Miller, Herbert Elmer 1914- *WhoAm 94*
Miller, Herbert John 1894- *WhAm 10*
Miller, Herbert John, Jr. 1924- *WhoAm 94*
Miller, Herbert Samuel 1943- *WhoAm 94*
Miller, Herman 1919- *WhoAm 94*
Miller, Herman Lunden 1924- *WhoScEn 94*
Miller, Hilary Duppa 1929- *Who 94*
Miller, Hope Ridings *WhoAm 94*
Miller, Horatio C. 1949- *WhoBlA 94*
Miller, Horrie, Mrs. *Who 94*
Miller, Howard G. 1955- *WhoAmP 93*
Miller, Howard M. 1929- *WhoBlA 94*
Miller, Howard S. 1943- *WhoMW 93*
Miller, Hugh d1976 *WhoHol 92*
Miller, Hugh 1937- *WrDr 94*
Miller, Hugh J. d1956 *WhoHol 92*
Miller, Hugh Thomas 1951- *WhoFI 94, WhoMW 93, WhoScEn 94*
Miller, Hyman M. *WhoAmP 93*
Miller, I. George 1937- *WhoAm 94*
Miller, Ian 1946- *EncSF 93*
Miller, Ian 1952- *WrDr 94*
Miller, Ian Reed 1962- *WhoFI 94*
Miller, Inge Morath *WhoAmA 93*
Miller, Ira *WhoHol 92*
Miller, Iris Ann 1938- *WhoAm 94*
Miller, Irving Franklin 1934- *WhoAm 94*
Miller, Isaac H., Jr. 1920- *WhoBlA 94*
Miller, Isabel *GayLL*
Miller, Isabelle d1957 *WhoHol 92*
Miller, Israel 1918- *WhoAm 94*
Miller, Ivan d1967 *WhoHol 92*
Miller, Ivan Lawrence 1914- *WhoAm 94*
Miller, J(ohn) D(onald) Bruce 1922- *Who 94, WrDr 94*
Miller, J. Gregg 1944- *WhoAmL 94*
Miller, J(oseph) Hillis 1928- *WrDr 94*
Miller, J. J. 1947- *WhoIns 94*
Miller, J. Philip 1937- *WhoAm 94*
Miller, J. Sturgis 1923- *WhoAmP 93*
Miller, Jack d1928 *WhoHol 92*
Miller, Jack d1941 *WhoHol 92*
Miller, Jack David 1945- *WhoIns 94*
Miller, Jack David R. 1930- *WhoAm 94*
Miller, Jack Everett 1921- *WhoAmL 94*
Miller, Jack R. 1916- *CngDr 93*
Miller, Jack Richard 1916- *WhoAm 94, WhoAmL 94*
Miller, Jacqueline Elizabeth 1935- *WhoBlA 94*
Miller, Jacqueline Winslow 1935- *WhoAm 94*
Miller, Jacques Francis 1931- *IntWW 93*
Miller, Jacques Francis Albert Pierre 1931- *Who 94*
Miller, Jake C. 1929- *WhoBlA 94*
Miller, James *WhoBlA 94*
Miller, James 1934- *Who 94, WhoAm 94*
Miller, James, Sr. 1944- *WhoBlA 94*
Miller, James Alexander 1915- *WhoAm 94*
Miller, James Arthur 1944- *WhoBlA 94*
Miller, James C., III *WhoAmP 93*
Miller, James Christopher 1951- *WhoFI 94*
Miller, James Clifford, III 1942- *IntWW 93, WhoAm 94, WhoFI 94*
Miller, James Davis *WhoFI 94*
Miller, James E. 1927- *WhoAmP 93*
Miller, James Edward 1940- *WhoScEn 94*
Miller, James Edward 1942- *WhoMW 93*
Miller, James Edward 1945- *WrDr 94*
Miller, James Edwin, (Jr.) 1920- *WrDr 94*
Miller, James Edwin, Jr. 1920- *WhoAm 94*
Miller, James Eugene 1946- *WhoMW 93*
Miller, James Frederick 1943- *WhoScEn 94*
Miller, James Gegan 1942- *WhoAm 94*
Miller, James Gormly 1914- *WhoAm 94*
Miller, James Hugh, Jr. 1922- *WhoAm 94*
Miller, James Hugh, III 1949- *WhoAmL 94*
Miller, James Lynn 1951- *WhoAm 94, WhoAmL 94, WhoWest 94*
Miller, James M. 1950- *WhoAmL 94*
Miller, James Monroe 1948- *WhoAmL 94*
Miller, James R. *IntMPA 94*
Miller, James Robert 1947- *WhoAm 94, WhoAmL 94*
Miller, James S. 1923- *WhoBlA 94*
Miller, James S. 1924- *WhoBlA 94*
Miller, James Vince 1920- *WhoAm 94*
Miller, James Wilkinson d1993 *NewYTBS 93*
Miller, Jan *WhoHol 92*
Miller, Jan Dean 1942- *WhoAm 94, WhoScEn 94*
Miller, Jane *DrAPF 93*
Miller, Jane Andrews 1952- *WhoFI 94*
Miller, Janel Howell 1947- *WhoScEn 94*
Miller, Janet 1954- *WhoAmA 93*
Miller, Janet Dawn Hoover 1941- *WhoMW 93*
Miller, Janet Jenkins 1937- *WhoAmP 93*
Miller, Janise Luevenia Monica 1956- *WhoAmL 94*
Miller, Jason 1932- *WrDr 94*
Miller, Jason 1939- *ConDr 93, IntMPA 94, WhoAm 94, WhoHol 92*
Miller, Jay Alan 1928- *WhoMW 93*
Miller, Jay Dante 1961- *WhoAmL 94*
Miller, Jean Carolyn Wilder 1932- *WhoBlA 94*
Miller, Jean Johnston 1918- *WhoAmA 93*
Miller, Jean Ruth 1927- *WhoWest 94*
Miller, Jeanne-Marie A. 1937- *WhoBlA 94*
Miller, Jeff 1941- *WhoAmP 93*
Miller, Jeffrey Charles 1954- *WhoAmP 93*
Miller, Jeffrey Clark 1943- *WhoAm 94*
Miller, Jeffrey Grant 1941- *WhoAm 94*
Miller, Jeffrey Robert 1941- *WhoAm 94*
Miller, Jeffrey Steven 1958- *WhoScEn 94*
Miller, Jeremy 1976- *WhoHol 92*
Miller, Jerome Gilbert 1931- *WhoAm 94*
Miller, Jerome K. 1931- *WhoWest 94*
Miller, Jerry 1939- *WhoMW 93*
Miller, Jerry A. 1935- *WhoWest 94*
Miller, Jerry D. 1942- *WhoAmP 93*
Miller, Jerry Floyd 1946- *WhoMW 93*
Miller, Jerry Huber 1931- *WhoAm 94, WhoWest 94*
Miller, Jerry J. 1933- *WhoAmP 93*
Miller, Jerry W. *WhoAmL 94*
Miller, Jesse D. 1930- *WhoAm 94*
Miller, Jesse L., Jr. 1942- *WhoAmP 93*
Miller, Jim Wayne *DrAPF 93*
Miller, Jim Wayne 1936- *TwCYAW, WrDr 94*
Miller, Jimmy *EncSF 93*
Miller, Joan d1988 *WhoHol 92*
Miller, Joan G. 1949- *WhoScEn 94*
Miller, Joan I(rene) 1944- *ConAu 41NR*
Miller, Joan L. 1930- *WhoAmA 93*
Miller, Joan Vita 1946- *WhoAmA 93*
Miller, Joel Lawrence 1935- *WhoAm 94*
Miller, Joel Steven 1944- *WhoScEn 94*
Miller, Johann Samuel 1779-1830 *DcNaB MP*
Miller, John d1968 *WhoHol 92*
Miller, John 1954- *WhoAmA 93*
Miller, John (Mansel) 1919- *Who 94*
Miller, John Albert 1939- *WhoAm 94*
Miller, John B. 1952- *WhoAmL 94*
Miller, John B., Jr. 1945- *WhoAmL 94*
Miller, John Bryan Peter Duppa- 1903- *Who 94*
Miller, John C. H., Jr. 1944- *WhoAmL 94*
Miller, John Cameron 1949- *WhoScEn 94*
Miller, John David 1923- *WhoAm 94*
Miller, John David 1945- *WhoAm 94*
Miller, John E. *DrAPF 93*
Miller, John E. 1929- *WhoAmP 93*
Miller, John Eddie 1945- *WhoAmL 94*
Miller, John Edward 1941- *WhoAm 94*
Miller, John Francis 1908- *WhoAm 94*
Miller, John Franklin 1940- *WhoAmA 93*
Miller, John Grider 1935- *WrDr 94*
Miller, John H. 1917- *WhoBlA 94*
Miller, John Harmsworth 1930- *Who 94*
Miller, John Holmes 1925- *Who 94*
Miller, John Ireland 1912- *Who 94*
Miller, John Joseph 1928- *Who 94*
Miller, John Kent 1944- *WhoAmL 94*
Miller, John Laurence 1947- *WhoAm 94, WhoWest 94*
Miller, John Leed 1949- *WhoAmL 94*
Miller, John Nelson 1948- *WhoFI 94, WhoWest 94*
Miller, John Paul 1918- *WhoAmA 93*
Miller, John Pendleton 1931- *WhoFI 94*
Miller, John R. 1938- *WhoAmP 93*
Miller, John R. 1946- *WhoFI 94*
Miller, John Randolph 1946- *WhoAmL 94*
Miller, John Richard 1927- *WhoAm 94*
Miller, John Richard 1944- *WhoScEn 94*
Miller, John Robert 1937- *WhoAm 94*
Miller, John T., Jr. 1922- *WhoAmL 94*
Miller, John Ulman 1914- *WhoAm 94*
Miller, John Wesley, III 1941- *WhoAmL 94*
Miller, John William, Jr. 1942- *WhoAm 94*
Miller, Jon H. 1938- *IntWW 93*
Miller, Jon Philip 1944- *WhoWest 94*
Miller, Jonathan 1934- *WhoHol 92*
Miller, Jonathan (Wolfe) 1934- *NewGrDO, WrDr 94*
Miller, Jonathan Wolfe 1934- *IntWW 93, Who 94, WhoAm 94*
Miller, Jordan *DrAPF 93*
Miller, Jordan Yale 1919- *WrDr 94*
Miller, Josef M. 1937- *WhoScEn 94*
Miller, Joseph Arthur 1933- *WhoScEn 94, WhoWest 94*
Miller, Joseph Calder 1939- *WhoAm 94*
Miller, Joseph Edward, Jr. 1945- *WhoWest 94*
Miller, Joseph Herman 1930- *WhoBlA 94*
Miller, Joseph Hillis 1928- *WhoAm 94*
Miller, Joseph Irwin 1909- *WhoAm 94, WhoMW 93*
Miller, Joseph James 1912- *WhoAmP 93*
Miller, Joseph Owen 1949- *WhoAmP 93*
Miller, Josephine Welder 1942- *WhoAmP 93*
Miller, Joshua *WhoHol 92*
Miller, JP 1919- *IntMPA 94*
Miller, Judith 1936- *WhoAmP 93*
Miller, Judith 1948- *ConAu 140*
Miller, Judith Ann 1968- *WhoFI 94*
Miller, Judith Ayoung 1965- *WhoFI 94*
Miller, Judith Henderson 1951- *Who 94*
Miller, Judson Frederick 1924- *WhoAm 94*
Miller, Julian Creighton 1895- *WhAm 10*
Miller, K(eith) Bruce 1927- *WrDr 94*
Miller, Karen 1944- *WhoAmL 94*
Miller, Karen A. 1946- *WhoMW 93*
Miller, Karin R. 1964- *WhoFI 94*
Miller, Karl (Fergus Connor) 1931- *WrDr 94*
Miller, Karl A. 1931- *WhoFI 94*
Miller, Karl F. *DrAPF 93*
Miller, Karl Fergus Connor 1931- *IntWW 93, Who 94*
Miller, Kathleen *WhoHol 92*
Miller, Kathleen Elizabeth 1942- *WhoAm 94*
Miller, Kathleen Roberts 1947- *WhoAmP 93*
Miller, Kathryn 1935- *WhoAmA 93*
Miller, Keith 1938- *WhoFI 94*
Miller, Keith Lloyd 1951- *WhoAmL 94, WhoMW 93*
Miller, Keith Wyatt 1941- *WhoAm 94*
Miller, Ken Leroy 1933- *WhoAm 94*
Miller, Kenneth A. 1944- *WhoWest 94*
Miller, Kenneth Allan Glen 1926- *Who 94*
Miller, Kenneth E 1926- *WrDr 94*
Miller, Kenneth Edward 1929- *WhoAm 94*
Miller, Kenneth Edward 1951- *WhoScEn 94, WhoWest 94*
Miller, Kenneth Gregory 1944- *WhoAm 94*
Miller, Kenneth Hayes 1876-1952 *WhoAmA 93N*
Miller, Kenneth James 1954- *WhoWest 94*
Miller, Kenneth Jim 1953- *WhoFI 94*
Miller, Kenneth Merrill 1930- *WhoFI 94*
Miller, Kenneth Michael 1921- *WhoAm 94, WhoFI 94*
Miller, Kenneth Roy 1902- *WhoAm 94*
Miller, Kenneth William 1947- *WhoAm 94, WhoFI 94*
Miller, Kenny *WhoHol 92*
Miller, Kent Dunkerton 1941- *WhoWest 94*
Miller, Kerby A. 1944- *WrDr 94*
Miller, Kerry Lee 1955- *WhoAmL 94*
Miller, Kevin D. 1949- *WhoMW 93*
Miller, Kevin D. 1966- *WhoBlA 94*
Miller, Kevin Grey 1930- *WhoAmP 93*
Miller, Kimberley Jean 1957- *WhoWest 94*
Miller, Kimberly Clarke 1965- *WhoFI 94, WhoMW 93*
Miller, Kirk *WhoAm 94*
Miller, Kristie 1944- *ConAu 142*
Miller, L. Martin 1939- *WhoAm 94, WhoFI 94*
Miller, Lajos 1940- *IntWW 93, NewGrDO*
Miller, Lamar Perry 1925- *WhoBlA 94*
Miller, Lane Franklin 1949- *WhoFI 94*
Miller, Larry *WhoHol 92*
Miller, Larry 1944- *WhoAmA 93*
Miller, Larry 1946- *BasBi*
Miller, Larry H. *WhoWest 94*
Miller, Larry J. 1954- *WhoAmP 93*
Miller, Larry Joseph 1932- *WhoAm 94*
Miller, Laura Hendrix-Branch 1951- *WhoMW 93*

Miller, Laurel Milton 1935- *WhoBlA 94*
Miller, Laurence Glenn 1948- *WhoAm 94, WhoAmA 93*
Miller, Lawrence A. 1946- *WhoAm 94*
Miller, Lawrence A., Jr. 1951- *WhoBlA 94*
Miller, Lawrence Edward 1944- *WhoAm 94*
Miller, Lawrence Edward 1950- *WhoBlA 94*
Miller, Lawrence G. *WhoAmP 93*
Miller, Lee d1977 *WhoHol 92*
Miller, Lee Ann 1957- *WhoAmL 94*
Miller, Lee Anne *WhoAm 94*
Miller, Lee Denmar 1935- *WhoAm 94*
Miller, Lee Edward 1951- *WhoAmL 94*
Miller, Lee Edward 1962- *WhoAmL 94*
Miller, Lee I. 1947- *WhoAmL 94*
Miller, Leland Bishop, Jr. 1931- *WhoAm 94*
Miller, Lenore 1932- *WhoAm 94, WhoFI 94*
Miller, Leon Gordon 1917- *WhoAmA 93*
Miller, Leonard David 1930- *WhoAm 94*
Miller, Leonard Doy 1941- *WhoAm 94, WhoScEn 94*
Miller, Leonard Martin 1941- *WhoAm 94*
Miller, Leonard Paul 1947- *WhoMW 93*
Miller, Leroy Benjamin 1931- *WhoAm 94*
Miller, Lesley, Jr. 1951- *WhoAmP 93*
Miller, Lesley James, Jr. 1951- *WhoBlA 94*
Miller, Leslie Adrienne *DrAPF 93*
Miller, Leslie Adrienne 1956- *WhoMW 93*
Miller, Leslie Anne 1951- *WhoAmL 94*
Miller, Leslie Haynes 1914-1989 *WhAm 10*
Miller, Lester Livingston, Jr. 1930- *WhoWest 94*
Miller, Levi 1944- *WhoMW 93*
Miller, Lewis Eugene 1961- *WhoAmL 94*
Miller, Lewis Nelson, Jr. 1944- *WhoAm 94*
Miller, Linda 1942- *WhoHol 92*
Miller, Linda B. 1937- *WhoAm 94*
Miller, Linda Patterson 1946- *WrDr 94*
Miller, Liz Rodriguez 1954- *WhoAm 94*
Miller, Lloyd Daniel 1916- *WhoAm 94*
Miller, Lloyd Ivan 1924-1990 *WhAm 10*
Miller, Loren, Jr. 1937- *WhoBlA 94*
Miller, Lori E. 1959- *WhoBlA 94*
Miller, Lori Meens 1961- *WhoMW 93*
Miller, Lorraine d1978 *WhoHol 92*
Miller, Lou d1993 *NewYTBS 93*
Miller, Lou Ann Margaret 1952- *WhoMW 93*
Miller, Louis Howard 1935- *WhoAm 94*
Miller, Louis Rice 1914- *WhoAm 94*
Miller, Louise 1936- *WhoAmP 93, WhoWomW 91*
Miller, Louise (Rolfe) 1940- *SmATA 76 [port]*
Miller, Louise T. 1919- *WhoBlA 94*
Miller, Lowell Donald 1933- *WhoAm 94*
Miller, Loye Wheat, Jr. 1930- *WhoAm 94*
Miller, Lu d1941 *WhoHol 92*
Miller, Luvenia C. 1909- *WhoBlA 94*
Miller, Lydia J. *WhoAmP 93*
Miller, Lyle G. *WhoWest 94*
Miller, Lyman Lee 1952- *WhoMW 93*
Miller, Lynn C. 1938- *WhoIns 94*
Miller, Lynn Fieldman 1938- *WhoAmL 94*
Miller, Lynn H. 1937- *WrDr 94*
Miller, Lynne Marie 1951- *WhoFI 94, WhoScEn 94*
Miller, M. Hughes 1913-1989 *WhAm 10*
Miller, M. Joy 1934- *WhoFI 94, WhoWest 94*
Miller, M. Sammye 1947- *WhoBlA 94*
Miller, Malcolm Henry 1934- *WhoMW 93*
Miller, Malcolm Lee 1923- *WhoAm 94*
Miller, Mandy 1944- *WhoHol 92*
Miller, Maposure T. 1934- *WhoBlA 94*
Miller, Marc Eric 1947- *WhoAmL 94*
Miller, Marc H. 1946- *WhoAmA 93*
Miller, Marcia M. 1948- *WhoBlA 94*
Miller, Marcus Hay 1941- *Who 94*
Miller, Margaret 1940- *WhoAmP 93*
Miller, Margaret Bannon 1944- *WhoAmL 94*
Miller, Margaret Elizabeth Battle 1934- *WhoBlA 94*
Miller, Margaret Greer 1934- *WhoBlA 94*
Miller, Margaret Haigh 1915- *WhoAm 94*
Miller, Margery K. 1947- *WhoAm 94, WhoAmL 94*
Miller, Margie-Jo 1964- *WhoFI 94*
Miller, Mariko Terasaki *WhoAmP 93*
Miller, Marilyn d1936 *WhoHol 92*
Miller, Marilyn Joan 1943- *WhoMW 93*
Miller, Marilyn Lea *WhoAm 94*
Miller, Marion 1913- *WhoWest 94*
Miller, Marjorie 1922- *WhoAmP 93*
Miller, Marjorie Lynne 1967- *WhoMW 93*
Miller, Mark *WhoAm 94, WhoFI 94, WhoMW 93*
Miller, Mark 1925- *WhoHol 92*
Miller, Mark Lee 1955- *WhoAmL 94*
Miller, Mark Steven 1967- *WhoAmP 93*
Miller, Marquis David 1959- *WhoBlA 94*
Miller, Marsha Ann 1950- *WhoMW 93*
Miller, Marshall Lee 1942- *WhoAm 94, WhoAmL 94*
Miller, Martha Escabí 1945- *WhoHisp 94*
Miller, Martiey Marie 1954- *WhoWest 94*
Miller, Martin d1969 *WhoHol 92*
Miller, Martin John 1943- *WhoAm 94*
Miller, Martin John 1946- *Who 94*
Miller, Marvin *WrDr 94*
Miller, Marvin d1985 *WhoHol 92*
Miller, Marvin 1917- *EncABHB 9*
Miller, Marvin Edward 1929- *WhoAm 94*
Miller, Mary 1942- *WhoAmP 93*
Miller, Mary Alice 1941- *WhoWest 94*
Miller, Mary Angela 1956- *WhoMW 93*
Miller, Mary Durack, Dame 1913- *WrDr 94*
Miller, Mary Elizabeth H. *Who 94*
Miller, Mary Grace Arbour 1950- *WhoAmL 94*
Miller, Mary Jeannette 1912- *WhoFI 94*
Miller, Mary Rita 1918- *WhoAmP 93*
Miller, Maryanne Cunningham 1931- *WhoAmP 93*
Miller, Mattie Sherryl 1933- *WhoBlA 94*
Miller, Maurice James 1926- *WhoAm 94*
Miller, Maurice Solomon 1920- *Who 94*
Miller, Max d1963 *WhoHol 92*
Miller, Max Arnold 1896- *WhAm 10*
Miller, Max B. 1937- *IntMPA 94*
Miller, Max Dunham, Jr. 1946- *WhoAm 94, WhoAmL 94*
Miller, May *DrAPF 93*
Miller, May 1899- *BlkWr 2, ConAu 142*
Miller, Maynard *WhoAmP 93*
Miller, Maynard Malcolm 1921- *WhoAm 94, WhoScEn 94, WhoWest 94*
Miller, Maynard R., Jr. 1947- *WhoAmL 94*
Miller, Melissa Wren 1951- *WhoAmA 93*
Miller, Melvin Allen 1950- *WhoBlA 94*
Miller, Melvin B. 1934- *WhoBlA 94*
Miller, Melvin Eugene 1949- *WhoFI 94*
Miller, Melvin Orville, Jr. 1937- *WhoAmA 93*
Miller, Merle Leroy 1922- *WhoScEn 94*
Miller, Merton (Howard) 1923- *WrDr 94*
Miller, Merton H. 1923- *NobelP 91 [port]*
Miller, Merton Howard 1923- *IntWW 93, Who 94, WhoAm 94, WhoFI 94, WhoMW 93*
Miller, Michael d1983 *WhoHol 92*
Miller, Michael 1933- *Who 94*
Miller, Michael 1937- *WhoAmL 94*
Miller, Michael A. *Who 94*
Miller, Michael Adam 1966- *WhoFI 94*
Miller, Michael Beach 1958- *WhoScEn 94*
Miller, Michael Carl 1955- *WhoMW 93, WhoScEn 94*
Miller, Michael Chilcott d'Elboux 1929- *WhoAm 94*
Miller, Michael David 1935- *WhoFI 94*
Miller, Michael David 1940- *WhoFI 94*
Miller, Michael David 1947- *WhoFI 94*
Miller, Michael Everett 1941- *WhoAm 94*
Miller, Michael Gabriel 1945- *WhoMW 93*
Miller, Michael I. 1937- *WhoAm 94*
Miller, Michael Jeffrey 1958- *WhoFI 94*
Miller, Michael Patiky 1944- *WhoAmL 94*
Miller, Michael Paul 1938- *WhoAm 94, WhoFI 94*
Miller, Michael R. d1993 *NewYTBS 93*
Miller, Michael Stephen 1938- *WhoAmA 93*
Miller, Mike 1951- *WhoAmP 93*
Miller, Mildred *WhoAm 94*
Miller, Millicent d1990 *WhoHol 92*
Miller, Milton Allen 1954- *WhoAmL 94*
Miller, Milton David 1911- *WhoScEn 94, WhoWest 94*
Miller, Milton Howard 1927- *WhoAm 94*
Miller, Miranda 1950- *EncSF 93, WrDr 94*
Miller, Mitch 1911- *ConMus 11 [port], WhoHol 92*
Miller, Monty Lee 1952- *WhoMW 93*
Miller, Morgan Lincoln 1924- *WhoAm 94*
Miller, Morris d1957 *WhoHol 92*
Miller, Morris Folsom 1919- *WhoAm 94*
Miller, Morris Henry 1954- *WhoAmL 94*
Miller, Mortimer Michael 1929- *WhoAmP 93*
Miller, Murray Henry 1931- *WhoScEn 94*
Miller, Nan Louise 1948- *WhoAm 94*
Miller, Nancy Ann 1960- *WhoFI 94*
Miller, Nancy Tokar 1941- *WhoAmA 93*
Miller, Naomi 1928- *WhoAm 94*
Miller, Nathan 1743-1790 *WhAmRev*
Miller, Nathan 1927- *WrDr 94*
Miller, Nathan H. 1943- *WhoAmP 93*
Miller, Neal Elgar 1909- *IntWW 93, WhoAm 94*
Miller, Neal Louis 1959- *WhoFI 94*
Miller, Neil 1945- *GayLL*
Miller, Neil Austin 1932- *WhoAm 94*
Miller, Neil S. 1958- *WhoAm 94, WhoFI 94*
Miller, Newton E. 1919- *WhoAmP 93*
Miller, Newton Edd, Jr. 1920- *WhoAm 94*
Miller, Nicholas G. 1950- *WhoAmL 94*
Miller, Nicole Gabrielle 1962- *WhoScEn 94*
Miller, Nicole Jacqueline 1951- *WhoAm 94*
Miller, Nona Lee 1958- *WhoMW 93*
Miller, Norma Adele 1919- *WhoBlA 94*
Miller, Norman 1933- *WhoAm 94*
Miller, Norman Charles, Jr. 1934- *WhoAm 94*
Miller, Norman L. 1928- *WhoBlA 94*
Miller, Norman L. 1936- *WhoFI 94*
Miller, Norman Richard 1922- *WhoAm 94*
Miller, Norman Samuel 1943- *WhoAmL 94, WhoFI 94*
Miller, Oliver *WhoBlA 94*
Miller, Oliver Chester 1898- *WhAm 10*
Miller, Oliver O. 1944- *WhoBlA 94*
Miller, Orlando Jack 1927- *WhoAm 94*
Miller, (Hanson) Orlo 1911- *WrDr 94*
Miller, Otis Louis 1933- *WhoMW 93*
Miller, Owen Thomas 1927- *WhoAmP 93*
Miller, P(eter) Schuyler 1912-1974 *EncSF 93*
Miller, Pam 1938- *WhoAmP 93*
Miller, Pamela *DrAPF 93*
Miller, Pat *WhoAmP 93*
Miller, Patricia 1947- *WhoAmP 93*
Miller, Patricia Ann 1933- *WhoMW 93*
Miller, Patricia Ann 1958- *WhoMW 93*
Miller, Patricia Elizabeth Cleary 1939- *WhoMW 93*
Miller, Patricia Frances 1943- *WhoMW 93*
Miller, Patricia G. 1933- *WhoAm 94, WhoAmL 94*
Miller, Patricia L. 1936- *WhoAmP 93*
Miller, Patricia Louise 1936- *WhoMW 93*
Miller, Patricia Palmer 1941- *WhoMW 93*
Miller, Patrick Dwight, Jr. 1935- *WhoAm 94*
Miller, Patrick William 1947- *WhoAm 94*
Miller, Patsy Ruth 1904- *WhoHol 92*
Miller, Paul *WhoFI 94*
Miller, Paul 1906-1991 *WhAm 10*
Miller, Paul Albert 1924- *WhoAm 94, WhoFI 94*
Miller, Paul Andrew 1959- *WhoScEn 94*
Miller, Paul Ausborn 1917- *WhoAm 94*
Miller, Paul Dean 1941- *WhoScEn 94*
Miller, Paul Fetterolf, Jr. 1927- *WhoAm 94*
Miller, Paul George 1922- *WhoAm 94*
Miller, Paul J. 1929- *WhoAm 94, WhoAmL 94*
Miller, Paul James 1939- *WhoAm 94, WhoFI 94*
Miller, Paul Lukens 1919- *IntWW 93, WhoAm 94*
Miller, Paul Neil 1950- *WhoWest 94*
Miller, Paul O., III 1943- *WhoAmL 94*
Miller, Paul Samuel 1939- *WhoAm 94, WhoAmL 94*
Miller, Paul William 1918- *Who 94*
Miller, Pearson L. 1936- *WhoMW 93*
Miller, Peggy *WhoHol 92*
Miller, Peggy McLaren 1931- *WhoMW 93*
Miller, Peggy Suzanne 1952- *WhoWest 94*
Miller, Penelope Ann 1964- *IntMPA 94, WhoAm 94, WhoHol 92*
Miller, Percy Hugh 1922- *WhoFI 94*
Miller, Perry Gilbert Eddy 1905- *DcAmReB 2*
Miller, Peter (North) 1930- *Who 94*
Miller, Peter Francis Nigel 1924- *Who 94*
Miller, Peter J. 1919- *WhoAmP 93*
Miller, Peter North 1930- *IntWW 93*
Miller, Peter Paul 1895- *WhAm 10*
Miller, Peter Spencer 1938- *WhoAmP 93*
Miller, Petr 1941- *IntWW 93*
Miller, Phebe Condict 1949- *WhoAm 94, WhoAmL 94*
Miller, Philip *DrAPF 93*
Miller, Philip Boyd 1938- *WhoAm 94, WhoFI 94*
Miller, Philip Francis 1921- *WhoFI 94*
Miller, Philip William 1948- *WhoMW 93*
Miller, Phillip Edward 1935- *WhoScEn 94*
Miller, Phyllis (Steinfurth) 1920- *WrDr 94*
Miller, R. Craig 1946- *WrDr 94*
Miller, R(ichard) Dewitt 1910-1958 *EncSF 93*
Miller, R. Terry 1947- *WhoAmL 94*
Miller, Ralph d1966 *WhoHol 92*
Miller, Ralph 191-?- *BasBi*
Miller, Ralph Bradley 1953- *WhoAmL 94, WhoAmP 93*
Miller, Ralph Harris 1932- *WhoFI 94*
Miller, Ralph I. 1947- *WhoAmL 94*
Miller, Ralph Menno 1925- *WhoWest 94*
Miller, Ralph Ross 1934- *WhoAmP 93*
Miller, Randall William 1954- *WhoMW 93*
Miller, Randolph Crump 1910- *WrDr 94*
Miller, Randolph Latourette 1947- *WhoFI 94*
Miller, Randy 1946- *WhoAmP 93*
Miller, Ranger Bill d1939 *WhoHol 92*
Miller, Ranne B. 1940- *WhoAmL 94*
Miller, Ray 1949- *WhoAmP 93*
Miller, Ray, Jr. 1949- *WhoBlA 94*
Miller, Raymond Edward 1928- *WhoAm 94*
Miller, Raymond Edwin 1937- *WhoMW 93*
Miller, Raymond Herbert 1923- *WhoMW 93*
Miller, Raymond Jarvis 1934- *WhoAm 94, WhoScEn 94*
Miller, Raymond Vincent, Jr. 1954- *WhoAmL 94*
Miller, Raymond Wiley 1895- *WhAm 10*
Miller, Reed 1918- *WhoAm 94*
Miller, Reginald Wayne 1965- *WhoBlA 94*
Miller, Rene Harcourt 1916- *WhoAm 94*
Miller, Reuben George 1930- *WhoAm 94*
Miller, Rhoda Evangeline 1930- *WhoWest 94*
Miller, Richard *WhoHol 92*
Miller, Richard (Connelly) 1925- *EncSF 93*
Miller, Richard Alan 1931- *WhoAm 94, WhoFI 94*
Miller, Richard Alan 1939- *WhoAm 94*
Miller, Richard Alan 1944- *WhoWest 94*
Miller, Richard Allan 1947- *WhoAmL 94*
Miller, Richard Allen 1944- *WhoAmL 94*
Miller, Richard Allen 1945- *WhoAmL 94*
Miller, Richard Archibald 1927- *WhoAm 94*
Miller, Richard Arthur 1925-1988 *WhAm 10*
Miller, Richard Charles, Jr. 1947- *WhoBlA 94*
Miller, Richard Clark 1955- *WhoAmL 94*
Miller, Richard Dwight 1929- *WhoAm 94*
Miller, Richard Franklin 1927- *WhoWest 94*
Miller, Richard Gregg 1964- *WhoMW 93*
Miller, Richard H. 1926- *WhoAmP 93*
Miller, Richard Hamilton 1931- *WhoAm 94*
Miller, Richard Harold 1942- *WhoAmP 93*
Miller, Richard Harris 1943- *WhoIns 94*
Miller, Richard Henry 1946- *WhoMW 93*
Miller, Richard Irwin 1924- *WhoAm 94*
Miller, Richard Jackson 1946- *WhoAm 94, WhoAmL 94*
Miller, Richard Jerome 1939- *WhoAm 94, WhoFI 94*
Miller, Richard Joseph 1941- *WhoAmL 94*
Miller, Richard Keith 1949- *WhoScEn 94*
Miller, Richard Kidwell 1930- *WhoAm 94, WhoAmA 93*
Miller, Richard Lawrence 1949- *WrDr 94*
Miller, Richard Lee 1945- *WhoScEn 94*
Miller, Richard Mark 1952- *WhoAmL 94*
Miller, Richard McDermott 1922- *WhoAm 94, WhoAmA 93*
Miller, Richard Morgan 1931- *Who 94*
Miller, Richard Nelson 1929- *WhoFI 94*
Miller, Richard Sherwin 1930- *WhoAm 94, WhoAmL 94*
Miller, Richard Steven 1951- *WhoAm 94, WhoAmL 94*
Miller, Richard Wesley 1940- *WhoAm 94, WhoFI 94*
Miller, Richards Thorn 1918- *WhoScEn 94*
Miller, Richmond Wayne 1945- *WhoMW 93*
Miller, Rob Hollis *DrAPF 93*
Miller, Robert 1923- *WhoAm 94*
Miller, Robert A. 1931- *WhoFI 94*
Miller, Robert A. 1939- *WhoAmP 93*
Miller, Robert Alan 1943- *WhoScEn 94*
Miller, Robert Alexander Gavin D. *Who 94*
Miller, Robert Allen 1945- *WhoAm 94*
Miller, Robert Allen 1946- *WhoScEn 94*
Miller, Robert Arthur 1939- *WhoAm 94, WhoAmL 94, WhoMW 93*
Miller, Robert Barry 1953- *WhoFI 94*
Miller, Robert Branson, Jr. 1935- *WhoAm 94*
Miller, Robert C. 1930- *WhoFI 94*
Miller, Robert Carl 1936- *WhoAm 94*
Miller, Robert Carl 1943- *WhoFI 94*
Miller, Robert Carmi, Jr. 1942- *WhoAm 94*
Miller, Robert Charles 1925- *WhoAm 94*
Miller, Robert Charles, Sr. 1927- *WhoAmP 93*

Miller, Robert Daniel 1960- *WhoAmL 94, WhoFI 94*
Miller, Robert David 1932- *WhoFI 94, WhoIns 94*
Miller, Robert David 1941- *WhoAmP 93*
Miller, Robert Earl 1932- *WhoAm 94*
Miller, Robert Ellis 1932- *IntMPA 94*
Miller, Robert Francis 1939- *WhoScEn 94*
Miller, Robert Frank 1925- *WhoScEn 94*
Miller, Robert G. 1944- *WhoAm 94, WhoFI 94, WhoWest 94*
Miller, Robert H. 1944- *WhoAm 94, WhoMW 93*
Miller, Robert Haskins 1919- *WhoAm 94, WhoAmP 93, WhoMW 93*
Miller, Robert Henry 1938- *WhoAm 94*
Miller, Robert Hopkins 1927- *WhoAmP 93*
Miller, Robert Hugh 1941- *WhoAmL 94*
Miller, Robert Hugh 1944- *WhoAmP 93*
Miller, Robert J. 1945- *WhoAmP 93*
Miller, Robert James 1923- *WhoAm 94*
Miller, Robert James 1926- *WhoAm 94*
Miller, Robert James 1933- *WhoAm 94*
Miller, Robert Jennings 1949- *WhoWest 94*
Miller, Robert Joseph 1945- *WhoAm 94, WhoWest 94*
Miller, Robert L. *WhoAm 94*
Miller, Robert L., Jr. 1950- *WhoAm 94, WhoAmL 94, WhoMW 93*
Miller, Robert Laverne 1953- *WhoBlA 94*
Miller, Robert Lindsey 1933- *WhoWest 94*
Miller, Robert Llewellyn 1929- *WhoMW 93*
Miller, Robert Louis 1926- *WhoAm 94*
Miller, Robert Morton 1927- *WhoWest 94*
Miller, Robert Nolen 1940- *WhoAm 94*
Miller, Robert Peter 1939- *WhoAmA 93*
Miller, Robert Ryal 1923- *WhoWest 94*
Miller, Robert Scott 1947- *WhoWest 94*
Miller, Robert Steven 1963- *WhoFI 94, WhoWest 94*
Miller, Robert Stevens, Jr. 1941- *IntWW 93, WhoAm 94, WhoFI 94, WhoWest 94*
Miller, Robert T. *WhoAmP 93*
Miller, Robert T. 1920- *WhoAm 94*
Miller, Robert Victor 1936- *WhoWest 94*
Miller, Robert Watt, Mrs. 1898- *WhoAmA 93*
Miller, Robert Wayne 1941- *WhoAmL 94*
Miller, Robert Wiley 1928- *WhoAm 94*
Miller, Robert William 1922- *WhoAm 94, WhoFI 94*
Miller, Roberta Balstad 1940- *WhoAm 94*
Miller, Roberta Davis 1931- *WhoAm 94*
Miller, Robin Anthony 1937- *Who 94*
Miller, Robin Feuer 1947- *WrDr 94*
Miller, Rodger Dale 1945- *WhoWest 94*
Miller, Roger 1936- *WhoHol 92*
Miller, Roger 1936-1992 *AnObit 1992, CurBio 93N*
Miller, Roger Allen 1934- *WhoScEn 94*
Miller, Roger Dean 1936-1992 *WhAm 10*
Miller, Roger James 1947- *WhoAmL 94*
Miller, Roger Pierce 1951- *WhoMW 93*
Miller, Roland B., III 1946- *WhoAmL 94*
Miller, Ron 1932- *WhoAmP 93*
Miller, Ronald Alan 1947- *WhoAm 94*
Miller, Ronald Alfred 1943- *WhoAm 94*
Miller, Ronald Andrew Baird 1937- *Who 94*
Miller, Ronald Anthony 1940- *WhoFI 94*
Miller, Ronald Baxter 1948- *WhoBlA 94*
Miller, Ronald Eugene 1933- *WhoAm 94*
Miller, Ronald Kinsman 1929- *Who 94*
Miller, Ronald Knox 1943- *WhoAmP 93*
Miller, Ronald Lewis 1946- *WhoScEn 94*
Miller, Ronald M. 1944- *WhoAm 94*
Miller, Ronald W. 1933- *IntMPA 94*
Miller, Rosalind Elaine 1929- *WhoAm 94*
Miller, Ross Charles 1943- *WhoFI 94*
Miller, Ross Hays 1923- *WhoAm 94*
Miller, Ross M. 1954- *WhoFI 94*
Miller, Ross M., Jr. 1928- *WhoBlA 94*
Miller, Roy F. 1912- *WhoAmP 93*
Miller, Roy Frank 1935- *Who 94*
Miller, Roy Phillip 1945- *WhoAmP 93*
Miller, Roy Raymond 1929- *WhoMW 93*
Miller, Royal DeVere, Jr. 1938- *WhoWest 94*
Miller, Ruby d1976 *WhoHol 92*
Miller, Ruby M. 1911- *ConAu 141*
Miller, Russell 1938- *WrDr 94*
Miller, Russell Bryan 1940- *WhoAm 94*
Miller, Russell L., Jr. 1939- *WhoBlA 94*
Miller, Russell Loyd, Jr. 1939- *WhoAm 94*
Miller, Russell Rowland 1937- *WhoFI 94, WhoIns 94*
Miller, Ruth d1981 *WhoHol 92*
Miller, Ruth 1919-1969 *BlmGWL*
Miller, Ruth 1931- *WhoAmL 94, WhoWest 94*
Miller, Ruth Ann 1930- *WhoAmA 93*
Miller, Sam Scott 1938- *WhoAm 94*
Miller, Samuel 1769-1850 *DcAmReB 2*
Miller, Samuel Carroll, III 1948- *WhoAmL 94*
Miller, Samuel Clifford 1930- *WhoAm 94, WhoAmA 93*
Miller, Samuel Martin 1938- *WhoAm 94, WhoFI 94*
Miller, Samuel O. 1931- *WhoBlA 94*
Miller, Samuel R. 1948- *WhoAmL 94*
Miller, Sanderson 1716-1780 *DcNaB MP*
Miller, Sanford Allen 1951- *WhoIns 94*
Miller, Sara Billow 1948- *WhoAm 94*
Miller, Sarabeth 1927- *WhoMW 93*
Miller, Scott *WhoHol 92*
Miller, Scott Joseph 1964- *WhoMW 93*
Miller, Seton I. d1974 *WhoHol 92*
Miller, Seton I. 1902-1974 *IntDcF 2-4*
Miller, Seumas 1953- *ConAu 141*
Miller, Seymour Michael 1922- *WhoAm 94*
Miller, Sharon DeAnn 1938- *WhoMW 93*
Miller, Sheila M. *WhoAmP 93*
Miller, Shelby Alexander 1914- *WhoMW 93, WhoScEn 94*
Miller, Shelley *DrAPF 93*
Miller, Sherre 1958- *WhoBlA 94*
Miller, Sidney 1916- *WhoHol 92*
Miller, Sidney Israel 1923- *WhoMW 93*
Miller, Sidney James 1943- *Who 94*
Miller, Stanford 1913- *WhoAm 94*
Miller, Stanley Allen 1928- *WhoAmP 93*
Miller, Stanley Custer, Jr. 1926- *WhoAm 94*
Miller, Stanley Lloyd 1930- *IntWW 93, WorScD*
Miller, Stanley Ray 1940- *WhoWest 94*
Miller, Stella Grobel 1941- *WhoMW 93*
Miller, Stephen (James Hamilton) 1915- *Who 94*
Miller, Stephen Douglas 1948- *WhoScEn 94*
Miller, Stephen E. *WhoHol 92*
Miller, Stephen M. *DrAPF 93*
Miller, Stephen Marcelles 1952- *WhoMW 93*
Miller, Stephen Paul *DrAPF 93*
Miller, Stephen Raben 1928- *WhoAm 94*
Miller, Stephen Ralph 1950- *WhoAm 94, WhoAmL 94*
Miller, Stevan A. 1952- *WhoAmL 94*
Miller, Steve *WhoAm 94, WhoAmA 93, WhoWest 94*
Miller, Steve 1949- *WhoAmP 93*
Miller, Steve 1950- *EncSF 93*
Miller, Steven L. 1958- *WhoMW 93*
Miller, Steven Lawrence 1940- *WhoAmP 93*
Miller, Steven Michael 1954- *WhoMW 93*
Miller, Steven Scott 1947- *WhoAmL 94*
Miller, Steven William 1949- *WhoMW 93*
Miller, Stewart Edward 1918-1990 *WhAm 10*
Miller, Stuart C(reighton) 1927- *WrDr 94*
Miller, Sue 1943- *WrDr 94*
Miller, Sue S. 1930- *WhoAmA 93*
Miller, Susan 1944- *ConDr 93, WrDr 94*
Miller, Susan Elizabeth 1951- *WhoAmP 93*
Miller, Susan Heilmann 1945- *WhoAm 94*
Miller, Susan Wise 1941- *WhoWest 94*
Miller, Sylvia Alberta Gregory 1919- *WhoBlA 94*
Miller, Tanfield Charles 1947- *WhoAm 94*
Miller, Telly Hugh 1939- *WhoBlA 94*
Miller, Terence George 1918- *IntWW 93, Who 94*
Miller, Terrance M. 1947- *WhoAm 94, WhoAmL 94*
Miller, Terrie Sue 1961- *WhoMW 93*
Miller, Terry Alan 1943- *WhoScEn 94*
Miller, Terry Dennis 1941- *WhoWest 94*
Miller, Terry Ellis 1945- *WhoMW 93*
Miller, Terry James 1949- *WhoAmP 93*
Miller, Terry Morrow 1947- *WhoAm 94*
Miller, Tevie 1928- *WhoAm 94*
Miller, Thelma Delmoor 1921- *WhoBlA 94*
Miller, Theodore A. 1921- *WhoAmL 94*
Miller, Theodore H. 1905- *WhoBlA 94*
Miller, Theodore Norman 1942- *WhoAm 94, WhoAmL 94*
Miller, Theodore Robert 1907- *WhoAm 94*
Miller, Theresa Ann 1945- *WhoAm 94, WhoMW 93*
Miller, Thomas d1942 *WhoHol 92*
Miller, Thomas Albert 1940- *WhoScEn 94*
Miller, Thomas B. 1929- *WhoAmP 93*
Miller, Thomas B. 1933- *WhoMW 93*
Miller, Thomas Burk 1929- *WhoAmL 94*
Miller, Thomas Cecil 1951- *WhoWest 94*
Miller, Thomas Edward 1948- *WhoAmL 94*
Miller, Thomas Eugene 1929- *WhoAmL 94, WhoWest 94*
Miller, Thomas Herman 1950- *WhoFI 94*
Miller, Thomas Hulbert, Jr. 1923- *WhoAm 94*
Miller, Thomas J. 1944- *WhoAm 94, WhoAmP 93*
Miller, Thomas Marshall 1910- *WhoAm 94*
Miller, Thomas Nathan 1954- *WhoScEn 94*
Miller, Thomas Robbins 1938- *WhoAm 94*
Miller, Thomas V. Mike, Jr. *WhoAmP 93*
Miller, Thomas Williams 1930- *WhoAm 94*
Miller, Thomasene 1942- *WhoBlA 94*
Miller, Thormund Aubrey 1919- *WhoAm 94*
Miller, Tice Lewis 1938- *WhoMW 93*
Miller, Timothy Alden 1938- *WhoAm 94*
Miller, Todd Q. 1957- *WhoScEn 94*
Miller, Tom H. 1925- *WhoAmP 93*
Miller, Tom Polk 1914- *WhoAm 94*
Miller, Toni M. Andrews 1949- *WhoMW 93*
Miller, Trudy Joyce *WhoMW 93*
Miller, Ty *WhoHol 92*
Miller, Valerie d1989 *WhoHol 92*
Miller, Valerie Ann 1956- *WhoAmL 94*
Miller, Vance D. 1948- *WhoAmL 94*
Miller, Vassar *DrAPF 93*
Miller, Vassar (Morrison) 1924- *WrDr 94*
Miller, Vernon DuBose 1955- *WhoMW 93*
Miller, Vernon Richard 1939- *WhoAmP 93*
Miller, Vic 1951- *WhoAmP 93*
Miller, Vincent Joseph *WhoAmP 93*
Miller, Virgil 1887-1974 *IntDcF 2-4*
Miller, W. Christie d1922 *WhoHol 92*
Miller, W. Marshall, II 1953- *WhoFI 94*
Miller, Wade 1920- *WrDr 94*
Miller, Walter d1940 *WhoHol 92*
Miller, Walter D. 1925- *WhoAmP 93*
Miller, Walter Dale 1925- *WhoAm 94, WhoMW 93*
Miller, Walter Edward 1936- *WhoScEn 94*
Miller, Walter Geoffrey Thomas 1934- *IntWW 93*
Miller, Walter George 1932- *Who 94*
Miller, Walter James *DrAPF 93*
Miller, Walter M(ichael) 1922- *EncSF 93*
Miller, Walter M(ichael), Jr. 1923- *WrDr 94*
Miller, Walter Neal 1929- *WhoAm 94*
Miller, Walter Richard, Jr. 1934- *WhoAm 94, WhoFI 94*
Miller, Walther Martin 1895- *WhAm 10*
Miller, Wanda Gough 1934- *WhoAmP 93*
Miller, Ward Beecher 1954- *WhoBlA 94*
Miller, Warner Allen 1959- *WhoScEn 94*
Miller, Warren 1921-1966 *BlkWr 2, EncSF 93*
Miller, Warren Baker 1917- *WhoAmP 93*
Miller, Warren C. *DrAPF 93*
Miller, Warren E 1924- *WrDr 94*
Miller, Warren Edward 1924- *WhoAm 94, WhoWest 94*
Miller, Warren F., Jr. 1943- *WhoBlA 94*
Miller, Warren Lloyd 1944- *WhoAm 94, WhoAmL 94*
Miller, Wayne Howard 1952- *WhoScEn 94*
Miller, Wendell Smith 1925- *WhoAm 94, WhoScEn 94, WhoWest 94*
Miller, Wesley A. *WhoAmP 93*
Miller, Wilbur Hobart 1915- *WhoAm 94, WhoFI 94, WhoScEn 94*
Miller, Wilbur J. 1928- *WhoBlA 94*
Miller, Wilbur Randolph 1932- *WhoAm 94*
Miller, Willard, Jr. 1937- *WhoAm 94*
Miller, William *IntWW 93, Who 94, WhoAm 94*
Miller, William 1782-1849 *AmSocL, DcAmReB 2*
Miller, William 1940- *WhoScEn 94*
Miller, William Alvin 1931- *WhoMW 93*
Miller, William C. d1922 *WhoHol 92*
Miller, William Charles 1937- *WhoAm 94, WhoFI 94, WhoWest 94*
Miller, William Charles 1940- *WhoAm 94*
Miller, William Dawes d1993 *NewYTBS 93*
Miller, William Dawes 1919- *WhoFI 94*
Miller, William Elwood 1919- *WhoWest 94*
Miller, William Evans, Jr. 1923- *WhoAm 94*
Miller, William Frederick 1925- *WhoAm 94, WhoFI 94, WhoWest 94*
Miller, William Frederick 1946- *WhoAmL 94*
Miller, William Green 1931- *WhoAmP 93*
Miller, William H. 1941- *WhoAm 94*
Miller, William Hughes 1941- *WhoAm 94, WhoScEn 94, WhoWest 94*
Miller, William J. 1946- *WhoWest 94*
Miller, William Jack 1927- *WhoAm 94*
Miller, William Jones 1938- *WhoAm 94*
Miller, William L. 1943- *WrDr 94*
Miller, William Lawrence 1937- *WhoAm 94*
Miller, William McD., III 1945- *WhoAmL 94*
Miller, William McKinley 1896- *WhAm 10*
Miller, William Napier Cripps 1930- *WhoAm 94*
Miller, William Nathaniel 1947- *WhoBlA 94*
Miller, William O. 1934- *WhoBlA 94*
Miller, William Paul 1943- *WhoMW 93*
Miller, William Richey, Jr. 1947- *WhoAm 94, WhoAmL 94, WhoFI 94*
Miller, William Robert 1928- *WhoAm 94, WhoFI 94*
Miller, William Talbot 1943- *WhoAm 94, WhoAmL 94*
Miller, Wilma Hildruth 1936- *WrDr 94*
Miller, Winston 1910- *WhoHol 92*
Miller, Winston E. 1946- *WhoAmL 94*
Miller, Yvonne Bond 1934- *WhoAmP 93, WhoBlA 94*
Miller, Zell Bryan 1932- *IntWW 93, WhoAm 94, WhoAmP 93*
Miller, Zoya Dickins 1923- *WhoWest 94*
Miller and Lyles *WhoCom*
Miller Cavanagh, Virginia Lee 1952- *WhoWest 94*
Miller-Clark, Denise *WhoAmA 93*
Miller-Duggan, Devon *DrAPF 93*
Miller-Girson, Eileen Bonnie 1953- *WhoMW 93*
Millerick, Eugene J. *WhoAmP 93*
Miller Jones, Hon. Mrs. *Who 94*
Miller-Jones, Dalton 1940- *WhoBlA 94*
Miller-Lane, Barbara 1934- *WhoAm 94*
Miller-Lewis, S. Jill *WhoBlA 94*
Miller of Glenlee, Stephen (William Macdonald) 1953- *Who 94*
Miller of Hendon, Baroness 1933- *Who 94*
Miller Parker, Agnes *Who 94*
Miller-Reid, Dora Alma *WhoBlA 94*
Millerson, Gerald (Edward Thomas) 1923- *WrDr 94*
Miller Stewart, Maria W. 1803-1879 *WomPubS*
Milles-Lade *Who 94*
Milleson, Ronald Kinsey 1934- *WhoAmP 93*
Millet, Blaine William 1954- *WhoFI 94*
Millet, Christian *WhoHol 92*
Millet, Clarence 1897-1959 *WhoAmA 93N*
Millet, Pierre Georges Louis 1922- *IntWW 93*
Milletaire, Carl *WhoHol 92*
Millett, Anthea Christine 1941- *Who 94*
Millett, Arthur d1952 *WhoHol 92*
Millett, Caroline Dunlop 1939- *WhoAmA 93*
Millett, John *WrDr 94*
Millett, John (Antill) 1922- *ConAu 43NR*
Millett, John D. d1993 *NewYTBS 93*
Millett, Kate 1934- *BlmGWL, GayLL, WrDr 94*
Millett, Katherine Murray 1934- *WhoAm 94*
Millett, Knolly E. 1922- *WhoBlA 94*
Millett, Martin J(ohn) 1955- *WrDr 94*
Millett, Merlin Lyle 1923- *WhoScEn 94, WhoWest 94*
Millett, Mervyn (Richard Oke) 1910- *WrDr 94*
Millett, Peter (Julian) 1932- *Who 94*
Millett, Ralph Linwood, Jr. 1919- *WhoAm 94*
Millett, Ricardo A. 1945- *WhoBlA 94*
Millette, Ted J. 1930- *WhoAmP 93*
Milley, Jane Elizabeth 1940- *WhoAm 94*
Millgate, Michael Henry 1929- *Who 94, WhoAm 94*
Millgram, Abraham E(zra) 1901-1993 *WrDr 94N*
Millhauser, Marguerite Sue 1953- *WhoAmL 94*
Millhiser, Marlys 1938- *WrDr 94*
Millhiser, Thomas McNally 1949- *WhoAmL 94*
Millhollen, Gary Lloyd 1941- *WhoMW 93*
Millhollin, James 1920- *WhoHol 92*
Milli, Robert 1932- *WhoHol 92*
Millian, Kathleen Lillian 1960- *WhoAmL 94*
Millian, Kenneth Young 1927- *WhoAm 94*
Millican, Arthenia J. Bates 1920- *WhoBlA 94*
Millican, Arthenia Jackson Bates 1920- *BlkWr 2*
Millican, Bill T. 1925- *WhoFI 94*
Millican, David Wayne 1959- *WhoScEn 94*
Millican, George Everett 1897- *WhAm 10*
Millican, James d1955 *WhoHol 92*
Millican, Mike *WhoAmP 93*
Millichamp, Stephen *WhoHol 92*
Millichap, Joseph Gordon 1918- *WhoAm 94*

Millichap, Paul Anthony 1952- WhoAm 94
Millichip, Frederick Albert 1914- Who 94
Millico, (Vito) Giuseppe 1737-1802 NewGrDO
Millie, Elena Gonzalez WhoAmA 93
Milligan, Hon. Lord 1934- Who 94
Milligan, Alice 1866-1953 BlmGWL
Milligan, Andy HorFD
Milligan, Arthur Achille 1917- WhoAm 94
Milligan, Bruce R. 1956- WhoIns 94
Milligan, Frederick James 1906- WhoAmL 94, WhoMW 93
Milligan, Gatewood Carlisle 1907- WhoWest 94
Milligan, Glenn Ellis 1919- WhoAm 94
Milligan, Hugh D. 1931- WhoBlA 94
Milligan, Iain Anstruther 1950- Who 94
Milligan, James 1928-1961 NewGrDO
Milligan, James George Who 94
Milligan, John Drane 1924- WhoAm 94
Milligan, Lawrence Drake, Jr. 1936- WhoAm 94
Milligan, Mancil Wood 1934- WhoAm 94
Milligan, Mary 1935- WhoAm 94
Milligan, Min d1966 WhoHol 92
Milligan, Nancy Patricia 1958- WhoWest 94
Milligan, Randall Andre 1961- WhoBlA 94
Milligan, Robert H. 1927- WhoAmP 93
Milligan, Robert Lee, Jr. 1934- WhoFI 94, WhoMW 93
Milligan, Spike 1918- EncSF 93, IntWW 93, WhoCom, WhoHol 92, WrDr 94
Milligan, Stephen David Wyatt 1948- Who 94
Milligan, Terence Alan (Spike) 1918- Who 94
Milligan, Thomas DrAPF 93
Milligan, Thomas Stuart 1934- WhoAmP 93
Milligan, Timothy James 1940- Who 94
Milligan, Unav Opal Wade WhoBlA 94
Milligan, Veronica Jean Kathleen d1989 Who 94N
Milligan, Victor 1929- WhoScEn 94
Milligan, Wyndham Macbeth Moir 1907- Who 94
Milligram, Steven Irwin 1953- WhoAmL 94
Millikan, Clark Harold 1915- WhoAm 94
Millikan, James Rolens 1950- WhoFI 94
Millikan, Larry Edward 1936- WhoScEn 94
Millikan, Robert Andrews 1868-1953 WorScD
Millikan, Roger Conant 1931- WhoAm 94
Milliken, Alexander Fabbri 1947- WhoAmA 93
Milliken, Charles Buckland 1931- WhoAmL 94
Milliken, Frank Roscoe 1914-1991 WhAm 10
Milliken, Gibbs 1935- WhoAmA 93
Milliken, Herselle E. Jackson 1915- WhoAmP 93
Milliken, John Geddes 1945- WhoAmP 93
Milliken, John Gordon 1927- WhoAm 94, WhoAmP 93, WhoWest 94
Milliken, Roger 1915- WhoAm 94, WhoFI 94
Milliken, Susan Johnstone 1922- WhoAm 94
Milliken, William Grawn 1922- WhoAmP 93
Milliken, William M. 1889-1978 WhoAmA 93N
Millikin, Severance Allen 1895- WhAm 10
Milliman, Carole Lynn 1950- WhoMW 93
Milliman, John D. 1938- WhoScEn 94
Millimet, Erwin 1925- WhoAm 94, WhoAmL 94
Millimet, Joseph Allen 1914- WhoAm 94
Millimet, Stanley 1928- WhoFI 94
Millin, Henry Allan WhoBlA 94
Millin, Laura J. 1954- WhoWest 94
Millin, Sarah Gertrude 1888-1968 BlmGWL
Millinder, Lucky d1966 WhoHol 92
Milling Who 94
Milling, Bert William, Jr. 1946- WhoAm 94, WhoAmL 94
Milling, Peter Francis Who 94
Milling, Roswell King 1940- WhoAm 94
Millington, (Terence) Alaric 1922- WrDr 94
Millington, Anthony Nigel Raymond 1945- Who 94
Millington, Barry 1951- ConAu 43NR
Millington, Ernest Rogers 1916- Who 94
Millington, Mary d1979 WhoHol 92
Millington, Rodney d1989 WhoHol 92
Million, E. Z. 1940- WhoAmP 93
Million, Elmer Mayse 1912-1990 WhAm 10
Million, Kenneth Rhea 1939- WhoFI 94, WhoMW 93
Milliones, Jake 1940-1993 WhoBlA 94N
Milliron, John Patrick 1947- WhoAmP 93
Millirons, Vivian Sue 1942- WhoAmP 93
Millis, David Howard 1958- WhoBlA 94
Millis, Mark Arthur 1955- WhoMW 93
Millis, Mark Matthew 1940- WhoAmP 93
Millis, Robert Lowell 1941- WhoScEn 94
Millisor, Kenneth Ray 1937- WhoMW 93
Millkey, John Michael 1945- WhoAmL 94
Millman, Bruce Russell 1948- WhoAmL 94
Millman, Edward 1907-1964 WhoAmA 93N
Millman, Jacob 1911-1991 WhAm 10
Millman, Joan DrAPF 93
Millman, Joan (M.) 1931- WrDr 94
Millman, Jode Susan 1954- WhoAm 94, WhoAmL 94
Millman, Linda Robin 1945- WhoAmL 94
Millman, Peter MacKenzie 1906-1990 WhAm 10
Millman, Richard George 1925- WhoAm 94
Millman, Robert Barnet 1939- WhoAm 94, WhoScEn 94
Millman, Ronald Burton 1934- WhAm 10
Millman, Sheila Kay 1943- WhoAmP 93
Millman, William d1937 WhoHol 92
Millner, Cork 1931- WrDr 94
Millner, Dianne Maxine 1949- WhoAmL 94, WhoBlA 94
Millner, Marietta d1929 WhoHol 92
Millner, Ralph 1912- Who 94
Millner, Robert B. 1950- WhoAm 94, WhoAmL 94
Millner, Wallace B., III 1939- WhoAm 94
Millner, Wayne d1976 ProFbHF
Millo, Aprile 1958- NewGrDO
Millo, Aprile Elizabeth 1958- WhoAm 94
Millocker, Carl 1842-1899 NewGrDO
Milloff, Mark David 1953- WhoAmA 93
Millon, Charles 1945- IntWW 93
Millon, Delecta Gay 1943- WhoMW 93
Millon, Henry Armand 1927- WhoAm 94
Milloss, Aurel (von) 1906-1988 IntDcB
Millot, Charles WhoHol 92
Milloy, Frank Joseph, Jr. 1924- WhoMW 93
Mills, Viscount 1956- Who 94
Mills, A(nthony) R(eginald) WrDr 94
Mills, Agnes WhoAmA 93
Mills, Alan Benjamin 1945- WhoWest 94
Mills, Alan Bernard 1966- WhoBlA 94
Mills, Alan Oswald Gawler d1992 Who 94N
Mills, Alex 1960- WhoFI 94
Mills, Alley 1952- WhoHol 92
Mills, Alyce WhoHol 92
Mills, Andrew Geoffrey 1952- WhoAm 94, WhoFI 94
Mills, Anna M. 1949- WhoFI 94
Mills, Anthony David 1918- Who 94
Mills, Barbara Jean Lyon 1940- Who 94
Mills, Barry 1950- WhoAmL 94
Mills, Barton Adelbert 1942- WhoWest 94
Mills, Benjamin Fay 1857-1916 DcAmReB 2
Mills, Bernard Yarnton 1920- Who 94
Mills, Billy d1971 WhoHol 92
Mills, Billy G. 1929- WhoBlA 94
Mills, Bob d1934 WhoHol 92
Mills, Bradford 1926- WhoAm 94
Mills, Brooke WhoHol 92
Mills, Bruce Randall 1963- WhoFI 94
Mills, C. Corey d1993 NewYTBS 93
Mills, C.J. EncSF 93
Mills, Carol Andrews 1943- WhoAmP 93
Mills, Carol Diane 1955- WhoAmL 94
Mills, Carol Margaret 1943- WhoFI 94, WhoWest 94
Mills, Cassandra E. 1959- WhoBlA 94
Mills, Cecil E. 1934- WhoAmP 93
Mills, Celeste Louise 1952- WhoAm 94
Mills, Charles (Piercy) 1914- Who 94
Mills, Charles Bright 1896- WhAm 10
Mills, Charles G. 1935- WhoAm 94, WhoFI 94
Mills, Charles Gardner 1940- WhoAmL 94
Mills, Christine Anne 1954- WhoFI 94
Mills, Craig David 1953- WhoAmL 94
Mills, Crispian 1970- WhoHol 92
Mills, Daniel Quinn 1941- WhoAm 94
Mills, David B. WhoAm 94
Mills, David Charles 1948- WhoMW 93
Mills, David Harlow 1932- WhoAm 94
Mills, David Michael 1942- WhoScEn 94
Mills, Debra 1963- WhoAmP 93
Mills, Derek Maitland 1942- WhoWest 94
Mills, Don Harper 1927- WhoAm 94
Mills, Donald 1915- WhoBlA 94, WhoHol 92
Mills, Donna WhoAm 94
Mills, Donna 1944- WhoHol 92
Mills, Donna 1945- IntMPA 94
Mills, Dudley Holbrook 1894- WhAm 10
Mills, Earl Lee 1925- WhoAmP 93
Mills, Edith d1962 WhoHol 92
Mills, Edward (David) 1915- Who 94
Mills, Edward D(avid) 1915- WrDr 94
Mills, Edward James 1954- WhoAmL 94
Mills, Edwin d1981 WhoHol 92
Mills, Edwin Smith 1928- WhoMW 93
Mills, Eleanor Pendleton 1937- WhoAmP 93
Mills, Elizabeth Stilz 1925- WhoAm 94
Mills, Eric Robertson 1918- Who 94
Mills, Eric William 1920- Who 94
Mills, Eugene Sumner 1924- WhoAm 94
Mills, Florence d1927 WhoHol 92
Mills, Florence 1895-1927 AfrAmAl 6
Mills, Frances Jones WhoAm 94, WhoAmP 93
Mills, Frank d1921 WhoHol 92
Mills, Frank d1973 WhoHol 92
Mills, Frank 1923- IntWW 93, Who 94
Mills, Freddie d1965 WhoHol 92
Mills, Frederick Van Fleet 1925- WhoAmA 93
Mills, Gary Wayne 1941- WhoWest 94
Mills, George Alexander 1914- WhoAm 94
Mills, George Marshall 1923- WhoAm 94, WhoFI 94
Mills, George William 1939- WhoAmP 93
Mills, Giles Hallam 1922- Who 94
Mills, Gladys Hunter 1923- WhoBlA 94
Mills, Glen Earl 1908- WhAm 10
Mills, Glenn B., Jr. 1948- WhoBlA 94
Mills, Gordon Lawrence 1933- WhoAm 94, WhoFI 94
Mills, Grace d1972 WhoHol 92
Mills, Grant d1973 WhoHol 92
Mills, Harlan Duncan 1919- WhoAm 94
Mills, Harold Hernshaw 1938- Who 94
Mills, Harry d1982 WhoHol 92
Mills, Harvey Wayland 1926- WhoAmP 93
Mills, Hayley 1946- IntMPA 94, WhoHol 92
Mills, Hayley Cathrine Rose Vivien 1946- IntWW 93
Mills, Herbert d1989 WhoHol 92
Mills, Howard McIlroy 1935- WhoAm 94
Mills, Hughie E. 1924- WhoBlA 94
Mills, Iain Campbell 1940- Who 94
Mills, Ian Who 94
Mills, (George) Ian 1935- Who 94
Mills, Ivor 1929- Who 94
Mills, Ivor Henry 1921- Who 94
Mills, James (Spencer) 1932- WrDr 94
Mills, James E. d1976 WhoHol 92
Mills, James Eugene 1935- WhoAmP 93
Mills, James Niland 1937- WhoAm 94
Mills, James Spencer 1932- WhoAm 94
Mills, James Stephen 1936- WhoAm 94
Mills, James Thoburn 1923- WhoFI 94
Mills, James Willard 1962- WhoAmP 93
Mills, Janet Marsico 1924- WhoAmP 93
Mills, Janet Trafton 1947- WhoAmP 93
Mills, Jay d1951 WhoHol 92
Mills, Jeffery N. WhoAmP 93
Mills, Jerry Woodrow 1940- WhoAm 94
Mills, Jim d1980 WhoHol 92
Mills, Joe d1935 WhoHol 92
Mills, Joey Richard 1950- WhoBlA 94
Mills, John Who 94
Mills, John 1908- ConTFT 11, IntMPA 94, IntWW 93, WhoHol 92
Mills, John 1956- WhoBlA 94
Mills, John, Sr. d1968 WhoHol 92
Mills, John, Jr. d1936 WhoHol 92
Mills, (Laurence) John 1920- Who 94
Mills, John (Lewis Ernest Watts) 1908- Who 94
Mills, John F. F. P. Who 94
Mills, John Francis 1949- WhoAm 94
Mills, John Frederick 1950- Who 94
Mills, John James 1939- WhoScEn 94
Mills, John L. WhoBlA 94
Mills, John Robert 1916- Who 94
Mills, John William 1914- Who 94
Mills, Jon K. WhoAm 94
Mills, Jon L. 1947- WhoAmP 93
Mills, Juan J. 1956- WhoHisp 94
Mills, Juliet 1941- IntMPA 94, WhoHol 92
Mills, Karen R. 1940- WhoAmP 93
Mills, Kathi 1948- WrDr 94
Mills, Kevin Paul 1961- WhoAmL 94
Mills, Larry Glenn 1951- WhoBlA 94
Mills, Laurin Howard 1957- WhoAmL 94
Mills, Lawrence 1932- WhoAmL 94, WhoFI 94, WhoWest 94
Mills, Lawrence William Robert 1934- Who 94
Mills, Leif Anthony 1936- Who 94
Mills, Leonard Sidney 1914- Who 94
Mills, Lester Stephen 1958- WhoScEn 94
Mills, Lev Timothy 1940- WhoAmA 93
Mills, Linda S. 1951- WhoAm 94, WhoFI 94
Mills, Liston Oury 1928- WhoAm 94
Mills, Lloyd L. DrAPF 93
Mills, Lois Jean 1939- WhoMW 93
Mills, Lois R. 1946- WhoMW 93
Mills, Lois Terrell 1958- WhoBlA 94
Mills, Margaret A(nn) 1946- ConAu 141
Mills, Mary Bell McMillan Who 94
Mills, Mary Elizabeth 1926- WhoBlA 94
Mills, Mary Lee 1912- WhoBlA 94
Mills, Mervyn 1906- WrDr 94
Mills, Michael Albert Farleigh 1934- WhoWest 94
Mills, Michael Paul 1956- WhoAmP 93
Mills, Mike WhoAm 94
Mills, Morris Hadley 1927- WhoAmP 93, WhoMW 93
Mills, Mort WhoHol 92
Mills, Murray John Who 94
Mills, Neil McLay 1923- Who 94
Mills, Norm 1924- WhoAmP 93
Mills, Olan, II 1930- WhoAm 94, WhoFI 94
Mills, Paul Chadbourne 1924- WhoAmA 93
Mills, Paul L. DrAPF 93
Mills, Peter 1598-1670 DcNaB MP
Mills, Peter (Frederick Leighton) 1924- Who 94
Mills, Peter McLay d1993 Who 94N
Mills, Peter Richard 1939- WhoAm 94
Mills, Peter William 1942- Who 94
Mills, Ralph J(oseph), Jr. 1931- WrDr 94
Mills, Richard Henry 1929- WhoAm 94, WhoAmL 94, WhoMW 93
Mills, Richard Michael 1931- Who 94
Mills, Robert 1936- WhoBlA 94
Mills, Robert A. 1934- WhoAm 94
Mills, Robert E. EncSF 93
Mills, Robert Ferris 1939- Who 94
Mills, Robert Gail 1924- WhoAm 94
Mills, Robert Laurence 1927- WhoAm 94, WhoScEn 94
Mills, Robert Lee 1916- WhoAm 94
Mills, Robert P(ark) 1920-1986 EncSF 93
Mills, Rodney Daniel 1942- WhoScEn 94
Mills, Samuel Davis, Jr. 1959- WhoAm 94
Mills, Samuel John 1783-1818 DcAmReB 2
Mills, Shirley 1926- WhoHol 92
Mills, Stanley Edwin Druce 1913- Who 94
Mills, Stanley Robert, Jr. 1929- WhoAmL 94, WhoFI 94
Mills, Stephanie 1959- WhoBlA 94
Mills, Stephen (Paul) 1952- WrDr 94
Mills, Stratton Who 94
Mills, (William) Stratton 1932- Who 94
Mills, Sumner Amos 1895- WhAm 10
Mills, Terence N. 1945- WhoFI 94
Mills, Terry, III 1946- WhoScEn 94
Mills, Terry Richard 1967- WhoBlA 94
Mills, Tessa Jane Helen Douglas Who 94
Mills, Theodore Mason 1920- WhoAm 94
Mills, Thomas C. H. 1949- WhoWest 94
Mills, Thomas Cooke 1955- WhoWest 94
Mills, Thomas R. d1953 WhoHol 92
Mills, Wilbur 1909-1992 AnObit 1992
Mills, Wilbur Daigh 1909-1992 WhAm 10
Mills, William Fredrick 1946- WhoAmL 94
Mills, William Harold, Jr. 1939- WhoAm 94
Mills, William Hayes 1931- WhoAm 94
Mills, William P. 1947- WhoAmP 93
Mills, Wyman Fellers 1924- WhoWest 94
Millsap, John E. 1960- WhoAmP 93
Millsap, Mike 1948- WhoAmP 93
Millsaps, Bryant 1947- WhoAm 94, WhoAmP 93
Millsaps, Fred Ray 1929- WhoAm 94
Millsaps, Knox IntWW 93N
Millsaps, Knox 1921- WhAm 10
Millsaps, Luther Lee 1926- WhoAmP 93
Millsfield, Charles d1962 WhoHol 92
Millslagle, Jeffrey Glenn 1960- WhoMW 93
Mills-Malet, Vincent EncSF 93
Millsom, Williams Erwin 1938- WhoFI 94
Millson, John Albert 1918- Who 94
Millson, John Arthur 1952- WhoAm 94, WhoMW 93
Millson, Rory Oliver 1950- WhoAm 94, WhoAmL 94
Millsop, Thomas E. 1898-1967 EncABHB 9 [port]
Millspaugh, Ben P. 1936- SmATA 77 [port]
Millspaugh, Martin Laurence 1925- WhoAm 94
Millspaugh, Richard Paul 1958- WhoMW 93
Millspaugh, Robert Wahl 1930- WhoMW 93
Millstein, David J. 1953- WhoAmL 94
Millstein, Ira M. 1926- WhoAm 94, WhoFI 94
Millstein, Richard Allen 1945- WhoAm 94
Millstone, David J. 1946- WhoAm 94, WhoAmL 94
Millu, Liana 1915- ConAu 141

Millum, Trevor 1945- WrDr 94
Millward, Dawson d1926 WhoHol 92
Millward, Eric (Geoffrey William) 1935- WrDr 94
Millward, William 1909- Who 94
Millwood, Kenneth L. 1947- WhoAmL 94
Milly d1980 WhoHol 92
Milly, Raymond Anthony 1930- WhoAmL 94
Milman, Andree Who 94
Milman, Claudio Daniel 1961- WhoMW 93
Milman, Derek 1918- Who 94
Milman, Donald S. 1924- WrDr 94
Milmine, Douglas 1921- Who 94
Milmo, John Boyle Martin 1943- Who 94
Milmo, Patrick Helenus 1938- Who 94
Milmoe, J. Gregory 1947- WhoAmL 94
Milmore, Benno Karl 1914- WhoWest 94
Milne, Baron 1909- Who 94
Milne, A. A. 1882-1956 BlmGEL
Milne, Alasdair David Gordon 1930- IntWW 93, Who 94
Milne, Alexander Taylor 1906- Who 94
Milne, Andrew McNicoll 1937- Who 94
Milne, Berkeley Who 94
Milne, (Alexander) Berkeley 1924- Who 94
Milne, Bruce Thomas 1957- WhoWest 94
Milne, Christopher Robin 1920- WrDr 94
Milne, David Calder 1945- Who 94
Milne, Denys Gordon 1926- IntWW 93, Who 94
Milne, Donald George 1934- WhoAmP 93
Milne, Douglas Graeme 1919- Who 94
Milne, Garth LeRoy 1942- WhoAm 94
Milne, Ian Innes 1912- Who 94
Milne, James L. Who 94
Milne, John 1850-1913 DcNaB MP
Milne, John 1952- WrDr 94
Milne, John (Drummond) 1924- Who 94
Milne, John Drummond 1924- IntWW 93
Milne, Kenneth Lancelot 1915- Who 94
Milne, Larry 1940- WrDr 94
Milne, Lennox d1980 WhoHol 92
Milne, Lorus J. SmATA 18AS [port]
Milne, Lorus J(ohnson) WrDr 94
Milne, Margery SmATA 18AS [port]
Milne, Margery (Joan Greene) WrDr 94
Milne, Maurice 1916- Who 94
Milne, Nanette Lilian Margaret 1942- Who 94
Milne, Norman 1915- Who 94
Milne, Patricia R. 1948- WhoAmP 93
Milne, Peter Alexander 1935- Who 94
Milne, Robert David 1930- WhoAm 94
Milne, Robert Duncan (Gordon) 1844-1899 EncSF 93
Milne, Seumas 1958- WrDr 94
Milne, William Gordon 1921-1989 WhAm 10
Milne Home, Archibald John Fitzwilliam d1993 Who 94N
Milne Home, John Gavin 1916- Who 94
Milner Who 94
Milner, Anthony Francis Dominic 1925- IntWW 93
Milner, Arthur John Robin Gorell 1934- Who 94
Milner, Brenda (Atkinson) 1918- Who 94
Milner, Brenda Atkinson Langford 1918- WhoAm 94
Milner, Charles Fremont, Jr. 1942- WhoFI 94
Milner, Eddie James, Jr. 1955- WhoBlA 94
Milner, Edward 1819-1884 DcNaB MP
Milner, Esther 1918- WrDr 94
Milner, Franklin 1956- WhoFI 94
Milner, Harold William 1934- WhoAm 94
Milner, Henry Ernest 1845-1906 DcNaB MP
Milner, Howard M. 1937- WhoAm 94
Milner, Ian Frank George 1911- WrDr 94
Milner, Irvin Myron 1916- WhoAm 94
Milner, Jack 1910- IntMPA 94
Milner, Jay 1938- WrDr 94
Milner, Jean Shepard 1893- WhAm 10
Milner, Jessamine d1983 WhoHol 92
Milner, Joanne R. 1957- WhoAmP 93
Milner, Joe W. 1929- WhoWest 94
Milner, Joseph 1922- Who 94
Milner, Marion 1900- WrDr 94
Milner, Martin 1927- WhoHol 92
Milner, Martin 1931- IntMPA 94
Milner, Martin 1952- WhoWest 94
Milner, Max 1914- WhoAm 94
Milner, Michael Edwin 1952- WhoBlA 94
Milner, Mordaunt Who 94
Milner, (George Edward) Mordaunt 1911- Who 94
Milner, Peter Marshall 1919- WhoAm 94
Milner, Ralph Who 94
Milner, Robert Joseph 1950- WhoMW 93
Milner, Ron(ald) 1938- ConDr 93, WrDr 94
Milner, Ronald DrAPF 93
Milner, Ronald James 1927- Who 94
Milner, Susan Jeanne 1947- WhoWest 94
Milner, Thirman L. 1933- WhoAmP 93, WhoBlA 94
Milner-Barry, (Philip) Stuart 1906- Who 94
Milner-Brage, John Richard 1944- WhoMW 93
Milner of Leeds, Baron 1923- Who 94
Milnes, Arthur George 1922- WhoAm 94
Milnes, Robert Winston 1948- WhoAmA 93
Milnes, Rodney Who 94
Milnes, Rodney 1936- NewGrDO
Milnes, Sherill 1935- IntWW 93
Milnes, Sherrill (Eustace) 1935- NewGrDO
Milnes, Sherrill Eustace 1935- WhoAm 94
Milnes, William Robert, Jr. 1946- WhoFI 94
Milnes Coates, Anthony (Robert) 1948- Who 94
Milne-Watson, Michael 1910- IntWW 93
Milne-Watson, Sir Michael 1910- Who 94
Milnikel, Robert Saxon 1926- WhoAm 94
Milnor, William Robert 1920- WhoAm 94
Milo, Albert Javier, Jr. 1951- WhoHisp 94
Milo, Frank Anthony 1946- WhoScEn 94
Milo, Ronnie 1949- IntWW 93
Milo, Sandra 1935- WhoHol 92
Milom, W. Michael 1942- WhoAmL 94
Milona, Costa 1889-1949 NewGrDO
Milonas, Herodotos WhoAmA 93
Milonas, Minos 1936- WhoAmA 93
Milone, Anthony M. 1932- WhoAm 94, WhoWest 94
Milone, Eugene Frank 1939- WhoScEn 94, WhoWest 94
Milone, Francis Michael 1947- WhoAm 94, WhoAmL 94
Milongo, Andre IntWW 93
Milord, Susan 1954- SmATA 74 [port]
Milos, Milos d1966 WhoHol 92
Milosevic, Slobodan 1941- IntWW 93
Milosh, Eugene John 1933- WhoAm 94
Miloslavsky, Dimitry T. Who 94
Milosz, Czeslaw 1911- ConWorW 93, IntWW 93, PoeCrit 8 [port], Who 94, WhoAm 94, WhoWest 94
Milow, Keith 1945- IntWW 93
Milrad, Aaron M. 1935- WhoAmA 93
Milrod, Eve Meredith 1962- WhoFI 94
Milrod, Jonathan Craig 1957- WhoWest 94
Milrod, Linda Jane 1953- WhoWest 94
Milroy, Dominic Liston 1932- Who 94
Milsap, Ronnie WhoAm 94
Mil'shtein, Samson 1940- WhoScEn 94
Milsom, Charles Henry 1926- WrDr 94
Milsom, Robert Cortlandt 1924- WhoAm 94, WhoFI 94
Milsom, Stroud Francis Charles 1923- IntWW 93, Who 94, WrDr 94
Milstead, Roderick Leon, Jr. 1969- WhoBlA 94
Milsted, David 1954- WrDr 94
Milstein, Albert 1946- WhoAm 94, WhoAmL 94
Milstein, Cesar 1927- IntWW 93, Who 94, WhoAm 94, WhoScEn 94
Milstein, Laurence Bennett 1942- WhoAm 94
Milstein, Michael Craig 1966- WhoWest 94
Milstein, Monroe Gary 1927- WhoFI 94
Milstein, Nathan d1992 IntWW 93N, Who 94N
Milstein, Nathan 1903-1992 AnObit 1992
Milstein, Nathan 1904-1992 CurBio 93N
Milstein, Richard Craig 1946- WhoAmL 94
Milstein, Richard Sherman 1926- WhoAm 94
Milsten, David Randolph 1903- WhoAm 94
Milsten, Robert B. 1932- WhoAm 94
Miltern, John d1937 WhoHol 92
Miltner, Robert Francis 1949- WhoMW 93
Milton, Viscount 1839-1877 WhWE
Milton, Barbara DrAPF 93
Milton, Billy d1989 WhoHol 92
Milton, Bob d1983 WhoHol 92
Milton, Chad Earl 1947- WhoAmL 94
Milton, Christian Michel 1947- WhoFI 94
Milton, Christopher Hull 1947- WhoAm 94
Milton, David Q. DrAPF 93
Milton, Derek Francis 1935- IntWW 93, Who 94
Milton, Edith DrAPF 93
Milton, Ernest d1974 WhoHol 92
Milton, Georges d1970 WhoHol 92
Milton, Harry d1965 WhoHol 92
Milton, Henry 1918- WhoBlA 94
Milton, Israel Henry 1929- WhoBlA 94
Milton, John 1608-1674 BlmGEL, DcLB 131 [port]
Milton, John Charles Douglas 1924- WhoAm 94
Milton, John R. DrAPF 93
Milton, John R 1924- WrDr 94
Milton, John Ronald 1924- WhoAm 94
Milton, Joyce DrAPF 93
Milton, Joyce 1946- WrDr 94
Milton, LeRoy 1924- WhoBlA 94
Milton, Louette d1930 WhoHol 92
Milton, Maud d1945 WhoHol 92
Milton, Morris Wilbert 1943- WhoAmP 93
Milton, Octavia Washington 1933- WhoBlA 94
Milton, Peter Winslow 1930- WhoAm 94, WhoAmA 93
Milton, Richard Henry 1938- WhoAm 94
Milton, Robert Mitchell 1920- WhoAm 94
Milton, Sue 1942- WhoAmP 93
Milton-Thompson, Godfrey (James) 1930- Who 94
Milton-Thompson, James 1930- IntWW 93
Milu, Constantin Gheorghe 1943- WhoScEn 94
Milvenan, Richard D. 1959- WhoAmL 94
Milverton, Baron 1930- Who 94
Milward, Alan S 1935- WrDr 94
Milward, Alan Steele 1935- Who 94
Milyukov, Oleg Vadimovich 1936- LngBDD
Milyutin, Yury Sergeyevich 1903-1968 NewGrDO
Milz, Mary Elizabeth 1961- WhoMW 93
Mim, Adrienne C. 1931- WhoAmA 93
Mimiaga, Robert Joaquin 1937- WhoHisp 94
Mimica, Vatroslav 1923-1972 IntDcF 2-4
Mimieux, Yvette 1939- IntMPA 94
Mimieux, Yvette 1941- WhoHol 92
Mimms, Maxine Buie 1929- WhoBlA 94
Mimna, Curtis John 1943- WhoFI 94
Mims, Beverly Carol 1955- WhoBlA 94
Mims, Cedric Arthur 1924- IntWW 93, Who 94
Mims, Edward Trow 1948- WhoFI 94
Mims, Forrest Marion, III 1944- WhoAm 94
Mims, George E. 1932- WhoBlA 94
Mims, George L. 1934- WhoBlA 94
Mims, Hornsby 1926- WhoIns 94
Mims, Lambert Carter 1930- WhoAmP 93
Mims, Luke d1933 WhoHol 92
Mims, Marjorie Joyce 1926- WhoBlA 94
Mims, Oscar Lugrie 1934- WhoBlA 94
Mims, Raymond Everett, Sr. 1938- WhoBlA 94
Mims, Robert Bradford 1934- WhoBlA 94
Mims, Thomas Jerome 1899- WhoAm 94, WhoFI 94, WhoIns 94
Mims, William WhoHol 92
Mims, William C. 1957- WhoAmP 93
Mims, William Thomas 1963- WhoAmP 93
Mims-Rich, Robin Eleanor 1965- WhoWest 94
Min, David Ilki 1951- WhoAsA 94
Min, Hokey 1954- WhoAsA 94, WhoFI 94
Min, K. Jo 1961- WhoAsA 94
Min, Kyung Ho 1935- WhoAsA 94
Min, Linda Lou 1945- WhoMW 93
Min, Nancy-Ann WhoAmP 93
Min, Pyong-Gap 1942- WhoAsA 94
Min, Sung Sik 1942- WhoFI 94
Min, Yong Soon 1953- WhoAmA 93, WhoAsA 94
Minac, Vladimir 1922- IntWW 93
Minah, Francis Misheck 1929- IntWW 93
Minahan, Daniel F. 1929- WhoAm 94, WhoAmL 94, WhoFI 94
Minahan, John A. 1956- ConAu 142
Minahan, John C., Jr. 1943- WhoAm 94, WhoAmL 94
Minahan, John English 1933- WhoAm 94
Minahan, Peter M. 1945- WhoAmP 93
Minahen, Timothy Malcolm 1955- WhoScEn 94
Minakov, Yury Aleksandrovich 1945- LngBDD
Minami, Robert Yoshio 1919- WhoWest 94
Mina-Mora, Dorise Olson 1932-1991 WhoAmA 93N
Mina-Mora, Raul Jose 1914- WhoAmA 93
Minamoto, Jennifer Noriko 1950- WhoAsA 94
Minamoto Yoritomo 1147-1199 HisWorL [port]
Minard, B. Gail 1952- WhoMW 93
Minard, Everett Lawrence, III 1949- WhoAm 94
Minard, Frank Pell Lawrence 1945- WhoAm 94
Minard, Joseph M. 1932- WhoAmP 93
Minard, Michael Kent 1944- WhoWest 94
Minard, Robert George 1956- WhoMW 93
Minardi, Richard A., Jr. 1943- WhoAmL 94
Minardos, Nico WhoHol 92
Minarik, Else H(olmelund) 1920- WrDr 94
Minarik, John Paul DrAPF 93
Minarik, Joseph John 1949- WhoAm 94
Minarik, Stephen J., III 1960- WhoAmP 93
Minasi, Anthony 1948- WhoFI 94
Minassian, Michael G. DrAPF 93
Minasy, Arthur John 1925- WhoScEn 94
Minato, Nicolo c. 1627-1698 NewGrDO
Minc, Henryk 1919- WhoAm 94
Mincer, Jacob 1922- IntWW 93, WhoAm 94, WhoFI 94
Mincey, W. James 1947- WhoBlA 94
Minch, Lawrence Norman 1948- WhoAmL 94
Minch, Virgil Adelbert 1924- WhoFI 94
Minch, Walter Edward 1926- WhoAmP 93
Minchejmer, Adam 1830-1904 NewGrDO
Minchew, John Randall 1957- WhoAmL 94
Minchin, Michael M., Jr. 1926- WhoFI 94
Minchinton, Walter Edward 1921- Who 94, WrDr 94
Minciotti, Esther d1962 WhoHol 92
Minciotti, Silvio d1961 WhoHol 92
Minck, Richard V. 1932- WhoIns 94
Minckwitz, Bernard von 1944- IntWW 93
Minco, Marga 1920- BlmGWL [port]
Mincy, Lisa Jo 1960- WhoMW 93
Minczeski, John DrAPF 93
Mindel, Laurence Brisker 1937- WhoFI 94
Mindell, Arnold 1940- WhoWest 94
Mindell, Earl Lawrence 1940- WhoWest 94
Mindell, Eugene Robert 1922- WhoAm 94
Minden, R. Doyle 1933- WhoWest 94
Mindes, Gayle Dean 1942- WhoMW 93
Mindham, Richard Hugh Shiels 1935- Who 94
Mindiola, Tatcho, Jr. WhoHisp 94
Mindlin, Michael 1923- WrDr 94
Mindlin, Richard Barnett 1926- WhoAm 94
Mindling, Martin John 1947- WhoFI 94, WhoWest 94
Mindrum, G. Scott 1958- WhoMW 93
Minear, Beth 1939- WhoAmA 93
Minear, Paul Sevier 1906- WrDr 94
Minear, Richard Hoffman 1938- WrDr 94
Minear, Roger Allan 1939- WhoScEn 94
Minear, William Loris 1910- WhoWest 94
Mineka, Susan 1948- WhoMW 93
Minelli, Giovanni Battista 1687?-1735? NewGrDO
Min Enze WhoPRCh 91
Mineo, Ronald William 1953- WhoFI 94
Mineo, Sal d1976 WhoHol 92
Miner, A. Bradford 1947- WhoAm 94
Miner, Alice E. 1956- WhoMW 93
Miner, Bert Dean 1926- WhoWest 94
Miner, David Morris 1962- WhoAmP 93
Miner, Debra Riggs 1953- WhoMW 93
Miner, Dennis Kane 1944- WhoFI 94
Miner, Don Jones 1951- WhoAmL 94
Miner, Donald 1913- WhoAmP 93
Miner, Doris P. WhoAmP 93
Miner, Dorothy Eugenia 1906-1973 WhoAmA 93N
Miner, Earl (Roy) 1927- WrDr 94
Miner, Earl Howard 1923- WhoAm 94
Miner, Earl Roy 1927- WhoAm 94
Miner, Harold WhoBlA 94
Miner, Horace Mitchell 1912- WhoAm 94
Miner, Jan 1917- WhoAm 94, WhoHol 92
Miner, John Burnham 1926- WhoAm 94, WhoFI 94
Miner, John Edward 1937- WhoWest 94
Miner, John Ronald 1938- WhoAm 94, WhoScEn 94, WhoWest 94
Miner, Mark Alan 1961- WhoFI 94
Miner, Robbin Kay 1948- WhoMW 93
Miner, Robert Gordon 1923- WhoAm 94
Miner, Roger Jeffrey 1934- WhoAm 94, WhoAmL 94, WhoAmP 93
Miner, Ruth 1920- WhoAmP 93
Miner, Steve 1951- HorFD, IntMPA 94
Miner, Thomas Hawley 1927- WhoAm 94
Miner, Valerie DrAPF 93
Miner, William Gerard 1950- WhoBlA 94
Minerbi, Luciano Mario Lauro 1941- WhoWest 94
Mines, Cynthia J. 1955- WhoMW 93
Mines, Denise Carol 1956- WhoAmL 94
Mines, Herbert Thomas 1929- WhoFI 94
Mines, Michael 1929- WhoAmL 94, WhoWest 94
Mines, Richard Oliver, Jr. 1953- WhoScEn 94
Mines, Samuel 1909- EncSF 93
Mineta, Norman Y. 1931- CngDr 93
Mineta, Norman Yoshio 1931- WhoAm 94, WhoAmP 93, WhoAsA 94, WhoWest 94
Minett, John Charles 1965- WhoAmL 94

Minette, Dennis Jerome 1937- WhoFI 94, WhoScEn 94
Minette, William F. 1921- WhoAmP 93
Minetti, G. Joseph d1993 NewYTBS 93 [port]
Minetti, Maria d1971 WhoHol 92
Minevitch, Borrah d1955 WhoHol 92
Minewski, Alex 1917-1979 WhoAmA 93N
Minford, (Anthony) Patrick (Leslie) 1943- IntWW 93, Who 94
Ming, Donald George K. WhoBlA 94
Ming, Moy Luke d1964 WhoHol 92
Ming, Si-Chun 1922- WhoAm 94, WhoScEn 94
Ming, William Paul 1950- WhoAsA 94
Mingay, G(ordon) E(dmund) 1923- WrDr 94
Mingay, James 1752-1812 DcNaB MP
Mingay, (Frederick) Ray 1938- Who 94
Ming Cho Lee 1930- NewGrDO
Minge, David 1942- CngDr 93, WhoAm 94, WhoAmP 93, WhoMW 93
Minge, James 1949- WhoAmL 94
Mingee, James Clyde, III 1943- WhoAmL 94
Minger, Terrell John 1942- WhoFI 94, WhoWest 94
Minghella, Anthony 1954- ConDr 93, WrDr 94
Mingione, Enzo 1947- ConAu 141
Mingle, John Orville 1931- WhoAm 94
Minglin, Michael Alan 1951- WhoAmP 93
Mingo WhAmRev
Mingo, James William Edgar 1926- WhoAm 94
Mingo, Pauline Hylton 1945- WhoBlA 94
Mingos, David Michael Patrick 1944- IntWW 93, Who 94
Mingotti, Pietro c. 1702-1759 NewGrDO
Mingotti, Regina 1722-1808 NewGrDO
Min Guirong WhoPRCh 91
Mingus, Charles d1979 WhoHol 92
Mingus, Charles 1922-1979 AfrAmAl 6 [port]
Ming Yang 1916- WhoPRCh 91 [port]
Ming Zhen WhoPRCh 91 [port]
Minhas, Faqir Ullah 1924- WhoFI 94, WhoWest 94
Minhinnick, Robert 1952- WrDr 94
Minic, Milos 1914- IntWW 93
Minichello, Dennis 1952- WhoAm 94
Minick, Michael 1945- WhoAm 94
Minick, Roger 1944- WhoAmA 93
Minick, W. Ted 1940- WhoAmL 94
Minicucci, Richard Francis 1947- WhoAm 94, WhoAmL 94
Minicucci, Robert A. 1952- WhoAm 94
Miniear, J. Dederick 1959- WhoMW 93
Minikes, Michael 1943- WhoFI 94
Minikes, Stephan Michael 1938- WhoAm 94
Minin, Evgeny Georgievich 1938- LngBDD
Mininberg, David T. 1936- WhoScEn 94
Minion, Mia 1960- WhoBlA 94
Minirth, Frank B. WrDr 94
Minisci, Brenda (Eileen) 1939- WhoAmA 93
Minish, Joseph George 1916- WhoAmP 93
Minish, Robert Arthur 1938- WhoAm 94
Minisi, Anthony S. 1926- WhoAm 94
Minister, Michael E. 1944- WhoAm 94, WhoAmL 94
Ministeri, George d1986 WhoHol 92
Ministry ConMus 10 [port]
Miniter, Margaret E. WhoAmL 94
Minium, Edward W. 1917- WrDr 94
Miniutti, John Roberts 1937- WhoFI 94
Miniutti, Robert Leonard 1962- WhoScEn 94
Mink, Eric P. 1947- WhoAm 94
Mink, John c. 1850-1943 EncNAR
Mink, John Robert 1927- WhoAm 94
Mink, Lawrence B. 1943- WhoAmL 94
Mink, Lyle R. 1944- WhoAmL 94
Mink, Patsy T. 1927- CngDr 93
Mink, Patsy Takemoto 1927- WhoAm 94, WhoAmP 93, WhoAsA 94, WhoWest 94
Minkel, Edward Joseph 1921- WhoAmP 93
Minkel, Herbert Philip, Jr. 1947- WhoAm 94, WhoAmL 94
Minker, Jack 1927- WhoAm 94
Minkoff, Jack 1925- WhoAm 94
Minkoff, Randy 1949- ConAu 141
Minkoff, Sandra Rita 1936- WhoMW 93
Minkov, Svetoslav 1902-1966 EncSF 93
Minkow, Rosalie 1927- WrDr 94
Minkowitz, Martin 1939- WhoAm 94
Minkowitz, Norma 1937- WhoAmA 93
Minkowski, Alexandre 1915- IntWW 93
Minkowski, Jan Michael 1916-1991 WhAm 10
Minkowycz, W. J. 1937- WhoAm 94, WhoScEn 94
Minks, Wilfried 1930- IntWW 93
Minkus, Barbara 1943- WhoHol 92
Minkus, Leon 1826-1917 IntDcB
Minkus, Raymond David 1953- WhoAm 94
Minn, Young Key 1938- WhoScEn 94
Minne, Lona A. WhoAmP 93
Minne, Nels 1901-1991 WhAm 10
Minnegerode, Cuthbert Powell 1876-1951 WhoAmA 93N
Minnelli, Liza 1946- IntMPA 94, IntWW 93, WhoAm 94, WhoHol 92
Minner, Kathryn d1969 WhoHol 92
Minner, Ruth Ann 1935- WhoAm 94, WhoAmP 93
Minnerly, Robert Ward 1935- WhoWest 94
Minnerop, Henry 1937- WhoAm 94
Minnes, Frederick D. 1948- WhoAmL 94
Minneste, Viktor, Jr. 1932- WhoMW 93
Minnette, Rhonda Williams 1952- WhoFI 94
Minney, Michael Jay 1948- WhoAmL 94, WhoAmP 93
Minnich, Diane Kay 1956- WhoAmL 94, WhoWest 94
Minnich, Joseph Edward 1932- WhoFI 94, WhoWest 94
Minnich, Virginia 1910- WhoAm 94
Minnick, Bruce Alexander 1943- WhoAmL 94
Minnick, Carlton Printess, Jr. 1927- WhoAm 94
Minnick, Daniel James, Jr. 1925- WhoAmP 93
Minnick, Esther Tress WhoAmA 93
Minnick, Joseph H. WhoAmP 93
Minnick, Malcolm David 1946- WhoAm 94, WhoAmL 94
Minnick, Sylvia Sun 1941- WhoAsA 94
Minnick, Walter Clifford 1942- WhoAm 94
Minnie, Mary Virginia 1922- WhoWest 94
Minnig, William Paul 1950- WhoAsA 94
Minnig, William Robert 1938- WhoFI 94
Minnigerode, Gunther von 1929- IntWW 93
Minnion, John (Lawrence) 1939- WrDr 94
Minnis, M. John WhoAmP 93
Minnitt, Robert John 1913- Who 94
Minnix, Bruce Milton 1923- WhoAm 94
Minns, Albert d1985 WhoHol 92
Minns, Clement d1978 WhoHol 92
Minns, Ellis Hovell 1874-1953 DcNaB MP
Minns, Susan 1839-1938 DcLB 140
Mino, Carlos Felix 1932- WhoHisp 94
Minocha, Harish C. 1932- WhoAsA 94
Minogue, Kenneth Robert 1930- Who 94, WrDr 94
Minogue, Kylie WhoHol 92
Minogue, Patrick John O'Brien 1922- Who 94
Minogue, Robert Brophy 1928- WhoAm 94
Minogue, Thomas John 1954- WhoAmL 94
Minogue, Valerie Pearson 1931- WrDr 94
Minoja, Ambrogio 1752-1825 NewGrDO
Minoletti, Paul Gerard 1957- WhoAmL 94
Minor, Bernice F. 1932- WhoAmP 93
Minor, Billy Joe 1938- WhoBlA 94
Minor, Bob 1944- WhoHol 92
Minor, Charles Daniel 1927- WhoAm 94
Minor, Cynthia A. 1957- WhoAmL 94
Minor, David M. 1947- WhoBlA 94
Minor, Edward Colquitt 1942- WhoFI 94
Minor, Emma Lucille 1925- WhoBlA 94
Minor, George Gilmer, III 1940- WhoFI 94
Minor, Hugh David 1955- WhoMW 93
Minor, James DrAPF 93
Minor, Jessica WhoBlA 94
Minor, John S. 1948- WhoBlA 94
Minor, John Threecivelous, III 1950- WhoWest 94
Minor, Joseph Edward 1938- WhoAm 94
Minor, Marcia Marie Carnicelli 1948- WhoMW 93
Minor, Mark William 1956- WhoScEn 94
Minor, Melvin G. 1937- WhoAmP 93
Minor, Raleigh Colston 1936- WhoAm 94
Minor, Robert Allen 1948- WhoAm 94, WhoAmL 94
Minor, Robert Walter 1919- WhoAm 94
Minor, Tracey L. 1963- WhoBlA 94
Minor, Vicki Beize 1938- WhoBlA 94
Minor, William WhoAmP 93
Minor, William Ernst 1954- WhoMW 93
Minor, Willie 1951- WhoBlA 94
Minoso, Minnie 1922- WhoHisp 94
Minot, Anna WhoHol 92
Minot, Stephen DrAPF 93
Minot, Stephen 1927- WrDr 94
Minot, Susan 1956- WrDr 94
Minot, Winthrop Gardner 1951- WhoAmL 94
Minotis, Alexis d1990 WhoHol 92
Minotti, Felice d1963 WhoHol 92
Minovitch, Michael A. 1935- WhoWest 94
Minow, Josephine Baskin 1926- WhoAm 94
Minow, Newton N. 1926- IntWW 93
Minow, Newton N(orman) 1926- WrDr 94
Minow, Newton Norman 1926- WhoAm 94, WhoAmP 93
Minow, Terry Lynn 1954- WhoAmP 93
Minowa, Noboru 1924- IntWW 93
Minozzi, Rosanna 1942- WhoWomW 91
Minshall, Greg 1952- WhoScEn 94
Minshall, Vera 1924- WrDr 94
Minshall, William Edwin, Jr. 1911-1990 WhAm 10
Minsker, Andrew Claude 1962- WhoWest 94
Minsker, Robert Stanley 1911- WhoAm 94, WhoFI 94
Minsky, Betty Jane 1932- WrDr 94
Minsky, Howard Alan 1946- WhoAmL 94
Minsky, Marvin Lee 1927- WhoScEn 94
Minsky, Richard 1947- WhoAmA 93
Minster, Norman Edgar 1922- WhoMW 93
Minta, Stephen 1947- WrDr 94
Minteer, Daniel C. 1949- WhoAmL 94
Minter, Alan 1951- IntWW 93
Minter, Charles Laskey 1941- WhoFI 94
Minter, David Edward 1946- WhoScEn 94
Minter, David Lee 1935- WhoAm 94, WrDr 94
Minter, Drew 1955- NewGrDO
Minter, Eloise Devada 1928- WhoBlA 94
Minter, Jerry Burnett 1913- WhoAm 94
Minter, Kendall Arthur 1952- WhoAmL 94, WhoBlA 94
Minter, Kristin WhoHol 92
Minter, Marilyn A. 1948- WhoAmA 93
Minter, Mary Miles d1984 WhoHol 92
Minter, Philip Clayton 1928- WhoAm 94
Minter, Steven Alan 1938- WhoAm 94, WhoBlA 94
Minter, Thomas Kendall 1924- WhoBlA 94
Minter, Wilbert Douglas, Sr. 1946- WhoBlA 94
Minter, William Fred d1937 WhoHol 92
Mintich, Mary Ringelberg WhoAmA 93
Minto, Earl of 1928- Who 94
Minto, Alfred 1928- Who 94
Minto, Clive 1945- WhoAm 94, WhoFI 94
Minto, Dorothy 1888- WhoHol 92
Minto, William 1845-1893 EncSF 93
Mintoff, Dominic 1916- IntWW 93, Who 94
Minton, Dwight Church 1934- WhoAm 94, WhoFI 94
Minton, Frank WhoIns 94
Minton, Graydon Blair 1966- WhoFI 94
Minton, Helena DrAPF 93
Minton, Jerry Davis 1928- WhoAm 94
Minton, John Dean 1921- WhoAm 94
Minton, John Peter 1934-1990 WhAm 10
Minton, Joseph Paul 1924- WhoAm 94
Minton, Michael B. 1953- WhoAmL 94
Minton, O. R., Jr. 1950- WhoAmP 93
Minton, Paul Christopher 1933- WhoMW 93
Minton, Thomas Wayne 1952- WhoWest 94
Minton, Torri 1956- WhoWest 94
Minton, Yvonne (Fay) 1938- NewGrDO
Minton, Yvonne Fay Who 94, WhoAm 94
Minton, Yvonne Fay 1938- IntWW 93
Minty, Emil WhoHol 92
Minty, Judith DrAPF 93
Minty, Keith Larry 1933- WhoFI 94, WhoWest 94
Mintz, Alan Paul 1938- WhoMW 93
Mintz, Albert 1929- WhoAm 94
Mintz, Daniel Gordon 1948- WhoAmP 93
Mintz, Daniel Harvey 1930- WhoScEn 94
Mintz, Donald Edward 1932- WhoAm 94
Mintz, Douglas C. WhoAmP 93
Mintz, Eli d1988 WhoHol 92
Mintz, Harry 1909- WhoAm 94, WhoAmA 93
Mintz, Herbert H. 1946- WhoAmL 94
Mintz, Jack d1983 WhoHol 92
Mintz, Jeanne Shirley 1922- WhoAm 94
Mintz, Jeffry Alan 1943- WhoAmL 94
Mintz, Joel Alan 1949- WhoAmL 94
Mintz, Larry WhoHol 92
Mintz, Leigh Wayne 1939- WhoWest 94
Mintz, Lenore Chaice 1925- WhoFI 94
Mintz, M. J. 1940- WhoAm 94, WhoAmL 94
Mintz, Marshall G. 1947- WhoAm 94, WhoAmL 94
Mintz, Morton Abner 1922- WhoAm 94
Mintz, Nancy K. WhoAmL 94
Mintz, Norman Nelson 1934- WhoAm 94
Mintz, Phil DrAPF 93
Mintz, Reginold Lee WhoBlA 94
Mintz, Ronald Steven 1947- WhoAmL 94
Mintz, Ruth Finer DrAPF 93
Mintz, Ruth Finer 1919- WrDr 94
Mintz, Samuel I(saiah) 1923- WrDr 94
Mintz, Seymour Stanley 1912- WhoAm 94
Mintz, Shlomo 1957- IntWW 93, WhoAm 94
Mintz, Sidney Wilfred 1922- WhoAm 94
Mintz, Stephen Allan 1943- WhoAm 94, WhoFI 94
Mintz, Stuart Alan 1956- WhoWest 94
Mintz, Walter 1929- WhoAm 94
Mintzberg, Henry 1939- WhoAm 94
Mintzer, David 1926- WhoAm 94
Mintzer, Edward Carl, Jr. 1949- WhoAmL 94
Mintzer, Paul 1948- WhoScEn 94
Mintzer, Yvette DrAPF 93
Minudri, Regina Ursula 1937- WhoAm 94, WhoWest 94
Minus, Homer Wellington 1931- WhoBlA 94
Minuse, Catherine Jean 1951- WhoAmL 94
Minuti, Baldo d1958 WhoHol 92
Minyard, Handsel B. 1943- WhoBlA 94
Min Yimin WhoPRCh 91
Min Yu WhoPRCh 91 [port]
Minz, Alexander d1992 WhAm 10
Minzey, Frank d1949 WhoHol 92
Minzner, Dean Frederick 1945- WhoWest 94
Minzner, Dick 1943- WhoAmP 93
Miolon-Carvalho, Marie Caroline NewGrDO
Mion, Barbara Louise 1929- WhoMW 93
Mion, Charles-Louis 1698-1775 NewGrDO
Mion, Pierre Riccardo 1931- WhoAmA 93
Mioni, Fabrizio WhoHol 92
Miota, Margaret Elizabeth 1940- WhoMW 93
Miotke, Anne E. 1943- WhoAmA 93
Miotte, Jean 1926- WhoAmA 93
Miou Miou 1950- IntMPA 94, WhoHol 92
Miquel, Pierre Gabriel Roger 1930- IntWW 93
Miquel, Raymond Clive 1931- Who 94
Mir, Carl J. 1956- WhoHisp 94
Mir, Gasper, III 1946- WhoHisp 94
Mirabai fl. 16th cent.- BlmGWL
Mirabal, Carlos G. 1947- WhoHisp 94
Mirabal, George G. 1949- WhoHisp 94
Mirabeau, Count 1749-1791 HisWorL [port]
Mirabella, Francis Michael, Jr. 1943- WhoScEn 94
Mirabelli, Eugene DrAPF 93
Mirabelli, Eugene 1931- WrDr 94
Mirabelli, Mario V. 1939- WhoAm 94
Mirabello, Francis Joseph 1954- WhoAm 94, WhoAmL 94
Mirabello, Mark Linden 1955- WhoMW 93
Mirabile, Robert J. 1935- WhoIns 94
Mirabile, Russell Michael 1947- WhoAmL 94
Mirabito, Michael Mark 1956- WhoScEn 94
Mirabito, Paul S. 1915-1991 WhAm 10
Miracle, Gordon Eldon 1930- WhoAm 94
Miracle, Irene WhoHol 92
Miracle, James Franklin 1938- WhoFI 94
Miracle, Maria Rosa 1945- WhoScEn 94
Miracle, Robert Warren WhoAm 94
Miracle, Rocky Reed 1953- WhoFI 94
Mira Galiana, Jaime Jose Juan 1950- WhoScEn 94
Miraglio, Angela Maria 1944- WhoMW 93
Mirakhor, Abbas 1941- IntWW 93
Mira-Lani DrAPF 93
Miralda, Antoni 1942- WhoAmA 93
Miralles, Juan de 1738-1780 AmRev
Miramontes, Arnulfo 1882-1960 NewGrDO
Mirand, Edwin Albert 1926- WhoAm 94
Miranda, Andres, Jr. 1940- WhoHisp 94
Miranda, Aurora WhoHol 92
Miranda, Carmen d1955 WhoHol 92
Miranda, Christopher Adam 1957- WhoAmL 94
Miranda, Constancio Fernandes 1926- WhoAm 94
Miranda, Felix Antonio 1962- WhoMW 93
Miranda, Francisco de 1750-1816 HisWorL [port]
Miranda, Frederick Ralph 1940- WhoHisp 94
Miranda, Gary DrAPF 93
Miranda, Gloria P. 1962- WhoWest 94
Miranda, Guillermo, Jr. 1943- WhoHisp 94
Miranda, Hector, Sr. 1960- WhoHisp 94
Miranda, Isa d1982 WhoHol 92
Miranda, Javier ConAu 43NR, ConWorW 93
Miranda, John Anthony 1944- WhoAm 94
Miranda, Lalla 1874-1944 NewGrDO
Miranda, Lourdes WhoHisp 94
Miranda, Luis WhoHisp 94

Miranda, M. L. 1939- *WhoHisp 94*
Miranda, Manuel Robert 1939- *WhoHisp 94*
Miranda, Maria de L. 1960- *WhoHisp 94*
Miranda, Maria T. 1936- *WhoHisp 94*
Miranda, Mark Harland 1960- *WhoFI 94*
Miranda, Martin Luis 1963- *WhoFI 94*
Miranda, Robert *WhoHol 92*
Miranda, Robert A. *WhoHisp 94*
Miranda, Robert Julian 1952- *WhoHisp 94*
Miranda, Robert Nicholas 1934- *WhoAm 94, WhoFI 94*
Miranda, Soledad *WhoHol 92*
Miranda, Susana 1950- *WhoHol 92*
Miranda, William 1951- *WhoHisp 94*
Miranda de Lage, Ana *WhoWomW 91*
Mirando, Joseph Andrew 1955- *WhoAm 94*
Mirandola, Alberto 1942- *WhoScEn 94*
Mirandy d1974 *WhoHol 92*
Miransky, Peretz d1993 *NewYTBS 93*
Mirante, Linda Kay 1952- *WhoMW 93*
Mirate, Raffaele 1815-1895 *NewGrDO*
Mirbach, Henry William 1948- *WhoFI 94*
Mirchandaney, Arjan Sobhraj 1923- *WhoMW 93*
Mirchandani, Arjun Sobhraj 1943- *WhoAsA 94*
Mirchandani, Gagan 1932- *WhoAsA 94*
Mirchandani, Prakash *WhoAsA 94*
Mirdamadi, Hamid Reza 1961- *WhoScEn 94*
Mirdha, Ram Niwas 1924- *IntWW 93*
Mirecki, Franciszek 1791-1862 *NewGrDO*
Mirel, Amelia d1987 *WhoHol 92*
Mireles, Andy 1950- *WhoHisp 94*
Mireles, Oscar *DrAPF 93*
Mireles, R. Christina 1961- *WhoHisp 94*
Mireles, Raymond D. *WhoHisp 94*
Mirell, Douglas E. 1956- *WhoAmL 94*
Mirels, Harold 1924- *WhoAm 94*
Miremont, Comtesse de 1735-1811 *BlmGWL*
Miremont, Jacqueline de fl. 16th cent.- *BlmGWL*
Mires, Monty *WhoAmP 93*
Mires, Ronald E. 1930- *WhoWest 94*
Mirgazyamov, Marat Parisovich 1942- *LngBDD*
Mirich, David Gage 1956- *WhoWest 94*
Miricioiu, Nelly 1952- *IntWW 93, NewGrDO*
Mirick, Henry Dustin 1905- *WhoAm 94*
Mirick, Robert Allen 1957- *WhoScEn 94*
Mirikitani, Andrew Kotaro 1955- *WhoAmL 94*
Mirikitani, Andy 1955- *WhoAsA 94*
Mirikitani, Janice *DrAPF 93*
Miripol, Jerilyn Elise *WhoMW 93*
Mirisch, David 1935- *IntMPA 94*
Mirisch, Marvin E. 1918- *IntMPA 94*
Mirisch, Marvin Elliot 1918- *WhoAm 94*
Mirisch, Walter 1921- *IntDcF 2-4, IntMPA 94*
Mirisch, Walter Mortimer 1921- *WhoAm 94*
Mirisola, Lisa Heinemann 1963- *WhoWest 94*
Mirk, Judy Ann 1944- *WhoWest 94*
Mirkil, Jay R. 1954- *WhoIns 94*
Mirkin, Abraham d1986 *WhoHol 92*
Mirkin, Abraham Jonathan 1910- *WhoAm 94*
Mirkin, Bernard Leo 1928- *WhoAm 94*
Mirman, Irving R. 1915- *WhoAm 94*
Mirman, Joel Harvey 1941- *WhoAm 94*
Mirman, Merrill Jay 1941- *WhoScEn 94*
Mirman, Sophie 1956- *Who 94*
Mirmiran, Amir 1961- *WhoScEn 94*
Miro, Henri 1879-1950 *NewGrDO*
Miro, Joseph E. 1946- *WhoHisp 94*
Miro, Pilar *BlmGWL*
Miroglio, Francis 1924- *NewGrDO*
Mirojnick, Ellen *ConTFT 11*
Miron, Amihai 1953- *WhoScEn 94*
Miron, Murray Samuel 1932- *WhoScEn 94*
Miron, Wilfrid Lyonel 1913- *Who 94*
Mironack, Michael Walter 1960- *WhoFI 94*
Mironov, Nikolai Efimovich 1936- *LngBDD*
Mironov, Valery Ivanovich 1943- *LngBDD*
Mironov, Vladimir Nikolaevich 1954- *LngBDD*
Mironovich, Alex 1952- *WhoAm 94*
Miro Romero, Pilar 1940- *IntWW 93*
Miroshnichenko, Yevgeniya (Semyonovna) 1931- *NewGrDO*
Miroslava d1955 *WhoHol 92*
Mirowitz, Howard David 1951- *WhoFI 94*
Mirowski, Philip Edward 1951- *WhoAm 94*
Mirra *WhoAmA 93*
Mirra, Carlo 1963- *WhoScEn 94*
Mirra, Joseph Meredith 1937- *WhoWest 94*
Mirren, Helen 1945- *IntWW 93*
Mirren, Helen 1946- *IntMPA 94, WhoHol 92*
Mirrielees, James Fay, III 1939- *WhoAm 94*
Mirrlees, James Alexander 1936- *IntWW 93, Who 94*
Mirrlees, Robin Ian Evelyn Stuart de la Lanne- 1925- *Who 94*
Mirsaidov, Shukrullo Rakhmatovich 1939- *LngBDD*
Mirsaidov, Shukurulla Rakhmatovich 1938- *IntWW 93*
Mirse, Ralph Thomas 1924- *WhoAm 94*
Mirsky, Arthur 1927- *WhoAm 94*
Mirsky, Mark *DrAPF 93*
Mirsky, Mark (Jay) 1939- *WrDr 94*
Mirsky, Sonya Wohl 1925- *WhoAm 94*
Mirtala 1929- *WhoAmA 93*
Mirtallo, Jay Matthew 1953- *WhoMW 93*
Mirvahabi, Farin *WhoAmL 94*
Mirvis, Theodore Neal 1951- *WhoAmL 94*
Mirvish, David 1944- *IntWW 93*
Mirvish, Edwin 1914- *Who 94*
Mirvish, Edwin (Ed.) 1914- *IntWW 93*
Miry, Karel 1823-1889 *NewGrDO*
Mirza, David Brown 1936- *WhoAm 94, WhoFI 94*
Mirza, M. Saeed *WhoScEn 94*
Mirza, Shaukat 1936- *WhoScEn 94*
Mirzabekov, Abdurazak Mardanovich 1938- *LngBDD*
Mirzabekov, Andrei Daryevich 1937- *IntWW 93*
Mirzabekov, Andrey Daryevich 1937- *WhoScEn 94*
Mirzai, Mohammed 1945- *WhoFI 94*
Mirzai, Pirooz 1953- *WhoAm 94*
Mirzoeff, Edward 1936- *Who 94*
Mirzoev, Akbar 1939- *LngBDD*
Mirzoyan, Edvard Mikhailovich 1921- *IntWW 93*
Misa, Kenneth Franklin 1939- *WhoAm 94, WhoWest 94*
Misamore, Bruce Kelvern 1950- *WhoFI 94*
Misasi, Riccardo 1932- *IntWW 93*
Misawa, Eduardo Akira 1956- *WhoScEn 94*
Misawa, Susumu 1951- *WhoScEn 94*
Misbrener, Joseph Michael 1924- *WhoWest 94*
Miscampbell, Norman Alexander 1925- *Who 94*
Misch, Allene K. 1928- *WhoAmA 93*
Misch, Robert Jay 1905-1990 *WhAm 10*
Mischel, Harriet Nerlove 1936- *WhoScEn 94*
Mischer, Don 1941- *IntMPA 94*
Mischer, Donald Leo 1940- *WhoAm 94*
Mischer, Walter M. 1923- *WhoAm 94*
Mischka, Tre 1961- *WhoFI 94*
Mischke, Carl Herbert 1922- *WhoAm 94, WhoMW 93*
Mischke, Charles Russell 1927- *WhoMW 93, WhoScEn 94*
Mischke, Frederick Charles 1930- *WhoAm 94, WhoFI 94*
Mischke, Richard Evans 1940- *WhoScEn 94*
Mischler, Norman Martin 1920- *Who 94*
Mischnick, Wolfgang 1921- *IntWW 93*
Mischou, Gregory Lee 1961- *WhoFI 94*
Miscovich, Timothy Joseph 1958- *WhoMW 93*
Miselman, Michael D. 1942- *WhoAmL 94*
Miselson, Alex J. Jacob 1926- *WhoFI 94*
Misener, Helen d1960 *WhoHol 92*
Misenko, Albert Edward 1930- *WhoMW 93*
Miser, Hugh Jordan 1917- *WhoAm 94*
Miser, Randall E. 1938- *WhoAmP 93*
Mises, Richard von 1883-1953 *WorScD*
Misfeldt, Michael Lee 1950- *WhoScEn 94*
Mish, Charles C(arroll) 1913-1992 *ConAu 140*
Mish, Frederick Crittenden 1938- *WhoAm 94*
Mish, Jo *DrAPF 93*
Misha *EncSF 93*
Mishan, E.J 1917- *WrDr 94*
Mishcon, Baron 1915- *Who 94*
Mishell, Daniel R., Jr. 1931- *WhoAm 94*
Misher, Allen 1933- *WhoAm 94*
Misher, Norman J. 1951- *WhoAmL 94*
Mishima, Masao d1973 *WhoHol 92*
Mishima, Yukio d1970 *WhoHol 92*
Mishima, Yukio 1925-1970 *GayLL*
Mishima Yukio 1925-1970 *RfGShF*
Mishin, Vasiliy Pavlovich 1917- *IntWW 93*
Mishkin, Barbara Friedman 1936- *WhoAmL 94*
Mishkin, Edwin B. 1937- *WhoAm 94*
Mishkin, Frederic Stanley 1951- *WhoFI 94, WhoScEn 94*
Mishkin, Jeffrey Alan 1948- *WhoAm 94, WhoAmL 94*
Mishkin, Julia *DrAPF 93*
Mishkin, Marc Paul 1946- *WhoAmL 94*
Mishkin, Marjorie Wong 1940- *WhoWest 94*
Mishkin, Mortimer 1926- *WhoAm 94, WhoScEn 94*
Mishkin, Paul J. 1927- *WhoAm 94*
Mishkin, Philip 1915- *WhoAmP 93*
Mishler, Clifford Leslie 1939- *WhoAm 94*
Mishler, Jacob 1911- *WhoAm 94, WhoAmL 94*
Mishler, John Milton 1946- *WhoAm 94*
Mishler, William, II 1947- *WhoAm 94*
Mishoe, Luna I., II 1948- *WhoAmP 93*
Mishra, Ajay Kumar 1960- *WhoScEn 94*
Mishra, Arun Kumar 1945- *WhoScEn 94*
Mishra, Brajendra 1959- *WhoScEn 94*
Mishra, Brajesh Chandra 1928- *IntWW 93*
Mishra, Shitala P. 1938- *WhoAsA 94*
Mishra, Vishnu S. 1956- *WhoScEn 94*
Misiaita, Asora 1951- *WhoAmP 93*
Miskimen, George William 1930- *WhoAm 94*
Miskimin, Harry Alvin 1932- *WhoAm 94*
Miskin, James (William) 1925- *Who 94*
Miskin, Raymond John 1928- *Who 94*
Miskovitch, Milorad 1928- *IntDcB [port]*
Miskovitz, Paul Frederick 1949- *WhoScEn 94*
Miskovsky, George, Sr. 1910- *WhoAm 94, WhoAmL 94*
Miskowski, Lee R. 1932- *WhoAm 94*
Miskus, Michael Anthony 1950- *WhoFI 94*
Misla Aldarondo, Edison *WhoAmP 93, WhoHisp 94*
Mislivecek, Josef *NewGrDO*
Mislow, Kurt Martin 1923- *WhoAm 94*
Misner, Charles William 1932- *WhoAm 94*
Misner, Robert David 1920- *WhoScEn 94*
Mison, Luis c. 1727-1766 *NewGrDO*
Mi Sook, Ahn 1959- *WhoAmA 93*
Misora, Hibari d1989 *WhoHol 92*
Mis-Quona-Queb fl. 170-?-180-? *EncNAR*
Misra, Alok C. 1950- *WhoAsA 94*
Misra, Dwarika Nath 1933- *WhoAsA 94*
Misra, Jayadev 1947- *WhoAm 94, WhoScEn 94*
Misra, Prabhakar 1955- *WhoAsA 94*
Misra, Prasanta Kumar 1935- *WhoScEn 94*
Misra, Raghunath Prasad 1928- *WhoAm 94*
Misra, Vaidyanath *ConWorW 93*
Misrach, Richard Laurence 1949- *WhoAm 94, WhoAmA 93*
Misrok, Irwin Roger 1932- *WhoFI 94*
Miss, Mary 1944- *WhoAm 94*
Missal, Joshua M. 1915- & Missal, Pegge 1923- *WhoAmA 93*
Missal, Joshua Morton 1915- *WhoWest 94*
Missal, Pegge *WhoAmA 93*
Missal, Pegge 1923-
See Missal, Joshua M. 1915- & Missal, Pegge 1923- *WhoAmA 93*
Missal, Stephen J. 1948- *WhoAmA 93*
Missan, Richard Sherman 1933- *WhoAm 94, WhoAmL 94*
Missar, Charles Donald 1925- *WhoAm 94*
Misselbrook, (Bertram) Desmond 1913- *Who 94*
Misshore, Joseph O., Jr. *WhoBlA 94*
Missimore, Maureen Margaret 1959- *WhoMW 93*
Miss Lou *BlkWr 2*
Missman, Jeffrey Stephan 1944- *WhoFI 94*
Missner, David N. 1941- *WhoAmL 94*
Missoffe, Francois 1919- *IntWW 93*
Missoffe, Helene 1927- *WhoWomW 91*
Missouri River fl. 19th cent.- *EncNAR*
Mistal, Karen *WhoHol 92*
Mistele, Thomas Martin 1953- *WhoAmL 94*
Mister, Melvin Anthony 1938- *WhoBlA 94*
Mistinguette d1956 *WhoHol 92*
Mistral, Bengo *EncSF 93*
Mistral, Frederic 1830-1914 *TwCLC 51 [port]*
Mistral, (Jean-Etienne-)Frederic 1830-1914 *NewGrDO*
Mistral, Gabriela *BlkWr 2*
Mistral, Gabriela 1889-1957 *BlmGWL, HispLC [port]*
Mistral, Jorge d1972 *WhoHol 92*
Mistry, Dhruva 1957- *IntWW 93, Who 94*
Mistry, Jayanthi 1952- *WhoAsA 94*
Mistry, Kishorkumar Purushottamdas 1953- *WhoScEn 94*
Mistry, Rohinton 1952- *ConAu 141*
Misuraca, Thomas L. 1950- *WhoAmL 94*
Misurec, Rudolf 1924- *WhoScEn 94*
Miszuga, Oleksandr *NewGrDO*
Mita, Itura 1929- *WhoScEn 94*
Mita, Katsushige 1924- *IntWW 93*
Mital, Naveen Kumar 1947- *WhoAsA 94*
Mitamura, Ron W. 1957- *WhoAsA 94*
Mitarai, Osamu 1950- *WhoScEn 94*
Mitau, Lee R. 1948- *WhoAm 94, WhoAmL 94*
Mitby, John Chester 1944- *WhoAmL 94*
Mitby, Norman Peter 1916- *WhoAm 94*
Mitchal, Saundra Marie 1949- *WhoBlA 94*
Mitcham, Constance 1947- *WhoWomW 91*
Mitcham, Heather d1993 *Who 94N*
Mitcham, Julius Jerome 1941- *WhoFI 94*
Mitchel, Frederick Kent 1927- *WhoAm 94*
Mitchel, Lawrence T. 1933- *WhoIns 94*
Mitchel, Les d1975 *WhoHol 92*
Mitchelhill, James Moffat 1912- *WhoScEn 94*
Mitchell, Abbie d1960 *WhoHol 92*
Mitchell, Abbie 1884-1960 *AfrAmAl 6*
Mitchell, Adrian 1932- *ConDr 93, EncSF 93, Who 94, WrDr 94*
Mitchell, Alec Burton 1924- *Who 94*
Mitchell, Aletha *WhoHol 92*
Mitchell, Alexander Graham 1923- *Who 94*
Mitchell, Alfred R. 1888-1972 *WhoAmA 93N*
Mitchell, Andrea 1946- *WhoAm 94*
Mitchell, Andrew John Bower 1956- *Who 94*
Mitchell, Angus *Who 94*
Mitchell, (John) Angus (Macbeth) 1924- *Who 94*
Mitchell, Arlene Harris 1940- *WhoMW 93*
Mitchell, Arnold 1918- *WrDr 94*
Mitchell, Arthur 1934- *AfrAmAl 6, IntDcB [port], IntWW 93, WhoAm 94, WhoBlA 94*
Mitchell, Arthur Harris 1916- *WhoAm 94*
Mitchell, Arthur W. 1883-1968 *AfrAmAl 6 [port]*
Mitchell, Augustus William 1913- *WhoBlA 94*
Mitchell, Austin Vernon 1934- *Who 94*
Mitchell, Barbara d1977 *WhoHol 92*
Mitchell, Barbara Jean 1950- *WhoFI 94*
Mitchell, Basil George 1917- *IntWW 93, Who 94*
Mitchell, Belle d1979 *WhoHol 92*
Mitchell, Bennie Robert, Jr. 1948- *WhoBlA 94*
Mitchell, Bert Breon 1942- *WhoAm 94*
Mitchell, Bert Norman 1938- *WhoBlA 94*
Mitchell, Beverly Tierney 1951- *WhoAmL 94*
Mitchell, Billy 1879-1936 *HisWorL [port]*
Mitchell, Billy Joel 1934- *WhoAmP 93*
Mitchell, Billy M. 1926- *WhoBlA 94*
Mitchell, Bob *Who 94*
Mitchell, Bobby *ProFbHF*
Mitchell, Bradford W. 1927- *WhoIns 94*
Mitchell, Bradford William 1927- *WhoAm 94*
Mitchell, Brenda K. *WhoAm 94*
Mitchell, Brenda K. 1943- *WhoBlA 94*
Mitchell, Brenda King 1943- *WhoAmP 93*
Mitchell, Briane Nelson 1953- *WhoAm 94*
Mitchell, Bruce d1952 *WhoHol 92*
Mitchell, Bruce Handiside 1908-1963 *WhoAmA 93N*
Mitchell, Bruce Logan 1947- *WhoFI 94*
Mitchell, Bruce Tyson 1928- *WhoAm 94, WhoAmP 93*
Mitchell, Bryan Franklin 1927- *WhoAmP 93*
Mitchell, Burley Bayard, Jr. 1940- *WhoAm 94, WhoAmL 94, WhoAmP 93*
Mitchell, Burton A. 1953- *WhoAmL 94*
Mitchell, Byron Lynwood 1936- *WhoBlA 94*
Mitchell, C. MacNeil 1942- *WhoAmL 94*
Mitchell, Cameron 1918- *IntMPA 94, WhoHol 92*
Mitchell, Carlton S. 1950- *WhoBlA 94*
Mitchell, Carol 1941- *WhoMW 93*
Mitchell, Carol Ann 1957- *WhoAmL 94*
Mitchell, Carol Greene 1960- *WhoBlA 94*
Mitchell, Carolyn d1966 *WhoHol 92*
Mitchell, Charles, Jr. 1938- *WhoBlA 94*
Mitchell, Charles Archie 1926- *WhoFI 94*
Mitchell, Charles E. 1925- *WhoBlA 94*
Mitchell, Charles Hill 1924- *WhoFI 94*
Mitchell, Charles J. d1929 *WhoHol 92*
Mitchell, Charles Julian Humphrey *Who 94*
Mitchell, Charles Mason d1930 *WhoHol 92*
Mitchell, Charles Wellman 1954- *WhoAmP 93*
Mitchell, Charlotte *WhoHol 92*
Mitchell, Cheryl Elaine 1951- *WhoFI 94*
Mitchell, Chuck 1927- *WhoHol 92*

Mitchell, Claybourne, Jr. 1923- WhoAm 94
Mitchell, Clifford 1925- WhoAmA 93
Mitchell, Clyde EncSF 93
Mitchell, Colin Campbell 1925- Who 94
Mitchell, Corinne Howard 1914- WhoBlA 94
Mitchell, Craig Martin 1962- WhoWest 94
Mitchell, Cranston J. 1946- WhoBlA 94
Mitchell, Dana Covington, Jr. 1918- WhoAmA 93
Mitchell, Daniel B. 1941- WhoBlA 94
Mitchell, Daniel Ray 1939- WhoFI 94
Mitchell, Danny Ray 1943- WhoAmP 93
Mitchell, David (Bower) 1928- Who 94
Mitchell, David (John) 1924- WrDr 94
Mitchell, David Campbell 1957- WhoFI 94, WhoWest 94
Mitchell, David E. WhoFI 94
Mitchell, David Ira 1932- WhoAm 94
Mitchell, David T. 1942- WhoAm 94, WhoFI 94, WhoWest 94
Mitchell, David Walker 1935- WhoAm 94
Mitchell, David William 1933- Who 94
Mitchell, Dean Lamont 1957- WhoAmA 93
Mitchell, Deborah Jane 1964- WhoScEn 94
Mitchell, Delmer Roy 1941- WhoAmL 94
Mitchell, Denis WhoScEn 94
Mitchell, Dennis Who 94, WhoAm 94
Mitchell, (Arthur) Dennis 1918- Who 94
Mitchell, Dennis A. 1966- WhoBlA 94
Mitchell, Derek 1922- IntWW 93
Mitchell, Derek (Jack) 1922- Who 94
Mitchell, Diane B. 1947- WhoAmL 94
Mitchell, Dianne WhoWest 94
Mitchell, Dianne (Ball) WhoAmA 93
Mitchell, Dodson d1939 WhoHol 92
Mitchell, Dolphus Burl 1922- WhoBlA 94
Mitchell, Don DrAPF 93
Mitchell, Don 1943- WhoHol 92
Mitchell, Don G. d1993 NewYTBS 93 [port]
Mitchell, Donald 1943- WhoBlA 94
Mitchell, Donald Hearin 1959- WhoScEn 94
Mitchell, Donald J. 1923- WhoAm 94, WhoAmP 93
Mitchell, Donald Wayne 1946- WhoFI 94
Mitchell, Douglas 1948- WhoBlA 94
Mitchell, Douglas Farrell 1940- WhoAm 94
Mitchell, Douglas Svard 1918- Who 94
Mitchell, Duke d1981 WhoHol 92
Mitchell, Duncan 1941- IntWW 93
Mitchell, Dwayne Oscar 1959- WhoBlA 94
Mitchell, Earl Douglass, Jr. 1938- WhoBlA 94
Mitchell, Earl Nelson 1926- WhoAm 94
Mitchell, Eddie 1947- WhoWest 94
Mitchell, Eddy WhoHol 92
Mitchell, Edward B. 1943- WhoAmL 94
Mitchell, Edward Franklin 1931- WhoFI 94
Mitchell, Edward James 1949- WhoAmL 94
Mitchell, Edward John 1937- WhoAm 94
Mitchell, Edward Lee 1932- WhoIns 94
Mitchell, Edward Page 1852-1927 EncSF 93
Mitchell, Edwin H., Sr. 1921- WhoBlA 94
Mitchell, Ehrman Burkman, Jr. 1924- WhoAm 94
Mitchell, Eleanor 1907- WhoAmA 93N
Mitchell, Eleyne 1913- BlmGWL
Mitchell, Elizabeth Allen 1957- WhoWest 94
Mitchell, Elizabeth H. 1940- WhoAmP 93
Mitchell, Ella Pearson 1917- WhoBlA 94
Mitchell, Ellin Hobbins d1993 NewYTBS 93
Mitchell, (Sibyl) Elyne (Keith) 1913- WrDr 94
Mitchell, Emerson Blackhorse DrAPF 93
Mitchell, Emmitt W. WhoBlA 94
Mitchell, Eric WhoHol 92
Mitchell, Eric, Mrs. Who 94
Mitchell, Eric Ignatius 1948- WhoBlA 94
Mitchell, Erica 1944- WrDr 94
Mitchell, Eugene Alexander 1953- WhoScEn 94
Mitchell, Ewan Who 94
Mitchell, Ewing d1988 WhoHol 92
Mitchell, Frank Who 94, WhoAmP 93
Mitchell, Frank d1991 WhoHol 92
Mitchell, Frank 1881-1967 EncNAR
Mitchell, Fred 1923- WhoAmA 93
Mitchell, Gary C. 1950- WhoAmP 93
Mitchell, Gary David 1940- WhoWest 94
Mitchell, Gary Earl 1935- WhoAm 94
Mitchell, Geneva d1949 WhoHol 92
Mitchell, Geneva Brooke 1929- WhoWest 94
Mitchell, Geoffrey Charles 1921- Who 94
Mitchell, Geoffrey Duncan 1921- WrDr 94
Mitchell, Geoffrey Sewell 1940- WhoAm 94, WhoAmL 94
Mitchell, George d1972 WhoHol 92
Mitchell, George Allen 1946- WhoMW 93
Mitchell, George Archibald Grant d1993 Who 94N
Mitchell, George B. 1940- WhoIns 94
Mitchell, George Ernest, Jr. 1930- WhoAm 94
Mitchell, George Francis 1912- IntWW 93
Mitchell, George Francis (Frank) 1912- Who 94
Mitchell, George Hall 1939- WhoAm 94
Mitchell, George J. 1933- CngDr 93, NewYTBS 93 [port]
Mitchell, George J(ohn) 1933- ConAu 141
Mitchell, George John 1933- IntWW 93, WhoAm 94, WhoAmP 93
Mitchell, George L. WhoBlA 94
Mitchell, George P. 1919- WhoAm 94, WhoFI 94
Mitchell, George Trice 1914- WhoMW 93
Mitchell, George Washington, Jr. 1917- WhoAm 94
Mitchell, Gladys 1901-1983 BlmGWL
Mitchell, Glen 1894-1972 WhoAmA 93N
Mitchell, Gordon WhoHol 92
Mitchell, Graham Richard 1938- WhoAm 94, WhoFI 94
Mitchell, Grant d1957 WhoHol 92
Mitchell, Gregory Roderick 1960- WhoFI 94
Mitchell, Guy 1925- WhoHol 92
Mitchell, Guy W., III 1944- WhoAmL 94
Mitchell, Gwenn WhoHol 92
Mitchell, Harry 1930- Who 94
Mitchell, Harry 1940- WhoAmP 93
Mitchell, Harry E. 1940- WhoWest 94
Mitchell, Heather WhoHol 92
Mitchell, Helen d1945 WhoHol 92
Mitchell, Helen Josephine Who 94
Mitchell, Henry (Clay, II) 1923- WrDr 94
Mitchell, Henry (Weber) 1915-1980 WhoAmA 93N
Mitchell, Henry B. 1918- WhoBlA 94
Mitchell, Henry Clay 1923- WhoAm 94
Mitchell, Henry Heywood 1919- WhoBlA 94
Mitchell, Herbert Hall 1916- WhoAm 94
Mitchell, Homer DrAPF 93
Mitchell, Horace 1944- WhoBlA 94
Mitchell, Howard d1958 WhoHol 92
Mitchell, Howard Estill 1921- WhoAm 94
Mitchell, Huey P. 1935- WhoBlA 94
Mitchell, Hugh Burnton 1907- WhoAmP 93
Mitchell, Iain Grant 1951- Who 94
Mitchell, Ian Edward 1932- Who 94
Mitchell, Irving d1969 WhoHol 92
Mitchell, Iverson O., III 1943- WhoBlA 94
Mitchell, J(ames) Leslie 1901-1935 EncSF 93
Mitchell, Jacob Bill 1932- WhoBlA 94
Mitchell, James 1920- WhoHol 92
Mitchell, James 1926- Who 94
Mitchell, James 1943- WhoAmP 93
Mitchell, James (William) 1926- WrDr 94
Mitchell, James Austin 1941- WhoAm 94, WhoFI 94, WhoIns 94
Mitchell, James Benjamin 1924- WhoAmP 93
Mitchell, James Clyde 1918- Who 94
Mitchell, James Fitzallen 1931- IntWW 93, Who 94
Mitchell, James H. 1948- WhoBlA 94
Mitchell, James Herbert 1946- WhoWest 94
Mitchell, James Kenneth 1930- WhoAm 94, WhoScEn 94, WhoWest 94
Mitchell, James Lowry 1937- WhoAm 94, WhoAmL 94
Mitchell, James Richard 1946- IntWW 93
Mitchell, James Robert 1953- WhoAmL 94
Mitchell, James Wesley 1950- WhoAmP 93
Mitchell, James Winfield 1943- WhoAm 94, WhoBlA 94
Mitchell, Janet Brew 1949- WhoScEn 94
Mitchell, Jay ConAu 41NR
Mitchell, Jere Holloway 1928- WhoScEn 94
Mitchell, Jere Rodney 1948- WhoMW 93
Mitchell, Jeremy George Swale Hamilton 1929- Who 94
Mitchell, Jerome 1935- WrDr 94
Mitchell, Jerry Calvin 1938- WhoScEn 94
Mitchell, Jo Kathryn 1934- WhoFI 94
Mitchell, Joan d1992 IntWW 93N
Mitchell, Joan 1926- WhoAmA 93N
Mitchell, Joan 1926-1992 AnObit 1992, CurBio 93N, WhAm 10
Mitchell, Joan E. 1920- WrDr 94
Mitchell, Joan Eileen 1920- Who 94
Mitchell, Joan Elizabeth WhoAmA 93
Mitchell, Joan LaVerne 1947- WhoScEn 94
Mitchell, Joann 1956- WhoBlA 94
Mitchell, Joanne 1938- WhoBlA 94
Mitchell, Joe H. DrAPF 93
Mitchell, Joel Stephenson 1898-1989 WhAm 10
Mitchell, John A(mes) 1845-1918 EncSF 93
Mitchell, John Anthony 1940- WhoFI 94
Mitchell, John Blair 1921- WhoAmA 93
Mitchell, John Cameron WhoHol 92
Mitchell, John Gall 1931- Who 94
Mitchell, John Hanson 1940- ConAu 142
Mitchell, John Henderson 1933- WhoAm 94, WhoWest 94
Mitchell, John Howard 1921- WrDr 94
Mitchell, John Logan 1947- Who 94
Mitchell, John Matthew 1925- Who 94
Mitchell, John Murray, Jr. 1928-1990 WhAm 10
Mitchell, John Noyes, Jr. 1930- WhoScEn 94, WhoWest 94
Mitchell, John Patrick 1945- WhoAm 94
Mitchell, John Phillimore 1918- WrDr 94
Mitchell, John Wesley 1913- Who 94, WhoAm 94
Mitchell, John William 1944- WhoWest 94
Mitchell, Johnny d1951 WhoHol 92
Mitchell, Jonathan James 1951- Who 94
Mitchell, Joni 1943- IntWW 93, WhoAm 94, WhoHol 92
Mitchell, Joseph 1803-1883 DcNaB MP
Mitchell, Joseph 1908- WrDr 94
Mitchell, Joseph (Quincy) 1908- IntWW 93
Mitchell, Joseph A. 1942- WhoAmP 93
Mitchell, Joseph B(rady) 1915-1993 ConAu 140
Mitchell, Joseph Christopher 1922- WhoBlA 94
Mitchell, Joseph Nathan 1922- WhoAm 94
Mitchell, Joseph Patrick 1939- WhoScEn 94, WhoWest 94
Mitchell, Joseph Quincy 1908- WhoAm 94
Mitchell, Joseph Rodney 1914- Who 94
Mitchell, Joseph Rudolph 1938- WhoBlA 94
Mitchell, Juanita Jackson 1913-1992 WhoBlA 94N
Mitchell, Judson, Jr. 1941- WhoBlA 94
Mitchell, JudyLynn 1951- WhoBlA 94
Mitchell, Julian 1935- IntWW 93, Who 94
Mitchell, (Charles) Julian 1935- WrDr 94
Mitchell, (Charles) Julian (Humphrey) 1935- ConDr 93
Mitchell, Julien d1954 WhoHol 92
Mitchell, Juliet 1940- WrDr 94
Mitchell, Julius P. 1941- WhoBlA 94
Mitchell, Katherine 1944- WhoAmA 93
Mitchell, Katherine Phillips 1943- WhoBlA 94
Mitchell, Kathleen Ann 1948- WhoWest 94
Mitchell, Katie IntWW 93
Mitchell, Keith Clarudius IntWW 93
Mitchell, Keith Kirkman 1927- Who 94
Mitchell, Kelly Karnale 1928- WhoBlA 94
Mitchell, Kendall WhoAm 94, WhoMW 93
Mitchell, Kevin Darrell 1962- WhoAm 94, WhoMW 93, WhoWest 94
Mitchell, Kieron Breon 1968- WhoMW 93
Mitchell, Kirk (John) 1950- EncSF 93
Mitchell, Langdon (Elwyn) 1862-1935 IntDcT 2
Mitchell, Langdon Elwyn, Mrs. d1944 WhoHol 92
Mitchell, Lansing Leroy 1914- WhoAm 94, WhoAmL 94
Mitchell, Larry WhoAmP 93
Mitchell, Larry Randell 1950- WhoAmP 93
Mitchell, Laura Ellen 1959- WhoWest 94
Mitchell, Laurie WhoHol 92
Mitchell, Lee Hartley 1941- WhoFI 94
Mitchell, Lee Mark 1943- WhoAm 94, WhoMW 93
Mitchell, LeMonte Felton 1939- WhoBlA 94
Mitchell, Leona 1949- AfrAmAl 6 [port], NewGrDO, WhoBlA 94
Mitchell, Leona Pearl 1949- WhoAm 94
Mitchell, Les d1965 WhoHol 92
Mitchell, Leslie d1985 WhoHol 92
Mitchell, Lilyann Jackson 1933- WhoBlA 94
Mitchell, Lindell Marvin 1937- WhoFI 94
Mitchell, Loften 1919- AfrAmAl 6, ConDr 93, WhoBlA 94, WrDr 94
Mitchell, Loretta Ann WhoMW 93
Mitchell, Louise WhoBlA 94
Mitchell, Lucius Quinn 1959- WhoFI 94
Mitchell, Lynn Lee 1945- WhoWest 94
Mitchell, Madeleine Enid 1941- WhoWest 94
Mitchell, Malcolm Stuart 1937- WhoAm 94
Mitchell, Margaret 1900-1945 BlmGWL
Mitchell, Margaret (Munnerlyn) 1900-1949 TwCYAW
Mitchell, Margaretta 1935- WrDr 94
Mitchell, Margaretta K. 1935- WhoAmA 93
Mitchell, Maria DrAPF 93
Mitchell, Maria 1818-1889 WorScD [port]
Mitchell, Marian Bartlett 1941- WhoBlA 94
Mitchell, Mark Halferty 1949- WhoAm 94, WhoMW 93
Mitchell, Mark Randolph 1955- WhoBlA 94
Mitchell, Mark T. 1952- WhoAmL 94
Mitchell, Martha Mallard 1940- WhoBlA 94
Mitchell, Martin Who 94
Mitchell, (James Lachlan) Martin 1929- Who 94
Mitchell, Maryann WhoAmP 93
Mitchell, Maurice B. 1915- WhoAm 94
Mitchell, Maurice Edward 1921- WhoWest 94
Mitchell, Maurice McClellan, Jr. 1929- WhoAm 94, WhoScEn 94
Mitchell, Melvin J. 1904- WhoBlA 94
Mitchell, Melvin Lester 1939- WhoBlA 94
Mitchell, Memory F 1924- WrDr 94
Mitchell, Michael Creswell 1950- WhoWest 94
Mitchell, Michael Sherman 1953- WhoAmL 94
Mitchell, Michael Stuart 1948- WhoAm 94
Mitchell, Mike 1956- BasBi
Mitchell, Mike Anthony 1956- WhoBlA 94
Mitchell, Mike P. 1925- WhoAmP 93
Mitchell, Millard d1953 WhoHol 92
Mitchell, Milton 1916- WhoAm 94
Mitchell, Mitch 1940- WhoAm 94
Mitchell, Mona (Ann) 1938- Who 94
Mitchell, N. Donald 1922- WhoAmA 93
Mitchell, Nathaniel 1753-1814 WhAmRev
Mitchell, Neil Charles 1964- WhoScEn 94
Mitchell, Nelli L. WhoBlA 94
Mitchell, Norma d1967 WhoHol 92
Mitchell, Norman WhoHol 92
Mitchell, Norval d1972 WhoHol 92
Mitchell, Olin Jackson 1931-1992 WhAm 10
Mitchell, Orlan E. 1933- WhoAm 94
Mitchell, Orrin Dwight 1946- WhoBlA 94
Mitchell, Ossie Ware 1919- WhoBlA 94
Mitchell, Otis Clinton, Jr. 1935- WhoAm 94
Mitchell, P(hilip) M(arshall) 1916- ConAu 43NR
Mitchell, Parren James 1922- WhoAmP 93, WhoBlA 94
Mitchell, Patrick John 1958- WhoFI 94
Mitchell, Patrick Reynolds 1930- Who 94
Mitchell, Paula Levin 1951- WhoScEn 94
Mitchell, Paula Rae 1951- WhoAm 94, WhoScEn 94
Mitchell, Peter 1920-1992 AnObit 1992
Mitchell, Peter Dennis 1920-1992 WhAm 10
Mitchell, Peter Kenneth, Jr. 1949- WhoAm 94
Mitchell, Peter McQuilkin 1934- WhoAm 94
Mitchell, Peter Todd 1929- WhoAmA 93
Mitchell, Peter W. 1942- WhoWest 94
Mitchell, Peter William 1950- WhoFI 94
Mitchell, Philip Michael 1953- WhoScEn 94
Mitchell, Philip W. 1941- WhoIns 94
Mitchell, Quitman J. WhoBlA 94
Mitchell, R. Clayton, Jr. WhoAmP 93
Mitchell, Randy WhoAmP 93
Mitchell, Rebecca Lou 1953- WhoMW 93
Mitchell, Reid 1955- ConAu 140
Mitchell, Rhea d1957 WhoHol 92
Mitchell, Richard Boyle 1947- WhoAm 94
Mitchell, Richard Charles 1927- Who 94
Mitchell, Richard Charles 1953- WhoFI 94
Mitchell, Richard LeRoy 1954- WhoWest 94
Mitchell, Richard Scott 1929-1988 WhAm 10
Mitchell, Robby K 1916- WrDr 94
Mitchell, Robert 1913- Who 94
Mitchell, Robert Alan 1953- WhoMW 93
Mitchell, Robert Buchanan d1993 NewYTBS 93
Mitchell, Robert C. WhoAm 94, WhoAmL 94
Mitchell, Robert C. 1935- WhoBlA 94
Mitchell, Robert Campbell 1940- WhoWest 94
Mitchell, Robert Curtis 1928- WhoScEn 94
Mitchell, Robert Dale 1910- WhoAm 94

Mizrahi, Abraham Mordechay 1929- *WhoAm 94, WhoScEn 94*
Mizrahi, Gerard 1952- *WhoFI 94*
Mizrahi, Isaac 1961- *IntWW 93, WhoAm 94*
Mizrahi, Michael *WhoHol 92*
Mizroch, John F. 1948- *WhoAm 94*
Mizsak, Stephen Andrew 1939- *WhoScEn 94*
Mizuguchi, Norman 1939- *WhoAmP 93*
Mizuno, Kiyoshi *IntWW 93*
Mizuno, Nobuko Shimotori 1916- *WhoAsA 94, WhoWest 94*
Mizuno, Seiichi 1905- *IntWW 93*
Mizuno, Shuko 1934- *NewGrDO*
Mizutani, Hiroshi 1949- *WhoScEn 94*
Mizutani, Junya 1932- *WhoScEn 94*
Mizutani, Satoshi 1937- *WhoAsA 94, WhoScEn 94*
Mizutani, Yaeko d1979 *WhoHol 92*
Mizuta Tamae 1929- *BlmGWL*
Mizzell, William Clarence 1949- *WhoBlA 94*
Mjolsness, Eric Daniel 1958- *WhoScEn 94*
Mkapa, Benjamin William 1938- *IntWW 93*
Mkhatshwa, Smangaliso 1939- *IntWW 93*
Mkona, Callisto Matekenya 1930- *Who 94*
Mladenov, Peter Toshev 1936- *IntWW 93*
Mladenovic, Nikola Sreten 1958- *WhoScEn 94*
Mlakar, Roy A. 1953- *WhoAm 94, WhoWest 94*
Mlay, Marian 1935- *WhoAm 94*
Mleziva, Dennis John 1950- *WhoAmP 93*
Mlinaric, David 1939- *Who 94*
Mlkvy, Bill 1931- *BasBi*
Mlocek, Frances Angeline 1934- *WhoFI 94*
Mlsna, Kathryn Kimura 1952- *WhoAmL 94*
Mlsna, Timothy Martin 1947- *WhoAm 94, WhoAmL 94*
Mlynar, Linda Herren *DrAPF 93*
Mlynarski, Emil 1870-1935 *NewGrDO*
Mmari, Geoffrey Raphael Vehaeli 1934- *IntWW 93*
Mnacko, Ladislav 1919- *ConWorW 93*
M'Naughten, Daniel d1865 *EncSPD*
Mnookin, James Paul 1945- *WhoFI 94*
Mnookin, Robert H(arris) 1942- *ConAu 140*
Mnookin, Robert Harris 1942- *WhoAm 94*
Mnookin, Wendy M. *DrAPF 93*
Mnouchkine, Alexander 1908-1993 *NewYTBS 93*
Mnouchkine, Ariane *IntWW 93*
Mnouchkine, Ariane 1939?- *CurBio 93 [port]*
Mo, Hugh H. 1950- *WhoAmL 94, WhoAsA 94*
Mo, Jiaqi 1937- *WhoScEn 94*
Mo, Luke W. 1934- *WhoAsA 94*
Mo, Luke Wei 1934- *WhoAm 94*
Mo, Roger Shih-Yah 1939- *WhoScEn 94*
Mo, Suchoon 1932- *WhoAsA 94*
Mo, Timothy 1950- *IntWW 93*
Mo, Timothy 1953- *WrDr 94*
Mo, Timothy Peter 1950- *Who 94*
Moak, Robert Warren 1958- *WhoAmP 93*
Moakley, John Joseph 1927- *CngDr 93, WhoAm 94, WhoAmP 93*
Moak-Mazur, Connie J. 1947- *WhoAm 94*
Moan, Raymond Charles 1942- *WhoAmP 93*
Moaney, Eric R. 1934- *WhoBlA 94*
Moat, Douglas Clarkson 1931- *WhoIns 94*
Moat, John 1936- *WrDr 94*
Moate, Roger (Denis) 1938- *Who 94*
Moates, G. Paul 1947- *WhoAm 94, WhoAmL 94*
Moates, Marianne Merrill *DrAPF 93*
Moats, John Edwin 1935- *WhoMW 93*
Moatts, Morris 1930- *WhoAmP 93*
Moav, Ram *EncSF 93*
Moawad, Atef 1935- *WhoAm 94, WhoScEn 94*
Moazzami, Sara 1960- *WhoScEn 94*
Mobbs, Michael Hall 1948- *WhoAm 94, WhoAmL 94*
Mobbs, (Gerald) Nigel 1937- *IntWW 93, Who 94*
Moberg, Clifford Allen 1951- *WhoMW 93, WhoScEn 94*
Moberg, David O. 1922- *WrDr 94*
Moberg, David Oscar 1922- *WhoAm 94*
Moberg, Dorothy Rood 1924- *WhoAmP 93*
Moberly, Harry, Jr. 1950- *WhoAmP 93*
Moberly, John (Campbell) 1925- *Who 94*
Moberly, Linden Emery 1923- *WhoWest 94*
Moberly, Michael Dean 1956- *WhoAmL 94*
Moberly, Patrick (Hamilton) 1928- *Who 94*
Moberly, Richard James 1906- *Who 94*
Moberly, Robert d1988 *WhoHol 92*
Moberly, Robert Blakely 1941- *WhoAm 94, WhoFI 94*
Moberly, Stephen C. 1941- *WhoAmP 93*
Mobley, Barbara J. 1947- *WhoAmP 93*
Mobley, Charles Alfred 1943- *WhoAmP 93*
Mobley, Charles Lamar 1932- *WhoBlA 94*
Mobley, Charles Murray 1954- *WhoWest 94*
Mobley, Cleon Marion, Jr. 1942- *WhoScEn 94*
Mobley, Clifton Arvil 1922- *WhoAmP 93*
Mobley, Emily Ruth *WhoAm 94, WhoMW 93*
Mobley, Emily Ruth 1942- *WhoBlA 94*
Mobley, Eugenia L. 1921- *WhoBlA 94*
Mobley, Joan Thompson 1944- *WhoBlA 94*
Mobley, John Homer, II 1930- *WhoAm 94, WhoAmL 94, WhoFI 94*
Mobley, John O., Jr. *WhoAmP 93*
Mobley, Jonniepat 1932- *WhoWest 94*
Mobley, Karen R. *WhoAmA 93*
Mobley, Karen Ruth 1961- *WhoWest 94*
Mobley, Lenora Washington 1940- *WhoAmP 93*
Mobley, Lucille Johanna 1944- *WhoWest 94*
Mobley, Mary Ann 1939- *WhoHol 92*
Mobley, Michael Howard 1945- *WhoAm 94*
Mobley, Roger 1951- *WhoHol 92*
Mobley, Stacey J. 1945- *WhoBlA 94*
Mobley, Sybil C. 1925- *WhoBlA 94*
Mobley, Tony Allen 1938- *WhoAm 94*
Mobley, Walt *ConAu 42NR*
Mobley, William Hodges 1941- *WhoAm 94*
Mobraaten, William Lawrence 1929- *WhoAm 94*
Mobutu, Joseph 1930- *HisWorL [port]*
Mobutu Sese Seko 1930- *News 93 [port]*
Mobutu Sese Seko, Marshal 1930- *IntWW 93*
Mocabee, James David 1958- *WhoAmP 93*
Moch, Lawrence E. 1929- *WhoBlA 94*
Moch, Robert Gaston 1914- *WhoAm 94*
Mochaikin, Aleksandr Gennadevich 1948- *LngBDD*
Mocharla, Raman 1953- *WhoMW 93*
Mochary, Mary Veronica 1942- *WhoAm 94*
Mochel, Myron George 1905- *WhoScEn 94*
Mochi, Ugo 1894-1977 *WhoAmA 93N*
Mochisanu, Alexandru 1932- *IntWW 93*
Mochizuki, Kiichi 1937- *WhoFI 94*
Mochizuki, Yuko d1977 *WhoHol 92*
Mochon, Donald 1916- *WhoAmA 93N*
Mochrie, Dottie 1966- *WhoAm 94*
Mochrie, Richard D. 1928- *WhoAm 94*
Mociuk, Yar W. 1927- *IntMPA 94*
Mock, Alice d1972 *WhoHol 92*
Mock, Alois 1934- *IntWW 93*
Mock, David Clinton, Jr. 1922- *WhoAm 94*
Mock, Dean R. *WhoAmP 93*
Mock, Frank Mackenzie 1944- *WhoAm 94*
Mock, Gary Norman 1942- *WhoScEn 94*
Mock, George Andrew 1886- *WhoAmA 93N*
Mock, Henry Byron 1911- *WhoAm 94*
Mock, Henry P. *WhoAmP 93*
Mock, James E. 1940- *WhoBlA 94*
Mock, James Richard 1951- *WhoFI 94*
Mock, John Edwin 1925- *WhoScEn 94*
Mock, Lawrence Edward 1917- *WhoAm 94*
Mock, Lawrence Edward, Jr. 1946- *WhoFI 94*
Mock, Peter Allen 1959- *WhoScEn 94*
Mock, Randall Don 1943- *WhoAmL 94*
Mock, Richard Basil 1944- *WhoAmA 93*
Mock, Robert Claude 1928- *WhoAm 94, WhoFI 94, WhoScEn 94*
Mock, Sally 1943- *WhoAmL 94*
Mock, Sandra Ford 1944- *WhoAmL 94*
Mock, Stanley Clyde 1946- *WhoFI 94*
Mock, Theodore Jaye 1941- *WhoAm 94*
Mockaitis, Algis Peter 1942- *WhoScEn 94*
Mockaitis, Joseph Peter 1942- *WhoScEn 94*
Mockary, Peter Ernest 1931- *WhoWest 94*
Mockbee, David W. 1949- *WhoAmL 94*
Mockler, Colman Michael, Jr. 1929-1991 *WhAm 10*
Mockler, E. Jayne 1957- *WhoAmP 93, WhoWest 94*
Mockler, Edward Joseph 1954- *WhoFI 94*
Mockler, John Barry 1941- *WhoWest 94*
Mockus, Joseph Frank 1965- *WhoMW 93*
Mocky, Jean-Pierre 1929- *WhoHol 92*
Moctezuma, II c. 1480-1520 *HisWorL [port]*
Moctezuma, Carlos Lopez *WhoHol 92*
Moczulski, Leszek 1930- *IntWW 93*
Moczygemba, George Anthony 1939- *WhoScEn 94*
Modai, Itzhak 1926- *IntWW 93*
Modak, Chintamani Krishna 1947- *WhoScEn 94*
Modano, Michael 1970- *WhoAm 94*
Modarressi, Anne *Who 94*
Modarressi, Hossein 1942- *WhoAm 94*
Modarressi, Taghi (M.) 1931- *WrDr 94*
Modderman, Melvin Earl 1940- *WhoAm 94*
Mode, Carol A. 1943- *WhoAmA 93*
Mode, Charles J. 1927- *WhoAm 94*
Mode, Paul J., Jr. 1938- *WhoAm 94, WhoAmL 94*
Modean, Jayne 1958- *WhoHol 92*
Modeen, Thor d1950 *WhoHol 92*
Modeer, Victor Albert, Jr. 1955- *WhoScEn 94*
Model, Elisabeth D. *WhoAmA 93*
Model, Elisabeth Dittmann *WhoAm 94*
Model, Evsa 1901-1976 *WhoAmA 93N*
Model, Peter 1933- *WhoAm 94*
Modell, Arthur B. 1925- *WhoAm 94, WhoMW 93*
Modell, Charles Scott 1953- *WhoAmL 94*
Modell, Edward G. 1946- *WhoAmL 94*
Modell, Frank *WhoAm 94*
Modell, Jerome Herbert 1932- *WhoAm 94*
Modell, John 1941- *WhoAm 94*
Modell, Michael Steven 1953- *WhoAm 94*
Moder, John Joseph 1948- *WhoAm 94*
Moder, Kenneth Philip 1954- *WhoMW 93*
Moderacki, Edmund Anthony 1946- *WhoAm 94*
Moderi, William E. 1950- *WhoAmL 94*
Moderow, Joseph Robert 1948- *WhoAm 94, WhoAmL 94, WhoFI 94*
Modert, (Betty) Jo 1921- *WrDr 94*
Modery, Richard Gillman 1941- *WhoFI 94*
Modesitt, L(eland) E(xton, Jr.) 1943- *EncSF 93*
Modeste, Leon Edgar 1926- *WhoBlA 94*
Modestino, James William 1940- *WhoAm 94, WhoScEn 94*
Modesto, Phillip *WhoHisp 94*
Modesto, Ruby 1913-1980 *EncNAR [port]*
Modi, Shailesh 1963- *WhoAsA 94*
Modi, Sohrab d1984 *WhoHol 92*
Modi, Vinay Kumar 1943- *IntWW 93*
Modiano, Patrick 1945- *ConWorW 93*
Modiano, Patrick Jean 1945- *IntWW 93*
Modiano-Revah, Manuel 1957- *WhoHisp 94*
Modic, Stanley John 1936- *WhoAm 94*
Modie, Ruth Rowell 1905- *WhoAmP 93*
Modigliani, Franco 1918- *IntWW 93, Who 94, WhoAm 94, WhoFI 94, WrDr 94*
Modine, Matthew 1959- *IntMPA 94, WhoAm 94*
Modine, Matthew 1960- *WhoHol 92*
Modise, Joe 1929- *IntWW 93*
Modisette, Ruth 1946- *WhoAmL 94*
Modi-Vitale, Lydia *WhoAmA 93*
Modjeska, Drusilla 1946- *BlmGWL*
Modjeska, Felix d1940 *WhoHol 92*
Modjeski, Mark Anton 1958- *WhoFI 94*
Modl, Martha *IntWW 93*
Modl, Martha 1912- *NewGrDO [port]*
Modleski, Tania 1949- *BlmGWL*
Modley, Albert d1979 *WhoHol 92*
Modlin, George Matthews 1903- *WhoAm 94*
Modlin, Howard S. 1931- *WhoAm 94, WhoAmL 94, WhoFI 94*
Modlin, James Michael 1955- *WhoScEn 94*
Modlinski, Neal David 1958- *WhoMW 93, WhoScEn 94*
Modot, Gaston d1970 *WhoHol 92*
Modrow, Hans 1928- *IntWW 93*
Mody, Mukund V. 1940- *WhoAsA 94*
Mody, Rustomji Hormusji 1918- *WhoFI 94*
Modzelewski, Stutz 1920- *BasBi*
Moe, Andrew Irving 1927- *WhoWest 94*
Moe, Chesney Rudolph 1908- *WhoAm 94*
Moe, Christian H(ollis) 1929- *WrDr 94*
Moe, Donald M. 1942- *WhoAmP 93*
Moe, Doug 1938- *BasBi*
Moe, George Cecil Rawle 1932- *IntWW 93*
Moe, Gordon Kenneth 1915-1989 *WhAm 10*
Moe, Henry Allen 1894-1975 *WhoAmA 93N*
Moe, John Arthur, II 1950- *WhoAmL 94*
Moe, Michael K. 1937- *WhoScEn 94*
Moe, Orville Leroy 1936- *WhoFI 94, WhoWest 94*
Moe, Osborne Kenneth 1925- *WhoScEn 94*
Moe, Palmer L. 1944- *WhoFI 94*
Moe, Richard 1936- *WhoAmP 93*
Moe, Richard D. 1928- *WhoAmA 93*
Moe, Richard Palmer 1936- *WhoAm 94, WhoAmL 94*
Moe, Roger Deane 1944- *WhoAmP 93*
Moe, Stanley Allen 1914- *WhoWest 94*
Moe, Thomas O. 1938- *WhoAm 94*
Moe, Thorvald 1940- *IntWW 93*
Moe, Vida Delores 1928- *WhoMW 93*
Moebus, Hans d1976 *WhoHol 92*
Moeck, Walter F. 1922- *WhoAm 94*
Moeckel, Bill Reid 1925- *WhoAm 94*
Moe-Fishback, Barbara Ann 1955- *WhoMW 93*
Moehl, Karl J. 1925- *WhoAmA 93*
Moehle, Jack P. *WhoScEn 94*
Moehlman, Michael Scott 1938- *WhoAm 94*
Moehlmann, Nicholas Bruce 1938- *WhoAmP 93*
Moehring, Fred Adolf 1935- *WhoFI 94*
Moehring, Kansas d1968 *WhoHol 92*
Moel, Steven Allen 1943- *WhoWest 94*
Moelhman, Amy J. 1954- *WhoMW 93*
Moeling, Walter Goos, IV 1943- *WhoAm 94, WhoAmL 94, WhoFI 94*
Moelis, Herbert Irwin 1931- *WhoFI 94*
Moelleken, Wolfgang Wilfried 1934- *WhoAm 94*
Moellenbeck, Albert John, Jr. 1934- *WhoScEn 94*
Moellenberg, Roland D. 1936- *WhoAmP 93*
Moeller, Achim Ferdinand Gerd 1942- *WhoFI 94*
Moeller, Armin J., Jr. 1947- *WhoAmL 94*
Moeller, Audrey Carolyn 1935- *WhoAm 94*
Moeller, Bernd 1931- *IntWW 93*
Moeller, Dade William 1927- *WhoAm 94*
Moeller, Donald Joseph 1933- *WhoAm 94*
Moeller, Eileen *DrAPF 93*
Moeller, Galen Ashley 1950- *WhoAmL 94*
Moeller, Gary *WhoAm 94*
Moeller, James *WhoAmP 93*
Moeller, James 1933- *WhoAm 94, WhoAmL 94, WhoWest 94*
Moeller, Jeanette 1926- *WhoAmP 93*
Moeller, Jerry G. *WhoAm 94*
Moeller, Linda Kay 1945- *WhoMW 93*
Moeller, Michael 1947- *WhoAmP 93*
Moeller, Peter H. 1939- *WhoIns 94*
Moeller, Richard Jon 1939- *WhoAm 94*
Moeller, Robert Charles, III 1938- *WhoAm 94, WhoAmA 93*
Moeller, Robert John 1938- *WhoAm 94*
Moeller, Ronald Scott 1963- *WhoScEn 94*
Moellering, John Henry 1938- *WhoAm 94*
Moellering, John J. 1952- *WhoAmL 94*
Moellering, Robert Charles, Jr. 1936- *WhoAm 94, WhoScEn 94*
Moelmann, Lawrence R. 1947- *WhoAm 94, WhoAmL 94*
Moe Moe (Inya) 1944-1990 *BlmGWL*
Moen, Diana Irene 1954- *WhoMW 93*
Moen, Rodney C. 1937- *WhoAmP 93*
Moen, Rodney Charles 1937- *WhoMW 93*
Moen, Timothy Paul 1952- *WhoMW 93*
Moens, Peter B. 1931- *WhoAm 94*
Moens, Thomas Odin 1961- *WhoMW 93*
Moenssens, Andre A. 1930- *WrDr 94*
Moeran, Edward Warner 1903- *Who 94*
Moerbeek, Stanley Leonard 1951- *WhoAmL 94, WhoWest 94*
Moerdani, Leonardus Benjamin 1932- *IntWW 93*
Moerdler, Charles Gerard 1934- *WhoAm 94, WhoAmL 94, WhoFI 94*
Moerdyk, Charles Conrad 1948- *WhoMW 93*
Moeri, Louise 1924- *TwCYAW*
Moerkerke, James Albert 1954- *WhoFI 94*
Moerner, Magnus 1924- *WrDr 94*
Moero fl. 4th cent.BC-3rd cent.BC *BlmGWL*
Moerpratomo, A. Sulasikin 1927- *WhoWomW 91*
Moersch, Karl 1926- *IntWW 93*
Moerschel, Chiara *WhoAmA 93*
Moersfelde, Edward M. 1946- *WhoAmL 94*
Moertel, Charles George 1927- *IntWW 93*
Moertono, Amir *IntWW 93*
Moeschl, Stanley Francis 1931- *WhoScEn 94*
Moese, Mark Douglas 1954- *WhoScEn 94*
Moesel, Rodd Alan 1954- *WhoAmP 93*
Moesgen, Karl John 1949- *WhoScEn 94*
Moewe, James A. 1946- *WhoAmL 94*
Mofenson, David Joel 1943- *WhoAmP 93*
Moffard, Rose 1922- *WhoWomW 91*
Moffat, Alistair Murray 1950- *Who 94*
Moffat, Brian Scott 1939- *Who 94*
Moffat, (William) Cameron 1929- *Who 94*
Moffat, Donald 1930- *IntMPA 94, WhoHol 92*
Moffat, Gwen 1924- *WrDr 94*
Moffat, John Lawrence 1916- *WrDr 94*
Moffat, John William 1932- *WhoAm 94*
Moffat, Kenneth M. 1932- *WhoIns 94*

Moffat, Margaret d1942 WhoHol 92
Moffat, Marian MacIntyre 1947- WhoAmL 94
Moffat, Mary 1795-1871 WhWE
Moffat, MaryBeth 1951- WhoFI 94
Moffat, Nancy 1951- WhoAmP 93
Moffat, Richard Howe 1931- WhoAmL 94
Moffat, Robert 1795-1883 WhWE
Moffat, Robert John 1927- WhoAm 94
Moffat, Terry Haldyn 1940- WhoFI 94
Moffat, W. Graham 1866- EncSF 93
Moffatt, David John 1939- WhoAm 94
Moffatt, David Lloyd 1927- WhoMW 93
Moffatt, Graham d1965 WhoHol 92
Moffatt, Graham, Mrs. d1943 WhoHol 92
Moffatt, Henry Keith 1935- IntWW 93, Who 94
Moffatt, Hugh McCulloch, Jr. 1933- WhoScEn 94, WhoWest 94
Moffatt, James 1922- EncSF 93
Moffatt, John 1922- IntWW 93, Who 94, WhoHol 92
Moffatt, John Myrick 1940- WhoFI 94
Moffatt, Joyce Anne 1936- WhoAm 94, WhoWest 94
Moffatt, Katy 1950- WhoAm 94
Moffatt, Robert Henry 1930- WhoWest 94
Moffeit, Tony DrAPF 93
Moffeit, Tony Archie 1942- WhoWest 94
Moffet, Donald Pratt 1932- WhoAm 94
Moffet, Hugh Lamson 1932- WhoAm 94, WhoMW 93
Moffet, Kenneth William 1959- WhoAmL 94
Moffet, Margaret J. 1953- WhoAm 94
Moffet, Thomas 1553-1604 DcLB 136 [port]
Moffett, Anthony 1944- WhoAmP 93
Moffett, Charles Simonton 1945- WhoAm 94
Moffett, Cleveland Langston 1863-1926 EncSF 93
Moffett, D. W. WhoHol 92
Moffett, Frank Cardwell 1931- WhoWest 94
Moffett, George Larry 1936- WhoMW 93
Moffett, James Robert 1938- WhoAm 94, WhoFI 94
Moffett, Jonathan Phillip 1954- WhoAm 94, WhoWest 94
Moffett, Judith DrAPF 93
Moffett, Judith 1942- EncSF 93, WrDr 94
Moffett, Kenworth William 1934- WhoAmA 93
Moffett, Mark Beyer 1935- WhoScEn 94
Moffett, Ross E. 1888-1971 WhoAmA 93N
Moffett, Samuel Hugh 1916- WrDr 94
Moffett, Terrill Kay 1949- WhoAmL 94
Moffett, Theresa Kay 1960- WhoMW 93
Moffett, Todd Stuart 1960- WhoFI 94
Moffett, William Andrew 1933- WhoAm 94, WhoWest 94
Moffie, Robert Wayne 1950- WhoWest 94
Moffit, George Seth 1947- WhoAm 94
Moffitt, Charles William 1932- WhoAm 94
Moffitt, Christopher Edward 1966- WhoScEn 94
Moffitt, David Louis 1953- WhoMW 93
Moffitt, Donald (Anthony) 1936- EncSF 93
Moffitt, Donald Eugene 1932- WhoAm 94, WhoFI 94, WhoWest 94
Moffitt, Donald L. 1947- WhoAmP 93
Moffitt, George, Jr. 1918- WhoAm 94
Moffitt, H. Lee 1941- WhoAmP 93
Moffitt, John Francis 1940- WhoAmA 93
Moffitt, Kevin David 1957- WhoWest 94
Moffitt, Phillip William 1946- WhoAm 94, WhoWest 94
Moffo, Anna IntWW 93
Moffo, Anna 1932- NewGrDO
Moffo, Anna 1934- WhoHol 92
Mofford, Rose 1922- IntWW 93, WhoAmP 93
Mofsky, James Steffan 1935- WhAm 10
Moftah, Mounir Amin 1922- WhoScEn 94
Mog, Aribert d1941 WhoHol 92
Mogabgab, William Joseph 1921- WhoAm 94
Mogador, Celeste 1824-1909 BlmGWL
Mogae, Festus Gontebanye 1939- IntWW 93
Mogami, Cynthia WhoWomW 91
Mogavero, Michael James 1950- WhoAmA 93
Mogel, William Allen 1942- WhoAmL 94
Mogelever, Bernard 1940- WhoAm 94
Mogensen, Paul 1941- WhoAmA 93
Mogenson, Gordon James 1931-1991 WhAm 10
Moger, Christopher Richard Derwent 1949- Who 94
Moger, Carolie Ann 1950- WhoMW 93
Moger, Stanley H. 1936- IntMPA 94
Mogg Who 94

Mogg, Donald Whitehead 1924- WhoWest 94
Mogg, John 1913- Who 94
Mogg, John Frederick 1943- Who 94
Moggach, Deborah 1948- WrDr 94
Moggi, Pietro NewGrDO
Moggie, Leo 1941- IntWW 93
Moggridge, Harry Traherne 1936- Who 94
Moghaddamjoo, Alireza 1953- WhoMW 93
Moghissi, Kamran S. 1925- WhoMW 93
Mogi, Max d1970 WhoHol 92
Mogielski, Phyllis Ann 1964- WhoMW 93
Mogil, Bernard Marc 1949- WhoAm 94
Mogill, Kenneth Marc 1948- WhoAmL 94
Moginie, Jim
  See Midnight Oil ConMus 11
Mogk, John Edward 1939- WhoAm 94
Moglia, James John 1959- WhoFI 94
Mogol, Alan Jay 1946- WhoAm 94, WhoAmL 94
Mogul, Emil d1993 NewYTBS 93
Mogulof, Melvin Bernard 1926- WhoWest 94
Mogwe, Archibald Mooketsa 1921- IntWW 93
Mohamad, Encik Mustaffa bin 1941- IntWW 93
Mohamed, Gary William 1963- WhoFI 94
Mohamed, Gerald R., Jr. 1948- WhoBlA 94
Mohamed, Ollie 1925- WhoAmP 93
Mohamed Ali, Ibrahim 1932- Who 94
Mohamed Kamil, Abdallah 1936- IntWW 93
Mohammad 560?-632 EncEth
Mohammad, Nazar 1935- IntWW 93
Mohammad, Shaikh Noor 1946- WhoScEn 94
Mohammed 570?-632 BlmGEL
Mohammed, Ali Mahdi IntWW 93
Mohammed, Amadu Nayaya 1935- IntWW 93
Mohammed, Kamaluddin 1927- IntWW 93
Mohammed Zahir Shah 1914- IntWW 93
Mohan, Chandra 1950- WhoAsA 94
Mohan, D. Mike 1945- WhoAm 94, WhoFI 94
Mohan, Earl d1928 WhoHol 92
Mohan, J. Patrick 1948- WhoAm 94, WhoFI 94
Mohan, John J. 1945- WhoAm 94, WhoAmL 94
Mohan, Prem 1954- WhoMW 93
Mohan, Ramesh 1920- IntWW 93
Mohan, Subburaman 1951- WhoWest 94
Mohan, William F. 1943- WhoAmP 93
Mohanazadeh, Farajollah Bakhtiari 1957- WhoScEn 94
Mohanti, Prafulla 1936- WrDr 94
Mohanty, Ajaya K. 1952- WhoScEn 94
Mohanty, Sashi B. 1932- WhoAsA 94
Mohanty, Udayan WhoScEn 94
Mohapatra, Rabindra N. 1944- WhoAsA 94
Mohar, John 1949- WhoAmP 93
Mohatt, Dennis Francis 1954- WhoMW 93
Mohaupt, Richard 1904-1957 NewGrDO
Moher, Frank 1955- WrDr 94
Mohica, Victor WhoHol 92
Mohieddin, Zakaria 1918- IntWW 93
Mohiuddin, A.H.G. 1940- IntWW 93
Mohiuddin, Syed Maqdoom 1934- WhoAm 94
Mohl, Anthony Steven 1961- WhoAm 94
Mohl, David Bruce 1968- WhoScEn 94
Mohl, James Brian 1957- WhoScEn 94
Mohle, Brenda Simonson 1959- WhoAmA 93
Mohlenbrock, Robert Herman, Jr. 1931- WhoAm 94, WhoScEn 94
Mohler, Brian Jeffery 1948- WhoAm 94
Mohler, James Aylward 1923- WrDr 94
Mohler, James William 1955- WhoWest 94
Mohler, Mary Gail 1948- WhoAm 94
Mohler, Ronald Rutt 1931- WhoAm 94
Mohler, Stanley Ross 1927- WhoAm 94
Mohler, Stanley Ross, Jr. 1961- WhoScEn 94
Mohler, Terence John WhoMW 93, WhoScEn 94
Mohlie, Raymond Eugene 1928- WhoAm 94
Mohlman, Don T. 1936- WhoAmL 94
Mohn, Cheri (Ann) 1936- WhoAmA 93
Mohn, George William, Jr. 1935- WhoFI 94
Mohn, Melvin Paul 1926- WhoAm 94
Mohn, Reinhard 1921- IntWW 93
Mohn, Walter Rosing 1948- WhoMW 93
Mohner, Carl 1921- WhoHol 92
Mohney, Franklin Walter 1927-1991 WhAm 10
Mohney, Ralph Wilson 1918- WhoAm 94
Moholland, Fred W. WhoAmP 93

Moholy, Noel Francis 1916- WhoAm 94
Mohorita, Vasil 1952- IntWW 93
Mohorovicic, Andrija WorScD
Mohr, Alice Marie 1932- WhoMW 93
Mohr, Anthony James 1947- WhoAmL 94
Mohr, Bill DrAPF 93
Mohr, Charles 1929-1989 WhAm 10
Mohr, Charlotte Lorraine 1922- WhoAmP 93
Mohr, Diane Louise 1951- WhoBlA 94
Mohr, Ellen G. 1942- WhoMW 93
Mohr, Gerald d1968 WhoHol 92
Mohr, Hal 1894-1974 IntDcF 2-4 [port]
Mohr, James William, Jr. 1948- WhoAmL 94
Mohr, Jay Preston 1937- WhoAm 94
Mohr, Jayne Holly 1954- WhoMW 93
Mohr, John Luther 1911- WhoAm 94, WhoScEn 94, WhoWest 94
Mohr, K(aren) Lee 1954- WhoAmA 93
Mohr, Karen 1963- WhoMW 93
Mohr, Marilyn DrAPF 93
Mohr, Mary Hull 1934- WhoMW 93
Mohr, Nicholasa 1935- BlmGWL, HispLC [port]
Mohr, Nicholasa 1938- TwCYAW, WhoHisp 94
Mohr, Paul B. 1931- WhoBlA 94
Mohr, Pauline Catherine 1948- WhoAmA 93
Mohr, Raymond Phillip 1959- WhoMW 93
Mohr, Richard D(rake) 1950- ConAu 140
Mohr, Richard Drake 1950- WhoMW 93
Mohr, Roger John 1931- WhoAm 94, WhoFI 94
Mohr, Selby 1918- WhoWest 94
Mohr, Siegfried Heinrich 1930- WhoScEn 94, WhoWest 94
Mohrdick, Eunice Marie WhoWest 94
Mohrfeld, Richard Gentel 1945- WhoAm 94
Mohrhaus, Robert Ambrose 1931- WhoMW 93
Mohrherr, Carl Joseph 1944- WhoScEn 94
Mohring, Monsieur c. 1700-1733? NewGrDO
Mohring, Andrew Herbert 1959- WhoAmL 94
Mohring, Herbert 1928- WhoFI 94
Mohrman, Kathryn WhoWest 94
Mohrmann, Leonard Edward, Jr. 1940- WhoScEn 94
Mohrmann, Robert E. 1945- WhoAm 94, WhoFI 94
Mohrt, Michel 1914- IntWW 93
Mohs, Frederic Edward 1910- WhoAm 94
Mohtashami, Ali Akbar 1946- IntWW 93
Mohun, Michael 1616?-1684 BlmGEL
Mohyeddin, Zia 1931- Who 94
Mohyeddin, Zia 1933- WhoHol 92
Moi, Daniel Arap 1924- IntWW 93, Who 94
Moi, Toril 1953- BlmGWL
Moilanen, Michael David 1968- WhoScEn 94
Moilanen, Robert C. 1951- WhoAm 94
Moilanen, Thomas Alfred 1944- WhoMW 93
Moily, Jaya Padubidri 1951- WhoAm 94
Moinet, Eric Emil 1952- WhoFI 94
Moinot, Pierre 1920- IntWW 93
Moinuddin, Masood A. 1963- WhoAsA 94
Moir, Alfred 1924- WhoAmA 93
Moir, Alfred Kummer 1924- WhoAm 94
Moir, Ernest Ian Royds 1925- Who 94
Moir, (George) Guthrie 1917- Who 94
Moir, James William Charles 1941- Who 94
Moir, Margaret 1941- WhoWomW 91
Moir, Richard WhoHol 92
Moir, Robert Jesse 1942- WhoAmL 94
Moira, Earl of WhAmRev
Moirao, Daniel R. 1952- WhoWest 94
Moir Carey, D. M. Who 94
Moise, Edwin E(variste) 1946- WrDr 94
Moise, Edwin Evariste 1918- WhoAm 94
Moiseev, Mikhail Alekseevich 1939- LngBDD
Moiseev, Nikita Nikolaevich 1917- LngBDD
Moiseiwitsch, Benjamin Lawrence 1927- IntWW 93, Who 94
Moiseiwitsch, Benno d1963 WhoHol 92
Moiseiwitsch, Tanya 1914- Who 94
Moiseyev, Igor 1906- IntDcB
Moiseyev, Igor Aleksandrovich 1906- IntWW 93
Moiseyev, Mikhail Alekseevich 1939- IntWW 93
Moishezon, Boris G. d1993 NewYTBS 93 [port]
Moisi, Dominique 1946- IntWW 93
Moissi, Alexander d1935 WhoHol 92
Moivre, Abraham de 1667-1754 WorScD
Moix, Ana Maria 1947- BlmGWL, DcLB 134 [port]

Moize, Jerry Dee 1934- WhoAmL 94
Moja, Hella d1937 WhoHol 92
Mojave, King d1973 WhoHol 92
Mojcik, Christopher Francis 1959- WhoScEn 94
Mojica, Aurora 1939- WhoHisp 94
Mojica, Jose d1974 WhoHol 92
Mojica, Jose 1896-1974 NewGrDO
Mojonnier, Timothy Marchant 1949- WhoFI 94
Mojsilov, Ilene Krug 1952- WhoAmA 93
Mojsisovics(-Mojsvar), Roderich 1877-1953 NewGrDO
Mojsov, Lazar 1920- IntWW 93
Mojtabai, A. G. DrAPF 93
Mojtabai, Ann Grace 1937- WhoAm 94
Mok, Carson Kwok-Chi 1932- WhoFI 94, WhoScEn 94
Mokae, Zakes WhoHol 92
Mokae, Zakes 1935- IntMPA 94
Mokama, Moleleki Didwell 1933- Who 94
Mo-Keen, Loki c. 1830-1934 EncNAB
Mokhov, Oleg Ivanovich 1959- WhoScEn 94
Mokhtarzadeh, Ahmad Agha 1933- WhoScEn 94
Mokodean, Michael John 1923- WhoAm 94
Mokodopo, Jean-Paul IntWW 93
Mokoroane, Morena Moletsane 1932- IntWW 93
Mokrasch, Lewis Carl 1930- WhoAm 94
Mokray, Bill 1907- BasBi
Mokriski, J. Charles 1942- WhoAmL 94
Mokrzycki, Andrew Gustav 1899- WhAm 10
Mokrzynski, Jerzy Boguslaw 1909- IntWW 93
Mokyr, Joel 1946- WrDr 94
Mol, Hans ConAu 43NR
Mol, J(ohannis) J(acob) 1922- ConAu 43NR
Mol, Johannis (Hans) J(acob) 1922- WrDr 94
Mola, Richard Arthur 1936- WhoAmP 93
Moland, Willie C. 1931- WhoBlA 94
Molander, Julia A. 1952- WhoAmL 94
Molander, Olof d1966 WhoHol 92
Molapo, Mooki Motsarapane 1928- Who 94
Molaro, Robert S. WhoAmP 93
Molarsky, Maurice 1885-1950 WhoAmA 93N
Molatto, Ronald H. 1948- WhoIns 94
Molberg, Maxine 1921- WhoAmP 93
Molby, Douglas Steven 1958- WhoWest 94
Molchanov, Kirill Vladimirovich 1922-1982 NewGrDO
Moldanado, Swarnalatha Adusumilli WhoWest 94
Moldaw, Stuart G. 1927- WhoFI 94
Molde, David Lawrence 1959- WhoWest 94
Moldea, Dan E. 1950- WrDr 94
Molden, Anna Jane WhoMW 93
Molden, Herbert George 1912- WhoAm 94
Moldenaers, Paula Fernande 1957- WhoScEn 94
Moldenhauer, Judith A. 1951- WhoAm 94
Moldenhauer, William Calvin 1923- WhoAm 94
Moldin, Steven Owen 1961- WhoMW 93
Moldovan, Ioan 1948- IntWW 93
Moldovan, Jeff WhoHol 92
Moldovan, Roman 1911- IntWW 93
Moldoveanu, Eugenia 1944- NewGrDO
Moldoveanu, Vasile 1935- NewGrDO
Moldover, Edward David 1926- WhoAmL 94
Moldoski, Al R. 1928- WhoAmA 93
Moldt, Ewald 1927- IntWW 93
Mole, David Richard Penton 1943- Who 94
Mole, John 1941- ConAu 41NR, WrDr 94
Mole, Joseph N. 1948- WhoAmL 94
Mole, Juliette WhoHol 92
Mole, Richard Jay 1951- WhoMW 93
Molefe, Popo Simon 1952- IntWW 93
Molen, Jerry WhoHol 92
Molen, John Klauminzer 1952- WhoAm 94, WhoAmL 94
Molenaar, Allan John 1931- WhoMW 93
Molenbeek, Robert Gerrit 1944- WhoFI 94, WhoMW 93
Molendorp, Dayton H. 1947- WhoIns 94
Molenkamp, Charles Richard 1941- WhoWest 94
Molenkamp, Onno d1990 WhoHol 92
Moler, Donald Lewis 1918- WhoMW 93
Moler, Edward Harold 1923- WhoAm 94
Moler, Elizabeth Anne 1949- WhoAm 94, WhoAmP 93
Molese, Michele 1936-1989 WhAm 10
Molesworth, Viscount 1907- Who 94
Molesworth, Allen Henry Neville 1931- Who 94

Monahan, Willian Welsh, Jr. 1929- *WhoAmP 93*
Mo Naiqun 1911- *WhoPRCh 91 [port]*
Monakhof, Nikolai d1936 *WhoHol 92*
Monakhov, Vladimir Georgievich 1947- *LngBDD*
Monan, James Donald 1924- *WhoAm 94*
Monanni, Angelo c. 1740-1796 *NewGrDO*
Monarch, Joel R. 1950- *WhoMW 93*
Monarchi, David Edward 1944- *WhoWest 94*
Monari, Clemente c. 1660-1729? *NewGrDO*
Monas, Sidney 1924- *WhAm 10*
Monasee, Charles Arthur 1924- *WhoAm 94*
Monash, Curt Alfred 1960- *WhoFI 94*
Monash, Paul 1917- *IntMPA 94*
Monash, Peter Ernest 1924- *WhoMW 93*
Monat, William Robert 1924- *WhoAm 94*
Monbart, Marie-Josephine de Lescun 1758- *BlmGWL*
Monberg, George d1925 *WhoHol 92*
Monberg, Jay Peter 1935- *WhoFI 94, WhoMW 93*
Monberg, Torben Axel 1929- *IntWW 93*
Monbiot, George (Joshua) 1963- *WrDr 94*
Moncachtape fl. 1850?- *WhWE*
Moncada, Rogelio N. 1933- *WhoHisp 94*
Moncada, Salvador Enrique 1944- *Who 94*
Moncarraz, Raúl *WhoHisp 94*
Moncaster, John Anthony 1939- *Who 94*
Moncayo Garcia, Jose Pablo 1912-1958 *NewGrDO*
Monce, Raymond Eugene 1924- *WhoAmP 93*
Moncel, Robert William 1917- *Who 94*
Monchak, Ronald W. *WhoAm 94*
Moncharsh, Jane Kline 1943- *WhoMW 93*
Moncharsh, Philip Isaac 1948- *WhoAmL 94*
Moncher, Daniel Joseph 1960- *WhoMW 93*
Moncier, Herbert Sanford 1946- *WhoAmL 94*
Moncion, Francisco *WhoHol 92*
Moncion, Francisco 1922- *IntDcB [port]*
Moncivais, Emil Ray 1942- *WhoHisp 94*
Monck, Viscount *Who 94*
Monck, Harry Nelson, IV 1958- *WhoAmL 94*
Monck, Mary c. 1680-1715 *BlmGWL*
Monck, Nicholas Jeremy 1935- *Who 94*
Monckton *Who 94*
Monckton, Christopher Walter 1952- *Who 94*
Monckton, Henry 1740-1778 *WhAmRev*
Monckton, (John) Lionel (Alexander) 1861-1924 *NewGrDO*
Monckton, Robert 1726-1782 *WhAmRev*
Monckton, Sidney 1888- *WhoHol 92*
Monckton-Arundell *Who 94*
Monckton of Brenchley, Viscount 1915- *Who 94*
Monclova, Felix d1977 *WhoHol 92*
Moncreiff, Baron 1915- *Who 94*
Moncreiff, Robert P. 1930- *WhoAm 94*
Moncrief, Keith W. 1958- *WhoAmP 93*
Moncrief, Michael J. 1943- *WhoAmP 93*
Moncrief, Sidney A. 1957- *WhoBlA 94*
Moncrieff, Alan Aird 1901-1971 *DcNaB MP*
Moncrieff, Gladys 1892-1976 *NewGrDO*
Moncrieff, James 1744-1793 *AmRev, WhAmRev*
Moncrieff, Murray d1949 *WhoHol 92*
Moncrieff, Peter *WhoBlA 94*
Moncrieff, William S. *Who 94*
Moncries, Edward d1938 *WhoHol 92*
Moncrif, Francois-Augustin Paradis de 1687-1770 *NewGrDO*
Moncton, Archbishop of 1930- *Who 94*
Moncure, Albert F. 1924- *WhoBlA 94*
Moncure, James Ashby 1926- *WhoAm 94*
Moncure, John Lewis 1930- *WhoAm 94*
Moncure, Lisa *WhoHol 92*
Moncure, Thomas McCarty, Jr. 1951- *WhoAmP 93*
Moncus, Mary Lynn 1934- *WhoWest 94*
Mond *Who 94*
Monda, Marilyn 1956- *WhoWest 94*
Mondal, Kalyan 1951- *WhoAsA 94*
Mondale, Joan Adams 1930- *WhoAm 94, WhoAmA 93, WhoMW 93*
Mondale, Ted A. 1957- *WhoAmP 93*
Mondale, Walter Frederick 1928- *IntWW 93, Who 94, WhoAm 94, WhoAmP 93, WhoMW 93*
Mondanaro, Philip J. 1950- *WhoIns 94*
Mondani, Thomas P. 1934- *WhoAmP 93*
Mondavi, Robert Gerald *WhoAm 94, WhoWest 94*
Monday, Horace Reginald 1907- *Who 94*
Monday, John Christian 1925- *WhoAm 94, WhoWest 94*
Mondello, John Paul 1948- *WhoFI 94*
Mondello, Joseph N. 1938- *WhoAmP 93, WhoHisp 94*
Mondesi, Raul 1971- *WhoHisp 94*
Mondini, Gregory Francis 1948- *WhoWest 94*
Mondjo, Nicolas 1933- *IntWW 93*
Mondlin, Marvin 1927- *WhoFI 94*
Mondo, Peggy d1991 *WhoHol 92*
Mondonville, Jean-Joseph Cassanea de 1711-1772 *NewGrDO*
Mondor, Kenneth James 1949- *WhoAm 94*
Mondose, Alex d1972 *WhoHol 92*
Mondragon, Chris 1936- *WhoHisp 94*
Mondragon, Clarence 1940- *WhoHisp 94*
Mondragón, Delfi 1941- *WhoHisp 94*
Mondragon, Fred Eloy 1942- *WhoAmP 93*
Mondragon, James I. *WhoHisp 94*
Mondragon, Nadine 1945- *WhoAmP 93*
Mondragón, Norbert L. 1960- *WhoHisp 94*
Mondragón, Roberto A. 1940- *WhoHisp 94*
Mondre, Richard D. 1945- *WhoAmL 94*
Mondrian, Piet 1872-1944 *ModArCr 4 [port]*
Mondry, Eugene *WhoAm 94, WhoFI 94*
Mondry, Ira *WhoAm 94, WhoFI 94*
Mondry, Paul Michael 1953- *WhoAmL 94*
Mondul, Donald David 1945- *WhoAmL 94, WhoMW 93*
Mondy, Pierre *WhoHol 92*
Mone, John Aloysius *Who 94*
Mone, Mathias Edward 1940- *WhoAm 94*
Mone, Michael Edward 1942- *WhoAmL 94*
Mone, Peter John 1940- *WhoAm 94*
Mone, Robert Paul 1934- *WhoAm 94*
Monek, Donna Marie 1947- *WhoScEn 94*
Monek, Francis Herman 1913- *WhoAm 94*
Monell, Paul Cabot 1947- *WhoMW 93*
Monelli, Raffaele 1782-1859 *NewGrDO*
Monerawela, Chandra 1937- *IntWW 93, Who 94*
Mones, Arthur 1919- *WhoAmA 93*
Monesson, Harry S. 1935- *WrDr 94*
Monet, Jacques 1930- *WrDr 94*
Moneta, Giuseppe 1754-1806 *NewGrDO*
Monette, Louis Gayle 1925- *WhoMW 93*
Monette, Paul 1945- *GayLL*
Money, Eldon A. 1930- *WhoAmP 93*
Money, Ernle (David Drummond) 1931- *Who 94*
Money, George Gilbert 1914- *Who 94*
Money, J. B. 1921- *WhoAmP 93*
Money, John (William) 1921- *ConAu 41NR*
Money, John William 1921- *WhoAm 94*
Money, Keith 1935- *WrDr 94*
Money, Margaret Sarah 1942- *WhoMW 93*
Money, Peter *DrAPF 93*
Money, Zoot *WhoHol 92*
Money-Coutts *Who 94*
Money-Coutts, David (Burdett) 1931- *Who 94*
Money-Coutts, David Burdett 1931- *IntWW 93*
Money-Coutts, Francis Burdett (Thomas Nevill) 1852-1923 *NewGrDO*
Moneypenny, Edward William 1942- *WhoAm 94*
Monfils, Yvonne Ruth 1954- *WhoMW 93*
Monforton, Gerard Roland 1938- *WhoScEn 94*
Monfre, Joseph Paul 1956- *WhoScEn 94*
Mong, Robert William, Jr. 1949- *WhoAm 94*
Mong, Seymour 1951- *WhoAsA 94*
Mong, William V. d1940 *WhoHol 92*
Mongan, Agnes 1905- *WhoAm 94, WhoAmA 93*
Mongan, James John 1942- *WhoAm 94*
Mongardi, Gianfranco 1933- *WhoIns 94*
Mongarella, Georgene Hughes 1951- *WhoAm 94*
Mongbe, Rene Valery 1939- *IntWW 93*
Monge, Gaspard 1746-1818 *WorScD*
Monge, Jay Parry 1943- *WhoAm 94, WhoAmL 94*
Monge, Luis Alberto 1925- *IntWW 93*
Monge-Rafuls, Pedro 1943- *WhoHisp 94*
Mongini, Pietro 1839-1874 *NewGrDO*
Mongo Beti 1932- *IntWW 93*
Mongold, Carmella Sue 1955- *WhoMW 93*
Mongold, Sandra K. 1947- *WhoMW 93*
Mongrain, Claude 1948- *WhoAmA 93*
Monguno, Alhaji Shettima Ali 1926- *IntWW 93*
Mon'hin Thin Ge c. 1800-c. 1880 *EncNAR*
Moniba, Harry Fumba 1937- *Who 94*
Monica, Corbett 1922- *WhoHol 92*
Monica, John C. 1941- *WhoAm 94, WhoAmL 94*
Monical, Robert Duane 1925- *WhoAm 94*
Monicelli, Mario 1915- *IntMPA 94, IntWW 93*
Monier-Williams, Evelyn Faithfull 1920- *Who 94*
Moniglia, Giovanni Andrea 1624-1700 *NewGrDO*
Monin, Lawrence Owen 1942- *WhoFI 94*
Moninger, Edward George, Jr. 1943- *WhoWest 94*
Monismith, Carl Leroy 1926- *WhoAm 94, WhoScEn 94*
Monita, Jose C. 1943- *WhoHisp 94*
Moniuszko, Stanislaw 1819-1872 *NewGrDO*
Moniz, Egas (Antonio Caetano de Abrere Freire) 1874-1955 *EncSPD*
Moniz, Ernest Jeffrey 1944- *WhoScEn 94*
Moniz, Henry Thomas Adams 1964- *WhoAmL 94*
Moniz, J. Webb 1941- *WhoAmL 94*
Moniz, Joseph A. 1947- *WhoAmL 94*
Monize, Robert Ray 1942- *WhoWest 94*
Monje, Andrew, Jr. 1928- *WhoHisp 94*
Monjo, Christel fl. 1720-1729 *NewGrDO*
Monjo, John C. 1931- *WhoAmP 93*
Monk, Alec *Who 94*
Monk, (David) Alec (George) 1942- *Who 94*
Monk, Alice Kemp d1954 *WhoHol 92*
Monk, Allan James 1942- *WhoAm 94*
Monk, Anthony John 1923- *Who 94*
Monk, Art 1957- *WhoAm 94, WhoBlA 94*
Monk, Arthur James 1924- *Who 94*
Monk, Charles O., II 1949- *WhoAmL 94*
Monk, Darilyn Anita 1951- *WhoMW 93*
Monk, Debra *WhoAm 94*
Monk, Diana Charla 1927- *WhoWest 94*
Monk, Edd Dudley 1898- *WhoBlA 94*
Monk, Elizabeth Margaret *Who 94*
Monk, Gregory Brittain 1942- *WhoWest 94*
Monk, James Russell 1947- *WhoAmP 93, WhoMW 93*
Monk, Janice Jones 1937- *WhoWest 94*
Monk, Julius *WhoHol 92*
Monk, Meredith *WhoAmA 93*
Monk, Meredith Jane 1942- *WhoAm 94*
Monk, Nancy 1951- *WhoAmA 93*
Monk, Raymond 1925- *WrDr 94*
Monk, Richard Hunley, Jr. 1939- *WhoFI 94*
Monk, Robert C 1930- *WrDr 94*
Monk, Robert Evan, Jr. 1950- *WhoAmA 93*
Monk, Thelonious d1982 *WhoHol 92*
Monk, Thelonious 1917-1982 *AfrAmAl 6 [port]*
Monk, Thelonious Sphere 1920-1982 *AmCulL [port]*
Monk, Thomas d1956 *WhoHol 92*
Monk Bretton, Baron 1924- *Who 94*
Monke, Edwin John 1925- *WhoAm 94, WhoScEn 94*
Monkees, The *WhoHol 92*
Monkewitz, Peter Alexis 1943- *WhoScEn 94, WhoWest 94*
Monkhouse, Bob 1928- *IntMPA 94, WhoHol 92*
"Monk" Lewis 1775-1818 *BlmGEL*
Monkman, Cheryl Ann 1962- *WhoFI 94*
Monkman, Phyllis d1976 *WhoHol 92*
Monkman, Richard Drake 1954- *WhoAmL 94*
Monks, James *WhoHol 92*
Monks, John, Jr. 1910- *IntMPA 94*
Monks, John L. 1924- *WhoAmP 93*
Monks, John Michael 1957- *WhoAmL 94*
Monks, John Stephen 1945- *Who 94*
Monks, Robert A. G. 1933- *WhoAmP 93*
Monks, Robert Augustus Gardner 1933- *WhoAm 94*
Monkswell, Baron 1947- *Who 94*
Monlaur, Yvonne *WhoHol 92*
Monleone, Domenico 1875-1942 *NewGrDO*
Monlux, Stanton Del 1964- *WhoWest 94*
Monmart, Berthe c. 1924- *NewGrDO*
Monmonier, Mark 1943- *WhoAm 94*
Monmouth, Bishop of 1950- *Who 94*
Monmouth, Dean of *Who 94*
Monmouth, James Scott, Duke of 1649-1685 *BlmGEL*
Monnar, Marlene Mercedes 1953- *WhoHisp 94*
Monné, Noelia 1948- *WhoHisp 94*
Monnet, Jean 1703-1785 *NewGrDO*
Monnet, Marie Moreau 1752-1798 *BlmGWL*
Monnier, Claude Michel 1938- *IntWW 93*
Monnier, Jacqueline Matisse *WhoAmA 93*
Monnin, Robert D. 1941- *WhoAmL 94*
Monning, Ben Prater, III 1951- *WhoAmL 94*
Monning, W. Bruce 1948- *WhoAmL 94*
Monninger, Robert Harold George 1918- *WhoAm 94, WhoMW 93, WhoScEn 94*
Monod, Jacques Lucien *WorScD*
Monod, Jerome 1930- *IntWW 93*
Monod, Theodore 1902- *Who 94*
Monod, Theodore Andre 1902- *IntWW 93*
Monongye, Preston Lee 1927-1988 *WhoAmA 93N*
Monopoli, Giacomo *NewGrDO*
Monory, Jacques 1934- *IntWW 93, WhoAmA 93*
Monory, Rene Claude Aristide 1923- *IntWW 93*
Monoson, Lawrence *WhoHol 92*
Monoyios, Ann 1949- *NewGrDO*
Monplaisir, Emma 1918- *BlmGWL*
Monpou, (Francois Louis) Hippolyte 1804-1841 *NewGrDO*
Monrad, Elizabeth A. 1954- *WhoIns 94*
Monrad, Ernest Ejner 1930- *WhoAm 94, WhoFI 94*
Monreal, Diane Wiemer 1948- *WhoMW 93*
Monreal Luque, Alberto 1928- *IntWW 93*
Monro, Hector (Seymour Peter) 1922- *Who 94*
Monro, Hugh *Who 94*
Monro, (Andrew) Hugh 1950- *Who 94*
Monro, James Alexander, Jr. 1949- *WhoFI 94*
Monro, Matt d1985 *WhoHol 92*
Monroche, Andre Victor Jacques 1941- *WhoScEn 94*
Monro Davies, William Llewellyn 1927- *Who 94*
Monroe, Annie Lucky 1933- *WhoBlA 94*
Monroe, Ark, III 1942- *WhoAmL 94*
Monroe, Betty Iverson 1922- *WhoAmA 93*
Monroe, Brooks 1925- *WhoAm 94*
Monroe, Bryan K. 1965- *WhoBlA 94*
Monroe, Burt Leavelle, Jr. 1930- *WhoAm 94*
Monroe, C. Robert 1946- *WhoAmL 94*
Monroe, Carl Dean, III 1960- *WhoAmL 94*
Monroe, Charles Edward 1950- *WhoBlA 94*
Monroe, Daniel Milton, Jr. 1943- *WhoScEn 94*
Monroe, Debra 1958- *WrDr 94*
Monroe, Denise Angela Bakema 1961- *WhoMW 93*
Monroe, Earl 1944- *BasBi, WhoBlA 94*
Monroe, Eric George 1944- *WhoFI 94, WhoWest 94*
Monroe, Eve Valin 1920- *WhoAmA 93*
Monroe, Frank d1937 *WhoHol 92*
Monroe, Frederick Leroy 1942- *WhoScEn 94*
Monroe, Gerald 1926- *WhoAmA 93*
Monroe, Gerald J. *WhoAmP 93*
Monroe, Haskell M., Jr. 1931- *WhoAm 94, WhoMW 93*
Monroe, James 1758-1831 *AmRev, HisWorL [port], WhAmRev*
Monroe, James H. 1946- *WhoBlA 94*
Monroe, James W. 1942- *AfrAmG [port], WhoBlA 94*
Monroe, James Walter 1936- *WhoAm 94, WhoFI 94*
Monroe, John Robert 1960- *WhoScEn 94*
Monroe, Keith *WhoWest 94*
Monroe, Kendyl Kurth 1936- *WhoAm 94, WhoAmL 94*
Monroe, Kenneth Anthony 1951- *WhoMW 93*
Monroe, Kenneth Edward, Jr. 1928- *WhoAmP 93*
Monroe, L. A. J. 1919- *WhoAm 94*
Monroe, Lee Alexander 1932- *WhoAm 94*
Monroe, Lillie Mae 1948- *WhoBlA 94*
Monroe, Linda Roach 1952- *WhoHisp 94*
Monroe, Lyle *EncSF 93*
Monroe, Marilyn d1962 *WhoHol 92*
Monroe, Melrose 1919- *WhoAm 94, WhoFI 94*
Monroe, Murray Shipley 1925- *WhoAm 94, WhoAmL 94, WhoMW 93*
Monroe, Ned L. 1961- *WhoAmP 93*
Monroe, Robert Alex *WhoBlA 94*
Monroe, Robert Rawson 1927- *WhoAm 94*
Monroe, Roger George 1934- *WhoMW 93*
Monroe, Russell Alan 1960- *WhoFI 94*
Monroe, Russell Ronald 1920- *WhoAm 94*
Monroe, Stanley Edwin 1902- *WhoWest 94*
Monroe, Sylvester 1951- *WhoWest 94*
Monroe, Thomas Edward 1947- *WhoAm 94*
Monroe, Vaughn d1973 *WhoHol 92*
Monroe, Vernon Earl, Jr. 1944- *WhoAm 94*
Monroe, Virginia Marie 1933- *WhoMW 93*
Monroe, W. Rod 1942- *WhoAmP 93*
Monroe, Walter Harris, III 1944- *WhoAm 94, WhoAmL 94*
Monroe, William Lewis 1941- *WhoAm 94, WhoFI 94*
Monroe, William R., Jr. *WhoAmP 93*
Monroe, William Smith 1911- *WhoAm 94*

Monroig, Antonio 1944- *WhoAmP 93, WhoHisp 94*
Monrreal, Samuel 1961- *WhoHisp 94*
Monsaingeon, Bruno 1943- *ConAu 142*
Monsalve, Martha Eugenia 1968- *WhoScEn 94*
Monsarrat, Ann Whitelaw 1937- *WrDr 94*
Monsarrat, Nicholas 1910-1979 *EncSF 93*
Monsees, James Eugene 1937- *WhoAm 94*
Monsees, Janet Louise 1943- *WhoAmP 93*
Monsell, Viscount 1905- *Who 94*
Monsen, Elaine Ranker 1935- *WhoAm 94*
Monsen, Raymond Joseph, Jr. 1931- *WhoAm 94*
Monserda de Macia, Dolors 1845-1919 *BlmGWL*
Monserrat, Leonardo G. 1948- *WhoHisp 94*
Monsigny, Pierre-Alexandre 1729-1817 *NewGrDO*
Monsky, John Bertrand 1930- *WhoAm 94*
Monsky, Michael David Wolf Von Sommer 1947- *WhoFI 94*
Monsma, Robbie Elizabeth 1952- *WhoFI 94*
Monsman, Gerald 1940- *WhoWest 94*
Monson, Baron 1932- *Who 94*
Monson, Angela Zoe 1955- *WhoAmP 93*
Monson, Arch, Jr. 1913- *WhoAm 94, WhoAmP 93*
Monson, Carl d1988 *WhoHol 92*
Monson, David Carl 1950- *WhoAmP 93*
Monson, David S. 1945- *WhoAmP 93*
Monson, David Smith 1945- *WhoAm 94*
Monson, Dianne Lynn 1934- *WhoMW 93*
Monson, Forrest Truman 1915- *WhoAm 94*
Monson, James Edward 1932- *WhoAm 94, WhoWest 94*
Monson, Joyce Loraine 1938- *WhoAmP 93*
Monson, (William Bonnar) Leslie d1993 *Who 94N*
Monson, Raymond Edwin 1957- *WhoScEn 94*
Monson, Thomas Spencer 1927- *WhoAm 94, WhoWest 94*
Monson, William Bonnar Leslie 1912- *IntWW 94*
Monsor, Barbara Allen 1923- *WhoAmP 93*
Monsour, Michael Anton 1952- *WhoHisp 94*
Monstein, Marline Berta 1955- *WhoHisp 94*
Montacute, Mervyn Charles 1946- *Who 94*
Montag, David Moses 1939- *WhoWest 94*
Montag, John Joseph, II 1948- *WhoAm 94*
Montag, Mordechai 1925- *WhoScEn 94*
Montag, Tom 1947- *WrDr 94*
Montagna, Gilberto Luis Humberto 1936- *IntWW 93*
Montagna, William 1913- *WhoAm 94, WhoScEn 94*
Montagnana, Antonio fl. 1730- *NewGrDO*
Montagnani, Renzo *WhoHol 92*
Montagne, Edward J. 1912- *IntMPA 94*
Montagne, John 1920- *WhoWest 94*
Montagne Sanchez, Ernesto 1916- *IntWW 93*
Montagnier, Luc 1932- *IntWW 93, Who 94*
Montagu *Who 94*
Montagu, Ashley 1905- *Who 94, WhoAm 94, WrDr 94*
Montagu, Charles Greville 1741-1784 *AmRev*
Montagu, Elizabeth 1720-1800 *BlmGEL, BlmGWL*
Montagu, Jennifer (Iris Rachel) 1931- *WrDr 94*
Montagu, Jennifer Iris Rachel 1931- *Who 94*
Montagu, John *AmRev, WhAmRev*
Montagu, John Edward Hollister 1943- *Who 94*
Montagu, Mary *WorScD*
Montagu, Mary Wortley 1689-1762 *BlmGEL*
Montagu, Mary Wortley 1689-1792 *BlmGWL*
Montagu, Montague Francis Ashley *Who 94*
Montagu, Nicholas Lionel John 1944- *Who 94*
Montagu, Victor *Who 94*
Montagu, (Alexander) Victor (Edward Paulet) 1906- *Who 94*
Montagu Douglas Scott *Who 94*
Montagu-Douglas-Scott, Douglas Andrew *Who 94*
Montague *Who 94*
Montague, Brian John 1951- *WhoAm 94*
Montague, Christina P. 1952- *WhoBlA 94*
Montague, Diana 1953- *IntWW 93, NewGrDO*
Montague, Fred d1919 *WhoHol 92*
Montague, Gary Leslie 1939- *WhoWest 94*

Montague, George T(homas) 1929- *WrDr 94*
Montague, H. Dixon 1952- *WhoAmL 94*
Montague, James L. 1906- *WhoAmA 93*
Montague, John (Patrick) 1929- *WrDr 94*
Montague, Kenneth C., Jr. 1942- *WhoAmP 93*
Montague, Lee 1927- *WhoHol 92*
Montague, Lee 1929- *WhoBlA 94*
Montague, Michael Jacob 1932- *Who 94*
Montague, Michael James 1947- *WhoScEn 94*
Montague, Monte d1959 *WhoHol 92*
Montague, Nelson C. 1929- *WhoBlA 94*
Montague, Richard Mark 1938- *WhoWest 94*
Montague, Rita d1962 *WhoHol 92*
Montague, Robert Joel 1948- *Who 94*
Montague, Robert T., Jr. 1943- *WhoAmL 94*
Montague, Ruth Mary Bryceson 1939- *Who 94*
Montague, Sidney James 1950- *WhoWest 94*
Montague Browne, Anthony Arthur Duncan 1923- *Who 94*
Montague-Jones, Ronald 1909- *Who 94*
Montagu of Beaulieu, Baron 1926- *Who 94*
Montagu of Beaulieu, Lord 1926- *WrDr 94*
Montagu-Pollock, Giles Hampden *Who 94*
Montagu-Pollock, William Horace d1993 *Who 94N*
Montagu-Stuart-Wortley *Who 94*
Montaigne, Michel de 1533-1592 *BlmGEL*
Montaigne, Michel (Eyquem) de 1533-1592 *EncEth*
Montaigne, Michel Eyquem de 1533-1592 *GuFrLit 2*
Montaigne, Ortiz *WhoBlA 94*
Montaiuti, Sandra 1956- *WhoHol 92*
Montalban, Carlos d1991 *WhoHol 92*
Montalban, Ricardo 1920- *IntMPA 94, WhoAm 94, WhoHisp 94, WhoHol 92*
Montalban-Anderssen, Romero Anton, XIV 1960- *WhoHisp 94*
Montalbano, Joseph A. 1954- *WhoAmP 93*
Montalbano, Mark M. *WhoAmP 93*
Montalbano, William Daniel 1940- *WhoWest 94*
Montali, Dennis 1940- *WhoAm 94, WhoAmL 94*
Montalto, Joseph Gerard 1951- *WhoAmP 93*
Montalvan, Celia d1958 *WhoHol 92*
Montalvo, Ana E. 1948- *WhoHisp 94*
Montalvo, Consuelo *WhoHisp 94*
Montalvo, Frank A. 1950- *WhoHisp 94*
Montalvo, Gary G. 1952- *WhoHisp 94*
Montalvo, Harry 1961- *WhoHisp 94*
Montalvo, LaRee Holloway 1959- *WhoFI 94*
Montalvo, Leo *WhoHisp 94*
Montalvo, Louis Anthony 1922- *WhoHisp 94*
Montalvo, María Antonia 1951- *WhoHisp 94*
Montalvo, Socorro Inmaculada 1954- *WhoHisp 94*
Montana, Anthony James 1950- *WhoScEn 94*
Montana, Bob 1920-1975 *WhoAmA 93N*
Montana, Bull d1950 *WhoHol 92*
Montana, Claude *IntWW 93*
Montana, James Samuel, Jr. 1943- *WhoAm 94*
Montana, Jordi 1949- *WhoFI 94*
Montana, Joseph, Jr. 1956- *IntWW 93, WhoAm 94, WhoMW 93*
Montana, Lenny d1984 *WhoHol 92*
Montana, Montie 1910- *WhoHol 92*
Montana, Patrick Joseph *WhoAm 94*
Montana, Patsy *WhoAm 94*
Montana, Pietro 1890-1978 *WhoAmA 93N*
Montana, Priscila A. C. 1948- *WhoHisp 94*
Montanari, John Richard 1944- *WhoWest 94*
Montanari Fornari, Nanda 1934- *WhoWomW 91*
Montanaro, Frank A. 1961- *WhoAmP 93*
Montanclos, Marie-Emilie Maryon de 1736-1812 *BlmGWL*
Montand, Yves 1921- *WhoHol 92*
Montand, Yves 1921-1991 *WhAm 10*
Montané, Carlos H. 1933- *WhoHisp 94*
Montane, David 1960- *WhoWest 94*
Montané, Diana Emilia 1946- *WhoHisp 94*
Montané, Jean Joseph 1961- *WhoScEn 94*
Montané, Olga González 1927- *WhoHisp 94*
Montanelli, Indro 1909- *IntWW 93*

Montanez, Pablo I. 1958- *WhoHisp 94*
Montanez, William Joseph 1952- *WhoHisp 94*
Montano, Carlos Xavier 1955- *WhoHisp 94*
Montano, George John 1927- *WhoAmP 93*
Montaño, Johnnie Anthony 1936- *WhoHisp 94*
Montano, Jorge 1945- *IntWW 93, WhoAm 94*
Montano, Linda (Mary) 1942- *WhoAmA 93*
Montano, Louis R. 1928- *WhoHisp 94*
Montaño, Mary 1949- *WhoHisp 94*
Montant, Jane *WhoAm 94*
Montanye, James Alan 1946- *WhoFI 94*
Montarsolo, Paolo 1925- *NewGrDO*
Montau, Michele d1989 *WhoHol 92*
Montaudo, Giorgio 1934- *WhoScEn 94*
Montayne, John D. *WhoAmP 93*
Montazeri, Ayatollah Hussein Ali 1923- *IntWW 93*
Montblern, Saint-Simon *WhAmRev*
Montcalm, Norman Joseph 1945- *WhoAm 94*
Montchrestien, Antoine de 1575?-1621 *GuFrLit 2*
Monte, Mysie d1983 *WhoHol 92*
Monte, Ralph 1960- *WhoHisp 94*
Monteagle of Brandon, Baron 1926- *Who 94*
Monteagudo, Eduardo 1953- *WhoHisp 94*
Monteagudo, Gene M. 1966- *WhoHisp 94*
Monteagudo, Lourdes María 1955- *WhoHisp 94*
Montealegre, Jose Ramiro 1959- *WhoScEn 94*
Montealegre, Lily Bendaña 1961- *WhoHisp 94*
Montecchi, Elena 1954- *WhoWomW 91*
Monteclair, Michel Pignolet de c. 1667-1737 *NewGrDO*
Montecorvino, John Of *WhWE*
Montedonico, Joseph 1937- *WhoAmL 94*
Montefiore, Harold Henry S. *Who 94*
Montefiore, Hugh (William) 1920- *WrDr 94*
Montefiore, Hugh William 1920- *IntWW 93, Who 94*
Montegriffo, Peter Cecil Patrick 1960- *IntWW 93*
Monteiro, Antonio Mascarenhas *IntWW 93*
Monteiro, Isaac 1938- *WhoAmA 93*
Monteiro, Jeronimo *EncSF 93*
Monteiro, Lois Ann 1934- *WhoAm 94*
Monteiro, Luis (Infante de la Cerda) de Sttau 1926-1993 *ConAu 142*
Monteiro, Marilyn D.S. 1941- *WhoBlA 94*
Monteiro, Renato Duarte Carneiro 1959- *WhoScEn 94*
Monteiro, Sergio Lara 1945- *WhoScEn 94*
Monteiro, Thomas 1939- *WhoBlA 94*
Monteiro-Riviere, Nancy Ann 1954- *WhoScEn 94*
Monteith, Charles Montgomery 1921- *Who 94*
Monteith, David Keith Brisson 1959- *WhoScEn 94*
Monteith, George Rae 1904- *Who 94*
Monteith, Henry C. 1937- *WhoBlA 94*
Monteith, John Lennox 1929- *Who 94*
Monteith, Kelly *WhoHol 92*
Monteith, Larry King 1933- *WhoAm 94*
Monteith, Robert Charles Michael 1914- *Who 94*
Monteith, Stanley Kimball 1929- *WhoWest 94*
Monteith, Walter Henry, Jr. 1930- *WhoFI 94*
Monteith, William Frederick 1941- *WhoMW 93*
Montejano, Rodolfo 1938- *WhoHisp 94*
Montejo, Francisco de 1479-1549 *WhWE*
Montejo, Francisco De 1508-1574 *WhWE*
Monteleone, Raymond R. 1947- *WhoAm 94*
Monteleone, Thomas F. 1946- *WrDr 94*
Monteleone, Thomas F(rancis) 1946- *EncSF 93*
Montell, Lisa 1933- *WhoHol 92*
Montelongo, Delia C. 1940- *WhoHisp 94*
Montelongo, Michael *WhoAm 94*
Montelongo, Michael 1955- *WhoHisp 94*
Montemarano, Francis Anthony 1944- *WhoFI 94*
Montemayor, Carlos Rene 1945- *WhoHisp 94*
Montemayor, Edilberto F. 1950- *WhoHisp 94*
Montemayor, Jesus Samson 1939- *WhoScEn 94*
Montemayor, Raymond 1946- *WhoHisp 94*
Montemezzi, Italo 1875-1952 *NewGrDO*
Montemuro, Frank J., Jr. 1925- *WhoAmL 94, WhoAmP 93*

Montenaro, Regina Lynne 1947- *WhoMW 93*
Montenegro, Conchita 1912- *WhoHol 92*
Monterey, Carlotta d1970 *WhoHol 92*
Montero, Ana M. 1949- *WhoHisp 94*
Montero, Darrel Martin 1946- *WhoWest 94*
Montero, Emily Bernal 1953- *WhoHisp 94*
Montero, Faustino, Jr. 1963- *WhoHisp 94*
Montero, Fernan Gonzalo 1948- *WhoAm 94, WhoHisp 94*
Montero, Jose Angel 1832-1881 *NewGrDO*
Montero, Juan Murillo, II 1942- *WhoAsA 94*
Montero, Pedro d1987 *WhoHol 92*
Montero, Rosa 1951- *BlmGWL*
Monterrosa, Jose Napoleon 1953- *WhoWest 94*
Monterroso, Amalia *WhoHisp 94*
Monterroza, Adiel Abisay 1957- *WhoHisp 94*
Montes, Andres Eugene 1962- *WhoHisp 94*
Montes, Diego J. 1955- *WhoHisp 94*
Montes, Elis *WhoHol 92*
Montes, Jess Henry 1944- *WhoHisp 94*
Montes, Lina d1984 *WhoHol 92*
Montes, Mary *WhoHisp 94*
Montes, Richard *WhoHisp 94*
Montes, Virginia E. 1943- *WhoHisp 94*
Montesano, Aldo Maria 1939- *WhoScEn 94*
Montesano, Enrico *WhoHol 92*
Montesanto, Luigi 1887-1954 *NewGrDO*
Montesco, Liliana 1934- *WhoHisp 94*
Montes De Oca, Alberto R. 1952- *WhoHisp 94*
Montes de Oca Ricks, Maria Helena 1947- *WhoHisp 94*
Montes Huidobro, Matías 1931- *WhoHisp 94*
Montesino, Paul V. 1937- *WhoHisp 94*
Montesquieu, baron de 1689-1755 *EncEth*
Montesquieu, Charles-Louis de Secondat, Baron de 1689-1755 *GuFrLit 2*
Montesson, Marquise de 1738-1806 *BlmGWL*
Monteux, Pierre 1875-1964 *NewGrDO*
Montevecchi, Liliane *WhoHol 92*
Montevecchi, Liliane 1933- *ConTFT 11*
Monteverde, Ronald Peter 1947- *WhoWest 94*
Monteverdi, Claudio (Zuan Antonio) c. 1567-1643 *NewGrDO*
Monteverdi, Giulio Cesare c. 1573-1630? *NewGrDO*
Monteverdi, Mark Victor 1963- *WhoBlA 94*
Montez, Chris 1943- *WhoHisp 94*
Montez, Maria d1951 *WhoHol 92*
Montez, Noel Peña 1965- *WhoHisp 94*
Montezuma, Carlos c. 1865-1923 *AmSocL, HisWorL [port]*
Montford, John T. 1943- *WhoAmP 93*
Montfort, Auguste 1913- *ConAu 41NR*
Montfort, Peter de c. 1205-1265 *DcNaB MP*
Montgolfier, Jacques 1745-1799 *WorInv*
Montgolfier, Joseph 1740-1810 *WorInv*
Montgomerie *Who 94*
Montgomerie, Lord 1966- *Who 94*
Montgomerie, Bruce Mitchell 1946- *WhoAm 94*
Montgomery *Who 94*
Montgomery, Alan Everard 1938- *Who 94*
Montgomery, Alpha LeVon, Sr. 1919- *WhoBlA 94*
Montgomery, Andrew Stuart 1960- *WhoFI 94, WhoMW 93*
Montgomery, Barbara 1939- *WhoHol 92*
Montgomery, Barbara Curry 1939- *WhoBlA 94*
Montgomery, Belinda J. 1950- *WhoHol 92*
Montgomery, Bernard 1887-1976 *HisWorL [port]*
Montgomery, Betty d1922 *WhoHol 92*
Montgomery, Betty D. *WhoAmP 93, WhoMW 93*
Montgomery, Billy W. 1937- *WhoAmP 93*
Montgomery, Brian Walter 1957- *WhoBlA 94*
Montgomery, Carl Robert 1939- *WhoAmP 93*
Montgomery, Carol Artman *DrAPF 93*
Montgomery, Catherine Lewis *WhoBlA 94*
Montgomery, Charles Barry 1937- *WhoAmL 94, WhoMW 93*
Montgomery, Charles Franklin 1910-1978 *WhoAmA 93N*
Montgomery, Charles Howard 1930- *WhoAm 94*
Montgomery, Charlotte A. *WhoMW 93*
Montgomery, Clark Taylor 1941- *WhoAm 94*
Montgomery, Claude 1912-1990 *WhoAmA 93N*
Montgomery, David *Who 94*

Montgomery, David d1917 *WhoHol 92*
Montgomery, David 1927- *Who 94*
Montgomery, David 1937- *IntWW 93*
Montgomery, (Basil Henry) David 1931-
Who 94
Montgomery, David Bruce 1938-
WhoAm 94, WrDr 94
Montgomery, David Campbell 1936-
WhoAm 94
Montgomery, David Craig 1870-1917
See Montgomery and Stone *WhoCom*
Montgomery, David John 1948-
IntWW 93, Who 94
Montgomery, David Paul *WhoAm 94*
Montgomery, Deane *IntWW 93N*
Montgomery, Deane 1909-1992 *WhAm 10*
Montgomery, Desmond Alan Dill 1916-
Who 94
Montgomery, Don W. 1925- *WhoIns 94*
Montgomery, Donald Joseph 1917-
WhoAm 94
Montgomery, Donald L. *WhoAmP 93*
Montgomery, Donald Russell 1920-
WhoAm 94
Montgomery, Douglass d1966 *WhoHol 92*
Montgomery, Dwight Ray 1950-
WhoBlA 94
Montgomery, Earl d1966 *WhoHol 92*
Montgomery, Earl d1987 *WhoHol 92*
Montgomery, Earline 1944- *WhoBlA 94*
Montgomery, Earline Robertson 1944-
WhoBlA 94
Montgomery, Edward Alembert, Jr. 1934-
WhoAm 94
Montgomery, Edward Benjamin 1915-
WhoAm 94
Montgomery, Elizabeth *ConAu 42NR*
Montgomery, Elizabeth d1993
NewYTBS 93 [port]
Montgomery, Elizabeth 1933- *IntMPA 94,
WhoHol 92*
Montgomery, Elizabeth Ann 1957-
W hoScEn 94
Montgomery, Elizabeth Rider
ConAu 42NR
Montgomery, Ethel Constance 1931-
WhoBlA 94
Montgomery, Evangeline J. 1933-
AfrAmAl 6
Montgomery, Evangeline Juliet 1933-
WhoBlA 94
Montgomery, Fergus *Who 94*
Montgomery, (William) Fergus 1927-
Who 94
Montgomery, Florence d1950 *WhoHol 92*
Montgomery, Frances Trego 1858-1925
EncSF 93
Montgomery, Frank E. (a.k.a. Frank E.
Monty) d1944 *WhoHol 92*
Montgomery, Fred O. 1922- *WhoBlA 94*
Montgomery, G. V. *CngDr 93*
Montgomery, Gary 1957- *WhoMW 93*
Montgomery, Gary Lee 1942-
WhoAmL 94, WhoAmP 93
Montgomery, George *DrAPF 93*
Montgomery, George 1916- *IntMPA 94,
WhoHol 92*
Montgomery, George Cranwell 1944-
WhoAm 94, WhoAmL 94, WhoAmP 93
Montgomery, George Franklin 1921-
WhoAm 94
Montgomery, George Lightbody d1993
Who 94N
Montgomery, George Louis, Jr. 1934-
WhoBlA 94
Montgomery, George Rodgers 1910-
Who 94
Montgomery, Gillespie V. *WhoAmP 93*
Montgomery, Gillespie V. 1920-
WhoAm 94
Montgomery, Glenn A. *WhoAm 94*
Montgomery, Goodee d1978 *WhoHol 92*
Montgomery, Gregory B. 1946-
WhoBlA 94
Montgomery, Harold Hench 1959-
WhoFI 94
Montgomery, Harold Ronnie 1938-
WhoAmP 93
Montgomery, Harry J. 1939- *WhoBlA 94*
Montgomery, Harry Sheffie 1926-
WhoAmP 93
Montgomery, Harry Thomas 1909-1991
WhAm 10
Montgomery, Henry DuBose, Jr. 1949-
WhoFI 94
Montgomery, Henry Irving 1924-
WhoFI 94, WhoMW 93
Montgomery, Hugh Bryan Greville 1929-
Who 94
Montgomery, J. W., III 1946-
WhoAmL 94
Montgomery, Jack d1962 *WhoHol 92*
Montgomery, James d1955 *WhoHol 92*
Montgomery, James C. 1918- *WhoBlA 94*
Montgomery, James Fischer 1934-
WhoAm 94, WhoFI 94, WhoWest 94
Montgomery, James Huey 1942-
WhoMW 93

Montgomery, James Morton 1931-
WhoAm 94
Montgomery, Jeffrey Thomas 1962-
WhoAm 94, WhoMW 93
Montgomery, Jim 1937- *WhoAmP 93*
Montgomery, Joe Elliott 1942- *WhoBlA 94*
Montgomery, John *IntWW 93, Who 94*
Montgomery, John 1722-1808 *WhAmRev*
Montgomery, (Charles) John 1917-
IntWW 93, Who 94
Montgomery, John Alan 1944-
WhoWest 94
Montgomery, John Atterbury 1924-
WhoAm 94
Montgomery, John B. 1943- *WhoAmL 94*
Montgomery, John D 1920- *WrDr 94*
Montgomery, John Dickey 1920-
WhoAm 94
Montgomery, John Duncan 1928- *Who 94*
Montgomery, John Grey 1940-
WhoMW 93
Montgomery, John Harold 1955-
WhoScEn 94
Montgomery, John Henry 1937-
WhoFI 94, WhoScEn 94
Montgomery, John Matthew 1930-
Who 94
Montgomery, John Osborn 1921-
WhoFI 94
Montgomery, John Rupert Patrick 1913-
Who 94
Montgomery, John Warwick 1931-
WhoAmL 94
Montgomery, Johnny Lester 1934-
WhoAm 94
Montgomery, Joseph 1733-1794
WhAmRev
Montgomery, Joseph William 1951-
WhoFI 94
Montgomery, Julie *WhoHol 92*
Montgomery, Kathleen Rae 1950-
WhoMW 93
Montgomery, Keesler H. 1917-
WhoBlA 94
Montgomery, Keith Norris, Sr. 1951-
WhoAmP 93
Montgomery, Kenneth 1943- *NewGrDO*
Montgomery, Kirby Vincent 1953-
WhoIns 94
Montgomery, L. M. 1874-1942
Au&Arts 12 [port], TwCLC 51 [port]
Montgomery, Lee *WhoHol 92*
Montgomery, Leslie David 1939-
WhoAm 94
Montgomery, Linda Kay 1951-
WhoAmP 93
Montgomery, Lucy Maud 1874-1942
BlmGWL
Montgomery, Marian d1977 *WhoHol 92*
Montgomery, Marion *DrAPF 93*
Montgomery, Marion 1925- *WrDr 94*
Montgomery, Martha *WhoHol 92*
Montgomery, Michael B. 1936-
WhoAmP 93
Montgomery, Mildren M. 1929-
WhoBlA 94
Montgomery, Oliver R. 1929- *WhoBlA 94*
Montgomery, Oscar Lee 1949- *WhoBlA 94*
Montgomery, Parker Gilbert 1928-
WhoAm 94
Montgomery, Patrick Matthew 1957-
WhoIns 94
Montgomery, Paula Kay 1946-
WhoAm 94
Montgomery, Payne 1933- *WhoBlA 94*
Montgomery, Peggy *WhoHol 92*
Montgomery, Philip O'Bryan, Jr. 1921-
WhoScEn 94
Montgomery, Ralph d1980 *WhoHol 92*
Montgomery, Ray 1919- *WhoHol 92*
Montgomery, Ray Hillman 1935-
WhoAmP 93
Montgomery, Rex 1923- *WhoAm 94*
Montgomery, Richard 1738-1775 *AmRev,
WhAmRev [port]*
Montgomery, Robert d1981 *WhoHol 92*
Montgomery, Robert E. 1948- *WhoBlA 94*
Montgomery, Robert E., Jr. 1939-
WhoAmL 94
Montgomery, Robert F. 1933-
WhoWest 94
Montgomery, Robert Floyd 1933-
WhoAmP 93
Montgomery, Robert Harold 1959-
WhoAm 94
Montgomery, Robert Humphrey, Jr.
1923- *WhoAm 94*
Montgomery, Robert Louis 1935-
WhoWest 94
Montgomery, Robert Morel, Jr. 1930-
WhoAm 94
Montgomery, Robert Raynor 1943-
WhoFI 94
Montgomery, Robert Renwick 1943-
WhoScEn 94
Montgomery, Roger 1925- *WhoAm 94*
Montgomery, Ronald Eugene 1937-
WhoAm 94

Montgomery, Roy Delbert 1926-
WhoAm 94
Montgomery, Royal Ewert 1896-
WhAm 10
Montgomery, Ruth 1927- *WhoAmP 93*
Montgomery, Ruth Shick *WhoAm 94*
Montgomery, Rutherford George 1896-
WhAm 10
Montgomery, Seth D. *WhoAmP 93*
Montgomery, Seth David 1937-
WhoAm 94, WhoAmL 94, WhoWest 94
Montgomery, Shirley Kay 1935-
WhoMW 93
Montgomery, Sonny 1920- *WhoAm 94*
Montgomery, Susan Barbieri 1949-
WhoAmL 94
Montgomery, Terry Gray 1953-
WhoScEn 94
Montgomery, Theodore Ashton 1923-
WhoAm 94
Montgomery, Toni-Marie 1956-
WhoBlA 94
Montgomery, Trent *WhoBlA 94*
Montgomery, Velmanette *WhoAmP 93,
WhoBlA 94*
Montgomery, Walter George 1945-
WhoAm 94, WhoFI 94
Montgomery, Wendell Cabel 1947-
WhoMW 93
Montgomery, Willard Wayne 1949-
WhoScEn 94
Montgomery, William 1736-1816
WhAmRev
Montgomery, William Adam 1933-
WhoAm 94, WhoAmL 94
Montgomery, William J. 1930-
WhoAm 94
Montgomery, William R. 1924-
WhoBlA 94
Montgomery, William Wayne 1923-
WhoAm 94
Montgomery, Willie Henry 1939-
WhoBlA 94
Montgomery and Stone *WhoCom*
Montgomery Cuninghame, John
Christopher Foggo 1935- *Who 94*
Montgomery-Davis, Joseph 1940-
WhoScEn 94
Montgomery-Meissner, Kathryn 1952-
NewGrDO
Montgomery of Alamein, Viscount 1928-
Who 94
Montgomery-Smith, Stephen John 1963-
WhoMW 93
Montgomery Watt, William *Who 94*
Montgrain, Noel 1933- *WhoAm 94*
Monthan, Guy 1925- *WhoAmA 93*
Montherlant, Henry (Millon) de
1896-1972 *IntDcT 2 [port]*
Monthyl, Marcelle d1950 *WhoHol 92*
Monti, Gaetano c. 1750-1816? *NewGrDO*
Monti, Innocenzo 1909- *IntWW 93*
Monti, John 1957- *WhoAmA 93*
Monti, Laura c. 1704-1760 *NewGrDO*
Monti, Laura Anne 1959- *WhoMW 93,
WhoScEn 94*
Monti, Marianna 1730-1814 *NewGrDO*
Monti, Stephen Arion 1939- *WhoAm 94*
Monti, Thomas Anthony 1950- *WhoFI 94*
Monticciolo, Joseph Domenick 1937-
WhoFI 94
Monticelli, Angelo Maria c. 1712-1758?
NewGrDO
Monticelli, Anna-Maria *WhoHol 92*
Monticelli Novelli, Antonio Felice
NewGrDO
Monticello, Roberto 1954- *ConAu 142*
Montiel, Jose R. *WhoHisp 94*
Montiel, Jose Ramon *WhoHisp 94*
Montiel, Miguel 1942- *WhoHisp 94*
Montiel, Roberto C. *WhoHisp 94*
Montiel, Sarita 1927- *WhoHol 92*
Monti Family *NewGrDO*
Montifoeud, Marc de *BlmGWL*
Montigny, Mark C. *WhoAmP 93*
Montijo, Ben 1940- *WhoHisp 94*
Montijo, Ralph Elias, Jr. 1928-
*WhoAm 94, WhoFI 94, WhoHisp 94,
WhoScEn 94*
Montilla, Cesar Alberto, Jr. 1942-
WhoAmP 93
Montion, Louis Herrera, Jr. 1943-
WhoHisp 94
Montlack, Edith *WhoAmA 93*
Montlake, Henry Joseph 1930- *Who 94*
Montle, Paul Joseph 1947- *WhoAm 94*
Montminy, Tracy 1911- *WhoAmA 93*
Montmorency, Arnold Geoffroy de
Who 94
Montmorin, Armand, Comte de
WhAmRev
Montolieu, Pauline 1751-1832 *BlmGWL*
Montoliu, Jesus 1919- *WhoScEn 94*
Montondon, Mark D. 1955- *WhoFI 94*
Montone, Kenneth Alan 1938-
WhoWest 94
Montone, Liber Joseph 1919-
WhoScEn 94

Montoni, Lorin Marc 1962- *WhoAmP 93*
Montoriol i Puig, Carme 1893-1966
BlmGWL
Montour, Esther *WhAmRev*
Montoya, A. R. *WhoHisp 94*
Montoya, Abran Felipe, Jr. 1948-
WhoHisp 94
Montoya, Alex d1970 *WhoHol 92*
Montoya, Alfredo C. 1921- *WhoHisp 94*
Montoya, Alicea Navarro 1947-
WhoAmP 93
Montoya, Alvaro 1942- *WhoHisp 94*
Montoya, Ana-Patricia *WhoHisp 94*
Montoya, Benjamin F. *WhoHisp 94*
Montoya, Carlos 1903-1993
NewYTBS 93 [port], News 93
Montoya, Carlos (Garcia) 1903-1993
CurBio 93N
Montoya, Carole McCauley 1944-
WhoMW 93
Montoya, Charles William 1937-
WhoHisp 94
Montoya, David *WhoHisp 94*
Montoya, David, Jr. 1934- *WhoHisp 94*
Montoya, Delilah M. 1955- *WhoHisp 94*
Montoya, Demetrio H. 1937- *WhoHisp 94*
Montoya, Dennis William 1954-
WhoWest 94
Montoya, Felipe d1955 *WhoHol 92*
Montoya, Frieda M. 1923- *WhoHisp 94*
Montoya, Gilbert John 1944- *WhoHisp 94*
Montoya, Herbert Patricio 1942-
WhoAmP 93
Montoya, Isaac D. 1950- *WhoHisp 94*
Montoya, John J. 1945- *WhoHisp 94*
Montoya, Johnny Lee 1966- *WhoHisp 94*
Montoya, Jorge P. 1946- *WhoHisp 94*
Montoya, Joseph O. 1945- *WhoHisp 94*
Montoya, Juan F. 1945- *WhoAm 94*
Montoya, Julio César 1942- *WhoHisp 94*
Montoya, Linda L. 1947- *WhoHisp 94*
Montoya, Louis *WhoHisp 94*
Montoya, Malaquias 1938- *WhoHisp 94*
Montoya, Marco 1944- *WhoHisp 94*
Montoya, Margaret E. 1948- *WhoHisp 94*
Montoya, Max *WhoHisp 94*
Montoya, Nancy Lucero 1954-
WhoHisp 94
Montoya, Pres L. 1954- *WhoAm 94,
WhoHisp 94*
Montoya, Regina T. 1953- *WhoAm 94,
WhoHisp 94*
Montoya, Richard 1960- *WhoHisp 94*
Montoya, Ronald E. 1940- *WhoHisp 94*
Montoya, Ruben Ortiz 1923- *WhoHisp 94*
Montoya, Sam John 1946- *WhoHisp 94*
Montoya, Thomas Paul 1953-
WhoHisp 94
Montoya, Tom 1932- *WhoHisp 94*
Montoya, Velma *WhoHisp 94*
Montoya-Rael, Lillian Josephine 1966-
WhoWest 94
Montpensier, Duchesse de 1627-1693
BlmGWL
Montreal, Archbishop of 1936- *Who 94*
Montreal, Bishop of 1938- *Who 94*
Montrelay, Michele *BlmGWL*
Montremy, Philipe Marie Waldruche de
1913- *IntWW 93*
Montresor, Beni 1926- *NewGrDO*
Montresor, John 1736-1799 *AmRev,
WhAmRev*
Montrone, Paul Michael 1941-
WhoAm 94, WhoFI 94
Montrose, Duke of 1935- *Who 94*
Montrose, Belle d1964 *WhoHol 92*
Montrose, Donald W. 1923- *WhoAm 94,
WhoWest 94*
Montrose, James Graham, Marquess of
1612-1650 *BlmGEL*
Montrose, James Karl 1954- *WhoWest 94*
Mont'Ros-Mendoza, Theresa 1952-
WhoHisp 94
Montross, Albert Edward 1936- *WhoFI 94*
Montross, Franklin, IV 1956- *WhoIns 94*
Montross, W. Scott 1947- *WhoAmL 94*
Monts, David Lee 1951- *WhoScEn 94*
Montsalvatge, Xavier 1912- *NewGrDO*
Montt, Christina d1969 *WhoHol 92*
Montuori, Deborah Jane 1948-
WhoMW 93
Montvid, Aleksandra Stanislavovna
1845- *BlmGWL*
Montville, Thomas Joseph 1953-
WhoScEn 94
Montwill, Alexander 1935- *IntWW 93*
Monty, Charles Embert 1927- *WhoAm 94*
Monty, Frank E. d1944 *WhoHol 92*
Monty, Gloria *WhoAm 94*
Monty, Jean Claude 1947- *WhoAm 94,
WhoFI 94*
Monty, Richard Arthur 1935-
WhoScEn 94
Monty, Robert 1944- *WhoAmP 93*
Monty Python *WhoHol 92*
Monty Python's Flying Circus *WhoCom*
Monyak, Wendell Peter 1931-
WhoMW 93, WhoScEn 94

Monyake, Lengolo Bureng 1930- IntWW 93
Monyer, Pete, Jr. 1944- WhoHisp 94
Monza, Carlo c. 1735-1801 NewGrDO
Monza, Carlo Ignazio d1739 NewGrDO
Monza, Maria fl. 1729-1741 NewGrDO
Monzen, Mitsugi 1918- IntWW 93
Monzon-Aguirre, Victor J. 1949- WhoHisp 94
Mood, John 1932- WhoWest 94
Moodera, Jagadeesh Subbaiah WhoAsA 94
Moodhe, Joseph Patrick 1955- WhoAmL 94
Moodie, Dahlia Maria 1959- WhoBlA 94
Moodie, Graeme Cochrane 1924- WrDr 94
Moodie, Susanna 1803-1885 BlmGWL
Moody, Ann BlmGWL
Moody, Anne 1940- WhoBlA 94
Moody, Anthony Merald 1932- WhoAmP 93
Moody, Brian Wayne 1955- WhoScEn 94
Moody, Charles David, Sr. 1932- WhoBlA 94
Moody, Charles Russell 1956- WhoWest 94
Moody, Christopher Marlin 1954- WhoAmL 94
Moody, David Edward 1950- WhoWest 94
Moody, Denman, Jr. 1942- WhoFI 94
Moody, Dwight L. 1837-1899 HisWorL [port]
Moody, Dwight Lyman 1837-1899 AmSocL [port], DcAmReB 2
Moody, Edward H. WhoAmP 93
Moody, Elizabeth C. 1944- WhoAmA 93
Moody, Eric Orlando 1951- WhoBlA 94
Moody, Evelyn Wilie WhoFI 94
Moody, Fanny 1866-1945 NewGrDO
Moody, Florence Elizabeth 1932- WhoAm 94
Moody, Frederick Jerome 1935- WhoAm 94
Moody, Fredreatha E. 1941- WhoBlA 94
Moody, G. William 1928- WhoAm 94, WhoFI 94
Moody, Gene Byron 1933- WhoScEn 94
Moody, George Ernest 1938- WhoFI 94
Moody, George Franklin 1930- IntWW 93
Moody, Graham Blair 1925- WhoAm 94
Moody, Harold L. 1932- WhoBlA 94
Moody, Helen Wills Who 94
Moody, Helen Wills 1905- BuCMET [port]
Moody, Hiram Frederick, Jr. 1935- WhoAm 94
Moody, Howard Craig 1951- WhoAmP 93
Moody, Ian Charles Hugh 1928- Who 94
Moody, J. William 1947- WhoAmP 93
Moody, James WhAmRev
Moody, James 1744-1809 AmRev
Moody, James L., Jr. 1931- WhoAm 94, WhoFI 94
Moody, James P. 1935- WhoAmP 93
Moody, James Tyne 1938- WhoAm 94, WhoAmL 94, WhoMW 93
Moody, John 1759-1781 WhAmRev
Moody, John (Percivale) 1906- NewGrDO
Moody, John Percivale d1993 Who 94N
Moody, Joseph M. 1928- WhoAmP 93
Moody, King WhoHol 92
Moody, Lamon Lamar, Jr. 1924- WhoAm 94, WhoScEn 94
Moody, Leslie Howard 1922- Who 94
Moody, Linda Dawn 1965- WhoMW 93
Moody, Lizabeth Ann 1934- WhoAmL 94
Moody, Lynne WhoHol 92
Moody, Lynne Gatlin WhoBlA 94
Moody, Maxwell, Jr. 1921- WhoScEn 94
Moody, Michael Jay 1958- WhoFI 94, WhoWest 94
Moody, Peter Edward 1918- Who 94
Moody, Peter R(ichard), Jr. 1943- WrDr 94
Moody, R. Bruce DrAPF 93
Moody, Ralph d1971 WhoHol 92
Moody, Robert Adams 1934- WhoAm 94
Moody, Robert J. 1942- WhoAmP 93
Moody, Robert M. WhoMW 93
Moody, Rodger DrAPF 93
Moody, Roger Wayne 1956- WhoScEn 94
Moody, Roland Herbert 1916- WhoAm 94
Moody, Ron 1924- WhoHol 92
Moody, Shirley DrAPF 93
Moody, Susan (Elizabeth Howard) WrDr 94
Moody, Willard James, Sr. 1924- WhoAmL 94, WhoAmP 93
Moody, William Dennis 1948- WhoBlA 94
Moody, William Vaughn 1869-1910 IntDcT 2
Moody-Lawrence, Bessie WhoAmP 93
Moody-Stewart, Mark 1940- IntWW 93
Moody-Stuart, Mark 1940- Who 94
Mooers, Christopher Northrup Kennard 1935- WhoAm 94, WhoScEn 94
Mooers, Daniel William 1943- WhoAmL 94
Mooers, De Sacia d1960 WhoHol 92
Mooers, Douglas Francis 1949- WhoWest 94
Mooers, Philip F. 1940- WhoIns 94
Moog, Heinz d1989 WhoHol 92
Moog, Mary Ann Pimley 1952- WhoAmL 94
Mook, William Harry, Jr. 1953- WhoMW 93
Mookerjee, Birendra Nath 1899- Who 94
Mookini, Esther T. 1928- WrDr 94
Moollan, Cassam (Ismael) 1927- Who 94
Moollan, (Abdool) Hamid (Adam) 1933- Who 94
Moomaw, Max WhoAmP 93
Moomaw, Ronald Lee 1943- WhoAm 94
Moon, Billy G. 1961- WhoScEn 94
Moon, Brenda Elizabeth 1931- Who 94
Moon, Byung Hwa 1956- WhoAsA 94
Moon, Carl 1879-1948 WhoAmA 93N
Moon, Charlotte Digges 1840-1912 DcAmReB 2
Moon, Chung-In 1951- WhoAsA 94
Moon, Danny Ray 1947- WhoWest 94
Moon, Deborah Joan 1956- WhoAmL 94
Moon, Donald Lee 1936- WhoMW 93
Moon, Donna d1918 WhoHol 92
Moon, Elizabeth 1945- WrDr 94
Moon, Elizabeth (N.) 1945- EncSF 93
Moon, George d1961 WhoHol 92
Moon, Gordon Ray WhoAmP 93
Moon, Harley William 1936- WhoAm 94, WhoScEn 94
Moon, Inso John 1938- WhoAsA 94
Moon, Jim 1928- WhoAmA 93
Moon, John Henry, Sr. 1937- WhoFI 94
Moon, John Scafa 1960- WhoWest 94
Moon, John Wesley 1940- WhoWest 94
Moon, Jung Suk 1944- WhoAsA 94
Moon, Kee Suk 1959- WhoAsA 94
Moon, Keith d1978 WhoHol 92
Moon, Marc 1923- WhoAmA 93
Moon, Maria Elena 1945- WhoHisp 94
Moon, Marjorie Ruth 1926-1991 WhAm 10
Moon, Marla Lynn 1956- WhoScEn 94
Moon, Mary Marjorie 1932- Who 94
Moon, Peter Wilfred Giles Graham- 1942- Who 94
Moon, Philip WhoHol 92
Moon, Philip Burton 1907- Who 94
Moon, Roger 1914- Who 94
Moon, Ronald T. WhoAmP 93
Moon, Ronald T. Y. 1940- WhoAmL 94, WhoWest 94
Moon, Ronald Tae-yang 1940- WhoAsA 94
Moon, Tag-Young 1931- WhoMW 93
Moon, Walter D. 1940- WhoBlA 94
Moon, Warren 1956- WhoAm 94, WhoBlA 94
Moon, Warren G. 1945-1992 WhAm 10
Moon, William D. 1947- WhoAmL 94
Moon, Young B. 1958- WhoAsA 94
Moonan, Thomas P. 1933- WhoAm 94
Moonan, Timothy James 1959- WhoFI 94
Moonchild EncSF 93
Moone, James Clark 1940- WhoBlA 94
Moone, Wanda Renee 1956- WhoBlA 94
Moonelis, Judith C. 1953- WhoAmA 93
Mooney, Bel 1946- Who 94
Mooney, Christopher F. d1993 NewYTBS 93
Mooney, Christopher F(rancis) 1925-1993 ConAu 142
Mooney, Christopher Francis 1925- WrDr 94
Mooney, Debra WhoHol 92
Mooney, Dennis John 1949- WhoScEn 94
Mooney, Donald James, Jr. 1950- WhoAm 94, WhoAmL 94
Mooney, Douglas G. 1950- WhoAmL 94
Mooney, Edward 1951- WrDr 94
Mooney, Edward Joseph, Jr. 1941- WhoAm 94
Mooney, Harold Alfred 1932- IntWW 93, WhoWest 94
Mooney, James Hugh 1929- WhoAm 94
Mooney, James Pierce 1943- WhoAm 94
Mooney, Jerome Henri 1944- WhoAmL 94, WhoWest 94
Mooney, John Allen 1918- WhoAm 94, WhoFI 94, WhoMW 93
Mooney, John Bradford, Jr. 1931- WhoAm 94, WhoScEn 94
Mooney, John Joseph 1930- WhoAmP 93
Mooney, John M. 1943- WhoAmL 94
Mooney, Joseph Patrick 1960- WhoAmL 94
Mooney, Justin David 1932- WhoFI 94
Mooney, Kevin Xavier 1933- WhoIns 94
Mooney, Laura WhoHol 92
Mooney, Margaret M. 1946- WhoAmL 94
Mooney, Marilyn 1952- WhoAm 94, WhoAmL 94
Mooney, Martha Vaughan 1952- WhoMW 93
Mooney, Martin E. 1952- WhoAmL 94
Mooney, Michael Edward 1945- WhoAm 94, WhoAmL 94
Mooney, Michael J. WhoAmA 93
Mooney, Michael Joseph 1942- WhoAm 94
Mooney, Patricia Kathryn 1955- WhoWest 94
Mooney, Patrick Haik 1962- WhoFI 94
Mooney, Richard E. 1927- WhoAm 94
Mooney, Robert Michael 1945- WhoScEn 94
Mooney, Steven Lee, Sr. 1948- WhoFI 94
Mooney, Ted 1951- EncSF 93, WhoAm 94
Mooney, Thomas d1978 WhoHol 92
Mooney, Walter Doherty 1951- WhoWest 94
Mooney, William 1936- WhoHol 92
Mooney, William Piatt 1936- WhoAm 94
Mooneyham, Walter Stanley 1926-1991 WhAm 10
Mooneyhan, Esther Louise 1920- WhoAm 94, WhoScEn 94
Moonie, Clyde Wickliffe 1918- WhoAm 94
Moonie, Lewis George 1947- Who 94
Moonie, Liana WhoAmA 93
Moonjean, Hank IntMPA 94
Moonman, Eric 1929- Who 94, WrDr 94
Moon-Meier, Delia Ann 1965- WhoMW 93
Moons, Charles M. J. A. 1917- IntWW 93
Moonves, Leslie 1949- WhoAm 94
Moor, Bill 1931- WhoHol 92
Moor, Cherie WhoHol 92
Moor, Emanuel 1863-1931 NewGrDO
Moor, Karel 1873-1945 NewGrDO
Moor, Manly Eugene, Jr. 1923- WhoAm 94
Moor, Roy Edward 1924- WhoAm 94
Moor, William fl. 174-?- WhWE
Moor, William Chattle 1941- WhoWest 94
Mooradian, Arshag Dertad 1953- WhoMW 93
Mooradian, Gregory Charles 1947- WhoScEn 94
Moorbath, Stephen Erwin 1929- IntWW 93, Who 94
Moorcock, Michael (John) 1939- EncSF 93, WrDr 94
Moorcraft, Dennis Harry 1921- Who 94
Moorcroft, William c. 1765-1825 WhWE
Moore Who 94
Moore, Viscount 1983- Who 94
Moore, Acel 1940- WhoAm 94, WhoBlA 94
Moore, Alan See Judas Priest ConMus 10
Moore, Alan 1953- EncSF 93
Moore, Alan Edward 1936- Who 94
Moore, Alan Willard 1951- WhoAmA 93
Moore, Albert 1952- WhoBlA 94
Moore, Albert Cunningham 1931- WhoAm 94
Moore, Albert Lawrence 1956- WhoMW 93
Moore, Alexander Wyndham Hume S. Who 94
Moore, Alfred 1755-1810 WhAmRev
Moore, Alfred 1956- WhoBlA 94
Moore, Alfred Anson 1925- WhoAm 94
Moore, Alfred Michael 1936- WhoFI 94
Moore, Alice d1960 WhoHol 92
Moore, Alice Evelyn 1933- WhoBlA 94
Moore, Alstork Edward 1940- WhoBlA 94
Moore, Alvin O'Brien 1912- WhoAmL 94
Moore, Alvy 1921- WhoHol 92
Moore, Andrea S. WhoAmP 93
Moore, Andrew 1752-1821 WhAmRev
Moore, Andrew G. T., II 1935- WhoAmP 93
Moore, Andrew Given Tobias, II 1935- WhoAm 94, WhoAmL 94
Moore, Andrew Michael, Jr. 1940- WhoFI 94
Moore, Andrew Taylor, Jr. 1940- WhoAm 94
Moore, Ann Dombourian 1939- WhoMW 93
Moore, Anne Frances 1946- WhoAm 94
Moore, Annie Jewell 1919- WhoBlA 94
Moore, Anthony Louis 1946- WhoBlA 94
Moore, Anthony R. 1950- WhoAm 94, WhoAmL 94
Moore, Antony Ross 1918- Who 94
Moore, Arch Alfred, Jr. 1923- IntWW 93
Moore, Archibald Lee Wright 1916- WhoBlA 94
Moore, Archie 1913- WhoHol 92
Moore, Archie Bradford, Jr. 1933- WhoBlA 94
Moore, Arnold D. 1916- WhoBlA 94
Moore, Arthur Cotton 1935- WhoAm 94, WhoAmA 93
Moore, Arthur James 1922- WhoAm 94
Moore, Barbara 1934- WrDr 94
Moore, Benjamin 1945- WhoWest 94
Moore, Benjamin E. 1929- WhoAmP 93
Moore, Benjamin Powell 1952- WhoAmA 93
Moore, Bessie 1876-1959 BuCMET
Moore, Betty Jean 1927- WhoAm 94
Moore, Beveridge 1915- WhoAmA 93
Moore, Beverly WhoBlA 94
Moore, Beverly Ann 1934- WhoWest 94
Moore, Beverly Cooper 1909- WhoAm 94
Moore, Billie Lee 1931- WhoFI 94
Moore, Bob Stahly 1936- WhoAm 94, WhoFI 94
Moore, Bobby d1993 NewYTBS 93 [port]
Moore, Bobby 1949- WhoAm 94, WhoBlA 94
Moore, Brenda Carol 1945- WhoBlA 94
Moore, Brian DrAPF 93
Moore, Brian 1921- ConAu 42NR, EncSF 93, IntWW 93, Who 94, WhoAm 94, WrDr 94
Moore, Brian Baden 1932- Who 94
Moore, Brian Clive 1945- WhoFI 94
Moore, Bridget Liane 1957- WhoAmA 93
Moore, Brooke Noel 1943- WhoAm 94
Moore, Bruce Alan 1952- WhoMW 93
Moore, Bryan Reid 1962- WhoMW 93
Moore, C. Bradley 1939- WhoAm 94, WhoWest 94
Moore, C(atherine) L(ucille) 1911-1987 EncSF 93
Moore, Calvin 1951- WhoAmP 93
Moore, Calvin C. 1936- WhoAm 94
Moore, Carey Armstrong 1930- WrDr 94
Moore, Carl Gordon 1922- WhoScEn 94
Moore, Carl R. 1930- WhoAmP 93
Moore, Carleton Bryant 1932- WhoScEn 94, WhoWest 94
Moore, Carlyle, Sr. d1924 WhoHol 92
Moore, Carlyle, Jr. d1977 WhoHol 92
Moore, Carman 1936- WrDr 94
Moore, Carman Leroy 1936- WhoBlA 94
Moore, Carol 1945- WhoAmP 93
Moore, Carol Louise 1943- WhoBlA 94
Moore, Carole Irene 1944- WhoAm 94
Moore, Carole Rinne 1944- IntWW 93
Moore, Carolyn Dabbs 1931- WhoAmP 93
Moore, Carolyn Lannin 1945- WhoMW 93
Moore, Caryn Gay 1952- WhoMW 93
Moore, Charles WhoHol 92
Moore, Charles d1993 NewYTBS 93
Moore, Charles A. 1950- WhoAmL 94
Moore, Charles August, Jr. 1944- WhoWest 94
Moore, Charles D. 1906- WhoBlA 94
Moore, Charles Edward 1948- WhoAmL 94
Moore, Charles Garrett Ponsonby NewGrDO
Moore, Charles Hewes, Jr. 1929- WhoAm 94
Moore, Charles Hilary 1956- IntWW 93, Who 94
Moore, Charles J. WhoFI 94
Moore, Charles Julian 1931- WhoAm 94
Moore, Charles R. d1947 WhoHol 92
Moore, Charles Stuart 1910- Who 94
Moore, Charles W. 1923- WhoBlA 94
Moore, Charles W(illard) 1925- WrDr 94
Moore, Charles Willard 1925- AmCulL, WhoAm 94, WhoScEn 94
Moore, Charlie W. 1926- WhoBlA 94
Moore, Christine WhoHol 92
Moore, Christine James 1930- WhoBlA 94
Moore, Christopher Barry 1938- WhoScEn 94
Moore, Cicely Frances Who 94
Moore, Clarence (Duke) d1976 WhoHol 92
Moore, Clarence Eugene 1931- WhoFI 94
Moore, Clay Randolph 1928- WhoAmL 94
Moore, Clayton 1914- WhoHol 92
Moore, Cleo d1973 WhoHol 92
Moore, Cleotha Franklin 1942- WhoBlA 94
Moore, Cleve d1954 WhoHol 92
Moore, Coban Cheek 1922- WhoAmP 93
Moore, Colin A. 1944- WhoBlA 94
Moore, Colleen d1988 WhoHol 92
Moore, Conrad Lee 1937- WhoAm 94
Moore, Constance 1919- WhoHol 92
Moore, Constance 1922- IntMPA 94
Moore, Cornell Leverette 1939- WhoBlA 94
Moore, Cynthia M. 1963- WhoBlA 94
Moore, Dalton, Jr. 1918- WhoAm 94, WhoFI 94, WhoScEn 94
Moore, Dan Sterling 1956- WhoWest 94
Moore, Dana Elizabeth 1960- WhoAmP 93
Moore, Daniel A., Jr. WhoAmP 93
Moore, Daniel Alton, Jr. 1933- WhoAm 94, WhoAmL 94, WhoWest 94
Moore, Daniel Charles 1918- WhoAm 94
Moore, Daniel Elliott 1953- WhoFI 94
Moore, Daniel Horatio 1959- WhoFI 94
Moore, Daniel Joseph 1959- WhoAmL 94

Moore, David *WhoMW 93*
Moore, David Austin 1935- *WhoFI 94, WhoScEn 94, WhoWest 94*
Moore, David Bernard, II 1940- *WhoBlA 94*
Moore, David C. 1941- *WhoIns 94*
Moore, David Graham 1918- *WhoAm 94*
Moore, David James Ladd 1937- *Who 94*
Moore, David Joseph 1941- *WhoMW 93*
Moore, David Lewis 1931- *WhoWest 94*
Moore, David Lowell 1930- *WhoAm 94*
Moore, David M. 1955- *WhoBlA 94*
Moore, David M., II 1944- *WhoAmL 94*
Moore, David Markley 1954- *WhoWest 94*
Moore, David Max 1949- *WhoMW 93*
Moore, David Robert 1959- *WhoAmL 94*
Moore, David Sumner 1939- *WhoScEn 94*
Moore, Debra Ponder 1957- *WhoBlA 94*
Moore, Del d1970 *WhoHol 92*
Moore, Demi *IntWW 93*
Moore, Demi 1962- *CurBio 93 [port], IntMPA 94, WhoAm 94, WhoHol 92*
Moore, Denise Marie 1949- *WhoMW 93*
Moore, Dennie 1907- *WhoHol 92*
Moore, Dennis d1964 *WhoHol 92*
Moore, Dennis Paul 1946- *WhoFI 94*
Moore, Derek William 1931- *Who 94*
Moore, Derrith Rachelle 1964- *WhoWest 94*
Moore, Derry *Who 94*
Moore, Dianne J. Hall 1936- *WhoMW 93*
Moore, Dianne Jo 1946- *WhoMW 93*
Moore, Dianne Lea 1949- *WhoWest 94*
Moore, Dianne Taylor 1950- *WhoMW 93*
Moore, Dickie 1925- *IntMPA 94, WhoHol 92*
Moore, Don A. 1928- *WhoAmP 93*
Moore, Don Allen 1952- *WhoMW 93*
Moore, Donald *WhoAmP 93*
Moore, Donald Eugene 1928- *WhoAm 94*
Moore, Donald Francis 1937- *WhoAm 94*
Moore, Donald Paul 1926- *WhoMW 93*
Moore, Donald Torian 1933- *WhoBlA 94*
Moore, Donald Walter 1942- *WhoWest 94*
Moore, Donald Willard 1928- *WhoWest 94*
Moore, Dorothy A. 1929- *WhoAmP 93*
Moore, Dorothy Rudd 1940- *AfrAmAl 6*
Moore, Dorsey Jerome 1935- *WhoAm 94*
Moore, Douglas Matthew, Jr. 1939- *WhoAmL 94*
Moore, Douglas S(tuart) 1893-1969 *NewGrDO*
Moore, Dudley 1919- *BasBi*
Moore, Dudley 1935- *IntMPA 94, WhoHol 92*
See Also Cook and Moore *WhoCom*
Moore, Dudley L., Jr. 1936- *WhoIns 94*
Moore, Dudley Lester, Jr. 1936- *WhoFI 94*
Moore, Dudley Stuart John 1935- *IntWW 93, Who 94, WhoAm 94*
Moore, Duncan 1941- *WhoAm 94*
Moore, Duncan Thomas 1946- *WhoScEn 94*
Moore, Dwayne Harrison 1958- *WhoBlA 94*
Moore, Dwight Terry 1948- *WhoAmL 94*
Moore, Earl B. 1930- *WhoBlA 94*
Moore, Earle Kennedy 1921- *WhoAm 94*
Moore, Eddie N., Jr. *WhoAm 94, WhoBlA 94*
Moore, Edmund Harvey 1961- *WhoScEn 94*
Moore, Edna Ruth 1911- *WhoAmP 93*
Moore, Edward D. *WhoAmP 93*
Moore, Edward Forrest 1925- *WhoAm 94*
Moore, Edward Francis Butler 1906- *Who 94*
Moore, Edward Frederick 1900- *WhAm 10*
Moore, Edward J. *WhoHol 92*
Moore, Edward Kent 1943- *WhoAmL 94*
Moore, Edward Stanton d1992 *Who 94N*
Moore, Edwin Earl 1894-1965 *EncABHB 9*
Moore, Eileen *WhoHol 92*
Moore, Eileen 1930- *WhoHol 92*
Moore, Elizabeth A. 1938- *WhoAmP 93*
Moore, Elizabeth D. 1954- *WhoBlA 94*
Moore, Elizabeth Jane 1940- *WhoWest 94*
Moore, Ellis 1924- *IntMPA 94*
Moore, Ellis Oglesby 1924- *WhoAm 94*
Moore, Emanuel A. 1941- *WhoBlA 94*
Moore, Emerson J. 1938- *WhoBlA 94*
Moore, Emma Sims 1937- *WhoMW 93*
Moore, Emmett Burris, Jr. 1929- *WhoAm 94*
Moore, Ernest C. 1922- *WhoAmP 93*
Moore, Ernest Carroll, III 1944- *WhoAmL 94*
Moore, Ernest Eugene, Jr. 1946- *WhoAm 94*
Moore, Eugene *WhoAmP 93*
Moore, Eulabelle d1964 *WhoHol 92*
Moore, Eva d1955 *WhoHol 92*
Moore, Evan Gregory 1923- *WhoBlA 94*
Moore, Evelyn Dzurilla 1962- *WhoAmL 94*
Moore, Evelyn K. 1937- *WhoBlA 94*
Moore, Fay *WhoAmA 93*
Moore, Fay Linda 1942- *WhoScEn 94*
Moore, Faye Halford 1941- *WhoFI 94*
Moore, Fletcher Brooks 1926- *WhoAm 94*
Moore, Floreese Naomi 1940- *WhoBlA 94*
Moore, Florence d1935 *WhoHol 92*
Moore, Florian Howard 1929- *WhoMW 93*
Moore, Francis Daniels 1913- *IntWW 93, WhoAm 94*
Moore, Francis Daniels, Jr. 1950- *WhoScEn 94*
Moore, Frank d1924 *WhoHol 92*
Moore, Frank 1946- *WhoHol 92*
Moore, Frank Charles 1896- *WhAm 10*
Moore, Frank D. *DrAPF 93*
Moore, Frank N. 1953- *WhoAmP 93*
Moore, Franklin Hall, Jr. 1937- *WhoAm 94*
Moore, Franklin Shearer 1960- *WhoFI 94*
Moore, Fred Henderson 1934- *WhoBlA 94*
Moore, Fred Thurman 1921- *WhoAmP 93*
Moore, Frederick Alvin 1952- *WhoBlA 94*
Moore, Frederick C. 1933- *WhoFI 94*
Moore, Frederick David 1902- *Who 94*
Moore, Frederick V. 1956- *WhoAmL 94*
Moore, Frontis H. 1894- *WhAm 10*
Moore, G. E. 1873-1958 *BlmGEL*
Moore, G(eorge) E(dward) 1873-1958 *EncEth*
Moore, Gar 1920- *WhoHol 92*
Moore, Garland Curtis 1954- *WhoAmL 94*
Moore, Garry 1915- *IntMPA 94, WhoCom*
Moore, Garry 1915-1993 *NewYTBS 93 [port]*
Moore, Garry A. 1949- *WhoAmP 93*
Moore, Gary E. 1962- *WhoBlA 94*
Moore, Gary Ray 1948- *WhoMW 93*
Moore, Gary Richard Nielsen 1944- *WhoAmL 94*
Moore, Gary Thomas 1945- *WhoScEn 94*
Moore, Geoffrey H(oyt) 1914- *ConAu 41NR*
Moore, Geoffrey Herbert 1920- *Who 94*
Moore, Geoffrey Hoyt 1914- *WhoAm 94*
Moore, George 1852-1933 *BlmGEL, DcLB 135 [port]*
Moore, George 1913- *Who 94*
Moore, George 1923- *Who 94*
Moore, George (Augustus) 1852-1933 *RfGShF*
Moore, George Anthony 1914- *WhoBlA 94*
Moore, George Crawford Jackson *WhoAm 94*
Moore, George Edgar 1907- *Who 94*
Moore, George Emerson, Jr. 1914- *WhoAm 94*
Moore, George Eugene 1920 *WhoAm 94*
Moore, George Herbert d1993 *Who 94N*
Moore, George Paul 1907- *WhoScEn 94*
Moore, George Thomas 1945- *WhoBlA 94*
Moore, Gerald d1954 *WhoHol 92*
Moore, Gerald L. 1933- *WhoBlA 94*
Moore, Gordon Charles 1928- *Who 94*
Moore, Gordon E. 1929- *WhoAm 94, WhoFI 94, WhoWest 94*
Moore, Grace d1947 *WhoHol 92*
Moore, Grace 1898-1947 *NewGrDO*
Moore, Gregory B. 1962- *WhoBlA 94*
Moore, Gregory James 1964- *WhoScEn 94*
Moore, Guerry R. 1944- *WhoAmL 94*
Moore, Gwen *WhoAmP 93, WhoBlA 94, WhoWomW 91*
Moore, Gwendolynne Sophia 1951- *WhoAmP 93*
Moore, Gwyneth 1923- *WrDr 94*
Moore, H(enry) Coleman, Jr. 1893- *WhAm 10*
Moore, H. Mathew 1953- *WhoAmL 94*
Moore, Hal G. 1929- *WhoAm 94, WhoWest 94, WrDr 94*
Moore, Harold C. (Dinty) d1976 *WhoHol 92*
Moore, Harold Earl, Jr. 1954- *WhoBlA 94*
Moore, Harold Gregory 1951- *WhoFI 94*
Moore, Harris *EncSF 93*
Moore, Harry 1915- *Who 94*
Moore, Hazel Stamps 1924- *WhoBlA 94*
Moore, Helen D. S. 1932- *WhoBlA 94*
Moore, Helen Elizabeth 1920- *WhoMW 93*
Moore, Henderson Alfred, Jr. 1912- *WhoFI 94*
Moore, Henrietta d1973 *WhoHol 92*
Moore, Henry J. 1949- *WhoBlA 94*
Moore, Henry Roderick *Who 94*
Moore, Henry Rogers 1916- *WhoAm 94, WhoFI 94*
Moore, Henry Trumbull, Jr. 1932- *WhoAmL 94*
Moore, Henry Wylie 1923- *Who 94*
Moore, Herbert Bell 1926- *WhoAm 94*
Moore, Herff Leo, Jr. 1937- *WhoFI 94*
Moore, Hilda d1929 *WhoHol 92*
Moore, Hilliard T., Sr. 1925- *WhoBlA 94*
Moore, Hiram Beene 1914- *WhoBlA 94*
Moore, Honor *DrAPF 93*
Moore, Howard d1993 *NewYTBS 93*
Moore, Howard, Jr. 1932- *WhoBlA 94*
Moore, Hugh Jacob, Jr. 1944- *WhoAmL 94*
Moore, Ida d1964 *WhoHol 92*
Moore, Ina May 1920- *WhoAmA 93*
Moore, J. Lawrence 1917- *WhoAmP 93*
Moore, J. T. 1939- *WhoAm 94*
Moore, Jack Kenneth 1921- *WhoAmP 93*
Moore, Jack Leslie 1947- *WhoFI 94*
Moore, Jack William 1939- *WhoMW 93*
Moore, Jackson Watts 1948- *WhoFI 94*
Moore, Jacqueline Shaleem 1937- *WhoMW 93*
Moore, James *DrAPF 93*
Moore, James 1737-1777 *WhAmRev*
Moore, James Alfred 1915- *WhoAm 94*
Moore, James Allan 1939- *WhoScEn 94*
Moore, James C. *WhoAmP 93*
Moore, James Collins 1941- *WhoAm 94, WhoWest 94*
Moore, James E. 1935- *WhoAmP 93*
Moore, James E. 1936- *WhoAmL 94, WhoAmP 93*
Moore, James Edward 1934- *WhoFI 94*
Moore, James Everett, Jr. 1950- *WhoAmL 94*
Moore, James F. 1928- *WhoIns 94*
Moore, James Fredrick 1958- *WhoBlA 94*
Moore, James L. *WhoBlA 94*
Moore, James L., Jr. 1942- *WhoAm 94, WhoFI 94*
Moore, James Mendon 1925- *WhoAm 94*
Moore, James Neal 1959- *WhoScEn 94*
Moore, James Patrick, Jr. 1953- *WhoAm 94*
Moore, James R. 1944- *WhoAm 94, WhoAmL 94*
Moore, James Richard 1955- *WhoWest 94*
Moore, James Robert 1925- *WhoAm 94*
Moore, Jane Bond 1938- *WhoBlA 94*
Moore, Jane Elizabeth 1738- *BlmGWL*
Moore, Jane Ross 1929- *WhoAm 94*
Moore, Janet 1935- *WhoAmP 93*
Moore, Janice Kay 1948- *WhoScEn 94*
Moore, Janice Townley *DrAPF 93*
Moore, Jean E. *WhoBlA 94*
Moore, Jean Oliver 1925-1992 *WhAm 10*
Moore, Jean S. *WrDr 94*
Moore, Jeffrey Clyde 1962- *WhoWest 94*
Moore, Jeffrey Lee 1960- *WhoMW 93*
Moore, Jellether Marie 1949- *WhoBlA 94*
Moore, Jeremy *Who 94*
Moore, (John) Jeremy 1928- *IntWW 93, Who 94*
Moore, Jerry A., Jr. 1918- *WhoBlA 94*
Moore, Jerry Luke 1959- *WhoWest 94*
Moore, Joan Elizabeth 1951- *WhoAm 94, WhoFI 94*
Moore, Joan L. 1935- *WhoScEn 94*
Moore, Joan Willard 1929- *WhoMW 93*
Moore, Joanna 1937- *WhoHol 92*
Moore, Joanna Elizabeth 1937- *WhoFI 94*
Moore, Joanne Iweita 1928- *WhoAm 94*
Moore, Joe d1926 *WhoHol 92*
Moore, Joe Wayne, Jr. 1959- *WhoFI 94*
Moore, John *WhAmRev, WhoHol 92*
Moore, John c. 1599-1650 *DcNaB MP*
Moore, John 1753- *AmRev*
Moore, John (Cochrane) 1915- *Who 94*
Moore, John (Michael) 1921- *Who 94*
Moore, John A(lexander) 1915- *IntWW 93*
Moore, John Arnold 1965- *WhoAmL 94*
Moore, John Arthur 1939- *WhoAm 94*
Moore, John C. 1943- *WhoAmL 94*
Moore, John Cordell 1912- *WhoAm 94, WhoMW 93*
Moore, John Crosby Brown d1993 *NewYTBS 93*
Moore, John D. 1937- *WhoFI 94, WhoWest 94*
Moore, John David 1943- *Who 94*
Moore, John Denis Joseph 1910-1988 *WhAm 10*
Moore, John Dennis 1931- *WhoAm 94*
Moore, John Edward 1920- *WhoFI 94, WhoMW 93*
Moore, John Edward, II 1961- *WhoMW 93*
Moore, John Edwin, Jr. 1942- *WhoAm 94*
Moore, John Evelyn 1921- *IntWW 93, Who 94*
Moore, John George, Jr. 1917- *WhoAm 94*
Moore, John Hampton 1935- *WhoAm 94*
Moore, John Hays 1941- *WhoScEn 94*
Moore, John Hebron 1920- *WhoAm 94*
Moore, John Henry, II 1929- *WhoAm 94, WhoAmL 94*
Moore, John J. 1941- *WhoAmA 93*
Moore, John James Cunningham 1948- *WhoScEn 94*
Moore, John Joseph 1933- *WhoAm 94*
Moore, John Lovell, Jr. 1929- *WhoAm 94*
Moore, John Michael 1935- *Who 94, WrDr 94*
Moore, John N(orton) 1937- *WrDr 94*
Moore, John Newton 1920- *WhoAm 94*
Moore, John Norton 1937- *WhoAm 94*
Moore, John Porfilio 1934- *WhoAm 94, WhoAmL 94, WhoAmP 93, WhoWest 94*
Moore, John Ronald 1935- *WhoAm 94*
Moore, John Royston 1921- *Who 94*
Moore, John Runyan 1929- *WhoAm 94*
Moore, John Seabrook, III 1949- *WhoWest 94*
Moore, John T. 1949- *WhoAmL 94*
Moore, John Travers 1908- *WhoAm 94*
Moore, John W. *WhoMW 93*
Moore, John W. 1947- *WhoAm 94, WhoAmL 94*
Moore, John Wesley, Jr. 1948- *WhoBlA 94*
Moore, John William 1939- *WhoAm 94*
Moore, John Wilson 1920- *WhoAm 94*
Moore, Johnnie Adolph 1929- *WhoBlA 94*
Moore, Johnny 1958- *BasBi*
Moore, Johnny Brian 1958- *WhoBlA 94*
Moore, Jonathan 1932- *WhoAm 94, WhoAmP 93*
Moore, Jonathan Guy J. *Who 94*
Moore, Joseph 1920- *WhoFI 94*
Moore, Joseph A. 1958- *WhoAmP 93*
Moore, Joseph H. 1938- *WhoAmL 94*
Moore, Joseph L. 1935- *WhoBlA 94*
Moore, Joseph Lavon 1944- *WhoWest 94*
Moore, Joseph P. d1993 *NewYTBS 93 [port]*
Moore, Josephine Carroll 1925- *WhoMW 93*
Moore, Josiah d1993 *NewYTBS 93*
Moore, Jossie A. 1947- *WhoBlA 94*
Moore, Joyce A. 1949- *WhoMW 93*
Moore, Joyce Kristina 1955- *WhoFI 94*
Moore, Joyce West 1936- *WhoWest 94*
Moore, Juanita 1922- *WhoBlA 94, WhoHol 92*
Moore, Judy I. 1940- *WhoMW 93*
Moore, Julia A. 1847-1920 *BlmGWL*
Moore, Julian Keith 1945- *Who 94*
Moore, Julianne Bay 1964- *WhoMW 93*
Moore, Julie Louise 1941- *WhoWest 94*
Moore, Justin Edward 1952- *WhoWest 94*
Moore, Karen Marie W. 1963- *WhoMW 93*
Moore, Karen Mueller 1950- *WhoAmL 94*
Moore, Katherine Bell 1941- *WhoBlA 94*
Moore, Kathleen *WhoAm 94*
Moore, Kathryn d1983 *WhoHol 92*
Moore, Kay 1948- *WrDr 94*
Moore, Kenneth Cameron 1947- *WhoAm 94, WhoAmL 94*
Moore, Kenneth Edwin 1933- *WhoAm 94*
Moore, Kenneth James 1957- *WhoMW 93*
Moore, Kenny *WhoHol 92*
Moore, Kenya *WhoBlA 94*
Moore, Kermit 1929- *AfrAmAl 6, WhoBlA 94*
Moore, Kerwin Lamar 1970- *WhoBlA 94*
Moore, Kevin L. 1960- *WhoScEn 94*
Moore, Kevin Michael 1951- *WhoAm 94, WhoAmL 94*
Moore, Kieron 1924- *WhoHol 92*
Moore, Kieron 1925- *IntMPA 94*
Moore, Larry Eugene 1947- *WhoAmP 93*
Moore, Larry Gale 1954- *WhoAmL 94*
Moore, Larry Louis 1954- *WhoBlA 94*
Moore, Laurence 1919- *WhAm 10*
Moore, Laurence John 1938- *WhoAm 94*
Moore, Laurens *WhoHol 92*
Moore, Lawrence Jack 1926- *WhoAmL 94*
Moore, Lenard D. *DrAPF 93*
Moore, Lenard Duane 1958- *WhoBlA 94*
Moore, Lenny Edward 1933- *WhoBlA 94*
Moore, Leonard *ProFbHF*
Moore, Leslie Rowsell 1912- *Who 94*
Moore, Lewis Calvin 1935- *WhoBlA 94*
Moore, Linda Perigo 1946- *WhoMW 93*
Moore, Lisa d1989 *WhoHol 92*
Moore, Lloyd Evans 1931- *WhoAmL 94*
Moore, Lois Jean *WhoAm 94*
Moore, Lois Jean 1935- *WhoBlA 94*
Moore, Lorrie *DrAPF 93*
Moore, Lorrie 1957- *WrDr 94*
Moore, Louis 1946- *WrDr 94*
Moore, Lucille Sanders 1920- *WhoBlA 94*
Moore, M. Elizabeth Gibbs *WhoBlA 94*
Moore, Mabel d1978 *WhoHol 92*
Moore, Majorie Louise 1917- *WhoAmP 93*
Moore, Malcolm A. S. 1944- *WhoAm 94*
Moore, Malcolm Arthur 1937- *WhoAm 94*
Moore, Marc Anthony 1928- *WhoAm 94*
Moore, Marcellus Harrison 1939- *WhoBlA 94*
Moore, Marcia M. 1928-1979 *AstEnc*
Moore, Marcus Lamar 1965- *WhoScEn 94*
Moore, Margo *WhoHol 92*
Moore, Marian J. *WhoBlA 94*
Moore, Marianna Gay 1939- *WhoAmL 94*
Moore, Marianne 1887-1972 *BlmGWL*

Moore, Marianne Craig 1887-1972 *AmCulL*
Moore, Marjorie *WhoHol 92*
Moore, Marjorie 1944- *WhoAmA 93*
Moore, Mark Harrison 1947- *WhoAm 94*
Moore, Mark Vincent 1962- *WhoMW 93*
Moore, Markita A. 1958- *WhoFI 94*
Moore, Marshall Walter 1929- *WhoAmP 93*
Moore, Martha Christine *WhoWomW 91*
Moore, Martha W. *WhoAmP 93*
Moore, Mary *Who 94, WhoFI 94*
Moore, Mary d1919 *WhoHol 92*
Moore, Mary d1931 *WhoHol 92*
Moore, Mary 1938- *WhoAmP 93*
Moore, (Georgina) Mary 1930- *IntWW 93, Who 94*
Moore, Mary (Louise) Carr 1873-1957 *NewGrDO*
Moore, Mary Evelyn 1942- *WhoMW 93*
Moore, Mary French 1938- *WhoWest 94*
Moore, Mary Tyler 1936- *IntMPA 94, WhoAm 94, WhoCom, WhoHol 92*
Moore, Matt d1960 *WhoHol 92*
Moore, Matthew Emerson 1964- *WhoWest 94*
Moore, Maureen 1952- *WhoHol 92*
Moore, Maureen (Audrey) 1943- *WrDr 94*
Moore, Maurice 1735-1777 *WhAmRev*
Moore, (James) Mavor 1919- *ConDr 93, WrDr 94*
Moore, McPherson Dorsett 1947- *WhoAm 94, WhoAmL 94, WhoMW 93*
Moore, Mechlin Dongan 1930- *WhoAm 94, WhoFI 94*
Moore, Melanie Anne 1950- *WhoBlA 94*
Moore, Melba 1945- *WhoBlA 94, WhoHol 92*
Moore, Melba 1947- *WhoAm 94*
Moore, Melinda Guzman 1963- *WhoAmL 94*
Moore, Michael 1911- *WrDr 94*
Moore, Michael 1925- *WhoHol 92*
Moore, Michael Antony Claes 1942- *Who 94*
Moore, Michael Arthur 1943- *Who 94*
Moore, Michael C. 1942- *WhoAmL 94*
Moore, Michael D. 1939- *WhoAm 94, WhoFI 94*
Moore, Michael E. 1950- *WhoAmL 94*
Moore, Michael Kenneth 1949- *IntWW 93, Who 94*
Moore, Michael M. 1943- *WhoAm 94, WhoAmL 94*
Moore, Michael Patrick 1956- *WhoMW 93*
Moore, Michael Rodney Newton 1936- *Who 94*
Moore, Michael S. *Who 94*
Moore, Michael Scott 1943- *WhoAm 94*
Moore, Michael T. 1948- *WhoAm 94, WhoAmL 94*
Moore, Michael Thomas 1934- *WhoAm 94*
Moore, Michael Wallace 1951- *WhoAmL 94*
Moore, Mike *WhoAm 94, WhoAmL 94, WhoAmP 93*
Moore, Milo Anderson 1942- *WhoAm 94, WhoFI 94*
Moore, Milton Donald, Jr. 1953- *WhoBlA 94*
Moore, Mitchell Jay 1954- *WhoAmL 94*
Moore, Monette d1962 *WhoHol 92*
Moore, Myreen 1940- *WhoAmA 93*
Moore, N. Webster 1913- *WhoBlA 94*
Moore, Nancy Jean 1946- *WhoAmP 93*
Moore, Nancy Newell 1939- *WhoMW 93*
Moore, Nat 1951- *WhoBlA 94*
Moore, Nathan 1931- *WhoBlA 94*
Moore, Nicholas 1915- *WrDr 94*
Moore, Noah Watson, Jr. 1902- *WhoBlA 94*
Moore, Noel Ernest Ackroyd 1928- *Who 94*
Moore, Norma 1935- *WhoHol 92*
Moore, Norman Slawson 1901- *WhoAm 94*
Moore, Norman Winfrid 1923- *Who 94*
Moore, O. Otto 1896- *WhAm 10*
Moore, Olga *WhoAmA 93*
Moore, Olive B. 1916- *WhoAmP 93*
Moore, Oliver Semon, III 1942- *WhoAm 94*
Moore, Omar Khayyam 1920- *WhoScEn 94, WhoWest 94*
Moore, Oscar James, Jr. *WhoBlA 94*
Moore, Oscar William, Jr. 1938- *WhoBlA 94*
Moore, Owen d1939 *WhoHol 92*
Moore, Parlett Longworth 1907- *WhoBlA 94*
Moore, Pat Howard 1930- *WhoAm 94, WhoFI 94*
Moore, Patricia Ann 1954- *WhoFI 94*
Moore, Patrick (Alfred) 1923- *EncSF 93*
Moore, Patrick (Alfred Caldwell-) 1923- *WrDr 94*
Moore, Patrick (William Eisdell) 1918- *Who 94*
Moore, Patrick Alfred Caldwell- 1923- *Who 94*
Moore, Patrick Caldwell- 1923- *IntWW 93*
Moore, Paul, Jr. 1919- *WhoAm 94*
Moore, Paul Brian 1940- *WhoMW 93*
Moore, Paul D. 1951- *WhoAmL 94*
Moore, Pauline 1914- *WhoHol 92*
Moore, Pearl B. 1936- *WhoAm 94*
Moore, Peggy Braden 1944- *WhoAmL 94*
Moore, Peggy Sue 1942- *WhoMW 93*
Moore, Penelope Ann 1944- *WhoScEn 94*
Moore, Percy d1945 *WhoHol 92*
Moore, Peter d1993 *NewYTBS 93*
Moore, Peter 1932- *WhoAmA 93*
Moore, Peter Bartlett 1939- *WhoAm 94*
Moore, Peter Clement 1924- *Who 94*
Moore, Peter Gerald 1928- *Who 94*
Moore, Peter Innisfree 1932- *WhoAm 94*
Moore, Peter Melville 1939- *WhoAm 94*
Moore, Philip John 1943- *Who 94*
Moore, Philip Walsh 1920- *WhoAm 94, WhoFI 94*
Moore, Powell Allen 1938- *WhoAm 94, WhoAmP 93*
Moore, Quincy L. 1949- *WhoBlA 94*
Moore, Randy 1949- *WhoAmP 93*
Moore, Ray A. 1912- *WhoAmP 93*
Moore, Rayburn Sabatzky 1920- *WhoAm 94, WrDr 94*
Moore, Raylyn *DrAPF 93*
Moore, Raylyn 1928- *EncSF 93*
Moore, Raymond Robert 1943- *WhoAmL 94*
Moore, Raymond S. 1915- *WrDr 94*
Moore, Reid Francis, Jr. 1934- *WhoAmP 93*
Moore, Rex d1975 *WhoHol 92*
Moore, Rich Blaise 1961- *WhoMW 93*
Moore, Richard *DrAPF 93*
Moore, Richard 1927- *WhoWest 94, WrDr 94*
Moore, Richard A. 1914- *IntWW 93*
Moore, Richard A., Jr. 1946- *WhoAmL 94*
Moore, Richard Alan 1930- *WhoAm 94*
Moore, Richard Alan 1948- *WhoMW 93*
Moore, Richard Albert 1915-1991 *WhAm 10*
Moore, Richard Allan 1924- *WhoAm 94*
Moore, Richard Anthony 1914- *WhoAm 94, WhoAmP 93*
Moore, Richard Baxter 1943- *WhoBlA 94*
Moore, Richard Earl 1940- *WhoAm 94*
Moore, Richard Earle 1916- *WhoBlA 94*
Moore, Richard Hancock 1960- *WhoAmP 93*
Moore, Richard Harlan 1945- *WhoAm 94*
Moore, Richard John 1951- *WhoMW 93*
Moore, Richard Kerr 1923- *WhoAm 94, WhoScEn 94*
Moore, Richard Lawrence 1934- *WhoScEn 94*
Moore, Richard Thomas 1943- *WhoAmP 93*
Moore, Richard V. 1906- *WhoBlA 94*
Moore, Richard Valentine 1916- *Who 94*
Moore, Robert *EncSF 93*
Moore, Robert d1984 *WhoHol 92*
Moore, Robert d1993 *Who 94N*
Moore, Robert 1915- *Who 94*
Moore, Robert 1941-1993 *WorESoc*
Moore, Robert Andrew 1953- *WhoBlA 94*
Moore, Robert Clay 1934- *WhoAmL 94*
Moore, Robert Condit 1921- *WhoAm 94*
Moore, Robert Edward 1923- *WhoAm 94*
Moore, Robert Eric 1927- *WhoAmA 93*
Moore, Robert F. d1993 *IntWW 93N*
Moore, Robert F. 1944- *WhoBlA 94*
Moore, Robert Henry 1940- *WhoAm 94, WhoIns 94*
Moore, Robert James 1922- *WhoAmA 93*
Moore, Robert Lowell, Jr. 1925- *WhoAm 94*
Moore, Robert Madison 1925- *WhoAm 94, WhoAmL 94*
Moore, Robert Stuart 1924- *WhoFI 94*
Moore, Robert William 1924- *WhoAm 94*
Moore, Robert William, Jr. *WhoAm 94*
Moore, Robert Yates 1931- *WhoAm 94*
Moore, Robin 1950- *WrDr 94*
Moore, Robin James 1934- *IntWW 93*
Moore, Roger 1927- *IntMPA 94, IntWW 93, Who 94, WhoHol 92*
Moore, Roger Allan 1931-1990 *WhAm 10*
Moore, Roger George 1927- *WhoAm 94*
Moore, Roger Lea 1936- *WhoMW 93*
Moore, Roger Stephenson 1939- *WhoScEn 94*
Moore, Ronald Clark 1949- *WhoWest 94*
Moore, Rosalie *DrAPF 93*
Moore, Roscoe Michael, Jr. 1944- *WhoBlA 94*
Moore, Rourke A. *WhoAmP 93*
Moore, Rowena Geneva 1910- *WhoAmP 93*
Moore, Roy Dean 1940- *WhoAm 94*
Moore, Roy Worsham, III 1941- *WhoAmL 94*
Moore, Rudy Ray *WhoHol 92*
Moore, Russell Eugene 1965- *WhoFI 94*
Moore, Russell James 1947- *WhoAmA 93*
Moore, Ruth d1952 *WhoHol 92*
Moore, S. Clark 1924- *WhoAmL 94*
Moore, Sabra 1943- *WhoAmA 93*
Moore, Sally Falk 1924- *WhoAm 94, WhoScEn 94*
Moore, Sam *WhoHol 92*
Moore, Sam 1935- *WhoBlA 94*
Moore, Sandra 1945- *WhoScEn 94*
Moore, Sandra Kay 1957- *WhoFI 94*
Moore, Scott d1967 *WhoHol 92*
Moore, Scott 1951- *WhoAmL 94*
Moore, Scott 1960- *WhoAmP 93*
Moore, Scott Martin 1949- *WhoAmA 93*
Moore, Scott Michael 1958- *WhoAmL 94, WhoFI 94*
Moore, Sean 1926- *WhoAm 94*
Moore, Sharon Pauline 1949- *WhoScEn 94*
Moore, Sheila Frances 1956- *WhoWest 94*
Moore, Shelley Lorraine 1950- *WhoBlA 94*
Moore, Sidney Dwayne 1938- *WhoWest 94*
Moore, Sonia 1902- *WhoAm 94*
Moore, Stanford *WorScD*
Moore, Stanley Ray 1946- *WhoAm 94*
Moore, Stanley William 1944- *WhoAmL 94*
Moore, Stephen 1937- *WhoHol 92*
Moore, Stephen Gates 1923- *WhoAm 94*
Moore, Stephen James 1947- *WhoAmL 94*
Moore, Steven Carroll 1949- *WhoFI 94*
Moore, Steven Dana 1951- *WhoMW 93*
Moore, Sue d1966 *WhoHol 92*
Moore, Susan 1953- *WhoAmA 93*
Moore, Susie M. 1918- *WhoBlA 94*
Moore, Tanna Lynn 1954- *WhoFI 94, WhoMW 93*
Moore, Terence 1931- *Who 94*
Moore, Terri Bonita 1956- *WhoMW 93*
Moore, Terris 1908- *WhoAm 94*
Moore, Terry 1929- *IntMPA 94, WhoHol 92*
Moore, Terry Jack 1956- *WhoAm 94*
Moore, Terry Wayne 1957- *WhoWest 94*
Moore, Thomas 1779-1852 *BlmGEL, NewGrDO*
Moore, Thomas (William) 1940- *WrDr 94*
Moore, Thomas A. 1951- *WhoFI 94*
Moore, Thomas Carrol 1936- *WhoAm 94*
Moore, Thomas Charles 1934- *WhoAm 94*
Moore, Thomas Clarence 1943- *WhoAmP 93*
Moore, Thomas David 1937- *WhoAm 94*
Moore, Thomas E. *WhoAm 94*
Moore, Thomas Edwin 1930- *WhoScEn 94*
Moore, Thomas Gale 1930- *WhoAm 94*
Moore, Thomas H. 1927- *WhoBlA 94*
Moore, Thomas J. 1947- *WhoAmL 94*
Moore, Thomas James, III 1942- *WhoMW 93*
Moore, Thomas Joseph 1939- *WhoScEn 94*
Moore, Thomas Joseph 1943- *WhoFI 94*
Moore, Thomas Kail 1938- *WhoAm 94, WhoAmL 94*
Moore, Thomas L. 1926- *WhoBlA 94*
Moore, Thomas L. 1950- *WhoAmP 93*
Moore, Thomas Lloyd 1942- *WhoAm 94*
Moore, Thomas O., III 1947- *WhoAmL 94*
Moore, Thomas Paul 1928- *WhoAm 94, WhoMW 93*
Moore, Thomas R. 1932- *WhoAm 94, WhoAmL 94*
Moore, Thomas W. *IntMPA 94*
Moore, Thomas William 1925- *Who 94*
Moore, Thomasine Elizabeth 1949- *WhoAmP 93*
Moore, Thurston Roach 1946- *WhoAm 94, WhoAmL 94*
Moore, Tillman Marion 1927- *WhoWest 94*
Moore, Tim 1887-1958 *WhoCom*
Moore, Timothy James 1949- *WhoFI 94*
Moore, Todd *DrAPF 93*
Moore, Todd Somers 1952- *WhoAmA 93*
Moore, Tom d1955 *WhoHol 92*
Moore, Tom 1943- *WhoAm 94*
Moore, Tom Loyd 1926- *WhoWest 94*
Moore, Trudy S. 1957- *WhoBlA 94*
Moore, U. A. Presnell 1925- *WhoAmP 93*
Moore, Undine Smith 1904-1989 *AfrAmAl 6*
Moore, Undine Smith 1907- *WhoBlA 94*
Moore, Vernon John, Jr. 1942- *WhoMW 93*
Moore, Vernon Lee 1928- *WhoAm 94*
Moore, Victor d1962 *WhoHol 92*
Moore, Vin d1949 *WhoHol 92*
Moore, Virgil Clinton 1933- *WhoAmP 93*
Moore, Virginia d1993 *NewYTBS 93*
Moore, W. Allen 1945- *WhoAmP 93*
Moore, W. E(dward) C. 1927- *IntWW 93*
Moore, W. Edgar 1910- *WhoAmP 93*
Moore, W. Henson 1939- *WhoAmP 93*
Moore, W. James 1916- *WhoScEn 94*
Moore, W. Taylor 1939- *WhoAmP 93*
Moore, Wallace *EncSF 93*
Moore, Walter (John) 1918- *WrDr 94*
Moore, Walter Calvin 1910- *WhoScEn 94*
Moore, Walter Dengel 1936- *WhoFI 94, WhoWest 94*
Moore, Walter Emil, Jr. 1925- *WhoMW 93*
Moore, Walter Louis 1946- *WhoBlA 94*
Moore, Walter M. 1920- *WhoAmP 93*
Moore, Walter Parker, Jr. 1937- *WhoScEn 94*
Moore, (Joseph) Ward 1903-1978 *EncSF 93*
Moore, Ward Frederick 1922-1989 *WhAm 10*
Moore, Ward Wilfred 1924- *WhoAm 94*
Moore, Warfield, Jr. 1934- *WhoBlA 94*
Moore, Wayland D. 1935- *WhoAmA 93*
Moore, Wayne V. 1942- *WhoScEn 94*
Moore, Wenda Weekes 1941- *WhoBlA 94*
Moore, Wesley Craig 1946- *WhoAm 94*
Moore, William *WhoHol 92*
Moore, William (Roger Clotworthy) 1927- *Who 94*
Moore, William B. 1941- *WhoAmL 94*
Moore, William D., Jr. 1917- *WhoAmP 93*
Moore, William E., III 1934- *WhoAmP 93*
Moore, William Edward 1949- *WhoIns 94*
Moore, William Evan 1925- *WhoFI 94*
Moore, William Gower Innes 1951- *WhoScEn 94*
Moore, William Graham 1922- *WhoAmP 93*
Moore, William Grover, Jr. *WhoAm 94, WhoFI 94*
Moore, William Henry 1848-1923 *EncABHB 9 [port]*
Moore, William Howard 1942- *WhoWest 94*
Moore, William J. *WhoAmP 93*
Moore, William James 1943- *WhoWest 94*
Moore, William Jason 1938- *WhoAm 94*
Moore, William John Myles 1924- *WhoAm 94*
Moore, William Kent 1955- *WhoAmL 94*
Moore, William Leroy, Jr. 1934- *WhoAm 94*
Moore, William Luther d1931 *EncNAR*
Moore, William Rudy, Jr. 1943- *WhoAmP 93*
Moore, William S., Jr. 1947- *WhoAmP 93*
Moore, William Vincent 1949- *WhoScEn 94*
Moore, Willis Henry Allphin 1940- *WhoWest 94*
Moore, Willson Carr, Jr. 1928- *WhoAmL 94*
Moore, Winston E. *WhoBlA 94*
Moore, Yvette 1958- *WrDr 94*
Moore, Yvonne Laughlin Howard Richardson 1943- *WhoFI 94*
Moore-Bentley, Mary Ann *EncSF 93*
Moore-Bick, Martin James 1946- *Who 94*
Moore-Brabazon *Who 94*
Moore-Carroll, Patricia Susan 1957- *WhoMW 93*
Moore-Colyer, Richard 1945- *ConAu 141*
Moorefield, Geddings Crawford 1962- *WhoAmL 94*
Moorefield, James Lee 1922- *WhoAm 94*
Moorehead, Agnes d1974 *WhoHol 92*
Moorehead, Bobbie Wooten 1937- *WhoBlA 94*
Moorehead, Caroline 1944- *WrDr 94*
Moorehead, Emery Matthew 1954- *WhoBlA 94*
Moorehead, Eric K. 1958- *WhoBlA 94*
Moorehead, John c. 1760-1804 *NewGrDO*
Moorehead, Justin Leslie 1947- *WhoBlA 94*
Moorehead, Thomas 1944- *WhoBlA 94*
Moore Of Lower Marsh, Baron 1937- *IntWW 93, Who 94*
Moore Of Wolvercote, Baron 1921- *Who 94*
Moorer, Admiral Thomas Hinman 1912- *IntWW 93*
Moorer, Thomas Hinman 1912- *Who 94, WhoAm 94*
Moore-Riesbeck, Susan Moore 1963- *WhoMW 93*
Moores, Anita Jean Young 1944- *WhoScEn 94*
Moores, Brian, Mrs. *Who 94*
Moores, Eldridge Morton 1938- *WhoScEn 94*
Moores, Frank Duff 1933- *Who 94*
Moores, Hervey Cuthrell 1926- *WhoAmP 93*
Moores, John d1993 *NewYTBS 93, Who 94N*
Moores, John 1896- *IntWW 93*

Moores, John 1928- *Who 94*
Moores, Michael Wayne 1960- *WhoMW 93*
Moores, Peter 1932- *Who 94*
Moores, Yvonne 1941- *Who 94*
Moore-Stovall, Joyce 1948- *WhoBlA 94*
Moorey, Adrian Edward 1946- *Who 94*
Moorey, Peter Roger Stuart 1937- *WrDr 94*
Moorey, (Peter) Roger (Stuart) 1937- *IntWW 93, Who 94*
Moorhead, Andrea *DrAPF 93*
Moorhead, Carlos J. 1922- *CngDr 93, WhoAm 94, WhoAmP 93, WhoWest 94*
Moorhead, Diana 1940- *WrDr 94*
Moorhead, Gerald Lee 1947- *WhoAm 94*
Moorhead, Hugh S. 1922- *WrDr 94*
Moorhead, John (Anthony) 1948- *ConAu 142*
Moorhead, John B. 1945- *WhoAm 94, WhoAmL 94*
Moorhead, John Couper 1949- *WhoWest 94*
Moorhead, John Dane 1941- *WhoFI 94*
Moorhead, John Leslie 1942- *WhoBlA 94*
Moorhead, Joseph H. 1921- *WhoBlA 94*
Moorhead, Michael John 1943- *WhoWest 94*
Moorhead, Natalie 1901- *WhoHol 92*
Moorhead, Paul Sidney 1924- *WhoAm 94*
Moorhead, Sarah Parsons fl. 1741-1742 *BlmGWL*
Moorhead, Sylvester Andrew 1920- *WhoAm 94*
Moorhead, Thomas Burch 1934- *WhoAm 94*
Moorhouse, Bert d1954 *WhoHol 92*
Moorhouse, Douglas Cecil 1926- *WhoAm 94, WhoFI 94, WhoWest 94*
Moorhouse, Frank 1938- *RfGShF*
Moorhouse, Geoffrey 1931- *Who 94, WrDr 94*
Moorhouse, James *Who 94*
Moorhouse, (Cecil) James (Olaf) 1924- *Who 94*
Moorhouse, Linda Virginia 1945- *WhoMW 93*
Moorhouse, Peter William 1938- *Who 94*
Moorhouse, (Kathleen) Tessa 1938- *Who 94*
Mooring, F. Paul 1921- *WhoMW 93*
Mooring, Kittye D. 1932- *WhoBlA 94*
Moorjani, Kishin 1935- *WhoScEn 94*
Moorland, Jesse Edward 1863-1940 *AfrAmAl 6*
Moorman, Clinton R. 1924- *WhoBlA 94*
Moorman, Holsey Alexander 1938- *WhoBlA 94*
Moorman, James Douglas 1939- *WhoMW 93*
Moorman, James Watt 1937- *WhoAmP 93*
Moorman, Mary Caroline 1905- *Who 94*
Moorman, Thomas Samuel, Jr. 1940- *WhoAm 94*
Moorman, William Jacob 1923- *WhoScEn 94*
Moorman van Kappen, Olav 1937- *IntWW 93*
Moorshead, John Earl 1939- *WhoMW 93*
Moorstein, Mark Alan 1949- *WhoAmL 94*
Moorthy, Arambamoorthy Thedchana 1928- *Who 94*
Moos, Christopher Robin 1954- *WhoWest 94*
Moos, Eugene *WhoAm 94*
Moos, Michael *DrAPF 93*
Moos, Trude d1969 *WhoHol 92*
Moos, Walter A. 1926- *WhoAmA 93*
Moosavian, Seid Hossein 1925- *WhoMW 93*
Moosbruker, Jane Barbara 1938- *WhoFI 94*
Moosdorf, Johanna 1911- *BlmGWL*
Moose, Charles A. 1953- *WhoWest 94*
Moose, George E. 1944- *WhoAm 94, WhoAmP 93, WhoBlA 94*
Moose, Philip Anthony 1921- *WhoAmA 93*
Moose, Ruth *DrAPF 93*
Moose, Talmadge Bowers 1933- *WhoAmA 93*
Mooser, Stephen 1941- *SmATA 75 [port]*
Moosonee, Bishop of 1941- *Who 94*
Mooson Kwauk *WhoPRCh 91*
Moossa, A. R. 1939- *WhoAm 94*
Moossy, John 1925- *WhoAm 94*
Moot, John Rutherford 1922- *WhoAmP 93*
Moot, Welles Van Ness, Jr. 1917- *WhoFI 94*
Moote, A. Lloyd 1931- *WhoAm 94, WrDr 94*
Mootham, Orby Howell 1901- *Who 94*
Mootry, Charles 1948- *WhoBlA 94*
Mooty, Bruce Wilson 1955- *WhoAmL 94*
Mooty, David Nelson 1953- *WhoAmL 94*
Mooty, John William 1922- *WhoAm 94, WhoMW 93*
Moo-Young, Louise L. 1942- *WhoBlA 94*
Mooz, Elizabeth Dodd 1939- *WhoScEn 94*
Mooz, R. Peter 1940- *WhoAmA 93*
Mooz, Ralph Peter 1940- *WhoAm 94*
Moquin, Richard Attilio 1934- *WhoAmA 93*
Mora, Abraham Martin 1954- *WhoAm 94*
Mora, Christiane Marie-Lys 1938- *WhoWomW 91*
Mora, David Richard 1945- *WhoHisp 94*
Mora, E. Kelly *WhoAmP 93, WhoHisp 94*
Mora, Emilio Chavez 1928- *WhoHisp 94*
Mora, Francisco 1922- *WhoAm 94*
Mora, Homer *WhoHisp 94*
Mora, James Ernest 1935- *WhoAm 94*
Mora, Kathleen Rita 1948- *WhoFI 94*
Mora, Maria-Alicia 1959- *WhoHisp 94*
Mora, Narciso Andres 1934- *WhoHisp 94*
Mora, Pat 1942- *HispLC [port], WhoHisp 94, WhoMW 93*
Mora, Philippe *HorFD [port]*
Mora, Thomas, Jr. 1954- *WhoHisp 94*
Morabito, Bruno Paul 1922- *WhoAm 94*
Morabito, David Robertson, Sr. 1954- *WhoAmL 94*
Moraczewski, Robert Leo 1942- *WhoAm 94*
Moradi, Ahmad F. 1955- *WhoFI 94*
Morado, David F. 1949- *WhoHisp 94*
Moraes, Dom 1938- *Who 94*
Moraes, Dom(inic Frank) 1938- *WrDr 94*
Moraes, Dominic 1938- *IntWW 93*
Moraff, Barbara *DrAPF 93*
Moraff, Howard 1936- *WhoScEn 94*
Moraga, Cherrie *DrAPF 93*
Moraga, Cherrie 1952- *BlmGWL, GayLL, WhoHisp 94*
Moraga, Peter 1926- *WhoHisp 94*
Moragne, Lenora *WhoBlA 94*
Moragne, Rudolph 1933- *WhoBlA 94*
Morahan, Christopher Thomas 1929- *Who 94*
Morahan, Thomas P. 1931- *WhoAmP 93*
Morahan-Martin, Janet May 1944- *WhoScEn 94*
Morain, Mary Stone Dewing 1911- *WhoWest 94*
Morais, Manuel Antonio 1939- *WhoFI 94*
Morais, Sabato 1823-1897 *DcAmReB 2*
Moraitis, Karen Karl 1943- *WhoFI 94*
Moral, Pablo del fl. 1765-1805 *NewGrDO*
Morales, Alejandro 1944- *WhoHisp 94*
Morales, Alex 1966- *WhoHisp 94*
Morales, Alvino 1950- *WhoHisp 94*
Morales, Angel E. 1953- *WhoHisp 94*
Morales, Angel L. 1952- *WhoHisp 94*
Morales, Anthony Russell 1960- *WhoHisp 94*
Morales, Antonio 1937- *WhoHisp 94*
Morales, Antonio Gil *WhoHisp 94*
Morales, Armando 1927- *IntWW 93, WhoAmA 93*
Morales, Armando 1932- *WhoWest 94*
Morales, Arturo Esteban 1949- *WhoHisp 94*
Morales, Cecillo José, Jr. 1952- *WhoHisp 94*
Morales, Charles S. 1946- *WhoHisp 94*
Morales, Claudio H. 1945- *WhoHisp 94*
Morales, Cynthia Torres 1952- *WhoScEn 94*
Morales, Dan *WhoAm 94, WhoAmL 94*
Morales, Dan 1956- *WhoHisp 94*
Morales, Daniel C. 1956- *WhoAmP 93*
Morales, David *WhoHisp 94*
Morales, David 1953- *WhoHisp 94*
Morales, Deborah 1952- *WhoHisp 94*
Morales, Dionicio *WhoHisp 94*
Morales, Ed 1956- *WhoHisp 94*
Morales, Enrique 1946- *WhoHisp 94*
Morales, Esai 1962- *WhoHol 92*
Morales, Esai 1963- *WhoHisp 94*
Morales, Esy d1950 *WhoHol 92*
Morales, Felicita 1951- *WhoHisp 94*
Morales, Frank 1941- *WhoHisp 94*
Morales, Fred 1924- *WhoHisp 94*
Morales, Gerard 1947- *WhoAm 94*
Morales, Gilbert 1965- *WhoHisp 94*
Morales, Hector *WhoHol 92*
Morales, Ibra 1945- *WhoHisp 94*
Morales, Jaime E. 1947- *WhoIns 94*
Morales, Jenny 1949- *WhoHisp 94*
Morales, Jorge Francisco 1948- *WhoHisp 94*
Morales, Jorge Juan 1945- *WhoHisp 94*
Morales, Jorge Luis 1930- *WhoHisp 94*
Morales, Jose 1945- *WhoHisp 94*
Morales, José 1952- *WhoHisp 94*
Morales, Jose Alberto *WhoHisp 94*
Morales, José Oscar 1933- *WhoHisp 94*
Morales, Joseph M. 1955- *WhoHisp 94*
Morales, Juan M. 1928- *WhoHisp 94*
Morales, Juan M. 1956- *WhoHisp 94*
Morales, Judy 1941- *WhoHisp 94*
Morales, Julio, Jr. 1942- *WhoHisp 94*
Morales, Julio K. 1948- *WhoAmL 94*
Morales, Magda Hernández 1943- *WhoHisp 94*
Morales, Manuel Francisco 1919- *WhoHisp 94*
Morales, Margo Melinda 1958- *WhoWest 94*
Morales, Mark
See Fat Boys, The *WhoHol 92*
Morales, Melesio 1838-1908 *NewGrDO*
Morales, Michael 1963- *WhoHisp 94*
Morales, Mike 1949- *WhoAmP 93*
Morales, Milsa 1952- *WhoHisp 94*
Morales, Noro d1964 *WhoHol 92*
Morales, Nydia 1955- *WhoHisp 94*
Morales, Ophelia C. 1928- *WhoHisp 94*
Morales, Pablo *WhoAm 94*
Morales, Pablo 1965- *WhoHisp 94*
Morales, Pablo A. 1918- *WhoAm 94*
Morales, Pete, Jr. 1950- *WhoHisp 94*
Morales, Ralph, Jr. 1940- *WhoHisp 94*
Morales, Ramon Villeda 1908-1971 *HisWorL*
Morales, Raul 1935- *WhoHisp 94*
Morales, Raul Hector 1963- *WhoScEn 94*
Morales, Raymond C. *WhoHisp 94*
Morales, Raymond Chacon 1946- *WhoHisp 94*
Morales, Richard 1938- *WhoHisp 94*
Morales, Richard 1949- *WhoHisp 94*
Morales, Richard 1958- *WhoScEn 94*
Morales, Rodolfo 1925- *WhoAmA 93*
Morales, Sylvia *WhoHisp 94*
Morales, Thomas Frime, Jr. 1947- *WhoHisp 94*
Morales-Acevedo, Arturo 1934- *WhoScEn 94*
Morales Bermudez, Francisco 1921- *IntWW 93*
Morales Bermudez Pedraglio, Remigio 1947- *IntWW 93*
Morales-Caban, Alex Antonio 1946- *WhoHisp 94*
Morales-Couvertier, Angel Luis 1919- *WhoHisp 94*
Morales Dunn, Nancy Barbara 1950- *WhoHisp 94*
Morales-Galarreta, Julio 1936- *WhoMW 93*
Morales-Lebrón, Mariano 1935- *WhoHisp 94*
Morales-Loebl, Maria 1953- *WhoHisp 94*
Morales-Nadal, Milga 1947- *WhoHisp 94*
Morales-Nieves, Alfredo 1956- *WhoHisp 94*
Morales-Pereira, Antonio 1928- *WhoHisp 94*
Morales-Rivas, Alice 1961- *WhoHisp 94*
Morales-Rosario, Mario 1955- *WhoHisp 94*
Morales Solis, Rafael Armando 1962- *WhoHisp 94*
Moralez, Joselyn Hope 1966- *WhoHisp 94*
Moralt, Rudolf 1902-1958 *NewGrDO*
Moran, Baron 1924- *IntWW 93, Who 94*
Moran, Anne E. 1953- *WhoAmL 94*
Moran, Barbara Burns 1944- *WhoAm 94*
Moran, Charles A. 1943- *WhoAm 94, WhoFI 94*
Moran, Charles F., Jr. 1931- *WhoAmP 93*
Moran, Charles R. 1945- *WhoAmL 94*
Moran, Daniel *EncSF 93*
Moran, Daniel Austin 1936- *WhoAm 94*
Moran, Daniel Keys 1962- *EncSF 93*
Moran, Dolores d1982 *WhoHol 92*
Moran, Edmond J. d1993 *NewYTBS 93 [port]*
Moran, Edmund Benedict, Jr. 1947- *WhoAmL 94*
Moran, Edward Kevin 1964- *WhoAmL 94*
Moran, Edward V. 1953- *WhoAmP 93*
Moran, Erin 1960- *WhoHol 92*
Moran, Frank d1967 *WhoHol 92*
Moran, Frank Sullivan 1918- *WhoFI 94*
Moran, Frederick Augustus 1942- *WhoFI 94*
Moran, George d1949 *WhoHol 92*
Moran, Gordon William 1938- *WhoAm 94*
Moran, J. Terry 1941- *WhoAmL 94*
Moran, Jackie d1990 *WhoHol 92*
Moran, James 1929- *WhoAmP 93*
Moran, James Boyan 1943- *WhoAmL 94*
Moran, James Byron 1930- *WhoAm 94, WhoAmL 94, WhoMW 93*
Moran, James J., Jr. *WhoAm 94, WhoAmL 94*
Moran, James P. 1945- *CngDr 93, WhoAmP 93*
Moran, James Patrick 1945- *WhoAm 94*
Moran, Jeffrey W. 1946- *WhoAmP 93*
Moran, Jerry *WhoAmP 93*
Moran, John A. 1932- *WhoAm 94*
Moran, John Bernard 1936- *WhoAm 94*
Moran, John Henry, Jr. 1923- *WhoAm 94*
Moran, John Joseph 1916- *WhoAm 94*
Moran, John Thomas, Jr. 1943- *WhoAmL 94*
Moran, Joseph John 1942- *WhoScEn 94*
Moran, Joseph Michael 1944- *WhoMW 93*
Moran, Joseph Milbert 1929- *WhoAm 94, WhoAmL 94*
Moran, Joyce E. 1948- *WhoBlA 94*
Moran, Julie Lumpkin 1963- *WhoAmL 94*
Morán, Julio *WhoHisp 94*
Moran, Kenneth Joseph 1946- *WhoAmL 94*
Moran, Kim 1935- *WhoAmP 93*
Moran, Lee d1961 *WhoHol 92*
Moran, Lois d1990 *WhoHol 92*
Moran, M. Michael 1944- *WhoAmL 94*
Moran, Manolo d1967 *WhoHol 92*
Moran, Manus Francis 1927- *Who 94*
Moran, Marcus, Jr. 1943- *WhoFI 94*
Moran, Mark Edward 1950- *WhoFI 94*
Moran, Martin Joseph 1930- *WhoAm 94, WhoFI 94*
Moran, Mary *DrAPF 93*
Moran, Mary Anne 1947- *WhoWest 94*
Moran, Michael c. 1794-1846 *DcNaB MP*
Moran, Monsignor John 1929- *Who 94*
Moran, Pat d1965 *WhoHol 92*
Moran, Patricia Genevieve 1945- *WhoAm 94*
Moran, Patrick G. 1950- *WhoAmL 94*
Moran, Patsy d1968 *WhoHol 92*
Moran, Paul James 1947- *WhoAm 94*
Moran, Peggy 1918- *WhoHol 92*
Moran, Percy d1952 *WhoHol 92*
Moran, Polly d1952 *WhoHol 92*
Moran, Polly 1883-1952 *WhoCom*
Moran, Rachel 1956- *WhoAm 94, WhoAmL 94, WhoWest 94*
Moran, Ricardo Julio 1939- *WhoFI 94, WhoScEn 94*
Moran, Robert (Leonard) 1937- *NewGrDO*
Moran, Robert Daniel 1929- *WhoAm 94*
Moran, Robert E., Sr. 1921- *WhoBlA 94*
Moran, Robert Joseph 1951- *WhoAmL 94*
Moran, Samuel Joseph 1929- *WhoMW 93*
Moran, Sharon Joyce 1946- *WhoScEn 94*
Moran, Thomas Francis 1936- *WhoAm 94*
Moran, Thomas Francis 1943- *WhoWest 94*
Moran, Thomas Harry 1937- *WhoWest 94*
Moran, Thomas J. 1920- *WhoAmP 93*
Moran, Thomas Joseph 1920- *WhoAm 94, WhoMW 93*
Moran, Thomas P. 1937- *WhoFI 94*
Moran, Timothy 1918- *WhoAmP 93*
Moran, Victor John, III 1951- *WhoIns 94*
Moran, Vincent 1932- *IntWW 93*
Moran, W. Dennis 1940- *WhoAm 94*
Moran, William Madison 1948- *WhoFI 94*
Moran and Mack *WhoCom*
Morancie, Horace L. *WhoBlA 94*
Morancy, Elizabeth 1941- *WhoAmP 93*
Morand, Blaise E. 1932- *WhoWest 94*
Morand, M. R. d1922 *WhoHol 92*
Morand, Peter 1935- *WhoAm 94, WhoScEn 94*
Morandi, Pietro 1745-1815 *NewGrDO*
Morandi, Rosa (Paolina) 1782-1824 *NewGrDO*
Morandini, Giuliana 1941- *BlmGWL*
Morando, Marta Lucile Hope 1952- *WhoAmL 94*
Morane, Jacqueline d1972 *WhoHol 92*
Morang, Alfred Gwynne 1901-1958 *WhoAmA 93N*
Morani, Lorenzo *NewGrDO*
Moranis, Rick 1953- *WhoCom, WhoHol 92*
Moranis, Rick 1954- *IntMPA 94*
Moran Lopez, Fernando 1926- *IntWW 93*
Morano, Michael L. 1915- *WhoAmP 93*
Morant, Frederick d1956 *WhoHol 92*
Morant, Mack Bernard 1946- *WhoBlA 94*
Morant, Ricardo Bernardino 1926- *WhoAm 94*
Morant, Richard *WhoHol 92*
Morante, Elsa 1912-1985 *BlmGWL*
Morante, Laura *WhoHol 92*
Morante, Milburn d1964 *WhoHol 92*
Morante, Rosemary Anne 1949- *WhoAmP 93*
Morantes, Rafael Ernesto 1954- *WhoHisp 94*
Moranzoni, Roberto 1880-1959 *NewGrDO*
Morari, Lorenzo fl. 1703- *NewGrDO*
Morari, Manfred 1951- *WhoAm 94, WhoScEn 94*
Morata, Larry P. 1953- *WhoHisp 94*
Moratelli, Sebastiano 1640-1706 *NewGrDO*
Morath, Inge 1923- *WhoAm 94, WhoAmA 93*
Morath, Ingeborg Hermine 1923- *IntWW 93*
Morath, Max Edward 1926- *WhoAm 94*
Moratin, Leandro Fernandez de *IntDcT 2*
Morauta, Mekere 1946- *Who 94*
Moravcsik, Edith Andrea 1939- *WhoMW 93*
Moravcsik, Julius Matthew 1931- *WhoWest 94*

Moravec, Hans P(eter) 1948- *ConAu 142*
Moravec, Michael R. 1945- *WhoAmL 94*
Moravec, Milan 1940- *WhoWest 94*
Moravia, Alberto 1907-1990 *RfGShF*
Moravia, Alberto (Pincherle) 1907-1990 *WhAm 10*
Moravy, L. Joe 1950- *WhoAm 94, WhoFI 94*
Morawetz, Cathleen Synge 1923- *WhoAm 94, WhoScEn 94*
Morawetz, Herbert 1915- *WhoAm 94*
Morawicz, Marion Agnes 1957- *WhoAmL 94*
Morawski-Dabrowa, Eugeniusz 1876-1948 *NewGrDO*
Moray, Earl of 1928- *Who 94*
Moray, Edward Bruce D. *Who 94*
Moray, Ross And Caithness, Dean of *Who 94*
Moraytis, Louis J. 1947- *WhoAmL 94*
Moray Williams, Ursula 1911- *WrDr 94*
Morazan, Francisco 1792-1842 *HisWorL [port]*
Morbey, Graham Kenneth 1935- *WhoScEn 94*
Morby, Jacqueline 1937- *WhoAm 94*
Morby, Jeffrey Lewis 1937- *WhoAm 94*
Morch, Dea Trier *ConWorW 93*
Morcillo, Jose d1949 *WhoHol 92*
Morcom, Anthony John 1916- *Who 94*
Morcom, Christopher 1939- *Who 94*
Morcom, Claudia House *WhoBlA 94*
Morcom, John Brian 1925- *Who 94*
Morcos, Maher N. 1946- *WhoAmA 93*
Morcos-Asaad, Fikry Naguib 1930- *Who 94*
Morcott, Southwood J. 1939- *WhoAm 94, WhoFI 94, WhoMW 93*
Mord, Irving Conrad, II 1950- *WhoAmL 94*
Morda Evans, Raymond John *Who 94*
Mordant, Edwin d1942 *WhoHol 92*
Mordant, Grace d1952 *WhoHol 92*
Mordasky, John David 1925- *WhoAmP 93*
Mordaunt, Richard (Nigel Charles) 1940- *Who 94*
Mordden, Ethan 1947- *WrDr 94*
Mordden, Ethan (Christopher) 1947- *GayLL*
Mordecai, Benjamin 1944- *WhoAm 94*
Mordecai, Pamela 1942- *BlmGWL*
Mordecai, Pamela (Claire) 1942- *WrDr 94*
Mordechai, Shaul 1941- *WhoScEn 94*
Morden, John Reid 1941- *WhoAm 94*
Mordkin, Mikhail 1880-1944 *IntDcB [port]*
Mordkovitch, Lydia 1944- *IntWW 93*
Mordo, Jean Henri 1945- *WhoAm 94*
Mordue, Richard Eric 1941- *Who 94*
Mordvinoff, Nicolas 1911-1973 *WhoAmA 93N*
Mordvinov, Nikolai d1966 *WhoHol 92*
Mordy, James Calvin 1927- *WhoAm 94, WhoAmL 94, WhoFI 94, WhoMW 93*
Mordyukova, Nonna (Noyabrina) Viktorovna 1925- *IntWW 93*
More, Camilla *WhoHol 92*
More, Douglas McLochlan 1926- *WhoAm 94*
Moré, Eduardo A. 1929- *WhoHisp 94*
More, Hannah 1745-1833 *BlmGEL [port], BlmGWL*
More, Hermon 1887-1968 *WhoAmA 93N*
More, John Herron *WhoAmL 94*
More, Kane Jean 1953- *WhoScEn 94*
More, Kenneth d1982 *WhoHol 92*
More, Mary d1713? *BlmGWL*
More, Norman 1921- *Who 94*
More, Philip Jerome 1911- *WhoAm 94*
More, Syver Wakeman 1950- *WhoScEn 94*
More, Thomas 1477?-1535 *DcLB 136*
More, Thomas 1478-1535 *BlmGEL, EncSF 93, HisWorL [port]*
More, Timothy T. 1945- *WhoAmL 94*
More, Unity d1981 *WhoHol 92*
More, William 1520-1600 *DcNaB MP*
Moreau, David Merlin 1927- *WrDr 94*
Moreau, Doug 1945- *WhoAmL 94*
Moreau, Fanchon 1668-1743? *NewGrDO*
Moreau, Hugues Andre 1948- *WhoScEn 94*
Moreau, Jean-Baptiste 1656-1733 *NewGrDO*
Moreau, Jeanne 1928- *IntMPA 94, IntWW 93, Who 94, WhoHol 92*
Moreau, Louise 1921- *WhoWomW 91*
Moreau, Louison 1668?-1692? *NewGrDO*
Moreau de Tours, Jacques Joseph 1804-1884 *EncSPD*
Morecambe, Eric d1984 *WhoHol 92*
Morecock, Earle Monroe 1898- *WhAm 10*
Morecroft, Michael John 1942- *WhoFI 94*
Moreell, Ben 1892-1978 *EncABHB 9 [port]*
Morefield, Michael Thomas 1956- *WhoFI 94*
Morefield, Richard Watts 1961- *WhoAmL 94*
Moreh, Shmuel 1932- *ConAu 141*
Morehart, Donald Hadley 1938- *WhoAm 94*
Morehart, James Henry 1959- *WhoScEn 94*
Morehart, Thomas Berton 1942- *WhoWest 94*
Morehead, Annette Marie *WhoWest 94*
Morehead, Charles Richard 1947- *WhoAm 94, WhoIns 94*
Morehead, Florida Mae 1948- *WhoBlA 94*
Morehead, Harry Edward 1934- *WhoFI 94*
Morehead, James Caddall, Jr. 1913- *WhoAm 94*
Morehead, John Woodson 1948- *WhoMW 93*
Morehouse, Carl Edward 1951- *WhoWest 94*
Morehouse, David Frank 1943- *WhoScEn 94*
Morehouse, James Ernest 1944- *WhoFI 94*
Morehouse, Joyce Louise 1935- *WhoMW 93*
Morehouse, Lawrence Glen 1925- *WhoAm 94, WhoScEn 94*
Morehouse, William Paul 1929- *WhoAmA 93*
Morein, Joseph A. *WhoAm 94*
Moreira, Antonio Leal 1758-1819 *NewGrDO*
Moreira, Domingo R. *WhoHisp 94*
Moreira, Jorge Washington 1955- *WhoHisp 94*
Moreira, Marcilio Marques 1932- *IntWW 93*
Moreira, Marcio Martins 1947- *WhoAm 94, WhoFI 94*
Moreira Neves, Lucas 1925- *IntWW 93*
Morel, Madame de *BlmGWL*
Morel, Benedict Augustin 1809-1873 *EncSPD*
Morel, Edmund Dene 1873-1924 *DcNaB MP*
Morel, Francois M.M. 1944- *WhoScEn 94*
Morel, Genevieve *WhoHol 92*
Morel, Jean (Paul) 1903-1975 *NewGrDO*
Morel, John L. 1938- *WhoAmL 94*
Morel, Nina *ConAu 142*
Morel-Almonte, Rafael 1948- *WhoFI 94*
Morelan, Paula Kay 1949- *WhoAm 94*
Moreland, Alvin Franklin 1931- *WhoAm 94*
Moreland, C. L. *WhoAmP 93*
Moreland, Dana A. 1951- *WhoAmP 93*
Moreland, Jane P. *DrAPF 93*
Moreland, Jesse Earl 1897- *WhAm 10*
Moreland, Lois Baldwin *WhoBlA 94*
Moreland, Mantan d1973 *WhoHol 92*
Moreland, Michael *WhoAmP 93*
Moreland, Michael Joseph 1962- *WhoMW 93*
Moreland, Richard C. 1953- *WrDr 94*
Moreland, Richard James 1947- *WhoAm 94*
Moreland, Robert John 1941- *Who 94*
Moreland, Sallie V. *WhoBlA 94*
Moreland, Thomas H. 1943- *WhoAmL 94*
Moreland-Young, Curtina 1949- *WhoBlA 94*
Morell, Andre d1978 *WhoHol 92*
Morella, Constance A. 1931- *CngDr 93*
Morella, Constance Albanese 1931- *WhoAm 94, WhoAmP 93*
Morelle, Joseph D. *WhoAmP 93*
Morellet, Francois Charles Alexis Albert 1926- *IntWW 93*
Morelli, Anthony Frank 1956- *WhoMW 93*
Morelli, Carmen 1922- *WhoAmL 94, WhoAmP 93, WhoFI 94*
Morelli, Joseph Gabriel, Jr. 1953- *WhoWest 94*
Morelli, Mike d1976 *WhoHol 92*
Morelli, Rina d1976 *WhoHol 92*
Morelli, William Annibale, Sr. 1938- *WhoAm 94, WhoMW 93*
Morello, Joseph Albert 1928- *WhoAm 94*
Morello, Josephine A. 1936- *WhoScEn 94*
Morello, Michael 1923- *WhoAmP 93*
Morelock, James Crutchfield 1920- *WhoAm 94*
Morelos, Alfredo, Jr. 1952- *WhoHisp 94*
Morelos, Raymond Perez, Jr. 1944- *WhoHisp 94*
Morel-Seytoux, Hubert Jean 1932- *WhoWest 94*
More-Molyneux, James Robert 1920- *Who 94*
Moren, Halldis *ConWorW 93*
Moren, Leslie Arthur 1914- *WhoScEn 94*
Moren, Sergio R. 1944- *WhoHisp 94*
Moren, William A. 1944- *WhoIns 94*
Morena, Berta 1878-1952 *NewGrDO*
Morena, John Joseph 1937- *WhoFI 94*
Morena, Sena d1925 *WhoHol 92*
Morency, Barbe-Suzanne-Aimable Giroux de 1770- *BlmGWL*
Morency, Paula J. 1955- *WhoAmL 94*
Morency, Robert d1937 *WhoHol 92*
Moreno, Alejandro, Jr. 1947- *WhoAmP 93, WhoHisp 94*
Moreno, Alfredo A., Jr. 1919- *WhoHisp 94*
Moreno, Anthony Ernest 1954- *WhoWest 94*
Moreno, Antonio d1967 *WhoHol 92*
Moreno, Antonio 1918- *WrDr 94*
Moreno, Antonio Elósegui 1918- *WhoHisp 94*
Moreno, Antonio L., Sr. 1945- *WhoHisp 94*
Moreno, Armando 1920- *WhoWest 94*
Moreno, Arturo *WhoHisp 94*
Moreno, Arturo 1934- *WhoHisp 94*
Moreno, Barry Marco Adolfo 1965- *WhoHisp 94*
Moreno, Belita *WhoHol 92*
Moreno, Benita 1792-1872 *NewGrDO*
Moreno, C. Eduardo 1941- *WhoHisp 94*
Moreno, Carlos Julio 1946- *WhoHisp 94*
Moreno, Carlos W. 1936- *WhoHisp 94*
Moreno, Cecilia May *WhoHisp 94*
Moreno, Clara Triay 1942- *WhoHisp 94*
Moreno, Dario d1968 *WhoHol 92*
Moreno, Dario Vincent 1958- *WhoHisp 94*
Moreno, Dorinda *DrAPF 93*
Moreno, Elida 1944- *WhoHisp 94*
Moreno, Ernest Henry 1946- *WhoHisp 94*
Moreno, Eugene 1947- *WhoHisp 94*
Moreno, Federico Antonio 1952- *WhoAm 94, WhoAmL 94*
Moreno, Federico Antonio, Sr. 1952- *WhoHisp 94*
Moreno, Fernando *WhoHisp 94*
Moreno, Fernando 1946- *WhoHisp 94*
Moreno, Fernando, Jr. 1955- *WhoHisp 94*
Moreno, Francisco 1827-c. 1905 *WhWE*
Moreno, Frank Javier 1961- *WhoWest 94*
Moreno, Frank Javier, Jr. 1961- *WhoHisp 94*
Moreno, Gilberto 1936- *WhoHisp 94*
Moreno, Glen Richard 1943- *WhoAm 94*
Moreno, H. Paul *WhoHisp 94*
Moreno, Hilda *WhoHol 92*
Moreno, Jaime Ricardo 1958- *WhoHisp 94*
Moreno, José Antonio 1928- *WhoHisp 94*
Moreno, Jose Elias d1969 *WhoHol 92*
Moreno, Jose Guillermo 1951- *WhoHisp 94*
Moreno, Juan Carlos 1954- *WhoHisp 94*
Moreno, Luis Fernando 1951- *WhoHisp 94*
Moreno, Luis G., Jr. 1955- *WhoHisp 94*
Moreno, Manuel 1945- *WhoHisp 94*
Moreno, Manuel D. 1930- *WhoAm 94, WhoHisp 94, WhoWest 94*
Moreno, Marcelino, Jr. 1961- *WhoHisp 94*
Moreno, Marguerite d1948 *WhoHol 92*
Moreno, Mariano 1778-1811 *HisWorL [port]*
Moreno, Mario 1911-1993 *NewYTBS 93 [port]*
Moreno, Mario Francisco, Jr. 1953- *WhoHisp 94*
Moreno, Mary A. *WhoHisp 94*
Moreno, Michael Rafael 1954- *WhoHisp 94*
Moreno, Miguel Angel 1949- *WhoHisp 94*
Moreno, Orlando Julio 1944- *WhoHisp 94*
Moreno, Oscar *WhoHisp 94*
Moreno, Paco d1941 *WhoHol 92*
Moreno, Patricia Jean *WhoAmP 93*
Moreno, Paul 1931- *WhoHisp 94*
Moreno, Paul Cruz 1931- *WhoAmP 93*
Moreno, Rachael E. 1941- *WhoHisp 94*
Moreno, Rafael 1949- *WhoHisp 94*
Moreno, Richard *WhoHisp 94*
Moreno, Richard D. 1940- *WhoHisp 94*
Moreno, Richard Mills 1938- *WhoWest 94*
Moreno, Rita 1931- *IntMPA 94, WhoAm 94, WhoHisp 94, WhoHol 92*
Moreno, Rogelio *WhoHisp 94*
Moreno, Rosita 1910- *WhoHol 92*
Moreno, Rudolfo 1933- *WhoHisp 94*
Moreno, Vaughn M. 1947- *WhoHisp 94*
Moreno, Victor John 1955- *WhoHisp 94*
Moreno, Virginia R. 1925- *BlmGWL*
Moreno, William *WhoHisp 94*
Moreno-Black, Geraldine 1946- *WhoHisp 94*
Moreno-Cabral, Carlos Eduardo 1951- *WhoHisp 94*
Moreno Iruegas, Maria de los Angeles *WhoWomW 91*
Moreno-Lopez, Jorge 1941- *WhoScEn 94*
Morenon, Elise 1939- *WhoAmA 93*
Moreno Rodriguez, Gilberto 1936- *WhoAmP 93*
Moreno Torroba, Federico 1891-1982 *NewGrDO*
Morera, Enric 1865-1942 *NewGrDO*
Morera, Osvaldo Francisco 1966- *WhoHisp 94*
Moreschi, Roger P. 1938- *WhoIns 94*
Moreschi, Roger Patrick 1938- *WhoFI 94*
Moresi, Alfonso J. 1947- *WhoAmL 94*
Moresi, Remo P. 1952- *WhoScEn 94*
Moresky, Lana 1946- *WhoAmP 93*
Moress, Helen Rae 1934- *WhoAmP 93*
Morest, Donald Kent 1934- *WhoAm 94*
Moret, Louis F. 1944- *WhoAmP 93, WhoHisp 94*
Moreton *Who 94*
Moreton, Lord 1981- *Who 94*
Moreton, Alfred E., III *WhoAmL 94*
Moreton, John 1921- *WrDr 94*
Moreton, John (Oscar) 1917- *Who 94*
Moreton, N. Edwina 1950- *WrDr 94*
Morett, Angela Marie 1952- *WhoHisp 94*
Moretti, August Joseph 1950- *WhoAm 94, WhoAmL 94*
Moretti, Ferdinando d1807 *NewGrDO*
Moretti, Jay Donald 1947- *WhoAmL 94*
Moretti, Nanni *WhoHol 92*
Moretz, William Henry 1914-1989 *WhAm 10*
Morey, Albert Anderson 1903-1991 *WhAm 10*
Morey, Anthony Bernard Nicholas 1936- *Who 94*
Morey, Bill 1923- *WhoHol 92*
Morey, Carl Reginald 1934- *WhoAm 94*
Morey, Harry T. d1936 *WhoHol 92*
Morey, Henry A. d1929 *WhoHol 92*
Morey, James Newman 1933- *WhoAm 94*
Morey, Leo d1965 *EncSF 93*
Morey, Marion Louise 1926- *WhoMW 93*
Morey, Philip Stockton, Jr. 1937- *WhoScEn 94*
Morey, Robert Hardy 1956- *WhoFI 94, WhoWest 94*
Morey, Samuel 1762-1843 *WorInv*
Morey, Walt 1907-1992 *AnObit 1992*
Morey, Walt(er Nelson) 1907-1992 *WrDr 94N*
Morey, Walter Nelson 1907-1992 *WhAm 10*
Morey, William Calvin 1949- *WhoWest 94*
Morf, Darrel Arle 1943- *WhoAmL 94*
Morf, Doris 1927- *WhoWomW 91*
Morfeld, Martin R. 1950- *WhoAmL 94*
Morfogen, George *WhoHol 92*
Morfopoulos, V. 1937- *WhoScEn 94*
Morford, Douglas Harry 1944- *WhoAmL 94*
Morford, Lynn Ellen 1953- *WhoMW 93*
Morford-Burg, JoAnn 1956- *WhoMW 93*
Morford-Burg, Joann Marie 1956- *WhoAmP 93*
Morga Bellizzi, Celeste 1921- *WhoAm 94*
Morgado, Arnold 1952- *WhoAmP 93*
Morgado, Richard Joseph 1946- *WhoFI 94*
Morgado, Robert *WhoAm 94, WhoFI 94*
Morgan *Who 94*
Morgan, Lady *BlmGWL*
Morgan, Alan D. *WhoAm 94, WhoWest 94*
Morgan, Alan Vivian 1943- *WhoAm 94, WhoScEn 94*
Morgan, Alan Wyndham *Who 94*
Morgan, Alice Johnson Parham 1943- *WhoBlA 94*
Morgan, Alison M. 1930- *WrDr 94*
Morgan, Andre 1952- *IntMPA 94*
Morgan, Andrew Wesley 1922- *WhoAm 94*
Morgan, Anne Carne 1964- *WhoAmL 94*
Morgan, Annette N. 1938- *WhoAmP 93*
Morgan, Anthony Hugh 1931- *Who 94*
Morgan, Anthony Ian 1938- *WhoAm 94*
Morgan, Ardys Nord 1946- *WhoMW 93*
Morgan, Arlene Notoro 1945- *WhoAm 94*
Morgan, Arthur C. 1904- *WhoAmA 93*
Morgan, Arthur Edward 1929- *WhoAm 94*
Morgan, Arthur William Crawford 1931- *Who 94*
Morgan, Audrey 1931- *WhoScEn 94, WhoWest 94*
Morgan, Austen 1949- *WrDr 94*
Morgan, Barbara 1900-1992 *AnObit 1992*
Morgan, Barbara Brooks 1900- *WhoAmA 93*
Morgan, Barbara Doolittle 1929- *WhoAmL 94*
Morgan, Barbara Janette 1916- *WhoMW 93*
Morgan, Barbara Joan 1940- *WhoMW 93*
Morgan, Barry Cennydd *Who 94*
Morgan, Beverly 1952- *NewGrDO*
Morgan, Beverly Carver 1927- *WhoAm 94*
Morgan, Bill *Who 94*
Morgan, Booker T. 1926- *WhoBlA 94*
Morgan, Boyd d1988 *WhoHol 92*
Morgan, Brinley John 1916- *Who 94*
Morgan, Bruce 1945- *Who 94*

Morgan, Bruce Blake 1946- WhoFI 94, WhoMW 93
Morgan, Bruce Ray 1932- WhoAm 94
Morgan, Buck d1981 WhoHol 92
Morgan, Byron d1963 WhoHol 92
Morgan, Carol M. 1944- WhoHisp 94
Morgan, Carol Marie 1942- WhoAm 94
Morgan, Carole DrAPF 93
Morgan, Chandos Clifford Hastings Mansel d1993 Who 94N
Morgan, Charles Christopher 1939- Who 94
Morgan, Charles Edward Phillip 1916- WhoWest 94
Morgan, Charles Oxford, Jr. 1940- WhoAmL 94
Morgan, Charles Russell 1946- WhoAmL 94, WhoFI 94
Morgan, Charles Sumner 1915- WhoAm 94
Morgan, Charlie O. 1931- WhoAmP 93
Morgan, Chris 1946- EncSF 93
Morgan, Cindy 1955- WhoHol 92
Morgan, Claire GayLL
Morgan, Claire 1921- WrDr 94
Morgan, Clarence (Edward) 1950- WhoAmA 93
Morgan, Clarence Edward, III 1945- WhoAmP 93
Morgan, Clark WhoHol 92
Morgan, Claudia d1974 WhoHol 92
Morgan, Clifford Isaac 1930- Who 94
Morgan, Clinton Gerard, Jr. 1897- WhAm 10
Morgan, Clyde Alafiju 1940- WhoBlA 94
Morgan, Clyde Nathaniel 1923- WhoAmP 93
Morgan, Constance Louise 1941- WhoFI 94
Morgan, Cyril Dion 1917- Who 94
Morgan, Dale Eugene 1930- WhoAmP 93
Morgan, Dan WhoAmP 93
Morgan, Dan d1975 WhoHol 92
Morgan, Dan 1925- EncSF 93, WrDr 94
Morgan, Daniel 1736-1802 AmRev, WhAmRev [port]
Morgan, Daniel Carl 1954- WhoScEn 94
Morgan, Dave EncSF 93
Morgan, David Allen 1962- WhoWest 94
Morgan, David Ernest 1942- WhoFI 94
Morgan, David Forbes 1930- WhoWest 94
Morgan, David Gethin 1929- Who 94
Morgan, David Glyn 1933- Who 94
Morgan, David John H. Who 94
Morgan, David Thomas 1946- Who 94
Morgan, Debbi WhoBlA 94, WhoHol 92
Morgan, Deloris Jackson 1947- WhoFI 94
Morgan, Dennis 1910- IntMPA 94, WhoHol 92
Morgan, Dennis Richard 1942- WhoAmL 94, WhoMW 93
Morgan, Dewi d1993 Who 94N
Morgan, Dewi 1916-1993 WrDr 94N
Morgan, Dolores Parker WhoBlA 94
Morgan, Donald Crane 1940- WhoAmL 94
Morgan, Donald George 1931- WhoScEn 94
Morgan, Donald M. 1942- ConTFT 11
Morgan, Donna Jean 1955- WhoMW 93, WhoScEn 94
Morgan, Douglas 1936- Who 94
Morgan, Dudley Who 94
Morgan, (David) Dudley 1914- Who 94
Morgan, Edmund Sears 1916- WhoAm 94
Morgan, Edward L., Jr. 1943- WhoIns 94
Morgan, Edward P. d1993 NewYTBS 93
Morgan, Edward P(addock) 1910-1993 ConAu 140, CurBio 93N
Morgan, Edwin (George) 1920- ConAu 43NR, Who 94, WrDr 94
Morgan, Edwin John 1927- Who 94
Morgan, Elaine (Neville) 1920- WrDr 94
Morgan, Eldridge Gates 1925- WhoBlA 94
Morgan, Elizabeth DrAPF 93
Morgan, Elizabeth d1987 WhoHol 92
Morgan, Elizabeth 1947- WhoAm 94
Morgan, Elliott Wayne 1957- WhoWest 94
Morgan, Ellis 1916- Who 94
Morgan, Elmo Rich 1913- WhoAm 94
Morgan, Ernest (Dunstan) 1896- Who 94
Morgan, Ernest R. AfrAmG [port]
Morgan, Evan 1930- WhoScEn 94
Morgan, Fletcher, Jr. 1920- WhoBlA 94
Morgan, Frances Irene 1958- WhoFI 94
Morgan, Frank d1949 WhoHol 92
Morgan, Frank Brown Webb, Jr. 1935- WhoAm 94
Morgan, Frank Edward, II 1952- WhoAm 94, WhoAmL 94
Morgan, Frederick 1922- WhoAm 94
Morgan, (George) Frederick 1922- WrDr 94
Morgan, Garfield 1931- WhoHol 92
Morgan, Garret A. 1877-1963 AfrAmAl 6 [port]
Morgan, Garret Augustus 1875-1963 WorInv [port]
Morgan, Gary WhoHol 92
Morgan, Gary B. 1943- WhoWest 94
Morgan, Gary Patrick 1944- WhoScEn 94
Morgan, Gemmell Who 94
Morgan, (Henry) Gemmell 1922- Who 94
Morgan, Gene d1940 WhoHol 92
Morgan, Geoffrey Thomas 1931- Who 94
Morgan, George 1742-1810 AmRev
Morgan, George 1743-1810 WhAmRev
Morgan, George Douglas 1953- WhoWest 94
Morgan, George Emir, III 1953- WhoFI 94, WhoScEn 94
Morgan, George Jefferson 1908- WhoAm 94
Morgan, George Lewis Bush 1925- Who 94
Morgan, George William 1935- WhoFI 94
Morgan, Geraint Who 94
Morgan, (William) Geraint (Oliver) 1920- Who 94
Morgan, Gladys B. 1899-1981 WhoAmA 93N
Morgan, Gordon D. 1931- WhoBlA 94
Morgan, Gretna Faye 1927- WhoFI 94
Morgan, Gwyn Who 94
Morgan, (John) Gwyn(fryn) 1934- Who 94
Morgan, H(oward) G(ethin) 1934- WrDr 94
Morgan, Harold George 1943- WhoAmP 93
Morgan, Harry 1915- IntMPA 94, WhoCom, WhoHol 92
Morgan, Harry 1926- WhoBlA 94
Morgan, Harvey Bland 1930- WhoAmP 93
Morgan, Haywood, Sr. 1936- WhoBlA 94
Morgan, Hazel C. Brown 1930- WhoBlA 94
Morgan, Helen d1941 WhoHol 92
Morgan, Helen (Gertrude Louise) 1921- WrDr 94
Morgan, Henry 1915- WhoAm 94, WhoCom, WhoHol 92
Morgan, Henry Coke, Jr. 1935- WhoAm 94, WhoAmL 94, WhoAmP 93
Morgan, Henry J. 1924- WhoAmL 94
Morgan, Herbert Doyle 1929- WhoAmP 93
Morgan, Howard Campbell 1935- WhoAm 94, WhoMW 93
Morgan, Howard DeWitt 1962- WhoFI 94
Morgan, Howard Edwin 1927- WhoAm 94
Morgan, Hugh Jackson, Jr. 1928- WhoAm 94
Morgan, J.M. EncSF 93
Morgan, J. Ronald 1952- WhoScEn 94
Morgan, Jack M. 1924- WhoWest 94
Morgan, Jack Mac Gee 1924- WhoAmP 93
Morgan, Jacob 1879-1950 EncNAR
Morgan, Jacob Richard 1925- WhoScEn 94
Morgan, Jacqueline Dee 1944- WhoMW 93
Morgan, Jacqui 1939- WhoAm 94
Morgan, James A. WhoFI 94
Morgan, James Allen 1934- WhoAm 94
Morgan, James C. 1938- WhoAm 94, WhoFI 94, WhoScEn 94, WhoWest 94
Morgan, James Durward 1936- WhoAm 94, WhoFI 94
Morgan, James Franklin 1943- WhoAmP 93
Morgan, James G. 1939- WhoFI 94
Morgan, James Hanly 1937- WhoAmP 93
Morgan, James Jay 1942- WhoAm 94
Morgan, James John 1932- WhoAm 94
Morgan, James L. 1947- WhoAmA 93
Morgan, James Leonard, III 1958- WhoAmP 93
Morgan, James N. 1918- IntWW 93
Morgan, James Newton 1918- WhoAm 94
Morgan, Jane d1972 WhoHol 92
Morgan, Jane Brennan 1955- WhoAmL 94
Morgan, Jane Hale 1925- WhoBlA 94
Morgan, Jane Hale 1926- WhoAm 94, WhoMW 93
Morgan, Janet Who 94, WhoHol 92
Morgan, Janet 1945- WrDr 94
Morgan, Jaye P. 1929- WhoHol 92
Morgan, Jeanne WhoHol 92
Morgan, Jeff 1954- WhoScEn 94
Morgan, Jeffrey David 1959- WhoMW 93
Morgan, Jim 1937- WhoAmP 93
Morgan, Jim Lee 1943- WhoWest 94
Morgan, Jimmy D. 1945- WhoAmP 93
Morgan, Jo Valentine, Jr. 1920- WhoAmL 94
Morgan, Joan 1905- WhoHol 92
Morgan, Joe 1943- WhoBlA 94
Morgan, Joe Leonard 1943- WhoAm 94, WhoWest 94
Morgan, John DrAPF 93
Morgan, John 1735-1789 AmRev, WhAmRev
Morgan, John (Albert Leigh) 1929- Who 94
Morgan, John Adrian 1952- WhoWest 94
Morgan, John Alfred 1931- Who 94
Morgan, John Ambrose 1934- Who 94
Morgan, John Augustine 1934- WhoFI 94
Morgan, John Bruce 1919- WhoAm 94
Morgan, John Davis 1921- WhoAm 94
Morgan, John Davis 1955- WhoScEn 94
Morgan, John Derald 1939- WhoAm 94, WhoWest 94
Morgan, John Jordan 1947- WhoAmP 93
Morgan, John Lewis 1919- Who 94
Morgan, John Paul 1929- WhoBlA 94
Morgan, John Pierpont 1837-1913 DcLB 140 [port], EncABHB 9 [port]
Morgan, John Pierpont, Jr. 1867-1943 DcLB 140 [port]
Morgan, John Stephen 1963- WhoAmP 93
Morgan, John William 1959- WhoMW 93
Morgan, John William Harold 1927- Who 94
Morgan, Joseph C. 1921- WhoBlA 94
Morgan, Joseph L. 1936- WhoBlA 94
Morgan, Juanita Kennedy 1911- WhoBlA 94
Morgan, Judith A. 1939- WhoAmL 94
Morgan, Julia 1872-1957 AmCulL
Morgan, Karen Sue 1944- WhoWest 94
Morgan, Keith John 1929- IntWW 93, Who 94
Morgan, Kenneth 1928- Who 94
Morgan, Kenneth 1945- WhoScEn 94
Morgan, Kenneth Owen 1934- IntWW 93, Who 94
Morgan, Kenneth Smith 1925- Who 94
Morgan, Lael 1936- WrDr 94
Morgan, Larry Douglas 1943- WhoFI 94
Morgan, Larry Ronald 1936- WhoAm 94
Morgan, Lee d1967 WhoHol 92
Morgan, Lee Morey 1943- WhoMW 93
Morgan, Leland J. WhoAmP 93
Morgan, Leon Alford 1934- WhoAm 94, WhoFI 94
Morgan, Leon M. 1940- WhoBlA 94
Morgan, Leslie Who 94
Morgan, (Frank) Leslie 1926- Who 94
Morgan, Lewis Henry 1818-1881 AmSocL
Morgan, Lewis Render 1913- WhoAm 94, WhoAmL 94
Morgan, Linda Claire 1958- WhoScEn 94
Morgan, Linda Rogers 1950- WhoAm 94
Morgan, Lorrie 1959- ConMus 10 [port], WhoAm 94
Morgan, Lucy W. 1940- WhoAm 94
Morgan, Lynda M. 1949- WhoAmP 93
Morgan, Mack J., III 1955- WhoAmL 94
Morgan, Madel Jacobs 1918- WhoAm 94
Morgan, Marabel 1937- WhoAm 94
Morgan, Margaret d1926 WhoHol 92
Morgan, Margo d1962 WhoHol 92
Morgan, Maria Chan 1941- WhoMW 93
Morgan, Marilyn WhoHol 92
Morgan, Marilyn 1947- WhoAm 94, WhoAmL 94, WhoWest 94
Morgan, Marilynne Ann 1946- Who 94
Morgan, Maritza Leskovar 1921- WhoAmA 93
Morgan, Marjorie 1915- WrDr 94
Morgan, Mark 1906- WrDr 94
Morgan, Mark Allen 1957- WhoWest 94
Morgan, Mark Quenten 1950- WhoWest 94
Morgan, Mary 1943- WrDr 94
Morgan, Mary H. Ethel 1912- WhoBlA 94
Morgan, Mary Louise Fitzsimmons 1946- WhoFI 94
Morgan, Meli'sa (Joyce) 1964- WhoBlA 94
Morgan, Melvin 1918- WhoAmP 93
Morgan, Meredith Walter 1912- WhoWest 94
Morgan, Michael 1957- AfrAmAl 6, WhoBlA 94
Morgan, Michael Brewster 1953- WhoWest 94
Morgan, Michael David 1942- Who 94
Morgan, Michael Dennis 1947- WhoMW 93
Morgan, Michael E. 1949- WhoAmL 94
Morgan, Michael Hugh 1925- Who 94
Morgan, Michael Joseph 1953- WhoScEn 94
Morgan, Michele 1920- IntMPA 94, IntWW 93, WhoHol 92
Morgan, Mike d1958 WhoHol 92
Morgan, Millett Granger 1941- WhoAm 94
Morgan, Monica Alise 1963- WhoBlA 94
Morgan, Monroe 1921- WhoAm 94
Morgan, Myra J. 1938- WhoAmA 93
Morgan, Nancy 1949- WhoHol 92
Morgan, Neil 1924- WhoAm 94, WhoWest 94, WrDr 94
Morgan, Norma Gloria WhoAmA 93
Morgan, P. J. WhoAm 94, WhoAmP 93, WhoMW 93
Morgan, Patricia Ann 1949- WhoMW 93
Morgan, Patrick 1944- Who 94
Morgan, Patrick Michael 1940- WhoWest 94
Morgan, Paul d1939 WhoHol 92
Morgan, Paul Hyacinth 1952- Who 94
Morgan, Paul Winthrop 1911-1992 WhAm 10
Morgan, Paula WhoHol 92
Morgan, (Colin) Pete(r) 1939- WrDr 94
Morgan, Peter Trevor Hopkin 1919- Who 94
Morgan, Peter William Lloyd 1936- IntWW 93, Who 94
Morgan, Philip 1930- IntWW 93, Who 94
Morgan, Pierr 1952- SmATA 77 [port]
Morgan, Priscilla WhoHol 92
Morgan, Raleigh, Jr. 1916- WhoAm 94, WhoBlA 94
Morgan, Ralph d1956 WhoHol 92
Morgan, Randall Collins, Sr. 1917- WhoBlA 94
Morgan, Ray d1975 WhoHol 92
Morgan, Raymond F. 1948- WhoAm 94
Morgan, Raymond Scott 1949- WhoFI 94
Morgan, Raymond Victor, Jr. 1942- WhoAm 94
Morgan, Read 1930- WhoHol 92
Morgan, Rebecca Q. 1938- WhoAmP 93
Morgan, Rebecca Quinn 1938- WhoWest 94
Morgan, Rena V. d1956 WhoHol 92
Morgan, Rex d1989 WhoHol 92
Morgan, Rhelda Elnola 1947- WhoMW 93
Morgan, Rhodri Who 94
Morgan, (Hywel) Rhodri 1939- Who 94
Morgan, Ric 1949- WhoWest 94
Morgan, Richard DrAPF 93, WhoAmP 93
Morgan, Richard Ernest 1937- WhoAm 94
Morgan, Richard Greer 1943- WhoAmL 94
Morgan, Richard H., Jr. 1944- WhoBlA 94
Morgan, Richard Martin 1940- Who 94
Morgan, Richard Thomas 1937- WhoAm 94, WhoFI 94
Morgan, Richard W. 1946- WhoAmL 94
Morgan, Rion WhoHol 92
Morgan, Robbi WhoHol 92
Morgan, Robert DrAPF 93
Morgan, Robert d1979 WhoHol 92
Morgan, Robert 1921- ConAu 42NR, WrDr 94
Morgan, Robert 1944- WrDr 94
Morgan, Robert, Jr. 1954- WhoBlA 94
Morgan, Robert Arthur 1918- WhoAm 94
Morgan, Robert B. 1934- WhoAm 94, WhoFI 94
Morgan, Robert Bruce 1934- WhoIns 94
Morgan, Robert Burren 1925- WhoAmP 93
Morgan, Robert Coolidge 1943- WhoAmA 93
Morgan, Robert Dale 1912- WhoAm 94, WhoAmL 94, WhoMW 93
Morgan, Robert Edward 1924- WhoAm 94, WhoAmL 94
Morgan, Robert George 1941- WhoFI 94
Morgan, Robert Hall 1950- WhoAmL 94
Morgan, Robert Lee 1934- WhoBlA 94
Morgan, Robert Marion 1930- WhoAm 94
Morgan, Robert Peter 1934- WhoAm 94
Morgan, Robert Steve 1945- WhoScEn 94
Morgan, Robert W., II 1932- WhoBlA 94
Morgan, Robin DrAPF 93
Morgan, Robin 1941- WhoHol 92
Morgan, Robin Evonne 1941- WhoAm 94
Morgan, Robin Milne 1930- Who 94
Morgan, Robin Richard 1953- Who 94
Morgan, Roger Who 94
Morgan, (Evan) Roger 1945- Who 94
Morgan, Roger Hugh Vaughan Charles 1926- Who 94
Morgan, Roger John 1942- WhoMW 93, WhoScEn 94
Morgan, Roger Pearce 1932- Who 94
Morgan, Ronald William 1951- WhoWest 94
Morgan, Rose WhoBlA 94
Morgan, Rose Marie 1935- WhoMW 93, WhoScEn 94
Morgan, Rosemarie (Anne Louise) 1938- WrDr 94
Morgan, Rudolph Courtney 1950- WhoBlA 94
Morgan, Russ d1969 WhoHol 92
Morgan, Russell Orin 1959- WhoFI 94
Morgan, Ruth Prouse 1934- WhoAm 94
Morgan, Sally 1951- BlmGWL
Morgan, Sally (Jane) 1951- WrDr 94
Morgan, Samuel Pope 1923- WhoAm 94, WhoFI 94
Morgan, Sarah (Nicola) 1959- WrDr 94
Morgan, Scott EncSF 93
Morgan, Shannon Thomas 1950- WhoWest 94

Morgan, Sidney L. 1948- *WhoFI 94*
Morgan, Speer *DrAPF 93*
Morgan, Stafford *WhoHol 92*
Morgan, Stanley Douglas 1955- *WhoBlA 94*
Morgan, Stanley Leins 1918- *WhoAm 94, WhoMW 93*
Morgan, Stephen Charles 1946- *WhoAm 94, WhoWest 94*
Morgan, Steven Gaines 1952- *WhoScEn 94*
Morgan, Steven Michael 1954- *WhoAm 94*
Morgan, Steven Robert 1948- *WhoFI 94*
Morgan, Susan 1953- *WhoAmA 93*
Morgan, Sybil Andrews *WhoAmA 93*
Morgan, Sydney d1931 *WhoHol 92*
Morgan, Ted 1932- *WrDr 94*
Morgan, Terence 1921- *WhoHol 92*
Morgan, Terrell Alan 1957- *WhoMW 93*
Morgan, Theodora *WhoAmA 93*
Morgan, Theodore 1910- *WhoFI 94, WhoMW 93, WrDr 94*
Morgan, Thomas Bruce 1926- *WhoAm 94*
Morgan, Thomas Ellsworth 1906- *WhoAmP 93*
Morgan, Thomas Hunt 1866-1945 *WorScD*
Morgan, Thomas Michael 1953- *WhoWest 94*
Morgan, Thomas Oliver *Who 94*
Morgan, Thomas Oliver 1944- *WhoWest 94*
Morgan, Thomas Rowland 1930- *WhoAm 94*
Morgan, Timi Sue 1953- *WhoAmL 94*
Morgan, Timothy Ian 1955- *WhoMW 93*
Morgan, Todd Michael 1947- *WhoAm 94*
Morgan, Tom 1914- *Who 94*
Morgan, Tony *Who 94*
Morgan, Vaughan Frederick John 1931- *Who 94*
Morgan, Vicki d1983 *WhoHol 92*
Morgan, Victor d1933 *WhoHol 92*
Morgan, Virginia 1938- *WrDr 94*
Morgan, Wallace 1873-1948 *WhoAmA 93N*
Morgan, Walter 1921- *WhoScEn 94*
Morgan, Walter Edward 1940- *WhoAm 94*
Morgan, Walter Thomas James 1900- *IntWW 93, Who 94*
Morgan, Warren W. *WhoBlA 94*
Morgan, Wayne Philip 1942- *WhoAm 94*
Morgan, Wendy *WhoHol 92*
Morgan, Will(iam) d1944 *WhoHol 92*
Morgan, William 1944- *WhoAmA 93*
Morgan, William Alfred 1931- *WhoMW 93*
Morgan, William Basil 1927- *Who 94*
Morgan, William Bruce 1926- *WhoAm 94*
Morgan, William Douglass 1925- *WhoAm 94*
Morgan, William Gwyn 1914- *Who 94*
Morgan, William J. 1947- *WhoAm 94*
Morgan, William James 1914- *Who 94*
Morgan, William Lionel, Jr. 1927- *WhoAm 94*
Morgan, William Robert 1924- *WhoAm 94*
Morgan, William T. 1928- *WhoFI 94*
Morgan, William Wilson 1906- *IntWW 93, WhoAm 94*
Morgan-Cato, Charlotte Theresa 1938- *WhoBlA 94*
Morgan-Fadness, Corrina May 1963- *WhoWest 94*
Morgan-Giles, Morgan (Charles) 1914- *Who 94*
Morgan-Grenville, Gerard (Wyndham) 1931- *WrDr 94*
Morgan Hughes, David *Who 94*
Morgan-Owen, John Gethin 1914- *Who 94*
Morgan-Price, Veronica Elizabeth 1945- *WhoBlA 94*
Morganroth, Fred 1938- *WhoAmL 94, WhoMW 93*
Morganroth, Mayer 1931- *WhoAmL 94, WhoMW 93*
Morgan-Smith, Sylvia *WhoBlA 94*
Morganstern, Anne McGee 1936- *WhoAmA 93*
Morganstern, Daniel Robert 1940- *WhoAm 94*
Morganstern, James 1936- *WhoAmA 93*
Morganstern, Mark *DrAPF 93*
Morganstern, Myrna Dorothy 1946- *WhoAmL 94*
Morganthaler, John Richard 1921- *WhoWest 94*
Morganti, Fausta Simona *WhoWomW 91*
Morganti, Peter Anthony 1946- *WhoAmL 94*
Morgan-Washington, Barbara 1953- *WhoBlA 94*
Morgan-Welch, Beverly Ann 1952- *WhoBlA 94*
Morgan-Witts, Max 1931- *WrDr 94*
Morgenlander, Ella Kramer 1931- *WhoAmA 93*
Morgenroth, Earl Eugene 1936- *WhoFI 94, WhoWest 94*
Morgens, Howard J(oseph) 1910- *IntWW 93*
Morgensen, Jerry Lynn 1942- *WhoWest 94*
Morgenstein, William 1933- *WhoAm 94, WhoFI 94*
Morgenstern, Brian D. *WhoScEn 94*
Morgenstern, Conrad J. 1924- *WhoMW 93*
Morgenstern, Dan Michael 1929- *WhoAm 94*
Morgenstern, Hans George 1936- *WhoFI 94*
Morgenstern, Leon 1919- *WhoAm 94*
Morgenstern, Norbert Rubin 1935- *WhoAm 94, WhoScEn 94, WhoWest 94*
Morgenstern, S. 1931- *WrDr 94*
Morgenstern, Sheldon Jon 1938- *WhoAm 94*
Morgentaler, Abraham 1956- *WhoScEn 94*
Morgenthal, Becky Holz 1947- *WhoFI 94*
Morgenthaler, Alisa Marie 1960- *WhoAmL 94*
Morgenthaler, Ann Welke 1962- *WhoScEn 94*
Morgenthaler, John Herbert 1929- *WhoScEn 94, WhoWest 94*
Morgenthau, Robert Morris 1919- *IntWW 93, WhoAm 94, WhoAmL 94*
Morgera, Salvatore Domenic 1946- *WhoAm 94*
Morgese, James N. 1951- *WhoWest 94*
Morgison, F. Edward 1940- *WhoFI 94*
Morgner, Aurelius 1917- *WhoAm 94*
Morgner, Irmtraud 1933-1990 *BlmGWL*
Morhardt, Josef Emil, IV 1942- *WhoScEn 94*
Morhardt, Sia S. *WhoScEn 94*
Mori, Allen Anthony 1947- *WhoWest 94*
Mori, Claudia *WhoHol 92*
Mori, Hanae *IntWW 93*
Mori, Hanae 1926- *WhoAm 94*
Mori, Haruki d1988 *Who 94N*
Mori, Haruki 1911- *IntWW 93*
Mori, Hideo 1925- *IntWW 93*
Mori, John P. 1951- *WhoAsA 94*
Mori, Joseph Hidenobu 1922- *WhoWest 94*
Mori, Jun 1929- *WhoAm 94*
Mori, Kazuhisa 1926- *IntWW 93*
Mori, Koichi 1956- *WhoWest 94*
Mori, Masayuki 1911- *WhoHol 92*
Mori, Nobuko 1932- *WhoWomW 91*
Mori, Paola d1986 *WhoHol 92*
Mori, Sandy Ouye *WhoAsA 94*
Mori, Shigejumi *WhoScEn 94*
Mori, Shigeya 1926- *WhoScEn 94*
Mori, Taikichiro *IntWW 93*
Mori, Taikichiro d1993 *NewYTBS 93 [port]*
Mori, Taisuke 1920- *IntWW 93*
Mori, Toshia 1913- *WhoHol 92*
Mori, Toshio 1910-1980 *RfGShF*
Mori, William Guido 1929- *WhoAmP 93*
Mori, Yoshiro *IntWW 93*
Morial, Ernest Nathan 1929-1989 *WhAm 10*
Morial, Marc H. 1958- *WhoAmP 93*
Morial, Sybil Haydel 1932- *WhoBlA 94*
Moriani, Napoleone 1806?-1878 *NewGrDO*
Moriarity, Judith K. 1942- *WhoAm 94*
Moriarty, Cathy 1960- *IntMPA 94*
Moriarty, Cathy 1961- *WhoHol 92*
Moriarty, Donald Peter, II 1935- *WhoWest 94*
Moriarty, Donald William, Jr. 1939- *WhoAm 94*
Moriarty, Frederic Barstow 1940- *WhoAm 94*
Moriarty, Frederick L 1913- *WrDr 94*
Moriarty, George Marshall 1942- *WhoAm 94, WhoAmL 94*
Moriarty, Gerald Evelyn 1928- *Who 94*
Moriarty, James *WhoHol 92*
Moriarty, Jeanne Marie 1944- *WhoAm 94*
Moriarty, Joan Olivia Elsie 1923- *Who 94*
Moriarty, Joanne d1964 *WhoHol 92*
Moriarty, John 1930- *WhoAm 94, WhoWest 94*
Moriarty, John Alden 1938- *WhoAm 94*
Moriarty, Judith K. 1942- *WhoAmP 93*
Moriarty, Judith Kay Spry 1942- *WhoMW 93*
Moriarty, Marcus d1916 *WhoHol 92*
Moriarty, Michael 1941- *IntMPA 94, WhoAm 94, WhoHol 92*
Moriarty, Michael Allen 1954- *WhoMW 93*
Moriarty, Michael David 1950- *WhoAmL 94*
Moriarty, Michael John 1930- *Who 94*
Moriarty, Pat d1962 *WhoHol 92*
Moriarty, Richard William 1939- *WhoAm 94*
Moriarty, William E., Jr. 1952- *WhoIns 94*
Moribayashi, Mikio 1940- *WhoAsA 94*
Moribondo, Thomas Peter 1954- *WhoAmL 94*
Morice, Dave *DrAPF 93*
Morice, James 1539-1597 *DcNaB MP*
Morice, Joseph Richard 1923- *WhoAm 94*
Morice, Peter Beaumont 1926- *Who 94*
Morichelli, Anna c. 1750-1800 *NewGrDO*
Morici, Peter George, Jr. 1948- *WhoFI 94*
Morie, G. Glen *WhoAmL 94*
Morien, Lyle J. 1944- *WhoIns 94*
Morier, Dean Michael 1960- *WhoScEn 94*
Morier-Genoud, Philippe *WhoHol 92*
Morigi, Pietro Antonio Filippo c. 1710-1772? *NewGrDO*
Morihara, David 1959- *WhoAmP 93*
Morikawa, Dennis J. 1946- *WhoAm 94, WhoAmL 94*
Morikawa, Kosuke 1942- *IntWW 93*
Morike, Eduard 1804-1873 *DcLB 133 [port]*
Morikis, Dimitrios 1960- *WhoScEn 94*
Mori Mari 1903-1987 *BlmGWL*
Morimoto, Carl Noboru 1942- *WhoAm 94, WhoWest 94*
Morimoto, Roderick Blaine 1961- *WhoScEn 94*
Morin, Alberto d1989 *WhoHol 92*
Morin, Anita 1945- *WhoMW 93*
Morin, Carlton Paul 1932- *WhoAm 94*
Morin, Charles *NewGrDO*
Morin, Edgar 1921- *IntWW 93*
Morin, Edward *DrAPF 93*
Morin, France *WhoAmA 93*
Morin, James Corcoran 1953- *WhoAmA 93*
Morin, Jean 1916- *IntWW 93*
Morin, Jean-Baptiste 1583-1656 *AstEnc*
Morin, Patrick Joyce 1938- *WhoAm 94*
Morin, Penny B. *WhoHisp 94*
Morin, Peter B. 1955- *WhoAmP 93*
Morin, Pierre Jean 1931- *WhoAm 94*
Morin, Richard Michael 1936- *WhoAmP 93*
Morin, Roland Louis 1932- *IntWW 93*
Morin, Thomas Edward 1934- *WhoAmA 93*
Morin, William Raymond 1949- *WhoAm 94, WhoMW 93*
Morin, Yves-Charles 1944- *WhoAm 94*
Morine, Bruce Phillip 1947- *WhoFI 94*
Morinelli, Karen Maryellen 1954- *WhoAmL 94*
Morinello, Carmen Angelo 1955- *WhoAmL 94*
Moring, John Frederick 1935- *WhoAm 94, WhoAmL 94*
Morini, Erica 1910- *Who 94*
Morinigo, Higinio 1897- *IntWW 93*
Morin-Labrecque, Albertine (Rosalie Odile) 1886-1957 *NewGrDO*
Morin-Miller, Carmen A. *WhoAmA 93*
Morin-Postel, Christine 1946- *WhoScEn 94*
Morioka, Sharon Emi 1959- *WhoWest 94*
Morioka, Ted T. 1921- *WhoAmP 93*
Morios, Armando *WhoHisp 94*
Moris, Lamberto Giuliano 1944- *WhoWest 94*
Morisaki Kazue 1927- *BlmGWL*
Morisawa, Marie Ethel 1919- *WhoAsA 94*
Morisey, Patricia Garland 1921- *WhoBlA 94*
Morishige, Fukumi 1925- *WhoScEn 94*
Morishima, Akira 1930- *WhoScEn 94*
Morishima, Isao 1942- *WhoScEn 94*
Morishima, Michio 1923- *IntWW 93, Who 94*
Morishita, Etsuo 1949- *WhoScEn 94*
Morishita, Joyce Chizuko 1944- *WhoAmA 93*
Morishita, Teresa Yukiko *WhoScEn 94*
Morishita, Yoko 1948- *IntDcB [port]*
Morisi, Guido d1951 *WhoHol 92*
Morisky, Martin Jerome 1948- *WhoFI 94*
Morison, Hon. Lord 1931- *Who 94*
Morison, Elsie (Jean) 1924- *NewGrDO*
Morison, Elting Elmore 1909- *WhoAm 94*
Morison, Hugh 1943- *Who 94*
Morison, Jack 1954- *WhoWest 94*
Morison, John Hopkins 1913- *WhoAm 94*
Morison, Lindsay d1917 *WhoHol 92*
Morison, Patricia 1914- *WhoHol 92*
Morison, Richard 1514?-1556 *DcLB 136*
Morison, Richard Trevor *Who 94*
Morison, Thomas Richard Atkin 1939- *Who 94*
Morisseau, Gerald Paul 1942- *WhoAmP 93*
Morisset, Gerard 1898-1970 *WhoAmA 93N*
Morita, Akio 1921- *IntWW 93, Who 94, WhoAm 94*
Morita, Ichiko T. *WhoAsA 94*
Morita, John Takami 1943- *WhoAmA 93, WhoAsA 94*
Morita, Kazutoshi 1937- *WhoScEn 94*
Morita, Noriyuki 1932- *IntMPA 94, WhoHol 92*
Morita, Pat 1932- *WhoAsA 94*
Morita, Richard Yukio 1923- *WhoAm 94, WhoAsA 94*
Morita, Shigemitsu 1927- *WhoAm 94*
Morits, Iunna Petrovna 1937- *BlmGWL*
Morits, Yunna Petrovna 1937- *IntWW 93*
Moritsugu, Kenneth Paul 1945- *WhoAm 94*
Moritz, Albert F. *DrAPF 93*
Moritz, Charles Fredric 1917- *WhoAm 94*
Moritz, Charles Worthington 1936- *WhoAm 94, WhoFI 94*
Moritz, Claire Louise 1954- *WhoAmL 94*
Moritz, Donald Brooks 1927- *WhoAm 94*
Moritz, Donald I. 1927- *WhoAm 94, WhoFI 94*
Moritz, Edward 1920- *WhoAm 94*
Moritz, James R. 1945- *WhoFI 94*
Moritz, John Matthew, Jr. 1962- *WhoFI 94*
Moritz, John Reid 1951- *WhoAmL 94*
Moritz, Louisa *WhoHol 92*
Moritz, Michael Everett 1933- *WhoAm 94, WhoAmL 94*
Moritz, Milton Edward 1931- *WhoAm 94, WhoFI 94*
Moritz, Milton I. 1933- *IntMPA 94*
Moriwaki, Clarence *WhoAsA 94*
Moriyama, Mayumi 1927- *WhoWomW 91*
Moriyama, Mayumi 1928- *IntWW 93*
Moriyama, Raymond 1929- *IntWW 93, WhoAm 94*
Morizet, Jacques 1921- *IntWW 93*
Morizumi, S. James 1923- *WhoAsA 94*
Morizumi, Shigenori James 1923- *WhoScEn 94*
Mork, Dianne Jeannette 1942- *WhoMW 93*
Mork, Gordon Robert 1938- *WhoMW 93*
Mork, Nicholas Joseph 1946- *WhoMW 93*
Morka, Madeleine d1985 *WhoHol 92*
Morkoc, Hadis 1947- *WhoScEn 94*
Morkovsky, John Louis 1909-1990 *WhAm 10*
Morlacchi, Francesco (Giuseppe Baldassarre) 1784-1841 *NewGrDO*
Morlaine, Jacques d1983 *WhoHol 92*
Morlan, George K(olmer) 1904- *WrDr 94*
Morland, Dick 1936- *EncSF 93, WrDr 94*
Morland, John Kenneth 1916- *WhoAm 94*
Morland, Martin Robert 1933- *Who 94*
Morland, Michael 1929- *Who 94*
Morland, Robert (Kenelm) 1935- *Who 94*
Morlay, Gaby d1964 *WhoHol 92*
Morley *Who 94*
Morley, Earl of 1923- *Who 94*
Morley, Annabel 1946- *WhoHol 92*
Morley, Barbara Jane 1946- *WhoMW 93*
Morley, Cecil Denis 1911- *Who 94*
Morley, Christopher (Darlington) 1890-1957 *EncSF 93*
Morley, David 1923- *WrDr 94*
Morley, Donald *WhoHol 92*
Morley, Edward Williams 1838-1923 *WorScD*
Morley, Elliot Anthony 1952- *Who 94*
Morley, Eric Douglas *Who 94*
Morley, Felix 1894-1982 *EncSF 93*
Morley, George William 1923- *WhoAm 94*
Morley, Harold Hall 1943- *WhoFI 94*
Morley, Harold Keith 1920- *WhoFI 94*
Morley, Harry Thomas, Jr. 1930- *WhoAm 94*
Morley, Herbert 1919- *Who 94*
Morley, Hilda *DrAPF 93*
Morley, Iris 1910-1953 *DcNaB MP*
Morley, Jay d1976 *WhoHol 92*
Morley, John d1949 *WhoHol 92*
Morley, John 1924- *Who 94*
Morley, John C. 1931- *WhoAm 94, WhoFI 94*
Morley, John Edward 1946- *WhoMW 93*
Morley, John F(rancis) 1936- *WrDr 94*
Morley, John Harwood 1933- *Who 94*
Morley, Karen 1905- *WhoHol 92*
Morley, Kay *WhoHol 92*
Morley, Lawrence Whitaker 1920- *WhoAm 94*
Morley, Leslie Sydney Dennis 1924- *Who 94*
Morley, Lloyd Albert 1940- *WhoAm 94*
Morley, Malcolm d1966 *WhoHol 92*
Morley, Malcolm 1931- *IntWW 93, WhoAmA 93*
Morley, Malcolm A. 1931- *Who 94, WhoAm 94*
Morley, Margaret 1941- *ConAu 140*
Morley, Michael B. 1935- *WhoAm 94*
Morley, Pat *See* Soul Asylum *ConMus 10*

Morley, Patrick Robert 1950- WhoAmL 94
Morley, Richard Kevin 1963- WhoAmL 94
Morley, Robert d1992 IntWW 93N
Morley, Robert 1908- WhoHol 92
Morley, Robert 1908-1992 AnObit 1992, ConTFT 11
Morley, Robert James d1952 WhoHol 92
Morley, Roger Hubert 1931- IntWW 93
Morley, Ruth 1926?-1991 ConTFT 11
Morley, Sheridan (Robert) 1941- WrDr 94
Morley, Sheridan Robert 1941- Who 94
Morley, Steve 1953- WrDr 94
Morley, Thomas Mark 1948- WhoFI 94
Morley, Wilfred Owen EncSF 93
Morley, William Fenton 1912- Who 94
Morley-John, Michael d1993 Who 94N
Morling, Leonard Francis 1904- Who 94
Morling, Norton Arthur 1909- Who 94
Morlock, Carl Grismore 1906- WhoAm 94
Mormino, August Charles 1924- WhoMW 93
Morne, Maryland d1935 WhoHol 92
Mornell, Pierre 1935- WrDr 94
Morner, Stanley WhoHol 92
Mornin, Daniel 1956- ConDr 93
Morning, John 1932- WhoAm 94
Morning, John Frew, Jr. 1932- WhoBlA 94
Morninghouse, Sundaira BlkWr 2, ConAu 141
Mornington, Earl of 1978- Who 94
Moro, Domenico d1976 WhoHol 92
Moro, Elisabetta fl. 1723-1741 NewGrDO
Moro, Maria Fida 1946- WhoWomW 91
Moro, Peter 1911- IntWW 93, Who 94
Moro, Vincenzo 1922- IntWW 93
Moro-Bishop, Diana Lynn 1961- WhoAmL 94
Morocco, King of IntWW 93
Moroff, Shelley Susan 1948- WhoAmL 94
Moroi, Makoto 1930- NewGrDO
Moroles, Jesus Bautista 1950- WhoAmA 93, WhoHisp 94
Morone, James A. 1951- ConAu 142
Morones, Anthony 1955- WhoHisp 94
Moroney, E. J. WhoHol 92
Moroney, Linda L. S. 1943- WhoAmL 94
Moroney, Michael John 1940- WhoAmL 94, WhoWest 94
Moroney, Michael Vincent 1930- WhoWest 94
Moroni, Aldo Leonard, Jr. 1953- WhoAmA 93
Moroni, Antonio 1953- WhoScEn 94
Moroni, Fabrizio WhoHol 92
Morosan, Ron 1947- WhoAmA 93
Morosani, John Warrington 1953- WhoAm 94, WhoFI 94
Morosco, B. Anthony 1936- WhoAmL 94
Morosco, Walter d1948 WhoHol 92
Morosky, Robert Harry 1941- WhoAm 94
Moross, Jerome 1913-1983 NewGrDO
Moross, Manfred David 1931- IntWW 93
Morot-Sir, Edouard d1993 NewYTBS 93 [port]
Morowitz, Harold J WrDr 94
Morowitz, Harold Joseph 1927- WhoAm 94, WhoScEn 94
Moroye, Lester Yoshio 1947- WhoWest 94
Moroz, Mychajlo 1904- WhoAmA 93
Moroz, Oleksandr Oleksandrovych 1944- LngBDD
Morozko, Luka dc. 1699 WhWE
Morozov, Konstantin Petrovich 1944- IntWW 93
Morozov, Konstantin Petrovych 1944- LngBDD
Morozov, Vladimir Mikhailovich 1933- IntWW 93
Morozov, Yury Valentinovich 1955- LngBDD
Morozova, Olga 1949- BuCMET
Morpeth, Viscount 1949- Who 94
Morpeth, Douglas (Spottiswoode) 1924- Who 94
Morphesis, Jim 1948- WhoAmA 93
Morphet, David Ian 1940- Who 94
Morphet, Richard Edward 1938- Who 94
Morphy, James Calvin 1954- WhoAmL 94
Morphy, John 1947- WhoAm 94
Morpurgo, J(ack) E(ric) 1918- WrDr 94
Morpurgo, Jack Eric 1918- Who 94
Morpurgo Davies, Anna Elbina Who 94
Morr, James Earl 1946- WhoAmL 94
Morra, Bernadette 1961- WhoAm 94
Morre, D. James 1935- WhoAm 94
Morre, Dorothy Marie 1935- WhoMW 93
Morreau, James Earl, Jr. 1955- WhoAmL 94
Morrel, Judith Harper 1946- WhoMW 93
Morrel, William Griffin, Jr. 1933- WhoAm 94, WhoFI 94
Morrell, Arthur A. 1943- WhoAmP 93
Morrell, Chuck WhoHol 92
Morrell, David DrAPF 93
Morrell, David d1974 WhoHol 92
Morrell, David 1943- ConAu 43NR
Morrell, David Cameron 1929- Who 94
Morrell, David William James 1933- Who 94
Morrell, Diane Marie 1966- WhoAmL 94
Morrell, Donald Richard 1958- WhoFI 94
Morrell, Frances Maine 1937- Who 94
Morrell, Gene Paul 1932- WhoAm 94
Morrell, George d1955 WhoHol 92
Morrell, James George 1923- Who 94
Morrell, James Herbert Lloyd 1907- Who 94
Morrell, James Wilson 1931- WhoAm 94
Morrell, Leslie James 1931- Who 94
Morrell, Louis d1945 WhoHol 92
Morrell, Michael Preston 1948- WhoAm 94, WhoFI 94
Morrell, Ottoline 1873-1938 BlmGWL
Morrell, Patty Lou 1951- WhoWest 94
Morrell, Peter Richard 1944- Who 94
Morrell, Valerie WhoHol 92
Morrell, Wayne (Beam) 1923- WhoAmA 93
Morrell, William Who 94
Morrell, (Herbert) William (James) 1915- Who 94
Morrel-Samuels, Palmer 1951- WhoScEn 94
Morressy, John DrAPF 93
Morressy, John 1930- EncSF 93, WrDr 94
Morrey, John Rolph 1930- WhoWest 94
Morrey, Walter Thomas 1946- WhoScEn 94
Morrical, Glenn Edwin 1952- WhoAm 94, WhoAmL 94
Morrice, J(ames) K(enneth) W(att) 1924- ConAu 41NR
Morrice, Ken ConAu 41NR
Morrice, Norman Who 94
Morrice, Norman 1931- IntDcB
Morrice, Norman Alexander 1931- IntWW 93
Morrice, Philip 1943- Who 94
Morrice, Roger c. 1628-1702 DcNaB MP
Morricone, Ennio 1928- IntDcF 2-4, IntMPA 94, IntWW 93
Morrill, David Earl 1932- WhoAm 94
Morrill, John S(tephen) 1946- WrDr 94
Morrill, John Stephen 1946- IntWW 93
Morrill, Priscilla 1927- WhoHol 92
Morrill, Ralph Alfred 1930- WhoWest 94
Morrill, Richard Leland 1934- WhoAm 94
Morrill, Richard Leslie 1939- WhoAm 94
Morrill, Rowena EncSF 93
Morrill, Thomas Clyde 1909- WhoAm 94
Morrill, William Ashley 1930- WhoAm 94
Morrin, Peter Patrick 1945- WhoAm 94, WhoAmA 93
Morrin, Thomas Harvey 1914- WhoAm 94, WhoScEn 94, WhoWest 94
Morrin, Virginia White 1913- WhoWest 94
Morrione, Paolo WhoFI 94
Morris Who 94
Morris, Baron 1937- Who 94
Morris, A. Burr 1924- WhoAmP 93
Morris, A.G. EncSF 93
Morris, Adrian d1941 WhoHol 92
Morris, Albert 1934- Who 94
Morris, Albert Jeff 1945- WhoMW 93
Morris, Albert Jerome 1919- WhoAm 94
Morris, Alec 1926- Who 94
Morris, (Arnold) Alec Who 94
Morris, Alfred EncSF 93
Morris, Alfred 1928- Who 94
Morris, Alfred Cosier 1941- Who 94
Morris, Alice S. d1993 NewYTBS 93
Morris, Alvin Lee 1920- WhoScEn 94, WhoWest 94
Morris, Alvin Leonard 1927- WhoAm 94
Morris, Anita 1932- WhoHol 92
Morris, Anita 1943- IntMPA 94
Morris, Anthony Lee 1957- WhoAmP 93
Morris, Anthony Paul 1948- Who 94
Morris, Archie, III 1938- WhoBlA 94
Morris, Arlene Myers 1951- WhoFI 94
Morris, Aubrey WhoHol 92
Morris, Barboura d1975 WhoHol 92
Morris, Barry Livingston 1947- WhoFI 94
Morris, Bernard Alexander 1937- WhoBlA 94
Morris, Bernard Ross d1993 NewYTBS 93
Morris, Betty Sue 1941- WhoAmP 93
Morris, Bevan Howell 1949- WhoMW 93
Morris, Bill 1924- WhoAmP 93
Morris, Bill 1945- WhoAmP 93
Morris, Bill 1952- ConLC 76 [port]
Morris, Brewster Hillard 1909-1990 WhAm 10
Morris, Bruce L. WhoAmP 93
Morris, Burlene 1935- WhoAmP 93
Morris, Byron Frederick 1943- WhoWest 94
Morris, C. Timothy 1950- WhoIns 94
Morris, Cadwalader 1741-1795 WhAmRev
Morris, Calvin S. 1941- WhoBlA 94
Morris, Carl d1993 NewYTBS 93
Morris, Carl 1911- WhoAmA 93
Morris, Carloss 1915- WhoAm 94
Morris, Carol DrAPF 93
Morris, Carolyn Sue 1958- WhoMW 93
Morris, Cedric Lockwood 1889-1982 DcNaB MP
Morris, Celeste 1949- WhoBlA 94
Morris, Charles (William) 1903-1979 WrDr 94N
Morris, Charles Edward, Jr. 1931- WhoBlA 94
Morris, Charles Elliot 1929- WhoAm 94
Morris, Charles Joseph, Jr. 1940- WhoAm 94
Morris, Charles R WrDr 94
Morris, Charles Richard 1926- Who 94
Morris, Charles Robert 1924-1986 WhAm 10
Morris, Cheryl-Ann 1958- WhoMW 93
Morris, Chester d1970 WhoHol 92
Morris, Chris 1946- EncSF 93
Morris, Chris(topher Crosby) 1946- WrDr 94
Morris, Christopher Who 94
Morris, Christopher David 1957- WhoAmL 94
Morris, Christopher Hugh 1938- WrDr 94
Morris, Christopher Vernard 1966- WhoBlA 94
Morris, Clara d1925 WhoHol 92
Morris, Clifton 1937- WhoBlA 94
Morris, Colin 1929- Who 94
Morris, Corbett d1951 WhoHol 92
Morris, Dale L. WhoWest 94
Morris, Daniel Kearns 1954- WhoAm 94
Morris, David Who 94
Morris, David d1960 WhoHol 92
Morris, (William) David 1936- Who 94
Morris, David Brian 1946- WhoScEn 94
Morris, David Brown 1942- WhoMW 93
Morris, David Clyde 1927- WhoMW 93
Morris, David Elwyn 1920- Who 94
Morris, David Griffiths 1940- Who 94
Morris, David Hargett 1920- WhoAm 94
Morris, David Hugh 1941- WhoAm 94, WhoMW 93
Morris, David John 1945- WhoWest 94
Morris, David Mark 1949- WhoFI 94
Morris, David Richard 1930- Who 94
Morris, David Richard 1934- Who 94
Morris, David William 1937- Who 94
Morris, Denis Edward 1907- Who 94
Morris, Denise d1969 WhoHol 92
Morris, Derek James 1945- Who 94
Morris, Desmond WhoAm 94
Morris, Desmond 1928- WrDr 94
Morris, Desmond John 1928- IntWW 93, Who 94
Morris, Desmond Victor 1926- Who 94
Morris, Dewey Blanton 1938- WhoAm 94
Morris, Diana d1961 WhoHol 92
Morris, Dolores N. 1948- WhoBlA 94
Morris, Dolores Orinskia WhoBlA 94
Morris, Don Melvin 1946- WhoScEn 94
Morris, Donald 1945- WhoFI 94
Morris, Donald Arthur Adams 1934- WhoAm 94
Morris, Donald Charles 1951- WhoWest 94
Morris, Donald Fischer 1925- WhoAmA 93
Morris, Donald James 1933- WhoWest 94
Morris, Donald Wayne 1941- WhoAmP 93
Morris, Doris Caldwell 1933- WhoWest 94
Morris, Dorothy 1922- WhoHol 92
Morris, Dudley H., Jr. 1912-1966 WhoAmA 93N
Morris, E(llis) Theodore 1898- WhAm 10
Morris, Earl Scott 1966- WhoBlA 94
Morris, Earle E., Jr. 1928- WhoAmP 93
Morris, Edmund 1940- WrDr 94
Morris, Edward Allan 1910- Who 94
Morris, Edward James 1915- Who 94
Morris, Edward James, Jr. 1936- WhoFI 94, WhoWest 94
Morris, Edward William, Jr. 1943- WhoAmL 94
Morris, Edwin Alexander 1903- WhoAm 94
Morris, Edwin Bateman, III 1939- WhoAm 94
Morris, Edwin Thaddeus 1912- WhoAm 94
Morris, Effie Lee WhoBlA 94
Morris, Elise L. 1916- WhoBlA 94
Morris, Elizabeth J. DrAPF 93
Morris, Elizabeth Treat 1936- WhoWest 94
Morris, Ella Lucille 1923- WhoBlA 94
Morris, (Clifford) Eric 1940- WrDr 94
Morris, Ernest Brougham 1908-1991 WhAm 10
Morris, Ernest Roland 1942- WhoBlA 94
Morris, Estelle 1952- Who 94
Morris, Eugene 1939- WhoBlA 94
Morris, Eugene Jerome 1910- WhoAm 94
Morris, Florence Marie 1928- WhoAmA 93
Morris, Frances 1908- WhoHol 92
Morris, Francis Edward 1942- WhoAmL 94
Morris, Frank Charles, Jr. 1948- WhoAm 94, WhoAmL 94
Morris, Frank Eugene 1923- WhoAm 94, WhoFI 94
Morris, Frank Lorenzo, Sr. 1939- WhoBlA 94
Morris, Frank Rockwell, Jr. 1929- WhoAm 94
Morris, Frederick W. 1947- WhoAmL 94
Morris, G. Ronald 1936- WhoAm 94, WhoFI 94
Morris, Gareth Who 94
Morris, Gareth (Charles Walter) 1920- Who 94
Morris, (John) Gareth 1932- Who 94
Morris, Garrett 1937- IntMPA 94, WhoBlA 94, WhoHol 92
Morris, Garrett 1944- WhoAm 94
Morris, Gene Terry 1926- WhoAmP 93
Morris, George Allen, III 1958- WhoWest 94
Morris, George Ford d1960 WhoAmA 93N
Morris, George L. K. 1905-1975 WhoAmA 93N
Morris, George N. 1930- WhoIns 94
Morris, George Norton 1930- WhoAm 94
Morris, Gerald Francis 1943- WhoFI 94
Morris, Gertrude Elaine 1924- WhoBlA 94
Morris, Glenn d1974 WhoHol 92
Morris, Glory Huckins d1987 WhAm 10
Morris, Gordon d1940 WhoHol 92
Morris, Gordon James 1942- WhoFI 94
Morris, Gouverneur 1752-1816 AmRev, WhAmRev [port]
Morris, Gouverneur 1876-1953 EncSF 93
Morris, Grant Harold 1940- WhoAm 94
Morris, Greg 1933- WhoBlA 94
Morris, Greg 1934- WhoHol 92
Morris, Greg Arthur 1953- WhoAmL 94
Morris, Greg James 1956- WhoMW 93
Morris, Gregg 1951- WhoAmA 93
Morris, H. Ramsey, Jr. 1940- WhoAmP 93
Morris, Harold Leon 1929- WhoWest 94
Morris, Harry DrAPF 93
Morris, Harry 1924- WrDr 94
Morris, Harvey 1946- WrDr 94
Morris, Haviland WhoHol 92
Morris, Henry Allen, Jr. 1940- WhoAm 94
Morris, Henry Arthur, Jr. 1923- WhoFI 94, WhoWest 94
Morris, Henry Madison, Jr. 1918- WhoAm 94
Morris, Henry Madison, III 1942- WhoFI 94, WhoWest 94
Morris, Herman, Jr. 1951- WhoBlA 94
Morris, Hilda d1991 WhoAmA 93N
Morris, Horace W. 1928- WhoBlA 94
Morris, Howard 1919- IntMPA 94, WhoCom, WhoHol 92
Morris, Howard Eugene 1934- WhoFI 94
Morris, Howard Redfern 1946- Who 94
Morris, Hubert Andrew 1946- WhoMW 93
Morris, Ivor Gray 1911- Who 94
Morris, Jack Austin, Jr. 1939- WhoAmA 93
Morris, Jack Pershing 1918- WhoAm 94
Morris, James Who 94
Morris, James 1936- Who 94
Morris, James 1947- NewGrDO
Morris, James (Humphry) IntWW 93
Morris, James Aloysius 1918- WhoAm 94
Morris, James Bruce 1943- WhoScEn 94
Morris, James C. DrAPF 93
Morris, James Carl 1930- WhoFI 94
Morris, James Edward 1937- WhoFI 94
Morris, James Francis 1943- WhoAmL 94
Morris, James Grant 1930- WhoWest 94
Morris, James Malachy 1952- WhoAmL 94, WhoFI 94
Morris, James Matthew 1935- WhoAm 94
Morris, James Paxton 1935- WhoAmP 93
Morris, James Peppler 1947- IntWW 93, WhoAm 94
Morris, James Russell 1944- WhoFI 94
Morris, James Shepherd 1931- Who 94
Morris, James Spencer 1942- WhoAmL 94
Morris, James Thomas 1943- WhoAm 94
Morris, James Thomas 1960- WhoIns 94
Morris, Jamie Walter 1965- WhoBlA 94
Morris, Jan 1926- IntWW 93, Who 94, WrDr 94
Morris, Jane Elizabeth 1940- WhoMW 93
Morris, Janet E(llen) 1946- EncSF 93
Morris, Jason WhoAm 94
Morris, Jay Kevin 1959- WhoScEn 94
Morris, (Margaret) Jean 1924- WrDr 94

Morris, Jed William 1954- *WhoAmL 94*
Morris, Jeff *WhoHol 92*
Morris, Jeffrey Selman 1948- *WhoMW 93*
Morris, Jeremy Noah 1910- *Who 94*
Morris, Jerry Dean 1935- *WhoAm 94*
Morris, Jim 1940- *EncSF 93*
Morris, Joe 1960- *WhoBlA 94*
Morris, Joe Alex 1904-1990 *WhAm 10*
Morris, John *IntMPA 94, WhoHol 92*
Morris, John 1926- *WrDr 94*
Morris, John 1931- *IntWW 93, Who 94*
Morris, John Barton 1910- *WhoFI 94*
Morris, John E. 1916- *WhoAmL 94*
Morris, John Evan A. *Who 94*
Morris, John H., Jr. 1953- *WhoAmL 94*
Morris, John Hite 1942- *WhoAm 94, WhoFI 94*
Morris, John James, Jr. 1896- *WhAm 10*
Morris, John McLean d1993 *NewYTBS 93 [port]*
Morris, John Michael 1949- *WhoScEn 94*
Morris, John Michael Douglas 1935- *Who 94*
Morris, John N. *DrAPF 93*
Morris, John Nickerson 1942- *WhoWest 94*
Morris, John S. *DrAPF 93*
Morris, John Selwyn 1925- *WhoAm 94*
Morris, John Steven 1947- *WhoFI 94*
Morris, John Theodore 1929- *WhoWest 94*
Morris, John Woodland 1921- *WhoAm 94*
Morris, Johnnie d1969 *WhoHol 92*
Morris, Joseph Allan 1951- *WhoAmL 94, WhoAmP 93*
Morris, Joseph Anthony 1918- *WhoFI 94*
Morris, Judy *WhoHol 92*
Morris, Julian 1916- *WrDr 94*
Morris, Justin Roy 1937- *WhoScEn 94*
Morris, KaAnne Marie 1952- *WhoFI 94*
Morris, Katharine *WrDr 94*
Morris, Keith Elliot Hedley 1934- *Who 94*
Morris, Kelso B. *WhoBlA 94*
Morris, Kenneth 1947- *Who 94*
Morris, Kenneth Baker 1922- *WhoAm 94*
Morris, Kenneth Donald 1946- *WhoAm 94, WhoAmL 94*
Morris, Kevin Perry 1957- *WhoMW 93*
Morris, Kirk *WhoHol 92*
Morris, Kyle Randolph 1918-1979 *WhoAmA 93N*
Morris, L. Daniel, Jr. 1939- *WhoAmL 94*
Morris, Lana 1930- *WhoHol 92*
Morris, Larry Brungard 1939- *WhoAmP 93*
Morris, Larry Kenneth 1948- *WhoFI 94*
Morris, Lawrence 1896- *WhAm 10*
Morris, LeAnne Allen 1949- *WhoWest 94*
Morris, Lee d1933 *WhoHol 92*
Morris, Leibert Wayne 1950- *WhoBlA 94*
Morris, Leigh Edward 1934- *WhoAm 94*
Morris, Leon (Lamb) 1914- *ConAu 43NR*
Morris, Leon Lamb 1914- *WrDr 94*
Morris, Leonard *WhoAmP 93*
Morris, Leonard Leslie 1914- *WhoWest 94*
Morris, Lester Joseph 1915- *WhoFI 94*
Morris, Lewis 1726-1798 *WhAmRev*
Morris, Lewis R. 1926- *WhoBlA 94*
Morris, Lily d1952 *WhoHol 92*
Morris, Lorri Karen 1961- *WhoFI 94*
Morris, Mac Glenn 1922- *WhoAm 94*
Morris, Major 1921- *WhoBlA 94*
Morris, Margaret d1968 *WhoHol 92*
Morris, Margaret Hill 1737-1816 *BlmGWL, WhAmRev*
Morris, Margaret Lindsay 1950- *WhoBlA 94*
Morris, Maria Antonia 1940- *WhoFI 94, WhoWest 94*
Morris, Marjorie Hale 1940- *WhoAm 94*
Morris, Mark *WhoAm 94*
Morris, Mark 1956- *IntDcB [port]*
Morris, Mark Loren d1993 *NewYTBS 93*
Morris, Mark Ronald 1941- *WhoAm 94*
Morris, Mark William 1956- *IntWW 93*
Morris, Marlene C. 1933- *WhoBlA 94*
Morris, Marshall Jay 1959- *WhoFI 94*
Morris, Marta Zetina 1946- *WhoFI 94*
Morris, Mary *DrAPF 93*
Morris, Mary d1970 *WhoHol 92*
Morris, Mary d1988 *WhoHol 92*
Morris, Mary 1862-1938 *DcNaB MP*
Morris, Mary 1947- *WrDr 94*
Morris, Mary Ann 1946- *WhoFI 94*
Morris, Mary Elizabeth 1913-1986 *WhAm 10*
Morris, Mary Helen *WhoBlA 94*
Morris, Max *Who 94*
Morris, Max F. 1943- *WhoAm 94, WhoAmL 94*
Morris, Melanie Marie 1963- *WhoMW 93*
Morris, Mellasenah Y. 1947- *WhoBlA 94*
Morris, Melvin 1937- *WhoBlA 94*
Morris, Mervyn 1937- *WrDr 94*
Morris, Michael *WhoHol 92*
Morris, Michael (Spence Lowdell) 1940- *WrDr 94*
Morris, Michael Allen 1953- *WhoFI 94*
Morris, Michael D. 1941- *WhoAmP 93*
Morris, Michael David 1939- *WhoScEn 94*
Morris, Michael Howard 1938- *WhoAm 94*
Morris, Michael Sachs 1924- *Who 94*
Morris, Michael Wolfgang Laurence 1936- *Who 94*
Morris, Nigel Godfrey 1908- *Who 94*
Morris, Norma Frances 1935- *Who 94*
Morris, Norman Frederick 1920- *Who 94*
Morris, Norval 1923- *WhoAmL 94*
Morris, Oswald 1915- *IntDcF 2-4, IntMPA 94*
Morris, Owen Glenn 1927- *WhoAm 94*
Morris, Owen Humphrey 1921- *Who 94*
Morris, Paul Ray 1949- *WhoFI 94*
Morris, Peter *Who 94*
Morris, (James) Peter 1926- *Who 94*
Morris, Peter Christopher West 1937- *Who 94*
Morris, Peter Frederick 1932- *IntWW 93*
Morris, Peter John 1934- *IntWW 93, Who 94*
Morris, Peter T. *Who 94*
Morris, Phil 1959- *WhoHol 92*
Morris, Philip d1949 *WhoHol 92*
Morris, Philip John 1946- *WhoAm 94*
Morris, Phyllis d1982 *WhoHol 92*
Morris, Phyllis Sutton 1931- *WhoMW 93*
Morris, Ralph *EncSF 93*
Morris, Ralph Odell 1917- *WhoWest 94*
Morris, Ralph William 1928- *WhoAm 94*
Morris, Raymond Philip 1904-1990 *WhAm 10*
Morris, Rebecca Robinson 1945- *WhoAm 94, WhoAmL 94*
Morris, Reggie d1928 *WhoHol 92*
Morris, Richard *Who 94*
Morris, Richard d1924 *WhoHol 92*
Morris, Richard 1924- *IntMPA 94*
Morris, (James) Richard (Samuel) 1925- *Who 94*
Morris, Richard (Ward) 1939- *WrDr 94*
Morris, Richard Brandon 1904-1989 *WhAm 10*
Morris, Richard Herbert 1928- *WhoAm 94*
Morris, Richard Jeffery 1953- *WhoMW 93*
Morris, Richard Keith 1947- *Who 94*
Morris, Richard Louis 1940- *WhoMW 93*
Morris, Richard Stratton 1937- *WhoWest 94*
Morris, Richard W. *DrAPF 93*
Morris, Richard Ward 1939- *WhoWest 94*
Morris, Robert 1734-1806 *AmRev, WhAmRev [port]*
Morris, Robert 1745-1815 *WhAmRev*
Morris, Robert 1915- *WhoAm 94*
Morris, Robert 1923- *WhoIns 94*
Morris, Robert 1931- *WhoAm 94, WhoAmA 93*
Morris, Robert (Byng) 1913- *Who 94*
Morris, Robert C. 1942- *WrDr 94*
Morris, Robert Christian 1948- *WhoAm 94*
Morris, Robert Clarke 1931- *WhoAmA 93*
Morris, Robert DuBois 1956- *WhoScEn 94*
Morris, Robert Gemmill 1929- *WhoAm 94*
Morris, Robert John 1950- *WhoFI 94*
Morris, Robert Julian, Jr. 1932- *WhoAm 94, WhoMW 93*
Morris, Robert K. 1933- *WrDr 94*
Morris, Robert Lee 1947- *WhoAm 94*
Morris, Robert Louis 1932- *WhoAm 94*
Morris, Robert Mark 1957- *WhoMW 93*
Morris, Robert Matthew 1937- *Who 94*
Morris, Robert V., Sr. 1958- *WhoBlA 94*
Morris, Roger 1695-1749 *DcNaB MP*
Morris, Roger 1727-1794 *WhAmRev*
Morris, Roger 1938- *ConAu 140*
Morris, Roger Dale 1947- *WhoAmA 93*
Morris, Roger Oliver 1932- *Who 94*
Morris, Ronald James Arthur 1915- *Who 94*
Morris, Roy Leslie *WhoAmL 94*
Morris, Russell Norman, Jr. 1951- *WhoAmP 93*
Morris, Rusty Rolland d1986 *WhoHol 92*
Morris, Samuel Cary 1942- *WhoScEn 94*
Morris, Samuel Solomon, Jr. 1916-1989 *WhAm 10*
Morris, Samuel W. 1918- *WhoAmP 93*
Morris, Samuel W., Jr. 1943- *WhoAmL 94*
Morris, Sandra Joan 1944- *WhoAmL 94*
Morris, Sara 1922- *WrDr 94*
Morris, Scott Lee 1947- *WhoAmL 94*
Morris, Seth Irwin 1914- *WhoAm 94*
Morris, Sharon Louise Stewart 1956- *WhoFI 94*
Morris, Shayne O'Neal 1970- *WhoMW 93*
Morris, Shelia Elaine 1959- *WhoMW 93*
Morris, Shirley Lou 1930- *WhoAmP 93*
Morris, Simon C. *Who 94*
Morris, Stanley E. 1942- *WhoAmP 93*
Morris, Stanley E., Jr. 1944- *WhoBlA 94*
Morris, Stanley M. 1942- *WhoAm 94, WhoScEn 94*
Morris, Stephen d1964 *WhoHol 92*
Morris, Stephen 1935- *WrDr 94*
Morris, Stephen 1957- *See* New Order *ConMus 11*
Morris, Stephen Blaine 1951- *WhoScEn 94*
Morris, Stephen Burritt 1943- *WhoAm 94*
Morris, Stephen James Michael 1934- *WhoAm 94*
Morris, Steve *WhoAmP 93*
Morris, Steven Lynn 1952- *WhoWest 94*
Morris, Stevland 1950- *WhoAm 94*
Morris, Terence Patrick 1931- *Who 94*
Morris, Terry 1914-1993 *NewYTBS 93*
Morris, Terry Lesser 1914-1993 *ConAu 142*
Morris, Thomas 1914- *Who 94*
Morris, Thomas A., Jr. 1947- *WhoAmL 94*
Morris, Thomas Bateman, Jr. 1936- *WhoAm 94*
Morris, Thomas Dallam 1913- *WhoAmP 93*
Morris, Thomas Quinlan 1933- *WhoAm 94*
Morris, Thomas William 1944- *WhoAm 94*
Morris, Timothy David 1948- *Who 94*
Morris, Timothy Denis 1935- *Who 94*
Morris, Trefor Alfred 1934- *Who 94*
Morris, Trevor Raymond 1930- *Who 94*
Morris, Twila Kathleen 1953- *WhoMW 93*
Morris, Vance Blom, II 1949- *WhoAmP 93*
Morris, Victor Franklin, Jr. 1947- *WhoAm 94*
Morris, Vincent Edwin 1967- *WhoMW 93*
Morris, W. Howard 1960- *WhoBlA 94*
Morris, W. Patrick 1940- *WhoAmP 93*
Morris, Walter Frederick 1914- *Who 94*
Morris, Walter Scott 1912- *WhoAm 94*
Morris, Wayne d1959 *WhoHol 92*
Morris, Wayne Lee 1954- *WhoBlA 94*
Morris, William *WhoAmP 93*
Morris, William d1936 *WhoHol 92*
Morris, William 1834-1896 *BlmGEL [port], EncSF 93*
Morris, William 1913- *WhoAm 94*
Morris, William 1938- *IntWW 93, Who 94*
Morris, William 1941- *WhoAm 94, WhoAmL 94*
Morris, William Allan 1933- *WhoScEn 94*
Morris, William Charles 1938- *WhoAm 94*
Morris, William E. d1948 *WhoHol 92*
Morris, William H., Jr. 1929- *WhoAmP 93*
Morris, William Howard 1960- *WhoFI 94*
Morris, William Ian Clinch 1907- *Who 94*
Morris, William James 1925- *Who 94*
Morris, William Joseph 1923- *WhoAm 94*
Morris, William L. *DrAPF 93*
Morris, William Noel, Jr. 1932- *WhoAm 94*
Morris, William Otis, Jr. 1922- *WhoAm 94*
Morris, William Shivers, III 1934- *WhoAm 94*
Morris, William Sparkes 1916-1983 *ConAu 141*
Morris, Willie 1934- *IntWW 93, WhoAm 94, WrDr 94*
Morris, Wolfe *WhoHol 92*
Morris, Wright *DrAPF 93*
Morris, Wright 1910- *WhoAm 94, WhoAmA 93*
Morris, Wright (Marion) 1910- *WrDr 94*
Morris, Wyn 1929- *Who 94*
Morris Archinal, Gretchen Suzanne 1963- *WhoFI 94, WhoMW 93*
Morrisey, Jimmy 1922- *WhoBlA 94*
Morrisey, Michael A. 1952- *WhoFI 94*
Morrish, Allan Henry 1924- *WhoAm 94*
Morrish, John Edwin 1915- *Who 94*
Morris-Hale, Walter 1933- *WhoBlA 94*
Morris-Jones, Ifor Henry 1922- *Who 94*
Morris-Jones, Wyndraeth Humphreys 1918- *Who 94, WrDr 94*
Morris of Castle Morris, Baron 1930- *Who 94*
Morris of Kenwood, Baron 1928- *Who 94*
Morrison *Who 94*
Morrison, Baron 1914- *Who 94*
Morrison, Adrian Russell 1935- *WhoScEn 94*
Morrison, Adrienne d1940 *WhoHol 92*
Morrison, Alexander Fraser 1948- *Who 94*
Morrison, Alexander John Henderson 1927- *Who 94*
Morrison, Alexia 1948- *WhoAmL 94*
Morrison, Alice Louise 1921- *WhoAmP 93*
Morrison, Angus Curran 1919- *WhoAm 94, WhoScEn 94*
Morrison, Angus Hugh 1935- *WhoAmP 93*
Morrison, Ann d1978 *WhoHol 92*
Morrison, Anna Marie d1972 *WhoHol 92*
Morrison, Arthur d1950 *WhoHol 92*
Morrison, Arthur 1863-1945 *DcLB 135 [port]*
Morrison, Ashton Byrom 1922- *WhoAm 94*
Morrison, Barbara *WhoHol 92*
Morrison, Barbara A. 1949- *WhoMW 93*
Morrison, Bee 1908- *WhoAmA 93*
Morrison, Benjamin Franklin, III 1943- *WhoAmP 93*
Morrison, Bill 1935- *WrDr 94*
Morrison, Bill 1940- *ConDr 93, WrDr 94*
Morrison, Blake *Who 94*
Morrison, (Philip) Blake 1950- *Who 94, WrDr 94*
Morrison, Boone M. 1941- *WhoAmA 93*
Morrison, Bradford Cary 1944- *WhoWest 94*
Morrison, Bradley Paul 1956- *WhoFI 94*
Morrison, Bret d1978 *WhoHol 92*
Morrison, Bruce A. 1944- *WhoAmP 93*
Morrison, Carole Lynne 1946- *WhoMW 93*
Morrison, Charles (Andrew) 1932- *Who 94*
Morrison, Charles Clayton 1874-1966 *DcAmReB 2*
Morrison, Charles Edward 1943- *WhoBlA 94*
Morrison, Charles John 1944- *WhoMW 93*
Morrison, Chester d1975 *WhoHol 92*
Morrison, Chick (Charles) d1924 *WhoHol 92*
Morrison, Clarence Christopher 1939- *WhoBlA 94*
Morrison, Clinton 1915- *WhoAm 94*
Morrison, Connie 1935- *WhoAmP 93*
Morrison, Constance Faith *WhoMW 93*
Morrison, Corinne Ann 1947- *WhoAmL 94*
Morrison, Curtis Angus 1945- *WhoBlA 94*
Morrison, Darrel Gene 1937- *WhoAm 94*
Morrison, David Campbell 1941- *WhoAm 94*
Morrison, David Fred 1953- *WhoAm 94*
Morrison, David Lee 1933- *WhoAm 94*
Morrison, De Lesseps S., Jr. 1944- *WhoAmP 93*
Morrison, Debra Lynn 1956- *WhoFI 94*
Morrison, Dennis John 1942- *Who 94*
Morrison, Dennis Patrick 1949- *WhoMW 93*
Morrison, Donald Alexander Campbell 1916- *Who 94*
Morrison, Donald Franklin 1931- *WhoAm 94*
Morrison, Donald Graham 1939- *WhoAm 94*
Morrison, Donald Mackay 1897- *WhAm 10*
Morrison, Donald William 1926- *WhoAm 94*
Morrison, Doris *WhoAmA 93*
Morrison, Dorothy *WhoHol 92*
Morrison, Dudley Butler 1937- *WhoFI 94*
Morrison, Elizabeth d1960 *WhoHol 92*
Morrison, Ernest 1912-1989 *See* East Side Kids *WhoCom*
Morrison, Ernie d1989 *WhoHol 92*
Morrison, Florence *WhoHol 92*
Morrison, Francis Henry 1947- *WhoAm 94, WhoAmL 94*
Morrison, Francis Secrest 1931- *WhoAm 94*
Morrison, Frank 1918- *WhoAm 94*
Morrison, Frank Brenner, Jr. 1937- *WhoAmP 93*
Morrison, Fred Beverly 1927- *WhoAm 94*
Morrison, Fritzi Mohrenstecher *WhoAmA 93*
Morrison, Garfield E., Jr. 1939- *WhoBlA 94*
Morrison, Gary Brent 1952- *WhoAm 94, WhoMW 93*
Morrison, Gary William *WhoMW 93*
Morrison, George 1919- *WhoAmA 93*
Morrison, George Ernest 1862-1920 *DcNaB MP*
Morrison, George Harold 1921- *WhoAm 94, WhoScEn 94*
Morrison, George Thornton 1924- *WhoWest 94*
Morrison, Gerald Lee 1951- *WhoScEn 94*
Morrison, Gilbert Caffall 1931- *WhoAm 94*
Morrison, Gordon Mackay, Jr. 1930- *WhoAm 94, WhoFI 94*
Morrison, Gregg Scott 1964- *WhoFI 94*
Morrison, Gwendolyn Christine Caldwell 1949- *WhoBlA 94*

Morrison, Harriet Barbara 1934- *WhoMW 93*
Morrison, Harry 1937- *WhoAm 94, WhoScEn 94*
Morrison, Harry L. 1932- *WhoBlA 94*
Morrison, Harvey Lee, Jr. 1947- *WhoAmL 94*
Morrison, Helen Dubino 1926- *WhoAmP 93*
Morrison, Herbert S. 1888-1965 *HisDcKW*
Morrison, Howard (Leslie) 1935- *Who 94*
Morrison, Howard Irwin 1929- *WhoFI 94*
Morrison, Hugh A. 1935- *WhoAmP 93*
Morrison, Ian Gordon 1914- *Who 94*
Morrison, Jack d1948 *WhoHol 92*
Morrison, Jacqueline 1951- *WhoBlA 94*
Morrison, James *WhoHol 92*
Morrison, James d1974 *WhoHol 92*
Morrison, James 1932- *Who 94*
Morrison, James Douglas 1924- *IntWW 93*
Morrison, James Frederick 1933- *WhoAm 94, WhoFI 94*
Morrison, James Ian 1930- *Who 94*
Morrison, James Ian 1952- *WhoAm 94, WhoWest 94*
Morrison, James Mark, Jr. 1959- *WhoMW 93*
Morrison, James R. 1924- *WhoAm 94*
Morrison, James W., Jr. 1936- *WhoBlA 94*
Morrison, Jeanette Helen 1927- *WhoAm 94*
Morrison, Jim *WhoAmP 93*
Morrison, Jim d1971 *WhoHol 92*
Morrison, Jo Ann 1953- *WhoMW 93*
Morrison, Joan 1922- *WrDr 94*
Morrison, John (Gordon) 1904- *RfGShF*
Morrison, John A. 1943- *WhoAm 94*
Morrison, John Anthony 1938- *Who 94*
Morrison, John Gill 1914- *WhoAm 94*
Morrison, John Horton 1933- *WhoAm 94, WhoAmL 94*
Morrison, John Lamb Murray 1906- *Who 94*
Morrison, John Peirce 1956- *WhoAmL 94*
Morrison, John Sinclair 1913- *Who 94*
Morrison, John Stuart 1947- *WhoWest 94*
Morrison, John W. 1934- *WhoAm 94*
Morrison, John Washburn 1922- *WhoAm 94*
Morrison, Johnny Edward 1952- *WhoBlA 94*
Morrison, Joline Parsoneault 1958- *WhoMW 93*
Morrison, Joseph Young 1951- *WhoFI 94*
Morrison, Juan LaRue, Sr. 1943- *WhoBlA 94*
Morrison, Julia *DrAPF 93*
Morrison, K. C. 1946- *WhoBlA 94*
Morrison, K. Jaydene 1933- *WhoAmP 93*
Morrison, Karen Margaret 1963- *WhoMW 93*
Morrison, Karl Frederick 1936- *WhoAm 94*
Morrison, Keith Anthony 1942- *WhoAmA 93, WhoBlA 94*
Morrison, Kenneth Douglas 1918- *WhoAm 94*
Morrison, Kristin Diane 1934- *WrDr 94*
Morrison, Lillian *DrAPF 93*
Morrison, Linda Smith 1950- *WhoAmP 93*
Morrison, Lonny D. *WhoAmL 94*
Morrison, Louis d1946 *WhoHol 92*
Morrison, Madison *DrAPF 93*
Morrison, Manley Glenn 1915- *WhoAm 94*
Morrison, Marcy 1935- *WhoAmP 93*
Morrison, Margaret 1924- *Who 94*
Morrison, Mark William 1957- *WhoFI 94*
Morrison, Martha A. 1948- *SmATA 77*
Morrison, Martha Kaye 1955- *WhoWest 94*
Morrison, Martin Earl 1947- *WhoAm 94*
Morrison, Mary Anne 1937- *Who 94*
Morrison, Meta d1982 *WhoHol 92*
Morrison, Michael d1993 *NewYTBS 93 [port]*
Morrison, Michael Gordon 1937- *WhoAm 94, WhoMW 93*
Morrison, Michael P. 1944- *WhoAm 94, WhoAmL 94*
Morrison, Michelle Williams 1947- *WhoWest 94*
Morrison, Murdo Donald 1919- *WhoWest 94*
Morrison, Nigel Murray Paton 1948- *Who 94*
Morrison, Nona Lou 1930- *WhoAmP 93*
Morrison, Paul Leslie 1899-1991 *WhAm 10*
Morrison, Perry 1959- *WrDr 94*
Morrison, Perry David 1919- *WhoAm 94*
Morrison, Pete d1973 *WhoHol 92*
Morrison, Peter (Hugh) 1944- *Who 94*
Morrison, Portia Owen 1944- *WhoAm 94*
Morrison, Priestly d1938 *WhoHol 92*

Morrison, R(obert) H(ay) 1915- *WrDr 94*
Morrison, R. J. 1795-1874 *AstEnc*
Morrison, Randi Val 1964- *WhoAmL 94*
Morrison, Raymond Edward 1958- *WhoFI 94*
Morrison, Reginald Joseph Gordon 1909- *Who 94*
Morrison, Richard *EncSF 93*
Morrison, Richard David 1910- *WhoBlA 94*
Morrison, Richard Pearce 1954- *WhoWest 94*
Morrison, Rick 1957- *WhoBlA 94*
Morrison, Robert *EncSF 93*
Morrison, Robert B., Jr. 1954- *WhoBlA 94*
Morrison, Robert Clifton 1924- *WhoAmA 93*
Morrison, Robert E. 1948- *WhoAmL 94*
Morrison, Robert Haywood 1927- *WrDr 94*
Morrison, Robert J. *WhoAmA 93*
Morrison, Robert Leroy 1931- *WhoMW 93*
Morrison, Robert Lewin 1947- *WhoAm 94*
Morrison, Robert Lord, Jr. 1944- *WhoAmL 94*
Morrison, Robert Scheck 1942- *WhoAm 94, WhoFI 94*
Morrison, Robert Thomas 1918- *WhoScEn 94*
Morrison, Robert William 1941- *WhoIns 94*
Morrison, Roberta 1910- *WrDr 94*
Morrison, Roger Barron 1914- *WhoAm 94, WhoFI 94, WhoScEn 94, WhoWest 94*
Morrison, Rollin John 1937- *WhoScEn 94*
Morrison, Ronald E. 1949- *WhoBlA 94*
Morrison, Samuel F. 1936- *WhoBlA 94*
Morrison, Sara Antoinette Sibell Frances 1934- *Who 94*
Morrison, Shelley 1936- *WhoAm 94, WhoHisp 94, WhoHol 92*
Morrison, Shirley Linden 1935- *WhoWest 94*
Morrison, Sid 1933- *WhoAmP 93*
Morrison, Stephen Roger 1947- *Who 94*
Morrison, Stuart Love 1922- *Who 94*
Morrison, Susan M. *WhoAm 94*
Morrison, Temuera *WhoHol 92*
Morrison, Theodore Davidson 1947- *WhoFI 94*
Morrison, Theodore V., Jr. 1935- *WhoAmP 93*
Morrison, Thomas Allen 1947- *WhoAmL 94*
Morrison, Thomas L. *WhoAmP 93*
Morrison, Tommy 1969- *WhoHol 92*
Morrison, Toni *DrAPF 93, NewYTBS 93 [port]*
Morrison, Toni 1931- *AfrAmAl 6 [port], BlkWr 2, BlmGWL [port], ConAu 42NR, ConLC 81 [port], DcLB Y93 [port], IntWW 93, TwCYAW, WhoAm 94, WhoBlA 94, WrDr 94*
Morrison, Travis 1948- *WhoAmP 93*
Morrison, Trudi Michelle 1950- *WhoBlA 94*
Morrison, Van 1945- *WhoAm 94*
Morrison, Vera *WhoHol 92*
Morrison, Walton Stephen 1907- *WhoAmL 94, WhoFI 94*
Morrison, Wanda Stalcup 1934- *WhoAmP 93*
Morrison, Wilbur H(oward) 1915- *WrDr 94*
Morrison, William Charles Carnegie 1938- *Who 94*
Morrison, William David 1940- *WhoAm 94*
Morrison, William Edward 1951- *WhoWest 94*
Morrison, William Fosdick 1935- *WhoWest 94*
Morrison, William Fowler, Jr. 1928- *WhoAm 94*
Morrison, William Garth 1943- *Who 94*
Morrison, William Leo 1931- *WhoAm 94*
Morrison, Wynona Marvel *WhoWest 94*
Morrison-Bell, William (Hollin Dayrell) 1956- *Who 94*
Morrison-Low, James *Who 94*
Morriss, Ann 1918- *WhoHol 92*
Morriss, Cynthia Matus 1953- *WhoHisp 94*
Morriss, Frank 1923- *WrDr 94*
Morriss, Frank Howard, Jr. 1940- *WhoAm 94*
Morriss, Mary Rachel *WhoAmA 93*
Morrissette, Bruce Archer 1911- *WhoAm 94*
Morrissette, Jean Fernand 1942- *WhoScEn 94*
Morrissette, Roland A. 1916- *WhoAmP 93*
Morrissey 1959- *ConMus 10 [port]*
Morrissey, Betty d1944 *WhoHol 92*

Morrissey, Charles Thomas 1933- *WhoAm 94*
Morrissey, Dolores Josephine *WhoAm 94*
Morrissey, Edmond Joseph 1943- *WhoAm 94*
Morrissey, Francis Daniel 1930- *WhoAm 94, WhoAmL 94*
Morrissey, George Michael 1941- *WhoAmL 94*
Morrissey, J(oseph) L(awrence) 1905- *EncSF 93*
Morrissey, James Robert 1949- *WhoAm 94*
Morrissey, John d1941 *WhoHol 92*
Morrissey, John Carroll 1914- *WhoAm 94, WhoAmL 94, WhoWest 94*
Morrissey, John J. d1993 *NewYTBS 93*
Morrissey, Kymberlee Anne 1957- *WhoWest 94*
Morrissey, Leo 1958- *WhoAmA 93*
Morrissey, LeRoy Edward 1925- *WhoWest 94*
Morrissey, Mary Jane 1951- *WhoAmP 93*
Morrissey, Michael J. 1948- *WhoAmL 94*
Morrissey, Michael W. 1954- *WhoAmP 93*
Morrissey, Paul 1939- *IntMPA 94*
Morrissey, Peter A. 1953- *WhoAm 94, WhoFI 94*
Morrissey, Richard Timothy 1961- *WhoFI 94*
Morrissey, Robert John 1944- *WhoAm 94*
Morrissey, Spencer W. 1951- *WhoAmP 93*
Morrissey, Thomas Jerome *WhoFI 94*
Morrissey, Will d1957 *WhoHol 92*
Morrissey, William Thomas 1950- *WhoFI 94, WhoWest 94*
Morris-Tatum, Johnnie 1951- *WhoAmP 93*
Morris Williams, Christine Margaret *Who 94*
Morritt, (Robert) Andrew 1938- *Who 94*
Morritt, Hope 1930- *WrDr 94*
Morro, Henry J. *DrAPF 93*
Morrocco, Alberto 1917- *Who 94*
Morrocco, Alfred Frederick, Jr. 1947- *WhoAmP 93*
Morrogh, Henton 1917- *Who 94*
Morrone, Edward P. 1950- *WhoAmP 93*
Morroni, John Michael 1955- *WhoAmP 93*
Morrow, Andrew Nesbit 1929- *WhoAm 94*
Morrow, Ann Patricia *WrDr 94*
Morrow, Barry 1948- *ConTFT 11*
Morrow, Barry Nelson 1948- *WhoAm 94*
Morrow, Benjamin Francis 1891-1958 *WhoAmA 93N*
Morrow, Bill *WhoAmP 93*
Morrow, Bradford *DrAPF 93*
Morrow, Brian L. 1957- *WhoAmL 94*
Morrow, Bruce 1935- *WhoHol 92*
Morrow, Bruce W. 1946- *WhoFI 94, WhoScEn 94*
Morrow, Byron *WhoHol 92*
Morrow, Charles G., III 1956- *WhoBlA 94*
Morrow, Charles Gay, III 1956- *WhoAmP 93, WhoMW 93*
Morrow, Charles Tabor 1917- *WhoAm 94*
Morrow, Charlie *DrAPF 93*
Morrow, Christopher Brian 1955- *WhoFI 94*
Morrow, David 1948- *WhoIns 94*
Morrow, David Austin, III 1935- *WhoAm 94*
Morrow, Dennis Robert 1951- *WhoMW 93*
Morrow, Dion Griffith 1932- *WhoBlA 94*
Morrow, Donald L. 1951- *WhoAmL 94*
Morrow, Doretta d1968 *WhoHol 92*
Morrow, E. Frederic 1909- *WhoAm 94, WhoBlA 94*
Morrow, Elizabeth 1947- *WhoAm 94, WhoMW 93*
Morrow, Emily May 1959- *WhoAm 94*
Morrow, Floyd Lee 1933- *WhoAmP 93*
Morrow, George Lester 1922- *WhoAm 94*
Morrow, George Telford, II 1943- *WhoAmL 94*
Morrow, Grant, III 1933- *WhoScEn 94*
Morrow, Gray 1934- *EncSF 93*
Morrow, Hugh 1915-1991 *WhAm 10*
Morrow, Ian (Thomas) 1912- *Who 94*
Morrow, Ian Thomas 1912- *IntWW 93*
Morrow, Jack B. 1927- *WhoWest 94*
Morrow, James (Kenneth) 1947- *EncSF 93*
Morrow, James Benjamin 1926- *WhoAm 94*
Morrow, James Franklin 1944- *WhoAm 94, WhoAmL 94*
Morrow, James Kirven 1941- *WhoWest 94*
Morrow, James Ward 1964- *WhoAmP 93*
Morrow, Jane d1925 *WhoHol 92*
Morrow, Jeff d1993 *NewYTBS 93*
Morrow, Jeff 1907- *IntMPA 94*
Morrow, Jeff 1913- *WhoHol 92*
Morrow, Jesse *WhoBlA 94*

Morrow, Jo 1939- *WhoHol 92*
Morrow, Joan Schieferstein 1949- *WhoAmL 94*
Morrow, John Calhoun 1960- *WhoAmL 94*
Morrow, John Charles, III 1924-1989 *WhAm 10*
Morrow, John Ellsworth 1943- *WhoAm 94, WhoAmL 94*
Morrow, John Howard 1910- *WhoAm 94*
Morrow, John Howard, Jr. 1944- *WhoBlA 94*
Morrow, John L. *WhoAmP 93*
Morrow, John W., Jr. 1922- *WhoAmP 93*
Morrow, John Watson 1931- *IntWW 93*
Morrow, Johnny M. 1942- *WhoAmP 93*
Morrow, Joseph Eugene 1935- *WhoScEn 94*
Morrow, Lance 1939- *WhoAm 94*
Morrow, Laura Annette 1958- *WhoFI 94*
Morrow, Laverne 1954- *WhoBlA 94*
Morrow, Lydia Ann 1962- *WhoMW 93*
Morrow, Martin S. 1923- *Who 94*
Morrow, Nelson William, Jr. 1960- *WhoMW 93*
Morrow, Neyle *WhoHol 92*
Morrow, Patricia 1944- *WhoHol 92*
Morrow, Paul Edward 1922- *WhoAm 94*
Morrow, Paul Lowell 1949- *WhoScEn 94*
Morrow, Phillip Henry 1943- *WhoBlA 94*
Morrow, Ralph Ernest 1920- *WhoAm 94*
Morrow, Richard Martin 1926- *WhoAm 94, WhoFI 94, WhoMW 93*
Morrow, Richard Raymond 1939- *WhoAmP 93*
Morrow, Richard Towson 1926- *WhoAm 94*
Morrow, Rob 1962- *IntMPA 94, WhoAm 94, WhoHol 92*
Morrow, Robert Dowden 1896- *WhAm 10*
Morrow, Robert Earl 1917- *WhoAmA 93*
Morrow, Robert Maxwell 1946- *WhoAm 94*
Morrow, Rosanne Surina 1956- *WhoWest 94*
Morrow, Roy Wayne 1942- *WhoScEn 94*
Morrow, Samuel P., Jr. 1928- *WhoBlA 94*
Morrow, Samuel Roy, III 1949- *WhoAm 94, WhoBlA 94*
Morrow, Sharon M. 1953- *WhoMW 93*
Morrow, Skip 1952- *WrDr 94*
Morrow, Susan 1931- *WhoHol 92*
Morrow, Susan Dagmar 1932- *WhoWest 94*
Morrow, Terry 1939- *WhoAmA 93*
Morrow, Tracey *WhoBlA 94*
Morrow, Vic d1982 *WhoHol 92*
Morrow, Walter Edwin, Jr. 1928- *WhoAm 94, WhoScEn 94*
Morrow, Wayne 1956- *WhoAmP 93*
Morrow, Webb B., III 1948- *WhoAmL 94*
Morrow, William Clarence 1935- *WhoAm 94*
Morrow, William Earl, Jr. 1930- *WhoAmP 93*
Morrow, William John Woodroofe 1949- *WhoScEn 94*
Morrow, Winston Vaughan 1924- *WhoAm 94, WhoAmL 94, WhoFI 94, WhoWest 94*
Morry, G. Richard 1943- *WhoAmL 94*
Mors, Walter B. 1920- *IntWW 93*
Morsberger, Emory *WhoAmP 93*
Morsberger, Louis Phillip 1929- *WhoAmP 93*
Morsch, Thomas Harvey 1931- *WhoAm 94*
Morsching, Germaine Ann 1934- *WhoFI 94, WhoMW 93*
Morse, Aaron Holt 1946- *WhoScEn 94*
Morse, Adrian Osborn 1895- *WhAm 10*
Morse, Alan Richard, Jr. 1938- *WhoFI 94*
Morse, Annie Ruth W. *WhoBlA 94*
Morse, Barry 1919- *WhoHol 92*
Morse, Bart J. 1938- *WhoAmA 93*
Morse, Bradford *IntWW 93*
Morse, Carl *DrAPF 93*
Morse, Carleton E. 1901-1993 *NewYTBS 93 [port]*
Morse, Carol 1908- *WrDr 94*
Morse, Christopher Jeremy 1928- *Who 94*
Morse, David 1953- *IntMPA 94, WhoHol 92*
Morse, David A. 1907-1990 *WhAm 10*
Morse, Donald E 1936- *WrDr 94*
Morse, Dorothy B. 1906-1979 *WhoAmA 93N*
Morse, Edmond Northrop 1922- *WhoAm 94*
Morse, Edward Lewis 1942- *WhoFI 94*
Morse, Ella Mae 1923- *WhoHol 92*
Morse, Ernest Lee 1922- *WhoAmP 93*
Morse, Eva Mae 1938- *WhoAmP 93*
Morse, F. Bradford 1921- *IntWW 93*
Morse, F. D., Jr. 1928- *WhoScEn 94*
Morse, Frank Bradford 1921- *WhoAmP 93*
Morse, Garlan, Jr. 1947- *WhoAm 94*

Morse, Gerald Ira 1909- *WhoAmP 93*
Morse, Glenn Tilley 1870-1950 *WhoAmA 93N*
Morse, Hayward *WhoHol 92*
Morse, Helen *WhoHol 92*
Morse, J. Mitchell 1912- *WrDr 94*
Morse, Jack Hatton 1923- *WhoAm 94*
Morse, James Buckner 1930- *WhoAm 94*
Morse, James L. *WhoAmP 93*
Morse, James L. 1940- *WhoAm 94, WhoAmL 94*
Morse, Jedidiah 1761-1826 *DcAmReB 2, EncNAR*
Morse, Jeremy *IntWW 93, Who 94*
Morse, (Christopher) Jeremy 1928- *IntWW 93*
Morse, Joann T. 1919- *WhoAmP 93*
Morse, Joel Niles *WhoFI 94*
Morse, John E. *WhoBlA 94*
Morse, John Harleigh 1910- *WhoAm 94*
Morse, John Lougee 1932- *WhoAm 94*
Morse, John Moore 1911- *WhoAm 94*
Morse, Joseph Ervin 1940- *WhoBlA 94*
Morse, Judy Hamilton 1946- *WhoAmL 94*
Morse, Karen Williams 1940- *WhoAm 94, WhoWest 94*
Morse, Karl d1936 *WhoHol 92*
Morse, Kenneth Pratt 1905- *WhoAm 94*
Morse, Kingsley G. d1993 *NewYTBS 93*
Morse, L(arry) A(lan) 1945- *WrDr 94*
Morse, Lee d1954 *WhoHol 92*
Morse, Leon William 1912- *WhoAm 94, WhoFI 94, WhoMW 93*
Morse, Lowell Wesley 1937- *WhoWest 94*
Morse, Luis C. 1940- *WhoAmP 93, WhoHisp 94*
Morse, Marcia Roberts 1944- *WhoAmA 93*
Morse, Martin A. 1957- *WhoScEn 94*
Morse, Marvin Henry 1929- *WhoAm 94*
Morse, Maryanne 1944- *WhoWomW 91*
Morse, Maryanne H. 1944- *WhoAmP 93*
Morse, Michael David 1952- *WhoWest 94*
Morse, Mildred S. 1942- *WhoBlA 94*
Morse, Mitchell Ian 1926- *WhoAmA 93*
Morse, Oliver 1922- *WhoBlA 94*
Morse, Peter 1935- *WhoAmA 93*
Morse, Peter Hodges 1935- *WhoAm 94*
Morse, Philip Dexter, II 1944- *WhoScEn 94*
Morse, R. C. *DrAPF 93*
Morse, Richard 1922- *WhoAm 94*
Morse, Richard Alan 1954- *WhoFI 94*
Morse, Richard Jay 1933- *WhoAm 94, WhoFI 94, WhoWest 94*
Morse, Richard McGee 1922- *WhoAm 94, WrDr 94*
Morse, Robert 1931- *IntMPA 94, WhoHol 92*
Morse, Robert Alan 1931- *WhoAm 94*
Morse, Robert Warren 1921- *WhoAm 94*
Morse, Robin d1958 *WhoHol 92*
Morse, Rory *DrAPF 93*
Morse, Samuel Finley Breese 1791-1872 *WorInv [port]*
Morse, Saul Julian 1948- *WhoAmL 94, WhoMW 93*
Morse, Scott David 1950- *WhoWest 94*
Morse, Scott N. 1950- *WhoAmL 94*
Morse, Stephan A. 1947- *WhoAmP 93*
Morse, Stephen Scott 1951- *WhoScEn 94*
Morse, Steven 1957- *WhoAmP 93*
Morse, True Delbert 1896- *WhoAm 94*
Morse, Warren W. 1912- *WhoBlA 94*
Morsell, Fred *WhoHol 92*
Morsell, Frederick Albert 1940- *WhoBlA 94*
Morselli, Adriano fl. 1676- *NewGrDO*
Morselli, Guido *EncSF 93*
Morsellino, Joseph P. 1939- *WhoAmL 94*
Morse Riley, Barbara Lyn 1958- *WhoBlA 94*
Morshchakov, Fedor Mikhailovich *LngBDD*
Morshchakova, Tamara Georgievna 1936- *LngBDD*
Morshead, Richard Williams 1931- *WhoAm 94*
Morshed, Md Moqbul 1962- *WhoFI 94*
Morshower, Glenn *WhoHol 92*
Morson, Basil Clifford 1921- *Who 94*
Morson, Gary Saul 1948- *WhoMW 93*
Morstein, Jay I. 1946- *WhoAmL 94*
Morston, Gary Scott 1960- *WhoBlA 94*
Mort, Jo-Ann *DrAPF 93*
Mort, John Ernest Llewelyn 1915- *Who 94*
Mort, (Margaret) Marion 1937- *Who 94*
Mortari, Virgilio 1902- *NewGrDO*
Mortazawi, Amir 1962- *WhoScEn 94*
Mortel, Rodrigue 1933- *WhoBlA 94*
Mortellari, Michele c. 1750-1807 *NewGrDO*
Mortellito, Domenico 1906- *WhoAmA 93*
Mortensen, Arvid LeGrande 1941- *WhoAm 94, WhoFI 94*
Mortensen, Davis K. *WhoFI 94*
Mortensen, Eugene Phillips 1941- *WhoAm 94*
Mortensen, Gordon Louis 1938- *WhoAm 94, WhoAmA 93*
Mortensen, H. Grant *WhoAmP 93*
Mortensen, James Dean 1967- *WhoWest 94*
Mortensen, James E. 1925- *WhoAm 94*
Mortensen, James Michael 1937- *WhoIns 94*
Mortensen, Kenneth Peter 1955- *WhoScEn 94*
Mortensen, Kjeld 1925- *IntWW 93*
Mortensen, Mary Ellen 1951- *WhoMW 93*
Mortensen, Max Christian *WhoAmP 93*
Mortensen, Peter 1935- *WhoAm 94*
Mortensen, Philip Stephen 1947- *WhoAmL 94*
Mortensen, Richard Edgar 1935- *WhoScEn 94, WhoWest 94*
Mortensen, Robert Henry 1939- *WhoAm 94*
Mortensen, Stanley John 1949- *WhoMW 93*
Mortensen, Susan Marie 1950- *WhoWest 94*
Mortensen, Viggo *WhoHol 92*
Mortensen, William Henry 1903-1990 *WhAm 10*
Mortensen, William S. 1932- *WhoAm 94, WhoFI 94, WhoWest 94*
Mortenson, Thomas Theodore 1934- *WhoFI 94*
Mortham, Sandra Barringer 1951- *WhoAmP 93*
Mortier, Gerard 1943- *IntWW 93, NewGrDO*
Mortier, Roland F. J. 1920- *IntWW 93*
Mortimer, Angela 1932- *BuCMET*
Mortimer, Armine Kotin 1943- *ConAu 41NR*
Mortimer, Barry *Who 94*
Mortimer, (John) Barry 1931- *Who 94*
Mortimer, Caroline 1942- *WhoHol 92*
Mortimer, Charles d1964 *WhoHol 92*
Mortimer, Clifford Hiley 1911- *Who 94*
Mortimer, Delores M. *WhoBlA 94*
Mortimer, Dorothy d1950 *WhoHol 92*
Mortimer, Doyle M. 1954- *WhoAmP 93*
Mortimer, Doyle Moss 1954- *WhoWest 94*
Mortimer, Ed (Edmund) d1944 *WhoHol 92*
Mortimer, G. F. *WhoAmP 93*
Mortimer, Gerald James 1918- *Who 94*
Mortimer, Gregory Keith 1954- *WhoAmP 93*
Mortimer, Henry d1952 *WhoHol 92*
Mortimer, Henry Tilford, Jr. 1942- *WhoAm 94*
Mortimer, J. Thomas 1939- *WhoAm 94, WhoMW 93, WhoScEn 94*
Mortimer, James Edward 1921- *IntWW 93, Who 94, WrDr 94*
Mortimer, James Edward 1947- *Who 94*
Mortimer, James Winslow 1955- *WhoScEn 94*
Mortimer, John (Clifford) 1923- *ConDr 93, IntDcT 2, Who 94, WrDr 94*
Mortimer, John Clifford 1923- *IntWW 93*
Mortimer, John Robert 1825-1911 *DcNaB MP*
Mortimer, Katharine Mary Hope 1946- *Who 94*
Mortimer, Kenneth P. *WhoWest 94*
Mortimer, Penelope 1918- *BlmGWL*
Mortimer, Penelope (Ruth) 1918- *Who 94, WrDr 94*
Mortimer, Penelope Ruth 1918- *IntWW 93*
Mortimer, Peter M. 1943- *WhoAm 94*
Mortimer, Ruth 1931- *WhoAm 94*
Mortimer, Wendell Reed, Jr. 1937- *WhoAm 94, WhoWest 94*
Mortimer, William James 1932- *WhoAm 94, WhoWest 94*
Mortimore, Peter John 1942- *Who 94*
Mortimore, Simon Anthony 1950- *Who 94*
Mortlock, Herbert Norman 1926- *Who 94*
Mortlock, Robert Paul 1931- *WhoAm 94, WhoScEn 94*
Mortmain, J. D. 1936- *WrDr 94*
Mortola, Edward Joseph 1917- *WhoAm 94*
Morton *Who 94*
Morton, Earl of 1927- *Who 94*
Morton, Alastair *IntWW 93, Who 94*
Morton, (Robert) Alastair 1938- *IntWW 93*
Morton, (Robert) Alastair (Newton) 1938- *Who 94*
Morton, Albert G. 1931- *WhoAmP 93*
Morton, Allan Harvey 1946- *WhoMW 93*
Morton, Andrew 1953- *ConAu 141*
Morton, Andrew Queen 1919- *Who 94*
Morton, Anthony (Storrs) 1923- *Who 94*
Morton, Arthur 1908- *IntMPA 94*
Morton, Arthur 1915- *Who 94*
Morton, Bernard Walter 1929- *WhoMW 93*
Morton, Bernice Finley 1923- *WhoMW 93*
Morton, Brenda *WrDr 94*
Morton, Bridget Balthrop *DrAPF 93*
Morton, Bruce Rutherfurd 1926- *WrDr 94*
Morton, Carlos *DrAPF 93*
Morton, Carlos 1947- *WhoHisp 94*
Morton, Charles Brinkley 1926- *WhoAm 94, WhoWest 94*
Morton, Charles E. 1926- *WhoBlA 94*
Morton, Chesley Venable, Jr. 1951- *WhoAmP 93*
Morton, Clive d1975 *WhoHol 92*
Morton, Craig Richard 1942- *WhoMW 93*
Morton, Crichton Charles 1912- *Who 94*
Morton, Cynthia Neverdon 1944- *WhoBlA 94*
Morton, David 1929- *IntWW 93, WhoAm 94, WhoFI 94*
Morton, David Christopher 1943- *Who 94*
Morton, David Ray 1948- *WhoFI 94*
Morton, Deborah Burwell 1953- *WhoAmL 94*
Morton, Don Townley 1933- *WhoWest 94*
Morton, Donald Charles 1933- *IntWW 93, WhoAm 94, WhoScEn 94*
Morton, Donald John 1931- *WhoAm 94*
Morton, Edward James 1926- *WhoAm 94*
Morton, Ferdinand 1890-1941 *AfrAmAl 6 [port]*
Morton, Frank 1906- *Who 94*
Morton, Frederic 1924- *ConAu 43NR, WhoAm 94*
Morton, Garnett Fry 1947- *WhoAmP 93*
Morton, Gary 1917- *WhoHol 92*
Morton, George Martin 1940- *Who 94*
Morton, Gregory d1986 *WhoHol 92*
Morton, Hank d1963 *WhoHol 92*
Morton, Harold Coleman 1895- *WhAm 10*
Morton, Harold Sylvanus, Jr. 1924- *WhoScEn 94*
Morton, Harry B. *WhoAmP 93*
Morton, Harvey Leon 1941- *WhoAmP 93*
Morton, Henry W 1929- *WrDr 94*
Morton, Herbert Charles 1921- *WhoAm 94*
Morton, Herwald Hutchins 1931- *WhoAm 94*
Morton, Hugh *WhoHol 92*
Morton, Hughes Gregory 1923- *WhoFI 94, WhoWest 94*
Morton, J(ohn Cameron Audrieu) B(ingham Michael) 1893-1979 *EncSF 93*
Morton, James (Severs) 1938- *WrDr 94*
Morton, James A. 1929- *WhoBlA 94*
Morton, James C. d1942 *WhoHol 92*
Morton, James Davis 1928- *WhoAm 94*
Morton, James Irwin 1935- *WhoAm 94*
Morton, Jay Robert 1914- *WhAm 10*
Morton, Jeffrey Bruce 1941- *WhoAm 94*
Morton, Jelly Roll 1885-1941 *AmCulL [port]*
Morton, Joe 1947- *IntMPA 94, WhoBlA 94, WhoHol 92*
Morton, John 1724-1777 *WhAmRev*
Morton, John, Jr. 1967- *WhoBlA 94*
Morton, John, III 1943- *WhoAm 94, WhoFI 94*
Morton, John Duggan, Sr. 1937- *WhoAmP 93*
Morton, John H. 1923- *WhoAm 94*
Morton, John Hall 1940- *WhoAm 94*
Morton, Kathryn Mary Stuart 1946- *Who 94*
Morton, Keith William 1930- *Who 94*
Morton, Kenneth Valentine Freeland 1907- *Who 94*
Morton, Leland Clure 1916- *WhoAm 94, WhoAmL 94*
Morton, Linda 1944- *WhoAm 94, WhoWest 94*
Morton, Lorraine H. *WhoBlA 94*
Morton, Margaret E. 1924- *WhoBlA 94*
Morton, Margaret E. Woods 1924- *WhoAmP 93*
Morton, Marie Etta 1926- *WhoAmP 93*
Morton, Marilyn M. 1946- *WhoBlA 94*
Morton, Marilyn Miller 1929- *WhoAm 94*
Morton, Mark Edward 1956- *WhoFI 94*
Morton, Marshall Nay 1945- *WhoAm 94, WhoFI 94*
Morton, Michael Ray 1952- *WhoFI 94*
Morton, Mickey *WhoHol 92*
Morton, Norman 1938- *WhoBlA 94*
Morton, Patricia Ann *Who 94*
Morton, Patsy Jennings 1951- *WhoBlA 94*
Morton, Ree 1936-1977 *WhoAmA 93N*
Morton, Richard Albert Dunlap 1932- *WhoFI 94*
Morton, Richard Everett 1930- *WrDr 94*
Morton, Richard G. 1918- *WhoAmP 93*
Morton, Richard H. 1921- *WhoAmA 93*
Morton, Robert Alan 1934- *WhoAmA 93*
Morton, Robert Allen 1954- *WhoFI 94*
Morton, Robert Steel 1917- *WrDr 94*
Morton, Roy Jay 1897- *WhAm 10*
Morton, Russell H. 1939- *WhoAmL 94*
Morton, Sarah Wentworth Apthorp 1759-1846 *BlmGWL*
Morton, Stephen Dana 1932- *WhoMW 93, WhoScEn 94*
Morton, Terry Wayne 1957- *WhoScEn 94*
Morton, Tex d1983 *WhoHol 92*
Morton, Thomas Hellman 1947- *WhoWest 94*
Morton, Thomas Jackson 1955- *WhoAmL 94*
Morton, Walter Graydon 1946- *WhoWest 94*
Morton, Warren Allen 1924- *WhoAmP 93*
Morton, William *WorScD*
Morton, William (David) 1926- *Who 94*
Morton, William Burton 1961- *WhoFI 94*
Morton, William Edwards 1929- *WhoWest 94*
Morton, William Gilbert 1906- *WhoAm 94*
Morton, William Gilbert, Jr. 1937- *WhoAm 94, WhoFI 94*
Morton, William Stanley 1947- *WhoBlA 94*
Morton Boyd, John *Who 94*
Morton Jack, David 1935- *Who 94*
Morton of Shuna, Baron 1930- *Who 94*
Morton-Saner, Robert 1911- *Who 94*
Mortonson, Christopher Albert 1952- *WhoMW 93*
Mortus, Cynthia A. *DrAPF 93*
Mortvedt, John Jacob 1932- *WhoAm 94*
Moruedi *BlmGWL*
Morvan, Roger Georges d1993 *NewYTBS 93*
Morwick, Carolyn Hammond 1942- *WhoAmP 93*
Mory, Douglas Clayton 1943- *WhoMW 93*
Moryan, Jeffrey W. 1954- *WhoAmL 94*
Mosak, Barbara Marcia 1950- *WhoMW 93*
Mosakowski, Kenneth Robert 1946- *WhoAmP 93*
Mosander, Carl Gustaf 1797-1858 *WorScD*
Mosar, Nicolas 1927- *Who 94*
Mosbacher, Emil, Jr. 1922- *IntWW 93, WhoAmP 93*
Mosbacher, Georgette c. 1947- *News 94-2 [port]*
Mosbacher, Martin Bruce 1951- *WhoAm 94, WhoFI 94*
Mosbacher, Peter d1977 *WhoHol 92*
Mosbacher, Robert A., Sr. 1927- *WhoAmP 93*
Mosbacher, Robert A., Jr. 1951- *WhoAmP 93*
Mosbacher, Robert Adam 1927- *IntWW 93, WhoAm 94*
Mosbaek, Craig Hall 1961- *WhoWest 94*
Mosbakk, Kurt 1934- *IntWW 93*
Mosby, Aline 1922- *WrDr 94*
Mosby, Carolyn Lewis 1937- *WhoBlA 94*
Mosby, Dewey Franklin 1942- *WhoAmA 93*
Mosby, Dorothea Susan 1948- *WhoWest 94*
Mosby, John Davenport, III 1956- *WhoAm 94, WhoFI 94*
Mosby, John Singleton, Jr. 1950- *WhoMW 93*
Mosby, Nathaniel 1929- *WhoBlA 94*
Mosby, William Harry 1898-1964 *WhoAmA 93N*
Mosca, August 1907- *WhoAmA 93*
Mosca, Giuseppe 1772-1839 *NewGrDO*
Mosca, Luigi 1775-1824 *NewGrDO*
Mosca, Ugo *IntWW 93N*
Moscarino, George J. 1934- *WhoAm 94*
Moscato, Anthony Charles 1945- *WhoAm 94, WhoAmL 94*
Moscato, Nicholas, Jr. 1942- *WhoAm 94, WhoFI 94*
Moscatt, Paul N. 1931- *WhoAmA 93*
Moschella, Samuel L. 1921- *WhoAm 94*
Mosches, Julio Cesar 1912- *WhoHisp 94*
Moschin, Gastone 1929- *WhoHol 92*
Moschin, Susan Kamin 1945- *WhoMW 93*
Moschine fl. 4th cent.BC- *BlmGWL*
Moschos, Demitrios Mina 1941- *WhoAmL 94*
Moscona, Aron Arthur 1922- *WhoAm 94*
Moscona, Jodi Anthony 1953- *WhoAmP 93*
Moscona, Nicola 1907-1975 *NewGrDO*
Mosconi, Willie 1913-1993 *CurBio 93N, NewYTBS 93 [port]*
Moscoso, Eloy 1935- *WhoHisp 94*
Moscoso, Luis De fl. 153-?-154-? *WhWE*
Moscoso, Pedro Fermin 1928- *WhoHisp 94*
Moscoso Del Prado Y Munoz, Javier 1934- *IntWW 93*
Moscovitch, Maurice d1940 *WhoHol 92*
Moscow, David 1975- *WhoHol 92*

Moscow, Warren 1908-1992 *WhAm 10*
Moscowitz, Albert Joseph 1929- *WhoAm 94, WhoScEn 94*
Moscowitz, Jennie d1953 *WhoHol 92*
Mosdell, Lionel Patrick 1912- *Who 94*
Mose, Carl C. 1903-1973 *WhoAmA 93N*
Mosebar, Donald Howard 1961- *WhoAm 94, WhoBlA 94, WhoWest 94*
Moseby, Lloyd Anthony 1959- *WhoBlA 94*
Mosee, Jean C. 1927- *WhoBlA 94*
Moseka, Aminata *WhoBlA 94*
Mosel, Darrel *WhoAmP 93*
Mosel, Ignaz Franz von 1772-1844 *NewGrDO*
Mosel, Tad 1922- *ConDr 93, WrDr 94*
Moseley, Barbara M. 1938- *WhoBlA 94*
Moseley, Bill *WhoHol 92*
Moseley, Calvin Edwin, Jr. 1906- *WhoBlA 94*
Moseley, Carlos DuPre 1914- *WhoAm 94*
Moseley, Chris Rosser 1950- *WhoAm 94*
Moseley, David Barton, Jr. 1946- *WhoAmL 94*
Moseley, Edward H(olt) 1931- *WrDr 94*
Moseley, Elwyn Rhys 1943- *Who 94*
Moseley, Frances Kenney 1949- *WhoBlA 94*
Moseley, Frank S. 1942- *WhoAmL 94*
Moseley, Frederick Strong, III 1928- *WhoAm 94, WhoFI 94*
Moseley, George (Walker) 1925- *Who 94*
Moseley, Henry Gwyn Jeffreys 1887-1915 *WorScD*
Moseley, (Thomas) Hywel 1936- *Who 94*
Moseley, Jack Edwin 1936- *WhoAm 94*
Moseley, James Francis 1936- *WhoAm 94, WhoAmL 94, WhoFI 94*
Moseley, James Orville B. 1909- *WhoBlA 94*
Moseley, James R. 1948- *WhoAmP 93*
Moseley, Jerry Lynn 1957- *WhoAmP 93*
Moseley, Joe *WhoAmP 93*
Moseley, Joe Lynn 1949- *WhoMW 93*
Moseley, John Marshall 1911- *WhoScEn 94*
Moseley, Marc Robards 1954- *WhoFI 94*
Moseley, Mark DeWayne 1948- *WhoAm 94*
Moseley, Martin Edward 1930- *WhoAmP 93*
Moseley, Phillip Duane 1946- *WhoAmP 93*
Moseley, Roger Lester 1949- *WhoIns 94*
Moseley, Vickie Marie 1956- *WhoAmP 93*
Moseley, William *DrAPF 93*
Moseley-Braun, Carol 1947- *CngDr 93, WhoAm 94, WhoMW 93*
Moseley Braun, Carol Elizabeth 1947- *WhoBlA 94*
Moselsio, Simon 1890- *WhoAmA 93N*
Mosely, Jack Meredith 1917- *WhoWest 94*
Mosely, John de Sola 1933- *WhoWest 94*
Mosely, Kenneth *WhoBlA 94*
Mosely, Linda Hays 1941- *WhoAm 94*
Moseman, Mildred Mae 1917- *WhoMW 93*
Mosemann, Lloyd Kenneth, II 1936- *WhoAm 94*
Mosenthal, Charlotte Dembo *WhoAmA 93*
Mosenthal, Salomon Hermann, Ritter von 1821-1877 *NewGrDO*
Moser, Alicia Kay 1969- *WhoMW 93*
Moser, Barbara Walsh 1958- *WhoAmL 94*
Moser, Barry 1940- *WhoAmA 93*
Moser, C. Thomas 1947- *WhoAmL 94*
Moser, Claus (Adolf) 1922- *Who 94*
Moser, Claus Adolf 1922- *IntWW 93*
Moser, Dean Joseph 1942- *WhoWest 94*
Moser, Donald Bruce 1932- *WhoAm 94*
Moser, Edda (Elisabeth) 1938- *NewGrDO*
Moser, Elizabeth Marie 1957- *WhoAmL 94*
Moser, Frank H. 1886-1964 *WhoAmA 93N*
Moser, Frank Hans 1907- *WhoMW 93*
Moser, Gregg Anthony 1954- *WhoMW 93*
Moser, Hans d1964 *WhoHol 92*
Moser, Harold Dean 1938- *WhoAm 94*
Moser, Hugo Wolfgang 1924- *WhoAm 94*
Moser, Jane Webb 1950- *WhoWest 94*
Moser, Joann *WhoAmA 93*
Moser, Joann Gail 1948- *WhoAm 94*
Moser, John Richard 1927- *WhoAmP 93*
Moser, Jurgen K. 1928- *IntWW 93*
Moser, Kenneth Allen 1942- *WhoAmL 94*
Moser, Kenneth Miles 1929- *WhoAm 94, WhoScEn 94*
Moser, Larry Edward 1952- *WhoFI 94*
Moser, Margot 1930- *WhoHol 92*
Moser, Martin Peter 1928- *WhoAm 94, WhoAmL 94*
Moser, Marvin 1924- *WhoAm 94*
Moser, Michael Matthew 1953- *WhoAm 94*
Moser, Milton John 1942- *WhoFI 94*
Moser, Norman *DrAPF 93*
Moser, Paul 1895- *WhAm 10*
Moser, Paul Kenneth 1957- *WhoMW 93*
Moser, Raymond 1931- *WhoAmP 93*
Moser, Robert Harlan 1923- *WhoAm 94, WhoWest 94*
Moser, Royce, Jr. 1935- *WhoAm 94, WhoScEn 94, WhoWest 94*
Moser, Suzan Anne 1959- *WhoWest 94*
Moser, Thomas 1945- *NewGrDO*
Moser, William Oscar Jules 1927- *WhoAm 94*
Moserova, Jaroslava 1930- *WhoWomW 91*
Moses 1525BC-1405BC *HisWorL [port]*
Moses, Abe Joseph 1931- *WhoAm 94*
Moses, Alan George 1945- *Who 94*
Moses, Albert 1937- *WhoHol 92*
Moses, Alfred Henry 1929- *WhoAm 94, WhoAmL 94*
Moses, Alice J. 1929- *WhoBlA 94*
Moses, Andrew M. 1926- *WhoBlA 94*
Moses, Anna Mary Robertson 1860-1961 *WhoAmA 93N*
Moses, Beth Herman 1955- *WhoFI 94*
Moses, Bette J. *WhoAmA 93*
Moses, Bob *NewYTBS 93 [port]*
Moses, Carl 1929- *WhoAmP 93*
Moses, Charles Alexander 1923- *IntMPA 94*
Moses, Charles T. 1952- *WhoBlA 94*
Moses, Claire Goldberg 1941- *ConAu 43NR*
Moses, David *WhoHol 92*
Moses, Ed 1926- *WhoAmA 93*
Moses, Edward Crosby *WhoAm 94*
Moses, Edwin *DrAPF 93*
Moses, Edwin 1955- *IntWW 93, WhoAm 94, WhoBlA 94, WhoWest 94*
Moses, Elbert Raymond, Jr. 1908- *WhoScEn 94, WhoWest 94, WrDr 94*
Moses, Eric George Rufus 1914- *Who 94*
Moses, Forrest (Lee), Jr. 1934- *WhoAmA 93*
Moses, Forrest King 1893-1974 *WhoAmA 93N*
Moses, Franklin Maxwell 1918- *WhoAm 94*
Moses, Gilbert 1942- *IntMPA 94, WhoAm 94*
Moses, Gilbert, III 1942- *WhoBlA 94*
Moses, Grandma d1961 *WhoHol 92*
Moses, Gregory Allen 1950- *WhoScEn 94*
Moses, Gregory Hayes, Jr. 1933- *WhoAm 94*
Moses, Hamilton, III 1950- *WhoScEn 94*
Moses, Harold Webster 1949- *WhoBlA 94*
Moses, Henry A. 1939- *WhoBlA 94*
Moses, Irving Byron 1925- *WhoAm 94*
Moses, Joel 1941- *WhoAm 94*
Moses, John Henry 1938- *Who 94*
Moses, Johnnie, Jr. 1939- *WhoBlA 94, WhoScEn 94*
Moses, Kenneth d1992 *Who 94N*
Moses, Lincoln E. 1921- *WhoAm 94*
Moses, Lincoln Ellsworth 1921- *IntWW 93*
Moses, MacDonald 1936- *WhoBlA 94*
Moses, Marion *WhoHol 92*
Moses, Mark *WhoHol 92*
Moses, Michael Howard 1940- *WhoIns 94*
Moses, Michael James 1956- *WhoFI 94*
Moses, Milton E. 1939- *WhoBlA 94*
Moses, Paul Davis 1938- *WhoAm 94*
Moses, Raphael Jacob 1913- *WhoAm 94*
Moses, Rick *WhoHol 92*
Moses, Robert 1888-1981 *AmSocL*
Moses, Robert 1935- *HisWorL*
Moses, Robert Davis 1919- *WhoAm 94*
Moses, Robert Edward 1936- *WhoAm 94*
Moses, Robert Jeffrey 1955- *WhoAmL 94*
Moses, Ronald Elliot 1930- *WhoAm 94*
Moses, Scott 1952- *WhoFI 94*
Moses, W. R. *DrAPF 93*
Moses, Walter 1898- *WhAm 10*
Moses, William R. 1959- *WhoHol 92*
Moses, Wilson Jeremiah 1942- *WhoBlA 94*
Moses, Winfield C., Jr. 1943- *WhoAmP 93, WhoMW 93*
Moses, Yolanda *WhoBlA 94*
Mosettig, Michael David 1942- *WhoAm 94*
Moshanu, Aleksandru 1932- *IntWW 93*
Mosheim, Grete d1986 *WhoHol 92*
Mo Shen 1951- *WhoPRCh 91 [port]*
Mosher, Alan Dale 1963- *WhoScEn 94*
Mosher, Anne Therese 1951- *WhoMW 93*
Mosher, Donald Joseph 1935- *WhoAmP 93*
Mosher, Donald Raymond 1930- *WhoScEn 94*
Mosher, Frederick Camp 1913-1990 *WhAm 10*
Mosher, Frederick Kenneth 1943- *WhoScEn 94*
Mosher, George Allan 1939- *WhoAm 94*
Mosher, Geraldine Louise 1939- *WhoWest 94*
Mosher, Gregory Dean 1949- *IntWW 93, WhoAm 94*
Mosher, Harry Stone 1915- *WhoScEn 94*
Mosher, Lawrence Forsyth 1929- *WhoAm 94*
Mosher, Loren Cameron 1938- *WhoWest 94*
Mosher, Michael Raymond 1955- *WhoWest 94*
Mosher, Paul H. 1936- *WhoAm 94*
Mosher, Ruth Suzanne 1945- *WhoMW 93*
Mosher, Sally Ekenberg 1934- *WhoAmL 94, WhoWest 94*
Mosher, Sol 1928- *WhoAmP 93*
Mosher, Steven Westley 1948- *WhoWest 94*
Moshier, Juanita Chavez 1955- *WhoMW 93*
Moshier, Terry Allen 1936- *WhoAmP 93*
Moshinsky, Elijah 1946- *IntWW 93, NewGrDO, Who 94*
Moshiri, Farrokh 1961- *ConAu 142*
Moshman, David Stewart 1951- *WhoMW 93*
Moshman, Jack 1924- *WhoAm 94*
Moshoeshoe, II 1938- *IntWW 93*
Mosich, Anelis Nick 1928- *WhoAm 94*
Mosick, Marian Perry d1973 *WhoHol 92*
Mosier, Frank Eugene 1930- *IntWW 93*
Mosier, Harry David, Jr. 1925- *WhoAm 94*
Mosier, Jacob Eugene 1924- *WhoAm 94*
Mosier, Stephen Russell 1942- *WhoScEn 94*
Mosimann, Anton 1947- *ConAu 141, IntWW 93, Who 94*
Mosinyi, Ester *WhoWomW 91*
Mosjidis, Cecilia O'Hara 1960- *WhoScEn 94*
Mosjoukine, Ivan d1939 *WhoHol 92*
Mosk, Richard Mitchell 1939- *WhoAm 94, WhoAmL 94*
Mosk, Stanley 1912- *WhoAm 94, WhoAmL 94, WhoAmP 93, WhoWest 94*
Moskal, Joseph Russell 1950- *WhoScEn 94*
Moskal, Robert M. 1937- *WhoAm 94, WhoMW 93*
Moskalski, Elton Alfred 1939- *WhoWest 94*
Moskin, John Robert 1923- *WhoAm 94*
Moskin, Morton 1927- *WhoAm 94*
Moskos, Charles C. 1934- *WhoAm 94*
Moskovchenko, Nikolai Mikhailovich 1954- *LngBDD*
Moskovitz, Irving 1912- *WhoAm 94*
Moskovitz, Ronald B. 1943- *WhoAmL 94*
Moskovitz, Stuart Jeffrey 1949- *WhoAmL 94*
Moskow, Michael H. 1938- *WhoAm 94, WrDr 94*
Moskowitz, Arnold X. 1944- *WhoAm 94*
Moskowitz, Bette Ann *DrAPF 93*
Moskowitz, David Alexander 1959- *WhoWest 94*
Moskowitz, Faye *DrAPF 93*
Moskowitz, Herbert 1935- *WhoAm 94*
Moskowitz, Ira 1912- *WhoAmA 93*
Moskowitz, Ivan William 1945- *WhoAmL 94*
Moskowitz, Jay 1943- *WhoAm 94*
Moskowitz, Joel Steven 1947- *WhoAm 94*
Moskowitz, Richard 1938- *WhoScEn 94*
Moskowitz, Richard Scott 1964- *WhoAmL 94*
Moskowitz, Robert S. 1935- *WhoAmA 93*
Moskowitz, Ronald 1939- *WhoScEn 94*
Moskowitz, Sam 1920- *EncSF 93, WhoAm 94*
Moskowitz, Shirley 1920- *WhoAmA 93*
Moskowitz, Stanley Alan 1956- *WhoFI 94*
Moskowitz, Stuart Stanley 1955- *WhoAmL 94*
Moskowsky, Moritz *NewGrDO*
Moskus, Jerry Ray 1942- *WhoWest 94*
Moskvin, Andrei 1901-1961 *IntDcF 2-4 [port]*
Mosler, Hermann 1912- *IntWW 93*
Mosler, John 1922- *WhoAm 94*
Mosley *Who 94*
Mosley, Bryan 1931- *WhoHol 92*
Mosley, Carolyn W. 1952- *WhoBlA 94*
Mosley, Christopher D. 1960- *WhoBlA 94*
Mosley, Edna Wilson 1925- *WhoBlA 94*
Mosley, Edward R. *WhoBlA 94*
Mosley, Elwood A. 1943- *WhoBlA 94*
Mosley, Eugene Lyter 1942- *WhoAmP 93*
Mosley, George Hinson 1932- *WhoAmP 93*
Mosley, Geraldine B. 1920- *WhoBlA 94*
Mosley, John William *WhoBlA 94*
Mosley, Lawrence Edward, Sr. 1953- *WhoBlA 94*
Mosley, Leonard 1913- *WrDr 94*
Mosley, Marie Oleatha 1941- *WhoBlA 94*
Mosley, Maurice B. 1946- *WhoAmP 93, WhoBlA 94*
Mosley, Max Rufus 1940- *IntWW 93*
Mosley, Nicholas *IntWW 93, Who 94*
Mosley, Nicholas 1923- *ConAu 41NR, WrDr 94*
Mosley, Philip 1947- *WrDr 94*
Mosley, Roger E. *IntMPA 94, WhoHol 92*
Mosley, Steven 1952- *WrDr 94*
Mosley, Tracey Ray 1960- *WhoBlA 94*
Mosley, Walter *WhoBlA 94*
Mosley, Walter 1952- *BlkWr 2, ConAu 142, ConBlB 5 [port]*
Mosley, Weldon V. 1924- *WhoIns 94*
Mosley, Zack d1993 *NewYTBS 93*
Mosley, Zack T. 1906- *WhoAmA 93*
Mosley, Zack Terrell 1906- *WhoAm 94*
Mosolov, Alexander Vasil'yevich 1900-1973 *NewGrDO*
Mosonyi, Mihaly 1815-1870 *NewGrDO*
Mosqueda, Joe J. 1954- *WhoHisp 94*
Mosqueira, Charlotte Marianne 1937- *WhoWest 94*
Mosquini, Marie d1983 *WhoHol 92*
Moss, Alfred A., Jr. 1943- *WhoBlA 94*
Moss, Ambler Holmes, Jr. 1937- *WhoAm 94, WhoAmP 93*
Moss, Anni R. *WhoBlA 94*
Moss, Arnold d1989 *WhoHol 92*
Moss, Arnold 1910-1989 *WhAm 10*
Moss, Arthur Henshey 1930- *WhoAm 94*
Moss, Barbara 1946- *WrDr 94*
Moss, Basil Geoffrey d1935 *WhoHol 92*
Moss, Basil Stanley 1918- *Who 94*
Moss, Bernard 1937- *WhoAm 94, WhoScEn 94*
Moss, Bill Ralph 1950- *WhoAmL 94, WhoFI 94*
Moss, Bradley Allen 1969- *WhoMW 93*
Moss, Charles 1938- *WhoAm 94, WhoFI 94*
Moss, Charles James 1917- *Who 94*
Moss, Charles Joseph, III 1953- *WhoMW 93*
Moss, Charles Norman 1914- *WhoScEn 94, WhoWest 94*
Moss, Cruse Watson 1926- *WhoAm 94*
Moss, Cynthia 1940- *CurBio 93 [port]*
Moss, Cynthia J(ane) 1940- *WrDr 94*
Moss, Daniel Calvin, Jr. 1933-1983 *WhoBlA 94N*
Moss, David Christopher 1946- *Who 94*
Moss, David John E. *Who 94*
Moss, David Joseph 1938- *IntWW 93, Who 94*
Moss, Debra Lee 1952- *WhoWest 94*
Moss, Donna Anderson 1954- *WhoAmP 93*
Moss, Douglas Mabbett 1954- *WhoWest 94*
Moss, Edward Herbert St. George 1918- *Who 94*
Moss, Elaine Dora 1924- *Who 94*
Moss, Estella Mae 1928- *WhoBlA 94*
Moss, Frank Edward 1911- *WhoAmP 93*
Moss, Frank L. 1913- *IntMPA 94*
Moss, Gabriel Stephen 1949- *Who 94*
Moss, Gary Curtis 1944- *WhoAm 94*
Moss, Gaylin d1979 *WhoHol 92*
Moss, Guy B. 1944- *WhoAm 94, WhoAmL 94*
Moss, Harry Mark 1919- *WhoAmP 93*
Moss, Harvey 1951- *WhoAmP 93*
Moss, Herbert Irwin 1932- *WhoScEn 94*
Moss, Irene *WhoAmA 93*
Moss, Irwin *IntMPA 94*
Moss, Jacqueline *WhoAmA 93*
Moss, James A. 1949- *WhoAmL 94*
Moss, James B., Jr. 1924- *WhoAmP 93*
Moss, James Edward 1949- *WhoBlA 94*
Moss, James R. *WhoAmP 93*
Moss, James Richard Frederick 1916- *Who 94*
Moss, James Taylor 1947- *WhoAm 94*
Moss, Jane Hope *Who 94*
Moss, Jeff *NewYTBS 93 [port]*
Moss, Jeff(rey) *ConAu 140*
Moss, Joe (Francis) 1933- *WhoAmA 93*
Moss, Joe Albaugh 1925- *WhoAm 94*
Moss, Joe Francis 1933- *WhoAm 94*
Moss, Joel 1946- *WhoScEn 94*
Moss, John Emerson 1915- *WhoAm 94*
Moss, John Ringer 1920- *Who 94*
Moss, Joseph S., Jr. 1898- *WhAm 10*
Moss, Karen Canner 1944- *WhoAmA 93*
Moss, Kenneth Wayne 1950- *WhoScEn 94*
Moss, Larry W. 1946- *WhoMW 93*
Moss, Lawrence Craig 1952- *WhoAmL 94*
Moss, Lawrence Kenneth 1927- *WhoAm 94*
Moss, Leonard Godfrey 1932- *Who 94*
Moss, Leslie Otha 1952- *WhoAm 94, WhoFI 94, WhoMW 93*
Moss, Lynda Bourque 1950- *WhoWest 94*
Moss, Maitland d1967 *WhoHol 92*
Moss, Malcolm Douglas 1943- *Who 94*
Moss, Martin Grenville 1923- *Who 94*
Moss, Marvin 1929- *WhoWest 94*
Moss, Michael *Who 94*
Moss, Michael 1943- *WhoFI 94*

Moss, (John) Michael 1936- *Who 94*
Moss, Michael Eric 1947- *WhoAm 94*
Moss, Miriam 1955- *SmATA 76 [port]*
Moss, Myra E. 1937- *WhoWest 94*
Moss, Nancy 1903- *WrDr 94*
Moss, Norman J. *Who 94*
Moss, Otis, Jr. 1935- *WhoBlA 94*
Moss, (Victor) Peter (Cannings) 1921- *WrDr 94*
Moss, Randy Hays 1953- *WhoMW 93*
Moss, Richard L. 1947- *WhoMW 93*
Moss, Robert 1903- *WrDr 94*
Moss, Robert C., Jr. 1939- *WhoBlA 94*
Moss, Robert Drexler 1909- *WhoAm 94*
Moss, Robert Earl 1940- *WhoAmP 93*
Moss, Robert Wayne 1938- *WhoFI 94*
Moss, Roberta 1903- *WrDr 94*
Moss, Roger William, Jr. 1940- *WhoAm 94*
Moss, Ronald Jay 1930- *WhoAm 94*
Moss, Ronald Trevor 1942- *Who 94*
Moss, Ronn *WhoHol 92*
Moss, Rose *DrAPF 93*
Moss, Rose 1937- *WrDr 94*
Moss, Roy Oran, Jr. 1937- *WhoAmL 94*
Moss, Sandra Hughes 1945- *WhoAmL 94*
Moss, Scott Francis 1954- *WhoFI 94*
Moss, Simeon F. 1920- *WhoBlA 94*
Moss, Simon Charles 1934- *WhoScEn 94*
Moss, Stanley *DrAPF 93*
Moss, Stanley 1935- *WhoAm 94, WrDr 94*
Moss, Stephen B. 1943- *WhoAm 94, WhoAmL 94*
Moss, Stephen Edward 1940- *WhoAmL 94*
Moss, Stewart 1938- *WhoHol 92*
Moss, Stirling 1929- *IntWW 93, Who 94, WrDr 94*
Moss, Sylvia *DrAPF 93*
Moss, Tanya Jill 1958- *WhoBlA 94*
Moss, Thomas Edward, Sr. 1934- *WhoBlA 94*
Moss, Thomas Henry 1939- *WhoAm 94, WhoAmP 93*
Moss, Thomas Warren, Jr. 1928- *WhoAm 94, WhoAmP 93*
Moss, Tobey C. 1928- *WhoAmA 93*
Moss, Trevor Simpson 1921- *Who 94*
Moss, Truett W. 1930- *WhoAmP 93*
Moss, Victoria Biedebach 1964- *WhoAmL 94*
Moss, Warwick *WhoHol 92*
Moss, Wayne B. 1960- *WhoBlA 94*
Moss, William John 1921- *WhoAm 94*
Moss, Wilmar Burnett, Jr. 1928- *WhoBlA 94*
Moss, Winston *WhoBlA 94*
Mossakowski, Miroslaw 1929- *IntWW 93*
Mossavar-Rahmani, Bijan 1952- *WhoFI 94, WhoScEn 94*
Mossawir, Harve H., Jr. 1942- *WhoAm 94, WhoAmL 94*
Mossbauer, Rudolf 1929- *IntWW 93*
Mossbauer, Rudolf L. 1929- *Who 94*
Mossbauer, Rudolf Ludwig *WorScD*
Mossbauer, Rudolf Ludwig 1929- *WhoScEn 94*
Mossbrucker, Tom *WhoAm 94*
Mosse, George L. 1918- *WhoAm 94, WrDr 94*
Mosse, Peter John Charles 1947- *WhoAm 94, WhoFI 94*
Mosselmans, Carel Maurits 1929- *Who 94*
Mosselmans, Jean-Marc 1963- *WhoScEn 94*
Mosser, Frederick William 1945- *WhoAm 94*
Mosser, Hans Matthias 1955- *WhoScEn 94*
Mosser, Terri Barziza 1958- *WhoAmL 94*
Mosser, Thomas Joseph 1944- *WhoAm 94, WhoFI 94*
Mossiman, Ary 1925- *WhoFI 94*
Mossinghoff, Gerald Joseph 1935- *WhoAm 94, WhoAmL 94, WhoAmP 93*
Mossman, Albert Pruitt 1937- *WhoWest 94*
Mossman, Robert Gillis, IV 1960- *WhoMW 93*
Mossman, Stuart Alan 1931- *WhoAm 94*
Mossman, Thomas Mellish, Jr. 1938- *WhoAm 94*
Mossner, Joachim 1950- *WhoScEn 94*
Mosso, David 1926- *WhoAm 94*
Mossoff, Jeffrey 1948- *WhoWest 94*
Moss-Vreeland, Patricia 1951- *WhoAmA 93*
Most, Donald 1953- *WhoHol 92*
Most, Jack Lawrence 1935- *WhoAmL 94*
Most, Johnny d1993 *NewYTBS 93*
Most, Nathan 1914- *WhoAm 94*
Most, Robert Bernard 1952- *WhoWest 94*
Mostafapour, M. Kazem 1937- *WhoMW 93*
Mostart, August Egbert Laurent Marie 1951- *WhoAm 94*
Mostel, Josh 1946- *IntMPA 94, WhoHol 92*
Mostel, Zero d1977 *WhoHol 92*
Mostel, Zero 1915-1977 *WhoCom [port]*
Mosteller, Frederick 1916- *IntWW 93, WhoAm 94, WhoScEn 94*
Mosteller, Glenn Randolph 1932- *WhoFI 94*
Mosteller, James Wilbur, III 1940- *WhoWest 94*
Mostert, P(aul) S(tallings) 1927- *WrDr 94*
Mostert, Paul Stallings 1927- *WhoAm 94*
Mostiler, John L. 1923- *WhoAmP 93*
Mostiler, Johnny Baxter 1947- *WhoAmL 94*
Mostillo, Ralph 1944- *WhoFI 94, WhoScEn 94*
Mostoff, Allan Samuel 1932- *WhoAm 94*
Mostofi, Khosrow 1921-1992 *WhAm 10*
Mostovoy, Marc Sanders 1942- *WhoAm 94*
Mostow, George Daniel 1923- *IntWW 93, WhoAm 94, WhoScEn 94*
Mostyn, Baron 1920- *Who 94*
Mostyn, David *Who 94*
Mostyn, (Joseph) David (Frederick) 1928- *Who 94*
Mostyn, Marge Lois Irwin 1947- *WhoMW 93*
Mostyn, William Basil John 1975- *Who 94*
Moszkowski, Alexandr 1851-1934 *EncSF 93*
Moszkowski, Lena Iggers 1930- *WhoWest 94*
Moszkowski, Moritz 1854-1925 *NewGrDO*
Moszynski, Andrew *WhoAmA 93*
Mota, Hector D. *WhoHisp 94*
Mota, Manny 1938- *WhoHisp 94*
Mota-Altman, Norma Patricia 1952- *WhoHisp 94*
Mota de Freitas, Duarte Emanuel 1957- *WhoMW 93*
Mote, Clayton Daniel, Jr. 1937- *WhoAm 94, WhoScEn 94, WhoWest 94*
Mote, Harold Trevor 1919- *Who 94*
Motejunas, Gerald William 1950- *WhoAmL 94*
Moten, Birdia B. 1934- *WhoBlA 94*
Moten, Chauncey Donald 1933- *WhoBlA 94*
Moten, Emmett S., Jr. 1944- *WhoBlA 94*
Moten, Etta *WhoHol 92*
Moten, Sarah Elizabeth 1941- *WhoAm 94*
Motenko, Neil Philip 1951- *WhoAm 94, WhoAmL 94*
Motes, Carl Dalton 1949- *WhoAmL 94*
Motesiczky, Marie-Louise von 1906- *IntWW 93*
Motheo, Artur de Jesus 1952- *WhoScEn 94*
Mother Mariia 1891-1945 *BlmGWL*
Mothershead, Charles Ivan, III 1948- *WhoAmP 93*
Mothershead, John Leland, Jr. 1908-1991 *WhAm 10*
Mothershed, Spaesio W. 1925- *WhoBlA 94*
Motherway, Joseph Edward 1930- *WhoAm 94*
Motherway, Robert T. *WhoAmP 93*
Motherwell, Bishop of 1937- *Who 94*
Motherwell, Cathryn 1957- *WrDr 94*
Motherwell, Phil *WhoHol 92*
Motherwell, Robert 1915-1991 *AmCulL, WhAm 10, WhoAmA 93N*
Mothkur, Sridhar Rao 1950- *WhoAsA 94, WhoMW 93, WhoScEn 94*
Motihar, Kamla Mansharamani 1933- *WhoAsA 94*
Motilall, Makeshwar Fip 1961- *WhoAsA 94*
Motin, Revell Judith 1941- *WhoFI 94, WhoScEn 94*
Motion, Andrew *WrDr 94*
Motion, Andrew 1952- *IntWW 93, Who 94*
Motley, Annette *WrDr 94*
Motley, Archibald 1891-1980 *AfrAmAl 6 [port]*
Motley, Constance Baker 1921- *AfrAmAl 6 [port], WhoAm 94, WhoAmL 94*
Motley, Constance Baker, Sr. 1921- *WhoBlA 94*
Motley, David Lynn 1958- *WhoBlA 94*
Motley, John H. 1942- *WhoBlA 94*
Motley, John Paul 1927- *WhoAm 94, WhoFI 94*
Motley, Langhorne A. 1938- *WhoAmP 93*
Motley, Marion *ProFbHF [port]*
Motley, Ronald Clark 1954- *WhoBlA 94*
Motloch, Chester George 1948- *WhoScEn 94*
Motoba, Toshio 1944- *WhoScEn 94*
Motorhead *ConMus 10 [port]*
Motroni, Hector John 1943- *WhoFI 94*
Motschenbacher, Steven Peter 1956- *WhoWest 94*
Motsett, Charles Bourke 1949- *WhoFI 94*
Motsinger, Carl Daniel 1956- *WhoAmL 94*
Motsinger, John Kings 1947- *WhoAmL 94*
Motsinger, Linda Sue 1947- *WhoMW 93*
Motsinger, Linda Susan Baumgardner 1941- *WhoMW 93*
Motsko, Lucinda M. 1950- *WhoAmL 94*
Motsuenyane, Samuel Mokgethi 1927- *IntWW 93*
Mott, Charles Davis 1914- *WhoScEn 94*
Mott, Charles Stewart Harding 1906-1989 *WhAm 10*
Mott, Elaine *DrAPF 93*
Mott, Evelyn Clarke 1962- *SmATA 75 [port]*
Mott, Gregory George Sidney 1925- *Who 94*
Mott, J. Thomas 1949- *WhoAmP 93*
Mott, John (Harmar) 1922- *Who 94*
Mott, John Charles Spencer 1926- *Who 94*
Mott, John Raleigh 1865-1955 *DcAmReB 2*
Mott, Joseph M. 1953- *WhoAmL 94*
Mott, June Marjorie 1920- *WhoWest 94*
Mott, Lucretia 1793-1880 *HisWorL [port]*
Mott, Lucretia Coffin 1793-1880 *AmSocL [port], DcAmReB 2*
Mott, Mary Elizabeth 1931- *WhoMW 93*
Mott, Michael *DrAPF 93*
Mott, Michael Duncan 1940- *Who 94*
Mott, Nevill 1905- *WhoAm 94, WhoScEn 94*
Mott, Nevill (Francis) 1905- *Who 94*
Mott, Nevill Francis 1905- *IntWW 93*
Mott, Peter Andrew 1959- *WhoScEn 94*
Mott, Philip Charles 1948- *Who 94*
Mott, Roger Alan 1950- *WhoAmP 93*
Mott, Stewart Rawlings 1937- *WhoAm 94*
Mott, Stokes E., Jr. 1947- *WhoBlA 94*
Mott, Vincent Valmon 1916- *WhoAm 94*
Mott, William Chamberlain 1911- *WhoAm 94*
Mott, William Penn, Jr. 1909-1992 *AnObit 1992*
Motta, Bess *WhoHol 92*
Motta, Dick 1931- *BasBi, WrDr 94*
Motta, John Joseph 1949- *WhoFI 94, WhoWest 94*
Motta, Zeze *WhoHol 92*
Motte, Diether de la 1928- *NewGrDO*
Motte, Isaac 1738-1795 *WhAmRev*
Mottek, Carl T. 1928- *WhoFI 94, WhoWest 94*
Motteler, Zane Clinton 1935- *WhoWest 94*
Mottelson, Ben R. 1926- *Who 94, WhoScEn 94*
Motter, Klara 1935- *WhoWomW 91*
Mottershead, Frank William 1911- *Who 94*
Mottet, Norman Karle 1924- *WhoAm 94*
Motteux, Peter Anthony 1663-1718 *NewGrDO*
Motteville, Francoise Bertaut, Madame de 1616?-1689 *BlmGWL*
Mottin de la Balme, Augustin 1736-1780 *WhAmRev*
Mottistone, Baron 1920- *Who 94*
Mottistone, Lord 1920- *IntWW 93*
Mottl, Felix (Josef) 1856-1911 *NewGrDO*
Mottl, Ronald M. 1934- *WhoMW 93*
Mottl, Ronald M., Sr. 1934- *WhoAmP 93*
Mottley, Eva d1985 *WhoHol 92*
Mottley, J. Donald *WhoAmP 93*
Motto, Jerome Arthur 1921- *WhoAm 94*
Mottola, Gary F. 1947- *WhoAm 94, WhoAmL 94*
Mottola, John T. 1945- *WhoIns 94*
Motton, Gregory 1961- *ConDr 93*
Mott-Radclyffe, Charles Edward d1992 *Who 94N*
Mottram, Buster 1955- *BuCMET*
Mottram, Eric *WrDr 94*
Mottram, John Frederick 1930- *Who 94*
Mottram, Joy 1928- *BuCMET*
Mottram, Linda 1957- *BuCMET*
Mottram, R(alph) H(ale) 1883-1971 *EncSF 93*
Mottram, Richard Clive 1946- *Who 94*
Mottram, Tony 1920- *BuCMET*
Mottram-Doss, Renee 1939- *WhoAm 94, WhoFI 94*
Mott-Smith, May 1879-1952 *WhoAmA 93N*
Motulsky, Arno Gunther 1923- *IntWW 93, WhoAm 94, WhoWest 94*
Moty, Eleanor H. *WhoAmA 93*
Motyer, John Alexander 1924- *Who 94*
Motz, John Frederick 1942- *WhoAm 94, WhoAmL 94*
Motz, Kenneth Earl 1960- *WhoFI 94*
Motz, Kenneth Lee 1922- *WhoAm 94*
Motzenbecker, Helen Kenny 1929- *WhoFI 94*
Mo Tzu 4th cent.BC- *EncEth*
Mou, Lan 1957- *WhoWest 94*
Mouatt, (Richard) Brian 1936- *Who 94*
Mouch, Frank Messman *WhoAm 94*
Mouchaty, Georges 1950- *WhoScEn 94*
Mouchet, Catherine 1959- *WhoHol 92*
Mouchly-Weiss, Harriet 1942- *WhoFI 94*
Moudgil, Brij Mohan 1945- *WhoAsA 94*
Moudgil, Virinder K. *WhoAsA 94*
Moudy, Walter (Frank) 1929-1973 *EncSF 93*
Moufarrege, Nicholas A. 1947- *WhoAmA 93N*
Mouftah, Hussein Talaat 1947- *WhoAm 94*
Moughler, John Harvey 1923- *WhoAmP 93*
Mouhot, Henri 1826-1861 *WhWE*
Moukawsher, Thomas G. *WhoAmP 93*
Moul, Dale Allen 1947- *WhoMW 93*
Moul, Francis Dean 1940- *WhoAmP 93*
Moul, Maxine *WhoAm 94*
Moul, Maxine B. *WhoAmP 93*
Moul, Maxine Burnett 1947- *WhoMW 93*
Moul, William Charles 1940- *WhoAm 94*
Moulan, Frank d1939 *WhoHol 92*
Moulaye, Mohamed 1936- *IntWW 93*
Mould, Bob 1961- *ConMus 10 [port]*
Mould, Daphne D(esiree) C(harlotte) Pochin 1920- *WrDr 94*
Mould, Edwin 1914- *WrDr 94*
Moulden, Fred Albert, Jr. 1960- *WhoMW 93*
Moulder, Christopher Charles 1951- *WhoMW 93*
Moulder, James Edwin 1926- *WhoAm 94*
Moulder, Walter d1967 *WhoHol 92*
Moulder, William H. 1938- *WhoMW 93*
Moulder-Brown, John 1945- *WhoHol 92*
Moulding, Colin
See XTC *ConMus 10*
Moulds, John F. *WhoAmL 94*
Moule, Charles Francis Digby 1908- *IntWW 93, Who 94, WrDr 94*
Moulijn, Jacob A. 1942- *WhoScEn 94*
Moulin, Annie 1946- *ConAu 140*
Moulin, Marie-Annie *ConAu 140*
Moulin, Velma Lyon d1982 *WhoHol 92*
Moulinghen, Jean-Baptiste d1812 *NewGrDO*
Moulinghen, Louis-Charles fl. 1768- *NewGrDO*
Mou Lingsheng 1931- *WhoPRCh 91 [port]*
Moulins, Max 1914- *IntWW 93*
Mouloudji, Marcel 1922- *WhoHol 92*
Moulson, (Roger) Harry 1944- *Who 94*
Moult, Ted d1986 *WhoHol 92*
Moulthrop, Edward Allen 1916- *WhoAm 94*
Moulthrop, James Sylvester 1939- *WhoScEn 94*
Moulthrop, Samuel Parker 1951- *WhoAm 94, WhoAmL 94*
Moulton, Alexander Eric 1920- *IntWW 93, Who 94*
Moulton, Buck (Edwin) d1959 *WhoHol 92*
Moulton, Edward Quentin 1926- *WhoAm 94*
Moulton, Herbert F. 1936- *WhoIns 94*
Moulton, Horace Platt 1907-1991 *WhAm 10*
Moulton, Hugh Geoffrey 1933- *WhoAm 94, WhoAmL 94, WhoFI 94*
Moulton, James Louis 1906- *Who 94, WrDr 94*
Moulton, James Roger 1950- *WhoFI 94*
Moulton, Jean Ann 1949- *WhoAmP 93*
Moulton, Joy Wade 1928- *WhoMW 93*
Moulton, Leslie Howard 1915- *Who 94*
Moulton, Linda Ann 1955- *WhoFI 94*
Moulton, Peter Franklin 1946- *WhoAm 94*
Moulton, Robert c. 1591-1652 *DcNaB MP*
Moulton, Rosalind Kimball 1941- *WhoAmA 93*
Moulton, Susan Gene 1944- *WhoAmA 93*
Moulton, Wilbur Wright, Jr. 1935- *WhoAm 94*
Moultrie, Fred 1923- *WhoAm 94*
Moultrie, James Bertram 1944- *IntWW 93*
Moultrie, John 1729-1798 *WhAmRev*
Moultrie, Roy D. *WhoAmP 93*
Moultrie, William 1730-1805 *WhAmRev [port]*
Mouly, Eileen Louise 1955- *WhoFI 94*
Moumin, Amini Ali 1944- *IntWW 93*
Moumouni, Aissata *WhoWomW 91*
Mound, Fred 1932- *IntMPA 94*
Mound, Laurence Alfred 1934- *Who 94*
Mound, Trevor Ernest John 1930- *Who 94*
Mounds, Leona Mae Reed 1945- *WhoWest 94*
Mounds, Monica *EncSF 93*
Mounet-Sully, Jean d1916 *WhoHol 92*
Moungar, Fidele *IntWW 93*
Mounger, Scott Edwin 1951- *WhoFI 94, WhoWest 94*
Mounsey, John Patrick David 1914- *Who 94*
Mount, Christopher John 1913- *Who 94*

Mount, Cindy Kay 1960- *WhoWest 94*
Mount, David Allen 1943- *WhoFI 94*
Mount, Ferdinand *Who 94*
Mount, (William Robert) Ferdinand 1939- *IntWW 93, Who 94*
Mount, James (William Spencer) 1908- *Who 94*
Mount, John Wallace 1946- *WhoWest 94*
Mount, Karl A. 1945- *WhoAm 94, WhoFI 94*
Mount, Marsha Louise 1962- *WhoFI 94*
Mount, Marshall Ward 1927- *WhoAmA 93*
Mount, Peggy 1916- *WhoHol 92*
Mount, Rick 1947- *BasBi*
Mount, Thom 1948- *IntMPA 94*
Mount, Thomas Henderson 1948- *WhoAm 94*
Mount, Ward *WhoAmA 93*
Mount, William Malcolm d1993 *Who 94N*
Mountain, Clifton Fletcher 1924- *WhoAm 94, WhoScEn 94*
Mountain, Denis Mortimer 1929- *Who 94*
Mountain, Rosemond c. 1768-1841 *NewGrDO*
Mountain, Worrall Frederick 1909-1992 *WhAm 10*
Mountain Wolf Woman 1884-1960 *EncNAR [port]*
Mountbatten *Who 94*
Mountbatten Of Burma, Countess 1924- *Who 94, WhoWomW 91*
Mountcastle, Katharine Babcock 1931- *WhoAm 94*
Mountcastle, Kenneth Franklin, Jr. 1928- *WhoAm 94, WhoFI 94*
Mountcastle, Vernon Benjamin 1918- *WhoAm 94*
Mountcastle, Vernon Benjamin, Jr. 1918- *IntWW 93*
Mountcastle, William Wallace, Jr. 1925- *WhoAm 94*
Mount Charles, Earl of 1951- *Who 94*
Mount Edgcumbe, Earl of 1939- *Who 94*
Mount Edgcumbe, Richard 1764-1839 *NewGrDO*
Mounteer, Thomas R. 1961- *WhoAmL 94*
Mounter, Julian D'Arcy 1944- *IntWW 93*
Mountevans, Baron 1943- *Who 94*
Mountfield, David 1938- *WrDr 94*
Mountfield, Peter 1935- *Who 94*
Mountfield, Robin 1939- *Who 94*
Mountford, Arnold Robert 1922- *Who 94*
Mountford, Helen Turner 1942- *WhoAmL 94*
Mountfort, Guy Reginald 1905- *Who 94*
Mountgarret, Viscount 1936- *Who 94*
Mountjoy, Richard 1932- *WhoAmP 93*
Mountjoy, Roberta Jean 1913- *WrDr 94*
Mounts, Lynda S. 1946- *WhoAmL 94*
Mountz, Louise Carson Smith 1911- *WhoAm 94, WhoMW 93*
Mountz, Timothy Wilson 1955- *WhoAmL 94*
Mountz, Wade 1924- *WhoAm 94*
Mountzoures, H. L. *DrAPF 93*
Moura, Jose Manuel Fonseca 1946- *WhoAm 94*
Moura, Paul E. 1956- *WhoAmP 93*
Mourant, A(rthur) E(rnest) 1904- *WrDr 94*
Mourant, Arthur Ernest 1904- *IntWW 93, Who 94*
Moure, Erin 1955- *BlmGWL*
Moureaux, Philippe 1939- *IntWW 93*
Mourek, Joseph Edward 1910- *WhoAm 94*
Mourelatos, Alexander Phoebus Dionysiou 1936- *WhoAm 94*
Mouret, Jean-Joseph 1682-1738 *NewGrDO*
Mouri, Michael Patrick 1955- *WhoWest 94*
Mourning, Alonzo *WhoBlA 94*
Mourning, Alonzo 1970- *News 94-2 [port]*
Mourning Dove 1888-1936 *BlmGWL*
Moursund, Albert Wadel, III 1919- *WhoAmL 94, WhoFI 94*
Mousa, Alyaa Mohammed Ali 1964- *WhoScEn 94*
Mousel, Craig Lawrence 1947- *WhoAmL 94*
Mousel, Donald Kee 1932- *WhoWest 94*
Mouser, Deanna Jean *WhoAmL 94*
Moushey, Nora Eyre 1949- *WhoFI 94*
Moushoutas, Constantine 1928- *IntWW 93*
Mousnier, Roland Emile d1993 *IntWW 93N*
Mousnier, Roland Emile 1907- *IntWW 93*
Moussa, Khalil Mahmoud 1959- *WhoScEn 94*
Moussa, Pierre L. 1922- *IntWW 93*
Moussavi, Mir Hussein 1942- *IntWW 93*
Moussavou Missambo, Paulette *WhoWomW 91*
Mousseau, Doris Naomi Barton 1934- *WhoMW 93*
Moustache d1987 *WhoHol 92*
Moustafa, Fikry Sayed 1944- *WhoFI 94*
Moustiers, Pierre Jean (Rossi) 1924- *IntWW 93*
Mout, Marianne Elisabeth Henriette Nicolette 1945- *IntWW 93*
Moutaery, Khalaf Reden 1949- *WhoScEn 94*
Mouton, Benjamin *WhoHol 92*
Mouton, John Olivier 1944- *WhoAm 94*
Mouton, Peter Randolph 1958- *WhoScEn 94*
Moutoussamy, Claude Louis 1949- *WhoMW 93*
Moutoussamy, John Warren 1922- *WhoAm 94, WhoBlA 94*
Moutza-Martinengou, Elisavet 1801-1832 *BlmGWL*
Mouvet, Maurice d1927 *WhoHol 92*
Mouw, Irma Marian 1928- *WhoMW 93*
Mou Yongbin *WhoPRCh 91*
Mouzakes-Siler, Helen Harriet 1929- *WhoMW 93*
Movalli, Charles Joseph 1945- *WhoAmA 93*
Movar, Dunja d1963 *WhoHol 92*
Movchan, Pavlo Mykhailovych 1939- *LngBDD*
Moverley, Gerald *Who 94*
Movita 1914- *WhoHol 92*
Movius, Geoffrey *DrAPF 93*
Movshin, Lawrence J. 1949- *WhoAmL 94*
Mow, Bill 1936- *WhoAsA 94*
Mow, Chao-chow 1930- *WhoAsA 94*
Mow, Douglas Farris 1928- *WhoAm 94*
Mow, Robert Henry, Jr. 1938- *WhoAm 94, WhoAmL 94*
Mow, Van C. 1939- *WhoAm 94, WhoScEn 94*
Mowat, Barbara Adams 1934- *WhoAm 94*
Mowat, Claire (Angel Wheeler) 1933- *WrDr 94*
Mowat, David 1943- *ConDr 93, ConTFT 11*
Mowat, David McIvor 1939- *Who 94*
Mowat, Farley (McGill) 1921- *ConAu 42NR, TwCYAW, WrDr 94*
Mowat, Farley McGill 1921- *IntWW 93, WhoAm 94*
Mowat, John Stuart 1923- *Who 94*
Mowatt, Anna Cora 1819-1870 *BlmGWL, IntDcT 2*
Mowatt, Oswald Victor *WhoBlA 94*
Mowatt, Zeke 1961- *WhoBlA 94*
Mowbray, Alan d1969 *WhoHol 92*
Mowbray, Carol Beatrice Thiessen 1948- *WhoMW 93*
Mowbray, Henry d1960 *WhoHol 92*
Mowbray, John 1916- *Who 94*
Mowbray, John Code 1918- *WhoAm 94, WhoAmL 94, WhoAmP 93, WhoWest 94*
Mowbray, John Robert 1932- *Who 94*
Mowbray, Robert Norman 1935- *WhoScEn 94*
Mowbray, William John 1928- *Who 94*
Mowbray, Segrave and Stourton, Baron 1923- *Who 94*
Mowday, Richard Thomas 1947- *WhoAm 94*
Mowder, Gary Leroy 1940- *WhoAm 94*
Mowe, Gregory Robert 1946- *WhoAm 94, WhoAmL 94*
Mowell, John Byard 1934- *WhoFI 94*
Mo Wenxiang 1923- *IntWW 93, WhoPRCh 91 [port]*
Mower, Brian Leonard d1993 *Who 94N*
Mower, Jack d1965 *WhoHol 92*
Mower, Patrick 1940- *WhoHol 92*
Mower, Scarlett Sue 1941- *WhoAmP 93*
Mowery, Anna Renshaw 1931- *WhoAmP 93*
Mowery, Bob Lee 1920- *WhoAm 94*
Mowery, Harold F., Jr. 1930- *WhoAmP 93*
Mowery, Mark Roth 1960- *WhoMW 93*
Mowery, Morris Everett 1942- *WhoAmP 93*
Mowitt, John 1952- *ConAu 140*
Mowl, Colin John 1947- *Who 94*
Mowlam, Marjorie 1949- *IntWW 93, Who 94, WhoWomW 91*
Mowll, Christopher Martyn 1932- *Who 94*
Mowrer, Glen Freeman, Jr. 1940- *WhoAmL 94*
Mowrer, Gordon Brown 1936- *WhoAmP 93*
Mowrey, Robert T. 1952- *WhoAmL 94*
Mowrey, Timothy James 1958- *WhoFI 94, WhoScEn 94*
Mowrey-McKee, Mary Flowers 1941- *WhoScEn 94*
Mowry, Daniel, Jr. 1729-1806 *WhAmRev*
Mowry, James Brian 1954- *WhoMW 93*
Mowry, Jess 1960- *WrDr 94*
Mowry, Robert Dean 1945- *WhoAm 94*
Mowry, Robert Wilbur 1923- *WhoAm 94, WhoScEn 94*
Moxey, Hugh *WhoHol 92*
Moxey, Patricio Keith Fleming 1943- *WhoAmA 93*
Moxley, F(rank) Wright 1889-1937 *EncSF 93*
Moxley, Frank O. 1908- *WhoBlA 94*
Moxley, John Howard, III 1935- *IntWW 93, WhoAm 94, WhoAmP 93*
Moxley, Joseph M. *DrAPF 93*
Moxon, (Roland) James 1920- *WrDr 94*
Moxon, John Sawyer 1939- *WhoFI 94*
Moxon, Michael Anthony 1942- *Who 94*
Moxon, (Edward) Richard 1941- *IntWW 93, Who 94*
Moxon Browne, Robert William 1946- *Who 94*
Moy, Celeste Marie 1950- *WhoBlA 94*
Moy, Curt Wayne 1961- *WhoAmL 94*
Moy, Donald 1955- *WhoAsA 94*
Moy, Edmund 1957- *WhoAsA 94*
Moy, George S. 1939- *WhoAsA 94*
Moy, Henry 1955- *WhoAmA 93, WhoAsA 94*
Moy, James S. 1948- *WhoAsA 94*
Moy, James Yee Kin 1934- *WhoAsA 94*
Moy, Jeffery Fei 1962- *WhoAsA 94*
Moy, Mamie Wong 1929- *WhoAsA 94*
Moy, Mary Anastasia 1964- *WhoAmL 94*
Moy, May (Wong) 1913- *WhoAmA 93*
Moy, Naomi Ogawa 1949- *WhoAsA 94*
Moy, Richard Henry 1931- *WhoAm 94*
Moy, Robert Carl 1958- *WhoAsA 94*
Moy, Ronald Leonard 1957- *WhoScEn 94*
Moy, Seong 1921- *WhoAmA 93*
Moy, Stan Yip 1948- *WhoAsA 94*
Moya, (John) Hidalgo 1920- *IntWW 93, Who 94*
Moya, Jose C. 1952- *WhoHisp 94*
Moya, P. Robert 1944- *WhoHisp 94*
Moya, Patrick Robert 1944- *WhoAm 94, WhoAmL 94*
Moya, Sara Dreier 1945- *WhoWest 94*
Moya de Guerra, Elvira 1947- *WhoScEn 94*
Mo Yan 1956- *WhoPRCh 91 [port]*
Moya Palencia, Lic. Mario 1933- *IntWW 93*
Moya Soto, Roberto 1935- *WhoAmA 93*
Moye, Anthony Joseph 1933- *WhoWest 94*
Moye, Catherine 1960- *WrDr 94*
Moye, Charles Allen, Jr. 1918- *WhoAm 94, WhoAmL 94*
Moye, Eric Vaughn 1954- *WhoAmL 94*
Moye, James M. 1921- *WhoAmP 93*
Moye, John Edward 1944- *WhoAm 94*
Moye, Judy Henley 1944- *WhoAmP 93*
Moyer, Alan Dean 1928- *WhoAm 94, WhoWest 94*
Moyer, Albert J. 1943- *WhoFI 94*
Moyer, Bruce Shore 1960- *WhoMW 93*
Moyer, Carl Frederick 1954- *WhoAmL 94*
Moyer, Craig Alan 1955- *WhoAmL 94, WhoWest 94*
Moyer, David Lee 1940- *WhoScEn 94*
Moyer, David S. 1952- *WhoFI 94*
Moyer, Dean LaRoche 1925- *WhoWest 94*
Moyer, Dennis K. 1952- *WhoAmL 94*
Moyer, F. Stanton 1929- *WhoAm 94*
Moyer, Glenn Roydon 1929- *WhoAmP 93*
Moyer, Holley Marker 1947- *WhoAmL 94*
Moyer, Homer Edward, Jr. 1942- *WhoAmL 94*
Moyer, James D. 1949- *WhoAmL 94*
Moyer, James Russell, Jr. 1963- *WhoMW 93*
Moyer, James Wallace 1919- *WhoScEn 94*
Moyer, Jay Edward 1940- *WhoAmL 94*
Moyer, Jennifer *DrAPF 93*
Moyer, Jerry Mills 1940- *WhoFI 94*
Moyer, John A. *WhoAmP 93*
Moyer, John Arthur 1922- *WhoWest 94*
Moyer, John Henry, III 1917- *WhoScEn 94*
Moyer, K. E 1919- *WrDr 94*
Moyer, Kenneth Evan 1919- *WhoAm 94*
Moyer, Kermit 1943- *WrDr 94*
Moyer, Kristin Lynn 1969- *WhoMW 93*
Moyer, Lane Richard 1963- *WhoMW 93*
Moyer, Marina Pavlova 1952- *WhoAmA 93*
Moyer, Mike 1956- *WhoMW 93*
Moyer, Ralph Owen, Jr. 1936- *WhoScEn 94*
Moyer, Raymond J. *WhoAmP 93*
Moyer, Robert Paul 1955- *WhoFI 94*
Moyer, Robert Theodore 1948- *WhoAm 94, WhoMW 93*
Moyer, Roy 1921- *WhoAmA 93*
Moyer, Samuel c. 1609-1683 *DcNaB MP*
Moyer, Thomas E. 1952- *WhoAmP 93*
Moyer, Thomas J. 1939- *WhoAm 94, WhoAmL 94, WhoAmP 93, WhoMW 93*
Moyer, Thomas Phillip 1946- *WhoScEn 94*
Moyers, Bill 1934- *IntMPA 94*
Moyers, Bill D. 1934- *IntWW 93, Who 94, WhoAm 94*
Moyers, Lowell Duane 1930- *WhoWest 94*
Moyers, William 1916- *WhoAmA 93*
Moyers, William Taylor 1916- *WhoWest 94*
Moyes, Kenneth Jack 1918- *Who 94*
Moyes, Patricia 1923- *TwCYAW, WrDr 94*
Mo Yingfeng 1938- *WhoPRCh 91 [port]*
Moylan, Catherine d1969 *WhoHol 92*
Moylan, (John) David (FitzGerald) 1915- *Who 94*
Moylan, James Harold 1930- *WhoAmP 93*
Moylan, James Joseph 1948- *WhoAmL 94*
Moylan, Jay Richard 1950- *WhoFI 94*
Moylan, Kurt S. 1939- *WhoAmP 93*
Moylan, Stephan 1737-1811 *AmRev*
Moylan, Stephen 1734-1811 *WhAmRev*
Moylan, Stephen Craig 1952- *WhoMW 93*
Moylan, Tom *EncSF 93*
Moylan-Jones, Roger Charles 1940- *Who 94*
Moylan-Torruella, Trish 1953- *WhoHisp 94*
Moyle, Bennett Isaac 1946- *WhoFI 94*
Moyle, Colin James 1929- *IntWW 93*
Moyle, Lawrence A. 1952- *WhoIns 94*
Moyle, Michael R. 1948- *WhoAmL 94*
Moyle, Oscar Wood, III 1938- *WhoAmL 94*
Moyle, Peter Briggs 1942- *WhoAm 94*
Moyle, Roland (Dunstan) 1928- *Who 94*
Moyler, Freeman William, Jr. 1931- *WhoBlA 94*
Moyles, Lois *DrAPF 93*
Moynahan, John Daniel, Jr. 1935- *WhoAm 94, WhoFI 94*
Moynahan, Julian (Lane) 1925- *WrDr 94*
Moynahan, Julian Lane 1925- *WhoAm 94*
Moynahan, Molly 1957- *WrDr 94*
Moynahan, Thomas A. 1938- *WhoAmP 93*
Moyne, Baron d1992 *IntWW 93N*
Moyne, Baron 1930- *Who 94*
Moyne, Jean-Baptiste *NewGrDO*
Moyne, John Abel 1920- *WhoAm 94*
Moynet, Andre 1921- *IntWW 93*
Moynihan, Colin Berkeley 1955- *IntWW 93, Who 94*
Moynihan, Daniel P(atrick) 1927- *ConAu 43NR*
Moynihan, Daniel Patrick 1927- *CngDr 93, IntWW 93, NewYTBS 93 [port], Who 94, WhoAm 94, WhoAmP 93, WrDr 94*
Moynihan, James Francis 1952- *WhoAmP 93*
Moynihan, John Bignell 1933- *WhoAmL 94*
Moynihan, John Dominic 1932- *WrDr 94*
Moynihan, Jonathan Patrick 1948- *WhoAm 94*
Moynihan, Kenneth James 1944- *WhoAmP 93*
Moynihan, Martin John 1916- *Who 94*
Moynihan, Maurice (Gerard) 1902- *WrDr 94*
Moynihan, Michael Emmet 1952- *WhoMW 93*
Moynihan, Michael J. 1946- *WhoMW 93*
Moynihan, Noel (Henry) 1916- *Who 94*
Moynihan, Patrick Joseph 1930- *WhoAmL 94*
Moynihan, Rosemary 1943- *WhoAmP 93*
Moynihan, Ruth B(arnes) 1933- *ConAu 41NR*
Moynihan, Timothy 1941- *WhoAmP 93*
Moyo, Yvette Jackson 1953- *WhoBlA 94*
Moyola, Baron 1923- *IntWW 93, Who 94*
Moyse, Alexis d1991 *IntWW 93N*
Moyse, Hermann, Jr. 1921- *WhoAm 94*
Moyse, Sophia *WhoHol 92*
Moyser, George H. 1945- *WrDr 94*
Moyski, Stephen Marek 1965- *WhoWest 94*
Moyzes, Alexander 1906-1984 *NewGrDO*
Mozaffari, Mojtaba 1952- *WhoScEn 94*
Mozart, George 1947- *WhoHol 92*
Mozart, (Johann Chrysostom) Wolfgang Amadeus 1756-1791 *NewGrDO*
Mozden, Stanley Walter, Jr. 1940- *WhoAmP 93*
Mozdzer, Henry Anthony 1924-1988 *WhAm 10*
Mozdziak, Paul Edward 1967- *WhoScEn 94*
Mozeen, Mrs. *NewGrDO*
Mozena, John Daniel 1956- *WhoScEn 94, WhoWest 94*
Mozes, Sanford K. 1955- *WhoAmL 94*
Mozeson, Isaac Elchanan *DrAPF 93*
Mozhayev, Boris Andreyevich 1923- *IntWW 93*
Mozhukhin, Ivan d1939 *WhoHol 92*
Mozian, Gerard Paul 1945- *WhoAm 94*
Mozley, Anita Ventura 1928- *WhoAmA 93*
Mozley, Paul David 1928- *WhoAm 94*
Mozurkewich, George, Jr. 1953- *WhoFI 94*
Mozzi, Pietro fl. 1686- *NewGrDO*

Mpetha, Oscar 1909- *IntWW 93*
Mphahlele, Es'kia *BlkWr 2*
Mphahlele, Es'kia 1919- *IntWW 93, RfGShF*
Mphahlele, Ezekiel *DrAPF 93*
Mphahlele, Ezekiel 1919- *BlkWr 2, WrDr 94*
Mpherson, Philip Keith 1927- *Who 94*
Mpinga Kasenda 1937- *IntWW 93*
Mpuchane, Samuel Akuna 1943- *Who 94*
M'Rabet, Fadela *BlmGWL*
Mrachek, L. Louis 1946- *WhoAmL 94*
Mracky, Ronald Sydney 1932- *WhoFI 94, WhoWest 94*
Mraczek, Joseph Gustav 1878-1944 *NewGrDO*
Mravina, Yevgeniya Konstantinovna 1864-1914 *NewGrDO*
Mrazek, Robert J. 1945- *WhoAmP 93*
Mrazek, Robert Vernon 1936-1990 *WhAm 10*
Mrdjenovich, Donald 1936- *WhoMW 93*
Mrkonic, George Ralph, Jr. 1952- *WhoAm 94, WhoFI 94*
Mroudjae, Ali *IntWW 93*
Mrouweh, Adnan 1936- *IntWW 93*
Mroz, Michael Allen 1956- *WhoAmL 94*
Mrozek, Donald L. 1947- *WhoAm 94, WhoAmL 94*
Mrozek, Slawomir 1930- *ConWorW 93, EncSF 93, IntDcT 2, IntWW 93*
Mruk, Charles Karzimer 1926- *WhoScEn 94*
Mruk, Eugene Robert 1927- *WhoFI 94*
Mruk, James Andrew 1949- *WhoMW 93*
Mrvan, Frank, Jr. *WhoAmP 93*
Mshonaji, Bibi 1939- *WhoBlA 94*
Mshvelidze, Shalva Mikhaylovich 1904-1984 *NewGrDO*
Msuya, Cleopa David 1931- *IntWW 93*
Mtawali, Bernard Brenm 1935- *Who 94*
Mtekateka, Josiah 1903- *Who 94*
Mtesa, Love 1942- *Who 94*
Mtewa, Mekki 1946- *WhoAm 94*
Mtoto, Pepo 1935- *WhoBlA 94*
Mtshali, Oswald (Joseph) 1940- *WrDr 94*
Mtshali, Oswald Mbuyiseni 1940- *BlkWr 2, ConAu 142*
Mtwa, Percy *ConDr 93*
Mu, Albert T. 1959- *WhoWest 94*
Mu, Eduardo 1957- *WhoScEn 94*
Mualla, Rashid bin Ahmad Al 1930- *IntWW 93*
Muan, Arnulf 1923-1990 *WhAm 10*
Muathen, Hussni Ahmad 1956- *WhoScEn 94*
Mubarak, (Muhammad) Hosni 1928- *IntWW 93*
Mubayi, Vinod 1941- *WhoScEn 94*
Mucari, Carlo *WhoHol 92*
Mucci, Gary Louis 1946- *WhoAmL 94*
Mucci, Patrick John 1947- *WhoFI 94*
Muccia, Joseph William 1948- *WhoAmL 94, WhoFI 94*
Mucciano, Stephanie Lyons 1944- *WhoFI 94*
Mucciante, Mary F. *WhoMW 93*
Muccilli, Jay Edward 1941- *WhoWest 94*
Muccio, John J. 1900-1989 *HisDcKW*
Muccio, John Joseph 1900-1989 *WhAm 10*
Muccioli, Anna Maria 1922- *WhoAmA 93*
Much, Ian Fraser Robert 1944- *Who 94*
Much, Kathy Lynn 1957- *WhoAmL 94*
Mucha, Jiri 1915- *WrDr 94*
Mucha, John Frank 1950- *WhoFI 94, WhoScEn 94*
Mucha, Patty *DrAPF 93*
Mucha, Susan Elizabeth 1958- *WhoWest 94*
Muchin, Allan B. 1936- *WhoAm 94*
Muchin, Arden Archie 1920- *WhoAmL 94*
Muchinguri, O.C.Z. *WhoWomW 91*
Muchmore, Carolin M. 1944- *WhoFI 94*
Muchmore, Charles J. 1950- *WhoAm 94, WhoAmL 94*
Muchmore, Clyde A. 1942- *WhoAmL 94*
Muchmore, Don Moncrief 1922- *WhoAm 94*
Muchmore, John Stephen 1945- *WhoScEn 94*
Muchmore, Robert Boyer 1917- *WhoAm 94*
Muchmore, William Breuleux 1920- *WhoAm 94*
Muchnic, Suzanne *WhoAmA 93*
Muchnick, Richard Stuart 1942- *WhoScEn 94*
Muchnij, Gregory P. 1962- *WhoWest 94*
Mu Chong 1905-1951? *HisDcKW*
Muci Kuchler, Karim Heinz 1964- *WhoScEn 94*
Muck, Carl 1859-1940 *NewGrDO*
Muck, George Arthur 1937- *WhoAm 94*
Muckelroy, William Lawrence 1945- *WhoBlA 94*
Muckenfuss, Cantwell Faulkner, III 1945- *WhoAm 94*
Muckenhoupt, Benjamin 1933- *WhoAm 94*
Muckerman, Norman James 1917- *WhoAm 94*
Muckian, Michael Patrick 1952- *WhoMW 93*
Muckler, Carl Henry 1941- *WhoAmP 93*
Muckler, John *WhoAm 94, WhoWest 94*
Mudar, Marian Jean *WhoScEn 94*
Mudd, (William) David 1933- *Who 94*
Mudd, E. Virginia d1979 *WhoHol 92*
Mudd, Emily H(artshorne) 1898- *WrDr 94*
Mudd, Harvey (Seeley, II) 1940- *WrDr 94*
Mudd, John Brian 1929- *WhoScEn 94*
Mudd, John Philip 1932- *WhoAm 94, WhoAmL 94, WhoFI 94*
Mudd, Louis L. 1943- *WhoBlA 94*
Mudd, Roger 1928- *IntMPA 94*
Mudd, Roger Harrison 1928- *IntWW 93, WhoAm 94*
Mudd, Sidney Peter 1917- *WhoAm 94*
Mudd, Steve *EncSF 93*
Mudd, Therese M. 1931- *WhoAmP 93*
Muddiman, Henry 1629-1692 *DcNaB MP*
Muddiman, John 1947- *WrDr 94*
Muddimer, Robert Michael 1933- *Who 94*
Muddock, J(oyce) E(mmerson) Preston 1843-1934 *EncSF 93*
Muddy Waters 1915-1983 *AmCulL [port]*
Mudek, Arthur Peter *WhoScEn 94*
Mudenda, Elijah Haatukali Kaiba 1927- *IntWW 93*
Mudford, Grant Leighton 1944- *WhoAmA 93*
Mudge, Augustine B. d1952 *WhoHol 92*
Mudge, Dirk *IntWW 93*
Mudge, Edmond Webster, Jr. 1904-1984 *WhoAmA 93N*
Mudge, Edmund W. 1870-1949 *EncABHB 9 [port]*
Mudge, Lewis Seymour 1929- *WhoAm 94*
Mudgeon, Apeman 1932- *WrDr 94*
Mudgett, Herman W. *EncSF 93*
Mudgett, Theresa Inez 1952- *WhoAmP 93*
Mudie, Charles Edward 1818-1890 *BlmGEL*
Mudie, George Edward 1945- *Who 94*
Mudie, Leonard d1965 *WhoHol 92*
Mudie, Michael (Winfield) 1914-1962 *NewGrDO*
Mudimbe, V.Y. 1941- *BlkWr 2, ConAu 141*
Mudry, Michael 1926- *WhoFI 94*
Mudundi, Ramakrishna Raju 1931- *WhoAsA 94*
Muecke, Charles Andrew 1918- *WhoAm 94, WhoAmL 94, WhoWest 94*
Muedeking, George Herbert 1915- *WhoAm 94*
Muegge, Paul 1936- *WhoAmP 93*
Mueh, Hans Juergen 1944- *WhoWest 94*
Muehl, Lois Baker 1920- *WrDr 94*
Muehlbauer, James Herman 1940- *WhoAm 94, WhoFI 94*
Muehleisen, Gene Sylvester 1915- *WhoAm 94*
Muehlemann, Kathy 1950- *WhoAmA 93*
Muehlenthal, Clarice Kelman 1924-1989 *WhAm 10*
Muehlner, Suanne Wilson 1943- *WhoAm 94*
Muehrcke, Juliana Obright 1945- *WhoMW 93*
Muehsam, Gerd 1913-1979 *WhoAmA 93N*
Mueller, Allan George 1942- *WhoAmP 93*
Mueller, Anne Elisabeth 1930- *Who 94*
Mueller, Anne O'Quin 1929- *WhoAmP 93*
Mueller, Barbara d1967 *WhoHol 92*
Mueller, Barbara Ruth 1925- *WhoAm 94, WhoMW 93*
Mueller, Betty Jeanne 1925- *WhoAm 94*
Mueller, Bonnie Mae 1944- *WhoWest 94*
Mueller, Carl Gustav, Jr. 1929- *WhoAm 94*
Mueller, Carl Richard 1931- *WhoAm 94*
Mueller, Charles Barber 1917- *WhoAm 94*
Mueller, Charles Leonard 1939- *WhoAmP 93*
Mueller, Charles William 1938- *WhoAm 94*
Mueller, Cookie d1989 *WhoHol 92*
Mueller, Dennis Warren 1946- *WhoScEn 94*
Mueller, Diane Mayne 1934- *WhoAmL 94*
Mueller, Don Sheridan 1927- *WhoMW 93*
Mueller, Donald Dean 1937- *WhoAm 94, WhoWest 94*
Mueller, Donald Scott 1947- *WhoScEn 94*
Mueller, Edward Albert 1923- *WhoAm 94*
Mueller, Elisabeth 1926- *WhoHol 92*
Mueller, Gail Delories 1957- *WhoWest 94*
Mueller, Gary Alfred 1950- *WhoWest 94*
Mueller, George Bernard 1939- *WhoMW 93*
Mueller, George E. 1918- *WhoScEn 94*
Mueller, Gerd Dieter 1936- *WhoAm 94*
Mueller, Gerda d1951 *WhoHol 92*
Mueller, Gerhard Gottlob 1930- *WhoAm 94*
Mueller, Gerhardt *ConAu 42NR*
Mueller, Gregory M 1953- *WhoAm 94*
Mueller, H. Carl 1944- *WhoMW 93*
Mueller, Henrietta Waters 1915- *WhoAmA 93, WhoWest 94*
Mueller, Inez Lee 1916- *WhoAmP 93*
Mueller, Ingo 1942- *ConAu 142*
Mueller, James Bernhard 1952- *WhoAm 94*
Mueller, James Paul 1954- *WhoAmL 94*
Mueller, Janel M(ulder) 1938- *WrDr 94*
Mueller, Janel Mulder 1938- *WhoAm 94*
Mueller, Jeannette Sue 1965- *WhoMW 93*
Mueller, Jeffrey Paul 1957- *WhoMW 93*
Mueller, John Alfred 1906- *WhoAm 94*
Mueller, John C. 1952- *WhoAm 94*
Mueller, John E. 1937- *WhoAm 94*
Mueller, John Edward 1939- *WhoMW 93*
Mueller, John Frederick Jack 1941- *WhoAmP 93*
Mueller, John Robert 1952- *WhoMW 93*
Mueller, Joseph Henry 1935- *WhoAmL 94*
Mueller, Joseph M. 1894- *WhAm 10*
Mueller, Karl *See* Soul Asylum *ConMus 10*
Mueller, Kathleen T. 1955- *WhoAmL 94*
Mueller, Keith John *WhoMW 93*
Mueller, Kenneth Howard 1940- *WhoScEn 94*
Mueller, Lisel *DrAPF 93*
Mueller, Lisel 1924- *WrDr 94*
Mueller, Lothar 1927- *IntWW 93*
Mueller, M. Gerardine Op *WhoAmA 93*
Mueller, Margaret Reid 1929- *WhoMW 93*
Mueller, Mark Christopher 1945- *WhoAmL 94*
Mueller, Marnie *DrAPF 93*
Mueller, Marnie Wagstaff 1937- *WhoAm 94*
Mueller, Maureen *WhoHol 92*
Mueller, Melinda *DrAPF 93*
Mueller, Paul 1939- *WhoScEn 94*
Mueller, Paul Henry 1917- *WhoAm 94, WhoFI 94*
Mueller, Peter Klaus *WhoWest 94*
Mueller, Peter Sterling 1930- *WhoAm 94, WhoScEn 94*
Mueller, Raymond Jay 1959- *WhoAm 94, WhoScEn 94, WhoWest 94*
Mueller, Richard Andrew 1950- *WhoMW 93*
Mueller, Richard Edward 1927- *WhoAm 94, WhoAmL 94*
Mueller, Robert Emmett 1925- *WrDr 94*
Mueller, Robert Kirk 1913- *WhoAm 94*
Mueller, Robert Raymond 1947- *WhoMW 93*
Mueller, Robert Swan, III 1944- *WhoAm 94, WhoAmL 94, WhoAmP 93*
Mueller, Robert William 1964- *WhoScEn 94*
Mueller, Ronald Raymond 1947- *WhoAm 94*
Mueller, Roy Clement 1930- *WhoFI 94*
Mueller, Rudhard Klaus 1936- *WhoScEn 94*
Mueller, Rudolf Gottfried 1934- *Who 94*
Mueller, Stephan 1930- *WhoScEn 94*
Mueller, Trude *WhoAmA 93*
Mueller, Walt 1925- *WhoAmP 93*
Mueller, Willard Fritz 1925- *WhoAm 94, WhoFI 94*
Mueller, William Martin 1917- *WhoAm 94*
Mueller, William R(andolph) 1916- *WrDr 94*
Mueller, Willys Francis, Jr. 1934- *WhoMW 93*
Mueller, Wolfgang d1960 *WhoHol 92*
Mueller-Heubach, Eberhard August 1942- *WhoAm 94*
Mueller-Stahl, Armin 1930- *ConTFT 11, WhoHol 92*
Mueller-Westerhagen, Marius *WhoHol 92*
Muellner, John Phillip 1936- *WhoMW 93*
Muellner, William Charles 1944- *WhoAm 94, WhoScEn 94*
Muench, John 1914- *WhoAmA 93*
Muench, John E. 1948- *WhoAm 94*
Muenster, Karen *WhoAmP 93*
Muesing Ellwood, Edith Elizabeth 1947- *WhoAm 94*
Muessig, Siegfried 1922- *WhoWest 94*
Mueth, Joseph Edward 1935- *WhoAm 94*
Muethel, Lothar d1964 *WhoHol 92*
Muezzinoglu, Ziya 1919- *IntWW 93*
Muff *Who 94*
Muff, Alfred 1949- *NewGrDO*
Muff, Stephen Carl 1962- *WhoFI 94*
Muffat, Georg 1653-1704 *NewGrDO*
Mufson, Maurice Albert 1932- *WhoAm 94, WhoScEn 94*
Mufti, Aftab A. 1940- *WhoScEn 94*
Mufti, Navaid Ahmed 1967- *WhoScEn 94*
Mufti, Siraj Islam 1938- *WhoWest 94*
Muftic, Michael 1933- *WhoAmP 93*
Mu Fu 1933- *WhoPRCh 91*
Mug, Thomas Hugh 1951- *WhoAmL 94*
Mugabe, Robert Gabriel 1924- *IntWW 93, Who 94*
Mugalian, Richard Aram 1922- *WhoAmP 93*
Mugan, Daniel Joseph 1933- *WhoHisp 94*
Mugar, Martin Gienandt 1949- *WhoAmA 93*
Mugavero, Francis J. 1914-1991 *WhAm 10*
Muggenburg, Bruce Al 1937- *WhoWest 94*
Muggeridge, Malcolm d1990 *WhoHol 92*
Muggeridge, Malcolm 1903-1990 *WhAm 10*
Muggeson, Margaret Elizabeth 1942- *WrDr 94*
Mugglebee, Michael Joseph 1951- *WhoIns 94*
Muggs, DJ c. 1970- *See* Cypress Hill *ConMus 11*
Mugica, Richard *WhoHisp 94*
Mugica Herzog, Enrique 1932- *IntWW 93*
Mugler, Dale Henry 1948- *WhoMW 93*
Mugler, Frederick, Jr. *DrAPF 93*
Mugler, Larry George 1946- *WhoWest 94*
Mugler, Thierry 1946- *IntWW 93*
Mugnone, Leopoldo 1858-1941 *NewGrDO*
Mugnozza, Carlo S. *Who 94*
Mugny, Gabriel 1949- *ConAu 140*
Mugo, Micere Githae 1942- *BlmGWL*
Mugot, Hazel (de Silva) 1947- *BlmGWL*
Mu Guozheng 1939- *WhoPRCh 91 [port]*
Muguruza, Francisco J. *WhoHisp 94*
Muha, George Joseph 1961- *WhoMW 93*
Muhammad *EncEth*
Muhammad c. 570-632 *HisWorL [port]*
Muhammad, Abdul Wazir d1991 *WhoBlA 94N*
Muhammad, Ali Nasser 1939- *IntWW 93*
Muhammad, Askiaa 1945- *WhoBlA 94*
Muhammad, Elijah 1897-1975 *AfrAmAl 6, AmSocL [port], DcAmReB 2*
Muhammad, Khalil Abdul 1962- *WhoFI 94*
Muhammad, M. Akbar 1951- *WhoBlA 94*
Muhammad, Marita 1943- *WhoBlA 94*
Muhammad, Raquel Annissa 1932- *WhoWest 94*
Muhammad, Shirley M. 1938- *WhoBlA 94*
Muhammad, Valencia *WhoBlA 94*
Muhammad, Wallace D. 1933- *WhoAm 94, WhoBlA 94*
Muhammad, Warith Deen 1933- *WhoBlA 94*
Muhammadullah 1921- *IntWW 93*
Muhando, Penina 1948- *BlmGWL*
Muhe, Erich 1938- *WhoScEn 94*
Muheim, Franz Emmanuel 1931- *IntWW 93, Who 94*
Muhieddin *IntWW 93*
Muhl, Edward E. 1907- *IntMPA 94*
Muhlanger, Erich 1941- *WhoFI 94*
Muhlbach, Luise 1814-1873 *BlmGWL, DcLB 133 [port]*
Muhlbach, Robert Arthur 1946- *WhoAmL 94*
Muhlbauer, Louis J. 1929- *WhoAmP 93*
Muhlberger, Richard Charles 1938- *WhoAm 94, WhoAmA 93*
Muhleman, Janet Christie 1951- *WhoAm 94*
Muhlenberg, Frederick Augustus Conrad 1750-1801 *WhAmRev*
Muhlenberg, Henry Melchior 1711-1787 *DcAmReB 2*
Muhlenberg, John Peter Gabriel 1746-1807 *AmRev, WhAmRev [port]*
Muhlenberg, William Augustus 1796-1877 *DcAmReB 2*
Muhlenbruch, Carl W. 1915- *WhoAm 94, WhoFI 94, WhoMW 93, WhoScEn 94*
Muhlenfeld, Michael J. 1952- *WhoFI 94*
Muhlenkamp, Ronald Henry 1944- *WhoFI 94*
Muhlert, Christopher Layton 1933- *WhoAmA 93*
Muhlert, Jan Keene 1942- *WhoAm 94, WhoAmA 93*
Muhs, Robert Keith, Sr. 1926- *WhoAmP 93*
Mui, Constance L. 1959- *WhoAsA 94*
Mui, Jimmy Kun 1958- *WhoFI 94*
Mui, Lorna H(olbrook) 1915- *WrDr 94*
Muilenburg, Robert Henry 1941- *WhoAm 94*
Muir, Alec Andrew 1909- *Who 94*
Muir, Alexander Laird 1937- *Who 94*
Muir, Brockett 1905- *WhoAmL 94*
Muir, David *WhoHol 92*
Muir, E. Roger 1918- *IntMPA 94*
Muir, Edwin 1887-1959 *BlmGEL*
Muir, Emily Lansingh *WhoAmA 93*
Muir, Esther 1903- *WhoHol 92*
Muir, Frank 1920- *Who 94, WrDr 94*
Muir, Gavin d1972 *WhoHol 92*

Muir, Georgette 1947- *WhoHol 92*
Muir, Helen d1934 *WhoHol 92*
Muir, Helen 1937- *WrDr 94*
Muir, (Isabella) Helen (Mary) 1920- *IntWW 93, Who 94*
Muir, Herman Stanley, III 1949- *WhoScEn 94*
Muir, J. Dapray 1936- *WhoAm 94, WhoAmL 94*
Muir, Jean 1911- *WhoHol 92*
Muir, Jean Elizabeth *IntWW 93, Who 94*
Muir, John 1838-1914 *AmSocL [port], EnvEnc [port]*
Muir, John (Harling) 1910- *Who 94*
Muir, Kenneth 1907- *Who 94*
Muir, Kenneth (Arthur) 1907- *IntWW 93, WrDr 94*
Muir, Kevin Dean 1962- *WhoFI 94*
Muir, Laurence (Macdonald) 1925- *Who 94*
Muir, Malcolm 1914- *WhoAm 94, WhoAmL 94*
Muir, Patricia Susan 1953- *WhoScEn 94*
Muir, Richard 1943- *WrDr 94*
Muir, Richard John Sutherland 1942- *Who 94*
Muir, Robert Bruce 1954- *WhoFI 94*
Muir, Robert Eugene 1934- *WhoAmL 94*
Muir, Ruth Brooks 1924- *WhoMW 93*
Muir, Steven Philip 1958- *WhoFI 94*
Muir, Tom 1936- *Who 94*
Muir, Ward 1878-1927 *EncSF 93*
Muir, Warren R. 1945- *WhoAm 94*
Muir, William Horace 1902-1965 *WhoAmA 93N*
Muir, William Ker, Jr. 1931- *WhoAm 94, WhoWest 94*
Muir, William Lloyd, III 1948- *WhoMW 93*
Muir Beddall, Hugh Richard *Who 94*
Muirden, Bruce Wallace 1928-1991 *WrDr 94N*
Muirhead, Alexander 1848-1920 *DcNaB MP*
Muirhead, David (Francis) 1918- *Who 94*
Muirhead, Douglas James 1951- *WhoAmL 94*
Muirhead, Vincent Uriel 1919- *WhoAm 94*
Muir Mackenzie, Alexander (Alwyne Henry Charles Brinton) 1955- *Who 94*
Muirshiel, Viscount d1992 *IntWW 93N*
Muir Wood, Alan (Marshall) 1921- *IntWW 93, Who 94*
Muise, Roxana 1935- *AstEnc*
Mujica, Alba d1983 *WhoHol 92*
Mujica, Mauro E. 1941- *WhoFI 94*
Mujuru, Joyce *WhoWomW 91*
Mujuru, Joyce Teurai-Ropa 1955- *IntWW 93*
Muka, Betty Loraine Oakes 1929- *WhoAmL 94, WhoFI 94*
Mukai, Francis Ken 1956- *WhoAsA 94*
Mukai, Franklin K. 1940- *WhoAmL 94*
Mukai, Hiroaki *WhoAsA 94*
Mukai, Robert G. 1951- *WhoAmL 94*
Mukai, Robert L. 1945- *WhoAsA 94*
Mukai, Stanley Y. 1932- *WhoAm 94*
Mukai, Yoshiko 1941- *WhoAsA 94*
Mukamal, Steven Sasoon 1940- *WhoAmL 94*
Mukamal, Stuart Sasson 1951- *WhoAmP 93*
Mukasey, Michael B. 1941- *WhoAm 94, WhoAmL 94*
Mukerjee, Pasupati 1932- *WhoAm 94, WhoAsA 94*
Mukha, Vitaly Petrovich 1936- *LngBDD*
Mukhamadiev, Rinat Safievich 1948- *LngBDD*
Mukhamedov, Irek *IntWW 93*
Mukhamedov, Irek 1960- *IntDcB [port]*
Mukhametshin, Farid Khairullovich 1949- *LngBDD*
Mukhammad, Sodyk Mukhammad Yusuf 1952- *LngBDD*
Mukherjea, Arunava 1941- *WhoAsA 94*
Mukherjee, Bharati 1938- *BlmGWL*
Mukherjee, Bharati 1940- *WhoAsA 94, WrDr 94*
Mukherjee, Bharati 1950- *IntWW 93*
Mukherjee, Geeta 1924- *WhoWomW 91*
Mukherjee, Kalinath 1932- *WhoAm 94*
Mukherjee, Kanak 1921- *WhoWomW 91*
Mukherjee, Pranab Kumar 1935- *IntWW 93, Who 94*
Mukherjee, Tapan Kumar 1929- *WhoAsA 94*
Mukherjee, Tara Kumar 1923- *Who 94*
Mukherjee, Trishit 1934- *WhoScEn 94*
Mukhopadhyay, Nimai C. 1942- *WhoAsA 94*
Mukhtar, Sheikh d1980 *WhoHol 92*
Mukoda Kuniko 1929-1981 *BlmGWL*
Mukoyama, James Hidefumi, Jr. 1944- *WhoAm 94*
Mukubenov, Maksim Bembeevich 1940- *LngBDD*

Mula, Avni 1926- *NewGrDO*
Mulaik, Stanley Allen 1935- *WhoScEn 94*
Mulamba Nyunyi Wa Kadima, (Leonard) 1928- *IntWW 93*
Mulanix, Mitchell Scott 1965- *WhoWest 94*
Mularz, Theodore Leonard 1933- *WhoAm 94, WhoFI 94*
Mulase, Motohico 1954- *WhoScEn 94, WhoWest 94*
Mulberry, Richard 1920- *WhoAmP 93*
Mulcahey, Richard Thomas 1935- *WhoAmP 93*
Mulcahy, Charles Chambers 1937- *WhoAmL 94*
Mulcahy, Daniel J. 1946- *WhoAmL 94*
Mulcahy, Daniel J. 1947- *WhoIns 94*
Mulcahy, Daniel Michael 1953- *WhoWest 94*
Mulcahy, Edward William 1921- *WhoAmP 93*
Mulcahy, Geoffrey John 1942- *IntWW 93, Who 94*
Mulcahy, John Michael, Jr. 1954- *WhoFI 94*
Mulcahy, Kathleen 1950- *WhoAmA 93*
Mulcahy, Michael D. 1947- *WhoAmL 94*
Mulcahy, Robert Edward 1932- *WhoAm 94*
Mulcahy, Robert William 1951- *WhoAm 94*
Mulcaster, G. H. d1964 *WhoHol 92*
Mulcay, Jimmy d1968 *WhoHol 92*
Mulchinock, David Steward 1945- *WhoAmL 94*
Mulckhuyse, Jacob John 1922- *WhoScEn 94*
Mulcock, James B., Jr. *WhoFI 94*
Muldary, Patrick Farrell 1951- *WhoWest 94*
Muldaur, Diana 1938- *IntMPA 94*
Muldaur, Diana 1943- *WhoHol 92*
Muldaur, Diana Charlton 1938- *WhoAm 94*
Mulder, Bernard J. 1896- *WhAm 10*
Mulder, David S. 1938- *WhoAm 94*
Mulder, Donald Gerrit 1924- *WhoAm 94*
Mulder, Donald William 1917- *WhoAm 94*
Mulder, Eldon Paul 1957- *WhoAmP 93*
Mulder, Thomas J. 1944- *WhoAmL 94*
Mulder de Draumer, Elisabeth 1904- *BlmGWL*
Mulderig, Robert A. 1953- *WhoIns 94*
Muldoon, Brian 1947- *WhoAm 94, WhoAmL 94*
Muldoon, Catherine Riesgo *WhoHisp 94*
Muldoon, Francis Creighton 1930- *WhoAmL 94*
Muldoon, Joseph Arthur, III 1955- *WhoAmL 94*
Muldoon, Nancy Knight 1938- *WhoWest 94*
Muldoon, Paul 1951- *BlmGEL, WrDr 94*
Muldoon, Paul Benedict 1951- *IntWW 93*
Muldoon, Robert 1921-1992 *AnObit 1992*
Muldoon, Robert David d1992 *IntWW 93N*
Muldoon, Robert David 1921-1992 *WhAm 10*
Muldoon, Robert Joseph, Jr. 1936- *WhoAm 94*
Muldoon, Roland 1941- *WhoHol 92*
Muldoon, Thea (Dale) 1927- *Who 94*
Muldoon, William Gene 1937- *WhoFI 94*
Muldoon, William Henry, III 1935- *WhoWest 94*
Muldowney, Diane Ellen *Who 94*
Muldowney, Dominic John 1952- *IntWW 93, Who 94*
Muldowney, Jerome Thomas 1945- *WhoIns 94*
Muldrow, Catherine 1931- *WhoBlA 94*
Muldrow, James Christopher 1945- *WhoBlA 94*
Muldrow, Lee J. 1946- *WhoAmL 94*
Mule, Giuseppe 1885-1951 *NewGrDO*
Mule, Margaret Mary Falcon 1941- *WhoAmP 93*
Mulford, David Campbell 1937- *WhoAmP 93*
Mulford, Donald Lewis 1918-1990 *WhAm 10*
Mulford, Hewett Probasco, Jr. 1937- *WhoMW 93*
Mulford, Maxene Fabe *DrAPF 93*
Mulford, Rand Perry 1943- *WhoWest 94*
Mulford, Scott 1952- *WhoMW 93*
Mulford, Wendy 1941- *BlmGWL, WrDr 94*
Mulgaonkar, Ranjit P. 1957- *WhoWest 94*
Mulgrave, Earl of 1954- *Who 94*
Mulgrew, Kate 1955- *IntMPA 94, WhoHol 92*
Mulhall, Jack d1979 *WhoHol 92*
Mulhall, Jack, Mrs. d1921 *WhoHol 92*
Mulhare, Edward *WhoHol 92*
Mulhauser, James d1939 *WhoHol 92*

Mulhearn, Cynthia Ann 1963- *WhoScEn 94*
Mulheran, John Thomas 1952- *WhoFI 94*
Mulhern, Edwin Joseph 1927- *WhoAmL 94*
Mulhern, Elsa Paine 1909- *WhoAmP 93*
Mulhern, John David 1928- *WhoAm 94*
Mulhern, Joseph Patrick 1921- *WhoAm 94*
Mulhern, Matt *WhoHol 92*
Mulhern, Matt 1960- *IntMPA 94*
Mulhern, Maureen *DrAPF 93*
Mulhern, Michael *WhoAmA 93*
Mulherne, Scott *WhoHol 92*
Mulhollan, Paige Elliott 1934- *WhoAm 94, WhoMW 93*
Mulholland *Who 94*
Mulholland, Angela Broadway 1957- *WhoAm 94, WhoMW 93*
Mulholland, Clare 1939- *Who 94*
Mulholland, Declan *WhoHol 92*
Mulholland, Kenneth Leo, Jr. 1943- *WhoAm 94*
Mulholland, Robert E. 1933- *IntMPA 94*
Mulholland, Robert Edge 1933- *WhoAm 94*
Mulholland, S. Grant 1936- *WhoAm 94*
Mulholland, Susan Collins 1955- *WhoMW 93*
Mulholland, Terence John 1963- *WhoAm 94*
Mulich, Steve Francis 1934- *WhoMW 93, WhoScEn 94*
Mulich, William *WhoAmP 93*
Mulin Chi *BlmGWL*
Mulisch, Harry *EncSF 93*
Mulisch, Harry (Kurt Victor) 1927- *ConWorW 93*
Mulitauaopele, Alamoana S. *WhoAmP 93*
Mulitauaopele, Ivi *WhoAmP 93*
Mulitauaopele, Ivi S. Alamoana 1939- *WhoAmP 93*
Muljadi, Eduard Benedictus 1957- *WhoScEn 94*
Mulkearns, Ronald Austin *Who 94*
Mulkeen, James P. 1945- *WhoAmL 94*
Mulkern, John 1931- *Who 94*
Mulkerns, Val 1925- *BlmGWL*
Mulkey, Charles Eric 1955- *WhoFI 94*
Mulkey, Chris *WhoHol 92*
Mulkey, Jack Clarendon 1939- *WhoAm 94*
Mulkey, Sharon Renee 1954- *WhoWest 94*
Mulks, Martha Huard 1950- *WhoMW 93*
Mull, Gale W. 1945- *WhoAmL 94*
Mull, Gerald S. *Who 94*
Mull, Martin 1943- *IntMPA 94, WhoAm 94, WhoCom, WhoHol 92*
Mull, Richard L. 1952- *WhoAmL 94*
Mull, Sandra Sue 1943- *WhoMW 93*
Mullach, Al d1970 *WhoAm 94*
Mullaley, Robert Charles 1926 *WhoAm 94*
Mullally, Frederic 1920- *EncSF 93*
Mullally, Megan *WhoHol 92*
Mullally, Pierce Harry 1918- *WhoFI 94, WhoMW 93*
Mullaly, Terence Frederick Stanley 1927- *Who 94*
Mullan, Bob 1947- *WrDr 94*
Mullan, Charles Heron 1912- *Who 94*
Mullan, David George 1951- *WrDr 94*
Mullan, James Boyd 1903- *WhoAm 94*
Mullan, John Francis 1925- *WhoAm 94*
Mullane, Denis Francis 1930- *WhoAm 94, WhoFI*
Mullane, Donald A. 1938- *WhoAm 94*
Mullane, John Francis 1937- *WhoAm 94*
Mullaney, Dora Aileen 1943- *WhoMW 93*
Mullaney, Jack d1982 *WhoHol 92*
Mullaney, Joseph E. 1933- *WhoAm 94, WhoAmL 94, WhoFI 94*
Mullaney, Thomas Joseph 1946- *WhoAmL 94*
Mullaney, Thomas Patrick, III 1953- *WhoAmL 94*
Mullard, Arthur 1912- *WhoHol 92*
Mullard, Chris(topher Paul) 1944- *WrDr 94*
Mullare, Thomas Kenwood, Jr. 1939- *WhoAm 94, WhoAmL 94*
Mullarkey, Mary J. *WhoAmP 93*
Mullarkey, Mary J. 1943- *WhoAm 94, WhoAmL 94, WhoWest 94*
Mullarkey, Maureen 1942- *WhoAmA 94*
Mullarkey, Thomas F. X. d1993 *NewYTBS 93*
Mullavey, Greg 1939- *WhoHol 92*
Mullen, Alexander 1945- *WhoScEn 94*
Mullen, Ann A. 1935- *WhoAmP 93*
Mullen, Barbara d1979 *WhoHol 92*
Mullen, Claude Robert, Jr. 1931- *WhoWest 94*
Mullen, Daniel Robert 1941- *WhoAm 94*
Mullen, David Clarence 1947- *WhoFI 94*
Mullen, Edward John, Jr. 1942- *WhoAm 94*

Mullen, Eileen Anne 1943- *WhoFI 94*
Mullen, Frederick J. 1951- *WhoAmL 94*
Mullen, Graham C. 1940- *WhoAm 94, WhoAmL 94*
Mullen, Harryette *DrAPF 93*
Mullen, J. Thomas 1940- *WhoAm 94, WhoAmL 94*
Mullen, James Gentry 1933- *WhoAm 94*
Mullen, James Hanna 1924-1989 *WhAm 10*
Mullen, James Martin 1935- *WhoAmA 94*
Mullen, Jo (Stauffer) 1908- *WhoAmA 93*
Mullen, John W. 1947- *WhoIns 94*
Mullen, John Wilfred 1924-1991 *WhAm 10*
Mullen, Joseph Patrick 1957- *WhoAm 94*
Mullen, Ken Ian 1955- *WhoScEn 94*
Mullen, Laura *DrAPF 93*
Mullen, Martin P. 1921- *WhoAmP 93*
Mullen, Michael Francis 1915- *WhoFI 94*
Mullen, Michael G. 1949- *WhoAmL 94*
Mullen, Michael Richard 1947- *WhoMW 93*
Mullen, Peter P. 1928- *WhoAm 94*
Mullen, Philip Edward 1942- *WhoAmA 93*
Mullen, R(ichard) D(ale) 1915- *EncSF 93*
Mullen, Ron 1939- *WhoAm 94*
Mullen, Sanford Allen 1925- *WhoAm 94*
Mullen, Stanley 1911-1973 *EncSF 93*
Mullen, Thomas Edgar 1936- *WhoFI 94, WhoMW 93*
Mullen, Timothy Bailey 1966- *WhoMW 93*
Mullen, William Joseph, III 1937- *WhoAm 94*
Mullenax, Charles Howard 1932- *WhoMW 93, WhoScEn 94*
Mullenbach, Linda Herman 1948- *WhoAmL 94*
Mullenbach, Philip 1912-1989 *WhAm 10*
Mullendore, Herbert Jack 1920- *WhoAmP 93*
Mullendore, James Myers 1919-1989 *WhAm 10*
Mullendore, Walter Edward 1940- *WhoAm 94*
Mullenix, Linda Susan 1950- *WhoAmL 94*
Mullenix, Ted 1945- *WhoAmP 93*
Mullenix, Travis H. 1931- *WhoFI 94*
Mullennex, Ronald Hale 1949- *WhoScEn 94*
Mullens, Anthony (Richard Guy) 1936- *Who 94*
Mullens, Delbert W. 1944- *WhoBlA 94*
Mullens, Jeffrey I. 1948- *WhoAmL 94*
Mullens, Johnnie d1978 *WhoHol 92*
Mullens, William Reese 1921- *WhoAm 94*
Muller, Achim 1938- *WhoScEn 94*
Muller, Adolf 1801-1886 *NewGrDO*
Muller, Alex *Who 94*
Muller, (Karl) Alex 1927- *Who 94*
Muller, Barbara J. 1954- *WhoAmL 94*
Muller, Carolina Fredrika 1755-1826 *NewGrDO*
Muller, Charles E., II 1951- *WhoAmL 94*
Muller, Charles William 1930- *WhoAmL 94*
Muller, Charlotte Feldman 1921- *WhoAm 94*
Muller, Christian Friedrich 1752-1827 *NewGrDO*
Muller, Clara 1861-1905 *BlmGWL*
Muller, Claudya Barbara 1946- *WhoMW 93*
Muller, Claus 1920- *IntWW 93*
Muller, Daniel 1953- *WhoScEn 94*
Muller, David Webster *WhoWest 94*
Muller, Dietrich Alfred Helmut 1936- *WhoAm 94, WhoScEn 94*
Muller, Edward Robert 1952- *WhoAm 94, WhoAmL 94, WhoFI 94*
Muller, Ernest H. 1923- *WhoAm 94*
Muller, Frank 1930- *WhoFI 94*
Muller, Frank B. 1926- *WhoAm 94*
Muller, Franz Joseph 1938- *Who 94*
Muller, Frederick Arthur 1937- *WhoAmL 94*
Muller, Gary William *WhoFI 94*
Muller, George F. 1866-1958 *WhoAmA 93N*
Muller, Gerhard 1929- *IntWW 93*
Muller, Gerhard 1939- *NewGrDO*
Muller, Gerhard 1945- *WorESoc [port]*
Muller, Harrison *WhoHol 92*
Muller, Heiner 1929- *ConWorW 93, IntDcT 2*
Muller, Helen B. 1922- *WhoAmA 93*
Muller, Henry James 1947- *WhoAm 94*
Muller, Henry John 1919- *WhoAm 94*
Muller, Henry Nicholas, III 1938- *WhoAm 94, WhoMW 93*
Muller, Hermann Joseph 1890-1967 *WorScD*
Muller, Hugh Walter 1944- *WhoFI 94*
Muller, Ingo *ConAu 142*

Mundin, Herbert d1939 *WhoHol 92*
Mundinger, Donald Charles 1929- *WhoAm 94*
Mundinger, Tom George 1950- *WhoMW 93*
Mundis, Hester *DrAPF 93*
Mundis, Hester (Jane) 1938- *WrDr 94*
Mundis, Jerrold *DrAPF 93*
Mundlak, Yair 1927- *WhoAm 94, WhoScEn 94*
Mundo, April Jean 1951- *WhoMW 93*
Mundschau, Michael Victor 1955- *WhoMW 93*
Mundt, Arley David 1959- *WhoMW 93*
Mundt, Barry Maynard 1936- *WhoAm 94*
Mundt, Ernest Karl 1905- *WhoAmA 93*
Mundt, Gary Harold 1943- *WhoAmP 93*
Mundt, Ray B. 1928- *WhoAm 94, WhoFI 94*
Mundt, Theodor 1808-1861 *DcLB 133 [port]*
Mundy, Carl Epting, Jr. 1935- *WhoAm 94*
Mundy, Edward d1962 *WhoHol 92*
Mundy, Ethel Frances d1964 *WhoAmA 93N*
Mundy, Gardner Marshall 1934- *WhoAmL 94*
Mundy, John Hine 1917- *WhoAm 94*
Mundy, John Jeffery 1962- *WhoAmL 94*
Mundy, Louise Easterday 1870-1952 *WhoAmA 93N*
Mundy, Mark J. 1942- *WhoAm 94*
Mundy, Max 1918- *WrDr 94*
Mundy, Meg 1923- *WhoHol 92*
Mundy, Phillip Carl *WhoScEn 94*
Mundy, Phyllis 1948- *WhoAmP 93*
Mundy, Rodney O. 1941- *WhoAmL 94*
Mundy, Talbot 1879-1940 *EncSF 93*
Mundy, William Greg 1950- *WhoAm 94, WhoAmL 94*
Munera, Gerard Emmanuel 1935- *WhoAm 94*
Munford, Christopher *DrAPF 93*
Munford, Dillard d1993 *NewYTBS 93*
Munford, Dillard 1918- *WhoAmP 93*
Munford, Joan Hardie 1933- *WhoAmP 93*
Munford, Luther Townsend 1949- *WhoAm 94*
Munford, Robert Watson 1925-1991 *WhoAmA 93N*
Munford, Walter F. 1900-1959 *EncABHB 9*
Munford, William Arthur 1911- *Who 94, WrDr 94*
Mungai, Njoroge 1926- *IntWW 93*
Mungan, Necmettin 1934- *WhoScEn 94*
Munger, Benson Scott 1942- *WhoAm 94*
Munger, Bryce L. 1933- *WhoAm 94*
Munger, Charles T. 1924- *WhoFI 94*
Munger, Edwin Stanton 1921- *WhoAm 94, WhoWest 94*
Munger, Elmer Lewis 1915- *WhoAm 94, WhoScEn 94*
Munger, Harold Charles 1929- *WhoAm 94, WhoMW 93, WhoScEn 94*
Munger, Harold Hawley, II 1947- *WhoMW 93*
Munger, James Guy 1951- *WhoFI 94*
Munger, John Francis 1946- *WhoAmP 93*
Munger, Molly 1948- *WhoAmL 94*
Munger, Paul R. 1932- *WhoAm 94, WhoScEn 94*
Munger, Theodore Thornton 1830-1910 *DcAmReB 2*
Munger, Willard M. 1911- *WhoAmP 93*
Mungia, Salvador Alejo, Jr. 1959- *WhoAmL 94*
Mungin, Horace *DrAPF 93*
Munguia, Gus *WhoHisp 94*
Munhall, Edgar 1933- *WhoAm 94*
Munhall, Ruth Beatrice 1929- *WhoFI 94*
Munhollon, Samuel Clifford 1948- *WhoFI 94*
Muni, Indu A. 1942- *WhoAsA 94*
Muni, Paul d1967 *WhoHol 92*
Munic, Martin Daniel 1959- *WhoAmL 94*
Munier, Alfred E. d1993 *NewYTBS 93*
Munier, Ferdinand d1945 *WhoHol 92*
Munif, 'Abd al-Rahman 1933- *ConWorW 93*
Munik, Janusz 1950- *WhoFI 94*
Munim, Mohammad Abdul 1935- *IntWW 93*
Muniot, Barbara King *WhoAmA 93*
Munir, Ashley Edward 1934- *Who 94*
Munir, Mohammad Idrees 1954- *WhoWest 94*
Munisteri, Joseph George 1930- *WhoAm 94*
Munitz, Barry 1941- *WhoAm 94, WhoWest 94*
Munitz, Gerald F. 1933- *WhoAm 94*
Muniz, Benigno, Jr. 1958- *WhoScEn 94*
Muniz, Carlos Manuel 1922- *IntWW 93*
Muniz, Eddy 1960- *WhoHisp 94*
Muñiz, Herminio 1928- *WhoHisp 94*
Muniz, Nicolas Jose 1962- *WhoAmL 94*
Muñiz Arrambide, Isabel 1960- *WhoHisp 94*
Muñiz Rivera, Edgardo Luis 1964- *WhoHisp 94*
Muñiz-Torres, Oscar 1947- *WhoHisp 94*
Munizzi, Pamela Annette 1954- *WhoAmP 93*
Munk, Frank 1901- *IntWW 93*
Munk, Jens Eriksen 1579-1628 *WhWE*
Munk, Kaj (Harald Leininger) 1898-1944 *IntDcT 2*
Munk, Peter 1927- *WhoAm 94, WhoFI 94*
Munk, Walter Heinrich 1917- *WhoAm 94, WhoScEn 94, WhoWest 94*
Munkacsy, Janos *EncSF 93*
Munk Andersen, Jens 1928- *IntWW 93*
Munkejord, Svein 1948- *IntWW 93*
Munker, Ariane *WhoHol 92*
Munk Olsen, Birger 1935- *IntWW 93*
Munley, Annette E. 1936- *WhoAmP 93*
Munn, Cecil Edwin 1923- *WhoAm 94*
Munn, James 1920- *Who 94*
Munn, Janet Teresa 1952- *WhoAmL 94*
Munn, Russell Dean 1970- *WhoMW 93*
Munn, Stephen P. *WhoAm 94*
Munn, William Charles, II 1938- *WhoWest 94*
Munneke, Gary Arthur 1947- *WhoAmL 94*
Munneke, Russell Edward 1946- *WhoMW 93*
Munnell, Alicia Haydock 1942- *WhoAm 94*
Munnich, Lee William, Jr. 1945- *WhoAmP 93*
Munninger, Michael Joseph 1948- *WhoWest 94*
Munno, Maurice William 1948- *WhoAmL 94*
Munns, Paul Robert 1963- *WhoAmP 93*
Munns, Victor George 1926- *Who 94*
Muno, Richard Carl 1939- *WhoAmA 93*
Munonye, John 1929- *WrDr 94*
Munowitz, Ken 1936-1978 *WhoAmA 93N*
Munoz, Adan, Jr. 1948- *WhoHisp 94*
Muñoz, Adolfo Homero, III 1945- *WhoHisp 94*
Munoz, Anthony 1958- *WhoBlA 94, WhoHisp 94*
Munoz, Artemio Zaragosa 1944- *WhoHisp 94*
Munoz, Aurelio *WhoHisp 94*
Muñoz, Braulio 1946- *WhoHisp 94*
Muñoz, Carlos, Jr. 1939- *WhoHisp 94, WhoWest 94*
Muñoz, Carlos Ramón *WhoHisp 94*
Munoz, Carlos Ramon 1935- *WhoAm 94, WhoFI 94*
Munoz, Carmen 1936- *WhoHisp 94*
Muñoz, Cecilia *WhoHisp 94*
Munoz, Celia Alvarez 1937- *WhoAmA 93, WhoHisp 94*
Munoz, Edward 1927- *WhoHisp 94*
Muñoz, Edward H. 1944- *WhoHisp 94*
Muñoz, Elias Miguel 1954- *WhoHisp 94*
Munoz, Enrique M. 1951- *WhoHisp 94*
Munoz, Ernesto *WhoHisp 94*
Muñoz, Frances *WhoHisp 94*
Munoz, George 1951- *WhoHisp 94*
Muñoz, Grisel 1957- *WhoHisp 94*
Munoz, Joanne Maura, Sister *WhoHisp 94*
Muñoz, John Anthony *WhoHisp 94*
Munoz, John Joaquin 1918- *WhoAm 94, WhoHisp 94*
Munoz, John Joseph 1932- *WhoWest 94*
Munoz, John Richard 1948- *WhoHisp 94*
Munoz, Jose Francisco 1946- *WhoHisp 94*
Muñoz, José Luis 1945- *WhoHisp 94*
Muñoz, Joseph 1940- *WhoHisp 94*
Muñoz, Juan H. 1944- *WhoHisp 94*
Munoz, Julian Daniel 1946- *WhoFI 94*
Munoz, Julio Alex 1922- *WhoHisp 94*
Munoz, Leonel 1953- *WhoHisp 94*
Munoz, Manuel Anthony 1945- *WhoFI 94, WhoHisp 94*
Munoz, Mario Alejandro 1928- *WhoMW 93*
Muñoz, Memo 1955- *WhoHisp 94*
Munoz, Michael Anthony 1958- *WhoAm 94*
Muñoz, Michael John 1963- *WhoHisp 94*
Munoz, Mike 1965- *WhoHisp 94*
Munoz, Moises Garcia 1922- *WhoHisp 94*
Munoz, Pedro Javier 1968- *WhoHisp 94*
Muñoz, Raúl 1932- *WhoHisp 94*
Muñoz, Raul Enrique 1939- *WhoHisp 94*
Munoz, Ricardo *WhoAmP 93*
Munoz, Ricardo Felipe 1950- *WhoWest 94*
Munoz, Rie *WhoAmA 93*
Munoz, Robert I. 1930- *WhoHisp 94*
Munoz, Romeo Solano 1933- *WhoMW 93*
Munoz, Sergio *WhoAmP 93, WhoHisp 94*
Muñoz, Victoria *WhoHisp 94*
Muñoz, Willy Oscar 1949- *WhoHisp 94*
Munoz-Blanco, Maria M. 1963- *WhoHisp 94*
Muñoz-Dones, Eloísa 1922- *WhoHisp 94*
Munoz Ledo, Porfirio 1933- *IntWW 93*
Muñoz-Sandoval, Ana Felicia 1947- *WhoHisp 94*
Muñoz-Solá, Haydeé S. 1943- *WhoHisp 94*
Munoz Vega, Pablo 1903- *IntWW 93*
Munro, Alan (Gordon) 1935- *IntWW 93, Who 94*
Munro, Alice 1931- *BlmGWL [port], IntWW 93, RfGShF, WhoAm 94, WrDr 94*
Munro, Alison *Who 94*
Munro, Caroline 1950- *WhoHol 92*
Munro, Charles Rowcliffe 1902- *Who 94*
Munro, Charles Wesley 1946- *WhoMW 93*
Munro, Colin Andrew 1946- *Who 94*
Munro, Colin William Gordon R. *Who 94*
Munro, Dana Gardner 1892-1990 *WhAm 10*
Munro, Donald J(acques) 1931- *WrDr 94*
Munro, Donald Jacques 1931- *WhoAm 94*
Munro, Douglas d1924 *WhoHol 92*
Munro, Duncan H. *EncSF 93*
Munro, Eleanor 1928- *WhoAmA 93*
Munro, Ellen Kane 1943- *WhoAmL 94*
Munro, Graeme Neil 1944- *Who 94*
Munro, H.H. *EncSF 93*
Munro, Hamish Nisbet 1915- *IntWW 93, WhoAm 94*
Munro, Hector Hugh *RfGShF*
Munro, Henry 1730-1802 *WhAmRev*
Munro, Ian Arthur Hoyle 1923- *Who 94*
Munro, J. Richard 1931- *IntWW 93, WhoAm 94, WhoFI 94*
Munro, James 1926- *WrDr 94*
Munro, Janet d1972 *WhoHol 92*
Munro, Janet Andrea 1949- *WhoAmA 93*
Munro, John 1849-1930 *EncSF 93*
Munro, John Bennet Lorimer 1905- *Who 94*
Munro, John Henry Alexander 1938- *WhoAm 94*
Munro, John M(urchison) 1932- *WrDr 94*
Munro, Joseph Barnes, Jr. 1930- *WhoAmL 94*
Munro, Nan 1905- *WhoHol 92*
Munro, Ralph Davies 1943- *WhoAm 94, WhoAmP 93, WhoWest 94*
Munro, Robert *WhoHol 92*
Munro, Robert (Lindsay) 1907- *Who 94*
Munro, Robert Allan 1932- *WhoAmL 94, WhoMW 93*
Munro, Roderick Anthony 1955- *WhoMW 93*
Munro, Rona 1959- *ConDr 93*
Munro, Ronald Eadie 1933- *WrDr 94*
Munro, Sydney Douglas G. *Who 94*
Munro, Thomas 1897-1974 *WhoAmA 93N*
Munro, William d1992 *Who 94N*
Munroe, David A. 1938- *WhoAmP 93*
Munroe, Donna Scott 1945- *WhoFI 94, WhoWest 94*
Munroe, George Barber 1922- *WhoAm 94*
Munroe, Lydia Darlene 1933- *WhoWest 94*
Munroe, Pat 1916- *WhoAm 94*
Munroe, Tapan *WhoAsA 94*
Munro of Foulis, Patrick 1912- *Who 94*
Munro of Foulis-Obsdale, Ian Talbot 1929- *Who 94*
Munro of Lindertis, Alasdair (Thomas Ian) 1927- *Who 94*
Munro of Novar, Hugh Andrew Johnstone c. 1797-1864 *DcNaB MP*
Munrow, Roger Davis 1929- *Who 94*
Muns Albuixech, Joaquin 1935- *IntWW 93*
Munsat, Stanley Morris 1939- *WhoAm 94*
Munsat, Theodore L. 1930- *WhoAm 94*
Munsch, Martha Hartle 1948- *WhoAm 94, WhoAmL 94*
Munsch, Richard John 1946- *WhoAmL 94*
Munsch, Robert 1945- *WrDr 94*
Munsel, Patrice 1925- *WhoHol 92*
Munsel, Patrice (Beverly) 1925- *NewGrDO*
Munsell, Elsie Louise 1939- *WhoAm 94*
Munsell, Susan Grimes *WhoAmP 93*
Munsell, Susan Grimes 1951- *WhoMW 93*
Munsey, David Morrill 1942- *WhoFI 94*
Munsey, Everard 1933- *WhoAmP 93*
Munsey, Frank A(ndrew) 1854-1925 *EncSF 93*
Munsey, Margaret Ruth 1924- *WhoWest 94*
Munsey, Rodney Roundy 1932- *WhoAm 94*
Munsey, Virdell Everard, Jr. 1933- *WhoAm 94*
Munshin, Jules d1970 *WhoHol 92*
Munsinger, Roger Alan 1948- *WhoScEn 94*
Munslow, Barry 1950- *ConAu 41NR*
Munson, Alex Robert 1941- *WhoAmL 94*
Munson, Arthur Julius 1907- *WhoAmP 93*
Munson, Bruce N. *WhoAmP 93*
Munson, Cheryl Denise 1954- *WhoBlA 94*
Munson, David Roy 1942- *WhoAmP 93*
Munson, Donald E. *WhoAmP 93*
Munson, Donald Francis 1937- *WhoAmP 93*
Munson, Earl Henry 1935- *WhoAmL 94*
Munson, Eddie Ray 1950- *WhoBlA 94*
Munson, Eric Bruce 1943- *WhoAm 94*
Munson, Harold Lewis 1923- *WhoAm 94*
Munson, Howard G. 1924- *WhoAm 94*
Munson, James Calfee 1944- *WhoAm 94, WhoAmL 94*
Munson, Janis Elizabeth Tremblay 1948- *WhoScEn 94*
Munson, John B. 1914- *WhoAmP 93*
Munson, John Backus 1933- *WhoAm 94*
Munson, John Christian 1926- *WhoAm 94*
Munson, Lawrence Shipley 1920- *WhoAm 94*
Munson, Leon J. 1939- *WhoFI 94*
Munson, Lucille Marguerite 1914- *WhoFI 94, WhoWest 94*
Munson, Mark Parr 1957- *WhoAmL 94*
Munson, Martha d1949 *WhoHol 92*
Munson, Nancy Kay 1936- *WhoAmL 94, WhoFI 94*
Munson, Norma Frances 1923- *WhoMW 93, WhoScEn 94*
Munson, Ona d1955 *WhoHol 92*
Munson, Paul Lewis 1910- *WhoAm 94*
Munson, Ralph Andrew 1950- *WhoWest 94*
Munson, Ray Eugene 1927- *WhoWest 94*
Munson, Richard Howard 1948- *WhoAm 94*
Munson, Robert Dean 1927- *WhoMW 93*
Munson, Robert H. 1931- *WhoBlA 94*
Munson, Thomas Nolan 1924- *WrDr 94*
Munson, Virginia Aldrich 1932- *WhoMW 93*
Munson, William Leslie 1941- *WhoAm 94*
Munster, Earl of 1926- *Who 94*
Munster, Andrew Michael 1935- *WhoAm 94*
Munster, Edward W. *WhoAmP 93*
Munsterberg, Hugo 1916- *WhoAmA 93*
Munsterteiger, Kay Diane 1956- *WhoWest 94*
Munt, Donna S. 1950- *WhoIns 94*
Munter, Godfrey L(eon) 1897- *WhAm 10*
Munter, Pamela Osborne 1943- *WhoFI 94*
Munts, Mary Louise 1924- *WhoAmP 93*
Muntwyler, Urs Walter 1958- *WhoScEn 94*
Muntyan, Mikhail 1943- *IntWW 93*
Muntz, Eric Phillip 1934- *WhoAm 94, WhoScEn 94*
Muntz, Ernest Gordon 1923- *WhoAm 94*
Muntz, Palmer Hayden 1960- *WhoWest 94*
Muntz, Richard Robert 1941- *WhoScEn 94*
Muntzing, Lewis Manning 1934- *WhoAm 94*
Muntzinger, Robert Wilson 1928- *WhoMW 93*
Muny, Keith Walter 1965- *WhoFI 94*
Munyer, Edward A. 1936- *WhoAm 94, WhoScEn 94*
Munyon, William Harry, Jr. 1945- *WhoFI 94*
Munz, Peter 1921- *WrDr 94*
Munzer, Cynthia Brown 1948- *WhoAm 94*
Munzer, Martha E. 1899- *WrDr 94*
Munzer, Martha Eiseman 1899- *WhoScEn 94*
Munzer, Stephen Ira 1939- *WhoAmL 94*
Munzer, Stephen R. 1944- *WhoAm 94*
Munzinger, Judith Montgomery 1944- *WhoMW 93*
Munzner, Aribert 1930- *WhoAmA 93*
Munzner, Robert Frederick 1936- *WhoScEn 94*
Muoto, Oliver Chukwudi 1965- *WhoWest 94*
Mupanga, Joyce *WhoWomW 91*
Mu Qing 1921- *IntWW 93, WhoPRCh 91 [port]*
Mur, Raphael 1927- *WhoAm 94*
Mura, Corinna d1965 *WhoHol 92*
Mura, David *DrAPF 93*
Mura, David 1952- *WhoAsA 94*
Mura, Toshio 1925- *WhoAm 94, WhoAsA 94*
Murabayashi, Harris Nozomu 1928- *WhoWest 94*
Murad, Ferid 1936- *WhoAm 94*
Murad, John Louis 1932- *WhoAm 94*
Murad, Sohail 1953- *WhoAsA 94*
Murad, Tariq 1936- *WhoMW 93*
Muradeli, Vano Il'ich 1908-1970 *NewGrDO*
Muradian, Vazgen 1921- *WhoAm 94*
Muradin-Szweykowska, Maria 1952- *WhoScEn 94*

Muradov, Sakhat Nepesovich 1932- *IntWW 93, LngBDD*
Murai, Norimoto 1944- *WhoAsA 94*
Murai, Shinji 1938- *WhoScEn 94*
Muraire, Louis fl. 1715- *NewGrDO*
Murakami, Edahiko 1922- *WhoScEn 94*
Murakami, Haruki 1949- *EncSF 93*
Murakami, Jeffrey Hisakazu 1962- *WhoAsA 94*
Murakami, Masakuni *IntWW 93*
Murakami, Pamela S. 1951- *WhoAsA 94*
Murakami, Richard M. 1932- *WhoAsA 94*
Murakami, Toshio *WhoWest 94*
Murakami Haruki 1949- *ConWorW 93*
Muraki, Yoshiro 1924- *IntDcF 2-4*
Murakishi, Steve 1949- *WhoAmA 93*
Muramatsu, Ichiro *WhoScEn 94*
Muranaka, Allen Tokuo 1956- *WhoWest 94*
Muranaka, Hideo 1946- *WhoAmA 93*
Muranaka, Ken-ichiro 1958- *WhoScEn 94*
Murane, William Edward 1933- *WhoAm 94*
Murante, David Alan 1946- *WhoAmL 94*
Muranyi, Gustave 1872-1961 *WhoAmA 93N*
Murao, Kenji 1946- *WhoScEn 94*
Muraoka, Dennis Dean 1952- *WhoWest 94*
Muraoka, Sadakatsu 1910- *IntWW 93*
Muraoka, Takakatsu 1938- *IntWW 93*
Murase, Jiro 1928- *WhoAm 94*
Murase, Mike 1947- *WhoAsA 94*
Murashima, Kumiko *WhoAmA 93*
Muraski, Anthony Augustus 1946- *WhoAmL 94, WhoFI 94, WhoMW 93*
Murasugi, Kunio 1929- *WhoAm 94*
Murat, Comtesse de 1670-1716 *BlmGWL*
Murat, Jean d1968 *WhoHol 92*
Murat, Jean-Louis *WhoHol 92*
Murat, William M. 1957- *WhoAmP 93*
Murata, Hiroshi 1941- *WhoAmA 93*
Murata, Keijiro 1924- *IntWW 93*
Murata, Kiyoaki 1922- *IntWW 93*
Murata, Makoto 1926- *IntWW 93*
Murata, Margaret K. 1946- *WhoAsA 94*
Murata, Masachika 1906- *IntWW 93*
Murata, Ryohei 1929- *IntWW 93*
Murata, Tadao 1938- *WhoAm 94*
Murata, Yasuo 1931- *WhoScEn 94*
Murata, Yuji 1942- *WhoAsA 94*
Muratore, Lucien d1954 *WhoHol 92*
Muratore, Lucien 1876-1954 *NewGrDO*
Muratore, Peter Frederick 1932- *WhoAm 94*
Muratore, Robert Peter 1957- *WhoAm 94*
Muratori, Fred *DrAPF 93*
Muratori, Jack R. 1929- *WhoAmP 93*
Muratova, Kira Georgievna 1934- *IntWW 93*
Muravchik, Joshua 1947- *WrDr 94*
Muravschi, Valeriu *IntWW 93*
Muravyova, Irina *WhoHol 92*
Murawski, Elisabeth *DrAPF 93*
Murayama, Makio 1912- *WhoAm 94, WhoScEn 94*
Murayama, Tatsuo *IntWW 93*
Murazawa, Tadashi 1940- *WhoScEn 94*
Murcell, George 1925- *WhoHol 92*
Murcelo, Karmin *WhoHol 92*
Murch, Anna Valentina 1948- *WhoAmA 93*
Murch, Everett Lloyd 1935- *WhoFI 94, WhoMW 93*
Murch, Walter *IntDcF 2-4*
Murch, Walter 1907-1967 *WhoAmA 93N*
Murch, Walter Scott 1943- *WhoAm 94*
Murchake, John 1922- *WhoFI 94*
Murchie, Donald John 1943- *WhoAmA 93*
Murchie, Douglas Robertson 1962- *WhoFI 94*
Murchie, Guy 1907- *ConAu 19AS [port], WhoAm 94, WhoFI 94*
Murchie, James Skiffington *WhoFI 94*
Murchie, John Ivor 1928- *Who 94*
Murchison, Craig Brian 1943- *WhoMW 93*
Murchison, David Claudius 1923- *WhoAm 94, WhoAmL 94, WhoFI 94*
Murchison, David Roderick 1948- *WhoAm 94, WhoAmL 94, WhoFI 94*
Murchison, John D. 1921-1979 *WhoAmA 93N*
Murciano, Marianne 1957- *WhoHisp 94*
Murcko, Donald Leroy 1953- *WhoMW 93*
Murcray, Frank James 1950- *WhoScEn 94*
Murdic, Thomas Edward 1953- *WhoAmP 93*
Murdin, Paul Geoffrey 1942- *Who 94*
Burdocco, Vince *WhoHol 92*
Murdoch, Bernard Constantine 1917- *WhoAm 94*
Murdoch, Brian (Oliver) 1944- *ConAu 141*
Murdoch, David Armor 1942- *WhoAm 94, WhoAmL 94, WhoFI 94*
Murdoch, Elisabeth (Joy) 1909- *Who 94*
Murdoch, Iris *Who 94*

Murdoch, Iris 1919- *BlmGEL [port], BlmGWL, WhoAm 94, WrDr 94*
Murdoch, (Jean) Iris 1919- *ConAu 43NR, ConDr 93, IntWW 93, Who 94*
Murdoch, John Derek Walter 1945- *Who 94*
Murdoch, Lawrence Corlies, Jr. 1926- *WhoAm 94*
Murdoch, Richard d1990 *WhoHol 92*
Murdoch, Robert 1911- *Who 94*
Murdoch, Robert Edward 1966- *WhoFI 94*
Murdoch, Robert Waugh 1942- *WhoAm 94, WhoFI 94*
Murdoch, Robert Whitten 1937- *WhoAmL 94, WhoFI 94*
Murdoch, Rupert *Who 94*
Murdoch, Rupert 1931- *IntMPA 94, WhoAm 94, WhoFI 94*
Murdoch, (Keith) Rupert 1931- *IntWW 93, Who 94*
Murdoch, William Richard 1931- *WhoWest 94*
Murdoch, William Ridley Morton 1917- *Who 94*
Murdoch-Kitt, Norma Hood 1947- *WhoScEn 94*
Murdock, Ann d1939 *WhoHol 92*
Murdock, Bruce 1956- *WhoScEn 94*
Murdock, Charles William 1935- *WhoAm 94, WhoAmL 94*
Murdock, David H. 1923- *WhoAm 94, WhoFI 94, WhoWest 94*
Murdock, Deborah Dale 1943- *WhoAmP 93*
Murdock, Denis Ray 1948- *WhoWest 94*
Murdock, Donald Dean 1928- *WhoAmP 93*
Murdock, Douglas William 1950- *WhoAmL 94*
Murdock, Eric Lloyd 1968- *WhoBlA 94*
Murdock, Eugene C 1921- *WrDr 94*
Murdock, Gary Allen 1960- *WhoMW 93*
Murdock, George *WhoHol 92*
Murdock, Greg 1954- *WhoAmA 93*
Murdock, Jack 1925- *WhoHol 92*
Murdock, James *WhoHol 92*
Murdock, Kermit d1981 *WhoHol 92*
Murdock, Larry Lee 1942- *WhoMW 93*
Murdock, M(elinda) S(eabrooke) 1947- *EncSF 93*
Murdock, Mary-Elizabeth 1930- *WhoAm 94*
Murdock, Michele 1942- *WhoFI 94*
Murdock, Mickey L. 1942- *WhoIns 94*
Murdock, Mickey Lane 1942- *WhoFI 94*
Murdock, Norman A. 1931- *WhoAmP 93*
Murdock, Pamela Ervilla 1940- *WhoFI 94, WhoAmL 94*
Murdock, Phelps Dubois, Jr. 1944- *WhoFI 94, WhoAmA 93*
Murdock, Robert Mead 1941- *WhoAm 94, WhoAmA 93*
Murdock, Steven Kent 1946- *WhoFI 94, WhoWest 94*
Murdock, Stuart Laird 1926- *WhoAm 94*
Murdock, Veronica 1963- *WhoWest 94*
Murdock, William d1978 *WhoHol 92*
Murdock, William 1754-1839 *WorInv*
Murdy, James L. *WhoFI 94*
Murdy, Louise Baughan 1935- *WrDr 94*
Murdy, Wayne William 1944- *WhoAm 94*
Mure, Kenneth Nisbet 1947- *Who 94*
Muren, Dennis E. 1946- *WhoAm 94*
Murena, H. A. 1923- *IntWW 93*
Murensky, Rick, III 1953- *WhoAmP 93*
Murerwa, Herbert Muchemwa 1941- *IntWW 93, Who 94*
Muresan, Ana *WhoWomW 91*
Muresanu, Violeta Ana 1942- *WhoScEn 94*
Murfet, Ian Campbell 1934- *WhoScEn 94*
Murfin, Donald Leon 1943- *WhoAm 94*
Murfin, Jane 1893-1955 *IntDcF 2-4 [port]*
Murfin, Ross C 1948- *WhoAm 94*
Murfree, Mary Noailles 1850-1922 *BlmGWL*
Murga, Jesse SantiEsteban 1958- *WhoAmL 94*
Murgatroyd, Eric Neal 1950- *WhoFI 94*
Murgatroyd, George William 1948- *WhoAmL 94*
Murgatroyd, Walter 1921- *Who 94*
Murger, Henry 1822-1861 *NewGrDO*
Murguia, Alejandro *DrAPF 93*
Murguia, D. Edward 1943- *WhoHisp 94*
Murguia, Dana M. 1967- *WhoHisp 94*
Murguia, Filiberto 1932- *WhoHisp 94*
Murguia, Joaquin Florentino 1958- *WhoWest 94*
Murgulescu, Ilie d1991 *IntWW 93N*
Muria i Romani, Anna 1904- *BlmGWL*
Murian, Richard Miller 1937- *WhoWest 94*
Murie, Margaret E(lizabeth) 1902- *WrDr 94*
Muriel, Nun of Wilton fl. 11th cent.- *BlmGWL*

Muriera, Helen Bautista 1926- *WhoAsA 94*
Murillo, Alice 1954- *WhoHisp 94*
Murillo, Christine *WhoHol 92*
Murillo, John J., Jr. 1964- *WhoHisp 94*
Murillo, Velda Jean 1943- *WhoWest 94*
Murillo-Rohde, Ildaura M. *WhoHisp 94*
Murillo-Rohde, Ildaura Maria *WhoAm 94*
Murino, Vincent S. d1993 *NewYTBS 93*
Muris, Timothy Joseph 1949- *WhoAm 94, WhoAmP 93*
Murkett, Philip Tillotson 1931- *WhoFI 94*
Murkowski, Frank H. 1933- *CngDr 93, WhoAmP 93*
Murkowski, Frank Hughes 1933- *IntWW 93, WhoAm 94, WhoWest 94*
Murley, John Tregarthen 1928- *Who 94*
Murley, Reginald (Sydney) 1916- *Who 94*
Murnaghan, Francis D. 1893- *WhAm 10*
Murnaghan, Francis D., Jr. *WhoAmP 93*
Murnaghan, Francis Dominic, Jr. 1920- *WhoAm 94, WhoAmL 94*
Murname, Allan d1950 *WhoHol 92*
Murnane, Edward David 1944- *WhoMW 93*
Murnane, George Thomas, Jr. 1921- *WhoFI 94*
Murnane, Gerald 1939- *EncSF 93, WrDr 94*
Murnane, Thomas George 1926- *WhoAm 94*
Murnau, F. W. 1888-1931 *TwCLC 53 [port]*
Murney, Christopher *WhoHol 92*
Murnik, James Michael 1934- *WhoMW 93*
Murnik, Mary Rengo 1942- *WhoMW 93, WhoScEn 94*
Muro, Bernardo de *NewGrDO*
Muro, Gertrude Hilda 1939- *WhoHisp 94*
Muro, Roy Alfred 1942- *WhoAm 94, WhoFI 94*
Muroff, Lawrence Ross 1942- *WhoAm 94, WhoScEn 94*
Murofushi, Minoru *IntWW 93*
Muroga, Saburo 1925- *WhoAm 94*
Murolo, Roberto *WhoHol 92*
Murotake, Thomas Hisashi 1955- *WhoWest 94*

Murph
See Dinosaur Jr. *ConMus 10*
Murphey, Arthur Gage, Jr. 1927- *WhoAm 94*
Murphey, Elmer, III 1945- *WhoAmL 94*
Murphey, Joseph Colin *DrAPF 93*
Murphey, Michael Martin 1945- *WhoAm 94*
Murphey, Murray Griffin 1928- *WhoAm 94*
Murphey, Rhoads 1919- *WhoAm 94, WhoMW 93, WrDr 94*
Murphey, Robert Stafford 1921- *WhoAm 94*
Murphey, Robert William 1933- *WhoWest 94*
Murphree, Henry Bernard Scott 1927- *WhoAm 94*
Murphy, Ada d1961 *WhoHol 92*
Murphy, Albert Thomas 1924- *WhoAm 94*
Murphy, Allen Forrest, III 1954- *WhoFI 94*
Murphy, Alma d1978 *WhoHol 92*
Murphy, Alvin Hugh 1930- *WhoBlA 94*
Murphy, Alvin Leo 1934- *WhoAm 94*
Murphy, Andrew J., Jr. *WhoMW 93*
Murphy, Andrew John 1946- *Who 94*
Murphy, Andrew Phillip, Jr. 1922- *WhoFI 94*
Murphy, Anne Marie 1926-1989 *WhAm 10*
Murphy, Anthony Albert 1924- *Who 94*
Murphy, Arnold Leo 1925- *WhoWest 94*
Murphy, Arthur G. 1929- *WhoBlA 94*
Murphy, Arthur John, Jr. 1950- *WhoAm 94*
Murphy, Arthur Lister 1906-1985 *ConDr 93*
Murphy, Arthur Thomas 1929- *WhoAm 94*
Murphy, Arthur William 1922- *WhoAm 94*
Murphy, Audie d1971 *WhoHol 92*
Murphy, Austin de la Salle 1917- *WhoAm 94, WhoFI 94*
Murphy, Austin J. 1927- *CngDr 93*
Murphy, Austin John 1927- *WhoAm 94, WhoAmP 93*
Murphy, Barbara Beasley *DrAPF 93*
Murphy, Barbara Joan 1936- *WhoAmP 93*
Murphy, Barri *WhoHol 92*
Murphy, Barry Ames 1938- *WhoAm 94*
Murphy, Barry John 1940- *WhoAm 94*
Murphy, Beatrice M. 1908- *WhoBlA 94*
Murphy, Beatrice M. 1908-1992 *BlkWr 2*
Murphy, Ben 1942- *IntMPA 94, WhoHol 92*

Murphy, Benjamin Edward 1942- *WhoAm 94*
Murphy, Bernard Thomas 1932- *WhoAm 94*
Murphy, Bette Jane Manion 1931- *WhoAmP 93*
Murphy, Betty Jane Southard *WhoAm 94, WhoAmP 93*
Murphy, Beverley Elaine Pearson 1929- *WhoAm 94*
Murphy, Bob d1948 *WhoHol 92*
Murphy, Brenda Fettig 1942- *WhoAm 94*
Murphy, Brian 1933- *WhoHol 92*
Murphy, Brian Taunton, Mrs. *Who 94*
Murphy, Brian Thomas 1955- *WhoAmL 94*
Murphy, Brooke S. 1945- *WhoAmL 94*
Murphy, C. L. 1924- *WrDr 94*
Murphy, C(harles) Thorne 1895- *WhAm 10*
Murphy, Calvin 1948- *BasBi*
Murphy, Calvin Jerome 1948- *WhoBlA 94*
Murphy, Carolyn Louise 1944- *WhoIns 94*
Murphy, Caryle Marie 1946- *WhoAm 94*
Murphy, Catherine 1946- *WhoAm 94*
Murphy, Catherine E. 1946- *WhoAmA 93*
Murphy, Charles *WhoHol 92*
Murphy, Charles A. 1932- *WhoBlA 94*
Murphy, Charles Arnold 1932- *WhoAm 94*
Murphy, Charles B. d1942 *WhoHol 92*
Murphy, Charles Franklin 1933- *WhoAm 94*
Murphy, Charles Haywood, Jr. 1920- *WhoAm 94, WhoFI 94*
Murphy, Charles Joseph 1947- *WhoAm 94, WhoFI 94*
Murphy, Charles Q. *WhoHol 92*
Murphy, Charles S. 1909-1983 *HisDcKW*
Murphy, Charles William 1929- *WhoBlA 94, WhoMW 93*
Murphy, Chester Glenn 1907- *WhoAmA 93*
Murphy, Christopher Philip Yorke 1947- *Who 94*
Murphy, Claire Rudolf 1951- *SmATA 76 [port]*
Murphy, Clyde Everett 1948- *WhoBlA 94*
Murphy, Colleen Frances 1960- *WhoMW 93*
Murphy, Colleen Patricia 1943- *WhoFI 94*
Murphy, Cornelius McCaffrey 1936- *Who 94*
Murphy, Dan
See Soul Asylum *ConMus 10*
Murphy, Daniel Howard 1944- *WhoBlA 94*
Murphy, Daniel Ignatius 1927- *WhoAmL 94*
Murphy, Daniel Patrick 1966- *WhoMW 93*
Murphy, David 1948- *WhoAmL 94*
Murphy, David Chandler 1962- *WhoMW 93*
Murphy, David Ridgeway 1945- *WhoAm 94*
Murphy, David Thomas 1929- *WhoAm 94*
Murphy, David William 1954- *WhoFI 94*
Murphy, Deborah June 1955- *WhoAmL 94*
Murphy, Deborah Lask 1946- *WhoAmP 93*
Murphy, Delbert S. 1929- *WhoAmP 93*
Murphy, Della Mary 1935- *WhoBlA 94*
Murphy, Dennis F. 1937- *WhoAm 94*
Murphy, Dennis Jasper *EncSF 93*
Murphy, Dennis Joseph 1946- *WhoAm 94, WhoAmL 94, WhoMW 93*
Murphy, Dennis Michael 1962- *WhoAmP 93*
Murphy, Dennis Raymond 1946- *WhoAmL 94*
Murphy, Dervla 1931- *BlmGWL, Who 94*
Murphy, Dervla Mary 1931- *IntWW 93, WrDr 94*
Murphy, Diana E. 1934- *WhoAm 94, WhoAmL 94, WhoMW 93*
Murphy, Diane Alyce 1949- *WhoMW 93*
Murphy, Donald *WhoHol 92*
Murphy, Donald Richard 1938- *WhoBlA 94*
Murphy, Douglas Blakeney 1945- *WhoScEn 94*
Murphy, Dudley C. 1940- *WhoAmA 93*
Murphy, E. Jefferson 1926- *WrDr 94*
Murphy, Eddie 1951- *IntWW 93*
Murphy, Eddie 1961- *AfrAmAl 6, IntMPA 94, WhoAm 94, WhoBlA 94, WhoCom [port], WhoHol 92*
Murphy, Edmund Michael 1936- *WhoAm 94*
Murphy, Edna d1974 *WhoHol 92*
Murphy, Edrie Lee 1953- *WhoMW 93*
Murphy, Edward P. *WhoAm 94*
Murphy, Edward Patrick, Jr. 1943- *WhoAm 94*

Murphy, Edward Thomas 1947- *WhoScEn 94*
Murphy, Eileen *WhoHol 92*
Murphy, Elaine Romaine *DrAPF 93*
Murphy, Eleanor M. *WhoAmP 93*
Murphy, Elizabeth *WhoAmP 93*
Murphy, Ellis *WhoAm 94, WhoFI 94*
Murphy, Emily Gowan 1868-1933 *BlmGWL*
Murphy, Eugene F. 1936- *WhoAm 94, WhoScEn 94*
Murphy, Eugene Francis 1913- *WhoAm 94*
Murphy, Evelyn F. 1940- *WhoAmP 93*
Murphy, Evelyn Frances 1940- *WhoAm 94*
Murphy, Ewell Edward, Jr. 1928- *WhoAm 94, WhoAmL 94*
Murphy, Frances L., II *WhoBlA 94*
Murphy, Frances Louise, II *WhoFI 94*
Murphy, Francis 1932- *WhoAm 94*
Murphy, Francis 1959- *WhoMW 93*
Murphy, Francis Patrick 1948- *WhoAmL 94*
Murphy, Francis Seward 1914- *WhoWest 94*
Murphy, Francis Xavier, Jr. 1948- *WhoFI 94*
Murphy, Frank *DrAPF 93*
Murphy, Franklin David 1916- *IntWW 93, WhoAm 94; WhoWest 94*
Murphy, Gene 1956- *WhoBlA 94*
Murphy, George d1941 *WhoHol 92*
Murphy, George 1902- *WhoHol 92*
Murphy, George A. 1923- *WhoAmP 93*
Murphy, George B., Jr. 1905-1987 *WhoBlA 94N*
Murphy, George E., Jr. *DrAPF 93*
Murphy, George William 1941- *WhoIns 94*
Murphy, Gerald 1938- *WhoAm 94, WhoFI 94*
Murphy, Gerald D. 1928- *WhoFI 94*
Murphy, Gerald Patrick 1934- *WhoAm 94*
Murphy, Geraldine Joanne 1920-1990 *WhAm 10*
Murphy, Gerard Norris 1950- *WhoFI 94*
Murphy, Gervase *Who 94*
Murphy, (John) Gervase (Maurice Walker) 1926- *Who 94*
Murphy, Gladys Wilkins 1907-1985 *WhoAmA 93N*
Murphy, Glen *WhoHol 92*
Murphy, Glenn Edgar, Jr. 1949- *WhoFI 94*
Murphy, Gordon J. 1927- *WrDr 94*
Murphy, Gordon John 1927- *WhoAm 94*
Murphy, Gordon Laurence 1935- *WhoFI 94*
Murphy, Gregory Gerard 1954- *WhoAm 94*
Murphy, Harold *WhoAmP 93*
Murphy, Harold Loyd 1927- *WhoAm 94, WhoAmL 94*
Murphy, Harriet Louise M. *WhoBlA 94*
Murphy, Hass 1950- *WhoAmA 93*
Murphy, Helen 1962- *WhoFI 94*
Murphy, Herbert A. 1911- *WhoAmA 93*
Murphy, Horace d1975 *WhoHol 92*
Murphy, Ian Patrick 1949- *Who 94*
Murphy, Ira H. 1928- *WhoBlA 94*
Murphy, J. Kevin 1927- *WhoAm 94*
Murphy, Jack Redmond 1912- *WhoAmP 93*
Murphy, Jacqueline Adell 1948- *WhoWest 94*
Murphy, Jacquelyn Maria 1952- *WhoMW 93*
Murphy, James A. d1993 *NewYTBS 93*
Murphy, James Burton, Jr. 1954- *WhoAmL 94*
Murphy, James F. 1933- *WhoAm 94, WhoMW 93*
Murphy, James Gilmartin 1959- *WhoAmL 94*
Murphy, James Jackson 1944- *WhoAm 94*
Murphy, James Jerome 1923- *WhoWest 94*
Murphy, James Jerome, Jr. 1936- *WhoAmP 93*
Murphy, James Lawson 1951- *WhoWest 94*
Murphy, James Lee 1939- *WhoAm 94, WhoFI 94*
Murphy, James Michael 1947- *WhoAm 94*
Murphy, James Patrick 1932- *Who 94*
Murphy, James Paul 1944- *WhoAm 94, WhoAmL 94*
Murphy, James S. 1934- *WrDr 94*
Murphy, James W. 1936- *WhoIns 94*
Murphy, James William 1936- *WhoAmP 93*
Murphy, Jane *WhoAmP 93*
Murphy, Jeanette Carol 1931- *WhoMW 93*
Murphy, Jeanne Claire 1929- *WhoBlA 94*
Murphy, Jeffrey Joseph 1954- *WhoAmL 94*

Murphy, Jenny Dee 1932- *WhoMW 93*
Murphy, Jill (Frances) 1949- *WrDr 94*
Murphy, Jill Lucille 1946- *WhoMW 93*
Murphy, Jim 1925- *WhoAmP 93*
Murphy, Jim 1947- *SmATA 77*
Murphy, Jimmy *WhoHol 92*
Murphy, Jo Anne *WhoMW 93*
Murphy, Joe d1961 *WhoHol 92*
Murphy, John A. 1905- *Who 94*
Murphy, John A. 1929- *IntWW 93*
Murphy, John Aloysius 1905- *IntWW 93*
Murphy, John Arthur 1929- *WhoAm 94*
Murphy, John Carter 1921- *WhoAm 94, WhoFI 94, WhoScEn 94*
Murphy, John Clark 1954- *WhoAmL 94*
Murphy, John Condron, Jr. 1945- *WhoAm 94, WhoAmL 94*
Murphy, John Cullen 1919- *WhoAm 94*
Murphy, John Daly d1934 *WhoHol 92*
Murphy, John E., Jr. 1943- *WhoAmP 93*
Murphy, John F. 1905- *IntMPA 94*
Murphy, John F. 1954- *WhoAmL 94*
Murphy, John Francis *WhoHol 92*
Murphy, John Francis 1923- *WhoAmP 93*
Murphy, John Francis 1938- *WhoAmP 93*
Murphy, John H., III 1916- *WhoBlA 94*
Murphy, John Henry 1840-1922 *AfrAmAl 6 [port]*
Murphy, John Joseph 1931- *WhoAm 94, WhoFI 94*
Murphy, John Joseph 1936- *WhoIns 94*
Murphy, John Joseph, Jr. 1951- *WhoFI 94*
Murphy, John Matthew, Jr. 1935- *WhoBlA 94*
Murphy, John Michael 1945- *IntWW 93*
Murphy, John Patrick 1945- *WhoIns 94*
Murphy, John T. d1955 *WhoHol 92*
Murphy, John Thomas 1928- *WhoAmL 94*
Murphy, John W. 1937- *WhoFI 94*
Murphy, Joseph E., Jr. 1930- *WrDr 94*
Murphy, Joseph Edward, Jr. 1930- *WhoAm 94*
Murphy, Joseph F. 1915- *WhoAm 94*
Murphy, Joseph S. 1933- *WhoAm 94*
Murphy, Judith Chisholm 1942- *WhoFI 94*
Murphy, Kathleen Jane 1962- *WhoScEn 94*
Murphy, Kathleen Mary 1945- *WhoAmL 94, WhoFI 94*
Murphy, Kay A. *DrAPF 93*
Murphy, Kevin Dion 1963- *WhoBlA 94*
Murphy, Kevin Robert 1949- *WhoAmL 94*
Murphy, Larry 1952- *WhoAmP 93*
Murphy, Lawrence Martin 1941- *WhoWest 94*
Murphy, Lawrence Thomas 1961- *WhoAm 94*
Murphy, Leslie (Frederick) 1915- *Who 94*
Murphy, Leslie Frederick 1915- *IntWW 93*
Murphy, Lester Fuller 1936- *WhoAmL 94*
Murphy, Lewis Curtis 1933- *WhoAm 94, WhoAmP 94*
Murphy, Lexa *WhoHol 92*
Murphy, Lois Barclay 1902- *ConAu 41NR*
Murphy, Margaret H. *WhoAmP 93*
Murphy, Margaret H. 1948- *WhoAm 94, WhoAmL 94*
Murphy, Margaret Humphries *WhoBlA 94*
Murphy, Margaret Marie 1944- *WhoMW 93*
Murphy, Marilyn L. 1950- *WhoAmA 93*
Murphy, Martha W(atson) 1951- *WrDr 94*
Murphy, (Gavin) Martin (Hedd) 1934- *WrDr 94*
Murphy, Martin Joseph, Jr. 1942- *WhoAm 94, WhoScEn 94*
Murphy, Mary 1931- *WhoHol 92*
Murphy, Mary Ann 1943- *WhoWest 94*
Murphy, Mary C. *WhoMW 93*
Murphy, Mary Catherine *WhoAmP 93*
Murphy, Mary Kathryn 1941- *WhoFI 94, WhoMW 93*
Murphy, Mary Lillie 1919- *WhoAmP 93*
Murphy, Mary Therese 1957- *WhoMW 93*
Murphy, Matt *WhoHol 92*
Murphy, Matthew J., Jr. 1926- *WhoAmP 93*
Murphy, Maureen *WhoAmP 93*
Murphy, Maurice d1978 *WhoHol 92*
Murphy, Maurice J., Jr. *WhoAmP 93*
Murphy, Maurice Thomas 1935- *WhoAmP 93*
Murphy, Max Ray 1934- *WhoAmL 94, WhoMW 93*
Murphy, Michael *DrAPF 93*
Murphy, Michael 1938- *IntMPA 94, WhoHol 92*
Murphy, Michael Ansell 1943- *WhoWest 94*
Murphy, Michael Conlon 1937- *WhoAm 94*
Murphy, Michael E. 1939- *WhoAmL 94*
Murphy, Michael Emmett 1936- *WhoAm 94, WhoFI 94*

Murphy, Michael J. 1940- *WhoAm 94, WhoAmL 94*
Murphy, Michael Lee *WhoMW 93*
Murphy, Michael McKay 1946- *WhoBlA 94*
Murphy, Michele Susan 1949- *WhoMW 93*
Murphy, Mike 1932- *WhoAmP 93*
Murphy, Nancy L. 1929- *WhoAmP 93*
Murphy, Napoleon Bonaparte 1921- *WhoAmP 93*
Murphy, Neil *Who 94*
Murphy, Nyla A. 1931- *WhoAmP 93*
Murphy, P. D. *DrAPF 93*
Murphy, P(eter) J(ohn) 1946- *WrDr 94*
Murphy, Pamela 1945- *WhoHol 92*
Murphy, Pat *DrAPF 93*
Murphy, Pat 1955- *EncSF 93*
Murphy, Pat 1959- *WhoAmP 93*
Murphy, Patrick Francis 1960- *WhoAmP 93*
Murphy, Patrick Hale 1948- *WhoAmP 93*
Murphy, Patrick James 1931- *Who 94*
Murphy, Patrick Joseph 1949- *WhoAmP 93*
Murphy, Patrick Joseph 1959- *WhoMW 93*
Murphy, Patrick M. *WhoAmP 93*
Murphy, Patrick Wallace 1944- *Who 94*
Murphy, Patrick William 1957- *WhoMW 93*
Murphy, Paul M. 1946- *WhoAmL 94*
Murphy, Paul Peter 1948- *Who 94*
Murphy, Paul Robert 1913- *WhoMW 93*
Murphy, Paula Christine 1950- *WhoBlA 94*
Murphy, Peter Connacher, Jr. 1936- *WhoAmP 93*
Murphy, Peter E. *DrAPF 93*
Murphy, Philip Edward 1945- *WhoFI 94, WhoWest 94*
Murphy, Rae Allan 1935- *ConAu 142*
Murphy, Ralph d1967 *WhoHol 92*
Murphy, Ramon Birkett 1935- *WhoFI 94*
Murphy, Randall Kent 1943- *WhoFI 94*
Murphy, Raymond 1937- *WhoAmP 93*
Murphy, Raymond E. 1898- *WhAm 10*
Murphy, Raymond M. 1927- *WhoBlA 94*
Murphy, Reg 1934- *WhoAm 94*
Murphy, Ric 1951- *WhoBlA 94*
Murphy, Rich *DrAPF 93*
Murphy, Richard d1993 *IntMPA 94N, NewYTBS 93*
Murphy, Richard 1927- *WrDr 94*
Murphy, Richard Alan 1938- *WhoScEn 94*
Murphy, Richard Carden 1947- *WhoFI 94*
Murphy, Richard David 1938- *WhoScEn 94*
Murphy, Richard E. 1931- *WhoAmP 93*
Murphy, Richard Gray 1930- *WhoMW 93*
Murphy, Richard Holmes 1915- *Who 94*
Murphy, Richard James 1929- *WhoAmP 93*
Murphy, Richard L. 1951- *WhoAm 94, WhoAmL 94*
Murphy, Richard Patrick 1943- *WhoMW 93*
Murphy, Richard Patrick 1954- *WhoAmL 94*
Murphy, Richard Thomas 1908- *WrDr 94*
Murphy, Richard Vanderburgh 1951- *WhoAmL 94*
Murphy, Richard William 1929- *WhoAm 94, WhoAmP 93*
Murphy, Robert Blair 1931- *WhoAm 94, WhoFI 94*
Murphy, Robert Brady Lawrence 1905- *WhoAm 94, WhoMW 93*
Murphy, Robert C. 1926- *WhoAmP 93*
Murphy, Robert Carl 1944- *WhoWest 94*
Murphy, Robert Charles 1926- *WhoAm 94, WhoAmL 94*
Murphy, Robert D. 1894-1978 *HisDcKW*
Murphy, Robert E. 1918- *WhoAmP 93*
Murphy, Robert Earl 1941- *WhoAm 94, WhoScEn 94*
Murphy, Robert Francis 1924-1990 *WhAm 10*
Murphy, Robert Francis 1953- *WhoScEn 94*
Murphy, Robert Harry 1938- *WhoAm 94*
Murphy, Robert L. 1935- *WhoBlA 94*
Murphy, Robert Owen, Sr. 1926- *WhoFI 94*
Murphy, Roderick Patrick 1939- *WhoAmP 93*
Murphy, Roland Edmund 1917- *WrDr 94*
Murphy, Romallus O. 1928- *WhoBlA 94*
Murphy, Rosemary *WhoAm 94*
Murphy, Rosemary 1927- *WhoHol 92*
Murphy, Rowley Walter 1891-1975 *WhoAmA 93N*
Murphy, Sandra Robison 1949- *WhoAm 94, WhoAmL 94*
Murphy, Scott L. 1947- *WhoAmL 94*
Murphy, Sean *WhoHol 92*
Murphy, Sharon Margaret 1940- *WhoAm 94*

Murphy, Shaun Edward 1961- *WhoFI 94*
Murphy, Sheila E. *DrAPF 93*
Murphy, Shirley R(ousseau) 1928- *WrDr 94*
Murphy, Shirley Rousseau 1928- *SmATA 18AS [port], TwCYAW*
Murphy, Stephan David 1948- *WhoScEn 94*
Murphy, Stephen P. 1926- *WhoFI 94*
Murphy, Stephen P. 1950- *WhoAm 94*
Murphy, Steve L. 1957- *WhoAmP 93*
Murphy, Steven Patrick 1960- *WhoWest 94*
Murphy, Susan 1950- *WhoAm 94, WhoAmA 93*
Murphy, Suzanne 1941- *NewGrDO*
Murphy, Sylvia 1937- *WrDr 94*
Murphy, Terence M. 1943- *WhoAmL 94*
Murphy, Terence Martin 1942- *WhoAm 94*
Murphy, Teresa Ann 1957- *WhoWest 94*
Murphy, Terry Laurence 1942- *WhoAmP 93*
Murphy, Thomas *WhoHol 92*
Murphy, Thomas 1915- *IntWW 93*
Murphy, Thomas 1928- *Who 94*
Murphy, Thomas 1935- *WrDr 94*
Murphy, Thomas A(quinas) 1915- *Who 94*
Murphy, Thomas Aquinas 1915- *IntWW 93, WhoAm 94*
Murphy, Thomas Bailey 1924- *WhoAm 94, WhoAmP 93*
Murphy, Thomas Francis 1905- *WhoAm 94*
Murphy, Thomas Frank 1948- *WhoMW 93*
Murphy, Thomas J. 1944- *WhoIns 94*
Murphy, Thomas James 1956- *Who 94*
Murphy, Thomas John 1931- *WhoAm 94*
Murphy, Thomas Joseph 1932- *WhoAm 94, WhoWest 94*
Murphy, Thomas Joseph 1941- *WhoScEn 94*
Murphy, Thomas Joseph 1944- *WhoAmP 93*
Murphy, Thomas Joseph 1945- *WhoAm 94*
Murphy, Thomas Patrick 1952- *WhoAm 94*
Murphy, Thomas S. 1925- *WhoAm 94, WhoFI 94*
Murphy, Thomas S. 1932- *WhoIns 94*
Murphy, Thomas W. 1953- *WhoAmP 93*
Murphy, Thomas William, Jr. 1942- *WhoAmP 93*
Murphy, Tim Hugh 1962- *WhoMW 93*
Murphy, Timothy 1751-1818 *AmRev, WhAmRev*
Murphy, Timothy Donald 1950- *WhoAmP 93*
Murphy, Timothy J. 1947- *WhoAmL 94*
Murphy, Timothy James 1946- *WhoAmP 93*
Murphy, Timothy Patrick d1988 *WhoHol 92*
Murphy, Tom 1935- *ConDr 93, IntWW 93*
Murphy, Tom (Bernard) 1935- *IntDcT 2*
Murphy, Walter Francis 1929- *WhoAm 94, WrDr 94*
Murphy, Walter Joseph, Jr. 1930- *WhoAmL 94*
Murphy, Walter Young 1930- *WhoAm 94, WhoFI 94*
Murphy, Warren (B.) 1933- *EncSF 93*
Murphy, Warren Burton 1933- *WhoAm 94*
Murphy, Warren Charles 1944- *WhoWest 94*
Murphy, Wendell H. 1938- *WhoAmP 93*
Murphy, William 1823?-1872 *DcNaB MP*
Murphy, William Beverly 1907- *WhoAm 94*
Murphy, William Celestin 1920- *WhoAmL 94*
Murphy, William Frances 1951- *WhoFI 94*
Murphy, William Francis 1906- *WrDr 94*
Murphy, William Host 1926- *WhoMW 93*
Murphy, William J. 1963- *WhoAmP 93*
Murphy, William James 1927- *WhoAm 94*
Murphy, William Joseph 1949- *WhoAmL 94*
Murphy, William K. *DrAPF 93*
Murphy, William Malcolm, Jr. 1927- *WhoAmP 93*
Murphy, William Michael 1916- *WhoAm 94*
Murphy, William P. d1987 *NobelP 91N*
Murphy, William Robert 1927- *WhoAmL 94*
Murphy, William Tayloe, Jr. 1933- *WhoAmP 93*
Murphy, William Theodore 1928- *WhoMW 93*
Murphy, Wilma Louise Bryant 1947- *WhoMW 93*

Murphy-Barrera, Linda Frances 1956- WhoHisp 94
Murphy-O'Connor, Cormac Who 94
Murphy-O'Connor, Cormac 1932- IntWW 93
Murphy Rose d1989 WhoHol 92
Murra, John Victor 1916- WhoAm 94
Murrain, Godfrey H. 1927- WhoBlA 94
Murrain, Samuel Urbane, Sr. 1930- WhoHisp 94
Murrain, William A. 1945- WhoBlA 94
Murray Who 94
Murray, Bishop of The 1931- Who 94
Murray, Rt. Hon. Lord 1922- Who 94
Murray, A. Brean 1937- WhoAm 94
Murray, A. Rosemary 1913- IntWW 93
Murray, Albert 1916- WrDr 94
Murray, Albert (Ketcham) 1906-1992 WhoAmA 93N
Murray, Albert L. 1916- BlkWr 2, WhoAm 94, WhoBlA 94
Murray, Albert R. 1946- WhoBlA 94
Murray, Alexander 1754-1821 WhAmRev
Murray, Alexander Douglass 1929- WhoMW 93
Murray, Alexander William Charles Oliphant 1870-1920 DcNaB MP
Murray, Alice Pearl 1932- WhoFI 94
Murray, Allen Edward 1929- IntWW 93, WhoAm 94, WhoFI 94
Murray, Andrew Robin 1941- Who 94
Murray, Ann 1949- NewGrDO
Murray, Ann Dennison 1945- WhoMW 93
Murray, Anna Martin WhoBlA 94
Murray, Anne 1945- WhoAm 94
Murray, Anthony 1937- WhoAm 94
Murray, Antony Who 94
Murray, (John) Antony (Jerningham) 1921- Who 94
Murray, Archibald R. 1933- WhoAmL 94, WhoBlA 94
Murray, Arthur 1895-1991 WhAm 10
Murray, Arthur Joseph 1954- WhoScEn 94
Murray, Athol Laverick 1930- Who 94
Murray, Barbara 1929- IntMPA 94, WhoHol 92
Murray, Barbara Bateman 1933- WhoFI 94
Murray, Beatrice 1944- WrDr 94
Murray, Beth Ann 1948- WhoFI 94
Murray, Betty Jean Kafka 1935- WhoMW 93
Murray, Bill 1950- IntMPA 94, IntWW 93, WhoAm 94, WhoCom, WhoHol 92
Murray, Brian 1933- Who 94
Murray, Brian 1937- WhoHol 92
Murray, Brian Doyle WhoHol 92
Murray, Bryan Clarence 1942- WhoAm 94
Murray, Carlos William, Jr. 1942- WhoAmL 94
Murray, Carole DrAPF 93
Murray, Caroline Fish 1920- WhoAm 94
Murray, Cecil Leonard 1929- WhoBlA 94
Murray, Cecil Wayne 1950- WhoFI 94
Murray, Charles (Alan) 1943- WrDr 94
Murray, Charles Alan 1943- IntWW 93
Murray, Charles Edward 1928- WhoAmP 93
Murray, Charles Henry 1917- Who 94
Murray, Charlie d1941 WhoHol 92
Murray, Chic d1985 WhoHol 92
Murray, Claude Robert, Jr. 1947- WhoAmL 94
Murray, Constance Ann 1929- WhoAm 94
Murray, Craig W. 1947- WhoAmL 94
Murray, Dale Stephen 1956- WhoFI 94
Murray, Dan DrAPF 93
Murray, Daniel Richard 1946- WhoAm 94, WhoAmL 94, WhoMW 93
Murray, Dave 1958- See Iron Maiden ConMus 10
Murray, David WhAmRev
Murray, David 1925- WhoAm 94
Murray, David 1953- WhoFI 94, WhoMW 93
Murray, David (J.) 1945- WrDr 94
Murray, David Edward 1951- Who 94
Murray, David Eugene 1936- WhoAmL 94
Murray, David George 1930- WhoAm 94
Murray, David Mitchell d1923 WhoHol 92
Murray, Delbert Milton 1941- WhoFI 94, WhoMW 93, WhoScEn 94
Murray, Diane Elizabeth 1942- WhoAm 94
Murray, Don 1929- IntMPA 94, WhoHol 92
Murray, Donald (Bruce) 1923- Who 94
Murray, Donald (Frederick) 1924- Who 94
Murray, Donnie Ray WhoAmL 94
Murray, Dwight D. 1944- WhoAmL 94
Murray, Eddie Clarence 1956- WhoAm 94, WhoBlA 94
Murray, Edgar d1959 WhoHol 92
Murray, Edna McClain 1918- WhoBlA 94
Murray, Edward Rock 1947- WhoFI 94
Murray, Edwin Rene 1960- WhoAmP 93
Murray, Eileen M. 1959- WhoAmA 93
Murray, E'Lane Carlisle DrAPF 93
Murray, Elizabeth d1914 WhoHol 92
Murray, Elizabeth d1946 WhoHol 92
Murray, Elizabeth 1940- WhoAm 94, WhoAmA 93
Murray, Elizabeth Davis Reid 1925- WhoAm 94
Murray, Ernest Don 1930- WhoAm 94
Murray, Ethel Ann 1932- WhoAmP 93
Murray, Fiona 1911- WrDr 94
Murray, Florence K. 1916- WhoAmP 93
Murray, Florence Kerins 1916- WhoAm 94, WhoAmL 94
Murray, Floretta May WhoAmA 93
Murray, Frances WhoAmA 93
Murray, Frances 1928- WrDr 94
Murray, Francis W. WhoAm 94
Murray, Francis William 1921- WhoWest 94
Murray, Francis Wisner, III 1928- WhoFI 94
Murray, Frank Waldo 1884-1956 WhoAmA 93N
Murray, Fred(erick) d1950 WhoHol 92
Murray, Fred E. WhoAmP 93
Murray, Frederick Franklin 1950- WhoAm 94, WhoAmL 94, WhoFI 94
Murray, G. E. DrAPF 93
Murray, Gale Barbara 1945- ConAu 140
Murray, Gary S. WhoBlA 94
Murray, George E. 1923- WhoAmP 93
Murray, George E. 1954- WhoAmL 94
Murray, George Hopkins, III 1940- WhoFI 94
Murray, George Sargent 1924- Who 94
Murray, George Washington 1853-1926 WorInv
Murray, (George) Gilbert (Aime) 1866-1957 EncSF 93
Murray, Glenn Richard, Jr. 1930- WhoAm 94
Murray, Gordon 1935- Who 94
Murray, Gregory S. 1949- WhoAm 94
Murray, Gregory Vincent 1949- WhoAm 94, WhoAmL 94
Murray, Grover Elmer 1916- WhoAm 94
Murray, Harlan W. WhoFI 94
Murray, Haydn Herbert 1924- WhoAm 94
Murray, Herbert Frazier 1923- WhoAm 94, WhoAmL 94
Murray, Hyde H. 1930- WhoAmP 93
Murray, Ian Paul 1964- WhoFI 94
Murray, Ian Stewart 1951- WhoAmA 93
Murray, J. Alec G. 1936- WhoAm 94, WhoFI 94
Murray, J. Harold d1940 WhoHol 92
Murray, J. Ralph 1931- WhoBlA 94
Murray, Jack R. 1929- WhoAmP 93
Murray, Jacquelyn Ann 1940- WhoMW 93
Murray, James d1936 WhoHol 92
Murray, James c. 1751-1811 WhAmRev
Murray, James 1919- Who 94
Murray, James Alan 1942- WhoFI 94
Murray, James Cunningham, Jr. 1944- WhoAm 94, WhoAmL 94
Murray, James Dickson 1931- Who 94
Murray, James Doyle 1938- WhoAm 94, WhoFI 94
Murray, James Edward 1915- WhoWest 94
Murray, James Hamilton 1933- WhoBlA 94
Murray, James Joseph, III 1933- WhoAm 94
Murray, James Kirtis, Jr. 1935- WhoAm 94, WhoFI 94
Murray, James Michael 1944- WhoAm 94, WhoAmL 94
Murray, James P. 1946- WhoBlA 94
Murray, James Patrick d1993 Who 94N
Murray, James Patrick 1919- WhoAm 94, WhoWest 94
Murray, Jan 1917- IntMPA 94, WhoCom, WhoHol 92
Murray, Jane Cairns 1960- WhoAmL 94
Murray, Jean Carolyn 1927- WhoAm 94
Murray, Jeanne WhoAm 94
Murray, Jeanne Morris 1925- WhoAm 94, WhoScEn 94
Murray, Jennifer Susan 1950- Who 94
Murray, Joan DrAPF 93
Murray, Joan 1927- WhoAmA 93
Murray, Joan Nina 1938- WhoWest 94
Murray, Joel WhoHol 92
Murray, John WhAmRev, Who 94, WhoHol 92
Murray, John 1732-1809 AmRev
Murray, John 1741-1815 WhAmRev
Murray, John 1778-1843 BlmGEL
Murray, John, IV d1993 NewYTBS 93
Murray, John A. 1932- WhoAm 94
Murray, John Arnaud Robin Grey d1993 Who 94N
Murray, John B. 1943- WhoWest 94
Murray, John Courtney 1904-1967 DcAmReB 2
Murray, John D. WhoIns 94
Murray, John Edward, Jr. 1932- WhoAm 94
Murray, John Einar 1918- WhoAm 94
Murray, John Frederic 1927- WhoAm 94, WhoWest 94
Murray, John Joseph 1915- WhoAm 94, WrDr 94
Murray, John Joseph, Jr. 1914- WhoAmP 93
Murray, John Michael 1931- WhoAmA 93
Murray, John Patrick 1943- WhoAm 94
Murray, John Ralph 1916- WhoAm 94
Murray, John Stevenson 1939- WhoAmP 93
Murray, John T. d1957 WhoHol 92
Murray, John W. 1921- WhoBlA 94
Murray, Joseph 1916- WhoScEn 94
Murray, Joseph E. 1919- NobelP 91 [port]
Murray, Joseph Edward 1919- IntWW 93, Who 94, WhoAm 94, WhoScEn 94
Murray, Joseph James, Jr. 1930- WhoAm 94, WhoScEn 94
Murray, Joseph William 1944- WhoAm 94
Murray, Judith 1941- WhoAmA 93
Murray, Judith Sargent 1751-1820 BlmGWL
Murray, Julia Killin 1951- WhoMW 93
Murray, Katherine Maud Elisabeth 1909- Who 94
Murray, Kathleen Ann 1952- WhoIns 94
Murray, Kathleen Ellen 1946- WhoFI 94
Murray, Kathryn Hazel 1906- WhoAm 94
Murray, Kay L. 1938- WhoBlA 94
Murray, Ken d1988 WhoHol 92
Murray, Kenneth 1930- Who 94
Murray, Kenneth Alexander George 1916- Who 94
Murray, Kenneth Malcolm, Jr. 1925- WhoMW 93
Murray, Kenneth Richard 1938- WhoAm 94, WhoFI 94
Murray, Lawrence 1939- WhoFI 94
Murray, Lawrence N(ewbold) 1894- WhAm 10
Murray, Leland WhoHol 92
Murray, Leo Gerard 1943- Who 94
Murray, Leo Joseph 1927- Who 94
Murray, Leonard Hugh 1913- WhoAm 94
Murray, Les(lie) (Allan) 1938- WrDr 94
Murray, Linda WrDr 94
Murray, Lindley 1892-1970 BuCMET
Murray, Lionel Philip, Jr. 1958- WhoMW 93
Murray, Lowell 1936- IntWW 93, WhoAm 94
Murray, Mabel Lake 1935- WhoBlA 94
Murray, Mae d1965 WhoHol 92
Murray, Marion d1951 WhoHol 92
Murray, Marita Diane 1935- WhoMW 93
Murray, Martin J(ulius) 1945- WrDr 94
Murray, Mary Aileen 1914- WhoMW 93
Murray, Mary Jeanette WhoAmP 93
Murray, Mary Katherine 1956- WhoScEn 94
Murray, Michael Patrick 1930- WhoAmL 94
Murray, Michael Peter 1946- WhoAm 94, WhoFI 94
Murray, Michael Webster 1935- WhoAmP 93
Murray, Mick WhoHol 92
Murray, Nigel 1944- Who 94
Murray, Noreen Elizabeth 1935- IntWW 93, Who 94
Murray, Pamela Alison 1955- WhoScEn 94
Murray, Patrick (Ian Keith) 1965- Who 94
Murray, Patrick Robert 1948- WhoScEn 94
Murray, Patty 1950- CngDr 93, IntWW 93, WhoAm 94, WhoWest 94
Murray, Patty L. 1950- WhoAmP 93
Murray, Paul Brady 1923- WhoAm 94, WhoFI 94
Murray, (Anna) Pauli(ne) 1910-1985 BlkWr 2
Murray, Peg 1925- WhoHol 92
Murray, Peggy d1976 WhoHol 92
Murray, Peter 1915- Who 94
Murray, Peter 1920- WhoAm 94, WhoFI 94, WhoScEn 94
Murray, Peter 1925- WhoHol 92
Murray, Peter (John) 1920- WrDr 94
Murray, Peter Allen 1959- WhoAmL 94
Murray, Peter Bryant 1927- WhoAm 94
Murray, Peter Loos 1943- WhoAm 94
Murray, Peter Tom 1941- WhoFI 94
Murray, Philip 1886-1952 AmSocL, EncABHB 9 [port]
Murray, Philip Edmund, Jr. 1950- WhoAmL 94
Murray, Philip Richard 1949- WhoFI 94
Murray, Raymond C. 1929- ConAu 142
Murray, Raymond Carl 1929- WhoAm 94
Murray, Raymond Harold 1925- WhoAm 94
Murray, Raymond Le Roy 1920- WhoAm 94
Murray, Rebecca Brake 1949- WhoAmL 94
Murray, Reuben WhoAmA 93
Murray, Richard Bennett 1928- WhoAm 94
Murray, Richard Charles 1949- WhoAmP 93
Murray, Richard Maximilian 1922- WhoAm 94
Murray, Richard Newton 1942- WhoAmA 93
Murray, Robert (Gray) 1936- WhoAmA 93
Murray, Robert A. 1948- WhoAmP 93
Murray, Robert Allen 1929- WrDr 94
Murray, Robert F. 1931- WhoBlA 94
Murray, Robert Fox 1952- WhoAmL 94
Murray, Robert Fulton, Jr. 1931- WhoAm 94
Murray, Robert Gray 1936- WhoAm 94
Murray, Robert J. 1941- WhoFI 94
Murray, Robert Wallace 1928- WhoAm 94, WhoScEn 94
Murray, Robin MacGregor 1944- Who 94
Murray, Roger 1936- Who 94
Murray, Roger Franklin 1911- WhoAm 94
Murray, Rona 1924- WrDr 94
Murray, Ronald 1931- WhoFI 94
Murray, Ronald King Who 94
Murray, Ronald Ormiston 1912- Who 94
Murray, Rosemary IntWW 93, Who 94
Murray, (Alice) Rosemary 1913- Who 94
Murray, Rowland William Patrick 1910- Who 94
Murray, Royce Wilton 1937- WhoAm 94, WhoScEn 94
Murray, Russell, II 1925- WhoAm 94, WhoAmP 93, WhoScEn 94
Murray, Scott Lee 1955- WhoFI 94
Murray, Simon 1940- IntWW 93
Murray, Spencer J., III 1964- WhoBlA 94
Murray, Stephen d1983 WhoHol 92
Murray, Stephen James 1943- WhoAmL 94, WhoFI 94
Murray, Stephen M. 1947- WhoAmL 94
Murray, Steven Nelsen 1944- WhoScEn 94
Murray, Sylvester 1941- WhoBlA 94
Murray, Sylvester Charles 1956- WhoAmL 94
Murray, T(homas) C(ornelius) 1873-1959 IntDcT 2
Murray, Terrence 1939- WhoAm 94, WhoFI 94
Murray, Terry 1950- WhoAm 94
Murray, Thad S. 1919- WhoAmP 93
Murray, Theresa Marie 1961- WhoMW 93
Murray, Therese WhoAmP 93
Murray, Thomas Azel 1929- WhoBlA 94
Murray, Thomas Francis 1910- WhoAm 94
Murray, Thomas John 1938- WhoAm 94
Murray, Thomas Joseph 1924- WhoAm 94
Murray, Thomas Michael 1944- WhoAm 94
Murray, Thomas Michael 1945- WhoAm 94, WhoAmL 94
Murray, Thomas Reed 1924- WhoScEn 94
Murray, Thomas W., Jr. 1935- WhoBlA 94
Murray, Tim(othy Douglas Gordon) 1938- WhoAmA 93
Murray, Timothy Vincent 1930- IntWW 93
Murray, Tom d1935 WhoHol 92
Murray, Tracy 1940- WhoFI 94
Murray, Tracy 1971- WhoBlA 94
Murray, Ty WhoAm 94
Murray, Virgie W. 1931- WhoBlA 94
Murray, Virginia R. DrAPF 93
Murray, Wallace Shordon 1921- WhoAm 94
Murray, Warren James 1936- WhoAm 94
Murray, Will 1953- EncSF 93
Murray, Willard H., Jr. WhoAmP 93
Murray, William DrAPF 93
Murray, William 1935- NewGrDO
Murray, William 1936- WhoAm 94, WhoFI 94, WhoScEn 94
Murray, William Aloysius, Jr. 1927- WhoWest 94
Murray, William Colman 1899-1977 WhoAmA 93N
Murray, William D. 1935- WhoFI 94
Murray, William Daniel 1908- WhoAm 94, WhoWest 94
Murray, William F. 1948- WhoAmL 94

Murray, William Gregory 1931- *WhoAmL 94*
Murray, William Hutchison 1913- *WrDr 94*
Murray, William J. 1948- *WhoIns 94*
Murray, William James 1933- *WhoScEn 94*
Murray, William Michael 1953- *WhoAmL 94*
Murray, William Richard 1949- *WhoAmL 94*
Murray, Winston Lloyd, Jr. 1952- *WhoBlA 94*
Murray, Zon d1979 *WhoHol 92*
Murray-Hill, Peter d1957 *WhoHol 92*
Murray of Blackbarony, Nigel Andrew Digby 1944- *Who 94*
Murray Of Epping Forest, Baron 1922- *IntWW 93, Who 94*
Murray Of Newhaven, Baron 1903- *IntWW 93, Who 94*
Murrel, Betty Elaine 1937- *WhoMW 93*
Murrell, Barbara Curry 1938- *WhoBlA 94*
Murrell, Carlton D. 1945- *WhoAmA 93*
Murrell, Geoffrey David George 1934- *Who 94*
Murrell, Jim 1934- *WrDr 94*
Murrell, John 1945- *ConDr 93, IntDcT 2, WrDr 94*
Murrell, John Norman 1932- *Who 94*
Murrell, Kenneth Darwin 1940- *WhoScEn 94*
Murrell, Kenneth Lynn 1945- *WhoFI 94*
Murrell, Peter C. 1920- *WhoBlA 94*
Murrell, Robert George 1932- *WhoAmL 94*
Murrell, Sam Edwin, Jr. 1927- *WhoAmL 94*
Murrell, Sylvia Marilyn 1947- *WhoBlA 94*
Murrell, Thomas W., III 1948- *WhoAm 94, WhoAmL 94*
Murren, Doug(las) 1951- *WrDr 94*
Murren, Douglas Edward 1951- *WhoWest 94*
Murret, Eugene John, Sr. 1932- *WhoAmL 94*
Murrey, Joseph Huffmaster, Jr. 1926- *WhoAmP 93*
Murrey, Thomas Whitelaw, Jr. 1959- *WhoWest 94*
Murrian, Robert Phillip 1945- *WhoAm 94, WhoAmL 94*
Murrie, William (Stuart) 1903- *Who 94*
Murrill, Gwynn 1942- *WhoAmA 93*
Murrill, Paul Whitfield 1934- *WhoAm 94*
Murrin, Regis Doubet 1930- *WhoAm 94*
Murrin, Thomas Edward 1923- *WhoAm 94*
Murrish, Charles Howard 1940- *WhoAm 94*
Murrow, Edward R. d1965 *WhoHol 92*
Murrow, Edward Roscoe 1908-1965 *AmSocL*
Murrow, Joseph Samuel 1835-1929 *EncNAR*
Murrow, Liza Ketchum *DrAPF 93*
Murry, Barbara R. 1950- *WhoMW 93*
Murry, Calvin *DrAPF 93*
Murry, Charles Emerson 1924- *WhoAm 94*
Murry, Colin Middleton *EncSF 93*
Murry, Colin Middleton 1926- *WrDr 94*
Murry, Harold David, Jr. 1943- *WhoAm 94, WhoAmL 94*
Murry, John Middleton 1889-1957 *BlmGEL*
Murry, Katherine Middleton 1925- *WrDr 94*
Mursell, Peter 1913- *Who 94*
Murska, Ilma di *NewGrDO*
Murstein, Denis 1952- *WhoMW 93*
Mursten, Michael Richard 1964- *WhoFI 94*
Murta, Jack Burnett *IntWW 93*
Murta, Kenneth Hall 1929- *Who 94*
Murtagh, Frederick, Jr. 1917- *WhoAm 94*
Murtagh, James P. 1911- *WhoAmL 94*
Murtagh, John Edward 1936- *WhoScEn 94*
Murtagh, Kate *WhoHol 92*
Murtagh, Marion *Who 94*
Murtagh, Thomas R. 1944- *WhoAmL 94*
Murtaugh, Christopher David 1945- *WhoAm 94, WhoAmL 94*
Murtaugh, John Brian 1937- *WhoAmP 93*
Murtaugh, John Patrick 1952- *WhoAmL 94*
Murtaugh, Maureen Ann 1961- *WhoMW 93*
Murtaugh, Michael K. 1944- *WhoAm 94, WhoAmL 94*
Murtaugh, Michael Paul 1951- *WhoMW 93*
Murtaugh, Rodger W. 1938- *WhoFI 94*
Murtaza, Ghulam 1955- *WhoScEn 94*
Murtaza, Sherkham 1932- *LngBDD*
Murth, Florence d1934 *WhoHol 92*
Murtha, John Francis 1930- *WhoAm 94*

Murtha, John P. *CngDr 93*
Murtha, John Patrick *WhoAmP 93*
Murtha, John Patrick 1932- *WhoAm 94*
Murtha, John Stephen 1913- *WhoAm 94*
Murtha, Selena Kimberly 1963- *WhoAmL 94*
Murtha, Thomas Michael 1955- *WhoAmL 94*
Murthy, A. Kumaresa S. 1943- *WhoAsA 94*
Murthy, Kamalakara Akula 1950- *WhoScEn 94*
Murthy, Krishna Kesava 1950- *WhoScEn 94*
Murthy, Srinivasa 1949- *WhoAsA 94*
Murthy, Srinivasa K. 1949- *WhoAm 94, WhoFI 94, WhoScEn 94*
Murthy, Sudha Akula 1957- *WhoScEn 94*
Murthy, Vadiraja Venkatesa 1940- *WhoScEn 94*
Murthy, Vanukuri Radha Krishna 1928- *WhoScEn 94*
Murthy, Veeraraghavan Krishna 1934- *WhoWest 94*
Murto, Patty L. 1950- *WhoMW 93*
Murto, Patty Lila 1950- *WhoAmP 93*
Murton *Who 94*
Murton, Lionel 1915- *WhoHol 92*
Murton of Lindisfarne, Baron 1914- *Who 94*
Murty, Katta Gopalakrishna 1936- *WhoAsA 94*
Murty, Komanduri Srinivasa 1956- *WhoAsA 94*
Musa, Gilda 1926- *BlmGWL*
Musa, John Davis 1933- *WhoAm 94*
Musa, Mahmoud Nimir 1943- *WhoMW 93*
Musa, Samuel Albert *WhoAm 94*
Musacchia, Xavier Joseph 1923- *WhoAm 94*
Musante, Tony *IntMPA 94, WhoAm 94*
Musante, Tony 1936- *WhoHol 92*
Musapeta, Hari 1952- *WhoAsA 94*
Musaphia, Joseph 1935- *ConDr 93, WrDr 94*
Musburger, Brent Woody 1939- *WhoAm 94*
Muscardini, Cristiana 1948- *WhoWomW 91*
Muscardini, Michael Carl 1950- *WhoWest 94*
Muscarella, Patricia A. 1952- *WhoAmP 93*
Muscarella, Vincent Alfred 1937- *WhoWest 94*
Muscarella, Vincent T. *WhoAmP 93*
Muscarelle, Joseph Louis 1903-1989 *WhAm 10*
Muscatello, Anthony Curtis 1950- *WhoWest 94*
Muscatine, Charles 1920- *WhoAm 94*
Muscato, Andrew 1953- *WhoAm 94, WhoAmL 94*
Musch, David Charles 1954- *WhoMW 93*
Muschel, Louis Henry 1916- *WhoAm 94*
Muschenheim, Frederick 1932- *WhoScEn 94*
Muschenheim, William Emil 1902-1990 *WhAm 10*
Muschg, Adolf 1934- *IntWW 93*
Muschler, James Arthur 1958- *WhoFI 94*
Musci, Teresa Stella 1960- *WhoScEn 94*
Musco, Angelo d1937 *WhoHol 92*
Muscroft, Harold Colin 1924- *Who 94*
Muse, Clarence d1979 *WhoHol 92*
Muse, Clarence 1889-1979 *AfrAmAl 6*
Muse, Ewell Henderson, III 1938- *WhoAm 94*
Muse, Harry Rogers, III 1955- *WhoFI 94*
Muse, Marshall Grove, III 1941- *WhoFI 94*
Muse, Martha Twitchell 1926- *WhoAm 94*
Muse, McGillivray 1909- *WhoAm 94*
Muse, Patricia *DrAPF 93*
Muse, Paul Forest 1905-1989 *WhAm 10*
Muse, William Brown, Jr. 1918- *WhoBlA 94*
Muse, William Van 1939- *WhoAm 94*
Muse, William Wayne 1948- *WhoAmL 94*
Museles, Melvin 1929- *WhoAm 94*
Muserlian, Charles A. 1932- *WhoFI 94*
Muses, Charles Arthur 1919- *WrDr 94*
Museus, Robert Allen 1955- *WhoMW 93*
Museveni, Yoweri Kaguta 1944- *IntWW 93*
Museveni, Yoweri Kaguta 1945- *Who 94*
Musfelt, Duane Clark 1951- *WhoAm 94, WhoAmL 94*
Musgrave, Charles Edward 1932- *WhoAm 94, WhoMW 93*
Musgrave, Christopher (Patrick Charles) 1949- *Who 94*
Musgrave, David Leslie 1952- *WhoWest 94*
Musgrave, Dennis Charles 1921- *WhoAm 94*

Musgrave, John Reynolds 1941- *WhoAmL 94*
Musgrave, R. Kenton 1927- *CngDr 93, WhoAm 94, WhoAmL 94*
Musgrave, Richard Abel 1910- *WhoAm 94, WhoFI 94, WhoWest 94*
Musgrave, Richard James 1922- *Who 94*
Musgrave, Rosanne Kimble 1952- *Who 94*
Musgrave, Shirley H. 1935- *WhoAmA 93*
Musgrave, Story 1935- *WhoAm 94*
Musgrave, Susan 1951- *BlmGWL, WrDr 94*
Musgrave, Thea 1928- *IntWW 93, NewGrDO, Who 94, WhoAm 94*
Musgrave, Thomas 1738-1812 *WhAmRev*
Musgrave, William c. 1506-1544 *DcNaB MP*
Musgrave, William Kenneth Rodgerson 1918- *Who 94*
Musgrove, A. J. *WhoAmA 93N*
Musgrove, D. Ronald 1956- *WhoAmP 93*
Musgrove, Frank 1922- *Who 94, WrDr 94*
Musgrove, Gertrude 1912- *WhoHol 92*
Musgrove, Harold John 1930- *Who 94*
Musgrove, John 1920- *Who 94*
Musgrove, John Conner 1929- *WhoFI 94*
Musgrove, Judy Autry 1946- *WhoFI 94*
Musgrove, Margaret Wynkoop 1943- *WhoBlA 94*
Musgrove, Stephen Ward 1949- *WhoAmA 93*
Musha, Toshimitsu 1931- *WhoScEn 94*
Mushel', Georgy 1909- *NewGrDO*
Mushik, Corliss *WhoMW 93*
Mushik, Corliss Dodge *WhoAmP 93*
Mushin, William Woolf d1993 *Who 94N*
Mushinsky, Mary M. *WhoAmP 93*
Mushketik, Yuri Mikhailovich 1929- *IntWW 93*
Mushkin, Leonard Barton 1944- *WhoWest 94*
Musi, Maria Maddalena 1669-1751 *NewGrDO*
Musial, Stanley 1920- *WhoAm 94*
Musicaro, John R., Jr. 1949- *WhoAmL 94*
Musick, Robert Lawrence, Jr. 1947- *WhoAmL 94*
Musidora d1957 *WhoHol 92*
Musielak, Zdzislaw Edward 1950- *WhoScEn 94*
Musihin, Konstantin K. 1927- *WhoScEn 94, WhoWest 94*
Musikas, Claude 1937- *WhoScEn 94*
Musiker, Reuben 1931- *WrDr 94*
Musil, Robert 1880-1942 *RfGShF*
Musillo, Joseph H. 1949- *WhoScEn 94*
Muske, Carol *DrAPF 93*
Muske-Dukes, Carol Anne 1945- *WhoWest 94*
Muskelly, Anna Marie *WhoBlA 94*
Muskerry, Baron *Who 94*
Musket, Ronald George 1940- *WhoWest 94*
Muskie, Edmund Sixtus 1914- *IntWW 93, Who 94, WhoAm 94, WhoAmP 93*
Muskin, Victor Philip 1942- *WhoAmL 94*
Musland, Roy Allan 1961- *WhoMW 93*
Musler, George T. 1929- *WhoAmP 93*
Muslin, Steven Barry 1949- *WhoAmL 94*
Musmann, Klaus 1935- *WhoWest 94*
Musmanni, Sergio 1960- *WhoScEn 94*
Musokotwane, Kebby Sililo Kambulu 1946- *IntWW 93*
Musolf, DeAnne Margaret 1960- *WhoWest 94*
Musolf, Lloyd D(aryl) 1919- *WrDr 94*
Musolf, Lloyd Daryl 1919- *WhoAm 94*
Musolino, Vincenzo d1969 *WhoHol 92*
Muson, Howard Henry 1935- *WhoAm 94*
Musone, Fred James 1944- *WhoAm 94*
Musorgsky, Modest Petrovich 1839-1881 *NewGrDO*
Muspratt, Edmund Knowles 1833-1923 *DcNaB MP*
Muspratt, Max 1872-1934 *DcNaB MP*
Muss, Hyman d1993 *NewYTBS 93*
Mussa, Michael 1944- *IntWW 93*
Mussehl, Allan Arthur 1942- *WhoMW 93*
Mussehl, Robert Clarence 1936- *WhoAm 94*
Musselman, Darwin B. 1916- *WhoAmA 93, WhoWest 94*
Musselman, Elizabeth Ann 1954- *WhoWest 94*
Musselman, Francis Haas 1925- *WhoAm 94*
Musselman, Jamie Boothe 1950- *WhoFI 94*
Musselman, Merle Mcneil 1915-1990 *WhAm 10*
Musselman, Raymond *WhoAmP 93*
Musselman, Robert Carl 1942- *WhoWest 94*
Musselman, Robert Metcalfe 1914- *WhoAmL 94*
Musselwhite, Marvin D., Jr. 1938- *WhoAmP 93*

Mussenden, Georg Antonio 1959- *WhoScEn 94*
Mussenden, Gerald 1941- *WhoScEn 94*
Mussenden, Maria Elisabeth 1949- *WhoScEn 94*
Musser, Alice 1929- *WhoAmP 93*
Musser, C. Walton 1909- *WhoAm 94, WhoWest 94*
Musser, Joe 1936- *WrDr 94*
Musser, Margaret Morris 1962- *WhoMW 93*
Musser, Sandra G. 1944- *WhoAmL 94*
Musser, Stanton Richard 1936- *WhoAm 94*
Musser, Terry M. 1947- *WhoAmP 93*
Musser, Tharon 1925- *WhoAm 94*
Musser, William Wesley, Jr. 1918- *WhoAm 94, WhoAmL 94*
Musserian, John Richard 1961- *WhoFI 94*
Musset, (Louis-Charles-) Alfred de 1810-1857 *IntDcT 2 [port]*
Mussette, Charles d1939 *WhoHol 92*
Mussey, Francine d1933 *WhoHol 92*
Mussey, Joseph Arthur 1948- *WhoAm 94*
Mussey, Virginia T. H. 1910- *WrDr 94*
Musshoff, Karl Albert 1910- *WhoScEn 94*
Mussina, Michael Cole 1968- *WhoAm 94*
Mussio, Emanuele *NewGrDO*
Mussman, Michael Steven 1954- *WhoWest 94*
Mussman, William Edward 1919- *WhoAmL 94*
Mussman, William Edward, III 1951- *WhoAmL 94*
Mussmann, Linda L. 1947- *WhoAmA 93*
Musso, Elizabeth Ann *WhoWest 94*
Musso, George *ProFbHF [port]*
Musso, Michael Anthony 1945- *WhoFI 94*
Mussolini, Alessandra 1964- *WhoHol 92*
Mussolini, Benito 1883-1945 *HisWorL [port]*
Musson, Alfred Henry 1900- *Who 94*
Musson, Bennet d1946 *WhoHol 92*
Musson, Donald George 1950- *WhoScEn 94*
Musson, Geoffrey (Randolph Dixon) 1910- *Who 94*
Musson, John Geoffrey Robin 1939- *Who 94*
Musson, John Nicholas Whitaker 1927- *Who 94*
Musson, Steven Harrison 1947- *WhoMW 93*
Mustacchi, Piero 1920- *WhoAm 94, WhoWest 94*
Mustache, James 1904- *EncNAR*
Mustaf, Jerrod (Terrah) 1949- *WhoBlA 94*
Mustafa, Ali Syed 1935- *WhoMW 93*
Mustafa, Mohammad Ghulam 1940- *WhoWest 94*
Mustafa, Nasr El-Din 1930- *Who 94*
Mustafa, Shams 1952- *WhoAsA 94, WhoMW 93*
Mustain, Brian Clark 1945- *WhoMW 93*
Mustakallio, Kimmo Kalervo 1931- *WhoScEn 94*
Mustapha Bin Datu Harun, Tun Datu 1918- *IntWW 93*
Mustard, James Fraser 1927- *WhoAm 94, WhoScEn 94*
Mustard, John Fraser 1961- *WhoScEn 94*
Mustard, Mary Carolyn 1948- *WhoMW 93*
Muste, Abraham John 1885-1967 *AmSocL*
Musters, George Chaworth 1841-1879 *WhWE*
Mustian, Middleton Truett 1921- *WhoAm 94*
Mustill, Baron 1931- *IntWW 93, Who 94*
Mustin, Burt d1977 *WhoHol 92*
Mustin, Lloyd Montague, II 1959- *WhoFI 94*
Musto, Barry 1930- *WrDr 94*
Musto, David Franklin 1936- *WhoAm 94*
Musto, Joseph J. 1943- *WhoAmL 94*
Musto, Michael 1955- *WrDr 94*
Musto, Michael J. *IntMPA 94*
Musto, Raphael J. 1929- *WhoAmP 93*
Mustoe, Anne 1933- *Who 94*
Mustokoff, Michael Mark 1947- *WhoAm 94, WhoAmL 94*
Muston, Gerald Bruce 1927- *Who 94*
Mustone, Amelia P. 1928- *WhoAmP 93, WhoWomW 91*
Musulin, Anne 1959- *WhoAmL 94*
Musuraca, Nicholas 1892-1975 *IntDcF 2-4*
Musyl, Marc J. 1952- *WhoAm 94*
Mutale, Elaine Butler 1943- *WhoBlA 94*
Mutalibov, Ayaz Niyazi Ogly 1938- *IntWW 93*
Mutallab, Alhaji Umaru Abdul 1939- *IntWW 93*
Mutalov, Abdulkhashim 1947- *LngBDD*
Mutch, Duane Olen 1925- *WhoAmP 93*
Mutch, James Donald 1943- *WhoScEn 94, WhoWest 94*

Mutch, Patricia Black 1943- *WhoMW 93*
Mutch, William Edward Scott 1925- *Who 94*
Mutcheruon, James Albertus, Jr. 1941- *WhoBlA 94*
Mutchie, Marjorie Ann *WhoHol 92*
Mutchler, Calvin Kendal 1926- *WhoScEn 94*
Mutebi, Ronald Muwenda, II *NewYTBS 93 [port]*
Mutel, Cornelia F. 1947- *SmATA 74 [port]*
Muth, George Edward 1906- *WhoAm 94*
Muth, John Francis 1918- *WhoAm 94*
Muth, John Fraser 1930- *WhoAm 94*
Muth, Jon R. 1945- *WhoAmL 94*
Muth, Michael Raymond 1950- *WhoAmL 94*
Muth, Richard F(erris) 1927- *WrDr 94*
Muth, Richard Ferris 1927- *WhoAm 94, WhoFI 94*
Muth, Robert James 1933- *WhoAm 94*
Muthukrishnan, Subbaratnam 1942- *WhoAsA 94*
Muthuswamy, Petham Padayatchi 1945- *WhoMW 93*
Muti, Ornella 1955- *WhoHol 92*
Muti, Riccardo 1941- *IntWW 93, NewGrDO, Who 94, WhoAm 94*
Mutio, Ricardo d1957 *WhoHol 92*
Mutkins, Helen *WhoHol 92*
Muto, Kabun 1926- *IntWW 93*
Muto, Peter 1924- *WhoAmP 93*
Muto, Susan Annette 1942- *WhoAm 94*
Mutombo, DiKembe 1966- *WhoAm 94, WhoBlA 94, WhoWest 94*
Mutsch, Lydia 1961- *WhoWomW 91*
Mutschler, Carlfried 1926- *IntWW 93*
Mutschler, Herbert Frederick 1919- *WhoAm 94, WhoWest 94*
Mutsuhito 1852-1912 *HisWorL [port]*
Mutt, Viktor 1923- *IntWW 93*
Mutter, Anne-Sophie 1963- *IntWW 93*
Mutterperl, William Charles 1946- *WhoAmL 94*
Mutters, David Ray 1949- *WhoFI 94*
Mutz, John M. *WhoAmP 93*
Mutz, John Massie 1935- *WhoAm 94*
Mutz, Oscar Ulysses 1928- *WhoAm 94*
Mutzebaugh, Richard Frances 1933- *WhoAmP 93*
Mutzenberger, Marv *WhoAmP 93*
Mutziger, John Charles 1949- *WhoScEn 94*
Mutziger, Judy Lynn 1947- *WhoFI 94*
Muuss, Rolf Eduard 1924- *WhoAm 94, WrDr 94*
Muwakkil, Salim 1947- *WhoBlA 94*
Muxlow, Keith 1933- *WhoAmP 93*
Muybridge, Eadweard James 1830-1904 *WorInv*
Mu Yongji 1932- *WhoPRCh 91 [port]*
Muyselaar, Piet d1978 *WhoHol 92*
Muyumba, Francois N. 1939- *WhoBlA 94*
Muyunda, Mavis *WhoWomW 91*
Muzenda, Simon Vengai 1922- *IntWW 93*
Muzii, Ronald Carl, Jr. 1961- *WhoFI 94*
Muzio, Claudia 1889-1936 *NewGrDO [port]*
Muzio, (Donnino) Emanuele 1821-1890 *NewGrDO*
Muzorewa, Abel Tendekayi 1925- *IntWW 93*
Muzquiz, Carlos d1960 *WhoHol 92*
Muzyka, Donald Richard 1938- *WhoAm 94*
Muzzillo, Rachel Evelyn Sheeley 1966- *WhoAm 94, WhoMW 93*
Muzzy, James F. 1939- *WhoIns 94*
Mveng, Engelbert 1930- *IntWW 93*
Mvungi, Martha *BlmGWL*
Mwaanga, Vernon Johnson 1939- *IntWW 93*
Mwakawago, Daudi Ngelautwa 1939- *IntWW 93*
Mwale, Siteke Gibson 1929- *IntWW 93*
Mwalimu, Charles 1953- *WhoAmL 94*
Mwamba, Zuberi I. 1937- *WhoBlA 94*
Mwanawasa, Levy Patrick 1948- *IntWW 93*
Mwangi, Meja 1948- *BlkWr 2*
Mwinyi, Ali Hassan 1925- *IntWW 93*
Mwinyi, Ndugu Ali Hassan 1925- *Who 94*
Myart, James Willie, Jr. 1954- *WhoAmP 93*
Myatt, Gordon J. 1928- *WhoBlA 94*
Myatt, Greely 1952- *WhoAmA 93*
Mybeck, Richard Raymond 1928- *WhoAmL 94, WhoWest 94*
Mycielski, Jan 1932- *WhoAm 94*
Mycock, Frederick Charles 1943- *WhoAmL 94*
Mycue, Edward *DrAPF 93*
Mycue, Edward 1937- *WhoWest 94*
Mydland, Gordon James 1922- *WhoAm 94*
Mydland, M. Lavonne 1923- *WhoAmP 93*
Myer, Elizabeth Gallup *WhoAm 94*
Myer, Howard S. 1947- *WhoAmL 94*
Myer, John Andrew 1956- *WhoFI 94*
Myer, John Daniel, II 1950- *WhoFI 94*
Myer, Jon Harold 1922- *WhoWest 94*
Myer, Paul Joseph 1954- *WhoMW 93*
Myer, Peter Livingston 1934- *WhoAmA 93*
Myer, Sidney Baillieu 1926- *Who 94*
Myer, Yash Paul 1932- *WhoAsA 94*
Myerberg, Marcia 1945- *WhoAm 94, WhoFI 94*
Myerburg, Robert Jerome 1937- *WhoAm 94*
Myers, A. Ross 1949- *WhoAm 94*
Myers, Adrian Marvyn 1951- *WhoIns 94*
Myers, Al 1922- *WhoFI 94, WhoWest 94*
Myers, Albert Aldrich, III 1963- *WhoAmL 94*
Myers, Albert G., Jr. 1917- *WhoAm 94*
Myers, Andrew Gordon 1959- *WhoScEn 94*
Myers, Anthony Maurice 1940- *WhoAm 94*
Myers, Arthur B. 1917- *WhoAm 94*
Myers, Barry Lee 1943- *WhoAmL 94, WhoFI 94*
Myers, Barton 1934- *IntWW 93, WhoWest 94*
Myers, Bernard S. d1993 *NewYTBS 93*
Myers, Bernard S(amuel) 1908-1993 *ConAu 140*
Myers, Bernard Samuel 1949- *WhoBlA 94*
Myers, Beth Ann 1957- *WhoAmL 94*
Myers, Bob *DrAPF 93*
Myers, Bradley Lawrence 1961- *WhoWest 94*
Myers, Byron Lee 1946- *WhoAm 94, WhoAmL 94*
Myers, C. Stowe 1906- *WhoAmA 93*
Myers, Carmel d1980 *WhoHol 92*
Myers, Carol Ann 1949- *WhoMW 93*
Myers, Carole *WhoAmA 93*
Myers, Carole Ann 1934- *WhoAmA 93*
Myers, Carrell *WhoHol 92*
Myers, Carroll Jean 1928- *WhoAmP 93*
Myers, Catherine R. 1934- *WhoAm 94*
Myers, Charles Andrew 1913- *WhoAm 94*
Myers, Charles Franklin 1942- *WhoAmL 94*
Myers, Clark Everett 1915- *WhoAm 94*
Myers, Clay 1927- *WhoAm 94, WhoAmP 93*
Myers, Connie Jean 1946- *WhoWest 94*
Myers, Dale D. 1922- *WhoAmP 93*
Myers, Dale Dehaven 1922- *IntWW 93, WhoScEn 94*
Myers, Dane Jacob 1948- *WhoAmL 94*
Myers, Daniel Lee 1961- *WhoScEn 94*
Myers, Daniel William, II 1931- *WhoAm 94*
Myers, Daryl Ronald 1948- *WhoScEn 94*
Myers, David Francis 1959- *WhoScEn 94*
Myers, David Milton 1911- *Who 94*
Myers, David N. 1900- *WhoAm 94*
Myers, David Richard 1948- *WhoFI 94*
Myers, Debra J. 1952- *WhoBlA 94*
Myers, Debra Lea 1959- *WhoMW 93*
Myers, Dee Dee *WhoAmP 93*
Myers, Dee Dee 1961- *WhoAm 94*
Myers, Dennis Gillford 1953- *WhoWest 94*
Myers, Denys Peter, Jr. 1916- *WhoAm 94*
Myers, Don *WhoAmP 93*
Myers, Donald B. 1944- *WhoAmL 94*
Myers, Donald Brenton 1937- *WhoFI 94*
Myers, Donald Earl 1931- *WhoWest 94*
Myers, Donald J. 1943- *WhoAmL 94*
Myers, Donald Richard 1951- *WhoScEn 94*
Myers, Dorothy Roatz 1921- *WhoAmA 93*
Myers, Douglas George 1949- *WhoAm 94, WhoWest 94*
Myers, Douglas Mark 1946- *WhoAmP 93*
Myers, Earl T. 1930- *WhoBlA 94*
Myers, Edmund Charles Wolf 1906- *Who 94*
Myers, Edward d1993 *NewYTBS 93*
Myers, Edward E. 1925- *WhoScEn 94*
Myers, Eldon Woodrow, Jr. 1953- *WhoAm 94*
Myers, Elisabeth P 1918- *WrDr 94*
Myers, Elizabeth Rouse 1923- *WhoWest 94*
Myers, Elmer 1926- *WhoWest 94*
Myers, Emma McGraw 1953- *WhoBlA 94*
Myers, Eric Arthur 1958- *WhoScEn 94*
Myers, Ernest Ray *WhoBlA 94*
Myers, Ethel K. 1881-1960 *WhoAmA 93N*
Myers, Eugene Nicholas 1933- *WhoAm 94*
Myers, Evelyn Stephenson 1922- *WhoAm 94*
Myers, Forrest Warden 1941- *WhoAmA 93*
Myers, Frances 1938- *WhoAm 94, WhoAmA 93*
Myers, Frances Althea 1957- *WhoBlA 94*
Myers, Frank B. 1941- *WhoAm 94*
Myers, Frank Harmon 1899-1956 *WhoAmA 93N*
Myers, Franklin 1952- *WhoAm 94, WhoAmL 94*
Myers, Fred A. 1937- *WhoAmA 93N*
Myers, Fred Arthur 1937-1991 *WhAm 10*
Myers, Geoffrey 1930- *Who 94*
Myers, Geoffrey Morris Price 1927- *Who 94*
Myers, George, Jr. *DrAPF 93*
Myers, George Carleton 1931- *WhoAm 94*
Myers, George Hewitt 1865-1957 *WhoAmA 93N*
Myers, Gerald E. 1923- *WhoAm 94*
Myers, Gloria J. 1949- *WhoMW 93*
Myers, Gordon Elliot 1929- *Who 94*
Myers, Gregory Alan 1961- *WhoFI 94*
Myers, Gregory Edwin 1960- *WhoFI 94, WhoScEn 94, WhoWest 94*
Myers, Gretchen Hardy Godar 1958- *WhoAmL 94*
Myers, Gwen McHaney 1925- *WhoAmP 93*
Myers, Hardy 1939- *WhoAmP 93*
Myers, Harold Mathews 1915- *WhoAm 94*
Myers, Harry d1938 *WhoHol 92*
Myers, Harry Eric 1914- *Who 94*
Myers, Harry J., Jr. 1931- *WhoAm 94*
Myers, Helen Dee *WhoWest 94*
Myers, Helen Lunz 1942- *WhoMW 93*
Myers, Holly *WhoAmP 93*
Myers, Homer Samuel 1916- *WhoWest 94*
Myers, Howard L. 1930-1971 *EncSF 93*
Myers, Howard Milton 1923- *WhoAm 94*
Myers, Howard Nathaniel 1939- *WhoMW 93*
Myers, Ira Lee 1924- *WhoAm 94*
Myers, Ira Thomas 1925- *WhoMW 93*
Myers, Israel 1950- *WhoFI 94*
Myers, Jack *DrAPF 93*
Myers, Jack (Elliott) 1941- *WrDr 94*
Myers, Jack Edgar 1913- *WhoAm 94*
Myers, Jack Fredrick 1927- *WhoAmA 93*
Myers, Jack Kay 1946- *WhoFI 94*
Myers, Jacob M(artin) 1904- *WrDr 94*
Myers, Jacob Martin 1904- *WhAm 10*
Myers, Jacqualine Desmona 1951- *WhoBlA 94*
Myers, Jacqueline M. 1951- *WhoMW 93*
Myers, James Nelson 1941- *WhoAm 94*
Myers, James R. 1952- *WhoAm 94*
Myers, Jay Scott 1921- *WhoAmP 93*
Myers, Jeffrey Donald 1955- *WhoWest 94*
Myers, Jerome Joseph *WhoFI 94*
Myers, Jerome Keeley 1921- *WhoAm 94*
Myers, Jerry Alan 1958- *WhoScEn 94*
Myers, Jesse Jerome 1940- *WhoAm 94*
Myers, Jo Ann 1946- *WhoFI 94*
Myers, Joel Norman 1939- *WhoAm 94*
Myers, Joel Philip 1934- *WhoAmA 93*
Myers, John 1895- *WhAm 10*
Myers, John David 1937- *Who 94*
Myers, John Eldridge 1917- *WhoMW 93*
Myers, John Herman 1945- *WhoAm 94*
Myers, John Jay 1948- *WhoAm 94*
Myers, John Joseph 1941- *WhoAm 94, WhoMW 93*
Myers, John L. 1958- *ConAu 141*
Myers, John Lytle 1929- *WhoAm 94*
Myers, John Moore 1946- *WhoMW 93*
Myers, John Richard 1945- *WhoFI 94, WhoWest 94*
Myers, John Robert 1947- *WhoWest 94*
Myers, John T. 1927- *CngDr 93, WhoAmP 93*
Myers, John Thomas 1927- *WhoAm 94, WhoMW 93*
Myers, John Wescott 1911- *WhoAm 94*
Myers, Jon D. *WhoAmP 93*
Myers, Jonathan Jay 1960- *WhoAmL 94*
Myers, Joyce Anne 1948- *WhoFI 94*
Myers, Julian F. 1918- *IntMPA 94*
Myers, Kenneth (Ben) 1907- *Who 94*
Myers, Kenneth Alan 1942- *WhoScEn 94*
Myers, Kenneth Ellis 1932- *WhoAm 94, WhoMW 93*
Myers, Kenneth M. 1933- *WhoAm 94*
Myers, Kenneth Morton 1933- *WhoAmP 93*
Myers, Kenneth Raymond 1939- *WhoAm 94*
Myers, Kim 1966- *WhoHol 92*
Myers, L. Leonard 1933- *WhoBlA 94*
Myers, Lawrence Stanley, Jr. 1919- *WhoScEn 94*
Myers, Legh 1916- *WhoAmA 93*
Myers, Lena Wright *WhoBlA 94*
Myers, Lenora d1950 *WhoHol 92*
Myers, Leopold Hamilton 1881-1944 *BlmGEL*
Myers, Lewis Horace 1946- *WhoBlA 94*
Myers, Lonn William 1946- *WhoAm 94*
Myers, Lou(is) 1915- *WrDr 94*
Myers, Malcolm Haynie 1917- *WhoAm 94, WhoAmA 93*
Myers, Marc Edward 1951- *WhoAmL 94*
Myers, Marcus Norville 1928- *WhoScEn 94*
Myers, Margaret A. 1957- *WhoMW 93*
Myers, Marlee S. 1950- *WhoAm 94, WhoAmL 94*
Myers, Martin 1951- *WhoAmA 93*
Myers, Martin Trevor 1941- *Who 94*
Myers, Mary Jane 1963- *WhoMW 93*
Myers, Mary Kathleen 1945- *WhoAm 94*
Myers, Mary Lynn 1945- *WhoAm 94*
Myers, Michele Tolela 1941- *WhoAm 94, WhoMW 93*
Myers, Mike 1963- *WhoAm 94*
Myers, Mike 1964?- *ConTFT 11*
Myers, Miller Franklin 1929- *WhoFI 94*
Myers, Mindy Morawetz 1955- *WhoWest 94*
Myers, Minor, Jr. 1942- *WhoAm 94, WhoMW 93, WrDr 94*
Myers, Morey M. 1927- *WhoAm 94*
Myers, Morey Mayer 1927- *WhoAmL 94*
Myers, Neil *DrAPF 93*
Myers, Norman 1934- *CurBio 93 [port]*
Myers, Norman Allan 1935- *WhoAm 94, WhoFI 94*
Myers, Norman W. *WhoAmP 93*
Myers, Orie Eugene, Jr. 1920- *WhoAm 94*
Myers, Patricia Ann 1955- *WhoIns 94*
Myers, Paul 1932- *WrDr 94*
Myers, Paulene *WhoHol 92*
Myers, Peter d1968 *WhoHol 92*
Myers, Peter C. 1931- *WhoAm 94*
Myers, Peter Douglas 1953- *WhoMW 93*
Myers, Peter S. 1923- *IntMPA 94*
Myers, Philip (Alan) 1931- *Who 94*
Myers, Phillip Fenton 1935- *WhoAm 94, WhoFI 94*
Myers, Phillip Ward 1939- *WhoAm 94*
Myers, Ralph Chandler 1933- *WhoAm 94*
Myers, Randall Kirk 1962- *WhoAm 94*
Myers, Raymond 1938- *NewGrDO*
Myers, Rex Charles 1945- *WhoAm 94*
Myers, Richard Alan 1953- *WhoWest 94*
Myers, Richard Lee 1939- *WhoMW 93*
Myers, Rita 1947- *WhoAmA 93*
Myers, Robert C. 1942- *WhoAmL 94*
Myers, Robert David 1937- *WhoAm 94*
Myers, Robert Durant 1931- *WhoAm 94*
Myers, Robert Eugene 1924- *WhoWest 94*
Myers, Robert Eugene 1928- *WhoMW 93*
Myers, Robert Eugene 1953- *WhoMW 93*
Myers, Robert Gilbert 1932- *WhoAm 94, WhoFI 94*
Myers, Robert Jay 1934- *WhoAm 94, WhoFI 94*
Myers, Robert John 1924- *WhoAm 94*
Myers, Robert Julius 1912- *WhoAmP 93*
Myers, Robert L., Jr. *WhoBlA 94*
Myers, Robert Lee 1923- *WhAm 10*
Myers, Robert Louis, II 1956- *WhoWest 94*
Myers, Robert Manson 1921- *WhoAm 94, WrDr 94*
Myers, Robert Norman, Jr. 1949- *WhoFI 94*
Myers, Rolland Graham 1945- *WhoAm 94, WhoFI 94*
Myers, Ronald Eugene 1947- *WhoMW 93, WhoScEn 94*
Myers, Ronald Kosty 1946- *WhoFI 94*
Myers, Roy *EncSF 93*
Myers, Rufus, Jr. 1942- *WhoAmP 93*
Myers, Rupert (Horace) 1921- *Who 94*
Myers, Samuel L. 1919- *WhoBlA 94*
Myers, Samuel L., Jr. 1949- *WhoBlA 94*
Myers, Samuel Lloyd 1919- *WhoAm 94*
Myers, Sean *WhoHol 92*
Myers, Seldy d1939 *WhoHol 92*
Myers, Sere Spaulding 1930- *WhoBlA 94*
Myers, Sherry Ransford 1948- *WhoMW 93*
Myers, Stanley *IntMPA 94*
Myers, Stanley 1933- *ConTFT 11*
Myers, Stephanie E. 1950- *WhoBlA 94*
Myers, Stephen Hawley 1953- *WhoAmL 94*
Myers, Susan *WhoHol 92*
Myers, Susan Kay Gunness 1949- *WhoMW 93*
Myers, Terry 1945- *WhoAmL 94*
Myers, Terry R. 1965- *WhoAmA 93*
Myers, Theodore Ash 1930- *WhoAm 94*
Myers, Thomas Andrew 1966- *WhoWest 94*
Myers, Thomas Everett 1954- *WhoAmL 94*
Myers, Thomas F. 1937- *WhoAmL 94*
Myers, Vernon C. 1911-1990 *WhAm 10*
Myers, Victoria Christina 1943- *WhoBlA 94, WhoMW 93*
Myers, Virginia Anne 1927- *WhoAmA 93, WhoMW 93*
Myers, Walter Dean *DrAPF 93*
Myers, Walter Dean 1937- *BlkWr 2, ConAu 42NR, TwCYAW, WhoBlA 94, WrDr 94*
Myers, Walter M. *BlkWr 2, ConAu 42NR*

Myers, Warren Powers Laird 1921-
WhoAm 94
Myers, Wayne Alan 1931- *WhoAm 94*
Myers, William 1939- *WrDr 94*
Myers, William George 1930-
WhoAmP 93
Myers, William Killeen 1938-
WhoMW 93
Myers, William S. *WhoAm 94*
Myers, Woodrow Augustus, Jr. 1954-
WhoAm 94, WhoBlA 94
Myers Medeiros, Patricia Jo 1942-
WhoFI 94
Myerson, Alan 1936- *WhoAm 94*
Myerson, Albert Leon 1919- *WhoAm 94, WhoScEn 94*
Myerson, Allan Stuart 1952- *WhoScEn 94*
Myerson, Arthur Levey 1928- *Who 94*
Myerson, Bernard 1918- *IntMPA 94*
Myerson, Eleanor 1922- *WhoAmP 93*
Myerson, Jacob M. 1926- *IntWW 93*
Myerson, Jacob Myer 1926- *WhoAm 94*
Myerson, Joel 1945- *ConAu 41NR*
Myerson, Joel Arthur 1945- *WhoAm 94*
Myerson, Paul E. 1922- *WhoAmL 94, WhoFI 94*
Myerson, Paul Graves 1914- *WhoAm 94*
Myerson, Raymond King 1917-
WhoWest 94
Myerson, Roger Bruce 1951- *WhoAm 94, WhoFI 94*
Myerson, Toby Salter 1949- *WhoAm 94, WhoAmL 94*
Myford, James C. 1940- *WhoAmA 93*
Mygatt, Susan Hall 1947- *WhoAm 94, WhoAmL 94*
Myhand, Wanda Reshel 1963-
WhoMW 93
Myhers, John 1924- *WhoHol 92*
Myhre, Byron Arnold 1928- *WhoAm 94*
Myhre, Deanna Shirley 1938-
WhoAmL 94
Myhre, Oyvind *EncSF 93*
Myhre-Hollerman, Janet Marlene 1932-
WhoWest 94
Myhren, Trygve Edward 1937-
WhoAm 94, WhoFI 94, WhoWest 94
Myia *BlmGWL*
Myia fl. 3rd cent.BC- *BlmGWL*
Myint, Than Htun 1949- *WhoAsA 94*
Myint Maung, U. 1921- *IntWW 93*
Mykkanen, Donald Lee 1932-
WhoWest 94
Mykytiuk, Alex P. *WhoScEn 94*
Myland, Howard David 1929- *Who 94*
Mylar, James Lewis 1940- *WhoScEn 94*
Myler, Lok *EncSF 93*
Myler, Russell Clinton 1944- *WhoMW 93*
Myles, Bruce *WhoHol 92*
Myles, David Fairlie 1925- *Who 94*
Myles, Eileen *DrAPF 93*
Myles, Ernestine 1921- *WhoBlA 94*
Myles, Herbert John 1923- *WhoBlA 94*
Myles, Kevin Michael 1934- *WhoMW 93, WhoScEn 94*
Myles, Meg *WhoHol 92*
Myles, Stan, Jr. 1943- *WhoBlA 94*
Myles, Symon 1949- *WhoAm 94, WrDr 94*
Myles, Wilbert 1935- *WhoBlA 94*
Myles, William 1936- *WhoBlA 94*
Mylett, Jeffrey d1986 *WhoHol 92*
Mylius, Ralph *EncSF 93*
Mylius-Erichsen, Ludwig 1872-1907
WhWE
Myllent, Peter *Who 94*
Mylne, Nigel James 1939- *Who 94*
Mylnechuk, Larry Herbert 1948-
WhoFI 94
Mylod, Robert Joseph 1939- *WhoAm 94, WhoFI 94*
Mylonakis, Stamatios Gregory 1937-
WhoFI 94, WhoScEn 94
Mylong, John d1975 *WhoHol 92*
Mylott, Dan H. 1942- *WhoAmP 93*
Mylroie, Willa Wilcox 1917- *WhoAm 94*
Mynatt, John Rupert, Jr. 1937- *WhoFI 94*
Mynne, George fl. 1614-1648 *DcNaB MP*
Mynors, Richard (Baskerville) 1947-
Who 94
Myntti, Jon Nicholas 1940- *WhoMW 93*
Myoda, Toshio Timothy 1929-
WhoAsA 94, WhoScEn 94
Myra, Harold Lawrence 1939- *WhoAm 94*
Myrat, Dimitris d1991 *WhoHol 92*
Myrberg, Arthur August, Jr. 1933-
WhoAm 94
Myrdal, Gunnar d1987 *NobelP 91N*
Myrdal, Jan 1927- *ConWorW 93, IntWW 93*
Myrdal, Karl Gunnar 1898- *WhAm 10*
Myrdal, Rosemarie C. 1929- *WhoAmP 93*
Myrdal, Rosemarie Caryle 1929-
WhoAm 94, WhoMW 93
Myre, David E., Jr. 1951- *WhoAmL 94*
Myren, David James 1960- *WhoMW 93*
Myren, Richard Albert 1924- *WhoAm 94*
Myrer, Anton Olmstead 1922- *WhoAm 94*

Myres, John Antony Lovell 1936- *Who 94*
Myrick, Clarissa 1954- *WhoBlA 94*
Myrick, David F. *WrDr 94*
Myrick, Howard A., Jr. 1934- *WhoBlA 94*
Myrick, Julian 1880-1969 *BuCMET*
Myrick, Katherine S. *WhoAmA 93N*
Myrick, Ronald Ernest 1943-
WhoAmL 94
Myrick, Sue 1941- *WhoAm 94, WhoAmP 93, WhoWomW 91*
Myricks, Noel 1935- *WhoBlA 94*
Myrin, Alarik F. 1946- *WhoAmP 93*
Myron, Robert 1928- *WhoAmA 93*
Myrtetus, William Kane 1934-
WhoAmP 93
Myrtil, Odette d1978 *WhoHol 92*
Myrtiotissa *BlmGWL*
Myrtis fl. 6th cent.BC-5th cent.BC
BlmGWL
Myrtle, Andrew Dewe 1932- *Who 94*
Mysak, Edward Damien 1930-1989
WhAm 10
Mysak, Lawrence Alexander 1940-
WhoAm 94
Mysels, Karol Joseph 1914- *WhoWest 94*
Mysen, Bjorn O. 1947- *IntWW 93*
Myslewski, Rik 1950- *WhoWest 94*
Myslik, Edward Joseph, Jr. 1932-
WhoFI 94
Myslinski, Norbert Raymond 1947-
WhoScEn 94
Myslivecek, Josef 1737-1781 *NewGrDO*
Mysliwiec, Ronald P. 1947- *WhoAmL 94*
Mysliwiec, Stephen R. 1948- *WhoAmL 94*
Myszuga, Aleksander 1853-1922
NewGrDO
Mytelka, Arnold Krieger 1937-
WhoAmL 94
Myung, John Y. 1964- *WhoAsA 94*
Mzali, Mohamed 1925- *IntWW 93*
Mzilikazi c. 1792-1868 *HisWorL [port]*

N

Na, Hu 1963- *BuCMET*
Naaden, Lawrence L. *WhoAmP 93*
Naar, Harry I. 1946- *WhoAmA 93*
Naas, Lord 1985- *Who 94*
Naatanen, Risto Kalervo 1939- *IntWW 93*
Nabakowski, Ronald Lee 1942-
  WhoAmP 93
Nabarro, Frank Reginald Nunes 1916-
  IntWW 93, Who 94
Nabarro, John (David Nunes) 1915-
  Who 94
Nabb, Magdalen 1947- *WrDr 94*
Nabers, Drayton, Jr. 1940- *WhoAm 94,*
  WhoFI 94, WhoIns 94
Nabers, J. Lynn 1940- *WhoAmL 94*
Nabers, Lynn 1940- *WhoAmP 93*
Nabholz, Joseph Vincent 1945-
  WhoScEn 94
Nabholz-Haidegger, Zollikon 1944-
  WhoWomW 91
Nabi, Mohamed 1935- *IntWW 93*
Nabi, Stanley Andrew 1930- *WhoAm 94*
Nabiev, Rakhman d1993 *IntWW 93N*
Nabiev, Rakhmon Nabievich 1931-
  LngBDD
Nabirahni, David M.A. 1956-
  WhoScEn 94
Nabiyev, Rakhman N. 1930-1993
  NewYTBS 93 [port]
Nabokov, Dmitri 1934- *WrDr 94*
Nabokov, Nicolas 1903-1978 *NewGrDO*
Nabokov, Peter (Francis) 1940- *WrDr 94*
Nabokov, Vladimir 1899-1977 *AmCulL,*
  EncSF 93, RfGShF
Nabors, James Thurston 1930-
  WhoAm 94
Nabors, Jesse Lee, Sr. 1940- *WhoBlA 94*
Nabors, Jim 1930- *WhoHol 92*
Nabors, Jim 1932- *IntMPA 94, WhoCom*
Nabors, John C. 1944- *WhoAmL 94*
Nabrit, James M., Jr. 1900- *WhoBlA 94*
Nabrit, James M., III 1932- *WhoBlA 94*
Nabrit, Samuel M. 1905- *WhoBlA 94*
Nabseth, Lars 1928- *IntWW 93*
Nace, Barry John 1944- *WhoAmL 94*
Nace, Harold Russ 1921- *WhoAm 94*
Nace, Theodore Keifer 1925- *WhoAmP 93*
Nachbar, James Milton 1956-
  WhoWest 94
Nachbaur, Franz (Ignaz) 1835-1902
  NewGrDO
Nache, Maria-Luisa 1924-1985 *NewGrDO*
Nachman, David Charles 1944- *WhoFI 94*
Nachman, Erwin Behr 1934- *WhoAmL 94*
Nachman, Gerald Weil 1938- *WhoAm 94*
Nachman, James L. 1942- *WhoAm 94*
Nachman, Leonard R. 1945- *WhoAmL 94*
Nachman, Merton Roland, Jr. 1923-
  WhoAm 94, WhoAmL 94
Nachman, Norman Harry *WhoAm 94,*
  WhoAmL 94, WhoMW 93
Nachreiner, Michael Leo 1944-
  WhoAmP 93
Nacht, Daniel Joseph 1915- *WhoAm 94*
Nacht, Sergio 1934- *WhoScEn 94,*
  WhoWest 94
Nacht, Steve Jerry 1948- *WhoWest 94*
Nachtigal, Gustav 1834-1885 *WhWE*
Nachtigal, Patricia 1946- *WhoAm 94,*
  WhoFI 94
Nachtigal, Ralph E. 1933- *WhoAmP 93*
Nachtigall, Dieter 1927- *IntWW 93*

Nachtrieb, Norman Harry 1916-1991
  WhAm 10
Nachwalter, Michael 1940- *WhoAmL 94*
Nackel, John George 1951- *WhoAm 94*
Nacol, Mae 1944- *WhoAmL 94*
Nad, Leon Marion 1927-1991 *WhAm 10*
Nadal, Jose Miguel, Jr. 1947- *WhoHisp 94*
Nadalini, (Louis Ernest) 1927-
  WhoAmA 93
Nadas, Alexander Sandor 1913-
  WhoAm 94
Nadas, John Adalbert 1949- *WhoMW 93*
Nadasdy, Leonard John 1930-
  WhoAmP 93
Nadasi, Ferenc 1893-1966 *IntDcB*
Naddafi, Nancy Lee 1947- *WhoFI 94*
Naddod fl. 86-?-87-? *WhWE*
Nadeau, Bertin F. 1940- *WhoAm 94,*
  WhoFI 94
Nadeau, Eleanor Saxe 1909- *WhoAm 94*
Nadeau, Gregory Guy 1957- *WhoAmP 93*
Nadeau, Guy R. 1956- *WhoAmP 93*
Nadeau, John 1934- *WhoFI 94,*
  WhoMW 93
Nadeau, Joseph Eugene 1937- *WhoFI 94*
Nadeau, Nadine *WhoHol 92*
Nadeau, Robert Bertrand, Jr. 1950-
  WhoAmL 94
Nadeau, Steven C. 1954- *WhoAmL 94*
Nadel, Ann Honig 1940- *WhoAmA 93*
Nadel, Edwin 1928- *WhoIns 94*
Nadel, Elliott 1945- *WhoAm 94,*
  WhoFI 94
Nadel, Laurie 1948- *SmATA 74*
Nadel, Mark Alan 1945- *WhoAm 94*
Nadel, Marvin 1926- *WhoAm 94*
Nadel, Norman Allen 1927- *WhoAm 94,*
  WhoScEn 94
Nadel, Roger 1950- *WhoMW 93*
Nadell, Andrew Thomas 1946-
  WhoWest 94
Nadelson, Carol Cooperman 1936-
  WhoAm 94
Naden, Vernon Dewitt 1947- *WhoMW 93*
Nader, G(eorge) A(lbert) 1940- *WrDr 94*
Nader, George 1921- *IntMPA 94,*
  WhoHol 92
Nader, Michael 1945- *WhoHol 92*
Nader, Ralph 1934- *AmSocL [port],*
  EnvEnc, IntWW 93, Who 94,
  WhoAm 94, WrDr 94
Nader, Robert Alexander 1928-
  WhoAm 94, WhoAmP 93
Nader, Suzanne Nora Beurer 1947-
  WhoMW 93
Naderi, Jamie Benedict 1951- *WhoFI 94*
Nadesan, Pararajasingam 1917- *Who 94*
Nadherny, Ernst d1966 *WhoHol 92*
Nadherny, Ferdinand *WhoAm 94,*
  WhoFI 94
Nadi, Aldo d1965 *WhoHol 92*
Nadich, Judah 1912- *WhoAm 94*
Nadig, Gerald George 1945- *WhoAm 94,*
  WhoFI 94, WhoMW 93
Nadim, Ali 1962- *WhoScEn 94*
Nadin, Alice Klicker 1954- *WhoMW 93*
Nadir, Zakee *DrAPF 93*
Nadiri, M. Ishaq 1936- *WhoAm 94*
Nadir Shah 1688-1747 *HisWorL [port]*
Nadkarni, Girish Vishwanath 1957-
  WhoFI 94
Nadkarni, Prakash Dattatraya 1941-
  WhoMW 93

Nadkarni, Sudhir V. 1947- *WhoAsA 94*
Nadkarni, Suresh Shankar 1934-
  IntWW 93
Nadler, Ellen R. 1946- *WhoAmL 94*
Nadler, Gerald 1924- *WhoAm 94*
Nadler, Harris 1944- *WhoMW 93*
Nadler, Harry 1930-1990 *WhoAmA 93N*
Nadler, Henry Louis 1936- *WhoAm 94,*
  WhoMW 93
Nadler, Jerrold 1947- *CngDr 93*
Nadler, Jerrold Lewis 1947- *WhoAm 94,*
  WhoAmP 93
Nadler, Mark B. 1951- *WhoAm 94*
Nadler, Mark Steven 1956- *WhoAmL 94*
Nadler, Myron Jay 1923- *WhoAm 94*
Nadler, Sigmond Harold 1932-
  WhoAm 94
Nadler-Hurvich, Hedda Carol 1944-
  WhoFI 94
Nadley, Harris Jerome 1926- *WhoAm 94*
Nadolski, Linda 1944- *WhoAmP 93*
Nadolski, Stephanie Lucille 1945-
  WhoAmA 93
Nady, John 1945- *WhoWest 94*
Nadzick, Judith Ann 1948- *WhoFI 94*
Nadziejka, David E. 1946- *WhoMW 93*
Nae, Elena 1928- *WhoWomW 91*
Naefe, David Parker 1942- *WhoFI 94*
Naegele, Carl Joseph 1939- *WhoAm 94*
Naegele, Charles Joseph *WhoWest 94*
Naegele, Eugene Alexander 1946-
  WhoMW 93
Naegele, Philipp Otto 1928- *WhoAm 94*
Naegele, Timothy Duncan 1941-
  WhoAmL 94
Naegle, Montana 1940- *WhoAmA 93*
Naegle, Stephen Howard 1938-1981
  WhoAmA 93N
Naeser, Charles Wilbur 1940-
  WhoWest 94
Naeser, Margaret Ann 1944- *WhoScEn 94*
Naess, Arne 1912- *EnvEnc*
Naess, Erling Dekke d1993 *NewYTBS 93*
Naessens, James Michael 1952-
  WhoScEn 94
Naeve, Clifford Milo 1947- *WhoAmP 93*
Naeve, Milo M. 1931- *WhoAmA 93*
Naeve, Milo Merle 1931- *WhoAm 94*
Naeye, Richard L. 1929- *WhoAm 94*
Nafe, Alicia 1947- *NewGrDO*
Nafe, John Elliott 1914- *WhoAm 94*
Naffah, Fouad Georges 1925- *IntWW 93*
Nafie, Laurence Allen 1945- *WhoAm 94*
Naftalis, Gary Philip 1941- *WhoAm 94,*
  WhoAmL 94, WhoFI 94
Naftolin, Frederick 1936- *WhoAm 94*
Naftulin, Rose *WhoAmA 93*
Naftzinger, David J. 1948- *WhoAmL 94*
Nafzger, Samuel Henry 1939-
  WhoAm 94
Nafzger, Estel Wayne 1938- *WhoAm 94,*
  WhoFI 94
Nafziger, George F(rancis) 1949- *WrDr 94*
Nafziger, Pattie Lois *WhoAmP 93*
Nag, Asish Chandra 1932- *WhoScEn 94*
Nag, Ronjon 1962?- *WhoAsA 94*
Nagac, Emile de 1828-1899 *NewGrDO*
Nagai, Michio 1923- *IntWW 93*
Nagai, Nelson Kei 1950- *WhoAsA 94*
Nagai, Tsuneji 1933- *WhoScEn 94*
Nagakura, Saburo 1920- *IntWW 93*
Nagamiya, Shoji 1944- *WhoScEn 94*
Nagan, Peter Seymour 1920- *WhoAm 94*

Nagan, Winston Percival 1941-
  WhoBlA 94
Nagano, Kent (George) 1951- *NewGrDO*
Nagano, Kent George 1951- *WhoAsA 94*
Nagano, Paul Tatsumi 1938-
  WhoAmA 93, WhoAsA 94
Nagano, Shozo *WhoAmA 93*
Nagao, Makoto 1936- *WhoScEn 94*
Nagao, Norris Sadato 1954- *WhoWest 94*
Nagaoka, Michael M. 1946- *WhoAsA 94*
Nagaprasanna, Bangalore R. 1948-
  WhoFI 94
Nagar, Arvind 1939- *WhoMW 93*
Nagarajan, Ramakrishnan 1931-
  WhoAsA 94
Nagarajan, Sundaram 1962- *WhoScEn 94*
Nagarjun 1911- *ConWorW 93*
Nagarjuna c. 113-213 *EncEth*
Nagarkatti, Jai Prakash 1947-
  WhoScEn 94
Nagasaka, Kyosuke 1955- *WhoScEn 94*
Nagasawa, Yuko *WhoScEn 94*
Nagata, Hiroshi 1949- *WhoScEn 94*
Nagata, Isao 1942- *WhoMW 93,*
  WhoScEn 94
Nagata, Minoru 1933- *WhoScEn 94*
Nagata, Russel 1951- *WhoAmP 93*
Nagata, Takao 1911- *IntWW 93*
Nagata, Takesi 1913- *IntWW 93*
Nagatani, Scott A. 1956- *WhoAsA 94*
Nagatoshi, Konrad R. 1951- *WhoAsA 94*
Nagda, Kanti 1926- *Who 94*
Nagel, Anne d1966 *WhoHol 92*
Nagel, Beth d1936 *WhoHol 92*
Nagel, Candice *WhoAmP 93*
Nagel, Carl, III 1953- *WhoFI 94*
Nagel, Carol 1937- *WhoAmP 93*
Nagel, Charles 1899-1992 *WhAm 10*
Nagel, Conrad d1970 *WhoHol 92*
Nagel, Daryl David 1939- *WhoAm 94,*
  WhoWest 94
Nagel, Edward McCaul 1926- *WhoAm 94*
Nagel, Gunter 1936- *IntWW 93*
Nagel, Ivan 1931- *IntWW 93*
Nagel, Jerome Kaub 1923- *WhoWest 94*
Nagel, Joachim Hans 1948- *WhoAm 94,*
  WhoScEn 94
Nagel, Joane 1944- *WhoMW 93*
Nagel, Joel Matthew 1965- *WhoAmL 94*
Nagel, Louis 1908- *IntWW 93*
Nagel, Max Richard 1909- *WhoScEn 94*
Nagel, Monica *WhoWomW 91*
Nagel, Patricia 1942- *WhoAmP 93*
Nagel, Patricia Jo 1942- *WhoWest 94*
Nagel, Paul C. 1926- *WrDr 94*
Nagel, Paul Chester 1926- *WhoAm 94*
Nagel, Ronald Curtis 1961- *WhoWest 94*
Nagel, Sidney Robert 1948- *WhoAm 94*
Nagel, Stanley Blair 1928- *WhoFI 94,*
  WhoWest 94
Nagel, Stina 1918-1969 *WhoAmA 93N*
Nagel, Stuart 1934- *WrDr 94*
Nagel, William Lee 1949- *WhoFI 94*
Nagele, Rainer 1943- *WhoAm 94*
Nagelvoort, Terry L. 1942- *WhoFI 94*
Nagem, Alex Joseph 1954- *WhoFI 94*
Nagem, Monique F. 1941- *ConAu 140*
Nagenda, John 1938- *BlkWr 2,*
  ConAu 140
Nagengast, William Joseph 1934-
  WhoAmA 93
Nager, Norman 1936- *WhoWest 94*
Nagera, Humberto 1927- *WhoAm 94*

Nagey, David Augustus 1950- *WhoScEn 94*
Naghdi, Paul Mansour 1924- *WhoAm 94*
Nagibin, Yuriy Markovich 1920- *IntWW 93*
Nagin, Lawrence M. 1941- *WhoAmL 94, WhoFI 94*
Nagin, Mary D. 1953- *WhoAmA 93*
Nagin, Stephen E. 1946- *WhoAmL 94*
Nagle, Arlington, Jr. 1943- *WhoFI 94*
Nagle, David R. 1943- *WhoAm 94, WhoAmP 93*
Nagle, Edward John, Jr. 1941- *WhoFI 94*
Nagle, Hubert Troy, Jr. 1942- *WhoAm 94*
Nagle, Jack *WhoHol 92*
Nagle, James F. 1929- *WhoAmP 93*
Nagle, James Francis 1948- *WhoAmL 94*
Nagle, Jean Sue 1936- *WhoMW 93*
Nagle, Laura Jennifer 1962- *WhoAmL 94*
Nagle, Patricia Anne 1928- *WhoAmP 93*
Nagle, Peggy Jo 1955- *WhoMW 93*
Nagle, Raymond J. 1900-1991 *WhAm 10*
Nagle, Ron 1939- *WhoAmA 93*
Nagle, Terence John 1942- *Who 94*
Nagle, William P., Jr. 1951- *WhoAmP 93*
Nagler, Alois M. d1993 *NewYTBS 93*
Nagler, Alois Maria 1907-1993 *ConAu 141*
Nagler, Arnold Leon 1935- *WhoAm 94*
Nagler, Edith Kroger 1895-1986 *WhoAmA 93N*
Nagler, Fred 1891-1983 *WhoAmA 93N*
Nagler, Leon Gregory 1932- *WhoAm 94, WhoFI 94*
Nagler, Michael Nicholas 1937- *WhoWest 94*
Nagler, Stewart Gordon 1943- *WhoAm 94, WhoFI 94, WhoIns 94, WhoWest 94*
Naglestad, Frederic Allen 1929- *WhoWest 94*
Naglich, Donald R. 1951- *WhoMW 93*
Naglieri, Thomas Joseph 1937- *WhoAm 94*
Nagorski, Edward John 1943- *WhoFI 94*
Nagoshi, Craig Tetsuo 1956- *WhoWest 94*
Nagoshi, Douglas N. 1942- *WhoAsA 94*
Nagourney, Herbert 1926- *WhoAm 94*
Nagrodskaia, Evdokiia Apollonovna 1866-1930 *BlmGWL*
Nagurski, Bronko d1990 *ProFbHF [port]*
Nagy, Andrew Francis 1932- *WhoAm 94*
Nagy, Bartholomew Stephen 1927- *WhoAm 94*
Nagy, Bill d1973 *WhoHol 92*
Nagy, Christina *WhoHol 92*
Nagy, Clive Michael 1936- *WhoMW 93*
Nagy, Imre 1896-1958 *HisWorL [port]*
Nagy, Janos B. 1940- *NewGrDO*
Nagy, Janos L. *Who 94*
Nagy, Kenneth Alex 1943- *WhoWest 94*
Nagy, Louis Leonard 1942- *WhoAm 94*
Nagy, Robert 1929- *NewGrDO*
Nagy, Robert David 1929- *WhoAm 94*
Nagy, Steven 1936- *WhoAm 94*
Nagy, Zoltan 1933- *WhoMW 93*
Nagyne, G. *WhoWomW 91*
Nagys, Elizabeth Ann *WhoMW 93, WhoScEn 94*
Naha, Ed 1950- *EncSF 93, WrDr 94*
Naha, Raymond d1975 *WhoAmA 93N*
Nahal, Chaman 1927- *WrDr 94*
Nahan, Stu *WhoHol 92*
Nahar, Sultana Nurun 1955- *WhoScEn 94*
Naharro-Calderon, Jose Maria 1953- *WhoHisp 94*
Nahas, Dominique Francois 1951- *WhoAmA 93*
Nahas, Gabriel G(eorges) 1920- *WrDr 94*
Nahas, Gabriel Georges 1920- *WhoAm 94*
Nahas, Walter N. 1938- *WhoWest 94*
Nahat, Dennis F. 1946- *WhoAm 94, WhoMW 93*
Nahata, Milap Chand 1950- *WhoAsA 94*
Nahata, Suparas M. 1943- *WhoAsA 94*
Nahavandi, Amir Nezameddin 1924- *WhoAm 94*
Nahayan, Zayed bin al- 1918- *IntWW 93*
Naheed, Kishwar 1940- *BlmGWL*
Nahigian, Alma Louise 1936- *WhoFI 94*
Nahigian, Robert John 1956- *WhoFI 94*
Nahill, Charles F., Jr. 1938- *WhoAmP 93*
Nahm, Moon H. 1948- *WhoAsA 94*
Nahman, Norris Stanley 1925- *WhoAm 94, WhoWest 94*
Nahmias, Andre Joseph 1930- *WhoAm 94*
Nahmias, Victor Jay 1951- *WhoWest 94*
Nahm-Mijo, Trina 1949- *WhoWest 94*
Nahon, Paul G. 1933- *WhoAmP 93*
Nahrwold, David Lange 1935- *WhoAm 94*
Nahrwold, James Lange 1939- *WhoIns 94, WhoMW 93*
Naiburg, Irving B., Jr. 1942- *WhoAm 94*
Naiden, James *DrAPF 93*
Naiden, James 1943- *WrDr 94*
Naidenov, Assen 1899- *NewGrDO*
Naides, Stanley Jay 1951- *WhoMW 93*
Naidoo, Beverley 1943- *TwCYAW*
Naidoo, Bobby d1967 *WhoHol 92*
Naidoo, Jay 1954- *IntWW 93*
Naidorf, Louis Murray 1928- *WhoAm 94*
Naidu, Sarojini 1879-1949 *BlmGWL*
Naidu, Seetala Veeraswamy 1957- *WhoAsA 94*
Naifeh, James O. 1939- *WhoAm 94*
Naifeh, Jimmy 1939- *WhoAmP 93*
Naifeh, Steven Woodward 1952- *WhoAm 94*
Naify, Marshall 1920- *IntMPA 94*
Naify, Robert *IntMPA 94*
Naik, Datta Vittal 1947- *WhoAsA 94*
Naik, Tarun Ratilal 1940- *WhoAsA 94*
Nail, Jimmy *WhoHol 92*
Nail, Joanne *WhoHol 92*
Nail, Olin Wesley 1930- *WhoFI 94*
Nail, Paul Reid 1952- *WhoScEn 94*
Nailatikau, Ratu Epeli 1941- *Who 94*
Nailor, Gerald Lloyde 1917-1952 *WhoAmA 93N*
Nailor, Jerry L. 1946- *WhoAmP 93*
Nailor, Peter 1928- *Who 94*
Nails, John Walker 1947- *WhoBlA 94*
Nails, Kenneth H. 1942- *WhoIns 94*
Nails, Odell 1929-1993 *WhoBlA 94N*
Naim, Shamim 1937- *WhoMW 93*
Naiman, Lee *WhoAmA 93*
Naimark, Arnold 1933- *WhoAm 94*
Naimark, George Modell 1925- *WhoAm 94, WhoFI 94, WhoScEn 94*
Naimark, Richard Wythes 1951- *WhoFI 94*
Naimi, Shapur 1928- *WhoAm 94, WhoScEn 94*
Naimoli, Raymond Anthony 1942- *WhoAm 94*
Naimoli, Vincent Joseph 1937- *WhoAm 94, WhoFI 94*
Nainby, Robert d1948 *WhoHol 92*
Nainoa, Sam K., Jr. 1944- *WhoHisp 94*
Nain Singh fl. 186-?-187-? *WhWE*
Naioti, Leo John, Jr. 1959- *WhoFI 94*
Naipaul, V. S. 1932- *BlmGEL*
Naipaul, V(idiadhar) S(urajprasad) 1932- *RfGShF, WrDr 94*
Naipaul, Vidiadhar Surajprasad 1932- *IntWW 93, Who 94, WhoAm 94*
Nair, C. V. Devan *IntWW 93*
Nair, Chandra K. 1944- *WhoAsA 94*
Nair, Chandra Kunju Pillai 1944- *WhoScEn 94*
Nair, Chengara Veetil Devan 1923- *Who 94*
Nair, K. M. 1933- *WhoAsA 94*
Nair, K. Manikantan 1933- *WhoScEn 94*
Nair, Madhavan Puthiya Veethil 1943- *WhoMW 93, WhoScEn 94*
Nair, Mia 1957- *IntMPA 94*
Nair, Mira 1957- *CurBio 93 [port], WhoAsA 94*
Nair, Raghavan D. 1951- *WhoAm 94*
Nair, Sudhakar Edayillam 1944- *WhoScEn 94*
Nair, V. Krishnan 1941- *WhoAsA 94*
Nair, Velayudhan 1928- *WhoAm 94, WhoScEn 94*
Nair, Velupillai Krishnan 1941- *WhoScEn 94*
Nairn, James Francis 1945- *WhoMW 93*
Nairn, Kenneth Gordon 1898- *Who 94*
Nairn, Margaret 1924- *Who 94*
Nairn, Martin John L. *Who 94*
Nairn, Michael 1938- *Who 94*
Nairn, Robert Arnold S. *Who 94*
Nairn, Roderick 1951- *WhoMW 93*
Nairne, Lady 1912- *Who 94*
Nairne, Alexander Robert 1953- *Who 94*
Nairne, Patrick (Dalmahoy) 1921- *Who 94*
Nairne, Patrick Dalmahoy 1921- *IntWW 93*
Nairne, Sandy *Who 94*
Nairobi, Archbishop of 1923- *Who 94*
Naisbitt, John 1929- *WrDr 94*
Naisby, Alan 1956- *WhoMW 93*
Naish, Bronwen 1939- *IntWW 93*
Naish, (Charles) David 1940- *Who 94*
Naish, J. Carrol d1973 *WhoHol 92*
Naishtat, Elliott 1945- *WhoAmP 93*
Naismith, James 1861-1939 *BasBi*
Naismith, James Pomeroy 1936- *WhoScEn 94*
Naismith, Laurence 1908- *WhoHol 92*
Naito, Herbert K. 1942- *WhoAsA 94*
Naito, Lisa 1955- *WhoAmP 93*
Naito, Michael K. 1948- *WhoAsA 94*
Naito, Samuel Teruhide 1921- *WhoAsA 94*
Naito, Takeshi 1929- *WhoAm 94*
Naitove, Matthew Henry 1949- *WhoAm 94*
Naj, Amal K. 1951- *ConAu 140*
Najar, Leo Michael 1953- *WhoAm 94, WhoMW 93*
Najarian, John Sarkis 1927- *IntWW 93, WhoAm 94, WhoScEn 94*
Najarian, Peter *DrAPF 93, WrDr 94*
Najder, Kenneth John 1960- *WhoAmL 94*
Najder, Zdzislaw 1930- *IntWW 93*
Najee *WhoBlA 94*
Najera, Edmund L. 1936- *WhoHisp 94*
Najera, Esteban, Jr. 1963- *WhoHisp 94*
Najera, Rafael 1938- *WhoScEn 94*
Najera, Richard *WhoHisp 94*
Najera, Richard Almeraz 1937- *WhoHisp 94*
Najibullah, Maj.-Gen. 1947- *IntWW 93*
Najita, Tetsuo 1936- *WhoAm 94, WhoAsA 94*
Najjar, Edward Robert 1951- *WhoHisp 94*
Najjoum, Linda Lemmon 1946- *WhoAmL 94*
Najm, Farid Nasri 1960- *WhoMW 93*
Najm, Issam Nasri 1963- *WhoScEn 94*
Nakabayashi, Nicholas Takateru 1920- *WhoFI 94, WhoWest 94*
Nakadai, Tatsuya 1930- *WhoHol 92*
Nakadegawa, Roy *WhoAsA 94*
Nakae, Toshitada 1929- *IntWW 93*
Nakae, Yosuke 1922- *IntWW 93*
Nakagaki, Masayuki 1923- *WhoScEn 94*
Nakagawa, Allen Donald 1955- *WhoWest 94*
Nakagawa, Cressey *WhoAsA 94*
Nakagawa, Eileen Chiyo 1959- *WhoWest 94*
Nakagawa, Jean Harue 1943- *WhoAm 94*
Nakagawa, John Edward 1962- *WhoScEn 94*
Nakagawa, Kiyoshi 1945- *WhoScEn 94*
Nakagawa, Yuzo 1932- *WhoScEn 94*
Nakaguchi, Richard T. 1938- *WhoAsA 94*
Nakahara, Masayoshi 1927- *WhoScEn 94*
Nakahara, Shohei 1942- *WhoAsA 94*
Nakahata, Tadaka 1924- *WhoWest 94*
Nakai, Hiroshi 1935- *WhoScEn 94*
Nakaidoklini d1881 *EncNAR*
Nakajima, Amane 1961- *WhoScEn 94*
Nakajima, Fumio 1904- *IntWW 93*
Nakajima, Gentaro 1929- *IntWW 93*
Nakajima, Hiroshi *IntWW 93*
Nakajima, Hiroshi 1928- *Who 94*
Nakajima, Mamoru *IntWW 93*
Nakajima, Nobuyuki 1923- *WhoAsA 94*
Nakajima, Takeshi 1924- *IntWW 93*
Nakajo, Steve *WhoAsA 94*
Nakamizo, Fuji 1889- *WhoAmA 93N*
Nakamoto, Donald Jiro 1955- *WhoAsA 94*
Nakamoto, Jon Masao 1958- *WhoWest 94*
Nakamoto, Kazuo 1922- *WhoMW 93*
Nakamoto, Tetsuo 1939- *WhoAsA 94, WhoScEn 94*
Nakamura, Hajime 1912- *IntWW 93*
Nakamura, Hiroshi 1933- *WhoScEn 94*
Nakamura, Hisao 1923- *IntWW 93*
Nakamura, Ichiro 1926- *IntWW 93*
Nakamura, James I. 1919- *WhoAm 94*
Nakamura, Kaneo 1922- *IntWW 93*
Nakamura, Kanzaburo d1988 *WhoHol 92*
Nakamura, Karen Tsuneko 1944- *WhoAsA 94*
Nakamura, Kazuo 1926- *WhoAm 94, WhoAmA 93*
Nakamura, Kishiro *IntWW 93*
Nakamura, Leonard Isamu 1948- *WhoFI 94*
Nakamura, Michael S. *WhoAsA 94, WhoWest 94*
Nakamura, Mitsuru James 1926- *WhoAm 94, WhoAsA 94*
Nakamura, Patricia Akemi Kosugi 1948- *WhoAsA 94*
Nakamura, Robert Motoharu 1927- *WhoAm 94*
Nakamura, Royden 1939- *WhoAsA 94*
Nakamura, Russell Koichi 1953- *WhoAsA 94*
Nakamura, Shozaburo *IntWW 93*
Nakamura, Taro 1920- *IntWW 93*
Nakamura, Tatsuo 1925- *IntWW 93*
Nakamura, Yoshio 1950- *WhoAm 94*
Nakamura, Yoshiro 1926- *WhoAmP 93*
Nakanishi, Alan 1940- *WhoWest 94*
Nakanishi, Don Toshiaki 1949- *WhoAsA 94*
Nakanishi, Koji 1925- *WhoAm 94, WhoScEn 94*
Nakanishi, Tamako 1919- *WhoWomW 91*
Nakanishi, Tsutomu 1939- *WhoAm 94, WhoScEn 94*
Nakano, Desmond *WrDr 94*
Nakano, Francis 1938- *WhoAsA 94*
Nakano, Frank Hiroshi 1935- *WhoAsA 94*
Nakano, George *WhoAsA 94*
Nakano, Mei Takaya 1924- *WhoAsA 94*
Nakano, Tatsuhiko 1925- *WhoScEn 94*
Nakano-Matsumoto, Naomi Namiko 1960- *WhoWest 94*
Nakao, Eiichi 1930- *IntWW 93*
Nakaoka, James Tatsumi 1952- *WhoFI 94, WhoWest 94*
Nakaoka, John Tatsuya 1952- *WhoFI 94*
Nakasato, Dennis M. 1947- *WhoAmP 93*
Nakasato, George *WhoAsA 94*
Nakash, Joseph 1943- *WhoAm 94*
Nakashima, George Katsutoshi 1905-1990 *WhAm 10*
Nakashima, Joanne P. 1937- *WhoAmP 93*
Nakashima, Joanne Pumphrey 1937- *WhoWest 94*
Nakashima, Mitsugi 1929- *WhoAsA 94*
Nakashima, Nobuo 1931- *WhoAmP 93*
Nakashima, Patricia Hatsuye 1943- *WhoWest 94*
Nakashima, Tom Vincent 1941- *WhoAsA 94*
Nakasone, Bob 1940- *WhoAmP 93*
Nakasone, Robert C. 1947- *WhoAm 94, WhoAsA 94, WhoFI 94*
Nakasone, Yasuhiro 1917- *IntWW 93*
Nakasone, Yasuhiro 1918- *Who 94*
Nakata, Herbert Minoru 1930- *WhoAm 94, WhoAsA 94*
Nakatani, Alan Isamu 1957- *WhoScEn 94*
Nakatani, Chiyoko 1930-1981 *ChlLR 30 [port]*
Nakatani, Corey 1970?- *WhoAsA 94*
Nakatani, Henry Masatoshi 1942- *WhoAsA 94*
Nakatani, Roy Eiji 1918- *WhoAm 94, WhoAsA 94*
Nakatsuji, Norio 1950- *WhoScEn 94*
Nakatsuka, Lawrence Kaoru 1920- *WhoAsA 94*
Nakatsukasa, Pedro Taiskan 1943- *WhoAmP 93*
Nakayama, Harvey Kiyoshi 1944- *WhoAsA 94*
Nakayama, Paula A. *WhoAmP 93*
Nakayama, Paula Aiko 1953- *WhoAmL 94*
Nakayama, Randall Shige 1957- *WhoAsA 94*
Nakayama, Shigeru 1928- *WrDr 94*
Nakayama, Tadashi 1932- *WhoFI 94*
Nakayama, Taro 1924- *IntWW 93*
Nakayama, Toshio *IntWW 93*
Nakayama, Wataru 1936- *WhoScEn 94*
Nakazato, Hiroshi 1941- *WhoScEn 94*
Nakazato, Hitoshi 1936- *WhoAmA 93*
Nakazawa, Anthony Tadashi 1949- *WhoAsA 94*
Nakazawa, Mitsuru 1956- *WhoScEn 94*
Nakazawa, Yoshio 1917-1990 *WhAm 10*
Nakazono, Benito Lopez 1946- *WhoAsA 94*
Naker, Mary Leslie 1954- *WhoFI 94, WhoMW 93*
Nakfoor, Karen M. 1955- *WhoAmL 94*
Nakhla, Atif Mounir 1946- *WhoScEn 94*
Nakhleh, Emile A. 1938- *WhoAm 94*
Nakhnikian, George 1920- *WrDr 94*
Nakicenovic, Nebojsa 1949- *WhoScEn 94*
Nakkim, Lynn Boerner Kalama 1937- *WhoWest 94*
Nakoneczny, Michael 1952- *WhoAmA 93*
Nakou, Lilika 1903- *BlmGWL*
Nakszynski, Nikolaus Gunther *WhAm 10*
Nakujima, Hideyuki *WhoAsA 94*
Nalbach, Daniel *WhoHol 92*
Nalbandyan, Dmitriy Arkadiyevich 1906- *IntWW 93*
Nalcioglu, Orhan 1944- *WhoAm 94, WhoWest 94*
Nalder, Crawford David 1910- *Who 94*
Nalder, Eric Christopher 1946- *WhoWest 94*
Naldi, Giuseppe 1770-1820 *NewGrDO*
Naldi, Nita d1961 *WhoHol 92*
Naldrett, Anthony James 1933- *WhoAm 94*
Nalecz, Maciej 1922- *IntWW 93*
Nalen, Craig Anthony 1930- *WhoAm 94*
Nalewaja, Donna *WhoAmP 93, WhoMW 93*
Nalewako, Mary Anne 1934- *WhoAm 94*
Naleway, John Joseph 1954- *WhoWest 94*
Nalipinski, Daniel Anthony 1943- *WhoFI 94*
Nall, Alvin James, Jr. 1960- *WhoBlA 94*
Nall, Barry T(homas) 1948- *ConAu 141*
Nall, Michael (Joseph) 1921- *Who 94*
Nall, Sandra Lillian 1943- *WhoFI 94*
Nall-Cain *Who 94*
Nalle, Billy 1921- *IntMPA 94*
Nalle, Peter Devereux 1947- *WhoAm 94*
Nallet, Henri Pierre 1939- *IntWW 93*
Nalley, Charles Lee 1949- *WhoFI 94*
Nally, William d1929 *WhoHol 92*
Naltner, Louis Justis 1930- *WhoMW 93*
Nam, Charles Benjamin 1926- *WhoAm 94*
Nam, Jung Wan 1927- *WhoScEn 94*
Nam, Sang Boo 1936- *WhoAm 94*
Nam, Sangboo 1936- *WhoAsA 94*
Nam, Sehyun 1949- *WhoAsA 94*
Nam, Sunwoo 1938- *WhoAmL 94*
Nam, Tin 1961- *WhoScEn 94*
Nam, Wonki Kim 1940- *WhoAsA 94*
Nama, George Allen 1939- *WhoAmA 93*
Namaliu, Rabbie Langanai 1947- *IntWW 93, Who 94*
Namara, Marguerite d1974 *WhoHol 92*
Namath, Joe *ProFbHF*

Namath, Joe 1943- *IntMPA 94, WhoHol 92*
Namath, Joseph William 1943- *WhoAm 94*
Namazova, Adila Avaz kyzy *WhoWomW 91*
Namba, Brian J. 1952- *WhoAmP 93*
Namba, Tatsuji 1927- *WhoAm 94, WhoScEn 94*
Namboodiri, Krishnan 1929- *WhoAm 94, WhoScEn 94*
Namboodiri, Krishnan 1953- *WhoScEn 94*
Namboodri, Chettoor Govindan 1968- *WhoScEn 94*
Nambu, Yoichiro 1921- *WhoAm 94, WhoAsA 94*
Namdari, Bahram 1939- *WhoFI 94, WhoMW 93, WhoScEn 94*
Nam Duck-Woo 1924- *IntWW 93*
Namey, Lee A. 1945- *WhoAmP 93*
Namgyal 1933- *WhoPRCh 91 [port]*
Namias, Jerome 1910- *IntWW 93, WhoAm 94, WrDr 94*
Nam Il 1913-1976 *HisDcKW*
Namingha, Dan 1950- *WhoAmA 93*
Namini, Ahmad Hossein 1961- *WhoScEn 94*
Namioka, Lensey 1929- *TwCYAW*
Namir, Ora 1930- *IntWW 93*
Namir, Ora 1933- *WhoWomW 91*
Namjoshi, Suniti 1941- *BlmGWL*
Namorato, Cono R. 1942- *WhoAmL 94*
Namour, Michel Alexandre 1935- *WhoAm 94*
Namphy, Henri *IntWW 93*
Namuth, Hans 1915-1990 *WhAm 10, WhoAmA 93N*
Nana Opoku Ware, II *IntWW 93*
Nanassy, Louis C(harles) 1913- *ConAu 41NR*
Nance, Allan Taylor 1933- *WhoAm 94, WhoAmL 94*
Nance, Betty Love 1923- *WhoAm 94*
Nance, Booker Joe, Sr. 1933- *WhoBlA 94*
Nance, Cecil Boone, Jr. 1925- *WhoAm 94*
Nance, Earl Edward, Jr. 1953- *WhoMW 93*
Nance, Francis James 1915- *Who 94*
Nance, Harold Wade 1924- *WhoFI 94*
Nance, Herbert Charles, Sr. 1946- *WhoBlA 94*
Nance, Jack *WhoHol 92*
Nance, James Clifton 1957- *WhoMW 93*
Nance, James Homer 1931- *WhoAmL 94*
Nance, James W. 1921- *WhoAmP 93*
Nance, Jesse J., Jr. 1939- *WhoBlA 94*
Nance, Jim 1942-1992 *AnObit 1992*
Nance, John J. 1946- *WrDr 94*
Nance, Joseph Milton 1913- *WhoAm 94*
Nance, Kenneth Robert 1941- *WhoAmP 93*
Nance, Larry 1959- *BasBi*
Nance, Larry Donell 1959- *WhoBlA 94*
Nance, Larry Donnell 1959- *WhoAm 94, WhoMW 93*
Nance, Lars Franklin 1954- *WhoAmL 94*
Nance, M. Maceo, Jr. 1925- *WhoBlA 94*
Nance, Peter M. 1944- *WhoIns 94*
Nance, Richard Damian 1951- *WhoScEn 94*
Nance, Robert Lewis 1936- *WhoWest 94*
Nance, Sandra Michel 1946- *WhoWest 94*
Nance, Thomas Alexander 1939- *WhoFI 94*
Nance, Tony Max-Perry 1955- *WhoAm 94*
Nance, W. A. 1918- *WhoAmP 93*
Nanda, Bal Ram 1917- *WrDr 94*
Nanda, Navin Chandar 1937- *WhoAsA 94*
Nanda, Ravindra 1943- *WhoAsA 94*
Nanda, Ved Prakash 1934- *WhoAm 94, WhoAmL 94*
Nanda, Vir A. 1942- *WhoAsA 94*
Nandagopal, Mallur R. 1938- *WhoScEn 94, WhoWest 94*
Nandivada, Nagendra Nath 1950- *WhoScEn 94*
Nandkumar, Nuggehalli Balmukund 1949- *WhoAsA 94*
Nandor, William Francis 1942- *WhoWest 94*
Nandwana, Ashok Lakhaji 1951- *WhoWest 94*
Nandy, Dipak 1936- *Who 94*
Nandy, Pritish 1947- *WrDr 94*
Nandy, Subas 1957- *WhoScEn 94*
Nangle, John Francis 1922- *WhoAm 94, WhoAmL 94, WhoMW 93*
Nania, Anthony J. *WhoAmP 93*
Nank, Lois Rae *WhoFI 94*
Nankivell, Owen 1927- *Who 94*
Nanne, Louis Vincent 1941- *WhoAm 94*
Nannen, Henri 1913- *IntWW 93*
Nannery, Michael Alan 1967- *WhoScEn 94*
Nannes, John M. 1948- *WhoAmL 94*
Nannes, Michael Edward 1953- *WhoAm 94*
Nannestad, Elizabeth 1956- *BlmGWL*
Nanney, Arthur Preston 1945- *WhoIns 94*
Nanney, David Ledbetter 1925- *WhoAm 94, WhoMW 93*
Nanney, Herbert Boswell 1918- *WhoAm 94*
Nannichi, Yasuo 1933- *WhoScEn 94*
Nannini, Livia Dorotea fl. 1695-1726 *NewGrDO*
Nannini, Lucia Vittoria *NewGrDO*
Nannis, Lawrence Stewart 1948- *WhoFI 94*
Nano, Fatos Thanas 1952- *IntWW 93*
Nanola, Frank G. *WhoHisp 94*
Nanook d1925 *WhoHol 92*
Nansen, Betty d1943 *WhoHol 92*
Nansen, Fridtjof 1861-1930 *HisWorL [port], WhWE [port]*
Nansen, Richard Ray 1956- *WhoWest 94*
Nantais, Thomas Stewart 1956- *WhoFI 94*
Nantell, Timothy James 1945- *WhoAm 94*
Nantier-Didiee, Constance (Betzy Rosabella) 1831-1867 *NewGrDO*
Nanto, Roxanna Lynn 1952- *WhoWest 94*
Nanty, Isabelle *WhoHol 92*
Nanula, Savino P. *WhoFI 94*
Nanus, Burton Benjamin 1936- *WhoAm 94*
Nanz, Claus Ernest 1934- *WhoScEn 94*
Nanz, Robert Hamilton 1923- *WhoAm 94*
Nan Zhenzhong *WhoPRCh 91*
Naoroji, Dadabhai 1825-1917 *DcNaB MP*
Napadensky, Hyla Sarane 1929- *WhoAm 94*
Naparstek, Arthur J. 1938- *WhoAm 94*
Napeshnee, Joseph c. 1800-1870 *EncNAR*
Naphier, Joe L. 1940- *WhoBlA 94*
Naphtali, Ashirah Sholomis 1950- *WhoBlA 94*
Napier *Who 94*
Napier, Lord 1930- *Who 94*
Napier, Master of 1962- *Who 94*
Napier, Alan *DrAPF 93*
Napier, Alan d1988 *WhoHol 92*
Napier, Austin 1947- *WhoAm 94*
Napier, Barbara Langmuir 1914- *Who 94*
Napier, Bill 1940- *WrDr 94*
Napier, Charles *WhoHol 92*
Napier, Diana d1982 *WhoHol 92*
Napier, Douglas William 1951- *WhoAmL 94*
Napier, Francis 1758-1823 *WhAmRev*
Napier, Gary L. 1947- *WhoMW 93*
Napier, J. B. 1928- *WhoAmP 93*
Napier, John *WhoHol 92*
Napier, John 1550-1617 *WorScD*
Napier, John 1944- *Who 94*
Napier, John Archibald Lennox 1946- *Who 94*
Napier, John Light 1947- *WhoAm 94, WhoAmL 94, WhoAmP 93*
Napier, Lennox Alexander Hawkins 1928- *Who 94*
Napier, Lois Christine 1942- *WhoMW 93*
Napier, Lonnie 1940- *WhoAmP 93*
Napier, Marita 1939- *NewGrDO*
Napier, Mark 1922- *WrDr 94*
Napier, Marshall *WhoHol 92*
Napier, Mary 1932- *WrDr 94*
Napier, Oliver John 1935- *Who 94*
Napier, Paul *WhoHol 92*
Napier, Richard Hanes 1951- *WhoIns 94*
Napier, Richard Stephen 1949- *WhoAm 94, WhoWest 94*
Napier, Robert Jon 1934- *WhoAm 94*
Napier, Robert Stewart 1947- *Who 94*
Napier, Robin (Surtees) 1932- *Who 94*
Napier, Russell d1975 *WhoHol 92*
Napier, Wilfrid Fox 1941- *IntWW 93*
Napier of Magdala, Baron 1940- *Who 94*
Naples, Caesar Joseph 1938- *WhoWest 94*
Naples, Gerard S. 1937- *WhoAmP 93*
Napley, David 1915- *IntWW 93, Who 94*
Napodano, Rudolph Joseph 1933- *WhoAm 94*
Napolean, Harry Nelson 1922- *WhoBlA 94*
Napoleon, I 1769-1821 *BlmGEL*
Napoleon, III 1808-1873 *BlmGEL, HisWorL [port]*
Napoleon, Benny Nelson 1955- *WhoBlA 94*
Napoleon Bonaparte 1769-1821 *BlmGEL*
Napoleon Bonaparte, I 1769-1821 *HisWorL [port]*
Napoles, Veronica Kleeman 1951- *WhoAm 94, WhoAmA 93*
Napoli, Donald J. 1941- *WhoMW 93*
Napoli, Jacopo 1911- *IntWW 93, NewGrDO*
Napoli, William Joseph 1960- *WhoWest 94*
Napoliello, Michael John 1942- *WhoAm 94*
Napolitan, Leonard 1919- *Who 94*
Napolitano, Alexander Lewis 1932- *WhoMW 93*
Napolitano, Grace *WhoHisp 94*
Napolitano, Grace F. 1936- *WhoAmP 93*
Napolitano, Janet Ann 1957- *WhoAmL 94*
Napolitano, Leonard Michael 1930- *WhoAm 94*
Napolitano, Pat 1916- *WhoFI 94*
Napolitano, Ralph Joseph 1942- *WhoMW 93*
Napolitano, Samuel Joseph *WhoFI 94*
Naponic, Tony 1954- *WhoAmA 93*
Napora, Joseph *DrAPF 93*
Napper, Berenice Norwood 1916- *WhoBlA 94*
Napper, Brian William 1960- *WhoWest 94*
Napper, Hyacinthe T. 1928- *WhoBlA 94*
Napper, James Wilbur 1917- *WhoBlA 94*
Napper, John (Pelham) 1916- *Who 94*
Napravnik, Eduard (Frantsevich) 1839-1916 *NewGrDO*
Napsiah Bte Omar, Dato' 1943- *WhoWomW 91*
Napue, O'Dell Christell 1927- *WhoMW 93*
Naqvi, Sarwar 1943- *WhoScEn 94*
Nara, Harry Raymond 1921- *WhoAm 94*
Nara, Mitsue d1977 *WhoHol 92*
Narahara, Hiromichi T. 1923- *WhoAsA 94*
Narahashi, Toshio 1927- *WhoAm 94, WhoAsA 94, WhoScEn 94*
Narain, Jagdish 1926- *IntWW 93*
Narain, Sase 1925- *Who 94*
Naraja, Robert *WhoAmP 93*
Naramore, James Joseph 1949- *WhoWest 94*
Narang, Gopi Chand 1931- *WrDr 94*
Naranjo, Anthony *WhoHisp 94*
Naranjo, Carmen 1931- *BlmGWL*
Naranjo, Emilio *WhoAmP 93, WhoHisp 94*
Naranjo, José de J. 1957- *WhoHisp 94*
Naranjo, Michael A. 1944- *WhoWest 94*
Naranjo, Michael Alfred 1944- *WhoAmA 93*
Narasaki, Hisatake 1933- *WhoScEn 94*
Narasimha, Roddam 1933- *Who 94, WhoScEn 94*
Narasimham, Maidavolu 1927- *IntWW 93*
Narasimhan, Chakravarthi Vijayaraghava 1915- *Who 94*
Narasimhan, Lakshmi Sourirajan 1952- *WhoMW 93*
Narasimhan, Ram 1947- *WhoAm 94*
Narasimhan, Sridhar 1956- *WhoAsA 94*
Narasimhan, Subha 1948- *WhoAsA 94*
Narasimha Rao, P. V. 1921- *IntWW 93*
Narath, Albert 1933- *WhoAm 94, WhoScEn 94, WhoWest 94*
Narayan, Irene Jai 1932- *WhoWomW 91*
Narayan, Jagdish *WhoScEn 94*
Narayan, Kavassesy Sureswaran 1964- *WhoScEn 94*
Narayan, Kirin 1959- *WhoAsA 94*
Narayan, Kocheril Raman 1921- *Who 94*
Narayan, R. K. 1906- *BlmGEL, Who 94*
Narayan, R(asipuram) K(rishnaswamy) 1906- *RfGShF*
Narayan, R(asipuran) K(rishnaswami) 1907- *WrDr 94*
Narayan, Ramesh 1950- *WhoScEn 94*
Narayan, Rasipuram Krishnaswamy 1906- *IntWW 93*
Narayan, Rudy 1938- *Who 94*
Narayanamurti, Venkatesh 1939- *WhoAm 94, WhoAsA 94, WhoFI 94, WhoWest 94*
Narayanan, A. Sampath 1941- *WhoAsA 94*
Narayanan, Kocheril Raman 1921- *IntWW 93*
Narayanan, Palayil Pathazapurayil 1923- *IntWW 93*
Narayanan, Sunder 1959- *WhoFI 94*
Narayanaswamy, Onbathiveli S. 1936- *WhoAsA 94*
Narber, Gregg R. 1946- *WhoIns 94*
Narber, Gregg Ross 1946- *WhoAmL 94*
Narciso, Anthony J., Jr. 1947- *WhoIns 94*
Narciso, Grazia d1967 *WhoHol 92*
Nardella, Michael Anthony 1948- *WhoFI 94*
Nardelli, George d1973 *WhoHol 92*
Nardelli-Olkowska, Krystyna Maria 1939- *WhoAm 94*
Nardello, Robert A. 1937- *WhoFI 94*
Nardi, Dann 1950- *WhoAmA 93*
Nardi, Joseph B. 1944- *WhoIns 94*
Nardi, Peter Michael 1947- *WhoWest 94*
Nardi, Theodora P. 1922- *WhoAmP 93*
Nardin, Mario 1940- *WhoAmA 93*
Nardini, James *WhoHol 92*
Nardini, Joseph D. *WhoAmP 93*
Nardini, Tom 1945- *WhoHol 92*
Nardino, Gary 1935- *IntMPA 94, WhoAm 94*
Nardi Riddle, Clarine 1949- *WhoAm 94, WhoAmL 94*
Nardone, Colleen Ann 1940- *WhoAmP 93*
Nardone, Don D. 1924- *WhoFI 94*
Nardone, Richard 1945- *WhoAmL 94*
Nardone, Robert Carmen 1953- *WhoScEn 94*
Nardone, Robert L. 1953- *WhoAmP 93*
Nardone, Vincent Joseph 1937- *WhoAmA 93*
Nardone, William Andrew 1954- *WhoAmL 94*
Nardulli, Joseph J. 1947- *WhoAmL 94*
Narduzzi, David 1953- *WhoFI 94*
Narea, Hernan Tomas 1960- *WhoFI 94*
Narefsky, David 1955- *WhoAmL 94*
Naremore, James Otis 1941- *WhoMW 93*
Narendra, Kumpati Subrahmanya 1933- *WhoAm 94, WhoScEn 94*
Nares, Anna d1915 *WhoHol 92*
Nares, George Strong 1831-1915 *WhWE*
Nares, Owen d1943 *WhoHol 92*
Narigan, Harold W. 1925- *WhoAm 94*
Narin, Francis 1934- *WhoScEn 94*
Narin, Stephen B. 1929- *WhoAm 94*
Narisi, Stella Maria 1950- *WhoAmL 94*
Narita, George M. 1928- *WhoAsA 94*
Narita, Hiro 1941- *WhoAm 94*
Narita, Yoriaki *IntWW 93*
Narizzano, Dino d1987 *WhoHol 92*
Narizzano, Silvio 1927- *IntMPA 94*
Narjes, Karl-Heinz 1924- *IntWW 93, Who 94*
Narke, Robin *WhoHol 92*
Narkis, Robert Joseph 1934- *WhoAm 94*
Narlikar, Jayant Vishnu 1938- *IntWW 93*
Narodick, Kit Gordon 1937- *WhoAmL 94*
Narodick, Sally G. 1945- *WhoAm 94*
Narogin, Mudrooroo 1938- *WrDr 94*
Narolin, Mikhail Tikhonov 1933- *LngBDD*
Narotzky, Norman David 1928- *WhoAmA 93*
Narr, Karl Josef 1921- *IntWW 93*
Narramore, Jimmy Charles 1949- *WhoScEn 94*
Narron, James Wiley *WhoAmP 93*
Narska, Robert 1948- *IntWW 93*
Narueput, Owart S. *Who 94*
Narula, Chaitanya Kumar 1955- *WhoMW 93*
Narula, Mohan Lal 1939- *WhoWest 94*
Narula, Subhash Chander 1944- *WhoAsA 94*
Narusis, Kathleen Marie *WhoFI 94*
Narutis, Vytas 1950- *WhoScEn 94*
Narvaez, Panfilo De c. 1470-c. 1528 *WhWE*
Narver, John Colin 1935- *WhoAm 94*
Narveson, Robert Donald 1930- *WhoMW 93*
Narwani, Dru Hassaram 1948- *WhoFI 94*
Narwold, Lewis Lammers 1921- *WhoAm 94*
Narwold, William Henry 1952- *WhoAmL 94*
Nary, William Lloyd Mossman 1960- *WhoWest 94*
Nasar, Syed Abu 1932- *WhoAm 94*
Nasby, Bruce Allen 1948- *WhoWest 94*
Nasby, David Asher 1939- *WhoMW 93*
Naschy, Paul *WhoHol 92*
Nascimento, Edson Arantes do *IntWW 93*
Nascimento, Lopo Fortunato Ferreira do 1940- *IntWW 93*
Naser, Najih A. 1962- *WhoScEn 94*
Nasereddin, M.F. Richard 1946- *WhoFI 94*
Nasgaard, Roald 1941- *WhoAm 94, WhoAmA 93*
Nash, Abner 1740-1786 *WhAmRev*
Nash, Ada Ruth 1925- *WhoAmP 93*
Nash, Aldon James 1923- *WhoAmP 93*
Nash, Alice Louise 1915- *WhoAmA 93*
Nash, Bernard Elbert 1922- *WhoAm 94*
Nash, Bradley DeLamater 1900- *WhoAm 94*
Nash, Brian 1956- *WhoHol 92*
Nash, Charles 1951- *IntWW 93*
Nash, Charles Presley 1932- *WhoAm 94*
Nash, Chris *WhoHol 92*
Nash, Clarence d1985 *WhoHol 92*
Nash, Curtis 1946- *WhoBlA 94*
Nash, Daniel Alphonza, Jr. 1942- *WhoBlA 94*
Nash, David 1945- *IntWW 93*
Nash, David John 1942- *WhoAm 94*
Nash, Donald Gene 1945- *WhoAm 94*
Nash, Edward L. 1936- *WhoAm 94*
Nash, Edward Thomas 1943- *WhoAm 94*
Nash, Elizabeth (Hamilton) 1934- *ConAu 142*
Nash, (Denis Frederic) Ellison 1913- *Who 94*
Nash, Eva L. 1925- *WhoBlA 94*
Nash, Florence d1950 *WhoHol 92*
Nash, Francis c. 1742-1777 *WhAmRev*
Nash, Frank Erwin 1916- *WhoAm 94*
Nash, Gary B 1933- *WrDr 94*
Nash, Gary Baring 1933- *WhoAm 94*
Nash, George d1944 *WhoHol 92*

Nash, George T., III 1935- *WhoBlA 94*
Nash, Gerald D(avid) 1928- *WrDr 94*
Nash, Gerald David 1928- *WhoAm 94*
Nash, Gordon Bernard, Jr. 1944- *WhoAmL 94*
Nash, Graham William 1942- *WhoAm 94*
Nash, Heddle 1894?-1961 *NewGrDO*
Nash, Helen E. 1921- *WhoBlA 94*
Nash, Henry Gary 1952- *WhoBlA 94*
Nash, Henry Warren 1927- *WhoAm 94*
Nash, Howard Allen 1937- *WhoAm 94, WhoScEn 94*
Nash, J. Frank 1958- *WhoMW 93*
Nash, Jay Robert, III 1937- *WhoAm 94*
Nash, Jean d1980 *WhoHol 92*
Nash, John Arthur 1938- *WhoAm 94, WhoFI 94, WhoMW 93*
Nash, John Edward 1925- *Who 94*
Nash, John N. 1946- *WhoAm 94*
Nash, Johnny 1940- *WhoHol 92*
Nash, Jonathon Michael 1942- *WhoAm 94*
Nash, June d1979 *WhoHol 92*
Nash, Kim Alan 1956- *WhoWest 94*
Nash, (Cyril) Knowlton 1927- *WrDr 94*
Nash, Lawrence F. 1937- *WhoAmP 93*
Nash, Lee J. 1939- *WhoAm 94, WhoFI 94*
Nash, Lee Marten 1927- *WhoWest 94*
Nash, Leon Albert 1912- *WhoBlA 94*
Nash, Leonard Kollender 1918- *WhoAm 94*
Nash, LeRoy T. 1925- *WhoBlA 94*
Nash, Lillian Dorothy 1931- *WhoScEn 94*
Nash, M. Elizabeth 1960- *WhoWest 94*
Nash, Manning 1924- *WhoMW 93*
Nash, Marilyn *WhoHol 92*
Nash, Mark Wixom 1948- *WhoAmL 94*
Nash, Mary d1976 *WhoHol 92*
Nash, Mary 1951- *WhoAmA 93*
Nash, Mattie Lee *WhoAmP 93*
Nash, Maxine d1938 *WhoHol 92*
Nash, Michaux, Jr. 1933- *WhoAm 94*
Nash, Mildred J. *DrAPF 93*
Nash, N. Richard 1913- *IntMPA 94*
Nash, Nicholas David 1939- *WhoAm 94*
Nash, Noreen *WhoHol 92*
Nash, Patrick Gerard 1933- *WrDr 94*
Nash, Paul *WhoAm 94*
Nash, Paul 1924- *WhoAmA 93, WrDr 94*
Nash, Paul LeNoir 1931- *WhoAm 94, WhoAmL 94*
Nash, Peter G. d1993 *NewYTBS 93*
Nash, Peter Gillette 1937- *WhoAmP 93*
Nash, Peter Hugh John 1921- *WhoAm 94*
Nash, Peter Theodore 1953- *WhoMW 93*
Nash, Philip 1930- *Who 94*
Nash, Philip Tajitsu 1956- *WhoAsA 94*
Nash, Ray 1905-1982 *WhoAmA 93N*
Nash, Richard Eugene 1954- *WhoWest 94*
Nash, Robert Coutts 1944- *WhoAmL 94*
Nash, Robert Fred 1933- *WhoAm 94*
Nash, Robert Johnson 1929- *WhoBlA 94*
Nash, Robert Peter 1955- *WhoMW 93*
Nash, Robert R. 1947- *WhoAm 94*
Nash, Roderick 1939- *WrDr 94*
Nash, Ronald Herman 1936- *WhoAm 94*
Nash, Ronald Peter 1946- *Who 94*
Nash, Simon *ConAu 42NR*
Nash, Stella B. 1942- *WhoWest 94*
Nash, Steven Alan 1944- *WhoAmA 93*
Nash, Sylvia Dotseth 1945- *WhoAm 94*
Nash, Thomas 1919- *WhoBlA 94*
Nash, Thomas Arthur Manly d1993 *Who 94N*
Nash, Trevor Gifford 1930- *Who 94*
Nash, Valery *DrAPF 93*
Nash, Victoria C. 1915- *WhoAmP 93*
Nash, William Arthur 1922- *WhoAm 94*
Nash, William Bradford 1958- *WhoAmL 94*
Nash, William George 1920- *WrDr 94*
Nash, William Wray, Jr. 1928- *WhoScEn 94*
Nasha, Margaret Nnananyana 1947- *Who 94*
Nashan, Joy Ortiz 1948- *WhoFI 94*
Nashe, Carol *WhoAm 94*
Nashe, Thomas 1567-1601 *BlmGEL*
Nasher, Raymond Donald 1921- *WhoAmA 93*
Nashif, Anne Marie 1964- *WhoMW 93*
Nashman, Alvin Eli 1926- *WhoAm 94, WhoScEn 94*
Nasi, Giovanni 1918- *IntWW 93*
Nasi, John Roderick 1940- *WhoWest 94*
Nasio, Brenda *DrAPF 93*
Nasir, Agha 1937- *IntWW 93*
Nasir, Amir Ibrahim 1926- *IntWW 93*
Nasisse, Andy S. 1946- *WhoAmA 93*
Naske, Claus-Michael 1935- *WhoWest 94*
Nasky, Harold Gregory 1942- *WhoAmL 94, WhoWest 94*
Naslund, Sena Jeter *DrAPF 93*
Nasmith *Who 94*
Nasmyth, James 1808-1890 *WorInv*
Nasmyth, Kim Ashley 1952- *Who 94*
Naso, Valerie Joan 1941- *WhoWest 94*
Nasolini, Sebastiano 1768?-1798? *NewGrDO*
Nason, Charles T. 1946- *WhoIns 94*
Nason, Charles Tuckey 1946- *WhoAm 94, WhoFI 94*
Nason, Danton Scott 1952- *WhoMW 93*
Nason, Dolores Irene 1934- *WhoFI 94, WhoScEn 94, WhoWest 94*
Nason, Freda Lee 1944- *WhoFI 94*
Nason, Gertrude 1890- *WhoAmA 93N*
Nason, John Charles 1945- *WhoAmP 93*
Nason, John William 1905- *IntWW 93, WhoAm 94*
Nason, Justin Patrick Pearse 1937- *Who 94*
Nason, Leonard Yoshimoto 1954- *WhoAmL 94*
Nason, Patricia Anne Woodward 1932- *WhoWest 94*
Nason, Robert E. 1936- *WhoAm 94, WhoFI 94*
Nason, Tema *DrAPF 93*
Nason, Thomas W. 1889-1971 *WhoAmA 93N*
Nasr, Farouk Sayf an- 1922- *IntWW 93*
Nasr, Kameel 1949- *ConAu 141*
Nasr, Nabil Zaki 1954- *WhoFI 94*
Nasr, Seyyed Hossein 1933- *WrDr 94*
Nasr, Suhayl Jose *WhoMW 93*
Nasr, Walid Merwan 1948- *WhoWest 94*
Nasralla, Emily 1938- *BlmGWL*
Nass, David Alan, Jr. 1956- *WhoFI 94*
Nass, Randall Kenneth 1958- *WhoMW 93*
Nass, Stephen L. 1952- *WhoAmP 93*
Nassar, Eugene Paul 1935- *WrDr 94*
Nassau, Michael Jay 1935- *WhoAm 94*
Nassauer, Rudolf 1924- *WrDr 94*
Nassberg, Richard T. 1942- *WhoAm 94, WhoAmL 94*
Nasser, Essam 1931- *WhoScEn 94*
Nasser, Gamel Abdel 1918-1970 *HisWorL [port]*
Nasser, William Kaleel 1933- *WhoMW 93*
Nassif, Joseph Gerard 1949- *WhoAmL 94*
Nassif, Thomas Anthony 1941- *WhoAm 94*
Nassikas, James Achilles 1927- *WhoFI 94*
Nassikas, John Nicholas 1917- *WhoAm 94, WhoAmP 93*
Nassirharand, Amir 1961- *WhoScEn 94*
Nassour, Ellis (Michael) 1941- *ConAu 43NR*
Nast, Dianne Martha 1944- *WhoAm 94, WhoAmL 94*
Nast, Minnie 1874-1956 *NewGrDO*
Nast, Thomas 1840-1902 *AmSocL*
Nastali, Bernadette Theresa 1933- *WhoMW 93*
Nastanovich, Robert Andrew 1937- *WhoAmP 93*
Nastas, George, III 1944- *WhoFI 94*
Nastase, Adrian 1950- *IntWW 93*
Nastase, Adriana *WhoScEn 94*
Nastase, Ilie 1946- *BuCMET [port], IntWW 93, WhoAm 94*
Nastav, Ann 1946- *WrDr 94*
Nastro, Charles Paul 1942- *WhoAm 94*
Nasu, Shoichi 1933- *WhoScEn 94*
Nat, Lucien d1972 *WhoHol 92*
Nat, Marie-Jose 1940- *WhoHol 92*
Natadze, Nodar 1929- *IntWW 93*
Natal, Bishop of 1934- *Who 94*
Natale, Samuel Michael 1943- *WhoAm 94*
Natale-Howard, Anne-Marie 1952- *WhoFI 94*
Natalicio, Diana S. 1939- *WhoAm 94*
Natalie, Ronald Bruce 1935- *WhoAm 94, WhoAmL 94*
Natan, Benveniste 1954- *WhoScEn 94*
Natanson, Maurice (Alexander) 1924- *WrDr 94*
Natanson, Maurice Alexander 1924- *WhoAm 94*
Nataraj, Chandrasekhar 1959- *WhoScEn 94*
Natarajan, Jayanthl 1954- *WhoWomW 91*
Natarajan, Lalgudi Vaidyanath 1943- *WhoMW 93*
Natarajan, Paramasivam 1940- *WhoScEn 94*
Natarajan, Thyagarajan 1942- *WhoScEn 94*
Natarus, Burton F. 1933- *WhoAmP 93*
Natcher, Stephen Darlington 1940- *WhoAm 94, WhoAmL 94, WhoFI 94*
Natcher, William H. *WhoAmP 93*
Natcher, William H. 1909- *CngDr 93*
Natcher, William Huston 1909- *WhoAm 94*
Natchez, Gladys 1915- *WrDr 94*
Natella, Arthur A(ristides), Jr. 1941- *ConAu 43NR*
Natelson, Stephen Ellis 1937- *WhoAm 94*
Nater, Swen 1950- *BasBi*
Nates, Jerome Harvey 1945- *WhoAmL 94*
Nath, Amar 1929- *WhoAsA 94*
Nath, Dhurma Gian 1934- *IntWW 93*
Nath, (Dhurma) Gian 1934- *Who 94*
Nath, Joginder 1932- *WhoAm 94, WhoAsA 94*
Nath, Mahendra 1940- *WhoMW 93*
Nath, Ravinder 1942- *WhoScEn 94*
Nathan, Baron 1922- *Who 94*
Nathan, Adele d1986 *WhoHol 92*
Nathan, Carl Francis 1946- *WhoAm 94*
Nathan, David 1926- *WrDr 94*
Nathan, David Gordon 1929- *WhoAm 94, WhoScEn 94*
Nathan, Donald Solomon 1945- *WhoAmL 94*
Nathan, Franklin Jay 1945- *WhoMW 93*
Nathan, Frederic Solis 1922- *WhoAm 94, WhoAmL 94*
Nathan, George Jean 1881-1958 *AmCulL [port]*
Nathan, George Jean 1882-1958 *DcLB 137 [port]*
Nathan, Helmuth Max 1901-1979 *WhoAmA 93N*
Nathan, Irvin B. 1943- *WhoAmL 94*
Nathan, Isaac 1790-1864 *NewGrDO*
Nathan, J. Andrew 1947- *WhoAmL 94*
Nathan, James Robert 1946- *WhoAm 94*
Nathan, Jean 1926- *WrDr 94*
Nathan, Jerry E. 1948- *WhoAmL 94*
Nathan, Jody Rae 1957- *WhoAmL 94*
Nathan, John E. 1942- *WhoAmL 94*
Nathan, Kenneth Craig 1946- *WhoMW 93*
Nathan, Lawrence Charles 1944- *WhoWest 94*
Nathan, Leonard *DrAPF 93*
Nathan, Leonard 1924- *WrDr 94*
Nathan, Leonard Edward 1924- *WhoAm 94, WhoWest 94*
Nathan, Marshall Ira 1933- *WhoAm 94*
Nathan, Norman *DrAPF 93*
Nathan, Norman 1915- *WrDr 94*
Nathan, Ove 1926- *IntWW 93*
Nathan, Paul S. 1913- *WhoAm 94*
Nathan, Peter 1914- *WrDr 94*
Nathan, Peter E. 1935- *WhoAm 94*
Nathan, Richard Arnold 1944- *WhoAm 94, WhoFI 94*
Nathan, Richard Perle 1935- *WhoAm 94, WhoAmP 93*
Nathan, Robert d1985 *WhoHol 92*
Nathan, Robert (Gruntal) 1894-1985 *EncSF 93*
Nathan, Robert Stuart *DrAPF 93*
Nathan, Stephen 1949- *WhoHol 92*
Nathan, Stephen Andrew 1947- *Who 94*
Nathan, Theodora Nathalia 1923- *WhoAmP 93*
Nathan, Theodore Reade d1993 *NewYTBS 93*
Nathan, Tony Curtis 1956- *WhoBlA 94*
Nathan, Vivian 1921- *WhoHol 92*
Nathan, William Israel 1896- *WhAm 10*
Nathaniel 1940- *WhoMW 93*
Nathaniel, His Grace Bishop 1940- *WhoAm 94*
Nathaniel, Isabel *DrAPF 93*
Nathanielsz, Peter William 1941- *WhoScEn 94*
Nathans, Daniel 1928- *IntWW 93, Who 94, WhoAm 94, WhoScEn 94*
Nathans, Rhoda R. 1940- *WhoAmA 93*
Nathanson, Carol (Edna) 1922- *WrDr 94*
Nathanson, Harvey Charles 1936- *WhoAm 94*
Nathanson, James A 1947- *WhoScEn 94*
Nathanson, James E. *WhoAmP 93*
Nathanson, Leonard 1942- *WhoAmL 94*
Nathanson, Leonard Mark 1929- *WhoAmL 94*
Nathanson, Linda Sue 1946- *WhoFI 94, WhoScEn 94*
Nathanson, Marc Bennett 1945- *WhoFI 94*
Nathanson, Melvyn Bernard 1944- *WhoAm 94*
Nathanson, Michael *WhoAm 94*
Nathanson, Nancy Louise 1951- *WhoAmP 93*
Nathanson, Neal 1927- *WhoAm 94*
Nathanson, Paul 1947- *ConAu 140*
Nathanson, Tenney *DrAPF 93*
Nathanson, Theodore Herzl 1923- *WhoWest 94*
Nathanson, Wayne Richard 1934- *WhoMW 93*
Nathe, Dennis Gerhardt 1938- *WhoWest 94*
Natheaux, Louis d1942 *WhoHol 92*
Nathenson, Stanley Gail 1933- *WhoAm 94*
Nathenson, Zoe *WhoHol 92*
Nathiri, N. Y. 1948- *ConAu 141*
Nathwani, Bharat Narottam 1945- *WhoScEn 94, WhoWest 94*
Naticchia, Alfred Dale 1952- *WhoAmL 94*
Nation, Carry 1846-1911 *AmSocL [port]*
Nation, Earl F. 1910- *WhoAm 94*
Nation, Floyd Reuben 1946- *WhoAmL 94*
Nation, James Edward 1933- *WhoAm 94*
Nation, John Arthur 1935- *WhoAm 94, WhoScEn 94*
Nation, Laura Crockett 1957- *WhoFI 94, WhoScEn 94*
Nation, Noel H. 1944- *WhoAmL 94*
Nation, Terry 1930- *EncSF 93*
Nations, Howard Lynn 1938- *WhoAm 94, WhoAmL 94*
Nations, Opal Louis *DrAPF 93*
Natividad, Irene 1948- *WhoAmP 93, WhoAsA 94*
Natkie, John L. *DrAPF 93*
Natkiewicz, Jan *DrAPF 93*
Natkin, Alvin Martin 1928- *WhoAm 94*
Natkin, Robert 1930- *WhoAmA 93*
Natoli, Joseph P. 1943- *WrDr 94*
Natoli, Sarah *WhoHol 92*
Natori, Josie Cruz 1947- *WhoAm 94, WhoAsA 94*
Natow, Annette Baum 1933- *WhoAm 94*
Natowitz, Joseph B. 1936- *WhoScEn 94*
Natsios, Nicholas Andrew 1920- *WhoAm 94*
Natsoulas, Anthony 1959- *WhoAmA 93*
Natsoulas, Thomas 1932- *WhoScEn 94*
Natsukari, Naoki 1952- *WhoScEn 94*
Natt, Calvin 1957- *BasBi*
Natta, Alessandro 1917- *IntWW 93*
Natta, Clayton Lyle 1932- *WhoBlA 94*
Natta, Giulio 1903-1979 *WorInv*
Natter, Jeff 1956- *WhoWest 94*
Nattiel, Ricky Rennard 1966- *WhoBlA 94*
Nattier, Frank Emile, Jr. 1915- *WhoAmL 94*
Nattkemper, C. Don 1947- *WhoAmP 93*
Nattle, Robert Dale 1924- *WhoAmP 93*
Natusch, Sheila 1926- *WrDr 94*
Natwar-Singh, K 1931- *WrDr 94*
Natwar-Singh, Kanwar 1931- *Who 94*
Natwick, Mildred 1908- *IntMPA 94, WhoHol 92*
Natzka, Oscar 1912-1951 *NewGrDO*
Natzke, Paulette Ann 1943- *WhoMW 93*
Natzler, Gertrud 1908-1971 *WhoAmA 93N*
Natzler, Greta *WhoHol 92*
Natzler, Otto 1908- *WhoAm 94, WhoAmA 93*
Natzmer, Cheryl Lynn 1947- *WhoAmA 93*
Nau, Henry R(ichard) 1941- *WrDr 94*
Nau, Maria(-Dolores-Benedicta-Josephine) 1818-1891 *NewGrDO*
Naubert, Christiane Benedikte Eugenie 1756-1819 *BlmGWL*
Naud, Melinda *WhoHol 92*
Naude, Adele 1910-1981 *BlmGWL*
Naude, (Christiaan) Beyers 1915- *IntWW 93*
Naudin, Emilio 1823-1890 *NewGrDO*
Nauen, Elinor *DrAPF 93*
Nauert, Charles Garfield 1928- *WhoMW 93*
Nauert, Peter W. 1943- *WhoIns 94*
Nauert, Peter William 1943- *WhoAm 94*
Nauert, Roger Charles 1943- *WhoAm 94, WhoScEn 94*
Nauful, Ernest Joseph, Jr. 1941- *WhoAmL 94*
Naughten, Robert Norman 1928- *WhoWest 94*
Naughter, Patrick M. 1943- *WhoIns 94*
Naughtie, (Alexander) James 1951- *Who 94*
Naughton, Bill 1910-1992 *AnObit 1992, ConDr 93, WrDr 94N*
Naughton, Charlie d1976 *WhoHol 92*
Naughton, David 1951- *IntMPA 94*
Naughton, David 1952- *WhoHol 92*
Naughton, Eileen Slattery 1945- *WhoAmP 93*
Naughton, James 1945- *IntMPA 94, WhoAm 94, WhoHol 92*
Naughton, James Martin 1938- *WhoAm 94*
Naughton, Jim 1957- *WrDr 94*
Naughton, John M. 1936- *WhoAm 94*
Naughton, John Patrick 1933- *WhoAm 94, WhoScEn 94*
Naughton, Philip Anthony 1943- *Who 94*
Naughty by Nature *ConMus 11 [port]*
Naugle, Jim 1954- *WhoAmP 93*
Naugle, John J., Jr. 1922- *WhoAmP 93*
Naugle, Robert Paul 1951- *WhoMW 93*
Nauheim, Stephen Alan 1942- *WhoAmL 94*
Naulls, Willie 1934- *BasBi*
Nault, Fernand 1921- *WhoAm 94*
Nault, Lowell Raymond 1940- *WhoMW 93*
Nault, William Henry 1926- *WhoAm 94*
Nauman, Bruce 1941- *IntWW 93, WhoAmA 93*
Nauman, Gerald Marston 1931- *WhoIns 94*
Naumann, Emil 1827-1888 *NewGrDO*
Naumann, Francis M. 1948- *WhoAmA 93*

Naumann, Hans Juergen 1935- *WhoAm 94*
Naumann, Johann Gottlieb 1741-1801 *NewGrDO*
Naumann, Klaus 1939- *IntWW 93*
Naumann, Michael 1941- *IntWW 93*
Naumann, Richard Walter 1946- *WhoFI 94*
Naumann, Robert Bruno Alexander 1929- *WhoAm 94, WhoScEn 94*
Naumann, William Carl 1938- *WhoFI 94*
Naumann, William L. 1911- *IntWW 93*
Naumer, Helmuth 1907- *WhoAmA 93*
Naumer, Helmuth Jacob 1934- *WhoAm 94*
Naumes, Patrick Edward 1947- *WhoWest 94*
Naumoff, Jerry 1957- *WhoMW 93*
Naumoff, Philip 1914- *WhoAm 94*
Naumov, Vladimir Naumovich 1927- *IntWW 93*
Naunton, Ralph Frederick 1921- *WhoAm 94*
Naurath, David Allison 1927- *WhoScEn 94, WhoWest 94*
Nauseda, Ann Jura 1950- *WhoAm 94*
Nauta, Walle Jetze Harinx 1916- *IntWW 93*
Nava, Cynthia D. *WhoAmP 93*
Nava, Diana d1988 *WhoHol 92*
Nava, Eloy Luis 1942- *WhoAm 94*
Nava, Gregory James 1949- *WhoHisp 94*
Nava, Julian 1927- *WhoHisp 94*
Nava, Michael 1954- *WhoHisp 94*
Nava, Pedro B., Jr. 1940- *WhoHisp 94*
Nava, Robert Joseph, Jr. 1954- *WhoHisp 94*
Nava-Carrillo, German 1930- *IntWW 93*
Nava Hamaker, Mary Lou *WhoHisp 94*
Navajas, Gonzalo 1946- *WhoWest 94*
Navajas-Mogro, Hugo 1923- *IntWW 93, WhoAm 94*
Navales, Ana Maria 1945?- *BlmGWL*
Navalkar, Ramchandra Govindrao 1924- *WhoAm 94*
Navangul, Himanshoo Vishnu Bhat 1940- *WhoAsA 94*
Navar, Luis Gabriel 1941- *WhoAm 94*
Navaretta, Cynthia *WhoAmA 93*
Navarre, James Earl 1931- *WhoWest 94*
Navarre, Marguerite de *GuFrLit 2*
Navarre, Mike 1956- *WhoAmP 93*
Navarre, Yves Henri Michel 1940- *IntWW 93*
Navarrete, Jorge Eduardo 1940- *Who 94*
Navarrete, Juan Fernandez de 1526-1579 *EncDeaf*
Navarrete, Yolanda 1960- *WhoAmL 94*
Navarrette, Llorente Fred 1966- *WhoHisp 94*
Navarrini, Francesco 1853-1923 *NewGrDO*
Navarro, Anna *WhoHol 92*
Navarro, Antonio 1922- *WhoHisp 94*
Navarro, Antonio Luis 1922- *WhoAm 94*
Navarro, Artemio Edward 1950- *WhoHisp 94, WhoWest 94*
Navarro, Aurora d1977 *WhoHol 92*
Navarro, Beltran 1945- *WhoHisp 94*
Navarro, Bruce Charles 1954- *WhoAm 94, WhoAmL 94*
Navarro, Carlos d1969 *WhoHol 92*
Navarro, Carlos Salvador 1946- *WhoHisp 94*
Navarro, Diego Jose *AmRev*
Navarro, Edward Fernando 1950- *WhoHisp 94*
Navarro, Eugenia Marie 1944- *WhoAmL 94*
Navarro, Flor Hernandez 1939- *WhoHisp 94*
Navarro, Jaime 1968- *WhoHisp 94*
Navarro, Janyte Janene 1935- *WhoFI 94*
Navarro, Jesus d1960 *WhoHol 92*
Navarro, Jose 1944- *WhoHisp 94*
Navarro, Joseph Anthony 1927- *WhoAm 94*
Navarro, Luis A. 1958- *WhoHisp 94*
Navarro, Maria Esperanza d1978 *WhoHol 92*
Navarro, Marlene *NewYTBS 93 [port]*
Navarro, Mary Louise 1933- *WhoHisp 94*
Navarro, Max *WhoHisp 94*
Navarro, Miguel 1928- *WhoHisp 94*
Navarro, Mireya 1957- *WhoHisp 94*
Navarro, Nestor J., Jr. 1947- *WhoHisp 94*
Navarro, Octavio R. 1959- *WhoHisp 94*
Navarro, Pedro 1948- *WhoHisp 94*
Navarro, Rafael A. 1935- *WhoHisp 94*
Navarro, Ralph C. 1949- *WhoAmL 94*
Navarro, Richard A. 1955- *WhoHisp 94*
Navarro, Richard H. 1951- *WhoHisp 94*
Navarro, Robert 1939- *WhoHisp 94*
Navarro, Robert David 1941- *WhoHisp 94*
Navarro, Samara Heros 1956- *WhoHisp 94*
Navarro, Santiago Raul 1954- *WhoWest 94*
Navarro, Steven Raymond 1948- *WhoFI 94*
Navarro, Theodore 1923-1950 *AfrAmAl 6*
Navarro, Victoria *WhoHisp 94*
Navarro, Wilfred, Jr. *WhoHisp 94*
Navarro, Wilfred, III 1956- *WhoHisp 94*
Navarro Alicea, Jorge *WhoAmP 93*
Navarro-Alicea, Jorge L. 1937- *WhoHisp 94*
Navarro-Bermudez, Francisco Jose 1935- *WhoHisp 94*
Navas, Deborah *DrAPF 93*
Navas, Elizabeth S. 1895- *WhoAmA 93N*
Navas, Linda Moore 1949- *WhoFI 94*
Navas, William A., Jr. *WhoHisp 94*
Navas, William Antonio, Jr. 1942- *WhoAm 94*
Navasky, Victor 1932- *WrDr 94*
Navasky, Victor Saul 1932- *IntWW 93, WhoAm 94*
Navatta, Anna Paula 1956- *WhoAmL 94*
Nava-Villarreal, Hector Rolando 1943- *WhoHisp 94*
Nave, Eric d1993 *NewYTBS 93*
Nave, Thomas George 1950- *WhoAmL 94*
Navedo, Angel C., Sr. 1941- *WhoHisp 94*
Naveira Marie De Rodon, Miriam 1934- *WhoAmP 93*
Navejas, Kathleen Mello 1954- *WhoHisp 94*
Navero, William *DrAPF 93*
Naves, Larry J. *WhoBlA 94*
Navia, Juan M. 1927- *WhoHisp 94*
Navia, Juan Marcelo 1927- *WhoAm 94*
Navia, Luis E. 1940- *WhoHisp 94*
Navin, William Henry 1945- *WhoAm 94*
Navis, Glen Edward 1950- *WhoMW 93*
Navoigille, Julien c. 1749-1811? *NewGrDO*
Navon, Ionel Michael 1940- *WhoAm 94*
Navon, Itzhak 1921- *IntWW 93*
Navrat, Den(nis Edward) 1942- *WhoAmA 93*
Navratil, Amy *WhoAmA 93*
Navratil, Gerald Anton 1951- *WhoScEn 94*
Navratil, Robert Norman *WhoAmP 93*
Navratilova, Martina 1956- *BuCMET [port], IntWW 93, Who 94, WhoAm 94*
Navrotsky, Alexandra *WhoAm 94, WhoScEn 94*
Navumcyk, Siarhiej Iosifavic 1961- *LngBDD*
Navy Blues Sextette *WhoHol 92*
Nawara, Jim 1945- *WhoAmA 93*
Nawara, Lucille Procter 1941- *WhoAmA 93*
Nawaz, Asif d1993 *IntWW 93N*
Nawaz, S. Shah 1917- *IntWW 93*
Nawaz Sharif, Mian 1949- *IntWW 93*
Nawn, John Anthony 1964- *WhoFI 94*
Nawrath, William Michael 1947- *WhoAmP 93*
Nawrocki, Henry Franz 1931- *WhoScEn 94*
Nawrocki, Thomas Dennis 1942- *WhoAmA 93*
Nawrocky, Roman Jaroslaw 1932- *WhoScEn 94*
Nawy, Edward George 1926- *WhoAm 94, WhoScEn 94*
Nay, Mary Spencer d1993 *NewYTBS 93*
Nay, Mary Spencer 1913- *WhoAmA 93*
Nay, Samuel Wesley 1914- *WhoWest 94*
Nayak, Bhagchand D. 1937- *WhoAsA 94*
Nayak, Tapan Kumar 1957- *WhoAsA 94*
Nayar, Baldev Raj 1931- *WhoAm 94*
Nayar, Kuldip 1924- *Who 94*
Nayar, Sushila 1914- *IntWW 93*
Nayden, Denis J. 1954- *WhoAm 94, WhoFI 94*
Nayder, Linda Ann 1962- *WhoFI 94, WhoMW 93*
Nayef Ibn Abdul Aziz, H.R.H. Prince 1933- *IntWW 93*
Nayer, Louise *DrAPF 93*
Nayfeh, Jamal Faris 1960- *WhoScEn 94*
Nayfeh, Munir Hasan 1945- *WhoScEn 94*
Nayler, Georgina Ruth 1959- *Who 94*
Naylon, Betsy Zimmermann 1934- *WhoAmA 93*
Naylor, Aubrey Willard 1915- *WhoAm 94*
Naylor, Bernard 1938- *Who 94*
Naylor, Bruce Gordon 1950- *WhoAm 94*
Naylor, Charles Douglas 1949- *WhoAmL 94*
Naylor, David Murray 1938- *Who 94*
Naylor, Ernest 1931- *Who 94*
Naylor, Frank W., Jr. 1939- *WhoAmP 93*
Naylor, George LeRoy 1915- *WhoAm 94, WhoAmL 94, WhoFI 94, WhoMW 93, WhoWest 94*
Naylor, Gloria *DrAPF 93*
Naylor, Gloria 1950- *AfrAmAl 6, BlkWr 2, BlmGWL, CurBio 93 [port], WhoBlA 94, WrDr 94*
Naylor, Grant *EncSF 93*
Naylor, Harry Brooks 1914- *WhoAm 94*
Naylor, James Charles 1932- *WhoAm 94*
Naylor, James Lamont, III 1954- *WhoMW 93*
Naylor, Jean Ann 1948- *WhoFI 94*
Naylor, John *Who 94*
Naylor, (Charles) John 1943- *Who 94*
Naylor, John Albert 1940- *WhoFI 94*
Naylor, John Geoffrey 1928- *WhoAmA 93*
Naylor, John Lewis, Jr. 1927- *WhoAm 94*
Naylor, John Thomas 1913- *WhoAm 94*
Naylor, Lauretta *WhoBlA 94*
Naylor, Malcolm Neville 1926- *Who 94*
Naylor, Maurice *Who 94*
Naylor, (William) Maurice 1920- *Who 94*
Naylor, Paul Donald 1925- *WhoAmL 94*
Naylor, Peter Brian 1933- *Who 94*
Naylor, Phyllis Reynolds *DrAPF 93*
Naylor, Phyllis Reynolds 1933- *TwCYAW, WhoAm 94, WrDr 94*
Naylor, Robert Ernest, Jr. 1932- *WhoAm 94*
Naylor, Robert W. 1944- *WhoAmL 94*
Naylor, Robert Wesley 1944- *WhoAmP 93*
Naylor, Ruth Eileen Bundy 1934- *WhoMW 93*
Naylor, Scott Jordan 1952- *WhoWest 94*
Naylor, Thomas Everett 1939- *WhoFI 94*
Naylor, Thomas Herbert 1936- *WhoAm 94*
Naylor, William Edward 1943- *WhoWest 94*
Naylor-Jackson, Jerry 1939- *WhoFI 94, WhoWest 94*
Naylor-Leyland, Philip (Vyvian) 1953- *Who 94*
Nayman, Robbie L. 1937- *WhoBlA 94*
Naymark, Sherman 1920- *WhoAm 94*
Nayyar, Harsh *WhoHol 92*
Nayyar, Sarv P. 1941- *WhoAsA 94*
Naza 1955- *WhoAmA 93*
Nazarbaev, Nursultan Abishevich 1940- *LngBDD*
Nazarbayev, Nursultan Abishevich 1940- *IntWW 93*
Nazarenko, Bonnie Coe 1933- *WhoAmA 93*
Nazareth, Annette LaPorte 1956- *WhoFI 94*
Nazareth, Gerald Paul 1932- *Who 94*
Nazareth, Peter Francis 1940- *WhoMW 93*
Nazar'eva, Kapitolina Valer'iaovna 1847-1900 *BlmGWL*
Nazarian, Iradj Haskell 1937- *WhoWest 94*
Nazarian, John 1932- *WhoAm 94*
Nazario, Carlos D., Jr. 1951- *WhoHisp 94*
Nazario, Luis A. 1948- *WhoHisp 94*
Nazario-Guirau, Armando L. 1954- *WhoHisp 94*
Nazarkin, Yury Konstantinovich 1932- *LngBDD*
Nazarov, Aleksandr Viktorovich 1951- *LngBDD*
Nazarro, Cliff d1961 *WhoHol 92*
Nazem, Fereydoun F. 1940- *WhoAm 94*
Nazer, Hisham Mohi ed-Din 1932- *IntWW 93*
Nazette, Richard Follett 1919- *WhoAm 94*
Nazimova, Alla d1945 *WhoHol 92*
Nazir-Ali, Michael 1949- *Who 94*
Nazir-Ali, Michael James 1949- *IntWW 93*
Nazmetdinova, Minrauza Minikhazievna 1940- *LngBDD*
Nazmy, Aly Sadek 1955- *WhoScEn 94*
Nazos, Demetri Eleftherios 1949- *WhoMW 93, WhoScEn 94*
Nazzari, Amedeo d1979 *WhoHol 92*
Nazzaro, David Alfred 1940- *WhoWest 94*
Ncholson, Rodney Dale 1944- *WhoMW 93*
Ncube, Bernard, Sister 1935- *WhoWomW 91*
Ndamase, Tutor Nyangilizwe 1921- *IntWW 93*
Ndegwa, Duncan Nderitu 1925- *IntWW 93*
N'Diaye, Babacar 1937- *IntWW 93*
Ndiaye, Marie 1967- *BlmGWL*
Ndiaye, Ndioro *WhoWomW 91*
Ndlovu, Callistus P. 1936- *WhoBlA 94*
N'Dong, Leon 1935- *IntWW 93*
Ndungane, Winston Njongonkulu 1941- *IntWW 93*
Neafsey, John Patrick 1939- *WhoFI 94*
Neagle, Dame Anna d1986 *WhoHol 92*
Neagley, Ross (L.) 1907- *WrDr 94*
Neagu, Paul 1938- *IntWW 93*
Neaher, Edward Raymond 1912- *WhoAm 94, WhoAmL 94*
Neal, A. Curtis 1922- *WhoAm 94, WhoAmL 94, WhoFI 94*
Neal, Alimam Butler 1947- *WhoBlA 94*
Neal, Angela Marie 1960- *WhoMW 93*
Neal, Ann Parker *WhoAmA 93*
Neal, Ann Parker 1934- *WhoAm 94*
Neal, Avon 1922- *WhoAm 94*
Neal, (Minor) Avon 1922- *WhoAmA 93*
Neal, Bernard George 1922- *Who 94*
Neal, Bonnie Jean 1930- *WhoMW 93*
Neal, Brenda Jean 1952- *WhoBlA 94*
Neal, Charlie 1944- *WhoBlA 94*
Neal, Curly 1942- *WhoBlA 94*
Neal, Curtis Emerson, Jr. 1931- *WhoBlA 94*
Neal, Dale K. 1948- *WhoAmL 94*
Neal, Darwina Lee 1942- *WhoAm 94*
Neal, David L. 1938- *WhoMW 93*
Neal, David Scott 1952- *WhoFI 94*
Neal, Earl 1928- *WhoAmP 93*
Neal, Earl Langdon 1928- *WhoBlA 94*
Neal, Earlene Traylor 1944- *WhoMW 93*
Neal, Eddie 1943- *WhoBlA 94*
Neal, Edna D. 1943- *WhoBlA 94*
Neal, Edward Garrison 1940- *WhoAmL 94*
Neal, Eric (James) 1924- *Who 94*
Neal, Eric James 1924- *IntWW 93*
Neal, Ernest Gordon 1911- *WrDr 94*
Neal, Frances 1921- *WhoHol 92*
Neal, Frank d1955 *WhoHol 92*
Neal, Frank 1932- *WrDr 94*
Neal, Fred Roy, III 1950- *WhoWest 94*
Neal, Fred Warner 1915- *WhoAm 94, WrDr 94*
Neal, Frederic Douglas 1942- *WhoBlA 94*
Neal, Frederick Albert 1932- *Who 94*
Neal, Gerald A. 1945- *WhoAmP 93*
Neal, Gerald J. 1943- *WhoAm 94*
Neal, Green Belton 1946- *WhoBlA 94*
Neal, Harry *EncSF 93*
Neal, Harry Edward d1993 *NewYTBS 93*
Neal, Harry Edward 1906- *WrDr 94*
Neal, Harry Edward 1906-1993 *ConAu 141, SmATA 76*
Neal, Harry Morton 1931- *Who 94*
Neal, Herman Joseph 1923- *WhoBlA 94*
Neal, Homer Alfred 1942- *WhoAm 94, WhoBlA 94*
Neal, Ira Tinsley 1931- *WhoBlA 94*
Neal, Irene 1936- *WhoAmA 93*
Neal, James Madison, Jr. 1925- *WhoWest 94*
Neal, James Preston 1935- *WhoAmP 93*
Neal, James S. 1922- *WhoBlA 94*
Neal, James Thomas 1921- *WhoAmP 93*
Neal, Jeff *WhoMW 93*
Neal, Jerry Eugene 1941- *WhoFI 94*
Neal, Jerry R. 1933- *WhoAmL 94*
Neal, John Anthony 1955- *WhoAmP 93*
Neal, John Eric 1950- *WhoAm 94, WhoFI 94*
Neal, Jon Charles 1955- *WhoFI 94*
Neal, Joseph C., Jr. 1941- *WhoBlA 94*
Neal, Joseph H. *WhoAmP 93*
Neal, Joseph M., Jr. 1935- *WhoAmP 93*
Neal, Joyce Olivia 1943- *WhoFI 94*
Neal, LaVelle E., III 1965- *WhoBlA 94*
Neal, Leonard (Francis) 1913- *Who 94*
Neal, Leonard Francis 1913- *IntWW 93*
Neal, Lloyd d1952 *WhoHol 92*
Neal, Louise Kathleen 1951- *WhoAm 94*
Neal, Margaret Ruth 1944- *WhoMW 93*
Neal, Marie Augusta 1921- *WrDr 94*
Neal, Mario Lanza 1951- *WhoBlA 94*
Neal, Michael David 1927- *Who 94*
Neal, Miriam Louise 1941- *WhoMW 93*
Neal, Patricia 1926- *IntMPA 94, IntWW 93, WhoHol 92*
Neal, Phil Hudson, Jr. 1926- *WhoAm 94*
Neal, Philip *WhoAm 94*
Neal, Philip Mark 1940- *WhoAm 94, WhoWest 94*
Neal, Reginald H. 1909-1992 *WhoAmA 93N*
Neal, Richard *WhoBlA 94*
Neal, Richard E. 1949- *CngDr 93*
Neal, Richard Edmund 1949- *WhoAm 94, WhoAmP 93*
Neal, Richard Edward 1925- *WhoFI 94*
Neal, Robert B. 1938- *WhoIns 94*
Neal, Robert Paul 1939- *WhoAmP 93*
Neal, Sarah Lee 1924- *WhoAmP 93*
Neal, Shirley Anne 1936- *WhoAmP 93*
Neal, Stephen C. 1949- *WhoAm 94, WhoAmL 94*
Neal, Stephen L. 1934- *CngDr 93*
Neal, Stephen Lybrook 1934- *WhoAm 94, WhoAmP 93*
Neal, Stephen Wayne 1964- *WhoScEn 94*
Neal, Steven George 1949- *WhoAm 94*
Neal, Sylvester 1943- *WhoBlA 94*
Neal, Tom d1972 *WhoHol 92*
Neal, Tom, Jr. 1957- *WhoHol 92*
Neal, William Henry 1896- *WhAm 10*
Neal, William Weaver 1932- *WhoAm 94*
Neal, Wilmer Lewis 1934- *WhoAm 94*
Neale, Alan (Derrett) 1918- *Who 94*
Neale, Betty Irene 1930- *WhoAmP 93*
Neale, Chinyere 1953- *WhoBlA 94*

Neale, Earle d1973 *ProFbHF [port]*
Neale, Ernest Richard Ward 1923- *WhoAm 94*
Neale, Gary Lee 1940- *WhoAm 94, WhoFI 94*
Neale, Gerrard Anthony 1941- *Who 94*
Neale, John Robert Geoffrey 1926- *Who 94*
Neale, Keith Douglas 1947- *Who 94*
Neale, Kenneth James 1922- *Who 94*
Neale, Michael Churton 1958- *WhoScEn 94*
Neale, Michael Cooper 1929- *Who 94*
Neale, Timothy Arthur 1948- *WhoAm 94*
Neale, Walter Castle 1925- *WrDr 94*
Nealey, Darwin R. *WhoAmP 93*
Nealey, Sue C. 1949- *WhoMW 93*
Neall, Robert Raymond 1948- *WhoAmP 93*
Nealon, Arthur Vincent 1946- *WhoAmL 94*
Nealon, Catherina Theresa *Who 94*
Nealon, James Francis 1955- *WhoFI 94*
Nealon, Kevin 1953- *WhoHol 92*
Nealon, William Joseph, Jr. 1923- *WhoAm 94, WhoAmL 94*
Neals, Felix 1929- *WhoBlA 94*
Neals, Huerta C. 1914- *WhoBlA 94*
Neals, Otto 1930- *WhoAmA 93*
Neaman, Brycene Allen 1955- *WhoWest 94*
Neaman, Mark Robert 1950- *WhoAm 94, WhoMW 93*
Neame, Alan John 1924- *WrDr 94*
Neame, Christopher *WhoHol 92*
Neame, Robert Harry Beale 1934- *Who 94*
Neame, Ronald 1911- *IntMPA 94, IntWW 93, Who 94, WhoAm 94*
Neandross, Sigurd 1869-1958 *WhoAmA 93N*
Neaoutiyne, Paul 1952- *IntWW 93*
Near, Holly *WhoHol 92*
Near, James W. 1938- *WhoAm 94, WhoFI 94*
Near, Robert Keith 1945- *WhoFI 94*
Nearchus c. 360BC-312BC *WhWE*
Nearing, Homer, Jr. 1915- *EncSF 93*
Nearing, Scott 1883-1983 *EnvEnc*
Nearn, Arnold Dorsey, Jr. 1949- *WhoBlA 94*
Nearne, Jacqueline d1982 *WhoHol 92*
Nears, Colin Gray 1933- *Who 94*
Neary, Brian Joseph 1951- *WhoAmL 94*
Neary, Colleen 1952- *WhoAm 94*
Neary, Dennis Patrick 1944- *WhoAmP 93*
Neary, Jeffrey Andrew 1958- *WhoAmL 94, WhoAmP 93*
Neary, John F. 1947- *WhoAmL 94*
Neary, Martin Gerard James 1940- *IntWW 93, Who 94*
Neary, Pamela 1955- *WhoAmP 93*
Neary, Patricia 1942- *IntDcB [port]*
Neary, Patricia Elinor *WhoAm 94*
Neary, Robert D. *WhoAm 94, WhoFI 94*
Neas, John Theodore 1940- *WhoAm 94, WhoFI 94*
Nease, Allan Bruce 1954- *WhoScEn 94*
Nease, Martha Leann 1955- *WhoAmP 93*
Nease, Stephen Wesley 1925- *WhoAm 94*
Neason, Hazel d1920 *WhoHol 92*
Neate, Kenneth 1914- *NewGrDO*
Neathawk, Roger Delmore *WhoAm 94*
Neathery, Bret Roy 1964- *WhoMW 93*
Neaton, Robert Alan 1956- *WhoAmP 93*
Neave, Julius Arthur Sheffield 1919- *Who 94*
Neave, Paul (Arundell) 1948- *Who 94*
Neaves, Robert Louis 1935- *WhoWest 94*
Neaves, William Barlow 1943- *WhoAm 94*
Neavon, Joseph Roy 1928- *WhoBlA 94*
Nebbia, Joseph James 1930- *WhoFI 94*
Nebeker, Frank Q. *CngDr 93*
Nebeker, Frank Quill 1930- *WhoAm 94, WhoAmL 94, WhoAmP 93*
Nebeker, Stephen Bennion 1929- *WhoAmL 94*
Nebel, Berthold 1889-1964 *WhoAmA 93N*
Nebel, Gerard Thomas 1950- *WhoAmL 94*
Nebel, Henry Martin, Jr. 1921- *WhoAm 94*
Nebel, Kai Allen 1932- *WhoAm 94*
Nebelkopf, Ethan 1946- *WhoScEn 94, WhoWest 94*
Nebenzahl, Paul 1954- *WhoMW 93*
Nebergall, Donald Charles 1928- *WhoFI 94, WhoMW 93*
Nebergall, Robert William 1954- *WhoScEn 94*
Nebergall, Roger Ellis 1926- *WhoAm 94*
Nebert, Daniel Walter 1938- *WhoAm 94*
Nebgen, Mary Kathryn 1946- *WhoWest 94*
Nebil, Corinne Elizabeth 1918- *WhoAm 94*
Neblett, Carol 1946- *NewGrDO, WhoAm 94*
Neblett, Richard F. 1925- *WhoBlA 94*
Neblett, Stewart Lawrence 1948- *WhoAmL 94*
Nebolsky, Peggy Ellen 1947- *WhoMW 93*
Nebout, Claire *WhoHol 92*
Nebra (Blasco), Jose (Melchor de) 1702-1768 *NewGrDO*
Nebuchadnezzar fl. 605BC-562BC *BlmGEL*
Nebuchadnezzar, II fl. 605BC-562BC *HisWorL [port]*
Necarsulmer, Henry 1914- *WhoAm 94*
Necco, Alexander David 1936- *WhoAmL 94*
Nechaev, Andrei Alekseevich 1953- *LngBDD*
Nechaev, Eduard Aleksandrovich 1934- *LngBDD*
Nechaev, Konstantin Vladimirovich 1926- *LngBDD*
Nechayev, Andrey Alekseevich 1953- *IntWW 93*
Nechemias, Stephen Murray 1944- *WhoAm 94, WhoAmL 94*
Neches, Richard Brooks 1955- *WhoScEn 94*
Nechin, Herbert Benjamin 1935- *WhoAm 94*
Nechis, Barbara 1937- *WhoAmA 93*
Necho, II d593BC *WhWE*
Nechvatal, Joseph James 1951- *WhoAmA 93*
Neck, Medicine *EncNAR*
Necker, Suzanne Cruchod 1737-1794 *BlmGWL*
Neckermann, Peter J. 1935- *WhoIns 94*
Neckermann, Peter Josef 1935- *WhoAm 94, WhoMW 93*
Neckers, Douglas Carlyle 1938- *WhoMW 93*
Necula, Nicholas 1940- *WhoScEn 94*
Nedbal, Oskar 1874-1930 *NewGrDO*
Nedd, (Robert) Archibald 1916- *Who 94*
Nedd, Jerome d1976 *WhoHol 92*
Nedd, Johnnie Colemon *WhoBlA 94*
Nedd, Stuart d1971 *WhoHol 92*
Neddeau, Donald Frederick Price 1913- *WhoAmA 93*
Nedelin, Gennady Pavlovich 1938- *LngBDD*
Nedell, Bernard d1972 *WhoHol 92*
Nederkoorn, Erik Jan 1943- *IntWW 93*
Nederlander, James Morton 1922- *IntWW 93, WhoAm 94*
Nederlander, Marjorie Smith 1922- *WhoMW 93*
Nederlander, Robert E. 1933- *WhoAm 94, WhoAmP 93*
Nederveld, Ruth Elizabeth 1933- *WhoFI 94*
Nedoluha, Alfred Karl Franz 1928- *WhoScEn 94*
Nedom, H. Arthur 1925- *WhoAm 94*
Nedreaas, Torborg 1906-1987 *BlmGWL*
Nedwek, Thomas Wayne 1933- *WhoAm 94, WhoAmL 94, WhoMW 93*
Nedwell, Robin 1946- *WhoHol 92*
Nedwin, Glenn E. 1955- *WhoWest 94*
Nedza, Edward A. 1927- *WhoAmP 93*
Nedza, Sandra Louise 1951- *WhoMW 93*
Nee, Frank Walter 1936- *WhoAm 94*
Nee, Mary Coleman 1917- *WhoAm 94*
Nee, Michael Wei-Kuo 1955- *WhoAsA 94*
Nee, Owen D., Jr. 1943- *WhoAm 94*
Neeb, Martin John 1933- *WhoWest 94*
Need, James Don 1944- *WhoMW 93*
Needel, Stephen Paul 1955- *WhoFI 94*
Needham *Who 94*
Needham, Charles William 1936 *WhoAm 94, WhoScEn 94*
Needham, Daniel 1922- *WhoAmP 93*
Needham, George Austin 1943- *WhoAm 94, WhoFI 94*
Needham, Glen Ray 1951- *WhoMW 93*
Needham, Gretchen Fentress d1993 *NewYTBS 93*
Needham, Hal 1931- *IntMPA 94, WhoAm 94, WhoHol 92*
Needham, Hal 1937- *IntDcF 2-4 [port]*
Needham, James *WhoHol 92*
Needham, James d1673 *WhWE*
Needham, James J. 1926- *IntWW 93*
Needham, James Joseph 1926- *WhoAm 94*
Needham, James Robert 1944- *WhoMW 93*
Needham, Joseph 1900- *IntWW 93, Who 94, WhoAm 94, WhoScEn 94*
Needham, Kathleen Ann 1944- *WhoMW 93*
Needham, Lucien Arthur 1929- *WhoAm 94*
Needham, Nancy Jean 1941- *WhoFI 94*
Needham, Noel Joseph Terence Montgomery *Who 94*
Needham, Paul Wesley 1921- *WhoFI 94*
Needham, Phillip 1940- *Who 94*
Needham, Richard Francis 1942- *Who 94*
Needham, Richard Henshaw d1993 *NewYTBS 93*
Needham, Richard Lee 1939- *WhoAm 94*
Needham, Roger Michael 1935- *Who 94*
Needham, William Felix, Jr. 1926- *WhoAmP 93*
Needle, Andrew 1953- *WhoAmL 94*
Needle, Jan 1943- *TwCYAW, WrDr 94*
Needle, Jeffrey Lowell 1947- *WhoAmL 94*
Needleman, Alan 1944- *WhoAm 94*
Needleman, Harry 1949- *WhoAm 94, WhoFI 94*
Needleman, Jacob 1934- *IntWW 93, WhoAm 94, WrDr 94*
Needler, George Treglohan 1935- *WhoAm 94*
Needler, Mabel Glidden *WhoAmA 93*
Needler, Martin Cyril 1933- *WhoWest 94*
Needles, Belverd Earl, Jr. 1942- *WhoMW 93*
Needles, Nique *WhoHol 92*
Neef, Elton T. *EncSF 93*
Neefe, Christian Gottlob 1748-1798 *NewGrDO*
Neefe, Douglas Charles 1944- *WhoAm 94, WhoWest 94*
Neel, Alice 1900- *WhAm 10*
Neel, Alice 1900-1984 *WhoAmA 93N*
Neel, Charles Norman 1941- *WhoAmP 93*
Neel, Harry Bryan, III 1939- *WhoAm 94*
Neel, James Van Gundia 1915- *IntWW 93, WhoAm 94*
Neel, Judy Murphy 1926- *WhoAm 94*
Neel, Louis Eugene Felix 1904- *IntWW 93, Who 94, WhoScEn 94*
Neel, Richard Eugene 1932- *WhoAm 94*
Neel, Roy M. 1945- *WhoAm 94*
Neel, Roy Meeks 1945- *WhoAmP 93*
Neel, Samuel Ellison 1914- *WhoAm 94*
Neel, Spurgeon Hart, Jr. 1919- *WhoAm 94*
Neelakantan, Ganapathy Subramanian 1965- *WhoScEn 94*
Neeland, Roger Philip 1942- *WhoWest 94*
Neeld, Elizabeth Harper 1940- *ConAu 141*
Neeld, Judith *DrAPF 93*
Neeld, Vaughn DeLeath 1943- *WhoMW 93*
Neeley, Ted 1943- *WhoHol 92*
Neelin, J. David 1959- *WhoWest 94*
Neels, Betty 1909- *WrDr 94*
Neels, John Thomas 1958- *WhoFI 94*
Neely, Cam 1965- *WhoAm 94*
Neely, Charles B., Jr. 1943- *WhoAmL 94*
Neely, Charles Lea, Jr. 1927- *WhoAm 94*
Neely, Daniel H. 1940- *WhoAmL 94*
Neely, David E. *WhoBlA 94*
Neely, Demetries Jo 1957- *WhoBlA 94*
Neely, Edgar Adams, Jr. 1910- *WhoAm 94*
Neely, Henry Mason 1942- *WhoBlA 94*
Neely, Mark *WhoHol 92*
Neely, Mark E., Jr. 1944- *WhoAm 94*
Neely, Mary Ruth 1928- *WhoAmP 93*
Neely, Noel Anne 1943- *WhoAmP 93*
Neely, Paul 1946- *WhoAm 94*
Neely, R. Hortensia 1947- *WhoHisp 94*
Neely, Richard *WrDr 94*
Neely, Richard 1802-1828 *EncNAR*
Neely, Richard 1941- *WhoAm 94, WhoAmL 94, WhoAmP 93*
Neely, Sally Schultz 1948- *WhoAm 94, WhoAmL 94*
Neely, Thomas Emerson 1943- *WhoAm 94*
Ne'Eman, Yuval 1925- *IntWW 93, WhoAm 94*
Neenan, Thomas Francis 1923- *WhoMW 93*
Neeper, Cary 1937- *EncSF 93*
Neeper, Frederic Allen 1946- *WhoWest 94*
Neer, Charles Sumner, II 1917- *WhoAm 94, WhoScEn 94*
Neera 1846-1918 *BlmGWL*
Neergaard, Preben d1990 *WhoHol 92*
Neerhout, John, Jr. 1931- *WhoFI 94*
Nees, Lawrence 1949- *WhoAmA 93*
Neese, A. Scott 1950- *WhoFI 94*
Neese, C. G. 1916-1989 *WhAm 10*
Neese, Elbert Haven 1923- *WhoAm 94*
Neese, Ronald Dwain 1948- *WhoWest 94*
Neesemann, Carroll E. 1940- *WhoAmL 94*
Neeskens, Johan 1951- *WorESoc*
Neeson, Liam *IntWW 93*
Neeson, Liam 1952- *IntMPA 94, News 93 [port], WhoHol 92*
Neeson, Paul A. 1935- *WhoFI 94*
Neeson, Richard G. 1946- *WhoAmP 93*
Neet, Sharon Eileen 1954- *WhoMW 93*
Neetzel, Raymond John 1937- *WhoMW 93*
Nef, Evelyn Stefansson 1913- *WhoAm 94*
Nefedov, Oleg Matveyevich 1931- *IntWW 93*
Neff, A. Guy 1951- *WhoAmL 94*
Neff, Arlene Merle 1946- *WhoFI 94*
Neff, Bonita Dostal 1942- *WhoMW 93*
Neff, Carole Cukell 1951- *WhoAmL 94*
Neff, Craig *WhoAm 94*
Neff, Daniel A. 1953- *WhoAmL 94*
Neff, Donald Leroy 1950- *WhoWest 94*
Neff, Donald Lloyd 1930- *WhoAm 94*
Neff, Edith 1943- *WhoAmA 93*
Neff, Edward August 1947- *WhoAm 94*
Neff, Edwin, Jr. 1942- *WhoFI 94*
Neff, Francine Irving 1925- *WhoAm 94, WhoAmP 93*
Neff, Fred Leonard 1948- *WhoAmL 94, WhoFI 94, WhoMW 93*
Neff, Gregory Pall 1942- *WhoFI 94, WhoScEn 94*
Neff, Harold Parker 1933- *WhoScEn 94*
Neff, Harry Richard 1933- *WhoFI 94*
Neff, Hildegarde 1925- *IntMPA 94, WhoHol 92*
Neff, Jack Kenneth 1938- *WhoAm 94*
Neff, John 1951- *WhoAm 94, WhoWest 94*
Neff, John A. 1926- *WhoAmA 93*
Neff, John Hallmark 1944- *WhoAmA 93*
Neff, John Michael 1932- *WhoWest 94*
Neff, Joseph 1900-1969 *WhoAmA 93N*
Neff, Kenneth D. 1929- *WhoMW 93*
Neff, Lester Leroy 1923- *WhoWest 94*
Neff, Mark Edward 1950- *WhoAmL 94*
Neff, Myrna May 1943- *WhoMW 93*
Neff, Ondrej *EncSF 93*
Neff, P. Sherrill 1951- *WhoAm 94, WhoFI 94*
Neff, Ralph d1973 *WhoHol 92*
Neff, Ray Quinn 1928- *WhoFI 94, WhoScEn 94*
Neff, Robert Arthur 1931- *WhoAm 94*
Neff, Robert Clark 1921- *WhoAmL 94, WhoMW 93*
Neff, Robert Wilbur 1936- *WhoAm 94*
Neff, Thomas J. *NewYTBS 93*
Neff, Thomas Joseph 1937- *WhoAm 94, WhoFI 94*
Neff, Vern C. 1927- *WhoAmP 93*
Neff, Walter Perry 1927- *WhoFI 94*
Neff, William DuWayne 1912- *WhoAm 94*
Neff, William L. 1947- *WhoAmL 94*
Neffati, Chedly 1946- *IntWW 93*
Neffson, Robert 1949- *WhoAmA 93*
Neft, David Samuel 1937- *WhoAm 94*
Neft, Else d1968 *WhoHol 92*
Nefzger, Anna Marie 1926- *WhoAmP 93*
Nefzger, Charles LeRoy 1944- *WhoScEn 94*
Nefzger, Tristan Robert 1950- *WhoWest 94*
Negabanat, Noel c. 1600-1666 *EncNAR*
Negahban, Ezatollah 1926- *IntWW 93*
Negahnquet, Albert 1874-1944 *EncNAR*
Negandhi, Anant 1929- *WrDr 94*
Negara Brunei Darussalam, Sultan of 1946- *Who 94*
Negas, Christos d1981 *WhoHol 92*
Negele, John William 1944- *WhoAm 94, WhoScEn 94*
Negishi, Takashi 1933- *IntWW 93*
Negitsoc, Neg 1929- *WrDr 94*
Negless, Markam Gerald 1961- *WhoFI 94*
Negoda, Natalya 1963- *WhoHol 92*
Negre, Louis-Pascal 1928- *IntWW 93*
Negrea, Martian 1893-1973 *NewGrDO*
Negrepontis, Michael Timothy 1930- *WhoAm 94, WhoMW 93*
Negret, Francois *WhoHol 92*
Negrete, Jorge d1953 *WhoHol 92*
Negrete, Louis Richard 1934- *WhoHisp 94*
Negri, Ada 1870-1945 *BlmGWL*
Negri, Cesare c. 1536-c. 1604 *IntDcB*
Negri, Gino 1919-1991 *NewGrDO*
Negri, Maria Caterina fl. 1720- *NewGrDO*
Negri, Maria Rosa c. 1715-1760 *NewGrDO*
Negri, Pola d1987 *WhoHol 92*
Negri, Robert Joseph 1926- *WhoAm 94*
Negri, Rocco Antonio 1932- *WhoAmA 93*
Negrin, Carl Michael 1958- *WhoHisp 94*
Negrini (Villa), Carlo 1826-1865 *NewGrDO*
Negri-Pouget, Fernanda d1955 *WhoHol 92*
Negri Sembilan, Yang di-Pertuan Besar 1922- *IntWW 93*
Negritoiu, Misu 1950- *IntWW 93*
Negron, Edna *WhoAmP 93, WhoHisp 94*
Negron, Guillermo Mendez *WhoAmP 93*
Negron, Taylor *WhoHol 92*
Negron, Theresa A. McDevitt 1957- *WhoAmL 94*
Negron, Victor 1949- *WhoAmP 93*
Negron, Victor H., Jr. 1953- *WhoAm 94*
Negrón, Yolanda 1963- *WhoHisp 94*
Negron-Garcia, Antonio S. 1940- *WhoAmL 94, WhoAmP 93*
Negroni, Peter J. 1942- *WhoHisp 94*
Negron Munoz, Mercedes *BlmGWL*
Negrón-Olivieri, Francisco A. 1933- *WhoHisp 94*
Negroponte, George 1953- *WhoAmA 93*
Negroponte, John D. *WhoAmP 93*
Negroponte, John Dimitri 1939- *IntWW 93, WhoAm 94*
Negrusz, Adam 1957- *WhoMW 93*

Negstad, Richard B. WhoAmP 93
Negulesco, Jean d1993 IntMPA 94N
Negulesco, Jean 1900- IntMPA 94
Negulesco, Jean 1900-1993 NewYTBS 93
Negulesco, Julian 1946- WhoHol 92
Negus, Norma Florence 1932- Who 94
Negus, Richard 1927- Who 94
Negus-de Wys, Jane B. 1924- WhoWest 94
Nehamas, Alexander 1946- WhoAm 94
Nehamkin, Arieh 1925- IntWW 93
Nehart, William James 1954- WhoMW 93
Neher, Carola d1936? WhoHol 92
Neher, (Rudolf Ludwig) Caspar 1897-1962 NewGrDO
Neher, Erwin 1944- IntWW 93, NobelP 91 [port], Who 94, WhoScEn 94
Neher, Fred 1903- WhoAmA 93
Neher, Fred Wendell 1903- WhoWest 94
Neher, John d1972 WhoHol 92
Neher, Lawrence T. 1952- WhoAmL 94
Neher, Leonardo 1922- WhoAmP 93
Neher, Leslie Irwin 1906- WhoFI 94, WhoMW 93, WhoScEn 94
Neher, Richard P. WhoAmP 93
Neher, Ross James 1949- WhoAmA 93
Neher, Susan 1959- WhoHol 92
Nehmer, Stanley 1920- WhoAm 94
Nehra, Gerald Peter 1940- WhoAmL 94
Nehrbass, Seth Martin 1960- WhoAmL 94
Nehring, Irvin Lloyd 1948- WhoMW 93
Nehring, James 1958- ConAu 140
Nehring, William H. 1915- WhoAmP 93
Nehrling, Arno Herbert, Jr. 1928- WhoFI 94
Nehrt, Lee C(harles) 1926- WrDr 94
Nehrt, Lee Charles 1926- WhoAm 94
Nehru, Arun IntWW 93
Nehru, Braj Kumar 1909- IntWW 93, Who 94
Nehru, Jawaharlal 1889-1964 HisWorL [port], HisDcKW
Nehru, Motilal 1861-1931 HisWorL [port]
Neibaur, Mack William 1922- WhoAmP 93
Neibel, Oliver Joseph, Jr. 1927- WhoMW 93
Neiburger, Judith A. WhoAmP 93
Neideffer, Carole Elaine 1944- WhoAmP 93
Neideffer, David Lee 1944- WhoAmP 93
Neidel, Charles G. d1962 WhoHol 92
Neidell, Martin H. 1946- WhoAm 94, WhoAmL 94
Neidell, Norman Samson 1939- WhoScEn 94
Neiderbach, Shelley DrAPF 93
Neidert, Kalo Edward 1918- WhoAm 94, WhoFI 94
Neidhardt, Carl Richard 1921- WhoAmA 93
Neidhardt, Frederick Carl 1931- WhoAm 94, WhoMW 93
Neidhardt, Jean Sliva 1956- WhoScEn 94
Neidhardt, Richard Joseph 1942- WhoFI 94
Neidhart, James Allen 1940- WhoAm 94
Neidhart von Reuental c. 1185-c. 1240 DcLB 138 [port]
Neidich, George Arthur 1950- WhoAmL 94
Neidig, Donald Foster, Jr. 1944- WhoWest 94
Neidigh, Kim L. DrAPF 93
Neidlinger, Gustav 1910-1991 NewGrDO
Neidorf, David WhoHol 92
Neidorf, Ross Lee d1989 WhoHol 92
Neidpath, Lord 1948- Who 94
Neier, Aryeh 1937- WhoAm 94
Neier, Reinhard Werner 1950- WhoScEn 94
Neiertz, Veronique 1942- WhoWomW 91
Neifeld, James Paul 1948- WhoScEn 94
Neighbors, Dolores Maria WhoBlA 94
Neighbors, P. M. Roy 1923- WhoAmP 93
Neighbour, Oliver Wray 1923- Who 94
Neighbour, Ralph W(ebster, Sr.) 1906- WrDr 94
Neighbours, John T. 1949- WhoAmL 94
Neiheisel, Thomas Henry 1953- WhoFI 94, WhoMW 93
Neiiendam, Sigrid d1955 WhoHol 92
Neikirk, Joseph Randolph 1928- WhoAm 94
Neikirk, William Robert 1938- WhoAm 94, WhoFI 94
Neikrug, Marjorie WhoAmA 93
Neil, Andrew Ferguson 1949- IntWW 93, Who 94
Neil, Carl Reynold 1933- WhoAmL 94
Neil, Cleveland Oswald 1931- WhoBlA 94
Neil, Fred Applestein 1933- WhoFI 94
Neil, Gary Lawrence 1940- WhoAm 94, WhoScEn 94
Neil, George Randall 1948- WhoScEn 94
Neil, Herbert Edward, Jr. 1931- WhoFI 94
Neil, Hildegard 1942- WhoHol 92
Neil, Iain Alexander 1956- WhoWest 94
Neil, J. M. 1937- WhoAmA 93
Neil, John Malcolm 1965- WhoWest 94
Neil, Matthew 1917- Who 94
Neil, Randolph Laning 1941- WhoAm 94
Neil, Richard H. 1932- WhoIns 94
Neil, Ronald John Baille 1942- Who 94
Neil, Sylvia Markowicz WhoAmL 94, WhoMW 93
Neil, Thomas 1913- Who 94
Neil, William 1954- WhoAm 94
Neilan, Marshall d1958 WhoHol 92
Neilan, Sarah WrDr 94
Neiland, Brendan Robert 1941- Who 94
Neilans, Joanne M. 1947- WhoFI 94
Neild, Robert Ralph 1924- IntWW 93, Who 94
Neile, Paul 1613-1685? DcNaB MP
Neill, A(lexander) S(utherland) 1883-1973 EncSF 93
Neill, Alistair 1932- Who 94
Neill, Ben E. 1914- WhoAmA 93
Neill, Benjamin Stowe, Jr. 1930- WhoAmP 93
Neill, Bob WhoHol 92
Neill, Brian (Thomas) 1923- Who 94
Neill, Brian (Thomas) Neill 1923- IntWW 93
Neill, Bruce Ferguson 1941- Who 94
Neill, Denis Michael 1943- WhoAm 94
Neill, Derrick James 1922- Who 94
Neill, Don Samuel 1949- WhoAmP 93
Neill, Francis Patrick 1926- IntWW 93
Neill, Gary Alvis 1951- WhoAmP 93
Neill, Hugh Who 94
Neill, (James) Hugh 1921- Who 94
Neill, Ivan 1906- Who 94
Neill, Ivan Delacherois 1912- Who 94
Neill, James d1931 WhoHol 92
Neill, Joe 1944- WhoAmA 93
Neill, John Robert Winder Who 94
Neill, K. Patrick 1946- WhoAmL 94
Neill, Noel 1920- WhoHol 92
Neill, Patrick Who 94
Neill, (Francis) Patrick 1926- Who 94
Neill, Peter DrAPF 93
Neill, Richard d1970 WhoHol 92
Neill, Richard Robert 1925- WhoAm 94
Neill, Robert 1908-1987 WhAm 10
Neill, Robert D. 1932- WhoScEn 94
Neill, Robert Harold 1930- WhoWest 94
Neill, Rolfe 1932- WhoAm 94
Neill, Ronald H. 1944- WhoAmL 94
Neill, Roy William d1946 WhoHol 92
Neill, Sam 1947- IntMPA 94, WhoAm 94
Neill, Sam 1949- WhoHol 92
Neill, Thomas Taylor 1903-1988 WhAm 10
Neill, William Alexander 1957- WhoAm 94
Neilly, Andrew Hutchinson, Jr. 1923- WhoAm 94
Neils, Betty Jo 1919- WhoAmP 93
Neils, Christopher B. 1944- WhoAmL 94
Neils, Howard William 1929- WhoAmP 93
Neilsen, Inga WhoHol 92
Neilsen, Tom WhoAmP 93
Neilson, Alasdair Hewitt 1932- WhoScEn 94
Neilson, Benjamin Reath 1938- WhoAm 94, WhoAmL 94
Neilson, Bruce John 1943- WhoAmP 93
Neilson, Catherine WhoHol 92
Neilson, Denny Woodall WhoAmP 93
Neilson, Elizabeth Anastasia 1913- WhoAm 94
Neilson, Ian (Godfrey) 1918- Who 94
Neilson, James Warren 1933- WrDr 94
Neilson, John 1745-1833 WhAmRev
Neilson, Katherine B. 1902-1977 WhoAmA 93N
Neilson, Keith (Townsend Olaf) 1935- EncSF 93
Neilson, Kenneth Thomas 1948- WhoAm 94
Neilson, Melany 1958- WrDr 94
Neilson, Nigel Fraser 1919- Who 94
Neilson, Perlita 1933- WhoHol 92
Neilson, Raymond P. R. 1881-1964 WhoAmA 93N
Neilson, Richard Alvin 1937- Who 94
Neilson, Ronald Price 1949- WhoScEn 94
Neilson, Winthrop Cunningham, III 1934- WhoAm 94
Neilson-Terry, Dennis d1932 WhoHol 92
Neilson-Terry, Julia d1957 WhoHol 92
Neilson-Terry, Phyllis d1977 WhoHol 92
Neiman, Dennis R. 1945- WhoAmL 94
Neiman, Jeffrey Charles 1953- WhoAmL 94
Neiman, Joan 1920- WhoWomW 91
Neiman, John Hammond 1917- WhoAm 94
Neiman, LeRoy 1927- News 93-3 [port], WhoAm 94, WhoAmA 93
Neiman, Lionel Joseph 1921- WhoAm 94
Neiman, Norma 1923- WhoMW 93
Neiman, Norman 1935- WhoFI 94
Neiman, Tanya Marie 1949- WhoAmL 94
Neimanas, Joyce WhoAmA 93
Neimann, Albert Alexander 1939- WhoWest 94
Neimark, Paul G. 1934- WrDr 94
Neimark, Philip John 1939- WhoFI 94, WhoMW 93
Neimark, Sheridan 1935- WhoAm 94
Neimark, Vassa 1954- WhoMW 93, WhoScEn 94
Neims, Allen Howard 1938- WhoAm 94
Nein, Scott R. WhoAmP 93
Neinas, Charles Merrill 1932- WhoAm 94
Neiner, Andrew Joseph 1950- WhoAm 94, WhoFI 94, WhoMW 93
Neira, Daniel Alejandro 1955- WhoHisp 94
Neira, Gail Elizabeth WhoHisp 94
Neis, Arnold Hayward 1938- WhoAm 94
Neis, Arthur Veral 1940- WhoFI 94
Neis, James M. 1946- WhoAm 94
Neise, George WhoHol 92
Neiser, Brent Allen 1954- WhoAm 94, WhoFI 94, WhoWest 94
Neiser, Richard William 1938- WhoFI 94
Neish, Francis Edward 1925- WhoFI 94
Neishlos, Arye Leon 1955- WhoScEn 94
Neiss, Hubert 1935- IntWW 93
Neisser, Ulric 1928- WhoAm 94
Neiswanger, Marjorie Bull 1929- WhoFI 94
Neiter, Gerald Irving 1933- WhoAm 94
Neitz, David Allan 1961- WhoScEn 94
Neitzel, Charlotte Louise 1953- WhoAm 94
Neitzel, Shirley 1941- SmATA 77 [port]
Neitzer, William Bryan 1958- WhoFI 94
Neiworth, Trish Latrissa Lee 1959- WhoWest 94
Neizer, Meredith Ann 1956- WhoBlA 94
Neizvestny, Ernst Iosifovich 1925- IntWW 93
Nejaime, Nabih 1935- WhoAmP 93
NeJame, Adele DrAPF 93
Nejedly, Vit 1912-1945 NewGrDO
Nejelski, Paul Arthur 1938- WhoAm 94
Nekoba, Devon M. T. 1968- WhoAmP 93
Nekola, Louis William 1954- WhoMW 93
Nekrich, Aleksandr M. d1993 NewYTBS 93
Nekrich, Aleksandr Moiseyevich 1920- IntWW 93
Nekritz, Barry B. 1938- WhoAm 94, WhoAmL 94
Nekritz, Edward Steven 1965- WhoAmL 94
Nelan, Augustine Philip d1993 NewYTBS 93
Nelder, John Ashworth 1924- IntWW 93, Who 94
Nelhybel, Vaclav 1919- NewGrDO
Neligan, Desmond West Edmund d1993 Who 94N
Neligan, Michael Hugh Desmond 1936- Who 94
Nelipovich, Sandra Grassi 1939- WhoWest 94
Nelis, Denise 1927- WhoWomW 91
Nelissen, Roelof J. 1931- IntWW 93
Nelken i Mausberger, Margarita 1898-1936 BlmGWL
Nelkin, Dorothy 1933- WhoAm 94, WhoScEn 94
Nelkin, Stacey WhoHol 92
Nell, Edward John 1935- WhoFI 94
Nell, Janine Marie 1959- WhoScEn 94
Nell, Nathalie 1950- WhoHol 92
Nell, Roger Eric 1965- WhoAmL 94
Nell, Victor 1935- WrDr 94
Nellams, Jane Harris 1955- WhoWest 94
Nellemose, Knud 1908- IntWW 93
Nellermoe, Leslie C. 1954- WhoAm 94
Nelles, Maurice 1906- WhoAm 94
Nelli, D. James 1917- WhoFI 94
Nelligan, Kate 1951- IntMPA 94, IntWW 93, WhoAm 94, WhoHol 92
Nelligan, Kenneth Egan 1952- WhoAmL 94
Nelligan, William David 1926- WhoAm 94
Nellington, Blaine 1951- WhoWest 94
Nellis, James F., Jr. 1946- WhoAmL 94
Nellis, Jennifred Gene WhoAmA 93
Nellist, David 1952- Who 94
Nellum, Albert L. 1932- WhoBlA 94
Nellums, Michael Wayne 1962- WhoBlA 94
Nelms, Charlie WhoMW 93
Nelms, Ommie Lee 1942- WhoBlA 94
Nelms, Robert E. 1960- WhoAmP 93
Nelms, Sheryl L. DrAPF 93
Neloms, Henry WhoBlA 94
Nelon, Robert Dale 1946- WhoAmL 94
Nelsen, Betty Jo 1935- WhoAmP 93
Nelsen, Hart Michael 1938- WhoAm 94
Nelsen, Timothy Alan 1947- WhoAm 94
Nelsen, William Cameron 1941- WhoAm 94
Nelson Who 94
Nelson, Bishop of 1941- Who 94
Nelson, Earl 1941- Who 94
Nelson, Adam Phillip 1960- WhoWest 94
Nelson, Alan Barry 1956- WhoFI 94
Nelson, Alan C. 1933- WhoAmP 93
Nelson, Alan Curtis 1933- WhoAm 94
Nelson, Alan Ray 1933- WhoAm 94
Nelson, Albert Louis, III 1938- WhoFI 94, WhoMW 93
Nelson, A'Lelia 1918- WhoBlA 94
Nelson, Alfred John 1922- WhoAm 94, WhoScEn 94
Nelson, Alfred W. WhoAmP 93
Nelson, Alice (Ruth) Moore Dunbar 1875-1935 BlmGWL
Nelson, Allyn Howard 1928- WhoMW 93
Nelson, Anna 1943- WhoAmP 93
Nelson, Anthony Who 94
Nelson, (Richard) Anthony 1948- Who 94
Nelson, Antonya DrAPF 93
Nelson, Arlene B. 1925- WhoAmP 93
Nelson, Arnold Bernard 1922- WhoAm 94
Nelson, Arthur Alexander, Jr. 1946- WhoAm 94, WhoWest 94
Nelson, Arthur Hunt 1923- WhoAm 94, WhoFI 94
Nelson, Artie Cortez 1955- WhoBlA 94
Nelson, Barbara Anne 1951- WhoAmL 94
Nelson, Barry 1920- WhoHol 92
Nelson, Barry 1923- IntMPA 94
Nelson, Barry Vernon 1939- WhoWest 94
Nelson, Basha Ruth WhoAmA 93
Nelson, Ben, Jr. 1942- WhoAm 94
Nelson, Bernard Edward 1950- WhoAm 94
Nelson, Bernard William 1935- WhoAm 94, WhoWest 94
Nelson, Bertram James 1925- Who 94
Nelson, Betty Henry 1932- WhoAmP 93
Nelson, Betty Palmer 1938- WrDr 94
Nelson, Bill d1973 WhoHol 92
Nelson, Bill 1942- WhoAmP 93
Nelson, Billy d1979 WhoHol 92
Nelson, Brent Christopher 1957- WhoWest 94
Nelson, Bruce WhoAmP 93
Nelson, Bruce Richard 1953- WhoFI 94
Nelson, Bruce Sherman 1951- WhoAm 94, WhoFI 94
Nelson, Bryan Eugene 1946- WhoAmL 94
Nelson, Bryan Herbert 1956- WhoWest 94
Nelson, Bryan Maynard 1949- WhoAmL 94
Nelson, Bud 1931- WhoAmP 93
Nelson, Byron 1912- NewYTBS 93 [port]
Nelson, Carey Boone WhoAmA 93
Nelson, Carl Michael 1956- WhoScEn 94
Nelson, Carl R. 1945- WhoAmL 94
Nelson, Carl Roger 1915- WhoAm 94
Nelson, Carl Vincent 1947- WhoMW 93
Nelson, Carolyn Callenbach 1937- WhoAmP 93
Nelson, Cassandra Ann 1957- WhoMW 93
Nelson, Chad Matthew 1965- WhoScEn 94
Nelson, Charles 1925- WhoAmP 93
Nelson, Charles Arthur 1922- WhoAm 94
Nelson, Charles Edward 1930- WhoAm 94
Nelson, Charles Frederick 1947- WhoAmL 94
Nelson, Charles Gustaf 1937- WhoMW 93
Nelson, Charles J. 1920- WhoAm 94, WhoBlA 94
Nelson, Chester Ervin, Jr. 1939- WhoMW 93
Nelson, Christine d1988 WhoHol 92
Nelson, Christopher WhoHol 92
Nelson, Clair L. 1940- WhoAmP 93
Nelson, Clayton H. 1937- WhoIns 94
Nelson, Cleopatra McClellan 1914- WhoBlA 94
Nelson, Clifford Arnold 1923- WhoAm 94
Nelson, Clifford H., Jr. 1952- WhoAmL 94
Nelson, Clifford Lee, Jr. 1936- WhoWest 94
Nelson, Cordner 1918- WrDr 94
Nelson, Craig Alan 1961- WhoAm 94, WhoWest 94
Nelson, Craig Richard WhoHol 92
Nelson, Craig T. WhoHol 92
Nelson, Craig T. 1946- IntMPA 94, WhoAm 94
Nelson, Curtis Jerome 1940- WhoAm 94, WhoMW 93
Nelson, Dan Karl 1947- WhoAmL 94
Nelson, Daniel 1941- WrDr 94
Nelson, Daniel R. 1938- WhoWest 94
Nelson, Daniel W. 1952- WhoAmL 94
Nelson, Darby WhoAmP 93
Nelson, Darrell Wayne 1939- WhoAm 94, WhoScEn 94
Nelson, Darrin Milo 1959- WhoBlA 94
Nelson, Darryl James 1950- WhoWest 94
Nelson, David 1936- IntMPA 94, WhoHol 92

Nelson, David A. *WhoAmP 93*
Nelson, David Aldrich 1932- *WhoAm 94, WhoAmL 94, WhoMW 93*
Nelson, David Brian 1940- *WhoScEn 94*
Nelson, David E. 1944- *WhoBlA 94*
Nelson, David Edward 1930- *WhoAm 94*
Nelson, David J. *DrAPF 93*
Nelson, David Leonard 1930- *WhoAm 94*
Nelson, David Lloyd d1987 *WhoHol 92*
Nelson, David Loren 1956- *WhoScEn 94*
Nelson, David Michael 1962- *WhoFI 94*
Nelson, David Robert 1942- *WhoMW 93*
Nelson, David Robert 1951- *WhoAm 94*
Nelson, David S. 1933- *WhoAm 94, WhoAmL 94, WhoBlA 94*
Nelson, David Scott 1953- *WhoAmL 94*
Nelson, David W. 1945- *WhoAmL 94*
Nelson, David Wallace 1951- *WhoFI 94*
Nelson, Debra J. 1957- *WhoBlA 94*
Nelson, Debra L. 1958- *WhoFI 94*
Nelson, Dennis Gene 1955- *WhoMW 93*
Nelson, Dennis George Anthony 1954- *WhoScEn 94*
Nelson, Diana Walker 1941- *WhoAmP 93*
Nelson, Doeg M. 1931- *WhoBlA 94*
Nelson, Don 1940- *BasBi*
Nelson, Don Jerome 1930- *WhoMW 93, WhoScEn 94*
Nelson, Dona Rae 1947- *WhoAmA 93*
Nelson, Donald Anders Fuller 1949- *WhoMW 93*
Nelson, Donald Arvid 1940- *WhoAm 94, WhoWest 94*
Nelson, Donald R. 1939- *WhoAmP 93*
Nelson, Donald T. 1935- *WhoAmP 93*
Nelson, Dorothy Patricia 1921- *WhoAm 94*
Nelson, Dorothy W. *WhoAmP 93*
Nelson, Dorothy Wright 1928- *WhoAm 94, WhoAmL 94, WhoWest 94*
Nelson, Dotson McGinnis, Jr. 1915- *WhoAm 94*
Nelson, Douglas A. 1927- *WhoAm 94*
Nelson, Douglas Lee 1944- *WhoFI 94*
Nelson, Drew 1952- *SmATA 77 [port]*
Nelson, Drew Vernon 1947- *WhoWest 94*
Nelson, Dwight Alan 1963- *WhoMW 93*
Nelson, E. Benjamin 1941- *WhoAm 94, WhoAmP 93, WhoIns 94, WhoMW 93*
Nelson, Ed 1928- *WhoHol 92*
Nelson, Edward Alexander, Jr. 1934- *WhoMW 93*
Nelson, Edward Gage 1931- *WhoAm 94*
Nelson, Edward Humphrey 1918- *WhoAm 94*
Nelson, Edward O. 1925- *WhoBlA 94*
Nelson, Edward Sheffield 1941- *WhoAm 94, WhoAmL 94*
Nelson, Edwin Clarence 1922- *WhoAm 94*
Nelson, Edwin L. 1940- *WhoAm 94, WhoAmL 94*
Nelson, Eileen F. *WhoBlA 94*
Nelson, Elmer Kingsholm, Jr. 1922- *WhoAm 94*
Nelson, Emmanuel S(ampath) 1954- *ConAu 142*
Nelson, Eric Douglas Mackinlay 1912- *Who 94*
Nelson, Eric Mark 1959- *WhoAmL 94*
Nelson, Eric Michael 1947- *WhoAmL 94*
Nelson, Eric Victor 1927- *Who 94*
Nelson, Erland Nels Peter 1897- *WhAm 10*
Nelson, Estella Newman 1960- *WhoFI 94*
Nelson, Evelyn d1923 *WhoHol 92*
Nelson, Flora Sue 1930- *WhoBlA 94*
Nelson, Ford R., Jr. 1942- *WhoAmL 94*
Nelson, Frank d1932 *WhoHol 92*
Nelson, Frank d1986 *WhoHol 92*
Nelson, Frank Eugene 1909- *WhoWest 94*
Nelson, Frank V. 1919- *WhoAmP 93*
Nelson, Freda Nell Hein 1929- *WhoMW 93*
Nelson, Frederick Carl 1932- *WhoAm 94, WhoScEn 94*
Nelson, Frederick Dickson 1958- *WhoAm 94, WhoAmL 94, WhoMW 93*
Nelson, Fredric C. 1945- *WhoAmL 94*
Nelson, Garrett R. *WhoAm 94, WhoFI 94, WhoWest 94*
Nelson, Gary 1936- *WhoWest 94*
Nelson, Gary Alfred 1936- *WhoAmP 93*
Nelson, Gary Dean 1935- *WhoAmP 93*
Nelson, Gary J. *WhoAmP 93*
Nelson, Gary Michael 1951- *WhoAmL 94*
Nelson, Gary Rohde 1942- *WhoScEn 94*
Nelson, Gary Steven 1952- *WhoFI 94*
Nelson, Gayle Vance 1946- *WhoMW 93*
Nelson, Gaylord Anton 1916- *IntWW 93, WhoAm 94, WhoAmP 93*
Nelson, Gene 1920- *IntMPA 94, WhoHol 92*
Nelson, Gene Alan 1952- *WhoMW 93*
Nelson, Gene Edward 1944- *WhoWest 94*
Nelson, Geoffrey Kenneth 1923- *WrDr 94*
Nelson, George Driver 1950- *WhoScEn 94*
Nelson, George Laurence 1887-1978 *WhoAmA 93N*
Nelson, George Leonard 1897- *WhoAm 94*
Nelson, George N. 1932- *WhoWest 94*
Nelson, George R. 1944- *WhoAmL 94*
Nelson, Gerald Kenneth 1922- *WhoAm 94*
Nelson, Gilbert L. 1942- *WhoBlA 94*
Nelson, Glen David 1937- *WhoAm 94, WhoFI 94*
Nelson, Glen Edward 1961- *WhoFI 94*
Nelson, Gordon d1956 *WhoHol 92*
Nelson, Gordon Lee 1936- *WhoAmP 93, WhoMW 93*
Nelson, Gordon Leigh 1943- *WhoAm 94, WhoFI 94, WhoScEn 94*
Nelson, Gordon Leon 1919- *WhoAm 94, WhoScEn 94*
Nelson, Gordon Leon, Jr. 1943- *WhoScEn 94*
Nelson, Gordon M. 1941- *WhoAmP 93*
Nelson, Grant Steel 1939- *WhoAm 94*
Nelson, Gregory James 1965- *WhoWest 94*
Nelson, Gwen d1990 *WhoHol 92*
Nelson, H. H. 1912- *WhoIns 94*
Nelson, H. Viscount, Jr. 1939- *WhoBlA 94*
Nelson, Harold d1937 *WhoHol 92*
Nelson, Harold B. 1947- *WhoAmA 93*
Nelson, Harold Bernhard 1947- *WhoAm 94, WhoWest 94*
Nelson, Harold D. 1921- *WhoAmP 93*
Nelson, Harold E. *WhoBlA 94*
Nelson, Harriet *WhoHol 92*
Nelson, Harriet 1914- *IntMPA 94*
Nelson, Harriet Hilliard 1914- *WhoAm 94*
Nelson, Harry 1923- *WhoAm 94*
Nelson, Harry Donald 1933- *WhoAm 94*
Nelson, Harry William 1908-1989 *WhAm 10*
Nelson, Harvey F., Jr. 1924- *WhoAmP 93*
Nelson, Harvey Frans, Jr. 1924- *WhoAm 94*
Nelson, Havelock 1917- *NewGrDO*
Nelson, Haywood 1960- *WhoHol 92*
Nelson, Hedwig Potok 1954- *WhoFI 94*
Nelson, Helaine Queen 1945- *WhoMW 93*
Nelson, Henry Alan 1957- *WhoMW 93*
Nelson, Herbert d1990 *WhoHol 92*
Nelson, Herbert Leroy 1922- *WhoAm 94*
Nelson, Hilda d1919 *WhoHol 92*
Nelson, Horatio 1758-1805 *BlmGEL, HisWorL [port], WhAmRev*
Nelson, Howard *DrAPF 93*
Nelson, Howard 1947- *WrDr 94*
Nelson, Howard Joseph 1919- *WhoAm 94*
Nelson, Ivory Vance 1934- *WhoBlA 94, WhoWest 94*
Nelson, J. Bryan 1932- *WrDr 94*
Nelson, J. Garnett 1939- *WhoIns 94*
Nelson, J. Robert 1920- *WrDr 94*
Nelson, J. Robert 1944- *WhoAm 94, WhoAmL 94*
Nelson, Jack 1882- *WhoHol 92*
Nelson, Jack D. 1929- *WhoAmA 93*
Nelson, Jack Ewald 1936- *WhoFI 94*
Nelson, Jack H. 1930- *WhoIns 94*
Nelson, Jack Lee 1932- *WhoAm 94, WrDr 94*
Nelson, Jack Raymond 1934- *WhoWest 94*
Nelson, James Alan 1950- *WhoWest 94*
Nelson, James Albert 1941- *WhoAm 94*
Nelson, James Alonzo 1938- *WhoScEn 94*
Nelson, James C. *WhoAmP 93*
Nelson, James Carmer, Jr. 1921- *WhoAm 94*
Nelson, James F. 1927- *WhoAm 94*
Nelson, James Frederick, Jr. 1945- *WhoAmP 93*
Nelson, James Graham 1929- *WrDr 94*
Nelson, James Harold 1936- *WhoScEn 94*
Nelson, James Lee 1935- *WhoAmP 93*
Nelson, James P. 1949- *WhoAmA 93*
Nelson, James Randall 1955- *WhoAmL 94*
Nelson, James Wilbur 1925- *WhoWest 94*
Nelson, Jamie (Charles Vernon Hope) 1949- *Who 94*
Nelson, Jan Craig 1951- *WhoAmL 94*
Nelson, Jane 1951- *WhoAmP 93*
Nelson, Jane Gray 1928- *WhoAmA 93*
Nelson, Janice Eileen 1943- *WhoAmL 94*
Nelson, Jeanne Francess 1933- *WhoScEn 94*
Nelson, Jeffrey Hale 1946- *WhoMW 93*
Nelson, Jeffrey Owen 1956- *WhoMW 93*
Nelson, Jeremy E. *WhoAmP 93*
Nelson, Jill 1952- *ConBlB 6 [port]*
Nelson, Jill E. 1952- *WhoMW 93*
Nelson, Jo *DrAPF 93*
Nelson, Joan 1958- *WhoAmA 93*
Nelson, John *AstEnc, Who 94*
Nelson, John 1936- *WhoAmP 93*
Nelson, John 1941- *NewGrDO*
Nelson, (Eustace) John (Blois) 1912- *Who 94*
Nelson, John Allen *WhoHol 92*
Nelson, John Carl 1958- *WhoFI 94*
Nelson, John Graeme 1947- *Who 94*
Nelson, John Henry 1919- *WhoAmP 93*
Nelson, John Herbert 1897- *WhAm 10*
Nelson, John Howard 1929- *WhoAm 94*
Nelson, John Howard 1930- *WhoAm 94, WhoScEn 94*
Nelson, John Keith 1943- *WhoAm 94*
Nelson, John Marshall 1941- *WhoFI 94*
Nelson, John Martin 1931- *WhoAm 94, WhoFI 94*
Nelson, John Robert 1920- *WhoAm 94*
Nelson, John Thilgen 1921- *WhoAm 94*
Nelson, John Walter, Jr. 1923- *WhoFI 94*
Nelson, John Wilton 1941- *WhoAm 94*
Nelson, John Woolard 1928- *WhoAm 94*
Nelson, Jon Allen 1936- *WhoAmA 93*
Nelson, Jonathan P. 1939- *WhoBlA 94*
Nelson, Joni Lysett 1938- *WhoAm 94*
Nelson, Joseph Conrad 1926- *WhoAm 94*
Nelson, Judd 1959- *IntMPA 94, WhoAm 94, WhoHol 92*
Nelson, Judith 1939- *IntWW 93, NewGrDO*
Nelson, Kathleen Veenstra 1932- *WhoWest 94*
Nelson, Kay LeRoi 1926- *WhoWest 94*
Nelson, Kay Yarborough 1945- *WhoScEn 94*
Nelson, Keithe Eugene 1935- *WhoAm 94, WhoAmL 94*
Nelson, Ken 1936- *WhoAmP 93*
Nelson, Kendall Ray 1952- *WhoMW 93*
Nelson, Kenneth d1993 *NewYTBS 93 [port]*
Nelson, Kenneth 1930- *WhoHol 92*
Nelson, Kenneth Arthur 1942- *WhoWest 94*
Nelson, Kenneth Edward 1948- *WhoAm 94*
Nelson, Kent *DrAPF 93*
Nelson, Kent C. 1937- *WhoAm 94, WhoFI 94*
Nelson, Kenwyn Gordon 1926- *WhoAm 94*
Nelson, Kim L. 1948- *WhoAmP 93*
Nelson, Kirk Richard 1956- *WhoWest 94*
Nelson, Kirk William 1953- *WhoWest 94*
Nelson, Knox 1926- *WhoAmP 93*
Nelson, Kristin 1945- *WhoHol 92*
Nelson, L. Clair 1918- *WhoAmP 93*
Nelson, Larry Ardean 1952- *WhoAmP 93*
Nelson, Larry James 1949- *WhoMW 93*
Nelson, Larry Keith 1948- *WhoScEn 94*
Nelson, Lars-Erik 1941- *WhoAm 94*
Nelson, Lauren Kathryn 1955- *WhoMW 93*
Nelson, Lawrence Barclay 1931- *WhoAm 94*
Nelson, Lawrence Evan 1932- *WhoAm 94*
Nelson, Lawrence Merle 1947- *WhoScEn 94*
Nelson, Lawrence Olaf 1926- *WhoAm 94, WhoWest 94*
Nelson, Leon T. 1938- *WhoBlA 94*
Nelson, Leonard 1912- *WhoAmA 93*
Nelson, Leonard 1920- *WhoAm 94*
Nelson, Leonard Earl 1944- *WhoFI 94*
Nelson, Leonard Martin 1935- *WhoAmL 94*
Nelson, Lester 1928- *WhoAmL 94*
Nelson, Lewis Clair 1918- *WhoAm 94*
Nelson, Linda *WhoAmP 93*
Nelson, Linda Ann 1955- *WhoAmP 93*
Nelson, Linda Ann 1959- *WhoWest 94*
Nelson, Linda J. 1942- *WhoAmP 93*
Nelson, Linda Ruth 1944- *WhoWest 94*
Nelson, Lindsey 1919- *WhoAm 94*
Nelson, Lloyd Steadman 1922- *WhoAm 94*
Nelson, Lori 1933- *IntMPA 94, WhoHol 92*
Nelson, Lottie d1966 *WhoHol 92*
Nelson, Lowell A. 1940- *WhoAmP 93*
Nelson, Lowry, Jr. 1926- *WhoAm 94, WrDr 94*
Nelson, Lyle Morgan 1918- *WhoAm 94*
Nelson, Magnus Charles 1938- *WhoWest 94*
Nelson, Marcia Marie 1950- *WhoAmL 94*
Nelson, Margaret Mogensen 1947- *WhoMW 93*
Nelson, Mark *WhoHol 92*
Nelson, Mark 1926- *WrDr 94*
Nelson, Mark Bruce 1921- *WhoAm 94*
Nelson, Mark David 1949- *WhoAmP 93*
Nelson, Mark Edward 1954- *WhoMW 93*
Nelson, Mark K. 1942- *WhoAmP 93*
Nelson, Mark T. 1951- *WhoAmL 94*
Nelson, Marshall J. 1943- *WhoAm 94, WhoAmL 94*
Nelson, Martha 1923- *WrDr 94*
Nelson, Martha Jane 1952- *WhoAm 94*
Nelson, Marvin Bernard 1931- *WhoFI 94*
Nelson, Marvin Ray 1926- *WhoAm 94*
Nelson, Mary Carroll 1929- *WhoAmA 93, WhoWest 94*
Nelson, Mary Elizabeth 1955- *WhoBlA 94*
Nelson, Mary Ellen Dickson 1933- *WhoMW 93*
Nelson, Mary Lou 1932- *WhoAmP 93*
Nelson, Mary S. 1943- *WhoAmP 93*
Nelson, Maxine Evelyn 1947- *WhoWest 94*
Nelson, Merle Royte 1935- *WhoAmP 93*
Nelson, Merlin Edward 1922- *WhoAm 94*
Nelson, Merrill F. 1955- *WhoAmP 93*
Nelson, Michael Edward 1929- *Who 94*
Nelson, Michael Fall 1950- *WhoAmP 93*
Nelson, Michael Gordon 1951- *WhoScEn 94*
Nelson, Michael S. 1942- *WhoAmL 94*
Nelson, Michael Underhill 1932- *WhoAm 94*
Nelson, Mike 1947- *WhoAmP 93*
Nelson, Mildred *DrAPF 93*
Nelson, Morton 1930- *WhoMW 93*
Nelson, Nancy Eleanor 1933- *WhoAm 94, WhoScEn 94, WhoWest 94*
Nelson, Nate d1984 *WhoHol 92*
Nelson, Nathaniel W. 1921- *WhoBlA 94*
Nelson, Nels Robert 1923- *WhoAm 94*
Nelson, Nette Adaline 1939- *WhoFI 94*
Nelson, Nevin Mary 1941- *WhoWest 94*
Nelson, Nicholas 1947- *Who 94*
Nelson, Norman Crooks 1929- *WhoAm 94*
Nelson, Norman Roy 1944- *WhoAmL 94*
Nelson, Norton 1910-1990 *WhAm 10*
Nelson, Novella C. 1939- *WhoBlA 94*
Nelson, O. Edward 1935- *WhoWest 94*
Nelson, Oliver Evans, Jr. 1920- *WhoAm 94*
Nelson, Otha Curtis, Sr. 1947- *WhoBlA 94*
Nelson, Ozzie d1975 *WhoHol 92*
Nelson, Pamela *WhoMW 93*
Nelson, Pamela A. *WhoAmP 93*
Nelson, Pamela Hudson 1947- *WhoAmA 93*
Nelson, Patricia Ann 1955- *WhoBlA 94*
Nelson, Paul *DrAPF 93*
Nelson, Paul Donald 1932- *WhoBlA 94*
Nelson, Paul Douglas 1948- *WhoAmL 94*
Nelson, Paul James 1932- *WhoFI 94*
Nelson, Paul Raymond 1951- *WhoMW 93*
Nelson, Paul Richard 1947- *WhoAm 94*
Nelson, Paula Morrison Bronson 1944- *WhoWest 94*
Nelson, Peter *WhoHol 92*
Nelson, Peter E. *DrAPF 93*
Nelson, Peter Edward 1953- *WhoScEn 94*
Nelson, Peter Martin 1954- *WhoAmL 94*
Nelson, Peter N. 1953- *ConAu 140*
Nelson, Philip Edwin 1934- *WhoScEn 94*
Nelson, Philip Francis 1928- *WhoAm 94*
Nelson, Portia *WhoHol 92*
Nelson, Prince Rogers 1958- *WhoAm 94, WhoBlA 94*
Nelson, R. P. *WhoAmP 93*
Nelson, Ralph d1987 *WhoHol 92*
Nelson, Ralph Alfred 1927- *IntWW 93, WhoAm 94*
Nelson, Ralph Lowell 1926- *WhoAm 94*
Nelson, Ralph Stanley 1943- *WhoAmL 94*
Nelson, Ramona M. 1950- *WhoBlA 94*
Nelson, Randall Cleaver 1945- *WhoAmL 94*
Nelson, Randall Erland 1948- *WhoWest 94*
Nelson, Ray 1931- *EncSF 93, WrDr 94*
Nelson, Ray Faraday *DrAPF 93*
Nelson, Raymond John 1917- *WhoAm 94*
Nelson, Raymond John 1938- *WhoAm 94*
Nelson, Raymond Milford 1928- *WhoWest 94*
Nelson, Richard *Who 94*
Nelson, Richard 1938- *WhoAm 94*
Nelson, Richard 1950- *ConDr 93, WrDr 94*
Nelson, (Sidney) Richard (Carlyle) 1907- *Who 94*
Nelson, Richard Arthur 1947- *WhoAm 94, WhoAmL 94*
Nelson, Richard Burton 1911- *WhoAm 94*
Nelson, Richard Copeland 1930- *WhoAm 94*
Nelson, Richard David 1940- *WhoAm 94, WhoMW 93*
Nelson, Richard David 1945- *WhoScEn 94*
Nelson, Richard Henry 1939- *WhoAm 94, WhoFI 94*
Nelson, Richard Lawrence 1953- *WhoMW 93*
Nelson, Richard Leland 1945- *WhoWest 94*
Nelson, Richard M. 1925- *WhoAmP 93*
Nelson, Richard Y., Jr. 1939- *WhoBlA 94*
Nelson, Rick(y) d1985 *WhoHol 92*
Nelson, Rick Knut 1952- *WhoFI 94*
Nelson, Ricky Eugene 1956- *WhoFI 94, WhoMW 93*
Nelson, Ricky Lee 1959- *WhoBlA 94*
Nelson, Robert *WhoAmP 93*
Nelson, Robert 1743-1818 *WhAmRev*
Nelson, Robert Bruce 1935- *WhoAm 94*
Nelson, Robert Charles 1924- *WhoAm 94*

Nessim, Barbara 1939- *WhoAmA 93*
Nessler, Viktor E(rnst) 1841-1890 *NewGrDO*
Nessmith, Herbert Alva 1935- *WhoScEn 94*
Nesson, H. Richard 1932- *WhoAm 94*
Nestande, Bruce 1938- *WhoAmP 93*
Nestell, Bill d1966 *WhoHol 92*
Nester, Eugene William 1930- *WhoScEn 94*
Nester, William Raymond, Jr. 1928- *WhoAm 94, WhoMW 93*
Nesterenko, Eric *WhoHol 92*
Nesterenko, Yevgeniy Yevgeniyevich 1938- *IntWW 93*
Nesterenko, Yevgeny (Yevgen'yevich) 1938- *NewGrDO*
Nesterikhin, Yuri Efremovich 1930- *IntWW 93*
Nestle, Jack d1978 *WhoHol 92*
Nestle, Joan *DrAPF 93*
Nestle, Joan 1940- *GayLL*
Nestor, Jack *DrAPF 93*
Nestor, John Charles 1956- *WhoMW 93*
Nestor, Lewis Ronal 1956- *WhoFI 94*
Nestor, Lula B. *WhoAmA 93*
Nestor, Lula B. 1935- *WhoMW 93*
Nestor, Tod Andrew 1963- *WhoFI 94*
Nestroy, Johann 1801-1862 *DcLB 133 [port], NinCLC 42 [port]*
Nestroy, Johann Nepomuk 1801-1862 *IntDcT 2 [port]*
Nestroy, Johann Nepomuk (Eduard Ambrosius) 1801-1862 *NewGrDO*
Nestvold, Elwood Olaf 1932- *WhoScEn 94*
Nesty, Glenn Albert 1911- *WhoWest 94*
Nesutan, Job d1675 *EncNAR*
Nesvadba, Josef 1926- *EncSF 93*
Net, Juan Antonio *WhoHisp 94*
Netanyahu, Benjamin 1949- *IntWW 93*
Netelenbos, Tineke 1944- *WhoWomW 91*
Netemeyer, Margaret 1950- *WhoAmL 94*
Neter, John 1923- *WhoAm 94*
Nethercut, Philip Edwin 1921- *WhoAm 94*
Nethercut, William Robert 1936- *WhoAm 94*
Nethercutt, Rolla Douglas 1968- *WhoMW 93*
Netherlands, H.R.H. Prince of the 1911- *IntWW 93*
Netherthorpe, Baron 1964- *Who 94*
Netherton, Jane 1945- *WhoFI 94*
Nethery, John Jay 1941- *WhoAm 94*
Nething, David E. *WhoAmP 93*
Neto, Antonio *WhoHisp 94*
Neto, Sebastiao De Souza Mattos 1951- *WhoAm 94*
Netravali, Arun N. 1946- *WhoAm 94*
Netsch, Dawn Clark 1926- *WhoAmP 93*
Nett, Carl Anthony 1941- *WhoAmP 93*
Nettelbeck, F. A. *DrAPF 93*
Nettels, Elsa 1931- *WhoAm 94*
Nettels, George E., Jr. 1927- *WhoAmP 93*
Nettels, George Edward, Jr. 1927- *WhoAm 94*
Netter, Cornelia Ann 1933- *WhoFI 94*
Netter, Douglas 1955?- *IntMPA 94*
Netter, Kurt Fred 1919- *WhoAm 94, WhoFI 94*
Netters, Tyrone Homer 1954- *WhoBlA 94*
Netterstrom, Henrik Munck 1924- *IntWW 93*
Netterville, George Leon, Jr. 1907- *WhoBlA 94*
Nettesheim, Christine Cook 1944- *CngDr 93, WhoAm 94, WhoAmL 94*
Netti, Giovanni Cesare 1649-1686 *NewGrDO*
Netting, Robert M. 1934- *WhoAm 94, WhoScEn 94, WhoWest 94*
Nettl, Bruno 1930- *WhoAm 94*
Nettle, Robert Dale 1924- *WhoMW 93*
Nettlefold, Joseph Henry 1827-1881 *DcNaB MP*
Nettleford, Rex Milton 1933- *WhoBlA 94*
Nettles, Albert Alexander, Jr. 1936- *WhoFI 94*
Nettles, Clem M. 1930- *WhoAmP 93*
Nettles, Eugene Leroy, Jr. 1954- *WhoAmP 93*
Nettles, John Barnwell 1922- *WhoAm 94*
Nettles, John Spratt 1943- *WhoBlA 94*
Nettles, Joseph Lee 1954- *WhoScEn 94*
Nettles, Louis David 1954- *WhoAmL 94*
Nettles, Nora Lee 1955- *WhoWest 94*
Nettles, Willard, Jr. 1944- *WhoBlA 94*
Nettleton, Asahel 1783-1844 *DcAmReB 2*
Nettleton, David *WhoAm 94*
Nettleton, John 1929- *WhoHol 92*
Nettleton, Lois 1930- *WhoHol 92*
Nettleton, Lois 1931- *IntMPA 94*
Netz, Charles Vail 1897- *WhAm 10*
Netzel, Paul Arthur 1941- *WhoFI 94, WhoWest 94*
Netzer, Dick 1928- *WhoAm 94*
Netzer, Lanore Agnes 1916- *WhoAm 94*
Netzky-Jolly, Wendy Heather 1955- *WhoWest 94*
Netzley, Robert E. 1922- *WhoAmP 93*
Netzloff, Michael Lawrence 1942- *WhoAm 94, WhoMW 93*
Neu, Arthur Alan 1933- *WhoAmP 93*
Neu, Carl Herbert, Jr. 1937- *WhoAm 94, WhoWest 94*
Neu, Charles Eric 1936- *WhoAm 94*
Neu, Harold Conrad 1934- *WhoAm 94*
Neubarth, Sanford L. 1948- *WhoIns 94*
Neubauer, Alex(ander) 1959- *WrDr 94*
Neubauer, Charles Frederick 1950- *WhoAm 94*
Neubauer, Franz Christoph c. 1760-1795 *NewGrDO*
Neubauer, Jeffrey S. 1955- *WhoAmP 93*
Neubauer, John Walter 1960- *WhoMW 93*
Neubauer, Joseph 1941- *WhoAm 94, WhoFI 94*
Neubauer, Mark Alan 1950- *WhoWest 94*
Neubauer, Michael Gerald 1954- *WhoWest 94*
Neubauer, Peter Bela 1913- *WhoAm 94*
Neubauer, Richard A. 1933- *WhoAm 94*
Neubauer, Werner George 1930- *WhoScEn 94*
Neuber, Friedel 1935- *IntWW 93*
Neuberger, Albert 1908- *IntWW 93, Who 94*
Neuberger, David Edmond 1948- *Who 94*
Neuberger, Egon 1925- *WhoAm 94, WhoFI 94*
Neuberger, Julia 1950- *WrDr 94*
Neuberger, Julia Babette Sarah 1950- *Who 94*
Neuberger, Maurine Brown 1964- *WhoAmP 93*
Neuberger, Michael Samuel 1953- *Who 94*
Neuberger, Rabbi Julia Babette Sarah 1950- *IntWW 93*
Neuberger, Roy R. 1903- *WhoAm 94, WhoAmA 93, WhoFI 94*
Neubert, George W. 1942- *WhoAm 94, WhoMW 93*
Neubert, George Walter 1942- *WhoAmA 93*
Neubert, Michael (John) 1933- *Who 94*
Neubert, Ralph Lewis 1922- *WhoFI 94*
Neubig, Herbert F. 1934- *WhoFI 94*
Neubohn, Naneen Hunter 1939- *WhoAm 94*
Neudeck, Gerold Walter 1936- *WhoAm 94*
Neudecker, Monsieur c. 1700-1733? *NewGrDO*
Neudoerffer, Volkmar Caj 1941- *WhoIns 94*
Neuefeind, Wilhelm 1939- *WhoAm 94, WhoFI 94*
Neuendorff, Adolph (Heinrich Anton Magnus) 1843-1897 *NewGrDO*
Neuenfels, Hans 1941- *NewGrDO*
Neuenschwander, Bob 1948- *WhoAmP 93*
Neuer, Kathleen *DrAPF 93*
Neuer, Philip David 1946- *WhoAmL 94*
Neufeld, Amos *DrAPF 93*
Neufeld, Arline E. 1952- *WhoHisp 94*
Neufeld, Edward P. 1937- *WhoMW 93*
Neufeld, Edward Peter 1927- *WhoAm 94*
Neufeld, Elizabeth Fondal 1928- *WhoAm 94*
Neufeld, Henry T. 1888-1968 *EncNAR*
Neufeld, John 1938- *Au&Arts 11 [port]*
Neufeld, John (Arthur) 1938- *TwCYAW*
Neufeld, Mace 1928- *IntMPA 94, WhoAm 94*
Neufeld, Melvin J. *WhoAmP 93*
Neufeld, Murray Jerome 1930- *WhoScEn 94*
Neufeld, Ronald David 1947- *WhoScEn 94*
Neuffer, Meredith Bowman d1993 *NewYTBS 93*
Neuffer, Myron Gerald 1922- *WhoMW 93*
Neufvic, Madame de fl. 17th cent.- *BlmGWL*
Neufville, Mortimer H. 1939- *WhoBlA 94*
Neugarten, Bernice Levin 1916- *IntWW 93, WhoAm 94*
Neugebauer, Gerry 1932- *WhoAm 94, WhoScEn 94, WhoWest 94*
Neugebauer, Joy Lois 1927- *WhoAmP 93*
Neugebauer, Marcia 1932- *WhoAm 94*
Neugebauer, Robert D. 1949- *WhoAmL 94*
Neugeberger, Margot 1929-1986 *WhoAmA 93N*
Neugeboren, Jay *DrAPF 93*
Neugeboren, Jay 1938- *WrDr 94*
Neuger, Sanford 1925- *WhoMW 93, WhoScEn 94*
Neugroschel, Arnost 1942- *WhoAm 94*
Neugroschel, Joachim *DrAPF 93*
Neuhard, James Richard 1944- *WhoAmL 94*
Neuhart, David M. 1952- *WhoAmL 94*
Neuharth, Allen H. 1924- *IntWW 93*
Neuharth, Allen Harold 1924- *WhoAm 94*
Neuharth, Daniel J., II 1953- *WhoWest 94*
Neuhaus, Cable 1947- *WhoWest 94*
Neuhaus, Max 1939- *WhoAm 94, WhoAmA 93*
Neuhaus, Otto Wilhelm 1922- *WhoAm 94*
Neuhaus, Philip Ross 1919- *WhoAm 94*
Neuhaus, Richard J(ohn) 1936- *WrDr 94*
Neuhaus, Rudolf 1914-1990 *NewGrDO*
Neuhausen, Benjamin Simon 1950- *WhoAm 94*
Neuhauser, Charles William, Jr. 1952- *WhoFI 94*
Neuhauser, Duncan von Briesen 1939- *IntWW 93, WhoAm 94*
Neuhauser, Mary 1934- *WhoAmP 93*
Neuhoff, Kathleen Toepp 1953- *WhoMW 93*
Neukirchen, Karl-Josef 1942- *IntWW 93*
Neukomm, Sigismund 1778-1858 *NewGrDO*
Neumaier, Gerhard John 1937- *WhoAm 94, WhoFI 94, WhoScEn 94*
Neumaier, Mark Adam 1958- *WhoAmL 94*
Neumaier, Robert Harold 1942- *WhoMW 93*
Neumaier, Robert Joseph 1951- *WhoAmP 93*
Neuman, B. Clifford 1963- *WhoWest 94*
Neuman, Charles P. 1940- *WhoAm 94, WhoScEn 94*
Neuman, Joan 1926- *WhoHol 92*
Neuman, K. Sidney 1936- *WhoAm 94*
Neuman, K. William 1945- *WhoAmL 94*
Neuman, Larry A. 1942- *WhoAmL 94*
Neuman, Linda 1948- *WhoAmP 93*
Neuman, Linda K. 1948- *WhoMW 93*
Neuman, Linda Kinney *WhoAmL 94, WhoMW 93*
Neuman, Michael Robert 1938- *WhoScEn 94*
Neuman, Nancy Adams Mosshammer 1936- *WhoAm 94*
Neuman, Robert Henry 1936- *WhoAm 94*
Neuman, Robert S. 1926- *WhoAmA 93*
Neuman, Robert Sterling 1926- *WhoAm 94*
Neuman, Shlomo P. 1938- *WhoAm 94*
Neuman, Ted 1946- *WhoAmP 93*
Neuman, William Lawrence, Jr. 1950- *WhoMW 93*
Neumann, Andrew Conrad 1933- *WhoAm 94, WhoScEn 94*
Neumann, Angelo 1838-1910 *NewGrDO*
Neumann, Arie Zodok 1961- *WhoFI 94*
Neumann, Bernhard Hermann 1909- *IntWW 93, Who 94, WhoScEn 94*
Neumann, Carl A. 1942- *WhoAmL 94*
Neumann, Charles August 1935- *WhoWest 94*
Neumann, Charles Henry 1943- *WhoFI 94*
Neumann, Donald Lee 1945- *WhoScEn 94*
Neumann, Dorothy *WhoHol 92*
Neumann, Eugene d1956 *WhoHol 92*
Neumann, Frantisek 1874-1929 *NewGrDO*
Neumann, Frederick Lloyd 1949- *WhoMW 93*
Neumann, Frederick Loomis 1930- *WhoAm 94, WhoFI 94*
Neumann, Gerhard *WhoScEn 94*
Neumann, Gerhard 1917- *WrDr 94*
Neumann, H. Denis 1938- *WhoWest 94*
Neumann, Harry 1930- *WhoAm 94*
Neumann, Herman Ernest 1931- *WhoWest 94*
Neumann, Herschel 1930- *WhoAm 94, WhoWest 94*
Neumann, Horst *NewGrDO*
Neumann, J. B. 1887-1961 *WhoAmA 93N*
Neumann, John Nepomucene 1811-1860 *DcAmReB 2*
Neumann, John von 1903-1957 *WorInv, WorScD [port]*
Neumann, Kurt d1958 *WhoHol 92*
Neumann, Nancy Ruth 1948- *WhoWest 94*
Neumann, Peter Gabriel 1932- *WhoScEn 94, WhoWest 94*
Neumann, Renee Anne 1951- *WhoWest 94*
Neumann, Rita 1944- *WhoAmL 94*
Neumann, Robert Gerhard 1916- *IntWW 93, WhoAm 94, WhoAmP 93*
Neumann, Robert William 1952- *WhoScEn 94*
Neumann, Roy Covert 1921- *WhoAm 94*
Neumann, Thomas William 1951- *WhoScEn 94*
Neumann, Vaclav 1920- *IntWW 93, NewGrDO*
Neumann, Vera d1993 *NewYTBS 93 [port]*
Neumann, Wilhelm Paul 1926- *WhoScEn 94*
Neumann, William 1934- *WhoMW 93*
Neumann, William A. 1924-1985 *WhoAmA 93N*
Neumann, William Allen 1944- *WhoAmL 94, WhoMW 93*
Neumann, Wolfgang 1945- *NewGrDO*
Neumann-Spallart, Gottfried 1915-1983 *NewGrDO*
Neumark, Dustin E. 1943- *WhoAmL 94*
Neumark, Michael Harry 1945- *WhoAm 94, WhoAmL 94, WhoMW 93*
Neumeier, John 1942- *IntDcB [port], IntWW 93, WhoAm 94*
Neumeier, Matthew Michael 1954- *WhoAmL 94, WhoFI 94, WhoMW 93*
Neumeier, Richard L. 1946- *WhoAmL 94*
Neumeyer, Alfred 1901-1973 *WhoAmA 93N*
Neumeyer, Jeffrey Daymon 1963- *WhoAmL 94*
Neumeyer, John Leopold 1930- *WhoScEn 94*
Neumeyer, Peter *DrAPF 93*
Neumeyer, Peter 1929- *WrDr 94*
Neumeyer, Peter Florian 1929- *WhoWest 94*
Neumiller, Louis Bontz 1896- *WhAm 10*
Neumiller, Phillip Joseph, III 1939- *WhoScEn 94*
Neuner, George William 1943- *WhoAmL 94*
Neurath, Hans 1909- *IntWW 93, WhoAm 94, WhoWest 94*
Neuringer, Leo J. d1993 *NewYTBS 93*
Neurrisse, Andre 1916- *IntWW 93*
Neus, Daniel Duane 1966- *WhoFI 94*
Neus, Michael Christopher 1961- *WhoAmL 94*
Neusner, Jacob 1932- *WhoAm 94, WrDr 94*
Neusom, Thomas G. 1922- *WhoBlA 94*
Neuspiel, Daniel Robert 1952- *WhoScEn 94*
Neuss, Karl Heinrich d1935 *WhoHol 92*
Neuss, Wolfgang d1989 *WhoHol 92*
Neustadt, Barbara Mae 1922- *WhoAm 94*
Neustadt, David Harold 1925- *WhoAm 94*
Neustadt, Richard E. 1919- *WrDr 94*
Neustadt, Richard Elliott 1919- *IntWW 93, WhoAm 94*
Neustein, Joshua 1940- *WhoAmA 93*
Neuthaler, Paul David 1942- *WhoAm 94*
Neutra, Richard 1892-1970 *WhoAmA 93N*
Neutra, Richard Josef 1892-1970 *AmCulL*
Neuts, Marcel Fernand 1935- *WhoWest 94*
Neutzling, Virginia Ruth 1942- *WhoMW 93*
Neutzsky-Wulff, Erwin *EncSF 93*
Neuville, Thomas M. 1950- *WhoAmP 93, WhoMW 93*
Neuvo, Yrjo A. 1943- *IntWW 93*
Neuwirth, Alan James 1943- *WhoAm 94, WhoAmL 94*
Neuwirth, Barbara *EncSF 93*
Neuwirth, Bebe *WhoAm 94, WhoHol 92*
Neuwirth, Bob *WhoHol 92*
Neuwirth, Eric 1957- *WhoFI 94*
Neuwirth, Lucien 1924- *IntWW 93*
Neuwirth, Robert Samuel 1933- *WhoAm 94*
Neva, Franklin Allen 1922- *WhoAm 94, WhoScEn 94*
Nevada, Emma 1859-1940 *NewGrDO*
Nevada, Mignon 1886-1971 *NewGrDO*
Nevai, Lucia *DrAPF 93*
Nevai, Paul 1948- *WhoMW 93*
Nevanlinna, Eero Olavi 1948- *IntWW 93*
Nevarez, Hector O. 1940- *WhoHisp 94*
Nevarez, Juan A. 1951- *WhoHisp 94*
Nevarez, Miguel A. 1937- *WhoHisp 94*
Nevas, Alan Harris 1928- *WhoAm 94, WhoAmL 94*
Neve, David Lewis d1992 *Who 94N*
Neveloff, Jay A. 1950- *WhoAm 94, WhoAmL 94*
Nevelskoy, Gennady Ivanovich 1814-1876 *WhWE*
Nevelson, Louise 1899-1988 *AmCulL, ModArCr 4 [port]*
Nevelson, Mike 1922- *WhoAmA 93*
Nevens, Paul *WhoHol 92*
Neverov, Valery Ivanovich 1952- *LngBDD*
Nevers, Ernie d1976 *ProFbHF*
Neverson, Norman Carl 1943- *WhoAmP 93*
Neves, Kerry Lane 1950- *WhoAmL 94*
Neves-Perman, Maria 1937- *WhoHisp 94*
Neveu, Raymond Philip 1938- *WhoFI 94*
Nevia, (Joseph Shepperd Rogers) *WhoAmA 93*
Neviaser, Robert Jon 1936- *WhoAm 94*
Nevil, Margaret d1993 *NewYTBS 93*
Nevil, Steve *WhoHol 92*
Nevile, Henry (Nicholas) 1920- *Who 94*
Nevill *Who 94*
Nevill, Bernard Richard 1934- *Who 94*
Nevill, Cosmo Alexander Richard 1907- *Who 94*
Nevill, Dorothy Fanny 1826-1913 *DcNaB MP*
Nevill, William Albert 1929- *WhoAm 94*
Neville *Who 94*

Ne Win, U. 1911- *IntWW 93*
Newing, John Frederick 1940- *Who 94*
Newing, Kenneth Albert 1923- *Who 94*
Newington, Michael (John) 1932- *Who 94*
Newinski, Dennis R. 1944- *WhoAmP 93*
Newis, Kenneth 1916- *Who 94*
Newitt, John Garwood, Jr. 1941- *WhoAmL 94, WhoFI 94*
Newkirk, Frank, Jr. 1957- *WhoAmP 93*
Newkirk, George L. 1941- *WhoAmP 93*
Newkirk, Gwendolyn *WhoBlA 94*
Newkirk, Inez Doris 1921- *WhoBlA 94*
Newkirk, John Burt 1920- *WhoAm 94*
Newkirk, Raymond Leslie 1944- *WhoFI 94, WhoWest 94*
Newkirk, Thomas Charles 1942- *WhoAmL 94*
Newkirk, Thomas H. 1929- *WhoBlA 94*
Newlan, Paul d1973 *WhoHol 92*
Newland, Anna Dewey d1967 *WhoHol 92*
Newland, Chester Albert 1930- *WhoAm*
Newland, David Edward 1936- *Who 94*
Newland, Douglass d1951 *WhoHol 92*
Newland, John 1917- *IntMPA 94, WhoHol 92*
Newland, Joseph Nelson 1953- *WhoAmA 93*
Newland, Julianna Marie 1958- *WhoMW 93*
Newland, Larry J. 1935- *WhoAm 94*
Newland, Mary 1905- *WhoHol 92*
Newland, Matthew J. 1967- *WhoAmP 93*
Newland, Ruth Laura 1949- *WhoFI 94, WhoWest 94*
Newland, Zachary Jonas 1954- *WhoBlA 94*
Newlands, Anthony 1926- *WhoHol 92*
Newlands, John Alexander Reina 1837-1898 *DcNaB MP*
Newley, Anthony 1931- *IntMPA 94, WhoHol 92*
Newley, (George) Anthony 1931- *Who 94*
Newley, Edward Frank 1913- *Who 94*
Newlin, Charles Fremont 1953- *WhoAm 94, WhoAmL 94*
Newlin, Douglas Randal 1940- *WhoWest 94*
Newlin, Lyman Wilbur 1910- *WhoAm 94, WhoFI 94*
Newlin, Margaret Rudd 1925- *WrDr 94*
Newlin, Michael H. 1926- *WhoAmP 93*
Newlin, Mike 1949- *BasBi*
Newlin, Rufus K. *WhoBlA 94*
Newlin, Sharon Dianne 1962- *WhoWest 94*
Newlin, William Rankin 1940- *WhoAm 94, WhoAmL 94*
Newling, Donald William 1941- *WhoScEn 94*
Newlove, John (Herbert) 1938- *WrDr 94*
Newman, Alfred d1970 *WhoHol 92*
Newman, Alfred 1901-1970 *IntDcF 2-4*
Newman, Alfred S. *IntMPA 94*
Newman, Amy S. 1961- *WhoAmL 94*
Newman, Anabel Powell *WhoMW 93*
Newman, Andrea 1938- *WrDr 94*
Newman, Andrew Edison 1944- *WhoAm 94, WhoFI 94, WhoMW 93*
Newman, Angela 1979 *WhoHol 92*
Newman, Anne *WhoHol 92*
Newman, Arnold 1918- *WhoAm 94, WhoAmA 93*
Newman, Aubrey N 1927- *WrDr 94*
Newman, Barbara 1953- *WhoMW 93*
Newman, Barbara (Pollock) 1939- *WrDr 94*
Newman, Barbara Mae 1932- *WhoMW 93*
Newman, Barnett 1905-1970 *AmCulL, WhoAmA 93N*
Newman, Barry 1938- *IntMPA 94, WhoHol 92*
Newman, Barry Hilton 1926- *Who 94*
Newman, Barry Ingalls 1932- *WhoAm 94*
Newman, Barry Marc 1951- *WhoMW 93*
Newman, Bernard 1897-1968 *EncSF 93*
Newman, Bernard 1907- *CngDr 93*
Newman, Betty Louise 1946- *WhoFI 94*
Newman, Bobby Gene 1926- *WhoAmP 93*
Newman, Bradley Presnell 1958- *WhoFI 94*
Newman, Brett 1961- *WhoScEn 94*
Newman, Bruce Allen 1943- *WhoAmP 93*
Newman, Bruce Lee 1936- *WhoAm 94*
Newman, C(oleman) J. 1935- *WrDr 94*
Newman, Candy d1966 *WhoHol 92*
Newman, Carol L. 1949- *WhoAm 94, WrDr 94*
Newman, Charles 1938- *WhoAm 94*
Newman, Charles (Hamilton) 1938- *WrDr 94*
Newman, Charles Andrew 1949- *WhoAm 94, WhoAmL 94*
Newman, Charles Forrest 1937- *WhoAmL 94*
Newman, Charles Judson 1950- *WhoFI 94*
Newman, Cliff 1942- *WhoAmP 93*
Newman, Colleen A. 1942- *WhoBlA 94*

Newman, Constance Berry 1935- *WhoBlA 94*
Newman, Cynthia Stair 1922- *WhoAmP 93*
Newman, Cyril Wilfred Francis 1937- *Who 94*
Newman, Daisy *WrDr 94*
Newman, Daniel F. *WhoAmP 93*
Newman, David *IntMPA 94*
Newman, David 1937- *IntMPA 94*
Newman, David, Jr. 1932- *WhoBlA 94*
Newman, David Wheeler 1952- *WhoAm 94*
Newman, Della M. 1932- *WhoAmP 93*
Newman, Denis 1930- *WhoAm 94, WhoFI 94*
Newman, Dennis Collins, Sr. 1932- *WhoFI 94*
Newman, Dennis Nathan 1946- *WhoAm 94*
Newman, Diana S. 1943- *WhoAm 94*
Newman, Don Melvin 1923- *WhoAm 94*
Newman, Donald John 1939- *WhoMW 93*
Newman, Donald Joseph 1924-1990 *WhAm 10*
Newman, Donald Rudd 1913- *WhoMW 93*
Newman, Doris Jean 1943- *WhoFI 94*
Newman, Dorothy G. 1917- *WhoAmP 93*
Newman, Edgar Leon 1939- *WhoWest 94*
Newman, Edward 1953- *Who 94*
Newman, Edwin 1919- *IntMPA 94*
Newman, Edwin (Harold) 1919- *WrDr 94*
Newman, Edwin Harold 1919- *IntWW 93, WhoAm 94*
Newman, Edwin Stanley 1922- *WhoAmL 94, WhoFI 94*
Newman, Elias 1903- *WhoAm 94*
Newman, Elizabeth H. *WhoAmA 93*
Newman, Elsie Louise 1943- *WhoMW 93, WhoScEn 94*
Newman, Eric Pfeiffer 1911- *WhoAm 94*
Newman, Ernest 1868-1959 *NewGrDO*
Newman, Ernest Wilbur 1928- *WhoBlA 94*
Newman, Felice *DrAPF 93*
Newman, Francis (Hugh Cecil) 1963- *Who 94*
Newman, Frank Cecil 1917- *WhoAm 94*
Newman, Frank Neil 1942- *WhoAm 94, WhoFI 94, WhoWest 94*
Newman, Fred C. 1931- *WhoIns 94*
Newman, Frederick Edward Fry 1916- *Who 94*
Newman, Fredric Samuel 1945- *WhoAm 94, WhoAmL 94*
Newman, G(ordon) F 1946- *WrDr 94*
Newman, G(ordon) F. 1947- *ConDr 93*
Newman, Geoffrey (Robert) 1947- *Who 94*
Newman, Geoffrey W. 1946- *WhoBlA 94*
Newman, George Michael 1941- *Who 94*
Newman, Gerald 1931-1992 *WhAm 10*
Newman, Geraldine Anne *WhoAm 94*
Newman, Gerard Kevin 1959- *WhoWest 94*
Newman, Gordon Harold 1933- *WhoAmL 94*
Newman, Grant Howard 1931- *WhoMW 93*
Newman, Gregory Alan 1953- *WhoWest 94*
Newman, Hank d1978 *WhoHol 92*
Newman, Harold Tolman 1916- *WhoAmP 93*
Newman, Harry Alan 1956- *WhoFI 94*
Newman, Harry Rudolph 1909- *WhoAm 94*
Newman, Howard Julian 1950- *WhoAm 94*
Newman, Howard Neal 1935- *WhoAm 94*
Newman, J. Robert 1928- *WhoWest 94*
Newman, Jack 1902- *Who 94*
Newman, James Michael 1946- *WhoAmL 94*
Newman, James Michael 1949- *WhoAm 94*
Newman, James Roy 1948- *WhoFI 94*
Newman, James Wilson 1909- *WhoAm 94*
Newman, Jan Bristow 1951- *WhoScEn 94*
Newman, Jane 1947- *WhoAm 94*
Newman, Janice Marie 1951- *WhoFI 94*
Newman, Jeffrey Hugh 1944- *WhoAmL 94*
Newman, Jeffrey Paul 1942- *WhoAmL 94*
Newman, Jeffrey Richard 1955- *WhoWest 94*
Newman, Jerrold Mitchell 1954- *WhoFI 94*
Newman, Jewel J. *WhoAmP 93*
Newman, Joan Meskiel 1947- *WhoAm 94, WhoAmL 94*
Newman, Jocelyn Margaret 1937- *WhoWomW 91*
Newman, Joe 1922-1992 *WhoBlA 94N*
Newman, Joel *DrAPF 93*
Newman, John *EncSF 93, WhoAmA 93*
Newman, John Beatty 1933- *WhoAmA 93*
Newman, John Dennis 1940- *WhoScEn 94*
Newman, John Henry 1801-1890 *BlmGEL, HisWorL [port]*

Newman, John Hughes 1945- *WhoScEn 94*
Newman, John Kevin 1928- *WhoAm 94*
Newman, John Koch d1927 *WhoHol 92*
Newman, John M., Jr. 1944- *WhoAm 94, WhoAmL 94*
Newman, John Nicholas 1935- *WhoAm 94*
Newman, John Robert 1932-1990 *WhAm 10*
Newman, John Scott 1938- *WhoAm 94*
Newman, John Sylvester, Jr. 1963- *WhoBlA 94*
Newman, Jon O. *WhoAmP 93*
Newman, Jon O. 1932- *WhoAm 94, WhoAmL 94*
Newman, Joseph H. 1928- *WhoAm 94*
Newman, Joseph James 1933- *WhoFI 94*
Newman, Joseph M. 1909- *IntMPA 94*
Newman, Joy *WhoHol 92*
Newman, Joyce Kligerman 1927- *WhoAm 94*
Newman, Julian M. 1927- *WhoIns 94*
Newman, Karen d1979 *WhoHol 92*
Newman, Karl Max 1919- *Who 94*
Newman, Karol Lyn 1949- *WhoAmL 94*
Newman, Katharine Dealy 1911- *WhoWest 94*
Newman, Kenneth (Leslie) 1926- *IntWW 93, Who 94*
Newman, Kenneth E. 1946- *WhoAm 94, WhoAmL 94*
Newman, Kenneth J. 1944- *WhoBlA 94*
Newman, Kim (James) 1959- *EncSF 93*
Newman, L(ouis) L(eon) 1898- *WhAm 10*
Newman, Laraine 1952- *IntMPA 94, WhoHol 92*
Newman, Lawrence 1931- *WhoAm 94*
Newman, Lawrence Walker 1935- *WhoAm 94, WhoAmL 94, WhoFI 94*
Newman, LeGrand 1940- *WhoBlA 94*
Newman, Leonard Jay 1927- *WhoFI 94*
Newman, Leslea *DrAPF 93*
Newman, Leslea 1955- *GayLL*
Newman, Leslie *DrAPF 93*
Newman, Libby *WhoAmA 93*
Newman, Linnaea Rose 1953- *WhoMW 93*
Newman, Lisa Ann 1952- *WhoScEn 94*
Newman, Lois d1987 *WhoHol 92*
Newman, Lois Mae 1942- *WhoWest 94*
Newman, Lotte Therese 1929- *Who 94*
Newman, Louis 1947- *WhoAmA 93*
Newman, Louis Benjamin 1951- *WhAm 10*
Newman, Malcolm 1946- *Who 94*
Newman, Marc Alan 1955- *WhoScEn 94, WhoWest 94*
Newman, Margaret 1926- *WrDr 94*
Newman, Marie Stefanini 1951- *WhoAmL 94*
Newman, Marion d1982 *WhoHol 92*
Newman, Mark M 1935- *WhoAmP 93*
Newman, Melissa *WhoHol 92*
Newman, Melvin Spencer 1908- *IntWW 93, WhoAm 94*
Newman, Michael 1948- *WhoAmL 94*
Newman, Michael Rodney 1945- *WhoAmL 94, WhoWest 94*
Newman, Miller Maurice 1941- *WhoBlA 94*
Newman, Monroe 1929- *WhoAm 94*
Newman, Morris 1924- *WhoAm 94*
Newman, Muriel Kallis Steinberg 1914- *WhoAm 94*
Newman, Murray Arthur 1924- *WhoAm 94, WhoWest 94*
Newman, Nancy Marilyn 1941- *WhoWest 94*
Newman, Nanette *IntWW 93*
Newman, Nanette 1932- *WhoHol 92*
Newman, Nanette 1934- *IntMPA 94*
Newman, Nanette 1939- *Who 94*
Newman, Nathaniel 1942- *WhoBlA 94*
Newman, Neil Jay 1939- *WhoAmL 94*
Newman, Nell d1931 *WhoHol 92*
Newman, Nicholas C. 1939- *WhoAmL 94*
Newman, Nigel Kevin 1941- *WhoMW 93*
Newman, Norman 1952- *WhoAm 94, WhoAmL 94*
Newman, Oscar 1935- *WrDr 94*
Newman, Otto 1922- *WhoWest 94*
Newman, P. B. *DrAPF 93*
Newman, P(aul) B(aker) 1919- *WrDr 94*
Newman, Paul *WhoHol 92*
Newman, Paul 1925- *IntMPA 94, IntWW 93, Who 94, WhoAm 94, WhoHol 92*
Newman, Paul Dean 1938- *WhoBlA 94*
Newman, Paul Richard 1947- *WhoScEn 94*
Newman, Paul Wayne 1955- *WhoScEn 94*
Newman, Pauline *WhoAmP 93*
Newman, Pauline 1927- *CngDr 93, WhoAm 94, WhoAmL 94*
Newman, Peter (Charles) 1929- *WrDr 94*
Newman, Peter C. 1929- *IntWW 93*
Newman, Peter Charles 1929- *WhoAm 94*

Newman, Peter Kenneth 1928- *WhoAm 94*
Newman, Philip Harker 1911- *Who 94*
Newman, Philip Robert 1942- *WhoMW 93*
Newman, Phillip Barbour, III 1932- *WhoAm 94*
Newman, Phyllis 1933- *WrDr 94*
Newman, Phyllis 1935- *WhoHol 92*
Newman, Rachel 1938- *WhoAm 94*
Newman, Ralph Geoffrey 1911- *WhoAm 94*
Newman, Randy 1943- *IntMPA 94, WhoAm 94*
Newman, Raymond Melvin 1956- *WhoMW 93, WhoScEn 94*
Newman, Rebecca *DrAPF 93*
Newman, Richard Alan 1930- *WhoAm 94*
Newman, Richard Charles 1938- *WhoAmA 93*
Newman, Richard Oakley 1920- *WhoAm 94*
Newman, Rick G. 1958- *WhoAmP 93*
Newman, Robert Gabriel 1937- *WhoAm 94*
Newman, Robert Joseph 1928- *WhoAm 94*
Newman, Robert Melville 1963- *WhoWest 94*
Newman, Robert William 1933- *WhoAm 94*
Newman, Robert Wyckoff 1951- *WhoScEn 94*
Newman, Roger *WhoHol 92*
Newman, Roy (Thomas) 1936- *Who 94*
Newman, Samuel 1938- *WhoAm 94*
Newman, Sanders David 1930- *WhoAmL 94*
Newman, Sarah Casey 1946- *WhoMW 93*
Newman, Sarah Winans 1941- *WhoMW 93*
Newman, Scott d1978 *WhoHol 92*
Newman, Scott David 1947- *WhoAm 94, WhoAmL 94*
Newman, Sharan (Hill) 1949- *WrDr 94*
Newman, Sheldon Oscar 1923- *WhoAm 94*
Newman, Simon Louis 1947- *WhoScEn 94*
Newman, Simon Philip 1963- *WhoFI 94*
Newman, Slater Edmund 1924- *WhoAm 94*
Newman, Sol *DrAPF 93*
Newman, Sophie 1925- *WhoAmA 93*
Newman, Stanley Ray 1923- *WhoScEn 94, WhoWest 94*
Newman, Stephen Alexander 1938- *WhoAm 94*
Newman, Stephen D. 1964- *WhoAmP 93*
Newman, Stephen L. 1952- *WrDr 94*
Newman, Stephen Michael 1945- *WhoAm 94, WhoAmL 94*
Newman, Steven H. 1943- *WhoIns 94*
Newman, Steven Harvey 1943- *WhoAm 94*
Newman, Stuart 1947- *WhoAm 94, WhoAmL 94*
Newman, Stuart (Richard) 1919- *Who 94*
Newman, Susan Kendall 1953- *WhoHol 92*
Newman, Suzanne Dinkes 1949- *WhoFI 94*
Newman, Sydney *IntMPA 94*
Newman, Sydney Cecil 1917- *Who 94*
Newman, Terrie Lynne *WhoFI 94*
Newman, Terry E. 1947- *WhoAm 94, WhoAmL 94*
Newman, Theodore R., Jr. 1934- *WhoAmP 93*
Newman, Theodore Roosevelt, Jr. 1934- *WhoAm 94, WhoBlA 94*
Newman, Thomas *WhoHol 92*
Newman, Thomas G. 1931- *WhoAmP 93*
Newman, Thomas Rubin 1933- *WhoAm 94, WhoAmL 94*
Newman, Wade *DrAPF 93*
Newman, Wade Davis 1936- *WhoAm 94*
Newman, Walter Andrews, Jr. 1930- *WhoAmA 93*
Newman, Walter Brown 1920- *IntMPA 94*
Newman, William 1926- *WhoAm 94, WhoFI 94*
Newman, William Bernard, Jr. 1950- *WhoAm 94, WhoAmL 94, WhoFI 94*
Newman, William Daniel 1963- *WhoWest 94*
Newman, William Louis 1920- *WhoAm 94*
Newman, William Morris, Jr. 1949- *WhoAmL 94*
Newman, William S. 1912- *WrDr 94*
Newman, William Stein 1912- *WhoAm 94*
Newman, William Thomas, Jr. 1950- *WhoBlA 94*
Newman-Gordon, Pauline 1925- *WhoAm 94*
Newman-Rice, Nancy 1950- *WhoAmA 93*
Newmar, Julie 1933- *IntMPA 94*
Newmar, Julie 1935- *WhoHol 92*

Newmarch, Michael George 1938-
IntWW 93, Who 94
Newmarch, Rosa 1857-1940 NewGrDO
Newmark, Emanuel 1936- WhoAm 94,
WhoScEn 94
Newmark, Herbert Lawrence 1924-
WhoWest 94
Newmark, Howard 1944- WhoFI 94
Newmark, Leonard 1929- WrDr 94
Newmark, Leonard Daniel 1929-
WhoAm 94
Newmark, Marilyn 1928- WhoAmA 93
Newmark, Milton Maxwell 1916-
WhoAmL 94
Newmark, Richard Alan 1940-
WhoMW 93
Newmeyer, Frederick Jaret 1944-
WhoAm 94
Newnam, Brian Emerson 1941-
WhoWest 94
Newnham, Ian Frederick Montague
d1993 Who 94N
Newnham, Robert Everest 1929-
WhoAm 94
Newns, (Alfred) Foley (Francis Polden)
1909- Who 94
New Order ConMus 11 [port]
Newpher, James Alfred, Jr. 1930-
WhoMW 93
Newport, Viscount 1980- Who 94
Newport, Brian John 1958- WhoScEn 94
Newport, Christopher c. 1565-1617
WhWE
Newport, John Paul 1917- WhoAm 94
Newquist, Don 1943- WhoAm 94
Newquist, Don E. WhoAmP 93
Newquist, Donald Stewart 1953-
WhoWest 94
Newry and Morne, Viscount 1966-
Who 94
News, Kathryn Anne 1934- WhoAm 94
Newsam, Peter (Anthony) 1928- Who 94
Newsom, Barbara Ylvisaker 1926-
WhoAmA 93
Newsom, Carolyn Cardall 1941-
WhoAm 94
Newsom, Carroll Vincent 1904-1990
WhAm 10
Newsom, David A. 1946- WhoAmL 94
Newsom, David D. 1918- WhoAmP 93
Newsom, David Dunlop 1918- IntWW 93,
WhoAm 94
Newsom, Douglas Ann Johnson 1934-
WhoAm 94
Newsom, George Edward 1919-
WhoAmP 93
Newsom, Gerald Higley 1939- WhoAm 94
Newsom, James T. 1944- WhoAm 94
Newsom, John H. 1961- WhoFI 94
Newsom, Lionel Hodge 1919-1991
WhAm 10
Newsom, Melvin Max 1931- WhoAm 94
Newsom, Will Roy 1912- WhoAm 94
Newsom-Davis, John Michael 1932-
Who 94
Newsome, Burnell 1938- WhoBlA 94
Newsome, Clarence Geno 1950-
WhoBlA 94
Newsome, Cola King 1925- WhoBlA 94
Newsome, David Hay 1929- Who 94,
WrDr 94
Newsome, Elisa C. 1964- WhoBlA 94
Newsome, Emanuel T. 1942- WhoBlA 94
Newsome, George Lane, Jr. 1923-
WhoAm 94
Newsome, George Marvin 1919-
WhoAmL 94
Newsome, Joseph E. 1955- WhoAmP 93
Newsome, Moses, Jr. 1944- WhoBlA 94
Newsome, Ozzie 1956- WhoBlA 94
Newsome, Paula Renee 1955- WhoBlA 94
Newsome, Randall Jackson 1950-
WhoAm 94, WhoAmL 94, WhoWest 94
Newsome, Ronald Wright 1949-
WhoBlA 94
Newsome, Steven Cameron 1952-
WhoBlA 94
Newsome, Vincent Karl 1961- WhoBlA 94
Newsome, William Antony 1919- Who 94
Newsome, William Roy, Jr. 1934-
WhoAm 94
Newson, Roosevelt, Jr. 1946- WhoBlA 94
Newson, Warren Dale 1964- WhoBlA 94
Newson-Smith, John (Kenneth) 1911-
Who 94
Newstead, Robert Richard 1935-
WhoWest 94
Newsetter, Wilber Irvin 1896- WhAm 10
Newte, Horace (Wykeham Can)
1870-1949 EncSF 93
Newth, Rebecca DrAPF 93
Newton, Baron 1950- Who 94
Newton, A. Edward 1864-1940
DcLB 140 [port]
Newton, Alexander Worthy 1930-
WhoAmL 94
Newton, Andrew E., Jr. 1943- WhoBlA 94
Newton, Antony Harold 1937- Who 94

Newton, Antony Harold (Tony) 1937-
IntWW 93
Newton, Barry Hamilton 1932- Who 94
Newton, Benjamin Wills 1807-1899
DcNaB MP
Newton, Bert WhoHol 92
Newton, Blake Tyler, III 1942- WhoAm 94
Newton, Carl Elbridge 1898-1989
WhAm 10
Newton, Charles d1926 WhoHol 92
Newton, Charles Chartier 1933-
WhoAm 94
Newton, Charles Oliver 1947-
WhoAmP 93
Newton, Christopher WhoAm 94
Newton, Christopher 1938- IntWW 93
Newton, Clive Trevor 1931- Who 94
Newton, Crystal Hoffman 1956-
WhoScEn 94
Newton, D(wight) B(ennett) 1916-
WrDr 94
Newton, David A. 1942- IntWW 93
Newton, David C. EncSF 93
Newton, David E(dward) 1933- WrDr 94
Newton, David G. 1935- WhoAmP 93
Newton, Demetrius C. WhoAmP 93
Newton, Demetrius C. 1928- WhoBlA 94
Newton, Derek Arnold 1930- WhoAm 94
Newton, Derek Henry 1933- Who 94
Newton, Douglas 1920- WhoAm 94,
WhoAmA 93
Newton, Douglas Anthony d1993
Who 94N
Newton, Earle Williams 1917- WhoAm 94,
WhoAmA 93
Newton, Eric Christopher 1965-
WhoBlA 94
Newton, Ernest E., II 1956- WhoBlA 94
Newton, Ernest Eugene, II 1956-
WhoAmP 93
Newton, Floyd Childs, III 1955-
WhoAmL 94
Newton, Francis 1917- WrDr 94
Newton, Frank Cota-Robles 1946-
WhoHisp 94
Newton, Gale JoAnn 1954- WhoFI 94
Newton, George Addison 1911-
WhoAm 94, WhoMW 93
Newton, George Durfee, Jr. 1931-
WhoAm 94, WhoFI 94
Newton, George Washington 1947-
WhoIns 94
Newton, Gordon Who 94
Newton, (Leslie) Gordon 1907-
IntWW 93, Who 94
Newton, Grace Hamilton d1958
WhoAmA 93N
Newton, Helmut 1920- IntWW 93
Newton, Huey P. 1942-1989
AfrAmAl 6 [port], HisWorL
Newton, Huey Percy 1942-1989 AmSocL
Newton, Ian Who 94
Newton, Ian 1940- Who 94
Newton, (Robert Edward) Ian 1946-
Who 94
Newton, Irving d1980 WhoHol 92
Newton, Isaac 1642-1727 AstEnc,
BlmGEL, WorScD [port]
Newton, Jacqueline L. WhoBlA 94
Newton, James Christopher 1970-
WhoAmP 93
Newton, James Douglas, Jr. 1949-
WhoBlA 94
Newton, James E. 1941- WhoBlA 94
Newton, James Quigg, Jr. 1911-
WhoAm 94
Newton, Jean S. 1952- WhoMW 93
Newton, Jeffrey F. WhoScEn 94
Newton, John 1925- WhoHol 92
Newton, John Anthony 1930- Who 94
Newton, John David 1921- Who 94
Newton, John Edward, Jr. 1954-
WhoAmL 94, WhoFI 94
Newton, John Michael 1935- Who 94
Newton, John Milton 1929- WhoAm 94
Newton, John Neil 1933- WhoAmA 93
Newton, John Oswald 1924- IntWW 93
Newton, John Thomas 1936- WhoFI 94
Newton, John Wharton, III 1953-
WhoAmL 94
Newton, Jon P. WhoAmL 94
Newton, Joseph Fort 1876-1950
DcAmReB 2
Newton, Julius P. EncSF 93
Newton, Kenneth 1940- WrDr 94
Newton, Kenneth (Garnar) 1918- Who 94
Newton, Lisa Haenlein 1939- WhoAm 94
Newton, Margaret 1893-1960
WhoAmA 93N
Newton, Margaret 1927- Who 94
Newton, Maxwell 1929-1990 WhAm 10
Newton, Melvin T. d1991 WhoBlA 94N
Newton, Michael Who 94
Newton, (Harry) Michael (Rex) 1923-
Who 94
Newton, Niles Rumely 1923- WhoAm 94
Newton, Norman Lewis 1929- WrDr 94

Newton, Norman Thomas (King)
1898-1992 WhAm 10
Newton, Oliver A., Jr. 1925- WhoBlA 94
Newton, Oscar Lee, Jr. 1927- WhoIns 94
Newton, Peter Marcus 1942- Who 94
Newton, Pynkerton Dion 1960-
WhoMW 93
Newton, Ralph d1977 WhoHol 92
Newton, Ray Clyde 1935- WhoWest 94
Newton, Rhonwen Leonard 1940-
WhoFI 94, WhoScEn 94
Newton, Richard Aaron 1935- WhoAm 94
Newton, Richard Edward 1948-
WhoAmA 93
Newton, Richard Howard 1932-
WhoWest 94
Newton, Richard James 1927- Who 94
Newton, Richard Wayne 1948-
WhoScEn 94
Newton, Robert d1956 WhoHol 92
Newton, Robert 1944- WhoBlA 94
Newton, Robert Eugene 1917- WhoAm 94
Newton, Robert George 1948-
WhoMW 93
Newton, Robert James 1946- WhoWest 94
Newton, Robert Park, Jr. 1913-1988
WhAm 10
Newton, Robin Caprice 1957- WhoBlA 94
Newton, Ronald Gordon 1912- IntWW 93
Newton, Sean Curry 1959- WhoScEn 94
Newton, Stacy d1987 WhoHol 92
Newton, Steven Lopez 1953- WhoHisp 94
Newton, Suzanne DrAPF 93
Newton, Suzanne 1936- SmATA 77 [port],
WrDr 94
Newton, Thandie WhoHol 92
Newton, Theodore d1963 WhoHol 92
Newton, Thomas Howard 1962-
WhoFI 94
Newton, Trevor 1943- Who 94
Newton, V. Miller 1938- WhoScEn 94
Newton, Verne W. 1944- ConAu 141
Newton, Verne Wester 1944- WhoAm 94
Newton, Virginia 1938- WhoAm 94
Newton, W(ilfrid) Douglas 1884-1951
EncSF 93
Newton, Warren S., Jr. 1938- WhoIns 94
Newton, Wayne 1942- ConTFT 11,
WhoAm 94, WhoHol 92, WhoWest 94
Newton, Wilfrid Who 94
Newton, (Charles) Wilfrid 1928-
IntWW 93, Who 94
Newton, William Allen, Jr. 1923-
WhoAm 94
Newton-Clare, Herbert Mitchell 1922-
Who 94
Newton Dunn, William Francis 1941-
Who 94
Newton-John, Olivia 1948- IntMPA 94,
IntWW 93, WhoAm 94, WhoHol 92
Newton-John, Rona WhoHol 92
Newton-Skelley, Martha Louise 1949-
WhoFI 94
Newtson, Richard Evan 1950-
WhoMW 93
Newtz, Joseph Clem 1965- WhoFI 94
New Zealand, Primate and Archbishop of
1934- Who 94
Nex, Andre WhoHol 92
Nexon, Hubert Henry 1917-1990
WhAm 10
Nexsen, Julian Jacobs 1924- WhoAm 94
Ney, Edward 1920- IntWW 93
Ney, Edward N. 1925- WhoAm 94,
WhoAmP 93
Ney, Edward Noonan 1925- IntWW 93
Ney, Ferenc EncSF 93
Ney, James Walter Edward Colby 1932-
WhoAm 94
Ney, Jenny 1824-1886 NewGrDO
Ney, Marie d1981 WhoHol 92
Ney, Michael Vincent 1947- WhoMW 93
Ney, Richard 1915- WhoHol 92
Ney, Richard 1917- IntMPA 94
Ney, Robert Terrence 1944- WhoAm 94,
WhoAmL 94
Ney, Robert William 1954- WhoAmP 93
Ney, Ronald Ellroy, Jr. 1936-
WhoScEn 94
Neyens, Deborah M. 1965- WhoAmL 94
Neyer, Joseph 1913-1989 WhAm 10
Neyhouse, Rose M. 1948- WhoMW 93
Neylan, John Francis, III 1953-
WhoScEn 94
Neylan, Kathleen Mary 1944-
WhoAmP 93
Neyland, Leedell Wallace 1921-
WhoBlA 94
Neylon, James M. DrAPF 93
Neylon, Martin Joseph 1920- WhoAm 94
Neyts-Uytterbroeck, Anne-Marie 1944-
WhoWoW 91
Nezadal, Maria 1897- NewGrDO
Nezeritis, Andreas 1897- IntWW 93
Nezeritis, Andreas 1897-1980 NewGrDO
Nezhad, Hameed Gholam 1941-
WhoScEn 94

Nezhdanova, Antonina 1873-1950
NewGrDO
Nezu, Christine Maguth 1952-
WhoScEn 94
Nezval, Jiri 1941- IntWW 93
N.F.B.A. BlmGWL
Ng, Anastacio C. 1933- WhoAsA 94
Ng, Assunta C. M. 1951- WhoAsA 94
Ng, David 1934- WhoAsA 94
Ng, Fae Myenne DrAPF 93
Ng, Fae Myenne 1957?- ConLC 81 [port]
Ng, Frank Mang Leang 1950- WhoAsA 94
Ng, Gerald Joe Lup 1946- WhoWest 94
Ng, Jeanne H. 1950- WhoAsA 94
Ng, Jeffrey C. F. 1953- WhoAsA 94
Ng, Kam Wing 1951- WhoAsA 94
Ng, Kheng Siang 1960- WhoScEn 94
Ng, Kwok-Wai 1958- WhoScEn 94
Ng, Lawrence Chen-Yim 1946-
WhoWest 94
Ng, Lawrence Ming-Loy 1940-
WhoWest 94
Ng, Lewis Yok-Hoi 1955- WhoMW 93,
WhoScEn 94
Ng, Martin K. 1952- WhoAsA 94
Ng, May-May Donna Lee 1952-
WhoAsA 94
Ng, Michael Wai-Man 1960- WhoAsA 94
Ng, Patrick 1944- WhoAsA 94
Ng, Peter A. 1941- WhoAsA 94
Ng, Rebecca P. 1962- WhoAsA 94
Ng, Richard 1964- WhoAsA 94
Ng, Richard Yut 1952- WhoAsA 94
Ng, Rita Mei-Ching 1958- WhoAsA 94
Ng, Tang-Tat Percy 1960- WhoAsA 94
Ng, Thomas WhoAsA 94
Ng, Vincent W. 1954- WhoAsA 94
Ng, Wing 1956- WhoAsA 94
Ng, Wing Chiu 1947- WhoFI 94,
WhoWest 94
Ng, Yuk-Chow 1955- WhoAsA 94
Ngai, Ka-Leung 1950- WhoMW 93,
WhoScEn 94
Ngai, Kia Ling 1940- WhoAsA 94
Ngai, Shih Hsun 1920- WhoAsA 94
Ngaiza, Christopher Pastor 1930- Who 94
Ngapoi Cedan Zhoigar 1919-
WhoPRCh 91 [port]
Ngapoi Ngawang Jigme 1911-
WhoPRCh 91 [port]
Ngapoi Ngawang Jigmi, Lieut.-Gen.
1911- IntWW 93
Ngapo Ngawang-Jigme IntWW 93
Ngata, Henare Kohere 1917- Who 94
Ng-Breckwoldt, May Sue 1958-
WhoAsA 94
Ng Cheng Kiat, Encik 1941- IntWW 93
Ngcobo, Lauretta 1932- BlmGWL
Ngei, Paul 1923- IntWW 93
Ngema, Mbongeni ConDr 93
Ngema, Mbongeni 1955- BlkWr 2
Ng'ethe Njoroge Who 94
Nghiem, Long Xuan 1952- WhoScEn 94
Nghiem, Son Van WhoScEn 94
Ngo, David 1960- WhoAsA 94
Ngo Dinh Diem 1901-1963
HisWorL [port]
Ngo Dinh Nhu, Madame IntWW 93
Ngonda, Putteho Muketoi 1936-
IntWW 93, Who 94
Ngor, Haing S. ConTFT 11, WhoAsA 94
Ngor, Haing S. 1950- IntMPA 94,
WhoHol 92
Nguema Mbasogo, Teodoro Obiang
IntWW 93
Ngugi, J(ames) T. 1938- WrDr 94
Ngugi, James T(hiong'o) BlkWr 2
Ngugi, wa Thiong'o 1938- ConDr 93,
IntWW 93
Ngugi wa Thiong'o 1938- BlkWr 2,
IntDcT 2, WrDr 94
Ngurukie, Pat Wambui 1948- BlmGWL
Nguya, Lydiah Mumbi BlmGWL
Nguyen, An H. 1950- WhoAsA 94
Nguyen, Anh Mai 1957- WhoAsA 94
Nguyen, Ann Cac Khue WhoScEn 94,
WhoWest 94
Nguyen, Ann Thi WhoFI 94
Nguyen, Ban Mau 1933- WhoAsA 94
Nguyen, Bao Gia 1954- WhoAsA 94
Nguyen, Bao T. WhoAsA 94
Nguyen, Benjamin Ban 1933- WhoAsA 94
Nguyen, Bong Van 1954- WhoAsA 94
Nguyen, Cam 1954- WhoAsA 94
Nguyen, Caroline P. 1962- WhoAsA 94
Nguyen, Charles C. 1956- WhoAsA 94
Nguyen, Charles Cuong 1956- WhoFI 94
Nguyen, Chris Cuong Manh 1947-
WhoAsA 94
Nguyen, Chuong Van 1957- WhoAsA 94
Nguyen, Cu D. 1954- WhoAsA 94
Nguyen, Cuong Phu 1964- WhoAsA 94
Nguyen, Duc Ba 1963- WhoAsA 94
Nguyen, Dung Dang 1950- WhoAsA 94
Nguyen, Hao Marc 1967- WhoScEn 94
Nguyen, Henry Thien 1954- WhoAsA 94
Nguyen, Hien Vu 1943- WhoAsA 94
Nguyen, Ho Ngoc 1946- WhoAsA 94

Nguyen, Hue Le 1968- WhoWest 94
Nguyen, Hue Thi 1951- WhoAsA 94
Nguyen, Kim-Oanh Thi 1960- WhoAsA 94
Nguyen, King Xuan 1930- WhoWest 94
Nguyen, Long 1958- WhoAmA 93, WhoAsA 94
Nguyen, Luu Thanh 1954- WhoAsA 94
Nguyen, Manh-Hung 1937- WhoAsA 94
Nguyen, Mike Chi 1956- WhoAsA 94
Nguyen, Nghia Van 1941- WhoAsA 94
Nguyen, Ngoc-Diep Thi 1958- WhoAsA 94
Nguyen, Philong 1956- WhoScEn 94
Nguyen, Quan A. 1960- WhoScEn 94
Nguyen, Tan Dinh 1956- WhoWest 94
Nguyen, Thinh Van 1948- WhoWest 94
Nguyen, Thuan Ke WhoAsA 94
Nguyen, Tien Manh 1957- WhoScEn 94, WhoWest 94
Nguyen, Tinh 1948- WhoScEn 94
Nguyen, Tony C. 1948- WhoAsA 94
Nguyen, Tri Huu 1936- WhoAsA 94
Nguyen, Truc Chinh 1960- WhoScEn 94
Nguyen, Trung Duc 1951- WhoWest 94
Nguyen, Tuan Anh 1956- WhoWest 94
Nguyen, Van Thanh 1946- WhoFI 94
Nguyen, Vu Linh 1966- WhoWest 94
Nguyen, Vung Duy 1938- WhoAsA 94
Nguyen, Xe V. 1948- WhoAsA 94
Nguyen Cao Ky, Air Vice-Marshal 1930- IntWW 93
Nguyen Co Thach 1923- IntWW 93
Nguyen-Dinh, Thanh 1950- WhoScEn 94
Nguyen-huu, Xuong 1933- WhoAsA 94
Nguyen Huu Tho 1910- IntWW 93
Nguyen Khanh, Lieut.-Gen. 1927- IntWW 93
Nguyen Phu Duc 1924- IntWW 93
Nguyen Thi Binh 1927- WhoWomW 91
Nguyen Thi Binh, Madame 1927- IntWW 93
Nguyen-Trong, Hoang 1936- WhoScEn 94
Nguyen Van Linh 1913- IntWW 93
Nguyen Van Loc 1922- IntWW 93
Nguyen Van Thieu, Lt.-Gen. 1923- IntWW 93
Nguyen Van Vy, Lt.-Gen. 1916- IntWW 93
Nguza Karl-I-Bond 1938- IntWW 93
Nhu, Madame IntWW 93
Ni, Preston C. 1964- WhoAsA 94
Ni, Wayne Weijen 1961- WhoWest 94
Niagara, Bishop of 1932- Who 94
Niall, Horace Lionel Richard 1904- Who 94
Nian Weisi WhoPRCh 91
Niarchos, Stavros Spyros 1909- IntWW 93, Who 94
Niare, Seydou 1933- IntWW 93
Niasse, Cheikh Moustapha 1939- IntWW 93
Niatum, Duane DrAPF 93
Niazi, Maulana Kausar 1934- IntWW 93
Nibbelink, Cynthia DrAPF 93
Nibbering, Nicolaas Martinus Maria 1938- IntWW 93
Nibbs, Alphonse, Sr. 1947- WhoBlA 94
Niblack, Terry L. WhoScEn 94
Niblett, Gary Lawrence 1943- WhoAmA 93
Niblett, William Roy WrDr 94
Niblett, William Roy 1906- Who 94
Nibley, Andrew Mathews 1951- WhoAm 94
Nibley, Robert Ricks 1913- WhoAm 94, WhoAmL 94, WhoWest 94
Niblo, Fred d1948 WhoHol 92
Niblock, Henry 1911- Who 94
Niblock, James Stewart 1959- WhoMW 93
Niblock, Phill 1933- WhoAmA 93
Niblock, Walter Raymond 1927- WhoAm 94
Niboyet, Eugenie 1797-1883 BlmGWL
Nic, Eileen d1993 NewYTBS 93
Nicandros, Constantine Stavros 1933- WhoAm 94, WhoFI 94
Nicastro, David Harlan 1961- WhoScEn 94
Nicastro, Francesco Vito Mario 1953- WhoScEn 94
Nicastro, Francis Efisio 1942- WhoAm 94
Nicastro, Michelle WhoHol 92
Nicaud, Philippe 1926- WhoHol 92
Nicco-Annan, Lionel WhoBlA 94
Niccolini, Drew George 1945- WhoScEn 94
Niccolini, Giuseppe NewGrDO
Niccolino NewGrDO
Niccum, Thomas Milton 1957- WhoMW 93
Nice, Carter 1940- WhoAm 94, WhoWest 94
Nice, Charles Monroe, Jr. 1919- WhoAm 94
Nice, Don 1932- WhoAmA 93
Nice, Geoffrey 1945- Who 94
Nice, James William 1948- WhoWest 94
Nice, Pamela Michele 1949- WhoMW 93
Nice, Robert Harold 1950- WhoFI 94
Niceley, Frank S. 1947- WhoAmP 93
Nicely, Constance Marie 1955- WhoMW 93
Nicely, Kip W. 1954- WhoAmP 93
Nicely, Philip A. 1942- WhoAmL 94
Nicely, Timothy 1944- WhoWest 94
Nicely, William Perry Amos 1922- WhoAmP 93
Nicewander, Dan Leon 1941- WhoAm 94
Nicewander, Walter Alan 1939- WhoScEn 94
Nichaus, Manfred 1933- NewGrDO
Nichetti, Maurizio WhoHol 92
Ni Chih-Fu IntWW 93
Nichol, Alice J. 1939- WhoAmP 93
Nichol, Douglas 1947- WhoScEn 94
Nichol, Doyle L. 1952- WhoAmP 93
Nichol, Duncan (Kirkbride) 1941- Who 94
Nichol, Francis David 1897- WhAm 10
Nichol, Fred Joseph 1912- WhoAm 94
Nichol, Henry Ferris 1911- WhoAm 94
Nichol, Lawrence Walter 1935- IntWW 93, Who 94
Nichol, Norman J. 1944- WhoAm 94
Nichol, Patricia Who 94
Nichol, (Daphne) Patricia 1932- Who 94
Nichol, Victor E., Jr. WhoAm 94, WhoFI 94
Nichol, William E. 1918- WhoAmP 93
Nicholas, St. BlmGEL
Nicholas, II 1868-1918 HisWorL [port]
Nicholas, Arthur Soterios 1930- WhoAm 94
Nicholas, Barry Who 94
Nicholas, (John Keiran) Barry (Moylan) 1919- IntWW 93, Who 94
Nicholas, Brenda L. 1953- WhoBlA 94
Nicholas, Carol Lynn 1938- WhoAmL 94
Nicholas, David 1930- IntWW 93, Who 94
Nicholas, David Cole 1944- WhoMW 93
Nicholas, David Durell 1930- WhoAmP 93
Nicholas, David M(ansfield) 1939- WrDr 94
Nicholas, David R. 1941- WhoAmP 93
Nicholas, Denise 1944- WhoBlA 94
Nicholas, Denise 1945- IntMPA 94
Nicholas, Denise 1946- WhoHol 92
Nicholas, Donna Lee 1938- WhoAmA 93
Nicholas, Eugene J. WhoAmP 93
Nicholas, Eugene Joseph 1945- WhoMW 93
Nicholas, Fayard 1914- & Nicholas, HaroldLloyd 1921- WhoHol 92
Nicholas, Fayard 1917- AfrAmAl 6
Nicholas, Fayard Antonio 1914- WhoAm 94, WhoBlA 94
Nicholas, Frederick M. 1920- WhoAmL 94, WhoWest 94
Nicholas, Gwendolyn Smith 1951- WhoBlA 94
Nicholas, Harold 1924- AfrAmAl 6
Nicholas, Harold Lloyd 1921- WhoHol 92
Nicholas, HaroldLloyd 1921- See Nicholas, Fayard 1914- & Nicholas, HaroldLloyd 1921- WhoHol 92
Nicholas, Harry Who 94
Nicholas, Herbert George 1911- IntWW 93, Who 94, WrDr 94
Nicholas, Herbert Richard 1905- Who 94
Nicholas, James Thomas 1956- WhoScEn 94
Nicholas, Jane Who 94
Nicholas, (Angela) Jane (Udale) 1929- Who 94
Nicholas, John (William) 1924- Who 94
Nicholas, Laurie Stevens 1959- WhoWest 94
Nicholas, Lawrence Bruce 1945- WhoFI 94
Nicholas, Mary Burke WhoBlA 94
Nicholas, Mary Kathryn 1956- WhoMW 93
Nicholas, Mike 1931- IntWW 93
Nicholas, Nicholas John, Jr. 1939- IntWW 93
Nicholas, Nicholas Soterios 1917- WhoAm 94
Nicholas, Nickie Lee 1938- WhoScEn 94
Nicholas, Paul 1945- WhoHol 92
Nicholas, Philip, Sr. 1954- WhoBlA 94
Nicholas, Ralph Wallace 1934- WhoAm 94, WhoScEn 94
Nicholas, Robert B. 1944- WhoAm 94
Nicholas, Rosemary Theresa 1943- WhoMW 93
Nicholas, Samuel 1744-1790 AmRev, WhAmRev
Nicholas, Thomas Andrew 1934- WhoAm 94, WhoAmA 93
Nicholas, Thomas Peter 1948- WhoAm 94, WhoWest 94
Nicholas, William Ford 1923- Who 94
Nicholas, William Richard 1934- WhoAm 94, WhoAmL 94
Nicholas Brothers, The WhoHol 92
Nicholaw, George 1927- WhoWest 94
Nicholia, Irene 1956- WhoAmP 93
Nicholia, Irene Kay 1956- WhoWest 94
Nicholl, Anthony John David 1935- Who 94
Nicholl, Nobes Einsel, Jr. 1936- WhoFI 94
Nicholls Who 94
Nicholls, Agnes 1877-1959 NewGrDO
Nicholls, Allan WhoHol 92
Nicholls, Anthony d1977 WhoHol 92
Nicholls, Brian 1928- Who 94
Nicholls, (Francis) Brian (Price) B. Who 94
Nicholls, Bruce Gilbert 1955- WhoAmL 94
Nicholls, C(hristine) S(tephanie) 1943- WrDr 94
Nicholls, Christine Stephanie 1943- Who 94
Nicholls, Clive Victor 1932- Who 94
Nicholls, Colin Alfred Arthur 1932- Who 94
Nicholls, David Alan 1931- Who 94
Nicholls, David G. 1965- WhoAm 94
Nicholls, Donald (James) 1933- Who 94
Nicholls, Grant T. 1946- WhoIns 94
Nicholls, John Who 94
Nicholls, John (Moreton) 1926- Who 94
Nicholls, John Graham 1929- Who 94
Nicholls, Josias 1553-1639 DcNaB MP
Nicholls, Michael William Newbery 1931- Who 94
Nicholls, Nigel Hamilton 1938- Who 94
Nicholls, Patrick Charles Martyn 1948- Who 94
Nicholls, Patti WhoHol 92
Nicholls, Peter (Douglas) 1939- EncSF 93
Nicholls, Philip 1914- Who 94
Nicholls, Phoebe WhoHol 92
Nicholls, Ralph William 1926- WhoAm 94, WhoScEn 94
Nicholls, Richard Aurelius 1941- WhoScEn 94
Nicholls, Richard H. 1938- WhoAm 94
Nicholls, Robert Michael 1939- Who 94
Nicholls, Thomas Maurice 1960- WhoMW 93
Nicholls, Vernon Sampson 1917- Who 94
Nichols, Alan Hammond 1940- WhoAmL 94, WhoWest 94
Nichols, Albert L. 1951- WhoFI 94
Nichols, Alfred Glen 1952- WhoBlA 94
Nichols, Andrew W. 1937- WhoAmP 93
Nichols, Andrew Wilkinson 1937- WhoWest 94
Nichols, Ann Huey 1943- WhoAmP 93
Nichols, Anne d1966 WhoHol 92
Nichols, Anthony Howard Who 94
Nichols, Avis Belle 1913- WhoAmP 93
Nichols, Barbara d1976 WhoHol 92
Nichols, Bruce W. 1930-1990 WhAm 10
Nichols, Buford Lee, Jr. 1931- WhoScEn 94
Nichols, C. Walter, III 1937- WhoAm 94, WhoFI 94
Nichols, C. William 1927- WhoAm 94, WhoMW 93
Nichols, Carl Michael 1961- WhoFI 94
Nichols, Carl Wheeler 1923- WhoAm 94
Nichols, Carol D. WhoAm 94
Nichols, Charles Harold 1919- WhoBlA 94
Nichols, Charles Warren 1939- WhoAm 94
Nichols, Chris 1971- WhoAmP 93
Nichols, Claude Alan 1947- WhoScEn 94
Nichols, Clement Roy 1909- Who 94
Nichols, Conrad WhoHol 92
Nichols, Dandy d1986 WhoHol 92
Nichols, David 1956- WrDr 94
Nichols, David A. 1917- WhoAmP 93
Nichols, David Arthur 1917- WhoAm 94, WhoAmL 94
Nichols, David Harry 1925- WhoAm 94
Nichols, David L. 1941- WhoAm 94, WhoFI 94
Nichols, David Michael 1950- WhoAmL 94
Nichols, David Norton 1954- WhoWest 94
Nichols, Dimaggio 1951- WhoBlA 94
Nichols, Dinah Alison 1943- Who 94
Nichols, Donald Arthur 1940- WhoAm 94, WhoFI 94
Nichols, Donald Edward 1922-1987 WhoAmA 93N
Nichols, Donald George 1943- WhoWest 94
Nichols, Donald Richardson 1911- WhoAm 94, WhoMW 93
Nichols, Dorothy Naddelle 1923- WhoAmP 93
Nichols, Dudley 1895-1960 IntDcF 2-4
Nichols, Edie Diane 1939- WhoFI 94
Nichols, Edward Edson 1929- WhoAmA 93
Nichols, Edward K., Jr. 1918- WhoBlA 94
Nichols, Edwin J. 1931- WhoBlA 94
Nichols, Elaine 1952- WhoBlA 94
Nichols, Eleanor Cary 1903-1988 WhoAmA 93N
Nichols, Eugene Douglas 1923- WhoAm 94, WhoScEn 94
Nichols, Evelin Gertraud 1931- WhoAmP 93
Nichols, Francis N., II WhoAmA 93
Nichols, Frederic Hone 1937- WhoScEn 94
Nichols, Frederick Harris 1936- WhoAmL 94
Nichols, George d1927 WhoHol 92
Nichols, George, Jr. d1939 WhoHol 92
Nichols, Grace 1950- BlmGEL, BlmGWL [port], WrDr 94
Nichols, Greg M. 1967- WhoMW 93
Nichols, Guy d1928 WhoHol 92
Nichols, Guy W. 1925- WhoAm 94
Nichols, Harold James 1945- WhoMW 93
Nichols, Harold Neil 1937- WhoAm 94
Nichols, Henry Eliot 1924- WhoAm 94, WhoAmL 94, WhoFI 94
Nichols, Henry Louis 1916- WhoAm 94
Nichols, Hobart 1869-1962 WhoAmA 93N
Nichols, Horace Elmo 1912- WhoAm 94
Nichols, Hugh 1936- WhoWest 94
Nichols, Irby Coghill, Jr. 1926- WhoAm 94
Nichols, Irene Delores 1938- WhoMW 93
Nichols, J. Hugh 1930- WhoAm 94, WhoAmP 93
Nichols, Jack Britt 1936- WhoAmL 94
Nichols, James Donald 1946- WhoMW 93
Nichols, James Harold 1921- WhoAmL 94
Nichols, James Phillip 1944- WhoFI 94
Nichols, James R. DrAPF 93
Nichols, James Richard 1923- WhoAm 94
Nichols, James Robbs 1926- WhoScEn 94
Nichols, James William 1928- WhoAmA 93
Nichols, Janet (Louise) 1952- WrDr 94
Nichols, Jenny WhoHol 92
Nichols, Jeremy Gareth Lane 1943- Who 94
Nichols, Joan Kane DrAPF 93
Nichols, John Who 94
Nichols, John 1940- WrDr 94
Nichols, (Kenneth) John (Heastey) 1923- Who 94
Nichols, John D. 1930- WhoAm 94, WhoFI 94, WhoMW 93
Nichols, John Gordon 1930- WrDr 94
Nichols, John Julian 1941- WhoAmL 94
Nichols, John M. WhoAmP 93
Nichols, John Winfrith de Lisle 1919- Who 94
Nichols, Johnnie Juanita 1908- WhoAmP 93
Nichols, Jose Angel 1960- WhoAmL 94
Nichols, Josephine WhoHol 92
Nichols, Joy WhoHol 92
Nichols, Kenneth David 1907- WhoAm 94
Nichols, Kyra 1958- WhoAm 94
Nichols, Kyra 1959- IntDcB
Nichols, Leigh EncSF 93, TwCYAW
Nichols, Leigh 1945- WrDr 94
Nichols, LeRoy 1924- WhoBlA 94
Nichols, Marguerite d1941 WhoHol 92
Nichols, Marjorie d1970 WhoHol 92
Nichols, Mary Elizabeth 1955- WhoMW 93
Nichols, Maxine McClendon WhoAmA 93
Nichols, Michael Lowery 1945- WhoWest 94
Nichols, Michele Marie 1954- WhoFI 94
Nichols, Mike 1931- IntMPA 94, WhoAm 94, WhoHol 92
See Also Nichols and May WhoCom
Nichols, Nancy Jean 1939- WhoAmP 93
Nichols, Nathan Lankford 1917-1991 WhAm 10
Nichols, Nellie V. d1971 WhoHol 92
Nichols, Nichelle WhoBlA 94
Nichols, Nichelle 1933- WhoHol 92
Nichols, Nichelle 1936- IntMPA 94
Nichols, Nick 1944- WhoBlA 94
Nichols, Nina Da Vinci DrAPF 93
Nichols, Owen D. 1929- WhoBlA 94
Nichols, Pamela Marjorie Who 94
Nichols, Patsy W. 1949- WhoAmL 94
Nichols, Paul 1939- WhoBlA 94
Nichols, Peter 1927- BlmGEL
Nichols, Peter (Richard) 1927- ConDr 93, IntDcT 2, WrDr 94
Nichols, Peter Richard 1927- IntWW 93, Who 94
Nichols, Philip, Jr. 1907-1990 WhAm 10
Nichols, Philip Martin 1960- WhoAmL 94
Nichols, Philip Vance 1934- WhoAmP 93
Nichols, Phyllis D'Ambrosio 1956- WhoWest 94
Nichols, R. Eugene 1914- WrDr 94
Nichols, Ralph Arthur 1919- WhoAm 94
Nichols, Red d1965 WhoHol 92
Nichols, Richard WhoHol 92
Nichols, Richard Dale 1926- WhoAm 94, WhoAmP 93, WhoMW 93

Nichols, Richard Everard 1938- *Who 94*
Nichols, Richard Maurice 1905- *WhoAm 94*
Nichols, Robert *WhoHol 92*
Nichols, Robert (Malise Bowyer) 1893-1944 *EncSF 93*
Nichols, Robert Edmund 1925- *WhoAm 94, WhoWest 94*
Nichols, Robert Lee 1924- *WhoAm 94*
Nichols, Robert Leighton 1926- *WhoAm 94*
Nichols, Rocky 1969- *WhoAmP 93*
Nichols, Rodney Wayson 1937- *WhoAm 94*
Nichols, Roger 1939- *WrDr 94*
Nichols, Roger Louis 1933- *WhoWest 94*
Nichols, Ron *WhoAmP 93*
Nichols, Ronald Augustus 1956- *WhoBlA 94*
Nichols, Ronald Lee 1941- *WhoAm 94, WhoScEn 94*
Nichols, Roy Calvin 1918- *WhoBlA 94*
Nichols, Roy Franklin 1896- *WhAm 10*
Nichols, Rudy J. 1945- *WhoAm 94*
Nichols, Ruth 1948- *BlmGWL, WrDr 94*
Nichols, Scott Tillman 1968- *WhoMW 93*
Nichols, Shuford Reinhardt 1909-1989 *WhAm 10*
Nichols, Spencer B. 1875-1950 *WhoAmA 93N*
Nichols, Stephen *WhoHol 92*
Nichols, Stephen George 1936- *WhoAm 94*
Nichols, Steven Parks 1950- *WhoScEn 94*
Nichols, Sylvia A. 1925- *WhoBlA 94*
Nichols, Thomas Robert 1948- *WhoScEn 94*
Nichols, Victoria (Sorensen) 1944- *WrDr 94*
Nichols, Vincent Gerard 1945- *IntWW 93, Who 94*
Nichols, Virginia Violet 1928- *WhoFI 94, WhoMW 93*
Nichols, Wade Hampton, III 1942- *WhoFI 94*
Nichols, Walter LaPlora 1938- *WhoBlA 94*
Nichols, Ward H. 1930- *WhoAmA 93*
Nichols, William Allyn 1942- *WhoAmA 93*
Nichols, William Curtis, Jr. 1929- *WhoAm 94*
Nichols, William David 1947- *WhoMW 93*
Nichols, William Deming 1924- *WhoAm 94*
Nichols, William Ford, Jr. 1934- *WhoAm 94*
Nichols, William Henry 1913- *Who 94*
Nichols, William Reginald 1912- *Who 94*
Nichols and May *WhoCom [port]*
Nicholsen, James Therman 1950- *WhoMW 93*
Nicholson, Aleathia Dolores 1937- *WhoBlA 94*
Nicholson, Alfred 1936- *WhoBlA 94*
Nicholson, Angus Archibald Norman 1919- *Who 94*
Nicholson, Anthony Thomas Cuthbertson 1929- *Who 94*
Nicholson, Ben 1894-1982 *WhoAmA 93N*
Nicholson, Bradford L. *WhoAmP 93*
Nicholson, Brent Bentley 1954- *WhoAmL 94*
Nicholson, Brian Thomas Graves 1930- *Who 94*
Nicholson, Bruce *WhoAm 94*
Nicholson, Bryan Hubert 1932- *IntWW 93, Who 94*
Nicholson, Carol Avery 1951- *WhoAmL 94*
Nicholson, Charles (Edward) 1946- *WrDr 94*
Nicholson, Charles Christian 1941- *Who 94*
Nicholson, Charles William 1929- *WhoAm 94, WhoFI 94*
Nicholson, Christina 1930- *WrDr 94*
Nicholson, David (Eric) 1904- *Who 94*
Nicholson, David C. 1941- *WhoAmL 94*
Nicholson, David John 1944- *Who 94*
Nicholson, David Lee 1947- *WhoAmP 93*
Nicholson, Dinah Schild 1952- *WhoFI 94*
Nicholson, Douglas Robert 1921- *WhoAm 94*
Nicholson, Dwight Roy 1947-1991 *WhAm 10*
Nicholson, E. Penn 1940- *WhoAmL 94*
Nicholson, E(rnest) W(ilson) 1938- *WrDr 94*
Nicholson, Earl G. *WhoAmP 93*
Nicholson, Emma Harriet 1941- *Who 94, WhoWomW 91*
Nicholson, Ernest Wilson 1938- *IntWW 93, Who 94*
Nicholson, Geoff 1953- *WrDr 94*
Nicholson, Geoffrey 1929- *WrDr 94*
Nicholson, George 1941- *WhoAmL 94*

Nicholson, George Albert, Jr. 1908- *WhoAm 94*
Nicholson, Gerald Lee 1944- *WhoMW 93*
Nicholson, Glen Ira 1925- *WhoAm 94, WhoWest 94*
Nicholson, Gordon *Who 94*
Nicholson, (Charles) Gordon (Brown) 1935- *Who 94*
Nicholson, Howard 1912- *Who 94*
Nicholson, Hubert 1908- *WrDr 94*
Nicholson, Isadore 1925- *WhoWest 94*
Nicholson, J.S. *EncSF 93*
Nicholson, Jack 1937- *ConTFT 11, IntMPA 94, IntWW 93, Who 94, WhoAm 94, WhoHol 92*
Nicholson, James c. 1736-1804 *WhAmRev*
Nicholson, James Allen 1948- *WhoScEn 94*
Nicholson, James Frederick 1945- *Who 94*
Nicholson, James Lloyd 1943- *WhoMW 93*
Nicholson, Jessie R. *WhoBlA 94*
Nicholson, John d1934 *WhoHol 92*
Nicholson, John Norris d1993 *Who 94N*
Nicholson, Joseph *DrAPF 93*
Nicholson, Joseph Bruce 1940- *WhoAm 94*
Nicholson, Joyce Elaine 1956- *WhoMW 93*
Nicholson, Lawrence E. 1915- *WhoBlA 94*
Nicholson, Leland Ross 1924- *WhoAm 94*
Nicholson, Lewis Frederick 1918- *Who 94*
Nicholson, Lillian d1949 *WhoHol 92*
Nicholson, Lisa Loechler 1963- *WhoMW 93*
Nicholson, Margaret Beda *Who 94*
Nicholson, Marion Crawford 1917- *WhoAmP 93, WhoFI 94, WhoMW 93*
Nicholson, Mark William 1960- *WhoAmL 94*
Nicholson, Max *Who 94*
Nicholson, (Edward) Max 1904- *Who 94*
Nicholson, Michael *Who 94*
Nicholson, Michael 1936- *WhoAmL 94*
Nicholson, (James) Michael (Anthony) 1973- *Who 94*
Nicholson, Michael Constantine 1932- *Who 94*
Nicholson, Morris Emmons, Jr. 1916- *WhoAm 94*
Nicholson, Myreen Moore *WhoAmA 93*
Nicholson, Natasha 1945- *WhoAmA 93*
Nicholson, Nick d1982 *WhoHol 92*
Nicholson, Nora d1973 *WhoHol 92*
Nicholson, Pamela 1945- *WhoWomW 91*
Nicholson, Patrick James 1920- *WhoAm 94*
Nicholson, Paul d1935 *WhoHol 92*
Nicholson, Paul (Douglas) 1938- *Who 94*
Nicholson, Paul Ewing *WhoWest 94*
Nicholson, R. James 1938- *WhoAmP 93*
Nicholson, R. Stephen 1926- *WhoAm 94*
Nicholson, Ralph Lambton Robb 1924- *Who 94*
Nicholson, Ranald 1931- *WrDr 94*
Nicholson, Richard Joseph 1932- *WhoAm 94*
Nicholson, Richard Selindh 1938- *WhoAm 94*
Nicholson, Robert 1920- *Who 94*
Nicholson, Robert Arthur 1923- *WhoAm 94*
Nicholson, Robert Douglas 1952- *WhoAm 94*
Nicholson, Robin (Buchanan) 1934- *Who 94*
Nicholson, Robin Buchanan 1934- *IntWW 93*
Nicholson, Roy S. 1903- *WhoAm 94*
Nicholson, Roy William 1943- *WhoAmA 93*
Nicholson, Rupert *Who 94*
Nicholson, (Edward) Rupert 1909- *Who 94*
Nicholson, Ruth *WhoAmP 93*
Nicholson, Samuel 1743-1811 *WhAmRev*
Nicholson, Shelia Elaine 1963- *WhoFI 94*
Nicholson, Thomas D. 1922- *WhoAmA 93N*
Nicholson, Thomas Dominic 1922-1991 *WhAm 10*
Nicholson, Thomas Laurence 1923- *WhoAm 94*
Nicholson, Victor Alvin 1941- *WhoMW 93*
Nicholson, Walter 1942- *WhoAm 94*
Nicholson, Will Faust, Jr. 1929- *WhoAm 94, WhoFI 94, WhoWest 94*
Nicholson, William 1872-1949 *DcLB 141 [port]*
Nicholson, William Joseph 1938- *WhoScEn 94, WhoWest 94*
Nicholson, William Mac 1918- *WhoScEn 94*
Nicholson, William Noel 1936- *WhoMW 93*

Nicholson, William Thomas 1944- *WhoAm 94*
Nicholson, (Rosa) Winifred 1893-1981 *DcNaB MP*
Nicholson-Guthrie, Catherine S. *WhoAm 94*
Ni Chonaill, Eibhlin Dubh c. 1743-c. 1800 *BlmGWL*
Nichter, Larry Steven 1951- *WhoWest 94*
Nichtern, Claire Joseph *WhoAm 94*
Ni Chuilleanain, Eilean 1942- *BlmGWL, WrDr 94*
Nicita, Rick *WhoAm 94*
Nick, George 1927- *WhoAmA 93*
Nick, Richard James 1943- *WhoFI 94*
Nickard, Gary Laurence 1954- *WhoAmA 93*
Nickel, Albert George 1943- *WhoAm 94, WhoFI 94*
Nickel, Dieter H. 1936- *WhoAmP 93*
Nickel, Donald Lloyd 1933- *WhoAm 94*
Nickel, Edward Henry 1957- *WhoFI 94*
Nickel, Hans Erich 1928- *WhoAm 94*
Nickel, Helen Wessel *WrDr 94*
Nickel, Henry V. 1943- *WhoAmL 94*
Nickel, Herman W. 1928- *IntWW 93, WhoAmP 93*
Nickel, Horst Wilhelm 1929- *WhoScEn 94*
Nickel, James Wesley 1943- *WhoWest 94*
Nickel, Janet Marlene Milton 1940- *WhoMW 93*
Nickel, Melvin Edwin 1915- *WhoMW 93*
Nickell, Christopher Shea 1959- *WhoAmL 94*
Nickell, Paul *IntMPA 94*
Nickell, Stephen John 1944- *Who 94*
Nickels, Christa 1952- *WhoWomW 91*
Nickels, Gregory James 1955- *WhoAmP 93*
Nickels, John L. *WhoAmL 94, WhoAmP 93, WhoMW 93*
Nickens, Jacks Clarence 1949- *WhoAm 94*
Nickerson, Albert Lindsay 1911- *IntWW 93, Who 94, WhoAm 94*
Nickerson, Bruce William 1941- *WhoAmL 94*
Nickerson, Dawn *WhoHol 92*
Nickerson, Don Carlos 1951- *WhoBlA 94*
Nickerson, Eileen Tressler 1927- *WhoAm 94*
Nickerson, Eugene H. 1918- *WhoAm 94, WhoAmL 94*
Nickerson, Eugene Hoffman 1918- *WhoAmP 93*
Nickerson, Gary Allan 1951- *WhoAmL 94*
Nickerson, Gary Lee 1942- *WhoMW 93*
Nickerson, Hardy Otto 1965- *WhoBlA 94*
Nickerson, James Findley 1910- *WhoAm 94*
Nickerson, Jerry Edgar Alan 1936- *WhoAm 94*
Nickerson, John Henry 1939- *WhoAmA 93*
Nickerson, John Mitchell 1937- *WhoAm 94*
Nickerson, Louisa Talcott 1961- *WhoAmL 94*
Nickerson, Mark William 1948- *WhoAmL 94*
Nickerson, Raymond Stephen 1931- *WhoScEn 94*
Nickerson, Richard Gorham 1927- *WhoFI 94*
Nickerson, Roy I. *WhoAmP 93*
Nickerson, Ruth 1905- *WhoAm 94, WhoAmA 93*
Nickerson, Sheila *DrAPF 93*
Nickerson, Sheila B(unker) 1942- *ConAu 43NR*
Nickerson, William *WorInv*
Nickerson, William Ernest 1908- *WhoWest 94*
Nickerson, William H. 1939- *WhoAmP 93*
Nickerson, William Milnor 1933- *WhoAm 94, WhoAmL 94*
Nickerson, Willie Curtis 1926- *WhoBlA 94*
Nickford, Juan 1925- *WhoAm 94, WhoAmA 93*
Nickinello, Louis R. 1940- *WhoAmP 93*
Nickisch, Willard Wayne 1939- *WhoMW 93*
Nicklas, John G. 1944- *WhoScEn 94*
Nicklas, Nancy Anne 1942- *WhoMW 93*
Nicklas, Robert Bruce 1932- *WhoAm 94*
Nicklaus, Charles Edward 1915- *WhoAm 94*
Nicklaus, Frederick *DrAPF 93*
Nicklaus, Frederick d1993 *NewYTBS 93*
Nicklaus, Jack William 1940- *IntWW 93, Who 94, WhoAm 94*
Nickle, Dennis Edwin 1936- *WhoAm 94, WhoFI 94, WhoScEn 94*
Nickle, Robert W. 1919-1980 *WhoAmA 93N*
Nickles, Don 1948- *CngDr 93*
Nickles, Donald 1948- *WhoAm 94*

Nickles, Donald Lee 1948- *IntWW 93, WhoAmP 93*
Nickles, Fredrick P. 1948- *WhoAmP 93*
Nicklin, Emily 1953- *WhoAm 94*
Nicklin, George Leslie, Jr. 1925- *WhoAm 94*
Nickol, Steven R. 1950- *WhoAmP 93*
Nickolaus, Darrell Ray 1936- *WhoMW 93*
Nickols, Herbert Arthur 1926- *Who 94*
Nickon, Alex 1927- *WhoAm 94*
Nicks, Paul Todd 1964- *WhoAmL 94*
Nicks, Stevie 1948- *IntWW 93, WhoAm 94*
Nicks, William James, Sr. 1905- *WhoBlA 94*
Nicksay, David *IntMPA 94*
Nickson, David (Wigley) 1929- *Who 94*
Nickson, David Wigley 1929- *IntWW 93*
Nickson, Francis 1929- *Who 94*
Nickson, Graham G. 1946- *WhoAmA 93*
Nickson, Julia 1958- *WhoHol 92*
Nickson, Milton Scott, Jr. 1934- *WhoAmL 94*
Nickson, Richard *DrAPF 93*
Nickson, Sheila Joan 1936- *WhoBlA 94*
Nickum, Gary John 1948- *WhoFI 94*
Nickum, James Daniel 1949- *WhoMW 93*
Nico d1988 *WhoHol 92*
Nicoara, John Paul 1948- *WhoAmL 94*
Nicodemi, Aldo d1963 *WhoHol 92*
Nicodemus *WhoHol 92*
Nicodemus, Chester Roland 1901- *WhoAmA 93*
Nicodemus, Matthew David 1960- *WhoWest 94*
Nicodim, Ion 1932- *IntWW 93*
Nicol, Baroness 1923- *Who 94, WhoWomW 91*
Nicol, Abioseh 1924- *WrDr 94*
Nicol, Alex 1916- *WhoHol 92*
Nicol, Alex 1919- *IntMPA 94*
Nicol, Angus Sebastian Torquil Eyers 1933- *Who 94*
Nicol, Betty Lou 1922- *WhoAmP 93*
Nicol, Davidson 1924- *WrDr 94*
Nicol, Davidson Sylvester Hector Willoughby 1924- *IntWW 93, Who 94*
Nicol, Donald MacGillivray 1923- *IntWW 93, Who 94, WrDr 94*
Nicol, James T. 1937- *WhoAmP 93*
Nicol, Joseph Arthur Colin 1915- *IntWW 93, Who 94*
Nicol, Joseph E. d1926 *WhoHol 92*
Nicol, Malcolm F. 1939- *WhoWest 94*
Nicol, Marjorie Carmichael 1929- *WhoScEn 94*
Nicol, William *Who 94*
Nicol, William c. 1768-1851 *DcNaB MP, WorInv*
Nicol, (Andrew) William 1933- *Who 94*
Nicola, Andrée 1948- *WrDr 94*
Nicola, Lewis 1717-1807 *AmRev, WhAmRev*
Nicoladis, Michael Frank 1960- *WhoFI 94, WhoScEn 94*
Nicolae, Dan 1945- *IntWW 93*
Nicolaeff, Ariadne 1915- *WrDr 94*
Nicolai, Claudio 1929- *NewGrDO*
Nicolai, Elena 1905- *NewGrDO*
Nicolai, Eugene Ralph 1911- *WhoFI 94, WhoWest 94*
Nicolai, (Carl) Otto (Ehrenfried) 1810-1849 *NewGrDO*
Nicolai, Paul Peter 1953- *WhoAmL 94*
Nicolai, Thomas R. 1943- *WhoAmL 94*
Nicolaides, Cristino 1925- *IntWW 93*
Nicolaides, Mary 1927- *WhoAmL 94*
Nicolaou, Kyriacos Costa 1946- *WhoScEn 94, WhoWest 94*
Nicolas, Ernest *NewGrDO*
Nicolas, George 1755-1799 *WhAmRev*
Nicolas, Georges Spiridon 1952- *WhoFI 94*
Nicolau, Antonio 1858-1933 *NewGrDO*
Nicolay, Janice K. *WhoAmP 93*
Nicolay, Jean Honore 1920- *WhoScEn 94*
Nicolay, Robert Richard, III 1957- *WhoMW 93*
Nicolazzi, Franco 1924- *IntWW 93*
Nicole, Christopher 1930- *WrDr 94*
Nicole, Mylene *WhoHol 92*
Nicole, Pierre 1625-1695 *GuFrLit 2*
Nicolesco, Mariana 1948- *NewGrDO*
Nicolet, Claude 1930- *IntWW 93*
Nicolet, Jean c. 1598-1642 *WhWE*
Nicolette, Archie John 1918- *WhoMW 93*
Nicoletti, Frank Medici 1944- *WhoAm 94, WhoAmL 94*
Nicoletti, Joseph A. *WhoAmP 93*
Nicoletti, Joseph Daniel 1930- *WhoFI 94*
Nicoletti, Louis A. d1969 *WhoHol 92*
Nicoletti, Paul Lee 1932- *WhoAm 94*
Nicoletti, Susi *WhoHol 92*
Nicoli, Eric Luciano 1950- *IntWW 93, Who 94*
Nicolin, Curt Rene 1921- *IntWW 93*
Nicolini c. 1673-1732 *NewGrDO [port]*
Nicolini, Ernest 1834-1898 *NewGrDO*

Nicolini, Giuseppe 1762-1842 NewGrDO
Nicolini, Mariano fl. 1731- NewGrDO
Nicolis, Gregoire 1939- WhoScEn 94
Nicolis, Nick George 1956- WhoMW 93
Nicolitz, Ernst 1947- WhoAm 94
Nicoll, Charles Samuel 1937- WhoAm 94
Nicoll, Douglas Robertson 1920- Who 94
Nicoll, Helen 1937- WrDr 94
Nicoll, William 1927- Who 94
Nicolle, Anthony William 1935- Who 94
Nicolle, Hilary Ann 1945- Who 94
Nicollet, Joseph Nicolas 1786-1843 WhWE
Nicolo NewGrDO
Nicolodi, Daria WhoHol 92
Nicolosi, Joseph 1893-1961 WhoAmA 93N
Nicolosi, Vincent F. WhoAmP 93
Nicols, Rosemary WhoHol 92
Nicolson Who 94
Nicolson, Charles White 1931- WhoAm 94
Nicolson, David (Lancaster) 1922- Who 94
Nicolson, David Lancaster 1922- IntWW 93
Nicolson, Gerda WhoHol 92
Nicolson, Harold (George) 1886-1968 EncSF 93
Nicolson, Ian 1928- WrDr 94
Nicolson, James AmRev
Nicolson, Malise Allen 1921- Who 94
Nicolson, Marjorie Hope 1894-1981 EncSF 93
Nicolson, Nigel 1917- Who 94, WrDr 94
Nicolson, Roy Macdonald 1944- Who 94
Nicoson, Steven Wayne 1959- WhoScEn 94
Nicotra, Joseph Charles 1931- WhoAmA 93
Nicuesa, Diego De d1511 WhWE
Niculescu, Stefan 1927- IntWW 93
Nida, Eugene Albert 1914- WhoAm 94
Nida, Jane Bolster 1918- WhoAm 94
Nidecki, Tomasz Napoleon 1807-1852 NewGrDO
Nidetz, Myron Philip 1935- WhoFI 94, WhoMW 93
Ni Dhomhnaill, Nuala 1952- BlmGWL
Ni Dhuibhne, Ellis 1954- BlmGWL [port]
Nido, Rafael Juan, III 1969- WhoHisp 94
Nie Bichu 1928- IntWW 93, WhoPRCh 91 [port]
Nie Binglin WhoPRCh 91
Niebla, Elvia Elisa 1945- WhoHisp 94
Niebla, J. Fernando 1939- WhoHisp 94
Niebruegge, Michael E. 1952- WhoAm 94
Niebuhr, Carsten 1733-1815 WhWE
Niebuhr, Christopher 1965- WhoScEn 94
Niebuhr, Helmut Richard 1894-1962 DcAmReB 2
Niebuhr, Karl Paul Reinhold 1892-1971 DcAmReB 2
Niebuhr, Reinhold 1892-1971 AmSocL, EncEth
Niebuhr, Richard Reinhold 1926- WhoAm 94
Niebuhr, Sigismund 1631-1699 WhWE
Niebur, Ernst Dietrich 1955- WhoScEn 94
Nieburg, H(arold) L(eonard) 1927- WrDr 94
Nied, Harriet Therese 1923- WhoMW 93
Nied, Thomas H. 1942- WhoAm 94
Nie Dajiang 1930- WhoPRCh 91 [port]
Niedecker, Charles William 1913- WhoIns 94
Niedel, James E. 1944- WhoAm 94
Nieder, Michael Louis 1956- WhoMW 93
Niederbrach, Jon 1966- WhoWest 94
Niederdrenk, Klaus 1950- WhoScEn 94
Niederer, Carl 1927- WhoAmA 93
Niedergeses, James D. 1917- WhoAm 94
Niederhofer, Laurence John 1932- WhoFI 94
Niederhuber, John Edward 1938- WhoAm 94
Niederjohn, Russell James 1944- WhoAm 94
Niederland, William G. d1993 NewYTBS 93
Niederland, William G(uglielmo) 1904-1993 CurBio 93N
Niederland, William G(ugliemo) 1904-1993 ConAu 142
Niederlehner, Leonard 1914-1991 WhAm 10
Niederman, James Corson 1924- WhoAm 94
Niedermeier, Christine Marie 1951- WhoAmL 94
Niedermeyer, (Abraham) Louis 1802-1861 NewGrDO
Niederreiter, Harald Guenther 1944- WhoAm 94, WhoScEn 94
Niederstadt, Roland G. 1943- WhoAmP 93
Niedner, Kathryn Ellen 1946- WhoMW 93
Nieduszynski, Anthony John 1939- Who 94
Niedzialek, Terry 1956- WhoAmA 93
Niedzielski, Henri Zygmunt 1931- WhoAm 94, WhoWest 94
Niefeld, Jaye Sutter 1924- WhoAm 94, WhoFI 94
Niefeld, Jo Ann R. 1929- WhoAmP 93
Nie Fengzhi 1914- IntWW 93, WhoPRCh 91 [port]
Niefer, Werner d1993 NewYTBS 93
Nieforth, Karl Allen 1936- WhoAm 94
Nie Gongcheng WhoPRCh 91
Niehans, Daniel J. 1949- WhoAm 94, WhoAmL 94
Niehaus, James William 1955- WhoMW 93
Niehaus, Merle H. 1933- WhoAm 94
Niehaus, Robert James 1930- WhoAm 94
Niehaus, William Scott 1954- WhoMW 93
Nieh Hualing 1925- BlmGWL
Nieh Jung-Chen, Marshal IntWW 93
Nieh K'Uei-Chu IntWW 93
Niehm, Bernard Frank 1923- WhoAm 94
Niehoff, Beatrice c. 1952- NewGrDO
Niehoff, Harry Charles Buck 1947- WhoAmL 94
Niehoff, K. Richard B. 1943- WhoAm 94, WhoFI 94
Niehoff, Leonard Marvin 1957- WhoAmL 94
Niehoff, Philip John 1959- WhoAmL 94
Niehouse, Oliver Leslie 1920- WhoFI 94
Niehuis, Edith 1950- WhoWomW 91
Niekamp, Thomas John 1948- WhoFI 94
Niekisch, Ernst 1889-1967 HisWorL
Nie Kuiju 1926- WhoPRCh 91 [port]
Nie Kuiju, Vice-Adm. 1929- IntWW 93
Niel, Jean-Baptiste 169-?-1775? NewGrDO
Nield, Basil Edward 1903- Who 94
Nield, David A. 1938- WhoIns 94
Nield, Howard (Kingsley) 1949- WrDr 94
Nield, Lawrence C. 1942- WhoIns 94
Nield, Wade Middleton 1958- WhoFI 94
Nield, William (Alan) 1913- Who 94
Nields, John W., Jr. 1942- WhoAmL 94
Nie Li 1930- WhoPRCh 91 [port]
Nie Li, Maj.-Gen. 1930- IntWW 93
Nielsen, Aksel Christopher W. Who 94
Nielsen, Aldon Dale 1922- WhoAm 94
Nielsen, Aldon Lynn 1950- WrDr 94
Nielsen, Alice 1876-1943 NewGrDO
Nielsen, Alvin Herborg 1910- WhoAm 94
Nielsen, Arthur 1897-1980 BuCMET
Nielsen, Asta d1972 WhoHol 92
Nielsen, Barbara WhoAmP 93
Nielsen, Barbara S. WhoAm 94
Nielsen, Ben R. 1945- WhoAmP 93
Nielsen, Brian 1948- WhoAm 94
Nielsen, Brigitte 1963?- ConTFT 11
Nielsen, Brigitte 1964- WhoHol 92
Nielsen, Carl (August) 1865-1931 NewGrDO
Nielsen, Christian Bayard 1954- WhoAmL 94
Nielsen, Christian Eric 1960- WhoFI 94
Nielsen, Corbett A. WhoIns 94
Nielsen, David J. 1947- WhoAmL 94
Nielsen, Donald Rodney 1931- WhoAm 94, WhoWest 94
Nielsen, Edward Herman 1946- WhoAmL 94
Nielsen, Eloise Wilma 1923- WhoMW 93
Nielsen, Emiel Theodore, Jr. 1914- WhoAm 94
Nielsen, Erik H. 1924- IntWW 93, Who 94
Nielsen, Forrest Harold 1941- WhoScEn 94
Nielsen, Frederick Park 1953- WhoFI 94
Nielsen, Gail Ann 1947- WhoMW 93
Nielsen, George Lee 1937- WhoAm 94
Nielsen, Glade 1926- WhoAmP 93
Nielsen, Glade Benjamin 1926- WhoWest 94
Nielsen, Greg Ross 1947- WhoAm 94, WhoAmL 94
Nielsen, Hans d1967 WhoHol 92
Nielsen, Harald Christian 1930- WhoAm 94
Nielsen, Helen (Berniece) 1918- WrDr 94
Nielsen, Inga WhoHol 92
Nielsen, Inga 1946- NewGrDO
Nielsen, Ingvard d1975 WhoHol 92
Nielsen, Jakob 1957- WhoScEn 94
Nielsen, James Nick 1942- WhoMW 93
Nielsen, James Wiley 1944- WhoAmP 93
Nielsen, Jens Rud 1894- WhAm 10
Nielsen, John Merle 1959- WhoMW 93
Nielsen, John T. 1941- WhoAmL 94
Nielsen, Jon Scott 1950- WhoMW 93
Nielsen, Joyce 1933- WhoAmP 93
Nielsen, Kenneth Andrew 1949- WhoScEn 94
Nielsen, Kenneth Burton 1929- WhoAmP 93
Nielsen, Lawrence Emory 1946- WhoWest 94
Nielsen, Lawrence Ernie 1917-1992 WhAm 10
Nielsen, Leland C. 1919- WhoWest 94
Nielsen, Leslie NewYTBS 93 [port]
Nielsen, Leslie 1922- WhoCom, WhoHol 92
Nielsen, Leslie 1926- ConTFT 11, IntMPA 94, WhoAm 94
Nielsen, (Carl Henrik) Ludolf 1876-1939 NewGrDO
Nielsen, Lynn Carol 1950- WhoFI 94
Nielsen, Mark D. 1964- WhoAmP 93
Nielsen, Mark Joseph 1959- WhoFI 94, WhoWest 94
Nielsen, Monica WhoHol 92
Nielsen, Niels Christian, Jr. 1921- WhoAm 94, WrDr 94
Nielsen, Niels E. EncSF 93
Nielsen, Niels F., Jr. 1927- WhoAmP 93
Nielsen, Niels Laurids 1863-1941 EncNAR
Nielsen, Nina I. M. 1940- WhoAmA 93
Nielsen, Norman L. 1935- WhoAmP 93
Nielsen, Norman Russell 1941- WhoWest 94
Nielsen, Otto R. 1905-1991 WhAm 10
Nielsen, Peter Eigil 1951- WhoScEn 94
Nielsen, Ray 1916- WhoAmP 93
Nielsen, Riccardo 1908-1982 NewGrDO
Nielsen, Stephen James 1951- WhoWest 94
Nielsen, Stu WhoAmP 93
Nielsen, Stuart Dee 1932- WhoWest 94
Nielsen, Vigo Gilbert, Jr. 1942- WhoAmL 94
Nielsen, William Fremming 1934- WhoAm 94, WhoAmL 94, WhoWest 94
Nielsen-Bohlman, Lynn Tracy 1958- WhoScEn 94
Nielson, Howard C. 1924- WhoAmP 93
Nielson, Howard Curtis 1924- WhoAm 94, WhoWest 94
Nielson, Nancy J. 1951- SmATA 77 [port]
Nieman, John Francis 1949- WhoAm 94
Nieman, Richard Hovey 1922- WhoWest 94
Niemann, Albert 1831-1917 NewGrDO [port]
Niemann, Bernard John, Jr. 1937- WhoAm 94
Niemann, David Arthur 1946- WhoMW 93
Niemann, Edmund E. WhoAmA 93
Niemann, Harry C. 1932- WhoIns 94
Niemann, James Alan 1965- WhoMW 93
Niemann, Kurt Max Walter 1932- WhoAm 94
Niemann, Lewis Keith 1930- WhoAm 94
Niemann, Linda (Grant) 1946- WrDr 94
Niemann, Nicholas Kent 1956- WhoAmL 94, WhoMW 93
Niemczyk, Julian M. WhoAmP 93
Niemeth, Charles Frederick 1939- WhoAm 94
Niemeyer, Arnold Matthew 1913- WhoAmA 93
Niemeyer, August Herman 1934- WhoFI 94
Niemeyer, David John 1961- WhoMW 93
Niemeyer, Gerhart 1907- IntWW 93, WhoAm 94
Niemeyer, Glenn Alan 1934- WhoAm 94
Niemeyer, James Robert 1950- WhoFI 94
Niemeyer, Joe d1965 WhoHol 92
Niemeyer, Oscar 1907- IntWW 93, Who 94
Niemeyer, Paul Victor 1941- WhoAm 94, WhoAmL 94, WhoAmP 93
Niemeyer, Richard James 1957- WhoFI 94
Niemi, Bruce Edward 1949- WhoAmP 93
Niemi, Gregory Allen 1956- WhoFI 94
Niemi, Irmeli 1931- IntWW 93
Niemi, Janice WhoAmP 93
Niemi, Janice 1928- WhoWest 94
Niemi, Lisa 1957- WhoHol 92
Niemi, Peter G. 1937- WhoAm 94
Niemi, Richard Gene 1941- WhoAm 94
Niemi, Robert John 1961- WhoWest 94
Niemiec, David Wallace 1949- WhoAm 94, WhoFI 94
Niemiec, Edward Walter 1936- WhoAm 94
Niemira, Michael Paul 1955- WhoFI 94
Niemoller, Arthur B. 1912- WhoFI 94, WhoMW 93, WhoScEn 94
Niemoller, Klaus 1929- IntWW 93
Nienaber, Harry Allen 1942- WhoMW 93
Nienburg, George Frank 1938- WhoAm 94
Nienhuis, Arthur Wesley 1941- WhoScEn 94
Nienow, James Anthony 1953- WhoScEn 94
Nienstedt, Gerd 1932- NewGrDO
Nienstedt, John F 1938- WhoWest 94
Nie Ou 1948- WhoPRCh 91
Niepce, Joseph Nicephore 1765-1833 WorInv
Nier, Alfred O(tto) C(arl) 1911- IntWW 93
Nier, Alfred Otto Carl 1911- WhoAm 94, WhoScEn 94
Nierenberg, Gerard I 1923- WrDr 94
Nierenberg, Norman 1919- WhoFI 94, WhoWest 94
Nierenberg, Roger 1947- WhoAm 94
Nierenberg, William Aaron 1919- IntWW 93, WhoWest 94
Nierman, Leonardo M. 1932- WhoAmA 93
Nierman, Leonardo Mendelejis 1932- WhoAm 94
Nierman, Lyndy Ann 1947- WhoAm 94
Nie Ronggui 1932- WhoPRCh 91 [port]
Nie Rongzhen d1992 IntWW 93N
Nie Rongzhen 1899- WhoPRCh 91 [port]
Niersbach, Donald Charles 1928- WhoAmL 94
Nierste, Joseph Paul 1952- WhoMW 93
Nies, Helen W. WhoAmP 93
Nies, Helen Wilson 1925- CngDr 93, WhoAm 94, WhoAmL 94
Niesar, Gerald V. 1940- WhoAmL 94
Niese, Hansi d1933 WhoHol 92
Niese, Henry Ernst 1924- WhoAmA 93
Niesen, Gertrude d1975 WhoHol 92
Nieset, James Robert 1942- WhoAmL 94
Niesluchowski, Witold S. 1944- WhoWest 94
Niesman, Kenneth M. 1950- WhoAmL 94
Nietes, Linda Maria WhoAsA 94
Nieto, Ernesto 1940- WhoHisp 94
Nieto, Eva Margarita WhoHisp 94
Nieto, Eva Maria 1922- WhoHisp 94
Nieto, Fred H. 1940- WhoHisp 94
Nieto, John W. 1936- WhoAmA 93
Nieto, Jose d1982 WhoHol 92
Nieto, Luis P., Jr. 1955- WhoHisp 94
Nieto, Maria Refugio 1949- WhoHisp 94
Nieto, Michael Martin 1940- WhoHisp 94
Nieto, Minerva 1948- WhoHisp 94
Nieto, Ofelia 1900-1931 NewGrDO
Nieto, Pedro 1942- WhoAmP 93
Nieto, Ramon Dante 1957- WhoHisp 94
Nieto, Rebecca Ann 1962- WhoHisp 94
Nieto, Rey J. WhoHisp 94
Nieto, Reynaldo WhoAmP 93
Nieto, Rodrigo Rapatalo 1962- WhoFI 94
Nieto, Sonia 1943- WhoHisp 94
Nieto, William, Jr. 1948- WhoHisp 94
Nieto del Rio, Juan Carlos 1962- WhoAm 94, WhoHisp 94
Nieto Gallo, Gratiniano 1917- IntWW 93
Nieto-Roig, Juan Jose 1958- WhoScEn 94
Nietzsche, Friedrich 1844-1900 DcLB 129 [port], EncEth
Nietzsche, Friedrich (Wilhelm) 1844-1900 NewGrDO
Nietzsche, Friedrich Wilhelm 1844-1900 BlmGEL
Nieuwsma, Milton John 1941- WhoFI 94, WhoMW 93
Nieva, Francisco 1927- ConWorW 93
Nievergelt, Jurg 1938- WhoAm 94
Nieves, Agustin Alberto 1963- WhoHisp 94
Nieves, Alvaro Lezcano 1944- WhoHisp 94
Nieves, Evelyn J. 1960- WhoHisp 94
Nieves, Felix D. 1942- WhoHisp 94
Nieves, Javier Alfonso 1958- WhoAmP 93, WhoHisp 94
Nieves, Juan Manuel 1965- WhoHisp 94
Nieves, Julie A. 1947- WhoHisp 94
Nieves, Marysol 1965- WhoHisp 94
Nieves, Melvyn Louis 1960- WhoHisp 94
Nieves, Michael D. WhoHisp 94
Nieves, Miguel, Jr. 1928- WhoHisp 94
Nieves, Robert 1945- WhoHisp 94
Nieves, Theresa 1952- WhoHisp 94
Nieves, Wilfredo 1949- WhoHisp 94
Nieves-Cruz, Bedford 1961- WhoHisp 94
Nieves-Gonzalez, Orlando 1961- WhoHisp 94
Nieves-Martínez, Ileana 1955- WhoHisp 94
Nie Weiping 1952- WhoPRCh 91 [port]
Niewiarowski, Stefan 1926- WhoAm 94, WhoScEn 94
Niewiarowski, Waclaw 1942- IntWW 93
Niewoehner, Gerald Joseph 1945- WhoMW 93
Niewyk, Anthony 1941- WhoAm 94
Nie Xinsen 1948- WhoPRCh 91 [port]
Niezer, Thomas Maurice 1959- WhoAmL 94
Niflis, Michael DrAPF 93
Nigah, Zehra BlmGWL
Nigam, Bishan Perkash 1928- WhoAm 94, WhoScEn 94, WhoWest 94
Nigar 1862-1918 BlmGWL
Nigeria, Metropolitan Archbishop of Who 94
Nigg, Benno M. 1938- WhoScEn 94
Nigh, George 1927- WhoAm 94

Nitta, Sandra Haruye 1949- *WhoAsA 94*
Nitti, Mary d1978 *WhoHol 92*
Nittoli, Thomas 1963- *WhoScEn 94*
Nittoly, Paul Gerard 1948- *WhoAm 94, WhoAmL 94*
Nitz, Frederic William 1943- *WhoFI 94, WhoScEn 94, WhoWest 94*
Nitz, P. Kenneth, Jr. 1940- *WhoIns 94*
Nitze, Paul 1907- *HisDcKW*
Nitze, Paul H(enry) 1907- *ConAu 140*
Nitze, Paul Henry 1907- *IntWW 93, WhoAmP 93*
Nitze, William Albert 1942- *WhoAm 94, WhoAmL 94*
Nitzsche, Elsa Koenig 1880-1952 *WhoAmA 93N*
Nitzsche, Fred 1953- *WhoScEn 94*
Nitzschke, Dale Frederick 1937- *WhoAm 94*
Niu, David 1960- *WhoAmL 94*
Niu, Keishiro 1929- *WhoScEn 94*
Niu Han 1923- *WhoPRCh 91 [port]*
Niu Maosheng 1939- *WhoPRCh 91 [port]*
Niumata, Malo L. *WhoAmP 93*
Niu Shucai 1908- *IntWW 93*
Niu Zhenhuan 1950- *BlmGWL*
Nivelle de la Chaussee, Pierre-Claude 1691?-1754 *GuFrLit 2*
Niven, Alastair (Neil Robertson) 1944- *WrDr 94*
Niven, Alastair Neil Robertson 1944- *Who 94*
Niven, Colin Harold Robertson 1941- *Who 94*
Niven, David d1983 *WhoHol 92*
Niven, David, Jr. 1942- *IntMPA 94*
Niven, Ian *Who 94*
Niven, John Robertson 1919- *Who 94*
Niven, Kip 1945- *WhoHol 92*
Niven, Larry *DrAPF 93*
Niven, Larry 1938- *EncSF 93, WrDr 94*
Niven, Laurence Van Cott 1938- *WhoAm 94*
Niven, Margaret Graeme 1906- *Who 94*
Niven, (Cecil) Rex d1993 *Who 94N*
Niven, (Cecil) Rex, Sir 1898- *WrDr 94*
Niven, Susan d1981 *WhoHol 92*
Niven, Vern *GayLL*
Nivens, Beatryce Thomasinia 1948- *WhoBlA 94*
Nivison *Who 94*
Nivison, David Shepherd 1923- *WhoAm 94*
Niwano, Nikkyo 1906- *IntWW 93*
Nix, Beverly Ann 1951- *WhoAm 94, WhoFI 94*
Nix, Charles Ray *WhoAmP 93*
Nix, Dennis Keith 1941- *WhoAm 94*
Nix, Edmund Alfred 1929- *WhoAm 94*
Nix, Gary William 1941- *WhoWest 94*
Nix, James Kelly 1934- *WhoAmP 93*
Nix, James Rayford 1938- *WhoWest 94*
Nix, John Sydney 1927- *Who 94*
Nix, Kenneth Owen 1939- *WhoAmP 93*
Nix, Martin Eugene 1951- *WhoScEn 94*
Nix, Nancy Jean *WhoWest 94*
Nix, Pat 1931- *WhoAmP 93*
Nix, Patricia (Lea) *WhoAmA 93*
Nix, Rick 1950- *WhoBlA 94*
Nix, Robert N. C., Jr. 1928- *WhoAmP 93, WhoBlA 94*
Nix, Robert Nelson Cornelius, Jr. 1928- *WhoAm 94, WhoAmL 94*
Nix, Robert Royal, II 1947- *WhoAmL 94*
Nix, Roscoe Russa 1921- *WhoBlA 94*
Nix, Theophilus Richard 1925- *WhoBlA 94*
Nix, Theophilus Richard, Jr. 1953- *WhoBlA 94*
Nix, William Dale 1936- *WhoAm 94, WhoScEn 94*
Nix, William Patterson 1948- *IntMPA 94*
Nixon, Agnes 1927- *IntMPA 94*
Nixon, Agnes Eckhardt *WhoAm 94*
Nixon, Allan *WhoHol 92*
Nixon, Anne Nims 1916- *WhoAmP 93*
Nixon, Arundel d1949 *WhoHol 92*
Nixon, Baunita T. 1932- *WhoAmP 93*
Nixon, Carol Holladay 1937- *WhoAmP 93*
Nixon, Charles William 1929- *WhoScEn 94*
Nixon, Clint d1937 *WhoHol 92*
Nixon, Corwin M. 1916- *WhoAmP 93*
Nixon, Cynthia 1966- *IntMPA 94, WhoHol 92*
Nixon, David Lee 1932- *WhoAmL 94*
Nixon, David Michael *DrAPF 93*
Nixon, Edwin (Ronald) 1925- *Who 94*
Nixon, Edwin Ronald 1925- *IntWW 93*
Nixon, Elliott Bodley 1921-1992 *WhAm 10*
Nixon, Eugene Ray 1919- *WhoAm 94*
Nixon, Felix Nathaniel 1918- *WhoBlA 94*
Nixon, George W. 1935- *WhoBlA 94*
Nixon, Gladys 1920-1992 *WhoBlA 94N*
Nixon, Glenford Delacy 1956- *WhoBlA 94*
Nixon, Harold L. 1939- *WhoBlA 94*
Nixon, Harvey 1931- *WhoAm 94*
Nixon, James I., Jr. 1933- *WhoBlA 94*
Nixon, James Joseph, III 1947- *WhoFI 94, WhoWest 94*
Nixon, James Melvin *WhoBlA 94*
Nixon, Jeremiah Jay 1956- *WhoAm 94*
Nixon, Jeremiah W. 1956- *WhoAmL 94, WhoMW 93*
Nixon, Jeremiah Willson 1956- *WhoAmP 93*
Nixon, Joan Lowery 1927- *Au&Arts 12 [port], TwCYAW, WhoAm 94, WrDr 94*
Nixon, John 1725-1815 *AmRev*
Nixon, John 1727-1815 *WhAmRev*
Nixon, John 1733-1808 *WhAmRev*
Nixon, John Forster 1937- *IntWW 93*
Nixon, John Harmon 1915- *WhoWest 94*
Nixon, John Trice 1933- *WhoAm 94, WhoAmL 94*
Nixon, John William 1922- *WhoBlA 94*
Nixon, Kenneth Michael John Basil 1919- *Who 94*
Nixon, Leslie C. 1956- *WhoAmP 93*
Nixon, Lester d1962 *WhoHol 92*
Nixon, Louise Aldrich 1897- *WhAm 10*
Nixon, Marian d1983 *WhoHol 92*
Nixon, Marni 1930- *NewGrDO, WhoAm 94*
Nixon, Marni 1931- *WhoHol 92*
Nixon, Mojo 1956- *WhoHol 92*
Nixon, Nichols 1947- *WhoAmA 93*
Nixon, Norm 1955- *BasBi*
Nixon, Norm Ellard 1955- *WhoBlA 94*
Nixon, Otis Junior 1959- *WhoBlA 94*
Nixon, Pat 1912-1993 *NewYTBS 93 [port], News 94-1*
Nixon, Patricia 1912-1993 *CurBio 93N*
Nixon, Patrick Michael 1944- *Who 94*
Nixon, Raymond Blalock 1903- *WhoAm 94*
Nixon, Richard (Milhous) 1913- *WrDr 94*
Nixon, Richard M. 1913- *HisWorL [port], HisDcKW, Who 94, WhoAmP 93*
Nixon, Richard Milhous 1913- *IntWW 93, WhoAm 94*
Nixon, Richard Neal 1942- *WhoAmL 94*
Nixon, Robert James 1930- *WhoAm 94*
Nixon, Robert Obey, Sr. 1922- *WhoFI 94, WhoWest 94*
Nixon, Robert Pleasants 1913- *WhoAm 94*
Nixon, Sallie *DrAPF 93*
Nixon, Scott West 1943- *WhoAm 94*
Nixon, Tamara Friedman 1938- *WhoFI 94*
Nixson, Frederick Ian 1943- *WrDr 94*
Niyazov, Saparmurad 1940- *IntWW 93*
Niyazov, Saparmurad Ataevich 1940- *LngBDD*
Niyungeko, Jonathas 1946- *IntWW 93*
Niza, Marcos De c. 1495-1558 *WhWE*
Nizami, Shafiq Ahmed 1956- *WhoAsA 94*
Nizamuddin, Khawaja 1960- *WhoMW 93, WhoScEn 94*
Nizer, Louis 1902- *IntMPA 94*
Ni Zhengjian *WhoPRCh 91*
Ni Zhengyu 1906- *IntWW 93, WhoPRCh 91 [port]*
Ni Zhifu 1932- *WhoPRCh 91 [port]*
Ni Zhifu 1933- *IntWW 93*
Nizin, Joel Scott 1953- *WhoScEn 94*
Nizio, Frank 1948- *WhoAmL 94*
Nizze, Judith Anne 1942- *WhoWest 94*
Njau, Rebecca *BlkWr 2, ConAu 142*
Njau, Rebeka 1932- *BlkWr 2, BlmGWL, ConAu 142*
Njeri, Itabari (Lord) *BlkWr 2*
N'jie, Louise *WhoWomW 91*
Njonjo, Charles E. G. H. 1920- *IntWW 93*
Njoroge, J(ames) K(ingangi) 1933- *BlkWr 2*
Njoroge, Mbugua J. 1944- *WhoBlA 94*
Nkabinde, Thulani *DrAPF 93*
Nkala, Enos 1933- *IntWW 93*
Nkemnji, John F. 1950- *WhoMW 93*
Nkomo, Joshua 1917- *HisWorL [port], IntWW 93*
Nkongola, Muyumba Wa 1939- *WhoBlA 94*
Nkonyansa, Osafuhin Kwaku 1938- *WhoBlA 94*
Nkosi, Lewis 1936- *ConDr 93, WrDr 94*
Nkrumah, Kwame 1909-1972 *BlkWr 2, HisWorL [port]*
Nnamani-Ferguson, Ngozi Ori 1962- *WhoFI 94*
N'Namdi, Carmen Ann 1949- *WhoBlA 94*
N'Namdi, George Richard 1946- *WhoBlA 94*
Nnolim, Charles E. 1939- *WhoBlA 94*
Noa, Florence 1941-1989 *WhoAmA 93N*
Noa, Manfred d1930 *WhoHol 92*
Noack, Carol Lynn 1935- *WhoFI 94*
Noack, Harold Quincy, Jr. 1931- *WhoAmL 94*
Noack, Joseph Patrick 1948- *WhoAmL 94*
Noad, Kenneth (Beeson) 1900- *Who 94*
Noah, Douglas True 1962- *WhoAmL 94*
Noah, Harold J. 1925- *WrDr 94*
Noah, Harold Julius 1925- *IntWW 93*
Noah, Hope Ellen 1943- *WhoAm 94*
Noah, Leroy Edward 1934- *WhoBlA 94*
Noah, Raymond Douglas 1932- *WhoAmP 93*
Noah, Steven Craig 1948- *WhoAmP 93*
Noah, Tim *WhoHol 92*
Noah, Yannick 1960- *BuCMET*
Noailles, Anna de 1876-1933 *BlmGWL*
Noailles, Louis Marie, Vicomte de 1756-1804 *WhAmRev*
Noakes, George 1924- *IntWW 93, Who 94*
Noakes, John Edward 1935- *Who 94*
Noakes, Michael 1933- *IntWW 93, Who 94*
Noakes, Philip Reuben 1915- *Who 94*
Noakes, Sheila Valerie *Who 94*
Noakes, Sidney Henry d1993 *Who 94N*
Noakes, Vivien 1937- *WrDr 94*
Noall, Nancy Ann 1957- *WhoAmL 94, WhoMW 93*
Noall, Roger 1935- *WhoAm 94, WhoFI 94*
Noar, Mark David 1953- *WhoScEn 94*
Noback, Charles Robert 1916- *WhoAm 94*
Noback, Richardson Kilbourne 1923- *WhoAm 94*
Nobay, (Avelino) Robert 1942- *Who 94*
Nobbs, David Gordon 1935- *Who 94*
Nobbs, Kenneth John 1938- *WhoFI 94*
Nobe, Ken 1925- *WhoAm 94*
Nobel, Alfred 1833-1896 *WorInv*
Nobel, Jerry 1937- *WhoAmP 93*
Nobel, Joel J. 1934- *WhoAm 94, WhoFI 94, WhoScEn 94*
Nobel, Phil *EncSF 93*
Nobes, (Charles) Patrick 1933- *Who 94*
Nobes, Peter John 1935- *Who 94*
Nobile, John Frank 1940- *WhoFI 94*
Nobile, Umberto 1885-1978 *WhWE*
Nobili, Lili de *NewGrDO*
Nobis, Elizabeth Ann 1916- *WhoAmP 93*
Noble, Adrian 1950- *ConTFT 11*
Noble, Adrian Keith *Who 94*
Noble, Adrian Keith 1950- *IntWW 93*
Noble, Alistair William 1954- *Who 94*
Noble, Andrew J., III 1950- *WhoAmL 94*
Noble, Barrie Paul 1938- *Who 94*
Noble, Chelsea 1964- *WhoHol 92*
Noble, Cherrie Saile 1953- *WhoMW 93*
Noble, Christopher L. 1944- *WhoAmL 94*
Noble, Chuck 1931- *BasBi*
Noble, Dan D. *WhoAmP 93*
Noble, David 1923- *Who 94*
Noble, David 1929- *Who 94*
Noble, David (Brunel) 1961- *Who 94*
Noble, David J. 1931- *WhoIns 94*
Noble, Denis 1936- *IntWW 93, Who 94*
Noble, Dennis 1899-1966 *NewGrDO*
Noble, Douglas Ross 1945- *WhoAm 94*
Noble, Ernest Pascal 1929- *WhoAm 94*
Noble, Fraser *Who 94*
Noble, (Thomas Alexander) Fraser 1918- *Who 94*
Noble, Gloria *WhoHol 92*
Noble, Harold J. 1903-1953 *HisDcKW*
Noble, Harry d1966 *WhoHol 92*
Noble, Helen (Harper) 1922- *WhoAmA 93*
Noble, Iain (Andrew) 1935- *Who 94*
Noble, James 1922- *WhoHol 92*
Noble, James Kendrick, Jr. 1928- *WhoAm 94, WhoFI 94, WhoScEn 94*
Noble, James Wilkes 1922- *WhoAm 94*
Noble, Jeffrey V. *WhoBlA 94*
Noble, John A. 1913- *WhoAmA 93*
Noble, John A. 1913-1983 *WhoAmA 93N*
Noble, John Charles 1941- *WhoBlA 94*
Noble, John Merris 1956- *WhoAmL 94*
Noble, John Pritchard 1931- *WhoBlA 94*
Noble, Joseph Veach 1920- *WhoAm 94, WhoAmA 93*
Noble, Kenneth Albert *Who 94*
Noble, Kevin 1952- *WhoAmA 93*
Noble, Mark *EncSF 93*
Noble, Merrill Emmett 1923- *WhoAm 94*
Noble, Peter *IntMPA 94*
Noble, Phil 1935- *WrDr 94*
Noble, Phillip D. 1946- *WhoAmL 94*
Noble, R. Elaine 1944- *WhoAmP 93*
Noble, Ray d1978 *WhoHol 92*
Noble, Regina Catherine 1963- *WhoMW 93*
Noble, Richard Lloyd 1939- *WhoAm 94, WhoWest 94*
Noble, Robert Tyrol 1940- *WhoFI 94*
Noble, Stuart Harris 1941- *WhoWest 94*
Noble, Sunny A. 1940- *WhoFI 94*
Noble, Thom *ConTFT 11*
Noble, Trisha *WhoHol 92*
Noble, William Charles 1935- *WrDr 94*
Nobles, Dollie d1930 *WhoHol 92*
Nobles, Edward *DrAPF 93*
Nobles, Laurence Hewit 1927- *WhoAm 94*
Nobles, Lewis 1925- *WhoAm 94*
Nobles, Milton d1924 *WhoHol 92*
Nobles, Milton, Jr. d1925 *WhoHol 92*
Nobles, Patricia Joyce 1955- *WhoBlA 94*
Noblin, Bobby Gene 1937- *WhoAmP 93*
Noblin, Charles Donald 1933- *WhoScEn 94*
Noblit, Betty Jean 1948- *WhoWest 94*
Noblitt, Floyd Wilson 1923- *WhoAmP 93*
Noblitt, Harding Coolidge 1920- *WhoAm 94, WhoMW 93*
Noblitt, Nancy Anne 1959- *WhoScEn 94*
Noboa, Junior 1964- *WhoHisp 94*
Noboa-Polanco, Julio 1949- *WhoHisp 94*
Nobrega, Isabel da 1925- *BlmGWL*
Nobriga, Ted d1981 *WhoHol 92*
Nocas, Andrew James 1941- *WhoAmL 94*
Noce, Gerard Thomas 1951- *WhoAmL 94*
Noce, Robert Henry 1914- *WhoAm 94, WhoScEn 94, WhoWest 94*
Noce, Walter William, Jr. 1945- *WhoAm 94*
Nocera, John Anthony 1952- *WhoAmL 94*
Nocerino, Kathryn *DrAPF 93*
Nochimson, David 1943- *WhoAm 94*
Nochlin, Linda (Pommer) 1931- *WhoAmA 93*
Nochlin, Linda Weinberg 1931- *WrDr 94*
Nochman, Lois Wood Kivi 1924- *WhoMW 93*
Noci, Giovanni Enrico 1955- *WhoScEn 94*
Nock, O(swald) S(tevens) 1905- *WrDr 94*
Nocker, Hans Gunter 1927- *NewGrDO*
Nocks, James Jay 1943- *WhoAm 94, WhoScEn 94*
Nocks, Randall Ian 1969- *WhoScEn 94*
Noda, Takayo *WhoAmA 93*
Noda, Takayo 1934- *WhoAsA 94*
Noda, Takeshi *IntWW 93*
Noda, Tetsuya 1940- *IntWW 93*
Noda, Yutaka 1937- *WhoScEn 94*
Nodal, Adolfo Victoriano 1950- *WhoHisp 94*
Nodder, Timothy Edward 1930- *Who 94*
Nodel, Sol 1912-1976 *WhoAmA 93N*
Nodelman, Jared Robert 1937- *WhoFI 94, WhoWest 94*
Nodiff, Bradley 1965- *WhoFI 94*
Nodine, Jane Allen 1954- *WhoAmA 93*
Nodset, Joan L. *WrDr 94*
Nodset, Joan L. 1913- *WrDr 94*
Nodtvedt, Donald Paul 1951- *WhoMW 93*
Noe, David Clifford 1964- *WhoFI 94, WhoWest 94*
Noe, Elnora 1928- *WhoMW 93*
Noe, Frances Elsie 1923- *WhoMW 93*
Noe, Guy 1934- *WhoAm 94*
Noe, James Alva 1932- *WhoAmL 94*
Noe, James Kirby 1951- *WhoMW 93*
Noe, Jerre Donald 1923- *WhoAm 94*
Noe, Jerry Lee 1940- *WhoAmA 93*
Noe, Paul Robert 1962- *WhoAmL 94*
Noe, Randolph 1939- *WhoAmL 94*
Noe, Robert d1988 *WhoHol 92*
Noe, Roger C. 1949- *WhoAmP 93*
Noebe, Ronald Dean 1961- *WhoMW 93, WhoScEn 94*
Noehren, Robert 1910- *WhoAm 94*
Noel *Who 94*
Noel, Alan d1977 *WhoHol 92*
Noel, Ann Harting 1944- *WhoAmP 93*
Noel, Atanielle Annyn 1947- *EncSF 93*
Noel, Bernard d1970 *WhoHol 92*
Noel, Chris 1942- *WhoHol 92*
Noel, Conrad le Despenser Roden 1869-1942 *DcNaB MP*
Noel, Curtis I. 1964- *WhoFI 94*
Noel, Dale Leon 1936- *WhoScEn 94*
Noel, David Bobbitt, Jr. 1950- *WhoAmL 94*
Noel, Donald Claude 1930- *WhoAmA 93*
Noel, Edwin Lawrence 1946- *WhoAm 94, WhoAmL 94*
Noel, Eldon Keith 1929- *WhoAmP 93*
Noel, Emile 1922- *IntWW 93*
Noel, Franklin Linwood 1951- *WhoAm 94, WhoAmL 94*
Noel, Gambier John Byng 1914- *Who 94*
Noel, Geoffrey Lindsay James 1923- *Who 94*
Noel, Georges 1924- *WhoAmA 93*
Noel, Gerald T., Sr. 1934- *WhoBlA 94*
Noel, Gerard Eyre Wriothesley 1926- *Who 94*
Noel, James Latane, Jr. 1909- *WhoAmL 94*
Noel, Jean 1940- *WhoAmA 93*
Noel, John 1930- *WrDr 94*
Noel, Laurent 1920- *WhoAm 94*
Noel, Lynton Cosmas 1928- *Who 94*
Noel, Magali 1932- *WhoHol 92*
Noel, Michael Lee 1941- *WhoFI 94*
Noel, Nicholas, III 1952- *WhoAmL 94*
Noel, Patrick Adolphus 1940- *WhoBlA 94*
Noel, Randall Deane 1953- *WhoAm 94, WhoAmL 94*
Noel, Sterling 1903-1984 *EncSF 93*
Noel, Tallulah Ann 1945- *WhoMW 93*
Noel, Victoire *NewGrDO*
Noel-Baker, Francis Edward 1920- *Who 94*
Noel-Buxton, Baron 1940- *Who 94*

Norcross, Marvin Augustus 1931- *WhoAm 94, WhoScEn 94*
Nord, Carol Ann *DrAPF 93*
Nord, David Paul 1947- *WhoMW 93*
Nord, David Wayne 1962- *WhoMW 93*
Nord, Eric Thomas 1917- *WhoAm 94*
Nord, Hans Robert 1919- *IntWW 93*
Nord, Harold Emil, Jr. 1928- *WhoFI 94*
Nord, Henry J. 1917- *WhoAm 94*
Nord, Paul Elliott 1936- *WhoAm 94*
Nord, Robert Eamor 1945- *WhoAm 94, WhoAmL 94*
Nord, Walter Robert 1939- *WhoAm 94*
Nordal, Johannes 1924- *IntWW 93*
Nordberg, Ivar 1933- *IntWW 93*
Nordberg, John Albert 1926- *WhoAm 94, WhoAmL 94*
Nordberg, Nils Lovering 1934- *WhoAmP 93*
Nordbo, Eldrid 1942- *WhoWomW 91*
Nordbrandt, Henrik 1945- *ConWorW 93*
Nordby, Eugene Jorgen 1918- *WhoAm 94, WhoMW 93, WhoScEn 94*
Nordby, Gene Milo 1926- *WhoAm 94*
Nordbye, Rodger Lincoln 1918- *WhoAm 94*
Norddahl, Birgir Valson 1947- *WhoFI 94*
Nordell, Emma Parker *WhoAmA 93N*
Nordell, Hans Roderick 1925- *WhoAm 94*
Norden, Bengt Johan Fredrik 1945- *WhoScEn 94*
Norden, Christine d1988 *WhoHol 92*
Norden, Denis 1922- *Who 94*
Norden, Dennis Arthur 1945- *WhoAmL 94*
Norden, Eric *EncSF 93*
Norden, K. Elis 1921- *WhoFI 94*
Norden, Tommy 1953- *WhoHol 92*
Nordenberg, Mark Alan 1948- *WhoAm 94*
Nordenskjold, Nils Adolf Erik 1832-1901 *WhWE*
Nordenskjold, Nils Otto Gustaf 1869-1928 *WhWE*
Nordgren, Ronald Paul 1936- *WhoAm 94, WhoScEn 94*
Nordgren, Sharon L. 1943- *WhoAmP 93*
Nordgren, William Bennett 1960- *WhoWest 94*
Nordhagen, Hallie Huerth 1914- *WhoMW 93*
Nordhagen, Per Jonas 1929- *IntWW 93*
Nordhaug, Odd 1953- *ConAu 140*
Nordhaus, Jean *DrAPF 93*
Nordhausen, A. Henry 1901- *WhoAmA 93*
Nordhoff, Charles Gilbert 1959- *WhoWest 94*
Nordica, Lillian 1857-1914 *NewGrDO [port]*
Nordin, Paul 1929- *WhoScEn 94*
Nordin, Phyllis E. *WhoAmA 93*
Nordin, Phyllis Eck *WhoMW 93*
Nordin, Vidar John 1924- *WhoAm 94*
Nordland, Gerald *WhoAm 94*
Nordland, Gerald John *WhoAmA 93*
Nordlander, Jan Peter Arne 1955- *WhoScEn 94*
Nordley, Gerald David 1947- *WhoWest 94*
Nordli, Odvar 1927- *IntWW 93*
Nordlie, Robert Conrad 1930- *WhoAm 94, WhoScEn 94*
Nordling, Bernard Erick 1921- *WhoAm 94, WhoAmL 94, WhoFI 94*
Nordling, Carl 1931- *IntWW 93*
Nordlinger, Eric Allen 1939- *WhoAm 94*
Nordlund, Donald Craig 1949- *WhoAm 94, WhoWest 94*
Nordlund, Donald Elmer 1922- *WhoAm 94, WhoFI 94*
Nordlund, James John 1939- *WhoAm 94*
Nordlund, James Robert 1952- *WhoAmP 93*
Nordlund, William Chalmers 1954- *WhoAm 94, WhoAmL 94*
Nordman, Christer Eric 1925- *WhoAm 94*
Nordman, Richard D. 1946- *WhoAm 94*
Nordmark, Glenn Everett 1929- *WhoScEn 94*
Nordmeyer, George 1912-1990 *WhAm 10*
Nordmeyer, Mary Betsy 1939- *WhoWest 94*
Nordquist, Myron Harry 1940- *WhoAm 94*
Nordquist, Stephen Glos 1936- *WhoAmL 94*
Nordqvist, Erik Askbo 1943- *WhoAm 94, WhoFI 94*
Nordstrand, Nathalie Johnson *WhoAmA 93*
Nordstrand, Raymond William 1932- *WhoAm 94*
Nordstrand, Scott Jeffery 1958- *WhoAmL 94*
Nordstrom, Bruce A. 1933- *WhoAm 94, WhoFI 94, WhoWest 94*
Nordstrom, Clarence d1968 *WhoHol 92*
Nordstrom, Elmer J. d1993 *NewYTBS 93*
Nordstrom, James F. 1940- *WhoFI 94, WhoWest 94*
Nordstrom, James Philip 1944- *WhoAmL 94*
Nordstrom, James William 1929- *WhoMW 93, WhoScEn 94*
Nordstrom, John N. 1937- *WhoAm 94, WhoFI 94, WhoWest 94*
Nordstrom, Richard Dean 1933- *WhoWest 94*
Nordstrom, Torkel 1910- *IntWW 93*
Nordtvedt, Kenneth L., Jr. 1939- *WhoAmP 93*
Nordwald, Charles 1955- *WhoAmP 93*
Noreault, Terry Robert 1953- *WhoMW 93*
Noreika, Joseph Casimir 1950- *WhoMW 93*
Noreika, Louise A. 1923- *WhoAmP 93*
Norek, Frances Therese 1947- *WhoAmL 94*
Norell, Henry d1990 *WhoHol 92*
Norell, Jacob Solomon 1927- *Who 94*
Norell, Mark Allen 1957- *WhoScEn 94*
Norelli, Martina Roudabush 1942- *WhoAmA 93*
Norelputus dc. 1902 *EncNAR*
Norem, Allen John 1941- *WhoAmP 93*
Norem, Richard Frederick, Sr. 1931- *WhoAm 94*
Noren, Lars 1944- *ConWorW 93, IntDcT 2*
Norena, Eide 1884-1968 *NewGrDO*
Norena, Maria Claudia 1963- *WhoHisp 94*
Norfleet, Barbara Pugh *WhoAmA 93*
Norfleet, Janet 1933- *WhoBlA 94*
Norfleet, Robert F., Jr. 1940- *WhoAm 94*
Norfolk, Archdeacon of *Who 94*
Norfolk, Duke of 1915- *IntWW 93, Who 94*
Norfolk, Edward Matheson 1921- *Who 94*
Norfolk, Lavinia, Duchess of 1916- *Who 94*
Norfolk, Lawrence 1963- *ConLC 76 [port]*
Norfolk, Leslie William 1911- *Who 94*
Norfolk, Neveda Brooks 1929- *WhoAmP 93*
Norfolk, William Ray 1941- *WhoAm 94, WhoAmL 94*
Norford, George E. 1918- *WhoBlA 94*
Norgaard, Carl Aage 1924- *IntWW 93*
Norgaard, Ivar 1922- *IntWW 93*
Norgaard, Richard Bruce 1943- *WhoWest 94*
Norgard, John Davey 1914- *Who 94*
Norgard, Michael Vincent 1951- *WhoScEn 94*
Norgard, Per 1932- *NewGrDO*
Norgle, Charles Ronald, Sr. 1937- *WhoAm 94, WhoAmL 94*
Norgon, Loretta Ann Mitchell *WhoMW 93*
Norgren, C. Neil 1923- *WhoAm 94, WhoWest 94*
Norgren, Constance *DrAPF 93*
Norgren, Ralph 1943- *WhoScEn 94*
Norholm, Ib 1931- *NewGrDO*
Nori, Dattatreyudu *WhoAsA 94*
Norick, Ronald 1941- *WhoAm 94*
Norick, Ronald J. 1941- *WhoAmP 93*
Noriega, Antonio 1940- *IntWW 93*
Noriega, Chon A. 1961- *ConAu 141*
Noriega, Eduardo 1918- *WhoHol 92*
Noriega, Edward Manuel L. 1960- *WhoHisp 94*
Noriega, Richard, Jr. 1950- *WhoHisp 94*
Noriega, Roger F. A. 1959- *WhoHisp 94*
Noriega, Saturnino N. 1939- *WhoHisp 94*
Noriega Rodriguez, David *WhoAmP 93, WhoHisp 94*
Norins, Arthur Leonard 1928- *WhoAm 94, WhoScEn 94*
Norinsky, Marvin 1927- *WrDr 94*
Noris, Assia 1912- *WhoHol 92*
Noris, Matteo d1714 *NewGrDO*
Nork, William Edward 1934- *WhoAmL 94*
Norkin, Mark Mitchell 1955- *WhoWest 94*
Norkus, Michael 1946- *WhoAm 94*
Norland, Donald Richard 1924- *WhoAm 94*
Norland, Otto Realf 1930- *Who 94*
Norlander, John Allen 1930- *WhoAm 94, WhoFI 94*
Norling, Bengt Olov 1925- *IntWW 93*
Norling, Bernard 1924- *WrDr 94*
Norling, Irwin Denison 1916- *WhoMW 93*
Norling, James A. *WhoFI 94*
Norling, Richard Arthur 1945- *WhoMW 93*
Norlund, Evy 1938- *WhoHol 92*
Norman, Albert George, Jr. 1929- *WhoAm 94, WhoAmL 94, WhoFI 94*
Norman, Alex James 1931- *WhoBlA 94*
Norman, Amber d1972 *WhoHol 92*
Norman, Anthony Mansfeldt 1934- *Who 94*
Norman, Anthony Westcott 1938- *WhoAm 94*
Norman, Archibald John 1954- *Who 94*
Norman, Archibald Percy 1912- *Who 94*
Norman, Arnold McCallum, Jr. 1940- *WhoScEn 94*
Norman, Arthur (Gordon) 1917- *Who 94*
Norman, Arthur Gordon 1917- *IntWW 93*
Norman, Barry *IntMPA 94*
Norman, Barry 1933- *EncSF 93*
Norman, Barry (Leslie) 1933- *Who 94*
Norman, Barry Leslie 1933- *IntWW 93*
Norman, Bobby Don 1933- *WhoBlA 94*
Norman, Bruce (Anthony John) 1936- *WrDr 94*
Norman, Calvin Haines 1923- *WhoBlA 94*
Norman, Charles Henry 1920- *WhoMW 93*
Norman, Clarence, Jr. 1951- *WhoAmP 93*
Norman, Clifford P. 1943- *WhoBlA 94*
Norman, Colin Arthur 1948- *WhoAm 94*
Norman, David A. 1935- *WhoFI 94*
Norman, David Mark 1941- *WhoAm 94*
Norman, Denis 1931- *IntWW 93*
Norman, Desmond *Who 94*
Norman, (Nigel) Desmond 1929- *Who 94*
Norman, Diana 1935- *WrDr 94*
Norman, Donald Arthur 1935- *WhoAm 94, WhoWest 94*
Norman, Dorothy (S.) 1905- *WhoAmA 93*
Norman, Dudley Kent 1949- *WhoAm 94*
Norman, E. Gladys 1933- *WhoFI 94, WhoScEn 94, WhoWest 94*
Norman, Edward R(obert) 1938- *WrDr 94*
Norman, Edward Robert 1938- *Who 94*
Norman, Eric *EncSF 93*
Norman, Eugene 1928- *WhoMW 93*
Norman, (John) Frank 1930-1980 *ConDr 93*
Norman, Geoffrey 1935- *Who 94*
Norman, Geoffrey Robert 1944- *WhoAm 94*
Norman, George Alfred B. *Who 94*
Norman, George Buford, Jr. 1945- *WhoAm 94*
Norman, George Emerson, Jr. 1914-1990 *WhAm 10*
Norman, Georgette M. 1946- *WhoBlA 94*
Norman, Gertrude d1943 *WhoHol 92*
Norman, Greg 1955- *WhoAm 94*
Norman, Greg(ory John) 1955- *WrDr 94*
Norman, Gurney *DrAPF 93*
Norman, Jack *WhoHol 92*
Norman, James H. 1948- *WhoBlA 94*
Norman, James Harold 1942- *WhoScEn 94*
Norman, Jessye 1945- *AfrAmAl 6 [port], ConBlB 5 [port], IntWW 93, NewGrDO, Who 94, WhoAm 94, WhoBlA 94*
Norman, Jett *WhoHol 92*
Norman, Jim 1935- *WhoAmP 93*
Norman, Joe G., Jr. 1947- *WhoAm 94*
Norman, John *Who 94*
Norman, John c. 1748-1817 *WhAmRev*
Norman, John 1931- *EncSF 93, WrDr 94*
Norman, (Herbert) John (La French) 1932- *Who 94*
Norman, John Barstow, Jr. 1940- *WhoAm 94, WhoWest 94*
Norman, John C. 1930- *WhoBlA 94*
Norman, John Edward 1922- *WhoFI 94, WhoWest 94*
Norman, Josephine d1951 *WhoHol 92*
Norman, Judith McDonald 1936- *WhoAmL 94*
Norman, Karyl d1947 *WhoHol 92*
Norman, Kenneth Darnel 1964- *WhoBlA 94*
Norman, Kenneth Roy 1925- *Who 94*
Norman, Kim Karen 1961- *WhoMW 93*
Norman, LaLander Stadig 1912- *WhoAm 94*
Norman, Larry Ellis 1952- *WhoAmP 93*
Norman, Lilith 1927- *WrDr 94*
Norman, Lindsay Dean, Jr. 1937- *WhoWest 94*
Norman, Lucille 1926- *WhoHol 92*
Norman, Maidie 1914- *WhoHol 92*
Norman, Maidie Ruth 1912- *WhoBlA 94*
Norman, Mark (Annesley) 1927- *Who 94*
Norman, Mark Richard 1910- *Who 94*
Norman, Marsha 1947- *BlmGWL, ConAu 41NR, ConDr 93, IntDcT 2, WhoAm 94, WrDr 94*
Norman, Millie Thomas 1953- *WhoMW 93*
Norman, Moses C. *WhoBlA 94*
Norman, Norman B. 1914- *WhAm 10*
Norman, P. Roosevelt 1933- *WhoBlA 94*
Norman, Patricia 1947- *WhoBlA 94*
Norman, Perry d1945 *WhoHol 92*
Norman, Peter Minert 1932- *WhoMW 93*
Norman, Philip Sidney 1924- *WhoAm 94*
Norman, Ralph David 1915- *WhoAm 94*
Norman, Ralph Louis 1933- *WhoAm 94*
Norman, Richard Arthur 1915- *WhoAm 94*
Norman, Richard Oswald Chandler d1993 *Who 94N*
Norman, Richard Oswald Chandler 1932- *IntWW 93*
Norman, Robert (Henry) 1914- *Who 94*
Norman, Robert (Wentworth) 1912- *Who 94*
Norman, Roy A. 1941- *WhoBlA 94*
Norman, Stephen Peckham 1942- *WhoAm 94, WhoFI 94*
Norman, Vesey *Who 94*
Norman, (Alexander) Vesey (Bethune) 1930- *Who 94*
Norman, Wallace 1962- *WhoBlA 94*
Norman, William Caffey, III 1953- *WhoAmL 94*
Norman, William H. 1946- *WhoBlA 94*
Norman, William James 1922- *WhoAmP 93*
Norman, William S. 1938- *WhoBlA 94*
Norman, William Stanley 1938- *WhoAm 94, WhoFI 94*
Norman, Willoughby Rollo *Who 94*
Norman, Willoughby Rollo 1909- *IntWW 93*
Norman, Wyatt Thomas, III 1952- *WhoFI 94*
Norman, Zack *WhoHol 92*
Normanby, Marquis of 1912- *Who 94*
Normand, Charles William Blyth 1889-1982 *DcNaB MP*
Normand, Edmund Alonso 1965- *WhoAmL 94*
Normand, James Arthur 1953- *WhoAmP 93*
Normand, Mabel d1930 *WhoHol 92*
Normand, Mabel 1930- *WhoCom*
Normand, Robert 1936- *WhoAm 94*
Normandeau, Andre Gabriel 1942- *WhoAm 94*
Normandin, Kurt A. 1957- *WhoAmP 93*
Normant, Henri 1907- *IntWW 93*
Normanton, Earl of 1945- *Who 94*
Normanton, Tom 1917- *Who 94*
Norment, Thomas K., Jr. 1946- *WhoAmP 93*
Normile, Michael T. 1949- *WhoAm 94*
Normington, David John 1951- *Who 94*
Normington, John 1937- *WhoHol 92*
Normyx *EncSF 93*
Norniella, Jesús, Jr. 1940- *WhoHisp 94*
Noro, Kyoichi 1919- *IntWW 93*
Noro, Line d1985 *WhoHol 92*
Norodom Sihanouk, Samdech Preah 1922- *IntWW 93*
Norona, Richard Owen, Jr. 1940- *WhoHisp 94*
Noronha, Francisco de Sa 1820-1881 *NewGrDO*
Norquist, John O. 1949- *WhoAmP 93*
Norquist, John Olof 1949- *WhoAm 94, WhoMW 93*
Norrander, Barbara 1954- *ConAu 141*
Norrback, Johan Ole 1941- *IntWW 93*
Norrby, Johannes 1936- *WhoIns 94*
Norrell, Mary Patricia *WhoMW 93*
Norrell-Nance, Rosalind Elizabeth 1950- *WhoBlA 94*
Norrell-Thomas, Sondra 1941- *WhoBlA 94*
Norreys, Lord 1958- *Who 94*
Norrgard, Clyde L. *WhoAmP 93*
Norrgard, Kristin Ann 1957- *WhoAm 94*
Norrie, Baron 1936- *Who 94*
Norrie, Anna d1957 *WhoHol 92*
Norrie, Claude d1916 *WhoHol 92*
Norrie, Marian Farrow 1940- *Who 94*
Norrington, Humphrey Thomas 1936- *Who 94*
Norrington, Roger (Arthur Carver) 1934- *NewGrDO*
Norrington, Roger Arthur Carver 1934- *IntWW 93, Who 94*
Norris, Alan E. 1935- *WhoAmP 93*
Norris, Alan Eugene 1935- *WhoAm 94, WhoAmL 94, WhoMW 93*
Norris, Albert Stanley 1926- *WhoAm 94*
Norris, Alfred Lloyd 1938- *WhoWest 94*
Norris, Andrea Spaulding 1945- *WhoAm 94, WhoAmA 93, WhoMW 93*
Norris, Arthur Mae 1911- *WhoBlA 94*
Norris, (Robert) Ben 1910- *WhoAmA 93*
Norris, Benjamin Franklin, Jr. 1870-1902 *AmCulL*
Norris, Charles L., Sr. 1926- *WhoBlA 94*
Norris, Charles R. 1925- *WhoAmP 93*
Norris, Charley William 1933- *WhoMW 93*
Norris, Chester E., Jr. 1927- *WhoAmP 93*
Norris, Christopher 1953- *WhoHol 92*
Norris, Christopher Neil F. *Who 94*
Norris, Chuck *NewYTBS 93 [port], WhoAm 94*
Norris, Chuck 1939- *WhoHol 92*
Norris, Chuck 1940- *IntMPA 94*
Norris, Clarence E. 1910- *WhoAmP 93*
Norris, Clay Allen 1957- *WhoMW 93*
Norris, Curtis Bird 1927- *WhoAm 94*
Norris, Curtis H. 1913- *WhoBlA 94*
Norris, Cynthia Clarice 1956- *WhoBlA 94*

Norris, D. Wayne 1939- *WhoWest 94*
Norris, Darell Forest 1928- *WhoAm 94*
Norris, Dave Noel 1942- *WhoAmP 93*
Norris, David Byrd 1933- *WhoAmP 93*
Norris, David Joseph 1922- *Who 94*
Norris, David Stuart 1938- *WhoAm 94*
Norris, Dennis E. *WhoMW 93*
Norris, Dolores June 1938- *WhoScEn 94*
Norris, Donna M. 1943- *WhoBlA 94*
Norris, Edward 1910- *WhoHol 92*
Norris, Edward Patrick 1940- *WhoAm 94*
Norris, Edwin L. 1946- *WhoAm 94*
Norris, Eleanor 1919- *WhoHol 92*
Norris, Elizabeth fl. 1748-1752 *NewGrDO*
Norris, Eric (George) 1918- *Who 94*
Norris, Eric Alexander 1959- *WhoWest 94*
Norris, Eric George 1918- *IntWW 93*
Norris, Ethel Maureen 1956- *WhoBlA 94*
Norris, Floyd Hamilton 1908- *WhoAmL 94*
Norris, Frances McMurtray 1946- *WhoAmP 93*
Norris, Franklin Gray 1923- *WhoAm 94, WhoScEn 94*
Norris, Fred Arthur, Jr. 1945- *WhoBlA 94*
Norris, Geoffrey 1937- *WhoAm 94*
Norris, Geoffrey 1947- *WrDr 94*
Norris, Gilbert Frank 1916- *Who 94*
Norris, Graham Alexander 1913- *Who 94*
Norris, Gunilla *DrAPF 93*
Norris, H. Thomas 1934- *WhoAm 94*
Norris, James Arnold 1937- *WhoAm 94*
Norris, James Ellsworth Chiles 1932- *WhoBlA 94*
Norris, James Harrold 1953- *WhoAm 94*
Norris, James Rufus, Jr. 1941- *WhoMW 93, WhoScEn 94*
Norris, James W. 1930- *WhoAmP 93*
Norris, Janet Clare 1952- *WhoAmL 94*
Norris, Joan *DrAPF 93*
Norris, John Anthony 1946- *WhoAm 94, WhoFI 94*
Norris, John Franklyn 1877-1952 *DcAmReB 2*
Norris, John Hallam Mercer 1929- *Who 94*
Norris, John Hart 1942- *WhoAm 94, WhoAmL 94, WhoMW 93*
Norris, John Robert 1932- *Who 94*
Norris, John Robert 1967- *WhoScEn 94*
Norris, John Windsor, Jr. 1936- *WhoAm 94, WhoFI 94*
Norris, Karen *WhoHol 92*
Norris, Karl Howard 1921- *WhoScEn 94*
Norris, Kathleen *DrAPF 93*
Norris, Ken *WhoHol 92*
Norris, Ken 1951- *WrDr 94*
Norris, Kenneth Michael 1952- *WhoAmL 94*
Norris, LaVena M. *WhoBlA 94*
Norris, Leonard Matheson 1913- *WhoAmA 93*
Norris, Leslie 1921- *WrDr 94*
Norris, Martin Joseph 1907- *WhoAm 94*
Norris, Mary Beth 1950- *WhoWest 94*
Norris, Melvin 1931- *WhoAm 94*
Norris, Merry *WhoAmA 93*
Norris, Michael David 1964- *WhoFI 94*
Norris, Mike 1962- *WhoHol 92*
Norris, Pamela 1946- *WhoScEn 94*
Norris, Patricia *ConTFT 11*
Norris, Patricia Kilmer 1933- *WhoAmL 94*
Norris, Peter Edward 1942- *WhoScEn 94*
Norris, Phyllis Irene 1909- *WrDr 94*
Norris, Pippa 1953- *WrDr 94*
Norris, Richard d1943 *WhoHol 92*
Norris, Richard Anthony 1943- *WhoAm 94*
Norris, Richard Earl 1926- *WhoWest 94*
Norris, Richard Patrick 1944- *WhoAm 94*
Norris, Robert F. 1922- *WhoFI 94*
Norris, Robert Fogg 1905- *WhoAm 94*
Norris, Robert Matheson 1921- *WhoAm 94*
Norris, Robert Wheeler 1932- *WhoAm 94, WhoAmL 94*
Norris, Ruth Ann 1955- *WhoMW 93*
Norris, Scott Alan 1966- *WhoAmL 94*
Norris, Steven John 1945- *Who 94*
Norris, Sydney George 1937- *Who 94*
Norris, Thomas Clayton 1938- *WhoAm 94, WhoFI 94*
Norris, Thomas Weirich 1951- *WhoMW 93*
Norris, Timothy Jon 1947- *WhoAmL 94*
Norris, Tracy Hopkins 1927- *WhoFI 94, WhoMW 93*
Norris, Vicki Jane 1948- *WhoMW 93*
Norris, Walter, Jr. 1945- *WhoBlA 94*
Norris, William d1929 *WhoHol 92*
Norris, William A. *WhoAmP 93*
Norris, William A. 1927- *WhoAmA 93*
Norris, William Albert 1927- *WhoAm 94, WhoAmL 94, WhoWest 94*
Norris, William E. *WhoBlA 94*
Norriss, Peter Coulson 1944- *Who 94*
Norsa, Hannah d1785 *NewGrDO*
Norse, Harold *DrAPF 93*
Norse, Harold 1916- *ConAu 18AS [port], WrDr 94*
Norst, Joel *EncSF 93*
Norstad, Lauris 1907-1988 *HisDcKW*
Norstein, Yuri 1942- *IntDcF 2-4*
Norstrand, Iris Fletcher 1915- *WhoScEn 94*
Norsworthy, Elizabeth Krassovsky 1943- *WhoAmL 94*
Norsworthy, Lamar 1946- *WhoFI 94*
North *Who 94*
North, Lord 1971- *Who 94*
North, Alan *WhoHol 92*
North, Alastair Macarthur 1932- *IntWW 93*
North, Alex 1910-1991 *IntDcF 2-4, WhAm 10*
North, Andrew *EncSF 93, TwCYAW*
North, Andrew 1912- *WrDr 94*
North, Anne Via 1939- *WhoWest 94*
North, Anthony *TwCYAW*
North, Arielle 1932- *WrDr 94*
North, Carol Sue 1954- *WhoMW 93*
North, Charles *DrAPF 93*
North, Charles d1936 *WhoHol 92*
North, Charles A. 1941- *WhoIns 94*
North, Colin *ConAu 42NR*
North, David *EncSF 93*
North, David Lee 1947- *WhoScEn 94*
North, Douglass C. *NewYTBS 93 [port]*
North, Douglass Cecil 1920- *WhoAm 94*
North, Edmund Hall 1911-1990 *WhAm 10*
North, Elizabeth (Stewart) 1932- *WrDr 94*
North, Eric 1884-1968 *EncSF 93*
North, Frederick 1732-1792 *AmRev*
North, Frederick, Lord 1732-1792 *WhAmRev [port]*
North, Harper Qua 1917-1989 *WhAm 10*
North, Heather 1950- *WhoHol 92*
North, Helen Florence *WhoAm 94*
North, Henry Ringling d1993 *NewYTBS 93 [port]*
North, Hope *WhoHol 92*
North, Jay 1952- *WhoHol 92*
North, Joe d1945 *WhoHol 92*
North, John Adna, Jr. 1944- *WhoFI 94*
North, John David 1934- *IntWW 93*
North, John E., Jr. 1952- *WhoAmL 94*
North, John Joseph 1926- *Who 94*
North, John Ringling d1985 *WhoHol 92*
North, John Thomas 1842-1896 *DcNaB MP*
North, Jonathan *Who 94*
North, (William) Jonathan (Frederick) 1931- *Who 94*
North, Judy 1937- *WhoAmA 93*
North, Kenneth Earl 1945- *WhoAmL 94, WhoFI 94, WhoMW 93*
North, Kevin A. 1952- *WhoIns 94*
North, Mark Huntington 1946- *WhoWest 94*
North, Mary d1976 *WhoHol 92*
North, Mary Hayne *DrAPF 93*
North, May d1949 *WhoHol 92*
North, Milou *ConAu 41NR*
North, Oliver *NewYTBS 93 [port]*
North, Oliver L. 1943- *IntWW 93*
North, Oliver L(aurence) 1943- *ConAu 142*
North, Peter Machin 1936- *IntWW 93, Who 94*
North, Phil Record 1918- *WhoAm 94*
North, Phillip J. 1949- *WhoAm 94*
North, Richard Alan 1944- *WhoScEn 94*
North, Robert d1976 *WhoHol 92*
North, Robert 1916- *WrDr 94*
North, Robert 1945- *IntDcB, Who 94*
North, Robert Carver 1914- *WhoAm 94*
North, Robert John 1935- *WhoAm 94, WhoScEn 94*
North, Sheree 1933- *IntMPA 94, WhoHol 92*
North, Simeon 1765-1852 *WorInv*
North, Sterling 1906-1974 *TwCYAW*
North, Steven Edward 1941- *WhoAmL 94*
North, Susan Lynne 1953- *WhoMW 93*
North, Ted 1916- *WhoHol 92*
North, Thomas 1535?-1601? *BlmGEL*
North, Thomas (Lindsay) 1919- *Who 94*
North, Valentine *EncSF 93*
North, Virginia *WhoHol 92*
North, Warren James 1922- *WhoAm 94*
North, Wheeler James 1922- *WhoAm 94, WhoWest 94*
North, Wilfred d1935 *WhoHol 92*
North, William 1755-1836 *WhAmRev*
North, William Carlton 1945- *WhoAmL 94*
North, William Charles 1925- *WhoAm 94*
North, William Haven 1926- *WhoAm 94*
North, Zeme *WhoHol 92*
Northampton, Archdeacon of *Who 94*
Northampton, Bishop of 1925- *Who 94*
Northampton, Marquess of 1946- *Who 94*
Northard, John Henry 1926- *IntWW 93, Who 94*
Northbourne, Baron 1926- *Who 94*
Northbrook, Baron 1954- *Who 94*
Northcliffe, Alfred Harmsworth, Viscount 1865-1922 *BlmGEL*
Northcote *Who 94*
Northcote, Donald Henry 1921- *IntWW 93, Who 94*
Northcote, Peter 1912- *WrDr 94*
Northcote, Peter Colston 1920- *Who 94*
Northcott, Douglas (Geoffrey) 1916- *WrDr 94*
Northcott, Douglas Geoffrey 1916- *Who 94*
Northcross, David C. 1917- *WhoBlA 94*
Northcross, Deborah Ametra 1951- *WhoBlA 94*
Northcross, Wilson Hill, Jr. 1946- *WhoBlA 94*
Northcutt, Carol Sue 1955- *WhoFI 94*
Northcutt, Clarence Dewey 1916- *WhoAm 94, WhoAmL 94*
Northcutt, Helene Louise Berking 1916- *WhoWest 94*
Northcutt, Robert Hull, Jr. 1934- *WhoAm 94*
Northcutt, Wanda L. 1937- *WhoAmP 93*
North-Eastern Caribbean and Aruba, Bishop of *Who 94*
Northen, Charles Swift, III 1937- *WhoAm 94*
Northenor, Doris Jean 1932- *WhoAmP 93, WhoMW 93*
Northern, Richard 1948- *WhoAmL 94*
Northern, Robert A. 1934- *WhoBlA 94*
Northern Argentina, Bishop of 1937- *Who 94*
Northern Territory (Australia), Bishop of the 1940- *Who 94*
Northesk, Earl of 1926- *Who 94*
Northfield, Baron 1923- *Who 94*
Northington, David K. *WhoAm 94, WhoScEn 94*
Northland, Viscount *Who 94*
Northnagel, E. W. *DrAPF 93*
Northolt, Archdeacon of *Who 94*
Northover, Vernon Keith 1934- *WhoBlA 94*
Northpole, John d1964 *WhoHol 92*
Northrip, Robert Earl 1939- *WhoAm 94, WhoAmL 94*
Northrop, Carl Wooden 1950- *WhoAm 94, WhoAmL 94*
Northrop, Douglas Anthony 1935- *WhoAm 94*
Northrop, Edward Harriman 1943- *WhoFI 94*
Northrop, Edward Skottowe 1911- *WhoAm 94, WhoAmL 94*
Northrop, Filmer S.C. 1893-1992 *AnObit 1992*
Northrop, Filmer Stuart Cuckow 1893- *WhAm 10*
Northrop, Glenn Allen 1953- *WhoWest 94*
Northrop, John H. d1987 *NobelP 91N*
Northrop, John Howard 1891-1987 *WorScD*
Northrop, Monroe 1931- *WhoAm 94*
Northrop, Stuart Johnston 1925- *WhoAm 94, WhoFI 94*
Northrup, Harry d1936 *WhoHol 92*
Northrup, Harry E. *WhoHol 92*
Northrup, Herbert Roof 1918- *WhoAm 94*
Northrup, Kevin Lyle 1942- *WhoMW 93*
Northrup, Sandra Joan 1938- *WhoWest 94*
Northumberland, Archdeacon of *Who 94*
Northumberland, Duke of 1953- *Who 94*
Northup, Anne Meagher 1948- *WhoAmP 93*
Northup, Brian Keith 1958- *WhoScEn 94*
Northup, John David 1910- *WhoAm 94*
Northup, T. Eugene *WhoScEn 94*
Northway, Eileen Mary 1931- *Who 94*
Northway, Wanda I. 1942- *WhoMW 93*
Northwick, Baron 1769-1859 *DcNaB MP*
Nortje, (Kenneth) Arthur 1942-1970 *BlkWr 2, ConAu 141*
Nortman, M. Judith Haworth 1959- *WhoMW 93*
Norton *Who 94*
Norton, Baron d1993 *Who 94N*
Norton, Baron 1915- *Who 94*
Norton, Andre 1912- *EncSF 93, TwCYAW*
Norton, Andre (Alice) 1912- *WrDr 94*
Norton, Andre Alice *WhoAm 94*
Norton, Andrew Lee 1958- *WhoFI 94*
Norton, Andrew McCall 1962- *WhoAmP 93*
Norton, Andrews 1786-1853 *DcAmReB 2*
Norton, Ann W. d1982 *WhoAmA 93N*
Norton, Augustus Richard 1946- *WhoAm 94, WrDr 94*
Norton, Aurelia Evangeline 1932- *WhoBlA 94*
Norton, Barry d1956 *WhoHol 92*
Norton, Caroline 1808-1877 *BlmGWL*
Norton, Charles Leroy, Jr. 1964- *WhoAmL 94*
Norton, Cliff *WhoHol 92*
Norton, Clifford Charles 1918- *WhoAm 94*
Norton, Dale Hamilton 1948- *WhoFI 94*
Norton, Dave Kenneth 1949- *WhoFI 94*
Norton, David C. 1946- *WhoAm 94, WhoAmL 94*
Norton, David William 1944- *WhoWest 94*
Norton, Delmar Lynn 1944- *WhoAm 94*
Norton, Desmond Anthony 1942- *WhoScEn 94*
Norton, Diana Mae 1945- *WhoFI 94, WhoMW 93*
Norton, Donald 1920- *Who 94*
Norton, Donald Linn *WhoWest 94*
Norton, Donn H. 1942- *WhoFI 94*
Norton, Douglas Ray 1933- *WhoFI 94, WhoWest 94*
Norton, Edgar d1953 *WhoHol 92*
Norton, Edward Worthington 1938- *WhoBlA 94*
Norton, Elda d1947 *WhoHol 92*
Norton, Eleanor Holmes *WhoAmP 93*
Norton, Eleanor Holmes 1937- *CngDr 93, WhoAm 94, WhoAmL 94*
Norton, Eleanor Holmes 1938- *AfrAmAl 6, WhoBlA 94*
Norton, Elizabeth Wychgel 1933- *WhoAmL 94*
Norton, Eunice 1908- *WhoAm 94*
Norton, Fay-Tyler Murray 1925- *WhoMW 93*
Norton, Fletcher d1941 *WhoHol 92*
Norton, Floyd Ligon, IV 1950- *WhoAm 94*
Norton, Frank Louis 1942- *WhoAmP 93*
Norton, Fred Carl 1938- *WhoAmP 93*
Norton, Frederick d1946 *WhoHol 92*
Norton, Gale 1954- *WhoAm 94, WhoAmL 94, WhoWest 94*
Norton, Gale Ann 1954- *WhoAmP 93*
Norton, George Dawson 1930- *WhoAm 94*
Norton, George Haseltine, Jr. 1914- *WhoFI 94*
Norton, Gerald Patrick 1940- *WhoAm 94*
Norton, Gerard Ross 1915- *Who 94*
Norton, Gregory c. 1603-1652 *DcNaB MP*
Norton, Harry N(eugebauer) 1922- *ConAu 142*
Norton, Harry Neugebauer 1922- *WhoScEn 94*
Norton, Heather Gaye 1967- *WhoMW 93*
Norton, Howard Cherrington 1955- *WhoWest 94*
Norton, Howard Melvin 1911- *WhoAm 94*
Norton, Hugh Edward 1936- *IntWW 93, Who 94*
Norton, Hugh Stanton 1921- *WhoAm 94*
Norton, Jack d1958 *WhoHol 92*
Norton, James 1931- *Who 94*
Norton, James Adolphus 1922- *WhoAm 94*
Norton, James J. 1930- *WhoAm 94, WhoFI 94*
Norton, Janice Elizabeth 1967- *WhoWest 94*
Norton, Jenny 1945- *WhoAmP 93*
Norton, Jerry Don 1958- *WhoScEn 94*
Norton, Jim 1938- *WhoHol 92*
Norton, Jody 1943- *WhoMW 93*
Norton, John *DrAPF 93*
Norton, John Hise 1952- *WhoAmL 94*
Norton, John Justin 1932- *WhoAmL 94*
Norton, John L. *WhoAmP 93*
Norton, John Lindsey 1935- *Who 94*
Norton, Judy *WhoAm 94*
Norton, Judy 1957- *WhoHol 92*
Norton, Karen Ann 1950- *WhoWest 94*
Norton, Kay d1985 *WhoHol 92*
Norton, Ken 1945- *WhoHol 92*
Norton, Kenneth Howard, Jr. 1966- *WhoBlA 94*
Norton, Lewis Franklin 1930- *WhoIns 94*
Norton, Lloyd Darrell 1953- *WhoMW 93*
Norton, Mark d1982 *WhoHol 92*
Norton, Mary 1903-1992 *AnObit 1992, WrDr 94N*
Norton, Mary Beth 1943- *WhoAm 94*
Norton, Mary Joyce *WhoAmA 93*
Norton, Mary Katherine *WhoAmL 94*
Norton, Michael Jeffrey 1938- *WhoAmP 93*
Norton, Ned d1961 *WhoHol 92*
Norton, Norman James 1933- *WhoAm 94*
Norton, Omar P. *WhoAmP 93*
Norton, Paul Allen 1913- *WhoAm 94*
Norton, Paul Foote 1917- *WhoAmA 93*
Norton, Peter Bowes 1929- *WhoAm 94, WhoFI 94, WhoMW 93*
Norton, Philip *EncSF 93*
Norton, Philip 1951- *WrDr 94*
Norton, Robert Anthony 1939- *IntWW 93*
Norton, Robert Leo, Sr. 1939- *WhoScEn 94*
Norton, Robert W. 1923- *WhoAmP 93*
Norton, Roy (E.) 1869-1942 *EncSF 93*
Norton, Stephen Allen 1940- *WhoAm 94*

Norton, Steven David 1965- *WhoMW 93, WhoScEn 94*
Norton, Thomas C. 1934- *WhoAmP 93*
Norton, Thomas Carter 1948- *WhoMW 93*
Norton, Thomas Edmond 1940- *WhoAm 94*
Norton, Tom E. 1940- *WhoAmP 93*
Norton, Victor Thane 1904-1989 *WhAm 10*
Norton, William George 1951- *WhoAmP 93*
Norton-Griffiths, John 1938- *Who 94*
Nortz, H. Robert 1932- *WhoAmP 93*
Norum, David P. 1931- *WhoFI 94*
Norup, Kim Stefan 1945- *WhoScEn 94*
Norvel, William Leonard 1935- *WhoBlA 94*
Norvell, G. Todd 1942- *WhoAm 94, WhoAmL 94*
Norvell, James David 1939- *WhoAmP 93*
Norvell, Patsy 1942- *WhoAmA 93*
Norvell, Ralph, Jr. 1921- *WhoAmL 94*
Norvelle, Norman Reese 1946- *WhoScEn 94*
Norvil, Manning *EncSF 93*
Norville, Craig Hubert 1944- *WhoAm 94, WhoAmL 94, WhoFI 94*
Norville, Deborah 1958- *WhoAm 94*
Norville, Herbert *WhoHol 92*
Norvo, Red 1908- *WhoHol 92*
Norwalk, Thomas Sawyer 1930- *WhoMW 93*
Norwell, John August 1946- *WhoFI 94*
Norwich, Archdeacon of *Who 94*
Norwich, Bishop of 1933- *Who 94*
Norwich, Dean of *Who 94*
Norwich, Viscount 1929- *IntWW 93, Who 94*
Norwich, Isaac of c. 1170-1235? *DcNaB MP*
Norwich, John Julius (Cooper) 1929- *WrDr 94*
Norwick, Braham 1916- *WhoScEn 94*
Norwick, Kenneth P. 1941- *WhoAmL 94*
Norwood, Bernard 1922- *WhoAm 94*
Norwood, Bernice N. 1917- *WhoBlA 94*
Norwood, Calvin Coolidge 1927- *WhoBlA 94*
Norwood, Carol Ruth 1949- *WhoScEn 94*
Norwood, Colvin Gamble, Jr. 1947- *WhoAm 94, WhoAmL 94*
Norwood, Deborah Anne 1950- *WhoAmL 94*
Norwood, Edward Andrew 1962- *WhoAmL 94*
Norwood, Eille d1948 *WhoHol 92*
Norwood, Elizabeth Lee 1912- *WhoBlA 94*
Norwood, Frederick Abbott 1914- *ConAu 42NR*
Norwood, Frederick Reyes 1939- *WhoWest 94*
Norwood, Geoffrey Alexander 1950- *WhoAm 94*
Norwood, George Joseph 1938- *WhoAm 94*
Norwood, Grover Carroll 1942- *WhoFI 94*
Norwood, Jack Mitchell 1930- *WhoAmP 93*
Norwood, Jack Roy 1926- *WhoFI 94*
Norwood, James Alan 1944- *WhoFI 94*
Norwood, Janet L. *WhoAmP 93*
Norwood, Janet Lippe 1923- *WhoAm 94, WhoFI 94*
Norwood, John F. 1927- *WhoBlA 94*
Norwood, Keith Edward 1963- *WhoScEn 94*
Norwood, Lily *WhoHol 92*
Norwood, Malcolm Mark 1928- *WhoAmA 93*
Norwood, Ronald Eugene 1952- *WhoBlA 94, WhoWest 94*
Norwood, Suzanne Freda 1926- *Who 94*
Norwood, Tom 1943- *WhoBlA 94*
Norwood, Victor (George Charles) 1920-1983 *EncSF 93*
Norwood, Walter (Neville) 1907- *Who 94*
Norwood, Warren *DrAPF 93*
Norwood, Warren 1945- *WrDr 94*
Norwood, Warren C(arl) 1945- *EncSF 93*
Norwood, William R. 1936- *WhoBlA 94*
Norworth, Jack d1959 *WhoHol 92*
Norz, Charles Henry 1937- *WhoFI 94*
Nosaka, Sanzo d1993 *NewYTBS 93*
NosE, Yukihiko 1932- *WhoScEn 94*
Nosek, Thomas Michael 1947- *WhoScEn 94*
Nosher, Edith d1929 *WhoHol 92*
Noshpitz, Joseph Dove 1922- *WhoAm 94*
Nosiglia, Enrique 1949- *IntWW 93*
Nosille, Nalrah *EncSF 93*
Noske, Frits (Rudolf) 1920- *NewGrDO*
Noskowski, Zygmunt 1846-1909 *NewGrDO*
Nosler, Robert Amos 1946- *WhoWest 94*
Nosov, Yevgeny Ivanovich 1925- *IntWW 93*
Nosratian, Farshad Joseph 1956- *WhoWest 94*
Noss, John Bramble 1935- *IntWW 93, Who 94*
Nossal, Gustav (Joseph Victor) 1931- *Who 94, WrDr 94*
Nossal, Gustav Joseph Victor 1931- *IntWW 93*
Nosseck, Martin d1981 *WhoHol 92*
Nosseck, Max d1972 *WhoHol 92*
Nosseck, Noel 1943- *IntMPA 94*
Nossek, Ralph *WhoHol 92*
Nossen, Bram d1983 *WhoHol 92*
Nossett, Paula Marie 1937- *WhoMW 93*
Nossis fl. 4th cent.BC-3rd cent.BC *BlmGWL*
Nossiter, Bernard 1926-1992 *AnObit 1992*
Nossiter, Bernard Daniel 1926-1992 *WhAm 10*
Nostlinger, Christine 1936- *BlmGWL, TwCYAW*
Nostrand, Howard Lee 1910- *WrDr 94*
Nostrand, Jennifer *DrAPF 93*
Nostrand, S. *DrAPF 93*
Nosworthy, Harold George 1908- *Who 94*
Nota, Kenneth Joseph 1962- *WhoAmL 94*
Nota, Ronald John 1948- *WhoFI 94*
Notarbartolo, Albert *WhoAmA 93*
Notarbartolo, Albert 1934- *WhoAm 94*
Notari, Guido d1957 *WhoHol 92*
Notari, Paul Celestin 1926- *WhoAm 94*
Notarianni, Philip Frank 1948- *WhoWest 94*
Notario, Vicente 1952- *WhoScEn 94*
Notaro, Anthony 1915-1984 *WhoAmA 93N*
Notaro, Michael R. 1914- *WhoAm 94*
Notch, James Stephen 1950- *WhoFI 94*
Note, Jean 1859-1922 *NewGrDO*
Notebaert, Richard C. *WhoAm 94, WhoFI 94*
Noterdaeme, Paul M. J. 1929- *IntWW 93*
Notestein, Barbara 1949- *WhoAmP 93*
Notestein, David Albert 1953- *WhoIns 94*
Notestine, Dorothy J. 1921- *WhoAmA 93*
Notestine, Kerry E. 1956- *WhoAmL 94*
Notestine, Tom W. 1919- *WhoAmA 93*
Notestine, Wilbur Edmund 1931- *WhoAm 94, WhoAmL 94*
Noth, Christopher *WhoHol 92*
Noth, Heinrich 1928- *IntWW 93*
Nothem, James M. 1942- *WhoIns 94*
Nothmann, Gerhard Adolf 1921- *WhoAm 94*
Nothmann, Rudolf S. 1907- *WhoAmL 94, WhoFI 94, WhoWest 94*
Nothnagel, Eugene Alfred 1952- *WhoScEn 94*
Nothomb, Charles Ferdinand 1936- *IntWW 93*
Notice, Guy Symour 1929- *WhoBlA 94*
Notkin, David 1955- *WhoWest 94*
Notkin, Leonard Sheldon 1931 *WhoAm 94*
Notkin, Richard T. 1948- *WhoAmA 93, WhoWest 94*
Notkins, Abner Louis 1932- *WhoScEn 94*
Notley, Alice *DrAPF 93*
Notley, Alice 1945- *WrDr 94*
Notley, Charles Roland Sykes 1939- *Who 94*
Notman, Mark Edward 1953- *WhoMW 93*
Noto, Aldo 1964- *WhoAmL 94*
Noto, Lore(nzo) 1923- *WrDr 94*
Noto, Robert Arthur 1952- *WhoAmL 94*
Notopoulos, Alexander Anastasios, Jr. 1953- *WhoAm 94, WhoAmL 94*
Notosusanto, Nugroho 1931- *IntWW 93*
Notowidigdo, Musinggih Hartoko 1938- *WhoMW 93, WhoScEn 94*
Nott, Charles Robert Harley 1904- *Who 94*
Nott, John (William Frederic) 1932- *Who 94*
Nott, John William Frederic 1932- *IntWW 93*
Nott, Kathleen 1909- *BlmGWL*
Nott, Kathleen (Cecilia) 1909- *EncSF 93*
Nott, Kathleen Cecilia *Who 94*
Nott, Peter John *Who 94*
Nott, Peter John 1933- *IntWW 93*
Nottage, Raymond Frederick Tritton 1916- *Who 94*
Nottara, Constantin C(onstantin) 1890-1950 *NewGrDO*
Nottingham, Archdeacon of *Who 94*
Nottingham, Bishop of 1925- *Who 94*
Nottingham, Edward Willis, Jr. 1948- *WhoAm 94, WhoAmL 94, WhoWest 94*
Nottingham, Pamela M. 1949- *WhoFI 94*
Nottingham, R. Kendall 1938- *WhoIns 94*
Nottingham, Robinson Kendall 1938- *WhoAm 94, WhoFI 94*
Nottingham, William Jesse 1927- *WhoMW 93*
Notz, John Kranz, Jr. 1932- *WhoAm 94*
Noue, Charles-Edouard De La 1624-1691 *WhWE*
Nouel, Philippe 1926- *IntWW 93*
Nougues, Jean(-Charles) 1875-1932 *NewGrDO*
Nouira, Hedi d1993 *IntWW 93N*
Nouira, Hedi 1911-1993 *NewYTBS 93 [port]*
Noulton, John David 1939- *Who 94*
Noumazalay, Ambroise 1933- *IntWW 93*
Nour, Samir 1935- *WhoWest 94*
Nouri, Michael 1945- *IntMPA 94, WhoHol 92*
Nouri-Moghadam, Mohamad Reza 1949- *WhoScEn 94*
Nourissier, Francois 1927- *IntWW 93*
Nourrit, Adolphe 1802-1839 *NewGrDO [port]*
Nourrit, Louis 1780-1831 *NewGrDO*
Nourse, Alan E(dward) 1928-1992 *EncSF 93, WrDr 94N*
Nourse, Allen *WhoHol 92*
Nourse, Hugh Oliver 1933- *WhoFI 94*
Nourse, Martin (Charles) 1932- *Who 94*
Nourse, Thomas Miller 1922- *WhoFI 94*
Nourse, Vincent Kevin 1953- *WhoFI 94*
Nousiainen, Jaakko Ilmari 1931- *IntWW 93*
Nouvel, Jean 1945- *IntWW 93*
Nouwen, Henri J(osef Machiel) 1932- *WrDr 94*
Nova, Craig *DrAPF 93*
Nova, Craig 1945- *WhoAm 94*
Nova, Lou 1920- *WhoHol 92*
Nova, Vangjo 1927-1992 *NewGrDO*
Novacek, Jay McKinley 1962- *WhoAm 94*
Novack, Alvin John 1925- *WhoAm 94*
Novack, David Jay 1950- *WhoAmL 94*
Novack, George 1905-1992 *WrDr 94N*
Novack, Kenneth Joseph 1941- *WhoAm 94*
Novack, Paul David 1958- *WhoAmL 94*
Novack, Robert 1953- *WhoAmL 94*
Novack, Shelly d1978 *WhoHol 92*
Novacky, Anton J. 1933- *WhoMW 93*
Novak, Alfred 1915- *WhoAm 94*
Novak, Barbara *WhoAm 94, WhoAmA 93*
Novak, Blaine *WhoHol 92*
Novak, Bruce A. 1946- *WhoFI 94*
Novak, Charles R. 1957- *WhoScEn 94*
Novak, Drew Edmund 1941- *WhoAmL 94*
Novak, Edward Frank 1947- *WhoAm 94, WhoAmL 94*
Novak, Edward Richard 1917- *WhoMW 93*
Novak, Eugene Francis 1925- *WhoAm 94*
Novak, Eva d1988 *WhoHol 92*
Novak, Francis Alphonsus 1923- *WhoMW 93*
Novak, Helga 1935- *BlmGWL*
Novak, J. G. *WhoAmP 93*
Novak, James B., III 1913- *WhoAmP 93*
Novak, James Michael 1944- *WhoAm 94*
Novak, Jane d1990 *WhoHol 92*
Novak, Jo-Ann Stout 1956- *WhoFI 94*
Novak, John Luther *EncSF 93*
Novak, John Philip 1946- *WhoAmP 93*
Novak, John Robert 1944- *WhoAm 94*
Novak, Josef 1905- *IntWW 93*
Novak, Joseph Donald 1930- *WhoAm 94*
Novak, Kim 1933- *IntMPA 94, WhoAm 94, WhoHol 92*
Novak, Lawrence Peter 1951- *WhoAmP 93*
Novak, Leslie Howard 1944- *WhoAmL 94, WhoMW 93*
Novak, Maximillian Erwin 1930- *WrDr 94*
Novak, Michael *DrAPF 93*
Novak, Michael 1933- *IntWW 93, WrDr 94*
Novak, Michael John 1933- *WhoAm 94*
Novak, Michael Paul *DrAPF 93*
Novak, Milan Vaclav 1907-1992 *WhAm 10*
Novak, Paul 1946- *WhoFI 94*
Novak, Paul Martin 1944- *WhoMW 93*
Novak, Peter John 1939- *WhoAm 94, WhoAmL 94*
Novak, Raymond Francis 1946- *WhoAm 94, WhoScEn 94*
Novak, Robert David Sanders 1931- *WhoAm 94*
Novak, Robert Louis 1928- *WhoScEn 94*
Novak, Steven G. 1949- *WhoAmP 93*
Novak, Terry Lee 1940- *WhoAm 94, WhoWest 94*
Novak, Theodore J. 1940- *WhoAmL 94*
Novak, Victor Anthony 1930- *WhoAm 94, WhoFI 94*
Novak, Vitezslav 1870-1949 *NewGrDO*
Novak, William Arnold 1948- *WhoAm 94*
Novakova, Tereza 1835-1912 *BlmGWL*
Novakovic, Branko Mane 1940- *WhoScEn 94*
Novakovich, Josip *DrAPF 93*
Noval, Michele M. *WhoHisp 94*
Novales, Ronald Richards 1928- *WhoAm 94*
Novara, Mauro 1957- *WhoScEn 94*
Novara, Medea *WhoHol 92*
Novarina, Maurice Paul Joseph 1907- *IntWW 93*
Novarro, Ramon d1968 *WhoHol 92*
Novas, Alfred Robert 1963- *WhoMW 93*
Novas, Joseph, Jr. 1921- *WhoAm 94*
Nova Scotia, Assistant Bishop of *Who 94*
Nova Scotia, Bishop of 1935- *Who 94*
Novatney, John F., Jr. 1930- *WhoAm 94*
Nove, Alec 1915- *WrDr 94*
Nove, Alexander 1915- *IntWW 93*
Nove, Alexander, Prof. 1915- *Who 94*
Novecento, Nick d1987 *WhoHol 92*
Novek, Minda *DrAPF 93*
Novelli, Amleto d1924 *WhoHol 92*
Novelli, Ermete d1919 *WhoHol 92*
Novelli, (Antonio) Felice fl. 1717- *NewGrDO*
Novellino, Anthony Ronald 1949- *WhoAm 94*
Novello, Antonia 1944- *WhoAmP 93*
Novello, Antonia Coello 1944- *WhoAm 94, WhoHisp 94, WhoScEn 94*
Novello, Don *WhoCom*
Novello, Don 1943- *IntMPA 94, WhoAm 94, WhoHol 92*
Novello, Ivor d1951 *WhoHol 92*
Novello, Ivor 1893-1951 *NewGrDO*
Novello, Jay d1982 *WhoHol 92*
November, Robert Stephen 1936- *WhoAm 94*
November, Sharyn *DrAPF 93*
Novembre, Tom *WhoHol 92*
Novenstern, Samuel 1926- *WhoAm 94, WhoFI 94*
Nover, Naomi *WhoAm 94*
Noverre, Jean-Georges 1727-1810 *IntDcB [port], NewGrDO*
Novetzke, Sally Johnson 1932- *WhoAm 94, WhoAmP 93*
Novich, Bruce Eric 1957- *WhoScEn 94*
Novich, Carolynn Mary 1957- *WhoWest 94*
Novick, Andrew Carl 1948- *WhoAm 94*
Novick, David 1926- *WhoAm 94*
Novick, Julius Lerner 1939- *WhoAm 94*
Novick, Marian *DrAPF 93*
Novick, Marvin 1931- *WhoAm 94, WhoAmP 93*
Novick, Nelson Lee 1949- *WhoAm 94*
Novick, Peter 1934- *WhoAm 94*
Novick, Robert 1923- *WhoAm 94*
Novick, Ronald Padrov 1957- *WhoScEn 94*
Novick, Sheldon M. 1941- *WhoAm 94*
Novick, Stuart Allan 1944- *WhoFI 94, WhoWest 94*
Novick, Stuart J. 1950- *WhoAmL 94*
Novick, Tom 1957- *WhoAmP 93*
Novik, Jay A. 1944- *WhoIns 94*
Novikoff, Harold Stephen 1951- *WhoAmL 94*
Novikov, Sergey Petrovich 1938- *IntWW 93*
Novin, Donald 1936- *WhoAm 94*
Novinc, Judith Kaye 1947- *WhoMW 93*
Novinger, Cathy Blackburn 1949- *WhoFI 94*
Novinski, Lyle Frank 1932- *WhoAmA 93*
Novinsky, Alex d1960 *WhoHol 92*
Novis, Donald d1966 *WhoHol 92*
Novitch, Mark 1932- *WhoAm 94, WhoFI 94*
Novitski, Charles Edward 1946- *WhoScEn 94*
Novitz, Charles Richard 1934- *WhoAm 94*
Novoa, Jose I. *WhoHisp 94*
Novoa, Julio Cesar 1941- *WhoHisp 94*
Novoa Carcacia, Maria del Pilar 1957- *WhoWomW 91*
Novoa-Sancho, Nydia Marle 1944- *WhoHisp 94*
Novodvorskaya, Valeriya Ilinichna 1950- *LngBDD*
Novogradac, Michael Joseph 1961- *WhoFI 94, WhoWest 94*
Novogrod, Nancy Ellen 1949- *WhoAm 94*
Novosielski, Michael 1750-1795 *NewGrDO*
Novotna, Jarmila 1907- *NewGrDO, WhoHol 92*
Novotney, Norman Edward 1960- *WhoMW 93*
Novotny, David Joseph 1953- *WhoAm 94, WhoAmL 94, WhoMW 93*
Novotny, Deborah Ann 1964- *WhoFI 94, WhoMW 93*
Novotny, Donald Wayne 1934- *WhoAm 94*
Novotny, Elmer Ladislaw 1909- *WhoAmA 93*
Novotny, Jiri 1943- *WhoScEn 94*
Novotny, Milos V. *WhoScEn 94*
Novovich, Serge 1932- *WhoAm 94, WhoAmL 94*
Novros, David 1941- *WhoAmA 93*
Novy, Diane Marie *WhoScEn 94*
Nowack, Wayne Kenyon 1923- *WhoAmA 93*

Nowacki, James Nelson 1947- *WhoAm 94, WhoAmL 94*
Nowaczynski, Ana Patricia 1954- *WhoHisp 94*
Nowak, Chester John, Jr. 1941- *WhoFI 94, WhoMW 93, WhoScEn 94*
Nowak, Chester Joseph 1923- *WhoMW 93*
Nowak, Felicia Veronika *WhoScEn 94*
Nowak, G. Philip 1944- *WhoAmL 94*
Nowak, Gerald L. 1930- *WhoMW 93*
Nowak, Glen Joseph 1960- *WhoFI 94*
Nowak, Gregory Joseph 1959- *WhoAmL 94*
Nowak, Henry James 1935- *WhoAmP 93*
Nowak, Jacquelyn Louise 1937- *WhoAm 94*
Nowak, Jan Zdzislaw 1913- *WhoAm 94*
Nowak, John E. 1947- *WhoAm 94, WhoAmL 94, WhoMW 93*
Nowak, Joseph J. 1931- *WhoFI 94*
Nowak, Leo 1907- *WhoAmA 93*
Nowak, Patricia Rose 1946- *WhoMW 93*
Nowak, Robert Michael 1930- *WhoAm 94*
Nowak, Romuald 1957- *WhoScEn 94*
Nowakowski, Kenneth R. 1955- *WhoAmL 94*
Nowar, Ma'an Abu 1928- *Who 94*
Nowatzki, Robert E. *WhoAmP 93*
Nowee, Paul d1993 *NewYTBS 93*
Nowel, David John 1935- *WhoWest 94*
Nowell, Ken 1956- *WhoAmP 93*
Nowell, Peter Carey 1928- *WhoAm 94*
Nowell, Tommy Lynn 1947- *WhoFI 94*
Nowell, Wedgewood d1957 *WhoHol 92*
Nowell, William Robert, III 1949- *WhoWest 94*
Nowell-Smith, Patrick Horace 1914- *Who 94*
Nowell-Smith, Simon Harcourt 1909- *Who 94*
Nowick, Abraham d1993 *NewYTBS 93*
Nowick, Arthur Stanley 1923- *WhoAm 94*
Nowicki, George Lucian 1926- *WhoAm 94*
Nowicki, Susan Ann 1945- *WhoMW 93*
Nowicki, William Ian 1957- *WhoWest 94*
Nowina-Konopka, Piotr 1949- *IntWW 93*
Nowlan, George Joseph 1925- *WhoAm 94*
Nowlan, Godfrey S. *WhoScEn 94*
Nowlan, Philip Francis 1888-1940 *EncSF 93*
Nowland, James Ferrell 1942- *WhoAmL 94*
Nowland, William Sims, II 1941- *WhoAmL 94*
Nowlin, Herman d1951 *WhoHol 92*
Nowlin, James Robertson 1937- *WhoAm 94, WhoAmL 94*
Nowlin, Joseph E. 1945- *WhoAmL 94*
Nowotny, Janusz 1936- *WhoScEn 94*
Nowowiejski, Feliks 1877-1946 *NewGrDO*
Nowra, Louis 1950- *ConDr 93, IntDcT 2, IntWW 93*
Nowytski, (Slavko) Sviatoslav 1934- *WhoAmA 93*
Nox, Andre d1946 *WhoHol 92*
Noy, Wilfred 1883- *WhoHol 92*
Noya, Scott Anthony 1960- *WhoAmL 94*
Noyce, James William 1955- *WhoIns 94*
Noyce, Philip 1950- *IntMPA 94*
Noyce, Robert N. 1927-1990 *WorInv*
Noyce, Robert Norton 1927-1990 *WhAm 10*
Noye, Fred Charles 1946- *WhoAmP 93*
Noyer-Weidner, Alfred 1921- *IntWW 93*
Noyes, Alfred 1880-1958 *EncSF 93*
Noyes, Betty d1987 *WhoHol 92*
Noyes, Eliot 1910-1977 *WhoAmA 93N*
Noyes, Guy Emerson d1993 *NewYTBS 93*
Noyes, Henry (Halsey) 1910- *WrDr 94*
Noyes, Henry Pierre 1923- *WhoAm 94*
Noyes, John Humphrey 1811-1886 *AmSocL, DcAmReB 2*
Noyes, Judith Gibson 1941- *WhoAm 94*
Noyes, Michael Lance 1946- *WhoAmL 94*
Noyes, Pierrepont B(urt) 1870-1959 *EncSF 93*
Noyes, Pierrepont T. 1914-1992 *WhAm 10*
Noyes, Ralph *EncSF 93*
Noyes, Ralph Norton 1923- *Who 94*
Noyes, Richard *WhoAmP 93*
Noyes, Richard Francis 1952- *WhoMW 93*
Noyes, Richard Hall 1930- *WhoAm 94*
Noyes, Richard Macy 1919- *IntWW 93, WhoAm 94, WhoScEn 94, WhoWest 94*
Noyes, Robert Edwin 1925- *WhoAm 94*
Noyes, Ronald T. 1937- *WhoScEn 94*
Noyes, Sandy 1941- *WhoAmA 93*
Noyes, Skeets d1936 *WhoHol 92*
Noyes, Stanley *DrAPF 93*
Noyes, Stanley 1924- *WrDr 94*
Noyes, Walter Omar 1929- *WhoScEn 94*
Noz, Marilyn Eileen 1939- *WhoScEn 94*
Nozaki, Kenzie 1916- *WhoAsA 94*
Nozaki, Shinji 1953- *WhoScEn 94*
Nozato, Ryoichi 1926- *WhoScEn 94*
Nozhikov, Yury Abramovich 1934- *LngBDD*
Nozick, Robert 1938- *IntWW 93, WhoAm 94, WrDr 94*
Nozieres, Philippe Pierre Gaston Francois 1932- *IntWW 93*
Nozik, Arthur Jack 1936- *WhoWest 94*
Nozik, Robert Alan 1934- *WhoWest 94*
Noziska, Charles Brant 1953- *WhoAmL 94, WhoWest 94*
Nozoe, Tetsuo 1902- *WhoScEn 94*
Nozzari, Andrea 1775-1832 *NewGrDO*
Nozzolio, Michael F. 1951- *WhoAmP 93*
Nriagu, Jerome O. 1942- *WrDr 94*
Nsekela, Amon James 1930- *IntWW 93, Who 94*
N'Singa Udjuu Ongwabeki Untube 1934- *IntWW 93*
Nsubuga, Emmanuel 1914-1991 *WhAm 10*
Ntiwane, Nkomeni Douglas 1933- *Who 94*
Ntsanwisi, Hudson d1993 *NewYTBS 93*
Nu, U. 1907- *IntWW 93*
Nua, Mailo S. T. *WhoAmP 93*
Nua, Sao T. 1948- *WhoAmP 93*
Nuber, Philip William 1939- *WhoAm 94*
Nuber, Richard H. 1943- *WhoAmP 93*
Nuber, Richard Howard 1943- *WhoAm 94*
Nucci, John A. 1952- *WhoAmP 93*
Nucci, Joseph E., Jr. 1962- *WhoWest 94*
Nucci, Leo 1942- *NewGrDO, WhoAm 94*
Nucciarone, A. Patrick 1947- *WhoAm 94, WhoAmL 94*
Nucci Mauro, Anna Maria 1943- *WhoWomW 91*
Nuccitelli, Saul Arnold 1928- *WhoAm 94, WhoFI 94, WhoMW 93, WhoScEn 94*
Nuce, Madonna Marie 1952- *WhoWest 94*
Nuchow, William Haywood 1928- *WhoAmP 93*
Nucklos, Shirley 1949- *WhoMW 93*
Nuckolls, Billie Jean 1943- *WhoAmP 93*
Nuckolls, Hugh Paul 1941- *WhoAmP 93*
Nuckolls, John Hopkins 1930- *WhoAm 94, WhoScEn 94*
Nuckolls, Kenneth Russell 1921- *WhoAmP 93*
Nuckolls, Leonard Arnold 1917- *WhoAm 94*
Nuckolls, Robert Theodore 1933- *WhoAm 94*
Nuckols, Frank Joseph 1926- *WhoScEn 94*
Nudel, Ida 1931- *WrDr 94*
Nudelman, Sidney 1938- *WhoAmL 94*
Nuderscher, Frank Bernard 1880-1959 *WhoAmA 93N*
Nuechterlein, Michael F. 1942- *WhoAmL 94*
Nueman, Joan d1987 *WhoHol 92*
Nuernberg, Susan Marie 1946- *WhoMW 93*
Nuernberg, William Richard 1946- *WhoAm 94, WhoAmL 94*
Nuesse, Celestine Joseph 1913- *WhoAm 94*
Nuetzel, Charles (Alexander) 1934- *EncSF 93*
Nuffer, David Ogden 1952- *WhoAmL 94*
Nugee, Edward George 1928- *Who 94*
Nugee, Rachel Elizabeth 1926- *Who 94*
Nugent *Who 94*
Nugent, Arthur William 1891-1975 *WhoAmA 93N*
Nugent, Bob L. 1947- *WhoAmA 93*
Nugent, Carol *WhoHol 92*
Nugent, Charles Arter 1924- *WhoAm 94*
Nugent, Daniel Eugene 1927- *WhoAm 94, WhoFI 94, WhoMW 93*
Nugent, Debbie Lee 1963- *WhoWest 94*
Nugent, Edward 1904- *WhoHol 92*
Nugent, Elliott d1980 *WhoHol 92*
Nugent, Elliott (John) 1899-1980 *ConDr 93*
Nugent, Frank S. 1908-1965 *IntDcF 2-4*
Nugent, G. Eugene 1927- *WhoAm 94*
Nugent, Gregory 1911-1992 *WhAm 10*
Nugent, J. C. d1947 *WhoHol 92*
Nugent, James E. *WhoAmP 93*
Nugent, Jane Kay 1925- *WhoMW 93*
Nugent, John (Edwin Lavallin) 1933- *Who 94*
Nugent, John Joseph 1942- *WhoFI 94*
Nugent, Johnny 1939- *WhoMW 93*
Nugent, Johnny Wesley 1939- *WhoAmP 93*
Nugent, Kathleen Shirley 1941- *WhoFI 94*
Nugent, Matthew Alfred 1961- *WhoScEn 94*
Nugent, Moya d1954 *WhoHol 92*
Nugent, Neill 1947- *WrDr 94*
Nugent, Nelle 1939- *WhoAm 94*
Nugent, Paul Allen 1962- *WhoAmL 94*
Nugent, Peter Daniel 1938- *WhoMW 93*
Nugent, Peter Walter James 1920- *Who 94*
Nugent, Robert Emmet 1955- *WhoAmP 93*
Nugent, Robert Emmet, III 1955- *WhoAmL 94*
Nugent, Robert J., Jr. 1942- *WhoFI 94*
Nugent, Robert Leon 1920- *WhoMW 93*
Nugent, Robin (George Colborne) 1925- *Who 94*
Nugent, Shane Vincent 1962- *WhoAmL 94, WhoMW 93*
Nugent, Theodore Anthony 1948- *WhoAm 94*
Nugent, Thomas D. 1943- *WhoAm 94*
Nugent, Walter T. K. 1935- *WrDr 94*
Nugent, Walter Terry King 1935- *WhoAm 94, WhoMW 93*
Nugent of Guildford, Baron 1907- *Who 94*
Nugteren, Cornelius 1928- *WhoAm 94*
Nuibo, Augustin 1874-1948 *NewGrDO*
Nuiry, Octavio Emilio 1958- *WhoHisp 94*
Nuitter, Charles-Louis-Etienne 1828-1899 *NewGrDO*
Nujoma, Sam Shafilshuna 1929- *IntWW 93*
Nuki 1919-1984 *WhoAmA 93N*
Nuland, Anthony C. J. 1943- *WhoAmL 94*
Null, Gary G. 1950- *WhoAmL 94*
Null, Jack Elton 1938- *WhoWest 94*
Null, Michael Elliot 1947- *WhoAmL 94*
Null, Miriam Pincus 1926- *WhoAmL 94*
Null, Roberta Lee 1934- *WhoMW 93*
Nulton, William Clements 1931- *WhoAm 94*
Nulty, George P. 1942- *WhoFI 94*
Nulty, William H(arry) 1932- *WrDr 94*
Numai, Takahiro 1961- *WhoScEn 94*
Numairi, Gaafar al- *IntWW 93*
Numan, Yasin Said *IntWW 93*
Numata, Nobuo 1954- *WhoFI 94*
Numbere, Daopu Thompson 1951- *WhoScEn 94*
Numbers, Ronald Leslie 1942- *WhoMW 93*
Numrich, Robert P. 1947- *WhoAmL 94*
Nunan, Manus 1926- *Who 94*
Nunan, Terence S. 1949- *WhoAmL 94*
Nunberg, Noah 1950- *WhoAmL 94*
Nunburnholme, Baron 1928- *Who 94*
Nuncio, Pete N. 1942- *WhoHisp 94*
Nunery, Gladys Cannon 1904- *WhoBlA 94*
Nunery, Leroy David 1955- *WhoBlA 94*
Nunes, Claude 1924- *EncSF 93, WrDr 94*
Nunes, Gary Howard 1956- *WhoAmL 94*
Nunes, Geoffrey 1930- *WhoAmL 94, WhoFI 94*
Nunes, Gordon Maxwell 1914- *WhAm 10*
Nunes, Lygia Bojunga 1932- *ConAu 142, SmATA 75 [port]*
Nunes, Manuel Jacinto 1926- *IntWW 93*
Nunes, Maria Natalia 1921- *BlmGWL*
Nunes, Paul Vincent 1952- *WhoAmL 94*
Nuñez, Albert, Jr. 1946- *WhoHisp 94*
Nuñez, Albert S. 1932- *WhoHisp 94*
Nuñez, Alex 1938- *WhoHisp 94*
Nuñez, Ana Rosa 1926- *WhoHisp 94*
Núñez, Antonio Alberto 1948- *WhoHisp 94*
Nunez, Edwin 1963- *WhoHisp 94*
Nuñez, Elpidio *WhoHisp 94*
Nunez, Frank 1931- *WhoAmP 93*
Núñez, Germán 1948- *WhoHisp 94*
Nunez, Gus 1934- *WhoHisp 94*
Nunez, Jose 1964- *WhoHisp 94*
Nunez, Jose Alberto *WhoAmP 93*
Nuñez, Juan Solomon, Jr. 1945- *WhoHisp 94*
Nuñez, Julio V. 1960- *WhoHisp 94*
Núñez, Louis *WhoHisp 94*
Nunez, Mario 1948- *WhoHisp 94*
Nunez, Miguel A., Jr. *WhoHol 92*
Nunez, Paulino A. *WhoHisp 94*
Nunez, Peter Kent 1942- *WhoHisp 94*
Nunez, Ralph *WhoHisp 94*
Nunez, Raul R. *WhoHisp 94*
Nuñez, Rene Jose 1941- *WhoHisp 94*
Nunez, Samuel B., Jr. 1930- *WhoAmP 93, WhoHisp 94*
Nunez, Stephen Christopher 1961- *WhoScEn 94*
Nunez, Yolanda 1952- *WhoHisp 94*
Nunez-Centella, Ramon Antonio 1946- *WhoScEn 94*
Nuñez-del Toro, Orlando 1940- *WhoHisp 94*
Núñez de Villavicencio, Orlando 1940- *WhoHisp 94*
Nunez-Lawton, Miguel G. 1949- *WhoFI 94*
Nuñez Ledo, Mercedes 1955- *WhoHisp 94*
Núñez-Molina, Mario A. 1957- *WhoHisp 94*
Nunez-Portuondo, Rica-do 1933- *WhoAm 94*
Núñez Santos, Dulcinia Rosa 1950- *WhoHisp 94*
Nunez-Wormack, Elsa *WhoHisp 94*
Nungesser, Charles d1927 *WhoHol 92*
Nungesser, Roland 1925- *IntWW 93*
Nungesser, William Aicklen 1929- *WhoAmP 93*
Nunis, Doyce B(lackman), Jr. 1924- *ConAu 42NR, WrDr 94*
Nunis, Doyce Blackman, Jr. 1924- *WhoAm 94*
Nunn, Alice d1988 *WhoHol 92*
Nunn, Bill *WhoHol 92*
Nunn, Bobbie B. *WhoBlA 94*
Nunn, Freddie Joe 1962- *WhoBlA 94*
Nunn, Frederic 1879- *WhoAmA 93N*
Nunn, Frederick McKinley 1937- *WrDr 94*
Nunn, G. Raymond 1918- *WrDr 94*
Nunn, Grady Harrison 1918- *WhoAm 94*
Nunn, J. Roy 1962- *WhoAmL 94*
Nunn, James Ross 1940- *WhoScEn 94*
Nunn, Jenny Wren 1944- *WhoScEn 94*
Nunn, John 1955- *WrDr 94*
Nunn, John, Jr. 1953- *WhoBlA 94*
Nunn, John Francis 1925- *IntWW 93, Who 94*
Nunn, John Richard Danford 1925- *Who 94*
Nunn, Leslie Edgar 1941- *WhoAmL 94, WhoWest 94*
Nunn, Louie B. 1924- *WhoAmP 93*
Nunn, Morris J. 1945- *WhoAmL 94*
Nunn, Robert Warne 1950- *WhoAm 94*
Nunn, Robinson S. 1944- *WhoBlA 94*
Nunn, Sam 1938- *CngDr 93, IntWW 93, NewYTBS 93 [port], WhoAmP 93*
Nunn, Samuel 1938- *WhoAm 94*
Nunn, Stephen R. 1952- *WhoAmP 93*
Nunn, Trevor 1940- *ConTFT 11*
Nunn, Trevor Robert 1940- *IntWW 93, Who 94, WhoAm 94*
Nunn, Wayne d1947 *WhoHol 92*
Nunn, William B. 1942- *WhoMW 93*
Nunn, William Curtis 1908- *WrDr 94*
Nunn, William Goldwin, Jr. *WhoBlA 94*
Nunnally, David H., Sr. 1929- *WhoBlA 94*
Nunnally, Don Lynn 1949- *WhoWest 94*
Nunnally, Gary Douglas 1955- *WhoMW 93*
Nunnally, James David 1945- *WhoAmP 93*
Nunnally, Knox Dillon 1943- *WhoAm 94, WhoAmL 94*
Nunnally, Phillip L. 1946- *WhoAmL 94*
Nunnally, Stephens Watson 1927- *WhoScEn 94*
Nunneley, Charles Kenneth Roylance 1936- *Who 94*
Nunneley, John Hewlett 1922- *Who 94*
Nunnelley, Robert B. 1929- *WhoAmA 93*
Nunnery, Willie James 1948- *WhoBlA 94*
Nuño, Jose Pablo 1956- *WhoHisp 94*
Nunz, Gregory Joseph 1934- *WhoScEn 94*
Nuon, Samuel 1945- *WhoAsA 94*
Nuorvala, Aarne Johannes 1912- *IntWW 93*
Nuovo, Betty A. 1931- *WhoAmP 93*
Nupen, Barry Dean 1953- *WhoWest 94*
Nurczyk, Mark Eric 1950- *WhoMW 93*
Nurdin, Mark Gregory 1961- *WhoFI 94*
Nurenberg, David 1939- *WhoAm 94*
Nurenberg, Thelma *ConAu 42NR*
Nureyev, Rudolf d1993 *IntMPA 94N*
Nureyev, Rudolf 1938- *IntMPA 94, WhoHol 92*
Nureyev, Rudolf 1938-1993 *IntDcB [port] NewYTBS 93 [port]*
Nureyev, Rudolf (Hametovich) d1993 *IntWW 93N*
Nureyev, Rudolf (Hametovich) 1938-1993 *CurBio 93N*
Nureyev, Rudolf Hametovich d1993 *Who 94N*
Nureyev, Rudolf Hametovich 1938-1993 *WhAm 10*
Nurhussein, Mohammed Alamin 1942- *WhoScEn 94*
Nurick, Gilbert 1906- *WhoAm 94*
Nurjadin, Roesmin 1930- *Who 94*
Nur Khan, M. 1923- *IntWW 93*
Nurkin, Sidney J. 1941- *WhoAmL 94*
Nurkse, D. *DrAPF 93*
Nurmagambetov, Sagadat Kozhakhmetovich 1924- *LngBDD*
Nurmela, Kari 1933-1984 *NewGrDO*
Nurmohemaiti Reyisi *WhoPRCh 91*
Nurnberg, Walter 1907-1991 *WrDr 94N*
Nurnberger, Gunther 1948- *WhoScEn 94*
Nurnberger, John I., Jr. 1946- *WhoScEn 94*
Nurnberger, Thomas Salisbury, Jr. 1918- *WhoFI 94*
Nurney, Fred d1973 *WhoHol 92*
Nurock, Robert Jay 1937- *WhoAm 94*
Nurre, Joseph Henry 1960- *WhoScEn 94*
Nursaw, James 1932- *Who 94*
Nursaw, William George 1903- *Who 94*
Nurse, Paul Maxime 1949- *IntWW 93, Who 94*
Nurse, Richard A. 1939- *WhoBlA 94*
Nurse, Robert Earl 1942- *WhoBlA 94*

O

O, Cao Kinh *WhoAsA 94*
O, San Luong 1949- *WhoAsA 94*
Oak, Claire Morisset 1921- *WhoWest 94*
Oak, Ronald Stuart 1956- *WhoScEn 94*
Oakar, Mary Rose 1940- *WhoAm 94, WhoAmP 93, WhoWomW 91*
Oakchiah c. 1810-1849 *EncNAR*
Oakeley, John (Digby Atholl) 1932- *Who 94*
Oakeley, Mary 1913- *Who 94*
Oakerhater, David Pendleton 1844-1931 *EncNAR*
Oakes, Carlton Elsworth 1966- *WhoScEn 94*
Oakes, Christopher 1949- *Who 94*
Oakes, Donald R. 1940- *WhoIns 94*
Oakes, Ellen Ruth 1919- *WhoScEn 94*
Oakes, Gordon James 1931- *Who 94*
Oakes, Henry Smith 1927- *WhoFI 94*
Oakes, James 1953- *WrDr 94*
Oakes, James L. 1924- *WhoAm 94, WhoAmL 94, WhoAmP 93*
Oakes, John Bertram 1913- *IntWW 93, WhoAm 94*
Oakes, John Warren 1941- *WhoAmA 93*
Oakes, Joseph Stewart 1919- *Who 94*
Oakes, Lester Cornelius 1923- *WhoAm 94*
Oakes, Maria Spachner 1947- *WhoMW 93*
Oakes, Melvin Ervin Louis 1936- *WhoAm 94, WhoScEn 94*
Oakes, Philip 1928- *Who 94*
Oakes, R. Michael 1957- *WhoMW 93*
Oakes, Randi 1952- *WhoHol 92*
Oakes, Robert Gibson 1918- *WhoFI 94*
Oakes, Robert James 1936- *WhoAm 94*
Oakes, Robert Roy 1951- *WhoAm 94*
Oakes, Roy Sidney 1928- *WhoAmP 93*
Oakes, Terry Louis 1953- *WhoWest 94*
Oakes, Thomas Wyatt 1950- *WhoScEn 94*
Oakes, Timothy Wayne 1938- *WhoFI 94*
Oakes, Walter Jerry 1946- *WhoAm 94*
Oakes, William Larry 1944- *WhoAmA 93*
Oakeshott, Gordon Blaisdell 1904- *WhoAm 94, WhoScEn 94, WhoWest 94*
Oakeson, David Oscar 1965- *WhoScEn 94*
Oakeson, Ralph Willard 1963- *WhoScEn 94*
Oakey, John Martin, Jr. 1935- *WhoAm 94*
Oakford, Lawrence Xavier 1953- *WhoScEn 94*
Oakham, Archdeacon of *Who 94*
Oakie, Jack d1978 *WhoHol 92*
Oakie, Jack 1903-1978 *WhoCom*
Oakie, Joe d1983 *WhoHol 92*
Oakland, Simon d1983 *WhoHol 92*
Oakland, Vivian d1958 *WhoHol 92*
Oakland, Will d1956 *WhoHol 92*
Oakley, Andrew Arthur 1958- *WhoMW 93*
Oakley, Ann 1944- *WrDr 94*
Oakley, Annie d1926 *WhoHol 92*
Oakley, Brian Wynne 1927- *IntWW 93, Who 94*
Oakley, Carolyn Le 1942- *WhoAmP 93, WhoWest 94*
Oakley, Charles 1963- *WhoBlA 94*
Oakley, Charles Allen 1900- *WrDr 94*
Oakley, Christopher John 1941- *Who 94*
Oakley, Diane 1953- *WhoFI 94*
Oakley, Florence d1956 *WhoHol 92*

Oakley, Francis Christopher 1931- *WhoAm 94*
Oakley, Graham 1929- *WrDr 94*
Oakley, James William, Jr. 1935- *WhoAmP 93*
Oakley, John Davidson 1921- *Who 94*
Oakley, Keith 1957- *WhoAmP 93*
Oakley, Laura d1957 *WhoHol 92*
Oakley, Marta Tlapova 1948- *WhoScEn 94*
Oakley, Robert Alan 1946- *WhoAm 94*
Oakley, Robert B. *WhoAmP 93*
Oakley, Robin Francis Leigh 1941- *Who 94*
Oakley, Stewart Philip 1931- *WrDr 94*
Oakley, Violet 1874-1960 *WhoAmA 93N*
Oakley, Wilfrid George 1905- *Who 94*
Oakman, Sondra A. 1943- *WhoMW 93*
Oakman, Wheeler d1949 *WhoHol 92*
Oaks, B. Ann 1929- *WhoAm 94*
Oaks, Dallin H. 1932- *WrDr 94*
Oaks, Dallin Harris 1932- *WhoAm 94, WhoWest 94*
Oaks, David Keith 1954- *WhoAmP 93*
Oaks, John Adams 1942- *WhoMW 93*
Oaks, Margaret Marlene 1940- *WhoWest 94*
Oaks, Maurice David 1934- *WhoFI 94*
Oaks, Nathaniel T. *WhoAmP 93*
Oaks, Robert C. *WhoAmP 93*
Oaks, Robert C. 1936- *WhoAm 94*
Oaks, Steven Clark 1938- *WhoAmP 93*
Oaksey, Baron 1880-1971 *DcNaB MP*
Oaksey, Baron 1929- *Who 94*
Oaksey, Lord 1929- *WrDr 94*
Oakshott, Anthony (Hendrie) 1929- *Who 94*
Oana, Harry Jerome 1957- *WhoScEn 94*
Oas, John Gilbert 1958- *WhoScEn 94*
Oates, Adam R. 1962- *WhoAm 94*
Oates, Caleb E. 1917- *WhoBlA 94*
Oates, Carl Everette 1931- *WhoAm 94, WhoAmL 94*
Oates, Cicely d1934 *WhoHol 92*
Oates, (Edward Ernest) David (Michael) 1927- *Who 94*
Oates, James G. *WhoAm 94*
Oates, James Maclay 1946- *WhoAm 94*
Oates, John 1930- *Who 94*
Oates, John Alexander, III 1932- *WhoAm 94*
Oates, John Francis 1934- *WhoAm 94*
Oates, Johnny 1946- *WhoAm 94*
Oates, Joyce Carol *DrAPF 93*
Oates, Joyce Carol 1938- *BlmGWL, DcLB 130 [port], IntWW 93, RfGShF, WhoAm 94, WrDr 94*
Oates, (John) Keith 1942- *Who 94*
Oates, Laurence Campbell 1946- *Who 94*
Oates, Stephen B(aery) 1936- *WrDr 94*
Oates, Stephen Baery 1936- *WhoAm 94*
Oates, Thomas 1917- *Who 94*
Oates, Titus 1649-1705 *BlmGEL*
Oates, Wallace Eugene 1937- *WhoFI 94, WrDr 94*
Oates, Wanda Anita 1942- *WhoBlA 94*
Oates, Warren d1982 *WhoHol 92*
Oates, William Armstrong, Jr. 1942- *WhoAm 94*
Oathout, Brenda Halm 1960- *WhoMW 93*
Oatis, Kathleen Ann 1951- *WhoAmP 93*
Oatley, Brian 1935- *Who 94*

Oatley, Charles (William) 1904- *IntWW 93, Who 94*
Oatley, Michael Charles 1935- *Who 94*
Oatman, Michael Clifton 1939- *WhoMW 93*
Oats, Bart Steven 1958- *WhoAm 94*
Oats, Charles S. 1931- *WhoFI 94*
Oatway, Francis Carlyle 1936- *WhoAm 94*
Oaxaca, Fernando 1927- *WhoHisp 94*
Oaxaca, Jaime 1931- *WhoHisp 94*
Obadia, Andre Isaac 1927- *WhoScEn 94*
Obaid, Fikri Makram 1916- *IntWW 93*
Obaldia, Rene de 1918- *IntDcT 2*
O'Ballance, Edgar 1918- *WrDr 94*
Oba Minako 1930- *BlmGWL*
Oban, Provost of *Who 94*
Oban, William Ernest 1947- *WhoAmP 93*
Obando y Bravo, Miguel 1926- *IntWW 93*
O'Banion, Nance 1949- *WhoAmA 93*
O'Banner-Owens, Jeanette *WhoBlA 94*
O'Bannon, Dan 1946- *HorFD [port]*
O'Bannon, David J. 1938- *WhoAm 94*
O'Bannon, Don Tella, Jr. 1957- *WhoAmL 94*
O'Bannon, Donna Edwards 1957- *WhoBlA 94*
O'Bannon, Frank Lewis 1930- *WhoAm 94, WhoAmP 93, WhoMW 93*
Obara, John Paul 1954- *WhoFI 94*
O'Barr, Bobby Gene 1932- *WhoAmL 94*
O'Barr, William McAlston 1942- *WhoAm 94*
Obasanjo, Olusegun 1937- *ConBlB 5 [port], IntWW 93, Who 94*
Obasi, Godwin Olu Patrick 1933- *IntWW 93, Who 94*
Obata, Gyo 1923- *WhoAsA 94*
Obayuwana, Alphonsus Osarobo 1948- *WhoBlA 94*
Obear, Frederick Woods 1935- *WhoAm 94*
O'Beck, Ferd d1929 *WhoHol 92*
Obed, Ellen Bryan 1944- *SmATA 74 [port]*
Obee, Kent 1942- *WhoAm 94*
Obeegadoo, (Louis) Claude 1928- *Who 94*
Obeid, Atef *IntWW 93*
Obeidat, Ahmad Abdul-Majeed 1938- *IntWW 93*
O'Beil, Hedy *WhoAmA 93*
O'Beirne Ranelagh, John 1947- *Who 94*
Obejas, Achy 1956- *WhoHisp 94*
Obenauer, John Charles 1967- *WhoScEn 94*
Obenberger, Thomas E. 1942- *WhoAmL 94*
Obeng, Letitia Eva 1925- *IntWW 93*
Obenhaus, Victor 1903- *WhoAm 94*
Obenour, Jerry Lee *WhoScEn 94*
Obenshain, Helen Wilkins 1934- *WhoAmP 93*
Obenshain, Mark Dudley 1962- *WhoAmP 93*
Obenshain, Scott Alan 1964- *WhoFI 94*
Obenson, Philip 1948- *WhoScEn 94*
Ober, Ann Morgan 1916- *WhoAmP 93*
Ober, Douglas Gary 1946- *WhoAm 94*
Ober, Eric W. *WhoAm 94*
Ober, George d1912 *WhoHol 92*
Ober, Philip d1982 *WhoHol 92*
Ober, Richard Francis, Jr. 1943- *WhoAm 94, WhoAmL 94*
Ober, Robert d1950 *WhoHol 92*

Ober, Russell John, Jr. 1948- *WhoAm 94, WhoAmL 94*
Ober, Stephen Henry 1949- *WhoWest 94*
Ober, Stuart Alan 1946- *WhoAm 94*
Ober, William 1920-1993 *DcLB Y93N [port]*
Ober, William B. d1993 *NewYTBS 93*
Obera, Marion L. 1947- *WhoBlA 94*
Oberbeck, Arthur William 1912-1989 *WhAm 10*
Oberdank, Lawrence Mark 1935- *WhoAmL 94*
Oberdier, Ronald Ray 1945- *WhoAmL 94*
Oberdorf, John J. 1946- *WhoAmL 94*
Oberdorfer, Eugene, II 1932- *WhoIns 94*
Oberdorfer, Franz 1951- *WhoScEn 94*
Oberdorfer, John L. 1944- *WhoAmL 94*
Oberdorfer, Louis F. 1919- *WhoAm 94, WhoAmL 94*
Oberdorfer, Louis Falk 1919- *CngDr 93*
Oberender, Frederick Garrett 1933- *WhoAm 94*
Oberg, Brooke Rae 1949- *WhoMW 93*
Oberg, Danny 1951- *WhoAmP 93*
Oberg, Kjell Erik 1946- *WhoScEn 94*
Oberg, Owen Henry 1925- *WhoWest 94*
Oberg, Roger Winston 1919- *WhoAm 94*
Oberhardt, William 1882-1958 *WhoAmA 93N*
Oberhausen, Joyce Ann Wynn 1941- *WhoFI 94*
Oberholtzer, Jay Roy 1930- *WhoFI 94*
Oberholtzer, Kenneth E. d1993 *NewYTBS 93*
Oberhuber, Konrad Johannes 1935- *WhoAm 94*
Oberlander, Ronald Y. *WhoAm 94, WhoFI 94*
Oberle, Florence d1943 *WhoHol 92*
Oberle, Frank 1932- *IntWW 93*
Oberle, Joseph 1958- *WrDr 94*
Oberle, William Albert, Jr. 1949- *WhoAmP 93*
Oberlies, John William 1939- *WhoAm 94*
Oberlin, David W. 1920- *WhoAmP 93*
Oberlin, Earl Clifford, III 1956- *WhoFI 94*
Oberlin, Russell (Keys) 1928- *NewGrDO*
Oberly, Charles M., III *WhoAmP 93*
Oberly, Charles Monroe, III 1946- *WhoAm 94, WhoAmL 94*
Oberly, Robert Peters 1931- *WhoAm 94*
Oberman, Michael Stewart 1947- *WhoAm 94, WhoAmL 94*
Oberman, Norman Charles 1929- *WhoWest 94*
Obermann, Allison Karen 1965- *WhoAmL 94*
Obermann, C. Esco 1904- *WhoAm 94*
Obermann, George 1935- *WhoMW 93*
Obermann, Richard Michael 1949- *WhoFI 94*
Obermayer, Herman Joseph 1924- *WhoFI 94*
Obermeyer, Nancy Joan 1955- *WhoMW 93*
Obermier, Norman W. 1915- *WhoAmP 93*
Obernauer, Marne 1919- *WhoAm 94*
Obernauer, Marne, Jr. 1943- *WhoAm 94*
Oberndorf, Meyera E. *WhoAm 94, WhoAmP 93, WhoWomW 91*
Oberon, Merle d1979 *WhoHol 92*
Oberquell, Diane *WhoAmP 93*

Oberreit, Walter William 1928- *WhoAm 94, WhoAmL 94, WhoFI 94*
O'Berry, Carl Gerald 1936- *WhoAm 94*
O'Berry, Phillip Aaron 1933- *WhoAm 94*
Oberst, Paul 1914- *WhoAm 94, WhoAmL 94*
Oberst, Robert John 1929- *WhoFI 94*
Oberstar, Helen Elizabeth *WhoFI 94*
Oberstar, James L. 1934- *CngDr 93, WhoAm 94, WhoAmP 93, WhoMW 93*
Oberstein, Marydale 1942- *WhoWest 94*
Obert, Charles Frank 1937- *WhoAm 94*
Obert, Edward Fredric 1910- *WhoAm 94*
Obert, Paul Richard 1928- *WhoAm 94, WhoAmL 94, WhoFI 94*
Oberth, Hermann *WorInv*
Oberti, Sylvia Marie Antoinette 1952- *WhoWest 94*
Oberts, William J. 1944- *WhoAmL 94*
Oberwager, Frances Robertson 1923- *WhoAmP 93*
Obey, Andre 1892-1975 *IntDcT 2*
Obey, Andre(-Alexis) 1892-1975 *NewGrDO*
Obey, David R. 1938- *CngDr 93, WhoAmP 93*
Obey, David Ross 1938- *WhoAm 94, WhoMW 93*
Obi, James E. 1942- *WhoBlA 94*
Obi, Onyeabo C. 1938- *IntWW 93*
Obie, Brian B. *WhoAmP 93*
Obiedo, Ray Anthony 1952- *WhoHisp 94*
Obin, Louis-Henri 1820-1895 *NewGrDO*
Obinna, Eleazu S. 1934- *WhoBlA 94*
Obiols, Mariano 1809-1888 *NewGrDO*
Obis, Paul Barrett Luty, Jr. 1951- *WhoAm 94*
O'Biso, Carol (Anne) 1953- *WrDr 94*
Oblad, Alexander Golden 1909- *WhoAm 94*
Oblak, John Byron 1942- *WhoAm 94*
Obledo, Mario Guerra 1932- *WhoHisp 94*
O'Blenes, Carole 1942- *WhoAmL 94*
Obler, Geri 1942- *WhoAmA 93*
Obligado, Lilian (Isabel) 1931- *WrDr 94*
Oblinger, Josephine Kneidl 1913- *WhoAmP 93*
O'Block, Robert Paul 1943- *WhoAm 94, WhoFI 94*
Oblong, Harold *WhoHol 92*
Obloy, Edward Joseph 1948- *WhoAmL 94*
Obninsky, Victor Peter 1944- *WhoAmL 94, WhoWest 94*
Obolensky, Dimitri 1918- *IntWW 93, Who 94*
Obolensky, Ivan 1925- *WhoAm 94*
Obolensky, Marilyn Wall 1929- *WhoAm 94*
Oboroc, Constantin Mihail 1950- *LngBDD*
Obote, (Apollo) Milton 1924- *IntWW 93, Who 94*
Oboukhoff, Anatole 1896-1962 *IntDcB [port]*
Oboukhov, Alexei Aleksandrovich 1938- *IntWW 93*
O'Boyle, James Bernard 1928- *WhoAm 94*
O'Boyle, R. James 1945- *WhoIns 94*
O'Boyle, Robert L. 1935- *WhoAm 94*
O'Bradovich, Robert E. d1993 *NewYTBS 93*
Obrams, Gunta Iris 1953- *WhoScEn 94*
Obraztsov, Ivan Filippovich 1920- *IntWW 93*
Obraztsova, Yelena (Vasil'yevna) 1937- *NewGrDO*
Obraztsova, Yelena Vasiliyevna 1939- *IntWW 93*
Obrecht, Jas 1952- *WrDr 94*
Obrecht, Kenneth William 1933- *WhoFI 94, WhoMW 93*
Obregon, Alejandro 1920- *IntWW 93*
Obregon, Alvaro 1880-1928 *HisWorL [port]*
Obregon, Carlos Daniel 1959- *WhoHisp 94*
Obregon, Richard Rivera 1951- *WhoHisp 94*
Obregón, Valentin 1953- *WhoHisp 94*
Obregon Tapia, Alvaro 1916-1993 *NewYTBS 93*
Obremski, Walter Joseph 1947- *WhoFI 94*
O'Briain, Niall P. *WhoAm 94, WhoFI 94*
O'Brian, Frank 1939- *WrDr 94*
O'Brian, Hugh 1925- *WhoHol 92*
O'Brian, Hugh 1930- *IntMPA 94*
O'Brian, Jack 1921- *WhoAm 94*
O'Brian, Patrick 1914- *NewYTBS 93 [port]*
O'Brian, Robert Enlow 1895- *WhAm 10*
O'Briant, Jennifer Lynne 1963- *WhoWest 94*
O'Briant, Walter H(erbert) 1937- *WrDr 94*
O'Brien *Who 94*
O'Brien, Albert James 1914- *WhoAm 94, WhoFI 94*
O'Brien, Ana Colomar *WhoHisp 94*
O'Brien, Andrew M. 1952- *WhoIns 94*
O'Brien, Ann Marie 1965- *WhoAmL 94*
O'Brien, Anna Belle Clement *WhoAmP 93*
O'Brien, Anne Sibley 1952- *WrDr 94*
O'Brien, Barry d1961 *WhoHol 92*
O'Brien, Beatrice *DrAPF 93*
O'Brien, Bernard Francis 1914- *WhoAmP 93*
O'Brien, Bradford Carl 1949- *WhoAm 94*
O'Brien, Brian 1898- *IntWW 93*
O'Brien, Brian Murrough Fergus 1931- *Who 94*
O'Brien, Brien Michael 1957- *WhoMW 93*
O'Brien, Carol Jean 1939- *WhoMW 93*
O'Brien, Charles G. 1931- *WhoFI 94*
O'Brien, Charles H. 1920- *WhoAm 94, WhoAmL 94*
O'Brien, Charles Maryon, Jr. 1943- *WhoAm 94*
O'Brien, Charles Michael 1919- *Who 94*
O'Brien, Charles O. 1929- *WhoFI 94*
O'Brien, Charles Patrick 1936- *WhoIns 94*
O'Brien, Charles Richard 1934- *WhoMW 93*
O'Brien, Chet 1911- *WhoHol 92*
O'Brien, Claudine Michele Niedzielski 1953- *WhoAmL 94*
O'Brien, Clay 1961- *WhoHol 92*
O'Brien, Conan c. 1963- *News 94-1 [port], WhoAm 94*
O'Brien, Conor Cruise 1917- *IntWW 93, Who 94, WrDr 94*
O'Brien, Dale 1916-1988 *WhAm 10*
O'Brien, Daniel Joseph 1931- *WhoMW 93*
O'Brien, Daniel Mark 1949- *WhoFI 94*
O'Brien, Daniel William 1926- *WhoAm 94*
O'Brien, Darcy 1939- *WhoAm 94*
O'Brien, Dave d1969 *WhoHol 92*
O'Brien, David *EncSF 93*
O'Brien, David A. 1958- *WhoAmL 94*
O'Brien, David Alfred 1958- *WhoAmP 93*
O'Brien, David Peter 1941- *WhoAm 94, WhoFI 94*
O'Brien, David Vincent 1932-1989 *WhAm 10*
O'Brien, David Wright 1918-1944 *EncSF 93*
O'Brien, Dean D. *EncSF 93*
O'Brien, Denis Patrick 1939- *Who 94*
O'Brien, Dennis M. *WhoAmP 93*
O'Brien, Dermod Patrick 1939- *Who 94*
O'Brien, Donal Clare, Jr. 1934- *WhoAm 94*
O'Brien, Donald Eugene 1923- *WhoAm 94, WhoAmL 94, WhoMW 93*
O'Brien, Donnell d1970 *WhoHol 92*
O'Brien, Dorothy Merrie 1936- *WhoAmP 93*
O'Brien, E.G. *EncSF 93*
O'Brien, Edmond d1985 *WhoHol 92*
O'Brien, Edna *Who 94*
O'Brien, Edna 1932- *BlmGEL [port], BlmGWL, RfGShF, WrDr 94*
O'Brien, Edna 1936- *ConAu 41NR, IntWW 93*
O'Brien, Edward Ignatius 1928- *WhoAm 94*
O'Brien, Ellen 1937- *WhoMW 93*
O'Brien, Ellen K. 1954- *WhoScEn 94*
O'Brien, Elmer 1911- *WrDr 94*
O'Brien, Elmer John 1932- *WhoAm 94*
O'Brien, Erin *WhoHol 92*
O'Brien, Eugene d1966 *WhoHol 92*
O'Brien, Fifi d1941 *WhoHol 92*
O'Brien, Fitz-James 1828-1862 *EncSF 93*
O'Brien, Flann 1911-1966 *EncSF 93*
O'Brien, Francis Anthony 1936- *WhoAm 94*
O'Brien, Francis X. 1941- *WhoAmL 94*
O'Brien, Frank *WhoHol 92*
O'Brien, Frank B. 1926- *WhoAm 94*
O'Brien, Frank B. 1946- *WhoAm 94*
O'Brien, Frederick (William Fitzgerald) 1917- *Who 94*
O'Brien, G. Robert 1936- *WhoAm 94, WhoFI 94*
O'Brien, George d1985 *WhoHol 92*
O'Brien, George 1945- *WrDr 94*
O'Brien, George Aloysius, Jr. 1948- *WhoFI 94*
O'Brien, George Dennis 1931- *WhoAm 94*
O'Brien, George Donoghue, Jr. 1938- *WhoWest 94*
O'Brien, George E., Jr. 1947- *WhoAmL 94*
O'Brien, Gerald James 1923- *WhoAm 94*
O'Brien, Gregory Francis 1950- *WhoFI 94*
O'Brien, Gregory Michael St. Lawrence 1944- *IntWW 93*
O'Brien, Harold Aloysius, Jr. 1936- *WhoWest 94*
O'Brien, Henry Xavier 1903-1990 *WhAm 10*
O'Brien, Herbert John 1930- *WhoAmP 93*
O'Brien, Holly 1946- *WhoWest 94*
O'Brien, J. Dennis 1942- *WhoAmL 94*
O'Brien, J. Willard 1930- *WhoAm 94*
O'Brien, Jacquelyn K. 1931- *WhoAmP 93*
O'Brien, Jacquelyn Kirtley 1931- *WhoMW 93*
O'Brien, James Aloysius 1936- *WhoAm 94*
O'Brien, James D., Jr. 1947- *WhoAmL 94*
O'Brien, James Edward 1912-1992 *WhAm 10*
O'Brien, James Jerome 1929- *WhoAm 94*
O'Brien, James Joseph 1930- *Who 94*
O'Brien, James Joseph 1935- *WhoAm 94, WhoScEn 94*
O'Brien, James K., Jr. 1951- *WhoAmP 93*
O'Brien, James Patrick 1961- *WhoWest 94*
O'Brien, James Phillip 1949- *WhoAm 94*
O'Brien, James V. 1955- *WhoAmL 94*
O'Brien, Janet W. *WhoAmP 93*
O'Brien, Jeremiah 1744-1818 *AmRev, WhAmRev*
O'Brien, Joan 1936- *WhoHol 92*
O'Brien, John *DrAPF 93*
O'Brien, John 1888-1967 *BasBi*
O'Brien, John 1921- *WhoAmP 93*
O'Brien, John 1953- *WrDr 94*
O'Brien, John Aeneas 1920- *WhoAmP 93*
O'Brien, John Augustine 1941- *WhoAmL 94*
O'Brien, John Conway *WhoAm 94, WhoScEn 94*
O'Brien, John D., Jr. *WhoAmP 93*
O'Brien, John F. 1943- *WhoIns 94*
O'Brien, John F., Jr. *WhoAm 94, WhoFI 94*
O'Brien, John Feighan 1936- *WhoAm 94, WhoFI 94*
O'Brien, John Fitzgerald 1928- *WhoAmP 93*
O'Brien, John Francis 1962- *WhoScEn 94*
O'Brien, John Gartland 1941- *WhoFI 94*
O'Brien, John Graham 1948- *WhoAmL 94*
O'Brien, John Joseph 1948- *WhoScEn 94*
O'Brien, John L. 1911- *WhoAmP 93*
O'Brien, John M. 1942- *WhoAm 94*
O'Brien, John Steininger 1936- *WhoScEn 94*
O'Brien, John Steven 1960- *WhoWest 94*
O'Brien, John W. 1931- *Who 94*
O'Brien, John Wilfrid 1931- *WhoAm 94*
O'Brien, John William, Jr. 1937- *WhoFI 94*
O'Brien, Joseph Arthur 1950- *WhoAmL 94*
O'Brien, Joseph E. 1940- *WhoIns 94*
O'Brien, Joseph Edward 1933- *WhoScEn 94*
O'Brien, Joseph M. 1917- *WhoAmP 93*
O'Brien, Joseph Patrick, Jr. 1940- *WhoAm 94*
O'Brien, Joseph William, Jr. 1929- *WhoAmP 93*
O'Brien, Judith A. 1944- *WhoAmL 94*
O'Brien, Kate 1897-1974 *BlmGWL [port]*
O'Brien, Katharine *DrAPF 93*
O'Brien, Katharine E 1901- *WrDr 94*
O'Brien, Kathleen Ann 1945- *WhoAmP 93*
O'Brien, Kathleen Ann 1948- *WhoMW 93*
O'Brien, Keith Michael 1954- *WhoWest 94*
O'Brien, Keith Michael Patrick *Who 94*
O'Brien, Keith Michael Patrick 1938- *IntWW 93*
O'Brien, Kenneth d1985 *WhoHol 92*
O'Brien, Kenneth John, Jr. 1960- *WhoAm 94*
O'Brien, Kenneth R. 1951- *WhoAm 94*
O'Brien, Kenneth Robert 1937- *WhoAm 94, WhoFI 94*
O'Brien, Kevin *Who 94*
O'Brien, (Thomas) Kevin 1923- *Who 94*
O'Brien, Kevin Charles 1957- *WhoWest 94*
O'Brien, Kevin E. 1952- *WhoAmL 94*
O'Brien, Kevin J. 1934- *WhoAm 94*
O'Brien, Kevin James 1954- *WhoAm 94*
O'Brien, Kieran *WhoHol 92*
O'Brien, Lawrence Francis 1917-1990 *WhAm 10*
O'Brien, Lawrence Francis, III 1945- *WhoAm 94, WhoAmL 94*
O'Brien, Lawrence John 1949- *WhoFI 94*
O'Brien, Leo, Jr. 1931- *WhoAmP 93*
O'Brien, Liam *WhoHol 92*
O'Brien, Liam 1913- *IntMPA 94*
O'Brien, Lisa Marie 1969- *WhoHisp 94*
O'Brien, Margaret 1937- *WhoHol 92*
O'Brien, Margaret 1938- *IntMPA 94*
O'Brien, Maria 1950- *WhoHol 92*
O'Brien, Marianne *WhoHol 92*
O'Brien, Mark *DrAPF 93*
O'Brien, Mark D. 1939- *WhoAmP 93*
O'Brien, Mark Stephen 1933- *WhoAm 94*
O'Brien, Mary *WhoHol 92*
O'Brien, Mary Blichfeldt 1952- *WhoMW 93*
O'Brien, Mary Devon 1944- *WhoFI 94*
O'Brien, Michael *DrAPF 93, WhoAmP 93*
O'Brien, Michael 1954- *Who 94*
O'Brien, Michael C. 1947- *WhoAmL 94*
O'Brien, Michael Dan 1955- *WhoAmL 94*
O'Brien, Michael J. *WhoIns 94*
O'Brien, Michael J. 1942- *WhoAmP 93*
O'Brien, Michael James 1961- *WhoMW 93*
O'Brien, Michael John 1930- *WhoAm 94*
O'Brien, Neal Ray 1937- *WhoAm 94*
O'Brien, Niall *WhoHol 92*
O'Brien, Orin Ynez 1935- *WhoAm 94*
O'Brien, Oscar 1892-1958 *NewGrDO*
O'Brien, Oswald 1928- *Who 94*
O'Brien, Pat d1920 *WhoHol 92*
O'Brien, Pat d1983 *WhoHol 92*
O'Brien, Patricia Jean 1937- *WhoAmP 93*
O'Brien, Patrick J. 1947- *WhoIns 94*
O'Brien, Patrick K. 1932- *WrDr 94*
O'Brien, Patrick Karl 1932- *IntWW 93, Who 94*
O'Brien, Patrick Michael 1943- *WhoAm 94*
O'Brien, Patrick William 1927- *WhoAm 94, WhoAmL 94*
O'Brien, Patrick William 1945- *Who 94*
O'Brien, Paul Herbert 1930- *WhoAm 94*
O'Brien, Paul Jerry 1925- *WhoAm 94, WhoWest 94*
O'Brien, Philip Michael 1940- *WhoWest 94*
O'Brien, Randall Eugene 1956- *WhoMW 93*
O'Brien, Raymond Francis 1922- *WhoAm 94, WhoFI 94, WhoWest 94*
O'Brien, Raymond Francis 1936- *Who 94*
O'Brien, Raymond Timothy 1948- *WhoMW 93*
O'Brien, Raymond Vincent, Jr. 1927- *WhoAm 94, WhoFI 94*
O'Brien, Rhonda A. 1956- *WhoAmL 94*
O'Brien, Richard d1983 *WhoHol 92*
O'Brien, Richard 1920- *Who 94*
O'Brien, Richard Desmond 1929- *WhoAm 94*
O'Brien, Richard Francis 1942- *WhoAm 94*
O'Brien, Richard Frank 1921-1989 *WhAm 10*
O'Brien, Richard Lee 1934- *WhoAm 94*
O'Brien, Robert Brownell, Jr. 1934- *WhoAm 94*
O'Brien, Robert C. 1918-1973 *TwCYAW*
O'Brien, Robert C(arroll) 1922-1973 *EncSF 93*
O'Brien, Robert Emmet 1923- *WhoFI 94*
O'Brien, Robert Francis 1942- *WhoAmL 94*
O'Brien, Robert John, Jr. 1935- *WhoAm 94*
O'Brien, Robert Kenneth 1934- *WhoAm 94*
O'Brien, Robert Peter 1941- *Who 94*
O'Brien, Robert S. 1918- *WhoAm 94, WhoWest 94*
O'Brien, Robert Thomas 1941- *WhoFI 94*
O'Brien, Romaine M. 1936- *WhoMW 93*
O'Brien, Rory 1955- *WhoHol 92*
O'Brien, Seamus d1977 *WhoHol 92*
O'Brien, Sean 1952- *WrDr 94*
O'Brien, Sean Dennis 1956- *WhoAmL 94*
O'Brien, Shannon P. *WhoAmP 93*
O'Brien, Sheila d1983 *WhoHol 92*
O'Brien, (Robert) Stephen 1936- *Who 94*
O'Brien, Sylvia *WhoHol 92*
O'Brien, Teddy *WhoHol 92*
O'Brien, Terence d1970 *WhoHol 92*
O'Brien, Terence John 1921- *IntWW 93, Who 94*
O'Brien, Thomas Francis 1938- *WhoAm 94*
O'Brien, Thomas G. 1954- *WhoAmL 94*
O'Brien, Thomas George, III 1942- *WhoAm 94, WhoAmL 94*
O'Brien, Thomas Henry 1937- *WhoAm 94, WhoFI 94*
O'Brien, Thomas Herbert 1921- *WhoFI 94*
O'Brien, Thomas Ignatius 1925- *WhoAmL 94, WhoFI 94*
O'Brien, Thomas Joseph 1935- *WhoAm 94, WhoWest 94*
O'Brien, Thomas Patrick 1956- *WhoMW 93*
O'Brien, Thomas William 1939- *WhoAm 94, WhoAmL 94*
O'Brien, Tim 1946- *WrDr 94*
O'Brien, Timothy Andrew 1943- *WhoAm 94*
O'Brien, Timothy Brian 1929- *Who 94*
O'Brien, Timothy James 1945- *WhoAm 94*
O'Brien, Timothy John 1958- *Who 94*
O'Brien, Timothy Martin 1944- *WhoAm 94*
O'Brien, Tom d1947 *WhoHol 92*
O'Brien, Turlough Aubrey 1907- *Who 94*
O'Brien, Vince(nt) *WhoHol 92*

O'Connor, (Mary) Flannery 1925-1964 *ConAu 41NR, RfGShF*
O'Connor, Francine Marie 1930- *WhoAm 94, WhoMW 93*
O'Connor, Francis Brian 1932- *Who 94*
O'Connor, Francis P. 1927- *WhoAmP 93*
O'Connor, Francis Patrick 1927- *WhoAmL 94*
O'Connor, Francis V. *DrAPF 93*
O'Connor, Francis V(alentine) 1937- *WrDr 94*
O'Connor, Francis Valentine 1937- *WhoAmA 93*
O'Connor, Francis X. 1929- *WhoAm 94*
O'Connor, Frank d1959 *WhoHol 92*
O'Connor, Frank 1903-1966 *BlmGEL, RfGShF*
O'Connor, Gayle McCormick 1956- *WhoAmL 94*
O'Connor, Genevieve A. 1914- *SmATA 75 [port]*
O'Connor, George Aquin, Sr. 1921- *WhoAm 94*
O'Connor, George Richard 1928- *WhoAm 94*
O'Connor, Gertrude Theresa, Sister 1939- *WhoMW 93*
O'Connor, Gillian Rose 1941- *Who 94*
O'Connor, Ginger Hobba 1951- *WhoMW 93*
O'Connor, Glynnis 1955- *IntMPA 94*
O'Connor, Glynnis 1956- *WhoHol 92*
O'Connor, Gwendolyn Marie 1928- *WhoAmP 93*
O'Connor, Harry d1971 *WhoHol 92*
O'Connor, Hazel *WhoHol 92*
O'Connor, Herbert d1933 *WhoHol 92*
O'Connor, Jack d1955 *WhoHol 92*
O'Connor, James John 1937- *WhoAm 94, WhoFI 94, WhoMW 93, WhoScEn 94*
O'Connor, James Joseph 1930- *WhoAm 94*
O'Connor, James Michael 1942- *WhoAmL 94*
O'Connor, John d1941 *WhoHol 92*
O'Connor, John 1920- *IntWW 93*
O'Connor, John Arthur 1940- *WhoAmA 93*
O'Connor, John D. 1946- *WhoAmL 94*
O'Connor, John Dennis 1942- *WhoAm 94*
O'Connor, John Edward, Jr. 1942- *WhoAm 94*
O'Connor, John Francis 1926- *WhoAm 94*
O'Connor, John Jay, III 1930- *WhoAm 94*
O'Connor, John Joseph 1950- *WhoMW 93*
O'Connor, John Joseph 1959- *WhoFI 94, WhoWest 94*
O'Connor, John Joseph, Jr. 1913- *WhoAm 94*
O'Connor, John Joseph Cardinal 1920- *WhoAm 94*
O'Connor, John Killeen 1932- *WhoAm 94*
O'Connor, John Morris, III 1937- *WhoAm 94*
O'Connor, John Paul 1939- *WhoMW 93*
O'Connor, John Paul 1963- *WhoAmL 94*
O'Connor, John Thomas 1944- *WhoFI 94*
O'Connor, Joseph A., Jr. 1937- *WhoAm 94, WhoAmL 94*
O'Connor, Joseph B. 1896- *WhAm 10*
O'Connor, Joseph W. 1942- *WhoIns 94*
O'Connor, Joseph William 1942- *WhoAm 94*
O'Connor, Judith 1936- *WhoAmP 93*
O'Connor, Karl William 1931- *WhoAm 94, WhoAmL 94, WhoWest 94*
O'Connor, Kathleen d1957 *WhoHol 92*
O'Connor, Kathleen Lucille 1944- *WhoWest 94*
O'Connor, Kathryn d1965 *WhoHol 92*
O'Connor, Kay F. 1941- *WhoAmP 93*
O'Connor, Kevin d1993 *Who 94N*
O'Connor, Kevin 1938-1991 *WhoHol 92*
O'Connor, Kevin J. 1964- *WhoHol 92*
O'Connor, Kevin Myles 1952- *WhoMW 93*
O'Connor, Kevin Neal 1953- *WhoScEn 94*
O'Connor, Kevin Patrick 1951- *WhoAmL 94*
O'Connor, Kevin Patrick 1966- *WhoScEn 94*
O'Connor, Kevin Thomas 1950- *WhoFI 94, WhoWest 94*
O'Connor, Kevin Washburn 1955- *WhoAmL 94*
O'Connor, Kim Claire 1960- *WhoScEn 94*
O'Connor, L. J. d1959 *WhoHol 92*
O'Connor, Laurence P. *WhoIns 94*
O'Connor, Lawrence Joseph, Jr. 1914- *WhoAm 94, WhoFI 94*
O'Connor, Leo F. 1936- *ConAu 141*
O'Connor, Margaret 1927- *WhoAmP 93*
O'Connor, Mary 1947- *WrDr 94*
O'Connor, Mary Beth *DrAPF 93*
O'Connor, Mary Flannery 1925-1964 *AmCulL*
O'Connor, Mary Patricia 1937- *WhoAmP 93*
O'Connor, Mary Scranton 1942- *WhoAm 94*
O'Connor, Maureen 1946- *WhoWest 94*
O'Connor, Maureen Frances 1946- *WhoWomW 91*
O'Connor, Michael *Who 94, WhoAmP 93*
O'Connor, (Brian) Michael (McDougal) 1942- *Who 94*
O'Connor, Michael E. 1948- *WhoAmL 94*
O'Connor, Michael Gerard 1949- *WhoAmP 93*
O'Connor, Michael John 1946- *WhoFI 94*
O'Connor, Michael Joseph 1928- *WhoAmP 93*
O'Connor, Michael Patrick *DrAPF 93*
O'Connor, Nancy Morrison 1951- *WhoAm 94*
O'Connor, Neal William 1925- *WhoAm 94*
O'Connor, Pat 1943- *IntMPA 94*
O'Connor, Patricia W. 1931- *WrDr 94*
O'Connor, Patrick 1949- *WrDr 94*
O'Connor, Patrick J. *WhoAmP 93*
O'Connor, Patrick Joseph 1914- *Who 94*
O'Connor, Patrick Lyman 1956- *WhoAmP 93*
O'Connor, Patrick McCarthy 1914- *Who 94*
O'Connor, Patrick Michael Joseph 1949- *Who 94*
O'Connor, Patsy 1929- *WhoHol 92*
O'Connor, Paul Daniel 1936- *WhoAm 94*
O'Connor, Paul Myron 1962- *WhoMW 93*
O'Connor, Peggy Lee 1953- *WhoMW 93*
O'Connor, Philip F. *DrAPF 93*
O'Connor, R. D. *WhoAm 94*
O'Connor, R. Dennis *WhoFI 94*
O'Connor, Ralph Sturges 1926- *WhoAm 94*
O'Connor, Raymond *WhoHol 92*
O'Connor, Raymond G(ish) 1915- *WrDr 94*
O'Connor, Raymond James 1926- *IntWW 93*
O'Connor, Raymond Joseph 1944- *WhoScEn 94*
O'Connor, Raymond Vincent, Jr. 1951- *WhoAmL 94*
O'Connor, Richard 1962- *WhoFI 94*
O'Connor, Richard Donald 1931- *WhoAm 94, WhoFI 94*
O'Connor, Richard M. 1953- *WhoAmP 93*
O'Connor, Robert 1959- *ConAu 140*
O'Connor, Robert B. d1993 *NewYTBS 93*
O'Connor, Robert Emmet 1919- *WhoAm 94*
O'Connor, Robert Emmett d1962 *WhoHol 92*
O'Connor, Robert Emmett 1945- *WhoAmP 93*
O'Connor, Rod 1934- *WhoAm 94*
O'Connor, Rodney Earl 1950- *WhoBlA 94*
O'Connor, Rory 1925- *Who 94*
O'Connor, Sandra Ann 1943- *WhoAmP 93*
O'Connor, Sandra Day 1930- *CngDr 93, IntWW 93, Who 94, WhoAm 94, WhoAmL 94, WhoAmP 93, WhoWomW 91*
O'Connor, Sara Andrews 1932- *WhoMW 93*
O'Connor, Sinead 1966- *WhoAm 94*
O'Connor, Stanley James *WhoAmA 93*
O'Connor, Stephen *DrAPF 93*
O'Connor, Thom 1937- *WhoAmA 93*
O'Connor, Thomas F., Jr. 1947- *WhoBlA 94*
O'Connor, Thomas P. 1944- *WhoIns 94*
O'Connor, Thomas Patrick 1944- *WhoAm 94, WhoFI 94*
O'Connor, Tim 1925- *WhoHol 92*
O'Connor, Timothy J., Jr. *WhoAmP 93*
O'Connor, Tom 1942- *WhoAm 94*
O'Connor, Una d1959 *WhoHol 92*
O'Connor, William Charles 1943- *WhoWest 94*
O'Connor, William Cody 1927- *WhoMW 93*
O'Connor, William E. 1922- *WrDr 94*
O'Connor, William Matthew 1955- *WhoAmL 94*
O'Connor, William Michael 1947- *WhoFI 94*
O'Connor, William Stewart 1953- *WhoMW 93*
O'Connor Howe, Josephine Mary 1924- *Who 94*
O'Conor, Herbert R., III 1948- *WhoAmL 94*
O'Conor, Hugh 1975- *WhoHol 92*
O'Conor, Joseph 1916- *WhoHol 92*
Oconostota c. 1710-1785 *WhAmRev*
Oconostota c. 1712-1783 *AmRev*
Ocque, James Peter 1937- *WhoAmP 93*
Ocrant, Ian 1954- *WhoScEn 94*
O'Crotty, Peter d1987 *WhoHol 92*
Octavia *BlmGEL*
October, John *EncSF 93*
Oculi, Okello 1942- *BlkWr 2*
Ocvirk, Andrej 1942- *WhoScEn 94*
Ocvirk, Otto G. 1922- *WhoAmA 93*
Ocvirk, Otto George 1922- *WhoAm 94*
Ocwirk, Ernst 1926- *WorESoc [port]*
Oda, Masayuki 1950- *WhoAmA 93*
Oda, Mayumi 1941- *WhoAmA 93*
Oda, Shigeru 1924- *IntWW 93*
Oda, Takuzo 1923- *WhoAm 94, WhoScEn 94*
Oda, Yoshio 1933- *WhoWest 94*
Odabasi, Halis 1931- *WhoScEn 94*
Odaga, Asenath (Bole) 1937- *BlkWr 2, ConAu 43NR*
Odaga, Asenath (Bole) 1938- *WrDr 94*
Odaga, Asenath Bole *BlmGWL*
Odak, Krsto 1888-1965 *NewGrDO*
Odaldi, Suor Annalena 1572-1638 *BlmGWL*
O'Daly, William Anthony 1951- *WhoWest 94*
Odam, John W. 1943- *WhoAmL 94*
Odam, Joyce *DrAPF 93*
O'Daniel, Ed, Jr. 1938- *WhoAmP 93*
O'Daniel, Janet *WrDr 94*
O'Daniel, William L. 1923- *WhoAmP 93*
O'Dare, Peggy *WhoHol 92*
Odasso, James Victor 1966- *WhoWest 94*
Odate, Toshio 1930- *WhoAmA 93*
Odavic, Ranko 1931- *WhoScEn 94*
O'Davoren, Vesey d1989 *WhoHol 92*
Odawara, Ken'ichi 1933- *WhoScEn 94*
O'Day, Alice d1937 *WhoHol 92*
O'Day, Anita 1919- *WhoHol 92*
O'Day, Anita Belle Colton 1919- *WhoAm 94*
O'Day, Dawn *WhoHol 92*
O'Day, Edward Joseph, Jr. 1932- *WhoMW 93*
O'Day, John Edward 1954- *WhoFI 94*
O'Day, John Hervey, Jr. 1953- *WhoMW 93*
O'Day, Joseph F. *WhoAmP 93*
O'Day, Kathleen Louise 1951- *WhoScEn 94*
O'Day, Maginnis d1964 *WhoHol 92*
O'Day, Molly 1911- *WhoHol 92*
O'Day, Nell d1989 *WhoHol 92*
O'Day, Paul Thomas 1935- *WhoAm 94, WhoFI 94*
O'Day, Peggy d1964 *WhoHol 92*
O'Day, Royal Lewis 1913- *WhoAm 94*
O'Day, Stephen E. 1953- *WhoAmL 94*
Odd, Gilbert 1902- *WrDr 94*
Odden, Allan Robert 1943- *WhoMW 93*
Oddershede, Jens Norgaard 1945- *WhoScEn 94*
Oddi, Silvio 1910- *IntWW 93*
Oddie, Christopher Ripley 1929- *Who 94*
Oddie, Guy Barrie 1922- *Who 94*
Oddie, James Henry 1964- *WhoMW 93*
Oddis, Joseph Anthony 1928- *WhoAm 94*
Oddo, Thomas Charles 1944-1989 *WhAm 10*
Oddsson, David 1948- *IntWW 93*
Oddy, Christine Margaret 1955- *Who 94, WhoWomW 91*
Oddy, Revel 1922- *Who 94*
Oddy, William Andrew 1942- *Who 94*
Ode, Connie 1951- *WhoAmL 94*
Ode, Eric d1983 *WhoHol 92*
O'Dea, Constance Louise 1946- *WhoFI 94*
O'Dea, Denis d1978 *WhoHol 92*
O'Dea, Dennis Michael 1946- *WhoAm 94, WhoAmL 94*
O'Dea, Eric Allen 1965- *WhoFI 94*
O'Dea, G. Kelly 1948- *WhoAm 94*
O'Dea, Jimmy d1965 *WhoHol 92*
O'Dea, John 1965- *WhoAmP 93*
O'Dea, John P. 1938- *WhoAmL 94*
O'Dea, Joseph d1968 *WhoHol 92*
O'Dea, Patrick Jerad 1918- *Who 94*
Odegaard, Charles Edwin 1911- *WhoAm 94*
Odegaard, Gary Martin 1940- *WhoAmP 93*
Odegard, Daniel James 1945- *WhoMW 93*
Odegard, Karen Ann 1950- *WhoMW 93*
Odegard, Margaret Bond 1925- *WhoMW 93*
Odegard, Mark Erie 1940- *WhoWest 94*
Odegard, Richard Erwin 1940- *WhoAm 94*
Odeh, Aziz Salim 1925- *WhoAm 94*
Odekirk, Bruce 1951- *WhoWest 94*
Odeku, Emmanuel Latunde 1927- *BlkWr 2*
Odell, Alexandra Robinson 1947- *WhoWest 94*
Odell, Andrew L. 1946- *WhoAmL 94*
O'Dell, Arvin Carlon 1954- *WhoMW 93*
O'Dell, Charlene Anne Audrey 1963- *WhoAmL 94*
O'Dell, Charles Robert 1937- *WhoAm 94*
O'Dell, "Digger" *WhoHol 92*
Odell, Donald Austin 1925- *WhoAm 94, WhoFI 94*
O'Dell, Edna d1987 *WhoHol 92*
O'Dell, Edward Thomas, Jr. 1935- *WhoAm 94*
O'Dell, Erin (Anne) 1938- *WhoAmA 93*
Odell, Frank Harold 1922- *WhoAm 94*
O'Dell, Georgia d1950 *WhoHol 92*
Odell, Herbert 1937- *WhoAm 94, WhoAmL 94*
O'Dell, James E. *WhoAm 94*
O'Dell, Joan Elizabeth 1932- *WhoAmL 94*
Odell, John H. 1955- *WhoWest 94*
Odell, John William *Who 94*
Odell, Jonathan 1737-1818 *WhAmRev*
O'Dell, June Patricia 1929- *Who 94*
Odell, Leonard E. 1945- *WhoIns 94*
O'Dell, Lynn Marie Luegge 1938- *WhoMW 93*
Odell, Mats *IntWW 93*
Odell, Maude d1937 *WhoHol 92*
Odell, Patrick Lowry 1930- *WhoAm 94*
Odell, Peter R(andon) 1930- *WrDr 94*
Odell, Peter Randon 1930- *Who 94*
Odell, Robert P., Jr. 1943- *WhoAmP 93*
Odell, Robert Stewart 1898- *WhAm 10*
Odell, Robin Ian 1935- *WrDr 94*
Odell, Samuel W. 1864-1948 *EncSF 93*
O'Dell, Scott 1898-1989 *TwCYAW, WhAm 10*
Odell, "Shorty" d1924 *WhoHol 92*
Odell, Stanley (John) 1929- *Who 94*
Odell, Stuart Irwin 1940- *WhoAm 94, WhoAmL 94*
O'Dell, Tony *WhoHol 92*
Odell, William Douglas 1929- *WhoAm 94, WhoScEn 94, WhoWest 94*
O'Dell, William Francis 1909- *WhoAm 94*
O'Dell, William H. 1938- *WhoAmP 93*
Odem, Charles David 1954- *WhoAmL 94*
Oden, David H. 1951- *WhoAmL 94*
Oden, Gloria *DrAPF 93*
Oden, Gloria 1923- *WhoBlA 94*
Oden, Howard Wayne 1929- *WhoFI 94*
Oden, Jean Phifer 1936- *WhoMW 93*
Oden, John Tinsley 1936- *WhoScEn 94*
Oden, Svante *EnvEnc*
Oden, Thomas C(lark) 1931- *ConAu 43NR*
Oden, Walter Eugene 1935- *WhoBlA 94*
Oden, William Arthur 1920- *WhoWest 94*
Oden, William Bryant 1935- *WhoAm 94*
Odendaal, Welma 1951- *BlmGWL*
Odendahl, Doris Frieda 1933- *WhoWomW 91*
Odenkirchen, Carl Josef 1921- *WhoAm 94*
Odenwald, Neil G. 1935- *ConAu 141*
Odenweller, Robert Paul 1938- *WhoAm 94*
Oder, Frederic Carl Emil 1919- *WhoAm 94*
Oder, Kenneth William 1947- *WhoAm 94*
Oder, Robin Roy 1934- *WhoScEn 94*
Oderman, Jeffrey M. 1949- *WhoAmL 94*
Odermatt, Bruno George 1956- *WhoIns 94*
Odermatt, Robert Allen 1938- *WhoAm 94, WhoWest 94*
Odescalchi, Edmond Pery 1928- *WhoFI 94*
Odets, Clifford d1963 *WhoHol 92*
Odets, Clifford 1906-1963 *AmCulL, IntDcT 2*
Odetta 1930- *WhoHol 92*
Odette, Mary 1901- *WhoHol 92*
Odeyale, Charles Olajide 1950- *WhoScEn 94*
Odgers, Christopher Reynold 1955- *WhoWest 94*
Odgers, Graeme David William 1934- *IntWW 93, Who 94*
Odgers, Paul Randell 1915- *Who 94*
Odgers, Richard William 1936- *WhoAmL 94*
Odie-Ali, Stella *WhoWomW 91*
Odin, Susan d1975 *WhoHol 92*
Odinet, Kenneth L. 1930- *WhoAmP 93*
Odinga, A. Oginga 1911- *IntWW 93*
Odink, Debra Alida 1963- *WhoScEn 94*
Odinot, Nicolas-Medard *NewGrDO*
Odio, Cesar H. *WhoHisp 94*
Odio Benito, Elizabeth *WhoWomW 91*
Odiorne, George Stanley 1920-1992 *WhAm 10*
Odiorne, Thomas H. d1993 *NewYTBS 93*
Odiorne, Virginia d1978 *WhoHol 92*
Odjig, Daphne 1919- *IntWW 93*
Odland, George Fisher 1922- *WhoAm 94*
Odland, Gerald Clark 1946- *WhoAm 94*
Odle, E(dwin) V(incent) 1890-1942 *EncSF 93*
Odle, Robert C., Jr. 1944- *WhoAmP 93*
Odle, Robert Charles, Jr. 1944- *WhoAm 94*
Odle, Stanley Gene 1926-1990 *WhAm 10*
Odlin, Richard Bingham 1934- *WhoAm 94*
Odling, Thomas George 1911- *Who 94*

OFORI-KYEI 842 Biography and Genealogy Master Index 1995

Ofori-Kyei, Mark Kwame 1966- *WhoWest 94*
Ofosu, Mildred Dean 1946- *WhoScEn 94*
Ofte, Donald 1929- *WhoAm 94, WhoFI 94, WhoWest 94*
Oftedahl, Marilyn J. 1937- *WhoMW 93*
Ofuchi, Kinuko 1944- *WhoWomW 91*
Ofverholm, Stefan 1936- *WhoFI 94, WhoScEn 94*
Ofwod, Stephen 1564-c. 1635 *DcNaB MP*
Ogaard, Louis Adolph 1947- *WhoScEn 94*
Ogaki, Masao 1958- *WhoFI 94*
Ogali, Ogali A(gu) 1931- *BlkWr 2*
O'Gallagher, Eamonn 1906-1982 *NewGrDO*
Ogan, Russell Griffith 1923- *WhoAm 94*
O'Gara, James Vincent 1953- *WhoAmL 94*
O'Gara, Patrick Denis 1941- *WhoAm 94, WhoMW 93*
O'Gara, William B. *WhoAmP 93*
Ogarkov, Nikolay Vasiliyevich 1917- *IntWW 93*
Ogasawara, Sadako 1920- *WhoWomW 91*
Ogata, Jeffery Morimasa 1954- *WhoAsA 94*
Ogata, Katsuhiko 1925- *WhoAm 94*
Ogata, Ken *WhoHol 92*
Ogata, Sadako *NewYTBS 93 [port]*
Ogata, Sadako 1927- *IntWW 93, Who 94*
Ogata, Shijuro 1927- *IntWW 93*
O'Gatty, Jimmy d1966 *WhoHol 92*
Ogawa, Dennis M. 1943- *WrDr 94*
Ogawa, Frank Hirao 1917- *WhoAsA 94*
Ogawa, Heiji 1910- *IntWW 93*
Ogawa, Heishiro 1916- *IntWW 93*
Ogawa, Joseph Minoru 1925- *WhoAsA 94*
Ogawa, Makio 1940- *WhoAm 94*
Ogawa, Osamu 1945- *WhoFI 94*
Ogawa, Patrick *WhoAsA 94*
Ogawa, Pelorhankhe Ai *DrAPF 93*
Ogawa, Seiichiro 1937- *WhoScEn 94*
Ogawa, Tomoya 1939- *WhoScEn 94*
Ogawara, Saburo 1931- *IntWW 93*
Ogbaa, Kalu 1945- *BlkWr 2, ConAu 141*
Ogbonnaya, Chuks Alfred 1953- *WhoScEn 94*
Ogburn, Charlton 1911- *WhoAm 94, WrDr 94*
Ogburn, Derial L. 1949- *WhoAmP 93*
Ogburn, Hugh Bell 1923- *WhoAm 94*
Ogburn, Roy 1942- *WhoAmP 93*
Ogburn, Wayne Lee 1947- *WhoAm 94*
Ogdahl, W. Wallace 1945- *WhoAmL 94*
Ogden, Aaron 1756-1839 *WhAmRev [port]*
Ogden, Alfred 1909- *WhoAm 94*
Ogden, Ann *WhoMW 93*
Ogden, C. Robert 1923- *WhoIns 94*
Ogden, Chester Robert 1923- *WhoFI 94*
Ogden, Chris 1945- *WrDr 94*
Ogden, David 1707-1800 *WhAmRev*
Ogden, Dayton *WhoAm 94, WhoFI 94*
Ogden, Eric 1923- *Who 94*
Ogden, Gerald Alan 1945- *WhoMW 93*
Ogden, Harry Peoples 1949- *WhoAmL 94*
Ogden, Howard 1947- *WrDr 94*
Ogden, Hugh *DrAPF 93*
Ogden, Isaac *WhAmRev*
Ogden, James d1781 *WhAmRev*
Ogden, James Douglas 1950- *WhoWest 94*
Ogden, Jean Lucille 1950- *WhoWest 94*
Ogden, Jerome Christopher 1943- *WhoAm 94*
Ogden, Joanne 1941- *WhoFI 94*
Ogden, John Hamilton 1951- *WhoAmL 94*
Ogden, Joseph Patrick 1956- *WhoFI 94*
Ogden, Matthias 1754-1791 *WhAmRev*
Ogden, Maureen B. 1928- *WhoAmP 93*
Ogden, Michael *Who 94*
Ogden, (Edward) Michael 1926- *Who 94*
Ogden, Michael Richard 1965- *WhoScEn 94*
Ogden, Peter James 1947- *WhoAm 94*
Ogden, Peter Skene 1794-1854 *WhWE*
Ogden, Ralph E. d1974 *WhoAmA 93N*
Ogden, Ralph Lindsey 1941- *WhoAm 94*
Ogden, Steve 1950- *WhoAmP 93*
Ogden, Sylvester O. 1935- *WhoFI 94*
Ogden, Valeria Juan 1924- *WhoWest 94*
Ogden, Valeria M. 1924- *WhoAmP 93*
Ogden, Vivia d1952 *WhoHol 92*
Ogden, Willard LeRoi 1929- *WhoFI 94*
Ogdon, Thomas Hammer 1935- *WhoAm 94*
Ogdon, Wilbur 1921- *WhoAm 94*
Ogesen, Robert Bruce 1934- *WhoMW 93*
Ogg, George Wesley 1932- *WhoAm 94*
Ogg, Jack Clyde 1933- *WhoAmP 93*
Ogg, James Elvis 1924- *WhoAm 94, WhoScEn 94*
Ogg, Oscar 1908-1971 *WhoAmA 93N*
Ogg, Wilson Reid 1928- *WhoAm 94, WhoAmL 94, WhoFI 94, WhoWest 94*
Ogi, Adolf 1942- *IntWW 93*
Ogida, Mikio 1938- *WhoAm 94*
Ogier, Bulle 1939- *WhoHol 92*
Ogier, Pascale d1984 *WhoHol 92*
Ogier, Walter Thomas 1925- *WhoAm 94, WhoWest 94*
Ogilby, Lyman Cunningham 1922-1990 *WhAm 10*
Ogilvie, Alec (Drummond) 1913- *Who 94*
Ogilvie, Bridget Margaret 1938- *IntWW 93, Who 94*
Ogilvie, Bruce Campbell 1944- *WhoFI 94, WhoMW 93*
Ogilvie, Donald Gordon 1943- *WhoAm 94*
Ogilvie, Elisabeth (May) 1917- *WrDr 94*
Ogilvie, Elisabeth May 1917- *ConAu 42NR*
Ogilvie, Kelvin Kenneth 1942- *WhoAm 94, WhoScEn 94*
Ogilvie, Richard Ian 1936- *WhoAm 94*
Ogilvie, Thomas Francis 1929- *WhoAm 94*
Ogilvie, Will 1901-1989 *WhoAmA 93N*
Ogilvie, William G(eorge) 1899- *WrDr 94*
Ogilvie-Grant *Who 94*
Ogilvie-Laing of Kinkell, Gerald 1936- *Who 94*
Ogilvie Thompson, Julian 1934- *IntWW 93, Who 94*
Ogilvy *Who 94*
Ogilvy, Lord 1958- *Who 94*
Ogilvy, Master of *Who 94*
Ogilvy, Alexandra 1936- *IntWW 93*
Ogilvy, Angus (James Bruce) 1928- *Who 94*
Ogilvy, C. Stanley 1913- *WrDr 94*
Ogilvy, David Mackenzie 1911- *IntWW 93, Who 94, WhoAm 94*
Ogilvy, Francis (Gilbert Arthur) 1969- *Who 94*
Ogilvy, Ian 1943- *WhoHol 92*
Ogilvy-Wedderburn, Andrew John Alexander 1952- *Who 94*
Ogimachi, Naomi Neil 1925- *WhoWest 94*
Oginski, Michal Kazimierz 1728-1800 *NewGrDO*
Oginz, Richard 1944- *WhoAmA 93*
Ogle, Alice Nichols 1925- *WhoAmP 93*
Ogle, Charles d1940 *WhoHol 92*
Ogle, Edward Proctor, Jr. 1935- *WhoFI 94*
Ogle, Joseph Womack 1902- *WhoWest 94*
Ogle, Natalie *WhoHol 92*
Ogle, Robert Lloyd, Jr. 1955- *WhoWest 94*
Ogles, D. Johnson 1961- *WhoAmL 94*
Ogles, Mark R. 1962- *WhoAmP 93*
Oglesbee, Frank William 1937- *WhoMW 93*
Oglesby, Clarkson Hill 1908-1992 *WhAm 10*
Oglesby, James Robert 1941- *WhoBlA 94*
Oglesby, Joe 1947- *WhoBlA 94*
Oglesby, Peter Rogerson 1922- *Who 94*
Oglesby, Ray Thurmond 1932- *WhoAm 94*
Oglesby, Sabert, Jr. 1921- *WhoAm 94*
Oglesby, Tony B. 1954- *WhoBlA 94*
Ogletree, Charles J., Jr. 1952- *WhoBlA 94*
Ogletree, John D., Jr. 1952- *WhoBlA 94*
Ogletree, Thomas Warren 1933- *WrDr 94*
Ogley, William David 1955- *Who 94*
Ogliaruso, Michael Anthony 1938- *WhoAm 94*
Oglivie, Benjamin A. 1949- *WhoBlA 94*
Ogmore, Baron 1931- *Who 94*
Ognall, Harry Henry 1934- *Who 94*
Ognibene, Andre John 1931- *WhoAm 94*
Ognibene, Frederick Peter 1953- *WhoScEn 94*
Ognibene, Thomas V. *WhoAmP 93*
Ognivtsev, Alexander Pavlovich 1920- *NewGrDO*
O'Gorman, Frank 1940- *WrDr 94*
O'Gorman, James Francis 1933- *WhoAmA 93*
O'Gorman, Ned *DrAPF 93*
O'Gorman, Ned 1929- *WrDr 94*
O'Gorman, Patricia Ann 1946- *WhoAmL 94*
O'Gorman, Peter Joseph 1938- *WhoFI 94*
O'Gorman, Richard 1953- *WhoAm 94*
O'Gorman, William d1966 *WhoHol 92*
Ogorodnikov, Aleksandr Ioilevich 1950- *LngBDD*
Ogot, Grace *WhoWomW 91*
Ogot, Grace 1930- *BlkWr 2, ConAu 142*
Ogot, Grace Akinyi 1930- *BlmGWL*
Ogra, Pearay L. 1939- *WhoAm 94*
O'Grady, Dennis Joseph 1943- *WhoAm 94, WhoAmL 94*
O'Grady, Desmond (James Bernard) 1935- *WrDr 94*
O'Grady, Francis William 1925- *Who 94*
O'Grady, Gail *WhoHol 92*
O'Grady, John Joseph, III 1933- *WhoAm 94*
O'Grady, Lani *WhoHol 92*
O'Grady, Rohan 1922- *WrDr 94*
O'Grady, Thomas James 1942- *WhoAmL 94*
O'Grady, Tom *DrAPF 93*
O'Grady, Tom d1942 *WhoHol 92*
O'Grady, Walter John 1926- *WhoAmP 93*
Ogrean, David William 1953- *WhoWest 94*
O'Green, Jennifer *ConAu 41NR*
O'Green, Jennifer Roberson *ConAu 41NR*
Ogren, Carroll Woodrow 1927- *WhoAm 94*
Ogren, Robert Edward 1922- *WhoAm 94*
Ogren, William Lewis 1938- *WhoAm 94*
Ogris, Werner 1935- *IntWW 93*
Ogston, Alexander George 1911- *IntWW 93, Who 94*
Ogston, Derek 1932- *Who 94*
O'Guin, Christopher Dwayne 1954- *WhoAmP 93*
O'Guinn, Jo Lynn 1954- *WhoBlA 94*
Ogul, Morris Samuel 1931- *WhoAm 94*
Ogundipe-Leslie, Molara *BlmGWL*
Oguniesi, Adebayo O. *WhoBlA 94*
Ogunseitan, Oladele Abiola 1961- *WhoWest 94*
Oguntoye, Ferdinand Abayomi 1949- *WhoScEn 94*
Ogunyemi, Wale 1939- *BlkWr 2, ConDr 93*
Ogura, Takekazu 1910- *IntWW 93*
Ogurak, Melvin 1929- *WhoAmL 94*
Ogut, Ali 1949- *WhoScEn 94*
Oh, Angela 1955- *WhoAsA 94*
Oh, Chan Soo 1938- *WhoAsA 94*
Oh, Chang H. 1946- *WhoAsA 94*
Oh, Eunsoon 1962- *WhoMW 93*
Oh, Harry K. 1935- *WhoAsA 94*
Oh, John Kie-Chiang 1930- *WhoAm 94*
Oh, Joseph 1943- *WhoAsA 94*
Oh, Keytack Henry 1938- *WhoAsA 94*
Oh, Kook Sang 1936- *WhoScEn 94*
Oh, Matthew InSoo 1938- *WhoAmL 94*
Oh, May Buong Yu Lau 1940- *WhoAmL 94, WhoFI 94*
Oh, Nam Hwan 1950- *WhoScEn 94*
Oh, Soon-Teck *WhoHol 92*
Oh, Tae Hee 1939- *WhoAsA 94*
Oh, Taesung 1947- *WhoAsA 94*
Oh, Tai Keun 1934- *WhoFI 94*
Oh, William 1931- *WhoAm 94*
Ohadi, Michael M. 1954- *WhoScEn 94*
O'Hagan, Baron 1945- *Who 94*
O'Hagan, Desmond 1909- *Who 94*
O'Hagan, Desmond Brian 1959- *WhoAmA 93*
O'Hagan, James Joseph 1936- *WhoAm 94*
O'Hagan, Joan 1926- *WrDr 94*
O'Hagan, William Gordon 1943- *WhoWest 94*
O'Hagin-Estrada, Isabel Barbara 1954- *WhoHisp 94*
O'Hair, John D. 1929- *WhoAmL 94*
O'Haire, Karen A. 1953- *WhoAmL 94*
Ohala, John Jerome 1941- *WhoAm 94*
Ohalete, Carol Lynn Schuster 1947- *WhoWest 94*
O'Hali, Abdulaziz A. 1937- *IntWW 93*
O'Hallion, Sheila 1942- *WrDr 94*
O'Halloran, Charles Ernest d1993 *Who 94N*
O'Halloran, Jack *WhoHol 92*
O'Halloran, Michael d1976 *WhoHol 92*
O'Halloran, Michael 1947- *WhoIns 94*
O'Halloran, Michael Joseph 1933- *Who 94*
O'Halloran, Thomas Alphonsus, Jr. 1931- *WhoAm 94, WhoWest 94*
Ohama, Yoshihiko 1937- *WhoAm 94, WhoScEn 94*
Ohan 1922- *WrDr 94*
Ohana, Maurice 1914- *NewGrDO*
O'Handley, Douglas Alexander 1937- *WhoScEn 94*
Ohanesian, David 1927- *NewGrDO*
Ohanian, Bernard Jay 1956- *WhoWest 94*
Ohanian, John B. 1937- *WhoWest 94*
Ohanian, Krekor 1925- *WhoAm 94*
O'Hanlon, Daniel J. 1919-1992 *AnObit 1992*
O'Hanlon, George d1989 *WhoHol 92*
O'Hanlon, George, Jr. *WhoHol 92*
O'Hanlon, James Barry 1927- *WhoAm 94*
O'Hanlon, Richard E. 1906-1985 *WhoAmA 93N*
O'Hanlon, Rory 1934- *IntWW 93*
Ohanneson, Joan 1930- *WrDr 94*
Ohannessian, Harry Haroutune 1919- *WhoFI 94*
O'Hannession, Dick d1966 *WhoHol 92*
Ohara, Akito 1948- *WhoScEn 94*
O'Hara, Alfred Peck 1919- *WhoAm 94*
O'Hara, Barry d1979 *WhoHol 92*
O'Hara, Bill 1929- *Who 94*
O'Hara, Catherine 1954- *IntMPA 94, WhoAm 94, WhoHol 92*
O'Hara, Charles 1740-1802 *AmRev, WhAmRev*
O'Hara, Derek Ive 1928- *Who 94*
O'Hara, Edward 1937- *Who 94*
O'Hara, Edwin Vincent 1881-1956 *DcAmReB 2*
O'Hara, Eliot 1890-1969 *WhoAmA 93N*
O'Hara, Eugene Michael 1937- *WhoAm 94, WhoFI 94*
O'Hara, Fiske d1945 *WhoHol 92*
O'Hara, Francis Patrick 1951- *WhoFI 94*
O'Hara, Frank 1926-1965 *GayLL*
O'Hara, Frank 1926-1966 *ConLC 78 [port]*
O'Hara, (James) Frederick 1904-1980 *WhoAmA 93N*
O'Hara, George d1966 *WhoHol 92*
O'Hara, Gerry 1924- *IntMPA 94*
O'Hara, James 1752-1819 *WhAmRev*
O'Hara, James Grant 1925-1989 *WhAm 10*
O'Hara, James Patrick 1955- *WhoAmL 94*
O'Hara, James Thomas 1936- *WhoAm 94, WhoAmL 94*
O'Hara, Jenny 1944- *WhoHol 92*
O'Hara, Jessee A. *WhoAmP 93*
O'Hara, Jill 1947- *WhoHol 92*
O'Hara, Jim (James) *WhoHol 92*
O'Hara, John d1929 *WhoHol 92*
O'Hara, John d1970 *WhoHol 92*
O'Hara, John (Henry) 1905-1970 *RfGShF*
O'Hara, John Henry 1905-1970 *AmCulL*
O'Hara, John Patrick 1930- *WhoAm 94, WhoAmL 94*
Ohara, Jun-Ichi 1950- *WhoWest 94*
O'Hara, Kenneth *EncSF 93*
O'Hara, Kenneth 1924- *WrDr 94*
O'Hara, Kevin Thomas 1960- *WhoAmL 94*
O'Hara, Leon P. 1920- *WhoBlA 94*
Ohara, Maricarmen 1954- *WhoHisp 94*
Ohara, Mariko *EncSF 93*
O'Hara, Marion Malone 1932- *WhoIns 94*
O'Hara, Marjorie (Doreen) 1928- *WrDr 94*
O'Hara, Maureen 1920- *WhoHol 92*
O'Hara, Maureen 1921- *IntMPA 94*
O'Hara, Michael James 1953- *WhoAmL 94*
O'Hara, Michael James 1956- *WhoWest 94*
O'Hara, Michael John 1933- *IntWW 93, Who 94*
O'Hara, Morgan 1941- *WhoAmA 93*
O'Hara, Patrick Joseph 1960- *WhoFI 94*
O'Hara, Paul M. 1946- *WhoFI 94*
O'Hara, Paul Vincent 1943- *WhoMW 93*
O'Hara, Quinn 1941- *WhoHol 92*
O'Hara, Robert James 1959- *WhoScEn 94*
O'Hara, Sheila Mary 1953- *WhoAmA 93*
O'Hara, Shirley d1979 *WhoHol 92*
O'Hara, Thomas Edwin 1915- *WhoAm 94*
O'Hara, Thomas Patrick 1947- *WhoAm 94*
O'Hara, William James 1930- *WhoAm 94*
Ohara Tomie 1912- *BlmGWL*
O'Hara Wood, Arthur *BuCMET*
O'Hara Wood, Pat 1891-1961 *BuCMET*
Ohardieno, Roger d1959 *WhoHol 92*
O'Hare, Daniel John 1955- *WhoMW 93*
O'Hare, Dean Raymond 1942- *WhoAm 94, WhoFI 94, WhoIns 94*
O'Hare, Don R. 1922- *WhoFI 94*
O'Hare, James Raymond 1938- *WhoAm 94, WhoFI 94*
O'Hare, John Mitchell 1946- *WhoAm 94*
O'Hare, Joseph Aloysius 1931- *IntWW 93, WhoAm 94*
O'Hare, Linda Parsons 1947- *WhoAm 94*
O'Hare, Patrick K. 1946- *WhoAm 94, WhoAmL 94*
O'Hare, Robert Joseph Michael, Jr. 1943- *WhoFI 94, WhoIns 94*
O'Hare, Terrence Dean 1946- *WhoAmL 94*
O'Hare, Thomas Edward 1928- *WhoWest 94*
O'Hare, William S., Jr. 1952- *WhoAmL 94*
Oharenko, Maria T. 1950- *WhoWest 94*
O'Harra, Catherine 1956- *WhoAmL 94*
Ohashi, Alan Joseph 1949- *WhoAsA 94*
Ohashi, Wataru 1944- *WhoAsA 94*
O'Haver, Thomas J. 1941- *WhoIns 94*
O'Hayer, Matthew 1955- *WhoFI 94*
Ohayon, Roger Jean 1942- *WhoScEn 94*
Ohberg, Ake 1905- *WhoHol 92*
Ohe, Katie (Minna) 1937- *WhoAmA 93*
Ohe, Shuzo 1938- *WhoAm 94, WhoScEn 94*
O'Heaney, Caitlin *WhoHol 92*
O'Hearn, Michael John 1952- *WhoAmL 94, WhoWest 94*
O'Hearn, Paul Burke 1947- *WhoAmL 94*
O'Hearn, Robert Raymond 1921- *WhoAm 94*
O'Hearn, William Wilson 1914- *WhoAmL 94*
O'Hearne, John Joseph 1922- *WhoAm 94*
O'Hehir, Diana *DrAPF 93*
Ohene-Frempong, Kwaku *WhoBlA 94*

Olah, George Andrew 1927- *WhoAm 94, WhoScEn 94, WhoWest 94*
Olah, Nancy Lynne 1955- *WhoIns 94*
Olah, Pamela Marie 1959- *WhoMW 93*
Olajuwon, Akeem Abdul 1963- *BasBi*
Olajuwon, Hakeem 1963- *CurBio 93 [port]*
Olajuwon, Hakeem Abdul 1963- *WhoAm 94, WhoBlA 94*
Olan, Susan Torian *EncSF 93*
Oland, Mark 1947- *WhoAmL 94*
Oland, S. M. *WhoAm 94, WhoFI 94*
Oland, Warner d1938 *WhoHol 92*
Olander, Jimmy
See Diamond Rio *ConMus 11*
Olander, Joseph D. 1939- *EncSF 93*
Olander, Per August 1824-1886 *NewGrDO*
Olander, Ray Gunnar 1926- *WhoAm 94, WhoFI 94*
Olang', Festo Habakkuk 1914- *IntWW 93, Who 94*
Olanow, Charles Warren 1941- *WhoScEn 94*
O'Laoghaire, Liam 1910-1992 *WrDr 94N*
Olapo, Olaitan 1956- *WhoBlA 94*
Olasov, David Michael 1945- *WhoAm 94, WhoAmL 94*
Olasz, Richard D. 1930- *WhoAmP 93*
O'Laughlin, Jeanne 1929- *WhoAm 94*
O'Laughlin, Marjorie Hartley *WhoAmP 93, WhoMW 93*
Olav, V, King of Norway 1903-1991 *WhAm 10*
Olaves, Jorge L. 1956- *WhoHisp 94*
Olawumi, Bertha Ann 1945- *WhoBlA 94*
Olayan, Suliman Saleh 1918- *Who 94*
Olazabal, Gary Steven Coyote 1953- *WhoWest 94*
Olazagasti-Segovia, Elena 1952- *WhoHisp 94*
Olberg, Harley 1941- *WhoAmP 93*
Olbrantz, Don Lee 1951- *WhoScEn 94*
Olbrechts, Guy Robert 1935- *WhoWest 94*
Olbyrchski, Daniel *WhoHol 92*
Olcay, Osman 1924- *IntWW 93*
Olchak, Lawrence Stephen 1955- *WhoFI 94*
Olcott, Henry Steel 1832-1907 *DcAmReB 2*
Olcott, Joanne Elizabeth 1958- *WhoWest 94*
Olcott, Richard Jay 1940- *WhoScEn 94*
Olcott, Sidney d1949 *WhoHol 92*
Olcott, William Alfred 1931- *WhoAm 94*
Olczak, Paul Vincent 1943- *WhoScEn 94*
Old, Bruce Scott 1913- *WhoAm 94*
Old, John Edward 1964- *WhoAmL 94*
Old, Lloyd John 1933- *WhoAm 94*
Old, Walter Gorn 1864-1919 *AstEnc*
Oldaker, Bruce Gordon 1950- *WhoScEn 94*
Oldaker, Guy Brooklyn, III 1950- *WhoFI 94*
Oldaker, William Henry 1931- *WhoWest 94*
Oldani, Christine D. 1950- *WhoAmL 94*
Oldcastle, John 1378-1417 *BlmGEL*
Olden, Kenneth 1938- *WhoAm 94, WhoScEn 94*
Oldenbourg, Zoe 1916- *IntWW 93*
Oldenbourg-Idalie, Zoe 1916- *Who 94*
Oldenburg, Carl 1932- *WrDr 94*
Oldenburg, Claes 1929- *IntWW 93*
Oldenburg, Claes Thure 1929- *AmCulL, WhoAm 94, WhoAmA 93*
Oldenburg, Ray 1932- *WrDr 94*
Oldenburg, Richard Erik 1933- *IntWW 93, Who 94, WhoAm 94, WhoAmA 93*
Oldenburg, Ronald Troy 1935- *WhoWest 94*
Oldenburg, Wayne C. 1947- *WhoAmL 94*
Oldenburg, William D. 1958- *WhoAmP 93*
Oldendorf, Lawrence Edward 1934- *WhoMW 93*
Oldendorf, William H. 1925-1992 *NewYTBS 93*
Older, Jack Stanley 1934- *WhoAm 94*
Older, Julia *DrAPF 93*
Oldershaw, Louis Frederick 1917- *WhoAm 94*
Oldewurtel, F. Keith 1957- *WhoMW 93*
Oldfather, Charles Eugene 1927- *WhoAm 94, WhoAmL 94*
Oldfield, Anne 1683?-1730 *BlmGEL*
Oldfield, Arthur Barney 1909- *WhoWest 94*
Oldfield, Barney d1946 *WhoHol 92*
Oldfield, Bruce 1950- *Who 94*
Oldfield, Bruce 1956- *IntWW 93*
Oldfield, E. Lawrence 1944- *WhoAmL 94, WhoMW 93*
Oldfield, Edward Charles, Jr. 1919- *WhoAm 94*
Oldfield, James Edmund 1921- *WhoAm 94, WhoScEn 94*
Oldfield, Jenny 1949- *WrDr 94*
Oldfield, John Richard Anthony 1899- *Who 94*
Oldfield, Michael 1950- *WrDr 94*
Oldfield, Michael Gordon 1953- *Who 94*
Oldfield, Pamela 1931- *WrDr 94*
Oldfield, Russell Miller 1946- *WhoAmL 94*
Oldham, Algie Sidney, Jr. 1927- *WhoBlA 94*
Oldham, Arthur Charles Godolphin 1905- *Who 94*
Oldham, Bill W. 1934- *WhoAm 94*
Oldham, Christopher Russell 1946- *WhoWest 94*
Oldham, Dale Ralph 1943- *WhoAm 94*
Oldham, Darius Dudley 1941- *WhoAm 94, WhoAmL 94*
Oldham, Derek d1968 *WhoHol 92*
Oldham, Dortch 1919- *WhoAmP 93*
Oldham, (Charles Herbert) Geoffrey 1929- *Who 94*
Oldham, J. Thomas 1948- *WhoAmL 94*
Oldham, Jawann 1957- *WhoBlA 94*
Oldham, John d1981 *WhoHol 92*
Oldham, John 1653-1683 *BlmGEL, DcLB 131 [port]*
Oldham, John Michael 1940- *WhoAm 94*
Oldham, John William 1952- *WhoAmP 93*
Oldham, Kevin 1960-1993 *NewYTBS 93*
Oldham, Lea Leever 1931- *WhoMW 93*
Oldham, Lucian Kenneth 1922- *WhoAmP 93*
Oldham, Maurice *WhoBlA 94*
Oldham, Maxine Jernigan 1923- *WhoFI 94, WhoWest 94*
Oldham, Pamela Sue 1946- *WhoMW 93*
Oldham, Perry *DrAPF 93*
Oldham, Phyllis Virginia Kidd 1926- *WhoMW 93*
Oldham, Richard Dixon 1858-1936 *DcNaB MP, WorScD*
Oldham, Ronald Wayne 1949- *WhoAmP 93*
Oldham, Theodore H. 1936- *WhoAmL 94*
Oldham, Timothy Richard 1947- *WhoScEn 94*
Oldham, Todd 1960- *WhoAm 94*
Oldham, Warren *WhoAmP 93*
Oldham, William George 1938- *WhoAm 94*
Oldham, William M. 1942- *WhoAmL 94*
Oldknow, Antony *DrAPF 93*
Oldknow, Samuel 1756-1828 *DcNaB MP*
Oldland, Lilian *WhoHol 92*
Oldman, Cecil Bernard 1894-1969 *DcNaB MP*
Oldman, Gary 1958- *IntMPA 94, IntWW 93, WhoAm 94, WhoHol 92*
"Old Marie" d1927 *WhoHol 92*
Oldmeadow, Ernest (James Francis) 1867-1949 *EncSF 93*
Oldmixon, Lady *NewGrDO*
Old Pretender, The 1688-1766 *BlmGEL*
Olds, Elizabeth 1896-1991 *WhAm 10*
Olds, Elizabeth Fay 1933- *WhoAmP 93*
Olds, Glenn Alvero 1921- *WhoAm 94*
Olds, Irving S. 1887-1963 *EncABHB 9 [port]*
Olds, Jennifer *DrAPF 93*
Olds, John Theodore 1943- *WhoAm 94*
Olds, Roger Alan 1951- *WhoWest 94*
Olds, Sharon *DrAPF 93*
Olds, Sharon 1942- *ConAu 41NR, WrDr 94*
Oldsey, Bernard *DrAPF 93*
Oldsey, Bernard S. 1923- *WrDr 94*
Oldshue, James Y. 1925- *WhoAm 94, WhoFI 94, WhoScEn 94*
Oldshue, Mary Holl 1951- *WhoFI 94*
Oldshue, Paul Frederick 1949- *WhoFI 94, WhoWest 94*
Oldson, William Orville 1940- *WhoAm 94*
Oldweiler, Thomas Patrick 1961- *WhoAmL 94*
Olea, Greg Manuel 1959- *WhoHisp 94*
Olea, Ricardo Antonio 1942- *WhoScEn 94*
Olearchyk, Andrew S. 1935- *WhoAm 94, WhoScEn 94*
O'Leary 1909- *WrDr 94*
O'Leary, Arthur Francis 1924- *WhoAm 94*
O'Leary, Bill d1954 *WhoHol 92*
O'Leary, Byron d1970 *WhoHol 92*
O'Leary, Cornelius Peter 1944- *WhoAmP 93*
O'Leary, Daniel Edmund 1950- *WhoFI 94, WhoWest 94*
O'Leary, Daniel Francis 1923- *WhoAm 94*
O'Leary, Daniel J. 1946- *WhoFI 94*
O'Leary, Daniel Vincent, Jr. 1942- *WhoAm 94, WhoAmL 94*
O'Leary, Dawn *DrAPF 93*
O'Leary, Denis Joseph 1924- *WhoAm 94*
O'Leary, Dennis Joseph 1941- *WhoAm 94*
O'Leary, Dennis Sophian 1938- *WhoAm 94, WhoScEn 94*
O'Leary, Edward Cornelius 1920- *WhoAm 94*
O'Leary, Frank J. 1953- *WhoAm 94*
O'Leary, Hazel 1937- *AfrAmAl 6, ConBlB 6 [port], IntWW 93, News 93 [port], WhoBlA 94*
O'Leary, Hazel R. *NewYTBS 93, WhoAmP 93*
O'Leary, Hazel R. 1937- *CngDr 93, WhoAm 94, WhoFI 94*
O'Leary, James John 1914- *WhoAm 94*
O'Leary, Jean 1948- *AmSocL*
O'Leary, John *WhoHol 92*
O'Leary, John Joseph, Jr. 1947- *WhoAmL 94*
O'Leary, John R. 1954- *WhoAmP 93*
O'Leary, Joseph Evans 1945- *WhoAm 94*
O'Leary, Kevin d1982 *WhoHol 92*
O'Leary, Liam 1910-1992 *WrDr 94N*
O'Leary, Marion Hugh 1941- *WhoAm 94*
O'Leary, Michael *WhoHol 92*
O'Leary, Michael 1936- *Who 94*
O'Leary, Michael 1938- *IntWW 93*
O'Leary, Patrick 1920- *WrDr 94*
O'Leary, Patrick J. 1951- *WhoAm 94*
O'Leary, Paul Francis 1945- *WhoAmP 93*
O'Leary, Paul Gerard 1935- *WhoAm 94, WhoFI 94*
O'Leary, Peggy Rene 1951- *WhoWest 94*
O'Leary, Peter Leslie 1929- *Who 94*
O'Leary, Prentice L. 1942- *WhoAmL 94*
O'Leary, Robert W. 1944- *WhoAm 94, WhoFI 94*
O'Leary, Rosemary 1955- *WhoAmL 94*
O'Leary, Terence Daniel 1928- *IntWW 93, Who 94*
O'Leary, Thomas Howard 1934- *WhoAm 94, WhoFI 94, WhoWest 94*
O'Leary, Thomas Michael 1944- *WhoAm 94, WhoAmL 94*
O'Leary, Thomas Michael 1948- *WhoAm 94*
O'Leary, Timothy F. 1945- *WhoAmP 93*
O'Leary, Timothy Francis 1948- *WhoMW 93*
O'Leary, Timothy Michael 1946- *WhoFI 94, WhoMW 93*
O'Leary, Wilfred Leo 1906- *WhoAm 94*
O'Leary, William *WhoHol 92*
O'Leary, William d1973 *WhoHol 92*
Olechowski, Tadeusz 1926- *IntWW 93*
Oleck, Howard L. 1911- *WhoAm 94, WrDr 94*
Oleen, Lana 1949- *WhoMW 93*
Oleen, Lana P. 1949- *WhoAmP 93*
Oleen-Burkey, MerriKay Adelle 1949- *WhoMW 93*
Oleinik, Vladimir Ivanovich 1936- *LngBDD*
Olejer, Andrew Joseph 1925- *WhoFI 94*
Olejko, Mitchell J. 1951- *WhoAmL 94*
Oleksey, Vicky Joyce 1952- *WhoFI 94, WhoMW 93*
Oleksiw, Daniel Philip 1921- *WhoAm 94*
Oleksiw, Susan (Prince) 1945- *ConAu 141*
Oleksy, Stephen A., II 1951- *WhoIns 94*
Olender, Beatrijs Tobi 1941- *WhoWest 94*
Olendorf, Bill *ConAu 41NR*
Olendorf, William 1924- *ConAu 41NR*
Olendorf, William Carr 1924- *WhoAmA 93*
Olendorf, William Carr, Jr. 1945- *WhoFI 94*
Olenick, David Charles 1947- *WhoAmA 93*
Oleniewski, Walter A. 1944- *WhoAmL 94*
Olenka *BlmGWL*
Olenski, Susan C. 1949- *WhoMW 93*
Oler, Howard Warren 1929- *WhoFI 94*
Oler, Wesley Marion, III 1918- *WhoAm 94, WhoScEn 94*
Olerich, Henry 1851- *EncSF 93*
Olerud, John Garrett 1968- *WhoAm 94*
Oles, Carole *DrAPF 93*
Oles, Henry J. 1943- *WhoFI 94*
Oles, Paul Stevenson 1936- *WhoAm 94, WhoFI 94*
Oles, Stuart Gregory 1924- *WhoAmL 94, WhoWest 94*
Olesen, Aase 1934- *IntWW 93, WhoWomW 91*
Olesen, Douglas Eugene 1939- *WhoAm 94, WhoFI 94, WhoScEn 94*
Olesen, Jens 1943- *WhoAm 94, WhoFI 94*
Olesen, Mogens Norgaard 1948- *WhoScEn 94*
Olesen, Poul 1939- *IntWW 93*
Oleskey, Stephen H. 1942- *WhoAmL 94*
Oleskiewicz, Francis S. 1928- *WhoIns 94*
Oleskiewicz, Francis Stanley 1928- *WhoAm 94*
Oleskowicz, Jeanette 1956- *WhoScEn 94*
Oleson, John Stanley 1947- *WhoMW 93*
Oleson, Otto H. 1915- *WhoAmP 93*
Oleszko, Patricia 1947- *WhoAmA 93*
Olevin, Beverly *DrAPF 93*
Olevskii, Victor Marcovich 1925- *WhoScEn 94*
Olexa, George Ronald 1955- *WhoWest 94*
Olexy, Peter D. 1943- *WhoAmL 94*
Olfield, Robert *WhAm 10*
Olga, Duchess d1953 *WhoHol 92*
Olgaard, Anders 1926- *IntWW 93*
Olguin, Dolores C. 1939- *WhoHisp 94*
Olguin, John Patrick 1959- *WhoWest 94*
Olguin, M. Michael 1948- *WhoHisp 94*
Olguin, Michael *WhoAmP 93*
Olguin, Ronald G. 1941- *WhoHisp 94*
Olguin, Ronald Gerald 1941- *WhoAmP 93*
Olhaye, Roble 1944- *IntWW 93*
Olhoft, John Ernest 1943- *WhoWest 94*
Olhoft, Wayne Lee 1951- *WhoAmP 93*
Olian, Robert Martin 1953- *WhoAm 94, WhoAmL 94*
Oliansky, Joel 1935- *WhoAm 94, WrDr 94*
Oliart Saussol, Alberto 1928- *IntWW 93*
Olick, Arthur Seymour 1931- *WhoAm 94*
Olick, Philip Stewart 1936- *WhoAm 94*
Olien, Neil Arnold 1935- *WhoAm 94*
Oliensis, Sheldon 1922- *WhoAm 94*
Oliinyk, Borys Illich 1935- *LngBDD*
Oliker, Vladimir 1945- *WhoAm 94*
Olila, Oscar Gesta 1955- *WhoScEn 94*
Olimpio, J. Lisbeth *WhoAmP 93*
Olin, Elisabeth 1740-1828 *NewGrDO*
Olin, Ferris *WhoAmA 93*
Olin, James Randolph 1920- *WhoAmP 93*
Olin, Ken 1954- *IntMPA 94, WhoHol 92*
Olin, Ken 1955- *WhoAm 94*
Olin, Kent Oliver 1930- *WhoAm 94*
Olin, Lena 1955- *IntMPA 94, WhoHol 92*
Olin, Lena 1956- *ConTFT 11*
Olin, Robert Floyd 1948- *WhoAm 94*
Olin, Stephen 1797-1851 *DcAmReB 2*
Olin, Stig 1920- *WhoHol 92*
Olin, Thomas Franklin 1928- *WhoAm 94*
Olin, William Harold 1924- *WhoAm 94*
Olinger, Chad Tracy 1962- *WhoScEn 94*
Olinger, David Y., Jr. 1948- *WhoBlA 94*
Olinger, Glenn Slocum 1929- *WhoAm 94*
Olins, Robert Abbot 1942- *WhoAm 94*
Olins, Wallace 1930- *Who 94*
Olinsky, Ivan G. 1878-1962 *WhoAmA 93N*
Olinsky, Wendy Rose 1960- *WhoAmL 94*
Olinto, Angela Villela 1961- *WhoMW 93*
Olipares, Hubert Barut 1957- *WhoScEn 94*
Oliphant, Betty 1918- *WhoAm 94*
Oliphant, Charles Frederick, III 1949- *WhoAmL 94*
Oliphant, Charles Romig 1917- *WhoScEn 94, WhoWest 94*
Oliphant, Dave *DrAPF 93*
Oliphant, David Nigel Kington B. *Who 94*
Oliphant, Ernie L. 1934- *WhoFI 94, WhoWest 94*
Oliphant, James S. 1945- *WhoAm 94, WhoAmL 94*
Oliphant, Jay Thomas 1959- *WhoFI 94*
Oliphant, Margaret 1828-1897 *BlmGEL, BlmGWL, RfGShF*
Oliphant, Mark 1901- *Who 94*
Oliphant, Mark Laurence Elwin 1901- *IntWW 93*
Oliphant, Patrick 1935- *IntWW 93, WhoAm 94, WhoAmA 93*
Oliphant, Robert *DrAPF 93*
Oliphant, Robert Thompson 1924- *WhoWest 94*
Oliphint, Benjamin Ray 1924- *WhoAm 94*
Olisah, Sunday Okenwa 1936-1964 *BlkWr 2*
Olitski, Jules 1922- *IntWW 93, WhoAm 94, WhoAmA 93*
Olitzka, Rosa 1873-1949 *NewGrDO*
Oliu, Ramon 1923- *WhoScEn 94*
Oliva, Dolores Maria 1944- *WhoHisp 94*
Oliva, Francesca 1671-1736 *NewGrDO*
Oliva, L. Jay 1933- *WrDr 94*
Oliva, Lawrence Jay 1933- *WhoAm 94*
Oliva, Robert Rogelio 1946- *WhoHisp 94*
Oliva, Stephen Edward 1946- *WhoWest 94*
Oliva, Tony 1940- *WhoHisp 94*
Oliva, Vincent Anthony 1950- *WhoFI 94*
Olivares, Julian, (Jr.) 1940- *ConAu 42NR*
Olivares, Julian, Jr. 1940- *WhoHisp 94*
Olivares, Luis d1993 *NewYTBS 93, WhoHisp 94N*
Olivares, Olga 1939- *WhoHisp 94*
Olivares, Omar 1967- *WhoHisp 94*
Olivares, Rafael A. 1944- *WhoHisp 94*
Olivares Del Valle, Francisco Javier 1950- *WhoScEn 94*
Olivarez, Jose Maurilio, Jr. 1966- *WhoHisp 94*
Olivarez, Stanley 1954- *WhoHisp 94*
Olivarez-Mason, Marylou *WhoHisp 94*
Olivas, Adolf 1956- *WhoAmP 93, WhoHisp 94*
Olivas, Daniel A. 1959- *WhoAmL 94, WhoWest 94*
Olivas, David Antonio 1952- *WhoWest 94*

Olivas, Guadalupe Soto 1952- *WhoHisp 94*
Olivas, Louis 1947- *WhoHisp 94*
Olivas, Maria Lucy 1943- *WhoHisp 94*
Olivas, Marian Jayne 1957- *WhoMW 93*
Olivas, Michael A. *WhoHisp 94*
Olivas, Ramon Rodriguez, Jr. 1949- *WhoHisp 94*
Olive, Chris Wiley 1958- *WhoAmP 93*
Olive, David Ian 1937- *IntWW 93, Who 94*
Olivé, Diego Eduardo 1949- *WhoHisp 94*
Olive, Edyth d1956 *WhoHol 92*
Olive, Elaine Carol 1957- *WhoMW 93*
Olive, J. Fred, II 1916- *WhoAmP 93*
Olive, Lindsay Shepherd 1917-1988 *WhAm 10*
Oliveira, Araken de *IntWW 93*
Oliveira, Elmar 1950- *WhoAm 94*
Oliveira, Gaspar *WhoHisp 94*
Oliveira, Manoel de 1908- *IntWW 93*
Oliveira, Marli de 1935- *BlmGWL*
Oliveira, Nathan 1928- *WhoAm 94, WhoAmA 93*
Oliveira, Rene Orlando 1955- *WhoAmP 93, WhoHisp 94*
Oliveira, Ronald Eugene 1935- *WhoAmL 94*
Oliveira, Sharon *WhoHisp 94*
Oliveira Campos, Narcisa Amalia de *BlmGWL*
Olivella, Barry James 1947- *WhoAm 94*
Oliver *Who 94*
Oliver, Al, Jr. 1946- *WhoBlA 94*
Oliver, Alexander R. 1944- *WhoAm 94*
Oliver, Andre d1993 *NewYTBS 93 [port]*
Oliver, Andrew c. 1707-1774 *WhAmRev*
Oliver, Ann Elizabeth 1953- *WhoFI 94*
Oliver, Anthony 1922- *WrDr 94*
Oliver, Anthony 1923- *WhoHol 92*
Oliver, Anthony Thomas, Jr. 1929- *WhoAmL 94, WhoWest 94*
Oliver, Barret *WhoHol 92*
Oliver, Benjamin Rhys 1928- *Who 94*
Oliver, Bernard More 1916- *WhoAm 94, WhoScEn 94*
Oliver, Bobbie 1949- *WhoAmA 93*
Oliver, Brian Darnell 1968- *WhoBlA 94*
Oliver, Bruce Lawrence 1951- *WhoFI 94, WhoScEn 94*
Oliver, Chad 1928- *EncSF 93*
Oliver, (Symmes) Chad(wick) 1928- *WrDr 94*
Oliver, Clarence Paul 1898- *WhAm 10*
Oliver, Clinton Paul 1922- *WhoAmP 93*
Oliver, Covey Thomas 1913- *WhoAmP 93*
Oliver, Daily E. 1942- *WhoBlA 94*
Oliver, Dale Hugh 1947- *WhoAmL 94*
Oliver, Dan David 1952- *WhoWest 94*
Oliver, Daniel 1939- *WhoAm 94, WhoAmP 93*
Oliver, Daniel Anthony 1939- *WhoScEn 94*
Oliver, David *WhoHol 92*
Oliver, David Edwin 1956- *WhoScEn 94*
Oliver, David Field 1952- *WhoAmL 94*
Oliver, David Jarrell 1954- *WhoScEn 94*
Oliver, David Keightley Rideal 1949- *Who 94*
Oliver, Dennis Stanley 1926- *Who 94*
Oliver, Diann 1951- *WhoAm 94*
Oliver, Douglas Alan 1957- *WhoFI 94*
Oliver, Eddie d1976 *WhoHol 92*
Oliver, Edna May d1942 *WhoHol 92*
Oliver, Edward C. 1930- *WhoAmP 93*
Oliver, Edward Carl 1930- *WhoFI 94, WhoMW 93*
Oliver, Egbert S(amuel) 1902- *WrDr 94*
Oliver, Elena 1942- *WhoHisp 94*
Oliver, Elizabeth Kimball 1918- *WhoAm 94*
Oliver, (Frederick) Ernest 1900- *Who 94*
Oliver, Everett Ahmad 1961- *WhoBlA 94*
Oliver, Fernando 1949- *WhoHisp 94*
Oliver, Francis Richard 1932- *WrDr 94*
Oliver, Frank d1939 *WhoHol 92*
Oliver, Frank Louis 1922- *WhoAmP 93, WhoBlA 94*
Oliver, Frederick Spencer *EncSF 93*
Oliver, George Benjamin 1938- *WhoAm 94, WhoMW 93*
Oliver, Gerald Clifford 1940- *WhoAm 94*
Oliver, Gloria Craig 1947- *WhoBlA 94*
Oliver, Gordon 1910- *WhoHol 92*
Oliver, Grayden 1894- *WhAm 10*
Oliver, Guy d1932 *WhoHol 92*
Oliver, Harry Maynard, Jr. 1921- *WhoAm 94*
Oliver, J. Van 1949- *WhoAmL 94*
Oliver, Jack Ertle 1923- *WhoAm 94*
Oliver, James L. 1934- *WhoBlA 94*
Oliver, James V. *WhoAmP 93*
Oliver, James William 1947- *WhoIns 94*
Oliver, Janne Rae 1951- *WhoMW 93*
Oliver, Jerry Alton, Sr. 1947- *WhoBlA 94*
Oliver, Jerry Joseph 1947- *WhoFI 94*
Oliver, Jesse Dean 1944- *WhoAmP 93, WhoBlA 94*
Oliver, John Andrew 1913- *Who 94*
Oliver, John E(dward) 1933- *WrDr 94*
Oliver, John Edward 1951- *WhoFI 94, WhoWest 94*
Oliver, John J., Jr. 1945- *WhoBlA 94*
Oliver, John Keith *Who 94*
Oliver, John Laurence 1910- *Who 94*
Oliver, John Michael 1939- *Who 94*
Oliver, John Oliver William 1911- *Who 94*
Oliver, John Percy, II 1942- *WhoAmL 94*
Oliver, John Preston 1934- *WhoAm 94*
Oliver, John Thomason, Jr. 1929- *WhoAm 94*
Oliver, John Watkins 1914-1990 *WhAm 10*
Oliver, Joseph 1885-1938 *AfrAmAl 6*
Oliver, Joseph McDonald, Jr. 1946- *WhoAm 94, WhoAmL 94*
Oliver, Joyce Anne 1958- *WhoFI 94, WhoWest 94*
Oliver, Kenneth A(rthur) 1912- *WrDr 94*
Oliver, Kenneth L., Jr. 1945- *WhoAmL 94*
Oliver, Kenneth Nathaniel 1945- *WhoBlA 94*
Oliver, Kenneth Steven 1954- *WhoAmL 94*
Oliver, Larry d1973 *WhoHol 92*
Oliver, LeAnn Michelle 1955- *WhoFI 94*
Oliver, Louis, III 1966- *WhoBlA 94*
Oliver, Maria Antonia 1946- *BlmGWL*
Oliver, Marian Parker 1924- *WhoAmP 93*
Oliver, Marie *ConAu 142*
Oliver, Mark 1927- *WrDr 94*
Oliver, Mark 1957- *WhoFI 94*
Oliver, Mark A. 1958- *WhoIns 94*
Oliver, Marvin E. *WhoAmA 93*
Oliver, Mary *DrAPF 93*
Oliver, Mary d1938 *WhoHol 92*
Oliver, Mary 1935- *ConAu 43NR, WhoAm 94, WrDr 94*
Oliver, Mary Margaret 1948- *WhoAmP 93*
Oliver, Mary Wilhelmina 1919- *WhoAm 94, WhoAmL 94*
Oliver, Melvin L. 1950- *WhoBlA 94*
Oliver, Michael *WhoHol 92*
Oliver, Michael Francis 1925- *Who 94*
Oliver, Michael Paul 1954- *WhoAmL 94*
Oliver, Michael Randolph 1961- *WhoFI 94*
Oliver, Michael Thomas 1943- *WhoFI 94*
Oliver, Nathan Jon 1965- *WhoWest 94*
Oliver, Nyra J. 1951- *WhoMW 93*
Oliver, Paul 1927- *WrDr 94*
Oliver, Pauline Ann 1947- *Who 94*
Oliver, Peter *AmRev*
Oliver, Peter 1713-1791 *WhAmRev*
Oliver, Peter Richard 1917- *Who 94*
Oliver, Raymond Davies 1936- *WhoAm 94*
Oliver, Rice Donald 1933- *WhoWest 94*
Oliver, Richard Alexander Cavaye 1904- *Who 94*
Oliver, Richard Bruce 1942-1983 *WhoAmA 93N*
Oliver, Richard Wayne 1946- *WhoFI 94*
Oliver, Robert *WhoHol 92*
Oliver, Robert Bruce 1931- *WhoAm 94*
Oliver, Robert G. 1927- *WhoAmP 93*
Oliver, Robert L. 1944- *WhoAmL 94*
Oliver, Robert Lee 1949- *WhoBlA 94*
Oliver, Robert T. 1909- *HisDcKW*
Oliver, Robert T(arbell) 1909- *ConAu 41NR*
Oliver, Robert Tarbell 1909- *WrDr 94*
Oliver, Robert W. 1922- *WrDr 94*
Oliver, Robert Warner 1922- *WhoAm 94, WhoFI 94, WhoWest 94*
Oliver, Rochelle 1937- *WhoHol 92*
Oliver, Roland 1923- *IntWW 93*
Oliver, Roland Anthony 1923- *Who 94, WrDr 94*
Oliver, Ronald 1949- *WhoBlA 94*
Oliver, Ronald Daniel 1946- *WhoBlA 94*
Oliver, Ronald Martin 1929- *Who 94*
Oliver, Roseann 1947- *WhoAmL 94*
Oliver, Rufus W., III 1947- *WhoAm 94, WhoAmL 94*
Oliver, Samuel William, Jr. 1935- *WhoAmL 94*
Oliver, Sandi *WhoAmA 93*
Oliver, Sandra 1941- *WhoAmA 93*
Oliver, Shirley (Louise Dawkins) 1958- *SmATA 74 [port]*
Oliver, Shirling d1971 *WhoHol 92*
Oliver, Stephanie Stokes *WhoAm 94*
Oliver, Stephen *WhoHol 92*
Oliver, Stephen 1950-1992 *NewGrDO*
Oliver, Stephen John 1948- *Who 94*
Oliver, Stephen John Lindsay 1938- *Who 94*
Oliver, Stephen Ronald 1947- *WhoWest 94*
Oliver, Steven Wiles 1947- *WhoAm 94, WhoFI 94*
Oliver, Susan d1990 *WhoHol 92*
Oliver, Susan 1937-1990 *ConTFT 11*
Oliver, Sy d1988 *WhoHol 92*
Oliver, Ted d1957 *WhoHol 92*
Oliver, Terry D. 1947- *WhoAmP 93*
Oliver, Terry Vincent 1951- *WhoWest 94*
Oliver, Thelma *WhoHol 92*
Oliver, Thomas d1808 *WhAmRev*
Oliver, Thomas William 1939- *WhoAm 94*
Oliver, Thornal Goodloe 1934- *WhoAm 94*
Oliver, Vic d1964 *WhoHol 92*
Oliver, Virgil d1988 *WhoHol 92*
Oliver, Walter Frederick 1962- *WhoMW 93*
Oliver, William Albert, Jr. 1926- *WhoAm 94*
Oliver, William Henry 1915- *WhoBlA 94*
Oliver, William John 1925- *WhoAm 94*
Oliver, William Langdon 1954- *WhoFI 94*
Olivera, Beatriz Maria 1956- *WhoHisp 94*
Olivera, Herbert Ernest 1923- *WhoBlA 94*
Olivera, Mercedes 1948- *WhoHisp 94*
Oliveras, Rene Martin 1943- *WhoHisp 94*
Oliveras-Soto, Gilberto 1959- *WhoHisp 94*
Olivera Williams, Maria Rosa 1955- *WhoMW 93*
Olivere, Marilyn Hess 1949- *WhoWest 94*
Oliverez, Manuel *WhoHisp 94*
Oliveri, Alfred d1977 *WhoHol 92*
Oliveri, Cesare *NewGrDO*
Oliveri, Kristin Ann 1952- *WhoAmL 94*
Oliveri, Sal *WhoAmP 93*
Oliverio, Michael Angelo, II 1963- *WhoAmP 93*
Olivero, John Joseph, Jr. 1941- *WhoScEn 94*
Olivero, Magda 1912- *NewGrDO*
Oliver of Aylmerton, Baron 1921- *IntWW 93, Who 94*
Oliveros, Chuck *DrAPF 93*
Oliveros, Gilda C. 1949- *WhoHisp 94*
Olives Chávez, Marcia Lynn 1953- *WhoHisp 94*
Oliveto, Frank Louis 1956- *WhoAm 94, WhoFI 94*
Olivette, Marie d1959 *WhoHol 92*
Olivette, Nina d1971 *WhoHol 92*
Olivier, Lady *Who 94*
Olivier, Christine *BlmGWL*
Olivier, Henry 1914- *Who 94*
Olivier, Jason Thomas 1961- *WhoAmL 94*
Olivier, Julie-Kate 1966- *WhoHol 92*
Olivier, Laurence d1989 *WhoHol 92*
Olivier, Laurence 1907-1989 *BlmGEL*
Olivier, Laurence Kerr 1907-1989 *WhAm 10*
Olivier, Louis 1923- *IntWW 93*
Olivier, Maricruz d1984 *WhoHol 92*
Olivier, Paul d1948 *WhoHol 92*
Olivier, Tarquin 1937- *WhoHol 92*
Olivieri, Angelo fl. 1678-1691 *NewGrDO*
Olivieri, Cesare fl. 1776-1792 *NewGrDO*
Olivieri, Joseph John 1923- *WhoMW 93*
Olivieri, Robert John 1950- *WhoAmL 94*
Olivo, Dora F. 1943- *WhoAmP 93*
Olivo, Efren 1936- *WhoHisp 94*
Olivo, Juan Ramiro 1946- *WhoHisp 94*
Olivo, Margaret Ellen Anderson 1941- *WhoAm 94*
Olkewicz, Walter *WhoHol 92*
Olkinetzky, Sam 1919- *WhoAm 94, WhoAmA 93*
Olkon, Ellis 1939- *WhoAmP 93*
Olkon, Nancy Katherine 1941- *WhoAmP 93*
Olkonen, Elsie Swan 1917- *WhoAmP 93*
Olkowski, Zbigniew Lech 1938- *WhoScEn 94*
Ollard, Richard 1923- *WrDr 94*
Ollard, Richard Laurence 1923- *Who 94*
Ollee, Mildred W. 1936- *WhoBlA 94*
Olleman, Roger Dean 1923- *WhoAm 94*
Ollendorf, Fritz 1912-1977 *NewGrDO*
Oller, William Maxwell 1924- *WhoAm 94*
Ollerenshaw, Kathleen 1912- *WrDr 94*
Ollerenshaw, Kathleen (Mary) 1912- *Who 94*
Ollestad, Norman d1979 *WhoHol 92*
Olley, Robert Edward 1933- *WhoAm 94, WhoWest 94*
Ollhoff, Barbara Jean 1947- *WhoMW 93*
Ollie, C. Arthur 1941- *WhoAmP 93*
Ollie, Clifford Arthur 1941- *WhoMW 93*
Ollier, Claude *EncSF 93*
Ollier, Cliff(ord) David 1931- *WrDr 94*
Ollila, Esko Juhani 1940- *IntWW 93*
Ollila, Jorma 1950- *IntWW 93*
Ollinger, W. James 1943- *WhoAm 94, WhoAmL 94*
Ollis, James Bruce 1934- *WhoAmP 93*
Ollis, May d1985 *WhoHol 92*
Ollis, William David 1924- *Who 94*
Ollison, Ruth Allen 1954- *WhoBlA 94*
Olliver, Denis G. 1940- *WhoFI 94*
Ollman, Arthur L. 1947- *WhoAmA 93*
Ollman, Susan Harriett 1954- *WhoMW 93*
Ollmann, Kurt 1957- *NewGrDO*
Ollone, Max(imilien-Paul-Marie-Felix) d' 1875-1959 *NewGrDO*
Olloqui, Jose Juan de 1931- *IntWW 93*
Ollwerther, William Raymond 1950- *WhoAm 94*
Olman, Maryellen 1946- *WhoFI 94*
Olmeda, Carmen Nydia 1938- *WhoHisp 94*
Olmedo, Alberto d1988 *WhoHol 92*
Olmedo, Alex 1936- *BuCMET*
Olmedo, Irma Maria 1943- *WhoHisp 94*
Olmedo, Kim Ellen 1959- *WhoHisp 94*
Olmer, Henry 1887-1950 *WhoAmA 93N*
Olmer, Lionel Herbert 1934- *WhoAm 94*
Olmert, Ehud 1945- *IntWW 93*
Olmert, Michael 1940- *ConAu 140*
Olmi, Ermanno 1931- *IntMPA 94, IntWW 93*
Olmo, Ralph James 1946- *WhoAmP 93*
Olmos, Antonio Garcia 1963- *WhoHisp 94*
Olmos, David R. 1957- *WhoHisp 94*
Olmos, Edward James 1947- *IntMPA 94, WhoAm 94, WhoHisp 94, WhoHol 92*
Olmos, Mico *WhoHol 92*
Olmstead, Cecil Jay 1920- *WhoAm 94*
Olmstead, Clarence Walter, Jr. 1943- *WhoAm 94, WhoAmL 94*
Olmstead, David 1943- *WhoAmL 94*
Olmstead, Dennis John 1957- *WhoAmL 94*
Olmstead, Francis Henry, Jr. 1938- *WhoAm 94*
Olmstead, Gertrude d1975 *WhoHol 92*
Olmstead, Marjorie Ann 1958- *WhoWest 94*
Olmstead, Paul Smith 1897- *WhoFI 94*
Olmstead, Robert 1954- *WrDr 94*
Olmstead, Tommy C. 1929- *WhoAmP 93*
Olmstead, Van Dregge, Jr. 1943- *WhoFI 94*
Olmstead, William Edward 1936- *WhoAm 94, WhoScEn 94*
Olmsted, Frederick Law 1822-1903 *AmCulL*
Olmsted, George Hamden 1901- *WhoAm 94*
Olmsted, Gideon 1749-1845 *WhAmRev*
Olmsted, Jared 1811-1843 *EncNAR*
Olmsted, Jerauld Lockwood 1938- *WhoAm 94*
Olmsted, Mildred Scott d1990 *WhAm 10*
Olmsted, Nelson *WhoHol 92*
Olmsted, Robert Amson 1924- *WhoScEn 94*
Olmsted, Robert W(alsh) 1936- *WrDr 94*
Olmsted, Ronald David 1937- *WhoWest 94*
Olmsted, Suzanne M. 1956- *WhoAmA 93*
Ol'nem 1872- *BlmGWL*
Olner, William John 1942- *Who 94*
Olney, James 1933- *WhoAm 94*
Olney, Peter Butler, Jr. 1924- *WhoAm 94*
Olney, Robert C. 1926- *WhoAm 94*
Olney, Ross R(obert) 1929- *WrDr 94*
Olofson, Tom William 1941- *WhoAm 94, WhoFI 94, WhoMW 93*
Ologboni, Tejumola F. 1945- *WhoBlA 94*
O'Loghlen, Colman (Michael) 1916- *Who 94*
O'Loingsigh, Padraig *WhoHol 92*
O'Loughlin, Earl T. 1930- *WhoAm 94*
O'Loughlin, Franklin Dennis 1951- *WhoAmL 94*
O'Loughlin, Gerald S. 1921- *WhoHol 92*
O'Loughlin, Gerald Stuart 1921- *IntMPA 94*
O'Loughlin, James William, III 1955- *WhoAmP 93*
O'Loughlin, Jane Frances 1960- *WhoMW 93*
O'Loughlin, John Kirby 1929- *WhoAm 94, WhoFI 94*
O'Loughlin, Sandra S. 1942- *WhoAmL 94*
Olovsson, Ivar 1928- *IntWW 93*
Olowu, (Claudius) Dele 1952- *WrDr 94*
Olphin, Philip Bruce 1954- *WhoFI 94*
Olpin, A(lbert) Ray 1898- *WhAm 10*
Olpin, Glen W. 1950- *WhoFI 94*
Olpin, Owen 1934- *WhoAm 94*
Olpin, Robert Spencer 1940- *WhoAmA 93, WhoWest 94*
Olsa, Jaroslav, Jr. 1964- *EncSF 93*
Olsak, Ivan Karel 1933- *WhoScEn 94*
Olsavsky, John George 1966- *WhoScEn 94*
Olsby, Gregory Scott *WhoWest 94*
Olscamp, Paul James 1937- *WhoMW 93*
Olscheske, Thomas John 1950- *WhoMW 93*
Olschwang, Alan Paul 1942- *WhoAm 94, WhoAmL 94, WhoFI 94, WhoWest 94*
Olsem, Jean-Pierre 1942- *WhoScEn 94*
Olsen, Alfred Jon 1940- *WhoAm 94*
Olsen, Allen Neil 1934- *WhoScEn 94*
Olsen, Alvin Gordon 1927- *WhoAm 94*
Olsen, Arthur Martin 1909- *WhoAm 94*
Olsen, Bob 1884-1956 *EncSF 93*

Olsen, C. Arild 1898- *WhAm 10*
Olsen, Carol M. 1946- *WhoIns 94*
Olsen, Chris John 1952- *WhoFI 94*
Olsen, Christine M. 1949- *WhoAmL 94*
Olsen, Christopher 1946- *WhoHol 92*
Olsen, Christopher Ted 1964- *WhoAmL 94, WhoWest 94*
Olsen, Clifford Wayne 1936- *WhoScEn 94, WhoWest 94*
Olsen, Dagne B. 1933- *WhoAmP 93, WhoMW 93*
Olsen, Daniel Paul 1952- *WhoWest 94*
Olsen, Daren Wayne 1965- *WhoScEn 94*
Olsen, David *DrAPF 93*
Olsen, David Alexander 1937- *WhoAm 94*
Olsen, David Magnor 1941- *WhoScEn 94, WhoWest 94*
Olsen, David Walter 1963- *WhoAmL 94*
Olsen, Don Lee 1928- *WhoWest 94*
Olsen, Donald Bert 1930- *WhoAm 94, WhoScEn 94*
Olsen, Donald Emmanuel 1919- *WhoAm 94*
Olsen, Donald Paul 1938- *WhoScEn 94*
Olsen, Edward Gustave 1908- *WhoAm 94*
Olsen, Edward John 1927- *WhoAm 94*
Olsen, Einar Arthur 1917-1985 *WhAm 10*
Olsen, Ernest Moran 1910- *WhoAmA 93*
Olsen, Ernfred Michael 1957- *WhoFI 94*
Olsen, Eugene Field 1896- *WhAm 10*
Olsen, Evan L. 1932- *WhoAmP 93*
Olsen, Frances Elisabeth 1945- *WhoAmL 94*
Olsen, Francine Wozniak 1952- *WhoMW 93*
Olsen, Francis Richard 1933-1991 *WhAm 10*
Olsen, Frederick L. 1938- *WhoAmA 93*
Olsen, Gary *WhoHol 92*
Olsen, Gary Alvin 1949- *WhoMW 93, WhoScEn 94*
Olsen, George d1971 *WhoHol 92*
Olsen, George Allen 1928- *WhoFI 94*
Olsen, George Edward 1924- *WhoMW 93*
Olsen, Glenn Warren 1938- *WhoWest 94*
Olsen, Hans Peter 1940- *WhoAm 94, WhoAmL 94*
Olsen, Harold 1895-1953 *BasBi*
Olsen, Harold Fremont 1920- *WhoAm 94*
Olsen, Harold William 1931- *WhoScEn 94*
Olsen, Harris Leland 1947- *WhoFI 94, WhoWest 94*
Olsen, Herb 1905-1973 *WhoAmA 93N*
Olsen, Jack 1925- *WhoAm 94*
Olsen, John Sigvard 1892-1963 *See* Olsen and Johnson *WhoCom*
Olsen, Kathie Lynn 1952- *WhoScEn 94*
Olsen, Kenneth Allen 1953- *WhoAmL 94*
Olsen, Kenneth Harold 1930- *WhoScEn 94*
Olsen, Kenneth Harry 1926- *WhoAm 94*
Olsen, Kurt 1924- *WhoAm 94*
Olsen, Lance *DrAPF 93*
Olsen, Larry 1939- *WhoHol 92*
Olsen, Lauritz d1955 *WhoHol 92*
Olsen, Lon Christopher 1966- *WhoMW 93*
Olsen, M. Kent 1948- *WhoAmL 94, WhoWest 94*
Olsen, Mark Norman 1947- *WhoFI 94*
Olsen, Marvin Elliott 1936-1992 *WhAm 10*
Olsen, Merlin *ProFbHF [port]*
Olsen, Merlin 1940- *WhoHol 92*
Olsen, Merlin Jay 1940- *WhoAm 94*
Olsen, Michael David 1946- *WhoAmL 94*
Olsen, Michael Erik 1959- *WhoWest 94*
Olsen, Moroni d1954 *WhoHol 92*
Olsen, Niels-Erik 1948- *WhoFI 94*
Olsen, Olaf 1928- *IntWW 93*
Olsen, Ole d1963 *WhoHol 92*
Olsen, Ole 1850-1927 *NewGrDO*
Olsen, Oscar Marken 1925- *WhoFI 94*
Olsen, Otto H. 1925- *WrDr 94*
Olsen, Phillip Buck 1931- *WhoWest 94*
Olsen, Rex Norman 1925- *WhoAm 94*
Olsen, Richard Galen 1945- *WhoFI 94, WhoScEn 94*
Olsen, Richard George 1937- *WhoScEn 94*
Olsen, Richard Scott 1954- *WhoScEn 94*
Olsen, Richard W. 1952- *WhoAm 94*
Olsen, Robert Arthur 1943- *WhoFI 94, WhoWest 94*
Olsen, Robert John 1928- *WhoAm 94, WhoFI 94*
Olsen, Robert Stephen 1946- *WhoWest 94*
Olsen, Roger E. 1946- *WhoWest 94*
Olsen, Roger Milton 1942- *WhoAm 94*
Olsen, Sally *WhoAmP 93*
Olsen, Sheila Ann 1938- *WhoAmP 93*
Olsen, Sondra Spatt *DrAPF 93*
Olsen, Stanley John 1919- *WhoWest 94*
Olsen, Stanley Severn 1944- *WhoMW 93*
Olsen, Stephen Edward 1952- *WhoMW 93*
Olsen, Susan 1961- *WhoHol 92*
Olsen, T. Fred *WhoFI 94*
Olsen, T(heodore) V(ictor) 1932- *WrDr 94*
Olsen, Theodora Morgan *WhoAmA 93*
Olsen, Theodore Alan 1953- *WhoAmL 94*
Olsen, Thomas Richard, Sr. 1934- *WhoAm 94*
Olsen, Thomas William 1952- *WhoScEn 94*
Olsen, Tillie *DrAPF 93*
Olsen, Tillie c. 1912- *RfGShF, WhoAm 94*
Olsen, Tillie 1913- *BlmGWL, ConAu 43NR, WrDr 94*
Olsen, Torkil 1922- *IntWW 93*
Olsen, W. Scott *DrAPF 93*
Olsen and Johnson *WhoCom*
Olsen Bergman, Ciel 1938- *WhoAmA 93*
Olsen-Darst, Sandra Annette 1963- *WhoMW 93*
Olshan, Bernard 1921- *WhoAmA 93*
Olshan, Kenneth S. 1932- *WhoAm 94*
Olshen, Abraham Charles 1913- *WhoFI 94, WhoWest 94*
Olshin, Lewis R. 1951- *WhoAmL 94*
Olshove, Dennis *WhoAmP 93*
Olsinski, Peter Kevin 1942- *WhoAm 94*
Olson, Alan J. 1940- *WhoAm 94*
Olson, Alec Gehard 1930- *WhoAmP 93*
Olson, Alice Adele 1928- *WhoAmP 93*
Olson, Alice Wicks d1993 *NewYTBS 93*
Olson, Allen Ingvar 1938- *IntWW 93, WhoAmP 93*
Olson, Arielle North 1932- *WrDr 94*
Olson, Barry Gay 1933- *WhoFI 94, WhoMW 93*
Olson, Bettye Johnson 1923- *WhoAmA 93*
Olson, Bob Moody 1934- *WhoAm 94*
Olson, Bruce Allan 1947- *WhoFI 94*
Olson, Cal Oliver 1939- *WhoWest 94*
Olson, Carl Alexius 1919- *WhoWest 94*
Olson, Carl Eric 1914- *WhoAmL 94*
Olson, Carl Marcus 1911- *WhoScEn 94*
Olson, Clarence Elmer, Jr. 1927- *WhoAm 94*
Olson, Clifford Larry 1946- *WhoAm 94, WhoFI 94, WhoMW 93*
Olson, Clinton L. 1916- *WhoAmP 93*
Olson, Clinton Louis 1916- *WhoAm 94*
Olson, Craig Lee 1951- *WhoMW 93*
Olson, Craig William 1934- *WhoAmP 93*
Olson, Craig William 1956- *WhoAm 94*
Olson, Dale C. 1934- *IntMPA 94, WhoAm 94*
Olson, Dan 1955- *WhoAmP 93*
Olson, Daniel Anthony 1951- *WhoAmP 93*
Olson, Darin S. 1964- *WhoScEn 94*
Olson, David A. 1953- *WhoAmL 94*
Olson, David Alan 1962- *WhoMW 93*
Olson, David John 1941- *WhoAm 94, WhoWest 94*
Olson, David Mark 1934- *WhoWest 94*
Olson, David P. 1956- *WhoScEn 94*
Olson, David Peter 1958- *WhoAmL 94*
Olson, David R. 1938- *WhoAm 94*
Olson, David Richard 1935- *WrDr 94*
Olson, David Wendell 1938- *WhoMW 93*
Olson, Dennis Oliver 1947- *WhoAmL 94*
Olson, Donald Ernest 1921- *WhoAm 94*
Olson, Donald George 1941- *WhoMW 93*
Olson, Donald Harold, Jr. 1949- *WhoWest 94*
Olson, Donald Richard 1917- *WhoAm 94*
Olson, Douglas Bernard 1945- *WhoWest 94*
Olson, Douglas John 1934- *WhoAmA 93*
Olson, Edgar L. 1937- *WhoAmP 93*
Olson, Edward Warren 1946- *WhoMW 93*
Olson, Edwin W., Jr. *WhoAmP 93*
Olson, Elder (James) 1909- *WrDr 94*
Olson, Elder James 1909-1992 *WhAm 10*
Olson, Elizabeth Kirk 1955- *WhoFI 94*
Olson, Elliott D. 1941- *WhoAmL 94*
Olson, Eric *WhoHol 92*
Olson, Eugene Rudolph 1926- *WhoAm 94*
Olson, Evan Edward 1927- *WhoFI 94*
Olson, Everett Claire 1910- *WhoAm 94*
Olson, Ferron Allred 1921- *WhoScEn 94, WhoWest 94*
Olson, Frances Allene 1914- *WhoAmP 93*
Olson, Frank Albert 1932- *WhoAm 94, WhoFI 94*
Olson, Frederick Irving 1916- *WhoAm 94*
Olson, Gail Diane 1954- *WhoMW 93*
Olson, Gary 1943- *WhoAm 94, WhoAmL 94*
Olson, Gary Duane 1939- *WhoMW 93*
Olson, Gary Miles 1931- *WhoAmP 93*
Olson, Gen 1938- *WhoAmP 93*
Olson, Gene 1926- *WhoAmP 93*
Olson, Gene Edward 1937- *WhoMW 93*
Olson, Gene Russel 1949- *WhoAmA 93*
Olson, George Edward 1935- *WhoMW 93*
Olson, Gerald Nels 1948- *WhoAmL 94*
Olson, Gerald Theodore 1928- *WhoWest 94*
Olson, Harold Dean 1946- *WhoMW 93*
Olson, Harry Andrew, Jr. 1923- *WhoAm 94*
Olson, Hector Monroy 1959- *WhoScEn 94*
Olson, Hilding Harold 1916- *WhoAm 94*
Olson, Horace Andrew 1925- *IntWW 93*
Olson, Howard Halfdan 1927- *WhoAmP 93*
Olson, Jack Benjamin 1920- *WhoAmP 93*
Olson, Jack Francis 1925- *WhoAm 94*
Olson, James 1930- *IntMPA 94, WhoHol 92*
Olson, James Allen 1924- *WhoMW 93*
Olson, James Chester 1907-1992 *WhAm 10*
Olson, James Clifton 1917- *WhoAm 94*
Olson, James Duane, II 1943- *WhoAm 94*
Olson, James Edward 1933- *WhoWest 94*
Olson, James Hilding 1965- *WhoScEn 94*
Olson, James R. *DrAPF 93*
Olson, James Richard 1941- *WhoAm 94*
Olson, James Robert 1940- *WhoAm 94*
Olson, James William Park 1940- *WhoAm 94*
Olson, Janice Lynn 1946- *WhoWest 94*
Olson, John Frederick 1939- *WhoAm 94*
Olson, John Karl 1949- *WhoAmL 94*
Olson, John Marshall 1949- *WhoAm 94, WhoAmL 94*
Olson, John Michael 1947- *WhoAmL 94, WhoAmP 93, WhoMW 93*
Olson, Joseph Olaf *WhoAmA 93*
Olson, Judith Reedy 1939- *WhoAmP 93*
Olson, Julie Ann 1957- *WhoMW 93*
Olson, Karl 1952- *WhoAmL 94*
Olson, Kathy Rae 1950- *WhoMW 93*
Olson, Katy 1928- *WhoAmP 93*
Olson, Kay Melchisedech 1948- *WhoAm 94*
Olson, Keith Waldemar 1931- *WhoAm 94*
Olson, Kenneth Harvey 1927- *WhoWest 94*
Olson, Kenneth Paul 1935- *WhoWest 94*
Olson, Kent Charles 1956- *WhoAmL 94*
Olson, Kirby *DrAPF 93*
Olson, Lawrence 1918-1992 *WhAm 10*
Olson, Lawrence E. Gene 1926- *WhoMW 93*
Olson, Leroy Calvin 1926- *WhoAm 94*
Olson, Lester C. 1955- *ConAu 142*
Olson, Loren Donald 1947- *WhoMW 93*
Olson, Lute 1934- *WhoAm 94, WhoWest 94*
Olson, Lyndon Lowell, Jr. 1947- *WhoAmP 93*
Olson, Lynn 1952- *WhoMW 93*
Olson, Lynnette Gail 1945- *WhoMW 93*
Olson, Mancur (Lloyd), Jr. 1932- *WrDr 94*
Olson, Mancur Lloyd 1932- *WhoAm 94*
Olson, Marian *DrAPF 93*
Olson, Marian Edna 1923- *WhoMW 93, WhoScEn 94*
Olson, Marian Katherine 1933- *WhoFI 94, WhoWest 94*
Olson, Mark 1955- *WhoAmP 93*
Olson, Mark S. 1950- *WhoAmL 94*
Olson, Marlin Lee 1927- *WhoMW 93*
Olson, Maurice Alan 1926- *WhoAmP 93*
Olson, Maxine 1931- *WhoAmA 93*
Olson, Mel *WhoAmP 93*
Olson, Nancy 1928- *WhoHol 92*
Olson, Nancy 1929- *IntMPA 94*
Olson, Nancy Suzanne 1955- *WhoWest 94*
Olson, Neil Chester 1950- *WhoScEn 94*
Olson, Norman Fredrick 1931- *WhoAm 94, WhoScEn 94*
Olson, Orlin A. 1926- *WhoAmP 93*
Olson, Paul Buxton 1937- *WhoMW 93*
Olson, Paul Lester Herman 1950- *WhoFI 94*
Olson, Paul Richard 1925- *WhoAm 94*
Olson, Peter Wesley 1950- *WhoAm 94*
Olson, Phillip David LeRoy 1940- *WhoWest 94*
Olson, Randall J. 1947- *WhoAm 94*
Olson, Rex Melton 1940- *WhoFI 94, WhoScEn 94*
Olson, Richard Anthony 1951- *WhoMW 93*
Olson, Richard David 1944- *WhoAm 94*
Olson, Richard Dean 1949- *WhoAm 94, WhoScEn 94*
Olson, Richard Earl 1953- *WhoAmP 93, WhoWest 94*
Olson, Richard George 1940- *WhoAm 94*
Olson, Richard Gottlieb 1922- *WhoMW 93*
Olson, Richard Hall 1898- *WhAm 10*
Olson, Richard W. 1938- *WhoAmA 93*
Olson, Rick 1950- *WhoAmA 93*
Olson, Robert 1930- *WhoAmP 93*
Olson, Robert Allan 1954- *WhoMW 93*
Olson, Robert Edward 1927- *WhoAm 94*
Olson, Robert Eugene 1919- *WhoAm 94*
Olson, Robert Goodwin 1924- *WhoAm 94*
Olson, Robert Grant 1952- *WhoAm 94*
Olson, Robert Howard 1934- *WhoFI 94*
Olson, Robert Howard 1944- *WhoAm 94, WhoWest 94*
Olson, Robert Leonard 1930- *WhoAm 94*
Olson, Robert W(illiam) 1940- *WrDr 94*
Olson, Robert Wyrick 1945- *WhoAm 94, WhoAmL 94*
Olson, Roberta Dawn 1960- *WhoMW 93*
Olson, Roberta Jeanne Marie 1947- *WhoAm 94, WhoAmA 93*
Olson, Roger Norman 1936- *WhoWest 94*
Olson, Ronald Charles 1937- *WhoWest 94*
Olson, Ronald Dale 1947- *WhoAm 94*
Olson, Ronald Dean 1934- *WhoWest 94*
Olson, Ronald Leroy 1941- *WhoAm 94*
Olson, Roy Arthur 1938- *WhoMW 93*
Olson, Roy Edwin 1931- *WhoScEn 94*
Olson, Rue Eileen 1928- *WhoMW 93*
Olson, Russell A. *WhoAmP 93*
Olson, Russell L. 1933- *WhoAm 94*
Olson, Sharon *DrAPF 93*
Olson, Sigmund Lars 1935- *WhoAm 94*
Olson, Stanley William 1914- *WhoAm 94*
Olson, Stephen Edward 1941- *WhoFI 94*
Olson, Stephen Michael 1948- *WhoAm 94, WhoAmL 94*
Olson, Steven Stanley 1950- *WhoWest 94*
Olson, Susan Jane 1958- *WhoMW 93*
Olson, Sylvester Irwin 1907- *WhoAm 94, WhoWest 94*
Olson, Theodore Alexander 1904- *WhoAm 94*
Olson, Theodore Bevry 1940- *WhoAm 94, WhoAmP 93*
Olson, Thomas Francis, II 1948- *WhoAm 94*
Olson, Thomas Michael 1946- *WhoIns 94*
Olson, Thomas W. 1947- *WhoAmL 94*
Olson, Toby *DrAPF 93*
Olson, Toby 1937- *WrDr 94*
Olson, Vincent *WhoAmP 93*
Olson, Walter Gilbert 1924- *WhoAm 94*
Olson, Walter Justus, Jr. 1941- *WhoAm 94*
Olson, Walter K. 1954- *WhoFI 94, WrDr 94*
Olson, Walter Steven 1941- *WhoMW 93*
Olson, Walter Theodore 1917- *WhoAm 94*
Olson, Warren Kinley 1943- *WhoMW 93*
Olson, Wilbert Orin 1947- *WhoMW 93*
Olson, William Clinton 1920- *WhoAm 94*
Olson, William Henry 1936- *WhoAm 94, WhoScEn 94*
Olson, William Jeffrey 1949- *WhoAmL 94, WhoAmP 93*
Olson, William Thomas 1940- *WhoFI 94, WhoWest 94*
Olson-Hellerud, Linda Kathryn 1947- *WhoMW 93*
Olsson, Ann-Margret 1941- *WhoAm 94*
Olsson, Carl Alfred 1938- *WhoAm 94*
Olsson, Curt G. 1927- *IntWW 93*
Olsson, Curt Gunnar 1927- *Who 94*
Olsson, George Carl Phillip 1903-1991 *WhAm 10*
Olsson, Hagar 1893-1978 *BlmGWL*
Olsson, Karl Erik 1938- *IntWW 93*
Olsson, Nils Urban 1959- *WhoScEn 94*
Olsson, Nils William 1909- *WhoAm 94*
Olsson, Ronald Arthur 1955- *WhoFI 94, WhoScEn 94, WhoWest 94*
Olstad, Roger Gale 1934- *WhoAm 94*
Olsten, Jann L. 1948- *WhoAmP 93*
Olsten, Stuart *WhoFI 94*
Olsten, William 1919-1991 *WhAm 10*
Olston, Mary Kay 1949- *WhoMW 93*
Olstowski, Franciszek 1927- *WhoFI 94, WhoScEn 94*
Olszewska, Maria 1892-1969 *NewGrDO*
Olszewski, Edward John 1937- *WhoAm 94*
Olszewski, James Frederick 1948- *WhoScEn 94*
Olszewski, Jan 1930- *IntWW 93, Who 94*
Olszewski, Jerzy Adam 1929- *WhoScEn 94*
Olszewski, Laurence Michael 1938- *WhoAm 94*
Olszewski, Lee Michael 1935- *WhoScEn 94*
Olszewski, Liliana 1965- *WhoHisp 94*
Olt, John Edward 1913- *WhoMW 93*
Oltion, Jerry B. 1957- *EncSF 93*
Oltman, C. Dwight 1936- *WhoAm 94*
Oltman, Henry George, Jr. 1927- *WhoAm 94*
Oltman, James Harvey 1930- *WhoAm 94*
Olton, Roy 1922- *WhoAm 94*
Oltrabella, Augusta 1897-1981 *NewGrDO*
Oltrogge, Keith Duane 1951- *WhoFI 94*
Oltz, Richard John 1945- *WhoAm 94*
Oludhe-Macgoye, Marjorie 1928- *WrDr 94*
Olufosoye, Timothy d1992 *Who 94N*
Olufosoye, Timothy Omotayo d1992 *IntWW 93N*
Olugebefola, Ademola 1941- *WhoBlA 94*
Oluleye, James Johnson 1937- *IntWW 93*
Olum, Paul 1918- *WhoAm 94*
Olver, Frank William John 1924- *WhoAm 94*
Olver, John W. 1936- *CngDr 93*

Olver, John Walter 1936- *WhoAm 94, WhoAmP 93*
Olver, Stephen (John Linley) 1916- *Who 94*
Olvera, Joe *DrAPF 93*
Olvera, Joe E. 1944- *WhoHisp 94*
Olvera, Jose Jesus 1935- *WhoHisp 94*
Olwin, John Hurst 1907- *WhoAm 94*
Olyott, Leonard Eric 1926- *Who 94*
Olyphant, David 1936- *WhoAm 94*
Olzacki, James Joseph 1949- *WhoIns 94*
Olzman, Saul 1920- *WhoAm 94*
O'Madigan, Isabel d1951 *WhoHol 92*
Omahana, Robin Joseph 1950- *WhoAmL 94*
O'Mahoney, Jacques *WhoHol 92*
O'Mahoney, Robert M. 1925- *WhoAm 94*
O'Mahony, Jeremiah Francis 1946- *WhoAm 94, WhoFI 94*
O'Maley, David Boyers 1946- *WhoAm 94*
O'Malley, Bert William 1936- *WhoAm 94, WhoScEn 94*
O'Malley, Carlon Martin 1929- *WhoAm 94, WhoAmL 94*
O'Malley, Charles d1958 *WhoHol 92*
O'Malley, Charles Acheson 1917-1989 *WhAm 10*
O'Malley, Comerford J. 1902-1991 *WhAm 10*
O'Malley, Cornelia Leary 1906- *WhoAmL 94*
O'Malley, Desmond Joseph 1939- *IntWW 93*
O'Malley, Dianemarie *DrAPF 93*
O'Malley, Edward 1926- *WhoAm 94*
O'Malley, Edward Joseph, Jr. 1942- *WhoFI 94*
O'Malley, Emanuela *DrAPF 93*
O'Malley, Eugene Francis 1950- *WhoFI 94*
O'Malley, Grania d1973 *WhoHol 92*
O'Malley, J. Pat d1985 *WhoHol 92*
O'Malley, James, Jr. 1910- *WhoAm 94*
O'Malley, James Terence 1950- *WhoAm 94, WhoAmL 94*
O'Malley, Jason *WhoHol 92*
O'Malley, John d1945 *WhoHol 92*
O'Malley, John Daniel 1926- *WhoAm 94*
O'Malley, John Edward 1942- *WhoAm 94*
O'Malley, John J. 1947- *WhoAm 94, WhoFI 94*
O'Malley, John P. d1959 *WhoHol 92*
O'Malley, Joseph James 1923- *WhoAm 94*
O'Malley, Kathleen *EncSF 93, WhoHol 92*
O'Malley, Kevin Francis 1947- *WhoAm 94, WhoAmL 94*
O'Malley, Lilian Wilkes d1976 *WhoHol 92*
O'Malley, Mary 1941- *WrDr 94*
O'Malley, Mary (Josephine) 1941- *ConDr 93*
O'Malley, Mary Kay 1959- *WhoMW 93*
O'Malley, Michael John 1954- *WhoAmL 94*
O'Malley, Pat d1966 *WhoHol 92*
O'Malley, Patrick J. *WhoAmP 93*
O'Malley, Patrick Lawrence 1911- *WhoAm 94*
O'Malley, Peter 1937- *WhoAm 94, WhoWest 94*
O'Malley, Rex d1976 *WhoHol 92*
O'Malley, Robert Edmund, Jr. 1939- *WhoAm 94*
O'Malley, Shaun F. 1935- *WhoAm 94, WhoFI 94*
O'Malley, Stephen Keppel 1940- *Who 94*
O'Malley, Steven Craig 1956- *WhoMW 93*
O'Malley, Susan *WhoAm 94*
O'Malley, Thomas d1926 *WhoHol 92*
O'Malley, Thomas D. 1941- *WhoAm 94, WhoFI 94*
O'Malley, Thomas Patrick 1930- *WhoAm 94, WhoWest 94*
O'Malley, William David 1947- *WhoScEn 94*
Oman, David A. 1952- *WhoAmP 93*
Oman, Deborah Sue 1948- *WhoMW 93*
Oman, Douglas A. 1944- *WhoAmP 93*
Oman, Glenn Earl, Jr. 1960- *WhoFI 94*
Oman, Henry 1918- *WhoScEn 94*
Oman, Julia Trevelyan 1930- *IntWW 93, NewGrDO, Who 94*
Oman, Paul Richard 1956- *WhoScEn 94*
Oman, Ralph 1940- *WhoAm 94, WhoAmL 94*
Oman, Richard Heer 1926- *WhoAm 94*
Oman, Sidney Maynard 1928- *WhoAmP 93*
Omaña, Julio Alfredo, Sr. 1938- *WhoHisp 94*
Omand, David Bruce 1947- *Who 94*
Omang, Joanne (Brenda) 1943- *WrDr 94*
Omann, Bernie *WhoAmP 93*
Omar, Abu Hassan Bin Haj 1940- *IntWW 93*
Omar, Ameenah E.P. 1941- *WhoMW 93*
Omar, Husam Anwar 1959- *WhoScEn 94*
Omar, Margit 1941- *WhoAmA 93*
Omar, Napsiah binti 1943- *IntWW 93*
Omar, Samira Ahmad 1950- *WhoWest 94*
O'Mara, James Wright 1940- *WhoAmL 94*
O'Mara, John Aloysius 1924- *WhoAm 94, WhoMW 93*
O'Mara, Joseph 1861-1927 *NewGrDO*
O'Mara, Kate 1939- *WhoHol 92*
O'Mara, Margaret 1951- *Who 94*
O'Mara, Marilyn Mae 1942- *WhoMW 93*
O'Mara, Robert Edmund George 1933- *WhoAm 94*
O'Mara, Thomas Patrick 1937- *WhoAm 94*
Omari, Dunstan Alfred 1922- *IntWW 93*
O'Marie, Carol Anne, Sister 1933- *WrDr 94*
Omata, Richard J. 1946- *WhoAmL 94*
Omata, Robert Rokuro 1920- *WhoAsA 94*
Omberg, Arthur Chalmers, Jr. 1939- *WhoFI 94*
Ombres, Rossana 1931- *BlmGWL*
Omdahl, Becky Lynn 1958- *WhoMW 93*
Omdahl, Lloyd B. 1931- *WhoAmP 93, WhoMW 93*
O'Meallie, Kitty 1916- *WhoAm 94, WhoAmA 93*
O'Meally, Robert G(eorge) 1948- *WrDr 94*
O'Meara, David Collow 1929- *WhoAm 94*
O'Meara, Deidre d1987 *WhoHol 92*
O'Meara, Edward S. *WhoAmP 93*
O'Meara, Edward Thomas 1921-1992 *WhAm 10*
O'Meara, Frederick Augustus 1814-1888 *EncNAR*
O'Meara, John Corbett 1933- *WhoAm 94*
O'Meara, John Joseph 1915- *WrDr 94*
O'Meara, Joseph 1898- *WhAm 10*
O'Meara, Onorato Timothy 1928- *WhoAm 94, WhoMW 93, WhoScEn 94*
O'Meara, Patrick O. 1938- *WhoAm 94, WhoMW 93*
O'Meara, Robert James, Jr. 1959- *WhoMW 93*
O'Meara, Thomas Franklin 1935- *WhoAm 94*
O'Meara, Vicki A. 1957- *WhoAmL 94, WhoMW 93*
O'Meara, Walter Andrew 1897-1989 *WhAm 10*
O'Meara Browne, Debra Rae 1960- *WhoFI 94*
Omelchenko, Hryhorii Omelianovych 1951- *LngBDD*
O'Melia, Charles Richard 1934- *WhoAm 94*
Omenn, Gilbert Stanley 1941- *WhoAm 94, WhoWest 94*
Omens, Estelle d1983 *WhoHol 92*
Omer, George Elbert, Jr. 1922- *WhoAm 94, WhoScEn 94, WhoWest 94*
Omer, Robert Wendell 1948- *WhoAm 94, WhoFI 94*
Omernick, Raymond John 1923- *WhoAmP 93*
Omholt, Bruce Donald 1943- *WhoFI 94*
Omholt, Elmer V. 1920- *WhoAmP 93*
Ominami Pascual, Carlos 1951- *IntWW 93*
Ominsky, Alan Jay 1938- *WhoAmL 94*
Ominsky, Harris 1932- *WhoAm 94, WhoAmL 94*
Omiros, George James 1956- *WhoFI 94, WhoScEn 94*
Omland, Tov 1923- *WhoScEn 94*
Omlor, John Joseph 1935- *WhoAm 94*
Ommaya, Ayub Khan 1930- *WhoAm 94*
Ommodt, Donald Henry 1931- *WhoAm 94, WhoMW 93*
Omoifo-Okoh, Julie *BlmGWL*
Omolade, Barbara 1942- *WhoBlA 94*
Omole, Gabriel Gbolabo 1940- *WhoFI 94*
Omolecki, Leonard Roman, Jr. 1962- *WhoAmL 94*
Omolodun, John Olatunji 1935- *Who 94*
O'Moore, Barry d1945 *WhoHol 92*
O'Moore, Patrick d1983 *WhoHol 92*
O Morain, Donall 1923- *IntWW 93*
O'Morchoe, Charles Christopher Creagh 1931- *WhoAm 94, WhoMW 93*
O'Morchoe, David Nial Creagh 1928- *Who 94*
Omori, Alvin I. 1948- *WhoAsA 94*
Omori, Morio 1921- *WhoAmL 94*
Omori, Yoshiaki 1961- *WhoAsA 94*
Omorogbe, Oluyinka Osayame 1957- *IntWW 93*
O'Morrison, Kenny *WhoHol 92*
Omoto, Loren Daikichi 1957- *WhoMW 93*
Omotoso, Kole 1943- *BlkWr 2*
Omron, Sam 1956- *WhoWest 94*
Omura, George Adolf 1938- *WhoAm 94*
Omura, James Matsumoto 1912- *WhoAm 94*
Omura, Jimmy Kazuhiro 1940- *WhoAm 94, WhoWest 94*
Omura, Mark Christopher 1956- *WhoAsA 94*
Omura, Tsuneo 1930- *WhoScEn 94*
Omurtag, Yildirim Bill 1939- *WhoAm 94*
Omwake, Eo, Jr. 1946- *WhoAmA 93*
Onak, Thomas Philip 1932- *WhoAm 94, WhoWest 94*
O'Nan, Martha 1921- *WhoAm 94*
Onana-Awana, Charles 1923- *IntWW 93*
Onaral, Banu Kum 1949- *WhoScEn 94*
Onasakenrat, Joseph 1845-1881 *EncNAR*
Onasch, Donald Carl 1927- *WhoFI 94, WhoWest 94*
Onassis, Jacqueline Bouvier Kennedy 1929- *WhoAm 94*
Onassis, Jacqueline Lee Bouvier 1929- *IntWW 93*
Onate, Juan De c. 1550-1630 *WhWE*
Onaya, Toshimasa 1935- *WhoScEn 94*
Oncina, Juan 1925- *NewGrDO*
Oncken, Henry Kuck 1938- *WhoAm 94*
Oncley, John Lawrence 1910- *WhoAm 94, WhoScEn 94*
Ondaatje, Michael 1943- *ConLC 76 [port], CurBio 93 [port], IntWW 93, WhoAm 94, WrDr 94*
Ondaatje, (Philip) Michael 1943- *ConAu 42NR*
Ondarts, Raul Agustin 1915- *IntWW 93*
Ondeck, Thomas Paul 1946- *WhoAm 94*
Ondejko, Michael Raymond 1960- *WhoMW 93*
Onderdonk, Mike *WhoAmP 93*
Ondetti, Miguel Angel 1930- *WhoAm 94, WhoScEn 94*
Ondine d1989 *WhoHol 92*
Ondo, Purificacion Angue *WhoWomW 91*
Ondra, Anny d1987 *WhoHol 92*
Ondrasik, Paul John, Jr. 1950- *WhoAm 94, WhoAmL 94*
Ondrejack, John Joseph 1954- *WhoScEn 94*
Ondrejka, Ronald 1932- *WhoAm 94, WhoMW 93*
Ondricek, Miroslav 1933- *IntDcF 2-4*
Ondrovich, Peggy Ann Chnupa 1952- *WhoMW 93*
Ondrusek, David Francis 1955- *WhoFI 94*
One, Ernest G. 1929- *WhoIns 94*
O'Neal, Anne d1971 *WhoHol 92*
O'Neal, B. F., Jr. 1922- *WhoAmP 93*
O'Neal, Bob H. 1934- *WhoAm 94, WhoFI 94*
O'Neal, Connie Murry 1951- *WhoBlA 94*
O'Neal, Dennis Lee 1951- *WhoScEn 94*
O'Neal, Earl L. 1928- *WhoAmP 93*
O'Neal, Eddie S. 1935- *WhoBlA 94*
O'Neal, Edgar Carl 1939- *WhoAm 94*
Oneal, Elizabeth 1934- *WrDr 94*
O'Neal, Forest Hodge 1917-1991 *WhAm 10*
O'Neal, Frederick 1905- *AfrAmAl 6, WhoHol 92*
O'Neal, Frederick 1905-1992 *AnObit 1992, WhAm 10*
O'Neal, Frederick Douglas 1905-1992 *WhoBlA 94N*
O'Neal, Fredrick William, Jr. 1948- *WhoBlA 94*
O'Neal, Griffin 1964 *WhoHol 92*
O'Neal, Hank 1940- *WrDr 94*
O'Neal, Kathleen Len 1953- *WhoFI 94, WhoScEn 94*
O'Neal, Kathleen M. *EncSF 93*
O'Neal, Kevin 1945- *WhoHol 92*
O'Neal, Larry R. 1947- *WhoAmL 94*
O'Neal, Malinda King 1929- *WhoBlA 94*
O'Neal, Michael R. 1951- *WhoAmP 93*
O'Neal, Michael Ralph 1951- *WhoAmL 94, WhoMW 93*
O'Neal, Michael Scott, Sr. 1948- *WhoAm 94, WhoAmL 94*
O'Neal, Patrick 1927- *IntMPA 94, WhoHol 92*
O'Neal, Perry Ernest 1893- *WhAm 10*
O'Neal, Raymond W., Sr. 1940- *WhoBlA 94*
O'Neal, Reagan *ConAu 140*
O'Neal, Regina *WhoBlA 94*
O'Neal, Roland Lenard 1948- *WhoAmA 93*
O'Neal, Ron 1937- *IntMPA 94, WhoHol 92*
O'Neal, Ryan 1941- *IntMPA 94, IntWW 93, WhoAm 94, WhoHol 92*
O'Neal, Shaquille Rashaun 1972- *WhoAm 94, WhoBlA 94*
O'Neal, Stanley *WhoBlA 94*
O'Neal, Stephen Michael 1955- *WhoScEn 94*
O'Neal, Tatum 1963- *IntMPA 94, IntWW 93, WhoAm 94, WhoHol 92*
O'Neal, William B. 1907- *WhoAm 94*
O'Neal, Winston James, Jr. 1948- *WhoFI 94*
O'Neal, Zelma 1907- *WhoHol 92*
Oneal, Zibby 1934- *TwCYAW, WrDr 94*
O'Neall, Barry Scott 1962- *WhoMW 93*
Onegin, (Elisabeth Elfriede Emilie) Sigrid 1889-1943 *NewGrDO*
O'Neil, Alexander Henry *Who 94*
O'Neil, Barbara d1980 *WhoHol 92*
O'Neil, Barry d1918 *WhoHol 92*
O'Neil, Bonnie Irene 1955- *WhoWest 94*
O'Neil, Brian Stephen 1952- *WhoFI 94*
O'Neil, Bruce William 1942- *WhoAmA 93*
O'Neil, Chris 1956- *BuCMET*
O'Neil, Cleora Tanner 1946- *WhoFI 94*
O'Neil, Colette *WhoHol 92*
O'Neil, Cyril F., Jr. d1993 *NewYTBS 93*
O'Neil, Daniel Joseph 1942- *WhoAm 94, WhoScEn 94*
O'Neil, Desmond (Henry) 1920- *Who 94*
O'Neil, Harold Francis, Jr. 1943- *WhoScEn 94*
O'Neil, James E. 1939- *WhoAmP 93*
O'Neil, James Peter 1944- *WhoAm 94*
O'Neil, John 1915- *WhoAm 94, WhoAmA 93*
O'Neil, John Joseph 1932- *WhoAmA 93*
O'Neil, John Joseph 1943- *WhoAm 94, WhoAmL 94, WhoFI 94*
O'Neil, John Patrick 1921- *WhoAm 94*
O'Neil, Joseph Francis 1934- *WhoAm 94*
O'Neil, Kathleen Kay 1947- *WhoMW 93*
O'Neil, Leo E. 1928- *WhoAm 94*
O'Neil, Lisa M. 1964- *WhoAmP 93*
O'Neil, Mary Agnes 1926- *WhoAm 94*
O'Neil, Michael A. 1940- *WhoAmL 94*
O'Neil, Michael Edward 1952- *WhoFI 94*
O'Neil, Nance d1965 *WhoHol 92*
O'Neil, Robert A. d1951 *WhoHol 92*
O'Neil, Robert Marchant 1934- *WhoAm 94, WhoAmL 94*
O'Neil, Roger 1938- *Who 94*
O'Neil, Sally d1968 *WhoHol 92*
O'Neil, Shane 1947- *WhoAm 94*
O'Neil, Stephen Edward 1932- *WhoAm 94*
Oneil, Susan Jean 1952- *WhoMW 93*
O'Neil, Thomas 1922- *WhoAmP 93*
O'Neil, Thomas F. 1915- *IntMPA 94*
O'Neil, Thomas Francis 1915- *IntWW 93*
O'Neil, Thomas Francis, III 1957- *WhoAmL 94*
O'Neil, Thomas Michael 1940- *WhoScEn 94*
O'Neil, Tricia 1945- *WhoHol 92*
O'Neil, Wayne 1931- *WhoAm 94*
O'Neil, William Andrew 1927- *IntWW 93*
O'Neil, William Francis 1936- *WhoAm 94*
O'Neill *Who 94*
O'Neill, Baron 1933- *Who 94*
O'Neill, Albert Clarence, Jr. 1939- *WhoAm 94, WhoAmL 94*
O'Neill, Alice 1937- *WhoWest 94*
O'Neill, Angela *WhoHol 92*
O'Neill, Ann Renee 1959- *WhoAmL 94, WhoMW 93*
O'Neill, Arthur J. 1917- *WhoAm 94, WhoMW 93*
O'Neill, Arthur J. 1952- *WhoAmP 93*
O'Neill, Bernard V., Jr. 1937- *WhoAmL 94*
O'Neill, Brian 1940- *WhoAm 94, WhoIns 94*
O'Neill, Brian Boru 1947- *WhoAm 94, WhoAmL 94*
O'Neill, Brian Dennis 1946- *WhoAm 94, WhoAmL 94, WhoFI 94*
O'Neill, Brian Francis 1929- *WhoAm 94*
O'Neill, Brian J. 1949- *WhoAmP 93*
O'Neill, Charles K. 1947- *WhoAmL 94*
O'Neill, Charles Kelly 1933- *WhoAm 94*
O'Neill, Christina Marie 1953- *WhoAmP 93*
O'Neill, Con *WhoHol 92*
O'Neill, Daniel 1938- *WhoHisp 94*
O'Neill, Daniel J. 1937- *WhoAm 94*
O'Neill, David Michael *WhoHol 92*
O'Neill, Dennis 1948- *NewGrDO*
O'Neill, Dennis William 1939- *WhoFI 94*
O'Neill, Dick *WhoHol 92*
O'Neill, Donald Edmund 1926- *WhoAm 94, WhoFI 94*
O'Neill, Ed 1945- *WhoHol 92*
O'Neill, Ed 1946- *IntMPA 94*
O'Neill, Edward 1867- *WhoHol 92*
O'Neill, Edward 1946- *WhoAm 94*
O'Neill, Eileen 1941- *WhoHol 92*
O'Neill, Eugene 1888-1953 *TwCLC 49 [port]*
O'Neill, Eugene (Gladstone) 1888-1953 *IntDcT 2 [port], NewGrDO*
O'Neill, Eugene Francis 1918- *WhoAm 94*
O'Neill, Eugene Gladstone 1888-1953 *AmCulL [port]*
O'Neill, Eugene Milton 1925- *WhoAm 94*
O'Neill, Francis X., Jr. *WhoAmP 93*
O'Neill, Francis Xavier, III 1953- *WhoAm 94*

O'Neill, Gary Marshall 1952- *WhoWest 94*
O'Neill, Gerald J. 1938- *WhoAmL 94*
O'Neill, Gerard K. *EncSF 93*
O'Neill, Gerard Kitchen 1927-1992 *WhAm 10*
O'Neill, Harry J. J. 1959- *WhoAmL 94*
O'Neill, Harry William 1929- *WhoAm 94*
O'Neill, Hector *WhoAmP 93, WhoHisp 94*
O'Neill, Henry d1961 *WhoHol 92*
O'Neill, Hugh (Detmar Torrens) 1939- *Who 94*
O'Neill, Hugh Bernard 1939- *WhoMW 93*
O'Neill, J. Norman, Jr. 1943- *WhoAmL 94*
O'Neill, James d1920 *WhoHol 92*
O'Neill, James d1938 *WhoHol 92*
O'Neill, James, Jr. d1923 *WhoHol 92*
O'Neill, James E., Jr. 1929- *WhoAmP 93*
O'Neill, James Francis 1943- *WhoScEn 94*
O'Neill, James J. 1934- *WhoFI 94*
O'Neill, James Michael 1954- *WhoAmP 93*
O'Neill, James William 1958- *WhoScEn 94*
O'Neill, Jennifer 1949- *IntMPA 94, WhoHol 92*
O'Neill, Jimmy 1940- *WhoHol 92*
O'Neill, John H. 1946- *WhoAm 94*
O'Neill, John Joseph 1920- *WhoAm 94*
O'Neill, John Joseph, Jr. 1919- *WhoAm 94*
O'Neill, John Patrick 1929- *WhoWest 94*
O'Neill, John Patton 1942- *WhoAmA 93*
O'Neill, John Robert 1937- *WhoAm 94*
O'Neill, John T. 1944- *WhoAm 94, WhoFI 94*
O'Neill, Johnny d1930 *WhoHol 92*
O'Neill, Joseph 1886-1953 *EncSF 93*
O'Neill, Joseph Dean *WhoAmL 94, WhoFI 94*
O'Neill, Judith (Beatrice) 1930- *TwCYAW*
O'Neill, Judith (Lyall) 1930- *WrDr 94*
O'Neill, Katherine Templeton 1949- *WhoMW 93*
O'Neill, Kathryn J. 1942- *WhoMW 93*
O'Neill, Lawrence Daniel 1946- *WhoAm 94, WhoAmL 94*
O'Neill, Lawrence T. *DrAPF 93*
O'Neill, Maire d1952 *WhoHol 92*
O'Neill, Mark Joseph 1946- *WhoScEn 94*
O'Neill, Martin (John) 1945- *Who 94*
O'Neill, Matt 1937- *WhoAmP 93*
O'Neill, Maura Louise 1956- *WhoWest 94*
O'Neill, Maureen C. 1945- *WhoAmL 94*
O'Neill, Maureen Kelly 1968- *WhoWest 94*
O'Neill, Michael *ConDr 93, WhoHol 92*
O'Neill, Michael 1953- *WrDr 94*
O'Neill, Michael C(ornelius) 1898- *WhAm 10*
O'Neill, Michael Foy 1943- *WhoWest 94*
O'Neill, Michael James 1922- *WhoAm 94*
O'Neill, Michael James 1958- *WhoScEn 94*
O'Neill, Michael Joseph 1956- *WhoAmL 94*
O'Neill, Michael Joseph 1960- *WhoFI 94*
O'Neill, Michael Joyce 1922-1989 *WhAm 10*
O'Neill, Michael Wayne 1940- *WhoScEn 94*
O'Neill, Norah Ellen 1949- *WhoWest 94*
O'Neill, Onora Sylvia 1941- *IntWW 93, Who 94*
O'Neill, Patrick Geoffrey 1924- *Who 94, WrDr 94*
O'Neill, Patrick Henry 1915- *WhoAm 94*
O'Neill, Patrick J. *WhoIns 94*
O'Neill, Patrick J. 1949- *WhoScEn 94*
O'Neill, Patrick Thomas 1957- *WhoFI 94*
O'Neill, Paul H. 1935- *IntWW 93*
O'Neill, Paul Henry 1935- *WhoAm 94, WhoFI 94*
O'Neill, Peggy d1945 *WhoHol 92*
O'Neill, Peter Thadeus 1957- *WhoScEn 94*
O'Neill, Philip Daniel, Jr. 1951- *WhoAm 94, WhoAmL 94*
O'Neill, Phoebe Joan 1934- *WhoAmL 94*
O'Neill, Richard J. 1923- *WhoAmP 93*
O'Neill, Robert Charles 1923- *WhoAm 94*
O'Neill, Robert Edward 1925- *WhoAm 94*
O'Neill, Robert James 1932- *IntWW 93, Who 94*
O'Neill, Robert John 1936- *IntWW 93, Who 94, WrDr 94*
O'Neill, Russell Richard 1916- *WhoAm 94, WhoScEn 94*
O'Neill, Sallie Boyd 1926- *WhoWest 94*
O'Neill, Scott *EncSF 93*
O'Neill, Shawn Thomas 1958- *WhoScEn 94*
O'Neill, Sheila *WhoHol 92*
O'Neill, Stephen Vincent 1948- *WhoFI 94*
O'Neill, Terence Patrick 1938- *IntWW 93*
O'Neill, Thomas J. 1946- *WhoAmL 94*
O'Neill, Thomas J. 1952- *WhoFI 94*
O'Neill, Thomas Newman, Jr. 1928- *WhoAm 94, WhoAmL 94*
O'Neill, Thomas P., Jr. 1912- *WhoAm 94, WhoAmP 93*
O'Neill, Thomas P., III 1944- *WhoAmP 93*
O'Neill, Thomas P(hilip), Jr. 1912- *Who 94*
O'Neill, Thomas Patrick, Jr. 1953- *WhoFI 94, WhoMW 93*
O'Neill, Thomas Philip, Jr. 1912- *IntWW 93*
O'Neill, Timothy G. 1960- *WhoAmL 94*
O'Neill, Timothy P. 1940- *WhoAmL 94*
O'Neill, Virginia Alice 1941- *WhoAmP 93*
O'Neill, William A. 1930- *WhoAmP 93*
O'Neill, William Atchison 1930- *IntWW 93*
O'Neill, William C. 1931- *WhoAmP 93*
O'Neill, William Gordon 1926- *WhoAmL 94*
O'Neill, William Joseph 1960- *WhoAmL 94*
O'Neill, William L. 1935- *WrDr 94*
O'Neill, William Lawrence 1935- *WhoAm 94*
O'Neill, William Patrick 1951- *WhoAm 94*
O'Neill, William Robert 1950- *WhoAm 94, WhoAmL 94*
O'Neill Bidwell, Katharine Thomas 1937- *WhoAm 94*
O'Neill-Contini, Anita *WhoAmA 93*
Onek, Joseph N. 1942- *WhoAmP 93*
Onek, Joseph Nathan 1942- *WhoAm 94, WhoAmL 94*
Onesti, Silvio Joseph 1926- *WhoAm 94*
"Onesyme" d1946 *WhoHol 92*
Onet, Virginia 1939- *WhoMW 93, WhoScEn 94*
Onetti, Juan Carlos 1909- *ConWorW 93, IntWW 93, RfGShF*
Ong, Beng Soo 1962- *WhoAsA 94*
Ong, Boon Kheng 1935- *WhoScEn 94*
Ong, Chee-Mun 1944- *WhoAm 94, WhoAsA 94*
Ong, Cynthia 1931- *WhoAsA 94*
Ong, Cynthia K. Char 1953- *WhoAsA 94*
Ong, Dana d1948 *WhoHol 92*
Ong, Edward Frank 1952- *WhoAsA 94*
Ong, Georgina 1946- *WhoAsA 94*
Ong, Haji Omar Yoke-Lin 1917- *IntWW 93*
Ong, James M. 1934- *WhoAsA 94*
Ong, James Shaujen 1957- *WhoMW 93*
Ong, John Doyle 1933- *IntWW 93, WhoAm 94, WhoFI 94, WhoMW 93*
Ong, Nai-Phuan 1948- *WhoAsA 94*
Ong, Owh Kian 1957- *WhoAsA 94*
Ong, Romualdo Anover 1939- *IntWW 93*
Ong, Say Kee 1956- *WhoScEn 94*
Ong, Sing-Cheong 1952- *WhoAsA 94*
Ong, Walter J(ackson) 1912- *WrDr 94*
Ong, Walter Jackson 1912- *WhoAm 94*
Ongania, Juan Carlos 1914- *IntWW 93*
Ongarelli, Rosa *NewGrDO*
Ongaro Basaglia, Franca 1928- *WhoWomW 91*
Ongena, Steven R. G. 1963- *WhoWest 94*
Ongert, Steven Walter 1945- *WhoAmL 94*
Ongley, Amy d1926 *WhoHol 92*
Ongley, Joseph (Augustine) 1918- *Who 94*
Ongman, John Will 1951- *WhoAm 94*
Ong Pang Boon 1929- *IntWW 93*
Ong Teng Cheong 1936- *IntWW 93*
Onhon, Candemir 1933- *IntWW 93, Who 94*
O'Niel, Colette d1975 *WhoHol 92*
O'Nions, Robert Keith 1944- *IntWW 93, Who 94*
Onishi, Akira 1929- *WhoFI 94, WhoScEn 94*
Onishi, Hironori 1936- *WhoAsA 94*
Onishi, Ryoichi 1955- *WhoScEn 94*
Onishi, Yasuo 1943- *WhoScEn 94, WhoWest 94*
Onkelinx, Laurette 1958- *WhoWomW 91*
Onken, George Marcellus 1914- *WhoAm 94*
Onken, Henry Dralle 1932- *WhoMW 93*
Onken, Richard Ray 1951- *WhoFI 94, WhoIns 94*
Onley, Toni 1928- *WhoAmA 93*
Onli, Turtel 1952- *WhoBlA 94*
Onn, Carrie *EncSF 93*
Onnen, Tony 1938- *WhoAmP 93*
Onnerfors, Alf 1925- *IntWW 93*
Onnes, Heike Kamerlingh *WorScD*
Onnis, Toto *WhoHol 92*
Onno, Ferdinand d1970 *WhoHol 92*
Ono, Akira 1928- *IntWW 93*
Ono, Hugh Yoshio 1942- *WhoFI 94*
Ono, Jon Ryoichi 1946- *WhoAmP 93*
Ono, Kanji 1938- *WhoAsA 94*
Ono, Kiyoko 1936- *WhoWomW 91*
Ono, Richard Dana 1953- *WhoAsA 94*
Ono, Yoko 1933- *ConMus 11 [port], WhoAmA 93, WhoAsA 94, WhoHol 92*
Ono, Yoneo 1925- *WhoWest 94*
Ono, Yuriko 1942- *WhoWomW 91*
Onodera, Sho d1974 *WhoHol 92*
Onoe, Morio 1926- *IntWW 93*
Onofre Jarpa Reyes, Sergio 1921- *IntWW 93*
Onokpise, Oghenekome Ukrakpo 1951- *WhoScEn 94*
Ononye, Daniel Chuka 1948- *WhoAm 94*
Onorati, Peter *WhoHol 92*
Onorato, Alfred John 1939- *WhoAmP 93*
Onorato, George *WhoAmP 93*
Onorato, Giovanni d1960 *WhoHol 92*
Onorato, Nicholas Louis 1925- *WhoAm 94*
Onorato, Ronald Joseph 1949- *WhoAmA 93*
Onsager, Jerome Andrew 1936- *WhoScEn 94*
Onslow, Earl of 1938- *Who 94*
Onslow, Cranley (Gordon Douglas) 1926- *Who 94*
Onslow, Cranley Gordon Douglas 1926- *IntWW 93*
Onslow, (Andre) Georges (Louis) 1784-1853 *NewGrDO*
Onslow, John (Roger Wilmot) 1932- *Who 94*
Onslow Ford, Gordon M. 1912- *WhoAmA 93*
Onslow Ford, Gordon Max 1912- *WhoAm 94, WhoWest 94*
Onstad, David O. 1939- *WhoWest 94*
Onstine Wood, Mary Louise 1963- *WhoFI 94, WhoWest 94*
Onstott, Edward Irvin 1922- *WhoAm 94, WhoScEn 94, WhoWest 94*
Onstott, Mark Douglas 1954- *WhoWest 94*
Ontario, Bishop of 1943- *Who 94*
Ontario, Metropolitan of *Who 94*
Ontiveros, Robert *WhoHisp 94*
Ontiveros, Steve 1961- *WhoHisp 94*
Ontjes, David Ainsworth 1937- *WhoAm 94*
Ontkean, Michael 1950- *IntMPA 94, WhoHol 92*
Ontto, Donald Edward 1952- *WhoScEn 94*
Onufrak, Joseph J. 1949- *WhoAm 94*
Onufrock, Richard Shade 1934- *WhoScEn 94*
Onuki, Hideo 1943- *WhoScEn 94*
Onunkwo, Emmanuel Nwafor 1933- *WhoFI 94*
Onur, Leyla 1945- *WhoWomW 91*
Onusko, Thomas J. 1952- *WhoAmL 94*
Onwudiwe, Ebere 1952- *WhoBlA 94*
Onwueme, Tess 1955- *BlmGWL*
Onwumechili, Cyril Agodi 1932- *IntWW 93*
Onyeama, Charles Dadi 1917- *IntWW 93*
Onyeama, Dillibe 1951- *WrDr 94*
Onyejekwe, Chike Onyekachi 1960- *WhoBlA 94*
Onyonka, Zachary 1939- *IntWW 93, WhoScEn 94*
Onyszchuk, Mario 1930- *WhoAm 94*
Onyszkiewicz, Janusz 1937- *IntWW 93*
Ooka, Makoto 1931- *IntWW 93*
Oolie, Sam 1936- *WhoFI 94*
Oommen, George 1942- *WhoAm 94*
Ooms, J. Wesley 1929- *WhoMW 93*
Ooms, Van Doorn 1934- *WhoAm 94*
Oorzhak, Sherig-ool Dizizhikovich 1942- *LngBDD*
Oort, Abraham Hans 1934- *WhoAm 94, WhoScEn 94*
Oort, Jan 1900-1992 *AnObit 1992*
Oort, Jan Hendrick 1900- *WorScD*
Oort, Jan Hendrik d1992 *IntWW 93N*
Oort, Jan Hendrik 1900-1992 *CurBio 93N*
Oosten, Roger Lester 1937- *WhoFI 94*
Oosterom, Richard H. 1955- *WhoAmA 93*
Opabajo, Olutoyin Olushina 1960- *WhoFI 94*
O'Pake, Michael Allen 1940- *WhoAmP 93*
Opala, Marian Peter 1921- *WhoAm 94, WhoAmL 94, WhoAmP 93*
Oparil, Richard James 1960- *WhoAmL 94*
Oparil, Suzanne 1941- *WhoAm 94*
Opaskar, Janet Marie 1955- *WhoMW 93*
Opatoshu, David 1918- *IntMPA 94, WhoHol 92*
Opatz, Joe *WhoAmP 93*
Opava-Stitzer, Susan Catherine 1947- *WhoScEn 94*
Opdycke, Leonard 1895-1977 *WhoAmA 93N*
Opedahl, Olaf E. 1912- *WhoAmP 93*
Opeka, John Frank 1940- *WhoFI 94*
Opel, Arthur William, Jr. 1943- *WhoAm 94*
Opel, James C. 1945- *WhoAmL 94*
Opel, John R. 1925- *WhoAm 94, WhoFI 94*
Opel, John Roberts 1925- *IntWW 93*
Opelt, Rilla Anne *WhoAmP 93*
Opelt, Rilla Anne 1939- *WhoMW 93*
Opengart, Bea *DrAPF 93*
Openshaw, Caroline Jane *Who 94*
Openshaw, Dale Kim 1950- *WhoWest 94*
Openshaw, (Charles) Peter (Lawford) 1947- *Who 94*
Opfell, John Burton 1924- *WhoWest 94*
Opfer, Darrell William 1941- *WhoAmP 93*
Opfer, Darrell Williams 1941- *WhoMW 93*
Opfer, Neil David 1954- *WhoWest 94*
Opferkuch, Paul Raymond 1938- *WhoAmP 93*
Opfermann, Myron William 1946- *WhoFI 94*
Ophir, Shai K. *WhoHol 92*
Ophuls, Marcel 1927- *IntMPA 94, WhoAm 94*
Ophuls, William 1934- *WrDr 94*
Opie, Alan 1945- *NewGrDO*
Opie, Alan John 1945- *Who 94*
Opie, Amelia 1769-1853 *BlmGWL*
Opie, Geoffrey James 1939- *Who 94*
Opie, Iona 1923- *WrDr 94*
Opie, Iona Margaret Balfour 1923- *Who 94*
Opie, Jane Maria 1961- *WhoScEn 94*
Opie, John Mart 1936- *WhoAmA 93*
Opie, Julian Gilbert 1958- *IntWW 93*
Opie, June 1926- *WrDr 94*
Opie, Lionel Henry 1933- *IntWW 93*
Opie, Roger Gilbert 1927- *Who 94*
Opie, William Robert 1920- *WhoAm 94*
Opihory, Kathleen Ann 1946- *WhoMW 93*
Opitz, Bernard Francis, Jr. 1947- *WhoFI 94*
Opitz, David Wilmer 1945- *WhoAmP 93*
Opitz, John Marius 1935- *WhoAm 94, WhoWest 94*
Opitz, Martin 1597-1639 *NewGrDO*
Opitz, May *BlkWr 2*
Ople, Blas F. 1927- *IntWW 93*
Opoku, Evelyn 1946- *WhoBlA 94*
Opotowsky, Maurice Leon 1931- *WhoAm 94, WhoWest 94*
Opotowsky, Stan 1923- *IntMPA 94*
Opotowsky, Stuart Berger 1935- *WhoAm 94, WhoFI 94*
Opp, Julie d1921 *WhoHol 92*
Oppe, Thomas Ernest 1925- *Who 94*
Oppedahl, Gillian Coyro 1955- *WhoWest 94*
Oppedahl, John Fredrick 1944- *WhoAm 94, WhoWest 94*
Oppedahl, Phillip Edward 1935- *WhoWest 94*
Oppel, Andrew John 1952- *WhoWest 94*
Oppel, Jerald J. 1941- *WhoAmL 94*
Oppel, Richard Alfred 1943- *WhoAm 94*
Oppenheim, Alan Victor 1937- *WhoAm 94*
Oppenheim, Alexander 1903- *IntWW 93, Who 94*
Oppenheim, Alfred 1915- *WhAm 10*
Oppenheim, Antoni Kazimierz 1915- *WhoAm 94*
Oppenheim, David Jerome 1922- *WhoAm 94*
Oppenheim, David John 1923- *WhoWest 94*
Oppenheim, Dennis A. 1938- *IntWW 93, WhoAmA 93*
Oppenheim, Donald J. 1950- *WhoAmL 94*
Oppenheim, Duncan (Morris) 1904- *Who 94*
Oppenheim, Duncan Morris 1904- *IntWW 93*
Oppenheim, E(dward) Phillips 1866-1946 *EncSF 93*
Oppenheim, Felix E. 1913- *WrDr 94*
Oppenheim, Irwin 1929- *WhoScEn 94*
Oppenheim, Menasha d1973 *WhoHol 92*
Oppenheim, Phillip Anthony Charles Lawrence 1956- *Who 94*
Oppenheim, Samuel Aaron 1940- *WhoWest 94*
Oppenheim, Samuel Edmund 1901-1992 *WhoAmA 93N*
Oppenheim, Saul Chesterfield 1897- *WhAm 10*
Oppenheim, Victor Eduard 1906- *WhoScEn 94*
Oppenheim-Barnes, Baroness 1930- *Who 94*
Oppenheim-Barnes, Sally 1930- *IntWW 93*
Oppenheimer, Alan *WhoHol 92*
Oppenheimer, Andres Miguel 1951- *WhoHisp 94*
Oppenheimer, David Benjamin 1950- *WhoAmL 94*
Oppenheimer, Franz Martin 1919- *WhoAm 94*
Oppenheimer, Fritz Ernest 1898- *WhAm 10*

Oppenheimer, Harry Frederick 1908- *IntWW 93, Who 94*
Oppenheimer, (Laetitia) Helen 1926- *Who 94*
Oppenheimer, J. Robert *WorInv*
Oppenheimer, J. Robert 1904-1967 *WorScD [port]*
Oppenheimer, James Richard 1921- *WhoAm 94*
Oppenheimer, Jane Marion 1911- *WhoAm 94*
Oppenheimer, Jerry L. 1937- *WhoAm 94*
Oppenheimer, Joel K. 1957- *WhoScEn 94*
Oppenheimer, Joseph 1927- *WhoAm 94*
Oppenheimer, Julius Robert 1904-1967 *AmSocL [port]*
Oppenheimer, Larry Eric 1942- *WhoScEn 94*
Oppenheimer, Martin J. 1933- *WhoAm 94*
Oppenheimer, Max, Jr. 1917- *WhoAm 94*
Oppenheimer, Max Stul 1947- *WhoAmL 94*
Oppenheimer, Michael 1946- *WhoAm 94*
Oppenheimer, Michael (Bernard Grenville) 1924- *Who 94*
Oppenheimer, Michael Anthony 1946- *Who 94*
Oppenheimer, Michael Frank 1945- *WhoAm 94*
Oppenheimer, Monroe 1904-1990 *WhAm 10*
Oppenheimer, Nicholas Frank 1945- *IntWW 93*
Oppenheimer, Nicola Anne 1950- *Who 94*
Oppenheimer, Peter Morris 1938- *Who 94*
Oppenheimer, Philip (Jack) 1911- *Who 94*
Oppenheimer, Preston Carl 1958- *WhoScEn 94, WhoWest 94*
Oppenheimer, Randolph Carl 1954- *WhoAmL 94*
Oppenheimer, Rex Maurice 1949- *WhoWest 94*
Oppenheimer, Selma L. 1898- *WhoAmA 93N*
Oppenheimer, Suzi 1934- *WhoAmP 93*
Oppenheimer, Tom Lucius 1943- *WhoFI 94*
Oppenlander, Karl Heinrich 1932- *IntWW 93*
Oppenlander, Robert 1923- *WhoAm 94*
Oppenlander, Robert Kirk 1952- *WhoFI 94*
Opper, Don 1949- *WhoHol 92*
Opper, John 1908- *WhoAmA 93*
Opper, Susanna 1940- *WhoFI 94*
Opperman, Danny Gene 1938- *WhoScEn 94*
Opperman, Dwight Darwin 1923- *WhoAm 94, WhoFI 94, WhoMW 93*
Opperman, Henry J. d1993 *NewYTBS 93*
Opperman, Hubert (Ferdinand) 1904- *Who 94*
Opperthauser, Earl Charles 1925- *WhoAmP 93*
Oppliger, David E. 1956- *WhoAmP 93*
Oppliger, Pearl Laviolette 1942- *WhoMW 93*
Opplt, Jan Jiri 1921- *WhoMW 93, WhoScEn 94*
Oppolzer, Wolfgang 1937- *IntWW 93*
Oprandy, John Jay 1956- *WhoScEn 94*
Opre, Thomas Edward 1943- *WhoAm 94*
Oprea, Gheorghe 1927- *IntWW 93*
Opsahl, Torkel 1931- *IntWW 93*
Opsal, Philip Mason 1931- *WhoWest 94*
Opsal, Scott D. 1960- *WhoIns 94*
Opsitnick, Allan Joseph 1953- *WhoAmL 94*
Opton, Frank G. 1906-1989 *WhAm 10*
Oquendo, Jose Manuel 1963- *WhoHisp 94*
Oquendo, Tony *WhoHisp 94*
O'Quinn, Terry *IntMPA 94, WhoHol 92*
Orabona, John 1943- *WhoAmP 93*
Oral, Sumer 1938- *IntWW 93*
Oram, Baron 1913- *Who 94*
Oram, Clifton (Albert) 1917- *WrDr 94*
Oram, John L. 1944- *WhoFI 94*
Oram, Kenneth Cyril 1919- *Who 94*
Oram, Neil 1938- *EncSF 93*
Oram, Robert W. 1922- *WhoAm 94*
Oramas-Oliva, Oscar 1936- *IntWW 93*
O'Ramey, Georgia d1928 *WhoHol 92*
Oran, Gary Carl 1948- *WhoScEn 94*
Oran, Stuart I. 1950- *WhoAmL 94*
Orange, Larry Jay 1942- *WhoAm 94*
O'Rangers, John Joseph 1936- *WhoScEn 94*
Oranmore And Browne, Baron 1901- *Who 94*
Orans, Ren 1959- *WhoWest 94*
Orantes, Manolo 1949- *BuCMET*
Oraon, Smt Sumati 1935- *WhoWomW 91*
Oras, Christine Futrell 1965- *WhoMW 93*
Orazem, Mark Edward 1954- *WhoScEn 94*
Orazem, Peter Francis 1955- *WhoFI 94*
Orazio, Angelo Frank 1926- *WhoAmP 93*
Orazio, Joan Politi 1930- *WhoFI 94*
Orazio, Paul Vincent 1957- *WhoFI 94*
Orbach, Jerry 1935- *IntMPA 94, WhoAm 94, WhoHol 92*
Orbach, Raymond Lee 1934- *WhoAm 94, WhoWest 94*
Orbach, Susie 1946- *ConAu 42NR*
Orban *EncSF 93*
Orban, Edmond Henry 1925- *WhoAm 94*
Orban, Kurt 1916- *WhoAm 94*
Orbe, Monica Patricia 1968- *WhoHisp 94*
Orbe, Octavius Anthony 1927- *WhoAm 94*
Orbeck, Edmund N. 1915- *WhoAmP 93*
Orbelian, Konstantin Agaparonovich 1928- *IntWW 93*
Orbell, John Donald 1949- *WhoScEn 94*
Orbell, Margaret 1934- *BlmGWL*
Orben, Jack Richard 1938- *WhoAm 94, WhoFI 94*
Orben, Robert 1927- *WhoAm 94*
Orben, Robert Allen 1936- *WhoAm 94*
Orbetzova, Verbka Tzekova 1938- *WhoWomW 91*
Orbigny, Alcide-Charles-Victor Des-Salines D' 1802-1857 *WhWE*
Orbison, David Vaillant 1952- *WhoScEn 94*
Orbison, James Graham 1953- *WhoScEn 94*
Orbison, Roy d1988 *WhoHol 92*
Orbison, Roy Kelton 1936-1988 *AmCulL*
Orbon, Margaret J. 1951- *WhoAm 94, WhoAmL 94*
Orbuch, Allen Harold 1928- *WhoAm 94*
Orce, Kenneth William 1943- *WhoAm 94, WhoAmL 94*
Orchard, (William) Arundell 1867-1961 *NewGrDO*
Orchard, Dennis Frank 1912- *WrDr 94*
Orchard, Donna Lee 1931- *WhoMW 93*
Orchard, Edward Eric 1920- *Who 94*
Orchard, Henry John 1922- *WhoAm 94*
Orchard, John *WhoHol 92*
Orchard, Julian d1979 *WhoHol 92*
Orchard, Peter Francis d1993 *IntWW 93N, Who 94N*
Orchard, Robert John 1946- *WhoAm 94*
Orchard, Stephen Michael 1944- *Who 94*
Orchard, William fl. 1468-1504 *DcNaB MP*
Orchard-Lisle, Paul David 1938- *Who 94*
Orci, Norma 1944- *WhoHisp 94*
Orcutt, Guy Henderson 1917- *WhoAm 94, WhoFI 94*
Orcutt, Joellen Lindh 1940- *WhoAmP 93*
Orcutt, Steven Glenn 1955- *WhoMW 93*
Orczy, Baroness 1865-1947 *EncSF 93*
Ord, Andrew James B. *Who 94*
Ordal, Caspar Reuben 1922- *WhoAm 94*
Ordanza, Bonagrace Francisco 1965- *WhoAsA 94*
Ordaz, Diego De 1480-1535 *WhWE*
Ordaz, Phillip A. 1934- *WhoHisp 94*
Orde, A.J. *EncSF 93*
Orde, Beryl d1966 *WhoHol 92*
Orde, Denis Alan 1932- *Who 94*
Orde, John (Alexander) Campbell 1943- *Who 94*
Orden, Susan Rabinowitz 1920- *WhoMW 93*
Orde-Powlett *Who 94*
Order, Trudy 1944- *WhoAmA 93*
Ordin, Andrea Sheridan *WhoAm 94*
Ordin, Andrea Sheridan 1940- *WhoHisp 94*
Ordish, George 1906-1992 *WrDr 94N*
Ordman, Alfred Bram 1948- *WhoMW 93*
Ordonez, Carlo d' 1734-1786 *NewGrDO*
Ordóñez, Michael Andrew 1954- *WhoHisp 94*
Ordonez, Nelson Gonzalo 1944- *WhoAm 94, WhoScEn 94*
Ordóñez, Ricardo 1959- *WhoHisp 94*
Ordonez, Sedfrey A. 1921- *IntWW 93*
Ordonneau, Maurice 1854-1916? *NewGrDO*
Ordonova, Hanka d1950 *WhoHol 92*
Ordorica, Steven Anthony 1957- *WhoScEn 94*
Ordover, Abraham Philip 1937- *WhoAm 94, WhoAmL 94*
Ordower, Ilene *WhoAmP 93*
Ordung, Philip Franklin 1919- *WhoAm 94*
Orduno, Robert Daniel 1933- *WhoAmA 93, WhoWest 94*
Orduño, Robert Octavio 1933- *WhoHisp 94*
Ordway, Frederick I., III 1927- *WrDr 94*
Ordway, Frederick Ira, III 1927- *WhoAm 94*
Ore, Rebecca 1948- *EncSF 93*
O'Reagan, Kevin Patrick 1960- *WhoFI 94*
O'Rear, Caine 1950- *WhoAmL 94*
O'Rear, Edgar Allen, III 1953- *WhoScEn 94*
Orear, Jay 1925- *WhoAm 94*
O'Reare, James *WhoHol 92*
Orebaugh, Phoebe May 1935- *WhoAmP 93*
Orechio, Carl A. 1914- *WhoAmP 93*
Orechio, Carmen A. 1926- *WhoAmP 93*
O'Ree, Willie 1935- *AfrAmAl 6, ConBlB 5 [port]*
Orefice, Paul F(austo) 1927- *IntWW 93*
Orefice, Paul Fausto 1927- *WhoFI 94, WhoMW 93*
Orefice, Antonio fl. 1708- *NewGrDO*
Orefice, Gary *WhoAmP 93*
Orefice, Giacomo 1865-1922 *NewGrDO*
O'Regan, (John) Barry 1915- *Who 94*
O'Regan, (Andrew) Brendan 1917- *IntWW 93*
O'Regan, Charles Robert *WhoAmP 93*
O'Regan, Deborah 1953- *WhoAmL 94*
O'Regan, Katherine Victoria 1946- *WhoWomW 91*
O'Regan, Kathleen 1903- *WhoHol 92*
O'Regan, Richard Arthur 1919- *WhoAm 94*
Oregel, Alicia M. 1949- *WhoHisp 94*
O'Reilly, Anthony J. F. 1936- *IntWW 93*
O'Reilly, Anthony John Francis 1936- *Who 94, WhoAm 94, WhoFI 94*
O'Reilly, Charles Terrance 1921- *WhoAm 94*
O'Reilly, Christine 1968-1993 *NewYTBS 93*
O'Reilly, Colm *Who 94*
O'Reilly, Cyril *WhoHol 92*
O'Reilly, Edward 1948- *IntWW 93*
O'Reilly, Erin *WhoHol 92*
O'Reilly, Francis Joseph 1922- *IntWW 93, Who 94*
O'Reilly, Gregory William 1958- *WhoMW 93*
O'Reilly, Hugh Joseph 1936- *WhoMW 93*
O'Reilly, Jackson *ConAu 140*
O'Reilly, James Thomas 1947- *WhoAmL 94*
O'Reilly, John B. 1930- *WhoAmA 93*
O'Reilly, John Bernard 1918- *WhoAmP 93*
O'Reilly, John Boyle 1844-1890 *DcAmReB 2, EncSF 93*
O'Reilly, John F. 1945- *WhoWest 94*
O'Reilly, John Joseph 1959- *WhoScEn 94*
O'Reilly, Kenneth William 1953- *WhoMW 93*
O'Reilly, Lawrence Patrick 1937- *WhoAm 94*
O'Reilly, Michael Joseph 1958- *WhoMW 93*
O'Reilly, Richard Brooks 1941- *WhoAm 94*
O'Reilly, Robert Bray fl. 1789- *NewGrDO*
O'Reilly, Rosann Tagliaferro 1948- *WhoMW 93*
O'Reilly, T. Mark 1944- *WhoAmL 94*
O'Reilly, Thomas Eugene 1932- *WhoAm 94*
O'Reilly, Thomas Patrick 1938- *WhoAmP 93*
O'Reilly, Timothy Patrick 1945- *WhoAm 94, WhoAmL 94*
O'Reilly, William John 1919- *Who 94*
O'Reilly, William R., Jr. 1955- *WhoAmL 94*
Oreja Aguirre, Marcelino 1935- *IntWW 93, Who 94*
Orek, Osman Nuri 1925- *IntWW 93*
Orel, Ann Elizabeth 1955- *WhoScEn 94*
Orel, Harold 1926- *ConAu 43NR, WhoAm 94, WhoMW 93, WrDr 94*
Oreli, Diana Margherita *NewGrDO*
Orellana, Carlos d1960 *WhoHol 92*
Orellana, Francisco De c. 1511-1546 *WhWE*
Orellana, Manuel M. 1947- *WhoHisp 94*
Orellana, Nicolás Alberto 1954- *WhoHisp 94*
Orellana, Rolando 1942- *WhoHisp 94*
Orelup, Elizabeth A. 1953- *WhoAmL 94*
Orem, Joseph Clifton 1944- *WhoWest 94*
Orem, Sandra Elizabeth 1940- *WhoFI 94*
Oren, Bruce Clifford 1952- *WhoAm 94*
Oren, Frederic Lynn 1934- *WhoWest 94*
Oren, John Birdsell 1909- *WhoAm 94*
Oren, Thomas Clayton 1951- *WhoMW 93*
Orendain, Antonio 1930- *WhoHisp 94*
Orens, Elaine Frances 1929- *WhoAmA 93*
Orensanz, Angel L. 1941- *WhoAmA 93*
Orenshein, Herbert 1931- *WhoIns 94*
Orenstein, Gloria Feman 1938- *WhoAmA 93*
Orenstein, Harold David 1936- *WhoAmP 93*
Orenstein, Howard 1955- *WhoAmP 93*
Orenstein, Michael 1939- *WhoFI 94, WhoWest 94*
Orenstein, Morton Henry 1936- *WhoWest 94*
Orenstein, Theodore Paul 1943- *WhoAmL 94*
Orent, Gerard M. 1931- *WhoAm 94, WhoFI 94*
Orentas, Rodney Raymond 1958- *WhoFI 94*
Orentlicher, John 1943- *WhoAmA 93*
Oresanya, Sasaenia Adedeji 1946- *IntWW 93*
Orescanin, Bogdan 1916- *Who 94*
Oresick, Peter *DrAPF 93*
Oreskes, Irwin 1926- *WhoAm 94*
Oreskes, Naomi 1958- *WhoScEn 94*
Oresman, Donald 1925- *WhoAm 94, WhoAmL 94, WhoFI 94*
Oresman, Stephen B. 1932- *WhoFI 94*
Oreste 1926- *WhoHol 92*
Orfalea, Gregory *DrAPF 93*
Orfaly, Alexander d1979 *WhoHol 92*
Orfei, Liana *WhoHol 92*
Orfei, Moira *WhoHol 92*
Orff, Carl 1895-1982 *NewGrDO*
Orfield, Adrienne Adams 1953- *WhoWest 94*
Orfield, Myron Willard, Jr. 1961- *WhoAmP 93, WhoMW 93*
Orfila, Alejandro 1925- *IntWW 93*
Orfuss, Mitchell Alan 1949- *WhoAm 94, WhoFI 94*
Orgad, Ben Zion 1926- *IntWW 93*
Organ, (Harold) Bryan 1935- *IntWW 93, Who 94*
Organ, Dennis Michael 1944- *WhoAm 94*
Organ, Joseph B. 1951- *WhoAm 94*
Organ, Troy Wilson 1912- *WrDr 94N*
Organski, A(bramo) F(imo) K(enneth) 1923- *WrDr 94*
Organski, Abramo Fimo Kenneth 1923- *WhoAm 94*
Orgebin-Crist, Marie-Claire 1936- *WhoAm 94*
Orgel, Doris 1929- *TwCYAW, WrDr 94*
Orgel, Irene *DrAPF 93*
Orgel, Leslie Eleazer 1927- *Who 94, WhoWest 94*
Orgel, Robert B. 1955- *WhoAmL 94*
Orgel, Stephen Kitay 1933- *WhoWest 94*
Orgeni, Aglaja 1841-1926 *NewGrDO*
Orgiani, Teofilo d1725 *NewGrDO*
Orgill, Douglas (William) *EncSF 93*
Orgitano, Raffaele c. 1770-1812 *NewGrDO*
Orgitano, Vincenzo c. 1735-1807? *NewGrDO*
Orhelm, Paul Joseph 1950- *WhoAmP 93*
Orhon, Necdet Kadri 1928- *WhoMW 93, WhoScEn 94*
Ori, Kan 1933- *WhoScEn 94*
Oriaku, Ebere Agwu 1951- *WhoFI 94, WhoScEn 94*
Oriana *BlmGEL*
Oriani, Ana Gloria 1953- *WhoHisp 94*
Oriani, Richard Anthony 1920- *WhoAm 94*
Orians, George Harrison 1900-1985 *WhAm 10*
Orians, Gordon Howell 1932- *WhoAm 94*
Orient, Jane Michel 1946- *WhoWest 94*
Orihel, Thomas Charles 1929- *WhoAm 94*
Orimenko, Martin Paul 1956- *WhoMW 93*
Orin, David Edward 1949- *WhoScEn 94*
Oringdulph, Robert E. 1932- *WhoAm 94*
O'Riordan, Cait *WhoHol 92*
O'Riordan, John Patrick Bruce 1936- *Who 94*
O'Riordan, Timothy 1942- *IntWW 93, Who 94*
O'Riordan, William Hugh 1947- *WhoAm 94, WhoAmL 94*
Orjas, Jose d1983 *WhoHol 92*
Orkand, Donald Saul 1936- *WhoAm 94, WhoFI 94*
Orkeny, Istvan 1912-1979 *IntDcT 2, RfGShF*
Orkin, Ad 1922- *IntMPA 94*
Orkin, Leonard 1932- *WhoAm 94*
Orkin, Louis Richard 1915- *WhoAm 94*
Orkin, Ruth 1921-1985 *WhoAmA 93N*
Orkney, Earl of c. 1080-1116 *DcNaB MP*
Orkney, Earl of 1919- *Who 94*
Orkow, Ben (Harrison) 1896- *EncSF 93*
Orkwis, Paul David 1962- *WhoScEn 94*
Orla, Resel d1931 *WhoHol 92*
Orlamond, William d1957 *WhoHol 92*
Orland, Frank Jay 1917- *WhoAm 94, WhoMW 93, WhoScEn 94*
Orland, Ted N. *WhoAmA 93*
Orland, Ted Norcross 1941- *WhoWest 94*
Orlandi, Chiara fl. 1717- *NewGrDO*
Orlandi, Elisa 1811-1834 *NewGrDO*
Orlandi, Felice *WhoHol 92*
Orlandi, Ferdinando 1774-1848 *NewGrDO*
Orlandi, Nicoleta 1961- *WhoWomW 91*
Orlandi, Santi d1619 *NewGrDO*
Orlandi Contucci, Corrado 1914- *IntWW 93*
Orlandi Malaspina, Rita 1937- *NewGrDO*
Orlandini, Giuseppe Maria 1676-1760 *NewGrDO*
Orlandini, Luca *WhoHol 92*

Orlando, Carl 1915- *WhoScEn 94*
Orlando, Danielle *WhoAm 94*
Orlando, Don d1987 *WhoHol 92*
Orlando, Ferdinando *NewGrDO*
Orlando, George Joseph 1944- *WhoAm 94*
Orlando, Kathy Reber 1942- *WhoFI 94*
Orlando, Margaret Ann 1939- *WhoMW 93*
Orlando, Mariano Alex 1962- *WhoFI 94*
Orlando, Quentin R. *WhoAmP 93*
Orlando, Tony 1944- *WhoHisp 94*
Orlans, Harold 1921- *WrDr 94*
Orlansky, Grace Suydam 1925- *WhoAmP 93*
Orlean, Susan 1955- *WrDr 94*
Orlebar, Michael Keith Orlebar S. *Who 94*
Orlebeke, Charles J. 1934- *WhoAmP 93*
Orlebeke, William Ronald 1933- *WhoAmL 94, WhoFI 94, WhoWest 94*
Orledge, Robert 1948- *WrDr 94*
Orlen, Joel 1924- *WhoAm 94, WhoScEn 94*
Orlen, Steve *DrAPF 93*
Orlett, Edward J. 1933- *WhoAmP 93*
Orlev, Uri 1931- *ChlLR 30 [port], TwCYAW*
Orlich, Rose *DrAPF 93*
Orlidge, Leslie Arthur 1953- *WhoScEn 94*
Orlik, Peter Blythe 1944- *WhoAm 94*
Orlik, Randy Phillip 1952- *WhoAmL 94*
Orlin, Karen J. 1948- *WhoAmL 94*
Orling, Anne d1988 *WhoAmA 93N*
Orlins, Stephen A. 1950- *WhoFI 94*
Orlinsky, Harry M. 1908-1992 *AnObit 1992*
Orlitzky, Robert 1960- *WhoScEn 94*
Orlob, Gerald T. 1924- *WhoAm 94*
Orlock, Carol *DrAPF 93*
Orloff, Chet 1949- *WhoWest 94*
Orloff, Gary William 1946- *WhoAm 94, WhoAmL 94*
Orloff, Jack 1921-1988 *WhAm 10*
Orloff, Lily 1908-1957 *WhoAmA 93N*
Orloff, Neil 1943- *WhoAm 94, WhoWest 94*
Orloski, Richard John 1947- *WhoAmP 93*
Orlov, Aleksei Ivanovich 1937- *LngBDD*
Orlov, Darlene 1949- *WhoFI 94*
Orlov, Dmitriy N. d1955 *WhoHol 92*
Orlov, Yuri Fedorovich 1924- *IntWW 93*
Orlova, Alexandra (Anatol'evna) 1911- *WrDr 94*
Orlova, Lyubov d1975 *WhoHol 92*
Orlovsky, Donald Albert 1951- *WhoAmL 94*
Orlovsky, Peter *DrAPF 93*
Orlowski, Stanislaw Tadeusz 1920- *WhoScEn 94*
Orlowsky, Lillian 1914- *WhoAmA 93*
Orlowsky, Martin L. 1941- *WhoFI 94*
Orlyk, Harry V. 1947- *WhoAmA 93*
Orman, Arthur Allen 1932- *WhoAm 94*
Orman, David Allen 1943- *WhoWest 94*
Orman, John Leo 1949- *WhoWest 94*
Orman, Leonard Arnold 1930- *WhoAm 94*
Orman, Roscoe *WhoHol 92*
Orman, Stanley 1935- *Who 94*
Ormandy, Eugene d1985 *WhoHol 92*
Ormasa, John 1925- *WhoAmL 94, WhoFI 94, WhoScEn 94, WhoWest 94*
Orme, Antony Ronald 1936- *WhoAm 94*
Orme, Denis Arthur 1946- *WhoAm 94, WhoFI 94*
Orme, Edward 1775-1848 *DcNaB MP*
Orme, Eliza 1848-1937 *DcNaB MP*
Orme, Jeremy David 1943- *Who 94*
Orme, Lila Morton *WhoAmP 93*
Orme, Lydia Gardner d1963 *WhoAmA 93N*
Orme, Maynard Evan 1936- *WhoWest 94*
Orme, Robert Thomas Neil 1947- *Who 94*
Orme, Stanley 1923- *IntWW 93, Who 94*
Orme-Johnson, Rhoda Frances 1940- *WhoMW 93*
Ormerod, Alec William 1932- *Who 94*
Ormerod, Pamela Catherine *Who 94*
Ormerod, Roger *WrDr 94*
Ormesson, Jean d' 1925- *IntWW 93, Who 94*
Ormeville, Carlo d' *NewGrDO*
Ormiston, James Joseph 1962- *WhoAmL 94*
Ormiston, Thomas 1826-1882 *DcNaB MP*
Ormiston, Timothy Shawn 1958- *WhoScEn 94*
Ormond, John (Davies Wilder) 1905- *Who 94*
Ormond, Judith 1946- *WhoMW 93*
Ormond, Mark Richard 1955- *WhoMW 93*
Ormond, Richard Louis 1939- *IntWW 93, Who 94*
Ormonde, Marquess of 1899- *Who 94*
Ormonde, Eugene d1922 *WhoHol 92*
Ormondroyd, Edward 1925- *WrDr 94*
Ormondroyd, Jesse 1897- *WhAm 10*
Ormos, Maria 1930- *IntWW 93*
Ormoy, Charlotte Chaumet, Mme presidente d' 1732?-1791 *BlmGWL*
Orms, Howard Raymond 1920- *WhoAm 94, WhoMW 93*
Ormsbee, Allen Ives 1926- *WhoAm 94*
Ormsbee, David 1907- *WrDr 94*
Ormsbee, David Marc 1956- *WhoMW 93*
Ormsby, Eric Linn 1941- *WhoAm 94*
Ormsby, Frank 1947- *WrDr 94*
Ormsby, Stephanie *BlmGWL*
Ormsby, William M. *WhoBlA 94*
Ormsby Gore *Who 94*
Orn, Einar *See* Sugarcubes, The *ConMus 10*
Ornauer, Richard Lewis 1922- *WhoAm 94*
Ornburn, Kristee Jean 1956- *WhoMW 93*
Orndorff, Charles Lewis 1952- *WhoAmP 93*
Orndorff, Mark Christian 1957- *WhoAmL 94*
Ornduff, Robert 1932- *WhoAm 94*
Ornelas, Michael Raul 1952- *WhoHisp 94*
Ornelas, Victor F. 1948- *WhoHisp 94*
Ornellas, Donald Louis 1932- *WhoScEn 94, WhoWest 94*
Ornellas, Norman d1975 *WhoHol 92*
Orner, William Richards 1948- *WhoMW 93*
Ornish, Dean 1953- *ConAu 142*
Ornitz, Richard Martin 1945- *WhoAm 94*
Ornolfsdottir, Margret *See* Sugarcubes, The *ConMus 10*
Ornstein, Alexander Thomas 1944- *WhoAmL 94*
Ornstein, Bruce *WhoHol 92*
Ornstein, Donald Samuel 1934- *IntWW 93, WhoAm 94, WhoWest 94*
Ornstein, Judith 1951- *WhoAmA 93*
Ornstein, Norman Jay 1948- *WhoAm 94*
Ornstein, Robert 1925- *WhoAm 94, WrDr 94*
Ornstein-Galicia, Jacob Leonard 1915- *WhoAm 94*
Orodeckis, Edward J. 1948- *WhoIns 94*
Orona, Josef L. 1948- *WhoHisp 94*
Orona, Manuel Jimenez 1946- *WhoHisp 94*
Orona, Nelly 1931- *WhoHisp 94*
Oronsky, Arnold Lewis 1940- *WhoAm 94*
Oropallo, Deborah 1954- *WhoAmA 93*
Oropallo, Michael Anthony 1959- *WhoAmL 94*
O'Rorke, James Francis, Jr. 1936- *WhoAm 94, WhoAmL 94*
Oros, Ernest L. 1923- *WhoAmP 93*
Orosco, Jesse 1957- *WhoHisp 94*
Orosco, Pedro Ramon 1945- *WhoHisp 94*
O'Ross, Ed *WhoHol 92*
Orosz, Janet E. Foley 1956- *WhoMW 93*
O'Rourke, Andrew 1931- *IntWW 93, Who 94*
O'Rourke, Andrew Patrick 1933- *WhoAm 94*
O'Rourke, Barnay d1977 *WhoHol 92*
O'Rourke, Brefni d1946 *WhoHol 92*
O'Rourke, Brian Jay 1946- *WhoWest 94*
O'Rourke, C. Larry 1937- *WhoAm 94, WhoAmL 94*
O'Rourke, Daniel 1947- *WhoAm 94*
O'Rourke, Dennis 1914- *WhoAm 94*
O'Rourke, Eugene d1917 *WhoHol 92*
O'Rourke, Heather d1988 *WhoHol 92*
O'Rourke, J. A. d1937 *WhoHol 92*
O'Rourke, J. Tracy 1935- *WhoAm 94, WhoFI 94, WhoWest 94*
O'Rourke, Jack 1937- *WhoFI 94*
O'Rourke, James Scofield, IV 1946- *WhoMW 93*
O'Rourke, Jim *WhoAmP 93*
O'Rourke, Joan B. Doty Werthman 1933- *WhoMW 93*
O'Rourke, Joanne A. 1939- *WhoAmP 93*
O'Rourke, John J. 1922- *IntMPA 94*
O'Rourke, John Raymond, Jr. 1951- *WhoAmL 94*
O'Rourke, Margaret Cookson 1927- *WhoAmP 93*
O'Rourke, Mary 1937- *IntWW 93, WhoWomW 91*
O'Rourke, Michael d1981 *WhoHol 92*
O'Rourke, Michael J. 1951- *WhoAm 94*
O'Rourke, Michael James 1944- *WhoAmL 94*
O'Rourke, Michell Lynn 1969- *WhoMW 93*
O'Rourke, P. J. 1947- *WhoAm 94, WrDr 94*
O'Rourke, P(atrick) J(ake) 1947- *ConAu 41NR*
O'Rourke, Ronald Eugene 1957- *WhoScEn 94, WhoWest 94*
O'Rourke, Stephen Charles 1916- *WhoAmP 93*
O'Rourke, Thomas Denis 1948- *WhoAm 94, WhoScEn 94*
O'Rourke, Thomas Joseph 1931- *WhoScEn 94*
O'Rourke, William *DrAPF 93*
O'Rourke, William 1945- *WrDr 94*
O'Rourke, William Andrew 1945- *WhoAm 94*
Orowan, Egon 1902-1989 *WhAm 10*
Orowitz, Eugene Maurice *WhAm 10*
Oroyan, Susanna Elizabeth 1942- *WhoWest 94*
Oroza, Ileana 1950- *WhoHisp 94*
Orozco, Carmen F. 1936- *WhoHisp 94*
Orozco, Frank *WhoHisp 94*
Orozco, John Alfred 1959- *WhoHisp 94*
Orozco, Jose A. 1949- *WhoHisp 94*
Orozco, Joseph William 1921- *WhoAmP 93*
Orozco, Luz Maria, Sister 1933- *WhoHisp 94*
Orozco, Mary Lee 1933- *WhoHisp 94*
Orozco, Mauricio J. 1960- *WhoHisp 94*
Orozco, Olga 1920- *BlmGWL*
Orozco, Raymond E. 1933- *WhoAm 94, WhoHisp 94, WhoMW 93*
Orozco, Ronald Avelino 1951- *WhoHisp 94*
Orphanides, Gus George 1947- *WhoScEn 94*
Orphee, Elvira 1930- *BlmGWL*
Orr, A. Lorraine 1921- *WhoAmP 93*
Orr, Allen L. 1949- *WhoAmL 94*
Orr, Arthur (Leslie) 1938- *WhoAmA 93*
Orr, Bobby 1948- *WhoAm 94*
Orr, Bobby Joe 1935- *WhoFI 94*
Orr, Carl Robert 1954- *WhoFI 94*
Orr, Carol Wallace 1933- *WhoAm 94*
Orr, Cheryl Denise 1963- *WhoAmL 94*
Orr, Clyde 1921- *WrDr 94*
Orr, Clyde Hugh 1931- *WhoBlA 94*
Orr, Daniel B. 1919- *WhoAmP 93*
Orr, David (Alexander) 1922- *Who 94*
Orr, David Alexander 1922- *IntWW 93*
Orr, David Duvall 1944- *WhoAmP 93*
Orr, David L. 1946- *WhoAm 94*
Orr, Dennis Patrick 1952- *WhoAmL 94*
Orr, Dorothy *WhoBlA 94*
Orr, Douglass Winnett 1905- *WhAm 10*
Orr, E. Wycliffe *WhoAmP 93*
Orr, Elliot 1904- *WhoAmA 93*
Orr, Forrest d1963 *WhoHol 92*
Orr, George J. *WhoAmP 93*
Orr, Gregory *DrAPF 93*
Orr, Gregory (Simpson) 1947- *WrDr 94*
Orr, Gregory Simpson 1947- *WhoAm 94*
Orr, Hugh 1715-1798 *WhAmRev*
Orr, Iain Campbell 1942- *Who 94*
Orr, Jack DeMilt 1952- *WhoWest 94*
Orr, James Bernard Vivian 1917- *Who 94*
Orr, James F., III 1943- *WhoAm 94, WhoFI 94*
Orr, James Francis 1945- *WhoMW 93*
Orr, James H. d1993 *NewYTBS 93*
Orr, James Henry 1927- *Who 94*
Orr, James Steele 1945- *WhoMW 93*
Orr, Jean Fergus Henderson 1920- *Who 94*
Orr, Jean Wopat 1946- *WhoFI 94*
Orr, Joel Nathaniel 1947- *WhoAm 94*
Orr, John Henry 1918- *Who 94*
Orr, John M. 1943- *WhoAmL 94*
Orr, Joseph Charles 1949- *WhoAmA 93*
Orr, Kay A. 1939- *IntWW 93, WhoAmP 93*
Orr, Kenneth Bradley 1933- *WhoAm 94*
Orr, L. Glenn, Jr. 1940- *WhoAm 94, WhoFI 94*
Orr, Linda *DrAPF 93*
Orr, Louis M. 1958- *WhoBlA 94*
Orr, Marcia 1949- *WhoFI 94, WhoScEn 94*
Orr, Mary 1918- *WhoHol 92*
Orr, Michael P. 1947- *WhoAm 94, WhoFI 94, WhoWest 94*
Orr, Michael Terence 1961- *WhoMW 93*
Orr, Owen *WhoHol 92*
Orr, Parker Murray 1927- *WhoAm 94*
Orr, Ray 1953- *WhoBlA 94*
Orr, Richard Tuttle 1915- *WhoAm 94*
Orr, Robert Dunkerson 1917- *IntWW 93, WhoAmP 93*
Orr, Robert Richmond 1930- *WrDr 94*
Orr, Robin 1909- *Who 94*
Orr, Robin (Kemsley) 1909- *NewGrDO*
Orr, Ronald S. 1946- *WhoAm 94*
Orr, Ronald Stewart 1946- *WhoAmL 94*
Orr, Roy Lee 1932- *WhoAmP 93*
Orr, San Watterson, Jr. 1941- *WhoAm 94, WhoFI 94*
Orr, Scott J. 1951- *WhoAmP 93*
Orr, Stanley d1968 *WhoHol 92*
Orr, Terrence S. 1943- *WhoAm 94*
Orr, Thomas S. 1948- *WhoIns 94*
Orr, Verlena *DrAPF 93*
Orr, Virgil 1923- *WhoAmP 93*
Orr, William 1917- *WhoHol 92*
Orr-Cahall, Christina 1947- *WhoAm 94*
Orr-Chall, Anona Christina *WhoAmA 93*
Orrego, George Humberto 1950- *WhoHisp 94*
Orrego-Salas, Juan (Antonio) 1919- *NewGrDO*
Orrego-Salas, Juan Antonio 1919- *WhoAm 94*
Orrego Vicuna, Francisco 1942- *IntWW 93, Who 94*
Orrell, James Francis Freestone 1944- *Who 94*
Orr-Ewing, Baron 1912- *Who 94*
Orr Ewing, Edward Stuart 1931- *Who 94*
Orr-Ewing, Hamish 1924- *IntWW 93, Who 94*
Orr Ewing, Ronald Archibald 1912- *Who 94*
Orrey, (Gilbert) Leslie 1908-1981 *NewGrDO*
Orrick, David d1979 *WhoHol 92*
Orrick, William Horsley, Jr. 1915- *WhoAm 94, WhoAmL 94, WhoAmP 93*
Orridge, Jeffrey Lyndon 1960- *WhoBlA 94*
Orrigoni, Marc'Antonio fl. 1677- *NewGrDO*
Orringer, Mark B. 1943- *WhoAm 94*
Orris *BlmGWL*
Orris, Daryl Joseph 1947- *WhoFI 94*
Orris, William LeRoy, Jr. 1941- *WhoMW 93*
Orrison, Carrol Payton 1929- *WhoAmP 93*
Orrock, Nancy Gorgan 1943- *WhoAmP 93*
Orrock, R. Dennis 1943- *WhoAmP 93*
Orrock, Robert Dickson 1955- *WhoAmP 93*
Orrok, Francene Feldman 1937- *WhoWest 94*
Orry-Kelly 1897-1964 *IntDcF 2-4*
Orsak, Joseph Cyril 1928- *WhoScEn 94*
Orsatti, Alfred Kendall 1932- *WhoAm 94, WhoWest 94*
Orsatti, Ernest Benjamin 1949- *WhoAmL 94*
Orsbon, Richard Anthony 1947- *WhoAm 94, WhoAmL 94*
Orsell, Renee d1988 *WhoHol 92*
Orser, Earl Herbert 1928- *WhoAm 94, WhoFI 94*
Orsetti, Christian Ernest 1923- *IntWW 93*
Orsillo, James Edward 1939- *WhoAm 94, WhoScEn 94*
Orsini, Flavio 1620-1698 *NewGrDO*
Orsini, Louis *WhoAmP 93*
Orsini, Marina *WhoHol 92*
Orsini, Umberto *WhoHol 92*
Orson, Rasin Ward 1927- *Who 94*
Orszag, Steven Alan 1943- *WhoAm 94, WhoScEn 94*
Orszulak, David John 1959- *WhoFI 94*
Orszulak, Richard Stewart 1957- *WhoFI 94*
Ort, Rosalyn Maria 1942- *WhoWest 94*
Orta, Teresa Margarida da Silva e 1712?-1793 *BlmGWL*
Ortal, Jose Casimiro, Jr. 1952- *WhoHisp 94*
Ortal-Miranda, Yolanda *WhoHisp 94*
Ortega, Anthony David 1958- *WhoHisp 94, WhoWest 94*
Ortega, Augusto Cesar 1927- *WhoHisp 94*
Ortega, Belén 1918- *WhoHisp 94*
Ortega, Blanca Rosa 1948- *WhoHisp 94*
Ortega, David Fernando 1940- *WhoHisp 94*
Ortega, Deborah L. 1955- *WhoHisp 94*
Ortega, Dimitrio *WhoHisp 94*
Ortega, Ernest Eugene 1940- *WhoHisp 94*
Ortega, Ernest W. 1945- *WhoHisp 94*
Ortega, German E. 1933- *WhoHisp 94*
Ortega, Jacobo 1929- *WhoHisp 94*
Ortega, James 1924- *WhoHisp 94*
Ortega, James McDonough 1932- *WhoAm 94*
Ortega, Jesús 1940- *WhoHisp 94*
Ortega, Katherine Davalos *WhoHisp 94*
Ortega, Kenny *IntMPA 94, WhoHisp 94*
Ortega, Lawrence A. 1948- *WhoHisp 94*
Ortega, Linda Dolores 1951- *WhoHisp 94*
Ortega, Lorraine G. 1940- *WhoAmP 93*
Ortega, M. Alice 1960- *WhoHisp 94*
Ortega, Manuel 1943- *WhoHisp 94*
Ortega, Manuel Anthony 1953- *WhoHisp 94*
Ortega, Manuel J., Jr. 1948- *WhoHisp 94*
Ortega, Oscar 1956- *WhoHisp 94*
Ortega, Oscar J. *WhoHisp 94*
Ortega, Patricia L. 1956- *WhoHisp 94*
Ortega, Rafael Enrique 1952- *WhoHisp 94*
Ortega, Ray 1940- *WhoHisp 94*
Ortega, Reuben A. 1941- *WhoHisp 94*
Ortega, Robert, Jr. 1947- *WhoHisp 94*
Ortega, Ruben *WhoAmP 93*
Ortega, Rubén 1939- *WhoHisp 94*
Ortega, Ruben Baptista 1939- *WhoWest 94*
Ortega, Ruben Francisco 1956- *WhoWest 94*
Ortega, Ruben Francisco, Jr. 1956- *WhoHisp 94*
Ortega, Santos d1976 *WhoHol 92*
Ortega, Sergio 1938- *NewGrDO*

Ortega, Silver 1949- *WhoHisp 94*
Ortega, Tony 1958- *WhoHisp 94*
Ortega Carter, Dolores 1950- *WhoHisp 94*
Ortega Chamorro, Guillermo 1909- *WhoHisp 94*
Ortega-Davey, María Belén 1918- *WhoHisp 94*
Ortega del Villar, Aniceto 1825-1875 *NewGrDO*
Ortega De Santis, Diana 1952- *WhoHisp 94*
Ortega-Rubio, Alfredo 1956- *WhoScEn 94*
Ortega Saavedra, Daniel 1945- *IntWW 93*
Ortega y Gasset, Jose 1883-1955 *HispLC [port]*
Ortego, Art d1960 *WhoHol 92*
Ortego, Gilda Baeza 1952- *WhoHisp 94, WhoWest 94*
Ortego, Joseph John 1954- *WhoHisp 94*
Ortego, Philip D. *DrAPF 93*
Ortego y Gasca, Felipe de 1926- *WhoHisp 94*
Ortelius, Abraham 1527-1598 *WhWE [port]*
Ortelli, Dyana *WhoHol 92*
Orten, Betty 1927- *WhoAmP 93*
Ortenberg, Elisabeth Claiborne 1929- *WhoAm 94*
Ortengren, John 1931- *WhoFI 94*
Ortese, Anna Maria 1914- *BlmGWL*
Ortez, Donald Jeronimo 1941- *WhoHisp 94*
Orth, David Nelson 1933- *WhoAm 94*
Orth, Frank d1962 *WhoHol 92*
Orth, Robert D. 1935- *WhoAmP 93*
Orthwein, James B. *WhoAm 94*
Orthwein, William Coe 1924- *WhoAm 94*
Orticke, Leslie Ann *WhoBlA 94*
Ortin, Miguel d1978 *WhoHol 92*
Ortinau, David Joseph 1948- *WhoFI 94*
Ortino, Hector Ruben 1942- *WhoFI 94, WhoHisp 94, WhoMW 93*
Ortique, Revius Oliver, Jr. 1924- *WhoAm 94, WhoAmL 94, WhoBlA 94*
Ortiz, Alfonso A. 1939- *WrDr 94*
Ortiz, Alfonso Alex 1939- *AmSocL*
Ortiz, Alfredo Tomas 1948- *WhoHisp 94*
Ortiz, Andrew F. 1969- *WhoHisp 94*
Ortiz, Andrew Flores 1969- *WhoFI 94*
Ortiz, Angel L. *WhoAmP 93, WhoHisp 94*
Ortiz, Antonio G. *DrAPF 93*
Ortiz, Antonio Ignacio 1961- *WhoFI 94, WhoWest 94*
Ortiz, Araceli 1937- *WhoHisp 94*
Ortiz, Augusto 1917- *WhoHisp 94*
Ortiz, Beatriz E. 1959- *WhoHisp 94*
Ortiz, Carlos *WhoAmA 93*
Ortiz, Carlos A. 1946- *WhoHisp 94*
Ortiz, Carlos Guillermo 1956- *WhoHisp 94*
Ortiz, Carlos Roberto 1946- *WhoHisp 94*
Ortiz, Carmen D. *WhoHisp 94*
Ortiz, Charles Francis 1951- *WhoWest 94*
Ortiz, Charles Leo 1941- *WhoHisp 94*
Ortiz, Clemencia 1942- *WhoHisp 94*
Ortiz, Cristina 1950- *IntWW 93*
Ortiz, Daniel Antonio 1953- *WhoHisp 94*
Ortiz, Daniel Zapata 1954- *WhoHisp 94*
Ortiz, Delia 1924- *WhoBlA 94*
Ortiz, Edgardo 1926- *WhoHisp 94*
Ortiz, Emanuel *WhoHisp 94*
Ortiz, Enrique O. *WhoHisp 94*
Ortiz, Francis R. 1955- *WhoHisp 94*
Ortiz, Francis Robert 1955- *WhoAmL 94*
Ortiz, Francis V., Jr. 1926- *WhoHisp 94*
Ortiz, Francis Vincent, Jr. 1926- *WhoAm 94*
Ortiz, Frank P. 1939- *WhoHisp 94*
Ortiz, Frank Vincent 1926- *IntWW 93*
Ortiz, Frank Xavier 1949- *WhoHisp 94*
Ortiz, George 1942- *WhoHisp 94*
Ortiz, Gonzalo Reyes 1949- *WhoHisp 94*
Ortiz, Hector *WhoHisp 94*
Ortiz, Herminio, Jr. 1949- *WhoHisp 94*
Ortiz, Isidro D. 1949- *WhoHisp 94*
Ortiz, Jack *WhoHisp 94*
Ortiz, James A. *WhoHisp 94*
Ortiz, James George 1961- *WhoWest 94*
Ortiz, Jay Richard Gentry 1945- *WhoAmL 94*
Ortiz, Jesus, Jr. 1942- *WhoHisp 94*
Ortiz, Jose Anibal 1957- *WhoHisp 94*
Ortiz, José G. 1955- *WhoHisp 94*
Ortiz, Jose Ramon *WhoHisp 94*
Ortiz, Joseph Vincent 1956- *WhoHisp 94, WhoScEn 94*
Ortiz, Julia Cristina 1955- *WhoHisp 94*
Ortiz, Junior 1959- *WhoHisp 94*
Ortiz, Leonardo Cesar 1943- *WhoHisp 94*
Ortiz, Lourdes 1943- *BlmGWL*
Ortiz, Luis Enrique 1949- *WhoMW 93*
Ortiz, Luis Tony 1955- *WhoHisp 94*
Ortiz, Manuel, Jr. 1938- *WhoHisp 94*
Ortiz, María C. 1959- *WhoHisp 94*
Ortiz, María Elena 1946- *WhoHisp 94*
Ortiz, Mario 1942- *WhoHisp 94*
Ortiz, Maritza 1956- *WhoHisp 94*
Ortiz, Maritza 1958- *WhoHisp 94*
Ortiz, Mary Theresa 1957- *WhoScEn 94*
Ortiz, Mecha d1987 *WhoHol 92*
Ortiz, Miguel 1954- *WhoHisp 94*
Ortiz, Miguel A. *DrAPF 93*
Ortiz, Norma I. 1955- *WhoHisp 94*
Ortiz, Nydia 1951- *WhoHisp 94*
Ortiz, Olivia Frances, Sister 1926- *WhoHisp 94*
Ortiz, Pablo Francis 1948- *WhoHisp 94*
Ortiz, Pedro 1949- *WhoHisp 94*
Ortiz, Peter *WhoAmP 93*
Ortiz, Rachael 1941- *WhoHisp 94*
Ortiz, Rafael Montanez 1934- *WhoHisp 94*
Ortiz, Ramon *WhoHisp 94*
Ortiz, Raphael Montanez 1934- *WhoAm 94, WhoAmA 93*
Ortiz, Raquel 1945- *WhoHisp 94*
Ortiz, Raymond Z. 1953- *WhoHisp 94*
Ortiz, Rene Genaro 1941- *IntWW 93*
Ortiz, Reynaldo U. 1946- *WhoHisp 94*
Ortiz, Ronald Antonio 1930- *WhoHisp 94*
Ortiz, Rosa Milagros 1949- *WhoHisp 94*
Ortiz, S. M. *WhoHisp 94*
Ortiz, Samuel Luis 1950- *WhoHisp 94*
Ortiz, Simon J. *DrAPF 93*
Ortiz, Simon J. 1941- *WrDr 94*
Ortiz, Solomon P. 1937- *WhoAm 94*
Ortiz, Solomon P. 1938- *CngDr 93*
Ortiz, Solomon Porfirio 1937- *WhoHisp 94*
Ortíz, Sylvia Margarita 1968- *WhoHisp 94*
Ortiz, Tino G. *WhoHisp 94*
Ortiz, Victor 1946- *WhoBlA 94*
Ortiz, Vilma 1954- *WhoHisp 94*
Ortiz, Ydalia 1916- *WhoHisp 94*
Ortiz-Alvarez, Jorge L. 1952- *WhoHisp 94*
Ortiz-Arduan, Alberto 1963- *WhoScEn 94*
Ortiz-Blanco, Gloria Esther 1951- *WhoHisp 94*
Ortiz-Brunet, Jorge 1940- *WhoHisp 94*
Ortiz-Buonafina, Marta 1933- *WhoHisp 94*
Ortiz-Cotto, Pablo 1929- *WhoHisp 94*
Ortiz-Del Valle, Sandra 1951- *WhoHisp 94*
Ortiz de Montellano, Bernard Ramon, V 1938- *WhoHisp 94*
Ortiz de Montellano, Paul Richard *WhoHisp 94*
Ortiz De Rozas, Carlos 1926- *IntWW 93, Who 94*
Ortiz de Zarate, Eleodoro 1865-1952 *NewGrDO*
Ortiz Diaz, Tomas 1944- *WhoHisp 94*
Ortiz-Franco, Luis 1946- *WhoHisp 94*
Ortiz-Gordils, Edgardo 1926- *WhoHisp 94*
Ortiz-Griffin, Julia L. *WhoHisp 94*
Ortiz-Leduc, William 1951- *WhoScEn 94*
Ortiz-Macri, Veronica Cecilia 1937- *WhoHisp 94*
Ortiz Mena, Antonio 1912- *IntWW 93*
Ortiz-Suarez, Humberto J. 1941- *WhoHisp 94*
Ortiz Velazquez, Rolando 1960- *WhoAmP 93*
Ortiz-White, Aleene J. 1953- *WhoHisp 94*
Ortleb, Rainer 1944- *IntWW 93*
Ortli, Patricia Gravatt 1938- *WhoMW 93*
Ortlieb, Robert Eugene 1925- *WhoAm 94, WhoAmA 93*
Ortlip, Mary Krueger *WhoAmA 93*
Ortlip, Paul Daniel 1926- *WhoAm 94, WhoAmA 93*
Ortloff, George Christian 1947- *WhoAmP 93*
Ortloff, Todd Wayne 1968- *WhoWest 94*
Ortman, Candy Jay 1954- *WhoMW 93*
Ortman, Eldon E. 1934- *WhoAm 94*
Ortman, George Earl 1926- *WhoAm 94, WhoAmA 93*
Ortman, Glen L. 1947- *WhoAmL 94*
Ortmeyer, Thomas Howard 1949- *WhoScEn 94*
Ortner, Charles B. 1945- *WhoAmL 94*
Ortner, Everett Howard 1919- *WhoAm 94*
Ortner, Robert 1927- *WrDr 94*
Ortner, Sherry B(eth) 1941- *WrDr 94*
Ortner, Toni *DrAPF 93*
Ortner, Toni 1941- *ConAu 42NR*
Ortner-Zimmerman, Toni *ConAu 42NR*
Ortolani, Minot Henry 1929- *WhoAm 94*
Ortolano, Leonard 1941- *WhoAm 94*
Ortolano, Ralph J. *WhoScEn 94*
Ortoli, Francois-Xavier 1925- *IntWW 93, Who 94*
Ortoll, Javier *WhoHisp 94*
Orton, Bill *WhoAmP 93*
Orton, Bill 1948- *CngDr 93*
Orton, Colin George 1938- *WhoAm 94*
Orton, George Frederick 1941- *WhoAm 94, WhoScEn 94*
Orton, Joe 1933-1967 *BlmGEL, GayLL, IntDcT 2 [port]*
Orton, John Stewart 1949- *WhoAmL 94*
Orton, Luther Kent 1946- *WhoAmL 94*
Orton, Stewart 1915- *WhoAm 94*
Orton, William H 1948- *WhoAm 94, WhoWest 94*
Orton, William Rolen, Jr. 1922-1990 *WhAm 10*
Orttung, William Herbert 1934- *WhoAm 94*
Ortwerth, Joseph Robert 1956- *WhoAmP 93*
Orullian, B. LaRae 1933- *WhoWest 94*
Orvieto, Laura 1876-1953 *BlmGWL*
Orville, Albert D' 1621-1662 *WhWE*
Orville, Richard Edmonds 1936- *WhoAm 94*
Orvin, George Henry 1922- *WhoScEn 94*
Orwell, George 1903-1950 *BlmGEL [port], EncSF 93, TwCLC 51 [port], TwCYAW*
Orwoll, Gregg S. K. 1926- *WhoAm 94, WhoAmL 94, WhoFI 94, WhoMW 93*
Orwoll, Robert Arvid 1940- *WhoAm 94*
Ory, Carlos Edmundo de 1923- *DcLB 134 [port]*
Ory, Edward d1973 *WhoHol 92*
Ory, Edward 1886-1973 *AfrAmAl 6*
Ory, Marcia G. 1950- *ConAu 141*
Ory, Robert L(ouis) 1925- *ConAu 142*
Oryshkevich, Roman Sviatoslav 1928- *WhoAm 94, WhoMW 93*
Orza, Vincent Frank 1950- *WhoFI 94*
Orzazekewski, Kasia d1956 *WhoHol 92*
Orze, Joseph John 1932- *WhoAmA 93*
Orzech, Ann Dorothy 1950- *WhoFI 94*
Orzel, Michael Dale 1952- *WhoAmL 94*
Orzel, Ronald F. 1934- *WhoMW 93*
Orzeszkowa, Eliza 1841-1910 *BlmGWL*
Osaki, Mark *DrAPF 93*
Osakwe, Christopher 1942- *WhoBlA 94*
Osar, Robert Leonard 1947- *WhoAmL 94*
Osato, Sono 1919- *IntDcB [port], WhoHol 92*
Osbaldeston, Gordon Francis 1930- *IntWW 93, WhoAm 94*
Osbeck, Kenneth W. 1924- *ConAu 41NR*
Osberg, Timothy M. 1955- *WhoAm 94, WhoScEn 94*
Osbey, Brenda Marie *DrAPF 93*
Osborn, Andrew d1985 *WhoHol 92*
Osborn, Ann George 1933- *WhoScEn 94*
Osborn, Bonita Genevieve 1941- *WhoFI 94*
Osborn, Carolyn *DrAPF 93*
Osborn, Clayton F. *WhoAmP 93*
Osborn, David (D.) 1923- *WrDr 94*
Osborn, Donald Robert 1929- *WhoAm 94*
Osborn, Elburt Franklin 1911- *WhoAm 94*
Osborn, Elodie C. (Mrs. Robert Osborn) 1911- *WhoAmA 93*
Osborn, Eric Francis 1922- *IntWW 93, WrDr 94*
Osborn, Frederic Adrian 1941- *Who 94*
Osborn, Guy A. 1936- *WhoAm 94, WhoFI 94*
Osborn, Henry Fairfield 1887-1969 *EnvEnc*
Osborn, Holly Ann 1959- *WhoMW 93*
Osborn, James Henshaw 1941- *WhoScEn 94*
Osborn, Janet Lynn 1952- *WhoMW 93*
Osborn, Joe Allen 1932- *WhoAmL 94*
Osborn, John (Holbrook) 1922- *Who 94*
Osborn, John David 1948- *WhoMW 93*
Osborn, John Jay *DrAPF 93*
Osborn, John Simcoe, Jr. 1926- *WhoAm 94*
Osborn, Jones *WhoAmP 93*
Osborn, June Elaine 1937- *WhoAm 94*
Osborn, Kenneth Louis 1946- *WhoMW 93*
Osborn, Kevin Russell 1951- *WhoAmA 93*
Osborn, Larry Lee 1943- *WhoMW 93*
Osborn, Leslie Andrewartha 1906- *WhoAm 94*
Osborn, Lyn d1958 *WhoHol 92*
Osborn, Malcolm Everett 1928- *WhoAmL 94*
Osborn, Mark Eliot 1950- *WhoMW 93*
Osborn, Marvin Griffing, Jr. 1922- *WhoAm 94*
Osborn, Mary Jane Merten 1927- *WhoAm 94*
Osborn, Nancy Jo 1950- *WhoMW 93*
Osborn, Ralph Stephen 1952- *WhoWest 94*
Osborn, Richard (Henry Danvers) 1958- *Who 94*
Osborn, Robert 1904- *WhoAmA 93*
Osborn, Robert Chesley 1904- *WhoAm 94*
Osborn, Ronald Edwin 1917- *WhoAm 94, WrDr 94*
Osborn, Sarah Haggar Wheaten 1714-1796 *BlmGWL*
Osborn, Simeon James 1958- *WhoWest 94*
Osborn, Terry Wayne 1943- *WhoAm 94*
Osborn, Theodore L., Jr. 1910- *WhoIns 94*
Osborn, Timothy Richard 1951- *WhoAm 94, WhoAmL 94*
Osborn, Torie 1950- *NewYTBS 93 [port]*
Osborn, William George 1925- *WhoAm 94*
Osborn, Hon. Lord 1937- *Who 94*
Osborne, Adrienne *NewGrDO*
Osborne, Alfred E., Jr. 1944- *WhoBlA 94*
Osborne, Anthony David 1935- *Who 94*
Osborne, Bud d1964 *WhoHol 92*
Osborne, Burl 1937- *WhoAm 94*
Osborne, Charles 1927- *WrDr 94*
Osborne, Charles (Thomas) 1927- *NewGrDO, Who 94*
Osborne, Clayton Henriquez 1945- *WhoBlA 94*
Osborne, Coles Alexander 1896- *Who 94*
Osborne, Conrad L(eon) 1934- *NewGrDO*
Osborne, Cynthia A. 1947- *WhoAmA 93*
Osborne, Cynthia Monteiro 1951- *WhoAmL 94*
Osborne, Daniel Lloyd 1946- *WhoScEn 94*
Osborne, David *EncSF 93*
Osborne, David 1935- *WrDr 94*
Osborne, Dee S. 1930- *WhoAm 94*
Osborne, Denis Gordon 1932- *IntWW 93, Who 94*
Osborne, Dorothy 1627-1695 *BlmGEL, BlmGWL*
Osborne, Douglas Leonard 1940- *Who 94*
Osborne, Earl Thomas 1920- *WhoAmP 93*
Osborne, Edward Beryl 1919- *WhoAmP 93*
Osborne, Elizabeth 1936- *WhoAmA 93*
Osborne, Ernest L. 1932- *WhoBlA 94*
Osborne, F. Edward 1925- *WhoAmP 93*
Osborne, Frederick Spring, Jr. 1940- *WhoAm 94*
Osborne, Gayla Marlene 1956- *WhoFI 94*
Osborne, Gayle Ann 1951- *WhoWest 94*
Osborne, George Delano 1938- *WhoAm 94*
Osborne, George H. *WhoAmP 93*
Osborne, Gregory *WhoAm 94*
Osborne, Gregory 1955- *IntWW 93*
Osborne, Gwendolyn Eunice 1949- *WhoBlA 94*
Osborne, Hamilton, Jr. 1943- *WhoAmL 94*
Osborne, Harold Wayne 1930- *WhoAm 94*
Osborne, Helena *Who 94*
Osborne, Herbert John 1897- *WhAm 10*
Osborne, Hugh Stancill 1918- *WhoBlA 94*
Osborne, James Alfred 1927- *WhoAm 94*
Osborne, James L. 1928- *WhoIns 94*
Osborne, James William 1928- *WhoAm 94*
Osborne, Jeffrey Linton 1948- *WhoBlA 94*
Osborne, John 1929- *BlmGEL, IntMPA 94, WhoHol 92*
Osborne, John (James) 1929- *ConDr 93, IntDcT 2, Who 94, WrDr 94*
Osborne, John Hampton 1945- *WhoMW 93*
Osborne, John James 1929- *IntWW 93*
Osborne, John Phillip 1951- *WhoAmA 93*
Osborne, John Walter 1927- *WhoAm 94*
Osborne, Kenneth Hilton *Who 94*
Osborne, Marie *WhoHol 92*
Osborne, MaryHelen 1936- *WhoMW 93*
Osborne, Mason Scott 1946- *WhoScEn 94*
Osborne, Michael John 1942- *Who 94*
Osborne, Michael Piers 1946- *WhoScEn 94*
Osborne, Miles *WhoHol 92*
Osborne, Milton (Edgeworth) 1936- *WrDr 94*
Osborne, Nigel 1948- *NewGrDO*
Osborne, Oliver Hilton 1931- *WhoBlA 94*
Osborne, Paul Douglas 1943- *WhoAm 94*
Osborne, Peter (George) 1943- *Who 94*
Osborne, Phillip Lee 1959- *WhoWest 94*
Osborne, Quinton Albert 1951- *WhoMW 93*
Osborne, Richard de Jongh 1934- *IntWW 93, WhoAm 94, WhoFI 94*
Osborne, Richard Hazelet 1920- *WhoAm 94*
Osborne, Richard Jay 1951- *WhoAm 94, WhoFI 94*
Osborne, Robert 1936- *Who 94*
Osborne, Robert Lee 1928- *WhoAmA 93*
Osborne, Robin William 1944- *WhoScEn 94*
Osborne, Roland d1920 *WhoHol 92*
Osborne, Ronald Walter 1946- *WhoAm 94*
Osborne, Scott B. 1949- *WhoAmL 94*
Osborne, Stanley de Jongh 1905- *WhoAm 94*
Osborne, Thomas Burr 1859-1929 *WorScD*
Osborne, Thomas Cramer 1927- *WhoAm 94*
Osborne, Thomas Joe 1942- *WhoWest 94*
Osborne, Thomas Walker 1961- *WhoWest 94*
Osborne, Tom 1937- *WhoAm 94*
Osborne, Trevor 1943- *Who 94*
Osborne, Vivienne d1961 *WhoHol 92*

Ostrom, Donald Irving 1939- WhoAmP 93
Ostrom, Douglas Roy 1946- WhoFI 94
Ostrom, Elinor 1933- WhoAm 94
Ostrom, Hans DrAPF 93
Ostrom, John H. 1928- WhoAm 94
Ostrom, Meredith Eggers 1930- WhoAm 94
Ostrom, Philip Gardner 1942- WhoWest 94
Ostrom, Thomas Marshall 1936- WhoAm 94
Ostrom, Vincent Alfred 1919- WhoAm 94, WhoMW 93
Ostromecki, Ronald Roman 1941- WhoMW 93
Ostroot, Timothy Vincent 1960- WhoAmL 94
Ostroski, Richard J. 1938- WhoMW 93
Ostrovsky, Alexander Nikolayevich 1823-1886 IntDcT 2, NewGrDO
Ostrovsky, Alexey 1953- WhoScEn 94
Ostrovsky, Mikhail Arkadievich 1935- IntWW 93
Ostrovsky, Victor 1949- ConAu 140
Ostrow, Andrew Alexander 1949- WhoAmL 94
Ostrow, Bonnie Susan 1940- WhoAmP 93
Ostrow, David Gene 1947- WhoMW 93
Ostrow, Jay Donald 1930- WhoScEn 94
Ostrow, Joanna DrAPF 93
Ostrow, Joseph W. 1933- WhoAm 94, WhoFI 94
Ostrow, Michael Jay 1934- WhoAmL 94
Ostrow, Richard David 1931- WhoAm 94
Ostrow, Ronald J. 1931- WrDr 94
Ostrow, Stephen Edward 1932- WhoAmA 93
Ostrow, Stuart WhoAm 94
Ostrow, Winston Alexander 1950- WhoAmL 94
Ostrower, Fayga 1920- IntWW 93
Ostrowski, Joan Lorraine Who 94
Ostrowski, Peter Phillip 1940- WhoScEn 94
Ostrum, Dean Gardner 1922- WhoAm 94
Ostry, Bernard 1927- WhoAm 94
Ostry, Sylvia WhoAm 94, WhoScEn 94
Ostry, Sylvia 1927- IntWW 93
Ostuni, Peter W. 1908-1992 WhoAmA 93N
Ostwald, Friedrich Wilhelm 1853-1932 WorScD
Ostwald, Martin 1922- WhoAm 94
Ostwald, Venice Eloise Varner 1928- WhoWest 94
O'Sullevan, Peter John 1918- Who 94
O'Sullivan, Arthur d1981 WhoHol 92
O'Sullivan, Brendan Patrick 1930- WhoAm 94, WhoAmL 94
O'Sullivan, Clifford 1897- WhAm 10
O'Sullivan, Daniel Edward 1929-1990 WhAm 10
O'Sullivan, Daniel Joseph 1940- WhoAmA 93
O'Sullivan, Denis 1868-1908 NewGrDO
O'Sullivan, Eugene Henry 1942- WhoAm 94
O'Sullivan, Gerald Joseph 1941- WhoMW 93
O'Sullivan, Gerry 1959- WrDr 94
O'Sullivan, James 1917- Who 94
O'Sullivan, John Who 94
O'Sullivan, John 1878-1955 NewGrDO
O'Sullivan, John 1942- IntWW 93
O'Sullivan, (Carrol Austin) John (Naish) 1915- Who 94
O'Sullivan, Judith Roberta 1942- WhoAmA 93, WhoAmL 94
O'Sullivan, Kevin WhoAmP 93
O'Sullivan, Kevin P. 1928- IntMPA 94
O'Sullivan, Lynda Troutman 1952- WhoAm 94, WhoAmL 94
O'Sullivan, Mary Ann WhoAmP 93
O'Sullivan, Mary F. DrAPF 93
O'Sullivan, Maureen 1911- IntMPA 94, WhoHol 92
O'Sullivan, Michael d1971 WhoHol 92
O'Sullivan, Michael Anthony 1960- WhoScEn 94
O'Sullivan, Patrick Edmund 1937- Who 94
O'Sullivan, Paul Kevin 1938- WhoAm 94
O'Sullivan, Richard 1943- WhoHol 92
O'Sullivan, Richard John 1938-1990 WhAm 10
O'Sullivan, Roger Francis 1946- WhoAmP 93
O'Sullivan, Sally Angela 1949- Who 94
O'Sullivan, Thomas J. 1940- WhoAm 94
O'Sullivan, Timothy 1945- WrDr 94
O'Sullivan, Timothy Patrick WhoAmP 93
O'Sullivan, Tony d1920 WhoHol 92
O'Sullivan, Vincent (Gerald) 1937- ConDr 93
O'Sullivan, Vincent (Gerard) 1937- WrDr 94
Osumi, Kenichiro 1904- IntWW 93
Osumi, Masato 1942- WhoFI 94, WhoScEn 94
Osuna, Jess 1928- WhoHol 92
Osuna, Rafe 1938-1969 BuCMET
Osunkhirhine, Pierre Paul fl. 1830-1849 EncNAR
Osver, Arthur 1912- WhoAm 94, WhoAmA 93
Oswaks, Roy Michael 1945- WhoScEn 94
Oswald, Delmont Richard 1940- WhoWest 94
Oswald, Eleazer 1755-1795 AmRev, WhAmRev
Oswald, Ernest John DrAPF 93
Oswald, George Charles WhoAm 94
Oswald, Gerd d1989 WhoHol 92
Oswald, James Marlin 1935- WhoFI 94
Oswald, John Henry 1949- WhoAm 94
Oswald, John (Julian) Robertson 1933- IntWW 93
Oswald, Joseph Michael 1959- WhoAmL 94
Oswald, (John) Julian (Robertson) 1933- Who 94
Oswald, Lori Jo DrAPF 93
Oswald, Neville Christopher 1910- Who 94
Oswald, Richard 1705-1784 WhAmRev
Oswald, Richard Anthony 1941- Who 94
Oswald, Robert Bernard 1932- WhoAm 94
Oswald, Rudolph A. 1932- WhoAm 94, WhoFI 94
Oswald, Stanton S. 1927- WhoAm 94
Oswald, William Jack 1927- WhoFI 94
Oswald, William Richard Michael 1934- Who 94
Oswalda, Ossi d1948 WhoHol 92
Oswalt, Aria Lucinda 1953- WhoMW 93
Oswalt, Bill G. 1933- WhoIns 94
Oswalt, Edna Rickey 1897- WhAm 10
Osyczka, Bohdan Danny WhoAmA 93
Osze, Andrew E. 1909- WhoAmA 93
Oszurek, Paul John 1959- WhoScEn 94
Ota, Dean 1950- WhoAsA 94
Ota, Henry Yasushi 1942- WhoAmL 94, WhoAsA 94
Ota, Isaac I. 1943- WhoAsA 94
Ota, Mabel Takako 1916- WhoAsA 94
Ota, Roy Tsuneo 1942- WhoWest 94
Otaka, Tadaaki 1947- IntWW 93
Otaka, Yoshiko 1920- WhoWomW 91
Otani, June 1934- WhoAmA 93
Otani, Mike 1945- WhoFI 94, WhoScEn 94
Otani, Sachio 1924- IntWW 93
Otava, Zdenek 1902-1980 NewGrDO
Otchakovsky-Laurens, Paul 1944- IntWW 93
Oteiba, Mana Saeed al- 1946- IntWW 93
Otenasek, Mildred 1914- WhoAmP 93
Otero, Agustin F. 1932- WhoHisp 94
Otero, Antonio Jacinto 1938- WhoHisp 94
Otero, Armando J. 1968- WhoFI 94
Otero, Blas de 1916-1979 DcLB 134 [port]
Otero, Carmen 1933- WhoHisp 94
Otero, Felicia A. 1956- WhoHisp 94
Otero, Ingrid 1959- WhoHisp 94
Otero, Jack 1934- WhoAmP 93
Otero, James WhoHisp 94
Otero, Joaquin Francisco 1934- WhoHisp 94
Otero, José Alejandro 1926- WhoHisp 94
Otero, José U. 1930- WhoHisp 94
Otero, Joseph A. 1926- WhoHisp 94
Otero, Richard J. 1939- WhoHisp 94
Otero, Rolando 1957- WhoHisp 94
Otero De Ramos, Mercedes WhoAmP 93
Otero Rosario, Ismael WhoHisp 94
Otero-Smart, Ingrid 1959- WhoHisp 94
Otescu, Ion Nonna 1888-1940 NewGrDO
Otey, Flem B., III 1935- WhoBlA 94
Otey, Orlando 1925- WhoAm 94
Othersen, Cheryl Lee 1948- WhoFI 94
Othersen, Henry Biemann, Jr. 1930- WhoAm 94
Othman, Abdul Manan bin 1935- IntWW 93
Othman Bin Wok 1924- IntWW 93
Othmer, Donald Frederick 1904- IntWW 93, WhoAm 94, WhoFI 94, WhoScEn 94
Otho, Henry d1940 WhoHol 92
Otho de Grandson, Sir c. 1238-1328 DcNaB MP
Othon, Arthur B. 1949- WhoHisp 94
Oths, Richard Philip 1935- WhoAm 94
Otieno-Ayim, Larban Allan 1940- WhoBlA 94
Otis, Amos Joseph 1947- WhoBlA 94
Otis, Arthur Brooks 1913- WhoAm 94
Otis, Carre WhoHol 92
Otis, Elisha Graves 1811-1861 WorInv
Otis, Elita Proctor d1927 WhoHol 92
Otis, Glenn Kay 1929- WhoAm 94
Otis, Jack 1923- WhoAm 94
Otis, James 1725-1783 WhAmRev [port]
Otis, James, Jr. 1931- WhoAm 94
Otis, John James 1922- WhoFI 94, WhoScEn 94
Otis, Mary WhoHol 92
Otis, Michael John 1949- WhoAmP 93
Otis, Samuel Allyne 1740-1814 WhAmRev
Otis, Todd H. 1945- WhoAmP 93
Otis-Lewis, Alexis WhoBlA 94
Otkan, John d1942 WhoHol 92
Otlowski, George J. 1912- WhoAmP 93
Otman Assed, Mohamed 1922- IntWW 93
Otokpa, Augustine Emmanuel Ogaba, Jr. 1945- WhoScEn 94
Otomo, Katsuhiro 1954- EncSF 93
Otomo, Stacy Akio 1955- WhoWest 94
O'Toole fl. 1870- EncNAR
O'Toole, Allan Thomas 1925- WhoAm 94
O'Toole, Annette 1953- IntMPA 94, WhoHol 92
O'Toole, Austin Martin 1935- WhoAm 94, WhoAmL 94, WhoFI 94
O'Toole, Edward Michael 1935- WhoAmL 94
O'Toole, Francis J. 1944- WhoAm 94, WhoAmL 94
O'Toole, G(eorge) J(oseph) A(nthony) 1936- ConAu 141
O'Toole, James Joseph 1945- WhoAm 94
O'Toole, Jim WhoAmP 93
O'Toole, John Dudley 1921- WhoAm 94
O'Toole, John E. 1929- WhoAm 94, WhoFI 94
O'Toole, John Peter 1962- WhoAmL 94
O'Toole, Joseph William 1931- WhoWest 94
O'Toole, Judith Hansen 1953- ConAu 142
O'Toole, Kate 1960- WhoHol 92
O'Toole, Marianne Therese 1963- WhoAmL 94
O'Toole, Marilyn B. 1944- WhoAmL 94
O'Toole, Martin William 1957- WhoAmL 94
O'Toole, Patrick Francis 1948- WhoAmP 93
O'Toole, Peter 1932- IntMPA 94, WhoAm 94, WhoHol 92
O'Toole, (Seamus) Peter 1932- Who 94
O'Toole, Peter Seamus 1932- IntWW 93
O'Toole, Robert John, II 1951- WhoWest 94
O'Toole, Robert Joseph 1941- WhoAm 94, WhoFI 94
O'Toole, Stanley IntMPA 94
O'Toole, Terrence J. 1946- WhoAm 94, WhoAmL 94
O'Toole, Timothy T. 1955- WhoFI 94
O'Toole, Timothy Terrence 1955- WhoAmL 94
Otooni, Monde A. 1933- WhoScEn 94
Otorowski, Christopher Lee 1953- WhoAmL 94
Otoshi, Tom Yasuo 1931- WhoScEn 94, WhoWest 94
Ots, Charles 1776-1845 NewGrDO
Ots, Georg (Karlovich) 1920-1975 NewGrDO
Otsason, Rein 1931- IntWW 93
Otstott, Charles Paddock 1937- WhoAm 94
Otsuka, Hideaki 1947- WhoScEn 94
Otsuka, Kanji 1935- WhoScEn 94
Otsuka, Yuji 1929- IntWW 93
Ott, Alexander Reginald 1931- WhoAmP 93
Ott, Alvin Robert, Jr. 1949- WhoAmP 93
Ott, Bob E. WhoAmP 93
Ott, David Michael 1952- WhoAm 94, WhoScEn 94, WhoWest 94
Ott, David N. 1937- WhoAmP 93
Ott, Fred d1936 WhoHol 92
Ott, George William, Jr. 1932- WhoAm 94
Ott, Gil DrAPF 93
Ott, Gilbert Russell, Jr. 1943- WhoAm 94, WhoAmL 94, WhoFI 94
Ott, Jack M. 1931- WhoAm 94
Ott, James Forgan 1935- WhoAm 94
Ott, Jennifer Johanna 1961- WhoMW 93
Ott, Jerry 1947- WhoAmA 93
Ott, John Harlow 1944- WhoAm 94
Ott, Karl Otto 1925- WhoAm 94, WhoScEn 94
Ott, Kent A. 1955- WhoAmP 93
Ott, M. Scott 1953- WhoMW 93
Ott, Michael Duane 1948- WhoAm 94
Ott, Michael E. 1945- WhoAmA 93
Ott, Richard B. 1897- WhAm 10
Ott, Robert William 1934- WhoAmA 93
Ott, Sabina 1955- WhoAmA 93
Ott, Walter Richard 1943- WhoAm 94
Ott, Warrene WhoHol 92
Ott, Wayne Robert 1940- WhoAm 94, WhoScEn 94, WhoWest 94
Ott, Wendell Lorenz 1942- WhoAm 94, WhoAmA 93
Ottani, Bernardo 1736-1827 NewGrDO
Ottani, Gaetano c. 1736-1808 NewGrDO
Ottawa, Archbishop of Who 94
Ottawa, Archbishop of 1931- Who 94
Ottaway, Cynda C. 1953- WhoAmL 94
Ottaway, James 1908- WhoHol 92
Ottaway, James Haller, Jr. 1938- WhoAm 94, WhoFI 94
Ottaway, Marina (Seassaro) 1943- ConAu 142
Ottaway, Richard Geoffrey James 1945- Who 94
Otte, A. Ray 1929- WhoIns 94
Otte, Carl 1923- WhoAmP 93
Otte, Clifford 1933- WhoAmP 93, WhoMW 93
Otte, Henri Rolf d1930 WhoHol 92
Otte, Paul John 1943- WhoAm 94
Otte, Paul Joseph 1923- WhoAmP 93
Otte, Ray M., Jr. 1946- WhoAmP 93
Otte, Ruth L. WhoAm 94
Otte, Stephen B. 1943- WhoIns 94
Ottein, Angeles 1895-1981 NewGrDO
Otten, Arthur Edward, Jr. 1930- WhoAmL 94, WhoWest 94
Otten, Charlotte F(ennema) 1926- WrDr 94
Otten, Charlotte Fennema 1926- WhoMW 93
Otten, Don 1921- BasBi
Otten, Kathleen Kay 1955- WhoMW 93
Otten, Thomas WhoAm 94
Ottenberg, James Simon 1918- WhoAm 94
Ottenberg, Simon 1923- WhoAm 94, WhoWest 94, WrDr 94
Ottendorf, Nicolas Dietrich WhAmRev
Ottenheimer, Albert M. d1980 WhoHol 92
Ottenheimer, Harriet Joseph 1941- WhoMW 93
Ottensmeyer, David Joseph 1930- WhoAm 94, WhoScEn 94
Ottensmeyer, Peter 1939- WhoAm 94
Ottensoser, Samuel F. 1942- WhoAmL 94
Ottenweller, Albert Henry 1916- WhoAm 94
Otter, Anne-Sofie von 1955- NewGrDO
Otter, Clement Leroy 1942- WhoAm 94, WhoAmP 93, WhoWest 94
Otter, John Martin, III 1930- WhoAm 94
Otter, Victor Charles 1914- Who 94
Otterbacher, Eric Wayne 1954- WhoMW 93
Otterbein, Philip Wilhelm 1726-1813 DcAmReB 2
Otterbourg, Robert Kenneth 1930- WhoAm 94
Otterholt, Barry L. 1953- WhoAm 94
Otterman, Kenneth James 1949- WhoFI 94
Otterman, Robert James 1932- WhoAmP 93
Otterson, David V. 1953- WhoAmL 94
Otteson, Schuyler Franklin 1917- WhoAm 94
Ottewill, Ronald Harry 1927- IntWW 93, Who 94
Otth, Edward John, Jr. 1925- WhoAm 94
Ottiano, John William 1926- WhoAmA 93
Ottiano, Rafaela d1942 WhoHol 92
Ottinger, Edward E. 1934- WhoAmP 93
Ottinger, Richard Lawrence 1929- WhoAmP 93
Ottino, Jolou Trujillo 1963- WhoHisp 94
Ottino, Julio Mario 1951- WhoAm 94
Ottley, Athniel C. 1941- WhoAmP 93
Ottley, Austin H. 1918- WhoBlA 94
Ottley, Jerold Don 1934- WhoAm 94, WhoWest 94
Ottley, Neville 1926- WhoBlA 94
Ottley, Roi (Vincent) 1906-1960 BlkWr 2
Ottman, John Budlong 1922- WhoFI 94
Ottmann, Klaus 1954- WhoAmA 93
Otto, Albert Dean 1939- WhoMW 93
Otto, Arthur d1918 WhoHol 92
Otto, Barry WhoHol 92
Otto, Bodo 1711-1787 AmRev, WhAmRev
Otto, Charles Edward 1946- WhoAm 94, WhoFI 94
Otto, Frank WhoHol 92
Otto, Fred Bishop 1934- WhoScEn 94
Otto, Frederick Joseph 1948- WhoAmL 94
Otto, Frei P(aul) 1925- IntWW 93
Otto, George John 1904- WhoAm 94
Otto, Glenn E. 1924- WhoAmP 93
Otto, Harry Claude 1957- WhoWest 94
Otto, Henry d1952 WhoHol 92
Otto, Ingolf Helgi Elfried 1920- WhoFI 94
Otto, James Daniel 1949- WhoAmL 94
Otto, Jean Hammond 1925- WhoAm 94
Otto, Jim ProFbHF [port]
Otto, John Edward 1955- WhoFI 94
Otto, John Francis, Jr. 1937- WhoMW 93
Otto, John Henry 1946- WhoAmL 94
Otto, Kenneth Lee 1930- WhoAm 94, WhoFI 94
Otto, Lawrence James 1941- WhoIns 94
Otto, Linda McHenry 1941- WhoMW 93
Otto, Lisa 1919- NewGrDO
Otto, Lon DrAPF 93
Otto, Lon 1948- WrDr 94

Otto, Ludwig 1934- *WhoFI 94*
Otto, Luther B(enedict) 1937- *WrDr 94*
Otto, Margaret Amelia 1937- *WhoAm 94*
Otto, Mary Castrop 1920- *WhoAmP 93*
Otto, Melitta 1842-1893 *NewGrDO*
Otto, Miranda *WhoHol 92*
Otto, Nikolaus August 1832-1891 *WorInv*
Otto, Paul d1943 *WhoHol 92*
Otto, Richard E. 1928- *WhoIns 94*
Otto, Teo 1904-1968 *NewGrDO*
Otto, Wayne Raymond 1931- *WhoAm 94*
Otto, Whitney 1955- *ConAu 140*
Ottoboni, Pietro 1667-1740 *NewGrDO*
Ottolina, Rhona *WhoWomW 91*
Ottoman, Richard Edward 1910- *WhAm 10*
Ottomme, Robert *WhoAmP 93*
Otton, Geoffrey (John) 1927- *Who 94*
Otton, Philip (Howard) 1933- *Who 94*
Otton, William G. d1930 *WhoHol 92*
Otto-Peters, Louise 1819-1895 *BlmGWL, DcLB 129 [port]*
Ottoson, Gary C. 1938- *WhoAmL 94*
Ottoson, Howard Warren 1920- *WhoAm 94*
Otto the Great, I 912-973 *HisWorL [port]*
Otts, James K. 1930- *WhoAmP 93*
Ottum, Bob 1925?-1986 *EncSF 93*
Ottumwa, Salvador 1945- *WhoHisp 94*
Ottwein, Merrill William George 1929- *WhoMW 93*
Otu, Joseph Obi 1957- *WhoScEn 94*
Otudeko, Adebisi Olusoga 1935- *WhoBlA 94*
Otumfuo Nana Opoku Ware, II 1919- *IntWW 93*
Otunga, Maurice *Who 94*
Otunga, Maurice 1923- *IntWW 93*
Otvos, Laszlo Istvan, Jr. 1955- *WhoScEn 94*
Otway, Thomas 1652-1685 *BlmGEL, IntDcT 2*
Otwell, Ralph Maurice 1926- *WhoAm 94*
Otwell, Ronnie Ray 1929- *IntMPA 94*
Ou, Ching-Nan 1945- *WhoAsA 94*
Ou, Hsien-Wang 1949- *WhoAsA 94*
Ou, Jing-hsiung James 1954- *WhoWest 94*
Ou, Shukong 1952- *WhoAsA 94*
Ou, Thuok 1940- *WhoAsA 94*
Ouattara, Alassane D. 1942- *IntWW 93*
Oubre, Hayward Louis *WhoAmA 93, WhoBlA 94*
Oubre, Linda Seiffert 1958- *WhoBlA 94*
Ouchi, Tsutomu 1918- *IntWW 93*
Ouchi, William George 1943- *WhoAm 94*
Oudart, Felix d1956 *WhoHol 92*
Ouderkirk, Mason James 1953- *WhoAmL 94*
Oudin, Eugene (Esperance) 1858-1894 *NewGrDO*
Oudinot, Nicolas-Medard *NewGrDO*
Oudney, Walter 1790-1824 *WhWE*
Oudrid (y Segura), Cristobal (Domingo) 1825-1877 *NewGrDO*
Oueddei, Goukouni 1944- *IntWW 93*
Ouedraogo, Gerard Kango 1925- *IntWW 93*
Ouedraogo, Idrissa *IntWW 93*
Ouedraogo, Idrissa 1954?- *CurBio 93 [port]*
Ouellet, Andre 1939- *IntWW 93*
Ouellette, Bernard Charles 1936- *WhoAm 94*
Ouellette, Robert O. 1949- *WhoAmP 93*
Oughton, James Henry, Jr. 1913- *WhoMW 93*
Oughton, Jerrie 1937- *SmATA 76*
Oughton, John Raymond Charles 1952- *Who 94*
Oughton, Winifred d1956 *WhoHol 92*
Oughtred, William *WorInv*
Ouida 1839-1908 *BlmGEL, BlmGWL*
Ouimet, Cecily Ramos *WhoHisp 94*
Ouimet, Gilles Philippe 1944- *WhoFI 94*
Oujesky, Helen M. 1930- *WhoAm 94*
Ould, Chris 1959?- *EncSF 93*
Ould Mohamed Mahmoud, Mohamedou 1944- *WhoAm 94*
Oulton, Brian 1908- *WhoHol 92*
Oulton, (Antony) Derek (Maxwell) 1927- *Who 94*
Oulton, Wilfrid Ewart 1911- *Who 94*
Oumarou, Ide 1937- *IntWW 93*
Oumarou, Mamane *IntWW 93*
Oumlil, Abderrahman Ben 1957- *WhoFI 94, WhoMW 93*
Oung Mean d1993 *NewYTBS 93*
Ounjian, Marilyn J. 1947- *WhoAm 94*
Ounsted, John 1919- *Who 94*
Ourada, Thomas D. 1958- *WhoAmP 93*
Ourant, Edwin L. 1933- *WhoFI 94*
Ourisson, Guy 1926- *IntWW 93*
Oursler, Fulton, Jr. 1932- *WhoAm 94*
Oursler, Tony 1957- *WhoAmA 93*
Oury, Gerard 1919- *WhoHol 92*
Ouseley, Duncan Brian Walter 1950- *Who 94*
Ouseley, William Norman 1935- *WhoMW 93*
Ousley, Harold Lomax 1929- *WhoBlA 94*
Ousmane, Sembene 1923- *ConWorW 93, IntWW 93*
Ouspenskaya, Maria d1949 *WhoHol 92*
Oussani, James John 1920- *WhoAm 94, WhoFI 94*
Ou Tangliang 1914- *WhoPRCh 91 [port]*
Outcalt, David Lewis 1935- *WhoAm 94, WhoMW 93*
Outcalt, Merlin Brewer 1928- *WhoMW 93*
Outerbridge, Mary 1852-1886 *BuCMET*
Outerino, Felix C. *Who 94*
Outhuok, T. 1940- *WhoAsA 94*
Outhwaite, (Richard) William 1949- *WrDr 94*
Outka, Gene Harold 1937- *WhoAm 94*
Outland, Orland T 1923- *WhoWest 94*
Outland, Wendy Helen 1953- *WhoAmA 93*
Outlaw, Arthur R. 1926- *WhoAmP 93*
Outlaw, John d1993 *NewYTBS 93*
Outlaw, Lucius T., Jr. 1944- *WhoBlA 94*
Outlaw, Patricia Anne *WhoBlA 94*
Outlaw, Sitnotra 1957- *WhoBlA 94*
Outlaw, Warren Gregory 1951- *WhoBlA 94*
Outler, Albert Cook 1908- *WhAm 10*
Outler, Albert Cook 1908-1989 *DcAmReB 2*
Outram, Alan James 1937- *Who 94*
Outram, Dorinda 1949- *IntWW 93, WrDr 94*
Outten, Elmer Stuart, Jr. 1944- *WhoAmP 93*
Outterbridge, John Wilfred 1933- *AfrAmAl 6, WhoAmA 93, WhoBlA 94*
Ouvrieu, Jean-Bernard 1939- *IntWW 93*
Ouwehand, William 1932- *WhoWest 94*
Ouyang Chuping *WhoPRCh 91*
Ouyang Shan 1908- *IntWW 93, WhoPRCh 91 [port]*
Ouyang Wen 1912- *WhoPRCh 91 [port]*
Ouyang Zhongmou *WhoPRCh 91*
Ouzts, Dale Keith 1941- *WhoMW 93*
Ovaert, Timothy Christopher 1959- *WhoScEn 94*
Ovard, A. R. 1921- *WhoAmP 93*
Ovard, Glen F. 1928- *WrDr 94*
Ovbiagele, Helen *BlmGWL*
Ovchinikov, Vladimir Pavlovich 1958- *IntWW 93*
Ovchinnikov, Lev Nikolayevich 1913- *IntWW 93*
Ovchinnikov, Yuri Anatoliyevich 1934-1988 *WhAm 10*
Ove, Peter 1930- *WhoAm 94*
Ovelmen, Richard J. 1952- *WhoAmL 94*
Ovenden, Graham Stuart 1943- *IntWW 93*
Ovenden, John Frederick 1942- *Who 94*
Ovens, Patrick John 1922- *Who 94*
Over, Jana Thais 1956- *WhoScEn 94*
Overall, Gene 1947- *WhoMW 93*
Overall, James Carney, Jr. 1937- *WhoAm 94*
Overall, John (Wallace) 1913- *Who 94*
Overall, John E. 1929- *WhoAm 94*
Overall, Manard 1939- *WhoBlA 94*
Overall, Park 1957?- *ConTFT 11, WhoHol 92*
Overall, Richard Palmer 1946- *WhoWest 94*
Overbea, Luix Virgil 1923- *WhoBlA 94*
Overbeck, Bud d1970 *WhoHol 92*
Overbeck, Egon 1918- *IntWW 93*
Overbeck, Gene Edward 1929- *WhoAm 94, WhoFI 94*
Overbeek, Jan Theodoor Gerard 1911- *IntWW 93*
Overberg, Paul Joseph 1926- *WhoAm 94*
Overbey, Charles Brown, Jr. 1915- *WhoMW 93*
Overbury, (Henry) Colin (Barry) 1931- *Who 94*
Overbury, Thomas 1581-1613 *BlmGEL*
Overby, Charles Frederick 1959- *WhoAmL 94*
Overby, Lacy Rasco 1920- *WhoAm 94*
Overby, Osmund Rudolf 1931- *WhoAm 94*
Overby, Veriti Page 1964- *WhoScEn 94*
Overbye, Dennis 1944- *ConAu 142*
Overbye, Thomas Jeffrey 1960- *WhoMW 93*
Overcash, Michael Ray 1944- *WhoScEn 94*
Overcash, Reece A., Jr. 1926- *WhoAm 94, WhoFI 94*
Overduin, Henk 1943-1988 *WhAm 10*
Overend, (William) George 1921- *Who 94*
Overend, William George 1921- *WrDr 94*
Overfelt, Clarence Lahugh 1935- *WhoAmL 94*
Overgaard, Mary Ann 1951- *WhoAmL 94*
Overgaard, Mitchell Jersild 1931- *WhoAm 94*
Overgaard, Robert Milton 1929- *WhoAm 94*
Overgaard, Willard Michele 1925- *WhoAm 94, WhoWest 94*
Overhauser, Albert Warner 1925- *IntWW 93, WhoAm 94, WhoMW 93, WhoScEn 94*
Overholser, Wayne D. 1906- *WrDr 94*
Overholt, Hugh Robert 1933- *WhoAm 94, WhoAmL 94*
Overholt, Miles Harvard 1921- *WhoFI 94, WhoWest 94*
Overholt, Miles Harvard, III 1948- *WhoAm 94, WhoFI 94*
Overholtzer, Phyllis Jo 1954- *WhoWest 94*
Overhouse, Madge Virginia 1924- *WhoAmP 93*
Overington, John 1946- *WhoAmP 93*
Overlan, Lawrence A. 1949- *WhoAmP 93*
Overland, Carlton Edward 1942- *WhoAmA 93*
Overlock, Frances Frost 1926- *WhoAmP 93*
Overlock, Willard Joseph, Jr. 1946- *WhoFI 94*
Overman, Dean Lee 1943- *WhoAm 94, WhoAmL 94*
Overman, Edwin Scott 1922- *WhoIns 94*
Overman, Glenn Delbert 1916- *WhoAm 94*
Overman, Jack d1950 *WhoHol 92*
Overman, Jerry Grey 1949- *WhoAm 94*
Overman, Lynne d1943 *WhoHol 92*
Overmyer, Daniel Lee 1935- *WhoAm 94*
Overmyer, Eric 1951- *ConDr 93*
Overmyer, Robert Franklyn 1936- *WhoScEn 94*
Overmyer, Scott Paul 1952- *WhoMW 93*
Overn, Alfred Victor 1893- *WhAm 10*
Overschmidt, Francis S. *WhoAmP 93*
Overseth, Oliver Enoch 1928- *WhoAm 94*
Overskei, David 1948- *WhoScEn 94*
Overson, Brent C. 1950- *WhoAmP 93*
Overstreet, Bonaro (Wilkinson) 1902-1985 *ConAu 142*
Overstreet, Everett Louis *WhoBlA 94*
Overstreet, Harry L. 1938- *WhoBlA 94*
Overstreet, James Wilkins *WhoScEn 94*
Overstreet, Morris *WhoBlA 94*
Overstreet, Raymond D. 1942- *WhoAmP 93*
Overton, Ben F. 1926- *WhoAmP 93*
Overton, Benjamin Frederick 1926- *WhoAm 94, WhoAmL 94*
Overton, Betty Jean 1949- *WhoBlA 94*
Overton, Bruce 1941- *WhoAm 94*
Overton, Edwin Dean 1939- *WhoWest 94*
Overton, Evart d1949 *WhoHol 92*
Overton, Frank d1967 *WhoHol 92*
Overton, George Washington 1918- *WhoAm 94, WhoAmL 94, WhoFI 94*
Overton, Hall 1920-1972 *NewGrDO*
Overton, James Martin 1942- *WhoMW 93*
Overton, Jane Vincent Harper 1919- *WhoAm 94*
Overton, Jenny (Margaret Mary) 1942- *WrDr 94*
Overton, Jerry 1933- *WhoAmP 93*
Overton, John Blair 1949- *WhoAmL 94*
Overton, Lewis Marvin, Jr. 1937- *WhoWest 94*
Overton, Marcus Lee 1943- *WhoAm 94*
Overton, Max *EncSF 93*
Overton, Norris W. 1926- *AfrAmG [port]*
Overton, Patrick Miles 1948- *WhoMW 93*
Overton, Richard Cleghorn 1907-1988 *WhAm 10*
Overton, Rick *WhoHol 92*
Overton, Ron *DrAPF 93*
Overton, Santford Vance 1949- *WhoScEn 94*
Overton, Volma Robert 1924- *WhoBlA 94*
Overton, William Samuels 1949- *WhoFI 94*
Overton, William Ward, Jr. 1897- *WhAm 10*
Overweg, Adolf 1822-1852 *WhWE*
Overweg, Norbert Ido Albert *WhoScEn 94*
Overy, Paul (Vivian) 1940- *WrDr 94*
Ovesen, Ellis *ConAu 42NR, DrAPF 93*
Oveson, W. Val 1952- *WhoAmP 93*
Oveson, Wilford Val 1952- *WhoAm 94, WhoWest 94*
Ovett, Stephen Michael 1955- *IntWW 93*
Ovey, George d1951 *WhoHol 92*
Oviatt, Larry Andrew 1939- *WhoWest 94*
Ovid 43BC-17AD *BlmGEL, NewGrDO*
Oviedo, Marco Antonio 1948- *WhoHisp 94*
Oviedo, Ollie O. 1956- *WhoHisp 94*
Oviedo y Valdez, Gonzalo Fernandez De 1478-1557 *WhWE*
Ovitsky, Steven Alan 1947- *WhoAm 94, WhoMW 93*
Ovitz, Judy *WhoHol 92*
Ovitz, Michael 1946- *IntMPA 94, IntWW 93*
Ovitz, Michael S. 1946- *WhoAm 94*
Ovsenik, Edward Charles 1956- *WhoAmL 94*
Ovshinsky, Stanford 1922- *WorInv*
Ovshinsky, Stanford Robert 1922- *WhoAm 94*
Ovsiew, Fred 1949- *WhoMW 93*
Ovstedal, Barbara *WrDr 94*
Owada, Hisashi 1932- *IntWW 93*
Owada, Masako *NewYTBS 93 [port]*
Owano, Mary Beth 1963- *WhoMW 93*
Owe, Aage Williand 1894- *WhAm 10*
Oweiss, Ibrahim Mohamed 1931- *WhoAm 94*
Owen, Baron 1938- *IntWW 93, Who 94*
Owen, Alun 1919- *Who 94*
Owen, Alun 1925- *IntMPA 94, WhoHol 92*
Owen, Alun (Davies) 1925- *ConDr 93, Who 94, WrDr 94*
Owen, Amy 1944- *WhoAm 94*
Owen, Annie 1949- *SmATA 75*
Owen, Aron 1919- *Who 94*
Owen, Bernard Laurence 1925- *Who 94*
Owen, Bill 1914- *ConTFT 11, IntMPA 94*
Owen, Bill 1915- *WhoHol 92*
Owen, Brad *WhoAmP 93*
Owen, Bruce Douglas 1927- *WhoScEn 94*
Owen, Carol Thompson 1944- *WhoWest 94*
Owen, Catherine Dale d1965 *WhoHol 92*
Owen, Cecil d1928 *WhoHol 92*
Owen, Charles 1915- *WrDr 94*
Owen, Christina L. 1946- *WhoAm 94*
Owen, Claude Bernard, Jr. 1945- *WhoAm 94, WhoAmL 94, WhoFI 94*
Owen, Clive *WhoHol 92*
Owen, Cynthia Carol 1943- *WhoFI 94*
Owen, Dave 1931- *WhoAmP 93*
Owen, David *Who 94*
Owen, David 1940- *WhoAmP 93*
Owen, David 1955- *WrDr 94*
Owen, David 1968- *WhoWest 94*
Owen, (Alfred) David 1936- *Who 94*
Owen, David (Anthony Llewellyn) 1938- *WrDr 94*
Owen, David Harold Owen 1933- *Who 94*
Owen, David Lanyon Ll. *Who 94*
Owen, Dean *EncSF 93*
Owen, Deborah K. *WhoAm 94, WhoFI 94*
Owen, Derek 1931- *WhoAmP 93*
Owen, Derwyn (Randulph Grier) 1914- *WrDr 94*
Owen, Douglas David Roy 1922- *WrDr 94*
Owen, Duncan Shaw, Jr. 1935- *WhoAm 94, WhoScEn 94*
Owen, Edmund 1931- *WrDr 94*
Owen, Edwin 1910- *Who 94*
Owen, Eileen *DrAPF 93*
Owen, Frank 1939- *WhoAmA 93*
Owen, Fred Wynne 1928- *WhoAm 94*
Owen, Frederick 1869-1959 *WhoAmA 93N*
Owen, Gareth 1922- *Who 94*
Owen, Gareth 1936- *ChlLR 31 [port]*
Owen, (John) Gareth 1936- *WrDr 94*
Owen, Garry d1951 *WhoHol 92*
Owen, Gary 1944- *WhoAmP 93*
Owen, Geoffrey (David) 1934- *IntWW 93, Who 94*
Owen, Gerald Victor 1922- *Who 94*
Owen, Gilbert Eugene 1949- *WhoWest 94*
Owen, Gordon Michael William 1937- *Who 94*
Owen, Granville *WhoHol 92*
Owen, H. Martyn 1929- *WhoAm 94, WhoAmL 94, WhoFI 94*
Owen, Harry 1911- *Who 94*
Owen, Henry 1920- *WhoAm 94*
Owen, Henry David 1920- *WhoAmP 93*
Owen, Henry Robert, IV 1958- *WhoMW 93*
Owen, Herbert Rodney 1935- *WhoAm 94*
Owen, Howard (Wayne) 1949- *ConAu 141*
Owen, Hugh (Bernard Pilkington) 1915- *Who 94*
Owen, Hugo Dudley C. *Who 94*
Owen, Idris Wyn 1912- *Who 94*
Owen, Ivor Henri 1930- *Who 94*
Owen, James Churchill 1901- *WhAm 10*
Owen, James Churchill, Jr. 1926- *WhoAm 94*
Owen, James Paige 1942- *WhoAmP 93*
Owen, John 1929- *WhoAm 94, WhoWest 94*
Owen, John (Arthur Dalziel) 1925- *Who 94*
Owen, John Atkinson, Jr. 1924- *WhoAm 94*
Owen, John Aubrey 1945- *Who 94*
Owen, John Benjamin Brynmor 1910- *Who 94*
Owen, John Gethin M. *Who 94*
Owen, John Halliwell 1935- *Who 94*
Owen, John Ivor Headon 1922- *Who 94*
Owen, John Joseph Thomas 1934- *Who 94*
Owen, John Laverty 1923- *WhoFI 94*
Owen, John Simpson 1912- *Who 94*
Owen, John V. *Who 94*
Owen, John Wyn 1942- *Who 94*

Owen, John Wynne 1939- *Who 94*
Owen, Karen Cordelia 1943- *WhoFI 94*
Owen, Karen Michelle 1952- *WhoFI 94*
Owen, Kathy Jan 1966- *WhoAmL 94*
Owen, Kenneth Dale 1938- *WhoScEn 94*
Owen, Kenneth Frederick 1935- *IntWW 93*
Owen, Larry d1979 *WhoHol 92*
Owen, Loyd Eugene, Jr. 1943- *WhoAmL 94*
Owen, Lynn 1946- *WhoAmP 93*
Owen, Lynn Rasmussen *WhoAm 94*
Owen, Marc Conley 1948- *WhoAmL 94*
Owen, Maureen A. *DrAPF 93*
Owen, Michael *WhoAm 94, WhoScEn 94*
Owen, Milton d1969 *WhoHol 92*
Owen, Myrfyn 1943- *Who 94*
Owen, Nancy N. 1935- *WhoAmP 93*
Owen, Nathan Richard 1919- *WhoAm 94, WhoFI 94*
Owen, Nicholas David Arundel 1947- *Who 94*
Owen, Nora 1945- *WhoWomW 91*
Owen, P. John 1947- *WhoAmL 94*
Owen, Patricia *Who 94*
Owen, Peter Francis 1940- *Who 94*
Owen, Philip Loscombe Wintringham 1920- *Who 94*
Owen, Ray David 1915- *IntWW 93, WhoAm 94, WhoScEn 94*
Owen, Reginald d1972 *WhoHol 92*
Owen, Richard 1922- *WhoAm 94, WhoAmL 94*
Owen, Richard Arthur James 1910- *Who 94*
Owen, Richard Wilfred 1932- *Who 94*
Owen, Robert 1771-1858 *BlmGEL*
Owen, Robert Barry 1943- *WhoWest 94*
Owen, Robert Dale 1801-1877 *AmSocL*
Owen, Robert Dewit 1948- *WhoAmL 94*
Owen, Robert Hubert 1928- *WhoAm 94*
Owen, Robert John Richard 1940- *IntWW 93, Who 94*
Owen, Robert Michael 1944- *Who 94*
Owen, Robert Penrhyn 1918- *Who 94*
Owen, Robert Roy 1921- *WhoAm 94*
Owen, Robert Vaughan 1920- *WhoAm 94*
Owen, Roberts Bishop 1926- *WhoAm 94*
Owen, Roderic 1921- *WrDr 94*
Owen, Rowland Hubert 1903- *Who 94*
Owen, Samuel Griffith 1925- *Who 94*
Owen, Scott Arnold 1961- *WhoWest 94*
Owen, Seena d1966 *WhoHol 92*
Owen, Stephen Lee 1952- *WhoAm 94*
Owen, Steve d1964 *ProFbHF [port]*
Owen, Sue *DrAPF 93*
Owen, Thomas Arfon 1933- *Who 94*
Owen, Thomas Barron 1920- *WhoAm 94*
Owen, Thomas Edward 1954- *WhoScEn 94*
Owen, Thomas Edwin 1931- *WhoScEn 94*
Owen, Thomas J. 1949- *WhoScEn 94*
Owen, Thomas Joseph 1946- *WhoScEn 94*
Owen, Thomas Llewellyn, Sr. 1928- *WhoAm 94, WhoFI 94*
Owen, Thomas Walker 1925- *WhoAm 94, WhoFI 94*
Owen, Tim *WhoHol 92*
Owen, Trevor Bryan 1928- *Who 94*
Owen, Tudor d1978 *WhoHol 92*
Owen, Ursula Margaret 1937- *Who 94*
Owen, Virginia 1921- *WhoMW 93*
Owen, Virginia Lee 1941- *WhoMW 93*
Owen, W. Masters *WhoAmP 93*
Owen, Walter Shepherd 1920- *Who 94, WhoAm 94*
Owen, Warren Herbert 1927- *WhoAm 94, WhoFI 94*
Owen, Warwick (Jack Burgoyne) 1916- *WrDr 94*
Owen, Wilfred 1893-1918 *BlmGEL*
Owen, Wilfred 1912- *WhoFI 94*
Owen, Wilfred (Edward Salter) 1893-1918 *ConAu 141, GayLL*
Owen, Wilfred Edward Salter 1893-1918 *DcNaB MP*
Owen, William Cone 1942- *WhoAm 94, WhoAmL 94*
Owen, William Frederick 1947- *WhoWest 94*
Owen, Yvonne 1923- *WhoHol 92*
Owenby, Mae S. *WhoAmP 93*
Owendoff, Stephen Peter 1943- *WhoAmL 94*
Owen-Jones, John Eryl 1912- *Who 94*
Owen-Jones, Lindsay 1946- *IntWW 93*
Owen-Jones, Lindsay Harwood 1946- *Who 94*
Owen-Riesch, Anna Lou 1919- *WhoWest 94*
Owens, Albert Henry, Jr. 1926- *WhoScEn 94*
Owens, Albert Thomas 1948- *WhoFI 94*
Owens, Andi 1934- *WhoBlA 94*
Owens, Angle B., Jr. 1922- *WhoBlA 94*
Owens, Arley E., Jr. 1948- *WhoBlA 94*
Owens, Arnold Dean 1943- *WhoAmL 94*
Owens, Bernard Charles 1928- *Who 94*
Owens, Billy E. 1969- *WhoBlA 94*
Owens, Bonnie 1933- *WhoHol 92*
Owens, Brigman 1943- *WhoBlA 94*
Owens, Buck 1929- *WhoAm 94*
Owens, Carol 1931- *WhoAmP 93*
Owens, Charles Clinton 1942- *WhoBlA 94*
Owens, Charles Edward 1938- *WhoBlA 94*
Owens, Charles Vincent, Jr. 1927- *WhoAm 94*
Owens, Curtis 1938- *WhoBlA 94*
Owens, David Kenneth 1948- *WhoBlA 94*
Owens, Debbie A. 1956- *WhoBlA 94*
Owens, Delia *News 93-3 [port]*
Owens, Doris A. 1950- *WhoWest 94*
Owens, Douglas Wayne 1937- *WhoAmP 93*
Owens, Edward Henry 1945- *WhoScEn 94*
Owens, Edwin Chandler 1935- *WhoIns 94*
Owens, Edwin Geynet 1953- *WhoScEn 94*
Owens, Emmett Hennington *WhoAmP 93*
Owens, Ernest Sibley, III 1945- *WhoWest 94*
Owens, F. Joseph, Jr. 1946- *WhoAmL 94*
Owens, Frank Arthur Robert 1912- *Who 94*
Owens, Frank Henry 1928- *WhoAm 94*
Owens, Fredric Newell 1941- *WhoAm 94*
Owens, Garland Chester 1922- *WhoAm 94, WhoFI 94*
Owens, Gary *WhoAm 94*
Owens, Gary 1936- *WhoHol 92*
Owens, Gary Mitchell 1949- *WhoScEn 94*
Owens, Gaylon 1934- *WhoAmP 93*
Owens, Genevra Irene 1917- *WhoAmP 93*
Owens, Geoffrey *WhoBlA 94*
Owens, George A. 1919- *WhoBlA 94*
Owens, Grady D., Sr. 1938- *WhoBlA 94*
Owens, Gregory Randolph 1948- *WhoScEn 94*
Owens, Gwendolyn Jane 1954- *WhoAmA 93*
Owens, Gwendolyn Rennetta 1940- *WhoWest 94*
Owens, Harry d1986 *WhoHol 92*
Owens, Howard T., Jr. 1934- *WhoAmP 93*
Owens, Hugh Franklin 1909- *WhAm 10*
Owens, Hugo Armstrong, Sr. 1916- *WhoBlA 94*
Owens, Iris *DrAPF 93*
Owens, Isaiah H. 1920- *WhoBlA 94*
Owens, Jack Byron 1944- *WhoAm 94*
Owens, James Cuthbert 1916- *WhoAm 94*
Owens, James E. 1937- *WhoBlA 94*
Owens, James Hilliard 1920- *WhoMW 93*
Owens, Janice Louise 1939- *WhoMW 93*
Owens, Jay R. 1944- *WhoBlA 94*
Owens, Jefferson Pleas 1917- *WhoBlA 94*
Owens, Jerry Sue 1947- *WhoBlA 94*
Owens, Jesse 1913-1980 *AfrAmAl 6 [port]*
Owens, Jimmy 1943- *WhoBlA 94*
Owens, Jo Ann Faye 1947- *WhoAmP 93*
Owens, Joan Murrell 1933- *WhoBlA 94*
Owens, John Franklin 1935- *WhoFI 94*
Owens, John Ridland 1932- *Who 94*
Owens, Joseph 1908- *WhoAm 94, WrDr 94*
Owens, Joseph E. *WhoAmP 93*
Owens, Joseph Francis 1949- *WhoMW 93*
Owens, Joseph Francis, III 1946- *WhoScEn 94*
Owens, Joseph Herron 1937- *WhoAmL 94*
Owens, Judith Myoli 1940- *WhoBlA 94*
Owens, June *DrAPF 93*
Owens, Justine Elizabeth 1953- *WhoScEn 94*
Owens, K. Buck 1949- *WhoWest 94*
Owens, Keith Alan 1958- *WhoBlA 94*
Owens, Kenneth, Jr. 1939- *WhoBlA 94*
Owens, Kimo d1979 *WhoHol 92*
Owens, Lewis E. 1934- *WhoAm 94*
Owens, Lillie Anne 1935- *WhoBlA 94*
Owens, Louis *DrAPF 93*
Owens, Luvie Moore 1933- *WhoAm 94, WhoMW 93*
Owens, Lynda Gayle 1956- *WhoBlA 94*
Owens, Major 1936- *ConBlB 6 [port]*
Owens, Major R. 1936- *CngDr 93, WhoAmP 93, WhoBlA 94*
Owens, Major Robert Odell 1936- *WhoAm 94*
Owens, Marian D. 1936- *WhoAmP 93*
Owens, Mark *News 93-3 [port]*
Owens, Mark Ernest 1956- *WhoAmL 94*
Owens, Mark Jeffrey 1955- *WhoScEn 94*
Owens, Marvin Franklin, Jr. 1916- *WhoAm 94*
Owens, Mary 1935- *WhoAmA 93*
Owens, Michael *WhoAm 94*
Owens, Michael Joseph *WorInv*
Owens, Nathaniel Davis 1948- *WhoBlA 94*
Owens, O'dell M. *WhoBlA 94*
Owens, Patricia 1927- *WhoHol 92*
Owens, Paul Thomas 1943- *WhoFI 94*
Owens, Phyllis Eileen Padilla 1952- *WhoHisp 94*
Owens, Robert G. 1923- *WrDr 94*
Owens, Robert Lee 1932- *WhoBlA 94*
Owens, Robert Leon, III 1925- *WhoBlA 94*
Owens, Robert Patrick 1954- *WhoAmL 94, WhoWest 94*
Owens, Robin Maria 1956- *WhoFI 94*
Owens, Rochelle *DrAPF 93*
Owens, Rochelle 1936- *ConDr 93, WhoAm 94, WrDr 94*
Owens, Rodney Joe 1950- *WhoAmL 94*
Owens, Ronald 1930- *WhoBlA 94*
Owens, Ronald C. 1936- *WhoBlA 94*
Owens, Scott Andrew 1958- *WhoFI 94, WhoMW 93*
Owens, Stephen J. 1955- *WhoAmL 94*
Owens, Stephen Thomas 1948- *WhoAm 94*
Owens, Steve *WhoAmP 93*
Owens, Steven Ralph 1950- *WhoWest 94*
Owens, Tennys Bowers 1940- *WhoAmA 93*
Owens, Thomas C., Jr. 1922- *WhoBlA 94*
Owens, Thomas M. 1937- *WhoAm 94, WhoFI 94*
Owens, Treka Elaine 1953- *WhoBlA 94*
Owens, Tyler Benjamin 1944- *WhoScEn 94*
Owens, Victor Allen 1945- *WhoBlA 94*
Owens, Wallace, Jr. *WhoAmA 93, WhoBlA 94*
Owens, Walter *WhoAmP 93*
Owens, Warner Barry 1939- *WhoWest 94*
Owens, Wayne 1937- *WhoAm 94*
Owens, Wilbur Dawson, Jr. 1930- *WhoAm 94, WhoAmL 94*
Owens, William d1926 *WhoHol 92*
Owens, William 1937- *WhoAmP 93, WhoBlA 94*
Owens, William A. 1905-1990 *WhAm 10*
Owens, William Arthur 1940- *WhoAm 94*
Owens, William Clarence 1947- *WhoAmP 93*
Owens, William Don 1939- *WhoAm 94*
Owens, William F. 1950- *WhoAmP 93*
Owensby, Earl 1935- *IntMPA 94*
Owensby, Earl 1936- *WhoHol 92*
Owens-Hicks, Shirley *WhoAmP 93*
Owens-Hicks, Shirley 1942- *WhoBlA 94*
Owenson, Sydney c. 1775-1859 *BlmGWL*
Owens-Smith, Joyce Latrell 1949- *WhoBlA 94*
Owens-Wilson, Gwendolyn Ann 1938- *WhoMW 93*
Ower, David Cheyne 1931- *Who 94*
Owers, Anne Elizabeth 1947- *Who 94*
Owers, Brian Charles 1934- *WhoAm 94*
Owings, Donald Henry 1943- *WhoAm 94, WhoWest 94*
Owings, Francis Barre 1941- *WhoAm 94*
Owings, George W., III 1945- *WhoAmP 93*
Owings, Malcolm William 1925- *WhoAm 94*
Owings, Margaret Wentworth 1913- *WhoAm 94, WhoWest 94*
Owings, Mark 1945- *EncSF 93*
Owings, Nathaniel Alexander 1903-1984 *AmCulL*
Owings, Todd Andrew 1967- *WhoMW 93*
Owl, W. David 1893-c. 1981 *EncNAR*
Owles, James W. d1993 *NewYTBS 93 [port]*
Ownbey, Lenore F. Daly *WhoFI 94*
Ownby, Jere Franklin, III 1956- *WhoAmL 94*
Ownby, Jerry Steve 1939- *WhoAm 94*
Owo, The Olowo of *Who 94*
Owren, Michael J. 1955- *WhoWest 94*
Owron, Roberta d1979 *WhoHol 92*
Owsley, Alvin 1926- *WhoAm 94, WhoFI 94*
Owsley, Betty Joan *WhoBlA 94*
Owsley, David Thomas 1929- *WhoAm 94, WhoAmA 93*
Owsley, Monroe d1937 *WhoHol 92*
Owsley, Norman Lee 1941- *WhoAm 94*
Owsley, Ray 1932- *WhoAmP 93*
Owsley, William Clinton, Jr. 1923- *WhoAm 94*
Owsley Coffey, Lesia Mae 1957- *WhoMW 93*
Owusu, Martin 1943- *ConDr 93*
Owusu, Victor 1923- *IntWW 93*
Owusu-Ansah, Twum 1935- *WhoScEn 94*
Owyoung, Steven David 1947- *WhoAm 94*
Ox, Jack 1948- *WhoAmA 93*
Oxburgh, Ernest Ronald 1934- *IntWW 93*
Oxburgh, (Ernest) Ronald 1934- *Who 94*
Oxbury, Harold Frederick 1903- *Who 94*
Oxenberg, Catherine 1961- *IntMPA 94, WhoHol 92*
Oxenbould, Ben *WhoHol 92*
Oxenbould, Moffatt 1943- *NewGrDO*
Oxenburg, Allen Sven 1927-1992 *WhAm 10*
Oxenbury, Dame Shirley (Ann) 1936- *Who 94*
Oxender, Glenn S. 1943- *WhoAmP 93*
Oxendine, John Edward 1943- *WhoBlA 94*
Oxendine, Willie H., Jr. 1963- *WhoAm 94*
Oxenford, John 1812-1877 *NewGrDO*
Oxenham, Thomas Henry, III 1950- *WhoAmL 94*
Oxenhandler, David 1958- *WhoWest 94*
Oxenhandler, Neal 1926- *WhoAm 94*
Oxenreiter, Maurice Frank 1924- *WhoAm 94*
Oxer, John Paul Daniell 1950- *WhoScEn 94*
Oxford, Archdeacon of *Who 94*
Oxford, Bishop of 1936- *Who 94*
Oxford, Charles William 1921- *WhoAm 94*
Oxford, Hubert, III 1938- *WhoAmL 94*
Oxford, Kenneth (Gordon) 1924- *Who 94*
Oxford, Patrick C. 1942- *WhoAmL 94*
Oxford And Asquith, Earl of 1916- *Who 94*
Oxfuird, Master of 1969- *Who 94*
Oxfuird, Viscount of 1934- *Who 94*
Oxilia, Jose (Giuseppe) 1861-1919 *NewGrDO*
Oxlade, Zena Elsie 1929- *Who 94*
Oxlee, Colin Hamilton 1935- *Who 94*
Oxley, Ann 1924- *WhoMW 93*
Oxley, David 1929- *WhoHol 92*
Oxley, Geraldine Motta 1930- *WhoAm 94*
Oxley, Humphrey Leslie Malcolm 1909- *Who 94*
Oxley, James Keith R. *Who 94*
Oxley, John Joseph William Molesworth 1783-1828 *WhWE*
Oxley, John Thurman 1909- *WhoAm 94*
Oxley, Julian Christopher 1938- *Who 94*
Oxley, Leo Lionel 1934- *WhoBlA 94*
Oxley, Margaret Carolyn Stewart 1930- *WhoMW 93*
Oxley, Michael G. 1944- *CngDr 93*
Oxley, Michael Garver 1944- *WhoAm 94, WhoAmP 93, WhoMW 93*
Oxley, Myron B. *WhoAmP 93*
Oxley, Philip 1922- *WhoAm 94*
Oxley, William 1939- *WrDr 94*
Oxman, David Craig 1941- *WhoAm 94*
Oxman, Katja *WhoAmA 93*
Oxman, Mark 1940- *WhoAmA 93*
Oxman, Stephen A. *WhoAm 94*
Oxmantown, Lord 1969- *Who 94*
Oxnam, Garfield Bromley 1891-1963 *DcAmReB 2*
Oxnard, Charles (Ernest) 1933- *ConAu 42NR*
Oxnard, Charles Ernest 1933- *WhoAm 94, WhoScEn 94*
Oxner, Glenn Ruckman 1938- *WhoFI 94*
Oxorn, Harry 1920- *ConAu 42NR*
Oxtoby, David William 1951- *WhoAm 94*
Oxtoby, John Corning 1910-1991 *WhAm 10*
Oxtoby, Robert Boynton 1921- *WhoAm 94, WhoAmL 94*
Oyalowo, Tunde O. 1953- *WhoBlA 94*
Oyama, Joseph Hikaru 1939- *WhoMW 93*
Oyamo *DrAPF 93*
OyamO 1943- *ConDr 93*
Oyangen, Gunhild 1947- *IntWW 93, WhoWomW 91*
Oyarzun, Emilia Pincheira *BlmGWL*
Oyarzun, Mila 1912- *BlmGWL*
Oye, Harald Arnljot 1935- *IntWW 93*
Oyekan, Soni Olufemi 1946- *WhoScEn 94*
Oye-Mba, Casimir 1942- *IntWW 93*
Oyer, Sanford Charles 1925- *WhoMW 93*
Oyeshiku, Patricia Delores Worthy 1944- *WhoBlA 94*
Oyewole, Saundra Herndon 1943- *WhoBlA 94*
Oyibo, Gabriel A. 1950- *WhoScEn 94*
Oyler, Gregory Kenneth 1953- *WhoAm 94*
Oyler, James Russell, Jr. 1946- *WhoFI 94*
Oyola, Eliezer 1944- *WhoHisp 94*
Oyola, Gerardo *WhoHisp 94*
Oyono, Ferdinand Leopold 1929- *IntWW 93*
Oyono-Mbia, Guillaume 1939- *ConWorW 93*
Oysher, Moishe d1958 *WhoHol 92*
Oyster, Carol Kathleen 1948- *WhoMW 93*
Oyugi, Joseph H. d1993 *NewYTBS 93*
Oz, Amos 1939- *ConWorW 93, IntWW 93, RfGShF*
Oz, Frank 1944- *IntMPA 94, WhoAm 94, WhoHol 92*
Ozaki, Satoshi 1929- *WhoScEn 94*
Ozaki, Yoji 1922- *WhoAsA 94*
Ozal, Semra *WhoWomW 91*
Ozal, Turgut d1993 *IntWW 93N, NewYTBS 93 [port]*
Ozal, Turgut 1927-1993 *CurBio 93N*
Ozalis, Sheila A. 1962- *WhoAmL 94*
Ozanich, Charles George 1933- *WhoWest 94*
Ozanne, Dominic L. 1953- *WhoBlA 94*
Ozanne, Leroy *WhoBlA 94*
Ozanne Marsh, Richard 1959- *WhoWest 94*
Ozar, Milton Bernard 1924- *WhoMW 93*

Ozarow, Kent Jorgensen *DrAPF 93*
Ozato, Keiko 1941- *WhoAsA 94*
Ozato, Sadatoshi 1930- *IntWW 93*
Ozawa, Galen M. 1937- *WhoAsA 94*
Ozawa, Ichiro *IntWW 93*
Ozawa, Keiya 1953- *WhoScEn 94*
Ozawa, Martha Naoko 1933- *WhoAm 94,
    WhoAsA 94*
Ozawa, Seiji 1935- *IntWW 93, NewGrDO,
    Who 94, WhoAm 94, WhoAsA 94*
Ozawa, Tatsuo *IntWW 93*
Ozawa, Terutomo 1935- *WhoAsA 94,
    WhoFI 94*
Ozbek, (Ibrahim Mehmet) Rifat 1953-
    IntWW 93
Ozbun, Jim L. *WhoAm 94, WhoMW 93*
Ozelli, Tunch 1938- *WhoFI 94,
    WhoScEn 94*
Ozenda, Paul 1920- *IntWW 93*
Ozendo, Pierre L. 1950- *WhoIns 94*
Ozenfant, Amedee J. 1886-1966
    WhoAmA 93N
Ozenne, Jean *WhoHol 92*
Ozer, Bernard 1930-1991 *WhAm 10*
Ozeray, Madeleine d1989 *WhoHol 92*
Ozernoy, Leonid Moissey 1939-
    WhoAm 94, WhoScEn 94, WhoWest 94
Ozero, Brian John 1932- *WhoAm 94*
Ozerov, Mikhail Vitalevich 1944-
    LngBDD
Ozick, Cynthia *DrAPF 93*
Ozick, Cynthia 1928- *BlmGWL,
    IntWW 93, RfGShF, WhoAm 94,
    WrDr 94*
Ozier, Irving 1938- *WhoAm 94*
Ozier, William Nelson 1944- *WhoAmL 94*
Ozim, Francis Taiino 1946- *WhoBlA 94*
Ozim, Igor 1931- *IntWW 93*
Ozinga, Suzanne 1935- *WhoMW 93*
Ozio, David *WhoAm 94*
Ozkan, Umit Sivrioglu 1954-
    WhoMW 93, WhoScEn 94
Ozker, Eren d1993 *NewYTBS 93*
Ozmen, Atilla 1941- *WhoScEn 94*
Ozment, Dennis Dean 1945- *WhoAmP 93*
Ozment, James Franklin 1962-
    WhoAmL 94
Ozment, Steven 1939- *WhoAm 94*
Ozmon, Howard 1935- *WrDr 94*
Ozmon, Kenneth Lawrence 1931-
    WhoAm 94
Oznowicz, Frank Richard 1944-
    WhoAm 94
Ozog, Edward J. 1948- *WhoAm 94,
    WhoAmL 94*
Ozonoff, Ida 1904- *WhoAmA 93*
Ozsoyoglu, Zehra Meral 1951-
    WhoMW 93
Ozuna, George, Jr. 1930- *WhoHisp 94*
Ozzard, Janet Lucile 1927- *WhoAm 94*

P

Paabo, Svante 1955- *WhoScEn 94*
Paalen, Bella 1881-1964 *NewGrDO*
Paalman, Maria Elisabeth Monica 1951-
WhoScEn 94
Paalz, Anthony L. 1924- *WhoAm 94*
Paalzow, Henriette von 1788-1847
BlmGWL
Paananen, Victor Niles 1938- *WhoAm 94*
Paar, Jack 1918- *IntMPA 94, IntWW 93,
WhoCom, WhoHol 92*
Paar, Randy 1949- *WhoAmL 94*
Paarmann, Larry Dean 1941-
WhoScEn 94
Paarz, Robert Emil 1948- *WhoAmL 94*
Paasio, Pertti Kullervo 1939- *IntWW 93*
Paaswell, Robert Emil 1937- *WhoAm 94,
WhoScEn 94*
Pa-ba-la Zhuo-lie Lang-jie *WhoPRCh 91*
Pablo 1934- *WhoAmA 93*
Pablo, Luis de 1930- *NewGrDO*
Pablos, Rolando 1939- *WhoHisp 94*
Pabon, Iris *WhoHisp 94*
Pabón-Price, Noemi 1950- *WhoHisp 94*
Pabst, Adolf 1899-1990 *WhAm 10*
Pabst, Edmund G. 1916- *WhoAm 94*
Pabst, G. W. d1967 *WhoHol 92*
Pabst, Michael John 1945- *WhoScEn 94*
Pabst, Ralph Malcom 1920- *WhoWest 94*
Paca, William 1740-1799 *WhAmRev*
Pacal, Joseph Frank 1952- *WhoWest 94*
Pacala, Leon 1926- *WhoAm 94*
Pacavira, Manuel Pedro 1939- *IntWW 93*
Paccagnini, Angelo 1930- *NewGrDO*
Pacchierotti, Gasparo 1740-1821
NewGrDO
Paccolat, Monique 1954- *WhoWomW 91*
Pace, Alicia Guzmán 1949- *WhoHisp 94*
Pace, Benny Clint 1947- *WhoAmL 94*
Pace, Brooks 1942- *WhoWest 94*
Pace, Carolina Jolliff 1938- *WhoFI 94*
Pace, Charles Robert 1912- *WhoAm 94*
Pace, David 1944- *WrDr 94*
Pace, Denny F. 1926- *WhoWest 94*
Pace, Eric 1936- *WrDr 94*
Pace, Eric Dwight 1936- *WhoAm 94*
Pace, Frank 1912-1988 *HisDcKW*
Pace, Henry Alexander 1914- *WhoMW 93*
Pace, James Robert 1958- *WhoAmA 93*
Pace, Judy *WhoHol 92*
Pace, Kay Robertine *WhoBlA 94*
Pace, Leonard 1924- *WhoAm 94*
Pace, Lorin Nelson 1925- *WhoAmP 93,
WhoWest 94*
Pace, Margaret Bosshardt *WhoAmA 93*
Pace, Nathan Leon 1943- *WhoAm 94*
Pace, Owen *WhoHol 92*
Pace, Ralph Wayne 1931- *WhoAm 94*
Pace, Richard Alan 1945- *WhoAm 94*
Pace, Richard Randall 1940- *WhoAm 94*
Pace, Robert Kelley, Jr. 1957-
WhoWest 94
Pace, Robert Scott 1904-1989 *WhAm 10*
Pace, Rosalind *DrAPF 93*
Pace, Rosella *DrAPF 93*
Pace, Stanley Carter 1921- *IntWW 93,
WhoAm 94, WhoWest 94*
Pace, Stanley Dan 1947- *WhoAmL 94*
Pace, Stephen S. 1918- *WhoAmA 93*
Pace, Stephen Shell 1918- *WhoAm 94*
Pace, Thomas 1951- *WhoAmL 94*
Pace, Thomas M. 1952- *WhoAm 94*
Pacea, Ion 1924- *IntWW 93*
Pace-Hinton, Lanita 1958- *WhoBlA 94*

Pacela, Allan Fred 1938- *WhoWest 94*
Pacella, Bernard Leonardo 1912-
WhoAm 94
Pacelli, Angela DeFlorio *WhoAmP 93*
Pacelli, Henry Paul *WhoAmP 93*
Pace-Perry, Lorelei 1950- *WhoMW 93*
Pacernick, Gary Bernard *DrAPF 93*
Pacetti, Iva 1898-1981 *NewGrDO*
Pacetti, James M. 1960- *WhoFI 94*
Pach, Chester Joseph, Jr. 1949-
WhoMW 93
Pach, Magda F. 1884-1950 *WhoAmA 93N*
Pach, Walter 1883-1958 *WhoAmA 93N*
Pach, Zsigmond Pal 1919- *IntWW 93*
Pachariyangkun, Upadit 1920- *IntWW 93*
Pache, Bernard 1934- *IntWW 93*
Pachecho, Maximo 1953- *IntWW 93*
Pacheco, Adonio W., Jr. 1956-
WhoHisp 94
Pacheco, Alex *WhoHisp 94*
Pacheco, Andres Leopoldo 1960-
WhoHisp 94
Pacheco, Benny Sena, Jr. 1951-
WhoHisp 94
Pacheco, Catherine Chapman 1927-
WrDr 94
Pacheco, Ceferino *WhoHisp 94*
Pacheco, Daniel J. 1956- *WhoHisp 94*
Pacheco, Donald Norman, Jr. 1959-
WhoHisp 94
Pacheco, Duarte dc.1530 *WhWE*
Pacheco, Evelyn 1950- *WhoHisp 94*
Pacheco, Ferdie 1927- *WhoHisp 94*
Pacheco, Henry Joe 1943- *WhoHisp 94*
Pacheco, Javier *DrAPF 93*
Pacheco, Joe B. 1937- *WhoHisp 94*
Pacheco, José 1942- *WhoHisp 94*
Pacheco, Jose Emilio 1939- *ConWorW 93,
HispLC*
Pacheco, Luis Novoa 1956- *WhoHisp 94*
Pacheco, Manuel Trinidad 1941-
WhoAm 94, WhoHisp 94, WhoWest 94
Pacheco, Marc R. *WhoAmP 93*
Pacheco, Mary Ann 1950- *WhoHisp 94*
Pacheco, Richard 1924- *WhoAmP 93,
WhoHisp 94*
Pacheco, Richard, Jr. 1927- *WhoHisp 94*
Pacheco, Robert Charles 1944-
WhoWest 94
Pacheco, Sammy Lawrence 1952-
WhoHisp 94
Pacheco Areco, Jorge 1920- *IntWW 93*
Pacheco-Ransanz, Arsenio 1932-
WhoAm 94
Pa Chin *ConWorW 93*
Pachios, Harold Christy 1936-
WhoAm 94, WhoAmP 93
Pachman, Daniel J. 1911- *WhoAm 94*
Pachner, William 1915- *WhoAmA 93*
Pachniak, Char Kay 1953- *WhoMW 93*
Pachol, Wayne C. 1955- *WhoFI 94*
Pacholski, Richard Francis 1947-
WhoAm 94
Pachon, Harry 1945- *WhoHisp 94*
Pachon, Harry Peter 1945- *WhoAmP 93*
Pachter, Irwin Jacob 1925- *WhoAm 94*
Pachter, Jonathan Alan 1957-
WhoScEn 94
Pachter, Josh 1951- *WrDr 94*
Pachter, Larry Hugh 1957- *WhoAmL 94*
Pachter, Victor 1921- *WhoFI 94*
Pacific, Joseph Nicholas, Jr. 1950-
WhoWest 94

Pacifico, Albert Dominick 1940-
WhoAm 94
Pacifico, Carl 1921- *WrDr 94*
Pacini, Andrea c. 1690-1764 *NewGrDO*
Pacini, Giovanni 1796-1867 *NewGrDO*
Pacini, Regina 1871-1965 *NewGrDO*
Pacino, Al 1940- *IntMPA 94, IntWW 93,
News 93 [port], WhoAm 94, WhoHol 92*
Paciocco, Anthony 1944- *WhoFI 94*
Paciorkiewicz, Tadeusz 1916- *NewGrDO*
Pacius, Fredrik 1809-1891 *NewGrDO*
Pack, Allen S. 1930- *WhoAm 94*
Pack, Arthur Newton 1893- *WhAm 10*
Pack, Charles Lloyd *WhoHol 92*
Pack, Donald Cecil 1920- *Who 94*
Pack, Doris 1942- *WhoWomW 91*
Pack, Emily Lloyd 1971- *WhoAm 94*
Pack, Janet 1952- *SmATA 77 [port]*
Pack, Judy Kay Daniels 1943-
WhoAmP 93
Pack, Leonard Brecher 1944- *WhoAm 94*
Pack, Phoebe Katherine Finley 1907-
WhoWest 94
Pack, Richard Morris 1915- *WhoAm 94*
Pack, Robert *DrAPF 93*
Pack, Robert 1929- *WrDr 94*
Pack, Robert John, Jr. 1969- *WhoBlA 94*
Pack, Roger A(mbrose) 1907- *WrDr 94*
Pack, Roger Lloyd *WhoHol 92*
Pack, Roy Sanghun 1964- *WhoFI 94*
Pack, Russell T 1937- *WhoWest 94*
Pack, Spencer J. 1953- *ConAu 140,
WhoFI 94*
Packard, Barbara Baugh 1938- *WhoAm 94*
Packard, Bonnie B. 1946- *WhoAmP 93*
Packard, Clayton d1931 *WhoHol 92*
Packard, David 1912- *IntWW 93,
WhoAm 94, WhoFI 94, WhoScEn 94,
WhoWest 94*
Packard, (Charles) Douglas 1903- *Who 94*
Packard, Elizabeth Parsons Ware *EncSPD*
Packard, George Randolph 1932-
WhoAm 94
Packard, John Mallory 1920- *WhoAm 94*
Packard, Julie *WhoAm 94, WhoWest 94*
Packard, Peter Kim 1938- *WhoAm 94*
Packard, Robert 1916- *WrDr 94*
Packard, Robert Charles 1919-
WhoAm 94, WhoAmL 94
Packard, Robert Goodale, III 1951-
WhoWest 94
Packard, Ron 1931- *CngDr 93,
WhoAmP 93*
Packard, Ronald 1931- *WhoAm 94,
WhoWest 94*
Packard, Sandra Podolin 1942-
WhoAm 94, WhoMW 93
Packard, Shermañ A. 1949- *WhoAmP 93*
Packard, Stephen Michael 1953-
WhoAmL 94
Packard, Susan Leigh 1963- *WhoFI 94*
Packard, Vance 1914- *IntWW 93,
WrDr 94*
Packard, Vance (Oakley) 1914- *Who 94*
Packard, Vance Oakley 1914- *WhoAm 94*
Packard, William *DrAPF 93*
Packer, Arnold Herman 1935-
WhoAmP 93
Packer, B(arbara) L(ee) 1947- *WrDr 94*
Packer, Beverly White 1930- *WhoAmP 93*
Packer, Boyd K. *WhoWest 94*
Packer, Clair Lange 1901-1978
WhoAmA 93N

Packer, Daniel Fredric, Jr. 1947-
WhoBlA 94
Packer, David *WhoHol 92*
Packer, Doris *WhoHol 92*
Packer, Eve *DrAPF 93*
Packer, Francis H. 1873-1957
WhoAmA 93N
Packer, Fred L. 1886-1956 *WhoAmA 93N*
Packer, Greg A. *WhoAmP 93*
Packer, James Innell 1926- *WrDr 94*
Packer, John Richard 1946- *Who 94*
Packer, Joy 1905-1977 *BlmGWL*
Packer, Karen Gilliland 1940-
WhoMW 93, WhoScEn 94
Packer, Katherine Helen 1918-
WhoAm 94
Packer, Kenneth John 1938- *Who 94,
WhoScEn 94*
Packer, Kerry Francis Bullmore 1937-
IntWW 93, Who 94
Packer, Lawrence Frank *WhoBlA 94*
Packer, Mark Barry 1944- *WhoAm 94,
WhoAmL 94, WhoWest 94*
Packer, Michael Ray 1951- *WhoAmL 94*
Packer, Netta d1962 *WhoHol 92*
Packer, Rekha Desai 1955- *WhoAm 94*
Packer, Richard John 1944- *Who 94*
Packer, Rosetta B. 1954- *WhoAmL 94*
Packer, Russell Howard 1951- *WhoFI 94*
Packer, Vin *TwCYAW*
Packer, William John 1940- *Who 94*
Packert, Gayla Beth 1953- *WhoAmL 94*
Packett, Charles Neville 1922- *WrDr 94*
Packett, Robert Lee 1952- *WhoMW 93*
Packey, Daniel J. 1952- *WhoScEn 94*
Packnett, Don Stevenson 1931-
WhoWest 94
Packo, Joseph John 1925- *WhoFI 94*
Packshaw, Robin David 1933- *Who 94*
Packwood, Bob 1932- *CngDr 93,
IntWW 93, WhoAm 94, WhoAmP 93,
WhoWest 94*
Packwood, Robert W. *NewYTBS 93 [port]*
Pacome, Maria *WhoHol 92*
Pacosz, Christina V. *DrAPF 93*
Pacter, Paul Allan 1943- *WhoAm 94*
Pacula, Joanna 1958- *WhoHol 92*
Pacumbaba, R.P. 1935- *WhoScEn 94*
Pacun, Norman 1932- *WhoAm 94*
Pacy, James Steven 1930- *WhoAm 94*
Paczesny, Edmunette 1933- *WhoAm 94*
Paczkowski, Jerzy 1946- *WhoScEn 94*
Paczynski, Bohdan 1940- *WhoAm 94,
WhoScEn 94*
Padavan, Frank *WhoAmP 93*
Padberg, Ann Marie 1943- *WhoMW 93*
Padberg, Daniel Ivan 1931- *WhoAm 94*
Padberg, Helen Swan *WhoMW 93*
Padbury, Wendy 1947- *WhoHol 92*
Padden, Mike 1946- *WhoAmP 93*
Padden, Robin Reinhard 1951-
WhoWest 94
Padden, Sarah d1967 *WhoHol 92*
Paddick, Hugh *WhoHol 92*
Paddio, Gerald *WhoBlA 94*
Paddio-Johnson, Eunice Alice 1928-
WhoBlA 94
Paddock, Anthony Conaway 1935-
WhoAm 94
Paddock, Austin Joseph 1908- *WhoAm 94*
Paddock, Charles d1943 *WhoHol 92*
Paddock, John *WhoAm 94, WhoMW 93*
Paddock, John Allen 1916- *WhoAmP 93*

Paddock, Robert Young 1917- *WhoMW 93*
Paddock, Stephen William 1953- *WhoMW 93*
Paddock, Stuart R., Jr. *WhoMW 93*
Paddock, Susan Mary 1946- *WhoMW 93*
Paddock, Willard Dryden 1873-1956 *WhoAmA 93N*
Padel, Ruth 1946- *WrDr 94*
Paden, Carolyn Eileen Belknap 1953- *WhoMW 93*
Paden, Kimbra Lea Kahle 1960- *WhoMW 93*
Paden, William E. 1939- *ConAu 142*
Paderewski, Clarence Joseph 1908- *WhoAm 94*
Paderewski, Ignace d1941 *WhoHol 92*
Paderewski, Ignace Jan 1860-1941 *HisWorL [port]*
Paderewski, Ignacy Jan 1860-1941 *NewGrDO*
Padfield, Nicholas David 1947- *Who 94*
Padfield, Peter 1932- *WrDr 94*
Padgaonkar, Dileep 1944- *IntWW 93*
Padget, John E. 1948- *WhoWest 94*
Padgett, (Mary) Abigail 1942- *ConAu 141*
Padgett, Alan Gregory 1955- *WhoWest 94*
Padgett, Bobby Lee, II 1966- *WhoScEn 94*
Padgett, Chance Robert 1946- *WhoMW 93*
Padgett, David Ramon 1956- *WhoMW 93*
Padgett, Dorothy B. 1927- *WhoAmP 93*
Padgett, Douglas Ralph Xavier 1942- *WhoAmL 94*
Padgett, Frank D. 1923- *WhoAmP 93*
Padgett, Frank David 1923- *WhoAm 94, WhoWest 94*
Padgett, George Arthur 1932- *WhoAm 94*
Padgett, Gregory Lee 1959- *WhoAmL 94*
Padgett, James A. 1948- *WhoBlA 94*
Padgett, John Dwain, II 1968- *WhoWest 94*
Padgett, Joy *WhoAmP 93*
Padgett, Kenneth W. 1929- *WhoAmP 93*
Padgett, Lewis *EncSF 93*
Padgett, Lucas C., Jr. 1946- *WhoAmL 94*
Padgett, Mark Jonathan 1956- *WhoMW 93*
Padgett, Mike 1923- *WhoAmP 93*
Padgett, Paul Marvin *WhoAmP 93*
Padgett, Richard Brinkley 1958- *WhoFI 94*
Padgett, Ron *DrAPF 93*
Padgett, Ron 1942- *WrDr 94*
Padgett, Shelton Edward 1948- *WhoAm 94, WhoAmL 94*
Padgett, Tom *DrAPF 93*
Padia, Anna Marie 1945- *WhoHisp 94*
Padian, Kevin 1951- *WhoWest 94*
Padilla (Lorenzo), Heberto 1932- *ConWorW 93*
Padilla, Alonzo J. 1953- *WhoHisp 94*
Padilla, Amado Manuel 1942- *WhoHisp 94*
Padilla, Charlie B. 1920- *WhoAmP 93*
Padilla, Corrine *WhoHisp 94*
Padilla, David Joseph, Jr. 1944- *WhoHisp 94*
Padilla, David P. 1949- *WhoHisp 94*
Padilla, Ema d1966 *WhoHol 92*
Padilla, Ernest 1944- *WhoHisp 94*
Padilla, Ernest A. *WhoHisp 94*
Padilla, Felix M. *WhoHisp 94*
Padilla, Genaro M. *WhoHisp 94*
Padilla, George Alonso 1945- *WhoHisp 94*
Padilla, George Jasso 1934- *WhoHisp 94*
Padilla, Gilbert 1929- *WhoHisp 94*
Padilla, Gilberto Cruz 1939- *WhoHisp 94*
Padilla, Heberto 1932- *WhoHisp 94*
Padilla, Hernan 1938- *WhoAmP 93, WhoHisp 94*
Padilla, Isaac F. *WhoHisp 94*
Padilla, James Earl 1953- *WhoAm 94, WhoAmL 94*
Padilla, James J. *WhoHisp 94*
Padilla, Jose 1889-1960 *NewGrDO*
Padilla, Juan De c. 1500-1542 *WhWE*
Padilla, Kevin Joseph 1964- *WhoHisp 94*
Padilla, Leocadio Joseph 1927- *WhoHisp 94*
Padilla, Manuel, Jr. 1956- *WhoHol 92*
Padilla, Maria Luisa 1947- *WhoHisp 94*
Padilla, Mariam *WhoHisp 94*
Padilla, Michael A. *WhoHisp 94*
Padilla, Michael James 1945- *WhoHisp 94*
Padilla, Nancy A. 1950- *WhoHisp 94*
Padilla, Nancy Ann 1950- *WhoAmP 93*
Padilla, Patrick J. 1950- *WhoHisp 94*
Padilla, Paula Jeanette 1953- *WhoHisp 94*
Padilla, Raymond V. *WhoHisp 94*
Padilla, Raymond V. 1944- *WrDr 94*
Padilla, Richard 1949- *WhoHisp 94*
Padilla, Rita M. 1951- *WhoHisp 94*
Padilla, Robert *WhoHol 92*
Padilla, Rudy 1940- *WhoHisp 94*
Padilla, Sally G. 1937- *WhoHisp 94*
Padilla, Wanda Maria 1948- *WhoHisp 94*
Padilla, William Joseph 1956- *WhoHisp 94*
Padilla Arancibia, David *IntWW 93*
Padilla Nervo, Luis 1898- *HisDcKW*
Padilla-Taylor, Laura M. 1962- *WhoHisp 94*
Padiyara, Anthony 1921- *IntWW 93*
Padjeon, Jack d1960 *WhoHol 92*
Padmanabhan, Mahesh 1962- *WhoMW 93, WhoScEn 94*
Padmore, (Thomas), Lady *Who 94*
Padmore, Elaine Marguirite 1947- *Who 94*
Padmore, Thomas 1909- *Who 94*
Padoa-Schioppa, Tommaso 1940- *IntWW 93*
Pados, Frank John, Jr. 1944- *WhoAm 94*
Padova, John R. 1935- *WhoAm 94, WhoAmL 94*
Padovan, John Mario Faskally 1938- *Who 94*
Padovani, Lea 1920- *WhoHol 92*
Padovanis, Domenicos 1817-1892 *NewGrDO*
Padovano, Anthony John 1933- *WhoAmA 93*
Padovano, Anthony T. 1934- *WrDr 94*
Padovano, Anthony Thomas 1934- *WhoAm 94*
Padovano, John d1973 *WhoHol 92*
Padre, Marc Cruz 1937- *WhoAsA 94*
Padrick, Kevin D. 1955- *WhoAmL 94*
Padron, D. Lorenzo 1945- *WhoHisp 94*
Padrón, Eduardo J. 1945- *WhoHisp 94*
Padron, Elida R. 1954- *WhoHisp 94*
Padron, Maria de Los Angeles 1955- *WhoHisp 94*
Padron, Peter E. *WhoHisp 94*
Padron, Raymond Vincent 1956- *WhoFI 94*
Padron Quero, Marisela *WhoWomW 91*
Paduano, Joseph 1953- *WhoFI 94*
Padula, Fred David 1937- *WhoAm 94, WhoAmA 93*
Padula, Marguerita d1957 *WhoHol 92*
Padula, Mary L. *WhoAmP 93*
Padula, Vicente d1967 *WhoHol 92*
Padulo, Louis 1936- *WhoAm 94, WhoBlA 94*
Padva, Genrikh Pavlovich 1931- *IntWW 93*
Padve, Martha Bertonneau *WhoWest 94*
Padway, Robert Alan 1945- *WhoAmL 94*
Padwe, Carol 1944- *WhoWest 94*
Paeff, Bash Ka 1893-1979 *WhoAmA 93N*
Paek, Chisun Jim 1967- *WhoAsA 94*
Paek, James Joon-Hong 1958- *WhoScEn 94*
Paek, Min *WhoAsA 94*
Paek Song-uk 1897-1981 *HisDcKW*
Paemel, Monika van 1945- *BlmGWL*
Pae Myung-In 1932- *IntWW 93*
Paer, Ferdinando 1771-1839 *NewGrDO*
Paessun, Michael Anthony 1959- *WhoMW 93*
Paetro, Maxine 1946- *WrDr 94*
Paez, Pedro 1564-1622 *WhWE*
Paez, Richard A. *WhoHisp 94*
Paffard, Michael (Kenneth) 1928- *WrDr 94*
Paffard, Ronald Wilson 1904- *Who 94*
Paffenbarger, Ralph Seal 1894- *WhAm 10*
Paffenbarger, Ralph Seal, Jr. 1922- *WhoAm 94*
Pafford, John Henry Pyle 1900- *IntWW 93, Who 94, WrDr 94*
Pafford, John Walter 1949- *WhoAmL 94*
Paffrath, Hans-Georg 1922- *IntWW 93*
Pagala, Murali Krishna 1942- *WhoScEn 94*
Pagán, Ana Ivelise 1957- *WhoHisp 94*
Pagan, Antonio *WhoAmP 93*
Pagán, Antonio 1963- *WhoHisp 94*
Pagan, Fernando L. 1943- *WhoHisp 94*
Pagan, John 1951- *WhoAmP 93*
Pagan, Richard 1954-1989 *WhoAmA 93N*
Pagán, Sam 1959- *WhoHisp 94*
Pagan-Ayala, Benjamin 1928- *WhoHisp 94*
Paganelli, Giuseppe Antonio 1710-c. 1763 *NewGrDO*
Paganelli, Robert P. 1931- *WhoAmP 93*
Pagani, Albert Louis 1936- *WhoWest 94*
Pagani, Beverly Darlene 1937- *WhoWest 94*
Paganini, Maria Angiola fl. 1742- *NewGrDO*
Paganis, K. George 1937- *WhoIns 94*
Pagano, Alfred H. 1930- *WhoAmP 93*
Pagano, Alphonse Frederick 1909- *WhoScEn 94*
Pagano, Anthony Frank 1948- *WhoAmL 94*
Pagano, Bartolomeo d1947 *WhoHol 92*
Pagano, Filippo Frank 1939- *WhoFI 94*
Pagano, Gino 1921- *IntWW 93*
Pagano, Jon Alain 1958- *WhoMW 93*
Pagano, Joseph Stephen 1931- *WhoScEn 94*
Pagano, Marina d1990 *WhoHol 92*
Pagano, Yolanda Frances 1965- *WhoAmL 94*
Pagan-Saez, Heriberto 1933- *WhoAm 94*
Paganucci, Paul Donnelly 1931- *WhoAm 94, WhoFI 94*
Pagay, Sophie d1937 *WhoHol 92*
Pagbalha Geleg Namgyai 1940- *IntWW 93, WhoPRCh 91 [port]*
Pagden, Leonard d1928 *WhoHol 92*
Pagdon, William Harry 1962- *WhoScEn 94*
Page *Who 94*
Page, Alan *ProFbHF*
Page, Alan d1987 *WhoHol 92*
Page, Alan C. 1945- *WhoAmP 93*
Page, Alan Cedric 1945- *WhoAmL 94, WhoBlA 94, WhoMW 93*
Page, Albert Lee 1927- *WhoAm 94*
Page, Alexander Warren d1993 *IntWW 93N, Who 94N*
Page, Alexander Warren 1914- *IntWW 93*
Page, Alfred Emil, Jr. 1938- *WhoAmL 94*
Page, Anita 1910- *WhoHol 92*
Page, Ann 1958- *WhoFI 94*
Page, Anne Ruth 1949- *WhoAm 94*
Page, Annette 1932- *Who 94*
Page, Anthony 1935- *IntMPA 94*
Page, Anthony (Frederick Montague) 1935- *Who 94*
Page, Armand Ernest 1955- *WhoScEn 94*
Page, Arthur d1968 *WhoHol 92*
Page, Arthur Anthony 1922- *WhoScEn 94*
Page, Ashley 1956- *IntDcB, Who 94*
Page, Austin P. 1936- *WhoAm 94, WhoFI 94*
Page, Benjamin Ingrim 1940- *WhoAm 94*
Page, Bertram Samuel 1904- *Who 94*
Page, Bob d1943 *WhoHol 92*
Page, Bradley *WhoHol 92*
Page, Bruce 1936- *IntWW 93, Who 94*
Page, Carolyn *DrAPF 93*
Page, Cedric Daniel 1945- *WhoBlA 94*
Page, Charles Edward 1920- *Who 94*
Page, Charles H. 1909- *WrDr 94*
Page, Charles Hunt 1909-1992 *WhAm 10*
Page, Clarence E. 1947- *WhoAm 94, WhoMW 93*
Page, Curtis Matthewson 1946- *WhoWest 94*
Page, Cyril Leslie 1916- *Who 94*
Page, Debra Kay 1953- *WhoAmL 94*
Page, Dennis 1932- *WhoScEn 94*
Page, Dennis Fountain 1919- *Who 94*
Page, Don Nelson 1948- *WhoScEn 94, WhoWest 94*
Page, Dozzie Lyons 1921- *WhoMW 93*
Page, Earl Michael 1950- *WhoFI 94*
Page, Edward Crozer, Jr. 1919- *WhoScEn 94*
Page, Ellis Batten 1924- *WhoAm 94*
Page, Emma *WrDr 94*
Page, Ernest 1927- *WhoAm 94*
Page, Ewan Stafford 1928- *IntWW 93, Who 94*
Page, Frederick (William) 1917- *Who 94*
Page, Frederick West 1932- *WhoAm 94*
Page, Gale d1983 *WhoHol 92*
Page, Genevieve 1927- *IntWW 93*
Page, Genevieve 1940- *WhoHol 92*
Page, Geoff(rey Donald) 1940- *WrDr 94*
Page, George Keith 1917- *WhoAm 94*
Page, Geraldine d1987 *WhoHol 92*
Page, Gertrude 1873-1922 *BlmGWL*
Page, Grant *WhoHol 92*
Page, Gregory 1689-1775 *DcNaB MP*
Page, Gregory Oliver 1950- *WhoBlA 94*
Page, Grover 1893-1958 *WhoAmA 93N*
Page, Harrison *WhoHol 92*
Page, Harrison Eugene 1941- *WhoBlA 94*
Page, Harry Robert 1915- *WhoAm 94*
Page, Howard William Barrett 1943- *Who 94*
Page, Irvine Heinly 1901-1991 *WhAm 10*
Page, J. Boyd 1948- *WhoAmL 94*
Page, J. D. 1952- *WhoAmL 94*
Page, Jack Randall 1956- *WhoAmL 94*
Page, Jake 1936- *WhoWest 94*
Page, James Allen 1918- *WhoBlA 94*
Page, James E. d1930 *WhoHol 92*
Page, James Francis, Jr. 1947- *WhoAmL 94*
Page, Janice Ellen 1948- *WhoAm 94*
Page, Jean Jepson 1924- *WhoAmA 93*
Page, Jennifer Anne 1944- *Who 94*
Page, Jimmy 1944-
See Yardbirds, The *ConMus 10*
Page, John *Who 94*
Page, John 1743-1808 *WhAmRev*
Page, (Arthur) John 1919- *Who 94*
Page, John (Joseph Joffre) 1915- *Who 94*
Page, John Boyd 1938- *WhoWest 94*
Page, John Brangwyn 1923- *Who 94*
Page, John C. 1924- *WhoAmP 93*
Page, John Henry, Jr. 1923- *WhoAm 94, WhoAmA 93*
Page, John Humphrey 1923- *Who 94*
Page, John Kenneth 1924- *Who 94*
Page, John Sheridan, Jr. 1942- *WhoBlA 94*
Page, Joy 1921- *WhoHol 92*
Page, Katherine Hall 1947- *WrDr 94*
Page, Kathy 1958- *EncSF 93, WrDr 94*
Page, Ken 1954- *WhoHol 92*
Page, Kenneth *Who 94*
Page, (Edwin) Kenneth 1898- *Who 94*
Page, Kenneth R. 1946- *WhoAmL 94*
Page, Kirby 1890-1957 *DcAmReB 2*
Page, Larry Keith 1933- *WhoAm 94*
Page, LaWanda 1920- *WhoHol 92*
Page, Lawrence Merle 1944- *WhoScEn 94*
Page, Leslie Andrew 1924- *WhoWest 94*
Page, Lewis Wendell, Jr. 1947- *WhoAmL 94*
Page, Linda Kay 1943- *WhoAm 94, WhoFI 94*
Page, Lorne Albert 1921- *WhoAm 94, WhoScEn 94*
Page, Louise 1955- *ConAu 140, ConDr 93, WrDr 94*
Page, Lucille d1964 *WhoHol 92*
Page, Mann 1749-1781 *WhAmRev*
Page, Marcus William 1937- *WhoAm 94*
Page, Marguerite A. *WhoBlA 94*
Page, Martha Poitevin 1948- *WhoWest 94*
Page, Matthew John 1929- *WhoAmP 93*
Page, Michel 1940- *WhoAm 94*
Page, Norman d1935 *WhoHol 92*
Page, Norman 1930- *WrDr 94*
Page, Norman B. 1951- *WhoAmL 94*
Page, Norvell W. 1904-1961 *EncSF 93*
Page, Oscar C. 1939- *WhoAm 94*
Page, P. K. 1916- *WrDr 94*
Page, Patricia Ann 1941- *WhoAmL 94*
Page, Patricia K. 1916- *BlmGWL*
Page, Patti 1927- *ConMus 11 [port], IntMPA 94, WhoHol 92*
Page, Paul d1974 *WhoHol 92*
Page, Penny B(ooth) 1949- *ConAu 140*
Page, Philip Ronald 1951- *WhoScEn 94*
Page, Pierre *WhoAm 94*
Page, Pippa 1955- *WhoHol 92*
Page, Raymond Ian 1924- *Who 94*
Page, Richard Allen 1952- *WhoScEn 94*
Page, Richard Lewis 1941- *Who 94*
Page, Rita d1954 *WhoHol 92*
Page, Robert Henry 1927- *WhoAm 94*
Page, Robert Wesley 1927- *WhoAm 94*
Page, Robin 1943- *WrDr 94*
Page, Rodney Fred 1946- *WhoAm 94, WhoAmL 94*
Page, Rosemary Saxton 1927- *WhoBlA 94*
Page, Rosewell, III 1939- *WhoAmL 94*
Page, Roy Christopher 1932- *WhoAm 94, WhoScEn 94*
Page, Ruth 1899?-1991 *IntDcB [port], WhAm 10*
Page, Ruth Joanne 1945- *WhoMW 93*
Page, Sallie *DrAPF 93*
Page, Sally Jacquelyn 1943- *WhoMW 93*
Page, Sandra Rector 1946- *WhoAmP 93*
Page, Simon Richard 1934- *Who 94*
Page, Stephen Allen 1952- *WhoAmP 93*
Page, Stephen Franklin 1940- *WhoAm 94*
Page, Thomas (Walker, IV) 1942- *EncSF 93*
Page, Thomas Alexander 1933- *WhoWest 94*
Page, Thomas R. 1951- *WhoAmL 94*
Page, Thornton Leigh 1913- *WhoAm 94*
Page, Tom *DrAPF 93*
Page, Tonya Fair 1956- *WhoScEn 94*
Page, Troy Edward 1938- *WhoMW 93*
Page, William *DrAPF 93*
Page, William Marion 1917- *WhoAm 94*
Page, Willie F. 1929- *WhoBlA 94*
Page, Willis *WhoAm 94*
Pagel, Bernard Ephraim Julius 1930- *Who 94*
Pagel, William Rush 1901- *WhoAm 94*
Pagels, Elaine *WrDr 94*
Pagels, Elaine Hiesey *WhoAm 94*
Pagels, Jurgen Heinrich 1925- *WhoAm 94*
Pagent-Fredericks, J. Rous-Marten 1905-1963 *WhoAmA 93N*
Pageotte, Donald P. 1926- *WhoAmP 93*
Pagery, Francois *EncSF 93*
Pages, Ernest Alexander 1959- *WhoHisp 94*
Pages, Jean 1907-1977 *WhoAmA 93N*
Paget *Who 94*
Paget, Alfred d1925 *WhoHol 92*
Paget, David Christopher John 1942- *Who 94*
Paget, Debra 1933- *IntMPA 94, WhoHol 92*
Paget, Joel Hathaway 1945- *WhoAmL 94*
Paget, John *EncSF 93*
Paget, John Arthur 1922- *WhoWest 94*
Paget, Julian (Tolver) 1921- *Who 94, WrDr 94*
Paget, Peter d1976 *WhoHol 92*
Paget, Richard (Herbert) 1957- *Who 94*
Paget, Richard Moscrop 1913-1991 *WhAm 10*
Paget, Violet *BlmGWL, GayLL*
Paget-Bowman, Cicely 1910- *WhoHol 92*

Paget De Beaudesert, Lord 1986- Who 94
Pagett, Gary WhoHol 92
Pagett, Nicola 1945- IntMPA 94, WhoHol 92
Pagett, Nicola Mary 1945- Who 94
Pagetti, Carlo 1945- EncSF 93
Paget-Wilkes, Michael Jocelyn James 1941- Who 94
Page Wood, Anthony John 1951- Who 94
Paglia, Camille 1947- IntWW 93, WhoAm 94
Paglia, Camille (Anna) 1947- ConAu 140
Pagliardi, Giovanni Maria 1637-1702 NewGrDO
Pagliarini, James WhoWest 94
Pagliarini, Ronald James 1957- WhoAmP 93
Pagliaro, Frank Joseph, Jr. 1940- WhoAmP 93
Pagliaro, Harold Emil 1925- WhoAm 94
Pagliaro, James Domenic 1951- WhoAm 94
Pagliero, Marcello d1980 WhoHol 92
Paglio, Lydia Elizabeth WhoAm 94
Pagliuca, Giuseppe fl. 1775-1805 NewGrDO
Pagliughi, Gloria F. WhoAmP 93
Pagliughi, Lina 1907-1980 NewGrDO
Pagnamenta, Peter John 1941- Who 94
Pagnani, Andreina d1981 WhoHol 92
Pagni, Patrick John 1942- WhoAm 94
Pagnol, Jacqueline 1926- WhoHol 92
Pagnozzi, Richard Douglas 1947- WhoIns 94
Pagnucci, Gianfranco DrAPF 93
Pagonis, William G. NewYTBS 93 [port]
Pagonis, William Gust 1941- WhoAm 94
Pagter, Carl Richard 1934- WhoAm 94, WhoAmL 94
Pagu BlmGWL
Pahadia, Shanti 1936- WhoWomW 91
Pahang, H.H. Sultan of 1930- IntWW 93
Pahides, Ann-Marie MacDonald 1961- WhoAmL 94
Pahissa, Jaime 1880-1969 NewGrDO
Pahlavi, Farah Diba 1938- IntWW 93
Pahls, Margaret Ellen 1932- WhoMW 93
Pahr, Willibald P. 1930- IntWW 93
Pai, Anantha M. 1931- WhoAm 94
Pai, Anna Chao 1935- WhoAsA 94
Pai, David Hsien-Chung 1936- WhoAsA 94
Pai, Devdas Mizar 1960- WhoFI 94
Pai, Gregory Gi Yong 1945- WhoAsA 94
Pai, K. Vasanth 1933- WhoAsA 94
Pai, Kenneth Y. 1947- WhoAsA 94
Pai, Lisa Koonghui Kim 1960- WhoAsA 94
Pai, Sadanand V. 1937- WhoAsA 94, WhoMW 93
Pai, Suzee 1962- WhoHol 92
Pai, Venkatrao K. 1939- WhoAsA 94
Pai, Young WhoMW 93
Paiba, Denis Anthony 1926- Who 94
Paice, Clifford 1938- Who 94
Paice, Ian 1948- See Deep Purple ConMus 11
Paice, James Edward Thornton 1949- Who 94
Paice, Karlo Bruce 1906- Who 94
Paicopolos, Michael F. 1920- WhoAmP 93
Paidosh, Chris Jonathan 1955- WhoMW 93
Paidoussis, Michael Pandeli 1935- WhoAm 94
Paier, Adolf Arthur 1938- WhoAm 94, WhoFI 94
Paige, Alan d1988 WhoHol 92
Paige, Alfred Lee 1950- WhoWest 94
Paige, Alvin 1934- WhoBlA 94
Paige, Connie 1945- WrDr 94
Paige, David Alwin 1947- WhoAmL 94
Paige, Edward George Sydney 1930- Who 94
Paige, Emmett, Jr. 1931- AfrAmG [port], WhoBlA 94
Paige, Glenn Durland 1929- WhoAm 94, WhoWest 94
Paige, Hilliard Wegner 1919- WhoAm 94
Paige, Janis 1922- WhoHol 92
Paige, Janis 1923- IntMPA 94
Paige, Jean d1990 WhoHol 92
Paige, Leroy d1982 WhoHol 92
Paige, Leroy Robert 1906-1982 AfrAmAl 6
Paige, Lowell J. 1919- WhoWest 94
Paige, Mabel d1954 WhoHol 92
Paige, Michael 1941- WhoAmL 94
Paige, Michele Anna 1969- ConAu 141
Paige, Nancy E. 1941- WhoAmL 94
Paige, Norma 1922- WhoFI 94
Paige, Norman WhoAm 94
Paige, Patsy d1963 WhoHol 92
Paige, Paul 1934- WhoWest 94
Paige, Peggy d1974 WhoHol 92
Paige, Raymond d1965 WhoHol 92
Paige, Richard EncSF 93
Paige, Richard Bruce 1949- WhoAm 94
Paige, Richard Collings 1911- Who 94
Paige, Robert d1987 WhoHol 92
Paige, Roderick 1935- WhoBlA 94
Paige, Stephone 1961- WhoBlA 94
Paige, Susanne Lynn 1950- WhoFI 94
Paige, Susanne Ruiz 1952- WhoAmL 94
Paige, Victor Grellier 1925- IntWW 93, Who 94
Paige, Victoria Hahne 1965- WhoWest 94
Paige, Vivian Jo-Ann 1960- WhoFI 94
Paige, Wayne Leo 1944- WhoAmA 93
Paige, Windell 1950- WhoBlA 94
Paigen, Kenneth 1927- WhoAm 94
Paik, Ho Jung 1944- WhoAsA 94
Paik, John Kee 1934- WhoScEn 94
Paik, Kun Woo 1946- IntWW 93
Paik, Nam June 1932- IntWW 93, ModArCr 4 [port], WhoAmA 93
Paik, Woon Ki 1925- WhoAsA 94
Paik, Young-Ki 1953- WhoScEn 94
Paikowsky, Sandra R. 1945- WhoAmA 93
Paikowsky, Sandra Roslyn 1945- WhoAm 94
Paik Son-yup 1920- HisDcKW
Paik Tu Chin 1908- HisDcKW
Pailen, Donald 1941- WhoBlA 94
Pain, Barry 1864-1928 DcLB 135 [port]
Pain, Barry (Eric Odell) 1864-1928 EncSF 93
Pain, Barry Newton 1931- Who 94
Pain, Charles Leslie 1913- WhoAm 94
Pain, Didier WhoHol 92
Pain, Emil Abramovich 1948- LngBDD
Pain, Gillian Margaret 1936- Who 94
Pain, Peter (Richard) 1913- Who 94
Pain, Rollo Who 94
Pain, (Horace) Rollo (Squarey) 1921- Who 94
Painchaud, Brian d1986 WhoHol 92
Paine, Albert B(igelow) 1861-1937 EncSF 93
Paine, Augustus G., II d1993 NewYTBS 93
Paine, Barbara Gordon DrAPF 93
Paine, Bruce Edwin 1933- WhoFI 94
Paine, Charles F. 1920- IntMPA 94
Paine, Charles William Eliot 1936- WhoAm 94
Paine, Christopher Hammon 1935- Who 94
Paine, Denise Langdon 1960- WhoMW 93
Paine, Ephraim 1730-1785 WhAmRev
Paine, Harry d1941 WhoHol 92
Paine, James Carriger 1924- WhoAm 94, WhoAmL 94
Paine, John Knowles 1839-1906 NewGrDO
Paine, Lauran (Bosworth) 1916- EncSF 93
Paine, Louis Burr, Jr. 1932- WhoAm 94
Paine, Marylin J. 1931- WhoAmP 93, WhoWomW 91
Paine, Peter Stanley 1921- Who 94
Paine, Ralph Delahaye 1906-1991 WhAm 10
Paine, Richard Earl 1953- WhoMW 93
Paine, Robert T. 1900-1965 WhoAmA 93N
Paine, Robert Treat 1731-1814 AmRev, WhAmRev
Paine, Robert Treat 1944- WhoWest 94
Paine, Roger Edward 1943- Who 94
Paine, Stephen William 1908-1992 WhAm 10
Paine, Thomas 1737-1808 EncEth
Paine, Thomas 1737-1809 AmRev, BlmGEL, DcAmReB 2, HisWorL [port], WhAmRev [port]
Paine, Thomas O. 1921-1992 AnObit 1992
Paine, Thomas Otten 1921-1992 WhAm 10
Paine, Timothy Francis 1965- WhoWest 94
Pa'-Ingya fl. 1887-1894 EncNAR
Paino, Frankie DrAPF 93
Paintal, Autar Singh 1925- IntWW 93, Who 94
Painter, Amelia Ann 1946- WhoWest 94
Painter, Ann B. 1920- WhoAmP 93
Painter, Carl Eric 1946- WhoAm 94, WhoFI 94
Painter, Charlotte DrAPF 93, WrDr 94
Painter, Daniel ConAu 42NR
Painter, Eleanor d1947 WhoHol 92
Painter, Gamaliel 1743-1819 WhAmRev
Painter, George Duncan 1914- Who 94
Painter, Helen (Welch) 1913- WrDr 94
Painter, Henry WhoAm 94
Painter, Jack Timberlake 1930- WhoAm 94
Painter, John 1935- WrDr 94
Painter, John Cecil 1943- WhoAm 94
Painter, John Hoyt 1934- WhoAm 94
Painter, Joseph T. 1927- WhoAm 94
Painter, Mark Philip 1947- WhoAmL 94, WhoMW 93
Painter, Michael A. 1939- WhoAmL 94
Painter, Michael Robert 1935- WhoAm 94
Painter, Nell Irvin 1942- WhoBlA 94
Painter, Pamela DrAPF 93
Painter, Paul Wain, Jr. 1945- WhoAmL 94
Painter, Samuel Franklin 1946- WhoAmL 94
Painter, Terence James 1935- Who 94
Painter, Thomas EncSF 93
Painter, Thomas Jay 1944- WhoFI 94
Painter, William 1540?-1594 DcLB 136
Painter, William Hall 1927- WhoAm 94
Painting, Rodger T. 1938- WhoIns 94
Paintog WhoPRCh 91
Painton, Ira Wayne 1917- WhoAm 94
Painton, Russell Elliott 1940- WhoAm 94, WhoAmL 94
Pai Pei-Ying IntWW 93
Pairault, Pierre EncSF 93
Pairo, Preston (A., III) 1958- ConAu 142
Pais, Abraham 1918- IntWW 93, WhoAm 94, WhoScEn 94
Pais, Arie 1930- IntWW 93
Pais, Mara Devine 1959- WhoAmL 94
Paischer, Edith-Maria 1929- WhoWomW 91
Paisiello, Giovanni 1740-1816 NewGrDO
Paisley, Bishop of 1929- Who 94
Paisley, David Duane 1961- WhoWest 94
Paisley, Ian Richard Kyle 1926- IntWW 93
Paisley, Ian Richard Kyle 1979- Who 94
Paisley, Keith W. 1928- WhoAmP 93, WhoMW 93
Paisley, Melvyn R. 1924- WhoAmP 93
Paisley, Robert 1919- Who 94
Paisner, Bruce Lawrence 1942- WhoAm 94
Paisner, Dina WhoHol 92
Paita, Giovanni fl. 1708- NewGrDO
Paiva, Apolinario Souza d1993 NewYTBS 93
Paiva, Joseph Moura 1955- WhoFI 94
Paiva, Nestor d1966 WhoHol 92
Paiva-Weed, M. Teresa 1959- WhoAmP 93
Paivio, Allan Urho 1925- WhoAm 94
Pajak, David Joseph 1956- WhoAmL 94
Pajak, Penelope Anne 1947- WhoAmP 93
Pajari, Roger Nelson 1941- WhoAm 94
Pajaud, William E. 1925- WhoBlA 94
Pajcic, Steve WhoAmP 93
Pajestka, Jozef 1924- IntWW 93
Pajil, Cheryl V. 1949- WhoHisp 94
Pajor, Robert E. 1936- WhoFI 94
Pajot, Gilles-Etienne 1958- WhoFI 94
Pak, Hyung Woong 1932- WhoAm 94
Pak, Koon Yan 1950- WhoAsA 94
Pak, Peter Hui-Mun 1963- WhoAsA 94
Pak, Ronald Yu-Sang 1957- WhoAsA 94
Pak, William Louis 1932- WhoMW 93
Pak, Yong Chin WhoAsA 94
Pakdemirli, Ekrem IntWW 93
Pake, George Edward 1924- IntWW 93, WhoAm 94
Pakenham Who 94
Pakenham, Elizabeth Who 94
Pakenham, Henry Desmond Verner 1911- Who 94
Pakenham, Michael Aidan 1943- Who 94
Pakenham, Thomas (Frank Dermot) 1933- Who 94, WrDr 94
Pakenham-Walsh, John 1928- Who 94
Pakes, Steven P. 1934- WhoScEn 94
Pak Hon-Yong 1900-1955 HisDcKW
Pakington Who 94
Pakiser, Louis Charles, Jr. 1919- WhoAm 94, WhoWest 94
Pakkinen, Saara-Maria 1941- WhoWomW 91
Pakrasi, Himadri Bhusan 1953- WhoMW 93
Pakula, Alan J. 1928- IntMPA 94, IntWW 93, WhoAm 94
Pakula, Alan J(ay) 1928- WrDr 94
Pakvasa, Sandip 1935- WhoAsA 94, WhoWest 94
Pal, George 1908-1980 EncSF 93, IntDcF 2-4
Pal, Lenard 1925- IntWW 93
Pal, Prabir Kumar 1936- WhoAm 94
Pal, Pratapaditya 1935- WhoAm 94, WhoAmA 93, WhoAsA 94, WrDr 94
Pal, Sibtosh 1963- WhoScEn 94
Palace, Johnny d1980 WhoHol 92
Palace, Thomas Michael 1956- WhoMW 93
Palacio, Eduardo J. 1968- WhoFI 94
Palacios, Arturo 1961- WhoHisp 94
Palacios, Frances M. 1954- WhoHisp 94
Palacios, Herman T. WhoAmP 93
Palacios, Ignacio G. 1957- WhoHisp 94
Palacios, Jaime 1963- WhoHisp 94
Palacios, Jeannette C. De 1946- WhoHisp 94
Palacios, Joaquin Alquisira 1943- WhoScEn 94
Palacios, Lucila 1902- BlmGWL
Palacios, Luis E. 1956- WhoHisp 94
Palacios, Magno WhoHisp 94
Palacios, May Husni 1926- WhoMW 93
Palacios, Pedro Pablo 1953- WhoAmL 94, WhoWest 94
Palacios, Rafael R. WhoHisp 94
Palacios, Vicente 1963- WhoHisp 94
Palacios De Vizzio, Sergio 1936- IntWW 93
Palacioz, Joe John 1948- WhoHisp 94
Palade, George WorScD
Palade, George Emil 1912- IntWW 93, Who 94, WhoAm 94, WhoScEn 94, WhoWest 94
Paladilhe, Emile 1844-1926 NewGrDO
Paladino, Albert Edward 1932- WhoFI 94
Paladino, Daniel R. WhoAm 94, WhoAmL 94, WhoFI 94
Paladino, Joseph Anthony 1953- WhoAm 94, WhoScEn 94
Palaia, Franc (Dominic) 1949- WhoAmA 93
Palaia, Joseph A. 1927- WhoAmP 93
Palaima, Thomas Gerard 1951- WhoAm 94
Palamand, Krishna 1933- WhoAsA 94
Palamara, Francis Joseph 1925- WhoAm 94
Palamara, Joseph WhoAmP 93
Palan, Perry 1943- WhoAmL 94
Palanca, Peter Michael 1951- WhoMW 93
Palance, Brooke 1951- WhoHol 92
Palance, Cody 1955- WhoHol 92
Palance, David Michael 1960- WhoScEn 94
Palance, Holly 1950- WhoHol 92
Palance, Ines d1962 WhoHol 92
Palance, Jack WhoAm 94
Palance, Jack 1920- IntMPA 94, WhoHol 92
Palangio, Thomas A. 1962- WhoAmP 93
Palans, Lloyd Alex 1946- WhoAm 94, WhoAmL 94
Palast, Geri D. WhoAm 94
Palasthy, Alexander d1948 WhoHol 92
Palasty, Irene WhoHol 92
Palatiello, John Michael 1955- WhoFI 94
Palatine, Madame 1652-1722 BlmGWL
Palau d1966 WhoHol 92
Palau, Luis 1934- IntWW 93, WhoHisp 94
Palau, Marta 1934- WhoAmA 93
Palau, Pierre d1966 WhoHol 92
Palay, Elliot 1948- NewGrDO
Palay, Gilbert 1827- WhoFI 94
Palay, Sanford Louis 1918- WhoAm 94, WhoScEn 94
Palazuelos, Ramon 1929- WhoHisp 94
Palazzi, Giovanni fl. 1718- NewGrDO
Palazzi, Joseph Lazarro 1947- WhoAm 94, WhoFI 94
Palazzi, Matilde 1802-1842 NewGrDO
Palazzini, Pietro 1912- IntWW 93
Palazzo, Frank J. 1917- WhoAmP 93
Palazzo, Mark James 1961- WhoFI 94
Palazzola, Guy 1919-1978 WhoAmA 93N
Palazzolo, Carl 1945- WhoAmA 93
Palazzolo, Linda A. 1948- WhoAmL 94
Palazzolo, Paul Gerard 1966- WhoMW 93
Palchesko, David Alan 1955- WhoMW 93
Palcy, Euzhan WhoBlA 94
Palcy, Euzhan 1957- IntMPA 94
Palczynski, Richard W. 1947- WhoIns 94
Paldus, Josef 1935- WhoAm 94
Palecek, George Thomas 1952- WhoWest 94
Palella, Antonio 1692-1761 NewGrDO
Palen, Theodore Edward 1954- WhoWest 94
Palencia, Elaine Fowler DrAPF 93
Palencia, Elaine Fowler 1946- ConAu 142
Palencia, Isabel de 1878-1960? BlmGWL
Palencia-Roth, Michael 1946- WhoHisp 94
Palentrotti, Melchior dc. 1618 NewGrDO
Paleokrassas, Yannis 1934- IntWW 93
Paleologos, Nicholas Arthur 1953- WhoAmP 93
Paleos, Constantinos Marcos 1941- WhoScEn 94
Palepu, Krishna Gour 1954- WhoFI 94
Palermino, Anthony J. WhoAmP 93
Palermo, Anthony Robert 1929- WhoAm 94, WhoAmL 94
Palermo, Christopher John 1962- WhoScEn 94
Palermo, Gregory Sebastian 1946- WhoAm 94
Palermo, Joseph 1917- WhoAm 94
Palermo, Norman Anthony 1937- WhoAmL 94
Palermo, Peter M., Jr. 1941- WhoAm 94
Palester, Roman 1907-1989 NewGrDO
Palethorpe-Todd, Richard Andrew Who 94
Palette, John 1928- Who 94
Palevsky, Max 1924- WhoAm 94

Paley, Alan H. 1950- *WhoAmL 94*
Paley, Albert Raymond 1944- *WhoAm 94, WhoAmA 93*
Paley, Alfred Irving 1927- *WhoAm 94*
Paley, David d1993 *NewYTBS 93*
Paley, Gerald Larry 1939- *WhoAm 94*
Paley, Grace *DrAPF 93*
Paley, Grace 1922- *BlmGWL, IntWW 93, RfGShF, WhoAm 94, WrDr 94*
Paley, Hiram 1933- *WhoMW 93*
Paley, Karl Robert d1993 *NewYTBS 93 [port]*
Paley, Maggie *DrAPF 93*
Paley, Natalie (Princess) d1981 *WhoHol 92*
Paley, Petronia *WhoHol 92*
Paley, Richard Thomas 1936- *WhoFI 94*
Paley, Steven Jann 1955- *WhoScEn 94*
Paley, Vivian Gussin 1929- *WrDr 94*
Paley, William 1743-1805 *EncEth*
Paley, William S. 1901-1990 *WhAm 10, WhoAmA 93N*
Paley, William S., Mrs. *WhoAmA 93N*
Palffy-Muhoray, Peter 1944- *WhoScEn 94*
Palfi, Lotta *WhoHol 92*
Palfrey, Joey 1915- *BuCMET*
Palfrey, Lee 1909-1987 *BuCMET*
Palfrey, Mianne 1911- *BuCMET*
Palfrey, Polly 1906- *BuCMET*
Palfrey, Sarah 1912- *BuCMET*
Palfrey, Thomas Rossman 1895- *WhAm 10*
Palgrave, William Gifford 1826-1888 *WhWE*
Paliashvili, Zakhary Petrovich 1871-1933 *NewGrDO*
Paliganoff, David James 1941- *WhoMW 93*
Palihnich, Nicholas Joseph, Jr. 1939- *WhoAm 94*
Palik, James N. 1941- *WhoAmL 94*
Palik, Robert Richard 1923- *WhoScEn 94*
Palillo, Ron 1954- *WhoHol 92*
Palin, Michael 1943- *IntMPA 94, WhoCom, WhoHol 92*
Palin, Michael (Edward) 1943- *WrDr 94*
Palin, Michael Edward 1943- *IntWW 93, Who 94*
Palin, Roger Hewlett *Who 94*
Palincsar, Steven Edward 1958- *WhoMW 93*
Paling, Helen Elizabeth 1933- *Who 94*
Palinkas, James Thomas 1945- *WhoFI 94*
Palisano, John Raymond 1947- *WhoScEn 94*
Palisano, Samuel J. 1947- *WhoAmL 94*
Palisca, Claude Victor 1921- *WhoAm 94*
Palisi, Anthony Thomas 1930- *WhoAm 94*
Palisi, Joseph John d1993 *NewYTBS 93*
Palissot de Montenoy, Charles 1730-1814 *GuFrLit 2*
Palitz, Clarence Yale, Jr. 1931- *WhoAm 94*
Palitzsch, Peter 1918- *IntWW 93*
Paliwoda, Stanley Joseph 1948- *WhoWest 94*
Palizzi, Anthony N. 1942- *WhoAmL 94*
Palk, Anna d1990 *WhoHol 92*
Palkhivala, Nani Ardeshir 1920- *IntWW 93*
Palko, Michael James 1936- *WhoAm 94, WhoFI 94*
Pall, David B. 1914- *WhoAm 94, WhoFI 94, WhoScEn 94*
Palladino, Nunzio Joseph 1916- *WhoAm 94*
Palladino, Vincent Neil 1950- *WhoAm 94*
Palladino, Vincent Oliver 1929- *WhoAmP 93*
Palladino-Craig, Allys 1947- *WhoAm 94, WhoAmA 93*
Palladio, Andrea 1508-1580 *BlmGEL*
Pallakoff, Owen E. 1930- *WhoAm 94*
Pallam, John James 1940- *WhoAmL 94*
Pallander, Edwin *EncSF 93*
Pallant, Cheryl *DrAPF 93*
Pallant, Layeh *DrAPF 93*
Pallares, Mariano 1943- *WhoHisp 94*
Pallas, Christopher William 1956- *WhoScEn 94*
Pallas, Gregory 1951- *WhoAmP 93*
Pallasch, B. Michael 1933- *WhoAm 94, WhoAmL 94, WhoMW 93*
Pallasch, Thomas John 1936- *WhoWest 94*
Pallavicini, Giovanni Domenico fl. 1702- *NewGrDO*
Pallavicini, Vincenzo d1756? *NewGrDO*
Pallavicino, Carlo c. 1640-1688 *NewGrDO*
Pallavicino, Stefano Benedetto 1672-1742 *NewGrDO*
Pallay, Fran d1981 *WhoHol 92*
Pallen, Conde B(enoist) 1858-1929 *EncSF 93*
Pallenberg, Anita 1942- *WhoHol 92*
Pallenberg, Max d1934 *WhoHol 92*
Pallenik, Gary Alan 1948- *WhoFI 94*
Paller, Gary 1953- *WhoAmA 93*
Pallette, Eugene d1954 *WhoHol 92*
Palley, Claire Dorothea Taylor 1931- *Who 94*
Pallin, Irving M. 1910- *WhoAm 94*
Palli-Petralia, Fani *WhoWomW 91*
Palliser, Charles 1947- *WhoAm 94, WrDr 94*
Palliser, Hugh c. 1722-1796 *AmRev*
Palliser, Hugh 1723-1796 *WhAmRev*
Palliser, John 1807-1887 *WhWE*
Palliser, (Arthur) Michael 1922- *IntWW 93, Who 94*
Pallister, Janis *DrAPF 93*
Pallmeyer, Rebecca Ruth 1954- *WhoAm 94, WhoAmL 94*
Pallo, Imre 1891-1978 *NewGrDO*
Pallone, Adrian Joseph 1928- *WhoAm 94*
Pallone, Dave 1951- *ConAu 140*
Pallone, Frank, Jr. 1951- *CngDr 93, WhoAm 94, WhoAmP 93*
Pallone, Joseph Andrew 1947- *WhoFI 94*
Pallot, Arthur Keith 1918- *Who 94*
Pallot, E. Albert 1908- *WhoAm 94, WhoAmL 94*
Pallotti, Marianne Marguerite 1937- *WhoAm 94*
Pallottino, Massimo 1909- *IntWW 93*
Palm, Ed 1934- *WhoAmP 93*
Palm, Gary Howard 1942- *WhoAm 94, WhoAmL 94*
Palm, Gerald Albert 1942- *WhoAm 94, WhoAmL 94*
Palm, Marion *DrAPF 93*
Palm, William John 1944- *WhoScEn 94*
Palma, Andrea d1987 *WhoHol 92*
Palma, Bernard John, Jr. 1955- *WhoMW 93*
Palma, Dolores Patricia *WhoAm 94*
Palma, Felip *BlmGWL*
Palma, Henry, Sr. 1933- *WhoHisp 94*
Palma, Jack D. 1946- *WhoAmL 94*
Palma, Nicholas James 1953- *WhoAmL 94*
Palma, Raúl Arnulfo 1925- *WhoHisp 94*
Palma, Robert Michael 1946- *WhoAmL 94*
Palma, Silvestro 1754-1834 *NewGrDO*
Palmar, Derek (James) 1919- *IntWW 93, Who 94*
Palmar, Lorna d1928 *WhoHol 92*
Palmarez, Sulema E. 1957- *WhoHisp 94*
Palmatier, Malcolm Arthur 1922- *WhoWest 94*
Palme, Ulf *WhoHol 92*
Palmeiro, Rafael Corrales 1964- *WhoHisp 94*
Palmer *Who 94*
Palmer, Baron 1951- *Who 94*
Palmer, A. Laure *WhoAmA 93*
Palmer, Ada Margaret 1940- *WhoFI 94*
Palmer, Adrian Oliver 1950- *Who 94*
Palmer, Alan 1936 *WhoWest 94*
Palmer, Alan Kenneth 1941- *WhoAm 94*
Palmer, Alan Michael 1958- *WhoScEn 94*
Palmer, Alan Warwick 1926- *WrDr 94*
Palmer, Alice 1939- *WhoAmP 93*
Palmer, Alice Eugenia 1910- *WhoAm 94*
Palmer, Alice J. 1939- *WhoMW 93*
Palmer, Allen Ingels 1910-1950 *WhoAmA 93N*
Palmer, Andrew Eustace 1937- *Who 94*
Palmer, Angela 1957- *Who 94*
Palmer, Ann Therese Darin 1951- *WhoAmL 94, WhoFI 94*
Palmer, Anthony *WhoHol 92*
Palmer, Anthony Thomas Richard *Who 94*
Palmer, Anthony Wheeler 1936- *Who 94*
Palmer, Arnold 1929- *WhoHol 92*
Palmer, Arnold Daniel 1929- *IntWW 93, Who 94, WhoAm 94*
Palmer, Arthur E. d1993 *NewYTBS 93 [port]*
Palmer, Arthur Eugene 1923- *WhoMW 93*
Palmer, Arthur Montague Frank 1912- *Who 94*
Palmer, Ashley Joanne 1951- *WhoScEn 94*
Palmer, Belinda *WhoHol 92*
Palmer, Benjamin Morgan 1818-1902 *DcAmReB 2*
Palmer, Bernard Harold Michael 1929- *Who 94*
Palmer, Bert d1980 *WhoHol 92*
Palmer, Betsy 1926- *IntMPA 94*
Palmer, Betsy 1929- *WhoHol 92*
Palmer, Beverly Blazey 1945- *WhoWest 94*
Palmer, Brent David 1959- *WhoMW 93, WhoScEn 94*
Palmer, Brian Desmond 1939- *Who 94*
Palmer, Brian Eugene 1948- *WhoAm 94, WhoAmL 94*
Palmer, Bud *WhoHol 92*
Palmer, Byron 1925- *WhoHol 92*
Palmer, C. Earl 1897- *WhAm 10*
Palmer, (John) Carey (Bowden) 1943- *WrDr 94*
Palmer, Charlene Noel *DrAPF 93*
Palmer, Charles d1976 *WhoHol 92*
Palmer, Charles B. 1935- *WhoAmP 93*
Palmer, Charles E., Jr. 1933- *WhoAmL 94*
Palmer, Charles F. 1946- *WhoAm 94*
Palmer, Charles Francis 1946- *WhoAmL 94*
Palmer, Charles Harvey 1919- *WhoScEn 94*
Palmer, Charles Lee 1931- *WhoAmL 94*
Palmer, Charles Ray 1940- *WhoWest 94*
Palmer, Charles Richard, Jr. 1959- *WhoAmL 94*
Palmer, Charles Stuart William 1930- *Who 94*
Palmer, Charles William 1945- *Who 94*
Palmer, Corliss d1952 *WhoHol 92*
Palmer, Cruise 1917- *WhoAm 94*
Palmer, Curtis Ray *WhoFI 94, WhoMW 93*
Palmer, Daisy Ann *WhoFI 94*
Palmer, Daniel Lee 1958- *WhoWest 94*
Palmer, Darlene Tolbert 1946- *WhoBlA 94*
Palmer, Darwin L. 1930- *WhoAm 94*
Palmer, Dave Richard 1934- *WhoAm 94*
Palmer, David *DrAPF 93, WhoHol 92*
Palmer, David (Reay) 1941- *EncSF 93*
Palmer, David Brent 1946- *WhoAm 94*
Palmer, David Erroll Prior 1941- *Who 94*
Palmer, David Gilbert 1945- *WhoAm 94, WhoAmL 94*
Palmer, David Michael Oliver 1962- *WhoScEn 94*
Palmer, David Richard 1945- *WhoFI 94*
Palmer, David Vereker 1926- *Who 94*
Palmer, Dawson d1972 *WhoHol 92*
Palmer, Deborah Jean 1947- *WhoAm 94, WhoAmL 94*
Palmer, Delos 1891-1961 *WhoAmA 93N*
Palmer, Dennis, III 1914- *WhoBlA 94*
Palmer, Dennis Alan 1953- *WhoWest 94*
Palmer, Dennis Dale 1945- *WhoAm 94, WhoAmL 94*
Palmer, Derek George 1928- *Who 94*
Palmer, Diana *ConAu 141*
Palmer, Don 1905- *WrDr 94*
Palmer, Doreen P. 1949- *WhoBlA 94*
Palmer, Douglas Harold 1951- *WhoBlA 94*
Palmer, Douglas S., Jr. 1945- *WhoAmL 94*
Palmer, E. Reed 1932- *WhoAmP 93*
Palmer, Edgar Bernard 1953- *WhoBlA 94*
Palmer, Edward *WhoHol 92*
Palmer, Edward 1928- *WhoBlA 94*
Palmer, Edward 1937- *WhoBlA 94*
Palmer, Edward Emery 1945- *WhoScEn 94*
Palmer, Edward Eugene 1923- *WhoAmP 93*
Palmer, Edward Hurry 1912- *Who 94*
Palmer, Edward Lewis 1917- *WhoAm 94*
Palmer, Effie d1942 *WhoHol 92*
Palmer, Elihu 1764-1806 *DcAmReB 2*
Palmer, Elizabeth 1942- *ConAu 142*
Palmer, Elliott B., Sr. 1933- *WhoBlA 94*
Palmer, Felicity (Joan) 1944- *NewGrDO*
Palmer, Felicity Joan 1944- *Who 94*
Palmer, Forrest Charles 1924- *WhoAm 94*
Palmer, Francis Harvey 1930- *Who 94*
Palmer, Frank Robert 1922- *IntWW 93, Who 94, WrDr 94*
Palmer, Frank William 1940- *WhoAm 94*
Palmer, G., Jr. *DrAPF 93*
Palmer, Gary Andrew 1953- *WhoAm 94*
Palmer, Gary Charles 1950- *WhoMW 93*
Palmer, Geoffrey 1927- *WhoHol 92*
Palmer, Geoffrey (Christopher John) 1936- *Who 94*
Palmer, Geoffrey (Winston Russell) 1942- *Who 94*
Palmer, Geoffrey Winston Russell 1942- *IntWW 93*
Palmer, George 1740-1795 *DcNaB MP*
Palmer, George D(avid), Jr. 1897- *WhAm 10*
Palmer, George Josiah 1828-1892 *DcNaB MP*
Palmer, Gregg 1927- *IntMPA 94, WhoHol 92*
Palmer, Hans Christian 1933- *WhoAm 94*
Palmer, Hap 1942- *WrDr 94*
Palmer, Harvey John 1946- *WhoAm 94*
Palmer, Henrietta *BlmGWL*
Palmer, Henry Robinson 1795-1844 *DcNaB MP*
Palmer, Herbert Bearl 1915- *WhoAmA 93*
Palmer, Horace Anthony 1937- *Who 94*
Palmer, Howell M., III 1951- *WhoIns 94*
Palmer, Inda d1923 *WhoHol 92*
Palmer, Irene Sabelberg 1923- *WhoAm 94*
Palmer, Jack d1928 *WhoHol 92*
Palmer, James Alvin 1945- *WhoAm 94*
Palmer, James D. 1928- *WhoBlA 94*
Palmer, James Daniel 1930- *WhoAm 94, WhoScEn 94*
Palmer, James Daniel 1936- *WhoWest 94*
Palmer, James E. 1938- *WhoBlA 94*
Palmer, James Edward 1935- *WhoAm 94*
Palmer, James Leon 1948- *WhoAmL 94*
Palmer, Jane 1946- *EncSF 93*
Palmer, Janice Maude 1951- *WhoAmL 94*
Palmer, Jean May *WhoFI 94*
Palmer, Jeffress Gary 1921- *WhoAm 94*
Palmer, Jeffrey Donald 1955- *WhoMW 93*
Palmer, Jocelyn Beth 1927- *WhoMW 93*
Palmer, Joe *Who 94*
Palmer, Joe 1951- *WhoBlA 94*
Palmer, John *WhoAmP 93*
Palmer, John 1928- *Who 94*
Palmer, John (Chance) 1920- *Who 94*
Palmer, John (Edward Somerset) 1926- *Who 94*
Palmer, John A. 1944- *WhoBlA 94*
Palmer, John Albert, Jr. 1933- *WhoAmP 93*
Palmer, John Bernard, III 1952- *WhoAm 94, WhoAmL 94*
Palmer, John C., Jr. 1934- *WhoAmL 94*
Palmer, John J. 1939- *WhoIns 94*
Palmer, John Jacob 1939- *WhoAm 94*
Palmer, John James Ellis 1913- *WhoAm 94*
Palmer, John L. 1943- *WhoAm 94*
Palmer, John Marshall 1906- *WhoAm 94, WhoAmL 94, WhoMW 93*
Palmer, John William 1950- *WhoMW 93*
Palmer, Joseph 1716-1788 *AmRev, WhAmRev*
Palmer, Judith Grace 1948- *WhoAmL 94*
Palmer, Juliette 1930- *WrDr 94*
Palmer, June *WhoHol 92*
Palmer, Kenneth A. 1939- *WhoIns 94*
Palmer, Langdon 1928- *WhoAm 94*
Palmer, Laura Olivia 1955- *WhoBlA 94*
Palmer, Leslie *DrAPF 93*
Palmer, Leslie Robert d1992 *Who 94N*
Palmer, Lilli d1986 *WhoHol 92*
Palmer, Linda L. 1947- *WhoAmP 93*
Palmer, Linwood E., Jr. 1921- *WhoAmP 93*
Palmer, Lori *WhoAmP 93*
Palmer, Lorraine R. 1929- *WhoAmP 93*
Palmer, Lucie MacKay 1913- *WhoAmA 93*
Palmer, Mabel (Evelyn) 1903- *WhoAmA 93*
Palmer, Marcia Ann 1951- *WhoMW 93*
Palmer, Marcus 1795- *EncNAR*
Palmer, Maria d1981 *WhoHol 92*
Palmer, Mark *Who 94*
Palmer, (Charles) Mark 1941- *Who 94*
Palmer, Mark A. *WhoAmP 93*
Palmer, Martha Jane 1947- *WhoMW 93, WhoScEn 94*
Palmer, Max d1984 *WhoHol 92*
Palmer, Melville Louis 1924- *WhoAm 94, WhoScEn 94*
Palmer, Meredith Ann 1951- *WhoAmA 93*
Palmer, Michael *DrAPF 93, Who 94*
Palmer, Michael 1943- *WrDr 94*
Palmer, (Joseph) Michael 1928- *Who 94*
Palmer, Michael Andrew 1942- *WhoAmA 93*
Palmer, Michael Charles 1931- *WhoAm 94*
Palmer, Michael Denison 1933- *WrDr 94*
Palmer, Michael Don 1950- *WhoMW 93*
Palmer, Michael Erik 1968- *WhoMW 93*
Palmer, Michael Julian Barham 1933- *Who 94*
Palmer, Michael Paul 1944- *WhoAmL 94*
Palmer, Mike *WhoAmP 93*
Palmer, Miles R 1953- *WhoScEn 94*
Palmer, Milton Meade 1916- *WhoAm 94*
Palmer, Miriam *DrAPF 93*
Palmer, Monroe Edward 1938- *Who 94*
Palmer, Nathan d1777 *WhAmRev*
Palmer, Nathaniel Brown 1799-1877 *WhWE*
Palmer, Nettie 1885-1964 *BlmGWL*
Palmer, Nigel Fenton 1946- *Who 94*
Palmer, Noel 1926- *WhoBlA 94*
Palmer, Norman d1986 *WhoHol 92*
Palmer, Norman D. 1909- *WrDr 94*
Palmer, Norman D(unbar) 1909- *ConAu 41NR*
Palmer, Norman Dunbar 1909- *WhoAm 94*
Palmer, Norman Kitchener 1928- *Who 94*
Palmer, Patricia d1964 *WhoHol 92*
Palmer, Patricia Ann Texter 1932- *WhoWest 94*
Palmer, Patricia Eileen 1934- *WhoMW 93*
Palmer, Patrick *Who 94*
Palmer, Patrick 1936- *IntMPA 94*
Palmer, (Charles) Patrick (Ralph) 1933- *Who 94*
Palmer, Patrick Asa 1943- *WhoFI 94*
Palmer, Patrick Edward 1940- *WhoAm 94*
Palmer, Paul Mathew 1954- *WhoMW 93*
Palmer, Paula LaRaine 1954- *WhoWest 94*
Palmer, Peter 1931- *WhoHol 92*

Palmer, Peter John 1932- *ConAu 42NR, WrDr 94*
Palmer, Philip Edward Stephen 1921- *WhoAm 94*
Palmer, Philip Francis 1903- *Who 94*
Palmer, Phoebe Worrall 1807-1874 *DcAmReB 2*
Palmer, Rayetta J. 1949- *WhoScEn 94*
Palmer, Raymond A. 1939- *WhoAm 94*
Palmer, Raymond A(rthur) 1910-1977 *EncSF 93*
Palmer, Reginald (Oswald) 1923- *Who 94*
Palmer, Renzo *WhoHol 92*
Palmer, Richard A. 1941- *WhoAmL 94*
Palmer, Richard Alan 1935- *WhoAm 94*
Palmer, Richard N. *WhoAmP 93*
Palmer, Richard N. 1950- *WhoAmL 94*
Palmer, Richard Ware 1919- *WhoAm 94, WhoAmL 94*
Palmer, Richard William 1933- *Who 94*
Palmer, Robert 1949- *WhoHol 92*
Palmer, Robert Alan 1948- *WhoAmL 94*
Palmer, Robert Arthur 1948- *WhoWest 94*
Palmer, Robert B. *WhoFI 94*
Palmer, Robert B. 1941- *WhoAm 94*
Palmer, Robert Baylis 1938- *WhoAm 94*
Palmer, Robert Erwin 1934- *WhoAm 94*
Palmer, Robert Henry Stephen 1927- *Who 94*
Palmer, Robert Joseph 1934- *WhoAm 94*
Palmer, Robert L. 1946- *WhoAmL 94*
Palmer, Robert L., II 1943- *WhoBlA 94*
Palmer, Robert Leslie 1957- *WhoAmL 94*
Palmer, Robert P. 1945- *WhoAmL 94*
Palmer, Robert R. 1950- *WhoMW 93*
Palmer, Robert Roswell 1909- *WhoAm 94*
Palmer, Robert Towne 1947- *WhoAmL 94, WhoFI 94, WhoMW 93*
Palmer, Robert W. 1946- *WhoAmL 94*
Palmer, Robie Marcus Hooker Mark 1941- *WhoAm 94*
Palmer, Rodney James 1945- *WhoAmP 93*
Palmer, Roger Farley 1931- *WhoAm 94*
Palmer, Roger Raymond 1926- *WhoAm 94*
Palmer, Ronald Alan 1950- *WhoScEn 94*
Palmer, Ronald D. 1932- *WhoAmP 93*
Palmer, Ronald DeWayne 1932- *WhoBlA 94*
Palmer, Ronald DeWayne Faisal 1932- *WhoAm 94*
Palmer, Ronald J. *WhoAmL 94*
Palmer, Ronald Leigh 1939- *WhoAm 94*
Palmer, Russell Eugene 1934- *WhoAm 94, WhoFI 94*
Palmer, Samuel Copeland, III 1934- *WhoAm 94*
Palmer, Sidney John 1913- *Who 94*
Palmer, Singleton 1912-1993 *NewYTBS 93*
Palmer, Stanley H. 1944- *WrDr 94*
Palmer, Stephen 1954- *WhoFI 94*
Palmer, Stephen Eugene 1896-1992 *WhAm 10*
Palmer, Stephen Eugene, Jr. 1923- *WhoAm 94*
Palmer, Stuart Hunter 1924- *WhoAm 94*
Palmer, Susann(a Louisa) 1923- *WrDr 94*
Palmer, Terry Wayne 1962- *WhoBlA 94*
Palmer, Thomas *WhoHol 92*
Palmer, Thomas Allan 1946- *WhoAmL 94*
Palmer, Thomas Earl 1939- *WhoAmL 94*
Palmer, Thomas Joseph 1931- *IntWW 93, Who 94*
Palmer, Thomas Stuart 1947- *WhoFI 94*
Palmer, Toni *WhoHol 92*
Palmer, Tony 1941- *Who 94*
Palmer, Tony Brian 1930- *Who 94*
Palmer, Vincent Allan 1913- *WhoWest 94*
Palmer, Walter L. d1993 *NewYTBS 93*
Palmer, Walter Lincoln 1896- *WhAm 10*
Palmer, William Alan 1947- *WhoScEn 94*
Palmer, William D. *WhoAmL 94*
Palmer, William Darrell 1935- *WhoAmP 93*
Palmer, William Hassell 1945- *WhoMW 93*
Palmer, William J. 1943- *WrDr 94*
Palmer, William James, Jr. 1956- *WhoFI 94*
Palmer, William Jay 1946- *WhoAmL 94*
Palmer, William John d1993 *Who 94N*
Palmer, William Joseph 1934- *WhoFI 94, WhoWest 94*
Palmer-Beard, Donna 1948- *WhoMW 93*
Palmer-Hildreth, Barbara Jean 1941- *WhoBlA 94*
Palmeri, Victor R. 1926- *WhoHisp 94*
Palmerini, Giovanni Battista fl. 1722-1728 *NewGrDO*
Palmerston, Lord 1784-1865 *HisWorL [port]*
Palmerton, Patricia Ruby 1949- *WhoMW 93*
Palmes, Peter Manfred Jerome 1920- *Who 94*
Palmese, Ernesto d1960 *WhoHol 92*
Palmese, Richard Dominick 1947- *WhoAm 94, WhoFI 94*
Palmese, Rose Marie d1953 *WhoHol 92*
Palmeter, N. David 1938- *WhoAm 94*
Palmgren, Donald Gene 1938- *WhoAmA 93*
Palmgren, Selim 1878-1951 *NewGrDO*
Palmier, Marina *WhoHol 92*
Palmieri, Carmen J. 1938- *WhoHisp 94*
Palmieri, Deborah Anne 1953- *WhoWest 94*
Palmieri, Dennis Anthony 1956- *WhoAmL 94*
Palmieri, Eddie 1936- *WhoHisp 94*
Palmieri, Edmund Louis 1907-1989 *WhAm 10*
Palmieri, Guy Joseph 1936- *WhoFI 94, WhoMW 93*
Palmieri, Nicola Walter 1935- *WhoAmL 94*
Palmieri, Ralph J. 1947- *WhoIns 94*
Palmieri, Rodney August 1944- *WhoWest 94*
Palmieri, Victor Henry 1930- *WhoAm 94*
Palmisano, Paul Anthony 1929- *WhoScEn 94*
Palmore, Fred W., III 1945- *WhoAm 94*
Palmore, Fred Wharton, III 1945- *WhoAmL 94*
Palmore, John Stanley, Jr. 1917- *WhoAm 94, WhoAmP 93*
Palmore, Lynne A. Janifer 1952- *WhoBlA 94*
Palmore, Roderick Alan 1952- *WhoAm 94, WhoAmL 94*
Palmore, Russell V., Jr. 1946- *WhoAmL 94*
Palmquist, Donald Leonard 1936- *WhoMW 93*
Palms, John Michael 1935- *WhoAm 94*
Palms, Roger Curtis 1936- *WhoAm 94*
Palms, Stephen Gerard 1951- *WhoAm 94*
Palo, Nicholas Edwin 1945- *WhoAm 94*
Palomarez, Nat 1937- *WhoHisp 94*
Palomba, Antonio 1705-1769 *NewGrDO*
Palomba, Giuseppe fl. 1765-1825 *NewGrDO*
Palombi, Barbara Jean 1949- *WhoWest 94*
Palombo, Bernardo Alfredo 1948- *WhoHisp 94*
Palombo, Joseph 1928- *WhoMW 93*
Palomino, Carlos 1950- *WhoHisp 94*
Palomino, Jose 1755-1810 *NewGrDO*
Palomino Roedel, Jose 1937- *IntWW 93*
Palomo, Antonio M. 1931- *WhoAmP 93*
Palomo, Juan R. 1946- *WhoHisp 94*
Palos, Frank G. 1948- *WhoHisp 94*
Palos, James Joseph 1961- *WhoHisp 94*
Palou, Francisco 1723-1789 *EncNAR*
Palous, Radim 1924- *IntWW 93*
Palovcik, Reinhard Anton 1950- *WhoScEn 94*
Paloyan, Edward 1932- *WhoAm 94*
Pals, Daniel L. 1946- *WhoAm 94*
Pals, Dean Clifford 1938- *WhoFI 94*
Palser, Barbara F. 1916- *WhoAm 94*
Palsikar, Nana d1984 *WhoHol 92*
Palsma, Mary Jacobson 1942- *WhoWest 94*
Palsson, Hermann 1921- *WrDr 94*
Palsson, Thorsteinn 1947- *IntWW 93*
Paltauf, Rudolf Charles 1930- *WhoScEn 94*
Paltenghi, David d1961 *WhoHol 92*
Palter, Robert Monroe 1924- *WhoAm 94*
Paltock, Robert 1697-1767 *EncSF 93*
Paltridge, Garth William 1940- *IntWW 93*
Paltrow, Bruce 1943- *IntMPA 94*
Paludi, Michele A. 1954- *ConAu 140*
Palumbo, Baron 1935- *Who 94*
Palumbo, Dennis (James) 1929- *EncSF 93*
Palumbo, Dennis J. 1929- *WrDr 94*
Palumbo, Jacques 1939- *WhoAmA 93*
Palumbo, James Fredrick 1950- *WhoFI 94*
Palumbo, Mario Joseph 1933- *WhoAmP 93*
Palumbo, Michael Arnold 1945- *WhoWest 94*
Palumbo, Michael R. 1946- *WhoAmL 94*
Palumbo, Pasquale John 1932- *WhoMW 93*
Palumbo, Peter Garth 1935- *IntWW 93*
Palumbo, Ralph H. 1947- *WhoAmL 94*
Palumbo, Richard A. 1938- *WhoAmP 93*
Palumbo, Ruth Ann 1949- *WhoAmP 93*
Palumbo, Thomas G. 1956- *WhoAmP 93*
Palumbo, Vincent J., Jr. 1956- *WhoAmP 93*
Paluselli, Stefan 1748-1805 *NewGrDO*
Paluszek, John L. 1933- *WhoAm 94, WhoFI 94*
Paluzzi, Luciana 1931- *WhoHol 92*
Palvino, Jack Anthony 1934- *WhoAm 94*
Pam, Jerry 1926- *IntMPA 94*
Pama, Cornelis 1916- *WrDr 94*
Pamenter, Robert Gerald 1954- *WhoMW 93*
Pamfilova, Ella Aleksandrovna 1953- *LngBDD*
Pamies, Teresa 1919- *BlmGWL*
Pamon, Patricia E. 1952- *WhoMW 93*
Pampani, Antonio Gaetano c. 1705-1775 *NewGrDO*
Pampanini, Rosetta 1896-1973 *NewGrDO*
Pampanini, Silvana 1925- *IntMPA 94, WhoHol 92*
Pampel, Fred C. 1950- *ConAu 141*
Pampel, Joseph Philip Stevenson 1932- *WhoAm 94*
Pampel, Roland D. 1935- *WhoScEn 94*
Pamperin, Keith Arnold 1945- *WhoMW 93*
Pamphila fl. 1st cent.- *BlmGWL*
Pamphili, Benedetto 1653-1730 *NewGrDO*
Pamplin, Robert Boisseau, Sr. 1911- *WhoAm 94, WhoWest 94*
Pamplin, Robert Boisseau, Jr. 1941- *WhoAm 94*
Pampusch, Anita Marie 1938- *WhoAm 94*
Pamuk, Orhan 1952- *ConAu 142, ConWorW 93*
Pan *EncSF 93*
P'an, Albert Yuan 1941- *WhoAm 94*
Pan, Coda H. T. 1929- *WhoAm 94, WhoScEn 94*
Pan, David Han-Kuang 1954- *WhoScEn 94*
Pan, Dawning 1945- *WhoAsA 94*
Pan, Elizabeth Lim 1941- *WhoAm 94*
Pan, Fung-Shine 1951- *WhoAsA 94*
Pan, Guang-Wen 1944- *WhoMW 93*
Pan, Henry Yue-Ming 1946- *WhoAm 94, WhoScEn 94*
Pan, Hermes d1990 *WhoHol 92*
Pan, Hermes 1909-1990 *WhAm 10*
Pan, Hermes 1910-1990 *IntDcF 2-4*
Pan, Huo-Hsi 1918- *WhoScEn 94*
Pan, Theodore (Ion) *WhoAmA 93*
Pan, Tzu-Ming 1947- *WhoScEn 94*
Pan, Wei-Ping 1954- *WhoAsA 94*
Pan, William Jiawei 1935- *WhoFI 94, WhoWest 94*
Pan, Yi 1960- *WhoMW 93*
Pan, Yuh-Kang 1936- *WhoAsA 94*
Pan, Zhengda 1944- *WhoScEn 94*
Pana, Doru *IntWW 93*
Panaeva, Avdot'ia Iakovlevna 1819?-1893 *BlmGWL*
Panagiotakos, Steven C. 1959- *WhoAmP 93*
Panagiotopoulos, Panagiotis Dionysios 1950- *WhoScEn 94*
Panagiotopoulos, Vasos-Peter John, II 1961- *WhoFI 94*
Panama, Charles A. 1925- *IntMPA 94*
Panama, Norman *IntMPA 94*
Panama, Norman 1914- *See* Frank, Melvin 1913-1988 *IntDcF 2-4*
Panard, Pierre Marie Maurice 1916- *IntWW 93*
Panarese, William C. 1929- *WhoAm 94*
Panaretos, John 1948- *WhoScEn 94*
Panarites, John Peter 1939- *WhoFI 94*
Panaro, Victor Anthony 1928- *WhoAm 94*
Panas, Eustace G. 1924- *IntWW 93*
Panasci, Henry d1993 *NewYTBS 93*
Panasci, Nancy Ervin 1954- *WhoWest 94*
Panatta, Adriano 1950- *BuCMET*
Panayides, Tasos Christou 1934- *Who 94*
Panayides Christou, Tasos 1934- *IntWW 93*
Panayiotou, Constantinos 1951- *WhoScEn 94*
Panayiotou, Gergios Kyriakou 1963- *WhoAm 94*
Panayirci, Sharon Lorraine 1957- *WhoMW 93*
Panayotacos, Constantine P. 1918- *IntWW 93*
Panayotovich, Sam 1946- *WhoAmP 93*
Pan Beilei 1941- *WhoPRCh 91*
Pancake, Breece D'J 1952-1979 *DcLB 130 [port]*
Pancero, Jack Blocher 1923- *WhoMW 93*
Panchanathan, Viswanathan 1939- *WhoScEn 94*
Pan Chengdong *WhoPRCh 91*
Pancheri, Eugene Joseph 1947- *WhoScEn 94*
Panciera, David J. 1944- *WhoAmP 93*
Panciera, Frederick Lee 1937- *WhoIns 94*
Panciroli, Romeo 1923- *IntWW 93*
Pancoast, Edwin C. 1925- *WhoAm 94*
Pancoast, Terrence Russell 1942- *WhoAm 94*
Panczenko, Russell 1947- *WhoAm 94, WhoAmA 93, WhoMW 93*
Panda, Markandeswar 1952- *WhoScEn 94*
Panday, Kedar 1920- *IntWW 93*
Pande, Gyan Shanker 1932- *WhoAsA 94*
Pande, Krishna P. 1946- *WhoAsA 94*
Pande, Krishna Prasad 1946- *WhoAm 94*
Pande, Mrinal 1946- *BlmGWL*
Pandelidis, Ioannis O. 1957- *WhoScEn 94*
Pandey, Bishun Deo 1954- *WhoMW 93*
Pandey, Dhirendra Kumar 1951- *WhoAm 94*
Pandey, Ishwari Raj 1934- *Who 94*
Pandey, Lakshmi Narayan 1956- *WhoScEn 94*
Pandey, Manorama 1932- *WhoWomW 91*
Pandey, Raghvendra Kumar 1937- *WhoScEn 94*
Pandey, Ramesh Chandra 1938- *WhoScEn 94*
Pandey, Ras Bihari 1953- *WhoAsA 94*
Pandeya, Nirmalendu Kumar 1940- *WhoMW 93, WhoScEn 94*
Pandiarajan, Vijayakumar 1961- *WhoScEn 94*
Pandina, Robert John 1945- *WhoScEn 94*
Pandini, Davide 1961- *WhoScEn 94*
Pandit, Grish Roy 1955- *WhoAsA 94*
Pandit, Jasraj 1930- *IntWW 93*
Pandit, Sudhakar Madhavrao 1939- *WhoAsA 94, WhoScEn 94*
Pandit, Vijaya Lakshmi 1900-1990 *HisDcKW*
Pando, Alan Oscar 1931- *WhoAm 94, WhoFI 94, WhoWest 94*
Pandolfe, John Thomas, Jr. 1941- *WhoAmL 94*
Pandolfi, Filippo Maria 1927- *IntWW 93, Who 94*
Pandolfi, Francis R. *WhoAm 94*
Pandolfini, Angelica 1871-1959 *NewGrDO*
Pandolfini, Francesco 1833-1916 *NewGrDO*
Pandolfini, Turi d1962 *WhoHol 92*
Pandolfo, Steven Philip 1945- *WhoAm 94*
Pandozy, Raffaele Martini *WhoAmA 93*
Pan Duo 1938- *WhoPRCh 91 [port]*
Pandurangi, Ananda Krishna 1951- *WhoScEn 94*
Pandya, Amit Anant 1950- *WhoAsA 94*
Pandya, Deepak N. 1932- *WhoAsA 94*
Pandya, Harish C. 1945- *WhoBlA 94*
Pane, Remigio Ugo 1912- *WhoAm 94*
Panebianco, Richard 1971- *WhoHol 92*
Panec, William Joseph 1937- *WhoAmL 94*
Panehal, Francine Mary 1925- *WhoAmP 93*
Panek, Jan 1930- *WhoAm 94*
Panelli, Edward A. 1931- *WhoAmP 93*
Panelli, Edward Alexander 1931- *WhoAmL 94, WhoWest 94*
Panelli, Juan A. 1962- *WhoHisp 94*
Panenka, James Brian Joseph 1942- *WhoMW 93*
Panerai, Rolando 1924- *NewGrDO*
Panes, Jack Samuel 1925- *WhoAm 94*
Panessa, Heather Ashley Behr 1967- *WhoFI 94*
Paneth, Donald J. 1927- *WhoAm 94*
Paneth, Thomas 1926- *WhoScEn 94*
Panethiere, Henry Andrea 1914- *WhoAmP 93*
Panetta, Joseph Daniel 1954- *WhoWest 94*
Panetta, Leon 1938- *IntWW 93*
Panetta, Leon E. 1938- *CurBio 93 [port]*
Panetta, Leon Edward 1938- *WhoAm 94, WhoAmP 93, WhoFI 94, WhoWest 94*
Panetti, Ramon Stanley 1931- *WhoWest 94*
Paneyko, Stephen Hobbs 1942- *WhoAm 94*
Pan Ezhang 1906- *WhoPRCh 91 [port]*
Panfilov, Gleb Anatolyevich 1934- *IntWW 93*
Panfilova, Ella Aleksandrovna 1953- *IntWW 93*
Pang, Chap Aik 1959- *WhoAsA 94*
Pang, Herbert George 1922- *WhoAm 94, WhoScEn 94, WhoWest 94*
Pang, James 1959- *WhoAsA 94*
Pang, Joshua Keun-Uk 1924- *WhoFI 94, WhoMW 93*
Pang, Keum Y. *WhoAsA 94*
Pang, Kevin D. *WhoWest 94*
Pang, Kin Man 1948- *WhoWest 94*
Pang, Peter Chiusing 1952- *WhoAmL 94*
Pang, Rubye-Huey 1929- *WhoAsA 94*
Pang, Seng Puang 1953- *WhoAsA 94*
Pang, Su-Seng 1958- *WhoAsA 94*
Pang, Wilma 1940- *WhoAsA 94*
Pangalos, Theodoros 1938- *IntWW 93*
Pang Bing'an 1934- *WhoPRCh 91 [port]*
Pangborn, Edgar 1909-1976 *EncSF 93*
Pangborn, Franklin d1958 *WhoHol 92*
Pangborn, Franklin 1893-1958 *WhoCom*
Pangelinan, Vicente C. *WhoAmP 93*
Pangerapan, Bob George 1938- *WhoFI 94*
Panggabean, Maraden Saur Halomoan 1922- *IntWW 93*
Pangle, Charles Lee 1941- *WhoAmP 93*
Pango Vildoso, Grover 1947- *IntWW 93*
Pangrazi, Ronald Joseph 1961- *WhoScEn 94*
Pang Tao *WhoPRCh 91 [port]*
Pang Weiqiang *WhoPRCh 91*
Pang Xianzhi 1929- *WhoPRCh 91 [port]*

Pang Yuan 1944?- *WhoPRCh 91*
Panhofer, Walter 1910- *IntWW 93*
Pan Hong *WhoPRCh 91 [port]*
Pan Hong 1954- *IntWW 93*
Pani, Corrado *WhoHol 92*
Paniagua, Santos Donato *WhoHisp 94*
Paniagua y Vasques, Cenobio 1821-1882 *NewGrDO*
Panic, Milan 1929- *CurBio 93 [port], IntWW 93*
Paniccia, Mario Domenic 1948- *WhoFI 94*
Paniccia, Patricia Lynn 1952- *WhoAmL 94*
Panich, Danuta Bembenista 1954- *WhoAm 94*
Panichas, George A(ndrew) 1930- *WrDr 94*
Panichas, George Andrew 1930- *IntWW 93*
Panici, Charles *WhoAmP 93*
Panicker, Mathew Mathai 1945- *WhoScEn 94*
Panides, Elias 1959- *WhoScEn 94*
Panigrahi, Chintamani 1922- *IntWW 93*
Panigrahi, Sanjukta 1944- *IntWW 93*
Panikkar, Sardar K. M. 1893-1963 *HisDcKW*
Panin, Fabio Massimo 1957- *WhoScEn 94*
Panin, Vasily Ivanovich 1934- *LngBDD*
Panioto, Ronald Angelo 1935- *WhoAmL 94*
Panish, Morton B. 1929- *WhoAm 94*
Paniszczyn, John Francis 1958- *WhoAmL 94*
Panitch, Leo (Victor) 1945- *WrDr 94*
Panitch, Lois Ponnock Krebs 1938- *WhoFI 94*
Panitch, Michael B. 1939- *WhoAm 94, WhoFI 94*
Panitt, Merrill 1917- *WhoAm 94*
Panitz, Lawrence Herbert 1941- *WhoAm 94, WhoAmL 94*
Panitz, Murray Wolfe 1925-1989 *WhAm 10*
Panizza, Hector 1875-1967 *NewGrDO*
Panizza, Michael 1946- *WhoScEn 94*
Panjehpour, Masoud 1958- *WhoScEn 94*
Pan Jiacheng *WhoPRCh 91*
Pan Jiazheng *WhoPRCh 91*
Pan Jiezi 1915- *WhoPRCh 91 [port]*
Pan Jiguang 1940?- *WhoPRCh 91 [port]*
Pan Jiluan 1927- *WhoPRCh 91 [port]*
Pan Jinpei *WhoPRCh 91*
Pan Jionghua *WhoPRCh 91*
Panjwani, Vishnu 1950- *WhoAsA 94*
Pank, (John) David (Graham) 1935- *Who 94*
Pank, Dorian Christopher L. *Who 94*
Pankau, Carole *WhoAmP 93*
Panken, Peter Michael 1936- *WhoAm 94, WhoAmL 94*
Pankey, Edgar Edward 1916- *WhoAm 94*
Pankey, George Atkinson 1933- *WhoAm 94*
Pankey, Phil 1928- *WhoAmP 93*
Pankhurst, Christabel *BlmGWL*
Pankhurst, Christabel 1888-1958 *HisWorL*
Pankhurst, Emmeline *BlmGWL*
Pankhurst, Emmeline d1928 *WhoHol 92*
Pankhurst, Emmeline 1858-1928 *HisWorL [port]*
Pankhurst, Leonard Thomas 1902- *Who 94*
Pankhurst, Richard (Keir Pethick) 1927- *WrDr 94*
Pankhurst, Sylvia *BlmGWL*
Pankhurst, Sylvia 1882-1960 *HisWorL*
Pankhurst, (Estelle) Sylvia 1882-1960 *DcNaB MP*
Pankiewicz, Tadeusz d1993 *NewYTBS 93*
Pankin, Boris Dmitrievich 1931- *LngBDD*
Pankin, Boris Dmitriyevich *IntWW 93*
Pankin, Jayson Darryl 1957- *WhoFI 94*
Pankin, Stuart *WhoHol 92*
Pankin, Stuart 1946- *IntMPA 94*
Pankok, Thomas A. 1931- *WhoAmP 93*
Pankopf, Arthur, Jr. 1931- *WhoAm 94, WhoAmL 94, WhoAmP 93*
Pankopf, John F. 1935- *WhoAmL 94*
Pankove, Jacques Isaac 1922- *WhoAm 94, WhoWest 94*
Pankow, John 1954- *WhoHol 92*
Pankowski, Elsie *DrAPF 93*
Pankratz, Henry J. 1939- *WhoAm 94*
Pan Liansheng 1932- *WhoPRCh 91 [port]*
Panlilio, Adelisa Lorna 1949- *WhoAsA 94*
Pan Lufu *WhoPRCh 91*
Pann, Peter d1948 *WhoHol 92*
Pannain, Guido 1891-1977 *NewGrDO*
Pannell, James H. 1920- *WhoAmP 93*
Pannell, James L. *WhoAmP 93*
Pannell, Nita *WhoHol 92*
Pannell, Patrick Weldon 1936- *WhoBlA 94*
Pannell, Raymond 1935- *NewGrDO*
Pannell, Robert D. 1942- *WhoAmL 94*
Pannell, William E. 1929- *WhoBlA 94*
Pannenberg, Wolfhart Ulrich 1928- *IntWW 93*
Panner, Bernard J. 1928- *WhoAm 94*
Panner, Owen M. 1924- *WhoAm 94, WhoAmL 94, WhoWest 94*
Panneton, Jacques 1943- *WhoAm 94*
Pannett, Juliet Kathleen *Who 94*
Panni, Marcello 1940- *IntWW 93*
Pannick, David 1956- *WrDr 94*
Pannick, David Philip 1956- *Who 94*
Pannier, Clyde Robert 1930- *WhoFI 94*
Pannill, William Presley 1940- *WhoAmL 94*
Pannke, Peggy M. *WhoMW 93*
Pannone, Rodger John 1943- *Who 94*
Pannos, Michael *WhoAmP 93*
Pannu, Dave S. 1941- *WhoAsA 94*
Panofka, Heinrich 1807-1887 *NewGrDO*
Panofsky, Wolfgang Kurt Hermann 1919- *IntWW 93, WhoAm 94, WhoScEn 94*
Panopoulos, Linda Louise 1949- *WhoWest 94*
Panos, Louis G. 1925- *WrDr 94*
Panos Schmitt, Athanasia Nancy 1951- *WhoFI 94*
Panoutsopoulos, Basile 1956- *WhoScEn 94*
Panov, Valery 1938- *IntDcB [port]*
Panov, Valery Matveyevich 1940- *IntWW 93*
Panova, Vera Fedorovna 1905-1973 *BlmGWL*
Pan Qichang *WhoPRCh 91*
Pan Qiongxiong 1930- *WhoPRCh 91 [port]*
Pan Rongwen 1931- *IntWW 93*
Pan Ruizheng 1914- *WhoPRCh 91 [port]*
Pansa Cedronio, Paolo 1915- *IntWW 93*
Panseron, Auguste (Mathieu) 1796-1859 *NewGrDO*
Panshin, Alexei 1940- *WrDr 94*
Panshin, Alexei (A.) 1940- *EncSF 93*
Panshin, Cory (Seidman) 1947- *EncSF 93*
Pansini, Michael Samuel 1928- *WhoAm 94*
Pansky, Ben 1928- *WhoScEn 94*
Pansky, Emil John 1921- *WhoWest 94*
Panson, Gilbert Stephen 1920- *WhoAm 94*
Pant, Apasaheb Balasaheb d1992 *IntWW 93N, Who 94N*
Pant, Krishna Chandra 1931- *IntWW 93*
Pant, Sumitranandan 1900- *IntWW 93*
Pantages, Louis James 1916- *WhoAm 94*
Pantaleoni, Adriano 1837-1908 *NewGrDO*
Pantaleoni, Romilda 1847-1917 *NewGrDO*
Pantazelos, Peter George 1930- *WhoAm 94, WhoFI 94*
Pantel, Glenn Steven 1953- *WhoAm 94, WhoAmL 94*
Pantel, Stan Roy 1950- *WhoAm 94*
Pantelakos, Laura C. 1935- *WhoAmP 93*
Pantelides, Sokrates Theodore 1948- *WhoFI 94*
Pantelis, John Andrew, Jr. 1956- *WhoScEn 94*
Pantell, Richard Keith 1951- *WhoAmA 93*
Pantenburg, Michel 1926- *WhoAm 94*
Panter, Gary 1950- *WhoAmA 93*
Panter-Downes, Mollie Patricia 1906- *Who 94*
Pantin, Anthony *Who 94*
Pantin, Leslie, Jr. 1948- *WhoHisp 94*
Pantin, Martha Sanchez 1957- *WhoHisp 94*
Pantlin, Dick (Hurst) 1919- *Who 94*
Pantling, Mary *Who 94*
Panto, Salvatore Joseph 1951- *WhoAmP 93*
Pantoja, Antonia *WhoHisp 94*
Pantoja, Rene V. 1960- *WhoHisp 94*
Pantoliano, Joe 1953- *WhoHol 92*
Pantoliano, Joe 1954- *IntMPA 94*
Panton, Alastair Dyson *Who 94*
Panton, Francis Harry 1923- *Who 94*
Panton, Verner 1926- *IntWW 93*
Panton, William c. 1740-1801 *AmRev*
Panton, William 1742-1801 *WhAmRev*
Pantos, William Pantazes 1957- *WhoScEn 94, WhoWest 94*
Pantridge, (James) Frank 1916- *Who 94*
Pantschak, Vera *WhoMW 93*
Pantuso, Vincent Joseph 1940- *WhoAm 94*
Panuccio, Anthony John 1930- *WhoAmP 93*
Panufnik, Andrzej 1914-1991 *WhAm 10*
Panuschka, Gerhard 1959- *WhoScEn 94*
Panuska, Joseph Allan 1927- *WhoAm 94*
Panuzio, Nicholas Arthur 1935- *WhoAmP 93*
Pany, Kurt Joseph 1946- *WhoAm 94, WhoWest 94*
Pan Yan 1916- *WhoPRCh 91 [port]*
Pan Yao 1927- *WhoPRCh 91 [port]*
Panyarachun, Anand 1932- *IntWW 93*
Pan Yiqing 1936- *WhoPRCh 91 [port]*
Panza, Georgene Sfraga 1950- *WhoFI 94*
Panza, Giuliano Francesco 1945- *WhoScEn 94*
Panzacchi, Domenico c. 1730-1805 *NewGrDO*
Panza di Biumo, Giuseppe 1923- *IntWW 93*
Panzarella, John Edward 1960- *WhoScEn 94*
Panzer, Hans Peter 1922- *WhoScEn 94*
Panzer, Joel Russell 1958- *WhoWest 94*
Panzer, Mary E. 1951- *WhoAmP 93*
Panzer, Mary Ellen 1951- *WhoMW 93*
Panzer, Mitchell Emanuel 1917- *WhoAm 94*
Panzer, Paul d1958 *WhoHol 92*
Panzer, Thomas Phillip 1939- *WhoFI 94*
Pan Zhiyuan *WhoPRCh 91*
Panzone, Rafael 1932- *WhoScEn 94*
Pao, Chia-Ven 1933- *WhoAsA 94*
Pao, Yih-Hsing 1930- *WhoAm 94*
Pao, Yoh-Han *WhoAm 94*
Paoletta, Leonard S. 1934- *WhoAmP 93*
Paoletta, Mark R. A. 1962- *WhoAm 94*
Paoli, Antonio 1871-1946 *NewGrDO*
Paoli, Betty 1814-1894 *BlmGWL*
Paolini, Gilbert *WhoAm 94*
Paolini, Robert Michael 1949- *WhoAmP 93*
Paolini Massimi, Petronilla 1663-1726 *BlmGWL*
Paolino, Joseph Robert, Jr. 1955- *WhoAmP 93*
Paolino, Raymond T. *WhoAmP 93*
Paolino, Richard Francis 1945- *WhoAm 94, WhoFI 94*
Paolino, Thomas Joseph 1905- *WhoAmP 93*
Paolis, Alessio de *NewGrDO*
Paolo c. 13th cent.- *BlmGEL*
Paolozzi, Eduardo (Luigi) 1924- *Who 94*
Paolozzi, Eduardo Luigi 1924- *IntWW 93*
Paolucci, Anne *DrAPF 93*
Paolucci, Anne Attura *WhoAm 94*
Paolucci, Henry *WhoAm 94*
Paolucci, Steven Lee *WhoFI 94*
Paone, Peter 1936- *WhoAm 94, WhoAmA 93*
Papa, Anthony Emil 1914- *WhoAm 94*
Papa, Vincent T. 1946- *WhoAm 94, WhoFI 94*
Papacek, James Thomas 1942- *WhoMW 93*
Papaconstantinou, Theophylactos 1905- *IntWW 93*
Papacostea, Serban 1928- *IntWW 93*
Papadakis, Constantine N. 1946- *WhoAm 94, WhoMW 93, WhoScEn 94*
Papadakis, Emmanuel Philippos 1934- *WhoAm 94*
Papadakos, Nicholas P. 1925- *WhoAmP 93*
Papadakos, Nicholas Peter 1925- *WhoAm 94, WhoAmL 94*
Papadakos, Peter John 1957- *WhoScEn 94*
Papadat-Bengescu, Hortensia 1876-1955 *BlmGWL*
Papadimitriou, Christos *WhoScEn 94*
Papadimitriou, Dimitri Basil 1946- *WhoFI 94*
Papadimitriou, Yiorghos D. 1916- *IntWW 93*
Papadongonas, Alexandros 1931- *IntWW 93*
Papadopoulo, Nicolas 1962- *WhoIns 94*
Papadopoulos, Achilles Symeon 1923- *Who 94*
Papadopoulos, Dimitrios 1914-1991 *WhAm 10*
Papadopoulos, Georgios 1919- *IntWW 93*
Papadopoulos, Konstantinos 1921- *IntWW 93*
Papadopoulos, Nicholas Constantinos 1939- *WhoFI 94*
Papadopoulos, Stelios B. 1940- *WhoAm 94, WhoFI 94*
Papadopoulou, Alexandra 1867-1906 *BlmGWL*
Papaeliou, Louis 1953- *WhoMW 93*
Papageorge, Tod 1940- *WhoAm 94, WhoAmA 93*
Papageorghiou, Panikkos 1946- *IntWW 93*
Papageorgiou, John Constantine 1935- *WhoAm 94*
Papagiannis, Michael Dimitrios 1932- *WhoAm 94*
Papaioannou, Evangelia-Lilly 1963- *WhoScEn 94*
Papakyriakou, Michael John 1958- *WhoScEn 94*
Papaleo, Anthony 1928- *WhoAm 94*
Papaleo, Joseph *DrAPF 93*
Papaleo, Louis Anthony 1953- *WhoFI 94*
Papalexopoulos, Alex Democrates 1957- *WhoScEn 94*
Papalia, Diane Ellen 1947- *WhoAm 94*
Papaligouras, Panayotis 1917- *IntWW 93*
Papalini, Joseph I. 1941- *WhoAmL 94*
Papan, Louis J. *WhoAmP 93*
Papana, Alex d1946 *WhoHol 92*
Papanastasiou, Tasos Charilaou 1953- *WhoScEn 94*
Papandopulo, Boris 1906-1991 *NewGrDO*
Papandrea, John Francis 1934- *WhoAmP 93*
Papandrea, Patsy, Jr. 1941- *WhoAmP 93*
Papandreou, Andreas George 1919- *IntWW 93, Who 94*
Papandreou, Constantine 1939- *WhoScEn 94*
Papandreou, Vasso *Who 94*
Papandreou, Vasso 1944- *IntWW 93, WhoWomW 91*
Papanek, Gustav Fritz 1926- *WhoAm 94*
Papanek, Jan 1896-1991 *WhAm 10*
Papanek, Victor 1926- *WhoAm 94*
Papanickolas, Emmanuel N. 1934- *WhoAmL 94*
Paparazzo, Ernesto 1950- *WhoScEn 94*
Paparella, Michael M. 1933- *WhoAm 94*
Paparelli, Angelo A. 1949- *WhoAm 94, WhoAmL 94*
Paparian, Michael 1955- *WhoWest 94*
Papas, Andreas Michael 1942- *WhoScEn 94*
Papas, George Nick 1961- *WhoFI 94, WhoMW 93*
Papas, Irene 1924- *WhoHol 92*
Papas, Irene 1926- *IntMPA 94*
Papas, Robert Felton 1939- *WhoMW 93*
Papas, William 1927- *WrDr 94*
Papasani, Subbaiah Venkata 1943- *WhoAsA 94*
Papashvily, George 1898-1978 *WhoAmA 93N*
Papasian, Jack C. 1878-1957 *WhoAmA 93N*
Papathanasiou, Athanasios George 1957- *WhoScEn 94*
Papathanassiou, Aspassia 1944- *IntWW 93*
Papatheofanis, Frank John 1959- *WhoScEn 94*
Papatzacos, Paul George 1941- *WhoScEn 94*
Papavassiliou, Athanasios George 1961- *WhoScEn 94*
Papavoine c. 1720-1793 *NewGrDO*
Papay, Lillian D. *WhoAmP 93*
Papayannapoulos, Dionyssis d1984 *WhoHol 92*
Papazian, Dennis Richard 1931- *WhoAm 94, WhoMW 93*
Papazian, Mary Arshagouni 1959- *WhoMW 93*
Papcun, George 1939- *WhoWest 94*
Pape, Arnis Weston 1950- *WhoWest 94*
Pape, Arthur Edward 1939- *WhoAm 94*
Pape, Barbara Harris 1936- *WhoAmL 94*
Pape, Greg *DrAPF 93*
Pape, (Jonathan) Hector (Carruthers) d1993 *Who 94N*
Pape, Lionel d1944 *WhoHol 92*
Pape, Patricia Ann 1940- *WhoMW 93*
Pape, Paul *WhoHol 92*
Pape, Richard (Bernard) 1916- *EncSF 93*
Pape, Stuart M. 1948- *WhoAmL 94*
Pape, Thomas Emil 1959- *WhoWest 94*
Pape, William James, II 1931- *WhoAm 94*
Papell, Helen *DrAPF 93*
Papen, Frank O'Brien 1909- *WhoAmP 93*
Papen, George William 1893- *WhAm 10*
Papenfuse, Edward Carl, Jr. 1943- *WhoAm 94*
Papenfuss, Tony *WhoHol 92*
Paper, Lewis J. 1946- *WhoAm 94, WhoAmL 94*
Paperin, Stewart Jules 1948- *WhoAm 94*
Papernik, Joel Ira 1944- *WhoAm 94, WhoAmL 94, WhoFI 94*
Paperno, Herbert 1933- *WhoWest 94*
Paperny, Vladimir 1944- *WhoWest 94*
Papert, Seymour Aubrey 1928- *WhoScEn 94*
Papet, Louis M. 1933- *WhoScEn 94*
Papi, Gennaro 1886-1941 *NewGrDO*
Papiano, Neil Leo 1933- *WhoAm 94*
Papier, Bruce Lee 1940- *WhoWest 94*
Papier, Maurice Anthony 1940- *WhoAmA 93*
Papier, Philip Britton, Jr. 1929- *WhoAmL 94, WhoFI 94*
Papiernik-Berkhauer, Emile 1936- *IntWW 93*
Papike, James Joseph 1937- *WhoScEn 94, WhoWest 94*
Papilian, Victor *EncSF 93*
Papillon, Bryan E. 1954- *WhoFI 94*
Papillon, Scott James 1949- *WhoMW 93*
Papillon de la Ferte, Denis Pierre Jean 1725-1794 *NewGrDO*
Papin, Denis 1647-1712 *WorInv*
Papin, Jean-Pierre 1963- *WorESoc*
Papineau, David 1947- *WrDr 94*

Papineau-Couture, Jean 1916- *WhoAm 94*
Papini, Mauricio Roberto 1952- *WhoScEn 94*
Papitto, Ralph Raymond 1926- *WhoAm 94, WhoFI 94*
Papke, David Ray 1947- *WhoMW 93*
Papkin, Robert David 1933- *WhoAm 94*
Papo, Iso 1925- *WhoAmA 93*
Papon, Christiane 1924- *WhoWomW 91*
Papon, Maurice Arthur Jean 1910- *IntWW 93*
Papon, Monique Genevieve Elizabeth 1934- *WhoWomW 91*
Papoulias, George Dimitrios 1927- *IntWW 93, Who 94*
Papoulias, Sotiri Aris 1953- *WhoFI 94*
Papoulis, Athanasios 1921- *WhoAm 94*
Papounhan d1775 *EncNAR*
Papoutsis, Demetri d1993 *NewYTBS 93*
Papp, Desiderius 1897- *EncSF 93*
Papp, James Michael 1953- *WhoFI 94*
Papp, Joseph 1921-1991 *AmCulL*
Papp, Joseph 1922-1991 *WhAm 10*
Papp, Laszlo 1926- *IntWW 93*
Papp, Laszlo George 1929- *WhoAm 94, WhoFI 94, WhoScEn 94*
Pappafava, Premo John 1926- *WhoFI 94*
Pappagianis, Demosthenes 1928- *WhoAm 94*
Pappajohn, John G. 1928- *WhoIns 94*
Pappalardo, A. John *WhoAmL 94*
Pappalardo, Salvatore 1918- *IntWW 93*
Pappano, John Amedeo 1958- *WhoAmL 94*
Pappano, Robert Daniel 1942- *WhoAm 94, WhoFI 94*
Pappas, Alceste Thetis 1945- *WhoAm 94*
Pappas, Anne Kerr 1934- *WhoAmP 93*
Pappas, Costas Ernest 1910- *WhoAm 94, WhoScEn 94, WhoWest 94*
Pappas, David Christopher 1936- *WhoAmL 94*
Pappas, Edward Harvey 1947- *WhoAm 94, WhoAmL 94, WhoMW 93*
Pappas, George 1929- *WhoAmA 93*
Pappas, George Demetrios 1926- *WhoAm 94, WhoMW 93*
Pappas, George Frank 1950- *WhoAm 94, WhoAmL 94*
Pappas, John 1957- *WhoScEn 94*
Pappas, John Stephen 1943- *WhoWest 94*
Pappas, Leah Aglala 1936- *WhoAmP 93*
Pappas, Michael 1940- *WhoFI 94*
Pappas, Nicholas 1937- *WhoWest 94*
Pappas, Peter 1936- *WhoMW 93*
Pappas, Philip James 1954- *WhoMW 93*
Pappas, Sandra L. 1949- *WhoAmP 93, WhoMW 93*
Pappas, Stanley Robert 1922- *WhoAmL 94*
Pappas, Ted Phillip 1934- *WhoAm 94*
Pappas, Theodore George 1956- *WhoMW 93*
Pappas, Theresa *DrAPF 93*
Pappas, Toni 1943- *WhoAmP 93*
Pappas, William G. 1952- *WhoAmL 94*
Pappas, William John 1937- *WhoMW 93*
Pappas-Speairs, Nina *WhoFI 94*
Pappenheim, Marie 1882-1966 *NewGrDO*
Pappenheimer, Alwin M., Jr. 1908- *IntWW 93*
Pappenheimer, Alwin Max, Jr. 1908- *WhoAm 94*
Pappenheimer, Will D. 1954- *WhoAmA 93*
Papper, Emanuel Martin 1915- *WhoAm 94*
Pappillion, Glenda M. 1951- *WhoBlA 94*
Pappone, Michael J. 1948- *WhoAmL 94*
Papps, Peter E. *WhoAmL 94*
Paprocki, Thomas John 1952- *WhoAmL 94*
Paproski, Ronald James 1966- *WhoScEn 94*
Papsidero, Joseph Anthony 1929- *WhoAm 94*
Papua New Guinea, Archbishop of 1927- *Who 94*
Papy, Charles C. 1952- *WhoAm 94*
Paquet, Gary Michael Sebastian, VIII 1943- *WhoHisp 94*
Paquet, Gilles 1936- *WhoAm 94*
Paquet, Jean-Guy 1938- *Who 94*
Paquet-Sevigny, Therese 1934- *IntWW 93*
Paquette, Jack Kenneth 1925- *WhoAm 94*
Paquette, Joseph F., Jr. 1934- *WhoAm 94, WhoFI 94*
Paquette, Mark Alfred 1956- *WhoMW 93*
Paquette, Rodolphe G. 1913- *WhoAmP 93*
Paquin, Edward H. 1953- *WhoAmP 93*
Paquin, Jeffrey Dean 1960- *WhoAmL 94*
Paquin, Leo d1993 *NewYTBS 93 [port]*
Paquin, Leo Francis 1947- *WhoMW 93*
Paquin, Paul Peter 1943- *WhoAm 94, WhoFI 94*
Parabellum *EncSF 93*
Parac, Ivo 1890-1954 *NewGrDO*
Parachini, Thomas G. 1944- *WhoAmL 94*
Parada, Jaime Alfonso 1957- *WhoScEn 94*
Paradice, Sammy Irwin 1952- *WhoFI 94*
Paradies, (Pietro) Domenico 1707-1791 *NewGrDO*
Paradies, Hasko Henrich 1940- *WhoScEn 94*
Paradis, Adrian Alexis 1912- *WrDr 94*
Paradis, Andre 1938- *WhoAm 94*
Paradis, Eugene J. 1923- *WhoAmP 93*
Paradis, Judy 1944- *WhoAmP 93, WhoWomW 91*
Paradis, Maria Theresia von 1759-1824 *NewGrDO*
Paradis, Patrick Eugene 1953- *WhoAmP 93*
Paradis, Philip *DrAPF 93*
Paradis, Richard Robert 1956- *WhoScEn 94*
Paradis, Vanessa 1972- *WhoHol 92*
Paradise, Phil (Herschel) 1905- *WhoAmA 93*
Paradise, Philip Herschel 1905- *WhoAm 94*
Paradise, Robert Richard 1934- *WhoAm 94, WhoFI 94*
Paradowski, Robert John 1940- *WhoScEn 94*
Parady, John Edward 1939- *WhoWest 94*
Paraense, Wladimir Lobato 1914- *IntWW 93*
Paragano, Vincent Dominick 1956- *WhoAmL 94*
Paraguay, Bishop of 1940- *Who 94*
Parain, Brice d1971 *WhoHol 92*
Paral, Vladimir *EncSF 93*
Páramo, Constanza Gisella 1956- *WhoHisp 94*
Paramo, Guadalupe Rodriguez 1917- *WhoHisp 94*
Paramo, James K. 1966- *WhoHisp 94*
Paramo, Robert Keith 1943- *WhoHisp 94*
Paramore, James Martin 1928- *WhoWest 94*
Paran, Mark Lloyd 1953- *WhoAm 94, WhoAmL 94, WhoFI 94*
Paranjpe, Raja d1979 *WhoHol 92*
Pararajasingam, Sangarapillai *Who 94N*
Paras, Nicholas Andrew 1942- *WhoFI 94*
Parascos, Edward Themistocles 1931- *WhoFI 94*
Paraskakis, Michael Emanuel 1930- *WhoFI 94*
Paraskevopoulos, Nicholas George 1960- *WhoScEn 94*
Parate, Natthu Sonbaji 1936- *WhoAsA 94*
Paratore, Jean 1949- *WhoMW 93*
Paravati, Michael Peter 1949- *WhoScEn 94*
Paravisini-Gebert, Lizabeth 1953- *WhoHisp 94*
Parayre, Jean-Paul-Christophe 1937- *IntWW 93, Who 94*
Parazzoli, Ferruccio *EncSF 93*
Parberry, Edward Allen 1941- *WhoScEn 94*
Parbo, Arvi (Hillar) 1926- *Who 94*
Parbo, Arvi Hillar 1926- *IntWW 93*
Parcel, Toby Lee 1949- *WhoMW 93*
Parcells, Bill *NewYTBS 93 [port]*
Parcells, Bill 1941- *WhoAm 94*
Parcells, Margaret R. 1930- *WhoAmP 93*
Parch, Grace Dolores *WhoAm 94*
Parcher, James Vernon 1920- *WhoAm 94*
Parcher, Joan Ann 1956- *WhoAmA 93*
Pardave, Alberto Catala d1989 *WhoHol 92*
Pardave, Joaquin d1955 *WhoHol 92*
Pardave, Jose d1970 *WhoHol 92*
Pardee, Arthur Beck 1921- *IntWW 93, WhoAm 94, WhoScEn 94*
Pardee, Doc d1975 *WhoHol 92*
Pardee, Jack 1936- *WhoAm 94*
Pardee, Jean *WhoAmP 93*
Pardee, Otway O'Meara 1920- *WhoAm 94*
Pardee, Scott Edward 1936- *WhoAm 94, WhoFI 94*
Pardee, William Hearne 1946- *WhoAmA 93*
Parden, Robert James 1922- *WhoAm 94*
Pardes, Herbert 1934- *WhoAm 94, WhoScEn 94*
Pardi, Justin A. 1898-1951 *WhoAmA 93N*
Pardieck, Roger Lee 1937- *WhoAmL 94*
Pardieck, Sherrie Chan 1953- *WhoMW 93*
Pardinek, Mary Therese 1958- *WhoFI 94*
Pardington, Ralph Arthur 1938- *WhoAmA 93*
Pardo, Bruce Edward 1947- *WhoHisp 94*
Pardo, Dominick George 1918- *WhoAm 94*
Pardo, Don *WhoHol 92*
Pardo, J. Robert 1958- *WhoHisp 94*
Pardo, James Aaron, Jr. 1952- *WhoAmL 94*
Pardo, James William 1964- *WhoHisp 94*
Pardo, Jose Victor 1954- *WhoHisp 94*
Pardo, Luis Maria de Pablo 1914- *IntWW 93*
Pardo, Robert Edward 1951- *WhoMW 93*
Pardo, Scott Albert 1957- *WhoWest 94*
Pardo Bazan, Emilia 1851-1921 *BlmGWL, RfGShF*
Pardoe, Alan Douglas William 1943- *Who 94*
Pardoe, Geoffrey Keith Charles 1928- *Who 94*
Pardoe, John George Magrath *Who 94*
Pardoe, John Wentworth 1934- *Who 94*
Pardoe, M(argot Mary) 1902- *WrDr 94*
Pardon, Earl B. 1926-1991 *WhoAmA 93N*
Pardue, A. Michael 1931- *WhoWest 94*
Pardue, Dwight Edward 1928- *WhoAm 94, WhoFI 94*
Pardue, Larry G. 1944- *WhoAm 94*
Pardue, Mary Lou 1933- *WhoAm 94*
Pardus, Donald Gene 1940- *WhoAm 94, WhoFI 94*
Pare, Ambrose 1510-1590 *WorInv, WorScD*
Pare, Jean-Jacques 1929- *WhoAm 94*
Pare, Michael 1959- *IntMPA 94, WhoHol 92*
Pare, Richard 1948- *WhoAmA 93*
Paredes, Agustin Vincent 1926- *WhoHisp 94*
Paredes, Alfonso 1926- *WhoAm 94*
Paredes, Americo 1915- *WhoAm 94, WhoHisp 94*
Paredes, Bert 1947- *WhoWest 94*
Paredes, Eduardo 1957- *WhoScEn 94*
Paredes, Frank C., Jr. 1949- *WhoHisp 94*
Paredes, Ismael S. 1942- *WhoHisp 94*
Paredes, James Anthony 1939- *WhoAm 94, WhoHisp 94*
Paredes, Limon Mariano 1912-1979 *WhoAmA 93N*
Paredes, Maria Luisa 1930- *WhoHisp 94*
Paredes, Miguel Angel 1942- *WhoHisp 94*
Paredes, Raymund A. *WhoHisp 94*
Paredes, Ruben Dario 1931- *IntWW 93*
Pareja-Heredia, Diego 1939- *WhoScEn 94*
Parejko, Ronald Anthony 1940- *WhoMW 93*
Parekh, Bhikhu Chhotalal 1935- *Who 94*
Parekh, Navnit M. 1935- *WhoAsA 94*
Parell, Mary Little 1946- *WhoAm 94, WhoAmL 94*
Parella, Albert Lucian 1909- *WhoAmA 93*
Parella, Gaetano D. 1922- *WhoAmP 93*
Parella, Mary A. 1927- *WhoAmP 93*
Parello, Laura Jean 1965- *WhoAmL 94*
Parent, Edward George 1957- *WhoScEn 94*
Parent, Elizabeth Anne 1941- *WhoWest 94*
Parent, James E. 1939- *WhoAm 94*
Parent, Paul *WhoAmP 93*
Parent, Richard Alfred 1935- *WhoScEn 94*
Parent, Rodolphe Jean 1937- *WhoAm 94*
Parent, Roger O. *WhoAmP 93*
Parente, Emil J. 1930- *WhoAm 94*
Parente, Joseph D. 1959- *WhoMW 93*
Parente, Marie J. *WhoAmP 93*
Parente, Michael 1941- *WhoAm 94*
Parente, Stephen Thomas 1965- *WhoFI 94*
Parente, William Joseph 1937- *WhoAm 94*
Parenti, Franco d1989 *WhoHol 92*
Parenti, Kathy Ann 1957- *WhoWest 94*
Parenti, Paolo Francesco 1764-1821 *NewGrDO*
Parepa(-Rosa), Euphrosyne 1836-1874 *NewGrDO*
Parer, Julian Thomas 1934- *WhoWest 94*
Parera, Valentin *WhoHol 92*
Pares, Richard 1902-1958 *DcNaB MP*
Parés-Avila, José Agustín 1964- *WhoHisp 94*
Paret, Peter 1924- *IntWW 93, WhoAm 94*
Pareto, Graziella 1889-1973 *NewGrDO*
Parets, Eric 1948- *WhoFI 94*
Paretsky, David 1918- *WhoAm 94*
Paretsky, Sara 1947- *WrDr 94*
Paretsky, Sara N. 1947- *BlmGWL [port], WhoAm 94*
Paretzky, Raymond Paul 1962- *WhoAmL 94*
Parfaict, Francois 1698-1753 *NewGrDO*
Parfenoff, Michael S. 1926- *WhoAmA 93*
Parfet, Donald Reid 1952- *WhoFI 94*
Parfet, William Upjohn 1946- *WhoAm 94, WhoFI 94*
Parfit, Derek Antony 1942- *Who 94*
Parfit, Gavin J. 1947- *WhoAm 94*
Parfitt, Judy 1935- *WhoHol 92*
Parfitt, Tudor (Vernon) 1944- *WrDr 94*
Parfrey, Adam 1957- *WhoWest 94*
Parfrey, Woodrow d1984 *WhoHol 92*
Pargeter, Edith 1913- *IntWW 93, Who 94, WrDr 94*
Pargeter, Edith Mary 1913- *ConAu 41NR*
Pargeter, Philip 1933- *Who 94*
Pargoff, Robert Michael 1961- *WhoMW 93*
Parham, Bobby Eugene 1941- *WhoAmP 93*
Parham, Brenda Joyce 1944- *WhoBlA 94*
Parham, Charles Fox 1873-1929 *DcAmReB 2*
Parham, David L. 1945- *WhoAmL 94*
Parham, Deborah L. 1955- *WhoBlA 94*
Parham, Frederick Russell 1953- *WhoBlA 94*
Parham, James Robert 1921- *WhoAm 94*
Parham, Jiles 1944- *WhoFI 94*
Parham, Johnny Eugene, Jr. 1937- *WhoBlA 94*
Parham, Marjorie B. *WhoBlA 94*
Parham, Nancy McRoberts 1960- *WhoAmL 94*
Parham, Robert *DrAPF 93*
Parham, Samuel Levenus 1905- *WhoBlA 94*
Parham, Samuel M. 1930- *WhoAmP 93*
Parham, Thomas David, Jr. 1920- *WhoBlA 94*
Parham, William Harold, Jr. 1960- *WhoFI 94*
Parham, William Thomas 1913- *WrDr 94*
Parhi, Keshab Kumar 1959- *WhoMW 93*
Pariati, Pietro 1665-1733 *NewGrDO*
Pariente, Rene Guillaume 1929- *WhoScEn 94*
Parigi, Giulio 1571-1635 *NewGrDO*
Parikh, Dilip 1948- *WhoScEn 94*
Parikh, Hemant Bhupendra 1951- *WhoAsA 94, WhoScEn 94*
Parikh, Indu 1937- *WhoAsA 94*
Parikh, Kirit Girishchandra 1942- *WhoAsA 94*
Parikh, Manor Madanmohan 1964- *WhoScEn 94*
Parikh, Parimal Jashwantlal 1949- *WhoFI 94*
Parikh, Prashant H. 1965- *WhoMW 93*
Parikh, Pravin P. 1929- *WhoAsA 94*
Parikh, Rajeev N. 1950- *WhoAsA 94*
Parikh, Rohit J. 1936- *WhoAsA 94*
Parikh, Rupesh N. 1963- *WhoAsA 94*
Parikh, Shrikant Navnitlal 1956- *WhoFI 94*
Parillaud, Anne *WhoHol 92*
Parini, Jay 1948- *WrDr 94*
Parins, Robert James 1918- *WhoAm 94, WhoMW 93*
Paris, Archbishop of *Who 94*
Paris, Bernard Jay 1931- *WrDr 94*
Paris, Bubba (William) 1960- *WhoBlA 94*
Paris, Calvin Rudolph 1932- *WhoBlA 94*
Paris, David Andrew 1962- *WhoScEn 94, WhoWest 94*
Paris, Demetrius Theodore 1928- *WhoAm 94*
Paris, Edward Marvin 1951- *WhoWest 94*
Paris, Felipe Sanchez 1941- *WhoHisp 94*
Paris, Franklin D. 1933- *WhoAmP 93*
Paris, George d1976 *WhoHol 92*
Paris, George M., Sr. *WhoAmP 93*
Paris, Guillaume-Alexis 1756?-1840 *NewGrDO*
Paris, Harold Persico 1925-1979 *WhoAmA 93N*
Paris, I. Mark 1950- *ConAu 141*
Paris, James Lawrence, Jr. 1965- *WhoFI 94*
Paris, Jeanne C. *WhoAmA 93*
Paris, Jerry d1986 *WhoHol 92*
Paris, Judith *WhoHol 92*
Paris, Kathleen Anne 1948- *WhoMW 93*
Paris, Kenneth Joel 1947- *WhoWest 94*
Paris, Lucille M. 1928- *WhoAmA 93*
Paris, Lucille Marie 1928- *WhoAm 94*
Paris, Manuel d1959 *WhoHol 92*
Paris, Matthew *DrAPF 93*
Paris, Michael 1949- *WrDr 94*
Paris, Michael Anthony 1970- *WhoMW 93*
Paris, Nicola fl. 1645- *NewGrDO*
Paris, Paul Croce 1930- *WhoAm 94*
Paris, Peter Junior 1933- *WhoAm 94*
Paris, Pierre-Adrien 1745-1819 *NewGrDO*
Paris, Richard Wayne 1956- *WhoWest 94*
Paris, Sam 1957- *WhoMW 93*
Paris, Simone *WhoHol 92*
Paris, Stephen J. 1938- *WhoAm 94*
Paris, Steven Mark 1956- *WhoFI 94*
Paris, Tania de Faria Gellert 1951- *WhoScEn 94*
Paris, Zachary T. 1948- *WhoAm 94, WhoAmL 94*
Parise, Marc Robert 1953- *WhoFI 94*
Pariseau, Judy Louise 1941- *WhoAmP 93*
Pariseau, Patricia 1936- *WhoAmP 93, WhoMW 93*
Pariser, Robert Jay 1948- *WhoScEn 94*
Parish, Barbara Shirk *DrAPF 93*
Parish, Daniel M. 1919- *WhoAmP 93*
Parish, Darrell Joe 1934- *WhoMW 93*
Parish, David (Elmer) W. *Who 94*
Parish, Gary E. 1947- *WhoAmL 94*

Parish, J. Michael 1943- *WhoAm 94, WhoAmL 94*
Parish, James (Robert) 1944- *WrDr 94*
Parish, James Robert 1944- *IntMPA 94, WhoAm 94*
Parish, Jeffrey J. 1944- *WhoAmL 94*
Parish, John Cook 1910- *WhoAm 94*
Parish, Lawrence Charles 1938- *WhoAm 94*
Parish, Louis Leon 1925- *WhoFI 94*
Parish, Mitchell 1900-1993 *NewYTBS 93 [port]*
Parish, Richard Lee 1945- *WhoScEn 94*
Parish, Robert 1953- *WhoBlA 94*
Parish, Suzanne Upjohn DeLano 1922- *WhoMW 93*
Parisi, Franklin Joseph 1945- *WhoAm 94*
Parisi, Georgianna Inez 1953- *WhoAmL 94*
Parisi, Giorgio *WhoScEn 94*
Parisi, Joseph Anthony 1944- *WhoAm 94*
Parisian, Edward Franklin 1949- *WhoAm 94*
Parisot, Pierre 1940- *Who 94*
Parisy, Andrea *WhoHol 92*
Pariza, Michael Willard 1943- *WhoScEn 94*
Parizeau, Jacques 1930- *CurBio 93 [port], IntWW 93*
Parizek, Eldon Joseph 1920- *WhoAm 94*
Parizek, Jaro 1934- *WhoAmA 93*
Parizhsky, Vladimir Georg 1958- *WhoMW 93*
Parizo, Bernard Ernest 1932- *WhoAmP 93*
Parizo, Mary-Ann 1934- *WhoAmP 93*
Park *Who 94*
Park, Andrew Edward Wilson 1939- *Who 94*
Park, Byeong-Jeon 1934- *WhoScEn 94*
Park, Byiung Jun 1934- *WhoScEn 94*
Park, Byung-Soo 1930- *WhoScEn 94*
Park, Byungwoo 1958- *WhoAsA 94*
Park, Carole Roper 1939- *WhoAmP 93*
Park, Caroline 1932- *WhoAmP 93*
Park, Chan Ho 1973?- *WhoAsA 94*
Park, Chang Gi 1953- *WhoMW 93*
Park, Chang Ho *WhoAsA 94*
Park, Chang Hwan 1946- *WhoScEn 94*
Park, Charles Rawlinson 1916- *IntWW 93*
Park, Chui Suh 1941- *WhoWest 94*
Park, Chul 1934- *WhoAsA 94*
Park, Chung I. 1938- *WhoAsA 94*
Park, Chung Il 1938- *WhoMW 93*
Park, Chung Uk 1940- *WhoAsA 94*
Park, Dale, Jr. 1935- *WhoAm 94*
Park, Daniel Joseph 1934- *WhoAmL 94*
Park, David Allen 1919- *WhoAm 94*
Park, David Duck-Young 1942- *WhoFI 94, WhoWest 94*
Park, Duk-Won 1945- *WhoAsA 94*
Park, Edna Mae 1936- *WhoMW 93*
Park, Edward Cahill, Jr. 1923- *WhoWest 94*
Park, George Maclean 1914- *Who 94*
Park, Glen Dell 1949- *WhoMW 93*
Park, Gordon L. 1937- *WhoAmP 93*
Park, Hoon 1948- *WhoAsA 94*
Park, Hugh (Eames) 1910- *Who 94*
Park, Hun Young 1951- *WhoAsA 94*
Park, Ian Grahame 1935- *Who 94*
Park, J. Stephen 1941- *WhoAmP 93*
Park, Jae Young 1930- *WhoAsA 94*
Park, James Theodore 1922- *WhoAm 94*
Park, James Wallace 1934- *WhoFI 94*
Park, Jangyul 1942- *WhoMW 93*
Park, Jeannie 1962- *WhoAsA 94*
Park, Jinwoo 1957- *WhoAsA 94*
Park, John Chong-Soon 1925- *WhoFI 94*
Park, John Thornton 1935- *WhoMW 93*
Park, Jon Keith 1938- *WhoScEn 94*
Park, Joon B. 1944- *WhoAsA 94*
Park, Joseph Chul Hui 1937- *WhoWest 94*
Park, June Sung 1954- *WhoMW 93*
Park, Kang H. 1946- *WhoAsA 94*
Park, Kap Yung 1957- *WhoAsA 94*
Park, Keith F. 1946- *WhoAmL 94*
Park, Keith Harrison 1947- *WhoAmL 94*
Park, Kinam 1952- *WhoMW 93*
Park, Kiri *Who 94*
Park, Kwan Il 1950- *WhoScEn 94*
Park, Laura Heyong 1969- *WhoAsA 94*
Park, Leland Madison 1941- *WhoAm 94*
Park, Lisa Clay 1960- *WhoFI 94*
Park, Madeleine F. 1891-1960 *WhoAmA 93N*
Park, Merle 1937- *IntDcB [port]*
Park, Merle (Florence) 1937- *Who 94*
Park, Merle Florence 1937- *IntWW 93*
Park, Michael *Who 94*
Park, (Ian) Michael (Scott) 1938- *Who 94*
Park, Min-Yong 1955- *WhoScEn 94*
Park, Mungo 1771-1806 *WhWE [port]*
Park, Myung Kun 1934- *WhoAsA 94*
Park, O Ok 1954- *WhoScEn 94*
Park, Ounyoung 1949- *WhoAsA 94*
Park, Patricia Weill 1939- *WhoFI 94*
Park, Paul (Claiborne) 1954- *EncSF 93*
Park, Post d1955 *WhoHol 92*
Park, Reg *WhoHol 92*
Park, Robert 1933- *IntWW 93*
Park, Robert C., Jr. 1946- *WhoAmL 94*
Park, Robert Ezra 1864-1944 *AmSocL*
Park, Roderic Bruce 1932- *WhoAm 94, WhoScEn 94, WhoWest 94*
Park, Roy Hampton d1993 *NewYTBS 93 [port]*
Park, Roy Hampton 1910- *WhoAm 94, WhoWest 94*
Park, Ruth c. 1923- *BlmGWL [port]*
Park, (Rosina) Ruth (Lucia) *TwCYAW, WrDr 94*
Park, Sang-Chul 1949- *WhoScEn 94*
Park, Sang Oh 1930- *WhoAsA 94*
Park, Seung Kook 1957- *WhoWest 94*
Park, Seung-Kyoon 1936- *WhoAsA 94*
Park, Siyoung 1945- *WhoAsA 94*
Park, Steven Lynn 1957- *WhoMW 93*
Park, Su-Moon 1941- *WhoAsA 94*
Park, Sung-Il 1940- *WhoAsA 94*
Park, Sung Jae 1937- *WhoAm 94*
Park, Sung-won Sam 1953- *WhoAsA 94*
Park, Tae Sung 1947- *WhoAsA 94*
Park, Ted S. 1956- *WhoAsA 94*
Park, Thomas 1908-1992 *WhAm 10*
Park, Thomas Joseph 1958- *WhoScEn 94*
Park, Trevor 1927- *Who 94*
Park, Virginia Lawhon 1937- *WhoAmP 93*
Park, William Wynnewood 1947- *WhoAm 94, WhoAmL 94*
Park, Won-Hoon 1940- *WhoScEn 94*
Park, Won J. 1935- *WhoAsA 94*
Park, Yong-Tae 1941- *WhoScEn 94*
Park, Young Whan 1936- *WhoAsA 94*
Parkany, John 1921- *WhoAm 94, WhoFI 94*
Park Choong-Hoon, Maj.-Gen. 1919- *IntWW 93*
Parke, David W., II 1951- *WhoScEn 94*
Parke, Dennis Vernon William 1922- *Who 94*
Parke, Dorothy *WhoHol 92*
Parke, Jo Anne Mark 1941- *WhoAm 94*
Parke, John 1754-1789 *WhAmRev*
Parke, John Grubb 1827-1900 *WhWE*
Parke, John Shepard 1933- *WhoFI 94*
Parke, Keol-bai 1946- *WhoAsA 94*
Parke, Lowell William 1925- *WhoAmP 93*
Parke, MacDonald d1960 *WhoHol 92*
Parke, Robert Leon 1940- *WhoFI 94*
Parke, Ross Duke 1938- *WhoScEn 94*
Parke, Terry R. 1944- *WhoAmP 93*
Parke, Walter Simpson 1909- *WhoAmA 93*
Parke, William, Sr. d1941 *WhoHol 92*
Parker *Who 94*
Parker, A(gnes) Miller 1895- *Who 94*
Parker, Adele Von Ohl d1966 *WhoHol 92*
Parker, Agnes Gust d1935 *WhoHol 92*
Parker, Alan 1944- *IntMPA 94*
Parker, Alan John 1944- *WhoAm 94*
Parker, Alan Leslie, II 1952- *WhoMW 93*
Parker, Alan William 1944- *IntWW 93, Who 94, WhoAm 94*
Parker, Albert d1974 *WhoHol 92*
Parker, Alberta West 1917- *WhoWest 94*
Parker, Alfred 1906-1985 *WhoAmA 93N*
Parker, Alfred Browning 1916- *WhoAm 94*
Parker, Alice Anne 1939- *WhoWest 94*
Parker, Allan Leslie 1938- *WhoMW 93*
Parker, Angelo Pan 1945- *WhoAm 94, WhoAmL 94*
Parker, Ann 1934- *WhoAm 94, WhoAmA 93*
Parker, Antonina B. 1921- *WhoAmP 93*
Parker, Arnita Walden 1905- *WhoBlA 94*
Parker, Averette Mhoon 1939- *WhoBlA 94*
Parker, Barnett d1941 *WhoHol 92*
Parker, Barrett 1908- *WrDr 94*
Parker, Barrington D. 1915-1993 *NewYTBS 93 [port], WhoBlA 94N*
Parker, Barrington D., Jr. 1944- *WhoAmL 94*
Parker, Barry James Charles 1947- *WhoFI 94*
Parker, Barry T. 1932- *WhoAmP 93*
Parker, Bernard F., Jr. 1949- *WhoBlA 94*
Parker, Beth Harrison 1955- *WhoAmL 94*
Parker, Billie Ida 1952- *WhoFI 94*
Parker, Bobby Eugene, Sr. 1925- *WhoAm 94*
Parker, Brent Mershon 1927- *WhoAm 94*
Parker, Brian Prescott 1929- *WhoWest 94*
Parker, Cameron Holdsworth 1932- *Who 94*
Parker, Carl Allen 1934- *WhoAmP 93*
Parker, Carl Harold 1923- *WhoAmP 93*
Parker, Carolyn Johnson 1942- *WhoAmA 93*
Parker, Catherine Langloh c. 1855-1940 *BlmGWL*
Parker, Catherine M. 1921- *WhoAmP 93*
Parker, Catherine Susanne 1934- *WhoAm 94, WhoWest 94*
Parker, Cecil d1971 *WhoHol 92*
Parker, Cecilia d1993 *NewYTBS 93*
Parker, Cecilia 1914- *WhoHol 92*
Parker, Charles A. *WhoAm 94, WhoFI 94*
Parker, Charles Christopher, Jr. 1920-1955 *AmCulL*
Parker, Charles Dean, Jr. 1954- *WhoScEn 94*
Parker, Charles Edward 1927- *WhoAmL 94, WhoWest 94*
Parker, Charles McCrae 1930- *WhoBlA 94*
Parker, Charles Thomas 1918- *WhoBlA 94*
Parker, Charles Walter, Jr. 1922- *WhoAm 94*
Parker, Charlie 1920-1955 *AfrAmAl 6*
Parker, Charlyn DeEtte 1947- *WhoWest 94*
Parker, Christopher *DrAPF 93, WhoHol 92*
Parker, Christopher William 1947- *WhoAm 94, WhoAmL 94*
Parker, Christopher William Oxley 1920- *Who 94*
Parker, Claire 1907-1980 *See* Alexeieff, Alexander 1901-1979 *IntDcF 2-4*
Parker, Clare Ward 1933- *WhoMW 93*
Parker, Clarence *ProFbHF*
Parker, Claude A. 1938- *WhoBlA 94*
Parker, Clea Edward 1927- *WhoAm 94*
Parker, Clifford Frederick 1920- *Who 94*
Parker, Corey 1966- *WhoHol 92*
Parker, Craig Stephen 1949- *WhoWest 94*
Parker, Daniel 1781-1844 *DcAmReB 2*
Parker, Daniel 1925- *WhoAmP 93*
Parker, Daniel 1925-1992 *WhAm 10*
Parker, Daniel Louis 1924- *WhoAmL 94, WhoFI 94*
Parker, Darwin Carey 1956- *WhoBlA 94*
Parker, David 1941- *WrDr 94*
Parker, David 1954- *WhoAmP 93*
Parker, David 1956- *WhoScEn 94*
Parker, David B. 1947- *WhoAmL 94*
Parker, David B. 1956- *WrDr 94*
Parker, David Forster 1934- *WhoAm 94*
Parker, David Gene 1951- *WhoBlA 94*
Parker, David Hiram 1951- *WhoScEn 94*
Parker, David Martin 1939- *WhoFI 94*
Parker, David Raymond 1943- *WhoFI 94*
Parker, David Russell 1950- *WhoBlA 94*
Parker, David Shannon 1953- *WhoAm 94*
Parker, David Stuart 1919-1990 *WhAm 10*
Parker, Davis Raff 1927-1989 *WhAm 10*
Parker, Delmas Espy, Jr. 1938- *WhoAmP 93*
Parker, Denise Renee 1964- *WhoWest 94*
Parker, Dennis d1985 *WhoHol 92*
Parker, Dennis Gene 1956- *WhoMW 93*
Parker, Derek 1932- *WrDr 94*
Parker, Diane Michelle 1964- *WhoAmL 94*
Parker, Donald d1981 *WhoHol 92*
Parker, Donald Emory 1933- *WhoIns 94*
Parker, Donald Fred 1934- *WhoAm 94*
Parker, Donald Henry 1912- *WhoAm 94*
Parker, Donald Howard 1922- *WhoAm 94*
Parker, Donald Irwin 1921- *WhoAmP 93*
Parker, Donald Samuel 1948- *WhoAmL 94*
Parker, Donn Blanchard 1929- *WhoWest 94*
Parker, Dorian Leigh 1920- *WhoHol 92*
Parker, Doris S. 1931- *WhoBlA 94*
Parker, Dorothy 1893-1967 *BlmGWL, RfGShF*
Parker, Douglas D. *Who 94*
Parker, Douglas Granger 1919- *Who 94*
Parker, Douglas Martin 1935- *WhoAm 94*
Parker, E. Charmaine Roberts 1956- *WhoBlA 94*
Parker, Earle Leroy 1943- *WhoFI 94*
Parker, Ed d1990 *WhoHol 92*
Parker, Edna G. 1930- *CngDr 93, WhoAm 94, WhoAmL 94*
Parker, Edwin d1960 *WhoHol 92*
Parker, Eleanor 1922- *IntMPA 94, WhoHol 92*
Parker, Ellis Jackson, III 1932- *WhoAm 94, WhoAmL 94, WhoFI 94*
Parker, Emily Ann 1949- *WhoAm 94*
Parker, Eric (Wilson) 1933- *Who 94*
Parker, Eric Wilson 1933- *IntWW 93*
Parker, Erwin d1987 *WhoHol 92*
Parker, Eugene N. 1927- *IntWW 93*
Parker, Eugene Newman 1927- *WhoAm 94, WhoMW 93, WhoScEn 94*
Parker, Everett Carlton 1913- *WhoAm 94*
Parker, Everett Hoitt 1930- *WhoAm 94, WhoAmL 94*
Parker, Fess 1924- *IntMPA 94*
Parker, Fess 1925- *WhoHol 92*
Parker, Flora d1950 *WhoHol 92*
Parker, Frank 1916- *BuCMET*
Parker, Frank 1932- *WhoAm 94*
Parker, Frank C., III 1945- *WhoAmP 93*
Parker, Frank Leon 1926- *WhoAm 94*
Parker, Frank R. 1940- *WrDr 94*
Parker, Franklin d1962 *WhoHol 92*
Parker, Franklin 1921- *IntWW 93, WhoAm 94, WrDr 94*
Parker, Fred I. 1938- *WhoAm 94, WhoAmL 94*
Parker, Fred Lee Cecil 1923- *WhoBlA 94*
Parker, Fred Wayne 1951- *WhoAmP 93*
Parker, Frederick John 1927- *Who 94*
Parker, Frederick L. 1939- *WhoAmP 93*
Parker, G. John *WhoWest 94*
Parker, G. John, Sr. 1941- *WhoBlA 94*
Parker, G. Preston 1943- *WhoAmP 93*
Parker, Gary *WhoAmP 93*
Parker, Gary Wayne 1945- *WhoIns 94*
Parker, Geoffrey *Who 94*
Parker, (James) Geoffrey 1933- *Who 94*
Parker, (Noel) Geoffrey 1943- *Who 94*
Parker, Geoffrey Alan 1944- *Who 94*
Parker, Geoffrey John 1937- *Who 94*
Parker, George 1929- *WhoAm 94, WhoAmP 93*
Parker, George Anthony 1952- *WhoBlA 94, WhoFI 94*
Parker, George Edgar 1946- *WhoAmL 94*
Parker, George Edward, III 1934- *WhoAm 94*
Parker, George Priestley, Jr. 1943- *WhoAmL 94*
Parker, George Waller 1888-1957 *WhoAmA 93N*
Parker, Gerald Edward 1944- *WhoMW 93*
Parker, Gerald William 1929- *WhoAm 94*
Parker, Gilbert d1932 *WhoHol 92*
Parker, Glenn 1898- *WhAm 10*
Parker, Glenn Charles 1928- *WhoAmL 94*
Parker, Gordon 1940- *WrDr 94*
Parker, Gordon Rae 1935- *WhoAm 94, WhoFI 94*
Parker, Graham 1950- *ConMus 10 [port]*
Parker, Gregory E. 1947- *WhoFI 94*
Parker, H. Lawrence 1926- *WhoAm 94*
Parker, H. Wallace 1941- *WhoBlA 94*
Parker, Harold Talbot 1907- *WhoAm 94*
Parker, Harry John 1923- *WhoAm 94*
Parker, Harry Lambert 1935- *WhoAm 94*
Parker, Harry Lee 1944- *WhoAm 94*
Parker, Harry S., III 1939- *WhoAm 94, WhoAmA 93, WhoWest 94*
Parker, Henry Ellsworth 1928- *WhoBlA 94*
Parker, Henry Griffith, III 1926- *WhoAm 94, WhoIns 94*
Parker, Henry H. 1933- *WhoBlA 94*
Parker, Herbert Gerald 1929- *WhoBlA 94*
Parker, Herbert John Harvey *Who 94*
Parker, Horatio (William) 1863-1919 *NewGrDO*
Parker, Howard 1931- *WhoAmP 93*
Parker, Hugh 1919- *Who 94*
Parker, Hyde 1714-1782 *WhAmRev*
Parker, Hyde, Jr. 1739-1807 *WhAmRev*
Parker, Israel Frank 1917- *WhoAm 94*
Parker, Jack *Who 94*
Parker, Jack Royal 1919- *WhoAm 94, WhoScEn 94*
Parker, Jack Steele 1918- *WhoAm 94*
Parker, Jacquelyn Heath *WhoBlA 94*
Parker, James 1924- *WhoAm 94*
Parker, James Aubrey 1937- *WhoAm 94, WhoAmL 94, WhoWest 94*
Parker, James Edward 1938- *WhoFI 94*
Parker, James Floyd 1946- *WhoMW 93*
Parker, James Francis 1947- *WhoAmL 94*
Parker, James Gordon 1952- *Who 94*
Parker, James Grady 1960- *WhoFI 94*
Parker, James L. 1923- *WhoBlA 94*
Parker, James Mavin 1934- *Who 94*
Parker, James Ray 1956- *WhoFI 94*
Parker, James Roger 1936- *WhoScEn 94*
Parker, James Roland Walter 1919- *Who 94*
Parker, James Thomas 1934- *WhoBlA 94*
Parker, James Varner 1925- *WhoAmA 93*
Parker, James William 1951- *WhoWest 94*
Parker, Jameson 1947- *IntMPA 94, WhoHol 92*
Parker, Janet Lee *WhoHol 92*
Parker, Jannette *WhoAmP 93*
Parker, Jean *Who 94*
Parker, Jean 1912- *WhoHol 92*
Parker, (Diana) Jean 1932- *Who 94*
Parker, Jean L. 1923- *WhoBlA 94*
Parker, Jeff d1984 *WhoHol 92*
Parker, Jeff, Sr. 1927- *WhoBlA 94*
Parker, Jeffrey Scott 1952- *WhoAmL 94*
Parker, Jennifer Ware 1959- *WhoAm 94*
Parker, Jerry P. 1943- *WhoBlA 94*
Parker, Jim *ProFbHF [port]*
Parker, Jim 1944- *WhoAmP 93*
Parker, Joan 1935- *WhoAm 94*
Parker, John *Who 94*
Parker, John 1725-1775 *AmRev*
Parker, John 1729-1775 *WhAmRev*
Parker, John 1759-1832 *WhAmRev*
Parker, (Thomas) John 1942- *IntWW 93, Who 94*

Parker, (Wilfred) John 1915- *Who 94*
Parker, John Brian 1959- *WhoFI 94, WhoWest 94*
Parker, John Calvin 1961- *WhoMW 93*
Parker, John F. 1907- *WhoAmP 93*
Parker, John Garrett 1947- *WhoAm 94*
Parker, John Hill 1944- *WhoAmL 94*
Parker, John Malcolm 1920- *WhoFI 94*
Parker, John Marchbank 1920- *WhoWest 94*
Parker, John P. 1827-1900 *WorInv*
Parker, John Paul *WhoAmP 93*
Parker, John R. 1967- *WhoScEn 94*
Parker, John Thomas 1950- *ConAu 41NR*
Parker, John Victor 1928- *WhoAm 94, WhoAmL 94*
Parker, John William 1931- *WhoAm 94, WhoWest 94*
Parker, Jon Irving 1944- *WhoScEn 94*
Parker, Jonathan (Frederic) 1937- *Who 94*
Parker, Jonathan Edward 1936- *WhoFI 94*
Parker, Joseph B., Jr. 1916- *WhoAm 94*
Parker, Joseph Caiaphas, Jr. 1952- *WhoBlA 94*
Parker, Joseph Mayon 1931- *WhoAm 94, WhoAmP 93, WhoFI 94*
Parker, Joseph Orville 1908-1991 *WhAm 10*
Parker, Josephus Derward 1906- *WhoScEn 94*
Parker, Joyce Linda 1944- *WhoBlA 94*
Parker, Joyce Steinfeld 1946- *WhoWest 94*
Parker, Judith Koehler 1940- *WhoAmP 93*
Parker, Julia Lynne 1966- *WhoWest 94*
Parker, Julius, Jr. 1934- *AfrAmG [port]*
Parker, Kai J. 1939- *WhoBlA 94*
Parker, Karl Theodore d1992 *IntWW 93N*
Parker, Kathryn M. *WhoMW 93*
Parker, Keith Dwight 1954- *WhoBlA 94*
Parker, Keith John 1940- *Who 94*
Parker, Kellis E. 1942- *WhoBlA 94*
Parker, Kenneth Alfred Lamport 1912- *Who 94*
Parker, Kenneth Blades 1945- *Who 94*
Parker, Kenneth Dean 1935- *WhoWest 94*
Parker, Kenneth L(croy) 1954- *WrDr 94*
Parker, Kevin James *WhoScEn 94*
Parker, Kimberly Jane 1958- *WhoWest 94*
Parker, Kristin Luan Martin 1967- *WhoWest 94*
Parker, Lara *WhoHol 92*
Parker, Larry James 1942- *WhoAmP 93*
Parker, Larry Lee 1938- *WhoFI 94, WhoScEn 94, WhoWest 94*
Parker, Lee 1949- *WhoBlA 94*
Parker, Lee Fischer 1932- *WhoMW 93*
Parker, Lee S. 1946- *WhoAmL 94*
Parker, Leon Douglas 1920- *WhoAmP 93*
Parker, Leonard *WhoHol 92*
Parker, Leslie *ConAu 140*
Parker, Lew d1972 *WhoHol 92*
Parker, Lewis Wardlaw, Jr. 1928- *WhoAmP 93*
Parker, Lisa Maureen 1955- *WhoAmP 93*
Parker, Lucy d1947 *WhoHol 92*
Parker, Lutrelle Fleming 1924- *WhoBlA 94*
Parker, Lydia Leach 1948- *WhoFI 94*
Parker, Lyn 1952- *Who 94*
Parker, Lynn Rosanne 1961- *WhoFI 94*
Parker, Maceo *WhoAm 94*
Parker, Margaret Annette McCrie Johnston *Who 94*
Parker, Marietta *WhoAmL 94*
Parker, Marion d1920 *WhoHol 92*
Parker, Martha Ann 1948- *WhoFI 94*
Parker, Martin Leonard 1921- *WhoAmP 93*
Parker, Marvin Grant 1934- *WhoMW 93*
Parker, Mary d1966 *WhoHol 92*
Parker, Mary 1925- *WhoHol 92*
Parker, Mary Ann fl. 1795- *BlmGWL*
Parker, Mary Ann 1953- *WhoAmL 94*
Parker, Mary Anne 1929- *WhoMW 93*
Parker, Mary Evelyn 1920- *WhoAm 94*
Parker, Mary Lou 1945- *WhoAmL 94*
Parker, Mary Louise 1964- *WhoHol 92*
Parker, Mary Patrice 1952- *WhoFI 94*
Parker, Maryland Mike 1926- *WhoBlA 94*
Parker, Matthew 1504-1575 *BlmGEL*
Parker, Matthew 1945- *WhoBlA 94*
Parker, Maynard Michael 1940- *IntWW 93, WhoAm 94, WhoFI 94*
Parker, Mel 1949- *WhoAm 94*
Parker, Melanie *WhoHol 92*
Parker, Michael *Who 94*
Parker, Michael 1949- *WhoAm 94*
Parker, Michael 1959- *ConAu 140*
Parker, (John) Michael (Avison) 1920- *Who 94*
Parker, Michael Andrew 1949- *WhoScEn 94*
Parker, Michael Clynes 1924- *Who 94*

Parker, Michael David 1954- *WhoWest 94*
Parker, Michael George 1951- *WhoMW 93*
Parker, Michael John 1941- *Who 94*
Parker, Michael Joseph Bennett 1931- *Who 94*
Parker, Michael St. J. *Who 94*
Parker, Michael Tracy 1961- *WhoAmL 94*
Parker, Mike 1949- *CngDr 93, WhoAmP 93*
Parker, Monica *WhoHol 92*
Parker, Nancy W(inslow) 1930- *WrDr 94*
Parker, Nancy Winslow 1930- *WhoAm 94, WhoAmA 93*
Parker, Nathaniel 1962- *WhoHol 92*
Parker, Noelle *WhoHol 92*
Parker, Norman *WhoHol 92*
Parker, Norman Neil, Jr. 1949- *WhoScEn 94*
Parker, Olivia 1941- *WhoAm 94, WhoAmA 93*
Parker, Omar Sigmund, Jr. 1945- *WhoAm 94*
Parker, Ora Dean Simmons 1939- *WhoAm 94*
Parker, Pat 1944-1989 *BlkWr 2, ConAu 42NR*
Parker, Pat (Cook) 1944-1989 *GayLL*
Parker, Patrick Johnston 1931- *WhoFI 94, WhoWest 94*
Parker, Patrick Streeter 1929- *WhoAm 94, WhoFI 94, WhoMW 93*
Parker, Paul E. 1935- *WhoBlA 94*
Parker, Paul Henry 1949- *WhoWest 94*
Parker, Percy Spurlark 1940- *BlkWr 2*
Parker, Peter *Who 94*
Parker, Peter 1721-1811 *WhAmRev [port]*
Parker, Peter 1924- *IntWW 93, Who 94*
Parker, Peter (Robert Nevill) 1954- *WrDr 94*
Parker, (William) Peter (Brian) 1950- *Who 94*
Parker, Peter D.M. 1936- *WhoScEn 94*
Parker, Pierson 1905- *WhoAm 94*
Parker, Quanah 1845?-1911 *DcAmReB 2, EncNAR*
Parker, R. Joseph 1944- *WhoAm 94, WhoAmL 94*
Parker, Ralph 1919- *WhoAmP 93*
Parker, Ralph Douglas 1898- *WhAm 10*
Parker, Ralph Halstead 1909-1990 *WhAm 10*
Parker, Ray, Jr. 1954- *WhoBlA 94*
Parker, Ray, Jr. 1956- *WhoHol 92*
Parker, Raymond d1987 *WhoHol 92*
Parker, Raymond d1993 *NewYTBS 93*
Parker, Raymond 1922-1990 *WhAm 10, WhoAmA 93N*
Parker, Reginald Boden 1901- *Who 94*
Parker, Richard 1915- *EncSF 93*
Parker, Richard A. d1993 *NewYTBS 93 [port]*
Parker, Richard Alexander 1898- *WhAm 10*
Parker, Richard Bennett 1925- *WhoAm 94*
Parker, Richard Bordeaux 1923- *WhoAmP 93*
Parker, Richard Edmund 1947- *WhoAm 94*
Parker, Richard Edward 1947- *WhoAmL 94*
Parker, Richard (William) Hyde 1937- *Who 94*
Parker, Richard Michael 1945- *WhoAmL 94*
Parker, Richard Ralph 1948- *WhoAmL 94*
Parker, Richard Wilson 1943- *WhoAmL 94*
Parker, Robert Aaron 1948- *WhoWest 94*
Parker, Robert Allan Ridley 1936- *WhoAm 94, WhoScEn 94*
Parker, Robert Andrew 1927- *WhoAm 94, WhoAmA 93*
Parker, Robert Andrew 1946- *WhoScEn 94*
Parker, Robert B. 1932- *CurBio 93 [port]*
Parker, Robert B(rown) 1932- *WrDr 94*
Parker, Robert Brown 1932- *WhoAm 94*
Parker, Robert Chauncey Humphrey 1941- *WhoFI 94, WhoMW 93*
Parker, Robert Daniel 1945- *WhoWest 94*
Parker, Robert Frederic 1907- *WhoAm 94*
Parker, Robert George 1925- *WhoAm 94*
Parker, Robert Hallett 1922- *WhoAm 94, WhoScEn 94*
Parker, Robert Lee, Sr. 1923- *WhoAm 94*
Parker, Robert Lee, Jr. 1948- *WhoAm 94*
Parker, Robert M. 1937- *WhoAm 94, WhoAmL 94*
Parker, Robert Rudolph 1927- *WhoMW 93*
Parker, Robert Samuel 1924- *WhoAmL 94*
Parker, Robert Stewart 1915- *WrDr 94*
Parker, Robert Stewart 1949- *Who 94*

Parker, Rodney Edwin 1931- *WhoAmP 93*
Parker, Roger (Jocelyn) 1923- *Who 94*
Parker, Roger (Leslie) 1951- *NewGrDO*
Parker, Ronald William 1909- *Who 94*
Parker, Roy Alfred 1930- *WhoWest 94*
Parker, Roy Turnage 1920- *WhoAm 94*
Parker, Rudolph 1934- *WhoAmP 93*
Parker, Sachi 1956- *WhoHol 92*
Parker, Samuel Murray 1936- *WhoAmA 93*
Parker, Sara Ann 1939- *WhoAm 94*
Parker, Sarah Elizabeth 1942- *WhoAmL 94, WhoAmP 93*
Parker, Sarah Jessica 1965- *IntMPA 94, WhoHol 92*
Parker, Scott Lane 1946- *WhoAm 94*
Parker, "Seth" d1975 *WhoHol 92*
Parker, Shirley *WhoHol 92*
Parker, Sidney Baynes 1922- *WhoBlA 94*
Parker, Stafford W. 1935- *WhoBlA 94*
Parker, Stanley Lewis 1956- *WhoMW 93*
Parker, Stanley R. 1927- *WrDr 94*
Parker, Stanley R. 1950- *WhoAmL 94*
Parker, Stephen A. *WhoBlA 94*
Parker, Steven L. 1960- *WhoAmL 94*
Parker, (James) Stewart 1941-1988 *ConDr 93, IntDcT 2*
Parker, Stuart I. 1943- *WhoAmL 94*
Parker, Sue Ellen 1950- *WhoAmP 93*
Parker, Susan Brooks 1945- *WhoAm 94*
Parker, Susan Huggard 1939- *WhoFI 94*
Parker, Suzy 1933- *IntMPA 94, WhoHol 92*
Parker, Theodore 1810-1860 *DcAmReB 2*
Parker, Theodore A., III d1993 *NewYTBS 93 [port]*
Parker, Theodore Clifford 1929- *WhoFI 94, WhoScEn 94, WhoWest 94*
Parker, Thomas 1904-1967 *WhoAmA 93N*
Parker, Thomas (Henry Louis) 1916- *WrDr 94*
Parker, Thomas Aaron 1965- *WhoMW 93*
Parker, Thomas E., Jr. 1916- *WhoBlA 94*
Parker, Thomas Edwin, III 1944- *WhoBlA 94*
Parker, Thomas Gooch 1925- *WhoWest 94*
Parker, Thomas Lee 1921- *WhoAm 94*
Parker, Thomas Sherman 1945- *WhoScEn 94*
Parker, Tim *WhoAmP 93*
Parker, Tom *ConAu 41NR*
Parker, Tom 1943- *WrDr 94*
Parker, Una-Mary 1930- *ConAu 140*
Parker, "Uncle Murray" d1965 *WhoHol 92*
Parker, V. M. 1915- *WhoAmP 93*
Parker, Virginia Lee 1935- *WhoMW 93*
Parker, Vivian d1974 *WhoHol 92*
Parker, W. Dale 1925- *WrDr 94*
Parker, W(illiam) H(enry) 1912- *WrDr 94*
Parker, Wallace Crawford 1937- *WhoWest 94*
Parker, Walteen Carter 1946- *WhoAmP 93*
Parker, Walter Gee 1933- *WhoBlA 94*
Parker, Warren d1976 *WhoHol 92*
Parker, Wayne Charles 1956- *WhoWest 94*
Parker, Wes 1945- *WhoHol 92*
Parker, Will 1944- *WhoAmA 93*
Parker, Willard 1912- *WhoHol 92*
Parker, William *WhoAmP 93*
Parker, William 1943-1993 *NewYTBS 93 [port]*
Parker, William C., Jr. 1939- *WhoBlA 94*
Parker, William Dale 1925- *WhoFI 94*
Parker, William Elbridge 1913- *WhoWest 94*
Parker, William H., III 1937- *WhoAm 94*
Parker, William Hartley 1947- *WhoBlA 94*
Parker, William Harvey 1946- *WhoFI 94*
Parker, William Hayes, Jr. 1947- *WhoBlA 94*
Parker, William Jerry 1931- *WhoAmL 94*
Parker, William Nelson 1919- *WhoAm 94*
Parker, William Thomas 1928- *WhoAmP 93*
Parker, Wilma 1941- *WhoAmA 93*
Parker, Winifred Ellis 1960- *WhoWest 94*
Parker-Jervis, Roger 1931- *Who 94*
Parker-Robinson, D. LaVerne 1949- *WhoBlA 94*
Parker-Sawyers, Paula *WhoBlA 94*
Parkerson, John 1945- *WhoAmP 93*
Parkerson, Michelle (Denise) 1953- *BlkWr 2*
Parkerson, William Francis, Jr. 1920- *WhoAmP 93*
Parkes, Alexander 1813-1890 *WorInv*
Parkes, Basil (Arthur) d1993 *Who 94N*
Parkes, Ed. 1904- *IntWW 93*
Parkes, Edward d1985 *WhoHol 92*
Parkes, Edward (Walter) 1926- *IntWW 93, Who 94*
Parkes, Gerard *WhoHol 92*

Parkes, Henry 1815-1896 *HisWorL [port]*
Parkes, John Alan 1939- *Who 94*
Parkes, John Hubert 1930- *Who 94*
Parkes, Kenneth Carroll 1922- *WhoAm 94*
Parkes, Lucas *EncSF 93*
Parkes, Malcolm Beckwith 1930- *Who 94*
Parkes, Margaret 1925- *Who 94*
Parkes, Norman James 1912- *Who 94*
Parkes, Roger Graham 1933- *WrDr 94*
Parkes, Walter F. *IntMPA 94*
Parkes, Walter F. 1952?- *ConTFT 11*
Parkey, Glen *WhoAmP 93*
Parkey, Robert Wayne 1938- *WhoScEn 94*
Parkhie, Mukund R. 1933- *WhoAsA 94*
Parkhill, Harold Loyal 1928- *WhoMW 93*
Parkhill, Miriam May 1913- *WhoMW 93*
Parkhouse, James 1927- *Who 94*
Parkhouse, Peter 1927- *Who 94*
Parkhurst, Charles 1913- *WhoAm 94, WhoAmA 93*
Parkhurst, Charles Henry 1842-1933 *AmSocL [port], DcAmReB 2*
Parkhurst, Charles Lloyd 1943- *WhoScEn 94, WhoWest 94*
Parkhurst, David Frank 1942- *WhoMW 93*
Parkhurst, Frances d1969 *WhoHol 92*
Parkhurst, Gary Stephen 1951- *WhoFI 94*
Parkhurst, George Leigh 1907-1990 *WhAm 10*
Parkhurst, Lindsay A. 1963- *WhoAmL 94*
Parkhurst, Raymond Thurston 1898- *Who 94*
Parkhurst, Todd Sheldon 1941- *WhoAm 94, WhoAmL 94, WhoMW 93*
Parkin, David John 1940- *Who 94*
Parkin, Evelyn Hope 1910- *WhoFI 94*
Parkin, Gerard Francis Ralph 1959- *WhoScEn 94*
Parkin, James Lamar 1939- *WhoAm 94*
Parkin, Joe L. d1993 *NewYTBS 93*
Parkin, John Mackintosh 1920- *Who 94*
Parkin, Molly 1932- *WrDr 94*
Parkin, Sara Lamb 1946- *Who 94*
Parkington, Beulah d1958 *WhoHol 92*
Parkins, Barbara 1942- *WhoHol 92*
Parkins, Barbara 1943- *IntMPA 94*
Parkins, Frederick Milton 1935- *WhoAm 94*
Parkins, Graham Charles 1942- *Who 94*
Parkins, Lenard M. 1949- *WhoAmL 94*
Parkinson, Baron 1931- *Who 94*
Parkinson, Benjamin Henry, Jr. 1922- *WhoAmL 94*
Parkinson, C. Northcote 1909-1993 *NewYTBS 93 [port]*
Parkinson, C(yril) Northcote d1993 *IntWW 93N*
Parkinson, C(yril) Northcote 1909-1993 *ConAu 140, CurBio 93N*
Parkinson, Cecil Edward 1931- *IntWW 93*
Parkinson, Charles Arden, Jr. d1976 *WhoHol 92*
Parkinson, Chuck d1988 *WhoHol 92*
Parkinson, Claire Lucille 1948- *WhoScEn 94*
Parkinson, Cliff d1950 *WhoHol 92*
Parkinson, Cyril Northcote d1993 *Who 94N*
Parkinson, Cyril Northcote 1909-1993 *WrDr 94N*
Parkinson, Dan 1935- *WrDr 94*
Parkinson, David Hardress 1918- *Who 94*
Parkinson, Del R. 1948- *WhoWest 94*
Parkinson, Dennis 1927- *WhoAm 94*
Parkinson, Desmond Frederick 1920- *Who 94*
Parkinson, Desmond John 1913- *Who 94*
Parkinson, Don 1942- *WhoAmP 93*
Parkinson, Dwight Maughan 1963- *WhoFI 94*
Parkinson, Elizabeth Bliss 1907- *WhoAmA 93*
Parkinson, Ethelyn Minerva 1906- *WhoAm 94*
Parkinson, Ewart West 1926- *Who 94*
Parkinson, Fred 1929- *WhoAmP 93*
Parkinson, Georgina 1938- *WhoAm 94*
Parkinson, Graham Edward 1937- *Who 94*
Parkinson, Greg Thomas 1950- *WhoAm 94, WhoMW 93*
Parkinson, H(arold) F(rederick) *EncSF 93*
Parkinson, Howard Evans 1936- *WhoFI 94*
Parkinson, James 1755-1824 *EncSPD*
Parkinson, James Christopher 1920- *Who 94*
Parkinson, James Thomas, III 1940- *WhoFI 94*
Parkinson, John David 1929- *WhoFI 94*
Parkinson, Kenneth Wells 1927- *WhoAmL 94*
Parkinson, Mark V. 1957- *WhoAmP 93*
Parkinson, Michael *WrDr 94*

Parkinson, Michael 1935- *IntWW 93, Who 94*
Parkinson, Nicholas (Fancourt) 1925- *Who 94*
Parkinson, Paul K. 1952- *WhoAmL 94*
Parkinson, Ronald Dennis 1945- *Who 94*
Parkinson, Thomas *DrAPF 93*
Parkinson, Thomas (Francis) 1920-1992 *WrDr 94N*
Parkinson, Thomas Brian 1935- *WhoWest 94*
Parkinson, Thomas Francis 1920-1992 *WhAm 10*
Parkinson, Thomas Harry 1907- *Who 94*
Parkinson, Thomas Ignatius, Jr. 1914- *WhoAm 94, WhoFI 94*
Parkinson, Thomas Paul 1921- *WhoMW 93*
Parkinson, William Charles 1918- *WhoAm 94*
Parkinson, William Quillian 1957- *WhoScEn 94*
Parkison, Roger Clyde 1949- *WhoWest 94*
Park Li, Gimmy 1945- *WhoAsA 94*
Park of Monmouth, Baroness 1921- *Who 94*
Parks, Albert Lauriston 1935- *WhoAmL 94*
Parks, Alfred G., Jr. 1951- *WhoBlA 94*
Parks, Andrew *WhoHol 92*
Parks, Arnold Grant 1939- *WhoBlA 94*
Parks, Bernard 1944- *WhoBlA 94*
Parks, Bert 1914- *WhoHol 92*
Parks, Bert 1914-1992 *AnObit 1992, WhAm 10*
Parks, Carrie Anne 1955- *WhoAmA 93*
Parks, Catherine M. *WhoAmP 93*
Parks, Charles Cropper 1922- *WhoAm 94, WhoAmA 93*
Parks, Corrine Frances 1934- *WhoMW 93*
Parks, David Allan 1961- *WhoFI 94*
Parks, Del 1941- *WhoAmP 93*
Parks, Dorothy Patricia 1956- *WhoWest 94*
Parks, Ed Horace, III 1948- *WhAm 10*
Parks, Edna Dorintha 1910- *WrDr 94*
Parks, George B. 1925- *WhoBlA 94*
Parks, George Richard 1935- *WhoAm 94*
Parks, Gerald Barttett *DrAPF 93*
Parks, Gerald Thomas, Jr. 1944- *WhoWest 94*
Parks, Gilbert R. 1944- *WhoBlA 94*
Parks, Gordon 1912- *AfrAmAl 6 [port], IntMPA 94*
Parks, Gordon (Alexander Buchanan) 1912- *BlkWr 2, WrDr 94*
Parks, Gordon A. 1912- *WhoBlA 94*
Parks, Gordon Roger Alexander Buchanan 1912- *WhoAm 94*
Parks, Harold Francis 1920- *WhoAm 94*
Parks, Harold Raymond 1949- *WhoScEn 94, WhoWest 94*
Parks, Henry G. 1916- *AfrAmAl 6*
Parks, Henry Green 1916-1989 *WhAm 10*
Parks, Herbert Louis 1925- *WhoFI 94, WhoIns 94*
Parks, Hildy 1924- *WhoHol 92*
Parks, James Clinton, Jr. 1944- *WhoBlA 94*
Parks, James Dallas 1906- *WhoBlA 94*
Parks, James Edgar 1939- *WhoScEn 94*
Parks, James Edward 1946- *WhoBlA 94*
Parks, James Franklin, Jr. 1942- *WhoAm 94*
Parks, James Thomas 1947- *WhoAm 94, WhoFI 94*
Parks, Jane deLoach 1927- *WhoAmL 94*
Parks, Jeffrey A. 1948- *WhoAm 94, WhoAmP 93*
Parks, Joe B. 1915- *WhoAmP 93*
Parks, John Lindsay 1929- *WhoIns 94*
Parks, John Robert 1952- *WhoAm 94, WhoAmL 94*
Parks, Larry d1975 *WhoHol 92*
Parks, Laurence Hall 1946- *WhoMW 93*
Parks, Lloyd Lee 1929- *WhoAm 94*
Parks, Louis 1955- *WhoFI 94*
Parks, Louise d1990 *WhoHol 92*
Parks, Madelyn N. *WhoAm 94*
Parks, Mary June 1926- *WhoIns 94*
Parks, Matthew William 1925- *WhoAm 94*
Parks, Michael 1938- *IntMPA 94, WhoHol 92*
Parks, Michael Christopher 1943- *WhoAm 94, WhoWest 94*
Parks, Norman Houston 1949- *WhoAmL 94*
Parks, Opal *WhoAmP 93*
Parks, Patricia J. 1945- *WhoAm 94, WhoAmL 94*
Parks, Paul 1923- *WhoBlA 94*
Parks, Raymond G. 1939- *WhoAmP 93*
Parks, Richard Keith 1947- *WhoWest 94*
Parks, Robert Edson 1942- *WhoScEn 94*
Parks, Robert Emmett, Jr. 1921- *WhoAm 94, WhoScEn 94*
Parks, Robert Henry 1924- *WhoAm 94*
Parks, Robert Howard, Jr. 1943- *WhoWest 94*
Parks, Robert Keith 1927- *WhoAm 94*
Parks, Robert Myers 1927- *WhoAm 94, WhoFI 94*
Parks, Rodney Keith 1962- *WhoScEn 94*
Parks, Rosa 1913- *WhoBlA 94*
Parks, Rosa Louise McCauley 1913- *AfrAmAl 6, AmSocL*
Parks, Sherman A. 1924- *WhoBlA 94*
Parks, Steven James 1965- *WhoScEn 94*
Parks, Suzan-Lori *ConDr 93*
Parks, Thelma Reece 1923- *WhoBlA 94*
Parks, Thomas Norville 1950- *WhoWest 94*
Parks, Tim 1954- *WrDr 94*
Parks, Tom Harris 1932- *WhoWest 94*
Parks, Vincent Joseph 1928- *WhoScEn 94*
Parks, William Anthony, Jr. 1947- *WhoAmP 93*
Parks, William Hamilton 1934- *WhoWest 94*
Parks-Duncanson, Louise 1929- *WhoBlA 94*
Park Sung Sang 1923- *IntWW 93*
Park-Taylor, Sonya Sunnah 1967- *WhoAsA 94*
Parkyakarkus d1958 *WhoHol 92*
Parkyakarkus 1904-1958 *WhoCom*
Parkyn, Brian (Stewart) 1923- *Who 94*
Parkyn, John Duwane 1944- *WhoMW 93*
Parkyn, John William 1931- *WhoAm 94*
Parl, Steen Allan 1945- *WhoAm 94*
Parla, JoAnn Oliveros 1948- *WhoHisp 94*
Parlakian, Nishan 1925- *WrDr 94*
Parlamagni, Antonio 1759-1838 *NewGrDO*
Parlato, Lisa Marie 1961- *WhoAmL 94*
Parlee, Randy Steven 1954- *WhoAmL 94*
Parler, William Carlos 1929- *WhoAm 94, WhoAmL 94*
Parlett, James *DrAPF 93*
Parlett, John Knight 1937- *WhoAmP 93*
Parlette, Carol Holland 1944- *WhoWest 94*
Parlin, Charles C., Jr. 1928- *WhoAm 94, WhoAmL 94*
Parlo, Dita *WhoHol 92*
Parlos, Alexander George 1961- *WhoScEn 94*
Parly, Ticho 1928- *NewGrDO*
Parma, Florence Virginia 1940- *WhoWest 94*
Parma, Ildebrando da *NewGrDO*
Parma, Viktor 1858-1924 *NewGrDO*
Parmakelis, John 1932- *WhoAmA 93*
Parmeggiani, Ettore 1895-1960 *NewGrDO*
Parmelee, Arthur Hawley, Jr. 1917- *WhoAm 94*
Parmelee, David Freeland 1924- *WhoAm 94*
Parmelee, Harold J. 1937- *WhoFI 94*
Parmelee, Ken 1940- *WhoAmP 93*
Parmelee, Walker Michael 1952- *WhoMW 93, WhoScEn 94*
Parment, William J. 1942- *WhoAmP 93*
Parmenter, Charles Stedman 1933- *WhoAm 94, WhoMW 93, WhoScEn 94*
Parmenter, Lonnie LeRoy 1944- *WhoMW 93*
Parmenter, Robert Haley 1925- *WhoAm 94, WhoWest 94*
Parmer, Dan Gerald 1926- *WhoScEn 94*
Parmer, Edgar Alan 1928- *WhoScEn 94*
Parmer, Hugh Q. 1939- *WhoAmP 93*
Parmerlee, Mark S. 1955- *WhoFI 94*
Parmesani, Rolando Romano 1960- *WhoScEn 94*
Parmet, Herbert S. 1929- *WrDr 94*
Parmet, Herbert Samuel 1929- *WhoAm 94*
Parmeter, Diana Lynn 1963- *WhoWest 94*
Parmiter, James Darlin 1934- *WhoAm 94*
Parmley, Loren Francis, Jr. 1921- *WhoAm 94, WhoScEn 94*
Parmley, Robert James 1950- *WhoAmL 94*
Parmoor, Baron 1929- *Who 94*
Parms, Edwin L. 1937- *WhoBlA 94*
Parnaby, John 1937- *Who 94*
Parnall, Edward 1904- *WhoWest 94*
Parnas, David Lorge 1941- *WhoAm 94*
Parnell *Who 94*
Parnell, Albert Hunter 1941- *WhoAmL 94*
Parnell, Arnold W. 1936- *WhoBlA 94*
Parnell, Bernard d1981 *WhoHol 92*
Parnell, Charles L. 1938- *WhoMW 93*
Parnell, Charles Stewart 1846-1891 *BlmGEL, HisWorL [port]*
Parnell, Dale Paul 1928- *WhoAm 94*
Parnell, David Russell 1925- *WhoAmP 93*
Parnell, Effie d1987 *WhoHol 92*
Parnell, Emory d1979 *WhoHol 92*
Parnell, Francis *EncSF 93*
Parnell, Francis William, Jr. 1940- *WhoAm 94*
Parnell, Gregory Elliott 1953- *WhoWest 94*
Parnell, James d1961 *WhoHol 92*
Parnell, John G. 1945- *WhoAmL 94*
Parnell, John Vaze, III 1944- *WhoBlA 94*
Parnell, Mary Davies 1936- *ConAu 140*
Parnell, (David) Michael 1934- *WrDr 94*
Parnell, Pat *WhoAmP 93*
Parnell, Sean R. 1962- *WhoAmP 93*
Parnell, Thomas 1679-1718 *BlmGEL*
Parnell, Thomas Alfred 1931- *WhoAm 94*
Parnell, William Cornellus, Jr. 1940- *WhoBlA 94*
Parnes, Alan P. 1952- *WhoAmL 94*
Parness, Charles 1945- *WhoAmA 93*
Parnicky, William 1921- *WhoWest 94*
Parnis, Alexander Edward Libor 1911- *Who 94*
Parnis, Mollie 1905-1992 *AnObit 1992*
Parnok, Sofiia Iakovlevna 1885-1933 *BlmGWL*
Parnok, Sophia (Yakovlevna) 1885-1932 *GayLL*
Parnov, Eremei (Iudovich) 1935- *EncSF 93*
Paro, Tom Edward 1923- *WhoAm 94*
Parobek, Drew Thomas 1957- *WhoAmL 94*
Parodi, Anton Gaetano 1923- *IntWW 93*
Parodi, Oscar S. 1932- *WhoHisp 94*
Parodi, Teresa 1827-1878? *NewGrDO*
Paroisse-Pougin, Arthur *NewGrDO*
Parola, Fredrick Edson, Jr. 1946- *WhoAmP 93*
Paroni, Genevieve Marie Swick 1926- *WhoWest 94*
Parotti, Phillip 1941- *WrDr 94*
Parpia, Zakir Husain 1948- *WhoWest 94*
Parque, Richard *DrAPF 93*
Parquette, Jack Robert 1934- *WhoWest 94*
Parr, Albert Eide 1900-1991 *WhAm 10*
Parr, Carolyn Miller *CngDr 93*
Parr, Carolyn Miller 1937- *WhoAm 94, WhoAmL 94*
Parr, Catherine 1512-1548 *BlmGWL [port]*
Parr, Catherine 1513?-1548 *DcLB 136 [port]*
Parr, Charles Theodore d1923 *WhoHol 92*
Parr, (Thomas) Donald 1930- *Who 94*
Parr, Ferdinand Van Siclen, Jr. 1908- *WhoAm 94*
Parr, Grant Van Siclen 1942- *WhoAm 94*
Parr, James David 1951- *WhoMW 93*
Parr, James Gordon 1927- *WhoAm 94*
Parr, Katharine *WhoHol 92*
Parr, Lloyd Byron 1931- *WhoAm 94*
Parr, Richard Arnold, II 1958- *WhoAmL 94, WhoFI 94*
Parr, Robert Ghormley 1921- *IntWW 93, WhoAm 94, WhoScEn 94*
Parr, Royse Milton 1935- *WhoAm 94*
Parr, Susanna fl. 1659- *BlmGWL*
Parr, Thurmond Charles, Jr. 1925- *WhoFI 94*
Parra, Carmen 1944- *WhoAmA 93*
Parra, Jose *WhoHisp 94*
Parra, Mike *WhoHisp 94*
Parra, Nicanor 1914- *ConWorW 93, HispLC [port], IntWW 93*
Parra, Raul O. 1954- *WhoHisp 94*
Parra, Teresa de La 1889-1936 *BlmGWL*
Parra, Teresita J. 1934- *WhoHisp 94*
Parra, Tim *WhoHisp 94*
Parra, Tony 1948- *WhoAmP 93*
Parra, Violeta 1917-1967 *BlmGWL*
Parra, William Charles 1942- *WhoHisp 94*
Parra-Diaz, Dennisse 1961- *WhoScEn 94*
Parraguirre, Ronald David 1959- *WhoAmL 94*
Parra Herrera, German *IntWW 93*
Parramore, John Andrew, II 1955- *WhoAm 94*
Parran, John Thomas, Jr. 1926- *WhoAmP 93*
Parratt, James Roy 1933- *IntWW 93*
Parravani, James V. 1962- *WhoAmL 94*
Parravano, Amelia Elizabeth 1951- *WhoFI 94*
Parravicini, Giannino 1910- *IntWW 93*
Parren, Kallirroi 1861-1940 *BlmGWL*
Parrenas, Cecilia Salazar 1945- *WhoWest 94*
Parrett, John d1992 *Who 94N*
Parrett, Sherman O. 1943- *WhoAm 94*
Parretti, Giancarlo 1941- *IntMPA 94*
Parrigin, Elizabeth Ellington 1932- *WhoAmL 94, WhoMW 93*
Parrinder, (Edward) Geoffrey (Simons) 1910- *Who 94*
Parrinder, (John) Patrick 1944- *EncSF 93*
Parrinello, James R. 1949- *WhoAmL 94*
Parrino, George 1942- *WhoAmA 93*
Parriott, James Deforis, Jr. 1923- *WhoAm 94*
Parriott, Joseph D. 1933- *WhoAmP 93*
Parris, Alvin, III 1951- *WhoBlA 94*
Parris, Charles Deighton 1922- *WhoScEn 94*
Parris, Don 1944- *WhoAmL 94*
Parris, Luther Allen 1955- *WhoScEn 94*
Parris, Matthew 1949- *IntWW 93*
Parris, Matthew (Francis) 1949- *WrDr 94*
Parris, Matthew Francis 1949- *Who 94*
Parris, Nina Gumpert 1927- *WhoAmA 93*
Parris, Robert 1924- *WhoAm 94*
Parris, Stanford E. 1929- *WhoAm 94, WhoFI 94*
Parris, Vincent Dumont 1948- *WhoMW 93*
Parrish, Alvin Edward 1922- *WhoAm 94*
Parrish, Barry Jay 1946- *WhoAm 94, WhoFI 94*
Parrish, Benjamin Emmitt, II 1945- *WhoFI 94*
Parrish, Bobby Lee 1931- *WhoFI 94*
Parrish, Clarence R. 1921- *WhoBlA 94*
Parrish, Clyde Robin, III 1952- *WhoScEn 94*
Parrish, Danny Earl d1976 *WhoHol 92*
Parrish, David Buchanan 1939- *WhoAmA 93*
Parrish, David Walker, Jr. 1923- *WhoAm 94, WhoAmL 94*
Parrish, Edgar Lee 1948- *WhoAm 94*
Parrish, Edward Alton, Jr. 1937- *WhoScEn 94*
Parrish, Frank 1929- *WrDr 94*
Parrish, Frank Jennings 1923- *WhoAm 94*
Parrish, Gigi *WhoHol 92*
Parrish, Harry Jacob 1922- *WhoAmP 93*
Parrish, Helen d1959 *WhoHol 92*
Parrish, James L. d1978 *WhoHol 92*
Parrish, James Nathaniel 1939- *WhoBlA 94*
Parrish, James W. 1908-1991 *WhoBlA 94N*
Parrish, James W. 1946- *WhoAmP 93*
Parrish, James Wesley 1946- *WhoMW 93*
Parrish, Jay 1921- *WhoAm 94*
Parrish, Jean 1911- *WhoAmA 93*
Parrish, Jimmy David 1947- *WhoAmP 93*
Parrish, John 1957- *WhoAmP 93*
Parrish, John Albert 1939- *WhoScEn 94*
Parrish, John Bishop 1911- *WhoAm 94*
Parrish, John Brett 1934- *WhoAm 94*
Parrish, John Henry 1924- *WhoBlA 94*
Parrish, John Wesley, Jr. 1941- *WhoScEn 94*
Parrish, Julie 1939- *WhoHol 92*
Parrish, Larry J. 1941- *WhoAmP 93*
Parrish, Laura d1977 *WhoHol 92*
Parrish, Lemar 1947- *WhoBlA 94*
Parrish, Leslie 1935- *WhoHol 92*
Parrish, Margaret Ann 1941- *WhoMW 93*
Parrish, Mary Catherine d1951 *WhoHol 92*
Parrish, Mary-Frances 1908-1992 *ConLC 76*
Parrish, Maurice Drue 1950- *WhoBlA 94*
Parrish, Maxfield 1870-1966 *WhoAmA 93N*
Parrish, Michael E(merson) 1942- *ConAu 43NR*
Parrish, Nancy Elaine 1948- *WhoAmP 93*
Parrish, Overton Burgin, Jr. 1933- *WhoAm 94, WhoFI 94*
Parrish, Patt 1942- *WrDr 94*
Parrish, Richard B. 1938- *WhoFI 94*
Parrish, Robert 1916- *WhoHol 92*
Parrish, Robert 1953- *BasBi*
Parrish, Robert Alton 1930- *WhoAm 94*
Parrish, Robert Ambrose 1927- *WhoAmP 93*
Parrish, Robert R. 1916- *IntMPA 94*
Parrish, Rufus H. *WhoBlA 94*
Parrish, Stephen Bennett 1951- *WhoMW 93*
Parrish, Steve *WhoHol 92*
Parrish, Teresa Lynette 1951- *WhoAmL 94*
Parrish, Thomas Dennison 1935- *WhoScEn 94*
Parrish, Thomas Kirkpatrick, III 1930- *WhoAm 94*
Parrish, Virginia Kay 1953- *WhoAmP 93*
Parrish, William E. 1931- *WrDr 94*
Parrish, William Earl 1931- *WhoAm 94*
Parrish, William M. 1953- *WhoAmL 94*
Parro, Douglas Arthur 1954- *WhoWest 94*
Parron, Delores L. 1944- *WhoBlA 94*
Parrot, Kenneth D. 1947- *WhoFI 94*
Parrott, Alonzo Leslie 1922- *WhoAm 94*
Parrott, Andrew Haden 1947- *IntWW 93, Who 94*
Parrott, Carl Leonard 1922- *WhoAmP 93*
Parrott, Charles *WhoHol 92*
Parrott, Dennis Beecher 1929- *WhoFI 94, WhoWest 94*
Parrott, Dennis Kirk 1954- *WhoAmP 93*
Parrott, Ian 1916- *WrDr 94*
Parrott, (Horace) Ian 1916- *NewGrDO*
Parrott, James Alfred 1952- *WhoFI 94*
Parrott, Mary Ellen 1943- *WhoAmP 93*
Parrott, Nancy Sharon 1944- *WhoAmL 94*
Parrott, Paul d1939 *WhoHol 92*
Parrott, Robert Harold 1923- *WhoAm 94*
Parroy, Michael Picton 1946- *Who 94*
Parruchiera, La *NewGrDO*

Pascarella, Perry James 1934- WhoAm 94
Pascarelli, Fred Joseph 1950- WhoWest 94
Pasch, Alan 1925- WhoAm 94
Pasch, Anne Dudley 1936- WhoWest 94
Pasch, Maurice Bernard 1910- WhoAm 94
Pasch, Reginald d1965 WhoHol 92
Paschal, Beverly Jo 1955- WhoAmL 94
Paschal, Eloise Richardson 1936- WhoBlA 94
Paschal, Willie L. 1926- WhoBlA 94
Paschall, Evita Arneda 1951- WhoAmL 94, WhoBlA 94
Paschall, Gael Penland 1949- WhoFI 94
Paschall, Jo Anne 1949- WhoAmA 93
Paschall, Lee McQuerter 1922- WhoAm 94
Paschall, Winford Lee 1945- WhoFI 94
Paschang, John Linus 1895- WhoAm 94
Paschang, Lisa Gale 1957- WhoMW 93
Paschke, Donald Vernon 1929- WhoAm 94
Paschke, Edward F. 1939- WhoAm 94, WhoAmA 93
Paschke, Fritz 1929- IntWW 93
Pasco, Barton Cheves 1954- WhoFI 94
Pasco, Frances d1978 WhoHol 92
Pasco, Hansell Merrill 1915- WhoAm 94
Pasco, Richard 1926- WhoHol 92
Pasco, Richard Edward 1926- IntWW 93, Who 94
Pasco, Rowanne 1938- Who 94
Pascoe, Alan Peter 1947- Who 94
Pascoe, Charles Milton 1936- WhoMW 93
Pascoe, D. Monte 1935- WhoAmP 93
Pascoe, Edmund Normoyle 1948- WhoIns 94
Pascoe, Edward Rudy 1948- WhoMW 93
Pascoe, Michael William 1930- Who 94
Pascoe, Nigel Spencer Knight 1940- Who 94
Pascoe, Pat 1935- WhoAmP 93
Pascoe, Patricia Hill 1935- WhoWest 94
Pascoe, Peggy 1954- WrDr 94
Pascoe, Robert (Alan) 1932- Who 94
Pasco Sam dc. 1920 EncNAR
Pascotto, Alvaro 1949- WhoAmL 94, WhoWest 94
Pascover, James Roger 1945- WhoMW 93
Pascrell, William J., Jr. 1937- WhoAmP 93
Pascual, Hugo 1935- WhoHisp 94
Pascual, Ramon 1942- IntWW 93
Pascual, Virginia 1951- WhoHisp 94
Pascucci, John Joseph 1949- WhoScEn 94
Pascucci, Joseph Robert 1966- WhoFI 94
Pasculli, Mark Andre 1962- WhoWest 94
Pascuzzi, Robert Mark 1953- WhoMW 93
Pasdar, Adrian 1965- WhoHol 92
Pasek, Jeffrey Ivan 1951- WhoAmL 94
Pasen, Robert Martin 1945- WhoMW 93
Paseneaux, Carolyn 1938- WhoAmP 93
Pasero, Tancredi 1893-1983 NewGrDO
Pasetta, Marty 1932- IntMPA 94
Pasetti, Louis Oscar 1916- WhoScEn 94
Pasetti, Peter 1916- IntWW 93
Pasewark, William Robert 1924- WhoAm 94, WrDr 94
Pash, Mary Margaret 1934- WhoMW 93
Pasha, Kalla d1933 WhoHol 92
Pasha, Mehmed Emin WhWE
Pashayan, Charles, Jr. 1941- WhoAmP 93
Pashby, Gary J. 1941- WhoAmL 94
Pashchenko, Andrey Filippovich 1885-1972 NewGrDO
Pashek, Robert Donald 1921- WhoAm 94
Pashennaya, Vera d1962 WhoHol 92
Pashgian, M. Helen WhoAmA 93
Pashkevich, Vasily Alexeyevich c. 1742-1797 NewGrDO
Pashkin-Boyer, Rona Linda 1946- WhoAm 94
Pashley, Donald William 1927- IntWW 93, Who 94
Pashley, Eugene W., Jr. 1954- WhoFI 94, WhoMW 93
Pasi, Antonio fl. 1704- NewGrDO
Pasich, Kirk Alan 1955- WhoAmL 94, WhoWest 94
Pasick, Robert 1946- WrDr 94
Pasillas, Diane WhoHisp 94
Pasin, Selena Ann 1963- WhoWest 94
Pasinetti, Luigi Lodovico 1930- IntWW 93
Pasinetti, Pier Maria 1913- WhoAm 94
Pasini, Debbie Dobbins 1956- WhoMW 93
Pasini, Laura 1894-1942 NewGrDO
Pasini, Roy 1927- WhoIns 94
Pasini-Vitale, Lina 1872-1959 NewGrDO
Pasinski, Irene 1923- WhoAmA 93
Pask, Joseph Adam 1913- WhoAm 94
Pask, Raymond Frank 1944- WrDr 94
Paskai, Laszlo 1927- IntWW 93
Paskalis, Kostas 1929- NewGrDO
Paskavich, Christine Adams 1956- WhoMW 93
Paskay, Alexander L. 1922- WhoAm 94, WhoAmL 94
Paskewitz, Bill, Jr. 1953- WhoAmA 93
Paskin, Arthur 1924- WhoScEn 94
Pasley, James Michael 1953- WhoMW 93
Pasley, (John) Malcolm (Sabine) 1926- Who 94
Paslov, Eugene WhoAm 94, WhoWest 94
Pasma, James Jay 1933- WhoAmP 93
Pasman, James S., Jr. 1930- WhoFI 94
Pasmanick, Kenneth 1924- WhoAm 94
Pasmanik, Wolf DrAPF 93
Pasmore, (Edwin John) Victor 1908- IntWW 93, Who 94
Pasnick, Raymond Wallace 1916- WhoAm 94
Paso, Alfonso d1978 WhoHol 92
Paso, Fernando del 1935- ConWorW 93
Pasolini, Pier Paolo d1975 WhoHol 92
Pasolini, Pier Paolo 1922-1975 GayLL
Pasour, Ernest Caleb, Jr. 1932- WhoFI 94
Pasqua, Charles Victor 1927- IntWW 93
Pasqua, Giuseppina 1855-1930 NewGrDO
Pasqua, Thomas M(ario), Jr. 1938- WrDr 94
Pasqua, Thomas Mario, Jr. 1938- WhoWest 94
Pasqual, Lluis 1951- IntWW 93
Pasquale, Frank Anthony 1954- WhoFI 94, WhoScEn 94
Pasquali, Bernice de 1880-1925 NewGrDO
Pasqualigo, Benedetto fl. 1706- NewGrDO
Pasqualini, Marc'Antonio c. 1614-1691 NewGrDO [port]
Pasquarelli, Joseph J. 1927- WhoAm 94, WhoFI 94
Pasquel, Joaquin 1960- WhoScEn 94
Pasquerilla, Frank James 1926- WhoAm 94
Pasquier, Evelyn Wood 1930- WhoAmL 94
Pasquier, Joel 1943- WhoAm 94
Pasquill, Frank 1914- Who 94
Pasquine, Ruth 1948- WhoAmA 93
Pasquini, Bernardo 1637-1710 NewGrDO
Pasquini, Giovanni Claudio 1695-1763 NewGrDO
Pass, Bobby Clifton 1931- WhoAm 94
Pass, Lenny d1989 WhoHol 92
Pass, Robert W. 1949- WhoAmL 94
Passage, David 1942- WhoAm 94, WhoAmP 93
Passailaigue, Ernest L., Jr. 1947- WhoAmP 93
Passalacqua, Angela Virginia 1961- WhoAmL 94
Passanante, Paul Jasper 1951- WhoAmL 94
Passaneau, Robert J. 1937- WhoAm 94, WhoFI 94
Passannante, William F. 1920- WhoAmP 93
Passano, Edward Magruder 1904- WhoAm 94
Passantino, Anthony WhoHol 92
Passantino, Benjamin Arthur 1956- WhoFI 94
Passantino, George Christopher WhoAmA 93
Passarella, Art d1981 WhoHol 92
Passarella, Daniel 1953- WorESoc
Passarella, Lee DrAPF 93
Passarella, Louis Anthony 1964- WhoScEn 94
Passarelli, John P. 1955- WhoAmL 94
Passarelli, Joseph WhoHol 92
Passarelli-Stamper, Phyllis 1944- WhoMW 93
Passarinho, Jarbas Goncalves 1920- IntWW 93
Passarini, Francesco fl. 1696- NewGrDO
Passaro, Andrea fl. 1829- NewGrDO
Passaro, Vincent DrAPF 93
Passavant, William Alfred 1821-1894 DcAmReB 2
Passenheim, Burr Charles 1941- WhoWest 94
Passer, Dirch d1980 WhoHol 92
Passer, Ivan 1933- IntMPA 94
Passerello, John B. DrAPF 93
Passerini, Christina fl. 1750- NewGrDO
Passero, James Joseph 1934- WhoFI 94
Passes, Alan 1943- EncSF 93
Passey, George Edward 1920- WhoAm 94
Passicot Callier, Andres 1937- IntWW 93
Passidomo, John Michael 1952- WhoAm 94, WhoAmL 94
Passion, Robert DrAPF 93
Passlof, Pat WhoAmA 93
Passman, Stephen Lee 1942- WhoWest 94
Passmore, Howard Clinton, Jr. 1942- WhoAm 94
Passmore, Jan William 1940- WhoAm 94, WhoMW 93
Passmore, John A. 1914- EnvEnc
Passmore, John Arthur 1914- IntWW 93
Passmore, Juanita Carter 1926- WhoBlA 94
Passmore, Mark Richard 1933- WhoMW 93
Passmore, William A. 1929- WhoBlA 94
Passner, Albert 1938- WhoScEn 94
Passon, Betty Jane 1931- WhoAmP 93
Passon, Richard Henry 1939- WhoAm 94
Passoni, Irma Rossetto 1943- WhoWomW 91
Passovoy, Susan Jane 1946- WhoAmL 94, WhoWest 94
Passow, A. Harry 1920- WrDr 94
Passow, Aaron Harry 1920- WhoAm 94
Passuntino, Peter Zaccaria 1936- WhoAmA 93
Passwater, Richard Albert 1937- WhoAm 94, WhoScEn 94
Pasta, Carlo Enrico 1817-1898 NewGrDO
Pasta, Giuditta (Angiola Maria Costanza) 1797-1865 NewGrDO [port]
Pastan, Ira Harry 1931- WhoScEn 94
Pastan, Linda DrAPF 93
Pastan, Linda 1932- WrDr 94
Pastega, Richard Louis 1936- WhoAmP 93, WhoFI 94, WhoWest 94
Pastell, George WhoHol 92
Paster, Benjamin G. 1947- WhoAmL 94
Paster, Gary M. 1943- IntMPA 94
Paster, Howard WhoAm 94
Paster, Howard G. 1944- NewYTBS 93 [port]
Paster, Janice D. 1942- WhoAmP 93, WhoWest 94
Pasterfield, Philip John 1920- Who 94
Pasternack, Robert Francis 1936- WhoAm 94, WhoScEn 94
Pasternack, Robert Harry 1949- WhoWest 94
Pasternak, Boris (Leonidovich) 1890-1960 RfGShF
Pasternak, Derick Peter 1941- WhoAm 94, WhoWest 94
Pasternak, Joe 1901-1991 ConTFT 11, IntDcF 2-4
Pasternak, Joseph 1901-1991 WhAm 10
Pasteur, Alfred Bernard 1947- WhoBlA 94
Pasteur, Louis 1822-1895 WorScD [port]
Pasteur, Marie Laurent WorScD
Pasteur, Nicole 1944- WhoScEn 94
Pastin, Mark Joseph 1949- WhoAm 94, WhoFI 94, WhoWest 94
Pastine, Maureen Diane 1944- WhoAm 94
Pastinen, Ilkka 1928- Who 94
Pastinen, Ilkka Olavi 1928- IntWW 93
Paston-Bedingfeld, Edmund George Felix 1915- Who 94
Paston-Bedingfeld, Henry Edgar 1943- Who 94
Paston Brown, Beryl 1909- Who 94
Pastor, Ed 1943- CngDr 93, WhoAm 94, WhoWest 94
Pastor, Ed Lopez 1943- WhoHisp 94
Pastor, Edward Lopez 1943- WhoAmP 93
Pastor, Ned DrAPF 93
Pastor, Richard Walter 1951- WhoScEn 94
Pastor, Selma R. WhoAmP 93
Pastor, Stephen Daniel 1947- WhoScEn 94
Pastor, Tony d1969 WhoHol 92
Pastor De La Torre, Celso 1914- IntWW 93
Pastore, Joseph Michael, Jr. 1941- WhoAm 94
Pastore, Michael Anthony 1932- WhoWest 94
Pastore, Peter Nicholas 1907- WhAm 10
Pastore, Peter Nicholas, Jr. 1950- WhoFI 94
Pastore, Robert L. 1946- WhoAmP 93
Pastore, Thomas Michael 1959- WhoFI 94, WhoWest 94
Pastorek, Norman Joseph 1939- WhoAm 94
Pastorelle, Peter John 1933- WhoAm 94
Pastorelli, Robert WhoAm 94
Pastorelli, Robert 1955- WhoHol 92
Pastorini, Dan WhoHol 92
Pastorino, Franco d1959 WhoHol 92
Pastorino, Robert Stephen 1940- WhoAm 94, WhoAmP 93
Pastorino Viscardi, Enrique Juan 1918- IntWW 93
Pastorius, Francis Daniel 1651-1720? DcAmReB 2
Pastoriza, Jorge 1952- WhoHisp 94
Pastor-Klucens, Caridad 1962- WhoHisp 94
Pastrana Borrero, Misael 1923- IntWW 93
Pastreich, Peter 1938- WhoAm 94, WhoWest 94
Pastrick, Robert A. 1927- WhoAmP 93
Pastrnak, Candy Kay 1958- WhoAmL 94
Pastukhov, Boris Nikolayevich 1933- IntWW 93
Pastuszak, William Theodore 1946- WhoScEn 94
Paszthory, Casimir von 1886-1966 NewGrDO
Patachou WhoHol 92
Patai, Raphael 1910- WhoAm 94, WrDr 94
Pataki, Andrew 1927- WhoAm 94, WhoMW 93
Pataki, George 1945- WhoAmP 93
Pataki, Michael 1938- WhoHol 92
Pataky, Kalman 1896-1964 NewGrDO
Patallo, Indalecio WhoHisp 94
Patane, Giuseppe 1931- IntWW 93
Patane, Giuseppe 1932-1989 NewGrDO
Patane, I. Edward 1935- WhoIns 94
Patankar, Suhas V. WhoScEn 94
Patasse, Ange 1937- IntWW 93
Patcevitch, Iva Sergei Voidato d1993 NewYTBS 93 [port]
Patch, Lauren Nelson 1951- WhoAm 94, WhoFI 94, WhoIns 94
Patch, Wally d1970 WhoHol 92
Patchan, Joseph 1922- WhoAm 94
Patchen, Joseph John 1960- WhoAmL 94
Patchett, Arthur Allan 1929- WhoScEn 94
Patchett, M(ary Osborne) E(lwyn) 1897- EncSF 93
Patchett, R. Dale 1950- WhoAmP 93
Patchett, Terry 1940- Who 94
Pate, Christopher 1953- WhoHol 92
Pate, Findlay Moye 1941- WhoScEn 94
Pate, Jacqueline Hail 1930- WhoFI 94
Pate, James Leonard 1935- WhoAm 94, WhoFI 94
Pate, James Wynford 1928- WhoAm 94
Pate, Joan Seitz WhoAm 94, WhoAmL 94
Pate, John d1704 NewGrDO
Pate, John Stewart 1932- IntWW 93, Who 94
Pate, John W., Sr. 1923- WhoBlA 94
Pate, Linda Kay 1949- WhoFI 94, WhoWest 94
Pate, Michael 1920- WhoHol 92
Pate, Michael Lynn 1951- WhoAm 94
Pate, Paul Danny 1958- WhoAmP 93, WhoMW 93
Pate, Robert Hewitt, Jr. 1938- WhoAm 94
Pate, Samuel Ralph 1937- WhoScEn 94
Pate, Stephen Patrick 1958- WhoAmL 94
Pate, Thomas L. 1926- WhoAmP 93
Pate, William Earl 1953- WhoFI 94
Pate, Zack Taylor, Jr. 1936- WhoAm 94
Patee, Doris S. 1897- WhAm 10
Patel, Anil J. 1952- WhoAsA 94
Patel, Anil S. 1939- WhoAsA 94
Patel, Appasaheb R. 1931- WhoAsA 94
Patel, Arvindkumar Motibhai 1937- WhoAsA 94
Patel, Ashok R. 1942- WhoAsA 94
Patel, Bhagvan H. 1942- WhoAsA 94
Patel, Bhagwandas Mavjibhai 1938- WhoAsA 94
Patel, Bharat R. 1947- WhoAsA 94
Patel, Bhavin R. 1963- WhoScEn 94
Patel, Bhulabhai C. 1948- WhoAsA 94
Patel, Bhupen N. 1941- WhoAsA 94
Patel, Chandra Kumar Naranbhai 1938- WhoAm 94, WhoAsA 94, WhoScEn 94
Patel, Chandrakant B. 1959- WhoAsA 94
Patel, Chandrakant J. 1947- WhoAsA 94
Patel, Chandu K. 1931- WhoAsA 94
Patel, Chandu M. 1937- WhoAsA 94
Patel, Deepak M. 1948- WhoAsA 94
Patel, Dilip Natubhai 1940- WhoMW 93
Patel, Dilipkumar Z. 1957- WhoAsA 94
Patel, Dinesh 1936- WhoAsA 94
Patel, Gieve 1940- WrDr 94
Patel, Hiren S. 1950- WhoAsA 94
Patel, Homi Burjor 1949- WhoAm 94, WhoFI 94
Patel, Indraprasad Gordhanbhai 1924- IntWW 93, Who 94
Patel, Indravadan R. 1942- WhoAsA 94
Patel, Jay M. 1953- WhoAsA 94
Patel, Jayant P. 1957- WhoAsA 94
Patel, Jayant Ramanlal 1946- WhoScEn 94
Patel, Jayanti R. 1947- WhoAsA 94
Patel, Jeram 1930- IntWW 93
Patel, Jitendra B 1942- WhoAsA 94
Patel, Jyoti Shivabhai 1943- WhoWest 94
Patel, Kalyani 1965- WhoAsA 94
Patel, Kamla 1929- WhoAsA 94
Patel, Kanaiyalal Ramdas 1949- WhoMW 93
Patel, Kanti L. 1951- WhoAsA 94
Patel, Kanti Shamjibhai 1938- WhoScEn 94
Patel, Kantilal P. 1935- WhoAsA 94
Patel, Kiran K. 1955- WhoAsA 94
Patel, Kiritkumar Natwerbhai 1946- WhoScEn 94
Patel, Kishor Manubhai 1953- WhoScEn 94
Patel, Kishor N. 1955- WhoAsA 94
Patel, Magan 1937- WhoFI 94
Patel, Manu Ambalal 1943- WhoScEn 94
Patel, Marilyn Hall 1938- WhoAm 94, WhoAmL 94, WhoWest 94

Patel, Mitesh K. 1965- WhoAsA 94
Patel, Mukesh M. 1950- WhoAsA 94
Patel, Mukul B. 1954- WhoAsA 94
Patel, Mukund R. 1942- WhoAsA 94
Patel, Mukund Ranchhodlal 1942- WhoScEn 94
Patel, Nagin K. 1932- WhoAsA 94
Patel, Narayan G. 1928- WhoAsA 94
Patel, Narendra D. 1949- WhoAsA 94
Patel, Naresh Maganlal 1965- WhoWest 94
Patel, Navin J. 1949- WhoWest 94
Patel, Praful Raojibhai Chaturbhai 1939- IntWW 93, Who 94
Patel, Pratibha A. WhoAsA 94
Patel, Raj-Rajendra Ambalal 1949- WhoMW 93
Patel, Rajendra Ishwarlal 1953- WhoMW 93
Patel, Rakesh WhoAsA 94
Patel, Ramesh Babubhai 1940- WhoFI 94
Patel, Ramesh D. 1937- WhoAsA 94
Patel, Ramesh Manibhai 1935- WhoFI 94
Patel, Ramesh P. 1944- WhoAsA 94
Patel, Ramesh V. 1951- WhoAsA 94
Patel, Ray J. WhoAsA 94
Patel, Ray L. 1945- WhoAsA 94
Patel, Roger 1950- WhoAsA 94
Patel, Ronald Anthony 1947- WhoAm 94
Patel, Sanjay Vrajlal 1964- WhoAsA 94
Patel, Sarla M. 1939- WhoAsA 94
Patel, Shailesh R. 1953- WhoAsA 94
Patel, Shirish A. 1942- WhoAsA 94
Patel, Suresh 1953- WhoScEn 94
Patel, Tarun R. 1952- WhoScEn 94
Patel, Vipin A. 1939- WhoAsA 94
Patel, Virendra Chaturbhai 1938- WhoAm 94, WhoAsA 94
Patell, Mahesh 1937- WhoScEn 94
Pateman, Jack Edward 1921- Who 94
Pateman, John Arthur 1926- IntWW 93
Pateman, John Arthur Joseph 1926- Who 94
Pateman, Trevor John 1947- WrDr 94
Patent, Dorothy Hinshaw 1940- WhoAm 94
Pater, Michael John 1957- WhoAmL 94
Pater, Walter Horatio 1839-1894 BlmGEL
Paterniti, Thomas H. 1929- WhoAmP 93
Paterno, Joseph Vincent 1926- WhoAm 94
Paternosto, Cesar Pedro 1931- WhoAmA 93
Paternotte, William Leslie 1945- WhoAm 94, WhoFI 94
Paternotte de la Vaillee, Alexandre E. M. L. G. C. 1923- IntWW 93
Patero, Joseph D. 1932- WhoAmP 93
Paterson, Alan Leonard Tuke 1944- WhoAm 94
Paterson, Alexander Craig 1924- Who 94
Paterson, Alistair (Ian Hughes) 1929- WrDr 94
Paterson, Allen Peter 1933- WhoAm 94
Paterson, Anthony R. 1934- WhoAmA 93
Paterson, Basil Alexander 1926- WhoAm 94, WhoAmP 93, WhoBlA 94
Paterson, Betty (Fraser Ross) 1916- Who 94
Paterson, Bill Who 94, WhoHol 92
Paterson, Caroline WhoHol 92
Paterson, David A. 1955- WhoAmP 93
Paterson, David Grant 1954- WhoAmL 94
Paterson, Dennis (Craig) 1930- Who 94
Paterson, Dennis Craig 1930- IntWW 93
Paterson, Eileen 1939- WhoScEn 94
Paterson, Francis 1930- Who 94
Paterson, Frank David 1918- Who 94
Paterson, George (Mutlow) 1906- Who 94
Paterson, Ian Veitch 1911- Who 94
Paterson, James WhAmRev
Paterson, James Hunter 1947- WhoAm 94
Paterson, James Rupert 1932- Who 94
Paterson, James Veitch 1928- Who 94
Paterson, John 1744-1808 WhAmRev
Paterson, John (Valentine) J. Who 94
Paterson, John M. R. 1944- WhoAmL 94
Paterson, John Mower Alexander 1920- Who 94
Paterson, John Munn Kirk 1922- Who 94
Paterson, John Thomas Farquhar 1938- Who 94
Paterson, Katherine (Womeldorf) 1932- TwCYAW, WrDr 94
Paterson, Katherine Womeldorf 1932- WhoAm 94
Paterson, Lee T. 1941- WhoAmL 94
Paterson, Mervyn Silas 1925- IntWW 93
Paterson, Neil Who 94
Paterson, Neil 1916- WrDr 94
Paterson, (James Edmund) Neil 1915- Who 94
Paterson, Pat d1978 WhoHol 92
Paterson, Richard Denis 1942- WhoAm 94
Paterson, Robert E. 1926- WhoAm 94
Paterson, Robert Lancelot 1918- Who 94
Paterson, Ronald (William Keith) 1933- WrDr 94
Paterson, William 1745-1806 WhAmRev
Paterson, William Alexander Who 94
Paterson, William Tulloch 1945- Who 94
Paterson-Brown, June 1932- Who 94
Pates, Gordon 1916-1988 WhAm 10
Pates, Harold WhoBlA 94
Pates, James Morgan 1950- WhoAmP 93
Patey, Edward Henry 1915- Who 94
Pathak, Dev S. 1942- WhoScEn 94
Pathak, Raghunandan Swarup 1924- Who 94
Pathak, Rahunandan Swarup 1924- IntWW 93
Pathak, Sen 1940- WhoAsA 94
Pathak, Sunit Rawly 1953- WhoAm 94, WhoFI 94
Pathak, Vibhav Gautam 1964- WhoScEn 94, WhoWest 94
Pathe, Charles 1863-1957 IntDcF 2-4
Patheske fl. 1850- EncNAR
Pati, A. Kumar 1954- WhoAsA 94
Patience, Andrew 1941- Who 94
Patience, John Francis 1951- WhoScEn 94
Patil, Popat N. WhoAsA 94
Patil, Popat Narayan 1934- WhoMW 93
Patil, Prabhakar Bapusaheb 1950- WhoScEn 94
Patil, Pralhad T. 1943- WhoAsA 94
Patil, Pratibha Devisingh 1934- WhoWomW 91
Patil, Smita d1986 WhoHol 92
Patil, Suryakanta Jayawantrao 1948- WhoWomW 91
Patil, Veerendra 1924- IntWW 93
Patillo, Maria WhoHol 92
Patin, Joseph Patrick 1937- WhoBlA 94
Patin, Jude W. P. 1940- WhoBlA 94
Patin, Jude Wilmot Paul 1940- AfrAmG [port]
Patin, Robert W. 1942- WhoIns 94
Patin, Robert White 1942- WhoAm 94
Patinkin, Don 1922- IntWW 93
Patinkin, Mandy 1952- IntMPA 94, WhoAm 94, WhoHol 92
Patinkin, Mark 1953- WrDr 94
Patino, Douglas Xavier 1939- WhoAm 94
Patino, Hugo 1952- WhoScEn 94
Patino, Isidro Frank 1943- WhoWest 94
Patino, Manuel Luis 1933- WhoWest 94
Patkin, Izhar 1955- WhoAmA 93
Patler, Louis DrAPF 93
Patmagrian, Ethelia M. WhoAmA 93
Patman, Carrin Mauritz 1932- WhoAmP 93
Patman, Harold C. 1935- WhoIns 94
Patman, Philip Franklin 1937- WhoAmL 94
Patman, William N. 1927- WhoAmP 93
Patmon, Claude 1941- WhoBlA 94
Patmore, (John) Allan 1931- Who 94
Patmore, Coventry Kersey Dighton 1823-1896 BlmGEL
Patmore, Geraldine Mary WhoWest 94
Patmos, Adrian Edward 1914- WhoAm 94
Patnaik, Amiya K. 1930- WhoAsA 94
Patnaik, Bijoyananda 1916- IntWW 93
Patnaik, Janaki Ballav 1927- IntWW 93
Patnaik, Promode K. 1939- WhoAm 94
Patnaude, William E. 1937- WhoAm 94
Patner, Richard 1946- WhoWest 94
Patnett, John Henry 1948- WhoBlA 94
Patnick, (Cyril) Irvine 1929- Who 94
Patnode, J. Scott 1945- WhoAmA 93
Patnode, Michael E. 1955- WhoFI 94
Paton, Alasdair Chalmers 1944- Who 94
Paton, Angus IntWW 93, Who 94
Paton, (Thomas) Angus (Lyall) 1905- IntWW 93, Who 94
Paton, Ann Who 94
Paton, Boris Evgenovich 1918- LngBDD
Paton, Boris Yevgeniyevich 1918- IntWW 93
Paton, Charles d1970 WhoHol 92
Paton, David Macdonald 1913- WrDr 94
Paton, Douglas Shaw F. Who 94
Paton, Douglas Stuart 1926- Who 94
Paton, Frank EncSF 93
Paton, John EncSF 93
Paton, Laurie WhoHol 92
Paton, Leland B. 1943- WhoAm 94, WhoFI 94
Paton, Mary Anne NewGrDO
Paton, Mary Margaret 1918- WhoMW 93
Paton, Michael John Macdonald 1922- Who 94
Paton, N.E., Jr. 1931- WhoMW 93
Paton, (Frederick) Ronald N. Who 94
Paton, Stuart d1944 WhoHol 92
Paton, William (Drummond Macdonald) 1917- Who 94
Paton Walsh, Jill 1937- Au&Arts 11 [port], TwCYAW, Who 94, WhoAm 94, WrDr 94
Patorzhinsky, Ivan (Sergeyevich) 1896-1960 NewGrDO
Patoski, Joe Nick 1951- ConAu 141
Patra, Sushant Kumar 1939- WhoFI 94
Patric, Gil d1971 WhoHol 92
Patric, Jason 1966- IntMPA 94, WhoHol 92
Patricelli, Robert E. 1939- WhoAm 94
Patricio, Rui Manuel de Medeiros d'Espiney 1932- IntWW 93
Patrick, St. c. 389- BlmGEL
Patrick, Saint c. 396-459 HisWorL [port]
Patrick, Alan K. 1942- WhoAmA 93
Patrick, Allan 1946- WhoFI 94
Patrick, Billy Wayne 1955- WhoAmP 93
Patrick, Butch 1953- WhoHol 92
Patrick, C. L. 1918- IntMPA 94
Patrick, Carl Lloyd 1918- WhoAm 94
Patrick, Casimir C., II 1939- WhoAmL 94
Patrick, Charles Namon, Jr. 1949- WhoBlA 94
Patrick, Charles William 1937- WhoAmA 93
Patrick, Charles William, Jr. 1954- WhoAmL 94
Patrick, Craig 1946- WhoAm 94
Patrick, Dane Herman 1960- WhoAmL 94
Patrick, Darryl L. 1936- WhoAmA 93
Patrick, Dennis 1918- WhoAm 94, WhoHol 92
Patrick, Dennis R. 1951- WhoAmP 93
Patrick, Deval Laurdine 1956- WhoAmL 94
Patrick, Dorothy d1987 WhoHol 92
Patrick, Edwin Hill 1901-1964 DcLB 137 [port]
Patrick, Ethel d1944 WhoHol 92
Patrick, Gail Who 94
Patrick, Gail d1980 WhoHol 92
Patrick, (Lilian) Gail 1941- Who 94
Patrick, Genie Hudson 1938- WhoAmA 93
Patrick, George Milton 1920- WhoFI 94, WhoMW 93
Patrick, George W. 1942- WhoAm 94, WhoAmL 94
Patrick, Graham McIntosh 1921- Who 94
Patrick, Gregory WhoHol 92
Patrick, H. Hunter 1939- WhoAmL 94
Patrick, Isadore W., Jr. 1951- WhoBlA 94
Patrick, James L. 1919- WhoBlA 94
Patrick, Jane Austin 1930- WhoFI 94, WhoMW 93
Patrick, Janet Cline 1934- WhoScEn 94
Patrick, Jennie R. 1949- WhoBlA 94
Patrick, Jerome d1923 WhoHol 92
Patrick, John 1903- WrDr 94
Patrick, John 1905- ConDr 93
Patrick, John Bowman 1916- Who 94
Patrick, John Joseph 1935- WhoAm 94, WhoMW 93
Patrick, Joseph Alexander 1938- WhoAmA 93
Patrick, Julius, Jr. 1938- WhoBlA 94
Patrick, Kerry WhoAmP 93
Patrick, Lawrence Clarence, Jr. 1945- WhoBlA 94
Patrick, Lee d1982 WhoHol 92
Patrick, Leslie Dayle 1951- WhoWest 94
Patrick, Lory 1938- WhoHol 92
Patrick, Lynda Lee 1938- WhoWest 94
Patrick, Lynn Allen 1935- WhoAm 94
Patrick, Margaret Kathleen 1923- Who 94
Patrick, Marty 1949- WhoAmL 94
Patrick, Matthew 1955- IntMPA 94
Patrick, Maxine 1942- WrDr 94
Patrick, (James) McIntosh 1907- Who 94
Patrick, Michael W. 1950- IntMPA 94
Patrick, Michael Wynn 1950- WhoAm 94
Patrick, Nigel d1981 WhoHol 92
Patrick, Odessa R. 1933- WhoBlA 94
Patrick, Opal Lee Young 1929- WhoBlA 94
Patrick, Pat d1954 WhoHol 92
Patrick, Randal WhoHol 92
Patrick, Ransom R. 1906-1971 WhoAmA 93N
Patrick, Robert WhoHol 92
Patrick, Robert 1937- ConDr 93, GayLL, WrDr 94
Patrick, Robert John, Jr. 1934-1992 WhAm 10
Patrick, Robert Winton, Jr. 1940- WhoAm 94
Patrick, Ruth WhoScEn 94
Patrick, Ruth 1907- EnvEnc [port]
Patrick, Susan 1921- WrDr 94
Patrick, Thomas H. 1944- WhoFI 94
Patrick, Ueal Eugene 1929- WhoAm 94
Patrick, Vincent Jerome 1959- WhoBlA 94
Patrick, Ward Douglas 1948- WhoMW 93
Patrick, William DrAPF 93
Patrick, William Bradshaw 1923- WhoAmL 94, WhoMW 93
Patrick, William Hardy, Jr. 1925- WhoAm 94
Patrick, William Samuel 1927- WhoAm 94
Patricks, Edward J. 1958- WhoMW 93
Patricola, Tom d1950 WhoHol 92
Patrie, Peter Hugo 1946- WhoWest 94
Patrik, Gary Steven 1944- WhoIns 94
Patrikis, Ernest T. 1943- WhoAm 94
Patriquin, David Ashley 1927- WhoAm 94
Patriquin, Edward Leroy, Jr. 1958- WhoWest 94
Patrizio, Frank, Jr. 1933- WhoMW 93
Patrollo, Patricia 1951- WhoAmP 93
Patron, Susan 1948- SmATA 76 [port]
Patronella, David M. 1957- WhoAmP 93
Patronik, Richard Stephen 1956- WhoIns 94
Patrow, Kristine Lydal 1963- WhoMW 93
Patry, Marcel Joseph 1923- WhoAm 94
Patsakos, George 1942- WhoWest 94
Patsalides, Andreas 1922- IntWW 93
Patscot, Michelle Patrice 1966- WhoMW 93
Patston, Doris d1957 WhoHol 92
Patt, Gideon 1933- IntWW 93
Pattakos, Stylianos 1912- IntWW 93
Patte, George David, Jr. 1945- WhoAmL 94
Pattee, Gordon Burleigh 1948- WhoAm 94
Patten, Bebe Harrison 1913- WhoAm 94, WhoWest 94
Patten, Bebe Rebecca 1950- WhoWest 94
Patten, Bernard Michael 1941- WhoScEn 94
Patten, Brian 1946- ConAu 43NR, Who 94, WrDr 94
Patten, Charles Anthony 1920- WhoAm 94
Patten, Charles Louis 1951- WhoAmP 93
Patten, Chris NewYTBS 93 [port]
Patten, Chris 1944- CurBio 93 [port]
Patten, Christopher 1944- IntWW 93, News 93-3 [port]
Patten, Christopher (Francis) 1944- Who 94
Patten, David L(ongfellow) 1894- WhAm 10
Patten, Dorothy d1975 WhoHol 92
Patten, Duncan Theunissen 1934- WhoAm 94
Patten, Edward Roy 1939- WhoBlA 94
Patten, Gerland Paul 1907- WhoAm 94
Patten, John 1746-1800 WhAmRev
Patten, John (Haggitt Charles) 1945- Who 94
Patten, John W. 1930- WhoAm 94, WhoFI 94
Patten, Karl DrAPF 93
Patten, Lanny Ray 1934- WhoAm 94, WhoFI 94
Patten, Luana 1938- WhoHol 92
Patten, Martha Ann 1956- WhoAmL 94
Patten, Maurine Diane 1940- WhoMW 93
Patten, Nicholas John 1950- Who 94
Patten, Richard E. 1953- WhoWest 94
Patten, Robert WhoHol 92
Patten, Robert L. WhoAmP 93
Patten, Robert Lowry 1939- WhoAm 94
Patten, Ronald James 1935- WhoAm 94, WhoMW 93
Patten, Thomas H., (Jr.) 1929- WrDr 94
Patten, Thomas Henry, Jr. 1929- WhoAm 94
Patten, Thomas Louis 1945- WhoAm 94, WhoAmL 94
Patten, Tom 1926- Who 94
Patten, William Hazel, III 1957- WhoMW 93
Patten, William Russell 1954- WhoAmL 94
Patten-Benham, Priscilla Carla 1950- WhoAm 94
Pattenden, Gerald 1940- Who 94
Patterson, Alan Bruce 1953- WhoAm 94
Patterson, Albert WhoHol 92
Patterson, Alonzo B. 1937- WhoBlA 94
Patterson, Arthur 1906- Who 94
Patterson, Arthur Gordon 1917- Who 94
Patterson, Barbara Ann WhoBlA 94
Patterson, Ben Who 94
Patterson, Beverley Pamela Grace 1956- WhoFI 94
Patterson, Bill WhoHol 92
Patterson, Bradley H., Jr. 1921- WrDr 94
Patterson, Bruce D. 1952- WhoMW 93
Patterson, Carl N., Jr. 1951- WhoAmL 94
Patterson, Cathleen Erin 1958- WhoMW 93
Patterson, Cecil Booker, Jr. 1941- WhoBlA 94
Patterson, Cecil Lloyd 1917- WhoBlA 94
Patterson, Charles 1935- ConAu 41NR
Patterson, Charles Darold 1928- WhoAm 94
Patterson, Charles Ernest 1941- WhoAm 94, WhoAmL 94
Patterson, Charles Jerry 1925- WhoBlA 94
Patterson, Charles Robert 1875-1958 WhoAmA 93N
Patterson, Cheryl Ann 1957- WhoBlA 94
Patterson, Chester March 1894- WhAm 10

Patton, Thomas Earl 1940- WhoAm 94, WhoAmL 94
Patton, Thomas F. 1903- EncABHB 9 [port]
Patton, Thomas James 1948- WhoMW 93
Patton, Thomas Kirby 1954- WhoFI 94
Patton, Thomas William Saunderson 1914- Who 94
Patton, Tom 1954- WhoAmA 93
Patton, Virginia 1925- WhoHol 92
Patton, Wendell Melton, Jr. 1922- WhoAm 94
Patton, Will 1954- IntMPA 94, WhoHol 92
Patton, William L. 1943- WhoAmL 94
Patton, William Wallace, Jr. 1923- WhoWest 94
Pattullo, Andrew 1917- WhoAm 94
Pattullo, (David) Bruce 1938- Who 94
Pattullo, Douglas Ernest 1947- WhoAm 94
Patty, Budge 1924- BuCMET
Patty, Claibourne Watkins, Jr. 1934- WhoAm 94
Patty, William A. 1889-1961 WhoAmA 93N
Pattyn, Remi Ceasar 1922- WhoAm 94
Paturis, Emmanuel Michael 1933- WhoAmL 94, WhoFI 94
Paty, Donald Winston 1936- WhoAm 94
Patyra, Marek Jerzy 1954- WhoMW 93
Patz, Arnall 1920- WhoAm 94
Patz, Edward Frank 1932- WhoAm 94
Patz, Lawrence Charles 1932- WhoIns 94
Patzaichin, Ivan 1949- IntWW 93
Patzak, Julius d1974 WhoHol 92
Patzak, Julius 1898-1974 NewGrDO [port]
Patzelt, Paul 1932- WhoScEn 94
Patzer, Eric John 1949- WhoWest 94
Patzig, Guenther 1926- IntWW 93
Patzke, Frank Thomas 1950- WhoMW 93
Patzke, Richard Joseph 1941- WhoAm 94
Patzman, Stephen Narr 1942- WhoIns 94
Pau, Louis-Francois 1948- IntWW 93
Pauer, Jiri 1919- NewGrDO
Paugh, Patricia Lou 1948- WhoAmL 94
Paugh, Thomas Francis 1929- WhoAm 94
Pauk, Gyorgy 1936- IntWW 93, Who 94
Pauk, Walter 1914- WrDr 94
Pauken, Thomas Weir 1944- WhoAmP 93
Pauker, Guy Jean 1916- WhoWest 94
Pauker, Ted 1917- WrDr 94
Paul dc. 64 HisWorL [port]
Paul, Adrian WhoHol 92
Paul, Alan Roderick 1950- Who 94
Paul, Alexandra 1963- WhoHol 92
Paul, Alice 1885-1977 AmSocL
Paul, Allen E. WhoMW 93
Paul, Allen Edward 1945- WhoAmP 93
Paul, Alvin, III 1941- WhoBlA 94
Paul, Ann Whitford 1941- SmATA 76 [port]
Paul, Anton Dilo 1951- WhoScEn 94
Paul, Ara Garo 1929- WhoAm 94
Paul, Arthur 1925- WhoAm 94, WhoAmA 93
Paul, Augustus John, III 1946- WhoWest 94
Paul, Barbara WrDr 94
Paul, Barbara 1931- WrDr 94
Paul, Barbara (Jeanne) 1931- EncSF 93
Paul, Beatrice 1943- WhoBlA 94
Paul, Benjamin David 1911- WhoAm 94
Paul, Betty 1921- WhoHol 92
Paul, Biraja Bilash 1933- WhoScEn 94
Paul, Boris Dupont 1901- WhoAmA 93N
Paul, Bruce Charles 1951- WhoMW 93
Paul, Carl Ellsworth Worthy, Jr. 1951- WhoAmL 94
Paul, Celeste 1952- ConAu 140
Paul, Charles d1980 WhoHol 92
Paul, Charles S. 1949- WhoAm 94, WhoFI 94
Paul, Christian Thomas 1926- WhoAm 94
Paul, Courtland Price 1927- WhoAm 94
Paul, Daniel Opdyke 1927- WhoAmP 93
Paul, David Jacob 1932- WhoWest 94
Paul, David Manuel d1993 Who 94N
Paul, David Patrick 1959- WhoWest 94
Paul, Deborah Ann 1954- WhoMW 93
Paul, Denny Kent 1941- WhoAm 94
Paul, Don Michael WhoHol 92
Paul, Donald Ross 1939- WhoAm 94, WhoScEn 94
Paul, Douglas Allan 1949- WhoAm 94, WhoFI 94
Paul, Eldor Alvin 1931- WhoAm 94
Paul, Elias 1919- WhoAm 94
Paul, Eve W. 1930- WhoAm 94, WhoAmL 94
Paul, Floyd W(alter) 1893- WhAm 10
Paul, Frank 1924- WhoAm 94
Paul, Frank E. 1934- WhoAmP 93
Paul, Frank R(udolph) 1884-1963 EncSF 93
Paul, Frank Waters 1938- WhoAm 94, WhoScEn 94
Paul, Fred 1880- WhoHol 92
Paul, Gabriel 1910- WhoAm 94
Paul, Gary Gene 1953- WhoMW 93
Paul, Geoffrey David 1929- Who 94
Paul, George William 1940- Who 94
Paul, Gerard John Christopher 1907- Who 94
Paul, Gloria WhoHol 92
Paul, Gordon Lee 1935- WhoAm 94
Paul, Gordon Wilbur 1933- WhoAm 94, WhoFI 94
Paul, Grace 1908- WhoMW 93
Paul, H. Edward 1942- WhoAmL 94
Paul, Herbert Morton WhoAm 94, WhoAmL 94, WhoFI 94
Paul, Herman Louis, Jr. 1912- WhoFI 94
Paul, Howard A. d1993 NewYTBS 93
Paul, Hugh Glencairn B. Who 94
Paul, Irving Buddy 1947- WhoAmL 94
Paul, Jack Davis 1927- WhoMW 93
Paul, James Caverly Newlin 1926- WhoAm 94
Paul, James Francis 1946- WhoMW 93
Paul, James Robert 1934- WhoAm 94
Paul, James William 1945- WhoAm 94, WhoAmL 94
Paul, Joanna 1945- BlmGWL
Paul, John 1921- WhoHol 92
Paul, John (Warburton) 1916- Who 94
Paul, John Douglas 1928- Who 94
Paul, John F. 1934- WhoBlA 94
Paul, John Joseph 1918- WhoAm 94, WhoMW 93
Paul, John Warburton 1916- IntWW 93
Paul, Jon C. 1948- WhoMW 93
Paul, Justin, Jr. 1966- WhoWest 94
Paul, Justus Fredrick 1938- WhoAm 94
Paul, Ken (Hugh) 1938- WhoAmA 93
Paul, Lee WhoHol 92
Paul, Lee Gilmour 1907- WhoAm 94
Paul, Leendert Cornelis 1946- WhoScEn 94
Paul, Les 1915- WhoAm 94, WhoHol 92
Paul, Logan d1932 WhoHol 92
Paul, M. B. 1909- IntMPA 94
Paul, M. Lee 1951- WhoAm 94
Paul, Mara 1961- WhoFI 94
Paul, Martin Ambrose 1910- WhoAm 94
Paul, Maurice M. 1932- WhoAm 94, WhoAmL 94
Paul, Mimi WhoHol 92
Paul, Noel Strange 1914- Who 94
Paul, Norman R. 1927- WhoAmP 93
Paul, Oglesby 1916- WhoAm 94
Paul, Rene d1968 WhoHol 92
Paul, Richard WhoHol 92
Paul, Richard A. 1948- WhoAmL 94
Paul, Richard Joseph WhoHol 92
Paul, Richard Stanley 1941- WhoAm 94, WhoAmL 94, WhoFI 94
Paul, Richard William 1937- WhoWest 94
Paul, Richard Wright 1953- WhoAm 94, WhoAmL 94
Paul, Rick W. 1945- WhoAmA 93
Paul, Robert 1931- WhoAmL 94
Paul, Robert Arthur 1937- WhoAm 94, WhoFI 94
Paul, Robert Cameron 1935- IntWW 93, Who 94
Paul, Robert Carey 1950- WhoAm 94, WhoAmL 94
Paul, Robert David 1928- WhoAm 94
Paul, Robert Dennis 1941- WhoAm 94
Paul, Robin Elizabeth 1955- WhoWest 94
Paul, Roderick Sayers 1935- Who 94
Paul, Roland Arthur 1937- WhoAm 94, WhoAmL 94
Paul, Ron 1935- WhoAmP 93
Paul, Ronald Ian S. Who 94
Paul, Ronald Neale 1934- WhoAm 94
Paul, Ronald Stanley 1923- WhoAm 94
Paul, Rosemary WhoHol 92
Paul, Sandra Koodin 1938- WhoFI 94
Paul, Shale 1931- WhoWest 94
Paul, Sherman 1920- WhoAm 94, WhoMW 93
Paul, Stephen Howard 1947- WhoAm 94, WhoAmL 94
Paul, Steven 1958- IntMPA 94, WhoHol 92
Paul, Steven M. WhoScEn 94
Paul, Stuart 1956- WhoHol 92
Paul, Susan L. 1944- WhoAm 94
Paul, Swraj 1931- Who 94
Paul, Thomas A. WhoAm 94
Paul, Thomas Francis 1924- WrDr 94
Paul, Thomas Frank 1925- WhoAmL 94
Paul, Val(entine) d1962 WhoHol 92
Paul, Vera Maxine 1940- WhoBlA 94, WhoScEn 94
Paul, Vivian 1925- WhoAmL 94
Paul, William 1926- WhoAm 94, WhoScEn 94
Paul, William D., Jr. 1934- WhoAmA 93
Paul, William Erwin 1936- WhoAm 94, WhoScEn 94
Paul, William F. WhoFI 94
Paul, William George 1930- WhoAm 94, WhoAmL 94, WhoFI 94
Paul, William McCann 1951- WhoAm 94, WhoAmL 94
Paul, Wolfgang 1913- IntWW 93, NobelP 91 [port], Who 94, WhoScEn 94
Paul, Wolfgang 1913-1993 NewYTBS 93 [port]
Paulauskas, Edmund Walter 1937- WhoAm 94, WhoFI 94
Paulding, John 1758-1818 WhAmRev
Paulding, Perry d1976 WhoHol 92
Paule, Lawrence David 1960- WhoWest 94
Paulet Who 94
Pauley, Bruce Frederick 1937- WhoAm 94
Pauley, Claude A(rlington) 1898- WhAm 10
Pauley, Jane 1950- IntMPA 94, WhoAm 94
Pauley, Jim G. 1932- WhoAmP 93
Pauley, Paul d1938 WhoHol 92
Pauley, Rhoda Anne 1939- WhoFI 94
Pauley, Richard Heim 1932- WhoFI 94
Pauley, Robert Reinhold 1923- WhoAm 94
Pauley, Stanley Frank 1927- WhoAm 94, WhoFI 94
Pauli, Chris Henry 1957- WhoFI 94
Pauli, Wolfgang 1900-1958 WorScD
Paulig, Albert d1933 WhoHol 92
Paulikas, George Algis 1936- WhoAm 94
Paulin, Andrej 1939- WhoScEn 94
Paulin, Henry Sylvester 1927- WhoAm 94
Paulin, Richard Calkins 1928- WhoAmA 93
Paulin, Roger Cole 1937- Who 94
Paulin, Scott WhoHol 92
Paulin, Tom 1949- WrDr 94
Paulina-Murl, Lianne 1944- WhoWomW 91
Pauling, Linus 1901- WorScD [port]
Pauling, Linus (Carl) 1901- Who 94, WrDr 94
Pauling, Linus Carl 1901- AmSocL [port], IntWW 93, WhoAm 94, WhoScEn 94, WhoWest 94
Pauling, Ned Bower d1993 NewYTBS 93
Paulino, Cleotilde Camacho 1927- WhoAmP 93
Paulinus, Suetonius dc. 70 WhWE
Paulk, James Lane 1949- WhoAmP 93
Paulk, William R. 1931- WhoAmP 93
Paull, George William, Jr. 1947- WhoAmL 94
Paull, Lawrence G. 1946- ConTFT 11
Paull, Mary 1940- WhoAmP 93
Paull, Morgan WhoHol 92
Paull, Richard Allen 1930- WhoAm 94
Paull, William Bernard 1952- WhoScEn 94
Paullin, JoAnn Marie 1946- WhoWest 94
Paulling, John Randolph, Jr. 1930- WhoAm 94
Pau-Llosa, Ricardo DrAPF 93
Pau-Llosa, Ricardo Manuel 1954- WhoHisp 94
Paulmuller, Herbert d1939 WhoHol 92
Paulos, John A(llen) 1945- WrDr 94
Paulos, Peter Ernest 1943- WhoWest 94
Pauls, Raymond 1936- IntWW 93
Pauls, Rolf Friedemann 1915- IntWW 93
Paulsen, Albert 1929- WhoHol 92
Paulsen, Anne M. WhoAmP 93
Paulsen, Arno d1969 WhoHol 92
Paulsen, Borge Regnar 1915- WhoFI 94
Paulsen, Brian Oliver 1941- WhoAmA 93
Paulsen, Elizabeth Robertson 1954- WhoMW 93
Paulsen, Frank Robert 1922- WhoAm 94
Paulsen, Gary 1939- TwCYAW, WrDr 94
Paulsen, Gary James DrAPF 93
Paulsen, Gary Melvin 1939- WhoAm 94
Paulsen, Herald d1954 WhoHol 92
Paulsen, James Walter 1954- WhoAmL 94
Paulsen, Kathryn DrAPF 93
Paulsen, Kevin Michael 1960- WhoFI 94
Paulsen, Lina d1932 WhoHol 92
Paulsen, Martin Raymond 1895- WhAm 10
Paulsen, Pat 1926- WhoHol 92
Paulsen, Pat 1927- WhoCom
Paulsen, Serenus Glen 1917- WhoAm 94
Paulsen, Vivian 1942- WhoAm 94, WhoWest 94
Paulson, A. B. DrAPF 93
Paulson, Belden Henry 1927- WhoAm 94
Paulson, Bernard Arthur 1928- WhoAm 94
Paulson, Christopher Robert 1947- WhoAmP 93
Paulson, David E. 1931- WhoAmP 93
Paulson, Donald Robert 1943- WhoAm 94, WhoWest 94
Paulson, Gaylord Dean 1937- WhoMW 93
Paulson, Gerrie Ellyn 1948- WhoMW 93
Paulson, Glenn 1941- WhoAm 94
Paulson, Gregory Stephen 1955- WhoWest 94
Paulson, James Marvin 1923- WhoAm 94
Paulson, John Daniel 1950- WhoScEn 94
Paulson, John Doran 1915- WhoAm 94
Paulson, John Frederick 1929- WhoScEn 94
Paulson, Kenneth Michael 1945- WhoFI 94
Paulson, Lawrance L. 1946- WhoAmL 94
Paulson, Lawrence Clifford 1951- WhoAmL 94
Paulson, Marilyn Elizabeth 1931- WhoMW 93
Paulson, Mary Alice 1962- WhoMW 93
Paulson, Michael WhoAmA 93N
Paulson, Moses 1897-1991 WhAm 10
Paulson, Paul Joseph 1932- WhoAm 94
Paulson, Peter John 1928- WhoAm 94
Paulson, Ronald (Howard) 1930- WrDr 94
Paulson, Ronald Howard 1930- WhoAm 94
Paulson, Stanley Fay 1920- WhoAm 94
Paulson, Terry Lee 1945- WhoWest 94
Paulson, William Lee 1913- WhoAmP 93
Paulson-Ehrhardt, Patricia Helen 1956- WhoWest 94
Paulsrud, Eric David 1960- WhoAmL 94
Paulston, Christina Bratt 1932- WhoAm 94
Paulston, Rolland G. 1929- WrDr 94
Paul, the Apostle, Saint 5-67? EncEth
Paultre, Patrick WhoScEn 94
Paultz, Billy 1948- BasBi
Paulu, Burton 1910- WrDr 94
Paulu, Frances Brown 1920- WhoMW 93
Paulus d1908 WhoHol 92
Paulus, Harold Edward 1929- WhoAm 94
Paulus, John Richard 1933- WhoFI 94
Paulus, Judith K. 1947- WhoFI 94
Paulus, Michael Damien 1965- WhoMW 93
Paulus, Norma J. 1933- WhoAmP 93
Paulus, Norma Jean Petersen 1933- WhoAm 94, WhoWest 94
Paulus, Sharon Marie 1949- WhoAmL 94
Paulus, Stephen (Harrison) 1949- NewGrDO
Paulus, Stephen Harrison 1949- WhoAm 94
Paulus, Wilma Florence 1930- WhoMW 93
Paulusz, Jan Gilbert 1929- Who 94
Pauly, Ann 1943- WhoAmL 94
Pauly, Bruce Henry 1920- WhoAm 94
Pauly, David F. 1952- WhoIns 94
Pauly, James Ross 1927- WhoWest 94
Pauly, John Edward 1927- WhoAm 94
Pauly, Rose 1894-1975 NewGrDO
Pauly, Sidney J. 1933- WhoAmP 93
Paumgarten, Nicholas Biddle 1945- WhoAm 94, WhoFI 94
Paumgartner, Bernhard 1887-1971 NewGrDO
Paumgartner, Gustav 1933- WhoScEn 94
Paumier, Alfred d1951 WhoHol 92
Paun, Radu 1915- IntWW 93
Pauncefort, Bernard Edward 1926- Who 94
Pauncefort, Claire d1924 WhoHol 92
Pauncefort, George d1942 WhoHol 92
Pauncefort-Duncombe, Philip Who 94
Paunio, Jouko Juhani Kyosti 1928- IntWW 93
Paup, Martin Arnold 1930- WhoWest 94
Paup, Michael Lee 1941- WhoAm 94, WhoAmL 94, WhoFI 94
Paupanakiss, Edward 1840-1911 EncNAR
Paupini, Giuseppe 1907- IntWW 93
Pausa, Clements Edward 1930- WhoAm 94
Paust, Marian 1908- WrDr 94
Paustenbach, Dennis James 1952- WhoScEn 94
Pautler, Paul F. 1945- WhoAmL 94
Pautler, Richard J. 1954- WhoAmL 94
Pauwels, Jean-Englebert 1768-1804 NewGrDO
Pauwels, Louis 1920- IntWW 93
Pauzus, Gerald Xavier 1943- WhoAmP 93
Pavalon, Eugene Irving 1933- WhoAm 94, WhoAmL 94, WhoMW 93
Pavan, Marisa 1932- IntMPA 94, WhoHol 92
Pavan, Pietro IntWW 93
Pavan, Robert David John 1929- WhoFI 94
Pavane, Lisa 1961- IntDcB [port]
Pavanelli, Livio d1958 WhoHol 92
Pavao, Leonel Maia 1934- WhoAm 94
Pavarotti, Luciano 1935- IntWW 93, NewGrDO, Who 94, WhoAm 94, WhoHol 92
Pavek, Charles Christopher 1955- WhoFI 94
Pavelic, Zlatko P. 1943- WhoScEn 94
Pavelka, Elaine Blanche WhoMW 93, WhoScEn 94
Paven, Nathan Samuel 1925- WhoAmL 94
Pavese, Cesare 1908-1950 RfGShF

Pavesi, Stefano 1779-1850 *NewGrDO*
Pavetti, Francis James 1931- *WhoAmL 94*
Pavey, Don 1922- *WrDr 94*
Pavey, Janet Sue 1954- *WhoWest 94*
Pavey, Martin Christopher 1940- *Who 94*
Pavia, George M. 1928- *WhoAmL 94*
Pavia, Louis, Jr. 1950- *WhoFI 94*
Pavic, Milorad 1929- *ConWorW 93, IntWW 93*
Pavich, Emil Sam 1931- *WhoAmP 93*
Pavie, Auguste-Jean-Marie 1847-1925 *WhWE*
Pavik, Malvin A. 1932- *WhoAm 94, WhoFI 94*
Pavilanis, Vytautas 1920- *WhoAm 94*
Pavilon, Michael Douglas 1945- *WhoFI 94*
Pavin, Corey *WhoAm 94*
Pavin, Randall Brooke 1953- *WhoWest 94*
Pavis, Jesse Andrew 1919- *WhoScEn 94*
Pavitt, William Hesser, Jr. 1916- *WhoAmL 94*
Pavlac, Diana Lynne 1956- *WhoMW 93*
Pavlak, Frank James 1947- *WhoWest 94*
Pavlak, John J. 1945- *WhoAmL 94*
Pavlath, Attila Endre 1930- *WhoWest 94*
Pavlicek, Frantisek 1923- *IntWW 93*
Pavlich, Walter *DrAPF 93*
Pavlick, Harvey Naylor 1942- *WhoFI 94, WhoWest 94*
Pavlick, Walter Eugene 1934- *WhoFI 94*
Pavlik, James William 1937- *WhoAm 94*
Pavlik, John M. 1939- *IntMPA 94*
Pavlik, Nancy 1935- *WhoWest 94*
Pavlik, Thomas Joseph 1951- *WhoScEn 94*
Pavlik, William Bruce 1932- *WhoAm 94*
Pavlikova, Jirina *WhoWomW 91*
Pavlis, Alfred Ulmer 1958- *WhoAmL 94*
Pavlista, Alexander Dimitri 1947- *WhoMW 93*
Pavloff, Wilma De *WhoAmA 93*
Pavlov, Ivan 1849-1936 *EncSPD*
Pavlov, Ivan Petrovitch 1849-1936 *WorScD [port]*
Pavlov, Nikolai Aleksandrovich 1951- *LngBDD*
Pavlov, Valentin Sergeevich 1937- *LngBDD*
Pavlov, Valentin Sergeyevich 1937- *IntWW 93*
Pavlov, Vladimir Yakovlevich 1923- *IntWW 93*
Pavlova, Anna d1931 *WhoHol 92*
Pavlova, Anna 1881-1931 *DcNaB MP, IntDcB [port]*
Pavlova, Karolina Karlovna 1807-1893 *BlmGWL [port]*
Pavlova, Nadezhda 1955- *IntDcB [port]*
Pavlovic, Milija N. 1950- *WhoScEn 94*
Pavlovic, Miodrag 1928- *ConWorW 93*
Pavlovich, Donald 1957- *WhoScEn 94*
Pavlovich, Robert John 1929- *WhoAmP 93*
Pavlovskaya, Emiliya Karlovna 1853-1935 *NewGrDO*
Pavlovsky, Eduardo 1933- *IntDcT 2*
Pavlow, Muriel 1921- *IntMPA 94, WhoHol 92*
Pavlowitch, Stevan K. 1933- *WrDr 94*
Pavlychko, Dmytro Vasylovych 1929- *IntWW 93, LngBDD*
Pavone, Elizabeth Ann 1962- *WhoAmL 94*
Pavony, William H. 1940- *WhoAm 94*
Pavord, Anna 1940- *Who 94*
Pavsek, Daniel Allan 1945- *WhoAm 94*
Pavy, Octave 1844-1884 *WhWE*
Pawar, Sharadchandra Govindrao 1940- *IntWW 93*
Pawel, Ernst 1920- *WrDr 94*
Pawelec, Graham Peter 1951- *WhoScEn 94*
Pawelec, William John 1917- *WhoFI 94*
Pawelski, James Gerard 1964- *WhoMW 93*
Pawlak, Mark *DrAPF 93*
Pawle, Lennox d1936 *WhoHol 92*
Pawlenty, Tim 1960- *WhoAmP 93*
Pawley, Edward d1988 *WhoHol 92*
Pawley, Godfrey Stuart 1937- *Who 94*
Pawley, Martin (Edward) 1938- *WrDr 94*
Pawley, Nancy *WhoHol 92*
Pawley, Ray Lynn 1935- *WhoMW 93*
Pawley, Robert John 1939- *Who 94*
Pawley, Thomas D., III 1917- *WhoBlA 94*
Pawley, William d1952 *WhoHol 92*
Pawlicki, Clarence Francis 1930- *WhoAmL 94*
Pawliczko, George Ihor 1950- *WhoAm 94, WhoFI 94*
Pawlik, James David 1958- *WhoAmL 94, WhoMW 93*
Pawlik, Robert Altenloh 1940- *WhoAm 94*
Pawlikowski, John Thaddeus 1940- *WrDr 94*
Pawlikowski, Priscilla Marie 1950- *WhoMW 93*
Pawling, Albert *WhAmRev*
Pawlitschek, Donald Paul 1941- *WhoMW 93*
Pawlson, Leonard Gregory 1943- *WhoAm 94*
Pawnee, Bill, Jr. d1947 *WhoHol 92*
Pawsey, James Francis 1933- *Who 94*
Pawson, Hargrave d1945 *WhoHol 92*
Pawula, Kenneth John 1935- *WhoAm 94, WhoWest 94*
Pax, James *WhoHol 92*
Paxinou, Katina d1973 *WhoHol 92*
Paxman, Jeremy Dickson 1950- *IntWW 93, Who 94*
Paxon, Bill 1954- *CngDr 93, WhoAmP 93*
Paxon, L. William 1954- *WhoAm 94*
Paxson, James Malone 1912- *WhoAmP 93*
Paxson, Jim 1957- *BasBi*
Paxson, Lowell White 1935- *WhoFI 94*
Paxton, Albert Elwyn 1902- *WhoMW 93*
Paxton, Alexander G(allatin) 1896- *WhAm 10*
Paxton, Bill 1955- *IntMPA 94*
Paxton, Brady Ralph 1947- *WhoAmP 93*
Paxton, Charles 1707-1788 *WhAmRev*
Paxton, Dan Richards 1947- *WhoFI 94*
Paxton, George d1914 *WhoHol 92*
Paxton, Gertrude Garnes 1931- *WhoBlA 94*
Paxton, Jane P. *WhoAmP 93*
Paxton, Jeffrey C. 1959- *WhoAmL 94*
Paxton, Joan Susan 1963- *WhoMW 93*
Paxton, John 1911-1985 *IntDcF 2-4*
Paxton, John 1923- *Who 94, WrDr 94*
Paxton, John Wesley 1937- *WhoAm 94, WhoScEn 94*
Paxton, Lois 1916- *WrDr 94*
Paxton, Peter James 1923- *Who 94*
Paxton, Phyllis Ann 1942- *WhoBlA 94*
Paxton, Ralph Robert 1920- *WhoScEn 94*
Paxton, Robert James 1928- *WhoAmP 93*
Paxton, Robert O(wen) 1932- *ConAu 42NR*
Paxton, Robert Owen 1932- *WhoAm 94*
Paxton, Sidney d1930 *WhoHol 92*
Paxton, Tom 1937- *WhoAm 94*
Paxton, William 1955- *WhoHol 92*
Pay, Howard Richard 1951- *WhoWest 94*
Pay, William *IntMPA 94*
Payack, Peter *DrAPF 93*
Payan, Art *WhoHisp 94*
Payan, Gustavo L. 1954- *WhoHisp 94*
Payan, Ilka Tanya *NewYTBS 93 [port]*
Payan, Ilka Tanya 1943- *WhoHisp 94*
Payan, Jean-Jacques 1935- *IntWW 93*
Payant, Lee d1976 *WhoHol 92*
Payant, V. Robert 1932- *WhoAmL 94, WhoWest 94*
Paycheck, Johnny 1941- *WhoAm 94*
Payden, Henry J., Sr. 1923- *WhoBlA 94*
Paydos, Charles J. 1940- *WhoFI 94*
Paye, Jean-Claude 1934- *IntWW 93, Who 94*
Payea, Norman Philip, II 1949- *WhoWest 94*
Payen, Anselme 1795-1871 *WorInv*
Payer, Julius Von 1842-1915 *WhWE*
Paykel, Eugene Stern 1934- *Who 94*
Payment, Robert C. 1934- *WhoAm 94*
Paymer, David 1954- *IntMPA 94*
Payn, Clyde Francis 1952- *WhoAm 94, WhoScEn 94*
Payn, Graham 1918- *WhoHol 92*
Payn, James 1830-1898 *EncSF 93*
Payne, Alan *ConAu 43NR*
Payne, Alan 1932- *WrDr 94*
Payne, Alan Jeffrey 1933- *Who 94*
Payne, Allen *WhoHol 92*
Payne, Allison Griffin 1964- *WhoBlA 94*
Payne, Ancil Horace 1921- *WhoAm 94, WhoWest 94*
Payne, Ancil Newton, Jr. 1935- *WhoAmL 94*
Payne, Anita Hart 1926- *WhoScEn 94*
Payne, Anthony Edward 1936- *IntWW 93*
Payne, Anthony Glen 1955- *WhoScEn 94*
Payne, Arthur Lee 1946- *WhoAmP 93*
Payne, Arthur Stanley 1930- *Who 94*
Payne, Barbara Jeanette 1947- *WhoMW 93*
Payne, Basil *DrAPF 93*
Payne, Billy *WhoAm 94, WhoFI 94, WhoWest 94*
Payne, Brown H. 1915- *WhoBlA 94*
Payne, Bruce *WhoHol 92*
Payne, Bruce 1911- *WhoAm 94, WrDr 94*
Payne, Carl A., II *WhoHol 92*
Payne, Carr 1898- *WhAm 10*
Payne, Christopher Charles 1946- *Who 94*
Payne, Christopher Frederick 1930- *Who 94*
Payne, Claire Margaret 1943- *WhoScEn 94, WhoWest 94*
Payne, Craig William 1943- *WhoMW 93*
Payne, Cynthia Paulette 1958- *WhoBlA 94*
Payne, Daniel Alexander 1811-1893 *AfrAmAl 6, DcAmReB 2*
Payne, Darrell Lee 1948- *WhoWest 94*
Payne, David d1987 *WhoHol 92*
Payne, David Marlin *WhoAmP 93*
Payne, David N. *WhoScEn 94*
Payne, David Neil 1944- *Who 94*
Payne, Deborah Anne 1952- *WhoFI 94*
Payne, Donald 1934- *WhoAmP 93*
Payne, Donald Gordon 1924- *WrDr 94*
Payne, Donald M. 1934- *CngDr 93, WhoAm 94, WhoBlA 94*
Payne, Douglas d1965 *WhoHol 92*
Payne, Douglas G. 1928- *WhoAmP 93, WhoMW 93*
Payne, Edith K. 1942- *WhoAmL 94*
Payne, Edmund d1914 *WhoHol 92*
Payne, Edna d1953 *WhoHol 92*
Payne, Edward Carlton 1928- *WhoAm 94*
Payne, Elvis *WhoHol 92*
Payne, Eugene C., III 1947- *WhoAmL 94*
Payne, Eugene Edgar 1942- *WhoAm 94*
Payne, Frances Anne 1932- *WhoAm 94*
Payne, Fred J. 1922- *WhoScEn 94*
Payne, Fred Ray 1931- *WhoAm 94*
Payne, Freda 1943- *WhoHol 92*
Payne, Freda 1944- *WhoBlA 94*
Payne, Gary D. 1948- *WhoBlA 94*
Payne, George Frederick 1941- *WhoAm 94*
Payne, Gerald Lew 1938- *WhoMW 93*
Payne, Gerald Oliver 1930- *WhoAm 94*
Payne, Gerrye *DrAPF 93*
Payne, Harry Charles 1947- *WhoAm 94*
Payne, Harry E., Jr. *WhoAmP 93*
Payne, Harry Morse, Jr. 1922- *WhoAm 94*
Payne, Henry Salusbury Legh D. *Who 94*
Payne, Homer Lemuel 1910- *WhoMW 93*
Payne, Howard James 1940- *WhoMW 93*
Payne, Ian 1926- *Who 94*
Payne, (Trevor) Ian *Who 94*
Payne, J. Gregory 1949- *WrDr 94*
Payne, J. Mark 1956- *WhoAmL 94*
Payne, James A. 1945- *WhoAmL 94*
Payne, James Floyd 1943- *WhoBlA 94*
Payne, James L. *WhoFI 94*
Payne, James Leroy 1936- *WhoAm 94*
Payne, James Richmond 1921- *Who 94*
Payne, James S. 1937- *WhoAm 94*
Payne, Jane Marian *Who 94*
Payne, Janet Anne 1948- *WhoAmP 93*
Payne, Jerry Oscar 1953- *WhoBlA 94*
Payne, Jesse James 1947- *WhoBlA 94*
Payne, John d1989 *WhoHol 92*
Payne, John D. 1934- *WhoAmA 93*
Payne, John Harman 1955- *WhoWest 94*
Payne, John Howard 1951- *WhoWest 94*
Payne, John Ross 1941- *WhoAm 94*
Payne, Julie 1940- *WhoHol 92*
Payne, June Evelyn 1948- *WhoBlA 94*
Payne, Keith 1933- *Who 94*
Payne, Kenneth Eugene 1936- *WhoAm 94*
Payne, Kenneth Victor 1966- *WhoBlA 94*
Payne, L. F. 1945- *WhoAmP 93*
Payne, Ladell 1933- *WhoAm 94, WrDr 94*
Payne, Laurence 1919- *WhoHol 92, WrDr 94*
Payne, Lawrence Edward 1923- *WhoAm 94*
Payne, Leigh Ann 1956- *WhoMW 93*
Payne, Leonard Sidney 1925- *Who 94*
Payne, Leslie 1941- *WhoAm 94, WhoBlA 94*
Payne, Lewis F., Jr. 1945- *CngDr 93*
Payne, Lewis Franklin, Jr. 1945- *WhoAm 94*
Payne, Linda Cohen 1953- *WhoFI 94*
Payne, Lisa R. 1962- *WhoBlA 94*
Payne, Louis d1953 *WhoHol 92*
Payne, Lucy Ann Salsbury 1952- *WhoAmL 94*
Payne, Margaret Anne 1947- *WhoAmL 94*
Payne, Margaret Ralston 1946- *WhoBlA 94*
Payne, Maxwell Carr, Jr. 1927- *WhoAm 94*
Payne, Melvin Monroe 1911-1990 *WhAm 10*
Payne, Michael *WhoAmP 93, WhoHol 92*
Payne, Michael 1969- *WhoWest 94*
Payne, Michael David 1941- *WhoAm 94*
Payne, Mitchell Howard 1950- *WhoBlA 94*
Payne, N. Joyce 1941- *WhoBlA 94*
Payne, Nicholas *Who 94*
Payne, Nicholas 1945- *IntWW 93*
Payne, (Geoffrey John) Nicholas 1945- *Who 94*
Payne, Norman 1939- *IntMPA 94*
Payne, Norman (John) 1921- *Who 94*
Payne, Norman John 1921- *IntWW 93*
Payne, Osborne Allen 1925- *WhoBlA 94*
Payne, Patricia 1942- *NewGrDO*
Payne, Patty Anne 1961- *WhoHisp 94*
Payne, Peggy *DrAPF 93*
Payne, Peter Charles John 1928- *Who 94*
Payne, Robert c. 1596-1651 *DcNaB MP*
Payne, (Pierre Stephen) Robert 1911-1983 *EncSF 93*
Payne, Robert E. 1941- *WhoAm 94, WhoAmL 94*
Payne, Robert M. 1935- *WhoAm 94*
Payne, Robert Somers *WhoIns 94*
Payne, Robert Walter 1925- *WhoAm 94*
Payne, Roger Lee 1946- *WhoAm 94*
Payne, Ronnie E. 1940- *WhoBlA 94*
Payne, Roy Steven 1952- *WhoAm 94, WhoAmL 94*
Payne, Samuel, Sr. 1919- *WhoBlA 94*
Payne, Sidney Stewart 1932- *WhoAm 94*
Payne, (Sidney) Stewart *Who 94*
Payne, Tyson Elliott, Jr. 1927- *WhoAm 94*
Payne, Vernon 1945- *WhoBlA 94*
Payne, Warren Gilbert 1954- *WhoWest 94*
Payne, Wilford Alexander 1945- *WhoBlA 94*
Payne, William d1967 *WhoHol 92*
Payne, William Bruce 1943- *WhoAm 94, WhoAmL 94*
Payne, William Jackson 1925- *WhoAm 94*
Payne, William Sanford 1946- *WhoFI 94*
Payne, William Spencer 1926- *WhoAm 94*
Payne, William T., Jr. 1927- *WhoAm 94*
Payne, William Thomas 1953- *WhoAmL 94*
Payne, William Thomas 1956- *WhoMW 93*
Payne, Winfield Scott 1917- *WhoScEn 94*
Payne-Butler, George William 1919- *Who 94*
Payne-Gallwey, Philip (Frankland) 1935- *Who 94*
Payne-Thomas, Janice Lynn 1960- *WhoAmL 94*
Paynter, Corona d1986 *WhoHol 92*
Paynter, David B. 1943- *WhoAmL 94*
Paynter, David H. 1921- *WrDr 94*
Paynter, Donald G. 1946- *WhoAmL 94*
Paynter, Harry Alvin 1923- *WhoAm 94*
Paynter, John Frederick 1931- *Who 94*
Paynter, John Philip 1928- *WhoAm 94*
Paynter, Mary 1931- *WhoMW 93*
Paynter, Noel Stephen 1898- *Who 94*
Paynter, Robert 1928- *IntMPA 94*
Pays, Amanda 1959- *IntMPA 94, WhoHol 92*
Pays, Howard 1927- *WhoHol 92*
Payson, Blanche d1964 *WhoHol 92*
Payson, Henry Edwards 1925- *WhoAm 94*
Payson, John Whitney 1940- *WhoAmA 93*
Payson, Martin D. 1936- *IntMPA 94*
Payson, Martin David 1936- *WhoAm 94, WhoFI 94*
Payson, Martin Fred 1940- *WhoAm 94, WhoAmL 94*
Payson, Mary Wold 1915- *WhoAmP 93*
Payte, J. Michael 1946- *WhoFI 94*
Payton, Albert Levern 1944- *WhoBlA 94*
Payton, Barbara d1967 *WhoHol 92*
Payton, Benjamin F. 1932- *AfrAmAl 6*
Payton, Benjamin Franklin 1932- *WhoAm 94, WhoBlA 94*
Payton, Carolyn Robertson 1925- *WhoBlA 94*
Payton, Claude d1955 *WhoHol 92*
Payton, Corse d1934 *WhoHol 92*
Payton, Denis *WhoHol 92*
Payton, Edgar Lee 1950- *WhoMW 93*
Payton, Gary Dwayne 1968- *WhoBlA 94*
Payton, James Edward, Jr. 1957- *WhoWest 94*
Payton, Jeff 1946- *WhoBlA 94*
Payton, Lawrence 1938-
See Four Tops, The *ConMus 11*
Payton, Lew d1945 *WhoHol 92*
Payton, Lucy d1969 *WhoHol 92*
Payton, Michael A. 1940- *WhoAmP 93*
Payton, Nolan H. 1919- *WhoBlA 94*
Payton, Stanley Walden 1921- *Who 94*
Payton, Thomas William 1946- *WhoAm 94*
Payton, Victor Emmanuel 1948- *WhoBlA 94*
Payton, Walter 1954- *AfrAmAl 6 [port], WhoAm 94, WhoMW 93*
Payton, Walter Jerry 1954- *WhoBlA 94*
Payton, Willis Conwell 1923- *WhoBlA 94*
Payton-France, JoMarie *WhoBlA 94, WhoHol 92*
Payton-Wright, Pamela 1941- *WhoHol 92*
Payuk, Edward William 1948- *WhoMW 93*
Payyapilli, John 1947- *WhoScEn 94*
Payzant, Thomas *WhoAm 94*
Paz, Denis George 1945- *WhoHisp 94*
Paz, Francis Xavier 1931- *WhoHisp 94*
Paz, Jennifer C. *WhoAsA 94*
Paz, Nils 1950- *WhoScEn 94*
Paz, Octavio 1914- *ConWorW 93, HispLC [port], IntWW 93, NobelP 91 [port], Who 94, WhoAm 94*
Paz, Rudy J. 1938- *WhoHisp 94*
Paz, Yamile C. 1967- *WhoHisp 94*
Paz Estenssoro, Victor 1907- *IntWW 93*
Pazicky, Edward Paul 1946- *WhoFI 94*
Pazik, George James 1921- *WhoAm 94*
Pazirandeh, Mahmood 1932- *WhoMW 93*
Paznyak, Zenyon *IntWW 93*
Pazos, Carlos Agustin 1956- *WhoAmL 94*

Pazovsky, Ary Moiseyevich 1887-1953 NewGrDO

Paz Paredes, Margarita 1922- BlmGWL

Paz-Pujalt, Gustavo Roberto 1954- WhoScEn 94

Pazuhanich, Mark Peter 1956- WhoAmL 94

Pazur, John Howard 1922- WhoAm 94

Paz Zamora, Jaime 1939- IntWW 93

P'Bitek, Okot 1931-1982 BlkWr 2

Pe, Maung Hla 1920- WhoAsA 94

Peabody, Abner 1906-1978
See Lum and Abner WhoCom

Peabody, Amelia 1890-1984 WhoAmA 93N

Peabody, Eddie d1970 WhoHol 92

Peabody, Elizabeth Palmer 1804-1894 AmSocL

Peabody, Francis Greenwood 1847-1936 DcAmReB 2

Peabody, George 1795-1869 AmSocL

Peabody, Joel R. EncSF 93

Peabody, Joseph 1757-1844 WhAmRev

Peabody, Maryanne 1946- WhoFI 94

Peabody, Nathaniel 1742-1823 WhAmRev

Peabody, Richard 1925- WhoHol 92

Peabody, Richard, Jr. DrAPF 93

Peabody, Robert Lee 1931- WrDr 94

Peabody, William Tyler, Jr. 1921- WhoAm 94

Peace, Bernie (Kinzel) 1933- WhoAmA 93

Peace, Charles Frederick 1832-1879 DcNaB MP

Peace, David Brian 1915- Who 94

Peace, Eula H. 1920- WhoBlA 94

Peace, G. Earl, Jr. 1945- WhoBlA 94

Peace, H. W., II 1935- WhoAm 94

Peace, Richard (Arthur) 1933- WrDr 94

Peace, Scott Parker 1942- WhoAmP 93

Peace, Steve 1953- WhoAmP 93

Peach, Benjamin Neeve 1842-1926 DcNaB MP

Peach, Charles Lindsay K. Who 94

Peach, Denis Alan 1928- Who 94

Peach, Guthlac Ceri Klaus 1939- Who 94

Peach, John Andrew 1948- WhoMW 93

Peach, Leonard (Harry) 1932- Who 94

Peach, Mary 1934- WhoHol 92

Peach, Philip Ray 1956- WhoWest 94

Peaches, Daniel 1940- WhoAmP 93

Peachey, Lee DeBorde 1932- WhoAm 94

Peaco, Joyce Lorane WhoAm 94

Peacock, Alan 1922- IntWW 93

Peacock, Alan (Turner) 1922- Who 94, WrDr 94

Peacock, Alvin Ward 1929- WhoAm 94, WhoFI 94

Peacock, Andrew Sharp 1939- IntWW 93, Who 94

Peacock, Carlos (Charles Hanbury) WrDr 94

Peacock, Cassius L., Jr. 1920- WhoAmP 93

Peacock, Clifton 1953- WhoAmA 93

Peacock, Daniel WhoHol 92

Peacock, Douglas W. 1938- WhoFI 94

Peacock, Elizabeth Joan 1937- Who 94, WhoWomW 91

Peacock, Enoch Benjamin 1947- WhoFI 94

Peacock, Erle Ewart, Jr. 1926- WhoAm 94

Peacock, George Rowatt 1923- WhoAm 94

Peacock, Georgine Geraldine 1936- WhoFI 94

Peacock, Hugh Anthony 1928- WhoScEn 94

Peacock, Ian Douglas 1934- Who 94

Peacock, James Daniel 1930- WhoAm 94

Peacock, Judith Ann 1939- WhoAm 94

Peacock, Keith d1966 WhoHol 92

Peacock, Kim d1966 WhoHol 92

Peacock, Lamar Batts 1920- WhoAm 94

Peacock, Lelon James 1928- WhoAm 94

Peacock, Lillian d1918 WhoHol 92

Peacock, Lucy 1947- NewGrDO

Peacock, Markham Lovick, Jr. 1903- WhoAm 94

Peacock, Mary Willa 1942- WhoAm 94

Peacock, Michael Who 94

Peacock, (Ian) Michael 1929- Who 94

Peacock, Molly DrAPF 93

Peacock, Molly 1947- WrDr 94

Peacock, Neal Dow 1897- WhAm 10

Peacock, Richard Beck 1933- WhoWest 94

Peacock, Ronald d1993 Who 94N

Peacock, Ronald 1907- IntWW 93, WrDr 94

Peacock, Ronald 1907-1993 ConAu 141

Peacock, Thomas Love 1785-1866 BlmGEL, RfGShF

Peacock, Tom DrAPF 93

Peacock, Trevor 1931- WhoHol 92

Peacock, Valerie Lynn 1962- WhoAmL 94

Peacock, William James 1937- IntWW 93, Who 94

Peacock, Arthur Robert 1924- Who 94

Peacocke, Christopher Arthur Bruce 1950- IntWW 93, Who 94

Peacocke, Cuthbert Irvine 1903- Who 94

Peacocke, Isabel Maud 1881-1973 BlmGWL

Peacocke, Thomas WhoHol 92

Peagler, Frederick Douglass 1922- WhoBlA 94

Peagler, Owen F. 1931- WhoAmP 93

Peagler, Owen F. 1935- WhoBlA 94

Peagler, Owen F. 1936- WhoAm 94

Peak, David 1941- WhoScEn 94

Peak, David 1953- WhoAm 94

Peak, Elizabeth Jayne 1952- WhoAmA 93

Peak, Gary Don 1962- WhoAmL 94

Peak, Robert d1992 WhoAmA 93N

Peake Who 94

Peake, Channing 1910-1991 WhoAmA 93N

Peake, Charles Franklin 1933- WhoFI 94

Peake, David Alphy Edward Raymond 1934- Who 94

Peake, Edward James, Jr. 1933- WhoBlA 94

Peake, Felicity (Hyde) 1913- Who 94

Peake, George 1722-1827 WorInv

Peake, John Fordyce 1933- Who 94

Peake, John Morris 1924- Who 94

Peake, Kirby 1915-1991 WhAm 10

Peake, Lilian Who 94

Peake, Mervyn 1911-1968 BlmGEL

Peake, Mervyn (Laurence) 1911-1968 EncSF 93

Peake, Richard Henry, Jr. 1934- WhoAm 94

Peake, Thaddeus Andrew, III 1948- WhoScEn 94

Peaker, E. J. IntMPA 94

Peaker, E. J. 1940- WhoHol 92

Peaker, Malcolm 1943- Who 94

Peale, Charles Willson 1741-1827 AmCulL, AmRev, WhAmRev

Peale, James 1749-1831 WhAmRev

Peale, Norman Vincent 1898- WhoAm 94, WrDr 94

Peale, Norman Vincent 1898-1993 NewYTBS 93

Peale, Ruth Stafford 1906- WhoAm 94

Peale, Stanton Jerrold 1937- WhoAm 94, WhoScEn 94

Peanasky, Robert Joseph 1927- WhoAm 94

Peapples, George Alan 1940- WhoAm 94, WhoFI 94

Pear, David (Adrian) 1957- ConAu 141

Pearce, Al d1961 WhoHol 92

Pearce, Alice d1966 WhoHol 92

Pearce, Andrew 1937- Who 94

Pearce, Austin (William) 1921- Who 94

Pearce, Austin William 1921- IntWW 93

Pearce, Betty McMurray 1926- WhoFI 94

Pearce, Brenda 1935- EncSF 93

Pearce, Brian Who 94

Pearce, (John) Brian 1935- Who 94

Pearce, Brian Louis 1933- ConAu 42NR, WrDr 94

Pearce, Cary Jack 1934- WhoAmL 94

Pearce, Christopher 1943- IntMPA 94

Pearce, Colman Cormac 1938- WhoAm 94

Pearce, David Harry 1943- WhoAm 94

Pearce, David William 1941- IntWW 93

Pearce, Donald Joslin 1924- WhoAm 94

Pearce, Drue 1951- WhoAmP 93, WhoWest 94

Pearce, Eli M. 1929- WhoScEn 94

Pearce, Eric (Herbert) 1905- Who 94

Pearce, George d1940 WhoHol 92

Pearce, George 1921- Who 94

Pearce, George Hamilton 1921- WhoAm 94

Pearce, Guy WhoHol 92

Pearce, H. E., Jr. 1936- WhoAmP 93

Pearce, Harry Jonathan 1942- WhoAmL 94

Pearce, Howard John Stredder 1949- Who 94

Pearce, Howard Spencer 1924- Who 94

Pearce, Idris Who 94

Pearce, (Daniel Norton) Idris 1933- IntWW 93, Who 94

Pearce, Jacqueline WhoHol 92

Pearce, James Wishart 1916-1992 WhAm 10

Pearce, Janice 1931- WhoWest 94

Pearce, John WhoHol 92

Pearce, John Dalziel Wyndham 1904- Who 94

Pearce, John Stedman 1940- WhoAmP 93

Pearce, John Trevor Archdall 1916- Who 94

Pearce, John Y. 1948- WhoAmL 94

Pearce, Kevin E. WhoIns 94

Pearce, Leslie Arthur 1918- Who 94

Pearce, Lester WhoAmP 93

Pearce, Llewellyn Gregory, Jr. 1948- WhoAm 94

Pearce, Lupe 1942- WhoHisp 94

Pearce, Margaret Tranne 1946- WhoAmL 94

Pearce, Martha Flores 1953- WhoHisp 94

Pearce, Mary E. 1932- WrDr 94

Pearce, Muriel d1984 WhoHol 92

Pearce, Neville John Lewis 1933- Who 94

Pearce, Paul Francis 1928- WhoAm 94

Pearce, Peggy d1964 WhoHol 92

Pearce, Philippa EncSF 93, Who 94

Pearce, (Ann) Philippa Who 94

Pearce, (Ann) Philippa 1920- WrDr 94

Pearce, Richard 1943- IntMPA 94

Pearce, Richard Allen 1951- WhoBlA 94

Pearce, Richard William, Jr. 1941- WhoIns 94

Pearce, Robert Harmon 1938- WhoMW 93

Pearce, Robert Penrose 1924- Who 94

Pearce, Robert Wayne 1944- WhoWest 94

Pearce, Ronald 1920- WhoAm 94

Pearce, Roy Harvey 1919- WrDr 94

Pearce, Ruth Anne 1942- WhoWest 94

Pearce, Susan Miriam 1937- WhoAm 94

Pearce, Vera d1966 WhoHol 92

Pearce, William Joseph 1925- WhoAm 94

Pearce, William Martin 1913- WhoAm 94

Pearce-Percy, Henry Thomas 1947- WhoScEn 94

Pearcy, Patricia WhoHol 92

Pearcy, Robert Woodwell 1941- WhoAm 94

Peard, Kenyon (Harry Terrell) 1902- Who 94

Peardon, Patricia d1993 NewYTBS 93 [port]

Pearl, Barry WhoHol 92

Pearl, Bernard Harold 1933- WhoMW 93

Pearl, David 1944- WrDr 94

Pearl, David Stephen 1944- Who 94

Pearl, Elliot David 1932- WhoWest 94

Pearl, George Clayton 1923- WhoAm 94

Pearl, Helen Zalkan 1938- WhoAmL 94

Pearl, Irwin d1980 WhoHol 92

Pearl, Jack d1982 WhoHol 92

Pearl, Jack 1895-1982 WhoCom

Pearl, James G. 1941- WhoIns 94

Pearl, James Hildred 1937- WhoAmL 94

Pearl, Marilyn WhoAmA 93

Pearl, Melvin E. 1936- WhoAm 94

Pearl, Minnie 1912- WhoAm 94, WhoCom, WhoHol 92

Pearl, Valerie Louise 1926- IntWW 93, Who 94

Pearl, William Richard Emden 1944- WhoScEn 94

Pearle, Lynn K. 1943- WhoAmL 94

Pearl Jam News 94-2 [port]

Pearlman, Bill DrAPF 93

Pearlman, Charlotte Blehert 1919- WhoAmP 93

Pearlman, Craig Stuart 1952- WhoAmL 94

Pearlman, David Samuel 1934- WhoAm 94

Pearlman, Edith DrAPF 93

Pearlman, Etta S. 1930- WhoAmA 93

Pearlman, Henry 1895-1974 WhoAmA 93N

Pearlman, Henry Bernard 1901-1991 WhAm 10

Pearlman, Jerry Kent 1939- WhoAm 94, WhoFI 94

Pearlman, Louis Jay 1954- WhoFI 94

Pearlman, Marshall M. 1936- WhoAmL 94

Pearlman, Michael WhoHol 92

Pearlman, Michael Allen 1946- WhoAmL 94

Pearlman, Mickey 1938- WrDr 94

Pearlman, Moshe 1911- WrDr 94

Pearlman, Peter Steven 1946- WhoAmL 94

Pearlman, Ronald Alan 1940- WhoAm 94, WhoAmP 93

Pearlman, Samuel Segel 1942- WhoAmL 94

Pearlman, Seth Leonard 1956- WhoScEn 94

Pearlman, Stephen WhoHol 92

Pearlman, Valerie Anne 1936- Who 94

Pearlmutter, Florence Nichols 1914- WhoScEn 94

Pearlson, Fredda S. DrAPF 93

Pearlstein, Alix 1983- WhoAmA 93

Pearlstein, Andrew M. 1955- WhoAmL 94

Pearlstein, Leonard WhoAm 94

Pearlstein, Marvin B. 1949- WhoAmL 94

Pearlstein, Philip 1924- IntWW 93, WhoAm 94, WhoAmA 93

Pearlstein, Seymour 1923- WhoAm 94, WhoAmA 93

Pearlstine, Norman 1942- WhoAm 94, WhoFI 94

Pearman, James (Eugene) 1904- Who 94

Pearman, James Elwood, Jr. 1948- WhoFI 94

Pearman, Katharine K. 1893-1961 WhoAmA 93N

Pearman, Raven-Symone Christina 1985- WhoBlA 94

Pearman, Reginald James 1923- WhoAm 94

Pearman, Sara Jane 1940- WhoAmA 93

Pearman, Virgil L. 1933- WhoAmP 93

Pearn, Victor DrAPF 93

Pears, David Francis 1921- IntWW 93, Who 94

Pears, Iain (George) 1955- WrDr 94

Pears, Peter (Neville Luard) 1910-1986 NewGrDO

Pearsall, Derek (Albert) 1931- WrDr 94

Pearsall, George Wilbur 1933- WhoAm 94

Pearsall, Glenn Lincoln 1949- WhoFI 94

Pearsall, Harry James 1916- WhoMW 93, WhoScEn 94

Pearsall, Henry Batterman 1934- WhoAm 94

Pearsall, Otis Pratt 1932- WhoAm 94

Pearsall, Phyllis Isobel 1906- Who 94

Pearsall, Ronald 1927- WrDr 94

Pearsall, Rosellen Dee 1945- WhoFI 94

Pearsall, Sam Haff 1923- WhoScEn 94

Pearsall, Thomas Perine 1945- WhoWest 94

Pearsall Stipek, Cathy Rae 1932- WhoAmP 93

Pearse, Anthony Guy Everson 1916- IntWW 93, Who 94

Pearse, Barbara Mary Frances 1948- IntWW 93, Who 94

Pearse, Brian Gerald 1933- IntWW 93, Who 94

Pearse, George Ancell, Jr. 1930- WhoScEn 94

Pearse, James Newburg 1930- WhoScEn 94

Pearse, John Roger Southey G. Who 94

Pearse, Patrick Henry 1879-1916 DcNaB MP

Pearse, Richard DrAPF 93

Pearse, Richard William 1952- WhoAmL 94

Pearse, Robert Francis 1916- WhoAm 94

Pearse, Warren Harland 1927- WhoAm 94

Pearson Who 94

Pearson, Alastair Stevenson 1915- Who 94

Pearson, Albert Marchant 1916- WhoAm 94

Pearson, Allen 1925- WhoAm 94

Pearson, Anthony John 1944- WhoAm 94

Pearson, Beatrice 1920- WhoHol 92

Pearson, Belinda Kemp 1931- WhoAm 94, WhoWest 94

Pearson, Bill 1922- WrDr 94

Pearson, Bob d1986 WhoHol 92

Pearson, Brett WhoHol 92

Pearson, Brian William 1949- Who 94

Pearson, Carol Lynn 1939- WrDr 94

Pearson, Charles I. 1917- WhoAm 94

Pearson, Charles Thomas, Jr. 1929- WhoAm 94, WhoAmL 94

Pearson, Clarence Edward 1925- WhoAm 94

Pearson, Claude Meredith 1921- WhoWest 94

Pearson, Clifton 1948- WhoAmA 93, WhoBlA 94

Pearson, Craig Alan 1950- WhoMW 93

Pearson, Daniel S. 1930- WhoAm 94, WhoAmL 94

Pearson, Dave Lee 1950- WhoAmP 93

Pearson, David Compton Froome 1931- Who 94

Pearson, David Petri 1926- WhoAm 94

Pearson, Derek Leslie 1921- Who 94

Pearson, Diane (Margaret) 1931- WrDr 94

Pearson, Donald Emanual 1914- WhoAm 94

Pearson, Donald Stuart 1905-1989 WhAm 10

Pearson, Douglas N. WhoFI 94

Pearson, Drew 1951- WhoBlA 94

Pearson, Erwin Gale 1932- WhoWest 94

Pearson, Frain Garfield 1936- WhoWest 94

Pearson, Gary Dean 1952- WhoWest 94

Pearson, Gayle 1947- WrDr 94

Pearson, George Burton, Jr. 1905- WhoFI 94

Pearson, Gerald Leon 1925- WhoAm 94

Pearson, Gertrude B. WhoAmP 93

Pearson, Graham Scott 1935- Who 94

Pearson, Gregory A. 1941- WhoAmL 94

Pearson, Henry C. 1914- WhoAmA 93

Pearson, Henry Charles 1914- WhoAm 94

Pearson, Henry Clyde 1925- WhoAm 94, WhoAmL 94

Pearson, Herbert Macdonald d1992 Who 94N

Pearson, Herman B. 1947- WhoBlA 94

Pearson, (Edward) Hesketh (Gibbons) 1887-1964 DcNaB MP

Pearson, Hugh Stephen 1931- WhoFI 94, WhoScEn 94

Pearson, J. Richmond 1930- WhoAmP 93

Pearson, James A. 1925- *WhoBlA 94*
Pearson, James B. *WhoAmP 93*
Pearson, James Boyd, Jr. 1930- *WhoAm 94*
Pearson, James Douglas 1911- *Who 94*
Pearson, James Eugene 1939- *WhoAmA 93*
Pearson, Jean *DrAPF 93*
Pearson, Jeremiah W., III 1938- *WhoAm 94, WhoScEn 94*
Pearson, Jerome 1938- *WhoMW 93*
Pearson, Jesse d1979 *WhoHol 92*
Pearson, Jesse S. 1923- *WhoBlA 94*
Pearson, Jim Berry 1924-1990 *WhAm 10*
Pearson, Jim Berry, Jr. 1948- *WhoFI 94*
Pearson, John *Who 94, WhoAmA 93*
Pearson, John 1923- *WhoAm 94, WhoScEn 94, WhoWest 94*
Pearson, John 1930- *WrDr 94*
Pearson, John 1934- *WrDr 94*
Pearson, (Edward) John (David) 1938- *Who 94*
Pearson, John Edward 1946- *WhoAm 94, WhoAmL 94*
Pearson, John King 1945- *WhoAm 94, WhoAmL 94*
Pearson, John Mark 1950- *WhoFI 94, WhoScEn 94*
Pearson, John William 1920- *Who 94*
Pearson, John Y., Jr. 1942- *WhoAmL 94*
Pearson, Jonathan P. 1951- *WhoAmL 94*
Pearson, Joseph T., Jr. 1876-1951 *WhoAmA 93N*
Pearson, Judy Cornelia 1946- *WhoMW 93*
Pearson, Karl 1857-1936 *WorScD*
Pearson, Keith David *WrDr 94*
Pearson, Keith Laurence 1929- *WhoWest 94*
Pearson, Keith Philip 1941- *Who 94*
Pearson, Kit 1947- *SmATA 77 [port], TwCYAW*
Pearson, Larry Jay 1945- *WhoFI 94*
Pearson, Larry Lester 1942- *WhoAm 94, WhoWest 94*
Pearson, Lennart Jon 1942- *WhoAmL 94*
Pearson, Lester B. 1897-1972 *HisDcKW*
Pearson, Linley E. *WhoAmP 93*
Pearson, Lionel (Ignatius Cusack) 1908- *WrDr 94*
Pearson, Lloyd d1966 *WhoHol 92*
Pearson, Lorentz Clarence 1924- *WhoAmP 93*
Pearson, Louise Mary 1919- *WhoFI 94, WhoMW 93*
Pearson, Margit Linnea 1950- *WhoAm 94*
Pearson, Marilyn Ruth 1955- *WhoBlA 94*
Pearson, Mark Landell 1940- *WhoScEn 94*
Pearson, Martin *EncSF 93*
Pearson, Michael David 1941- *WhoAmP 93*
Pearson, Michael Novel 1956- *WhoBlA 94*
Pearson, Michael P. 1953- *WhoAmL 94*
Pearson, Molly d1959 *WhoHol 92*
Pearson, Nathan Williams 1911- *WhoAm 94*
Pearson, Nathan Williams 1951- *WhoFI 94*
Pearson, Nels Kenneth 1918- *WhoFI 94, WhoMW 93*
Pearson, Nicholas *Who 94*
Pearson, (Francis) Nicholas (Fraser) 1943- *Who 94*
Pearson, Norman 1928- *WhoFI 94, WhoMW 93*
Pearson, Norman Ralston 1939- *WhoMW 93*
Pearson, Olof Hjalmer 1913-1990 *WhAm 10*
Pearson, Oscar Harris 1902- *WhoAm 94*
Pearson, Paul Brown 1905- *WhoAm 94*
Pearson, Paul David 1940- *WhoAm 94, WhoAmL 94*
Pearson, Paul Guy 1926- *WhoAm 94, WhoMW 93*
Pearson, Paul Hammond *WhoAm 94*
Pearson, Paul Holding 1940- *WhoAm 94*
Pearson, Phillip Theodore 1932- *WhoAm 94*
Pearson, Preston James 1945- *WhoBlA 94*
Pearson, Ra-Nelle Lynn 1952- *WhoAmP 93*
Pearson, Ralph Gottfrid 1919- *WhoAm 94, WhoScEn 94*
Pearson, Ralph Gottfried 1919- *IntWW 93*
Pearson, Ralph M. 1883-1958 *WhoAmA 93N*
Pearson, Ramona Henderson 1952- *WhoBlA 94*
Pearson, Richard 1731-1806 *WhAmRev*
Pearson, Richard 1918- *WhoHol 92*
Pearson, Richard Allen 1942- *WhoMW 93*
Pearson, Richard Joseph 1938- *WhoAm 94*
Pearson, Richard L. 1955- *WhoAmL 94*
Pearson, Ridley 1953- *WrDr 94*
Pearson, Robert Allen 1946- *WhoWest 94*
Pearson, Robert Greenlees 1917- *WhoAm 94*
Pearson, Roger 1927- *WhoAm 94*
Pearson, Roger Alan 1956- *WhoScEn 94*
Pearson, Roger Lee 1940- *WhoAm 94*
Pearson, Ronald Dale 1940- *WhoFI 94, WhoMW 93*
Pearson, Ronald Matthew 1925- *Who 94*
Pearson, Roy 1914- *WrDr 94*
Pearson, Roy Laing 1939- *WhoAm 94*
Pearson, Roy Messer, Jr. 1914- *WhoAm 94*
Pearson, Scott Roberts 1938- *WhoFI 94, WhoScEn 94, WrDr 94*
Pearson, Sharon Ann 1961- *WhoMW 93*
Pearson, Stanley E. 1949- *WhoBlA 94*
Pearson, Sybil Angela Margaret *Who 94*
Pearson, T(homas) R(eid) 1956- *WrDr 94*
Pearson, Ted d1961 *WhoHol 92*
Pearson, Theodore Richard 1951- *WhoAmP 93*
Pearson, Thomas (Cecil Hook) 1914- *Who 94*
Pearson, Thomas Arthur 1950- *WhoScEn 94*
Pearson, Thomas Owen 1947- *WhoFI 94*
Pearson, Thomas S(pencer) 1949- *WrDr 94*
Pearson, Vernon R. *WhoAmP 93*
Pearson, Virginia d1958 *WhoHol 92*
Pearson, Wallace M. 1895- *WhAm 10*
Pearson, Walter Donald 1916- *WhoAm 94*
Pearson, Walter Howard 1946- *WhoWest 94*
Pearson, Warren Thomas 1929- *WhoWest 94*
Pearson, Willard 1915- *WhoAm 94*
Pearson, Willard John 1942- *WhoAm 94*
Pearson, William Hardy 1956- *WhoMW 93*
Pearson, William James 1938- *WhoAm 94*
Pearson, William Rowland 1923- *WhoScEn 94*
Pearson of Rannoch, Baron 1942- *Who 94*
Peart, Brian 1925- *Who 94*
Peart, Jerry Linn 1948- *WhoAmA 93*
Peart, Michael John 1943- *Who 94*
Peart, (William) Stanley 1922- *IntWW 93, Who 94*
Pearthree, Pippa *WhoHol 92*
Pearton, Stephen John 1957- *WhoScEn 94*
Peary, Harold *WhoCom*
Peary, Harold d1985 *WhoHol 92*
Peary, Robert Edwin 1856-1920 *WhWE*
Peary, Timothy H. 1943- *WhoAmP 93*
Peasback, David R. *WhoAm 94, WhoFI 94*
Pease *Who 94*
Pease, Carol Helene 1949- *WhoAm 94*
Pease, David G. 1932- *WhoAmA 93*
Pease, David Gordon 1932- *WhoAm 94*
Pease, Deborah *DrAPF 93*
Pease, Denise Louise 1953- *WhoBlA 94*
Pease, Donald E. 1936- *WhoAm 94, WhoFI 94*
Pease, Donald James 1931- *WhoAm 94, WhoAmP 93*
Pease, Edward Allan 1951- *WhoAmP 93, WhoMW 93*
Pease, Howard 1894- *WhAm 10*
Pease, (Clarence) Howard 1894-1974 *ConAu 41NR*
Pease, Howard Franklin 1939- *WhoScEn 94*
Pease, James 1916-1967 *NewGrDO*
Pease, John *EncSF 93*
Pease, Louise McNeill 1911-1993 *NewYTBS 93*
Pease, Marita LuAnn 1958- *WhoMW 93*
Pease, Nickolas Allen 1954- *WhoWest 94*
Pease, Rendel Sebastian 1922- *IntWW 93, Who 94*
Pease, Richard Thorn 1922- *Who 94*
Pease, Robert *DrAPF 93*
Pease, Robert John Claude 1922- *Who 94*
Pease, Roger Fabian Wedgwood 1936- *WhoAm 94*
Pease, Roland F., Jr. *DrAPF 93*
Pease, Rosamund Dorothy Benson 1935- *Who 94*
Pease, Vincent *Who 94*
Pease, (Alfred) Vincent 1926- *Who 94*
Peasland, Bruce Randall 1945- *WhoFI 94, WhoWest 94*
Peaslee, David Chase 1922- *WhoScEn 94*
Peaslee, James M. 1952- *WhoAm 94, WhoAmL 94*
Peaslee, Janice L. 1935- *WhoAmP 93*
Peaslee, Kent Dean 1956- *WhoScEn 94*
Peaslee, Margaret Mae Hermanek 1935- *WhoAm 94*
Peaslee, Maurice Keenan 1950- *WhoAmL 94*
Peaslee, Richard Cutts 1930- *WhoAm 94*
Peat, F. David 1938- *WrDr 94*
Peat, Gerrard (Charles) 1920- *Who 94*
Peat, Lawrence Joseph 1928- *Who 94*
Peat, Michael Charles Gerrard 1949- *Who 94*
Peat, Randall Dean 1935- *WhoAm 94*
Peat, (William Wood) Watson 1922- *Who 94*
Peattie, Lisa Redfield 1924- *WhoAm 94*
Peattie, Yvonne d1990 *WhoHol 92*
Peavey, John T. *WhoAmP 93*
Peavler, Nancy Jean 1951- *WhoAm 94*
Peavler, Terry J. 1942- *WrDr 94*
Peavy, Homer Louis, Jr. 1924- *WhoFI 94, WhoMW 93*
Peavy, James Edwin 1920- *WhoAmP 93*
Peavy, John W., Jr. 1943- *WhoBlA 94*
Peavy, Linda *DrAPF 93*
Peavy, Robert A. 1938- *WhoAm 94, WhoAmL 94*
Peavy, S. Lanny 1938- *WhoIns 94*
Peay, Francis *WhoBlA 94*
Peay, Isaac Charles, Sr. 1910- *WhoBlA 94*
Peay, Samuel 1939- *WhoBlA 94*
Pebbles 1965- *WhoBlA 94*
Pebereau, Georges Alexandre 1931- *IntWW 93*
Pecano, Donald Carl 1948- *WhoAm 94*
Peccarelli, Anthony Marando 1928- *WhoAmL 94, WhoMW 93*
Peccei, Roberto Daniele 1942- *WhoWest 94*
Pecchenino, J. Ronald 1932- *WhoAmA 93*
Peccorini, Francisco Letona 1915-1989 *WhAm 10*
Peche, Dale C. 1928- *WhoAmA 93*
Pecheur, Bruce d1973 *WhoHol 92*
Pecheur, Sierra *WhoHol 92*
Pechewlys, Charles 1949- *WhoAmL 94*
Pechilis, William John 1924- *WhoAm 94*
Pechillo, Jerome Arthur 1919-1991 *WhAm 10*
Pechman, Joseph Aaron 1918-1989 *WhAm 10*
Pechmann, Cornelia Ann Rachel 1959- *WhoWest 94*
Pechner, Gerhard 1903-1969 *NewGrDO*
Pechous, Robert C. *WhoAmP 93*
Pecht, Gerard G. 1953- *WhoAmL 94*
Pechtel, Curtis Theodore 1920- *WhoWest 94*
Pechter, Steven Jerome 1958- *WhoFI 94*
Pechukas, Philip 1942- *WhoAm 94*
Pecina, Ludmila Symonauna 1950- *LngBDD*
Peck, A. William 1938- *WhoScEn 94*
Peck, Abraham 1945- *WhoAm 94*
Peck, Arthur John, Jr. 1940- *WhoAm 94*
Peck, Austin H., Jr. 1913- *WhoAm 94*
Peck, Barbara May 1926- *WhoAmP 93*
Peck, Bernard Sidney 1915- *WhoAm 94*
Peck, Bob *WhoHol 92*
Peck, Brian *WhoHol 92*
Peck, Cecilia 1958- *WhoHol 92*
Peck, Charles Edward 1925- *WhoAm 94*
Peck, Charles S. 1947- *WhoWest 94*
Peck, Curtiss Steven 1947- *WhoMW 93*
Peck, Dale 1968?- *ConLC 81 [port]*
Peck, Dallas Lynn 1929- *WhoAm 94, WhoScEn 94*
Peck, Daniel Farnum 1927- *WhoAm 94*
Peck, David *WhoHol 92*
Peck, David (Edward) 1917- *Who 94*
Peck, David Warner 1902-1990 *WhAm 10*
Peck, Deana S. 1947- *WhoAm 94, WhoAmL 94*
Peck, Dianne Kawecki 1945- *WhoScEn 94*
Peck, Donald Harvey 1945- *WhoWest 94*
Peck, Donald Vincent 1930- *WhoAm 94*
Peck, Douglas Edward 1961- *WhoAmL 94*
Peck, Douglas Robert 1960- *WhoBlA 94*
Peck, Ed *WhoHol 92*
Peck, Edmund James 1850-1924 *EncNAR*
Peck, Edward d1970 *WhoAmA 93N*
Peck, Edward (Heywood) 1915- *Who 94*
Peck, Edward L. 1944- *WhoAmL 94*
Peck, Edward Lionel 1929- *WhoAm 94, WhoAmP 93*
Peck, Edwin Russell 1931- *WhoAm 94*
Peck, Ellie Enriquez 1934- *WhoAmP 93, WhoHisp 94, WhoWest 94*
Peck, Ernest James, Jr. 1941- *WhoWest 94*
Peck, Fred Neil 1945- *WhoAm 94, WhoFI 94, WhoScEn 94*
Peck, Frederic C(arleton) 1894- *WhAm 10*
Peck, Gail J. *DrAPF 93*
Peck, Gaillard Ray, Jr. 1940- *WhoFI 94, WhoScEn 94, WhoWest 94*
Peck, Garnet Edward 1930- *WhoAm 94*
Peck, George 1950- *WhoHol 92*
Peck, Gregory 1916- *IntMPA 94, IntWW 93, Who 94, WhoAm 94, WhoHol 92*
Peck, Gregory Lester 1952- *WhoBlA 94*
Peck, J. Eddie *WhoHol 92*
Peck, James d1993 *NewYTBS 93 [port]*
Peck, James Edward 1907- *WhoAmA 93*
Peck, James M. 1945- *WhoAmL 94*
Peck, James Stevenson 1923- *WhoAm 94*
Peck, Jeffrey A. 1946- *WhoAmL 94*
Peck, Joan Kay 1959- *WhoScEn 94*
Peck, John *DrAPF 93*
Peck, John (Frederick) 1941- *WrDr 94*
Peck, John (Howard) 1913- *Who 94*
Peck, John Mason 1789-1858 *DcAmReB 2*
Peck, John Thomas 1950- *WhoWest 94*
Peck, John W. 1913- *WhoAm 94, WhoAmL 94, WhoMW 93*
Peck, John Weld 1944- *WhoAmL 94*
Peck, Judith 1930- *WhoAmA 93*
Peck, Lee Barnes 1942- *WhoAmA 93*
Peck, Leontyne Clay 1958- *WhoBlA 94*
Peck, Louis P. 1918- *WhoAmP 93*
Peck, M(organ) Scott 1936- *WrDr 94*
Peck, Maryly VanLeer 1930- *WhoAm 94*
Peck, Merton Joseph 1925- *WrDr 94*
Peck, Michael Dickens 1953- *WhoScEn 94*
Peck, Michael Patrick 1949- *WhoAmL 94*
Peck, Morgan Scott 1936- *WhoAm 94*
Peck, Neil 1939- *WhoAm 94, WhoAmL 94*
Peck, Paul Arthur 1926- *WhoAm 94*
Peck, Paul Lachlan 1928- *WhoWest 94*
Peck, Ralph Brazelton 1912- *WhoAm 94*
Peck, Ray L. 1926- *WhoAmP 93*
Peck, Raymond A., Jr. *WhoAmP 93*
Peck, Raymond Charles, Sr. 1937- *WhoWest 94*
Peck, Richard *DrAPF 93*
Peck, Richard (Wayne) 1934- *TwCYAW, WrDr 94*
Peck, Richard Cleon 1917- *WhoAm 94, WhoAmL 94*
Peck, Richard E(arl) 1936- *EncSF 93*
Peck, Richard Earl 1936- *WhoAm 94, WhoWest 94*
Peck, Richard Leslie 1937- *Who 94*
Peck, Richard Wayne 1934- *WhoAm 94*
Peck, Robert 1924- *WhoAmP 93*
Peck, Robert David 1929- *WhoAm 94*
Peck, Robert McCracken 1952- *WhoScEn 94*
Peck, Robert Newton 1928- *TwCYAW, WrDr 94*
Peck, Robert S(tephen) 1953- *ConAu 141*
Peck, Rodney R. 1945- *WhoAmL 94*
Peck, Russell 1956- *WhoMW 93*
Peck, Russell A. 1933- *WhoAm 94*
Peck, Shauna Arlene 1955- *WhoWest 94*
Peck, Stanley Edwards 1916- *Who 94*
Peck, Stephen B. 1951- *WhoAmL 94*
Peck, Stephen John 1956- *WhoFI 94*
Peck, Steven *WhoHol 92*
Peck, Sylvia *DrAPF 93*
Peck, Sylvia 1953- *WrDr 94*
Peck, Templeton 1908- *WhoAm 94*
Peck, Theodore Richard 1931- *WhoMW 93*
Peck, Tony 1957- *WhoHol 92*
Peck, Vivian Rosetta 1924- *WhoAmP 93*
Peck, William Arno 1933- *WhoAm 94*
Peck, William Henry 1932- *WhoAm 94, WhoAmA 93*
Peck, William R., III 1931- *WhoAmP 93*
Peckar, Robert S. 1946- *WhoAmL 94*
Peckenpaugh, Angela *DrAPF 93*
Peckenpaugh, Robert Earl 1926- *WhoAm 94, WhoFI 94*
Pecker, David J. 1951- *WhoAm 94, WhoFI 94*
Pecker, Jean-Claude 1923- *IntWW 93*
Peckerman, Bruce Martin 1949- *WhoAmL 94*
Peckford, (Alfred) Brian 1942- *IntWW 93, Who 94*
Peckham, Arthur John 1920- *Who 94*
Peckham, Donald Eugene 1922- *WhoAm 94*
Peckham, Frances Miles d1959 *WhoHol 92*
Peckham, Howard Henry 1910- *WhoAm 94*
Peckham, John Munroe, III 1933- *WhoAm 94*
Peckham, Michael John 1935- *IntWW 93, Who 94*
Peckham, Morse 1914- *WrDr 94*
Peckham, Nicholas 1940- *WhoAmA 93*
Peckham, P. Hunter 1944- *WhoScEn 94*
Peckham, Robert Dabney 1946- *WhoAm 94*
Peckham, Robert F. d1993 *NewYTBS 93 [port]*
Peckham, Rufus Wheeler, Jr. 1928- *WhoAmP 93*
Peckinpah, Sam d1984 *WhoHol 92*
Peckinpaugh, Jack *WhoIns 94*
Peckinpaugh, William Eugene 1947- *WhoFI 94*
Peckolick, Alan 1940- *WhoAm 94*
Peckover, Richard Stuart 1942- *Who 94*
Pecora, Frank Anthony 1930- *WhoAmP 93*
Pecora, Louis Michael 1947- *WhoScEn 94*
Pecora, Robert 1938- *WhoAm 94, WhoWest 94*

Pendergast, Edward G. 1938- *WhoIns 94*
Pendergast, Edward Gaylord 1938- *WhoAm 94*
Pendergast, James *DrAPF 93*
Pendergast, John Joseph, III 1936- *WhoAm 94*
Pendergast, Russell A. d1993 *NewYTBS 93*
Pendergast, William Ross 1931- *WhoAm 94*
Penderghast, Thomas Frederick 1936- *WhoWest 94*
Pendergraft, Michele M. 1954- *WhoBlA 94*
Pendergraft, Norman Elveis 1934- *WhoAmA 93*
Pendergraft, Phyllis M. 1937- *WhoAmP 93*
Pendergrass, Emma H. *WhoBlA 94*
Pendergrass, Eugene P. 1895- *WhAm 10*
Pendergrass, Henry Pancoast 1925- *WhoAm 94*
Pendergrass, Margaret E. 1912- *WhoBlA 94*
Pendergrass, Teddy 1950- *WhoAm 94, WhoHol 92*
Pendergrass, Theodore D. 1950- *WhoBlA 94*
Penders, John Patrick 1942- *WhoAmL 94*
Pendexter, Joan Marie 1947- *WhoAmP 93*
Pendle, Karin 1939- *ConAu 141*
Pendlebury, Edward 1925- *Who 94*
Pendleton, Austin 1940- *IntMPA 94, WhoHol 92*
Pendleton, Barbara Jean 1924- *WhoAm 94, WhoMW 93*
Pendleton, Bill *WhoAmP 93*
Pendleton, Billy 1934- *WhoAmP 93*
Pendleton, Brian Clarke 1941- *WhoAmP 93*
Pendleton, Clarence McClane, Jr. 1930-1988 *AfrAmAl 6 [port]*
Pendleton, Dave *WhoHol 92*
Pendleton, Don(ald Eugene) 1927- *EncSF 93, WrDr 94*
Pendleton, Edmund 1721-1803 *WhAmRev*
Pendleton, Edmund E. 1922- *WhoAmP 93*
Pendleton, Elmer Dean, Jr. 1927- *WhoAm 94*
Pendleton, Eugene Barbour, Jr. 1913- *WhoAm 94*
Pendleton, Florence Howard *WhoAmP 93, WhoBlA 94*
Pendleton, Gary Herman 1947- *WhoAm 94*
Pendleton, Gaylord (Steve) *WhoHol 92*
Pendleton, Joan Marie 1954- *WhoScEn 94*
Pendleton, Joey 1946- *WhoAmP 93*
Pendleton, Mary Caroline *WhoAmA 93*
Pendleton, Mary Catherine 1940- *WhoAm 94*
Pendleton, Moses Robert Andrew 1949- *WhoAm 94*
Pendleton, Nat d1967 *WhoHol 92*
Pendleton, Othniel Alsop 1911- *WhoFI 94, WhoWest 94*
Pendleton, Peggy A. *WhoAmP 93*
Pendleton, Ralph Cooper 1895- *WhAm 10*
Pendleton, Ronald Kenneth 1940- *WhoWest 94*
Pendleton, Sumner Alden 1918- *WhoAm 94*
Pendleton, Terry Lee 1960- *WhoAm 94, WhoBlA 94*
Pendleton, Verne H., Jr. 1945- *WhoScEn 94, WhoWest 94*
Pendleton, Wyman 1916- *WhoHol 92*
Pendley, Donald Lee 1950- *WhoFI 94*
Pendley, William Tyler 1936- *WhoAm 94*
Pendower, John Edward Hicks 1927- *Who 94*
Pendray, (George) Edward 1901-1987 *EncSF 93*
Pendred, Piers Loughnan 1943- *Who 94*
Pendrill, Viviana *WhoHisp 94*
Pendry, John Brian 1943- *Who 94*
Pendry, Thomas 1934- *Who 94*
Pendse, Sripad Narayan 1913- *ConWorW 93*
Pendygraft, George William 1946- *WhoAmL 94*
Penecilla, Gerard Ledesma 1956- *WhoScEn 94*
Pene du Bois, William (Sherman) 1916-1993 *ConAu 41NR*
Penegar, Kenneth Lawing 1932- *WhoAm 94*
Penelas, Alex 1961- *WhoHisp 94*
Penella (Moreno), Manuel 1880-1939 *NewGrDO*
Penella, Emma 1930- *WhoHol 92*
Penelton, Barbara Spencer 1937- *WhoBlA 94*
Penfield, Paul Livingstone, Jr. 1933- *WhoAm 94*
Penfold, Merimeri 1924- *BlmGWL*
Penfold, Nita *DrAPF 93*
Penfold, Robert Bernard 1916- *Who 94*
Peng, Chang-Shyh 1961- *WhoAsA 94*
Peng, Dachung Pat 1946- *WhoAsA 94*
Peng, George Tso Chih 1928- *WhoAsA 94*
Peng, Jen-Chieh 1949- *WhoAsA 94*
Peng, Liang-Chuan 1936- *WhoFI 94, WhoScEn 94*
Peng, Syd S. 1939- *WhoAsA 94*
Peng, Ying-shin Christine 1945- *WhoAsA 94*
Peng, Zhong 1946- *WhoWest 94*
Peng Chong 1909- *IntWW 93*
Peng Chong 1915- *WhoPRCh 91 [port]*
Peng Deqing 1915- *WhoPRCh 91*
Peng Di *WhoPRCh 91 [port]*
Peng Dixian 1909- *WhoPRCh 91 [port]*
Pengelly, Richard Anthony 1925- *Who 94*
Peng Gang *WhoPRCh 91*
Peng Gongge *WhoPRCh 91*
Peng Guanghan *WhoPRCh 91*
Penghlis, Thaao *WhoHol 92*
Peng Huanwu 1915- *IntWW 93*
Peng Huanwu 1925- *WhoPRCh 91*
Pengilly, Brian William 1930- *WhoAm 94*
Peng Jiaqing 1909- *WhoPRCh 91 [port]*
Peng Jinzhang *WhoPRCh 91*
Penglase, Frank Dennis 1940- *WhoAm 94*
Peng Peiyun 1929- *IntWW 93, WhoPRCh 91 [port], WhoWomW 91*
Peng Qingyuan 1920- *WhoPRCh 91 [port]*
Peng Qingyun *WhoPRCh 91*
Peng Shaoyi 1917- *WhoPRCh 91*
Peng Shilu 1925- *IntWW 93, WhoPRCh 91 [port]*
Peng Teh-Huai 1898-1974 *HisDcKW*
Peng Xiaolian 1953- *WhoPRCh 91 [port]*
Peng Xuefu 1940- *WhoPRCh 91*
Peng Yaoming *WhoPRCh 91*
Peng Yingming *WhoPRCh 91*
Peng Youjin 1914- *WhoPRCh 91 [port]*
Peng Yu 1941- *WhoPRCh 91 [port]*
Peng Zhaoqin 1963- *WhoPRCh 91 [port]*
Peng Zhen 1902- *IntWW 93, WhoPRCh 91 [port]*
Penha, James W. *DrAPF 93*
Penha, Joseph De La fl. 168-?-169-? *WhWE*
Penhale, Polly Ann 1947- *WhoScEn 94*
Penhaligon, Annette 1946- *Who 94*
Penhaligon, Susan 1949- *WhoHol 92*
Penhall, Bruce *WhoHol 92*
Penhallow, Richard 1906- *WhoAmP 93*
Penherski, Zbigniew 1935- *NewGrDO*
Penhune, John Paul 1936- *WhoAm 94, WhoScEn 94, WhoWest 94*
Penick, George Dial, Jr. 1948- *WhoAm 94*
Penick, Joe Edward 1920- *WhoAm 94*
Penikett, Antony David John 1945- *WhoAm 94*
Penington, David Geoffrey 1930- *IntWW 93, Who 94*
Penisten, Gary D. 1931- *WhoAmP 93*
Penisten, Gary Dean 1931- *WhoAm 94, WhoFI 94*
Peniston, CeCe *WhoBlA 94*
Peniston, Louis Tandy 1919- *WhoAmP 93*
Penix, Bill 1922- *WhoAmP 93*
Penkava, Robert Ray 1942- *WhoAm 94*
Penke, Cynthia Marie 1963- *WhoMW 93*
Penkethman, William d1725 *BlmGEL*
Penkoff, Diane Witmer 1945- *WhoWest 94*
Penkoff, Ronald Peter 1932- *WhoAmA 93*
Penland, Arnold Clifford, Jr. 1933- *WhoAm 94*
Penland, John Thomas 1930- *WhoAm 94*
Penley, Deborah Williamson 1949- *WhoMW 93*
Penley, William Henry 1917- *Who 94*
Penlington, Ross Grange 1931- *Who 94*
Penman, Ian Dalgleish 1931- *Who 94*
Penman, John 1913- *Who 94*
Penman, Lea d1962 *WhoHol 92*
Penman, Paul Duane 1937- *WhoScEn 94*
Penn, Alvin W. *WhoAmP 93*
Penn, Arthur 1922- *IntMPA 94, IntWW 93*
Penn, Arthur (Hiller) 1922- *WrDr 94*
Penn, Arthur Hiller 1922- *WhoAm 94*
Penn, Charles E. 1928- *WhoBlA 94*
Penn, Christopher *IntMPA 94*
Penn, Christopher 1966- *WhoHol 92*
Penn, Eric d1993 *NewYTBS 93, Who 94N*
Penn, Gerald Melville 1937- *WhoMW 93*
Penn, Hannah Callowhill 1671-1726 *BlmGWL*
Penn, Irving 1917- *IntWW 93, WhoAm 94, WhoAmA 93*
Penn, John *WrDr 94*
Penn, John 1729-1795 *WhAmRev*
Penn, John 1740-1788 *WhAmRev*
Penn, John Garrett 1932- *CngDr 93, WhoAm 94, WhoAmL 94, WhoBlA 94*
Penn, John Hull 1944- *WhoMW 93*
Penn, John S. 1926- *WhoAmP 93*
Penn, Leo 1921- *WhoHol 92*
Penn, Leonard d1975 *WhoHol 92*
Penn, Luther 1924-1977 *WhoBlA 94N*
Penn, Matthew *WhoHol 92*
Penn, Mindell Lewis 1944- *WhoBlA 94*
Penn, Nolan E. 1928- *WhoBlA 94*
Penn, Richard 1945- *Who 94*
Penn, Richard, Jr. 1736-1811 *WhAmRev*
Penn, Robert Clarence 1943- *WhoBlA 94*
Penn, Ronald Hulen 1951- *WhoMW 93*
Penn, Sean 1960- *CurBio 93 [port], IntMPA 94, WhoAm 94, WhoHol 92*
Penn, Shelton C. 1925- *WhoBlA 94*
Penn, Sherry Eve 1941- *WhoScEn 94*
Penn, Stanley William 1928- *WhoAm 94*
Penn, William 1644-1718 *AmSocL [port], DcAmReB 2, HisWorL [port]*
Penn, William S. *DrAPF 93*
Penn, Zachary Owen 1968- *WhoWest 94*
Penna, Nancy Sue 1956- *WhoMW 93*
Penna, Sandro 1906-1977 *GayLL*
Pennak, Robert William 1912- *WhoWest 94*
Penn and Teller *WhoCom, WhoHol 92*
Pennaneach-Biova-Soumi, Bruno Samuel 1941- *IntWW 93*
Pennant *Who 94*
Pennant, David Edward Thornton 1912- *Who 94*
Pennant, Edmund *DrAPF 93*
Pennant-Rea, Rupert Lascelles 1948- *IntWW 93, Who 94*
Pennarini, Aloys 1870-1927 *NewGrDO*
Pennario, Leonard 1924- *WhoAm 94*
Penn-Atkins, Barbara A. 1935- *WhoBlA 94*
Pennebaker, D. A. 1926- *IntMPA 94*
Pennebaker, John David 1943- *WhoAmP 93*
Pennel, John d1993 *NewYTBS 93 [port]*
Pennell, Jon *WhoHol 92*
Pennell, Larry *WhoHol 92*
Pennell, (James Henry) Leslie 1906- *Who 94*
Pennell, Nicholas *WhoHol 92*
Pennell, R. O. d1934 *WhoHol 92*
Pennell, William Brooke 1935- *WhoAm 94, WhoAmL 94*
Penneman, Robert Allen 1919- *WhoAm 94*
Penner, Fred 1946- *ConMus 10 [port]*
Penner, Fred (Ralph Cornelius) 1946- *WrDr 94*
Penner, Hans Henry 1934- *WhoAm 94*
Penner, Harry Harold Hamilton, Jr. 1945- *WhoAm 94*
Penner, Joe d1941 *WhoHol 92*
Penner, Joe 1904-1941 *WhoCom*
Penner, Jonathan *DrAPF 93*
Penner, Jonathan 1940- *WrDr 94*
Penner, Karen Marie 1972- *WhoScEn 94*
Penner, Leona Joyce 1944- *WhoMW 93*
Penner, Roland 1924- *WhoAm 94*
Penner, Rudolph Gerhard 1936- *WhoAm 94*
Penner, Stanford Solomon 1921- *WhoAm 94, WhoWest 94*
Penner, Vernon D. 1939- *WhoAmP 93*
Penner, William A. 1933- *WhoAm 94*
Penney, Allan *WhoHol 92*
Penney, Alphonsus Liguori 1924- *Who 94, WhoAm 94*
Penney, Bryan Le Roy Humphrey 1954- *WhoWest 94*
Penney, Charles Rand 1923- *WhoAm 94, WhoAmA 93, WhoAmL 94, WhoFI 94*
Penney, David Wright 1954- *WhoMW 93*
Penney, Edmund F. 1926- *WrDr 94*
Penney, Edward Thomas 1935- *WhoAm 94*
Penney, Ian 1960- *SmATA 76 [port]*
Penney, Jacqueline 1930- *WhoAmA 93*
Penney, James 1910-1982 *WhoAmA 93N*
Penney, James John 1946- *WhoMW 93*
Penney, Jennifer Beverly 1946- *Who 94*
Penney, Penelope Anne 1942- *Who 94*
Penney, Reginald John 1919- *Who 94*
Penney, Robert Allan 1959- *WhoScEn 94*
Penney, Sherry Hood 1937- *WhoAm 94*
Pennfield, Edward B. 1945- *WhoAmL 94*
Penni, Serafina fl. 1743- *NewGrDO*
Pennica, Diane 1951- *WhoScEn 94*
Pennick, Aurie Alma 1947- *WhoBlA 94*
Pennick, Jack d1964 *WhoHol 92*
Pennick, Ronald *WhoHol 92*
Pennicott, Brian Thomas 1938- *Who 94*
Pennie, Hester 1931- *WrDr 94*
Pennie, Michael William 1936- *IntWW 93*
Penniman, Clara 1914- *WhoAm 94*
Penniman, Nicholas Griffith, IV 1938- *WhoAm 94, WhoFI 94, WhoMW 93*
Penniman, Richard Wayne 1932- *WhoAm 94, WhoBlA 94*
Penniman, W. David 1937- *WhoAm 94*
Penniman, William Howard 1948- *WhoAmL 94*
Pennine, Anthony P. 1927- *WhoAmP 93*
Penninger, Johannes Mathieu L. 1942- *WhoScEn 94*
Penninger, William Holt, Jr. 1954- *WhoAmL 94, WhoMW 93*
Penning-Rowsell, Edmund Lionel 1913- *Who 94*
Pennington, Ann d1971 *WhoHol 92*
Pennington, Beverly Melcher 1931- *WhoFI 94, WhoMW 93*
Pennington, Bruce 1944- *EncSF 93*
Pennington, Bruce Carter 1932- *WhoFI 94*
Pennington, Catherine Ann 1950- *WhoAmL 94*
Pennington, Dorothy Carolyn 1921- *WhoWest 94*
Pennington, Edith Mae d1974 *WhoHol 92*
Pennington, Edward Charles 1956- *WhoScEn 94*
Pennington, Eliberto Escamilla 1958- *WhoHisp 94*
Pennington, Estill Curtis 1950- *WhoAmA 93*
Pennington, J. Gordon 1927- *WhoAmP 93*
Pennington, James William Charles 1809-1870 *DcAmReB 2*
Pennington, Jesse C. 1938- *WhoBlA 94*
Pennington, Lee *DrAPF 93*
Pennington, Leenette Morse 1936- *WhoBlA 94*
Pennington, Mary Anne 1943- *WhoAm 94, WhoAmA 93*
Pennington, Mary Engle 1872-1952 *WorInv*
Pennington, Michael 1943- *ConTFT 11*
Pennington, Michael Richard 1961- *WhoAmL 94*
Pennington, Michael Vivian Fyfe 1943- *Who 94*
Pennington, Olin Oliver, Jr. 1939- *WhoAmL 94*
Pennington, Randy 1940- *WhoAmP 93*
Pennington, Richard Maier 1926- *WhoAm 94*
Pennington, Ricky Lewis 1959- *WhoMW 93*
Pennington, Robert Roland 1927- *Who 94*
Pennington, Rodney Edward 1956- *WhoScEn 94*
Pennington, Rodney Lee 1946- *WhoScEn 94*
Pennington, Sally 1953- *WhoAmA 93*
Pennington, Thomas K. 1936- *WhoIns 94*
Pennington, Walter Carter 1957- *WhoFI 94*
Pennington, William Sandford 1757-1826 *WhAmRev*
Pennisi, Francesco 1934- *NewGrDO*
Pennison, Clifford Francis 1913- *Who 94*
Pennisten, John William 1939- *WhoAm 94, WhoFI 94, WhoScEn 94*
Penniston, Gregory Kent 1957- *WhoWest 94*
Pennock, Baron d1993 *IntWW 93N, Who 94N*
Pennock, Cecil Alan 1946- *WhoWest 94*
Pennock, Christopher *WhoHol 92*
Pennock, David Lawson 1944- *WhoMW 93*
Pennock, Donald William 1915- *WhoAm 94, WhoFI 94, WhoScEn 94*
Pennock, George Tennant 1912- *WhoAm 94*
Pennock, James Roland 1906- *WhoAm 94*
Pennoyer, A. Sheldon 1888-1957 *WhoAmA 93N*
Pennoyer, Paul Geddes, Jr. 1920- *WhoAm 94*
Pennoyer, Robert M. 1925- *WhoAm 94*
Pennoyer, Russell Parsons 1951- *WhoFI 94*
Pennuto, James William 1936- *WhoAmA 93*
Penny *Who 94*
Penny, Aubrey John Robert 1917- *WhoAmA 93*
Penny, Charles Richard 1934- *WhoAm 94*
Penny, (Francis) David 1918- *Who 94*
Penny, David G(eorge) *EncSF 93*
Penny, Donald Charles 1935- *WhoAmA 93*
Penny, Frank d1946 *WhoHol 92*
Penny, James M., Jr. 1946- *WhoAmL 94*
Penny, Jennifer 1946- *IntDcB [port]*
Penny, Joe 1957- *WhoHol 92*
Penny, Joseph Noel Bailey 1916- *Who 94*
Penny, Nicholas Beaver 1949- *Who 94*
Penny, Robert 1935- *WhoBlA 94*
Penny, Robert L. 1940- *WhoBlA 94*
Penny, Roger Pratt 1936- *WhoAm 94, WhoFI 94*
Penny, Sydney 1971- *WhoHol 92*
Penny, Timothy J. 1951- *CngDr 93, WhoAmP 93*
Penny, Timothy Joseph 1951- *WhoAm 94, WhoMW 93*
Penny, William Lewis 1953- *WhoAmL 94*
Pennycuick, Colin James 1933- *Who 94*
Pennypacker, Barbara White 1946- *WhoScEn 94*
Pennypacker, James S. 1951- *WhoAmA 93*
Pennywell, Phillip, Jr. 1941- *WhoBlA 94*

Penot Lombart, Louis-Pierre 1744-c. 1800 *WhAmRev*
Penot Lombart de Noirmont, Rene-Hippolyte 1750-1792 *WhAmRev*
Penoyer, Ronald Joseph 1951- *WhoMW 93*
Penraat, Jaap 1918- *WhoScEn 94*
Penrhyn, Baron 1908- *Who 94*
Penrice, Arthur *EncSF 93*
Penrice, Geoffrey 1923- *Who 94*
Penrith, Bishop Suffragan of 1928- *Who 94*
Penrod, James Wilford 1934- *WhoAm 94*
Penrod, Kenneth Earl 1916- *WhoAm 94*
Penrose, Hon. Lord 1938- *Who 94*
Penrose, Charles d1952 *WhoHol 92*
Penrose, Charles, Jr. 1921- *WhoAm 94*
Penrose, Cynthia C. 1939- *WhoFI 94*
Penrose, Edith Tilton 1914- *IntWW 93, Who 94*
Penrose, George William *Who 94*
Penrose, John d1983 *WhoHol 92*
Penrose, John Hubert 1916- *Who 94*
Penrose, Oliver 1929- *IntWW 93, Who 94*
Penrose, Roger 1931- *IntWW 93, Who 94, WhoScEn 94, WrDr 94*
Penry, Deborah L. 1957- *WhoScEn 94*
Penry, James Kiffin 1929- *WhoAm 94, WhoScEn 94*
Penry, Kathryn Jane 1952- *WhoMW 93*
Penry, Walter E., Jr. *WhoAmP 93*
Penry-Davey, David Herbert 1942- *Who 94*
Pense, Alan Wiggins 1934- *WhoAm 94, WhoScEn 94*
Pensinger, John Lynn 1949- *WhoAmL 94*
Pensis, Henri Bram 1927- *WhoMW 93*
Pensis, Sharon B. 1964- *WhoMW 93*
Penskar, Mark Howard 1953- *WhoAm 94*
Penslar, Derek J(onathan) 1958- *WrDr 94*
Pensler, Jay Michael 1954- *WhoMW 93*
Penson, Edward Martin 1927- *WhoAm 94*
Penta, Virginia *WhoHol 92*
Pentak, Stephen 1951- *WhoAmA 93*
Pentas, Herodotos Antreas 1955- *WhoScEn 94*
Pentecost, David Henry 1938- *Who 94*
Pentecoste, Joseph C. 1918- *WhoBlA 94*
Pentelovitch, Robert Alan 1955- *WhoAmA 93*
Pentelow, Arthur 1924- *WhoHol 92*
Pentima, Vincent J. 1947- *WhoAmL 94*
Pentiuk, Randall Alan 1955- *WhoAmL 94, WhoMW 93*
Pentland, Barbara Lally 1912- *WhoAm 94*
Penton, Theo David, Jr. 1950- *WhoFI 94*
Pentony, DeVere Edwin 1924- *WhoWest 94*
Pentz, Donald Robert 1940- *WhoAmA 93*
Pentz, Martin Charles 1958- *WhoAmL 94*
Pentz, Paul 1940- *WhoAm 94, WhoFI 94*
Penuelas, Marcelino Company 1916- *WhoAm 94*
Penwarden, Duncan d1930 *WhoHol 92*
Penwell, Jones Clark 1921- *WhoWest 94*
Penz, Anton Jacob 1906- *WhoAm 94*
Penzavecchia, James *DrAPF 93*
Penzer, Geoffrey Ronald 1943- *Who 94*
Penzer, Mark 1932- *WhoAm 94*
Penzias, Arno Allan 1933- *IntWW 93, Who 94, WhoAm 94, WhoFI 94, WhoScEn 94, WorScD*
Penzien, Joseph 1924- *WhoAm 94*
Penzl, Herbert 1910- *WhoAm 94*
Peoples, Don *WhoAmP 93*
Peoples, Earl F., Sr. 1930- *WhoBlA 94*
Peoples, Erskine L. 1931- *WhoBlA 94*
Peoples, Florence W. 1940- *WhoBlA 94*
Peoples, Gregory Allan 1951- *WhoBlA 94*
Peoples, Harrison Promis, Jr. 1940- *WhoBlA 94*
Peoples, John *WhoAmP 93*
Peoples, John Arthur, Jr. 1926- *WhoAm 94, WhoBlA 94*
Peoples, John Derrick, Jr. 1951- *WhoBlA 94*
Peoples, Joyce P. 1937- *WhoBlA 94*
Peoples, Lucille Kimberly 1945- *WhoMW 93*
Peoples, Morgan D. 1919- *WrDr 94*
Peoples, Sesser R. 1934- *WhoBlA 94*
Peoples, Thomas Edward 1915- *WhoAm 94*
Peoples, Veo, Jr. 1947- *WhoBlA 94*
Pepe, Barbara Eilene 1951- *WhoWest 94*
Pepe, Frank A. 1931- *WhoAm 94*
Pepe, Louis Robert 1943- *WhoAmL 94, WhoAmP 93*
Pepe, Stephen Phillip 1943- *WhoAm 94, WhoAmL 94*
Pepe, Steven Douglas 1943- *WhoAmL 94*
Pepe, Teri-Anne 1967- *WhoScEn 94*
Peper, Christian Baird 1910- *WhoAm 94, WhoAmL 94, WhoFI 94, WhoMW 93*
Peper, George Frederick 1950- *WhoAm 94*
Peper, John H. 1952- *WhoAmL 94*
Pepich, Bruce Walter 1952- *WhoAm 94, WhoAmA 93*
Pepin, Jean-Luc 1924- *IntWW 93, WhoAm 94*
Pepin, John Nelson 1946- *WhoScEn 94*
Pepin, Lucie 1936- *IntWW 93*
Pepin, Marcel 1941- *WhoAm 94*
Pepin, Richard G., Jr. 1940- *WhoAmL 94*
Pepin, Timothy Leroy 1942- *WhoFI 94*
Pepine, Carl John 1941- *WhoAm 94*
Pepino, Leo P. 1927- *WhoAmP 93*
Pepito d1975 *WhoHol 92*
Pepitone, Byron Vincent 1918- *WhoAm 94*
Peplau, Hildegard Elizabeth 1909- *WhoAm 94*
Peplinski, Daniel Raymond 1951- *WhoScEn 94*
Peploe, Clare *IntMPA 94*
Peploe, Denis Frederic Neil d1993 *Who 94N*
Pepoli, Allesandro 1757-1796 *NewGrDO*
Pepoli, Carlo 1795-1881 *NewGrDO*
Pepoli, Sicinio 1684-1750 *NewGrDO*
Peponis, Harold Arthur 1928- *WhoMW 93*
Peponis, James Arthur 1934- *WhAm 10*
Peppard, Blaylock A. 1952- *WhoAmA 93*
Peppard, George 1928- *IntMPA 94, IntWW 93, WhoAm 94, WhoHol 92*
Peppard, Nadine Sheila 1922- *Who 94*
Peppas, Nikolaos Athanassiou 1948- *WhoAm 94*
Peppe, M. John 1941- *WhoIns 94*
Peppe, Rodney (Darrell) 1934- *SmATA 74 [port], WrDr 94*
Peppel, Heidi Karen Ross 1960- *WhoMW 93*
Pepper, Allan Michael 1943- *WhoAm 94, WhoAmL 94*
Pepper, Art d1982 *WhoHol 92*
Pepper, Barbara d1969 *WhoHol 92*
Pepper, Beverly 1924- *WhoAm 94, WhoAmA 93*
Pepper, Buddy 1922- *WhoHol 92*
Pepper, Buddy 1922-1993 *NewYTBS 93*
Pepper, Charles Hovey 1864-1950 *WhoAmA 93N*
Pepper, Claude Denson 1900-1989 *WhAm 10*
Pepper, Cynthia 1940- *WhoHol 92*
Pepper, Daniel Allen 1951- *WhoMW 93*
Pepper, Darrell Weldon 1946- *WhoWest 94*
Pepper, David Charles 1917- *IntWW 93*
Pepper, David J. 1962- *WhoScEn 94*
Pepper, David M. 1949- *WhoAm 94, WhoWest 94*
Pepper, Dorothy Mae 1932- *WhoScEn 94*
Pepper, Eugene Melvin 1934- *WhoAmL 94*
Pepper, Gordon Terry 1934- *Who 94*
Pepper, Helsey James d1928 *WhoHol 92*
Pepper, Ian L. 1946- *WhoAm 94*
Pepper, Jack d1979 *WhoHol 92*
Pepper, John Ennis, Jr. 1938- *IntWW 93, WhoAm 94, WhoFI 94*
Pepper, John Roy 1937- *WhoWest 94*
Pepper, Jonathon Lester 1955- *WhoAm 94*
Pepper, Kathleen Daly *WhoAmA 93*
Pepper, Kenneth Bruce 1913- *Who 94*
Pepper, Lawrence Anthony, Jr. 1943- *WhoAmP 93*
Pepper, Lennard J. 1931- *WhoAmP 93*
Pepper, Mark Jay 1957- *WhoFI 94*
Pepper, Michael 1942- *IntWW 93, Who 94*
Pepper, Robert d1964 *WhoHol 92*
Pepper, Steven A. 1955- *WhoAmL 94*
Pepper, Thomas Mark 1939- *WhoFI 94*
Pepper, William Burton, Jr. *WhoScEn 94*
Peppercorn, John Edward 1937- *WhoFI 94, WhoWest 94*
Pepperdene, Margaret Williams 1919- *WhoAm 94*
Pepperl, Joanne Margaret 1952- *WhoAmL 94, WhoMW 93*
Pepperman, Walter Leon, II 1939- *WhoAmL 94*
Peppers, Jerry P. 1946- *WhoAm 94, WhoAmL 94*
Peppers, Mary Jean 1955- *WhoMW 93*
Peppiatt, Hugh Stephen Kenneth 1930- *Who 94*
Peppiatt, Michael 1941- *ConAu 42NR*
Peppitt, John Raymond 1931- *Who 94*
Pepple, Daniel P. 1947- *WhoAmL 94*
Peppler, Daniel Darcy 1944- *WhoAm 94*
Peppler, William Norman 1925- *WhoAm 94*
Pepples, Ernest 1935- *WhoAm 94*
Peppmeier, John Dean 1944- *WhoMW 93*
Pepusch, Johann Christoph 1667-1752 *NewGrDO*
Pepyne, Edward Walter 1925- *WhoAm 94, WhoAmL 94*
Pepys *Who 94*
Pepys, Samuel 1633-1703 *BlmGEL*
Pera, Isabella 1945- *WhoAmA 93*
Pera, Rod James 1941- *WhoAmL 94*
Peradotto, John Joseph 1933- *WhoAm 94*
Peragallo, Mario 1910- *NewGrDO*
Perahia, Murray 1947- *ConMus 10 [port], IntWW 93, Who 94, WhoAm 94*
Perak, H.H. Sultan of 1928- *IntWW 93*
Perakis, Robert Anthony 1953- *WhoAmP 93*
Perakos, Sperie P. 1915- *IntMPA 94*
Perales, Cesar A. 1940- *WhoHisp 94*
Perales, Christopher Oscar 1962- *WhoHisp 94*
Perales, Eduardo *WhoHisp 94*
Perales, Jorge Inocente 1951- *WhoHisp 94*
Perales, Mirta de *WhoHisp 94*
Peralta, Angela 1845-1883 *NewGrDO*
Peralta, Everett Figueroa 1954- *WhoWest 94*
Peralta, Frank Carlos 1946- *WhoHisp 94*
Peralta, Frederick A. *WhoAmP 93*
Peralta, Frederick A., Jr. *WhoHisp 94*
Peralta, Gabriel d1977 *WhoHol 92*
Peralta, Ignacio Diego 1949- *WhoHisp 94*
Peralta, Mauro G. 1947- *WhoHisp 94*
Peralta, Richard Carl 1949- *WhoHisp 94, WhoWest 94*
Peralta Azurdia, Enrique 1908- *IntWW 93*
Peranda, Marco Gioseppe c. 1625-1675 *NewGrDO*
Peranich, Diane C. 1940- *WhoAmP 93*
Peranski, Robert Zigmunt 1935- *WhoIns 94*
Peranteau, Michael 1951- *WhoAmA 93*
Perara, Mitchell Mebane 1924- *WhoBlA 94*
Perard, Victor S. 1867-1957 *WhoAmA 93N*
Peratt, Anthony Lee 1940- *WhoScEn 94, WhoWest 94*
Peratt, Karen Lee 1954- *WhoWest 94*
Peraza-Labrador, Luis Francisco 1958- *WhoHisp 94*
Perazzo, Glen Thomas 1963- *WhoWest 94*
Perben, Dominique 1945- *IntWW 93*
Percas de Ponseti, Helena 1921- *WhoAm 94*
Perceval *Who 94*
Perceval, Viscount 1934- *Who 94*
Perceval, John de Burgh 1923- *IntWW 93*
Perceval, Michael 1936- *Who 94*
Perceval, Robert Westby 1914- *Who 94*
Perchard, Colin William 1940- *Who 94*
Perche Rivas, Emilio *WhoHisp 94*
Perchik, Benjamin Ivan 1941- *WhoScEn 94*
Perchik, Simon *DrAPF 93*
Percier, Charles 1764-1838 *NewGrDO*
Percival, Anthony (Edward) 1910- *Who 94*
Percival, Horace d1961 *WhoHol 92*
Percival, Ian 1921- *Who 94*
Percival, (Walter) Ian *Who 94*
Percival, Ian Colin 1931- *Who 94*
Percival, John 1927- *Who 94*
Percival, John 1937- *Who 94*
Percival, Lance 1933- *WhoHol 92*
Percival, Robert C. 1908- *WrDr 94*
Percival, Robert Clarendon 1908- *Who 94*
Percival, Walter d1934 *WhoHol 92*
Percival-Prescott, Westby William 1923- *Who 94*
Percival Smith, Anthony Michael *Who 94*
Percle, Lori Dupre 1961- *WhoFI 94*
Percoto, Caterina 1812-1887 *BlmGWL*
Percovich Roca, Luis *IntWW 93*
Percus, Jerome Kenneth 1926- *WhoAm 94, WhoScEn 94*
Percy *BlmGEL, Who 94*
Percy, Algernon Eustace Hugh H. *Who 94*
Percy, Ann Buchanan 1940- *WhoAm 94, WhoAmA 93*
Percy, Charles Harting 1919- *IntWW 93, WhoAm 94, WhoAmP 93*
Percy, Charles Henry *BlmGWL*
Percy, Eileen d1973 *WhoHol 92*
Percy, Esme d1957 *WhoHol 92*
Percy, F. Walker 1916-1990 *EncSF 93*
Percy, Hugh 1742-1817 *AmRev, WhAmRev [port]*
Percy, John Howard 1945- *WhoAmL 94*
Percy, John Pitkeathly 1942- *Who 94*
Percy, John R(ees) 1941- *ConAu 140*
Percy, Lee Edward 1953- *WhoWest 94*
Percy, Richard Bruce 1947- *WhoMW 93*
Percy, Rodney Algernon 1924- *Who 94*
Percy, Thomas 1729-1811 *BlmGEL*
Percy, W. S. d1946 *WhoHol 92*
Percy, Walker 1916-1990 *WhAm 10*
Perdang, Jean Marcel 1940- *WhoScEn 94*
Perdigó, Luisa Marina 1947- *WhoHisp 94*
Perdomo, Eduardo *WhoHisp 94*
Perdomo, George Luis 1961- *WhoHisp 94*
Perdreau, Cornelia *WhoBlA 94*
Perdue, Beverly Moore 1948- *WhoAmP 93*
Perdue, Charles L., Jr. 1930- *WrDr 94*
Perdue, Christine H. 1949- *WhoAm 94, WhoAmL 94*
Perdue, Derelys *WhoHol 92*
Perdue, Franklin P. *WhoAm 94, WhoFI 94*
Perdue, Franklin Roosevelt 1944- *WhoBlA 94*
Perdue, Garland Day 1926- *WhoAm 94*
Perdue, George *WhoAmP 93, WhoBlA 94*
Perdue, George 1946- *WhoAmP 93*
Perdue, James Everett 1916- *WhoAm 94*
Perdue, John F. 1912- *WhoBlA 94*
Perdue, Julia M. Ward 1938- *WhoBlA 94*
Perdue, Melina Dee 1951- *WhoFI 94*
Perdue, Pamela Price 1962- *WhoScEn 94*
Perdue, Richard Gordon 1910- *Who 94*
Perdue, Theda 1949- *WhoAm 94*
Perdunn, Richard Francis 1915- *WhoAm 94*
Perdurabo, Frater *GayLL*
Perea, Alicia 1955- *WhoHisp 94*
Perea, Juan F. 1955- *WhoHisp 94*
Perea, Sylvia Jean 1941- *WhoHisp 94*
Perea, Toribio 1944- *WhoHisp 94*
Perec, Georges 1936-1982 *ConAu 141*
Pereda, Delfina Haydeé 1921- *WhoHisp 94*
Pereda, Francisco Eugenio 1923- *WhoHisp 94*
Pereda, John *WhoHisp 94*
Peregoff, Lee Steven 1959- *WhoFI 94*
Peregoy, Calvin *EncSF 93*
Peregrin, Magda Elizabeth 1923- *WhoAmA 93, WhoWest 94*
Peregrina, La *BlmGWL*
Peregrina, Eddie d1977 *WhoHol 92*
Peregrine, David 1954-1989 *WhAm 10*
Peregrine, David Seymour 1921- *WhoScEn 94*
Peregrine, Gwilym Rhys 1924- *Who 94*
Peregrino, Hugo *WhoHisp 94*
Perehudoff, William W. 1919- *WhoAmA 93*
Pereira, Alvaro Javier 1963- *WhoHisp 94*
Pereira, Angelo R. *WhoFI 94*
Pereira, Aristides Maria 1923- *IntWW 93*
Pereira, Arthur Leonard 1906- *Who 94*
Pereira, Carmen *WhoWomW 91*
Pereira, Charles *Who 94*
Pereira, (Herbert) Charles 1913- *IntWW 93, Who 94*
Pereira, Edmund S. 1921- *WhoAmP 93*
Pereira, Enrique A. *WhoHisp 94*
Pereira, Francisca *WhoWomW 91*
Pereira, Frederick A. 1942- *WhoHisp 94*
Pereira, Helio Gelli 1918- *IntWW 93, Who 94*
Pereira, I. Rice 1901-1971 *WhoAmA 93N*
Pereira, Jacobo Rodriguez 1715-1780 *EncDeaf*
Pereira, Jose Francisco 1935- *WhoScEn 94*
Pereira, Julio Cesar 1944- *WhoHisp 94*
Pereira, Luis G. 1962- *WhoHisp 94*
Pereira, Margaret 1928- *Who 94*
Pereira, Sarah Martin 1909- *WhoBlA 94*
Pereira, Sergio 1944- *WhoHisp 94*
Pereira, Teresinka *DrAPF 93*
Pereira, W(ilfred) D(ennis) 1921- *ConAu 42NR, EncSF 93*
Pereira Burgos, Cesar 1929- *IntWW 93*
Pereira Dos Santos, Adalberto 1905- *IntWW 93*
Pereira Gray, Denis John *Who 94*
Pereira Lira, Paulo H. 1930- *IntWW 93*
Pereira Mendes, H(enry) 1852-1937 *EncSF 93*
Pereira-Mendoza, Vivian 1917- *Who 94*
Pereiras Garcia, Manuel 1950- *WhoHisp 94*
Perek, Lubos 1919- *IntWW 93*
Perek, Patricia Jean 1948- *WhoFI 94*
Perel, Jane Lunin *DrAPF 93*
Perell, Edward Andrew 1940- *WhoAm 94*
Perell, William Simon 1952- *WhoWest 94*
Perella, Joseph Robert 1941- *IntWW 93*
Perella, Susanne Brennan 1936- *WhoAm 94*
Perelle, Ira B. 1925- *WhoAm 94*
Perelman, Bob 1947- *WrDr 94*
Perelman, Leon Joseph 1911- *WhoAm 94, WhoFI 94*
Perelman, Melvin 1930- *WhoAm 94, WhoFI 94, WhoMW 93*
Perelman, Rachel Greenspan 1938- *WhoAmP 93*
Perelman, Ronald Owen 1943- *IntWW 93, WhoAm 94, WhoFI 94*
Perelman, S(idney) J(oseph) 1904-1979 *ConDr 93*
Perelmuter, Rosa 1948- *WhoHisp 94*
Perelson, Glenn Howard 1954- *WhoWest 94*
Perenchio, Andrew J. 1930- *IntMPA 94*
Perenchio, Andrew Jerrold 1930- *WhoAm 94*
Pereny, George *DrAPF 93*
Perenyi, Eleanor (Spencer Stone) 1918- *WrDr 94*
Perenyi, Miklos 1948- *IntWW 93*
Perera, Ana María 1925- *WhoHisp 94*
Perera, George A. 1911- *WhoAm 94*

Perera, Hilda 1926- *WhoHisp 94*
Perera, Lawrence Thacher 1935- *WhoAm 94, WhoAmL 94*
Perera, Liyanage Henry Horace 1915- *IntWW 93*
Perera, Padma *BlmGWL, DrAPF 93*
Perera, Uduwanage Dayaratna 1945- *WhoScEn 94*
Perera, Victor *DrAPF 93*
Perera, Victor H. 1934- *WhoHisp 94*
Perera, Vicumpriya Sriyantha 1961- *WhoMW 93*
Perera, Wahalatantrige D.R. 1928- *IntWW 93*
Perera-Pfeifer, Isabel *WhoHisp 94*
Peres, Judith May 1946- *WhoAm 94*
Peres, Shimon 1923- *IntWW 93, Who 94*
Peress, Gilles 1946- *WhoAm 94, WhoAmA 93*
Peress, Maurice 1930- *WhoAm 94*
Peresypkin, Oleg Gerasimovich *IntWW 93*
Peretti, Frank E. 1951- *WrDr 94*
Peretti, Niccolo fl. 1762- *NewGrDO*
Peretti, Serge 1910- *IntDcB*
Peretz, David Lindsay Corbett 1943- *IntWW 93, Who 94*
Peretz, Don 1922- *ConAu 41NR*
Peretz, Susan *WhoHol 92*
Peretz, Yitzhak Haim 1939- *IntWW 93*
Peretzky, Cathy Sue 1954- *WhoMW 93*
Perey, Bernard Jean Francois 1930- *WhoAm 94*
Perey, Ron 1943- *WhoAmL 94*
Pereyra-Suarez, Charles Albert 1947- *WhoAm 94, WhoAmL 94, WhoHisp 94, WhoWest 94*
Pereyra-Suárez, Esther 1925- *WhoHisp 94*
Perez, Albert Pena 1940- *WhoHisp 94*
Pérez, Alberto Julián 1948- *WhoHisp 94*
Perez, Alejandro 1940- *WhoHisp 94*
Perez, Alejandro Raymundo 1936- *WhoHisp 94*
Perez, Alfredo R. 1955- *WhoAmL 94*
Perez, Alicia 1953- *WhoHisp 94*
Perez, Alicia S. 1931- *WhoHisp 94*
Perez, Alonzo 1956- *WhoHisp 94*
Perez, Altagracia 1961- *WhoBlA 94*
Perez, Amanda Carrales 1932- *WhoHisp 94*
Perez, Angel Alvarez *WhoAm 94, WhoFI 94*
Perez, Angie Vigil *WhoAmP 93*
Perez, Anna 1952- *WhoBlA 94*
Perez, Anthony David 1948- *WhoHisp 94*
Perez, Anthony Martin, Jr. 1953- *WhoAmL 94, WhoWest 94*
Perez, Antonio *WhoHisp 94*
Perez, Arturo *WhoHisp 94*
Perez, Atilano V. 1937- *WhoFI 94*
Perez, Bernard Lucio 1948- *WhoHisp 94*
Pérez, Bernardo Matias 1939- *WhoHisp 94*
Perez, Bertin John 1939- *WhoFI 94*
Perez, Betty Weiss *WhoAmA 93*
Perez, Carlos 1950- *WhoHisp 94*
Perez, Carlos A. 1934- *WhoAm 94, WhoHisp 94*
Perez, Carlos Jesus 1959- *WhoHisp 94*
Pérez, Carmelo *WhoHisp 94*
Perez, Carmen *WhoAmP 93, WhoHisp 94*
Pérez, Carmen González 1956- *WhoHisp 94*
Perez, Carmen O. *WhoHisp 94*
Perez, Celis 1939- *WhoAmA 93*
Perez, Daniel Edward 1963- *WhoHisp 94*
Perez, Daniel Francisco 1958- *WhoAmL 94*
Perez, Dario 1941- *WhoHisp 94*
Perez, David 1711-1778 *NewGrDO*
Perez, David 1948- *WhoHisp 94*
Perez, David Douglas 1937- *WhoHisp 94*
Perez, Edgar 1948- *WhoHisp 94*
Perez, Edith A. 1956- *WhoHisp 94*
Perez, Elio 1938- *WhoHisp 94*
Perez, Elizabeth 1961- *WhoHisp 94*
Perez, Elva A. *WhoHisp 94*
Perez, Emiliano 1935- *WhoHisp 94*
Perez, Emilio 1940- *WhoHisp 94*
Perez, Enrique Manuel 1957- *WhoHisp 94*
Perez, Eustolia *WhoHisp 94*
Perez, Felix *WhoHisp 94*
Pérez, Francisco Luis 1950- *WhoHisp 94*
Pérez, Francisco R. 1938- *WhoHisp 94*
Perez, Frank S. 1929- *WhoHisp 94*
Perez, George *WhoHisp 94*
Perez, Gerald S. A. 1943- *WhoAm 94*
Perez, Gerard Vincent 1946- *WhoFI 94, WhoMW 93*
Perez, Gilbert Bernal 1950- *WhoHisp 94*
Perez, Gilberto Guillermo 1943- *WhoHisp 94*
Perez, Guido Oscar 1938- *WhoHisp 94*
Perez, Guillermo 1957- *WhoHisp 94*
Perez, Gustavo 1928- *WhoHisp 94*
Perez, Hector 1957- *WhoHisp 94*
Perez, Hector Antonio Tico 1962- *WhoAmL 94*
Perez, Herbert John 1959- *WhoHisp 94*
Perez, Ignacio *WhoHisp 94*
Pérez, Irma Rossana 1958- *WhoHisp 94*
Perez, Isidro *WhoHisp 94*
Perez, James Benito *WhoHisp 94*
Perez, James Rudolph 1936- *WhoHisp 94*
Perez, Jane R. 1943- *WhoHisp 94*
Perez, Jean-Yves 1945- *WhoScEn 94*
Perez, Jim 1957- *WhoHisp 94*
Perez, John Carlos 1941- *WhoScEn 94*
Perez, Jorge David 1964- *WhoHisp 94*
Perez, Jorge L. 1962- *WhoHisp 94*
Perez, Jorge Luis 1945- *WhoFI 94*
Perez, Jose *WhoHisp 94*
Perez, Jose d1981 *WhoHol 92*
Perez, Jose 1939- *WhoHisp 94*
Perez, Jose Antonio 1951- *WhoHisp 94*
Perez, Jose Luis 1951- *WhoMW 93, WhoScEn 94*
Perez, Jose Miguel *WhoHisp 94*
Perez, Jose R., Jr. 1948- *WhoHisp 94*
Perez, Joseph Dominique 1942- *WhoAm 94*
Perez, Joseph E. 1946- *WhoHisp 94*
Perez, Joseph Peter 1944- *WhoHisp 94*
Pérez, Juan Ovidio 1954- *WhoHisp 94*
Perez, Julian Ernesto 1933- *WhoHisp 94*
Pérez, Julio E. 1958- *WhoHisp 94*
Pérez, Julio Edgardo 1950- *WhoHisp 94*
Perez, Laura Alonso 1962- *WhoHisp 94*
Perez, Leo 1958- *WhoHisp 94*
Perez, Lillian 1957- *WhoAm 94, WhoHisp 94*
Perez, Lombardo *WhoHisp 94*
Perez, Louie *WhoHisp 94*
Perez, Louis G. 1946- *WhoHisp 94*
Perez, Louis Michael 1946- *WhoAm 94*
Perez, Luis 1928- *WhoHisp 94*
Perez, Luis 1940- *WhoHisp 94*
Perez, Luis A. *WhoHisp 94*
Perez, Luis A. 1947- *WhoHisp 94*
Perez, Luis Alberto 1956- *WhoAmL 94, WhoHisp 94*
Perez, Luz Lillian 1946- *WhoScEn 94*
Pérez, Lydia 1947- *WhoHisp 94*
Perez, Lydia Tena 1955- *WhoHisp 94*
Perez, Manuel 1939- *WhoHisp 94*
Perez, Maria E. 1928- *WhoHisp 94*
Perez, Mariano Martin 1964- *WhoHisp 94*
Perez, Mario 1940- *WhoHisp 94*
Perez, Mario Alberto 1958- *WhoHisp 94*
Perez, Maritza E. 1947- *WhoHisp 94*
Perez, Maritza Ivonne 1957- *WhoHisp 94*
Pérez, Marlene 1959- *WhoHisp 94*
Perez, Martin *WhoHisp 94*
Perez, Mary A. *WhoHisp 94*
Perez, Melido T 1966- *WhoAm 94, WhoHisp 94*
Perez, Melvyn James 1936- *WhoHisp 94*
Perez, Mike 1964- *WhoHisp 94*
Perez, Minerva 1955- *WhoHisp 94*
Pérez, Nancy 1953- *WhoHisp 94*
Perez, Nelida *WhoHisp 94*
Perez, Nicolas J. 1943- *WhoAmP 93, WhoHisp 94*
Perez, Nilsa Ivette 1968- *WhoFI 94*
Perez, Pablo 1936- *WhoHisp 94*
Perez, Pedro *WhoHisp 94*
Perez, Pedro 1936- *WhoHisp 94*
Perez, Pedro L., Sr. 1935- *WhoHisp 94*
Perez, Pepito d1975 *WhoHol 92*
Perez, Pete *WhoHisp 94*
Perez, Peter Felix 1948- *WhoAmP 93*
Perez, Peter Manuel 1940- *WhoAm 94, WhoFI 94*
Perez, Rafael R. *WhoHisp 94*
Perez, Raul, Jr. 1946- *WhoHisp 94*
Perez, Raul Ramon 1942- *WhoHisp 94*
Perez, Ray *WhoHisp 94*
Perez, Reinaldo Joseph 1957- *WhoScEn 94, WhoWest 94*
Perez, Renato 1946- *WhoAmL 94*
Perez, Renato Eduardo 1937- *WhoHisp 94*
Perez, Rey *WhoHisp 94*
Perez, Richard 1947- *WhoHisp 94*
Perez, Richard Lee 1940- *WhoHisp 94*
Perez, Richard Lee 1946- *WhoAmL 94, WhoWest 94*
Perez, Richard Patrick 1941- *WhoHisp 94*
Perez, Richard Raymond 1934- *WhoHisp 94*
Perez, Robert *WhoHisp 94*
Perez, Robert 1942- *WhoHisp 94*
Perez, Robert Antony 1955- *WhoHisp 94*
Perez, Roberto 1959- *WhoHisp 94*
Perez, Roger 1943- *WhoHisp 94*
Perez, Roger A. *WhoAmP 93*
Perez, Roger Anthony 1959- *WhoHisp 94*
Perez, Roland W. 1943- *WhoHisp 94*
Perez, Rolando 1957- *WhoHisp 94*
Perez, Romulo 1954- *WhoHisp 94*
Perez, Ronald A. 1949- *WhoHisp 94*
Perez, Ronald A. 1961- *WhoScEn 94*
Perez, Rosie *News 94-2 [port], WhoHisp 94, WhoHol 92*
Perez, Salvador Stephen 1965- *WhoHisp 94*
Perez, Santiago, Jr. 1938- *WhoHisp 94*
Perez, Segundo, Jr. 1949- *WhoHisp 94*
Perez, Severo, Jr. 1941- *WhoHisp 94*
Perez, Sigifredo, Jr. 1937- *WhoHisp 94*
Pérez, Sory 1948- *WhoHisp 94*
Perez, Stephen Manuel 1947- *WhoHisp 94*
Perez, Steven Randall 1960- *WhoWest 94*
Perez, Timothy Allen 1961- *WhoWest 94*
Perez, Tony 1942- *WhoHisp 94*
Perez, Tony David 1948- *WhoHisp 94*
Perez, Toraldo Casimiro, Jr. 1936- *WhoHisp 94*
Perez, Victor 1930- *WhoScEn 94*
Perez, Victor O. 1947- *WhoHisp 94*
Perez, Vincent *WhoHol 92*
Perez, Vincent 1938- *WhoAmA 93*
Perez, Vincent R. 1938- *WhoHisp 94*
Perez, Waldo D. 1946- *WhoHisp 94*
Perez, William Charles 1944- *WhoHisp 94*
Perez, Yorkis Miguel 1967- *WhoHisp 94*
Perez-Aguilera, Jose Raul 1961- *WhoHisp 94*
Pérez Aucar, Manuel A. 1922- *WhoHisp 94*
Perez-Blanco, Horacio 1951- *WhoHisp 94*
Pérez-Bustillo, Camilo *WhoHisp 94*
Pérez-Captoe, Juan M. 1938- *WhoHisp 94*
Perez-Colon, Roberto 1949- *WhoHisp 94*
Perez De Cuellar, Javier 1920- *IntWW 93, Who 94, WhoAm 94*
Pérez del Rió, José Joaquín 1941- *WhoHisp 94*
Pérez-Diaz, Carmen María 1953- *WhoHisp 94*
Perez-Eguis, Jose Juan de Dios 1954- *WhoFI 94*
Pérez-Erdelyi, Mireya 1942- *WhoHisp 94*
Perez Esquivel, Adolfo 1931- *IntWW 93, Who 94*
Pérez-Farfante, Isabel C. 1916- *WhoHisp 94*
Pérez-Feria, Richard M. 1964- *WhoHisp 94*
Perez Fernandez, Pedro 1949- *IntWW 93*
Perez Firmat, Gustavo 1950- *WhoHisp 94*
Perez-Gimenez, Juan Manuel 1941- *WhoAm 94, WhoAmL 94, WhoHisp 94*
Perez Godoy, Ricardo Pio 1905- *IntWW 93*
Perez Hernandez, Juan Josef c. 1725-1775 *WhWE*
Perez-Hernandez, Manny *WhoHisp 94*
Perez Jimenez, Marcos 1914- *IntWW 93*
Perez-Llorca, Jose Pedro 1940- *IntWW 93*
Perez-Lopez, Rene 1945- *WhoHisp 94*
Perez Marin, Andres 1961- *WhoHisp 94*
Perez-Mendez, Victor 1923- *WhoAm 94, WhoHisp 94, WhoWest 94*
Perez-Mireles, Guadalupe Louisa 1951- *WhoHisp 94*
Perez Mon, Coynthia 1958- *WhoHisp 94*
Perez-Ramirez, Bernardo 1960- *WhoScEn 94*
Perez Rivera, Harry Luis *WhoAmP 93*
Perez Rodriguez, Carlos Andres 1922- *IntWW 93*
Perez-Rodriguez, Carolyn Delfina 1951- *WhoHisp 94*
Pérez Rodriguez, Roberto J. 1947- *WhoHisp 94*
Perez Sanchez, Ezequiel 1911-1986 *WhAm 10*
Perez-Sanz, Jose Ramon 1952- *WhoHisp 94*
Perez Soriano, Agustin 1846-1907 *NewGrDO*
Pérez-Stable, Eliseo Joaquín 1952- *WhoHisp 94*
Pérez-Stable, María Adelaida 1954- *WhoHisp 94, WhoMW 93*
Pérez-Stansfield, María Pilar *WhoHisp 94*
Perez-Tulla, Maritza Ivonne 1957- *WhoHisp 94*
Perez-Vega, Elsa 1953- *WhoHisp 94*
Pérez y Mena, Andrés I. 1948- *WhoHisp 94*
Perfall, Karl von 1824-1907 *NewGrDO*
Perfido, Ruth S. 1941- *WhoAm 94, WhoAmL 94*
Pergam, Albert Steven d1993 *NewYTBS 93*
Pergam, Albert Steven 1938- *WhoAm 94, WhoAmL 94*
Pergericht, Frances Lee 1952- *WhoAmL 94*
Pergolesi, Giovanni Battista 1710-1736 *NewGrDO*
Perhach, James Lawrence 1943- *WhoAm 94*
Perham, Richard Nelson 1937- *Who 94*
Perham, Roy Gates 1916- *WhoAmA 93*
Perham, Roy Gates, III 1958- *WhoScEn 94*
Perheentupa, Jaakko Pentti 1934- *WhoScEn 94*
Peri, Achille 1812-1880 *NewGrDO*
Peri, Jacopo 1561-1633 *NewGrDO*
Perich, Michael Joseph 1957- *WhoScEn 94*
Perich, Shawn Casey 1959- *WhoMW 93*
Perich, Thomas J. 1945- *WhoAmL 94*
Peric-Knowlton, Wlatka 1955- *WhoWest 94*
Pericles *BlmGEL*
Pericles c. 495BC-429BC *HisWorL [port]*
Periconi, James Joseph 1948- *WhoAmL 94*
Perictione fl. 4th cent.?BC-2nd cent.BC *BlmGWL*
Perier, Francois *WhoHol 92*
Perier, Francois 1919- *IntWW 93*
Perier, Jean (Alexis) 1869-1954 *NewGrDO*
Perier, Jean Pierre d1966 *WhoHol 92*
Peri Fagerstrom, Rene Alberto 1926- *IntWW 93*
Perigot, Francois 1926- *IntWW 93*
Perilla *BlmGWL*
Perilla, Alejandro 1965- *WhoHisp 94*
Perillo, Lucia Maria *DrAPF 93*
Perilloux, Bruce Edgar 1961- *WhoWest 94*
Perilstein, Fred Michael 1945- *WhoScEn 94*
Perin, Donald Wise, Jr. 1915- *WhoAm 94*
Perin, Francois 1921- *IntWW 93*
Perin, Roberto 1948- *WrDr 94*
Perinal, Georges 1897-1965 *IntDcF 2-4 [port]*
Perinat, Marques de 1923- *Who 94*
Perinat, Luis Guillermo 1923- *IntWW 93*
Perine, James L. 1943- *WhoBlA 94*
Perine, Martha Levingston 1948- *WhoBlA 94*
Perine, Robert Heath 1922- *WhoAmA 93*
Perinet, Joachim 1763-1816 *NewGrDO*
Perini, David B. 1937- *WhoAm 94, WhoFI 94*
Perini, Flora 1887-1975 *NewGrDO*
Perini, Joseph R. 1930- *WhoFI 94*
Periolot, George d1940 *WhoHol 92*
Periquin d1957 *WhoHol 92*
Peri Rossi, Christina 1941- *BlmGWL*
Peri Rossi, Cristina 1941- *ConWorW 93*
Perish, Melanie *DrAPF 93*
Perisho, Russell L. 1953- *WhoAm 94*
Perisic, Zoran 1940- *IntWW 93*
Perisin, Ivo 1925- *IntWW 93*
Perissich, Riccardo 1942- *IntWW 93*
Peritore, Norman Patrick 1944- *WhoMW 93*
Peritz, Abraham Daniel 1940- *WhoAm 94, WhoFI 94*
Perkiel, Mitchel H. 1949- *WhoAm 94, WhoAmL 94*
Perkin, James Russell Conway 1928- *IntWW 93*
Perkin, Joan 1926- *WrDr 94*
Perkin, Reginald Lewis 1930- *WhoAm 94*
Perkin, William Henry 1838-1907 *WorInv*
Perkins, A. Alan 1915- *WhoAmA 93*
Perkins, A. William 1925- *WhoAm 94*
Perkins, Alan J. 1953- *WhoAm 94, WhoAmL 94*
Perkins, Alfred Lamont 1949- *WhoMW 93*
Perkins, Alice Elizabeth 1949- *Who 94*
Perkins, Ann 1915- *WhoAmA 93*
Perkins, Anna d1993 *NewYTBS 93 [port]*
Perkins, Anne Scarlett 1937- *WhoAmP 93*
Perkins, Anthony d1992 *IntMPA 94N*
Perkins, Anthony 1932- *WhAm 10, WhoHol 92*
Perkins, Anthony 1932-1992 *AnObit 1992, ConTFT 11*
Perkins, Anthony C. *WhoAmP 93*
Perkins, Barbara Gayle 1946- *WhoMW 93*
Perkins, Bernard James 1928- *Who 94*
Perkins, Bobby Frank 1929- *WhoAm 94*
Perkins, Bradford 1925- *WhoAm 94*
Perkins, Carl 1932- *WhoHol 92*
Perkins, Carl C. 1954- *WhoAmP 93*
Perkins, Carroll Mason 1929- *WhoAm 94*
Perkins, Charles, III 1952- *WhoAm 94*
Perkins, Charles Windell 1946- *WhoBlA 94*
Perkins, Cheryl Green 1945- *WhoWest 94*
Perkins, Constance M. 1913- *WhoAmA 93N*
Perkins, D. Michael 1950- *WhoMW 93*
Perkins, David *DrAPF 93*
Perkins, David D(exter) 1919- *IntWW 93*
Perkins, David Dexter 1919- *WhoAm 94*
Perkins, David Layne, Sr. 1925- *WhoAm 94*
Perkins, David Patrick 1957- *WhoAmL 94*
Perkins, Deborah Anne Kehley 1966- *WhoFI 94*
Perkins, Deborah Elaine 1951- *WhoMW 93*
Perkins, Dennis Lynn 1952- *WhoAmL 94*
Perkins, Derek Duncombe S. *Who 94*
Perkins, Dian R. 1946- *WhoAmP 93*
Perkins, Donald H. 1925- *IntWW 93*
Perkins, Donald Hill 1925- *Who 94*
Perkins, Dorothy A. 1926- *WhoAm 94, WhoAmP 93, WhoWest 94*

Perkins, Dwight Heald 1934- *WhoAm 94, WhoFI 94, WrDr 94*
Perkins, Edward 1928- *ConBlB 5 [port]*
Perkins, Edward A. 1928- *WhoAm 94*
Perkins, Edward J. 1928- *IntWW 93*
Perkins, Edward Joseph 1928- *WhoAmP 93, WhoBlA 94*
Perkins, Elizabeth 1960- *WhoHol 92*
Perkins, Elizabeth 1961- *IntMPA 94*
Perkins, Elizabeth Ann 1960- *WhoAm 94*
Perkins, (Useni) Eugene 1932- *BlkWr 2, ConAu 142*
Perkins, Floyd Jerry 1924- *WhoWest 94*
Perkins, Frances 1880-1965 *HisWorL [port]*
Perkins, Frances J. 1919- *WhoBlA 94*
Perkins, Francis Layton 1912- *Who 94*
Perkins, Frank Overton 1938- *WhoAm 94*
Perkins, G. Holmes 1904- *WhoAmA 93*
Perkins, Geoffrey *EncSF 93*
Perkins, George (Burton) 1930- *WrDr 94*
Perkins, George Holmes 1904- *WhoAm 94*
Perkins, George Walbridge 1862-1920 *EncABHB 9 [port]*
Perkins, George William, II 1926- *WhoAm 94*
Perkins, Gil *WhoHol 92*
Perkins, Gilbert Harold 1896- *WhAm 10*
Perkins, Gladys Patricia 1921- *WhoBlA 94, WhoWest 94*
Perkins, H. Jack 1950- *WhoMW 93*
Perkins, Heayron Calvin 1955- *WhoFI 94*
Perkins, Herbert Asa 1918- *WhoAm 94*
Perkins, Homer Guy 1916- *WhoAm 94*
Perkins, Huel D. 1924- *WhoBlA 94*
Perkins, Irwyn Morse 1920- *Who 94*
Perkins, Jack *WhoHol 92*
Perkins, Jack Edwin 1943- *WhoAm 94*
Perkins, Jacob 1766-1849 *WorInv*
Perkins, James (Alfred) 1911- *WrDr 94*
Perkins, James A. *DrAPF 93*
Perkins, James Alfred 1911- *IntWW 93, WhAm 10, Who 94*
Perkins, James Connelle 1951- *WhoBlA 94*
Perkins, James Eliab 1905-1990 *WhAm 10*
Perkins, James Francis 1924- *WhoScEn 94*
Perkins, James L. 1931- *WhoAm 94*
Perkins, James O. 1940- *WhoIns 94*
Perkins, James Patrick 1939- *WhoAm 94*
Perkins, James Winslow 1955- *WhoFI 94*
Perkins, James Wood 1924- *WhoAm 94*
Perkins, Jean d1922 *WhoHol 92*
Perkins, Jim 1949- *WhoAmP 93*
Perkins, John
See XTC *ConMus 10*
Perkins, John Allen 1919- *WhoAm 94*
Perkins, John M. *WhoBlA 94*
Perkins, Joseph John, Jr. 1954- *WhoAmL 94*
Perkins, Julie Anne Rate 1935- *WhoAmL 94*
Perkins, Kenneth 1926- *Who 94*
Perkins, Kenneth Earl 1950- *WhoMW 93*
Perkins, Kent *WhoHol 92*
Perkins, Leonard L. 1933- *WhoBlA 94*
Perkins, Lewis Bryant, Jr. *WhoBlA 94*
Perkins, Linda Marie 1950- *WhoAm 94, WhoBlA 94*
Perkins, Lois Bouthillier 1937- *WhoAmA 93*
Perkins, Louvenia Black 1948- *WhoBlA 94*
Perkins, Mable H. 1880-1974 *WhoAmA 93N*
Perkins, Malcolm Donald 1914- *WhoAm 94*
Perkins, Marion 1908-1961 *AfrAmAl 6 [port], WhoAmA 93N*
Perkins, Marvin Earl 1920- *WhoAm 94*
Perkins, Merle Lester 1919- *WhoAm 94, WhoMW 93*
Perkins, Michael *DrAPF 93, EncSF 93*
Perkins, Michael 1942- *WrDr 94*
Perkins, Mildred Kelley 1908- *WhoAmP 93*
Perkins, Millie 1936- *WhoHol 92*
Perkins, Millie 1938- *IntMPA 94*
Perkins, Myla Levy 1939- *WhoBlA 94*
Perkins, Nancy Jane 1949- *WhoFI 94, WhoMW 93*
Perkins, Osgood d1937 *WhoHol 92*
Perkins, Paul Bouthillier 1961- *WhoFI 94*
Perkins, Paul R. 1929- *WhoAmP 93*
Perkins, Philip R. d1968 *WhoAmA 93N*
Perkins, Phyllis Hartley 1934- *WhoWest 94*
Perkins, Ralph Linwood 1914- *WhoAm 94*
Perkins, Ray 1941- *WhoAm 94*
Perkins, Rebecca Daeda 1955- *WhoAmP 93*
Perkins, Richard Burle, II 1960- *WhoScEn 94*
Perkins, Richard D. 1961- *WhoAmP 93*
Perkins, Robert Bennett 1932- *WhoScEn 94*
Perkins, Robert E. 1944- *WhoAmL 94*
Perkins, Robert E. L. 1925- *WhoBlA 94*
Perkins, Robert Eugene 1931- *WhoAmA 93*
Perkins, Robert Louis 1931- *WhoAm 94*
Perkins, Roger Allan 1943- *WhoAmL 94*
Perkins, Ronald Dee 1935- *WhoAm 94*
Perkins, Roswell Burchard 1926- *WhoAm 94*
Perkins, Roy Frank 1918- *WhoWest 94*
Perkins, Sam Bruce 1961- *WhoBlA 94*
Perkins, Samuel 1948- *WhoAm 94, WhoAmL 94*
Perkins, Samuel Thomas 1946- *WhoAm 94*
Perkins, T. W. *DrAPF 93*
Perkins, Thomas Cole 1933- *WhoFI 94, WhoIns 94*
Perkins, Thomas James 1932- *WhoAm 94, WhoFI 94, WhoWest 94*
Perkins, Thomas Keeble 1932- *WhoAm 94*
Perkins, Thomas P. 1940- *WhoBlA 94*
Perkins, Thomas Ralph 1931- *WhoAmP 93*
Perkins, Tim 1958- *WhoWest 94*
Perkins, Van L. 1930- *WhoAm 94*
Perkins, Victoria Jane 1945- *WhoAm 94*
Perkins, Voltaire d1977 *WhoHol 92*
Perkins, Walter d1925 *WhoHol 92*
Perkins, Whitney Trow 1921- *WhoAm 94*
Perkins, William Allan, Jr. 1925- *WhoAm 94*
Perkins, William Clinton 1920- *WhoWest 94*
Perkins, William H., Jr. 1921- *WhoAm 94, WhoMW 93*
Perkins, William Hughes 1923- *WhoAm 94*
Perkins, William J., Sr. *WhoAmP 93*
Perkins, William O., Jr. 1926- *WhoBlA 94*
Perkins, William Randolph 1934- *WhoAm 94*
Perkins, Winston E. 1935- *WhoIns 94*
Perkins-Carpenter, Betty Lou 1931- *WhoFI 94*
Perkins-Frederick, Pamela M. *DrAPF 93*
Perkinson, Coleridge-Taylor 1932- *AfrAmAl 6*
Perkinson, Diana Agnes Zouzelka 1943- *WhoAm 94, WhoFI 94*
Perkinson, Robert Ronald 1945- *WhoMW 93*
Perkins-Ripley, Lucy Fairfield *WhoAmA 93N*
Perko, Brian M. 1953- *WhoAmL 94*
Perko, Walter Kim 1950- *WhoWest 94*
Perkoff, Gerald Thomas 1926- *IntWW 93, WhoAm 94*
Perkovic, Robert Branko 1925- *WhoAm 94*
Perkowitz, Sidney 1939- *WhoAm 94*
Perkowski, Casimir Anthony 1941- *WhoScEn 94*
Perkowski, Marek Andrzej 1946- *WhoWest 94*
Perks, (John) Clifford 1915- *Who 94*
Perks, Roger Ian 1921- *WhoAm 94*
Perkuhn, Gaylen Lee 1955- *WhoScEn 94*
Perky, Henry *WorInv*
Perl, Andras 1955- *WhoScEn 94*
Perl, Martin Lewis 1927- *IntWW 93*
Perl, Ronald L. 1951- *WhoAmL 94*
Perl, Ruth June 1929- *WrDr 94*
Perl, Stephen C. 1942- *WhoMW 93*
Perl, Teri (Hoch) 1926- *ConAu 42NR*
Perla, Randall Michael 1949- *WhoAmL 94*
Perlberg, Deborah *DrAPF 93*
Perlberg, Jules Martin 1931- *WhoAm 94*
Perlberg, Mark *DrAPF 93*
Perlberger, Martin 1928- *WhoWest 94*
Perle, Eugene Gabriel 1922- *WhoAm 94*
Perle, George 1915- *WhoAm 94*
Perle, Richard N. 1941- *WhoAmP 93*
Perle, Richard Norman 1941- *WhoAm 94*
Perlea, Jonel 1900-1970 *NewGrDO*
Perlemuter, Vlado 1904- *IntWW 93*
Perles, Julia 1914- *WhoAmL 94*
Perless, Ellen 1941- *WhoAm 94*
Perless, Robert 1938- *WhoAmA 93*
Perless, Robert L. 1938- *WhoAm 94*
Perley, Charles d1933 *WhoHol 92*
Perley, J. Dwight 1911- *WhoAm 94*
Perley, Merrill Ernest 1915- *WhoAmP 93*
Perley, Peter Ernest 1944- *WhoAmP 93*
Perli, Lisa *NewGrDO*
Perlick, Richard Allan 1947- *WhoFI 94*
Perlik, William R. 1925- *WhoAm 94*
Perlin, Arthur Saul 1923- *WhoAm 94*
Perlin, Bernard 1918- *WhoAmA 93*
Perlin, John 1944- *WrDr 94*
Perlin, Michael Louis 1946- *WhoAmL 94*
Perlin, Rae *WhoAmA 93*
Perlin, Ruth Rudolph *WhoAmA 93*
Perlin, Seymour 1925- *WhoAm 94*
Perlina, Nina U. 1939- *WhoMW 93*
Perlini, Richard Alan 1949- *WhoAmL 94*
Perlis, H.R.H. The Raja Of 1920- *IntWW 93*
Perlis, Alan J. 1922-1990 *WhAm 10*
Perlis, Donald M. 1941- *WhoAm 94*
Perlis, Michael Fredrick 1947- *WhoAm 94, WhoAmL 94, WhoFI 94, WhoWest 94*
Perlis, Michael Steven 1953- *WhoAm 94*
Perlman, Anne S. *DrAPF 93*
Perlman, B. Arthur 1959- *WhoAmL 94*
Perlman, Barry Stuart 1939- *WhoAm 94*
Perlman, Bennard Bloch 1928- *WhoAmA 93*
Perlman, Brett Alan 1959- *WhoAmL 94*
Perlman, Burton 1924- *WhoAm 94, WhoAmL 94*
Perlman, Daniel Hessel 1935- *WhoAm 94, WhoMW 93*
Perlman, David 1918- *WhoAm 94, WhoWest 94*
Perlman, David 1920- *WhoAm 94*
Perlman, David Stanley 1942- *WhoAmL 94*
Perlman, Henry H. d1993 *NewYTBS 93*
Perlman, Hirsch 1960- *WhoAmA 93*
Perlman, Itzhak 1945- *IntWW 93, Who 94, WhoAm 94*
Perlman, Jerald Lee 1947- *WhoAmL 94*
Perlman, Joel Leonard 1943- *WhoAmA 93*
Perlman, John Niels *DrAPF 93*
Perlman, Judy Platt 1949- *WhoAm 94, WhoAmL 94*
Perlman, Lawrence 1938- *WhoAm 94, WhoFI 94, WhoMW 93*
Perlman, Leonard G. 1932- *WhoAm 94*
Perlman, Mark 1923- *WhoAm 94*
Perlman, Mark A. 1950- *WhoAmA 93*
Perlman, Matthew Saul 1936- *WhoAm 94*
Perlman, Mitchel Dean 1955- *WhoWest 94*
Perlman, Rhea *WhoAm 94*
Perlman, Rhea 1948- *IntMPA 94, WhoHol 92*
Perlman, Richard Brian 1951- *WhoAmL 94*
Perlman, Richard Wilfred 1923- *WhoAm 94*
Perlman, Ron 1950- *IntMPA 94*
Perlman, Ron 1951- *WhoHol 92*
Perlman, Ronald S. 1948- *WhoAmL 94*
Perlman, Victor S. 1945- *WhoAmL 94*
Perlmuth, William Alan 1929- *WhoAm 94*
Perlmutter, Alvin Howard 1928- *WhoAm 94*
Perlmutter, David M. 1934- *IntMPA 94*
Perlmutter, Diane F. 1945- *WhoAm 94, WhoFI 94*
Perlmutter, Donna *WhoAm 94*
Perlmutter, Felice Davidson 1931- *WhoAm 94*
Perlmutter, Frank 1912- *WhoFI 94*
Perlmutter, Jack 1920- *WhoAm 94, WhoAmA 93*
Perlmutter, Jerome Herbert 1924- *WhoAm 94*
Perlmutter, Lawrence David 1936- *WhoScEn 94*
Perlmutter, Leonard Michael 1925- *WhoAm 94, WhoWest 94*
Perlmutter, Linda M. 1943- *WhoAmA 93*
Perlmutter, Louis 1934- *WhoAm 94, WhoFI 94*
Perlmutter, Lynn Susan 1954- *WhoWest 94*
Perlmutter, Mark Leeds 1949- *WhoAmL 94*
Perlmutter, Merle 1936- *WhoAmA 93*
Perlmutter, Milton Manuel 1956- *WhoScEn 94, WhoWest 94*
Perlmutter, Sandra Pauline 1952- *WhoAmP 93*
Perloff, Jean Marcosson 1942- *WhoAmL 94*
Perloff, Jeffrey Mark 1950- *WhoFI 94, WhoWest 94*
Perloff, Joseph Kayle 1924- *WhoAm 94*
Perloff, Marjorie (Gabrielle) 1931- *WrDr 94*
Perloff, Marjorie G. 1931- *WhoAmA 93*
Perloff, Marjorie Gabrielle 1931- *WhoAm 94*
Perloff, Robert 1921- *WhoAm 94, WhoScEn 94*
Perlongo, Bob *DrAPF 93*
Perlongo, Daniel James 1942- *WhoAm 94*
Perlos, Alexander Charles 1930- *WhoMW 93*
Perlot, Enzo 1933- *IntWW 93*
Perlov, Dadie 1929- *WhoAm 94, WhoFI 94*
Perlow, Katharina Rich *WhoAmA 93*
Perlow, Max d1993 *NewYTBS 93*
Perls, Frank (Richard) 1910-1975 *WhoAmA 93N*
Perls, Klaus G. 1912- *WhoAmA 93*
Perls, Klaus Gunther 1912- *WhoAm 94*
Perls, Robert A. 1957- *WhoAmP 93*
Perlstadt, Sidney Morris 1907- *WhoAm 94*
Perlstein, William James 1950- *WhoAmL 94*
Perlt, Walter E. *WhoAmP 93*
Perman, Martey Robert 1939- *WhoAmL 94*
Perman, Norman Wilford 1928- *WhoAm 94*
Permut, David A. 1952- *IntMPA 94*
Permutt, Solbert 1925- *WhoAm 94*
Perna, Frank, Jr. 1938- *WhoAm 94, WhoFI 94, WhoWest 94*
Pernas, James Francis 1965- *WhoFI 94*
Pernerstorfer, Alois 1912-1978 *NewGrDO*
Pernet, Andre 1894-1966 *NewGrDO*
Pernice, Gino *WhoHol 92*
Pernicone, Carl John 1958- *WhoAmL 94*
Pernicone, Nicola 1935- *WhoScEn 94*
Pernotto, James Angelo 1950- *WhoAmA 93*
Pernow, Bengt 1924- *IntWW 93*
Pero, Joseph John 1939- *WhoAm 94, WhoFI 94, WhoIns 94*
Pero, Michael Andrew 1941- *WhoIns 94*
Perocchi, Paul Patrick 1948- *WhoAm 94*
Peroff, Ronald Peter 1942- *WhoWest 94*
Perol, Gilbert 1926- *IntWW 93*
Peron, Eva d1952 *WhoHol 92*
Peron, Eva Maria Duarte de 1919-1952 *HisWorL*
Peron, Francois 1775-1810 *WhWE*
Peron, Juan Domingo 1895-1974 *HisWorL*
Peron, Maria Estela (Isabelita) *IntWW 93*
Perone, John Michael 1945- *WhoAmP 93*
Perosio, Ettore 1868-1919 *NewGrDO*
Perot, H. Ross 1930- *WhoAm 94, WhoFI 94*
Perot, H(enry) Ross 1930- *ConAu 142*
Perot, Ross *WhoAmP 93*
Perot, (Henry) Ross 1930- *IntWW 93*
Perotti, Giovanni Domenico 1761-1825 *NewGrDO*
Perotti, Rose Norma 1930- *WhoAmL 94, WhoFI 94, WhoMW 93*
Perouse, Jean-Francois De Galaup, Comte De La *WhWE*
Perovic, Latinka 1933- *WhoWomW 91*
Perowne, Benjamin Cubitt d1992 *Who 94N*
Perpener, Winifred Uveda 1929- *WhoBlA 94*
Perper, Joshua Arte 1932- *WhoScEn 94*
Perpetua fl. 3rd cent.- *BlmGWL*
Perpich, Rudy 1928- *IntWW 93*
Perpich, Rudy George 1928- *WhoAmP 93*
Perpina-Robert, Fernando 1937- *IntWW 93*
Perr, Irwin 1928- *WhoAm 94*
Perra, Margarita 1908-1984 *NewGrDO*
Perrault, Charles 1628-1703 *BlmGEL, GuFrLit 2*
Perrault, Dominique *IntWW 93*
Perrault, Georges Gabriel 1934- *WhoScEn 94*
Perrault, Pierre 1957- *WhoAmA 93*
Perrault, Raymond 1926- *WhoAm 94*
Perreau, Gerald *WhoHol 92*
Perreau, Gigi 1941- *IntMPA 94, WhoHol 92*
Perreau, Janine 1942- *WhoHol 92*
Perreault, Ellen *DrAPF 93*
Perreault, George *DrAPF 93*
Perreault, Jeanne 1929- *WhoAm 94*
Perreault, John *DrAPF 93*
Perreault, John 1937- *WhoAmA 93*
Perreault, Laura Cecile 1925- *WhoMW 93*
Perreault, William Daniel, Jr. 1948- *WhoAm 94*
Perreiah, Alan Richard 1937- *WhoAm 94*
Perrein, Michele *BlmGWL*
Perrein, Michele Marie-Claude 1929- *IntWW 93*
Perrella, Anthony Joseph 1942- *WhoFI 94, WhoScEn 94, WhoWest 94*
Perrella, Donald J. 1928- *WhoHisp 94*
Perrella, James Elbert 1935- *WhoFI 94*
Perrenoud, Jean Jacques 1947- *WhoScEn 94*
Perret, Donna C. 1949- *WhoAmA 93*
Perret, Ferdinand 1888-1960 *WhoAmA 93N*
Perret, Gene 1937- *SmATA 76 [port]*
Perret, Gerard Anthony, Jr. 1959- *WhoScEn 94*
Perret, Gloria McKinnon 1929- *WhoAmP 93*
Perret, Joseph Aloysius 1929- *WhoAm 94, WhoWest 94*
Perret, Leonce d1935 *WhoHol 92*
Perret, Nell Foster 1916-1986 *WhoAmA 93N*
Perret, Peter James 1941- *WhoAm 94*
Perreten, Frank Arnold 1927- *WhoScEn 94*
Perrett, Bryan 1934- *WrDr 94*

Perrett, Galen J. 1875-1949 *WhoAmA 93N*
Perrette, Jean Rene 1931- *WhoFI 94*
Perretti, Peter *WhoAmP 93*
Perretti, Peter N., Jr. 1931- *WhoAm 94*
Perrey, Mireille *WhoHol 92*
Perri, Fortunato *WhoAmP 93*
Perriam, Wendy 1940- *WrDr 94*
Perrich, Jerry Robert 1947- *WhoAm 94, WhoMW 93*
Perrie, Lynne 1931- *WhoHol 92*
Perrier, Barbara Sue 1937- *WhoWest 94*
Perrier, Mireille *WhoHol 92*
Perrier, Pierre Claude 1935- *WhoScEn 94*
Perrill, Frederick Eugene 1939- *WhoWest 94*
Perriman, Brett 1965- *WhoBlA 94*
Perrimon, Vivian Spence 1926- *WhoBlA 94*
Perrin, Arnold *DrAPF 93*
Perrin, Bill K. 1938- *WhoAmP 93*
Perrin, C. Robert 1915- *WhoAmA 93*
Perrin, Charles John 1940- *Who 94*
Perrin, David Thomas Perry 1951- *WhoBlA 94*
Perrin, Edward Burton 1931- *WhoAm 94, WhoWest 94*
Perrin, Francis *WhoHol 92*
Perrin, Francis 1901-1992 *AnObit 1992*
Perrin, Francis Henri Jean Siegfried d1992 *IntWW 93N*
Perrin, Gail 1938- *WhoAm 94*
Perrin, Harry A. 1953- *WhoAmL 94*
Perrin, Jack d1967 *WhoHol 92*
Perrin, Jacques *WhoHol 92*
Perrin, Jane Frances 1940- *WhoFI 94*
Perrin, Jean Baptiste 1870-1942 *WorScD*
Perrin, John Henry 1916- *Who 94*
Perrin, John Paul 1943- *WhoAm 94*
Perrin, Marco *WhoHol 92*
Perrin, Martha C. 1944- *WhoAmL 94*
Perrin, Michael Warren 1946- *WhoAmL 94*
Perrin, Noel 1927- *WhoAm 94*
Perrin, Norman 1920-1976 *DcAmReB 2*
Perrin, Norman Arthur 1930- *Who 94*
Perrin, Pierre c. 1620-1675 *NewGrDO*
Perrin, Richard William Edmund 1909- *WhAm 10*
Perrin, Robert 1925- *WhoAm 94*
Perrin, Robert Maitland 1950- *WhoAm 94*
Perrin, Tomas d1985 *WhoHol 92*
Perrin, Vic d1989 *WhoHol 92*
Perrin Du Lac, Francois-Marie 1766-1824 *WhWE*
Perrine, Laurence 1915- *WrDr 94*
Perrine, Richard Leroy 1924- *WhoAm 94*
Perrine, Valerie 1943- *IntMPA 94, WhoAm 94, WhoHol 92*
Perrine, William Everett 1933- *WhoAm 94*
Perring, Franklyn Hugh 1927- *Who 94*
Perring, John Raymond 1931- *Who 94*
Perring, Ralph (Edgar) 1905- *Who 94*
Perrino, Betty V. 1927- *WhoAmP 93*
Perrins, Christopher Miles 1935- *Who 94*
Perrins, Leslie d1962 *WhoHol 92*
Perris, David (Arthur) 1929- *Who 94*
Perris, Elizabeth L. 1951- *WhoAm 94, WhoAmL 94, WhoWest 94*
Perris, John Douglas 1928- *Who 94*
Perris, Terrence George 1947- *WhoAm 94, WhoAmL 94*
Perritt, Henry Hardy, Jr. 1944- *WhoAmL 94*
Perro, Mary Elizabeth 1964- *WhoWest 94*
Perron, James Patrick 1955- *WhoAmP 93*
Perron, Joachim du 1756-1814 *WhAmRev*
Perron, Karl 1858-1928 *NewGrDO*
Perron, Pierre O. 1939- *WhoAm 94, WhoScEn 94*
Perrone, Charles A. 1951- *WrDr 94*
Perrone, Jeff 1953- *WhoAmA 93*
Perrone, Joao Consani 1922- *IntWW 93*
Perrone, Nicholas 1930- *WhoAm 94*
Perrone, Stephen John 1952- *WhoFI 94*
Perros, Theodore Peter 1921- *WhoAm 94*
Perrot, Jules 1810-1892 *IntDcB [port]*
Perrot, Nicolas c. 1644-1717 *WhWE*
Perrot, Paul N. 1926- *WhoAmA 93*
Perrot, Paul Norman 1926- *WhoWest 94*
Perrott, Pamela Rundle 1941- *WhoWest 94*
Perrotta, Fioravante Gerald 1931- *WhoAm 94*
Perrotta, Giorgio 1940- *WhoScEn 94*
Perrotti, Barbara *WhoAmA 93*
Perrow, (Joseph) Howard 1923- *Who 94*
Perrow, Robert Dean 1948- *WhoAmL 94*
Perrucci, Michael J. 1953- *WhoAmP 93*
Perrucci, Robert 1931- *WhoAm 94*
Perry *Who 94*
Perry, Baron 1921- *IntWW 93*
Perry, Alan Joseph 1930- *Who 94*
Perry, Albert d1933 *WhoHol 92*
Perry, Albert J. 1935- *WhoAmP 93*
Perry, Alexis E. 1944- *WhoBlA 94*
Perry, Anne 1938- *WrDr 94*
Perry, Anthony 1929- *IntMPA 94*
Perry, Anthony John 1919- *WhoAm 94*
Perry, Antoinette d1946 *WhoHol 92*
Perry, Antoinette Krueger 1954- *WhoWest 94*
Perry, Aubrey M. 1937- *WhoBlA 94*
Perry, Barbara *WhoHol 92*
Perry, Benjamin 1939- *WhoBlA 94*
Perry, Benjamin L., Jr. 1918- *WhoBlA 94*
Perry, Beryl Henry, Jr. 1956- *WhoFI 94*
Perry, Billy Dwight 1933- *WhoAm 94*
Perry, Bonne Lu 1929- *WhoWest 94*
Perry, Bradley Wilbur 1938- *WhoAm 94*
Perry, Brenda L. 1948- *WhoBlA 94*
Perry, Carleton Flood 1931- *WhoAmP 93*
Perry, Carrie Saxon *WhoAm 94, WhoAmP 93, WhoBlA 94*
Perry, Charles Alling, Jr. 1957- *WhoMW 93*
Perry, Charles Bruce 1903- *Who 94*
Perry, Charles David 1955- *WhoFI 94*
Perry, Charles E. 1937- *WhoAm 94*
Perry, Charles Emmett d1967 *WhoHol 92*
Perry, Charles O. 1929- *WhoAmA 93*
Perry, Charles Owen 1929- *WhoAm 94*
Perry, Charles S. 1936- *WhoAm 94*
Perry, Charles Wayne 1951- *WhoAm 94*
Perry, Chris Nicholas 1945- *WhoAm 94*
Perry, Clifford, III 1945- *WhoBlA 94*
Perry, Craig Crane 1948- *WhoAm 94*
Perry, Cynthia Norton Shepard 1928- *WhoAm 94*
Perry, Cynthia Shepard *WhoAmP 93*
Perry, Dale Lynn 1947- *WhoAm 94*
Perry, Daniel Patrick 1945- *WhoScEn 94*
Perry, Danny Lamar, Sr. 1945- *WhoAmP 93*
Perry, David 1958- *WhoAmP 93*
Perry, David (Howard) 1931- *Who 94*
Perry, David Gordon 1937- *Who 94*
Perry, David Lee 1942- *WhoAmP 93*
Perry, David M. 1917- *WhoAmP 93*
Perry, David Niles 1940- *WhoWest 94*
Perry, David Norman *Who 94*
Perry, Dennis Gordon 1942- *WhoScEn 94*
Perry, Dennis Ralph 1951- *WhoMW 93*
Perry, Desmond d1985 *WhoHol 92*
Perry, Donald A. 1938- *WhoAm 94*
Perry, Donald Cleveland 1940- *WhoAmP 93*
Perry, Donald Dean 1939- *WhoAmA 93*
Perry, Donald Howard 1927- *WhoAm 94*
Perry, Donald Lester, II 1958- *WhoFI 94, WhoWest 94*
Perry, Douglas *WhoAm 94*
Perry, Ed 1946- *WhoAmP 93*
Perry, Edith Early 1943- *WhoAmP 93*
Perry, Edward Samuel 1937- *WhoAmA 93*
Perry, Edwin Charles 1931- *WhoAmL 94*
Perry, Eleanor 1915-1981 *IntDcF 2-4*
Perry, Elizabeth *DrAPF 93*
Perry, Emma Bradford *WhoBlA 94*
Perry, Erma Jackson McNeil *WhoAm 94*
Perry, Ernest George 1908- *Who 94*
Perry, Eston Lee 1936- *WhoAm 94, WhoMW 93*
Perry, Eugene Calvin, Jr. 1953- *WhoBlA 94*
Perry, Evelyn Reis *WhoFI 94*
Perry, Felix Edwin 1942- *WhoAmP 93*
Perry, Felton *WhoBlA 94, WhoHol 92*
Perry, Frances Mary 1907- *Who 94*
Perry, Francine Jackson 1956- *WhoAmL 94*
Perry, Francis J. 1918- *WhoAmP 93*
Perry, Frank 1923- *WhoAmA 93*
Perry, Frank 1930- *IntMPA 94, WhoAm 94, WhoHol 92*
Perry, Frank Anthony 1921- *WhoBlA 94*
Perry, Franklin D. *WhoBlA 94*
Perry, Fred 1909- *BuCMET [port]*
Perry, Fred(erick) John 1909- *IntWW 93*
Perry, Frederick John 1909- *Who 94*
Perry, Frederick Sayward, Jr. 1940- *WhoScEn 94*
Perry, Gail Walborn 1952- *WhoWest 94*
Perry, Gary W. 1952- *WhoBlA 94*
Perry, Gaylord Jackson 1938- *WhoAm 94*
Perry, George 1935- *WrDr 94*
Perry, George 1953- *WhoMW 93*
Perry, George Edward, Jr. 1936- *WhoAm 94*
Perry, George Henry 1920- *Who 94*
Perry, George Lewis 1934- *WhoAm 94*
Perry, George Williamson 1926- *WhoAmL 94*
Perry, George Wilson 1929- *WhoFI 94, WhoScEn 94*
Perry, Georgette *DrAPF 93*
Perry, Gerald 1960- *WhoBlA 94*
Perry, Glenn A. *AstEnc*
Perry, Glenn Earl 1940- *WhoMW 93*
Perry, Gordon E. 1932- *WhoAm 94, WhoFI 94*
Perry, Harold 1924- *WhoBlA 94*
Perry, Harold Otto 1921- *WhoAm 94*
Perry, Harold R. 1916-1991 *WhAm 10*
Perry, Harold Robert 1916- *AfrAmAl 6 [port]*
Perry, Harold Tyner 1926- *WhoMW 93*
Perry, Harry Montford 1943- *WhoScEn 94*
Perry, Hubert Carver 1911- *WhoWest 94*
Perry, I. Chet 1943- *WhoFI 94, WhoScEn 94*
Perry, Ida d1966 *WhoHol 92*
Perry, J. Warren 1921- *WhoAm 94*
Perry, Jack d1971 *WhoHol 92*
Perry, Jack Richard 1930- *WhoAmP 93*
Perry, Jacquelin 1918- *WhoAm 94*
Perry, James Alfred 1945- *WhoMW 93, WhoScEn 94*
Perry, James Benn 1950- *WhoAm 94*
Perry, James Frederic 1936- *WhoAm 94*
Perry, James Gregory 1952- *WhoFI 94, WhoWest 94*
Perry, Janet 1947- *NewGrDO*
Perry, Jean B. 1946- *WhoBlA 94*
Perry, Jean Louise 1950- *WhoWest 94*
Perry, Jerald Isaac, Sr. 1950- *WhoBlA 94*
Perry, Jerry Eileen *WhoAmP 93*
Perry, Jessie d1944 *WhoHol 92*
Perry, Joan 1915- *WhoHol 92*
Perry, Joe *ProFbHF*
Perry, John *Who 94*
Perry, John 1954- *WhoAmP 93, WhoWest 94*
Perry, (Rudolph) John 1936- *Who 94*
Perry, John B. 1945- *WhoBlA 94*
Perry, John Bennett 1941- *WhoHol 92*
Perry, John D. *WhoAmP 93*
Perry, John Freeman *Who 94*
Perry, John Neville 1920- *Who 94*
Perry, John Richard 1943- *IntWW 93, WhoAm 94*
Perry, John Spencer 1951- *WhoWest 94*
Perry, John Stephen 1931- *WhoScEn 94*
Perry, John Van Buren 1928- *WhoWest 94*
Perry, John William 1938- *Who 94*
Perry, Joseph *WhoHol 92*
Perry, Joseph James 1936- *WhoBlA 94*
Perry, Julia 1924-1979 *AfrAmAl 6*
Perry, Julia (Amanda) 1924-1979 *NewGrDO*
Perry, June Carter 1943- *WhoBlA 94*
Perry, June Martin 1947- *WhoBlA 94*
Perry, Kathryn 1902- *WhoHol 92*
Perry, Kathryn Powers 1948- *WhoAmA 93*
Perry, Kenneth Walter 1932- *WhoAm 94*
Perry, Kenneth Wilbur 1919- *WhoAm 94*
Perry, L. Tom *WhoWest 94*
Perry, Lallah Miles 1926- *WhoAmA 93*
Perry, Lansford Wilder 1955- *WhoFI 94*
Perry, Laval *WhoBlA 94*
Perry, Lee Charles, Jr. 1955- *WhoBlA 94*
Perry, Lee Rowan 1933- *WhoAm 94, WhoAmL 94, WhoFI 94, WhoWest 94*
Perry, Leland Charles 1942- *WhoScEn 94*
Perry, Leonard Douglas, Jr. 1952- *WhoBlA 94*
Perry, Lester Clayton 1950- *WhoMW 93*
Perry, Lewis Charles 1931- *WhoScEn 94*
Perry, Lewis Curtis 1938- *WhoAm 94*
Perry, Lincoln Frederick 1949- *WhoAmA 93*
Perry, Louis Barnes 1918- *WhoAm 94*
Perry, Lowell W. 1931- *WhoBlA 94*
Perry, Lowell Wesley, Jr. 1956- *WhoBlA 94*
Perry, Luke *WhoAm 94, WhoHol 92*
Perry, Luke 1966?- *ConTFT 11, IntMPA 94*
Perry, Malcolm Blythe 1930- *WhoAm 94*
Perry, Malcolm Oliver 1929- *WhoAm 94*
Perry, Margaret 1913- *WhoHol 92*
Perry, Margaret 1933- *WhoAm 94, WhoBlA 94, WrDr 94*
Perry, Margaret D. 1921- *WhoAmP 93*
Perry, Marilyn 1934- *WhoFI 94*
Perry, Marion *DrAPF 93*
Perry, Marion Walter 1911- *WhoFI 94*
Perry, Marney Dunman, Jr. 1926- *WhoAmP 93*
Perry, Marsha G. 1936- *WhoAmP 93*
Perry, Marvin Banks, Jr. 1918- *WhoAm 94*
Perry, Mary d1971 *WhoHol 92*
Perry, Mary Ethel 1929- *WhoAmP 93*
Perry, Matthew 1969- *WhoHol 92*
Perry, Matthew Calbraith 1794-1858 *HisWorL*
Perry, Matthew J., Jr. 1921- *WhoAm 94, WhoAmL 94*
Perry, Mervyn Francis 1923- *WhoAm 94*
Perry, Michael Charles 1933- *Who 94, WrDr 94*
Perry, Michael Clinton 1945- *WhoAm 94*
Perry, Michael Dean 1965- *WhoAm 94, WhoBlA 94, WhoMW 93*
Perry, Michael Dennis 1953- *WhoWest 94*
Perry, Michael Moore 1951- *WhoMW 93*
Perry, Michael Sydney 1934- *IntWW 93, Who 94*
Perry, Michael Thomas 1950- *WhoWest 94*
Perry, Morris 1925- *WhoHol 92*
Perry, N. Nick 1950- *WhoAmP 93*
Perry, Nancy Estelle 1934- *WhoMW 93*
Perry, Nancy Trotter 1935- *WhoFI 94*
Perry, Norman *Who 94*
Perry, Norman Henry 1944- *Who 94*
Perry, Norman L. 1928-1990 *WhAm 10*
Perry, Norman Robert 1929- *WhoAm 94*
Perry, Oliver Hazard 1785-1819 *HisWorL [port]*
Perry, Pamela Su 1948- *WhoMW 93*
Perry, Pascale d1953 *WhoHol 92*
Perry, Patsy Brewington 1933- *WhoBlA 94*
Perry, Paul 1926-1988 *WhAm 10*
Perry, Paul 1950- *ConAu 140*
Perry, Paul Alverson 1929- *WhoAm 94*
Perry, Peter George 1923- *Who 94*
Perry, R(alph) B(arton) 1876-1957 *EncEth*
Perry, Ralph Barton, III 1936- *WhoAm 94*
Perry, Raymond 1876-1960 *WhoAmA 93N*
Perry, Regenia Alfreda 1941- *WhoAmA 93*
Perry, Rhoda E. 1944- *WhoAmP 93*
Perry, Richard 1944- *WhoBlA 94*
Perry, Richard Lee 1930- *WhoWest 94*
Perry, Rick 1950- *WhoAmP 93*
Perry, Robert d1962 *WhoHol 92*
Perry, Robert Cephas 1946- *WhoBlA 94*
Perry, Robert Joseph 1932- *WhoAm 94*
Perry, Robert L. 1957- *WhoWest 94*
Perry, Robert Lee 1932- *WhoBlA 94, WhoMW 93, WhoScEn 94*
Perry, Robert Michael 1931- *WhoWest 94*
Perry, Robert Palese 1931- *IntWW 93, WhoAm 94*
Perry, Robert Ryan 1956- *WhoScEn 94*
Perry, Robin *DrAPF 93*
Perry, Roger *EncSF 93*
Perry, Roger 1933- *WhoHol 92*
Perry, Roger 1940- *Who 94*
Perry, Roger Lawrence 1923- *WhoAm 94*
Perry, Roland Rick 1958- *WhoFI 94, WhoHisp 94*
Perry, Ronald 1952- *WhoAm 94, WhoAmL 94*
Perry, Russell H. 1908-1988 *WhAm 10*
Perry, Samuel Victor 1918- *Who 94*
Perry, Sara d1959 *WhoHol 92*
Perry, Scott *WhoHol 92*
Perry, Seymour Monroe 1921- *IntWW 93, WhoAm 94, WhoScEn 94*
Perry, Sherryl Rosenbaum 1941- *WhoAmL 94*
Perry, Simon 1943- *IntMPA 94*
Perry, Spence William 1942- *WhoAm 94, WhoAmL 94*
Perry, Stephen Clay 1963- *WhoFI 94*
Perry, Stephen Clayton 1942- *WhoFI 94*
Perry, Steve 1947- *EncSF 93, SmATA 76 [port]*
Perry, Susan *WhoHol 92*
Perry, Suzanne Christl 1952- *WhoWest 94*
Perry, Thomas *WrDr 94*
Perry, Thornton Dudley 1941- *WhoAmP 93*
Perry, Tim 1958- *WhoAmP 93*
Perry, Timothy D. 1965- *WhoBlA 94*
Perry, Timothy J. 1929- *WhoWest 94*
Perry, Timothy Sewell 1947- *WhoAm 94, WhoAmL 94*
Perry, Val M. *WhoIns 94*
Perry, Victor d1974 *WhoHol 92*
Perry, Vincent Aloysius *WhoAm 94*
Perry, Walter d1934 *WhoHol 92*
Perry, Walter Copland 1814-1911 *EncSF 93*
Perry, Wanda d1985 *WhoHol 92*
Perry, Wayne D. 1944- *WhoBlA 94*
Perry, William Anthony 1962- *WhoBlA 94*
Perry, William Arthur 1937- *Who 94*
Perry, William Cox 1917-1988 *WhAm 10*
Perry, William E. 1932- *WhoBlA 94*
Perry, William James 1927- *WhoAm 94*
Perry, William Joseph 1930- *WhoWest 94*
Perry, William L. 1941- *WhoIns 94*
Perry, William Rodwell, III 1959- *WhoBlA 94*
Perry, William Walter 1949- *WhoFI 94*
Perry-Holston, Waltina D. 1959- *WhoBlA 94*
Perryman, Alford Armstrong d1985 *WhoHol 92*
Perryman, Bruce Clark 1939- *WhoWest 94*
Perryman, Diana d1979 *WhoHol 92*
Perryman, (Francis) Douglas 1930- *Who 94*
Perryman, James dc. 1882 *EncNAR*
Perryman, Jill 1933- *WhoHol 92*
Perryman, Joseph M. 1883- *EncNAR*
Perryman, Kent Michael 1940- *WhoWest 94*
Perryman, Lavonia Lauren *WhoBlA 94*
Perryman, Lloyd d1977 *WhoHol 92*

Perryman, Lorraine Bonner WhoAmP 93
Perryman, Robert 1964- WhoBlA 94
Perryman, Thomas Ward 1839-1903 EncNAR
Perry of Southwark, Baroness 1931- Who 94
Perry of Walton, Baron 1921- Who 94
Pers, Jessica S. 1950- WhoAmL 94
Persaud, Bishnodat 1933- WhoScEn 94
Persaud, Inder 1926- WhoBlA 94
Persaud, Lahkshmi BlmGWL
Persaud, Trivedi Vidhya Nandan 1940- WhoAm 94
Persavich, Warren Dale 1952- WhoAm 94
Perschbacher, Debra Bassett 1956- WhoAmL 94
Perschbacher, Rex Robert 1946- WhoAm 94
Perschetz, Arthur Driban 1943- WhoAmL 94, WhoIns 94
Perschetz, Martin L. 1952- WhoAm 94, WhoAmL 94
Perschy, Maria 1938- WhoHol 92
Perschy, Maria 1940- IntMPA 94
Perse, St.-John ConAu 43NR
Persekian, Tom WhoHol 92
Persell, Caroline Hodges 1941- WhoAm 94
Persellin, Robert Harold 1930- WhoAm 94
Pershan, Marion WhoAmA 93
Pershan, Richard Henry 1930- WhoAm 94
Pershe, Edward Richard 1924- WhoScEn 94
Pershing, David Walter 1948- WhoAm 94
Pershing, John J. 1860-1948 HisWorL [port]
Pershing, Lucille Virginia 1916- WhoAmP 93
Pershing, Robert George 1941- WhoAm 94, WhoMW 93
Persiani, Fanny NewGrDO
Persiani, Giuseppe c. 1799-1869 NewGrDO
Persichetti, Vincent 1915-1987 NewGrDO
Persico, Joseph E. 1930- WrDr 94
Persico, Joseph Edward 1930- WhoAm 94
Persico, Mario 1892-1977 NewGrDO
Persico, Vincent Anthony 1948- WhoAmP 93
Persina, William Eugene 1946- WhoAmL 94
Perske, Betty Joan 1924- WhoAm 94
Perskie, Steven Philip 1945- WhoAmP 93
Persky, Lester 1927- IntMPA 94, WhoAm 94
Persky, Lisa Jane 1955- WhoHol 92
Persky, Marilyn S. WhoHol 92
Persky, Robert S. 1930- WhoAmA 93
Persky, Victoria Weyler 1945- WhoMW 93
Persoff, Nehemiah 1919- IntMPA 94
Persoff, Nehemiah 1920- WhoHol 92
Person, Chuck Connors 1964- WhoBlA 94
Person, Curtis Standifer, Jr. 1934- WhoAmP 93
Person, Dawn Renee 1956- WhoBlA 94
Person, Donald Ames, Sr. 1938- WhoAm 94
Person, Earle G. 1928- WhoBlA 94
Person, Earle George, Jr. 1928- WhoAmP 93
Person, Evert Bertil 1914- WhoAm 94, WhoWest 94
Person, Leonard Alan 1943- WhoFI 94
Person, Leslie Robin 1962- WhoBlA 94
Person, Paula 1935- WhoMW 93
Person, Robert John 1927- WhoAm 94
Person, Thomas 1733-1800 WhAmRev
Person, Timothy David, Jr. 1954- WhoMW 93
Person, Tom DrAPF 93
Person, Victoria Bernadett 1958- WhoScEn 94
Person, Waverly J. 1926- WhoBlA 94
Person, William Alfred 1945- WhoBlA 94
Person, Willis Bagley 1928- WhoAm 94
Personick, Stewart David 1947- WhoAm 94
Persons, Daniel Jay 1962- WhoMW 93
Persons, J. Robert 1946- WhoAm 94, WhoAmL 94
Persons, Oscar N. 1939- WhoAm 94, WhoAmL 94
Persons, Oscar Newton 1939- WhoAmP 93
Persons, Stow Spaulding 1913- WhoAm 94
Persons, W. Ray 1953- WhoAmL 94, WhoBlA 94
Persoon, James Richard 1951- WhoFI 94
Persse, Thomas H. d1920 WhoHol 92
Persson, Erland Karl 1923- WhoAm 94
Persson, Essy WhoHol 92
Persson, Goran 1949- IntWW 93
Persson, Jorgen 1936- IntWW 93
Persson, Maria WhoHol 92
Persson, William Michael Dermot 1927- Who 94
Persuis, Louis-Luc Loiseau de 1769-1819 NewGrDO
Pert, Camille 1865-1952 BlmGWL
Pert, Candace WorScD
Pert, Edwin Harry 1933- WhoAmP 93
Pert, Michael 1947- Who 94
Perth, Archbishop of 1936- Who 94
Perth, Archbishop of 1937- Who 94
Perth, Assistant Bishop of Who 94
Perth, Earl of 1907- Who 94
Perth, Provost of Who 94
Perthou, Alison Chandler 1945- WhoWest 94
Perti, Giacomo Antonio 1661-1756 NewGrDO
Pertica, Alexander Jose 1961- WhoWest 94
Pertici, Caterina Brogi NewGrDO
Pertici, Pietro c. 1700-1768 NewGrDO
Pertile, Aureliano 1885-1952 NewGrDO
Pertini, Sandro 1896-1990 WhAm 10
Pertschuk, Michael 1933- WhoAmP 93
Pertwee, Bill 1926- WhoHol 92
Pertwee, Jon 1919- IntMPA 94, WhoHol 92
Pertwee, Michael (Henry Roland) 1916-1991 WrDr 94N
Pertwee, Roland d1963 WhoHol 92
Pertwee, Roland 1885-1963 EncSF 93
Peru and Bolivia, Bishop of 1949- Who 94
Perucci, Anna (Maria) NewGrDO
Peruggi, Regina S. WhoAm 94
Perumpral, John Verghese 1939- WhoScEn 94
Perun, John Joseph, Jr. 1963- WhoFI 94
Peruo, Marsha 1951- WhoAmA 93
Perusek, Wesley 1930- WhoMW 93
Perusso, Mario 1936- NewGrDO
Perutz, Kathrin DrAPF 93
Perutz, Leo 1882-1957 EncSF 93
Perutz, Max (Ferdinand) 1914- WrDr 94
Perutz, Max Ferdinand 1914- IntWW 93, Who 94, WhoAm 94, WhoScEn 94, WorScD
Peruzzi, Anna (Maria) fl. 1728- NewGrDO
Peruzzini, Giovanni 1815-1869 NewGrDO
Peruzzo, Albert Louis 1951- WhoFI 94, WhoMW 93
Pervin, William Joseph 1930- WhoAm 94
Pervyshin, Erlen Kirikovich 1932- IntWW 93
Pery Who 94
Pery, Nicole 1943- WhoWomW 91
Peryam, David Roger 1915-1992 WhAm 10
Perz, Sally WhoAmP 93
Perzek, Philip John 1960- WhoAmL 94
Perzel, John Michael 1950- WhoAmP 93
Pesacreta, George Joseph 1960- WhoScEn 94
Pesapane, John 1946- WhoWest 94
Pesaran, (Mohammad) Hashem 1946- Who 94
Pesaresi, Martin Hugo WhoAmL 94
Pescadero, Joey S. 1952- WrDr 94
Pescadero, Julia 1952- WrDr 94
Pescatore, Pierre 1919- IntWW 93
Pesce, Michael L. 1943- WhoAmP 93
Pescetti, Giovanni Battista c. 1704-1766 NewGrDO
Pesch, LeRoy Allen 1931- WhoAm 94, WhoFI 94
Peschka, Thomas Alan 1931- WhoAmL 94
Peschke, Donald B. 1947- WhoFI 94
Pesci, Frank Bernard, Sr. 1929- WhoAmP 93
Pesci, Joe 1943- IntMPA 94, WhoAm 94, WhoHol 92
Pesci, Timothy Louis 1944- WhoAmP 93
Pescia, Lisa WhoHol 92
Pescod, Mainwaring Bainbridge 1933- Who 94
Pescow, Donna 1954- IntMPA 94, WhoHol 92
Pesec, David John 1956- WhoMW 93
Pesek, Boris Peter 1926- WhoMW 93, WrDr 94
Pesek, James Robert 1941- WhoAm 94
Pesek, Libor 1933- IntWW 93, Who 94
Pesek, Ludek 1919- EncSF 93
Pesenti, Antonio 1910- IntWW 93
Peserik, James E. 1945- WhoScEn 94
Peseroff, Joyce DrAPF 93
Peseta, Tili BlmGWL
Pesetsky, Bette DrAPF 93
Pesetsky, Bette 1932- DcLB 130 [port], WrDr 94
Peshkin, Alan 1931- WhoAm 94
Peshkin, Murray 1925- WhoAm 94
Peshkin, Samuel David 1925- WhoAm 94, WhoAmL 94, WhoFI 94
Peshkov, Alexei Maximovich 1868-1936 ConAu 141
Pesic, Batric 1948- WhoFI 94
Peskett, Stanley Victor 1918- Who 94
Peskett, William 1952- WrDr 94
Peskin, Gary Lee 1952- WhoWest 94
Peskin, Kenneth WhoFI 94
Peskin, Matt Alan 1954- WhoAm 94
Peskin, Richard Martin 1944- Who 94
Peskin, Sheila Harriet 1935- WhoMW 93
Pesko, Zoltan 1937- NewGrDO
Pesmazoglu, John Stevens 1918- IntWW 93
Pesmen, Sandra 1931- WhoAm 94
Pesner, Carole Manishin 1937- WhoAm 94, WhoAmA 93
Pesner, Leon 1921- WhoAmP 93
Pesner, Steven M. 1945- WhoAmL 94
Pesola, Anja Helena 1947- IntWW 93
Pesola, William Ernest 1945- WhoFI 94, WhoMW 93
Pesqueira, Ralph Raymond WhoHisp 94
Pesqueira, Ralph Raymond 1935- WhoWest 94
Pesqueira, Richard E. 1937- WhoHisp 94
Pessard, Emile (Louis Fortune) 1843-1917 NewGrDO
Pessen, Edward 1920-1992 ConAu 140, WrDr 94N
Pessoa, Fernando 1888-1935 HispLC [port]
Pestalozzi, Johann 1746-1827 HisWorL [port]
Pestana, Alice BlmGWL
Pestana, Carla Gardina 1958- ConAu 141
Pestana, Carlos 1936- WhoAm 94
Pestana-Nascimento, Juan M. 1963- WhoScEn 94
Pestano, Gary Anthony 1966- WhoScEn 94
Pestell Who 94
Pestell, Catherine Eva Who 94
Pestell, Catherine Eva 1933- IntWW 93
Pestell, John Edmund 1930- Who 94
Pestell, John Richard 1916- Who 94
Pester, Jack Cloyd 1935- WhoFI 94
Pestillo, Peter John 1938- WhoFI 94
Pestle, John William 1948- WhoAm 94, WhoAmL 94
Peston, Baron 1931- Who 94
Pestronk, Alan 1946- WhoScEn 94
Pestureau, Pierre Gilbert 1933- WhoMW 93
Peszke, Michael Alfred 1932- WhoAm 94
Petaccia, Mario A. DrAPF 93
Petacque, Art 1924- WhoAm 94
Petacque, Arthur M. 1924- WhoMW 93
Petain, Henri-Philippe 1856-1951 HisWorL [port]
Petaja, Emil (Theodore) 1915- EncSF 93, WrDr 94
Petak, George WhoAmP 93
Petch, Barry Irvine 1933- Who 94
Petch, Norman James d1992 Who 94N
Petch, Norman James 1917- IntWW 93
Petchclai, Bencha 1937- WhoScEn 94
Petchler, John William 1956- WhoFI 94
Petelo, Tupuola WhoAmP 93
Petelos, Tony 1953- WhoAmP 93
Peter 1926- WhoAm 94
Peter, Arnold Philimon 1957- WhoAmL 94, WhoWest 94
Peter, Blume 1906-1992 AnObit 1992
Peter, Brunhilde 1925- WhoWomW 91
Peter, Carl Joseph 1932-1991 WhAm 10
Peter, Elias 1916- WrDr 94
Peter, Emmett, Jr. DrAPF 93
Peter, Frances Marchbank WhoAm 94
Peter, Friedrich Gunther 1933- WhoAmA 93
Peter, Gabor d1993 NewYTBS 93
Peter, George 1922- WhoAmA 93
Peter, Helmut W. 1932- WhoFI 94
Peter, Janos 1910- IntWW 93
Peter, Laurence Johnston 1919-1990 WhAm 10
Peter, Mac Nicol IntMPA 94
Peter, Martin August 1941- WhoMW 93
Peter, Phillips Smith 1932- WhoAm 94, WhoAmL 94, WhoFI 94
Peter, Richard Ector 1943- WhoAm 94
Peterborough, Bishop of 1925- Who 94
Peterborough, Dean of Who 94
Peter de Montfort c. 1205-1265 DcNaB MP
Peterdi, Gabor F. 1915- WhoAmA 93
Peterfreund, Sheldon Paul 1917- WhoAm 94
Peterfreund, Stuart DrAPF 93
Petering, David Harold 1942- WhoScEn 94
Petering, Janice Faye 1950- WhoAm 94
Petering, Ralph Edwin 1908-1990 WhAm 10
Peterken, Laurence Edwin 1931- Who 94
Peterkiewicz, Jerzy 1916- EncSF 93, Who 94, WrDr 94
Peterkin, DeWitt, Jr. 1913- WhoAm 94
Peterkin, George Alexander, Jr. 1927- WhoFI 94
Peterkin, Neville (Allan Mercer) 1915- Who 94
Peterle, Lozje 1948- IntWW 93
Peterle, Tony John 1925- WhoAm 94, WhoScEn 94
Peterlin, Boris Matija 1947- WhoScEn 94
Peterman, Bruce Edgar 1931- WhoAm 94
Peterman, Chris Allen 1952- WhoFI 94
Peterman, Leotis 1934- WhoBlA 94
Peterman, Mark H. 1947- WhoAm 94, WhoAmL 94
Peterman, Mynie Gustav 1896- WhAm 10
Peterman, Peggy M. 1936- WhoBlA 94
Peterman, Timothy Edward 1959- WhoMW 93
Petermann, August Heinrich 1822-1878 WhWE
Petermann, Gotz Eike 1941- WhoScEn 94
Peternal, Nancy Farrell 1929- WhoAmP 93
Peternel, Joan DrAPF 93
Peternell, Ben Clayton 1945- WhoFI 94
Peter of Cornwall c. 1140-1221 DcNaB MP
Peters, Aileen Marie d1978 WhoHol 92
Peters, Alan 1929- WhoAm 94, WhoScEn 94
Peters, Alexander Robert 1936- WhoMW 93
Peters, Alma Dorothy 1953- WhoMW 93
Peters, Alton Emil 1935- WhoAm 94
Peters, Andrea Jean 1947- WhoAmA 93
Peters, Andrew Warren 1929- WhoAmL 94
Peters, Ann d1965 WhoHol 92
Peters, Arthur Gordon Who 94
Peters, Arthur King 1919- WhoAm 94
Peters, Audrey WhoHol 92
Peters, Aulana Louise 1941- WhoAm 94, WhoAmL 94, WhoBlA 94
Peters, Barbara Humbird 1948- WhoWest 94
Peters, Barbara M. Stratton 1949- WhoWest 94
Peters, Bernadette 1948- IntMPA 94, WhoAm 94, WhoHol 92
Peters, Boyd Leon 1951- WhoMW 93
Peters, Brian 1919- WrDr 94
Peters, Brock 1927- IntMPA 94, WhoHol 92
Peters, Brock G. 1927- WhoBlA 94
Peters, Carl H. 1946- WhoMW 93
Peters, Carl W. 1897-1980 WhoAmA 93N
Peters, Carol Ann Dudycha 1938- WhoMW 93
Peters, Carol Beattie Taylor 1932- WhoScEn 94
Peters, Charles L., Jr. 1935- WhoBlA 94
Peters, Charles Martin 1955- WhoScEn 94
Peters, Charles William 1927- WhoAm 94
Peters, Cheryl Olga 1951- WhoIns 94
Peters, Clarke WhoHol 92
Peters, Connie 1933- WhoAmP 93
Peters, David EncSF 93
Peters, David Allen 1947- WhoAm 94
Peters, David Frankman 1941- WhoAm 94
Peters, David Keith 1938- Who 94
Peters, David Louis 1945- WhoFI 94
Peters, David M. 1954- WhoAmP 93
Peters, Deanna Jean 1964- WhoWest 94
Peters, Deborah Lynn 1954- WhoMW 93
Peters, Dennis Gail 1937- WhoAm 94
Peters, Diane (Peck) 1940- WhoAmA 93
Peters, Donald Cameron 1915- WhoAm 94
Peters, Donald Joseph 1959- WhoFI 94
Peters, Donald Mullen 1950- WhoAmL 94
Peters, Douglas Cameron 1955- WhoWest 94
Peters, Douglas Scott 1943- WhoAm 94
Peters, Edgar Eugene 1952- WhoFI 94
Peters, Edward Murray 1936- WhoAm 94
Peters, Elizabeth 1927- WrDr 94
Peters, Elizabeth Ann Hampton 1934- WhoMW 93
Peters, Ellen Ash WhoAmP 93
Peters, Ellen Ash 1930- WhoAm 94, WhoAmL 94
Peters, Ellis ConAu 41NR, IntWW 93, Who 94
Peters, Ellis 1913- WrDr 94
Peters, Ernest 1926- WhoAm 94
Peters, Erskine Alvin 1948- WhoBlA 94
Peters, Esther Caroline 1952- WhoScEn 94
Peters, Farnsley Lewellyn 1929- WhoAm 94
Peters, Fenton 1935- WhoBlA 94
Peters, Francis C. 1902-1977 WhoAmA 93N
Peters, Frank Albert 1931- WhoFI 94, WhoScEn 94
Peters, Frank Lewis, Jr. 1930- WhoAm 94
Peters, Fred d1963 WhoHol 92
Peters, Frederick Whitten 1946- WhoAmL 94
Peters, Galen Roger 1942- WhoMW 93
Peters, George Henry 1934- Who 94

Peters, George J. *WhoHol 92*
Peters, Gerald Richard 1932- *WhoMW 93*
Peters, Geraldine Joan *WhoWest 94*
Peters, Gordon Benes 1931- *WhoAm 94*
Peters, Gwendolyn Maxine 1954- *WhoMW 93*
Peters, Henry Augustus 1920- *WhoAm 94*
Peters, Henry Buckland 1916- *WhoAm 94*
Peters, Henry H. 1941- *WhoAmP 93, WhoWest 94*
Peters, Herbert David 1948- *WhoAmP 93*
Peters, House d1967 *WhoHol 92*
Peters, House, Jr. 1916- *WhoHol 92*
Peters, Howard Nevin 1938- *WhoAm 94*
Peters, J. Elbert 1933- *WhoAmP 93*
Peters, Jack d1993 *NewYTBS 93 [port]*
Peters, James Empson 1954- *WhoScEn 94*
Peters, James Ray 1946- *WhoAm 94*
Peters, James Sedalia, II *WhoBlA 94*
Peters, Jane *WhoHol 92*
Peters, Jean 1926- *WhoHol 92*
Peters, Joan K. *DrAPF 93*
Peters, John d1940 *WhoHol 92*
Peters, John 1740-1788 *WhAmRev*
Peters, John Edward 1931- *WhoAm 94*
Peters, John Eric 1962- *WhoWest 94*
Peters, John Lyon 1920- *WhoAmP 93*
Peters, John S. d1963 *WhoHol 92*
Peters, Johnnie Mae 1929- *WhoAmP 93*
Peters, Jon 1947- *IntMPA 94, WhoAm 94*
Peters, Jon Fleming 1945- *WhoWest 94*
Peters, Jonathan C. 1946- *IntWW 93*
Peters, Joyce Eileen 1953- *WhoWest 94*
Peters, Kay *WhoHol 92*
Peters, Kelly Jean *WhoHol 92*
Peters, Kenneth Darryl, Sr. 1949- *WhoBlA 94, WhoWest 94*
Peters, Kenneth Gerald d1993 *NewYTBS 93*
Peters, Kenneth Jamieson 1923- *Who 94*
Peters, Kenneth P. 1952- *WhoAmP 93*
Peters, Kevin Casey 1952- *WhoAmP 93*
Peters, Kurt Thomas 1950- *WhoMW 93*
Peters, Larry Dean 1938- *WhoAmA 93*
Peters, Laura Lee *WhoAmP 93*
Peters, Lauralee Milberg 1943- *WhoAm 94*
Peters, Lauri 1943- *WhoHol 92*
Peters, Lawrence *EncSF 93*
Peters, Lawrence H. 1945- *WhoAm 94*
Peters, Lenrie (Leopold) 1932- *WrDr 94*
Peters, Leo Francis 1937- *WhoScEn 94*
Peters, Leon, Jr. 1923- *WhoAm 94, WhoScEn 94*
Peters, Linda *SmATA 74*
Peters, Lisa Westberg 1951- *ConAu 141, SmATA 74 [port]*
Peters, Lori Susan 1958- *WhoFI 94, WhoMW 93*
Peters, Ludovic 1931-1984 *EncSF 93*
Peters, Margot (McCullough) 1933- *WrDr 94*
Peters, Marilyn A. 1952- *WhoAmL 94*
Peters, Marjorie Young 1928- *WhoAmP 93*
Peters, Martin Trevor 1936- *Who 94*
Peters, Mary Elizabeth 1939- *Who 94*
Peters, Matty d1983 *WhoHol 92*
Peters, Maureen 1935- *WrDr 94*
Peters, Melodie *WhoAmP 93*
Peters, Mercedes *WhoScEn 94*
Peters, Michael Bartley 1943- *WhoAm 94, WhoMW 93*
Peters, Michael Ray 1949- *WhoAmP 93*
Peters, Natasha *WrDr 94*
Peters, Page d1916 *WhoHol 92*
Peters, Patricia Ann 1938- *WhoAmP 93*
Peters, Paula Anne 1962- *WhoMW 93*
Peters, Perry 1931- *WhoAmP 93*
Peters, Peter d1955 *WhoHol 92*
Peters, R. Jonathan 1927- *WhoAmL 94*
Peters, Ralph d1959 *WhoHol 92*
Peters, Ralph 1952- *ConAu 140*
Peters, Ralph B. 1922- *WhoAmP 93*
Peters, Ralph Edgar 1923- *WhoFI 94*
Peters, Ralph Frew 1929- *WhoAm 94*
Peters, Ralph Irwin, Jr. 1947- *WhoScEn 94*
Peters, Ralph Martin 1926- *WhoAm 94*
Peters, Randal Craig 1956- *WhoFI 94*
Peters, Randy Alan 1953- *WhoScEn 94*
Peters, Raymond Eugene 1933- *WhoFI 94, WhoScEn 94, WhoWest 94*
Peters, Raymond Harry 1918- *Who 94*
Peters, Richard c. 1744-1828 *WhAmRev*
Peters, Richard Stanley 1919- *Who 94, WrDr 94*
Peters, Richard T. 1946- *WhoAm 94, WhoAmL 94*
Peters, Robert *DrAPF 93*
Peters, Robert 1924- *WrDr 94*
Peters, Robert Allen 1937- *WhoMW 93*
Peters, Robert G. *WhoAmP 93*
Peters, Robert Geoffrey 1940- *Who 94*
Peters, Robert Timothy 1946- *WhoAmL 94*
Peters, Robert Wayne 1950- *WhoFI 94, WhoWest 94*
Peters, Robert William 1921- *WhoScEn 94*
Peters, Roberta 1930- *NewGrDO, WhoAm 94, WhoHol 92*
Peters, Roscoe Hoffman, Jr. 1945- *WhoBlA 94*
Peters, S. Jeffrey 1924- *WhoFI 94*
Peters, Samuel 1735-1826 *WhAmRev*
Peters, Samuel A. 1934- *WhoBlA 94*
Peters, Samuel Anthony 1934- *WhoAmL 94*
Peters, Sarah Whitaker 1924- *WhoAm 94*
Peters, Scott *WhoHol 92*
Peters, Sheila Renee 1959- *WhoBlA 94*
Peters, Stanley Thomas 1934- *WhoAm 94*
Peters, Stanley W. 1927- *WhoAmP 93*
Peters, Steven 1948- *WhoFI 94*
Peters, Susan d1952 *WhoHol 92*
Peters, Theodore, Jr. 1922- *WhoScEn 94*
Peters, Theophilus 1921- *Who 94*
Peters, Thomas J. 1942- *WrDr 94*
Peters, Thomas Robert 1929- *WhoMW 93*
Peters, Virginia *WhoHol 92*
Peters, Virginia 1924- *WhoAm 94*
Peters, Wallace 1924- *IntWW 93, Who 94*
Peters, Werner d1972 *WhoHol 92*
Peters, William 1921- *WhoAm 94*
Peters, William 1923- *Who 94*
Peters, William Alfred 1940- *WhoBlA 94*
Peters, William C(allier) 1920- *WrDr 94*
Peters, William Frank 1934- *WhoWest 94*
Peters, William Henry 1928- *WhoAm 94*
Peters, William P. 1950- *WhoAm 94*
Peters, William R. 1946- *WhoAmL 94*
Peters, William Wesley 1912-1991 *WhAm 10*
Peters, Winston R. *IntWW 93*
Peters, Yanis 1939- *IntWW 93*
Petersdorf, Robert George 1926- *IntWW 93, WhoAm 94, WhoScEn 94*
Petersen, Allan Ernest 1918- *WhoBlA 94*
Petersen, Anne Cheryl 1944- *WhoAm 94*
Petersen, Arthur Everett, Jr. 1949- *WhoBlA 94*
Petersen, Arthur Meredith 1942- *WhoWest 94*
Petersen, Bent Edvard 1942- *WhoAm 94*
Petersen, Bruce *WhoIns 94*
Petersen, Bruce N. 1948- *WhoAmP 93*
Petersen, Catherine Holland 1951- *WhoAmL 94*
Petersen, Christian Peter 1946- *WhoFI 94*
Petersen, Colin 1946- *WhoHol 92*
Petersen, Daniel F. 1951- *WhoAmP 93*
Petersen, David c. 1650-1737 *NewGrDO*
Petersen, David L. *WhoAm 94, WhoAmL 94*
Petersen, Dean Mitchell 1950- *WhoFI 94*
Petersen, Donald *DrAPF 93*
Petersen, Donald Edward 1958- *WhoAmL 94*
Petersen, Donald Eugene 1926- *IntWW 93*
Petersen, Donald Felix 1928- *WhoFI 94, WhoWest 94*
Petersen, Donald Sondergaard 1929- *WhoAm 94*
Petersen, Douglas Arndt 1944- *WhoFI 94, WhoMW 93*
Petersen, Douglas W. *WhoAmP 93*
Petersen, Edwin L. 1944- *WhoWest 94*
Petersen, Eileen Ramona 1937- *WhoBlA 94*
Petersen, Elsa d1974 *WhoHol 92*
Petersen, Finn Bo 1951- *WhoWest 94*
Petersen, Forrest Silas 1922-1990 *WhAm 10*
Petersen, Frank E. 1932- *AfrAmG [port], AfrAmAl 6 [port]*
Petersen, Frank Emmanuel, Jr. 1932- *WhoBlA 94*
Petersen, Franklin G. 1940- *WhoAmA 93*
Petersen, Gene A. 1942- *WhoAmL 94*
Petersen, George Bouet 1933- *IntWW 93*
Petersen, Gregg Emil 1956- *WhoWest 94*
Petersen, Howard C. 1910- *IntWW 93*
Petersen, Howard Edwin 1932- *WhoAmL 94*
Petersen, James L. 1947- *WhoAm 94, WhoAmL 94*
Petersen, James M. 1942- *WhoAmL 94*
Petersen, Jeffrey (Charles) 1920- *Who 94*
Petersen, Jens 1923- *IntWW 93*
Petersen, Joan Marie 1942- *WhoMW 93*
Petersen, Johannes B. *Who 94*
Petersen, Kenneth Clarence 1936- *WhoAm 94*
Petersen, Kenneth James 1949- *WhoMW 93*
Petersen, Kent A. 1947- *WhoFI 94*
Petersen, Kim Eberhard 1956- *WhoFI 94*
Petersen, Lyndell 1931- *WhoAmP 93*
Petersen, Mark Dean 1951- *WhoAmL 94*
Petersen, Martin Eugene 1931- *WhoAm 94*
Petersen, Maureen Jeanette Miller 1956- *WhoFI 94, WhoMW 93*
Petersen, Michael Kevin 1959- *WhoWest 94*
Petersen, Niels Helveg 1939- *IntWW 93*
Petersen, Norman Richard, Jr. 1933- *WhoAm 94*
Petersen, Norman William 1933- *WhoFI 94*
Petersen, P(eter) J(ames) 1941- *TwCYAW*
Petersen, Pat 1967- *WhoHol 92*
Petersen, Paul 1945- *IntMPA 94, WhoHol 92*
Petersen, Perry Marvin 1933- *WhoScEn 94*
Petersen, Peter d1956 *WhoHol 92*
Petersen, Ralph Allen *WhoScEn 94*
Petersen, Raymond Joseph 1919- *WhoAm 94*
Petersen, Richard Herman 1934- *WhoScEn 94*
Petersen, Robin Mark 1956- *WhoAmL 94*
Petersen, Roland 1926- *WhoAm 94, WhoWest 94*
Petersen, Roland Conrad 1926- *WhoAmA 93*
Petersen, Stephen D. 1943- *WhoAmL 94*
Petersen, Stewart *WhoHol 92*
Petersen, Susan Jane 1944- *WhoAm 94*
Petersen, Toni 1933- *WhoAm 94, WhoAmA 93*
Petersen, Ulrich 1927- *WhoAm 94*
Petersen, Vernon Leroy 1926- *WhoWest 94*
Petersen, W. Harold 1928- *WhoIns 94*
Petersen, Will 1928- *WhoAmA 93*
Petersen, William 1953- *IntMPA 94, WhoHol 92*
Petersen, William Otto 1926- *WhoAm 94*
Petersen, Wolfgang 1941- *IntMPA 94*
Petersen-Frey, Roland 1937- *WhoFI 94*
Petersham, Viscount 1945- *Who 94*
Petersham, Miska 1888-1959 *WhoAmA 93N*
Petersmeyer, Charles Wrede 1919- *WhoAm 94*
Petersmeyer, John Clinton 1945- *WhoMW 93, WhoScEn 94*
Peterson, A. E. S. 1908-1984 *WhoAmA 93N*
Peterson, Adaire *WhoIns 94*
Peterson, Agnes Marie 1926- *WhoAmP 93*
Peterson, Alan Herbert 1948- *WhoBlA 94*
Peterson, Alan J. *WhoAmP 93*
Peterson, Alan Julius 1951- *WhoMW 93*
Peterson, Alan Reed 1940- *WhoAmP 93*
Peterson, Allan *DrAPF 93*
Peterson, Alphonse 1926- *WhoBlA 94*
Peterson, Amanda 1971- *WhoHol 92*
Peterson, Andrew C. 1941- *WhoAmL 94*
Peterson, Anita Ann *WhoWest 94*
Peterson, Ann-Marie *WhoHol 92*
Peterson, Ann Sullivan 1928- *WhoAm 94, WhoMW 93*
Peterson, Annamarie Jane 1936- *WhoMW 93*
Peterson, Arthur 1912- *WhoHol 92*
Peterson, Arthur Laverne 1926- *WhoAm 94*
Peterson, Audrey *WrDr 94*
Peterson, Audrey Clinton 1917- *WhoBlA 94*
Peterson, Barbara Ann Bennett 1942- *WhoWest 94*
Peterson, Barry Lockwood 1935- *WhoAmL 94*
Peterson, Benjamin 1942- *WhoBlA 94*
Peterson, Bergen Voros 1959- *WhoWest 94*
Peterson, Betty Ann 1929- *WhoAmP 93*
Peterson, Bill d1993 *NewYTBS 93*
Peterson, Bill 1954- *WhoAm 94, WhoWest 94*
Peterson, Bob d1981 *WhoHol 92*
Peterson, Bonnie Jean 1951- *WhoMW 93*
Peterson, Bradley Eugene 1961- *WhoFI 94, WhoMW 93*
Peterson, Brooke Alan 1949- *WhoAmL 94, WhoWest 94*
Peterson, Bruce Henry 1918- *WrDr 94*
Peterson, Bryan Charles 1956- *WhoScEn 94*
Peterson, Carl *WhoAm 94, WhoMW 93*
Peterson, Carl Adrian 1930- *WhoMW 93*
Peterson, Carl Eric 1944- *WhoAm 94*
Peterson, Carl Herbert 1922- *WhoWest 94*
Peterson, Carl M. 1914- *WhoBlA 94*
Peterson, Carl Roy 1930- *WhoAm 94*
Peterson, Carl Stuart 1966- *WhoWest 94*
Peterson, Carl William, Jr. 1932- *WhoAmL 94*
Peterson, Cary G. 1953- *WhoAmP 93*
Peterson, Cassandra 1951- *WhoHol 92*
Peterson, Cathryn J. 1952- *WhoIns 94*
Peterson, Cathryn Mary *Who 94*
Peterson, Charlene Marie 1953- *WhoMW 93*
Peterson, Charles E. 1914- *WhoAmP 93*
Peterson, Charles Emil 1906- *WhoAm 94*
Peterson, Charles Eric 1914- *WhoWest 94*
Peterson, Charles Gordon 1926- *WhoAm 94*
Peterson, Charles Hayes 1938- *WhoAm 94*
Peterson, Charles Lloyd 1927- *WhoMW 93*
Peterson, Charles Loren 1938- *WhoAm 94, WhoScEn 94*
Peterson, Charles Marquis 1943- *WhoScEn 94*
Peterson, Charles Roland 1935- *WhoAmP 93*
Peterson, Chase N. 1929- *WhoAm 94, WhoWest 94*
Peterson, Chris(tine Louise) 1957- *ConAu 141*
Peterson, Christian Mark 1954- *WhoMW 93*
Peterson, Christmas 1939- *WrDr 94*
Peterson, Clarence Josephus 1932- *WhoBlA 94*
Peterson, Colin Hampton 1923- *WhoFI 94*
Peterson, Colin Vyvyan 1932- *Who 94*
Peterson, Collin C. 1944- *CngDr 93, WhoAm 94, WhoMW 93*
Peterson, Collin Clark 1944- *WhoAmP 93*
Peterson, Courtland Harry 1930- *WhoAm 94*
Peterson, Craig A. 1947- *WhoAmP 93*
Peterson, Curtis Gerald 1952- *WhoWest 94*
Peterson, Curtis N. *WhoAmP 93*
Peterson, Dave *WhoHol 92*
Peterson, David 1943- *IntWW 93*
Peterson, David Andreas 1939- *WhoAm 94*
Peterson, David Charles 1949- *WhoAm 94, WhoMW 93*
Peterson, David Don 1957- *WhoFI 94*
Peterson, David Frederick 1937- *WhoAm 94, WhoAmP 93*
Peterson, David Maurice 1940- *WhoScEn 94*
Peterson, David Robert 1943- *Who 94, WhoAm 94*
Peterson, David Winfield 1913- *WhoAmA 93*
Peterson, Dawn Eileen 1955- *WhoMW 93*
Peterson, Dean McCormack 1931- *WhoWest 94*
Peterson, Debra Leigh Curtis 1953- *WhoMW 93*
Peterson, Delaine Charles 1936- *WhoAmL 94, WhoFI 94*
Peterson, Donald 1956- *WrDr 94*
Peterson, Donald C. *WhoAmP 93*
Peterson, Donald Curtis 1931- *WhoFI 94*
Peterson, Donald Franklin 1925- *WhoIns 94*
Peterson, Donald M. 1936- *WhoIns 94*
Peterson, Donald Matthew 1936- *WhoFI 94*
Peterson, Donald Robert 1923- *WhoAm 94*
Peterson, Donald Robert 1929- *WhoAm 94*
Peterson, Donald William 1925- *WhoWest 94*
Peterson, Donald Wilton 1929- *WhoAmL 94*
Peterson, Donn Neal 1942- *WhoMW 93, WhoScEn 94*
Peterson, Donna C. 1946- *WhoAmP 93*
Peterson, Dorothy d1979 *WhoHol 92*
Peterson, Dorothy (Hawkins) 1932- *WhoAmA 93*
Peterson, Dorothy Hawkins 1932- *WhoWest 94*
Peterson, Doug 1948- *WhoAmP 93*
Peterson, Douglas 1935- *WhoAm 94*
Peterson, Douglas Arthur 1945- *WhoMW 93, WhoScEn 94*
Peterson, Douglas S. 1966- *WhoAmP 93*
Peterson, Duane M. 1929- *WhoMW 93*
Peterson, Dwight Arthur 1948- *WhoAmP 93*
Peterson, Dwight Malcolm 1957- *WhoScEn 94*
Peterson, Edward Adrian 1941- *WhoAm 94, WhoAmL 94*
Peterson, Edward N. 1925- *WrDr 94*
Peterson, Edward Nohl 1930- *WhoAm 94, WhoMW 93*
Peterson, Edwin J. 1930- *WhoAm 94, WhoAmL 94, WhoAmP 93, WhoWest 94*
Peterson, Edwin Loose 1915- *WrDr 94*
Peterson, Elmer 1930- *WrDr 94*
Peterson, Elmor Lee 1938- *WhoAm 94*
Peterson, Eric Christian 1950- *WhoAm 94*
Peterson, Eric Follett 1960- *WhoScEn 94*
Peterson, Eric Scott 1962- *WhoScEn 94*
Peterson, Erle Vidaillet 1915- *WhoWest 94*
Peterson, Esther 1906- *WhoAm 94*
Peterson, Esther Eggertsen 1906- *WhoAmP 93*
Peterson, Frank Robert 1951- *WhoWest 94*

Peterson, Franklin Delano 1932- *WhoAmL 94*
Peterson, Fred McCrae 1936- *WhoAm 94*
Peterson, Fred W. 1932- *ConAu 140*
Peterson, Gale Eugene 1944- *WhoAm 94, WhoMW 93*
Peterson, Garry Freeman 1942- *WhoMW 93*
Peterson, Gary 1945- *WhoScEn 94*
Peterson, Gary Andrew 1940- *WhoAm 94*
Peterson, Geoff *DrAPF 93*
Peterson, George E. 1947- *WhoAmL 94*
Peterson, George Emanuel, Jr. 1931- *WhoAm 94*
Peterson, George P. 1930- *WhoAm 94, WhoScEn 94*
Peterson, Georgia Bodell *WhoAmP 93*
Peterson, Gerald Alvin 1931- *WhoAm 94*
Peterson, Gerald C. 1948- *WhoAm 94*
Peterson, Gerard M. 1932- *WhoBlA 94*
Peterson, Gil *WhoHol 92*
Peterson, Glenn Stephen 1952- *WhoScEn 94*
Peterson, Glenn Viggo 1928- *WhoWest 94*
Peterson, Gwen Entz 1938- *WhoAmA 93*
Peterson, Harold Albert 1908- *WhoAm 94*
Peterson, Harold Oscar 1909-1992 *WhAm 10*
Peterson, Harold Patrick 1935- *WhoAmA 93*
Peterson, Harries-Clichy 1924- *WhoAm 94*
Peterson, Harry Leroy 1940- *WhoWest 94*
Peterson, Harry W. 1923- *WhoBlA 94*
Peterson, Holger Martin 1912- *WhoFI 94, WhoScEn 94*
Peterson, Horace M., III 1945-1992 *WhoBlA 94N*
Peterson, Howard Cooper 1939- *WhoAmL 94, WhoFI 94, WhoWest 94*
Peterson, Howard George Finnemore 1951- *WhoAm 94, WhoWest 94*
Peterson, Indira Viswanathan *WhoAsA 94*
Peterson, Ingrid Janet 1935- *WhoMW 93*
Peterson, Irene Renie 1927- *WhoWest 94*
Peterson, Isobel Rose 1911- *WhoAmP 93*
Peterson, Jack Milton 1920- *WhoScEn 94*
Peterson, James A. 1935- *WhoAmP 93*
Peterson, James Algert 1915- *WhoAm 94, WhoScEn 94, WhoWest 94*
Peterson, James Alma 1950- *WhoWest 94*
Peterson, James August 1935- *WhoFI 94*
Peterson, James Kenneth 1934- *WhoAm 94*
Peterson, James Lincoln 1942- *WhoAm 94, WhoMW 93*
Peterson, James Robert 1927- *WhoAm 94*
Peterson, Jan Kent 1945- *WhoWest 94*
Peterson, Jane 1876-1965 *WhoAmA 93N*
Peterson, Janet Smyrl 1954- *WhoMW 93*
Peterson, Jerome *WhoAmP 93*
Peterson, Jim *DrAPF 93*
Peterson, JoAnne Elizabeth 1947- *WhoMW 93*
Peterson, John 1935- *WhoAmP 93*
Peterson, John Douglas 1939- *WhoAm 94, WhoAmA 93*
Peterson, John Dwight 1933- *WhoFI 94*
Peterson, John E. 1938- *WhoAmP 93*
Peterson, John Eric 1914- *WhoAm 94, WhoWest 94*
Peterson, John L. 1953- *WhoAmP 93*
Peterson, John Leonard 1933- *WhoAm 94, WhoAmL 94, WhoWest 94*
Peterson, John P. d1949 *WhoAmA 93N*
Peterson, Julie 1949- *WhoAmP 93*
Peterson, Karen *DrAPF 93*
Peterson, Keith *DrAPF 93*
Peterson, Keith James 1951- *WhoMW 93*
Peterson, Kenner Charles 1945- *WhoWest 94*
Peterson, Kenneth Allen, Sr. 1939- *WhoMW 93*
Peterson, Kent Wright 1943- *WhoAm 94*
Peterson, Kevin Bruce 1948- *WhoAm 94, WhoWest 94*
Peterson, Kevin Merle 1950- *WhoWest 94*
Peterson, Kirk Charles 1949- *WhoAm 94*
Peterson, Kristin 1954- *WhoAmA 93*
Peterson, Kristina *WhoAm 94*
Peterson, Lance Robert 1947- *WhoMW 93*
Peterson, Larry Charles 1940- *WhoWest 94*
Peterson, Larry D. 1935- *WhoAmA 93*
Peterson, Lauren Michael 1943- *WhoScEn 94*
Peterson, Lenka 1925- *WhoHol 92*
Peterson, Leroy 1930- *WhoWest 94*
Peterson, Leroy DeWayne 1941- *WhoAmP 93*
Peterson, Leslie Ernest *Who 94*
Peterson, Leslie Raymond 1923- *WhoAm 94*
Peterson, Levi Savage 1933- *WhoWest 94*
Peterson, Linda S. 1952- *WhoAm 94*
Peterson, Lisa Lee 1959- *WhoFI 94*
Peterson, Lloyd, Jr. 1958- *WhoBlA 94*
Peterson, Lorna Ingrid 1956- *WhoBlA 94*
Peterson, Louis (Stamford, Jr.) 1922- *BlkWr 2*
Peterson, Louis Robert 1923- *WhoAm 94*
Peterson, Lowell 1950- *WhoWest 94*
Peterson, Lowell S. 1937- *WhoAmP 93*
Peterson, M. Roger 1929- *WhoAm 94*
Peterson, Marcella Tandy *WhoBlA 94*
Peterson, Marilyn Ann Whitney 1933- *WhoMW 93*
Peterson, Marion 1923- *WhoAmP 93*
Peterson, Marjorie d1974 *WhoHol 92*
Peterson, Mark Bradley 1957- *WhoAmL 94*
Peterson, Martha 1916- *IntWW 93*
Peterson, Martin Lynn 1943- *WhoAmP 93*
Peterson, Martin Severin 1897- *WhAm 10*
Peterson, Mary *DrAPF 93*
Peterson, Mary Ellis *DrAPF 93*
Peterson, Mary Lou 1931- *WhoAmP 93*
Peterson, Maurice 1952- *WhoBlA 94*
Peterson, Merle Francis 1916- *WhoAmP 93*
Peterson, Merrill D. 1921- *WrDr 94*
Peterson, Merrill Daniel 1921- *WhoAm 94*
Peterson, Michael A. 1953- *WhoAmL 94*
Peterson, Michael Charles 1960- *WhoWest 94*
Peterson, Michael J. *WhoAmP 93*
Peterson, Michael K. 1960- *WhoAmP 93*
Peterson, Michelle Monica 1959- *WhoBlA 94*
Peterson, Mildred Othmer 1902- *WhoAm 94*
Peterson, Millie M. 1944- *WhoAmP 93, WhoWest 94*
Peterson, Monica *WhoAm 94, WhoHol 92*
Peterson, N. Curtis, Jr. 1922- *WhoAm 94, WhoAmP 93*
Peterson, Nad Alma 1926- *WhoAm 94, WhoFI 94*
Peterson, Nadeen 1934- *WhoAm 94, WhoFI 94*
Peterson, Nan *WhoHol 92*
Peterson, Nancy 1943- *WhoAmP 93*
Peterson, Nancy Ann 1947- *WhoFI 94*
Peterson, Nancy Jo 1955- *WhoFI 94*
Peterson, Norris Adrian 1953- *WhoFI 94*
Peterson, O. *WhoMW 93*
Peterson, Oscar 1925- *AfrAmAl 6 [port], ConMus 11 [port]*
Peterson, Oscar Emmanuel 1925- *IntWW 93, Who 94, WhoAm 94, WhoBlA 94*
Peterson, Oscar James, III 1935- *WhoAm 94*
Peterson, Osler Leopold 1946- *WhoAmL 94*
Peterson, P. Kurt 1949- *WhoAmL 94*
Peterson, Pamela Parrish 1954- *WhoFI 94*
Peterson, Patricia Elizabeth 1942- *WhoMW 93*
Peterson, Patricia Lynn 1952- *WhoMW 93*
Peterson, Patti McGill 1943- *WhoAm 94*
Peterson, Paul Ames 1928- *WhoAmL 94*
Peterson, Paul E. 1940- *IntWW 93*
Peterson, Paul Edward 1935- *WhoMW 93*
Peterson, Paul Michael 1954- *WhoScEn 94*
Peterson, Paul Murrey 1897- *WhAm 10*
Peterson, Paul Quayle 1912- *WhoAm 94*
Peterson, Perry 1908-1958 *WhoAmA 93N*
Peterson, Pete 1935- *CngDr 93, WhoAm 94, WhoAmP 93*
Peterson, Peter G. 1926- *IntWW 93, WhoAm 94, WhoFI 94*
Peterson, Philip Everett 1922- *WhoAm 94*
Peterson, Ralph 1924- *WhoAm 94*
Peterson, Ralph Edward 1932- *WhoAm 94*
Peterson, Randolph W. 1953- *WhoAmP 93*
Peterson, Ray E. 1938- *WhoAmP 93*
Peterson, Raymond A. *WhoAm 94, WhoFI 94*
Peterson, Renno Louis 1948- *WhoAmL 94*
Peterson, Richard 1928- *WhoAmP 93*
Peterson, Richard Austin 1932- *WrDr 94*
Peterson, Richard Edward 1946- *WhoWest 94*
Peterson, Richard Elton 1941- *WhoAm 94, WhoMW 93*
Peterson, Richard Hamlin 1914- *WhoAm 94*
Peterson, Richard Harold 1942- *WhoAm 94*
Peterson, Richard Hermann 1942- *WhoWest 94*
Peterson, Richard S(cot) 1938- *WrDr 94*
Peterson, Richard W. 1949- *IntMPA 94*
Peterson, Richard William 1925- *WhoAm 94, WhoAmL 94*
Peterson, Robert *DrAPF 93*
Peterson, Robert Allen 1944- *WhoAm 94*
Peterson, Robert Austin 1925- *WhoAm 94, WhoFI 94*
Peterson, Robert Byron *WhoAm 94, WhoFI 94*
Peterson, Robert Carl 1946- *WhoMW 93*
Peterson, Robert Donald 1919-1990 *WhAm 10*
Peterson, Robert Eugene 1930- *WhoAmP 93*
Peterson, Robert L. 1932- *WhoAm 94, WhoFI 94, WhoMW 93*
Peterson, Robert Marcellus 1944- *WhoAm 94*
Peterson, Robert W. 1929- *WhoAmP 93*
Peterson, Robert Williams 1925- *WhoWest 94*
Peterson, Robin Tucker 1937- *WhoAm 94*
Peterson, Robyn *WhoHol 92*
Peterson, Roderick William 1921- *WhoAm 94*
Peterson, Rodney Delos 1932- *WhoAm 94*
Peterson, Roger Eric 1937- *WhoAm 94, WhoFI 94*
Peterson, Roger Lyman 1938- *WhoMW 93*
Peterson, Roger Marshall 1936- *WhoFI 94*
Peterson, Roger Tory *NewYTBS 93 [port]*
Peterson, Roger Tory 1908- *IntWW 93, WhoAm 94, WhoAmA 93*
Peterson, Rohn Dale 1949- *WhoMW 93*
Peterson, Roland Oscar 1932- *WhoAm 94, WhoFI 94, WhoWest 94*
Peterson, Rolf Olin 1949- *WhoMW 93*
Peterson, Ronald Arthur 1920- *WhoAmL 94, WhoWest 94*
Peterson, Ronald C. 1945- *WhoAmL 94*
Peterson, Ronald Duane 1948- *WhoWest 94*
Peterson, Ronald John 1963- *WhoMW 93*
Peterson, Ronald Roger 1948- *WhoAm 94, WhoAmL 94*
Peterson, Roxanna Lee 1944- *WhoMW 93*
Peterson, Rudolph A. 1904- *IntWW 93, WhoAm 94*
Peterson, Russell Wilbur 1916- *IntWW 93, WhoAm 94, WhoAmP 93*
Peterson, S. Dean 1923- *IntMPA 94*
Peterson, Sally Lu 1942- *WhoMW 93*
Peterson, Scott Lee 1959- *WhoFI 94*
Peterson, Sharon Elizabeth 1958- *WhoWest 94*
Peterson, Sharon Lynn Craig 1945- *WhoMW 93*
Peterson, Shirley Ann 1935- *WhoAmP 93*
Peterson, Sonja Lynn 1957- *WhoAmL 94*
Peterson, Spencer Alan 1940- *WhoWest 94*
Peterson, Spiro 1922-1992 *WhAm 10*
Peterson, Stanley Lee 1949- *WhoWest 94*
Peterson, Stephen Cary 1960- *WhoScEn 94*
Peterson, Stephen Lee 1940- *WhoAm 94*
Peterson, Steven Walter 1956- *WhoFI 94*
Peterson, Susan *DrAPF 93*
Peterson, Susan Harnly 1925- *WhoAmA 93*
Peterson, Sushila Jane-Clinton 1952- *WhoBlA 94*
Peterson, Thage G. 1933- *IntWW 93*
Peterson, Theodore Bernard 1918- *WhoAm 94*
Peterson, Thomas Hull 1929- *WhoMW 93*
Peterson, Vance Tullin 1944- *WhoWest 94*
Peterson, Victor Lowell 1934- *WhoScEn 94, WhoWest 94*
Peterson, Virginia Beth 1946- *WhoMW 93*
Peterson, W. C. *WhoAmP 93*
Peterson, Wallace C(arroll) 1921- *WrDr 94*
Peterson, Wallace Carroll 1921- *WhoAmP 93*
Peterson, Wallace Carroll, Sr. 1921- *WhoAm 94*
Peterson, Walt *DrAPF 93*
Peterson, Walter 1922- *IntWW 93, WhoAmP 93*
Peterson, Walter Fritiof 1920- *WhoAm 94, WhoMW 93*
Peterson, Wayne E. 1947- *WhoAmL 94*
Peterson, Wayne Turner 1927- *WhoAm 94*
Peterson, Willard James 1938- *WhoAm 94*
Peterson, Willard James 1955- *WhoWest 94*
Peterson, William Allen 1934- *WhoAmL 94*
Peterson, William E. 1936- *WhoAmP 93*
Peterson, William Frank 1922- *WhoScEn 94*
Peterson, William G. 1944- *WhoAmP 93*
Peterson, William Herbert 1921- *WhoAm 94*
Peterson, Willie Diamond 1911- *WhoBlA 94*
Peterson, Willis Lester 1932- *WhoAm 94*
Peterson-Berger, Wilhelm 1867-1942 *NewGrDO*
Peterson-Henry, Terri A. 1962- *WhoMW 93*
Peterson-More, Diana Lewis 1950- *WhoAm 94*
Peters-Pike, Damaris Porter 1933- *WhoMW 93*
Peters Sisters, The *WhoHol 92*
Petersson, Bertil Ingemar 1949- *WhoFI 94*
Peter the Great 1672-1725 *HisWorL [port]*
Peterzell, Paul Robert 1961- *WhoFI 94, WhoWest 94*
Petesch, Natalie L. M. *DrAPF 93*
Petett, Freddye Webb 1943- *WhoBlA 94*
Pethachi, Muthiah Chidambaram 1933- *WhoScEn 94*
Pethahia Of Regensburg fl. 118-?-119-? *WhWE*
Petheo, Bela Francis 1934- *WhoAmA 93*
Petherbridge, Carol 1954- *WhoFI 94*
Petherbridge, Edward 1936- *Who 94*
Pethick, Christopher John 1942- *WhoAm 94*
Pethick, Geoffrey Loveston 1907- *Who 94*
Pethick-Lawrence, Emmeline 1867-1954 *DcNaB MP*
Pethrick, Richard Arthur 1942- *IntWW 93*
Pethtel, Dave 1951- *WhoAmP 93*
Pethybridge, Roger William 1934- *WrDr 94*
Peticolas, Warner Leland 1929- *WhoAm 94, WhoWest 94*
Petievich, Gerald 1944- *WrDr 94*
Petika, David M. 1945- *WhoAm 94*
Petillo, James Thomas 1944- *WhoAm 94*
Petillo, John Joseph, Jr. 1949- *WhoIns 94*
Petillon, Lee Ritchey 1929- *WhoAmL 94*
Petina, Irra 1914- *WhoHol 92*
Petinga, Charles Michael 1946- *WhoFI 94, WhoMW 93*
Petingi, Roberto 1953- *WhoHisp 94*
Petioni, Muriel M. 1914- *WhoBlA 94*
Petipa, (Joseph) Lucien 1815-1898 *NewGrDO*
Petipa, Marius 1818-1910 *IntDcB*
Petipa, (Victor) Marius (Alphonse) 1818-1910 *NewGrDO*
Petipas, Mlle d1739 *NewGrDO*
Petit, Albert d1963 *WhoHol 92*
Petit, Brenda Joyce 1939- *WhoFI 94*
Petit, Dinshaw Manockjee 1934- *Who 94*
Petit, Eugene Pierre *IntWW 93*
Petit, Magdalena 1903- *BlmGWL*
Petit, Parker Holmes 1939- *WhoAm 94*
Petit, Pascale 1938- *WhoHol 92*
Petit, Pierre 1922- *IntWW 93*
Petit, Roland 1924- *IntDcB [port], IntWW 93, Who 94, WhoHol 92*
Petit, Susan 1945- *ConAu 142*
Petit, Wanda *WhoHol 92*
Petit, William 1965- *WhoScEn 94*
Petitan, Debra Ann Burke 1932- *WhoMW 93*
Petitbon, Richie 1938- *WhoAm 94*
Petite, Yvonne Marie 1951- *WhoMW 93*
Petitmengin, Jacques 1928- *IntWW 93*
Petito, George Daniel 1941- *WhoFI 94*
Petitpierre, Eduard 1941- *WhoScEn 94*
Petitt, Gerald William 1945- *WhoAm 94, WhoFI 94*
Petitte, James Nicholas 1957- *WhoScEn 94*
Petka, Ed 1943- *WhoAmP 93*
Petkanics, Bryan G. 1955- *WhoAmL 94*
Petkevis, Edward Raymond 1960- *WhoAmL 94*
Petkov, Dimiter 1938- *NewGrDO*
Petkov, Petko Danev 1942- *IntWW 93*
Petkun, David S. 1947- *WhoAmL 94*
Petkun, Lisa B. 1951- *WhoAmL 94*
Petkus, Alan Francis 1956- *WhoMW 93*
Petley, Frank E. d1945 *WhoHol 92*
Petlin, Irving 1934- *WhoAmA 93*
Peto, Henry (George Morton) 1920- *Who 94*
Peto, John Frederick 1854-1907 *AmCulL*
Peto, Michael (Henry Basil) 1938- *Who 94*
Peto, Richard 1943- *Who 94*
Petok, Samuel 1922- *WhoAm 94*
Petosa, Jason Joseph 1939- *WhoAm 94*
Petr, Constance F. 1950- *WhoWest 94*
Petra, Hortense d1982 *WhoHol 92*
Petra, Yvon 1916-1984 *BuCMET*
Petracca, Mark Patrick 1955- *WhoWest 94*
Petracek, Michael Ray 1946- *WhoAm 94*
Petraitis, Rimtautas A. 1935- *WhoWest 94*
Petrak, William Allen 1918- *WhoAmP 93*
Petrakis, Harry Mark *DrAPF 93*
Petrakis, Harry Mark 1923- *WhoAm 94, WrDr 94*
Petrakis, Leonidas 1935- *WhoAm 94*
Petrakis, Nicholas Louis 1922- *WhoAm 94, WhoWest 94*
Petrakis, Peter 1951- *WhoAm 94, WhoAmL 94*
Petrakos, Chris *DrAPF 93*

Petrakov, Nikolai Yakovlevich 1937- *IntWW 93*
Petralia, Ronald Sebastian 1954- *WhoAm 94*
Petranovich, Milo 1950- *WhoAmL 94*
Petrarca, Joseph A. *WhoAmP 93*
Petrarca, Sandra Maria 1948- *WhoWest 94*
Petrarch 1304-1374 *BlmGEL, PoeCrit 8 [port]*
Petraro, Vincent L. 1956- *WhoAmL 94*
Petras, John W. 1940- *WrDr 94*
Petrash, Jeffrey Michael 1948- *WhoAm 94, WhoAmL 94*
Petrasich, John Moris 1945- *WhoAmL 94*
Petrassi, Goffredo 1904- *IntWW 93, NewGrDO*
Petrauskas, Kipras 1885-1968 *NewGrDO*
Petre, Baron 1942- *Who 94*
Petre, Francis Herbert Loraine 1927- *Who 94*
Petre, Gio 1937- *WhoHol 92*
Petre, Robert Edward 1742-1801 *DcNaB MP*
Petre, Zoe 1940- *IntWW 93*
Petree, Neil 1898- *WhAm 10*
Petrek, William Joseph 1928- *WhoAm 94*
Petrella, Clara 1914-1987 *NewGrDO*
Petrella, Errico 1813-1877 *NewGrDO*
Petrella, Mary Therese 1957- *WhoMW 93*
Petrelli, Joseph Lawrence 1951- *WhoIns 94*
Petremont, Clarice M. d1949 *WhoAmA 93N*
Petrenko, Aleksey Vasilevich 1938- *IntWW 93*
Petrenko, Yelizaveta Fyodorovna 1880-1951 *NewGrDO*
Petrequin, Harry Joseph, Jr. 1929- *WhoAm 94*
Petrescu, Cezar *EncSF 93*
Petri, Carl Axel Henrik 1929- *IntWW 93*
Petri, Gyorgy 1943- *ConWorW 93*
Petri, Mario d1985 *WhoHol 92*
Petri, Michala 1958- *IntWW 93*
Petri, Peter Alexander 1946- *WhoAm 94*
Petri, Thomas E. *WhoAmP 93*
Petri, Thomas E. 1940- *CngDr 93*
Petri, Thomas Everet 1940- *WhoAm 94, WhoMW 93*
Petrich, Beatrice Ann 1925- *WhoAm 94*
Petrich, John E. 1950- *WhoFI 94*
Petrich, Mark Anton 1961- *WhoScEn 94*
Petricioli, Gustavo 1928- *IntWW 93*
Petrick, Alfred, Jr. 1926- *WhoAm 94*
Petrick, Ernest Nicholas 1922- *WhoAm 94*
Petricoff, M. Howard 1949- *WhoAm 94, WhoAmL 94*
Petricola, Anthony John 1936- *WhoScEn 94*
Petrides, George Athan 1916- *WhoScEn 94*
Petridis, Petros Antonios 1959- *WhoScEn 94*
Petrie, Allan Kendrick 1928- *WhoWest 94*
Petrie, Bruce I., Jr. 1954- *WhoAmL 94*
Petrie, Bruce Inglis 1926- *WhoAmL 94*
Petrie, Daniel 1920- *IntMPA 94*
Petrie, Daniel Mannix 1920- *WhoAm 94*
Petrie, Donald Archibald 1921- *WhoAm 94, WhoFI 94*
Petrie, Donald Joseph 1921- *WhoAm 94*
Petrie, Ferdinand Ralph 1925- *WhoAm 94, WhoAmA 93*
Petrie, Garth F. 1938- *WhoAm 94*
Petrie, Geoff 1948- *BasBi*
Petrie, George *WhoHol 92*
Petrie, George Whitefield, III 1912- *WhoScEn 94*
Petrie, Gregory Steven 1951- *WhoAm 94*
Petrie, Hay d1948 *WhoHol 92*
Petrie, Howard d1968 *WhoHol 92*
Petrie, James Stanton 1936- *WhoAm 94*
Petrie, Joan Caroline 1920- *Who 94*
Petrie, John Daniel 1936- *WhAm 10*
Petrie, John Richard 1945- *WhoAm 94*
Petrie, Lucinda Alicia 1951- *WhoMW 93*
Petrie, Milton J. *WhoFI 94*
Petrie, Paul *DrAPF 93*
Petrie, Paul (James) 1928- *WrDr 94*
Petrie, Peter 1932- *IntWW 93*
Petrie, Peter (Charles) 1932- *Who 94*
Petrie, Rhona 1922- *WrDr 94*
Petrie, Roy H. 1940- *WhoAm 94*
Petrie, Susan *WhoHol 92*
Petrie, Sylvia Spencer 1931- *WhoAmA 93*
Petrie, William 1912- *WhoAm 94*
Petrignani, Rinaldo 1927- *IntWW 93*
Petrik, Alois Richard 1928- *WhoMW 93*
Petrikin, James Ronald 1946- *WhoAmL 94*
Petrilli, Giuseppe 1913- *IntWW 93*
Petrilli, Joseph R. 1942- *WhoAmP 93*
Petrillo, Carl Edward 1940- *WhoAm 94*
Petrillo, Leonard Philip 1941- *WhoAm 94, WhoFI 94*
Petrillo, Sammy *WhoHol 92*
Petrin, Helen Fite 1940- *WhoAmL 94*
Petrina, Anthony J. *WhoFI 94*
Petrine, Deborah Leigh Martin 1955- *WhoFI 94*
Petrinovich, Lewis F. 1930- *WhoAm 94*
Petrirena, Mario J. 1953- *WhoHisp 94*
Petris, Nicholas C. 1923- *WhoAmP 93*
Petro, Cheryl Ann 1945- *WhoMW 93*
Petro, James Michael 1948- *WhoAmL 94, WhoAmP 93, WhoMW 93*
Petro, Joe, III 1956- *WhoAmA 93*
Petro, John William 1930- *WhoMW 93*
Petro, Joseph (Victor), Jr. 1932- *WhoAmA 93*
Petro, Nicolai N. 1958- *WrDr 94*
Petrobelli, Francesco d1695 *NewGrDO*
Petrobelli, Pierluigi 1932- *NewGrDO*
Petrocelli, Americo William 1931- *WhoAm 94*
Petrocelli, Anthony Joseph 1937- *WhoFI 94*
Petrocelli, Marta Baez 1965- *WhoAmL 94*
Petroff, Paul d1981 *WhoHol 92*
Petrolati, Thomas M. *WhoAmP 93*
Petrolini, Ettore d1936 *WhoHol 92*
Petron, Donald Robert 1946- *WhoWest 94*
Petrone, Thomas C. 1937- *WhoAmP 93*
Petroni, Donald Victor 1931- *WhoAm 94*
Petroni, Romeo Geno 1929- *WhoAmP 93*
Petroniero, Vincent John 1943- *WhoFI 94*
Petronio, Ronald Anthony 1956- *WhoWest 94*
Petropoulos, Labros S. 1962- *WhoScEn 94*
Petros, Raymond Louis, Jr. 1950- *WhoAm 94, WhoAmL 94*
Petrosellini, Giuseppe 1727-c. 1797 *NewGrDO*
Petroskey, Belinda Wehner 1951- *WhoAmP 93*
Petroski, Catherine *DrAPF 93*
Petroski, Henry *DrAPF 93*
Petroski, Henry 1942- *WrDr 94*
Petrosky, Anthony *DrAPF 93*
Petrosky, Robert 1953- *WhoAmL 94*
Petross, Precious Doris *WhoBlA 94*
Petrou, David Michael 1949- *IntMPA 94*
Petrouske, Rosalie Sanara *DrAPF 93*
Petrov, Alan Michael 1949- *WhoAmL 94*
Petrov, Andrei Pavlovich 1930- *IntWW 93*
Petrov, Andrey Pavlovich 1930- *NewGrDO*
Petrov, Ivan d1963 *WhoHol 92*
Petrov, Ivan (Ivanovich) 1920- *NewGrDO*
Petrov, Michel 1945- *WrDr 94*
Petrov, Nicolas 1933- *WhoAm 94*
Petrov, Osip Afanas'yevich 1806?-1878 *NewGrDO [port]*
Petrov, Rem Viktorovich 1930- *IntWW 93*
Petrov, Vasily 1879-1937 *NewGrDO*
Petrov, Vladimir Ivanovich 1942- *LngBDD*
Petrov, Yuriy Vladimirovich 1932- *IntWW 93*
Petrov, Yury Vladimirovich 1939- *LngBDD*
Petrova, Anna Yakovlevna (Vorob'yova-) 1817-1901 *NewGrDO*
Petrova, Dimitrina Gueorguieva 1957- *WhoWomW 91*
Petrova, Olga d1977 *WhoHol 92*
Petrovic, Alexandre Gabriel 1925- *WhoScEn 94*
Petrovich, Janice 1946- *WhoHisp 94*
Petrovich, Stephen Christopher 1966- *WhoAmL 94*
Petrovics, Emil 1930- *IntWW 93, NewGrDO*
Petrovna, Sonia *WhoHol 92*
Petrovsky, Boris *GayLL*
Petrovsky, Boris Vasiliyevich 1908- *IntWW 93*
Petrovsky, Vladimir Fyodorovich 1933- *IntWW 93*
Petrovsky, Vladimir Petrovich 1933- *LngBDD*
Petrovykh, Mariia Sergeevna 1908-1979 *BlmGWL*
Petrowski, Daniel Thomas 1953- *WhoFI 94*
Petrowski, Gregory Lee 1962- *WhoFI 94*
Petrowski, Lawrence C. 1944- *WhoAmL 94*
Petrucci, Brizio 1737-1828 *NewGrDO*
Petrucci, Giovanni *WhoHol 92*
Petrucci, Jane Margaret 1955- *WhoScEn 94*
Petrucci, Russell Simon 1962- *WhoFI 94*
Petrucelli, James Michael 1949- *WhoAmL 94*
Petrucelli, Rocco Joseph, II 1943- *WhoAm 94*
Petrucelly, Jeffrey Paul 1946- *WhoAmL 94*
Petruno, Frank Delano 1932- *WhoFI 94*
Petrunoff, Vance T. 1956- *WhoWest 94*
Petrus, Robert Thomas 1957- *WhoFI 94*
Petrusenko, Oxana Andriivna 1900-1940 *NewGrDO*
Petrush, John Joseph 1942- *WhoAmL 94*
Petrushevskaia, Liudmila (Stefanovna) 1938- *ConWorW 93*
Petrushevskaia, Liudmila Stepanovna 1938- *BlmGWL*
Petrushevskaya, Lyudmila *ConWorW 93*
Petrushevskaya, Lyudmila (Stefanova) 1938- *IntDcT 2*
Petrushevskaya, Lyudmila Stefanovna 1938- *IntWW 93*
Petruska, Gregory James 1958- *WhoWest 94*
Petrusky, John W. 1935- *WhoFI 94*
Petruzzi, Anthony Joseph, Jr. 1946- *WhoFI 94*
Petruzzi, Christopher Robert 1951- *WhoFI 94, WhoWest 94*
Petruzzi, Guido *WhoAm 94, WhoFI 94*
Petruzzi, Julian d1967 *WhoHol 92*
Petry, Alice Hall 1951- *WrDr 94*
Petry, Ann *DrAPF 93*
Petry, Ann 1908- *AfrAmAl 6 [port], BlmGWL, WhoBlA 94*
Petry, Ann (Lane) 1908- *WrDr 94*
Petry, Carl Forbes 1943- *WhoMW 93*
Petry, Heinz 1919- *IntWW 93*
Petry, Heywood Megson 1952- *WhoScEn 94*
Petry, Paul E. 1946- *WhoIns 94*
Petry, Samuel Richard, II 1942- *WhoAmL 94*
Petry, Stanley Edward 1966- *WhoBlA 94*
Petry, Terence Michael 1962- *WhoFI 94*
Petry, Thomas Edwin 1939- *WhoAm 94, WhoFI 94*
Petrzilka, Henry 1920- *WhoWest 94*
Petschek, Albert George 1928- *WhoAm 94*
Pett, Raymond Austin 1941- *Who 94*
Pett, Saul d1993 *NewYTBS 93*
Pettaway, Charles, Jr. 1949- *WhoBlA 94*
Pettee, Daniel Starr 1925- *WhoScEn 94*
Pettengill, Gordon Hemenway 1926- *IntWW 93*
Pettengill, Harry Junior 1946- *WhoAm 94*
Pettengill, Kroger 1922- *WhoAm 94*
Petter, Bertha Elise Kinsinger 1872- *EncNAR*
Petter, Rodolphe Charles 1865-1947 *EncNAR*
Petters, Samuel Brian 1967- *WhoWest 94*
Pettersen, Bjorn Ragnvald 1950- *WhoScEn 94*
Pettersen, Kjell Will 1927- *WhoAm 94, WhoFI 94*
Pettersen, Mary J. *WhoAmP 93*
Pettersen, Oddrunn 1937- *IntWW 93, WhoWomW 91*
Pettersen, Thomas Morgan 1950- *WhoWest 94*
Petterson, Donald K. *WhoAmP 93*
Petterson, Donald K. 1930- *WhoAm 94*
Petterson, Steve D. *DrAPF 93*
Pettersson, Brigitta *WhoHol 92*
Pettersson, Hjordis *WhoHol 92*
Petterway, Jackie Willis *WhoBlA 94*
Pettes, Robert Carlton 1922- *WhoMW 93*
Pettet, Joanna 1944- *WhoHol 92*
Pettet, Simon *DrAPF 93*
Pettett, Deane H. 1920- *WhoIns 94*
Petteway, Samuel Bruce 1924- *WhoAm 94*
Pettey, Dix Hayes 1941- *WhoMW 93*
Pettey, Pat Higgins *WhoAmP 93*
Pettey, Walter Graves, III 1949- *WhoAm 94, WhoAmL 94*
Petteys, D. F. *DrAPF 93*
Petti, Edward Charles 1939- *WhoFI 94*
Pettibone, John Wolcott 1942- *WhoAmA 93*
Pettibone, Peter John 1939- *WhoAm 94, WhoAmL 94, WhoFI 94*
Pettibone, Richard H. 1938- *WhoAmA 93*
Pettie, George c. 1548-1589 *DcLB 136*
Pettiette, Alison Yvonne 1952- *WhoAmL 94, WhoFI 94*
Pettiette, Lawrence Wayne 1953- *WhoAmL 94*
Pettifer, Julian 1935- *Who 94, WrDr 94*
Pettifor, David Godfrey 1945- *Who 94*
Pettiford, Betty Irene 1928- *WhoAmP 93*
Pettiford, Oscar 1922-1960 *AfrAmAl 6*
Pettiford, Quentin H. 1929- *WhoBlA 94*
Pettiford, Reuben J., Jr. 1960- *WhoBlA 94*
Pettiford, Steven Douglas 1948- *WhoBlA 94*
Pettigrew, Amy Conklin 1950- *WhoMW 93*
Pettigrew, Anne Stone *WhoAmL 94*
Pettigrew, Carl Newton 1964- *WhoFI 94*
Pettigrew, Edward W. 1943- *WhoAmL 94*
Pettigrew, Grady L., Jr. 1943- *WhoAmL 94, WhoBlA 94*
Pettigrew, John Douglas 1943- *Who 94*
Pettigrew, L. Eudora 1928- *WhoAm 94, WhoBlA 94*
Pettigrew, Russell (Hilton) 1920- *Who 94*
Pettigrew, Steven Lee 1949- *WhoWest 94*
Pettigrew, Thomas Fraser 1931- *WhoAm 94, WhoWest 94, WrDr 94*
Pettijohn, Francis John 1904- *WhoAm 94*
Pettijohn, Fred Phillips 1917- *WhoAm 94*
Pettinella, Nicholas Anthony 1942- *WhoFI 94*
Pettinga, Cornelius Wesley 1921- *WhoAm 94*
Pettingel, Richard H. 1947- *WhoAmL 94*
Pettingell, Frank d1966 *WhoHol 92*
Pettingell, Richard Hilton 1947- *WhoAm 94*
Pettis, Dianne Hart 1957- *WhoMW 93*
Pettis, Francis Joseph, Jr. 1930- *WhoScEn 94*
Pettis, Gary George 1958- *WhoBlA 94*
Pettis, Joyce Owens 1946- *WhoBlA 94*
Pettis, Ronald Eugene 1939- *WhoAm 94, WhoWest 94*
Pettis, William Charles 1942- *WhoMW 93*
Pettis-Roberson, Shirley McCumber *WhoAm 94, WhoWest 94*
Pettit, Albert W. 1930- *WhoAmP 93*
Pettit, Alvin Dwight 1945- *WhoBlA 94*
Pettit, Arthur Edwin 1896- *WhAm 10*
Pettit, Bob 1932- *BasBi*
Pettit, Charles 1736-1806 *WhAmRev*
Pettit, Dale Alexander 1940- *WhoAm 94*
Pettit, Daniel (Eric Arthur) 1915- *Who 94*
Pettit, Frances Marie 1927- *WhoAmP 93*
Pettit, Frederick Sidney 1930- *WhoAm 94*
Pettit, George Robert 1929- *WhoScEn 94, WhoWest 94*
Pettit, Ghery DeWitt 1926- *WhoAm 94, WhoWest 94*
Pettit, Horace 1903- *WhoScEn 94*
Pettit, Hugh Boyd, III 1952- *WhoAmP 93*
Pettit, John W. 1942- *WhoAm 94*
Pettit, John Whitney 1935- *WhoAm 94*
Pettit, Lawrence K. *WhoBlA 94*
Pettit, Lawrence Kay 1937- *WhoAm 94*
Pettit, Manson Bowers 1902- *WhAm 10*
Pettit, Michael *DrAPF 93*
Pettit, Philip Noel 1945- *IntWW 93*
Pettit, Roger Lee 1946- *WhoAmL 94*
Pettit, Sara L. 1944- *WhoAmL 94*
Pettit, Tamara 1948- *WhoAmP 93*
Pettit, Thomas Henry 1929- *WhoAm 94*
Pettit, Tom 1859-1946 *BuCMET*
Pettit, Walter Fitch 1918- *WhoAm 94*
Pettit, Wendy Jean 1945- *WhoFI 94*
Pettit, William Dutton, Sr. 1920- *WhoFI 94*
Pettit, William Dutton, Jr. 1949- *WhoFI 94, WhoWest 94*
Pettit, William Thomas 1931- *WhoAm 94*
Pettite, William Clinton 1937- *WhoWest 94*
Pettiti, Louis Edmond 1916- *IntWW 93*
Pettitt, Gordon Charles 1934- *Who 94*
Pettitt, Jay S. 1926- *WhoAm 94*
Pettitt, Roger Carlyle 1927- *WhoAm 94*
Pettress, Andrew William 1937- *WhoBlA 94*
Pettus, Alvin Morris 1941- *WhoAm 94*
Pettus, Barbara Wyper 1947- *WhoAm 94*
Pettus, E. Lamar 1945- *WhoAmL 94*
Pettus, Jane M. 1908- *WhoAmA 93N*
Pettus, Willie Clinton 1944- *WhoAm 94*
Pettus-Bellamy, Brenda Karen 1957- *WhoBlA 94*
Pettway, Jo Celeste 1952- *WhoBlA 94*
Petty, Barrett Reed 1941- *WhoFI 94*
Petty, Bob 1940- *WhoBlA 94*
Petty, Bruce Anthony 1938- *WhoBlA 94*
Petty, Charles Sutherland 1920- *WhoAm 94*
Petty, Donald Griffin 1949- *WhoWest 94*
Petty, Douglas Cooper, Jr. 1931- *WhoAm 94*
Petty, Eric D. *WhoAmP 93*
Petty, Floyd Ernest 1928- *WhoAmP 93*
Petty, George Oliver 1939- *WhoAm 94, WhoAmL 94*
Petty, John 1919- *EncSF 93*
Petty, John Fitzmaurice 1935- *Who 94*
Petty, John Robert 1930- *WhoAm 94*
Petty, Joseph Taggart 1951- *WhoAmP 93*
Petty, Keith 1920- *WhoWest 94*
Petty, Kyle *WhoAm 94*
Petty, Lori *WhoHol 92*
Petty, Marge 1946- *WhoAmP 93, WhoMW 93*
Petty, Maximilian 1617-1662 *DcNaB MP*
Petty, Olive Scott 1895- *WhoScEn 94*
Petty, Phillip N. 1953- *WhoFI 94*
Petty, Rachel Monteith 1943- *WhoBlA 94*
Petty, Reginald E. 1935- *WhoBlA 94*
Petty, Richard *WhoAm 94*
Petty, Richard Edward 1951- *WhoScEn 94*
Petty, Robert Scott 1947- *WhoAmP 93*
Petty, Ronald Franklin 1947- *WhoFI 94*
Petty, Thomas Lee 1932- *WhoAm 94*
Petty, Tom *WhoHol 92*
Petty, Tom 1952- *WhoAm 94*
Petty, Travis Hubert 1928- *WhoAm 94*
Petty, W(illiam) H(enry) 1921- *WrDr 94*

Phelan, Thomas P. d1993 *NewYTBS 93*
Pheley, Alfred Maxmillion, III 1956- *WhoMW 93*
Phelps (Ward), Elizabeth Stuart 1844-1911 *BlmGWL*
Phelps, Anthony John 1922- *Who 94*
Phelps, Arthur Van Rensselaer 1923- *WhoScEn 94*
Phelps, Ashton, Jr. 1945- *WhoAm 94*
Phelps, Barry 1941- *ConAu 140*
Phelps, Buster d1983 *WhoHol 92*
Phelps, C. Kermit 1908- *WhoBlA 94*
Phelps, Carrie Lynn 1964- *WhoMW 93*
Phelps, Charles Frederick 1934- *Who 94*
Phelps, Constance Kay 1940- *WhoBlA 94*
Phelps, David D. 1947- *WhoAmP 93*
Phelps, Digger 1940- *BasBi*
Phelps, Donald Gayton 1929- *WhoBlA 94*
Phelps, Edith Catlin 1875-1961 *WhoAmA 93N*
Phelps, Edmund Strother 1933- *IntWW 93, WhoAm 94*
Phelps, Edna Mae 1920- *WhoAmP 93*
Phelps, Eleanor *WhoHol 92*
Phelps, Elizabeth Porter 1747-1817 *BlmGWL*
Phelps, Elizabeth Stuart 1815-1852 *BlmGWL*
Phelps, Esmond, II 1945- *WhoAmL 94*
Phelps, Fancher, Sr. d1972 *WhoHol 92*
Phelps, Flora Louise Lewis 1917- *WhoAm 94*
Phelps, Gilbert (Henry, Jr.) 1915- *EncSF 93, WrDr 94*
Phelps, Gilbert (Henry, Jr.) 1915-1993 *ConAu 141*
Phelps, Glenn Howard 1943- *WhoScEn 94*
Phelps, Harvey W. 1922- *WhoAmP 93*
Phelps, Howard Thomas Henry Middleton 1926- *Who 94*
Phelps, J(oseph) Alfred 1927- *WrDr 94*
Phelps, James Douglas 1955- *WhoAmP 93*
Phelps, James Edward 1952- *WhoScEn 94*
Phelps, James Solomon, III 1952- *WhoScEn 94*
Phelps, Judson Hewett 1942- *WhoAm 94*
Phelps, Lee d1953 *WhoHol 92*
Phelps, Leonard Thomas Herbert 1917- *Who 94*
Phelps, Malcom Elza 1905-1991 *WhAm 10*
Phelps, Maurice Arthur 1935- *Who 94*
Phelps, Michael Everett Joseph 1947- *WhoAm 94, WhoFI 94*
Phelps, Nan d1990 *WhoAmA 93N*
Phelps, Oliver 1749-1809 *WhAmRev*
Phelps, Orme Wheelock 1906- *WhoAm 94*
Phelps, Paul Michael 1933- *WhoAm 94, WhoMW 93*
Phelps, Paulding 1933- *WhoAm 94*
Phelps, Peter *WhoHol 92*
Phelps, Richard William 1946- *WhoFI 94*
Phelps, Richard Wintour 1925- *Who 94*
Phelps, Robert Frederick, Jr. 1956- *WhoAmL 94*
Phelps, Robin McCann 1957- *WhoWest 94*
Phelps, Susan Van Buren 1951- *WhoMW 93*
Phelps, W. Robert *WhoAmP 93*
Phelps, Willard *WhoWest 94*
Phelps, William Anthony 1964- *WhoBlA 94*
Phelps, William Cunningham 1934- *WhoIns 94*
Phelps Brown, Ernest Henry *Who 94*
Phelps-Patterson, Lucy 1931- *WhoBlA 94*
Phemister, Robert David 1936- *WhoAm 94*
Phemister, Thomas Alexander 1940- *WhoAm 94*
Phemonoe *BlmGWL*
Phenicie, Mark Elihu 1954- *WhoAmL 94, WhoAmP 93*
Phenix, Gloria Gayle 1956- *WhoMW 93*
Phenix, Philip Henry 1915- *WrDr 94*
Phibbs, Ciaran Sargent 1957- *WhoWest 94*
Phibbs, Clifford Matthew 1930- *WhoAm 94, WhoMW 93*
Phibbs, Harry Albert 1933- *WhoAm 94*
Phibbs, Roderic Henry 1930- *WhoAm 94*
Phifer, Ross S. 1941- *WhoIns 94*
Phil 1940- *WhoBlA 94*
Phil, Gary
See Boston *ConMus 11*
Philaenis fl. 3rd cent.?BC- *BlmGWL*
Philander, S. George H. 1942- *WhoBlA 94*
Philaret 1935- *IntWW 93*
Philbert, Robert Earl 1946- *WhoMW 93*
Philbin, Edward J. 1932- *WhoAmP 93*
Philbin, Edward James 1932- *WhoAm 94, WhoAmL 94, WhoFI 94*
Philbin, John *WhoHol 92*
Philbin, John Arthur 1934- *WhoAmL 94*
Philbin, Mary 1903- *WhoHol 92*
Philbin, Regis *WhoAm 94*
Philbin, Regis 1930- *WhoHol 92*
Philbrick, Donald Lockey 1923- *WhoAm 94*
Philbrick, Donald R. 1934- *WhoAmP 93*
Philbrick, Edward D. 1936- *WhoAmP 93*
Philbrick, Herbert A. d1993 *NewYTBS 93 [port]*
Philbrick, Herbert A(rthur) 1915-1993 *CurBio 93N*
Philbrick, Margaret Elder 1914- *WhoAm 94, WhoAmA 93*
Philbrick, Otis 1888-1973 *WhoAmA 93N*
Philbrick, Ralph 1934- *WhoAm 94*
Philbrick, Stephen *DrAPF 93*
Philbrick, William d1955 *WhoHol 92*
Philbrook, James d1982 *WhoHol 92*
Philbrook, Paula L. 1968- *WhoAmP 93*
Philby, Harry St. John Bridger 1885-1960 *WhWE*
Philibbosian, Khatchig Zaven 1966- *WhoFI 94*
Philidor, Francois-Andre Danican 1726-1795 *NewGrDO*
Philion, Norman Joseph, III 1946- *WhoAm 94*
Philip, Hon. Lord 1942- *Who 94*
Philip, II 1527-1598 *HisWorL [port]*
Philip, A. G. Davis 1929- *WhoAm 94, WhoScEn 94*
Philip, Alexander Morrison *Who 94*
Philip, James 1930- *WhoMW 93*
Philip, James Peyton, Jr. 1930- *WhoAmP 93*
Philip, John Robert 1927- *IntWW 93, Who 94*
Philip, Lotte Brand 1910- *WhoAmA 93N*
Philip, Marlene Nourbese 1947- *BlmGWL*
Philip, Peter Joseph 1937- *WhoAmP 93*
Philip, Peter Van Ness 1925- *WhoAm 94*
Philip, Sunny Koipurathu 1957- *WhoFI 94*
Philip, Thomas Peter 1933- *WhoFI 94*
Philip, William Warren 1926- *WhoAm 94, WhoFI 94, WhoWest 94*
Philip Augustus, II 1165-1223 *HisWorL [port]*
Philipp, Cyrus L. 1898- *WhAm 10*
Philipp, Elliot Elias 1915- *WrDr 94*
Philipp, John Joseph 1928- *WhoMW 93*
Philipp, Manfred Hans Wilhelm 1945- *WhoScEn 94*
Philipp, Marilyn Oetjen 1947- *WhoWest 94*
Philipp, Perry Fred 1913- *WhoFI 94*
Philipp, Robert 1895-1981 *WhoAmA 93N*
Philipp, Walter Viktor 1936- *WhoAm 94*
Philippe, Andre *WhoHol 92*
Philippe, Andre 1926- *IntWW 93*
Philippe, Andre J. 1926- *Who 94*
Philippe, Beatrice 1948- *WhoFI 94*
Philippe, Gerard d1959 *WhoHol 92*
Philippe, Michele d1972 *WhoHol 92*
Philippe de Bourbon 1674-1723 *NewGrDO*
Philippi, Edmond Jean 1936- *WhoScEn 94*
Philippi, Ervin William 1922- *WhoWest 94*
Philippou, Andreas N. 1944- *IntWW 93*
Philipps *Who 94*
Philipps, Edward William 1938- *WhoAm 94*
Philipps, Hanning *Who 94*
Philipps, (Richard) Hanning 1904- *Who 94*
Philipps, John c. 1666-1737 *DcNaB MP*
Philipps, John Michael 1946- *WhoMW 93*
Philipps, Louis Edward 1906- *WhoAm 94*
Philipps, Marion (Violet) 1908- *Who 94*
Philips, Alfredo 1935- *IntWW 93*
Philips, Ambrose 1675?-1749 *BlmGEL*
Philips, Barbara *WhoAmP 93*
Philips, Cyril (Henry) 1912- *Who 94, WrDr 94*
Philips, Cyril Henry 1912- *IntWW 93*
Philips, Daniel Joseph 1948- *WhoWest 94*
Philips, David 1939- *IntWW 93*
Philips, David Evan 1926- *WhoAm 94*
Philips, Emo 1956- *WhoCom*
Philips, Irving 1921-1992 *WhAm 10*
Philips, James Albert 1950- *WhoAmL 94*
Philips, Jesse 1914- *WhoAm 94*
Philips, John 1676-1709 *BlmGEL*
Philips, Julia Therese 1953- *WhoMW 93*
Philips, Julie *WhoHol 92*
Philips, Justin Robin Drew 1948- *Who 94*
Philips, Katherine 1632-1664 *BlmGWL, DcLB 131 [port]*
Philips, Lee 1927- *WhoHol 92*
Philips, Malcolm H. 1945- *WhoAm 94*
Philips, Mary d1975 *WhoHol 92*
Philipsborn, John Timothy 1949- *WhoAmL 94, WhoWest 94*
Philipsborn, Randall H. 1952- *WhoWest 94*
Philipse, Frederick c. 1719-1785 *WhAmRev*
Philipson, David 1862-1949 *DcAmReB 2*
Philipson, Garry 1921- *Who 94*
Philipson, Herman Louis, Jr. 1924- *WhoAm 94*
Philipson, John Trevor Graham 1948- *Who 94*
Philipson, Joseph 1918- *WhoWest 94*
Philipson, Lennart Carl 1929- *WhoScEn 94*
Philipson, Robert James d1992 *IntWW 93N*
Philipson, Willard Dale 1930- *WhoAm 94*
Philipson-Stow, Christopher 1920- *Who 94*
Phillabaum, Leslie Ervin 1936- *WhoAm 94*
Philliber, John d1944 *WhoHol 92*
Phillifent, John T(homas) 1916-1976 *EncSF 93*
Phillimore, Baron 1911- *Who 94*
Phillimore, John Gore 1908- *Who 94*
Phillip, Andy 1922- *BasBi*
Phillip, Arthur 1738-1814 *HisWorL [port]*
Phillip, Michael John 1929- *WhoBlA 94*
Phillip, White, III 1956- *WhoBlA 94*
"Phillipi" *WhoHol 92*
Phillipoff, Mark James 1951- *WhoAmL 94*
Phillippe, Mary Jane Barker Beaman 1919- *WhoAmP 93*
Phillippi, Wendell Crane 1918- *WhoAm 94*
Phillips, Baroness 1910- *WhoWomW 91*
Phillips, Acen L. 1935- *WhoBlA 94*
Phillips, Adolph d1937 *WhoHol 92*
Phillips, Adran Abner 1924- *WhoAm 94, WhoScEn 94*
Phillips, Adrian Alexander Christian 1940- *Who 94*
Phillips, Alan *Who 94*
Phillips, (David) Alan 1926- *Who 94*
Phillips, Alan Guy 1949- *WhoWest 94*
Phillips, Albert d1940 *WhoHol 92*
Phillips, Alex, Sr. d1977 *WhoHol 92*
Phillips, Alice Elizabeth 1939- *WhoMW 93*
Phillips, Alice Jane 1947- *WhoAmA 93*
Phillips, Alma Bercovitz 1923- *WhoWest 94*
Phillips, Almarin 1925- *WhoAm 94, WhoAmL 94*
Phillips, Alonzo *WorInv*
Phillips, Andrew Bassett 1945- *Who 94*
Phillips, Andrew Craig 1922- *WhoAmP 93*
Phillips, Anna 1936- *WhoWest 94*
Phillips, Anna Maria *NewGrDO*
Phillips, Anne *Who 94*
Phillips, Anthony *WhoScEn 94*
Phillips, Anthony Charles Julian 1936- *Who 94*
Phillips, Anthony Francis 1937- *WhoAm 94*
Phillips, Anthony George 1943- *WhoAm 94*
Phillips, Anthony Mark 1945- *WhoAm 94*
Phillips, Arthur 1948- *WhoIns 94*
Phillips, Arthur Morton, III 1947- *WhoScEn 94, WhoWest 94*
Phillips, Arthur William, Jr. 1915- *WhoAm 94, WhoScEn 94*
Phillips, Barbara 1936- *WhoBlA 94*
Phillips, Barbara Jean 1942- *WhoAmP 93*
Phillips, Barnet, IV 1948- *WhoAm 94, WhoAmL 94*
Phillips, Barney d1982 *WhoHol 92*
Phillips, Barry 1929- *WhoAm 94*
Phillips, Basil Oliphant 1930- *WhoBlA 94*
Phillips, Bertha 1940- *WhoBlA 94*
Phillips, Bertrand D. 1938- *WhoAmA 93, WhoBlA 94*
Phillips, Bessie Gertrude Wright *WhoScEn 94*
Phillips, Betty *DrAPF 93*
Phillips, Betty Lou *WhoAm 94, WhoWest 94*
Phillips, Billy Joe 1931- *WhoAmP 93*
Phillips, Billy Saxton 1915- *WhoWest 94*
Phillips, Bluebell Stewart 1904- *WrDr 94*
Phillips, Bobby *WhoAmP 93*
Phillips, Bonnie 1942- *WhoAmA 93*
Phillips, Brad d1993 *NewYTBS 93*
Phillips, Brent *WhoAm 94*
Phillips, Bubba d1993 *NewYTBS 93*
Phillips, Calbert Inglis 1925- *Who 94*
Phillips, Carl Maxey 1951- *WhoFI 94*
Phillips, Carter Glasgow 1952- *WhoAm 94, WhoAmL 94*
Phillips, Caryl 1958- *BlkWr 2, ConAu 141, ConDr 93, WrDr 94*
Phillips, Cecil Barton 1924- *WhoAm 94*
Phillips, Charles d1958 *WhoHol 92*
Phillips, Charles A. Speas 1922- *WhoAm 94*
Phillips, Charles Alan 1939- *WhoAm 94*
Phillips, Charles Eugene 1933- *WhoAmP 93*
Phillips, Charles Franklin 1910- *WhoAm 94*
Phillips, Charles Franklin, Jr. 1934- *WhoAm 94, WhoAmP 93*
Phillips, Charles Garrett 1916- *Who 94*
Phillips, Charles Gorham 1921- *WhoAm 94*
Phillips, Charles Richard 1947- *WhoWest 94*
Phillips, Christopher Hallowell 1920- *WhoAmP 93*
Phillips, Chynna 1967- *WhoHol 92*
Phillips, Clarence Edward 1950- *WhoAmP 93*
Phillips, Clarence W. *WhoAmP 93*
Phillips, Clifton J. 1919- *WhoAm 94*
Phillips, Colette Alice-Maude 1954- *WhoBlA 94*
Phillips, Conrad 1927- *WhoHol 92*
Phillips, Constance Ann 1941- *WhoBlA 94*
Phillips, Craig 1922- *WhoAm 94*
Phillips, Curtis Glen 1962- *WhoFI 94*
Phillips, Cyrus Eastman, IV 1944- *WhoAm 94*
Phillips, D. John 1909- *IntMPA 94*
Phillips, Dana Wayne 1951- *WhoAmL 94*
Phillips, Daniel Anthony 1938- *WhoAm 94*
Phillips, Daniel Miller 1933- *WhoAm 94*
Phillips, Daniel P. 1917- *WhoBlA 94*
Phillips, Darrell 1956- *WhoWest 94*
Phillips, David 1939- *Who 94*
Phillips, David (Chilton) 1924- *IntWW 93, Who 94*
Phillips, David I. 1962- *WhoMW 93*
Phillips, David Lee 1948- *WhoMW 93*
Phillips, David Morgan 1951- *WhoWest 94*
Phillips, David Parker 1934- *WhoWest 94*
Phillips, Deborah Faye 1953- *WhoAmP 93*
Phillips, Dennis *DrAPF 93*
Phillips, Dennis 1924- *WrDr 94*
Phillips, Dennis 1951- *ConAu 141*
Phillips, Derek L. 1934- *WrDr 94*
Phillips, Dewi Zephaniah 1934- *Who 94, WrDr 94*
Phillips, Diane Susan 1942- *Who 94*
Phillips, Dick 1933- *WhoAmA 93*
Phillips, Dilcia R. 1949- *WhoBlA 94*
Phillips, Donald Arthur 1945- *WhoAm 94*
Phillips, Donald James 1924- *WhoWest 94*
Phillips, Donald John 1930- *IntWW 93*
Phillips, Donald Lawrence 1935- *WhoAmL 94*
Phillips, Donald Lewis 1933- *WhoWest 94*
Phillips, Donald Lundahl 1952- *WhoScEn 94*
Phillips, Donald Ray 1938- *WhoFI 94*
Phillips, Donna Rose 1961- *WhoWest 94*
Phillips, Dorothy d1980 *WhoHol 92*
Phillips, Dorothy Kay 1945- *WhoAmL 94*
Phillips, Dorothy Reid 1924- *WhoWest 94*
Phillips, Dorothy W. 1906-1977 *WhoAmA 93N*
Phillips, Douglas Paul 1961- *WhoMW 93*
Phillips, Duncan 1886-1966 *WhoAmA 93N*
Phillips, Dutch, Jr. 1944- *WhoAmA 93*
Phillips, E. R. d1915 *WhoHol 92*
Phillips, Earl Norfleet, Jr. 1940- *WhoAm 94, WhoFI 94*
Phillips, Earl W. 1917- *WhoBlA 94*
Phillips, Earle Norman 1948- *WhoScEn 94*
Phillips, Earmia Jean 1941- *WhoBlA 94*
Phillips, Ed *WhoAmP 93*
Phillips, Edna d1952 *WhoHol 92*
Phillips, Edward d1944 *WhoHol 92*
Phillips, Edward d1965 *WhoHol 92*
Phillips, Edward Alexander 1942- *WhoBlA 94*
Phillips, Edward Everett 1927- *WhoAm 94, WhoFI 94*
Phillips, Edward John 1940- *WhoAm 94, WhoFI 94*
Phillips, Edward Martin 1935- *WhoBlA 94*
Phillips, Edward Thomas John 1930- *Who 94*
Phillips, Edwin d1981 *WhoHol 92*
Phillips, Edwin Arthur 1952- *WhoWest 94*
Phillips, Edwin Charles 1917- *WhoAm 94*
Phillips, Edwin William 1918- *Who 94*
Phillips, Edwina P. Dalton 1936- *WhoAmP 93*
Phillips, Eileen Werik *WhoAm 94*
Phillips, Eldon Franklin 1941- *WhoWest 94*
Phillips, Elizabeth Joan 1938- *WhoAm 94*
Phillips, Ellen Agnes 1950- *WhoMW 93*
Phillips, Elliott Hunter 1919- *WhoAm 94, WhoAmL 94*
Phillips, Ellis Laurimore, Jr. 1921- *WhoAm 94*
Phillips, Elvin Willis 1949- *WhoAmL 94*

Phillips, Eric Lawrance 1909- *Who 94*
Phillips, Eric McLaren, Jr. 1952- *WhoBlA 94*
Phillips, Ethan *WhoHol 92*
Phillips, Ethel C. *WhoAm 94*
Phillips, Euan Hywel 1928- *WhoAm 94*
Phillips, Eugenie Elvira 1918- *WhoBlA 94*
Phillips, Evan Jerome, Jr. 1946- *WhoFI 94*
Phillips, Everette A. 1960- *WhoFI 94*
Phillips, F. Allison 1937- *WhoBlA 94*
Phillips, Frances *DrAPF 93*
Phillips, Frances Caldwell 1923- *WhoBlA 94*
Phillips, Frances Evelyn 1947- *WhoAm 94, WhoAmL 94*
Phillips, Frances Marie 1918- *WhoAm 94*
Phillips, Frank Edward 1930- *WhoBlA 94*
Phillips, Frank Sigmund 1952- *WhoWest 94*
Phillips, Fred (Albert) 1918- *Who 94*
Phillips, Fred Ronald 1940- *WhoFI 94*
Phillips, Frederick Brian 1946- *WhoBlA 94*
Phillips, Frederick Falley 1946- *WhoMW 93*
Phillips, Frederick Stanley 1928- *WhoFI 94*
Phillips, Gabriel 1933- *WhoAm 94*
Phillips, Gail 1944- *WhoAmP 93*
Phillips, Gary L. 1951- *WhoMW 93*
Phillips, Gary Lynn 1947- *WhoFI 94*
Phillips, Gary W. 1947- *WhoScEn 94*
Phillips, Gayle Sarratt 1939- *WhoAmP 93*
Phillips, Geneva Ficker 1920- *WhoWest 94*
Phillips, Geoffrey Kent 1956- *WhoWest 94*
Phillips, George 1806-1877 *DcNaB MP*
Phillips, George L. 1949- *WhoAm 94, WhoAmL 94*
Phillips, George Mark 1961- *WhoAmL 94*
Phillips, George Michael 1947- *WhoAm 94*
Phillips, Gerald Baer 1925- *WhoAm 94*
Phillips, Gerald Cleveland 1922- *WhoAm 94*
Phillips, Gerald M(arvin) 1928- *WrDr 94*
Phillips, Gertrude Marilynn 1931- *WhoWest 94*
Phillips, Gifford 1918- *WhoAmA 93*
Phillips, Glen Edwin 1933- *WhoAmP 93*
Phillips, Glenn Owen 1946- *WhoBlA 94*
Phillips, Gordon *WhoHol 92*
Phillips, Graham Holmes 1939- *WhoFI 94*
Phillips, Gregory A. 1960- *WhoAmP 93*
Phillips, Harvey 1929- *WhoAm 94*
Phillips, Hayden *Who 94*
Phillips, (Gerald) Hayden 1943- *Who 94*
Phillips, Helen (Elizabeth) 1913- *WhoAmA 93*
Phillips, Helen M. 1926- *WhoBlA 94*
Phillips, Helena d1955 *WhoHol 92*
Phillips, Henry (Ellis Isidore) 1914- *Who 94*
Phillips, Henry Alan 1954- *WhoAm 94*
Phillips, Herbert Alvin, Jr. 1928- *WhoAm 94*
Phillips, Horace 1917- *IntWW 93, Who 94*
Phillips, Howard Mitchell 1943- *WhoAm 94*
Phillips, Howard William 1930- *WhoAm 94*
Phillips, Ian 1938- *Who 94*
Phillips, Irving W. 1905- *WhoAmA 93*
Phillips, J. Campbell 1873-1949 *WhoAmA 93N*
Phillips, Jack *Who 94*
Phillips, Jacqueline Loehler 1935- *WhoAmP 93*
Phillips, Jacqy *WhoHol 92*
Phillips, James 1929- *WhoAmA 93N*
Phillips, James Charles 1933- *WhoAm 94, WhoScEn 94*
Phillips, James D. 1933- *WhoAm 94*
Phillips, James D., Jr. *WhoAmP 93*
Phillips, James Daniel 1933- *WhoAmP 93*
Phillips, James Dickson, Jr. 1922- *WhoAm 94, WhoAmL 94*
Phillips, James Edgar 1947- *WhoAm 94, WhoAmL 94*
Phillips, James Lawrence 1932- *WhoBlA 94*
Phillips, James Linford 1943- *WhoAm 94*
Phillips, James M. 1946- *WhoAmA 93*
Phillips, James Macilduff 1916- *WhoAm 94, WhoScEn 94*
Phillips, Janet Colleen 1933- *WhoAm 94*
Phillips, Jay 1898- *WhAm 10*
Phillips, Jayne Anne *DrAPF 93*
Phillips, Jayne Anne 1952- *BlmGWL, WrDr 94*
Phillips, Jean d1970 *WhoHol 92*
Phillips, Jeffrey *WhoMW 93*
Phillips, Jeremy Patrick Manfred 1941- *Who 94*
Phillips, Jerry Juan 1935- *WhoAm 94*
Phillips, Jerry P. 1939- *WhoBlA 94*
Phillips, Jill Meta 1952- *WhoAm 94, WhoWest 94*
Phillips, Jobyna *WhoHol 92*
Phillips, Joe E. d1972 *WhoHol 92*
Phillips, John *WhoHol 92*
Phillips, John 1719-1795 *WhAmRev*
Phillips, John 1926- *Who 94*
Phillips, John A(llen) 1949- *WrDr 94*
Phillips, John Atlas, III 1944- *WhoScEn 94*
Phillips, John Benton 1959- *WhoScEn 94*
Phillips, John Bomar 1947- *WhoAmL 94*
Phillips, John C. 1948- *WhoAmL 94*
Phillips, John David 1920- *WhoAm 94*
Phillips, John David 1942- *WhoFI 94*
Phillips, John Davisson 1906- *WhoAm 94*
Phillips, John E. 1928- *WhoAmP 93*
Phillips, John E. 1939- *WhoAmL 94*
Phillips, John F. 1942- *AfrAmG [port], WhoAm 94*
Phillips, John Fleetwood Stewart 1917- *Who 94*
Phillips, John Francis 1911- *Who 94*
Phillips, John Goldsmith 1907-1992 *WhAm 10*
Phillips, John H. *WhoIns 94*
Phillips, John Jason, II 1938- *WhoBlA 94*
Phillips, John Lawrence, Jr. 1923- *WrDr 94*
Phillips, John R. 1946- *WhoAmL 94*
Phillips, John Randall 1940- *Who 94*
Phillips, John Reed 1944- *WhoAmL 94*
Phillips, John Richard 1934- *WhoAm 94, WhoWest 94*
Phillips, John Thomas, II 1954- *WhoAmP 93*
Phillips, John Walter 1918- *WhoMW 93*
Phillips, Josef Clayton 1908- *WhoAm 94*
Phillips, Joseph Brantley, Jr. 1931- *WhoAmL 94*
Phillips, Joseph C. 1962- *WhoBlA 94*
Phillips, Joy Lambert 1955- *WhoAmL 94*
Phillips, Julia 1944- *IntMPA 94*
Phillips, Julia (Miller) 1944- *ConAu 140*
Phillips, Julia Mae 1954- *WhoScEn 94*
Phillips, Julia Miller 1944- *WhoAm 94*
Phillips, Julianne 1960- *WhoHol 92*
Phillips, June M. J. 1941- *WhoBlA 94*
Phillips, Karen Ann 1944- *WhoMW 93*
Phillips, Karen Borlaug 1956- *WhoAm 94, WhoAmL 94, WhoAmP 93, WhoFI 94*
Phillips, Kate d1931 *WhoHol 92*
Phillips, Kate Johnson *DrAPF 93*
Phillips, Kenneth Higbie 1940- *WhoAm 94*
Phillips, Kenneth L. 1947- *WhoFI 94*
Phillips, Kevin Emil 1955- *WhoAmP 93*
Phillips, Kevin John 1948- *WhoFI 94, WhoScEn 94*
Phillips, Kevin Price 1940- *WhoAm 94*
Phillips, Larry 1951- *WhoAmP 93*
Phillips, Larry Alan 1957- *WhoAmP 93*
Phillips, Larry Duane 1948- *WhoFI 94*
Phillips, Larry Edward 1942- *WhoAm 94, WhoAmL 94, WhoFI 94*
Phillips, Larry H., II 1947- *WhoScEn 94*
Phillips, Laughlin 1924- *WhoAm 94, WhoAmA 93*
Phillips, Lawrence S. 1927- *WhoAm 94, WhoFI 94*
Phillips, Layn R. 1952- *WhoAm 94*
Phillips, Lee Trinkle 1918- *WhoAmP 93*
Phillips, Leo Augustus 1931- *WhoBlA 94*
Phillips, Leo Harold, Jr. 1945- *WhoAmL 94, WhoFI 94*
Phillips, Leon Francis 1935- *IntWW 93*
Phillips, Leroy Daniel 1935- *WhoBlA 94*
Phillips, Leslie 1924- *IntMPA 94, WhoHol 92*
Phillips, Lewis 1920- *WhoAmP 93*
Phillips, Lewis Milton 1921- *WhoAmP 93*
Phillips, Lloyd Garrison, Jr. 1941- *WhoBlA 94*
Phillips, Lou Diamond 1962- *IntMPA 94, WhoHol 92*
Phillips, Louis *DrAPF 93*
Phillips, Loyal 1905- *WhoAm 94*
Phillips, Lyman C. 1939- *WhoFI 94*
Phillips, Mackenzie 1959- *WhoHol 92*
Phillips, Mallory E., III 1954- *WhoAmL 94*
Phillips, Margaret d1984 *WhoHol 92*
Phillips, Marion 1881-1932 *DcNaB MP*
Phillips, Marisa 1932- *Who 94*
Phillips, Marjorie 1894-1985 *WhoAmA 93N*
Phillips, Mark *EncSF 93*
Phillips, Mark 1927- *WrDr 94*
Phillips, Mark 1933- *WrDr 94*
Phillips, Mark Anthony Peter 1948- *Who 94*
Phillips, Mark Douglas 1953- *WhoFI 94, WhoScEn 94*
Phillips, Martha Henderson 1942- *WhoAmP 93*
Phillips, Mary d1990 *WhoHol 92*
Phillips, Matt *WhoAmA 93*
Phillips, Maureen Kay 1944- *WhoMW 93*
Phillips, Max 1924- *Who 94*
Phillips, Mel 1945- *WhoAmP 93*
Phillips, Meredith *WhoHol 92*
Phillips, Merle H. 1928- *WhoAmP 93*
Phillips, Mervyn John 1930- *Who 94*
Phillips, Michael 1937- *WhoAmA 93*
Phillips, Michael 1943- *IntMPA 94*
Phillips, Michael C. 1950- *WhoAmL 94*
Phillips, Michael F. 1962- *WhoAmP 93*
Phillips, Michael Joseph *DrAPF 93*
Phillips, Michael Joseph 1937- *WrDr 94*
Phillips, Michael Keith 1943- *WhoAmP 93, WhoMW 93*
Phillips, Michael Lynn 1952- *WhoFI 94*
Phillips, Michelle 1944- *IntMPA 94, WhoHol 92*
Phillips, Minna d1963 *WhoHol 92*
Phillips, Montague F(awcett) 1885-1969 *NewGrDO*
Phillips, Morris Clayton, Jr. 1944- *WhoAmP 93*
Phillips, Murray d1993 *NewYTBS 93*
Phillips, Nathaniel Pope 1898- *WhAm 10*
Phillips, Neville Crompton 1916- *Who 94*
Phillips, Nicholas *WhoHol 92*
Phillips, Nicholas (Addison) 1938- *Who 94*
Phillips, Norma d1931 *WhoHol 92*
Phillips, Norman d1931 *WhoHol 92*
Phillips, Olin Ray 1934- *WhoAmP 93*
Phillips, Oliver Clyde, Jr. 1929- *WhoAm 94*
Phillips, Owen Martin 1930- *IntWW 93, Who 94, WhoAm 94*
Phillips, Owen Richard 1953- *WhoWest 94*
Phillips, Pamela Kim 1958- *WhoAmL 94, WhoFI 94*
Phillips, Patricia *WhoHol 92*
Phillips, Patrick Edward 1931- *WhoWest 94*
Phillips, Paul *WhoHol 92*
Phillips, Paul 1956- *WhoAmP 93*
Phillips, Paul David, Jr. 1950- *WhoAm 94, WhoAmL 94*
Phillips, Penelope Ann 1950- *WhoAmL 94*
Phillips, Peregrine fl. 1831- *DcNaB MP*
Phillips, Peter (John) 1930- *Who 94*
Phillips, Peter Charles Bonest 1948- *WhoAm 94*
Phillips, Philip Kay 1933- *WhoFI 94, WhoMW 93*
Phillips, Philip Sanford 1948- *WhoAmL 94*
Phillips, R(obert) A(rthur) J(ohn) 1922- *WrDr 94*
Phillips, Ralph Leonard 1925- *WhoBlA 94*
Phillips, Ralph Saul 1913- *WhoAm 94*
Phillips, Ralph Wilbur 1918- *WhAm 10*
Phillips, Ralph Willard 1931- *WhoAmL 94*
Phillips, Randall Clinger 1924- *WhoAm 94*
Phillips, Randel Eugene 1947- *WhoAmL 94*
Phillips, Randy Ernest 1950- *WhoAmP 93*
Phillips, Redmond *WhoHol 92*
Phillips, Rex Philip 1913- *Who 94*
Phillips, Richard 1964- *WhoAmP 93*
Phillips, Richard Anthony, Jr. 1956- *WhoFI 94*
Phillips, Richard Charles Jonathan 1947- *Who 94*
Phillips, Richard Edward 1936- *WhoMW 93*
Phillips, Richard Hart 1922- *WhoAm 94*
Phillips, Richard Loveridge 1939- *WhoAm 94*
Phillips, Richard Myron 1931- *WhoAm 94*
Phillips, Richard Wendell, Jr. 1929- *WhoAm 94*
Phillips, Robert *DrAPF 93, WhoHol 92*
Phillips, Robert (Schaeffer) 1938- *WrDr 94*
Phillips, Robert Hansbury 1924- *WhoBlA 94*
Phillips, Robert J. 1946- *WhoAmA 93*
Phillips, Robert James, Jr. 1955- *WhoFI 94*
Phillips, Robert Lee 1938- *WhoAmP 93*
Phillips, Robert Thomas 1945- *WhoAmP 93*
Phillips, Robin 1942- *Who 94, WhoHol 92, WhoWest 94*
Phillips, Robin Francis 1940- *Who 94*
Phillips, Roderick (Goler) 1947- *WrDr 94*
Phillips, Rog 1909-1965 *EncSF 93*
Phillips, Roger 1939- *WhoAm 94*
Phillips, Roger Julian Noel 1930- *IntWW 93*
Phillips, Romeo Eldridge 1928- *WhoBlA 94*
Phillips, Ronald Edward Ron 1937- *WhoWest 94*
Phillips, Ronald Frank 1934- *WhoAm 94, WhoAmL 94, WhoWest 94*
Phillips, Ronald Lewis 1940- *WhoAm 94*
Phillips, Rondall Van 1945- *WhoWest 94*
Phillips, Roscoe Wendell, Jr. 1927- *WhoAm 94*
Phillips, Rosemarye L. 1926- *WhoBlA 94*
Phillips, Roy G. 1934- *WhoBlA 94*
Phillips, Rufus 1929- *WhoAmP 93*
Phillips, Rufus Colfax, III 1929- *WhoAm 94*
Phillips, Russell Alexander, Jr. 1937- *WhoAm 94*
Phillips, S. E. *WhoAmL 94*
Phillips, Samuel Cochran 1921-1990 *WhAm 10*
Phillips, Sandra Sammataro *WhoWest 94*
Phillips, Scott Allen 1957- *WhoMW 93*
Phillips, Scott Douglas 1946- *WhoFI 94*
Phillips, Seth Harold 1951- *WhoAmP 93*
Phillips, Shelley 1934- *WhoScEn 94*
Phillips, Sian *IntWW 93, Who 94*
Phillips, Sian 1934- *WhoHol 92*
Phillips, Sidney Frederick 1933- *WhoAm 94*
Phillips, Simon
See Judas Priest *ConMus 10*
Phillips, Sky 1921- *ConAu 140*
Phillips, Spencer Kleckner 1914- *WhoMW 93*
Phillips, Stanton Earl 1954- *WhoAmL 94*
Phillips, Stephen Chase 1960- *WhoWest 94*
Phillips, Stephen Marshall 1962- *WhoScEn 94*
Phillips, Stephen S. 1946- *WhoAmL 94*
Phillips, Stevan D. 1945- *WhoAmL 94*
Phillips, Susan Elizabeth *ConAu 142*
Phillips, Susan M. 1944- *WhoFI 94*
Phillips, Susan Meredith 1944- *WhoAm 94, WhoAmP 93*
Phillips, T. Stephen 1941- *WhoAm 94*
Phillips, Ted Ray 1948- *WhoAm 94, WhoWest 94*
Phillips, Terry Lee 1951- *WhoAmP 93*
Phillips, Terry LeMoine 1938- *WhoMW 93*
Phillips, Theodore Locke 1933- *WhoAm 94*
Phillips, Thomas *EncSF 93*
Phillips, Thomas Dean 1954- *WhoScEn 94*
Phillips, Thomas Edworth, Jr. 1944- *WhoFI 94*
Phillips, Thomas John 1948- *WhoAm 94, WhoAmL 94*
Phillips, Thomas L. 1924- *IntWW 93, WhoAm 94*
Phillips, Thomas R. 1949- *WhoAmP 93*
Phillips, Thomas Royal 1949- *WhoAm 94, WhoAmL 94*
Phillips, Thomas Wade 1943- *WhoAm 94*
Phillips, Timothy James 1959- *WhoAmL 94*
Phillips, Tom 1937- *IntWW 93, Who 94*
Phillips, Tony 1937- *WhoAmA 93*
Phillips, Tony 1959- *WhoBlA 94*
Phillips, Tubby d1930 *WhoHol 92*
Phillips, Vel R. 1924- *WhoAmP 93*
Phillips, Velma 1894- *WhAm 10*
Phillips, Vernon Francis 1930- *Who 94*
Phillips, Vincent Mallory 1950- *WhoAmP 93*
Phillips, Virginia C. 1924- *WhoAmP 93*
Phillips, W. Thomas 1943- *WhoBlA 94*
Phillips, Wade 1947- *WhoAm 94, WhoWest 94*
Phillips, Walter J. *WhoAmP 93*
Phillips, Walter Mills, III 1947- *WhoScEn 94*
Phillips, Walter Ray 1932- *WhoAm 94*
Phillips, Warren Henry 1926- *IntWW 93, WhoAm 94*
Phillips, Wendell 1811-1884 *AmSocL [port]*
Phillips, Wendell K. 1907- *WhoHol 92*
Phillips, Wendy 1952- *WhoHol 92*
Phillips, Wilburn R. *WhoBlA 94*
Phillips, Will E. 1943- *WhoAmL 94*
Phillips, Willard L., Jr. 1941- *WhoAmP 93*
Phillips, William *IntWW 93, Who 94, WhoAm 94*
Phillips, William d1957 *WhoHol 92*
Phillips, William 1731-1781 *AmRev, WhAmRev*
Phillips, William c. 1906- *AmSocL, WrDr 94*
Phillips, William 1907- *DcLB 137 [port]*
Phillips, (Ronald) William 1949- *Who 94*
Phillips, William David 1952- *WhoIns 94*
Phillips, William Erwin 1947- *WhoAmP 93*
Phillips, William Eugene 1930- *WhoAm 94*
Phillips, William Evans 1962- *WhoAmL 94*
Phillips, William George 1920- *WhoAm 94*

Phillips, William K. 1936- *WhoIns 94*
Phillips, William M. 1942- *WhoIns 94*
Phillips, William Michael 1966- *WhoWest 94*
Phillips, William Ray, Jr. 1931- *WhoAm 94, WhoFI 94*
Phillips, William Revell 1929- *WhoWest 94*
Phillips, William Robert 1948- *WhoScEn 94*
Phillips, William Russell, Sr. 1948- *WhoAmL 94*
Phillips, William Thomas 1952- *WhoScEn 94*
Phillips, Winfred Marshall 1940- *WhoAm 94, WhoFI 94*
Phillips, Zaiga Alksnis 1934- *WhoWest 94*
Phillips-Garcia, Gary Lee 1948- *WhoHisp 94*
Phillips Griffiths, Allen *Who 94*
Phillips-Jones, Linda *WhoWest 94*
Phillips Narigon, Frances Marie 1934- *WhoMW 93*
Phillipson, David W. 1942- *WrDr 94*
Phillipson, Donald E. 1942- *WhoAmL 94*
Phillipson, John Samuel 1917- *WhoAm 94*
Phillipson, Michael 1940- *WrDr 94*
Phillipson, Paul Gustave 1947- *WhoWest 94*
Phillis, John Whitfield 1936- *WhoAm 94, WhoMW 93, WhoScEn 94*
Phillis, Marilyn Hughey 1927- *WhoAmA 93*
Phillis, Robert Weston 1945- *IntWW 93, Who 94*
Phillis, Yannis A. *DrAPF 93*
Phillpot, Clive James 1938- *WhoAm 94, WhoAmA 93*
Phillpotts, (Mary) Adelaide (Eden) 1896- *WrDr 94*
Phillpotts, (Mary) Adelaide Eden 1896- *Who 94*
Phillpotts, Ambrosine d1980 *WhoHol 92*
Phillpotts, Eden 1862-1960 *DcLB 135 [port], EncSF 93*
Phills, Bobby Ray, II 1969- *WhoBlA 94*
Philmus, Robert M(ichael) 1943- *EncSF 93, WrDr 94*
Philo, Gordon Charles George 1920- *Who 94*
Philogene, Bernard J. R. 1940- *WhoAm 94*
Philon, James Leon 1928- *WhoAm 94, WhoFI 94*
Philotheos 1924- *WhoAm 94*
Philp, Frank 1947- *WhoAmP 93*
Philp, Geoffrey *DrAPF 93*
Philp, (Dennis Alfred) Peter 1920- *WrDr 94*
Philp, Richard Nilson 1943- *WhoAm 94*
Philpot, John Lee 1935- *WhoScEn 94*
Philpot, John William Bill, Jr. 1942- *WhoWest 94*
Philpot, Joseph Henry *EncSF 93*
Philpot, Kenneth J. 1948- *WhoAmL 94*
Philpot, Nicholas Anthony John 1944- *Who 94*
Philpot, Oliver Lawrence Spurling d1993 *Who 94N*
Philpot, Timothy N. 1951- *WhoAmP 93*
Philpott, Albert Lee 1919-1991 *WhAm 10*
Philpott, Delbert Eugene 1923- *WhoWest 94*
Philpott, Harry Melvin 1917- *WhoAm 94*
Philpott, James Alvin, Jr. 1947- *WhoAm 94*
Philpott, John Davis 1931- *WhoAmP 93*
Philpott, Larry La Fayette 1937- *WhoAm 94, WhoWest 94*
Philpott, Lindsey 1948- *WhoWest 94*
Philps, Frank Richard 1914- *Who 94*
Philps, (Frank) Richard 1914- *WrDr 94*
Phinazee, Henry Charles 1956- *WhoMW 93*
Phinizy, Robert Burchall 1926- *WhoFI 94*
Phinney, William Charles 1930- *WhoAm 94, WhoScEn 94*
Phintys fl. 3rd cent.BC- *BlmGWL*
Phipps *Who 94*
Phipps, Allen Mayhew 1938- *WhoAm 94, WhoFI 94*
Phipps, Arthur Raymond 1931- *WhoFI 94*
Phipps, Benjamin Kimball, II 1933- *WhoAmL 94*
Phipps, Charles d1950 *WhoHol 92*
Phipps, Claude Raymond 1940- *WhoWest 94*
Phipps, Colin Barry 1934- *Who 94*
Phipps, Delores Cheryl 1946- *WhoMW 93*
Phipps, Donald Lee, Jr. 1939- *WhoFI 94*
Phipps, Gerald H. d1993 *NewYTBS 93*
Phipps, Herbert Edward 1941- *WhoAmP 93*
Phipps, John Randolph 1919- *WhoAm 94*
Phipps, John Tom 1937- *WhoAmL 94, WhoMW 93*
Phipps, Leslie William 1930- *Who 94*
Phipps, Max *WhoHol 92*
Phipps, Nicholas d1980 *WhoHol 92*
Phipps, Paul Frederick 1921- *WhoMW 93*
Phipps, Sally d1978 *WhoHol 92*
Phipps, Simon Wilton 1921- *Who 94*
Phipps, Wanda *DrAPF 93*
Phipps, William *WhoHol 92*
Phipps, William Eugene 1930- *WrDr 94*
Phipps, Wilma J. 1925- *WhoMW 93*
Phipson, Joan 1912- *WrDr 94*
Phipson, Joan (Margaret) 1912- *TwCYAW*
Phister, Montgomery, Jr. 1926- *WhoAm 94*
Phiz 1815-1882 *BlmGEL*
Phizackerley, Gerald Robert 1929- *Who 94*
Phlegar, Benjamin Focht 1921- *WhoAm 94*
Phleger, Atherton Macondray 1926-1988 *WhAm 10*
Pho, Hai B. *WhoAsA 94*
Phocas, George John 1927- *WhoAm 94, WhoAmL 94, WhoFI 94*
Phoebus, Edgar 1941- *WhoIns 94*
Phoenix, Antoinette Davis 1959- *WhoMW 93*
Phoenix, G. Keith 1946- *WhoAmL 94*
Phoenix, Leaf 1974- *WhoHol 92*
Phoenix, Patricia d1986 *WhoHol 92*
Phoenix, Paul Joseph 1928- *WhoAm 94, WhoFI 94*
Phoenix, Rainbow *WhoHol 92*
Phoenix, River *IntWW 93*
Phoenix, River d1993 *NewYTBS 93 [port]*
Phoenix, River 1970- *IntMPA 94, WhoAm 94, WhoHol 92*
Phoenix, River 1970-1993 *News 94-2*
Phoenix, Summer *WhoHol 92*
Phommasouvanh, Banlang 1946- *WhoAsA 94*
Phomvihane, Kaysone d1992 *IntWW 93N*
Phomvihane, Kaysone 1920-1992 *AnObit 1992*
Phooaphirom, Jatuphon d1981 *WhoHol 92*
Phoofolo, Monyane Paanya 1946- *IntWW 93*
Phounsavanh, Nouhak *IntWW 93*
Phripp, Matthew *WhAmRev*
Phung, Doan Lien 1940- *WhoAsA 94*
Phyfe, Duncan c. 1768-1854 *AmCulL*
Phyfe, James Duncan 1942- *WhoAmL 94*
Phypers, Dean Pinney 1929- *WhoAm 94*
Physick, John Frederick 1923- *Who 94*
Phythian, Brian A(rthur) 1932- *WrDr 94*
Pi, Wen-Yi Shih 1935- *WhoWest 94*
Piachaud, David Francois James 1945- *Who 94*
Piaf, Edith d1963 *WhoHol 92*
Piaggione, Rocky Joseph 1949- *WhoAmL 94*
Piaker, Philip Martin 1921- *WhoAm 94*
Pialat, Maurice 1925- *IntMPA 94*
Pian, Carlson Chao-Ping 1945- *WhoAsA 94*
Pian, Rulan Chao 1922- *WhoAm 94*
Pian, Theodore Hsueh-Huang 1919- *WhoAm 94, WhoAsA 94, WhoScEn 94*
Pianka, Eric R. 1939- *WrDr 94*
Pianko, Howard 1945- *WhoAmL 94*
Pianko, Theodore A. 1955- *WhoAm 94*
Piano, Girolamo fl. 1726- *NewGrDO*
Piano, Renzo 1937- *IntWW 93*
Piano, Vincent Carmine 1922- *WhoAm 94*
Piasecki, Bruce *DrAPF 93*
Piasecki, Jane B. 1953- *WhoAmA 93*
Piassick, Joel Bernard 1940- *WhoAm 94, WhoAmL 94*
Piat, Yann 1949- *WhoWomW 91*
Piatachenko, Hryhorii Oleksandrovych 1932- *LngBDD*
Piatek, Francis John 1944- *WhoAmA 93*
Piatetski-Shapiro, Ilya 1929- *WhoAm 94, WhoScEn 94*
Piatigorsky, Gregor d1976 *WhoHol 92*
Piatkowski, Steven Mark 1962- *WhoScEn 94*
Piatt, Jack Boyd 1928- *WhoAm 94*
Piatt, William McKinney, III 1918- *WhoAm 94*
Piattelli-Palmarini, Massimo 1942- *WhoScEn 94*
Piave, Francesco Maria 1810-1876 *NewGrDO*
Piazza, Antonio 1742-1825 *NewGrDO*
Piazza, Ben 1934-1991 *ConTFT 11, WhoHol 92*
Piazza, Carl Frank 1945- *WhoAmL 94*
Piazza, Dario d1974 *WhoHol 92*
Piazza, Duane Eugene 1954- *WhoWest 94*
Piazza, Jim *WhoHol 92*
Piazza, John *WhoFI 94*
Piazza, Lisa d1986 *WhoHol 92*
Piazza, Marguerite 1926- *WhoAm 94*
Piazza, Michael Joseph 1968- *WhoAm 94, WhoWest 94*
Pibulsonggram, Nitya 1941- *IntWW 93, WhoAm 94*
Pica, John Anthony, Jr. 1952- *WhoAmP 93*
Pica, Tina d1968 *WhoHol 92*
Picachy, Lawrence Trevor d1992 *IntWW 93N, Who 94N*
Picano, Felice *DrAPF 93*
Picano, Felice 1944- *GayLL*
Picard, Barbara Leonie 1917- *WrDr 94*
Picard, Cecil J. 1938- *WhoAmP 93*
Picard, Dennis J. *IntWW 93*
Picard, Dennis J. 1932- *WhoAm 94, WhoFI 94*
Picard, Howard Richard 1939- *WhoFI 94*
Picard, Jacques Jean 1934- *WhoFI 94*
Picard, Laurent 1927- *WhoAm 94*
Picard, Robert George 1951- *WhoWest 94*
Picard, Robert Real 1932- *WhoFI 94*
Picard, Roger A. 1957- *WhoAmP 93*
Picard, Thomas Joseph, Jr. 1933- *WhoFI 94*
Picarda, Hubert Alistair Paul 1936- *Who 94*
Picardi, Anthony Charles 1948- *WhoScEn 94*
Picardi, Ferdinand Louis 1930- *WhoAmL 94, WhoAmP 93*
Picardo, Robert 1953- *WhoHol 92*
Picariello, Pasquale 1959- *WhoAmL 94*
Picasso, Pablo d1973 *WhoHol 92*
Picasso, Pablo 1881-1973 *IntDcB [port]*
Picasso, Paloma 1949- *IntWW 93, WhoHisp 94*
Piccaluga, Nino (Filippo) 1890-1973 *NewGrDO*
Piccard, Auguste 1884-1962 *WorInv*
Piccard, Jacques 1922- *Who 94*
Piccard, Jacques Ernest Jean 1922- *IntWW 93*
Piccarreta, Carl Alan 1955- *WhoAmL 94*
Piccaver, Alfred 1884-1958 *NewGrDO*
Picchi, Mirto 1915-1980 *NewGrDO*
Picchione, Nicholas Everett 1928- *WhoFI 94*
Picciano, Lana *WhoAmA 93*
Piccillo, Joseph 1941- *WhoAm 94, WhoAmA 93*
Piccinini, Janice A. 1945- *WhoAmP 93*
Piccinini, Robert M. *WhoAm 94, WhoWest 94*
Piccinino, Linda Jeanne 1956- *WhoScEn 94*
Piccinni, Louis Alexandre 1779-1850 *NewGrDO*
Piccinni, Luigi 1764-1827 *NewGrDO*
Piccinni, (Vito) Niccolo (Marcello Antonio Giacomo) 1728-1800 *NewGrDO*
Piccinni, Patrizia *WhoHol 92*
Piccinni Family *NewGrDO*
Piccione, Anthony *DrAPF 93*
Piccione, John William 1947- *WhoFI 94*
Piccione, Nicolas Antonio 1925- *WhoScEn 94*
Piccirilli, Furio 1868-1949 *WhoAmA 93N*
Piccirilli, Robert James, Jr. 1943- *WhoMW 93*
Picco, Steven Joseph 1948- *WhoAmL 94*
Piccola, Jeffrey Early 1948- *WhoAmP 93*
Piccoli, Michel 1925- *IntMPA 94, IntWW 93, WhoHol 92*
Piccolo, C. A. Lance 1940- *WhoAm 94, WhoFI 94*
Piccolo, Joseph Anthony 1953- *WhoFI 94*
Piccolo, Ottavia 1949- *WhoHol 92*
Piccolo, Richard 1943- *WhoAmA 93*
Piccolomini, Marietta 1834-1899 *NewGrDO*
Piccone, Joseph Anthony 1935- *WhoWest 94*
Picerni, Paul 1922- *IntMPA 94, WhoHol 92*
Picha, Hermann d1936 *WhoHol 92*
Pichal, Henri Thomas 1923- *WhoScEn 94*
Pichardo, Hipolito 1969- *WhoHisp 94*
Pichardo, Nelson Alexander 1958- *WhoHisp 94*
Pichel, Irving d1954 *WhoHol 92*
Picher, Claude 1927- *WhoAmA 93*
Picher, Paul J. 1914- *WhoAmP 93*
Pichette, Claude 1936- *WhoAm 94, WhoScEn 94*
Pichini, Guido Michael 1952- *WhoFI 94*
Pichl, Vaclav 1741-1805 *NewGrDO*
Pichler, Johann Hanns 1936- *WhoScEn 94*
Pichler, Joseph A. 1939- *IntWW 93*
Pichler, Joseph Anton 1939- *WhoAm 94, WhoFI 94, WhoMW 93*
Pichler, Karoline 1769-1843 *BlmGWL*
Pichois, Claude 1925- *IntWW 93*
Pichon, Madame *NewGrDO*
Picirilli, Robert Eugene 1932- *WhoAm 94*
Pick, Amelie *WhoHol 92*
Pick, Arthur Joseph, Jr. 1931- *WhoWest 94*
Pick, Charles Samuel 1917- *Who 94*
Pick, Daniel Lloyd 1959- *WhoWest 94*
Pick, James Block 1943- *WhoScEn 94, WhoWest 94*
Pick, John Barclay 1921- *WrDr 94*
Pick, Kay Levi 1944- *WhoAmL 94*
Pick, Lupu d1931 *WhoHol 92*
Pick, Malcolm John 1945- *WhoFI 94*
Pick, Michael Claude 1931- *WhoAm 94*
Pick, Ralph Herbert Hans 1957- *WhoAmP 93*
Pick, Ruth 1913- *WhoAm 94*
Pick, W. Samuel *WhoAmP 93*
Pickands, James, III 1931- *WhoScEn 94*
Pickard, Albert Marshall 1922- *WhoAmP 93*
Pickard, Bob 1934- *WhoAmP 93*
Pickard, Cyril Stanley d1992 *IntWW 93N, Who 94N*
Pickard, David L. 1936- *WhoIns 94*
Pickard, Frank Clemence, III 1944- *WhoAm 94*
Pickard, Franklin George Thomas 1933- *WhoFI 94*
Pickard, George Lawson 1913- *WhoAm 94*
Pickard, Helena d1959 *WhoHol 92*
Pickard, Howard Brevard 1917- *WhoAmL 94*
Pickard, Huia Masters 1909- *Who 94*
Pickard, John *WhoHol 92*
Pickard, John Anthony 1934- *Who 94*
Pickard, John Benedict 1928- *WhoAm 94*
Pickard, John Douglas 1946- *Who 94*
Pickard, Joseph Alfred 1930- *WhoFI 94*
Pickard, Mary Ann 1942- *WhoAmP 93*
Pickard, Mary Jean 1946- *WhoMW 93*
Pickard, (John) Michael 1932- *IntWW 93, Who 94*
Pickard, Myrna Rae 1935- *WhoAm 94*
Pickard, Nancy 1945- *WrDr 94*
Pickard, Neil Edward William 1929- *Who 94*
Pickard, Nicholas *WhoHol 92*
Pickard, Obed d1954 *WhoHol 92*
Pickard, Tom 1946- *WrDr 94*
Pickard, Tony *Who 94*
Pickard, William Frank 1941- *WhoBlA 94*
Pickel, Frederick Hugh 1952- *WhoFI 94, WhoWest 94*
Pickell, Timothy Vernon 1952- *WhoAmL 94*
Pickels, John Curtis 1945- *WhoAmL 94*
Picken, George 1898-1971 *WhoAmA 93N*
Picken, Harry Belfrage 1916- *WhoScEn 94*
Picken, Laurence Ernest Rowland 1909- *Who 94*
Picken, R. David 1945- *WhoAmP 93*
Pickens, Alexander Legrand 1921- *WhoAm 94, WhoWest 94*
Pickens, Alton 1917-1991 *WhoAmA 93N*
Pickens, Andrew 1739-1817 *AmRev, WhAmRev [port]*
Pickens, Buford Lindsay 1906- *WhoAm 94*
Pickens, David Richard, Jr. 1920- *WhoAm 94*
Pickens, Ernestine W. McCoy 1936- *WhoBlA 94*
Pickens, Franklin Ace 1936- *WhoAm 94, WhoAmL 94*
Pickens, Helen *WhoHol 92*
Pickens, James, Jr. *WhoHol 92*
Pickens, Jane *WhoHol 92*
Pickens, Jimmy Burton 1935- *WhoScEn 94*
Pickens, Jo Ann 1950- *IntWW 93*
Pickens, Marion Lee 1932- *WhoAmP 93*
Pickens, Patti *WhoHol 92*
Pickens, Robert Bruce 1926- *WhoAm 94*
Pickens, Slim d1983 *WhoHol 92*
Pickens, Thomas Boone, Jr. 1928- *IntWW 93, WhoAm 94, WhoFI 94*
Pickens, William Garfield 1927- *WhoBlA 94*
Pickens, William H. 1946- *WhoWest 94*
Pickens Sisters, The *WhoHol 92*
Picker, Arnold Melville 1913-1989 *WhAm 10*
Picker, David V. 1931- *IntMPA 94*
Picker, Eugene d1993 *NewYTBS 93 [port]*
Picker, Eugene D. 1903- *IntMPA 94*
Picker, Marc 1954- *WhoAmL 94*
Picker, Martin 1929- *WrDr 94*
Picker, Sylvia d1981 *WhoHol 92*
Pickerell, James Howard 1936- *WhoAm 94*
Pickerill, Mary Lou 1931- *WhoAmP 93*
Pickering, Alice Marie d1938 *WhoHol 92*
Pickering, AvaJane 1951- *WhoWest 94*
Pickering, Barbara Ann 1949- *WhoScEn 94*
Pickering, Becky Ruth Thompson 1949- *WhoMW 93*
Pickering, Brian Thomas 1936- *Who 94*
Pickering, Charles W. 1937- *WhoAm 94, WhoAmL 94*
Pickering, Charles Willis 1937- *WhoAmP 93*
Pickering, Donald 1933- *WhoHol 92*
Pickering, Edward (Davies) 1912- *Who 94*

Pickering, Edward Davies 1912- *IntWW 93*
Pickering, Errol Neil 1938- *Who 94*
Pickering, Fred 1919- *Who 94*
Pickering, George Roscoe, Jr. 1912- *WhoAmP 93*
Pickering, George W. 1937- *WrDr 94*
Pickering, Harry J., Sr. 1919- *WhoAmP 93*
Pickering, Howard William 1935- *WhoAm 94*
Pickering, James Henry, III 1937- *WhoAm 94*
Pickering, John Frederick 1939- *Who 94*
Pickering, John Harold 1916- *WhoAm 94, WhoAmL 94*
Pickering, John Robertson 1925- *Who 94*
Pickering, Richard Edward Ingram 1929- *Who 94*
Pickering, Robert *WhoHol 92*
Pickering, Robert Easton 1934- *WrDr 94*
Pickering, Robert Perry 1950- *WhoBlA 94*
Pickering, Sara Reed d1977 *WhoHol 92*
Pickering, Sarah *WhoHol 92*
Pickering, Shelbie Jean 1939- *WhoFI 94*
Pickering, Thomas Clifford 1934- *WhoAm 94*
Pickering, Thomas Reeve 1931- *IntWW 93, Who 94, WhoAm 94, WhoAmP 93*
Pickering, Timothy 1745-1829 *AmRev, WhAmRev [port]*
Pickering, Victoria L. 1951- *WhoIns 94*
Pickering, William Hayward 1910- *IntWW 93, WhoAm 94*
Pickert, Robert Walter 1936- *WhoMW 93*
Pickett, Alvin L. 1930- *WhoBlA 94*
Pickett, Betty Horenstein 1926- *WhoAm 94*
Pickett, Bill d1932 *WhoHol 92*
Pickett, Bobby *WhoHol 92*
Pickett, Calder Marcus 1921- *WhoAm 94*
Pickett, Cindy 1947- *WhoHol 92*
Pickett, David Franklin, Jr. 1936- *WhoWest 94*
Pickett, Donn Philip 1952- *WhoAmL 94*
Pickett, Donna A. 1949- *WhoBlA 94*
Pickett, Dovie T. 1921- *WhoBlA 94*
Pickett, Dovie Theodosia 1921- *WhoAmP 93*
Pickett, Doyle Clay 1930- *WhoAm 94*
Pickett, Edwin Gerald 1946- *WhoAm 94, WhoFI 94*
Pickett, Garth E. 1943- *WhoAmL 94*
Pickett, Geraldine 1944- *WhoAmL 94*
Pickett, Henry B., Jr. 1938- *WhoBlA 94*
Pickett, Ingram d1963 *WhoHol 92*
Pickett, Jackson Brittain 1943- *WhoFI 94*
Pickett, James McPherson 1921- *WhoScEn 94*
Pickett, John Anthony 1945- *IntWW 93*
Pickett, John O., Jr. *WhoAm 94*
Pickett, Jolene Sue *WhoScEn 94*
Pickett, Keri L. *WhoAmA 93*
Pickett, Lawrence Kimball 1919- *WhoAm 94*
Pickett, Michael D. 1947- *WhoAm 94, WhoFI 94, WhoWest 94*
Pickett, Owen B. 1930- *CngDr 93, WhoAm 94*
Pickett, Owen Bradford 1930- *WhoAmP 93*
Pickett, Robert Clement 1928- *WhoAm 94*
Pickett, Robert E. 1936- *WhoBlA 94*
Pickett, Steven Harold 1946- *WhoMW 93*
Pickett, Theodore R., Jr. 1923- *WhoWest 94*
Pickett, Thomas 1912- *Who 94*
Pickett, Thomas William 1957- *WhoFI 94*
Pickett, Will Hays, Jr. 1955- *WhoAmP 93*
Pickett, William Francis 1894- *WhAm 10*
Pickett, William Lee 1941- *WhoAm 94*
Pickett, William Walter 1952- *WhoFI 94*
Pickett, Wilson 1941- *ConMus 10 [port]*
Pickford, Charlotte d1928 *WhoHol 92*
Pickford, David Michael 1926- *Who 94*
Pickford, Jack d1933 *WhoHol 92*
Pickford, Lottie d1936 *WhoHol 92*
Pickford, Mary *Who 94*
Pickford, Mary d1979 *WhoHol 92*
Pickford, Mary 1893-1979 *AmCulL [port]*
Pickford, (Lillian) Mary 1902- *Who 94*
Pickford, Rollin, Jr. *WhoAmA 93*
Pickhardt, Carl 1908- *WhoAmA 93*
Pickhardt, Carl Emile, Jr. 1908- *WhoAm 94*
Pickhardt, Carl Emile, III 1939- *WhoScEn 94*
Pickholtz, Raymond Lee 1932- *WhoAm 94*
Pickholz, Jerome Walter 1932- *WhoAm 94, WhoFI 94*
Pickholz, Marvin G. 1942- *WhoAm 94, WhoAmL 94*
Pickle, J. J. 1913- *CngDr 93, WhoAmP 93*
Pickle, James Jarrell 1913- *WhoAm 94*
Pickle, Jerry Richard 1947- *WhoAmL 94*
Pickle, Joseph Wesley, Jr. 1935- *WhoWest 94*
Pickle, Judith Ann 1935- *WhoWest 94*
Pickle, Linda Williams 1948- *WhoScEn 94*
Pickle, Ramona Lee 1931- *WhoAmP 93*
Pickle, Robert Douglas 1937- *WhoAm 94, WhoAmL 94, WhoFI 94, WhoMW 93*
Pickle, Willian Neel, II 1961- *WhoScEn 94*
Pickles, Carolyn *WhoHol 92*
Pickles, Christina *WhoHol 92*
Pickles, Eric Jack 1952- *Who 94*
Pickles, James 1925- *Who 94*
Pickles, James Oliver *WhoScEn 94*
Pickles, Vivian 1933- *WhoHol 92*
Pickles, Wilfred d1978 *WhoHol 92*
Picklesimer, Max Douglas 1951- *WhoAmL 94*
Pickman, Jerome 1916- *IntMPA 94*
Pickman, Phillip 1938- *WhoWest 94*
Pick-Mangiagalli, Riccardo 1882-1949 *NewGrDO*
Pickney, Charles Edward 1944- *WhoScEn 94*
Pickover, Clifford A. 1957- *ConAu 141*
Pickrel, Paul 1917- *WhoAm 94*
Pickrell, Thomas Richard 1926- *WhoAm 94, WhoScEn 94, WhoWest 94*
Pickrell, Timothy E. 1949- *WhoAm 94, WhoAmL 94*
Pickren, Stacey 1954- *WhoHol 92*
Pickthall, Colin 1944- *Who 94*
Pickthall, Marjorie 1883-1922 *BlmGWL*
Pickthorn, Charles (William Richards) 1927- *Who 94*
Pickton, Thomas Emil 1949- *WhoMW 93*
Pickup, David Cunliffe 1936- *Who 94*
Pickup, David Francis William 1953- *Who 94*
Pickup, Ronald 1941- *WhoHol 92*
Pickup, Ronald Alfred 1940- *Who 94*
Pickus, Albert Pierre 1931- *WhoAm 94*
Picó, Fernando 1941- *WhoHisp 94*
Pico, Rafael 1912- *WhoHisp 94*
Picón, Héctor Tomás, Jr. 1952- *WhoHisp 94*
Picon, Molly 1890-1992 *AnObit 1992*
Picon, Molly 1898- *WhoHol 92*
Picone, John, Jr. 1952- *WhoFI 94*
Picorri, John d1977 *WhoHol 92*
Picot, Genevieve *WhoHol 92*
Picot, Pierre 1948- *WhoAmA 93*
Picotte, Leonard Francis 1939- *WhoAm 94*
Picotte, Michael Bernard 1947- *WhoAm 94*
Picotte, Terri Rosella 1947- *WhoMW 93*
Picotte-Foley, Susan Gaynel 1948- *WhoMW 93*
Picou, Gary Lee 1957- *WhoScEn 94*
Picower, Warren Michael 1934- *WhoAm 94*
Picozzi, Anthony 1917- *WhoAm 94*
Picraux, Danice R. 1946- *WhoAmP 93*
Picraux, Samuel Thomas 1943- *WhoScEn 94*
Pictet, Francois-Charles 1929- *Who 94*
Picton, Bernard 1931- *WrDr 94*
Picton, Jacob Glyndwr 1912- *Who 94*
Picus, Joy *WhoAmP 93*
Piczak, John P. 1940- *WhoAmP 93*
Piddington, Jack Hobart 1910- *IntWW 93*
Piddington, Philip Michael 1931- *Who 94*
Pidgeon, Christopher William 1950- *WhoWest 94*
Pidgeon, John (Allan Stewart) 1926- *Who 94*
Pidgeon, John Anderson 1924- *WhoAm 94*
Pidgeon, Rebecca *WhoHol 92*
Pidgeon, Walter d1984 *WhoHol 92*
Pidhorets'ky, Borys Volodymyrovych 1873-1919 *NewGrDO*
Pidot, Jeffrey Robert 1947- *WhoAmL 94*
Pidot, Whitney Dean 1944- *WhoAmL 94*
Piecewicz, Walter Michael 1948- *WhoAm 94*
Piech, Ferdinand *IntWW 93*
Piech, Ferdinand 1937- *Who 94*
Piech, Mary Lou Rohling 1927- *WhoMW 93*
Piechuta, Michael Paul 1960- *WhoFI 94*
Piecuch, John M. 1943- *WhoFI 94*
Piedmont, Richard Stuart 1948- *WhoAmL 94*
Piedra, Alberto Martinez 1926- *WhoAmP 93*
Piedra, Francisco J. *WhoHisp 94*
Piedra, Silvia L. 1949- *WhoHisp 94*
Piedrahita, Raul Humberto 1954- *WhoScEn 94*
Piegai, Daniela *EncSF 93*
Piehl, Donald Herbert 1939- *WhoAm 94*
Piehl, Walter Jason, Jr. 1942- *WhoAmA 93*
Piekarczyk, Richard Joseph 1952- *WhoMW 93*
Piekarski, Stan *WhoAmP 93*
Piekarski, Victor J. 1950- *WhoAm 94, WhoAmL 94*
Piekos, Henry 1926- *WhoAmP 93*
Piel, Carolyn Forman 1918- *WhoAm 94*
Piel, Gerard 1915- *DcLB 137 [port], IntWW 93, WhoAm 94*
Piel, Harry d1963 *WhoHol 92*
Piel, Loren Allen 1961- *WhoAmL 94*
Piel, Robert John 1945- *WhoAmP 93*
Piel, William, Jr. 1909- *WhoAm 94*
Pielach, Martin 1951- *WhoFI 94*
Piele, Philip Kern 1935- *WhoAm 94*
Pielmeier, John 1949- *ConDr 93, WrDr 94*
Pielou, Evelyn C. *WhoAm 94*
Pien, Edward H. 1955- *WhoAsA 94*
Pien, Shyh-Jye John 1956- *WhoScEn 94*
Pienaar, Louis Alexander 1926- *IntWW 93*
Piene, Otto 1928- *IntWW 93, WhoAm 94, WhoAmA 93*
Pieniazek, Szczepan Aleksander 1913- *IntWW 93*
Pienkowski, Jan Michal 1936- *Who 94*
Piepenburg, Robert 1941- *WhoAmA 93*
Pieper, Darold D. 1944- *WhoAmL 94, WhoWest 94*
Pieper, Ernst 1928- *IntWW 93*
Pieper, Heinz Paul 1920- *WhoAm 94*
Pieper, Jay Brooks 1943- *WhoFI 94*
Pieper, Jeffrey Robert 1964- *WhoMW 93*
Pieper, John William 1935- *WhoAm 94*
Pieper, Martha Heineman 1941- *WhoMW 93*
Pieper, Nathaniel G.W. 1942- *WhoAmL 94*
Pieper, Patricia Rita 1923- *WhoAm 94*
Pieper, Wylie Bernard 1932- *WhoFI 94*
Piepho, Robert Walter 1942- *WhoAm 94*
Pieplu, Claude 1923- *WhoHol 92*
Pieracki, Jozef d1988 *WhoHol 92*
Pierami, Edward A. 1949- *WhoFI 94*
Pierard, Richard V. 1934- *WrDr 94*
Pieras, Jaime, Jr. 1924- *WhoAm 94, WhoAmL 94, WhoAmP 93, WhoHisp 94*
Pierce, Aaronetta Hamilton 1943- *WhoBlA 94*
Pierce, Alan Kraft 1931- *WhoAm 94*
Pierce, Allan Dale 1936- *WhoAm 94*
Pierce, Ann Trucksess 1931- *WhoAmA 93*
Pierce, Arthur d1987 *WhoHol 92*
Pierce, Benjamin Allen 1953- *WhoScEn 94*
Pierce, Bob *WhoAmP 93*
Pierce, Brenda Nielson 1954- *WhoIns 94*
Pierce, Charles *WhoHol 92*
Pierce, Charles B. *WhoHol 92*
Pierce, Charles Earl 1955- *WhoScEn 94*
Pierce, Charles Eliot, Jr. 1941- *WhoAm 94, WhoAmA 93*
Pierce, Charles R. 1922- *WhoAm 94*
Pierce, Charles Stephen 1945- *WhoFI 94*
Pierce, Chester Middlebrook 1927- *WhoAm 94, WhoBlA 94, WhoScEn 94*
Pierce, Clarence Albert, Jr. 1928- *WhoAmP 93*
Pierce, Cynthia Straker *WhoBlA 94*
Pierce, Daniel 1934- *WhoAm 94*
Pierce, Daniel Marshall 1928- *WhoAm 94, WhoAmP 93*
Pierce, Danny P. *WhoAmA 93*
Pierce, Danny P. 1920- *WhoAm 94*
Pierce, Darrell William 1955- *WhoAmL 94*
Pierce, David 1947- *ConAu 141*
Pierce, David A. 1957- *WhoAmP 93*
Pierce, David L. 1947- *WhoAmP 93, WhoMW 93*
Pierce, Deborah Mary *WhoWest 94*
Pierce, Delilah W. 1904- *WhoBlA 94N*
Pierce, Delilah W. 1904-1992 *WhoAmA 93N*
Pierce, Diane 1939- *WhoAmA 93*
Pierce, Donald (Benjamin) 1916- *WhoAmA 93*
Pierce, Donald Fay 1930- *WhoAmL 94*
Pierce, Donna L. 1952- *WhoAmL 94*
Pierce, Douglas Franklin 1924- *WhoFI 94*
Pierce, Earl S. 1942- *WhoBlA 94*
Pierce, Edward Charles 1930- *WhoAmP 93*
Pierce, Edward Franklin 1927- *WhoAm 94*
Pierce, Evelyn d1960 *WhoHol 92*
Pierce, Frances d1913 *WhoHol 92*
Pierce, Francis Casimir 1924- *WhoAm 94, WhoFI 94, WhoScEn 94*
Pierce, Francis Edmund, III 1954- *WhoAmL 94*
Pierce, Francis William 1915- *Who 94*
Pierce, Frank P. *WhoAmP 93*
Pierce, Frank Powell 1953- *WhoBlA 94*
Pierce, Frederick S. 1933- *IntMPA 94*
Pierce, Gary d1969 *WhoAmA 93N*
Pierce, George 1941- *WhoAmP 93*
Pierce, George Adams 1943- *WhoAm 94, WhoWest 94*
Pierce, George Foster, Jr. 1919- *WhoAm 94, WhoScEn 94*
Pierce, Germaine Rose Anne 1969- *WhoMW 93*
Pierce, Gregory Francis Augustine 1947- *WhoMW 93*
Pierce, Gregory W. 1957- *WhoBlA 94*
Pierce, Gretchen Natalie 1945- *WhoFI 94*
Pierce, Hilda *WhoAm 94, WhoWest 94*
Pierce, Hugh Humphrey 1931- *Who 94*
Pierce, Jack *WhoAm 94*
Pierce, Jack P. 1889-1968 *IntDcF 2-4 [port]*
Pierce, James 1900- *WhoHol 92*
Pierce, James Clarence 1929- *WhoAm 94*
Pierce, James Lee 1936- *WhoAm 94*
Pierce, James Robert 1933- *WhoAm 94*
Pierce, James Robinson d1993 *NewYTBS 93*
Pierce, Jeffrey Leo 1951- *WhoScEn 94, WhoWest 94*
Pierce, Jerry Thomas 1943- *WhoAmP 93*
Pierce, Joan Joy 1941- *WhoAmP 93*
Pierce, Joe E. 1924- *WrDr 94*
Pierce, Joel Farwell 1946- *WhoAm 94*
Pierce, John Alvin 1907- *WhoScEn 94*
Pierce, John Charles 1950- *WhoAmP 93*
Pierce, John J. *EncSF 93*
Pierce, John R(obinson) 1910- *EncSF 93, WrDr 94*
Pierce, John Robinson 1910- *IntWW 93, WhoAm 94*
Pierce, John Thomas 1949- *WhoScEn 94*
Pierce, Kenneth Ray 1934- *WhoAm 94*
Pierce, Kevin Michael 1958- *WhoAmL 94*
Pierce, Lambert Reid 1930- *WhoScEn 94*
Pierce, Lawrence Warren 1924- *WhoAm 94, WhoAmL 94, WhoBlA 94*
Pierce, Lee Roy, Jr. 1953- *WhoAmL 94*
Pierce, Leonard L. 1932- *WhoAmP 93*
Pierce, Lester Laurin 1907- *WhoWest 94*
Pierce, Lisa Margaret 1957- *WhoFI 94*
Pierce, Louis 1929- *WhAm 10*
Pierce, Maggie *WhoHol 92*
Pierce, Margaret Hunter 1910- *WhoAm 94*
Pierce, Marianne Louise 1949- *WhoFI 94*
Pierce, Mark Allen 1958- *WhoMW 93*
Pierce, Martin, Jr. 1940- *WhoAm 94*
Pierce, Mary Lee 1955- *WhoWest 94*
Pierce, Meredith Ann 1958- *TwCYAW, WrDr 94*
Pierce, Michael D(ale) 1940- *ConAu 142*
Pierce, Michael Patrick 1960- *WhoAmL 94*
Pierce, Morton Allen 1948- *WhoAm 94*
Pierce, Naomi Ellen 1954- *WhoAm 94, WhoScEn 94*
Pierce, Patricia Jobe 1943- *WhoAmA 93*
Pierce, Ponchitta A. 1942- *WhoBlA 94*
Pierce, Ponchitta Anne 1942- *WhoAm 94*
Pierce, Raymond O., Jr. 1931- *WhoBlA 94*
Pierce, Reuben G. 1926- *WhoBlA 94*
Pierce, Richard Austin 1918- *WhoWest 94, WrDr 94*
Pierce, Richard Herbert 1943- *WhoAmP 93*
Pierce, Richard Hilton 1935- *WhoAm 94*
Pierce, Ricklin Ray 1953- *WhoAmL 94*
Pierce, Ricky Charles 1959- *WhoAm 94, WhoBlA 94, WhoMW 93*
Pierce, Robert Lorne *WhoAm 94, WhoWest 94*
Pierce, Robert Nash 1931- *WhoAm 94*
Pierce, Robert Raymond 1914- *WhoMW 93, WhoScEn 94*
Pierce, Robert William 1940- *WhoWest 94*
Pierce, Ronald K. 1944- *ConAu 142*
Pierce, Ronald Lee 1939- *WhoWest 94*
Pierce, Roy 1923- *WhoAm 94, WrDr 94*
Pierce, Rudolph F. 1942- *WhoAmL 94, WhoBlA 94*
Pierce, Samuel R., Jr. *WhoAmP 93*
Pierce, Samuel R., Jr. 1922- *WhoBlA 94*
Pierce, Samuel Riley, Jr. 1922- *IntWW 93, WhoAm 94, WhoFI 94*
Pierce, Scott 1930- *WhoAm 94*
Pierce, Shelby Crawford 1932- *WhoMW 93, WhoScEn 94*
Pierce, Stack *WhoHol 92*
Pierce, Stanley 1933- *WhoAm 94*
Pierce, Steven D. 1949- *WhoAmP 93*
Pierce, Susan Resneck 1943- *WhoAm 94, WhoWest 94*
Pierce, Tamora 1954- *TwCYAW*
Pierce, Walter J. 1941- *WhoBlA 94*
Pierce, Walter Roy 1945- *WhoAmL 94*
Pierce, Walter S. 1920- *WhoAm 94*
Pierce, Webb d1991 *WhoHol 92*
Pierce, William Charles 1945- *WhoMW 93*
Pierce, William Cobb 1940- *WhoAm 94*
Pierce, William Dallas 1940- *WhoBlA 94*
Pierce, William Gamewell 1904- *WhoWest 94*
Pierce, William Henry 1856- *EncNAR*
Pierce, William James 1921- *WhoAm 94*
Pierce, William L. 1740-1789 *WhAmRev*
Pierce, William Rodgers 1915- *WhoWest 94*

Pierce, William Schuler 1937- *WhoAm 94, WhoScEn 94*
Pierceall, Gregory Micheal 1950- *WhoMW 93*
Pierce-French, Lynne Carol 1952- *WhoMW 93*
Pierce-Huxtable, Diane *WhoAmA 93*
Piercy, Baron 1946- *Who 94*
Piercy, Gordon Clayton 1944- *WhoWest 94*
Piercy, Joanna Elizabeth *Who 94*
Piercy, Marge *DrAPF 93*
Piercy, Marge 1936- *BlmGWL, ConAu 43NR, EncSF 93, WhoAm 94, WrDr 94*
Piercy, Penelope Katherine 1916- *Who 94*
Pierer, Heinrich von 1941- *IntWW 93*
Piereson, James Eugene 1946- *WhoAm 94*
Piergallini, Alfred A. 1946- *WhoAm 94, WhoFI 94*
Piergies, Barbara Alice 1958- *WhoMW 93*
Piergies, Kathi Ann 1958- *WhoFI 94*
Pieri, Maria Maddalena c. 1683-1753 *NewGrDO*
Pieri, (Maria) Teresa *NewGrDO*
Pieri, Vittorio d1926 *WhoHol 92*
Pierik, Marilyn Anne 1939- *WhoWest 94*
Pierlot, Francis d1955 *WhoHol 92*
Pierluisi, Pedro R. *WhoAmP 93*
Pierman, Carol J. *DrAPF 93*
Pierne, (Henri Constant) Gabriel 1863-1937 *NewGrDO*
Pierno, Anthony Robert 1932- *WhoAmL 94*
Pieroni, Leonard J. 1939- *WhoAm 94*
Pieropan, Joseph Antonio 1961- *WhoAmL 94*
Pieroth, Elmar 1934- *IntWW 93*
Pierotti, John William 1936- *WhoAmL 94*
Pierotti, Robert Amedeo 1931- *WhoAm 94*
Pierpoint, Powell 1922- *WhoAm 94*
Pierpont, Laura d1972 *WhoHol 92*
Pierpont, Robert 1932- *WhoAm 94*
Pierpont, Wilbur K. 1914- *WhoAm 94*
Pierre, Abbe *IntWW 93*
Pierre, Abbe 1912- *Who 94*
Pierre, Anatole d1926 *WhoHol 92*
Pierre, Clara 1939- *WrDr 94*
Pierre, Dallas 1933- *WhoBlA 94*
Pierre, Donald Arthur 1936- *WhoWest 94*
Pierre, Francoise *WhoScEn 94*
Pierre, Gerald P. 1951- *WhoBlA 94*
Pierre, Jennifer Casey 1953- *WhoBlA 94*
Pierre, Joseph Horace, Jr. 1929- *WhoWest 94*
Pierre, Percy Anthony 1939- *WhoBlA 94*
Pierre, Roger *WhoHol 92*
Pierre, Wilford *WhoAmP 93*
Pierre, William Henry 1898- *WhAm 10*
Pierre-Brossolette, Claude 1928- *IntWW 93*
Pierre-Louis, Constant 1939- *WhoBlA 94*
Pierre-Noel, Vergniaud 1910- *WhoAmA 93*
Pierrepoint, Albert 1905-1992 *AnObit 1992*
Pierret, Alain Marie 1930- *IntWW 93*
Pierro, Marina *WhoHol 92*
Piers, Charles Robert Fitzmaurice 1903- *Who 94*
Piers, Desmond William 1913- *Who 94*
Piersante, Denise 1954- *WhoFI 94, WhoMW 93*
Pierschbacher, Mary Lou Reynolds 1937- *WhoAmP 93*
Pierse, Lyn *WhoHol 92*
Pierse, Terence Joseph 1951- *WhoFI 94*
Piersen, Arthur d1975 *WhoHol 92*
Piersen, William D(illon) 1942- *WrDr 94*
Pierskalla, William Peter 1934- *WhoAm 94*
Piersol, Allan Gerald 1930- *WhoScEn 94*
Piersol, Lawrence L. 1940- *WhoAmP 93*
Pierson, Abraham 1609-1678 *EncNAR*
Pierson, Albert Chadwick 1914- *WhoAm 94*
Pierson, Anne Bingham 1929- *WhoAm 94*
Pierson, Arthur Tappan 1837-1911 *DcAmReB 2*
Pierson, Carol Anne 1945- *WhoWest 94*
Pierson, David Renick 1951- *WhoAm 94*
Pierson, Dennis *WhoAmP 93*
Pierson, Earl Wendell 1910-1989 *WhAm 10*
Pierson, Edward Joseph, Jr. 1948- *WhoFI 94*
Pierson, Edward Samuel 1937- *WhoAm 94*
Pierson, Elmer F. 1896- *WhAm 10*
Pierson, Frank 1925- *IntMPA 94*
Pierson, Gary Clinton 1959- *WhoAmL 94*
Pierson, George W. d1993 *NewYTBS 93*
Pierson, George Wilson 1904- *WhoAm 94, WrDr 94*
Pierson, H. Daniel 1950- *WhoFI 94*
Pierson, Henry Hugo 1815-1873 *NewGrDO*
Pierson, Jerry D. 1933- *WhoMW 93*
Pierson, Jim 1940- *WhoAmP 93*
Pierson, John Herman Groesbeck 1906- *WhoAm 94*
Pierson, John Kelly 1963- *WhoAmL 94*
Pierson, John Theodore, Jr. 1931- *WhoAm 94*
Pierson, Kathleen Mary 1949- *WhoMW 93*
Pierson, Margaret Rosalind 1941- *WhoMW 93*
Pierson, Richard Allen 1944- *WhoAm 94*
Pierson, Richard Norris, Jr. 1929- *WhoAm 94*
Pierson, Robert 1911-1989 *WrDr 94N*
Pierson, Robert David 1935- *WhoAm 94, WhoFI 94*
Pierson, Steve Douglas 1966- *WhoScEn 94*
Pierson, Wayne George 1950- *WhoFI 94*
Pierson, William George 1951- *WhoAmL 94*
Pierson, William R. 1930- *WhoScEn 94*
Pierzynski, Gary Michael 1959- *WhoMW 93*
Pies, Ronald E. 1940- *WhoWest 94*
Piester, David Lee 1947- *WhoAm 94, WhoAmL 94*
Piet, John Frances 1946- *WhoAmA 93*
Piet, John H. 1914- *WrDr 94*
Piet, Steven James 1956- *WhoWest 94*
Pietak, Raymond Adam 1933- *WhoMW 93*
Pieterse, Hendrik Johannes Christoffel 1936- *WhoAm 94*
Pietersen, William Gerard 1937- *WhoAm 94*
Pietikainen, Sirpa Maria 1959- *WhoWomW 91*
Pietra, Francesco 1933- *WhoScEn 94*
Pietragrua, Carlo *NewGrDO*
Pietragrua, Carlo Luigi *NewGrDO*
Pietrangeli, Nicky 1933- *BuCMET*
Pietri, Giuseppe 1886-1946 *NewGrDO*
Pietri, Pedro Juan *DrAPF 93*
Pietri, Pedro Juan 1943- *WhoHisp 94*
Pietri, Wayne R. 1942- *WhoFI 94*
Pietrini, Dan Harold 1942- *WhoMW 93*
Pietrobelli, Francesco *NewGrDO*
Pietrofesa, John Joseph 1940- *WhoMW 93*
Pietrowski, Robert Frank, Jr. 1945- *WhoAm 94*
Pietrus, Carol Lynn 1948- *WhoMW 93*
Pietruski, John Michael 1933- *IntWW 93*
Pietruski, John Michael, Jr. 1933- *WhoAm 94*
Pietrusza, David 1949- *WrDr 94*
Pietruszka, Michael F. 1956- *WhoAmL 94*
Pietrzak, Alfred Robert 1949- *WhoAm 94, WhoAmL 94, WhoFI 94*
Pietrzak, Ted S. 1952- *WhoAm 94*
Pietrzyk, Donald John 1934- *WhoAm 94*
Pietrzyk, Leslie *DrAPF 93*
Pietsch, Carl Walter 1930- *WhoAmP 93*
Piette, Edward James 1947- *WhoMW 93*
Piettre, Andre 1906- *IntWW 93*
Pieve, Carlos 1929- *WhoHisp 94*
Piez, William 1932- *WhoAm 94*
Pifarré, Juan Jorge 1942- *WhoHisp 94*
Pifer, Alan 1921- *WhoAm 94*
Pifer, Alan (Jay Parrish) 1921- *IntWW 93*
Piffle, John d1951 *WhoHol 92*
Piga, Franco 1927-1990 *WhAm 10*
Piga, Stephen Mulry 1929- *WhoAm 94*
Pigafetta, Francesco Antonio 1491-1535 *WhWE*
Pigarouich, Etienne fl. 17th cent.- *EncNAR*
Pigaut, Roger d1989 *WhoHol 92*
Pigeat, Henri Michel 1939- *IntWW 93*
Pigeon, Madame *NewGrDO*
Pigford, Robert Lamar 1917-1988 *WhAm 10*
Pigford, Thomas Harrington 1922- *WhoAm 94*
Pigg, Alexandra 1963- *WhoHol 92*
Piggford, Roland Rayburn 1926- *WhoAm 94*
Piggott, Alan (Derek) 1922- *WrDr 94*
Piggott, Donald James 1920- *Who 94*
Piggott, Francis James Claude 1910- *Who 94*
Piggott, Lester Keith 1935- *IntWW 93, Who 94*
Piggott, Stuart 1910- *IntWW 93, Who 94, WrDr 94*
Pigman, Jack Richard 1944- *WhoAm 94, WhoAmL 94*
Pigman, Paul Rine 1934- *WhoFI 94*
Pignal, Pierre Ivan 1961- *WhoScEn 94*
Pignanelli, Frank R. 1960- *WhoAmP 93*
Pignataro, Louis James 1923- *WhoAm 94, WhoScEn 94*
Pignatelli, Debora Becker 1947- *WhoAmP 93*
Pignatelli, Frank 1946- *Who 94*
Pignatta, Pietro Romulo dc. 1700 *NewGrDO*
Pigno, Antonia Quintana *DrAPF 93*
Pignolet, Keith Glenn 1956- *WhoMW 93*
Pignon, Edouard d1993 *IntWW 93N*
Pignon, Edouard 1905- *IntWW 93*
Pigot, George (Hugh) 1946- *Who 94*
Pigot, Robert 1720-1796 *AmRev, WhAmRev*
Pigot, Thomas Herbert 1921- *Who 94*
Pigott, Charles McGee 1929- *WhoAm 94, WhoFI 94, WhoWest 94*
Pigott, Christopher Donald 1928- *Who 94*
Pigott, (Berkeley) Henry (Sebastian) 1925- *Who 94*
Pigott, James M. 1894- *WhAm 10*
Pigott, John A. 1932- *WhoFI 94*
Pigott, Melissa Ann 1958- *WhoScEn 94*
Pigott, Robert 1924- *WhoAmP 93*
Pigott, Ronald Wellesley 1932- *Who 94*
Pigott, Tempe d1962 *WhoHol 92*
Pigott-Brown, William Brian 1941- *Who 94*
Pigott-Smith, Tim 1946- *IntMPA 94, IntWW 93, WhoHol 92*
Pigott-Smith, Timothy Peter 1946- *Who 94*
Pigozzi, Raymond Anthony 1928- *WhoAm 94*
Pih, Norman 1959- *WhoScEn 94*
Pihl, James Melvin 1943- *WhoScEn 94, WhoWest 94*
Pihl, Lawrence Edward 1944- *WhoScEn 94*
Pihl, Mary Mackenzie 1916- *Who 94*
Pihlaja, Maxine Muriel Mead 1935- *WhoWest 94*
Pihlajamaki, Veikko Jaako Uolevi 1922- *IntWW 93*
Pihlstrom, Bruce 1943- *WhoAm 94*
Pihos, Pete *ProFbHF [port]*
Piipari, (Kasurinen) Anna-Liisa 1940- *IntWW 93*
Piirto, Douglas Donald 1948- *WhoWest 94*
Piirto, Jane *DrAPF 93*
Pijanowski, Eugene M. 1938- *WhoAmA 93*
Pijper, Willem 1894-1947 *NewGrDO*
Pikaizen, Viktor Aleksandrovich 1933- *IntWW 93*
Pikarsky, Milton 1924-1989 *WhAm 10*
Pike, Baroness 1918- *Who 94, WhoWomW 91*
Pike, Allen W. *WhoFI 94*
Pike, Charles R. 1914- *WrDr 94*
Pike, Charles R. 1936- *WrDr 94*
Pike, Christopher *EncSF 93, TwCYAW, WrDr 94*
Pike, Christopher Doran 1953- *WhoWest 94*
Pike, Cornelia M. 1933- *IntMPA 94*
Pike, David Louis 1933- *WhoFI 94*
Pike, Don, Jr. d1978 *WhoHol 92*
Pike, Donald Wayne 1949- *WhoAmP 93*
Pike, Edward Roy 1929- *IntWW 93, Who 94*
Pike, George Harold, Jr. 1933- *WhoAm 94*
Pike, Harry J. d1919 *WhoHol 92*
Pike, Hew William Royston 1943- *Who 94*
Pike, James Albert 1913-1969 *DcAmReB 2*
Pike, James Maitland Nicholson 1916- *Who 94*
Pike, John 1911-1979 *WhoAmA 93N*
Pike, John Nazarian 1929- *WhoFI 94, WhoScEn 94*
Pike, John Robert 1931- *WhoFI 94, WhoMW 93*
Pike, John S. *WhoAm 94*
Pike, John S. 1946- *IntMPA 94*
Pike, Joyce Lee 1929- *WhoAmA 93*
Pike, Kenneth Lee 1912- *WhoAm 94*
Pike, Kermit Jerome 1941- *WhoAm 94*
Pike, Larry Samuel 1939- *WhoAm 94*
Pike, Laurence Bruce 1927- *WhoAm 94*
Pike, Michael (Edmund) 1931- *Who 94*
Pike, Nita d1954 *WhoHol 92*
Pike, Peter Leslie 1937- *Who 94*
Pike, Philip 1914- *IntWW 93*
Pike, Philip Ernest Housden 1914- *Who 94*
Pike, Richard Joseph, Jr. 1937- *WhoWest 94*
Pike, Robert William 1941- *WhoAm 94, WhoFI 94, WhoIns 94*
Pike, Ruth 1931- *WrDr 94*
Pike, St. John Surridge d1992 *Who 94N*
Pike, Stephen Michael 1953- *WhoAmL 94*
Pike, Thomas Harrison 1950- *WhoScEn 94*
Pike, William Edward 1929- *WhoAm 94, WhoFI 94*
Pike, William Gregory Huddleston d1993 *Who 94N*
Pike, Zebulon Montgomery 1779-1813 *WhWE*
Piket, Frederick 1903-1974 *NewGrDO*
Pikler, Charles *WhoAm 94*
Piklo, Charlene Lorraine 1954- *WhoFI 94*
Pikoraitis, Dale Edward 1957- *WhoMW 93*
Pikus, David Heller 1955- *WhoAmL 94*
Piland, Jeanne 1945- *NewGrDO*
PiLand, Neill Finnes 1943- *WhoFI 94*
Pilarcik, Kathleen Frances 1960- *WhoMW 93*
Pilarczyk, Daniel Edward 1934- *IntWW 93, WhoAm 94, WhoMW 93*
Pilarczyk, Helga (Kathe) 1925- *NewGrDO*
Pilarski, Adam Mark 1948- *WhoFI 94*
Pilarski, Judith Ann 1943- *WhoMW 93*
Pilarski, Laura P. 1926- *WrDr 94*
Pilate, Pontius *BlmGEL*
Pilato, Louis Peter 1944- *WhoAmL 94*
Pilavin, Selma F. 1908- *WhoAmA 93*
Pilbeam, David Roger 1940- *WhoAm 94, WhoScEn 94*
Pilbeam, Nova 1919- *WhoHol 92*
Pilbrow, Richard 1933- *WhoAm 94*
Pilbrow, Richard Hugh 1933- *Who 94*
Pilcer, Harry d1961 *WhoHol 92*
Pilcer, Sonia *DrAPF 93*
Pilcher, (Charlie) Dennis 1906- *Who 94*
Pilcher, George R. 1948- *WhoMW 93*
Pilcher, James Brownie 1929- *WhoAmL 94, WhoAmP 93*
Pilcher, Joshua 1790-1843 *WhWE*
Pilcher, Patricia *WhoAmP 93*
Pilcher, Percy Sinclair 1867-1899 *DcNaB MP*
Pilcher, Robin Sturtevant 1902- *Who 94*
Pilcher, Rosamunde 1924- *WrDr 94*
Pilcher, Tony 1936- *IntMPA 94*
Pilchik, Ely Emanuel 1913- *WhoAm 94*
Pildes, Sara *WhoAmA 93*
Pilditch, James George Christopher 1929- *Who 94*
Pilditch, Richard (Edward) 1926- *Who 94*
Pile, Frederick (Devereux) 1915- *Who 94*
Pile, James 1943- *WhoAmA 93*
Pile, Michael David Mc Kenzie 1954- *WhoBlA 94*
Pile, Robert Bennett 1918- *WhoAm 94*
Pile, Walter Mitchell, Jr. 1948- *WhoAm 94*
Pile, William (Dennis) 1919- *Who 94*
Pilecki, Paul Steven 1950- *WhoAm 94*
Pileggi, Mitch *WhoHol 92*
Pilger, John Richard 1939- *ConAu 141, Who 94*
Pilgrim, Anne *SmATA 75*
Pilgrim, Anne 1915- *WrDr 94*
Pilgrim, Cecil Stanley 1932- *Who 94*
Pilgrim, Derral 1928- *WrDr 94*
Pilgrim, Dianne Hauserman 1941- *WhoAm 94, WhoAmA 93*
Pilgrim, James F. 1941- *WhoAmA 93*
Pilgrim, James Rollins 1947- *WhoFI 94*
Pilgrim, Jessie V. 1958- *WhoAmP 93*
Pilgrim, Lonnie 1928- *WhoAm 94, WhoFI 94*
Pilgrim, Sidney Alfred Leslie 1933- *WhoScEn 94*
Pilibosian, Helene *DrAPF 93*
Pilic, Nikki 1939- *BuCMET*
Pilie, Louis M. 1898- *WhAm 10*
Pilinszky, Janos 1921-1981 *ConAu 142*
Pilipovic, Uladzimir Antonavic 1931- *LngBDD*
Pilipp, Frank 1961- *ConAu 141*
Pilisuk, Marc 1934- *WhoAm 94*
Pilkey, Dav 1966- *WrDr 94*
Pilkey, Orrin H. 1934- *WhoAm 94*
Pilkington, Alan Ralph 1943- *WhoAm 94*
Pilkington, Alastair *Who 94*
Pilkington, Antony (Richard) 1935- *Who 94*
Pilkington, Godfrey *Who 94*
Pilkington, (Richard) Godfrey 1918- *Who 94*
Pilkington, Kevin *DrAPF 93*
Pilkington, Laetitia c. 1708-1750 *BlmGWL*
Pilkington, Lawrence Herbert Austin 1911- *Who 94*
Pilkington, Lionel Alexander Bethune 1920- *IntWW 93, Who 94*
Pilkington, Lorraine 1975- *WhoHol 92*
Pilkington, Michael John 1937- *Who 94*
Pilkington, Muriel Norma 1941- *Who 94*
Pilkington, Paul d1918 *WhoHol 92*
Pilkington, Peter 1933- *Who 94*
Pilkington, Roger Windle 1915- *Who 94, WrDr 94*
Pilkington, Sandra Jayne 1943- *WhoWest 94*
Pilkington, Theo Clyde 1935- *WhoAm 94, WhoScEn 94*
Pilkington, Thomas Henry Milborne-Swinnerton- 1934- *Who 94*
Pilkington, Tom d1971 *WhoHol 92*
Pill, Malcolm (Thomas) 1938- *Who 94*
Pilla, Anthony Michael 1932- *WhoAm 94, WhoMW 93*
Pilla, Felix Mario 1932- *WhoAm 94*

Plank, Melinda 1942- *WhoHol 92*
Plank, Peggy Lynn 1954- *WhoAmL 94*
Plank, Scott *WhoHol 92*
Plano, Jack Charles 1921- *WrDr 94*
Plano, Richard James 1929- *WhoAm 94*
Planquette, (Jean) Robert 1848-1903 *NewGrDO*
Planson, Rollie Joe 1945- *WhoMW 93*
Plant *Who 94*
Plant, Al O. 1930- *WhoAmP 93*
Plant, Albin MacDonough 1937- *WhoAm 94*
Plant, Chris 1946- *WhoAmP 93*
Plant, David William 1931- *WhoAm 94*
Plant, Forrest Albert 1924- *WhoAm 94*
Plant, Mike c. 1950-c. 1992 *AnObit 1992*
Plant, Robert Anthony 1948- *WhoAm 94*
Planta, Louis von 1917- *IntWW 93*
Plantade, Charles-Henri 1764-1839 *NewGrDO*
Plante, David *DrAPF 93*
Plante, David (Robert) 1940- *WrDr 94*
Plante, Gaston *WorInv*
Plante, William Madden 1938- *WhoAm 94*
Plantey, Alain Gilles 1924- *IntWW 93*
Planting, Peter John 1937- *WhoWest 94*
Plantinga, Alvin 1932- *WhoAm 94*
Plantinga, Alvin (Carl) *WrDr 94*
Plantinga, John Everett 1923- *WhoFI 94*
Plant of Highfield, Baron 1945- *Who 94*
Plantu 1951- *IntWW 93*
Plantz, Christine Marie 1946- *WhoMW 93*
Planz, Allen *DrAPF 93*
Plaovic, Rasa d1977 *WhoHol 92*
Pla Pastor, Adela *WhoWomW 91*
Plapp, Bryce Vernon 1939- *WhoAm 94*
Plaschke, Friedrich 1875-1952 *NewGrDO*
Plasencio, Nellie E. 1925- *WhoHisp 94*
Plasier, Lee J. 1942- *WhoMW 93*
Plasier, Leroy J. 1942- *WhoAmP 93*
Plaskett, Frederick Joseph 1926- *Who 94*
Plaskett, Thomas G. 1943- *WhoAm 94*
Plaskett, Thomas George 1943- *IntWW 93*
Plassara, Katerina 1943- *BlmGWL*
Plassmeyer, Norbert Bernard 1938- *WhoAmP 93*
Plaster, Alice Marie *WhoAmA 93*
Plastow, David (Arnold Stuart) 1932- *Who 94*
Plastow, David Arnold Stuart 1932- *IntWW 93*
Plaszczak, Roman Thaddeus 1943- *WhoAmL 94*
Plat, Richard Vertin 1929- *WhoAm 94, WhoFI 94*
Plata, Armando Luis Carlos 1949- *WhoHisp 94*
Plata, Maximino 1937- *WhoHisp 94*
Platania, James Robert 1959- *WhoFI 94*
Platania, Pietro 1828-1907 *NewGrDO*
Plata-Salaman, Carlos Ramon 1959- *WhoScEn 94*
Plate, Andrea 1952- *WrDr 94*
Plate, Janet Margaret *WhoMW 93*
Plate, Nicolai A. 1934- *WhoScEn 94*
Plate, Thomas Gordon 1944- *WhoAm 94, WhoWest 94*
Plate, Walter 1925-1972 *WhoAmA 93N*
Platel, Elisabeth 1959- *IntDcB [port]*
Platen, Carl Henrik G:son von 1913- *IntWW 93*
Platen, Karl d1952 *WhoHol 92*
Plater, Alan (Frederick) 1935- *ConDr 93, WrDr 94*
Plater, Alan Frederick 1935- *Who 94*
Plater, Felix 1536-1614 *EncDeaf*
Plater, George 1735-1792 *WhAmRev*
Plater, William Marmaduke 1945- *WhoAm 94*
Plath, Iona 1907- *WhoAmA 93*
Plath, James *DrAPF 93*
Plath, James Walter 1950- *WhoMW 93*
Plath, Sylvia 1932-1963 *AmCulL, BlmGEL, BlmGWL, DcNaB MP, TwCYAW*
Platika, Doros 1953- *WhoScEn 94*
Platini, Michel 1955- *WorESoc*
Platis, James George 1927- *WhoMW 93*
Platner, Bronson 1946- *WhoAmP 93*
Platner, Warren 1919- *WhoAm 94*
Platnick, Norman I. 1951- *WhoAm 94*
Plato c. 430BC-347BC *EncEth*
Plato 428?BC-348?BC *BlmGEL*
Plato c. 429BC-347BC *EncSF 93*
Plato c. 427BC-c. 347BC *AstEnc*
Plato, Ann *BlmGWL*
Plato, Dana 1964- *WhoHol 92*
Platon, Nicolas 1909- *IntWW 93*
Platonov, Andrey (Platonovich) 1896-1951 *EncSF 93*
Platonov, Vladimir Petrovich 1939- *IntWW 93*
Platonova, Yuliya Fyodorovna 1841-1892 *NewGrDO*
Platou, Joanne Dode 1919- *WhoAm 94*
Platov, Mariquita *DrAPF 93*
Platowski, Andrew C. 1947- *WhoMW 93*
Platt *Who 94*
Platt, Alexander Hartley 1955- *WhoAmL 94*
Platt, Anthony Michael Westlake 1928- *Who 94*
Platt, Charles 1944- *WrDr 94*
Platt, Charles (Michael) 1945- *EncSF 93*
Platt, Charles Adams 1932- *WhoAm 94*
Platt, Colin 1934- *WrDr 94*
Platt, Colin Peter Sherard 1934- *Who 94*
Platt, Donald R. 1923- *WhoAmP 93*
Platt, Ed d1974 *WhoHol 92*
Platt, Eleanor 1910-1974 *WhoAmA 93N*
Platt, Eleanor Frances 1938- *Who 94*
Platt, Eugene *DrAPF 93*
Platt, Eugene (Robert) 1939- *WrDr 94*
Platt, Franklin Dewitt 1932- *WhoAm 94*
Platt, Harold Kirby 1942- *WhoAmL 94*
Platt, Harrison Gray 1902-1992 *WhAm 10*
Platt, Howard *WhoHol 92*
Platt, James Robert 1948- *WhoFI 94, WhoWest 94*
Platt, James Westlake 1897- *WhAm 10*
Platt, John 1817-1872 *DcNaB MP*
Platt, John Richard 1942- *Who 94*
Platt, John Stoddard 1943- *WhoWest 94*
Platt, Jonathan James 1950- *WhoAmL 94*
Platt, Joseph Beaven 1915- *WhoAm 94, WhoWest 94*
Platt, Judith Roberta 1939- *WhoScEn 94*
Platt, Kenneth Allan 1923-1988 *WhAm 10*
Platt, Kin 1911- *Au&Arts 11 [port], SmATA 17AS [port]*
Platt, Leslie A. 1944- *WhoAmL 94*
Platt, (Frank) Lindsey *Who 94*
Platt, Louise 1915- *WhoHol 92*
Platt, Lucian Brewster 1931- *WhoAm 94*
Platt, Marc 1913- *WhoHol 92*
Platt, Margaret *Who 94*
Platt, Mark E. *WhoFI 94*
Platt, Marsha R. *WhoAmP 93*
Platt, Mary Frances 1952- *WhoAmL 94*
Platt, Milt 1912- *IntMPA 94*
Platt, Milton d1992 *IntMPA 94N*
Platt, Nicholas 1936- *IntWW 93, WhoAm 94, WhoAmP 93*
Platt, Norman 1920- *NewGrDO, Who 94*
Platt, Oliver *WhoHol 92*
Platt, Peter 1924- *Who 94*
Platt, Peter Godfrey 1937- *WhoAm 94*
Platt, Richard A. *WhoBlA 94*
Platt, Robert Stevenson 1932- *WhoAmP 93*
Platt, Sherman Phelps, Jr. 1918- *WhoAm 94*
Platt, Stephen 1954- *Who 94*
Platt, Stuart Franklin 1933- *WhoWest 94*
Platt, Terence Charles 1936- *Who 94*
Platt, Thomas Collier, Jr. 1925- *WhoAm 94, WhoAmL 94*
Platt, Thomas Collier, III 1955- *WhoAmL 94*
Platt, Thomas E. 1949- *WhoAmL 94*
Platt, Trevor Charles 1942- *WhoAm 94*
Platt, Warren E. 1943- *WhoAmL 94*
Platt, William Henry 1940- *WhoAm 94, WhoAmL 94*
Platt, William James d1993 *Who 94N*
Platt, William Rady 1915- *WhoAm 94*
Platt, Zephaniah 1735-1807 *WhAmRev*
Platten, Donald Campbell 1918-1991 *WhAm 10*
Platten, Peter Michael, III 1939- *WhoAm 94, WhoFI 94*
Platten, Stephen George 1947- *Who 94*
Platters, The *WhoHol 92*
Platthy, Jeno 1920- *WhoAm 94, WhoFI 94, WhoMW 93*
Platthy, Terrance Lee 1950- *WhoMW 93*
Plattner, Phyllis 1940- *WhoAmA 93*
Plattner, Richard Serber 1952- *WhoAmL 94*
Platto, Charles 1945- *WhoAm 94, WhoAmL 94*
Platt of Writtle, Baroness 1923- *Who 94, WhoWomW 91*
Platts, Francis Holbrook 1939- *WhoScEn 94*
Platts, Todd R. 1962- *WhoAmP 93*
Plattsmier, Don C. 1943- *WhoAmL 94*
Platts-Mills, John Faithful Fortescue 1906- *Who 94*
Platts-Mills, Thomas Alexander E. 1941- *WhoAm 94*
Platz, George Arthur, III 1939- *WhoAm 94*
Platz, Howard Richard 1961- *WhoWest 94*
Platz, Joan Elnora 1951- *WhoFI 94, WhoMW 93*
Platz, Judith Rachel *DrAPF 93*
Platz, Terrance Oscar 1943- *WhoScEn 94*
Platzer, Ferdinand K. d1993 *NewYTBS 93*
Platzer, Joseph 1751-1806 *NewGrDO*
Platzker, Arnold C.G. 1936- *WhoWest 94*
Platzman, George William 1920- *WhoAm 94*
Plauger, P.J. 1944- *WhoScEn 94*
Plauger, P(hillip) J(ames) 1944- *EncSF 93*
Plaut, Eric Alfred 1927- *WhoAm 94*
Plaut, James S. 1912- *WhoAmA 93*
Plaut, James Sachs 1912- *WhoAm 94*
Plaut, Jonathan Victor 1942- *WhoAm 94*
Plaut, Marshall 1944- *WhoScEn 94*
Plaut, Nathan Michael 1917- *WhoAm 94*
Plaut, Roger David 1966- *WhoAm 94*
Plaut, W. Gunther 1912- *WrDr 94*
Plaut, Walter Sigmund 1923- *WhAm 10*
Plaut, Wolf Gunther 1912- *WhoAm 94*
Plautus, Titus Maccius 254?BC-184BC *BlmGEL, IntDcT 2*
Plautz, Jolene Marie 1956- *WhoAmP 93*
Plavcan, Joseph Michael 1908-1981 *WhoAmA 93N*
Plave, Lee Jonathan 1958- *WhoAmL 94*
Plavinsky, Dmitri Petrovich 1937- *IntWW 93*
Plavoukos, Spencer 1936- *WhoAm 94, WhoFI 94*
Plawecki, David Anthony 1947- *WhoAmP 93, WhoMW 93*
Plaxton, Cecil Andrew d1993 *Who 94N*
Player, David Arnott 1927- *Who 94*
Player, Denis Sydney 1913- *Who 94*
Player, Gary (Jim) 1935- *IntWW 93, Who 94*
Player, Gary Farnsworth 1943- *WhoWest 94*
Player, Gary Jim 1935- *WhoAm 94*
Player, Willa B. 1909- *WhoBlA 94*
Playfair, Edward (Wilder) 1909- *Who 94*
Playfair, Edward Wilder 1909- *IntWW 93*
Playfair, Giles 1910- *WrDr 94*
Playfair, James 1755-1794 *DcNaB MP*
Playfair, Nigel d1934 *WhoHol 92*
Playford, Jonathan Richard 1940- *Who 94*
Playle, Colin 1933- *Who 94*
Playten, Alice 1947- *WhoHol 92*
Playter, Wellington d1937 *WhoHol 92*
Plaza, Charito B. 1957- *WhoWomW 91*
Plaza, Sixto 1944- *WhoHisp 94*
Plaza, Wayne Frank 1945- *WhoAmL 94*
Plazak, Richard A. 1937- *WhoIns 94*
Plear, Scott 1952- *WhoAmA 93*
Pleas, John Roland 1938- *WhoBlA 94*
Pleasance, Angela *WhoHol 92*
Pleasance, Donald 1919- *WhoHol 92*
Pleasant, Albert E., III 1944- *WhoBlA 94*
Pleasant, James Scott 1943- *WhoAm 94, WhoAmL 94*
Pleasant, Mae Barbee Boone 1919- *WhoBlA 94*
Pleasant, Robert Dale 1946- *WhoFI 94, WhoMW 93*
Pleasants, Charles Wrenn 1937- *WhoBlA 94*
Pleasants, Frederick R. 1906- *WhoAmA 93N*
Pleasants, Henry 1910- *NewGrDO, WhoAm 94, WrDr 94*
Pleasants, Michael Francis 1942- *WhoAmL 94*
Pleasence, Donald 1919- *IntMPA 94, IntWW 93, Who 94, WhoAm 94*
Pleasure, Robert Jonathan 1942- *WhoAmL 94*
Pleban, C. John 1949- *WhoMW 93*
Pleban, Sarah Shelledy 1956- *WhoAmL 94*
Pleban, Uwe Frederik 1952- *WhoFI 94*
Pledger, Reginald Harrison, Jr. 1934- *WhoAmL 94*
Pledger, Verline S. 1927- *WhoBlA 94*
Pledger, Vernese Dianne 1958- *WhoBlA 94*
Plee, Steven Leonard 1951- *WhoScEn 94*
Pleeth, William 1916- *Who 94*
Pleggenkuhle, Lavern Ross 1942- *WhoMW 93*
Pleier, Der fl. c. 1250- *DcLB 138*
Pleijel, Agneta 1940- *BlmGWL*
Pleijel, Agneta (Christina) 1940- *ConAu 142*
Pleissner, Ogden Minton 1905-1983 *WhoAmA 93N*
Pleming, Nigel Peter 1946- *Who 94*
Pleming-Yocum, Laura Chalker 1913- *WhoWest 94*
Plena, Jose 1951- *WhoHisp 94*
Plender, Richard Owen 1945- *Who 94*
Plenderleith, Harold James 1898- *Who 94*
Plenderleith, Ian 1943- *Who 94*
Plenderleith, Thomas Donald 1921- *Who 94*
Plenge, Charles F. 1945- *WhoAmL 94*
Pleninger, Susan Elaine 1963- *WhoMW 93*
Plenk, Agnes Mero 1917- *WhoWest 94*
Plenk, Henry P. 1917- *WhoWest 94*
Plenty, Royal Homer 1918- *WhoAm 94*
Plenty Wolf, George c. 1901-1977 *EncNAR*
Plesec, William Thomas 1942- *WhoAm 94*
Pleshette, Eugene *IntMPA 94*
Pleshette, John *WhoHol 92*
Pleshette, Suzanne *WhoAm 94*
Pleshette, Suzanne 1937- *IntMPA 94, WhoHol 92*
Pleska, P. Michael 1942- *WhoAmL 94*
Pleskac, Karel *EncSF 93*
Pleskow, Eric 1924- *IntMPA 94*
Pleskow, Eric Roy *WhoFI 94*
Plesniak, Michael Walter 1961- *WhoMW 93*
Pless, John Edward 1938- *WhoAm 94*
Pless, Vera 1931- *WhoMW 93*
Plessen, Elisabeth 1944- *BlmGWL*
Plesser, Ronald L. 1945- *WhoAmL 94*
Plesset, Milton Spinoza 1908-1991 *WhAm 10*
Plessis, Thomas-Antoine 1753-1791 *WhAmRev*
Plessner, Yakir 1935- *IntWW 93*
Plessow, Ellen d1967 *WhoHol 92*
Pletcher, David Mitchell 1920- *WhoAm 94*
Pletcher, Eldon 1922- *WhoAm 94*
Pletcher, Eldon L(ee) 1922- *WrDr 94*
Pletcher, Gerry *WhoAmA 93*
Pletcher, Peggy Jo 1932- *WhoWest 94*
Pletcher, Rockney D. 1940- *WhoAmL 94*
Pletka, Paul 1946- *WhoAmA 93*
Pletnev, Mikhail Vasilievich 1957- *IntWW 93*
Pletsch, Carl Erich 1943- *WhoMW 93*
Pletscher, Josephine Marie *WhoAmA 93*
Pletz, Arthur C. 1943- *WhoIns 94*
Pletz, Karen L. 1947- *WhoAmL 94*
Pletz, Thomas Gregory 1943- *WhoAmL 94*
Plevan, Bettina B. 1945- *WhoAmL 94*
Plevan, Kenneth A. 1944- *WhoAmL 94*
Pleven, Rene d1993 *IntWW 93N*
Pleven, Rene 1901-1993 *CurBio 93N, NewYTBS 93 [port]*
Pleven, Rene Jean d1993 *Who 94N*
Plevin, Cynthia H. 1950- *WhoAmL 94*
Plevin, Steven M. 1948- *WhoAmL 94*
Plevnick, Vera *WhoHol 92*
Plevy, Arthur L. 1936- *WhoAmL 94*
Plewa, Casmere Joseph 1926- *WhoAmP 93*
Plewa, John Robert 1945- *WhoAmP 93, WhoMW 93*
Plewes, Steven Arthur 1954- *WhoFI 94*
Plexico, Clark *WhoAmP 93*
Pleydell-Bouverie *Who 94*
Pleyel, Ignace Joseph 1757-1831 *NewGrDO*
Pliatzky, Leo 1919- *IntWW 93, Who 94*
Plichta, Thomas Francis 1952- *WhoFI 94*
Plidor d1920 *WhoHol 92*
Plier, Robert Edwin 1947- *WhoFI 94*
Plimmer, Jack Reynolds 1927- *WhoMW 93*
Plimmer, Walter J. d1968 *WhoHol 92*
Plimpton, Calvin Hastings 1918- *WhoAm 94*
Plimpton, George 1927- *WhoHol 92*
Plimpton, George (Ames) 1927- *WrDr 94*
Plimpton, George Ames 1927- *IntWW 93, WhoAm 94*
Plimpton, Martha 1970- *IntMPA 94*
Plimpton, Martha 1971- *WhoHol 92*
Plimpton, Peggy Lucas 1931- *WhoFI 94*
Plimpton, Shelley *WhoHol 92*
Plimpton, Todd A. 1965- *WhoAmP 93*
Plimsoll, James 1917-1987 *HisDcKW*
Plinton, James O., Jr. 1914- *WhoBlA 94*
Pliny *BlmGEL*
Pliny The Elder c. 23-79 *WhWE [port]*
Plioplys, Audrius Vaclovas 1951- *WhoMW 93*
Plischke, Elmer 1914- *WhoAm 94, WrDr 94*
Plischke, Le Moyne Wilfred 1922- *WhoScEn 94*
Plisetskaya, Erika Michael 1929- *WhoScEn 94*
Plisetskaya, Maiya Mikhailovna 1925- *IntWW 93*
Plisetskaya, Maya *WhoHol 92*
Plisetskaya, Maya 1925- *IntDcB [port]*
Plishka, Paul 1941- *NewGrDO*
Plishner, Michael Jon 1948- *WhoAm 94, WhoAmL 94*
Pliska, Edward William 1935- *WhoWest 94*
Pliskin, Marvin Robert 1938- *WhoAm 94*
Pliskin, William Aaron 1920- *WhoAm 94*
Plisson, Marie-Prudence 1727-1788 *BlmGWL*
Plitt, Henry d1993 *IntMPA 94N*
Pliushch, Ivan Stepanovych *LngBDD*
Plochmann, Carolyn Gassan 1926- *WhoAmA 93*
Plochocki, Andrew Plato 1936- *WhoAm 94*
Plockinger, Erwin 1914- *IntWW 93*

Ploeser, Walter Christian 1907- WhoAmP 93
Ploetz, Lawrence Jeffrey 1946- WhoScEn 94
Plog, Michael Bellamy 1944- WhoMW 93
Plog, Stanley C. 1930- WhoWest 94
Ploger, Robert Riis 1915- WhoAm 94, WhoMW 93
Ploix, Helene Marie Joseph 1944- IntWW 93
Plomer, John c. 1410-1484 DcNaB MP
Plomer, William (Charles Franklyn) 1903-1973 NewGrDO, RfGShF
Plomgren, Ronald Arthur 1934- WhoFI 94
Plommet, Michel Georges 1927- WhoScEn 94
Plomp, Teunis 1938- WhoAm 94
Plonkey, Kenneth Dale 1937- WhoWest 94
Plonnies, Louise von 1803-1872 BlmGWL
Plonsey, Robert 1924- WhoAm 94
Ploog, Holli Ilene 1947- WhoAmP 93, WhoWest 94
Plopper, Charles George 1944- WhoAm 94, WhoWest 94
Plosser, Charles Irving 1948- WhoAm 94, WhoFI 94, WhoScEn 94
Plossu, Bernard 1945- WhoAmA 93
Plossu, Bernard Pierre 1945- WhoAm 94
Ploszaj, Stephen Charles 1949- WhoAm 94
Plotch, Walter 1932- WhoAm 94, WhoFI 94
Plotek, Leopold 1948- WhoAmA 93
Plothow, Roger Henry 1934- WhoWest 94
Plotinus BlmGEL
Plotinus c. 205-c. 270 AstEnc, EncEth
Plotkin, Bruce Andrew 1951- WhoWest 94
Plotkin, Gordon David 1946- Who 94
Plotkin, Harry Morris 1913- WhoAm 94
Plotkin, Irving Herman 1941- WhoFI 94
Plotkin, Linda 1938- WhoAmA 93
Plotkin, Lynn 1945- WhoAmA 93
Plotkin, Manuel D. WhoAm 94
Plotkin, Manuel D. 1923- WhoAmP 93
Plotkin, Martin 1922- WhoAm 94
Plotkin, Richard L. 1944- WhoAmL 94
Plotkin, Sylvia WhoAmA 93
Plotnick, Harvey Barry 1941- WhoAm 94
Plotnick, Paul William 1947- WhoAmL 94
Plotnik, Arthur 1937- WhoAm 94
Plotsky, Paul Mitchell 1952- WhoScEn 94
Plott, Charles R. 1938- WhoAm 94, WhoWest 94
Plott, Paula 1946- WhoAmA 93
Plotz, Charles Mindell 1921- WhoAm 94
Plouffe, Leo, Jr. 1957- WhoScEn 94
Plough, Charles Tobias, Jr. 1926- WhoWest 94
Plourde, Alphonse O. 1946- WhoAmP 93
Plourde, Charles C. 1945- WhoAmP 93
Plourde, Gerard 1916- WhoAm 94
Plourde, Joseph Aurele 1915- IntWW 93, Who 94
Plourde, Joseph Donald 1936- WhoAm 94
Plous, Phyllis WhoAmA 93
Plousadis, James 1960- WhoAmL 94
Plouviez, Peter William 1931- Who 94
Plovnick, Mark Stephen 1946- WhoWest 94
Plowden, Baron 1907- Who 94
Plowden, Lady Who 94
Plowden, Lady 1910- IntWW 93
Plowden, Alison (Margaret Chichele) 1931- WrDr 94
Plowden, David 1932- WhoAm 94, WhoAmA 93, WrDr 94
Plowden, Edwin Noel 1907- IntWW 93
Plowden, Roger d1960 WhoHol 92
Plowden, William Julius Lowthian 1935- Who 94
Plowden Roberts, Hugh Martin 1932- Who 94
Plowman, (John) Anthony d1993 Who 94N
Plowman, Debra D. WhoAmP 93
Plowman, Francis Wilds 1902- WhoAmP 93
Plowman, Jack Wesley 1929- WhoAm 94
Plowman, Jeffrey N. 1954- WhoAmL 94
Plowman, Joan Marie 1951- WhoAmP 93
Plowman, John (Robin) 1908- Who 94
Plowman, John Brent 1949- WhoMW 93
Plowman, R. Dean 1928- WhoAm 94, WhoScEn 94
Plowman, Stephanie 1922- WrDr 94
Plowright, David Ernest 1930- IntWW 93, Who 94
Plowright, Hilda d1973 WhoHol 92
Plowright, Joan 1929- ConTFT 11, IntMPA 94, WhoHol 92
Plowright, Joan Ann 1929- Who 94
Plowright, Joan Anne 1929- IntWW 93, WhoAm 94
Plowright, Rosalind (Anne) 1949- NewGrDO
Plowright, Rosalind Anne 1949- IntWW 93, Who 94
Plowright, Teresa 1952- EncSF 93
Plowright, Walter 1923- Who 94
Plucknett, Donald Lovelle 1931- WhoScEn 94
Plues, George d1953 WhoHol 92
Pluimer, Edward J. 1949- WhoAm 94, WhoAmL 94
Pluimer, Peggy Lee 1948- WhoMW 93
Plum, Bernard Mark 1952- WhoAmL 94
Plum, Charles Walden 1914- WhoAm 94
Plum, Jennifer 1938- WrDr 94
Plum, Kenneth Ray 1941- WhoAmP 93
Plum, Matthias, Jr. 1933- WhoFI 94
Plum, Patrick Who 94
Plum, Richard Eugene 1928- WhoWest 94
Plumb, Baron 1925- Who 94
Plumb, Eve 1958- WhoHol 92
Plumb, Hay d1960 WhoHol 92
Plumb, (Charles) Henry 1925- IntWW 93
Plumb, James Douglas 1941- WhoAmA 93
Plumb, John (Harold) 1911- Who 94, WrDr 94
Plumb, John Harold 1911- IntWW 93
Plumb, Pamela Pelton 1943- WhoAm 94
Plumb, Thomas John 1952- WhoAmP 93
Plumbly, Derek John 1948- Who 94
Plumbridge, Robin Allan 1935- IntWW 93
Plume, John Trevor 1914- Who 94
Plumez, Jean Paul 1939- WhoAm 94
Plumley, Don 1934- WhoHol 92
Plumley, Harold Johnson 1927- WhoFI 94
Plumley, Jack Martin 1910- Who 94
Plumley, Michael Alan 1950- WhoFI 94
Plumley, S. Patric 1949- WhoAm 94, WhoFI 94
Plumlovsky, Ignac 1703-1759 NewGrDO
Plumly, Daniel Harp 1953- WhoAmL 94
Plumly, Stanley DrAPF 93
Plumly, Stanley 1939- WrDr 94
Plumme, Don E. 1933- WrDr 94
Plummer Who 94
Plummer, Amanda 1957- IntMPA 94, WhoAm 94, WhoHol 92
Plummer, Ben ConAu 42NR
Plummer, Blaise R. WhoAmP 93
Plummer, Carlton B. WhoAmA 93
Plummer, Carol Ann 1952- WhoMW 93
Plummer, Cecil Eugene 1932- WhoFI 94
Plummer, Charles McDonald 1934- WhoWest 94
Plummer, Christopher Who 94
Plummer, Christopher 1927?- ConTFT 11, IntMPA 94
Plummer, Christopher 1929- WhoHol 92
Plummer, (Arthur) Christopher (Orme) 1929- IntWW 93, Who 94
Plummer, Christopher Orme 1929- WhoAm 94
Plummer, Daniel C. 1927- WhoIns 94
Plummer, Daniel Clarence, III 1927- WhoAm 94, WhoFI 94
Plummer, (Arthur) Desmond (Herne) 1914- WrDr 94
Plummer, Dirk Arnold 1930- WhoScEn 94
Plummer, Ernest Lockhart 1940- WhoScEn 94
Plummer, Gayther Lynn 1925- WhoScEn 94
Plummer, Gladys Emily Serena 1894- WhAm 10
Plummer, James D. WhoScEn 94
Plummer, James Walter 1920- WhoScEn 94
Plummer, Jerry L. 1941- WhoIns 94
Plummer, Joel 1933- WhoAmP 93
Plummer, John c. 1410-1484 DcNaB MP
Plummer, Joseph Thornton 1941- WhoAm 94, WhoFI 94
Plummer, Kenneth Alexander 1928- WhoMW 93
Plummer, Lawrence H. 1940- WhoAmP 93
Plummer, Leo Heathcote 1923- Who 94
Plummer, Lincoln d1928 WhoHol 92
Plummer, Marcie Stern 1950- WhoAm 94
Plummer, Matthew W., Sr. 1920- WhoBlA 94
Plummer, Michael Justin 1947- WhoBlA 94
Plummer, Michael Kenneth 1954- WhoFI 94
Plummer, Milton WhoBlA 94
Plummer, Ora B. 1940- WhoBlA 94
Plummer, Patricia Lynne Moore WhoMW 93
Plummer, Paul James 1946- WhoFI 94
Plummer, Peter Edward 1919- Who 94
Plummer, Risque Wilson 1910- WhoAm 94
Plummer, Rose d1955 WhoHol 92
Plummer of St. Marylebone, Baron 1914- Who 94
Plummer-Talley, Olga Ann 1934- WhoBlA 94
Plump, Leslie Z. 1934- WhoAmL 94
Plumpp, Sterling Dominic 1940- WhoBlA 94
Plumpton, Alan 1926- Who 94
Plumpton, Alfred fl. 1870-1891 NewGrDO
Plumptre Who 94
Plumstead, Isobel Mary 1947- Who 94
Plumstead, William Charles 1938- WhoScEn 94
Plungis, Barbara Marie 1938- WhoAm 94
Plunguian, Gina d1962 WhoAmA 93N
Plunk, Robert M. 1932- WhoIns 94
Plunket, Baron 1925- Who 94
Plunket, Daniel Clark 1929- WhoAm 94
Plunket, Robert WhoHol 92
Plunket Greene, Mary Who 94
Plunkett Who 94
Plunkett, Hugh V., III 1942- WhoAmL 94
Plunkett, Jack William 1950- WhoFI 94
Plunkett, James 1920- WrDr 94
Plunkett, Jim 1947- WhoHisp 94
Plunkett, John Meredith 1948- WhoFI 94
Plunkett, Lewin 1941- WhoAmL 94
Plunkett, Maryann 1953- WhoAm 94
Plunkett, Patricia 1928- WhoHol 92
Plunkett, Paul Edward 1935- WhoAm 94, WhoAmL 94, WhoMW 93
Plunkett, Robert 1919- WhoAm 94
Plunkett, Roy WorInv
Plunkett, Roy J. WhoScEn 94
Plunkett, Walter d1982 WhoHol 92
Plunkett, Walter 1902-1982 IntDcF 2-4
Plunkett, Warren Francis 1920- WhoIns 94
Plunkett, William Joseph 1921- Who 94
Plusk, Ronald Frank 1933- WhoAm 94
Plusquellic, Donald L. 1949- WhoAm 94, WhoAmP 93, WhoMW 93
Pluta, Stanley John 1966- WhoFI 94
Plutarch 46-120? BlmGEL
Pluth, Joseph John 1943- WhoScEn 94
Plyler, Aaron Wesley 1926- WhoAmP 93
Plymale, Robert H. 1955- WhoAmP 93
Plymat, William N. 1911- WhoIns 94
Plymate, Robert Russel 1936- WhoWest 94
Plymell, Charles DrAPF 93
Plymouth, Archdeacon of Who 94
Plymouth, Bishop of 1937- Who 94
Plymouth, Bishop Suffragan of 1939- Who 94
Plymouth, Earl of 1923- Who 94
Plyushch, Ivan 1941- IntWW 93
P. M. Dawn ConMus 11 [port]
Png, Margaret L.H. 1960- WhoAmL 94
Pniakowski, Andrew Frank 1930- WhoScEn 94
Po, Hung d1968 WhoHol 92
Poag, Charles N. WhoAmP 93
Poag, Coleman G. 1930- WhoAmP 93
Poague, Leland 1948- WrDr 94
Poague, Leland Allen 1948- WhoMW 93
Poananga, Brian Matauru 1924- Who 94
Poarch, Mary Hope Edmondson 1958- WhoScEn 94
Poat Rearick, Mary 1960- WhoMW 93
Poaty-Souchalaty, Alphonse Mouissou IntWW 93
Pober, Jordan S. 1949- WhoScEn 94
Pobo, Kenneth DrAPF 93
Poboisk, Donald Paul 1926-1989 WhAm 10
Poc, Sorya WhoAsA 94
Pocci, Franz 1807-1876 NewGrDO
Pocek-Matic, Mirjana 1932- WhoWomW 91
Poch, Herbert Edward 1927- WhoScEn 94
Poch, Stephen 1909- WhoFI 94
Pochath, Werner WhoHol 92
Poche, Marc B. 1934- WhoAmP 93
Pochi, Peter Ernest 1929- WhoAm 94
Pochick, Francis Edward 1931- WhoFI 94
Pochinok, Aleksandr Petrovich 1958- LngBDD
Pochmann, Virginia 1938- WhoAmA 93
Pochocki, Ethel (Frances) 1925- SmATA 76 [port]
Pochyly, Donald Frederick 1934- WhoAm 94
Pocius, Kenneth J. 1942- WhoAmL 94
Pockell, Leslie M. 1942- WhoAm 94
Pocker, Yeshayau 1928- WhoAm 94, WhoScEn 94, WhoWest 94
Pocklington, Peter H. 1941- WhoAm 94, WhoWest 94
Pocknett, Lawrence W. 1934- WhoIns 94
Pocknett, Lawrence Wendell 1934- WhoBlA 94
Pocock, Donald Arthur 1920- Who 94
Pocock, Frederick James 1923- WhoAm 94
Pocock, Gordon James 1933- Who 94
Pocock, John Greville Agard 1924- IntWW 93
Pocock, Kenneth Walter 1913- Who 94
Pocock, Leslie Frederick 1918- Who 94
Pocock, Tom 1925- WrDr 94
Pocrass, Richard Dale 1940- WhoFI 94
Podagrosi-Spratt, Jo-Ella 1959- WhoMW 93
Podboy, Alvin Michael, Jr. 1947- WhoAm 94, WhoAmL 94, WhoMW 93
Podboy, John Watts 1943- WhoWest 94
Podd, Ann WhoAm 94
Poddar, Ramendra Kumar 1930- IntWW 93, Who 94
Poddar, Shrikumar 1940- WhoFI 94
Podell, Albert N. 1937- IntMPA 94
Podell, Richard N. 1942- WhoAm 94
Podell, Rick WhoHol 92
Podest, Ludvik 1921-1968 NewGrDO
Podesta, Maria Esther d1983 WhoHol 92
Podesta, Robert Angelo 1912- WhoAm 94
Podesta, Roger E. 1947- WhoAmL 94
Podesta, Rossana 1934- WhoHol 92
Podewell, Cathy WhoHol 92
Podgor, Ellen Sue 1952- WhoAmL 94
Podgorecki, Adam 1925- WrDr 94
Podgoretsky, Boris Vladimirovich NewGrDO
Podgornov, Nikolai Mikhailovich 1949- LngBDD
Podgorny, George 1934- WhoAm 94
Podgorny, Richard Joseph 1944- WhoAm 94
Podgorski, Robert Paul 1943- WhoFI 94, WhoMW 93
Podhoretz, Norman 1930- AmSocL, IntWW 93, WhoAm 94, WrDr 94
Podhorzer, Munio 1911- IntMPA 94
Podhorzer, Nathan 1919- IntMPA 94
Podila, Gopi Krishna 1957- WhoScEn 94
Podkolzin, Evgeny Nikolaevich 1936- LngBDD
Podkowinski, Marian Aleksander 1909- IntWW 93
Podles, Eleanor Pauline 1920- WhoAmP 93
Podlesny, Laura Ann 1962- WhoMW 93
Podlin, Mark Joseph 1953- WhoMW 93
Podmokly, Patricia Gayle 1940- WhoFI 94, WhoMW 93
Podmore, Ian Laing 1933- Who 94
Podolny, Walter, Jr. 1929- WhoScEn 94
Podoloff, Maurice 1890-1985 BasBi
Podolske, Diane Lynne 1966- WhoMW 93
Podolsky, Andrea 1951- WhoAmL 94
Podoprigora, Vladimir Nikolaevich 1954- LngBDD
Podosek, Frank Anthony 1941- WhoAm 94
Podrazik, Mark Allen 1959- WhoMW 93
Podro, Michael (Isaac) 1931- WrDr 94
Podro, Michael Isaac 1931- Who 94
Poduska, John William, Sr. 1937- WhoAm 94
Poduska, Malinda Mae 1961- WhoMW 93
Poduska, T. F. 1925- WhoAmA 93
Podvin, Francis John 1941- WhoAmL 94
Podzamsky, John Edward 1947- WhoMW 93
Podziba, Susan Lisa 1960- WhoAmL 94
Podzimek, Jana 1956- WhoMW 93
Poe, Alfred WhoBlA 94
Poe, Booker 1936- WhoBlA 94
Poe, David Russell 1948- WhoAm 94, WhoAmL 94
Poe, Douglas Allan 1942- WhoAm 94, WhoAmL 94
Poe, Edgar Allan 1809-1849 AmCulL, BlmGEL, EncSF 93, NewGrDO, RfGShF
Poe, Fernando, Jr. WhoHol 92
Poe, Fred J. WhoBlA 94
Poe, H. Sadler 1944- WhoAm 94, WhoAmL 94
Poe, James M. 1949- WhoAmL 94
Poe, Jerry B. 1931- WhoAm 94
Poe, Linda J. 1950- WhoMW 93
Poe, Lugne (Aurelien-Marie) d1940 WhoHol 92
Poe, Luke Harvey, Jr. 1916- WhoAm 94
Poe, Reigh Kessen 1949- WhoAmL 94
Poe, Robert Alan 1951- WhoAmL 94
Poe, Stephen IntMPA 94
Poe, Wellon B. 1923- WhoAmP 93
Poe, William Edward 1923- WhoAmL 94
Poe, William Frederick 1931- WhoAm 94
Poedtke, Carl Henry George, Jr. 1938- WhoAm 94, WhoWest 94
Poehler, Theodore Otto 1935- WhoScEn 94
Poehlmann, Carl John 1950- WhoMW 93, WhoScEn 94
Poehlmann, Gerhard Manfred 1924- WhoScEn 94
Poehlmann, JoAnna 1932- WhoAm 94, WhoAmA 93
Poehls, Aileen Orianna 1951- WhoWest 94
Poehner, Raymond Glenn 1923- WhoFI 94, WhoWest 94
Poel, Robert Walter 1934- WhoAm 94
Poel, William 1852-1934 BlmGEL
Poelker, John Henry 1913-1990 WhAm 10
Poellnitz, Fred Douglas 1944- WhoBlA 94

Poelman, Ronald Stoddard 1953- WhoAmL 94
Poen, Monte M. 1930- WhoAm 94
Poepoe, Andrew Keliikuniaupuni 1935- WhoAmP 93
Poertner, David Michael 1946- WhoFI 94
Poertner, Lee Anne 1936- WhoWest 94
Poesch, Jessie Jean 1922- WhoAm 94
Poeschl, Brian K. 1964- WhoWest 94
Poettcker, Henry 1925- WhoAm 94
Poetter, Bruce E. 1951- WhoMW 93
Poettmann, Fred Heinz 1919- WhoAm 94
Poettmann, Frederick Heinz 1919- WhoScEn 94
Poetzsch, T. Peter 1941- WhoAmL 94
Poff, Bing C. 1936- WhoAmP 93
Poff, Lon d1952 WhoHol 92
Poff, Pamela Sue 1951- WhoAm 94
Poff, Richard H. 1923- WhoAmP 93
Poff, Richard Harding 1923- WhoAm 94, WhoAmL 94
Poff, William Beverly 1932- WhoAmL 94
Poffenberger, David John 1959- WhoWest 94
Poffenberger, Virginia 1934- WhoAmP 93
Pogach, Gerald WhoAmA 93
Poganski, Donald J. 1928- WrDr 94
Pogany, Gabor Laszlo 1957- WhoWest 94
Pogany, Miklos 1945- WhoAmA 93
Pogemiller, Lawrence J. 1951- WhoAmP 93
Poger, Ruth 1937- WhoAmP 93
Poggeler, Otto 1928- IntWW 93
Poggenpohl, Teresa Loyola 1961- WhoMW 93
Poggi, Antonio 1806-1875 NewGrDO
Poggi, Gianfranco 1934- WhoAm 94
Poggi, Gianni 1921?-1989 NewGrDO
Poggio, Gian Franco 1927- WhoAm 94
Poggio, Tomaso Armando 1947- WhoScEn 94
Poggione, P. Daniel 1939- WhoAmP 93
Poggione, William Joseph 1935- WhoWest 94
Poglazov, Boris Fedorovich 1930- WhoScEn 94
Poglietti, Alessandro d1683 NewGrDO
Pognonec, Yves Maurice 1948- WhoFI 94
Pogo, Beatriz Teresa Garcia-Tunon 1932- WhoAm 94
Pogorel, Barry Robert 1948- WhoWest 94
Pogorelich, Ivo 1958- IntWW 93
Pogorelov, Aleksey Vasiliyevich 1919- IntWW 93
Pogorelsky, Igor Vladislav 1946- WhoScEn 94
Pogrebin, Bertrand B. 1934- WhoAmL 94
Pogrebin, Letty Cottin 1939- WhoAm 94, WrDr 94
Pogue, Bill EncSF 93
Pogue, Brent Daryl 1954- WhoBlA 94
Pogue, D. Eric 1949- WhoBlA 94
Pogue, Forrest Carlisle 1912- WhoAm 94, WrDr 94
Pogue, Frank G., Jr. 1939- WhoBlA 94
Pogue, Kenneth WhoHol 92
Pogue, Lester Clarence 1943- WhoBlA 94
Pogue, Lloyd Welch 1899- WhoAm 94, WhoAmL 94
Pogue, Mark Allen 1955- WhoAmL 94
Pogue, Richard James 1943- WhoBlA 94
Pogue, Richard Welch 1928- WhoAm 94, WhoAmL 94, WhoMW 93
Pogue, Thomas d1941 WhoHol 92
Pogue, Thomas Franklin 1935- WhoMW 93
Pogue, (Lloyd) Welch 1899- IntWW 93
Pogue, William Reid 1930- WhoAm 94, WhoScEn 94
Pogutse, Oleg Pavlovich 1936- IntWW 93
Pohan, Armand 1944- WhoAm 94
Pohankova, Jana 1944- BlmGWL
Poher, Alain Emile Louis Marie 1909- IntWW 93
Pohjala, Toivo Topias 1931- IntWW 93
Pohjanoksa, Aino Sivia 1936- WhoWomW 91
Pohl, Carol EncSF 93
Pohl, David 1624-1695 NewGrDO
Pohl, Frederik DrAPF 93
Pohl, Frederik 1919- EncSF 93, WhoAm 94, WrDr 94
Pohl, Gunther Erich 1925- WhoAm 94
Pohl, Howard Herbert 1943- WhoFI 94
Pohl, Hugo David 1878-1960 WhoAmA 93N
Pohl, John Henning 1944- WhoWest 94
Pohl, John Joseph, Jr. 1927- WhoAm 94
Pohl, Karl Otto 1929- IntWW 93, Who 94
Pohl, Kathleen Sharon 1951- WhoMW 93
Pohl, Michael A. 1942- WhoAmL 94
Pohl, Paul Michael 1948- WhoAm 94, WhoAmL 94
Pohl, Richard 1826-1896 NewGrDO
Pohl, Richard Walter 1916- WhoAm 94
Pohl, Robert Otto 1929- WhoAm 94, WhoScEn 94
Pohl, Robert W. 1942- WhoAmL 94

Pohl, Victoria Mary 1930- WhoMW 93
Pohlad, Carl R. WhoAm 94, WhoMW 93
Pohland, Frederick George 1931- WhoScEn 94
Pohler, Susan J. 1955- WhoAmP 93
Pohlman, Carlyle George 1931- WhoMW 93
Pohlman, David Lawrence 1944- WhoWest 94
Pohlman, Randolph Allen 1944- WhoAm 94
Pohlman, William J. 1954- WhoMW 93
Pohlmann, Eric d1979 WhoHol 92
Pohlsander, Hans Achim 1927- WhoAm 94
Pohost, Gerald M. 1941- WhoAm 94, WhoScEn 94
Pohrer, Jack Edward 1940- WhoAmP 93
Poiesz, Bernard Joseph 1948- WhoScEn 94
Poile, David Robert 1949- WhoAm 94
Poinar, George Orlo, Jr. 1936- WhoAm 94, WhoScEn 94
Poincare, Jules-Henri 1854-1912 WorScD
Poindexter WhoHol 92
Poindexter, Buster WhoHol 92
Poindexter, Buster 1950- WhoAm 94
Poindexter, Charles L. L. 1932- WhoBlA 94
Poindexter, Christian Herndon 1938- WhoAm 94, WhoFI 94
Poindexter, Elinor Fuller WhoAmA 93
Poindexter, Gammiel Gray 1944- WhoBlA 94
Poindexter, John Bruce 1944- WhoAm 94, WhoFI 94
Poindexter, John Marlane IntWW 93
Poindexter, Joseph Boyd 1935- WhoMW 93
Poindexter, Kathleen A. Krause 1956- WhoMW 93
Poindexter, Kim M. 1955- WhoScEn 94
Poindexter, Larry WhoHol 92
Poindexter, Malcolm P. 1925- WhoBlA 94
Poindexter, Robert L. 1912- WhoBlA 94
Poindexter, William Green, IV 1944- WhoAmP 93
Poindexter, William Mersereau 1925- WhoAm 94
Poindexter, Zeb F. 1929- WhoBlA 94
Poinier, Arthur Best 1911- WhoAmA 93
Poinsett, Alexander C. 1926- WhoBlA 94
Poinsett, Alexander Caesar 1926- WhoAm 94
Poinsette, Donald Eugene 1914- WhoFI 94
Point, Nicholas 1799-1868 EncNAR
Pointer, Anita 1948- WhoHol 92
Pointer, Ann Margaret 1947- WhoAmL 94
Pointer, James Edgar, Jr. 1922- WhoAmP 93
Pointer, June 1954- WhoHol 92
Pointer, Noel 1956- WhoBlA 94
Pointer, Peter Leon 1934- WhoMW 93
Pointer, Priscilla WhoHol 92
Pointer, Richard H. 1944- WhoBlA 94
Pointer, Richard W(ayne) 1955- WrDr 94
Pointer, Ruth 1946- WhoHol 92
Pointer, Sam Clyde, Jr. 1934- WhoAm 94, WhoAmL 94
Pointer, Sidney d1955 WhoHol 92
Pointer, Tom Lee 1949- WhoFI 94
Pointer Sisters, The WhoHol 92
Pointon, Robert BlmGWL
Pointon, Robert 1914- WrDr 94
Points, David S. WhoAmP 93
Points, Roy Wilson 1940- WhoMW 93
Poiret, Jean 1926- WhoHol 92
Poiret, Jean 1926-1992 AnObit 1992
Poirie, Constant John 1940- WhoAmL 94
Poirier, Carol Sue 1963- WhoWest 94
Poirier, Frank Eugene 1940- WhoAm 94
Poirier, Kevin 1940- WhoAmP 93
Poirier, Louis ConWorW 93
Poirier, Louis Joseph 1918- WhoAm 94
Poirier, Paul N. 1948- WhoAmP 93
Poirier, Richard 1925- WhoAm 94
Poirier, Richard (William) 1925- WrDr 94
Poirier, Richard Oveila 1947- WhoWest 94
Poirier, Robert James 1947- WhoWest 94
Poirion, Daniel 1927- WhoAm 94
Poirot, James Wesley 1931- WhoAm 94, WhoFI 94, WhoScEn 94, WhoWest 94
Poirot-Delpech, Bertrand M.A.H. 1929- IntWW 93
Pois, Joseph 1905- WhoAm 94, WhoAmL 94, WhoFI 94
Pois, Robert August 1940- WhoAm 94
Poise, (Jean Alexandre) Ferdinand 1828-1892 NewGrDO
Poison ConMus 11 [port]
Poissant, Brian M. 1948- WhoAmL 94
Poissant, Charles-Albert 1925- WhoAm 94, WhoFI 94
Poissant, Margaret Anne 1959- WhoAm 94

Poissl, Johann Nepomuk 1783-1865 NewGrDO
Poisson, Gary Wayne 1953- WhoMW 93
Poisson, Simeon-Denis 1781-1840 WorScD
Poister, R(alph) S(eymour) 1893- WhAm 10
Poitevent, Edward Butts, II 1949- WhoAm 94, WhoAmL 94
Poitevint, Alec Loyd, II 1947- WhoAmP 93
Poitier, Jane 1736-1774? NewGrDO
Poitier, Sidney 1924- IntWW 93, WhoBlA 94, WhoHol 92
Poitier, Sidney 1927- AfrAmAl 6 [port], IntMPA 94, Who 94, WhoAm 94
Poitout, Dominique Gilbert M. 1946- WhoScEn 94
Poitras, Pierre 1934- WhoAm 94
Poivre, Annette WhoHol 92
Pojanowski, Joseph A., III 1948- WhoAmP 93
Pojeta, John, Jr. 1935- WhoAm 94
Poka Laenui 1946- WhoAmL 94
Pokaski, Daniel Francis 1949- WhoAmP 93
Pokelwaldt, Robert N. WhoFI 94
Pokempner, Joseph Kres 1936- WhoAm 94, WhoAmL 94
Pokka, Hannele 1952- WhoWomW 91
Poklemba, Ronald Steven 1947- WhoScEn 94
Pokorni, Orysia 1938- WhoMW 93
Pokornowski, Ronald Felix 1933- WhoMW 93
Pokorny, Alex Daniel 1918- WhoScEn 94
Pokorny, Fern Kathryn 1949- WhoAmP 93
Pokorny, Frank Joseph 1956- WhoMW 93
Pokorny, Gerold E. 1928- WhoAm 94
Pokorny, Jan Hird 1914- WhoAm 94
Pokorny, Wayne D. 1938- WhoMW 93
Pokotilow, Manny David 1938- WhoAmL 94
Pokras, Sheila Frances Grabelle 1935- WhoAmP 93
Pokross, David R., Jr. 1945- WhoAmL 94
Pokrovsky, Boris Aleksandrovich 1912- IntWW 93
Pokrovsky, Valentin Ivanovich 1929- IntWW 93
Pol, Talitha d1971 WhoHol 92
Pola, Isa d1984 WhoHol 92
Polac, Michel 1930- IntWW 93
Polacchine, Le NewGrDO
Polacco, Giorgio 1873-1960 NewGrDO
Polacco, Patricia 1944- SmATA 74 [port]
Polach, Jaroslav G(eorge) 1914- WrDr 94
Polach, Jaroslav George 1914- WhoFI 94
Polachek, Solomon William 1945- WhoFI 94
Polachek, Thomas A. 1942- WhoAmL 94
Poladian, Ara A. 1953- WhoWest 94
Polainer, Edward Joseph WhoMW 93
Polak, Andrew Joseph 1911- WhoAmP 93
Polak, Cornelia Julia 1908- Who 94
Polak, Elijah 1931- WhoAm 94
Polak, George 1923- WhoFI 94
Polak, Jacques Jacobus 1914- IntWW 93, WhoAm 94, WhoFI 94
Polak, John W. 1948- WhoIns 94
Polak, Julia Margaret 1939- Who 94
Polak, Michael Charles 1960- WhoAmP 93
Polak, Vivian Louise 1952- WhoAm 94, WhoAmL 94
Polak, Werner L. 1936- WhoAm 94
Polakoff, Abe WhoAm 94
Polakoff, Keith (Ian) 1941- WrDr 94
Polakoff, Keith Ian 1941- WhoAm 94, WhoWest 94
Polakoff, Moses 1896-1993 NewYTBS 93
Polakoff, Murray Emanuel 1922- WhoAm 94
Polakoff, Pedro Paul, II 1926- WhoScEn 94
Polan, Annette 1944- WhoAmA 93
Polan, Annette Lewis 1944- WhoAm 94
Polan, Charles M., Jr. 1913- WhoAmP 93
Polan, David Jay 1951- WhoAmL 94, WhoWest 94
Polan, Lincoln M. 1909- WhoAmA 93
Polan, Lou d1976 WhoHol 92
Polan, Morris 1924- WhoAm 94
Polan, Nancy Moore WhoAm 94, WhoAmA 93
Polanco, Richard 1951- WhoAmP 93
Polanco, Richard G. 1951- WhoHisp 94
Poland, Dorothy (Elizabeth Hayward) 1937- WrDr 94
Poland, Edmund Nicholas 1917- Who 94
Poland, Marguerite 1950- WrDr 94
Poland, Reginald 1893- WhAm 10
Poland, Richard Clayton 1947- WhoAmP 93
Poland, Richard Domville 1914- Who 94
Poland, Robert Glenn 1938- WhoMW 93
Poland, Robert Paul 1925- WhoAm 94

Poland, Todd M. 1947- WhoAmL 94
Polani, Girolamo fl. 1689- NewGrDO
Polani, Paul Emanuel 1914- Who 94
Polanski, Goury d1976 WhoHol 92
Polanski, Roman NewYTBS 93 [port]
Polanski, Roman 1933- HorFD [port], IntMPA 94, IntWW 93, WhoAm 94, WhoHol 92
Polansky, Larry Paul 1932- WhoAm 94
Polansky, Lois B. 1939- WhoAmA 93
Polansky, Sol 1926- WhoAmP 93
Polanyi, John Charles 1929- IntWW 93, Who 94, WhoAm 94, WhoScEn 94
Polarek, James Wallace 1957- WhoWest 94
Polascik, Mary Ann 1940- WhoMW 93
Polasek, Edward John 1927- WhoScEn 94
Polashek, David Clarence 1948- WhoMW 93
Polaski, Deborah 1949- NewGrDO
Polay, Bruce 1949- WhoMW 93
Polayes, Irving Marvin 1927- WhoAm 94
Polcari, Stephen 1945- WhoAmA 93
Polcelli, Luigia NewGrDO
Polcinski, Gene WhoAm 94
Polcz, Alaine 1921- BlmGWL
Poldini, Ede 1869-1957 NewGrDO
Pole Who 94
Pole, Jack Richon 1922- IntWW 93, Who 94, WrDr 94
Pole, Peter Van Notten 1921- Who 94
Pole, Reginald 1500-1558 DcLB 132 [port]
Polebaum, Elliot Edward 1950- WhoAm 94
Polebaum, Mark Neal 1952- WhoAmL 94
Poledouris, Basil ConTFT 11
Poledouris, Basil 1945- IntMPA 94
Polelle, Michael Joseph 1938- WhoAmL 94
Polemitou, Olga Andrea 1950- WhoFI 94
Polen, Nat d1981 WhoHol 92
Polenberg, Richard 1937- WhoAm 94, WrDr 94
Polen-Dorn, Linda Frances 1945- WhoFI 94
Polenov, Fedor Dmitrievich 1929- LngBDD
Polenske, Karen Rosel 1937- WhoAm 94
Poleri, David S(amuel) 1921-1967 NewGrDO
Polese, Richard Louis 1941- WhoWest 94
Poleskie, Stephen Francis 1938- WhoAm 94, WhoAmA 93
Polesky, Herbert Fred 1933- WhoAm 94
Polet, Herman 1930- WhoMW 93
Poletti, Alan Ronald 1937- IntWW 93
Poletti, Charles 1903- WhoAm 94
Poletti, Syria 1921- BlmGWL
Poletti, Ugo 1914- IntWW 93
Polezhaev, Leonid Konstantinovich 1940- LngBDD
Polfer, Lydie 1952- WhoWomW 91
Polfer, Mary Margaret WhoFI 94
Polgar, Judit 1976- News 93-3 [port]
Polgar, Laszlo 1947- IntWW 93, NewGrDO
Polgar, Tibor 1907- NewGrDO
Polgar, Timothy Thomas 1955- WhoMW 93
Polge, (Ernest John) Christopher 1926- Who 94
Polglase, Van Nest 1898-1968 IntDcF 2-4
Polhemus, Mary Irene 1937- WhoMW 93
Polhemus, Robert M(ackinlay) 1935- WrDr 94
Poli, Afro WhoHol 92
Poli, Kenneth Joseph 1921- WhoAm 94
Poliacof, Michael Mircea 1932- WhoScEn 94
Poliakoff, Gary A. 1944- WhoAmL 94
Poliakoff, Stephen IntWW 93, Who 94
Poliakoff, Stephen 1952- ConDr 93, IntDcT 2
Poliakoff, Stephen 1953- WrDr 94
Polian, Bill 1942- WhoAm 94
Poli Bortone, Adriana 1943- WhoWomW 91
Polic, Henry, II WhoHol 92
Polic, Mirko 1890-1951 NewGrDO
Policano, Andrew J. 1949- WhoAm 94, WhoFI 94
Policano, Joseph Daniel 1933- WhoAm 94
Polich, John Michael 1947- WhoScEn 94
Policoff, Leonard David 1918- WhoAm 94
Policoff, Stephen Phillip 1948- SmATA 77 [port]
Policoff, Susan Lewis DrAPF 93
Policy, Vincent Mark 1948- WhoAmL 94
Polidor d1977 WhoHol 92
Polidouri, Maria 1902-1930 BlmGWL
Polier, Marie-Elisabeth 1742-1817 BlmGWL
Polik, William Frederick 1960- WhoMW 93
Polikoff, Barbara G(arland) 1929- SmATA 77 [port]
Polikoff, Benet, Jr. 1936- WhoAm 94, WhoAmL 94

Polillo, Sergio 1917- IntWW 93
Polimita, D. BlmGWL
Polin, Alan Jay 1953- WhoAmL 94
Polin, Claire WhoAm 94
Polin, Jane Louise 1958- WhoAm 94
Poliner, Robert S. 1943- WhoAmP 93
Poling(-Kempes), Lesley 1954- WrDr 94
Poling, Christopher Alan 1961- WhoMW 93
Poling, Clark V. WhoAmA 93
Poling, Claudia Sue 1947- WhoMW 93
Poling, Harold Arthur 1925- IntWW 93, WhoAm 94, WhoFI 94
Poling, Kermit William 1941- WhoAm 94
Poling, Richard Duane 1955- WhoAmL 94
Polini, Emilie d1927 WhoHol 92
Polinsky, Janet 1930- WhoAmP 93
Polinsky, Joseph Thomas 1947- WhoScEn 94
Polinsky, Robert Alexander 1941- WhoAmP 93
Poli-Randaccio, Tina 1879-1956 NewGrDO
Polis, Michael Philip 1943- WhoAm 94
Polis, Samuel 1926- WhoWest 94
Polis, Sheri Helene 1956- WhoFI 94
Polisar, Barry Louis 1954- SmATA 77 [port]
Polisar, Leonard Myers 1929- WhoAm 94
Polisena, Joseph M. 1954- WhoAmP 93
Polish, John 1917- WhoAmP 93
Polishan, Paul Frank 1945- WhoFI 94
Polisi, Joseph William 1947- WhoAm 94
Politan, Nicholas H. 1935- WhoAm 94, WhoAmL 94
Politano, Victor Anthony 1919- WhoAm 94
Polite, Carlene Hatcher 1932- WhoBlA 94
Polite, Craig K. 1947- WhoBlA 94
Polite, Frank DrAPF 93
Polite, Marie Ann 1954- WhoBlA 94
Politella, Dario 1921- WrDr 94
Polites, Michael Edward 1944- WhoScEn 94
Politis, Dimitris Nicolas 1960- WhoMW 93
Politis, Timothy Jude 1944- WhoFI 94
Polito, Jon WhoHol 92
Polito, Joseph Michael 1950- WhoAm 94, WhoAmL 94
Polito, Sol 1892-1960 IntDcF 2-4
Politoff, Alberto Lifschitz 1935- WhoMW 93
Politte, John Leo 1935- WhoMW 93
Politz, Henry A. 1932- WhoAmP 93
Politz, Henry Anthony 1932- WhoAm 94, WhoAmL 94
Politz, Nyle Anthony 1953- WhoAmL 94
Politzer, Hugh David 1949- WhoAm 94
Politzer, S. Robert 1929- WhoAmP 93
Polivnick, Paul 1947- WhoAm 94
Polizoidis, Germanos d1993 NewYTBS 93
Polizotto, Bruce Alan 1941- WhoAm 94, WhoAmL 94
Polizzi, Jan WhoAmP 93
Polizzi, Jan Crandall 1949- WhoMW 93
Polizzi, Olga Who 94
Polk, Anthony Joseph 1941- WhoBlA 94
Polk, Benjamin Kauffman 1916- WhoWest 94
Polk, Benjamin Michael 1951- WhoAm 94
Polk, Carol Fultz 1952- WhoFI 94
Polk, Charles 1920- WhoAm 94
Polk, David d1987 WhoHol 92
Polk, Donna Lee 1943- WhoAmP 93
Polk, Eugene Steven, Sr. 1939- WhoBlA 94
Polk, Frank Frederick 1908- WhoAmA 93
Polk, Gene-Ann 1926- WhoBlA 94
Polk, George Douglas 1919- WhoBlA 94
Polk, Gordon d1960 WhoHol 92
Polk, Hiram Carey, Jr. 1936- WhoAm 94
Polk, James Hilliard 1911-1992 WhAm 10
Polk, James Ray 1937- WhoAm 94
Polk, Judith A. 1942- WhoAmP 93
Polk, Lee d1993 NewYTBS 93
Polk, Lee Thomas 1945- WhoAmL 94
Polk, Leonidas 1806-1864 DcAmReB 2
Polk, Leonidas Lafayette 1837-1892 AmSocL
Polk, Lorna Marie 1948- WhoBlA 94
Polk, Louis Frederick, Jr. 1930- WhoAm 94
Polk, Oscar d1949 WhoHol 92
Polk, Richard A. 1936- WhoBlA 94
Polk, Robert Edward, Jr. 1955- WhoMW 93
Polk, Robert Forrest 1947- WhoAm 94
Polk, Robert L. 1928- WhoBlA 94
Polk, Thomas 1732-1794 WhAmRev
Polk, Vernon C. d1981 WhoHol 92
Polk, William 1758-1834 WhAmRev [port]
Polk, William C. 1935- WhoBlA 94
Polk, William Merrill 1935- WhoAm 94, WhoAmP 93
Polka, Matthew Merle 1959- WhoAmL 94
Polke, Sigmar 1941- WhoAm 94
Polkes, Alan H. 1931- WhoAmA 93N
Polking, Kirk 1925- WrDr 94
Polking, Paul J. WhoAmL 94
Polkinghorne, John Charlton 1930- IntWW 93, Who 94
Polkosnik, Walter 1968- WhoScEn 94
Polkowski, Delphine Theresa 1930- WhoMW 93
Poll, David Ian Alistair 1950- WhoScEn 94
Poll, Heinz 1926- WhoAm 94, WhoMW 93
Poll, Martin H. 1926- IntMPA 94
Poll, Martin Harvey WhoAm 94
Poll, Robert Eugene, Jr. 1948- WhoAm 94
Polla, Pauline d1940 WhoHol 92
Pollack, Alan Myron 1958- WhoWest 94
Pollack, Anita Jean 1946- Who 94, WhoWomW 91
Pollack, Ben d1971 WhoHol 92
Pollack, Bruce 1951- WhoAm 94
Pollack, Dale WhoAm 94
Pollack, Daniel 1935- WhoAm 94
Pollack, Debra Winthrop 1952- WhoAmL 94
Pollack, Eileen DrAPF 93
Pollack, Erwin Wilburt 1935- WhoMW 93
Pollack, Gerald A. 1929- WhoAm 94, WhoFI 94
Pollack, Gerald Harvey 1940- WhoAm 94
Pollack, Gerald Leslie 1933- WhoAm 94, WhoScEn 94
Pollack, Henry Nathan 1936- WhoAm 94, WhoScEn 94
Pollack, Herbert 1905-1990 WhAm 10
Pollack, Howard Martin 1928- WhoScEn 94
Pollack, Ilana 1946- IntWW 93
Pollack, Irwin William 1927- WhoAm 94
Pollack, Jeffrey Lee 1945- WhoFI 94
Pollack, Joe 1931- WhoAm 94
Pollack, Joseph 1917- WhoAm 94
Pollack, Joseph 1939- WhoAm 94
Pollack, Lana 1942- WhoAmP 93, WhoMW 93, WhoWomW 91
Pollack, Louis 1920- WhoAm 94
Pollack, Louis 1921-1970 WhoAmA 93N
Pollack, Mark Joel 1957- WhoWest 94
Pollack, Martin D. 1951- WhoAmL 94
Pollack, Michael 1946- WhoAm 94, WhoAmL 94
Pollack, Michael Bruce 1958- WhoAmL 94
Pollack, Milton 1906- WhoAm 94
Pollack, Murray d1979 WhoHol 92
Pollack, Murray Michael 1947- WhoScEn 94
Pollack, Norman 1933- WhoAm 94
Pollack, Paul Robert 1941- WhoAm 94
Pollack, Peter 1911-1978 WhoAmA 93N
Pollack, Rachel DrAPF 93
Pollack, Rachel (Grace) 1945- EncSF 93
Pollack, Reginald 1924- WrDr 94
Pollack, Reginald Murray 1924- WhoAm 94, WhoAmA 93
Pollack, Richard W. WhoAmL 94
Pollack, Robert 1933- WhoIns 94
Pollack, Robert Elliot 1940- WhoAm 94, WhoScEn 94
Pollack, Robert William 1947- WhoScEn 94
Pollack, Ronald Frank 1944- WhoAm 94
Pollack, Roslyn Goold 1948- WhoAmL 94
Pollack, S. Thomas 1943- WhoAmL 94
Pollack, Sandra (Barbara) 1937- ConAu 43NR
Pollack, Seymour Victor 1933- WhoAm 94
Pollack, Solomon Robert 1934- WhoAm 94
Pollack, Stanley P. 1928- WhoAmL 94
Pollack, Stephen J. 1937- WhoAm 94
Pollack, Sydney 1934- IntMPA 94, IntWW 93, WhoAm 94, WhoHol 92
Pollack, Tessa Martinez WhoHisp 94
Pollack, Virginia Morris WhoAmA 93N
Pollak, Anna 1912- NewGrDO
Pollak, Cheryl 1967- WhoHol 92
Pollak, David Paul 1964- WhoAmL 94
Pollak, Edward Barry 1934- WhoAm 94, WhoFI 94
Pollak, Egon 1879-1933 NewGrDO
Pollak, James Stephen 1940- WhoAm 94
Pollak, Jay Mitchell 1937- WhoAmL 94
Pollak, Jerry Leslie 1929- WhoFI 94
Pollak, Joanne E. 1944- WhoAmL 94
Pollak, Kevin 1957- WhoHol 92
Pollak, Louis Heilprin 1922- WhoAm 94, WhoAmL 94
Pollak, Mark 1947- WhoAm 94, WhoAmL 94
Pollak, Martha 1951- WhoMW 93
Pollak, Martha D. 1941- ConAu 140
Pollak, Martin Marshall 1927- WhoAm 94
Pollak, Norman L. 1931- WhoFI 94, WhoWest 94
Pollak, Oliver Burt 1943- WhoMW 93
Pollak, Raymond 1950- WhoMW 93
Pollak, Richard 1934- WhoAm 94
Pollak, Robert Andrew 1938- WhoAm 94, WhoWest 94
Pollak, Theresa 1899- WhoAmA 93
Pollak, Tim WhoAm 94
Pollak, Vivian R. 1938- WrDr 94
Pollan, Carolyn Joan 1937- WhoAmP 93
Pollan, Stephen Michael 1929- WhoAmL 94, WhoFI 94
Pollan, Tracy 1960- IntMPA 94, WhoHol 92
Pollan-Cohen, Shirley B. DrAPF 93
Polland, Madeleine A(ngela) 1918- WrDr 94
Pollar, Gene d1971 WhoHol 92
Pollara, Bernard WhoAm 94
Pollard, A(nthony) J(ames) 1941- WrDr 94
Pollard, A. W. 1859-1944 BlmGEL
Pollard, Alexander d1950 WhoHol 92
Pollard, Alfonso McInham 1952- WhoBlA 94
Pollard, Alton Brooks, III 1956- WhoBlA 94
Pollard, Anthony John Griffin 1937- Who 94
Pollard, Arthur 1922- WrDr 94
Pollard, B. Tommy 1941- WhoAmP 93
Pollard, Barry Who 94
Pollard, (Charles) Barry 1927- Who 94
Pollard, Bernard 1927- Who 94
Pollard, Braxton 1908- WhAm 10
Pollard, Bud d1952 WhoHol 92
Pollard, Carl F. 1938- WhoAm 94, WhoFI 94
Pollard, Charles 1945- Who 94
Pollard, Charles William 1938- WhoAm 94, WhoFI 94
Pollard, Charles William 1957- WhoAm 94, WhoAmL 94
Pollard, Christopher Charles 1957- Who 94
Pollard, Daphne d1978 WhoHol 92
Pollard, David Edward 1927- WhoAm 94
Pollard, David W. 1948- WhoAmL 94
Pollard, Diane S. 1944- WhoBlA 94
Pollard, Donald Pence 1924- WhoAmA 93
Pollard, Emily Frances WhoBlA 94
Pollard, Eve Who 94
Pollard, Frank Edward 1932- WhoAmL 94
Pollard, Fred Don 1931- WhoAm 94
Pollard, Freeman Wallace 1922- WhoBlA 94
Pollard, G. B., Jr. 1931- WhoAmP 93
Pollard, George Marvin 1909- WhoAm 94
Pollard, Harry d1934 WhoHol 92
Pollard, Henry 1931- WhoAm 94, WhoAmL 94
Pollard, J. A. DrAPF 93
Pollard, Jann Diann 1942- WhoWest 94
Pollard, Jim d1993 NewYTBS 93 [port]
Pollard, Jim 1922- BasBi
Pollard, John (Richard Thornhill) 1914- WrDr 94
Pollard, John Oliver 1937- WhoAmL 94
Pollard, Joseph Augustine 1924- WhoAm 94, WhoFI 94
Pollard, Joseph Warren 1956- WhoFI 94
Pollard, Kenneth Michael 1952- WhoWest 94
Pollard, Latanya 1960- BasBi
Pollard, Michael J. 1939- IntMPA 94, WhoHol 92
Pollard, Michael Ross 1947- WhoAmL 94
Pollard, Morris 1916- WhoAm 94
Pollard, Muriel Ransom 1953- WhoBlA 94
Pollard, Odell 1927- WhoAmP 93
Pollard, Overton Price 1933- WhoAm 94, WhoAmL 94
Pollard, Percy Edward, Sr. 1943- WhoBlA 94
Pollard, Raymond J. 1932- WhoBlA 94
Pollard, Richard Frederick David 1941- Who 94
Pollard, Sidney 1925- Who 94, WrDr 94
Pollard, Snub d1962 WhoHol 92
Pollard, Snub 1886-1962 WhoCom
Pollard, Thomas Brown, Jr. 1933- WhoAmL 94
Pollard, Thomas Dean 1942- WhoAm 94, WhoScEn 94
Pollard, Thomas Evan 1921- WrDr 94
Pollard, Velma 1937- BlmGWL
Pollard, Warren Randolph 1898- WhAm 10
Pollard, William Albert 1946- WhoAmL 94
Pollard, William C. 1951- WhoAmL 94
Pollard, William E. 1915- WhoBlA 94
Pollard, William Lawrence 1944- WhoBlA 94
Pollard, William Sherman, Jr. 1925- WhoAm 94
Pollard Family NewGrDO
Pollari, Robert William 1925- WhoAmP 93
Pollaro, Paul WhoAmA 93
Pollarolo, (Giovanni) Antonio c. 1676-1746 NewGrDO
Pollarolo, Carlo Francesco c. 1653-1723 NewGrDO
Pollart, Dale Flavian 1932- WhoAm 94
Pollay, Richard L. 1932- WhoAm 94
Pollei, Dane F. WhoAmA 93
Pollen, Arabella Rosalind Hungerford 1961- IntWW 93
Pollen, Arthur Joseph Hungerford 1866-1937 DcNaB MP
Pollen, John Michael Hungerford 1919- Who 94
Pollen, Peregrine Michael Hungerford 1931- Who 94
Pollen, Raymond James 1956- WhoAmL 94
Poller, Jeri 1952- WhoAmL 94
Polles, Cynthia Dillon 1954- WhoMW 93
Pollet, Elizabeth DrAPF 93
Pollet, Francoise 1949- NewGrDO
Pollet, Joseph 1898-1979 WhoAmA 93N
Pollet, Richard WhoAm 94, WhoAmL 94, WhoFI 94
Pollet, Sylvester DrAPF 93
Pollexfen, Jack 1918- IntMPA 94
Polley, Alan Scott 1958- WhoAmL 94
Polley, Claudia Anne 1949- WhoMW 93
Polley, Dale Whitcomb 1949- WhoAm 94
Polley, Daryl William 1948- WhoFI 94
Polley, Edward Herman 1923- WhoAm 94
Polley, Ernest 1936- WhoAmP 93
Polley, Frederick 1875- WhoAmA 93N
Polley, Harvey Lee 1924- WhoWest 94
Polley, Howard Freeman 1913- WhoAm 94
Polley, Joseph Crawford 1897- WhAm 10
Polley, Judith Anne 1938- WrDr 94
Polley, Richard Donald 1937- WhoFI 94, WhoScEn 94
Polley, Sarah 1979- WhoHol 92
Polley, Terry Lee 1947- WhoAmL 94, WhoWest 94
Polley, William Alphonse 1942- WhoMW 93, WhoScEn 94
Polley, William Emory 1921- WhoBlA 94
Pollicino, Joseph Anthony 1939- WhoAm 94, WhoFI 94
Pollick, G. David 1947- WhoAm 94
Pollick, Marissa W. 1957- WhoAmL 94
Pollihan, Thomas Henry 1949- WhoAmL 94
Pollin, Abe 1923- WhoAm 94
Pollin, Pierre Louis 1947- WhoMW 93
Pollinger, William Joshua 1944- WhoAmL 94
Pollington, Viscount Who 94
Pollini, Francesco (Giuseppe) 1762-1846 NewGrDO
Pollini, Francis 1930- WhoAm 94
Pollini, Maurizio 1942- IntWW 93
Pollio, Ralph Thomas 1948- WhoAm 94
Pollitt, Jerome Jordan 1934- WhoAm 94, WhoAmA 93
Pollitt, John 1926- IntWW 93
Pollitt, Katha DrAPF 93
Pollitt, Michael WhoHol 92
Pollitt, Richard Malone, Jr. 1952- WhoAmP 93
Pollitzer, William Sprott 1923- WhoAm 94
Pollmer, Jost Udo 1954- WhoScEn 94
Pollmer, Wolfgang Gerhard 1926- WhoScEn 94
Pollner, Martin Robert 1934- WhoAm 94
Pollnow, Jan L. WhoIns 94
Pollock Who 94
Pollock, Adrian Anthony 1943- WhoScEn 94
Pollock, Alexander 1944- Who 94
Pollock, Alexander John 1943- WhoAm 94, WhoFI 94, WhoMW 93
Pollock, Allen 1948- WhoFI 94
Pollock, Bruce 1951- WhoAmA 93
Pollock, Bruce Gerald 1947- WhoAmL 94
Pollock, Craig Allen 1956- WhoFI 94
Pollock, Dale 1950- IntMPA 94, WrDr 94
Pollock, David John Frederick 1942- Who 94
Pollock, Davis Allen 1942-1990 WhAm 10
Pollock, Dee WhoHol 92
Pollock, Donald Kerr 1950- WhoScEn 94
Pollock, E. Jill 1946- WhoAm 94
Pollock, Earl Edward 1928- WhoAm 94
Pollock, Ellen 1903- WhoHol 92
Pollock, Ellen Clara 1902- Who 94
Pollock, George F(rederick) 1928- Who 94
Pollock, George Howard 1923- WhoAm 94
Pollock, Giles (Hampden) Montagu- 1928- Who 94
Pollock, Jack Paden 1920- WhoScEn 94
Pollock, Jackson 1912-1956 WhoAmA 93N

Pollock, James Arlin 1898-1949
  WhoAmA 93N
Pollock, Jeffrey Morrow 1961-
  WhoAmL 94
Pollock, John Albon 1936- WhoAm 94
Pollock, John Charles WrDr 94
Pollock, John Crothers, III 1943-
  WhoAm 94
Pollock, John Denton 1926- Who 94
Pollock, John Glennon 1943- WhoAm 94
Pollock, John Phleger 1920- WhoAm 94
  WhoAmL 94, WhoWest 94
Pollock, Karen Anne 1961- WhoMW 93
Pollock, Kenneth Hugh 1948-
  WhoScEn 94
Pollock, M. Duncan 1943- WhoAm 94
Pollock, Marilyn J. 1934- WhoMW 93
Pollock, Martin Rivers 1914- Who 94
Pollock, Marvin Erwin 1931- WhoAm 94
Pollock, Merlin F. 1905- WhoAmA 93
Pollock, Michael (Patrick) 1916-
  IntWW 93, Who 94
Pollock, Nancy R. d1979 WhoHol 92
Pollock, Neal Jay 1947- WhoFI 94,
  WhoScEn 94
Pollock, Oliver c. 1737-1823 AmRev,
  WhAmRev
Pollock, Paul Edward 1938- WhoIns 94
Pollock, Paul Jackson 1912-1956 AmCulL
Pollock, Peter Brian 1936- Who 94
Pollock, Phillip R. 1947- WhoAmL 94
Pollock, R. Jeffrey 1946- WhoAmL 94
Pollock, Raphael Etomar 1950-
  WhoScEn 94
Pollock, Richard Edwin 1928-
  WhoWest 94
Pollock, Robert Elwood 1936-
  WhoAm 94, WhoScEn 94
Pollock, Robert Michael 1926-
  WhoAmP 93
Pollock, Roy Van Horn 1949- WhoAm 94
Pollock, Sharon 1936- BlmGWL,
  ConAu 93, IntDcT 2, WrDr 94
Pollock, (Mary) Sharon 1936- ConAu 141
Pollock, Sheldon Ivan 1948- WhoAm 94
Pollock, Stephen Michael 1936-
  WhoAm 94
Pollock, Stewart G. 1932- WhoAmP 93
Pollock, Stewart Glasson 1932-
  WhoAm 94, WhoAmL 94
Pollock, Thomas 1943- IntMPA 94
Pollock, Thomas Alan 1946- WhoMW 93
Pollock, Thomas P. 1943- WhoAm 94,
  WhoFI 94
Pollock, Tony J. 1961- WhoMW 93
Pollock, Walter Herries EncSF 93
Pollock-O'Brien, Louise Mary 1948-
  WhoAm 94
Pollone, Maria Dominichina c.
  1700-1750? WhoGrDO
Polmann, Donald Jeffrey 1957-
  WhoScEn 94
Polo, Eddie d1961 WhoHol 92
Polo, James F. 1950- WhoHisp 94
Polo, Maffeo fl. 126-?-129-? WhWE
Polo, Marco 1254?-1324? BlmGEL,
  WhWE [port]
Polo, Niccolo fl. 126-?-129-? WhWE
Polo, Sam d1966 WhoHol 92
Polo, Teri WhoHol 92
Polome, Edgar Charles 1920- WhoAm 94
Polomskey, Harry 1927- WhoAmP 93
Polon, Ira H. 1943- WhoAmL 94
Polon, Linda Beth 1943- WhoWest 94
Polon, Martin Ishiah 1942- WhoFI 94
Polonia, Luis Andrew 1964- WhoHisp 94
Polonis, Douglas Hugh 1928- WhoAm 94
Polonsky, Abraham 1910- IntMPA 94
Polonsky, Antony (Barry) 1940- WrDr 94
Polonsky, Arthur 1925- WhoAm 94,
  WhoAmA 93
Polonsky, Helen 1936- WhoAmP 93
Polos, James 1944- WhoFI 94
Polosin, Vyacheslav Sergeevich 1956-
  LngBDD
Polotan, Kerima BlmGWL
Polovets, Alexander 1935- WhoAm 94
Polovinkin, Leonid Alexeyevich
  1894-1949 NewGrDO
Polovy, Marian 1952- WhoAmL 94
Polow, Bertram 1918- WhoAmL 94
Poloyac, Michael, II 1952- WhoAmP 93
Polozkov, Ivan Kuzmich 1935- IntWW 93
Polozkova, Lidia Pavlovna 1939-
  IntWW 93
Polozola, Frank Joseph 1942- WhoAm 94,
  WhoAmL 94
Polpetta, La NewGrDO
Pol Pot 1928- IntWW 93
Polsby, Nelson Woolf 1934- WhoAm 94
Polsfuss, Craig Lyle 1950- WhoFI 94,
  WhoMW 93
Polsinelli, Anthony Renato 1944-
  WhoFI 94
Polski, Robert William 1950- WhoFI 94
Polsky, Cynthia Hazen 1939-
  WhoAmA 93
Polsky, Michael Peter 1949- WhoScEn 94

Polson, Donald Allan 1911- WhoWest 94
Polson, Jerilyn Handel 1962- WhoAmL 94
Polson, John WhoHol 92
Polster, James DrAPF 93
Polstra, Larry John 1945- WhoAmL 94
Poltimore, Baron 1957- Who 94
Poltoranin, Mikhail Nikiforovich 1939-
  IntWW 93, LngBDD
Polukhina, Valentina 1936- WrDr 94
Polumbo, Anthony L. 1945- WhoAmP 93
Polumbus, Gary M. 1941- WhoAmL 94
Polunin, Nicholas IntWW 93, Who 94,
  WhoAm 94, WhoScEn 94, WrDr 94
Polunsky, Steven Michael 1959-
  WhoAmP 93
Polus, Judith Ann 1943- WhoWest 94
Poluyanov, Nikolai Andreevich 1952-
  LngBDD
Poluzzi, Amleto 1919- WhoScEn 94
Polvinen, Tuomo Ilmari 1931- IntWW 93
Polwarth, Baron 1916- IntWW 93
Polwarth, Lord 1916- Who 94
Polwarth, Master of 1947- Who 94
Polwhele, Elizabeth 1651?-1691 BlmGWL
Polya, John Bela 1914-1992 WrDr 94N
Polyakov, Vladimir Porfiriyevich 1931-
  IntWW 93
Polyanichko, Viktor P. d1993
  NewYTBS 93
Polyanin, Andrey GayLL
Polyansky, Anatoliy Trofimovich 1928-
  IntWW 93
Polydoris, Nicholas George 1930-
  WhoFI 94, WhoMW 93, WhoScEn 94
Polynesia, Bishop in 1935- Who 94
Polynice, Olden 1964- WhoBlA 94
Polyzos, George Constantine 1959-
  WhoWest 94
Polze, Werner 1931- IntWW 93
Polzelli, Luigia c. 1760-1830 NewGrDO
Polzer, Joseph 1929- WhoAmA 93
Polzin, Charles Henry 1954- WhoAmL 94
Polzin, John Theodore 1919- WhoAmL 94
Polzin, Paul Elmer 1943- WhoFI 94
Pomare, Eleo 1937- WhoBlA 94
Pombo, Manuel WhoHisp 94
Pombo, Pilar BlmGWL
Pombo, Richard 1961- WhoAm 94,
  WhoWest 94
Pombo, Richard W. 1961- CngDr 93,
  WhoAmP 93
Pomerance, Bernard 1940- ConDr 93,
  WrDr 94
Pomerance, Diane Linda 1951- WhoFI 94
Pomerance, Norman 1926- WhoAm 94
Pomerance, Ralph 1907- WhoAm 94
Pomerantz, Alan J. 1944- WhoAmL 94
Pomerantz, Edward DrAPF 93
Pomerantz, Ernest Harold 1941-
  WhoAm 94
Pomerantz, James Robert 1946-
  WhoAm 94, WhoScEn 94
Pomerantz, Jeff WhoHol 92
Pomerantz, Jerald Michael 1954-
  WhoAmL 94
Pomerantz, John J. 1933- WhoAm 94,
  WhoFI 94
Pomerantz, Laura 1948- WhoFI 94
Pomerantz, Mark F. 1951- WhoAmL 94
Pomerantz, Martin 1939- WhoAm 94
Pomerantz, Marvin Alvin 1930-
  WhoAm 94, WhoAmP 93, WhoFI 94
Pomeranz, Felix 1926- WhoAm 94,
  WhoFI 94
Pomeranz, Jerome Raphael 1930-
  WhoMW 93
Pomeranz, Yeshajahu 1922- WhoAm 94,
  WhoWest 94
Pomerene, James Herbert 1920-
  WhoAm 94
Pomerico, Thomas Michael 1954-
  WhoFI 94
Pomerleau, Luc 1955- EncSF 93
Pomeroy Who 94
Pomeroy, Benjamin Sherwood 1911-
  WhoAmP 93
Pomeroy, Bruce Marcel 1959-
  WhoMW 93
Pomeroy, David James 1951- WhoMW 93
Pomeroy, Duane Franklin 1952-
  WhoAmP 93
Pomeroy, Earl 1952- WhoAmP 93
Pomeroy, Earl R. 1952- WhoAm 94,
  WhoMW 93
Pomeroy, Earl Ralph 1952- CngDr 93
Pomeroy, Elwaine Franklin 1933-
  WhoAmP 93
Pomeroy, Frederick George 1924-
  WhoAmA 93
Pomeroy, Harlan 1923- WhoAm 94,
  WhoAmL 94
Pomeroy, Horace B. 1937- WhoAmP 93
Pomeroy, Horace Burton, III 1937-
  WhoWest 94
Pomeroy, James Caldwell 1945-1992
  WhoAmA 93N

Pomeroy, John Seltzer 1929- WhoWest 94
Pomeroy, Kent Lytle 1935- WhoScEn 94,
  WhoWest 94
Pomeroy, Lee Harris 1932- WhoAm 94
Pomeroy, Lyndon Fayne 1925-
  WhoAmA 93
Pomeroy, Mary Barnas 1921- WhoAmA 93
Pomeroy, Pete ConAu 140, SmATA 75
Pomeroy, Robert Corttis 1943-
  WhoAm 94
Pomeroy, Robert Lee 1938- WhoFI 94
Pomeroy, Robert M., Jr. 1951-
  WhoAmL 94
Pomeroy, Seth 1706-1776 AmRev
Pomeroy, Seth 1706-1777 WhAmRev
Pomeroy, Thomas Wilson, Jr. 1908-
  WhoAm 94
Pomeroy, Wyman Burdette 1932-
  WhoFI 94
Pomfret, John 1667-1702 BlmGEL
Pomfret, Richard 1948- ConAu 42NR
Pomicino, Paolo Cirino 1939- IntWW 93
Pomilio, Anthony Kenneth 1920-
  WhoAmL 94
Pommer, Erich 1889-1966 IntDcF 2-4
Pommer, Richard 1930-1992
  WhoAmA 93N
Pommerening, Grace M. 1956-
  WhoMW 93
Pommerville, Robert W. WhoFI 94
Pommier, Jean Bernard IntWW 93
Pomo, Roberto Dario 1949- WhoHisp 94
Pomodoro, Arnaldo 1926- IntWW 93
Pomorski, Stanislaw 1934- WhoAm 94
Pompa, James Robert 1937- WhoAm 94
Pompa, Jerry Paul 1956- WhoHisp 94
Pompadour, Madame de 1721-1764
  NewGrDO
Pompadur, I. Martin 1935- WhoAm 94
Pompan, Jack Maurice 1926- WhoFI 94
Pompea, Stephen M. 1953- WhoWest 94
Pompei, Giovanni fl. 1865-1880
  NewGrDO
Pompeia, Nuria 1938- BlmGWL
Pomper, Gerald M(arvin) 1935-
  ConAu 41NR
Pomper, Philip 1936- WhoAm 94
Pompey 106BC-48BC BlmGEL,
  HisWorL [port]
Pompey, Charles Spencer 1915-
  WhoBlA 94
Pompey, Sherman Lee 1930- WhoWest 94
Pomphrey, Michael Kevin 1947-
  WhoWest 94
Pomraning, Gerald Carlton 1936-
  WhoAm 94, WhoWest 94
Pomus, Doc 1925-1991 WhAm 10
Pon, Chew, Mrs. d1959 WhoHol 92
Pona, Charles Gerard 1960- WhoAmL 94
Ponazecki, Joe WhoHol 92
Pon-Brown, Kay Migyoku 1956-
  WhoScEn 94
Ponce, Carlos 1948- WhoHisp 94
Ponce, Christopher B. WhoHisp 94
Ponce, Frank Kalani 1955- WhoHisp 94
Ponce, Gabriel 1939- WhoHisp 94
Ponce, Gregorio A. 1963- WhoHisp 94
Ponce, Manuel León 1945- WhoHisp 94
Ponce, Merrihelen 1938- WhoHisp 94
Ponce, Tony 1925- WhoHisp 94
Ponce de León, Alicia WhoHisp 94
Ponce de Leon, Jose Maria 1846-1882
  NewGrDO
Ponce De Leon, Juan 1460-1521
  WhWE [port]
Ponce de Leon, Michael 1922- WhoAm 94,
  WhoAmA 93
Ponce de Leon, Pedro d1584 EncDeaf
Ponce Enrile, Juan 1924- IntWW 93
Poncelet, Christian 1928- IntWW 93
Poncelet, Jean Victor 1788-1867 WorScD
Poncet, Jean Andre F. Who 94
Ponchard, Louis(-Antoine-Eleonore)
  1787-1866 NewGrDO
Ponchard, Marie-Sophie 1792-1873
  NewGrDO
Ponchielli, Amilcare 1834-1886
  NewGrDO
Poncin, Marcel d1953 WhoHol 92
Poncy, Charles N. 1922- WhoAmP 93
Pond, Byron O. 1936- WhoFI 94
Pond, Carole Who 94
Pond, Clayton 1941- WhoAmA 93
Pond, Dana 1881-1962 WhoAmA 93N
Pond, Daniel James 1949- WhoAm 94,
  WhoWest 94
Pond, Donald H., Jr. 1943- WhoIns 94
Pond, Gideon EncNAR
Pond, Grace (Isabelle) 1910- WrDr 94
Pond, Jesse E., Jr. 1917- WhoAm 94
Pond, Joan DrAPF 93
Pond, Martin Allen 1912- WhoAm 94
Pond, Patricia Brown 1930- WhoAm 94
Pond, Peter 1740-1807 WhWE
Pond, Phyllis J. 1930- WhoAmP 93
Pond, Phyllis Joan 1930- WhoMW 93
Pond, Samuel W. 1808-1891 EncNAR

Pond, Thomas Alexander 1924-
  WhoAm 94
Pond, Willi Baze 1896-1947
  WhoAmA 93N
Ponder, Bruce Anthony John 1944-
  Who 94
Ponder, Eunice Wilson 1929- WhoBlA 94
Ponder, Henry 1928- WhoBlA 94
Ponder, Herman 1928- WhoAm 94
Ponder, Jack d1970 WhoHol 92
Ponder, Jacqueline Arrena 1946-
  WhoAmP 93
Ponder, Lester McConnico 1912-
  WhoAm 94, WhoAmL 94
Ponder, Marian Ruth 1932- WhoMW 93
Ponder, Patricia 1942- WrDr 94
Ponder, Randall Scott 1959- WhoWest 94
Ponder, Thomas C. 1921- WhoAm 94
Ponder, Zeno Herbert 1920- WhoAmP 93
Pondrom, Lee Girard 1933- WhoAm 94
Poneman, Daniel 1956- WrDr 94
Ponet, John 1516?-1556 DcLB 132
Pong, Schwe Fang 1936- WhoAsA 94
Pong, Ting-Chuen 1957- WhoAsA 94
Pongpanit, Montree 1943- IntWW 93
Pongratz, Alfred d1977 WhoHol 92
Pongsiri, Nutavoot 1961- WhoScEn 94
Poniatowska (Armor), Elena 1933-
  ConWorW 93
Poniatowska, Elena 1933- BlmGWL,
  HispLC [port]
Poniatowski, Jozef (Michal Ksawery
  Franciszek Jan) 1816-1873 NewGrDO
Poniatowski, Michel Casimir 1922-
  IntWW 93
Ponicini Zilioli, Francesco 1704-1782
  NewGrDO
Ponicsan, Darryl DrAPF 93
Poniman, S. 1926- IntWW 93
Ponitz, David H. 1931- WhoAm 94,
  WhoMW 93
Ponitz, John Allan 1949- WhoAm 94,
  WhoAmL 94
Ponka, Lawrence John 1949- WhoFI 94,
  WhoMW 93
Ponnamperuma, Cyril Andrew 1923-
  IntWW 93, WhoAm 94, WhoScEn 94,
  WorScD
Ponne, Nanci Teresa 1958- WhoFI 94
Ponnelle, Jean-Pierre 1932-1988
  NewGrDO
Ponomarev, Vladimir 1892-1951 IntDcB
Ponomariov, Nikolai Alexandrovich
  1918- IntWW 93
Ponoroff, Lawrence 1953- WhoAmL 94
Ponosov, Arcady Vladimirovitch 1957-
  WhoScEn 94
Pons, Joseph F. 1944- WhoMW 93
Pons, Lily d1976 WhoHol 92
Pons, Lily (Alice Josephine) 1898-1976
  NewGrDO
Pons, Victor Manuel, Jr. 1935-
  WhoAmP 93
Pon-Salazar, Francisco Demetrio 1951-
  WhoMW 93
Ponselle, Rosa (Melba) 1897-1981
  NewGrDO [port]
Ponseti, Ignacio Vives 1914- WhoAm 94
Ponsonby Who 94
Ponsonby, Ashley (Charles Gibbs) 1921-
  Who 94
Ponsonby, D(oris) A(lmon) 1907-
  WrDr 94
Ponsonby, Laura 1935- ConAu 140
Ponsonby, Myles Walter 1924- Who 94
Ponsonby, Robert Noel 1926- Who 94
Ponsonby, Sarah BlmGWL
Ponsonby of Shulbrede, Baron 1958-
  Who 94
Ponsor, Michael A. 1946- WhoAm 94,
  WhoAmL 94
Ponsot, Claude F. 1927- WhoAmA 93
Ponsot, Marie DrAPF 93
Pont. 1908-1940 DcNaB MP
Pont, John 1927- WhoAm 94
Pontarelli, John Michael 1950-
  WhoMW 93
Pontarelli, Thomas 1949- WhoIns 94
Pontarolo, Michael Joseph 1947-
  WhoAmL 94, WhoMW 93
Ponte, Charles Dennis 1953- WhoScEn 94
Ponte, Lowell Alton 1946- WhoHisp 94
Ponte, Manuel Louis 1931- WhoMW 93
Pontecorvo, Bruno d1993
  NewYTBS 93 [port]
Pontecorvo, Bruno Maksimovich 1913-
  IntWW 93
Pontecorvo, Gillo 1919- IntMPA 94,
  IntWW 93
Pontecorvo, Giulio 1923- WhoFI 94
Pontecorvo, Guido 1907- IntWW 93,
  Who 94
Pontefract, Archdeacon of Who 94
Pontefract, Bishop Suffragan of 1932-
  Who 94
Ponterio, Frank Julian 1961- WhoWest 94
Pontes, Henry A. WhoHisp 94
Ponti, Carlo 1910- IntDcF 2-4 [port]

Ponti, Carlo 1913- *IntMPA 94, IntWW 93*
Ponti, Carlo, Signora *Who 94*
Ponti, Michael 1937- *IntWW 93*
Pontiac c. 1720-1769 *HisWorL [port]*
Ponti-Aldo, Yusuf Benavil 1927- *WhoHisp 94*
Pontifex, David More 1922- *Who 94*
Pontikes, Kenneth Nicholas 1940- *WhoAm 94, WhoFI 94*
Pontin, Frederick William 1906- *Who 94*
Pontin, John Graham 1937- *Who 94*
Pontiroli, Antonio Ettore 1947- *WhoScEn 94*
Pontissara, John of c. 1240-1304 *DcNaB MP*
Pontius, John Samuels 1945- *WhoAmP 93*
Pontius, Madge Alma 1915- *WhoMW 93*
Ponto, Erich d1957 *WhoHol 92*
Pontois, Noella 1943- *IntDcB [port]*
Pontoise, John of c. 1240-1304 *DcNaB MP*
Ponton, Richard Edward 1937- *WhoAm 94*
Pontone, Kathleen 1950- *WhoAmL 94*
Pontrelli, Bernice d1993 *NewYTBS 93*
Pontremoli, David *WhoHol 92*
Ponty, Jean-Luc 1942- *WhoAm 94*
Pontynen, Arthur 1950- *WhoAmA 93*
Ponvert, Renny 1959- *WhoFI 94*
Ponziglione, Paul M. 1818-1900 *EncNAR*
Ponzini, Antony 1936- *WhoHol 92*
Ponzio, Peter Joseph 1954- *WhoMW 93*
Ponzo, Giuseppe fl. 1759-1791 *NewGrDO*
Ponzoni, Cochi *WhoHol 92*
Pool, Dan L. *WhoAmP 93*
Pool, Douglas Vernon 1945- *WhoAm 94*
Pool, Henry S. 1942- *WhoAmL 94*
Pool, Jeannie Gayle 1951- *WhoWest 94*
Pool, JoAnne 1952- *WhoAmL 94*
Pool, John Thomas 1943- *WhoWest 94*
Pool, Mary Jane *WhoAm 94, WhoFI 94*
Pool, Patricia Stewart 1946- *WhoAm 94*
Pool, Philip Bemis, Jr. 1954- *WhoAm 94*
Pool, Roger B. 1944- *WhoAmL 94*
Pool, Timothy Kevin 1954- *WhoFI 94*
Pool, Vera C. 1946- *WhoBlA 94*
Poole, Baron d1993 *Who 94N*
Poole, Baron 1911- *IntWW 93*
Poole, Baron 1945- *Who 94*
Poole, Abram 1882-1961 *WhoAmA 93N*
Poole, Anne *Who 94*
Poole, (Avril) Anne (Barker) 1934- *Who 94*
Poole, Anthony Cecil James 1927- *Who 94*
Poole, Barbara Ann 1935- *WhoWest 94*
Poole, Barbara Mills 1958- *WhoFI 94*
Poole, Cecil F. *WhoAm 94, WhoAmL 94, WhoAmP 93, WhoWest 94*
Poole, Cecil F. 1914- *WhoBlA 94*
Poole, D. Bruce 1959- *WhoAmP 93*
Poole, Darryl Vernon 1946- *WhoFI 94*
Poole, David Anthony 1938- *Who 94*
Poole, David Arthur Ramsay 1935- *Who 94*
Poole, David James 1931- *IntWW 93, Who 94*
Poole, Deborah Louise 1958- *WhoAmL 94*
Poole, Dillard M. 1939- *WhoBlA 94*
Poole, Donald C. 1942- *WhoAmL 94*
Poole, Earl Lincoln 1891-1972 *WhoAmA 93N*
Poole, Elizabeth fl. 1648- *BlmGWL*
Poole, Elizabeth 1820-1906 *NewGrDO*
Poole, Fiona Farrell 1947- *BlmGWL*
Poole, Frank S. 1913- *IntMPA 94*
Poole, Gordon Leicester 1926- *WhoAm 94*
Poole, Harry Wendell 1953- *WhoWest 94*
Poole, Henry Joe, Jr. 1957- *WhoWest 94*
Poole, Isobel Anne 1941- *Who 94*
Poole, James F. 1936- *WhoBlA 94*
Poole, John Bayard 1912-1989 *WhAm 10*
Poole, John Jordan 1906- *WhoAm 94*
Poole, Josephine 1933- *WrDr 94*
Poole, Leslie Donald 1942- *WhoAmA 93*
Poole, Marion L. 1921- *WhoBlA 94*
Poole, Marion Ronald 1936- *WhoScEn 94*
Poole, Nancy Geddes 1930- *WhoAm 94, WhoAmA 93*
Poole, Patricia Mary 1965- *WhoMW 93*
Poole, Phil 1959- *WhoAmP 93*
Poole, Rachel Irene 1924- *WhoBlA 94*
Poole, Richard 1945- *WrDr 94*
Poole, Richard John 1929- *Who 94*
Poole, Richard William 1927- *WhoAm 94, WhoFI 94, WhoScEn 94*
Poole, Robert Anthony 1944- *WhoWest 94*
Poole, Robert S. *DrAPF 93*
Poole, Roy d1986 *WhoHol 92*
Poole, Van B. 1935- *WhoAmP 93*
Poole, William 1937- *WhoAm 94*
Poole, William Daniel 1932- *WhoFI 94*
Poole, William M. 1944- *WhoAmL 94*
Pool-Eckert, Marquita Jones 1945- *WhoBlA 94*
Poole-Heard, Blanche Denise 1951- *WhoBlA 94*
Pooler, Catherine Mary 1954- *WhoAmL 94*
Poole-Wilson, Philip Alexander 1943- *Who 94*
Pooley, Beverley John 1934- *WhoAm 94*
Pooley, Derek 1937- *Who 94*
Pooley, Frederick Bernard 1916- *Who 94*
Pooley, James Henry Anderson 1948- *WhoAm 94, WhoAmL 94*
Pooley, Olaf *WhoHol 92*
Pooley, Peter 1936- *Who 94*
Pooley, Robert C(ecil) 1899- *WhAm 10*
Pooley, Robin 1936- *Who 94*
Poolman, Jim 1970- *WhoAmP 93*
Poolos, Pete Nick, Jr. 1933- *WhoMW 93*
Poon, Chi-Sang 1952- *WhoAsA 94, WhoScEn 94*
Poon, William Wai-Lik 1965- *WhoScEn 94*
Poon, Yi-Chong Sarina Chow 1944- *WhoAmA 93*
Poonawala, Ismail Kurbanhusein 1937- *WhoWest 94*
Pooni, Amardeep Singh 1963?-1993 *WhoAsA 94N*
Poonja, Mohamed 1948- *WhoFI 94, WhoWest 94*
Poons, Larry 1937- *WhoAm 94, WhoAmA 93*
Poons, Sylvain d1985 *WhoHol 92*
Poor, Anne 1918- *WhoAm 94, WhoAmA 93*
Poor, Clarence Alexander 1911- *WhoWest 94*
Poor, Enoch 1736-1780 *AmRev, WhAmRev*
Poor, Harold Vincent 1951- *WhoAm 94*
Poor, Henry Varnum 1888-1970 *WhoAmA 93N*
Poor, James T. 1932- *WhoIns 94*
Poor, Janet Meakin 1929- *WhoAm 94, WhoMW 93*
Poor, Peter Varnum 1926- *WhoAm 94*
Poor, Robert John 1931- *WhoAmA 93*
Poor, Salem c. 1747- *WhAmRev*
Poor Coyote dc. 1920 *EncNAR*
Poore, Duncan *Who 94*
Poore, (Martin Edward) Duncan 1925- *Who 94*
Poore, Herbert Edward 1930- *Who 94*
Poore, James Albert, III 1943- *WhoAmL 94*
Poor Man, Mercy c. 1922- *EncNAR*
Poorman, Omer Wayne 1949- *WhoFI 94*
Poorman, Paul Arthur 1930- *WhoAm 94*
Poorman, Robert Lewis 1926- *WhoAm 94*
Poortvliet, William G. 1931- *WhoIns 94*
Poos, George Ireland 1923- *WhoAm 94*
Poos, Jacques F. 1935- *IntWW 93*
Poos, L. R. 1954- *ConAu 141*
Poot, Anton 1929- *Who 94*
Poot, Marcel 1901-1988 *NewGrDO*
Poovey, Kenneth M. 1932- *WhoAmL 94*
Poovey, William Arthur 1913- *WrDr 94*
Pop, Emil 1939- *WhoScEn 94*
Pop, Iggy 1946- *WhoHol 92*
Pop, Iggy 1947- *WhoAm 94*
Pop, Julia *WhoHol 92*
Pop, Valeriu Eugen *IntWW 93*
Popa, Christina Marie 1963- *WhoMW 93*
Popa, Petru 1938- *WhoScEn 94*
Popa, Pretor 1922- *Who 94*
Popadiuk, Roman 1950- *WhoAm 94, WhoAmP 93*
Popcorn, Faith 1947?- *CurBio 93 [port]*
Pope d1690 *EncNAR*
Pope, His Holiness the *Who 94*
Pope, Abbie Hanscom 1858-1894 *DcLB 140*
Pope, Addison W. 1926- *WhoBlA 94*
Pope, Alexander 1688-1744 *BlmGEL [port]*
Pope, Alexander H. 1929- *WhoAm 94*
Pope, Andrew Jackson, Jr. 1913- *WhoAm 94, WhoAmL 94*
Pope, Andrew Lancelot d1993 *Who 94N*
Pope, Annie 1949- *WhoMW 93*
Pope, Bill Jordan 1922- *WhoAm 94*
Pope, C. H., Jr. 1946- *WhoAmL 94*
Pope, Carey Nat 1952- *WhoScEn 94*
Pope, Cathryn Mary 1957- *Who 94*
Pope, Christie Farnham 1937- *WhoMW 93*
Pope, Daniel James 1948- *WhoAm 94, WhoAmL 94*
Pope, David Bruce 1945- *WhoAmL 94*
Pope, David E. 1920- *WhoAm 94*
Pope, Deborah *DrAPF 93, WrDr 94*
Pope, Donna 1931- *WhoAmP 93*
Pope, Douglas Vanstone 1945- *WhoFI 94*
Pope, Dudley (Bernard Egerton) 1925- *WrDr 94*
Pope, Dudley Bernard Egerton 1925- *Who 94*
Pope, Durand L. 1946- *WhoMW 93*
Pope, Edward John Andrew 1962- *WhoFI 94, WhoWest 94*
Pope, Ernle *Who 94*
Pope, (John) Ernle 1921- *Who 94*
Pope, Fred Wallace, Jr. 1941- *WhoAmL 94*
Pope, Geoffrey George 1934- *Who 94*
Pope, George L., Jr. 1941- *WhoAmL 94*
Pope, Gregory James 1960- *Who 94*
Pope, Gustavus W. *EncSF 93*
Pope, Harrison Graham, Jr. 1947- *WhoAm 94, WhoScEn 94*
Pope, Henry 1922- *WhoBlA 94*
Pope, Howard E. *WhoIns 94*
Pope, Isaac S. 1939- *WhoBlA 94*
Pope, Jacqueline S. 1931- *WhoAmP 93*
Pope, James Arthur 1956- *WhoAmP 93*
Pope, James M. 1927- *WhoBlA 94*
Pope, Jeremy James Richard 1943- *Who 94*
Pope, Jerome W. 1951- *WhoAm 94, WhoAmL 94*
Pope, John Alexander 1906-1982 *WhoAmA 93N*
Pope, John B. 1822-1892 *WhWE*
Pope, John Charles 1949- *WhoAm 94, WhoFI 94*
Pope, John Clifford 1911- *Who 94*
Pope, John Edwin, III 1928- *WhoAm 94*
Pope, John William 1947- *WhoAmL 94, WhoWest 94*
Pope, Joseph (Albert) 1914- *Who 94*
Pope, Joseph N. *WhoBlA 94*
Pope, Kerig Rodgers 1935- *WhoAm 94*
Pope, Laurence E., II *WhoAm 94, WhoAmP 93*
Pope, Lawrence S. 1945- *WhoMW 93*
Pope, Leavitt Joseph 1924- *WhoAm 94*
Pope, Lena Elizabeth 1935- *WhoMW 93*
Pope, Marion Holden d1958 *WhoAmA 93N*
Pope, Mark Andrew 1952- *WhoAmL 94*
Pope, Martha S. *CngDr 93*
Pope, Marvin Hoyle 1916- *WhoAm 94*
Pope, Mary Ann Irwin 1932- *WhoAmA 93*
Pope, Mary Maude 1916- *WhoBlA 94*
Pope, Max Lyndell 1932- *WhoWest 94*
Pope, Michael 1924- *WhoAm 94*
Pope, Michael Arthur 1944- *WhoAmL 94*
Pope, Michael Donald K. *Who 94*
Pope, Michael Keith 1958- *WhoMW 93*
Pope, Mirian Artis 1952- *WhoBlA 94*
Pope, Peggy *WhoHol 92*
Pope, Peter T. 1934- *WhoAm 94, WhoWest 94*
Pope, Richard M. 1946- *WhoScEn 94*
Pope, Richard W. 1933- *WhoIns 94*
Pope, Robert Dean 1945- *WhoAm 94, WhoAmL 94*
Pope, Robert Glynn 1935- *WhoAm 94, WhoFI 94*
Pope, Robert William 1916- *Who 94*
Pope, Ruben Edward, III 1948- *WhoBlA 94*
Pope, Shawn Hideyoshi 1962- *WhoAmL 94*
Pope, Stephen Bailey 1949- *WhoAm 94*
Pope, Steven Francois 1948- *WhoAm 94*
Pope, Susan Lyon *DrAPF 93*
Pope, Theodore Campbell, Jr. 1932- *WhoFI 94*
Pope, Thomas H., III 1946- *WhoAmP 93*
Pope, Thomas Harrington, Jr. 1913- *WhoAm 94*
Pope, Tim 1957- *WhoAmP 93*
Pope, Virginia 1885-1978 *NewYTBS 93 [port]*
Pope, Wendell LaVon 1928- *WhoWest 94*
Pope, William David, III 1952- *WhoScEn 94*
Pope, William L. 1960- *WhoAmL 94*
Pope-Hennessy, John (Wyndham) 1913- *Who 94, WrDr 94*
Pope-Hennessy, John Wyndham 1913- *IntWW 93, WhoAm 94*
Popeil, Ron 1936- *WhoAm 94*
Popejoy, William J. 1938- *WhoAm 94, WhoFI 94, WhoWest 94*
Popek, Edwina Jane 1952- *WhoScEn 94*
Popek, John George 1945- *WhoFI 94*
Popel, Aleksander S. 1945- *WhoAm 94*
Popenoe, John 1929- *WhoAm 94*
Poperen, Jean Maurice 1925- *IntWW 93*
Popescu, Cara d1991 *WhoAmA 93N*
Popescu, Dan Mircea 1950- *IntWW 93*
Popescu, Dumitru Radu 1935- *IntWW 93*
Popescu, Ioan-Iovitz 1932- *IntWW 93*
Popescu-Gopo, Ion 1923-1990 *IntDcF 2-4*
Popham, Arthur Cobb, Jr. 1915- *WhoAm 94*
Popham, Christopher John 1927- *Who 94*
Popham, George c. 1550-1608 *WhWE*
Popham, Hugh 1920- *WrDr 94*
Popham, Lewis Charles, III 1928- *WhoAm 94*
Popham, Melinda *DrAPF 93*
Popham, Mervyn Reddaway 1927- *Who 94*
Popham, Wayne Gordon 1929- *WhoAm 94*
Popiela, Stanislawa *WhoWomW 91*
Popik, Charles Thomas 1935- *WhoFI 94*
Popinsky, Arnold Dave 1930- *WhoAmA 93*
Popjak, George Joseph 1914- *Who 94, WhoAm 94*
Popkave, Murray Warren 1941- *WhoAmL 94*
Popkes, Steven 1952- *EncSF 93*
Popkin, Carol Lederhaus 1944- *WhoScEn 94*
Popkin, Elsie Dinsmore 1937- *WhoAmA 93*
Popkin, Joel 1932- *WhoFI 94*
Popkin, Roy Sandor 1921- *WhoAm 94*
Poplar, Carl D. 1943- *WhoAmL 94*
Pople, John Anthony 1925- *IntWW 93, Who 94, WhoAm 94, WhoScEn 94*
Poploff, Michelle 1956- *WrDr 94*
Popoff, Frank Peter 1935- *IntWW 93, WhoAm 94, WhoFI 94, WhoMW 93*
Popofsky, Melvin Laurence 1936- *WhoAm 94*
PoPolizio, Vincent 1940- *WhoMW 93*
Popov, Aleksandr Stepanovich 1859-1906 *WorInv*
Popov, Alexander 1954- *EncSF 93*
Popov, Andrei d1983 *WhoHol 92*
Popov, Dmitar *IntWW 93*
Popov, Egor Paul 1913- *WhoAm 94, WhoScEn 94*
Popov, Elizabeth M. 1915- *WhoAmP 93*
Popov, Fyodot Alekseyev fl. 164-?- *WhWE*
Popov, Gavriil Kharitonovich 1936- *IntWW 93, LngBDD*
Popov, Oleg *WhoHol 92*
Popov, Oleg Konstantinovich 1930- *IntWW 93*
Popov, Viktor Ivanovich 1918- *IntWW 93, Who 94*
Popov, Yevgeniy Pavlovich 1914- *IntWW 93*
Popova, Nina 1922- *WhoAm 94*
Popovac, Gwynn 1948- *WhoAmA 93, WhoWest 94*
Popovic, Koca 1908-1992 *CurBio 93N*
Popovic, Nenad D. 1909- *WrDr 94*
Popovic, Tatyana (Vladana) 1928- *WrDr 94*
Popovich, Helen Houser 1935- *WhoAm 94*
Popovich, Peter S. 1920- *WhoAmP 93*
Popovich, Peter Stephen 1920- *WhoAm 94, WhoAmL 94, WhoMW 93*
Popovich, Robert P. 1939- *WhoScEn 94*
Popovici, Adrian 1942- *WhoAm 94*
Popovici, Doru 1932- *NewGrDO*
Popovici, Galina 1940- *WhoScEn 94*
Popovici-Bayreuth, Dimitrie 1860-1927 *NewGrDO*
Popovsky, Mark 1922- *ConAu 41NR*
Popp, Adelheid 1869-1939 *BlmGWL*
Popp, Carl J. 1941- *WhoScEn 94*
Popp, Charlotte Louise 1946- *WhoFI 94*
Popp, Dale D. 1923- *WhoScEn 94*
Popp, James Alan 1945- *WhoAm 94*
Popp, Lucia 1939- *IntWW 93, NewGrDO*
Popp, Lucia 1939-1993 *NewYTBS 93 [port]*
Popp, Nathaniel 1940- *WhoMW 93*
Popp, Nathaniel William George 1940- *WhoAm 94*
Poppa, Ryal Robert 1933- *WhoAm 94, WhoFI 94, WhoWest 94*
Poppe, Frances Winnie Perez 1942- *WhoFI 94*
Poppe, Fred Christoph 1923- *WhoAm 94*
Poppe, Gerald Wayne 1952- *WhoFI 94*
Poppe, Howard A. 1931- *WhoAmL 94*
Poppe, Wassily 1918- *WhoAm 94*
Poppel, Harvey Lee 1937- *WhoAm 94*
Poppel, Seth Raphael 1944- *WhoAm 94, WhoFI 94*
Poppen, Andrew Gerard 1965- *WhoScEn 94*
Poppen, Henry Alvin 1922- *WhoAmP 93*
Poppenhagen, Dennis Joseph 1938- *WhoAmP 93*
Poppenhagen, Ronald William 1948- *WhoMW 93*
Poppensiek, George Charles 1918- *WhoAm 94*
Popper, Arthur N. 1943- *WhoAm 94*
Popper, Charles William 1946- *WhoScEn 94*
Popper, Edward Thomas 1944- *WhoMW 93*
Popper, Frank James 1944- *WrDr 94*
Popper, Howard Robert 1930- *WhoAmL 94*
Popper, Karl (Raimund) 1902- *IntWW 93, Who 94, WrDr 94*
Popper, Karl Raimund 1902- *WhoScEn 94*
Popper, Robert 1932- *WhoAm 94*
Popper, Robert David 1927- *WhoAm 94*
Popper, Walter Lincoln 1920- *WhoFI 94*
Poppers, Paul Jules 1929- *WhoAm 94, WhoScEn 94*
Poppick, David Seth 1954- *WhoAmL 94*
Poppino, Allen Gerald 1925- *WhoFI 94*

Poppino, Kathryn *DrAPF 93*
Poppino, Rollie E(dward) 1922- *WrDr 94*
Poppitz, James 1957- *WhoAmA 93*
Poppler, Doris Swords 1924- *WhoAm 94, WhoAmL 94*
Poppler, Larry Stanley 1954- *WhoFI 94*
Popplestone, Robin John 1938- *WhoScEn 94*
Popplewell, Catharine Margaret 1929- *Who 94*
Popplewell, Oliver (Bury) 1927- *Who 94*
Poppoff, Ilia George 1924- *WhoWest 94*
Poprick, Mary Ann 1939- *WhoMW 93, WhoScEn 94*
Popstefanija, Ivan 1959- *WhoScEn 94*
Poptodurova-Petrova, Elena Borislavova *WhoWomW 91*
Poptsov, Oleg Maksimovich 1934- *LngBDD*
Popwell, Albert *WhoHol 92*
Popwell, Johnny *WhoHol 92*
Porad, Laurie Jo 1951- *WhoWest 94*
Porada, Edith 1912- *WhoAm 94, WhoAmA 93*
Poran, Chaim Jehuda 1952- *WhoScEn 94*
Poray, Stan P. 1888-1948 *WhoAmA 93N*
Porcaro, Jeff c. 1954-1992 *AnObit 1992*
Porcaro, Michael Francis 1948- *WhoFI 94, WhoWest 94*
Porcaro, Michael James 1950- *WhoAm 94*
Porcasi, Paul d1946 *WhoHol 92*
Porcelli, Fred *WhoHol 92*
Porcello, Leonard Joseph 1934- *WhoAm 94*
Porch, Douglas 1944- *WrDr 94*
Porch, Roger A. *WhoAmP 93*
Porche, Verandah *DrAPF 93*
Porche-Burke, Lisa 1954- *WhoBlA 94*
Porcher, Frank Bryan, II 1953- *WhoScEn 94*
Porcher, Michael Somerville 1921- *Who 94*
Porcher, Robert 1969- *WhoBlA 94*
Porchester, Lord 1956- *Who 94*
Porcile, Giuseppe *NewGrDO*
Porco, Carmen 1947- *WhoAmP 93*
Porcupine c. 1847-1929 *EncNAR*
Porcupine Standing Sideways c. 1771-1891 *EncNAR*
Pordenone, Odoric Of c. 1265-1331 *WhWE*
Pordenone, Ordoric Of *WhWE*
Pordon, William Philip 1925- *WhoWest 94*
Pordum, Francis J. *WhoAmP 93*
Pordy, David Andrew 1950- *WhoAmL 94*
Pordy, Leon 1919- *WhoAm 94*
Porel, Jacqueline *WhoHol 92*
Porel, Marc d1983 *WhoHol 92*
Porell, Richard D. 1933- *WhoIns 94*
Porete, Marguerite d1310 *BlmGWL*
Poretsky, Joel A. 1946- *WhoAm 94, WhoAmL 94*
Porfirii, Pietro fl. 1687- *NewGrDO*
Porges, Arthur 1915- *EncSF 93*
Porges, Heinrich 1837-1900 *NewGrDO*
Porges, Michael *DrAPF 93*
Porges, Walter Rudolf 1931- *WhoAm 94*
Pories, Walter Julius 1930- *WhoAm 94*
Porile, Norbert Thomas 1932- *WhoAm 94, WhoMW 93*
Porizkova, Paulina 1965- *WhoAm 94, WhoHol 92*
Porkert, Manfred Bruno 1933- *WhoScEn 94*
Porkolab, Miklos 1939- *WhoScEn 94*
Porn, (Gustav) Ingmar 1935- *WrDr 94*
Porosky, Michael 1930- *WhoWest 94*
Porosoff, Harold 1946- *WhoAm 94*
Porovskyi, Mykola Ivanovych 1956- *LngBDD*
Porphyrios, Demetri *IntWW 93*
Porpora, Nicola (Antonio) 1686-1768 *NewGrDO*
Porras, Jorge Enrique 1942- *WhoHisp 94*
Porras-Field, Esperanza 1954- *WhoHisp 94*
Porrata, Manuel Francisco, Jr. 1965- *WhoHisp 94*
Porreca, Vincent Joe 1941- *WhoAmP 93*
Porrero, Henry, Jr. 1945- *WhoWest 94*
Porretta, Emanuele Peter 1942- *WhoAm 94*
Porretta, Louis Paul 1926- *WhoMW 93*
Porrino, Ennio 1910-1959 *NewGrDO*
Porrino, Peter R. 1956- *WhoIns 94*
Porritt, Baron 1900- *Who 94*
Porritt, Arthur 1900- *IntWW 93*
Porritt, Jonathon (Espie) 1950- *IntWW 93, Who 94*
Porro, Michael John 1951- *WhoFI 94*
Porsile, Giuseppe 1680-1750 *NewGrDO*
Porsman, Frank O. 1905- *WhoAmA 93N*
Port, Sidney Charles 1935- *WhoAm 94*
Porta, Bernardo 1758-1829 *NewGrDO*
Porta, Giovanni c. 1675-1755 *NewGrDO*
Porta, Nunziato fl. 1770- *NewGrDO*
Porta, Sicna Gillann 1951- *WhoAmA 93*
Portal, Ellis *EncSF 93*
Portal, Ellis 1925- *WrDr 94*
Portal, Gilbert Marcel Adrien 1930- *WhoAm 94*
Portal, Jean-Claude 1941- *WhoScEn 94*
Portal, Jonathan (Francis) 1953- *Who 94*
Portal, Louise *WhoHol 92*
Portal, Marta 1930- *BlmGWL*
Portalatin, Maria 1937- *WhoHisp 94*
Portales, Diego 1793-1837 *HisWorL [port]*
Portales, Marco A. *WhoHisp 94*
Portales, Ramon, Sr. 1929- *WhoHisp 94*
Portanova, Joseph Domenico 1909-1979 *WhoAmA 93N*
Portarlington, Earl of 1938- *Who 94*
Portaro, Sam Anthony, Jr. 1948- *WhoMW 93*
Porte, Barbara Ann *DrAPF 93*
Porte, Daniel, Jr. 1931- *WhoScEn 94*
Porte, Joel Miles 1933- *WhoAm 94*
Portee, Frank, III 1955- *WhoBlA 94*
Portela, Antonio Gouvea 1918- *WhoScEn 94*
Portela, Rafael 1947- *WhoHisp 94*
Port Elizabeth, Bishop of 1929- *Who 94*
Portelli, Vincent George 1932- *WhoAm 94, WhoFI 94*
Porten, Anthony Ralph 1947- *Who 94*
Porten, Bezalel 1931- *WrDr 94*
Porten, Henny d1960 *WhoHol 92*
Portenier, Walter James 1927- *WhoScEn 94*
Porteous, Christopher 1921- *Who 94*
Porteous, Christopher Selwyn 1935- *Who 94*
Porteous, James 1926- *Who 94*
Porteous, Norman Walker 1898- *Who 94*
Porteous, Patrick Anthony 1918- *Who 94*
Porteous, Timothy 1933- *WhoAm 94*
Porter *Who 94*
Porter, A. Duane 1936- *WhoWest 94*
Porter, A(nthony) P(eyton) 1945- *WrDr 94*
Porter, Alastair Robert Wilson 1928- *Who 94*
Porter, Albert S. 1930- *WhoBlA 94*
Porter, Albert Wright 1923- *WhoAmA 93, WhoWest 94*
Porter, Alisan 1981- *WhoHol 92*
Porter, Amy R. 1944- *WhoAm 94, WhoAmL 94*
Porter, Andrew 1743-1813 *WhAmRev*
Porter, Andrew 1928- *IntWW 93, NewGrDO, WrDr 94*
Porter, Andrew (Ian) 1946- *EncSF 93*
Porter, Andrew Brian 1928- *Who 94*
Porter, Anna *WrDr 94*
Porter, Arleen Helen Boyda 1938- *WhoMW 93*
Porter, Arthur 1910- *Who 94, WhoAm 94*
Porter, Arthur L. 1940- *WhoBlA 94*
Porter, Arthur Reno 1918- *WhoAm 94*
Porter, Arthur T. 1956- *WhoScEn 94*
Porter, Arthur Thomas 1924- *Who 94*
Porter, Barry *Who 94*
Porter, Bern *DrAPF 93*
Porter, Bern 1911- *WrDr 94*
Porter, Bernard (John) 1941- *WrDr 94*
Porter, Beth *WhoHol 92*
Porter, Bill 1932- *WhoAmP 93*
Porter, Blaine Robert Milton 1922- *WhoAm 94*
Porter, Blanche Troullier 1933- *WhoBlA 94*
Porter, Brian 1938- *WhoAmP 93*
Porter, Brian (Ernest) 1928- *WrDr 94*
Porter, Brian Stanley 1938- *WhoWest 94*
Porter, Bruce Douglas 1952- *WhoAm 94*
Porter, Bruce Jackman 1954- *WhoScEn 94*
Porter, Burt *DrAPF 93*
Porter, Burton F. 1936- *WrDr 94*
Porter, Burton Frederick 1936- *WhoAm 94*
Porter, Caleb d1940 *WhoHol 92*
Porter, Carol Denise 1948- *WhoBlA 94*
Porter, Carolyn (Jane) 1946- *WrDr 94*
Porter, Charles Allan 1932- *WhoAm 94*
Porter, Charles O. 1919- *WhoAmP 93*
Porter, Charles Raleigh, Jr. 1922- *WhoAmL 94*
Porter, Charles William 1939- *WhoBlA 94*
Porter, Clarence A. 1939- *WhoBlA 94*
Porter, Cloyd Allen 1935- *WhoAmP 93, WhoMW 93*
Porter, Cole 1891-1964 *ConMus 10 [port], IntDcF 2-4*
Porter, Cole (Albert) 1891-1964 *NewGrDO*
Porter, Cole Albert 1891-1964 *AmCulL*
Porter, Colin Andrew 1956- *WhoScEn 94*
Porter, Connie (Rose) 1959- *BlkWr 2, ConAu 142*
Porter, Curtiss E. 1939- *WhoBlA 94*
Porter, Dale Wayne 1963- *WhoScEn 94*
Porter, Daniel Reed, III 1930- *WhoAm 94*
Porter, Darwin Fred 1937- *WhoAm 94, WhoFI 94*
Porter, (Edwin) David 1912- *WhoAmA 93*
Porter, David Brownfield d1993 *Who 94N*
Porter, David Hugh 1935- *WhoAm 94*
Porter, David John 1948- *Who 94*
Porter, David Lindsey 1941- *WhoAm 94*
Porter, David Stewart 1909-1989 *WhAm 10*
Porter, David Taylor 1951- *WhoWest 94*
Porter, Dean Allen 1939- *WhoAm 94, WhoMW 93*
Porter, Dennis Carl 1955- *WhoMW 93*
Porter, Dennis Dudley 1933- *WhoAm 94*
Porter, Dixie Lee 1931- *WhoFI 94, WhoWest 94*
Porter, Don 1912- *IntMPA 94, WhoHol 92*
Porter, Donald 1939- *WrDr 94*
Porter, Donald James 1921- *WhoAm 94, WhoMW 93*
Porter, Donald Richard 1944- *WhoMW 93*
Porter, Dorothea Noelle Naomi 1927- *Who 94*
Porter, Dorothy B. 1905- *WhoBlA 94*
Porter, Dubose 1953- *WhoAmP 93*
Porter, Dudley, Jr. 1915- *WhoAm 94*
Porter, Dwight Johnson 1916- *WhoAm 94*
Porter, E. Melvin 1930- *WhoBlA 94*
Porter, Edward d1939 *WhoHol 92*
Porter, Edward Samuel 1935- *WhoFI 94*
Porter, Edwin S. d1941 *WhoHol 92*
Porter, Eliot (Furness) 1901-1990 *ConAu 42NR*
Porter, Eliot Furness 1901-1990 *EnvEnc, WhAm 10, WhoAmA 93N*
Porter, Elisabeth Scott 1942- *WhoAm 94*
Porter, Ellis Nathaniel 1931- *WhoBlA 94*
Porter, Elmer Johnson 1907- *WhoAmA 93*
Porter, Elsa Allgood 1928- *WhoAm 94*
Porter, Eric 1928- *WhoHol 92*
Porter, Eric (Richard) 1928- *Who 94*
Porter, Eric Richard 1928- *IntWW 93*
Porter, Ernest Reed 1926- *WhoFI 94*
Porter, Everette M. 1910- *WhoBlA 94*
Porter, Fairfield 1907-1975 *WhoAmA 93N*
Porter, Fia *WhoHol 92*
Porter, Gareth 1942- *WrDr 94*
Porter, Gary *WhoAmP 93*
Porter, Gene Lavon 1935- *WhoWest 94*
Porter, Gene T. 1956- *WhoAmP 93*
Porter, George 1920- *WhoAm 94, WhoScEn 94, WrDr 94*
Porter, George Barrington 1939- *Who 94*
Porter, Gerald Joseph 1937- *WhoAm 94*
Porter, Geraldine Ruth 1932- *WhoAmP 93*
Porter, Glenn 1944- *WhoAm 94*
Porter, Gloria Jean 1951- *WhoBlA 94*
Porter, Grady J. 1918- *WhoBlA 94*
Porter, Gregory W. *WhoAmP 93*
Porter, Hal 1911-1984 *ConDr 93, RfGShF*
Porter, Harry Randall 1952- *WhoAmP 93*
Porter, Harvey 1931- *WhoFI 94*
Porter, Helen Viney 1935- *WhoAm 94*
Porter, Henry Homes, Jr. *WhoAm 94*
Porter, Henry Lee 1948- *WhoBlA 94*
Porter, Herschel Donovan 1924- *WhoMW 93*
Porter, Howard Charles 1913- *WhoAmP 93*
Porter, Howard Newton d1993 *NewYTBS 93*
Porter, Irene Rae 1961- *WhoScEn 94*
Porter, Irwin W. 1912- *WhoFI 94*
Porter, Ivan 1947- *WhoAm 94, WhoFI 94*
Porter, Ivor Forsyth 1913- *Who 94*
Porter, J. Robert *WhoHol 92*
Porter, J. Winston 1937- *WhoAm 94*
Porter, Jack A. 1945- *WhoAmL 94*
Porter, Jack Nusan 1944- *WhoAm 94*
Porter, James A. 1905-1971 *AfrAmAl 6*
Porter, James Alexander 1942- *WhoAm 94*
Porter, James Forrest 1928- *Who 94*
Porter, James H. 1933- *WhoBlA 94*
Porter, James Kenneth 1934- *WhoAmL 94*
Porter, James Morris 1931- *WhoAm 94, WhoAmL 94*
Porter, James Neil 1931- *WhoWest 94*
Porter, Jean 1925- *WhoHol 92*
Porter, Jeanne Chenault 1944- *WhoAmA 93*
Porter, Jessica Gettemy 1956- *WhoAmL 94*
Porter, Joe Ashby *DrAPF 93*
Porter, John Alan 1934- *Who 94*
Porter, John Andrew 1916- *Who 94*
Porter, John Byron 1896- *WhAm 10*
Porter, John Edward 1935- *CngDr 93, WhoAm 94, WhoAmP 93, WhoMW 93*
Porter, John Finley, Jr. 1927- *WhoAm 94*
Porter, John Henry 1950- *WhoBlA 94*
Porter, John Hill 1933- *WhoFI 94*
Porter, John Louis 1959- *WhoScEn 94*
Porter, John Richard 1932- *WhoBlA 94*
Porter, John Robert, Jr. 1935- *WhoAm 94*
Porter, John Simon H. *Who 94*
Porter, John Stephen 1932- *WhoAm 94*
Porter, John T. 1941- *WhoBlA 94*
Porter, John W. 1931- *WhoBlA 94*
Porter, John Wilson 1931- *WhoAm 94, WhoMW 93*
Porter, Jonathan 1938- *WhoWest 94*
Porter, Joseph Charles 1946- *WhoMW 93*
Porter, Joshua Roy 1921- *WrDr 94*
Porter, Joyce Klowden 1949- *WhoMW 93*
Porter, Judith Deborah Revitch 1940- *WhoAm 94*
Porter, Karen Collins 1953- *WhoMW 93*
Porter, Karl Hampton 1939- *AfrAmAl 6, WhoAm 94, WhoBlA 94*
Porter, Katherine Anne 1890-1980 *AmCulL, BlmGWL, RfGShF*
Porter, Kenneth *Who 94*
Porter, (Melvin) Kenneth (Drowley) 1912- *Who 94*
Porter, Kevin 1950- *BasBi, WhoBlA 94*
Porter, Lana Garner 1943- *WhoFI 94*
Porter, Leslie 1920- *IntWW 93, Who 94*
Porter, Liliana 1941- *WhoAmA 93*
Porter, Liliana Alicia 1941- *WhoAm 94, WhoHisp 94*
Porter, Lillian *WhoHol 92*
Porter, Linsey 1954- *WhoBlA 94*
Porter, Lionel 1943- *WhoBlA 94*
Porter, Lulu *WhoHol 92*
Porter, Lynn Keith 1929- *WhoAm 94*
Porter, Maibeth J. 1956- *WhoAmL 94*
Porter, Marguerite Ann 1948- *Who 94*
Porter, Mary E. 1946- *WhoAmL 94*
Porter, Max L. 1942- *WhoScEn 94*
Porter, Mia Lachone 1965- *WhoBlA 94*
Porter, Michael Arthur 1949- *WhoFI 94*
Porter, Michael Blair 1958- *WhoScEn 94*
Porter, Michael Charles 1953- *WhoBlA 94, WhoFI 94, WhoMW 93*
Porter, Michael E(ugene) 1947- *WrDr 94*
Porter, Michael LeRoy 1947- *WhoBlA 94*
Porter, Michael Pell 1940- *WhoAmL 94, WhoWest 94*
Porter, Milton 1911- *WhoAm 94*
Porter, Murray Victor d1993 *Who 94N*
Porter, Nancy Carol 1961- *WhoMW 93*
Porter, Neil Anthony 1930- *IntWW 93*
Porter, Nicolas Christopher *WhoAm 94*
Porter, Nina *WrDr 94*
Porter, Nyree Dawn *WhoHol 92*
Porter, Otha L. 1928- *WhoBlA 94*
Porter, Patricia L. 1940- *WhoAmP 93*
Porter, Patrick A. 1944- *WhoBlA 94*
Porter, Paul d1957 *WhoHol 92*
Porter, Peter 1929- *BlmGEL [port]*
Porter, Peter (Neville Frederick) 1929- *WrDr 94*
Porter, Peter Neville Frederick 1929- *IntWW 93, Who 94*
Porter, Philip Thomas 1930- *WhoAm 94*
Porter, Philip Wayland 1928- *WhoAm 94*
Porter, Reed d1979 *WhoHol 92*
Porter, Richard Arlen 1930- *WhoAmP 93*
Porter, Richard Ernest 1933- *WhoWest 94*
Porter, Richard Howard 1942- *WhoAm 94, WhoAmL 94*
Porter, Richard James 1950- *WhoAmA 93*
Porter, Richard Sterling 1929- *WhoAm 94*
Porter, Richard Sylvester 1923- *WhoBlA 94*
Porter, Robert 1932- *IntWW 93, Who 94*
Porter, Robert (Wilson) 1923- *Who 94*
Porter, Robert Carl, Jr. 1927- *WhoAmL 94*
Porter, Robert George 1924- *Who 94*
Porter, Robert H. 1952- *WhoAmP 93*
Porter, Robert Philip 1942- *WhoScEn 94*
Porter, Robert Stanley 1924- *Who 94*
Porter, Robert William 1926-1991 *WhAm 10*
Porter, Robert William 1938- *WhoScEn 94*
Porter, Robin 1933- *WhoAmP 93*
Porter, Roger B. 1946- *WrDr 94*
Porter, Roger Blaine 1946- *WhoAm 94, WhoAmP 93*
Porter, Roger John 1942- *WhoAm 94*
Porter, Roger Stephen 1928- *WhoAm 94*
Porter, Roy *Who 94*
Porter, (Joshua) Roy 1921- *Who 94*
Porter, Roy Lee 1923- *WhoBlA 94*
Porter, Russell d1987 *WhoHol 92*
Porter, Russell Dennis 1918- *WhoMW 93*
Porter, Samuel David 1934- *WhoMW 93*
Porter, Samuel Hamilton 1927- *WhoAm 94, WhoAmL 94*
Porter, Sarah fl. 1791- *BlmGWL*
Porter, Scott E. 1924- *WhoBlA 94*
Porter, Scott Gray 1931- *WhoMW 93*
Porter, Sheena 1935- *WrDr 94*
Porter, Shirley *WhoAmA 93*
Porter, Shirley 1930- *Who 94*
Porter, Stanley *Who 94*
Porter, (Walter) Stanley 1909- *Who 94*
Porter, Stephen Cummings 1934- *WhoAm 94*

Potsic, William Paul 1943- *WhoAm 94*
Pottakis, Yannis A. 1939- *IntWW 93*
Pottash, A. Carter 1948- *WhoAm 94*
Pottenger, Maritha 1952- *AstEnc*
Pottenger, Suzanne Marie 1960- *WhoAmL 94*
Pottenger, Thomas A. *WhoAmP 93*
Potter, A(rchibald) J(ames) 1918-1980 *NewGrDO*
Potter, Alfred Danielson 1926- *WhoMW 93*
Potter, Allan L. 1947- *WhoAmL 94, WhoAmP 93*
Potter, Allen Meyers 1924- *Who 94*
Potter, Anthony Nicholas, Jr. 1942- *WhoFI 94*
Potter, Arthur Kingscote 1905- *Who 94*
Potter, Barrett George 1929- *WhoAm 94*
Potter, Beatrix 1866-1943 *DcLB 141 [port]*
Potter, Beverly A(nn) 1944- *ConAu 43NR*
Potter, Beverly Ann 1944- *WhoFI 94*
Potter, Calvin 1945- *WhoAmP 93*
Potter, Carol *DrAPF 93*
Potter, Cary Nicholas 1939- *WhoAm 94, WhoFI 94*
Potter, Charles Jackson 1908-1990 *WhAm 10*
Potter, Charles L., Jr. 1946- *WhoAmL 94*
Potter, Clarkson Nott 1928- *WhoAm 94, WhoFI 94*
Potter, David Eric 1949- *WhoWest 94*
Potter, David Lynn 1938- *WhoMW 93*
Potter, David Roger William 1944- *Who 94*
Potter, David Samuel 1925- *WhoAm 94*
Potter, Dayna Mae 1954- *WhoWest 94*
Potter, Dennis 1935- *IntMPA 94*
Potter, Dennis (Christopher George) 1935- *ConDr 93, IntWW 93, Who 94, WrDr 94*
Potter, Dennis Arthur 1952- *WhoFI 94*
Potter, Don Howard 1926- *WhoMW 93*
Potter, Donald Charles 1922- *Who 94*
Potter, Douglas A. 1956- *ConAu 141*
Potter, Emma Josephine Hill 1921- *WhoFI 94*
Potter, Ernest Frank 1923- *Who 94*
Potter, Ernest Luther 1940- *WhoAm 94, WhoAmL 94*
Potter, Francis Malcolm 1932- *Who 94*
Potter, Frank 1936- *IntWW 93*
Potter, Frank N(ewton) 1911- *WrDr 94*
Potter, Fred Leon 1948- *WhoIns 94*
Potter, George Ernest 1937- *WhoAmL 94*
Potter, George Harris 1936- *WhoFI 94*
Potter, Glenn Edward 1943- *WhoAm 94, WhoMW 93*
Potter, Guy Dill 1928- *WhoAm 94*
Potter, Hamilton Fish, Jr. 1928- *WhoAm 94, WhoAmL 94*
Potter, Ian *Who 94*
Potter, (William) Ian 1902- *Who 94*
Potter, Jack Arthur 1917- *WhoMW 93*
Potter, James 1729-1789 *WhAmRev*
Potter, James Douglas 1944- *WhoAm 94*
Potter, James Earl 1933- *WhoAm 94*
Potter, James William 1957- *WhoAmL 94*
Potter, Jay Hill *WrDr 94*
Potter, Jeffrey Stewart 1943- *WhoWest 94*
Potter, Jennifer 1949- *WrDr 94*
Potter, Jeremy *Who 94*
Potter, Jeremy 1922- *WrDr 94*
Potter, (Ronald) Jeremy 1922- *Who 94*
Potter, Jeremy Patrick L. *Who 94*
Potter, John d1749 *BlmGEL*
Potter, John 1913- *Who 94*
Potter, John Francis 1925- *WhoAm 94*
Potter, John Herbert 1928- *Who 94*
Potter, John Howell 1954- *WhoWest 94*
Potter, John Leith 1923- *WhoAm 94*
Potter, John McEwen 1920- *Who 94*
Potter, John William 1918- *WhoAm 94, WhoAmL 94, WhoMW 93*
Potter, Judith Diggs 1941- *WhoBlA 94*
Potter, June Anita 1938- *WhoMW 93*
Potter, Karl Harrington 1927- *WhoAm 94*
Potter, Kenneth *WhoAmA 93*
Potter, (George) Kenneth 1926- *WhoAmA 93*
Potter, Kevin *WhoAmL 94*
Potter, Larry G. 1947- *WhoMW 93*
Potter, Lillian Florence 1912- *WhoAm 94*
Potter, Madeleine *IntMPA 94, WhoHol 92*
Potter, Malcolm *Who 94*
Potter, Marc Randall 1949- *WhoFI 94*
Potter, Margaret (Newman) 1926- *WrDr 94*
Potter, Margaret Ann 1948- *WhoAmL 94*
Potter, Mark Howard 1937- *Who 94*
Potter, Martin 1944- *WhoHol 92*
Potter, Maureen *WhoHol 92*
Potter, Michael 1924- *WhoScEn 94*
Potter, Michael William 1959- *WhoFI 94*
Potter, Miles M. 1945- *WhoFI 94*
Potter, Myrtle Stephens 1958- *WhoBlA 94*
Potter, Nancy *DrAPF 93*
Potter, Orlando B. 1928- *WhoAmP 93*
Potter, Osbert *WhoAmP 93*
Potter, Paul Edwin 1925- *WhoScEn 94*
Potter, Peter d1983 *WhoHol 92*
Potter, Philip Alford 1921- *Who 94*
Potter, Ralph Benajah, Jr. 1931- *WhoAm 94*
Potter, Raymond *Who 94*
Potter, Raymond 1933- *Who 94*
Potter, (Joseph) Raymond (Lynden) 1916- *Who 94*
Potter, Richard Clifford 1946- *WhoAmL 94*
Potter, Robert 1831- *EncSF 93*
Potter, Robert Daniel 1923- *WhoAm 94, WhoAmL 94*
Potter, Robert Joseph 1932- *WhoAm 94*
Potter, Robert R. 1948- *WhoAmL 94*
Potter, Roderick H. 1938- *WhoAmP 93*
Potter, Ronald Stanley James 1921- *Who 94*
Potter, Rosemary 1952- *WhoAmP 93*
Potter, Russell Sherwood 1897- *WhAm 10*
Potter, Suzanne *DrAPF 93*
Potter, Tanya Jean 1956- *WhoAmL 94*
Potter, Ted 1933- *WhoAmA 93*
Potter, Thomas D. 1939- *WhoFI 94, WhoIns 94*
Potter, Thomas Eugene 1933- *WhoAmP 93*
Potter, Trevor 1955- *WhoAmP 93*
Potter, Trevor Alexander McClurg 1955- *WhoAm 94, WhoAmL 94*
Potter, Vincent 1614-1661 *DcNaB MP*
Potter, Vincent G. 1928- *WrDr 94*
Potter, Wilfrid John *Who 94*
Potter, William Bartlett 1938- *WhoAm 94, WhoFI 94*
Potter, William Gray, Jr. 1950- *WhoAm 94*
Potter, William J. 1883-1964 *WhoAmA 93N*
Potter, William James 1948- *WhoAm 94, WhoFI 94*
Potter, Yerda McIntyre 1941- *WhoAmP 93*
Potterton, Homan 1946- *Who 94*
Potterton, John Paul 1951- *WhoMW 93*
Potthast, Milton Joseph 1957- *WhoAmP 93*
Pottie, David Laren 1952- *WhoFI 94*
Pottie, Roswell Francis 1933- *WhoAm 94*
Pottinger, Albert A. 1928- *WhoBlA 94*
Pottinger, (William) George 1916- *Who 94*
Pottinger, Henry 1789-1856 *WhWE*
Pottker, Janice Marie 1948- *ConAu 42NR, WhoFI 94*
Pottle, Harry 1925- *IntMPA 94*
Pottorff, Beau Backus 1959- *WhoScEn 94*
Pottorff, Jo Ann 1936- *WhoAmP 93, WhoMW 93*
Pottorff, William Thomas 1914- *WhoAmP 93*
Pottruck, David S. 1948- *WhoAm 94, WhoFI 94, WhoWest 94*
Potts, Albert M. 1914- *WhoScEn 94*
Potts, Annie 1952- *IntMPA 94, News 94-1 [port], WhoAm 94*
Potts, Annie 1953- *WhoHol 92*
Potts, Anthony Vincent 1945- *WhoMW 93*
Potts, Archibold 1932- *Who 94*
Potts, Barbara J. 1932- *WhoAmP 93*
Potts, Barbara Joyce 1932- *WhoAm 94, WhoMW 93*
Potts, Bernard 1915- *WhoAmL 94*
Potts, Charles *DrAPF 93*
Potts, Charles A. d1986 *WhoAmA 93N*
Potts, Cliff 1945- *WhoHol 92*
Potts, David Malcolm 1935- *WhoAm 94*
Potts, Dennis Walker 1945- *WhoAmL 94*
Potts, Douglas Gordon 1927- *WhoAm 94*
Potts, Erwin Rea 1932- *WhoWest 94*
Potts, Gerald Neal 1933- *WhoAm 94*
Potts, Grover C., Jr. 1944- *WhoAmL 94*
Potts, H. R., Jr. 1939- *WhoAmP 93*
Potts, Hank d1980 *WhoHol 92*
Potts, Harold E. 1921- *WhoBlA 94*
Potts, Harold Francis, Jr. 1955- *WhoFI 94*
Potts, (Francis) Humphrey 1931- *Who 94*
Potts, James Manning 1895- *WhAm 10*
Potts, Jean 1910- *WrDr 94*
Potts, Jeff 1951- *WhoAmP 93*
Potts, John Thomas, Jr. 1932- *WhoAm 94, WhoScEn 94*
Potts, Johnathan 1745-1781 *AmRev*
Potts, Jonathan 1745-1781 *WhAmRev*
Potts, Kevin T. 1928- *WhoAm 94*
Potts, Lyman Harvey 1952- *WhoFI 94*
Potts, Nell 1959- *WhoHol 92*
Potts, Peter 1935- *Who 94*
Potts, Ramsay Douglas 1916- *WhoAm 94*
Potts, Richard 1753-1808 *WhAmRev*
Potts, Richard 1938- *WrDr 94*
Potts, Richard Allen 1940- *WhoMW 93*
Potts, Robert Leslie 1944- *WhoAm 94*
Potts, Robert Lester 1923- *WhoBlA 94*
Potts, Robin 1944- *Who 94*
Potts, Sammie *WhoBlA 94*
Potts, Stephen Deaderick 1930- *WhoAm 94*
Potts, Thomas Edmund d1993 *Who 94N*
Potts, Walter d1943 *WhoHol 92*
Potuznik, Charles Laddy 1947- *WhoAm 94, WhoAmL 94*
Potvin, Alfred Raoul 1942- *WhoAm 94*
Potvin, George Albert 1948- *WhoAmP 93*
Potvin, Jane B. 1935- *WhoAmP 93*
Potvin, Pierre 1932- *WhoAm 94*
Potvin, Raymond Herve 1924- *WhoAm 94*
Poucher, Ralph Lee 1938- *WhoAmL 94*
Pouder, George Harry 1896- *WhAm 10*
Poudyal, Sri Ram 1950- *WhoScEn 94*
Pouget, Marie 1949- *WhoHisp 94*
Pough, Frederick Harvey 1906- *WhoAm 94, WhoWest 94*
Pough, W. Newton 1921- *WhoAmP 93*
Pougin, (Francois-Auguste-)Arthur 1834-1921 *NewGrDO*
Pougy, Liane de 1869-1950 *BlmGWL*
Poujade, Pierre 1920- *IntWW 93*
Poujouly, Georges *WhoHol 92*
Poul, Franklin 1924- *WhoAm 94*
Poulain, Mademoiselle fl. 18th cent.- *BlmGWL*
Poulenard, Isabelle 1961- *NewGrDO*
Poulenc, Francis 1899-1963 *IntDcB [port]*
Poulenc, Francis (Jean Marcel) 1899-1963 *NewGrDO*
Pouleur, Hubert Gustave 1948- *WhoScEn 94*
Poulides, Fotis George 1914- *IntWW 93*
Poulin, A., Jr. *DrAPF 93*
Poulin, A(lfred A.), Jr. 1938- *WrDr 94*
Poulin, John Roger 1946- *WhoFI 94*
Poulin, Marie-Paule 1945- *WhoAm 94*
Poulin, Robert Scott 1959- *WhoFI 94*
Poulin, Roland *WhoAmA 93*
Poulin, Thomas E. 1956- *WhoAmP 93*
Poulios, Nick Sotirios 1949- *WhoFI 94*
Pouliot, Roger M. 1937- *WhoAmP 93*
Pouliquen, Marcel Francois 1945- *WhoScEn 94*
Poulos, Basilios Nicholas 1941- *WhoAmA 93*
Poulos, Darwin Robert 1959- *WhoWest 94*
Poulos, Michael James 1931- *WhoAm 94, WhoFI 94*
Poulos, Peter Peter 1922- *WhoAmL 94*
Poulsen, Dennis Robert 1946- *WhoFI 94, WhoScEn 94, WhoWest 94*
Poulsen, Fern Sue 1959- *WhoMW 93*
Poulsen, Harold L. *WhoAmP 93*
Poulsen, Valdemar 1869-1942 *WorInv*
Poulshock, Normand Garber 1926- *WhoWest 94*
Poulson, Donald Frederick 1910-1989 *WhAm 10*
Poulson, Howard D. *WhoFI 94*
Poulson, Jeffrey Lee 1951- *WhoAmL 94*
Poulson, Richard J. M. 1938- *WhoAm 94*
Poulson, Robert Dean 1927- *WhoAm 94*
Poulson, Sandra Louise 1947- *WhoWest 94*
Poulter, Brian Henry 1941- *Who 94*
Poultney, David 1939- *ConAu 141*
Poulton, A. G. 1867- *WhoHol 92*
Poulton, Bruce Robert 1927- *WhoAm 94*
Poulton, Charles Edgar 1917- *WhoAm 94*
Poulton, Craig Kidd 1951- *WhoFI 94*
Poulton, Donna Lee 1945- *WhoFI 94*
Poulton, Mabel 1906- *WhoHol 92*
Poulton, Richard Christopher 1938- *Who 94*
Pouncey, Denys Duncan Rivers 1906- *Who 94*
Pouncey, Peter Richard 1937- *WhoAm 94*
Pound, Ezra 1885-1972 *BlmGEL*
Pound, Ezra (Loomis) 1885-1972 *NewGrDO*
Pound, Ezra Weston Loomis 1885-1972 *AmCulL*
Pound, John Bennett 1946- *WhoAmL 94, WhoWest 94*
Pound, John David 1946- *Who 94*
Pound, Keith Salisbury 1933- *Who 94*
Pound, Leland Earl 1945- *WhoWest 94*
Pound, Leslie 1926- *IntMPA 94*
Pound, Richard William Duncan 1942- *WhoAm 94*
Pound, Robert Vivian 1919- *IntWW 93, WhoAm 94, WhoScEn 94*
Pounder, C. C. H. 1952- *WhoBlA 94*
Pounder, CCH *WhoHol 92*
Pounder, Richard A. 1946- *WhoAm 94, WhoFI 94*
Pounds, Augustine Wright 1936- *WhoBlA 94*
Pounds, Billy Dean 1930- *WhoAmL 94*
Pounds, Courtice d1927 *WhoHol 92*
Pounds, (Charles) Courtice 1862-1927 *NewGrDO*
Pounds, Edgar George Derek 1922- *Who 94*
Pounds, Elaine 1946- *WhoBlA 94*
Pounds, Ernest Ray 1947- *WhoAmP 93*
Pounds, Kenneth Alwyne 1934- *IntWW 93, Who 94*
Pounds, Kenneth Ray 1942- *WhoBlA 94*
Pounds, Moses B. 1947- *WhoBlA 94*
Pounds, William Frank 1928- *WhoAm 94*
Poungui, Ange Edouard *IntWW 93*
Pounian, Albert Kachouni 1924- *WhoAmA 93*
Pountain, Eric (John) 1933- *Who 94*
Pountain, Eric John 1933- *IntWW 93*
Pountney, David (Willoughby) 1947- *NewGrDO*
Pountney, David Willoughby 1947- *IntWW 93, Who 94*
Poupard, James J. 1932- *WhoAm 94*
Poupard, Paul 1930- *IntWW 93*
Poupeney, Mollie *WhoAmA 93*
Pourakis, Cally *DrAPF 93*
Pouran *WhoHol 92*
Pourchot, Pat *WhoAmP 93*
Pourciau, Kerry L. 1951- *WhoBlA 94*
Pourciau, Lester John 1936- *WhoAm 94*
Pour-El, Marian Boykan *WhoAm 94*
Pourkermani, Mahmood 1944- *WhoMW 93*
Pournelle, Jerry (Eugene) 1933- *WrDr 94*
Pournelle, Jerry E(ugene) 1933- *EncSF 93*
Pournelle, Jerry Eugene 1933- *WhoAm 94, WhoWest 94*
Pourre, Eugenio *WhAmRev*
Pouschine, John Laurence 1957- *WhoFI 94*
Pousette-Dart, Joanna 1947- *WhoAmA 93*
Pousette-Dart, Nathaniel J. 1886-1965 *WhoAmA 93N*
Pousette-Dart, Richard 1916-1992 *AnObit 1992, WhAm 10, WhoAmA 93N*
Poussaint, Alvin F. 1934- *ConBlB 5 [port]*
Poussaint, Alvin Francis 1934- *WhoAm 94, WhoBlA 94*
Poussaint, Ann Ashmore 1942- *WhoBlA 94*
Poussaint, Renee Francine 1944- *WhoBlA 94*
Poussart, Denis Jean-Marie 1940- *WhoAm 94*
Poussette-Dart, Richard 1916-1992 *CurBio 93N*
Pousseur, Henri (Leon Marie Therese) 1929- *NewGrDO*
Pout, Harry Wilfrid 1920- *Who 94*
Poutsiaka, William J. 1952- *WhoIns 94*
Pouw, Stanley Siong-In 1942- *WhoAsA 94*
Pouyet, Eugene d1950 *WhoHol 92*
Povah, Phyllis 1902- *WhoHol 92*
Poveda, Carlos Manuel, III 1963- *WhoHisp 94*
Pover, Alan John 1933- *IntWW 93, Who 94*
Poverman, C. E. *DrAPF 93*
Povey, Keith 1943- *Who 94*
Povey, Thomas George 1920- *WhoAm 94, WhoFI 94*
Povhe, Thomas Jerome 1950- *WhoWest 94*
Povich, David 1935- *WhoAm 94, WhoAmL 94*
Povich, Maury 1939- *ConTFT 11*
Povich, Maury Richard 1939- *WhoAm 94*
Povich, Shirley Lewis 1905- *WhoAm 94*
Povish, Kenneth Joseph 1924- *WhoAm 94, WhoMW 93*
Povlsen, Shirley 1927- *WhoAmP 93*
Povman, Morton 1931- *WhoAmP 93*
Povod, Reinaldo 1959- *WrDr 94*
Povondra, William Frank, Jr. 1943- *WhoWest 94*
Pow, Tom 1950- *WrDr 94*
Powathil, Joseph 1930- *IntWW 93*
Powden, Carl D. 1954- *WhoAmP 93*
Powderly, Terence Vincent 1849-1924 *AmSocL*
Powderly, William H., III 1930- *WhoAm 94*
Powditch, Alan (Cecil Robert) 1912- *Who 94*
Powdrill, Gary Leo 1945- *WhoMW 93*
Powe, B(ruce) W. 1955- *WrDr 94*
Powe, Bruce 1925- *EncSF 93*
Powe, Bruce Allen 1925- *WrDr 94*
Powe, Joseph S. 1946- *WhoBlA 94*
Powe, Ralph Elward 1944- *WhoAm 94, WhoScEn 94*
Powe, Willaim A. 1937- *WhoAm 94, WhoFI 94*
Powell *Who 94*
Powell, Adam Clayton *WhoAmP 93*
Powell, Adam Clayton, Sr. 1865-1953 *AfrAmAl 6 [port]*
Powell, Adam Clayton, Jr. 1908-1972 *AfrAmAl 6 [port]*
Powell, Adam Clayton, Jr. 1945-1971 *AfrAmAl 6*
Powell, Adam Clayton, III 1946- *WhoBlA 94*
Powell, Addie Scott 1922- *WhoBlA 94*
Powell, Addison *WhoHol 92*

Powell, Alan 1928- WhoAm 94, WhoScEn 94
Powell, Alan T. 1951- WhoAmP 93
Powell, Albert Edward 1927- Who 94
Powell, Amy Purcell 1933- WhoAmP 93
Powell, Amy Tuck 1963- WhoAmP 93
Powell, Anice Carpenter 1928- WhoAm 94
Powell, Anne Elizabeth 1951- WhoAm 94
Powell, Anthony ConTFT 11
Powell, Anthony 1905- BlmGEL
Powell, Anthony (Dymoke) 1905- WrDr 94
Powell, Anthony Dymoke 1905- IntWW 93, Who 94
Powell, Archie James 1950- WhoBlA 94
Powell, Ardal 1958- ConAu 142
Powell, Arnold Joseph Philip Who 94
Powell, Arthur Barrington 1918- Who 94
Powell, Aston Wesley 1909- WhoBlA 94
Powell, Barry B. 1942- WrDr 94
Powell, Barry Bruce 1942- WhoAm 94
Powell, Benjamin H., III 1946- WhoAmL 94
Powell, Benjamin Harrison, IV 1915-1989 WhAm 10
Powell, Bernice Fletcher 1949- WhoBlA 94
Powell, Betty Jean 1928- WhoWest 94
Powell, Bill Jake 1936- WhoAm 94
Powell, Bolling Raines, Jr. 1910- WhoAm 94
Powell, Boone, Jr. 1937- WhoAm 94
Powell, Brian Hill 1962- WhoScEn 94
Powell, Bud 1924-1966 AfrAmAl 6
Powell, Burnele Venable 1947- WhoAm 94, WhoAmL 94
Powell, C. Clayton 1927- WhoAmP 93, WhoBlA 94
Powell, Carol Christine 1941- WhoMW 93
Powell, Cecil Frank 1903-1969 WorScD
Powell, Charles (David) 1941- Who 94
Powell, Charles David 1941- IntWW 93
Powell, Charles L., Jr. 1931- WhoBlA 94
Powell, Charles Law 1958- WhoAmL 94
Powell, Charles Lewis 1933- WhoAmP 93
Powell, Charles P. 1923- WhoBlA 94
Powell, Christopher Robert 1963- WhoScEn 94
Powell, Clarence Dean, Jr. 1939- WhoBlA 94
Powell, Clayton Jermiah, Jr. 1957- WhoAmL 94, WhoAmP 93
Powell, Clilan Bethany 1894- WhAm 10
Powell, Clinton Cobb 1918- WhoAm 94
Powell, Colin L. NewYTBS 93
Powell, Colin L. 1937- AfrAmG [port], AfrAmAl 6 [port], WhoAmP 93, WhoBlA 94
Powell, Colin Luther 1937- IntWW 93, Who 94, WhoAm 94
Powell, Craig 1940- WrDr 94
Powell, Dan T. 1950- WhoAmA 93
Powell, Dannye Romine DrAPF 93
Powell, Darlene Wright 1960- WhoBlA 94
Powell, Darrell Lee 1959- WhoBlA 94
Powell, David d1925 WhoHol 92
Powell, David 1914- Who 94
Powell, David 1925- ConAu 142
Powell, David Greatorex 1933- WhoAm 94, WhoFI 94
Powell, David L. 1938- WhoBlA 94
Powell, David Lee 1936- WhoMW 93
Powell, David Lee 1938- WhoMW 93
Powell, David M. 1944- WhoAmL 94
Powell, Diane Elaine 1955- WhoAmL 94
Powell, Dick d1948 WhoHol 92
Powell, Dick d1963 WhoHol 92
Powell, Dick, Jr. WhoHol 92
Powell, (Elizabeth) Dilys 1901- Who 94
Powell, Doane 1881-1951 WhoAmA 93N
Powell, Don Watson 1938- WhoAm 94
Powell, Drexel Dwane, Jr. 1944- WhoAm 94
Powell, Dudley Vincent 1917- WhoBlA 94
Powell, Durwood Royce 1951- WhoAm 94, WhoAmL 94
Powell, Earl Alexander, III 1943- IntWW 93, Who 94, WhoAm 94, WhoAmA 93, WhoWest 94
Powell, Eddie WhoHol 92
Powell, Edmund William 1922- WhoAm 94
Powell, Edward Lee 1941- WhoAmP 93
Powell, Edward Lee, I 1958- WhoMW 93
Powell, Eleanor d1982 WhoHol 92
Powell, Enid Levinger DrAPF 93
Powell, Enoch IntWW 93, Who 94
Powell, (John) Enoch 1912- IntWW 93, Who 94, WrDr 94
Powell, Ernestine Breisch 1906- WhoAm 94, WhoAmL 94, WhoFI 94
Powell, Francis Turner 1914- Who 94
Powell, Gary Allison 1954- WhoWest 94
Powell, Gayle Lett 1943- WhoBlA 94
Powell, Geoffrey Who 94
Powell, (John) Geoffrey 1928- Who 94
Powell, Geoffrey (Stewart) 1914- WrDr 94
Powell, Geoffry Charles Hamilton 1920- Who 94
Powell, George E. 1945- WhoAmP 93
Powell, George Everett, Jr. 1926- WhoFI 94
Powell, George Everett, III 1948- WhoAm 94, WhoFI 94, WhoMW 93
Powell, George Van Tuyl 1910- WhoAm 94
Powell, Georgette Seabrooke 1916- WhoBlA 94
Powell, Gordon 1947- WhoAmA 93
Powell, Gordon George 1911- WrDr 94
Powell, Grady Wilson 1932- WhoBlA 94
Powell, Gregory DrAPF 93
Powell, Hampton Oliver 1911- WhoAm 94
Powell, Harold 1932- WhoAm 94
Powell, Harry Allan Rose 1912- Who 94
Powell, Harvard Wendell 1915- WhoAm 94
Powell, Hazel Nunn 1935- WhoAmP 93
Powell, Herbert J. 1898- WhoAm 94
Powell, Horace W., Sr. 1932- WhoAmP 93
Powell, J. R. 1954- WhoAmL 94
Powell, Jack d1976 WhoHol 92
Powell, James 1942- WrDr 94
Powell, James Bobbitt 1938- WhoAm 94, WhoFI 94
Powell, James Corbley 1955- WhoAmL 94
Powell, James Henry 1928- WhoAm 94
Powell, James Kevin 1959- WhoFI 94
Powell, James Lawrence 1936- WhoAm 94
Powell, James Matthew 1930- WhoAm 94
Powell, James Richard 1944- WhoAm 94
Powell, Jane 1928- WhoHol 92
Powell, Jane 1929- IntMPA 94
Powell, Janet Frances 1942- WhoWomW 91
Powell, Jerry T. 1933- WhoAm 94
Powell, Jody 1943- WhoFI 94
Powell, John Alfred 1923- Who 94
Powell, John Allen 1947- WhoAmP 93
Powell, John Duane 1925- WhoAmP 93
Powell, John Frederick 1915- Who 94
Powell, John Lewis 1902- WhoBlA 94
Powell, John Lewis 1950- Who 94
Powell, John R. WhoAmP 93
Powell, John Wesley 1834-1902 AmSocL [port], EnvEnc [port], WhWE [port]
Powell, John William 1928- WhoAmP 93
Powell, Jonathan Leslie 1947- IntWW 93, Who 94
Powell, Joseph DrAPF 93
Powell, Joseph Hansford 1946- WhoBlA 94
Powell, Joseph Herbert 1926- WhoAm 94
Powell, Joseph Lester 1943- WhoFI 94
Powell, Joseph T. 1923- WhoBlA 94
Powell, Juan Herschel 1960- WhoBlA 94
Powell, Judith Carol 1949- WhoScEn 94
Powell, Julia Gertrude 1907- WhoWest 94
Powell, Julius Cherry 1926-1988 WhAm 10
Powell, Kenneth Alasandro 1945- WhoBlA 94
Powell, Kenneth Alger 1925- WhoMW 93
Powell, Kenneth Edward 1952- WhoAm 94, WhoAmL 94
Powell, Kenneth Grant 1960- WhoMW 93
Powell, Kevin 1966- WhoBlA 94
Powell, Lane Alan 1955- WhoWest 94
Powell, Larry Randall 1948- WhoAm 94
Powell, Larson Merrill 1932- WhoAm 94, WhoFI 94
Powell, Lawrenceson Fitzroy 1881-1975 DcNaB MP
Powell, Lawrie William 1934- Who 94
Powell, Lee d1944 WhoHol 92
Powell, Leola P. 1932- WhoBlA 94
Powell, Leslie Charles, Jr. 1927- WhoAm 94
Powell, Lewis F., Jr. 1907- WhoAmP 93
Powell, Lewis Franklin, Jr. 1907- CngDr 93, Who 94, WhoAm 94, WhoAmL 94
Powell, Lewis Franklin, III 1952- WhoAm 94, WhoAmL 94
Powell, Linda 1964- WhoHol 92
Powell, Lovelady WhoHol 92
Powell, Lydia Bond 1892-1978 WhoAmA 93N
Powell, Marcus WhoHol 92
Powell, Margaret Ann Simmons 1952- WhoScEn 94
Powell, Mark Thomas 1958- WhoFI 94
Powell, Martha Jane 1948- WhoScEn 94
Powell, Marvin 1955- WhoBlA 94
Powell, Mary Atkeson 1944- WhoMW 93
Powell, Mel 1923- WhoAm 94, WhoHol 92, WhoWest 94
Powell, Melchior Daniel 1935- WhoWest 94
Powell, Michael d1990 WhoHol 92
Powell, Michael 1905-1990 ConTFT 11
Powell, Michael James David 1936- IntWW 93, Who 94
Powell, Michael Vance 1946- WhoAm 94, WhoAmL 94
Powell, Mike 1963- CurBio 93 [port], WhoBlA 94
Powell, Mike 1964- WhoAm 94
Powell, Miles, Jr. 1926- WhoFI 94
Powell, Myrtis H. 1939- WhoBlA 94
Powell, Nancy Egan 1944- WhoMW 93
Powell, Neil 1948- WrDr 94
Powell, Nicholas (Folliott Douglas) 1935- Who 94
Powell, Norborne Berkeley 1914- WhoAm 94
Powell, Nosher WhoHol 92
Powell, Padgett DrAPF 93
Powell, Padgett 1952- WrDr 94
Powell, Patricia 1966- WhoBlA 94
Powell, Patricia Ann 1956- WhoScEn 94
Powell, Percival Hugh 1912- Who 94
Powell, Peter John 1928- EncNAR
Powell, Philip IntWW 93
Powell, Philip 1921- Who 94
Powell, (Arnold Joseph) Philip 1921- IntWW 93
Powell, Philip Melancthon, Jr. 1941- WhoBlA 94
Powell, Ralph Edwin 1946- WhoMW 93
Powell, Ramon Jesse 1935- WhoFI 94
Powell, Ray 1920- WhoAmP 93
Powell, Raymond 1928- Who 94
Powell, Raymond William 1944- WhoFI 94
Powell, Richard d1937 WhoHol 92
Powell, Richard (Royle) 1909- Who 94
Powell, Richard Clarence 1965- WhoMW 93
Powell, Richard Gordon 1918- WhoAm 94
Powell, Richard Grant 1938- WhoMW 93
Powell, Richard Maurice 1951- WhoBlA 94
Powell, Richard Pitts 1908- WhoAm 94
Powell, Richard Royle 1909- IntWW 93
Powell, Robert 1944- IntWW 93, WhoHol 92
Powell, Robert Dominick 1942- WhoAmL 94, WhoFI 94
Powell, Robert E. 1919- WhoBlA 94
Powell, Robert Ellis 1936- WhoAm 94
Powell, Robert Eugene 1955- WhoFI 94, WhoMW 93
Powell, Robert Lane B. Who 94
Powell, Robert Meaker 1930- WhoBlA 94
Powell, Robert William 1909- Who 94
Powell, Roberta A. 1952- WhoWest 94
Powell, Roger Gant 1949- WhoFI 94
Powell, Ronald James 1949- WhoWest 94
Powell, Ronald Mark 1957- WhoMW 93
Powell, Ronald Rowe 1944- WhoMW 93
Powell, Russell d1950 WhoHol 92
Powell, Sally Jane Who 94
Powell, Sandra Theresa 1944- WhoAm 94
Powell, Sandy d1982 WhoHol 92
Powell, Saul Reuben 1953- WhoScEn 94
Powell, Sharon Lee 1940- WhoFI 94
Powell, Shirley DrAPF 93
Powell, Sidney K. 1955- WhoAmL 94
Powell, Sonny EncSF 93
Powell, Stanley, Jr. 1917- WhoAm 94
Powell, Stephanie 1946- WhoWest 94
Powell, Stephen Douglas 1955- WhoFI 94
Powell, Stephen Joseph 1942- WhoAmL 94
Powell, Stephen Walter 1955- WhoAmL 94
Powell, Talmage 1920- WrDr 94
Powell, Ted Ferrell 1935- WhoWest 94
Powell, Templar d1949 WhoHol 92
Powell, Teresa Lynn 1949- WhoAmP 93
Powell, Theresa Ann 1956- WhoMW 93
Powell, Thomas Francis A. 1925- WhoBlA 94
Powell, Tim Who 94
Powell, Trevor John David 1948- WhoAm 94
Powell, Victor George Edward 1929- Who 94
Powell, Victoria WhoHol 92
Powell, Violet 1912- WrDr 94
Powell, Virginia W. 1948- WhoAm 94, WhoAmL 94
Powell, Walter E. 1931- WhoAmP 93
Powell, Walter Hecht 1915- WhoAm 94
Powell, (Dewi) Watkin 1920- Who 94
Powell, Watson, Jr. 1917- WhoIns 94
Powell, Wayne Hugh 1946- WhoBlA 94
Powell, Wendell WhoAmP 93
Powell, Will d1977 WhoHol 92
Powell, William d1984 WhoHol 92
Powell, William 1892-1984 WhoCom
Powell, William 1935- WhoBlA 94
Powell, William Albert 1935- WhoFI 94
Powell, William Arnold, Jr. 1929- WhoAm 94, WhoFI 94
Powell, William Council, Sr. 1948- WhoFI 94
Powell, William E. 1936- AfrAmG [port]
Powell, William J. 1908- WhoBlA 94
Powell, William O., Jr. 1934- WhoBlA 94
Powell, William Rhys 1948- Who 94
Powell, William Rossell, Jr. 1926- WhoAm 94
Powell, Yvonne Macon 1936- WhoBlA 94
Powell-Brown, Ann 1947- WhoMW 93
Powell-Cotton, Christopher 1918- Who 94
Powell-Jones, John E. 1925- IntWW 93
Powell-Jones, John Ernest 1925- Who 94
Powell-Smith, Vincent 1939- WrDr 94
Powelson, John Palen 1920- ConAu 41NR, WhoWest 94, WrDr 94
Powelson, Rosemary A. WhoAmA 93
Powelson, Steven E. 1954- WhoWest 94
Power, Alastair John Cecil 1958- Who 94
Power, Brian St. Quentin, Mrs. Who 94
Power, Dennis Michael 1941- WhoAm 94, WhoWest 94
Power, Dorothy K. 1932- WhoAmP 93
Power, Ed(ward) WhoHol 92
Power, Eugene B. d1993 NewYTBS 93
Power, Eugene Barnum 1905- Who 94, WhoAm 94
Power, F. William 1925- WhoAm 94
Power, Hartley d1966 WhoHol 92
Power, John Bruce 1936- WhoAm 94, WhoAmL 94, WhoFI 94, WhoWest 94
Power, John Paul 1958- WhoAmP 93
Power, Joseph Edward 1938- WhoAm 94
Power, Jule d1932 WhoHol 92
Power, Jules 1921- WhoAm 94
Power, M(aurice) S(tephen) 1935- WrDr 94
Power, Margaret (M.) SmATA 75 [port]
Power, Marjorie DrAPF 93
Power, Mark 1937- WhoAm 94, WhoAmA 93
Power, Mary Susan WhoAmP 93
Power, Mary Susan 1935- WhoAm 94
Power, Michael George 1924- Who 94
Power, Mimi 1935- WhoWest 94
Power, Noel Plunkett 1929- Who 94
Power, Paul d1968 WhoHol 92
Power, Richard B. d1993 NewYTBS 93
Power, Robert Cornelius 1922- WhoBlA 94
Power, Romina 1950- WhoHol 92
Power, S. Brenda Joan 1941- WhoAmA 93
Power, Taryn 1954- WhoHol 92
Power, Thomas G. WhoAmP 93
Power, Thomas Michael 1940- WhoAm 94
Power, Tyrone d1958 WhoHol 92
Power, Tyrone, Mrs. d1959 WhoHol 92
Power, Tyrone, Sr. d1931 WhoHol 92
Power, Tyrone, Jr. 1959- WhoHol 92
Power, Victor DrAPF 93
Power, Walter Robert 1924- WhoScEn 94
Powers, Alan 1955- ConAu 140
Powers, Alan Dale 1929- WhoWest 94
Powers, Allen Edward 1939- WhoAm 94
Powers, Anna Bertha Josephine 1912- WhoAmP 93
Powers, Anne 1913-1987 WrDr 94N
Powers, Anthony Richard, Jr. 1942- WhoMW 93
Powers, Arthur 1947- WhoAm 94
Powers, Arthur B. 1928- WhoAmP 93
Powers, Barry Richard 1962- WhoAmL 94
Powers, Basil L. 1932- WhoAmP 93
Powers, Ben WhoHol 92
Powers, Beverly WhoHol 92
Powers, Brenda d1967 WhoHol 92
Powers, Bruce Raymond 1927- WhoAm 94
Powers, Bruce Theodore 1934- WhoAmP 93
Powers, C. F., Jr. 1923- IntMPA 94
Powers, Charles F. DrAPF 93
Powers, Claudia M. WhoAmP 93
Powers, Clifford Blake, Jr. 1960- WhoScEn 94
Powers, David Leon 1932- WhoWest 94
Powers, David Richard 1939- WhoAm 94, WhoMW 93
Powers, Deane Fishburne, Jr. 1955- WhoFI 94
Powers, Dennis Alpha 1938- WhoAm 94
Powers, Donald T. 1950- WhoAmA 93
Powers, Doris Hurt 1927- WhoFI 94, WhoScEn 94
Powers, Dudley 1911- WhoAm 94
Powers, Edward Alton 1927- WhoAm 94
Powers, Edward Herbert 1942- WhoAmL 94
Powers, Edward Latell 1919- WhoAm 94
Powers, Edwin Malvin 1915- WhoWest 94
Powers, Eldon Nathaniel 1932- WhoFI 94, WhoScEn 94
Powers, Elizabeth Whitmel 1949- WhoAm 94
Powers, Eric Randall 1947- WhoAm 94
Powers, Ernest Michael 1942- WhoMW 93
Powers, Eva Agoston 1938- WhoScEn 94
Powers, Francis d1940 WhoHol 92
Powers, Gary Lee 1945- WhoFI 94
Powers, George Edward, Jr. 1952- WhoAmL 94
Powers, Georgia M. WhoBlA 94
Powers, Georgia M. 1923- WhoAmP 93

Powers, Gerard E., Jr. 1934- *WhoAmP 93*
Powers, Harris Pat 1934- *WhoAm 94*
Powers, Henry Martin, Jr. 1932- *WhoAm 94*
Powers, Hiram 1805-1873 *AmCulL*
Powers, Hurshal George 1933- *WhoWest 94*
Powers, J. F. 1917- *DcLB 130 [port]*
Powers, J(ames) F(arl) 1917- *RfGShF, WrDr 94*
Powers, J.L. *EncSF 93*
Powers, James *WhoFI 94*
Powers, James Bascom 1924- *WhoAm 94*
Powers, James Farl 1917- *WhoAm 94*
Powers, James J. 1936- *WhoIns 94*
Powers, JoAnne Patricia 1953- *WhoWest 94*
Powers, John d1941 *WhoHol 92*
Powers, John A. 1926- *IntWW 93*
Powers, John Austin 1926- *WhoFI 94*
Powers, John Dale 1936- *WhoAmL 94*
Powers, John Glenn, Jr. 1930- *WhoFI 94*
Powers, John Lewis 1943- *WhoAmL 94*
Powers, John R. 1945- *WhoAm 94*
Powers, John Y. 1929- *WhoAm 94, WhoAmL 94*
Powers, Johnny d1951 *WhoHol 92*
Powers, Kathleen Anne 1941- *WhoFI 94*
Powers, Kathryn Dolores 1929- *WhoMW 93*
Powers, Kim Dean 1962- *WhoScEn 94*
Powers, Leona d1970 *WhoHol 92*
Powers, Linda 1943- *WhoAmP 93*
Powers, Lucille d1981 *WhoHol 92*
Powers, M. L. 1919- *WrDr 94*
Powers, Mala 1931- *IntMPA 94, WhoHol 92*
Powers, Mamon, Sr. *WhoBlA 94*
Powers, Mamon M., Jr. 1948- *WhoBlA 94*
Powers, Marcus Eugene 1929- *WhoAm 94, WhoAmL 94, WhoWest 94*
Powers, Marie d1973 *WhoHol 92*
Powers, Marie 1910-1973 *NewGrDO*
Powers, Marilyn 1925-1976 *WhoAmA 93N*
Powers, Mark Healey 1954- *WhoAmP 93*
Powers, Mark Lyman 1955- *WhoAmL 94*
Powers, Martin Joseph 1948- *WhoMW 93*
Powers, Mary Swift 1885-1959 *WhoAmA 93N*
Powers, May d1961 *WhoHol 92*
Powers, Meredith A(nn) 1949- *ConAu 140*
Powers, Michael Kevin 1948- *WhoAm 94*
Powers, N. Thompson 1929- *WhoAm 94, WhoAmL 94*
Powers, Nan Margaret 1956- *WhoMW 93*
Powers, Nelson Roger 1946- *WhoScEn 94*
Powers, Nora *WrDr 94*
Powers, Odell Eugene 1928-1991 *WhAm 10*
Powers, Onie H. 1907- *WhoScEn 94*
Powers, Patrick Kenneth 1960- *WhoMW 93*
Powers, Paul J. 1935- *WhoAm 94, WhoMW 93*
Powers, Paul William 1962- *WhoMW 93*
Powers, Paullete 1941- *WhoWest 94*
Powers, Philip Hemsley 1937- *WhoAmL 94*
Powers, Pierce William, Jr. 1946- *WhoMW 93*
Powers, Pike, Jr. 1941- *WhoAm 94, WhoAmL 94*
Powers, Ramon Sidney 1939- *WhoAm 94*
Powers, Ray Lloyd 1929- *WhoAmP 93, WhoWest 94*
Powers, Richard d1963 *WhoHol 92*
Powers, Richard Augustine, III 1932- *WhoAm 94, WhoAmL 94*
Powers, Richard Dale 1927- *WhoAm 94*
Powers, Richard F., III 1946- *WhoAm 94, WhoFI 94*
Powers, Richard M. 1921- *EncSF 93*
Powers, Robert M. 1942- *WrDr 94*
Powers, Runas, Jr. 1938- *WhoBlA 94, WhoScEn 94*
Powers, Samuel Joseph, Jr. 1917-1991 *WhAm 10*
Powers, Sarah Ann 1958- *WhoAmL 94*
Powers, Sharon A. 1955- *WhoWest 94*
Powers, Stefanie 1942- *IntMPA 94, WhoHol 92*
Powers, Stefanie 1945- *WhoAm 94*
Powers, Stephen 1936- *WhoWest 94*
Powers, Stephen E. 1940- *WhoAmL 94*
Powers, Thomas Edward 1948- *WhoFI 94*
Powers, Thomas Moore 1940- *WhoAm 94*
Powers, Tim *WrDr 94*
Powers, Tim(othy) 1952- *EncSF 93*
Powers, Timothy Eugene 1955- *WhoAmL 94*
Powers, Tom d1955 *WhoHol 92*
Powers, W. Alex 1940- *WhoAmA 93*
Powers, Werner A. 1951- *WhoAmL 94*
Powers, William D. *WhoAmP 93*
Powers, William Francis 1940- *WhoAm 94*
Powers, William Jennings 1930- *WhoAm 94*
Powers, William Shotwell 1910- *WhoAmP 93*
Powers, William T. 1926- *WrDr 94*
Powers, Winston D. 1930- *AfrAmG [port]*
Powerscourt, Viscount 1935- *Who 94*
Powerscourt, Sheila, Viscountess 1906-1992 *WrDr 94N*
Powis, Earl of d1993 *Who 94N*
Powis, Earl of 1952- *Who 94*
Powis, Alfred 1930- *IntWW 93, WhoAm 94, WhoFI 94, WhoScEn 94*
Powis, Constance Gail 1946- *WhoAmL 94*
Powledge, Fred 1935- *WrDr 94*
Powlen, David Michael 1953- *WhoAm 94, WhoAmL 94*
Powles, Guy (Richardson) 1905- *Who 94*
Powles, John G. 1936- *WhoIns 94*
Powles, Peter B. 1936- *WhoAm 94*
Powless, David Griffin 1953- *WhoMW 93*
Powless, Kenneth Barnett 1917- *WhoMW 93*
Powlett *Who 94*
Powley, Bryan d1962 *WhoHol 92*
Powley, Donald 1955- *WhoAmA 93*
Powley, Elizabeth Anne 1950- *WhoMW 93*
Powley, John Albert 1936- *Who 94*
Powling, Chris 1943- *WrDr 94*
Pownall, David 1938- *ConAu 18AS [port], ConDr 93, ConTFT 11, WrDr 94*
Pownall, Frederick M. 1937- *WhoAmL 94*
Pownall, Henry Charles 1927- *Who 94*
Pownall, John Harvey 1933- *Who 94*
Pownall, John Lionel 1929- *Who 94*
Pownall, Leon *WhoHol 92*
Pownall, Leslie Leigh 1921- *Who 94*
Pownall, Malcolm Wilmor 1933- *WhoAm 94*
Pownall, Mary Ann *NewGrDO*
Pownall, Michael Graham 1949- *Who 94*
Pownall, Thomas 1722-1805 *WhAmRev*
Powney, Clare *WhoHol 92*
Powsner, Gary 1952- *WhoScEn 94*
Powter, Susan *NewYTBS 93 [port]*
Powys *Who 94*
Powys, John Cowper 1872-1963 *BlmGEL, EncSF 93*
Powys, Theodore Francis 1875-1953 *BlmGEL*
Poy, Glenn Derrick 1957- *WhoWest 94*
Poyarkov, Vasily Danilovich fl. 164-?- *WhWE*
Poydock, Mary Eymard 1910- *WhoAm 94*
Poyer, David *DrAPF 93*
Poyer, David C. 1949- *EncSF 93*
Poyer, Joe 1939- *EncSF 93, WrDr 94*
Poyner, James Marion 1914- *WhoAm 94*
Poyner, Ken *DrAPF 93*
Poynor, Deborah Ann 1952- *WhoMW 93*
Poynor, Lana Paulette 1963- *WhoWest 94*
Poynter, Bill Charles 1935- *WhoAmP 93*
Poynter, James Morrison 1939- *WhoWest 94*
Poynter, John Riddoch 1929- *IntWW 93*
Poynter, Judy Fensterbusch 1950- *WhoMW 93*
Poynter, Marion Knauss 1926- *WhoAm 94*
Poynter, Melissa Venable 1949- *WhoFI 94*
Poynter, Philip A. 1942- *WhoIns 94*
Poynton, (Arthur) Hilton 1905- *Who 94*
Poynton, (John) Orde 1906- *Who 94*
Poyntz, Samuel Greenfield *Who 94*
Poyntz, Samuel Greenfield 1926- *IntWW 93*
Poyo, Gerald E. 1950- *WhoHisp 94*
Poyser, Victoria *EncSF 93*
Poythress, David Bryan 1943- *WhoAm 94*
Poythress, Stephanie Lynn 1964- *WhoMW 93*
Poza, Ernesto J. 1950- *WhoFI 94*
Poza, Margarita 1948- *WhoHisp 94*
Pozdro, John Walter 1923- *WhoAm 94*
Pozefsky, William 1937- *WhoAmL 94*
Pozela, Juras 1925- *IntWW 93*
Pozen, Walter 1933- *WhoAm 94*
Poznanski, Andrew Karol 1931- *WhoAm 94*
Pozner, Louis-Jack 1946- *WhoAmL 94*
Pozner, Vladimir 1934- *WrDr 94*
Pozo-Diaz, Martha del Carmen 1965- *WhoAmL 94*
Pozorski, Joseph Michael, Jr. 1957- *WhoAmL 94*
Pozza, Clarence L. 1948- *WhoAm 94, WhoAmL 94*
Pozzatti, Rudy O. 1925- *WhoAmA 93*
Pozzatti, Rudy Otto 1925- *WhoAm 94*
Pozzessere, Heather Graham *ConAu 141, WrDr 94*
Pozzetto, Renato *WhoHol 92*
Pozzi, Angelo 1932- *WhoScEn 94*
Pozzi, Anna fl. 1776- *NewGrDO*
Pozzi, Antonia 1912-1938 *BlmGWL*
Pozzi, Lucio 1935- *WhoAmA 93*
Pozzo, Modesta *BlmGWL*
Pozzoni(-Anastasi), Antonietta 1846-1914 *NewGrDO*
Pozzuoli, Joseph Anthony 1953- *WhoAmL 94*
Praagh, Peggy van *IntDcB*
Prabhakar, Arati 1959- *WhoAm 94, WhoAmP 93, WhoAsA 94, WhoScEn 94*
Prabhjot Kaur 1924- *IntWW 93*
Prabhu, R. D. *WhoAsA 94*
Prabhudas, Mercy Ratnavathy 1960- *WhoScEn 94*
Prabhudesai, Mukund M. 1942- *WhoAsA 94, WhoMW 93*
Pracht, Drenda Kay 1952- *WhoMW 93*
Prachthauser, Don Carl 1951- *WhoAmL 94*
Prack, Rudolf d1981 *WhoHol 92*
Pracko, Bernard F., II 1945- *WhoAmA 93*
Pracko, Bernard Francis, II 1945- *WhoWest 94*
Pracy, Robert 1921- *Who 94*
Praczukowski, Edward Leon 1930- *WhoAmA 93*
Prada, Alfredo Sadi 1934- *WhoHisp 94*
Prada, Antonio J. 1946- *WhoHisp 94*
Prada, Jose Maria d1978 *WhoHol 92*
Prada, Michel Andre Jean Edmond 1940- *IntWW 93*
Pradal, Bruno *WhoHol 92*
Prade, Jean Noel Cresta 1946- *WhoFI 94*
Pradham, Sahana *WhoWomW 91*
Pradhan, Shekhar 1953- *WhoAsA 94*
Pradhan, Trilochan 1929- *IntWW 93*
Pradier, Henri Joseph Marie 1931- *IntWW 93*
Prado, Adelia 1936- *BlmGWL*
Prado, Bessie A. 1953- *WhoHisp 94*
Prado, Cesar, Jr. 1945- *WhoHisp 94*
Prado, Edward Charles 1947- *WhoAm 94, WhoAmL 94, WhoHisp 94*
Prado, Faustino Lucio 1946- *WhoHisp 94*
Prado, Gerald M. 1946- *WhoAm 94*
Prado, Holly *DrAPF 93*
Prado, Huberto Walterio 1940- *WhoHisp 94*
Prado, Jesus M. *WhoHisp 94*
Prado, Luis Antonio 1948- *WhoHisp 94*
Prado, Marcial 1933- *WhoHisp 94*
Prado, Maria Esther 1959- *WhoHisp 94*
Prado, Marta 1951- *WhoHisp 94*
Prado, Melvin Ralph 1955- *WhoHisp 94*
Prado, Neilton Goncalves 1940- *WhoScEn 94*
Prado, Perez d1989 *WhoHol 92*
Prado, Raul C. 1949- *WhoHisp 94*
Prado Aranguiz, Jorge Jose 1937- *IntWW 93*
Pradon, Jacques 1644-1698 *GuFrLit 2*
Prador, Irene 1912- *WhoHol 92*
Prados, David Michael 1957- *WhoAmL 94*
Prados, Emilio 1899-1962 *DcLB 134 [port]*
Prados, John William 1929- *WhoAm 94, WhoScEn 94*
Pradot, Marcelle d1982 *WhoHol 92*
Prado Vallejo, Julio 1924- *IntWW 93*
Prady, Norman 1933- *WhoAm 94, WhoMW 93*
Pradzynski, Andrzej Henryk 1924- *WhoScEn 94*
Praed, Michael *WhoHol 92*
Praed, Rosa 1851-1935 *BlmGWL*
Praeger, Frederick A. 1915- *WhoAmA 93*
Praeger, Frederick Amos 1915- *IntWW 93*
Praeger, Sandy 1944- *WhoAmP 93*
Praetorius, Johann Philipp 1696?-1766? *NewGrDO*
Praetorius, William Albert, Sr. 1924- *WhoAm 94*
Prag, Arthur Barry 1938- *WhoWest 94*
Prag, Derek 1923- *Who 94*
Prag, John *Who 94*
Prag, (Andrew) John (Nicholas Warburg) 1941- *Who 94*
Pragana, Rildo Jose Da Costa 1951- *WhoScEn 94*
Prager, Alice Heinecke 1930- *WhoAm 94*
Prager, David 1918- *WhoAm 94, WhoAmP 93*
Prager, David A. 1913- *WhoAmA 93*
Prager, Gary Joseph 1949- *WhoFI 94*
Prager, Jonas 1938- *WhoFI 94*
Prager, Michael Haskell 1948- *WhoScEn 94*
Prager, Stanley d1972 *WhoHol 92*
Prager, Stephen 1928- *WhoAm 94*
Prager, Susan Westerberg 1942- *WhoAm 94, WhoAmL 94, WhoWest 94*
Pragnell, Anthony William 1921- *Who 94*
Pragnell, Festus 1905-1965? *EncSF 93*
Prago, Albert d1993 *NewYTBS 93*
Prague, Edith G. 1925- *WhoAmP 93*
Prah, Pamela Marie 1963- *WhoAm 94*
Praher, Adelheid 1933- *WhoWomW 91*
Prais, Sigbert Jon 1928- *Who 94*
Prakapas, Dorothy 1928- *WhoAmA 93*
Prakapas, Eugene Joseph 1932- *WhoAm 94, WhoAmA 93*
Prakash, Louise 1943- *WhoScEn 94*
Prakash, Ravi 1941- *WhoAm 94*
Prakash, Ravi 1950- *WhoScEn 94*
Prakash, Satya 1938- *WhoAm 94*
Prakash, Shamsher 1933- *WhoAsA 94, WhoFI 94, WhoMW 93*
Prakke, Lucas 1938- *IntWW 93*
Prakup, Barbara Lynn 1957- *WhoFI 94, WhoMW 93*
Prall, Bert R. 1895- *WhAm 10*
Prall, Stuart E. 1929- *WrDr 94*
Pramer, David 1923- *WhoAm 94*
Pramoedya Ananta Toer 1925- *IntWW 93*
Pramoj, Mom Rachawongse Kukrit 1911- *IntWW 93*
Pramoj, Mom Rachawongse Seni 1905- *IntWW 93*
Pramuk, Edward Richard 1936- *WhoAmA 93*
Pran, Peter Christian 1935- *WhoAm 94*
Prance, Claude A(nnett) 1906- *ConAu 43NR*
Prance, Ghillean Tolmie 1937- *IntWW 93, Who 94*
Prandelli, Giacinto 1914- *NewGrDO*
Prandini, Giovanni 1943- *IntWW 93*
Prange, Arthur Jergen, Jr. 1926- *WhoAm 94*
Prange, Roy Leonard, Jr. 1945- *WhoAm 94*
Prange, Sally Bowen 1927- *WhoAmA 93*
Pranger, Robert (J.) 1931- *WrDr 94*
Pranger, Robert John 1931- *WhoAmP 93*
Prankerd, Thomas Arthur John 1924- *Who 94*
Pranses, Anthony Louis 1920- *WhoAm 94*
Prante, Franklin C. 1947- *WhoAmP 93*
Prantera, Amanda 1942- *WrDr 94*
Prapas Charusathira, General *IntWW 93*
Pras, Robert Thomas 1941- *WhoAm 94*
Prasad, Ananda Shiva 1928- *WhoAm 94*
Prasad, B.H. 1955- *WhoScEn 94*
Prasad, Birendra 1949- *WhoMW 93*
Prasad, Brij 1942- *WhoFI 94*
Prasad, Chandan 1941- *WhoScEn 94*
Prasad, Jayasimha Swamy 1948- *WhoWest 94*
Prasad, K. Venkatesh 1959- *WhoScEn 94*
Prasad, Marehalli Gopalan 1950- *WhoAsA 94, WhoScEn 94*
Prasad, Rajendra 1945- *WhoWest 94*
Prasad, Rameshwar 1936- *WhoAsA 94*
Prasad, Ramjee 1946- *WhoScEn 94*
Prasad, Ravi 1944- *WhoScEn 94*
Prasad, Satish Chandra 1944- *WhoScEn 94*
Prasad, Surya Sattiraju *WhoScEn 94*
Prasada, Krishna *Who 94N*
Prasasvinitchai, Sudhee 1931- *Who 94*
Prashar, Usha Kumari 1948- *Who 94*
Prassel, Allen William 1922- *WhoAmP 93*
Prasuhn, Alan Lee 1938- *WhoScEn 94*
Prat, Jordi, Jr. 1949- *WhoHisp 94*
Pratchett, Terence David John 1948- *Who 94*
Pratchett, Terry 1948- *EncSF 93, IntWW 93, WrDr 94*
Prate, Alain 1928- *IntWW 93*
Pratella, Francesco Balilla 1880-1955 *NewGrDO*
Prater, Arlene 1947- *WhoAmL 94*
Prater, Oscar L. *WhoBlA 94*
Prater, Walter Lloyd 1955- *WhoWest 94*
Prater, Willis Richard 1942- *WhoMW 93*
Prather, Brenda Joyce 1956- *WhoScEn 94*
Prather, Charles Edward 1938- *WhoWest 94*
Prather, Denzil Lewis 1921- *WhoScEn 94*
Prather, Donna Ruth 1957- *WhoMW 93*
Prather, Gerald L. 1935- *WhoAm 94*
Prather, Jeffrey Lynn 1941- *WhoBlA 94*
Prather, Joan 1951- *WhoHol 92*
Prather, John Gideon 1919- *WhoAmL 94*
Prather, John Gideon, Jr. 1946- *WhoAmL 94*
Prather, Joseph W. 1939- *WhoAmP 93*
Prather, Kenneth Earl 1933- *WhoAmL 94*
Prather, Lee d1958 *WhoHol 92*
Prather, Lenore L. 1931- *WhoAmP 93*
Prather, Lenore Loving 1931- *WhoAm 94, WhoAmL 94*
Prather, Lynnette Marie 1968- *WhoMW 93*
Prather, R. William, III 1962- *WhoMW 93*
Prather, Richard Scott 1921- *WrDr 94*
Prather, Rita Catherine 1948- *WhoScEn 94*
Prather, Thomas L., Jr. 1940- *WhoBlA 94*
Prather, Thomas Levi, Jr. 1940- *AfrAmG [port]*
Prati, Alessio 1750-1788 *NewGrDO*
Pratley, Alan Sawyer 1933- *Who 94*
Pratley, Clive William 1929- *Who 94*
Pratley, David Illingworth 1948- *Who 94*
Pratley, Gerald *IntMPA 94*

Prats, Christopher Thomas 1941- WhoHisp 94
Prats, Jorge J. 1945- WhoHisp 94
Prats, Michael 1925- WhoAm 94
Pratt Who 94
Pratt, Albert 1911- WhoAm 94
Pratt, Alexander H., Jr. 1945- WhoAmL 94
Pratt, Alexander Thomas 1938- WhoBlA 94
Pratt, Anthony Malcolm G. Who 94
Pratt, Camden Who 94
Pratt, (Richard) Camden 1947- Who 94
Pratt, Carroll Cornelius 1894- WhAm 10
Pratt, (John) Christopher 1935- IntWW 93
Pratt, Christopher Leslie 1947- Who 94
Pratt, Clara Collette 1948- WhoWest 94
Pratt, Cornelia Atwood d1929 EncSF 93
Pratt, Dallas 1914- WhoAmA 93
Pratt, Dan Edwin 1924- WhoAm 94
Pratt, Dana Joseph 1926- WhoAm 94
Pratt, David Lee 1957- WhoScEn 94
Pratt, David Terry 1934- WhoAm 94
Pratt, Diane Adele 1951- WhoAm 94, WhoMW 93
Pratt, Donald Henry 1937- WhoFI 94
Pratt, Donald Oliver 1944- WhoAmL 94
Pratt, Dudley 1897-1975 WhoAmA 93N
Pratt, E(dwin) J(ohn) 1883?-1964 ConAu 141
Pratt, Edmund T., Jr. 1927- IntWW 93
Pratt, Edmund Taylor, Jr. 1927- WhoAm 94, WhoFI 94
Pratt, Edward Taylor, Jr. 1923- WhoAm 94
Pratt, Elizabeth Southwick d1964 WhoAmA 93N
Pratt, Eugene Frank 1946- WhoFI 94
Pratt, (Murray) Fletcher 1897-1956 EncSF 93
Pratt, Frances 1913- WhoAmA 93
Pratt, (Arthur) Geoffrey 1922- Who 94
Pratt, (Ewart) George 1917- Who 94
Pratt, George Byington, III 1936- WhoMW 93
Pratt, George C. 1928- WhoAmP 93
Pratt, George Cheney 1928- WhoAm 94, WhoAmL 94
Pratt, George Janes, Jr. 1948- WhoWest 94
Pratt, Harold Irving 1937- WhoAmL 94
Pratt, Henry Lucius 1920- WhoWest 94
Pratt, Hugh MacDonald d1993 Who 94N
Pratt, Irene A. 1924- WhoAmP 93
Pratt, J. C. 1927- WhoBlA 94
Pratt, Jack d1938 WhoHol 92
Pratt, Jack E. WhoAmP 93
Pratt, Jeremy 1954- WhoScEn 94
Pratt, John d1986 WhoHol 92
Pratt, John Adams, Jr. 1930- WhoAm 94
Pratt, John Clark 1932- WhoWest 94, WrDr 94
Pratt, John Helm 1910- CngDr 93, WhoAm 94
Pratt, John Michael 1946- WhoAmP 93
Pratt, John Rolla 1940- WhoAm 94
Pratt, John Sherman 1952- WhoAm 94
Pratt, John Winsor 1931- WhoAm 94
Pratt, Joseph Hyde, Jr. 1911- WhoAm 94
Pratt, Judith A. 1941- WhoAmP 93
Pratt, Judson WhoHol 92
Pratt, Katharin 1947- WhoAmP 93
Pratt, Kerry D. 1960- WhoAmP 93
Pratt, Lawrence Arthur 1907- WhoAm 94
Pratt, Lawrence D. 1942- WhoAmP 93
Pratt, Leighton C. 1923- WhoAmP 93
Pratt, Linda Ray 1943- WhoMW 93
Pratt, Louis Hill 1937- WhoBlA 94
Pratt, Lynn d1930 WhoHol 92
Pratt, Mable 1943- WhoBlA 94
Pratt, Mark Ernest 1939- WhoScEn 94
Pratt, Matthew 1734-1805 WhAmRev
Pratt, Matthew Rick 1928- WhoAm 94
Pratt, Melvin Lemar 1946- WhoBlA 94
Pratt, Michael d1976 WhoHol 92
Pratt, Michael John 1933- Who 94
Pratt, Michael Theodore 1943- WhoAm 94
Pratt, Minnie Bruce DrAPF 93
Pratt, Minnie Bruce 1946- GayLL
Pratt, Parley Parker 1807-1857 DcAmReB 2
Pratt, Peter Lynn 1927- Who 94
Pratt, Philip Chase 1920- WhoAm 94
Pratt, Purnell d1941 WhoHol 92
Pratt, Randall Aden 1921- WhoFI 94, WhoWest 94
Pratt, Renee WhoAmP 93
Pratt, Richard Houghton 1934- WhoAm 94
Pratt, Richard T. 1937- WhoAmP 93
Pratt, Richardson, Jr. 1923- WhoAm 94
Pratt, Robert Cranford 1926- WhoAm 94
Pratt, Robert George 1943- WhoScEn 94
Pratt, Robert Wayne 1967- WhoFI 94
Pratt, Robert Windsor 1950- WhoAm 94, WhoAmL 94
Pratt, Ron d1987 WhoHol 92
Pratt, Ronald Franklin 1948- WhoFI 94, WhoWest 94
Pratt, Rosalie Rebollo 1933- WhoWest 94
Pratt, Ruth Jones 1923- WhoBlA 94
Pratt, S. Mason, Jr. 1938- WhoAmL 94
Pratt, Silas G(amaliel) 1846-1916 NewGrDO
Pratt, Stephen R. 1967- WhoFI 94
Pratt, Steven Harold 1946- WhoAmL 94
Pratt, Terrence Wendall 1940- WhoAm 94
Pratt, Timothy Jean Geoffrey 1934- Who 94
Pratt, Vernon Gaither 1940- WhoAmA 93
Pratt, Walden Penfield 1928- WhoWest 94
Pratt, Waldo Elliott, Jr. 1895- WhAm 10
Pratt, Warren Thomas 1949- WhoAmL 94
Pratt, William Crouch, Jr. 1927- WhoAm 94
Pratte, Lise 1950- WhoAm 94
Pratte, Robert John 1948- WhoAm 94
Pratter, Gene E. K. 1949- WhoAm 94, WhoAmL 94
Pratter, Robert L. 1945- WhoAmL 94
Prattis, Lawrence 1926- WhoBlA 94
Pratto, Felicia 1961- WhoScEn 94
Pratzel, Alan David 1952- WhoAmL 94
Prausnitz, John Michael 1928- WhoAm 94, WhoWest 94
Pravda, George d1985 WhoHol 92
Pravda, Muriel WhoAmA 93
Pravdenko, Serhii Makarovych 1949- LngBDD
Pravel, Bernarr Roe 1924- WhoAm 94, WhoAmL 94
Praw, Albert Z. 1948- WhoAm 94, WhoFI 94
Prawer, S(iegbert) S(alomon) 1925- WrDr 94
Prawer, Siegbert Salomon 1925- IntWW 93, Who 94
Prawer Jhabvala, Ruth Who 94
Prawiro, Radius 1928- IntWW 93
Praxilla fl. 5th cent.BC- BlmGWL
Praxmarer, Karin 1944- WhoWomW 91
Praxy, Raoul d1967 WhoHol 92
Pray, Carrel Myers 1919- WhoMW 93
Pray, Charles P. 1945- WhoAmP 93
Pray, David W. 1942- WhoIns 94
Pray, Donald Eugene 1932- WhoAmL 94
Pray, Donald George 1928- WhoScEn 94
Pray, John Allan 1949- WhoAmL 94
Pray, Lloyd Charles 1919- WhoAm 94, WhoScEn 94
Pray, Ralph Emerson 1926- WhoScEn 94, WhoWest 94
Pray, Ralph Marble, III 1938- WhoAm 94, WhoAmL 94
Prazenka, William, Jr. 1957- WhoFI 94
Preacher, Stephen Preston 1949- WhoWest 94
Preate, Ernest D., Sr. 1909- WhoAm 94
Preate, Ernest D., Jr. 1940- WhoAm 94, WhoAmL 94, WhoAmP 93
Preate, Joseph Gerard 1961- WhoFI 94
Prebble, David Lawrence 1932- Who 94
Prebble, John (Edward Curtis) 1915- WrDr 94
Prebble, John Edward Curtis 1915- Who 94
Prebble, Richard William 1948- IntWW 93
Prebil, Richard Louis 1951- WhoAmL 94
Preble, Darrell W. 1946- WhoScEn 94
Preble, Duane 1936- WhoWest 94
Preble, Edward 1761-1807 WhAmRev
Preble, Laurence George 1939- WhoAm 94, WhoAmL 94
Preble, Lou-Ann M. WhoAmP 93
Preble, Michael C. 1966- WhoAmP 93
Preble, Robert Curtis, Jr. 1922- WhoIns 94, WhoMW 93
Prebluda, Harry Jacob 1911-1990 WhAm 10
Prebula, Mary Aunita 1953- WhoAmL 94
Prechtl, Victor Lee 1946- WhoFI 94
Preciado, Steve Manuel 1954- WhoHisp 94
Preckwinkle, Toni WhoAmP 93
Precopio, Frank Mario 1925- WhoAm 94
Precourt, George Augustine 1934- WhoAm 94
Precourt, Lyman Arthur 1926- WhoAm 94
Preddy, Raymond Randall 1940- WhoAm 94
Predescu, Viorel N. 1950- WhoScEn 94
Predieri, Antonio c. 1650-1710 NewGrDO
Predieri, Luca Antonio 1688-1767 NewGrDO
Predpall, Daniel Francis 1946- WhoFI 94, WhoScEn 94
Preece, Betty P. WhoScEn 94
Preece, Derek Alan 1953- WhoWest 94
Preece, Grant 1943- WhoAmP 93
Preece, John Earl 1952- WhoMW 93
Preece, McCoy D. 1954- WhoWest 94
Preece, Nancy Ann 1960- WhoMW 93
Preece, Norma 1922- WhoWest 94
Preece, Raymond George 1927- WhoScEn 94
Preece, Warren Eversleigh 1921- WhoAm 94
Preede, Nydia 1926- WhoAmA 93
Preedom, Barry Mason 1940- WhoScEn 94
Preefer, John J. 1948- WhoAmL 94
Preeg, Ernest Henry 1934- WhoAm 94
Preeg, William Edward 1942- WhoAm 94, WhoScEn 94
Preer, Evalyn d1932 WhoHol 92
Preer, John Randolph, Jr. 1918- IntWW 93, WhoAm 94
Preetorius, Emil 1883-1973 NewGrDO
Prefontaine, Joan Wolf DrAPF 93
Pregardien, Christoph 1956- NewGrDO
Pregerson, Harry WhoAmP 93
Pregerson, Harry 1923- WhoAm 94, WhoAmL 94, WhoWest 94
Prehm, John Thomas, Jr. 1922- WhoFI 94, WhoMW 93
Preil, Gabriel d1993 NewYTBS 93
Preil, Gabriel (Joshua) 1911-1993 ConAu 141
Preis, Alfred 1911- WhoAmA 93
Preis, E. Frederick, Jr. 1949- WhoAmL 94
Preis, Mary Louise WhoAmP 93
Preis, Nancy Joan 1949- WhoFI 94
Preiser, Wolfgang Friedrich Ernst 1941- WhoAm 94
Preiskel, Barbara Scott 1924- WhoAm 94, WhoAmL 94, WhoBlA 94
Preiskel, Robert Howard 1922- WhoAm 94
Preiss, Alexandru Petre 1952- WhoAmA 93
Preiss, Beth 1954- WhoFI 94
Preiss, Byron (Cary) 1953- EncSF 93
Preiss, David Lee 1935- WhoAm 94
Preiss, Jack 1932- WhoAm 94, WhoMW 93, WhoScEn 94
Preiss, Wolfgang WhoHol 92
Preisser, Cherry d1964 WhoHol 92
Preisser, June d1984 WhoHol 92
Preissner, Edgar Daryl 1938- WhoScEn 94
Preissova, Gabriela 1862-1946 BlmGWL, NewGrDO
Preister, Donald G. 1946- WhoAmP 93, WhoMW 93
Prejean, Albert d1979 WhoHol 92
Prejean, Helen NewYTBS 93 [port]
Prejean, J. David 1940- WhoScEn 94
Prejean, Ruby D. 1925- WhoBlA 94
Prekop, Martin D. 1940- WhoAm 94
Prekop, Martin Dennis 1940- WhoAmA 93
Prell, Edward M. 1936- WhoMW 93
Prell, Joel James 1944- WhoWest 94
Prell, Martin 1918- WhoScEn 94
Prell, Michael Jack 1944- WhoAm 94
Prelle, Micheline WhoHol 92
Prelleur, Peter 1705?-1741 NewGrDO
Prelli, F. Philip 1948- WhoAmP 93
Prelog, Vladimir 1906- IntWW 93, Who 94, WhoScEn 94
Prelow, Arleigh 1953- WhoBlA 94
Prelutsky, Jack 1940- WrDr 94
Prem, F. Herbert, Jr. 1932- WhoAm 94, WhoAmL 94
Prem, Konald Arthur 1920- WhoAm 94
Premack, David 1925- WhoAm 94
Premadasa, Ranasinghe d1993 IntWW 93N, Who 94N
Premauer, Werner 1912- IntWW 93
Premcand 1880-1936 RfGShF
Prem Chand, D. 1916- IntWW 93
Preminger, Erik Lee WhoHol 92
Preminger, Erik Lee 1944- WrDr 94
Preminger, Otto d1986 WhoHol 92
Premo, Paul Mark 1942- WhoAm 94
Premont, Paul 1936- WhoFI 94
Prempree, Thongbliew 1935- WhoAm 94, WhoScEn 94
Premraj, A. N. 1945- WhoAsA 94
Prem Tinsulanonda, Gen. 1920- IntWW 93
Premus, Robert 1939- WhoFI 94, WhoScEn 94
Prendergast, (Christopher) Anthony 1931- Who 94
Prendergast, Brian 1948- WhoFI 94
Prendergast, Charles E. 1868-1948 WhoAmA 93N
Prendergast, George Aloysius 1933- WhoFI 94
Prendergast, James Francis 1917- WhoAmP 93
Prendergast, James T. d1993 NewYTBS 93
Prendergast, John Francis 1938- WhoMW 93
Prendergast, John Vincent d1993 Who 94N
Prendergast, Joseph Thomas, Jr. 1945- WhoAmP 93
Prendergast, Kieran Who 94
Prendergast, (Walter) Kieran 1942- IntWW 93, Who 94
Prendergast, Peter Thomas 1946- IntWW 93
Prendergast, Robert A. 1931- WhoScEn 94
Prendergast, Robert James Christie Vereker 1941- Who 94
Prendergast, Simone (Ruth) 1930- Who 94
Prendergast, Thomas A. 1933- WhoFI 94
Prendergast, Walter Gerard 1965- WhoScEn 94
Prendergast, William John 1942- WhoScEn 94, WhoWest 94
Prendes, Mercedes d1981 WhoHol 92
Preng, David Edward 1946- WhoAm 94, WhoFI 94
Prenovitz, Sheldon M. 1950- WhoFI 94
Prensky, Arthur Lawrence 1930- WhoAm 94
Prent, Mark 1947- WhoAmA 93
Prentice, Baron 1923- Who 94
Prentice, Ann Ethelynd 1933- WhoAm 94, WhoScEn 94
Prentice, Bridget Theresa 1952- Who 94
Prentice, Daniel David 1941- Who 94
Prentice, David Ramage 1943- WhoAmA 93
Prentice, Dixon Wright 1919- WhoAmP 93
Prentice, Eugene Miles, III 1942- WhoAm 94, WhoAmL 94, WhoFI 94
Prentice, Gordon 1951- Who 94
Prentice, James Stuart 1944- WhoAm 94
Prentice, (Hubert Archibald) John 1920- Who 94
Prentice, Keith 1940- WhoHol 92
Prentice, Margarita WhoAmP 93
Prentice, Margarita 1931- WhoHisp 94
Prentice, Norman Macdonald 1925- WhoAm 94
Prentice, Penelope DrAPF 93
Prentice, Reginald Ernest 1923- IntWW 93
Prentice, Robert A. 1945- WhoAmL 94
Prentice, Robert Craig 1951- WhoMW 93, WhoScEn 94
Prentice, Thomas 1919- Who 94
Prentice, Thomas Archer 1952- WhoAm 94
Prentice, Tim 1930- WhoAm 94
Prentice, William (Thomas) 1919- Who 94
Prentice, Winifred (Eva) 1910- Who 94
Prentiss, Ann WhoHol 92
Prentiss, C. J. WhoAmP 93
Prentiss, Charlotte EncSF 93
Prentiss, Ed WhoHol 92
Prentiss, Eleanor d1979 WhoHol 92
Prentiss, Lewis d1967 WhoHol 92
Prentiss, Paul E. 1943- WhoAmL 94
Prentiss, Paula 1939- IntMPA 94, WhoHol 92
Prentke, Richard Ottesen 1945- WhoAm 94, WhoAmL 94
Prenzlow, Elmer John-Charles, Jr. 1929- WhoMW 93
Preobrajenska, Olga 1871-1962 IntDcB [port]
Preobrazhenskaya, Olga 1871-1962 IntDcB [port]
Preobrazhenskaya, Olga Ivanova d1966 WhoHol 92
Preonas, George Elias 1943- WhoAm 94
Preovolos, Penelope Athene 1955- WhoAm 94, WhoWest 94
Preparata, Franco Paolo 1935- WhoAm 94
Presant, Sanford Calvin 1952- WhoAm 94, WhoAmL 94
Presas, Arturo WhoHisp 94
Presby, J. Thomas 1940- WhoAm 94
Presby, Shannon WhoHol 92
Preschlack, John Edward 1933- WhoAm 94
Prescod, Marsha BlmGWL
Prescot, Dray EncSF 93
Prescott, Caleb ConAu 42NR
Prescott, Casey 1946- WrDr 94
Prescott, David Marshall 1926- WhoAm 94, WhoWest 94
Prescott, Douglas W. 1951- WhoAmP 93
Prescott, Dray 1914- WrDr 94
Prescott, Harold Sturtevant, Jr. 1931- WhoFI 94
Prescott, J(ohn) R(obert) V(ictor) 1931- WrDr 94
Prescott, Jack GayLL
Prescott, Joel Henry 1941- WhoWest 94
Prescott, John Barry 1940- IntWW 93
Prescott, John F., Jr. 1950- WhoAmL 94
Prescott, John Herbert Dudley 1937- Who 94
Prescott, John Hernage 1935- WhoAm 94, WhoScEn 94
Prescott, John Leslie 1938- IntWW 93, Who 94

Prescott, John Mack 1921- WhoAm 94
Prescott, Kenneth Wade 1920- WhoAmA 93
Prescott, Lawrence Malcolm 1934- WhoScEn 94, WhoWest 94
Prescott, Mark 1948- Who 94
Prescott, Oliver 1731-1804 WhAmRev
Prescott, Peter George Addington 1924- Who 94
Prescott, Peter John 1936- Who 94
Prescott, Peter Richard Kyle 1943- Who 94
Prescott, Peter Sherwin 1935- WhoAm 94
Prescott, Richard 1725-1788 WhAmRev
Prescott, Richard Paul, Jr. 1939- WhoMW 93
Prescott, Robert 1725-1816 WhAmRev
Prescott, Samuel 1751-c. 1777 WhAmRev
Prescott, Wayne H. 1947- WhoAmL 94
Prescott, Westby William P. Who 94
Prescott, William 1726-1795 AmRev, WhAmRev
Presdorf, Karen Renwick 1955- WhoMW 93
Present, Arthur Jerome 1905-1989 WhAm 10
Present, Jess J. WhoAmP 93
Presgrave, Ralph 1898- WhAm 10
Preska, Loretta A. 1949- WhoAm 94, WhoAmL 94
Preska, Margaret Louise Robinson 1938- WhoAm 94, WhoMW 93
Presland, John David 1930- Who 94
Preslar, Len Broughton, Jr. 1947- WhoAm 94
Preslar-Eskew, Carolyn Elizabeth 1942- WhoMW 93
Presle, Micheline 1922- IntMPA 94, WhoHol 92
Presler, Gerald Allen 1945- WhoWest 94
Presler, Kristopher Keith 1968- WhoMW 93
Presley, Alice Ruth Weiss WhoScEn 94
Presley, Bobby W. 1931- WhoIns 94
Presley, Calvin Alonzo 1914- WhoBlA 94
Presley, Elvis d1977 WhoHol 92
Presley, Elvis Aaron 1935-1977 AmCulL [port]
Presley, Oscar Glen 1942- WhoBlA 94
Presley, Priscilla 1945- IntMPA 94, WhoAm 94, WhoHol 92
Presley, Robert B. 1924- WhoAmP 93
Presley, Robert Buel 1924- WhoWest 94
Presley, Stanley Patrick 1951- WhoAmP 93
Presnal, Billy Charles 1932- WhoAmP 93
Presnell, Gregory A. 1942- WhoAmL 94
Presnell, Harve 1933- WhoHol 92
Presner, Lewis A. 1945- ConAu 142
Press, Barry Harris Jay 1951- WhoWest 94
Press, Bill WhoAmP 93
Press, Charles 1922- WhoAm 94
Press, Edward 1913- WhoAm 94
Press, Fiona WhoHol 92
Press, Frank 1924- IntWW 93, Who 94, WhoAm 94, WhoAmP 93, WhoScEn 94, WrDr 94
Press, Harry Cody, Jr. 1931- WhoBlA 94
Press, Irving E. d1993 NewYTBS 93
Press, Jeffery Bruce 1947- WhoAm 94
Press, John (Bryant) 1920- WrDr 94
Press, John Bryant 1920- Who 94
Press, Lloyd Douglas, Jr. 1950- WhoWest 94
Press, Marvin d1968 WhoHol 92
Press, Michael S. 1948- WhoAmL 94
Press, O(tto) Charles 1922- WrDr 94
Press, Richard Stern 1939- WhoFI 94
Press, Santha WhoHol 92
Press, Simone Juda DrAPF 93
Press, Skip DrAPF 93
Press, Steve 1946- WhoAmP 93
Press, Tamara Natanovna 1937- IntWW 93
Press, Theodore L. 1943- WhoAmL 94
Press, William Henry 1948- WhoAm 94, WhoScEn 94
Pressel, Esther Joan 1937- WhoWest 94
Presser, Dorothy 1929- WhoAmP 93
Presser, Elena 1940- WhoAmA 93
Presser, Harriet Betty 1936- WhoAm 94
Presser, Josef 1907-1967 WhoAmA 93N
Presser, Leon 1940- WhoHisp 94
Presser, Stephen Bruce 1946- WhoAm 94, WhoAmL 94
Pressey, Junius Batten, Jr. 1947- WhoBlA 94
Pressey, Paul Matthew 1958- WhoBlA 94
Pressler, Herman Paul 1902- WhoAm 94
Pressler, Larry 1942- CngDr 93, IntWW 93, WhoAm 94, WhoAmP 93, WhoMW 93
Pressler, Philip Bernard 1946- WhoFI 94
Pressley, Fred G., Jr. 1953- WhoAm 94, WhoAmL 94
Pressley, James Ray 1946- WhoWest 94
Pressley, Stephen, Jr. 1947- WhoBlA 94
Pressly, Barbara B. 1937- WhoAmP 93
Pressly, Nancy Lee 1941- WhoAmA 93
Pressly, Thomas James 1919- WhoAm 94
Pressly, William Laurens 1944- WhoAmA 93
Pressman, Arthur Lewis 1945- WhoAmL 94
Pressman, Edward R. IntMPA 94, WhoHol 92
Pressman, Gregory P. 1944- WhoAmL 94
Pressman, J. J., Mrs. Who 94
Pressman, Judy Kolodny 1947- WhoAmL 94
Pressman, Lawrence 1939- IntMPA 94, WhoHol 92
Pressman, Michael 1950- IntMPA 94
Pressman, Norman W. 1948- WhoAmL 94
Pressman, Thane Andrew 1945- WhoWest 94
Pressmann, John F. 1952- WhoAmP 93
Presson, Ellis Wynn 1940- WhoAm 94
Presson, Francis Tennery 1925- WhoFI 94
Presson, Jason WhoHol 92
Prestage, James J. 1926- WhoBlA 94
Prestage, James Jordan 1926- WhoAm 94
Prestage, Jewel Limar 1931- WhoAm 94, WhoAmP 93, WhoBlA 94
Prestage, Terri WhoIns 94
Prestanski, Harry Thomas 1947- WhoMW 93
Prestbo, John Andrew 1941- WhoAm 94
Prestegaard, Peter 1942- WhoAm 94
Presti, Michael Richard 1955- WhoFI 94
Prestia, Michael Anthony 1931- WhoFI 94
Presting, Hartmut 1956- WhoScEn 94
Prestini, James Libero 1908- WhoAmA 93
Prestipino, Bart 1922- WhoAmP 93
Prestley, Peter Burgoyne 1945- WhoAmL 94
Preston Who 94
Preston, Alice Bolam 1889-1958 WhoAmA 93N
Preston, Andrew Joseph 1922- WhoAm 94, WhoScEn 94
Preston, Ann L. 1942- WhoAmA 93
Preston, Billy 1946- WhoBlA 94
Preston, Charles Bartley 1928- WhoFI 94
Preston, Charles Brian 1937- WhoScEn 94
Preston, Charles George 1940- WhoAmL 94
Preston, Charles R. WhoAmP 93
Preston, Colleen Ann 1955- WhoAmL 94
Preston, Daniel S. DrAPF 93
Preston, David Michael 1930- WhoAm 94
Preston, Dean Laverne 1953- WhoScEn 94
Preston, Donald 1941- WhoFI 94
Preston, Donald G. 1945- WhoFI 94
Preston, Douglas 1956- ConAu 141
Preston, Edward Lee 1925- WhoBlA 94
Preston, Eugene Anthony 1952- WhoBlA 94
Preston, F(rederick) Leslie 1903- Who 94
Preston, Faith 1921- WhoAm 94
Preston, Fayrene WrDr 94
Preston, Frances W. WhoAm 94
Preston, Franklin DeJuanette 1947- WhoBlA 94
Preston, Frederick Willard 1912- WhoAm 94
Preston, Geoffrey Averill 1924- Who 94
Preston, George Nelson 1938- WhoAmA 93, WhoBlA 94
Preston, Harriet Brown 1892-1961 WhoAmA 93N
Preston, Ian Mathieson Hamilton 1932- Who 94
Preston, Ivy (Alice) 1913- WrDr 94
Preston, J. A. WhoHol 92
Preston, James E. 1933- WhoAm 94, WhoFI 94
Preston, James M. 1874-1962 WhoAmA 93N
Preston, Jay Wilson 1956- WhoWest 94
Preston, Jean Rouse WhoAmP 93
Preston, Jeffrey William 1940- Who 94
Preston, Jerome 1898- WhAm 10
Preston, John DrAPF 93, WhoHol 92
Preston, John 1945- GayLL, WrDr 94
Preston, John Frederick, Jr. 1917-1988 WhAm 10
Preston, Joseph, Jr. WhoAmP 93
Preston, Joseph, Jr. 1947- WhoBlA 94
Preston, Karen Yvonne WhoMW 93
Preston, Kelly 1962- IntMPA 94, WhoHol 92
Preston, Kendall, Jr. 1927- WhoAm 94, WhoFI 94
Preston, Kenneth (Huson) 1901- Who 94
Preston, Lee 1944- WhoAmP 93
Preston, Leonard 1948- WhoBlA 94
Preston, Leslie Who 94
Preston, Lewis T. 1926- IntWW 93
Preston, Lewis Thompson 1926- WhoAm 94, WhoFI 94
Preston, Malcolm 1919- WhoAm 94
Preston, Malcolm H. 1920- WhoAmA 93
Preston, Mark 1956- WhoHisp 94
Preston, Mark I. 1938- WhoAm 94, WhoFI 94
Preston, Martha Sue 1952- WhoWest 94
Preston, Melvin Alexander 1921- WhoAm 94
Preston, Michael B. 1933- WhoBlA 94
Preston, Michael Richard 1927- Who 94
Preston, Mike WhoHol 92
Preston, Myles Park 1927- Who 94
Preston, Paul 1946- IntWW 93
Preston, Peter (Sansome) 1922- Who 94
Preston, Peter John 1938- IntWW 93, Who 94
Preston, R. Kevin 1959- WhoScEn 94
Preston, Ray 1947- WhoAmP 93
Preston, Reginald Dawson 1908- IntWW 93, Who 94, WrDr 94
Preston, Richard (Arthur) 1910- WrDr 94
Preston, Richard Arthur 1910- WhoAm 94
Preston, Richard Clark 1933- WhoBlA 94
Preston, Richard McCann 1954- WhoFI 94
Preston, Richard McKim 1947- WhoAm 94
Preston, Robert d1987 WhoHol 92
Preston, Robert Arthur 1944- WhoWest 94
Preston, Robert Bruce 1926- WhoAm 94
Preston, Robert F. 1929- WhoAmP 93
Preston, Robert Leslie 1942- WhoScEn 94
Preston, Robert Sheffey, III 1953- WhoFI 94
Preston, Ronald (Douglas Hildebrand) 1916- Who 94
Preston, Ronald Haydn 1913- Who 94
Preston, Rosalind 1935- Who 94
Preston, Samuel Hulse 1943- WhoAm 94
Preston, Seymour Stotler, III 1933- WhoAm 94, WhoFI 94
Preston, Simon John 1938- IntWW 93, Who 94
Preston, Swanee H. T., Jr. 1924- WhoBlA 94
Preston, Thomas 1537-1598 BlmGEL
Preston, Thomas c. 1730- WhAmRev
Preston, Thomas 1860-1900 DcNaB MP
Preston, Thomas Ronald 1936- WhoAm 94
Preston, Timothy William 1935- Who 94
Preston, Tobias James 1962- WhoWest 94
Preston, Walter James 1925- Who 94
Preston, Wayde 1930- WhoHol 92
Preston, William 1921- ConTFT 11
Preston, William Hubbard 1920- WhoAm 94
Prestopino, Frank J. 1949- WhoIns 94
Prestopino, Gregorio 1907- WhoAmA 93N
Prestowitz, Clyde Vincent 1941- WhoAm 94
Prestrud, Stuart H. 1919- WhoWest 94
Prestt, Arthur Miller 1925- Who 94
Prestt, Ian 1929- IntWW 93, Who 94
Prestwich, Michael (Charles) 1943- WrDr 94
Prestwich, Michael Charles 1943- Who 94
Prestwidge-Bellinger, Barbara Elizabeth 1945- WhoBlA 94
Prete, John Donald 1934- WhoAmP 93
Pretender BlmGEL
Preti, Luigi 1914- IntWW 93
Pretl, Michael Albert 1942- WhoAmL 94
Pretlow, James Gary 1949- WhoAmP 93
Pretlow, Theresa P. 1939- WhoMW 93
Pretoria, Bishop of 1936- Who 94
Preto-Rodas, Richard Anthony 1936- WhoAm 94
Pretre, Georges 1924- IntWW 93, NewGrDO
Pretti, Bradford Joseph 1930- WhoAm 94
Pretto-Ferro, Franklin David 1946- WhoHisp 94
Pretty, Arline d1978 WhoHol 92
Pretty, David Walter 1925- WhoIns 94
Pretty, Katharine Bridget 1945- Who 94
Prettyman, Elijah Barrett, Jr. 1925- WhoAm 94
Prettyman, Keith Arthur 1951- WhoIns 94
Prettyman, Quandra 1933- WhoBlA 94
Pretty-Shield c. 1857- EncNAR [port]
Preu, Dana WhoHol 92
Preuitt, James E. 1935- WhoAmP 93
Preus, David Walter 1922- WhoAm 94
Preus, Jacob Aall Ottesen 1920- WhoAm 94
Preuss, Arthur 1878-1944 NewGrDO
Preuss, Charles F. 1941- WhoAmL 94
Preuss, Gregory Edward 1946- WhoFI 94
Preuss, Paul 1942- EncSF 93, WrDr 94
Preuss, Roger 1922- WhoAmA 93
Preuss, Roger Emil 1922- WhoAm 94, WhoMW 93
Preuss, Ronald Stephen 1935- WhoAmL 94, WhoMW 93
Preusser, Joseph William 1941- WhoMW 93
Preusser, Robert Ormerod 1919- WhoAmA 93
Preval, Rene 1943- IntWW 93
Preve, Roberta Jean 1954- WhoAm 94
Prevedel, Frank 1932- WhoAmP 93
Prevedi, Bruno 1928-1988 NewGrDO
Prevelakis, Pandelis 1909-1986 IntDcT 2
Prevert, Jacques 1900-1977 IntDcF 2-4 [port]
Prevert, Pierre d1988 WhoHol 92
Previant, David 1910- WhoAmL 94
Previn, Andre 1929- IntDcF 2-4, IntMPA 94, WhoAm 94, WhoHol 92
Previn, Andre (George) 1929- Who 94, WrDr 94
Previn, Andre George 1929- IntWW 93
Previn, Charles d1973 WhoHol 92
Previs, John R. 1949- WhoAmL 94
Previtali, Fernando 1907-1985 NewGrDO
Previte, John Edward 1934- Who 94
Previte, Richard 1935- WhoWest 94
Prevo, Mary Ellen 1947- WhoWest 94
Prevor, Ruth Claire 1944- WhoScEn 94
Prevost, Antoine-Francois 1697-1763 NewGrDO
Prevost, Antoine-Francois, abbe 1697-1763 GuFrLit 2
Prevost, Augustine 1723-1786 WhAmRev
Prevost, Christopher (Gerald) 1935- Who 94
Prevost, Edward James 1941- WhoAm 94
Prevost, Eugene-Prosper 1809-1872 NewGrDO
Prevost, Francoise 1681-1741 IntDcB [port]
Prevost, Francoise 1930- WhoHol 92
Prevost, James A. d1993 NewYTBS 93
Prevost, James Mark WhAmRev
Prevost, Jeanne d1980 WhoHol 92
Prevost, Marie d1937 WhoHol 92
Prevost d'Exiles 1697-1763 GuFrLit 2
Prevot, Ferdinand c. 1800-1857? NewGrDO
Prevots, Naima 1935- WrDr 94
Prevoznik, Stephen Joseph 1929- WhoAm 94
Prew, Arthur Thomas, Jr. 1951- WhoMW 93
Prew, Diane Schmidt 1945- WhoScEn 94
Prewett, Gerd Birgitta 1955- WhoFI 94
Prewitt, Al Bert 1907- WhoBlA 94
Prewitt, Charles Thompson 1933- WhoAm 94, WhoScEn 94
Prewitt, Kenneth 1936- WhoAm 94, WrDr 94
Prewitt, Lena Voncille Burrell 1932- WhoBlA 94
Prewitt, Nathan Coleman 1964- WhoScEn 94
Prewitt, Thomas R., Jr. 1949- WhoAmL 94
Prewitt, William Chandler 1946- WhoFI 94
Prewoznik, Jerome Frank 1934- WhoAm 94, WhoAmL 94
Prey, Claude 1925- NewGrDO
Prey, Dick 1942- WhoIns 94
Prey, Hermann 1929- IntWW 93, NewGrDO, Who 94
Prey, Yvonne Mary 1945- WhoMW 93
Preyer, Lunsford Richardson 1919- WhoAmP 93
Preyer, Robert Otto 1922- WhoAm 94
Preysz, Louis Robert Fonss, III 1944- WhoFI 94
Prezeau, Louis E. 1943- WhoBlA 94
Prezeau, Maryse 1942- WhoBlA 94
Preziosi, Donald A. 1941- WhoAmA 93
Prezioso, Roman W., Jr. 1949- WhoAmP 93
Prezkop, John Joseph 1932- WhoFI 94
Prezzano, Wilbur John 1940- WhoAm 94
Prezzi, Wilma M. 1915- WhoAmA 93N
Prial, Nancy Beth 1957- WhoFI 94
Priaulx, Allan 1940- WhoAm 94
Priaulx, David Lloyd 1949- WhoFI 94
Pribanic, Victor Hunter 1954- WhoAmL 94
Pribble, Easton 1917- WhoAm 94, WhoAmA 93
Pribble, Edward David Lalor 1944- WhoAmL 94
Priber, Johann Gottlieb fl. 1734-1744 EncNAR
Pribilsky, Kevin Andrew 1963- WhoWest 94
Pribor, Hugo Casimer 1928- WhoScEn 94
Pribor, Jeffrey Douglas 1957- WhoFI 94
Pribram, Karl H(arry) WrDr 94
Pribram, Karl Harry 1919- WhoScEn 94
Pribramsky, Steven R. 1961- WhoFI 94
Pribyl, Vilem 1925-1990 NewGrDO
Pribylov, Gavrilo Loginovich fl. 178-?- WhWE
Prica, Srdja 1905- Who 94
Price, Adrian Hyde ConAu 140
Price, Alan 1942- WhoHol 92
Price, Alan Thomas 1949- WhoFI 94

Price, Albert H. 1922- *WhoBlA 94*
Price, Albert J. 1930- *WhoAmP 93*
Price, Alexander 1913- *WhoScEn 94*
Price, Alfred Douglas 1947- *WhoBlA 94*
Price, Alfred Lee 1935- *WhoAmL 94, WhoFI 94*
Price, Alice L. *DrAPF 93*
Price, Alonzo d1962 *WhoHol 92*
Price, Alvin Audis 1917- *WhoAm 94*
Price, Andrea R. 1959- *WhoBlA 94*
Price, Ann Hesse 1955- *WhoWest 94*
Price, Anne Kirkendall 1922- *WhoAmA 93*
Price, Anthony 1928- *WrDr 94*
Price, (Alan) Anthony 1928- *Who 94*
Price, Antony 1945- *IntWW 93*
Price, Arthur Richard 1951- *WhoAm 94, WhoFI 94, WhoWest 94*
Price, B. Byron *WhoAm 94*
Price, Barbara Gillette 1938- *WhoAmA 93*
Price, Barry *Who 94*
Price, (William Frederick) Barry 1925- *Who 94*
Price, Barry David Keith 1933- *Who 94*
Price, Bernard Albert 1944- *Who 94*
Price, Borden Bowne 1916- *WhoAmL 94*
Price, Brian *WhoHol 92*
Price, Bruce 1942- *WhoAmP 93*
Price, C. Hoyt 1918- *WhoFI 94*
Price, Caroline Leona 1947- *WhoFI 94*
Price, Cecil (John Layton) 1915-1991 *WrDr 94N*
Price, Cecil Ernest 1921- *Who 94*
Price, Charles 1940- *WhoBlA 94*
Price, Charles Eugene *WhoBlA 94*
Price, Charles H., II 1931- *IntWW 93, Who 94, WhoAm 94, WhoAmP 93, WhoMW 93*
Price, Charles (Keith Napier) Rugge- 1936- *Who 94*
Price, Charles Steven 1955- *WhoAmL 94*
Price, Charles T. *WhoAm 94*
Price, Charles T. 1944- *WhoAm 94*
Price, Charlton Reed 1927- *WhoMW 93*
Price, Chester B. 1885-1962 *WhoAmA 93N*
Price, Christopher 1932- *Who 94*
Price, Clara Sue 1953- *WhoAmP 93*
Price, Clayton S. 1874-1950 *WhoAmA 93N*
Price, Clifford Warren 1935- *WhoScEn 94*
Price, Curtis (Alexander) 1945- *NewGrDO*
Price, Curtis Alexander 1945- *Who 94*
Price, Cynthia Ann 1957- *WhoWest 94*
Price, Dafne *WhoHol 92*
Price, Dale *WhoAmP 93*
Price, Dalias Adolph 1913- *WhoAm 94*
Price, Dan Q. 1919- *WhoAmP 93*
Price, Dana Lynn 1965- *WhoMW 93*
Price, Daniel Martin 1955- *WhoAmL 94*
Price, David *Who 94*
Price, David (Ernest Campbell) 1924- *Who 94*
Price, (Maurice) David 1915- *Who 94*
Price, (Paul) David 1940- *WrDr 94*
Price, David B., Jr. 1945- *WhoBlA 94*
Price, David E. 1940- *CngDr 93*
Price, David Eugene 1940- *WhoAm 94, WhoAmP 93*
Price, David Lee 1934- *WhoBlA 94*
Price, Dennis d1973 *WhoHol 92*
Price, Dennis 1915-1973 *DcNaB MP*
Price, Dennis Lee 1930- *WhoAm 94, WhoScEn 94*
Price, Diane Miller 1943- *WhoAmA 93*
Price, Dolores Holland 1932- *WhoAmP 93*
Price, Dolores Rose 1961- *WhoAmP 93*
Price, Don K. 1910- *WhoAm 94*
Price, Don Krasher 1910- *IntWW 93*
Price, Donald Albert 1919- *WhoAm 94*
Price, Donald Ray 1939- *WhoAm 94, WhoScEn 94*
Price, Donald Wayne 1961- *WhoAmL 94*
Price, Doris C. *WhoAmA 93*
Price, Douglas Armstrong 1950- *WhoScEn 94*
Price, E. H. 1918- *WhoAmL 94*
Price, E(dgar) Hoffmann (Trooper) 1898-1988 *EncSF 93*
Price, Edgar Hilleary, Jr. 1918- *WhoAm 94*
Price, Edward Dean 1919- *WhoAm 94, WhoAmL 94, WhoWest 94*
Price, Edward J., III 1952- *WhoAmP 93*
Price, Elizabeth Cain 1934- *WhoScEn 94*
Price, Elizabeth Louise 1934- *WhoBlA 94*
Price, Eric Hardiman Mockford 1931- *Who 94*
Price, Faye Hughes *WhoBlA 94*
Price, Florence 1888-1953 *AfrAmAl 6*
Price, Francis (Caradoc Rose) 1950- *Who 94*
Price, Frank 1930- *IntMPA 94, IntWW 93, WhoAm 94, WhoWest 94*
Price, Frank (Leslie) 1922- *Who 94*
Price, Frederic Newlin 1884-1963 *WhoAmA 93N*
Price, Frederick Clinton 1927- *WhoScEn 94*
Price, Frederick Kenneth Cercie 1932- *WhoAm 94*
Price, Gail Elizabeth 1940- *WhoFI 94*
Price, Gail Elizabeth 1945- *WhoFI 94*
Price, Gail Mary 1935- *WhoAmP 93*
Price, Gareth 1939- *Who 94*
Price, Garrett 1897-1979 *WhoAmA 93N*
Price, Gary Paul 1948- *WhoMW 93*
Price, Gayl Baader 1949- *WhoFI 94, WhoWest 94*
Price, Geoffrey Alan *Who 94*
Price, George 1901- *WhoAmA 93*
Price, George (Cadle) 1919- *Who 94*
Price, George A. 1926- *WhoAmP 93*
Price, George Baker 1929- *AfrAmG [port], WhoBlA 94*
Price, George Cadle 1919- *IntWW 93*
Price, Georgie d1964 *WhoHol 92*
Price, Geraint *Who 94*
Price, (William) Geraint 1943- *Who 94*
Price, Gerald Alexander Lewin 1948- *Who 94*
Price, Glanville 1928- *WrDr 94*
Price, Glenda Delores 1939- *WhoBlA 94*
Price, Gordon A. 1947- *WhoFI 94*
Price, Griffith Baley, Jr. 1942- *WhoAm 94, WhoAmL 94*
Price, H. Joseph, Jr. 1953- *WhoAmL 94*
Price, Hal d1964 *WhoHol 92*
Price, Harold Archibald 1893-1990 *WhAm 10*
Price, Harrison Alan 1921- *WhoAm 94*
Price, Harry *WhoHol 92*
Price, Harry Steele, Jr. 1910- *WhoAm 94*
Price, Harvey Raymond 1947- *WhoMW 93*
Price, Henry J. 1937- *WhoAmL 94*
Price, Hilary Martin Connop 1912- *Who 94*
Price, Homer G. 1941- *WhoAmL 94*
Price, Hubert, Jr. *WhoAmP 93*
Price, Hugh B. 1941- *WhoAm 94*
Price, Hugh Bernard 1941- *WhoBlA 94*
Price, Humphrey Wallace 1954- *WhoWest 94*
Price, I. Edward 1942- *WhoFI 94*
Price, J(ohn) Maurice 1922- *Who 94*
Price, James D. *WhoAmP 93*
Price, James Gordon 1926- *IntWW 93, WhoAm 94, WhoMW 93*
Price, James H., III 1945- *WhoAmL 94*
Price, James Joseph 1911- *WhoAmP 93*
Price, James Melford 1921- *WhoScEn 94*
Price, James Newton 1947- *WhoAm 94*
Price, James Rogers 1942- *WhoBlA 94*
Price, James Thonen 1929- *WhoMW 93*
Price, James Tucker 1955- *WhoAmL 94*
Price, Janis *WhoMW 93*
Price, Jeannine Alleenica 1949- *WhoWest 94*
Price, Jeffrey Brian 1963- *WhoScEn 94*
Price, Joan Webster 1931- *WhoAmA 93*
Price, Joe 1935- *WhoAm 94, WhoWest 94*
Price, Joe (Allen) 1935- *WhoAmA 93*
Price, John d1987 *WhoHol 92*
Price, John Alan 1938- *Who 94*
Price, John Aley 1947- *WhoAm 94, WhoAmL 94*
Price, John Elwood 1935- *WhoBlA 94*
Price, John Lister Willis 1915- *Who 94*
Price, John Roy, Jr. 1938- *WhoAm 94*
Price, John Walter 1930- *Who 94*
Price, John William 1927- *WhoAm 94*
Price, Jonathan *DrAPF 93*
Price, Jonathan G. 1950- *WhoAm 94, WhoScEn 94*
Price, Joseph Charles 1854-1893 *AfrAmAl 6*
Price, Joseph Earl 1930- *WhoWest 94*
Price, Joseph Hubbard 1939- *WhoAm 94*
Price, Joseph L. 1931- *WhoBlA 94*
Price, Joseph Levering 1962- *WhoAm 94*
Price, Joseph Michael 1947- *WhoAm 94, WhoAmL 94*
Price, Joseph Sterling 1954- *WhoFI 94*
Price, Judith 1937- *WhoBlA 94*
Price, Jules Morton 1929- *WhoFI 94*
Price, Karen Overstreet 1964- *WhoScEn 94*
Price, Kate d1943 *WhoHol 92*
Price, Kathaleen Rae 1952- *WhoAmL 94*
Price, Kathleen McCormick 1932- *WhoWest 94*
Price, Keith Glenn 1941- *WhoWest 94*
Price, Kenneth 1935- *WhoAmA 93*
Price, Kingsley Blake 1917- *WrDr 94*
Price, Larry C. 1954- *WhoAm 94*
Price, Lawrence Craig 1953- *WhoWest 94*
Price, Lawrence Howard 1952- *WhoScEn 94*
Price, Leolin *Who 94*
Price, (Arthur) Leolin 1924- *Who 94*
Price, Leonard Russell 1942- *WhoAmP 93*
Price, Leonard Sidney 1922- *Who 94*
Price, Leontyne 1927- *AfrAmAl 6 [port], IntWW 93, Who 94, WhoAm 94, WhoBlA 94*
Price, (Mary Violet) Leontyne 1927- *NewGrDO [port]*
Price, Leslie Kenneth *WhoAmA 93*
Price, Leslie Victor 1920- *Who 94*
Price, Lisa DeNere 1958- *WhoMW 93*
Price, Lonny 1959- *WhoHol 92*
Price, Louis J. 1953- *WhoAmL 94*
Price, Lucy Key 1944- *WhoFI 94*
Price, Margaret (Berenice) 1941- *NewGrDO, Who 94*
Price, Margaret Berenice 1941- *IntWW 93*
Price, Margaret E. 1888- *WhoAmA 93N*
Price, Margaret P. *WhoAmP 93*
Price, Margaret Ruth 1956- *WhoWest 94*
Price, Marion Woodrow 1914- *WhoAm 94*
Price, Mark d1917 *WhoHol 92*
Price, Mark 1964- *WhoAm 94, WhoMW 93*
Price, Martin Burton 1928- *WhoAm 94*
Price, Mary Brent 1931- *WhoAmP 93*
Price, Megan D. 1954- *WhoAmP 93*
Price, Michael Benjamin 1940- *WhoAmA 93*
Price, Michael Scott 1966- *WhoMW 93*
Price, Minnie 1877-1957 *WhoAmA 93N*
Price, Mona Renita 1958- *WhoMW 93*
Price, Morgan Samuel 1947- *WhoAmA 93*
Price, Nancy *DrAPF 93*
Price, Nancy d1970 *WhoHol 92*
Price, Nicholas N. 1947- *WhoAmL 94*
Price, Nicholas Peter Lees 1944- *Who 94*
Price, Nick *WhoAm 94*
Price, Norman (Charles) 1915- *Who 94*
Price, Norman Mills 1877-1951 *WhoAmA 93N*
Price, Pamela Anita 1952- *WhoBlA 94*
Price, Pamela Odell 1945- *WhoAmL 94*
Price, Patricia Anne 1950- *WhoWest 94*
Price, Paul B. 1933- *WhoHol 92*
Price, Paul Buford 1932- *IntWW 93, WhoAm 94, WhoWest 94*
Price, Paul L. 1945- *WhoAmL 94*
Price, Paul Marnell 1959- *WhoAmL 94*
Price, Paul S. 1951- *WhoMW 93*
Price, Paul Sanford 1942- *WhoBlA 94*
Price, Pete c. 1868-1951 *EncNAR*
Price, Peter Bryan 1944- *Who 94*
Price, Peter Nicholas 1942- *Who 94*
Price, Peter Owen 1930- *Who 94*
Price, Peter S. *Who 94*
Price, Philip 1898-1989 *WhAm 10*
Price, Phillip G. *WhoBlA 94*
Price, Phyllis E. *DrAPF 93*
Price, Ralph *Who 94*
Price, (Llewelyn) Ralph 1912- *Who 94*
Price, Ramon B. 1933- *WhoBlA 94*
Price, Randall Craig 1960- *WhoAm 94*
Price, Ray 1926- *ConMus 11 [port], WhoAm 94*
Price, Raymond Alexander 1933- *WhoAm 94*
Price, Reynolds *DrAPF 93*
Price, Reynolds 1933- *WhoAm 94*
Price, (Edward) Reynolds 1933- *WrDr 94*
Price, Richard *DrAPF 93*
Price, Richard 1723-1791 *EncEth, WhAmRev*
Price, Richard 1941- *WhoAm 94*
Price, Richard George 1950- *WhoScEn 94*
Price, Richard Michael 1964- *WhoAmL 94*
Price, Richard Taft, Jr. 1954- *WhoFI 94, WhoWest 94*
Price, Rita F. *WhoAmA 93*
Price, Robert *IntWW 93, Who 94*
Price, Robert 1929- *WhoAm 94*
Price, Robert 1932- *WhoAm 94, WhoAmL 94, WhoFI 94*
Price, (James) Robert 1912- *IntWW 93, Who 94*
Price, Robert A. 1924- *WhoScEn 94*
Price, Robert Conrad, II 1958- *WhoWest 94*
Price, Robert Dale 1927- *WhoAmP 93*
Price, Robert E. 1942- *WhoAm 94, WhoFI 94, WhoWest 94*
Price, Robert Earle 1936- *WhoAmP 93*
Price, Robert Eben 1931- *WhoAm 94*
Price, Robert Edmunds 1926- *WhoScEn 94*
Price, Robert (John) G. *Who 94*
Price, Robert George 1928- *Who 94*
Price, Robert Ira 1921- *WhoAm 94*
Price, Robert Stanley 1937- *WhoAm 94*
Price, Roger d1990 *WhoHol 92*
Price, Roger (David) 1944- *WrDr 94*
Price, Roger (Taylor) 1921- *EncSF 93*
Price, Roger Allen 1952- *WhoMW 93*
Price, Roger Lawrence 1944- *WhoAmL 94*
Price, Roland John Stuart 1961- *WhoAm 94*
Price, Rollo Edward Crwys 1916- *Who 94*
Price, Ron *DrAPF 93*
Price, Ronald Francis 1926- *WrDr 94*
Price, Ronald Franklin 1948- *WhoScEn 94*
Price, Ronald James 1933- *WhoFI 94*
Price, Rosalie Pettus *WhoAmA 93*
Price, Roy Cantrell 1935- *WhoWest 94*
Price, Roy Kenneth 1916- *Who 94*
Price, S. David *DrAPF 93*
Price, Samuel d1992 *WhoBlA 94N*
Price, Sara J. *WhoAmA 93*
Price, Sherwood *WhoHol 92*
Price, Stanley d1955 *WhoHol 92*
Price, Stanley 1931- *WrDr 94*
Price, Stanley B. 1945- *WhoAmL 94*
Price, Stephen Richard 1952- *WhoFI 94*
Price, Stephen Richie 1955- *WhoAmP 93*
Price, Steven 1962- *WhoFI 94*
Price, Susan 1955- *WrDr 94*
Price, Susan M. 1950- *WhoMW 93*
Price, Suzanne Davis 1921- *WhoBlA 94*
Price, Ted d1928 *WhoHol 92*
Price, Terence *Who 94*
Price, (Benjamin) Terence 1921- *Who 94*
Price, Theodora Hadzisteliou 1938- *WhoMW 93*
Price, Thomas Allan 1944- *WhoMW 93*
Price, Thomas Benjamin 1920- *WhoAm 94*
Price, Thomas Emile 1921- *WhoAm 94, WhoMW 93*
Price, Thomas Frederick 1937- *WhoWest 94*
Price, Thomas Munro 1937- *WhoWest 94*
Price, Thomas Ransone 1934- *WhoAm 94, WhoScEn 94*
Price, Thomas Rowe 1898- *WhAm 10*
Price, Trevor Robert Pryce 1943- *WhoAm 94*
Price, V. B. *DrAPF 93*
Price, Victor (Henry John) 1930- *WrDr 94*
Price, Vincent 1911- *IntMPA 94, IntWW 93, WhoAmA 93, WhoHol 92*
Price, Vincent 1911-1993 *NewYTBS 93 [port], News 94-2*
Price, Vincent Leonard 1911- *WhoAm 94*
Price, Vivian William Cecil 1926- *Who 94*
Price, Wallace Walter 1921- *WhoBlA 94*
Price, Walter Lee 1914- *WhoAmL 94*
Price, Warren *WhoAmP 93*
Price, Warren, III 1943- *WhoAm 94, WhoAmL 94, WhoWest 94*
Price, Weldon R. *WhoAmP 93*
Price, Westcott Wilkin, III 1939- *WhoFI 94, WhoWest 94*
Price, William *DrAPF 93*
Price, William Anthony 1959- *WhoMW 93, WhoScEn 94*
Price, William Charles d1993 *Who 94N*
Price, William George 1934- *Who 94*
Price, William James 1918- *WhoAm 94*
Price, William James, IV 1924- *WhoAm 94*
Price, William John R. *Who 94*
Price, William R., Jr. 1952- *WhoAmP 93*
Price, William Ray, Jr. 1952- *WhoAmL 94, WhoMW 93*
Price, William S. 1942- *WhoAmL 94*
Price, William S., III 1923- *WhoBlA 94*
Price, William Sloane 1939- *WhoFI 94*
Price, Willis Joseph 1931- *WhoAm 94, WhoFI 94*
Price, Winford Hugh Protheroe 1926- *Who 94*
Price, Zane Herbert 1922- *WhoScEn 94*
Price Boday, Mary Kathryn 1945- *WhoFI 94*
Price-Curtis, William 1944- *WhoBlA 94*
Price Evans, David Alan *Who 94*
Price Jones, Laurel Galbraith 1948- *WhoMW 93*
Price-Mars, Jean 1875-1969 *BlkWr 2*
Pricer, Jamie Lee 1948- *WhoWest 94*
Pricer, Wayne Francis 1935- *WhoMW 93*
Pricer, Wilbur David 1935- *WhoAm 94*
Price Radford, Cheryl Lynn 1955- *WhoMW 93*
Prichard, E. Allen 1949- *WhoAmL 94*
Prichard, Edgar Allen 1920- *WhoAm 94*
Prichard, Harold Arthur 1871-1947 *EncEth*
Prichard, John Robert Stobo 1949- *WhoAm 94*
Prichard, Katharine Susannah 1883-1969 *BlmGWL [port], RfGShF*
Prichard, Mathew Caradoc Thomas 1943- *Who 94*
Prichard, Richard Augustin R. *Who 94*
Prichard, Richard Julian Paget 1915- *Who 94*
Prichard, Robert Alexander, Jr. 1953- *WhoScEn 94*
Prichard, Robert Allyn *WhoAmP 93*
Prichard, Robert Williams 1923- *WhoAm 94*
Prichard, Roger Kingsley 1944- *WhoScEn 94*
Prichard-Jones, John 1913- *Who 94*
Prickett, David Clinton 1918- *WhoScEn 94, WhoWest 94*

Prickett, Gordon Odin 1935- WhoMW 93, WhoScEn 94
Prickett, Maudie d1976 WhoHol 92
Prickett, Oliver 1905- WhoHol 92
Prickett, Roger Leon 1940- WhoFI 94
Prickett, Stephen 1939- WrDr 94
Prickett, (Alexander Thomas) Stephen 1939- Who 94
Prickett, Thomas (Other) 1913- Who 94
Prickett, William WhoIns 94
Prida, Dolores 1943- WhoHisp 94
Priddle, Robert John 1938- Who 94
Priddle, Roland 1933- WhoAm 94
Priddy, Dottie 1935- WhoAmP 93
Pride, Charley 1938- WhoBlA 94
Pride, Charley 1939- AfrAmAl 6 [port], WhoAm 94
Pride, Douglas Spencer 1959- WhoAm 94
Pride, Hemphill P., II 1936- WhoBlA 94
Pride, J. Thomas 1940- WhoBlA 94
Pride, John Bernard 1929- WrDr 94
Pride, John L. 1940- WhoBlA 94
Pride, Walter LaVon 1922- WhoBlA 94
Prideaux, Gary Dean 1939- WhoAm 94
Prideaux, Humphrey (Povah Treverbian) 1915- Who 94
Prideaux, Humphrey Povah Treverbian 1915- IntWW 93
Prideaux, John Denys Charles Anstice 1944- Who 94
Prideaux, John Francis d1993 IntWW 93N, Who 94N
Prideaux, Julian Humphrey 1942- Who 94
Prideaux, Tom d1993 NewYTBS 93
Prideaux, Tom 1908-1993 ConAu 141, SmATA 76
Prideaux, Walter Arbuthnot 1910- Who 94
Pridgen, Eugene C. 1946- WhoAmL 94
Pridham, Brian Robert 1934- Who 94
Pridham, Herbert H. 1929- WhoAm 94
Pridham, Kenneth Robert Comyn 1922- Who 94
Pridham, Thomas Grenville 1920- WhoScEn 94, WhoWest 94
Pridmore, Roy Davis 1925- WhoAm 94
Pridnia, John D. WhoAmP 93
Priebe, Berl E. 1918- WhoAmP 93
Priebe, Karl 1914-1976 WhoAmA 93N
Priebe, Stefan 1953- WhoScEn 94
Pries, Ralph W. 1919- IntMPA 94
Priesand, Sally Jane 1946- WhoAm 94
Priess, Howard K., II 1944- WhoAmL 94
Priest, Alan 1898-1968 WhoAmA 93N
Priest, Charles R. 1946- WhoAmP 93
Priest, Christopher (McKenzie) 1943- EncSF 93, WrDr 94
Priest, Colin Herbert Dickinson C. Who 94
Priest, Dan WhoHol 92
Priest, George L. 1947- WhoAm 94
Priest, Gregory A. WhoIns 94
Priest, Hartwell Wyse 1901- WhoAm 94, WhoAmA 93
Priest, Lisa 1964- ConAu 140
Priest, Marlon L. WhoBlA 94
Priest, Martin WhoHol 92
Priest, Melville Stanton 1912- WhoAm 94, WhoScEn 94
Priest, Natalie d1987 WhoHol 92
Priest, Pat 1936- WhoHol 92
Priest, Robert George 1933- Who 94
Priest, Sharon Devlin 1947- WhoAmP 93
Priest, Stephen 1954- ConAu 140
Priest, T. 1928- WhoAmA 93
Priester, Gayle Boller 1912- WhoScEn 94
Priester, Julian Anthony 1935- WhoBlA 94
Priestley, Carol Lynn 1943- WhoFI 94
Priestley, Charles Henry Brian 1915- Who 94
Priestley, Clive 1935- Who 94
Priestley, G. T. Eric 1942- WhoFI 94, WhoScEn 94
Priestley, J. B. 1894-1984 BlmGEL, DcLB 139 [port]
Priestley, J. B., Mrs. Who 94
Priestley, J(ohn) B(oynton) 1894-1983 ConDr 93
Priestley, J(ohn) B(oynton) 1894-1984 EncSF 93, IntDcT 2 [port]
Priestley, Jason WhoHol 92
Priestley, Jason 1969- IntMPA 94
Priestley, John Christopher, Rev. 1939- Who 94
Priestley, Joseph WorInv
Priestley, Joseph 1733-1804 BlmGEL, DcAmReB 2, WorScD [port]
Priestley, Leslie William 1933- Who 94
Priestley, Margaret 1919?- EncSF 93
Priestley, Maurice Bertram 1933- Who 94
Priestley, Philip John 1946- Who 94
Priestley, Robert Henry 1946- Who 94
Priestley, Thomas A. d1993 NewYTBS 93
Priestly, J. B. 1910- WrDr 94
Priestly, Jack 1926-1993 NewYTBS 93
Priestly, Jason WhoAm 94
Priestman, Brian 1927- NewGrDO
Priestman, Jane 1930- Who 94
Priestman, John David 1926- Who 94
Priestman, Martin 1949- WrDr 94
Priestner, Edward Bernard 1936- WhoAm 94, WhoFI 94
Prieto, Antonio L. 1965- WhoHisp 94
Prieto, Chula d1960 WhoHol 92
Prieto, Claudio R. 1933- WhoHisp 94
Prieto, Maria Cynthia WhoWomW 91
Prieto, Mercy WhoHisp 94
Prieto, Michael 1958- WhoAmL 94
Prieto, Miguel A. 1943- WhoHisp 94
Prieto, Robert 1954- WhoAm 94
Prieto-Fortun, Guillermo 1935- WhoFI 94
Prietto, Mario WhoHisp 94
Prieve, E. Arthur WhoMW 93
Prigent, Michel 1950- IntWW 93
Prigge, William F. d1993 NewYTBS 93
Prigmore, Charles Samuel 1919- WhoAm 94
Prignano, Stephen Michael 1961- WhoAmL 94
Prigogine, Ilya 1917- IntWW 93, Who 94, WrDr 94
Prigogine, Vicomte Ilya 1917- WhoAm 94, WhoScEn 94
Prigozhin, Lyutsian Abramovich 1926- NewGrDO
Prihoda, James Sheldon 1959- WhoScEn 94
Priley, Stephen Anthony 1947- WhoAmP 93
Prill, Arnold WhoFI 94
Prillaman, Terry Smith, Jr. 1959- WhoAmL 94
Prim, Natalie Flores 1945- WhoHisp 94
Prim, Suzy 1895- WhoHol 92
Prima, Louis d1978 WhoHol 92
Primack, Alice Lefler 1939- WhoScEn 94
Primack, Leonard 1936- WhoFI 94
Primack, Marvin Herbert 1931- WhoWest 94
Primakov, Evgeny Maksimovich 1929- LngBDD
Primakov, Yevgeniy Maksimovich 1929- IntWW 93
Primarolo, Dawn 1954- Who 94, WhoWomW 91
Primas, Melvin R., Jr. 1949- WhoAmP 93
Primatesta, Raul Francisco 1919- IntWW 93
Primavera, Carl S. 1953- WhoAmL 94
Prime, Benjamin 1733-1791 WhAmRev
Prime, Derek James 1931- WrDr 94
Prime, Henry Ashworth 1921- Who 94
Prime, Roger Carl 1938- WhoScEn 94
Prime, Samuel Irenaeus 1812-1885 DcAmReB 2
Primeau, Ernest John 1909-1989 WhAm 10
Primeau, Lawrence Steven 1947- WhoAmP 93
Primi, Don Alexis 1947- WhoFI 94
Primis, Lance Roy 1946- WhoAm 94
Primm, Beny Jene 1928- WhoBlA 94
Primmer, George Melvin, Jr. 1954- WhoFI 94
Primo, Marie Nash 1928- WhoMW 93
Primo, Quintin E., Jr. 1913- WhoBlA 94
Primous, Emma M. 1942- WhoBlA 94
Primps, William Guthrie 1949- WhoAm 94, WhoAmL 94
Primrose Who 94
Primrose, Daisy d1927 WhoHol 92
Primrose, Diana fl. 1630- BlmGWL
Primrose, John Ure 1960- Who 94
Primus ConMus 11 [port]
Primus, The Who 94
Primus, Barry 1938- IntMPA 94, WhoHol 92
Primus, Mary Jane Davis 1924- WhoMW 93
Primus, Pearl 1919- AfrAmAl 6, ConBlB 6 [port], WhoAm 94
Primus, Pearl E. 1919- WhoBlA 94
Primus-Cotton, Bobbie J. 1934- WhoBlA 94
Primuth, Richard A. 1945- WhoAmL 94
Prina, Louis Edgar 1917- WhoAm 94
Prina, Stephen James 1954- WhoAmA 93
Prince 1958- AfrAmAl 6 [port], IntMPA 94, IntWW 93, WhoAm 94, WhoBlA 94, WhoHol 92
Prince, Adelaide d1941 WhoHol 92
Prince, Alan Theodore 1915- WhoAm 94
Prince, Alexine 1938- WhoWest 94
Prince, Alison 1931- WrDr 94
Prince, Andrew Lee 1952- WhoBlA 94
Prince, Andrew Steven 1943- WhoAm 94
Prince, Anna Lou 1935- WhoFI 94
Prince, (Celestino) Anthony 1921- Who 94
Prince, Arnold 1925- WhoAmA 93
Prince, Arthur d1948 WhoHol 92
Prince, Carl E. 1934- WhoAm 94
Prince, Charles d1933 WhoHol 92
Prince, Charles O., III 1950- WhoAmL 94
Prince, Cheryl Patrice 1956- WhoBlA 94
Prince, Clayton WhoHol 92
Prince, Daniel Lloyd 1955- WhoAm 94
Prince, David 1948- Who 94
Prince, David Cannon 1950- WhoAmL 94
Prince, Edgar Oliver 1947- WhoBlA 94
Prince, Elsie 1902- WhoHol 92
Prince, Ernest S. 1942- WhoBlA 94
Prince, Eugene Augustus 1930- WhoAmP 93
Prince, F(rank) T(empleton) 1912- ConAu 43NR, WrDr 94
Prince, Frances Anne Kiely 1923- WhoMW 93
Prince, Frank Michael 1946- WhoAmL 94
Prince, Frank Templeton 1912- Who 94
Prince, Garnett B., Jr. 1949- WhoAm 94
Prince, George Edward 1921- WhoScEn 94
Prince, Ginger WhoHol 92
Prince, Gregory Smith, Jr. 1939- WhoAm 94
Prince, Harold 1928- IntMPA 94, WhoAm 94
Prince, Harold S. 1928- IntWW 93
Prince, Harold Smith 1928- Who 94
Prince, Henry James 1811-1899 DcNaB MP
Prince, Hugh Anthony 1911- Who 94
Prince, James W. 1953- WhoWest 94
Prince, Joan Marie 1954- WhoBlA 94
Prince, John Luther, III 1941- WhoAm 94
Prince, John T. d1937 WhoHol 92
Prince, Jonathan 1960- WhoHol 92
Prince, Julius S. 1911- WhoAm 94
Prince, Kathleen Corinne 1948- WhoWest 94
Prince, Kenneth Stephen 1950- WhoAm 94, WhoAmL 94
Prince, Larry Emerson 1950- WhoAmL 94
Prince, Larry L. 1937- WhoAm 94, WhoFI 94
Prince, Mary c. 1788- BlmGWL
Prince, Milton S. 1912- WhoAm 94
Prince, Morris David 1926- WhoAm 94
Prince, Morton Bronenberg 1924- WhoAm 94
Prince, Oliver Gilbert, Jr. 1953- WhoMW 93
Prince, Patricia 1959- WhoWest 94
Prince, Richard Edmund 1949- WhoAmA 93
Prince, Richard Everett 1947- WhoBlA 94
Prince, Robb Lincoln 1941- WhoAm 94
Prince, Robert Lanston 1954- WhoAmP 93
Prince, Robert Mason 1914- WhoFI 94
Prince, Stephen 1959- WhoScEn 94
Prince, Thomas 1687-1758 DcLB 140 [port]
Prince, Thomas Richard 1934- WhoAm 94
Prince, Warren Victor 1911- WhoFI 94, WhoScEn 94
Prince, William 1913- IntMPA 94, WhoHol 92
Prince, William B. 1949- WhoAmL 94
Prince, William Meade 1893-1951 WhoAmA 93N
Prince, William Taliaferro 1929- WhoAm 94, WhoAmL 94
Prince Be 197-?- See P. M. Dawn ConMus 11
Prince-Smith, (William) Richard 1928- Who 94
Princess Anne ConAu 140
Princess Baba 1917- WhoHol 92
Princess Indira d1979 WhoHol 92
Principal, Victoria 1950- IntMPA 94, WhoAm 94, WhoHol 92
Principato, Gregory Onofrio 1956- WhoAmP 93
Principe, Christopher 1958- WhoFI 94
Principe, Helen M. 1953- WhoWest 94
Principe, Joseph Vincent, Jr. 1946- WhoScEn 94
Principi, Anthony Joseph 1944- WhoAmL 94
Princz, Judith WhoAm 94
Prindeville, Charles Trego 1896-1989 WhAm 10
Prindiville, Jim 1941- WhoAmA 93
Prindle, Allen Merle 1947- WhoMW 93
Prindle, Barclay Ward 1938- WhoAmP 93
Prindle, Hazel Webster 1924- WhoAmP 93
Prindle, Robert William 1950- WhoWest 94
Prindle, William Roscoe 1926- WhoAm 94
Prine, Andrew 1936- IntMPA 94, WhoHol 92
Prine, John 1946- WhoAm 94
Prine, Stephen Brent 1952- WhoFI 94
Prineas, Ronald James 1937- WhoAm 94
Pring, Katherine 1940- NewGrDO
Pring, Martin fl. 1603-1606 WhWE
Pring, Richard Anthony 1938- Who 94
Pringle, Aileen d1989 WhoHol 92
Pringle, Barbara C. 1939- WhoAmP 93
Pringle, Barbara Carroll 1939- WhoMW 93
Pringle, Bruce D. 1944- WhoAm 94, WhoAmL 94, WhoWest 94
Pringle, Bryan 1935- WhoHol 92
Pringle, Charles (Norman Seton) 1919- Who 94
Pringle, Curt L. 1959- WhoAmP 93
Pringle, David (William) 1950- EncSF 93, WrDr 94
Pringle, Derek Hair 1926- Who 94
Pringle, Diana Kay 1961- WhoFI 94
Pringle, Donald Frank McKenzie 1930- IntWW 93
Pringle, Edward E. 1914- WhoAm 94, WhoAmP 93
Pringle, George Overton 1923- WhoFI 94
Pringle, James Robert Henry 1939- IntWW 93
Pringle, Joan 1945- WhoHol 92
Pringle, John d1929 WhoHol 92
Pringle, John 1938- NewGrDO
Pringle, John (Martin Douglas) 1912- WrDr 94
Pringle, John Martin Douglas 1912- IntWW 93, Who 94
Pringle, Laurence Patrick 1935- WhoAm 94
Pringle, Lewis Gordon 1941- WhoAm 94, WhoFI 94
Pringle, Margaret Ann 1946- Who 94
Pringle, Nell Rene 1952- WhoBlA 94
Pringle, Oran Allan 1923- WhoAm 94
Pringle, Robert Bernard 1944- WhoAm 94, WhoAmL 94
Pringle, Robert M. 1936- WhoAmP 93
Pringle, Robert Maxwell 1936- WhoAm 94
Pringle, Robert W. WhoIns 94
Pringle, Robert William 1920- Who 94
Pringle, Roberta Frances 1944- WhoWest 94
Pringle, Ronald Sandy Alexander 1945- WhoScEn 94
Pringle, Steuart (Robert) 1928- Who 94
Pringle, Terrence Michael 1947- WrDr 94
Pringle, Wendy d1978 WhoHol 92
Pring-Mill, Robert Duguid Forrest 1924- Who 94
Prinja, Anil Kant 1955- WhoScEn 94, WhoWest 94
Prins, David 1930- WhoAm 94
Prins, Robert Jack 1932- WhoAm 94
Prins-Grose, LaVonne Kay 1957- WhoFI 94, WhoMW 93
Prinster, Dan 1962- WhoAmP 93
Printemps, Yvonne d1977 WhoHol 92
Printemps, Yvonne 1894-1977 NewGrDO
Printy, Dennis Michael 1942- WhoFI 94
Printz, Bonnie Allen WhoAmA 93
Prinz, John Richard 1949- WhoMW 93
Prinz, LeRoy 1895-1983 IntDcF 2-4 [port]
Prinze, Freddie 1954-1977 WhoCom
Prinzi, Barbara Dolle 1938- WhoMW 93
Prinzing, Fred W. 1933- WhoMW 93
Prioleau, Diane Thys 1934- WhoAmP 93
Prioleau, Peter Sylvester 1949- WhoBlA 94
Prioleau, Sara Nelliene 1940- WhoBlA 94
Prior, Baron 1927- Who 94
Prior, Allan 1902- WhoHol 92
Prior, Allan 1922- WrDr 94
Prior, Arthur Norman 1914-1969 DcNaB MP
Prior, Boyd Thelman 1926- WhoFI 94
Prior, Christopher 1912- Who 94
Prior, David James 1943- WhoWest 94
Prior, Edwina M. 1910- WhoAmP 93
Prior, Gary L. 1943- WhoAm 94, WhoAmL 94
Prior, H. David 1944- WhoAm 94, WhoAmL 94
Prior, Harris King 1911-1975 WhoAmA 93N
Prior, Herbert d1954 WhoHol 92
Prior, James Michael Leathes 1927- IntWW 93
Prior, Joseph LaFayette 1935- WhoMW 93
Prior, Kenneth Francis William 1926- WrDr 94
Prior, Linda Gay 1942- WhoWest 94
Prior, Matthew 1664-1721 BlmGEL
Prior, Peter James 1919- Who 94
Prior, Reed Richard 1951- WhoFI 94
Prior, Robert Lee 1941- WhoMW 93
Prior, Ted WhoHol 92
Prior, William Howard 1941- WhoMW 93
Prior, William Johnson 1924- Who 94
Priore, Roger L. 1938- WhoAm 94
Priore, Vincent John d1981 WhoHol 92
Prioteasa, Paula WhoWomW 91
Prip, Janet 1950- WhoAmA 93
Prip, John A. 1922- WhoAmA 93
Prisbrey, Rex Prince 1922- WhoWest 94
Prisco, Douglas Louis 1945- WhoScEn 94
Prisco, Michele 1920- ConWorW 93

Pristavkin, Anatoliy Ignatevich 1931- *IntWW 93*
Pritam, Amrita 1919- *BlmGWL, ConWorW 93*
Pritan, Amrita 1919- *WhoWomW 91*
Pritcard, John Wallace 1912- *WrDr 94*
Pritchard, Baron 1910- *Who 94*
Pritchard, Arthur Alan 1922- *Who 94*
Pritchard, Arthur Osborn 1910- *WhoWest 94*
Pritchard, B. Holland 1951- *WhoAmL 94*
Pritchard, Claudius Hornby 1896- *WhAm 10*
Pritchard, Claudius Hornby, Jr. 1927- *WhoAm 94*
Pritchard, Constance Jenkins 1950- *WhoAm 94*
Pritchard, Dalton Harold 1921- *WhoAm 94*
Pritchard, Daron 1954- *WhoBlA 94*
Pritchard, David E. 1941- *IntWW 93*
Pritchard, David Edward 1941- *WhoAm 94, WhoScEn 94*
Pritchard, David Graham 1945- *WhoScEn 94*
Pritchard, David Ralph 1937- *WhoMW 93*
Pritchard, Donald William 1922- *WhoAm 94, WhoScEn 94*
Pritchard, Douglas Jack 1937- *WhoMW 93*
Pritchard, Gwynedd Idris 1924- *Who 94*
Pritchard, Gwynn *Who 94*
Pritchard, (Iorwerth) Gwynn 1946- *Who 94*
Pritchard, Hannah 1709-1768 *BlmGEL*
Pritchard, Hilary *WhoHol 92*
Pritchard, Hugh Wentworth 1903- *Who 94*
Pritchard, Huw Owen 1928- *WhoAm 94*
Pritchard, James Bennett 1909- *WhoAm 94*
Pritchard, James Robert 1947- *WhoMW 93*
Pritchard, Joel 1925- *WhoAm 94, WhoWest 94*
Pritchard, Joel M. 1925- *WhoAmP 93*
Pritchard, John (Michael) 1921-1989 *NewGrDO, WhAm 10*
Pritchard, John F. 1943- *WhoAmL 94*
Pritchard, Kathleen Jo 1951- *WhoMW 93*
Pritchard, Kenneth John 1926- *Who 94*
Pritchard, Kenneth William 1933- *Who 94*
Pritchard, Llewelyn G. 1937- *WhoAmL 94*
Pritchard, Marion K. Smith *WhoBlA 94*
Pritchard, Melissa *DrAPF 93*
Pritchard, Neil 1911- *Who 94*
Pritchard, Norman Henry, II *DrAPF 93*
Pritchard, Paul Clement 1944- *WhoAm 94*
Pritchard, R(obert) John 1945- *WrDr 94*
Pritchard, Robert Starling, II 1929- *WhoBlA 94*
Pritchard, Thomas Farnolls 1723-1777 *DcNaB MP*
Pritchard, Thomas Owen 1932- *Who 94*
Pritchard, Wilbur Louis 1923- *WhoAm 94*
Pritchard, William Baker 1950- *WhoAmP 93*
Pritchard, William Grady, Jr. 1927- *WhoIns 94*
Pritchard, William H. 1932- *WrDr 94*
Pritchard, William Roy 1924- *WhoAm 94*
Pritchard, William Winther 1951- *WhoAm 94*
Pritchatt, Henry Ian 1948- *WhoFI 94*
Pritchett, A. G. 1928- *WhoAmP 93*
Pritchett, Allen Monroe 1949- *WhoMW 93*
Pritchett, Bruce Michael, Sr. 1940- *WhoWest 94*
Pritchett, Charles Herman 1907- *WhoAm 94*
Pritchett, Joseph Everett 1948- *WhoFI 94, WhoMW 93*
Pritchett, Kay 1946- *WrDr 94*
Pritchett, Lafayette Bow 1934- *WhoAmL 94*
Pritchett, Paula *WhoHol 92*
Pritchett, Samuel Travis 1938- *WhoAm 94, WhoFI 94, WhoIns 94*
Pritchett, Thomas Ronald 1925- *WhoAm 94*
Pritchett, V. S. 1900- *BlmGEL, DcLB 139 [port], ShSCr 14 [port]*
Pritchett, V(ictor) S(awdon) 1900- *RfGShF, WrDr 94*
Pritchett, Victor (Sawdon) 1900- *Who 94*
Pritchett, Victor Sawdon 1900- *IntWW 93, WhoAm 94*
Pritikin, David T. 1949- *WhoAm 94, WhoAmL 94*
Pritikin, James B. 1939- *WhoAmL 94*
Pritikin, Marvin E. 1922- *WhoIns 94*
Pritikin, Roland I. 1906- *WhoAm 94*
Pritsker, A. Alan B. 1933- *WhoAm 94, WhoScEn 94*
Pritt, Charlotte J. 1949- *WhoAmP 93*
Prittie *Who 94*
Pritz, Michael Burton 1947- *WhoWest 94*
Pritz, Sandra Germond 1938- *WhoMW 93*
Pritzker, Andreas Eugen Max 1945- *WhoScEn 94*
Pritzker, Jay Arthur 1922- *WhoAm 94, WhoFI 94, WhoMW 93*
Pritzker, Leon 1922- *WhoAm 94*
Pritzker, Nicholas J. *WhoAm 94, WhoFI 94*
Pritzker, Robert Alan 1926- *WhoAm 94, WhoFI 94*
Pritzlaff, John, Jr. 1925- *WhoAmA 93*
Pritzlaff, John, Jr., Mrs. *WhoAmA 93*
Pritzlaff, John Charles, Jr. 1925- *WhoAm 94, WhoAmP 93*
Privat, Jeannette Mary 1938- *WhoAm 94*
Privateer, Paul Michael 1946- *WrDr 94*
Privett, Donald F. 1955- *WhoIns 94*
Privett, Howard J. 1929- *WhoAm 94*
Privette, Coy Clarence 1933- *WhoAmP 93*
Privitera, John Nathan 1944- *WhoFI 94*
Priz, Edward John 1952- *WhoFI 94, WhoMW 93*
Prizer, Charles John 1924- *WhoAm 94*
Prizzi, Jack Anthony 1935- *WhoAm 94*
Pro, Philip Martin 1946- *WhoAm 94, WhoAmL 94, WhoWest 94*
Proach, Henry d1986 *WhoHol 92*
Proast, Jonas c. 1642-1710 *DcNaB MP*
Proba fl. 4th cent.- *BlmGWL*
Probala, Andrew Eugene 1908- *WhoMW 93*
Probasco, Calvin Henry Charles 1926- *WhoAm 94*
Probasco, Dale Richard 1946- *WhoMW 93, WhoWest 94*
Probasco, Jeanetta *WhoBlA 94*
Probasco, Scott Livingston 1928- *WhoAm 94*
Prober, Alexandra Jaworski 1907- *WhoWest 94*
Prober, Joanne S. 1938- *WhoMW 93*
Probert, David Henry 1938- *Who 94*
Probert, (William) Ronald 1934- *Who 94*
Probert, Walter 1925- *WhoAm 94*
Probine, Mervyn Charles 1924- *Who 94*
Probst, Kevin Forbes 1950- *WhoWest 94*
Probst, Leslie J. 1949- *WhoMW 93*
Probst, Mark 1925- *WrDr 94*
Probst, Raymond R. 1919- *IntWW 93*
Probstein, Ronald Filmore 1928- *WhoAm 94*
Proby, Peter 1911- *Who 94*
Procacci, Annamaria 1949- *WhoWomW 91*
Procel, Guillermo, Jr. 1947- *WhoHisp 94*
Prochaska, Alice Marjorie Sheila 1947- *Who 94*
Prochaska, Donald Frank 1952- *WhoMW 93*
Prochaska, Otto 1933- *WhoScEn 94*
Prochaska, Robert *DrAPF 93*
Prochazka, F(rantisek) S(erafinsky) 1861-1939 *NewGrDO*
Prochazka, Karel 1947- *WhoScEn 94*
Prochnicka, Lidia *WhoHol 92*
Prochnow, Douglas Lee 1952- *WhoAm 94, WhoAmL 94, WhoMW 93*
Prochnow, Herbert Victor *IntWW 93*
Prochnow, Herbert Victor 1897- *WhoAm 94, WrDr 94*
Prochnow, Herbert Victor, Jr. 1931- *WhoAmL 94, WhoFI 94, WhoMW 93*
Prochnow, James R. 1943- *WhoAm 94, WhoAmL 94*
Prochnow, Jurgen 1941- *WhoHol 92*
Prochownik, Walter A. 1923- *WhoAmA 93*
Prockl, Ernst d1957 *WhoHol 92*
Prockop, Darwin Johnson 1929- *WhoAm 94, WhoScEn 94*
Procktor, Patrick 1936- *IntWW 93, Who 94*
Procope, John Levy 1925- *WhoBlA 94*
Procopio, Joseph Guydon 1940- *WhoAmL 94*
Procopio, Margarida *WhoWomW 91*
Procter, Adelaide 1825-1864 *BlmGWL*
Procter, Harvey Thornton, Jr. 1945- *WhoBlA 94*
Procter, Jane Hilary *Who 94*
Procter, John Ernest 1918- *WhoAm 94*
Procter, (Mary) Norma 1928- *Who 94*
Procter, Robert John Dudley 1935- *Who 94*
Procter, Sidney 1925- *Who 94*
Proctor, A. Phimister 1862-1950 *WhoAmA 93N*
Proctor, Anthony James 1931- *Who 94*
Proctor, Barbara Gardner *WhoAm 94, WhoBlA 94*
Proctor, Charles Lafayette, II 1954- *WhoScEn 94*
Proctor, David Ray 1956- *WhoAmL 94*
Proctor, David Victor 1930- *Who 94*
Proctor, Dean Wesley 1946- *WhoAm 94*
Proctor, Donald Frederick 1913- *WhoAm 94*
Proctor, Earl D. 1941- *WhoBlA 94*
Proctor, Edward George 1929- *WhoAmL 94*
Proctor, Geo(rge) W. *EncSF 93*
Proctor, George W. *WrDr 94*
Proctor, Harvey *Who 94*
Proctor, (Keith) Harvey 1947- *Who 94*
Proctor, James E., Jr. *WhoAmP 93*
Proctor, James Roscoe 1938- *WhoAmP 93*
Proctor, Jesse Harris, Jr. 1924- *WhoAm 94*
Proctor, Jesse Heighton 1908- *Who 94*
Proctor, Jessie d1975 *WhoHol 92*
Proctor, John Franklin 1931- *WhoAm 94*
Proctor, John P. 1942- *WhoAm 94, WhoAmL 94*
Proctor, Kenneth Donald 1944- *WhoAm 94, WhoAmL 94*
Proctor, Leonard D. 1919- *WhoBlA 94*
Proctor, Lister Hill 1938- *WhoAmP 93*
Proctor, Mark Alan 1948- *WhoFI 94*
Proctor, Marland d1988 *WhoHol 92*
Proctor, Michael Anthony 1961- *WhoAmL 94*
Proctor, Nancy Jean 1936- *WhoAmP 93*
Proctor, Nick Hobert 1941- *WhoMW 93*
Proctor, Philip *WhoHol 92*
Proctor, Richard J. 1931- *WhoScEn 94*
Proctor, Richard Jerome, Jr. 1941- *WhoFI 94*
Proctor, Richard Lee 1944- *WhoAmP 93*
Proctor, Richard Owen 1935- *WhoAm 94*
Proctor, Robert Neel 1954- *WhoScEn 94*
Proctor, Robert Swope 1922- *WhoAm 94*
Proctor, Samuel 1919- *WhoAm 94*
Proctor, Samuel D(eWitt) 1921- *WrDr 94*
Proctor, Samuel Dewitt 1921- *WhoBlA 94*
Proctor, Stanley Matthew 1920- *WhoMW 93*
Proctor, Timothy DeWitt 1949- *WhoBlA 94*
Proctor, Vernon Robert 1954- *WhoAmL 94*
Proctor, W. Thomas 1953- *WhoAmL 94*
Proctor, William H. 1945- *WhoBlA 94*
Proctor, William Lee 1933- *WhoAm 94*
Proctor, William Zinsmaster 1902- *WhoAm 94*
Proctor-Beauchamp, Christopher Radstock P. *Who 94*
Procunier, Richard Werner 1936- *WhoWest 94*
Prodan, Andrea *WhoHol 92*
Prodan, David d1992 *IntWW 93N*
Prodan, John 1924- *WhoMW 93*
Prodan, Richard Stephen 1952- *WhoScEn 94*
Proebsting, Edward Louis, Jr. 1926- *WhoScEn 94*
Proechel, Glen Fred 1938- *WhoMW 93*
Proefrock, Carl Kenneth 1928- *WhoAm 94*
Proensa, Comtesse de fl. 12th cent.- *BlmGWL*
Professor Backwards 1911-1976 *WhoCom*
Professor Dope *WhoCom*
Profet, Margie 1958- *WhoScEn 94*
Profeta, Salvatore, Jr. 1951- *WhoScEn 94*
Proffer, Kathleen Anne 1955- *WhoWest 94*
Proffer, Marvin E. 1931- *WhoAmP 93*
Proffit, William Robert 1936- *WhoAm 94*
Proffitt, A. James 1941- *WhoMW 93*
Proffitt, Alan Wayne 1956- *WhoScEn 94*
Proffitt, Charles G. 1896- *WhAm 10*
Proffitt, Curtis Ray 1935- *WhoAmP 93*
Proffitt, Donald *WhoHol 92*
Proffitt, John Richard 1930- *WhoAm 94, WhoFI 94*
Proffitt, John Roscoe, Jr. 1924- *WhoFI 94*
Proffitt, Lawrence Alan 1959- *WhoWest 94*
Proffitt, Waldo, Jr. 1924- *WhoAm 94*
Profit, Kirk A. 1952- *WhoAmP 93*
Proft, Pat 1947- *ConTFT 11*
Proft Cink, Cecilia Jo 1963- *WhoMW 93*
Profumo, John Dennis 1915- *IntWW 93, Who 94*
Profusek, Robert Alan 1950- *WhoAm 94, WhoAmL 94*
Progar, Dorothy 1924- *WhoAm 94*
Progelhof, Richard Carl 1936- *WhoAm 94*
Proger, Phillip A. 1948- *WhoAmL 94*
Progoff, Ira 1921- *WrDr 94*
Prohaska, Elena Anastasia 1946- *WhoAmA 93*
Prohaska, Felix 1912-1987 *NewGrDO*
Prohaska, Janos d1974 *WhoHol 92*
Prohaska, Jaro(slav) 1891-1965 *NewGrDO*
Prohaska, Karl 1869-1927 *NewGrDO*
Prohaska, Ray 1901-1981 *WhoAmA 93N*
Prokasy, William Frederick 1930- *WhoAm 94*
Prokhanov, Aleksandr Andreevich 1938- *LngBDD*
Prokhorov, Aleksandr *WorInv*
Prokhorov, Aleksandr Mikhailovich 1916- *IntWW 93, WhoScEn 94*
Prokhorov, Alexander Mikhailovich 1916- *Who 94*
Prokhorova, Violetta *Who 94*
Prokhovenko, Shanna *WhoHol 92*
Prokhovnik, Simon Jacques 1920- *WrDr 94*
Prokofiev, Sergei 1891-1953 *IntDcB, IntDcF 2-4*
Prokofiev, Sergey (Sergeyevich) 1891-1953 *NewGrDO*
Prokop, Ruth Timberlake *WhoAmP 93*
Prokop, Ruth Timberlake 1939- *WhoAmL 94*
Prokop, Stanley A. 1942- *WhoAmL 94*
Prokopis, Emmanuel Charles 1942- *WhoAm 94*
Prokopoff, Stephen 1929- *WhoAmA 93*
Prokopoff, Stephen Stephen 1929- *WhoAm 94, WhoMW 93*
Prokoshkin, Yuriy Dmitriyevich 1929- *IntWW 93*
Prokovsky, Andre 1939- *IntDcB [port]*
Prom, Stephen George 1954- *WhoAm 94, WhoAmL 94*
Promboin, Gail Betsy 1949- *WhoFI 94*
Prominski, Eileen 1938- *WhoMW 93*
Promis, Flo d1956 *WhoHol 92*
Promisel, Nathan E. 1908- *WhoAm 94*
Promislo, Daniel 1932- *WhoAm 94, WhoAmL 94*
Promutico, Jean 1936- *WhoAmA 93*
Promyslov, Vladimir F. d1993 *NewYTBS 93*
Pronk, Johannes Pieter 1940- *IntWW 93*
Pronko, Leonard Cabell 1927- *WhoWest 94*
Pronove-Irreverre, Pacita 1919- *WhoWest 94*
Pront, Peter E. 1950- *WhoAmL 94*
Pronzini, Bill 1943- *EncSF 93, WrDr 94*
Pronzini, Bill John 1943- *WhoAm 94, WhoWest 94*
Proom, William Arthur 1916- *Who 94*
Proops, Marjorie *Who 94, WrDr 94*
Proost, Robert Lee 1937- *WhoAm 94*
Proper, Stan *DrAPF 93*
Propersi, August J. 1926- *WhoAmA 93*
Propes, Victor Lee 1938- *WhoBlA 94*
Prophet, Arthur Shelley 1918- *Who 94*
Prophet, John 1931- *Who 94*
Prophet, Matthew Waller, Jr. 1930- *WhoWest 94*
Prophet, Melissa 1957- *WhoHol 92*
Prophet, Richard L., Jr. *WhoBlA 94*
Prophet-Compton, Debbie Jo 1956- *WhoMW 93*
Prophete, Beaumanoir 1920- *WhoBlA 94*
Prophete, John c. 1350-1416 *DcNaB MP*
Prophit, Penny Pauline 1939- *Who 94*
Propiac, (Catherine Joseph Ferdinand) Girard de 1759-1823 *NewGrDO*
Propp, Dale Hartley 1935- *WhoWest 94*
Propp, Seymour d1993 *NewYTBS 93*
Propper, Dan *DrAPF 93*
Propst, Catherine Lamb 1946- *WhoAm 94*
Propst, Floyd E. *WhoAmL 94*
Propst, Harold Dean 1934- *WhoAm 94*
Propst, Howard Benson 1923- *WhoAmP 93*
Propst, John Leake 1914- *WhoAm 94*
Propst, Michael Truman 1940- *WhoWest 94*
Propst, Robert Bruce 1931- *WhoAm 94, WhoAmL 94*
Prorok, Robert Francis 1952- *WhoAm 94, WhoAmL 94*
Prosch, Harry 1917- *WrDr 94*
Proschek, Eric Eugene 1949- *WhoAmL 94*
Prose, Francine 1947- *WrDr 94*
Prosen, Harry 1930- *WhoAm 94*
Prosen, Rose Mary *DrAPF 93*
Proshansky, Harold Milton 1920-1991 *WhAm 10*
Proskin, Arnold W. 1938- *WhoAmP 93*
Proskovec, Bernard Joseph 1952- *WhoMW 93*
Prosky, Robert 1930- *IntMPA 94*
Prosky, Robert 1931- *WhoHol 92*
Prosky, Robert Joseph 1930- *WhoAm 94*
Prosperi, Carola 1883-1975 *BlmGWL*
Prosperi, David Philip 1953- *WhoMW 93*
Prosperi, Louis Anthony 1954- *WhoAm 94, WhoAmL 94*
Prosperi, Robert 1942- *WhoFI 94*
Prospero and Caliban *EncSF 93, GayLL*
Pross, Lester Fred 1924- *WhoAmA 93*
Pross, Maureen Nell 1953- *WhoMW 93*
Prosser, Hon. Lord 1934- *Who 94*
Prosser, C. Ladd 1907- *IntWW 93, WhoAm 94*
Prosser, Daniel Lee 1951- *WhoMW 93*
Prosser, David John 1944- *Who 94*
Prosser, David Thomas, Jr. 1942- *WhoAmP 93, WhoMW 93*
Prosser, Eleanor Alice 1922- *WhAm 10*
Prosser, Franklin Pierce 1935- *WhoAm 94*

Prosser, Gabriel c. 1775-1800 *AfrAmAl 6*
Prosser, Harold Lee *DrAPF 93*
Prosser, Harold Lee 1944- *WrDr 94*
Prosser, Hugh d1952 *WhoHol 92*
Prosser, Ian Maurice Gray 1943- *IntWW 93, Who 94*
Prosser, (Elvet) John 1932- *Who 94*
Prosser, John Martin 1932- *WhoAm 94*
Prosser, Margaret Theresa 1937- *Who 94*
Prosser, Raymond Frederick 1919- *Who 94*
Prosser, William David *Who 94*
Prost, Alain Marie Pascal 1955- *IntWW 93*
Prost, Donald *WhoAmP 93*
Prost, James Leonard 1946- *WhoFI 94*
Prostak, Arnold S. 1929- *WhoScEn 94*
Prosterman, Roy L. 1935- *WhoAm 94*
Proszowska, Joanna *WhoWomW 91*
Prot, Felix-Jean 1747-1823 *NewGrDO*
Prota, Gabriele 1755-1843 *NewGrDO*
Prota, Giovanni c. 1786-1843 *NewGrDO*
Prota, Ignazio 1690-1748 *NewGrDO*
Prota, Tommaso 1727?-1768? *NewGrDO*
Protacio, Romeo Romualdo 1941- *WhoWest 94*
Prota Family *NewGrDO*
Prota-Giurleo, Ulisse 1886-1966 *NewGrDO*
Protagoras of Abdera c. 490BC-c. 421BC *EncEth*
Protan, John 1920- *WhoAmP 93*
Protas, Ron *WhoAm 94*
Protazanov, Yakov d1945 *WhoHol 92*
Protheroe, Alan Hackford 1934- *IntWW 93, Who 94*
Prothro, Edwin Terry 1919- *WhoScEn 94*
Prothro, Gerald Dennis 1942- *WhoBlA 94*
Prothro, Johnnie Watts 1922- *WhoBlA 94*
Prothro, Louise Robinson 1920-1981 *WhoBlA 94N*
Prothrow-Stith, Deborah Boutin 1954- *WhoBlA 94*
Protigal, Stanley Nathan 1950- *WhoAmL 94*
Proto, Neil Thomas 1945- *WhoAm 94, WhoAmL 94*
Protopapas, Nakos 1927- *IntWW 93*
Protschka, Josef 1944- *NewGrDO*
Protti, Aldo 1920- *NewGrDO*
Protti, Maria Evelyn 1957- *WhoAmL 94*
Protzman, Grant D. 1950- *WhoAmP 93*
Protzman, Grant Dale 1950- *WhoWest 94*
Proud, Clifford J. *WhoAmL 94*
Proud, Edward H. 1950- *WhoFI 94*
Proud, Eileen Mariel 1954- *WhoFI 94*
Proud, Gary 1943- *WhoAmP 93*
Proud, Harold John Granville Ellis 1906- *Who 94*
Proud, John (Seymour) 1907- *Who 94*
Proud, John Frederick 1942- *WhoWest 94*
Proudfoot, Bruce *Who 94*
Proudfoot, (Vincent) Bruce 1930- *Who 94*
Proudfoot, Bruce Falconer 1903- *Who 94*
Proudfoot, David W. 1940- *WhoAmL 94*
Proudfoot, James Michael 1955- *WhoWest 94*
Proudfoot, Wilfred *Who 94*
Proudfoot, (George) Wilfred 1921- *Who 94*
Proudfoot, William D. 1940- *WhoAmP 93*
Prough, Russell Allen 1943- *WhoAm 94*
Prough, Stephen W. 1945- *WhoWest 94*
Proulx, E. Annie 1935- *ConLC 81 [port]*
Proulx, Edna Annie 1935- *WhoAm 94*
Proulx, Ernest E. 1931- *WhoAmP 93*
Proulx, Michael John 1948- *WhoWest 94*
Proulx, Norman R. 1951- *WhoAmP 93*
Proumen, Henri-Jacques *EncSF 93*
Proust, Joseph Louis 1754-1826 *WorScD*
Proust, Marcel 1871-1922 *BlmGEL*
Proust, (Valentin-Louis-George-Eugene-) Marcel 1871-1922 *GayLL*
Prout, Brian
See Diamond Rio *ConMus 11*
Prout, Carl Wesley 1941- *WhoWest 94*
Prout, Christopher (James) 1942- *Who 94*
Prout, Curtis 1915- *IntWW 93, WhoAm 94*
Prout, George Russell, Jr. 1924- *WhoAm 94, WhoScEn 94*
Prout, Patrick M. 1941- *WhoBlA 94*
Prout, Ralph Eugene 1933- *WhoAm 94, WhoWest 94*
Prout, William 1785-1850 *WorScD*
Prout, William H., Jr. 1945- *WhoAmL 94*
Prouty, Chilton Eaton 1914- *WhoMW 93*
Prouty, Jed d1956 *WhoHol 92*
Prouty, Morton Dennison, Jr. 1918- *WhAm 10*
Prouty, Norman R. 1939- *WhoAm 94*
Proval, David 1943- *WhoHol 92*
Provan, James Lyal Clark 1936- *Who 94*
Provan, Marie *Who 94*
Provder, Carl 1933- *WhoAmA 93*
Provencal, Leo A. 1928- *WhoAmP 93*
Provencher, Roger Arthur 1923- *WhoAm 94*
Provencio, Dolores *WhoHisp 94*
Provencio, John H. 1933- *WhoHisp 94*
Provencio, Ricardo B. 1947- *WhoHisp 94*
Provensen, Alice Rose Twitchell *WhoAm 94*
Provenza, Paul 1958- *WhoHol 92*
Provenzale, Francesco c. 1626-1704 *NewGrDO*
Provenzale, Maryellen Kirby 1938- *WhoAm 94, WhoAmL 94*
Provenzo, Eugene (F.), Jr. 1949- *WrDr 94*
Providence, Wayne *DrAPF 93*
Provin, Cleo Elbert 1948- *WhoAmP 93*
Provine, Dorothy 1937- *IntMPA 94, WhoHol 92*
Provine, John C. 1938- *WhoAm 94, WhoAmL 94*
Provisor, Janis 1946- *WhoAmA 93*
Provist, d'Alain *BlkWr 2*
Provoost, Samuel 1742-1815 *DcAmReB 2*
Provorny, Frederick Alan 1946- *WhoAm 94, WhoAmL 94*
Provost, Caterina F. *DrAPF 93*
Provost, Etienne 1782-1850 *WhWE*
Provost, Gary (Richard) 1944- *WrDr 94*
Provost, Gilles R. 1945- *WhoAmP 93*
Provost, Jeanne d1980 *WhoHol 92*
Provost, Jon 1950- *WhoHol 92*
Provost, Lloyd 1931- *WhoIns 94*
Provost, Marsha Parks 1947- *WhoBlA 94*
Provost, Paul E. 1915- *WhoAmP 93*
Provost, Sarah *DrAPF 93*
Provow, Jeffrey Steven 1957- *WhoWest 94*
Provus, Barbara Lee 1949- *WhoAm 94, WhoFI 94*
Provvedi, Federico 1972- *WhoHol 92*
Prown, Jules David 1930- *WhoAmA 93*
Prowse, David 1941- *WhoHol 92*
Prowse, Florence Irene *Who 94*
Prowse, Juliet 1936- *WhoHol 92*
Prowse, Peter d1976 *WhoHol 92*
Prowse, Philip 1937- *NewGrDO*
Prowse, Philip (John) 1937- *Who 94*
Proxmire, William 1915- *IntWW 93, WhoAm 94, WhoAmP 93*
Proyect, Martin H. 1932- *WhoWest 94*
Prozan, Lawrence Ira 1961- *WhoFI 94*
Prozeller, Cecile Marie 1954- *WhoFI 94*
Prucha, John James 1924- *WhoAm 94*
Prucz, Jacky Carol 1949- *WhoScEn 94*
Prude, Agnes George de Mille 1905-1993 *ConAu 142*
Prude, Walter F., Mrs. *Who 94*
Pruden, Glenn Richard 1950- *WhoAmL 94*
Pruden, James Wesley 1935- *WhoAm 94*
Prudent 1780?- *NewGrDO*
Prud'homme, Albert Fredric 1952- *WhoFI 94*
Prud'homme, Cameron d1967 *WhoHol 92*
Prud'homme, Cindy Jo 1959- *WhoMW 93*
Prud'homme, George d1972 *WhoHol 92*
Prudhomme, Nellie Rose 1948- *WhoBlA 94*
Prudhomme, Ronald Edward 1941- *WhoWest 94*
Prudhomme, Shirley Mae 1941- *WhoMW 93*
Prudnikov, Viktor Alekseevich 1939- *LngBDD*
Pruedhomme de Borre, Philippe Hubert, Chevalier de 1717- *WhAmRev*
Prueitt, Melvin Lewis 1932- *WhoWest 94*
Pruess, David Louis 1938- *WhoScEn 94*
Prueter, James M. 1947- *WhoIns 94*
Pruett, Charles David 1948- *WhoScEn 94*
Pruett, Clayton Dunklin 1935- *WhoFI 94, WhoScEn 94*
Pruett, Helen Gorham 1919- *WhoMW 93*
Pruett, James Worrell 1932- *WhoAm 94*
Pruett, Jane McGill 1927- *WhoAmP 93*
Pruett, Jeanne *WhoAm 94*
Pruett, Jerome 1941- *NewGrDO*
Pruett, Kyle D(ean) 1943- *WrDr 94*
Pruett, Kyle Dean 1943- *WhoAm 94, WhoScEn 94*
Prugh, Dane Gaskill 1918- *WhAm 10*
Prugh, George Shipley 1920- *WhoAm 94*
Prugh, William Byron 1945- *WhoAm 94, WhoAmL 94*
Prugovecki, Eduard 1937- *WhoAm 94*
Pruis, John J. 1923- *WhoAm 94*
Pruitt, Alice Fay 1943- *WhoScEn 94*
Pruitt, Alonzo Clemons 1951- *WhoBlA 94*
Pruitt, Anne Loring 1929- *WhoAm 94*
Pruitt, Anne Smith *WhoBlA 94, WhoMW 93*
Pruitt, Basil Arthur, Jr. 1930- *WhoAm 94*
Pruitt, Charles Joseph 1946- *WhoAm 94, WhoAmL 94*
Pruitt, David Carl, III 1933- *WhoAmP 93*
Pruitt, Dean Garner 1930- *WhoAm 94*
Pruitt, Fred Roderic 1938- *WhoBlA 94*
Pruitt, George Albert 1946- *WhoAm 94, WhoBlA 94*
Pruitt, Glyndon C. 1928- *WhoAmP 93*
Pruitt, Gregory Donald 1951- *WhoBlA 94*
Pruitt, James Boubias 1964- *WhoBlA 94*
Pruitt, Ken 1957- *WhoAmP 93*
Pruitt, Lynn 1937- *WhoAmA 93*
Pruitt, Mary *WhoAmP 93*
Pruitt, Michael *WhoBlA 94*
Pruitt, Mike 1954- *WhoBlA 94*
Pruitt, Peter Taliaferro 1932- *WhoFI 94*
Pruitt, Robert Grady, III 1954- *WhoAmL 94*
Pruitt, Russell Clyde 1927- *WhoMW 93*
Pruitt, Wes *WhoAmP 93*
Pruitt, William *DrAPF 93*
Pruitt, William Edwin 1934- *WhoMW 93*
Pruitt, William O. 1922- *WrDr 94*
Pruneda, Max 1948- *WhoAmA 93*
Prunieres, Henry 1886-1942 *NewGrDO*
Prunskiene, Kazimiera 1943- *IntWW 93*
Prunty, Howard Edward *WhoBlA 94*
Prunty, Lyle Delmar 1945- *WhoMW 93*
Prunty, Paul E. 1943- *WhoAmP 93*
Prunty, Wyatt *DrAPF 93*
Prupas, Melvern Irving 1926- *WhoFI 94*
Prus, Joseph Stanley 1952- *WhoScEn 94*
Prus, Victor Marius 1917- *WhoAm 94*
Prusa, James Graham 1948- *WhoAm 94*
Prusak, Maximilian Michael 1943- *WhoAmL 94*
Prusak, Mikhail Mikhailovich 1960- *LngBDD*
Prusiner, Stanley Ben 1942- *WhoAm 94, WhoScEn 94, WhoWest 94*
Pruslin, Stephen (Lawrence) 1940- *NewGrDO*
Prusoff, William Herman 1920- *WhoAm 94*
Prussia, Leland S. 1929- *IntWW 93*
Prussin, Jeffrey A. 1943- *WhoFI 94*
Prussing, Laurel Lunt 1941- *WhoMW 93*
Prussing, Laurel Victoria Lunt 1941- *WhoAmP 93*
Prussing, Margaret d1944 *WhoHol 92*
Prusti, Riitta Anneli 1941- *WhoWomW 91*
Pruter, Karl Hugo 1920- *WhoAm 94*
Pruter, Margaret Franson *WhoMW 93*
Prutton, Douglas Allen 1957- *WhoAmL 94*
Prutton, Martin 1934- *WrDr 94*
Pruyn, Leonard 1898-1973 *EncSF 93*
Pruyn, William J. 1922- *WhoAm 94*
Pruzan, Irene 1949- *WhoMW 93*
Pruzansky, Joshua Murdock 1940- *WhoAmL 94*
Pryanishnikov, Ippolit Petrovich 1847-1921 *NewGrDO*
Prybil, Lawrence Dewey 1940- *WhoAm 94, WhoMW 93*
Prybyla, Jan S. 1927- *WrDr 94*
Pryce, Deborah 1951- *CngDr 93*
Pryce, Deborah D. 1951- *WhoAm 94, WhoMW 93*
Pryce, Deborah Denine 1951- *WhoAmP 93*
Pryce, Edward L. 1914- *WhoBlA 94*
Pryce, Edward Lyons 1914- *WhoAm 94*
Pryce, George Terry 1934- *IntWW 93*
Pryce, James Taylor 1936- *Who 94*
Pryce, Jonathan 1947- *IntMPA 94, IntWW 93, Who 94, WhoAm 94, WhoHol 92*
Pryce, Maurice Henry Lecorney 1913- *IntWW 93, Who 94*
Pryce, Richard James 1936- *WhoMW 93*
Pryce, Roy 1928- *Who 94*
Pryce, Terry *Who 94*
Pryce, (George) Terry 1934- *Who 94*
Pryce, William *WhoAmP 93*
Pryce, William Thornton 1932- *WhoAm 94*
Pryce-Jones, Alan Payan 1908- *IntWW 93, Who 94*
Pryce-Jones, David 1936- *WrDr 94*
Pryde, Arthur Edward 1946- *WhoBlA 94*
Pryer, (Eric) John 1929- *Who 94*
Pryjmak, Peter Gothart 1949- *WhoFI 94*
Pryke, David Dudley 1912- *Who 94*
Pryke, Roy Thomas 1940- *Who 94*
Pryn, William John 1928- *Who 94*
Prynne, J(eremy) H(alward) 1936- *WrDr 94*
Pryor, Adel 1918- *WrDr 94*
Pryor, Ainslie d1958 *WhoHol 92*
Pryor, Alan Mark 1949- *WhoAm 94, WhoFI 94*
Pryor, Ann G. 1941- *WhoAmP 93*
Pryor, Arthur John 1939- *Who 94*
Pryor, Bonnie H. 1942- *WrDr 94*
Pryor, Brian Hugh 1931- *Who 94*
Pryor, C. Robert 1945- *WhoMW 93*
Pryor, Calvin Caffey 1928- *WhoBlA 94*
Pryor, Carolyn Ann 1934- *WhoWest 94*
Pryor, Chester Cornelius, II 1930- *WhoBlA 94*
Pryor, David 1934- *CngDr 93*
Pryor, David Hampton 1934- *IntWW 93, WhoAm 94, WhoAmP 93*
Pryor, Douglas Keith 1944- *WhoScEn 94, WhoWest 94*
Pryor, Frederic L. 1933- *WhoFI 94*
Pryor, Harold S. 1920- *WhoAm 94*
Pryor, Hubert 1916- *WhoAm 94, WhoFI 94*
Pryor, Hugh d1963 *WhoHol 92*
Pryor, Jerry Dennis 1952- *WhoFI 94*
Pryor, John Pembro 1937- *Who 94*
Pryor, Joseph Ehrman 1918- *WhoAm 94*
Pryor, Julius, Jr. 1924- *WhoBlA 94*
Pryor, Lillian W. 1917- *WhoBlA 94*
Pryor, Malcolm D. *WhoBlA 94*
Pryor, Mark Allan 1954- *WhoWest 94*
Pryor, Mark L. 1963- *WhoAmP 93*
Pryor, Maureen d1977 *WhoHol 92*
Pryor, Nicholas 1935- *WhoHol 92*
Pryor, Peter Patrick 1946- *WhoAm 94, WhoWest 94*
Pryor, Richard *NewYTBS 93 [port]*
Pryor, Richard 1940- *AfrAmAl 6 [port], IntMPA 94, IntWW 93, WhoAm 94, WhoBlA 94, WhoCom [port], WhoHol 92*
Pryor, Richard James 1948- *WhoFI 94*
Pryor, Richard Walter 1932- *WhoAm 94*
Pryor, Robert Charles 1938- *Who 94*
Pryor, Roger d1974 *WhoHol 92*
Pryor, Ronald Roger 1945- *WhoMW 93*
Pryor, Samuel Frazier, III 1928- *WhoAm 94*
Pryor, Shepherd Green, III 1919- *WhoAmL 94*
Pryor, Tedmund Wylie 1956- *WhoFI 94*
Pryor, Thomas M. 1912- *IntMPA 94*
Pryor, Vanessa *EncSF 93*
Pryor, Vanessa 1942- *WrDr 94*
Pryor, Wayne Robert 1961- *WhoScEn 94*
Pryor, William Austin 1929- *WhoAm 94*
Pryor, William C. 1932- *WhoAmP 93*
Prysch, Peter 1962- *WhoScEn 94*
Prys-Davies, Baron 1923- *Who 94*
Pryse, Hugh d1955 *WhoHol 92*
Prystowsky, Harry 1925- *WhoAm 94*
Prystupa, Ester Ana 1956- *WhoFI 94*
Przelomski, Anastasia Nemenyi 1918- *WhoAm 94*
Przelozny, Zbigniew 1954- *WhoScEn 94*
Przemieniecki, Janusz Stanislaw 1927- *WhoAm 94*
Przhevalsky, Nikolay Mikhailovich 1839-1888 *WhWE*
Przybycien, Todd Michael 1962- *WhoScEn 94*
Przybysz, Kenneth Louis 1947- *WhoAmP 93*
Przybyszewska, Stanislawa 1901-1935 *IntDcT 2*
Przybyszewski, Anthony R. *WhoIns 94*
Psaltakis, Emanuel P. 1965- *WhoScEn 94*
Psaltis, Helen 1931- *WhoMW 93*
Psaltis, John Costas 1940- *WhoAm 94*
Psarakis, Emanuel Nicholas 1932- *WhoAm 94*
Psaris, Amy Celia 1963- *WhoScEn 94*
Pschunder, Willi 1944- *WhoScEn 94*
Pseudoman, Akkad 1886-1940 *EncSF 93*
Pshtissky, Yacov 1952- *WhoScEn 94*
Psilander, Valdemar d1917 *WhoHol 92*
Psomiades, Harry John 1928- *WhoAm 94*
Psuty, Norbert Phillip 1937- *WhoAm 94, WhoScEn 94*
Ptacek, William H. *WhoAm 94*
Ptak, Frank S. 1943- *WhoAm 94*
Ptak, John *IntMPA 94*
Ptashkin, Barry Irwin 1944- *WhoFI 94, WhoMW 93*
Ptashne, Mark Stephen 1940- *IntWW 93*
Ptasinski, Carol M. *WhoMW 93*
Ptasynski, Harry 1926- *WhoWest 94*
Ptaszek, Edward Gerald, Jr. 1950- *WhoAm 94, WhoAmL 94*
Ptasznik, Victor F. 1945- *WhoAmL 94*
Ptolemy c. 100-170 *WorScD*
Ptolemy fl. 2nd cent.- *BlmGEL*
Ptolemy, Claudius c. 90-c. 168 *WhWE*
Ptolemy, Claudius 100-178 *AstEnc*
Ptolemy Soter, I 367BC-285BC *HisWorL [port]*
Ptushko, Alexander 1900- *IntDcF 2-4*
Pualani, Gloria 1950- *WhoBlA 94*
Pu Anxiu 1918- *WhoPRCh 91 [port]*
Puapua, Tomasi 1938- *IntWW 93*
Pubillones, Jorge 1954- *WhoFI 94*
Public Enemy *AfrAmAl 6*
Puccetti, Roland (Peter) 1922- *EncSF 93*
Puccetti, Roland Peter 1924- *WhoAm 94*
Pucci, Emilio d1992 *IntWW 93N*
Pucci, Emilio 1914-1992 *AnObit 1992, CurBio 93N, WhAm 10*
Puccinelli, Leo John 1921- *WhoAmP 93*
Puccinelli, Raimondo 1904-1986 *WhoAmA 93N*
Puccinelli, Robert A. 1937- *WhoIns 94*
Puccini, Domenico (Vincenzo Maria) 1772-1815 *NewGrDO*
Puccini, Giacomo (Antonio Domenico Michele Secondo Maria) 1858-1924 *NewGrDO [port]*
Puccitelli, Virgilio 1599-1654 *NewGrDO*
Puccitta, Vincenzo *NewGrDO*
Pucel, Robert Albin 1926- *WhoAm 94*

Pu Chaozhu 1929- *IntWW 93, WhoPRCh 91 [port]*
Puchon, Madame c. 1700-1722? *NewGrDO*
Puchta, Charles George 1918- *WhoAm 94*
Pucitta, Vincenzo 1778-1861 *NewGrDO*
Puck, Eva d1979 *WhoHol 92*
Puck, Theodore Thomas 1916- *IntWW 93, WhoAm 94, WhoScEn 94, WhoWest 94*
Pucker, Bernard H. 1937- *WhoAmA 93*
Puckett, Allen Weare 1942- *WhoAm 94*
Puckett, Carlissa Roseann 1951- *WhoMW 93*
Puckett, Elbridge Gerry 1956- *WhoScEn 94*
Puckett, Elizabeth Ann 1943- *WhoAmL 94*
Puckett, Hoyle Brooks 1925- *WhoScEn 94*
Puckett, James Philip 1937- *WhoAmP 93*
Puckett, Kirby 1961- *WhoAm 94, WhoBlA 94, WhoMW 93*
Puckett, Richard Edward 1932- *WhoWest 94*
Puckett, Robert Hugh 1935- *WhoAm 94*
Puckette, Stephen Elliott 1927- *WhoAm 94*
Puck Hyah Toot 1878-1965? *EncNAR [port]*
Puckler-Muskau, Hermann von 1785-1871 *DcLB 133 [port]*
Puckorius, Theodore D. 1930- *WhoAm 94*
Puckrein, Gary Alexander 1949- *WhoBlA 94*
Puclik, Mark Steven 1955- *WhoAmL 94*
Puddephatt, Andrew Charles 1950- *Who 94*
Puddington, Ira Edwin 1911- *WhoAm 94*
Puddy, Donald Ray 1937- *WhoScEn 94*
Pudelek, Barbara Therese 1961- *WhoMW 93*
Pudles, Lynne 1951- *WhoMW 93*
Pudlin, Dave B. 1952- *WhoAmP 93*
Pudney, Gary Laurence 1934- *WhoAm 94, WhoWest 94*
Pudoje 1939- *WhoPRCh 91 [port]*
Pudovkin, Vsevolod d1953 *WhoHol 92*
Puech, Jean 1942- *IntWW 93*
Puechner, Ray 1935-1987 *WrDr 94N*
Puello, Andres D. 1932- *WhoHisp 94*
Puente, Antonio Enrique 1952- *WhoHisp 94*
Puente, John George 1930- *WhoAm 94*
Puente, Jose Garza 1949- *WhoWest 94*
Puente, Oralia 1944- *WhoHisp 94*
Puente, Robert R. 1958- *WhoAmP 93, WhoHisp 94*
Puente, Stephen L. *WhoHisp 94*
Puente, Sylvia Mary 1958- *WhoHisp 94*
Puente, Teresa Christina 1967- *WhoHisp 94*
Puente, Tito *WhoHol 92*
Puente, Tito 1923 *WhoHisp 94*
Puente, Tito Anthony 1923- *WhoAm 94*
Puente, Victor, Sr. *WhoHisp 94*
Puente, Yolanda 1964- *WhoHisp 94*
Puente-Duany, Hary P. 1944- *WhoHisp 94*
Puentes, Arnold 1956- *WhoHisp 94*
Puentes, Carlos Julian 1958- *WhoHisp 94*
Puentes, Charles Theodore, Jr. 1933- *WhoHisp 94*
Puentes, Roberto Santos 1929- *WhoHisp 94*
Puenzo, Luis 1949- *IntWW 93*
Puerner, John *WhoAm 94*
Puerner, Paul Raymond 1927- *WhoAmL 94*
Puertolas, Soledad 1947- *BlmGWL*
Puett, Garnett G. 1959- *WhoAmA 93*
Puette, William J. *DrAPF 93*
Puettjer, Gustav d1959 *WhoHol 92*
Puettmer, Marcus Armin 1964- *WhoScEn 94*
Puetz, William Charles 1950- *WhoScEn 94*
Pufahl, John K. 1942- *WhoAmA 93*
Pufendorf, Samuel, Freiherr von 1632-1694 *EncEth*
Puffer, Leonard Bruce, Jr. 1928- *WhoAm 94, WhoAmL 94*
Puffer, Richard Judson 1931- *WhoAm 94*
Puffer, Ruth Rice 1907- *WhoWest 94*
Puffy, Charles d1942 *WhoHol 92*
Puga, Francisco Javier 1942- *WhoHisp 94*
Puga, Rafael *WhoHisp 94*
Pugay, Jeffrey Ibanez 1958- *WhoFI 94, WhoScEn 94, WhoWest 94*
Pugel, Robert Joseph 1941- *WhoAmP 93*
Pugh, Alan Virgil 1952- *WhoAmP 93*
Pugh, Alastair Tarrant 1928- *Who 94*
Pugh, Andrew Cartwright 1937- *Who 94*
Pugh, Ann D. 1952- *WhoAmP 93*
Pugh, Arthur James 1937- *WhoAm 94, WhoFI 94*
Pugh, C. Emmett 1940- *WhoAmP 93*
Pugh, Charles Edward 1922- *Who 94*
Pugh, Clementine A. *WhoBlA 94*
Pugh, Coy 1952- *WhoAmP 93*
Pugh, Donald Ray 1953- *WhoMW 93*
Pugh, Edward Clevely 1937- *Who 94*
Pugh, Edwin William 1874-1930 *DcLB 135 [port]*
Pugh, Emerson Martindale 1896- *WhAm 10*
Pugh, Emerson William 1929- *WhoAm 94*
Pugh, G. Douglas 1923- *WhoBlA 94*
Pugh, George Willard, Jr. 1956- *WhoAmL 94*
Pugh, Grace Huntley 1912- *WhoAmA 93*
Pugh, Harold Valentine 1899- *Who 94*
Pugh, Helen Pedersen 1934- *WhoWest 94*
Pugh, Idwal (Vaughan) 1918- *Who 94*
Pugh, James Byron 1955- *WhoFI 94*
Pugh, Jamie Kathleen 1946- *WhoWest 94*
Pugh, Jess M. d1962 *WhoHol 92*
Pugh, John 1945- *WhoAmP 93*
Pugh, John Arthur 1920- *Who 94*
Pugh, John Stanley 1927- *Who 94*
Pugh, John Wilbur 1912- *WrDr 94*
Pugh, Keith E., Jr. 1937- *WhoAm 94*
Pugh, Kyle Mitchell, Jr. 1937- *WhoWest 94*
Pugh, Lawrence R. 1933- *WhoAm 94, WhoFI 94*
Pugh, Lionel Roger Price 1916- *Who 94*
Pugh, Marion Stirling 1911- *WhoAm 94*
Pugh, Mark Ashael 1955- *WhoMW 93*
Pugh, Marlana Patrice 1952- *WhoBlA 94*
Pugh, Michael Joel 1946- *WhoAmL 94*
Pugh, Patterson David Gordon d1993 *Who 94N*
Pugh, Paul Franklin 1922- *WhoScEn 94*
Pugh, Peter David S. *Who 94*
Pugh, Richard Crawford 1929- *WhoAm 94, WhoWest 94*
Pugh, Robert Gahagan 1924- *WhoAm 94*
Pugh, Robert William, Sr. 1926- *WhoBlA 94*
Pugh, Roderick W. 1919- *WhoBlA 94*
Pugh, Roderick Wellington 1919- *WhoAm 94*
Pugh, Roger Courtenay Beckwith 1917- *Who 94*
Pugh, Sheenagh 1950- *WrDr 94*
Pugh, Ted *Who 94*
Pugh, Thomas Jefferson 1917- *WhoBlA 94*
Pugh, Thomas W. 1949- *WhoAmP 93*
Pugh, Thomas Wilfred 1949- *WhoMW 93*
Pugh, Tim Francis, II 1963- *WhoScEn 94*
Pugh, Timothy J. 1945- *WhoAmL 94*
Pugh, Willard E. *WhoHol 92*
Pugh, William David 1904- *Who 94*
Pugh, William Whitmell Hill 1954- *WhoAmL 94*
Pughe, Bronwyn Ginger 1955- *WhoWest 94*
Pugin, Nikolai Andreyevich 1940- *IntWW 93*
Puglia, Frank d1975 *WhoHol 92*
Pugliese, Albert 1954- *WhoFI 94*
Pugliese, Juan Carlos 1915- *IntWW 93*
Pugliese, Robert Francis 1933- *WhoAm 94, WhoAmL 94*
Pugliese, Robert J. 1953- *WhoAm 94, WhoAmL 94*
Puglise, John Michael 1948- *WhoFI 94, WhoMW 93*
Puglisi, Anthony Joseph 1949- *WhoAm 94*
Puglisi, Frank Joseph 1931- *WhoAmL 94*
Puglisi, Philip James 1943- *WhoMW 93*
Pugmire, Gregg Thomas 1963- *WhoScEn 94, WhoWest 94*
Pugnani, Gaetano 1731-1798 *NewGrDO*
Pugni, Cesare 1802-1870 *IntDcB, NewGrDO*
Pugno, (Stephane) Raoul) 1852-1914 *NewGrDO*
Pugonowska-Jucha, Emilia *WhoWomW 91*
Pugsley, Alfred Grenvile 1903- *IntWW 93, Who 94*
Pugsley, David Philip 1944- *Who 94*
Pugsley, Frank Burruss 1920- *WhoAm 94*
Pu Guochang 1937- *WhoPRCh 91 [port]*
Pu Haiqing 1941- *WhoPRCh 91 [port]*
Puhakka, Matti Juhani 1945- *IntWW 93*
Puhala, James Joseph 1942- *WhoAm 94*
Puhk, Heino 1923- *WhoMW 93, WhoScEn 94*
Puhl, Nick Robert 1956- *WhoFI 94*
Puhr, Stephen Patrick 1959- *WhoFI 94*
Puhvel, Jaan 1932- *WhoAm 94*
Pui, Ching-Hon 1951- *WhoAsA 94*
Puig, Eva d1968 *WhoHol 92*
Puig, Gilberto, Jr. 1961- *WhoHisp 94*
Puig, James *WhoHol 92*
Puig, Manuel d1990 *IntWW 93N*
Puig, Manuel 1932-1990 *GayLL, HispLC [port]*
Puig, Nicolas 1952- *WhoHisp 94*
Puig, Vicente P. *WhoHisp 94*
Puig De La Bellacasa, Jose Joaquin 1931- *Who 94*
Puigdollers, Carmen *DrAPF 93*
Puisieux, Madeleine d'Arsant de 1720-1798 *BlmGWL*
Puja, Frigyes 1921- *IntWW 93*
Pujals, Humberto A., Jr. 1952- *WhoHisp 94*
Pujara, Subhash Somabhai 1946- *WhoAsA 94*
Pu Jiexiu 1907- *WhoPRCh 91 [port]*
Pujman, Ferdinand 1889-1961 *NewGrDO*
Pujol, Elliott 1943- *WhoAmA 93*
Pujol, Ernesto 1957- *WhoHisp 94*
Pujol I Soley, Jordi 1930- *IntWW 93*
Pulaski, Casimir 1747-1779 *WhAmRev [port]*
Pulaski, Charles Alexander, Jr. 1941- *WhoAm 94*
Pulaski, Kazimierz 1748-1779 *AmRev*
Pulaski, Lillian d1977 *WhoHol 92*
Pulaski, Mary Ann (Spencer) 1916-1992 *WrDr 94N*
Pulatov, Abdul Rahmid *IntWW 93*
Pulatov, Timur Iskhakovich 1939- *LngBDD*
Puleo, Frank Charles 1945- *WhoAm 94, WhoAmL 94*
Puleo, Johnny d1983 *WhoHol 92*
Pulford, Richard Charles 1944- *Who 94*
Pulford, Robert Jesse 1936- *WhoMW 93*
Pulfrey, Roy Allan 1953- *WhoMW 93*
Pulgram, Ernst 1915- *WhoAm 94*
Pulgram, William Leopold 1921- *WhoAm 94*
Puliafito, Carmen Anthony 1951- *WhoScEn 94*
Pulich, Warren Mark, Jr. 1946- *WhoScEn 94*
Pulido, Carlos Orlando 1949- *WhoScEn 94*
Pulido, Miguel A. *WhoHisp 94*
Pulido, Richard 1960- *WhoHisp 94*
Pulido, Rudolph Valentino, Sr. 1939- *WhoHisp 94*
Pulido, Victor Ismael 1961- *WhoHisp 94*
Puligandla, Viswanadham 1938- *WhoAsA 94*
Pulijal, Madhu V. 1949- *WhoAsA 94*
Pulis, Ralph Stephen 1944- *WhoIns 94*
Pulis, Stephen James 1968- *WhoMW 93*
Pulitzer, Emily S. Rauh 1933- *WhoAm 94*
Pulitzer, Joseph 1847-1911 *AmSocL*
Pulitzer, Joseph, Jr. 1913- *IntWW 93, WhoFI 94*
Pulitzer, Joseph, Jr. 1913-1993 *NewYTBS 93 [port]*
Pulitzer, Michael Edgar 1930- *WhoAm 94, WhoFI 94*
Pulitzer, Ralph, Mrs. *WhAm 10*
Pulitzer, Sam Clarence 1905-1989 *WhAm 10*
Pulkkinen, Gayla Sue 1946- *WhoAmP 93*
Pulkrabek, Larry Alster 1939- *WhoAm 94, WhoAmL 94, WhoFI 94*
Pulla, Armas J. *EncSF 93*
Pullan, Brian Sebastian 1935- *Who 94*
Pullan, John Marshall 1915- *Who 94*
Pullapilly, Elizabeth Antonnette 1944- *WhoMW 93*
Pullee, Ernest Edward 1907- *Who 94*
Pullein-Thompson, Christine 1930- *WrDr 94*
Pullein-Thompson, Denis *Who 94*
Pullein-Thompson, Diana *WrDr 94*
Pullein-Thompson, Josephine (Mary Wedderburn) *ConAu 43NR, WrDr 94*
Pullein-Thompson, Josephine Mary Wedderburn *Who 94*
Pullen, Edwin Wesley 1923- *WhoAm 94*
Pullen, Keats A., Jr. 1916- *WhoAm 94*
Pullen, Kent 1942- *WhoAmP 93*
Pullen, Kent Edward 1942- *WhoWest 94*
Pullen, Lucius Wilson 1927- *WhoAmL 94*
Pullen, Margaret I. 1950- *WhoScEn 94*
Pullen, Penny Lynne 1947- *WhoAmP 93*
Pullen, (William) Reginald (James) 1922- *Who 94*
Pullen, Richard Owen 1944- *WhoAmL 94, WhoFI 94*
Pullen, Roderick Allen 1949- *Who 94*
Pullen-Brown, Stephanie D. 1949- *WhoBlA 94*
Puller, Lewis B., Jr. 1945- *WhoAm 94*
Puller, Lewis B(urwell), Jr. 1945?- *ConAu 142*
Puller, Linda T. 1945- *WhoAmP 93*
Pulles, Gregory J. *WhoAmL 94*
Pulley, Clyde Wilson 1934- *WhoBlA 94*
Pulley, Lewis Carl 1954- *WhoAmL 94*
Pulley, Paul 1936- *WhoAmP 93*
Pulleyblank, Edwin George 1922- *Who 94, WhoAm 94, WrDr 94*
Pulleyn, Samuel Robert 1946- *WhoAm 94*
Pulli, Pietro c. 1710-1759? *NewGrDO*
Pulliainen, Erkki Ossi Olavi 1938- *WhoScEn 94*
Pulliam, Betty E. 1941- *WhoBlA 94*
Pulliam, Curtis Richard 1957- *WhoScEn 94*
Pulliam, Eugene Smith 1914- *WhoAm 94, WhoWest 94*
Pulliam, Francine Sarno 1937- *WhoWest 94*
Pulliam, Harvey Jerome, Jr. 1967- *WhoBlA 94*
Pulliam, Howard Ronald 1945- *WhoAm 94, WhoScEn 94*
Pulliam, Keshia Knight 1979- *WhoHol 92*
Pulliam, Mark Stephen 1955- *WhoAm 94, WhoAmL 94*
Pulliam, Norman F. 1942- *WhoAmP 93*
Pulliam, Robert P. 1936- *WhoAmP 93*
Pulliam, Sandra Brandt 1959- *WhoFI 94*
Pulliam, Steve Cameron 1948- *WhoFI 94*
Pulliam, Terry Lester 1949- *WhoScEn 94*
Pulliam, Yvonne Antoinette *WhoMW 93*
Pullin, Jorge Alfredo 1963- *WhoScEn 94, WhoWest 94*
Pulling, Ronald Wilson, Sr. 1919- *WhoAm 94*
Pulling, Thomas Leffingwell 1939- *WhoAm 94*
Pullinger, (Francis) Alan 1913- *Who 94*
Pullinger, John Elphick 1930- *Who 94*
Pullman, Bill 1954- *IntMPA 94, WhoHol 92*
Pullman, Maynard Edward 1927- *WhoAm 94*
Pullman, Philip 1946- *SmATA 17AS [port]*
Pullman, Philip (N.) 1946- *TwCYAW*
Pullman, Richard D. 1946- *WhoAmL 94*
Pullman, Robert A. 1926- *WhoAmP 93*
Pullum, Erin Lynn 1961- *WhoMW 93*
Pullum, Geoffrey Keith 1945- *WhoWest 94*
Pully, B. S. d1972 *WhoHol 92*
Pulman, Michael Barraclough 1933- *WrDr 94*
Pulos, Arthur Jon 1917- *WhoAm 94, WhoAmA 93*
Pulsford, Petronella 1946- *WrDr 94*
Pulsifer, Edgar Darling 1934- *WhoFI 94, WhoMW 93*
Pulsifer, Roy 1931- *WhoFI 94*
Pultrone, Anthony Joseph 1967- *WhoFI 94*
Pulver, Enid 1934- *WhoHol 92*
Pulver, Liselotte 1929- *WhoHol 92*
Pulver, Robin 1945- *SmATA 76 [port]*
Pulvermacher, Louis C. 1928- *WhoAmL 94*
Pulvertaft, David Martin 1938- *Who 94*
Pulvertaft, (Isobel) Lalage 1925- *WrDr 94*
Pulzer, Peter George Julius 1929- *Who 94, WrDr 94*
Puma, J. *WhoHisp 94*
Pumariega, JoAnne Buttacavoli 1952- *WhoScEn 94*
Pumfrey, Nicholas Richard 1951- *Who 94*
Pumper, Robert William 1921- *WhoAm 94*
Pumphrey, Fred Homer 1898- *WhAm 10*
Pumphrey, Gerald Robert 1947- *WhoAmL 94*
Pumphrey, Jean *DrAPF 93*
Pumphrey, (John) Laurence 1916- *Who 94*
Pun, Pattle Pak-Toe 1946- *WhoAsA 94*
Punch, Sandra Lee 1952- *WhoWest 94*
Punchard, Lionel 1952- *WhoWest 94*
Punch-McGregor, Angela 1953- *WhoHol 92*
Puncog Wangje 1921- *WhoPRCh 91 [port]*
Pundeff, Marin V. 1921- *WrDr 94*
Pundmann, Ed John, Jr. 1939- *WhoMW 93*
Pundt, Richard Arthur 1944- *WhoAmL 94*
Pung, Rosalyn Alyce 1948- *WhoMW 93*
Pungan, Vasile 1926- *Who 94*
Pungor, Erno 1923- *IntWW 93, WhoScEn 94*
Punia, Constance Edith *WhoAmA 93*
Puniello, Francoise Sara 1947- *WhoAmA 93*
Punj, Vikram 1957- *WhoFI 94*
Punjala, Shiv Shanker 1929- *IntWW 93*
Punnapayak, Hunsa 1951- *WhoScEn 94*
Punnett, Reginald Crundall 1875-1967 *DcNaB MP, WorScD*
Punnett, Robert Malcolm 1936- *WrDr 94*
Punsley, Bernard *WhoHol 92*
Punsly, Bernard 1922- *See* East Side Kids *WhoCom*
Punt, Leonard Cornelis 1940- *WhoMW 93*
Punt, Terry Lee 1949- *WhoAmP 93*
Punwani, Dharam Vir 1942- *WhoAsA 94*
Punzi, Henry Anthony 1958- *WhoHisp 94*
Puolanne, Ulla Kaija 1931- *IntWW 93, WhoWomW 91*
Puotinen, Arthur Edwin 1941- *WhoAm 94*
Pupo, Jorge I. 1960- *WhoHisp 94*
Pupo-Mayo, Gustavo Alberto 1955- *WhoHisp 94*
Puquin 1937- *WhoPRCh 91 [port]*
Pura, William Paul 1948- *WhoAmA 93*
Puracchio, Sheryl Leger 1957- *WhoMW 93*

Purandare, Yeshwant K. 1934- *WhoScEn 94*
Puravs, John Andris 1945- *WhoMW 93*
Purce, Thomas Les 1946- *WhoBlA 94*
Purcell, Alexander Holmes 1942- *WhoWest 94*
Purcell, Amelia Allerton 1953- *WhoFI 94*
Purcell, Ann 1941- *WhoAmA 93*
Purcell, Ann R. *WhoAmP 93*
Purcell, Arthur Henry 1944- *WhoAm 94*
Purcell, Bill 1953- *WhoAmP 93*
Purcell, Bradford Moore 1929- *WhoAm 94*
Purcell, Charles d1962 *WhoHol 92*
Purcell, Charles Kipps 1959- *WhoWest 94*
Purcell, Dale 1919- *WhoAm 94*
Purcell, Daniel c. 1660-1717 *NewGrDO*
Purcell, Dick d1944 *WhoHol 92*
Purcell, Edward Mills 1912- *Who 94, WhoAm 94, WhoScEn 94, WorScD*
Purcell, Ethel d1946 *WhoHol 92*
Purcell, Fenton Peter 1942- *WhoFI 94*
Purcell, Francis Jerome 1939- *WhoAm 94*
Purcell, Harry 1919- *Who 94*
Purcell, Henry 1658-1695 *BlmGEL, NewGrDO*
Purcell, Hugh D. 1915- *WhoAmA 93*
Purcell, Irene d1972 *WhoHol 92*
Purcell, James *WhoHol 92*
Purcell, James Francis 1920- *WhoAm 94*
Purcell, James Lawrence 1929- *WhoAm 94, WhoAmL 94*
Purcell, James Nelson 1938- *IntWW 93*
Purcell, James Nelson, Jr. 1938- *WhoAm 94*
Purcell, James Thomas 1968- *WhoMW 93*
Purcell, Jerry *WhoScEn 94*
Purcell, Joan *WhoWomW 91*
Purcell, John Baptist 1800-1883 *DcAmReB 2*
Purcell, John F. 1954- *WhoAmL 94*
Purcell, John W. 1948- *WhoAmL 94*
Purcell, Kenneth 1928- *WhoAm 94*
Purcell, Lee 1947- *WhoHol 92*
Purcell, (Robert) Michael 1923- *Who 94*
Purcell, Noel d1985 *WhoHol 92*
Purcell, Patrick B. 1943- *IntMPA 94, WhoAm 94, WhoFI 94*
Purcell, Patrick Joseph 1947- *WhoAm 94*
Purcell, Philip James 1943- *WhoAm 94, WhoFI 94*
Purcell, Richard Fick 1924- *WhoAm 94*
Purcell, Robert Harry 1935- *WhoAm 94, WhoScEn 94*
Purcell, Robert W. 1911-1991 *WhAm 10*
Purcell, Royal Ellis, III 1921- *WhoMW 93*
Purcell, Sally (Anne Jane) 1944- *WrDr 94*
Purcell, Steven Richard *WhoAm 94*
Purcell, Stuart McLeod, III 1944- *WhoFI 94, WhoWest 94*
Purcell, Thomas Owen, Jr. 1944- *WhoScEn 94*
Purcell, William 1909- *WrDr 94*
Purcell, William Ernest 1909- *Who 94*
Purcell, William Henry Samuel 1912- *Who 94*
Purcell, William O. 1941- *WhoAmL 94*
Purcell, William Paul 1935- *WhoAm 94*
Purcell, William Paxson, III 1953- *WhoAmL 94*
Purchas, Christopher Patrick Brooks 1943- *Who 94*
Purchas, Francis (Brooks) 1919- *Who 94*
Purchas, Robin Michael 1946- *Who 94*
Purchase, Brian *WhoHol 92*
Purchase, Kenneth 1939- *Who 94*
Purcifull, Dan Elwood 1935- *WhoAm 94, WhoScEn 94*
Purcifull, Robert Otis 1932- *WhoAm 94*
Purdee, Nathan *WhoHol 92*
Purdee, Nathan 1950- *WhoBlA 94*
Purdell, Reginald d1953 *WhoHol 92*
Purden, Roma Laurette 1928- *Who 94*
Purdes, Alice Marie 1931- *WhoMW 93*
Purdey, Gary Rush 1936- *WhoScEn 94*
Purdie, Robin Stanford 1940- *WhoWest 94*
Purdom, Billy Joe 1947- *WhoAmP 93*
Purdom, Edmund 1924- *IntMPA 94, WhoHol 92*
Purdom, Paul Walton, Jr. 1940- *WhoAm 94, WhoScEn 94*
Purdom, R. Don 1926- *WhoIns 94*
Purdom, Thomas James 1937- *WhoAm 94*
Purdom, Tom 1936- *EncSF 93*
Purdon, Corran William Brooke 1921- *Who 94*
Purdon, Kevin Eric 1955- *WhoFI 94*
Purdum, Rebecca 1959- *WhoAmA 93*
Purdum, Robert L. 1935- *IntWW 93, WhoAm 94, WhoFI 94*
Purdy, A(lfred) W(ellington) 1918- *WrDr 94*
Purdy, Al *ConAu 42NR*
Purdy, Al(fred Wellington) 1918- *ConAu 42NR*
Purdy, Alan Harris 1923- *WhoAm 94*
Purdy, Alan MacGregor 1940- *WhoAm 94*
Purdy, Alfred 1918- *IntWW 93*
Purdy, Carol 1943- *WrDr 94*
Purdy, Charles Robert 1937- *WhoAm 94*
Purdy, Constance d1960 *WhoHol 92*
Purdy, David Lawrence 1928- *WhoScEn 94*
Purdy, Dennis Gene 1946- *WhoFI 94*
Purdy, Donald Gilbert, Jr. 1953- *WhoScEn 94*
Purdy, Donald R. 1924- *WhoAmA 93*
Purdy, Douglas C. 1944- *WhoAmL 94*
Purdy, Dwight H(illiard) 1941- *WrDr 94*
Purdy, Henry Carl 1937- *WhoAmA 93*
Purdy, James *DrAPF 93*
Purdy, James 1923- *IntWW 93, WhoAm 94, WrDr 94*
Purdy, James (Amos) 1923- *GayLL*
Purdy, James Aaron 1941- *WhoMW 93*
Purdy, Joseph Donald 1942- *WhoWest 94*
Purdy, Ken W. 1913-1972 *DcLB 137 [port]*
Purdy, Marlene Ann 1941- *WhoAmP 93*
Purdy, Michael Waite 1945- *WhoMW 93*
Purdy, Ralph William 1924- *WhoAm 94*
Purdy, Richard Allan 1946- *WhoFI 94*
Purdy, Robert John 1916- *Who 94*
Purdy, William Crossley 1930- *WhoAm 94*
Purdy, William Marshall 1940- *WhoAm 94*
Purens, Ilmars *DrAPF 93*
Puretz, Donald Harris 1934- *WhoScEn 94*
Purfeerst, Clarence M. 1928- *WhoAmP 93*
Purgathofer, Werner 1955- *WhoScEn 94*
Puri, Ambrogio 1920- *IntWW 93*
Puri, Madan Lal 1929- *WhoAm 94, WhoMW 93*
Puri, Pratap 1938- *WhoAsA 94*
Puri, Pushpinder Singh 1946- *WhoScEn 94*
Puri, Shamlal 1951- *WrDr 94*
Puris, Martin Ford 1939- *WhoAm 94*
Puritz, David 1935- *WhoAmP 93*
Puritz, David A. *WhoAmP 93*
Purkey, Harry Robert 1934- *WhoAmP 93*
Purkinje, Jan Evangelista 1787-1869 *WorScD*
Purkis, Andrew James 1949- *Who 94*
Purkyne, Jan Evangelista 1787-1869 *WorScD*
Purl, Linda 1955- *IntMPA 94, WhoHol 92*
Purl, O. Thomas 1924- *WhoAm 94*
Purle, Charles Lambert 1947- *Who 94*
Purmort, Francis Walworth, Jr. 1930- *WhoIns 94*
Purnell, Carolyn J. 1939- *WhoBlA 94*
Purnell, Charles Giles 1921- *WhoAmL 94*
Purnell, Charles Rea 1922- *WhoAm 94, WhoAmL 94*
Purnell, Frank 1886-1953 *EncABHB 9 [port]*
Purnell, John H. 1941- *WhoAm 94*
Purnell, Louise 1942- *WhoHol 92*
Purnell, Lynet Jane 1954- *WhoMW 93*
Purnell, Mark W. 1957- *WhoBlA 94*
Purnell, Marshall E. 1950- *WhoBlA 94*
Purnell, Maurice Eugene, Jr. 1940- *WhoAm 94*
Purnell, Nicholas Robert 1944- *Who 94*
Purnell, Paul Oliver 1936- *Who 94*
Purnell, Ricky Duane 1962- *WhoMW 93*
Purney, Thomas 1695-1730 *DcNaB MP*
Puro, Michael Steven 1949- *WhoAmP 93*
Purohit, Milind Vasant 1957- *WhoAsA 94, WhoScEn 94*
Purohit, Sharad Chandra 1949- *WhoScEn 94*
Purpur, George Franklin, Jr. 1925- *WhoAm 94*
Purpura, Dominick P. 1927- *WhoAm 94, WhoScEn 94*
Purpura, Dominick Paul 1927- *IntWW 93*
Purpura, Joseph Matthew 1950- *WhoMW 93*
Purpura, Peter Joseph 1939- *WhoAm 94*
Purrington, Linwood N. *WhoAmP 93*
Purse, Charles Roe 1960- *WhoAm 94*
Purse, Hugh Robert Leslie 1940- *Who 94*
Pursel, Harold Max, Sr. 1921- *WhoWest 94*
Pursel, Robert Wayne, Jr. 1966- *WhoFI 94*
Pursell, Carl D. 1933- *WhoAmP 93*
Pursell, Carroll Wirth 1932- *WhoAm 94*
Pursell, Paul Dennis 1950- *WhoWest 94*
Pursell, Robert d1982 *WhoHol 92*
Purser, Donald Joseph 1954- *WhoAmL 94*
Purser, John W(hitley) 1942- *WrDr 94*
Purser, Philip (John) 1925- *WrDr 94*
Purser, Stuart Robert 1907-1986 *WhoAmA 93N*
Purses, Samuel D. 1942- *WhoAmP 93*
Pursey, Derek Lindsay 1927- *WhoAm 94*
Pursifull, Carmen Maria 1930- *WhoHisp 94*
Pursinger, Marvin Gavin 1923- *WhoAm 94, WhoFI 94, WhoWest 94*
Pursley, Evelyn Marie 1952- *WhoAmL 94*
Pursley, Michael Bader 1945- *WhoAm 94*
Pursley, Ricky Anthony 1954- *WhoAmL 94*
Pursoo, Eugene 1946- *IntWW 93*
Purssell, Anthony John Richard 1926- *Who 94*
Purtell, Dennis Joseph 1940- *WhoAmL 94*
Purtell, Lawrence Robert 1947- *WhoAm 94*
Purtill, Richard L. 1931- *WrDr 94*
Purtilo, Karen Elaine *WhoMW 93*
Purtle, Carol Jean 1939- *WhoAmA 93*
Purtle, John Ingram 1923- *WhoAm 94, WhoAmP 93*
Purves, Alan Carroll 1931- *WhoAm 94*
Purves, Daphne (Helen) 1908- *Who 94*
Purves, Elizabeth Mary 1950- *Who 94*
Purves, Libby 1950- *WrDr 94*
Purves, William 1931- *IntWW 93, Who 94*
Purves, William Kirkwood 1934- *WhoAm 94*
Purviance, Edna d1958 *WhoHol 92*
Purviance, Edna 1894-1958 *WhoCom*
Purvin, Robert Leman 1917-1991 *WhAm 10*
Purvines, Verne Ewald, Jr. 1945- *WhoAmL 94*
Purvis, Allen R. 1946- *WhoAmL 94*
Purvis, Archie C., Jr. 1939- *WhoBlA 94*
Purvis, George Dewey, III 1947- *WhoScEn 94*
Purvis, George Frank, Jr. 1914- *WhoAm 94, WhoFI 94, WhoIns 94*
Purvis, Henry R. *Who 94*
Purvis, Hoyt Hughes 1939- *WhoAm 94*
Purvis, Jack *WhoHol 92*
Purvis, John Anderson 1942- *WhoAmL 94, WhoWest 94*
Purvis, John Robert 1938- *Who 94*
Purvis, Lowell d1980 *WhoHol 92*
Purvis, Neville 1936- *Who 94*
Purvis, Perrin Hays 1918- *WhoAmP 93*
Purvis, Randall W. B. 1957- *WhoAmL 94*
Purvis, Ronald Scott 1928- *WhoFI 94*
Purvis, Stewart Peter 1947- *Who 94*
Puryear, Alvin N. 1937- *WhoBlA 94*
Puryear, Alvin Nelson 1937- *WhoAm 94*
Puryear, Byron Nelson 1913- *WhoAmP 93*
Puryear, Martin 1941- *AfrAmAl 6, IntWW 93, WhoAm 94, WhoAmA 93*
Pusack, George Williams 1920- *Who 94*
Pusateri, James Anthony 1938- *WhoAm 94, WhoAmL 94*
Pusateri, Lawrence Xavier 1931- *WhoAm 94, WhoAmL 94, WhoFI 94*
Pusateri, Paul Dennis 1952- *WhoAmL 94*
Puscas, Victor Stefan 1943- *LngBDD*
Pusch, William Gerard 1935- *WhoAm 94*
Puscheck, Herbert Charles 1936- *WhoAm 94*
Pusey, Arthur *WhoHol 92*
Pusey, Nathan Marsh 1907- *IntWW 93, Who 94*
Pusey, William Anderson 1936- *WhoAm 94*
Pusey, William Webb, III 1910- *WhoAm 94*
Pu Shan 1923- *IntWW 93, WhoPRCh 91 [port]*
Pushkar, Raymond Stephen Edward 1938- *WhoAm 94*
Pushkarev, Boris S. 1929- *WhoAm 94, WrDr 94*
Pushker, Gloria (Teles) 1927- *ConAu 142, SmATA 75 [port]*
Pushkin, Aleksandr 1907-1970 *IntDcB*
Pushkin, Aleksandr (Sergeevich) 1799-1837 *RfGShF*
Pushkin, Alexander (Sergeyevich) 1799-1837 *IntDcT 2*
Pushkin, Alexander Sergeyevich 1799-1837 *NewGrDO*
Pushman, Hovsep 1877-1966 *WhoAmA 93N*
Pusich, Antonia Gertrudes 1805-1883 *BlmGWL*
Pusinelli, (Frederick) Nigel (Moliere) 1919- *Who 94*
Puskas, Elek 1942- *WhoFI 94*
Puskas, Ferenc 1926- *WorESoc [port]*
Pusol, Jorge *WhoHisp 94*
Pust, David Richard 1940- *WhoWest 94*
Pustilnik, David Daniel 1931- *WhoAm 94, WhoAmL 94*
Pustilnik, Jean Todd 1932- *WhoAm 94*
Pustovar, Paul Thomas 1951- *WhoMW 93*
Puszynski, Jan Alojzy 1950- *WhoScEn 94*
Puta, Diane Fay 1947- *WhoMW 93, WhoScEn 94*
Pu Ta-Hai 1922- *IntWW 93*
Putatunda, Susil Kumar 1948- *WhoMW 93, WhoScEn 94*
Putch, John 1961- *WhoHol 92*
Putchakayala, Hari Babu 1949- *WhoScEn 94*
Puth, John Wells 1929- *WhoAm 94*
Puthenveetil, Jos Anthony 1947- *WhoFI 94*
Puthoff, Francis Urban 1922- *WhoMW 93*
Putinar, Mihai Ioan 1955- *WhoWest 94*
Putka, Andrew Charles 1926- *WhoAm 94*
Putman, Brenda 1890-1975 *WhoAmA 93N*
Putman, Carol Jean 1943- *WhoWest 94*
Putman, Dale Cornelius 1927- *WhoAm 94*
Putman, Dwight Frederick 1898- *WhAm 10*
Putman, Kathleen Harvey 1913- *WhoAmP 93*
Putman, Loucile Minnie 1929- *WhoAmP 93*
Putman, Michael 1948- *WhoAmL 94*
Putman, Thomas Harold 1930- *WhoScEn 94*
Putnam, Alfred Wynne 1919- *WhoAmL 94*
Putnam, Ashley (Elizabeth) 1952- *NewGrDO*
Putnam, Barrett Graham 1919- *WhoWest 94*
Putnam, Barry J. 1954- *WhoAmP 93*
Putnam, Clara Joyce 1943- *WhoWest 94*
Putnam, Constance E(lizabeth) 1943- *ConAu 140*
Putnam, David Frank 1932- *WhoWest 94*
Putnam, Ed M., II 1928- *WhoAmP 93*
Putnam, Elena Brown 1923- *WhoMW 93*
Putnam, Frank William 1917- *WhoAm 94*
Putnam, Frederick Warren, Jr. 1917- *WhoAm 94*
Putnam, George d1975 *WhoHol 92*
Putnam, George Endicott 1921- *WhoAm 94*
Putnam, George W., Jr. 1920- *WhoAm 94*
Putnam, Glendora M. 1923- *WhoBlA 94*
Putnam, Hilary 1926- *IntWW 93, WrDr 94*
Putnam, Hugh Dyer 1928- *WhoScEn 94*
Putnam, Israel 1718-1790 *AmRev, WhAmRev [port]*
Putnam, J. E. *WhoAmP 93*
Putnam, Jackson Keith 1929- *WhoWest 94*
Putnam, John 1904- *WrDr 94*
Putnam, John B., Mrs. 1903- *WhoAmA 93N*
Putnam, Julie Katherine 1952- *WhoMW 93*
Putnam, Linda Lee 1945- *WhoAm 94*
Putnam, Michael Courtney Jenkins 1933- *WhoAm 94*
Putnam, Nol 1934- *WhoAmA 93*
Putnam, Pamela Kay 1946- *WhoAmL 94*
Putnam, Peter Brock 1920- *WhoAm 94*
Putnam, Richard Johnson 1913- *WhoAm 94*
Putnam, Robert E. 1933- *ConAu 41NR, WhoAm 94*
Putnam, Robert Ervin 1927- *WhoScEn 94*
Putnam, Rufus 1738-1824 *AmRev, WhAmRev*
Putnam, Terry Michael 1954- *WhoAm 94, WhoAmL 94*
Putnam, Virginia Alice 1952- *WhoWest 94*
Putnam, William Lowell 1924- *WhoFI 94*
Putney, Gail J. 1927- *WrDr 94*
Putney, John A., Jr. 1939- *WhoIns 94*
Putney, John Alden, Jr. 1939- *WhoAm 94, WhoFI 94*
Putney, Lacey Edward 1928- *WhoAmP 93*
Putney, Mark William 1929- *WhoAm 94, WhoFI 94, WhoMW 93*
Putney, Mary Engler 1933- *WhoFI 94*
Putney, Paul William 1940- *WhoAm 94*
Pu Tongxiu *WhoPRCh 91*
Putriment, Pauline Titus 1922- *WhoAmP 93*
Putsep, Peeter Ervin 1955- *WhoScEn 94*
Putt, John Ward 1924- *WhoScEn 94*
Putt, S(amuel) Gorley 1913- *Who 94*
Puttenham, George d1590 *BlmGEL*
Putter, Irving 1917- *WhoAm 94*
Putterman, Florence Grace 1927- *WhoAm 94, WhoAmA 93*
Putterman, Louis G. 1952- *WhoAm 94*
Puttick, Richard George 1916- *Who 94*
Puttlitz, Karl Joseph, Sr. 1941- *WhoScEn 94*
Puttnam, David 1941- *IntDcF 2-4, IntMPA 94*
Puttnam, David Terence 1941- *IntWW 93, Who 94, WhoAm 94*
Putzel, Constance Kellner 1922- *WhoAm 94*
Putzel, Michael 1942- *WhoAm 94*
Putzell, Edwin Joseph, Jr. 1913- *WhoAm 94, WhoAmL 94, WhoFI 94*
Puxley, Ray 1948- *ConAu 142*
Puxon, (Christine) Margaret 1915- *Who 94*
Puyana, Rafael 1931- *IntWW 93*
Puyat-Reyes, Ma. Consuelo 1937- *WhoWomW 91*
Puyau, Francis Albert 1928- *WhoAm 94*
Puyi 1905-1967 *HisWorL*

Q

Qabbani, Nizar 1923- *BlmGWL,*
ConWorW 93
Qaboos Bin Said 1940- *IntWW 93*
Qaddafi, Mu'ammar al- *IntWW 93*
Qadhafi, Mu'ammar al- *IntWW 93*
Qadri, Syed Burhanullah 1949-
WhoScEn 94
Qaim, Syed Muhammad 1941-
WhoScEn 94
Qalbani, Askar A. 1948- *WhoMW 93*
Qamar, Nadi Abu 1917- *WhoBlA 94*
Qanba Dhili 1929- *WhoPRCh 91*
Qasim, Syed Reazul 1938- *WhoAm 94,*
WhoAsA 94
Qasimi, Saqr bin Muhammad Al 1920-
IntWW 93
Qaysi, Riyadh Mehmoud Sami al- 1939-
IntWW 93
Qazilbash, Imtiaz Ali 1934- *WhoFI 94,*
WhoScEn 94
Qerama, Thanas *EncSF 93*
Qian, Dahong 1965- *WhoScEn 94*
Qian, Wen-yuan 1936- *WhoMW 93*
Qian, Yongjia 1939- *WhoScEn 94*
Qian Baogong d1992 *IntWW 93N*
Qian Baogong 1916- *WhoPRCh 91*
Qian Benyuan *WhoPRCh 91*
Qian Bohai *WhoPRCh 91*
Qian Changkui *WhoPRCh 91*
Qian Dai *WhoPRCh 91*
Qian Fenyong 1930- *WhoPRCh 91 [port]*
Qian Fuxing *WhoPRCh 91*
Qiang-ba Chi-lai *WhoPRCh 91*
Qian Guoliang *WhoPRCh 91*
Qiang Xiaochu *IntWW 93,*
WhoPRCh 91 [port]
Qian Hao *WhoPRCh 91*
Qian Hong 1971- *WhoPRCh 91 [port]*
Qian Huimin 1911- *WhoPRCh 91*
Qian Jiadong *WhoPRCh 91*
Qian Jiaju 1909- *IntWW 93*
Qian Jiaju 1910- *WhoPRCh 91 [port]*
Qian Jiaming 1930- *WhoPRCh 91 [port]*
Qian Lingxi 1916- *IntWW 93,*
WhoPRCh 91 [port]
Qian Linzhao 1906- *IntWW 93*
Qian Linzhao 1907- *WhoPRCh 91 [port]*
Qian Liren 1924- *IntWW 93,*
WhoPRCh 91 [port]
Qianlong 1711-1799 *HisWorL [port]*
Qian Min 1915- *WhoPRCh 91 [port]*
Qian Qi'ao 1933- *WhoPRCh 91 [port]*
Qian Qichen 1928- *IntWW 93,*
WhoPRCh 91 [port]
Qian Renyuan 1917- *IntWW 93,*
WhoPRCh 91
Qian Sanqiang d1992 *IntWW 93N*
Qian Sanqiang 1913- *WhoPRCh 91 [port]*
Qian Shaojun *WhoPRCh 91*
Qian Shugen *WhoPRCh 91*
Qian Weichang 1912- *IntWW 93,*
WhoPRCh 91 [port]
Qian Xiaoping 1938- *WhoPRCh 91 [port]*
Qian Xinbo 1923- *IntWW 93,*
WhoPRCh 91
Qian Xinzhong 1911- *WhoPRCh 91 [port]*
Qian Xuesen 1910- *IntWW 93*
Qian Xuesen 1912- *WhoPRCh 91 [port]*
Qian Xuezhong 1933- *WhoPRCh 91 [port]*
Qian Yingqian *WhoPRCh 91*
Qian Yongchang 1933- *IntWW 93,*
WhoPRCh 91 [port]
Qian Yongnian 1933- *WhoPRCh 91 [port]*

Qian Yunlu 1944- *WhoPRCh 91 [port]*
Qian Yurong *WhoPRCh 91*
Qian Zhengying 1922- *IntWW 93*
Qian Zhengying 1923-
WhoPRCh 91 [port]
Qian Zhihong *WhoPRCh 91*
Qian Zhonghan 1911- *WhoPRCh 91 [port]*
Qian Zhongshu 1910- *ConWorW 93,*
IntWW 93, WhoPRCh 91 [port]
Qian Zhongtai *WhoPRCh 91*
Qiao Dianyun 1930- *WhoPRCh 91 [port]*
Qiao Mai 1939- *WhoPRCh 91 [port]*
Qiao Mingfu 1912- *WhoPRCh 91 [port]*
Qiao Peixin *WhoPRCh 91*
Qiao Shi 1924- *IntWW 93,*
WhoPRCh 91 [port]
Qiao Shiguang 1937- *IntWW 93*
Qiao Shiguang 1940?- *WhoPRCh 91 [port]*
Qiao Xiaoguang 1918- *IntWW 93,*
WhoPRCh 91 [port]
Qiao Xueheng 1928- *WhoPRCh 91 [port]*
Qiao Zonghuai 1944- *WhoPRCh 91*
Qi Feng *WhoPRCh 91*
Qi Gong 1912- *WhoPRCh 91 [port]*
Qi Guiyuan *WhoPRCh 91*
Qi Huaiyuan 1930- *IntWW 93,*
WhoPRCh 91 [port]
Qi Lianyun 1933- *WhoPRCh 91 [port]*
Qi Moujia 1933- *WhoPRCh 91 [port]*
Qin, Ning 1958- *WhoScEn 94*
Qin Boyi *WhoPRCh 91*
Qin Chuan 1919- *IntWW 93,*
WhoPRCh 91 [port]
Qin Daofu *WhoPRCh 91*
Qing-ge-er-tai *WhoPRCh 91*
Qinggeltai 1924- *WhoPRCh 91 [port]*
Qin Hezhen 1913- *IntWW 93*
Qin Huasun *WhoPRCh 91*
Qin Jianming 1942- *WhoPRCh 91 [port]*
Qin Jiwei 1914- *WhoPRCh 91 [port]*
Qin Jiwei, Gen. 1914- *IntWW 93*
Qin Kecai 1931- *WhoPRCh 91 [port]*
Qin Lingyun 1914- *WhoPRCh 91 [port]*
Qin Mu *WhoPRCh 91*
Qin Shi Huang-di 259BC-210BC
HisWorL [port]
Qin Wencai 1925- *IntWW 93*
Qin Xinghan *WhoPRCh 91*
Qin Yingji 1915- *WhoPRCh 91 [port]*
Qin Yizhi 1907- *WhoPRCh 91 [port]*
Qin Yuanyue 1940- *WhoPRCh 91*
Qin Zhaochen *WhoPRCh 91*
Qin Zhaoyang 1916- *IntWW 93,*
WhoPRCh 91 [port]
Qin Zhongda 1923- *IntWW 93,*
WhoPRCh 91 [port]
Qin Zhongfang *WhoPRCh 91*
Qin Zisheng *WhoPRCh 91*
Qiong Yao 1938- *BlmGWL*
Qi Ping 1935- *WhoPRCh 91 [port]*
Qiqin Gaowa 1941- *WhoPRCh 91 [port]*
Qi Qingcai *WhoPRCh 91*
Qiu, Shen Li 1947- *WhoScEn 94*
Qiu Deshu 1948- *WhoPRCh 91*
Qiu Fazu *WhoPRCh 91*
Qiu Fujian *WhoPRCh 91*
Qi Qing 1929- *WhoPRCh 91 [port]*
Qiu Weifan 1912- *WhoPRCh 91 [port]*
Qiu Wenyi 1927- *WhoPRCh 91 [port]*
Qi Yuanjing 1929- *IntWW 93,*
WhoPRCh 91 [port]
Qi Zhongtang *WhoPRCh 91*
Qizhongyi 1927- *WhoPRCh 91 [port]*

Quaal, Ward Louis 1919- *WhoAm 94,*
WhoFI 94, WhoMW 93
Quack, Martin 1948- *WhoScEn 94*
Quackenbush, Charles W. 1954-
WhoAmP 93
Quackenbush, David John 1951-
WhoFI 94
Quackenbush, Justin Lowe 1929-
WhoAm 94, WhoAmL 94, WhoWest 94
Quackenbush, Robert 1929- *WhoAmA 93*
Quackenbush, Robert L. *WhoAmP 93*
Quackenbush, Robert Mead 1929-
WhoAm 94
Quackenbush, Ronald Vern 1952-
WhoAmP 93
Quade, John *WhoHol 92*
Quade, Quentin Lon 1933- *WhoAm 94*
Quade, Victoria Catherine 1953-
WhoAm 94
Quadflieg, Will 1914- *IntWW 93*
Quadir, Kamal Uddin Mohammad 1951-
WhoFI 94
Quadra, Juan Francisco De La Bodega y
WhWE
Quadri, Argeo 1911- *NewGrDO*
Quadri, Fazle Rab 1948- *WhoAmL 94*
Quadrio, Francesco Saverio 1695-1756
NewGrDO
Quadrio Curzio, Alberto 1937- *IntWW 93*
Quadt, Raymond Adolph 1916-
WhoAm 94
Quagliano, Tony *DrAPF 93*
Quagliata, Narcissus 1942- *WhoAmA 93*
Quaglio Family *NewGrDO*
Quaid, Buddy d1987 *WhoHol 92*
Quaid, Buddy 1974- *WhoHol 92*
Quaid, Dennis 1954- *IntMPA 94,*
IntWW 93, WhoHol 92
Quaid, Dennis William 1954- *WhoAm 94*
Quaid, Randy 1950- *IntMPA 94,*
WhoAm 94, WhoHol 92
Quail, Beverly J. 1949- *WhoAmL 94*
Quail, John Wilson 1936- *WhoScEn 94*
Quain, Mitchell I. 1951- *WhoAm 94,*
WhoFI 94
Quaini, Duane C. 1945- *WhoAmL 94*
Quaintance, Charles, Jr. 1939-
WhoAmL 94
Quaintance, Robert Forsyth, Jr. 1950-
WhoAm 94
Quainton, Anthony Cecil Eden 1934-
WhoAm 94, WhoAmP 93
Quaison-Sackey, Alex(ander) 1924-1992
CurBio 93N
Quaison-Sackey, Alexander d1992
IntWW 93N
Quale, Andrew C., Jr. 1942- *WhoAm 94*
Quale, Andrew Christopher, Jr. 1942-
WhoAmL 94
Quale, G(ladys) Robina 1931- *WrDr 94*
Quale, John Carter 1946- *WhoAm 94,*
WhoAmL 94
Quale, Mark Christopher 1948-
WhoWest 94
Qualen, John d1987 *WhoHol 92*
Qualich, Cynthia Ann 1958- *WhoMW 93*
Quall, Dave *WhoAmP 93*
Qualley, Charles Albert 1930- *WhoAm 94,*
WhoWest 94
Qualls, Charles Wayne, Jr. 1949-
WhoScEn 94
Qualls, Robert Gerald 1952- *WhoScEn 94*
Qualls, Robert L. 1933- *WhoAm 94*

Qualls, Roxanne *WhoMW 93*
Qualls, Rudy Brock 1947- *WhoFI 94*
Qualset, Calvin Odell 1937- *WhoAm 94*
Qualter, Terence H. 1925- *WrDr 94*
Qualter, Terence Hall 1925- *WhoAm 94*
Qualters, Tot d1974 *WhoHol 92*
Quan, Hanson Wayne 1965- *WhoAsA 94*
Quan, Jonathan De 1971- *WhoHol 92*
Quan, Katie 1952- *WhoAsA 94*
Quan, Lisa Ling 1967- *WhoWest 94*
Quan, Ralph W. 1963- *WhoScEn 94*
Quan, William Chun 1953- *WhoAsA 94*
Quan, Xina 1957- *WhoAsA 94,*
WhoScEn 94
Quanbeck, Martin 1905-1991 *WhAm 10*
Quander, Rohulamin 1943- *WhoBlA 94*
Quandt, Bernhardt 1903- *IntWW 93*
Quandt, Elizabeth 1922- *WhoAmA 93*
Quandt, Richard (Emeric) 1930- *WrDr 94*
Quandt, Richard Emeric 1930-
WhoAm 94, WhoAmL 94
Quandt, Russell Jerome 1919-1970
WhoAmA 93N
Quandt, William Bauer 1941- *WhoAm 94,*
WrDr 94
Quang, David Sang 1939- *WhoFI 94*
Quang, Eiping 1957- *WhoScEn 94*
Quansah-Dankwa, Juliana Aba 1955-
WhoBlA 94
Quan Shuren 1930- *IntWW 93,*
WhoPRCh 91 [port]
Quanstrom, Walter Roy 1942-
WhoAm 94, WhoFI 94
Quant, Mary 1934- *IntWW 93, Who 94*
Quantrill, Malcolm 1931- *Who 94,*
WrDr 94
Quantrill, William Ernest 1939- *Who 94*
Quan Zhenghuan 1932- *IntWW 93,*
WhoPRCh 91 [port]
Quan Zihuai *WhoPRCh 91*
Quapaw, John d1928 *EncNAR*
Qu'appelle, Bishop of 1932- *Who 94*
Quaranta, Lydia d1928 *WhoHol 92*
Quaretti, Lea 1912- *BlmGWL*
Quarles, Benjamin A. 1904- *WhoBlA 94*
Quarles, Carroll Adair, Jr. 1938-
WhoAm 94
Quarles, Denise LaTressa *WhoAmL 94*
Quarles, Francis 1592-1644 *BlmGEL*
Quarles, George R. 1927- *WhoBlA 94*
Quarles, Herbert DuBois 1929-
WhoBlA 94
Quarles, James Cliv 1921- *WhoAm 94*
Quarles, James Linwood, III 1946-
WhoAm 94, WhoAmL 94
Quarles, John Rhodes 1897- *WhAm 10*
Quarles, Joseph James 1911- *WhoBlA 94*
Quarles, Norma 1936- *AfrAmAl 6 [port]*
Quarles, Norma R. 1936- *WhoBlA 94*
Quarles, Ruth Brett 1914- *WhoBlA 94*
Quarles, Steven Princeton 1942-
WhoAmL 94
Quarles, William Daniel 1948-
WhoAmL 94
Quarmby, David Anthony 1941- *Who 94*
Quarrelles, James Ivan 1926- *WhoBlA 94*
Quarren Evans, (John) Kerry 1926-
Who 94
Quarrie, Bruce 1947- *WrDr 94*
Quarrie, Donald 1951- *IntWW 93*
Quarrington, Paul (Lewis) 1953- *WrDr 94*
Quarry, Nick *WrDr 94*
Quarry, Robert *WhoHol 92*

Quartano, Ralph Nicholas 1927- *Who 94*
Quartararo, Florence 1922- *NewGrDO*
Quartaro, Nena d1985 *WhoHol 92*
Quartermain, James 1920- *WrDr 94*
Quartermaine, Charles d1958 *WhoHol 92*
Quartermaine, Leon d1967 *WhoHol 92*
Quartly, Reg d1983 *WhoHol 92*
Quarton, Jean Elsa Rulf 1942- *WhoMW 93*
Quarton, William Barlow 1903- *WhoAm 94*
Quartucci, Pedro d1983 *WhoHol 92*
Quasha, Alan G. 1950- *WhoFI 94*
Quasha, George *DrAPF 93*
Quasha, William Howard 1912- *WhoAm 94, WhoAmL 94, WhoFI 94*
Quasius, Chiyoko Taninari 1948- *WhoFI 94*
Quasius, Sharron G. 1948- *WhoAmA 93*
Quast, Philip *WhoHol 92*
Quat, Helen S. 1918- *WhoAmA 93*
Quate, Calvin Forrest 1923- *WhoAm 94, WhoScEn 94, WhoWest 94*
Quatermass, Martin 1948- *WrDr 94*
Quatman, George William 1958- *WhoAmL 94*
Quatrone, Rich *DrAPF 93*
Quattlebau, A. Marvin 1941- *WhoAmL 94*
Quattlebaum, Walter Emmett, Jr. 1922- *WhoFI 94*
Quattlebaum, William Franklin 1953- *WhoAmL 94*
Quattro, Mark Henry 1955- *WhoAmL 94*
Quattrocchi, Edmondo 1889-1966 *WhoAmA 93N*
Quattrocchi, Rocco Anthony 1927- *WhoAmP 93*
Quattrociocchi, Ralph *WhoAmP 93*
Quattrucci, Joseph 1925- *WhoAmP 93*
Quave, Gerald Joullian, Sr. 1933- *WhoFI 94*
Quay, Gregory Harrison 1937- *WhoMW 93*
Quay, Laurie Ann 1966- *WhoMW 93*
Quay, Paul Douglas 1949- *WhoScEn 94*
Quay, Thomas Emery 1934- *WhoAm 94, WhoAmL 94*
Quay, Wilbur Brooks 1927- *WhoScEn 94*
Quaye, Cofie 1947?- *BlkWr 2*
Quaye, Kofi *BlkWr 2*
Quayle, Anna 1937- *WhoHol 92*
Quayle, Anthony d1989 *WhoHol 92*
Quayle, (John) Anthony 1913- *WhAm 10*
Quayle, Eric 1921- *WrDr 94*
Quayle, Frederick MacDonald 1936- *WhoAmP 93*
Quayle, J. Danforth 1947- *WhoAmP 93*
Quayle, James Danforth 1947- *IntWW 93, Who 94, WhoAm 94, WhoMW 93*
Quayle, John Clare 1956- *WhoMW 93*
Quayle, John Rodney 1926- *Who 94*
Quayle, Marilyn Tucker *NewYTBS 93 [port]*
Quayle, Marilyn Tucker 1949- *WhoAm 94, WhoAmL 94, WhoMW 93*
Quayle, Thomas David Graham 1936- *Who 94*
Quaynor, Thomas Addo 1935- *WhoBlA 94*
Quaytman, Harvey 1937- *WhoAm 94, WhoAmA 93*
Quazzo, Marco Lorenzo 1962- *WhoAmL 94*
Quebe, Jerry Lee 1942- *WhoAm 94*
Quebec, Archbishop of 1926- *Who 94*
Quebec, Bishop of 1940- *Who 94*
Quebedeaux, Bruno 1941- *WhoAm 94*
Quedens, Eunice *WhoHol 92*
Queen, Brian Charles 1964- *WhoScEn 94*
Queen, Daniel 1934- *WhoScEn 94*
Queen, David D. 1947- *WhoAmL 94*
Queen, Ellery 1920- *WrDr 94*
Queen, Evelyn E. Crawford 1945- *WhoBlA 94*
Queen, Michael L. 1962- *WhoAmP 93*
Queen, Paul David 1950- *WhoMW 93*
Queen, Robert Calvin 1912- *WhoBlA 94*
Queen, Thomas W. 1949- *WhoAmL 94*
Queenan, Charles Joseph, Jr. 1930- *WhoAm 94*
Queenan, James F., Jr. *WhoAmL 94*
Queenan, Joe 1950- *ConAu 140*
Queenan, John William 1906-1992 *WhAm 10*
Queenan, Joseph Martin, Jr. 1950- *WhoAm 94*
Queeney, David 1957- *WhoScEn 94*
Queen Latifah *WhoBlA 94*
Queen Latifah 1970- *AfrAmAl 6*
Queensberry, Marquess of 1929- *Who 94*
Queensland, North, Bishop of 1926- *Who 94*
Queffelec, Anne 1948- *IntWW 93*
Queguiner, Jean 1921- *Who 94*
Que Hee, Shane Stephen 1946- *WhoWest 94*
Quehl, Gary Howard 1938- *WhoAm 94*
Queiros, Dina Silveira de 1911-1983 *BlmGWL*
Queiros, Raquel de 1910- *BlmGWL*
Queiroz, Rachel de 1910- *ConWorW 93*
Queizan, Maria Xose 1938- *BlmGWL*
Quelch, Henry 1858-1913 *DcNaB MP*
Queler, Eve *IntWW 93, WhoAm 94*
Queler, Eve 1936- *NewGrDO*
Quelle, Frederick William, Jr. 1934- *WhoAm 94*
Queller, Donald Edward 1925- *WhoAm 94*
Queller, Fred 1932- *WhoAmL 94*
Quellmalz, Frederick 1912- *WhoFI 94, WhoMW 93*
Quellmalz, Henry 1915- *WhoAm 94, WhoFI 94*
Quello, James H. 1921- *WhoAmP 93*
Quello, James Henry 1914- *WhoAm 94, WhoFI 94*
Quene, Theo 1930- *IntWW 93*
Queneau, Paul Etienne 1911- *WhoAm 94, WhoScEn 94*
Queneau, Raymond *EncSF 93*
Quennell, Joan Mary 1923- *Who 94*
Quennell, Nicholas 1935- *WhoAm 94*
Quennell, Peter 1905- *IntWW 93, Who 94*
Quennell, Peter C. d1993 *NewYTBS 93*
Quenneville, Freda *DrAPF 93*
Quenon, Robert Hagerty 1928- *WhoAm 94*
Quenroe, Robert Henry 1929- *WhoMW 93*
Quensel, Isa *WhoHol 92*
Quentel, Albert Drew 1934- *WhoAm 94*
Quentel, Holt 1961- *WhoAmA 93*
Quenzer, Mique 1943- *WhoWest 94*
Queral, Luis Emilio 1921- *WhoAmP 93*
Quercia, Peter Wade, Jr. 1954- *WhoWest 94*
Querejazu Calvo, Roberto 1913- *Who 94*
Quereshi, Mohammed Younus 1929- *WhoMW 93*
Querin, Phillip C. 1946- *WhoAmL 94*
Querio, Isa d1976 *WhoHol 92*
Querol Moreno, Cherie M. *WhoAsA 94*
Query, Jeffrey 1959- *WhoFI 94*
Query, Joy Marves Neale *WhoAm 94*
Querzoli Laschi, Anna Maira fl. 1737-1768 *NewGrDO*
Quesada, Angel Torres *EncSF 93*
Quesada, Antonio Patrick 1941- *WhoFI 94*
Quesada, Antonio R. 1948- *WhoHisp 94*
Quesada, Catalina 1944- *WhoHisp 94*
Quesada, E(lwood) R(ichard) 1904-1993 *CurBio 93N*
Quesada, Elwood R. 1904-1993 *NewYTBS 93 [port]*
Quesada, Gonzolo Jimenez De *WhWE*
Quesada, Jorge R. 1947- *WhoHisp 94*
Quesada, Mark Alejandro 1955- *WhoScEn 94*
Quesenberry, Kenneth Hays 1947- *WhoAm 94*
Quesnay de Beaurepaire, Alexandre-Marie 1755-1820 *WhAmRev*
Quesnel, Gregory L. 1948- *WhoAm 94, WhoFI 94*
Quesnel, (Louis) Joseph (Marie) 1746-1809 *NewGrDO*
Quest, Charles Francis 1904- *WhoAmA 93*
Quest, Dorothy (Johnson) 1909- *WhoAmA 93*
Quest, Erica 1919- *WrDr 94*
Quest, Erica 1924- *WrDr 94*
Quest, James Howard 1934- *WhoAm 94*
Questel, Joseph Raymond 1959- *WhoMW 93*
Questel, Mae 1908- *WhoAm 94, WhoHol 92*
Questel, Mae 1912- *WhoCom*
Quester, Aline Olson 1943- *WhoFI 94*
Quester, David J. 1964- *WhoFI 94*
Quester, George (Herman) 1936- *WrDr 94*
Quester, George Herman 1936- *WhoAm 94*
Questiaux, Nicole Francoise 1930- *IntWW 93*
Queston, Joanna (Marie) 1951- *WrDr 94*
Questrom, Allen I. 1941- *WhoAm 94, WhoFI 94*
Quevedo, Francisco de 1580-1645 *LitC 23*
Quevedo, Sylvestre Grado 1949- *WhoHisp 94*
Quezada, Leticia *WhoHisp 94*
Quezada, Maria E. 1967- *WhoFI 94*
Quezaire, Roy J., Jr. *WhoAmP 93*
Qu Geping 1930- *WhoPRCh 91 [port]*
Quiat, Gerald M. 1924- *WhoAm 94*
Quiban, Estelita Cabrera 1938- *WhoWest 94*
Quibano, Jairo Alfonso 1953- *WhoHisp 94*
Quick, Albert Thomas 1939- *WhoAm 94, WhoAmL 94*
Quick, Anthony Oliver Hebert 1924- *Who 94*
Quick, Barbara 1954- *WrDr 94*
Quick, Charles E. 1933- *WhoBlA 94*
Quick, Daryl Eugene 1947- *WhoFI 94*
Quick, Diana 1946- *WhoHol 92*
Quick, Dorothy 1944- *Who 94*
Quick, Edward E. 1935- *WhoAmP 93*
Quick, Edward Raymond 1943- *WhoAm 94, WhoAmA 93, WhoMW 93*
Quick, Eldon *WhoHol 92*
Quick, Elizabeth L. 1948- *WhoAmL 94*
Quick, George Kenneth 1947- *WhoBlA 94*
Quick, Jack Beaver 1947- *WhoFI 94*
Quick, James S. 1940- *WhoAm 94*
Quick, Joan B. *WhoAmP 93*
Quick, Leslie Charles, III 1953- *WhoAm 94, WhoFI 94*
Quick, Michelle Louise 1967- *WhoMW 93*
Quick, Mike 1959- *WhoBlA 94*
Quick, Norman 1922- *Who 94*
Quick, R. Edward 1927- *WhoBlA 94*
Quick, Robert Louis 1946- *WhoAmL 94*
Quick, Thomas Clarkson 1955- *WhoAm 94*
Quick, Valerie Anne 1952- *WhoWest 94*
Quick, W.T. *EncSF 93*
Quick, William Thomas 1946- *WhoFI 94, WhoWest 94*
Quicke, John (Godolphin) 1922- *Who 94*
Quickel, Kenneth Elwood, Jr. 1939- *WhoAm 94*
Quicksall, Carl Owen 1941- *WhoScEn 94*
Quidd, David Andrew 1954- *WhoAmL 94, WhoAmP 93*
Quie, Albert Harold 1923- *WhoAmP 93*
Quie, Paul Gerhardt 1925- *WhoAm 94, WhoMW 93*
Quigg, Donald James 1916- *WhoAm 94*
Quigg, Richard John 1930- *WhoMW 93*
Quigless, Milton Douglas, Jr. 1945- *WhoBlA 94*
Quigley, Anthony Leslie Coupland 1946- *Who 94*
Quigley, Austin Edmund 1942- *WhoAm 94*
Quigley, Charles d1964 *WhoHol 92*
Quigley, George *Who 94*
Quigley, (William) George (Henry) 1929- *IntWW 93, Who 94*
Quigley, Godfrey *WhoHol 92*
Quigley, Herbert Joseph, Jr. 1937- *WhoMW 93*
Quigley, Jack Allen 1914- *WhoAm 94*
Quigley, Jerome Harold 1925- *WhoFI 94*
Quigley, Joan 1927- *ConAu 43NR*
Quigley, Johanna Mary *Who 94*
Quigley, John Bernard 1940- *WhoAm 94, WhoMW 93*
Quigley, John Michael 1942- *WhoAm 94, WhoFI 94*
Quigley, Joseph John 1947- *WhoFI 94*
Quigley, Joseph Milton 1922-1990 *WhAm 10*
Quigley, Juanita 1931- *WhoHol 92*
Quigley, Kevin *WhoAmP 93*
Quigley, Kevin Walsh 1961- *WhoWest 94*
Quigley, Lane 1949- *WhoAmL 94*
Quigley, Leonard Vincent 1933- *WhoAm 94*
Quigley, Linnea *WhoHol 92*
Quigley, Martin *DrAPF 93*
Quigley, Martin, Jr. 1917- *IntMPA 94*
Quigley, Martin Schofield 1917- *WhoAm 94*
Quigley, Michael Allen 1950- *WhoAmA 93*
Quigley, Nancy Louise 1935- *WhoMW 93*
Quigley, Philip J. 1943- *WhoAm 94, WhoFI 94, WhoWest 94*
Quigley, Rita 1923- *WhoHol 92*
Quigley, Robert Charles 1949- *WhoFI 94*
Quigley, Robert Murvin 1934- *WhoAm 94*
Quigley, Robin L. 1947- *WhoAmA 93*
Quigley, Thomas J. 1923- *WhoAm 94, WhoAmL 94*
Quigley, William J. 1951- *IntMPA 94*
Quijada, Angelica Maria 1963- *WhoWest 94*
Quijano, Alfonso 1939- *WhoHisp 94*
Quijano, Raul Alberto 1923- *IntWW 93*
Quijas, Louis F., Jr. 1951- *WhoHisp 94*
Quiles, Paul 1942- *IntWW 93, WhoScEn 94*
Quiles Rodriguez, Edwin Rafael 1949- *WhoHisp 94*
Quilici, Joe 1925- *WhoAmP 93*
Quilico, Gino 1955- *NewGrDO*
Quilico, Jack Andrew *WhoWest 94*
Quilico, Louis 1929- *NewGrDO*
Quilico, Louis 1931- *WhoAm 94*
Quill, John *EncSF 93*
Quill, Monica 1929- *WrDr 94*
Quill, Tim *WhoHol 92*
Quillan, Eddie d1990 *WhoHol 92*
Quillan, John d1985 *WhoHol 92*
Quillan, Joseph d1962 *WhoHol 92*
Quillan, Marie 1911- *WhoHol 92*
Quillan, Sarah d1969 *WhoHol 92*
Quillen, Cecil Dyer, Jr. 1937- *WhoAm 94, WhoAmL 94, WhoFI 94*
Quillen, Edward Kenneth, III 1950- *WhoWest 94*
Quillen, Ford C. 1938- *WhoAmP 93*
Quillen, George Robert 1928- *WhoAmP 93*
Quillen, James H. 1916- *CngDr 93*
Quillen, James Henry 1916- *WhoAm 94, WhoAmP 93*
Quillen, Lloyd Douglas 1943- *WhoFI 94*
Quillen, William T. *WhoAmP 93*
Quillen, William Tatem 1935- *WhoAm 94*
Quiller, Andrew *EncSF 93*
Quiller, Andrew 1914- *WrDr 94*
Quiller, Stephen Frederick 1946- *WhoAmA 93*
Quiller-Couch, Arthur 1863-1944 *DcLB 135 [port], TwCLC 53 [port]*
Quilley, Denis 1927- *IntWW 93, WhoHol 92*
Quilley, Denis Clifford 1927- *Who 94*
Quilliam, Juan Pete 1915- *Who 94*
Quilliam, Peter *Who 94*
Quilliam, (James) Peter 1920- *Who 94*
Quillian, J. Kirk 1946- *WhoAmL 94*
Quillian, William Fletcher, Jr. 1913- *WhoAm 94*
Quilligan, Edward James 1925- *WhoAm 94, WhoWest 94*
Quillin, Patrick 1951- *WhoScEn 94*
Quilliot, Roger 1925- *IntWW 93*
Quilp, Jocelyn 1870-1932 *EncSF 93*
Quilter, Anthony (Raymond Leopold Cuthbert) 1937- *Who 94*
Quilter, David (Cuthbert) Tudway 1921- *Who 94*
Quilter, J. Barney 1919- *WhoAmP 93*
Quilter, Roger 1877-1935 *NewGrDO*
Quilty, Rafe 1943- *WrDr 94*
Quimby, Fred William 1945- *WhoScEn 94*
Quimby, George (Irving) 1913- *WrDr 94*
Quimby, George Irving 1913- *WhoAm 94, WhoScEn 94*
Quimby, Margaret d1963 *WhoHol 92*
Quimby, Robert Sherman 1916- *WhoAm 94, WhoMW 93*
Quimpo, Rafael Gonzales 1938- *WhoAsA 94*
Quin *Who 94*
Quin, Ann 1936-1973 *BlmGWL*
Quin, James 1693-1766 *BlmGEL*
Quin, Joseph Marvin 1947- *WhoFI 94*
Quin, Joyce Gwendolen 1944- *Who 94, WhoWomW 91*
Quin, Louis DuBose 1928- *WhoAm 94*
Quin, Mary Patricia 1953- *WhoFI 94*
Quinault, Jean-Baptiste-Maurice 1687-1745 *NewGrDO*
Quinault, Philippe 1635-1688 *IntDcT 2 [port], NewGrDO*
Quinby, Charles Edward, Jr. 1943- *WhoAm 94*
Quinby, Richard Emerson 1954- *WhoAmL 94*
Quinby, William Albert 1941- *WhoAm 94, WhoAmL 94*
Quince, Kevin 1950- *WhoBlA 94*
Quince, Louis d1954 *WhoHol 92*
Quince, Peter *Who 94*
Quincy, Edmund *DrAPF 93*
Quincy, Josiah 1744-1775 *WhAmRev*
Quincy, Ronald Lee 1950- *WhoBlA 94*
Quincy, Samuel 1735-1789 *WhAmRev*
Quindlen, Anna 1953- *CurBio 93 [port], WhoAm 94*
Quine, Judith Balaban 1932- *ConAu 140*
Quine, Richard d1989 *WhoHol 92*
Quine, Willard V(an Orman) 1908- *WrDr 94*
Quine, Willard Van Orman 1908- *IntWW 93, Who 94, WhoAm 94*
Quinell, Bruce Andrew 1949- *WhoAm 94*
Quinlan, Alan Geoffrey 1933- *Who 94*
Quinlan, David M. 1945- *WhoAmL 94*
Quinlan, Gertrude d1963 *WhoHol 92*
Quinlan, Guy Christian 1939- *WhoAm 94, WhoAmL 94*
Quinlan, Henry 1906- *Who 94*
Quinlan, James Joseph 1924- *WhoWest 94*
Quinlan, James Milton *WhoMW 93*
Quinlan, Joseph Charles 1930- *WhoMW 93*
Quinlan, Joseph Michael 1941- *WhoAm 94*
Quinlan, Kathleen 1954- *IntMPA 94, WhoHol 92*
Quinlan, Kenneth Paul 1930- *WhoScEn 94*
Quinlan, Michael (Edward) 1930- *Who 94*
Quinlan, Michael J. 1938- *WhoIns 94*
Quinlan, Michael Robert 1944- *WhoAm 94, WhoFI 94*
Quinlan, Patrick Albert 1947- *WhoFI 94*
Quinlan, Roger d1976 *WhoHol 92*
Quinlan, William Joseph, Jr. 1939- *WhoAm 94, WhoAmL 94*
Quinlan, William Louis 1930- *WhoAmP 93*

Quinlivan, Charles d1974 *WhoHol 92*
Quinn, A. Peter, Jr. 1923- *WhoIns 94*
Quinn, Aidan 1959- *IntMPA 94, WhoAm 94, WhoHol 92*
Quinn, Aileen 1971- *WhoHol 92*
Quinn, Alan d1944 *WhoHol 92*
Quinn, Alfred Thomas 1922- *WhoBlA 94*
Quinn, Andrew 1937- *Who 94*
Quinn, Andrew Peter, Jr. 1923- *WhoAm 94*
Quinn, Anthony 1915- *IntMPA 94, WhoHol 92*
Quinn, Anthony Rudolph Oaxaca 1915- *IntWW 93, WhoAm 94, WhoHisp 94*
Quinn, Barbara *WhoHol 92*
Quinn, Bayard Elmer 1915-1990 *WhAm 10*
Quinn, Bernetta *DrAPF 93*
Quinn, Betty Nye 1921- *WhoAm 94*
Quinn, Beverly Wilson 1943- *WhoAmP 93*
Quinn, Bill 1916- *WhoHol 92*
Quinn, Bob *WhoAm 94*
Quinn, Brian *Who 94*
Quinn, Brian 1936- *Who 94*
Quinn, (James Steven) Brian 1936- *Who 94*
Quinn, Brian Grant 1950- *WhoAmA 93*
Quinn, C. Jack 1929- *WhoAm 94*
Quinn, Charles Layton, Jr. 1951- *WhoScEn 94*
Quinn, Charles Nicholas 1930- *WhoAm 94*
Quinn, Cindy Lee 1949- *WhoWest 94*
Quinn, Daniel 1935- *EncSF 93*
Quinn, David (Beers) 1909- *WrDr 94*
Quinn, David Beers 1909- *Who 94*
Quinn, David W. *WhoFI 94*
Quinn, Deborah McLean 1953- *WhoAmL 94*
Quinn, Dennis B. 1928- *WhoAm 94*
Quinn, Diane C. 1942- *WhoBlA 94*
Quinn, Doris Marilyn 1923- *WhoAmP 93*
Quinn, Douglas E. 1953- *WhoAmL 94*
Quinn, Dwight Wilson 1917- *WhoAmP 93*
Quinn, Edward Francis, III 1944- *WhoScEn 94*
Quinn, Edward James 1911- *WhAm 10*
Quinn, Eugene Frederick 1935- *WhoAm 94*
Quinn, Francesco 1962- *WhoHol 92*
Quinn, Francis A. 1921- *WhoAm 94, WhoWest 94*
Quinn, Francis F. 1946- *WhoAmL 94*
Quinn, Frank P. d1986 *WhoHol 92*
Quinn, Galen Warren 1922- *WhoAm 94*
Quinn, Gerard A. 1927- *EncSF 93*
Quinn, Henrietta Reist 1918- *WhoAmA 93*
Quinn, J. C. *WhoHol 92*
Quinn, J. Terence 1946- *WhoMW 93*
Quinn, Jack d1929 *WhoHol 92*
Quinn, Jack 1951- *CngDr 93, WhoAm 94, WhoAmP 93*
Quinn, Jack J. *WhoAm 94, WhoMW 93*
Quinn, James *WhoHol 92*
Quinn, James d1919 *WhoHol 92*
Quinn, James Aiden O'Brien 1932- *Who 94*
Quinn, James Charles Frederick 1919- *Who 94*
Quinn, James L(ouis) *EncSF 93*
Quinn, James P. 1933- *WhoIns 94*
Quinn, James W. 1945- *WhoAm 94, WhoAmL 94*
Quinn, Jane Bryant c. 1939- *News 93, WhoAm 94*
Quinn, Jarus William 1930- *WhoAm 94, WhoScEn 94*
Quinn, Jimmy d1940 *WhoHol 92*
Quinn, Joe d1974 *WhoHol 92*
Quinn, John *DrAPF 93*
Quinn, John Albert 1932- *WhoAm 94, WhoScEn 94*
Quinn, John Collins 1925- *WhoAm 94, WhoFI 94*
Quinn, John E. 1950- *WhoAm 94, WhoAmL 94*
Quinn, John Edward 1947- *WhoWest 94*
Quinn, John Edward 1961- *WhoAmL 94*
Quinn, John F. *WhoAmP 93*
Quinn, John Henry, III 1946- *WhoAm 94, WhoAmL 94*
Quinn, John J. 1950- *WhoAmL 94*
Quinn, John M. 1949- *WhoAmL 94*
Quinn, John Michael 1946- *WhoScEn 94*
Quinn, John R. 1929- *WhoAm 94, WhoWest 94*
Quinn, John Robert 1948- *WhoAmP 93*
Quinn, Jonathan Stuart 1959- *WhoAmL 94*
Quinn, Joseph Michael 1937- *WhoAm 94*
Quinn, Joseph R. 1932- *WhoAmP 93*
Quinn, Kenneth (Fleming) 1920- *WrDr 94*
Quinn, LeBris Smith 1954- *WhoWest 94*
Quinn, Lorenzo 1966- *WhoHol 92*
Quinn, Louis d1988 *WhoHol 92*
Quinn, Martha *WhoHol 92*
Quinn, Martin *ConAu 43NR*
Quinn, Martin 1942- *WrDr 94*
Quinn, Mary Cynthia 1956- *WhoAmL 94, WhoFI 94*
Quinn, Mary Ellen 1923- *WhoScEn 94*
Quinn, Michael Desmond 1936- *WhoAm 94, WhoFI 94*
Quinn, Michael S. 1945- *WhoAmL 94*
Quinn, Michael William 1949- *WhoFI 94*
Quinn, Nancy d1993 *NewYTBS 93 [port]*
Quinn, Noel J. d1993 *NewYTBS 93*
Quinn, Noel Joseph 1915- *WhoAmA 93*
Quinn, Pat *WhoHol 92*
Quinn, Pat 1943- *WhoAm 94, WhoWest 94*
Quinn, Patrick *WhoAmP 93, WhoMW 93*
Quinn, Patrick James 1946- *WhoWest 94*
Quinn, Patrick Michael 1934- *WhoFI 94*
Quinn, Patrick William 1955- *WhoAmL 94*
Quinn, Paul Allan 1950- *WhoMW 93*
Quinn, Peter (John) 1941- *WrDr 94*
Quinn, Philip Lawrence 1940- *WhoAm 94, WhoMW 93*
Quinn, Phyllis Mary 1952- *WhoAm 94*
Quinn, R. Joseph *WhoAmP 93*
Quinn, Richard Kendall 1957- *WhoMW 93, WhoScEn 94*
Quinn, Richard M., Jr. 1965- *WhoAmP 93*
Quinn, Robert Hayes 1902-1962 *WhoAmA 93N*
Quinn, Robert Henry 1919- *WhoAm 94*
Quinn, Robert Joseph, Jr. 1956- *WhoAmP 93*
Quinn, Robert William 1912- *WhoScEn 94*
Quinn, Ruairi 1946- *IntWW 93*
Quinn, Sally 1941- *WhoAm 94*
Quinn, Sheila (Margaret Imelda) 1920- *Who 94*
Quinn, Simon *ConAu 43NR*
Quinn, Simon 1942- *WrDr 94*
Quinn, Stephen Paul 1952- *WhoMW 93*
Quinn, Teddy 1959- *WhoHol 92*
Quinn, Terence P. 1939- *WhoAmL 94*
Quinn, Terry Jay 1950- *WhoMW 93*
Quinn, Thomas *WhoHol 92*
Quinn, Thomas Patrick, Jr. 1938- *WhoAmA 93*
Quinn, Timothy Charles, Jr. 1936- *WhoAmL 94*
Quinn, Timothy J. 1947- *WhoAmL 94*
Quinn, Timothy R. 1950- *WhoAmL 94*
Quinn, Tom 1944- *WhoWest 94*
Quinn, Tony d1967 *WhoHol 92*
Quinn, Vincent Kevin 1931- *WhoIns 94*
Quinn, William 1929- *WhoAmA 93*
Quinn, William A. 1928- *WhoIns 94*
Quinn, William Francis 1919- *WhoAm 94*
Quinn, William Wilson 1907- *WhoAm 94*
Quinn, William Wilson, Jr. 1947- *WhoAmL 94*
Quinn, Yvonne Susan 1951- *WhoAm 94, WhoAmL 94*
Quinnan, Edward Michael 1935- *WhoAm 94*
Quinnan, Gerald Vincent, Jr. 1947- *WhoAm 94, WhoScEn 94*
Quinn-Cooper, Mary 1960- *WhoAmL 94*
Quinnell, Bruce Andrew 1949- *WhoFI 94*
Quinnen, Peter John 1945- *Who 94*
Quinney, John fl. 18th cent.- *EncNAR*
Quinney, Richard 1934- *WrDr 94*
Quinney, Seymour Joseph 1893- *WhAm 10*
Quinn-Judge, Paul Malachy 1949- *WhoAm 94*
Quinones, Adolfo 1955- *WhoHol 92*
Quinones, Alberto Louis 1956- *WhoHisp 94*
Quinones, Carlos Ramon 1951- *WhoFI 94*
Quinones, Edgar A. 1935- *WhoWest 94*
Quiñones, Edwin 1947- *WhoHisp 94*
Quiñones, John Manuel 1952- *WhoHisp 94*
Quinones, Jose Antonio 1939- *WhoScEn 94*
Quiñones, José Ramon, Jr. 1950- *WhoHisp 94*
Quinones, Louis Edward 1932- *WhoHisp 94*
Quinones, Luis Ignacio 1951- *WhoHisp 94*
Quinones, Magaly *DrAPF 93*
Quiñones, Mark A. 1931- *WhoHisp 94*
Quiñones, Migdalia 1960- *WhoHisp 94*
Quiñones, Samuel 1949- *WhoHisp 94*
Quiñones, Thomas 1955- *WhoHisp 94*
Quiñones, Wilfredo 1957- *WhoHisp 94*
Quinones Amezquita, Mario Rafael 1933- *IntWW 93*
Quiñones-Keber, Eloise *WhoHisp 94*
Quiñones Ortiz, María de los A. 1950- *WhoHisp 94*
Quinones Rivera, Victor 1948- *WhoHisp 94*
Quiñones-Suarez, Miguel Angel 1967- *WhoHisp 94*
Quiñonez, Naomi 1951- *WhoHisp 94*
Quinsac, Annie-Paule 1945- *WhoAmA 93*
Quinsey, Mary Beth 1948- *WrDr 94*
Quinsler, William Thomson 1924- *WhoAm 94*
Quinson, Bruno Andre 1938- *WhoAm 94*
Quint, Alexander Norman 1959- *WhoFI 94*
Quint, Arnold Harris 1942- *WhoAm 94, WhoAmL 94*
Quint, Ira 1930- *WhoAm 94*
Quint, Monique 1945- *WhoWomW 91*
Quintana, Alvina E. 1949- *WhoHisp 94*
Quintana, Betty J. 1946- *WhoHisp 94*
Quintana, Carlos Narcis 1965- *WhoHisp 94*
Quintana, Edward M. *WhoHisp 94*
Quintana, Henry, Jr. 1952- *WhoHisp 94*
Quintana, Jean 1951- *WhoWest 94*
Quintana, Jose Booth 1946- *WhoAm 94*
Quintana, Julio C. 1945- *WhoHisp 94*
Quintana, Leroy V. *DrAPF 93*
Quintana, Leroy V. 1944- *HispLC [port], WhoHisp 94*
Quintana, Luis Antonio 1960- *WhoHisp 94*
Quintana, M. V. 1953- *WhoHisp 94*
Quintana, Manuel E. 1947- *WhoHisp 94*
Quintana, Sammy J. 1949- *WhoAm 94*
Quintana, Sammy Joseph 1949- *WhoHisp 94*
Quintana, Yamilé 1940- *WhoHisp 94*
Quintana-Díaz, Julio C. 1945- *WhoHisp 94*
Quintanilla, Antonio Paulet 1927- *WhoMW 93, WhoScEn 94*
Quintanilla, Guadalupe C. 1937- *WhoHisp 94*
Quintanilla, Michael Ray 1954- *WhoHisp 94*
Quintavalle, Antonio fl. 1688- *NewGrDO*
Quintela, Abel R. 1946- *WhoHisp 94*
Quintela, Richard Gerard 1964- *WhoHisp 94*
Quinten, Christopher 1957- *WhoHol 92*
Quintero, Ana Helvia 1945- *WhoHisp 94*
Quintero, Conrad O. 1952- *WhoHisp 94*
Quintero, Frank, Jr. 1958- *WhoAmL 94*
Quintero, Hector Enrique 1951- *WhoScEn 94*
Quintero, Janneth Ivon 1960- *WhoHisp 94*
Quintero, Jess *WhoHisp 94*
Quintero, José 1923- *WhoHisp 94*
Quintero, Jose 1924- *WhoAm 94*
Quintero, Jose Benjamin 1924- *AmCulL*
Quintero, Orlando A. *WhoHisp 94*
Quintero, Ronald Gary 1954- *WhoAm 94, WhoFI 94*
Quintero, Ruben 1952- *WhoHisp 94*
Quintero, Ruben David 1949- *WhoHisp 94*
Quintian, Andres Rogelio 1920- *WhoFI 94*
Quintiere, Gary G. 1944- *WhoAm 94*
Quinto, P. Frank 1956- *WhoScEn 94*
Quinton, Baron 1925- *Who 94*
Quinton, Lord 1925- *WrDr 94*
Quinton, Amelia Stone 1833-1926 *EncNAR*
Quinton, Anthony Meredith 1925- *IntWW 93*
Quinton, Barbara A. 1941- *WhoBlA 94*
Quinton, John (Grand) 1929- *Who 94*
Quinton, John Grand 1929- *IntWW 93*
Quinton, Paul Marquis 1944- *WhoAm 94, WhoWest 94*
Quintrell, Lute A. 1952- *WhoMW 93*
Quintrell, Thomas A. 1920- *WhoAm 94*
Quintyne, Irwin Sinclair 1926- *WhoBlA 94*
Quirantes, Albert M. 1963- *WhoAmL 94*
Quirarte, Jacinto 1931- *WhoAm 94, WhoAmA 93, WhoHisp 94*
Quirico, Francis Joseph 1911- *WhoAm 94*
Quirin, Philip J. 1940- *WhoIns 94*
Quiring, Patti Lee *WhoMW 93*
Quirk, Billy d1926 *WhoHol 92*
Quirk, Cathleen *DrAPF 93*
Quirk, Deborah Hardin 1950- *WhoAmP 93*
Quirk, Desmond John 1929- *IntWW 93*
Quirk, Francis Joseph 1907-1974 *WhoAmA 93N*
Quirk, Frank Edward 1932- *WhoAmL 94*
Quirk, Frank Joseph 1941- *WhoAm 94, WhoScEn 94*
Quirk, James Patrick 1924- *IntWW 93*
Quirk, John A. 1951- *WhoAmP 93*
Quirk, John James 1943- *WhoAm 94*
Quirk, John Stanton S. *Who 94*
Quirk, Kenneth Paul 1953- *WhoFI 94*
Quirk, Peter Richard 1936- *WhoAm 94*
Quirk, Randolph 1920- *WrDr 94*
Quirk, (Charles) Randolph 1920- *IntWW 93, Who 94*
Quirk, Robert Emmett 1950- *WhoAm 94*
Quirk, Robert Joseph 1931- *WhoAmP 93*
Quirk, Thomas d1976 *WhoHol 92*
Quirk, Thomas Charles, Jr. 1922- *WhoAmA 93*
Quirk, Thomas Edward 1950- *WhoAmL 94*
Quirk, William E. 1950- *WhoAmL 94*
Quiroga (de Abarca), Elena 1921?- *ConWorW 93*
Quiroga, Carmen Lucila 1946- *WhoHisp 94*
Quiroga, Dario O. 1941- *WhoHisp 94*
Quiroga, Elena *IntWW 93*
Quiroga, Elena 1921- *BlmGWL*
Quiroga, Francisco Gracia *WhoHisp 94*
Quiroga, Francisco Gracia 1930- *WhoWest 94*
Quiroga, Horacio 1878-1937 *HispLC [port]*
Quiroga, Horacio (Sylvestre) 1878-1937 *RfGShF*
Quiroga, Indalecio Ruiz 1937- *WhoHisp 94*
Quiroga, Jorge Humberto 1950- *WhoHisp 94*
Quiroga, José A. 1959- *WhoHisp 94*
Quiroga, Robert *WhoHisp 94*
Quiroga, Roger *WhoHisp 94*
Quiros, Carlos Francisco 1946- *WhoWest 94*
Quiros, Pedro Fernandez De 1565-1614 *WhWE*
Quiróz, Alfred James 1944- *WhoHisp 94*
Quiroz, Jesse M. 1939- *WhoHisp 94*
Quiroz, Martin 1955- *WhoHisp 94*
Quirt, Walter 1902-1968 *WhoAmA 93N*
Quisenberry, Robert Max 1956- *WhoWest 94*
Quisgard, Liz Whitney 1929- *WhoAm 94, WhoAmA 93*
Quisling, Vidkun 1887-1945 *HisWorL [port]*
Quismorio, Francisco P., Jr. 1941- *WhoAsA 94, WhoWest 94*
Quist, Adrian 1913-1991 *BuCMET*
Quist, Allen J. 1944- *WhoAmP 93*
Quist, Edwin Arnold, Jr. 1951- *WhoAm 94*
Quist, George Robert 1920- *WhoIns 94*
Quist, Gordon Jay 1937- *WhoAm 94, WhoAmL 94, WhoMW 93*
Quist, Lisa d1981 *WhoHol 92*
Quist, Susan *DrAPF 93*
Quistgaard, Johan Waldemar De Rehling 1877-1962 *WhoAmA 93N*
Quisthoult-Rowohl, Godelieve 1947- *WhoWomW 91*
Quistorp, Eva 1945- *WhoWomW 91*
Quitak, Oscar 1926- *WhoHol 92*
Quitmeier, William Michael 1951- *WhoAmL 94*
Quittell, Frederic Charles 1948- *WhoFI 94*
Quittmeyer, Charles Loreaux 1917- *WhoAm 94*
Quittner, Arnold M. 1927- *WhoAm 94*
Quitugua, Antonio Ogo *WhoAmP 93*
Quitugua, Franklin Joseph 1933- *WhoAmP 93*
Quivar, Florence 1944- *NewGrDO*
Quivers, Eric Stanley 1955- *WhoBlA 94*
Quivers, William Wyatt, Sr. 1919- *WhoBlA 94*
Qu Mianyu 1925- *WhoPRCh 91*
Qu Mu d1992 *IntWW 93N*
Quo, Beulah *WhoHol 92*
Quo, Phillip C. 1930- *WhoScEn 94*
Quoirez, Francoise *ConWorW 93*
Quon, Check Yuen 1949- *WhoAsA 94*
Quon, Shun Wing 1950- *WhoAsA 94*
Quoss, Karen Rae 1950- *WhoMW 93*
Quotem, Caleb *WhAmRev*
Quoy, Jean-Rene-Constant 1790-1869 *WhWE*
Quoyeser, Clement Louis 1899- *WhoFI 94*
Qu Qinyue *WhoPRCh 91*
Quraishi, Abdul Aziz Bin Said Al 1930- *IntWW 93*
Quraishi, Marghoob A. 1931- *WhoFI 94, WhoWest 94*
Quraishi, Mohammed Sayeed 1924- *WhoAm 94*
Qureshey, Safi U. 1951- *WhoAm 94, WhoFI 94, WhoWest 94*
Qureshi, Iqbal Hussain 1936- *WhoScEn 94*
Qureshi, Ishtiaq Husain 1903- *IntWW 93*
Qureshi, Moeen Ahmad 1930- *IntWW 93*
Qureshi, Muquarrab Ahmed 1953- *WhoAsA 94*
Qureshi, Qadeer Ahmad 1957- *WhoAsA 94*
Qureshi, Sajjad Aslam 1954- *WhoScEn 94*
Qureshi, Shamim 1942- *WhoMW 93*
Qurratulain Haidar *ConWorW 93*
Qutar, Emir of *IntWW 93*
Qutub, Musa Yacub 1940- *WhoAm 94*
Qu Wei *WhoPRCh 91*
Qu Wu 1898- *WhoPRCh 91 [port]*
Qu Xiaosong 1953- *WhoPRCh 91 [port]*
Qu Xixian 1928?- *WhoPRCh 91 [port]*
Qu Yongshou 1929- *WhoPRCh 91 [port]*
Quyth, Gabriel 1928- *WrDr 94*
Qu Zhenmou 1925- *WhoPRCh 91 [port]*

R

Ra, Carol F. 1939- *SmATA 76 [port]*
Raab, Ada Dennett d1950 *WhoAmA 93N*
Raab, Cecilia Marie 1952- *WhoMW 93*
Raab, Elie *WhoHol 92*
Raab, Esther 1899-1981 *BlmGWL*
Raab, G. Kirk 1935- *WhoAm 94*
Raab, Gail B. 1934- *WhoAmA 93*
Raab, George Gregory 1947- *WhoAmP 93*
Raab, Harry Frederick, Jr. 1926- *WhoScEn 94*
Raab, Herbert Norman 1925- *WhoAm 94*
Raab, Ira Jerry 1935- *WhoAm 94, WhoAmL 94*
Raab, Irving W. *WhoAmA 93*
Raab, Kurt d1988 *WhoHol 92*
Raab, Lawrence *DrAPF 93*
Raab, Madeline Murphy 1945- *WhoWomW 91*
Raab, Paul Richard 1958- *WhoFI 94*
Raab, Rosemarie 1946- *WhoWomW 91*
Raab, Selwyn 1934- *WhoAm 94*
Raab, Sheldon 1937- *WhoAm 94, WhoAmL 94*
Raab, Vil'gel'mina Ivanovna 1848-1917 *NewGrDO*
Raab, Walter Ferdinand 1924- *WhoAm 94, WhoFI 94*
Raabe, Mark Douglas 1957- *WhoFI 94*
Raabe, Wilhelm 1831-1910 *DcLB 129 [port]*
Raabe, William Wallace 1928- *WhoWest 94*
Raad, Virginia 1925- *WhoAm 94*
Raaf, John Elbert 1905- *WhoAm 94*
Raaff, Anton c. 1714-1797 *NewGrDO [port]*
Raaflaub, Kurt A. 1941- *WhoAm 94*
Raamot, Kristin 1968- *WhoFI 94*
Raas, Daniel Alan 1947- *WhoAmL 94*
Raasch, Richard W. 1943- *WhoFI 94*
Raatama, Henry H., Jr. 1943- *WhoAmL 94*
Raats, Jaan 1932- *IntWW 93*
Rab, Mirza M. 1924- *WhoAsA 94*
Rabade, Jose Manuel 1922- *WhoHisp 94*
Rabaeus, Bengt 1917- *IntWW 93*
Rabagliati, Alberto d1974 *WhoHol 92*
Rabago, Antonio J. 1953- *WhoHisp 94*
Rábago, Karl R. 1957- *WhoHisp 94*
Rabago, Karl Roger 1957- *WhoAmL 94*
Rabal, Francisco 1925- *WhoHol 92*
Rabal, Teresa *WhoHol 92*
Rabalais, David Randall 1959- *WhoAmL 94*
Raban, Jonathan 1942- *IntWW 93, Who 94, WrDr 94*
Rabasa, Emilio O. 1925- *IntWW 93*
Rabassa, Albert Oscar 1936- *WhoHisp 94*
Rabassa, Gregory 1922- *IntWW 93, WhoAm 94, WhoHisp 94, WrDr 94*
Rabasse, Marie d1967 *WhoHol 92*
Rabaud, Henri 1873-1949 *NewGrDO*
Rabb, Bernard Paul 1939- *WhoAm 94*
Rabb, Bruce 1941- *WhoAm 94, WhoFI 94*
Rabb, Ellis 1930- *WhoAm 94*
Rabb, George Bernard 1930- *WhoAm 94, WhoWest 93, WhoScEn 94*
Rabb, Harriet Schaffer 1941- *WhoAmL 94*
Rabb, Irving W., Mrs. *WhoAmA 93*
Rabb, Jeannette *WhoAmA 93*
Rabb, Madeline M. *WhoAmA 93*
Rabb, Maurice F. *WhoBlA 94*

Rabb, Maxwell M. 1910- *WhoAm 94, WhoAmP 93*
Rabb, Theodore K. 1937- *WhoAm 94, WrDr 94*
Rabbai, Ronald Edward 1935- *WhoMW 93*
Rabbe, David Ellsworth 1955- *WhoFI 94*
Rabbett, Martin *WhoHol 92*
Rabbi, The Chief *Who 94*
Rabbideau, Richard E. 1938- *WhoAm 94*
Rabbit, Running *WhoAmA 93*
Rabbitt, Edward Thomas 1941- *WhoAm 94*
Rabbitt, Thomas *DrAPF 93*
Rabbitts, Terence Howard 1946- *Who 94*
Rabby, Pat *DrAPF 93*
Rabe, Berniece (Louise) 1928- *SmATA 77 [port], WrDr 94*
Rabe, David 1940- *WrDr 94*
Rabe, David (William) 1940- *ConDr 93, IntDcT 2*
Rabe, David William 1940- *IntMPA 94, WhoAm 94*
Rabe, John Earl d1943 *WhoHol 92*
Rabe, Jurgen P. 1955- *WhoScEn 94*
Rabe, William George 1896- *WhAm 10*
Rabel, William Huitt 1941- *WhoIns 94*
Rabelais, Francois 1494?-1553 *EncSF 93, GuFrLit 2*
Rabelais, Francois 1495?-1553 *BlmGEL*
Rabemananjara, Jacques 1913- *IntWW 93*
Raben, Daniel Max 1949- *WhoScEn 94*
Rabenseifner, Hanna Camille 1957- *WhoAmL 94*
Rabenstein, Dallas Leroy 1942- *WhoAm 94*
Raber, Marvin 1937- *WhoAm 94*
Rabetafika, Joseph Albert Blaise 1932- *IntWW 93*
Rabett, Catherine *WhoHol 92*
Rabi, I. I. d1988 *NobelP 91N*
Rabi, Isidor Isaac 1898-1988 *WorScD*
Rabideau, Peter Wayne 1940- *WhoAm 94, WhoScEn 94*
Rabier, Jean 1927- *IntDcF 2-4*
Rabikovitz, Dahlia *ConWorW 93*
Rabil, Albert, Jr. 1934- *WhoAm 94*
Rabil, Mitchell Joseph 1931- *WhoAm 94*
Rabin, A(lbert) I(srael) 1912- *ConAu 41NR*
Rabin, Aaron 1945- *WhoScEn 94*
Rabin, Brian Robert 1927- *Who 94*
Rabin, Bruce Stuart 1941- *WhoAm 94*
Rabin, Chaim 1915- *WrDr 94*
Rabin, Herbert 1928- *WhoAm 94*
Rabin, Jack 1930- *WhoAm 94, WhoFI 94*
Rabin, Joseph Harry 1927- *WhoFI 94, WhoMW 93*
Rabin, Michael O. 1931- *WhoScEn 94*
Rabin, Oskar 1928- *IntWW 93*
Rabin, Paul Irwin 1938- *WhoIns 94*
Rabin, Samuel d1993 *NewYTBS 93 [port]*
Rabin, Stanley Arthur 1938- *WhoAm 94, WhoFI 94*
Rabin, Yitzhak 1922- *IntWW 93, NewYTBS 93 [port], Who 94*
Rabinbach, Anson (Gilbert) 1945- *ConAu 142*
Rabineau, Louis 1924- *WhoAm 94*
Rabiner, Lawrence Richard 1943- *WhoAm 94*
Rabiner, Susan 1948- *WhoAm 94*

Rabinovich, Raquel 1929- *WhoAm 94, WhoAmA 93*
Rabinovich, Rhea Sanders *WhoAmA 93*
Rabinovich, Semyon 1922- *WhoWest 94*
Rabinovich, Sergio 1928- *WhoAm 94*
Rabinovitch, B(enton) Seymour 1919- *IntWW 93*
Rabinovitch, Benton Seymour 1919- *Who 94, WhoAm 94*
Rabinovitch, Max Joel 1929- *WhoFI 94*
Rabinovitch, William Avrum 1936- *WhoAmA 93*
Rabinovitz, Bruce H. 1945- *WhoAmL 94*
Rabinovitz, Jason *IntMPA 94*
Rabinovitz, Jason 1921- *WhoAm 94, WhoWest 94*
Rabinovitz, Joel 1939- *WhoAm 94*
Rabinovitz, Rubin 1938- *WrDr 94*
Rabinow, Jacob 1910- *WhoAm 94, WhoScEn 94, WorInv*
Rabinowicz, Ernest 1926- *WhoAm 94*
Rabinowicz, Mordka Harry 1919- *WrDr 94*
Rabinowicz, Theodore 1919- *WhoScEn 94*
Rabinowitch, David 1943- *WhoAmA 93*
Rabinowitch, David George 1943- *WhoAm 94*
Rabinowitch, Royden Leslie 1943- *WhoAmA 93*
Rabinowitz, Arthur Philip 1957- *WhoScEn 94*
Rabinowitz, Hannah *WhoHol 92*
Rabinowitz, Harry 1916- *IntWW 93, Who 94*
Rabinowitz, Howard K. 1946- *WhoAm 94*
Rabinowitz, Jack Grant 1927- *WhoAm 94*
Rabinowitz, Jay Andrew 1927- *WhoAm 94, WhoAmL 94, WhoAmP 93, WhoWest 94*
Rabinowitz, Jesse C. 1925- *IntWW 93*
Rabinowitz, Mario 1936- *WhoWest 94*
Rabinowitz, Mark Allan 1954- *WhoAm 94*
Rabinowitz, Marvin 1939- *WhoFI 94*
Rabinowitz, Mayer Elya 1939- *WhoAm 94*
Rabinowitz, Samuel Nathan 1932- *WhoAm 94*
Rabinowitz, Simon S. 1953- *WhoScEn 94*
Rabinowitz, Stanley Samuel 1917- *WhoAm 94*
Rabinowitz, Wilbur M. 1918- *WhoFI 94*
Rabins, Michael Jerome 1932- *WhoAm 94*
Rabish, Christopher Allan 1961- *WhoMW 93*
Rabjohn, Norman 1915- *WhoAm 94*
Rabkin, Eric S(tanley) 1946- *EncSF 93*
Rabkin, Lawrence B. 1948- *WhoAmL 94*
Rabkin, Leo 1919- *WhoAmA 93*
Rabkin, Mitchell T. 1930- *IntWW 93*
Rabkin, Mitchell Thornton 1930- *WhoAm 94*
Rable, George Calvin 1950- *WhoMW 93*
Rabl-Stadler, Helga 1948- *WhoWomW 91*
Rabo, Jule Anthony *WhoAm 94, WhoScEn 94*
Rabold, Barbara Ann 1939- *WhoMW 93*
Rabold, Robert E. H. *WhoIns 94*
Rabolt, John Francis 1949- *WhoScEn 94*
Rabon, Ronald Ray 1955- *WhoFI 94*
Rabon, Timothy Alan 1954- *WhoFI 94*
Rabon, Tom B., Jr. 1954- *WhoAmP 93*
Rabon, William James, Jr. 1931- *WhoAm 94, WhoScEn 94*

Raborg, Christopher Henry 1950- *WhoWest 94*
Raborg, Frederick A., Jr. *DrAPF 93*
Raborn, William Francis, Jr. 1905-1990 *WhAm 10*
Rabosky, Joseph George 1944- *WhoFI 94, WhoScEn 94*
Rabouin, E. Michelle 1956- *WhoBlA 94*
Rabovsky, Jean 1937- *WhoWest 94*
Rabow, Gerald 1928- *WrDr 94*
Raboy, Marc 1948- *WrDr 94*
Raboy, S. Caesar 1936- *WhoIns 94*
Rabson, Alan Saul 1926- *WhoAm 94, WhoScEn 94*
Rabson, Robert 1926- *WhoScEn 94*
Rabson, Thomas Avelyn 1923- *WhoScEn 94*
Rabstejnek, George John 1932- *WhoAm 94*
Rabuck, Bob 1944- *WhoAmP 93*
Rabuka, Sitiveni Ligamamada 1948- *IntWW 93*
Rabukawaqa, Josua Rasilau 1917- *IntWW 93, Who 94*
Rabun, John Brewton, Jr. 1946- *WhoAm 94*
Raby, Clyde T. 1934- *WhoBlA 94*
Raby, Derek (Graham) 1927- *WrDr 94*
Raby, Elizabeth *DrAPF 93*
Raby, William Louis 1927- *WhoAm 94, WhoWest 94*
Racan, Honorat de Bueil, Seigneur de 1589-1670 *GuFrLit 2*
Racaniello, Lori Kuck 1961- *WhoScEn 94*
Racaniello, Vincent Raimondi 1953- *WhoScEn 94*
Racca, Giuseppe Domenico 1957- *WhoScEn 94*
Race, George Justice 1926- *WhoAm 94*
Race, Howard Everett 1918- *WhoAmP 93*
Race, Hugo *WhoHol 92*
Race, Lisa Anne 1961- *WhoScEn 94, WhoWest 94*
Race, Paula Holmes *WhoMW 93*
Race, (Denys Alan) Reg 1947- *Who 94*
Race, Robert K. 1956- *WhoIns 94*
Race, Ruth Ann *Who 94*
Race, Steve 1921- *Who 94*
Racette, Francine *WhoHol 92*
Racey, Paul Adrian 1944- *Who 94*
Rachal, Patricia *DrAPF 93*
Rachel 1890-1931 *BlmGWL*
Rachel, Naomi *DrAPF 93*
Racheter, Donald Paul 1947- *WhoAmP 93*
Rachford, Fred *DrAPF 93*
Rachie, Cyrus 1908- *WhoAm 94*
Rachiele, Arthur Henry 1928- *WhoWest 94*
Rachilde 1860-1953 *BlmGWL*
Rachins, Alan *WhoAm 94*
Rachins, Alan 1942- *WhoHol 92*
Rachinsky, Joseph W. 1946- *WhoIns 94*
Rachleff, Owen Spencer 1934- *WhoAm 94*
Rachleff, Peter (J.) 1951- *ConAu 141*
Rachlin, Alan Sanders 1942- *WhoAmL 94*
Rachlin, Harvey Brant 1951- *WhoAm 94*
Rachlin, Howard 1935- *WhoScEn 94*
Rachlin, Nahid *DrAPF 93*
Rachlin, Stephen Leonard 1939- *WhoAm 94, WhoScEn 94*
Rachman, Stanley Jack 1934- *WrDr 94*
Rachmeler, Martin 1928- *WhoWest 94*

Rachofsky, David J. 1936- *WhoAm 94, WhoAmL 94*
Rachow, Louis August 1927- *WhoAm 94*
Rachow, Sharon Dianne 1939- *WhoMW 93*
Rachwalski, Frank Joseph, Jr. 1945- *WhoAm 94, WhoFI 94*
Racicot, Marc 1948- *WhoAmP 93*
Racicot, Marc F. 1948- *IntWW 93, WhoAm 94, WhoWest 94*
Racicot, Rachel I. 1968- *WhoAmP 93*
Racimo, Victoria *WhoHol 92*
Racina, Thom 1946- *WhoAm 94, WhoWest 94*
Racine, Douglas A. 1952- *WhoAmP 93*
Racine, Jean *BlmGEL*
Racine, Jean 1639-1699 *GuFrLit 2, IntDcT 2 [port], NewGrDO*
Racine, Jean Dorine 1944- *WhoAm 94*
Racine, Norman O. 1923- *WhoAmP 93*
Raciti, Cherie 1942- *WhoAm 94, WhoAmA 93, WhoWest 94*
Raciunas, Antanas 1905-1984 *NewGrDO*
Rackam, John d1720 *DcNaB MP*
Racker, Efraim 1913-1991 *WhAm 10*
Rackers, Patricia Kathryn 1957- *WhoMW 93*
Rackham, Arthur 1867-1939 *DcLB 141 [port]*
Rackham, John *EncSF 93*
Rackleff, Owen Spencer 1934- *WhoAm 94*
Rackley, Lurma M. 1949- *WhoBlA 94*
Rackmales, Robert 1937- *WhoAm 94*
Rackman, Joseph Robert 1948 *WhoAmL 94*
Rackman, Steve *WhoHol 92*
Rackover, Howard 1952- *WhoFI 94*
Rackow, Julian Paul 1941- *WhoAm 94, WhoAmL 94*
Rackus, George (Keistus) 1927- *WhoAmA 93*
Raclin, Ernestine Morris 1927- *WhoAm 94*
Ractliffe, Robert Edward George 1943- *WhoFI 94*
Racusen, Lorraine Claire 1947- *WhoScEn 94*
Racz, Andre 1916- *WhoAm 94, WhoAmA 93*
Racz-Clough, Victoria Elizabeth 1955- *WhoMW 93*
Raczkiewicz, Paul Edward 1944- *WhoAm 94*
Raczkowski, Cynthia Lea 1956- *WhoScEn 94*
Raczkowski, Waldemar Tadeusz 1964- *WhoMW 93*
Raczynski, Edward d1993 *Who 94N*
Raczynski, Edward 1891-1993 *NewYTBS 93 [port]*
Rada, Alexander 1923- *WhoWest 94*
Rada, Alexander Sverre 1955- *WhoWest 94*
Radabaugh, Michele Jo 1961 *WhoMW 93*
Radabaugh, Mike *WhoAmL 94*
Radan, George Tivadar 1923- *WhoAmA 93*
Radandt, Friedhelm K. 1932- *WhoAm 94*
Radanovic, Loretta Jane 1966- *WhoFI 94*
Radashaw, Sharon Lee 1937- *WhoWest 94*
Radavich, David *DrAPF 93*
Radcliff, William Franklin 1922- *WhoAm 94*
Radcliffe, Ann 1764-1823 *BlmGEL, BlmGWL*
Radcliffe, Anthony Frank 1933- *Who 94*
Radcliffe, Aubrey 1941- *WhoBlA 94*
Radcliffe, Charles W. 1925- *WhoAmP 93*
Radcliffe, Dale W. 1949- *WhoAmP 93*
Radcliffe, Donnie *WrDr 94*
Radcliffe, Francis Charles Joseph 1939- *Who 94*
Radcliffe, (Henry) Garnett 1899- *EncSF 93*
Radcliffe, George Grove 1924- *WhoAm 94*
Radcliffe, Gerald Eugene 1923- *WhoMW 93*
Radcliffe, Harry Southland 1894- *WhAm 10*
Radcliffe, Hugh John Reginald Joseph 1911- *Who 94*
Radcliffe, Jack d1967 *WhoHol 92*
Radcliffe, Janette *WhAm 10*
Radcliffe, Mary Ann c. 1746-c. 1810 *DcNaB MP*
Radcliffe, Michael T. 1948- *WhoAmL 94*
Radcliffe, R. Stephen 1945- *WhoIns 94*
Radcliffe, Redonia *WrDr 94*
Radcliffe, Redonia Wheeler *WhoAm 94*
Radcliffe, S. Victor 1927- *WhoAm 94*
Radcliffe, Sebastian Everard 1972- *Who 94*
Radcliffe, Timothy Peter Joseph 1945- *Who 94*
Radcliffe-Brown, Alfred Reginald 1881-1955 *DcNaB MP*
Radcliffe-Smallwood, Cynthia 1946- *WhoMW 93*
Radcliff-Umstead, Douglas 1944- *WrDr 94N*
Radcliff-Umstead, Douglas 1944-1992 *WhAm 10*
Radclyffe-Hall, Marguerite Antonia 1880-1943 *DcNaB MP*
Radd, Ronald d1976 *WhoHol 92*
Radda, George K. 1936- *Who 94*
Radda, George Karoly 1936- *IntWW 93*
Raddall, Thomas Head 1903- *WrDr 94*
Raddatz, Carl 1911- *WhoHol 92*
Radden, James David, Sr. 1945- *WhoAmP 93*
Radden, Lawrence Nathaniel 1956- *WhoAmL 94*
Radden, Thelma Gibson 1903- *WhoBlA 94*
Radding, Andrew 1944- *WhoAmL 94*
Radding, Charles Michael 1946- *WhoMW 93*
Radding, Paul Louis 1950- *WhoMW 93*
Radebaugh, Alan Paine 1952- *WhoWest 94*
Radebaugh, James Brewster 1947- *WhoFI 94*
Radebaugh, Ray 1939- *WhoWest 94*
Radecki, Anthony Eugene 1939- *WhoAm 94*
Radecki, Martin John 1948- *WhoAmA 93*
Radegonde, Sylvestre Louis 1956- *Who 94*
Radeka, Veljko 1930- *WhoAm 94*
Radelet, Michael L. 1950- *ConAu 140*
Radell, Nicholas John 1930- *WhoAm 94*
Rademacher, Betty Green 1935- *WhoMW 93*
Rademacher, Gary Edward 1954- *WhoMW 93*
Rademacher, Hollis William 1935- *WhoAm 94*
Rademacher, John Martin 1924- *WhoScEn 94*
Rademacher, Richard Joseph 1937- *WhoAm 94, WhoMW 93*
Rademaekers, Ed 1948- *WhoAm 94*
Rademaekers, Iwana 1962- *WhoAmL 94*
Rademaker, Stephen Geoffrey 1959- *WhoAm 94*
Rademaker Grunewald, Augusto Hamann 1905- *IntWW 93*
Raden, Louis 1929- *WhoAm 94, WhoFI 94, WhoMW 93*
Radenski, Atanas Atanassov 1950- *WhoMW 93*
Rader, Charles George 1946- *WhoAm 94, WhoScEn 94*
Rader, Charles Phillip 1935- *WhoMW 93*
Rader, Dotson *DrAPF 93*
Rader, Dotson Carlyle 1942- *WhoAm 94*
Rader, Ella Jane 1941- *WhoScEn 94*
Rader, Gene *WhoHol 92*
Rader, Hannelore 1937- *WhoAm 94, WhoMW 93*
Rader, Jack *WhoHol 92*
Rader, Joan Sperry d1993 *NewYTBS 93*
Rader, Joan Sperry 1934- *WhoAmP 93*
Rader, John L. 1927- *WhoAmP 93*
Rader, Larry William 1936- *WhoAmL 94*
Rader, Louis T. 1911- *WhoAm 94*
Rader, Ralph Terrance 1947- *WhoAm 94*
Rader, Ralph Wilson 1930- *WhoWest 94*
Rader, Randall R. 1949- *CngDr 93, WhoAmP 93*
Rader, Randall Ray 1949- *WhoAm 94, WhoAmL 94*
Rader, Robert Michael 1946- *WhoAm 94*
Rader, Steven Palmer 1952- *WhoAmL 94, WhoAmP 93*
Rader, William Sherman 1921- *WhoAmL 94*
Rades, William L. 1943- *WhoAmA 93*
Radespiel, Rolf Ernst 1957- *WhoScEn 94*
Radest, Howard Bernard 1928- *WhoAm 94*
Radev, Ivan Stefanov 1958- *WhoScEn 94*
Radewagen, Amata Coleman 1947- *WhoAmP 93*
Radewagen, Fred 1944- *WhoAm 94, WhoAmP 93*
Radey, Dona Lynn 1959- *WhoAmL 94*
Radez, David Charles 1946- *WhoFI 94*
Radford, Arthur W. 1896-1973 *HisDcKW*
Radford, Basil d1952 *WhoHol 92*
Radford, Courtenay Arthur Ralegh 1900- *IntWW 93*
Radford, Joseph 1918- *Who 94*
Radford, Linda Robertson 1944- *WhoScEn 94*
Radford, Norman DePue, Jr. 1943- *WhoAm 94, WhoAmL 94*
Radford, Ralegh *Who 94*
Radford, (Courtenay Arthur) Ralegh 1900- *Who 94*
Radford, Richard F. *DrAPF 93*
Radford, Robert 1874-1933 *NewGrDO*
Radford, Robert Edwin 1921- *Who 94*
Radford, Ronald (Walter) 1916- *Who 94*
Radford, Virginia Rodriguez 1917- *WhoMW 93*
Radford Sisters *NewGrDO*
Radha, M. R. d1979 *WhoHol 92*
Radhakrishnamurthy, Bhandaru 1928- *WhoAsA 94*
Radhakrishnan, Sarvepalli 1888-1975 *HisDcKW*
Radharamanan, Ramachandran 1948- *WhoFI 94*
Radi, Essam Radi Abd al-Hamid *IntWW 93*
Radic, Dusan 1929- *NewGrDO*
Radicati, Felice Alessandro 1775-1820 *NewGrDO*
Radice, Anne-Imelda 1948- *WhoAm 94*
Radice, Anne-Imelda Marino 1948- *WhoAmA 93*
Radice, Anthony M. 1945- *WhoAmL 94*
Radice, Edward Albert 1907- *Who 94*
Radice, Giles Heneage 1936- *Who 94*
Radice, Italo de Lisle 1911- *Who 94*
Radick, Barry G. 1941- *WhoAmL 94*
Radigan, Dennis M. 1938- *WhoAmP 93*
Radigan, J. Joseph 1929- *WhoAmP 93*
Radigan, Joseph Richard 1939- *WhoAm 94*
Radilack, Charles d1972 *WhoHol 92*
Radillo, Eduardo, Jr. 1928- *WhoHisp 94*
Radin, Alex 1921- *WhoAm 94*
Radin, Brian Jeremy 1961- *WhoFI 94*
Radin, Dan 1929- *WhoAmA 93*
Radin, Doris *DrAPF 93*
Radin, John William 1944- *WhoAm 94*
Radin, Marcia Beth 1947- *WhoMW 93*
Radin, Norman Samuel 1920- *WhoAm 94*
Radin, Paul 1913- *IntMPA 94*
Radin, Ruth Yaffe 1938- *WrDr 94*
Radisson, Pierre-Esprit 1636-1710 *WhWE [port]*
Radjai, Abbas 1950- *WhoAmA 93*
Radji, Parviz C(amran) 1936- *WrDr 94*
Radji, Parviz Camran 1936- *Who 94*
Radke, Dale Lee 1933- *WhoMW 93*
Radke, Dorothy Grace 1923- *WhoMW 93*
Radke, Rodney Owen 1942- *WhoAm 94*
Radke, William John 1947- *WhoScEn 94*
Radlauer, David G. 1954- *WhoAmL 94*
Radler, Franklin David 1942- *WhoAm 94, WhoFI 94, WhoWest 94*
Radler, Warren S. 1936- *WhoAm 94*
Radley, Eric John 1917- *WrDr 94*
Radley, Ken *WhoHol 92*
Radley, Sheila 1928- *WrDr 94*
Radley, Virginia Louise 1927- *WhoAm 94*
Radley-Smith, Eric John *Who 94*
Radloff, Robert Albert 1947- *WhoAm 94, WhoFI 94*
Radmacher, Sally Ann 1937- *WhoMW 93*
Radmer, Michael John 1945- *WhoAm 94, WhoAmL 94, WhoMW 93*
Radnai, Miklos 1892-1935 *NewGrDO*
Radnay, Paul Andrew 1913- *WhoAm 94*
Radner, Gilda d1989 *WhoHol 92*
Radner, Gilda 1946-1989 *WhAm 10, WhoCom*
Radner, Rebecca *DrAPF 93*
Radner, Roy 1927- *IntWW 93, WhoAm 94, WhoFI 94*
Radnitz, Robert B. 1924- *IntMPA 94*
Radnofsky, Barbara *WhoAmL 94*
Radnofsky, Barbara A. 1956- *WhoAmL 94*
Radnor, Earl of 1927- *Who 94*
Radnor, Alan T. 1946- *WhoAm 94, WhoAmL 94*
Rado, Ladislav Leland 1909- *WhoAm 94*
Radock, Michael 1917- *WhoAm 94*
Radoczy, Albert 1914- *WhoAmA 93*
Radoff, Leonard Irving 1927- *WhoAm 94*
Radojevic, Danilo 1957- *WhoAm 94*
Radolovich, Fred R. 1946- *WhoAmL 94*
Radomski, Jack London 1920- *WhoAm 94*
Radon, Jenik Richard 1946- *WhoAmL 94, WhoFI 94*
Radoux, Jean-Theodore 1835-1911 *NewGrDO*
Radoux-Rogier, Charles 1877-1952 *NewGrDO*
Radovich, Donald 1932- *WhoAmA 93*
Radowich, Jeffrey J. 1945- *WhoAmL 94*
Radowitz, Stuart P. *DrAPF 93*
Radtke, Fred Raymond 1938- *WhoMW 93*
Radtke, Jeffrey Lee 1962- *WhoMW 93*
Radtke, Randall James 1951- *WhoAmP 93*
Radtke, Rosetta *DrAPF 93*
Radtke, Schrade Fred 1919-1988 *WhAm 10*
Raduchel, William James 1946- *WhoFI 94*
Raduenz, Brian Dean 1966- *WhoMW 93*
Radugge, Phyllis Anne 1936- *WhoMW 93*
Radulescu, Gheorghe d1991 *IntWW 93N*
Radunsky, Aleksandr 1912- *IntDcB*
Radvanyi, Pierre Charles 1926- *WhoScEn 94*
Radway, Janice A. *BlmGWL*
Radway, Laurence Ingram 1919- *WhoAmP 93*
Radwin, Robert Gerry *WhoScEn 94*
Rady, Arnold I. 1948- *WhoAmL 94*
Rady, Elsa 1943- *WhoAm 94, WhoAmA 93*
Rady, Ernest S. 1938- *WhoAm 94, WhoFI 94, WhoWest 94*
Radycki, J(osephine) Diane 1946- *WhoAmA 93*
Radys, Raymond George 1940- *WhoScEn 94, WhoWest 94*
Radzicki, Michael Joseph 1958- *WhoFI 94*
Radziemski, Leon Joseph 1937- *WhoWest 94*
Radzinowicz, Leon 1906- *IntWW 93, Who 94*
Radzinowicz, Leon, Sir 1906- *WrDr 94*
Radzinowicz, Mary Ann 1925- *WhoAm 94*
Radzinskii, Edvard (Stanislavovich) 1936- *ConWorW 93*
Radzinsky, Edvard (Stanislavovich) 1936- *ConAu 142*
Radzinsky, Edvard Stanislavovich 1936- *IntWW 93*
Radzinsky, Edward *ConWorW 93*
Radziwit, Anna *WhoWomW 91*
Radzwill, Franciszka 1705-1753 *BlmGWL*
Rae, Alexander Lindsay 1923- *IntWW 93*
Rae, Alice d1944 *WhoHol 92*
Rae, Allan Alexander Sinclair 1925- *Who 94*
Rae, Barbara Davis 1943- *Who 94*
Rae, Charlotte 1926- *WhoHol 92*
Rae, Claire d1938 *WhoHol 92*
Rae, Douglas Whiting 1939- *WhoAm 94*
Rae, Henry Edward Grant 1925- *Who 94*
Rae, Hugh C(rawford) 1935- *WrDr 94*
Rae, John d1977 *WhoHol 92*
Rae, John 1813-1893 *WhWE*
Rae, John 1942- *Who 94*
Rae, John (Malcolm) 1931- *Who 94*
Rae, John Malcolm 1931- *WrDr 94*
Rae, Matthew Sanderson, Jr. 1922- *WhoAm 94, WhoAmL 94, WhoAmP 93, WhoFI 94, WhoWest 94*
Rae, Nicol C(ursiter) 1960- *WrDr 94*
Rae, Rita Emilia Anna 1950- *Who 94*
Rae, Robert Keith 1948- *IntWW 93, Who 94, WhoAm 94*
Rae, Robert Wright 1914- *Who 94*
Rae, Ronald Arthur R. *Who 94*
Rae, Wallace (Alexander Ramsay) 1914- *Who 94*
Rae, William McCulloch 1940- *Who 94*
Raeben, Jay E. d1993 *NewYTBS 93*
Raeburn, Andrew Harvey 1933- *WhoAm 94*
Raeburn, Antonia 1934- *WrDr 94*
Raeburn, Boyd d1966 *WhoHol 92*
Raeburn, David Antony 1927- *Who 94*
Raeburn, Digby *Who 94*
Raeburn, (William) Digby (Manifold) 1915- *Who 94*
Raeburn, Frances d1976 *WhoHol 92*
Raeburn, Henzie d1973 *WhoHol 92*
Raeburn, John Hay 1941- *WhoAm 94*
Raeburn, John Ross 1912- *Who 94*
Raeburn, Michael Edward Norman 1954- *Who 94*
Raeburn, Susan Adiel Ogilvie 1954- *Who 94*
Raedeke, Linda Dismore 1950- *WhoWest 94*
Raeder, Myrna Sharon 1947- *WhoAmL 94*
Raedler, Dorothy d1993 *NewYTBS 93*
Raedler, Dorothy Florence 1917- *WhoAm 94*
Rae-Dupree, Janet Sanderson 1962- *WhoWest 94*
Raeff, Marc 1923- *WrDr 94*
Rae-Hallcom, Judy 1945- *WhoWest 94*
Rael, Daniel A. 1959- *WhoHisp 94*
Rael, Henry Sylvester 1928- *WhoWest 94*
Rael, Jeannette G. 1954- *WhoHisp 94*
Rael, Juan Jose 1948- *WhoHisp 94*
Rael, Selimo C. 1946- *WhoHisp 94*
Raelson, Douglas A. 1948- *WhoAmL 94*
Raemer, Harold Roy 1924- *WhoAm 94*
Raeper, William 1959- *WrDr 94*
Raes, Hugo *EncSF 93*
Raeschild, Sheila *DrAPF 93*
Raese, John Reeves 1950- *WhoAmP 93*
Rae Smith, David Douglas 1919- *Who 94*
Raeth, Peter George 1951- *WhoMW 93*
Raether, Edward W. 1936- *WhoFI 94, WhoMW 93*
Raether, Scott Edward 1960- *WhoScEn 94*
Raetz, Gary Edward 1955- *WhoFI 94*
Raetz, Greg Christie 1949- *WhoAmP 93*
Raeuchle, John Steven 1955- *WhoMW 93*
Raeuchle, Thomas Michael 1956- *WhoMW 93*
Rafael, Gideon 1913- *IntWW 93, Who 94*
Rafael, Ruth Kelson 1929- *WhoAm 94, WhoWest 94*
Rafael Mares, Carmen de 1911- *BlmGWL*

Rafajko, Robert Richard 1931- *WhoAm 94, WhoFI 94*
Rafanelli, Kenneth Robert 1937- *WhoAm 94*
Rafanelli, Leda 1880-1971 *BlmGWL*
Rafano, Robert C. 1937- *WhoAmL 94*
RAF Casualty *ConAu 141*
Rafe, Stephen C. 1937- *WrDr 94*
Rafea, Ahmed Abdelwahed 1950- *WhoScEn 94*
Rafeedie, Edward 1929- *WhoAm 94, WhoAmL 94, WhoWest 94*
Rafelson, Bob 1933- *IntMPA 94, IntWW 93, WhoAm 94*
Rafelson, Max Emanuel, Jr. 1921- *WhoAm 94*
Rafelson, Peter 1961- *WhoHol 92*
Rafetto, John 1950- *WhoScEn 94*
Rafey, Larry Dean 1948- *WhoScEn 94*
Raff, David Alan 1945- *WhoAmL 94*
Raff, Gary *WhoHol 92*
Raff, Gilbert 1928- *WhoAm 94*
Raff, (Joseph) Joachim 1822-1882 *NewGrDO*
Raff, Joseph Allen 1933- *WhoAm 94*
Raff, Martin Charles 1938- *Who 94*
Raffa, Dominic C. 1918- *WhoAmP 93*
Raffa, Joseph *DrAPF 93*
Raffael, Joseph 1933- *WhoAm 94, WhoAmA 93*
Raffael, Judith K. *WhoAmA 93*
Raffaelli, Francesca *NewGrDO*
Raffalow, Janet Terry 1947- *WhoAmL 94*
Raffan, Keith William Twort 1949- *Who 94*
Raffanelli, Luigi 1752-1821 *NewGrDO*
Raffanielo, Robert Donald 1957- *WhoScEn 94*
Raffanti, Dano 1948- *NewGrDO*
Raffay, Stephen Joseph 1927- *WhoAm 94*
Raffeiner, Walter 1947- *NewGrDO*
Raffel, Burton *DrAPF 93*
Raffel, Jeffrey Allen 1945- *WhoAm 94*
Raffel, Leroy B. 1927- *WhoAm 94*
Raffel, Louis B. 1933- *WhoAm 94*
Raffeld, David *DrAPF 93*
Raffelson, Michael 1946- *WhoFI 94*
Rafferty, Anne Judith *Who 94*
Rafferty, Bob 1964- *WhoAmP 93*
Rafferty, Brian Joseph 1957- *WhoAm 94*
Rafferty, Chips d1971 *WhoHol 92*
Rafferty, Edson Howard 1943- *WhoAmL 94, WhoFI 94*
Rafferty, Frances 1922- *IntMPA 94, WhoHol 92*
Rafferty, James Patrick 1947- *WhoAm 94*
Rafferty, James Paul 1952- *WhoFI 94*
Rafferty, Jane Pauline 1946- *WhoMW 93*
Rafferty, Joanne Miller 1948- *WhoAmA 93*
Rafferty, John Knox 1938- *WhoAmP 93*
Rafferty, John Powell 1957- *WhoFI 94*
Rafferty, Joseph Anstice *Who 94*
Rafferty, Kevin Alfred 1953- *WhoWest 94*
Rafferty, Kevin Lawrence 1933- *Who 94*
Rafferty, Kevin Robert 1944- *Who 94*
Rafferty, Michael Robert 1949- *WhoAm 94*
Rafferty, Michael William 1961- *WhoFI 94*
Rafferty, Nancy Schwarz 1930- *WhoAm 94*
Rafferty, S. S. 1930- *WrDr 94*
Rafferty, William Bernard 1912- *WhoAm 94*
Raffetto, Michael d1990 *WhoHol 92*
Raffi 1948- *WhoAm 94, WrDr 94*
Raffill, Stewart *EncSF 93*
Raffin, Deborah 1953- *IntMPA 94, WhoHol 92*
Raffin, Thomas A. 1947- *WhoAm 94*
Raffler, Hans 1930- *WhoIns 94*
Raffman, Relly 1921-1988 *WhAm 10*
Raffo, Carlos 1927- *Who 94*
Raffo, Steve 1912- *WhoAm 94, WhoAmA 93*
Rafi, Malik Mohammed 1963- *WhoWest 94*
Rafi, Mohammed 1944- *IntWW 93*
Rafkin, Alan 1928- *WhoAm 94*
Rafkin, Louise *DrAPF 93*
Rafn, Eleanor Yolanda 1932- *WhoWest 94*
Rafsanjani, Hojatoleslam Ali Akhbar Hashemi 1934- *IntWW 93*
Rafshoon, Gerald Monroe 1934- *WhoAm 94*
Rafsky, Jessica C. 1924- *WhoAmA 93*
Rafsky, Robert d1993 *NewYTBS 93 [port]*
Rafsnider, Giles Thomas 1941- *WhoWest 94*
Raft, George d1980 *WhoHol 92*
Rafter, Michael Kevin 1968- *WhoFI 94*
Raftery, Barry Joseph 1944- *IntWW 93*
Raftery, J(ohn) Patrick 1957- *NewGrDO*
Raftery, Lawrence M. 1895- *WhAm 10*
Raftery, M. Daniel 1962- *WhoScEn 94*
Raftery, Peter Albert 1929- *Who 94*
Ragab, Mohamed Mahmoud 1952- *WhoWest 94*
Ragan, Charles Ransom 1947- *WhoAm 94, WhoAmL 94*
Ragan, David 1925- *WhoAm 94*
Ragan, Harold J. 1928- *WhoAmP 93*
Ragan, Hugh A. 1942- *WhoAmP 93*
Ragan, James *DrAPF 93*
Ragan, James Francis 1949- *WhoFI 94*
Ragan, James Otis 1942- *WhoScEn 94*
Ragan, James Thomas 1929- *WhoAm 94*
Ragan, Joseph Douglas 1940- *WhoAmP 93*
Ragan, Mike *WhoHol 92*
Ragan, Roy Allen 1929-1989 *WhAm 10*
Ragan, Samuel Talmadge 1915- *WhoAm 94*
Ragan, Seaborn Bryant Timmons 1929- *WhoFI 94*
Ragatz, Roland Andrew 1898- *WhAm 10*
Ragatz, Thomas George 1934- *WhoAm 94*
Ragen, Douglas M. 1942- *WhoAmL 94*
Ragen, Naomi 1949- *WrDr 94*
Ragent, Boris 1924- *WhoAm 94*
Rager, Richard Scott 1948- *WhoIns 94*
Rager, William Lewis 1947- *WhoMW 93*
Ragg, Theodore David Butler 1919- *Who 94*
Raggatt, Timothy Walter Harold 1950- *Who 94*
Raggi, Reena 1951- *WhoAm 94, WhoAmL 94*
Raggio, Carl W. *WhoAmP 93*
Raggio, Kenneth Gaylord 1949- *WhoAm 94, WhoAmL 94*
Raggio, Lisa *WhoHol 92*
Raggio, Louise Ballerstedt 1919- *WhoAm 94*
Raggio, Olga *WhoAmA 93*
Raggio, Thomas Louis 1946- *WhoAmL 94*
Raggio, William J. 1926- *WhoAmP 93*
Raggio, William John 1926- *WhoWest 94*
Raghavan, Sridhar A. 1950- *WhoAsA 94*
Raghavan, Srikant 1950- *WhoMW 93*
Raghavendra, Cauligi Srinivasa 1955- *WhoWest 94*
Ragheb, Osman *WhoHol 92*
Raghunathan, Raghu Srinivasan 1943- *WhoScEn 94*
Raghupathi, P. S. 1945- *WhoAm 94*
Ragin, Derek Lee 1958- *NewGrDO*
Ragin, John S. 1933- *WhoHol 92*
Raginsky, Nina *WhoAmA 93*
Raginsky, Nina 1941- *WhoAm 94*
Raglan, Baron 1927- *Who 94*
Raglan, James d1961 *WhoHol 92*
Raglan, Robert 1906- *WhoHol 92*
Ragland, Alwine Mulhearn 1913- *WhoAmL 94*
Ragland, Bob 1938- *WhoAmA 93*
Ragland, George A. 1943- *WhoAmL 94*
Ragland, Jack Whitney 1938- *WhoAm 94, WhoAmA 93*
Ragland, James Black 1917-1991 *WhAm 10*
Ragland, Michael Steven 1958- *WhoBlA 94*
Ragland, Rags d1946 *WhoHol 92*
Ragland, Robert Allen 1954- *WhoAmL 94*
Ragland, Robert Oliver 1931- *IntMPA 94*
Ragland, Samuel Connelly 1946- *WhoWest 94*
Ragland, Sherman Leon, II 1962- *WhoBlA 94*
Ragland, Tommy 1949- *WhoAmP 93*
Ragland, Wylheme Harold 1946- *WhoBlA 94*
Raglin, Fran 1939- *WhoBlA 94*
Ragno, Joseph *WhoHol 92*
Rago, Ann D'Amico 1957- *WhoAm 94*
Rago, Nicholas A. 1942- *WhoAm 94*
Rago, Rosalinde Teresa 1952- *WhoAm 94*
Ragon, Michel 1924- *IntWW 93*
Ragone, David Vincent 1930- *WhoAm 94*
Ragone, Lourdes Margarita 1939- *WhoHisp 94*
Ragsdale, Bertha Mae 1925- *WhoFI 94*
Ragsdale, Carl Vandyke 1925- *WhoAm 94*
Ragsdale, Charles Lea Chester 1929- *WhoBlA 94*
Ragsdale, Diane 1952- *WhoAmP 93*
Ragsdale, E.K. Easton 1951- *WhoFI 94*
Ragsdale, Edward Floyd 1939- *WhoAmP 93*
Ragsdale, George Robinson 1936- *WhoAm 94*
Ragsdale, James Marcus 1938- *WhoAm 94*
Ragsdale, Kathleen Mary 1964- *WhoWest 94*
Ragsdale, Lincoln Johnson 1926- *WhoBlA 94, WhoFI 94*
Ragsdale, Paul B. 1945- *WhoBlA 94*
Ragsdale, Paul Burdett 1945- *WhoAmP 93*
Ragsdale, Rex H. 1957- *WhoMW 93*
Ragsdale, Richard Elliot 1943- *WhoAm 94*
Ragsdale, William *WhoHol 92*
Ragudos, John L. 1948- *WhoAsA 94*
Rague, Louis-Charles c. 1760-1793? *NewGrDO*
Ragueneau, Paul 1608-1680 *EncNAR*
Raguenet, Francois c. 1660-1722 *NewGrDO*
Raguin, Virginia C. 1941- *WhoAmA 93*
Raguindin, Shirley Saoit 1964- *WhoWest 94*
Ragusa, Isa 1926- *WhoAmA 93*
Ragusa, Olga Maria 1922- *WhoAm 94*
Ragusa, Paul Carmen 1961- *WhoScEn 94*
Rahal, Mary G. 1946- *WhoIns 94*
Rahall, Nick, II 1949- *CngDr 93*
Rahall, Nick J. 1949- *WhoAmP 93*
Rahall, Nick J., II 1949- *WhoAm 94, WhoFI 94*
Raham, (R.) Gary 1946- *WrDr 94*
Rahdert, George Karl 1950- *WhoAmL 94*
Rahe, Maribeth Sembach 1948- *WhoAm 94, WhoMW 93*
Raheem
See Geto Boys, The *ConMus 11*
Rahenkamp, John Edward 1937- *WhoAm 94*
Raher, Patrick M. 1947- *WhoAmL 94*
Rahill, Alice Armstrong 1948- *WhoMW 93*
Rahill, Margaret Fish 1919- *WhoAmA 93*
Rahim, Haroon 1949- *BuCMET*
Rahimian, Ahmad 1955- *WhoScEn 94*
Rahja, Virginia Helga 1921- *WhoAmA 93*
Rahl, J. Andrew, Jr. 1948- *WhoAmL 94*
Rahl, James Andrew 1917- *WhoAm 94*
Rahl, Leslie Lynn 1950- *WhoFI 94*
Rahm, David Alan 1941- *WhoAm 94, WhoAmL 94, WhoFI 94*
Rahm, Knute Olaf d1957 *WhoHol 92*
Rahm, Susan Berkman 1943- *WhoAm 94, WhoAmL 94*
Rahman, Abdul *IntWW 93*
Rahman, Abul Khayer Mohammad Matiur 1952- *WhoFI 94*
Rahman, Ahmed Assem 1940- *WhoMW 93, WhoScEn 94*
Rahman, Anwarur 1929- *WhoScEn 94*
Rahman, (Mohammad) Azizur 1925- *IntWW 93*
Rahman, Fazlur 1919-1988 *WhAm 10*
Rahman, Hamood-Ur 1910- *IntWW 93*
Rahman, Khandaker Mohammad Abdur 1938- *WhoScEn 94*
Rahman, Mahdi Abdul 1942- *WhoBlA 94*
Rahman, Matiur 1940- *ConAu 141*
Rahman, Muhammad Abdur 1930- *WhoScEn 94*
Rahman, Omar Abdel- 1938- *News 93-3 [port]*
Rahman, Sami Ur 1962- *WhoScEn 94*
Rahman, Yueh-Erh 1928- *WhoAm 94, WhoAsA 94, WhoScEn 94*
Rahmani, Cherif 1945- *IntWW 93*
Rahman Khan, Ataur 1905- *IntWW 93*
Rahming, Norris 1886-1959 *WhoAmA 93N*
Rahmmings, Keith *DrAPF 93*
Rahn, Alvin Albert 1925- *WhoAm 94*
Rahn, George E., Jr. 1948- *WhoAmL 94*
Rahn, Gerald Alan 1947- *WhoMW 93*
Rahn, Hermann 1912-1990 *WhAm 10*
Rahn, Lawrence Joseph 1951- *WhoFI 94*
Rahn, Pete Kevin 1954- *WhoAmP 93*
Rahn, Richard William 1942- *WhoAm 94*
Rahn, Trudy Jo 1953- *WhoMW 93*
Rahnamai, Kourosh Jonathan 1955- *WhoScEn 94*
Rahoi, Richard John 1935- *WhoMW 93*
Rahojsa, Viaceslau Piatrovic 1942- *LngBDD*
Rahr, Tammy Sue 1958- *WhoWest 94*
Rahtz, Philip Arthur 1921- *Who 94*
Rahv, Philip 1908-1973 *AmSocL, DcLB 137 [port]*
Rai, Amarendra Kumar 1952- *WhoAsA 94*
Rai, Arti K. 1966- *WhoAsA 94*
Rai, Arun 1963- *WhoAsA 94*
Rai, Gauri S. 1944- *WhoAsA 94*
Rai, Vijai Narain 1941- *WhoAsA 94*
Raia, Joseph S. *WhoAmP 93*
Raible, Peter Spilman 1929- *WhoAm 94, WhoWest 94*
Raibley, Parvin Rudolph 1926- *WhoMW 93*
Raica, Robert 1954- *WhoAmP 93*
Raich, Abraham Leonard 1922- *WhoScEn 94*
Raiche, Maureen E. *WhoAmP 93*
Raiche, Robert Edward 1937- *WhoAmP 93*
Raichev, Alexander 1922- *NewGrDO*
Raichev, Peter 1887-1960 *NewGrDO*
Raichle, Marcus Edward 1937- *WhoAm 94*
Raiden, Norman H. *WhoAmL 94*
Raider, Louis 1913- *WhoScEn 94*
Raidi 1938- *IntWW 93, WhoPRCh 91 [port]*
Raifikesht, Vladimir Fedorovich 1951- *LngBDD*
Raifman, Irving 1924- *WhoScEn 94*
Raiford, Roger Lee 1942- *WhoBlA 94*
Raigoza, Jaime 1937- *WhoHisp 94*
Raihall, Denis T. 1941- *WhoIns 94*
Raikes, Charles FitzGerald 1930- *WhoAm 94, WhoAmL 94*
Raikes, Iwan (Geoffrey) 1921- *Who 94*
Railsback, Steve 1947- *WhoHol 92*
Railsback, Steve 1948- *IntMPA 94*
Railsback, Tom 1932- *WhoAmP 93*
Railton, Mary d1992 *Who 94N*
Railton, Ruth 1915- *Who 94*
Railton, William Scott 1935- *WhoAm 94, WhoAmL 94*
Raimi, Burton Louis 1938- *WhoAm 94, WhoAmL 94*
Raimi, Charles N. 1951- *WhoAmL 94*
Raimi, Sam *HorFD [port]*
Raimi, Sam 1959- *IntMPA 94*
Raimi, Samuel M. 1959- *WhoAm 94*
Raimi, Steven Aaron 1962- *WhoMW 93*
Raimo, Bernard, Jr. 1944- *WhoAmL 94*
Raimond, Jean-Bernard 1926- *IntWW 93*
Raimondi, Albert Anthony 1925- *WhoAm 94*
Raimondi, Anna Louise 1961- *WhoAmL 94*
Raimondi, Gianni 1923- *NewGrDO*
Raimondi, John 1948- *WhoAmA 93*
Raimondi, Peter John, III 1955- *WhoAmL 94, WhoFI 94*
Raimondi, Pietro 1786-1853 *NewGrDO*
Raimondi, Ruggero *WhoHol 92*
Raimondi, Ruggero 1941- *IntWW 93, NewGrDO, WhoAm 94*
Raimu d1946 *WhoHol 92*
Raimund, Ferdinand 1790-1836 *IntDcT 2 [port], NewGrDO*
Raimundo, Cris C. *WhoAsA 94*
Rain, Cheryl Ann 1950- *WhoMW 93*
Rain, Douglas *WhoHol 92*
Raina, Ashok K. 1942- *WhoAsA 94*
Raina, Rajesh 1963- *WhoScEn 94*
Rainaldi, Lidio G. *WhoHisp 94*
Rainbolt, C. Michael 1948- *WhoFI 94*
Rainboth, Frank d1951 *WhoHol 92*
Rainbow, (James) Conrad (Douglas) 1926- *Who 94*
Rainbow-Earhart, Kathryn Adeline 1921- *WhoBlA 94*
Raine, Adelaide d1978 *WhoHol 92*
Raine, Charles Herbert, III 1937- *WhoBlA 94*
Raine, Craig 1944- *BlmGEL, WrDr 94*
Raine, Craig Anthony 1944- *IntWW 93, Who 94*
Raine, Jack d1979 *WhoHol 92*
Raine, John Stephen 1941- *Who 94*
Raine, Kathleen 1908- *BlmGEL, BlmGWL*
Raine, Kathleen (Jessie) 1908- *WrDr 94*
Raine, Kathleen Jessie 1908- *IntWW 93, Who 94*
Raine, Neale *Who 94*
Raine, (Harcourt) Neale 1923- *Who 94*
Raine, Norman Reilly 1895-1971 *IntDcF 2-4*
Raine, Patricia *WhoHol 92*
Raine, Stanley M. 1949- *WhoAmL 94*
Raine, William Alexis 1959- *WhoScEn 94*
Rainer, John David 1921- *WhoAm 94*
Rainer, Luise *Who 94*
Rainer, Luise 1909- *WhoHol 92*
Rainer, Margrit d1982 *WhoHol 92*
Rainer, Rex Kelly 1924- *WhoAm 94*
Rainer, William Gerald 1927- *WhoAm 94*
Rainer, Yvonne 1934- *WrDr 94*
Raines, Colden Douglas 1915- *WhoBlA 94*
Raines, Cristina 1953- *WhoHol 92*
Raines, Ella d1988 *WhoHol 92*
Raines, Frances *WhoHol 92*
Raines, Franklin Delano 1949- *WhoAm 94, WhoFI 94*
Raines, Helon *DrAPF 93*
Raines, Howell Hiram 1943- *WhoAm 94*
Raines, Jeff 1943- *WhoAm 94*
Raines, Leonard Harley 1947- *WhoWest 94*
Raines, Lisa *WhoHol 92*
Raines, Mary Elizabeth 1951- *WhoAm 94*
Raines, Patricia Anne 1938- *WhoMW 93*
Raines, Ronald Bruce 1929- *WhoFI 94*
Raines, Theron 1927- *EncSF 93*
Raines, Tim 1959- *WhoAm 94, WhoMW 93*
Raines, Timothy 1959- *WhoBlA 94*
Raines, Walter R. 1940- *WhoBlA 94*
Rainey, Anthony Harold 1958- *WhoWest 94*
Rainey, Arthur H. 1943- *WhoAm 94, WhoAmL 94*
Rainey, Barbara Ann 1949- *WhoScEn 94, WhoWest 94*
Rainey, Bessye Coleman 1929- *WhoBlA 94*
Rainey, Christine Rose 1952- *WhoMW 93*

Rainey, Claude Gladwin 1923- *WhoAm 94*
Rainey, Donald Glenn 1931- *WhoAmP 93*
Rainey, Ford 1908- *WhoHol 92*
Rainey, Froelich (Gladstone) 1907-1992 *CurBio 93N*
Rainey, Gene Edward 1934- *WrDr 94*
Rainey, Gordon Fryer, Jr. 1940- *WhoAm 94, WhoAmL 94*
Rainey, Howard H. 1927- *WhoAmP 93*
Rainey, James Lynn 1952- *WhoAmL 94*
Rainey, Jean Osgood 1925- *WhoAm 94*
Rainey, John David 1945- *WhoAm 94, WhoAmL 94*
Rainey, Joseph H. 1832-1887 *AfrAmAl 6*
Rainey, Larry Bruce 1951- *WhoScEn 94*
Rainey, Ma 1886-1939 *AfrAmAl 6 [port]*
Rainey, Mary Teresa 1955- *WhoAm 94*
Rainey, Norman d1960 *WhoHol 92*
Rainey, Richard K. 1938- *WhoAmP 93*
Rainey, Robert Edward 1943- *WhoFI 94*
Rainey, Sylvia Valentine *WhoBlA 94*
Rainey, Thomas Orlando 1953- *WhoAmP 93*
Rainey, William Joel 1946- *WhoAm 94, WhoAmL 94, WhoFI 94*
Rainforth, Elizabeth 1814-1877 *NewGrDO*
Rainger, Peter 1924- *Who 94*
Rainier, III 1923- *IntWW 93*
Rainier, Robert Paul 1940- *WhoAm 94*
Rainis, Eugene Charles 1940- *WhoAm 94, WhoFI 94*
Rainolde, Richard c. 1530-1606 *DcLB 136*
Rainone, Michael Carmine 1918- *WhoAmL 94*
Rains, Albert 1902-1991 *WhAm 10*
Rains, Anthony John Harding 1920- *Who 94*
Rains, Claude d1967 *WhoHol 92*
Rains, Fred d1945 *WhoHol 92*
Rains, Harry Hano 1909- *WhoAm 94, WhoAmL 94*
Rains, Horace 1912- *WhoBlA 94*
Rains, Jack M. 1937- *WhoAmP 93*
Rains, Jessica 1938- *WhoHol 92*
Rains, Leon 1870-1954 *NewGrDO*
Rains, Mary Jo 1935- *WhoFI 94*
Rains, Merritt Neal 1943- *WhoAm 94, WhoAmL 94*
Rainsford, Bettis C. *WhoAm 94, WhoFI 94*
Rainsford, George Nichols 1928- *WhoAm 94*
Rainsford, Greta M. 1936- *WhoBlA 94*
Rainsford, Seymour Grome 1900- *Who 94*
Raintree, Diane *DrAPF 93*
Rainville, Paul d1952 *WhoAmA 93N*
Rainwater, Barry Lynn 1958- *WhoFI 94*
Rainwater, Janette 1922- *WhoWest 94*
Rainwater, Marjorie Akins 1927- *WhoAmP 93*
Rainwater, Nancy Gregg 1951- *WhoWest 94*
Rainwater, Wallace Eugene 1924- *WhoAmP 93*
Rairdin, Craig Allen 1959- *WhoFI 94, WhoMW 93*
Rais, Abdul J. *Who 94*
Raisa, Rosa d1963 *WhoHol 92*
Raisa, Rosa 1893-1963 *NewGrDO*
Raisanen, Heikki Martti 1941- *IntWW 93*
Raisani, Sardar Ghaus Bakhsh 1924- *IntWW 93*
Raisbeck, Gordon 1925- *WhoAm 94*
Raisbeck, James David 1936- *WhoAm 94, WhoScEn 94, WhoWest 94*
Raisch, Bill d1984 *WhoHol 92*
Raisch, William A. 1928- *WhoAmP 93*
Raiselis, Richard 1951- *WhoAmA 93*
Raish, David Langdon 1947- *WhoAm 94, WhoAmL 94*
Raisian, John 1949- *WhoAm 94, WhoWest 94*
Raisig, Paul Jones, Jr. 1932- *WhoAm 94*
Raisin, Catherine Alice 1855-1945 *DcNaB MP*
Raisler, Kenneth Mark 1951- *WhoAm 94*
Raisman, Allan Leslie 1952- *WhoScEn 94*
Raisman, John Michael 1929- *IntWW 93, Who 94*
Raison, John Charles Anthony 1926- *Who 94*
Raison, Timothy (Hugh Francis) 1929- *Who 94*
Raisor, Philip *DrAPF 93*
Rais-Rohani, Masoud 1960- *WhoScEn 94*
Raiter, Frank *WhoHol 92*
Raiter, George L. *WhoAmP 93*
Raitio, Vaino (Eerikki) 1891-1945 *NewGrDO*
Raitt, Alan William 1930- *Who 94, WrDr 94*
Raitt, Bonnie 1949- *WhoHol 92*
Raitt, Bonnie Lynn 1949- *WhoAm 94*
Raitt, David H. 1942- *WhoAmL 94*
Raitt, Jill 1931- *WhoMW 93*
Raitt, John 1917- *WhoHol 92*
Raitz, Vladimir Gavrilovich 1922- *Who 94*
Raiziss, Sonia *DrAPF 93*
Raj, Harkisan D. 1926- *WhoAsA 94*
Raj, Kakkadan Nandanath 1924- *Who 94*
Raja, Rajendran 1948- *WhoAsA 94*
Raja, Ravi Varma 1946- *WhoMW 93*
Rajabi-Asl, Ali 1963- *WhoFI 94, WhoWest 94*
Rajadurai, Pathmanathan 1953- *WhoScEn 94*
Rajagopal, Kumbakonam Ramamani 1950- *WhoAsA 94*
Rajagopal, Rangaswamy 1944- *WhoScEn 94*
Rajah, Arumugam Ponnu 1911- *Who 94*
Rajakaruna, Lalith Asoka 1958- *WhoScEn 94*
Rajakumar, Charles 1947- *WhoScEn 94*
Rajan, Frederick E. N. 1949- *WhoAsA 94*
Rajan, M(annarswamighala) S(reeranga) 1920- *WrDr 94*
Rajan, Mannaraswamighala Sreeranga 1920- *IntWW 93*
Rajan, Periasamy Karivaratha 1942- *WhoAsA 94*
Rajan, Raghuram Govind 1963- *WhoAsA 94*
Rajan, Shital 1946- *WhoFI 94*
Rajan, Tilottama 1951- *WrDr 94*
Rajani, Prem Rajaram 1949- *WhoAm 94, WhoAsA 94*
Rajapaksa, Yatendra Ramyakanthi Perera 1957- *WhoScEn 94*
Rajaram, Sanjaya 1943- *WhoAm 94*
Rajaratnam, Daniel 1955- *WhoFI 94*
Rajaratnam, Richard G. *WhoWest 94*
Rajaratnam, Sinnathamby 1915- *IntWW 93*
Rajaravivarma, Rathika 1961- *WhoScEn 94*
Rajasekhar, Amar 1963- *WhoAsA 94*
Rajbansi, Amichand 1942- *IntWW 93*
Rajchman, Jan Aleksander 1911-1989 *WhAm 10*
Rajendran, Narasimhan 1955- *WhoScEn 94*
Rajendran, Vazhaikkurichi M. 1952- *WhoAsA 94*
Rajic, Negovan 1923- *WrDr 94*
Rajicic, Stanojlo 1910- *NewGrDO*
Rajki, Walter Albert 1925- *WhoAm 94*
Rajkowski, Frank Joseph 1948- *WhoAmL 94*
Rajlich, Vaclav Thomas 1939- *WhoMW 93, WhoScEn 94*
Rajna, Thomas 1928- *IntWW 93*
Rajoppi, Joanne 1947- *WhoAmP 93*
Rajot, Pierre-Loup *WhoHol 92*
Rajotte, Ray V. 1942- *WhoScEn 94*
Rajski, Peggy *IntMPA 94*
Raju, Krishnam 1954- *WhoScEn 94*
Raju, Perumal Reddy 1952- *WhoScEn 94*
Raju, Poolla Tirupati 1904-1992 *WrDr 94N*
Raju, Puthankurissi Sankaranarayan 1950- *WhoFI 94*
Raju, Seshadri 1939- *WhoAsA 94*
Raju, Solomon Nalli, Sr. 1934- *WhoAsA 94*
R.A.K. *EncSF 93*
Rak, Lorraine Karen 1959- *WhoAmL 94*
Rakamoto 1960- *WhoAsA 94*
Rakay, William R. 1955- *WhoAm 94*
Rake, Alan 1933- *ConAu 142*
Rakel, Robert Edwin 1932- *WhoAm 94*
Raker, Lorin d1959 *WhoHol 92*
Rakers, Linda McWard 1947- *WhoMW 93*
Rakes, Ganas Kaye 1938- *WhoAm 94*
Rakestraw, Gregory Allen 1949- *WhoAmL 94*
Rakestraw, Kyle Damon 1961- *WhoBlA 94*
Rakestraw, Priscilla B. *WhoAmP 93, WhoWomW 91*
Rakestraw, Warren Vincent 1940- *WhoAm 94*
Rakhimov, Murtaza Gubaidullovich 1934- *LngBDD*
Rakhimova, Bikhodzhal Fatkhitdinovna *WhoWomW 91*
Rakhmaninov, Sergey Vasil'yevich 1873-1943 *NewGrDO*
Raki, Laya 1927- *WhoHol 92*
Rakic, Pasko 1933- *WhoAm 94*
Rakita, Louis 1922- *WhoAm 94*
Rakitov, Anatoly Ilich 1928- *LngBDD*
Rakocy, William (Joseph) 1924- *WhoAmA 93*
Rakoczy, Jacob David 1955- *WhoMW 93*
Rakoff, Alvin 1927- *WrDr 94*
Rakoff, Alvin 1937- *IntMPA 94*
Rakoff, Jed Saul 1943- *WhoAm 94, WhoAmL 94*
Rakoff, Vivian Morris 1928- *WhoAm 94*
Rakolta, John 1923- *WhoAm 94, WhoFI 94, WhoMW 93*
Rakosi, Carl *DrAPF 93*
Rakosi, Carl 1903- *WrDr 94*
Rakotoarijaona, Desire 1934- *IntWW 93*
Rakotoniaina, Justin 1933- *IntWW 93*
Rakovan, Lawrence Francis 1939- *WhoAm 94, WhoAmA 93*
Rakower, Joel A. 1958- *WhoFI 94*
Rakowski, Barbara Ann 1948- *WhoMW 93*
Rakowski, Dennis Thomas 1939- *WhoFI 94*
Rakowski, Mieczyslaw Franciszek 1926- *IntWW 93*
Rakowsky, Ronald John 1944- *WhoAmL 94*
Raksakulthai, Vinai 1942- *WhoMW 93*
Raksin, David 1912- *IntDcF 2-4, IntMPA 94*
Raksis, Joseph W. 1942- *WhoScEn 94*
Rakutis, Ruta 1939- *WhoScEn 94, WhoWest 94*
Rale, Nero *ConAu 42NR*
Rale, Sebastien 1657-1724 *EncNAR*
Ralegh, Walter 1552-1618 *BlmGEL*
Raleigh, Cecil Baring 1934- *WhoAm 94, WhoWest 94*
Raleigh, Henry Patrick 1931- *WhoAmA 93*
Raleigh, Jean Margaret Macdonald C. *Who 94*
Raleigh, Michael 1947- *ConAu 141*
Raleigh, Saba d1923 *WhoHol 92*
Raleigh, Walter 1552-1618 *BlmGEL, WhWE [port]*
Raleigh, Walter 1554-1618 *HisWorL [port]*
Rales, Mitchell P. 1956- *WhoFI 94*
Rales, Steven M. 1951- *WhoAm 94, WhoFI 94*
Raley, Charles Edward 1946- *WhoAmL 94*
Raley, David Marion 1938- *WhoFI 94*
Raley, John W., Jr. 1932- *WhoAmL 94*
Raley, Patti J. 1946- *WhoAmP 93*
Raley, Robert L. 1924- *WhoAmA 93*
Ralf, Oscar (Georg) 1881-1964 *NewGrDO*
Ralf, Torsten (Ivar) 1901-1954 *NewGrDO*
Rall, David Platt 1926- *IntWW 93, WhoAm 94*
Rall, J. Edward 1920- *IntWW 93*
Rall, Johann Gottlieb c. 1720-1776 *WhAmRev [port]*
Rall, Joseph Edward 1920- *WhoAm 94*
Rall, Lloyd Louis 1916- *WhoScEn 94*
Rall, Tommy 1929- *WhoHol 92*
Ralli, Constantine Pandia 1948- *WhoAm 94, WhoAmL 94*
Ralli, Giovanna 1935- *WhoHol 92*
Ralli, Godfrey (Victor) 1915- *Who 94*
Ralli, Paul d1953 *WhoHol 92*
Ralling, (Antony) Christopher 1929- *Who 94*
Rallis, George J. 1918- *IntWW 93*
Rallo, Douglas 1953- *WhoAmL 94*
Rallo, James Gilbert 1942- *WhoFI 94*
Ralls, Katherine 1939- *WhoAm 94*
Ralov, Kirsten 1922- *IntDcB [port]*
Ralph, Alan Edgar 1951- *WhoAmP 93*
Ralph, Anna *WhoHol 92*
Ralph, Arthur 1942- *WhoAmL 94*
Ralph, Colin John 1951- *Who 94*
Ralph, David Clinton 1922- *WhoMW 93*
Ralph, James R. 1933- *WhoScEn 94*
Ralph, Jessie d1944 *WhoHol 92*
Ralph, Richard Garrick 1935- *WhoFI 94*
Ralph, Richard Peter 1946- *Who 94*
Ralph, Roger Paul 1953- *WhoAm 94*
Ralph, Sheryl Lee 1956- *WhoBlA 94*
Ralph, Sheryl Lee 1957- *WhoHol 92*
Ralph, Thomas A. 1941- *WhoAm 94, WhoAmL 94*
Ralph, Thomas Joseph 1926- *WhoMW 93*
Ralph, William J. 1953- *WhoAm 94*
Ralphs, Enid Mary 1915- *Who 94*
Ralston, Anthony 1930- *WhoAm 94*
Ralston, David Edmund 1954- *WhoAmP 93*
Ralston, Denny 1942- *BuCMET*
Ralston, Edward J. 1938- *WhoBlA 94*
Ralston, Elreta Melton Alexander 1919- *WhoBlA 94*
Ralston, Esther 1902- *WhoHol 92*
Ralston, Gilbert Alexander 1912- *WhoWest 94*
Ralston, Henry J. d1993 *NewYTBS 93*
Ralston, Henry James, III 1935- *WhoAm 94*
Ralston, James Allen 1946- *WhoAmL 94*
Ralston, James Kenneth 1896-1987 *WhoAmA 93N*
Ralston, Joanne Smoot 1939- *WhoAm 94, WhoFI 94*
Ralston, Jobyna d1967 *WhoHol 92*
Ralston, John Peter 1951- *WhoScEn 94*
Ralston, Ken *WhoAm 94*
Ralston, Lenore Dale 1949- *WhoWest 94*
Ralston, Patricia A. Stark 1957- *WhoScEn 94*
Ralston, Rachel Walters 1915- *WhoWest 94*
Ralston, Richard H. 1942- *WhoAmL 94*
Ralston, Roy B. 1917- *WhoFI 94, WhoScEn 94, WhoWest 94*
Ralston, Steven Philip 1954- *WhoFI 94*
Ralston, Vera Hruba 1919- *WhoHol 92*
Ram, Chitta Venkata 1948- *WhoAm 94*
Ram, Michael Jay 1940- *WhoAmL 94*
Rama, Carlos M. 1921- *IntWW 93*
Rama, John C. 1958- *WhoAmP 93*
Ramachandra, Srinivas R. 1950- *WhoAsA 94*
Ramachandran, Cherubala Pathayapurayil 1936- *IntWW 93*
Ramachandran, Gopalasamudram Narayana 1922- *Who 94*
Ramachandran, M. G. d1987 *WhoHol 92*
Ramachandran, Nadaraja 1934- *WhoAsA 94*
Ramachandran, Narayanan 1958- *WhoScEn 94*
Ramachandran, Parthasarathi 1921- *IntWW 93*
Ramachandran, Rita 1963- *WhoAsA 94*
Ramachandran, Venkatanarayana Deekshit 1934- *WhoAm 94*
Ramadhani, John Acland *Who 94*
Ramadhani, John Acland 1932- *IntWW 93*
Ramadhyani, Satish 1949- *WhoAsA 94, WhoScEn 94*
Ramaema, Elias Phisoana 1933- *IntWW 93*
Ramage, Cecil d1988 *WhoHol 92*
Ramage, (James) Granville (William) 1919- *Who 94*
Ramage, Jerrie Keith 1947- *WhoMW 93*
Ramage, John c. 1748-1802 *WhAmRev*
Ramage, Lawson Paterson 1909-1990 *WhAm 10*
Ramage, Michael Roy 1951- *WhoAmL 94*
Ramage, Robert 1935- *Who 94*
Ramage, Robert Thomas 1928- *WhoAm 94*
Ramahatra, Victor 1945- *IntWW 93*
Ramakrishna 1836-1886 *HisWorL [port]*
Ramakrishna, Kilaparti *WhoAsA 94*
Ramakrishna, Medahalli V. 1954- *WhoMW 93*
Ramakrishnan, Ramani 1948- *WhoScEn 94*
Ramakrishnan, Terizhandur S. 1958- *WhoAsA 94*
Ramakrishnan, Venkataswamy 1929- *WhoAm 94, WhoFI 94, WhoScEn 94*
Ramakumar, Ramachandra Gupta 1936- *WhoAsA 94*
Ramaley, Judith Aitken 1941- *WhoAm 94*
Ramalingam, Mysore Loganathan 1954- *WhoAsA 94, WhoScEn 94*
Ramalingaswami, Vulimiri 1921- *IntWW 93*
Ramamurthy, Subramanian 1948- *WhoMW 93*
Raman, Aravamudhan 1937- *WhoAsA 94*
Raman, William D. 1952- *WhoAmL 94*
Ramanantsoa, Gabriel 1906- *IntWW 93*
Ramanarayanan, Madhava Prabhu 1945- *WhoAm 94*
Ramanathan, Kavasseri Vaidianatha 1932- *WhoAm 94*
Ramanathan, Veerabhadran 1944- *WhoAsA 94*
Ramanauskas, Dalia Irena 1936- *WhoAmA 93*
Ramani, Narayan 1942- *WhoScEn 94*
Ramani, Raja Venkat 1938- *WhoScEn 94*
Ramanuja, Jayalakshmi Krishnadesikachar 1945- *WhoMW 93*
Ramanuja, Teralandur Krishnaswamy 1941- *WhoMW 93, WhoScEn 94*
Ramanujam, Gopala 1916- *IntWW 93*
Ramanujan, A. K. *DrAPF 93*
Ramanujan, A(ttipat) K(rishnaswami) 1929- *WrDr 94*
Ramanujan, A(ttipat) K(rishnaswami) 1929-1993 *ConAu 141*
Ramanujan, Attipat Krishnaswami d1993 *NewYTBS 93 [port]*
Ramaphosa, Matamela Cyril 1953- *IntWW 93*
Ramaprasad, Kackadasam Raghavachar 1938- *WhoScEn 94*
Rama Rao, Nandamuri Taraka 1923- *IntWW 93*
Rama Rau, Santha 1923- *IntWW 93, Who 94*
Ramasamy, Ravichandran 1965- *WhoScEn 94*
Ramasamy, Savakkattu Muniappan 1942- *WhoWest 94*
Ramasubbu, Sunder 1953- *WhoScEn 94*
Ramaswami, Devabhaktuni 1933- *WhoMW 93*
Ramaswami, Vaidyanathan 1950- *WhoAsA 94*
Ramaswamy, Krishnamurthy 1941- *WhoMW 93*
Ramaswamy, Padmanabhan 1953- *WhoWest 94*

Ramay, James Charles, Jr. 1951- *WhoFI 94*
Ramazanov, Marat Davidovich 1939- *LngBDD*
Rambahadur Limbu, Captain 1939- *Who 94*
Rambeau, Marjorie d1970 *WhoHol 92*
Ramberg, Christina 1946- *WhoAm 94, WhoAmA 93*
Ramberg, Patricia Lynn 1951- *WhoFI 94, WhoMW 93*
Rambert, Charles Jean Julien 1924- *IntWW 93*
Rambert, Marie 1888-1982 *IntDcB [port]*
Rambin, W. Neil 1954- *WhoAmL 94*
Rambo, Bettye R. 1936- *WhoBlA 94*
Rambo, Dack 1947- *WhoHol 92*
Rambo, David L. *WhoAm 94*
Rambo, Dirk d1967 *WhoHol 92*
Rambo, G. Dan 1928- *WhoAmP 93*
Rambo, Sylvia H. 1936- *WhoAm 94, WhoAmL 94*
Rambova, Natacha d1966 *WhoHol 92*
Rambush, Niels Edvard 1889-1957 *DcNaB MP*
Ramchandani, Raj S. 1941- *WhoAsA 94*
Ramdin, Ron(ald Andrew) 1942- *WrDr 94*
Rame, Franca 1929- *BlmGWL*
Rameau, Emil d1957 *WhoHol 92*
Rameau, Jean-Philippe c. 1683-1764 *NewGrDO*
Rameau, Jean-Phillippe 1683-1763 *IntDcB*
Rameau, Pierre c. 1674-1748 *IntDcB*
Ramee, Marie Louise de la *BlmGWL*
Ramel, Stig 1927- *IntWW 93*
Ramelli, Rudolph R. 1952- *WhoAmL 94*
Ramelson, Baruch 1910- *Who 94*
Ramer, Bruce M. 1933- *WhoAm 94, WhoAmL 94, WhoWest 94*
Ramer, James LeRoy 1935- *WhoAm 94, WhoFI 94, WhoMW 93, WhoScEn 94*
Ramer, Lawrence Jerome 1928- *WhoAm 94*
Rames, Stanley Dodson 1923- *WhoAmA 93*
Ramesh, Kalahasti Subrahmanyam 1949- *WhoScEn 94*
Ramesh, Kaliat Thazhathveetil 1959- *WhoScEn 94*
Ramesh, Krishnan 1959- *WhoScEn 94*
Ramesh, Swaminathan 1949- *WhoScEn 94*
Ramette, Richard Wales 1927- *WhoAm 94*
Ramey, Adele Marie 1954- *WhoBlA 94*
Ramey, Carl Robert 1941- *WhoAm 94, WhoAmL 94*
Ramey, Cecil Edward, Jr. 1923- *WhoAm 94, WhoAmL 94*
Ramey, Craig T. *WhoScEn 94*
Ramey, Denny L. 1947- *WhoAm 94, WhoAmL 94, WhoFI 94*
Ramey, Drucilla Stender 1946- *WhoAmL 94*
Ramey, Felicenne H. *WhoBlA 94*
Ramey, Felicenne Houston *WhoWest 94*
Ramey, Harmon Hobson, Jr. 1930- *WhoScEn 94*
Ramey, Henry Jackson, Jr. 1925- *WhoAm 94, WhoScEn 94*
Ramey, James Melton 1928- *WhoScEn 94*
Ramey, John Mulvey 1952- *WhoFI 94*
Ramey, John Randall 1921- *WhoAmP 93*
Ramey, Joseph Frederick 1925- *WhoAm 94*
Ramey, Mary Price 1930- *WhoAmP 93*
Ramey, Melvin Richard 1938- *WhoAm 94*
Ramey, Robert Colin 1958- *WhoWest 94*
Ramey, Samuel (Edward) 1942- *NewGrDO*
Ramey, Samuel Edward 1942- *WhoAm 94*
Ramey, Steven A. 1952- *WhoAmP 93*
Ramezan, Massood 1956- *WhoScEn 94*
Ramfors, Bo C. E. 1936- *IntWW 93*
Ramharack, Roopram 1952- *WhoScEn 94*
Ramien, Th *GayLL*
Ramier, Douglas William 1958- *WhoWest 94*
Ramig, Alexander, Jr. 1941- *WhoAm 94*
Ramil, Mario R. 1946- *WhoAmL 94, WhoAsA 94*
Ramin, Kurt 1942- *WhoFI 94*
Ramin, Manfred, Mme. *Who 94*
Ramirez (Mercado), Sergio 1942- *ConWorW 93*
Ramirez, Alfred *WhoAmP 93, WhoHisp 94*
Ramirez, Alice *DrAPF 93*
Ramirez, Amelie G. 1951- *WhoHisp 94*
Ramirez, Anthony Benjamin 1937- *WhoHisp 94*
Ramirez, Antonio, Jr. 1955- *WhoHisp 94*
Ramirez, Arturo 1947- *WhoHisp 94*
Ramirez, Arturo J. 1960- *WhoHisp 94*
Ramirez, Baudelio 1941- *WhoHisp 94*
Ramirez, Berta C. 1942- *WhoHisp 94*
Ramírez, Blandina Cárdenas 1944- *WhoHisp 94*
Ramirez, Carlos d1986 *WhoHol 92*
Ramirez, Carlos 1957- *WhoHisp 94*
Ramírez, Carlos A. 1953- *WhoHisp 94*
Ramirez, Carlos D. 1946- *WhoHisp 94*
Ramirez, Carlos M. 1951- *WhoHisp 94*
Ramirez, Carmen Cecilia 1947- *WhoHisp 94*
Ramirez, Celso Lopez 1950- *WhoHisp 94*
Ramirez, Dan *WhoHisp 94*
Ramirez, David 1959- *WhoHisp 94*
Ramirez, David Eugene 1952- *WhoHisp 94*
Ramirez, David M. 1948- *WhoHisp 94*
Ramirez, David Michael 1950- *WhoAmL 94*
Ramirez, Domingo Victor 1932- *WhoAm 94, WhoHisp 94*
Ramirez, Donald E. 1943- *WhoHisp 94*
Ramirez, Enrique Rene 1930- *WhoHisp 94*
Ramirez, Ernest E. 1940- *WhoHisp 94*
Ramirez, Filomena R. 1944- *WhoHisp 94*
Ramirez, Gene Richard 1942- *WhoHisp 94*
Ramirez, Gilbert 1921- *WhoBlA 94, WhoHisp 94*
Ramirez, Gladys 1962- *WhoHisp 94*
Ramirez, Guillermo 1934- *WhoHisp 94*
Ramirez, Gus 1953- *WhoHisp 94*
Ramirez, Harold C. *WhoHisp 94*
Ramirez, Horacio S. *WhoHisp 94*
Ramírez, Hugo Alberto 1942- *WhoHisp 94*
Ramirez, Irene 1962- *WhoHisp 94*
Ramirez, J. Roberto 1941- *WhoHisp 94*
Ramirez, Jack 1939- *WhoAmP 93*
Ramirez, Joan 1961- *WhoHisp 94*
Ramirez, Joel Tito 1923- *WhoAmA 93, WhoHisp 94*
Ramirez, John 1943- *WhoHisp 94*
Ramirez, John Edward 1953- *WhoHisp 94*
Ramirez, Johnny 1957- *WhoHisp 94*
Ramirez, Jorge Hernan 1963- *WhoHisp 94*
Ramirez, Jose Lorenzo 1959- *WhoHisp 94, WhoMW 93*
Ramirez, Jose Luis 1936- *WhoHisp 94*
Ramirez, Jose Luis 1955- *WhoWest 94*
Ramirez, Jose M. 1955- *WhoHisp 94*
Ramirez, Jose S., Sr. 1919- *WhoHisp 94*
Ramirez, Joseph 1937- *WhoHisp 94*
Ramírez, Juan *WhoHisp 94*
Ramirez, Juan, Jr. 1945- *WhoHisp 94*
Ramirez, Juan A. 1961- *WhoHisp 94*
Ramírez, Julio Jesús 1955- *WhoHisp 94, WhoScEn 94*
Ramirez, Julio O. 1957- *WhoHisp 94*
Ramirez, Kevin Michael 1947- *WhoHisp 94*
Ramirez, Larry 1952- *WhoAmL 94*
Ramirez, Lewis 1942- *WhoHisp 94*
Ramirez, Linda Friedman 1952- *WhoAmL 94*
Ramírez, Luis Angel 1950- *WhoHisp 94*
Ramirez, Manuel A. *WhoHisp 94*
Ramirez, Maria Fiorini 1948- *WhoAm 94*
Ramírez, Mario E., Jr. 1950- *WhoHisp 94*
Ramirez, Mario Efrain 1926- *WhoAm 94, WhoHisp 94*
Ramirez, Mike 1954-1990 *WhoHisp 94N*
Ramirez, Olga 1936- *WhoHisp 94*
Ramírez, Oscar 1946- *WhoHisp 94*
Ramirez, Pedro Heberto 1943- *WhoHisp 94*
Ramirez, Pete Lopez 1949- *WhoHisp 94*
Ramírez, Rafael 1959- *WhoHisp 94*
Ramirez, Ralph Henry 1949- *WhoMW 93*
Ramirez, Ralph Roy 1937- *WhoHisp 94*
Ramirez, Raul 1953- *BuCMET*
Ramirez, Ràul Anthony 1944- *WhoAm 94, WhoAmL 94*
Ramirez, Ricardo 1936- *WhoAm 94, WhoHisp 94, WhoWest 94*
Ramirez, Richard 1954- *WhoHisp 94*
Ramirez, Richard G. 1952- *WhoHisp 94*
Ramirez, Richard Rogers 1952- *WhoHisp 94*
Ramirez, Robert T. 1948- *WhoHisp 94*
Ramirez, Roberto *WhoAmP 93, WhoHisp 94*
Ramirez, Rolando Ricardo 1958- *WhoHisp 94*
Ramirez, Roy Rene-Salvador 1959- *WhoHisp 94*
Ramirez, Ruben Ramirez 1953- *WhoHisp 94*
Ramirez, Samuel *WhoAmP 93, WhoHisp 94*
Ramirez, Saul, Jr. *WhoHisp 94*
Ramirez, Saul N., Jr. 1958- *WhoAmP 93*
Ramirez, Selma Angela 1955- *WhoHisp 94*
Ramirez, Stephen 1957- *WhoHisp 94*
Ramirez, Steven Adrian 1961- *WhoWest 94*
Ramirez, Susan E(lizabeth) 1946- *WrDr 94*
Ramirez, Susan Elizabeth 1946- *WhoHisp 94, WhoMW 93*
Ramirez, Tina *WhoHisp 94*
Ramirez, Victor E. *WhoHisp 94*
Ramírez-Arroyo, Manuel Fernando 1950- *WhoHisp 94*
Ramírez-Boulette, Teresa *WhoHisp 94*
Ramirez Cancel, Carlos Manuel 1944- *WhoScEn 94*
Ramirez-De-Arellano, Diana *DrAPF 93*
Ramirez de Arellano, Diana Teresa Clotilde 1919- *WhoHisp 94*
Ramirez de la Piscina, Julian 1956- *WhoFI 94*
Ramirez-Garcia, Eduardo Agustin 1950- *WhoScEn 94*
Ramirez-Garcia, Mari Carmen 1955- *WhoHisp 94*
Ramirez Mercado, Sergio 1942- *IntWW 93*
Ramirez Pantojas, Rosa M. *WhoHisp 94*
Ramirez-Rivera, Jose 1929- *WhoAm 94, WhoHisp 94*
Ramirez-Ronda, Carlos Hector 1943- *WhoHisp 94, WhoScEn 94*
Ramirez Vazquez, Pedro 1919- *IntWW 93*
Ramirez Vega, Adrian Nelson 1934- *WhoHisp 94*
Ramis, Guillermo J. 1945- *WhoHisp 94*
Ramis, Harold 1944- *IntMPA 94*
Ramis, Harold 1945- *WhoHol 92*
Ramis, Harold Allen 1944- *WhoAm 94*
Ramiscal, Elmer Febenito 1942- *WhoFI 94*
Ramjerdi, Jan Emily *DrAPF 93*
Ramjuttun, Dinesh 1946- *IntWW 93*
Ramke, Bin *DrAPF 93*
Ramler, Warren Joseph 1921- *WhoMW 93*
Ramm, (Norwyn) MacDonald 1924- *Who 94*
Ramm, Richard W. 1949- *WhoFI 94*
Rammelkamp, Julian Sturtevant 1917- *WhoMW 93*
Ramming, Michael Alexander 1940- *WhoMW 93*
Ramo, Roberta Cooper 1942- *WhoWest 94*
Ramo, Simon 1913- *IntWW 93, WhoAm 94, WhoFI 94, WhoScEn 94, WhoWest 94, WrDr 94*
Ramo, Virginia M. Smith *WhoAm 94, WhoWest 94*
Ramon, Angelo A. 1944- *WhoHisp 94*
Ramon, Haim 1950- *IntWW 93*
Ramón, Jaime *WhoHisp 94*
Ramón, José-María Crispin 1937- *WhoHisp 94*
Ramon, Leon *WhoHol 92*
Ramond, Charles Knight, II 1930- *WhoAm 94*
Ramondino, Fabrizia 1936- *BlmGWL*
Ramondon, Littleton 1684-1715? *NewGrDO*
Ramon y Cajal, Santiago 1852-1934 *WorScD*
Ramos, Abiud 1930- *WhoAm 94*
Ramos, Adam R. 1946- *WhoHisp 94*
Ramos, Albert A. 1927- *WhoWest 94*
Ramos, Angel L. Bulerin *WhoAmP 93*
Ramos, Angel Salvador *WhoScEn 94*
Ramos, Carlos d1969 *WhoHol 92*
Ramos, Charles Edward 1942- *WhoHisp 94*
Ramos, David J. *WhoHisp 94*
Ramos, Domingo 1958- *WhoHisp 94*
Ramos, Eva *WhoHisp 94*
Ramos, Fernando d1969 *WhoHol 92*
Ramos, Fidel 1928- *IntWW 93*
Ramos, Fred 1959- *WhoHisp 94*
Ramos, Fred M., Jr. 1949- *WhoHisp 94*
Ramos, George M. 1947- *WhoHisp 94*
Ramos, J. E., Jr. 1959- *WhoHisp 94*
Ramos, J. Mario 1956- *WhoAm 94, WhoWest 94*
Ramos, Jesus A. 1945- *WhoHisp 94*
Ramos, John Salias 1942- *WhoHisp 94*
Ramos, José S. 1950- *WhoHisp 94*
Ramos, Joseph Steven 1943- *WhoHisp 94*
Ramos, Juan Ignacio 1953- *WhoHisp 94*
Ramos, Julianne *WhoAmA 93*
Ramos, Kenneth S. 1956- *WhoHisp 94*
Ramos, Kimberley Ann 1966- *WhoMW 93*
Ramos, Linda Marie 1961- *WhoWest 94*
Ramos, Lolinda Daoang 1934- *WhoAmP 93*
Ramos, Lolita J. 1945- *WhoHisp 94*
Ramos, Luis Roberto 1964- *WhoWest 94*
Ramos, Lydia *WhoHisp 94*
Ramos, Manuel 1951- *WhoHisp 94*
Ramos, Mario Anthony 1953- *WhoHisp 94*
Ramos, Mary Angel 1959- *WhoHisp 94*
Ramos, Melvin John 1935- *WhoAm 94, WhoAmA 93*
Ramos, Nelson Herbert 1950- *WhoWest 94*
Ramos, Oreste, Jr. 1946- *WhoAmP 93*
Ramos, Philip M., Jr. *WhoHisp 94*
Ramos, Phillip V. 1949- *WhoHisp 94*
Ramos, Ramon Rolando 1946- *WhoHisp 94*
Ramos, Raúl 1946- *WhoHisp 94*
Ramos, Raul Antonio 1931- *WhoHisp 94*
Ramos, Richard *WhoHol 92*
Ramos, Robert Anthony *WhoHisp 94*
Ramos, Rosa Alicia 1953- *WhoHisp 94*
Ramos, Rudy 1950- *WhoHol 92*
Ramos, Tab 1967- *WhoHisp 94*
Ramos, Theodore 1928- *WhoAmA 93*
Ramos, Valeriano 1958- *WhoHisp 94*
Ramos, Vivian Eleanor 1946- *WhoMW 93*
Ramos, William *WhoHisp 94*
Ramos-Alamo, Sandra *WhoHisp 94*
Ramos Carrion, Miguel 1845-1915 *NewGrDO*
Ramos-Díaz, Oreste *WhoHisp 94*
Ramos-Escobar, Jose Luis 1950- *WhoHisp 94*
Ramos-Garcia, Luis A. 1945- *WhoHisp 94*
Ramos-Ledon, Leandro Juan 1924- *WhoScEn 94*
Ramos Martin, Jose 1892-1974 *NewGrDO*
Ramos Otero, Manuel 1948- *WhoHisp 94*
Ramos-Polanco, Bernardo 1946- *WhoHisp 94*
Ramp, Marjorie Jean Sumerwell 1924- *WhoMW 93*
Rampacek, Anne S. 1946- *WhoAmL 94*
Rampal, Jean-Pierre Louis 1922- *IntWW 93, Who 94, WhoAm 94*
Rampalli, Sitaram 1944- *WhoMW 93*
Rampersad, Arnold *WrDr 94*
Rampersad, Arnold 1941- *BlkWr 2, WhoBlA 94*
Rampersad, Peggy A. Snellings 1933- *WhoMW 93*
Ramphal, Shridath (Surendranath) 1928- *ConAu 141*
Ramphal, Shridath Surendranath 1928- *IntWW 93, Who 94*
Ramphele, Mamphela Aletta 1947- *IntWW 93*
Ramphul, Indurduth 1931- *IntWW 93, Who 94*
Rampil, Ira Jay 1953- *WhoWest 94*
Rampini, (Giovanni) Giacomo 1680-1760 *NewGrDO*
Rampino, Michael R. 1948- *WhoScEn 94*
Rampling, Anne *TwCYAW*
Rampling, Anne 1941- *WrDr 94*
Rampling, Charlotte 1946- *IntMPA 94, IntWW 93, WhoHol 92*
Ramponi, Virginia *NewGrDO*
Rampton, Calvin Lewellyn 1913- *WhoAmP 93*
Rampton, Jack (Leslie) 1920- *Who 94*
Ramqvist, Lars Henry 1938- *IntWW 93*
Rams, Armando Ignacio, Jr. 1962- *WhoHisp 94*
Ramsahoye, Lyttleton Estil 1930- *WhoScEn 94*
Ramsauer, Joseph Francis 1943- *WhoAmA 93*
Ramsauer, Kirk Lee 1947- *WhoFI 94*
Ramsaur, Allan Fields 1951- *WhoAmL 94*
Ramsay *Who 94*
Ramsay, Lord 1948- *Who 94*
Ramsay, Alexander William Burnett *Who 94*
Ramsay, Allan 1686-1758 *BlmGEL*
Ramsay, Allan (John Heppel Ramsay) 1937- *Who 94*
Ramsay, Charles Alexander 1936- *Who 94*
Ramsay, David 1749-1815 *AmRev, WhAmRev*
Ramsay, David Craig 1946- *WhoMW 93*
Ramsay, Donald Allan 1922- *IntWW 93, Who 94, WhoAm 94, WhoScEn 94*
Ramsay, Eric Guy 1927- *WhoWest 94*
Ramsay, Ernest Canaday 1939- *WhoAm 94*
Ramsay, Gustavus Remak 1937- *WhoAm 94*
Ramsay, Henry Thomas 1907- *Who 94*
Ramsay, J. Robert 1947- *WhoAmL 94*
Ramsay, Jack 1925- *BasBi*
Ramsay, Jay 1958- *WrDr 94*
Ramsay, John Barada 1929- *WhoWest 94*
Ramsay, John Graham 1931- *Who 94*
Ramsay, Louis Lafayette, Jr. 1918- *WhoAm 94, WhoAmL 94*
Ramsay, Margaret Ann 1935- *WhoAmP 93*
Ramsay, Marion Livingston 1897- *WhAm 10*
Ramsay, Martha Laurens 1759-1811 *BlmGWL*
Ramsay, Nathaniel 1741-1817 *AmRev, WhAmRev*
Ramsay, Norman James Gemmill 1916- *Who 94*
Ramsay, Patrick George Alexander 1926- *Who 94*
Ramsay, Remak 1937- *WhoHol 92*
Ramsay, Richard Alexander McGregor 1949- *Who 94*

Ramsay, Robert Henry 1925- *WhoFI 94, WhoWest 94*
Ramsay, Thomas (Meek) 1907- *Who 94*
Ramsay, Thomas Anderson 1920- *Who 94*
Ramsay, Tom 1939- *WhoAmP 93*
Ramsay, William 1852-1916 *WorScD*
Ramsay, William Charles 1930- *WhoAm 94*
Ramsay-Fairfax-Lucy, Edmund J.W.H.C. *Who 94*
Ramsay-Hill, C. S. d1967 *WhoHol 92*
Ramsay Rae, Ronald Arthur 1910- *Who 94*
Ramsbacher, Scott Blane 1960- *WhoScEn 94*
Ramsbotham *Who 94*
Ramsbotham, David (John) 1934- *Who 94*
Ramsbotham, Peter (Edward) 1919- *IntWW 93, Who 94*
Ramsbottom, John 1814-1897 *DcNaB MP*
Ramsbury, Area Bishop of 1930- *Who 94*
Ramsby, Mark Delivan 1947- *WhoWest 94*
Ramsdell, Richard Adoniram 1953- *WhoScEn 94*
Ramsdell, Vittz-James 1921- *WhoAm 94*
Ramsden, E. H. *WrDr 94*
Ramsden, Frances *WhoHol 92*
Ramsden, Herbert 1927- *Who 94, WrDr 94*
Ramsden, James Edward 1923- *Who 94*
Ramsden, John (Charles Josslyn) 1950- *Who 94*
Ramsden, John Andrew 1947- *WrDr 94*
Ramsden, Mary Catherine *WhoMW 93*
Ramsden, Michael *Who 94*
Ramsden, (John) Michael 1928- *Who 94*
Ramsden, Sally *Who 94*
Ramseier, Roger I. 1936- *WhoFI 94*
Ramsen, Al d1984 *WhoHol 92*
Ramses, II c. 1304BC-1213BC *HisWorL [port]*
Ramseur, Andre William 1949- *WhoBlA 94*
Ramseur, Donald E. 1919- *WhoBlA 94*
Ramseur, Isabelle R. 1906- *WhoBlA 94*
Ramseur, Walter Reid 1928- *WhoFI 94*
Ramsey, Alfred (Ernest) 1920- *Who 94*
Ramsey, Anne d1988 *WhoHol 92*
Ramsey, Anne Elizabeth *WhoHol 92*
Ramsey, Basil Albert Rowland 1929- *Who 94*
Ramsey, Bill 1931- *WhoAm 94*
Ramsey, Bonnie Jeanne 1952- *WhoScEn 94*
Ramsey, Bruce C. 1940- *WhoAmL 94*
Ramsey, Carl C. 1946- *WhoMW 93*
Ramsey, Charles Edward, Jr. 1956- *WhoBlA 94*
Ramsey, Charles Eugene 1923- *WhoAm 94*
Ramsey, Claude Swanson, Jr. 1925- *WhoAm 94*
Ramsey, David *WhoHol 92*
Ramsey, Donna Elaine 1941- *WhoBlA 94*
Ramsey, Dorothy J. 1935- *WhoAmA 93*
Ramsey, Doug(las A.) 1934- *WrDr 94*
Ramsey, Elizabeth M. d1993 *NewYTBS 93*
Ramsey, Forrest Gladstone, Jr. 1930- *WhoAm 94*
Ramsey, Frank 1931- *BasBi*
Ramsey, Frank Allen 1929- *WhoAm 94*
Ramsey, Frank Plumpton 1903-1930 *DcNaB MP*
Ramsey, Freeman, Jr. 1943- *WhoBlA 94*
Ramsey, Gael Kathleen 1942- *Who 94*
Ramsey, Glenn Eugene 1953- *WhoScEn 94*
Ramsey, Gordon d1993 *NewYTBS 93*
Ramsey, Gordon Clark 1941- *WrDr 94*
Ramsey, Henry, Jr. 1934- *WhoAm 94, WhoAmL 94, WhoBlA 94*
Ramsey, Ira Clayton 1931- *WhoAm 94*
Ramsey, J. W. 1934- *WhoAmP 93*
Ramsey, Jackson Eugene 1938- *WhoAmP 93*
Ramsey, James H. 1931- *WhoBlA 94*
Ramsey, James Rolla 1939- *WhoMW 93*
Ramsey, Jarold *DrAPF 93*
Ramsey, Jarold 1937- *WrDr 94*
Ramsey, Jarold William 1937- *WhoAm 94*
Ramsey, Jerome Capistrano 1953- *WhoBlA 94*
Ramsey, Jerry Virgil 1940- *WhoWest 94*
Ramsey, John Arthur 1942- *WhoAm 94, WhoAmL 94*
Ramsey, John Hansberry 1941- *WhoAm 94*
Ramsey, John Tyler 1946- *WhoMW 93*
Ramsey, Leland Jay 1956- *WhoScEn 94*
Ramsey, Leland Keith 1952- *WhoWest 94*
Ramsey, Liston Bryan 1919- *WhoAmP 93*
Ramsey, Lloyd Brinkley 1918- *WhoAm 94*
Ramsey, Logan 1921- *WhoHol 92*
Ramsey, Lucille Avra 1942- *WhoFI 94*
Ramsey, Marion *WhoHol 92*
Ramsey, Marjorie Elizabeth 1921- *WhoAm 94*
Ramsey, Martha *DrAPF 93*
Ramsey, Milton Worth 1848?-1906 *EncSF 93*
Ramsey, Nelda Jeanne 1937- *WhoFI 94*
Ramsey, Nelson d1929 *WhoHol 92*
Ramsey, Norman *WorInv*
Ramsey, Norman 1915- *WhoAm 94*
Ramsey, Norman F. 1915- *NobelP 91 [port], WhoScEn 94*
Ramsey, Norman F(oster) 1915- *WrDr 94*
Ramsey, Norman Foster 1915- *IntWW 93, Who 94*
Ramsey, Norman Park 1922- *WhoAm 94*
Ramsey, P. Virginia *WhoAmP 93*
Ramsey, Paul *DrAPF 93*
Ramsey, Paul 1924- *WrDr 94*
Ramsey, Paul Willard 1919- *WhoAm 94*
Ramsey, Peter Christie 1942- *WhoAm 94*
Ramsey, Richard David 1947- *WhoAmP 93*
Ramsey, Richard Ralph 1940- *WhoAmP 93*
Ramsey, Robert Lee 1929- *WhoAm 94*
Ramsey, Ronald L. 1955- *WhoAmP 93*
Ramsey, Ross LaMar 1937- *WhoWest 94*
Ramsey, Sally Ann Seitz 1931- *WhoFI 94*
Ramsey, Stephen Douglas 1947- *WhoAm 94, WhoAmL 94, WhoFI 94*
Ramsey, Thea d1987 *WhoHol 92*
Ramsey, Thomas R., III 1945- *WhoAmP 93*
Ramsey, Vivian Arthur 1950- *Who 94*
Ramsey, Waldo Emerson W. *Who 94*
Ramsey, Walter S. *WhoBlA 94*
Ramsey, William *WhoAm 94, WhoAmP 93*
Ramsey, William fl. 1323-1349 *DcNaB MP*
Ramsey, William Crites 1912- *WhoAmP 93*
Ramsey, William Dale, Jr. 1936- *WhoFI 94, WhoScEn 94*
Ramsey, William Edward 1931- *WhoAm 94*
Ramsey, William Ray 1926- *WhoAm 94*
Ramseyer, Paul Edwards 1927- *WhoAm 94*
Ramshaw, John David 1944- *WhoScEn 94*
Ramsland, Katherine 1953- *WrDr 94*
Ramstack, Tom Philip 1956- *WhoAmL 94*
Ramstad, Jim 1946- *CngDr 93, WhoAm 94, WhoAmL 94, WhoAmP 93, WhoMW 93*
Ramthun, Phillip Joseph 1953- *WhoAmL 94*
Ramudo, Olga *WhoHisp 94*
Ramunno, Charles A. 1940- *WhoAmL 94*
Ramunno, Thomas Paul 1952- *WhoMW 93*
Ramus, Nick *WhoHol 92*
Ramusack, Barbara Nell 1937- *WhoMW 93*
Ran, Chongwei 1956- *WhoScEn 94*
Ran, Josef 1947- *WhoScEn 94*
Ran, Shulamit 1949- *WhoAm 94, WhoMW 93*
Rana, Gurinder Mohan Singh 1946- *WhoAsA 94*
Rana, J. 1919- *WrDr 94*
Rana, Mohammed Waheed-uz-Zaman 1934- *WhoAsA 94*
Ranade, D. G. 1947- *WhoAsA 94*
Ranade, Madhukar G. 1953- *WhoAsA 94*
Ranahan-Zazueta, Fedro Sigmundo 1951- *WhoHisp 94*
Ranaldi, Frank d1933 *WhoHol 92*
Ranalli, Daniel 1946- *WhoAmA 93*
Ranalli, Daniel 1948- *WhoAm 94*
Ranalli, Michael Patrick 1933- *WhoAm 94, WhoFI 94*
Ranalow, Frederick d1953 *WhoHol 92*
Ranalow, Frederick (Baring) 1873-1953 *NewGrDO*
Ranard, Donald Louis 1917-1990 *WhAm 10*
Ranasinghe, (Kulatilaka Arthanayake) Parinda 1926- *Who 94*
Rance, Gerald Francis 1927- *Who 94*
Rance, Greig W. 1957- *WhoIns 94*
Rance, Joseph *ConAu 142*
Rance, Quentin E. 1935- *WhoWest 94*
Rance, Thomas P. 1961- *WhoWest 94*
Ranchhodlal, Chinubhai Madhowlal 1929- *Who 94*
Ranchod, Bhadra 1944- *IntWW 93*
Ranck, John Stevens 1945- *WhoFI 94, WhoWest 94*
Ranck, Sandra Ann 1962- *WhoMW 93*
Rancourt, James Daniel *WhoScEn 94*
Rancourt, John Herbert 1946- *WhoFI 94*
Ranczak, Hildegard 1895-1987 *NewGrDO*
Rand, A. Barry 1944- *ConBlB 6 [port]*
Rand, A. Barry 1945- *WhoBlA 94*
Rand, Anne M. *WhoAmP 93*
Rand, Anthony Eden 1939- *WhoAmP 93*
Rand, Archie 1949- *WhoAmA 93*
Rand, Ayn d1982 *WhoHol 92*
Rand, Ayn 1905-1982 *BlmGWL, ConLC 79 [port], EncSF 93, TwCYAW*
Rand, Calvin Gordon 1929- *WhoAm 94*
Rand, Carolyn 1938- *WhoFI 94*
Rand, Duncan D. 1940- *WhoAm 94*
Rand, Harold 1928- *IntMPA 94*
Rand, Harry 1947- *WhoAmA 93*
Rand, Harry Israel 1912- *WhoAm 94*
Rand, Harry Zvi 1947- *WhoAm 94*
Rand, J. H. 1944- *WrDr 94*
Rand, James Henry 1943- *WhoAm 94*
Rand, John d1940 *WhoHol 92*
Rand, John Fay 1932- *WhoAm 94*
Rand, Kathy Sue 1945- *WhoAm 94*
Rand, Kenneth Richard, Jr. 1937- *WhoFI 94*
Rand, Lawrence Anthony 1942- *WhoAm 94, WhoFI 94*
Rand, Leon 1930- *WhoAm 94, WhoMW 93*
Rand, Paul 1914- *WhoAm 94, WhoAmA 93*
Rand, Peter *DrAPF 93*
Rand, Phillip Gordon 1934- *WhoAm 94*
Rand, Richard M. 1955- *WhoAmL 94*
Rand, Rick W. 1957- *WhoAmP 93*
Rand, Robert Wheeler 1923- *WhoAm 94*
Rand, Sally d1979 *WhoHol 92*
Rand, Sidney Anders 1916- *WhoAm 94*
Rand, Silas Tertius 1810-1889 *EncNAR*
Rand, Stephen Colby 1949- *WhoScEn 94*
Rand, Steven Jay *WhoAmA 93*
Rand, Walter 1919- *WhoAmP 93*
Rand, William 1911- *WrDr 94*
Rand, William 1926- *WhoAm 94*
Randa, Rudolph Thomas 1940- *WhoAm 94, WhoAmL 94, WhoMW 93*
Randall, Addison d1945 *WhoHol 92*
Randall, Alan John 1944- *WhoFI 94*
Randall, Ann Knight *WhoBlA 94*
Randall, Ann Knight 1942- *WhoAm 94*
Randall, Anne *WhoHol 92*
Randall, Arthur Raymond 1927- *WhoFI 94*
Randall, Barbara Ann 1958- *WhoScEn 94*
Randall, Belle *DrAPF 93*
Randall, Bernard d1954 *WhoHol 92*
Randall, Bill 1932- *WhoAmP 93*
Randall, Bob 1937- *WhoAm 94*
Randall, Brett d1963 *WhoHol 92*
Randall, Charles H(enry) 1920- *WrDr 94*
Randall, Charles Richard 1920- *Who 94*
Randall, Claire 1919- *WhoAm 94, WhoBlA 94*
Randall, Clarence Belden 1891-1967 *EncABHB 9 [port]*
Randall, Clifford Wendell 1936- *WhoAm 94*
Randall, Craig 1957- *WhoFI 94*
Randall, Dale B(ertrand) J(onas) 1929- *WrDr 94*
Randall, David Anton 1905-1975 *DcLB 140 [port]*
Randall, David John 1938- *WhoAm 94, WhoScEn 94*
Randall, Dean Bowman 1920- *WhoAm 94*
Randall, Deborah 1957- *WrDr 94*
Randall, Donald Millard 1926- *WhoAmP 93*
Randall, Dudley *DrAPF 93*
Randall, Dudley 1914- *AfrAmAl 6, WrDr 94*
Randall, Dudley Felker 1914- *WhoBlA 94*
Randall, Edmund Laurence 1920- *Who 94*
Randall, Edwin Clarence 1949- *WhoAmP 93*
Randall, Elizabeth 1953- *WhoAmP 93*
Randall, Elizabeth Ellen 1915- *WhoMW 93*
Randall, Florence Engel 1917- *WrDr 94*
Randall, Francis Ballard 1931- *WhoAm 94, WrDr 94*
Randall, Fred d1933 *WhoHol 92*
Randall, Gary Lee 1943- *WhoAmP 93*
Randall, Gaye Powers 1946- *WhoMW 93*
Randall, Gerald J. 1931- *WhoAm 94, WhoFI 94*
Randall, Harry d1932 *WhoHol 92*
Randall, Henry Thomas 1914- *WhoAm 94*
Randall, James Grafton 1951- *WhoAmL 94*
Randall, James R. 1924- *WhoAm 94, WhoFI 94*
Randall, Janet 1919- *WrDr 94*
Randall, Janet Ann 1943- *WhoScEn 94, WhoWest 94*
Randall, Jeff William 1954- *Who 94*
Randall, Jerry *WhoHol 92*
Randall, Jim Allen 1950- *WhoAmP 93*
Randall, John Ernest 1924- *WhoWest 94*
Randall, John L(eslie) 1933- *WrDr 94*
Randall, Joshua 1951- *WrDr 94*
Randall, Julia *DrAPF 93*
Randall, Julia 1923- *WrDr 94*
Randall, Kenneth Allan 1932- *WhoAmP 93*
Randall, Leslie 1924- *WhoHol 92*
Randall, Lilian M. C. 1931- *WhoAmA 93*
Randall, Malcom 1916- *WhoAm 94*
Randall, Margaret *DrAPF 93*
Randall, Margaret 1936- *WrDr 94*
Randall, Marta 1948- *EncSF 93, WrDr 94*
Randall, Michael Bennett 1919- *IntWW 93*
Randall, Neil *EncSF 93*
Randall, Pat *WhoHol 92*
Randall, Patricia Mary 1948- *WhoFI 94*
Randall, (Lillian) Paula 1895-1985 *WhoAmA 93N*
Randall, Priscilla Richmond 1926- *WhoFI 94*
Randall, Queen F. 1935- *WhoBlA 94*
Randall, Rae d1934 *WhoHol 92*
Randall, Richard Harding, Jr. 1926- *WhoAm 94, WhoAmA 93*
Randall, Richard Rainier 1925- *WhoAm 94*
Randall, Robert *EncSF 93*
Randall, Robert 1927- *WrDr 94*
Randall, Robert Gordon 1966- *WhoWest 94*
Randall, Robert Lee 1936- *WhoAm 94, WhoFI 94, WhoScEn 94*
Randall, Roger Paul 1946- *WhoWest 94*
Randall, Rona *WrDr 94*
Randall, Ronald Fisher 1934- *WhoMW 93*
Randall, Sherri Lee 1959- *WhoFI 94*
Randall, Stephen F. *IntMPA 94*
Randall, Stuart *WhoHol 92*
Randall, Stuart 1938- *Who 94*
Randall, Sue d1984 *WhoHol 92*
Randall, Tony 1920- *IntMPA 94, WhoAm 94, WhoCom, WhoHol 92*
Randall, Willard Sterne 1942- *WrDr 94*
Randall, William B. 1921- *WhoAm 94, WhoFI 94, WhoWest 94*
Randall, William Clarence 1943- *WhoAmP 93*
Randall, William Edward 1920- *Who 94*
Randall, William Lovis 1930- *WhoMW 93*
Randall, William Seymour 1933- *WhoAm 94*
Randall, William Theodore 1931- *WhoAm 94, WhoWest 94*
Randax, Georges d1979 *WhoHol 92*
Randazzo, Samuel C. 1949- *WhoAmL 94*
Randazzo, Teddy *WhoHol 92*
Randegger, Alberto 1832-1911 *NewGrDO*
Randel, Ronald Dean 1938- *WhoAm 94*
Randell, Beverley 1931- *WrDr 94*
Randell, Linda L. 1950- *WhoAmL 94*
Randell, Peter Neil 1933- *Who 94*
Randell, Robert 1935- *WrDr 94*
Randell, Ron 1920- *WhoHol 92*
Randhawa, Bikkar Singh 1933- *WhoAm 94, WhoWest 94*
Randhawa, Ravinder 1953- *BlmGWL*
Randi, Ermanno d1951 *WhoHol 92*
Randi, James 1928- *WhoAm 94, WrDr 94*
Randinelli, Tracey Anne 1963- *WhoAm 94*
Randinitis, Edward John 1940- *WhoMW 93*
Randish, Joan Marie 1954- *WhoScEn 94*
Randisi, Elaine Marie 1926- *WhoWest 94*
Randisi, Robert J(oseph) 1951- *WrDr 94*
Randle, Berdine Caronell 1929- *WhoBlA 94*
Randle, Carver A. 1942- *WhoBlA 94*
Randle, Ellen Eugenia Foster 1948- *WhoWest 94*
Randle, Frank d1957 *WhoHol 92*
Randle, Kevin D. 1949- *EncSF 93*
Randle, Lucious A. 1927- *WhoBlA 94*
Randle, Michael Charles 1952- *WhoWest 94*
Randle, Philip (John) 1926- *Who 94*
Randle, Philip John 1926- *IntWW 93*
Randle, Rodger A. 1943- *WhoAmP 93*
Randle, Ronald Eugene 1946- *WhoScEn 94*
Randle, Thomas 1958- *NewGrDO*
Randle, William Crawford 1952- *WhoWest 94*
Randle, Wilma Jean-Elizabeth 1955- *WhoBlA 94*
Randles, Guy A. 1952- *WhoAmL 94*
Randles, Jennifer Christine 1951- *ConAu 142*
Randles, Jenny *ConAu 142*
Randlett, James Raymond 1942- *WhoAmP 93*
Randlett, Mary Willis 1924- *WhoAm 94, WhoAmA 93*
Randlev, Karen *DrAPF 93*
Randman, Barry I. 1958- *WhoFI 94*
Randol, George Cedric 1930- *WhoWest 94*
Randolf, Alma Louise 1957- *WhoBlA 94*
Randolf, Anders d1930 *WhoHol 92*
Randolph, A(sa) Philip 1889-1979 *BlkWr 2*
Randolph, A. Raymond 1943- *CngDr 93, WhoAmP 93*

Rao, Marepalli Bhaskara 1943- WhoMW 93
Rao, Mentreddi Anandha 1937- WhoAsA 94
Rao, Ming 1954- WhoScEn 94, WhoWest 94
Rao, Nagaraja R. 1942- WhoAsA 94
Rao, Nannapaneni Narayana WhoAm 94
Rao, P. V. Narasimha 1921- Who 94
Rao, Papineni S. 1937- WhoAsA 94
Rao, Potarazu Krishna 1930- WhoAsA 94
Rao, Raghav H. 1958- WhoAsA 94
Rao, Raja 1908- RfGShF
Rao, Raja 1909- IntWW 93
Rao, Ramachandra Adiseshappa 1939- WhoMW 93
Rao, Ramachandra Miryala 1953- WhoWest 94
Rao, Ramesh K. S. 1952- WhoAsA 94
Rao, Ramgopal P. 1942- WhoAsA 94
Rao, Sadasiva Madiraju 1953- WhoAsA 94
Rao, Singiresu Sambasiva 1944- WhoAsA 94
Rao, Spuma M. 1947- WhoAsA 94
Rao, Srikumar S. 1951- WhoAsA 94
Rao, T. K. Sreepada 1944- WhoAsA 94
Rao, Tanveer Hameed 1958- WhoMW 93
Rao, Taramanohar B. 1933- WhoAsA 94
Rao, Tejaswini 1949- WhoAsA 94
Rao, Vaman WhoAsA 94
Rao, Vaman 1933- WhoFI 94, WhoScEn 94
Rao, Venigalla Basaveswara 1954- WhoAsA 94, WhoScEn 94
Rao, Vincent P. d1993 NewYTBS 93
Rao, Vittal Srirangam 1944- WhoAm 94, WhoScEn 94
Rao, Yalamanchili Krishna 1941- WhoAsA 94
Rao-Arelli, A. P. 1948- WhoMW 93
Rao Qinzhi WhoPRCh 91
Raos, Predrag EncSF 93
Rao Shoukun 1915- WhoPRCh 91 [port]
Raoul, Alfred 1930- IntWW 93
Rao Xingli 1925- IntWW 93
Rao Yongyu WhoPRCh 91
Rapaccioli, Michel Antoine 1934- WhoAm 94, WhoFI 94
Rapanos, Judith Ann 1939- WhoAmP 93
Rapant, Larry DrAPF 93
Rapaport, David Alan 1942- WhoAm 94
Rapaport, Felix Theodosius 1929- WhoAm 94
Rapaport, Mark Samuel 1947- WhoAm 94, WhoAmL 94
Rapaport, Martin Baruch 1963- WhoScEn 94
Rapaport, Robert M. 1931- WhoAm 94
Rapaport, Ross Jay 1950- WhoMW 93
Rapaport, Walter 1895- WhAm 10
Rapeanu, Valeriu 1931- IntWW 93
Raper, Charles Albert 1926- WhoAm 94
Raper, (Alfred) Graham 1932- Who 94
Raper, Kenneth Bryan 1908- IntWW 93
Raper, William Burkette 1927- WhoAm 94
Raper, William Cranford 1946- WhoAm 94, WhoAmL 94
Raphael 1972- IntWW 93
Raphael, Adam Eliot Geoffrey 1938- Who 94
Raphael, Albert Ash, Jr. 1925- WhoAm 94
Raphael, Bernard Joseph 1935- WhoBlA 94
Raphael, Chaim 1908- Who 94, WrDr 94
Raphael, Coleman 1925- WhoAm 94
Raphael, Dan DrAPF 93
Raphael, David Daiches 1916- Who 94, WrDr 94
Raphael, Farid 1933- IntWW 93
Raphael, Frederic 1931- IntDcF 2-4, IntMPA 94
Raphael, Frederic (Michael) 1931- WrDr 94
Raphael, Frederic Michael DrAPF 93
Raphael, Frederic Michael 1931- IntWW 93, Who 94, WhoAm 94
Raphael, George Farid 1962- WhoFI 94, WhoScEn 94
Raphael, John Patrick 1955- WhoAmP 93
Raphael, Lennox DrAPF 93
Raphael, Lev 1954- GayLL, WrDr 94
Raphael, Martin George 1946- WhoWest 94
Raphael, Phyllis DrAPF 93
Raphael, Ralph Alexander 1921- Who 94
Raphael, Rick 1919- EncSF 93, WrDr 94
Raphael, Sally Jessy WhoAm 94
Raphael, Sally Jessy 1943- ConTFT 11
Raphael, Stuart A. 1964- WhoAmL 94
Raphael, Stuart I. 1938- WhoIns 94
Raphael, Timothy John 1929- Who 94
Raphaelson, Joel 1928- WhoAm 94
Raphaelson, Samson 1896-1983 IntDcF 2-4
Raphael the Painter BlmGEL
Raphan, Benjamin 1937- WhoAmL 94
Raphel, David 1925- IntMPA 94
Raphel, Jerome WhoHol 92
Raphoe, Bishop of 1940- Who 94
Rapidis, Alexander Demetrius 1948- WhoScEn 94
Rapidis, Petros A. 1951- WhoScEn 94
Rapien, Gerald J. 1943- WhoAmL 94
Rapier, Kenny 1936- WhoAmP 93
Rapier, Pascal Moran 1914- WhoScEn 94, WhoWest 94
Rapilly, Yves Georges 1931- IntWW 93
Rapin, Charles Rene Jules 1935- WhoScEn 94
Rapin, Isabelle 1927- WhoAm 94
Rapin, Lynn Suzanne 1946- WhoMW 93
Rapisarda, Joseph Paul, Jr. 1950- WhoAmL 94
Rapke, Jack WhoAm 94
Rapkin, Jerome 1929- WhoScEn 94
Rapoport, Alan M. 1942- WrDr 94
Rapoport, Anatol 1911- WhoAm 94
Rapoport, Bernard 1917- WhoAm 94, WhoFI 94, WhoIns 94
Rapoport, Bernard Robert 1919- WhoAm 94
Rapoport, David E. 1956- WhoAmL 94
Rapoport, Frank M. 1950- WhoAmL 94
Rapoport, Judith 1933- WhoScEn 94
Rapoport, Louis (Harvey) 1942- WrDr 94
Rapoport, Miles S. 1949- WhoAmP 93
Rapoport, Natalie 1927- WhoAmP 93
Rapoport, Robert Norman 1924- WrDr 94
Rapoport, Roger (Dale) 1946- WrDr 94
Rapoport, Ronald Jon 1940- WhoAm 94
Rapoport, Sonya WhoAm 94, WhoAmA 93
Raposo, Mario 1929- IntWW 93
Rapoza, Norbert Pacheco 1929- WhoScEn 94
Rapp, Anthony 1972- WhoHol 92
Rapp, Christian Ferree 1933- WhoFI 94
Rapp, Danny d1983 WhoHol 92
Rapp, Doris Jean 1940- WhoMW 93
Rapp, Fred 1929- WhoAm 94, WhoScEn 94
Rapp, Gene Edward 1930- WhoWest 94
Rapp, George 1757-1847 DcAmReB 2
Rapp, George (Robert), Jr. 1930- WrDr 94
Rapp, George Robert, Jr. 1930- WhoAm 94
Rapp, Gerald Duane 1933- WhoAm 94, WhoAmL 94, WhoFI 94, WhoMW 93
Rapp, James Allen 1946- WhoFI 94
Rapp, John Buswell 1936- WhoAm 94
Rapp, Larry WhoHol 92
Rapp, Larry P. 1948- WhoFI 94, WhoMW 93
Rapp, Lawrence Keith 1947- WhoWest 94
Rapp, Lea Bayers 1946- WhoFI 94
Rapp, Lois WhoAmA 93
Rapp, Richard Tilden 1944- WhoAm 94, WhoFI 94
Rapp, Robert Anthony 1934- WhoAm 94, WhoScEn 94
Rapp, Robert David 1950- WhoAmL 94
Rapp, Robert Neil 1947- WhoAm 94, WhoAmL 94
Rapp, Stephen John 1949- WhoAmP 93
Rapp, Wolfgang 1944- WhoFI 94
Rappa, Julianne Marie 1959- WhoFI 94
Rappaport, Allan H. 1946- WhoFI 94
Rappaport, Anna Maria 1940- WhoIns 94
Rappaport, Charles Owen 1950- WhoAm 94, WhoAmL 94
Rappaport, David d1990 WhoHol 92
Rappaport, Gary Burton 1937- WhoAm 94
Rappaport, James WhoAmP 93
Rappaport, Lawrence 1928- WhoAm 94, WhoScEn 94
Rappaport, Martin Paul 1935- WhoAm 94, WhoScEn 94
Rappaport, Paul Marc 1947- WhoFI 94
Rappaport, Richard J. 1943- WhoAmL 94
Rappaport, Richard Warren 1948- WhoAmL 94
Rappaport, Samuel 1932- WhoAmP 93
Rappaport, Stephen S. WhoAm 94
Rappaport, Steve 1948- WrDr 94
Rappaport, Stuart R. 1935- WhoAmL 94
Rappaport, Theodore Scott 1960- WhoScEn 94
Rappe, Virginia d1921 WhoHol 92
Rappeneau, Jean-Paul 1932- IntDcF 2-4 [port], IntWW 93
Rappeport, Ira J. 1954- WhoAm 94
Rapper, Irving 1904- IntMPA 94
Rappleye, Richard Kent 1940- WhoAm 94
Rappleyea, Clarence D. 1933- WhoAmP 93
Rappold, Charles Edward, II 1952- WhoAmL 94
Rappold, Marie 1873-1957 NewGrDO
Rappoport, David Steven 1957- WrDr 94
Rappoport, Gerald J. 1925- IntMPA 94
Rappoport, Ken 1935- ConAu 42NR
Rapport, Fred d1973 WhoHol 92
Rapport, Greg 1954- WhoFI 94
Rapport, Helena d1954 WhoHol 92
Rapport, Jack Michael 1952- WhoFI 94
Rapp-Svrcek, Paul S. 1955- WhoAmP 93
Rapson, Ralph 1914- IntWW 93
Rapson, Richard L. 1937- WhoAm 94, WhoWest 94, WrDr 94
Rapson, William Howard 1912- WhoAm 94
Raptakis, Leonidas Peter 1959- WhoAmP 93
Rapuano, Mary Anne 1934- WhoWest 94
Raquello, Edward d1976 WhoHol 92
Rarick, John Richard 1924- WhoAmP 93
Rarick, Joseph Francis, Sr. 1921-1989 WhAm 10
Raridon, Richard Jay 1931- WhoAm 94
Rarig, Frederick John 1915- WhAm 10
Ras, Eva WhoHol 92
Rasa, Lina Bruna 1907-1984 NewGrDO
Rasanen, Eric K. 1946- WhoIns 94
Rasband, Ronald A. 1951- WhoWest 94
Rasberry, Robert Eugene WhoBlA 94
Rascarini, Francesco Maria d1706 NewGrDO
Rascel, Renato d1991 WhoHol 92
Rasch, Albertina d1967 WhoHol 92
Rasch, Janet Smith 1962- WhoAmL 94
Rasch, Richard Guy Carne 1918- Who 94
Rasch, Stephen Christopher 1962- WhoAmL 94
Rasche, David 1944- WhoHol 92
Rasche, Frank 1946- WhoAmP 93
Rasche, J. David 1929- WhoMW 93
Rasche, Robert Harold 1941- WhoAm 94, WhoFI 94
Raschke, Carl Allan 1944- WhoWest 94
Raschko, Bettyann Bernadette 1925- WhoWest 94
Rasco, Albert 1925- WhoAmP 93
Rasco, Carol NewYTBS 93 [port]
Rasco, Carol Hampton 1948- WhoAm 94
Rasco, Kay Frances 1925- WhoMW 93
Rascoe, Stephanie WhoHol 92
Rascoe, Stephen Thomas 1924- WhoAmA 93
Rascon, Armando 1956- WhoAmA 93
Rasero, Lawrence Joseph, Jr. 1938- WhoAmP 93
Rasey, Jean WhoHol 92
Rash, Nancy 1940- WhoAmA 93
Rashad, Ahmad 1949- WhoAm 94, WhoBlA 94
Rashad, Johari M(ahasin) 1951- BlkWr 2
Rashad, Phylicia 1948- AfrAmAl 6, IntMPA 94, WhoBlA 94, WhoHol 92
Rashedi, Saeed WhoWest 94
Rasheed, Hassan (Ahmed) 1896-1969 NewGrDO
Rasheed, Howard S. 1953- WhoBlA 94
Rasheed, Suraiya 1936- WhoAsA 94
Rasher, George Joseph 1956- WhoWest 94
Rashford, David R. 1947- WhoScEn 94
Rashford, John Harvey 1947- WhoBlA 94
Rashid, Carl, Jr. 1948- WhoAm 94, WhoAmL 94
Rashid, Harun Ur 1954- WhoMW 93
Rashid, Kamal A. 1944- WhoScEn 94
Rashid, Saleha Abdul BlmGWL
Rashid, Zafar 1950- WhoIns 94
Rashid Bin Said Al-Maktum IntWW 93
Rashid Bin Said Al-Maktum, Sheikh WhAm 10
Rashish, Myer 1924- WhoAmP 93
Rashkovetsky, Leonid 1953- WhoScEn 94
Rashkow, Ronald 1940- WhoAm 94
Rashleigh, Richard (Harry) 1958- Who 94
Rashleigh Belcher, John Who 94
Rasi, Francesco 1574-1621 NewGrDO
Rasi, Humberto Mario 1935- WhoAm 94
Rasic, Janko 1938- WhoFI 94
Rasines, Isidoro 1927- WhoScEn 94
Rask, Michael Raymond 1930- WhoAm 94, WhoFI 94, WhoScEn 94, WhoWest 94
Raskin, A. H. 1911-1993 NewYTBS 93 [port]
Raskin, Ellen 1928-1984 TwCYAW
Raskin, Fred Charles 1948- WhoAm 94, WhoFI 94
Raskin, Jef 1943- WhoWest 94
Raskin, Judith 1928-1984 NewGrDO
Raskin, Marcus Goodman 1934- WhoAm 94
Raskin, Michael A. 1925- WhoAm 94
Raskin, Michael Mester 1942- WhoAmL 94
Raskin, Sarah Anne 1962- WhoWest 94
Raskin, Steven Allen 1953- WhoScEn 94
Raskind, Leo Joseph 1919- WhoAm 94
Raskind, Philis WhoAmA 93
Rasko, Maximilian A. 1884-1961 WhoAmA 93N
Rasky, Harry 1928- WhoAm 94
Rasley, Jeffrey Scott 1953- WhoAmL 94
Rasminsky, Louis 1908- Who 94
Rasmus, Daniel Wayne 1961- WhoWest 94
Rasmus, Henry Irving, Jr. 1894- WhAm 10
Rasmus, John A. 1954- WhoAm 94
Rasmus, John Charles 1941- WhoAmL 94
Rasmuson, Brent Jacobsen 1950- WhoWest 94
Rasmuson, Elmer Edwin 1909- WhoAm 94, WhoFI 94, WhoWest 94
Rasmuson, Judith Ellen 1948- WhoMW 93
Rasmussen, Alis A. 1958- EncSF 93
Rasmussen, Anders Fogh 1953- IntWW 93
Rasmussen, Anton Jesse 1942- WhoAmA 93
Rasmussen, Bruce David 1946- WhoAmP 93
Rasmussen, David George 1943- WhoAmL 94
Rasmussen, Dennis Loy 1940- WhoFI 94
Rasmussen, Dennis Robert 1949- WhoScEn 94
Rasmussen, Douglas John 1941- WhoAmL 94
Rasmussen, Eric Ashby 1956- WhoWest 94
Rasmussen, Frank Morris 1934- WhoAm 94
Rasmussen, Frederick Tatum 1943- WhoAmL 94
Rasmussen, Gail Maureen 1941- WhoWest 94
Rasmussen, Garret Garretson 1949- WhoAm 94
Rasmussen, Gerald Elmer 1935- WhoAm 94
Rasmussen, Gunnar 1925- WhoScEn 94
Rasmussen, Harry Paul 1939- WhoAm 94
Rasmussen, James Michael 1959- WhoScEn 94
Rasmussen, Janet Elaine 1949- WhoMW 93
Rasmussen, Jeffrey Gene 1960- WhoFI 94
Rasmussen, Jeri Wharton 1934- WhoAmP 93
Rasmussen, Jessie K. 1945- WhoAmP 93, WhoMW 93
Rasmussen, John Atwell 1946- WhoAm 94
Rasmussen, John Curtis, Jr. 1943- WhoAmP 93
Rasmussen, John Oscar 1926- WhoAm 94
Rasmussen, Karsten WhoAmP 93
Rasmussen, Knud Johan Victor 1879-1933 WhWE
Rasmussen, Leo Brown 1941- WhoAmP 93
Rasmussen, Marilyn WhoAmP 93
Rasmussen, Maud Truby Christian WhoAmP 93
Rasmussen, Michele Vincent 1963- WhoWest 94
Rasmussen, Mike Joseph 1947- WhoWest 94
Rasmussen, Neil Woodland 1926- WhoWest 94
Rasmussen, Niels Lee 1956- WhoScEn 94
Rasmussen, Norman Carl 1927- IntWW 93, WhoAm 94, WhoScEn 94
Rasmussen, Poul Norregaard 1922- IntWW 93
Rasmussen, Poul Nyrup 1943- IntWW 93
Rasmussen, Raun Jay 1928- WhoFI 94
Rasmussen, Richard Alan 1950- WhoIns 94
Rasmussen, Richard Robert 1946- WhoAmL 94
Rasmussen, Robert Adrian 1962- WhoFI 94
Rasmussen, Robert Dee 1936- WhoFI 94
Rasmussen, Robert Norman WhoAmA 93
Rasmussen, Roberta A. WhoAmP 93, WhoMW 93
Rasmussen, Ronald Dean 1930- WhoAmP 93
Rasmussen, Thomas Val, Jr. 1954- WhoWest 94
Rasmussen, Tom 1940- WhoAmP 93
Rasmusson, Donald C. WhoScEn 94
Rasmusson, Eric Dana 1961- WhoWest 94
Rasmusson, Eugene Martin 1929- WhoScEn 94
Rasnake, James Hamilton, Jr. 1935- WhoFI 94
Rasnake, Marshall Everett 1924- WhoAmP 93
Rasof, Henry Leplin 1946- WhoWest 94
Rasor, Dina Lynn 1956- WhoAm 94
Rasor, Elizabeth Ann 1962- WhoScEn 94
Rasor, Garry Girard 1943- WhoAm 94
Rasor, Robert D. 1948- WhoAm 94, WhoAmL 94
Rasouli, Firooz 1948- WhoScEn 94
Rasp, Fritz d1976 WhoHol 92
Rasp, John Cletus 1942- WhoAmL 94
Rasp, Renate 1935- BlmGWL
Raspail, Jean 1925- EncSF 93
Raspberry, William J. 1935- AfrAmAl 6 [port], WhoBlA 94

Rauschenbach, Henri S. *WhoAmP 93*
Rauschenberg, Robert 1925- *AmCulL [port], IntWW 93, WhoAm 94, WhoAmA 93*
Rauschenberger, Floyd Arthur, III 1954- *WhoAmP 93*
Rauschenberger, Steven J. *WhoAmP 93*
Rauschenbusch, Walter 1861-1918 *AmSocL, DcAmReB 2*
Rauscher, Frances Helen 1957- *WhoScEn 94*
Rauscher, Frank J., Jr. d1992 *NewYTBS 93 [port]*
Rauscher, Hannah Sarah 1925- *WhoAmP 93*
Rauscher, Tomlinson Gene 1946- *WhoAm 94*
Rauscher, William d196-? *WhoHol 92*
Rauschkolb, Roy Simpson 1933- *WhoWest 94*
Rauser, Vickie Sue 1959- *WhoWest 94*
Raushenbush, Stephen 1896-1991 *WhAm 10*
Raushenbush, Walter Brandeis 1928- *WhoAm 94*
Rausser, Gordon Clyde 1943- *WhoAm 94*
Raut, Kamalakar Balkrishna 1920- *WhoAsA 94*
Rautavaara, Einojuhani 1938- *NewGrDO*
Rautawaara, Aulikki 1906-1990 *NewGrDO*
Rautbord, Dorothy H. 1906- *WhoAmA 93*
Rautenberg, Robert Frank 1943- *WhoAm 94, WhoFI 94, WhoWest 94*
Rauth, William R., III 1944- *WhoAmL 94*
Rautio, James Clinton 1954- *WhoFI 94*
Rauzzini, Matteo 1754-1791 *NewGrDO*
Rauzzini, Venanzio 1746-1810 *NewGrDO*
Rava, Susan Roudebush 1939- *WhoMW 93*
Ravage, John William 1937- *WhoWest 94*
Raval, Dilip N. 1933- *WhoScEn 94*
Ravanel, Jean 1920- *IntWW 93*
Ravani, Kirit T. 1945- *WhoMW 93*
Ravarra, Patricia 1947- *WhoAmA 93*
Rave, John c. 1855-1917 *EncNAR*
Raveau, Alice 1884-1951 *NewGrDO*
Raveche, Harold Joseph 1943- *WhoAm 94, WhoScEn 94*
Ravel, Joanne Macow 1924- *WhoAm 94*
Ravel, Maurice 1875-1937 *IntDcB [port]*
Ravel, (Joseph) Maurice 1875-1937 *NewGrDO*
Ravel, Sandra d1954 *WhoHol 92*
Raveling, George *WhoAm 94, WhoWest 94*
Raveling, George Henry 1937- *WhoBlA 94*
Ravelle, Ray d1969 *WhoHol 92*
Ravelo, Daniel F. 1939- *WhoHisp 94*
Ravely, Victoria Alline 1946- *WhoWest 94*
Raven, Arlene 1944- *WhoAmA 93*
Raven, Bertram Herbert 1926- *WhoAm 94, WhoScEn 94, WhoWest 94*
Raven, Elsa *WhoHol 92*
Raven, Francis Harvey 1928- *WhoMW 93*
Raven, Gregory Kurt 1949- *WhoFI 94*
Raven, Jacques Robert 1933- *WhoAm 94, WhoFI 94*
Raven, John Albert 1941- *Who 94*
Raven, John Armstrong 1920- *Who 94*
Raven, Jonathan Ezra 1951- *WhoFI 94*
Raven, Kathleen 1910- *Who 94*
Raven, Larry Joseph 1939- *WhoAmP 93*
Raven, Mike *WhoHol 92*
Raven, Patricia Elaine 1943- *WhoAmP 93*
Raven, Peter Hamilton 1936- *IntWW 93, WhoAm 94, WhoMW 93*
Raven, Robert Dunbar 1923- *WhoAm 94, WhoAmL 94*
Raven, Ronald William 1904- *WrDr 94*
Raven, Simon (Arthur Noel) 1927- *Who 94, WrDr 94*
Raven, Simon Arthur Noel 1927- *IntWW 93*
Ravenal, Earl Cedric 1931- *WhoAm 94*
Ravenel, Arthur, Jr. 1927- *CngDr 93, WhoAm 94, WhoAmP 93*
Ravenel, Charles Dufort 1938- *WhoAmP 93*
Ravenel, Florence d1975 *WhoHol 92*
Ravenell, Joseph Phillip 1940- *WhoBlA 94*
Ravenell, Mildred 1944- *WhoBlA 94*
Ravenell, William Hudson 1942- *WhoBlA 94*
Ravenholt, Reimert Thorolf 1925- *WhoAm 94*
Ravens, Karl Friedrich 1927- *IntWW 93*
Ravenscroft, Bryan Dale 1951- *WhoScEn 94*
Ravenscroft, Edward c. 1643- *IntDcT 2*
Ravenscroft, Edward 1650?-1697 *BlmGEL*
Ravenscroft, Ellen 1876-1949 *WhoAmA 93N*
Ravenscroft, John Robert Parker 1939- *Who 94*
Ravenscroft, Ralph d1934 *WhoHol 92*
Ravenscroft, Raymond Lockwood 1931- *Who 94*
Ravenscroft, Vernon Frank 1920- *WhoWest 94*
Ravensdale, Baron 1923- *Who 94*
Ravensdale, Baron 1923- *IntWW 93*
Ravensworth, Baron 1924- *Who 94*
Raven-Symone 1985- *WhoBlA 94*
Raventos, Antolin 1925- *WhoAm 94*
Raventos, George 1939- *WhoHisp 94*
Raver, Leonard 1927-1992 *WhAm 10*
Raveson, Sherman Harold 1907-1974 *WhoAmA 93N*
Ravetch, Irving 1920- *ConTFT 11, IntDcF 2-4, IntMPA 94*
Ravett, Abraham 1947- *WhoAmA 93*
Ravetz, Alison 1930- *WrDr 94*
Ravey, Donald Lee 1929- *WhoWest 94*
Ravi, Vilupanur Alwar 1960- *WhoScEn 94*
Ravichandran, Kurumbail Gopalakrishnan 1960- *WhoScEn 94*
Ravichandran, Ramarathnam *WhoFI 94*
Ravikoff, Ronald B. 1948- *WhoAmL 94*
Ravikovitch, Dahlia 1936- *ConWorW 93*
Ravikovitch, Dalia 1936- *BlmGWL*
Ravikumar, Thanjavur Subramaniam 1950- *WhoScEn 94*
Ravilious, Robin 1944- *SmATA 77*
Ravin, Richard Michael 1943- *WhoIns 94*
Ravinal, Rosemary 1954- *WhoHisp 94*
Ravindra, Nuggehalli Muthanna 1955- *WhoAsA 94*
Ravindran, Nair N. 1934- *WhoAsA 94*
Raviola, D'Elia Giuseppina 1935-1986 *WhAm 10*
Raviola, Elio 1932- *WhoAm 94, WhoScEn 94*
Ravirosa Wade, Leandro 1920- *IntWW 93*
Ravis, Howard Shepard 1934- *WhoAm 94*
Ravitch, Beverly *WhoAmL 94*
Ravitch, Diane 1938- *IntWW 93*
Ravitch, Diane Silvers 1938- *WhoAm 94*
Ravitch, Mark Mitchell 1910-1989 *WhAm 10*
Ravitch, Norman 1936- *WhoAm 94, WrDr 94*
Ravitz, Abe (Carl) 1927- *WrDr 94*
Ravitz, John *WhoAmP 93*
Ravitz, Leonard J., Jr. *WhoAm 94, WhoScEn 94*
Ravitz, Mel 1924- *WhoAmP 93*
Ravitz, Robert Allan 1938- *WhoAm 94*
Raviv, Dan 1954- *ConAu 140*
Raviv, Moshe 1935- *IntWW 93, Who 94*
Ravnholt, Eiler Christian 1923- *WhoAmP 93*
Rawal, Darshan Lal 1934- *WhoMW 93*
Rawat, Arun Kumar 1945- *WhoAsA 94*
Rawat, Banmali Singh 1947- *WhoAsA 94, WhoWest 94*
Rawbone, Alfred Raymond 1923- *Who 94*
Rawcliffe, Derek Alec 1921- *Who 94*
Rawdin, Grant 1959- *WhoFI 94*
Rawdon, Francis 1754-1826 *AmRev*
Rawdon, Francis Rawdon-Hastings 1754-1826 *WhAmRev [port]*
Rawe, Barbara *WhoHol 92*
Rawes, Francis Roderick 1916- *Who 94*
Rawiri, Georges 1932- *IntWW 93*
Rawitch, Robert Joe 1945- *WhoAm 94, WhoWest 94*
Rawl, Alfred Victor 1946- *WhoAmP 93*
Rawl, Arthur Julian 1942- *WhoAm 94, WhoFI 94*
Rawl, Lawrence G. 1928- *WhoAm 94, WhoFI 94*
Rawl, Lawrence G. 1952- *IntWW 93*
Rawle, Anna fl. 1781- *BlmGWL*
Rawle, Jeff 1951- *WhoHol 92*
Rawlence, Christopher 1945- *WrDr 94*
Rawles, Edward Hugh 1945- *WhoAmL 94, WhoMW 93*
Rawles, Elizabeth Gibbs 1943- *WhoBlA 94*
Rawley, Alan David 1934- *Who 94*
Rawley, Ann Keyser 1923- *WhoMW 93*
Rawley, James *WhoHol 92*
Rawley, James A. 1916- *WrDr 94*
Rawley, James Albert 1916- *WhoAm 94*
Rawlings, Adrian *WhoHol 92*
Rawlings, Alice *WhoHol 92*
Rawlings, Boynton Mott 1935- *WhoAm 94, WhoAmL 94, WhoFI 94*
Rawlings, Calvin W(illiam) 1895- *WhAm 10*
Rawlings, George Chancellor, Jr. 1921- *WhoAmP 93*
Rawlings, Howard P. 1937- *WhoAmP 93*
Rawlings, Hunter Ripley, III 1944- *WhoAm 94, WhoMW 93*
Rawlings, James Scott 1922- *WhoAm 94*
Rawlings, Jerry 1947- *IntWW 93*
Rawlings, John Oren 1932- *WhoAm 94*
Rawlings, Margaret 1906- *Who 94, WhoHol 92*
Rawlings, Marilyn Manuela 1956- *WhoBlA 94*
Rawlings, Marjorie Kinnan 1896-1953 *BlmGWL, TwCYAW*
Rawlings, Martha 1942- *WhoBlA 94*
Rawlings, Monte Alamo d1988 *WhoHol 92*
Rawlings, Nicholas Arthur 1944- *WhoFI 94*
Rawlings, Noella A. 1955- *WhoAsA 94*
Rawlings, Norborne L. 1894- *WhAm 10*
Rawlings, Patricia Elizabeth 1939- *Who 94, WhoWomW 91*
Rawlings, Paul C. 1928- *WhoAm 94*
Rawlings, Rob Roy 1920- *WhoAmP 93*
Rawlings, Robert Hoag 1924- *WhoAm 94, WhoWest 94*
Rawlins, Benjamin W., Jr. 1938- *WhoAm 94, WhoFI 94*
Rawlins, C. L. *DrAPF 93*
Rawlins, Christopher John 1945- *WhoAm 94*
Rawlins, Colin Guy Champion 1919- *Who 94*
Rawlins, Elizabeth B. 1927- *WhoBlA 94*
Rawlins, Gordon John 1944- *Who 94*
Rawlins, John (Stuart Pepys) 1922- *Who 94*
Rawlins, John Stuart Pepys 1922- *IntWW 93*
Rawlins, Judy d1974 *WhoHol 92*
Rawlins, Lester d1988 *WhoHol 92*
Rawlins, Michael David 1941- *Who 94*
Rawlins, Peter Jonathan 1951- *IntWW 93, Who 94*
Rawlins, Sedrick John 1927- *WhoBlA 94*
Rawlins, Susan *DrAPF 93*
Rawlinson *Who 94*
Rawlinson, Anthony Henry John 1936- *Who 94*
Rawlinson, Charles Frederick Melville 1934- *Who 94*
Rawlinson, Dennis George Fielding 1919- *Who 94*
Rawlinson, Dennis Patrick 1947- *WhoAm 94, WhoAmL 94*
Rawlinson, Gerald 1904- *WhoHol 92*
Rawlinson, Gloria 1918- *BlmGWL*
Rawlinson, Helen Ann 1948- *WhoAm 94*
Rawlinson, Herbert d1953 *WhoHol 92*
Rawlinson, Jonlane Frederick 1940- *WhoAmA 93*
Rawlinson, Stuart Elbert 1950- *WhoWest 94*
Rawlinson Of Ewell, Baron 1919- *IntWW 93, Who 94*
Rawls, Eugenia *WhoAm 94*
Rawls, Frank Macklin 1952- *WhoAmL 94*
Rawls, George H. 1928- *WhoBlA 94*
Rawls, James C. 1948- *WhoAmL 94*
Rawls, James Jabus 1945- *WhoWest 94*
Rawls, John 1921- *EncEth, WrDr 94*
Rawls, Lou 1935- *WhoHol 92*
Rawls, Lou 1936- *WhoAm 94, WhoBlA 94*
Rawls, Louis 1905- *WhoBlA 94*
Rawls, Raleigh Richard 1925- *WhoBlA 94*
Rawls, Sol Waite, III 1948- *WhoAm 94*
Rawls, William D., Sr. *WhoBlA 94*
Rawls Bond, Charles Cynthia 1934- *WhoBlA 94*
Rawn, Byung Soon 1936- *WhoAsA 94*
Rawnsley, Hardwicke Drummond 1851-1920 *DcNaB MP*
Rawnsley, Howard Melody 1925- *WhoAm 94*
Rawnsley, John 1950- *NewGrDO*
Raworth, Tom 1938- *WrDr 94*
Rawski, Conrad Henry 1914- *WhoAm 94, WhoMW 93*
Rawski, Evelyn Sakakida 1939- *WhoAm 94*
Rawski, Thomas George 1943- *WhoAm 94*
Rawson, Bruce Strathearn 1935- *WhoAm 94*
Rawson, Christopher Selwyn Priestley 1928- *Who 94*
Rawson, Claude Julien 1935- *WrDr 94*
Rawson, David P. *WhoAmP 93*
Rawson, Eleanor S. *WhoAm 94*
Rawson, Jessica Mary 1943- *Who 94*
Rawson, Kay Thompson 1939- *WhoAmP 93*
Rawson, Kenneth John 1926- *Who 94*
Rawson, Kennett Longley 1911- *WhAm 10*
Rawson, Leonard Lee 1954- *WhoAmP 93*
Rawson, Nancy Ellen 1956- *WhoScEn 94*
Rawson, Peter *WhoAm 94*
Rawson, Ralph William 1916-1991 *WhAm 10*
Rawson, Raymond D. 1940- *WhoAmP 93, WhoWest 94*
Rawson, Robert H., Jr. 1944- *WhoAm 94, WhoAmL 94*
Rawson, Robert Orrin 1917- *WhoAm 94*
Rawson, Roger F. 1939- *WhoAmP 93*
Rawson, Tristan d1974 *WhoHol 92*
Rawson, William Robert 1925- *WhoAm 94*
Rawsthorne, Anthony Robert 1943- *Who 94*
Rawsthorne, John 1936- *Who 94*
Raxlen, Rick *WhoHol 92*
Ray, Ajit Nath 1912- *IntWW 93, Who 94*
Ray, Albert d1944 *WhoHol 92*
Ray, Aldo d1991 *WhoHol 92*
Ray, Allene d1979 *WhoHol 92*
Ray, Andrew 1939- *WhoHol 92*
Ray, Andrew 1948- *WhoBlA 94*
Ray, Anne d1986 *WhoHol 92*
Ray, Anthony 1934- *WhoHol 92*
Ray, Arliss Dean 1929- *WhoFI 94*
Ray, Austin H. 1943- *WhoBlA 94*
Ray, Barbara d1955 *WhoHol 92*
Ray, Benjamin Franklin 1965- *WhoFI 94*
Ray, Bill 1922- *WhoAmP 93*
Ray, Billy Victor 1958- *WhoFI 94*
Ray, Bradley Stephen 1957- *WhoAm 94*
Ray, Bruce David 1955- *WhoAmL 94, WhoWest 94*
Ray, Charles d1943 *WhoHol 92*
Ray, Charles 1953- *WhoAmA 93*
Ray, Charles Edwin 1953- *WhoAmL 94*
Ray, Charles Joseph 1911- *WhoMW 93*
Ray, Charles Kendall 1928- *WhoAm 94*
Ray, Christopher T. 1937- *WhoAmA 93*
Ray, Cortland T. 1953- *WhoIns 94*
Ray, Cread L., Jr. 1931- *WhoAm 94, WhoAmP 93*
Ray, Cyril 1908-1991 *WrDr 94N*
Ray, Dan Alan 1933- *WhoAmP 93*
Ray, David *DrAPF 93*
Ray, David 1932- *WrDr 94*
Ray, David Bruce 1953- *WhoBlA 94*
Ray, David Christian 1961- *WhoWest 94*
Ray, David Lewin 1929- *WhoAmL 94, WhoWest 94*
Ray, David Randolph 1946- *WhoAmL 94*
Ray, David Scott 1930- *WhoAm 94*
Ray, Deborah *WhoAmA 93*
Ray, Dixy Lee 1914- *IntWW 93, WrDr 94*
Ray, Donald Hensley 1952- *WhoAm 94*
Ray, Dorothy Jean 1919- *WrDr 94*
Ray, Douglas *WhoMW 93*
Ray, Eddye Robert 1941- *WhoFI 94*
Ray, Edgar Wayne, Jr. 1941- *WhoAm 94*
Ray, Edward Ernest 1924- *Who 94*
Ray, Edward John 1944- *WhoAm 94, WhoFI 94*
Ray, Ellen *WhoHol 92*
Ray, Emma d1935 *WhoHol 92*
Ray, Frank Allen 1949- *WhoAmL 94, WhoMW 93*
Ray, Frank David 1940- *WhoAm 94, WhoMW 93*
Ray, Fred Olen *HorFD*
Ray, Gary Alan 1958- *WhoMW 93*
Ray, Gene Anthony 1961- *WhoHol 92*
Ray, George Einar 1910- *WhoAm 94*
Ray, Gilbert T. 1944- *WhoAm 94, WhoAmL 94*
Ray, Gordon Norton 1915-1986 *DcLB 140 [port]*
Ray, Gordon Thompson 1928 *WhoAm 94, WhoScEn 94*
Ray, Greg Alan 1963- *WhoBlA 94*
Ray, H. M. 1924- *WhoAm 94*
Ray, Harold Byrd 1940- *WhoFI 94*
Ray, Helen d1965 *WhoHol 92*
Ray, Hugh d1956 *ProFbHF*
Ray, Hugh M. 1943- *WhoAmL 94*
Ray, Hugh Massey, Jr. 1943- *WhoAm 94, WhoAmL 94*
Ray, Isaac 1807-1881 *EncSPD*
Ray, Jack d1975 *WhoHol 92*
Ray, Jacqueline Walker 1944- *WhoBlA 94*
Ray, James d1988 *WhoHol 92*
Ray, James A. 1960- *WhoWest 94*
Ray, James Allen 1931- *WhoFI 94*
Ray, James Allen 1945- *WhoScEn 94*
Ray, James Edward 1922- *WhoAmP 93*
Ray, James Henry 1925- *WhoScEn 94*
Ray, James R., III 1963- *WhoBlA 94*
Ray, James William, Sr. 1939- *WhoAmP 93*
Ray, Jeanne Cullinan 1943- *WhoAm 94*
Ray, Jerry W. 1944- *WhoMW 93*
Ray, John 1943- *WhoAmP 93*
Ray, John Walker 1936- *WhoMW 93, WhoScEn 94*
Ray, Johnnie d1990 *WhoHol 92*
Ray, Johnny d1927 *WhoHol 92*
Ray, Johnny 1957- *WhoBlA 94*
Ray, Judith Diana 1946- *WhoBlA 94*
Ray, Judy *DrAPF 93*
Ray, Judy 1939- *WrDr 94*
Ray, Kelley *WhoAm 94*
Ray, Leah 1915- *WhoHol 92*
Ray, Leo Eldon 1937- *WhoWest 94*
Ray, Louis S. 1937- *WhoMW 93*
Ray, Man d1976 *WhoHol 92*
Ray, Marianne Yurasko 1934- *WhoWest 94*
Ray, Marilyn June 1950- *WhoFI 94*
Ray, Mario A. 1945- *WhoHisp 94*
Ray, Marjorie d1924 *WhoHol 92*
Ray, Mary (Eva Pedder) 1932- *WrDr 94*
Ray, Mary E. 1911- *WhoBlA 94*
Ray, Mary Louise Ryan 1954- *WhoAmL 94*

Ray, Mercer Z. 1911- *WhoBlA 94*
Ray, Michael Edwin 1949- *WhoAm 94, WhoAmL 94*
Ray, Michael Robert 1965- *WhoAmL 94*
Ray, Michael Thomas 1954- *WhoIns 94*
Ray, Michel 1947- *WhoHol 92*
Ray, Moses Alexander 1920- *WhoBlA 94*
Ray, Naomi d1966 *WhoHol 92*
Ray, Nicholas d1979 *WhoHol 92*
Ray, Norman Wilson 1942- *WhoAm 94*
Ray, Ola *WhoHol 92*
Ray, Pamela A. 1948- *WhoAmL 94*
Ray, Paul Leo 1946- *WhoWest 94*
Ray, Paul Richard, Jr. 1943- *WhoAm 94*
Ray, Philip Bicknell 1917- *Who 94*
Ray, Randy Wayne 1951- *WhoAm 94*
Ray, Rene d1993 *NewYTBS 93 [port]*
Ray, Rene 1912- *EncSF 93*
Ray, Renee 1912- *WhoHol 92*
Ray, Richard 1927- *WhoAmP 93*
Ray, Richard Eugene 1950- *WhoMW 93, WhoScEn 94*
Ray, Richard Rex 1942- *WhoBlA 94*
Ray, Richard Stanley 1937- *WhoWest 94*
Ray, Ricky 1977-1992 *AnObit 1992*
Ray, Robert 1928- *EncSF 93*
Ray, Robert 1935- *WhoAmP 93*
Ray, Robert (Donald) 1924- *WhoAmA 93*
Ray, Robert D. 1928- *IntWW 93, WhoAmP 93*
Ray, Robert Francis 1947- *IntWW 93, Who 94*
Ray, Robert Franklin 1949- *WhoAm 94*
Ray, Robert H. 1940- *WrDr 94*
Ray, Robert Landon 1950- *WhoScEn 94*
Ray, Robert Owen 1949- *WhoAm 94*
Ray, Robert W. 1961- *WhoFI 94*
Ray, Robin *Who 94*
Ray, Roger Buchanan 1935- *WhoAm 94*
Ray, Ronald Dudley 1942- *WhoAmL 94*
Ray, Rosalind Rosemary 1956- *WhoBlA 94*
Ray, Roy L. 1939- *WhoAmP 93*
Ray, Roy Lee 1939- *WhoMW 93*
Ray, Ruth 1919-1977 *WhoAmA 93N*
Ray, Sankar 1953- *WhoScEn 94, WhoWest 94*
Ray, Satyajit 1921-1992 *AnObit 1992, ConLC 76 [port], ConTFT 11, WhAm 10*
Ray, Sheila G(raham) 1930- *WrDr 94*
Ray, Shreela *DrAPF 93*
Ray, Sib Narayan 1921- *WrDr 94*
Ray, Siba Prasad 1944- *WhoAsA 94*
Ray, Siddhartha Sankar 1920- *IntWW 93*
Ray, Steven Hutter 1961- *WhoAmL 94*
Ray, Suzanne Judy 1939- *WhoMW 93*
Ray, Ted d1977 *WhoHol 92*
Ray, Terrance d1978 *WhoHol 92*
Ray, Timothy Britt 1939- *WhoAmL 94*
Ray, Timothy Frederick 1949- *WhoFI 94*
Ray, Tuhin 1963- *WhoMW 93*
Ray, W. Harmon 1940- *WhoAm 94*
Ray, Walter I., Jr. 1923- *WhoBlA 94*
Ray, Walter S. 1941- *WhoAmP 93*
Ray, William Benjamin *WhoBlA 94*
Ray, William F. 1915- *WhoAm 94, WhoFI 94*
Ray, William Jackson 1945- *WhoAm 94*
Ray, William Joel 1954- *WhoFI 94*
Raya, Nick S. d1950 *WhoHol 92*
Rayam, Curtis 1951- *NewGrDO*
Rayborn, William Lee 1936- *WhoAmP 93*
Raybould, Barry John 1956- *WhoWest 94*
Raybould, (Robert) Clarence 1886-1972 *NewGrDO*
Rayburn (Dale), Boyd 1942- *WhoAmA 93*
Rayburn, B. B. Sixty 1916- *WhoAmP 93*
Rayburn, Carole Mary Aida Ann 1938- *WhoAm 94*
Rayburn, Gene 1917- *IntMPA 94*
Rayburn, George Marvin 1920- *WhoAm 94*
Rayburn, James Chalmers, III 1945- *WhoWest 94*
Rayburn, Margaret 1927- *WhoWest 94*
Rayburn, Margaret Shaw 1927- *WhoAmP 93*
Rayburn, Ray Arthur 1948- *WhoScEn 94*
Rayburn, S. T. 1947- *WhoAmL 94*
Rayburn, Wendell Gilbert 1929- *WhoBlA 94*
Raychaudhuri, Tapan Kumar 1926- *Who 94*
Raydon, Alexander R. *WhoAmA 93*
Raye, Carol 1923- *WhoHol 92*
Raye, Jimmy *WhoBlA 94*
Raye, John 1941- *WhoBlA 94*
Raye, Martha 1916- *IntMPA 94, WhoCom, WhoHol 92*
Raye, Vance Wallace 1946- *WhoBlA 94*
Rayen, James Wilson 1935- *WhoAmA 93*
Rayer, Francis G(eorge) 1921-1981 *EncSF 93*
Rayes, Ghazi al 1935- *IntWW 93*
Rayfield, Allan Laverne 1935- *WhoAm 94*
Rayfield, Denise E. 1955- *WhoBlA 94*
Rayfield, (Patrick) Donald 1942- *WrDr 94*
Rayfield, Gordon Elliott 1950- *WhoAm 94*
Rayford, Brenda L. 1940- *WhoBlA 94*
Rayford, Floyd Kinnard 1957- *WhoBlA 94*
Rayford, Lee Edward 1935- *WhoBlA 94*
Rayford, Phillip Leon 1927- *WhoBlA 94*
Rayford, Zula M. 1941- *WhoBlA 94*
Ray-Goins, Jeanette 1933- *WhoBlA 94*
Rayher, Edward *DrAPF 93*
Rayl, Harris Ashton 1953- *WhoAm 94*
Rayl, Ruth Corena 1952- *WhoFI 94*
Rayleigh, Baron 1960- *Who 94*
Raylesberg, Alan Ira 1950- *WhoAm 94, WhoAmL 94*
Raylman, Raymond Robert 1961- *WhoMW 93*
Ray-Lynch, Leopold Augustus 1951- *WhoWest 94*
Raymaker, Herman d1944 *WhoHol 92*
Rayman, Steven Louis 1958- *WhoAmL 94*
Raymer, Donald George 1924- *WhoAm 94*
Raymer, Michael Robert 1917- *Who 94*
Raymond, Alex 1909-1956 *EncSF 93*
Raymond, Alexander 1909-1956 *WhoAmA 93N*
Raymond, Arthur *WhoAmP 93*
Raymond, Arthur 1923- *WhoAm 94*
Raymond, Arthur Charles 1933- *WhoAmP 93*
Raymond, Arthur Emmons 1899- *WhoScEn 94*
Raymond, B. Louis fl. 1785- *NewGrDO*
Raymond, Candy *WhoHol 92*
Raymond, Charles Walker, III 1937- *WhoFI 94*
Raymond, Clarinda Harriss *DrAPF 93*
Raymond, Cyril d1973 *WhoHol 92*
Raymond, Dale Rodney 1949- *WhoScEn 94*
Raymond, David Alan 1948- *WhoAm 94*
Raymond, David Walker 1945- *WhoAmL 94*
Raymond, Derek *EncSF 93*
Raymond, Derek 1931- *WrDr 94*
Raymond, Diana Joan 1916- *WrDr 94*
Raymond, Dorothy Gill 1954- *WhoAmL 94*
Raymond, E.V. *EncSF 93*
Raymond, Ellsworth 1912- *WrDr 94*
Raymond, Eugene Thomas 1923- *WhoScEn 94, WhoWest 94*
Raymond, Evelyn L. 1908- *WhoAmA 93*
Raymond, F. Douglas, III 1958- *WhoAmL 94*
Raymond, Ford d1960 *WhoHol 92*
Raymond, Frances d1961 *WhoHol 92*
Raymond, G. Alison *ConAu 142*
Raymond, Gary 1935- *WhoHol 92*
Raymond, Gene 1908- *IntMPA 94, WhoHol 92*
Raymond, George Gamble, Jr. 1921- *WhoAm 94*
Raymond, George Marc 1919- *WhoAm 94*
Raymond, George Thomas 1960- *WhoWest 94*
Raymond, Guy 1911- *WhoAm 94*
Raymond, Guy 1915- *WhoHol 92*
Raymond, Harvey Francis 1915- *WhoAm 94*
Raymond, Helen d1965 *WhoHol 92*
Raymond, Henry James, II 1957- *WhoBlA 94*
Raymond, Jack d1951 *WhoHol 92*
Raymond, Jack d1953 *WhoHol 92*
Raymond, Jack 1918- *WhoAm 94*
Raymond, Joan M. 1936- *WhoAm 94*
Raymond, John Charles 1948- *WhoScEn 94*
Raymond, Judith Ann 1938- *WhoAmP 93*
Raymond, Kenneth Norman 1942- *WhoAm 94, WhoWest 94*
Raymond, Lee R. 1938- *WhoAm 94, WhoFI 94*
Raymond, Lilo 1922- *WhoAmA 93*
Raymond, Lina *WhoHol 92*
Raymond, Lisa *NewYTBS 93 [port]*
Raymond, Monica E. *DrAPF 93*
Raymond, P.T. *EncSF 93*
Raymond, Patrick (Ernest) 1924- *WrDr 94*
Raymond, Paula 1923- *WhoHol 92*
Raymond, Paula 1925- *IntMPA 94*
Raymond, Pete d1927 *WhoHol 92*
Raymond, Phillip Gregory 1957- *WhoBlA 94*
Raymond, Ray d1927 *WhoHol 92*
Raymond, Richard 1960- *WhoAmP 93*
Raymond, Robert Edward 1936- *WhoWest 94*
Raymond, Robert H. 1923- *WhoFI 94*
Raymond, Robin *WhoHol 92*
Raymond, Ronald C. 1951- *WhoAmP 93*
Raymond, Roy d1993 *NewYTBS 93 [port]*
Raymond, Royal d1949 *WhoHol 92*
Raymond, Ruth *WhoHol 92*
Raymond, Spencer Henry 1926- *WhoAm 94*
Raymond, Stephen L. 1942- *WhoAmL 94*
Raymond, Susan Grant 1943- *WhoWest 94*
Raymond, William d1960 *WhoHol 92*
Raymond, William Francis 1922- *Who 94*
Raymond, William Marshall 1934- *WhoFI 94*
Raymonda, James Earl 1933- *WhoAm 94*
Raymont, Warwick Deane 1941- *WhoScEn 94*
Raymund, Steven 1955- *WhoFI 94*
Raymundo, Adelisa A. 1934- *WhoWomW 91*
Raynard, Shirley M. 1942- *WhoAmP 93*
Raynaud, Fernand d1973 *WhoHol 92*
Raynaud, Jean-Pierre 1939- *IntWW 93*
Raynaud, Pierre 1917- *IntWW 93*
Raynauld, Andre 1927- *WhoAm 94*
Rayne, Baron 1918- *Who 94*
Rayne, Max 1918- *IntWW 93*
Rayner, Baron 1926- *Who 94*
Rayner, Arno Alfred 1928- *WhoWest 94*
Rayner, Bonnie Lou 1940- *WhoMW 93*
Rayner, Bryan Roy 1932- *Who 94*
Rayner, Claire Berenice 1931- *Who 94*
Rayner, David Edward 1940- *Who 94*
Rayner, Derek George 1926- *IntWW 93*
Rayner, Edward John 1936- *Who 94*
Rayner, Gordon 1935- *WhoAmA 93*
Rayner, John Desmond 1924- *WrDr 94*
Rayner, Keith *Who 94*
Rayner, Mary (Yoma Grigson) 1933- *WrDr 94*
Rayner, Minnie d1941 *WhoHol 92*
Rayner, Robert Martin 1946- *WhoFI 94*
Rayner, William 1929- *WrDr 94*
Rayner, William Alexander 1929- *WhoAm 94*
Raynes, Edward Peter 1945- *IntWW 93, Who 94*
Raynham, Viscount 1945- *Who 94*
Raynham, Frank 1881- *WhoHol 92*
Raynolds, David Robert 1928- *WhoWest 94*
Raynolds, Harold, Jr. 1925- *WhoAm 94*
Raynolds, John F., III *WhoAm 94, WhoFI 94*
Raynolds, William Franklin 1820-1894 *WhWE*
Raynor, Henry (Broughton) 1917- *WrDr 94*
Raynor, Joe B. 1923- *WhoAmP 93*
Raynor, John Patrick 1923- *WhoAm 94*
Raynor, Lynn S. 1940- *IntMPA 94*
Raynor, Richard Benjamin 1928- *WhoAm 94*
Raynor, Robert G., Jr. 1954- *WhoBlA 94*
Raynor, Sheila *WhoHol 92*
Raynowska, Bernard J. 1925- *WhoAmP 93*
Raynsford, Nick *Who 94*
Raynsford, Robert Wayne, Jr. 1935- *WhoFI 94*
Raynsford, Wyvill Richard Nicolls 1945- *Who 94*
Rayon, Paul E., III 1950- *WhoBlA 94*
Rayport, Mark 1922- *WhoMW 93*
Rayson, Edwin Hope 1923- *WhoAm 94*
Rayson, Glendon Ennes 1915- *WhoScEn 94*
Rayson, Hannie 1957- *ConDr 93*
Rayson, Jack Henry 1931- *WhoAm 94*
Rayson, John Chandler 1949- *WhoAmP 93*
Rayward, Warden Boyd 1939- *WhoAm 94*
Raz, Hilda 1938- *WhoAm 94*
Raz, Joseph 1939- *IntWW 93, Who 94*
Raz, Robert Eugene 1942- *WhoAm 94, WhoMW 93*
Raz, Tzvi 1951- *WhoScEn 94*
Razafimahatratra, Victor 1921- *IntWW 93*
Razafimbahiny, Jules Alphonse 1922- *IntWW 93*
Razak, Mohamad Najib bin tun Haj Abdul 1954- *IntWW 93*
Razaleigh Hamzah, Tengku Tan Sri Datuk 1936- *IntWW 93*
Razborov, Alexander A. 1963- *WhoScEn 94*
Razetto, Stella d1948 *WhoHol 92*
Razgaitis, Anthony Richard 1944- *WhoMW 93*
Razin, Assaf 1941- *WrDr 94*
Raziuddin, Syed Husaini 1957- *WhoMW 93*
Razl, Stanislav 1920- *IntWW 93*
Raznoff, Beverly Shultz 1946- *WhoAm 94*
Razo, Jose H. 1951- *WhoHisp 94*
Razonable, John 1943- *WhoHisp 94*
Razook, Richard J. *WhoHisp 94*
Razouk, Rashad Elias 1911- *WhoScEn 94, WhoWest 94*
Razzaghi, Mahmoud 1951- *WhoScEn 94*
Razzall, Leonard Humphrey 1912- *Who 94*
Razzano, Frank Charles 1948- *WhoAm 94, WhoAmL 94*
Razzano, Pasquale Angelo 1943- *WhoAmL 94*
Razzouk, Akram 1953- *WhoMW 93*
Re, Edward D. 1920- *CngDr 93, WhoAm 94*
Re, Gustavo d1979 *WhoHol 92*
Re, Marisa Del *WhoAmA 93*
Re, Richard N. 1944- *WhoAm 94, WhoScEn 94*
Re, Vincenzo c. 1700-1762 *NewGrDO*
Rea, Baron 1928- *Who 94*
Rea, Amadeo Michael 1939- *WhoAm 94*
Rea, David K. 1942- *WhoMW 93*
Rea, Dorothy Callaway 1939- *WhoAmP 93*
Rea, Ernest 1945- *Who 94*
Rea, George Robert, Jr. 1939- *WhoAmP 93*
Rea, Jack D. 1933- *WhoAmP 93*
Rea, James Edmond 1935- *WhoFI 94*
Rea, James F. 1937- *WhoAmP 93*
Rea, James Taylor 1907- *Who 94*
Rea, John 1944- *NewGrDO*
Rea, John Rowland 1933- *Who 94*
Rea, Mabel Lillian d1968 *WhoHol 92*
Rea, Michael J., Jr. 1940- *WhoAmP 93*
Rea, Peggy *WhoHol 92*
Rea, Robert Hall 1934- *WhoWest 94*
Rea, Roger Kevin 1958- *WhoAmL 94*
Rea, Rupert Lascelles P. *Who 94*
Rea, Stephen *WhoAm 94*
Rea, Stephen 1949- *IntMPA 94*
Rea, Susan *DrAPF 93*
Rea, Tom *DrAPF 93*
Rea, William J. 1920- *WhoAm 94, WhoAmL 94, WhoWest 94*
Reachi, Santiago 1898- *WhoHisp 94*
Read, Alan Ernest Alfred 1926- *Who 94*
Read, Allan Alexander 1923- *Who 94, WhoAm 94*
Read, Anthony 1935- *WrDr 94*
Read, Antony *Who 94*
Read, (John) Antony (Jervis) 1913- *Who 94*
Read, Arthur Martin, II 1946- *WhoAmP 93*
Read, Arthur William 1930- *WhoAm 94*
Read, Barbara d1963 *WhoHol 92*
Read, Benjamin Huger d1993 *NewYTBS 93 [port]*
Read, Beverly Money 1919- *WhoAm 94*
Read, Brian 1927- *WrDr 94*
Read, Charles (Frederick) 1918- *Who 94*
Read, Charles Raymond, Sr. 1915- *WhoWest 94*
Read, Dale T. 1946- *WhoAmP 93*
Read, Daniel 1757-1836 *WhAmRev*
Read, Dave 1938- *WhoAmA 93*
Read, David (Haxton Carswell) 1910- *WrDr 94*
Read, David Haxton Carswell 1910- *Who 94, WhoAm 94*
Read, David John 1939- *Who 94*
Read, Didde d1932 *WhoHol 92*
Read, Dolly *WhoHol 92*
Read, Donald 1930- *WrDr 94*
Read, Dorothy Louise 1938- *WhoScEn 94*
Read, Elfreida 1920- *WrDr 94*
Read, Frank Henry 1934- *Who 94*
Read, Frank Thompson 1938- *WhoAm 94, WhoAmL 94, WhoWest 94*
Read, Frederick Wilson, Jr. 1908- *WhoAm 94*
Read, Gardner 1913- *WrDr 94*
Read, George 1733-1798 *WhAmRev*
Read, Gregory Charles 1942- *WhoAm 94, WhoAmL 94*
Read, Harold E. 1898- *WhAm 10*
Read, Harold Thomas 1938- *WhoFI 94*
Read, Harry 1924- *Who 94*
Read, Helen Appleton 1887-1974 *WhoAmA 93N*
Read, Herbert (Edward) 1893-1968 *EncSF 93*
Read, Imelda Mary 1939- *Who 94, WhoWomW 91*
Read, Jacob 1752-1816 *WhAmRev*
Read, James 1743-1822 *WhAmRev*
Read, James 1954- *WhoHol 92*
Read, Jan 1917- *WrDr 94*
Read, Jay Rollin 1936- *WhoMW 93*
Read, Joel *WhoFI 94*
Read, Joel, Sr. *WhoAm 94*
Read, John (Emms) 1918- *Who 94*
Read, John Conyers 1947- *WhoAm 94, WhoMW 93*
Read, John Emms 1918- *IntWW 93*
Read, John Leslie 1935- *Who 94*
Read, John O. *WhoAmP 93*
Read, Leonard Ernest 1925- *Who 94*
Read, Leslie Webster 1937- *WhoScEn 94*
Read, Lionel Frank 1929- *Who 94*
Read, Mel *Who 94*
Read, Miss *Who 94*
Read, Miss 1913- *WrDr 94*
Read, Opie (Percival) d1939 *WhoHol 92*
Read, Paul E. 1937- *WhoAm 94*
Read, Peter G. 1927- *ConAu 141*
Read, Peter Kip 1941- *WhoAm 94*
Read, Philip Lloyd 1932- *WhoAm 94*
Read, Piers Paul 1941- *IntWW 93, Who 94, WhoAm 94, WrDr 94*
Read, Robert Logan 1938- *WhoWest 94*

Read, Robert P., Jr. 1946- *WhoAmP 93*
Read, Sylvia Joan *WrDr 94*
Read, Thomas c. 1740-1788 *WhAmRev*
Read, Timothy Thomas 1957- *WhoAmL 94*
Read, William Brooks 1926- *WhoAmP 93*
Read, William Edgar 1927- *WhoAm 94*
Read, William Lawrence 1926- *WhoAm 94*
Read, William McClain 1918- *WhoAm 94*
Reade, Brian Anthony 1940- *Who 94*
Reade, Charles 1814-1884 *BlmGEL, IntDcT 2*
Reade, Claire Elizabeth 1952- *WhoAm 94*
Reade, Clyde Nixon 1906- *Who 94*
Reade, Hamish 1936- *WrDr 94*
Reade, Lewis Pollock 1932- *WhoAm 94*
Reade, Philip *EncSF 93*
Reade, Philip d1979 *WhoHol 92*
Reade, Randall Roger 1961- *WhoAmL 94*
Reade, Richard Sill 1913- *WhoAm 94*
Reade, Robert Mellor 1940- *WhoWest 94*
Reade, Roma 1877-1958 *WhoAmA 93N*
Reader, Alec Harold 1957- *WhoScEn 94*
Reader, Barbara 1955- *WhoAmL 94*
Reader, Dennis J. *DrAPF 93*
Reader, George Gordon 1919- *WhoAm 94, WhoScEn 94*
Reader, Joseph 1934- *WhoScEn 94*
Reader, Ralph d1982 *WhoHol 92*
Reader Harris, (Muriel) Diana 1912- *Who 94*
Readey, Bartley John, III 1943- *WhoAmL 94, WhoMW 93*
Readick, Bobby d1985 *WhoHol 92*
Readick, Frank M. d1924 *WhoHol 92*
Reading, Area Bishop of 1930- *Who 94*
Reading, Marquess of 1942- *Who 94*
Reading, Anthony John 1933- *WhoAm 94*
Reading, Bertice d1991 *WhoHol 92*
Reading, Bonnie Nelson 1943- *WhoAmL 94*
Reading, Harold G. *WhoScEn 94*
Reading, James Edward 1924- *WhoAm 94*
Reading, John fl. 1684- *NewGrDO*
Reading, Peter 1946- *WrDr 94*
Readinger, David M. 1935- *WhoAmP 93*
Readio, Wilfred A. 1895-1961 *WhoAmA 93N*
Readmond, Ronald Warren 1943- *WhoFI 94*
Ready, Catherine Murray 1916- *WhoBlA 94*
Ready, Elizabeth Mary 1953- *WhoAmP 93*
Ready, George Banks 1957- *WhoAmP 93*
Ready, John Fetsch 1932- *WhoMW 93*
Ready, Kevin E., Sr. 1952- *WhoAmL 94*
Ready, Leah Henriquez 1947- *WhoHisp 94*
Ready, Mike d1936 *WhoHol 92*
Ready, Robert James 1952- *WhoAm 94*
Ready, Thomas Wesley 1949- *WhoAmP 93*
Ready, William B(ernard) 1914-1981 *EncSF 93*
Reagan, Barbara Benton *WhoAm 94*
Reagan, Gary Don 1941- *WhoAmL 94, WhoAmP 93, WhoWest 94*
Reagan, Harry Edwin, III 1940- *WhoAm 94, WhoAmL 94*
Reagan, Janet Thompson 1945- *WhoWest 94*
Reagan, Joseph Bernard 1934- *WhoAm 94*
Reagan, Michael 1945- *WhoHol 92*
Reagan, Nancy Davis 1921- *IntWW 93*
Reagan, Nancy Davis 1923- *WhoAm 94, WhoWest 94, WrDr 94*
Reagan, Robert Brian 1943- *WhoAmL 94*
Reagan, Ron 1958- *WhoHol 92*
Reagan, Ronald 1911- *IntMPA 94, Who 94, WhoHol 92*
Reagan, Ronald Wilson 1911- *IntWW 93, WhoAm 94, WhoAmP 93, WhoWest 94*
Reagon, Bernice Johnson 1942- *WhoBlA 94*
Real, Betty d1969 *WhoHol 92*
Real, Manuel Lawrence 1924- *WhoAm 94, WhoAmL 94, WhoHisp 94, WhoWest 94*
Real, Thomas Michael 1962- *WhoScEn 94*
Reale, John P. 1949- *WhoAmL 94*
Reale, Nicholas Albert 1922- *WhoAmA 93N*
Reale, William A. 1933- *WhoAm 94*
Reals, William Joseph 1920- *WhoAm 94*
Ream, David Lowell 1940- *WhoMW 93*
Ream, Juliet Lynn 1963- *WhoAmL 94*
Ream, Norman Jacob 1912- *WhAm 10*
Ream, Robert R. 1936- *WhoAmP 93*
Reaman, Gregory Harold 1947- *WhoScEn 94*
Reames, Spencer Eugene 1946- *WhoScEn 94*
Reames, Thomas Eugene 1940- *WhoScEn 94*
Reames, Victor Leon 1945- *WhoFI 94*
Reamey, George Spottswood 1895- *WhAm 10*
Reams, Bernard Dinsmore, Jr. 1943- *WhoAm 94, WhoAmL 94, WhoFI 94, WhoMW 93*
Reams, Bill H. *WhoAmP 93*
Reams, Cynthia Lynette 1959- *WhoAmL 94*
Reamsbottom, Barry Arthur 1949- *Who 94*
Reamy, Tom 1935-1977 *EncSF 93*
Reaney, Gilbert 1924- *WhoAm 94*
Reaney, James 1926- *ConAu 42NR*
Reaney, James (Crerar) 1926- *ConDr 93, IntDcT 2, WrDr 94*
Reaney, James Crerar 1926- *WhoAm 94*
Reap, Mary Margaret 1941- *WhoAm 94*
Rea Price, (William) John 1937- *Who 94*
Reardanz, Leslie Elmer, III 1965- *WhoWest 94*
Rearden, Carole Ann 1946- *WhoWest 94*
Rearden, John B., Jr. 1942- *WhoAmL 94*
Rearden, Sara B. *WhoBlA 94*
Reardon, Barry 1931- *IntMPA 94*
Reardon, Bernard M(orris) G(arvin) 1913- *WrDr 94*
Reardon, Bill *WhoAmP 93*
Reardon, Bryan Peter 1928- *WhoAm 94*
Reardon, Casper d1941 *WhoHol 92*
Reardon, Daniel B. 1955- *WhoAmP 93*
Reardon, Dennis J. 1944- *ConDr 93, WrDr 94*
Reardon, Frank Emond 1953- *WhoAmL 94*
Reardon, Frederick Henry 1932- *WhoScEn 94*
Reardon, James 1880- *WhoHol 92*
Reardon, Jeffrey James 1955- *WhoAm 94, WhoMW 93*
Reardon, John 1930-1988 *NewGrDO*
Reardon, John Edward 1943- *WhAm 10*
Reardon, John Patrick 1933- *Who 94*
Reardon, Judy E. 1958- *WhoAmP 93*
Reardon, Martin Alan 1932- *Who 94*
Reardon, Mary A. *WhoAmA 93*
Reardon, Ned d1916 *WhoHol 92*
Reardon, Patrick Thomas 1949- *WhoMW 93*
Reardon, Raymond 1932- *IntWW 93*
Reardon, Robert Joseph 1928- *WhoAm 94, WhoFI 94*
Reardon, Steven Wayne 1952- *WhoMW 93*
Reardon, Susan B. 1956- *WhoMW 93*
Reardon, William J. 1941- *WhoAmP 93*
Reardon-Smith, William *Who 94*
Rearick, Carolyn Sue 1949- *WhoMW 93*
Rearick, James Isaac 1952- *WhoScEn 94*
Reark, John Benson 1923- *WhoScEn 94*
Reaser, Richard Lee 1932- *WhoWest 94*
Reason, Joseph Henry 1905- *WhoBlA 94*
Reason, Joseph Paul 1941- *AfrAmG [port]*
Reason, Patrick 1817-1852 *WhoAmA 93N*
Reason, Rex 1928- *IntMPA 94, WhoHol 92*
Reason, Rhodes 1930- *WhoHol 92*
Reasoner, Barrett Hodges 1964- *WhoAmL 94*
Reasoner, Donald J. 1940- *WhoScEn 94*
Reasoner, Harry 1923-1991 *WhAm 10*
Reasoner, Harry Max 1939- *WhoAm 94, WhoAmL 94*
Reasoner, Stephen M. 1944- *WhoAm 94, WhoAmL 94*
Reasoner, Willis Irl, III 1951- *WhoAm 94, WhoAmL 94*
Reasor, Jackson E., Jr. 1952- *WhoAmP 93*
Reath, George, Jr. 1939- *WhoAm 94, WhoAmL 94, WhoFI 94*
Reaume, David Michael 1941- *WhoFI 94*
Reaumur, Rene-A. F. de *WorInv*
Reaumur, Rene-Antoine Ferchault de 1683-1757 *WorScD*
Reaver, Chap 1935-1993 *ConAu 142, SmATA 77, TwCYAW*
Reaver, Herbert R. *ConAu 142*
Reaver, J. Russell 1915- *WrDr 94*
Reaves, Benjamin F. *WhoAm 94*
Reaves, Benjamin Franklin 1932- *WhoBlA 94*
Reaves, Charles William 1923- *WhoFI 94*
Reaves, Craig Charles 1952- *WhoAmL 94*
Reaves, Curtis Felton 1938- *WhoFI 94*
Reaves, Darryl 1960- *WhoAmP 93*
Reaves, E. Fredericka M. 1938- *WhoBlA 94*
Reaves, Franklin Carlwell 1942- *WhoBlA 94*
Reaves, Gibson 1923- *WhoWest 94*
Reaves, Ginevera N. 1925- *WhoBlA 94*
Reaves, Henry L. 1919- *WhoAmP 93*
Reaves, J. Michael 1950- *WrDr 94*
Reaves, J(ames) Michael 1950- *EncSF 93*
Reaves, John Daniel 1939- *WhoAm 94*
Reaves, Lacy H. 1947- *WhoAmL 94*
Reaves, Ray Donald 1935- *WhoFI 94*
Reavey, William Anthony, III 1944- *WhoAm 94, WhoAmL 94, WhoWest 94*
Reavill, David William 1948- *WhoWest 94*
Reavis, Anne Rivers 1955- *WhoAmL 94*
Reavis, Dick J. 1945- *WrDr 94*
Reavis, Hubert Gray, Jr. 1945- *WhoMW 93*
Reavis, John William, Jr. 1935- *WhoBlA 94*
Reavis, Lincoln 1933- *WhoAmL 94*
Reavis, Robert Arthur 1949- *WhoWest 94*
Reavis, Theodore Edward 1937- *WhoWest 94*
Reavley, Thomas Morrow 1921- *WhoAm 94, WhoAmL 94, WhoAmP 93*
Reavley, Thomas Wilson 1947- *WhoAmL 94*
Reay, Lord 1937- *Who 94*
Reay, Master of 1965- *Who 94*
Reay, Alan *Who 94*
Reay, (Hubert) Alan (John) 1925- *Who 94*
Reay, David William 1940- *Who 94*
Reay, John Sinclair Shewan 1932- *Who 94*
Reback, Joyce Ellen 1948- *WhoAm 94, WhoAmL 94*
Reback, Richard Neal 1954- *WhoAmL 94*
Rebagay, Teofila Velasco 1928- *WhoScEn 94*
Rebane, John T. 1946- *WhoAm 94*
Rebar, Alex *WhoHol 92*
Rebar, Robert William 1947- *WhoAm 94*
Rebata, Virginia Patricia 1953- *WhoHisp 94*
Rebay, Hilla 1890-1967 *WhoAmA 93N*
Rebay, Luciano 1928- *WhoAm 94*
Rebbeck, Denis 1914- *IntWW 93, Who 94*
Rebbeck, Lester James, Jr. 1929- *WhoAmA 93, WhoMW 93*
Rebe, Bernd Werner 1939- *IntWW 93*
Rebec, George Vincent 1949- *WhoAm 94*
Rebein, David James 1955- *WhoAmL 94*
Rebeiz, Constantin Anis 1936- *WhoAm 94, WhoScEn 94*
Rebek, Julius, Jr. 1949- *IntWW 93*
Rebel, Bernard d1964 *WhoHol 92*
Rebel, Francois 1701-1775 *NewGrDO*
Rebel, Jean-Fery c. 1666-1747 *NewGrDO*
Rebel, Jerome Ivo 1949- *WhoFI 94*
Rebel, Thomas P. 1947- *WhoAmL 94*
Rebelein, Paul Richard 1938- *WhoAmP 93*
Rebellon, Eduardo Rodriguez-Losada *NewGrDO*
Rebelo De Sousa, Baltasar 1922- *IntWW 93*
Rebelsky, Leonid 1956- *WhoScEn 94*
Rebenack, John Henry 1918- *WhoAm 94*
Rebenfeld, Ludwig 1928- *WhoAm 94, WhoScEn 94*
Reber, Clark L. 1937- *WhoAmP 93*
Reber, David James 1944- *WhoAmL 94*
Reber, Glenn B. 1952- *WhoAmP 93*
Reber, Grote 1911- *WorInv*
Reber, (Napoleon-)Henri 1807-1880 *NewGrDO*
Reber, Jane C. *WhoAmP 93*
Reber, Joseph E. 1940- *WhoAmL 94*
Reber, Martin Donald 1950- *WhoFI 94*
Reber, Mick 1942- *WhoAmA 93*
Reber, Raymond Andrew 1942- *WhoScEn 94*
Reber, Robert D., Jr. 1947- *WhoAmP 93*
Rebeyrol, Yvonne 1928- *IntWW 93*
Rebeyrolle, Paul 1926- *IntWW 93*
Rebhorn, James *WhoHol 92*
Rebhun, Pearl G. 1924- *WhoAmA 93*
Rebikov, Vladimir Ivanovich 1866-1920 *NewGrDO*
Rebillot, Chris Conrad 1952- *WhoFI 94*
Rebmann, Johann 1820-1876 *WhWE*
Rebocho Vaz, Camilo Augusto de Miranda 1920- *IntWW 93*
Rebolledo, Tey Diana 1937- *WhoHisp 94*
Rebollo-Lopez, Francisco *WhoAmL 94*
Rebollo-Lopez, Francisco 1938- *WhoAmP 93*
Reboredo, Pedro *WhoHisp 94*
Rebori, Robert Louis 1935- *WhoFI 94*
Reboul, Jaques Regis 1947- *WhoScEn 94*
Rebozo, Charles Gregory 1912- *WhoAm 94*
Rebstock, Irma Dell 1927- *WhoAmP 93*
Rebuck, Gail 1952- *IntWW 93*
Rebuck, Gail Ruth 1952- *Who 94*
Reby, Jacob W. 1947- *WhoAmL 94*
Recabo, Jaime Miguel 1950- *WhoAmL 94*
Recana, Mel Red *WhoAsA 94*
Recanati, Dina *WhoAmA 93*
Recanati, Elias Isaac 1932- *WhoFI 94*
Recanati, Raphael 1924- *WhoAm 94, WhoFI 94*
Recchi, Vincenzo 1945- *WhoScEn 94*
Recchia, Richard (Henry) 1885-1983 *WhoAmA 93N*
Recchion, Eugene Laverne 1918- *WhoFI 94*
Receveur, Betty Layman 1930- *WrDr 94*
Rech, Geza 1910- *NewGrDO*
Rechard, Ottis William 1924- *WhoAm 94, WhoWest 94*
Rechard, Paul Albert 1927- *WhoAm 94, WhoFI 94*
Rechcigl, Miloslav, Jr. 1930- *WhoAm 94*
Rechendorff, Torben 1937- *IntWW 93*
Rechholtz, Robert August 1937- *WhoFI 94*
Rechka, Mary Emily 1937- *WhoMW 93*
Recht, Phillip Edward 1945- *WhoAm 94, WhoAmL 94*
Rechter, Yacov 1924- *IntWW 93*
Rechtin, Eberhardt 1926- *WhoAm 94, WhoScEn 94, WhoWest 94*
Rechtsteiner, Steven Allen 1945- *WhoFI 94*
Rechtzeit, Seymour d1988 *WhoHol 92*
Rechtzigel, Sue Marie 1947- *WhoMW 93*
Rechy, John *DrAPF 93*
Rechy, John 1934- *HispLC [port]*
Rechy, John (Francisco) 1934- *GayLL, WrDr 94*
Rechy, John Francisco *WhoAm 94, WhoHisp 94*
Reck, Andrew Joseph 1927- *WhoAm 94, WrDr 94*
Reck, Francis James 1955- *WhoScEn 94*
Reck, Gregory Milton 1946- *WhoAm 94*
Reck, J. David *WhoAm 94*
Reck, Joel Marvin 1941- *WhoAm 94*
Reck, Richard Alan 1949- *WhoFI 94*
Reck, Waldo Emerson 1903- *WhoAm 94, WhoMW 93*
Reckamp, Douglas E. 1968- *WhoScEn 94*
Reckase, Mark Daniel 1944- *WhoScEn 94*
Reckdahl, Joan Marie 1936- *WhoAmP 93*
Recke, Elisabeth von der 1754-1833 *BlmGWL*
Recker, Catherine Rose 1950- *WhoMW 93*
Reckers, Philip Merle 1946- *WhoWest 94*
Reckitt, Basil Norman 1905- *Who 94*
Recklein, Linda Sue *WhoMW 93*
Recklinghausen, Marianne Von 1929- *WhoAmA 93*
Reckman, Robert Frederick 1922- *WhoAmP 93*
Recknagel, Richard Otto 1916-1991 *WhAm 10*
Reckord, Barry *ConDr 93*
Recktenwald, Fred William 1946- *WhoMW 93*
Record, Alice B. 1921- *WhoAmP 93*
Record, Lincoln Fredrick 1939- *WhoMW 93*
Record, Phillip Julius 1929- *WhoAm 94*
Record, Rush Hamil 1917- *WhoAmL 94*
Rectenwald, Gary Michael 1949- *WhoFI 94*
Rector, Baker R. 1949- *WhoAmL 94*
Rector, Brent Douglas 1949- *WhoAmL 94*
Rector, Bruce Alan 1963- *WhoAmL 94*
Rector, Bruce Johnson 1953- *WhoFI 94*
Rector, Clark Ellsworth 1934- *WhoFI 94*
Rector, Eugene Walter 1922- *WhoMW 93*
Rector, Floyd Clinton, Jr. 1929- *WhoAm 94*
Rector, Helen Carolyne 1929- *WhoMW 93*
Rector, John Michael 1943- *WhoAm 94, WhoAmL 94*
Rector, Lee Tate 1927- *WhoAmP 93*
Rector, Liam *DrAPF 93*
Rector, Milton Gage 1918- *WhoAm 94*
Rector, Nancy Lamp 1953- *WhoAmP 93*
Rector, Richard Robert 1925- *WhoAm 94*
Rector, Robert Wayman 1916- *WhoAm 94*
Rector, Shirley *WhoAmP 93*
Rector, William David 1953- *WhoMW 93*
Rector, William Gordon 1922- *WhoAmP 93*
Recznik, Mark Edward 1954- *WhoMW 93*
Reda, Robert Salvatore 1962- *WhoMW 93*
Redaelli Spreafico, Enrico 1911- *IntWW 93*
Redal, Javier *EncSF 93*
Redalen, Elton R. *WhoAmP 93*
Redalieu, Elliot 1939- *WhoScEn 94*
Redbone, Leon *WhoAm 94*
Redburn, Chris Richard 1950- *WhoAmL 94*
Redcay, Ronald C. 1949- *WhoAmL 94*
Redd, Albert Carter, Sr. 1917- *WhoBlA 94*
Redd, Charles Appleton 1954- *WhoAmL 94*
Redd, Charles Hardy 1936- *WhoAmP 93*
Redd, John Packard 1930- *WhoAmP 93*
Redd, Judy Ann 1939- *WhoMW 93*
Redd, M. Paul, Sr. 1928- *WhoBlA 94*
Redd, Mary-Robin *WhoHol 92*
Redd, Orial Anne 1924- *WhoBlA 94*
Redd, Richard James 1931- *WhoAmA 93*
Redd, Rudolph James 1924- *WhoScEn 94*
Redd, Thomasina A. 1941- *WhoBlA 94*
Redd, William L. 1950- *WhoBlA 94*
Redda, Kinfe Ken 1948- *WhoAm 94*
Reddall, H(enry) Hastings 1893-1989 *WhAm 10*
Reddan, Harold Jerome 1926- *WhoAm 94*
Reddaway, Brian *Who 94*
Reddaway, (William) Brian 1913- *Who 94*
Reddaway, David Norman 1953- *Who 94*

Reddaway, Norman *Who 94*
Reddaway, (George Frank) Norman 1918- *Who 94*
Reddaway, Peter (Brian) 1939- *WrDr 94*
Reddaway, William Brian 1913- *IntWW 93, WrDr 94*
Redd Ekks 1937- *WhoAmA 93*
Reddell, Donald Lee 1937- *WhoScEn 94*
Redden, Barry 1960- *WhoBlA 94*
Redden, Camille J. 1930- *WhoBlA 94*
Redden, David Normand 1949- *WhoAm 94*
Redden, Forrest Richard, Jr. 1937- *WhoFI 94*
Redden, Harral Arthur, Jr. 1936- *WhoFI 94*
Redden, Jack Allison 1926- *WhoAm 94*
Redden, James Anthony 1929- *WhoAm 94, WhoAmL 94, WhoAmP 93, WhoWest 94*
Redden, Joe Winston, Jr. 1951- *WhoAmL 94*
Redden, Kenneth Robert 1917- *WhoAm 94*
Redden, Lawrence Drew 1922- *WhoAm 94*
Redden, Roger Duffey 1932- *WhoAm 94*
Redder, Thomas H. 1948- *WhoAm 94*
Redder, Thomas Joseph *WhoAmP 93*
Reddi, A. Hari 1942- *WhoScEn 94*
Reddick, Alzo Jackson 1937- *WhoAmP 93, WhoBlA 94*
Reddick, Cecil d1986 *WhoHol 92*
Reddick, David Lowell 1959- *WhoFI 94*
Reddick, Linda H. 1916- *WhoBlA 94*
Reddick, Thomas J., Jr. 1919- *WhoBlA 94*
Reddien, Charles Henry, Jr. 1944- *WhoAmL 94, WhoWest 94*
Reddig, Walter Eduard 1936- *WhoMW 93*
Reddin, Jon Newcomb 1945- *WhoAmL 94*
Reddin, Keith 1956- *ConDr 93*
Redding, Arthur Francis 1964- *WhoMW 93*
Redding, Barbara J. 1938- *WhoMW 93*
Redding, David A(sbury) 1923- *WrDr 94*
Redding, Foster Kinyon 1929- *WhoAm 94*
Redding, Gregory J. 1948- *WhoWest 94*
Redding, John C. 1963- *WhoAmL 94*
Redding, Joseph Deighn 1859-1932 *NewGrDO*
Redding, Louis L. *WhoBlA 94*
Redding, Otis 1941-1967 *AfrAmAl 6 [port]*
Redding, Peter Stoddard 1938- *WhoFI 94*
Redding, Rogers Walker 1942- *WhoAm 94*
Reddington, Charles Leonard 1929- *WhoAmA 93*
Reddington, Joseph 1947- *WhoAm 94, WhoFI 94*
Reddington, (Clifford) Michael 1932- *Who 94*
Reddish, Vincent Cartledge 1926- *Who 94*
Reddix, Roscoe Chester 1933- *WhoAmA 93*
Reddoch, John B. 1956- *WhoAmL 94*
Reddoch, Mildred Lucas 1916- *WhoAm 94*
Reddway, Eddie d1919 *WhoHol 92*
Reddy, Bandaru S. 1932- *WhoAsA 94*
Reddy, C. Subba 1942- *WhoAsA 94*
Reddy, Chilecampalli Adinarayana 1941- *WhoScEn 94*
Reddy, Chilekampalli Adinarayana 1941- *WhoAsA 94*
Reddy, Churku Mohan 1942- *WhoAsA 94*
Reddy, Dhanireddy Ramalinga 1949- *WhoAsA 94*
Reddy, Eashwer K. 1944- *WhoAsA 94*
Reddy, Gudigopuram Bhaskar 1945- *WhoAsA 94*
Reddy, Gunda *WhoAsA 94*
Reddy, Guvvala Nagabhushana 1959- *WhoScEn 94*
Reddy, Helen 1941- *WhoHol 92*
Reddy, Helen 1942- *IntMPA 94*
Reddy, Helen Maxine 1941- *WhoAm 94*
Reddy, Indra Karan 1958- *WhoAsA 94*
Reddy, J. Narasimh *WhoScEn 94*
Reddy, Junuthula N. 1945- *WhoAsA 94*
Reddy, Kapuluru Chandrasekhara 1942- *WhoAsA 94*
Reddy, Kasu Brahmananda 1909- *IntWW 93*
Reddy, Krishna N. 1925- *WhoAmA 93*
Reddy, Krishna Narayana 1925- *WhoAm 94*
Reddy, Maureen T. 1955- *WrDr 94*
Reddy, Michael Bernard 1954- *WhoAmL 94*
Reddy, Nagendranath K. 1937- *WhoWest 94*
Reddy, Nallapu Narayan 1939- *WhoAsA 94*
Reddy, Narayana Muniswamy 1935- *WhoScEn 94*
Reddy, Narender Pabbathi 1947- *WhoAsA 94*
Reddy, Neelam Sanjiva 1913- *IntWW 93*
Reddy, Pannala Sathyanahayana 1950- *WhoAsA 94*
Reddy, Paul W. 1940- *WhoFI 94*
Reddy, Pradeep K. 1954- *WhoAsA 94*
Reddy, Pratap Chandupatla 1944- *WhoAm 94*
Reddy, Pratap P. 1950- *WhoAsA 94*
Reddy, Raj 1937- *WhoAsA 94*
Reddy, Rajasekara L. 1948- *WhoScEn 94*
Reddy, Ram Kadiri 1949- *WhoWest 94*
Reddy, Ramakrishna P. 1936- *WhoAsA 94*
Reddy, Robert Jackson 1937- *WhoAmP 93*
Reddy, (Neelam) Sanjiva 1913- *Who 94*
Reddy, Venkat Narsimha 1922- *WhoScEn 94*
Reddy, Yenemala Jaysimha 1968- *WhoFI 94*
Rede, George Henry 1952- *WhoHisp 94*
Redein, Alex S. 1912- *WhoAmA 93N*
Redeker, Allan Grant 1924- *WhoAm 94, WhoScEn 94*
Redeker, James Russell 1941- *WhoAm 94, WhoAmL 94*
Redeker, Jerrald Hale 1934- *WhoAm 94*
Redeker, Quinn 1936- *WhoHol 92*
Redelsperger, Kenneth 1940- *WhoAmP 93*
Redemann, Robert Paul 1951- *WhoAmL 94*
Redente, Edward Francis 1951- *WhoWest 94*
Reder, Bernard *WhAm 10*
Reder, Bernard 1897-1963 *WhoAmA 93N*
Reder, Lynne Marie 1950- *WhoScEn 94*
Redesdale, Baron 1967- *Who 94*
Redfern, John D. 1936- *WhoAm 94*
Redfern, John Joseph, III 1939- *WhoFI 94*
Redfern, Philip 1922- *Who 94*
Redfern, Richard Robert 1951- *WhoMW 93*
Redfern, Robert Seth 1933- *WhoAmP 93*
Redfield, Dennis *WhoHol 92*
Redfield, Edward W. 1869-1965 *WhoAmA 93N*
Redfield, Holland L., Jr. 1943- *WhoAmP 93*
Redfield, James Michael 1935- *WhoAm 94*
Redfield, John Duncan 1947- *WhoWest 94*
Redfield, Reuben Robert *WhoFI 94*
Redfield, Rochelle *WhoHol 92*
Redfield, William d1976 *WhoHol 92*
Red Fish d1928 *EncNAR*
Redford, Donald Bruce 1934- *WhoAm 94*
Redford, Donald Kirkman 1919- *Who 94*
Redford, Kent H(ubbard) 1955- *ConAu 141*
Redford, Robert *Who 94*
Redford, Robert 1937- *ConTFT 11, IntMPA 94, IntWW 93, WhoAm 94, WhoHol 92*
Redford, (Charles) Robert 1937- *Who 94*
Redgate, Edward Stewart 1925- *WhoScEn 94*
Redglare, Rockets 1949- *WhoHol 92*
Redgrave, Adrian Robert Frank 1944- *Who 94*
Redgrave, Corin 1939- *IntMPA 94, WhoHol 92*
Redgrave, Felicity 1920- *WhoAmA 93*
Redgrave, Jemma *WhoHol 92*
Redgrave, Lynn 1943- *IntMPA 94, IntWW 93, Who 94, WhoAm 94, WhoHol 92*
Redgrave, Michael d1985 *WhoHol 92*
Redgrave, Natasha 1963- *WhoHol 92*
Redgrave, Rachel *Who 94*
Redgrave, Roy Michael Frederick 1925- *Who 94*
Redgrave, Vanessa 1937- *IntMPA 94, IntWW 93, Who 94, WhoAm 94, WhoHol 92*
Redgrove, Peter 1932- *BlmGEL [port], WrDr 94*
Redgrove, Peter (William) 1932- *EncSF 93*
Redgrove, Peter William 1932- *IntWW 93, Who 94*
Redgwick, Hubert Arthur 1906- *WhoFI 94*
Red Hat, Edward 1898-1982 *EncNAR*
Red Hawk c. 1829- *EncNAR*
Redhead, Brian 1929- *Who 94*
Redhead, Michael Logan Gonne 1929- *Who 94*
Redhead, Paul Aveling 1924- *WhoAm 94*
Redheffer, Raymond Moos 1921- *WhoAm 94, WhoScEn 94, WhoWest 94*
Redican, Lois D. 1944- *WhoFI 94*
Redick, Eva Jane 1901- *WhoAm 94*
Redig, Dale Francis 1929- *WhoAm 94*
Rediger, Richard Kim 1950- *WhoAmL 94*
Rediker, Robert Harmon 1924- *WhoAm 94*
Reding, John A. 1944- *WhoAmL 94*
Reding, Leo J. 1924- *WhoAmP 93*
Reding, Sheila Marie 1942- *WhoMW 93*
Reding, Viviane 1951- *WhoWomW 91*
Redinger, James Collins 1937- *WhoFI 94*
Redinger, Walter Fred 1942- *WhoAmA 93*
Redington, Rowland Wells 1924- *WhoAm 94*
Redisch, Walter d1993 *NewYTBS 93 [port]*
Redish, Edward Frederick 1942- *WhoScEn 94*
Redl, Hans 1914- *BuCMET*
Redleaf, Diane Lynn 1954- *WhoAmL 94*
Redlich, Marc 1946- *WhoAmL 94*
Redlich, Norman 1925- *WhoAm 94*
Redlich, Robert Walter 1928- *WhoMW 93, WhoScEn 94*
Redlin, Rolland W. 1920- *WhoAmP 93*
Redlinger, Samuel Edward 1949- *WhoMW 93, WhoScEn 94*
Redman, Amanda *WhoHol 92*
Redman, Barbara Klug *WhoAm 94*
Redman, Charles E. 1943- *WhoAmP 93*
Redman, Clarence Owen 1942- *WhoAmL 94*
Redman, Denis Arthur Kay 1910- *Who 94*
Redman, Dewey 1931- *AfrAmAl 6*
Redman, Don d1964 *WhoHol 92*
Redman, Don 1900-1964 *AfrAmAl 6*
Redman, Eric 1948- *WhoAm 94, WhoAmL 94*
Redman, Henry fl. 1495-1528 *DcNaB MP*
Redman, James W. 1915- *WhoBlA 94*
Redman, John B. 1914- *IntWW 93*
Redman, Joyce 1918- *WhoHol 92*
Redman, Lister Appleton 1933- *WrDr 94*
Redman, Maurice 1922- *Who 94*
Redman, Peter 1935- *WhoAm 94*
Redman, Richard Elson 1938- *WhoAmP 93*
Redman, Robert Shelton 1935- *WhoScEn 94*
Redman, Steven Phillip 1965- *WhoScEn 94*
Redman, Sydney 1914- *Who 94*
Redman, Timothy Paul 1950- *WhoAm 94*
Redman, William Charles 1923- *WhoAm 94*
Redman, William W., Jr. 1933- *WhoAmP 93*
Redman-Johnson, Chloe Louise 1942- *WhoFI 94*
Redmayne, Clive 1927- *Who 94*
Redmayne, Nicholas (John) 1938- *Who 94*
Redmer, Alfred Willy, Jr. 1956- *WhoAmP 93*
Redmon, Ann Louise 1925- *WhoBlA 94*
Redmon, Harry Smith, Jr. 1934- *WhoAm 94, WhoAmL 94*
Redmon, Jeffrey Allen 1957- *WhoMW 93*
Redmon, John King 1920- *WhoFI 94*
Redmon, Wesley Scott 1966- *WhoMW 93*
Redmond, Barbara Wright 1960- *WhoMW 93*
Redmond, Darlene Leola 1963- *WhoAmL 94*
Redmond, David Dudley 1944- *WhoAmL 94*
Redmond, Donald Eugene, Jr. 1939- *WhoAm 94*
Redmond, Edward Crosby 1921- *WhoAmL 94*
Redmond, Elmer E. d1955 *WhoHol 92*
Redmond, Eugene B. *DrAPF 93*
Redmond, Eugene B. 1937- *BlkWr 2, WhoBlA 94*
Redmond, Frances Harrietta 1921- *WhoMW 93*
Redmond, Gail Elizabeth 1946- *WhoScEn 94*
Redmond, Gerald 1934- *WrDr 94*
Redmond, James 1918- *Who 94*
Redmond, James Melvin 1947- *WhoAm 94*
Redmond, James Ronald 1928- *WhoAm 94*
Redmond, Jane Smith 1948- *WhoBlA 94*
Redmond, John Charles 1931- *WhoAm 94*
Redmond, John Durham 1948- *WhoFI 94*
Redmond, Kelly Thomas 1952- *WhoWest 94*
Redmond, Liam 1913- *WhoHol 92*
Redmond, Marge *WhoHol 92*
Redmond, Martin 1937- *Who 94*
Redmond, Moira *WhoHol 92*
Redmond, Paul Anthony 1937- *WhoFI 94*
Redmond, Richard Anthony 1947- *WhoAmL 94*
Redmond, Robert 1934- *WhoAmL 94*
Redmond, Robert Francis 1927- *WhoScEn 94*
Redmond, Robert Spencer 1919- *Who 94*
Redmond, Rozze 1952- *WhoAmA 93*
Redmond, William d1954 *WhoHol 92*
Redmond, William A. 1908- *WhoAmP 93*
Redmond, William Joseph, Jr. 1958- *WhoFI 94*
Redmont, Bernard Sidney 1918- *WhoAm 94*
Redmore, Derek 1938- *WhoScEn 94*
Redmount, Ian H. 1956- *WhoMW 93, WhoScEn 94*
Red Nest, William *EncNAR*
Redo, David Lucien 1937- *WhoFI 94*
Redo, Maria E. 1925- *WhoAmP 93*
Redo, Martha Maria 1960- *WhoAmL 94*
Redo, Philip Lappano 1956- *WhoFI 94, WhoMW 93*
Redo, Saverio Frank 1920- *WhoAm 94*
Redon, Joel 1961- *WrDr 94*
Redon, Leonard Eugene 1951- *WhoBlA 94*
Redondo (Valencia), Marcos 1893-1976 *NewGrDO*
Redondo, Antonio 1948- *WhoWest 94*
Redondo, Diego Ramon 1964- *WhoScEn 94*
Redondo-Churchward, Irene 1942- *WhoHisp 94*
Redondo de Feldman, Susana 1913- *WhoHisp 94*
Redpath, John Thomas 1915- *Who 94*
Redrick, Virginia Pendleton 1945- *WhoBlA 94*
Redsell, Peter T. W. *WhoAm 94*
Redshaw, Peter Robert Gransden 1942- *Who 94*
Redshaw, Seymour Cunningham 1906- *Who 94*
Redshaw, Thomas Dillon *DrAPF 93*
Redsky, James, Sr. 1899- *EncNAR*
Red Star, Kevin 1943- *WhoAmA 93*
Redstone, Edward S. 1928- *IntMPA 94*
Redstone, Louis Gordon 1903- *WhoAm 94, WhoAmA 93*
Redstone, Sumner 1923- *News 94-1 [port]*
Redstone, Sumner Murray 1923- *IntMPA 94, WhoAm 94, WhoAmL 94, WhoFI 94*
Redus, Gary Eugene 1956- *WhoBlA 94*
Redway, Alan Arthur Sydney 1935- *WhoAm 94*
Red Weasel c. 1831- *EncNAR*
Redwine, Edward David 1947- *WhoAmP 93*
Redwine, Robert Allan 1942- *WhoAmL 94*
Red Wing, Princess d1974 *WhoHol 92*
Redwing, Rodd d1971 *WhoHol 92*
Redwood, John (Alan) 1951- *ConAu 41NR, WrDr 94*
Redwood, John Alan 1951- *Who 94*
Redwood, Peter (Boverton) 1937- *Who 94*
Redwood, Richard George 1936- *WhoAm 94*
Redzierska-Truszynska, Dobrochna *WhoWomW 91*
Ree, Donna 1950- *WhoMW 93*
Reece, Arley 1945- *NewGrDO*
Reece, Avalon B. 1927- *WhoBlA 94*
Reece, Beth Pauley 1945- *WhoFI 94, WhoMW 93*
Reece, Brian d1962 *WhoHol 92*
Reece, Charles (Hugh) 1927- *Who 94*
Reece, (James) Gordon 1930- *IntWW 93, Who 94*
Reece, Guy L., II *WhoBlA 94*
Reece, Joe Wilson 1935- *WhoAm 94*
Reece, Judith Fleur 1941- *WhoAmP 93*
Reece, Laurence Hobson, III 1952- *WhoAmL 94*
Reece, Marshall Philip 1954- *WhoMW 93*
Reece, Marynell D. 1920- *WhoAmP 93*
Reece, Maynard 1920- *WhoAmA 93*
Reece, Maynard Fred 1920- *WhoAm 94*
Reece, Monte Meredith 1945- *WhoAm 94, WhoAmL 94, WhoWest 94*
Reece, Paul Richard 1955- *WhoMW 93*
Reece, Paynter *Who 94*
Reece, (Edward Vans) Paynter 1936- *Who 94*
Reece, Robert William 1942- *WhoAm 94, WhoScEn 94*
Reece, Steven 1947- *WhoBlA 94*
Reece, Wayne 1957- *WhoAmP 93*
Reed, Adam Victor 1946- *WhoAm 94*
Reed, Addison W. 1929- *WhoBlA 94*
Reed, Adolphus Redolph 1912- *WhoBlA 94*
Reed, Adrian Harbottle 1921- *Who 94*
Reed, Alan d1977 *WhoHol 92*
Reed, Alan, Jr. 1938- *WhoHol 92*
Reed, Alan Barry 1940- *WhoAmP 93*
Reed, Alan L. 1933- *WhoAm 94*
Reed, Alec Edward 1934- *Who 94*
Reed, Alfonzo 1938- *WhoBlA 94*
Reed, Alfred 1921- *WhoAm 94*
Reed, Alfred Byron 1916- *WhoAm 94*
Reed, Allen Ralph 1959- *WhoAmL 94*
Reed, Allene Wallace *WhoBlA 94*
Reed, Alyson 1958- *WhoHol 92*
Reed, Andre Darnell 1964- *WhoAm 94, WhoBlA 94*
Reed, Andrew 1837-1914 *DcNaB MP*
Reed, April Anne 1930- *Who 94*
Reed, Barry St. George Austin 1931- *Who 94*
Reed, Beatrice M. 1916- *WhoBlA 94*
Reed, Berenice Anne 1934- *WhoFI 94*
Reed, Betty Lou 1927- *WhoAmP 93*
Reed, Billy d1974 *WhoHol 92*
Reed, Bruce Allen 1957- *WhoFI 94*
Reed, Bruce Cameron 1954- *WhoScEn 94*

Reed, Burness Jean 1930- WhoAmP 93
Reed, Carol d1976 WhoHol 92
Reed, Charles Allen 1912- WhoAm 94
Reed, Charles Bass 1941- IntWW 93, WhoAm 94
Reed, Charles Eli 1913- WhoScEn 94
Reed, Charles Emmett 1922- WhoAm 94
Reed, Charles Kenneth 1917- WhoScEn 94
Reed, Charles Ray 1944- WhoAmP 93
Reed, Christine Emerson 1944- WhoAmP 93
Reed, Christopher Robert 1948- WhoScEn 94
Reed, Clarence Hammit, III 1957- WhoBlA 94
Reed, Clarence Raymond 1932- WhoAm 94
Reed, Clarke Thomas 1928- WhoAmP 93
Reed, Cleota WhoAmA 93
Reed, Clifford C(ecil) 1911- EncSF 93
Reed, Constance Louise WhoMW 93
Reed, Cordell 1938- WhoBlA 94, WhoFI 94
Reed, Daisy Frye WhoBlA 94
Reed, Dale Devon 1931- WhoWest 94
Reed, Dallas John 1929- WhoWest 94
Reed, Darwin Cramer 1915- WhoAm 94
Reed, David 1945- Who 94
Reed, David 1946- WhoAm 94, WhoAmA 93
Reed, David Benson 1927- WhoAm 94
Reed, David Doss 1956- WhoMW 93
Reed, David George 1945- WhoFI 94, WhoWest 94
Reed, David V. 1924- EncSF 93
Reed, Dean d1986 WhoHol 92
Reed, Dennis James 1946- WhoAmA 93
Reed, Derryl L. WhoBlA 94
Reed, Diana Lynn 1943- WhoMW 93
Reed, Diane Gray 1945- WhoFI 94, WhoScEn 94
Reed, Diane Marie 1934- WhoScEn 94
Reed, Doel 1894- WhoAmA 93N
Reed, Dolores M. 1932- WhoAmP 93
Reed, Don S. 1945- See Statler Brothers, The WhoHol 92
Reed, Donald d1973 WhoHol 92
Reed, Donald Blackhall 1915- WhoAmP 93
Reed, Donald James 1930- WhoScEn 94
Reed, Donna d1986 WhoHol 92
Reed, Douglas Byron 1946- WhoFI 94
Reed, Douglas F. 1949- WhoFI 94
Reed, Dwayne Milton 1933- WhoScEn 94
Reed, Dwight Thomas 1955- WhoWest 94
Reed, Eddie 1945- WhoBlA 94
Reed, Edward Cornelius, Jr. 1924- WhoAm 94, WhoAmL 94, WhoWest 94
Reed, Edward John 1913- Who 94
Reed, Eliot 1909- WrDr 94
Reed, Emmett X. ConAu 41NR
Reed, Falani W. WhoAmP 93
Reed, Farie Mae 1931- WhoAmP 93
Reed, Flint Winter 1933- WhoAmA 93
Reed, Florence d1967 WhoHol 92
Reed, Florine 1905- WhoBlA 94
Reed, Floyd T. 1915- WhoBlA 94
Reed, Frank Fremont, II 1928- WhoWest 94
Reed, Frank Metcalf 1912- WhoFI 94, WhoWest 94
Reed, Frederick R. 1948- WhoAmL 94
Reed, Gary W. WhoAmP 93
Reed, Gavin d1990 WhoHol 92
Reed, Gavin Barras 1934- Who 94
Reed, Geoffrey WhoHol 92
Reed, George E. d1952 WhoHol 92
Reed, George Farrell 1922- WhoAm 94
Reed, George Ford, Jr. 1946- WhoFI 94
Reed, George Francis 1928- WhoAm 94
Reed, George Franklin 1935- WhAm 10
Reed, George H. d1952 WhoHol 92
Reed, Gerald Wilfred 1945- WhoMW 93
Reed, Geraldine Sumner 1917- WhoAmP 93
Reed, Gerard Alexander 1941- WhoWest 94
Reed, Glen Alfred 1951- WhoAm 94
Reed, Gordon Wies 1899- WhoAm 94
Reed, Gregory 1945- WhoAmL 94
Reed, Gregory J. 1948- WhoBlA 94
Reed, H. Carlyle 1915- WhoAm 94
Reed, H. Ellis d1938 WhoHol 92
Reed, H(erbert) Owen 1910- ConAu 42NR, NewGrDO, WrDr 94
Reed, Hal 1921- WhoAmA 93
Reed, Harold 1937- WhoAmA 93
Reed, Helen Bernice 1917- WhoWest 94
Reed, Helen Skuggedal 1948- WhoAmL 94, WhoMW 93
Reed, Horace Curtis 1917- WhoAm 94
Reed, Howard Alexander 1920- WhoAm 94
Reed, Ishmael 1938- AfrAmAl 6 [port], EncSF 93, WrDr 94
Reed, Ishmael (Scott) 1938- BlkWr 2
Reed, Ishmael Scott 1938- IntWW 93, WhoAm 94, WhoBlA 94
Reed, J. Walter 1933- WhoAm 94
Reed, Jack 1949- CngDr 93
Reed, James DrAPF 93
Reed, James 1723-1807 WhAmRev
Reed, James 1922- WrDr 94
Reed, James 1935- WhoBlA 94
Reed, James Alexander, Jr. 1930- WhoAmL 94
Reed, James Anthony 1939- WhoWest 94
Reed, James Donald 1940- WhoAm 94
Reed, James Earl 1957- WhoWest 94
Reed, James W. 1935- WhoBlA 94
Reed, James Wesley 1944- WhoAm 94
Reed, James Whitfield 1935- WhoAm 94
Reed, James William, Jr. 1947- WhoAmL 94
Reed, Jane Barbara Who 94
Reed, Jane Garson 1948- WhoMW 93
Reed, Janet 1916- IntDcB [port]
Reed, Janet Lynn 1951- WhoAm 94
Reed, Jasper Percell 1929- WhoBlA 94
Reed, Jeremy 1951- WrDr 94
Reed, Jerry 1937- WhoHol 92
Reed, Jesse Floyd 1920- WhoAmA 93
Reed, Joann 1939- WhoBlA 94
Reed, Joe 1945- WhoAmP 93
Reed, Joe Louis 1938- WhoAmP 93, WhoBlA 94
Reed, Joel Leston 1951- WhoAm 94, WhoFI 94
Reed, John Alan 1951- WhoAmL 94
Reed, John Alton 1931- WhoAm 94
Reed, John Charles 1930- WhoScEn 94
Reed, John Francis 1949- WhoAm 94, WhoAmP 93
Reed, John Franklin 1917- WhoAm 94
Reed, John G. 1929- WhoAm 94, WhoAmL 94
Reed, John H., III 1949- WhoAmP 93
Reed, John Hathaway 1921- WhoAm 94, WhoAmP 93
Reed, John Langdale 1931- Who 94
Reed, John R. DrAPF 93
Reed, John Shedd 1917- WhoAm 94, WhoMW 93
Reed, John Shepard 1939- WhoAm 94, WhoFI 94
Reed, John Silas 1887-1920 AmSocL [port]
Reed, John Squires, II 1949- WhoAm 94, WhoAmL 94
Reed, John Wesley 1918- WhoAm 94
Reed, Joseph 1741-1785 AmRev, WhAmRev [port]
Reed, Joseph V., Jr. 1937- WhoAmP 93
Reed, Joseph W. 1932- WrDr 94
Reed, Joseph Wayne 1932- WhoAm 94
Reed, Joyce Ann Borden 1939- WhoAm 94
Reed, Julian d1934 WhoHol 92
Reed, Kathleen Rand 1947- WhoBlA 94
Reed, Kathlyn Louise 1940- WhoAm 94
Reed, Keith Allen 1939- WhoAm 94, WhoAmL 94
Reed, Kenneth G. 1917- WhoAm 94
Reed, Kevin Francis 1948- WhoAm 94, WhoAmL 94
Reed, Kit DrAPF 93, WrDr 94
Reed, Kit 1932- EncSF 93
Reed, Lambert S., II 1937- WhoBlA 94
Reed, Larita D. 1960- WhoBlA 94
Reed, Laura Ann 1960- WhoMW 93
Reed, Laurance Douglas 1937- Who 94
Reed, Laurence A. 1939- WhoFI 94
Reed, Leon Samuel 1949- WhoFI 94
Reed, Leslie d1915 WhoHol 92
Reed, Leslie Edwin 1925- Who 94
Reed, Lester James 1925- WhoAm 94, WhoScEn 94
Reed, Liki, II 1954- WhoAmP 93
Reed, Lloyd H. 1922- WhoBlA 94
Reed, Lola N. 1923- WhoBlA 94
Reed, Lou 1942- IntWW 93, WhoAm 94, WhoHol 92
Reed, Lowell A., Jr. 1930- WhoAm 94, WhoAmL 94
Reed, Margaret WhoHol 92
Reed, Maria Dawn 1967- WhoMW 93
Reed, Marshall d1980 WhoHol 92
Reed, Mary Hutchings 1951- WhoAm 94
Reed, Mary Lou WhoAmP 93, WhoWest 94
Reed, Matthew WhoHol 92
Reed, Maurice L. 1924- WhoBlA 94
Reed, Maxwell d1974 WhoHol 92
Reed, Michael Alan 1953- WhoScEn 94
Reed, Michael E. 1942- WhoAmL 94
Reed, Michael Ernest 1949- WhoMW 93
Reed, Michael H. 1949- WhoBlA 94
Reed, Michael Haywood 1949- WhoAm 94, WhoAmL 94
Reed, Michael Robert 1953- WhoScEn 94
Reed, Nathaniel Pryor 1933- WhoAmP 93
Reed, Nicholas Rathburn 1943- WhoWest 94
Reed, Nigel (Vernon) 1913- Who 94
Reed, Norman Dee 1929- WhoMW 93
Reed, Oliver Who 94
Reed, Oliver 1938- IntMPA 94, IntWW 93, WhoHol 92
Reed, (Robert) Oliver 1938- Who 94
Reed, Orville L., III 1947- WhoAmL 94
Reed, Pamela 1949- WhoAm 94
Reed, Pamela 1950- WhoHol 92
Reed, Pamela 1953- IntMPA 94
Reed, Pat 1946- WhoAmP 93
Reed, Patrick Norman 1947- WhoWest 94
Reed, Paul WhoHol 92
Reed, Paul Allen 1919- WhoAm 94, WhoAmA 93
Reed, Peter EncSF 93
Reed, Peter N. WhoHisp 94
Reed, Philip 1908- WhoHol 92
Reed, Philip Dunham 1899-1989 WhAm 10
Reed, Ray Paul 1927- WhoScEn 94, WhoWest 94
Reed, Raymond Deryl 1930- WhoAm 94
Reed, Rebecca S. 1964- WhoWest 94
Reed, Rex 1938- WhoAm 94, WhoHol 92, WrDr 94
Reed, Rex Raymond 1922- WhoAm 94
Reed, Richard Addison WhoHol 92
Reed, Richard John 1922- IntWW 93, WhoAm 94
Reed, Rick 1947- WhoAmP 93
Reed, Robert 1932- WhoHol 92
Reed, Robert 1932-1992 AnObit 1992, ConTFT 11
Reed, Robert 1956- EncSF 93
Reed, Robert Alan 1942- WhoAm 94, WhoFI 94
Reed, Robert Daniel 1941- WhoAm 94
Reed, Robert Dixon, Sr. 1927- WhoFI 94
Reed, Robert George, III 1927- WhoAm 94, WhoFI 94, WhoWest 94
Reed, Robert Marshall 1941- WhoScEn 94
Reed, Robert Michael 1957- WhoFI 94
Reed, Robert Monroe 1932- WhoAm 94
Reed, Robert Phillip 1952- WhoAmL 94
Reed, Robi WhoBlA 94
Reed, Rodney J. 1932- WhoBlA 94
Reed, Sam Glen 1946- WhoAmP 93
Reed, Sam Sumner 1941- WhoAmP 93
Reed, Scott Warren 1949- WhoFI 94
Reed, Shanna 1955- WhoHol 92
Reed, Sharon Lee 1953- WhoScEn 94
Reed, Sheila A. 1958- WhoBlA 94
Reed, Sheldon Clark 1910- WhoMW 93
Reed, Sherman Kennedy 1919- WhoAm 94
Reed, Simon 1941- WrDr 94
Reed, Stanley 1911- WrDr 94
Reed, Stanley Foster 1917- WhoAm 94
Reed, Stanley William 1911- Who 94
Reed, Stephen Russell 1949- WhoAmP 93
Reed, Steven Mike 1946- WhoFI 94
Reed, Suellen WhoAmP 93
Reed, Susan 1927- WhoHol 92
Reed, T(erence) J(ames) 1937- WrDr 94
Reed, Talbot Baines 1852-1893 DcLB 141
Reed, Tammy Michelle 1966- WhoMW 93
Reed, Ted Brooks 1923- WhoAmP 93
Reed, Terence James 1937- Who 94
Reed, Theresa Greene 1923- WhoBlA 94
Reed, Thomas Brackett 1839-1902 HisWorL [port]
Reed, Thomas Care 1934- IntWW 93, WhoAm 94
Reed, Thomas Clayton 1951- WhoAm 94, WhoAmL 94
Reed, Thomas German 1817-1888 NewGrDO
Reed, Thomas J. 1927- WhoBlA 94
Reed, Thomas Thornton 1902- Who 94, WrDr 94
Reed, Tony Norman 1951- WhoAm 94
Reed, Tracy WhoHol 92
Reed, Tracy 1949- WhoHol 92
Reed, Travis Dean 1930- WhoAm 94
Reed, Van EncSF 93
Reed, Vincent Emory 1928- WhoAm 94, WhoBlA 94
Reed, Vivian WhoHol 92
Reed, Vivian d1989 WhoHol 92
Reed, W. Franklin 1946- WhoAm 94, WhoAmL 94
Reed, Wallace Allison 1916- WhoAm 94
Reed, Wallace Smart 1945- WhoFI 94
Reed, Walt Arnold 1917- WhoAmA 93
Reed, Walter 1851-1902 WorScD [port]
Reed, Walter 1916- WhoHol 92
Reed, Walter Gurnee Dyer 1952- WhoAm 94
Reed, Wilbur R. 1936- WhoBlA 94
Reed, William Arthur 1947- WhoWest 94
Reed, William Doyle 1897- WhAm 10
Reed, William F. WhoAmP 93
Reed, William N. 1950- WhoAmL 94
Reed, William Piper, Jr. 1942- WhoScEn 94
Reed, Willis 1942- BasBi, WhoAm 94, WhoBlA 94
Reed, Willis 1943- AfrAmAl 6
Reede, James William, Jr. 1952- WhoBlA 94
Reeder, Carolyn 1937- WrDr 94
Reeder, Charles Benton 1922- WhoAm 94
Reeder, Charles C. 1953- WhoAmL 94
Reeder, Colin (Dawson) 1938- ConAu 141, SmATA 74 [port]
Reeder, David Scott 1944- WhoMW 93
Reeder, Don David 1935- WhoMW 93
Reeder, F. Robert 1943- WhoAmL 94
Reeder, James Arthur 1933- WhoAmL 94
Reeder, Joe Robert 1947- WhoAm 94, WhoAmL 94
Reeder, John 1949- Who 94
Reeder, John P., Jr. 1937- WhoAm 94
Reeder, L. Martin, Jr. 1955- WhoAmL 94
Reeder, Mike Fredrick 1955- WhoScEn 94
Reeder, Odette Kehne 1930- WhoAmP 93
Reeder, Oliver Howard 1916- WhoAm 94
Reeder, Randy Marcelle 1956- WhoWest 94
Reeder, Richard W. 1961- WhoFI 94
Reeder, Robert Harry 1930- WhoAm 94, WhoAmL 94, WhoMW 93
Reeder, Robert R. 1944- WhoAmL 94
Reeder, Samuel Kenneth 1938- WhoWest 94
Reed-Graham, Lois L. 1933- WhoWest 94
Reed-Miller, Rosemary E. 1939- WhoBlA 94
Reed-Purvis, Henry 1928- Who 94
Reeds, Robert Terrill 1932- WhoWest 94
Reedstrom, Bradley Kent 1961- WhoFI 94
Reedy, Frances Starr 1948- WhoMW 93
Reedy, George E(dward) 1917- WrDr 94
Reedy, George Edward 1917- IntWW 93, WhoAm 94
Reedy, Jerry Edward 1936- WhoAm 94
Reedy, John J. 1927- WhoAmP 93
Reedy, Mitsuno Ishii 1941- WhoAmA 93
Reedy, Norris John 1934- Who 94
Reef, Arthur 1916- WhoAm 94
Reeg, Kurtis Bradford 1954- WhoAmL 94, WhoMW 93
Reeke, George Norman, Jr. WhoScEn 94
Reeker, Larry H. 1943- WhoScEn 94
Reekie, Charles Douglas WhoFI 94
Reekie, Henry Enfield 1907- Who 94
Reel, Shaun Delane 1964- WhoFI 94
Reel, Virginia WhoHol 92
Reeman, Douglas (Edward) 1924- WrDr 94
Reems, Harry 1947- WhoHol 92
Reen, Jeremiah Joseph 1942- WhoAm 94
Reen, Terry Peter 1951- WhoMW 93
Reents, James William 1948- WhoMW 93
Reents, Sue WhoWest 94
Reents, Sue 1946- WhoAmP 93
Reep, Edward Arnold 1918- WhoAm 94, WhoAmA 93
Reep, Robert Gregg 1954- WhoAmP 93
Rees Who 94
Rees, Baron 1926- Who 94
Rees, Alan WhoHisp 94
Rees, Albert 1921-1992 AnObit 1992
Rees, Albert (Everett) 1921-1992 WhAm 10
Rees, Alfred William 1925- WhoAm 94
Rees, Angharad 1949- WhoHol 92
Rees, Arthur d1960 WhoHol 92
Rees, Arthur Morgan 1912- Who 94
Rees, Barbara 1934- WrDr 94
Rees, Brian 1929- Who 94, WrDr 94
Rees, Brinley Roderick 1919- Who 94
Rees, Charles H. G. 1922- WhoAm 94
Rees, Charles Wayne 1927- IntWW 93, Who 94
Rees, Clifford Harcourt, Jr. 1936- WhoAm 94
Rees, David 1918- Who 94
Rees, David (Bartlett) 1936- WrDr 94
Rees, David (Bartlett) 1936-1993 GayLL
Rees, David Allan 1936- IntWW 93, Who 94
Rees, David Bartlett 1936-1993 ConAu 141, SmATA 76
Rees, David Charles 1958- WhoScEn 94
Rees, David William Edward 1936- WhoFI 94
Rees, Edward d1978 WhoHol 92
Rees, Edward Randolph d1976 WhoHol 92
Rees, Elaine 1940- WhoFI 94
Rees, Ennis DrAPF 93
Rees, Erica Sue 1956- WhoMW 93
Rees, Frank William, Jr. 1943- WhoFI 94, WhoScEn 94
Rees, Gomer DrAPF 93
Rees, Grover Joseph, III 1951- WhoAm 94
Rees, Gwendolen Who 94
Rees, (Florence) Gwendolen 1906- Who 94
Rees, Harland 1909- Who 94
Rees, Haydn Who 94
Rees, (Thomas Morgan) Haydn 1915- Who 94
Rees, Helen Blodwen 1960- Who 94

Rees, Henry 1916- *WrDr 94*
Rees, Hubert 1923- *IntWW 93, Who 94*
Rees, Hugh *Who 94*
Rees, (John Edward) Hugh 1928- *Who 94*
Rees, Hugh Francis E. *Who 94*
Rees, Ioan Bowen 1929- *WrDr 94*
Rees, Ivor *Who 94*
Rees, (John) Ivor *Who 94*
Rees, Joan d1983 *WhoHol 92*
Rees, Joan 1927- *WrDr 94*
Rees, John *Who 94, WhoHol 92*
Rees, (Anthony) John (David) 1943- *Who 94*
Rees, John Charles 1949- *Who 94*
Rees, John Robert 1930- *WhoAm 94*
Rees, John Samuel 1931- *Who 94*
Rees, Lane Charles *WhoAmP 93*
Rees, Lane Charles 1951- *WhoFI 94, WhoWest 94*
Rees, Lesley Howard 1942- *Who 94*
Rees, (George) Leslie (Clarke) 1905- *WrDr 94*
Rees, Leslie Lloyd 1919- *Who 94*
Rees, Linford *Who 94*
Rees, (William) Linford (Llewelyn) 1914- *Who 94*
Rees, Llewellyn *Who 94*
Rees, Llewellyn 1901- *WhoHol 92*
Rees, (Walter) Llewellyn 1901- *Who 94*
Rees, Martin (John) 1942- *Who 94*
Rees, Martin John 1942- *IntWW 93, WhoScEn 94*
Rees, Merlyn *IntWW 93*
Rees, Meuric *Who 94*
Rees, (Richard Ellis) Meuric 1924- *Who 94*
Rees, Michael *Who 94*
Rees, (Richard) Michael 1935- *Who 94*
Rees, Michael Joseph 1954- *WhoMW 93*
Rees, Mina Spiegel 1902- *WhoAm 94*
Rees, Natalie H. 1949- *WhoAmL 94*
Rees, Nigel (Thomas) 1944- *WrDr 94*
Rees, Owen 1934- *Who 94*
Rees, Paul Stromberg 1900- *WrDr 94*
Rees, Peter Magnall 1921- *Who 94*
Rees, Peter Wynne 1948- *Who 94*
Rees, Philip 1941- *Who 94*
Rees, Ray 1943- *Who 94*
Rees, Raymond F. 1944- *WhoWest 94*
Rees, Richard John William 1917- *Who 94*
Rees, Richard-Lewis 1950- *ConAu 142*
Rees, Rick Stephen 1953- *WhoFI 94*
Rees, Roger 1944- *IntMPA 94, WhoAm 94, WhoHol 92*
Rees, Rosemary 1876-1963 *BlmGWL*
Rees, Sherrel Jerry Evans 1926- *WhoAm 94*
Rees, Stanley *Who 94*
Rees, (Charles William) Stanley 1907- *Who 94*
Rees, Stephen J. 1947- *WhoAmP 93*
Rees, Thomas L. 1939- *WhoAmP 93*
Rees, Thomas M. 1925- *WhoAmP 93*
Rees, Tom 1947- *WhoAmP 93*
Rees, Warren David 1956- *WhoAmL 94*
Rees, William Howard Guest 1928- *Who 94*
Rees, William Hurst 1917- *Who 94*
Rees, William James 1922- *WhoWest 94*
Rees, William Linford (Llewelyn) 1914- *WrDr 94*
Reese, Albert Moore *WhoWest 94*
Reese, Alferd George 1934- *WhoMW 93*
Reese, Ann N. *WhoAm 94, WhoFI 94*
Reese, Bob L. 1929- *WhoAmP 93*
Reese, Charles L. 1862-1940 *WorInv*
Reese, Charles Lee, Jr. 1903-1989 *WhAm 10*
Reese, Colin Bernard 1930- *IntWW 93, Who 94, WhoScEn 94*
Reese, Colin Edward 1950- *Who 94*
Reese, Daniel G. 1927- *WhoAmP 93*
Reese, David 1961- *WhoAmL 94*
Reese, Della 1931- *ConBlB 6 [port], WhoAm 94, WhoBlA 94*
Reese, Della 1932- *IntMPA 94, WhoHol 92*
Reese, Douglas Wayne 1963- *WhoMW 93*
Reese, Errol Lynn 1939- *WhoAm 94*
Reese, Francis Edward 1919- *WhoAm 94*
Reese, Frederick D. 1929- *WhoBlA 94*
Reese, Gary Fuller 1938- *WhoWest 94*
Reese, Glenn G. *WhoAmP 93*
Reese, Gregory Lamarr 1949- *WhoBlA 94*
Reese, Harry Browne 1926-1991 *WhAm 10*
Reese, Harry Edwin, Jr. 1928- *WhoAm 94*
Reese, Hayne Waring 1931- *WhoAm 94*
Reese, Herschel Henry 1935- *WhoMW 93, WhoScEn 94*
Reese, Howard Fred 1947- *WhoFI 94*
Reese, James d1960 *WhoHol 92*
Reese, Janet Anne 1953- *WhoAmL 94*
Reese, Jim L. 1958- *WhoAmP 93*
Reese, John Rathbone 1944- *WhoAm 94*
Reese, John Robert 1939- *WhoAm 94*
Reese, Kenneth Wendell 1930-1991 *WhAm 10*
Reese, Kirk David 1948- *WhoAmL 94*
Reese, Lymon Clifton 1917- *WhoAm 94, WhoScEn 94*
Reese, Mamie Bynes *WhoBlA 94*
Reese, Mansel *Who 94*
Reese, (John) Mansel 1906- *Who 94*
Reese, Marcia Mitchell *WhoAmA 93*
Reese, Mary Anne 1956- *WhoAmL 94*
Reese, Matthew Anderson 1927- *WhoAmP 93*
Reese, Michelle *WhoHol 92*
Reese, Milous J. *WhoBlA 94*
Reese, Norma Carol 1946- *WhoMW 93*
Reese, Paul *WhoAmP 93*
Reese, Richard Bruce 1940- *WhoAm 94*
Reese, Robert J. 1947- *WhoAmP 93*
Reese, Robert Jenkins 1947- *WhoAmL 94, WhoWest 94*
Reese, Sammy d1985 *WhoHol 92*
Reese, (John) Terence 1913- *Who 94*
Reese, Tex 1935- *WhoMW 93*
Reese, Thomas Ford 1943- *WhoAmA 93*
Reese, Thomas Sargent 1935- *WhoScEn 94*
Reese, Tom *WhoHol 92*
Reese, Viola Kathryn 1953- *WhoBlA 94*
Reese, Virginia Dahlenburg 1924- *WhoMW 93*
Reese, William Albert, III 1932- *WhoScEn 94*
Reese, William Foster 1938- *WhoAmA 93*
Reese, William Harry 1947- *WhoFI 94*
Reese, William Lewis 1921- *WhoAm 94*
Reese, William Willis 1940- *WhoFI 94*
Reese, Willis Livingston Mesier 1913-1990 *WhAm 10*
Reeser, Jeannie G. *WhoHisp 94*
Reeser, Jeannie G. 1943- *WhoAmP 93*
Reeser, Robert D. 1931- *WhoAmA 93*
Reeser, Robert Duane 1931- *WhoWest 94*
Reesing, John Palmer, Jr. 1920-1990 *WhAm 10*
Rees-Jones, Geoffrey Rippon 1914- *Who 94*
Reeslund, Michael E. 1948- *WhoAmL 94*
Rees-Mogg, Baron 1928- *Who 94*
Rees-Mogg, William 1928- *ConAu 142, IntWW 93*
Rees-Williams *Who 94*
Rees-Williams, Jonathan 1949- *Who 94*
Reetz, Harold Frank, Jr. *WhoAm 94*
Reeve, Ada d1966 *WhoHol 92*
Reeve, Alison 1956- *WhoWest 94*
Reeve, Anthony 1938- *IntWW 93, Who 94*
Reeve, Arthur B(enjamin) 1880-1936 *EncSF 93*
Reeve, Christopher 1952- *IntMPA 94, IntWW 93, WhoAm 94, WhoHol 92*
Reeve, Clara 1729-1807 *BlmGWL*
Reeve, F. D. *DrAPF 93*
Reeve, F(ranklin) D(olier) 1928- *WrDr 94*
Reeve, Gary Preston 1946- *WhoMW 93*
Reeve, James Ernest 1926- *Who 94*
Reeve, James Key *WhoAmA 93*
Reeve, John 1944- *Who 94*
Reeve, John Newton 1947- *WhoAm 94*
Reeve, Lorraine Ellen 1951- *WhoScEn 94*
Reeve, Marjorie Frances *Who 94*
Reeve, Michael David 1943- *IntWW 93, Who 94*
Reeve, Robin Martin 1934- *Who 94*
Reeve, Ronald Cropper, Jr. 1943- *WhoAm 94*
Reeve, Roy Stephen 1941- *Who 94*
Reeve, Suzanne Elizabeth *Who 94*
Reeve, Thomas Burnell, Jr. 1947- *WhoAmL 94*
Reeve, Trevor *Who 94*
Reeve, (Charles) Trevor 1915- *Who 94*
Reeve, William 1757-1815 *NewGrDO*
Reeves, Alan M. *WhoBlA 94*
Reeves, Alexis Scott 1949- *WhoAm 94, WhoBlA 94*
Reeves, Alvin Frederick, II 1941- *WhoScEn 94*
Reeves, Andrew Louis 1924- *WhoMW 93*
Reeves, Anthony Henry 1940- *WhoFI 94*
Reeves, Barbara Ann 1949- *WhoAm 94, WhoAmL 94*
Reeves, Barry Lucas 1935- *WhoScEn 94*
Reeves, Billy d1943 *WhoHol 92*
Reeves, Billy Dean 1927- *WhoScEn 94*
Reeves, Bob d1960 *WhoHol 92*
Reeves, Bruce 1955- *WhoWest 94*
Reeves, C. Lee 1945- *WhoAmL 94*
Reeves, Carla Marianne 1949- *WhoWest 94*
Reeves, Charles Howell 1915- *WhoAm 94*
Reeves, Christopher Reginald 1936- *IntWW 93, Who 94*
Reeves, Dale Leslie 1936- *WhoMW 93*
Reeves, Dan *NewYTBS 93 [port]*
Reeves, Dan d1971 *ProFbHF*
Reeves, Daniel Edward 1944- *WhoAm 94*
Reeves, Daniel McDonough *WhoAmA 93*
Reeves, Dianne *WhoHol 92*
Reeves, Dianne 1956- *WhoBlA 94*
Reeves, Donald St. John 1934- *Who 94*
Reeves, Emery Irving 1929- *WhoWest 94*
Reeves, Esther May 1937- *WhoAmA 93*
Reeves, Faye Couch 1953- *SmATA 76 [port]*
Reeves, Frances Cowart 1919- *WhoAmP 93*
Reeves, Frank Blair 1922- *WhoAm 94*
Reeves, Gene 1930- *WhoAmL 94*
Reeves, George d1959 *WhoHol 92*
Reeves, George McMillan, Jr. 1921- *WhoAm 94*
Reeves, Gordon *Who 94*
Reeves, (William) Gordon 1938- *Who 94*
Reeves, Helen May 1945- *Who 94*
Reeves, Howell J. 1941- *WhoAmL 94*
Reeves, Hubert 1932- *WrDr 94*
Reeves, J. Mason 1898-1973 *WhoAmA 93N*
Reeves, James Doyle 1927- *WhoAmP 93*
Reeves, James Franklin 1946- *WhoAmA 93*
Reeves, James N. 1945- *WhoAmL 94*
Reeves, Jim d1964 *WhoHol 92*
Reeves, Jim d1971 *WhoHol 92*
Reeves, Jim 1923-1964 *ConMus 10 [port]*
Reeves, John Alexander 1938- *WhoAmA 93*
Reeves, John Allen 1950- *WhoWest 94*
Reeves, John Barrett 1928- *WhoFI 94*
Reeves, John Raymond 1957- *WhoAmP 93*
Reeves, Joyce 1911- *WrDr 94*
Reeves, Julius Lee 1961- *WhoBlA 94*
Reeves, Keanu 1964- *IntMPA 94, WhoAm 94, WhoAsA 94, WhoHol 92*
Reeves, Kynaston d1971 *WhoHol 92*
Reeves, L(ynette) P(amela) 1937- *EncSF 93*
Reeves, Linda Dono 1961- *WhoMW 93*
Reeves, Louise 1944- *WhoBlA 94*
Reeves, Lucy Mary 1932- *WhoMW 93*
Reeves, Marcia Ellen 1949- *WhoWest 94*
Reeves, Marjorie E. 1905- *WrDr 94*
Reeves, Marjorie E(thel) 1905- *ConAu 42NR*
Reeves, Marjorie Ethel 1905- *IntWW 93, Who 94*
Reeves, Martha Rose 1941- *WhoBlA 94*
Reeves, Marvin Coke 1911- *WhoFI 94*
Reeves, Marylou 1959- *WhoFI 94*
Reeves, Michael 1944-1969 *HorFD [port]*
Reeves, Michael S. 1935- *WhoBlA 94*
Reeves, Michael Stanley 1935- *WhoAm 94*
Reeves, Nigel Barrie Reginald 1939- *Who 94*
Reeves, Paul Alfred 1932- *IntWW 93, Who 94*
Reeves, Peggy 1941- *WhoAmP 93*
Reeves, Philip Thomas Langford 1931- *Who 94*
Reeves, Polly R. *WhoAmP 93*
Reeves, Ralph B., III 1947- *WhoAm 94*
Reeves, Richard d1967 *WhoHol 92*
Reeves, Richard Allen 1944- *WhoScEn 94*
Reeves, Robert Estill 1942- *WhoAmP 93*
Reeves, Robert Grier LeFevre 1920- *WhoAm 94, WhoScEn 94*
Reeves, Robert W. 1951- *WhoAmL 94*
Reeves, Roberta Anne d1981 *WhoHol 92*
Reeves, Rosser Scott, III 1936- *WhoAm 94*
Reeves, Sandra Lee 1942- *WhoAmP 93*
Reeves, Saskia *WhoHol 92*
Reeves, Scott *WhoHol 92*
Reeves, Sims 1818-1900 *NewGrDO*
Reeves, Steve 1926- *IntMPA 94, WhoHol 92*
Reeves, Susan Elizabeth 1956- *WhoWest 94*
Reeves, Thomas C. 1936- *WrDr 94*
Reeves, Trish *DrAPF 93*
Reeves, William Boyd 1932- *WhoAmL 94*
Reeves, William Desmond 1937- *Who 94*
Reeves, Willie Lloyd, Jr. 1949- *WhoBlA 94*
Reeves-Smith, George c. 1858-1914 *DcNaB MP*
Reeves-Smith, H. d1938 *WhoHol 92*
Reeves-Smith, Olive d1972 *WhoHol 92*
Reff, Theodore 1930- *WhoAm 94, WhoAmA 93*
Reffell, Derek (Roy) 1928- *Who 94*
Reffell, Derek Roy 1928- *IntWW 93*
Refice, Licinio 1883-1954 *NewGrDO*
Refinetti, Roberto 1957- *WhoScEn 94*
Refior, Everett Lee 1919- *WhoAm 94, WhoAmP 93*
Reflecting Man, John d1956 *EncNAR*
Refo, Patricia Lee 1958- *WhoAmL 94*
Refregier, Anton 1905-1979 *WhoAmA 93N*
Ref-Ren *WhAm 10*
Refshauge, William (Dudley) 1913- *Who 94*
Refshauge, William Dudley 1913- *IntWW 93*
Refsland, Gary Arlan 1944- *WhoAm 94, WhoWest 94*
Regal, Dorothea Weir 1946- *WhoAmL 94*
Regalado, Jose Marcelino, Jr. 1961- *WhoHisp 94*
Regalado, Raul L. 1945- *WhoAm 94, WhoHisp 94*
Regalado, Robert 1964- *WhoFI 94*
Regalbuto, Joe *WhoHol 92*
Regalbuto, Monica Cristina 1961- *WhoScEn 94*
Regalmuto, Nancy Marie 1956- *WhoFI 94*
Regamey, Constantin 1907-1982 *NewGrDO*
Regan, Ann Ellen 1962- *WhoWest 94*
Regan, Ann Kennedy 1923- *WhoAmP 93*
Regan, Ann W. 1948- *WhoAmL 94*
Regan, Barry d1956 *WhoHol 92*
Regan, Charles Maurice 1925- *Who 94*
Regan, David 1935- *WhoAm 94*
Regan, Dian Curtis 1950- *ConAu 142, SmATA 75 [port]*
Regan, Donald H. 1944- *WhoAm 94, WhoAmL 94*
Regan, Donald T. 1918- *WhoAmP 93*
Regan, Donald Thomas 1918- *IntWW 93, Who 94, WhoAm 94*
Regan, Edward V. *WhoAmP 93*
Regan, Gerald Augustine 1929- *IntWW 93, Who 94*
Regan, James Martin 1950- *WhoMW 93*
Regan, Jennifer *DrAPF 93*
Regan, Jerry 1911- *WrDr 94*
Regan, John B. 1934- *WhoAmP 93*
Regan, John Bernard Jack 1934- *WhoWest 94*
Regan, John J. 1929- *WhoAm 94, WhoAmL 94, WrDr 94*
Regan, John J. 1949- *WhoAmL 94*
Regan, John Ward 1950- *WhoScEn 94*
Regan, Joseph d1931 *WhoHol 92*
Regan, Mary *WhoHol 92*
Regan, Michael Dalrymple 1942- *Who 94*
Regan, Michael Patrick 1941- *WhoAmL 94*
Regan, Patty *WhoHol 92*
Regan, Paul Michael 1953- *WhoAmL 94*
Regan, Peter Francis, III 1924- *WhoAm 94*
Regan, Phil 1906- *WhoHol 92*
Regan, Purdy C. 1897- *WhAm 10*
Regan, Ray *WhoAmP 93*
Regan, Rich 1930- *BasBi*
Regan, Robert Charles 1930- *WhoAm 94*
Regan, Robert Martin 1930- *WhoAmP 93*
Regan, Robert P. 1936- *WhoAmP 93*
Regan, Stephen 1957- *ConAu 142*
Regan, Sylvia 1908- *WhoAm 94*
Regan, Timothy W. 1947- *WhoAmL 94*
Regan, Tom 1938- *EnvEnc*
Regan, Tony d1988 *WhoHol 92*
Regan, William Joseph, Jr. 1946- *WhoAm 94, WhoIns 94*
Regante, Mark L. 1951- *WhoAmL 94*
Regas, George d1940 *WhoHol 92*
Regas, Pedro d1974 *WhoHol 92*
Regat, Jean-Jacques Albert 1945- *WhoAmA 93*
Regat, Mary E. 1943- *WhoAmA 93*
Regazzi, John Henry 1921- *WhoAm 94, WhoFI 94*
Regazzi, John James, III 1948- *WhoAm 94*
Regazzi, Sabina *WhoHol 92*
Regdos, Shane Lawrence 1962- *WhoScEn 94*
Regehr, Duncan 1954- *WhoHol 92*
Regeimbal, Neil Robert, Sr. 1929- *WhoAm 94*
Regelbrugge, Roger Rafael 1930- *WhoAm 94, WhoFI 94*
Regele, Michael Bruce 1952- *WhoWest 94*
Regener, Victor H. 1913- *WhoScEn 94*
Regensburg, Pethahia Of *WhWE*
Regensburg, Sophy P. 1885-1974 *WhoAmA 93N*
Regenstein, Lewis Graham 1943- *WhoAm 94*
Regenstein, Louis 1912- *WhoAm 94*
Regensteiner, Else (Friedsam) 1906- *WhoAmA 93*
Regensteiner, Else Friedsam 1906- *WhoAm 94*
Regenstreif, Herbert 1935- *WhoAmL 94, WhoFI 94*
Regenstreif, S(amuel) Peter 1936- *WrDr 94*
Regenstreif, Samuel Peter 1936- *WhoAm 94*
Regent, Benoit *WhoHol 92*
Reger, Bill 1942- *WhoAmP 93*
Reger, Lawrence L. 1939- *WhoAmA 93*
Reger, Lawrence Lee 1939- *WhoAm 94*
Reges, Marianna Alice 1947- *WhoAm 94*
Regester, Charlotte *WhoAmA 93N*
Regester, John Dickinson 1897- *WhAm 10*
Regester, Michael 1947- *IntWW 93*

Regez, Rudolph Frederick 1942- *WhoFI 94*
Reggia, Frank 1921- *WhoAm 94*
Reggia, James Allen 1949- *WhoScEn 94*
Reggiani, Serge 1922- *IntWW 93, WhoHol 92*
Reggie, Doris Boustany 1930- *WhoAmP 93*
Reggie, Ed Michael 1952- *WhoFI 94*
Reggio, Vito Anthony 1929- *WhoFI 94, WhoMW 93*
Regier, Gail *DrAPF 93*
Regina, Archbishop of 1930- *Who 94*
Reginald *ConAu 42NR*
Reginald, R. *ConAu 42NR*
Reginald, R(obert) *ConAu 42NR*
Reginald, Robert 1948- *EncSF 93, WrDr 94*
Reginato, Peter 1945- *WhoAmA 93*
Reginato, Robert Joseph 1935- *WhoAm 94, WhoWest 94*
Regine 1932- *WhoHol 92*
Regino, Thomas Charles 1950- *WhoScEn 94*
Regio, Jose 1901-1969 *IntDcT 2*
Regiomontanus 1436-1476 *AstEnc*
Regis, Colette *WhoHol 92*
Regis, Edward, Jr. 1944- *WrDr 94*
Regis, John 1966- *IntWW 93*
Register, Jasper C. 1937- *WhoBlA 94*
Register, Richard Alan 1963- *WhoScEn 94*
Register, Ulma Doyle 1920- *WhoAm 94*
Reglein, Eugene B. 1918- *WhoMW 93*
Regnard, Jean-Francois 1655-1709 *GuFrLit 2, IntDcT 2*
Regnell, Barbara Caramella 1935- *WhoMW 93*
Regner, David Joseph 1931- *WhoAmP 93*
Regner, Sidney L. d1993 *NewYTBS 93*
Regnery, Alfred Scattergood 1942- *WhoAm 94*
Regnery, Henry 1912- *WhoAm 94*
Regnery, Marcia Joan 1962- *WhoMW 93*
Regnier, Charles *WhoHol 92*
Regnier, Charles 1914- *IntWW 93*
Regnier, Francois Jean 1933- *WhoFI 94*
Regnier, Linda Kay Moore 1939- *WhoMW 93*
Regnier, Marc Charles 1939- *WhoAm 94*
Regnier, Mathurin 1573-1613 *GuFrLit 2*
Regnier, Richard Adrian 1931- *WhoAmL 94*
Regnier, Richard Olin 1929- *WhoAmP 93*
Rego, George Browne 1934- *IntWW 93*
Rego, Lawrence *WhoHisp 94*
Rego, Paula 1935- *IntWW 93*
Rego, (Maria) Paula (Figueiroa) 1935- *Who 94*
Rego, Stephen Lawrence 1958- *WhoMW 93*
Rego, Vernon Joseph 1956- *WhoHisp 94*
Regoli, John W. *WhoAmP 93*
Regoord, Mark Stephan 1963- *WhoFI 94*
Regozin, Roy L. 1942- *WhoAmL 94*
Regueiro, Maria Cristina 1947- *WhoHisp 94*
Reguero, Edward Anthony 1960- *WhoFI 94, WhoWest 94*
Reguero, M. A. 1918- *WhoHisp 94*
Regula, Ralph 1924- *CngDr 93, WhoAm 94, WhoMW 93*
Regula, Ralph S. 1924- *WhoAmP 93*
Regy, Claude 1923- *IntWW 93*
Reh, John W. 1935- *WhoScEn 94*
Reh, Thomas Edward 1943- *WhoMW 93, WhoScEn 94*
Reha, Rose Krivisky 1920- *WhoMW 93*
Reha, William Christopher 1954- *WhoScEn 94*
Rehak, James Richard 1938- *WhoScEn 94*
Rehan, Mary d1963 *WhoHol 92*
Rehart, Burton Schyler 1934- *WhoWest 94*
Rehbein, Edna Aguirre 1955- *WhoHisp 94*
Rehbein, Edward Andrew 1947- *WhoFI 94*
Rehbein, William, Jr. 1948- *WhoAmP 93*
Rehberg, Dennis R. 1955- *WhoAm 94, WhoAmP 93, WhoWest 94*
Rehberger, Gustav 1910- *WhoAmA 93*
Rehbock, Richard Alexander 1946- *WhoAmL 94*
Reherman, Ronald Gilbert 1935- *WhoAm 94, WhoMW 93*
Rehfeld, Barry J. 1946- *WrDr 94*
Rehfeld, Curt d1934 *WhoHol 92*
Rehfeld, Jens Frederik 1941- *IntWW 93*
Rehfuss, Heinz (Julius) 1917-1988 *NewGrDO*
Rehfuss, Walter Guy 1936- *WhAm 10*
Rehg, Kenneth Lee 1939- *WhoWest 94*
Rehkemper, Heinrich 1894-1949 *NewGrDO*
Rehkope, Paul d1949 *WhoHol 92*
Rehkugler, Gerald Edwin 1935- *WhoAm 94, WhoScEn 94*
Rehlander, Monte D. 1939- *WhoAmP 93*
Rehm, Carl E. 1930- *WhoFI 94*
Rehm, Gary Gordon 1947- *WhoMW 93*
Rehm, George William 1941- *WhoMW 93*
Rehm, Gerald S. 1927- *WhoAmP 93*
Rehm, Jack Daniel 1932- *WhoAm 94, WhoFI 94*
Rehm, John Bartram 1930- *WhoAm 94*
Rehm, John Edwin 1924- *WhoMW 93*
Rehm, Leo Frank 1916- *WhoAm 94*
Rehm, Warren Stacey, Jr. 1907- *WhoAm 94*
Rehme, Robert G. 1935- *IntMPA 94*
Rehmus, Charles Martin 1926- *WhoAm 94*
Rehn, Elisabeth 1935- *WhoWomW 91*
Rehn, Jens *EncSF 93*
Rehn, Mildred d1989 *WhoHol 92*
Rehnquist, William H. 1924- *IntWW 93, Who 94*
Rehnquist, William H(ubbs) 1924- *ConAu 140*
Rehnquist, William Hubbs 1924- *CngDr 93, WhoAm 94, WhoAmL 94, WhoAmP 93*
Rehorn, Lois Marie Smith 1919- *WhoWest 94*
Rehrmann, Eileen Mary 1944- *WhoAmP 93*
Rehwald, Walther R. 1930- *WhoScEn 94*
Reiback, Earl M. 1948- *WhoAmA 93*
Reibel, Bertram 1901- *WhoAmA 93*
Reibel, Kurt 1926- *WhoAm 94*
Reibel, Paula *ConAu 41NR*
Reiber, Gregory Duane 1955- *WhoWest 94*
Reibman, Jeanette Fichman 1915- *WhoAm 94, WhoAmP 93*
Reibstein, Regina *DrAPF 93*
Reibstein, Richard Jay 1951- *WhoAm 94*
Reich, Abraham Charles 1949- *WhoAm 94, WhoAmL 94*
Reich, Alan Anderson 1930- *WhoAm 94*
Reich, Ali 1933- *WrDr 94*
Reich, Allan J. 1948- *WhoAm 94, WhoAmL 94*
Reich, Bernard 1926- *WhoAm 94*
Reich, Bernard 1941- *WhoAm 94*
Reich, Bruce P. 1956- *WhoIns 94*
Reich, Charles William 1930- *WhoAm 94*
Reich, David J. 1954- *WhoAmL 94*
Reich, David Lee 1930- *WhoAm 94*
Reich, Deborah 1960- *WrDr 94*
Reich, Edward Stuart 1936- *WhoAmL 94*
Reich, Ellen *DrAPF 93*
Reich, Garrett Wayne 1951- *WhoAmL 94*
Reich, Gary 1961- *WhoFI 94*
Reich, Gunter 1921-1989 *NewGrDO*
Reich, Herb *WhoAm 94*
Reich, Jack E. 1910- *WhoIns 94*
Reich, Jack Egan 1910- *WhoAm 94*
Reich, Jay A. 1948- *WhoAmL 94*
Reich, Joachim David 1952- *WhoMW 93*
Reich, Kenneth Alan 1946- *WhoAmL 94*
Reich, Kenneth Irvin 1938- *WhoAm 94*
Reich, Larry Sam 1946- *WhoAm 94, WhoAmL 94*
Reich, Lee 1947- *ConAu 142*
Reich, Morton Melvyn 1939- *WhoAm 94*
Reich, Nathaniel E. *WhoAmA 93*
Reich, Nathaniel Edwin 1907- *WhoAm 94*
Reich, Olive B. 1935- *WhoAmA 93*
Reich, Otto J. 1945- *WhoAmP 93*
Reich, Otto Juan 1945- *WhoAm 94*
Reich, Pauline Carole 1946- *WhoAm 94, WhoAmL 94*
Reich, Peter Gordon 1926- *Who 94*
Reich, Randi Ruth Novak 1954- *WhoScEn 94*
Reich, Richard Allen 1962- *WhoFI 94*
Reich, Robert B. *NewYTBS 93*
Reich, Robert B. 1946- *CngDr 93, ConAu 141, CurBio 93 [port], WhoAmP 93*
Reich, Robert Bernard 1946- *IntWW 93, WhoAm 94, WhoFI 94*
Reich, Robert Claude 1929- *WhoScEn 94*
Reich, Robert S. 1945- *WhoAmL 94*
Reich, Robert Sigmund 1913- *WhoAm 94*
Reich, Rose Marie 1937- *WhoMW 93*
Reich, Seymour David 1933- *WhoAm 94*
Reich, Sheldon 1931- *WhoAmA 93*
Reich, Simeon 1948- *WhoWest 94*
Reich, Steve 1936- *IntWW 93, WhoAm 94*
Reich, Thomas J. 1964- *WhoAmL 94*
Reich, Willi 1898-1980 *NewGrDO*
Reich, Yaron Z. 1950- *WhoAm 94, WhoAmL 94*
Reicha, Antoine(-Joseph) 1770-1836 *NewGrDO*
Reichard, David Wark 1948- *WhoWest 94*
Reichard, Hector, Jr. *WhoAmL 94*
Reichard, Hugo Manley 1918- *WhoAm 94*
Reichard, John Francis 1924- *WhoAm 94*
Reichard, Sherwood Marshall 1928- *WhoAm 94*
Reichard, Stephen Brantley 1949- *WhoAmA 93N*
Reichard, William Thomas, III 1943- *WhoAm 94*
Reichardt, Carl E. 1931- *WhoAm 94, WhoFI 94*
Reichardt, Delbert Dale 1927- *WhoAm 94*
Reichardt, Glenn Richard 1951- *WhoAm 94*
Reichardt, Harold William 1951- *WhoMW 93*
Reichardt, Johann Friedrich 1752-1814 *NewGrDO*
Reichardt, John Field 1948- *WhoAmP 93*
Reichardt, Robert Heinrich 1927- *IntWW 93*
Reichard-Zamora, Héctor 1910- *WhoHisp 94*
Reichart, Walter A. 1903- *WrDr 94*
Reichartz, W. Dan 1946- *WhoFI 94, WhoWest 94*
Reichbach, Naomi Estelle 1934- *WhoWest 94*
Reich-Berman, Eunice Thelma 1947- *WhoFI 94*
Reiche, Frank Perley 1929- *WhoAm 94*
Reiche, Marvin Gary 1949- *WhoWest 94*
Reiche, Momoe Malietoa von *BlmGWL*
Reichek, Elaine 1943- *WhoAmA 93*
Reichek, Jesse 1916- *WhoAm 94, WhoAmA 93, WhoWest 94*
Reichek, Morton Arthur 1924- *WhoAm 94*
Reichek, Nathaniel 1941- *WhoScEn 94*
Reichel, Aaron I(srael) 1950- *WrDr 94*
Reichel, Aaron Israel 1950- *WhoAmL 94*
Reichel, John Kento 1959- *WhoWest 94*
Reichel, Lee Elmer 1944- *WhoMW 93, WhoScEn 94*
Reichel, Myra 1951- *WhoAmA 93*
Reichel, Philip Lee 1946- *WhoWest 94*
Reichel, Sabine 1946- *WrDr 94*
Reichel, Walter Emil 1935- *WhoAm 94*
Reichelderfer, F(rancis) W(ilton) 1895- *WhAm 10*
Reichelt, Fred 1941- *WhoAm 94, WhoFI 94, WhoMW 93*
Reichen, Jurg 1946- *WhoScEn 94*
Reichenbach, Bruce 1943- *WrDr 94*
Reichenbach, Francois d1993 *NewYTBS 93 [port]*
Reichenbach, Stephen E. 1954- *WhoMW 93*
Reichenbach, Thomas 1947- *WhoScEn 94, WhoWest 94*
Reichenberg, Cherri Jann 1951- *WhoWest 94*
Reichenstein, William Robert 1952- *WhoFI 94*
Reicher, David M. 1952- *WhoAmL 94*
Reicher, Frank d1965 *WhoHol 92*
Reicher, Hedwiga d1971 *WhoHol 92*
Reicher, Robert Jay 1956- *WhoAmL 94*
Reicher, Seth Adam 1964- *WhoFI 94*
Reicher, Thomas Zachary 1949- *WhoAm 94*
Reicher-Kindermann, Hedwig 1853-1883 *NewGrDO*
Reichers, Helene d1957 *WhoHol 92*
Reichert, David 1929- *WhoAm 94*
Reichert, Donald Karl 1932- *WhoAmA 93*
Reichert, Heinz 1877-1940 *NewGrDO*
Reichert, Jack Frank 1930- *WhoAm 94, WhoFI 94, WhoMW 93*
Reichert, Joseph Frederick 1937- *WhoMW 93*
Reichert, Kittens d1990 *WhoHol 92*
Reichert, Leo Edmund, Jr. 1932- *WhoAm 94, WhoScEn 94*
Reichert, Marilyn F. *WhoAmA 93*
Reichert, Norman Vernon 1921- *WhoAm 94*
Reichert, Robert A. B. 1948- *WhoAmP 93*
Reichert, Willy d1973 *WhoHol 92*
Reichert-Facilides, Otto Ernst 1925- *WhoAm 94*
Reichgott, Ember D. 1953- *WhoAmP 93*
Reichgott, Ember Darlene 1953- *WhoAm 94, WhoMW 93*
Reichhardt, Irmgard 1935- *WhoWomW 91*
Reichhardt, Poul d1985 *WhoHol 92*
Reichhold, Henry 1901-1989 *WhAm 10*
Reichhold, Janet E. 1937- *WhoWest 94*
Reichl, Ruth Molly 1948- *WhoAm 94*
Reichle, David Edward 1938- *WhoScEn 94*
Reichlin, Louise 1941- *WhoWest 94*
Reichlin, Seymour 1924- *WhoAm 94*
Reichman, Dawn Leslie 1951- *WhoAmL 94*
Reichman, Fred 1925- *WhoAmA 93*
Reichman, Fredrick Thomas 1925- *WhoAm 94, WhoWest 94*
Reichman, George Albert 1925- *WhoScEn 94*
Reichman, Joe d1970 *WhoHol 92*
Reichman, Leah Carol 1951- *WhoAmA 93*
Reichman, Lee Brodersohn 1938- *WhoAm 94*
Reichman, Michael Alan 1957- *WhoFI 94*
Reichman, Walter 1938- *WhoAm 94*
Reichmanis, Elsa 1953- *WhoAm 94*
Reichmann, Paul 1930- *IntWW 93*
Reichmann, Peter Ivan 1942- *WhoScEn 94*
Reichmann, Theodor 1849-1903 *NewGrDO [port]*
Reichow, Otto 1904- *WhoHol 92*
Reichow, Werner d1973 *WhoHol 92*
Reich-Ranicki, Marcel 1920- *IntWW 93*
Reichstein, Tadeus 1897- *IntWW 93, Who 94, WhoAm 94, WhoScEn 94*
Reichstein, Tadeusz 1897- *WorScD*
Reichstetter, Arthur Charles 1946- *WhoAm 94, WhoFI 94*
Reicin, Ronald Ian 1942- *WhoAm 94, WhoAmL 94*
Reickert, Erick Arthur 1935- *WhoMW 93*
Reid, Agnes Nan d1987 *WhoHol 92*
Reid, Alan Clifford 1961- *WhoWest 94*
Reid, Alan Forrest 1931- *IntWW 93*
Reid, Alastair 1926- *WrDr 94*
Reid, Alexander (James) 1932- *Who 94*
Reid, Andrew H. 1940- *WrDr 94*
Reid, Andrew Milton 1929- *Who 94*
Reid, Antonio *WhoAm 94, WhoBlA 94*
Reid, Archibald Cameron 1915- *Who 94*
Reid, Barbara *DrAPF 93*
Reid, Barbara Addison 1943- *WhoFI 94*
Reid, Barry Jonathan 1957- *WhoFI 94, WhoWest 94*
Reid, Baxter Ellis, Jr. 1943- *WhoMW 93*
Reid, Belmont Mervyn 1927- *WhoFI 94, WhoWest 94*
Reid, Benjamin F. 1937- *WhoBlA 94*
Reid, Beryl 1918- *WhoHol 92*
Reid, Beryl 1920- *IntMPA 94, Who 94*
Reid, Bruce Eugene 1950- *WhoMW 93*
Reid, Carl Benton d1973 *WhoHol 92*
Reid, Charles 1937- *WhoAmA 93*
Reid, Charles Adams, III 1947- *WhoAm 94, WhoAmL 94*
Reid, Charles Clark 1937- *WhoAm 94*
Reid, Charles E. *WhoBlA 94*
Reid, Charles H. 1934- *WhoBlA 94*
Reid, Charles L. 1927- *WrDr 94*
Reid, Charles Phillip Patrick 1940- *WhoAm 94*
Reid, Christina 1942- *ConDr 93*
Reid, Christopher *WhoHol 92*
Reid, Christopher 1949- *WrDr 94*
Reid, Christopher (John) 1949- *ConAu 140*
Reid, Christy Eve 1951- *WhoAmL 94*
Reid, Clarice Wills 1931- *WhoBlA 94*
Reid, Clyde Henderson, Jr. 1928- *WrDr 94*
Reid, David Evans 1943- *WhoAm 94*
Reid, David Paul 1954- *WhoAmP 93*
Reid, David Wesley 1952- *WhoFI 94*
Reid, Desmond *EncSF 93*
Reid, Desmond 1939- *WrDr 94*
Reid, Dixie Lee 1942- *WhoWest 94*
Reid, Donald Bruce 1940- *WhoMW 93*
Reid, Dougal Gordon 1925- *Who 94*
Reid, Douglas William John 1934- *Who 94*
Reid, Duane Lee 1950- *WhoMW 93*
Reid, Ealnor Jean 1950- *WhoMW 93*
Reid, Edith C. *WhoBlA 94*
Reid, Edward Snover 1930- *WhoAm 94*
Reid, Elisabeth Jesser 1789-1866 *DcNaB MP*
Reid, Elizabeth Margaret 1947- *Who 94*
Reid, Elliott 1920- *WhoHol 92*
Reid, Ellis Edmund, III 1934- *WhoBlA 94*
Reid, Escott Meredith 1905- *IntWW 93*
Reid, Evans Burton 1913- *WhoAm 94*
Reid, F. Theodore, Jr. 1929- *WhoBlA 94*
Reid, Frances 1915- *WhoHol 92*
Reid, Frances Marion Pugh 1910- *WhoWest 94*
Reid, Frances P. 1910- *WrDr 94*
Reid, Francesca d1983 *WhoHol 92*
Reid, G. Kelley, Jr. 1941- *WhoAmL 94*
Reid, Gavin Hunter *Who 94*
Reid, George Agnew d1947 *WhoAmA 93N*
Reid, George Bernard, Jr. 1948- *WhoAm 94, WhoAmL 94*
Reid, George Kell 1918- *WhoAm 94*
Reid, George Newlands 1939- *Who 94*
Reid, George Oswald d1993 *Who 94N*
Reid, Gerald Alan 1961- *WhoWest 94*
Reid, Geraldine Wold 1944- *WhoMW 93*
Reid, Goldie Hartshorn 1913- *WhoBlA 94*
Reid, Gordon *Who 94*
Reid, (James) Gordon 1952- *Who 94*
Reid, Graham Livingstone 1937- *Who 94*
Reid, Hal d1920 *WhoHol 92*
Reid, Hal, Mrs. *WhoHol 92*
Reid, Harold Sherman 1941- *WhoBlA 94, WhoMW 93*
Reid, Harold W. 1939- *See* Statler Brothers, The *WhoHol 92*
Reid, Harry 1939- *CngDr 93, IntWW 93, WhoAm 94, WhoAmP 93, WhoWest 94*
Reid, Hoch 1909- *WhoAm 94*
Reid, Hugh 1933- *Who 94*
Reid, Iain 1942- *Who 94*

Reid, Ian George 1921- *Who 94*
Reid, Inez Smith 1937- *WhoAm 94, WhoBlA 94*
Reid, Irvin D. *WhoBlA 94*
Reid, Ivo *Who 94*
Reid, (Percy Fergus) Ivo 1911- *Who 94*
Reid, J. Don *WhoIns 94*
Reid, J. Frederick 1927- *WhoIns 94*
Reid, J. R. 1968- *WhoBlA 94*
Reid, J. Stephen 1939- *WhoWest 94*
Reid, Jack Powell 1936- *WhoFI 94*
Reid, Jack Richard 1947- *WhoScEn 94*
Reid, Jackson Brock 1921- *WhoAm 94*
Reid, James 1921- *Who 94*
Reid, James B. 1935- *WhoAmP 93*
Reid, James Dolan 1930- *WhoAm 94*
Reid, James Randolph 1750-1789 *WhAmRev*
Reid, James Robert 1943- *Who 94*
Reid, James Sims, Jr. 1926- *WhoAm 94, WhoFI 94, WhoMW 93*
Reid, Janet Warner 1944- *WhoScEn 94*
Reid, Janie Ellen 1950- *WhoBlA 94*
Reid, Jeff Goodwyn, Jr. 1951- *WhoAmP 93*
Reid, Jeffrey Tate 1961- *WhoFI 94*
Reid, Jim 1961- *See* Jesus and Mary Chain, The *ConMus 10*
Reid, Joan Evangeline 1932- *WhoAmL 94*
Reid, Joel Otto 1936- *WhoBlA 94*
Reid, John 1947- *Who 94*
Reid, John (James Andrew) 1925- *Who 94*
Reid, John (Kelman Sutherland) 1910- *WrDr 94*
Reid, John Boyd 1929- *Who 94*
Reid, John H., III 1944- *WhoAmL 94*
Reid, John Kelman Sutherland 1910- *Who 94*
Reid, John Low 1943- *Who 94*
Reid, John Mitchell 1926- *WhoAm 94, WhoScEn 94*
Reid, John P(hillip) 1930- *WrDr 94*
Reid, John Phillip 1930- *ConAu 41NR, WhoAm 94*
Reid, John Robert 1928- *Who 94*
Reid, John Spence 1942- *WhoAmP 93*
Reid, Joseph Lee 1923- *WhoAm 94, WhoScEn 94, WhoWest 94*
Reid, Juanin A. *WhoHisp 94*
Reid, Juliet Icilda 1949- *WhoFI 94*
Reid, Kate d1993 *IntMPA 94N, NewYTBS 93 [port]*
Reid, Kate 1930- *WhoHol 92*
Reid, Kate 1930-1993 *CurBio 93N*
Reid, Kenneth Bannerman Milne 1943- *Who 94*
Reid, Langhorne, III 1950- *WhoAm 94, WhoFI 94*
Reid, Lawrence Charles 1948- *WhoIns 94*
Reid, Lealaifuaneva Peter E. 1932- *WhoAmP 93*
Reid, Leslie d1917 *WhoHol 92*
Reid, Leslie 1919- *Who 94*
Reid, Leslie 1947- *WhoAmA 93*
Reid, Leslie Bancroft 1934- *WhoBlA 94*
Reid, Loren 1905- *WrDr 94*
Reid, Loren Dudley 1905- *WhoAm 94*
Reid, Lyle *WhoAmP 93*
Reid, Lyle 1930- *WhoAm 94, WhoAmL 94*
Reid, Lynne McArthur 1923- *Who 94, WhoAm 94*
Reid, Macgregor Stewart 1932- *WhoScEn 94*
Reid, Malcolm Herbert Marcus 1927- *Who 94*
Reid, Malissie Laverne 1953- *WhoBlA 94*
Reid, Margaret (Isabel) 1925- *WrDr 94*
Reid, Margaret Elizabeth 1935- *WhoWomW 91*
Reid, Marilyn J. *WhoMW 93*
Reid, Marilyn J. 1941- *WhoAmP 93*
Reid, Marion L. 1929- *WhoAm 94*
Reid, Marion Taylor 1944- *WhoWest 94*
Reid, Martin *Who 94*
Reid, Martin 1928- *IntWW 93*
Reid, (Harold) Martin (Smith) 1928- *Who 94*
Reid, Martin A. 1956- *WhoFI 94*
Reid, Mary d1979 *WhoHol 92*
Reid, Maude K. *WhoBlA 94*
Reid, Max d1969 *WhoHol 92*
Reid, Megan Beth 1954- *WhoWest 94*
Reid, Meta Mayne *WrDr 94*
Reid, Michael Edward 1950- *WhoAm 94*
Reid, Michael J. 1938- *WhoAm 94*
Reid, Michael J. 1954- *WhoAmP 93*
Reid, Miles Alvin 1931- *WhoBlA 94*
Reid, Milton 1917- *WhoHol 92*
Reid, Milton A. 1930- *WhoBlA 94*
Reid, Myke 1953- *WhoAmP 93*
Reid, Nanci Glick 1941- *WhoFI 94*
Reid, Norman (Robert) 1915- *Who 94*
Reid, Norman Robert 1915- *IntWW 93*
Reid, Ogden Rogers 1925- *IntWW 93, WhoAmP 93*
Reid, Peter Daer 1925- *Who 94*
Reid, Peter Ferdinand 1939- *WhoFI 94*
Reid, Philip *Who 94*
Reid, Ralph Benjamine 1950- *WhoAm 94, WhoAmL 94*
Reid, Ralph Ralston, Jr. 1934- *WhoAm 94, WhoScEn 94*
Reid, Ralph Waldo Emerson 1915- *WhoFI 94*
Reid, Randall *DrAPF 93*
Reid, Richard Alan 1938- *WhoWest 94*
Reid, Robert 1955- *WhoBlA 94*
Reid, Robert (Basil) 1921- *Who 94*
Reid, Robert Basil 1921- *IntWW 93*
Reid, Robert Clark 1924- *WhoAm 94*
Reid, Robert Dennis 1924- *WhoAm 94, WhoAmA 93, WhoBlA 94*
Reid, Robert Edward 1903- *WhoBlA 94*
Reid, Robert H. 1960- *WhoScEn 94*
Reid, Robert John 1942- *WhoAm 94*
Reid, Robert Lelon 1942- *WhoAm 94, WhoScEn 94*
Reid, Robert Paul 1934- *IntWW 93, Who 94*
Reid, Robert Philip 1933- *WhoAmP 93*
Reid, Roberto Elliott 1930- *WhoBlA 94*
Reid, Ronda Eunese 1955- *WhoBlA 94*
Reid, Rosemary K. 1933- *WhoAmP 93*
Reid, Ross 1917-1989 *WhAm 10*
Reid, Ross 1953- *WhoAm 94*
Reid, Rubin J. *WhoBlA 94*
Reid, Rust Endicott 1931- *WhoAm 94*
Reid, Ruth Hanford 1938- *WhoMW 93*
Reid, Sarah Layfield 1952- *WhoAm 94*
Reid, Selwyn Charles 1944- *WhoBlA 94*
Reid, Seona Elizabeth 1950- *Who 94*
Reid, Sheila *WhoHol 92*
Reid, Sina M. 1944- *WhoBlA 94*
Reid, Susan M. 1937- *WhoAmL 94*
Reid, Terence C. W. 1941- *WhoAm 94*
Reid, Thomas 1710-1796 *EncEth*
Reid, Thomas Fenton 1932- *WhoAm 94*
Reid, Tim 1944- *IntMPA 94, WhoBlA 94, WhoHol 92*
Reid, Timothy 1936- *WhoAm 94*
Reid, Timothy Escott 1936- *IntWW 93*
Reid, Trevor d1965 *WhoHol 92*
Reid, Vernon c. 1958- *See* Living Colour *News 93-3*
Reid, Vernon H. 1904- *WhoBlA 94*
Reid, Vic(tor Stafford) 1913- *WrDr 94*
Reid, Virginia d1955 *WhoHol 92*
Reid, Wallace d1923 *WhoHol 92*
Reid, Wallace, Mrs. d1977 *WhoHol 92*
Reid, Wallace, Jr. d1990 *WhoHol 92*
Reid, Whitelaw 1913- *Who 94*
Reid, Wilfred 1923- *WhoBlA 94*
Reid, Willard Malcolm 1910- *WhAm 10*
Reid, William 1921- *Who 94*
Reid, William 1926- *Who 94*
Reid, William 1958- *See* Jesus and Mary Chain, The *ConMus 10*
Reid, William Gordon 1943- *Who 94*
Reid, William Hill 1926- *WhoAm 94*
Reid, William James 1927- *WhoAm 94*
Reid, William James 1928- *WhoAm 94*
Reid, William James 1941- *WhoFI 94*
Reid, William Kennedy 1931- *Who 94*
Reid, William Macpherson 1938- *Who 94*
Reid, William Michael 1954- *WhoFI 94, WhoScEn 94*
Reid, William Stanford 1913- *IntWW 93*
Reid, Yolanda A. 1954- *WhoHisp 94*
Reida, Alvah 1920-1975 *EncSF 93*
Reida, Larry 1935- *WhoAmP 93*
Reid Banks, Lynne *Who 94*
Reid Banks, Lynne 1929- *SmATA 75 [port], TwCYAW, WrDr 94*
Reid Cabral, Donald J. 1923- *IntWW 93*
Reid-Crisp, Wendy *WhoAm 94*
Reide, Jerome L. 1954- *WhoBlA 94*
Reidelbach, Michael Joseph, Sr. 1946- *WhoMW 93*
Reidenbach, Thomas Victor 1946- *WhoMW 93*
Reidenbaugh, Lowell Henry 1919- *WhoAm 94*
Reidenberg, Louis Morton 1939- *WhoAmL 94*
Reidenberg, Marcus Milton 1934- *WhoAm 94*
Reider, George M., Jr. 1940- *WhoIns 94*
Reider, Harry Robert 1940- *WhoWest 94*
Reider, Marlyn 1935- *WhoMW 93*
Reidhaven, Viscount *Who 94*
Reidlinger, Charles Ronald 1929- *WhoWest 94*
Reid-Merritt, Patricia Ann 1950- *WhoBlA 94*
Reidy, Carolyn Kroll 1949- *IntWW 93, WhoAm 94*
Reidy, Charles Parnell, III 1942- *WhoAmL 94*
Reidy, Daniel Edward 1949- *WhoAmL 94*
Reidy, Edward Michael 1897- *WhAm 10*
Reidy, Frank J. 1914- *WhoAmP 93*
Reidy, Gerald Patrick 1929- *WhoAm 94, WhoFI 94*
Reidy, Joseph A., Jr. 1949- *WhoFI 94*
Reidy, Michael J. *WhoAmP 93*
Reidy, Richard Robert 1947- *WhoWest 94*
Reidy, Sue *BlmGWL*
Reidy, Thomas Anthony 1952- *WhoAm 94, WhoAmL 94*
Reierson, James Dutton 1941- *WhoScEn 94*
Reif, Arnold E. 1924- *WhoScEn 94*
Reif, David 1941- *WhoAm 94, WhoWest 94*
Reif, (F.) David 1941- *WhoAmA 93*
Reif, David Adams 1946- *WhoAmL 94, WhoAmP 93*
Reif, Eric Peter 1942- *WhoAm 94, WhoAmL 94*
Reif, John Henry 1951- *WhoAm 94, WhoFI 94*
Reif, John Steven 1940- *WhoWest 94*
Reif, Kathryn Louise 1952- *WhoMW 93*
Reif, Laurie Louise 1929- *WhoWest 94*
Reif, Louis Raymond 1923- *WhoAm 94, WhoFI 94*
Reif, Rudolf d1961 *WhoHol 92*
Reifel, Ben 1906-1990 *WhAm 10*
Reifenberg, Tom Perl 1930- *WhoMW 93*
Reifenheiser, Thomas V. 1935- *WhoAm 94*
Reifer, Sol S. 1952- *WhoAmL 94*
Reiff, A. E. *DrAPF 93*
Reiff, Arthur Frederick 1936- *WhoAmP 93*
Reiff, James Stanley 1935- *WhoMW 93*
Reiff, Robert Frank 1918-1982 *WhoAmA 93N*
Reiff, Robert L. *DrAPF 93*
Reiff, Robert Scott 1958- *WhoAmL 94*
Reiff, Sidney 1918- *WhoWest 94*
Reiff, Theodore Curtis 1942- *WhoFI 94, WhoWest 94*
Reiffel, Leonard 1927- *WhoAm 94*
Reifler, Clifford Bruce 1931- *WhoAm 94*
Reifler, Samuel *DrAPF 93*
Reifman, Jaques 1957- *WhoScEn 94*
Reifman, William J. 1952- *WhoAm 94*
Reifsnider, Kenneth Leonard 1940- *WhoAm 94, WhoScEn 94*
Reifsnyder, William Edward 1924- *WhoAm 94*
Reif-Stewart, Sheryl Louise 1965- *WhoMW 93*
Reig, June Wilson 1933- *WhoAm 94*
Reigate, Archdeacon of *Who 94*
Reigate, Baron 1905- *Who 94*
Reigbert, Claire d1957 *WhoHol 92*
Reiger, John Franklin 1943- *WhoMW 93*
Reighard, Clyde Waltz 1929- *WhoMW 93*
Reighard, Homer Leroy 1924- *WhoAm 94*
Reigrod, Robert Hull 1941- *WhoAm 94*
Reiher, Frederick (Bernard Carl) 1945- *Who 94*
Reijnders, Lucas 1946- *IntWW 93*
Reik, Rita Ann Fitzpatrick 1951- *WhoScEn 94*
Reiland, Earl D. 1944- *WhoAmL 94*
Reiland, Lowell Keith 1948- *WhoAm 94, WhoAmA 93*
Reile, Louis 1925- *WrDr 94*
Reiley, T. Phillip 1950- *WhoFI 94*
Reiley, Thomas Noel 1938- *WhoFI 94*
Reiling, Henry Bernard 1938- *WhoAm 94*
Reilley, James Clark 1919- *WhoFI 94*
Reilley, Kathleen Patricia 1948- *WhoWest 94*
Reilly, Bernard F. 1925- *ConAu 142*
Reilly, Bernard Francis 1950- *WhoAmA 93*
Reilly, Catherine d1982 *WhoHol 92*
Reilly, Charles James 1950- *WhoAmL 94*
Reilly, Charles Nelson 1931- *IntMPA 94, WhoHol 92*
Reilly, Christopher Aloysius 1942- *WhoMW 93*
Reilly, Conor Desmond 1952- *WhoAmL 94*
Reilly, Daniel Patrick 1928- *WhoAm 94*
Reilly, David Henry 1936- *WhoAm 94*
Reilly, Edward Arthur 1943- *WhoAm 94, WhoAmL 94*
Reilly, Edward F. 1954- *WhoAmL 94*
Reilly, Edward Francis, Jr. 1937- *WhoAm 94, WhoAmL 94, WhoAmP 93*
Reilly, Elvira 1899-1958 *WhoAmA 93N*
Reilly, Frank B., Jr. 1945- *WhoAmL 94*
Reilly, Frank Kelly 1935- *WhoAm 94, WhoMW 93*
Reilly, Frank Michael 1960- *WhoAmL 94*
Reilly, George 1934- *WhoAmL 94*
Reilly, George Love Anthony 1918- *WhoAm 94*
Reilly, Gerard Denis 1906- *WhoAm 94*
Reilly, Gregory B. 1945- *WhoAmL 94*
Reilly, Hugh *WhoHol 92*
Reilly, Jack 1950- *WhoAmA 93*
Reilly, Jad *DrAPF 93*
Reilly, James Richard 1945- *WhoAmP 93*
Reilly, Jane *WhoHol 92*
Reilly, Jeanette P. 1908- *WhoMW 93, WhoScEn 94*
Reilly, Jeremy (Calcott) 1934- *Who 94*
Reilly, Joan Rita 1947- *WhoMW 93*
Reilly, John 1940- *WhoHol 92*
Reilly, John Bernard 1947- *WhoAmL 94*
Reilly, John C. *WhoHol 92*
Reilly, John J. 1942- *WhoAmL 94*
Reilly, John Paul 1943- *WhoFI 94*
Reilly, Judith Gladding 1935- *WhoScEn 94*
Reilly, Karen Powers 1953- *WhoFI 94*
Reilly, Kevin Francis 1955- *WhoAmL 94, WhoFI 94*
Reilly, Kevin Michael 1938- *WhoAmL 94*
Reilly, Kevin P. 1928- *WhoAmP 93*
Reilly, Kevin Patrick 1963- *WhoMW 93*
Reilly, Kevin Thomas 1960- *WhoFI 94*
Reilly, Margaret Anne 1937- *WhoScEn 94*
Reilly, Mary Anne Sommers 1943- *WhoAm 94*
Reilly, Michael Atlee 1948- *WhoFI 94*
Reilly, Michael Thomas 1955- *WhoScEn 94*
Reilly, Nancy *DrAPF 93*
Reilly, Nancy 1927- *WhoAmA 93*
Reilly, Patrick *Who 94*
Reilly, (D'Arcy) Patrick 1909- *IntWW 93, Who 94*
Reilly, Patrick John 1925- *WhoFI 94*
Reilly, Peter C. 1907- *WhoAm 94, WhoFI 94, WhoMW 93, WhoScEn 94*
Reilly, Richard 1926- *WhoAmA 93*
Reilly, Robert Frederick 1952- *WhoAm 94, WhoFI 94, WhoMW 93*
Reilly, Robert Joseph 1936- *WhoWest 94*
Reilly, Robert Thomas 1922- *WrDr 94*
Reilly, (David) Robin 1928- *WrDr 94*
Reilly, Sean E. 1961- *WhoAmP 93*
Reilly, Stephen Archer 1947- *WhoAmL 94*
Reilly, Steven Michael 1961- *WhoFI 94*
Reilly, Susan Buckingham 1952- *WhoAmL 94*
Reilly, Timothy P. 1953- *WhoAmL 94*
Reilly, Tom 1960- *WhoHol 92*
Reilly, William Francis 1938- *WhoAm 94, WhoFI 94*
Reilly, William K. 1940- *EnvEnc [port]*
Reilly, William Kane 1940- *WhoAm 94, WhoAmP 93*
Reilly, William Patrick 1917-1991 *WhAm 10*
Reilly, William Thomas 1949- *WhoAm 94*
Reim, Ruthann 1943- *WhoWest 94*
Reiman, Donald Henry 1934- *Who 94, WhoAm 94*
Reiman, Elise d1993 *NewYTBS 93*
Reimann, Aribert 1936- *NewGrDO*
Reimann, Arline 1937- *WhoAmA 93*
Reimann, Bernhard Erwin Ferdinand 1922- *WhoWest 94*
Reimann, Brigitte 1933-1973 *BlmGWL*
Reimann, William P. 1935- *WhoAmA 93*
Reimann, William Page 1935- *WhoAm 94*
Reimer, Bennett 1932- *WhoAm 94*
Reimer, Borge R. 1931- *WhoFI 94*
Reimer, Dennis J. *WhoAm 94*
Reimer, Glenda Faith 1950- *WhoAmP 93*
Reimer, Neil Joseph 1954- *WhoWest 94*
Reimer, Rollin 1939- *WhoAmP 93*
Reimer, Steven James 1957- *WhoWest 94*
Reimers, Ed *WhoHol 92*
Reimers, Georg d1936 *WhoHol 92*
Reimnitz, Elroi 1948- *WhoWest 94*
Reimschuessel, Herbert Kurt 1921- *WhoScEn 94*
Rein, Bert Walter 1941- *WhoAm 94*
Rein, Catherine Amelia 1943- *WhoAm 94*
Rein, Harold *EncSF 93*
Rein, Martin L. 1915- *WhoIns 94*
Rein, Martin Louis 1915- *WhoAmL 94, WhoFI 94*
Rein, Stanley M. 1946- *WhoAm 94*
Rein, Wolfgang 1947- *WhoAm 94*
Reina, Domenico 1797-1843 *NewGrDO*
Reina, Nicholas Joseph 1948- *WhoHisp 94*
Reina, Nick J. 1956- *WhoHisp 94*
Reinagle, Alexander 1756-1809 *NewGrDO*
Reinard, Roy 1954- *WhoAmP 93*
Reinauer, Richard 1926- *IntMPA 94*
Reinberg, Deborah *IntMPA 94*
Reinbold, James S. *DrAPF 93*
Reinbold, Leo 1933- *WhoAmP 93*
Reince, Martha Mary 1962- *WhoWest 94*
Reincke, Rhonda 1958- *WhoMW 93*
Reindel, Carl *WhoHol 92*
Reindel, F. William 1953- *WhoAmL 94*
Reindel, William George 1871-1948 *WhoAmA 93N*
Reinders, James W. 1927- *WhoWest 94*
Reindl, Constantin 1738-1799 *NewGrDO*
Reindorf, Samuel 1914-1988 *WhoAmA 93N*
Reineck, Gay Beste *DrAPF 93*
Reinecke, Carl (Heinrich Carsten) 1824-1910 *NewGrDO*
Reinecke, David William 1957- *WhoAmL 94*
Reinecke, Ed 1924- *WhoAmP 93*

Reinecke, Manfred G. 1935- *WhoAm 94*
Reinecke, Mike Gerard 1960- *WhoAmL 94*
Reinecke, Robert Dale 1929- *WhoAm 94*
Reineke, Harold George 1897- *WhAm 10*
Reineker, Peter 1940- *WhoScEn 94*
Reinemund, Steven S. 1948- *WhoAm 94, WhoFI 94*
Reiner, Carl 1922- *WhoAm 94, WhoCom, WhoHol 92*
Reiner, Carl 1923- *IntMPA 94*
Reiner, Fritz d1963 *WhoHol 92*
Reiner, Fritz 1888-1963 *NewGrDO*
Reiner, Gladys & Reiner, Jules 1918- *WhoAmA 93*
Reiner, James Anthony 1958- *WhoWest 94*
Reiner, John 1947- *WhoAmL 94*
Reiner, Jules 1918- *See* Reiner, Gladys & Reiner, Jules 1918- *WhoAmA 93*
Reiner, Jules 1918- *WhoAmA 93*
Reiner, Rob 1945- *IntWW 93, WhoAm 94, WhoCom*
Reiner, Rob 1947- *IntMPA 94*
Reiner, Rob(ert) 1945- *WhoHol 92*
Reiner, Samuel Theodore 1933- *WhoAmL 94*
Reiner, Stuart 1943- *WhoFI 94*
Reiner, Tracy 1964- *WhoHol 92*
Reiners, Karlheinz 1950- *WhoScEn 94*
Reiners, Stephen Joseph 1956- *WhoFI 94*
Reiners, William Joseph 1923- *Who 94*
Reinert, Erik Steenfeldt 1949- *WhoScEn 94*
Reinert, Heinrich 1920- *IntWW 93*
Reinert, James A. 1944- *WhoScEn 94*
Reinert, Norbert Frederick 1928- *WhoAm 94*
Reinert, Pamela Ann 1952- *WhoAm 94*
Reinert, Paul Clare 1910- *WhoAm 94*
Reinert, Ronald *WhoAmP 93*
Reinertsen, Norman 1934- *WhoAm 94*
Reinertson, Lisa 1955- *WhoAmA 93*
Reines, Frederick 1918- *IntWW 93, WhoAm 94, WhoScEn 94, WorScD*
Reinfeld, Linda M. 1940- *ConAu 141*
Reinfeld, Stuart Glenn 1959- *WhoAmL 94*
Reinfelds, Juris 1936- *WhoWest 94*
Reinglass, Michelle Annette 1954- *WhoAmL 94*
Reingold, Haim 1910- *WhoAm 94*
Reingold, Michael H. *WhoAm 94*
Reingold, Nathan 1927- *ConAu 140, WhoAm 94*
Reinhard, Carolyn Jill 1961- *WhoAmL 94*
Reinhard, Christopher John 1953- *WhoAm 94*
Reinhard, Keith Leon 1935- *IntWW 93, WhoAm 94, WhoFI 94*
Reinhard, Marilyn Marjean 1933- *WhoMW 93*
Reinhard, Mary Marthe 1929- *WhoAm 94*
Reinhard, Norman Arthur 1939- *WhoMW 93*
Reinhard, Philip G. 1941- *WhoAm 94, WhoAmL 94, WhoMW 93*
Reinhard, Walter G. 1945- *WhoAmL 94*
Reinhardt, Ad F. 1913-1967 *WhoAmA 93N*
Reinhardt, Bruce Steven 1951- *WhoWest 94*
Reinhardt, Charles Francis 1933- *WhoScEn 94*
Reinhardt, Daniel Sargent 1949- *WhoAm 94, WhoAmL 94*
Reinhardt, David John 1954- *WhoFI 94*
Reinhardt, Delia 1892-1974 *NewGrDO*
Reinhardt, Domingo Haroldo 1952- *WhoWest 94*
Reinhardt, Gottfried 1911- *IntMPA 94*
Reinhardt, Heinrich 1865-1922 *NewGrDO*
Reinhardt, James Alec 1942- *WhoAm 94*
Reinhardt, John d1953 *WhoHol 92*
Reinhardt, John Edward 1920- *IntWW 93, WhoAm 94, WhoAmP 93, WhoBlA 94*
Reinhardt, Jon David 1943- *WhoAmP 93*
Reinhardt, Kenneth Gerald 1951- *WhoMW 93*
Reinhardt, Kurt 1920- *WhoScEn 94*
Reinhardt, Madge *DrAPF 93*
Reinhardt, Marion J. d1993 *NewYTBS 93*
Reinhardt, Max 1873-1943 *NewGrDO*
Reinhardt, Max 1915- *IntWW 93, Who 94*
Reinhardt, Richard R. 1934- *WhoAmP 93*
Reinhardt, Stephen *WhoAmP 93*
Reinhardt, Stephen Roy 1931- *WhoAm 94, WhoAmL 94, WhoWest 94*
Reinhardt, Uwe Ernst 1937- *WhoAm 94, WhoScEn 94*
Reinhardt, William Parker 1942- *WhoAm 94, WhoWest 94*
Reinhart, Bill 20th cent.- *BasBi*
Reinhart, Dietrich Thomas 1949- *WhoAm 94*
Reinhart, Kellee Connely 1951- *WhoAm 94*
Reinhart, Margaret Emily 1908- *WhoAmA 93*
Reinhart, Mary Ann 1942- *WhoAm 94, WhoScEn 94*
Reinhart, Peter 1950- *WrDr 94*
Reinhart, Peter Sargent 1950- *WhoAm 94*
Reinhart, Robert Karl 1962- *WhoScEn 94*
Reinhart, Robert Rountree, Jr. 1947- *WhoAm 94, WhoAmL 94*
Reinharz, Jehuda 1944- *WhoAm 94*
Reinheart, Alice d1993 *NewYTBS 93*
Reinheimer, Robert, Jr. 1917- *WhoAm 94*
Reinherz, Helen Zarsky 1923- *WhoAm 94*
Reinhold, Allen Kurt 1936- *WhoWest 94*
Reinhold, Frederick Charles 1737-1815 *NewGrDO*
Reinhold, Henry d1751 *NewGrDO*
Reinhold, Judge 1957- *IntMPA 94*
Reinhold, Judge 1958- *WhoHol 92*
Reinhold, Richard Lawrence 1951- *WhoAm 94, WhoAmL 94*
Reinholm, Gert 1926- *IntDcB*
Reinholt, George 1939- *WhoHol 92*
Reinhorn, Andrei M. 1945- *WhoAm 94*
Reinicke, Verle Arden 1942- *WhoMW 93*
Reinig, Christa 1926- *BlmGWL*
Reinig, Timothy Warren 1957- *WhoAmL 94*
Reiniger, Douglas Haigh 1948- *WhoAmL 94*
Reiniger, Lotte 1899-1981 *IntDcF 2-4*
Reining, Donald James 1923- *WhoWest 94*
Reining, Maria 1903-1991 *NewGrDO*
Reininghaus, Ruth 1922- *WhoAm 94, WhoAmA 93*
Reinisch, Bodo Walter 1936- *WhoScEn 94*
Reinisch, June Machover 1943- *WhoAm 94*
Reinisch, Lou 1954- *WhoScEn 94*
Reinisch, Marc Conrad 1963- *WhoFI 94*
Reinisch, Nancy Rae 1953- *WhoWest 94*
Reinke, Barbara Jean 1953- *WhoMW 93*
Reinke, Doris Marie 1922- *WhoMW 93*
Reinke, Leonard Herman 1918- *WhoAm 94*
Reinke, Ralph Louis 1927- *WhoAm 94*
Reinke, Stefan Michael 1958- *WhoAmL 94*
Reinke, William John 1930- *WhoAm 94, WhoAmL 94*
Reinking, Ann 1949- *WhoHol 92*
Reinmar, Hans 1895-1961 *NewGrDO*
Reinmar der Alte c. 1165-c. 1205 *DcLB 138 [port]*
Reinmar von Zweter c. 1200-c. 1250 *DcLB 138 [port]*
Reinmuth, James E. *WhoAm 94, WhoFI 94, WhoWest 94*
Reinmuth, Oscar MacNaughton 1927- *WhoAm 94*
Reino, Fernando 1929- *IntWW 93*
Reinoehl, Richard Louis 1944- *WhoAm 94*
Reinold, Bernard A. d1940 *WhoHol 92*
Reins, Ralph Erich 1940- *WhoAm 94, WhoFI 94*
Reinsberg-Duringsfeld, Ida von 1815-1876 *BlmGWL*
Reinsch, James Leonard 1908-1991 *WhAm 10*
Reinsch, William Alan 1946- *WhoAmP 93*
Reinschke, Kurt Johannes 1940- *WhoScEn 94*
Reinschmidt, Kenneth Frank 1938- *WhoAm 94*
Reinschmiedt, Anne Tierney 1932- *WhoFI 94, WhoScEn 94*
Reinsdorf, Jerry Michael 1936- *WhoAm 94, WhoFI 94, WhoMW 93*
Reinshagen, Gerlind 1926- *BlmGWL, IntWW 93*
Reinsma, Harold Lawrence 1928- *WhoMW 93, WhoScEn 94*
Reinsmith, Richard 1930- *EncSF 93*
Reinstein, Alan 1947- *WhoAm 94*
Reinstein, Alan Lee 1928- *WhoAmL 94*
Reinstein, Henry Allen 1922- *WhoWest 94*
Reinstein, Joel 1946- *WhoAm 94, WhoAmL 94*
Reinstein, Paul Michael 1952- *WhoAm 94*
Reinstein, Todd Bennett 1968- *WhoFI 94*
Reinstein, William George 1939- *WhoAmP 93*
Reinthaler, Karl (Martin) 1822-1896 *NewGrDO*
Reinthaler, Richard Walter 1949- *WhoAm 94*
Reintsema, Robert Arnold 1937- *WhoAmP 93*
Reinwald, Arthur Burton 1929- *WhoAm 94*
Reiplinger, John Edward 1942- *WhoFI 94*
Reiring, Janelle 1946- *WhoAmA 93*
Reis, Arthur Robert, Jr. 1916- *WhoAm 94*
Reis, Don 1927- *WhoAm 94*
Reis, Donald Jeffery 1931- *WhoAm 94, WhoScEn 94*
Reis, Frank Henry 1936- *WhoFI 94*
Reis, Jean Stevenson 1914- *WhoWest 94*
Reis, Joao Carlos Ribeiro 1945- *WhoScEn 94*
Reis, Judson Patterson 1942- *WhoAm 94*
Reis, Maria Firmina dos 1825-1917 *BlmGWL*
Reis, Mario 1953- *WhoAmA 93*
Reis, Muriel Henle *WhoAmL 94*
Reis, Patrick Joseph 1951- *WhoMW 93*
Reis, Robert John 1950- *WhoFI 94*
Reis, Victor H. *WhoScEn 94*
Reis, Wanda Mendes 1953- *WhoWomW 91*
Reisberg, Barry 1947- *WhoAm 94*
Reisberg, Leon Elton 1949- *WhoWest 94*
Reisch, Georg 1930- *IntWW 93*
Reisch, Harold Franklin 1920- *WhoAmP 93*
Reisch, Michael Stewart 1948- *WhoWest 94*
Reisch, Walter 1903-1983 *IntDcF 2-4*
Reischauer, Edwin Oldfather 1910-1990 *WhAm 10*
Reischman, Michael Mack 1942- *WhoScEn 94*
Reise, Barbara d1978 *WhoAmA 93N*
Reise, Jay 1950- *NewGrDO*
Reisen, Mark *NewGrDO*
Reisenauer, Kevin 1959- *WhoMW 93*
Reisenbach, Sanford E. *IntMPA 94*
Reiser, David Richard 1959- *WhoFI 94*
Reiser, Leroy Franklin, Jr. 1921- *WhoAm 94*
Reiser, Morton Francis 1919- *WhoAm 94*
Reiser, Paul *WhoAm 94*
Reiser, Paul 1956- *WhoHol 92*
Reiser, Paul 1957- *IntMPA 94*
Reisert, Charles Edward, Jr. 1941- *WhoMW 93*
Reisgies, Teresa (Maria) 1966- *SmATA 74 [port]*
Reisig, Martin I. 1945- *WhoAmL 94*
Reising, H. William 1942- *WhoAmL 94*
Reising, Richard P. *WhoAmL 94*
Reisinger, Barbara *NewGrDO*
Reisinger, George Lambert 1930- *WhoAm 94, WhoFI 94, WhoWest 94*
Reisinger, Joy Ann 1934- *WhoMW 93*
Reisinger, Robert Lee 1964- *WhoAmL 94*
Reisler, Helen Barbara 1933- *WhoFI 94*
Reisler, Raymond, Sr. 1907-1992 *WhAm 10*
Reisman, Arnold 1934- *WhoAm 94, WhoMW 93*
Reisman, Averil 1942- *WhoMW 93*
Reisman, Fredricka Kauffman 1930- *WhoAm 94*
Reisman, Philip 1904-1992 *WhoAmA 93N*
Reisman, Robert E. 1932- *WhoAm 94*
Reismann, Herbert 1926- *WhoAm 94*
Reismeyer, David W. 1957- *WhoFI 94*
Reisner, Allen *IntMPA 94*
Reisner, Andrew Douglas 1955- *WhoMW 93, WhoScEn 94*
Reisner, Barbara *DrAPF 93*
Reisner, John Henry, Jr. 1917- *WhoScEn 94*
Reisner, Larisa Mikhailovna 1895-1926 *BlmGWL*
Reisner, Milton 1934- *WhoScEn 94*
Reisner, Phyllis 1934- *WhoFI 94, WhoWest 94*
Reiss, Albert 1870-1940 *NewGrDO*
Reiss, Albert John, Jr. 1922- *WhoAm 94*
Reiss, Alvin 1932- *WhoAm 94*
Reiss, Barbara Eve *DrAPF 93*
Reiss, Betti 1944- *WhoScEn 94*
Reiss, Bonnie M.S. 1954- *WhoAm 94, WhoAmL 94*
Reiss, Dale Anne 1947- *WhoAm 94, WhoFI 94*
Reiss, Donald Andrew 1945- *WhoScEn 94*
Reiss, Elaine Serlin 1940- *WhoFI 94*
Reiss, Gertrude *DrAPF 93*
Reiss, Howard 1922- *IntWW 93, WhoAm 94, WhoScEn 94*
Reiss, Ira Leonard 1925- *WhoAm 94, WrDr 94*
Reiss, James *DrAPF 93*
Reiss, Jeffrey C. 1942- *IntMPA 94*
Reiss, Jeffrey Charles 1942- *WhoFI 94*
Reiss, Jerome 1924- *WhoAm 94*
Reiss, John Barlow 1939- *WhoAm 94, WhoAmL 94*
Reiss, John C. 1922- *WhoAm 94*
Reiss, John Henry 1918- *Who 94*
Reiss, Kathryn 1957- *SmATA 76 [port]*
Reiss, Kenneth William 1959- *WhoFI 94, WhoMW 93*
Reiss, Lionel S. 1929- *WhoAmA 93N*
Reiss, Martin Harold 1935- *WhoAm 94*
Reiss, Michael 1943- *WhoAm 94, WhoAmL 94*
Reiss, Paul Jacob 1930- *WhoAm 94*
Reiss, Raymond Henry 1897- *WhAm 10*
Reiss, Rhoda 1943- *WhoAmP 93*
Reiss, Roland 1929- *WhoAmA 93*
Reiss, Roland M. 1929- *WhoAm 94*
Reiss, Ronn 1932- *WhoFI 94*
Reiss, Sidney H. 1926- *WhoAm 94, WhoAmL 94*
Reiss, Steven Alan 1951- *WhoAm 94, WhoAmL 94*
Reiss, Stuart A. 1921- *IntMPA 94*
Reiss, Timothy James 1942- *IntWW 93, WhoAm 94*
Reissenweber, Beth Randerson 1961- *WhoMW 93*
Reissig, Martha Tilton 1929- *WhoMW 93*
Reissiger, Karl Gottlieb 1798-1859 *NewGrDO*
Reissmann, August (Friedrich Wilhelm) 1825-1903 *NewGrDO*
Reissner, Eric 1913- *WhoScEn 94*
Reissner, Eric Max Erich 1913- *WhoAm 94*
Reister, Raymond Alex 1929- *WhoAm 94, WhoAmL 94, WhoMW 93*
Reister, Ruth Alkema 1936- *WhoAm 94*
Reistle, Carl Ernest, Jr. 1901- *WhoAm 94*
Reiswig, Kay B. *WhoAmP 93*
Reisz, John P. 1944- *WhoAmL 94*
Reisz, Karel 1926- *IntMPA 94, IntWW 93, Who 94*
Reitan, Daniel Kinseth 1921- *WhoAm 94*
Reitan, Earl Aaron 1925- *WhoMW 93*
Reitan, Harold Theodore 1928- *WhoWest 94*
Reitan, Paul Hartman 1928- *WhoAm 94*
Reitemeier, George 1931- *WhoWest 94*
Reitemeier, Joseph Richard 1954- *WhoMW 93*
Reitemeier, Richard Joseph 1923- *WhoAm 94*
Reiten, Chester *WhoAmP 93*
Reiten, Eivind 1953- *IntWW 93*
Reiten, Richard 1939- *WhoAm 94, WhoFI 94, WhoWest 94*
Reitenour, Steven Lynn 1956- *WhoAmL 94*
Reiter, Bonnie Jean 1948- *WhoMW 93*
Reiter, Glenn Mitchell 1951- *WhoAm 94, WhoAmL 94*
Reiter, Harvey Leonard 1950- *WhoAmL 94*
Reiter, Janusz 1952- *IntWW 93*
Reiter, Josef 1862-1939 *NewGrDO*
Reiter, Joseph Henry 1929- *WhoAm 94, WhoAmL 94*
Reiter, Michael A. 1941- *WhoAm 94, WhoAmL 94*
Reiter, Nathan I., Jr. 1917- *WhoAmP 93*
Reiter, Richard Ronald 1938- *WhoAm 94*
Reiter, Robert Edward 1943- *WhoAm 94, WhoFI 94*
Reiter, Sheldon 1942- *WhoAmL 94*
Reiter, Stanley 1925- *WhoAm 94, WhoScEn 94*
Reiter, Susan K. 1942- *WhoAmL 94*
Reiter, Sydney Louise 1942- *WhoMW 93*
Reiter, Thomas *DrAPF 93*
Reiter, William Martin 1925- *WhoScEn 94*
Reith, Baron of *Who 94*
Reith, Carl Joseph 1914- *WhoAm 94*
Reith, Christopher John 1928- *Who 94*
Reith, Douglas 1919- *Who 94*
Reith, Martin 1935- *Who 94*
Reith, Peter 1950- *IntWW 93*
Reitinger, Thomas Anthony 1944- *WhoAm 94, WhoMW 93*
Reitman, Ivan 1946- *IntMPA 94, WhoAm 94*
Reitman, Jerry Irving 1938- *WhoAm 94*
Reitman, Judith 1951- *ConAu 142*
Reitman, Mitchell H. 1958- *WhoFI 94*
Reitman, Robert Stanley 1933- *WhoAm 94, WhoFI 94*
Reitmeister, Noel William 1938- *WhoFI 94*
Reitner, Barnet 1945- *WhoAmL 94*
Reitsma, Jan Harmen 1948- *WhoAmL 94*
Reitter, Charles Andrew 1956- *WhoAm 94*
Reitter, Rose *DrAPF 93*
Reitz, Barbara Maurer 1931- *WhoMW 93*
Reitz, Charles Edward 1946- *WhoMW 93*
Reitz, Curtis Randall *WhoAm 94*
Reitz, David Alan 1950- *WhoFI 94, WhoMW 93*
Reitz, Del *DrAPF 93*
Reitz, Edgar 1932- *IntWW 93*
Reitz, Elmer A. 1909- *WhoFI 94*
Reitz, Henry Matthew 1922- *WhoMW 93*
Reitz, Howard Wesley 1947- *WhoFI 94*
Reitz, J. Wayne 1908-1993 *NewYTBS 93*
Reitz, Richard Elmer 1938- *WhoAm 94, WhoScEn 94*
Reitz, Ronald Charles 1939- *WhoWest 94*
Reitze, David Howard 1961- *WhoScEn 94*
Reitzenstein, Reinhard 1949- *WhoAmA 93*
Reitzfeld, Robert 1938- *WhoAm 94*
Reizenstein, Franz (Theodor) 1911-1968 *NewGrDO*
Reizenstein, Peter Georg 1928- *WhoScEn 94*
Reizner, Lou d1978 *WhoHol 92*

Rejai, Mostafa 1931- *WhoAm 94, WrDr 94*
Rejane, Gabrielle d1920 *WhoHol 92*
Rekate, Albert C. 1916- *WhoAm 94*
Reker, Les 1951- *WhoAmA 93*
Rekert, Winston *WhoHol 92*
Rekkas, Christos Michail 1962- *WhoScEn 94*
Rekola, Esko Johannes 1919- *IntWW 93*
Rekowski, John Joseph 1951- *WhoAmP 93*
Rekstis, Walter J., III 1945- *WhoAm 94, WhoAmL 94*
Relangi d1975 *WhoHol 92*
Reldan, Robert Ronald 1942- *WhoAmL 94, WhoFI 94*
Relf, Keith 1943-1976
See Yardbirds, The *ConMus 10*
Relias, John Alexis 1946- *WhoAm 94, WhoAmL 94*
Religa, James Paul 1953- *WhoWest 94*
Relin, Marie-Therese *WhoHol 92*
Rell, M. Jodi *WhoWomW 91*
Rell, M. Jodi 1946- *WhoAmP 93*
Relle, Attila Tibor 1959- *WhoMW 93*
Relle, Ferenc Matyas 1922- *WhoAm 94, WhoMW 93, WhoScEn 94*
Reller, L. Barth *WhoScEn 94*
Rellie, Alastair James Carl Euan 1935- *Who 94*
Rellstab, (Heinrich Friedrich) Ludwig 1799-1860 *NewGrDO*
Relly, Gavin Walter Hamilton 1926- *IntWW 93, Who 94*
Relman, Arnold Seymour 1923- *WhoAm 94*
Relph, George d1960 *WhoHol 92*
Relph, Kaye B. 1918- *WhoAmP 93*
Relph, Michael *IntMPA 94, IntWW 93*
Relph, Michael Leighton George *Who 94*
Relph, Simon 1940- *IntMPA 94*
Relph, Simon George Michael 1940- *Who 94*
Relson, Morris 1915- *WhoAm 94*
Relton, Stanley 1923- *Who 94*
Relwani, Nirmalkumar Murlidhar 1954- *WhoScEn 94*
Relyea, Robert E. 1930- *IntMPA 94*
Relyea, Robert Gordon 1917- *WhoWest 94*
Rem, Joseph Paul, Jr. 1950- *WhoAmL 94*
Remacle, Rosemary 1942- *WhoWest 94*
Remak, Henry H.H. 1916- *WhoMW 93*
Remar, James 1953- *IntMPA 94, WhoHol 92*
Remar, Robert Boyle 1948- *WhoAmL 94*
Remarque, Erich Maria d1970 *WhoHol 92*
Rematt, Theodore J. *WhoAm 94*
Rembar, Charles 1915- *WrDr 94*
Rembar, Charles Isaiah 1915- *WhoAm 94*
Rembar, James Carlson 1949- *WhoScEn 94*
Rembe, Toni 1936- *WhoAm 94, WhoAmL 94*
Rembert, Donald Mosby 1939- *WhoFI 94*
Rembert, Emma White *WhoBlA 94*
Rembert, Virginia Pitts 1921- *WhoAm 94, WhoAmA 93*
Rembo, Sonja Marie Hillevi 1933- *WhoWomW 91*
Rembski, Stanislav *WhoAm 94, WhoAmA 93*
Rembusch, Trueman T. 1909- *IntMPA 94*
Remec, Thomas Michael 1946- *WhoMW 93*
Remedios, Alberto (Telisforo) 1935- *NewGrDO*
Remedios, Alberto Telisforo 1935- *IntWW 93, Who 94*
Remedios, Ramon 1940- *NewGrDO*
Remels, Keith Mitchell 1963- *WhoAmL 94*
Remeneski, Shirley Rodriguez 1938- *WhoHisp 94*
Remenick, Seymour 1923- *WhoAm 94, WhoAmA 93*
Remer, Donald Sherwood 1943- *WhoAm 94*
Remer, Vernon Ralph 1918- *WhoAm 94*
Remey, Ethel d1979 *WhoHol 92*
Remez, Aharon 1919- *Who 94*
Remick, Barbara R. 1938- *WhoAmP 93*
Remick, Forrest Jerome, Jr. 1931- *WhoAm 94*
Remick, Lee d1991 *WhoHol 92*
Remick, Lee 1935-1991 *WhAm 10*
Remick, Oscar Eugene 1932- *WhoAm 94*
Remillard, Gil 1944- *WhoAm 94*
Remillard, Richard Louis 1954- *WhoScEn 94*
ReMine, Debra Bjurquist 1956- *WhoAmL 94, WhoMW 93*
ReMine, William Hervey, Jr. 1918- *WhoAm 94, WhoScEn 94*
Reminger, Richard Thomas 1931- *WhoAm 94, WhoAmL 94, WhoMW 93*
Remington, Charles Bradford 1935- *WhoAm 94, WhoFI 94*
Remington, Clinton O., III 1945- *WhoAmP 93*
Remington, Deborah Williams 1935- *IntWW 93, WhoAm 94, WhoAmA 93*
Remington, Delwin Woolley 1950- *WhoFI 94, WhoScEn 94, WhoWest 94*
Remington, Jack Samuel 1931- *WhoAm 94*
Remington, Mark *ConAu 42NR*
Remington, Philipa M. 1949- *WhoAmL 94*
Remington, Scott Alan 1964- *WhoScEn 94*
Remini, Robert Vincent 1921- *WhoAm 94*
Remis, Margaret Helen *WhoMW 93*
Remis, Shepard M. 1943- *WhoAmL 94*
Remke, Richard Edwin 1943- *WhoFI 94*
Remkiewicz, Frank 1939- *SmATA 77 [port]*
Remley, Frank d1967 *WhoHol 92*
Remley, Ralph M. d1939 *WhoHol 92*
Remley, Theodore Phant, Jr. 1947- *WhoAm 94*
Remmelink, Jan 1922- *IntWW 93*
Remmenga, D. Elaine 1932- *WhoAmP 93*
Remmer, Harry Thomas, Jr. 1920- *WhoScEn 94*
Remmers, R. Wiley 1916- *WhoAmP 93*
Remmert, Pete 1934- *WhoAmP 93*
Remmey, Paul B. *WhoAmA 93N*
Remnant, Baron 1930- *Who 94*
Remond, Fritz d1976 *WhoHol 92*
Rempel, William C. 1947- *ConAu 141*
Remple, Timothy Kirk 1955- *WhoWest 94*
Remsberg, Stephen R. 1947- *WhoAmL 94*
Remsen, Bert 1925- *IntMPA 94, WhoHol 92*
Remsen, Charles Cornell, III 1937- *WhoScEn 94*
Remsen, Deborah d1977 *WhoHol 92*
Remsen, James Vanderbeek, Jr. 1949- *WhoScEn 94*
Remsen, John 1939- *WhoAmA 93*
Remsing, (Joseph) Gary 1946- *WhoAmA 93*
Remson, Anthony Terence 1952- *WhoBlA 94*
Remson, Irwin 1923- *WhoAm 94*
Remus, Edward W. 1942- *WhoAmL 94*
Remus, Eugene *WhoBlA 94*
Remus, Romola d1987 *WhoHol 92*
Remusat, Claire de 1780-1821 *BlmGWL*
Remy, Albert d1967 *WhoHol 92*
Remy, Dick, Sr. d1947 *WhoHol 92*
Remy, Pierre-Jean 1937- *IntWW 93*
Remy, Ray *WhoAm 94, WhoWest 94*
Remy, Robert E. 1952- *WhoIns 94*
Ren, Chung-Li 1931- *WhoScEn 94*
Ren, Shang Yuan 1940- *WhoAsA 94*
Renaldo, Duncan d1980 *WhoHol 92*
Renals, Stanley 1923- *Who 94*
Renant, Simone *WhoHol 92*
Renard, David d1973 *WhoHol 92*
Renard, Joseph 1938- *EncSF 93*
Renard, Ken *WhoHol 92*
Renard, Kenneth George 1934- *WhoAm 94*
Renard, Maurice 1875-1939 *EncSF 93*
Renard, Paul Steven 1934- *WhoMW 93*
Renard, Ronald Lee 1949- *WhoWest 94*
Renaud, Bernadette Marie Elise 1945- *WhoAm 94*
Renaud, Dennis L. 1942- *WhoAmP 93*
Renaud, Gilles *WhoHol 92*
Renaud, Line *WhoHol 92*
Renaud, Madeleine 1900- *IntWW 93, WhoHol 92*
Renaud, Madeleine 1903- *Who 94*
Renaud, Maurice (Arnold) 1860-1933 *NewGrDO*
Renaud, Pierre Jean Marie 1894- *WhAm 10*
Renaud, Ronald N. 1959- *WhoAmP 93*
Renauer, Albin (J.) 1959- *WrDr 94*
Renau I Manen, Maria Dolores 1935- *WhoWomW 91*
Renault, Camille d1976 *WhoHol 92*
Renault, Louis 1877-1944 *WorInv*
Renault, Mary 1905-1983 *BlmGWL, GayLL*
Renault, Michel d1993 *NewYTBS 93*
Renault, Michel 1927-1993 *IntDcB*
Renavent, Georges d1969 *WhoHol 92*
Renay, Liz 1926- *WhoHol 92*
Rench, Richard E. 1941- *WhoAmP 93*
Ren Chao *WhoPRCh 91*
Renchard, William S(hryock) 1908- *IntWW 93*
Renchard, William Shryock 1908- *WhoFI 94*
Renda, Dominic Phillip 1913- *WhoAm 94*
Renda, Randolph Bruce 1926- *WhoAm 94*
Rendall, David 1948- *NewGrDO*
Rendall, Peter Godfrey 1909- *Who 94*
Rendano, Alfonso 1853-1931 *NewGrDO*
Rendel, Betty J. *WhoAmP 93*
Rendel, David Digby 1949- *Who 94*
Rendel, Stuart 1834-1913 *DcNaB MP*
Rendell, Edward G. *WhoAmP 93*
Rendell, Edward Gene 1944- *WhoAm 94, WhoAmL 94*
Rendell, Joan *WrDr 94*
Rendell, Robert Sloat 1940- *WhoAm 94*
Rendell, Ruth 1930- *BlmGWL, IntWW 93, WrDr 94*
Rendell, Ruth Barbara 1930- *Who 94*
Rendell, William 1908- *Who 94*
Rendell-Baker, Leslie 1917- *WhoAm 94*
Render, Arlene *WhoAm 94, WhoAmP 93*
Render, Arlene 1943- *WhoBlA 94*
Render, Regina Alberta 1961- *WhoMW 93*
Render, William H. 1950- *WhoBlA 94*
Ren Deyao *WhoPRCh 91 [port]*
Rendina, George 1923- *WhoScEn 94*
Rendine, Robert J. *WhoAmP 93*
Rendl, M(ildred Marcus) 1928- *WhoAmA 93*
Rendle, Michael Russel 1931- *IntWW 93, Who 94*
Rendle, Peter Critchfield 1919- *Who 94*
Rendleman, Danny *DrAPF 93*
Rendleman, Nancy S. 1952- *WhoAmL 94*
Rendlen, Albert L. *WhoAmP 93*
Rendlen, Charles Earnest, Jr. 1919- *WhoAmP 93*
Rendlen, Charles Earnest, III 1950- *WhoAmP 93*
Rendlen, Charles Earnest Sketch, III 1950- *WhoAmL 94*
Rendlesham, Baron 1915- *Who 94*
Rendle-Short, John 1919- *WrDr 94*
Rendl-Marcus, Mildred 1928- *WhoFI 94*
Rendón, Armando B. 1939- *WhoHisp 94, WrDr 94*
Rendón, Florencio H. 1950- *WhoHisp 94*
Rendón, Josefina Muñiz 1949- *WhoHisp 94*
Rendon, Juan Jose, Sr. 1945- *WhoHisp 94*
Rendon, Mario Ivan 1938- *WhoHisp 94*
Rendon, Ruth Marie 1961- *WhoHisp 94*
Rendón, Sally *WhoHisp 94*
Rendon, Thomas Tipton 1958- *WhoMW 93*
Rendón, Uriel 1960- *WhoHisp 94*
Rendon-Herrero, Oswald 1937- *WhoHisp 94*
Rendu, Jean-Michel Marie 1944- *WhoScEn 94, WhoWest 94*
Rene, (France) Albert 1935- *IntWW 93, Who 94*
Rene, Louis 1918- *IntWW 93*
Reneau, Daniel D. *WhoAm 94, WhoScEn 94*
Reneberg, Richard 1965- *WhoAm 94*
Renee 1929- *BlmGWL, ConDr 93*
Renee, Lisabeth 1952- *WhoAmA 93*
Renee, Paula *WhoAmA 93*
Renehan, Edward J(ohn), Jr. 1956- *ConAu 140*
Renehan, Robert Francis Xavier 1935- *WhoAm 94*
Reneker, Maxine Hohman 1942- *WhoAm 94*
Renella, Pat *WhoHol 92*
Renetzky, Alvin 1940- *WhoWest 94*
Reney, Everett R. 1914- *WhoAmP 93*
Renfert, Blaine Rusy 1961- *WhoAmL 94*
Renfield, Richard Lee 1932- *WrDr 94*
Renford, Edward J. 1943- *WhoAm 94*
Renfrew *Who 94*
Renfrew, Charles Byron 1928- *WhoAmL 94, WhoFI 94*
Renfrew, (Andrew) Colin 1937- *WrDr 94*
Renfrew, Glen McGarvie 1928- *Who 94*
Renfrew, Malcolm MacKenzie 1910- *WhoAm 94*
Renfrew Of Kaimsthorn, Baron 1937- *IntWW 93, Who 94*
Renfrey, Lionel Edward William 1916- *Who 94*
Renfro, Charles Gilliland 1943- *WhoAm 94*
Renfro, Donald William 1931- *WhoWest 94*
Renfro, John Kevin 1961- *WhoAmL 94*
Renfro, Mary Frances 1965- *WhoAmL 94*
Renfro, Mel 1941- *WhoBlA 94*
Renfro, Rennie d1962 *WhoHol 92*
Renfro, Sally *DrAPF 93*
Renfro, William Leonard 1945- *WhoAmL 94*
Renfroe, Earl W. 1907- *WhoBlA 94*
Renfroe, Iona Antoinette 1953- *WhoBlA 94*
Renfrow, Edward 1940- *WhoAmP 93*
Rengarajan, Sembiam Rajagopal 1948- *WhoScEn 94, WhoWest 94*
Renge, I. Beth 1959- *WhoAsA 94*
Renger, Annemarie 1919- *IntWW 93, WhoWomW 91*
Renger, James Dietrich 1940- *WhoFI 94*
Renick, Carol Bishop 1956- *WhoFI 94*
Renick, Cecil Oren, Jr. 1944- *WhoAm 94*
Renick, James C. 1948- *WhoBlA 94*
Renick, Ralph Apperson 1928-1991 *WhAm 10*
Renick, Ruth d1984 *WhoHol 92*
Renick, William Jackson 1953- *WhoAmP 93*
Renier, Elizabeth 1916- *WrDr 94*
Renier, James J. 1930- *WhoAm 94, WhoFI 94, WhoMW 93*
Renier, Joseph Emile d1966 *WhoAmA 93N*
Renier, Yves *WhoHol 92*
Ren Jianxin 1925- *IntWW 93, WhoPRCh 91 [port]*
Ren Jiyu 1916- *WhoPRCh 91*
Renk, Kristin Yates 1959- *WhoFI 94*
Renk, Merry 1921- *WhoAmA 93*
Renka, Robert Joseph 1947- *WhoAm 94, WhoScEn 94*
Renke, John K. 1946- *WhoAmP 93*
Renken, Kevin James 1961- *WhoScEn 94*
Renken, Paul Brian 1956- *WhoFI 94*
Renken, Robert 1922- *WhoAmP 93*
Renko, Sheri Ann 1958- *WhoMW 93*
Ren Meie *IntWW 93*
Renn, Casey *ConAu 43NR*
Renn, Katharina d1975 *WhoHol 92*
Renn, Kurt Daniel 1964- *WhoFI 94*
Renna, Eugene A. *WhoFI 94*
Renna, John P. 1920- *WhoAmP 93*
Rennard, Deborah *WhoHol 92*
Renne, Janice Lynn 1952- *WhoWest 94*
Renne, Louise Hornbeck 1937- *WhoAmP 93*
Renne, Merlin Moulthrop 1945- *WhoAmP 93*
Rennebohm, J. Fred 1927- *WhoAm 94*
Rennecker, Anita Louise 1937- *WhoMW 93*
Renneke, Earl Wallace 1928- *WhoAmP 93*
Renneker, Frederick Weyman, III 1939- *WhoAm 94*
Rennell, Baron 1935- *Who 94*
Rennels, Marshall Leigh 1939- *WhoAm 94*
Renner, Barbara Jean 1957- *WhoMW 93*
Renner, Bruce *DrAPF 93*
Renner, Clarence E. 1922- *WhoAmL 94, WhoMW 93*
Renner, Daniel Segismundo 1953- *WhoWest 94*
Renner, Eric 1941- *WhoAmA 93*
Renner, George R. 1946- *WhoAmP 93*
Renner, John Wilson 1924- *WhAm 10*
Renner, Michael John 1957- *WhoScEn 94*
Renner, Richard Henry 1962- *WhoFI 94*
Renner, Robert George 1923- *WhoAm 94, WhoAmL 94, WhoMW 93*
Renner, Simon Edward 1934- *WhoAm 94*
Rennerfeldt, Earl R. 1938- *WhoAmP 93*
Rennerfeldt, Earl Ronald 1938- *WhoMW 93*
Rennert, Gunther 1911-1978 *NewGrDO*
Rennert, Owen Murray 1938- *WhoAm 94*
Rennert, Wolfgang 1922- *IntWW 93*
Renner-Tana, Patti *DrAPF 93*
Renneville, Sophie de 1772-1822 *BlmGWL*
Rennick, Kyme Elizabeth Wall 1953- *WhoAmL 94*
Rennie, Alexander Allan 1917- *Who 94*
Rennie, Archibald Louden 1924- *Who 94*
Rennie, Basil Cameron 1920- *WrDr 94*
Rennie, Carol Ann 1939- *WhoIns 94*
Rennie, Guy *WhoHol 92*
Rennie, James d1965 *WhoHol 92*
Rennie, James Douglas Milne 1931- *Who 94*
Rennie, John 1761-1821 *WorInv*
Rennie, John Chalmers 1907- *Who 94*
Rennie, John Coyne 1937- *WhoAm 94*
Rennie, John Shaw 1917- *Who 94*
Rennie, John Vernon Lockhart 1903- *IntWW 93*
Rennie, Kevin F. 1958- *WhoAmP 93*
Rennie, Michael d1971 *WhoHol 92*
Rennie, Robert Alvin 1917- *WhoFI 94*
Renninger, Katharine Steele 1925- *WhoAmA 93*
Renninger, Mary Karen 1945- *WhoAm 94*
Renno, Vincent d1955 *WhoHol 92*
Reno *NewYTBS 93 [port]*
Reno 1956- *WhoHisp 94*
Reno, Barbara Morrison 1946- *WhoAmP 93*
Reno, Douglas Walter 1937- *WhoAmL 94*
Reno, Janet *CngDr 93, WhoAmP 93*
Reno, Janet 1938- *CurBio 93 [port], IntWW 93, NewYTBS 93 [port], News 93-3 [port], Who 94, WhoAm 94, WhoAmL 94*
Reno, Jean *WhoHol 92*
Reno, John Findley 1939- *WhoAm 94, WhoFI 94*
Reno, June Mellies d1993 *NewYTBS 93*
Reno, Kelly 1966- *WhoHol 92*
Reno, Ottie Wayne 1929- *WhoAmL 94, WhoMW 93*
Reno, Roger 1924- *WhoAm 94, WhoAmL 94*
Reno, Russell Ronald, Jr. 1933- *WhoAm 94*

Reuter, James William 1948- *WhoAm 94, WhoAmL 94*
Reuter, John James Arnold 1944- *WhoMW 93*
Reuter, (Paul) Julius de 1816-1899 *DcNaB MP*
Reuter, Laurel J. 1943- *WhoAmA 93*
Reuter, Stewart Ralston 1934- *WhoAm 94*
Reutersward, Carl Fredrik 1934- *IntWW 93*
Reuther, David Louis 1946- *WhoAm 94*
Reuther, James Joseph 1950- *WhoMW 93*
Reuther, Terry Lee 1944- *WhoAmP 93*
Reuther, Walter 1911- *WhoAm 94, WhoWest 94*
Reuther, Walter Philip 1907-1970 *AmSocL*
Reutiman, Robert William, Jr. 1944- *WhoAmL 94*
Reutov, Oleg Aleksandrovich 1920- *IntWW 93*
Reutter, Eberhard Edmund, Jr. 1924- *WhoAm 94*
Reutter, (Johann Adam Joseph Karl) Georg (von) c. 1708-1772 *NewGrDO*
Reutter, Hermann 1900-1985 *NewGrDO*
Reutzel, Barry Lane 1951- *WhoAmP 93*
Revans, Reginald William 1907- *Who 94*
Reve, Gerard (Kornelis van het) 1923- *ConWorW 93*
Reveal, Ernest Ira 1915- *WhoAm 94*
Reveal, Ernest Ira, III 1948- *WhoAm 94, WhoAmL 94*
Revel, Comte de *WhAmRev*
Revel, Gary Neal 1949- *WhoFI 94*
Revel, Harry d1958 *WhoHol 92*
Revel, Jean-Francois 1924- *IntWW 93*
Revel, Mollie d1932 *WhoHol 92*
Reveles, Robert A. 1932- *WhoHisp 94*
Reveley, Edith 1930- *WrDr 94*
Reveley, Walter Taylor, III 1943- *WhoAm 94, WhoAmL 94*
Revell, Anthony Leslie 1935- *Who 94*
Revell, Donald *DrAPF 93*
Revell, Dorothy Evangeline Tompkins 1911- *WhoMW 93*
Revell, John Harold 1906- *WhoWest 94*
Revell, John Robert Stephen 1920- *WrDr 94*
Revell, Oliver Burgan 1938- *WhoAm 94*
Revell, Patsy Roberts 1928- *WhoAmP 93*
ReVelle, Charles S. 1938- *WhoAm 94*
Revelle, Donald Gene 1930- *WhoAm 94*
Revelle, Geoffrey George 1947- *WhoAmL 94*
Revelle, Hamilton d1958 *WhoHol 92*
Re Velle, Jack Boyer 1935- *WhoScEn 94*
Revelle, Randy 1941- *WhoAmP 93*
Revelle, Robert, Sr. 1947- *WhoBlA 94*
Revelle, Roger Randall Dougan 1909-1991 *WhAm 10*
Revelle, William Roger 1944- *WhoScEn 94*
Revelos, Constantine Nicholas 1938- *WhoAmL 94*
Revels, Hiram Rhodes 1827-1901 *AfrAmAl 6 [port]*
Revels, Mia Renea 1966- *WhoScEn 94*
Revels, Richard W., Jr. 1950- *WhoAmL 94*
Revelstoke, Baron 1863-1929 *DcNaB MP*
Revelstoke, Baron 1911- *Who 94*
Revely, William 1941- *WhoBlA 94*
Revens, John Cosgrove, Jr. 1947- *WhoAmP 93*
Reventlov, Franziska zu 1871-1918 *BlmGWL*
Reverand, Cedric Dwight, II 1941- *WhoWest 94*
Revercomb, George H. 1929- *CngDr 93*
Revercomb, George Hughes 1929- *WhoAm 94*
Revercomb, Horace Austin, III 1948- *WhoAmL 94*
Reverdin, Bernard J. 1919- *WhoAm 94*
Reverdin, Olivier 1913- *IntWW 93, Who 94*
Revere, Anne d1990 *WhoHol 92*
Revere, Anne 1903-1990 *WhAm 10*
Revere, Paul 1735-1818 *AmRev, WhAmRev [port]*
Reves, Efren d1968 *WhoHol 92*
Reviczky, Janos 1954- *WhoScEn 94*
Revier, Dorothy d1993 *NewYTBS 93 [port]*
Revier, Dorothy 1904- *WhoHol 92*
Revill, Clive 1930- *IntMPA 94, WhoHol 92*
Revilla, Carmen *WhoHisp 94*
Revilla Beltrán, Vincenne Maria 1952- *WhoHisp 94*
Reville, Alma d1982 *WhoHol 92*
Reville, Alma 1899-1982 *IntDcF 2-4*
Reville, Eugene Thomas 1932- *WhAm 10*
Revington, George D., III *WhoAmA 93N*
Revington Burdick, Betty *WhoAmA 93*
Revis, Nathaniel W. 1939- *WhoBlA 94*
Revish, Jerry 1949- *WhoBlA 94*
Revlock, Therese Cathleen 1965- *WhoMW 93*
Revnell, Ethel d1978 *WhoHol 92*
Revoile, Charles Patrick 1934- *WhoAm 94*
Revol, Jean-Pierre Charles 1948- *WhoScEn 94*
Revol, Max d1967 *WhoHol 92*
Revollo Bravo, Mario 1919- *IntWW 93*
Revor, Remy 1914- *WhoAmA 93*
Revsine, Lawrence 1942- *WhoAm 94*
Revuelta, Pedro *DrAPF 93*
Revy, Richard d1965 *WhoHol 92*
Revzen, Joel *WhoMW 93*
Rew, Paul Francis 1953- *Who 94*
Rew, William Edmund 1923- *WhoFI 94, WhoScEn 94*
Rewak, William John 1933- *WhoAm 94*
Rewald, John 1912- *WrDr 94*
Rewcastle, Neill Barry 1931- *WhoAm 94*
Rewey, Pamela S. 1946- *WhoMW 93*
Rex, David Lawrence 1935- *WhoFI 94*
Rex, Eugen d1943 *WhoHol 92*
Rex, Frances Lillian 1911- *WhoAmP 93*
Rex, Gerald Bartlett 1945- *WhoFI 94*
Rex, John Arderne 1925- *Who 94, WrDr 94*
Rex, Robert Richmond d1992 *Who 94N*
Rexach Benitez, Roberto 1929- *WhoAmP 93, WhoHisp 94*
Rexed, Bror A(nders) 1914- *IntWW 93*
Rexha, Lumturi *WhoWomW 91*
Rexine, John Efstratios 1929- *WhoAm 94*
Rexon, George Frederick *WhoFI 94*
Rexroat, Dee Ann 1960- *WhoMW 93*
Rexrodt, Gunter 1941- *IntWW 93*
Rexroth, Kenneth 1905-1982 *ConDr 93*
Rexroth, Nancy Louise 1946- *WhoAm 94, WhoAmA 93*
Rexroth-Berg, Natanael *NewGrDO*
Rey, Alberto Enrique 1960- *WhoHisp 94*
Rey, Alejandro d1987 *WhoHol 92*
Rey, Alvino 1916- *WhoHol 92*
Rey, Anita d1978 *WhoHol 92*
Rey, Antonia *WhoHol 92*
Rey, Antonia 1927- *WhoHisp 94*
Rey, Antonio B. 1940- *WhoHisp 94*
Rey, Bret *WrDr 94*
Rey, Carlos Raul 1959- *WhoFI 94*
Rey, Carmen Rosello 1923- *WhoAm 94*
Rey, Cemal Resit 1904-1985 *NewGrDO*
Rey, Daniel *WhoHisp 94*
Rey, (Louis-Etienne-)Ernest *NewGrDO*
Rey, Fernando *IntWW 93*
Rey, Fernando 1915- *WhoHol 92*
Rey, Fernando 1917- *IntMPA 94*
Rey, Frank, Jr. 1932- *WhoHisp 94*
Rey, H. A. 1898-1977 *WhoAmA 93N*
Rey, Harry d1910 *WhoHol 92*
Rey, Jean-Baptiste 1734-1810 *NewGrDO*
Rey, Jerry A. *WhoHisp 94*
Rey, John A. 1942- *WhoHisp 94*
Rey, Juan Carlos 1957- *WhoWest 94*
Rey, Justo, Jr. 1955- *WhoHisp 94*
Rey, Margret 1906- *WrDr 94*
Rey, Margret E. 1906- *WhoAm 94*
Rey, Roberto d1972 *WhoHol 92*
Rey, Rosa d1969 *WhoHol 92*
Rey, Russell *EncSF 93*
Reyburn, Harold Orbra 1915- *WhAm 10*
Reycraft, George Dewey 1924- *WhoAm 94, WhoAmL 94*
Reyen, Daniel Wordsworth 1945- *WhoMW 93*
Reyer, (Louis-Etienne-)Ernest 1823-1909 *NewGrDO*
Reyes, Adelaida 1930- *WhoAsA 94*
Reyes, Albert L. 1958- *WhoHisp 94*
Reyes, Andre *WhoAm 94*
Reyes, Angela Pedraza 1949- *WhoAmL 94*
Reyes, Antonio 1939- *WhoHisp 94*
Reyes, Aurora C. 1938- *WhoHisp 94*
Reyes, Ben *WhoHisp 94*
Reyes, Ben T. 1947- *WhoAmP 93*
Reyes, Benjamin 1952- *WhoHisp 94*
Reyes, Bienvenido Castro 1944- *WhoWest 94*
Reyes, Carlos *DrAPF 93*
Reyes, Carmencita O. *WhoWomW 91*
Reyes, Cecille Lizzette 1962- *WhoHisp 94*
Reyes, Cynthia Paula 1960- *WhoHisp 94*
Reyes, David Edward 1947- *WhoHisp 94*
Reyes, Delia *WhoHisp 94*
Reyes, Eduardo 1965- *WhoHisp 94*
Reyes, Edward 1944- *WhoHisp 94*
Reyes, Edward D. 1930- *WhoAmP 93*
Reyes, Emilio Alejandro 1959- *WhoHisp 94*
Reyes, Ernie, Jr. 1972- *WhoHol 92*
Reyes, Eugene Fernando, III 1942- *WhoHisp 94*
Reyes, Eva d1970 *WhoHol 92*
Reyes, Frank *WhoHisp 94*
Reyes, Frank Rodriguez 1934- *WhoHisp 94*
Reyes, Guillermo Agusto 1963- *WhoHisp 94*
Reyes, Harold E. 1954- *WhoHisp 94*
Reyes, Henry G. 1929- *WhoAmP 93*
Reyes, Hernan M. 1933- *WhoAsA 94*
Reyes, Janie 1940- *WhoAmP 93*
Reyes, Jesse G. 1952- *WhoHisp 94*
Reyes, Jorge d1985 *WhoHol 92*
Reyes, Jorge A. 1949- *WhoHisp 94*
Reyes, Jose Israel 1941- *WhoHisp 94*
Reyes, Jose M. *WhoHisp 94*
Reyes, José N., Jr. 1955- *WhoHisp 94*
Reyes, Leopoldo Guadalupe 1940- *WhoHisp 94*
Reyes, Lico 1946- *WhoHisp 94*
Reyes, Lillian Jenny 1955- *WhoAmL 94*
Reyes, Lucha d1944 *WhoHol 92*
Reyes, Luis *WhoHisp 94*
Reyes, Manuel, Jr. 1929- *WhoHisp 94*
Reyes, Manuel A. *WhoHisp 94*
Reyes, Marcia Stygles 1950- *WhoScEn 94*
Reyes, Marco Antonio 1955- *WhoHisp 94*
Reyes, Narciso G. 1914- *IntWW 93, Who 94*
Reyes, Nicholas Carlos 1953- *WhoAm 94*
Reyes, Oscar J. 1936- *WhoHisp 94*
Reyes, Pete P. *WhoAmP 93*
Reyes, Raul Gregorio 1928- *WhoFI 94*
Reyes, Raymond T. *WhoHisp 94*
Reyes, Richard Ellis 1951- *WhoHisp 94*
Reyes, Richard R. 1954- *WhoHisp 94*
Reyes, Robert *WhoHisp 94*
Reyes, Rodrigo Berenguer De Los 1924- *WhoIns 94*
Reyes, Rogelio 1931- *WhoHisp 94*
Reyes, Sarah Lorraine 1961- *WhoHisp 94*
Reyes, Tomas, Jr. *WhoHisp 94*
Reyes, Tony 1942- *WhoHisp 94*
Reyes, Victor Ioannis 1959- *WhoAmL 94*
Reyes, Victor M. F. 1931-1992 *WhoHisp 94N*
Reyes, Vinicio H. 1934- *WhoHisp 94*
Reyes-Báez, Gloria E. 1946- *WhoHisp 94*
Reyes-Cuevas, Carmen Elsa 1961- *WhoHisp 94*
Reyes de Ruiz, Neris B. *WhoHisp 94*
Reyes-Gavilan, Adelina Rosario 1959- *WhoHisp 94*
Reyes-Guerra, Antonio 1916- *WhoScEn 94*
Reyes-Guerra, Antonio, Jr. 1919- *WhoHisp 94*
Reyes-Guerra, David Richard 1933- *WhoHisp 94*
Reyes Kopack, Laura 1953- *WhoHisp 94*
Reymann, Patrick H. 1947- *WhoAmL 94*
Reyna, Carlos Fernando 1942- *WhoHisp 94*
Reyna, Felipe 1945- *WhoHisp 94*
Reyna, Jorge De *EncSF 93*
Reyna, Jose R. 1941- *WhoHisp 94*
Reyna, R. Michael 1964- *WhoHisp 94*
Reyna, Ralph *WhoHisp 94*
Reyna, Roberto 1941- *WhoHisp 94*
Reyna, Tadeo, Jr. 1947- *WhoHisp 94*
Reyna, Valerie F. 1955- *WhoHisp 94*
Reyna, Valerie Frances 1955- *WhoWest 94*
Reynaga, Jesse Richard 1951- *WhoHisp 94*
Reynard, Carolyn Cole 1934- *WhoAmA 93*
Reynard, Charles G. 1946- *WhoAmL 94*
Reynard, Grant T. 1887-1967 *WhoAmA 93N*
Reynard, Muriel Joyce 1945- *WhoAmL 94*
Reynardus, Jorge E. 1944- *WhoHisp 94*
Reyne, David *WhoHol 92*
Reyner, William Stanley, Jr. 1945- *WhoAm 94, WhoAmL 94*
Reynes, Stephen Alan 1946- *WhoAmP 93*
Reynick, Robert J. 1932- *WhoScEn 94*
Reynold, Frederic 1936- *Who 94*
Reynolds, A. Wanjiku H. *DrAPF 93*
Reynolds, A. William 1933- *WhoAm 94, WhoFI 94, WhoMW 93*
Reynolds, Abe d1955 *WhoHol 92*
Reynolds, Adeline De Walt d1961 *WhoHol 92*
Reynolds, Alan d1976 *WhoHol 92*
Reynolds, Alan (Munro) 1926- *Who 94*
Reynolds, Alan Anthony 1942- *WhoAm 94*
Reynolds, Albert 1933- *Who 94*
Reynolds, Albert 1935- *IntWW 93*
Reynolds, Albert Barnett 1931- *WhoAm 94*
Reynolds, Alva-Inez 1933- *WhoFI 94*
Reynolds, Andrew Buchanan 1939- *WhoBlA 94*
Reynolds, Anna 1931- *NewGrDO*
Reynolds, Anna 1936- *IntWW 93*
Reynolds, Audrey Lucile *WhoBlA 94*
Reynolds, Barbara 1914- *Who 94*
Reynolds, Barbara A. *WhoBlA 94*
Reynolds, Barrie 1932- *WrDr 94*
Reynolds, Benedict Michael 1925- *WhoAm 94*
Reynolds, Benjamin J. d1950 *WhoHol 92*
Reynolds, Billie I. 1929- *WhoAm 94*
Reynolds, Bradford Charles 1948- *WhoFI 94, WhoScEn 94*
Reynolds, Bruce C. 1948- *WhoAmP 93*
Reynolds, Bruce Howard 1935- *WhoBlA 94*
Reynolds, Burt 1935- *WhoHol 92*
Reynolds, Burt 1936- *IntMPA 94, IntWW 93, WhoAm 94*
Reynolds, Calvin 1928- *WhoAm 94*
Reynolds, Carl Christiansen 1934- *WhoAm 94*
Reynolds, Catherine Cox 1928- *WhoAmP 93*
Reynolds, Cathey Ann 1953- *WhoFI 94*
Reynolds, Charles *WhoAmP 93*
Reynolds, Charles H. *WhoAmL 94*
Reynolds, Charles McKinley, Jr. 1937- *WhoBlA 94*
Reynolds, Charles Patrick 1952- *WhoWest 94*
Reynolds, Christopher John 1947- *WhoAmL 94*
Reynolds, Claude Lewis, Jr. 1948- *WhoScEn 94*
Reynolds, Clay *DrAPF 93*
Reynolds, Collins James, III 1937- *WhoAm 94*
Reynolds, Craig d1949 *WhoHol 92*
Reynolds, Dale *WhoHol 92*
Reynolds, David George 1933- *WhoAm 94*
Reynolds, David James 1924- *Who 94*
Reynolds, David Parham 1915- *WhoAm 94, WhoFI 94*
Reynolds, David Robert *WhoIns 94*
Reynolds, Debbie 1932- *IntMPA 94, WhoAm 94, WhoHol 92*
Reynolds, Debra Kay 1952- *WhoMW 93*
Reynolds, Dennis Dean 1947- *WhoAm 94*
Reynolds, Dick *WhoAmP 93*
Reynolds, Dixon Jace 1956- *WhoAmL 94*
Reynolds, Don William 1926- *WhoFI 94, WhoScEn 94*
Reynolds, Donald Dean 1921- *WhoWest 94*
Reynolds, Donald W. 1906-1993 *NewYTBS 93*
Reynolds, Dorothy d1977 *WhoHol 92*
Reynolds, Dorothy L. 1928- *WhoAmP 93*
Reynolds, Douglas R. 1941- *WhoAm 94, WhoAmL 94*
Reynolds, E. Vivian d1952 *WhoHol 92*
Reynolds, Edward 1926- *WhoAm 94*
Reynolds, Edward 1942- *WhoBlA 94*
Reynolds, Edward Osmund Royle 1933- *Who 94*
Reynolds, Ellis W. 1932- *WhoScEn 94*
Reynolds, Eric Vincent d1992 *Who 94N*
Reynolds, Ernest West 1920- *WhoAm 94*
Reynolds, Eva Mary Barbara *Who 94*
Reynolds, Fiona Claire 1958- *Who 94*
Reynolds, Francis Martin Baillie 1932- *Who 94*
Reynolds, Frank Arrowsmith 1916- *Who 94*
Reynolds, Frank Everett 1930- *WhoAm 94*
Reynolds, Frank Miller 1917- *WhoAm 94*
Reynolds, Gary Alan 1943- *WhoAm 94*
Reynolds, Gary Kemp 1944- *WhoAm 94*
Reynolds, Gayle Marie 1943- *WhoAm 94*
Reynolds, Gene 1925- *WhoAm 94, WhoHol 92*
Reynolds, Genevieve d1922 *WhoHol 92*
Reynolds, George Thomas 1917- *WhoAm 94*
Reynolds, Gillian 1935- *Who 94*
Reynolds, Graham *Who 94*
Reynolds, Graham 1914- *WrDr 94*
Reynolds, (Arthur) Graham 1914- *Who 94*
Reynolds, Grant 1908- *WhoBlA 94*
Reynolds, Guy Edwin K. *Who 94*
Reynolds, H. C. 1920- *WhoAmP 93*
Reynolds, H. Gerald 1940- *WhoAmL 94*
Reynolds, Hanson Shallcross 1933- *WhoAm 94*
Reynolds, Harold d1972 *WhoHol 92*
Reynolds, Harold Craig 1960- *WhoBlA 94*
Reynolds, Harrington d1919 *WhoHol 92*
Reynolds, Harry G. 1915- *WhoBlA 94*
Reynolds, Harry Lincoln 1925- *WhoAm 94*
Reynolds, Harry Weatherly, Jr. 1946- *WhoFI 94*
Reynolds, Helen Elizabeth 1925- *WhoFI 94*
Reynolds, Helene d1990 *WhoHol 92*
Reynolds, Ida Manning 1946- *WhoBlA 94*
Reynolds, Jack d1977 *WhoHol 92*
Reynolds, Jack Raymond 1916- *Who 94*
Reynolds, Jack W. 1923- *WhoAm 94, WhoMW 93*
Reynolds, James 1908- *Who 94*
Reynolds, James A. 1929- *WhAm 10*
Reynolds, James E. 1943- *WhoAm 94, WhoAmL 94*
Reynolds, James Elwood 1926- *WhoAmA 93*
Reynolds, James F. 1914- *WhoBlA 94*
Reynolds, James Van 1946- *WhoBlA 94*
Reynolds, James W. 1944- *WhoBlA 94*
Reynolds, Jean Edwards 1941- *WhoAm 94*

Reynolds, Jerry 1962- *WhoBlA 94*
Reynolds, Jerry Lemuel 1949- *WhoFI 94*
Reynolds, Jerry Owen 1944- *WhoAm 94, WhoWest 94*
Reynolds, Jo-Anne Elaine 1956- *WhoWest 94*
Reynolds, Jock *WhoAmA 93*
Reynolds, Joe *GayLL*
Reynolds, John 1914- *WrDr 94*
Reynolds, John Charles 1933- *WhoAm 94*
Reynolds, John Curby 1948- *WhoWest 94*
Reynolds, John Francis 1921- *WhoAm 94, WhoMW 93*
Reynolds, John Hamilton 1796-1852 *BlmGEL*
Reynolds, John Hamilton 1923- *IntWW 93, WhoAm 94*
Reynolds, John J. d1993 *NewYTBS 93*
Reynolds, John W. 1921- *WhoAm 94*
Reynolds, Joseph Berchmans 1896- *WhAm 10*
Reynolds, Joseph Charles 1930- *WhoAmP 93*
Reynolds, Joseph Hurley 1946- *WhoAm 94*
Reynolds, Joshua 1723-1792 *BlmGEL*
Reynolds, Joyce 1924- *WhoHol 92*
Reynolds, Joyce Maire 1918- *IntWW 93, Who 94*
Reynolds, Julian A. *WhoAmP 93*
Reynolds, June M. 1925- *WhoAmP 93*
Reynolds, Kathleen Diane Foy 1946- *WhoWest 94*
Reynolds, Kay *WhoHol 92*
Reynolds, Kimberley (Griffith) 1955- *WrDr 94*
Reynolds, Kirk *Who 94*
Reynolds, (James) Kirk 1951- *Who 94*
Reynolds, Larry T(homas) 1938- *WrDr 94*
Reynolds, Lawrence Paul 1953- *WhoMW 93*
Reynolds, Leighton Durham 1930- *Who 94*
Reynolds, Leo Thomas 1945- *WhoFI 94*
Reynolds, Linda Richardson 1940- *WhoFI 94*
Reynolds, Lloyd (George) 1910- *WrDr 94*
Reynolds, Lloyd George 1910- *WhoAm 94*
Reynolds, Lloyd J. 1902-1978 *WhoAmA 93N*
Reynolds, Mack 1917-1983 *EncSF 93*
Reynolds, Madge 1914- *WrDr 94*
Reynolds, Margaret 1941- *WhoWomW 91*
Reynolds, Marian K. *WhoAmP 93*
Reynolds, Marjorie 1921- *IntMPA 94, WhoHol 92*
Reynolds, Marshall Truman 1937- *WhoAm 94*
Reynolds, Martin L. 1950- *WhoAmP 93*
Reynolds, Martin Richard Finch 1943- *Who 94*
Reynolds, Mary Trackett 1913- *WhoAm 94*
Reynolds, Mel *WhoAmP 93*
Reynolds, Mel 1952- *CngDr 93, WhoBlA 94*
Reynolds, Melvin J. 1952- *WhoAm 94, WhoMW 93*
Reynolds, Michael Emanuel 1931- *Who 94*
Reynolds, Michael Everett 1945- *WhoScEn 94*
Reynolds, Michael Floyd 1953- *WhoScEn 94*
Reynolds, Michael Frank 1930- *Who 94*
Reynolds, Michael J. *WhoHol 92*
Reynolds, Michael Joseph 1938- *WhoAm 94*
Reynolds, Micheal John 1958- *WhoFI 94*
Reynolds, Milton L. 1924- *WhoBlA 94*
Reynolds, Nancy Hubbard 1923- *WhoMW 93*
Reynolds, Nanette Lee 1946- *WhoBlA 94*
Reynolds, Neil S. 1952- *WhoMW 93*
Reynolds, Nicholas S. 1944- *WhoAm 94, WhoAmL 94*
Reynolds, Norman Eben 1919- *WhoAm 94, WhoAmL 94*
Reynolds, Osbourne 1842-1912 *WorScD*
Reynolds, Pamela Terese 1963- *WhoBlA 94*
Reynolds, Patricia Ellen 1934- *WhoAmA 93*
Reynolds, Patrick 1948- *WhoWest 94*
Reynolds, Patrick 1949- *WhoHol 92*
Reynolds, Paul George 1922- *WhoFI 94*
Reynolds, Peter d1975 *WhoHol 92*
Reynolds, Peter (William John) 1929- *Who 94*
Reynolds, Peter William John 1929- *IntWW 93*
Reynolds, Philip Alan 1920- *Who 94, WrDr 94*
Reynolds, Quentin d1965 *WhoHol 92*
Reynolds, R. J. 1960- *WhoBlA 94*
Reynolds, R. John 1936- *WhoAm 94*
Reynolds, Ralph Duane 1934- *WhoMW 93*
Reynolds, Ralph William 1905-1991 *WhoAmA 93N*
Reynolds, Randolph Nicklas 1941- *WhoFI 94*
Reynolds, Richard (Henry) 1913- *WhoAmA 93*
Reynolds, Richard Clyde 1929- *WhoAm 94*
Reynolds, Richard Henry 1913- *WhoWest 94*
Reynolds, Richard Louis 1953- *WhoAmL 94*
Reynolds, Richard Paulsen 1946- *WhoWest 94*
Reynolds, Richard Samuel, III 1934- *WhoAmP 93*
Reynolds, Ricky Scott (Derrick) 1965- *WhoBlA 94*
Reynolds, Robert 1936- *WhoAmA 93*
Reynolds, Robert Edgar 1938- *WhoAm 94*
Reynolds, Robert Harrison 1913- *WhoFI 94, WhoWest 94*
Reynolds, Robert Hugh 1937- *WhoAm 94, WhoMW 93*
Reynolds, Robert Joel 1944- *WhoAm 94, WhoFI 94, WhoScEn 94*
Reynolds, Robert Leonard, Jr. 1930- *WhoAmP 93*
Reynolds, Robert Lester 1917- *WhoAm 94*
Reynolds, Robert Louis 1939- *WhoAm 94, WhoFI 94*
Reynolds, Robert Webster 1941- *WhoFI 94*
Reynolds, Roger Lee 1934- *WhoAm 94*
Reynolds, Roy Gregory 1939- *Who 94*
Reynolds, Russel Burton 1894- *WhAm 10*
Reynolds, Russell Joseph 1941- *WhoAmP 93*
Reynolds, Ruth Carmen *WhoMW 93*
Reynolds, Sallie Blackburn 1940- *WhoMW 93*
Reynolds, Scott Walton 1941- *WhoAm 94*
Reynolds, Sheldon 1923- *IntMPA 94*
Reynolds, Stephen Francis 1950- *WhoAmA 93*
Reynolds, Stephen Philip 1948- *WhoWest 94*
Reynolds, Stephen Robert 1958- *WhoAmL 94*
Reynolds, Steve 1920- *WhoAmP 93*
Reynolds, Steven Lee 1952- *WhoWest 94*
Reynolds, Stuart 1907- *IntMPA 94*
Reynolds, Susan Mary Grace 1929- *Who 94*
Reynolds, Ted 1938- *EncSF 93*
Reynolds, Terry S(cott) 1946- *ConAu 43NR*
Reynolds, Terry Scott 1946- *WhoScEn 94*
Reynolds, Thomas A., Jr. 1928- *WhoAm 94*
Reynolds, Thomas A., III 1952- *WhoAm 94*
Reynolds, Thomas M. *WhoAmP 93*
Reynolds, Thomas P. 1952- *WhoFI 94*
Reynolds, Thomas Robert 1962- *WhoScEn 94*
Reynolds, Thomas Upton, II 1954- *WhoAmP 93*
Reynolds, Tim *DrAPF 93*
Reynolds, Tom d1942 *WhoHol 92*
Reynolds, Tommy d1986 *WhoHol 92*
Reynolds, Valrae 1944- *WhoAmA 93*
Reynolds, Vera d1962 *WhoHol 92*
Reynolds, Vernon 1935- *WrDr 94*
Reynolds, Vernon Glenn 1952- *WhoFI 94*
Reynolds, Viola J. 1925- *WhoBlA 94*
Reynolds, Wade 1929- *WhoAmA 93*
Reynolds, Warren Jay 1918- *WhoAm 94*
Reynolds, Wiley Richard 1917- *WhoAm 94*
Reynolds, William 1931- *WhoHol 92*
Reynolds, William Bradford 1942- *WhoAm 94, WhoAmP 93*
Reynolds, William Craig 1933- *WhoScEn 94, WhoWest 94*
Reynolds, William Francis 1930- *WhoAm 94*
Reynolds, William H. 1910- *IntDcF 2-4*
Reynolds, William Harold 1925- *WhoAm 94*
Reynolds, William J. 1956- *WrDr 94*
Reynolds, William James 1956- *WhoMW 93*
Reynolds, William Jay 1960- *WhoAmL 94*
Reynolds, William Leroy 1945- *WhoAm 94*
Reynolds, William MacKenzie, Jr. 1921- *WhoAmL 94*
Reynolds, William Oliver 1915- *Who 94*
Reynolds, William Roscoe 1942- *WhoAmL 94, WhoAmP 93*
Reynolds, Wynetka Ann 1937- *WhoAm 94*
Reynoldson, W. Ward 1920- *WhoAmP 93*
Reynoldson, Walter Ward 1920- *WhoAm 94*
Reynosa, Leo *WhoHisp 94*
Reynoso, Cruz 1931- *WhoHisp 94*
Reynoso, Jose *WhoHisp 94*
Reynoso, José S. 1953- *WhoHisp 94*
Reynoso, Jose Santos, Jr. 1954- *WhoHisp 94*
Reyntiens, Nicholas Patrick 1925- *Who 94*
Reyor, Rose Ann 1919- *WhoAmP 93*
Rey-Rosa, Rodrigo 1958- *WrDr 94*
Rey-Tejerina, Arsenio 1938- *WhoHisp 94*
Reyzen, Mark (Osipovich) 1895- *NewGrDO*
Reza, Jesus *WhoHisp 94*
Reza, Martha Ruth 1958- *WhoHisp 94*
Reza, Veronica Cristina 1962- *WhoHisp 94*
Rezac, Don M. 1940- *WhoAmP 93*
Rezac, Richard 1952- *WhoAmA 93*
Rezach, Brian Daniel 1957- *WhoFI 94*
Rezachek, David Allen 1950- *WhoScEn 94*
Rezaiyan, A. John 1955- *WhoScEn 94*
Rezak, Richard 1920- *WhoScEn 94*
Rezak, William David 1940- *WhoFI 94*
Rezash, Lawrence Joseph 1930- *WhoMW 93*
Rezek, Geoffrey Robert 1941- *WhoFI 94*
Rezek, Ivan Emil 1914- *WhoAmP 93*
Rezich, George F. 1927- *WhoFI 94*
Rezits, Joseph 1925- *WrDr 94*
Rezmerski, John Calvin *DrAPF 93*
Rezneck, Daniel Albert 1935- *WhoAm 94*
Reznicek, Anton Albert 1950- *WhoScEn 94*
Reznicek, Bernard William 1936- *WhoFI 94, WhoScEn 94*
Reznicek, E(mil) N(ikolaus) von 1860-1945 *NewGrDO*
Reznick, Charlotte 1950- *WhoWest 94*
Reznick, Scott Matthew 1946- *WhoFI 94*
Rezzonico, Renzo 1929- *WhoFI 94*
Rha, ChoKyun 1933- *WhoAm 94, WhoAsA 94, WhoScEn 94*
Rhallys, George J. *IntWW 93*
Rhame, Frank Scorgie 1942- *WhoMW 93*
Rhame, John E. 1928- *WhoAm 94, WhoFI 94*
Rhame, Thomas Gene 1941- *WhoAm 94*
Rhame, William Thomas 1915- *WhoAm 94*
Rhames, Ving *WhoHol 92*
Rhea, Alexander Dodson 1919- *Who 94*
Rhea, Ann Crawford 1940- *WhoWest 94*
Rhea, Claude Hiram, Jr. 1927-1990 *WhAm 10*
Rhea, Edward Buford, Jr. 1934- *WhoMW 93*
Rhea, Jerry Dwaine 1950- *WhoFI 94*
Rhea, Marcia Chandler 1956- *WhoFI 94*
Rhea, Michael 1946- *WhoBlA 94*
Rhead, Kim A. 1954- *WhoAmP 93, WhoMW 93*
Rheault, Lillian I. 1919- *WhoAmP 93*
Rhee, Chase Chonggwang 1942- *WhoAsA 94*
Rhee, Hahn-Kyou 1954- *WhoAsA 94*
Rhee, Hang Yul 1938- *WhoAsA 94*
Rhee, Hyun-Ku 1939- *WhoScEn 94*
Rhee, Jhoon Goo 1932- *WhoAsA 94*
Rhee, Khee Choon 1938- *WhoAsA 94*
Rhee, Phillip 1960- *WhoAsA 94*
Rhee, Sang Foon 1963- *WhoAsA 94*
Rhee, Song Nai 1935- *WhoAsA 94*
Rhee, Susan Byungsook 1937- *WhoAsA 94*
Rhee, Syngman 1875-1965 *HisWorL [port], HisDcKW*
Rhee, Yang Ho 1943- *WhoMW 93*
Rhee, Young Eun 1941- *WhoAsA 94*
Rheims, Maurice 1910- *IntWW 93*
Rhein, Mitchell d1977 *WhoHol 92*
Rhein, Murray Harold 1912- *WhoAm 94*
Rheinberger, Joseph (Gabriel) 1839-1901 *NewGrDO*
Rheinboldt, Werner Carl 1927- *WhoAm 94*
Rheiner, William Harris 1944- *WhoAmL 94*
Rheinheimer, Kurt *DrAPF 93*
Rheinish, Robert Kent 1934- *WhoWest 94*
Rhein-Schrading, Otto Franz d1952 *WhoHol 92*
Rheinstein, Peter Howard 1943- *WhoAm 94, WhoAmL 94, WhoScEn 94*
Rhett, Alicia *WhoHol 92*
Rhett, Haskell Emery Smith 1936- *WhoAm 94*
Rhett, John Taylor, Jr. 1925- *WhoAm 94*
Rhett, Michael 1954- *WhoBlA 94*
Rhetta, Helen L. *WhoBlA 94*
Rhiew, Francis Changnam 1938- *WhoScEn 94*
Rhim, Aesop 1933- *WhoAsA 94*
Rhim, Johng Sik 1930- *WhoAsA 94*
Rhimes, Richard David 1947- *WhoScEn 94*
Rhind, David William 1943- *Who 94*
Rhind, J. Christopher 1934- *WhoIns 94*
Rhind, James Thomas 1922- *WhoAm 94, WhoAmL 94*
Rhine, John E. 1952- *WhoAmL 94*
Rhine, Robley Dick 1930- *WhoWest 94*
Rhinehart, John Raymond 1916- *WhoMW 93*
Rhinehart, June Acie 1934- *WhoBlA 94*
Rhinehart, Luke 1932- *EncSF 93*
Rhinehart, Shelby Aaron 1927- *WhoAmP 93*
Rhinehart, Susan Oneacre 1938- *WrDr 94*
Rhinehart, Vernon Morel 1935- *WhoBlA 94*
Rhinelander, John Bassett 1933- *WhoAm 94, WhoAmP 93*
Rhines, Jesse Algeron 1948- *WhoBlA 94*
Rhines, Peter Broomell 1942- *IntWW 93, WhoAm 94*
Rhinesmith, Stephen Headley 1942- *WhoAm 94*
Rhoad, Richard Arthur 1935- *WhoMW 93*
Rhoad, Thomas Nathaniel 1923- *WhoAmP 93*
Rhoades, Barbara 1947- *WhoHol 92*
Rhoades, Douglas Duane 1960- *WhoScEn 94*
Rhoades, Floyd *WhoAm 94, WhoFI 94*
Rhoades, James J. 1941- *WhoAmP 93*
Rhoades, Jim *WhoAmP 93*
Rhoades, John Skylstead, Sr. 1925- *WhoAm 94, WhoAmL 94*
Rhoades, Jon Allen 1937- *WhoIns 94*
Rhoades, Marye Frances 1937- *WhoAmL 94*
Rhoades, Samuel Thomas 1946- *WhoBlA 94*
Rhoades, Warren A., Jr. 1924- *WhoAm 94*
Rhoads, Dean A. 1935- *WhoAmP 93*
Rhoads, Dean Allan 1935- *WhoWest 94*
Rhoads, Esther Biddle 1896- *WhAm 10*
Rhoads, Geraldine Emeline 1914- *WhoAm 94*
Rhoads, James Berton 1928- *IntWW 93, WhoAm 94*
Rhoads, John Edward, Jr. 1954- *WhoMW 93*
Rhoads, Jonathan Evans 1907- *WhoAm 94, WhoScEn 94*
Rhoads, Karroll G. 1948- *WhoAmP 93*
Rhoads, Kevin George 1951- *WhoScEn 94*
Rhoads, Mark Quentin 1946- *WhoAmP 93*
Rhoads, Nancy Glenn 1957- *WhoAmL 94*
Rhoads, Paul Kelly 1940- *WhoAm 94, WhoAmL 94*
Rhoads, Robert K. 1954- *WhoAmL 94, WhoFI 94*
Rhoads, Samuel 1711-1784 *WhAmRev*
Rhoads, Steven Eric 1939- *WhoAm 94*
Rhoads, Thomas John *WhoAmL 94*
Rhode, Alfred Shimon 1928- *WhoAm 94*
Rhode, Christopher *WhoHol 92*
Rhode, David Leland 1950- *WhoAm 94*
Rhode, Deborah Lynn 1952- *WhoAm 94*
Rhode, Edward Albert 1926- *WhoAm 94, WhoWest 94*
Rhode, Kenneth George 1909- *WhoIns 94*
Rhodeman, Clare M. 1932- *WhoBlA 94*
Rhoden, Grady Lamar 1937- *WhoAmP 93*
Rhoden, Harold Hugh 1943- *WhoAm 94*
Rhoden, John W. 1918- *WhoAmA 93*
Rhoden, Richard Allan 1930- *WhoBlA 94*
Rhodenbaugh, Suzanne *DrAPF 93*
Rhodes, Alfred d1948 *WhoHol 92*
Rhodes, Alfred William 1922- *WhoAm 94*
Rhodes, Andrew James 1911- *WhoAm 94*
Rhodes, Anne G. 1942- *WhoAmP 93*
Rhodes, Anne L. 1935- *WhoBlA 94*
Rhodes, Anthony 1916- *WrDr 94*
Rhodes, Arthur Delano 1960- *WhoAmL 94*
Rhodes, Ashby Marshall 1923- *WhoAm 94*
Rhodes, Basil (Edward) 1915- *Who 94*
Rhodes, Bessie M. L. 1935- *WhoBlA 94*
Rhodes, Betty Jane 1921- *WhoHol 92*
Rhodes, Billie d1988 *WhoHol 92*
Rhodes, Buck Austin 1935- *WhoFI 94*
Rhodes, C. Adrienne 1961- *WhoBlA 94*
Rhodes, Cecil 1853-1902 *HisWorL [port]*
Rhodes, Charles Harker, Jr. 1930- *WhoAm 94, WhoAmL 94*
Rhodes, Chester Allen *WhoAmP 93*
Rhodes, Chester Dusty 1921- *WhoAmP 93*
Rhodes, Christene Ford 1926- *WhoAmP 93*
Rhodes, Christopher d1964 *WhoHol 92*
Rhodes, Chuck William 1954- *WhoScEn 94*
Rhodes, Curtis A. 1939- *WhoAmA 93*
Rhodes, Cynthia 1956- *IntMPA 94*
Rhodes, Cynthia 1957- *WhoHol 92*
Rhodes, Donald Robert 1923- *WhoAm 94*
Rhodes, Donnelly *WhoHol 92*
Rhodes, Doug *WhoScEn 94*
Rhodes, Edward 1943- *WhoBlA 94*
Rhodes, Edward Thomas, Sr. 1933- *WhoBlA 94*
Rhodes, Eric Foster 1927- *WhoFI 94*
Rhodes, Erik d1990 *WhoHol 92*

Rhodes, Eugene Manlove 1869-1934 *TwCLC 53 [port]*
Rhodes, Frank 1950- *WhoAmP 93*
Rhodes, Frank E. *WhoAmP 93*
Rhodes, Frank Harold Trevor 1926- *IntWW 93, WhoAm 94*
Rhodes, Gail Sue 1947- *WhoMW 93*
Rhodes, George Harold Lancashire 1916- *Who 94*
Rhodes, George Milton 1898- *WhAm 10*
Rhodes, Gerald Lee 1954- *WhoWest 94*
Rhodes, Gordon Ellsworth 1927- *WhoIns 94*
Rhodes, Grandon d1987 *WhoHol 92*
Rhodes, Hari 1932- *WhoHol 92*
Rhodes, Helen Mary 1921- *WhoMW 93*
Rhodes, Horace Gibson 1927- *WhoAmL 94*
Rhodes, Ila 1918- *WhoHol 92*
Rhodes, Jacob A. 1949- *WhoBlA 94*
Rhodes, Jacqueline Yvonne 1949- *WhoMW 93*
Rhodes, James Allen 1909- *WhoAmP 93*
Rhodes, James Arthur 1939- *WhoMW 93*
Rhodes, James Lamar, Jr. 1948- *WhoWest 94*
Rhodes, James Mauran, Jr. 1937- *WhoWest 94*
Rhodes, James Melvin 1938- *WhoAmA 93*
Rhodes, James Richard 1945- *WhoScEn 94*
Rhodes, James T. 1941- *WhoAm 94, WhoFI 94*
Rhodes, James Whitfield 1945- *WhoAm 94*
Rhodes, Jane (Marie Andree) 1929- *NewGrDO*
Rhodes, Jeanne *WhoBlA 94*
Rhodes, Jeffrey Iver 1954- *WhoWest 94*
Rhodes, John (Christopher Douglas) 1946- *Who 94*
Rhodes, John Andrew 1949- *Who 94*
Rhodes, John Bower 1925- *WhoAm 94*
Rhodes, John David 1943- *Who 94*
Rhodes, John Ivor McKinnon 1914- *Who 94*
Rhodes, John J. 1916- *WhoAmP 93*
Rhodes, John Jacob 1916- *IntWW 93, WhoAm 94*
Rhodes, Jordan *WhoHol 92*
Rhodes, Joseph, Jr. 1947- *WhoBlA 94*
Rhodes, Karl Derrick 1968- *WhoBlA 94*
Rhodes, Kenneth Anthony, Jr. 1930- *WhoAmL 94*
Rhodes, Kent 1912-1991 *WhAm 10*
Rhodes, Kent Bertis 1958- *WhoWest 94*
Rhodes, Lelia G. *WhoBlA 94*
Rhodes, Marion 1907- *Who 94*
Rhodes, Marjorie d1979 *WhoHol 92*
Rhodes, Mary *WhoAm 94, WhoAmP 93*
Rhodes, Mitchell L. 1940- *WhoAm 94*
Rhodes, Paula R. 1949- *WhoBlA 94*
Rhodes, Percy d1956 *WhoHol 92*
Rhodes, Peregrine (Alexander) 1925- *Who 94*
Rhodes, Peter Edward 1942- *WhoAm 94*
Rhodes, Peter John 1940- *Who 94*
Rhodes, Philip 1922- *Who 94, WrDr 94*
Rhodes, Rathbun Kendrick 1952- *WhoMW 93*
Rhodes, Ray 1950- *WhoBlA 94*
Rhodes, Reginald Paul 1918- *Who 94*
Rhodes, Reilly Patrick 1941- *WhoAmA 93*
Rhodes, Richard *DrAPF 93*
Rhodes, Richard (Lee) 1937- *WrDr 94*
Rhodes, Richard David Walton 1942- *Who 94*
Rhodes, Richard L. 1937- *IntWW 93*
Rhodes, Richard Lee 1937- *WhoAm 94*
Rhodes, Robert Charles 1926- *WhoMW 93*
Rhodes, Robert Elliott 1945- *Who 94*
Rhodes, Robert Hunt 1937- *WrDr 94*
Rhodes, Robert LeRoy 1953- *WhoScEn 94*
Rhodes, Robert Shaw 1936- *WhoBlA 94*
Rhodes, Roberta Ann *WhoScEn 94*
Rhodes, Rondell Horace 1918- *WhoScEn 94*
Rhodes, Royal William 1946- *WhoMW 93*
Rhodes, Samuel 1941- *WhoAm 94*
Rhodes, Samuel Thomas 1944- *WhoAmP 93*
Rhodes, Stephen Michael 1949- *WhoFI 94*
Rhodes, Theodore Ernest 1943- *WhoAm 94, WhoAmL 94*
Rhodes, Thomas W. 1946- *WhoAmL 94*
Rhodes, Virgil O. *WhoAmP 93*
Rhodes, W(illiam) H(enry) 1822-1876 *EncSF 93*
Rhodes, Wanda E. 1916- *WhoAmP 93*
Rhodes, Wayne Robert 1951- *WhoScEn 94*
Rhodes, Willard 1901-1992 *WhAm 10*
Rhodes, William George, III 1956- *WhoScEn 94*
Rhodes, William Reginald 1935- *WhoAm 94, WhoFI 94*
Rhodes, Zandra 1940- *IntWW 93*
Rhodes, Zandra Lindsey 1940- *Who 94*
Rhodes-Haan, Nancy Ates 1955- *WhoFI 94*
Rhodes James, Robert (Vidal) 1933- *Who 94*
Rhodin, Anders G.J. 1949- *WhoScEn 94*
Rhody, Ronald Edward 1932- *WhoAm 94, WhoFI 94*
Rhomberg, Rudolf Robert 1922- *WhoFI 94*
Rhone, Douglas Pierce 1940- *WhoMW 93*
Rhone, Richard Wallace 1946- *WhoAmP 93*
Rhone, Sylvia M. 1952- *WhoBlA 94*
Rhone, Trevor D. 1940- *ConDr 93, WrDr 94*
Rhoodie, Eschel Mostert d1993 *NewYTBS 93 [port]*
Rhoton, Albert Loren, Jr. 1932- *WhoAm 94*
Rhue, Madlyn 1937- *WhoHol 92*
Rhue, Morton 1950- *WrDr 94*
Rhule, Homer A. 1921- *WhoIns 94*
Rhum, Susan Caroline 1932- *WhoAmP 93*
Rhykerd, Charles Loren 1929- *WhoMW 93*
Rhymes, Douglas Alfred 1914- *Who 94, WrDr 94*
Rhyne, Charles S. 1912- *WrDr 94*
Rhyne, Charles Sylvanus 1912- *WhoAm 94, WhoAmL 94, WhoFI 94*
Rhyne, Charles Sylvanus 1932- *WhoAmA 93*
Rhyne, Johnathan L., Jr. 1955- *WhoAmP 93*
Rhyne, Nancy 1926- *WrDr 94*
Rhyne, Philip Mark, Sr. 1957- *WhoFI 94*
Rhyne, Vernon Thomas, III 1942- *WhoAm 94*
Rhyne Marvin, Helen 1917- *WhoWomW 91*
Rhys *Who 94*
Rhys, Ioan 1929- *WrDr 94*
Rhys, Jack *EncSF 93*
Rhys, Jean 1890-1967 *BlmGWL*
Rhys, Jean 1890-1979 *RfGShF*
Rhys, Jean 1894-1979 *BlmGEL [port]*
Rhys, Paul 1963- *WhoHol 92*
Rhys-Davies, John 1944- *IntMPA 94, WhoHol 92*
Rhys Jones, Griffith 1953- *Who 94*
Rhys Williams, (Arthur) Gareth (Ludovic Emrys) 1961- *Who 94*
Rhythm Boys, The *WhoHol 92*
Riable, Mark J. 1955- *WhoAmP 93*
Riabouchinska, Tatiana 1916- *Who 94*
Riabouchinska, Tatiana 1917- *IntDcB [port]*
Riabov, Darelle Dee Lake 1951- *WhoFI 94*
Riach, Alan 1957- *ConAu 141*
Riach, Douglas Alexander 1919- *WhoFI 94, WhoWest 94*
Riach, Jennifer *WhoHol 92*
Riach, Peter Andrew 1937- *WhoScEn 94*
Riad, Mahmoud 1917- *WrDr 94*
Riahi, Daniel Nourollah 1943- *WhoMW 93*
Riahi-Belkaoui, Ahmed 1943- *ConAu 140*
Rial, Carol 1963- *WhoHisp 94*
Rial, Louise d1940 *WhoHol 92*
Rialson, Candice *WhoHol 92*
Rianhard, Carl Jory 1959- *WhoWest 94*
Riano, Renie d1971 *WhoHol 92*
Riasanovsky, Nicholas V(alentine) 1923- *WrDr 94*
Riasanovsky, Nicholas Valentine 1923- *WhoAm 94*
Riaume, Helen d1924 *WhoHol 92*
Riaz, Fahmida 1946- *BlmGWL*
Riaz, Rashid 1957- *WhoMW 93*
Riazi, Mohammad 1944- *WhoMW 93*
Riba, Paul F. 1912-1977 *WhoAmA 93N*
Ribak, Charles Eric 1950- *WhoWest 94*
Ribak, Louis 1902-1980 *WhoAmA 93N*
Ribalow, M. Z. *DrAPF 93*
Ribar, Dixie Lee 1938- *WhoMW 93*
Ribaric, Marijan 1932- *WhoScEn 94*
Ribas, Ivan Gene 1947- *WhoHisp 94*
Ribas, Jorge Luis 1942- *WhoAm 94*
Ribaudo, Anthony D. 1941- *WhoAmP 93*
Ribault, Jean c. 1520-1565 *WhWE*
Ribbans, Geoffrey Wilfrid 1927- *Who 94, WhoAm 94*
Ribbins, Gertrude 1924- *WhoBlA 94*
Ribble, John Charles 1931- *WhoAm 94*
Ribble, Michael Shannon 1966- *WhoMW 93*
Ribble, Ronald George 1937- *WhoScEn 94*
Ribbs, William Theodore, Jr. 1956- *WhoBlA 94*
Ribeiro, Antonio 1928- *IntWW 93*
Ribeiro, Frank Henry 1949- *WhoFI 94*
Ribeiro, Joao Ubaldo (Osorio Pimentel) 1941- *ConWorW 93*
Ribeiro, Joao Ubaldo Osorio Pimentel 1941- *IntWW 93*
Ribeiro, Joy d1972 *WhoHol 92*
Ribeiro, Leon 1854-1931 *NewGrDO*
Ribellia, Patrick A. 1947- *WhoAmP 93*
Ribenboim, Paulo 1928- *WhoAm 94*
Ribera, Anthony 1947- *WhoHisp 94*
Ribera, Anthony D. *WhoWest 94*
Ribera, Gilbert Joseph 1936- *WhoHisp 94*
Ribera, John E. 1944- *WhoHisp 94*
Ribera, Jose Antonio Moya 1946- *IntWW 93*
Riberholdt, Gunnar 1933- *IntWW 93*
Ribero, Michael A. 1956- *WhoHisp 94*
Ribero, Michael Antonio 1956- *WhoFI 94*
Ribicic, Mitja 1919- *IntWW 93*
Ribick, James Joseph 1947- *WhoFI 94*
Ribicoff, Abraham A. 1910- *IntWW 93, WhoAm 94, WhoAmP 93*
Rible, Morton 1938- *WhoAm 94, WhoAmL 94, WhoFI 94*
Ribman, Ronald (Burt) 1932- *ConDr 93, WrDr 94*
Ribman, Ronald Burt 1932- *WhoAm 94*
Ribner, Herbert Spencer 1913- *WhoAm 94*
Riboud, Antoine Amedee Paul 1918- *IntWW 93*
Ricanek, Carolyn Wright 1939- *WhoBlA 94*
Ricard, John H. 1940- *WhoBlA 94*
Ricardez, Mario L. 1929- *WhoHisp 94*
Ricardi, Leon Joseph 1924- *WhoAm 94, WhoWest 94*
Ricardo, Jack 1940- *ConAu 140*
Ricardo-Campbell, Rita 1920- *WhoAm 94, WhoFI 94, WhoHisp 94, WhoScEn 94, WhoWest 94*
Ricascio, Vincent Ranosa 1947- *WhoFI 94*
Riccardi, Carl'Antonio fl. 1663- *NewGrDO*
Riccardi, Lori 1964- *WhoFI 94*
Riccardi, Vincent Michael 1940- *WhoWest 94*
Riccardo, Carona d1917 *WhoHol 92*
Riccardo, Rick, Jr. d1977 *WhoHol 92*
Riccards, Michael Patrick 1944- *WhoAm 94*
Ricci, Brian Francis 1957- *WhoMW 93*
Ricci, Christina 1981- *WhoHol 92*
Ricci, Domenico c. 1700-1751 *NewGrDO*
Ricci, Federico 1809-1877 *NewGrDO*
Ricci, Francesco Benedetto fl. 1790- *NewGrDO*
Ricci, Giovanni Mario 1929- *WhoAm 94, WhoFI 94*
Ricci, Jerri *WhoAmA 93*
Ricci, Joseph Anthony 1962- *WhoAmL 94*
Ricci, Luigi 1805-1859 *NewGrDO*
Ricci, Marco 1676-1730 *NewGrDO*
Ricci, Matteo 1552-1610 *WhWE*
Ricci, Nora d1976 *WhoHol 92*
Ricci, Robert Ronald 1945- *WhoFI 94*
Ricci, Ruggiero 1918- *IntWW 93, WhoAm 94*
Ricci, Ulysses 1888-1960 *WhoAmA 93N*
Ricci, William J. 1953- *WhoAmL 94*
Ricciardelli, Carl F. 1931- *WhoIns 94*
Ricciardi, Antonio 1922- *WhoScEn 94*
Ricciardi, Catherine Marie 1946- *WhoMW 93*
Ricciardi, Christine Secola 1963- *WhoFI 94*
Ricciardi, Franc Mario 1923-1989 *WhAm 10*
Ricciardi, Lawrence R. *WhoAm 94, WhoAmL 94, WhoFI 94*
Ricciardi, Louis Michael 1959- *WhoFI 94*
Ricciardi, Patrice Joan 1956- *WhoFI 94*
Ricciardione, Salvatore J., Jr. 1948- *WhoIns 94*
Ricciarelli, Katia 1946- *NewGrDO, WhoAm 94*
Riccio, Benedetto 1678?-1710? *NewGrDO*
Riccio, Domenico *NewGrDO*
Riccio, George Peter, Jr. 1959- *WhoFI 94*
Riccio, Jerome Michael 1955- *WhoFI 94*
Riccio, John Charles 1958- *WhoAmL 94*
Riccioli, Guido d1958 *WhoHol 92*
Riccioni, Barbara fl. 1684- *NewGrDO*
Ricciuti, Renato Edmund 1916- *WhoAmP 93*
Ricco, Neil Raymond *DrAPF 93*
Ricco, Raymond Joseph, Jr. 1948- *WhoScEn 94, WhoWest 94*
Riccoboni, Marie-Jeanne Laboras de Mezieres 1713-1792 *BlmGWL*
Riccobono, Juanita Rae 1963- *WhoScEn 94*
Rice *Who 94*
Rice, A. Hamilton 1875-1956 *WhWE*
Rice, Albert R(ichard) 1951- *ConAu 142*
Rice, Allen Troy 1962- *WhoBlA 94*
Rice, Ann 1933- *WhoAm 94*
Rice, Anne *DrAPF 93*
Rice, Anne 1941- *BlmGWL, TwCYAW, WhoAm 94, WrDr 94*
Rice, Anthony Hopkins 1948- *WhoAmA 93*
Rice, Barbara Menen *See* Rice, M. Robert & Rice, Barbara Menen *WhoAmA 93*
Rice, Barbara Menen *WhoAmA 93*
Rice, Barbara Pollak 1937- *WhoWest 94*
Rice, Benjamin Manson, Jr. 1930- *WhoFI 94*
Rice, Bernard Francis 1949- *WhoMW 93*
Rice, Brian Keith 1932- *WrDr 94*
Rice, C(harles) David 1941- *ConAu 41NR*
Rice, C(harles) Duncan 1942- *WrDr 94*
Rice, Candace Kohles 1948- *WhoAm 94*
Rice, Carol *WhoAmP 93*
Rice, Charles Dale 1934- *WhoMW 93*
Rice, Charles Duncan 1942- *WhoAm 94*
Rice, Charles E. *WhoAmP 93*
Rice, Charles Edward 1936- *WhoAm 94, WhoFI 94*
Rice, Charles Howard 1925- *WhoAmP 93*
Rice, Charles Lane 1945- *WhoScEn 94*
Rice, Charles William 1955- *WhoMW 93*
Rice, Clare I. 1918- *WhoAm 94*
Rice, Condoleezza *NewYTBS 93 [port]*
Rice, Condoleezza 1954- *WhoBlA 94*
Rice, Condoleezza 1955- *WhoAm 94*
Rice, Constance Williams 1945- *WhoBlA 94*
Rice, Cora Lee 1926- *WhoBlA 94*
Rice, Darrel Alan 1947- *WhoAm 94, WhoAmL 94*
Rice, David 1733-1816 *DcAmReB 2*
Rice, David Ainsworth 1940- *WhoAm 94*
Rice, David Eugene, Jr. 1916- *WhoAm 94, WhoBlA 94*
Rice, David Lee 1929- *WhoMW 93*
Rice, Deckie M. 1924- *WhoAmP 93*
Rice, Denis Timlin 1932- *WhoAm 94, WhoWest 94*
Rice, Dennis George 1927- *Who 94*
Rice, Desmond (Hind Garrett) 1924- *Who 94*
Rice, Devereux Dunlap 1952- *WhoWest 94*
Rice, Don *DrAPF 93*
Rice, Donald B. 1939- *WhoAmP 93*
Rice, Donald Blessing 1939- *WhoAm 94*
Rice, Donald L. 1938- *WrDr 94*
Rice, Donald Sands 1940- *WhoAm 94*
Rice, Dorothy P. 1922- *IntWW 93*
Rice, Dorothy Pechman 1922- *WhoAm 94*
Rice, Douglas Edward 1962- *WhoFI 94*
Rice, Edward 1953- *WhoAmA 93*
Rice, Edward A. 1929- *WhoBlA 94*
Rice, Edward Earl 1909- *WhoAm 94*
Rice, Edward Everett 1848-1924 *NewGrDO*
Rice, Edward William 1911- *WhoWest 94*
Rice, Elmer 1892-1967 *EncSF 93, IntDcT 2 [port]*
Rice, Emily Marie 1922- *WhoAmL 94, WhoMW 93*
Rice, Emmett J. *WhoAmP 93, WhoBlA 94*
Rice, Eric Edward *WhoScEn 94*
Rice, Fanny d1936 *WhoHol 92*
Rice, Felix d1990 *WhoHol 92*
Rice, Ferill Jeane 1926- *WhoAm 94, WhoMW 93*
Rice, Florence d1974 *WhoHol 92*
Rice, Frank d1936 *WhoHol 92*
Rice, Fred 1926- *WhoBlA 94*
Rice, Frederick Colton 1938- *WhoFI 94*
Rice, Gail 1947- *WhoMW 93*
Rice, George Lawrence, III 1951- *WhoAmL 94*
Rice, Glen A. 1967- *WhoBlA 94*
Rice, Gordon Kenneth 1927- *Who 94*
Rice, Grantland d1954 *WhoHol 92*
Rice, Gregory Allen 1955- *WhoMW 93*
Rice, Harold Leon 1941- *WhoAmP 93*
Rice, Harold Randolph 1912-1987 *WhoAmA 93N*
Rice, Haynes 1932- *WhoBlA 94*
Rice, J. Andrew 1953- *WhoFI 94*
Rice, Jack d1968 *WhoHol 92*
Rice, Jack 1925- *WhoAmP 93*
Rice, James A. 1948- *WhoAm 94, WhoFI 94*
Rice, James Grundy 1946- *WhoMW 93*
Rice, James I. 1925- *WhoAmP 93*
Rice, James Robert 1940- *WhoAm 94*
Rice, Jerry 1962- *ConBlB 5 [port]*
Rice, Jerry Lee 1962- *WhoAm 94, WhoBlA 94, WhoWest 94*
Rice, Jim 1953- *WhoBlA 94*
Rice, Jim 1957- *WhoAmP 93*
Rice, Joan 1930- *WhoHol 92*
Rice, John Andrew 1944- *WhoScEn 94*
Rice, John C. d1915 *WhoHol 92*
Rice, John Holt 1777-1831 *DcAmReB 2*
Rice, John Joseph 1939- *WhoFI 94*
Rice, John Reynolds 1946- *WhoFI 94*
Rice, John Rischard 1934- *WhoAm 94, WhoMW 93*
Rice, John Thomas 1931- *WhoAm 94*
Rice, John W. *WhoAmP 93*
Rice, Jonathan C. 1916- *WhoWest 94*
Rice, Joseph Albert 1924- *WhoAm 94*
Rice, Joseph Lee, III 1932- *WhoAm 94*

Rice, Joy Katharine 1939- *WhoAm 94*
Rice, Julian Casavant 1924- *WhoAm 94, WhoAmL 94, WhoWest 94*
Rice, Kenneth Lloyd 1937- *WhoMW 93*
Rice, Kraig Josiah 1945- *WhoWest 94*
Rice, Lacy I., Jr. 1931- *WhoAm 94*
Rice, Larry Dean 1953- *WhoAmP 93*
Rice, Lester 1927- *WhoAm 94*
Rice, Linda Johnson *WhoAm 94*
Rice, Linda Johnson 1958- *WhoBlA 94*
Rice, Lois Dickson 1933- *WhoAm 94, WhoBlA 94, WhoFI 94*
Rice, Louis Albert 1895- *WhAm 10*
Rice, Louise Allen 1940- *WhoBlA 94*
Rice, Luther 1783-1836 *DcAmReB 2*
Rice, Lyle K. 1905- *WhoAmP 93*
Rice, M. Robert & Rice, Barbara Menen *WhoAmA 93*
Rice, Martha Helen 1949- *WhoAm 94*
Rice, Mary Alice d1989 *WhoHol 92*
Rice, Mary Esther 1926- *WhoScEn 94*
Rice, Mary M. 1938- *WhoMW 93*
Rice, Maureen *Who 94*
Rice, Maurice Ainsworth 1936- *WhoFI 94, WhoMW 93*
Rice, Michael Downey 1938- *WhoAmL 94*
Rice, Michael Lewis 1943- *WhoAm 94, WhoWest 94*
Rice, Mitchell F. 1948- *BlkWr 2, WhoBlA 94*
Rice, Nancy Newman *WhoAmA 93*
Rice, Nelson, Sr. 1932- *WhoAmP 93*
Rice, Noel Stephen Cracroft 1931- *Who 94*
Rice, Norman d1957 *WhoHol 92*
Rice, Norman 1943- *WhoAm 94, WhoAmP 93, WhoWest 94*
Rice, Norman Blann 1943- *WhoBlA 94*
Rice, Norman Lewis 1905- *WhoAmA 93*
Rice, Otis K(ermit) 1919- *WrDr 94*
Rice, Otis LaVerne 1922- *WhoFI 94, WhoMW 93*
Rice, Pamela Ann 1956- *WhoBlA 94*
Rice, Patricia Ann 1946- *WhoWest 94*
Rice, Paul *DrAPF 93*
Rice, Peter Alan 1942- *WhoScEn 94*
Rice, Peter Anthony Morrish 1928- *Who 94*
Rice, Peter D. *Who 94*
Rice, Peter Ronan d1992 *Who 94N*
Rice, Philip Joseph, Jr. 1917-1989 *WhAm 10*
Rice, Ramona Gail 1950- *WhoMW 93, WhoScEn 94*
Rice, Randolf James 1947- *WhoAmL 94*
Rice, Richard Campbell 1933- *WhoAm 94, WhoFI 94, WhoMW 93*
Rice, Richard Lee 1919- *WhoAm 94*
Rice, Richard Lee, Jr. 1967- *WhoWest 94*
Rice, Rick Blackburn 1954- *WhoFI 94*
Rice, Robert C. 1923- *WhoBlA 94*
Rice, Roger Douglas 1921- *WhoAm 94*
Rice, Roma Jean 1936- *WhoAm 94*
Rice, Ron d1964 *WhoHol 92*
Rice, Ronald Bart 1957- *WhoFI 94*
Rice, Ronald James 1944- *WhoAm 94*
Rice, Ronald L. 1945- *WhoAmP 93*
Rice, Roy d1966 *WhoHol 92*
Rice, Roy Warren 1934- *WhoScEn 94*
Rice, Sally 1949- *WhoAmP 93*
Rice, Sam d1946 *WhoHol 92*
Rice, Sheila 1947- *WhoAmP 93*
Rice, Shelley Enid 1950- *WhoAmA 93*
Rice, Shirley J. 1929- *WhoAmP 93*
Rice, Stan *DrAPF 93*
Rice, Stanley Arthur 1957- *WhoMW 93*
Rice, Stanley Travis, Jr. 1942- *WhoAm 94*
Rice, Stephen Landon 1941- *WhoAm 94*
Rice, Steven Dale 1947- *WhoScEn 94, WhoWest 94*
Rice, Steven J. 1949- *WhoAmL 94*
Rice, Stuart Alan 1932- *IntWW 93, WhoAm 94, WhoScEn 94*
Rice, Sue Ann 1934- *WhoAm 94*
Rice, Susan F. *WhoAm 94*
Rice, Susie Leon 1922- *WhoBlA 94*
Rice, Terrence Kevin 1955- *WhoMW 93*
Rice, Thomas E. P., Jr. 1923- *WhoAmP 93*
Rice, Thomas R. 1945- *WhoWest 94*
Rice, Tim(othy) Miles Bindon 1944- *IntWW 93*
Rice, Timothy Miles Bindon 1944- *Who 94, WhoAm 94*
Rice, Treva Kay 1951- *WhoScEn 94*
Rice, V(irgil) Thomas 1920- *WhoAmP 93*
Rice, Verdine D. 1918- *WhoAmP 93*
Rice, Victor Albert 1941- *IntWW 93, WhoAm 94, WhoFI 94*
Rice, Virgil Thomas 1920- *WhoAmL 94*
Rice, Virginia *WhoAmP 93*
Rice, W. R. 1924- *WhoAmP 93*
Rice, Wallace William 1936- *WhoWest 94*
Rice, Walter Herbert 1937- *WhoAm 94, WhoAmL 94, WhoMW 93*
Rice, William Clem 1937- *WhoWest 94*
Rice, William E. 1933- *WhoBlA 94*
Rice, William Edward 1938- *WhoAm 94*
Rice, William Phipps 1944- *WhoFI 94*
Rice, William Ross 1939- *WhoMW 93*
Rice, Winston Edward 1946- *WhoAmL 94*
Rice-Davies, Mandy 1944- *WhoHol 92*
Rice-Edwards, Sebastian *WhoHol 92*
Rice-Knight, Maureen 1958- *Who 94*
Rice-Oxley, James Keith 1920- *Who 94*
Ricevuto, Vincent Edmond 1966- *WhoFI 94*
Rich, Adam 1969- *WhoHol 92*
Rich, Adrienne *DrAPF 93*
Rich, Adrienne 1929- *BlmGWL [port], ConLC 76 [port], IntWW 93, WhoAm 94, WhoWest 94*
Rich, Adrienne (Cecile) 1929- *GayLL, WrDr 94*
Rich, Adrienne Cecile 1929- *AmCulL*
Rich, Alan 1924- *WhoAm 94, WhoWest 94*
Rich, Alexander 1924- *IntWW 93, WhoAm 94*
Rich, Allan *WhoHol 92*
Rich, Allen d1976 *WhoHol 92*
Rich, Andrew Michael 1945- *WhoFI 94*
Rich, Arthur Lowndes 1905- *WhoAm 94*
Rich, Barbara *EncSF 93*
Rich, Ben Arthur 1947- *WhoAm 94, WhoAmL 94, WhoWest 94*
Rich, Beverly Eileen 1950- *WhoAmP 93*
Rich, Bruce Allan 1939- *WhoAm 94*
Rich, Buddy d1987 *WhoHol 92*
Rich, Charles Allan 1932- *WhoAm 94*
Rich, Charles Anthony 1951- *WhoScEn 94*
Rich, Christopher 1657-1714 *BlmGEL*
Rich, Christopher 1953- *WhoHol 92*
Rich, Claude 1929- *WhoHol 92*
Rich, Clayton 1924- *IntWW 93*
Rich, Craig Robert 1954- *WhoMW 93*
Rich, Daniel Catton 1904-1976 *WhoAmA 93N*
Rich, Daniel Hulbert 1942- *WhoScEn 94*
Rich, David Barry 1952- *WhoWest 94*
Rich, David Lowell 1920- *IntMPA 94*
Rich, Dick d1967 *WhoHol 92*
Rich, Donald L. *WhoAmP 93*
Rich, Doris d1971 *WhoHol 92*
Rich, Elaine Sommers 1926- *WrDr 94*
Rich, Elizabeth Gamsky 1958- *WhoAmL 94*
Rich, Elizabeth Grace 1928- *WhoAmP 93*
Rich, Elizabeth Marie 1949- *WhoWest 94*
Rich, Eric 1921- *WhoAm 94, WhoFI 94*
Rich, Frances 1909- *WhoHol 92*
Rich, Frances L. 1910- *WhoAmA 93*
Rich, Frances Luther 1910- *WhoAm 94, WhoWest 94*
Rich, Frank Hart 1949- *WhoAm 94*
Rich, Frank Hart, Jr. 1949- *IntWW 93*
Rich, Freddie d1956 *WhoHol 92*
Rich, Gareth Edward 1961- *WhoWest 94*
Rich, Garry Lorence 1943- *WhoAmA 93*
Rich, Giles S. *WhoAmP 93*
Rich, Giles Sutherland 1904- *CngDr 93, WhoAm 94, WhoAmL 94*
Rich, Glenn Eugene 1949- *WhoAmP 93*
Rich, Harry E. 1940- *WhoAm 94, WhoFI 94*
Rich, Harry Louis 1917- *WhoScEn 94*
Rich, Helen d1963 *WhoHol 92*
Rich, Irene d1988 *WhoHol 92*
Rich, J. Peter 1953- *WhoAm 94*
Rich, James Edward 1951- *WhoAmP 93*
Rich, Jane C. 1942- *WhoAmP 93*
Rich, Jeffrey A. 1945- *WhoAmP 93*
Rich, John *IntMPA 94*
Rich, John 1692-1761 *BlmGEL, NewGrDO*
Rich, John 1925- *WhoAm 94*
Rich, John Martin 1931- *WhoAm 94*
Rich, John Rowland 1928- *IntWW 93, Who 94*
Rich, John Townsend 1943- *WhoAmL 94*
Rich, Joseph Ash 1943- *WhoWest 94*
Rich, Joseph John 1944- *WhoMW 93*
Rich, Jude T. 1943- *WhoAm 94*
Rich, Kenneth Malcolm 1946- *WhoAm 94*
Rich, Kerry *WhoAmP 93*
Rich, Lawrence Vincent 1951- *WhoFI 94*
Rich, Lee *WhoAm 94*
Rich, Lee 1926- *IntMPA 94*
Rich, Lillian d1954 *WhoHol 92*
Rich, Lorimer 1892-1978 *WhoAmA 93N*
Rich, Mary 1624-1678 *BlmGWL*
Rich, Matty 1971- *BlkWr 2, ConAu 140*
Rich, Matty 1972- *WhoBlA 94*
Rich, Michael Anthony 1931- *Who 94*
Rich, Michael David 1953- *WhoAm 94*
Rich, Michael Joseph 1945- *WhoAm 94, WhoAmL 94*
Rich, Michael Samuel 1933- *Who 94*
Rich, Myrtle May d1931 *WhoHol 92*
Rich, Nigel Mervyn Sutherland 1945- *Who 94*
Rich, Patrick J. J. *WhoAm 94, WhoFI 94*
Rich, Patrick Jean Jacques 1931- *IntWW 93*
Rich, Philip Dewey 1940- *WhoFI 94*
Rich, Raphael Z. 1929- *WhoScEn 94*
Rich, Robert Bruce 1949- *WhoAm 94, WhoAmL 94*
Rich, Robert E., Jr. 1941- *WhoFI 94*
Rich, Robert Edward 1944- *WhoAm 94, WhoAmL 94*
Rich, Robert F. *WhoAm 94, WhoMW 93, WhoScEn 94*
Rich, Robert G., Jr. 1930- *WhoAmP 93*
Rich, Robert Graham, Jr. 1930- *IntWW 93*
Rich, Robert Regier 1941- *WhoAm 94*
Rich, Robert Stephen 1938- *WhoAm 94, WhoAmL 94, WhoWest 94*
Rich, Roland Deaver 1936- *WhoAmP 93*
Rich, Rolla Ross 1945- *WhoWest 94*
Rich, Ron *WhoHol 92*
Rich, Rosan 1946- *WhoFI 94*
Rich, S. Judith *WhoAm 94*
Rich, Sharon Lee 1956- *WhoFI 94*
Rich, Stanley C. 1920- *WhoBlA 94*
Rich, Stanley Robert d1993 *NewYTBS 93 [port]*
Rich, Thomas Hewitt 1941- *WhoScEn 94*
Rich, Thomas Hurblut 1946- *WhoAm 94*
Rich, Vernon d1978 *WhoHol 92*
Rich, Vivian d1957 *WhoHol 92*
Rich, Wayne Schermerhorn 1912- *WhoAmP 93*
Rich, Wilbur C. 1939- *WhoBlA 94*
Rich, Willis Frank, Jr. 1919- *WhoAm 94*
Richard, Baron 1932- *IntWW 93, Who 94*
Richard, II fl. 1377-1399 *BlmGEL*
Richard, III 1452-1485 *HisWorL [port]*
Richard, III fl. 1483-1485 *BlmGEL*
Richard, Adrienne 1921- *WrDr 94*
Richard, Alexander *WhoAmP 93*
Richard, Alison *WhoAm 94*
Richard, Allen Joseph 1947- *WhoAmP 93*
Richard, Alvin J. 1932- *WhoBlA 94*
Richard, Anita Louise 1951- *WhoWest 94*
Richard, Arlene Castain 1955- *WhoBlA 94*
Richard, Barry Scott 1942- *WhoAmP 93*
Richard, Betti 1916- *WhoAm 94*
Richard, Christian Remi 1941- *IntWW 93*
Richard, Cliff 1940- *IntMPA 94, IntWW 93, Who 94, WhoHol 92, WrDr 94*
Richard, Edward H. 1937- *WhoAm 94*
Richard, Firmine *WhoHol 92*
Richard, Flossie d1976 *WhoHol 92*
Richard, Floyd Anthony 1952- *WhoBlA 94*
Richard, Frederick Hugh 1938- *WhoFI 94*
Richard, Frieda d1946 *WhoHol 92*
Richard, Fritz d1933 *WhoHol 92*
Richard, Henri-Claude 1944- *WhoBlA 94*
Richard, Howard 1921- *WhoAmL 94*
Richard, Howard M. 1944- *WhoAmL 94*
Richard, Jack 1922- *WhoAmA 93*
Richard, James L. 1917- *WhoBlA 94*
Richard, Jean *WhoHol 92*
Richard, Jean Barthelemy 1921- *IntWW 93*
Richard, Mark M. 1939- *WhoAm 94*
Richard, Marty 1940- *WhoWest 94*
Richard, Paul 1939- *WhoAm 94, WhoAmA 93*
Richard, Pierre 1934- *WhoHol 92*
Richard, R. Paul 1950- *WhoBlA 94*
Richard, Robert John 1947- *WhoAm 94, WhoWest 94*
Richard, Sandra Clayton *WhoFI 94*
Richard, Scott F. 1946- *WhoAm 94*
Richard, Susan *ConAu 142*
Richard, Susan 1933- *WrDr 94*
Richard, Susan Mathis 1949- *WhoAm 94*
Richard, Sylvan Joseph 1934- *WhoScEn 94*
Richard, Thomas Mark 1957- *WhoAmL 94*
Richard, Virginia Rynne 1943- *WhoAmL 94*
Richard, Wendy *WhoHol 92*
Richard, William 1937- *WhoMW 93*
Richard, William Ralph, Jr. 1922-1990 *WhAm 10*
Richard Coeur de Lion, I fl. 1189-1199 *BlmGEL*
Richarde, Tessa *WhoHol 92*
Richardet, Rodney James 1955- *WhoMW 93*
Richardi, Ralph Leonard 1947- *WhoAm 94*
Richard of Haldingham fl. 1260-1278 *DcNaB MP*
Richards *Who 94*
Richards, Addison d1964 *WhoHol 92*
Richards, Alayna 1944- *WrDr 94*
Richards, Alfred Bate 1820-1876 *EncSF 93*
Richards, Allan M. 1954- *WhoAmP 93*
Richards, Alun *Who 94*
Richards, (Richard) Alun 1920- *Who 94*
Richards, Ann *NewYTBS 93 [port]*
Richards, Ann 1918- *WhoHol 92*
Richards, Ann Willis 1933- *IntWW 93, WhoAm 94, WhoAmP 93, WhoWomW 91*
Richards, Archibald Banks 1911- *Who 94*
Richards, Arthur A. 1924- *WhoBlA 94*
Richards, Arthur Cyril 1921- *Who 94*
Richards, Arthur Lincoln 1907-1991 *WhAm 10*
Richards, Atherton 1894- *WhAm 10*
Richards, Aubrey *WhoHol 92*
Richards, Beah *BlkWr 2, IntMPA 94, WhoBlA 94, WhoHol 92*
Richards, Bernard 1927- *WhoAm 94*
Richards, Bertrand *Who 94*
Richards, (Edmund) Bertrand (Bamford) 1913- *Who 94*
Richards, Beverly Joan 1962- *WhoMW 93*
Richards, Bill 1936- *WhoAm 94, WhoAmA 93*
Richards, Bill 1944- *WhoAmA 93*
Richards, Brent C. 1937- *WhoAmP 93*
Richards, Brian Henry 1938- *Who 94*
Richards, Brian Mansel 1932- *Who 94*
Richards, Brooks *Who 94*
Richards, (Francis) Brooks 1918- *Who 94*
Richards, Burt *WhoHol 92*
Richards, Burt 1930- *WhoAm 94*
Richards, Carlyle Edward 1935- *WhoAm 94, WhoAmL 94*
Richards, Carmeleete A. 1948- *WhoFI 94*
Richards, Catherine Margaret d1993 *Who 94N*
Richards, Charles d1948 *WhoHol 92*
Richards, Charles Anthony Langdon 1911- *Who 94*
Richards, Christine Elizabeth 1948- *WhoAmL 94*
Richards, Christine-Louise 1910- *WrDr 94*
Richards, Christos 1957- *WhoWest 94*
Richards, Cicely d1933 *WhoHol 92*
Richards, Clare 1941- *WrDr 94*
Richards, Cully d1978 *WhoHol 92*
Richards, Cyndi *DrAPF 93*
Richards, Dale Scott 1952- *WhoWest 94*
Richards, David *ConAu 42NR*
Richards, David Alan 1945- *WhoAm 94, WhoAmL 94*
Richards, David Anthony Stewart 1951- *Who 94*
Richards, David Gleyre 1935- *WhoAm 94*
Richards, David Gordon 1928- *Who 94*
Richards, David John 1948- *WhoFI 94*
Richards, David Kimball 1939- *WhoAm 94*
Richards, David L. 1938- *WhoAmP 93*
Richards, DeLeon Marie 1976- *WhoBlA 94*
Richards, Denis Edward 1923- *Who 94*
Richards, Denis George 1910- *Who 94, WrDr 94*
Richards, Diana Lyn 1944- *WhoMW 93, WhoScEn 94*
Richards, Dick 1934- *IntMPA 94*
Richards, Donald d1953 *WhoHol 92*
Richards, Donald Allen 1948- *WhoFI 94*
Richards, Donald Crawford 1932- *WhoFI 94*
Richards, Eddie d1947 *WhoHol 92*
Richards, Edgar Lester 1942- *WhoAm 94*
Richards, Edward A. 1930- *WhoBlA 94*
Richards, Elfyn John 1914- *Who 94*
Richards, Ellen H. 1842-1911 *HisWorL [port]*
Richards, Emily-Mary Fisher 1948- *WhoFI 94*
Richards, Eric Albert Stephan 1965- *WhoWest 94*
Richards, Eric Scott 1961- *WhoAmL 94*
Richards, Ernest William 1960- *WhoScEn 94*
Richards, Eugene 1944- *WhoAmA 93*
Richards, Evan 1970- *WhoHol 92*
Richards, Evelyn E. 1927- *WhoAmP 93*
Richards, Francis Neville 1945- *Who 94*
Richards, Frank *WhoHol 92*
Richards, Fred Tracy 1914- *WhoAm 94*
Richards, Frederic Middlebrook 1925- *IntWW 93, WhoAm 94*
Richards, Frederick *WhoAmP 93*
Richards, Frederick Francis, Jr. 1936- *WhoFI 94*
Richards, Gale Lee 1918- *WhoAm 94*
Richards, Gary Thomas 1941- *WhoMW 93*
Richards, George Henry 1820-1896 *DcNaB MP*
Richards, Gerald Thomas 1933- *WhoAmL 94, WhoWest 94*
Richards, Glen Elvin 1938- *WhoMW 93*
Richards, Glenora 1909- *WhoAmA 93*
Richards, Gordon d1964 *WhoHol 92*
Richards, Gordon Waugh 1930- *Who 94*
Richards, Grant d1963 *WhoHol 92*
Richards, Gregg Rankin 1954- *WhoMW 93*
Richards, Guy 1905-1979 *EncSF 93*
Richards, Gwynfryn d1992 *Who 94N*
Richards, Henry *EncSF 93*
Richards, Herbert East 1919- *WhoAm 94, WhoWest 94*

Richards, Hilda 1936- *WhoAm 94, WhoBlA 94*
Richards, Howard Curtis 1938- *WhoAmL 94*
Richards, Hugh Taylor 1918- *WhoAm 94, WhoMW 93, WhoScEn 94*
Richards, I. A. 1893-1979 *BlmGEL*
Richards, Ira Steven 1948- *WhoScEn 94*
Richards, J. Scott *WhoScEn 94*
Richards, James Alan 1913- *Who 94*
Richards, James Maude 1907- *WrDr 94*
Richards, James R. 1933- *WhoAm 94, WhoAmL 94, WhoAmP 93*
Richards, James Ward 1933- *WhoAm 94*
Richards, James William 1921- *WhoWest 94*
Richards, Janet Radcliffe 1944- *WrDr 94*
Richards, Jeanne Herron *WhoAmA 93*
Richards, Jeanne Herron 1923- *WhoAm 94*
Richards, Jeff d1989 *WhoHol 92*
Richards, Jerry Lee 1939- *WhoAm 94*
Richards, Jim *WhoHol 92*
Richards, Jody 1938- *WhoAmP 93*
Richards, Joel 1937- *EncSF 93*
Richards, John 1933- *Who 94*
Richards, John (Charles Chisholm) 1927- *IntWW 93, Who 94*
Richards, John Arthur 1918- *Who 94*
Richards, John Deacon 1931- *Who 94*
Richards, John Harold 1950- *WhoAmP 93*
Richards, John Inigo 1728?-1810 *NewGrDO*
Richards, John Lewis 1943- *WhoScEn 94*
Richards, John M. 1937- *WhoFI 94, WhoWest 94*
Richards, John Wheeler 1936- *WhoFI 94*
Richards, John William, Jr. 1950- *WhoFI 94*
Richards, Johnetta Gladys 1950- *WhoBlA 94*
Richards, Jon d1988 *WhoHol 92*
Richards, Joseph Edward 1921- *WhoAm 94, WhoAmA 93*
Richards, Keith *WhoHol 92*
Richards, Keith d1987 *WhoHol 92*
Richards, Keith 1943- *ConMus 11 [port], IntWW 93, News 93-3 [port], WhoAm 94*
Richards, Ken *WhoHol 92*
Richards, Kenneth Edwin 1917- *WhoFI 94, WhoWest 94*
Richards, Kent Harold 1939- *WhoWest 94*
Richards, Kim 1964- *WhoHol 92*
Richards, Kyle *WhoHol 92*
Richards, LaClaire Lissetta Jones *WhoMW 93*
Richards, Larry *ConAu 42NR*
Richards, LaVerne W. 1947- *WhoBlA 94*
Richards, Lawrence O. 1931- *ConAu 42NR*
Richards, Leon 1945- *WhoBlA 94*
Richards, Leonard Martin 1935- *WhoFI 94*
Richards, Lisa *WhoHol 92*
Richards, Lisle Frederick 1909- *WhoAm 94*
Richards, Lloyd *ConTFT 11*
Richards, Lloyd G. *WhoBlA 94*
Richards, Lloyd George *WhoAm 94*
Richards, Loretta Theresa, Sister 1929- *WhoBlA 94*
Richards, Marilee *DrAPF 93*
Richards, Marilyn Jeanette 1957- *WhoWest 94*
Richards, Mark 1922- *WrDr 94*
Richards, Marta Alison 1952- *WhoAmL 94, WhoFI 94*
Richards, Max De Voe 1923- *WhoAm 94*
Richards, Melanie *DrAPF 93*
Richards, Merlon Foss 1920- *WhoAm 94*
Richards, Michael *WhoHol 92*
Richards, Michael 1915- *Who 94*
Richards, Michael c. 1949- *News 93 [port], WhoAm 94*
Richards, Michael Anthony 1926- *Who 94*
Richards, Morris Dick 1939- *WhoWest 94*
Richards, Norman Blanchard 1924- *WhoAm 94*
Richards, Pamela Motter 1950- *WhoAmL 94*
Richards, Paul d1974 *WhoHol 92*
Richards, Paul A. 1927- *WhoAmL 94, WhoWest 94*
Richards, Paul Granston 1943- *WhoAm 94*
Richards, Paul Linford 1934- *WhoAm 94, WhoWest 94*
Richards, Peter 1936- *Who 94*
Richards, Peter Graham Gordon 1939- *Who 94*
Richards, Randal William 1948- *WhoScEn 94*
Richards, Renee 1934- *BuCMET*
Richards, Reuben Francis 1929- *WhoAm 94, WhoFI 94*
Richards, Rex (Edward) 1922- *Who 94*
Richards, Rex Edward 1922- *IntWW 93*
Richards, Richard 1932- *WhoAmP 93*

Richards, Richard Meredyth 1920- *Who 94*
Richards, Riley Harry 1912- *WhoAm 94*
Richards, Robert Charles 1939- *WhoFI 94*
Richards, Robert L(aurence) 1898- *WhAm 10*
Richards, Robert Wadsworth 1921- *WhoAm 94*
Richards, Roderick 1947- *Who 94*
Richards, Ronald Edwin 1908- *Who 94*
Richards, Ronald Wayne 1931- *WhoFI 94*
Richards, Ross *EncSF 93*
Richards, Roy, Jr. *WhoAm 94, WhoFI 94*
Richards, Roy Clark 1942- *WhoMW 93*
Richards, Russell B. 1949- *WhoAmL 94*
Richards, Sabra *WhoAmA 93*
Richards, Sandra Lee 1946- *WhoBlA 94*
Richards, Sandra Louise 1934- *WhoWest 94*
Richards, Sindee Anne 1954- *WhoHol 92*
Richards, Stanford Harvey 1932- *WhoAm 94*
Richards, Stephen *WhoHol 92*
Richards, Stephen Price 1950- *Who 94*
Richards, Susan *WhoHol 92*
Richards, Susan 1948- *WrDr 94*
Richards, Suzanne K. 1947- *WhoAmL 94*
Richards, Suzanne V. 1927- *WhoAmL 94*
Richards, Tally *WhoAmA 93*
Richards, Theodore William 1868-1928 *WorScD*
Richards, Thomas Carl 1930- *WhoAm 94*
Richards, Thomas H. 1942- *WhoAmL 94*
Richards, Tom *WhoHol 92*
Richards, Valerie *WhoHol 92*
Richards, Victor 1918- *WhoAm 94*
Richards, Vikki 1949- *WhoHol 92*
Richards, Vincent *WhoHol 92*
Richards, Vincent Philip Haslewood 1933- *WhoAm 94, WhoWest 94*
Richards, Vinnie 1903-1959 *BuCMET*
Richards, Vivian *Who 94*
Richards, (Isaac) Vivian (Alexander) 1952- *Who 94*
Richards, (Isaac) Vivian Alexander 1952- *IntWW 93*
Richards, W. Michael 1946- *WhoAmL 94*
Richards, Walter DuBois 1907- *WhoAm 94, WhoAmA 93*
Richards, William Earl 1921- *WhoBlA 94*
Richards, William George 1920-1992 *WhAm 10*
Richards, William Sidney 1910- *WhoAmP 93*
Richards, Winn L. 1928- *WhoAmP 93*
Richards, Winston Ashton 1935- *WhoBlA 94*
Richards-Alexander, Billie J. *WhoBlA 94*
Richards-Brandt, Mary Robinson 1921- *WhAm 10*
Richards-Kortum, Rebecca Rae 1964- *WhoScEn 94*
Richards-Maldonado, Judy 1954- *WhoHisp 94*
Richards O'Gallagher, Mary Rose *WhoMW 93*
Richards O'Hare Cunningham, Kate 1876-1948 *WomPubS*
Richardson *Who 94*
Richardson, Baron 1910- *IntWW 93, Who 94, WrDr 94*
Richardson, Alan 1923- *WrDr 94*
Richardson, Albert Dion 1946- *WhoBlA 94*
Richardson, Alfred Lloyd 1927- *WhoBlA 94*
Richardson, Ann Bishop 1940- *WhoAm 94*
Richardson, Anne .1935- *WrDr 94*
Richardson, Anthony *Who 94*
Richardson, (Henry) Anthony 1925- *Who 94*
Richardson, Anthony (Lewis) 1950- *Who 94*
Richardson, Anthony W. 1957- *WhoBlA 94*
Richardson, Artemas Partridge 1918- *WhoAm 94*
Richardson, Arthur Bertholin Larsen 1935- *WhoWest 94*
Richardson, Arthur Leslie 1910- *WhoWest 94*
Richardson, Arthur Wilhelm 1963- *WhoAmL 94, WhoFI 94, WhoWest 94*
Richardson, Barbara Connell 1947- *WhoMW 93*
Richardson, Barbara Hull 1922- *WhoMW 93*
Richardson, Ben T. 1924- *WhoAmP 93*
Richardson, Betty H. *WhoAmL 94*
Richardson, Betty Hansen 1953- *WhoAmP 93*
Richardson, Beulah *BlkWr 2*
Richardson, Bill 1947- *CngDr 93, WhoAmP 93, WhoHisp 94*
Richardson, Billy *WhoAmP 93*
Richardson, Bingley G., Sr. 1935- *WhoAmP 93*

Richardson, Bob 1945- *WhoAmP 93*
Richardson, Bobby Harold 1944- *WhoAmP 93*
Richardson, Bonham C. 1939- *WrDr 94*
Richardson, Brenda 1942- *WhoAmA 93*
Richardson, Bryan Kevin 1959- *WhoScEn 94*
Richardson, Campbell 1930- *WhoAm 94, WhoAmL 94*
Richardson, Carl Colley, Jr. 1941- *WhoFI 94*
Richardson, Carlos Albert 1895- *WhAm 10*
Richardson, Carol Joan 1944- *WhoScEn 94*
Richardson, Carolyn Jane 1943- *WhoWest 94*
Richardson, Charles 1814-1896 *DcNaB MP*
Richardson, Charles (Leslie) *Who 94*
Richardson, Charles Clifton 1935- *WhoAm 94*
Richardson, Charles Lawrence 1935- *WhoWest 94*
Richardson, Charles Ronald 1949- *WhoBlA 94*
Richardson, Charles T. 1947- *WhoAm 94, WhoAmL 94*
Richardson, Charles Walter Philipps d1993 *Who 94N*
Richardson, Clint Dewitt 1956- *WhoBlA 94*
Richardson, Clinton Dennis 1949- *WhoAmL 94*
Richardson, Clyta Faith 1915- *WhoAm 94*
Richardson, Constance (Coleman) 1905- *WhoAmA 93*
Richardson, Cordell 1946- *WhoBlA 94*
Richardson, David 1928- *Who 94*
Richardson, David (Horsfall Stuart) 1942- *WrDr 94*
Richardson, David John 1943- *WhoAm 94*
Richardson, David Lee 1947- *WhoFI 94*
Richardson, David P., Jr. 1948- *WhoAmP 93*
Richardson, David Preston, Jr. 1948- *WhoBlA 94*
Richardson, David R. 1942- *WhoAmL 94*
Richardson, David Walthall 1925- *WhoAm 94*
Richardson, Dean Eugene 1927- *WhoAm 94*
Richardson, Deanna Ruth 1956- *WhoMW 93*
Richardson, Deborah Ruth 1950- *WhoScEn 94*
Richardson, Delroy M. 1938- *WhoBlA 94*
Richardson, Dennis Michael 1949- *WhoAmL 94*
Richardson, DeRutha Gardner 1941- *WhoBlA 94*
Richardson, Don Orland 1934- *WhoScEn 94*
Richardson, Donald Charles 1937- *WhoFI 94, WhoScEn 94*
Richardson, Donald Edward 1931- *WhoAm 94*
Richardson, Dorothy 1873-1957 *BlmGEL*
Richardson, Dorothy Miller 1873-1957 *BlmGWL [port], DcNaB MP*
Richardson, Douglas Fielding 1929- *WhoAm 94, WhoAmL 94, WhoFI 94*
Richardson, Earl Stanford 1943- *WhoBlA 94*
Richardson, Eddie Price, Jr. 1936- *WhoBlA 94*
Richardson, Edgar Preston 1902-1985 *WhoAmA 93N*
Richardson, Edward James 1954- *WhoAm 94*
Richardson, Elaine *WhoAmP 93*
Richardson, Eleanor Elizabeth 1948- *WhoFI 94*
Richardson, Eleanor L. *WhoAmP 93*
Richardson, Elisha R. 1931- *WhoBlA 94*
Richardson, Elliot Lee 1920- *IntWW 93, Who 94, WhoAm 94, WhoAmL 94*
Richardson, Elvenn James Alonzo 1953- *WhoFI 94*
Richardson, Emilie White *WhoFI 94*
Richardson, Eric *Who 94*
Richardson, (John) Eric 1905- *Who 94*
Richardson, Ernest A. 1925- *WhoBlA 94*
Richardson, Ethel *BlmGWL*
Richardson, Evelyn D. *WhoAmP 93*
Richardson, Everett Vern 1924- *WhoAm 94, WhoScEn 94*
Richardson, F. C. 1936- *WhoAm 94, WhoBlA 94*
Richardson, Frank d1962 *WhoHol 92*
Richardson, Frank 1950- *WhoBlA 94*
Richardson, Frank, Jr. 1950- *WhoAmA 93*
Richardson, Frank H. 1933- *IntWW 93, WhoAm 94, WhoFI 94*
Richardson, Frank Kellogg 1914- *WhoAm 94*
Richardson, Frank McLean 1904- *Who 94, WrDr 94*

Richardson, Fred L. 1942- *WhoAmP 93*
Richardson, Garland Dale 1931- *WhoWest 94*
Richardson, Gary Lee 1947- *WhoAmP 93*
Richardson, Geoffrey Alan 1936- *WrDr 94*
Richardson, George Barclay 1924- *IntWW 93, Who 94*
Richardson, George C. 1929- *WhoBlA 94*
Richardson, George Taylor 1924- *IntWW 93, Who 94*
Richardson, Gilda Faye 1926- *WhoBlA 94*
Richardson, Gisele 1929- *WhoAm 94*
Richardson, Gloster V. 1941- *WhoBlA 94*
Richardson, Gordon Banning 1937- *WhoAmP 93*
Richardson, Graham 1949- *IntWW 93*
Richardson, Greg Drexel 1955- *WhoAmL 94*
Richardson, H. L. 1927- *WhoAmP 93*
Richardson, Harold Edward 1922- *WhoBlA 94*
Richardson, Harry W(ard) 1938- *WrDr 94*
Richardson, Henry Handel 1870-1946 *BlmGEL, BlmGWL, RfGShF*
Richardson, Henry Hobson 1838-1886 *AmCulL*
Richardson, Henry J., III 1941- *WhoBlA 94*
Richardson, Herbert D. 1950- *WhoAmP 93*
Richardson, Herbert Heath 1930- *WhoAm 94*
Richardson, Horace Vincent 1913- *Who 94*
Richardson, Hugh Edward 1905- *Who 94*
Richardson, Ian 1934- *WhoHol 92*
Richardson, Ian William 1934- *IntWW 93, Who 94*
Richardson, Ivor (Lloyd Morgan) 1930- *Who 94*
Richardson, Jack *WhoAmP 93*
Richardson, Jack d1957 *WhoHol 92*
Richardson, Jack 1935- *WrDr 94*
Richardson, Jack (Carter) 1935- *ConDr 93, IntDcT 2*
Richardson, James *DrAPF 93*
Richardson, James 1806-1851 *WhWE*
Richardson, James Alexander 1943- *WhoMW 93*
Richardson, James Armstrong 1922- *Who 94*
Richardson, James David 1953- *WhoFI 94*
Richardson, James F. *WhoAmP 93*
Richardson, James Fairgrieve 1940- *WhoIns 94*
Richardson, James G. d1983 *WhoHol 92*
Richardson, James John 1941- *Who 94*
Richardson, James Lewis 1927- *WhoAmA 93N*
Richardson, James M. 1940- *WhoAmP 93*
Richardson, James R. 1944- *WhoAmL 94*
Richardson, James Troy 1941- *WhoWest 94*
Richardson, Jamie Irene 1952- *WhoAmL 94*
Richardson, Jasper Edgar 1922- *WhoScEn 94*
Richardson, Jay *WhoHol 92*
Richardson, Jay 1957- *WhoAmL 94*
Richardson, Jean 1940- *WhoAmA 93*
Richardson, Jerome Johnson 1936- *WhoAm 94, WhoFI 94*
Richardson, Jo 1923- *WhoWomW 91*
Richardson, Joanna *IntWW 93, Who 94, WrDr 94*
Richardson, Joely 1958- *IntWW 93*
Richardson, Joely 1965- *IntMPA 94, WhoHol 92*
Richardson, John 1787-1865 *WhWE*
Richardson, John 1921- *WhoAm 94*
Richardson, John 1924- *ConAu 140*
Richardson, John 1936- *WhoHol 92*
Richardson, John Adkins 1929- *WhoAmA 93*
Richardson, John Carroll 1932- *WhoAm 94*
Richardson, John Charles 1935- *Who 94*
Richardson, John Charles 1953- *WhoWest 94*
Richardson, John David Benbow 1919- *Who 94*
Richardson, John Edmon 1942- *WhoWest 94*
Richardson, John Eric 1916- *Who 94*
Richardson, John Flint 1906- *Who 94*
Richardson, John Francis 1934- *Who 94*
Richardson, John Francis 1952- *WhoFI 94*
Richardson, John Stephen 1950- *Who 94*
Richardson, John Thomas 1923- *WhoAm 94, WhoMW 93*
Richardson, John Vinson, Jr. 1949- *WhoAm 94, WhoWest 94*
Richardson, Johnny L. 1952- *WhoBlA 94*
Richardson, Joseph 1940- *WhoBlA 94*
Richardson, Joseph Ablett, Jr. 1928- *WhoAmL 94*

Richardson, Joseph Hill 1928- *WhoAm 94, WhoScEn 94*
Richardson, Joseph John, Sr. 1930- *WhoMW 93*
Richardson, Josephine *Who 94*
Richardson, Judith Benet 1941- *SmATA 77 [port]*
Richardson, Julieanna Lynn 1954- *WhoFI 94*
Richardson, K. Scott 1951- *WhoFI 94*
Richardson, Kathleen Margaret 1938- *Who 94*
Richardson, Kathy Kreag *WhoAmP 93*
Richardson, keith 1936- *IntWW 93*
Richardson, Kenneth Albert 1926- *Who 94*
Richardson, Kenneth Augustus 1939- *Who 94*
Richardson, Kenneth T., Jr. 1948- *WhoWest 94*
Richardson, Kermit W. 1929- *WhoAmP 93*
Richardson, Kevin William 1954- *WhoScEn 94*
Richardson, L. F. *WorScD*
Richardson, Lacy Franklin 1937- *WhoBlA 94*
Richardson, Laurel Walum 1938- *WhoAm 94*
Richardson, Lawrence 1923- *WhoAmP 93*
Richardson, Lawrence, Jr. 1920- *WhoAm 94*
Richardson, Lee *WhoHol 92*
Richardson, Leo 1931- *WhoBlA 94*
Richardson, Lester Edwin 1961- *WhoWest 94*
Richardson, Linda *EncSF 93*
Richardson, Linda Waters 1946- *WhoBlA 94*
Richardson, Linford Lawson 1941- *WhoWest 94*
Richardson, Louis M. 1927- *WhoBlA 94*
Richardson, Lovella Lee 1931- *WhoFI 94*
Richardson, Luns C. 1928- *WhoBlA 94*
Richardson, Mabel Lowe 1896- *WhoAmP 93*
Richardson, Madison Franklin 1943- *WhoBlA 94*
Richardson, Margaret Milner *WhoAmP 93*
Richardson, Margaret Milner 1943- *WhoAm 94, WhoFI 94*
Richardson, Marilyn 1936- *NewGrDO*
Richardson, Mark Allen 1950- *WhoMW 93*
Richardson, Mark Lee 1952- *WhoAmP 93*
Richardson, Mary Margaret 1932- *WhoBlA 94*
Richardson, Matthew Statisfield 1972- *WhoBlA 94*
Richardson, Mattie Lou 1924- *WhoAmP 93*
Richardson, Maurice Howe 1928- *WhoAmL 94*
Richardson, Maurine Janet 1944- *WhoMW 93*
Richardson, Melvin M. 1928- *WhoAmP 93*
Richardson, Michael 1947- *WhoHol 92*
Richardson, Michael (John de Rougemont) 1925- *IntWW 93, Who 94*
Richardson, Michael John 1946- *Who 94*
Richardson, Michael Oborne 1908- *Who 94*
Richardson, Michael Ray 1955- *BasBi*
Richardson, Midge Turk 1930- *WhoAm 94, WrDr 94*
Richardson, Mike Calvin 1961- *WhoBlA 94*
Richardson, Mildred Tourtillott 1907- *WhoMW 93*
Richardson, Miles 1932- *WrDr 94*
Richardson, Miranda 1958- *IntMPA 94, Who 94, WhoAm 94, WhoHol 92*
Richardson, Myrtle H. 1907- *WhoAmP 93*
Richardson, Nancy Lester 1934- *WhoMW 93*
Richardson, Natasha 1963- *IntMPA 94, NewYTBS 93 [port], WhoHol 92*
Richardson, Natasha Jane 1963- *Who 94, WhoAm 94*
Richardson, Nola Mae 1936- *WhoBlA 94*
Richardson, Nolan *WhoAm 94*
Richardson, Nolan 1941- *WhoBlA 94*
Richardson, Odis Gene 1940- *WhoBlA 94*
Richardson, Otis Alexander 1943- *WhoBlA 94*
Richardson, Patrick William 1925- *WhoAmL 94*
Richardson, Paul W. 1916- *WhoAmP 93*
Richardson, Peter *WhoHol 92*
Richardson, (George) Peter 1935- *ConAu 43NR*
Richardson, Peter Damian 1935- *IntWW 93, Who 94, WhoAm 94*
Richardson, Pooh (Jerome, Jr.) 1966- *WhoBlA 94*
Richardson, Ralph d1983 *WhoHol 92*
Richardson, Ralph Ernest 1927- *WhoAm 94*
Richardson, Ralph H. 1935- *WhoBlA 94*
Richardson, Ralph Herman 1935- *WhoMW 93*
Richardson, Ramona Grace 1928- *WhoMW 93*
Richardson, Randle *WhoAmP 93*
Richardson, Ray *WhoAmP 93*
Richardson, Rebecca fl. 1738- *BlmGWL*
Richardson, Rhonda Karen 1956- *WhoBlA 94*
Richardson, Richard Colby, Jr. 1933- *WhoWest 94*
Richardson, Richard Judson 1935- *WhoAm 94, WrDr 94*
Richardson, Richard Thomas 1933- *WhoAm 94*
Richardson, Robert (Francis) 1929- *Who 94*
Richardson, Robert Augustus 1912- *Who 94*
Richardson, Robert Charlwood, III 1918- *WhoAm 94*
Richardson, Robert Coleman 1937- *WhoScEn 94*
Richardson, Robert Dale, Jr. 1934- *WhoAm 94*
Richardson, Robert Edward 1955- *WhoMW 93*
Richardson, Robert Eugene 1941- *WhoBlA 94*
Richardson, Robert Galloway 1926- *WrDr 94*
Richardson, Robert S. *EncSF 93*
Richardson, Robin Ann 1955- *WhoFI 94*
Richardson, Roger Gerald 1953- *WhoBlA 94*
Richardson, Roger Glynn 1949- *WhoAmP 93*
Richardson, Ronald F. 1952- *WhoAm 94*
Richardson, Rory Fleming 1953- *WhoWest 94*
Richardson, Ross Frederick 1928- *WhoAm 94*
Richardson, Roy 1931- *WhoFI 94*
Richardson, Rudy James 1945- *WhoAm 94*
Richardson, Rupert Florence, Mrs. 1930- *WhoBlA 94*
Richardson, Ruth *IntWW 93*
Richardson, Ruth 1951- *WrDr 94*
Richardson, Ruth Margaret 1950- *Who 94, WhoWomW 91*
Richardson, Sally K. 1933- *WhoAmP 93*
Richardson, Sam 1934- *WhoAmA 93*
Richardson, Sam Scruton 1919- *Who 94*
Richardson, Samuel 1689-1761 *BlmGEL [port], BlmGWL*
Richardson, Scott Douglas 1956- *WhoMW 93*
Richardson, Scott H. *WhoAmP 93*
Richardson, Scovel 1912- *WhoBlA 94*
Richardson, Sheila J. 1948- *WhoWest 94*
Richardson, Simon Alaisdair S. *Who 94*
Richardson, Stewart Lee, Jr. 1940- *WhoAmP 93*
Richardson, Susan 1954- *WhoHol 92*
Richardson, Suzann 1939- *WhoAmP 93*
Richardson, Sy *WhoHol 92*
Richardson, Sylvia Onesti 1920- *WhoAm 94*
Richardson, Terry E., Jr. 1945- *WhoAmL 94*
Richardson, Thomas A. 1945- *WhoAmL 94*
Richardson, Thomas Andrew 1955- *WhoFI 94*
Richardson, Thomas Anthony 1922- *Who 94*
Richardson, Thomas Hampton 1941- *WhoMW 93, WhoScEn 94*
Richardson, Thomas James 1954- *WhoAmL 94*
Richardson, Thomas Legh 1941- *Who 94*
Richardson, Thomas Wilson 1940- *WhoWest 94*
Richardson, Timothy L. 1958- *WhoBlA 94*
Richardson, Timothy Mark 1955- *WhoFI 94*
Richardson, Tony *Who 94*
Richardson, Tony 1928-1991 *ConTFT 11, WhAm 10*
Richardson, Troy Kenneth 1962- *WhoMW 93*
Richardson, Valerie K. 1955- *WhoBlA 94*
Richardson, W. C. 1953- *WhoAmA 93*
Richardson, Walter John 1926- *WhoAm 94*
Richardson, Walter P. 1907- *WhoBlA 94*
Richardson, Wayne Michael 1948- *WhoBlA 94*
Richardson, William *WhoAmP 93*
Richardson, William d1937 *WhoHol 92*
Richardson, William 1916- *Who 94*
Richardson, (David) William d1993 *Who 94N*
Richardson, William Allen, Jr. 1932- *WhoAmP 93*
Richardson, William Blaine 1947- *WhoAm 94, WhoWest 94*
Richardson, William Chase 1940- *IntWW 93, WhoAm 94*
Richardson, William Eric 1915- *Who 94*
Richardson, William F. 1948- *WhoAm 94*
Richardson, William J. 1933- *WhoBlA 94*
Richardson, William R., Jr. 1952- *WhoAmL 94*
Richardson, William Sidney 1930- *WhoMW 93*
Richardson, William Winfree, III 1939- *WhoAmL 94*
Richardson, William York, III 1952- *WhoWest 94*
Richardson-Bunbury, (Richard David) Michael *Who 94*
Richardson Gonzales, James H. *WhoHisp 94*
Richardson Of Duntisbourne, Baron 1915- *IntWW 93, Who 94*
Richards-Stower, Nancy Ann 1951- *WhoAmP 93*
Richard the Lionheart, I 1157-1199 *HisWorL [port]*
Richart, Douglas Stephen 1931- *WhoFI 94, WhoScEn 94*
Richart, Frank Edwin, Jr. 1918- *WhoAm 94*
Richart, John Douglas 1947- *WhoAm 94*
Richburg, Billy Keith 1946- *WhoFI 94*
Riche, Alan *IntMPA 94*
Riche, Barnabe 1542-1617 *DcLB 136*
Riche, Claude-Antoine-Gaspard 1762-1797 *WhWE*
Riche, Pierre 1921- *IntWW 93*
Richelieu, Cardinal 1585-1642 *HisWorL [port]*
Richelson, Jeffrey T(albot) 1949- *ConAu 43NR*
Richelson, Paul William 1939- *WhoAm 94*
Richenburg, Robert Bartlett 1917- *WhoAm 94, WhoAmA 93*
Richens, Greg P. 1959- *WhoWest 94*
Richens, Muriel Whittaker *WhoWest 94*
Richepin, Jean d1926 *WhoHol 92*
Richer, Stephen Bruce 1946- *WhoAmP 93*
Richerson, Hal Bates 1929- *WhoAm 94, WhoMW 93*
Richert, John Louis 1931- *WhoAmL 94*
Richert, Paul 1948- *WhoAmL 94*
Riches, Derek (Martin Hurry) 1912- *Who 94*
Riches, Ian (Hurry) 1908- *Who 94*
Riches, Kenneth 1908- *Who 94*
Riches, Kenneth William 1962- *WhoScEn 94, WhoWest 94*
Richeson, Cena Golder *DrAPF 93*
Richeson, Cyndi *DrAPF 93*
Richeson, Hugh Anthony, Jr. 1947- *WhoAmL 94*
Richeson, James Grady 1928- *WhoWest 94*
Richet, Charles Robert 1850-1935 *WorScD*
Richette, Lisa Aversa 1928- *WhoAm 94*
Richetti, John J. 1938- *WrDr 94*
Richey, Charles R. *NewYTBS 93 [port]*
Richey, Charles R. 1923- *CngDr 93*
Richey, Charles Robert 1923- *WhoAm 94, WhoAmL 94*
Richey, Clarence Bentley 1910- *WhoScEn 94*
Richey, Cliff 1946- *BuCMET*
Richey, Edwin d1973 *WhoHol 92*
Richey, Everett Eldon 1923- *WhoAm 94, WhoWest 94*
Richey, Herbert Southall, II 1922- *WhoAm 94*
Richey, Herman G(lenn) 1897- *WhAm 10*
Richey, John O. 1929- *WhoMW 93*
Richey, Mary Ellen 1949- *WhoAmL 94*
Richey, Nancy 1942- *BuCMET*
Richey, P. Jerome 1949- *WhoAmL 94*
Richey, Phil Horace 1923- *WhoAm 94*
Richey, Robert Lee 1923- *WhoAm 94*
Richey, Rodney L. 1955- *WhoFI 94*
Richey, Thomas Adam 1934- *WhoAm 94*
Richey, Thomas S. 1944- *WhoAmL 94*
Richfield, Edwin d1990 *WhoHol 92*
Richgels, Jeffrey Scott 1962- *WhoMW 93*
Richichi, Joseph 1946- *WhoAmL 94*
Richie, Donald 1924- *WrDr 94*
Richie, Leroy C. 1941- *WhoAmL 94, WhoBlA 94, WhoFI 94*
Richie, Lionel 1949- *AfrAmAl 6*
Richie, Lionel B., Jr. 1949- *WhoAm 94*
Richie, Lionel Brockman, Jr. 1950- *WhoBlA 94*
Richie, Sharon Ivey 1949- *WhoBlA 94*
Richie, Winston Henry 1925- *WhoBlA 94*
Richings, (Mary) Caroline 1827-1882 *NewGrDO*
Richings, Lewis David George 1920- *Who 94*
Richins, Barry Lane 1941- *WhoWest 94*
Richkin, Barry Elliott 1944- *WhoFI 94*
Richkind, Melvyn 1939- *WhoWest 94*
Richland, W. Bernard 1909- *WhoAmL 94*
Richlen, Scott Lane 1949- *WhoFI 94*
Richler, Mordecai 1931- *IntWW 93, Who 94, WhoAm 94, WrDr 94*
Richlin, W. Gar 1945- *WhoFI 94*
Richman, Al(bert) d1936 *WhoHol 92*
Richman, Alan 1939- *WhoAm 94*
Richman, Alan Elliott 1949- *WhoAmL 94*
Richman, Anthony E. 1941- *WhoFI 94, WhoWest 94*
Richman, Charles d1940 *WhoHol 92*
Richman, David 1945- *WhoAmL 94*
Richman, David Bruce 1942- *WhoWest 94*
Richman, David Paul 1943- *WhoAm 94*
Richman, Elliot *DrAPF 93*
Richman, Frances Bragan *DrAPF 93*
Richman, Frances Sharpe 1947- *WhoMW 93*
Richman, Frederick Alexander 1945- *WhoAm 94, WhoAmL 94*
Richman, Harold Alan 1937- *WhoAm 94*
Richman, Harry d1972 *WhoHol 92*
Richman, Harry Bernard 1922- *WhoMW 93*
Richman, Herbert J. 1935- *WhoAm 94*
Richman, Jeffrey Alan 1956- *WhoMW 93*
Richman, Joan F. 1939- *WhoAm 94*
Richman, John Emmett 1951- *WhoFI 94, WhoMW 93, WhoScEn 94*
Richman, John Marshall 1927- *IntWW 93, WhoAm 94, WhoMW 93*
Richman, Kathleen Jacob 1957- *WhoAmP 93*
Richman, Lillian Beatrice 1924- *WhoAmL 94*
Richman, Marc Herbert 1936- *WhoAm 94*
Richman, Marion d1956 *WhoHol 92*
Richman, Martin Franklin 1930- *WhoAm 94*
Richman, Marvin Jordan 1939- *WhoAm 94, WhoFI 94, WhoWest 94*
Richman, Michael F. 1942- *WhoAmL 94*
Richman, Paul 1942- *WhoAm 94, WhoFI 94*
Richman, Peter 1927- *WhoAm 94*
Richman, Peter Mark 1927- *IntMPA 94, WhoAm 94, WhoHol 92*
Richman, Peter Speer 1957- *WhoWest 94*
Richman, Phyllis Chasanow 1939- *WhoAm 94*
Richman, Stella 1922- *Who 94*
Richman, Stephen Erik 1945- *WhoAm 94, WhoAmL 94*
Richman, Stephen I. 1933- *WhoAm 94, WhoAmL 94*
Richman, Steven Norman 1956- *WhoAmL 94*
Richman, William Sheldon 1921- *WhoAm 94*
Richmond, Archdeacon of *Who 94*
Richmond, Duke of 1929- *Who 94*
Richmond, Alan (James) 1919- *Who 94*
Richmond, Andrew John 1931- *Who 94*
Richmond, Ann White 1946- *WhoScEn 94*
Richmond, Anthony Henry 1925- *WhoAm 94, WrDr 94*
Richmond, Branscombe *WhoHol 92*
Richmond, Bruce E. 1938- *WhoAm 94*
Richmond, Clifford (Parris) 1914- *Who 94*
Richmond, David Walker 1914- *WhoAm 94*
Richmond, Delores Ruth 1951- *WhoBlA 94*
Richmond, Donald J. 1943- *WhoAmP 93*
Richmond, Fiona *WhoHol 92*
Richmond, Francis Henry Arthur *Who 94*
Richmond, Frederick W. 1923- *WhoAmP 93*
Richmond, George 1915- *WrDr 94*
Richmond, Gerald Martin 1914- *WhoWest 94*
Richmond, Harold Nicholas 1935- *WhoAmL 94*
Richmond, Herbert Bernard 1920- *WhoAmL 94*
Richmond, Hugh Macrae 1932- *WrDr 94*
Richmond, Isidor 1893- *WhAm 10*
Richmond, James Arthur 1940- *WhoScEn 94*
Richmond, James Ellis 1938- *WhoAm 94*
Richmond, John 1926- *Who 94*
Richmond, John (Frederick) 1924- *Who 94*
Richmond, John Melvyn 1939- *WhoFI 94*
Richmond, John P. 1811-1895 *EncNAR*
Richmond, Julius B. 1916- *IntWW 93*
Richmond, Julius Benjamin 1916- *WhoAm 94, WhoScEn 94*
Richmond, Kane d1973 *WhoHol 92*
Richmond, Laverne Ann 1935- *WhoAmP 93*
Richmond, Lawrence 1909-1978 *WhoAmA 93N*
Richmond, Leigh *WrDr 94*
Richmond, Leigh (Tucker) 1911- *EncSF 93*

Richmond, Leo C. d1979 *WhoHol 92*
Richmond, Lindell Bruce 1929- *WhoAmP 93*
Richmond, Luellen Josephine 1950- *WhoAmP 93*
Richmond, Marilyn Susan 1949- *WhoAm 94, WhoAmL 94*
Richmond, Mark (Henry) 1931- *Who 94*
Richmond, Mark Henry 1931- *IntWW 93*
Richmond, Mary 1903-1973 *EncSF 93*
Richmond, Michael Lloyd 1945- *WhoAmL 94*
Richmond, Mitch 1965- *WhoBlA 94*
Richmond, Myrian Patricia 1942- *WhoBlA 94*
Richmond, Norris L. 1931- *WhoBlA 94*
Richmond, Peter *WhoHol 92*
Richmond, Peter 1943- *Who 94*
Richmond, Peter Graham 1951- *WhoWest 94*
Richmond, Phyllis Allen 1921- *WhoAm 94*
Richmond, Raymond Dean 1958- *WhoScEn 94*
Richmond, Rebekah *WhoAmA 93*
Richmond, Richard Thomas 1933- *WhoAm 94, WhoMW 93*
Richmond, Robert Linn 1920- *WhoAm 94*
Richmond, Robert P. 1914- *WrDr 94*
Richmond, Robin 1951- *ConAu 142, SmATA 75 [port]*
Richmond, Rodney Welch 1940- *WhoBlA 94*
Richmond, Ronald LeRoy 1931- *WhoScEn 94*
Richmond, Samuel Bernard 1919- *WhoAm 94, WhoFI 94*
Richmond, Steve *DrAPF 93*
Richmond, Susan d1959 *WhoHol 92*
Richmond, Ted 1912- *IntMPA 94*
Richmond, Thomas G. 1957- *WhoAm 94, WhoWest 94*
Richmond, Tyronza R. 1940- *WhoBlA 94*
Richmond, Virginia Elizabeth 1947- *WhoFI 94*
Richmond, Walt(er R.) 1922-1977 *EncSF 93*
Richmond, Warner d1948 *WhoHol 92*
Richmond, William Frederick, Jr. 1943- *WhoAmL 94*
Richmond, William Patrick 1932- *WhoAm 94, WhoAmL 94*
Richnell, Donovan Thomas 1911- *Who 94*
Richstein, Abraham Richard 1919- *WhoAm 94*
Richtarich, Thomas Philip 1952- *WhoAmP 93*
Richter, Alan Marc 1955- *WhoFI 94*
Richter, Barbara Ann 1943- *WhoMW 93*
Richter, Barry 1935- *WhoAm 94, WhoFI 94*
Richter, Bernie *WhoAmP 93*
Richter, Burton 1931- *IntWW 93, Who 94, WhoAm 94, WhoScEn 94, WhoWest 94, WorScD*
Richter, Conrad (Michael) 1890-1968 *TwCYAW*
Richter, Deborah *WhoHol 92*
Richter, Denise Ann 1961- *WhoWest 94*
Richter, Don 1930- *WhoAmP 93*
Richter, Donald Paul 1924- *WhoAm 94, WhoAmL 94*
Richter, Dwight Edward 1945- *WhoAmP 93*
Richter, Earl Edward 1923- *WhoFI 94*
Richter, Edwin William 1922- *WhoScEn 94*
Richter, Elizabeth Dunlop 1944- *WhoMW 93*
Richter, Ferdinand Tobias 1651-1711 *NewGrDO*
Richter, George Robert, Jr. 1910- *WhoAm 94*
Richter, Gerhard 1932- *IntWW 93, WhoAm 94*
Richter, Gisela Marie Augusta 1882-1972 *WhoAmA 93N*
Richter, Haloli Q. *AstEnc*
Richter, Hank 1928- *WhoAmA 93*
Richter, Hans d1976 *WhoHol 92*
Richter, Hans 1843-1916 *NewGrDO*
Richter, Hans 1888-1976 *WhoAmA 93N*
Richter, Hans 1940- *WhoMW 93*
Richter, Hans Peter 1925- *TwCYAW*
Richter, Hans Werner 1908- *IntWW 93*
Richter, Harvena 1919- *WrDr 94*
Richter, Horst-Eberhard 1923- *IntWW 93*
Richter, James Michael 1950- *WhoAm 94*
Richter, Jean Louise 1953- *WhoWest 94*
Richter, Jeffrey Alan 1960- *WhoScEn 94*
Richter, Judith Anne 1942- *WhoAm 94*
Richter, Lawrence E., Jr. *WhoAmP 93*
Richter, Norman B. 1957- *WhoAmL 94*
Richter, Paul d1961 *WhoHol 92*
Richter, Peter Christian 1944- *WhoAm 94, WhoAmL 94*
Richter, Richard Paul 1931- *WhoAm 94*
Richter, Richard Wayne 1946- *WhoAmP 93*
Richter, Rotraut d1947 *WhoHol 92*
Richter, Samuel 1972- *WhoMW 93*
Richter, Scott 1943- *WhoAmA 93*
Richter, Susan Mary 1959- *WhoMW 93*
Richter, Sviatoslav Theofilovich 1915- *Who 94*
Richter, Svyatoslav Theofilovich 1915- *IntWW 93*
Richter, Tobin Marais 1944- *WhoAmL 94*
Richter, Todd Benjamin 1957- *WhoFI 94*
Richter, W. D. 1945- *IntMPA 94*
Richter-Frich, Ovre *EncSF 93*
Richtermeyer, Beverly Summers 1932- *WhoMW 93*
Richter Prada, Pedro *IntWW 93*
Richthofen, Ferdinand Paul Wilhelm, Baron Von 1833-1905 *WhWE*
Richthofen, Hermann, Freiherr von 1933- *IntWW 93*
Richtol, Herbert Harold 1932- *WhoAm 94*
Richwine, Maria *WhoHol 92*
Rick, Charles Madeira, Jr. 1915- *IntWW 93, WhoAm 94, WhoScEn 94*
Rickabaugh, Janet Fraley 1939- *WhoMW 93, WhoScEn 94*
Rickard, Cole 1928- *WrDr 94*
Rickard, David Leon 1928- *WhoAmP 93*
Rickard, John Hellyar 1940- *Who 94*
Rickard, Marcia Ruth 1948- *WhoMW 93*
Rickard, Norman Edward 1936- *WhoAm 94*
Rickard, Peter 1922- *Who 94*
Rickard, Ruth David 1926- *WhoMW 93*
Rickard, Vernon Edward d1983 *WhoHol 92*
Rickards, (Richard) Barrie 1938- *Who 94*
Rickards, Leonard Myron 1927- *WhoAm 94*
Rickards, Michael Anthony 1930- *WhoScEn 94*
Rickart, Charles Earl 1913- *WhoAm 94*
Ricke, David Louis 1942- *WhoMW 93*
Ricke, Larry Edward 1950- *WhoFI 94*
Ricke, P. Scott 1948- *WhoScEn 94, WhoWest 94*
Rickel, Annette Urso *WhoMW 93, WhoScEn 94*
Rickels, Karl 1924- *WhoAm 94*
Rickelt, Gustav d1946 *WhoHol 92*
Rickenbach, Francine Wolf 1950- *WhoMW 93*
Rickenbacker, Harry Lee 1943- *WhoAmP 93*
Ricker, Alison Scott 1953- *WhoMW 93, WhoScEn 94*
Ricker, Darlene Marie 1954- *WhoAmL 94*
Ricker, George F. 1930- *WhoAmP 93*
Ricker, Jeffrey Paul 1957- *WhoWest 94*
Ricker, Joanne Danette 1965- *WhoWest 94*
Ricker, John Boykin, Jr. 1917- *WhoAm 94*
Ricker, Louis W. 1941- *WhoAmL 94*
Ricker, Richard Edmond 1952- *WhoScEn 94*
Ricker, Robert S. *WhoAm 94*
Ricker, William Edwin 1908- *WhoAm 94, WhoScEn 94*
Rickerby, David George 1952- *WhoScEn 94*
Rickerd, Donald Sheridan 1931- *WhoAm 94*
Rickerson, Stuart Eugene 1949- *WhoAmL 94*
Rickert, Edwin Weimer 1914- *WhoFI 94*
Rickert, Florence Evelyn 1914- *WhoAmP 93*
Rickert, John F. 1924- *IntMPA 94*
Rickert, Jonathan Bradley 1937- *WhoAm 94*
Rickert, Richard Michael 1936- *WhoMW 93*
Rickert, Shirley Jean 1926- *WhoHol 92*
Rickets, Reginald Anthony Scott 1929- *Who 94*
Ricketson, Edward D., Jr. *WhoAmP 93*
Rickett, Denis Hubert Fletcher 1907- *IntWW 93, Who 94*
Rickett, Joseph Compton 1847-1919 *EncSF 93*
Rickett, Raymond (Mildmay Wilson) 1927- *Who 94*
Rickett, William Francis Sebastian 1953- *Who 94*
Ricketts, Abdy Henry Gough d1993 *Who 94N*
Ricketts, David William 1935- *WhoBlA 94*
Ricketts, Gary Eugene 1935- *WhoAm 94*
Ricketts, John F. *WhoFI 94*
Ricketts, Liese L. 1920- *WhoAmP 93*
Ricketts, Mac Linscott 1930- *WrDr 94*
Ricketts, Marijane G. *DrAPF 93*
Ricketts, Martin John 1948- *Who 94*
Ricketts, Michael Rodney 1923- *Who 94*
Ricketts, Philip F. 1945- *WhoAmL 94*
Ricketts, Ralph Robert 1902- *WrDr 94*
Ricketts, Robert (Cornwallis Gerald St. Leger) 1917- *Who 94*
Ricketts, Sondra Lou 1941- *WhoMW 93*
Ricketts, Theresa *Who 94*
Ricketts, (Anne) Theresa 1919- *Who 94*
Ricketts, Thomas Roland 1931- *WhoAm 94, WhoFI 94, WhoMW 93*
Ricketts, Tom d1939 *WhoHol 92*
Ricketts, Tristram *Who 94*
Ricketts, (Robert) Tristram 1946- *Who 94*
Rickey, Douglas Keith 1957- *WhoAmP 93*
Rickey, George W. 1907- *WhoAmA 93*
Rickey, George Warren 1907- *WhoAm 94*
Rickey, June Evelyn Million 1923- *WhoWest 94*
Rickey, Ronald Thomas 1940- *WhoAmP 93*
Rickford, Jonathan Braithwaite Keevil 1944- *Who 94*
Rickheit, Alan 1939- *WhoAmP 93*
Rickles, Don 1926- *IntMPA 94, WhoCom, WhoHol 92*
Rickles, Donald Jay 1926- *WhoAm 94*
Rickley, David Arthur 1956- *WhoWest 94*
Ricklin, Arthur H. 1934- *WhoAm 94*
Rickman, Alan *IntWW 93, Who 94, WhoAm 94*
Rickman, Alan 1946- *IntMPA 94, WhoHol 92*
Rickman, Geoffrey Edwin 1932- *Who 94*
Rickman, Hans Peter 1918- *WrDr 94*
Rickman, Herbert Paul 1931- *WhoAmP 93*
Rickman, Lewis Daniel, Sr. 1900- *WhoBlA 94*
Rickman, Ray 1948- *WhoAmP 93, WhoBlA 94*
Rickner, Gary J. 1948- *WhoAmL 94*
Ricks, Albert William 1900- *WhoBlA 94*
Ricks, Archie d1962 *WhoHol 92*
Ricks, Christopher 1933- *WrDr 94*
Ricks, Christopher Bruce 1933- *IntWW 93, Who 94*
Ricks, David Trulock 1936- *Who 94*
Ricks, Donald Jay 1936- *WhoAm 94*
Ricks, George R. 1924- *WhoBlA 94*
Ricks, J. Brent 1949- *WhoWest 94*
Ricks, John Paul 1955- *WhoFI 94*
Ricks, Joycia Camilla 1949- *WhoAmL 94*
Ricks, Lyndon Lee 1955- *WhoAmL 94*
Ricks, Mark G. 1924- *WhoAmP 93*
Ricks, Mary Frances 1939- *WhoWest 94*
Ricks, Robert Neville 1942- *Who 94*
Ricksen, Lucille d1925 *WhoHol 92*
Rickson, Gary Ames 1942- *WhoBlA 94*
Rickson, Joe (Joseph) d1958 *WhoHol 92*
Rickus, Gwenneth Margaret 1925- *Who 94*
Ricles, Robert E. 1929- *WhoAmP 93*
Rico, Francisco 1942- *IntWW 93*
Rico, Joseph John 1954- *WhoHisp 94*
Rico, Julie 1957- *WhoHisp 94*
Rico, Maura 1935- *WhoAmP 93*
Rico, Mona *WhoHol 92*
Ricoeur, Paul 1913- *EncEth*
Ricordi *NewGrDO*
Ricordi, Camillo 1957- *WhoScEn 94*
Ricotta, Vincenzo *WhoHol 92*
Ridabock, Ray 1904-1970 *WhoAmA 93N*
Ridd, John William Gregory 1931- *Who 94*
Riddagh, Robert W. 1914- *WhoAmP 93*
Riddel, Joseph Neill 1931- *WhAm 10, WrDr 94*
Riddell, George d1944 *WhoHol 92*
Riddell, Jacqueline Anne 1965- *WhoFI 94*
Riddell, John 1942- *ConAu 142*
Riddell, John (Charles Buchanan) 1934- *Who 94*
Riddell, Maria Woodley 1772-1808 *DcNaB MP*
Riddell, Matthew Donald Rutherford 1918- *WhoAm 94*
Riddell, Peter John Robert 1948- *Who 94*
Riddell, Richard Anderson 1940- *WhoAm 94*
Riddell, Richard Harry 1916- *WhoAm 94*
Riddell, Robert James, Jr. 1923- *WhoWest 94*
Riddell, Robert McAlpin 1919- *WhoWest 94*
Riddell-Webster, John Alexander 1921- *Who 94*
Riddelsdell, Mildred 1913- *Who 94*
Ridder, Bernard Herman, Jr. 1916- *WhoAm 94*
Ridder, Daniel Hickey 1922- *WhoAm 94, WhoWest 94*
Ridder, Elizabeth Sullivan d1993 *NewYTBS 93*
Ridder, Eric 1918- *WhoAm 94*
Ridder, Paul Anthony 1940- *WhoAm 94, WhoFI 94*
Ridder, Ruthe B. 1929- *WhoAmP 93*
Ridder, Walter Thompson 1917- *WhAm 10*
Ridder, William Henry, III 1957- *WhoWest 94*
Ridderbusch, Karl 1932- *NewGrDO*
Ridderheim, David Sigfrid 1936- *WhoAm 94, WhoMW 93*
Riddick, Andrea Celestine 1963- *WhoFI 94*
Riddick, Daniel Howison 1941- *WhoAm 94*
Riddick, Douglas Smith 1942- *WhoFI 94, WhoScEn 94*
Riddick, Eugene E. 1938- *WhoBlA 94*
Riddick, Frank Adams, Jr. 1929- *IntWW 93, WhoAm 94, WhoScEn 94*
Riddick, Graham Edward Galloway 1955- *Who 94*
Riddiford, Lynn Moorhead 1936- *WhoWest 94*
Riddle, Charles A. 1955- *WhoAmP 93*
Riddle, Charles Addison, III 1955- *WhoAmL 94*
Riddle, Clarine Nardi *WhoAmP 93*
Riddle, Donald Husted 1921- *WhoAm 94*
Riddle, Hal *WhoHol 92*
Riddle, Hugh Joseph 1912- *Who 94*
Riddle, John H. 1946- *WhoAmL 94*
Riddle, John Paul 1901-1989 *WhAm 10*
Riddle, John Thomas, Jr. 1933- *WhoAmA 93*
Riddle, Judith Lee 1950- *WhoAmL 94*
Riddle, Kay Williams 1933- *WhoAmP 93*
Riddle, Matthew Casey 1938- *WhoWest 94*
Riddle, Nelson d1985 *WhoHol 92*
Riddle, Rhonda Kiser 1960- *WhoMW 93*
Riddle, Sturgis Lee 1909- *WhoAm 94*
Riddle, Tohby 1965- *SmATA 74 [port]*
Riddle, Veryl Lee 1921- *WhoAm 94*
Riddoch, Gregory Lee 1945- *WhoWest 94*
Riddoch, Hilda Johnson 1923- *WhoWest 94*
Ride, Sally 1951- *IntWW 93*
Ride, Sally Kristen 1951- *WhoAm 94, WhoScEn 94*
Ride, W(illiam) D(avid) L(indsay) 1926- *WrDr 94*
Ridenhour, Joseph Conrad 1920- *WhoAm 94*
Ridenour, David Allen 1962- *WhoFI 94*
Ridenour, Jerry Lee 1958- *WhoFI 94*
Ridenour, Marcella V. 1945- *WhoScEn 94*
Ridenour, Richard Edward 1955- *WhoFI 94*
Ridenour, Windsor Allen 1938- *WhoAm 94*
Rideout, David Edward 1937- *WhoAm 94*
Rideout, Harry Freeman 1942- *WhoAmP 93*
Rideout, Joseph Alan 1951- *WhoAmL 94*
Rideout, Patricia Irene 1931- *WhoAm 94*
Rideout, Philip Munroe 1936- *WhoAm 94*
Rideout, Roger William 1935- *Who 94*
Rideout, Walter Bates 1917- *WhoAm 94*
Rider, Brian Clayton 1948- *WhoAm 94, WhoAmL 94*
Rider, Caroline Vreeland 1949- *WhoAmL 94*
Rider, Gregory Ashford 1949- *WhoFI 94*
Rider, Harry Durbin 1905- *WhoAmP 93*
Rider, J. R. *WhoBlA 94*
Rider, J. W. *ConAu 43NR*
Rider, Jane Louise 1919- *WhoWest 94*
Rider, Lynn Mariann 1966- *WhoMW 93*
Rider, Marilyn Ann 1941- *WhoFI 94*
Rider, Robert Alan 1937- *WhoMW 93*
Rider, Robert Farrington 1928- *WhoFI 94*
Ridge, Anthony Hubert 1913- *Who 94*
Ridge, David A. *WhoAmP 93*
Ridge, John L., Jr. 1939- *WhoAmL 94*
Ridge, Martin 1923- *WhoWest 94*
Ridge, Sterling *WhoAmP 93*
Ridge, Thomas J. 1945- *CngDr 93, WhoAmP 93*
Ridge, Thomas Joseph 1945- *WhoAm 94*
Ridge, William Pett 1859-1930 *DcLB 135 [port]*
Ridgel, Gus Tolver 1926- *WhoBlA 94*
Ridgely, Cleo d1962 *WhoHol 92*
Ridgely, John d1968 *WhoHol 92*
Ridgers, John Nalton Sharpe 1910- *Who 94*
Ridges, Stanley d1951 *WhoHol 92*
Ridges-Horton, Lee Esther 1951- *WhoBlA 94*
Ridgeway, Bill Tom 1927- *WhoBlA 94*
Ridgeway, Fritzi d1961 *WhoHol 92*
Ridgeway, Henry Dorman 1952- *WhoAmL 94*
Ridgeway, James Fowler 1936- *WhoAm 94*
Ridgeway, L. Don 1948- *WhoAmP 93*
Ridgeway, Luann *WhoAmP 93*
Ridgeway, Peter d1938 *WhoHol 92*
Ridgeway, William C. 1942- *WhoBlA 94*
Ridgewell, Audrey d1968 *WhoHol 92*
Ridgewell, Rosemary d1979 *WhoHol 92*
Ridgley, Sherry E. 1952- *WhoAm 94*
Ridgley, Thomas Brennan 1940- *WhoAm 94*
Ridgway, Brunilde Sismondo 1929- *WhoAm 94*

Ridgway, David Wenzel 1904- *WhoWest 94*
Ridgway, Jason 1928- *WrDr 94*
Ridgway, John 1938- *WrDr 94*
Ridgway, M(atthew) B(unker) 1895-1993 *CurBio 93N*
Ridgway, Marcella Davies 1957- *WhoMW 93, WhoScEn 94*
Ridgway, Matthew B. 1895- *HisDcKW, IntWW 93*
Ridgway, Matthew B. 1895-1993 *NewYTBS 93 [port]*
Ridgway, Matthew Bunker d1993 *Who 94N*
Ridgway, Patricia d1978 *WhoHol 92*
Ridgway, Rozanne L. *WhoAmP 93*
Ridgway, Rozanne LeJeanne 1935- *WhoAm 94*
Riding, Julia *EncSF 93*
Riding, Laura *EncSF 93, WhAm 10*
Riding, Laura 1901-1991 *WrDr 94N*
Ridings, C. Leslie, Jr. 1926- *WhoAmP 93*
Ridings, Dorothy Sattes 1939- *WhoAm 94*
Ridings, William John, Jr. 1948- *WhoAmL 94*
Ridington, Robin 1939- *WrDr 94*
Ridl, Jack *DrAPF 93*
Ridland, John M. *DrAPF 93*
Ridland, John Murray 1933- *WhoWest 94*
Ridlen, Julian 1940- *WhoAmP 93*
Ridlen, Samuel Franklin 1916- *WhoMW 93*
Ridler, Anne 1912- *BlmGWL*
Ridler, Anne (Barbara) 1912- *ConDr 93, NewGrDO, Who 94, WrDr 94*
Ridler, Vivian Hughes 1913- *Who 94*
Ridley, Viscount 1925- *Who 94*
Ridley, Adam (Nicholas) 1942- *Who 94*
Ridley, Alfred Denis 1948- *WhoBlA 94*
Ridley, Arnold d1984 *WhoHol 92*
Ridley, Arthur d1978 *WhoHol 92*
Ridley, Betty *Who 94*
Ridley, (Mildred) Betty 1909- *Who 94*
Ridley, Charles Robert 1948- *WhoBlA 94*
Ridley, Clarence Haverty 1942- *WhoAm 94, WhoAmL 94*
Ridley, Edward Alexander Keane 1904- *Who 94*
Ridley, Elizabeth J(ayne) 1966- *ConAu 142*
Ridley, Frank A(mbrose) c. 1896- *EncSF 93*
Ridley, Frederick Fernand 1928- *Who 94*
Ridley, Gordon 1921- *Who 94*
Ridley, Gregory D., Jr. 1925- *WhoAmA 93*
Ridley, Harold *Who 94*
Ridley, (Nicholas) Harold (Lloyd) 1906- *Who 94*
Ridley, Harry Joseph 1923- *WhoBlA 94*
Ridley, J. Dorsey 1953- *WhoAmP 93*
Ridley, Jasper (Godwin) 1920- *WrDr 94*
Ridley, Jasper Godwin 1920- *Who 94*
Ridley, John A. 1943- *WhoAmL 94*
Ridley, Mark 1956- *WrDr 94*
Ridley, May Alice *WhoBlA 94*
Ridley, Michael *Who 94*
Ridley, (Robert) Michael 1947- *Who 94*
Ridley, Michael Kershaw 1937- *Who 94*
Ridley, Nicholas d1993 *NewYTBS 93 [port]*
Ridley, Nicholas 1500?-1555 *BlmGEL*
Ridley, Nicholas 1929- *ConAu 141*
Ridley, Paula Frances Cooper 1944- *Who 94*
Ridley, Philip *ConAu 140*
Ridley, Philip Waller 1921- *Who 94*
Ridley, Sidney 1902- *Who 94*
Ridley, Tony Melville 1933- *Who 94*
Ridley, Vinton T. 1928- *WhoAmP 93*
Ridley, William Terence Colborne 1915- *Who 94*
Ridley of Liddesdale, Baron d1993 *IntWW 93N, Who 94N*
Ridley-Thomas, Mark *WhoAmP 93*
Ridley-Thomas, Roger 1939- *Who 94*
Ridloff, Richard 1948- *WhoAm 94*
Ridlon, James A. 1936- *WhoAmA 93*
Ridout, Alan (John) 1934- *NewGrDO*
Ridout, Godfrey 1918-1984 *NewGrDO*
Ridout, Ronald 1916- *WrDr 94*
Ridsdale, Julian (Errington) 1915- *Who 94*
Ridsdale, Victoire Evelyn Patricia 1921- *Who 94*
Rie, Lucie 1902- *Who 94*
Rieb, Mark David 1954- *WhoMW 93*
Riebe, Cynthia Morris 1946- *WhoWest 94*
Riebe, Mel 1920- *BasBi*
Riebe, Susan Jane 1955- *WhoScEn 94*
Riebel, Alan Chester 1927- *WhoAmP 93*
Rieber, Ruth B. 1924- *WhoAmA 93*
Rieber-Mohn, Georg Fredrik 1945- *IntWW 93*
Riebesehl, E. Allan 1938- *WhoFI 94*
Riechers, Inez Richardson 1926- *WhoAmP 93*
Riechmann, Fred B. 1915- *WhoAm 94*
Rieck, Charles Lange 1939- *WhoAm 94*
Rieck, Stephen Charles 1949- *WhoAmP 93*
Rieck, Thomas Booth 1951- *WhoFI 94*
Rieck, William Joseph 1944- *WhoIns 94*
Riecke, Hans Heinrich 1929- *WhoAm 94*
Riecken, Henry William 1917- *WhoAm 94*
Riecker, Margaret Ann 1933- *WhoAmP 93*
Ried, Aquinas c. 1810-1869 *NewGrDO*
Riede, David G(eorge) 1951- *WrDr 94*
Riede, Ronald Frederick, Jr. 1957- *WhoMW 93*
Riedeburg, Theodore 1912- *WhoAm 94*
Riedel, Alan Ellis 1930- *WhoAm 94*
Riedel, Bernard Edward 1919- *WhoAm 94*
Riedel, Charles Alan 1949- *WhoWest 94*
Riedel, David Thomas 1945- *WhoAmL 94*
Riedel, Deborah 1958- *NewGrDO*
Riedel, Paul Schreiter 1911- *WhoFI 94*
Riedel, Richard A. 1922- *WhoWest 94*
Rieder, Robert Werner, Jr. 1942- *WhoAmL 94*
Rieder, Ronald Frederick 1932- *WhoWest 94*
Rieders, Fredric 1922- *WhoAm 94*
Riedesel, Frederica Charlotte, Baroness von 1746-1807 *WhAmRev [port]*
Riedesel, Fredericke von 1746-1808 *AmRev*
Riedesel, Friedrich, Baron von 1738-1800 *WhAmRev*
Riedinger, Alan Blair 1926- *WhoScEn 94*
Riedinger, Edward Anthony 1944- *WhoMW 93*
Riedl, John Orth 1937- *WhoMW 93*
Riedlbauch, Vaclav 1947- *IntWW 93*
Riedlsperger, Max Ernst 1937- *WhoWest 94*
Riedmann, Agnes *DrAPF 93*
Riedner, Werner Ludwig Fritz 1924- *WhoScEn 94*
Riedthaler, William Allen 1948- *WhoMW 93*
Riedy, Mark Joseph 1942- *WhoAm 94*
Rief, Frank J., III 1944- *WhoAmL 94*
Riefe, Alan 1925- *WrDr 94*
Riefe, Barbara 1925- *WrDr 94*
Riefenstahl, Leni 1902- *IntWW 93, WhoHol 92*
Rieff, Philip 1922- *WrDr 94*
Riefler, Donald Brown 1927- *WhoAm 94, WhoFI 94*
Rieflin, William
See Ministry *ConMus 10*
Riegel, Arvilla Christena 1931- *WhoMW 93*
Riegel, Byron William 1938- *WhoAm 94, WhoScEn 94, WhoWest 94*
Riegel, Georgene Annette 1943- *WhoAmL 94*
Riegel, Gregg Mason 1953- *WhoScEn 94*
Riegel, John Kent 1938- *WhoAm 94*
Riegel, Kenneth 1938- *NewGrDO*
Riegel, Kurt Wetherhold 1939- *WhoAm 94, WhoScEn 94*
Riegel, Michael Byron 1946- *WhoAmA 93*
Riegel, Robert Edgar 1897- *WhAm 10*
Riegels, David Andrew 1944- *WhoAmL 94*
Riegels, Guy Anthony 1945- *WhoAm 94*
Riegels, Roy d1993 *NewYTBS 93 [port]*
Rieger, Carol T. 1941- *WhoAmL 94*
Rieger, Elaine June 1937- *WhoWest 94*
Rieger, Homer 1933- *WhoAmP 93*
Rieger, Mitchell Sheridan 1922- *WhoAm 94, WhoAmL 94, WhoMW 93*
Rieger, Philip Henri 1935- *WhoAm 94, WhoScEn 94*
Rieger, Phillip Warren 1948- *WhoScEn 94*
Rieger, Steven Arthur 1952- *WhoAmP 93, WhoWest 94*
Rieger, William W. 1922- *WhoAmP 93*
Riegert, Peter 1947- *IntMPA 94, WhoAm 94, WhoHol 92*
Riegert, Raymond Irwin 1947- *WhoWest 94*
Riegert, Robert Adolf 1923- *WhoAm 94, WhoAmL 94*
Riegle, Donald W., Jr. 1938- *CngDr 93, IntWW 93, WhoAmP 93*
Riegle, Donald W(ayne), Jr. 1938- *ConAu 43NR*
Riegle, Donald Wayne, Jr. 1938- *WhoAm 94, WhoMW 93*
Riegle, Linda B. 1948- *WhoAm 94, WhoAmL 94, WhoWest 94*
Riegle, Robert Mack 1924- *WhoAmA 93*
Riegler, Alan Martin 1946- *WhoFI 94*
Riegler, Josef 1938- *IntWW 93*
Riegner, Gerhart M. 1911- *IntWW 93*
Riegsecker, Marvin D. 1937- *WhoAmP 93*
Riegsecker, Marvin Dean 1937- *WhoMW 93*
Riehecky, Janet Ellen 1953- *WhoAm 94*
Riehl, Charles T., III 1944- *WhoAmL 94*
Riehl, Emil Joseph 1946- *WhoAmP 93*
Riehl, Kay d1988 *WhoHol 92*
Riehle, Helen S. 1950- *WhoAmP 93*
Riehle, James Ronald 1943- *WhoScEn 94*
Riehle, Marie B. 1948- *WhoAmL 94*
Riehle, Richard *WhoHol 92*
Riehle, Theodore Martin, III 1947- *WhoAmP 93*
Riehs, John Daryl 1953- *WhoScEn 94*
Rieke, Elizabeth Ann 1943- *WhoAm 94*
Rieke, Paul Victor 1949- *WhoAm 94, WhoAmL 94*
Rieke, Richard Davis 1935- *WhoWest 94*
Rieke, Robert W. 1954- *WhoAmL 94*
Rieke, William Oliver 1931- *WhoAm 94*
Rieken, Danny Michael 1967- *WhoScEn 94*
Riekenberg, Warren Glenn 1936- *WhoMW 93*
Rieker, Albert George 1889-1959 *WhoAmA 93N*
Riekert, Louis Albert 1935- *WhoFI 94*
Riel, Gordon Kienzie 1934- *WhoScEn 94*
Riel, Louis 1844-1885 *HisWorL [port]*
Riel, Pauline Skinner 1923- *WhoAmP 93*
Riel, Robert Joseph 1961- *WhoWest 94*
Riel, Steven *DrAPF 93*
Rielley, David Joseph, III 1938- *WhoAmL 94*
Rielly, John Edward 1932- *WhoAm 94*
Riemann, Georg Friedrich Bernhard 1826-1866 *WorScD*
Riemann, Johannes d1959 *WhoHol 92*
Riemenschneider, Albert Louis 1936- *WhoAm 94*
Riemenschneider, Paul Arthur 1920- *WhoAm 94*
Riemer, Ruby *DrAPF 93*
Riemke, Richard Allan 1944- *WhoAm 94*
Riemschneider, Johann Gottfried fl. 1720-1740 *NewGrDO*
Rienacker, Gunther 1904- *IntWW 93*
Riendeau, Russell Joseph 1958- *WhoFI 94*
Rienhoff, Otto 1949- *WhoScEn 94*
Rienne, Dozie Ignatius 1954- *WhoScEn 94*
Rienner, Lynne Carol 1945- *WhoAm 94, WhoWest 94*
Rienow, Leona (Train) 1903-1983 *EncSF 93*
Rienow, Robert *EncSF 93*
Riensche, Benjamin R. 1961- *WhoFI 94*
Riento, Virgilio d1959 *WhoHol 92*
Rienzi, Thomas Matthew Michael 1919- *WhoWest 94*
Riepe, Dale Maurice 1918- *WhoAm 94*
Riepe, James Sellers 1943- *WhoAm 94*
Riepe, Mark William 1964- *WhoMW 93*
Rieper, Alan George 1941- *WhoFI 94*
Riepl, Francis Joseph 1936- *WhoFI 94*
Rieppel, Ludwig 1861-1960 *WhoAmA 93N*
Rier, John Paul, Jr. 1925- *WhoBlA 94*
Riera, Carme 1949- *BlmGWL*
Rierson, James Hendrick 1940- *WhoMW 93*
Rierson, Robert Leak 1927- *WhoAm 94*
Ries, Barbara Ellen 1952- *WhoWest 94*
Ries, David P. 1938- *WhoAmL 94*
Ries, Edward Richard 1918- *WhoAm 94, WhoFI 94, WhoScEn 94*
Ries, Ferdinand c. 1784-1838 *NewGrDO*
Ries, Herman Elkan, Jr. 1911-1991 *WhAm 10*
Ries, Jonathan 1948- *WhoAmL 94*
Ries, Martin 1926- *WhoAm 94, WhoAmA 93*
Ries, Ronald Edward 1944- *WhoMW 93*
Ries, Stanley K. 1927- *WhoAm 94*
Ries, Thomas G. *WhoAmP 93*
Ries, William Campbell 1948- *WhoAm 94, WhoAmL 94*
Riesbeck, James Edward 1942- *WhoFI 94*
Riesco, German 1941- *IntWW 93, Who 94*
Riese, Arthur Carl 1955- *WhoFI 94, WhoScEn 94, WhoWest 94*
Riese, Beatrice *WhoAmA 93*
Riese, David John 1937- *WhoFI 94*
Riese, Friedrich Wilhelm *NewGrDO*
Rieselbach, Allen Newman 1931- *WhoAmL 94*
Riesen, Austin Herbert 1913- *WhoWest 94*
Riesenbach, Marvin S. 1929- *WhoFI 94*
Riesenberg, Daniel N. 1949- *WhoAmL 94*
Riesenberg, Peter 1925- *WhoMW 93*
Riesenberger, Frank Ralph 1897- *WhAm 10*
Riesenberger, John Richard 1948- *WhoMW 93, WhoScEn 94*
Riesenfeld, Stefan Albrecht 1908- *WhoWest 94*
Riesenhuber, Heinz Friedrich 1935- *IntWW 93, WhoScEn 94*
Rieser, Joseph A., Jr. 1947- *WhoAm 94, WhoAmL 94*
Rieser, Leonard Moos 1922- *WhoAm 94*
Rieser, Steven William 1954- *WhoFI 94*
Riesgo, Armando *WhoHisp 94*
Riesman, David 1909- *WhoAm 94, WrDr 94*
Riesner, Chuck d1962 *WhoHol 92*
Riesner, Dean 1918- *WhoHol 92*
Riess, Curt d1993 *NewYTBS 93*
Riess, Daniel Michael 1936- *WhoAmL 94*
Riess, George Febiger 1943- *WhoAmL 94*
Riess, Henri Gerard 1932- *WhoScEn 94*
Riess, Lore *WhoAmA 93*
Riess, Steven Allan 1947- *WhoMW 93*
Riesterer, William Mark 1952- *WhoMW 93*
Riesz, Peter Charles 1937- *WhoAm 94*
Rieth, David M. 1943- *WhoAmL 94*
Rieth, Michael Gerard 1956- *WhoMW 93*
Rieth, Peter Allan 1941- *WhoScEn 94*
Rieti, Vittorio 1898- *NewGrDO*
Rietti, Victor d1963 *WhoHol 92*
Rietty, Robert 1923- *WhoHol 92*
Rietveld, Thomas Alan 1951- *WhoWest 94*
Rietz, John Thomas 1933- *WhoFI 94*
Riew, Changkiu Keith 1928- *WhoMW 93*
Rifa'i, Zaid al- 1936- *IntWW 93*
Rifas, Leonard 1946- *WhoMW 93*
Rif'at, Alifa 1930- *BlmGWL*
Rifbjerg, Klaus 1931- *IntWW 93*
Rifbjerg, Klaus (Thorvald) 1931- *ConWorW 93, EncSF 93*
Rife, Anita 1946- *WhoBlA 94*
Rife, Jack 1943- *WhoAmP 93*
Rife, Jack Clark 1945- *WhoScEn 94*
Rife, Sarah Jane *WhoFI 94*
Rifenburgh, Richard Philip 1932- *WhoAm 94*
Riff, Emmanuel Raphael 1924- *WhoMW 93*
Riffaterre, Michael 1924- *WhoAm 94*
Riffe, Lovice Dee 1949- *WhoAmL 94*
Riffe, Vernal G., Jr. *WhoMW 93*
Riffe, Vernal G., Jr. 1925- *WhoAmP 93*
Riffel, Norman D. 1938- *WhoAmP 93*
Rifflard, Arthur James 1948- *WhoMW 93*
Riffle, Juanita Maria Annette 1952- *WhoMW 93*
Riffle, Kenneth H. 1945- *WhoAmP 93*
Rifkin, Arnold *WhoAm 94*
Rifkin, Arthur *DrAPF 93*
Rifkin, Bernard Murray 1924- *WhoAm 94*
Rifkin, Harmon 1942- *IntMPA 94*
Rifkin, Harold 1916- *WhoAm 94*
Rifkin, Jeremy 1945- *WrDr 94*
Rifkin, Joshua 1944- *IntWW 93*
Rifkin, Julian 1915- *IntMPA 94*
Rifkin, Julie Kaye *WhoAmP 93*
Rifkin, Ned 1949- *WhoAm 94*
Rifkin, Ron *WhoHol 92*
Rifkin, Shepard *DrAPF 93*
Rifkin, Shepard 1918- *WrDr 94*
Rifkin, Stuart G. 1955- *WhoAmL 94*
Rifkind, David Stuart 1963- *WhoAmL 94*
Rifkind, Malcolm (Leslie) 1946- *Who 94*
Rifkind, Malcolm Leslie 1946- *IntWW 93*
Rifkind, Robert Gore 1928- *WhoAmA 93*
Rifkind, Robert Singer 1936- *WhoAm 94*
Rifkind, Simon Hirsch 1901- *WhoAm 94, WhoAmL 94*
Riford, Lloyd Steve, Jr. 1924- *WhoAmP 93*
Riga, Nadine d1968 *WhoHol 92*
Rigali, Joseph Leo 1948- *WhoScEn 94*
Rigas, Anthony Leon 1931- *WhoMW 93*
Rigatti, Brian Walter 1968- *WhoScEn 94*
Rigattieri, Lisa 1953- *WhoIns 94*
Rigau, Marco Antonio, Jr. 1946- *WhoAmP 93*
Rigaud, George d1984 *WhoHol 92*
Rigaux, Christopher Michael 1960- *WhoFI 94*
Rigby, Arthur d1944 *WhoHol 92*
Rigby, Arthur d1971 *WhoHol 92*
Rigby, Bryan 1933- *Who 94*
Rigby, Christopher Palmer 1820-1885 *DcNaB MP*
Rigby, Edward d1951 *WhoHol 92*
Rigby, Harry d1985 *WhoHol 92*
Rigby, Ida Katherine 1944- *WhoAmA 93*
Rigby, Jean 1954- *NewGrDO*
Rigby, Jean Prescott *IntWW 93, Who 94*
Rigby, John *Who 94*
Rigby, (Hugh) John (Macbeth) 1914- *Who 94*
Rigby, Kenneth 1925- *WhoAmL 94*
Rigby, Martin L. 1964- *WhoWest 94*
Rigby, Melinda Bird 1965- *WhoAmL 94*
Rigby, Norman Leslie 1920- *Who 94*
Rigby, Paul Crispin 1924- *WhoAm 94*
Rigby, Perry Gardner 1932- *WhoAm 94*
Rigby, Peter William Jack 1947- *Who 94*
Rigby, Reginald Francis 1919- *Who 94*
Rigby, Terence 1937- *WhoHol 92*
Rigdon, Glenn Joseph 1950- *WhoMW 93*
Rigdon, Kevin 1956- *ConTFT 11*
Rigdon, Richard Levi 1945- *WhoAmP 93*
Rigdon, Sidney 1793-1876 *DcAmReB 2*
Rigel, Henri-Joseph 1741-1799 *NewGrDO*
Rigg, Carl *WhoHol 92*
Rigg, Diana 1938- *IntMPA 94, Who 94, WhoHol 92*
Rigg, (Enid) Diana (Elizabeth) 1938- *IntWW 93*

Rigg, Margaret Ruth 1929- *WhoAmA 93*
Rigg, Rebecca *WhoHol 92*
Rigg, Robert B. *EncSF 93*
Rigge, Marianne 1948- *Who 94*
Riggenbach, Duane Lee 1956- *WhoScEn 94*
Riggins, John Alfred, Jr. 1912-1986 *WhAm 10*
Riggins, Lester 1928- *WhoBlA 94*
Riggins, Ronald Stewart 1956- *WhoFI 94*
Riggins-Ezzell, Lois 1939- *WhoAm 94*
Riggio, Jerry d1971 *WhoHol 92*
Riggio, Stephen *WhoAm 94*
Riggle, Louise d1987 *WhoHol 92*
Riggleman, James David 1952- *WhoAm 94, WhoWest 94*
Riggs, Alfred Longley 1837-1916 *EncNAR*
Riggs, Anna Claire 1944- *WhoFI 94, WhoMW 93*
Riggs, Arthur Jordy 1916- *WhoAm 94, WhoAmL 94*
Riggs, Benjamin Clapp, Jr. 1945- *WhoAm 94*
Riggs, Betty *WhoHol 92*
Riggs, Bobby 1918- *BuCMET [port]*
Riggs, Byron Lawrence, Jr. 1931- *WhoAm 94, WhoMW 93*
Riggs, Conrad Albert 1963- *WhoWest 94*
Riggs, Dale Flint 1930- *WhoAmP 93*
Riggs, David (Ramsey) 1941- *WrDr 94*
Riggs, David Lee 1957- *WhoMW 93*
Riggs, David Lynn 1943- *WhoFI 94*
Riggs, Donald Eugene 1942- *WhoAm 94*
Riggs, Douglas A. 1944- *WhoAm 94*
Riggs, Elizabeth A. 1942- *WhoBlA 94*
Riggs, Enrique A. 1943- *WhoBlA 94*
Riggs, Frank D. 1950- *WhoAmP 93*
Riggs, Frank E., Jr. 1948- *WhoAmL 94*
Riggs, Frank Lewis 1937- *WhoFI 94*
Riggs, Gerald Antonio 1960- *WhoBlA 94*
Riggs, Harry L. 1914- *WhoBlA 94*
Riggs, Henry Earle 1935- *WhoAm 94, WhoWest 94*
Riggs, Jack d1978 *WhoHol 92*
Riggs, James Arthur 1936- *WhoAm 94*
Riggs, John Arthur 1946- *WhoAmP 93*
Riggs, John Forrest 1959- *WhoWest 94*
Riggs, John Hutton, Jr. 1936- *WhoAm 94*
Riggs, Karl Alton, Jr. 1929- *WhoFI 94*
Riggs, Lawrence Wilson 1943- *WhoFI 94*
Riggs, Leonard, II 1943- *WhoAm 94*
Riggs, Lorrin Andrews 1912- *IntWW 93, WhoAm 94*
Riggs, Marlon 1957- *ConBlB 5 [port]*
Riggs, Melvin David 1937- *WhoAmP 93*
Riggs, Michael David 1951- *WhoAm 94*
Riggs, Paula Detmer 1944- *WhoWest 94*
Riggs, Penny Kaye 1965- *WhoScEn 94*
Riggs, Ralph d1951 *WhoHol 92*
Riggs, Richard Alan 1949- *WhoAmL 94*
Riggs, Robert 1896-1970 *WhoAmA 93N*
Riggs, Robert E(dwon) 1927- *WrDr 94*
Riggs, Robert Edwon 1927- *WhoWest 94*
Riggs, Roderick Douglas 1931- *WhoAmP 93*
Riggs, Stephen Return 1812-1883 *DcAmReB 2, EncNAR*
Riggs, Steven Ray 1959- *WhoAmP 93*
Riggs, Thomas Jeffries, Jr. 1916- *WhoAm 94*
Riggs, Thomas Lawrence 1847-1940 *EncNAR*
Riggs, Tommy d1967 *WhoHol 92*
Riggs, Warren Elwood 1927- *WhoAmP 93*
Riggsby, Ernest Duward 1925- *WhoScEn 94*
Righenzi, Carlo fl. 1648- *NewGrDO*
Righetti, Geltrude 1793-1862 *NewGrDO*
Righi-Lambertini, Egano 1906- *IntWW 93*
Righini, Pietro 1683-1742 *NewGrDO*
Righini, Vincenzo 1756-1812 *NewGrDO*
Righter, Richard Scott 1894- *WhAm 10*
Righter, Walter Cameron 1923- *WhoAm 94*
Rightmire, G. Philip 1942- *WrDr 94*
Rigler, Lee George 1896- *WhAm 10*
Rigling, Richard Vaughn 1950- *WhoMW 93*
Rignault, Alexandre d1985 *WhoHol 92*
Rigney, E. Douglas 1958- *WhoScEn 94*
Rigney, Harlan 1933- *WhoAmP 93*
Rigney, Howard Ernest 1922- *Who 94*
Rigney, James Oliver, Jr. 1948- *ConAu 140*
Rigolosi, Vincent Paul 1932- *WhoAmP 93*
Rigolot, Francois 1939- *WhoAm 94*
Rigor, Bradley Glenn 1955- *WhoAmL 94*
Rigot, Joseph M. 1943- *WhoAmL 94*
Rigout, Marcel 1928- *IntWW 93*
Rigsbee, David *DrAPF 93*
Rigsbee, Stephen Reese 1956- *WhoFI 94*
Rigsby, Billy *WhoAmP 93*
Rigsby, Esther Martin *WhoBlA 94*
Rigsby, John Newton 1946- *WhoFI 94*
Rigual, Antonio Ramón 1946- *WhoHisp 94*
Riha, Bobby 1958- *WhoHol 92*
Riha, William Edwin 1943- *WhoScEn 94*
Rihani, Sarmad Albert 1954- *WhoScEn 94*
Riherd, John Arthur 1946- *WhoAmL 94*
Rihm, Paul Charles 1953- *WhoFI 94*
Rihm, Wolfgang 1952- *NewGrDO*
Riikola, Michael Edward 1951- *WhoAmL 94, WhoWest 94*
Riipi, Linda Ruth 1952- *WhoMW 93*
Riis, Jacob August 1849-1914 *AmSocL*
Riis, Povl 1925- *IntWW 93*
Riis, Sharon 1947- *BlmGWL, WrDr 94*
Rijken, Hedy L. 1958- *WhoAmP 93*
Rijo, José 1965- *WhoHisp 94*
Rijo, Jose Antonio 1965- *WhoBlA 94*
Rikanovic, Svetozar 1938- *Who 94*
Rikard, William L., Jr. 1945- *WhoAmL 94*
Rike, Linda Stokes 1949- *WhoFI 94*
Rikelman, Herman 1911- *WhoWest 94*
Riker, Joseph Thaddeus, III 1940- *WhoWest 94*
Riker, Walter F., Jr. 1916- *WhoAm 94*
Riker, William H. 1920- *IntWW 93*
Riker, William H(arrison) 1920-1993 *ConAu 141*
Riker, William Harrison d1993 *NewYTBS 93*
Riker, William Harrison 1920- *WhoAm 94*
Riker, William Kay 1925- *WhoAm 94*
Rikhiraj, Sadhu Singh 1942- *WhoAsA 94*
Rikhoff, Jean *DrAPF 93*
Rikleen, Lauren Stiller 1953- *WhoAmL 94*
Rikli, Arthur Eugene 1917- *WhoFI 94*
Rikli, Donald Carl 1927- *WhoAmL 94*
Riklis, Marcia *WhoFI 94*
Riklis, Meshulam 1923- *IntWW 93*
Rikon, Michael 1945- *WhoAmL 94*
Rikoski, Richard Anthony 1941- *WhoAm 94, WhoFI 94, WhoMW 93, WhoScEn 94*
Riles, Wilson Camanza 1917- *WhoAm 94, WhoAmP 93, WhoBlA 94, WhoWest 94*
Riley, Adele d1938 *WhoHol 92*
Riley, Ann J. *WhoAmP 93*
Riley, Ann L. 1950- *WhoWest 94*
Riley, Anthony William 1929- *WhoAm 94*
Riley, Antonio 1963- *WhoAmP 93*
Riley, Arch Wilson, Jr. 1957- *WhoAmL 94*
Riley, Avis Monica 1953- *WhoBlA 94*
Riley, Barbra Bayne 1949- *WhoAmA 93*
Riley, Benjamin Kneeland 1957- *WhoAmL 94, WhoWest 94*
Riley, Bernard Joseph 1911-1984 *WhoAmA 93N*
Riley, Beryl Elise 1960- *WhoBlA 94*
Riley, Bridget 1931- *IntWW 93*
Riley, Bridget Louise 1931- *Who 94*
Riley, C. Ronald 1938- *WhoIns 94*
Riley, Carole A. *WhoAm 94*
Riley, Carroll L. 1923- *WrDr 94*
Riley, Carroll Lavern 1923- *WhoAm 94, WhoScEn 94, WhoWest 94*
Riley, Catherine I. 1947- *WhoAmP 93*
Riley, Charlene Marie 1945- *WhoAmP 93*
Riley, Charles Logan 1946- *WhoWest 94*
Riley, Charles Michael 1939- *WhoAmL 94*
Riley, Charles W., Sr. 1950- *WhoBlA 94*
Riley, Christopher John 1947- *Who 94*
Riley, Clayton 1935- *WhoBlA 94*
Riley, Dan 1946- *WrDr 94*
Riley, Daniel Edward 1915- *WhoAm 94*
Riley, Daniel Jeffery 1949- *WhoMW 93*
Riley, David Ray 1955- *WhoMW 93*
Riley, David Richard 1940- *WhoWest 94*
Riley, Denise 1948- *BlmGWL*
Riley, Dennis 1943- *NewGrDO*
Riley, Dennis James 1948- *WhoAmL 94*
Riley, Dennis Lawrence 1945- *WhoAmP 93*
Riley, Dick 1946- *WrDr 94*
Riley, Doris J. 1929- *WhoAmP 93*
Riley, Dorothy B. 1925- *WhoAmP 93*
Riley, Dorothy Comstock 1924- *WhoAmL 94, WhoAmP 93, WhoHisp 94*
Riley, Dorothy Elaine *WhoMW 93*
Riley, Douglas Scott 1958- *WhoScEn 94*
Riley, Edward Calverley 1923- *WrDr 94*
Riley, Elaine 1923- *WhoHol 92*
Riley, Emile Edward 1934- *WhoBlA 94*
Riley, Eve Montgomery 1955- *WhoBlA 94*
Riley, Francena 1957- *WhoScEn 94*
Riley, Frances L. 1928- *WhoAmP 93*
Riley, Frank *EncSF 93*
Riley, Gary *WhoHol 92*
Riley, George d1972 *WhoHol 92*
Riley, Gerald Wayne 1950- *WhoWest 94*
Riley, Glenn Pleasants 1960- *WhoBlA 94*
Riley, Harold Euguene 1928- *WhoIns 94*
Riley, Harold John, Jr. 1940- *WhoAm 94*
Riley, Harris DeWitt, Jr. 1924- *WhoAm 94*
Riley, Helene Maria Kastinger 1939- *WhoAm 94*
Riley, Henry Charles 1932- *WhoAm 94*
Riley, Herbert James 1925- *WhoWest 94*
Riley, Ivers Whitman 1932- *WhoAm 94*
Riley, Jack d1933 *WhoHol 92*
Riley, Jack 1935- *WhoAm 94*
Riley, Jack 1937- *WhoHol 92*
Riley, Jack T., Jr. 1946- *WhoAmL 94*
Riley, James Alvin 1943- *WhoScEn 94*
Riley, James C. 1943- *WhoFI 94*
Riley, James Joseph 1919- *WhoMW 93*
Riley, James Kevin 1945- *WhoAmL 94*
Riley, James L. *WhoHisp 94*
Riley, James N. 1943- *WhoAmP 93*
Riley, James Whitcomb d1916 *WhoHol 92*
Riley, James Whitcomb 1849-1916 *TwCLC 51 [port]*
Riley, Janeway 1936- *WhoMW 93*
Riley, Jay Flash d1988 *WhoHol 92*
Riley, Jeannine 1941- *WhoHol 92*
Riley, Jeremiah Anthony 1951- *WhoAm 94*
Riley, Joan 1958- *BlmGWL [port]*
Riley, Jocelyn *DrAPF 93*
Riley, John F. 1943- *WhoIns 94*
Riley, John Francis 1927- *WhoWest 94*
Riley, John Graham 1945- *WhoAm 94, WhoFI 94*
Riley, John Roland Christopher 1925- *Who 94*
Riley, John Winchell, Jr. 1908- *WhoAm 94*
Riley, Joseph C. d1977 *WhoHol 92*
Riley, Joseph Harry 1922- *WhoAm 94*
Riley, Joseph Patrick, Jr. 1943- *WhoAmP 93*
Riley, Joshua Dean 1962- *WhoFI 94*
Riley, Kathleen 1945- *WhoMW 93*
Riley, Kathleen Ann 1945- *WhoFI 94*
Riley, Kenneth J. 1947- *WhoBlA 94*
Riley, Kenneth Joseph 1940- *Who 94*
Riley, Kevin Thomas 1943- *WhoIns 94*
Riley, Larry d1992 *WhoBlA 94N*
Riley, Larry 1952- *WhoHol 92*
Riley, Larry 1952-1992 *AnObit 1992*
Riley, Lawrence Joseph 1914- *WhoAm 94*
Riley, Lewis R. 1935- *WhoAmP 93*
Riley, Lynda Maree 1957- *WhoAmL 94*
Riley, Mack d1963 *WhoHol 92*
Riley, Madeleine (Veronica) 1933- *WrDr 94*
Riley, Margaret 1951- *WhoMW 93*
Riley, Marin *WhoHol 92*
Riley, Matilda White 1911- *WhoAm 94, WrDr 94*
Riley, Matthew Barker 1960- *WhoAmL 94*
Riley, Matthew Howard, Jr. *WhoAmP 93*
Riley, Maynard H. 1953- *WhoMW 93*
Riley, Michael *WhoHol 92*
Riley, Michael d1984 *WhoHol 92*
Riley, Michael D. *DrAPF 93*
Riley, Michael Eugene 1952- *WhoWest 94*
Riley, Michael Hylan 1951- *WhoAmL 94*
Riley, Michael Verity 1933- *WhoMW 93*
Riley, Mike *WhoAmP 93*
Riley, Mikel Ralph 1955- *WhoMW 93*
Riley, Nancy Mae 1939- *WhoMW 93*
Riley, Pat 1945- *BasBi*
Riley, Patrick Gavan Duffy 1927- *WhoAm 94*
Riley, Patrick James 1945- *WhoAm 94*
Riley, Patrick R. 1947- *WhoAmL 94*
Riley, Paul Eugene 1941- *WhoScEn 94*
Riley, Paul J. *WhoAmP 93*
Riley, Peter James 1956- *WhoAmL 94*
Riley, Ralph 1924- *IntWW 93, Who 94*
Riley, Randy James 1950- *WhoAm 94*
Riley, Richard W. 1933- *CngDr 93, CurBio 93 [port]*
Riley, Richard Wilson 1933- *WhoAm 94, WhoAmP 93*
Riley, Richard Wilson 1935- *IntWW 93*
Riley, Robert Annan, III 1955- *WhoFI 94*
Riley, Robert Bartlett 1931- *WhoAm 94*
Riley, Robert Coons 1921- *WhoFI 94*
Riley, Robert Edward 1930- *WhoAm 94*
Riley, Robert S. 1942- *WhoMW 93*
Riley, Rosetta Margueritte 1940- *WhoBlA 94*
Riley, Sam G. 1939- *WrDr 94*
Riley, Sarah Anne 1946- *WhoFI 94*
Riley, Stephen Thomas 1908- *WhoAm 94*
Riley, Sumpter Marion, Jr. 1903- *WhoBlA 94*
Riley, Teddy *WhoBlA 94*
Riley, Terry 1935- *WhoAm 94*
Riley, Terry Mitchell 1935- *IntWW 93*
Riley, Thomas Jackson 1933- *WhoAmL 94*
Riley, Thomas Leslie 1927- *WhoAm 94*
Riley, Timothy Crocker 1946- *WhoAmP 93*
Riley, Timothy Michael 1954- *WhoFI 94*
Riley, Tom *DrAPF 93*
Riley, Victor 1916- *Who 94*
Riley, Victor J., Jr. 1931- *WhoAm 94, WhoFI 94*
Riley, Wayne Joseph 1959- *WhoBlA 94*
Riley, William 1931- *WhoFI 94*
Riley, William A. 1924- *WhoAmP 93*
Riley, William Bell 1861-1947 *DcAmReB 2*
Riley, William Franklin 1925- *WhoAm 94, WhoScEn 94*
Riley, William Jay 1947- *WhoAmL 94*
Riley, William L. 1942- *WhoAmL 94*
Riley, William Lee 1944- *WhoFI 94*
Riley, William Scott 1940- *WhoBlA 94*
Riley-Land, Sarah 1947- *WhoAmA 93*
Riley-Scott, Barbara P. 1928- *WhoBlA 94*
Riley-Smith, Jonathan Simon Christopher 1938- *Who 94*
Rilinger, Dennis R. 1947- *WhoAmL 94*
Rill, Eli 1926- *WhoHol 92*
Rill, James Franklin 1933- *WhoAm 94*
Rilla, Walter 1895- *WhoHol 92*
Rillieux, Norbert 1806-1894 *AfrAmAl 6, WorInv*
Rilling, Helmuth 1933- *IntWW 93*
Rima, Ingrid Hahne *WhoAm 94*
Riman, Josef 1925- *WhoScEn 94*
Rimao, Ciro d1973 *WhoHol 92*
Rimbach, Evangeline Lois 1932- *WhoAm 94*
Rimbey, Peter Raymond 1947- *WhoScEn 94*
Rimel, Rebecca Webster *WhoAm 94*
Rimer, Barbara K. 1949- *WrDr 94*
Rimer, Colin Percy Farquharson 1944- *Who 94*
Rimer, J. Thomas *WrDr 94*
Rimer, John Thomas 1933- *WhoAm 94*
Rimerman, Ira Stephen 1938- *WhoAm 94, WhoFI 94*
Rimerman, Morton Walter 1929- *WhoAm 94*
Rimerman, Thomas W. 1934- *WhoFI 94*
Rimiller, Ronald Wayne 1949- *WhoScEn 94*
Rimington, Claude d1993 *NewYTBS 93, Who 94N*
Rimington, Claude 1902- *IntWW 93*
Rimington, John David 1935- *Who 94*
Rimington, Stella 1935- *IntWW 93, Who 94*
Rimkus, Steven *WhoHol 92*
Rimm, Byron Newton 1948- *WhoBlA 94*
Rimmer, Frederick William 1914- *Who 94*
Rimmer, Henry 1928- *Who 94*
Rimmer, Jack 1921- *WhoAm 94*
Rimmer, Shane *WhoHol 92*
Rimmereid, Arthur V. *WhoMW 93*
Rimmington, Gerald Thorneycroft 1930- *WrDr 94*
Rimoin, David Lawrence 1936- *WhoAm 94, WhoScEn 94*
Rimoldi, Adriano d1965 *WhoHol 92*
Rimpel, Auguste Eugene, Jr. 1939- *WhoAm 94, WhoFI 94*
Rimrott, Friedrich Paul Johannes 1927- *WhoAm 94*
Rimskaya-Korsakova, Yuliya Lazarevna *NewGrDO*
Rimsky-Korsakov, Nikolay Andreyevich 1844-1908 *NewGrDO*
Rimson, Ira Jay 1935- *WhoScEn 94*
Rimstidt, Diana Francis 1952- *WhoFI 94*
Rimsza, Skip *WhoAmP 93*
Rin, Zengi 1935- *WhoScEn 94*
Rinaldi, Alberto 1939- *NewGrDO*
Rinaldi, Ann 1934- *TwCYAW*
Rinaldi, Donald M. *WhoAmP 93*
Rinaldi, Elaine Marie 1957- *WhoAmL 94*
Rinaldi, Joseph A. 1948- *WhoFI 94*
Rinaldi, Margherita 1935- *NewGrDO*
Rinaldi, Michael G. 1946- *WhoAm 94*
Rinaldi, Nicholas M. *DrAPF 93*
Rinaldi, Ophelia Sandoval 1933- *WhoHisp 94*
Rinaldi, Peter M. d1993 *NewYTBS 93*
Rinaldini, Luis Emilio 1953- *WhoAm 94*
Rinaldo, Matthew John 1931- *WhoAmP 93*
Rinaldo, Richard F. 1945- *WhoAmL 94*
Rinaldo di, Capua c. 1710-c. 1780 *NewGrDO*
Rinaman, James Curtis, Jr. 1935- *WhoAm 94, WhoAmL 94*
Rinchin, Lodongiin 1929- *IntWW 93*
Rincon de Gautier, Felisa 1897- *WhoHisp 94*
Rind, Sherry *DrAPF 93*
Rinde, John Jacques 1935- *WhoScEn 94*
Rinder, George Greer 1921- *WhoAm 94*
Rinder, Virginia Hay 1920- *WhoMW 93*
Rinderle, Walter 1940- *ConAu 140*
Rindfleisch, Jan *WhoAmA 93*
Rindfleisch, Norval *DrAPF 93*
Rindfusz, Robert Dale 1946- *WhoAmL 94*
Rindge, Debora Anne 1956- *WhoAmA 93*
Rindlaub, Jean Wade 1904-1991 *WhAm 10*
Rindlaub, John Wade 1934- *WhoAm 94*
Rindler, Alan B. 1949- *WhoAm 94*
Rindler, Wolfgang 1924- *IntWW 93*
Rinearson, Peter Mark 1954- *WhoAm 94, WhoWest 94*
Rineberg, W. J. 1937- *WhoFI 94*
Rinefort, Foster Christian, Jr. 1932- *WhoMW 93*
Rinehart, Charles R. 1947- *WhoAm 94, WhoFI 94, WhoWest 94*

Rinehart, Dana G. *WhoAmP 93*
Rinehart, Frederick Roberts 1953- *WhoWest 94*
Rinehart, I. Lynn 1936- *WhoMW 93*
Rinehart, James Alan 1957- *WhoFI 94*
Rinehart, Jonathan 1930- *WhoAm 94, WhoFI 94*
Rinehart, Mary Roberts 1876-1958 *TwCLC 52 [port]*
Rinehart, Michael 1934- *WhoAmA 93*
Rinehart, Nita *WhoAmP 93, WhoWest 94*
Rinek, Larry Moffett 1947- *WhoWest 94*
Rinell, Susan *WhoHol 92*
Riner, James William 1936- *WhoAmL 94*
Riner, Tom 1946- *WhoAmP 93*
Rines, John Randolph 1947- *WhoAm 94, WhoFI 94, WhoMW 93*
Rines, Robert Harvey 1922- *WhoScEn 94*
Rines, S. Melvin 1924- *WhoAm 94*
Riney, Hal Patrick 1932- *WhoAm 94*
Riney, Richard Thomas 1896- *WhAm 10*
Rinfret, Gabriel-Edouard 1905- *Who 94*
Ring, Alvin Manuel 1933- *WhoAm 94*
Ring, Blanche d1961 *WhoHol 92*
Ring, Carolyn Louise 1926- *WhoAmP 93*
Ring, Cyril d1967 *WhoHol 92*
Ring, Douglas 1921- *WrDr 94*
Ring, Eddie Joseph 1965- *WhoFI 94*
Ring, Edward A. *WhoAmA 93*
Ring, Gerald J. 1928- *WhoAm 94*
Ring, Herbert Everett 1925- *WhoFI 94, WhoMW 93*
Ring, James 1927- *Who 94*
Ring, James Edward Patrick 1940- *WhoAm 94, WhoFI 94*
Ring, James Walter 1929- *WhoAm 94*
Ring, Jennifer *WhoAmP 93*
Ring, Jennifer 1948- *ConAu 140*
Ring, John James 1928- *WhoMW 93*
Ring, Leonard M. 1923- *WhoAm 94, WhoAmL 94, WhoMW 93*
Ring, Lindsay (Roberts) 1914- *Who 94*
Ring, Lindsay Roberts 1914- *IntWW 93*
Ring, Michael Wilson 1943- *WhoAm 94, WhoAmL 94*
Ring, Renee E. 1950- *WhoAm 94*
Ring, Rodney Everett 1927- *WhoAm 94*
Ring, Ronald Herman 1938- *WhoAmL 94*
Ring, Steven Jan 1949- *WhoAmL 94*
Ring, Victoria A. 1958- *WhoMW 93*
Ring, Wolfhard 1930- *IntWW 93*
Ringadoo, Veerasamy 1920- *IntWW 93, Who 94*
Ringbom, Sixten d1992 *IntWW 93N*
Ringel, Dean 1947- *WhoAm 94, WhoAmL 94*
Ringel, Fred Morton 1929- *WhoAmL 94*
Ringel, Harvey Norman 1903- *WhoMW 93*
Ringel, Robert Lewis 1937- *WhoAm 94, WhoMW 93*
Ringell, Marilyn Patricia Robinson 1946-1991 *WhoBlA 94N*
Ringen, Catherine Oleson 1943- *WhoAm 94*
Ringen, Sonja Gay 1953- *WhoWest 94*
Ringen, Stein 1945- *Who 94*
Ringer, James Milton 1943- *WhoAm 94, WhoAmL 94*
Ringer, Robert J. 1938- *WrDr 94*
Ringer, William F. 1948- *WhoAmL 94*
Ringert, William F. 1932- *WhoAmP 93*
Ringgold, Faith 1930- *AfrAmAl 6, WhoAm 94, WhoAmA 93, WhoBlA 94*
Ringgold, Faith 1934- *ChlLR 30 [port]*
Ringhofer, William Michael 1943- *WhoIns 94*
Ringius, Carl 1879-1950 *WhoAmA 93N*
Ringle, Brett Adelbert 1951- *WhoAm 94, WhoAmL 94*
Ringle, Dave d1965 *WhoHol 92*
Ringlee, Robert James 1926- *WhoAm 94*
Ringler, Daniel Howard 1941- *WhoScEn 94*
Ringler, James M. 1945- *WhoFI 94*
Ringler, Lenore *WhoAm 94*
Ringness, Charles Obert *WhoAmA 93*
Ringo, Betty Penfold 1924- *WhoMW 93*
Ringo, James Joseph 1935- *WhoFI 94*
Ringo, Jim *ProFbHF [port]*
Ringoir, Severin Maria Ghislenus 1931- *WhoScEn 94*
Ringold, Anthony F. 1931- *WhoAmL 94*
Ringold, Clay 1908- *WrDr 94*
Ringold, David Allan 1956- *WhoAmL 94*
Ringold, Francine *DrAPF 93*
Ringquist, Lynn Anne 1952- *WhoMW 93*
Ringrose, John Robert 1932- *Who 94*
Rings, Randall Eugene 1962- *WhoMW 93*
Rings, Roy Wilson 1916- *WhoMW 93*
Ringsak, Marnell Walter 1951- *WhoAmL 94*
Ringuette, David Aaron 1958- *WhoWest 94*
Ringwald, Molly 1968- *IntMPA 94, WhoHol 92*
Ringwood, Alfred Edward 1930- *IntWW 93, Who 94*
Ringwood, David Kilpatrick 1951- *WhoAmL 94*
Ringwood, Gwen Pharis 1910-1984 *BlmGWL*
Ringwood, Gwen(dolyn Margaret) Pharis 1910-1984 *IntDcT 2*
Ringwood, Michael Paul 1953- *WhoAmL 94*
Rinhart, Floyd (Lincoln) 1915- *WrDr 94*
Rinhart, Marion (Hutchinson) 1916- *WrDr 94*
Rini, Joseph Timothy, Jr. 1952- *WhoFI 94, WhoMW 93*
Rink, Christopher Lee 1952- *WhoScEn 94*
Rink, Lawrence Donald 1940- *WhoAm 94*
Rink, Margaret Joan *Who 94*
Rink, Thomas C. 1945- *WhoAmL 94*
Rink, Wesley Winfred 1922- *WhoAm 94*
Rinkel, Ralph Chris 1911- *WhoFI 94*
Rinkenberger, Richard Krug 1933- *WhoScEn 94*
Rinker, Al d1982 *WhoHol 92*
Rinker, Charles Washington, Jr. 1940- *WhoAmP 93*
Rinker, Earl A., III 1935- *WhoAmP 93*
Rinker, Marshall Edison, Sr. 1904- *WhoAm 94*
Rinker, Ruby Stewart 1936- *WhoAm 94*
Rinkevich, Charles Francis 1940- *WhoAm 94*
Rinkewich, Mindy *DrAPF 93*
Rinks, Randy *WhoAmP 93*
Rinne, Mark Douglas 1952- *WhoWest 94*
Rinnemaki, William Allen 1951- *WhoAmP 93*
Rinner, Chris L. 1951- *WhoMW 93*
Rinpoche *ConAu 42NR*
Rinpoche, Gelek *WhoAsA 94*
Rinsch, Charles Emil 1932- *WhoAm 94, WhoFI 94, WhoWest 94*
Rinsch, Maryann Elizabeth 1939- *WhoWest 94*
Rinser, Luise 1911- *BlmGWL, IntWW 93*
Rinsky, Arthur C. 1944- *WhoAmL 94*
Rinsky, David Stuart 1944- *WhoFI 94*
Rinsky, Joel Charles 1938- *WhoAmL 94, WhoFI 94*
Rinsky, Judith Lynn 1941- *WhoFI 94*
Rinsland, Roland D. 1933- *WhoBlA 94*
Rinsley, Donald Brendan 1928-1989 *WhAm 10*
Rintelmann, William Fred 1930- *WhoAm 94*
Rin-Tin-Tin d1932 *WhoHol 92*
Rintoul, David 1948- *WhoHol 92*
Rintzler, Marius 1932- *NewGrDO*
Rintzler, Marius Adrian 1932- *IntWW 93*
Rinuccini, Ottavio 1562-1621 *NewGrDO*
Rinzel, Daniel Francis 1942- *WhoAm 94*
Rinzler, Allan 1941- *WhoAm 94*
Rinzler, Carol Ann *WrDr 94*
Rinzler, Carol Gene Eisen 1941-1990 *WhAm 10*
Rinzler, Kenneth 1955- *WhoAmP 93*
Rinzler, Ralph 1934- *WhoAm 94*
Rio, Joanne d1984 *WhoHol 92*
Rio, Rita *WhoHol 92*
Riojas, Ana 1932- *WhoHisp 94*
Rio-Jelliffe, Rebecca 1922- *WhoAsA 94*
Riondino, David *WhoHol 92*
Riopelle, Arthur Jean 1920- *WhoAm 94*
Riopelle, Jean-Paul 1923- *IntWW 93*
Riordan, George Nickerson 1933- *WhoAm 94*
Riordan, James (William) 1936- *WrDr 94*
Riordan, James Quentin 1927- *WhoAm 94, WhoFI 94*
Riordan, James R. 1949- *WhoAmP 93*
Riordan, John Richard 1943- *WhoScEn 94*
Riordan, John Stephen 1965- *WhoWest 94*
Riordan, John Thomas 1937- *WhoAm 94*
Riordan, John Thomas 1945- *WhoAm 94*
Riordan, Joseph Edward 1953- *WhoFI 94*
Riordan, Kevin Michael 1958- *WhoFI 94*
Riordan, Marjorie 1921- *WhoHol 92*
Riordan, Richard *WhoAmP 93*
Riordan, Richard 1930- *News 93 [port]*
Riordan, Richard J. 1930- *WhoAm 94*
Riordan, Robert d1968 *WhoHol 92*
Riordan, Stephen Vaughan 1950- *Who 94*
Riordan, William F. 1941- *WhoAm 94, WhoAmP 93, WhoWest 94*
Riordan, William John 1955- *WhoScEn 94*
Riordon, John Arthur 1941- *WhoScEn 94*
Riordon, John Bernard 1947- *WhoAm 94*
Riordon, Michael 1944- *WrDr 94*
Rios, Alberto Alvaro *DrAPF 93*
Rios, Alberto Alvaro 1952- *WhoHisp 94, WhoWest 94*
Rios, Armando C., Jr. 1958- *WhoHisp 94*
Rios, Benjamin Bejarano 1931- *WhoHisp 94*
Rios, Diego Marcial 1962- *WhoWest 94*
Rios, Dolores Garcia 1964- *WhoHisp 94*
Rios, Edward C. *WhoHol 92*
Rios, Edwin Mundo *WhoAmP 93*
Rios, Elvira d1987 *WhoHol 92*
Rios, Evelyn Deerwester 1916- *WhoAm 94*
Rios, Francisco Gonzalez, Jr. 1950- *WhoHisp 94*
Rios, Freddy *WhoHisp 94*
Rios, Gilberto Ernesto 1951- *WhoHisp 94*
Rios, Irma Garcia 1938- *WhoHisp 94*
Rios, Isabella 1948- *WhoHisp 94*
Rios, Joe 1957- *WhoHisp 94*
Rios, Jorge C. 1953- *WhoHisp 94*
Rios, Joseph A. 1941- *WhoHisp 94*
Rios, Joseph Leon Cuerrero 1928- *WhoAmP 93*
Rios, Juan 1914- *IntWW 93*
Rios, Lalo d1973 *WhoHol 92*
Rios, Miguel, Jr. 1941- *WhoHisp 94*
Rios, Oscar *WhoHisp 94*
Rios, Peter 1949- *WhoHisp 94*
Rios, Peter D. 1949- *WhoAmP 93*
Rios, Ronald 1957- *WhoHisp 94*
Rios, Sandra Ann 1952- *WhoHisp 94*
Rios, Sylvia C. 1940- *WhoHisp 94*
Rios-Bustamante, Antonio 1948- *WhoHisp 94*
Rios de Betancourt, Ethel 1926- *WhoHisp 94*
Rios Montt, Efrain 1927- *IntWW 93*
Rios Olivares, Eddy O. 1942- *WhoHisp 94*
Rios-Rodriguez, Rafael 1956- *WhoHisp 94*
Riotte, Philipp Jakob 1776-1856 *NewGrDO*
Rioux (De Messimy), Deena (Coty) Des 1941- *WhoAmA 93*
Rioux, Roland A. *WhoAmP 93*
Ripa, Louis Carl 1927- *WhoFI 94*
Ripa Di Meana, Carlo 1929- *IntWW 93, Who 94*
Ripich, Stefan John 1957- *WhoWest 94*
Ripinsky-Naxon, Michael 1944- *WhoScEn 94, WhoWest 94*
Ripken, Calvin Edwin, Jr. 1960- *WhoAm 94*
Ripley, Alden Lassell 1896-1969 *WhoAmA 93N*
Ripley, Brian David 1952- *Who 94*
Ripley, Dillon *Who 94*
Ripley, (Sidney) Dillon 1913- *Who 94*
Ripley, Dorothy 1767-1831 *DcNaB MP*
Ripley, Earle Allison 1933- *WhoWest 94*
Ripley, Edward Franklin 1927- *WhoAm 94*
Ripley, George 1802-1880 *DcAmReB 2*
Ripley, Hilda L. 1942- *WhoHisp 94*
Ripley, Hugh 1916- *Who 94*
Ripley, Jack 1921- *WrDr 94*
Ripley, Karen *EncSF 93*
Ripley, Michael David 1952- *WrDr 94*
Ripley, Patricia 1926- *WhoHol 92*
Ripley, Randall B(utler) 1938- *ConAu 41NR*
Ripley, Randall Butler 1938- *WrDr 94*
Ripley, Ray d1938 *WhoHol 92*
Ripley, Robert L. d1949 *WhoHol 92*
Ripley, Robert L. 1893-1949 *WhoAmA 93N*
Ripley, Stuart McKinnon 1930- *WhoWest 94*
Ripley, Wayne E., Jr. 1946- *WhoAmL 94*
Ripling, Edward Joseph 1921- *WhoAm 94*
Ripoll, Edward Conrad 1924- *WhoAmP 93*
Ripon, Bishop of 1931- *Who 94*
Ripon, Dean of *Who 94*
Ripp, Bryan Jerome 1959- *WhoScEn 94*
Ripp, Michael Werner 1948- *WhoFI 94, WhoMW 93*
Ripp, William Robert 1924- *WhoAmP 93*
Rippa, Vincent Raymond *WhoAmP 93*
Rippe, Peter Marquart 1937- *WhoAm 94*
Rippel, Harry Conrad 1926- *WhoAm 94*
Rippel, Julius Alexander 1901-1991 *WhAm 10*
Rippel, M. 1930- *WhoAmA 93*
Rippengal, Derek 1928- *Who 94*
Ripper, Michael 1913- *WhoHol 92*
Ripper, Rita Jo 1950- *WhoWest 94*
Ripperda, Thomas Henry 1949- *WhoFI 94*
Rippert, Otto d1940 *WhoHol 92*
Rippeteau, Darrel Downing 1917- *WhoAm 94*
Rippey, Clayton 1923- *WhoAmA 93, WhoWest 94*
Rippey, Donald Taylor 1927- *WhoAm 94*
Rippie, Edward Grant 1931- *WhoMW 93*
Ripple, Kenneth F. 1943- *WhoAmP 93*
Ripple, Kenneth Francis 1943- *WhoAm 94, WhoAmL 94, WhoMW 93*
Ripple, William John 1952- *WhoWest 94*
Rippley, La Vern J. 1935- *WrDr 94*
Rippon *Who 94*
Rippon, Angela 1944- *IntWW 93*
Rippon, Michael 1938- *NewGrDO*
Rippon, Ruth Margaret 1927- *WhoAmA 93*
Rippon, Thomas Michael 1954- *WhoAm 94, WhoAmA 93*
Rippon, Thomas Richard 1946- *WhoAmP 93*
Rippon Of Hexham, Baron 1924- *IntWW 93, Who 94*
Rippons, Cleveland L. 1954- *WhoFI 94*
Ripps, Rodney *WhoAmA 93*
Rippy, James P. 1943- *WhoIns 94*
Rippy, Rodney Allen 1968- *WhoBlA 94*
Rips, Richard Maurice 1930- *WhoScEn 94*
Ripsch, Marjorie Mary 1927- *WhoMW 93*
Ripstein, Charles Benjamin 1913- *WhoAm 94*
Riquelme, Carlos 1912- *WhoHol 92*
Riquet, Michel d1993 *NewYTBS 93*
Ririe, Craig Martin 1943- *WhoAm 94, WhoWest 94*
Ririe, Thomas Robert 1964- *WhoFI 94*
Ris, Hans 1914- *IntWW 93, WhoAm 94, WhoMW 93*
Ris, William Krakow 1915- *WhoAm 94*
Risack, Rosa Negri *NewGrDO*
Risbeck, Philip Edward 1939- *WhoAmA 93*
Risberg, Robert Lawrence, Sr. 1935- *WhoFI 94, WhoScEn 94*
Risbrook, Arthur Timothy 1929- *WhoBlA 94*
RisCassi, Robert W. *WhoAm 94*
Risch, James E. 1943- *WhoAm 94, WhoAmP 93*
Risch, Martin Donald 1929- *WhoAm 94*
Risch, Maurice *WhoHol 92*
Risch, Richard William 1941- *WhoMW 93*
Rischel, Jorgen 1934- *IntWW 93*
Rischin, Moses 1925- *WhoWest 94, WrDr 94*
Rischiotto, Ann Marie 1957- *WhoWest 94*
Rischitelli, Donald Gary 1961- *WhoWest 94*
Riscoe, Arthur d1954 *WhoHol 92*
Risden, Arthur F. 1949- *WhoAmL 94*
Risdon, Elizabeth d1958 *WhoHol 92*
Risdon, Michael Paul 1946- *WhoMW 93*
Rise, John Ernest 1954- *WhoAmA 93*
Risebero, Bill 1938- *WrDr 94*
Risebrough, Doug 1954- *WhoAm 94, WhoWest 94*
Riseley, Martha Suzannah Heater 1916- *WhoMW 93, WhoScEn 94*
Riseley-Prichard, Richard Augustin 1925- *Who 94*
Riseling, Robert Lowell 1941- *WhoAmA 93*
Risen, Arnie 1924- *BasBi*
Risenhoover, Terry Jack, II 1965- *WhoWest 94*
Riser, Bruce L. 1950- *WhoScEn 94*
Riser, John W. *WhoAmP 93*
Rishe, Melvin 1940- *WhoAm 94*
Rishel, James Burton 1920- *WhoMW 93*
Rishel, Joseph John, Jr. 1940- *WhoAmA 93*
Rishel, Mary Ann Malinchak *DrAPF 93*
Rishel, Richard Clinton 1943- *WhoAm 94*
Rishell, Myrtle d1942 *WhoHol 92*
Rishell, Robert Clifford 1917-1976 *WhoAmA 93N*
Risher, Douglas James 1943- *WhoMW 93*
Risher, John R., Jr. 1938- *WhoBlA 94*
Risher, John Robert, Jr. 1938- *WhoAm 94*
Risher, Paul David 1935- *WhoFI 94*
Risher, Stephan Olaf 1951- *WhoMW 93*
Rishi, Satchidanand Raam 1933- *WhoAsA 94*
Rishtya, Kassim *IntWW 93*
Risi, Louis J., Jr. 1936- *WhoAm 94*
Risica, Loretta Cash 1930- *WhoFI 94*
Risik, Debra Joy 1956- *WhoFI 94*
Rising, William S. d1930 *WhoHol 92*
Risk, Douglas James 1941- *Who 94*
Risk, J. Fred 1928- *WhoAm 94*
Risk, Thomas (Neilson) 1922- *Who 94*
Risk, Thomas Neilson 1922- *IntWW 93*
Risk, William Symington 1909- *Who 94*
Riskas, Mike 1934- *WhoWest 94*
Riske, David Petzel 1951- *WhoMW 93*
Riske, William Kenneth 1949- *WhoAm 94*
Riskin, Adrian Boreas 1963- *WhoWest 94*
Riskin, Robert 1897-1955 *IntDcF 2-4*
Riskind, Kenneth Jay 1937- *WhoAm 94*
Risko, James Richard 1953- *WhoFI 94*
Risley, Allyn Wayne 1950- *WhoScEn 94*
Risley, Gregory Byron 1949- *WhoMW 93*
Risley, John Hollister 1919- *WhoAmA 93*
Risley, Larry L. *WhoAm 94, WhoFI 94, WhoWest 94*
Risley, Ralph G. 1937- *WhoWest 94*
Risley, Todd Robert 1937- *WhoAm 94, WhoWest 94*
Risman, Michael 1938- *WhoAm 94*
Risner, Paul Edward 1957- *WhoAmL 94*
Risness, Eric John 1927- *Who 94*
Risom, Jens 1916- *WhoAm 94*
Risom, Ole Christian 1919- *WhoAm 94*
Rison, Andre 1967- *WhoAm 94*
Rison, Andre Previn 1967- *WhoBlA 94*

Rison, Faye Rison 1942- *WhoBlA 94*
Rispo, Ronald A. 1943- *WhoAmL 94*
Rispoli, Salvatore c. 1736-1812 *NewGrDO*
Riss, Dan d1970 *WhoHol 92*
Riss, Eric 1929- *WhoAm 94*
Riss, Murray 1940- *WhoAm 94, WhoAmA 93*
Riss, Robert Bailey 1927- *WhoAm 94, WhoFI 94*
Risse, Carl c. 1810-1845? *NewGrDO*
Risse, Diana Marie 1957- *WhoMW 93*
Risse, Guenter Bernhard 1932- *WhoAm 94*
Risse, Klaus H. 1929- *WhoAm 94*
Risseeuw, John Lewis 1945- *WhoWest 94*
Risser, Fred A. 1927- *WhoAm 94, WhoAmP 93, WhoMW 93*
Risser, James K. 1947- *WhoAmA 93*
Risser, James Vaulx, Jr. 1938- *WhoAm 94*
Risser, Paul Gillan 1939- *WhoAm 94*
Rissetto, Harry A. 1943- *WhoAm 94, WhoAmL 94*
Rissien, Edward L. *IntMPA 94*
Rissing, Daniel Joseph 1944- *WhoAm 94, WhoMW 93*
Rissler, Niel Junior 1923- *WhoWest 94*
Rissling, Roy Gerard 1957- *WhoWest 94*
Rissman, Burton Richard 1927- *WhoAm 94*
Rissner, Danton 1940- *IntMPA 94*
Risso, Attilio d1967 *WhoHol 92*
Risso, Harry Francis 1929- *WhoHisp 94*
Risso, Patricia Ann *WhoWest 94*
Risso, Roberto 1926- *WhoHol 92*
Risson, Robert Joseph Henry d1992 *Who 94N*
Rissone, Checco d1985 *WhoHol 92*
Rissone, Giuditta d1977 *WhoHol 92*
Rist, Harold Ernest 1919- *WhoScEn 94*
Rist, Henry D. 1926- *WhoAmP 93*
Rist, John Michael 1936- *Who 94*
Rist, Louis G. 1888-1959 *WhoAmA 93N*
Rist, Robbie 1964- *WhoHol 92*
Rist, Susan E. *WhoBlA 94*
Ristau, Kenneth Eugene, Jr. 1939- *WhoAm 94*
Ristau, Mark Moody 1944- *WhoAmL 94*
Ristau, Toni Kae 1947- *WhoAmL 94*
Riste, Olav 1933- *IntWW 93, WrDr 94*
Ristelhueber, Joseph d1943 *WhoHol 92*
Ristich, Miodrag 1938- *WhoScEn 94*
Ristine, Thomas H. 1950- *WhoAmL 94*
Ristori, Giovanni Alberto 1692-1753 *NewGrDO*
Ristorini, Antonio Maria fl. 1690- *NewGrDO*
Ristorini, Caterina fl. 1757- *NewGrDO*
Ristorini, Giovanni Battista fl. 1750- *NewGrDO*
Ristorini, Giuseppe fl. 1724- *NewGrDO*
Ristorini, Luigi fl. 1741- *NewGrDO*
Ristow, Bruno 1940- *WhoWest 94*
Ristow, George Edward 1943- *WhoAm 94*
Ristow, Rodney Earl 1920- *WhoFI 94*
Ristow, Walter W. 1908- *WrDr 94*
Rit, Jean Qui *ConAu 142*
Ritardi, Albert Francis 1936- *WhoAm 94*
Ritblat, John Henry 1935- *IntWW 93, Who 94*
Ritch, Herald LaVern 1951- *WhoAm 94*
Ritch, Kathleen 1943- *WhoAm 94*
Ritchard, Cyril d1977 *WhoHol 92*
Ritcher, James Alexander 1958- *WhoAm 94*
Ritcheson, Charles Ray 1925- *Who 94*
Ritchey, Mercedes B. 1919- *WhoBlA 94*
Ritchey, Patrick William 1949- *WhoAm 94, WhoAmL 94*
Ritchey, Paul Andrew 1950- *WhoMW 93*
Ritchey, Samuel Donley, Jr. 1933- *WhoWest 94*
Ritchey, William Michael 1925- *WhoAm 94*
Ritchie *Who 94*
Ritchie, Lady 1837-1919 *BlmGWL*
Ritchie, Adele d1930 *WhoHol 92*
Ritchie, Albert 1939- *WhoAm 94*
Ritchie, Albert Edgar 1916- *Who 94*
Ritchie, Alexander James Otway 1928- *Who 94*
Ritchie, Andrew C. 1907-1978 *WhoAmA 93N*
Ritchie, (Celia) Ann 1934- *WhoAmA 93*
Ritchie, Anthony Elliot 1915- *Who 94*
Ritchie, Beedy Tatlow 1936- *WhoWest 94*
Ritchie, Billie d1921 *WhoHol 92*
Ritchie, Billie 1878-1921 *WhoCom*
Ritchie, Buzz 1947- *WhoAmP 93*
Ritchie, Cedric E. 1927- *IntWW 93*
Ritchie, Cedric Elmer 1927- *WhoAm 94, WhoFI 94*
Ritchie, Charles Stewart Almon 1906- *Who 94*
Ritchie, Clint *WhoHol 92*
Ritchie, Daniel Lee 1931- *WhoAm 94, WhoWest 94*
Ritchie, David Robert 1948- *Who 94*
Ritchie, Donald Andrew 1938- *Who 94*
Ritchie, Douglas Malcolm d1993 *Who 94N*
Ritchie, Elisavietta *DrAPF 93*
Ritchie, Eric Robert David 1942- *WhoWest 94*
Ritchie, Franklin d1918 *WhoHol 92*
Ritchie, Garry Harlan 1938- *WhoAm 94*
Ritchie, George Stephen 1914- *Who 94*
Ritchie, Horace David 1920- *Who 94*
Ritchie, Ian Carl 1947- *Who 94*
Ritchie, Ian Charles Stewart 1953- *Who 94*
Ritchie, Ian Russell 1953- *Who 94*
Ritchie, J. Murdoch 1925- *IntWW 93*
Ritchie, J(oseph) Murdoch 1925- *Who 94*
Ritchie, James I. 1918- *WhoFI 94*
Ritchie, James J. 1954- *WhoIns 94*
Ritchie, James Walter 1920- *Who 94*
Ritchie, Jean Harris 1947- *Who 94*
Ritchie, Jeffrey Scott 1954- *WhoFI 94*
Ritchie, Joe 1949- *WhoBlA 94*
Ritchie, John 1904-1988 *WhAm 10*
Ritchie, John Bennett 1924- *WhoWest 94*
Ritchie, John Hindle 1937- *Who 94*
Ritchie, Joseph c. 1788-1819 *WhWE*
Ritchie, June 1939- *WhoHol 92*
Ritchie, Kenneth Gordon 1921- *Who 94*
Ritchie, Louise Reid 1951- *WhoBlA 94*
Ritchie, Margaret 1903-1969 *NewGrDO*
Ritchie, Margaret Claire 1937- *Who 94*
Ritchie, Mark Ellis 1960- *WhoWest 94*
Ritchie, (James) Martin d1993 *Who 94N*
Ritchie, Michael 1938- *IntMPA 94*
Ritchie, Michael Brunswick 1938- *WhoAm 94*
Ritchie, P. Scott 1960- *WhoAmL 94*
Ritchie, Paul 1923- *EncSF 93*
Ritchie, Paul S. 1951- *WhoAmL 94*
Ritchie, Perry V. d1918 *WhoHol 92*
Ritchie, Richard Lee 1946- *WhoAm 94, WhoFI 94*
Ritchie, Robert Blackwood 1937- *Who 94*
Ritchie, Robert Field 1917- *WhoAm 94, WhoAmL 94*
Ritchie, Robert Jamieson 1944- *WhoAm 94*
Ritchie, Robert Oliver 1948- *WhoScEn 94, WhoWest 94*
Ritchie, Royal Daniel 1945- *WhoAm 94*
Ritchie, Shirley Anne 1940- *Who 94*
Ritchie, Thomas Harald 1962- *WhoWest 94*
Ritchie, Wayne *WhoAmP 93*
Ritchie, William 1941- *WhoAmA 93*
Ritchie, William M. d1937 *WhoHol 92*
Ritchie, William Paul 1946- *WhoAm 94*
Ritchie Of Dundee, Baron 1919- *Who 94*
Riter, Charles L. 1941- *WhoAmL 94*
Riter, Emanuel 1927- *WhoWest 94*
Riter, Stephen 1940- *WhoAm 94*
Rithauddeen Al-Haj Bin Tengku Ismail, Y.M. Tengku Ahmad 1932- *IntWW 93*
Ritholz, Jules 1925- *WhoAm 94*
Ritman, Barbara Ellen 1946- *WhoWest 94*
Ritman, Louis 1889-1963 *WhoAmA 93N*
Ritok, Joseph A., Jr. 1948- *WhoAmL 94*
Riton *WhoHol 92*
Ritorni, Carlo 1786-1860 *NewGrDO*
Ritsch, Frederick Field 1935- *WhoAm 94*
Ritschard, Hans Victor 1961- *WhoWest 94*
Ritschel, James Allan 1930- *WhoFI 94, WhoMW 93, WhoScEn 94*
Ritschel, William 1864-1949 *WhoAmA 93N*
Ritsema, Fredric A. 1951- *WhoAmL 94*
Ritt, Martin d1990 *WhoHol 92*
Ritt, Martin 1914-1991 *WhAm 10*
Ritt, Paul Edward 1928- *WhoAm 94*
Ritt, Roger M. 1950- *WhoAm 94*
Ritt, Roger Merrill 1950- *WhoAmL 94*
Rittberg, Eric Joseph 1962- *WhoAmP 93*
Rittenbach, Gail Sylvia 1948- *WhoWest 94*
Rittenberg, Marc A. 1945- *WhoWest 94*
Rittenburg, Thomas John 1953- *WhoAm 94*
Rittenhouse, Bruce Dean 1951- *WhoFI 94*
Rittenhouse, Carl Harris 1922- *WhoWest 94*
Rittenhouse, David 1732-1796 *AmRev, WhAmRev*
Rittenhouse, Diana Angela 1939- *WhoAmP 93*
Rittenhouse, Donna Jean 1934- *WhoWest 94*
Rittenhouse, Joseph Wilson 1917- *WhoAm 94*
Ritter, Alexander 1833-1896 *NewGrDO*
Ritter, Alfred 1923- *WhoAm 94*
Ritter, Alfred Francis, Jr. 1946- *WhoAm 94, WhoFI 94*
Ritter, Ann L. 1933- *WhoAmL 94, WhoFI 94*
Ritter, August *WhoAmP 93*
Ritter, Charles Edward 1938- *WhoAm 94*
Ritter, Dale F. 1932- *WhoAm 94, WhoScEn 94, WhoWest 94*
Ritter, Dale William 1919- *WhoWest 94*
Ritter, Daniel Benjamin 1937- *WhoAm 94, WhoFI 94*
Ritter, David Allen 1954- *WhoMW 93*
Ritter, Dianne Marie 1959- *WhoWest 94*
Ritter, Donald Lawrence 1940- *WhoAm 94, WhoAmP 93, WhoScEn 94*
Ritter, Doris Standring 1926- *WhoMW 93*
Ritter, Edward S. 1954- *WhoIns 94*
Ritter, Erica 1948- *BlmGWL*
Ritter, Erika 1948- *ConDr 93*
Ritter, Esther d1925 *WhoHol 92*
Ritter, Frank Nicholas 1928- *WhoAm 94*
Ritter, George d1919 *WhoHol 92*
Ritter, Gerald Lee 1939- *WhoScEn 94*
Ritter, Gerhard A. 1929- *IntWW 93*
Ritter, Grant L. 1955- *WhoScEn 94*
Ritter, Guy Franklin 1933- *WhoFI 94*
Ritter, James Anthony 1960- *WhoScEn 94*
Ritter, Jay Rial 1954- *WhoMW 93*
Ritter, Jerry E. 1935- *WhoAm 94, WhoFI 94*
Ritter, Johann Wilhelm 1776-1810 *WorScD*
Ritter, John 1948- *IntMPA 94, WhoHol 92*
Ritter, Johnathan Southworth 1948- *WhoAm 94*
Ritter, Jorge Eduardo 1950- *IntWW 93*
Ritter, Joseph M. 1950- *WhoIns 94*
Ritter, Julian 1909- *WhoAmA 93*
Ritter, Julian Stawska Fromm *WhoAmA 93*
Ritter, Karen A. 1953- *WhoAmP 93*
Ritter, Margaret Jean 1925- *WhoAmP 93*
Ritter, Mary Catherine 1943- *WhoMW 93*
Ritter, Michael Dean 1945- *WhoMW 93*
Ritter, Miriam Virginia 1957- *WhoAmP 93*
Ritter, Norman Richard 1929- *WhoFI 94*
Ritter, Paul Monroe 1953- *WhoAmL 94*
Ritter, Peter 1763-1846 *NewGrDO*
Ritter, Randall Eugene 1953- *WhoMW 93*
Ritter, Renee Gaylinn *WhoAmA 93*
Ritter, Richard Frederick, Jr. 1948- *WhoMW 93*
Ritter, Robert Forcier 1943- *WhoAm 94*
Ritter, Robert Joseph 1925- *WhoAm 94, WhoAmL 94, WhoFI 94*
Ritter, Rudolf d1966 *WhoHol 92*
Ritter, Rudolf 1878-1966 *NewGrDO*
Ritter, Russell Joseph 1932- *WhoWest 94*
Ritter, Terry Lee 1952- *WhoScEn 94*
Ritter, Tex d1974 *WhoHol 92*
Ritter, Thelma d1969 *WhoHol 92*
Ritter, Thomas D. *WhoAmP 93*
Ritter, Thomas J. 1922- *WhoBlA 94*
Ritter-Ciampi, Gabrielle 1886-1974 *NewGrDO*
Ritterhoff, Charles William 1921- *WhoAm 94*
Ritterman, Janet Elizabeth 1941- *Who 94*
Ritterman, Stuart I. 1937- *WhoAm 94*
Rittersband, Gerhard d1959 *WhoHol 92*
Ritterskamp, Douglas Dolvin 1948- *WhoAm 94*
Rittgers, Charles Henry 1951- *WhoAmL 94*
Ritthaler, Gerald Irvin 1930- *WhoAm 94*
Rittinger, Carolyne June 1942- *WhoAm 94, WhoMW 93*
Rittley, John Howard 1957- *WhoAmL 94*
Rittmann, Paul Douglas 1949- *WhoWest 94*
Rittmer, Elaine Heneke 1931- *WhoMW 93*
Rittmer, Sheldon 1928- *WhoMW 93*
Rittmer, Sheldon L. 1928- *WhoAmP 93*
Rittner, Edmund Sidney 1919- *WhoAm 94*
Rittner, Luke Philip Hardwick 1947- *IntWW 93, Who 94*
Rittner, Rudolf d1943 *WhoHol 92*
Ritts, Edwin Earl, Jr. 1948- *WhoAmA 93*
Ritvo, Edward Ross 1930- *WhoAm 94*
Ritvo, Harriet 1946- *WrDr 94*
Ritvo, Lucille B. 1920- *WhoAmP 93*
Ritvo, Roger Alan 1944- *WhoAm 94*
Ritz, Al d1965 *WhoHol 92*
Ritz, Al 1901-1965
See Ritz Brothers, The *WhoCom*
Ritz, Esther Leah 1918- *WhoAm 94*
Ritz, Harry d1986 *WhoHol 92*
Ritz, Harry 1907-1986
See Ritz Brothers, The *WhoCom*
Ritz, Harry Leonard 1932- *WhoMW 93*
Ritz, Jimmy d1985 *WhoHol 92*
Ritz, Jimmy 1904-1985
See Ritz Brothers, The *WhoCom*
Ritz, Kenneth Francis 1935- *WhoAmL 94*
Ritz, Lorna J. *WhoAmA 93*
Ritz, Richard Ellison 1919- *WhoAm 94*
Ritz Brothers, The *WhoCom [port]*
Ritzema, Rudolph *WhAmRev*
Ritzen, Jo 1945- *IntWW 93*
Ritzen, Jozef Maria Mathias 1945- *WhoScEn 94*
Ritzka, Timothy Joseph 1959- *WhoAmL 94*
Ritzlin, George 1942- *WhoMW 93*
Ritzo, Eugene 1919- *WhoAmP 93*
Riu, Victor 1887-1974 *WhoAmA 93N*
Riva, Emmanuele 1927- *WhoHol 92*
Riva, Maria 1925- *WhoHol 92*
Riva, Mario d1960 *WhoHol 92*
Rivadeneira, Luis E. 1937- *WhoHisp 94*
Rivalles, Rafael d1966 *WhoHol 92*
Rivani, Antonio d1686 *NewGrDO*
Rivard, David *DrAPF 93*
Rivard, Paul Edmund 1943- *WhoAm 94*
Rivard, Timothy Daniel 1956- *WhoFI 94*
Rivard, William Charles 1942- *WhoAm 94*
Rivarol, Antoine Rivaroli 1753-1801 *GuFrLit 2*
Rivarola, Alfonso 1591?-1640 *NewGrDO*
Rivas, Alejandro Alberto 1945- *WhoHisp 94*
Rivas, Armando *WhoHisp 94*
Rivas, Carlos *WhoHol 92*
Rivas, Charlie, Jr. 1953- *WhoHisp 94*
Rivas, Daniel E. 1945- *WhoHisp 94*
Rivas, David 1953- *WhoHisp 94*
Rivas, Edgar J. 1933- *WhoHisp 94*
Rivas, Eneida 1957- *WhoHisp 94*
Rivas, Fernando *WhoHisp 94*
Rivas, Henry Vasquez, Sr. 1952- *WhoHisp 94*
Rivas, Joseph M. 1951- *WhoHisp 94*
Rivas, Maggie *WhoHisp 94*
Rivas, Martin, Sr. *WhoHisp 94*
Rivas, Mercedes 1931- *WhoHisp 94*
Rivas, Milagros 1955- *WhoHisp 94*
Rivas, P. Rodolfo 1940- *WhoHisp 94*
Rivas, Ronald K. 1958- *WhoHisp 94*
Rivas, Wilfredo Jose 1949- *WhoHisp 94*
Riva Saleta, Luis Octavio 1949- *WhoHisp 94*
Rivas-Haddock, Carlos Manuel 1943- *WhoHisp 94*
Rivas-Mijares, Gustavo 1922- *IntWW 93*
Rive, Kenneth 1919- *IntMPA 94*
Rive, Richard (Moore) 1931-1989 *BlkWr 2, RfGShF*
Rivel, Charlie d1983 *WhoHol 92*
Rivela, Francisco G. *WhoHisp 94*
Rivele, Stephen J. 1949- *ConAu 142*
Rivelino, Roberto 1947- *WorESoc [port]*
Rivenbark, Rembert Reginald 1912- *WhoFI 94*
Rivenburg, Roy 1958- *WhoWest 94*
Riveness, Phillip J. 1947- *WhoAmP 93*
River, Louis Philip 1901-1991 *WhAm 10*
Rivera, Alvin D. *WhoHisp 94*
Rivera, Americo, Jr. 1928- *WhoHisp 94*
Rivera, Anastacio S., Father *WhoHisp 94*
Rivera, Angel Miguel 1955- *WhoHisp 94*
Rivera, Antonio T. *WhoIns 94*
Rivera, Armando Remonte 1940- *WhoScEn 94, WhoWest 94*
Rivera, Aurelio *WhoHisp 94*
Rivera, Ben 1968- *WhoHisp 94*
Rivera, Carlos 1955- *WhoHisp 94*
Rivera, Cecilia C. 1945- *WhoHisp 94*
Rivera, Chita *NewYTBS 93 [port]*
Rivera, Chita 1933- *IntMPA 94, WhoAm 94, WhoHisp 94, WhoHol 92*
Rivera, Craig Alan 1954- *WhoFI 94*
Rivera, Dennis 1950- *WhoHisp 94*
Rivera, Diana Huizar 1953- *WhoHisp 94*
Rivera, Don *WhoHisp 94*
Rivera, Eddy 1938- *WhoBlA 94*
Rivera, Edgardo 1953- *WhoHisp 94*
Rivera, Edward *DrAPF 93, WhoHisp 94*
Rivera, Edwin 1948- *WhoHisp 94*
Rivera, Edwin A. 1946- *WhoHisp 94*
Rivera, Eladio A., Jr. *WhoHisp 94*
Rivera, Elias J. 1937- *WhoAmA 93*
Rivera, Elliot 1938- *WhoHisp 94*
Rivera, Ernesto Rosado 1934- *WhoHisp 94*
Rivera, Etnairis *DrAPF 93*
Rivera, Evangelina 1953- *WhoHisp 94*
Rivera, Evelyn Margaret 1929- *WhoAsA 94*
Rivera, Evelyn Socias 1959- *WhoHisp 94*
Rivera, Ezequiel Ramirez 1942- *WhoHisp 94*
Rivera, Fanny 1953- *WhoHisp 94*
Rivera, Francisco Xavier 1961- *WhoHisp 94*
Rivera, Frank 1939- *WhoAmA 93*
Rivera, Frank E., Sr. 1928- *WhoHisp 94*
Rivera, George 1955- *WhoHisp 94*
Rivera, Geraldo 1943- *IntMPA 94, WhoAm 94*
Rivera, Geraldo Miguel 1943- *WhoHisp 94*
Rivera, Gianni 1943- *WorESoc*
Rivera, Hector 1951- *WhoHisp 94*
Rivera, Hector A. 1943- *WhoHisp 94*
Rivera, Hector L. *WhoHisp 94*
Rivera, Henry Michael 1946- *WhoAmL 94, WhoAmP 93, WhoHisp 94*
Rivera, Jaime *WhoHisp 94*
Rivera, Jaime Diego 1948- *WhoHisp 94*
Rivera, Jennifer Antoinette 1956- *WhoHisp 94*
Rivera, Jerry M. 1946- *WhoAmP 93*

Rivera, John 1945- *WhoHisp 94*
Rivera, John A. 1954- *WhoHisp 94*
Rivera, John David 1948- *WhoHisp 94*
Rivera, Jose 1938- *WhoAmP 93, WhoHisp 94*
Rivera, José J. 1951- *WhoHisp 94*
Rivera, Jose Luis 1946- *WhoHisp 94*
Rivera, Juan 1953- *WhoHisp 94*
Rivera, Juan B., II 1940- *WhoHisp 94*
Rivera, Juan M. 1944- *WhoHisp 94*
Rivera, Juan Manuel 1943- *WhoHisp 94*
Rivera, Julia E. 1949- *WhoHisp 94*
Rivera, Laura E. 1945- *WhoHisp 94*
Rivera, Lloyd David 1947- *WhoHisp 94*
Rivera, Louis Reyes *DrAPF 93*
Rivera, Louis Reyes 1945- *WhoHisp 94*
Rivera, Lucia 1938- *WhoHisp 94*
Rivera, Lucy 1937- *WhoHisp 94*
Rivera, Luis *WhoHol 92*
Rivera, Luis 1964- *WhoHisp 94*
Rivera, Luis Eduardo 1940- *WhoHisp 94*
Rivera, Luis Ernesto 1950- *WhoHisp 94*
Rivera, Luis J. 1953- *WhoHisp 94*
Rivera, Luis Ruben 1956- *WhoScEn 94*
Rivera, Marcelina 1962- *WhoHisp 94*
Rivera, Marcelino d1987 *WhoHol 92*
Rivera, Marco Antonio 1945- *WhoHisp 94*
Rivera, Marika *WhoHol 92*
Rivera, Mario Angel 1941- *WhoHisp 94*
Rivera, Martin Garcia 1963- *WhoHisp 94*
Rivera, Mercedes A. 1954- *WhoHisp 94*
Rivera, Migdalia Vazquez 1961- *WhoHisp 94*
Rivera, Miguel Primo de 1870-1930 *HisWorL [port]*
Rivera, Miquela C. 1954- *WhoHisp 94*
Rivera, Nancy J. 1964- *WhoHisp 94*
Rivera, Oscar R. 1956- *WhoAmL 94*
Rivera, Osvaldo *WhoHisp 94*
Rivera, Oswald 1944- *WhoHisp 94*
Rivera, Patrick 1956- *WhoHisp 94*
Rivera, Peter Angel 1933- *WhoHisp 94*
Rivera, Peter M. 1946- *WhoAmP 93*
Rivera, Rafael *WhoHisp 94*
Rivera, Rafael J. 1940- *WhoHisp 94*
Rivera, Rafael Rene 1950- *WhoHisp 94*
Rivera, Ramon Luis 1929- *WhoAmP 93, WhoHisp 94*
Rivera, Raul 1930- *WhoHisp 94*
Rivera, Ray *WhoHisp 94*
Rivera, Rhonda Rae 1938- *WhoMW 93*
Rivera, Richard E. 1947- *WhoAm 94, WhoFI 94, WhoHisp 94*
Rivera, Robert A. 1940- *WhoHisp 94*
Rivera, Roberto 1953- *WhoHisp 94*
Rivera, Ron *WhoHisp 94*
Rivera, Rosa M. 1950- *WhoHisp 94*
Rivera, Salvador *WhoHisp 94*
Rivera, Sandra Lynn 1955- *WhoHisp 94*
Rivera, Theodore Basiliso 1955- *WhoHisp 94*
Rivera, Thomas D. 1928- *WhoHisp 94*
Rivera, Tony A. 1944- *WhoHisp 94*
Rivera, Victor Manuel 1916- *WhoHisp 94, WhoWest 94*
Rivera, Vincent 1950- *WhoHisp 94*
Rivera, Walter 1955- *WhoAmL 94, WhoHisp 94*
Rivera, William McLeod 1934- *WhoHisp 94*
Rivera-Alequin, Ulpiano H. 1938- *WhoHisp 94*
Rivera-Alvarez, Miguel-Angel 1952- *WhoHisp 94*
Rivera Bigas, Juan 1929- *WhoHisp 94*
Rivera-Brenes, Luis 1916- *WhoAmP 93*
Rivera-Carlo, Roberto 1955- *WhoHisp 94*
Rivera-Colón, Angel Antonio 1947- *WhoHisp 94*
Rivera Cruz, Hector 1950- *WhoHisp 94*
Rivera Domenech, Angel L. 1940- *WhoHisp 94*
Rivera-García, Ignacio 1914- *WhoHisp 94*
Rivera-Izcoa, Carmen 1928- *WhoHisp 94*
Rivera-Lopez, Angel 1944- *WhoHisp 94*
Rivera-Matos, Noelia 1949- *WhoHisp 94*
Rivera-Morales, Roberto 1953- *WhoHisp 94*
Rivera Ortiz, Gilberto 1932- *WhoHisp 94*
Rivera-Pagán, Carmen A. 1923- *WhoHisp 94*
Rivera Perez, Efrain E. *WhoHisp 94*
Rivera-Ramos, Efrén 1947- *WhoHisp 94*
Rivera-Rivera, Felix A. 1948- *WhoHisp 94*
Rivera-Rodas, Hernan 1940- *WhoHisp 94*
Rivera-Viera, Diana T. 1949- *WhoHisp 94*
Riverdale, Baron 1901- *Who 94*
Rivere, Alec *EncSF 93*
Riverina, Bishop of 1939- *Who 94*
Riverman, Rylla Claire 1955- *WhoWest 94*
Rivero, Ana Margarita 1960- *WhoHisp 94*
Rivero, Andres *DrAPF 93*
Rivero, Andres 1936- *WhoHisp 94*
Rivero, Andres 1960- *WhoAmL 94*
Rivero, Eliana S. 1940- *WhoHisp 94*
Rivero, Emilio Adolfo 1947- *WhoHisp 94*
Rivero, George *WhoHol 92*
Rivero, Hector M. *WhoHisp 94*
Rivero, Jorge *WhoHol 92*
Rivero, Juan A. 1923- *WhoHisp 94*
Rivero, Julian d1976 *WhoHol 92*
Rivero, Marilyn Elaine Keith 1942- *WhoAmP 93*
Rivero, Marita Joy 1943- *WhoBlA 94*
Rivero, Ricardo A. 1962- *WhoHisp 94*
Riveron, Enrique 1902- *WhoAmA 93*
Rivers, Alfred J. 1925- *WhoBlA 94*
Rivers, Ann *DrAPF 93*
Rivers, Cheryl Pratt 1951- *WhoAmP 93*
Rivers, Clarence Joseph 1931- *WhoBlA 94*
Rivers, David Eugene 1943- *WhoBlA 94*
Rivers, Denovious Adolphus 1928- *WhoBlA 94*
Rivers, Donald Lee 1943- *WhoMW 93*
Rivers, Dorothy 1933- *WhoBlA 94*
Rivers, Elfrida *GayLL*
Rivers, Fernand d1960 *WhoHol 92*
Rivers, Francine (Sandra) 1947- *WrDr 94*
Rivers, G(eorge) L(amb) 1896- *WhAm 10*
Rivers, Gary C. 1951- *WhoBlA 94*
Rivers, Glenn Anton 1961- *WhoBlA 94*
Rivers, Griffin Harold 1939- *WhoBlA 94*
Rivers, Horace Kevin 1968- *WhoScEn 94*
Rivers, J. W. *DrAPF 93*
Rivers, Jessie Mae 1933- *WhoMW 93*
Rivers, Joan 1933- *IntMPA 94, WhoCom [port], WhoHol 92, WrDr 94*
Rivers, Joan 1937- *WhoAm 94*
Rivers, John Daniel 1966- *WhoFI 94*
Rivers, John Minott, Jr. 1945- *WhoAm 94*
Rivers, Johnny 1942- *WhoBlA 94*
Rivers, Johnny 1949- *WhoBlA 94*
Rivers, Kenneth Jay 1938- *WhoAmL 94*
Rivers, Larry 1923- *IntWW 93, WhoAm 94*
Rivers, Larry 1925- *WhoAmA 93*
Rivers, Lawrence Alan 1956- *WhoWest 94*
Rivers, Lee Walter 1929- *WhoScEn 94*
Rivers, Len *WhoBlA 94*
Rivers, Louis 1922- *WhoBlA 94*
Rivers, Lynn N. *WhoAmP 93*
Rivers, Marie Bie 1928- *WhoAm 94*
Rivers, Mavis 1929?-1992 *WhoAsA 94N*
Rivers, Mickey (John Milton) 1948- *WhoBlA 94*
Rivers, Patrick 1920- *WrDr 94*
Rivers, Philip R. 1948- *WhoAmP 93*
Rivers, Richard Davis 1934- *WhoAmL 94*
Rivers, Richard Douglas, Jr. 1956- *WhoWest 94*
Rivers, Richard Robinson 1942- *WhoAm 94, WhoAmL 94*
Rivers, Robert Alfred 1923- *WhoAm 94*
Rivers, Robert Allen 1951- *WhoScEn 94*
Rivers, Robert Joseph, Jr. 1931- *WhoBlA 94*
Rivers, Valerie L. 1952- *WhoBlA 94*
Rivers, Vernon Frederick 1933- *WhoBlA 94*
Rivers, Victoria Z. 1948- *WhoAmA 93*
Rivers, Wilga Marie 1919- *WhoAm 94*
Rivers, William Halse Rivers 1864-1922 *DcNaB MP*
Riverside, John *EncSF 93*
Rives, Stanley Gene 1930- *WhoAm 94, WhoMW 93*
Rives, Sterling Edwards, Jr. 1921- *WhoAmP 93*
Rives, William D. 1943- *WhoAm 94, WhoAmL 94*
Rives, William LeGrande 1940- *WhoFI 94*
Rivet, A(lbert) L(ionel) F(rederick) 1915-1993 *ConAu 142*
Rivet, Albert Lionel Frederick d1993 *Who 94N*
Rivet, Albert Lionel Frederick 1915- *IntWW 93, WrDr 94*
Rivet, Diana Wittmer 1931- *WhoAmL 94, WhoFI 94*
Rivett, Geoffrey Christopher 1932- *Who 94*
Rivett, Robert Wyman 1921- *WhoWest 94*
Rivett-Carnac, Miles James 1933- *Who 94*
Rivett-Carnac, (Thomas) Nicholas 1927- *Who 94*
Rivett-Drake, Jean (Elizabeth) 1909- *Who 94*
Rivette, Gerard Bertram 1932- *WhoAm 94*
Rivette, Jacques 1928- *IntWW 93*
Rivié, Daniel Juan 1964- *WhoHisp 94*
Riviello Bazan, Antonio 1926- *WhoAm 94*
Rivier, Joaquin 1937- *WhoHisp 94*
Riviere, Christopher Henry 1956- *WhoAmL 94*
Riviere, Fred d1935 *WhoHol 92*
Riviere, Marie 1956- *WhoHol 92*
Rivin, Ira G. 1948- *WhoAmL 94*
Rivington, James 1724-1802 *AmRev, WhAmRev [port]*
Rivira, Luis *WhoAmP 93*
Rivkin, Donald Herschel 1924- *WhoAm 94*
Rivkin, Ellis 1918- *WrDr 94*
Rivkin, J. F. *DrAPF 93*
Rivkin, Jack Leon 1940- *WhoAm 94*
Rivkin, Robert S. *WhoAmL 94*
Rivkind, Perry Abbot 1930- *WhoAm 94*
Rivlin, Alice M. 1931- *WhoAmP 93*
Rivlin, Alice Mitchell 1931- *WhoAm 94*
Rivlin, Benjamin 1921- *WhoAm 94*
Rivlin, Geoffrey 1940- *Who 94*
Rivlin, Liora *WhoHol 92*
Rivlin, Moshe 1925- *IntWW 93*
Rivlin, Richard Saul 1934- *WhoScEn 94*
Rivlin, Ronald Samuel 1915- *WhoAm 94*
Rivo, Shirley Winthrope 1925- *WhoAmA 93*
Rivoli, Paulina 1817-1881 *NewGrDO*
Rivoyre, Christine Berthe Claude Denis de 1921- *IntWW 93*
Rivoyre, Christine de 1921- *BlmGWL*
Rix, Baron 1924- *Who 94*
Rix, Bernard (Anthony) 1944- *Who 94*
Rix, Brian 1924- *WhoHol 92*
Rix, John 1917- *Who 94*
Rix, Steven John 1952- *WhoAmP 93*
Rix, Timothy John 1934- *IntWW 93, Who 94*
Rixon, Benjamin R. *WhoHol 92*
Rixon, Morris L. *WhoHol 92*
Ri Yong Tae *WhoPRCh 91*
Riza, Alper Ali 1948- *Who 94*
Rizai, Matthew M. 1956- *WhoFI 94*
Rizer, Franklin Morris 1953- *WhoMW 93*
Rizk, Waheeb 1921- *Who 94*
Rizkallah, Jihad Joseph 1954- *WhoMW 93*
Rizkin, Alexander 1936- *WhoScEn 94*
Rizo, Marco 1916- *WhoHisp 94*
Rizvi, Javed 1955- *WhoScEn 94*
Rizvi, Tanzeem R. 1949- *WhoWest 94*
Rizzello, Michael Gaspard 1926- *Who 94*
Rizzi, Deborah L. 1955- *WhoFI 94*
Rizzi, Domenico *NewGrDO*
Rizzi, James 1950- *WhoAmA 93*
Rizzi, Joseph Vito 1949- *WhoFI 94*
Rizzi, Teresa Marie 1964- *WhoWest 94*
Rizzie, Dan 1951- *WhoAmA 93*
Rizzo, Alfredo *WhoHol 92*
Rizzo, Anthony Augustine 1928-1991 *WhAm 10*
Rizzo, Carlo d1977 *WhoHol 92*
Rizzo, Francis 1936- *WhoAm 94*
Rizzo, Francis Lazzaro 1920-1991 *WhAm 10*
Rizzo, Geraldine Josephine 1942- *WhoMW 93*
Rizzo, Gianni *WhoHol 92*
Rizzo, Henry C. *WhoAmP 93*
Rizzo, James M. 1938- *WhoIns 94*
Rizzo, Jilly *WhoHol 92*
Rizzo, John J. 1947- *WhoAmL 94*
Rizzo, Joseph L. 1942- *WhoIns 94*
Rizzo, Richard C. 1944- *WhoAm 94, WhoAmL 94*
Rizzo, Richard David 1944- *WhoAm 94*
Rizzo, Ronald Stephen 1941- *WhoAm 94, WhoAmL 94, WhoMW 93*
Rizzo, Sandra Lee 1941- *WhoMW 93*
Rizzo, Steven J. 1954- *WhoFI 94*
Rizzo, Thomas Anthony 1958- *WhoScEn 94*
Rizzo, William Ober 1948- *WhoAm 94*
Rizzolatti, Giacomo 1937- *WhoScEn 94*
Rizzoli, Angelo 1943- *IntWW 93*
Rizzotto, Kathleen Marie 1959- *WhoAmL 94, WhoWest 94*
Rizzuto, Carmela Rita 1942- *WhoWest 94*
Rizzuto, Helen Morrissey *DrAPF 93*
Rizzuto, James T. 1945- *WhoAmP 93*
Rizzuto, Leandro Peter 1938- *WhoFI 94*
Roa, Benedicta B. 1929- *WhoWomW 91*
Roa Bastos, Augusto 1917- *HispLC [port], IntWW 93*
Roa Bastos, Augusto (Antonio) 1917- *ConWorW 93*
Roach, Arvid Edward, II 1951- *WhoAm 94, WhoAmL 94*
Roach, Bert d1971 *WhoHol 92*
Roach, Catherine B. 1942- *WhoAmL 94*
Roach, Dale Anthony 1945- *WhoMW 93*
Roach, Deloris 1944- *WhoBlA 94*
Roach, Edgar Mayo, Jr. 1948- *WhoAm 94, WhoAmL 94*
Roach, Gary Francis 1933- *Who 94*
Roach, Hal d1992 *IntMPA 94N*
Roach, Hal 1892-1992 *AnObit 1992, IntDcF 2-4 [port]*
Roach, Hildred Elizabeth 1937- *WhoBlA 94*
Roach, Hugh William 1945- *WhoFI 94*
Roach, Irene K. 1934- *WhoMW 93*
Roach, James Robert 1922- *WhoAm 94*
Roach, Jeanne 1934- *WhoAm 94*
Roach, John D. C. 1943- *WhoAm 94, WhoFI 94, WhoWest 94*
Roach, John Hendee, Jr. 1941- *WhoAm 94*
Roach, John Michael 1947- *WhoWest 94*
Roach, John Robert 1921- *WhoAm 94, WhoMW 93*
Roach, John Vinson, II 1938- *WhoAm 94, WhoFI 94*
Roach, Jon Gilbert 1944- *WhoAmL 94*
Roach, Karen E. 1953- *WhoMW 93*
Roach, Kathleen Lynn 1962- *WhoAmL 94*
Roach, Lee 1937- *WhoBlA 94*
Roach, Lonnie Calvin 1951- *WhoAmP 93*
Roach, Margaret d1964 *WhoHol 92*
Roach, Margot Ruth 1934- *WhoAm 94*
Roach, Max 1924- *WhoBlA 94*
Roach, Maxwell 1925- *AfrAmAl 6*
Roach, Maxwell Lemuel 1924- *IntWW 93, WhoAm 94*
Roach, Neal Edward 1963- *WhoMW 93*
Roach, Pamela Jean 1948- *WhoAmP 93*
Roach, Pat *WhoHol 92*
Roach, Patrick Joseph 1952- *WhoAm 94*
Roach, Randy 1951- *WhoAmP 93*
Roach, Robert Corwine, Jr. 1956- *WhoWest 94*
Roach, Robert Mahlon 1946- *WhoFI 94*
Roach, Robert Michael, Jr. 1955- *WhoAmL 94*
Roach, Russ 1947- *WhoAmP 93*
Roach, Steven Arthur 1961- *WhoAmL 94*
Roach, Thomas Adair 1929- *WhoAm 94, WhoAmL 94, WhoAmP 93*
Roach, Wesley Linville 1931- *WhoAm 94*
Roach, William D. 1931- *WhoAmP 93*
Roach, William Russell 1940- *WhoAm 94, WhoFI 94*
Roache, Edward Francis 1923- *WhoAm 94*
Roache, Francis Michael 1936- *WhoAm 94*
Roache, Patrick John 1938- *WhoWest 94*
Roache, Patrick Michael, Jr. 1946- *WhoFI 94*
Roache, Viola d1961 *WhoHol 92*
Roache, William 1932- *WhoHol 92*
Road, Mike *WhoHol 92*
Roaden, Arliss Lloyd 1930- *WhoAm 94*
Roades, John Leslie 1951- *WhoAmL 94, WhoAmP 93*
Roadman, Betty d1975 *WhoHol 92*
Roads, Christopher Herbert 1934- *Who 94*
Roads, Peter George 1917- *Who 94*
Roady, Stephen E. 1949- *WhoAmL 94*
Roaf, Clifton G. 1941- *WhoBlA 94*
Roa-Kouri, Raul 1936- *IntWW 93*
Roaldset, Elen 1944- *WhoScEn 94*
Roan, Forrest Calvin, Jr. 1944- *WhoAmL 94, WhoFI 94*
Roan, James Cortland, Jr. 1937- *WhoAm 94*
Roan, Vernon Parker, Jr. 1935- *WhoScEn 94*
Roane, David James, Jr. 1960- *WhoFI 94*
Roane, Glenwood P. 1930- *WhoBlA 94*
Roane, Philip Ransom, Jr. 1927- *WhoBlA 94*
Roanne, Andre d1959 *WhoHol 92*
Roar, Leif 1937- *NewGrDO*
Roark, Counsellor F. d1929 *WhoHol 92*
Roark, Dallas M. 1931- *WrDr 94*
Roark, Denis Darel 1943- *WhoWest 94*
Roark, Helen Wills 1905- *Who 94*
Roark, James E. 1945- *WhoAmP 93*
Roark, Terry Paul 1938- *WhoAm 94, WhoWest 94*
Roarke, Adam *WhoHol 92*
Roath, Stephen D. 1941- *WhoWest 94*
Roath, William Wesley 1934- *WhoMW 93*
Roatz *WhoAmA 93*
Roazen, Paul 1936- *WrDr 94*
Rob, Charles Granville 1913- *Who 94*
Rob, Peter 1940- *WhoAm 94*
Robach, Joseph E. *WhoAmP 93*
Robak, Jennie 1932- *WhoAmP 93*
Robards, Frank Benjamin, Jr. 1929- *WhoAm 94*
Robards, Jason 1922- *IntMPA 94, WhoHol 92*
Robards, Jason, Sr. d1963 *WhoHol 92*
Robards, Jason Nelson, Jr. 1922- *IntWW 93, WhoAm 94*
Robards, Karen 1954- *ConAu 42NR*
Robards, Sam *IntMPA 94*
Robards, Sam 1962- *WhoHol 92*
Robards, Willis d1921 *WhoHol 92*
Robart, James Louis 1947- *WhoAm 94, WhoAmL 94*
Robarts, Basil 1915- *Who 94*
Robarts, Julian *Who 94*
Robarts, (Anthony) Julian 1937- *Who 94*
Robathan, Andrew Robert George 1951- *Who 94*
Robb, Bruce 1919- *WhoAm 94*
Robb, Charles 1938- *WhoAmA 93*
Robb, Charles S. 1939- *CngDr 93, WhoAmP 93*
Robb, Charles Spittal 1939- *IntWW 93, WhoAm 94*
Robb, David 1947- *WhoHol 92*
Robb, David Metheny 1903-1990 *WhAm 10*
Robb, David Metheny, Jr. 1937- *WhoAm 94, WhoAmA 93*
Robb, Dean Allen, Sr. 1924- *WhoAmL 94, WhoMW 93*
Robb, Edgar S. 1937- *WhoAmP 93*
Robb, Felix Compton 1914- *WhoAm 94*
Robb, Gary Charles 1955- *WhoAmL 94*

Robb, James Alexander 1930- WhoAm 94
Robb, James Christie 1924- Who 94
Robb, James Harding 1920- WrDr 94
Robb, James Willis 1918- WhoAm 94
Robb, Jeffery Michael 1949- WhoScEn 94
Robb, John 1932- IntWW 93
Robb, John Donald 1892-1989 WhAm 10
Robb, John E. 1937- WhoAmP 93
Robb, John Weddell 1936- IntWW 93, Who 94
Robb, John Wesley 1919- WhoAm 94
Robb, Lawrence d1990 WhoHol 92
Robb, Lotus d1969 WhoHol 92
Robb, Michael S. WhoIns 94
Robb, Nathaniel Heyward, Jr. 1942- WhoAm 94
Robb, Patrick Kenneth 1955- WhoAmL 94
Robb, Peggy Hight 1924- WhoAmA 93
Robb, Richard Arlin 1942- WhoScEn 94
Robb, Robert Clifton, Jr. 1945- WhoAmP 93
Robb, Scott Hall 1944- WhoAmL 94
Robb, Walter Lee 1928- WhoAm 94, WhoFI 94, WhoScEn 94
Robbe, Joan Eda 1946- WhoAmP 93
Robbe-Grillet, Alain 1922- ConWorW 93, IntDcF 2-4 [port], IntWW 93, Who 94
Robbelen, Gerhard Paul Karl 1929- IntWW 93
Robberstad, James David, Jr. 1966- WhoMW 93
Robbert, Louise Buenger 1925- WhoMW 93
Robbie, Joseph 1916-1990 WhAm 10
Robbie, Timothy John 1955- WhoAm 94
Robbin, Anthony Stuart 1943- WhoAmA 93
Robbin, Tony 1943- ConAu 142, WhoAmA 93
Robbins, Aimee Carol 1953- WhoAmL 94
Robbins, Alan Ira 1953- WhoAmL 94
Robbins, Alfred S. 1925- WhoBlA 94
Robbins, Allen Bishop 1930- WhoAm 94, WhoScEn 94
Robbins, Anne Francis 1923- WhoAm 94, WhoWest 94
Robbins, Archie d1975 WhoHol 92
Robbins, Barbara WhoHol 92
Robbins, Brian WhoHol 92
Robbins, Bruce 1948- WhoAmA 93
Robbins, Chandler Seymour 1918- WhoAm 94
Robbins, Charles Dudley, III 1943- WhoWest 94
Robbins, Charles Edward 1906-1989 WhAm 10
Robbins, Charles Michael 1966- WhoScEn 94
Robbins, Cindy 1937- WhoHol 92
Robbins, Clyde W. 1926- WhoAmP 93
Robbins, Conrad W. 1921- WhoScEn 94, WhoWest 94
Robbins, Cornelius Van Vorse 1931- WhoAm 94
Robbins, Daniel 1933- WhoAm 94
Robbins, Daniel J. 1932- WhoAmA 93
Robbins, David A. 1957- WhoAmA 93
Robbins, David L. 1950- EncSF 93
Robbins, Donald Kenneth 1928- WhoFI 94
Robbins, Donald Michael 1935- WhoAm 94, WhoAmL 94
Robbins, Doren DrAPF 93
Robbins, Edith Schultz 1941- WhoAm 94
Robbins, Eugenia S. 1935- WhoAmA 93
Robbins, Frank 1917- WhoAmA 93N
Robbins, Frank Edward 1924- WhoAm 94, WhoAmL 94
Robbins, Fred Walker 1943- WhoMW 93
Robbins, Frederick C. 1916- Who 94
Robbins, Frederick Chapman 1916- IntWW 93, WhoAm 94, WhoMW 93, WhoScEn 94
Robbins, G. Arthur 1957- WhoAmL 94
Robbins, Gale d1980 WhoHol 92
Robbins, Gary 1940- WhoAmP 93
Robbins, Gary D. WhoAmP 93
Robbins, Harold 1912- WrDr 94
Robbins, Harold 1916- IntWW 93, Who 94, WhoAm 94
Robbins, Harvey Arnold 1922- WhoFI 94
Robbins, Henry Zane 1930- WhoAm 94, WhoMW 93
Robbins, Herman C. 1928- WhoBlA 94
Robbins, Hulda D. 1910- WhoAmA 93
Robbins, Hulda Dornblatt 1910- WhoAm 94
Robbins, Jack Howard 1957- WhoAmL 94, WhoWest 94
Robbins, Jackie Wayne Darmon 1940- WhoScEn 94
Robbins, James A. 1952- WhoIns 94
Robbins, James Edward 1931- WhoWest 94
Robbins, James Tate 1945- WhoFI 94
Robbins, Jane Borsch 1939- WhoAm 94
Robbins, Jane Marla WhoHol 92
Robbins, Jane Marla 1943- WrDr 94
Robbins, Jeffrey Howard 1941- WhoFI 94
Robbins, Jerome 1918- AmCulL, ConTFT 11, IntDcB [port], IntWW 93, Who 94, WhoAm 94
Robbins, Jerome David 1953- WhoMW 93
Robbins, Jerry Hal 1939- WhoAm 94
Robbins, Jessie Earl 1944- WhoScEn 94
Robbins, Joan Nash 1941- WhoAmA 93
Robbins, John Clapp 1921- WhoAm 94
Robbins, John Michael, Jr. 1947- WhoAm 94, WhoFI 94
Robbins, Joseph G. d1993 NewYTBS 93
Robbins, Kay WrDr 94
Robbins, Keith Cranston 1944- WhoScEn 94
Robbins, Keith Gilbert 1940- IntWW 93, Who 94
Robbins, Kenneth Carl 1917- WhoMW 93, WhoScEn 94
Robbins, Kenneth L. IntWW 93, WhoAm 94, WhoFI 94
Robbins, Kevin F. 1958- WhoBlA 94
Robbins, Lawrence H. 1938- ConAu 140
Robbins, Lawrence Harry 1938- WhoAm 94
Robbins, Lenore Rasmussen 1939- WhoWest 94
Robbins, Leonard 1955- WhoBlA 94
Robbins, Leroy (Southward) 1904- WhoAmA 93
Robbins, Lois WhoHol 92
Robbins, Marc d1931 WhoHol 92
Robbins, Marion Le Ron 1941- WhoScEn 94
Robbins, Martha Louise 1952- WhoMW 93
Robbins, Martin DrAPF 93
Robbins, Marty d1982 WhoHol 92
Robbins, Mary Ann 1944- WhoMW 93
Robbins, Matthew IntMPA 94
Robbins, Michael Who 94
Robbins, Michael 1930- WhoHol 92
Robbins, (Raymond Frank) Michael 1928- Who 94
Robbins, (Richard) Michael 1915- Who 94
Robbins, Millard D. 1919- WhoBlA 94
Robbins, Neville 1938- WhoWest 94
Robbins, Norman Nelson 1919- WhoAmL 94
Robbins, Orem O. 1915- WhoIns 94
Robbins, Peter 1956- WhoHol 92
Robbins, Peter Norman 1955- WhoWest 94
Robbins, Phillips Wesley 1930- WhoAm 94, WhoScEn 94
Robbins, Randall d1985 WhoHol 92
Robbins, Ray Charles 1920- WhoAm 94, WhoFI 94
Robbins, Rex WhoHol 92
Robbins, Richard DrAPF 93
Robbins, Richard d1969 WhoHol 92
Robbins, Richard 1940- IntMPA 94
Robbins, Richard Leroy, Jr. 1953- WhoMW 93
Robbins, Robert B. 1951- WhoAm 94
Robbins, Robert Dennis 1944- WhoAmP 93
Robbins, Robert J. 1924- WhoBlA 94
Robbins, Robert Marvin 1924- WhoMW 93
Robbins, Rossell Hope 1912-1990 WhAm 10
Robbins, Sara Ellen 1952- WhoAmL 94
Robbins, Sarah Ann 1955- WhoWest 94
Robbins, Sheila WhoHol 92
Robbins, Sheryl DrAPF 93
Robbins, "Skeeter" Bill d1933 WhoHol 92
Robbins, Stephen WhoAmP 93
Robbins, Stephen Douglas 1959- WhoFI 94
Robbins, Stephen J. M. 1942- WhoAmL 94, WhoWest 94
Robbins, Stuart DrAPF 93
Robbins, Thomas Owen 1937- WhoMW 93, WhoScEn 94
Robbins, Tim IntWW 93
Robbins, Tim 1958- IntMPA 94, WhoAm 94, WhoHol 92
Robbins, Tom 1936- CurBio 93 [port], IntWW 93, WhoAm 94, WrDr 94
Robbins, Trina 1938- WhoAmA 93
Robbins, Vernon Earl 1921- WhoAmL 94
Robbins, Virginia Ann 1936- WhoAmP 93
Robbins, Walt 1888- WhoHol 92
Robbins, Warren 1923- WhoBlA 94
Robbins, Warren M. 1923- WhoAmA 93
Robbins, Wayne Lindsey, Jr. 1965- WhoAmL 94
Robbins, Wendy 1960- WhoFI 94
Robblee, Richard Howard 1952- WhoWest 94
Robe, Thurlow Richard 1934- WhoAm 94
Robeck, Cecil Melvin, Jr. 1945- WhoWest 94
Robek, Mary Frances 1927- WhoAm 94
Robel, Ruth Ann 1937- WhoAmP 93
Robeling, Albin d1953 WhoHol 92
Robenalt, John Alton 1922- WhoAm 94
Robens Who 94
Robens Of Woldingham, Baron 1910- IntWW 93, Who 94
Robens of Woldingham, Lord 1910- WrDr 94
Rober, Richard d1952 WhoHol 92
Roberdeau, Daniel 1727-1795 WhAmRev
Roberg, Meir 1937- Who 94
Roberge, Fernand Adrien 1935- WhoScEn 94
Roberge, Lawrence Francis 1959- WhoScEn 94
Roberge, M. Sheila WhoAmP 93
Roberson, Alexis H. WhoWomW 91
Roberson, Alidean Slate 1927- WhoAmP 93
Roberson, Bruce H. 1941- WhoAm 94, WhoFI 94
Roberson, Charles Ed DrAPF 93
Roberson, Chuck d1988 WhoHol 92
Roberson, Dalton Anthony 1937- WhoBlA 94
Roberson, David Earle 1954- WhoFI 94
Roberson, Earl 1931- WhoBlA 94
Roberson, F. Alexis H. 1942- WhoBlA 94
Roberson, Fred O., Jr. 1947- WhoFI 94
Roberson, Gary WhoBlA 94
Roberson, Gloria Grant WhoBlA 94
Roberson, James Edward 1944- WhoWest 94
Roberson, Jennifer 1953- ConAu 41NR
Roberson, Lawrence R. 1946- WhoBlA 94
Roberson, Linda 1947- WhoAmL 94
Roberson, Lou d1966 WhoHol 92
Roberson, Nathan Russell 1930- WhoAm 94
Roberson, Patt Foster 1934- WhoAm 94
Roberson, Samuel Arndt 1939- WhoAmA 93
Roberson, Sandra Short 1950- WhoBlA 94
Roberson, William 1939- WhoAmA 93
Robert, Adrian WrDr 94
Robert, Debra Ann 1969- WhoScEn 94
Robert, Hans d1954 WhoHol 92
Robert, Henry Flood, Jr. 1943- WhoAmA 93
Robert, Jacques Frederic 1928- IntWW 93
Robert, Jean WhoAmA 93
Robert, Leslie Ladislas 1924- WhoScEn 94
Robert, Lionel 1935- WrDr 94
Robert, Louise-Felicite Guinement de Keralio 1758-1821 BlmGWL
Robert, Marie Anne Roumier 1705-1771 BlmGWL
Robert, Patricia Harrison 1939- IntMPA 94
Robert, Patrick 1937- WhoAm 94
Robert, Richard 1961- WhoWest 94
Robert, Scott Matthew 1962- WhoWest 94
Robert, Stephen 1940- WhoAm 94, WhoFI 94
Robert, William Henry, III 1945- WhoAmP 93
Robert, Yves 1920- WhoHol 92
Robert-Angelini, Enif 1886-1976 BlmGWL
Robert de Boron BlmGEL
Roberti, David A. 1939- WhoAmP 93
Roberti, Girolamo Frigimelica NewGrDO
Roberti, Lyda d1938 WhoHol 92
Roberti, Mario Andrew 1935- WhoAm 94, WhoFI 94
Robertiello, Richard C. 1923- WrDr 94
Roberto, Costantino 1700-1773 NewGrDO
Roberto, Holden IntWW 93
Roberto, Nicholas P. 1955- WhoIns 94
Roberton, Hugh Stevenson 1874-1952 DcNaB MP
Roberton, Kenneth Baillie 1895- WhAm 10
Roberts Who 94
Roberts, A. James, III 1938- WhoAmL 94
Roberts, Adam Who 94
Roberts, (Edward) Adam 1940- Who 94, WrDr 94
Roberts, Adele Marie 1941- WhoFI 94
Roberts, Alan Silverman 1939- WhoWest 94
Roberts, Albert d1941 WhoHol 92
Roberts, Albert 1908- Who 94
Roberts, Albert Roy 1944- WhoAm 94
Roberts, Alfred Lloyd, Sr. 1942- WhoBlA 94
Roberts, Alfred Wheeler, III 1938- WhoAm 94
Roberts, Allan Deverell 1950- Who 94
Roberts, Allen B. 1945- WhoAmL 94
Roberts, Allen Fraleigh 1945- WhoMW 93
Roberts, Allene 1928- WhoHol 92
Roberts, Alta Belle 1946- WhoMW 93
Roberts, Alwyn 1933- Who 94
Roberts, Amanda 1958- WhoWest 94
Roberts, Andrew 1963- WrDr 94
Roberts, Andrew Lyle 1938- Who 94
Roberts, Angela Dorrean 1960- WhoBlA 94
Roberts, Angus Thomas 1913- Who 94
Roberts, Ann Who 94
Roberts, Anna d1915 WhoHol 92
Roberts, Anthony 1940-1990 EncSF 93
Roberts, Antonette 1940- WhoMW 93
Roberts, Archibald Edward 1915- WhoWest 94
Roberts, Arnold d1986 WhoHol 92
Roberts, Arthur EncSF 93, WhoHol 92
Roberts, Arthur d1933 WhoHol 92
Roberts, Arthur Loten 1906- Who 94
Roberts, B. K. 1907- WhoAm 94, WhoAmL 94
Roberts, Barbara 1936- IntWW 93, WhoAm 94, WhoAmP 93, WhoWest 94, WhoWomW 91
Roberts, Barbara Haig Who 94
Roberts, Barbara Lea 1951- WhoAmP 93
Roberts, Bart WhoHol 92
Roberts, Benjamin d1947 WhoHol 92
Roberts, Benjamin Charles 1917- Who 94, WrDr 94
Roberts, Benjamin Titus 1823-1893 DcAmReB 2
Roberts, Bernard 1933- IntWW 93
Roberts, Bert C., Jr. 1942- WhoAm 94, WhoFI 94
Roberts, Bertie 1919- Who 94
Roberts, Betty B. 1932- WhoAmP 93
Roberts, Beverly 1914- WhoHol 92
Roberts, Beverly Nance 1954- WhoAm 94
Roberts, Beverly Randolph 1948- WhoMW 93
Roberts, Bill 1914-1978 WhoAmA 93N
Roberts, Bill Glen 1938- WhoAm 94
Roberts, Bip 1963- WhoBlA 94, WhoMW 93
Roberts, Blanche Elizabeth 1955- WhoBlA 94
Roberts, Bobby L. 1938- WhoBlA 94
Roberts, Brett WhoBlA 94
Roberts, Brian 1930- WrDr 94
Roberts, Brian Leon 1959- WhoFI 94
Roberts, Brian Michael 1957- WhoAmL 94
Roberts, Brian Stanley 1936- Who 94
Roberts, Bruce Elliott WhoAmA 93
Roberts, Bryan Clieve 1923- Who 94
Roberts, Bryndis Wynette 1957- WhoBlA 94
Roberts, Brynley Francis 1931- Who 94
Roberts, Burnell R. 1927- IntWW 93
Roberts, Burton Bennett 1922- WhoAm 94, WhoAmL 94
Roberts, C. Kenneth 1930- WhoAm 94, WhoAmL 94
Roberts, C. Patrick 1936- WhoAmP 93
Roberts, Carl Geoffrey 1948- WhoAm 94, WhoAmL 94
Roberts, Carroll Curtis 1896- WhAm 10
Roberts, Carter Dale 1944- WhoIns 94
Roberts, Catherine 1917- WrDr 94
Roberts, Cedric Kenelm 1918- Who 94
Roberts, Chalmers (McGeagh) 1910- WrDr 94
Roberts, Chalmers McGeagh 1910- IntWW 93, WhoAm 94
Roberts, Charles (Jack) d1927 WhoHol 92
Roberts, Charles Bren 1949- WhoAmL 94
Roberts, Charles G(eorge) D(ouglas) 1860-1943 EncSF 93, RfGShF
Roberts, Charles Joseph 1953- WhoAmP 93
Roberts, Charles L. 1943- WhoBlA 94
Roberts, Charles Morgan 1932- WhoWest 94
Roberts, Charles Patrick 1936- WhoAm 94, WhoMW 93
Roberts, Charles S. 1937- WhoScEn 94, WhoWest 94
Roberts, Charles W., Jr. 1962- WhoHisp 94
Roberts, Cheryl Dornita Lynn 1958- WhoBlA 94
Roberts, Chester Arthur 1948- WhoAmP 93
Roberts, Christian WhoHol 92
Roberts, Christopher William 1937- Who 94
Roberts, Cledge d1957 WhoHol 92
Roberts, Clete d1984 WhoHol 92
Roberts, Clyde Francis 1924- WhoAm 94
Roberts, Clyde Harry 1923- WhoAmA 93
Roberts, Cokie WhoAm 94
Roberts, Cokie 1943- News 93 [port]
Roberts, Colette (Jacqueline) 1910-1971 WhoAmA 93N
Roberts, Conrad WhoHol 92
Roberts, Corinne Boggs 1943- WhoAm 94
Roberts, Craige 1949- WhoMW 93
Roberts, Curtis IntMPA 94
Roberts, Curtis Bush 1933- WhoIns 94
Roberts, Dan 1912- WrDr 94
Roberts, Darryl WhoHol 92
Roberts, Darryl R. 1944- WhoAmP 93
Roberts, David WhoHol 92
Roberts, David Diehl 1918- WhoFI 94
Roberts, David Earl 1923- WhoAmP 93

Roberts, David Ewart 1921- Who 94
Roberts, David Francis 1941- Who 94
Roberts, David Glendenning 1928- WhoAm 94, WhoAmL 94, WhoAmP 93
Roberts, David Harrill 1944- WhoAm 94
Roberts, David Lowell 1954- WhoWest 94
Roberts, David Michael 1931- Who 94
Roberts, Davis WhoHol 92
Roberts, Davis d1993 NewYTBS 93
Roberts, Dawn C. 1941- WhoAmP 93
Roberts, Dellas Vernon 1934- WhoFI 94
Roberts, Denis Edwin 1917- Who 94
Roberts, Dennis William 1943- WhoWest 94
Roberts, Denys (Tudor Emil) 1923- Who 94, WrDr 94
Roberts, Denys Tudor Emil 1923- IntWW 93
Roberts, Derek Franklyn 1942- Who 94
Roberts, Derek Harry 1931- WrDr 94
Roberts, Derek Harry 1932- IntWW 93, Who 94
Roberts, Desmond d1968 WhoHol 92
Roberts, Dick d1966 WhoHol 92
Roberts, Don E. 1934- WhoFI 94
Roberts, Donald 1923- WhoAmA 93
Roberts, Donald Albert 1935- WhoAm 94, WhoFI 94
Roberts, Donald Duane 1929- WhoAmP 93
Roberts, Donald John 1945- WhoAm 94
Roberts, Donald Lee 1929- WhoBlA 94
Roberts, Donald Munier 1935- WhoAm 94
Roberts, Donna Joyce 1935- WhoAm 94
Roberts, Dora Sandlin 1939- WhoAmL 94
Roberts, Doris 1930- WhoAm 94, WhoHol 92
Roberts, Doris Emma 1915- WhoAm 94
Roberts, Dorothy d1993 NewYTBS 93
Roberts, Douglas B. WhoMW 93
Roberts, Dwight Loren 1949- WhoFI 94, WhoWest 94
Roberts, E. F. 1930- WhoAm 94
Roberts, Earl John 1913- WhoScEn 94
Roberts, Earlene WhoAmP 93
Roberts, Edd J. d1953 WhoHol 92
Roberts, Edgar 1946- WhoBlA 94
Roberts, Edith d1935 WhoHol 92
Roberts, Edward A. 1950- WhoBlA 94
Roberts, Edward Baer 1935- WhoAm 94, WhoFI 94, WhoScEn 94
Roberts, Edward Calhoun 1937- WhoAm 94, WhoAmL 94, WhoAmP 93
Roberts, Edward Eric 1911- Who 94
Roberts, Edward Graham WhoAm 94
Roberts, Edward James Keymer 1908- Who 94
Roberts, Edward Verne 1939- WhoWest 94
Roberts, Edwin Albert, Jr. 1932- WhoAm 94
Roberts, Eirlys Rhiwen Cadwaladr 1911- Who 94
Roberts, Elizabeth Madox BlmGWL
Roberts, Ella S. 1927- WhoBlA 94
Roberts, Elliott C., Sr. 1927- WhoAm 94
Roberts, Elton Neal 1928- WhoWest 94
Roberts, Enoch G. 1940- WhoIns 94
Roberts, Eric 1914- WrDr 94
Roberts, Eric 1956- IntMPA 94, WhoAm 94, WhoHol 92
Roberts, Eric Matthias 1914- Who 94
Roberts, Eric Stenius 1952- WhoScEn 94
Roberts, Ernest Alfred Cecil 1912- Who 94
Roberts, Ernst Edward 1926- WhoAm 94
Roberts, Evelyn d1962 WhoHol 92
Roberts, Ewan 1914- WhoHol 92
Roberts, Florence d1927 WhoHol 92
Roberts, Florence d1940 WhoHol 92
Roberts, Florence Smythe WhoHol 92
Roberts, Frances Cabaniss 1916- WhoAm 94
Roberts, Francis Donald 1938- WhoAm 94
Roberts, Francis Joseph 1918- WhoAm 94
Roberts, Francis Joy 1931- WhoAm 94
Roberts, Francis Stone 1944- WhoAm 94, WhoFI 94
Roberts, Frank (Kenyon) 1907- Who 94
Roberts, Frank Kenyon 1907- IntWW 93
Roberts, Frank Lester 1895- WhAm 10
Roberts, Frank Livezey 1915- WhoAmP 93
Roberts, Fred Clark 1943- WhoMW 93
Roberts, Fred T. 1941- WhoIns 94
Roberts, Gareth Gwyn 1940- Who 94
Roberts, Gary 1947- WhoAmL 94
Roberts, Gemma 1929- WhoHisp 94
Roberts, Gene WhoAmP 93
Roberts, Geoffrey Frank Ingleson 1926- Who 94
Roberts, Geoffrey Newland 1906- Who 94
Roberts, Geoffrey P. H. Who 94
Roberts, George DrAPF 93
Roberts, George d1930 WhoHol 92
Roberts, George A. 1919- IntWW 93
Roberts, George Adam 1919- WhoFI 94
Roberts, George Arnott 1930- Who 94
Roberts, George Bernard, Jr. 1939- WhoAm 94
Roberts, George Christopher 1936- WhoFI 94, WhoWest 94
Roberts, George Harrison 1944- WhoIns 94
Roberts, George R. WhoAm 94, WhoFI 94, WhoWest 94
Roberts, Gilbert 1899-1978 DcNaB MP
Roberts, Gilbert (Howland Rookehurst) 1934- Who 94
Roberts, Gilbert B. 1941- WhoAm 94
Roberts, Gillian DrAPF 93
Roberts, Gillian Frances 1944- Who 94
Roberts, Gilroy WhoAmA 93
Roberts, Glen d1974 WhoHol 92
Roberts, Glenn Dale 1943- WhoMW 93
Roberts, Godwin 1939- WhoScEn 94
Roberts, Gordon (James) 1921- Who 94
Roberts, Grady H., Jr. 1940- WhoBlA 94
Roberts, Granville Oral 1918- WhoAm 94
Roberts, Gwilym Who 94
Roberts, (David) Gwilym (Morris) 1925- Who 94
Roberts, Gwilym Edffrwd 1928- Who 94
Roberts, Hans d1954 WhoHol 92
Roberts, Harlan William, III 1931- WhoBlA 94
Roberts, Harold Ross 1930- WhoAm 94, WhoScEn 94
Roberts, Harry Morris, Jr. 1938- WhoAm 94, WhoAmL 94, WhoFI 94
Roberts, Harry Vivian 1923- WhoAm 94
Roberts, Haynes R. 1950- WhoAmL 94
Roberts, Helene Emylou 1931- WhoAmA 93
Roberts, Henry Reginald 1916- WhoAm 94
Roberts, Herbert Ray 1913-1992 AnObit 1992
Roberts, Herman 1924- WhoBlA 94
Roberts, Hermese E. 1913- WhoBlA 94
Roberts, Holly L. 1951- WhoAmA 93
Roberts, Howard Nick 1939- WhoWest 94
Roberts, Howard Richard 1932- WhoScEn 94
Roberts, Hugh Eifion Pritchard 1927- Who 94
Roberts, Hugh Evan 1923- WhoAm 94
Roberts, Hugh Martin P. Who 94
Roberts, Hyman Jacob 1924- WhoAm 94, WhoScEn 94
Roberts, I. M. 1925- WrDr 94
Roberts, Ian White 1927- Who 94
Roberts, Iolo Francis 1925- WrDr 94
Roberts, Irene 1925- WrDr 94
Roberts, Ivor 1925- WrDr 94
Roberts, Ivor Anthony 1946- Who 94
Roberts, J. H. d1961 WhoHol 92
Roberts, J. R. 1951- WrDr 94
Roberts, J. Wendell 1943- WhoAm 94, WhoAmL 94
Roberts, J. William 1942- WhoAm 94
Roberts, Jack d1980 WhoHol 92
Roberts, Jack Earl 1928- WhoAmP 93
Roberts, Jack Earle 1928- WhoAm 94
Roberts, Jacqueline Johnson 1944- WhoAmP 93, WhoBlA 94
Roberts, James Allen 1934- WhoAm 94
Roberts, James Allen 1947- WhoMW 93
Roberts, James C. 1945- WhoAmL 94
Roberts, James Carl 1953- WhoFI 94, WhoWest 94
Roberts, James Cleveland 1946- WhoAm 94
Roberts, James D(eotis, Sr.) 1927- WrDr 94
Roberts, James E. 1903- WhoBlA 94
Roberts, James E. 1938- WhoIns 94
Roberts, James G. 1922- WhoAm 94
Roberts, James H. 1932- WhoAmP 93
Roberts, James H. 1944- WhoAmL 94
Roberts, James Hall 1927- WrDr 94
Roberts, James Harold, III 1949- WhoAm 94
Roberts, James Hazelton 1925- WhoAmP 93
Roberts, James Lamar, Jr. 1945- WhoAmP 93
Roberts, James Lewis 1951- WhoScEn 94
Roberts, James McGregor 1923- WhoAm 94, WhoWest 94
Roberts, James Milnor, Jr. 1918- WhoAm 94
Roberts, James Owen 1930- WhoAm 94, WhoFI 94
Roberts, James Stanley 1954- WhoAmL 94
Roberts, James Thomas 1965- WhoAmP 93
Roberts, James William 1928- WhoAmP 93
Roberts, Jane Who 94
Roberts, Jane 1929-1984 EncSF 93
Roberts, (Priscilla) Jane (Stephanie) 1949- Who 94
Roberts, Janet DrAPF 93
Roberts, Janet Louise 1925- WhAm 10
Roberts, Janice L. 1959- WhoBlA 94
Roberts, Jay 1927- WhoAm 94
Roberts, Jean Reed 1939- WhoAmL 94, WhoWest 94
Roberts, Jeanne Addison WhoAm 94
Roberts, Jeremy Michael Graham 1941- Who 94
Roberts, Jim 1938- WhoAmP 93
Roberts, Jo Ann Wooden 1948- WhoMW 93
Roberts, Joan I. WhoAm 94
Roberts, Joan Ila 1935- WrDr 94
Roberts, Joetta Karen 1949- WhoMW 93
Roberts, John ConAu 42NR, EncSF 93, Who 94
Roberts, John c. 1853-1949 EncNAR
Roberts, (Anthony) John 1944- Who 94
Roberts, (David) John 1919- Who 94
Roberts, (Herbert) John 1919- Who 94
Roberts, John Anthony 1928- Who 94
Roberts, John Arthur 1917- Who 94
Roberts, John B. 1912- WhoBlA 94
Roberts, John Benjamin, II 1955- WhoAm 94
Roberts, John C(urtis) 1895- WhAm 10
Roberts, John Charles Quentin 1933- Who 94
Roberts, John Christopher 1944- WhoBlA 94
Roberts, John D. 1918- IntWW 93, WhoAm 94, WhoScEn 94, WhoWest 94
Roberts, John Derham 1942- WhoAm 94, WhoAmL 94, WhoWest 94
Roberts, John Edward 1946- Who 94
Roberts, John Eric 1907- Who 94
Roberts, John Frederick 1913- Who 94
Roberts, John Glover, Jr. 1955- WhoAm 94, WhoAmL 94
Roberts, John Harvey Polmear 1935- Who 94
Roberts, John Herbert 1933- Who 94
Roberts, John Houghton 1947- Who 94
Roberts, John J. 1946- WhoAm 94, WhoFI 94
Roberts, John Joseph 1922- WhoAm 94, WhoIns 94
Roberts, John Kenneth, Jr. 1936- WhoAm 94, WhoFI 94, WhoIns 94
Roberts, John Laing 1939- Who 94
Roberts, John Lewis 1928- Who 94
Roberts, John Maddox 1947- EncSF 93
Roberts, John Milton 1916-1990 WhAm 10
Roberts, John Morris 1928- IntWW 93, Who 94, WrDr 94
Roberts, John Oliver 1924- Who 94
Roberts, John Peter Lee 1930- WhoAm 94
Roberts, John S., Jr. 1938- WhoAmL 94
Roberts, John Todd d1979 WhoHol 92
Roberts, John William 1925- WhoWest 94
Roberts, Joseph d1923 WhoHol 92
Roberts, Joseph J., Jr. 1952- WhoAmP 93
Roberts, Judith L. L. 1939- WhoAmL 94
Roberts, Julia 1967- IntMPA 94, IntWW 93, WhoAm 94, WhoHol 92
Roberts, Julian Who 94
Roberts, (Richard) Julian 1930- Who 94
Roberts, Julie Ann 1965- WhoMW 93
Roberts, Kathleen Anne WhoAm 94
Roberts, Kathryn Dolliver 1942- WhoAmP 93
Roberts, Kay George 1950- AfrAmAl 6, WhoBlA 94
Roberts, Keith (John Kingston) 1935- EncSF 93, WrDr 94
Roberts, Keith Edward, Sr. 1928- WhoAmL 94, WhoMW 93
Roberts, Kenneth Allison 1912-1989 WhAm 10
Roberts, Kenneth Barris 1954- WhoAmL 94
Roberts, Kenneth E., Jr. 1944- WhoAmL 94
Roberts, Kenneth Lewis 1932- WhoAm 94
Roberts, Kevin 1940- WrDr 94
Roberts, Kevin Thomas 1957- WhoAmL 94
Roberts, Kim DrAPF 93
Roberts, Kim A. 1957- WhoBlA 94
Roberts, Larry 1934- WhoMW 93
Roberts, Larry D. 1946- WhoAmP 93
Roberts, Larry Paul 1950- WhoAm 94, WhoWest 94
Roberts, Larry Spurgeon 1935- WhoAm 94
Roberts, Lawrence 1941- WhoAmP 93
Roberts, Lawrence Darrell 1963- WhoAmL 94
Roberts, Lawrence R. 1955- WhoAmP 93
Roberts, Leigh Milton 1925- WhoAm 94, WhoMW 93, WhoScEn 94
Roberts, Len DrAPF 93
Roberts, Lenore d1978 WhoHol 92
Roberts, Leon Joseph, III 1963- WhoAm 94, WhoBlA 94
Roberts, Leona d1954 WhoHol 92
Roberts, Leonard H. 1949- WhoAm 94, WhoFI 94
Roberts, Lewis Edward John 1922- IntWW 93, Who 94
Roberts, Lewis H. WhoIns 94
Roberts, Lillian 1928- WhoBlA 94
Roberts, Liona Russell, Jr. 1928- WhoScEn 94, WhoWest 94
Roberts, Lionel EncSF 93
Roberts, Lois 1941- WhoHol 92
Roberts, Lonnie 1937- WhoAmP 93
Roberts, Lorin Watson 1923- WhoAm 94, WhoScEn 94, WhoWest 94
Roberts, Lorraine Marie 1930- WhoBlA 94
Roberts, Louis Douglas 1918- WhoAm 94, WhoScEn 94
Roberts, Louis Wright 1913- WhoAm 94, WhoBlA 94
Roberts, Louise Nisbet 1919- WhoAm 94
Roberts, Luanne WhoHol 92
Roberts, Lucille D. (Malkia) WhoAmA 93
Roberts, Lynn Springer 1943- WhoAm 94
Roberts, Lynne d1978 WhoHol 92
Roberts, M. Caldwell 1939- WhoAmL 94
Roberts, Malcolm Blair 1936- WhoAmP 93
Roberts, Malcolm John 1942- WhoScEn 94
Roberts, Margaret Harold 1928- WhoAm 94
Roberts, Margaret Mills 1936- WhoBlA 94
Roberts, Margaret Rose 1957- WhoAmL 94
Roberts, Margaret Ward 1934- WhoBlA 94
Roberts, Margie Lee Stewart 1927- WhoAmP 93
Roberts, Marie Dyer 1943- WhoFI 94, WhoScEn 94, WhoWest 94
Roberts, Mark WhoHol 92
Roberts, Mark Owen 1911- WhoIns 94
Roberts, Mark Scott 1951- WhoAmL 94, WhoWest 94
Roberts, Marke G. 1961- WhoMW 93
Roberts, Markley 1930- WhoAm 94
Roberts, Mary Linda 1944- WhoAmP 93
Roberts, Mary Lou 1950- WhoScEn 94
Roberts, Meade WhoHol 92
Roberts, Melville Parker, Jr. 1931- WhoAm 94, WhoScEn 94
Roberts, Merrill Joseph 1915- WhoAm 94
Roberts, Michael 1908- IntWW 93, Who 94, WrDr 94
Roberts, Michael D. WhoHol 92
Roberts, Michael J. 1944- WhoAmL 94
Roberts, Michael James 1936- WhoAm 94, WhoAmL 94
Roberts, Michael V. 1948- WhoBlA 94
Roberts, Michael Victor 1948- WhoAmP 93
Roberts, Michele 1949- BlmGEL, BlmGWL [port]
Roberts, Michele (Brigitte) 1949- EncSF 93
Roberts, Morris Henry, Jr. 1940- WhoAm 94
Roberts, Morton 1927-1964 WhoAmA 93N
Roberts, Morton Spitz 1926- WhoAm 94
Roberts, Nancy d1962 WhoHol 92
Roberts, Nancy 1938- WhoAm 94
Roberts, Nancy Correll 1924- WrDr 94
Roberts, Nancy Lee 1954- WhoMW 93
Roberts, Narlie 1931- WhoBlA 94
Roberts, Nathan Jay 1906- WhoWest 94
Roberts, Ned d1973 WhoHol 92
Roberts, Neil Fletcher 1914- WhoAm 94
Roberts, Nora 1950- WrDr 94
Roberts, Norbert Joseph 1916- WhAm 10
Roberts, Norman Frank 1931- WhoWest 94
Roberts, Norman Leslie 1935- WhoAmL 94
Roberts, Norman Stafford d1993 Who 94N
Roberts, Oral 1918- WhoAm 94
Roberts, Owen L. 1945- WhoAmL 94
Roberts, Owen W. 1924- WhoAmP 93
Roberts, P. Elaine 1944- WhoWest 94
Roberts, Paquita Hudson 1938- WhoBlA 94
Roberts, Pascale WhoHol 92
Roberts, Pat 1936- CngDr 93
Roberts, Patrick John 1942- Who 94
Roberts, Patrick Kent 1948- WhoMW 93
Roberts, Patrick Scott 1965- WhoMW 93
Roberts, Paul Craig 1939- WhoAmP 93
Roberts, Paul Craig, III 1939- WhoAm 94
Roberts, Paul Harry 1929- IntWW 93, Who 94
Roberts, Paul William 1950- ConAu 141
Roberts, Paula WrDr 94
Roberts, Percival R. 1935- WhoAmA 93N
Roberts, Percy Charles 1920- Who 94
Roberts, Pernell 1928- WhoHol 92
Roberts, Pernell 1930- IntMPA 94
Roberts, Peter DrAPF 93

Roberts, Peter A. 1951- *WhoAm 94, WhoFI 94*
Roberts, Peter Christopher Tudor 1945- *WhoScEn 94, WhoWest 94*
Roberts, Peter S. 1937- *WhoIns 94*
Roberts, Philip *Who 94*
Roberts, (George) Philip (Bradley) 1906- *Who 94*
Roberts, Philip Bedlington 1921- *Who 94*
Roberts, Philip Davies 1938- *WrDr 94*
Roberts, Philip John 1948- *WhoWest 94*
Roberts, Phyllida Katharine S. *Who 94*
Roberts, Priscilla Warren 1916- *WhoAm 94, WhoAmA 93*
Roberts, Rachel d1980 *WhoHol 92*
Roberts, Ralph d1944 *WhoHol 92*
Roberts, Ralph 1922- *WhoHol 92*
Roberts, Ralph Arthur d1940 *WhoHol 92*
Roberts, Ralph Joel 1920- *WhoAm 94, WhoFI 94*
Roberts, Randall E. 1953- *WhoAmL 94*
Roberts, Randolph *WhoHol 92*
Roberts, Randolph Wilson 1946- *WhoScEn 94*
Roberts, Randy (W.) 1951- *WrDr 94*
Roberts, Raymond Harcourt 1931- *Who 94*
Roberts, Rhonda *WhoAmP 93*
Roberts, Richard 1925- *WhoAmA 93*
Roberts, Richard 1938- *WhoScEn 94*
Roberts, Richard (David Hallam) 1931- *Who 94*
Roberts, Richard Douglas 1916- *Who 94*
Roberts, Richard Frederick Anthony 1932- *IntWW 93, Who 94*
Roberts, Richard Heilbron 1925- *WhoAm 94, WhoFI 94*
Roberts, Richard James 1922- *WhoAm 94*
Roberts, Richard John 1943- *WhoScEn 94*
Roberts, Richard Stewart 1945- *WhoAm 94*
Roberts, Robert, III 1930- *WhoAmL 94*
Roberts, Robert Cantwell 1935- *WhoWest 94*
Roberts, Robert Chadwick 1947- *WhoScEn 94*
Roberts, Robert Clark 1946- *WhoScEn 94*
Roberts, Robert Evan 1912- *Who 94*
Roberts, Robert Richard, III 1944- *WhoIns 94*
Roberts, Robert Thaddeus, Jr. 1952- *WhoAmL 94, WhoFI 94*
Roberts, Robert Winston 1932- *WhoAm 94*
Roberts, Robin 1960- *WhoBlA 94*
Roberts, Robin Wendell 1959- *WhoFI 94*
Roberts, Roger P. 1948- *WhoIns 94*
Roberts, Ron *WhoAmP 93*
Roberts, Ronald John 1941- *Who 94*
Roberts, Rosemary *DrAPF 93*
Roberts, Roy d1975 *WhoHol 92*
Roberts, Roy Ernest James d1993 *Who 94N*
Roberts, Roy Ernest James 1928- *IntWW 93*
Roberts, Roy J. 1940- *WhoBlA 94*
Roberts, Roy S. *WhoBlA 94*
Roberts, Ruby Altizer 1907- *WhoAm 94*
Roberts, Russell Hill 1937- *WhoAmL 94*
Roberts, Ruth *WhoHol 92*
Roberts, Sally 1935- *WrDr 94*
Roberts, Sally-Ann 1953- *WhoBlA 94*
Roberts, Samuel 1948- *Who 94*
Roberts, Samuel Alden 1930- *WhoMW 93*
Roberts, Samuel Kelton 1944- *WhoBlA 94*
Roberts, Samuel Smith 1936- *WhoAm 94*
Roberts, Sandra 1951- *WhoAm 94*
Roberts, Sandra Brown 1939- *WhoFI 94*
Roberts, Sara Jane d1968 *WhoHol 92*
Roberts, Scott 1961- *WhoAmL 94*
Roberts, Scott 1965- *WhoMW 93*
Roberts, Seymour M. 1934- *WhoAm 94*
Roberts, Sheila *DrAPF 93*
Roberts, Sheila 1937- *BlmGWL*
Roberts, Sherron Killingsworth 1957- *WhoMW 93*
Roberts, Sidney *Who 94*
Roberts, Sidney 1918- *WhoAm 94*
Roberts, (Edward Fergus) Sidney 1901- *Who 94*
Roberts, Sidney I. 1913- *WhoAm 94*
Roberts, Stanley Corvet 1970- *WhoBlA 94*
Roberts, Stephen d1982 *WhoHol 92*
Roberts, Stephen (James Leake) 1915- *Who 94*
Roberts, Stephen Pritchard 1949- *Who 94*
Roberts, Stephen Wandless 1939- *WhoAmP 93*
Roberts, Steven C. 1952- *WhoAmP 93, WhoBlA 94*
Roberts, Steven K. 1954- *WhoAmA 93*
Roberts, Steven L. 1952- *WhoAmL 94*
Roberts, Steven Victor 1943- *WhoAm 94*
Roberts, Susan 1945- *WhoAmL 94*
Roberts, Susan Ellen 1949- *WhoMW 93*
Roberts, Talmadge 1931- *WhoBlA 94*
Roberts, Tanya 1954- *WhoHol 92*
Roberts, Ted Blake 1952- *WhoAmP 93*
Roberts, Terence 1911-1973 *EncSF 93*
Roberts, Terrence James 1941- *WhoBlA 94*
Roberts, Thayer d1968 *WhoHol 92*
Roberts, Theodore d1928 *WhoHol 92*
Roberts, Theodore Harris 1929- *WhoAm 94, WhoMW 93*
Roberts, Thomas Carrol 1947- *WhoScEn 94*
Roberts, Thomas G. 1949- *WhoAm 94*
Roberts, Thomas George 1929- *WhoScEn 94*
Roberts, Thomas L. 1932- *WhoBlA 94*
Roberts, Thomas Michael 1952- *WhoAmP 93*
Roberts, Thomas Raymond 1947- *WhoAmL 94*
Roberts, Thomas Somerville 1911- *Who 94*
Roberts, Tom *WhoHol 92*
Roberts, Tom 1908- *WhoAmA 93*
Roberts, Tommy Ed 1940- *WhoAmP 93*
Roberts, Tony 1939- *IntMPA 94, WhoAm 94, WhoHol 92*
Roberts, Tracey *WhoHol 92*
Roberts, Trev 1925- *WrDr 94*
Roberts, Trish *WhoBlA 94*
Roberts, Tudy 1882-1957 *EncNAR*
Roberts, Victor 1944- *WhoAmL 94*
Roberts, Victoria Heintzelman 1950- *WhoAmL 94*
Roberts, Violet Kent 1880- *WhoAmA 93N*
Roberts, Virgil Dean 1922- *WhoAmP 93*
Roberts, Virgil Patrick 1947- *WhoAm 94, WhoBlA 94*
Roberts, Walter Arthur 1955- *WhoScEn 94*
Roberts, Walter Herbert Beatty 1915- *WhoAm 94*
Roberts, Walter Lenn 1962- *WhoAmP 93*
Roberts, Walter Orr 1915-1990 *WhAm 10*
Roberts, Walter Ronald 1916- *WhoAm 94*
Roberts, Warren Errol 1933- *WhoAm 94*
Roberts, Warren Hoyle, Jr. 1955- *WhoScEn 94*
Roberts, Wayne 1906- *WrDr 94*
Roberts, Wesley A. 1938- *WhoBlA 94*
Roberts, Wilbur Eugene 1942- *WhoMW 93, WhoScEn 94*
Roberts, Wilfred d1954 *WhoHol 92*
Roberts, William *IntMPA 94*
Roberts, William, Jr. 1942- *WhoAmL 94*
Roberts, William (James Denby) 1936- *Who 94*
Roberts, William B. 1939- *WhoAm 94*
Roberts, William Bailey 1950- *WhoAmL 94*
Roberts, William Edward 1941- *WhoAmA 93*
Roberts, William Everett 1926- *WhoAm 94*
Roberts, William H. 1945- *WhoIns 94*
Roberts, William Harrison 1921- *WhoWest 94*
Roberts, William Hugh 1917- *WhoAmP 93*
Roberts, William Hugh, III 1936- *WhoAm 94*
Roberts, William James Cynfab 1938- *WhoScEn 94*
Roberts, William L. 1891-1968 *HisDcKW*
Roberts, William Richard 1936- *WhoWest 94*
Roberts, Willo Davis 1928- *TwCYAW, WrDr 94*
Roberts, Wyn *Who 94*
Roberts, (Ieuan) Wyn (Pritchard) 1930- *Who 94*
Roberts, Y. Carol 1941- *WhoAmP 93*
Roberts-DeGennaro, Maria 1947- *WhoWest 94*
Robertshaw, Jerrold d1941 *WhoHol 92*
Roberts-Jones, Ivor 1913- *IntWW 93, Who 94*
Roberts-Lindsey, Carol Annette 1958- *WhoWest 94*
Robertson *Who 94*
Robertson, Hon. Lord 1912- *Who 94*
Robertson, A. Haeworth 1930- *WhoAm 94*
Robertson, Abel L., Jr. 1926- *WhoAm 94, WhoMW 93, WhoScEn 94*
Robertson, Adrian Andrew 1939- *WhoFI 94*
Robertson, Agnes *DrAPF 93*
Robertson, Alan 1920- *Who 94*
Robertson, Alan D. 1958- *WhoBlA 94*
Robertson, Alan S. 1941- *WhoAmP 93*
Robertson, Alexander, IV 1959- *WhoAmL 94, WhoWest 94*
Robertson, Alvin 1962- *BasBi*
Robertson, Alvin Cyrrale 1962- *WhoAm 94, WhoBlA 94, WhoMW 93*
Robertson, Andre *NewYTBS 93 [port]*
Robertson, Andre Levett 1957- *WhoBlA 94*
Robertson, Ann Eliza Worcester 1826-1905 *EncNAR*
Robertson, Anne Strachan *Who 94*
Robertson, Armand James, II 1937- *WhoAm 94*
Robertson, Barbara Anne 1931- *WrDr 94*
Robertson, Benjamin W. 1931- *WhoBlA 94*
Robertson, Beverly Carruth 1922- *WhoAm 94*
Robertson, Billy O'Neal 1930- *WhoAm 94*
Robertson, Bob Walter 1922- *WhoAmL 94*
Robertson, Brenda 1929- *WhoWomW 91*
Robertson, Brian
See Motorhead *ConMus 10*
Robertson, Brian Paul *DrAPF 93*
Robertson, Bryan Charles Francis 1925- *Who 94*
Robertson, C. Alton 1933- *WhoWest 94*
Robertson, Charles 1940- *Who 94*
Robertson, Charles Garland 1942- *WhoAm 94*
Robertson, Charles J. 1934- *WhoAmA 93*
Robertson, Charles Martin 1911- *Who 94*
Robertson, Charles Robert Suttie 1920- *Who 94*
Robertson, Cliff 1925- *IntMPA 94, WhoAm 94, WhoHol 92*
Robertson, Clifford Houston 1912- *WhoScEn 94*
Robertson, Dale 1923- *IntMPA 94, WhoHol 92*
Robertson, Dale 1954- *WhoAmP 93*
Robertson, Daniel Carlton 1951- *WhoWest 94*
Robertson, Daphne Jean Black 1937- *Who 94*
Robertson, Daryl Bruce 1954- *WhoAmL 94*
Robertson, David 1947- *WhoAm 94, WhoScEn 94*
Robertson, David Byres 1960- *WhoAmP 93*
Robertson, David Govan 1947- *WhoAm 94, WhoAmL 94*
Robertson, David Lars Manwaring 1917- *Who 94*
Robertson, David Werner 1955- *WhoAmP 93*
Robertson, Dawn Smith 1960- *WhoBlA 94*
Robertson, Dennis *WhoHol 92*
Robertson, Donald B. 1931- *WhoAmP 93*
Robertson, Donald Buchanan 1932- *Who 94*
Robertson, Doris S. *WhoHol 92*
Robertson, Douglas William d1993 *Who 94N*
Robertson, Durant Waite 1914-1992 *AnObit 1992*
Robertson, Durant Waite, Jr. 1914-1992 *WhAm 10*
Robertson, E(ileen) Arnot 1903-1961 *EncSF 93*
Robertson, E. Bruce 1955- *WhoAmA 93*
Robertson, Edward D. 1930- *WhoAmP 93*
Robertson, Edward D., Jr. 1952- *WhoAm 94, WhoAmL 94, WhoAmP 93, WhoMW 93*
Robertson, Edward Neil 1950- *WhoMW 93*
Robertson, Edwin (Hanton) 1912- *WrDr 94*
Robertson, Edwin David 1946- *WhoAm 94, WhoAmL 94, WhoFI 94*
Robertson, Elgin Barnett 1893- *WhAm 10*
Robertson, Elspeth 1928- *WrDr 94*
Robertson, Erle Shervinton 1962- *WhoScEn 94*
Robertson, Evelyn Crawford, Jr. 1941- *WhoBlA 94*
Robertson, Florence Winkler 1945- *WhoMW 93*
Robertson, Frances Jean d1942 *WhoHol 92*
Robertson, Garland L. *NewYTBS 93 [port]*
Robertson, Geoffrey Ronald 1946- *Who 94*
Robertson, George Beryl, Jr. 1943- *WhoFI 94*
Robertson, George Islay Macneill 1946- *Who 94*
Robertson, George Leonard 1922- *WhoAm 94*
Robertson, George Leven 1921- *WhoAm 94*
Robertson, George R. *WhoHol 92*
Robertson, Gertrude 1924- *WhoBlA 94*
Robertson, Graeme Alan 1945- *Who 94*
Robertson, Gregg Westland 1934- *WhoAm 94*
Robertson, Hamish 1931- *Who 94*
Robertson, Heather 1942- *BlmGWL*
Robertson, Henry 1816-1888 *DcNaB MP*
Robertson, Herbert Chapman, Jr. 1928- *WhoFI 94*
Robertson, Horace Bascomb, Jr. 1923- *WhoAm 94*
Robertson, Horace C. H. 1894-1960 *HisDcKW*
Robertson, Howard W. *DrAPF 93*
Robertson, Hugh Duff 1957- *WhoAm 94, WhoAmL 94, WhoWest 94*
Robertson, Iain Samuel 1945- *Who 94*
Robertson, Ian (Campbell) 1928- *WrDr 94*
Robertson, Ian George William 1922- *Who 94*
Robertson, Ian Gordon 1943- *Who 94*
Robertson, Ian Macdonald *Who 94*
Robertson, Imogene d1948 *WhoHol 92*
Robertson, Ivan Denzil, III 1951- *WhoScEn 94*
Robertson, J. Francis d1942 *WhoHol 92*
Robertson, J.R. *EncSF 93*
Robertson, Jack Clark 1943- *WhoAm 94*
Robertson, Jacqueline Lee 1947- *WhoWest 94*
Robertson, James *WhoHol 92*
Robertson, James d1936 *WhoHol 92*
Robertson, James 1717-1788 *AmRev*
Robertson, James c. 1720-1788 *WhAmRev*
Robertson, James 1740-c. 1812 *WhAmRev*
Robertson, James 1742-1814 *WhAmRev, WhWE*
Robertson, James c. 1751-1818 *WhAmRev*
Robertson, James 1912-1991 *NewGrDO*
Robertson, James 1938- *WhoAmL 94*
Robertson, James Alexander Rowland 1910- *Who 94*
Robertson, James Allen 1948- *WhoAmL 94, WhoFI 94*
Robertson, James B. 1940- *WhoBlA 94*
Robertson, James Cole 1929- *WhoFI 94*
Robertson, James Colvert 1932- *WhoAm 94, WhoFI 94*
Robertson, James David 1922- *WhoAm 94*
Robertson, James Downie 1931- *Who 94*
Robertson, James Erbie 1954- *WhoMW 93*
Robertson, James Geddes 1910- *Who 94*
Robertson, James I., Jr. 1930- *WrDr 94*
Robertson, James Irvin, Jr. 1930- *WhoAm 94*
Robertson, James L. 1940- *WhoAm 94*
Robertson, James Lawton 1940- *WhoAmP 93*
Robertson, James Mueller 1916- *WhoScEn 94*
Robertson, James Smith 1917- *Who 94*
Robertson, Jaquelin Taylor 1933- *WhoAm 94*
Robertson, Jean d1967 *WhoHol 92*
Robertson, Jean 1928- *Who 94*
Robertson, Jeffrey D. 1946- *WhoAm 94*
Robertson, Jenny *WhoHol 92*
Robertson, Jerry Earl 1932- *WhoAm 94*
Robertson, Jerry Lewis 1933- *WhoScEn 94*
Robertson, Jewell Lewis 1911- *WhoFI 94*
Robertson, Joan E. 1942- *WhoAmA 93*
Robertson, John Anderson 1931- *WhoAmP 93*
Robertson, John Archibald Law 1925- *WhoAm 94*
Robertson, John Bernard 1940- *WhoMW 93*
Robertson, John Carnegie 1917- *Who 94*
Robertson, John David H. *Who 94*
Robertson, John Francis 1949- *WhoMW 93*
Robertson, John Gilbert 1932-1992 *WhoBlA 94N*
Robertson, John Harvey 1941- *WhoScEn 94*
Robertson, John Keith 1926- *Who 94*
Robertson, John Patrick 1951- *WhoMW 93*
Robertson, John S. d1964 *WhoHol 92*
Robertson, John Windeler 1934- *Who 94*
Robertson, Joseph David 1944- *WhoAm 94*
Robertson, Joseph Edmond 1918- *WhoFI 94, WhoMW 93*
Robertson, Joseph Martin 1952- *WhoAmL 94*
Robertson, Julia Ann *Who 94*
Robertson, Karen A. *WhoBlA 94*
Robertson, Karen Lee 1955- *WhoWest 94*
Robertson, Keith (Carlton) 1914-1991 *TwCYAW, WrDr 94N*
Robertson, Kenneth McLeod 1957- *WhoScEn 94*
Robertson, Kimmy *WhoHol 92*
Robertson, Kirk *DrAPF 93*
Robertson, Larry Wayne 1947- *WhoScEn 94*
Robertson, Laurie Luissa 1960- *WhoScEn 94*
Robertson, Lawrence Marshall 1900-1988 *WhAm 10*
Robertson, Lawrence Marshall, Jr. 1932- *WhoWest 94*
Robertson, Leon H. 1934- *WhoAm 94*
Robertson, Leslie Earl 1928- *WhoAm 94*
Robertson, Lewis 1922- *IntWW 93, Who 94*
Robertson, Linda Lou 1940- *WhoAmL 94*

Robertson, Linwood Righter 1940-
WhoAm 94
Robertson, Lucretia Speziale 1944-
WhoAm 94
Robertson, Lynn E. 1921- WhoBlA 94
Robertson, Lynne Marie 1945- WhoFI 94
Robertson, Malcolm 1933- WhoHol 92
Robertson, Margaret Murray 1821-1897
BlmGWL
Robertson, Marian 1921- WrDr 94
Robertson, Marian Ella 1920- WhoFI 94,
WhoWest 94
Robertson, Martha R. 1952- WhoAmP 93
Robertson, Martha Rappaport 1952-
WhoMW 93
Robertson, Marvin Lee, Jr. 1960-
WhoAmL 94
Robertson, Mary Elsie DrAPF 93
Robertson, Mary Louise 1945- WhoAm 94
Robertson, Melvina 1934- WhoMW 93
Robertson, Michael John 1956-
WhoMW 93
Robertson, Michael S. 1935- WhoAmP 93
Robertson, Michael Swing 1935-
WhoAm 94
Robertson, Monica S. 1965- WhoWest 94
Robertson, Morgan (Andrew) 1861-1915
EncSF 93
Robertson, Nancy (Margaret) 1909-
Who 94
Robertson, Nancy Elizabeth WhoAmA 93
Robertson, Nat Clifton 1919- WhoAm 94
Robertson, Nelson Who 94
Robertson, (William) Nelson 1933-
Who 94
Robertson, Noel Farnie 1923- Who 94
Robertson, Norah d1982 WhoHol 92
Robertson, Norman Robert Ean 1931-
Who 94
Robertson, Orie O. d1964 WhoHol 92
Robertson, Oscar 1938- BasBi
Robertson, Oscar Palmer 1938-
WhoAm 94, WhoBlA 94, WhoFI 94
Robertson, Pat 1930- WhoAm 94
Robertson, Patrick Allan Pearson 1913-
Who 94
Robertson, Paul Chandler 1902-1961
WhoAmA 93N
Robertson, Paul Joseph 1946-
WhoAmP 93
Robertson, Peter James 1947- WhoAm 94
Robertson, Philip Scott 1943-
WhoAmP 93
Robertson, Philip W. 1934- WhoAmP 93
Robertson, Piedad F. WhoHisp 94
Robertson, Quincy L. 1934- WhoBlA 94
Robertson, Quindonell S. WhoBlA 94
Robertson, Rachel 1972- WhoHol 92
Robertson, Raymond Scott 1959- Who 94
Robertson, Rebecca 1964- WhoFI 94
Robertson, Reuben Buck, III 1939-
WhoAmL 94, WhoAm 94
Robertson, Richard Boyd 1936-
WhoAmP 93
Robertson, Richard Curtis 1929-
WhoFI 94
Robertson, Richard Earl 1933- WhoAm 94
Robertson, Richard Stuart 1942-
WhoAm 94, WhoFI 94
Robertson, Robbie 1943- WhoAm 94,
WhoHol 92
Robertson, Robert 1909- Who 94
Robertson, Robert Gordon 1917-
WhoAm 94
Robertson, Robert Henry 1929- Who 94
Robertson, Robert T. WhoAm 94
Robertson, (Harold) Rocke 1912- Who 94
Robertson, Ronald Wade WhoAmP 93
Robertson, Ross Who 94
Robertson, (Richard) Ross 1914- Who 94
Robertson, Russell Boyd 1932-
WhoAm 94
Robertson, Rutherford (Ness) 1913-
Who 94
Robertson, Rutherford Ness 1913-
IntWW 93
Robertson, Samuel Harry, III 1934-
WhoScEn 94
Robertson, Sandra Dee 1953- WhoFI 94
Robertson, Sara Jene 1934- WhoAmP 93
Robertson, Sara Stewart 1940- WhoFI 94
Robertson, Sarah M. d1948 WhoAmA 93N
Robertson, Sidney Park 1914- Who 94
Robertson, Stanley Stewart John 1938-
Who 94
Robertson, Stephen Lee 1949- WhoAm 94
Robertson, Stewart WhoAm 94
Robertson, (William) Strowan (Amherst)
1894-1955 DcNaB MP
Robertson, Stuart d1958 WhoHol 92
Robertson, T. W. 1829-1871 BlmGEL
Robertson, T(homas) W(illiam)
1829-1871 IntDcT 2 [port]
Robertson, Ted Walter 1942- WhoAmA 93
Robertson, Ted Z. WhoAmP 93
Robertson, Ted Zanderson 1921-
WhoAm 94
Robertson, Thomas E. WhoAmP 93

Robertson, Thomas Leo 1932- WhoFI 94
Robertson, Tim WhoHol 92
Robertson, Timothy Joel 1937-
WhoAm 94
Robertson, Timothy N. 1932-
WhoAmP 93
Robertson, Toby Who 94
Robertson, Vernon Colin 1922- Who 94
Robertson, Walter S. 1893-1970 HisDcKW
Robertson, Willard d1948 WhoHol 92
Robertson, William d1980 WhoHol 92
Robertson, William Bell, Jr. 1949-
WhoScEn 94
Robertson, William Bruce 1923- Who 94
Robertson, William Duncan 1922-
Who 94
Robertson, William Franklin 1917-
WhoAm 94
Robertson, William Osborne 1925-
WhoAm 94, WhoScEn 94
Robertson, William P. DrAPF 93
Robertson, William Richard 1941-
WhoAm 94, WhoFI 94, WhoMW 93
Robertson, William Ross, III 1942-
WhoAmL 94
Robertson, William Schenck 1820-1881
EncNAR
Robertson, William Withers 1941-
WhoAm 94, WhoAmL 94
Robertson of Brackla, Ian Argyll 1913-
Who 94
Robertson Of Oakridge, Baron 1930-
Who 94
Roberts-West, George Arthur Alston-
Who 94
Roberval, Jean-Francois De La Roque,
Sieur De c. 1500-1561 WhWE
Robeson, Eslanda d1965 WhoHol 92
Robeson, Eslanda Cardoza Goode
1896-1965 ConAu 141
Robeson, Kenneth EncSF 93
Robeson, Kenneth 1933- WrDr 94
Robeson, Paul d1976 WhoHol 92
Robeson, Paul 1898-1976 AfrAmAl 6 [port]
Robeson, Paul, Jr. NewYTBS 93 [port]
Robeson, Paul, Jr. 1927- WhoBlA 94
Robeson, Paul Leroy Bustill 1898-1976
AmSocL
Robespierre, Isidore Maximilien de
1758-1794 BlmGEL
Robespierre, Maximilien 1758-1794
HisWorL [port]
Robey, Douglas John Brett 1914- Who 94
Robey, George d1954 WhoHol 92
Robey, Margaret Durham 1898-
WhAm 10
Robey, Ronald Gerald 1952- WhoAmL 94
Robfogel, Susan Salitan 1943- WhoAm 94,
WhoAmL 94
Robi, Paul d1989 WhoHol 92
Robichaud, Julie-Marie WhoAmP 93
Robichaud, Louis Joseph 1925-
IntWW 93, WhoAm 94
Robichaux, Jolyn H. 1928- WhoBlA 94
Robida, Albert 1848-1926 EncSF 93
Robidoux, Antoine 1794-1860 WhWE
Robie, Clarence W. WhoBlA 94
Robie, Donna Jean 1966- WhoScEn 94
Robie, Fred Smith 1920- WhoMW 93
Robie, Ronald Boyd 1937- WhoAmL 94
Robillard, Florence 1926- WhoAmP 93
Robin, Arthur de Quetteville 1929-
WrDr 94
Robin, Dany 1927- IntMPA 94,
WhoHol 92
Robin, David Arthur 1960- WhoWest 94
Robin, Edward A. 1936- WhoFI 94
Robin, Gabriel Marie Louis 1929-
IntWW 93
Robin, Gordon de Quetteville 1921-
Who 94
Robin, Ian (Gibson) 1909- Who 94
Robin, Mado 1918-1960 NewGrDO
Robin, Michel WhoHol 92
Robin, Richard C. 1945- WhoAmL 94
Robin, Richard Shale 1926- WhoAm 94
Robin, Ruth d1987 WhoHol 92
Robin, Theodore Tydings, Jr. 1939-
WhoAm 94
Robiner, Donald Maxwell 1935-
WhoAm 94, WhoAmL 94
Robinet, Harriette Gillem 1931- BlkWr 2,
ConAu 42NR, WhoBlA 94
Robinet, Lee EncSF 93
Robinett, Ann 1949- WhoWest 94
Robinett, Betty Wallace 1919- WhoAm 94
Robinett, Stephen 1941- WrDr 94
Robinett, Stephen (Allen) 1941- EncSF 93
Robinett, Thomas A., Jr. WhoAmP 93
Robinette, David Michael 1949-
WhoFI 94
Robinette, Joseph A. 1939- WrDr 94
Robinow, Meinhard 1909- WhoMW 93
Robinowitz, Carolyn Bauer 1938-
WhoScEn 94
Robinowitz, Joe Reece 1950- WhoAm 94
Robinowitz, Stuart 1929- WhoAm 94
Robins, Ann-Lorraine 1958- WhoWest 94

Robins, Barry d1986 WhoHol 92
Robins, Charles W. 1939- WhoAmL 94
Robins, Corinne DrAPF 93
Robins, Corinne 1934- WhoAmA 93
Robins, Edward H. d1955 WhoHol 92
Robins, Edwin Claiborne, Sr. 1910-
WhoAm 94
Robins, Eli 1921- WhoAm 94,
WhoScEn 94
Robins, Elizabeth 1862-1952 BlmGEL,
DcNaB MP
Robins, Frank B. 1924- WhoAmP 93
Robins, Gerald Burns 1924- WhoAm 94
Robins, Henry Ian 1945- WhoMW 93
Robins, Laila WhoHol 92
Robins, Lawrence Arthur 1949-
WhoAm 94
Robins, Lee Nelken 1922- IntWW 93,
WhoAm 94
Robins, Leonard Edward 1921- Who 94
Robins, Malcolm Owen 1918- Who 94
Robins, Marjorie McCarthy 1914-
WhoMW 93
Robins, Michael H(arvey) 1941- WrDr 94
Robins, Natalie DrAPF 93
Robins, Norman Alan 1934- WhoAm 94
Robins, Oliver WhoHol 92
Robins, Patricia ConAu 42NR
Robins, Patricia 1921- WrDr 94
Robins, Ralph (Harry) 1932- IntWW 93,
Who 94
Robins, Robert Henry 1921- IntWW 93,
Who 94, WrDr 94
Robins, Robert Sidwar 1938- WhoAm 94
Robins, Ronald David 1957- WhoWest 94
Robins, Toby d1986 WhoHol 92
Robins, W. Ronald 1943- WhoAmL 94
Robins, William Edward Charles 1924-
Who 94
Robins, William John Pherrick 1941-
Who 94
Robinson Who 94
Robinson, A(ntony) M(eredith) Lewin
1916- WrDr 94
Robinson, Adelbert Carl 1926-
WhoAmL 94, WhoFI 94
Robinson, Adeline Black 1915-
WhoBlA 94
Robinson, Alan Hadley 1934-
WhoWest 94
Robinson, Alastair Who 94
Robinson, (Francis) Alastair (Lavie) 1937-
Who 94
Robinson, (Francis) Alastair Lavie 1937-
IntWW 93
Robinson, Albert (Edward Phineas) 1915-
Who 94
Robinson, Albert Arnold 1937-
WhoBlA 94
Robinson, Albert Edward Phineas 1915-
IntWW 93
Robinson, Albert Lee 1938- WhoAmP 93
Robinson, Albert M. WhoBlA 94
Robinson, Alcurtis WhoBlA 94
Robinson, Alcurtis 1940- WhoIns 94
Robinson, Alexander Jacob 1920-
WhoMW 93, WhoScEn 94
Robinson, Alfred B., Jr. WhoAmP 93
Robinson, Alfred G. 1928- WhoScEn 94
Robinson, Alfreda P. 1932- WhoBlA 94
Robinson, Allan Richard 1932-
WhoAm 94
Robinson, Alwyn Arnold 1929- Who 94
Robinson, Aminah Brenda Lynn 1940-
SmATA 77 [port], WhoMW 93
Robinson, Amy WhoHol 92
Robinson, Anastasia c. 1692-1755
NewGrDO
Robinson, Andrew WhoHol 92
Robinson, Andrew 1939- WhoBlA 94
Robinson, Angela Yvonne 1956-
WhoBlA 94
Robinson, Ann 1930- WhoHol 92
Robinson, Ann 1937- Who 94
Robinson, Ann Garrett 1934- WhoBlA 94
Robinson, Ann Turner d1741 NewGrDO
Robinson, Annette WhoAmP 93
Robinson, Annettmarie 1940- WhoFI 94,
WhoWest 94
Robinson, Anthony DrAPF 93
Robinson, Arnold 1929- WhoWest 94
Robinson, Arthur Alexander 1924-
Who 94
Robinson, Arthur Howard 1915-
WhoAm 94
Robinson, Aubrey E., Jr. 1922- CngDr 93
Robinson, Aubrey Eugene, Jr. 1922-
WhoAm 94, WhoBlA 94
Robinson, (Edward) Austin (Gossage)
d1993 Who 94N
Robinson, (Edward) Austin (Gossage)
1897- IntWW 93
Robinson, Barbara Jon 1944- WhoWest 94
Robinson, Barbara Paul 1941- WhoAm 94
Robinson, Barry Lane 1943- WhoBlA 94
Robinson, Barry Lee 1955- WhoFI 94
Robinson, Barry R. 1946- WhoAm 94,
WhoAmL 94

Robins, Barry d1986 WhoHol 92
Robinson, Bartlett d1986 WhoHol 92
Robinson, Basil William 1912- IntWW 93,
Who 94, WrDr 94
Robinson, Benjamin Ellison, III 1963-
WhoBlA 94
Robinson, Benjamin Harton 1934-
WhoAmP 93
Robinson, Bernard Leo 1924-
WhoAmL 94, WhoFI 94, WhoWest 94
Robinson, Bert Kris 1936- WhoAmL 94
Robinson, Beverley 1721-1792 AmRev,
WhAmRev [port]
Robinson, Beverly Jean 1957- WhoBlA 94
Robinson, Bill WhoHol 92
Robinson, Bill d1949 WhoHol 92
Robinson, Bill d1993 NewYTBS 93
Robinson, Bill 1878-1949 AfrAmAl 6,
AmCulL [port]
Robinson, Bill, Jr. 1943- WhoBlA 94
Robinson, Boardman 1876-1952
WhoAmA 93N
Robinson, Bob Leo 1933- WhoAm 94
Robinson, Brian Gordon 1947- Who 94
Robinson, Brian Lewis 1936- Who 94
Robinson, Brooks Calbert, Jr. 1937-
WhoAm 94
Robinson, Bruce WhoHol 92
Robinson, Bruce 1912- Who 94
Robinson, Bruce 1946- IntMPA 94,
WrDr 94
Robinson, Bruce Butler 1933-
WhoScEn 94
Robinson, C. N. 1928- WhoAmP 93
Robinson, Calvin Stanford 1920-
WhoAmL 94
Robinson, Cardew 1923- WhoHol 92
Robinson, Carl Cornell 1946- WhoBlA 94
Robinson, Carl Dayton 1942- WhoBlA 94
Robinson, Carl Terrell 1947- WhoAm 94
Robinson, Carol Evonne 1959-
WhoBlA 94
Robinson, Carol W. 1953- WhoBlA 94
Robinson, Carole Ann 1935- WhoFI 94,
WhoWest 94
Robinson, Carrie C. 1912- WhoBlA 94
Robinson, Cas 1935- WhoAmP 93
Robinson, Casey 1903-1979 IntDcF 2-4
Robinson, Catherine 1904- WhoBlA 94
Robinson, Cecelia Ann 1948- WhoBlA 94
Robinson, Charles WhoHol 92
Robinson, Charles d1980 WhoHol 92
Robinson, Charles 1940- WhoBlA 94
Robinson, Charles 1945- WhoHol 92
Robinson, Charles Alvin 1941- WhoAm 94
Robinson, Charles Arthur, II 1957-
WhoAmL 94
Robinson, Charles Clifton 1937-
WhoIns 94
Robinson, Charles David 1944- WhoFI 94
Robinson, Charles E. 1926- WhoBlA 94
Robinson, Charles E. 1933- WhoFI 94
Robinson, Charles Edwards 1939-
WhoAmP 93
Robinson, Charles Frederic 1942-
WhoAmL 94
Robinson, Charles Henry 1843-1930
EncSF 93
Robinson, Charles James 1958- WhoFI 94
Robinson, Charles James, Jr. 1951-
WhoMW 93
Robinson, Charles Knox WhoHol 92
Robinson, Charles Paul 1941- WhoAm 94,
WhoWest 94
Robinson, Charles Sherwood 1920-
WhoWest 94
Robinson, Charles Warren 1948-
WhoFI 94
Robinson, Charles Wesley 1919-
WhoWest 94
Robinson, Charlie Davis 1946-
WhoMW 93
Robinson, Charlotte 1924- WhoAmA 93
Robinson, Charlotte L. 1924- WhoBlA 94
Robinson, Chester Hersey 1918-
WhoAm 94
Robinson, Chris 1938- WhoHol 92
Robinson, Chris 1951- WhoAmA 93
Robinson, Christine Marie WhoAm 94,
WhoScEn 94
Robinson, Christopher John 1936-
Who 94
Robinson, Christopher Philipse 1938-
Who 94
Robinson, Christopher Thomas 1951-
WhoAm 94
Robinson, Chuck Frank 1956- WhoFI 94,
WhoMW 93
Robinson, Clare, Mrs. Who 94
Robinson, Clarence B. 1911- WhoAmP 93,
WhoBlA 94
Robinson, Clarence G. 1920- WhoBlA 94
Robinson, Clark Zachary 1961-
WhoWest 94
Robinson, Claudia WhoHol 92
Robinson, Cleveland L. 1914- WhoBlA 94
Robinson, Clifton Eugene Bancroft 1926-
Who 94

Robinson, Cloyd Erwin 1938-
WhoAmP 93
Robinson, Colin 1932- Who 94
Robinson, Curtis 1934- WhoBlA 94
Robinson, Curtis L. 1958- WhoBlA 94
Robinson, Daniel Baruch 1937-
WhoAm 94
Robinson, Daniel Lee 1923- WhoBlA 94
Robinson, Daniel Thomas 1925-
WhoAm 94
Robinson, Daphne McCaskey 1912-
WhoBlA 94
Robinson, Dar d1986 WhoHol 92
Robinson, Darren
See Fat Boys, The WhoHol 92
Robinson, David 1965- CurBio 93 [port],
WhoAm 94
Robinson, David Adair 1925- WhoAm 94
Robinson, David Allen 1956-
WhoScEn 94
Robinson, David Ashley 1954-
WhoScEn 94
Robinson, David B. 1943- WhoAm 94,
WhoAmL 94
Robinson, David Brooks 1939-
WhoAm 94, WhoWest 94
Robinson, David Howard 1948-
WhoAmL 94
Robinson, David Julien 1930- Who 94
Robinson, David Mason 1932-
WhoAm 94, WhoScEn 94
Robinson, David Maurice 1965-
WhoBlA 94
Robinson, David Roger 1951-
WhoWest 94
Robinson, David Weaver 1914-
WhoAm 94
Robinson, David Zav 1927- WhoAm 94
Robinson, Davis Rowland 1940-
WhoAm 94, WhoAmL 94
Robinson, Dawn WhoBlA 94
Robinson, Dawn c. 1969-
See En Vogue ConMus 10
Robinson, Dawn c. 1969-
See En Vogue News 94-1
Robinson, Dean Wentworth 1929-
WhoAm 94
Robinson, Deanna Adell 1945-
WhoBlA 94
Robinson, Debra Kay 1963- WhoMW 93
Robinson, Denauvo M. 1949- WhoBlA 94
Robinson, Derek 1932- Who 94, WrDr 94
Robinson, Derek Anthony 1942- Who 94
Robinson, Dewey d1950 WhoHol 92
Robinson, Donald Edward 1947-
WhoScEn 94
Robinson, Donald Keith 1932- WhoAm 94
Robinson, Donald Lee 1930- WhoBlA 94
Robinson, Donald Leonard 1936-
WhoAm 94
Robinson, Donald Louis 1936-
WhoAmP 93
Robinson, Donald Peter 1928-
WhoMW 93
Robinson, Donald Walter WhoAm 94
Robinson, Donald Wilford 1928-
WhoAm 94
Robinson, Donald William Bradley 1922-
IntWW 93, Who 94
Robinson, Dorlos 1935- WhoAmP 93
Robinson, Dorothy Carol Jones 1930-
WhoMW 93
Robinson, Dorothy K. 1951- WhoAmL 94
Robinson, Dorothy Mokuren 1951-
WhoWest 94
Robinson, Douglas 1930- WhoAm 94
Robinson, Douglas George 1943-
WhoAm 94, WhoAmL 94
Robinson, Duncan Who 94
Robinson, Duncan 1943- WhoAm 94,
WhoAmA 93
Robinson, (David) Duncan 1943- Who 94
Robinson, Dwight Parker, Jr. 1900-
WhAm 10
Robinson, E(dward) A. EncSF 93
Robinson, E. B., Jr. 1941- WhoAm 94,
WhoFI 94
Robinson, Earl, Jr. 1954- WhoFI 94
Robinson, Earl (Hawley) 1910-1991
ConAu 43NR, NewGrDO
Robinson, Earl Hawley 1910-1991
WhAm 10
Robinson, Eddie 1919- WhoBlA 94
Robinson, Eddie 1970- WhoBlA 94
Robinson, Eddie Gay WhoAm 94
Robinson, Edgar Allen 1933- WhoAm 94,
WhoFI 94
Robinson, Edith 1924- WhoBlA 94
Robinson, Edsel F. 1928- WhoBlA 94
Robinson, Edward A. 1935- WhoBlA 94
Robinson, Edward Ashton 1949-
WhoBlA 94
Robinson, Edward G. d1973 WhoHol 92
Robinson, Edward G., Jr. d1974
WhoHol 92
Robinson, Edward Joseph 1940-
WhoAm 94, WhoFI 94

Robinson, Edward Norwood, Jr. 1953-
WhoScEn 94
Robinson, Edward T., III 1932-
WhoAmL 94
Robinson, Edwin Arlington 1869-1935
AmCulL
Robinson, Edwin O., Jr. 1939- WhoAm 94
Robinson, Effie WhoBlA 94
Robinson, Eleanor EncSF 93
Robinson, Ella S. 1943- WhoBlA 94
Robinson, Ellen-Ann 1950- WhoAmP 93
Robinson, Emily Worth 1931-
WhoScEn 94
Robinson, Emyré Barrios 1926-
WhoHisp 94
Robinson, Enders Anthony 1930-
WhoAm 94, WhoScEn 94
Robinson, Eric WhoAmP 93
Robinson, Eric B. 1961- WhoBlA 94
Robinson, Eric Embleton 1927- Who 94
Robinson, Eric Larmuth 1912-
WhoWest 94
Robinson, Ermer d1982 WhoHol 92
Robinson, Ernest Preston, Sr. 1947-
WhoBlA 94
Robinson, Eunice Primus 1935-
WhoBlA 94
Robinson, Farrel Richard 1927-
WhoAm 94
Robinson, Faye 1943- NewGrDO
Robinson, Fisher J. 1929- WhoBlA 94
Robinson, Florence Claire Crim 1932-
WhoAm 94
Robinson, Florine Samantha 1935-
WhoFI 94
Robinson, Floyd A. 1936- WhoBlA 94
Robinson, Flynn 1941- BasBi
Robinson, (Peter) Forbes 1926-1987
NewGrDO
Robinson, Forrest d1924 WhoHol 92
Robinson, Frances d1971 WhoHol 92
Robinson, Francis E. 1909- WhoAmP 93
Robinson, Frank 1935- AfrAmAl 6,
WhoAm 94, WhoBlA 94
Robinson, Frank J. 1939- WhoBlA 94
Robinson, Frank M(alcolm) 1926-
EncSF 93, WrDr 94
Robinson, Frank Robert 1938-
WhoWest 94
Robinson, Franklin Kenneth 1929-
WhoFI 94
Robinson, Franklin W. 1939- WhoAmA 93
Robinson, Franklin Westcott 1939-
WhoAm 94
Robinson, Fred c. 1861-1941 EncNAR
Robinson, Fred Colson 1930- WhoAm 94
Robinson, G. Craig 1954- WhoAmL 94
Robinson, G. Wilse 1924- WhoAm 94
Robinson, Gail E. 1949- WhoAmA 93
Robinson, Gary Dale 1938- WhoAm 94,
WhoFI 94, WhoScEn 94, WhoWest 94
Robinson, Gary O. 1935-1992
WhoBlA 94N
Robinson, Genevieve 1940- WhoBlA 94
Robinson, Geoffrey Who 94
Robinson, Geoffrey 1938- Who 94
Robinson, (Arthur) Geoffrey 1917-
Who 94
Robinson, Geoffrey Walter 1945- Who 94
Robinson, George Ali 1939- WhoBlA 94
Robinson, George L. WhoBlA 94
Robinson, George S. 1945- WhoAmP 93
Robinson, Georgia May 1926-
WhoMW 93
Robinson, Gerrard Jude 1948- Who 94
Robinson, Gertrude d1962 WhoHol 92
Robinson, Gertrude Rivers 1927-
WhoBlA 94
Robinson, Gilbert A. 1928- WhoAmP 93
Robinson, Gilbert de Beauregard 1906-
WrDr 94
Robinson, Gill Doncelia 1948- WhoBlA 94
Robinson, Glenn Hugh 1912-
WhoMW 93, WhoScEn 94
Robinson, Glynne 1934- WhoAm 94
Robinson, Gordon Pringle 1911-
WhoWest 94
Robinson, Grove 1935- WhoAmA 93
Robinson, Grover C., III WhoAmP 93
Robinson, H(enry) Basil 1919- WrDr 94
Robinson, H. James 1949- WhoAmP 93
Robinson, Harold George Robert 1924-
Who 94
Robinson, Harold Nyle 1925-1985
WhAm 10
Robinson, Harold Wendell, Jr. 1937-
WhoScEn 94
Robinson, Harriet Burlingame Lewis
WhoAmP 93
Robinson, Harry, Jr. WhoBlA 94
Robinson, Harry G., III 1942- WhoBlA 94
Robinson, Harry Granville, III 1942-
WhoAm 94
Robinson, Harry T. d1946 WhoHol 92
Robinson, Henrietta 1919- WhoAmP 93
Robinson, Henry 1936- WhoBlA 94
Robinson, Henry Crabb 1775-1867
BlmGEL

Robinson, Herbert A. 1927- WhoBlA 94
Robinson, Herbert Henry, III 1933-
WhoWest 94
Robinson, Herbert William 1914-
WhoWest 94
Robinson, Hobart Krum 1937- WhoAm 94
Robinson, Holly 1965- WhoBlA 94
Robinson, Hubert Nelson 1909-
WhoBlA 94
Robinson, Hugh Granville 1932-
AfrAmG [port], WhoAm 94, WhoBlA 94,
WhoFI 94
Robinson, Hugh R. 1922- WhoAm 94
Robinson, Hurley 1925- WhoScEn 94,
WhoWest 94
Robinson, Ira Charles 1940- WhoBlA 94
Robinson, Irwin Jay 1928- WhoAm 94,
WhoAmL 94, WhoFI 94
Robinson, Isaiah E. 1924- WhoBlA 94
Robinson, J. Cordell 1940- WhoHisp 94
Robinson, J(ohn) Lewis 1918- WrDr 94
Robinson, J. Mack 1923- WhoIns 94
Robinson, Jack, Jr. 1942- WhoBlA 94
Robinson, Jack Albert 1930- WhoAm 94,
WhoFI 94, WhoMW 93
Robinson, Jack E. WhoBlA 94
Robinson, Jack E. 1960- WhoBlA 94
Robinson, Jack Errol, III 1960- WhoFI 94
Robinson, Jack Fay 1914- WhoMW 93
Robinson, Jackie d1972 WhoHol 92
Robinson, Jackie 1919-1972
AfrAmAl 6 [port], ConBlB 6 [port]
Robinson, Jacqueline J. WhoBlA 94
Robinson, Jacques Alan 1947- WhoAm 94
Robinson, Jacqui 1935- WhoBlA 94
Robinson, James WhoAm 94
Robinson, James Arthur 1932- WhoAm 94
Robinson, James Arthur 1949- WhoIns 94
Robinson, James D., III 1935- IntWW 93
Robinson, James Dixon, III 1935-
WhoAm 94
Robinson, James Edward 1943-
WhoBlA 94
Robinson, James G. IntMPA 94
Robinson, James Kenneth 1943-
WhoAm 94, WhoAmL 94
Robinson, James L. 1940- WhoBlA 94
Robinson, James LeRoy 1940-
WhoAm 94, WhoScEn 94
Robinson, James Walker WhoAmP 93
Robinson, James Waymond 1926-
WhoBlA 94
Robinson, James William 1919-
WhoAm 94
Robinson, Jancis Mary 1950- Who 94
Robinson, Jane Alexander 1931-
WhoBlA 94
Robinson, Janice Sheryl 1952-
WhoAmL 94
Robinson, Jason Guy 1934- WhoBlA 94
Robinson, Jay 1915- WhoAm 94
Robinson, Jay 1930- WhoHol 92
Robinson, Jay (Thurston) 1915-
WhoAmA 93
Robinson, Jayne G. 1912- WhoBlA 94
Robinson, Jean Marie WhoAmL 94
Robinson, Jeanne EncSF 93
Robinson, Jeffery Herbert 1956-
WhoFI 94, WhoScEn 94
Robinson, Jeffrey Adams 1956-
WhoAmL 94
Robinson, Jeremy DrAPF 93
Robinson, Jerome Lawrence 1922-
WhoFI 94
Robinson, Jerry H. 1932- WhoAm 94
Robinson, Jesse Lee 1912- WhoBlA 94
Robinson, Jill DrAPF 93
Robinson, Jim C. 1943- WhoBlA 94
Robinson, Joan 1963- WhoFI 94
Robinson, Joe WhoHol 92
Robinson, John DrAPF 93
Robinson, John d1979 WhoHol 92
Robinson, John 1615-1680 DcNaB MP
Robinson, John 1727-1802 WhAmRev
Robinson, John (James Michael Laud)
1943- Who 94
Robinson, John Abbott 1939-
WhoScEn 94
Robinson, John Alan 1930- WhoAm 94
Robinson, John Alexander 1935-
WhoWest 94
Robinson, John Armstrong 1925- Who 94
Robinson, John Beckwith 1922-
WhoAm 94
Robinson, John Bowers, Jr. 1946-
WhoAm 94, WhoFI 94
Robinson, John David 1937- WhoAm 94
Robinson, John E. 1942- WhoAm 94
Robinson, John Edmund 1924-1989
WhAm 10
Robinson, John F. 1944- WhoBlA 94
Robinson, John G. 1942- WhoBlA 94
Robinson, John George 1856-1943
DcNaB MP
Robinson, John Hamilton 1927-
WhoAm 94
Robinson, John Henry 1955- WhoAmP 93
Robinson, John L. 1930- WhoBlA 94

Robinson, John Lewis 1918- WhoAm 94
Robinson, John M. 1949- WhoBlA 94
Robinson, John William, IV 1950-
WhoAmL 94
Robinson, Johnathan Prather 1953-
WhoBlA 94
Robinson, Jonathan N. 1922- WhoBlA 94
Robinson, Jontyle Theresa 1947-
WhoBlA 94
Robinson, Joseph 1927- Who 94
Robinson, Joseph 1940- WhoBlA 94
Robinson, Joseph Albert 1938- WhoAm 94
Robinson, Joseph Edward 1925-
WhoAm 94
Robinson, Joseph William, Sr. WhoBlA 94
Robinson, Judson, III WhoAmP 93
Robinson, June Lyne 1941- WhoAmP 93
Robinson, Karen Denise 1956-
WhoBlA 94
Robinson, Kathleen Marian 1911- Who 94
Robinson, Kayne 1943- WhoAmP 93
Robinson, Keith Who 94
Robinson, (Leonard) Keith 1920- Who 94
Robinson, Kenneth 1911- Who 94
Robinson, Kenneth 1947- WhoBlA 94
Robinson, Kenneth Ernest 1914-
IntWW 93, Who 94
Robinson, Kenneth Eugene 1947-
WhoBlA 94
Robinson, Kenneth George, Jr. 1945-
WhoAmL 94
Robinson, Kenneth Larry 1944- WhoFI 94
Robinson, Kenneth Leonard, Jr. 1929-
WhoAm 94, WhoFI 94
Robinson, Kenneth Patrick 1933-
WhoAmL 94
Robinson, Kent W. 1952- WhoAmL 94
Robinson, Kim Stanley 1952- EncSF 93,
WrDr 94
Robinson, Kinsey Maxfield 1895-
WhAm 10
Robinson, Kitty 1921- WhoBlA 94
Robinson, Larry WhoAmP 93
Robinson, Larry 1968- WhoBlA 94
Robinson, Larry E. 1948- WhoMW 93
Robinson, Larry R. 1928- WhoMW 93
Robinson, Larry Robert 1936- WhoAm 94,
WhoFI 94, WhoIns 94
Robinson, Lauren Danielle 1964-
WhoBlA 94
Robinson, Lawrence B. 1919- WhoBlA 94
Robinson, Lawrence D. 1942- WhoBlA 94
Robinson, Lawrence Dewitt 1943-
WhoAm 94
Robinson, Lawrence Wiswall 1948-
WhoScEn 94
Robinson, Learthon Steven, Sr. 1925-
WhoBlA 94
Robinson, Lee Fisher 1923- Who 94
Robinson, Lee Harris 1939- WhoAm 94
Robinson, Legal d1919 WhoHol 92
Robinson, (Esme Stuart) Lennox
1886-1958 IntDcT 2
Robinson, Leonard H., Jr. 1943-
WhoAmP 93
Robinson, Leonard Harrison, Jr. 1943-
WhoAm 94, WhoBlA 94
Robinson, Leonard Wallace DrAPF 93
Robinson, Libby WhoAmA 93
Robinson, Lilien Filipovitch 1940-
WhoAmA 93
Robinson, Lillian S. DrAPF 93
Robinson, Linda Gosden 1953-
WhoAm 94, WhoFI 94
Robinson, Linda Parent 1943-
WhoAmP 93
Robinson, Lloyd Who 94
Robinson, Lois Hart 1927- WhoMW 93
Robinson, Lou DrAPF 93
Robinson, Louie, Jr. 1926- WhoBlA 94
Robinson, Luther D. 1922- WhoBlA 94
Robinson, Lynn B. 1955- WhoAm 94
Robinson, Madeleine 1916- WhoHol 92
Robinson, Manuel 1931- WhoBlA 94
Robinson, Marcus 1912- Who 94
Robinson, Margaret A. DrAPF 93
Robinson, Margaret King 1906-
WhoAmP 93
Robinson, Margot WhoAmA 93
Robinson, Marguerite S. 1935- WrDr 94
Robinson, Marguerite Stern 1935-
WhoAm 94
Robinson, Marie Rachelle G. 1919-1988
WhoAmA 93N
Robinson, Marietta Sebree 1951-
WhoAmL 94
Robinson, Marilyn BlmGWL
Robinson, Marilynne 1943- WrDr 94
Robinson, Mark Alexander, III 1941-
WhoFI 94
Robinson, Mark Leighton 1927-
WhoFI 94, WhoWest 94
Robinson, Mark Louis 1950- WhoScEn 94
Robinson, Mark Noel Foster 1946-
Who 94
Robinson, Mark William 1952- WhoFI 94
Robinson, Marshall Alan 1922-
WhoAm 94

Robinson, Martha Dolores 1956- WhoBlA 94
Robinson, Martha Stewart 1914- WhoAm 94
Robinson, Martin F. 1939- WhoAm 94
Robinson, Marvin Stuart 1933- WhoAm 94
Robinson, Mary 1944- IntWW 93, Who 94, WhoWomW 91
Robinson, Mary Ann 1923- WhoAmA 93
Robinson, Mary Elizabeth 1946- WhoBlA 94
Robinson, Mary Ellen 1948- WhoMW 93
Robinson, Mary Lou 1926- WhoAm 94, WhoAmL 94
Robinson, Mary Susan 1951- WhoWest 94
Robinson, Matilda Turner 1951- WhoBlA 94
Robinson, Matt 1937- WhoBlA 94
Robinson, Maude Eloise 1927- WhoBlA 94
Robinson, Maura 1956- WhoAmA 93
Robinson, Maurice C. 1932- WhoBlA 94
Robinson, Maurice Richard, Jr. 1937- WhoAm 94
Robinson, Max 1939-1988 AfrAmAl 6 [port]
Robinson, Melvin P. 1935- WhoBlA 94
Robinson, Melvyn Roland 1933- WhoScEn 94
Robinson, Michael Claire 1949- WhoMW 93
Robinson, Michael David 1953- WhoBlA 94
Robinson, Michael F(inlay) 1933- NewGrDO
Robinson, Michael Francis 1954- WhoFI 94
Robinson, Michael Hill 1929- WhoAm 94
Robinson, Michael Keith 1951- WhoMW 93
Robinson, Michael Lynn 1948- WhoAmL 94
Robinson, Michael Maurice Jeffries 1927- Who 94
Robinson, Mildred Wigfall 1944- WhoAm 94, WhoAmL 94
Robinson, Milton Bernidine 1913- WhoBlA 94
Robinson, Milton J. 1935- WhoBlA 94
Robinson, Moses 1742-1813 WhAmRev
Robinson, Moureen Ann Who 94
Robinson, Muriel F. Cox 1927- WhoBlA 94
Robinson, Myron Frederick 1943- WhoBlA 94
Robinson, Nancy L. 1965- WhoFI 94
Robinson, Nathaniel 1951- WhoBlA 94
Robinson, Neil 1929- Who 94
Robinson, Neil Cibley, Jr. 1942- WhoAmL 94
Robinson, Niall B. L. Who 94
Robinson, Nina 1943- WhoBlA 94
Robinson, Noah R. WhoBlA 94
Robinson, Norman T., Jr. 1918- WhoBlA 94
Robinson, Oliver John 1908- Who 94
Robinson, Ollie Ama 1924- WhoAmP 93
Robinson, Oswald Horsley 1926- Who 94
Robinson, Patricia Snyder 1952- WhoAmL 94
Robinson, Patrick William 1943- Who 94
Robinson, Paul Arnold 1940- WhoAm 94
Robinson, Paul Randall 1937- WhoAmP 93
Robinson, Paul William 1928- WhoFI 94
Robinson, Peggie Crose 1944- WhoMW 93
Robinson, Pete 1954- WhoAmP 93
Robinson, Peter 1922- Who 94
Robinson, Peter 1932- WhoAm 94, WhoWest 94
Robinson, Peter Clark 1938- WhoAm 94, WhoFI 94
Robinson, Peter Damian 1926- Who 94
Robinson, Peter David 1948- IntWW 93, Who 94
Robinson, Peter Eliot 1950- WhoMW 93
Robinson, Peter Lee, Jr. 1922- WhoBlA 94
Robinson, Peter M. 1957- WhoAm 94
Robinson, Peter Michael 1947- Who 94
Robinson, Phil Alden IntMPA 94
Robinson, Philip 1949- Who 94
Robinson, Philip Bedford 1926- EncSF 93
Robinson, Philip Henry 1926- Who 94
Robinson, Phillip Dean 1956- WhoAm 94
Robinson, Phyllis 1946- WhoAmP 93
Robinson, Prezell Russell 1922- WhoAm 94, WhoBlA 94
Robinson, R. David 1941- WhoBlA 94
Robinson, Rad d1988 WhoHol 92
Robinson, Randall S. WhoBlA 94
Robinson, Randall S. 1939- WhoBlA 94
Robinson, Randall S. 1942?- AfrAmAl 6 [port]
Robinson, Raphael Mitchel 1911- WhoWest 94
Robinson, Ray Charles 1930- WhoAm 94
Robinson, Raymond IntWW 93, Who 94
Robinson, (Arthur Napoleon) Raymond 1926- IntWW 93, Who 94
Robinson, Raymond Edwin 1932- WhoAm 94
Robinson, Renault A. 1942- WhoBlA 94
Robinson, Richard 1937- WhoAm 94
Robinson, Richard Allen, Jr. 1936- WhoWest 94
Robinson, Richard Dunlop 1921- WhoFI 94
Robinson, Richard Earl 1903- WhAm 10
Robinson, Richard Gary 1931- WhoFI 94
Robinson, Richard Lee 1958- WhoAmL 94
Robinson, Richard Russell 1925- WhoAmL 94
Robinson, Rick Lee 1952- WhoWest 94
Robinson, Rob 1955- WhoAm 94
Robinson, Robb 1922- WhoAmP 93
Robinson, Robert 1886-1975 WorScD
Robinson, Robert 1927- WrDr 94
Robinson, Robert Alan 1955- WhoScEn 94
Robinson, Robert Alexander 1914-1990 WhAm 10
Robinson, Robert Armstrong 1925- WhoAm 94, WhoFI 94
Robinson, Robert Blacque 1927- WhoAm 94, WhoWest 94
Robinson, Robert E. WhoAmP 93
Robinson, Robert G. 1943- WhoBlA 94
Robinson, Robert Hamilton, Jr. d1976 WhoHol 92
Robinson, Robert Henry 1927- Who 94
Robinson, Robert James 1935- WhoAm 94
Robinson, Robert L. WhoIns 94
Robinson, Robert L. 1936- WhoAm 94
Robinson, Robert Love, Jr. 1961- WhoBlA 94
Robinson, Rodney Joel 1943- WhoMW 93
Robinson, Roger 1940- WhoBlA 94, WhoHol 92
Robinson, Roger 1943- EncSF 93
Robinson, Roger James 1932- Who 94
Robinson, Roland (Edward) 1912- WrDr 94
Robinson, Ronald Alan 1952- WhoAm 94, WhoWest 94
Robinson, Ronald C. 1930- WhoAmP 93
Robinson, Ronald Edward 1920- Who 94
Robinson, Ronald James 1946- WhoFI 94
Robinson, Ronald Michael 1942- WhoAm 94, WhoFI 94
Robinson, Ronnie W. 1942- WhoBlA 94
Robinson, Rosalyn Karen 1946- WhoBlA 94
Robinson, Roscoe, Jr. d1993 NewYTBS 93 [port]
Robinson, Roscoe, Jr. 1928- AfrAmG [port], AfrAmAl 6, WhoBlA 94
Robinson, Roscoe Ross 1929- WhoAm 94
Robinson, Roxana (Barry) WrDr 94
Robinson, Rudyard Livingstone 1951- WhoScEn 94
Robinson, Rumeal James 1966- WhoBlA 94
Robinson, Russell Marable, II 1932- WhoAmL 94
Robinson, Ruth d1966 WhoHol 92
Robinson, Ruth 1949- WhoBlA 94
Robinson, Ruth M. 1921- WhoAmP 93
Robinson, S. Benton 1928- WhoBlA 94
Robinson, S. Yolanda 1946- WhoBlA 94
Robinson, Sally W. 1924- WhoAmA 93
Robinson, Samuel 1935- WhoBlA 94
Robinson, Samuel Francis, Jr. 1942- WhoAmL 94
Robinson, Samuel L. WhoFI 94
Robinson, Samuel Willis, Jr. 1927- WhoWest 94
Robinson, Sandra Hawkins 1951- WhoBlA 94
Robinson, Sandra Lawson 1944- WhoBlA 94
Robinson, Scott Douglas 1957- WhoFI 94
Robinson, Scott Hayden 1950- WhoAmL 94
Robinson, Shannon WhoAmP 93, WhoWest 94
Robinson, Sheila (Mary) 1928- WrDr 94
Robinson, Sherman 1932- WhoBlA 94
Robinson, Sherman 1942- WhoAm 94, WhoWest 94
Robinson, Smokey WhoAm 94
Robinson, Smokey 1940- AfrAmAl 6, WhoHol 92
Robinson, Smokey (William, Jr.) 1940- WhoBlA 94
Robinson, Spencer, Jr. 1942- WhoAm 94, WhoMW 93
Robinson, Spencer T. 1940- WhoMW 93
Robinson, Spencer T. Herk 1940- WhoAm 94
Robinson, Spider 1948- EncSF 93, TwCYAW, WrDr 94
Robinson, "Spike" d1942 WhoHol 92
Robinson, Spotswood W., III 1916- CngDr 93
Robinson, Spottswood William, III 1916- WhoBlA 94
Robinson, Stacy 1962- WhoBlA 94
Robinson, Stanford 1904-1984 NewGrDO
Robinson, Stanley Daniel 1926- WhoAm 94, WhoAmL 94
Robinson, Stanley Scott 1913- Who 94
Robinson, Stephen Brooks 1896- WhAm 10
Robinson, Stephen Joseph 1931- Who 94
Robinson, Stephen Michael 1942- WhoAm 94
Robinson, Steve Mark 1959- WhoMW 93
Robinson, Sue Lewis 1952- WhoAm 94, WhoAmL 94
Robinson, Sugar Ray d1989 WhoHol 92
Robinson, Sugar Ray 1920-1989 AfrAmAl 6
Robinson, Sugarchile 1940- WhoHol 92
Robinson, Sumner Martin 1928- WhoAm 94, WhoMW 93
Robinson, Susan Estes 1950- WhoScEn 94
Robinson, Susan Shelton 1941- WhoFI 94
Robinson, Suzanne Beth 1965- WhoMW 93
Robinson, Terry Earl 1949- WhoMW 93
Robinson, Thelma Maniece 1938- WhoBlA 94
Robinson, Theodore 1852-1896 WhoAmA 93N
Robinson, Theodore Curtis, Jr. 1916- WhoAmL 94
Robinson, Thomas Bullene 1917- WhoAm 94
Robinson, Thomas Christopher 1944- WhoAm 94
Robinson, Thomas Donald 1941- WhoBlA 94
Robinson, Thomas Hugh 1934- Who 94
Robinson, Thomas John 1935- WhoMW 93
Robinson, Thomas Lloyd 1912- IntWW 93, Who 94
Robinson, Thomas V. 1938- WhoAmA 93
Robinson, Thurston 1915- WhoAm 94
Robinson, Tommy F. 1942- WhoAmP 93
Robinson, Tony ConTFT 11
Robinson, Truck 1951- BasBi
Robinson, Vaughan 1957- WrDr 94
Robinson, Victor 1925- Who 94
Robinson, Vivian 1944- Who 94
Robinson, W. Bruce DrAPF 93
Robinson, W. Lee 1943- WhoAmP 93
Robinson, W(illiam) R(onald) 1927- WrDr 94
Robinson, Walker Lee 1941- WhoBlA 94
Robinson, Walter 1950- WhoAmA 93
Robinson, Walter F. 1950- WhoBlA 94
Robinson, Walter G. 1928- WhoBlA 94
Robinson, Walter George 1911- WhoAm 94
Robinson, Walter Kenneth 1926- WhoAmP 93
Robinson, Walter Lonzo, Jr. 1947- WhoAmP 93
Robinson, Walter Stitt, Jr. 1917- WhoAm 94
Robinson, Waverly Clyde 1956- WhoMW 93
Robinson, Wilbur R. 1916- WhoBlA 94
Robinson, Wilfred (Henry Frederick) 1917- Who 94
Robinson, Wilkes Coleman 1925- CngDr 93, WhoAm 94, WhoAmL 94
Robinson, Will WhoBlA 94
Robinson, William 1838-1935 DcNaB MP
Robinson, William 1920- WhoBlA 94
Robinson, William Andrew 1943- WhoBlA 94
Robinson, William David 1931- Who 94
Robinson, William Dwight 1943- WhoAmP 93
Robinson, William Earl 1940- WhoBlA 94
Robinson, William Earle 1940- WhoWest 94
Robinson, William Franklin 1916- WhoAm 94
Robinson, William G. 1926- WhoAmP 93
Robinson, William Good 1919- Who 94
Robinson, William H., Jr. 1943- WhoAmL 94
Robinson, William Henry 1922- WhoBlA 94
Robinson, William Hugh 1951- WhoFI 94
Robinson, William Ingraham 1909- WhoAm 94
Robinson, William J. 1918- WhoIns 94
Robinson, William J. 1951- WhoAmL 94
Robinson, William James 1916- Who 94
Robinson, William James 1933- WhoBlA 94
Robinson, William James 1953- WhoFI 94, WhoWest 94
Robinson, William M. 1941- WhoAm 94, WhoAmL 94
Robinson, William P. 1949- WhoAm 94
Robinson, William Peters, Jr. 1942- WhoAmP 93
Robinson, William Philip, III 1940- WhoAm 94, WhoAmL 94
Robinson, William Rhys Brunel 1930- Who 94
Robinson, William Russell WhoAmP 93
Robinson, William Spencer 1940- WhoMW 93
Robinson, William Wheeler 1918- WhoAm 94
Robinson, Willie C. 1934- WhoBlA 94
Robinson, Zelig 1934- WhoAmL 94
Robinson-Brown, Jeannette WhoBlA 94
Robinson-Ford, Denise Renee 1953- WhoBlA 94
Robinson-Walker, Mary P. WhoBlA 94
Robin-Vergeer, Bonnie Ilene 1965- WhoAmL 94
Robirds, Estel WhoAmP 93
Robison, Andrew 1940- WhoAmA 93
Robison, Barbara Jane 1924- WhoMW 93
Robison, Charles B. 1913- WhoIns 94
Robison, Clarence, Jr. 1924- WhoAm 94, WhoScEn 94
Robison, Frederick Mason 1934- WhoAm 94
Robison, J. C. DrAPF 93
Robison, James Everett 1915- WhoAm 94, WhoFI 94
Robison, John Jeffrey 1946- WhoFI 94
Robison, Kenneth L. 1936- WhoAmP 93
Robison, Mary DrAPF 93
Robison, Mary 1949- DcLB 130 [port], WrDr 94
Robison, Norman Glenn 1938- WhoScEn 94
Robison, Paul Frederick 1919- WhoAm 94
Robison, Paula Judith 1941- WhoAm 94
Robison, Peter Donald 1950- WhoScEn 94
Robison, Reid Edward 1944- WhoAmL 94
Robison, Robin Kim 1962- WhoFI 94
Robison, Shelba Cole DrAPF 93
Robison, Wilbur Gerald, Jr. 1933- WhoScEn 94
Robison, William Robert 1947- WhoAmL 94
Robitaille, Albert Leo 1958- WhoAmL 94
Robitaille, Luc 1966- WhoAm 94, WhoWest 94
Robkin, Maurice Abraham 1931- WhoAm 94
Roble, Carole Marcia 1938- WhoFI 94
Robledo, Angela L. 1954- WhoHisp 94
Robledo, Dan A. 1941- WhoHisp 94
Robledo, Jose L. 1947- WhoHisp 94
Robledo, Roberto Manuel 1951- WhoHisp 94
Robledo Montecel, María del Refugio 1953- WhoHisp 94
Roblek, Branko 1934- WhoScEn 94
Robles, Alejandro 1941- WhoHisp 94
Robles, Alfred A. DrAPF 93
Robles, Arturo 1948- WhoHisp 94
Robles, Bárbara J. 1957- WhoHisp 94
Robles, Emma F. 1933- WhoHisp 94
Robles, Ernest Marin 1956- WhoHisp 94
Robles, Ernest Z. WhoHisp 94
Robles, Felix 1945- WhoHisp 94
Robles, Frank M. 1925- WhoHisp 94
Robles, Humberto E. 1938- WhoHisp 94
Robles, John, Jr. 1941- WhoHisp 94
Robles, Josue, Jr. 1946- WhoHisp 94
Robles, Julian 1933- WhoAmA 93
Robles, Marisa 1937- IntWW 93, Who 94
Robles, Mauro P., Sr. WhoHisp 94
Robles, Mireya DrAPF 93
Robles, Neopito de Leon 1932- WhoHisp 94
Robles, Richard d1940 WhoHol 92
Robles, Rosalie Miranda 1942- WhoAm 94, WhoWest 94
Robles, Rudy d1970 WhoHol 92
Robles, Salvador A. 1943- WhoHisp 94
Robles, Victor L. 1945- WhoAmP 93, WhoHisp 94
Robles, Walter WhoHol 92
Robles De Witt, Vera WhoHisp 94
Robles Garcia, Yolanda 1949- WhoHisp 94
Robles Jimenez, Jose Esaul 1925- WhoAm 94
Robleto, Alfonso Alberto, Sr. 1941- WhoHisp 94
Roblin, Duff 1917- WhoAm 94
Roblin, Graham Henry 1937- Who 94
Roblin, Ross Peter 1956- WhoFI 94
Robling, Ronald Joe 1939- WhoAmP 93
Robnett, Melissa Beth 1958- WhoFI 94
Robnett, Nolan J. 1941- WhoAmP 93
Robock, Stefan Hyman 1915- WhoAm 94
Robohm, Peggy Adler 1942- WhoFI 94
Robohm, Richard Arthur 1936- WhoScEn 94
Robol, Richard Thomas 1952- WhoAmL 94
Robold, Alice Ilene 1928- WhoAm 94
Roborough, Baron 1940- Who 94
Robotham, Lascelles (Lister) 1923- Who 94

Robottom, John (Carlisle) *WrDr 94*
Robrecht, Raymond R. *WhoAmP 93*
Robreno, Eduardo C. 1945- *WhoAm 94, WhoAmL 94, WhoHisp 94*
Robrock, James Lawrence 1956- *WhoWest 94*
Robshaw, James Dale 1942- *WhoAm 94*
Robson *Who 94*
Robson, Andrew d1921 *WhoHol 92*
Robson, Anthony Emerson 1932- *WhoScEn 94*
Robson, Brian Ewart 1926- *Who 94*
Robson, Brian Turnbull 1939- *WrDr 94*
Robson, Bryan 1957- *IntWW 93*
Robson, Charles Baskervill, Jr. 1938- *WhoAm 94, WhoAmL 94*
Robson, Christopher 1953- *NewGrDO*
Robson, David Ernest Henry 1940- *Who 94*
Robson, Deborah *DrAPF 93*
Robson, Derek Ian 1935- *WrDr 94*
Robson, Dirk 1932- *WrDr 94*
Robson, Elizabeth Browel 1928- *Who 94*
Robson, Flora d1984 *WhoHol 92*
Robson, Frank Elms 1931- *Who 94*
Robson, Geoffrey Robert 1929- *WhoScEn 94*
Robson, Godfrey 1946- *Who 94*
Robson, (James) Gordon 1921- *Who 94*
Robson, James Gordon 1921- *IntWW 93*
Robson, James Scott 1921- *Who 94*
Robson, Jeremy 1939- *WrDr 94*
Robson, John (Adam) 1930- *Who 94*
Robson, John E. 1930- *WhoAmP 93*
Robson, John Merritt 1930- *WhoAm 94*
Robson, John Phillips 1932- *Who 94*
Robson, Judith B. 1939- *WhoAmP 93*
Robson, Judith Biros 1939- *WhoMW 93*
Robson, Lawrence Fendick d1992 *Who 94N*
Robson, Lucia St. Clair 1942- *WrDr 94*
Robson, Mark 1913-1978 *HorFD [port]*
Robson, May d1944 *WhoHol 92*
Robson, Michael John 1946- *WhoFI 94*
Robson, Nigel John d1993 *Who 94N*
Robson, Peter Neville 1930- *Who 94*
Robson, Philip d1919 *WhoHol 92*
Robson, Robert Michael 1935- *Who 94*
Robson, Robert William 1933- *Who 94*
Robson, Stephen Arthur 1943- *Who 94*
Robson, Stuart, Mrs. d1924 *WhoHol 92*
Robson, Stuart, Jr. d1946 *WhoHol 92*
Robson, Sybil Ann 1956- *WhoFI 94, WhoWest 94*
Robson, Terry Patrick 1943- *WhoFI 94*
Robson, William Michael 1912- *Who 94*
Robson, William Wallace d1993 *Who 94N*
Robson, Zuleika 1953- *WhoHol 92*
Robson Of Kiddington, Baroness 1919- *Who 94, WhoWomW 91*
Robu, Cornel 1938- *EncSF 93*
Robuchon, Joel 1945- *IntWW 93*
Robus, Hugo 1885-1964 *WhoAmA 93N*
Robustelli, Andy *ProFbHF*
Roby, Brian L. 1960- *WhoMW 93*
Roby, Christina Yen *WhoFI 94, WhoScEn 94*
Roby, Douglas Fergusson 1898-1992 *WhAm 10*
Roby, Edgar Maclin 1931- *WhoFI 94*
Roby, Frank Helmuth 1911- *WhAm 10*
Roby, Joe Lindell 1939- *WhoAm 94, WhoFI 94*
Roby, Lavelle *WhoHol 92*
Roby, Mary Elizabeth 1936- *WhoFI 94*
Roby, Mary Linn 1930- *WrDr 94*
Roby, Pamela Ann 1942- *WrDr 94*
Roby, Reggie Henry 1961- *WhoBlA 94*
Roby, Richard Joseph 1954- *WhoScEn 94*
Roby, Thomas E. *WhoAmP 93*
Robyn, (Johann) Alfred G(eorge) 1860-1935 *NewGrDO*
Robyn, Richard Courtney 1949- *WhoMW 93*
Robyns, William d1936 *WhoHol 92*
Roc, Patricia 1915- *WhoHol 92*
Roca, Carlos Manuel 1962- *WhoHisp 94*
Roca, Octavio 1949- *WhoHisp 94*
Roca, Rafael A. 1928- *WhoHisp 94, WhoIns 94*
Roca, Sergio G. 1944- *WhoHisp 94*
Rocaboy, Francoise Marie Jeanne 1962- *WhoScEn 94*
Rocamora, Jaume 1946- *WhoAmA 93*
Rocan, Jacquelyne Marie 1966- *WhoAmL 94*
Rocard, Michael Louis Leon 1930- *IntWW 93*
Rocard, Michel Louis Leon 1930- *Who 94*
Rocard, Pascale *WhoHol 92*
Roca Rosenfeld, Janice Irene 1965- *WhoHisp 94*
Rocca, Daniela *WhoHol 92*
Rocca, James Victor 1930- *WhoWest 94*
Rocca, Lodovico 1895-1986 *NewGrDO*
Rocca, Nicholas Francis 1955- *WhoWest 94*
Rocca, Sal 1946- *WhoAmP 93*
Roccaforte, Gaetano fl. 18th cent.- *NewGrDO*
Roccardi, Albert d1934 *WhoHol 92*
Rocco, Alex 1936- *IntMPA 94, WhoHol 92*
Rocco, John A. 1936- *WhoAmP 93*
Rocco, Kenneth A. *WhoAmP 93*
Rocco, Maurice d1976 *WhoHol 92*
Rocco, Ron 1953- *WhoAm 94, WhoAmA 93*
Rocek, Jan 1924- *WhoAm 94*
Roch, Ernst 1928- *WhoAmA 93*
Roch, Jean-Marc 1960- *WhoWest 94*
Roch, John (Ormond) 1934- *Who 94*
Roch, Lewis Marshall, III 1956- *WhoFI 94*
Roch, Muriel Elizabeth Sutcliffe 1916- *Who 94*
Rocha, Adolfo 1907- *ConAu 141*
Rocha, Armandino Cordeiro Dos Santos 1934- *WhoAm 94, WhoFI 94*
Rocha, Catherine T. 1944- *WhoHisp 94*
Rocha, Conrad Michael 1951- *WhoHisp 94*
Rocha, Guy Louis 1951- *WhoAm 94, WhoWest 94*
Rocha, Joseph Ramon, Jr. 1925- *WhoBlA 94*
Rocha, Juan 1943- *WhoHisp 94*
Rocha, Luis M. 1959- *WhoHisp 94*
Rocha, Mark William 1953- *WhoHisp 94*
Rocha, Octavio *WhoHisp 94*
Rocha, Pedro, Jr. 1939- *WhoHisp 94*
Rocha, Randolfo 1950- *WhoAmA 93*
Rocha, Red 1925- *BasBi*
Rocha, Rene *WhoHisp 94*
Rocha, Steven *WhoHisp 94*
Rocha, Veronica Rodrigues 1946- *WhoHisp 94*
Rocha, Victor *WhoHisp 94*
Rocha, Victoria Joan d1987 *WhoHol 92*
Rochaix, Francois 1942- *NewGrDO*
Rochaix, Jean-David *WhoScEn 94*
Rochambeau, Donatien Marie Joseph de Vimeur, Vicomte de 1750-1813 *WhAmRev*
Rochambeau, Jean-Baptiste-Donátien de Vimeur 1725-1807 *AmRev*
Rochambeau, Jean Baptiste Donatien de Vimeur, Comte de 1725-1807 *WhAmRev [port]*
Rochard, Henri 1921- *WrDr 94*
Rochas Da Costa, Celestino *IntWW 93*
Rochat, Jean-Paul 1943- *WhoFI 94*
Rochberg, George 1918- *NewGrDO, WhoAm 94*
Rochdale, Archdeacon of *Who 94*
Rochdale, Viscount d1993 *Who 94N*
Rochdale, Viscount 1906- *IntWW 93*
Rochdale, Viscount 1938- *Who 94*
Roche *Who 94*
Roche, Alain Andre 1948- *WhoScEn 94*
Roche, Barbara Maureen 1954- *Who 94*
Roche, Billy 1949- *ConDr 93*
Roche, David (O'Grady) 1947- *Who 94*
Roche, Douglas David 1936- *WhoAm 94*
Roche, Eugene 1929- *WhoHol 92*
Roche, Frank d1963 *WhoHol 92*
Roche, Frederick Lloyd d1992 *Who 94N*
Roche, George Augustine 1941- *WhoFI 94*
Roche, George Charles, III 1935- *WhoAm 94*
Roche, Gerard R. *NewYTBS 93*
Roche, Gerard Raymond 1931- *WhoFI 94*
Roche, James McMillan 1934- *WhoAm 94*
Roche, James Richard 1924- *WhoAm 94, WhoScEn 94*
Roche, Jean Casimir Henri Hilaire d1992 *IntWW 93N*
Roche, John d1952 *WhoHol 92*
Roche, John A. d1980 *WhoHol 92*
Roche, John Edward 1946- *WhoAm 94*
Roche, John J. *WhoAmL 94*
Roche, John James 1961- *WhoMW 93*
Roche, John Jefferson 1934- *WhoAm 94*
Roche, John P. 1923- *IntWW 93, WhoAm 94, WrDr 94*
Roche, Kerry Lee 1964- *WhoScEn 94*
Roche, Kevin *IntWW 93*
Roche, Kevin 1922- *WhoAm 94, WhoScEn 94*
Roche, (Eamonn) Kevin 1922- *IntWW 93*
Roche, Marcel 1920- *IntWW 93*
Roche, Marilyn M. 1939- *WhoAmP 93*
Roche, Mark William 1956- *WhoMW 93*
Roche, Mazo de la 1879-1961 *BlmGWL*
Roche, Paul 1928- *WrDr 94*
Roche, Robert (Richard) *WhoAmA 93*
Roche, Suzzy *WhoHol 92*
Roche, Thomas Gabriel 1909- *Who 94*
Roche, Tony 1945- *BuCMET*
Roche, William Joseph 1927- *WhoAm 94*
Rocheblave, Sieur de *WhAmRev*
Roche de Fermoy, Matthias *WhAmRev*
Rocheé, Arthur Stewart, Sr. 1933- *WhoHisp 94*
Rochefermoy, Mathieu Alexis de 1725-1782 *AmRev*
Rochefort, Christiane 1917- *BlmGWL, ConWorW 93*
Rochefort, Jean 1930- *WhoHol 92*
Rochefort, Jean-Baptiste 1746-1819 *NewGrDO*
Rochefort, John Spencer 1924- *WhoAm 94*
Rocheleau, Beth Ann 1963- *WhoFI 94*
Rocheleau, Dale Andre 1958- *WhoAmL 94*
Rocheleau, James Romig 1940- *WhoAm 94*
Rochell, Carlton Charles 1933- *WhoAm 94*
Rochelle, Claire d1981 *WhoHol 92*
Rochelle, Edwin d1977 *WhoHol 92*
Rochelle, Mercedes 1955- *ConAu 140*
Rochelle, Michael R. 1949- *WhoAmL 94*
Rochelle, Robert Thomas 1945- *WhoAmP 93*
Rochelle, William Curson 1937- *WhoScEn 94*
Rochen, Donald Michael 1943- *WhoMW 93*
Rocher, Edouard Yves 1932- *WhoScEn 94*
Rocher, Guy 1924- *IntWW 93*
Rocher, Ludo 1926- *WhoAm 94*
Roches, Catherine Fradonnet des 1542-1587 *BlmGWL*
Roches, Madeleine Neveu des 1520-1587 *BlmGWL*
Rochester *WhoHol 92*
Rochester, Archdeacon of *Who 94*
Rochester, Baron 1916- *Who 94*
Rochester, Bishop of 1935- *Who 94*
Rochester, Dean of *Who 94*
Rochester, Earl of 1647-1680 *DcLB 131 [port]*
Rochester, David John 1939- *WhoWest 94*
Rochester, Geof 1959- *WhoBlA 94*
Rochester, George Dixon 1908- *IntWW 93, Who 94*
Rochester, George E. *EncSF 93*
Rochester, J. W. 1861-1924 *BlmGWL*
Rochester, John Wilmot, Earl of 1647-1680 *BlmGEL*
Rochester, Mattilyn Talford 1941- *WhoAmP 93*
Rochester, Michael Grant 1932- *WhoAm 94*
Rochester, Nathaniel 1752-1831 *WhAmRev*
Rochette, Anne Monique 1957- *WhoAmA 93*
Rochette, Louis 1923- *WhoAm 94*
Rochetti, (Gaetano) Filippo fl. 1724- *NewGrDO*
Rochford, Joseph Patrick 1935- *WhoAmP 93*
Rochin, Paul d1964 *WhoHol 92*
Rochín-Rodriguez, Refugio Ismael 1941- *WhoHisp 94*
Rochkind, Louis Philipp 1948- *WhoAmL 94*
Rochkind, Rosalind Heideman 1948- *WhoAmL 94*
Rochlin, Doris *DrAPF 93*
Rochlin, Irma *WhoAmP 93*
Rochlis, Jeffrey Aaron 1945- *WhoWest 94*
Rochois, Marie Le *NewGrDO*
Rochon, Esther 1948- *EncSF 93*
Rochon, Jean 1938- *IntWW 93*
Rochon, John Philip 1951- *WhoAm 94, WhoFI 94*
Rochon, Lela *WhoBlA 94*
Rochon, Lela 1965- *WhoHol 92*
Rochwarger, Leonard *WhoAmP 93*
Rochwarger, Leonard 1925- *WhoAm 94*
Rock, Arthur 1926- *WhoAm 94, WhoFI 94*
Rock, Blossom d1978 *WhoHol 92*
Rock, Charles d1919 *WhoHol 92*
Rock, Chris 1968- *WhoBlA 94*
Rock, Clarence Warren d1960 *WhoHol 92*
Rock, Felippa *WhoHol 92*
Rock, George David d1988 *WhoHol 92*
Rock, Harold L. 1932- *WhoAmL 94*
Rock, Helga 1951- *WhoWomW 91*
Rock, Irvin 1922- *WhoScEn 94*
Rock, Joe d1984 *WhoHol 92*
Rock, John *WorInv*
Rock, John Aubrey 1946- *WhoAm 94*
Rock, Kenneth Willett 1938- *WhoAm 94*
Rock, Monte, III *WhoHol 92*
Rock, Paul Elliot 1943- *Who 94*
Rock, Philip Joseph 1937- *WhoAmP 93*
Rock, R. Rand, II 1949- *WhoAmP 93*
Rock, Richard R. 1924- *WhoAmP 93*
Rock, Richard Rand 1924- *WhoMW 93*
Rock, Warren d1960 *WhoHol 92*
Rock, William d1922 *WhoHol 92*
Rockart, John Fralick 1931- *WhoFI 94, WhoScEn 94*
Rock-Bailey, Jinni *WhoBlA 94*
Rockburne, Dorothea *IntWW 93, WhoAmA 93*
Rockburne, Dorothea G. *WhoAm 94*
Rocke, Alan J. 1948- *WhoMW 93*
Rocke, David Morton 1946- *WhoAm 94*
Rocke, John Roy Mansfield 1918- *Who 94*
Rockefeller, Blanchette Ferry Hooker 1909-1992 *AnObit 1992*
Rockefeller, Blanchette Hooker 1909-1992 *WhAm 10*
Rockefeller, David 1915- *IntWW 93, Who 94, WhoAm 94, WhoAmA 93*
Rockefeller, David, Mrs. *WhoAmA 93*
Rockefeller, Edwin Shaffer 1927- *WhoAm 94, WhoAmL 94*
Rockefeller, Happy *WhoAm 94*
Rockefeller, James S. 1902- *IntWW 93*
Rockefeller, James Stillman 1902- *Who 94*
Rockefeller, John D., IV 1937- *CngDr 93*
Rockefeller, John Davison 1839-1937 *AmSocL [port]*
Rockefeller, John Davison, III 1906-1978 *WhoAmA 93N*
Rockefeller, John Davison, IV 1937- *IntWW 93, WhoAm 94, WhoAmP 93, WhoScEn 94*
Rockefeller, Laurance S., Mrs. 1910- *WhoAmA 93*
Rockefeller, Laurance Spelman 1910- *IntWW 93, Who 94*
Rockefeller, Margaretta Fitler Murphy *WhoAm 94*
Rockefeller, Nelson Aldrich 1908-1979 *WhoAmA 93N*
Rockefeller, Sharon Percy 1944- *WhoAmP 93*
Rockefeller, William 1918-1990 *WhAm 10*
Rockefeller, Winthrop 1912-1973 *WhoAmA 93N*
Rockel, August 1814-1876 *NewGrDO*
Rockel, Joseph (August) 1783-1870 *NewGrDO*
Rockelman, Georgia Fowler Benz 1920- *WhoFI 94*
Rockensies, John William 1932- *WhoFI 94, WhoScEn 94*
Rockenstein, Walter Harrison, II *WhoAm 94, WhoAmL 94*
Rockenstein, William J. 1949- *WhoIns 94*
Rocker, Lee 1961- *See* Stray Cats, The *ConMus 11*
Rocker, Tracy Quinton 1966- *WhoBlA 94*
Rocket, Charles *WhoHol 92*
Rockett, Angus Alexander 1957- *WhoScEn 94*
Rockett, Carlton Lee 1941- *WhoAm 94*
Rockett, D. Joe 1942- *WhoAmL 94*
Rockett, Damon Emerson 1938- *WhoBlA 94*
Rockett, Rikki *See* Poison *ConMus 11*
Rockey, Dawn 1961- *WhoAm 94*
Rockey, Dawn E. 1961- *WhoAmP 93, WhoMW 93*
Rockey, Kenneth Henry 1894- *WhAm 10*
Rockey, Tobin F. *DrAPF 93*
Rockfern, Danielle 1931- *WrDr 94*
Rockhampton, Bishop of 1935- *Who 94*
Rockhill, Jack Kerrigan 1930- *WhoFI 94*
Rockhold, Lois M. *WhoAmP 93*
Rockin' Dopsie 1932-1993 *ConMus 10 [port]*
Rockingham, Marquis of 1730-1782 *AmRev*
Rockingham, Charles Watson-Wentworth, Marquis of 1730-1782 *WhAmRev [port]*
Rockland, Barry Clifford 1943- *WhoAm 94, WhoFI 94*
Rockland, Jeffrey *WhoHol 92*
Rockland, Michael Aaron 1935- *WrDr 94*
Rocklen, Kathy Hellenbrand 1951- *WhoAmL 94, WhoFI 94*
Rockler, Walter James 1920- *WhoAm 94*
Rockley, Baron 1934- *IntWW 93, Who 94*
Rockley, L(awrence) E(dwin) 1916- *WrDr 94*
Rocklin, David Samuel 1931- *Who 94*
Rocklin, Isadore J. 1907- *WhoAm 94*
Rocklin, Raymond 1922- *WhoAmA 93*
Rocklynne, Ross 1913-1988 *EncSF 93*
Rockne, Sue Lorentzen 1934- *WhoAmP 93*
Rockoff, S. David 1931- *WhoAm 94*
Rockower, Edward B. 1943- *WhoScEn 94*
Rockowitz, Noah Ezra 1949- *WhoAmL 94*
Rockrise, George Thomas 1916- *WhoAm 94*
Rockstein, Morris 1916- *WhoAm 94*
Rockstroh, Dennis John 1942- *WhoWest 94*
Rockstroh, Lenna M. 1924- *WhoAmP 93*
Rockwell, Alvin John 1908- *WhoAm 94*
Rockwell, Anne (Foote) 1934- *WrDr 94*
Rockwell, Benjamin Allen 1964- *WhoScEn 94*
Rockwell, Bruce McKee 1922- *WhoAm 94*
Rockwell, Burton Lowe 1920- *WhoAm 94*
Rockwell, David Hosmer 1944- *WhoAmL 94*
Rockwell, Don Arthur 1938- *WhoAm 94, WhoWest 94*
Rockwell, Elizabeth Adams 1928- *WhoAmP 93*

Rockwell, Elizabeth Dennis 1921- *WhoAm 94, WhoFI 94*
Rockwell, Florence d1964 *WhoHol 92*
Rockwell, George d1978 *WhoHol 92*
Rockwell, George Barcus 1926- *WhoAm 94*
Rockwell, Jack d1947 *WhoHol 92*
Rockwell, John Sargent 1940- *WhoAm 94*
Rockwell, Levon Irvin 1924- *WhoAmP 93*
Rockwell, Ned M. 1956- *WhoScEn 94*
Rockwell, Norman 1894-1978 *AmCulL [port], WhoAmA 93N*
Rockwell, Robert *WhoHol 92*
Rockwell, Robert Goode 1922- *WhoWest 94*
Rockwell, Ronald James, Jr. 1937- *WhoAm 94*
Rockwell, Steven Albert 1941- *WhoWest 94*
Rockwell, Theodore 1922- *WhoAm 94*
Rockwell, Theodore, (III) 1922- *ConAu 140*
Rockwell, Thomas 1933- *WrDr 94*
Rockwell, Willard Frederick, Jr. 1914-1992 *WhAm 10*
Rockwell, Winthrop Adams 1948- *WhoAm 94, WhoAmL 94*
Rockwood, Franklin Alexander 1936- *WhoFI 94, WhoMW 93*
Rockwood, Roy *EncSF 93*
Rockwood, Ruth H. 1906- *WhoAm 94*
Roco, Mihail Constantin 1947- *WhoScEn 94*
Rocque, John 1704?-1762 *DcNaB MP*
Rocque, Rebecca Homedew 1954- *WhoWest 94*
Rocque, Vincent Joseph 1945- *WhoAm 94*
Rod, Edouard 1857-1910 *TwCLC 52 [port]*
Roda 1926- *WhoAmA 93*
Roda, Roda d1945 *WhoHol 92*
Rodabaugh, David Joseph 1938- *WhoWest 94*
Rodahl, Kaare 1917- *WrDr 94*
Rodak, Ralph 1954- *WhoAmL 94*
Rodale, Robert David 1930-1990 *WhAm 10*
Rodan, Don 1950- *WhoAmA 93*
Rodann, Ziva 1937- *WhoHol 92*
Rodarmor, William 1942- *ConAu 140*
Rodarte, Joseph Robert 1938- *WhoHisp 94*
Rodarte, Pablo 1946- *WhoHisp 94*
Rodbard, Betty *WhoAmA 93*
Rodbard, David 1941- *WhoScEn 94*
Rodbell, Clyde Armand 1927- *WhoAm 94*
Rodbell, Martin 1925- *WhoAm 94*
Rodburg, Michael Lee 1946- *WhoAm 94, WhoAmL 94*
Rodd *Who 94*
Rodd, John 1905- *WrDr 94*
Rodd, Marcia 1940- *WhoHol 92*
Rodda, Emily 1948?- *ChlLR 32 [port]*
Rodda, James 1945- *Who 94*
Rodda, Luca 1960- *WhoFI 94, WhoScEn 94*
Roddam, Franc 1946- *IntMPA 94*
Roddan, Ray Gene 1947- *WhoMW 93*
Rodde, Anne-Marie 1946- *NewGrDO*
Rodden, John (Gallagher) 1956- *WrDr 94*
Rodden, Lois Mae 1928- *AstEnc*
Roddenberry, Eugene Wesley 1921-1991 *WhAm 10*
Roddenberry, Gene 1921-1991 *EncSF 93*
Roddenberry, Stephen Keith 1948- *WhoAmL 94*
Roddey, John Barber 1936- *WhoFI 94*
Roddick, Alan 1937- *WrDr 94*
Roddick, Anita *NewYTBS 93 [port]*
Roddick, Anita (Lucia) 1942- *ConAu 140*
Roddick, Anita Lucia 1942- *IntWW 93, Who 94*
Roddick, David Bruce 1948- *WhoFI 94, WhoWest 94*
Roddick, (George) Winston 1940- *Who 94*
Roddie, Ian Campbell 1928- *IntWW 93, Who 94*
Roddis, Louis Harry, Jr. 1918-1991 *WhAm 10*
Roddis, Richard Stiles Law 1930- *WhoAm 94, WhoIns 94*
Roddis, Winifred Mary Kim 1955- *WhoScEn 94*
Roddy, Edith Jeannette *WhoAmA 93N*
Roddy, Howard W. 1950- *WhoBlA 94*
Roddy, James D. d1986 *WhoHol 92*
Roddy, Lee 1921- *WrDr 94*
Rode, Anne Hathaway 1960- *WhoFI 94*
Rode, Helle 1954- *WhoAmL 94*
Rode, James Dean 1948- *WhoAm 94*
Rode, Larry Jon 1960- *WhoAmP 93*
Rode, Leif 1926- *WhoAm 94*
Rode, Meredith Eagon 1938- *WhoAmA 93*
Rode, Walter d1973 *WhoHol 92*
Rode, Wilhelm 1887-1959 *NewGrDO*
Rodeck, Charles Henry 1944- *Who 94*
Rodee, Bernard Leslie 1958- *WhoMW 93*
Rodefer, Jeffrey Robert 1963- *WhoAmL 94*
Rodefer, Stephen 1940- *WrDr 94*
Rodeffer, Michael Eugene 1967- *WhoMW 93*
Rodeffer, Stephanie Lynn Holschlag 1947- *WhoWest 94*
Rodeheaver, Homer Alvan 1880-1955 *DcAmReB 2*
Rodeiro, Jose Manuel 1949- *WhoAmA 93, WhoHisp 94*
Rodela, Leo E. 1932- *WhoAmP 93*
Rodell, Timothy Clarke 1951- *WhoWest 94*
Rodella, Debbie A. 1961- *WhoAmP 93*
Rodeman, Frederick Ernest 1938- *WhoMW 93*
Rodeman, Richard Dean 1953- *WhoAmL 94*
Rodemeyer, Michael Leonard, Jr. 1950- *WhoAmL 94*
Roden, Earl of 1909- *Who 94*
Roden, Johanna Wahl 1928- *WhoWest 94*
Rodenbach, Edward Francis 1951- *WhoAm 94, WhoAmL 94*
Rodenberger, Charles Alvard 1926- *WhoAm 94*
Rodenberg-Roberts, Mary Patricia 1963- *WhoAmL 94*
Rodenburg, Clifton Glenn 1949- *WhoAmL 94*
Rodenhuis, David Roy 1936- *WhoScEn 94*
Rodenkirk, Robert Francis, Jr. 1952- *WhoMW 93*
Rodensky, Shmuel d1989 *WhoHol 92*
Rodenstock, Rudolf 1917- *IntWW 93*
Roder, Heinrich 1952- *WhoScEn 94*
Roder, Mary Renee 1963- *WhoFI 94*
Roderick, Caerwyn Eifion 1927- *Who 94*
Roderick, Charles Edward Morys d1993 *Who 94N*
Roderick, David Milton *IntWW 93N*
Roderick, David Milton 1924- *EncABHB 9 [port]*
Roderick, Dorothy Paetel 1935- *WhoMW 93*
Roderick, George *WhoHol 92*
Roderick, Gerald John 1924- *WhoAmP 93*
Roderick, John R. 1926- *WhoAmP 93*
Roderick, Keith Richard 1953- *WhoMW 93*
Roderick, Richard Michael 1948- *WhoAm 94*
Roderick, Robert Lee 1925- *WhoAm 94*
Roderick, Robin M. 1961- *WhoMW 93*
Roderick, Stephen A 1944- *WhoAm 94*
Roderick, Sue *WhoHol 92*
Roderick, William Rodney 1933- *WhoMW 93*
Roderus, Frank 1942- *WrDr 94*
Rodes, John Edward 1923- *WrDr 94*
Rodeschin, Beverly T. 1936- *WhoAmP 93*
Rodewald, James Michael 1942- *WhoMW 93*
Rodewald, Paul Gerhard 1899- *WhoAm 94*
Rodewald, William Young 1928- *WhoAm 94*
Rodewig, John Stuart 1933- *WhoAm 94, WhoFI 94*
Rodey, Patrick Michael 1943- *WhoAmP 93, WhoWest 94*
Rodez, Andrew LaMarr 1931- *WhoBlA 94*
Rodger, Allan George 1902- *Who 94*
Rodger, Claire *WhoHol 92*
Rodger, George William Adam 1908- *IntWW 93*
Rodger, Patrick Campbell 1920- *Who 94*
Rodger, Struan *WhoHol 92*
Rodger Of Earlsferry, Baron 1944- *Who 94*
Rodgers *Who 94*
Rodgers, Aggie Guerard *WhoAm 94*
Rodgers, Alan *EncSF 93*
Rodgers, Alice Lynn 1942- *WhoFI 94*
Rodgers, Anthony D. *WhoAm 94*
Rodgers, Anthony Recarido, Sr. 1951- *WhoBlA 94*
Rodgers, Anton 1927- *WhoHol 92*
Rodgers, Augustus 1945- *WhoBlA 94*
Rodgers, Barbara Lorraine 1946- *WhoBlA 94*
Rodgers, Beverly 1954- *WhoAmP 93*
Rodgers, Buck 1938- *WhoAm 94, WhoWest 94*
Rodgers, Carolyn M. *DrAPF 93, WrDr 94*
Rodgers, Carolyn M(arie) 1945- *BlkWr 2*
Rodgers, Carolyn Marie 1943- *WhoBlA 94*
Rodgers, Charles 1941- *WhoBlA 94*
Rodgers, Dan d1993 *NewYTBS 93*
Rodgers, Daniel Tracy 1942- *WhoAm 94*
Rodgers, David A. 1945- *WhoIns 94*
Rodgers, Edward 1927- *WhoBlA 94*
Rodgers, Eugene d1919 *WhoHol 92*
Rodgers, Eugene 1939- *WhoAm 94, WrDr 94*
Rodgers, Frank 1927- *WhoAm 94*
Rodgers, Frederic Barker 1940- *WhoAm 94, WhoAmL 94, WhoWest 94*
Rodgers, G. Philip 1928- *WhoAmP 93*
Rodgers, George 1925- *Who 94*
Rodgers, Guy 1935- *BasBi*
Rodgers, Guy William, Jr. 1935- *WhoBlA 94*
Rodgers, Harold William 1907- *Who 94*
Rodgers, Horace J. 1925- *WhoBlA 94*
Rodgers, Ilona *WhoHol 92*
Rodgers, Imogene Sevin 1945- *WhoScEn 94*
Rodgers, Jack A. 1938- *WhoAmA 93*
Rodgers, James A(lexander) 1898- *WhAm 10*
Rodgers, James Earl 1943- *WhoScEn 94*
Rodgers, James Foster 1951- *WhoAm 94, WhoScEn 94*
Rodgers, James Joseph 1950- *WhoAmL 94*
Rodgers, James R. 1947- *WhoBlA 94*
Rodgers, Jerome Thomas 1943- *WhoFI 94*
Rodgers, Jimmie d1933 *WhoHol 92*
Rodgers, Jimmie 1933- *WhoHol 92*
Rodgers, Joan 1956- *IntWW 93*
Rodgers, Joe M. 1933- *IntWW 93, WhoAmP 93*
Rodgers, John 1723-1789 *WhAmRev*
Rodgers, John 1727-1811 *WhAmRev*
Rodgers, John 1914- *IntWW 93, WhoAm 94*
Rodgers, John (Charles) 1906- *WrDr 94*
Rodgers, John Charles d1993 *Who 94N*
Rodgers, John Hunter 1944- *WhoAm 94, WhoFI 94*
Rodgers, John M. 1928- *WhoAmP 93*
Rodgers, John Wesley *WhoHol 92*
Rodgers, Johnathan 1946- *ConBlB 6 [port], WhoAm 94, WhoMW 93*
Rodgers, Johnathan A. 1946- *WhoBlA 94*
Rodgers, Joseph James, Jr. 1939- *WhoBlA 94*
Rodgers, Julie Jack 1959- *WhoAmL 94*
Rodgers, La Sandra 1950- *WhoWest 94*
Rodgers, Lawrence Rodney 1920- *WhoAm 94*
Rodgers, Louis Dean 1930- *WhoMW 93*
Rodgers, Mary 1931- *WrDr 94*
Rodgers, Mary Columbro 1925- *WhoAm 94*
Rodgers, Melonee *WhoHol 92*
Rodgers, Napoleon *WhoBlA 94*
Rodgers, Nile *WhoBlA 94*
Rodgers, Nile 1952- *WhoAm 94*
Rodgers, Pamela 1945- *WhoHol 92*
Rodgers, Patricia Elaine Joan *IntWW 93*
Rodgers, Patricia Elaine Joan 1948- *Who 94*
Rodgers, Paul 1933- *WhoAm 94, WhoAmL 94*
Rodgers, Pepper 1931- *WrDr 94*
Rodgers, Peter H. 1948- *WhoAmL 94*
Rodgers, Piers *Who 94*
Rodgers, (Andrew) Piers (Wingate) 1944- *Who 94*
Rodgers, Ralph Emerson 1954- *WhoAmL 94*
Rodgers, Richard d1979 *WhoHol 92*
Rodgers, Richard (Charles) 1902-1979 *NewGrDO*
Rodgers, Richard Charles 1902-1979 *AmCulL*
Rodgers, Rod Audrian 1937- *WhoBlA 94*
Rodgers, Ronald Carl 1948- *WhoMW 93*
Rodgers, Sarah *DrAPF 93*
Rodgers, Sarah Jane 1927- *WhoAmP 93*
Rodgers, Shirley Marie 1948- *WhoBlA 94*
Rodgers, Thomas 1946- *WhoMW 93*
Rodgers, Tobias *Who 94*
Rodgers, (John Fairlie) Tobias 1940- *Who 94*
Rodgers, Vincent G. 1958- *WhoBlA 94*
Rodgers, Walter d1951 *WhoHol 92*
Rodgers, Warren Lee 1950- *WhoAmP 93*
Rodgers, Willard Lineus 1940- *WhoMW 93*
Rodgers, William Henry 1947- *WhoAm 94*
Rodgers, William J. 1943- *WhoAmL 94*
Rodgers, William Lee 1952- *WhoMW 93*
Rodgers, William M. 1926- *WhoAm 94*
Rodgers, William M., Jr. 1941- *WhoBlA 94*
Rodgers Of Quarry Bank, Baron 1928- *IntWW 93, Who 94*
Rodgman, Alan 1947- *WhoAm 94*
Rodham, Hugh E. d1993 *NewYTBS 93 [port]*
Rodi, Nelly 1918- *WhoWomW 91*
Rodibaugh, Robert Kurtz 1916- *WhoAm 94, WhoAmL 94*
Rodiger, W. Gregory, III 1959- *WhoFI 94*
Rodilak, Charles d1972 *WhoHol 92*
Rodimer, Frank Joseph 1927- *WhoAm 94*
Rodin, Alvin Eli 1926- *WhoAm 94*
Rodin, Ervin Yechiel Laszlo 1932- *WhoAm 94, WhoMW 93*
Rodin, Judith 1944- *IntWW 93*
Rodin, Judith Seitz 1944- *WhoAm 94*
Rodin, Michael F. 1954- *WhoAmL 94*
Rodino, Peter Wallace, Jr. 1909- *IntWW 93, WhoAm 94, WhoAmP 93*
Rodino, Vincent Louis 1929- *WhoFI 94*
Rodionov, Yury Nikolaevich 1938- *LngBDD*
Rodis, Rodel E. 1951- *WhoAsA 94*
Rodis, Theodore George 1947- *WhoMW 93*
Rodite, Robert R.R. 1942- *WhoFI 94*
Roditi, Edouard (Herbert) 1910- *WrDr 94*
Rodkin, Henry Hollison 1935- *WhoMW 93*
Rodley, Laura *DrAPF 93*
Rodman, Alpine Clarence 1952- *WhoFI 94, WhoWest 94*
Rodman, David Lawrence 1956- *WhoFI 94*
Rodman, Dennis Keith 1961- *WhoBlA 94*
Rodman, Eric *EncSF 93*
Rodman, Harry Eugene 1913- *WhoAm 94*
Rodman, James Purcell 1926- *WhoAm 94*
Rodman, John *WhoBlA 94*
Rodman, Leroy Eli 1914- *WhoAm 94*
Rodman, Maia *ConAu 41NR, DrAPF 93*
Rodman, Michael Worthington 1941- *WhoBlA 94*
Rodman, Nancy *WhoHol 92*
Rodman, Peter Warren 1943- *WhoAm 94*
Rodman, Roland Vere 1897- *WhAm 10*
Rodman, Ruth M. 1928- *WhoAmA 93*
Rodman, Selden 1909- *WhoAmA 93*
Rodman, Sue Arlene 1951- *WhoFI 94, WhoWest 94*
Rodman, Sumner 1915- *WhoAm 94*
Rodman, Victor d1965 *WhoHol 92*
Rodne, Kjell John 1948- *WhoMW 93*
Rodner, Stephen B. 1942- *WhoAmL 94*
Rodney, Baron d1992 *Who 94N*
Rodney, Baron 1953- *Who 94*
Rodney, Caesar 1728-1784 *HisWorL, WhAmRev*
Rodney, Earl 1933- *WhoFI 94*
Rodney, Earle d1932 *WhoHol 92*
Rodney, George Brydges 1718-1792 *AmRev, WhAmRev*
Rodney, Jack d1967 *WhoHol 92*
Rodney, Janet *DrAPF 93*
Rodney, Jim Anthony 1962- *WhoFI 94*
Rodney, Joel Morris 1937- *WhoAm 94*
Rodney, John 1916- *WhoHol 92*
Rodney, John Charles 1954- *WhoAmL 94*
Rodney, Karl Basil 1940- *WhoBlA 94*
Rodney, Martin Hurtus 1909- *WhoBlA 94*
Rodney, Thomas 1744-1811 *WhAmRev*
Rodney, William 1923- *WrDr 94*
Rodnick, Eliot Herman 1911- *WhoAm 94*
Rodnite, Andrew John 1935- *WhoAmL 94*
Rodnitzky, Robert Lee 1941- *WhoMW 93*
Rodnunsky, Sidney 1946- *WhoWest 94*
Rodolff, Dale Ward 1938- *WhoFI 94*
Rodolphe, Jean Joseph 1730-1812 *NewGrDO*
Rodoreda, Merce 1909-1983 *BlmGWL*
Rodoreda, Merce (i Gurgui) 1909-1983 *RfGShF*
Rodosovich, Peter 1959- *WhoAmP 93*
Rodovich, Andrew Paul 1948- *WhoAm 94, WhoAmL 94*
Rodowsky, Colby 1932- *SmATA 77 [port]*
Rodowsky, Lawrence F. *WhoAmP 93*
Rodowsky, Lawrence Francis 1930- *WhoAm 94, WhoAmL 94*
Rodricks, Daniel J. 1954- *WrDr 94*
Rodrigo, Thomas James 1950- *WhoHisp 94*
Rodrigo, Timothy 1947- *WhoHisp 94*
Rodrigue, Christine M. 1952- *WhoWest 94*
Rodrigue, George Pierre 1931- *WhoAm 94*
Rodrigues, Alberto 1911- *Who 94*
Rodrigues, Alfred Benjamin Kameeiamoku 1947- *WhoWest 94*
Rodrigues, Amalia 1920- *WhoHol 92*
Rodrigues, Antonio S. *WhoHisp 94*
Rodrigues, David M. 1945- *WhoHisp 94*
Rodrigues, Joseph E. 1936- *WhoAm 94, WhoFI 94*
Rodrigues, Mark 1948- *WhoWest 94*
Rodrigues, Nelson 1912-1980 *IntDcT 2*
Rodrigues, Percy 1924- *WhoHol 92*
Rodriguez, Abel Tomas, Sr. 1942- *WhoHisp 94*
Rodriguez, Abraham, Jr. *WhoHisp 94*
Rodriguez, Adna Rosa 1934- *WhoHisp 94*
Rodriguez, Agustin Antonio 1961- *WhoScEn 94*
Rodriguez, Agustín M. 1967- *WhoHisp 94*
Rodriguez, Aida *WhoHisp 94*
Rodriguez, Albert R. 1951- *WhoHisp 94*
Rodriguez, Albert Ray 1960- *WhoHisp 94*
Rodriguez, Albert S. 1933- *WhoHisp 94*
Rodriguez, Alberto F. 1945- *WhoIns 94*
Rodriguez, Alberto M. 1942- *WhoHisp 94*
Rodriguez, Aleida *DrAPF 93*
Rodriguez, Alfonso Camarillo 1938- *WhoHisp 94*
Rodriguez, Alfredo *WhoHisp 94*

Rodriguez, Alfredo M. 1957- *WhoHisp 94*
Rodriguez, Alma Delia 1965- *WhoHisp 94*
Rodriguez, Alonzo T. *WhoHisp 94*
Rodriguez, Amador *WhoHisp 94*
Rodriguez, Ana Milagros 1949- *WhoHisp 94*
Rodriguez, Andres 1924- *IntWW 93*
Rodriguez, Andres F. 1929- *WhoHisp 94*
Rodriguez, Angel Alfredo 1941- *WhoHisp 94*
Rodriguez, Angel Edgardo 1949- *WhoHisp 94*
Rodriguez, Angel R. 1934- *WhoHisp 94*
Rodriguez, Anthony Ellis 1961- *WhoAmL 94, WhoWest 94*
Rodriguez, Antonio David 1957- *WhoHisp 94*
Rodriguez, Antonio Jose 1944- *WhoAmL 94*
Rodriguez, Ariel A. 1947- *WhoHisp 94*
Rodriguez, Armando Antonio 1961- *WhoScEn 94*
Rodriguez, Armando Osorio 1929- *WhoHisp 94*
Rodriguez, Art A. 1958- *WhoHisp 94*
Rodriguez, Arturo Salvador, III 1949- *WhoHisp 94*
Rodriguez, Augusto 1954- *WhoHisp 94*
Rodriguez, Aurelio 1947- *WhoHisp 94*
Rodriguez, Aurora 1940- *WhoHisp 94*
Rodriguez, Bartolo G. *WhoHisp 94*
Rodriguez, Beatriz *WhoAm 94*
Rodriguez, Beatriz 1951- *WhoHisp 94*
Rodriguez, Belgica 1941- *WhoAm 94, WhoHisp 94*
Rodriguez, Ben *WhoHisp 94*
Rodriguez, Benjamin 1938- *WhoHisp 94*
Rodriguez, Benjamin, Jr. 1943- *WhoHisp 94*
Rodriguez, Carlos 1961- *WhoHisp 94*
Rodriguez, Carlos Augusto 1954- *WhoAmL 94*
Rodriguez, Carlos Eduardo 1941- *WhoHisp 94*
Rodríguez, Carlos Hermes 1953- *WhoHisp 94*
Rodriguez, Carlos J. 1941- *WhoHisp 94*
Rodriguez, Carmen M. 1950- *WhoHisp 94*
Rodriguez, Carmen N. 1957- *WhoHisp 94*
Rodriguez, Carolyn 1961- *WhoAmL 94*
Rodriguez, César 1945- *WhoHisp 94*
Rodriguez, Cesar O. 1952- *WhoHisp 94*
Rodriguez, Charles 1942- *WhoHisp 94*
Rodriguez, Charles 1947- *WhoHisp 94*
Rodriguez, Charles F. 1938- *WhoHisp 94*
Rodriguez, Charles J. *WhoHol 92*
Rodriguez, Chi Chi 1935- *WhoAm 94, WhoHisp 94*
Rodriguez, Cipriano Facundo 1907-1991 *WhoHisp 94N*
Rodriguez, Ciro D. 1946- *WhoAmP 93, WhoHisp 94*
Rodríguez, Clara Elsie 1944- *WhoHisp 94*
Rodriguez, Claudio 1934- *DcLB 134 [port]*
Rodriguez, Daniel 1965- *WhoHisp 94*
Rodriguez, Daniel J. *WhAmRev*
Rodriguez, Daniel R. 1935- *WhoHisp 94*
Rodriguez, Danny Fajardo 1949- *WhoHisp 94*
Rodriguez, David Arthur 1946- *WhoHisp 94*
Rodriguez, Debra Kay Nall 1955- *WhoMW 93*
Rodriguez, Desiderio, Sr. 1942- *WhoHisp 94*
Rodriguez, Domingo 1939- *WhoHisp 94*
Rodriguez, Domingo Antonio *WhoHisp 94*
Rodriguez, Don *WhoHisp 94*
Rodriguez, Doris L. 1927- *WhoBlA 94*
Rodriguez, Ed 1958- *WhoHisp 94*
Rodriguez, Edmundo 1935- *WhoHisp 94*
Rodriguez, Eduardo 1957- *WhoHisp 94*
Rodriguez, Eduardo Ariel 1955- *WhoAmL 94, WhoHisp 94*
Rodriguez, Eduardo L. 1944- *WhoHisp 94*
Rodriguez, Edward F. 1944- *WhoAmL 94*
Rodriguez, Eladio Rafael 1937- *WhoHisp 94*
Rodriguez, Elena Garcia 1944- *WhoFI 94*
Rodriguez, Eli Monserrate 1946- *WhoHisp 94*
Rodriguez, Elias *WhoHisp 94*
Rodriguez, Elias C. 1919- *WhoAmL 94*
Rodriguez, Eliott 1956- *WhoHisp 94*
Rodriguez, Elisa 1936- *WhoHisp 94*
Rodríguez, Elizabeth 1953- *WhoHisp 94*
Rodríguez, Elmer Arturo 1934- *WhoHisp 94*
Rodriguez, Eloy 1947- *WhoAm 94, WhoHisp 94*
Rodriguez, Emma Jean 1944- *WhoHisp 94*
Rodriguez, Eriberto G. 1928- *WhoHisp 94*
Rodriguez, Ernesto Angelo 1947- *WhoHisp 94*
Rodriguez, Ernesto Jesus 1954- *WhoHisp 94*
Rodriguez, Estelita d1966 *WhoHol 92*
Rodriguez, Eugene 1940- *WhoHisp 94*
Rodriguez, Eva I. 1948- *WhoHisp 94*
Rodriguez, F. Ann 1954- *WhoHisp 94*
Rodriguez, Fabio Enrique 1959- *WhoScEn 94*
Rodriguez, Federico G. 1939- *WhoHisp 94*
Rodriguez, Felipe, Jr. *WhoHisp 94*
Rodriguez, Felipe N. *WhoHisp 94*
Rodriguez, Ferdinand 1928- *WhoAm 94, WhoHisp 94, WhoScEn 94*
Rodríguez, Francisco 1959- *WhoHisp 94*
Rodriguez, Francisco 1966- *WhoHisp 94*
Rodriguez, Frank John 1920- *WhoAmP 93*
Rodriguez, Fred 1949- *WhoHisp 94*
Rodriguez, Freddie *WhoHisp 94*
Rodríguez, Frederick Marshall 1938- *WhoHisp 94*
Rodríguez, Galindo 1955- *WhoHisp 94*
Rodriguez, Geno 1940- *WhoAm 94, WhoAmA 93*
Rodriguez, Gerald P. 1940- *WhoHisp 94*
Rodriguez, Gilbert 1941- *WhoHisp 94*
Rodriguez, Gilda Ena 1952- *WhoAmL 94*
Rodriguez, Gloria G. 1948- *WhoHisp 94*
Rodriguez, Gloria R. 1954- *WhoHisp 94*
Rodriguez, Gregorio 1946- *WhoHisp 94*
Rodriguez, Guillermo 1956- *WhoHisp 94*
Rodriguez, Guillermo, Jr. 1968- *WhoHisp 94*
Rodriguez, Guisella 1959- *WhoHisp 94*
Rodriguez, Gustavo Adolfo 1949- *WhoHisp 94*
Rodriguez, Hector Philip 1956- *WhoHisp 94*
Rodriguez, Hector R. 1938- *WhoHisp 94*
Rodriguez, Henry 1952- *WhoHisp 94*
Rodriguez, Henry 1967- *WhoHisp 94*
Rodriguez, Henry, Jr. 1955- *WhoHisp 94*
Rodriguez, Henry Joseph, Jr. 1935- *WhoHisp 94*
Rodriguez, Heriberto, III 1958- *WhoHisp 94*
Rodriguez, Hiram *WhoHisp 94*
Rodriguez, Homer *WhoHisp 94*
Rodriguez, Humberto 1931- *WhoHisp 94*
Rodriguez, Isabel Lorraine *WhoHisp 94*
Rodriguez, Israel I. 1937- *WhoHisp 94*
Rodriguez, Ivan 1971- *WhoAm 94, WhoHisp 94*
Rodriguez, J. Louis 1920- *WhoScEn 94*
Rodriguez, Jacinto 1932- *WhoHisp 94*
Rodriguez, Jacqueline Caridad 1967- *WhoHisp 94*
Rodriguez, Jaime E. *WhoHisp 94*
Rodriguez, James 1956- *WhoHisp 94*
Rodriguez, Jay 1928- *WhoWest 94*
Rodriguez, Jeanette *WhoHisp 94*
Rodriguez, Jesse 1942- *WhoHisp 94*
Rodriguez, Jesus Gene 1952- *WhoHisp 94*
Rodriguez, Jesus Jorge 1946- *WhoHisp 94*
Rodriguez, Jesus Rafael 1960- *WhoHisp 94*
Rodriguez, Jesus Ybarra 1945- *WhoHisp 94*
Rodriguez, Joe D. 1943- *WhoHisp 94*
Rodriguez, John 1958- *WhoHisp 94*
Rodriguez, John C., Jr. 1930- *WhoHisp 94*
Rodriguez, John H. *WhoHisp 94*
Rodriguez, John Perez 1959- *WhoHisp 94*
Rodriguez, Johnny *WhoHisp 94*
Rodriguez, Johnny 1951- *WhoHol 92*
Rodriguez, Johnny 1952- *WhoHisp 94*
Rodriguez, Jorge 1950- *WhoHisp 94*
Rodriguez, Jorge 1956- *WhoHisp 94*
Rodriguez, Jorge Luis 1944- *WhoHisp 94*
Rodriguez, Jorge Luis 1953- *WhoHisp 94*
Rodriguez, Jorge Luis 1957- *WhoHisp 94*
Rodriguez, Jorge S. 1950- *WhoHisp 94*
Rodriguez, Jose 1949- *WhoHisp 94*
Rodriguez, Jose Enrique 1933- *WhoHisp 94*
Rodriguez, Jose Francisco 1942- *WhoWest 94*
Rodriguez, Jose G. 1945- *WhoHisp 94*
Rodriguez, Jose Gabriel 1945- *WhoAmL 94*
Rodriguez, Jose Luis *WhoHisp 94*
Rodriguez, José Manuel *WhoHisp 94*
Rodriguez, Jose Miguel *WhoHisp 94*
Rodriguez, Joseph 1942- *WhoHisp 94*
Rodriguez, Joseph H. *WhoHisp 94*
Rodriguez, Joseph H. 1930- *WhoAm 94, WhoAmL 94*
Rodríguez, Joseph Lawerence 1952- *WhoHisp 94*
Rodriguez, Juan Alfonso 1941- *WhoAm 94, WhoHisp 94*
Rodriguez, Juan Antonio, Jr. 1946- *WhoHisp 94*
Rodriguez, Juan G. 1920- *WhoHisp 94*
Rodriguez, Juan Guadalupe 1920- *WhoAm 94*
Rodriguez, Juan J. 1951- *WhoHisp 94*
Rodriguez, Juan N. 1948- *WhoHisp 94*
Rodriguez, Judith 1936- *BlmGWL*
Rodriguez, Judith (Green) 1936- *WrDr 94*
Rodriguez, Judith Rocio 1950- *WhoHisp 94*
Rodriguez, Julia Garced 1929- *WhoHisp 94*
Rodriguez, Julian Saenz 1938- *WhoHisp 94*
Rodriguez, Julio 1935- *WhoHisp 94*
Rodríguez, Julio R. 1938- *WhoHisp 94*
Rodriguez, Kenneth Leigh 1959- *WhoHisp 94*
Rodríguez, Kyrsis Raquel 1948- *WhoHisp 94*
Rodriguez, Leonard 1944- *WhoWest 94*
Rodriguez, Leonardo 1938- *WhoHisp 94*
Rodriguez, Lina S. 1949- *WhoHisp 94*
Rodriguez, Lorraine Ditzler 1920- *WhoScEn 94*
Rodriguez, Louis J. 1933- *WhoHisp 94*
Rodriguez, Louis Joseph 1933- *WhoAm 94*
Rodriguez, Lourdes de los Angeles 1957- *WhoAmL 94*
Rodríguez, Luis 1944- *WhoHisp 94*
Rodriguez, Luis A., Sr. 1933- *WhoHisp 94*
Rodriguez, Luis Francisco 1953- *WhoHisp 94*
Rodriguez, Luis J. 1954- *ConAu 142*
Rodriguez, Luis Javier 1954- *WhoHisp 94*
Rodríguez, Lula *WhoHisp 94*
Rodriguez, Lynne Roxanne 1954- *WhoBlA 94*
Rodriguez, Manuel *WhoHisp 94*
Rodriguez, Manuel H. 1930- *WhoHisp 94*
Rodriguez, Manuel J. 1935- *WhoHisp 94*
Rodriguez, Marcelino 1939- *WhoHisp 94*
Rodriguez, Marcos *WhoHisp 94*
Rodriguez, Maria Carla 1954- *WhoHisp 94*
Rodriguez, María del Pilar *WhoHisp 94*
Rodriguez, Maria Martinez 1945- *WhoHisp 94*
Rodriguez, Maria Teresa 1953- *WhoHisp 94*
Rodriguez, Marie R. 1961- *WhoHisp 94*
Rodriguez, Mario J. 1932- *WhoHisp 94*
Rodriguez, Mark Gregory 1957- *WhoHisp 94*
Rodriguez, Martha V. *WhoHisp 94*
Rodriguez, Matt L. *WhoAm 94, WhoMW 93*
Rodriguez, Matt L. 1936- *WhoHisp 94*
Rodríguez, Meriemil 1940- *WhoHisp 94*
Rodriguez, Michael Reynaldo 1957- *WhoHisp 94*
Rodriguez, Miguel *WhoHisp 94*
Rodriguez, Miguel 1931- *WhoAm 94*
Rodriguez, Miguel E., Jr. 1934- *WhoHisp 94*
Rodriguez, Mike Angel 1957- *WhoHisp 94*
Rodríguez, Milagros 1947- *WhoHisp 94*
Rodriguez, Milton A. 1951- *WhoHisp 94*
Rodriguez, Moises-Enrique 1962- *WhoScEn 94*
Rodriguez, Myrtle Mary 1939- *WhoAmL 94*
Rodriguez, Nancy E. 1953- *WhoHisp 94*
Rodriguez, Nicholas George 1953- *WhoWest 94*
Rodríguez, Nilda Ocasio de 1943- *WhoHisp 94*
Rodríguez, Norma Kristine 1966- *WhoHisp 94*
Rodriguez, Oscar *WhoHisp 94*
Rodriguez, Pablo 1955- *WhoHisp 94*
Rodriguez, Pascual *WhoHisp 94*
Rodriguez, Patricia Ann 1958- *WhoHisp 94*
Rodríguez, Paul *WhoHisp 94*
Rodriguez, Paul 1955- *WhoHol 92*
Rodriguez, Paul E. 1956- *WhoHisp 94*
Rodriguez, Paul Henry 1937- *WhoHisp 94*
Rodriguez, Paul Lopez 1939- *WhoHisp 94*
Rodriguez, Paul R. *WhoHisp 94*
Rodriguez, Pedro *WhoHisp 94*
Rodriguez, Peter 1926- *WhoHisp 94*
Rodriguez, Peter Ernest 1950- *WhoHisp 94*
Rodriguez, Plinio A. 1942- *WhoHisp 94*
Rodriguez, Rafo *WhoAmP 93*
Rodriguez, Ralph 1952- *WhoHisp 94*
Rodriguez, Ramon *WhoHisp 94*
Rodriguez, Ramon 1921- *WhoHisp 94*
Rodriguez, Ramon J. 1950- *WhoHisp 94*
Rodriguez, Ramon Joe 1934- *WhoHisp 94*
Rodriguez, Raul G. 1952- *WhoHisp 94*
Rodriguez, Ray *WhoHisp 94*
Rodriguez, Ray Cortez 1929- *WhoHisp 94*
Rodriguez, Raymond Mendoza *WhoHisp 94*
Rodriguez, Rene Mauricio 1946- *WhoHisp 94*
Rodriguez, Rene R., Jr. 1962- *WhoHisp 94*
Rodriguez, Renée Gonzalez *WhoHisp 94*
Rodriguez, Rich 1963- *WhoHisp 94*
Rodriguez, Richard 1944- *HispLC [port], WhoHisp 94*
Rodriguez, Richard Antonio 1942- *WhoHisp 94*
Rodriguez, Richard Fajardo 1945- *WhoHisp 94*
Rodriguez, Rick 1954- *WhoHisp 94*
Rodriguez, Rita D. 1956- *WhoHisp 94*
Rodriguez, Rita M. 1942- *WhoHisp 94*
Rodriguez, Rita Maria 1944- *WhoAm 94, WhoFI 94*
Rodriguez, Robert 1968- *WhoHisp 94*
Rodriguez, Robert A. 1946- *WhoHisp 94*
Rodriguez, Robert H. 1950- *WhoHisp 94*
Rodriguez, Robert J. 1962- *WhoHisp 94*
Rodriguez, Robert Wayne 1950- *WhoHisp 94*
Rodriguez, Roberto R. 1942- *WhoHisp 94*
Rodriguez, Rocío A. 1952- *WhoHisp 94*
Rodriguez, Rodd 1939- *WhoHisp 94*
Rodriguez, Rodney Tápanes 1946- *WhoHisp 94*
Rodriguez, Rodri Josefina 1955- *WhoHisp 94*
Rodriguez, Rolando Damian 1957- *WhoHisp 94*
Rodriguez, Roman 1951- *WhoAm 94, WhoWest 94*
Rodriguez, Romeo 1948- *WhoHisp 94*
Rodriguez, Ronald 1954- *WhoHisp 94*
Rodríguez, Rosa M. 1955- *WhoHisp 94*
Rodriguez, Rosario 1969- *WhoHisp 94*
Rodriguez, Ruben *WhoBlA 94, WhoHisp 94*
Rodriguez, Rudy, Jr. *WhoHisp 94*
Rodriguez, Russell A. 1957- *WhoHisp 94*
Rodriguez, Sabino, III 1953- *WhoAmL 94*
Rodriguez, Sebastian James 1936- *WhoHisp 94*
Rodriguez, Sergio 1930- *WhoHisp 94*
Rodriguez, Simon Yldefonso 1928- *WhoHisp 94*
Rodríguez, Sylvan Robert, Jr. 1948- *WhoHisp 94*
Rodríguez, Sylvia B. 1947- *WhoHisp 94*
Rodriguez, Sylvia G. 1941- *WhoAmP 93*
Rodriguez, Teresa *WhoHisp 94*
Rodriguez, Thomas Richard 1947- *WhoHisp 94*
Rodriguez, Tito d1973 *WhoHol 92*
Rodriguez, Tony *WhoHisp 94*
Rodriguez, Tulio *WhoHisp 94*
Rodríguez, Valerio Sierra 1922- *WhoHisp 94*
Rodriguez, Vicente *WhoHisp 94*
Rodriguez, Victor *WhoAmP 93*
Rodriguez, Victor 1937- *WhoHisp 94*
Rodriguez, Victor David 1942- *WhoHisp 94*
Rodriguez, Vincent Angel 1921- *WhoAm 94, WhoHisp 94*
Rodriguez, Waldemar Quiles 1940- *WhoAmP 93*
Rodriguez, Walter 1948- *ConAu 142*
Rodriguez, Walter Enrique 1948- *WhoHisp 94*
Rodriguez, Ward Arthur 1948- *WhoHisp 94*
Rodriguez, William Robert *DrAPF 93*
Rodriguez, Yolanda *WhoHisp 94*
Rodriguez-Arias, Jorge H. 1915- *WhoScEn 94*
Rodriguez-Arroyo, Jesus 1948- *WhoHisp 94, WhoScEn 94*
Rodriguez-Borges, Carlina 1952- *WhoHisp 94*
Rodriguez-Broatch, Carlos R. 1941- *WhoHisp 94*
Rodriguez-Camilloni, Humberto Leonardo 1945- *WhoAm 94, WhoHisp 94*
Rodríguez-Cintrón, William 1959- *WhoHisp 94*
Rodriguez-Collazo, Angel A. 1942- *WhoHisp 94*
Rodriguez Colon, Charles A. 1954- *WhoAmP 93*
Rodriguez de Hita, Antonio 1724?-1787 *NewGrDO*
Rodriguez-del Valle, Nuri 1945- *WhoAm 94, WhoHisp 94, WhoScEn 94*
Rodriguez De Yurre, Prudencio 1941- *WhoHisp 94*
Rodriguez-Diaz, Juan E. 1941- *WhoAmL 94*
Rodriguez-Erdmann, Franz 1935- *WhoAm 94, WhoHisp 94*
Rodriguez-Espi, Miguel Angel, Jr. 1968- *WhoHisp 94*
Rodriguez-Esquerdo, Brunilda Esperanza 1957- *WhoAmL 94*
Rodriguez-Florido, Jorge Julio 1943- *WhoHisp 94*
Rodriguez-Garcia, Frank 1934- *WhoAmP 93*
Rodriguez Garcia, Jose A. 1946- *WhoScEn 94*
Rodriguez-Gómez, Jose R. 1959- *WhoHisp 94*
Rodriguez Graf, Barbara Ann 1956- *WhoHisp 94*
Rodríguez Hernández, Aurea E. 1948- *WhoHisp 94*
Rodriguez-Holguin, Jeanette 1954- *WhoHisp 94*
Rodriguez-Howard, Mayra *WhoHisp 94*

Rodríguez-Jiménez, Saraí 1945- WhoHisp 94
Rodriguez Kimbell, Sylvia WhoHisp 94
Rodriguez Lara, Guillermo 1923- IntWW 93
Rodriguez-Losada Rebellon, Eduardo 1886-1973 NewGrDO
Rodriguez-Luis, Julio 1937- WhoHisp 94
Rodriguez-Mendoza, Amalia 1946- WhoHisp 94
Rodriguez Negron, Enrique WhoAmP 93, WhoHisp 94
Rodriguez-O, Jaime E. 1940- WhoHisp 94
Rodriguez-Orellana, Manuel 1948- WhoAmL 94
Rodríguez-Pagán, Juan Antonio 1942- WhoHisp 94
Rodriguez-Peralta, Carmen Laura 1956- WhoHisp 94
Rodríguez-Pérez, Hilda D. 1939- WhoHisp 94
Rodriguez-Poventud, Julie Rose 1953- WhoHisp 94
Rodriguez Remeneski, Shirley 1938- WhoAmP 93
Rodriguez-Rivera, Angel Luis 1947- WhoFI 94
Rodriguez Roche, José Antonio 1955- WhoHisp 94
Rodriguez Rodriguez, Carlos Rafael 1913- IntWW 93
Rodriguez-Roque, Victor Bernabe 1935- WhoHisp 94
Rodriguez-Sardiñas, Orlando 1938- WhoHisp 94
Rodríguez-Schieman, Hildegarde WhoHisp 94
Rodriguez-Sierra, Jorge Fernando 1945- WhoHisp 94
Rodríguez-Sosa, Sergio A. 1947- WhoHisp 94
Rodríguez Suárez, Roberto 1923- WhoHisp 94
Rodriguez-Thompson, Diana 1968- WhoHisp 94
Rodriquez, Ernesto Angelo 1947- WhoAmA 93
Rodrogues, Donald Frank 1938- WhoWest 94
Rodts, Gerald Edward 1934- WhoScEn 94
Rodulfo, Lillie M. 1947- WhoHisp 94
Rodutti, Esther C. 1933- WhoAmL 94, WhoFI 94
Rodway, Allan Edwin 1919- WrDr 94
Rodway, Norman 1929- WhoHol 92
Rodwell, Craig L. d1993 NewYTBS 93
Rodwell, Daniel Alfred Hunter 1936- Who 94
Rodwell, George (Herbert Bonaparte) 1800-1852 NewGrDO
Rodwell, John Dennis 1946- WhoAm 94
Rodwin, Lloyd 1919- ConAu 42NR, WrDr 94
Rodysill, Jerome Otto 1929- WhoAm 94, WhoFI 94
Rodzianko, Paul 1945- WhoAm 94, WhoFI 94
Rodzinski, Artur d1958 WhoHol 92
Rodzinski, Artur 1892-1958 NewGrDO
Rodzinski, Halina d1993 NewYTBS 93
Rodzinski, Halina 1904-1993 ConAu 141
Roe, Anthony Maitland 1929- Who 94
Roe, Arthur d1993 NewYTBS 93
Roe, Audrey R. 1946- WhoBlA 94
Roe, Barbara L(ouise) 1947- ConAu 141
Roe, Bassett d1934 WhoHol 92
Roe, Benson Bertheau 1918- WhoAm 94, WhoWest 94
Roe, Byron Paul 1934- WhoAm 94, WhoScEn 94
Roe, Charles Richard 1940- WhoAm 94, WhoWest 94
Roe, Clifford Ashley, Jr. 1942- WhoAm 94, WhoAmL 94
Roe, Daphne A. d1993 NewYTBS 93
Roe, Daphne A(nderson) 1923-1993 ConAu 142
Roe, Derek Arthur 1937- WrDr 94
Roe, Ernest 1920- WrDr 94
Roe, Geoffrey Eric 1944- Who 94
Roe, Georgeanne Thomas 1945- WhoScEn 94
Roe, Ivan EncSF 93
Roe, Jerry D. 1936- WhoAmP 93
Roe, John H. 1939- WhoAm 94, WhoFI 94
Roe, Keith WhoAmP 93
Roe, Kenneth Andrew 1916-1991 WhAm 10
Roe, Kenneth Keith 1945- WhoAm 94
Roe, Marion Audrey 1936- Who 94, WhoWomW 91
Roe, Marty See Diamond Rio ConMus 11
Roe, Matt WhoHol 92
Roe, Michael Dean 1951- WhoScEn 94
Roe, Michael Henry 1944- WhoFI 94
Roe, Norman John Edward 1922- WhoMW 93
Roe, Radie Lynn 1962- WhoFI 94, WhoMW 93
Roe, Raigh (Edith) 1922- Who 94
Roe, Ramona Jeraldean 1942- WhoAmL 94
Roe, Raymond WhoHol 92
Roe, Rex (David) 1925- Who 94
Roe, Richard C. 1930- WhoAm 94
Roe, Robert A. 1924- WhoAmP 93
Roe, Robert A. 1954- WhoAmP 93
Roe, Ryong-Joon 1929- WhoMW 93
Roe, Thomas c. 1581-1644 WhWE
Roe, Thomas Anderson 1927- WhoAm 94
Roe, Thomas Coombe 1914- WhoAm 94
Roe, Walter C. d1913 EncNAR
Roe, William Gordon Who 94
Roe, William Thomas 1944- WhoWest 94
Roebling, John 1806-1869 WorInv
Roebling, Mary G. 1905- WhoAmA 93
Roebling, Mary Gindhart WhoAm 94, WhoFI 94
Roebling, Paul WhoHol 92
Roebuck, Daniel WhoHol 92
Roebuck, Derek 1935- WrDr 94
Roebuck, Elmo D. 1934- WhoAmP 93
Roebuck, Gerard Francis 1953- WhoBlA 94
Roebuck, James Randolph, Jr. 1945- WhoAmP 93, WhoBlA 94
Roebuck, John Clifford 1950- WhoAm 94
Roebuck, Joseph Chester 1946- WhoFI 94
Roebuck, Roy Delville 1929- Who 94
Roebuck-Hayden, Marcia WhoBlA 94
Roebuck-Hoard, Marcia Veronica 1950- WhoBlA 94
Roeck, Thomas J., Jr. 1944- WhoAm 94
Roeckel, August NewGrDO
Roeckel, Joseph NewGrDO
Roecker, James Allen 1936- WhoMW 93
Roedder, Edwin Woods 1919- WhoAm 94
Roedder, William Chapman, Jr. 1946- WhoAmL 94
Roedel, Paul Robert 1927- WhoAm 94, WhoFI 94
Roedema, Charles Edward 1939- WhoAm 94
Roeder, Charles William 1942- WhoWest 94
Roeder, David Lowell 1939- WhoFI 94
Roeder, Gloria Jean 1945- WhoMW 93
Roeder, Rebecca Emily 1959- WhoMW 93
Roeder, Richard Kenneth 1948- WhoFI 94
Roeder, Robert Gayle 1942- WhoAm 94
Roeder, Stephen Bernhard Walter 1939- WhoAm 94, WhoWest 94
Roeder, William F., Jr. 1942- WhoAmL 94
Roederer, Juan Gualterio 1929- WhoAm 94
Roediger, David R(andall) 1952- ConAu 142
Roeding, Richard Louis 1930- WhoAmP 93
Roeg, Nicolas 1928- IntMPA 94
Roeg, Nicolas Jack 1928- IntWW 93, Who 94, WhoAm 94
Roeger, William Coley, Jr. 1947- WhoAmL 94
Roegner, George Peter 1932- WhoAm 94
Roehl, Kathleen Ann 1948- WhoMW 93
Roehl, Richard WhoAmP 93
Roehl, Wesley Scott 1959- WhoWest 94
Roehm, Carolyne Jane 1951- WhoAm 94
Roehm, Edward Charles 1946- WhoFI 94
Roehm, Frederick Wesley 1946- WhoMW 93
Roehm, James R. 1948- WhoIns 94
Roehm, MacDonell, Jr. 1939- WhoAm 94
Roehrenbeck, Paul William 1945- WhoScEn 94
Roehrick, John WhoAmP 93
Roehrig, Catharine H. 1949- WrDr 94
Roehrig, Charles Burns 1923- WhoAm 94
Roehrig, Frederick 1942- WhoMW 93
Roehrig, Terence Jerome 1955- WhoMW 93
Roehrkasse, Pauline Catherine Holtorf 1909- WhoMW 93
Roehrs, Robert Christian 1931- WhoWest 94
Roekk, Marika 1913- WhoHol 92
Roel, Edmundo Lorenzo 1917- WhoHisp 94
Roelke, Ada Ellen 1928- WhoWest 94
Roelker, Nancy Lyman d1993 NewYTBS 93
Roell, C. J., Mrs. 1955- WhoFI 94
Roelli, Kathleen Jane 1954- WhoMW 93
Roellig, Leonard Oscar 1927- WhoAm 94
Roelofs, Wendell Lee 1938- WhoAm 94, WhoScEn 94
Roels, Marcel d1973 WhoHol 92
Roels, Oswald Albert 1921- WhoAm 94
Roem, Mohammad 1908- IntWW 93
Roemer, Buddy 1943- WhoAmP 93
Roemer, Charles Elson, III 1943- IntWW 93
Roemer, Edward Pier 1908- WhoScEn 94, WhoWest 94
Roemer, Elaine Sloane 1938- WhoFI 94
Roemer, Elizabeth 1929- WhoAm 94, WhoScEn 94
Roemer, Ernest Albin, Jr. 1931- WhoAmP 93
Roemer, James W., Jr. 1944- WhoAmL 94
Roemer, Joan (Phylis Akre) 1933- WrDr 94
Roemer, John Alan 1949- WhoFI 94
Roemer, John E. 1945- WhoWest 94
Roemer, Milton Irwin 1916- WhoAm 94
Roemer, Olaus 1644-1710 WorScD [port]
Roemer, Tim 1956- WhoAm 94, WhoAmP 93
Roemer, Timothy J. 1956- CngDr 93, WhoMW 93
Roemer, William F., Jr. 1926- WrDr 94
Roemer, William Frederick 1933- WhoAm 94, WhoFI 94
Roemerman, Steven Dane 1951- WhoFI 94
Roeming, Robert Frederick 1911- WhoAm 94
Roemmele, Brian Karl 1961- WhoFI 94, WhoScEn 94, WhoWest 94
Roen, Sheldon R. WhoAm 94
Roenbaugh, Susan WhoAmP 93
Roenfeldt, Roger David 1938- WhoIns 94
Roenick, Jeremy 1970- WhoAm 94
Roentgen, Wilhelm Konrad WorScD
Roepe, Paul David 1960- WhoScEn 94
Roeper, Karen Bracey 1950- WhoMW 93
Roeper, Richard 1959- WhoAm 94
Roer, Robert David 1952- WhoAm 94
Roerick, William 1912- WhoHol 92
Roerick, William George 1912- WhoAm 94
Roes, Nicholas A. 1952- WhoFI 94
Roesch, Clarence Henry 1925- WhoAm 94
Roesch, Kurt (Ferdinand) 1905- WhoAmA 93N
Roesch, Lynda Eileen 1953- WhoAmL 94
Roesch, Raymond August 1914-1991 WhAm 10
Roesch, Robert Arthur 1946- WhoAmA 93
Roesch, Robert Eugene 1951- WhoMW 93
Roesch, Warren Dale 1945- WhoWest 94
Roesch, William Robert 1925-1983 EncABHB 9 [port]
Roese, Dennis J. 1943- WhoMW 93
Roeseler, William Gene 1943- WhoWest 94
Roeseler, Wolfgang Guenther Joachim 1925- WhoFI 94
Roeser, Kirk George 1943- WhoIns 94
Roeser, Ronald O. 1950- WhoAmL 94
Roeser, Ross Joseph 1942- WhoScEn 94
Roeske, Fiona WhoHol 92
Roeske, Paulette DrAPF 93
Roesky, Herbert W. 1935- IntWW 93
Roesky, Herbert Walter 1935- WhoScEn 94
Roesler, Alan Keith 1955- WhoMW 93
Roesler, Norbert Leonhard Hugo 1901- WhoAmA 93N
Roesler, Robert Harry 1927- WhoAm 94
Roesner, Larry August 1941- WhoAm 94, WhoFI 94
Roesner, Peter Lowell 1937- WhoAm 94
Roess, Roger Peter 1947- WhoAm 94
Roesser, Jean Wolberg 1930- WhoAmP 93
Roesset, Jose M. WhoAm 94
Roessig, John Robert 1947- WhoWest 94
Roessler, Ernest Christian 1941- WhoAm 94
Roessler, P. Dee 1941- WhoAmL 94
Roessler, Ronald James 1939- WhoAm 94, WhoAmL 94
Roessner, Roland Gommel 1911- WhoAm 94
Roessner, Vincent William 1948- WhoMW 93
Roestam, Soepardjo 1926- IntWW 93
Roeth, Frederick Warren 1941- WhoScEn 94
Roethe, James Norton 1942- WhoAm 94, WhoAmL 94
Roethel, David Albert Hill 1926- WhoAm 94
Roethenmund, Otto Emil 1928- WhoAm 94
Roethke, Richard Porter 1945- WhoFI 94
Roethke, Theodore Huebner 1908-1963 AmCulL
Roethlisberger, Eric M. 1934- IntWW 93
Roetman, Orvil M. 1925- WhoAm 94
Roett, Riordan 1938- WhoAm 94
Roettger, Norman Charles, Jr. 1930- WhoAm 94, WhoAmL 94
Roettger, Walter Barackman 1941- WhoAm 94
Roetzel, Danny Nile 1952- WhoAmL 94
Roeves, Maurice WhoHol 92
Roeves, Maurice 1937- IntMPA 94
Rofe, Barbara Dale 1946- WhoFI 94
Rofes, Eric Edward 1954- WrDr 94
Roff, Alan Lee 1936- WhoAmL 94
Roff, Derek Michael 1932- Who 94
Roff, Jill Robin 1946- WhoAmL 94
Roff, John Hugh, Jr. 1931- WhoAm 94
Roff, William Robert 1929- WhoAm 94
Roffe, Andrew S. WhoAmL 94
Roffers, Mary 1953- WhoAmP 93
Roffey, Harry Norman 1911- Who 94
Roffey, Robert Cameron, Jr. 1935- WhoIns 94
Roffman, Blaine Yale 1935- WhoMW 93
Roffman, Howard WhoAm 94
Roffman, Rosaly DeMaios DrAPF 93
Rogachev, Igor Alexeevich 1932- IntWW 93
Rogachevsky, Joseph 1891-1985 NewGrDO
Rogalin, Roger Richard 1949- WhoAm 94
Rogalla, Steve Leon 1953- WhoAmP 93
Rogallo, Francis Melvin 1912- WhoScEn 94
Rogalski, Edward J. 1942- WhoAm 94
Rogalski, Gary L. 1949- WhoMW 93
Rogalski, Jerzy Marian 1956- WhoScEn 94
Rogalski, Walter 1923- WhoAmA 93
Rogaly, (Henry) Joseph 1935- WrDr 94
Rogan, Beth WhoHol 92
Rogan, John 1928- Who 94
Rogan, Johnny 1953- WrDr 94
Rogan, Mary Lou 1956- WhoAmP 93
Rogan, Patrick Goode 1944- WhoAm 94, WhoAmL 94
Rogan, Richard A. 1950- WhoAmL 94
Rogan, Robert William WhoFI 94
Rogard, Pascale WhoHol 92
Rogasky, Barbara 1933- TwCYAW, WrDr 94
Rogat, Dorothy Shiff 1913- WhoFI 94
Rogatis, Francesco Saverio de NewGrDO
Rogatis, Pascual de 1880-1980 NewGrDO
Rogatnick, Joseph Hirsch 1917- WhoAm 94
Rogatz, Peter 1926- WhoAm 94
Rogaway, Betty Jane 1921- WhoWest 94
Roge, Pascal 1951- IntWW 93
Roge, Ronald William 1947- WhoFI 94
Rogel, Jose 1829-1901 NewGrDO
Rogel, Todd Stephen 1952- WhoAmL 94
Rogen, Mark Endre 1956- WhoAmP 93, WhoMW 93
Rogeness, Mary S. 1941- WhoAmP 93
Rogenski, Marion M. 1926- WhoAmP 93
Roger, Gustave-Hippolyte 1815-1879 NewGrDO
Roger, Kent M. 1955- WhoAmL 94, WhoHisp 94
Roger, Lee WhoHol 92
Roger, Noelle 1874-1953 EncSF 93
Roger, Victor 1853-1903 NewGrDO
Roger de Meuland c. 1215-1295 DcNaB MP
Roger-Ducasse, Jean (Jules Aimable) 1873-1954 NewGrDO
Rogerio, JoAnn 1967- WhoHisp 94
Rogero, David M. 1948- WhoAmL 94
Roger Of Taize, Brother 1915- IntWW 93
Rogers, Alan Francis Bright 1907- Who 94
Rogers, Alan Victor 1942- WhoAm 94
Rogers, Alfred R. 1931- WhoBlA 94
Rogers, Allan Ralph 1932- Who 94
Rogers, Alva 1923-1982 EncSF 93
Rogers, Andrew J., Jr. 1944- WhoAmP 93
Rogers, Archibald Coleman 1917- WhoAm 94
Rogers, Art 1948- WhoAmA 93
Rogers, Arthur Hamilton, III 1945- WhoAm 94, WhoAmL 94
Rogers, Arthur Merriam, Jr. 1941- WhoAm 94
Rogers, Arthur Rex 1931- WhoWest 94
Rogers, Barbara 1937- WhoAmA 93
Rogers, Barbara Ann 1941- WhoWest 94
Rogers, Barbara Radcliffe 1939- WhoAmP 93
Rogers, Benjamin D., Jr. 1919- WhoAmP 93
Rogers, Bernard 1893-1968 NewGrDO
Rogers, Bernard Rousseau 1944- WhoBlA 94
Rogers, Bernard William 1921- IntWW 93, Who 94, WhoAm 94
Rogers, Bertha DrAPF 93
Rogers, Bessie d1930 WhoHol 92
Rogers, Betty Gravitt 1945- WhoFI 94
Rogers, Brad Quin 1963- WhoAmL 94
Rogers, Bradley Barney 1957- WhoWest 94
Rogers, Brian Deane 1937- WhoAm 94
Rogers, Brian Douglas 1950- WhoAmP 93, WhoWest 94
Rogers, Brian Frederick 1923- Who 94
Rogers, Bruce DrAPF 93
Rogers, Bruce 1870-1957 WhoAmA 93N
Rogers, Bruce Holland DrAPF 93

Rogers, Bryan Leigh 1941- *WhoAm 94, WhoAmA 93*
Rogers, C(laude) Ambrose 1920- *Who 94*
Rogers, C. B. 1930- *WhoAm 94*
Rogers, C. B., Jr. 1929- *WhoIns 94*
Rogers, Carl D. d1965 *WhoHol 92*
Rogers, Carl Lindbergh Bernard 1928- *IntWW 93*
Rogers, Carleton Carson, Jr. 1935- *WhoFI 94*
Rogers, Carson 1924- *WhoAmP 93*
Rogers, Charles 1904- *IntMPA 94, WhoHol 92*
Rogers, Charles B. 1911-1987 *WhAm 10, WhoAmA 93N*
Rogers, Charles Calvin 1929- *AfrAmG [port]*
Rogers, Charles Clayton 1957- *WhoAm 94*
Rogers, Charles D. 1935- *WhoBlA 94*
Rogers, Charles Edwin 1929- *WhoAm 94*
Rogers, Charlie Ellic 1938- *WhoScEn 94*
Rogers, Chester Benjamin 1939- *WhoAmP 93*
Rogers, Chloe 1918- *WhoAmP 93*
Rogers, Christopher Bruce 1958- *WhoWest 94*
Rogers, Cindy Marie 1959- *WhoFI 94*
Rogers, Claudette J. 1939- *WhoAmP 93*
Rogers, Colonel Hoyt 1906- *WhoScEn 94*
Rogers, Craig Alan 1959- *WhoFI 94, WhoScEn 94*
Rogers, Cyril A(lfred) 1923-1993 *ConAu 141*
Rogers, Dale Arthur 1954- *WhoScEn 94*
Rogers, Daryl *DrAPF 93*
Rogers, David *WhoAm 94*
Rogers, David Anthony 1939- *WhoMW 93, WhoScEn 94*
Rogers, David Anthony 1952- *WhoAm 94*
Rogers, David Arthur 1921- *Who 94*
Rogers, David Bryan 1929- *Who 94*
Rogers, David Elliott 1926- *WhoAm 94*
Rogers, David Hale 1918- *WhoWest 94*
Rogers, David Hughes 1947- *WhoAm 94*
Rogers, David John 1960- *WhoAmL 94*
Rogers, David William 1959- *WhoBlA 94*
Rogers, Deborah Champion *WhoMW 93*
Rogers, Decatur Braxton *WhoBlA 94*
Rogers, Del Marie *DrAPF 93*
Rogers, Desiree Glapion 1959- *WhoBlA 94*
Rogers, Dianna *WhoBlA 94*
Rogers, Don 1928- *WhoAmP 93*
Rogers, Donald Burl 1936- *WhoAm 94*
Rogers, Donald Onis 1938- *WhoAm 94*
Rogers, Donald Patrick 1947- *WhoAm 94, WhoFI 94*
Rogers, Donald R. 1946- *WhoAmL 94*
Rogers, Donna Whitaker 1960- *WhoBlA 94*
Rogers, Douglas L. 1946- *WhoAmL 94*
Rogers, Dwane Leslie 1943- *WhoWest 94*
Rogers, Earl Leslie 1918- *WhoWest 94*
Rogers, Earline S. *WhoAmP 93*
Rogers, Earline S. 1934- *WhoBlA 94, WhoMW 93*
Rogers, Eddy J. 1940- *WhoAm 94*
Rogers, Edward 1909- *Who 94*
Rogers, Edward Samuel 1933- *WhoAm 94, WhoFI 94*
Rogers, Elijah Baby 1939- *WhoBlA 94*
Rogers, Elizabeth Barlow 1936- *WhoAm 94*
Rogers, Emma 1951- *SmATA 74 [port]*
Rogers, Eric William Evan 1925- *Who 94*
Rogers, Erika Palmer 1942- *WhoAmL 94*
Rogers, Ernest Mabry 1947- *WhoAm 94, WhoAmL 94*
Rogers, Eugene *WhoAmP 93*
Rogers, Eugene Charles 1932- *WhoAm 94*
Rogers, Eugene Herman 1957- *WhoAmP 93*
Rogers, Eugene Jack 1921- *WhoAm 94*
Rogers, Floyd *ConAu 43NR*
Rogers, Floyd 1923- *WrDr 94*
Rogers, Frank 1929- *WhoAmP 93*
Rogers, Frank (Jarvis) 1920- *Who 94*
Rogers, Frank B. d1959 *WhoHol 92*
Rogers, Frank Jarvis 1920- *IntWW 93*
Rogers, Franklin Robert 1921- *WrDr 94*
Rogers, Fred 1928- *IntMPA 94*
Rogers, Fred Baker 1926- *WhoAm 94*
Rogers, Fred McFeely 1928- *WhoAm 94*
Rogers, Freddie Clyde 1922- *WhoBlA 94*
Rogers, Frederick 1846-1915 *DcNaB MP*
Rogers, Gardner Spencer 1926- *WhoFI 94*
Rogers, Garth Winfield 1938- *WhoAmL 94*
Rogers, Gene d1919 *WhoHol 92*
Rogers, George d1942 *WhoHol 92*
Rogers, George 1935- *WhoAmP 93, WhoBlA 94*
Rogers, George, III 1947- *WhoBlA 94, WhoMW 93*
Rogers, George Edward 1897- *WhAm 10*
Rogers, George Ernest 1927- *IntWW 93*
Rogers, George Theodore 1919- *Who 94*
Rogers, George William 1917- *WrDr 94*
Rogers, George Winters, Jr. *WhoAmP 93*
Rogers, Gil *WhoHol 92*
Rogers, Gillum Harris 1947- *WhoWest 94*
Rogers, Ginger 1911- *IntMPA 94, IntWW 93, WhoAm 94, WhoHol 92*
Rogers, Gregory Parker 1964- *WhoAmL 94*
Rogers, Harold 1937- *CngDr 93*
Rogers, Harold Dallas 1937- *WhoAm 94, WhoAmP 93*
Rogers, Harry G. 1931- *WhoAm 94*
Rogers, Harvey W. 1945- *WhoAmL 94*
Rogers, Heidi 1963- *WhoMW 93*
Rogers, Henry Augustus 1918- *Who 94*
Rogers, Henry C. 1914- *IntMPA 94*
Rogers, Howard Gardner 1915- *WhoAm 94*
Rogers, Howard H. 1926- *WhoAm 94*
Rogers, Hubert 1898-1982 *EncSF 93*
Rogers, Isabel Wood 1924- *WhoAm 94*
Rogers, J. Jean 1943- *WhoAmP 93*
Rogers, J. Robert 1940- *WhoAmP 93*
Rogers, J. Stanley 1939- *WhoAmP 93*
Rogers, Jack David 1937- *WhoWest 94*
Rogers, Jacqueline Jeanette 1961- *WhoMW 93*
Rogers, Jalane *DrAPF 93*
Rogers, James Albert 1944- *WhoAm 94, WhoAmL 94*
Rogers, James Beeland, Jr. 1942- *WhoFI 94*
Rogers, James Devitt 1929- *WhoAm 94, WhoAmL 94*
Rogers, James Edward 1945- *WhoAm 94, WhoFI 94*
Rogers, James Edwin 1929- *WhoScEn 94*
Rogers, James Eugene, Jr. 1947- *WhoAm 94, WhoMW 93*
Rogers, James Frederick 1935- *WhoAm 94*
Rogers, James Gardiner 1952- *WhoFI 94*
Rogers, James Thomas 1941- *WhoAmL 94*
Rogers, James Virgil, Jr. 1922- *WhoAm 94, WhoScEn 94*
Rogers, Jay Lee 1962- *WhoFI 94*
Rogers, Jean d1991 *WhoHol 92*
Rogers, Jeffrey E. 1949- *WhoAmL 94*
Rogers, Jerry L. 1938- *WhoAm 94*
Rogers, Jimmy 1915- *WhoHol 92*
Rogers, Joel Augustus 1880?-1966 *BlkWr 2*
Rogers, John d1963 *WhoHol 92*
Rogers, John 1906-1985 *WhoAmA 93N*
Rogers, John 1934- *Who 94*
Rogers, John 1949- *IntWW 93*
Rogers, John (Robson) 1928- *Who 94*
Rogers, John D. 1940- *WhoAmP 93*
Rogers, John Ellsworth 1942- *WhoAm 94*
Rogers, John Francis William 1956- *WhoAmP 93*
Rogers, John H. *WhoAmP 93*
Rogers, John H. 1921- *WhoAmA 93*
Rogers, John I., III 1937- *WhoAmP 93*
Rogers, John James William 1930- *WhoAm 94, WhoScEn 94*
Rogers, John L., III 1948- *WhoAmL 94*
Rogers, John Michael Thomas 1938- *Who 94*
Rogers, John Russell 1929- *WhoMW 93, WhoScEn 94*
Rogers, John S. 1930- *WhoAm 94*
Rogers, John W. 1918- *WhoBlA 94*
Rogers, John W., Jr. *WhoAm 94, WhoBlA 94, WhoFI 94*
Rogers, John W., Jr. 1940- *WhoAmP 93*
Rogers, John W., Jr. 1958- *ConBlB 5 [port]*
Rogers, John William 1941- *WhoMW 93*
Rogers, John Willis 1929- *Who 94*
Rogers, Jon Martin 1942- *WhoFI 94*
Rogers, Jonathan 1928- *WhoAmP 93*
Rogers, Jonathan Grote 1953- *WhoAmL 94*
Rogers, Joseph John 1958- *WhoFI 94*
Rogers, Joseph Shepperd *WhoAmA 93*
Rogers, Josias 1755-1795 *WhAmRev*
Rogers, Judith W. *WhoAmL 94, WhoAmP 93*
Rogers, Justin Towner, Jr. 1929- *WhoAm 94, WhoFI 94, WhoMW 93*
Rogers, Kasey *WhoHol 92*
Rogers, Kate Ellen 1920- *WhoMW 93, WhoScEn 94*
Rogers, Katharine M. 1932- *WrDr 94*
Rogers, Katherine D. 1955- *WhoAmP 93*
Rogers, Keith 1925- *WrDr 94*
Rogers, Kenneth Norman 1931- *WhoAm 94*
Rogers, Kenneth R. *WhoAm 94*
Rogers, Kenneth Ray 1938- *WhoAm 94*
Rogers, Kenny 1938- *IntMPA 94, WhoHol 92*
Rogers, Kent d1944 *WhoHol 92*
Rogers, L. David 1928- *WhoMW 93*
Rogers, Larry James 1934- *WhoAmP 93*
Rogers, Laurence Steven 1950- *WhoAm 94*
Rogers, Lawrence F. 1937- *WhoBlA 94*
Rogers, Lawrence H., II 1921- *IntMPA 94, WhoAm 94*
Rogers, Lebbeus Harding 1847-1932 *EncSF 93*
Rogers, Lee Frank 1934- *WhoAm 94*
Rogers, Lee Jasper 1955- *WhoAm 94, WhoFI 94*
Rogers, Lela d1977 *WhoHol 92*
Rogers, Leo Paul, Jr. 1961- *WhoAmL 94*
Rogers, Linwood Arthur 1917- *WhoAmP 93*
Rogers, Lockhart Burgess 1917-1992 *WhAm 10*
Rogers, Lonnie Lee 1916- *WhoAmP 93*
Rogers, Lora d1948 *WhoHol 92*
Rogers, Lorene Lane 1914- *WhoAm 94*
Rogers, Malcolm Austin 1948- *Who 94*
Rogers, Margaret Esther 1873-1961 *WhoAmA 93N*
Rogers, Marian H. 1932- *ConAu 140*
Rogers, Marianne Gordon *WhoHol 92*
Rogers, Mark Charles 1942- *WhoAm 94*
Rogers, Martin Hartley Guy 1925- *Who 94*
Rogers, Martin John Wyndham 1931- *Who 94*
Rogers, Mary Joseph 1882-1955 *DcAmReB 2*
Rogers, Mary Martin 1945- *WhoAm 94*
Rogers, Maurice Arthur Thorold 1911- *Who 94*
Rogers, Mayrine D. 1925- *WhoAmP 93*
Rogers, McKinley Bradford 1955- *WhoScEn 94*
Rogers, Megan Elizabeth *WhoMW 93*
Rogers, Melinda Jane 1964- *WhoWest 94*
Rogers, Melva *EncSF 93*
Rogers, Meyric Reynold 1893-1972 *WhoAmA 93N*
Rogers, Michael *DrAPF 93, Who 94*
Rogers, Michael (Alan) 1951- *EncSF 93*
Rogers, (John) Michael 1935- *Who 94*
Rogers, Michael Alan 1950- *WhoWest 94*
Rogers, Michael Charles 1949- *WhoBlA 94*
Rogers, Michael Holmes 1949- *WhoWest 94*
Rogers, Michele Denise 1945- *WhoWest 94*
Rogers, Mildred d1973 *WhoHol 92*
Rogers, Millard Foster, Jr. 1932- *WhoAm 94, WhoAmA 93, WhoMW 93*
Rogers, Milton Bardstown 1939- *WhoFI 94, WhoWest 94*
Rogers, Mimi 1956- *IntMPA 94, WhoHol 92*
Rogers, Myrtle Beatrice 1925- *WhoAmP 93*
Rogers, Nadzaip 1871-1952 *EncNAR*
Rogers, Nat Stewart 1898-1990 *WhAm 10*
Rogers, Nathaniel Sims 1919- *WhoAm 94*
Rogers, Nigel (David) 1935- *NewGrDO*
Rogers, Nigel David 1935- *Who 94*
Rogers, Nolan Ray 1931- *WhoAmP 93*
Rogers, Norman 1931- *WhoBlA 94*
Rogers, Norman Charles 1916- *Who 94*
Rogers, Ormer, Jr. 1945- *WhoBlA 94*
Rogers, Oscar Allan, Jr. 1928- *WhoBlA 94*
Rogers, Otto Donald 1935- *WhoAmA 93*
Rogers, P. E., Mrs. *Who 94*
Rogers, P. J. *WhoAmA 93*
Rogers, Pamela 1927- *WrDr 94*
Rogers, Parry *Who 94*
Rogers, (Thomas Gordon) Parry 1924- *Who 94*
Rogers, Pat *EncSF 93*
Rogers, Pat 1938- *WrDr 94*
Rogers, Pattiann *DrAPF 93*
Rogers, Paul 1917- *IntWW 93, Who 94, WhoHol 92*
Rogers, Paul A'Court 1939- *WhoFI 94*
Rogers, Paul Grant 1921- *WhoAm 94, WhoAmP 93*
Rogers, Paul Scott 1949- *WhoAmP 93*
Rogers, Paul W. 1926- *WhoFI 94, WhoMW 93*
Rogers, Peaches Eleanor 1933- *WhoAmP 93*
Rogers, Peggy J. 1951- *WhoBlA 94*
Rogers, Percival Hallewell 1912- *Who 94*
Rogers, Peter 1916- *IntMPA 94*
Rogers, Peter Brian 1941- *Who 94*
Rogers, Peter Philips 1937- *WhoAm 94*
Rogers, Peter Richard 1939- *Who 94*
Rogers, Peter Wilfrid 1933- *WhoAmA 93*
Rogers, Philip (James) 1908- *Who 94*
Rogers, Ralph B. 1909- *WhoAm 94, WhoFI 94*
Rogers, Raymond Jesse 1941- *WhoAm 94*
Rogers, Raymond Thomas 1940- *Who 94*
Rogers, Rebecca Elizabeth 1959- *WhoMW 93*
Rogers, Rena d1966 *WhoHol 92*
Rogers, Rex Martin 1952- *WhoMW 93*
Rogers, Richard (George) 1933- *Who 94*
Rogers, Richard Adams 1930- *WhoAmP 93*
Rogers, Richard Annesley C. *Who 94*
Rogers, Richard C. d1993 *NewYTBS 93*
Rogers, Richard Dean 1921- *WhoAm 94, WhoAmL 94, WhoMW 93*
Rogers, Richard Edgar 1929- *WhoMW 93*
Rogers, Richard F. 1942- *WhoAm 94*
Rogers, Richard George 1933- *IntWW 93*
Rogers, Richard Gregory 1955- *WhoWest 94*
Rogers, Richard Hilton 1935- *WhoAm 94, WhoFI 94*
Rogers, Richard Hunter 1939- *WhoAm 94*
Rogers, Richard Michael 1944- *WhoAmL 94, WhoMW 93*
Rogers, Richard Raymond 1943- *WhoAm 94*
Rogers, Richard Wayne 1943- *WhoIns 94*
Rogers, Rick Alan 1953- *WhoFI 94, WhoWest 94*
Rogers, Robert d1916 *WhoHol 92*
Rogers, Robert 1731-1795 *AmRev, WhWE*
Rogers, Robert 1732-1795 *WhAmRev*
Rogers, Robert Burnett 1931- *WhoAm 94*
Rogers, Robert D. 1936- *WhoFI 94*
Rogers, Robert Ernest 1928- *WhoAm 94*
Rogers, Robert Francis 1931-1989 *WhAm 10*
Rogers, Robert H., Jr. 1928- *WhoAmP 93*
Rogers, Robert Mark 1933- *WhoAm 94*
Rogers, Robert Reed 1929- *WhoWest 94*
Rogers, Robert Stockton 1896- *WhoAmA 93N*
Rogers, Robert Wayne 1935- *WhoScEn 94*
Rogers, Robert Wentworth 1914-1992 *WhAm 10*
Rogers, Robert William *WhoFI 94*
Rogers, Rod d1983 *WhoHol 92*
Rogers, Roddy *WhoScEn 94*
Rogers, Rodney *WhoBlA 94*
Rogers, Rodney Albert 1926- *WhoAm 94*
Rogers, Rose Marie 1927- *WhoAmP 93*
Rogers, Rosemarie Dougherty 1958- *WhoMW 93*
Rogers, Rosemary 1932- *WhoAm 94, WrDr 94*
Rogers, Ross Frederick, III 1944- *WhoScEn 94*
Rogers, Roy 1911- *IntMPA 94, WhoAm 94*
Rogers, Roy 1912- *WhoHol 92*
Rogers, Roy, Jr. *WhoHol 92*
Rogers, Roy Steele, III 1940- *WhoMW 93*
Rogers, Ruth d1953 *WhoHol 92*
Rogers, Rutherford David 1915- *WhoAm 94*
Rogers, Samuel 1763-1855 *BlmGEL*
Rogers, Samuel Shepard 1943- *WhoAm 94*
Rogers, Sandra Louise 1947- *WhoAmP 93*
Rogers, Sarah Jeanne 1956- *WhoAm 94*
Rogers, Sharon J. 1941- *WhoAm 94*
Rogers, Sharyn Gail 1948- *WhoAmL 94*
Rogers, Shirley *WhoBlA 94*
Rogers, Stanley 1934- *WhoAmP 93*
Rogers, Stephen 1912- *WhoAm 94*
Rogers, Stephen H. 1930- *WhoAmP 93*
Rogers, Stephen Hitchcock 1930- *WhoAm 94*
Rogers, Steve 1945- *WhoAmA 93*
Rogers, Stuart *WhoHol 92*
Rogers, Susan 1949- *WhoFI 94*
Rogers, Teresa 1956- *WhoWest 94*
Rogers, Theodore Courtney 1934- *WhoAm 94, WhoFI 94*
Rogers, Theodore Otto, Jr. 1953- *WhoAmL 94*
Rogers, Thomas (Hunton) 1927- *WrDr 94*
Rogers, Thomas Charles 1924- *WhoAmP 93*
Rogers, Thomas Edward 1912- *Who 94*
Rogers, Thomas Francis 1923- *WhoAm 94*
Rogers, Thomas Hardin 1932- *WhoWest 94*
Rogers, Thomas Sydney 1954- *WhoAmL 94*
Rogers, Timmie *WhoBlA 94, WhoHol 92*
Rogers, Timothy Folk 1947- *WhoAmP 93*
Rogers, Timothy Revelle 1960- *WhoAmP 93*
Rogers, Tony *DrAPF 93*
Rogers, Vance Donald 1917- *WhoAm 94*
Rogers, Vern Child 1941- *WhoScEn 94, WhoWest 94*
Rogers, Verna Aileen 1930- *WhoScEn 94*
Rogers, Victor *WhoHol 92*
Rogers, Victor Alvin 1944- *WhoBlA 94*
Rogers, Victor W. 1962- *WhoHisp 94*
Rogers, Virgil Madison 1898-1990 *WhAm 10*
Rogers, Walter E. 1908- *WhoAmP 93*
Rogers, Warren Joseph, Jr. 1922- *WhoAm 94*
Rogers, Wayne 1933- *IntMPA 94, WhoHol 92*
Rogers, Werner *WhoAm 94*
Rogers, Werner 1941- *WhoAmP 93*
Rogers, Will d1935 *WhoHol 92*
Rogers, Will 1879-1935 *WhoCom [port]*
Rogers, Will, Jr. d1993 *IntMPA 94N*

Rogers, Will, Jr. 1911-1993 *CurBio 93N, NewYTBS 93 [port]*
Rogers, Will, Jr. 1912- *WhoHol 92*
Rogers, William (Cecil) 1919- *WrDr 94*
Rogers, William Cecil 1919- *WhoAm 94*
Rogers, William Cordell 1943- *WhoFI 94, WhoWest 94*
Rogers, William Dill 1927- *WhoAm 94*
Rogers, William Edward 1947- *WhoFI 94*
Rogers, William F., III 1916- *WhoAmP 93*
Rogers, William Fenna, Jr. 1912- *WhoFI 94*
Rogers, William P. 1913- *IntWW 93*
Rogers, William Pierce 1913- *Who 94, WhoAm 94, WhoAmL 94*
Rogers, William Raymond 1932- *WhoAm 94*
Rogers, William Richard, Jr. 1929- *WhoAmP 93*
Rogers, William Sherman 1951- *WhoAmL 94*
Rogers, William Shields, Jr. 1943- *WhoWest 94*
Rogers-Bell, Mamie Lee 1954- *WhoBlA 94*
Rogers-Grundy, Ethel W. 1938- *WhoBlA 94*
Rogers-Lafferty, Sarah 1956- *WhoAmA 93*
Rogers-Lomax, Alice Faye 1950- *WhoBlA 94*
Rogers Maddox, Donna 1964- *WhoAmL 94*
Rogersohn, William *EncSF 93*
Rogerson, Alan Thomas 1943- *WrDr 94*
Rogerson, Barry *Who 94*
Rogerson, Craig Allan 1956- *WhoFI 94*
Rogerson, Nicolas 1943- *Who 94*
Rogerson, Philip Graham 1945- *Who 94*
Rogerson, Susan *Who 94*
Rogg, Lionel 1936- *Who 94*
Rogg, Oskar G. *WhoAmP 93*
Rogge, Dwaine William 1938- *WhoFI 94*
Rogge, Everett Kurt 1968- *WhoMW 93*
Rogge, Mary Ellen 1942- *WhoMW 93*
Rogge, Richard Daniel 1926- *WhoWest 94*
Roggenkamp, Charles Lee 1949- *WhoMW 93*
Rogger, Hans Jack 1923- *WhoAm 94*
Roggero, Arnaldo 1934- *WhoScEn 94*
Roggero, Miguel Leonardo 1962- *WhoWest 94*
Roggeveen, Jakob 1659-1729 *WhWE*
Roggiano, Alfredo Angel 1919- *WhoHisp 94*
Rogich, Sig *WhoAm 94*
Rogin, Gilbert *DrAPF 93*
Rogin, Gilbert Leslie 1929- *WhoAm 94*
Rogin, Michael Paul 1937- *ConAu 43NR*
Rogister, Andre Lambert 1940- *WhoScEn 94*
Rogler, Charles Edward 1946- *WhoScEn 94*
Rogler, Lloyd H. 1930- *WhoHisp 94*
Rogler, Lloyd Henry 1930- *WrDr 94*
Rogliano, Aldo Thomas 1925- *WhoAm 94*
Rognan, Lloyd Norman *WhoAmA 93*
Rognan, Lorraine d1969 *WhoHol 92*
Rognan, Roy d1943 *WhoHol 92*
Rognoni, Paulina Amelia 1947- *WhoScEn 94*
Rognoni, Virginio 1924- *IntWW 93*
Rogo, Kathleen 1952- *WhoScEn 94*
Rogoff, Andrew R. 1952- *WhoAmL 94*
Rogoff, Barbara 1950- *ConAu 42NR*
Rogoff, Ilan 1943- *IntWW 93*
Rogoff, Jay *DrAPF 93*
Rogoff, Jerome Howard 1938- *WhoAm 94*
Rogoff, Kenneth S. 1953- *WhoFI 94*
Rogols, Saul 1933- *WhoFI 94*
Rogosheske, Walter Frederick 1914- *WhoAm 94*
Rogoski, Patricia Diana 1939- *WhoAm 94*
Rogovin, Lawrence H. 1932- *WhoAmL 94*
Rogovin, Mark 1946- *WhoAmA 93*
Rogovin, Milton 1909- *WhoAm 94, WhoAmA 93*
Rogovin, Mitchell 1930- *WhoAm 94, WhoAmL 94, WhoAmP 93*
Rogow, Arnold A(ustin) 1924- *WrDr 94*
Rogow, Bruce Joel 1945- *WhoAm 94*
Rogow, Roberta 1942- *ConAu 140*
Rogow, Zack *DrAPF 93*
Rogoway, Lawrence Paul 1932- *WhoScEn 94*
Rogowski, Ludomir Michal 1881-1954 *NewGrDO*
Rogowsky, Martin Lawrence 1948- *WhoAmP 93*
Rogoz, Adrian *EncSF 93*
Rogula, James Leroy 1933- *WhoAm 94*
Roh, Tae Woo 1932- *Who 94*
Rohack, John James 1954- *WhoScEn 94*
Rohadfox, Ronald Otto 1935- *WhoBlA 94*
Rohan, Michael Scott 1951- *EncSF 93*
Rohan, Robert J. *WhoAmP 93*
Rohan, Sue *WhoAmP 93*
Rohan-Vargas, Fred 1949- *WhoHisp 94*
Rohatgi, Pradeep K. 1943- *WhoAsA 94*
Rohatgi, Upendra Singh 1949- *WhoAsA 94*
Rohatgi, Vijay K. 1939- *WhoAsA 94*
Rohatsch, Ralph R., Jr. 1940- *WhoAm 94*
Rohatyn, Felix George 1928- *IntWW 93, WhoAm 94, WhoFI 94*
Rohatyn, Nicolas Streit 1960- *WhoAm 94, WhoFI 94*
Rohda, Rodney Raymond 1942- *WhoAm 94*
Rohde, Bruce C. 1948- *WhoAmL 94*
Rohde, David William 1944- *WhoAm 94*
Rohde, Gil C., Jr. 1948- *WhoIns 94*
Rohde, Gregory Joseph 1963- *WhoMW 93*
Rohde, Helmut 1925- *IntWW 93*
Rohde, James Vincent 1939- *WhoFI 94, WhoScEn 94, WhoWest 94*
Rohde, Juliet d1987 *WhoHol 92*
Rohde, Richard R. 1949- *WhoAmL 94*
Rohde, Suzanne Louise 1963- *WhoMW 93*
Rohde, Thomas Daulton 1940- *WhoMW 93*
Rohe, Jere Louis 1945- *WhoWest 94*
Rohe, Thomas Glenn 1955- *WhoFI 94*
Roheim, Paul Samuel 1925- *WhoScEn 94*
Rohila, Pritam Kumar 1935- *WhoAsA 94, WhoWest 94*
Rohland, Paul 1884-1953 *WhoAmA 93N*
Rohlf, F. James 1936- *WhoScEn 94*
Rohlf, Paul Leon 1937- *WhoMW 93*
Rohlfing, Christian 1916- *WhoAmA 93*
Rohlfing, Frederick W. 1928- *WhoAmP 93*
Rohlfing, Frederick William 1928- *WhoAm 94, WhoAmL 94, WhoWest 94*
Rohlfs, Friedrich Gerhard 1831-1896 *WhWE*
Rohm, Charles E. 1935- *WhoIns 94*
Rohm, Charles Edward 1935- *WhoAm 94*
Rohm, Eberhard 1940- *WhoAm 94*
Rohm, Maria 1949- *WhoHol 92*
Rohm, Robert 1934- *WhoAmA 93*
Rohm, Robert Hermann 1934- *WhoAm 94*
Rohmer, Eric 1920- *IntMPA 94, IntWW 93, Who 94, WhoAm 94*
Rohmer, Patrice *WhoHol 92*
Rohmer, Richard 1924- *WrDr 94*
Rohmer, Richard H. 1924- *EncSF 93*
Rohmer, Sax 1883-1959 *EncSF 93*
Rohn, Elizabeth Janda 1931- *WhoAmP 93*
Rohn, Gordon Frederick 1939- *WhoWest 94*
Rohn, Linda Joy 1954- *WhoMW 93*
Rohn, Robert Jones 1918- *WhoScEn 94*
Rohner, Clayton *WhoHol 92*
Rohner, Georges 1907- *IntWW 93*
Rohner, Ralph John 1938- *WhoAm 94, WhoAmL 94*
Rohner, Ronald P. 1935- *WrDr 94*
Rohner, Thomas John, Jr. 1936- *WhoAm 94*
Rohr, Brian P. 1947- *WhoIns 94*
Rohr, Daniel C. 1946- *WhoAm 94*
Rohr, David Baker 1933- *WhoAm 94*
Rohr, Davis Charles 1929- *WhoAm 94*
Rohr, Donald Gerard 1920- *WhoAm 94, WhoFI 94*
Rohr, James Edward 1948- *WhoAm 94, WhoFI 94*
Rohr, Leonard Carl 1921- *WhoBlA 94*
Rohr, Richard David 1926- *WhoAmL 94*
Rohrabacher, Dana 1947- *CngDr 93, WhoAm 94, WhoWest 94*
Rohrabacher, Dana Tyrone 1947- *WhoAmP 93*
Rohrbach, Eric John 1951- *WhoAmP 93*
Rohrbach, Jay William 1957- *WhoScEn 94*
Rohrbach, Larry 1946- *WhoAmP 93*
Rohrbach, Peter Thomas 1926- *WrDr 94*
Rohrbach, Roger Phillip 1942- *WhoScEn 94*
Rohrbach, Sharon Evelyn 1942- *WhoMW 93*
Rohrbach, William 1943- *WhoAmP 93*
Rohrback, Michael David 1954- *WhoWest 94*
Rohrback, Robert Lee, Jr. 1924- *WhoAmL 94*
Rohrbaugh, Lisa Anne 1956- *WhoMW 93*
Rohrbaugh, Randolph Lee 1950- *WhoIns 94*
Rohrberg, Roderick George 1925- *WhoWest 94*
Rohrbough, Keith James 1949- *WhoWest 94*
Rohrbough, Linda Jandecka 1947- *WhoFI 94, WhoMW 93*
Rohrbough, Malcolm Justin 1932- *WhoMW 93, WrDr 94*
Rohrer, George John 1931- *WhoAmL 94*
Rohrer, Grace Jemison 1924- *WhoAmP 93*
Rohrer, Heinrich *WorInv*
Rohrer, Heinrich 1933- *IntWW 93, Who 94, WhoAm 94, WhoScEn 94*
Rohrer, Richard Carl, Jr. 1946- *WhoFI 94*
Rohrer, Richard Joseph 1960- *WhoScEn 94*
Rohrer, Ronald Alan 1939- *WhoAm 94, WhoScEn 94*
Rohrer, Samuel E. *WhoAmP 93*
Rohrer, Warren 1927- *WhoAmA 93*
Rohrich, Rodney James 1953- *WhoScEn 94*
Rohrig, Timothy Patrick 1956- *WhoScEn 94*
Rohrig, Walter 1897?-1945 *IntDcF 2-4*
Rohrlich, George Friedrich 1914- *WhoAm 94, WhoFI 94, WhoScEn 94*
Rohrman, Douglass Frederick 1941- *WhoAmL 94, WhoFI 94*
Rohrman, Nicholas Leroy 1937- *WhoAm 94*
Rohrs, Alvin Wayne 1956- *WhoMW 93*
Rohrs, Elizabeth Vincent 1959- *WhoAmL 94*
Rohrs, Gustav Werner 1931- *WhoAm 94*
Rohrs, John Theodore, III 1955- *WhoAmL 94*
Rohrs, Karl 1910- *IntWW 93*
Rohs, Martha 1909-1963 *NewGrDO*
Rohsenow, Warren Max 1921- *WhoAm 94*
Roh Tae Woo 1932- *IntWW 93*
Rohwer, Bruce Steven 1951- *WhoAmP 93*
Roider, Karl Andrew, Jr. 1943- *WhoAm 94*
Roig, J. Adalberto, Sr. *WhoHisp 94*
Roig, J. Adalberto, Jr. *WhoHisp 94*
Roig, Montserrat 1946- *BlmGWL*
Roig, Randy Allen 1949- *WhoWest 94*
Roin, Howard James 1953- *WhoAm 94, WhoAmL 94*
Roiphe, Ann *DrAPF 93*
Roiphe, Anne *NewYTBS 93 [port]*
Roiphe, Anne Richardson 1935- *WrDr 94*
Roiphe, Katie *NewYTBS 93 [port]*
Roisler, Glenn Harvey 1952- *WhoFI 94*
Roisman, Roger M. 1950- *WhoAmL 94*
Roitberg, Bernard David 1953- *WhoScEn 94*
Roitblat, Herbert Lawrence 1952- *WhoWest 94*
Roiter, Eric D. 1948- *WhoAm 94*
Roith, Oscar 1927- *Who 94*
Roitt, Ivan Maurice 1927- *Who 94*
Roitz, Edward J. 1955- *WhoAmP 93*
Roitzsch, Ingrid 1940- *WhoWomW 91*
Roiz, Myriam 1938- *WhoWest 94*
Roizin, Leon 1912-1991 *WhAm 10*
Roiz-Leiva, Carmen Teresa 1936- *WhoHisp 94*
Roizman, Bernard 1929- *IntWW 93, WhoAm 94, WhoMW 93*
Roizman, Owen 1936- *IntDcF 2-4, IntMPA 94*
Roj, William Henry 1949- *WhoAm 94, WhoAmL 94*
Ro Jai-Dong *IntWW 93*
Rojak, Rebecca Lee 1957- *WhoMW 93*
Rojan Kovsky, Feodor Stepanovich 1891-1970 *WhoAmA 93N*
Rojas, Bill *WhoHisp 94*
Rojas, Carlos 1928- *WhoAm 94*
Rojas, Cookie 1939- *WhoHisp 94*
Rojas, Edward J. 1959- *WhoHisp 94*
Rojas, Fernando de 1465-1541 *LitC 23 [port]*
Rojas, Guillermo 1938- *WhoHisp 94*
Rojas, Jorge 1948- *WhoHisp 94*
Rojas, Luis Diaz 1964- *WhoHisp 94*
Rojas, Luis E. 1953- *WhoAmP 93, WhoHisp 94*
Rojas, Manuel Joseph 1948- *WhoHisp 94*
Rojas, Mel 1966- *WhoHisp 94*
Rojas, Paúl 1912- *WhoHisp 94*
Rojas, Richard Raimond 1931- *WhoAm 94*
Rojas, Robert R. 1927- *WhoHisp 94*
Rojas, Roland Samuel 1932- *WhoAmP 93*
Rojas, Steven Raymond 1952- *WhoHisp 94*
Rojas, Virginia *WhoWomW 91*
Rojas, Waldemar *WhoHisp 94, WhoWest 94*
Rojas De Moreno Diaz, Maria Eugenia 1934- *IntWW 93*
Rojek, Christine 1949- *WhoAmA 93*
Rojhantalab, Hossein Mohammad 1944- *WhoScEn 94*
Rojo, Gustavo 1926- *WhoHol 92*
Rojo, Javier 1951- *WhoHisp 94*
Rojo, Luis Angel 1934- *IntWW 93*
Rojo, Vicente 1932- *WhoAmA 93*
Rok, Natan R. 1935- *WhoHisp 94*
Rokach, Abraham Jacob 1948- *WhoScEn 94*
Rokahr, Theodore 1896- *WhAm 10*
Rokeach, Barrie 1947- *WhoAmA 93*
Roker, A.B. *EncSF 93*
Roker, Rennie *WhoHol 92*
Roker, Roxie 1929- *WhoBlA 94, WhoHol 92*
Rokes, Willis Park 1926- *WhoIns 94*
Roketsky, Leonid Yulianovich 1942- *LngBDD*
Rokhlin, Stanislav Iosef 1944- *WhoMW 93, WhoScEn 94*
Rokiatou Sow, Sow *WhoWomW 91*
Rokison, Kenneth Stuart 1937- *Who 94*
Rokita, Jan Maria 1959- *IntWW 93*
Rokitansky, Hans, Freiherr von 1835-1909 *NewGrDO*
Rokkan, Elizabeth 1925- *ConAu 140*
Rokke, Ervin Jerome 1939- *WhoAm 94*
Rokke, Mona 1940- *IntWW 93*
Rokoff, Gerald 1950- *WhoAmL 94*
Rokos, John Paul 1952- *WhoWest 94*
Rokosz, Susan Marie 1957- *WhoScEn 94*
Rokstad, Odd Arne 1935- *WhoScEn 94*
Rolan, Phidalia Lynn 1961- *WhoWest 94*
Roland, Madame 1754-1793 *HisWorL [port]*
Roland, Anne 1947- *WhoAm 94*
Roland, Benautrice, Jr. 1945- *WhoBlA 94*
Roland, Betty 1903- *BlmGWL*
Roland, Billy Ray 1926- *WhoFI 94*
Roland, Catherine Dixon 1936- *WhoFI 94*
Roland, Charles Gordon 1933- *WhoAm 94*
Roland, Craig Williamson 1935- *WhoAm 94*
Roland, David Leonard 1948- *WhoFI 94*
Roland, Donald Edward 1942- *WhoAm 94*
Roland, Frederick d1936 *WhoHol 92*
Roland, Gilbert 1905- *IntMPA 94, WhoHol 92*
Roland, Gilbert 1905-1994 *WhoHisp 94N*
Roland, Gyl *WhoHol 92*
Roland, Henry d1985 *WhoHol 92*
Roland, Jay 1905-1960 *WhoAmA 93N*
Roland, Johnny E. 1943- *WhoBlA 94*
Roland, Judi D. *WhoAmP 93*
Roland, Marie-Jeanne Philipon 1754-1793 *BlmGWL*
Roland, Marion d1966 *WhoHol 92*
Roland, Mary *ConAu 43NR*
Roland, Melissa Montgomery 1961- *WhoFI 94*
Roland, Nicholas *Who 94*
Roland, Raymond William 1947- *WhoAmL 94*
Roland, Richard Ralph 1952- *WhoAmL 94*
Roland, Ruth d1937 *WhoHol 92*
Roland, Steve *WhoHol 92*
Roland Holst, Henriette 1869-1952 *BlmGWL*
Rolandi, Gianna 1952- *NewGrDO, WhoAm 94*
Rolandi, Ulderico 1874-1951 *NewGrDO*
Rolandis, Nicos A. 1934- *IntWW 93*
Roland-Manuel 1891-1966 *NewGrDO*
Rolando, William Arthur *WhoAmP 93*
Roland Smith, Gordon 1931- *WrDr 94*
Rolant, Rene *EncSF 93*
Rolark, Calvin W. 1927- *WhoBlA 94*
Rolark, M. Wilhelmina *WhoBlA 94*
Rolark, Wilhelmina J. *WhoAmP 93*
Roldan, Charles Robert 1940- *WhoHisp 94*
Roldán, Hipolito *WhoHisp 94*
Roldan, Luis Gonzalez 1925- *WhoScEn 94*
Roldán, Nancy *WhoHisp 94*
Roldán, Paul *WhoHisp 94*
Rolde, Neil Richard 1931- *WhoAmP 93*
Rolett, Ellis Lawrence 1930- *WhoAm 94*
Roletta, Richard Peter 1939- *WhoWest 94*
Rolewicz, Robert John 1954- *WhoMW 93*
Rolf, David 1938- *WrDr 94*
Rolf, Erik d1957 *WhoHol 92*
Rolf, Frederick 1926- *WhoHol 92*
Rolf, Howard Leroy 1928- *WhoScEn 94*
Rolf, Percy Henry 1915- *Who 94*
Rolf, Tutta 1907- *WhoHol 92*
Rolfe, Cynthia Elaine 1953- *WhoFI 94*
Rolfe, Des d1979 *WhoHol 92*
Rolfe, Fr. *GayLL*
Rolfe, Frederick (William) 1860-1913 *EncSF 93*
Rolfe, Frederick (William Serafino Austin Lewis Mary) 1860-1913 *GayLL*
Rolfe, Frederick William 1860-1913 *DcNaB MP*
Rolfe, Guy 1915- *WhoHol 92*
Rolfe, Henry Cuthbert Norris 1908- *Who 94*
Rolfe, Hume B. *Who 94*
Rolfe, Marianne Teresa N. *Who 94*
Rolfe, Michael N. 1937- *WhoAm 94, WhoFI 94, WhoMW 93*
Rolfe, Robert Martin 1951- *WhoAm 94, WhoAmL 94*
Rolfe, Robin Ann 1949- *WhoAm 94*
Rolfe, Ronald Stuart 1945- *WhoAm 94, WhoAmL 94*
Rolfe, Sam d1993 *NewYTBS 93*
Rolfe, Stanley Theodore 1934- *WhoAm 94*
Rolfe, William David Ian 1936- *Who 94*
Rolfe Johnson, Anthony 1940- *IntWW 93, NewGrDO, Who 94*

Rolfes, Herman Harold 1936- *WhoWest 94*
Rolfing, Tom d1990 *WhoHol 92*
Rolfs, Edward C. *WhoAmP 93*
Rolfs, Kirk Alan 1962- *WhoScEn 94*
Rolfs, Thomas John 1922- *WhoFI 94*
Rolike, Hank *WhoHol 92*
Rolison, Jay P., Jr. 1929- *WhoAmP 93*
Roll *Who 94*
Roll, Barbara Honeyman 1910- *WhoWest 94*
Roll, Charles Weissert 1928- *WhoAmP 93*
Roll, David Lee 1940- *WhoAmL 94*
Roll, Irwin Clifford 1925- *WhoAm 94*
Roll, James (William Cecil) 1912- *Who 94*
Roll, John McCarthy 1947- *WhoAm 94, WhoAmL 94, WhoWest 94*
Rollan, Henri d1967 *WhoHol 92*
Rolland, Alvin Eugene 1930- *WhoAmP 93*
Rolland, Charles W. *WhoAmP 93*
Rolland, Christopher Lars 1947- *WhoAm 94*
Rolland, Erik 1961- *WhoWest 94*
Rolland, Ian McKenzie *WhoIns 94*
Rolland, Ian McKenzie 1933- *WhoAm 94, WhoFI 94, WhoMW 93*
Rolland, Jean-Claude d1967 *WhoHol 92*
Rolland, Jean-Louis *WhoHol 92*
Rolland, Lawrence Anderson Lyon 1937- *Who 94*
Rolland, Lucien G. 1916- *WhoAm 94, WhoFI 94*
Rolland, Peter George 1930- *WhoAm 94*
Rolland, Romain 1866-1944 *NewGrDO*
Rolland, Ronald Henri 1944- *WhoMW 93*
Rollans, James O. 1942- *WhoAm 94*
Rollason, W. Peter 1939- *WhoAm 94, WhoFI 94*
Rolle, Albert Eustace 1935- *WhoBlA 94*
Rolle, Andrew 1922- *WrDr 94*
Rolle, Andrew F. 1922- *WhoAm 94*
Rolle, Bridgette Deanne 1964- *WhoWest 94*
Rolle, Christopher Davies 1951- *WhoAm 94*
Rolle, Esther *WhoAm 94, WhoBlA 94, WhoHol 92*
Rolle, Esther 1922- *IntMPA 94*
Rolle, F. Robert 1939- *WhoScEn 94*
Rolle, Johann Heinrich 1716-1785 *NewGrDO*
Rolle, Myra Moss 1937- *WhoWest 94*
Rolle, Richard 1300-1349 *BlmGEL*
Rollence, Michele Lynette 1955- *WhoScEn 94*
Roller, Alfred 1864-1935 *NewGrDO*
Roller, Cleve *WhoHol 92*
Roller, Douglas P. 1944- *WhoAmL 94*
Roller, Duane Henry DuBose 1920- *WhoAm 94*
Roller, Herbert Alfred 1927- *WhoAm 94*
Roller, Marion Bender *WhoAmA 93*
Roller, Paul S. d1993 *NewYTBS 93*
Roller, Richard Allen 1956- *WhoScEn 94*
Roller, Robert Douglas, III 1928- *WhoAm 94*
Roller, Robert M. 1946- *WhoAmL 94*
Roller, Russell Kenneth 1938- *WhoAmA 93*
Roller, Susan Lorrayne 1954- *WhoWest 94*
Roller, Thomas Benjamin 1950- *WhoAm 94, WhoFI 94*
Roller, Wolfgang 1929- *IntWW 93*
Rollet, Marie Francois Louis Gand Leblanc *NewGrDO*
Rollett, Raymond d1961 *WhoHol 92*
Rolley, Alan W. 1933- *WhoFI 94*
Rollhaus, Philip Edward, Jr. 1934- *WhoAm 94, WhoFI 94*
Rolli, Paolo Antonio 1687-1765 *NewGrDO*
Rollin, Bernard Elliot 1943- *WhoAm 94*
Rollin, Betty *NewYTBS 93 [port]*
Rollin, Betty 1936- *WhoAm 94*
Rollin, Georges d1964 *WhoHol 92*
Rollin, Roger B. 1930- *WrDr 94*
Rollings, Gordon d1985 *WhoHol 92*
Rollings, JoAnn 1947- *WhoAm 94*
Rollins, Albert Williamson 1930- *WhoScEn 94*
Rollins, Alfred Brooks, Jr. 1921- *WhoAm 94*
Rollins, Amber *DrAPF 93*
Rollins, Avon William, Sr. 1941- *WhoBlA 94*
Rollins, Christopher D. *NewYTBS 93 [port]*
Rollins, David 1908- *WhoHol 92*
Rollins, Edward Tyler, Jr. 1922- *WhoAm 94*
Rollins, Ethel Eugenia 1932- *WhoBlA 94*
Rollins, Gary Wayne 1944- *WhoFI 94*
Rollins, Henry 1961- *ConMus 11 [port]*
Rollins, Henry Moak 1921- *WhoAm 94*
Rollins, Howard 1950- *IntMPA 94*
Rollins, Howard E., Jr. 1951- *WhoBlA 94, WhoHol 92*
Rollins, Howard Ellsworth, Jr. 1950- *WhoAm 94*
Rollins, Jack 1914- *IntMPA 94, WhoAm 94*
Rollins, Jack James 1922- *WhoWest 94*
Rollins, James Austin 1931- *WhoAm 94*
Rollins, James Gregory 1963- *WhoWest 94*
Rollins, James Richard 1939- *WhoWest 94*
Rollins, Jo Lutz 1896-1989 *WhoAmA 93N*
Rollins, John Charles 1958- *WhoFI 94*
Rollins, John William, Sr. 1916- *WhoAm 94*
Rollins, Lee Owen 1938- *WhoBlA 94*
Rollins, R. Randall *WhoFI 94*
Rollins, Reed Clark 1911- *IntWW 93*
Rollins, Richard Albert 1927- *WhoBlA 94*
Rollins, Scott Franklin 1959- *WhoScEn 94*
Rollins, Sherrie Sandy 1958- *WhoAm 94*
Rollins, Sonny 1929- *AfrAmAl 6 [port]*
Rollins, Sonny 1930- *WhoAm 94, WhoBlA 94*
Rollins, Tim 1955- *WhoAmA 93*
Rollins, Tree (Wayne Monte) 1955- *WhoBlA 94*
Rollins, Walter Theodore 1930- *WhoBlA 94*
Rollins, Wayne Gilbert 1929- *WrDr 94*
Rollinson, Mark 1935- *WhoAmL 94*
Rollison, Gerardo Roy 1954- *WhoAmL 94*
Rollison, John Adams, III 1950- *WhoAmP 93*
Rollman, Charlotte 1947- *WhoAmA 93*
Rollman, Steven Allan 1947- *WhoAm 94*
Rollo, Lord 1915- *Who 94*
Rollo, Master of 1943- *Who 94*
Rollo, F. David 1939- *WhoAm 94*
Rollo, Vera Foster 1924- *WrDr 94*
Rollock, Barbara T. d1992 *WhoBlA 94N*
Roll Of Ipsden, Baron 1907- *IntWW 93, Who 94, WrDr 94*
Rollow, Preston d1947 *WhoHol 92*
Rolls, Barbara Jean 1945- *WhoScEn 94*
Rolls, Brian *EncSF 93*
Rolls, Eric Charles 1923- *WrDr 94*
Rolls, John Allison 1941- *WhoFI 94*
Rolls, John Marland, Jr. 1937- *WhoAmL 94*
Rollwagen, John A. *NewYTBS 93 [port]*
Rollwagen, John A. 1940- *WhoAm 94, WhoFI 94, WhoScEn 94*
Rolly, Ronald Joseph 1937- *WhoAmA 93*
Rollyson, Christopher Shawn 1960- *WhoMW 93*
Rolo, Cyril Felix 1918- *Who 94*
Roloff, John Scott 1947- *WhoAmA 93*
Roloff, Karen Marie 1946- *WhoMW 93*
Roloff, Michael 1937- *WrDr 94*
Roloff, ReBecca Koenig 1954- *WhoIns 94*
Roloff, Thomas Paul 1965- *WhoScEn 94*
Roloff-Momin, Ulrich *IntWW 93*
Rolontz, Robert 1920- *WhoAm 94*
Rolph, C. H. 1901- *Who 94, WrDr 94*
Rolphe, Ben Richard, Jr. 1932- *WhoFI 94, WhoWest 94*
Rolshoven, Ross William 1954- *WhoMW 93*
Rolston, Holmes 1932- *EnvEnc [port]*
Rolston, Holmes, III 1932- *WhoAm 94, WhoScEn 94, WhoWest 94*
Rolston, Kenneth Stuart 1928- *WhoAm 94*
Rolston, Mark *WhoHol 92*
Rolston, Robert John 1944- *WhoFI 94*
Rolston, Robert Lee 1936- *WhoWest 94*
Rolt, Lionel Thomas Caswall 1910-1974 *DcNaB MP*
Rolvaag, Karl Fritjof 1913-1990 *WhAm 10*
Rolwes, Edward Joseph 1960- *WhoAmL 94*
Rom, Barbara 1949- *WhoAmL 94*
Rom, Martin 1946- *WhoAm 94*
Rom, Rebecca L. 1949- *WhoAmL 94*
Roma, Patrick 1949- *WhoAmP 93*
Romagosa, Elmo Lawrence 1924- *WhoAm 94*
Romaguera, Enrique 1942- *WhoFI 94, WhoMW 93*
Romaguera, Josefina 1955- *WhoHisp 94*
Romahi, Seif al-Wady al- 1938- *IntWW 93*
Romain, Roderick Jessel Anidjar 1916- *Who 94*
Romain, Yvonne 1938- *WhoHol 92*
Romaine, Elaine *DrAPF 93*
Romaine, George d1929 *WhoHol 92*
Romaine, Henry Simmons 1933- *WhoAm 94, WhoFI 94*
Romaine-Davis, Ada 1929- *ConAu 142*
Romalis, Carl 1948- *WhoAmL 94*
Roman, Andy, Jr. 1965- *WhoHisp 94*
Roman, Angel Luis 1950- *WhoAmP 93*
Roman, Angelo, Jr. 1954- *WhoHisp 94*
Roman, Cecelia Florence 1956- *WhoScEn 94*
Roman, Chris Leonard 1966- *WhoHisp 94*
Roman, Erasmo Tañón, Jr. 1932- *WhoHisp 94*
Roman, Freddie *WhoHol 92*
Román, Gilbert 1940- *WhoHisp 94*
Roman, Greg 1931- *WhoHol 92*
Roman, Herschel Lewis 1914-1989 *WhAm 10*
Roman, John Charles 1920- *WhoMW 93*
Roman, Joseph 1922- *WhoHol 92*
Roman, Kenneth, Jr. 1930- *WhoAm 94*
Roman, Lawrence 1921- *IntMPA 94*
Roman, Leticia 1941- *WhoHol 92*
Roman, Mary *WhoHisp 94*
Roman, Murray d1973 *WhoHol 92*
Roman, Norberto Nieves *WhoAmP 93*
Roman, Paul W., Jr. 1946- *WhoAmL 94*
Roman, Petre 1946- *IntWW 93*
Roman, Ric *WhoHol 92*
Roman, Roberto 1940- *WhoHisp 94*
Roman, Ronald Peter 1945- *WhoAmL 94*
Roman, Roy M. *WhoHisp 94*
Roman, Ruth 1922- *WhoHol 92*
Roman, Ruth 1924- *IntMPA 94*
Roman, Sheri Riley 1963- *WhoMW 93*
Roman, Shirley *WhoAmA 93*
Roman, Spencer Myles 1949- *WhoIns 94*
Roman, Stan G. 1954- *WhoAmL 94*
Roman, Stanford Augustus, Jr. *WhoScEn 94*
Roman, Stella 1904?-1992 *AnObit 1992, NewGrDO*
Román-Arroyo, Belinda 1962- *WhoHisp 94*
Roman-Barber, Helen 1946- *WhoAm 94*
Romance, Viviane 1909- *WhoHol 92*
Romanelli, Luigi 1751-1839 *NewGrDO*
Romanelli, Peter Nicholas 1948- *WhoWest 94*
Romanes, George John 1916- *Who 94*
Romani, Felice 1788-1865 *NewGrDO*
Romani, John Henry 1925- *WhoAm 94*
Romani, Pietro 1791-1877 *NewGrDO*
Romani, Stefano 1778-1850? *NewGrDO*
Romani Cignomi, Daniela 1956- *WhoWomW 91*
Romaniello, Charlotte *DrAPF 93*
Romanina, La 1550-162-? *NewGrDO*
Romanina, La fl. 1684-1707 *NewGrDO*
Romaniuk, Ryszard Stanislaw 1952- *WhoScEn 94*
Romankiw, Lubomyr Taras 1931- *WhoScEn 94*
Romano, Andy *WhoHol 92*
Romano, Benito 1949- *WhoAmL 94*
Romano, Charles Paul 1961- *WhoMW 93*
Romano, Clare Camille *WhoAmA 93*
Romano, Clifford Samuel 1951- *WhoWest 94*
Romano, Deane (Louis) 1927- *EncSF 93*
Romano, Emanuel Glicen 1897- *WhoAmA 93N*
Romano, Frank S., III 1961- *WhoFI 94*
Romano, Irene Marion 1950- *WhoAmP 93*
Romano, John 1908- *IntWW 93, WhoAm 94*
Romano, John 1948- *WrDr 94*
Romano, John A. 1923- *WhoAmP 93*
Romano, John Joseph 1942- *WhoAm 94*
Romano, John Joseph, Jr. 1947- *WhoWest 94*
Romano, Lalla 1909- *BlmGWL*
Romano, Larry *WhoHol 92*
Romano, Louis 1921- *WrDr 94*
Romano, Louis, Jr. 1945- *WhoFI 94*
Romano, Louis A. 1930- *WhoAmP 93*
Romano, Louis James 1950- *WhoScEn 94*
Romano, Renato *WhoHol 92*
Romano, Robert M. 1947- *WhoAmL 94*
Romano, Salvatore Michael 1925- *WhoAmA 93*
Romano, Sergio 1929- *IntWW 93*
Romano, Tony 1915- *WhoHol 92*
Romano, Xavier Eduardo 1960- *WhoHisp 94*
Romanoff, Marjorie Reinwald 1923- *WhoMW 93*
Romanoff, Mike d1971 *WhoHol 92*
Romanoff, Milford Martin 1921- *WhoAm 94*
Romanoff, Stanley M., Jr. 1948- *WhoFI 94, WhoMW 93*
Romanos, John, Jr. 1942- *WhoAm 94*
Romanos, Nabil Elias 1965- *WhoFI 94, WhoWest 94*
Romanov, Boris 1891-1957 *IntDcB*
Romanov, Mikhail Alekseevich 1936- *LngBDD*
Romanov, Natasha Galitzine d1989 *WhoHol 92*
Romano-V., Octavio I. 1932- *WhoHisp 94*
Romanov, Vladimir Kirillovich 1917-1992 *AnObit 1992*
Romanov Family *NewGrDO*
Romanow, Richard Brian 1953- *WhoAmP 93*
Romanow, Roy (John) 1939- *WrDr 94*
Romanow, Roy John *WhoAm 94, WhoWest 94*
Romanowitz, Byron Foster 1929- *WhoAm 94*
Romanowski, Hubert d1993 *NewYTBS 93*
Romanowski, Kenneth 1952- *WhoFI 94*
Romanowski, Robert Lee 1939- *WhoMW 93*
Romanowski, Thomas Andrew 1925- *WhoAm 94, WhoScEn 94*
Romanowski, William David 1954- *WhoMW 93*
Romanowsky, Richard d1968 *WhoHol 92*
Romans, Ann 1929- *WhoBlA 94*
Romans, Bernard 1720-1784 *AmRev, WhAmRev*
Romans, Charles John 1891-1973 *WhoAmA 93N*
Romans, Donald Bishop 1931- *WhoAm 94*
Romans, John Niebrugge 1942- *WhoAm 94, WhoAmL 94*
Romans, John Thomas 1933- *WhoFI 94*
Romans, Pat *WhoAmP 93*
Romans, Van Anthony 1944- *WhoAmA 93*
Romansky, Michael A. 1952- *WhoAm 94*
Romansky, Monroe James 1911- *IntWW 93, WhoAm 94*
Romanus, Richard *WhoHol 92*
Romanus, Robert *WhoHol 92*
Romanus, Sven Einar 1906- *IntWW 93*
Romanyak, James Andrew 1944- *WhoAmL 94*
Romanzini, Maria Theresa *NewGrDO*
Romary, John M. 1947- *WhoAmL 94*
Romashin, Anatoliy Vladimirovich 1931- *IntWW 93*
Romatowski, Peter J. 1950- *WhoAm 94*
Romay, Lina *WhoHol 92*
Rombauer, Marjorie Lorraine 1927- *WhoWest 94*
Romberg, Andreas Jakob 1767-1821 *NewGrDO*
Romberg, Bernhard Heinrich 1767-1841 *NewGrDO*
Romberg, Sigmund 1887-1951 *NewGrDO*
Romberger, John Albert 1925- *WhoScEn 94*
Rombough, Bartlett B. 1924- *WhoAm 94*
Rombout, Luke 1933- *WhoAm 94, WhoAmA 93*
Rombs, Vincent Joseph 1918- *WhoFI 94, WhoMW 93*
Rome, Alan Mackenzie 1930- *Who 94*
Rome, Alger *EncSF 93*
Rome, Anthony *WrDr 94*
Rome, Bert d1946 *WhoHol 92*
Rome, David 1910- *ConAu 142*
Rome, David 1938- *EncSF 93*
Rome, Donald Lee 1929- *WhoAm 94, WhoAmL 94, WhoFI 94*
Rome, Harold J. 1908-1993 *NewYTBS 93 [port]*
Rome, Harold Jacob 1908- *WhoAm 94*
Rome, John L. 1954- *WhoFI 94*
Rome, Marcus *DrAPF 93*
Rome, Margaret *WrDr 94*
Rome, Morton Eugene 1913- *WhoAmL 94*
Rome, Stewart d1965 *WhoHol 92*
Rome, Sydne 1947- *WhoHol 92*
Romee, Marcelle d1932 *WhoHol 92*
Romei, Adolph A. 1957- *WhoAmL 94*
Romei, Lura Knachel 1947- *WhoAm 94*
Romein-Verschoor, Annie 1895-1978 *BlmGWL*
Romeling, W. B. 1909- *WhoAmA 93*
Romens'ky, Mykhaylo Demyanovych 1887-1971 *NewGrDO*
Romeo, Luigi 1926- *WhoAm 94*
Romeo, Neola Fern 1914- *WhoAmP 93*
Romeo, Peter John 1942- *WhoAm 94, WhoAmL 94*
Romeo, Richard Patrick 1950- *WhoFI 94*
Romer, Emma 1814-1868 *NewGrDO*
Romer, Jeanne Geraldine 1939- *WhoFI 94*
Romer, (Louis) John 1941- *WrDr 94*
Romer, Leila d1944 *WhoHol 92*
Romer, Mark Lemon Robert 1927- *Who 94*
Romer, Robert Horton 1931- *WhoScEn 94*
Romer, Roy R. 1928- *IntWW 93, WhoAm 94, WhoAmP 93, WhoWest 94*
Romer, Tomi d1969 *WhoHol 92*
Romeri, Michael Niti 1954- *WhoAm 94*
Romeril, John 1945- *ConDr 93, IntDcT 2, WrDr 94*
Romero (Sarachaga), Federico 1886-1976 *NewGrDO*
Romero, Alberto C. 1950- *WhoHisp 94*
Romero, Benjamin Pedro 1912- *WhoHisp 94*
Romero, Carlos *WhoHol 92*
Romero, Cesar 1907- *IntMPA 94, WhoHol 92*
Romero, Cesar 1907-1994 *WhoHisp 94N*
Romero, Cesar 1943- *WhoHisp 94*
Romero, Craig F. *WhoAmP 93*
Romero, Daniel H. 1928- *WhoHisp 94*
Romero, Ed L. *WhoHisp 94*
Romero, Ed L. 1934- *WhoAmP 93*
Romero, Edgardo 1957- *WhoHisp 94*
Romero, Elmer 1956- *WhoHisp 94*

Romero, Emilio Felipe 1946- *WhoHisp 94, WhoScEn 94*
Romero, Esteban Enos 1951- *WhoHisp 94*
Romero, Filiberto Martimiano 1934- *WhoHisp 94*
Romero, Frank 1943- *WhoHisp 94*
Romero, Freddie Joseph 1956- *WhoAmL 94*
Romero, Georg L. 1954- *WhoHisp 94*
Romero, George A. 1939- *WhoAm 94*
Romero, George A. 1940- *EncSF 93, HorFD [port], IntMPA 94*
Romero, Gilbert E. *WhoHisp 94*
Romero, Gilbert E. 1955- *WhoAmP 93*
Romero, Hector R. 1942- *WhoHisp 94*
Romero, Henry, Jr. 1946- *WhoHisp 94*
Romero, Irene *WhoHisp 94*
Romero, Jeff 1945- *WhoAmL 94*
Romero, Joe *WhoHisp 94*
Romero, Joe d1978 *WhoHol 92*
Romero, Jorge Antonio 1948- *WhoScEn 94*
Romero, Jose T. *WhoAmA 93*
Romero, Juan Carlos 1937- *WhoHisp 94*
Romero, Juan De Jesus 1874-1978 *EncNAR*
Romero, Kenneth Phillip 1960- *WhoHisp 94*
Romero, Leo *DrAPF 93*
Romero, Leo 1950- *WhoHisp 94*
Romero, Leon A. 1951- *WhoHisp 94*
Romero, Leota V. 1921- *WhoHisp 94*
Romero, Lucille Bernadette 1955- *WhoHisp 94*
Romero, Martin E. *WhoHisp 94*
Romero, Megan H. 1942- *WhoAmA 93*
Romero, Miguel A. 1925- *WhoScEn 94*
Romero, Ned 1925- *WhoHol 92*
Romero, Orlando Arturo 1945- *WhoHisp 94*
Romero, Paul Anthony, Sr. 1961- *WhoHisp 94*
Romero, Paulo Armando 1943- *WhoHisp 94*
Romero, Pepe 1944- *IntWW 93*
Romero, Peter *WhoAmP 93*
Romero, Peter Frank 1949- *WhoAm 94*
Romero, Phil Andrew 1949- *WhoHisp 94*
Romero, Philip James 1953- *WhoHisp 94*
Romero, Philip Joseph 1957- *WhoWest 94*
Romero, Rachael L. 1953- *WhoAmA 93*
Romero, Ralph 1953- *WhoScEn 94*
Romero, Raymond G. 1954- *WhoHisp 94*
Romero, Richard Joseph 1955- *WhoHisp 94*
Romero, Richard M. *WhoAmP 93*
Romero, Richard Roy 1949- *WhoHisp 94*
Romero, Robert 1963- *WhoHisp 94*
Romero, Sandra S. *WhoAmP 93*
Romero, Scott Joseph 1956- *WhoWest 94*
Romero, Thomas Arthur 1939- *WhoAmP 93, WhoHisp 94*
Romero, Tino 1935- *WhoHisp 94*
Romero-Barcelo, Carlos 1932- *CngDr 93*
Romero-Barcelo, Carlos Antonio 1932- *IntWW 93, WhoAm 94, WhoAmP 93, WhoHisp 94*
Romero-Font, Luis Guillermo 1952- *WhoFI 94*
Romero Herrera, Carlos 1941- *IntWW 93*
Romero Kolbeck, Gustavo 1923- *IntWW 93*
Romero Mena, Carlos Humberto *IntWW 93*
Romes, Charles Michael 1954- *WhoBlA 94*
Romeu, Joost A. 1948- *WhoAmA 93*
Romeu, Jorge Luis *DrAPF 93*
Romey, William Dowden 1930- *WhoAm 94, WhoScEn 94*
Romeyn, Jane d1963 *WhoHol 92*
Romeyn, Richard Loren 1953- *WhoMW 93*
Romieu, Marie de 1545?-1590? *BlmGWL*
Romig, Alton Dale, Jr. 1953- *WhoScEn 94*
Romig, Lleuellen Dewight 1897- *WhAm 10*
Romig, Phillip Richardson 1938- *WhoAm 94*
Romilus, Arn *EncSF 93*
Romine, Charles Everett, Jr. 1936- *WhoAmP 93*
Romine, Richard Larimore 1946- *WhoMW 93*
Romine, Thomas Beeson, Jr. 1925- *WhoAm 94, WhoScEn 94*
Romine, Thomas Howard 1944- *WhoMW 93*
Rominger, James Corridon 1920- *WhoAmP 93*
Rominger, Richard 1927- *WhoAm 94*
Romino, Dominick Joseph 1911- *WhoAmP 93*
Romita, Pier Luigi 1924- *IntWW 93*
Romiti, Cesare 1923- *IntWW 93*
Romjue, Jane Murphy 1944- *WhoWest 94*
Romjue, Nickell *DrAPF 93*
Romley, Richard M. 1949- *WhoAmL 94*
Rommel, A. Ross, Jr. 1947- *WhoAmL 94*
Rommel, Erwin 1891-1944 *HisWorL [port]*
Romney, Earl of 1910- *Who 94*
Romney, Carl F. 1924- *WhoAm 94*
Romney, Clyde Anderson 1943- *WhoAmL 94*
Romney, Edana 1919- *WhoHol 92*
Romney, Edgar O. 1943- *WhoBlA 94*
Romney, G. Scott 1941- *WhoAmL 94*
Romney, George 1907- *WhoAm 94*
Romney, Hervin A. R. 1941- *WhoAmA 93*
Romney, Joseph Barnard 1935- *WhoWest 94*
Romney, Richard Bruce 1942- *WhoAm 94, WhoAmL 94*
Romney, Richard Miles 1952- *WhoWest 94*
Romney, Seymour Leonard 1917- *WhoAm 94*
Romney, Steve *ConAu 42NR*
Romney, W Mitt 1947- *WhoAm 94*
Romney-Brown, Cheryl *DrAPF 93*
Romo, Eloise R. 1948- *WhoHisp 94*
Romo, Gene David 1947- *WhoAm 94*
Romo, John B. 1946- *WhoHisp 94*
Romo, José León 1930- *WhoHisp 94*
Romo, Oscar I. 1929- *WhoHisp 94*
Romo, Paul J. 1936- *WhoHisp 94*
Romo, Ric 1958- *WhoHisp 94*
Romo, Ricardo 1943- *WhoHisp 94*
Romo, Rolando 1947- *WhoHisp 94*
Romo, Sylvia 1942- *WhoAmP 93*
Romoser, George Kenneth 1929- *WhoAm 94*
Romoser, Sally Beth 1958- *WhoWest 94*
Rompe, Robert 1905- *IntWW 93*
Rompf, Clifford G., Jr. 1930- *WhoFI 94*
Rompis, Robert James 1951- *WhoFI 94*
Romppanen, Eino Antti *WhoAmA 93*
Romsdahl, Marvin Magnus 1930- *WhoAm 94*
Romsey, Lord 1947- *Who 94*
Romtvedt, David *DrAPF 93*
Romualdez, Eduardo Z. 1909- *IntWW 93*
Romualdi, James Philip 1929- *WhoAm 94*
Romun, Isak *DrAPF 93*
Rona, Victor 1936- *IntDcB*
Ronald, Allan Ross 1938- *WhoAm 94*
Ronald, Bruce W(alton) 1931- *EncSF 93*
Ronald, Edith *Who 94*
Ronald, Peter 1926- *WhoAm 94*
Ronald, Thomas Iain 1933- *WhoAm 94, WhoFI 94*
Ronald, William 1926- *WhoAm 94, WhoAmA 93*
Ronaldshay, Earl of 1965- *Who 94*
Ronan, Alfred Gregory 1947- *WhoAmP 93*
Ronan, Colin Alistair 1920- *WrDr 94*
Ronan, Helen *DrAPF 93*
Ronan, John J. *DrAPF 93*
Ronan, Richard *DrAPF 93*
Ronan, Robert d1977 *WhoHol 92*
Ronan, Sean G. 1924- *IntWW 93*
Ronan, Timothy Dwyer 1959- *WhoWest 94*
Ronan, William John 1912- *WhoAm 94, WhoFI 94*
Ronaszegi, Miklos *EncSF 93*
Ronay, Edina *WhoHol 92*
Ronay, Egon *IntWW 93, Who 94*
Ronayne, Michael Richard, Jr. 1937- *WhoAm 94*
Ronbeck, Sissel 1950- *IntWW 93*
Ronca, Luciano Bruno 1935- *WhoAm 94*
Ronca, William E., III 1962- *WhoHisp 94*
Ronca-Battista, Melinda Jane 1959- *WhoWest 94*
Roncaglia, Francesco c. 1750-c. 1812 *NewGrDO*
Roncalio, Ceil *WhoAmP 93*
Roncallo, Angelo D. 1927- *WhoAmP 93*
Ronco, Bradley Eugene 1946- *WhoFI 94*
Ronco, Nicolas Dominique 1967- *WhoFI 94*
Ronconi, Giorgio 1810-1890 *NewGrDO*
Ronconi, Luca 1933- *NewGrDO*
Ronda, James P(aul) 1943- *WrDr 94*
Rondeau, Cheryl MaryAnn 1952- *WhoMW 93*
Rondeau, Clement Robert 1928- *WhoFI 94*
Rondeau, Doris Jean 1941- *WhoFI 94, WhoWest 94*
Rondeau, Jacques Antoine 1947- *WhoScEn 94*
Rondelli, Lucio 1924- *IntWW 93*
Rondepierre, Edmond F. 1930- *WhoIns 94*
Rondepierre, Edmond Francois 1930- *WhoAm 94, WhoAmL 94*
Rondi, Brunello d1989 *WhoHol 92*
Rondileau, Adrian 1912- *WhoAm 94*
Rondinelli, Dennis August 1943- *WhoFI 94*
Rondon, Edania Cecilia 1960- *WhoAmL 94*
Rondon, Fernando E. 1936- *WhoAmP 93*
Rondon-Tollens, Salomon *WhoHisp 94*
Rone, William Eugene, Jr. 1926- *WhoAm 94*
Ronell, Ann d1993 *NewYTBS 93*
Ronell, Avital 1956- *WrDr 94*
Ronen, Carol *WhoAmP 93*
Ronet, Maurice d1983 *WhoHol 92*
Roney, Harold Arthur 1899-1986 *WhoAmA 93N*
Roney, John Harvey 1932- *WhoAm 94, WhoAmL 94, WhoFI 94, WhoWest 94*
Roney, Lynn Karol 1946- *WhoScEn 94*
Roney, Paul Hitch 1921- *WhoAm 94, WhoAmL 94*
Roney, Raymond G. 1941- *WhoBlA 94*
Roney, Robert Kenneth 1922- *WhoAm 94*
Roney, Scott Allen 1964- *WhoMW 93*
Roney, Wallace 1960- *WhoAm 94*
Ronga, Luigi 1901-1983 *NewGrDO*
Rongey, Wesley Gregory 1961- *WhoMW 93*
Rong Gaotang 1912- *IntWW 93, WhoPRCh 91 [port]*
Rong Yi 1923- *WhoPRCh 91 [port]*
Rong Yiren 1916- *IntWW 93, WhoPRCh 91 [port]*
Rong Ziqing *WhoPRCh 91*
Ronhovde, Virginia S. 1909- *WhoAmP 93*
Roningen, Vernon Oley 1939- *WhoFI 94*
Ronk, Glenn Emery 1925- *WhoAm 94*
Ronn, Avigdor Meir 1938- *WhoScEn 94*
Ronn, Ehud Israel 1950- *WhoFI 94*
Ronnebeck, Arnold H. 1885-1947 *WhoAmA 93N*
Ronneberg, Norman J. 1947- *WhoAmL 94*
Ronneburger, Uwe 1920- *IntWW 93*
Ronnefeld, Peter 1935-1965 *NewGrDO*
Ronquillo, Marcos G. 1953- *WhoHisp 94*
Ronquillo, Pablo Javier 1932-1992 *WhoHisp 94N*
Ronsard, Pierre de 1524-1585 *BlmGEL, EncDeaf, GuFrLit 2*
Ronsch, Hannelore *WhoWomW 91*
Ronsley, Joseph 1931- *WrDr 94*
Ronsman, Wayne John 1938- *WhoWest 94*
Ronson, Gerald Maurice 1939- *IntWW 93, Who 94*
Ronson, Mick d1993 *NewYTBS 93*
Ronson, Raoul R. 1931- *WhoAm 94, WhoFI 94*
Ronstadt, Linda 1946- *WhoHol 92*
Ronstadt, Linda Marie 1946- *WhoAm 94, WhoHisp 94*
Rontgen, Wilhelm Konrad 1845-1923 *WorScD [port]*
Ronto, Gyorgyi 1934- *IntWW 93*
Ronzi De Begnis, Giuseppina 1800-1853 *NewGrDO*
Roobol, Norman Richard 1934- *WhoAm 94*
Rood, David S. 1940- *WhoAm 94*
Rood, Johannes Joseph Van 1926- *IntWW 93*
Rood, John 1906-1974 *WhoAmA 93N*
Rood, Kay 1945- *WhoAmA 93*
Rood, Paul 1894- *WhAm 10*
Rood, Robert Eugene 1951- *WhoScEn 94*
Roodkowsky, Alice May 1921- *WhoAmP 93*
Roodman, David A. 1962- *WhoAmL 94*
Roodman, Stanford Trent 1939- *WhoMW 93*
Rook, Clarence 1863-1915 *DcLB 135*
Rook, Edward F. 1870-1960 *WhoAmA 93N*
Rook, Peter Francis Grosvenor 1949- *Who 94*
Rook, Tony 1932- *WrDr 94*
Rooke, Allen Driscoll, Jr. 1924- *WhoAm 94, WhoScEn 94*
Rooke, Daphne 1914- *BlmGWL*
Rooke, Daphne (Marie) 1914- *WrDr 94*
Rooke, Daphne Marie 1914- *Who 94*
Rooke, David Lee 1923- *WhoAm 94*
Rooke, Denis (Eric) 1924- *Who 94*
Rooke, Denis Eric 1924- *IntWW 93*
Rooke, Fay Lorraine 1934- *WhoAmA 93*
Rooke, Giles Hugh 1930- *Who 94*
Rooke, Irene d1958 *WhoHol 92*
Rooke, James Smith 1916- *Who 94*
Rooke, Katerina Anghelaki *ConWorW 93*
Rooke, Leon *DrAPF 93*
Rooke, Leon 1934- *WrDr 94*
Rooke, Vera Margaret 1924- *Who 94*
Rooke, William Michael 1794-1847 *NewGrDO*
Rooker, Andrew D. 1945- *WhoAmL 94*
Rooker, Jeffrey William 1941- *Who 94*
Rooker, Leroy S. 1947- *WhoAmP 93*
Rooker, Michael 1954- *WhoHol 92*
Rooker, Michael 1955- *IntMPA 94*
Rooker, Michael Angelo 1743-1801 *NewGrDO [port]*
Rooklidge, William Charles 1957- *WhoAmL 94*
Rooks, Charles Shelby 1924- *WhoAm 94, WhoBlA 94*
Rooks, Conrad *WhoHol 92*
Rooks, Eleanor Knee 1927- *WhoAmP 93*
Rooks, James Orville 1922- *WhoAmP 93*
Rooks, Judith Pence 1941- *WhoWest 94*
Rooks, Sean Lester 1969- *WhoBlA 94*
Rooley, Anthony 1944- *Who 94*
Roomann, Hugo 1923- *WhoAm 94*
Roomberg, Lila Goldstein 1929- *WhoAm 94*
Roome, Oliver McCrea 1921- *Who 94*
Roomkin, Myron J. 1945- *WhoMW 93*
Roomsburg, Judy Dennis 1954- *WhoScEn 94*
Rooner, Charles d1954 *WhoHol 92*
Rooney, Andrew A. 1919- *IntMPA 94*
Rooney, Andrew A(itken) 1919- *WrDr 94*
Rooney, Andrew Aitken 1919- *WhoAm 94*
Rooney, Andy 1919- *WhoCom*
Rooney, Anne 1925- *WhoHol 92*
Rooney, Arthur Joseph d1988 *ProFbHF [port]*
Rooney, Brian Gordon 1954- *WhoMW 93*
Rooney, Carol Bruns 1940- *WhoMW 93*
Rooney, Daniel M. 1932- *WhoAm 94*
Rooney, Dean Michael 1952- *WhoAmL 94*
Rooney, Denis Michael Hall 1919- *IntWW 93, Who 94*
Rooney, Francis Xavier 1927- *IntWW 93*
Rooney, George Willard 1915- *WhoAmL 94*
Rooney, J. Patrick 1927- *WhoIns 94*
Rooney, James F. 1935- *WhoAmP 93*
Rooney, John Connell 1967- *WhoScEn 94*
Rooney, John Edward 1939- *WhoAmP 93*
Rooney, John Edward, Jr. 1942- *WhoAm 94*
Rooney, John Joseph 1915- *WhoAm 94, WhoAmP 93*
Rooney, John Philip 1932- *WhoAm 94, WhoAmL 94, WhoMW 93*
Rooney, Kathleen Dixon 1949- *WhoFI 94*
Rooney, Kevin D. 1944- *WhoAmP 93*
Rooney, Kevin Davitt 1944- *WhoAm 94*
Rooney, Lucy 1926- *WrDr 94*
Rooney, Matthew A. 1949- *WhoAm 94, WhoAmL 94*
Rooney, Michael, Jr. *WhoHol 92*
Rooney, Michael James 1947- *WhoAmL 94*
Rooney, Michael John 1944- *Who 94*
Rooney, Mickey *NewYTBS 93 [port]*
Rooney, Mickey 1920- *IntMPA 94, WhoAm 94, WhoCom, WhoHol 92*
Rooney, Pat d1933 *WhoHol 92*
Rooney, Pat d1962 *WhoHol 92*
Rooney, Pat, III d1979 *WhoHol 92*
Rooney, Paul C., Jr. 1943- *WhoAm 94*
Rooney, Paul George 1925- *WhoAm 94*
Rooney, Paul Monroe 1918- *WhoAm 94*
Rooney, Scott William 1961- *WhoAmL 94*
Rooney, Stephen Gerard 1955- *WhoAmL 94*
Rooney, Susan Kay 1946- *WhoFI 94*
Rooney, Teddy *WhoHol 92*
Rooney, Terence Henry 1950- *Who 94*
Rooney, Terence Joseph 1964- *WhoAmP 93*
Rooney, Tim *WhoHol 92*
Rooney, Wallace *WhoHol 92*
Rooney, William Richard 1938- *WhoAm 94*
Roop, Connie 1951- *WrDr 94*
Roop, Jack J. 1933- *WhoAmP 93*
Roop, James John 1949- *WhoAm 94, WhoFI 94, WhoMW 93*
Roop, Joseph McLeod 1941- *WhoScEn 94, WhoWest 94*
Roop, Mark Edward 1958- *WhoScEn 94*
Roop, Peter 1951- *WrDr 94*
Roop, Ralph Goodwin 1915- *WhoAm 94*
Roop, Robert Dickinson 1949- *WhoScEn 94*
Roope, Bruce Edward 1952- *WhoAmP 93*
Roope, Fay d1961 *WhoHol 92*
Roorbach, Bill *DrAPF 93*
Roorda, John Francis, Jr. 1923- *WhoAm 94*
Roorda, Walter John 1930- *WhoAmP 93, WhoMW 93*
Roork, Donald Wallace 1949- *WhoFI 94*
Roos, Casper 1925- *WhoAm 94*
Roos, Daniel 1939- *WhoAm 94*
Roos, David Bernard 1928- *WhoWest 94*
Roos, Eric Eugene 1941- *WhoAm 94*
Roos, Fred 1934- *IntMPA 94*
Roos, Frederick Ried 1934- *WhoAm 94*
Roos, George William 1932- *WhoWest 94*
Roos, Joanna d1989 *WhoHol 92*
Roos, Kathleen Marie 1962- *WhoMW 93*
Roos, Kelley 1911- *WrDr 94*
Roos, Leslie Jay 1947- *WhoAmL 94*
Roos, Michael 1945- *WhoAmP 93*
Roos, Michael Edward 1952- *WhoMW 93*
Roos, Murphre 1951- *WrDr 94*
Roos, Nestor Robert 1925- *WhoAm 94, WhoWest 94*
Roos, Noralou P. 1942- *WrDr 94*
Roos, Philip 1930- *WhoAm 94*
Roos, Richard c. 1410-1482 *DcNaB MP*

Roos, Sidney W. d1993 *NewYTBS 93*
Roos, Stephen 1945- *SmATA 77 [port]*
Roos, Thomas Bloom 1930- *WhoAm 94*
Roos, William 1911- *WrDr 94*
Roosa, Jan Bertorotta 1937- *WhoMW 93*
Roosa, Robert V. 1918- *IntWW 93*
Roosa, Robert V. 1939-1993 *NewYTBS 93 [port]*
Roose-Evans, James 1927- *WrDr 94*
Roose-Evans, James Humphrey 1927- *Who 94*
Roosen, Mia Westerlund 1942- *WhoAmA 93*
Roosen-Van Pelt, Riet (M.) J.J. 1934- *WhoWomW 91*
Roosevelt, Archibald Bulloch, Jr. 1918-1990 *WhAm 10*
Roosevelt, Buddy d1973 *WhoHol 92*
Roosevelt, Eleanor 1884-1962 *HisWorL [port]*
Roosevelt, Ellen 1868-1954 *BuCMET*
Roosevelt, Elliott 1910-1990 *WhAm 10*
Roosevelt, Franklin Delano 1882-1945 *HisWorL [port]*
Roosevelt, Haven C. 1940- *WhoAmL 94*
Roosevelt, James 1907-1991 *WhAm 10*
Roosevelt, James, Jr. 1945- *WhoAmL 94, WhoAmP 93*
Roosevelt, Mark 1955- *WhoAmP 93*
Roosevelt, Michael A. 1946- *WhoAmL 94*
Roosevelt, Selwa 1929- *WrDr 94*
Roosevelt, Theodore d1919 *WhoHol 92*
Roosevelt, Theodore 1858-1919 *EnvEnc [port], HisWorL [port]*
Roosevelt, Theodore, IV 1942- *WhoAm 94*
Roosma, Hubert 1929- *WhoFI 94*
Root, Alan Charles 1925- *WhoAm 94, WhoFI 94*
Root, Allen William 1933- *WhoAm 94*
Root, Blake Smith 1905-1990 *WhAm 10*
Root, Charles Joseph, Jr. 1940- *WhoWest 94*
Root, Daniel Reinhardt 1942- *WhoMW 93*
Root, Doris Smiley 1924- *WhoWest 94*
Root, Edward Lakin 1940- *WhoAm 94*
Root, Edward W., Mrs. *WhoAmA 93N*
Root, Edward Wales 1884-1956 *WhoAmA 93N*
Root, Elihu 1845-1937 *HisWorL [port]*
Root, Elisha King 1808-1865 *WorInv*
Root, Franklin Russell 1923- *WhoAm 94*
Root, George L., Jr. 1947- *WhoAmL 94*
Root, Howard Eugene 1926- *Who 94*
Root, Jesse 1737-1822 *WhAmRev*
Root, John Howard 1955- *WhoAmL 94*
Root, Judith *DrAPF 93*
Root, Kim Kelly 1953- *WhoMW 93*
Root, L. Allen *WhoAm 94*
Root, Lynal A. 1930- *WhoAm 94, WhoFI 94*
Root, M. Belinda 1957- *WhoScEn 94*
Root, Michael J. 1955- *WhoMW 93*
Root, Nile 1926- *WhoWest 94*
Root, Nina J. 1934- *WhoAm 94*
Root, Oren 1911- *WhoAm 94*
Root, Phyllis 1949- *WrDr 94*
Root, Richard Kay 1937- *WhoWest 94*
Root, Samuel I. 1930- *WhoMW 93*
Root, Stanley William, Jr. 1923- *WhoAm 94*
Root, Stuart Dowling 1932- *WhoAm 94*
Root, Wayne Allyn 1961- *WhoWest 94*
Root, Wells 1900- *IntMPA 94*
Root, William Alden 1923- *WhoAm 94*
Root, William Dixon 1951- *WhoWest 94*
Root, William Lucas 1919- *WhoAm 94*
Root, William Pitt *DrAPF 93*
Root, William Pitt 1941- *WhoAm 94, WrDr 94*
Root-Bernstein, Robert Scott 1953- *WhoAm 94, WrDr 94*
Rootes, Baron 1951- *Who 94*
Rooth, Robert Stephen 1949- *WhoAmL 94*
Rootham, Jasper (St. John) 1910-1990 *ConAu 41NR*
Roots, Ernest Frederick 1923- *WhoAm 94*
Roots, Garrison 1952- *WhoAmA 93*
Roots, Guy Robert Godfrey 1946- *Who 94*
Roots, John McCook 1903-1988 *WhAm 10*
Roots, Paul John 1929- *Who 94*
Roots, Peter Charles 1921- *WhoFI 94*
Rooy, Anton(ius Maria Josephus) van 1870-1932 *NewGrDO*
Roozen, Mary Louise 1921- *WhoMW 93*
Ropartz, Joseph Guy (Marie) 1864-1955 *NewGrDO*
Ropchan, Jim R. 1950- *WhoScEn 94*
Rope, Barry Stuart 1942- *WhoScEn 94*
Rope, William Frederick 1940- *WhoAm 94*
Roper *Who 94*
Roper, Birdie Alexander *WhoWest 94*
Roper, Bobby L. *WhoBlA 94*
Roper, Brian 1933- *WhoHol 92*
Roper, Burns Worthington 1925- *WhoAm 94*
Roper, Clinton Marcus 1921- *Who 94*
Roper, Clyde Forrest Eugene 1937- *WhoAm 94*
Roper, Donald Spencer 1960- *WhoFI 94*
Roper, Grace Trott 1925- *WhoBlA 94*
Roper, Gregory D. 1953- *WhoAmL 94*
Roper, Harry Joseph 1940- *WhoAmL 94*
Roper, Jack d1966 *WhoHol 92*
Roper, John (Francis Hodgess) 1935- *Who 94*
Roper, John Charles Abercromby 1915- *Who 94*
Roper, John Lonsdale, III 1927- *WhoAm 94*
Roper, John Marlin 1942- *WhoAm 94, WhoAmL 94*
Roper, L. V. Sam 1931- *WhoAmP 93*
Roper, Laura Wood 1911- *WrDr 94*
Roper, Margaret (More) 1505-1544 *BlmGWL*
Roper, Margaret More 1505-1544 *BlmGEL*
Roper, Michael 1932- *Who 94*
Roper, Paul Holmes 1932- *WhoAm 94*
Roper, Richard Walter 1945- *WhoBlA 94*
Roper, Robert Burnell 1921- *Who 94*
Roper, Robert Edward 1916- *WhoAmP 93*
Roper, Walter William 1945- *WhoWest 94*
Roper, Warren Richard 1938- *IntWW 93, Who 94*
Roper-Curzon *Who 94*
Ropes, Linda Brubaker 1942- *ConAu 140*
Rophar 1935- *WhoAmA 93*
Ropiequet, John Lee 1947- *WhoAmL 94, WhoMW 93*
Ropner, David *Who 94*
Ropner, (William Guy) David 1924- *Who 94*
Ropner, John (Bruce Woollacott) 1937- *Who 94*
Ropner, John Raymond 1903- *Who 94*
Ropner, Robert Douglas 1921- *Who 94*
Ropp, Ann L. 1939- *WhoAm 94*
Ropp, Ann L. 1946- *WhoAmA 93*
Ropp, Clarence Daniel Luther 1898- *WhAm 10*
Ropp, Gordon L. 1933- *WhoAmP 93*
Ropp, Richard Claude 1927- *WhoScEn 94*
Ropski, Gary Melchior 1952- *WhoAm 94, WhoAmL 94*
Roque, Margarita 1946- *WhoHisp 94*
Roque, Roberto Dizon 1929- *WhoAm 94*
Roque, Ruben 1957- *WhoHisp 94*
Roquelaure, A.N. *TwCYAW*
Roquelaure, A. N. 1941- *WrDr 94*
Roquemaurel, Ithier de 1914- *IntWW 93*
Roquemore, Henry d1943 *WhoHol 92*
Roquemour, Grayson 1942- *WhoFI 94*
Roqueplan, Nestor 1805-1870 *NewGrDO*
Roques, Jeanne *WhoHol 92*
Roques, (David) John (Seymour) 1938- *Who 94*
Roquevert, Noel d1973 *WhoHol 92*
Roraback, Thomas Joseph 1943- *WhoIns 94*
Rorabaugh, Joan 1928- *WhoAmP 93*
Rorem, Ned 1923- *GayLL, NewGrDO, WhoAm 94*
Rorer, John Whiteley 1930- *WhoFI 94*
Rorex, Robert Albright 1935- *WhoAmA 93*
Rorick, Alan Green 1918- *WhoAm 94*
Rorie, Roger L. 1947- *WhoAmP 93*
Rorig, Kurt Joachim 1920- *WhoAm 94*
Rorimer, James J. 1905-1966 *WhoAmA 93N*
Rorimer, Louis 1947- *WhoAm 94, WhoAmL 94*
Roripaugh, Robert (Alan) 1930- *WrDr 94*
Rork, Allen Wright 1944- *WhoIns 94*
Rork, Ann d1988 *WhoHol 92*
Rork, Peter Ernest 1953- *WhoWest 94*
Rorke, Hayden d1987 *WhoHol 92*
Rorke, Ina d1944 *WhoHol 92*
Rorke, John d1957 *WhoHol 92*
Rorke, John 1923- *Who 94*
Rorke, Kevin Hayden 1949- *WhoFI 94*
Rorke, Lucy Balian 1929- *WhoAm 94*
Rorke, Margaret Hayden d1969 *WhoHol 92*
Rorke, Mary d1938 *WhoHol 92*
Rorschach, Richard Gordon 1928- *WhoAm 94*
Rorty, Amelie Oskenberg 1932- *WrDr 94*
Rorty, Richard McKay 1931- *IntWW 93, WhoAm 94, WrDr 94*
Rory, Rossana 1930- *WhoHol 92*
Ros, Enrique Jorge 1927- *IntWW 93*
Rosa, Carl (August Nikolaus) 1842-1889 *NewGrDO*
Rosa, Clarence Henry 1912-1990 *WhAm 10*
Rosa, Fredric David 1946- *WhoFI 94, WhoWest 94*
Rosa, Joao Guimaraes *RfGShF*
Rosa, Josephine 1929- *WhoHisp 94*
Rosa, Margarita 1953- *WhoHisp 94*
Rosa, Maritza 1949- *WhoHisp 94*
Rosa, Marta T. 1957- *WhoHisp 94*
Rosa, Paul James, Jr. 1927- *WhoAmP 93*
Rosa, Peter Manuel 1946- *WhoFI 94*
Rosa, Raymond Ulric 1927- *WhoAm 94*
Rosa, Robby 1970- *WhoHol 92*
Rosa, Rosa 1894-1978 *BlmGWL*
Rosa, Rose Nelida 1939- *WhoHisp 94*
Rosa, Vicky Lynn 1953- *WhoMW 93*
Rosa, William 1948- *WhoHisp 94*
Rosado, Caleb 1942- *WhoHisp 94*
Rosado, David *WhoAmP 93, WhoHisp 94*
Rosado, Jose Francisco 1948- *WhoHisp 94*
Rosado, Julio Rosado, Jr. 1942- *WhoHisp 94*
Rosado, Maria *WhoHol 92*
Rosado, Nytza I. 1962- *WhoHisp 94*
Rosado, Raul *WhoHisp 94*
Rosado, Rossana 1961- *WhoHisp 94*
Rosado, Sonia *WhoHisp 94*
Rosado, Wanda I. 1962- *WhoHisp 94*
Rosado, Wilfredo 1961- *WhoHisp 94*
Rosado-Linera, Ramon Arturo 1963- *WhoHisp 94*
Rosado Mendez, Emilio 1911- *WhoHisp 94*
Rosado-Vila, Luis, II 1931- *WhoHisp 94*
Rosa-Gonzalez, Ferdinand 1940- *WhoHisp 94*
Rosa Guzman, Antonio *WhoHisp 94*
Rosaldo, Renato Ignacio, Jr. 1941- *WhoAm 94, WhoHisp 94*
Rosales, Antonio c. 1740-1801 *NewGrDO*
Rosales, Arabel Alva 1959- *WhoHisp 94*
Rosales, Daniel J. 1945- *WhoWest 94*
Rosales, Israel 1933- *WhoHisp 94*
Rosales, Javier Alberto 1965- *WhoHisp 94*
Rosales, John Albert 1956- *WhoHisp 94*
Rosales, Jose Antonio 1932- *WhoHisp 94*
Rosales, Luis 1910-1992 *DcLB 134 [port]*
Rosales, Maria E. 1961- *WhoHisp 94*
Rosales, Miguel 1943- *WhoHisp 94*
Rosales, Oscar Rafael 1959- *WhoHisp 94*
Rosalez, Ramon Sifuentes 1952- *WhoHisp 94*
Rosalie, Mlle. *NewGrDO*
Rosamalin *BlmGWL*
Rosamond, John Bell 1936- *WhoAm 94*
Rosan, Burton 1928- *WhoScEn 94*
Rosand, David 1938- *WhoAmA 93, WrDr 94*
Rosand, Ellen 1940- *NewGrDO*
Rosander, Arlyn Custer 1903- *WhoScEn 94, WhoWest 94*
Rosane, Edwin L. 1936- *WhoIns 94*
Rosanelli, Robert Damian 1952- *WhoAmL 94*
Rosanova, Rosa d1944 *WhoHol 92*
Rosapepe, James C. 1951- *WhoAmP 93*
Rosar, Annie d1963 *WhoHol 92*
Rosario 1920- *WhoHol 92*
Rosario, Anna G. 1953- *WhoHisp 94*
Rosario, Carlos *WhoHisp 94*
Rosario, Darlene 1964- *WhoHisp 94*
Rosario, Edgardo N. 1957- *WhoHisp 94*
Rosario, Lourdes M. 1961- *WhoHisp 94*
Rosario, Myra Odette 1960- *WhoScEn 94*
Rosario, Robert 1951- *WhoHisp 94*
Rosario, Ruben Amilcar 1954- *WhoHisp 94*
Rosario, Victor 1966- *WhoHisp 94*
Rosario, William 1951- *WhoHisp 94*
Rosario Collazo, Francisco 1931- *WhoHisp 94*
Rosario-García, Efraín 1938- *WhoHisp 94*
Rosario Guardiola, Reinaldo 1948- *WhoScEn 94*
Rosario Rodriguez, José Angel 1946- *WhoHisp 94*
Rosas, Carlos Augusto 1952- *WhoHisp 94*
Rosas, Cesar *WhoHisp 94*
Rosas, Joan Xicota 1958- *WhoFI 94*
Rosas, Jose Leopold 1944- *WhoHisp 94*
Rosas, Juan Manuel de 1793-1877 *HisWorL [port]*
Rosas, Laura 1957- *WhoHisp 94*
Rosas, Leo 1944- *WhoHisp 94*
Rosas, Lou Michael 1956- *WhoHisp 94*
Rosas, Maurice O. 1944- *WhoHisp 94*
Rosas, Mel 1950- *WhoAmA 93, WhoHisp 94*
Rosas, Roberto Garcia, Jr. 1957- *WhoHisp 94*
Rosas, Salvador Miguel 1950- *WhoHisp 94*
Rosas, Yolanda T. 1940- *WhoHisp 94*
Rosasco, William Sebastian, III 1929- *WhoAmP 93*
Rosas Vega, Gabriel 1939- *IntWW 93*
Rosati, Beth Ann 1964- *WhoMW 93*
Rosati, Carolina 1826-1905 *IntDcB [port]*
Rosati, Mario 1928- *WhoScEn 94*
Rosati, Mario M. 1946- *WhoAmL 94*
Rosato, Francis Ernest 1934- *WhoAm 94*
Rosato, Tony 1954- *WhoHol 92*
Rosay, Francoise d1974 *WhoHol 92*
Rosbaud, Hans 1895-1962 *NewGrDO*
Rosbe, William Louis 1944- *WhoAm 94, WhoAmL 94*
Rosberg, Carl Gustaf 1923- *WhoAm 94*
Rosberg, David William 1919- *WhoAm 94*
Rosberg, Rose *DrAPF 93*
Rosberg, Rose 1916- *WrDr 94*
Rosborough, Bradley James 1958- *WhoWest 94*
Rosbottom, Ronald Carlisle 1942- *WhoAm 94*
Rosca, Ninotchka *BlmGWL*
Rosch, John Thomas 1939- *WhoAm 94*
Rosch, Paul John 1927- *WhoAm 94*
Rosche, Terry Arnold 1957- *WhoFI 94*
Roscher, Marina L. *DrAPF 93*
Roscher, Nina Matheny 1938- *WhoAm 94*
Roschova, Anna 1951- *WhoWomW 91*
Roscius 126?BC-62BC *BlmGEL*
Roscoe, Alan d1933 *WhoHol 92*
Roscoe, Albert *WhoHol 92*
Roscoe, Charlotte Marie 1954- *WhoMW 93*
Roscoe, (John) Gareth 1948- *Who 94*
Roscoe, Lee *WhoHol 92*
Roscoe, Robert Bell 1906- *Who 94*
Roscoe, Stanley Nelson 1920- *WhoAm 94*
Roscoe, William 1753-1831 *BlmGEL*
Roscoe, Wilma J. 1938- *WhoBlA 94*
Roscommon, Wentworth Dillon, Earl of 1633?-1685 *BlmGEL*
Roscopf, Charles Buford 1928- *WhoAm 94*
Rosdeitcher, Sidney S. 1936- *WhoAm 94*
Rose, Adam Zachary 1948- *WhoAm 94*
Rose, Al *WhoHol 92*
Rose, Al 1916- *WrDr 94*
Rose, Alan Douglas 1945- *WhoAm 94, WhoAmL 94*
Rose, Albert 1910-1990 *WhAm 10*
Rose, Albert Schoenburg 1945- *WhoAmL 94*
Rose, Alex 1946- *ConTFT 11, IntMPA 94*
Rose, Alvin W. 1916- *WhoBlA 94*
Rose, Andrew *Who 94*
Rose, (Wilfred) Andrew 1916- *Who 94*
Rose, Andrew (Wyness) 1944- *WrDr 94*
Rose, Anthea Lorrainne 1946- *Who 94*
Rose, Arthur 1921- *WhoBlA 94*
Rose, Augustus Steele 1907-1989 *WhAm 10*
Rose, Axl *WhoAm 94*
Rose, Barbara 1937- *WhoAmA 93*
Rose, Barry 1923- *Who 94*
Rose, Barry Michael 1934- *Who 94*
Rose, Beatrice Schroeder 1922- *WhoAm 94*
Rose, Bernard Peter 1957- *WhoFI 94*
Rose, Bernard William George 1916- *Who 94*
Rose, Bessie L. 1958- *WhoBlA 94*
Rose, Blanche d1953 *WhoHol 92*
Rose, Bram 1907- *IntWW 93*
Rose, Brian 1930- *Who 94*
Rose, C. Kimball *WhoAmL 94*
Rose, C. Tanner, Jr. 1943- *WhoAmL 94*
Rose, Carl E. 1914- *WhoAmP 93*
Rose, Cecilia 1925- *WhoAm 94*
Rose, Charles *WhoAm 94*
Rose, Charles, III 1939- *WhoAmP 93*
Rose, Charles Frederick 1926- *Who 94*
Rose, Charles Grandison, III 1939- *WhoAm 94*
Rose, Charlie 1939- *CngDr 93*
Rose, Charlie 1943- *News 94-2 [port]*
Rose, Chester Alva, Jr. 1930- *WhoFI 94*
Rose, Chester Arthur 1941- *WhoFI 94*
Rose, Christine Brooke *Who 94*
Rose, Christopher (Dudley Roger) 1937- *Who 94*
Rose, Clifford *Who 94*
Rose, Clifford 1929- *WhoHol 92*
Rose, Clive (Martin) 1921- *IntWW 93, Who 94*
Rose, Cristine *WhoHol 92*
Rose, Daniel 1929- *WhoFI 94*
Rose, Daniel Asa *DrAPF 93*
Rose, David 1910- *WhoAmA 93*
Rose, David 1910-1990 *WhAm 10*
Rose, David Allan 1937- *WhoFI 94*
Rose, David Edward 1924- *Who 94*
Rose, David Louis 1931- *WhoAmL 94*
Rose, David William 1930- *WhoWest 94*
Rose, Davis Stuart 1961- *WhoMW 93*
Rose, Deborah Elizabeth 1956- *WhoMW 93*
Rose, Dennis Norman 1948- *WhoFI 94*
Rose, Donald Henry Gair 1926- *Who 94*
Rose, Donald James 1944- *WhoAm 94*
Rose, Donald McGregor 1933- *WhoAm 94*
Rose, Earl Forrest 1926- *WhoAmL 94*
Rose, Edward c. 1775-c. 1832 *WhWE*
Rose, Edward W. *WhoAm 94*
Rose, Elihu 1933- *WhoAm 94*
Rose, Elinor K. 1920- *WrDr 94*
Rose, Eliot Joseph Benn 1909- *IntWW 93, Who 94, WrDr 94*
Rose, Elizabeth 1941- *WhoAm 94*
Rose, Eric Allen 1951- *WhoAm 94*
Rose, Ernst 1932- *WhoMW 93*

Rose, Esther Mae 1916- *WhoMW 93*
Rose, Evans, Jr. 1932- *WhoAm 94, WhoAmP 93*
Rose, Evelyn (Gita) 1925- *WrDr 94*
Rose, F(rederick) Horace (Vincent) 1876- *EncSF 93*
Rose, Francois Jean-Baptiste Hubert Edouard Marie de T 1910- *IntWW 93*
Rose, Frank Anthony 1920-1991 *WhAm 10*
Rose, Frank Clifford 1926- *Who 94*
Rose, Gary Lee 1950- *WhoAmP 93*
Rose, Geoffrey Arthur 1926- *Who 94*
Rose, George d1988 *WhoHol 92*
Rose, George Walter 1920- *WhoAm 94*
Rose, Gerald (Hembdon Seymour) 1935- *ConAu 42NR*
Rose, Gerald Gershon 1921- *Who 94*
Rose, Gilbert Jacob 1923- *WhoScEn 94*
Rose, Graham Hunt 1937- *Who 94*
Rose, Graham John 1928- *Who 94*
Rose, Gregory Mancel 1953- *WhoWest 94*
Rose, Hanna Toby 1909-1976 *WhoAmA 93N*
Rose, Harold Bertram 1923- *Who 94*
Rose, Harold M. 1930- *WhoAm 94*
Rose, Harry d1975 *WhoHol 92*
Rose, Helen c. 1904-1985 *IntDcF 2-4 [port]*
Rose, Henry 1927- *WhoAm 94*
Rose, Henry C. 1940- *WhoAmP 93*
Rose, Henry Gerard 1949- *WhoAmL 94*
Rose, Herman 1909- *WhoAm 94, WhoAmA 93*
Rose, Horace Chapman 1907-1990 *WhAm 10*
Rose, Howard d1978 *WhoHol 92*
Rose, Hugh 1926- *WhoScEn 94*
Rose, Israel Harold 1917- *WhoAm 94*
Rose, Iver 1899-1972 *WhoAmA 93N*
Rose, Jack 1911- *IntMPA 94*
Rose, Jack 1917- *Who 94*
Rose, James *Who 94*
Rose, (Arthur) James *Who 94*
Rose, James McKinley, Jr. 1927- *WhoAm 94*
Rose, James Turner 1935- *WhoScEn 94*
Rose, James V. 1925-1989 *WhAm 10*
Rose, James W. 1935- *WhoAm 94*
Rose, Jamie 1960- *WhoHol 92*
Rose, Jane d1979 *WhoHol 92*
Rose, Jane A. 1940- *WhoFI 94*
Rose, Janet 1947- *WhoAmP 93*
Rose, Jeffrey David 1931- *Who 94*
Rose, Jeffrey Raymond 1946- *WhoAm 94*
Rose, Jennifer *WhoHol 92*
Rose, Jennifer Joan 1951- *WhoAmL 94*
Rose, Jerald Lyle 1935- *WhoWest 94*
Rose, Jerome Gerald 1926- *WhoAmL 94*
Rose, Jerzy Edwin 1909-1992 *WhAm 10*
Rose, Jewel d1970 *WhoHol 92*
Rose, Jim *Who 94, WhoAmP 93*
Rose, Joel *DrAPF 93*
Rose, Joel Alan 1936- *WhoAmL 94*
Rose, John c. 1621-1677 *DcNaB MP*
Rose, John 1929- *WhoAmP 93*
Rose, John A. 1940- *WhoAm 94, WhoAmP 93*
Rose, John Charles 1924- *WhoAm 94*
Rose, John Raymond 1934- *Who 94*
Rose, John Theodore 1934- *WhoAmP 93*
Rose, John Thomas 1943- *WhoAm 94, WhoFI 94*
Rose, John Timothy 1942- *WhoAmA 93*
Rose, Jonathan Chapman 1941- *WhoAm 94, WhoAmL 94*
Rose, Jonathan Charman 1941- *WhoAmP 93*
Rose, Joyce A. *DrAPF 93*
Rose, Joyce Dora Hester 1929- *Who 94*
Rose, Julian (Day) 1947- *Who 94*
Rose, Jurgen 1937- *NewGrDO*
Rose, Kathleen Blount 1908- *WhoAmP 93*
Rose, Kenneth (Vivian) 1924- *WrDr 94*
Rose, Kenneth Vivian 1924- *Who 94*
Rose, Lance Haden 1943- *WhoAm 94*
Rose, Larry Lee 1943- *WhoAm 94*
Rose, Laura Powell 1942- *WhoWest 94*
Rose, Laurence F. *EncSF 93*
Rose, Laurie *WhoHol 92*
Rose, Leatrice *WhoAmA 93*
Rose, Leatrice 1924- *WhoAm 94*
Rose, Lewis John 1935- *Who 94*
Rose, Lois Lynn Hall 1951- *WhoMW 93*
Rose, Louis Herbert 1954- *WhoMW 93*
Rose, Lucy McCombs 1940- *WhoScEn 94*
Rose, Lynne *DrAPF 93*
Rose, Marian Henrietta *WhoScEn 94*
Rose, Mark 1939- *EncSF 93*
Rose, Mark Allen 1939- *WhoAm 94*
Rose, Mark Willson 1924- *Who 94*
Rose, Martin E. 1949- *WhoAmL 94*
Rose, Mary Anne 1949- *WhoAmA 93*
Rose, Mary R. 1956- *WhoAmP 93*
Rose, Mason H., IV 1915- *WhoAm 94*
Rose, Matthew Adam 1959- *WhoAmA 93*
Rose, Melissa Eva Anderson 1959- *WhoFI 94*
Rose, Merrill 1955- *WhoMW 93*
Rose, Michael *Who 94, WhoAm 94, WhoFI 94*
Rose, Michael d1974 *WhoHol 92*
Rose, (Hugh) Michael 1940- *Who 94*
Rose, Michael (Simon) 1937- *WrDr 94*
Rose, Michael David 1942- *WhoFI 94*
Rose, Michael Dean 1937- *WhoAm 94*
Rose, Michael Thomas 1947- *WhoAmP 93*
Rose, Milton Curtiss 1904- *WhoAm 94*
Rose, Nancy A. 1934- *WrDr 94*
Rose, Nelson Henry 1945- *WhoMW 93*
Rose, Noel Richard 1927- *WhoAm 94, WhoScEn 94*
Rose, Norman *WhoHol 92*
Rose, Norman 1923- *WhoAmL 94*
Rose, Norman Anthony 1934- *WrDr 94*
Rose, Paul (Bernard) 1935- *Who 94, WrDr 94*
Rose, Paul Edward 1947- *WhoAm 94, WhoFI 94*
Rose, Pete *NewYTBS 93 [port]*
Rose, Pete 1938- *WhoFI 94*
Rose, Peter Edward 1941- *WhoAm 94*
Rose, Peter Henry 1935- *WhoAmA 93*
Rose, Peter I(saac) 1933- *WrDr 94*
Rose, Peter Isaac 1933- *WhoAm 94*
Rose, Phyllis 1942- *WhoAm 94, WrDr 94*
Rose, Phyllis Kay 1955- *WhoFI 94*
Rose, Polly d1971 *WhoHol 92*
Rose, Rachelle Sylvia 1946- *WhoBlA 94*
Rose, Raymond Allen 1951- *WhoScEn 94*
Rose, Raymond Edward 1926- *WhoBlA 94*
Rose, Reginald 1920- *ConAu 42NR, WhoAm 94*
Rose, Reginald 1921- *IntMPA 94*
Rose, Reva 1940- *WhoHol 92*
Rose, Richard 1933- *IntWW 93, Who 94, WrDr 94*
Rose, Richard Loomis 1936- *WhoAm 94, WhoAmL 94*
Rose, Richard Townsend, Jr. 1950- *WhoFI 94*
Rose, Robert d1936 *WhoHol 92*
Rose, Robert Carlisle 1917- *WhoAm 94*
Rose, Robert E. 1939- *WhoAm 94, WhoAmL 94, WhoWest 94*
Rose, Robert Edgar 1939- *WhoAmP 93*
Rose, Robert Gordon 1943- *WhoAm 94, WhoAmL 94*
Rose, Robert John 1930- *WhoAm 94, WhoMW 93*
Rose, Robert Lawrence 1945- *WhoAm 94*
Rose, Robert Leon 1920- *WhoWest 94*
Rose, Robert Michael 1937- *WhoAm 94*
Rose, Robert Neal 1951- *WhoAm 94, WhoFI 94*
Rose, Robert Paul 1966- *WhoWest 94*
Rose, Robert R., Jr. 1915- *WhoAm 94, WhoWest 94*
Rose, Robin Carlise 1946- *WhoAmA 93*
Rose, Ronald L. 1941- *WhoAmL 94*
Rose, Roslyn 1929- *WhoAmA 93*
Rose, Rubye Blevins *WhoAm 94*
Rose, Rudolph L. 1943- *WhoAmL 94*
Rose, Samuel 1941- *WhoAmA 93*
Rose, Scott A. 1953- *WhoAmL 94*
Rose, Selwyn H. 1933- *WhoAm 94*
Rose, Shelvie 1936- *WhoBlA 94*
Rose, Sherrie *WhoHol 92*
Rose, Stanley Jay 1918- *WhoFI 94*
Rose, Stephanie *WhoAmA 93*
Rose, Stephen *IntMPA 94*
Rose, (Thomas) Stuart d1993 *Who 94N*
Rose, Susan Porter 1941- *WhoAm 94*
Rose, Terry W. 1942- *WhoAmP 93*
Rose, Thoma Hadley 1942- *WhoScEn 94*
Rose, Thomas Albert 1942- *WhoAm 94, WhoAmA 93*
Rose, Veronica d1968 *WhoHol 92*
Rose, Vincent d1944 *WhoHol 92*
Rose, Virginia Rogers 1942- *WhoMW 93*
Rose, Wendy *DrAPF 93*
Rose, Wil 1931- *WhoAm 94*
Rose, Willi d1978 *WhoHol 92*
Rose, William 1919- *WhoMW 93*
Rose, William 1928- *WhAm 10*
Rose, William Allen, Jr. 1938- *WhoAm 94*
Rose, William B. 1929- *WhoAmP 93*
Rose, William Cudebec 1959- *WhoScEn 94*
Rose, William Cumming 1887-1985 *WorScD*
Rose, William Shepard, Jr. 1948- *WhoAm 94, WhoAmL 94*
Rose, Zeldon E. 1932- *WhoAm 94*
Rose-Ackerman, Susan 1942- *WhoAm 94, WhoFI 94*
Roseau, Maurice Edmond Adolphe 1925- *IntWW 93*
Roseberg, Carl Andersson 1916- *WhoAm 94, WhoAmA 93*
Rosebery, Earl of 1929- *Who 94*
Roseboro, Anthony Michael 1960- *WhoMW 93*
Roseborough, Teresa Wynn 1958- *WhoAmL 94*
Rosebrock, Charles A. 1946- *WhoAmL 94*
Rosebrough, Walter M., Jr. 1954- *WhoAm 94, WhoFI 94*
Rosebure, Gerald Frederick 1945- *WhoAm 94*
Rosebush, James Scott 1949- *WhoAm 94*
Rosecrance, Francis Chase 1897- *WhAm 10*
Rosecrance, Ralph Clayton 1893- *WhAm 10*
Rosecrance, Richard (Newton) 1930- *WrDr 94*
Rosedale, Peter Klaus 1931- *WhoAmP 93*
Roseff, Martin Hilliard 1941- *WhoMW 93*
Rosefielde, Steven Shelley 1942- *WhoFI 94*
Rosegger, Gerhard 1930- *WhoAm 94*
Rosegger, Peter 1843-1918 *DcLB 129 [port]*
Rose-Hansen, John 1937- *WhoScEn 94*
Rosehart, Robert George 1943- *WhoAm 94*
Rosehill, Lord 1954- *Who 94*
Rosehnal, Mary Ann 1943- *WhoWest 94*
Roseig, Esther Marian 1917- *WhoScEn 94*
Roseland, Harry Herman 1866-1950 *WhoAmA 93N*
Roseleigh, Jack d1940 *WhoHol 92*
Rosell, Antoinette Fraser 1926- *WhoAmP 93*
Rosell, Sharon Lynn 1948- *WhoScEn 94, WhoWest 94*
Rosella, John Daniel 1938- *WhoScEn 94*
Roselle, Anne 1894- *NewGrDO*
Roselle, David 1939- *IntWW 93*
Roselle, David Paul 1939- *WhoAm 94*
Roselle, Richard Donaldson 1916- *WhoScEn 94*
Roselle, William d1945 *WhoHol 92*
Roselle, William Charles 1936- *WhoAm 94*
Roselli, Richard Joseph 1954- *WhoAmL 94*
Rosellini, Albert D. 1910- *WhoAmP 93*
Roseman, Charles Sanford 1945- *WhoAmL 94, WhoWest 94*
Roseman, Jack 1931- *WhoFI 94*
Roseman, Jennifer Eileen 1952- *WhoBlA 94*
Roseman, Kenneth David 1939- *WrDr 94*
Roseman, Robert Drew 1947- *WhoAmL 94*
Roseman, Saul 1921- *IntWW 93, WhoAm 94*
Roseman, Susan Carol 1950- *WhoAmA 93*
Rose Marie 1923- *WhoCom*
Rose Marie 1925- *WhoHol 92*
Rosemarin, Carey Stephen 1950- *WhoAm 94*
Rosemberg, Eugenia 1918- *WhoAm 94, WhoScEn 94*
Rosemin, Neville Nathaniel 1957- *WhoFI 94*
Rosemond, Clinton d1966 *WhoHol 92*
Rosemond, John H. 1917- *WhoBlA 94*
Rosemond, John Henry 1917- *WhoAmP 93*
Rosemond, Lemuel Menefield 1920- *WhoBlA 94*
Rosemond, Manning Wyllard, Jr. 1918- *WhoBlA 94*
Rosemont, Norman 1924- *WhoAm 94*
Rosen, Al d1990 *WhoHol 92*
Rosen, Albert 1924- *IntWW 93*
Rosen, Alexander Carl 1923- *WhoScEn 94, WhoWest 94*
Rosen, Andrew Mayer 1951- *WhoAm 94*
Rosen, Annabeth 1957- *WhoAmA 93*
Rosen, Arthur Marvin 1930- *WhoAm 94*
Rosen, Barry 1944- *WrDr 94*
Rosen, Barry F. 1950- *WhoAmL 94*
Rosen, Barry Howard 1942- *WhoAm 94, WhoMW 93, WhoScEn 94*
Rosen, Benjamin Maurice 1933- *WhoAm 94, WhoFI 94*
Rosen, Benson 1942- *WhoAm 94*
Rosen, Bernard H. 1922- *WhoAm 94*
Rosen, Beth Dee 1945- *WhoFI 94*
Rosen, Carol M. *WhoAmA 93*
Rosen, Carol Mendes 1933- *WhoAm 94*
Rosen, Charles 1878-1950 *WhoAmA 93N*
Rosen, Charles 1927- *IntWW 93, Who 94*
Rosen, Charles, II 1925- *WhoAm 94*
Rosen, Charles Welles 1927- *WhoAm 94*
Rosen, Coleman William 1957- *WhoScEn 94*
Rosen, Daniel Allan 1952- *WhoAmL 94*
Rosen, David 1880-1960 *WhoAmA 93N*
Rosen, David 1938- *NewGrDO*
Rosen, David Allen 1955- *WhoWest 94*
Rosen, David Lawrence 1954- *WhoScEn 94*
Rosen, David Scott 1954- *WhoMW 93*
Rosen, Diane *WhoAmA 93*
Rosen, Dorothy 1916- *ConAu 43NR*
Rosen, Elsa Marianne von *IntDcB*
Rosen, Esther Yovits 1916- *WhoAmA 93*
Rosen, Eve Cutler 1952- *WhoAmL 94, WhoIns 94*
Rosen, Fred Saul 1930- *WhoAm 94*
Rosen, George *DrAPF 93*
Rosen, George 1920- *WhoAm 94*
Rosen, George M. 1936- *WhoAm 94, WhoFI 94, WhoWest 94*
Rosen, Georgy Fyodorovich *NewGrDO*
Rosen, Gerald *DrAPF 93*
Rosen, Gerald 1938- *WrDr 94*
Rosen, Gerald Ellis 1951- *WhoAm 94, WhoAmL 94, WhoMW 93*
Rosen, Gerald Harris 1933- *WhoAm 94*
Rosen, Gerald Robert 1930- *WhoAm 94*
Rosen, Haiim B. 1922- *IntWW 93*
Rosen, Harvey H. 1941- *WhoAmL 94*
Rosen, Harvey Sheldon 1949- *WhoAm 94*
Rosen, Herman 1935- *WhoScEn 94*
Rosen, Howard 1914- *WhoFI 94*
Rosen, Howard Robert 1960- *WhoAmL 94*
Rosen, Hy 1923- *WhoAmA 93*
Rosen, Israel 1911- *WhoAmA 93*
Rosen, James Mahlon 1933- *WhoAm 94, WhoAmA 93*
Rosen, Jeff 1955- *WhoAmP 93*
Rosen, Jeffrey Arnold 1961- *WhoWest 94*
Rosen, Jeffrey J. 1949- *WhoAmL 94*
Rosen, Jerome 1921- *WhoAm 94*
Rosen, Jimmy d1940 *WhoHol 92*
Rosen, Joan Fischman *WhoAmA 93*
Rosen, John *EncSPD*
Rosen, Jon Howard 1943- *WhoAmL 94, WhoWest 94*
Rosen, Joseph David 1935- *WhoScEn 94*
Rosen, Judah Ben 1922- *WhoAm 94*
Rosen, Kay *WhoAmA 93*
Rosen, Kenneth *DrAPF 93*
Rosen, Kenneth Roy 1950- *WhoIns 94*
Rosen, Lawrence 1941- *WhoAm 94*
Rosen, Lee Spencer 1961- *WhoAmL 94*
Rosen, Leo 1906-1989 *WhAm 10*
Rosen, Lester L. 1924- *WhoAmP 93*
Rosen, Louis 1918- *WhoAm 94, WhoScEn 94*
Rosen, Marcella Jung 1934- *WhoAm 94*
Rosen, Martin Jack 1931- *WhoAmL 94, WhoWest 94*
Rosen, Marvin Jerold 1929- *WhoWest 94*
Rosen, Marvin S. 1940- *WhoAmL 94*
Rosen, Matthew Stephen 1943- *WhoAm 94*
Rosen, Michael 1927- *Who 94*
Rosen, Michael (Wayne) 1946- *WrDr 94*
Rosen, Michael Howard 1943- *WhoFI 94*
Rosen, Michael J(oel) 1954- *WrDr 94*
Rosen, Milton William 1915- *IntWW 93*
Rosen, Moishe 1932- *WhoAm 94, WhoWest 94*
Rosen, Molly Ann 1941- *WhoAm 94*
Rosen, Mortimer Gilbert 1931-1992 *WhAm 10*
Rosen, Murray Hilary 1953- *Who 94*
Rosen, Myor 1917- *WhoAm 94*
Rosen, Nathaniel Kent 1948- *WhoAm 94*
Rosen, Norma *DrAPF 93*
Rosen, Norman Edward 1938- *WhoAm 94, WhoAmL 94, WhoFI 94*
Rosen, Paul Maynard 1943- *WhoAmL 94*
Rosen, Peter 1935- *WhoScEn 94*
Rosen, Rabbi Jeremy 1942- *Who 94*
Rosen, Ralph J. 1919- *WhoAmP 93*
Rosen, Raymond 1950- *WhoAm 94*
Rosen, Richard d1993 *NewYTBS 93*
Rosen, Richard (Dean) 1949- *WrDr 94*
Rosen, Richard Lewis 1943- *WhoAm 94, WhoAmL 94*
Rosen, Robert Arnold 1936- *WhoAm 94, WhoFI 94*
Rosen, Robert Charles 1945- *WhoAm 94*
Rosen, Robert L. 1937- *IntMPA 94*
Rosen, Robert Thomas 1941- *WhoScEn 94*
Rosen, Sam 1920- *WhoAm 94, WrDr 94*
Rosen, Samuel D. 1945- *WhoAmL 94*
Rosen, Sanford Jay 1937- *WhoAm 94, WhoAmL 94, WhoWest 94*
Rosen, Seth Lloyd 1956- *WhoAmL 94*
Rosen, Sherwin 1938- *WhoAm 94, WhoFI 94*
Rosen, Sidney 1916- *WrDr 94*
Rosen, Sidney Marvin 1939- *WhoAmL 94*
Rosen, Stanley Howard 1929- *WhoAm 94, WrDr 94*
Rosen, Stephen Louis 1937- *WhoMW 93*
Rosen, Steven 1950- *WhoAm 94*
Rosen, Steven O. 1949- *WhoAmL 94*
Rosen, Steven Terry 1952- *WhoScEn 94*
Rosen, Sylvia *DrAPF 93*
Rosen, Thomas E. 1948- *WhoAmL 94*
Rosen, Wendy Lee 1961- *WhoFI 94*
Rosen, William 1926- *WhoAm 94*
Rosen, William Warren 1936- *WhoAm 94, WhoAmL 94*
Rosenak, Chuck 1927- *WrDr 94*
Rosenak, Jan(ice M.) 1930- *WrDr 94*
Rosenau, Fred W. 1922- *WhoAmP 93*
Rosenau, James Nathan 1924- *WhoAm 94*

Rosenay, Charles F. 1962- *WhoFI 94*
Rosenbach, A. S. W. 1876-1952 *DcLB 140 [port]*
Rosenbauer, Mark A. 1950- *WhoAmP 93*
Rosenbaum, Allen 1937- *WhoAmA 93*
Rosenbaum, Arthur Elihu 1935- *WhoAm 94*
Rosenbaum, E. C. *WhoAmP 93*
Rosenbaum, Evelyn Eller *WhoAmA 93*
Rosenbaum, Glen A. 1948- *WhoAmL 94*
Rosenbaum, I. Alfred 1920- *WhoAmP 93*
Rosenbaum, Irving M. 1921- *WhoAm 94*
Rosenbaum, Jacob I. 1927- *WhoAm 94, WhoAmL 94*
Rosenbaum, James Michael 1944- *WhoAm 94, WhoAmL 94, WhoMW 93*
Rosenbaum, James Todd 1949- *WhoScEn 94*
Rosenbaum, Jan Susan 1956- *WhoMW 93*
Rosenbaum, Jean 1927- *WhoWest 94*
Rosenbaum, Joan H. *WhoAmA 93*
Rosenbaum, Jody Barbara 1954- *WhoAmL 94*
Rosenbaum, Jonathan 1943- *WrDr 94*
Rosenbaum, Joseph Irving 1947- *WhoAmL 94*
Rosenbaum, Lois Omenn 1950- *WhoAm 94*
Rosenbaum, Lynne Claire 1950- *WhoMW 93*
Rosenbaum, Martin M. 1923- *WhoIns 94*
Rosenbaum, Martin Michael 1923- *WhoAmL 94*
Rosenbaum, Michael A. 1953- *WhoAm 94, WhoFI 94*
Rosenbaum, Michael Francis 1959- *WhoWest 94*
Rosenbaum, Nathan 1897- *WhAm 10*
Rosenbaum, Paul William 1948- *WhoAmL 94*
Rosenbaum, Richard Merrill 1931- *WhoAm 94, WhoAmL 94, WhoAmP 93*
Rosenbaum, Robert Abraham 1915- *WhoAm 94*
Rosenbaum, Robert David 1943- *WhoAmL 94*
Rosenbaum, Steven Ira 1946- *WhoAm 94*
Rosenberg, A. Richard 1938- *WhoFI 94*
Rosenberg, Aaron Edward 1937- *WhoAm 94*
Rosenberg, Alan *WhoHol 92*
Rosenberg, Alan Stewart 1930- *WhoAm 94*
Rosenberg, Alberto 1937- *WhoScEn 94*
Rosenberg, Alex 1926- *WhoAm 94, WhoWest 94*
Rosenberg, Alex Jacob 1919- *WhoAm 94, WhoAmA 93*
Rosenberg, Alexander 1946- *WhoAm 94, WrDr 94*
Rosenberg, Alison P. 1945- *WhoAm 94*
Rosenberg, Amye 1950- *SmATA 74 [port]*
Rosenberg, Arthur James 1926- *WhoAm 94*
Rosenberg, Auria Eleanor *WhoAmP 93*
Rosenberg, Benjamin B. d1993 *NewYTBS 93*
Rosenberg, Bernard 1938- *WhoAmA 93*
Rosenberg, Bruce Alan 1934- *WhoAm 94, WrDr 94*
Rosenberg, Carole Halsband 1936- *WhoAmA 93*
Rosenberg, Carolyn Hope 1957- *WhoAmL 94*
Rosenberg, Charles Ernest 1936- *WhoAm 94*
Rosenberg, Charles Harvey 1919- *WhoScEn 94*
Rosenberg, Charles Martin 1942- *WhoAm 94, WhoAmL 94*
Rosenberg, Charles Michael 1945- *WhoAm 94, WhoAmA 93*
Rosenberg, Claude N., Jr. 1928- *WrDr 94*
Rosenberg, Claude Newman, Jr. 1928- *WhoAm 94*
Rosenberg, Dale Norman 1928- *WhoMW 93, WhoScEn 94*
Rosenberg, Dan Yale 1922- *WhoScEn 94, WhoWest 94*
Rosenberg, David *DrAPF 93*
Rosenberg, David Alan 1948- *WhoAm 94*
Rosenberg, David Howard 1941- *WhoAm 94*
Rosenberg, David Scott *WhoFI 94*
Rosenberg, David W. 1942- *WhoAmL 94*
Rosenberg, Dennis Melville Leo 1921- *WhoAm 94*
Rosenberg, Diane Lynne 1945- *WhoAmL 94*
Rosenberg, Donald Martin 1933- *WhoAm 94, WhoFI 94*
Rosenberg, Edgar 1925- *WhoAm 94*
Rosenberg, Eric William 1961- *WhoFI 94*
Rosenberg, Eva 1953- *WhoWest 94*
Rosenberg, Frank P. 1913- *IntMPA 94*
Rosenberg, Gary Aron 1940- *WhoAm 94, WhoFI 94, WhoMW 93*
Rosenberg, Gary Marc 1950- *WhoAmL 94*

Rosenberg, George *WhoAm 94, WhoFI 94*
Rosenberg, George 1896- *WhAm 10*
Rosenberg, George Stanley 1930- *WrDr 94*
Rosenberg, Gerald Alan 1944- *WhoAmL 94*
Rosenberg, Gerald Nelson 1954- *WhoMW 93*
Rosenberg, Grant E. 1952- *IntMPA 94*
Rosenberg, Harold 1906-1978 *WhoAmA 93N*
Rosenberg, Henry A., Jr. 1929- *WhoAm 94, WhoFI 94*
Rosenberg, Herb 1942- *WhoAmA 93*
Rosenberg, Hilding (Constantin) 1892-1985 *NewGrDO*
Rosenberg, Howard Alan 1927- *WhoWest 94*
Rosenberg, Irwin Harold 1935- *WhoScEn 94*
Rosenberg, Isaac 1890-1918 *BlmGEL, DcNaB MP*
Rosenberg, J. Mitchell 1906- *WrDr 94*
Rosenberg, Jack Michael 1958- *WhoMW 93*
Rosenberg, Jacob Joseph 1947- *WhoScEn 94*
Rosenberg, Jakob 1893-1980 *WhoAmA 93N*
Rosenberg, James Donald 1956- *WhoMW 93*
Rosenberg, James G. 1946- *WhoAmL 94*
Rosenberg, James Louis 1950- *WhoAm 94*
Rosenberg, Jane 1949- *WhoAmA 93*
Rosenberg, Jerome I. 1931- *WhoAm 94*
Rosenberg, Jerome Laib 1921- *WhoAm 94*
Rosenberg, Jerry Martin 1935- *WhoAm 94*
Rosenberg, Joel 1954- *EncSF 93*
Rosenberg, Joel Barry 1942- *WhoFI 94, WhoScEn 94*
Rosenberg, John Alan 1920- *WhoMW 93*
Rosenberg, John D(avid) 1929- *WrDr 94*
Rosenberg, John David 1929- *WhoAm 94*
Rosenberg, John K. 1945- *WhoAm 94, WhoAmL 94, WhoFI 94*
Rosenberg, John R. 1961- *WhoMW 93*
Rosenberg, Joseph Fredrick 1934- *WhoAmL 94*
Rosenberg, Joseph Lawrence 1949- *WhoFI 94*
Rosenberg, Kenneth Ira 1947- *WhoAmL 94*
Rosenberg, L. M. *DrAPF 93*
Rosenberg, Lee Evan 1952- *WhoFI 94*
Rosenberg, Leon E. 1933- *WhoAm 94*
Rosenberg, Leon Joseph 1918- *WhoAm 94*
Rosenberg, Leonard 1920- *WhoAm 94*
Rosenberg, Leroy Joseph 1940- *WhoAm 94*
Rosenberg, Liz *DrAPF 93*
Rosenberg, Liz 1958- *ConAu 142, SmATA 75 [port]*
Rosenberg, Manuel 1930- *WhoAm 94*
Rosenberg, Marilyn R. *WhoAmA 93*
Rosenberg, Marilyn R. 1934- *WhoAm 94*
Rosenberg, Mark d1992 *IntMPA 94N*
Rosenberg, Mark 1948-1992 *AnObit 1992*
Rosenberg, Marshal E. 1936- *WhoFI 94*
Rosenberg, Marvin *WrDr 94*
Rosenberg, Maurice 1919- *WhoAm 94, WhoAmL 94*
Rosenberg, Maxine B(erta) 1939- *ConAu 41NR*
Rosenberg, Michael d1972 *WhoHol 92*
Rosenberg, Michael 1937- *WhoAm 94, WhoAmL 94*
Rosenberg, Michael 1945- *WhoAmL 94*
Rosenberg, Michael Joseph 1928- *WhoAm 94*
Rosenberg, Michael L. 1944- *WhoAmL 94*
Rosenberg, Milton J. 1925- *WhoAm 94*
Rosenberg, Morris 1922- *WrDr 94*
Rosenberg, Morton Mervin 1930- *WhoMW 93*
Rosenberg, Morton Yale 1932- *WhoAm 94*
Rosenberg, Nancy Taylor 1946- *ConAu 140*
Rosenberg, Nathan 1927- *WhoAm 94*
Rosenberg, Neil Lloyd 1954- *WhoWest 94*
Rosenberg, Norman 1916- *WhoAm 94*
Rosenberg, Norman Jack 1930- *WhoAm 94*
Rosenberg, Paul 1910- *WhoAm 94*
Rosenberg, Peter David 1942- *WhoAmL 94*
Rosenberg, Pierre Max 1936- *IntWW 93, WhoAm 94*
Rosenberg, Ralph 1949- *WhoAmP 93*
Rosenberg, Richard Allan 1948- *WhoMW 93*
Rosenberg, Richard Henry 1949- *WhoAmL 94*
Rosenberg, Richard J. 1942- *WhoFI 94*
Rosenberg, Richard K. 1942- *IntMPA 94*
Rosenberg, Richard M. 1934- *WhoAm 94*
Rosenberg, Richard Morris 1930- *IntWW 93, Who 94, WhoAm 94, WhoFI 94, WhoWest 94*

Rosenberg, Rick *IntMPA 94*
Rosenberg, Robert Allen 1935- *WhoScEn 94*
Rosenberg, Robert Brinkmann 1937- *WhoAm 94*
Rosenberg, Robert C. 1942- *WhoAmL 94*
Rosenberg, Robert Jay 1947- *WhoAmL 94*
Rosenberg, Robert Michael 1938- *WhoAm 94*
Rosenberg, Roger Newman 1939- *WhoAm 94*
Rosenberg, Ruth Helen Borsuk 1935- *WhoAm 94, WhoAmL 94*
Rosenberg, Saemy *WhoAmA 93N*
Rosenberg, Samuel 1896-1972 *WhoAmA 93N*
Rosenberg, Samuel 1949- *WhoFI 94*
Rosenberg, Samuel I. 1950- *WhoAmP 93*
Rosenberg, Samuel Nathan 1936- *WhoAm 94*
Rosenberg, Sarah d1964 *WhoHol 92*
Rosenberg, Sarah Zacher 1931- *WhoAm 94*
Rosenberg, Saul Allen 1927- *WhoAm 94, WhoScEn 94*
Rosenberg, Seymour 1926- *WhoAm 94*
Rosenberg, Sheldon 1930- *WhoScEn 94*
Rosenberg, Sheli Zysman 1942- *WhoAm 94, WhoAmL 94, WhoFI 94*
Rosenberg, Sherman 1933- *WhoScEn 94*
Rosenberg, Shirley Sirota *WhoFI 94*
Rosenberg, Stanley C. *WhoAmP 93*
Rosenberg, Stephen Francis 1949- *WhoFI 94*
Rosenberg, Steven A. 1940- *IntWW 93*
Rosenberg, Steven Aaron 1940- *WhoAm 94, WhoScEn 94*
Rosenberg, Stuart 1927- *IntMPA 94, WhoAm 94*
Rosenberg, Susan Janette 1959- *WhoFI 94*
Rosenberg, Sydney J. 1914- *WhoFI 94*
Rosenberg, Terry 1954- *WhoAmA 93*
Rosenberg, Theodore Roy 1933- *WhoFI 94*
Rosenberg, Tina 1960- *WrDr 94*
Rosenberg, William Gordon 1938- *WhoMW 93*
Rosenberg, Wolfgang 1915- *WrDr 94*
Rosenberger, Bryan David 1950- *WhoAm 94, WhoAmL 94*
Rosenberger, Carol 1935- *WhoAm 94*
Rosenberger, David A. 1947- *WhoScEn 94*
Rosenberger, Ernst Hey 1931- *WhoAm 94*
Rosenberger, Franz Ernst 1933- *WhoScEn 94*
Rosenberger, Walter Emerson 1918- *WhoAm 94*
Rosenberry, William Kenneth 1946- *WhoAmL 94*
Rosenblatt, Abram B. 1960- *WhoWest 94*
Rosenblatt, Adolph 1933- *WhoAmA 93*
Rosenblatt, Albert Martin 1936- *WhoAm 94*
Rosenblatt, Arthur Isaac 1931- *WhoAm 94*
Rosenblatt, Arthur S. 1938- *WrDr 94*
Rosenblatt, Cy Hart 1954- *WhoAmP 93*
Rosenblatt, Frederic Thomas 1944- *WhoAmL 94*
Rosenblatt, Gerd Matthew 1933- *WhoAm 94, WhoScEn 94*
Rosenblatt, Howard Marshall 1947- *WhoAmL 94, WhoFI 94*
Rosenblatt, Hyman d1993 *NewYTBS 93 [port]*
Rosenblatt, Jay Seth 1923- *WhoScEn 94*
Rosenblatt, Jerrold Hall 1948- *WhoFI 94*
Rosenblatt, Joan Raup 1926- *WhoAm 94, WhoScEn 94*
Rosenblatt, Josef d1933 *WhoHol 92*
Rosenblatt, Joseph 1933- *WhoAm 94, WrDr 94*
Rosenblatt, Joseph David 1953- *WhoScEn 94*
Rosenblatt, Leonard 1929-1990 *WhAm 10*
Rosenblatt, Lester 1920- *WhoAm 94*
Rosenblatt, Martin *WhoHol 92*
Rosenblatt, Michael 1947- *WhoAm 94*
Rosenblatt, Murray 1926- *WhoAm 94, WhoScEn 94, WhoWest 94*
Rosenblatt, Paul Gerhardt 1928- *WhoAm 94, WhoAmL 94, WhoWest 94*
Rosenblatt, Peter Ronald 1933- *WhoAm 94, WhoAmP 93*
Rosenblatt, Roger 1940- *WhoAm 94*
Rosenblatt, Stephen Paul 1935- *WhoAm 94*
Rosenblatt, Stephen Woodburn 1948- *WhoAmL 94*
Rosenblatt, Steven 1938- *WhoMW 93*
Rosenblatt, Suzanne Maris 1937- *WhoAmA 93*
Rosenblatt, William Walter 1945- *WhoAmL 94*
Rosenbleeth, Michael *WhoIns 94*
Rosenbleeth, Richard Marvin 1932- *WhoAm 94*

Rosenblith, Walter Alter 1913- *IntWW 93, WhoAm 94*
Rosenblitt, Alice *DrAPF 93*
Rosenbloom, Allan M. 1943- *WhoAmL 94*
Rosenbloom, Arlan Lee 1934- *WhoAm 94*
Rosenbloom, Bert 1944- *WhoAm 94*
Rosenbloom, Daniel 1930- *WhoAm 94, WhoFI 94*
Rosenbloom, H. David 1941- *WhoAm 94, WhoAmL 94*
Rosenbloom, Jerry Samuel 1939- *WhoIns 94*
Rosenbloom, Joseph R. 1928- *WrDr 94*
Rosenbloom, Lewis Stanley 1953- *WhoAm 94, WhoAmL 94*
Rosenbloom, Morris Victor 1915- *WhoAm 94*
Rosenbloom, Noah H. 1915- *WrDr 94*
Rosenbloom, Norma Frisch 1925- *WhoAmL 94, WhoAmP 93*
Rosenbloom, Richard Selig 1933- *WhoAm 94*
Rosenbloom, Sanford M. 1928- *WhoAm 94*
Rosenbloom, Slapsie Maxie d1976 *WhoHol 92*
Rosenblueth, Emilio 1926- *WhoAm 94, WhoScEn 94*
Rosenblum, Arnold 1935- *WhoFI 94*
Rosenblum, Carla Nadine 1937- *WhoWest 94*
Rosenblum, Elizabeth 1954- *WhoAmA 93*
Rosenblum, Harold Arthur 1923- *WhoAm 94*
Rosenblum, Jay 1933-1989 *WhoAmA 93N*
Rosenblum, John William 1944- *WhoAm 94, WhoFI 94*
Rosenblum, Judith Barbara 1951- *WhoScEn 94*
Rosenblum, M. Edgar 1932- *WhoAm 94*
Rosenblum, Marc Joseph 1936- *WhoAmL 94*
Rosenblum, Martin Jack *DrAPF 93*
Rosenblum, Marvin 1926- *WhoAm 94, WhoScEn 94*
Rosenblum, Michael F. 1940- *WhoAm 94*
Rosenblum, Myron 1925- *WhoAm 94*
Rosenblum, Nancy L. 1947- *WrDr 94*
Rosenblum, Peter M. 1949- *WhoAmL 94*
Rosenblum, Ralph 1925- *IntDcF 2-4*
Rosenblum, Richard Mark 1950- *WhoWest 94*
Rosenblum, Richard Stephen 1940- *WhoAmA 93*
Rosenblum, Robert *WhoAm 94, WhoScEn 94*
Rosenblum, Robert 1927- *Who 94, WhoAm 94, WhoAmA 93, WrDr 94*
Rosenblum, Steven Louis 1963- *WhoFI 94, WhoMW 93*
Rosenblum, Victor Gregory 1925- *WhoAm 94*
Rosenblum, William F., Jr. 1935- *WhoAmL 94*
Rosenbluth, Marshall Nicholas 1927- *WhoAm 94*
Rosenbluth, Michael Albert 1930- *WhoAm 94*
Rosenbluth, Morton 1924- *WhoAm 94*
Rosenbluth, Nancy d1962 *WhoHol 92*
Rosenborg, Ralph Mozart 1913- *WhoAm 94*
Rosenbrock, Howard Harry 1920- *IntWW 93, Who 94*
Rosencrance, Daris Wilson, Jr. 1964- *WhoFI 94*
Rosencrans, Evan William 1926- *WhoAm 94*
Rosencrantz, James R. 1914- *WhoAmP 93*
Rosendahl, Bruce Ray 1946- *WhoScEn 94*
Rosendale, George William 1933- *WhoFI 94*
Rosendhal, Jeffrey David 1941- *WhoAm 94*
Rosendin, Edmund W. *WhoHisp 94*
Rosendin, Raymond J. 1929- *WhoHisp 94*
Rosendin, Raymond Joseph 1929- *WhoAm 94*
Rosendorff, Clive 1938- *WhoScEn 94*
Rosene, Linda Roberts 1938- *WhoFI 94*
Rosener, George d1945 *WhoHol 92*
Rosener, Ronald Dean 1952- *WhoAmL 94*
Rosenfeld, Aaron P. 1951- *WhoAmL 94*
Rosenfeld, Alfred John 1922- *Who 94*
Rosenfeld, Arnold Solomon 1933- *WhoAm 94*
Rosenfeld, Arthur H. 1930- *WhoAm 94, WhoFI 94*
Rosenfeld, Azriel 1931- *WhoAm 94, WhoScEn 94*
Rosenfeld, Eric 1932- *WhoAm 94*
Rosenfeld, Eric Stanley 1932- *WhoAm 94*
Rosenfeld, Gerhard 1931- *NewGrDO*
Rosenfeld, Harry Morris 1929- *WhoAm 94*
Rosenfeld, Joel 1957- *WhoMW 93, WhoScEn 94*

Rosenfeld, Joel Charles 1939- *WhoMW 93*
Rosenfeld, Leslie Karen 1955- *WhoWest 94*
Rosenfeld, Louis 1925- *WhoScEn 94*
Rosenfeld, Louis 1947- *WhoScEn 94*
Rosenfeld, Mark Kenneth 1946- *WhoAm 94, WhoFI 94*
Rosenfeld, Martin 1932- *WhoFI 94, WhoWest 94*
Rosenfeld, Martin Jerome 1944- *WhoAmL 94, WhoMW 93*
Rosenfeld, Mitchell Allan 1928- *WhoAmP 93*
Rosenfeld, Richard Joel 1940- *WhoAmA 93*
Rosenfeld, Ron Gershon 1946- *WhoScEn 94, WhoWest,94*
Rosenfeld, Samuel L. 1931- *WhoAmA 93*
Rosenfeld, Sharon 1954- *WhoAmA 93*
Rosenfeld, Stephen Samuel 1932- *WhoAm 94*
Rosenfeld, Steven B. 1943- *WhoAm 94, WhoAmL 94*
Rosenfeld, Steven Ira 1949- *WhoAm 94*
Rosenfeld, Susan Paula 1953- *WhoAmL 94*
Rosenfeld, Walter David, Jr. 1930- *WhoAm 94*
Rosenfeld, William *DrAPF 93*
Rosenfelder, Alfred S. 1916- *WhoIns 94*
Rosenfeldt, Stuart Alan 1955- *WhoAmL 94*
Rosenfelt, Frank E. 1921- *IntMPA 94*
Rosenfelt, Frank Edward 1921- *IntWW 93, WhoAm 94*
Rosenfelt, Scott 1955- *IntMPA 94*
Rosenfield, Allan 1933- *WhoAm 94*
Rosenfield, Bruce Alan 1951- *WhoAm 94, WhoAmL 94*
Rosenfield, Israel 1939- *WrDr 94*
Rosenfield, James Harold 1929- *WhoAm 94*
Rosenfield, James Steven 1962- *WhoWest 94*
Rosenfield, Jay Gary 1948- *WhoAm 94*
Rosenfield, John M. 1924- *WhoAmA 93*
Rosenfield, John Max 1924- *WhoAm 94*
Rosenfield, Jonas, Jr. 1915- *IntMPA 94*
Rosenfield, Richard Ernest 1915- *WhoScEn 94*
Rosenfield, Robert Lee 1934- *WhoAm 94*
Rosengarten, Ellen 1950- *WhoMW 93*
Rosengren, William R. 1934- *WhoAm 94, WhoFI 94*
Rosenhaft, Ann Williams 1926- *WhoAmP 93*
Rosenhain, Jacob 1813-1894 *NewGrDO*
Rosenhauer, James Joseph 1942- *WhoAm 94, WhoAmL 94*
Rosenheck, Jean Birnbaum 1930- *WhoFI 94*
Rosenheim, Donald Edwin 1926- *WhoAm 94*
Rosenheim, Edward Weil 1918- *WhoAm 94*
Rosenheim, Howard Harris 1915- *WhoAm 94*
Rosenheim, Margaret Keeney 1926- *WhoAm 94*
Rosenhoffer, Chris 1913- *WhoAmL 94, WhoMW 93*
Rosenhouse, Howard 1939- *WhoAmL 94*
Rosenhouse, Irwin *WhoAm 94*
Rosenhouse, Irwin 1924- *WhoAmA 93*
Rosenker, Mark Victor 1946- *WhoAm 94*
Rosenkilde, Carl Edward 1937- *WhoScEn 94, WhoWest 94*
Rosenkoetter, Gerald Edwin 1927- *WhoAm 94, WhoFI 94, WhoScEn 94*
Rosenkrans, Kenneth Ray 1951- *WhoWest 94*
Rosenkrantz, Barbara Gutmann 1923- *WhoAm 94*
Rosenkrantz, Daniel J. 1943- *WhoAm 94*
Rosenkrantz, Linda *DrAPF 93*
Rosenkrantz, Linda 1934- *WhoWest 94*
Rosenkrantz, Rita R. 1934- *WhoAmL 94*
Rosenkranz, Herbert S. 1933- *WhoAm 94*
Rosenkranz, Robert Bernard 1939- *WhoAm 94*
Rosenkranz, Stanley William 1933- *WhoAm 94*
Rosenman, Daniel 1930- *WhoFI 94*
Rosenman, Howard 1945- *IntMPA 94*
Rosenman, Howard Zui 1945- *WhoWest 94*
Rosenman, John B. *DrAPF 93*
Rosenman, Julian Gary 1945- *WhoAm 94*
Rosenman, Leonard 1924- *IntDcF 2-4, IntMPA 94*
Rosenman, Stephen J. 1955- *WhoAmL 94*
Rosenmann, Daniel 1959- *WhoScEn 94*
Rosenmeyer, Patricia A. 1958- *ConAu 142*
Rosenn, Harold 1917- *WhoAm 94, WhoAmL 94, WhoFI 94*
Rosenn, Keith Samuel 1938- *WhoAm 94*

Rosenn, Max 1910- *WhoAm 94, WhoAmL 94*
Rosenne, Meir 1931- *IntWW 93, WhoAm 94*
Rosenne, Shabtai 1917- *IntWW 93*
Rosenof, Howard Paul 1948- *WhoScEn 94*
Rosenow, Edward Carl, III 1934- *WhoAm 94*
Rosenow, John Edward 1949- *WhoAm 94, WhoFI 94*
Rosenow, John Henry 1913- *WhoAm 94*
Rosenow, Patricia E. 1959- *WhoFI 94*
Rosenquist, Glenn Carl 1931- *WhoAm 94*
Rosenquist, James 1933- *WhoAmA 93*
Rosenquist, James Albert 1933- *WhoAm 94*
Rosenquist, Marc H. 1955- *WhoAmA 93*
Rosenquit, Bernard 1923-1991 *WhAm 10, WhoAmA 93N*
Rosensaft, Lester Jay 1958- *WhoAmL 94*
Rosensaft, Menachem Z. 1948- *WrDr 94*
Rosensaft, Menachem Zwi 1948- *WhoAm 94, WhoAmL 94*
Rosenschein, Guy Raoul 1953- *WhoScEn 94*
Rosenshein, Neil 1947- *NewGrDO*
Rosenshine, Allen Gilbert 1939- *IntWW 93, WhoAm 94, WhoFI 94*
Rosenson, Robert Sidney 1956- *WhoMW 93*
Rosenspire, Karen Cheryl 1951- *WhoMW 93*
Rosensteel, George T. 1947- *WhoAm 94, WhoScEn 94*
Rosensteel, John William 1940- *WhoAm 94, WhoFI 94*
Rosenstein, Allen Bertram 1920- *WhoAm 94, WhoWest 94*
Rosenstein, Beryl Joel 1937- *WhoAm 94*
Rosenstein, Claude Houston 1893- *WhAm 10*
Rosenstein, Gertrude *IntMPA 94*
Rosenstein, Ira *DrAPF 93*
Rosenstein, James Alfred 1939- *WhoAm 94, WhoAmL 94*
Rosenstein, Marvin 1939- *WhoScEn 94*
Rosenstein, Robert Bryce 1954- *WhoAmL 94*
Rosenstein, Samuel M. 1909- *CngDr 93, WhoAm 94*
Rosenstein, Tony P. 1945- *WhoAmL 94*
Rosenstiel, Tom 1956- *ConAu 142*
Rosenstock, Elliot David 1932- *WhoFI 94*
Rosenstock, Joseph 1895-1985 *NewGrDO*
Rosenstock, Lawrence M. 1943- *WhoAmP 93*
Rosenstock, Lucille Simon 1924- *WhoAmL 94*
Rosenstraus, Maurice Jay 1951- *WhoScEn 94*
Rosensweig, Ronald Ellis 1932- *WhoAm 94*
Rosensweig, Stanley Harold 1918- *WhoAm 94*
Rosental, Ruben *WhoHisp 94*
Rosenthal, Aaron 1914- *WhoAm 94*
Rosenthal, Abby Jane *DrAPF 93*
Rosenthal, Abraham Michael 1922- *IntWW 93*
Rosenthal, Alan David 1949- *WhoAmL 94*
Rosenthal, Alan H., Mrs. d1990 *WhoAmA 93N*
Rosenthal, Alan Irwin 1947- *WhoScEn 94*
Rosenthal, Alan Sayre 1926- *WhoAm 94*
Rosenthal, Albert Jay 1928- *WhoAm 94*
Rosenthal, Albert Joseph 1919- *WhoAm 94*
Rosenthal, Alexander 1912- *WhoIns 94*
Rosenthal, Amnon 1934- *WhoAm 94*
Rosenthal, Arnold H. 1933- *WhoAm 94*
Rosenthal, Arthur Jesse 1919- *WhoAm 94*
Rosenthal, Barbara *DrAPF 93*
Rosenthal, Bernard G. 1922- *WrDr 94*
Rosenthal, Bernard G(ordon) 1922-1993 *ConAu 141*
Rosenthal, Bernard Gordon d1993 *NewYTBS 93*
Rosenthal, Bob *DrAPF 93*
Rosenthal, Bud 1934- *IntMPA 94*
Rosenthal, Carole *DrAPF 93*
Rosenthal, David 1876-1949 *WhoAmA 93N*
Rosenthal, David H. *DrAPF 93*
Rosenthal, Deborah Maly 1950- *WhoAmA 93*
Rosenthal, Donald A. 1942- *WhoAmA 93*
Rosenthal, Donald B. 1937- *WhoAm 94, WrDr 94*
Rosenthal, Donna 1950- *WhoWest 94*
Rosenthal, Doris d1971 *WhoAmA 93N*
Rosenthal, Douglas Eurico 1940- *WhoAm 94, WhoAmL 94*
Rosenthal, Earl Edgar 1921- *WhoAm 94, WhoAmA 93*
Rosenthal, Edward Leonard 1948- *WhoMW 93*

Rosenthal, Erwin (Isak Jacob) 1904- *WrDr 94*
Rosenthal, Evelyn Daoud *WhoAm 94*
Rosenthal, Frank S. 1944- *WhoMW 93*
Rosenthal, Frank Vernon 1908- *WhoIns 94*
Rosenthal, Franz 1914- *WhoAm 94*
Rosenthal, Gert 1935- *IntWW 93*
Rosenthal, Gertrude 1903-1989 *WhoAmA 93N*
Rosenthal, Gloria M. 1928- *WhoAmA 93*
Rosenthal, Gregory Alan 1964- *WhoAmL 94*
Rosenthal, Gustave Henri, Baron de 1753-1829 *WhAmRev*
Rosenthal, Harold D(avid) 1917-1987 *NewGrDO*
Rosenthal, Harold Leslie 1922- *WhoAm 94*
Rosenthal, Harry d1953 *WhoHol 92*
Rosenthal, Herbert Marshall *WhoAmL 94*
Rosenthal, Herschel 1918- *WhoAmP 93*
Rosenthal, Howard 1948- *WhoAmA 93*
Rosenthal, Howard Lewis 1939- *WhoAm 94*
Rosenthal, Ira Maurice 1920- *WhoAm 94*
Rosenthal, Irvin Harold 1927- *WhoAmL 94*
Rosenthal, Jack 1930- *WhoAm 94, WhoWest 94*
Rosenthal, Jack (Morris) 1931- *ConAu 140*
Rosenthal, Jack Morris 1931- *Who 94*
Rosenthal, Jacob 1935- *WhoAm 94*
Rosenthal, James D. 1932- *WhoAm 94*
Rosenthal, James Edward 1942- *WhoIns 94*
Rosenthal, Jean 1923- *IntWW 93*
Rosenthal, Joel 1946- *WhoAmP 93*
Rosenthal, John David 1950- *WhoWest 94*
Rosenthal, John Thomas 1949- *WhoScEn 94*
Rosenthal, John W. 1928- *WhoAmA 93, WhoMW 93*
Rosenthal, Judith-Ann Saks *WhoAmA 93*
Rosenthal, Julian Bernard 1908- *WhoAm 94*
Rosenthal, Lee H. 1952- *WhoAm 94, WhoAmL 94*
Rosenthal, Leighton A. 1915- *WhoAm 94*
Rosenthal, Liliana Hermosilla 1943- *WhoHisp 94*
Rosenthal, Lucy Gabrielle *WhoAm 94*
Rosenthal, Lyova Haskell 1931- *WhoAm 94*
Rosenthal, M. L. *DrAPF 93*
Rosenthal, M(acha) L(ouis) 1917- *WrDr 94*
Rosenthal, Macha Louis 1917- *WhoAm 94*
Rosenthal, Manuel 1904- *NewGrDO*
Rosenthal, Mara d1975 *WhoHol 92*
Rosenthal, Marilynn Mae 1930- *WhoMW 93*
Rosenthal, Mark 1945- *WrDr 94*
Rosenthal, Mark Elliott 1952- *WhoAm 94*
Rosenthal, Mark L. 1945- *WhoAmA 93*
Rosenthal, Mark W. 1961- *WhoMW 93*
Rosenthal, Marshall 1940- *WhoMW 93*
Rosenthal, Martin Sanford 1961- *WhoAmL 94*
Rosenthal, Maureen Diane *Who 94*
Rosenthal, Meyer Louis 1944- *WhoAmL 94*
Rosenthal, Michael Bruce 1955- *WhoAmL 94*
Rosenthal, Michael Ross 1939- *WhoAm 94*
Rosenthal, Milton Frederick 1913- *WhoAm 94, WhoFI 94*
Rosenthal, Murray Wilford 1926- *WhoAm 94*
Rosenthal, Myron Martin 1930- *WhoAm 94*
Rosenthal, Nan 1937- *WhoAm 94*
Rosenthal, Norman Leon 1944- *Who 94*
Rosenthal, Paul C. 1950- *WhoAm 94*
Rosenthal, Paul Edmond 1951- *WhoAm 94, WhoAmL 94*
Rosenthal, Peter 1946- *WhoAm 94*
Rosenthal, Philip 1916- *IntWW 93*
Rosenthal, Philip 1949- *WhoWest 94*
Rosenthal, Rachel 1926- *WhoAmA 93*
Rosenthal, Richard 1948- *WhoAmL 94*
Rosenthal, Richard Jay 1940- *WhoFI 94*
Rosenthal, Richard Morris 1961- *WhoAmL 94*
Rosenthal, Rick 1949- *IntMPA 94*
Rosenthal, Robert 1933- *ConAu 42NR, WhoAm 94, WhoScEn 94*
Rosenthal, Robert E. 1945- *WhoBlA 94*
Rosenthal, Robert S. 1947- *WhoAmL 94*
Rosenthal, Samuel Robert 1899- *WhoAm 94*
Rosenthal, Sandy d1987 *WhoHol 92*
Rosenthal, Seymour 1921- *WhoAmA 93*
Rosenthal, Sol 1934- *WhoAm 94, WhoWest 94*

Rosenthal, Sol Roy *WhoAm 94*
Rosenthal, Stanley Lawrence 1929- *WhoAm 94*
Rosenthal, Stephen 1935- *WhoAmA 93*
Rosenthal, Stephen D. 1950- *WhoAmP 93*
Rosenthal, Steven Siegmund 1949- *WhoAm 94, WhoAmL 94*
Rosenthal, Stuart Allan 1948- *WhoAm 94, WhoAmL 94*
Rosenthal, Susan Leslie 1956- *WhoMW 93, WhoScEn 94*
Rosenthal, Thomas Gabriel 1935- *IntWW 93, Who 94*
Rosenthal, Tony (Bernard) 1914- *WhoAmA 93*
Rosenthal, Tony Bernard 1914- *WhoAm 94*
Rosenthal, William Edward 1953- *WhoAmL 94*
Rosenthal, William Forshaw 1933- *WhoAm 94*
Rosenthal, William J. 1920- *WhoAm 94*
Rosenwald, Carol 1933- *WhoAmA 93*
Rosenwald, E. John, Jr. 1930- *WhoAm 94*
Rosenwald, John *DrAPF 93*
Rosenwald, John 1943- *WhoMW 93*
Rosenwald, Julius 1862-1932 *AmSocL*
Rosenwald, Lessing Julius 1891-1979 *WhoAmA 93N*
Rosenwald, William 1903- *WhoAm 94*
Rosenzweig, Barney 1937- *IntMPA 94*
Rosenzweig, Charles Leonard 1952- *WhoAmL 94*
Rosenzweig, Daphne Lange 1941- *WhoAmA 93*
Rosenzweig, David 1940- *WhoAm 94, WhoWest 94*
Rosenzweig, Geri *DrAPF 93*
Rosenzweig, Harry 1907- *WhoAmP 93*
Rosenzweig, Mark Richard 1922- *IntWW 93, WhoAm 94, WhoScEn 94, WhoWest 94*
Rosenzweig, Michael Leo 1941- *WhoScEn 94*
Rosenzweig, Norman 1924- *WhoAm 94, WhoMW 93, WhoScEn 94*
Rosenzweig, Peggy A. 1936- *WhoAmP 93*
Rosenzweig, Phyllis D. 1943- *WhoAmA 93*
Rosenzweig, Richard Stuart 1935- *WhoAm 94, WhoWest 94*
Rosenzweig, Robert Myron 1931- *WhoAm 94*
Rosenzweig, Saul 1907- *ConAu 141, WhoAm 94*
Rosenzweig-Diaz, Roberto de 1924- *IntWW 93*
Roser, Ce *WhoAmA 93, WhoAsA 94*
Roser, Franz de Paula 1779-1830 *NewGrDO*
Roser, Michael R. 1948- *WhoAmL 94*
Rosett, Ann Doyle 1955- *WhoAm 94, WhoWest 94*
Rosett, Arthur Irwin 1934- *WhoAm 94, WhoWest 94*
Rosett, Richard Nathaniel 1928- *WhoAm 94*
Rosette, Fabian Maria 1948- *WhoHisp 94*
Roseveare, Robert William 1924- *Who 94*
Rosewaenge, Helge d1972 *WhoHol 92*
Rosewall, Ken 1934- *BuCMET [port]*
Rosewarn, John 1940- *Who 94*
Rosewell, Edward Joseph 1928- *WhoAmP 93*
Roshal, Leonid Mikhailovich 1933- *IntWW 93*
Roshar, Michael L. 1949- *WhoAmL 94*
Roshel, John Albert, Jr. 1941- *WhoMW 93*
Roshell, Marvin J. 1932- *WhoAmP 93*
Rosher, Charles 1885-1974 *IntDcF 2-4 [port]*
Rosher, Dorothy *WhoHol 92*
Rosholt, (Aanon) Michael 1920- *IntWW 93*
Rosholt, Stephen 1946- *WhoAmL 94*
Roshon, George Kenneth 1942- *WhoAm 94, WhoFI 94*
Roshwald, Mordecai 1921- *WrDr 94*
Roshwald, Mordecai (Marceli) 1921- *EncSF 93*
Roshwald, Mordecai M. *DrAPF 93*
Rosi, Carolina 1966- *WhoHol 92*
Rosi, Eugene Joseph 1931- *WhoAm 94*
Rosi, Francesco 1922- *IntMPA 94, IntWW 93*
Rosica, Gabriel Adam 1940- *WhoAm 94*
Rosich, Rayner Karl 1940- *WhoWest 94*
Rosicky, Henry Charles, Jr. 1937- *WhoAm 94*
Rosiello, Michael 1950- *WhoAmL 94*
Rosier, David Lewis 1937- *WhoFI 94*
Rosier, Frederick (Ernest) 1915- *Who 94*
Rosier, Stanley Bruce 1928- *Who 94*
Rosillo, Salvador Edmundo 1936- *WhoHisp 94*
Rosin, Harry 1897-1973 *WhoAmA 93N*
Rosin, Walter L. *WhoAm 94*
Rosinek, Jeffrey 1941- *WhoAmL 94*

Rosing, Bodil d1941 *WhoHol 92*
Rosing, Vladimir 1890-1963 *NewGrDO*
Rosini, James Edward 1953- *WhoAmL 94*
Rosinski, Edwin Francis 1928- *WhoAm 94*
Rosinski, Joseph P. d1982 *WhoHol 92*
Rosiny, Frank Richard 1940- *WhoAmL 94*
Roskam, Jan 1930- *WhoAm 94*
Roskam, Peter *WhoAmP 93*
Roskamp, Karl Wilhelm 1923- *WhoFI 94, WrDr 94*
Roskell, John Smith 1913- *Who 94*
Roskens, Ronald W. *WhoAmP 93*
Roskens, Ronald William 1932- *WhoAm 94*
Roskies, Ethel 1933- *WhoAm 94*
Roskill, Baron 1911- *IntWW 93, Who 94*
Roskill, Mark Wentworth 1933- *WhoAmA 93, WrDr 94*
Roskill, Oliver Wentworth 1906- *Who 94*
Roskin, Lewis Ross 1920- *WhoAm 94*
Roskin, Michael Gary 1939- *WhoFI 94*
Roskind, E. Robert 1945- *WhoAm 94*
Rosko, John James 1947- *WhoScEn 94*
Rosko, Michael Daniel 1949- *WhoAm 94, WhoFI 94*
Roskoff, Allen N. 1950- *WhoAmP 93*
Roskoski, Robert, Jr. 1939- *WhoAm 94*
Roskothen, Michael S. 1936- *WhoFI 94*
Rosky, Burton Seymour 1927- *WhoAm 94, WhoAmL 94, WhoWest 94*
Rosky, Theodore Samuel 1937- *WhoAm 94*
Ros-Lehtinan, Ileana Carmen 1952- *WhoAmP 93, WhoWomW 91*
Ros-Lehtinen, Ileana 1952- *CngDr 93, WhoAm 94, WhoHisp 94*
Rosler, Endre 1904-1963 *NewGrDO*
Rosler, Lee 1923- *WhAm 10*
Rosler, Martha *DrAPF 93*
Rosler, Martha (Rose) 1943- *WhoAmA 93*
Rosley, Adrian d1937 *WhoHol 92*
Rosling, Derek Norman 1930- *Who 94*
Rosling, Peter Edward 1929- *Who 94*
Roslow, Sydney 1910- *WhoFI 94*
Roslund, Carol L. 1943- *WhoAmL 94*
Rosmer, Ernst 1866-1949 *NewGrDO*
Rosmer, Milton d1971 *WhoHol 92*
Rosmino, Gian Paolo d1982 *WhoHol 92*
Rosnack, Richard John 1959- *WhoFI 94*
Rosnay, Joel 1937- *IntWW 93*
Rosner, Ann 1935- *WhoAm 94*
Rosner, Arthur J. 1947- *WhoAmL 94*
Rosner, Bernat 1932- *WhoAmL 94*
Rosner, Daniel Eric 1958- *WhoAmL 94*
Rosner, Fred 1935- *WhoAm 94*
Rosner, Jonathan Levi 1932- *WhoAmL 94*
Rosner, Jonathan Lincoln 1941- *WhoAm 94*
Rosner, Jorge 1921- *WhoAm 94*
Rosner, Lisa 1958- *ConAu 140*
Rosner, Lydia S. 1933- *WhoAm 94*
Rosner, M. Norton 1931- *WhoAm 94*
Rosner, Robert 1947- *WhoAm 94*
Rosner, Robert Allan 1956- *WhoWest 94*
Rosner, Robin Lisa Ziskind 1956- *WhoMW 93*
Rosner, Ronald Alan 1967- *WhoScEn 94*
Rosner, Seth 1931- *WhoAmL 94*
Rosness, Betty June 1924- *WhoFI 94*
Rosny, J.H., aine 1856-1940 *EncSF 93*
Rosocha, Louis Andrew 1950- *WhoScEn 94*
Rosochacki, Daniel *DrAPF 93*
Rosoff, Leonard, Sr. 1912- *WhoAm 94*
Rosoff, William A. 1943- *WhoAm 94, WhoAmL 94, WhoFI 94*
Rosoff, William L. 1946- *WhoAmL 94*
Rosofsky, Seymour 1924- *WhoAmA 93N*
Rosoman, Leonard Henry 1913- *IntWW 93, Who 94*
Rosovsky, Henry 1927- *WhoAm 94*
Rosow, Jerome Morris 1919- *WhoAm 94, WhoAmP 93*
Rosow, Stuart L. 1950- *WhoAm 94, WhoAmL 94*
Rosowski, Robert Bernard 1940- *WhoAm 94, WhoFI 94*
Rospigliosi *Who 94*
Rospigliosi, Giulio 1600-1669 *NewGrDO*
Rosquellas, Pablo (Mariano) 1784-1859 *NewGrDO*
Rosqui, Tom d1991 *WhoHol 92*
Ross, Rt. Hon. Lord 1927- *IntWW 93, Who 94*
Ross, Adrian E. 1912- *WhoAm 94*
Ross, Alan 1922- *Who 94, WrDr 94*
Ross, Alan Marshall 1944- *WhoFI 94*
Ross, Alan O. 1921-1993 *NewYTBS 93*
Ross, Alan Otto 1921- *WhoAm 94*
Ross, Alexander 1742-1827 *WhAmRev*
Ross, Alexander 1783-1856 *WhWE*
Ross, Alexander 1907- *Who 94*
Ross, Alexander 1908- *WhAm 10*
Ross, Alexander 1908-1990 *WhoAmA 93N*
Ross, Allan Anderson 1939- *WhoAm 94*
Ross, Allan Michael 1939- *WhoAm 94*
Ross, Alvin 1920-1975 *WhoAmA 93N*
Ross, Alvin 1922- *WhoFI 94, WhoWest 94*
Ross, Amy Ann 1953- *WhoScEn 94*
Ross, Andre Louis Henry 1922- *IntWW 93*
Ross, Andrew Christian 1931- *Who 94*
Ross, Angus 1911- *WrDr 94*
Ross, Angus 1927- *WrDr 94*
Ross, Annie 1930- *WhoHol 92*
Ross, Anthony d1955 *WhoHol 92*
Ross, Anthony Roger 1953- *WhoBlA 94*
Ross, Archibald (David Manisty) 1911- *Who 94*
Ross, Archibald David Manisty 1911- *IntWW 93*
Ross, Arthur S. d1955 *WhoHol 92*
Ross, Austin 1929- *WhoAm 94*
Ross, Barney d1967 *WhoHol 92*
Ross, Beatrice Brook 1927- *WhoAm 94*
Ross, Bernard L. *EncSF 93*
Ross, Betsy 1752-1836 *AmRev, WhAmRev*
Ross, Betsy King d1989 *WhoHol 92*
Ross, Bettie Louise 1948- *WhoWest 94*
Ross, Betty Grace 1931- *WhoFI 94*
Ross, Beverly *WhoHol 92*
Ross, Bob d1982 *WhoHol 92*
Ross, Brian Elliott 1948- *WhoAm 94*
Ross, Bruce Mitchell 1925- *WhoScEn 94*
Ross, C. Chandler d1952 *WhoAmA 93N*
Ross, Carol Joyce Waller 1942- *WhoWest 94*
Ross, Carolyn Thayer 1948- *WhoAm 94*
Ross, Carson 1946- *WhoAmP 93*
Ross, Catherine 1919- *WrDr 94*
Ross, Catherine Jane 1949- *WhoAmL 94*
Ross, Catherine Laverne 1948- *WhoBlA 94*
Ross, Charles 1918- *WhoBlA 94*
Ross, Charles 1937- *WhoAm 94, WhoAmA 93*
Ross, Charles Alexander 1933- *WhoScEn 94*
Ross, Charles J. d1918 *WhoHol 92*
Ross, Charles R., Jr. 1956- *WhoAmP 93*
Ross, Charles Robert 1920- *WhoAm 94*
Ross, Charles Worthington, IV 1933- *WhoAm 94*
Ross, Charlotte *WhoHol 92*
Ross, Charlotte Pack 1932- *WhoAm 94*
Ross, Chelcie *WhoHol 92*
Ross, Chester Wheeler 1922- *WhoMW 93*
Ross, Chris d1970 *WhoHol 92*
Ross, Christopher Theodore William 1925- *WhoAmL 94*
Ross, Christopher Wade Stelyan 1943- *WhoAm 94, WhoAmP 93*
Ross, Churchilll d1962 *WhoHol 92*
Ross, Clarissa 1912- *WrDr 94*
Ross, Claude G. 1917- *WhoAmP 93*
Ross, Clifford 1952- *WhoAmA 93*
Ross, Coleman DeVane 1943- *WhoAm 94, WhoFI 94*
Ross, Conrad H. 1931- *WhoAmA 93*
Ross, Curlee 1929- *WhoBlA 94*
Ross, Dallas *EncSF 93*
Ross, Dana 1912- *WrDr 94*
Ross, Daniel I. *WhoAmP 93*
Ross, Daniel Manuel 1918- *WhoFI 94*
Ross, Daniel R. 1941- *WhoAm 94, WhoAmL 94*
Ross, David *DrAPF 93*
Ross, David d1975 *WhoHol 92*
Ross, David 1755-1800 *WhAmRev*
Ross, David A. 1949- *WhoAm 94*
Ross, David Anthony 1949- *WhoAmA 93*
Ross, David D. 1949?- *EncSF 93*
Ross, David G. 1945- *WhoAmL 94*
Ross, David Lee 1948- *WhoAmL 94*
Ross, David William, II *WhAm 10*
Ross, Deborah Dean 1946- *WhoMW 93*
Ross, Debra Benita 1956- *WhoFI 94, WhoMW 93*
Ross, Delmer Gerrard 1942- *WhoAm 94*
Ross, Dennis B. *NewYTBS 93*
Ross, Diana 1944- *AfrAmAl 6 [port], IntMPA 94, IntWW 93, WhoAm 94, WhoBlA 94, WhoHol 92*
Ross, Don R. 1941- *WhoAmP 93*
Ross, Donald, Jr. 1941- *WhoAm 94*
Ross, Donald Edward 1930- *WhoAm 94, WhoFI 94, WhoScEn 94*
Ross, Donald Edward 1939- *WhoAm 94*
Ross, Donald Hugh 1949- *WhoMW 93*
Ross, Donald Keith 1925- *WhoAm 94*
Ross, Donald Kenneth 1925- *WhoAm 94*
Ross, Donald MacArthur *Who 94*
Ross, Donald Nixon 1922- *Who 94*
Ross, Donald Roe 1922- *WhoAm 94, WhoAmL 94, WhoAmP 93, WhoMW 93*
Ross, Doris A. 1923- *WhoBlA 94*
Ross, Douglas 1948- *WhoAm 94, WhoFI 94*
Ross, Douglas Allan 1937- *WhoAmA 93*
Ross, Douglas C. 1953- *WhoAmL 94*
Ross, Douglas Taylor 1929- *WhoAm 94*
Ross, Duncan Alexander 1928- *Who 94*
Ross, E. R. 1937- *WhoIns 94*
Ross, Earle d1961 *WhoHol 92*
Ross, Edgar D. 1944- *WhoAmP 93*
Ross, Edna Genevieve 1916- *WhoAmP 93*
Ross, Edward 1937- *WhoAm 94, WhoBlA 94, WhoMW 93, WhoScEn 94*
Ross, Edward J. d1993 *NewYTBS 93*
Ross, Edward Joseph 1934- *WhoAm 94*
Ross, Edward W. *WhoMW 93*
Ross, Elinor 1932- *NewGrDO, WhoAm 94*
Ross, Elise Jane 1943- *WhoAm 94*
Ross, Elliott Daniel 1945- *WhoMW 93*
Ross, Elmer Pearl *WhoAmP 93*
Ross, Emma Jean 1945- *WhoBlA 94*
Ross, Eric Alan 1961- *WhoMW 93, WhoScEn 94*
Ross, Eric Peter 1960- *WhoFI 94*
Ross, Ernest 1942- *Who 94*
Ross, Euan Macdonald 1937- *WhoScEn 94*
Ross, Eve McClure d1966 *WhoHol 92*
Ross, Frances Margaret 1950- *WhoWest 94*
Ross, Frank d1990 *WhoHol 92*
Ross, Frank Howard, III 1946- *WhoMW 93*
Ross, Frank Kenneth 1943- *WhoBlA 94*
Ross, Fred *DrAPF 93*
Ross, Gary Earl *DrAPF 93*
Ross, George 1730-1779 *AmRev, WhAmRev*
Ross, George Campbell d1993 *Who 94N*
Ross, George Martin 1933- *WhoAm 94*
Ross, George William 1940- *WhoAm 94*
Ross, Gerald Elliott 1941- *WhoAmL 94*
Ross, Gerald Fred 1930- *WhoAm 94*
Ross, Geraldine M. Schneider Ryherd 1929- *WhoMW 93*
Ross, Gilbert Stuart 1930- *WhoAm 94*
Ross, Glenn Evan 1958- *WhoFI 94*
Ross, Gloria F(rankenthaler) 1923- *WhoAmA 93*
Ross, Glynn 1914- *WhoAm 94, WhoWest 94*
Ross, Glynn (William) 1914- *NewGrDO*
Ross, Graham Garland *Who 94*
Ross, Guy Matthews, Jr. 1933- *WhoAm 94*
Ross, Harold 1892-1951 *DcLB 137 [port]*
Ross, Harold Truslow 1895- *WhAm 10*
Ross, Harry *WhoHol 92*
Ross, Harry Scott 1960- *WhoAmP 93*
Ross, Hector *WhoHol 92*
Ross, Helaine 1915- *WrDr 94*
Ross, Henry Raymond 1919- *WhoAm 94*
Ross, Herbert d1934 *WhoHol 92*
Ross, Herbert 1927- *IntMPA 94*
Ross, Herbert David 1927- *WhoAm 94*
Ross, Hope Snider 1910- *WhoAmP 93*
Ross, Howard *WhoHol 92*
Ross, Howard Persing 1935- *WhoWest 94*
Ross, Howard Philip 1939- *WhoAmL 94, WhoFI 94*
Ross, Hugh Courtney 1923- *WhoAm 94, WhoFI 94, WhoWest 94*
Ross, I. Louise 1928- *WhoAmP 93*
Ross, Ian Gordon 1926- *IntWW 93*
Ross, Ian Kenneth 1930- *WhoWest 94*
Ross, Ian Munro 1927- *IntWW 93, WhoAm 94, WhoFI 94*
Ross, Jack Clifford 1945- *WhoWest 94*
Ross, Jack Lewis 1932- *WhoAm 94*
Ross, Jaime 1946- *WhoAmA 93*
Ross, James *EncSF 93*
Ross, James 1913- *Who 94*
Ross, James Alexander 1911- *Who 94*
Ross, James Barrett 1930- *WhoAm 94*
Ross, James Brent 1925-1989 *WhAm 10*
Ross, James Clark 1800-1862 *WhWE*
Ross, James E. 1921- *WhoAmP 93*
Ross, James Elmer 1931- *WhoAm 94*
Ross, James Francis 1931- *WhoAm 94*
Ross, James Neil, Jr. 1940- *WhoAm 94*
Ross, James Robert 1923- *WhoAmP 93*
Ross, James Ulric 1941- *WhoAmL 94*
Ross, Jane d1985 *WhoHol 92*
Ross, Janet 1914- *WhoWest 94*
Ross, Janice Koenig 1926- *WhoAmA 93*
Ross, Jean Marie 1942- *WhoAmP 93*
Ross, Jeffrey Allan 1947- *WhoAm 94*
Ross, Jeffrey Kenneth *WhoAm 94*
Ross, Jim Buck 1917- *WhoAmP 93*
Ross, Jimmy Douglas 1936- *WhoAm 94*
Ross, Joan M. 1931- *WhoAmA 93*
Ross, Joanne A. 1929- *WhoBlA 94*
Ross, Joe E. d1982 *WhoHol 92*
Ross, Joe E. 1914-1982 *WhoCom*
Ross, John *WhoHol 92*
Ross, John 1762-1789 *AmRev*
Ross, John 1777-1856 *WhWE*
Ross, John 1790-1866 *HisWorL [port]*
Ross, John 1926- *WhoAm 94, WhoScEn 94, WhoWest 94*
Ross, John, Jr. 1928- *WhoAm 94, WhoScEn 94*
Ross, John J. *WhoFI 94*
Ross, John Joseph 1927- *WhoAm 94*
Ross, John Mershon 1931- *WhoAmL 94, WhoFI 94*
Ross, John Michael 1919- *WhoAm 94*
Ross, John R., III 1955- *WhoScEn 94*
Ross, John Raymond 1923-1990 *WhAm 10*
Ross, John T. 1921- *WhoAmA 93*
Ross, John Thompson, Jr. 1942- *WhoAm 94*
Ross, Jonathan 1916- *WrDr 94*
Ross, Joseph 1929- *EncSF 93*
Ross, Joseph Comer 1927- *WhoAm 94, WhoScEn 94*
Ross, Joseph E. 1923- *WhoAm 94*
Ross, Joseph Foster 1910- *WhoAm 94, WhoWest 94*
Ross, Justin 1954- *WhoHol 92*
Ross, Katharine 1943- *IntMPA 94, WhoHol 92*
Ross, Kathleen Anne 1941- *WhoWest 94*
Ross, (James) Keith 1927- *Who 94*
Ross, Kenneth 1941- *IntMPA 94*
Ross, Kenneth Alexander 1949- *Who 94*
Ross, Kerry Lynn 1960- *WhoWest 94*
Ross, Kevin Arnold 1955- *WhoBlA 94*
Ross, Kristine Marie 1962- *WhoHisp 94*
Ross, Lanny d1988 *WhoHol 92*
Ross, Lanson Clifford, Jr. 1936- *WhoWest 94*
Ross, Lawrence John 1942- *WhoAm 94, WhoScEn 94*
Ross, Leon Thomas 1931- *WhoWest 94*
Ross, Leonard Lester 1927- *WhoAm 94*
Ross, Leonard Q. *Who 94*
Ross, Leonard Q. 1908- *WhoAm 94, WrDr 94*
Ross, Lesa Moore 1959- *WhoFI 94, WhoScEn 94*
Ross, Lillian Hammer 1925- *ConAu 140*
Ross, Louis *WhoMW 93*
Ross, Louis 1901-1963 *WhoAmA 93N*
Ross, Louis Robert 1932- *WhoAm 94, WhoFI 94*
Ross, Lowell William 1932- *WhoAmP 93*
Ross, Madelyn Ann 1949- *WhoAm 94*
Ross, Malcolm 1929- *WhoAm 94*
Ross, Malcolm 1932- *WrDr 94*
Ross, Malcolm (Harrison) 1895-1965 *EncSF 93*
Ross, Malcolm Keir 1910- *Who 94*
Ross, Maria Elena 1945- *WhoHisp 94*
Ross, Marilyn 1912- *WrDr 94*
Ross, Marilyn Ann 1939- *WhoWest 94*
Ross, Marion *WhoAm 94*
Ross, Marion 1928- *WhoHol 92*
Ross, Mark Alfred 1956- *WhoMW 93*
Ross, Mark Samuel 1957- *WhoAmL 94*
Ross, Mark Steven 1946- *WhoAm 94, WhoAmL 94*
Ross, Martha E. 1943- *WhoBlA 94*
Ross, Martin *RfGShF*
Ross, Martin 1861-1915 *BlmGWL*
Ross, Martin 1862-1915 *RfGShF*
See Also Somerville, Edith OEnone 1858-1949 *DcLB 135*
See Also Somerville, Edith 1858-1949 *TwCLC 51*
Ross, Mary Adelaide Eden 1896- *WrDr 94*
Ross, Mary C. 1923- *WhoAmP 93*
Ross, Mary Caslin 1953- *WhoFI 94*
Ross, Mary Harvey 1925- *WhoScEn 94*
Ross, Mary Olivia *WhoBlA 94*
Ross, Matthew 1953- *WhoAmL 94*
Ross, Maurice James 1908- *Who 94*
Ross, Merrie Lynn *WhoHol 92*
Ross, Michael *WhoHol 92*
Ross, Michael Aaron 1941- *WhoAm 94, WhoAmL 94*
Ross, Michael David 1946- *Who 94*
Ross, Michael E. 1949- *WhoAmL 94*
Ross, Michael Frederick 1950- *WhoAmL 94, WhoFI 94*
Ross, Michael Neil 1952- *WhoFI 94, WhoMW 93*
Ross, Mike 1937- *WhoAmP 93*
Ross, Mike 1961- *WhoAmP 93*
Ross, Molly Owings 1954- *WhoFI 94, WhoWest 94*
Ross, Monte 1932- *WhoAm 94*
Ross, Muriel Dorothy 1927- *WhoScEn 94*
Ross, Murray George 1910- *WhoAm 94, WrDr 94*
Ross, Murray Louis 1947- *WhoAm 94, WhoFI 94*
Ross, Myrna d1975 *WhoHol 92*
Ross, N. Rodney 1957- *WhoBlA 94*
Ross, Neil 1944- *WhoFI 94*
Ross, Nicholas, Mrs. *Who 94*
Ross, Nicholas David 1947- *Who 94*
Ross, Norman Alan 1942- *WhoAm 94*
Ross, Norman Alexander 1922- *WhoAm 94*
Ross, Otho Bescent 1951- *WhoAmL 94*
Ross, Patti Jayne 1946- *WhoScEn 94*
Ross, Paul 1927- *WhoAm 94*
Ross, Percy Nathan 1916- *WhoAm 94*
Ross, Peter J. 1953- *WhoFI 94*
Ross, Phyllis Harrison 1936- *WhoBlA 94*
Ross, Ralph M. 1936- *WhoBlA 94*
Ross, Randall Austin 1895- *WhAm 10*
Ross, Randolph Ernest 1955- *WhoFI 94*

Ross, Raymond J. EncSF 93
Ross, Regina D. 1948- WhoBlA 94
Ross, Reuben James, Jr. 1918- WhoScEn 94
Ross, Rhoda Honore 1941- WhoAmA 93
Ross, Richard IntWW 93, Who 94
Ross, Richard 1935- Who 94
Ross, Richard 1937- WhoFI 94
Ross, (Claud) Richard 1924- IntWW 93, Who 94
Ross, Richard A. WhoAm 94
Ross, Richard C. 1927- WhoAmL 94, WhoAmP 93
Ross, Richard Francis 1935- WhoAm 94, WhoMW 93
Ross, Richard Harris 1958- WhoFI 94
Ross, Richard Starr 1924- WhoAm 94
Ross, Richard Wayne 1953- WhoAmL 94
Ross, Rick Allen d1993 NewYTBS 93
Ross, Robert d1954 WhoHol 92
Ross, Robert 1912- Who 94
Ross, Robert Baldwin 1869-1918 DcNaB MP
Ross, Robert C. d1990 WhoHol 92
Ross, Robert Evan 1947- WhoFI 94, WhoMW 93
Ross, Robert Grierson, Jr. 1950- WhoFI 94
Ross, Robert Jeremy 1939- Who 94
Ross, Robert Joseph 1936- WhoAm 94, WhoWest 94
Ross, Robert King 1927- WhoWest 94
Ross, Robert Nathan 1941- WhoScEn 94
Ross, Robert Thomas 1924- WhoAm 94
Ross, Robinette Davis 1952- WhoAm 94
Ross, Roderic Henry 1930- WhoAm 94
Ross, Roger Scott 1946- WhoAmL 94
Ross, Ronald EncSF 93
Ross, Ronald 1857-1932 WorScD
Ross, Ronald Douglas 1920- Who 94
Ross, Russell 1929- WhoAm 94, WhoScEn 94, WhoWest 94
Ross, Russell Marion 1921- WhoAm 94
Ross, Sam 1912- WrDr 94
Ross, Sander B. 1948- WhoAmL 94
Ross, Scott Alan 1951- WhoAm 94
Ross, Scott Lamond 1948- WhoFI 94
Ross, Sheldon 1925- WhoAmA 93
Ross, Sheldon Jules 1924- WhoAm 94
Ross, Sherman 1919- WhoAm 94
Ross, Shirley d1975 WhoHol 92
Ross, Sinclair 1908- WrDr 94
Ross, (James) Sinclair 1908- RfGShF
Ross, Sophie Who 94
Ross, Stan WhoHol 92
Ross, Stanford G. 1931- WhoAm 94
Ross, Stanford Gordon 1931- WhoAmL 94
Ross, Stanley 1914-1992 WhAm 10
Ross, Stanley Ralph 1940- WhoAm 94
Ross, Steven Carter 1954- WhoMW 93
Ross, Steven Charles 1947- WhoWest 94
Ross, Steven J. d1992 IntMPA 94N, IntWW 93N
Ross, Steven J. 1927- WhoFI 94
Ross, Steven J. 1927-1992 AnObit 1992, News 93-3
Ross, Stuart B. 1937- WhoAm 94, WhoFI 94
Ross, Sueellen 1941- WhoAmA 93
Ross, Susan Louise WhoAmL 94
Ross, Ted WhoHol 92
Ross, Terence William 1935- WhoWest 94
Ross, Terrence DrAPF 93
Ross, Terry D. 1943- WhoAmL 94
Ross, Terry Joseph 1952- WhoWest 94
Ross, Thomas Bernard 1929- WhoAm 94
Ross, Thomas McCallum 1931- WhoFI 94
Ross, Thomas W. d1959 WhoHol 92
Ross, Thomas Warren 1950- WhoAmL 94
Ross, Timothy David M. Who 94
Ross, Tom M. 1933- WhoWest 94
Ross, Tony 1938- WrDr 94
Ross, Tracey WhoHol 92
Ross, Victor 1919- Who 94
Ross, Victor Julius 1935- WhoWest 94
Ross, Vonia Pearl 1942- WhoWest 94
Ross, W(illiam) D(avid) 1877-1971 EncEth
Ross, Walter Hugh Malcolm 1943- Who 94
Ross, Walter Marion 1903-1990 WhAm 10
Ross, Warren Howard 1927- WhoWest 94
Ross, Wayne Anthony 1943- WhoAmL 94
Ross, Wendy d1988 WhoHol 92
Ross, Wendy Clucas 1942- WhoAm 94
Ross, Wilbur Louis, Jr. 1937- WhoAm 94, WhoFI 94
Ross, Willard H. 1930- WhoAmP 93
Ross, William 1925- WhoFI 94
Ross, William 1936- Who 94
Ross, William (Edward Daniel) 1912- WrDr 94
Ross, William Alexander Jackson 1937- WhoBlA 94
Ross, William H. 1946- WhoAm 94, WhoFI 94, WhoWest 94
Ross, William Henry 1862-1944 DcNaB MP
Ross, William Jarboe 1930- WhoAmL 94
Ross, William Mackie 1922- Who 94
Ross, William Warfield 1926- WhoAm 94
Ross, Willie WhoHol 92
Ross, Winston A. 1941- WhoBlA 94
Ross, Yan Michael 1942- WhoAmL 94
Rossabi, Morris 1941- WrDr 94
Rossano, August Thomas 1916- WhoAm 94
Rossant, James Stephane 1928- WhoAm 94
Rossardi, Orlando 1938- WhoHisp 94
Rossato, Arturo 1882-1942 NewGrDO
Ross-Audley, Cheryl Yvonne 1950- WhoBlA 94
Rossavik, Ivar Kristian 1936- WhoScEn 94
Rossbach, Philip Edward 1959- WhoScEn 94
Rossberg, Robert Howard 1926- WhoAm 94
Rossby, Carl-Gustaf 1898-1957 WorScD
Rosse, Earl of 1936- Who 94
Rosse, Ian 1904-1987 WrDr 94N
Rosse, James Nelson 1931- WhoAm 94
Rosse, Maryvonne 1917- WhoAmA 93
Rossel, Eduard Ergartovich 1937- LngBDD
Rossel, Elisabeth-Paul-Edouard, Chevalier De 1765-1829 WhWE
Rossel, Guillermo Leonardo 1945- WhoHisp 94
Rossel, Seymour (H.) 1945- WrDr 94
Rosselli, Amelia 1930- BlmGWL
Rosselli, John 1927- NewGrDO
Rosselli, William Anthony 1947- WhoFI 94
Rossellini, Isabella 1952- IntMPA 94, IntWW 93, WhoAm 94, WhoHol 92
Rossellini, Renzo d1982 WhoHol 92
Rossellini, Renzo 1908-1982 NewGrDO
Rossello, Pedro WhoAm 94
Rossello, Pedro 1944- WhoAmP 93, WhoHisp 94
Rossen, Carol WhoHol 92
Rossen, Jordan 1934- WhoAm 94, WhoAmL 94
Rossen, Susan F. WhoAmA 93
Rosser, Annetta Hamilton 1913- WhoMW 93
Rosser, Charles D. 1935- WhoAm 94
Rosser, J. Allyn DrAPF 93
Rosser, James M. 1939- WhoBlA 94
Rosser, James Milton 1939- WhoWest 94
Rosser, John Barkley 1907- WhAm 10
Rosser, Malcolm Edward, IV 1955- WhoAmL 94
Rosser, Melvyn (Wynne) 1926- Who 94
Rosser, Pearl Lockhart 1935- WhoBlA 94
Rosser, Rachel Mary Who 94
Rosser, Richard Andrew 1944- Who 94
Rosser, Richard Franklin 1929- WhoAm 94
Rosser, Samuel Blanton 1934- WhoBlA 94
Rosset, Barnet Lee, Jr. 1922- WhoAm 94
Rosset, Lisa Krug 1952- WhoAm 94
Rosseter, Thomas Arthur 1935- WhoFI 94
Rossetti, Ana 1950- BlmGWL
Rossetti, Christina 1830-1894 BlmGWL, PoeCrit 7 [port]
Rossetti, Christina Georgina 1830-1894 BlmGEL
Rossetti, Dante Gabriel 1828-1882 BlmGEL
Rossetti, Donald David 1940- WhoAmL 94
Rossetti, Louis 1895- WhAm 10
Rossetti, Robert John 1947- WhoFI 94
Rossetti, Rosemarie 1953- WhoMW 93
Rossey, Paul William 1926- WhoAm 94
Rossi, Agnelo 1913- IntWW 93
Rossi, Aldo 1931- IntWW 93
Rossi, Alice S. 1922- WhoAm 94
Rossi, Amadeo Joseph 1954- WhoWest 94
Rossi, Anthony Gerald 1935- WhoAm 94
Rossi, Anthony T. d1993 NewYTBS 93 [port]
Rossi, Barbara WhoAmA 93
Rossi, Bruno d1993 NewYTBS 93 [port]
Rossi, Bruno 1905- WhoAm 94
Rossi, Bruno B. 1905- IntWW 93
Rossi, Cristina Peri ConWorW 93
Rossi, Dominick F., Jr. 1941- WhoAm 94
Rossi, Ennio C. 1931- WhoMW 93
Rossi, Ernest E. 1929- WhoMW 93
Rossi, Faust F. 1932- WhoAm 94, WhoAmL 94
Rossi, Francesco NewGrDO
Rossi, Gaetano 1774-1855 NewGrDO
Rossi, Giacomo fl. 1710-1731 NewGrDO
Rossi, Giovanni (Gaetano) 1828-1886 NewGrDO
Rossi, Guido Antonio 1944- WhoScEn 94
Rossi, Gustavo Alberto 1942- WhoHisp 94
Rossi, Guy Anthony 1952- WhoWest 94
Rossi, Harald Hermann 1917- WhoAm 94
Rossi, Hugh (Alexis Louis) 1927- Who 94
Rossi, Joseph O. WhoAmA 93
Rossi, Joseph Stephen 1951- WhoScEn 94
Rossi, Lauro 1812-1885 NewGrDO
Rossi, Lee DrAPF 93
Rossi, Leo WhoHol 92
Rossi, Luigi 1597?-1653 NewGrDO
Rossi, Luis Heber 1948- WhoHisp 94
Rossi, Mario Alexander 1931- WhoAm 94
Rossi, Michelangelo c. 1602-1656? NewGrDO
Rossi, Michelle WhoHol 92
Rossi, Miriam 1952- WhoScEn 94
Rossi, Paolo WhoHol 92
Rossi, Paolo 1956- WorESoc
Rossi, Peter Henry 1921- ConAu 41NR, WhoAm 94
Rossi, Ralph L. 1928- WhoFI 94
Rossi, Richard Joseph 1956- WhoWest 94
Rossi, Robert Andrew 1925- WhoFI 94
Rossi, Robert John 1928- WhoFI 94
Rossi, Roberta Marie 1957- WhoAmL 94
Rossi, Scot Alan 1960- WhoMW 93
Rossi, Steve WhoHol 92
Rossi, Steve 1932- See Allen and Rossi WhoCom
Rossi, Thomas J. 1946- WhoAmP 93
Rossi, Tino d1983 WhoHol 92
Rossi, William Matthew 1954- WhoAmL 94
Rossides, Eugene Telemachus 1927- WhoAm 94, WhoAmP 93
Rossi-Drago, Eleanora 1925- WhoHol 92
Rossi-Espagnet, Gianfranco 1947- WhoAm 94
Rossignol, Felix-Ludger NewGrDO
Rossignol, Roger John 1941- WhoScEn 94
Rossi-Lemeni, Nicola 1920-1991 NewGrDO
Rossin, Herbert Yale 1936- WhoWest 94
Rossing, Thomas D. 1929- WhoScEn 94
Rossington, David Ralph 1932- WhoAm 94
Rossington, Norman 1928- WhoHol 92
Rossini, Frederick Dominic 1899- IntWW 93
Rossini, Gioachino (Antonio) 1792-1868 NewGrDO [port]
Rossini, Jan WhoHol 92
Rossini, Joseph 1939- WhoAm 94
Rossinot, Andre 1939- IntWW 93
Rossio, Richard Dominic 1933- WhoFI 94, WhoMW 93
Rossiter, Alexander, Jr. 1936- WhoAm 94
Rossiter, Charles DrAPF 93
Rossiter, Clare 1936- WrDr 94
Rossiter, Eileen 1929- WhoWomW 91
Rossiter, (Anthony) Francis 1931- Who 94
Rossiter, Frank Raymond 1937-1989 WhAm 10
Rossiter, John 1916- WrDr 94
Rossiter, John 1918- WrDr 94
Rossiter, Leonard d1984 WhoHol 92
Rossiter, Margaret Walsh 1944- WhoAm 94
Rossiter, Michael Anthony 1935- WhoAmP 93
Rossiter, Oscar 1918- EncSF 93
Rossiter, Peter L. 1948- WhoAmL 94
Rossiter, Phyllis J. 1938- WhoMW 93
Rossiter, Robert E. 1946- WhoFI 94
Rossiter, Sarah DrAPF 93
Rossiter, Sarah 1942- WrDr 94
Rossitto, Angelo WhoHol 92
Ross-Jacobs, Ruth Ann 1934- WhoFI 94
Rosskamm, Alan 1950- WhoFI 94
Rosskamm, Martin 1915- WhoFI 94
Rosskothen, Heinz Dieter 1936- WhoScEn 94
Ross-Lee, Barbara WhoBlA 94
Rossler, Tini NewGrDO
Rossler, Willis Kenneth, Jr. 1946- WhoAm 94, WhoFI 94
Rossley, Paul R. 1938- WhoIns 94
Rossl-Majdan, Hilde(gard) 1921- NewGrDO
Rosslyn, Earl of WhAmRev
Rosslyn, Earl of 1958- Who 94
Ross-Macdonald, Malcolm (John) 1932- WrDr 94
Rossman, Chris Edmund 1950- WhoAmL 94
Rossman, Janet Kay 1954- WhoAm 94
Rossman, Michael 1941- WhoAmA 93
Rossman, Richard Alan 1939- WhoAm 94
Rossman, Robert Harris 1932- WhoFI 94
Rossman, Ruth Scharff WhoAm 94, WhoAmA 93
Rossmann, Charles Boris 1945- WhoMW 93, WhoScEn 94
Rossmann, Jack Eugene 1936- WhoAm 94
Rossmann, Michael George 1930- WhoAm 94
Rossmiller, George Eddie 1935- WhoAm 94, WhoScEn 94
Rossmore, Baron 1931- Who 94
Ross-Munro, Colin William Gordon 1928- Who 94
Ross-Murray, Carmin Danielle 1963- WhoAmL 94
Rossner, Judith DrAPF 93
Rossner, Judith 1935- WhoAm 94, WrDr 94
Rosso, Christine Hehmeyer 1947- WhoAmL 94
Rosso, Lewis T. 1909- IntMPA 94
Rosso, Louis T. 1933- WhoAm 94, WhoFI 94, WhoWest 94
Rosso, R. Jerry 1938- WhoFI 94
Rosso de Irizarry, Carmen 1947- WhoFI 94
Rossoff, Mack F. 1952- WhoAm 94, WhoFI 94
Ross of Newport, Baron d1993 Who 94N
Rossol, Monona 1936- ConAu 140
Rosson, Arthur d1960 WhoHol 92
Rosson, Glenn Richard 1937- WhoAm 94
Rosson, Hal 1895-1988 IntDcF 2-4
Rosson, Helene d1985 WhoHol 92
Rosson, Peggy 1935- WhoAmP 93
Rosson, Queenie d1978 WhoHol 92
Rosson, Renal B. 1919- WhoAmL 94
Rosson, Richard d1953 WhoHol 92
Rossoni, Giulio fl. 1665-1681 NewGrDO
Rossor, Martin Neil 1950- Who 94
Rossotti, Barbara Jill Margulies 1940- WhoAm 94
Rossotti, Charles Ossola 1941- WhoAm 94, WhoScEn 94
Rossotti, Hazel Swaine 1930- ConAu 142
Rossovich, Rick 1957- IntMPA 94
Rossovich, Rick 1958- WhoHol 92
Rossovich, Tim WhoHol 92
Rossow, William B. EncSF 93
Ross Russell, Graham 1933- Who 94
Rosston, Edward William 1918- WhoAm 94
Rossum, Ralph Arthur 1946- WhoAm 94
Rosswall, Thomas 1941- Who 94
Rost, David Edward 1955- WhoMW 93
Rost, Mark D. 1949- WhoFI 94
Rost, Miles Ernest 1891-1961 WhoAmA 93N
Rost, Peter 1959- WhoFI 94
Rost, Peter Lewis 1930- Who 94
Rost, Thomas Lowell 1941- WhoAm 94, WhoWest 94
Rost, William Joseph 1926- WhoAm 94
Rosta, Endre 1909- IntWW 93
Rostad, Kenneth Leif 1941- WhoWest 94
Rostagno, Derrick 1965- WhoAm 94
Rostand, Edmond (-Eugene) 1868-1918 IntDcT 2 [port]
Rostand, Michel 1895- WhoAmA 93N
Rostboll, Grethe Fogh 1941- WhoWomW 91
Rosteck, Paul Robert, Jr. 1949- WhoMW 93
Rosten, Irwin WhoAm 94
Rosten, Leo 1908- WrDr 94
Rosten, Leo C. 1908- Who 94
Rosten, Leo Calvin 1908- WhoAm 94
Rosten, Norman DrAPF 93
Rostenberg, Leona 1908- DcLB 140 [port]
Rostenkowski, Dan CngDr 93
Rostenkowski, Dan 1928- IntWW 93, NewYTBS 93 [port], WhoAm 94, WhoAmP 93, WhoMW 93
Roster, Fred Howard 1944- WhoAmA 93
Roster, Michael 1945- WhoAm 94, WhoAmL 94
Rostker, Skipper 1919- WhoAmP 93
Rostkowski, Margaret I. 1945- TwCYAW
Rostky, George Harold 1926- WhoAm 94
Rostler, Jefferson Paul 1945- WhoAm 94, WhoAmL 94
Rostohar, Raymond 1961- WhoScEn 94
Rostoker, Gordon 1940- WhoAm 94, WhoScEn 94
Rostoker, Michael David 1958- WhoAmL 94
Roston, Arnold 1923- WhoAm 94
Roston, David C. 1943- WhoAm 94, WhoAmL 94
Roston, Murray 1928- WrDr 94
Roston, Ruth DrAPF 93
Rostopchina, Evdokiia Petrovna 1811-1858 BlmGWL [port]
Rostov, Stefan WrDr 94
Rostow, Charles Nicholas 1950- WhoAm 94
Rostow, Elspeth Davies WhoAm 94
Rostow, Eugene V. 1913- WrDr 94
Rostow, Eugene Victor 1913- IntWW 93, Who 94, WhoAm 94
Rostow, Walt W. 1916- WrDr 94
Rostow, Walt Whitman 1916- IntWW 93, Who 94, WhoAm 94, WhoAmP 93
Rostropovich, Mstislav 1927- Who 94
Rostropovich, Mstislav (Leopol'dovich) 1927- NewGrDO
Rostropovich, Mstislav Leopoldovich 1927- IntWW 93, WhoAm 94

Rothschild, Paul Henry 1945- *WhoAmL 94*
Rothschild, Robert 1911- *IntWW 93, Who 94*
Rothschild, Shelly 1949- *WhoAm 94*
Rothschild, Steven James 1944- *WhoAm 94, WhoAmL 94*
Rothschild, V(ictor) Henry, II 1908- *WhAm 10*
Rothschild, William Edward 1933- *WhoFI 94*
Rothstein, Alan Roel 1941- *WhoAmL 94*
Rothstein, Anne Louise 1943- *WhoAm 94*
Rothstein, Arnold Joel 1928- *WhoScEn 94*
Rothstein, Arthur 1915-1985 *WhoAmA 93N*
Rothstein, Aser 1918- *WhoAm 94*
Rothstein, Barbara Jacobs 1939- *WhoAm 94, WhoAmL 94, WhoWest 94*
Rothstein, Barry Steven 1953- *WhoWest 94*
Rothstein, Charlotte M. 1924- *WhoAmP 93*
Rothstein, Cy 1934- *WhoWest 94*
Rothstein, Edward 1952- *WrDr 94*
Rothstein, Eric 1936- *WhoAm 94*
Rothstein, Fred H. *WhoAm 94*
Rothstein, Gerald Alan 1941- *WhoAm 94, WhoFI 94*
Rothstein, Howard 1935- *WhoScEn 94*
Rothstein, John A. 1953- *WhoAmL 94*
Rothstein, Morton 1926- *WhoAm 94, WhoWest 94*
Rothstein, Robert Richard 1944- *WhoAmL 94*
Rothstein, Ronald 1942- *WhoAm 94, WhoMW 93*
Rothstein, Ruth M. *WhoMW 93*
Rothstein, Samuel 1921- *WhoAm 94, WrDr 94*
Rothstein, Saul 1920- *Who 94*
Rothwarf, Allen 1935- *WhoAm 94, WhoScEn 94*
Rothweiler, Paul R. 1931- *WrDr 94*
Rothwell, Albert Falcon 1926- *WhoAm 94*
Rothwell, Geoffrey Scott 1953- *WhoFI 94*
Rothwell, Kenneth Sprague 1921- *WrDr 94*
Rothwell, Margaret Irene 1938- *Who 94*
Rothwell, Michael *WhoHol 92*
Rothwell, Robert *WhoHol 92*
Rothwell, Robert Alan 1939- *WhoWest 94*
Rothwell, Robert Clark 1939- *WhoAm 94*
Rothwell, Sheila Gwendoline 1935- *Who 94*
Rothwell, Timothy Gordon 1951- *WhoScEn 94*
Rothwell, Victor Howard 1945- *WrDr 94*
Roti, Contessa Anna *BlmGWL*
Roti, Fred B. 1920- *WhoAmP 93*
Roti, Thomas David 1945- *WhoAmL 94*
Rotier, Peter 1888- *WhoAmA 93N*
Rotimi, Ola 1938- *ConDr 93, WrDr 94*
Rotimi, (Emmanuel Gladstone) Ola(wale) 1938- *BlkWr 2, IntDcT 2*
Rotithor, Hemant Govind 1958- *WhoScEn 94*
Rotkin, Michael Eric 1945- *WhoWest 94*
Rotko, Bernard Benjamin 1908- *WhAm 10*
Rotman, Douglas Allen 1942- *WhoWest 94*
Rotman, Jesse Louis 1947- *WhoAm 94*
Rotman, Morris Bernard 1918- *WhoAm 94*
Rotner, Robert Alan 1944- *WhoAm 94*
Rotner, Shelley 1951- *SmATA 76*
Rotolo, Joseph A. 1931- *WhoAm 94*
Rotolo, Vilma Stolfi 1930- *WhoScEn 94*
Rotondi, Dorothy A. 1958- *WhoAmP 93*
Rotondi, Samuel 1946- *WhoAmP 93*
Rotondo, Gaetano Mario 1926- *WhoScEn 94*
Rotrou, Jean 1609-1650 *GuFrLit 2*
Rotrou, Jean (de) 1609-1650 *IntDcT 2*
Rotschafer, John Charles 1951- *WhoMW 93*
Rotsey, Martin
See Midnight Oil *ConMus 11*
Rotsler, William 1926- *EncSF 93, WrDr 94*
Rotstein, Robert H. 1951- *WhoAmL 94*
Rott, Nicholas 1917- *WhoAm 94, WhoScEn 94*
Rottas, Ray 1927- *WhoAmP 93*
Rotten, Johnny 1956- *WhoHol 92*
Rottensteiner, Franz 1942- *EncSF 93*
Rotter, Paul Talbott 1918- *WhoAm 94, WhoFI 94, WhoWest 94*
Rotter, Steve 1950- *WhoAm 94*
Rotterdam, Paul Z. 1939- *WhoAmA 93*
Rottger, Heinz 1909-1977 *NewGrDO*
Rottiers, Donald Victor 1938- *WhoScEn 94*
Rottler, Terry Robert 1951- *WhoAmP 93*
Rottman, Ellis 1930- *WhoAm 94*
Rottschaefer, William Andrew 1933- *WhoWest 94*
Rotunda, Donald Theodore 1945- *WhoFI 94*
Rotunda, Ronald Daniel 1945- *WhoAm 94*
Rotunno, Giuseppe 1923- *IntDcF 2-4, IntMPA 94*
Rotunno, Richard *WhoScEn 94*
Rotwitt, Jeffrey Brent 1950- *WhoAmL 94*
Rotz, Anna Overcash 1940- *WhoAmP 93*
Rotz, Jean c. 1505-c. 1560 *DcNaB MP*
Rotzoll, Kim Brewer 1935- *WhoAm 94*
Rouan, Brigitte *WhoHol 92*
Rouan, Gregory W. 1954- *WhoScEn 94*
Rouayheb, George Michael 1933- *WhoScEn 94*
Roub, Bryan Roger 1941- *WhoAm 94, WhoFI 94*
Roubal, William Theodore 1930- *WhoScEn 94, WhoWest 94*
Roubert, Matty d1973 *WhoHol 92*
Roubos, Gary Lynn 1936- *WhoAm 94, WhoFI 94*
Rouch, James *EncSF 93*
Rouch, Jean 1917- *IntWW 93*
Rouchell, John A. 1952- *WhoAmL 94*
Rouda, Mitchell Bruce 1957- *WhoAm 94*
Roudane, Charles 1927- *WhoFI 94*
Roudebush, George M. 1894-1992 *WhAm 10*
Roudebush, Richard L. 1918- *WhoAmP 93*
Roudinesco, Elisabeth 1944- *ConAu 142*
Roudy, Yvette *IntWW 93*
Roudy, Yvette 1929- *WhoWomW 91*
Roudybush, Franklin 1906- *WhoAm 94, WhoFI 94, WhoScEn 94*
Roueche, Berton *DrAPF 93*
Roueche, Berton 1911- *WhoAm 94, WrDr 94*
Roueche, John Edward, II 1938- *WhoAm 94*
Rouerie, Tuffin de la *WhAmRev*
Rouf, Mohammed Abdur 1933- *WhoAsA 94, WhoScEn 94*
Rougas, Michael *WhoHol 92*
Rougeau, Lynne Marie *WhoWest 94*
Rougeau, Weldon Joseph 1942- *WhoMW 93*
Rough, David S. 1933- *WhoFI 94*
Roughton, William Lemuel, Jr. 1947- *WhoAmL 94*
Roughwood, Owen d1947 *WhoHol 92*
Rougier, Charles Jeremy 1933- *Who 94*
Rougier, Richard George 1932- *Who 94*
Rougier-Chapman, Alwyn Spencer Douglas 1939- *WhoAm 94, WhoFI 94*
Rougraff, Maurice E. 1926- *WhoIns 94*
Rouhana, William Joseph, Jr. 1952- *WhoFI 94*
Rouillard, Zelda Jeanne 1929- *WhoWest 94*
Rouillon, Fernand 1920- *IntWW 93*
Rouilly, Jean 1943- *IntWW 93*
Roukema, Margaret Scafati 1929- *WhoAm 94*
Roukema, Marge 1929- *CngDr 93, WhoAmP 93, WhoWomW 91*
Roukes, Nicholas M. 1925- *WhoAmA 93*
Roulac, Stephen E. 1945- *WhoAm 94, WhoFI 94, WhoWest 94*
Rouleau, Joseph (Alfred) 1929- *NewGrDO*
Rouleau, Joseph-Alfred 1929- *IntWW 93*
Rouleau, Philippe *WhoHol 92*
Rouleau, Raymond d1981 *WhoHol 92*
Rouleau, Reynald 1935- *WhoMW 93*
Roulet, Norman Lawrence 1932- *WhoMW 93*
Roulhac, Edgar Edwin 1946- *WhoBlA 94*
Roulhac, Joseph D. 1916- *WhoBlA 94*
Roulhac, Nellie Gordon 1924- *WhoBlA 94*
Roulhac, Roy L. 1943- *WhoBlA 94*
Roulien, Raul *WhoHol 92*
Roulien, Tosca d1933 *WhoHol 92*
Roullet, Marie Francois Louis Gand Leblanc, Bailli du 1716-1786 *NewGrDO*
Roulston, David John 1936- *WhoScEn 94*
Roulston, Donald 1937- *WhoAmP 93*
Roulston, Thomas Henry 1933- *WhoAm 94*
Roulstone, Joan Margaret 1945- *Who 94*
Round, Dorothy 1909-1982 *BuCMET [port]*
Round, Frank E. *WhoScEn 94*
Round, Nicholas Grenville 1938- *Who 94*
Roundell, Henry J. 1947- *WhoAm 94, WhoFI 94*
Roundfield, Dan 1953- *BasBi*
Roundfield, Danny Thomas 1953- *WhoBlA 94*
Rounds, Bruce C. 1928- *WhoAmP 93*
Rounds, David d1983 *WhoHol 92*
Rounds, Donald Edwin 1926- *WhoAm 94*
Rounds, Donald Michael 1941- *WhoWest 94*
Rounds, Glen (Harold) 1906- *WrDr 94*
Rounds, Kevin Thomas 1951- *WhoAm 94*
Rounds, M. Michael *WhoAmP 93*
Roundtree, Eugene V. N. 1927- *WhoBlA 94*
Roundtree, Nicholas John 1956- *WhoBlA 94*
Roundtree, Richard 1937- *WhoHol 92*
Roundtree, Richard 1942- *AfrAmAl 6 [port], IntMPA 94, WhoBlA 94*
Rounick, Jack A. 1935- *WhoAm 94, WhoAmL 94, WhoFI 94*
Rounsaville, Guy, Jr. 1943- *WhoAmL 94*
Rounsaville, Lucious Brown, Jr. 1954- *WhoBlA 94*
Rounseville, Robert d1974 *WhoHol 92*
Rounsley, Robert Richard 1931- *WhoMW 93*
Rountree, Asa 1927- *WhoAm 94*
Rountree, Ella Jackson 1936- *WhoBlA 94*
Rountree, George Denton 1937- *WhoAm 94*
Rountree, Herbert Horton 1921- *WhoAmP 93*
Rountree, Janet Caryl 1937- *WhoAm 94*
Rountree, Linda Sue 1947- *WhoMW 93*
Rountree, Louise M. 1921- *WhoBlA 94*
Rountree, Owen 1932- *WrDr 94*
Rountree, Peter Charles Robert 1936- *Who 94*
Rountree, Ruthann Louise 1950- *WhoWest 94*
Rountree, Thomas J. 1927- *WrDr 94*
Rountree, William Clifford 1941- *WhoAmP 93*
Rountree, William M. 1917- *WhoAmP 93*
Roupe, James Paul 1957- *WhoFI 94*
Roupp, Albert Allen 1930- *WhoMW 93*
Roura, Andrés 1937- *WhoHisp 94*
Rourk, Christopher John 1962- *WhoScEn 94*
Rourke, Arlene Carol 1944- *WhoFI 94*
Rourke, Michael James 1934- *WhoAm 94*
Rourke, Mickey 1954- *WhoHol 92*
Rourke, Mickey 1956- *IntMPA 94, WhoAm 94*
Rourke, Mickey (Philip Andre) 1955- *IntWW 93*
Rourke, Russell Arthur 1931- *WhoAmP 93*
Rourke, Stanley Andrew 1936- *WhoFI 94*
Rourke, Susan F. 1954- *WhoAmP 93*
Rous *Who 94*
Rous, Stephen N. 1931- *ConAu 141*
Rous, Stephen Norman 1931- *WhoAm 94, WhoScEn 94*
Rous, William (Edward) 1939- *Who 94*
Rousakis, John Paul 1929- *WhoAm 94, WhoAmP 93*
Rouse, Andrew Miles 1928- *WhoAm 94*
Rouse, Anthony (Gerald Roderick) 1911- *Who 94*
Rouse, Christopher Chapman, III 1949- *WhoAm 94*
Rouse, Donald E. 1932- *WhoBlA 94*
Rouse, Doris Jane 1948- *WhoAm 94*
Rouse, E(dward) Clive 1901- *Who 94*
Rouse, Elaine Burdett 1915- *WhoAmP 93*
Rouse, Eloise Meadows 1931- *WhoAm 94*
Rouse, Gene Gordon, Sr. 1923- *WhoBlA 94*
Rouse, Gerald Edward 1944- *WhoMW 93*
Rouse, Gregory Stanley 1954- *WhoFI 94*
Rouse, Hallock d1930 *WhoHol 92*
Rouse, Irene *DrAPF 93*
Rouse, Irving 1913- *IntWW 93, WhoAm 94, WhoScEn 94, WrDr 94*
Rouse, Jacqueline Anne 1950- *WhoBlA 94*
Rouse, Jeff *WhoAm 94*
Rouse, John Wilson, Jr. 1937- *WhoAm 94, WhoFI 94, WhoScEn 94*
Rouse, Joseph P. 1944- *WhoAmL 94*
Rouse, Margaret Othmer 1953- *WhoWest 94*
Rouse, Mary A(mes) 1934- *ConAu 141*
Rouse, Parke Shepherd, Jr. 1915- *WrDr 94*
Rouse, Richard Hunter 1933- *WhoAm 94*
Rouse, Richard James 1954- *WhoAmP 93*
Rouse, Robert Hunter 1940- *WhoAmP 93*
Rouse, Robert Moorefield 1936- *WhoScEn 94*
Rouse, Robert Sumner 1930- *WhoAm 94*
Rouse, Ronald W. 1948- *WhoAmL 94*
Rouse, Roscoe, Jr. 1919- *WhoAm 94*
Rouse, Roy Dennis 1920- *WhoAm 94*
Rouse, Simon *WhoHol 92*
Rouse, Terrie 1952- *WhoBlA 94*
Rouse, Terrie Suzitte 1952- *WhoAm 94*
Rouse, William Bradford 1947- *WhoAm 94*
Roush, George Jonathan 1937- *WhoFI 94*
Roush, J. Edward 1920- *WhoAmP 93*
Roush, Mildred Jessianna 1920- *WhoMW 93*
Roush, Nancy Schmidt 1951- *WhoAmL 94*
Roush, Phillip Henry 1931- *WhoMW 93*
Rouson, Lee 1962- *WhoBlA 94*
Rouss, Ruth 1914- *WhoAm 94, WhoAmL 94, WhoFI 94*
Roussakis, Nicolas 1934- *WhoAm 94*
Rousseau, Conrad Ernest, Jr. 1937- *WhoIns 94*
Rousseau, Eugene Ellsworth 1932- *WhoAm 94*
Rousseau, Eva Rice 1944- *WhoAm 94*
Rousseau, George S. 1941- *WrDr 94*
Rousseau, Irene Victoria *WhoAm 94, WhoAmA 93*
Rousseau, Jean-Baptiste 1671-1741 *NewGrDO*
Rousseau, Jean-Jacques 1712-1778 *BlmGEL, EncEth, GuFrLit 2, NewGrDO*
Rousseau, Lucien G., Jr. 1945- *WhoAmP 93*
Rousseau, Marcel Samuel *NewGrDO*
Rousseau, Mark Owen 1940- *WhoMW 93*
Rousseau, Paul Emile 1929- *Who 94*
Rousseau, Robert G. 1950- *WhoAmP 93*
Rousseau, Ronald William 1943- *WhoAm 94*
Rousseau, Serge *WhoHol 92*
Rousseau, Theodore, Jr. 1912-1974 *WhoAmA 93N*
Rousseau, Victor 1879-1960 *EncSF 93*
Rousseau-Vermette, Mariette *WhoAmA 93*
Roussel, Albert (Charles Paul Marie) 1869-1937 *NewGrDO*
Roussel, Claude Patrice 1930- *WhoAmA 93*
Roussel, Lee Dennison 1944- *WhoAm 94*
Roussel, (Philip) Lyon 1923- *Who 94*
Roussel, Myriem 1962- *WhoHol 92*
Roussel, Robert Walter 1916- *WhoAmL 94*
Rousselet, Andre Claude Lucien 1922- *IntWW 93*
Rousseliere, Charles 1875-1950 *NewGrDO*
Roussell, Norman 1934- *WhoBlA 94*
Rousselle, Regis 1948- *IntWW 93*
Rousselot, John Harbin 1927- *WhoAmP 93*
Rousselot, Peter F. 1942- *WhoAm 94*
Rousselot, Peter Frese 1942- *WhoAmL 94*
Rousselot, Philippe *ConTFT 11*
Rousselot, Philippe 1945- *IntMPA 94*
Rousseu, Marie Christine *WhoHol 92*
Roussey, Robert Stanley 1935- *WhoAm 94*
Roussin, Andre d1987 *WhoHol 92*
Roussin, Michael 1939- *IntWW 93*
Rousso, Eli L. 1920- *WhAm 10*
Roussos, Stavros G. 1918- *Who 94*
Roustan, Yvon Dominique 1944- *WhoAmL 94*
Rout, Owen Howard 1930- *Who 94*
Routbort, Jules Lazar 1937- *WhoScEn 94*
Router, Paul Getty 1942- *WhoWest 94*
Routh, Donald Kent 1937- *WhoAm 94*
Routh, Donald Thomas 1936- *Who 94*
Routh, Francis John 1927- *WrDr 94*
Routh, John William 1957- *WhoAmL 94*
Routh, Joseph Isaac 1910- *WhoScEn 94*
Routh, Joseph P. 1893- *WhAm 10*
Routhier, Maurice 1913- *WhoAmP 93*
Routien, John Broderick 1913- *WhoAm 94*
Routledge, Alan 1919- *Who 94*
Routledge, Alison *WhoHol 92*
Routledge, Patricia 1929- *WhoHol 92*
Routledge, (Katherine) Patricia 1929- *Who 94*
Routon, David F. 1931- *WhoAmA 93*
Routson, Clell Dennis 1946- *WhoFI 94*
Routson, Samuel John 1949- *WhoAmP 93*
Routsong, Alma 1924- *GayLL*
Routte-Gomez, Eneid G. 1944- *WhoBlA 94*
Routti, Jorma Tapio 1938- *WhoScEn 94*
Rouvel, Catherine *WhoHol 92*
Rouvelas, Emanuel Larry 1944- *WhoAm 94, WhoAmL 94*
Rouverol, Jean *WhoHol 92*
Rouvillois, Philippe Andre Marie 1935- *IntWW 93, WhoScEn 94*
Rouw, Carla Sue Roberts 1968- *WhoMW 93*
Roux, Ambroise Marie Casimir 1921- *IntWW 93, WhoAm 94*
Roux, Bernard Georges Marie 1934- *IntWW 93*
Roux, David Gerhardus 1920- *IntWW 93*
Roux, Jacques 1907- *IntWW 93*
Roux, Jean-Louis 1923- *IntWW 93*
Roux, John *DrAPF 93*
Roux, Joseph Edward 1958- *WhoAm 94*
Roux, Michel 1924- *NewGrDO*
Roux, Michel Andre 1941- *Who 94*
Roux, Tony d1976 *WhoHol 92*
Roux, Vincent J. 1937- *WhoBlA 94*
Rouxel, Jean 1935- *IntWW 93*
Rouze, Jeffrey Alan 1952- *WhoFI 94, WhoMW 93*
Rovak, Stephen H. 1948- *WhoAmL 94*
Rove, Karl Christian 1950- *WhoAmP 93*
Rove, Olaf N(orberg) 1898- *WhAm 10*
Rovelstad, Mathilde Verner 1920- *WhoAm 94*
Rovelstad, Trygue A. d1990 *WhoAmA 93N*
Rovensky, Joseph d1937 *WhoHol 92*

Rover, Constance Mary 1910- *WrDr 94*
Rover, Edward Frank 1938- *WhoAm 94*
Rovere, Agostino 1804-1865 *NewGrDO*
Rovere, Gina *WhoHol 92*
Roveri, Ermanno d1968 *WhoHol 92*
Rovetta, Giovanni 1596?-1668 *NewGrDO*
Rovetti, Paul F. 1939- *WhoAmA 93*
Rovettino, Giovanni Battista *NewGrDO*
Rovine, Arthur William 1937- *WhoAm 94, WhoAmL 94*
Rovinsky, Joseph Judah 1927- *WhoAm 94*
Rovira, Joachim Jack 1945- *WhoHisp 94*
Rovira, Lois Ann 1937- *WhoAmP 93*
Rovira, Luis D. 1923- *WhoAmP 93, WhoHisp 94*
Rovira, Luis Dario 1923- *WhoAm 94, WhoAmL 94, WhoWest 94*
Rovira, Maritza *WhoHisp 94*
Rovira, Martino Francisco 1940- *WhoHisp 94*
Rovison, John Michael, Jr. 1959- *WhoScEn 94*
Rovit, Earl *DrAPF 93*
Rovit, Earl 1927- *WrDr 94*
Rovner, Arkady *DrAPF 93*
Rovner, David Richard 1930- *WhoAm 94*
Rovner, Ilana Kara Diamond 1938- *WhoAm 94, WhoAmL 94, WhoMW 93*
Rovner, Jack Alan 1946- *WhoAm 94*
Row, David 1949- *WhoAmA 93*
Row, John Alfred 1905- *Who 94*
Row, Peter L. *WhoAm 94*
Rowallan, Baron d1993 *Who 94N*
Rowallan, Baron 1947- *Who 94*
Rowan, Albert T. 1927- *WhoBlA 94*
Rowan, Andrew Nicholas 1946- *WhoScEn 94*
Rowan, Carl Thomas 1925- *AfrAmAl 6 [port], BlkWr 2, Who 94, WhoAm 94, WhoBlA 94*
Rowan, Dan d1987 *WhoHol 92*
Rowan, Dan 1922-1987
See Rowan and Martin *WhoCom*
Rowan, Danielle *IntMPA 94*
Rowan, Deirdre 1930- *WrDr 94*
Rowan, Dennis Michael 1938- *WhoAmA 93*
Rowan, Don d1966 *WhoHol 92*
Rowan, Edward Beatty 1898-1946 *WhoAmA 93N*
Rowan, Frances Physioc 1908- *WhoAmA 93*
Rowan, Gerald Burdette 1916- *WhoAm 94*
Rowan, Herman 1923- *WhoAmA 93*
Rowan, Hester 1928- *WrDr 94*
Rowan, John Patrick 1945- *WhoAmP 93*
Rowan, John Robert 1919- *WhoAm 94*
Rowan, M(arie) M. 1943- *WrDr 94*
Rowan, Patricia Adrienne *Who 94*
Rowan, (C.) Patrick 1937- *WhoAmA 93*
Rowan, Pelham Agee 1931-1983 *WhAm 10*
Rowan, Rena Jung 1928- *WhoAm 94*
Rowan, Richard Lamar 1931- *WhoAm 94*
Rowan, Ronald Thomas 1941- *WhoWest 94*
Rowan and Martin *WhoCom*
Rowand, Joseph Donn 1942- *WhoAmA 93*
Rowand, Nada *WhoHol 92*
Rowan-Legg, Allan Aubrey 1912- *Who 94*
Rowantree, Karen Smiley 1947- *WhoAmA 93*
Rowark, Maureen 1933- *WhoAm 94, WhoMW 93*
Rowat, Donald C(ameron) 1921- *ConAu 42NR, WrDr 94*
Rowbotham, Bill *ConTFT 11*
Rowbotham, David (Harold) 1924- *WrDr 94*
Rowbotham, Sheila 1943- *WrDr 94*
Rowcroft, Charles 1795?-1856 *EncSF 93*
Rowden, Gwen Alison 1954- *WhoAmL 94*
Rowden, Marcus Aubrey 1928- *WhoAm 94, WhoAmL 94*
Rowden, Todd Andrew 1964- *WhoAmL 94*
Rowden, William Henry 1930- *WhoAm 94*
Rowder, William Louis 1937- *WhoAm 94*
Rowe, Adrian Harold Redfern 1925- *Who 94*
Rowe, Albert P. 1934- *WhoBlA 94*
Rowe, Albert Prince 1934- *WhoAmP 93*
Rowe, Allan Duncan 1951- *WhoAm 94*
Rowe, Alvin George 1933- *WhoScEn 94*
Rowe, Andrew 1935- *Who 94*
Rowe, Anne E. 1944- *WhoAmP 93*
Rowe, Arthur Edgar 1929- *WhoAm 94, WhoFI 94*
Rowe, Bridget 1950- *Who 94*
Rowe, C(hristopher) J(ames) 1944- *WrDr 94*
Rowe, Carl Osborn 1944- *WhoFI 94, WhoWest 94*
Rowe, Carol Lipinsky 1957- *WhoAm 94*
Rowe, Charles Alfred 1934- *WhoAm 94, WhoAmA 93*
Rowe, Charles Spurgeon 1925- *WhoAm 94*
Rowe, Christa F. 1959- *WhoBlA 94*
Rowe, Clair Devere 1924- *WhoAm 94*
Rowe, Clarence John 1916- *WhoAm 94*
Rowe, Colon Harvey, Jr. 1939- *WhoAmP 93*
Rowe, Corinne d1965 *WhoAmA 93N*
Rowe, David John 1936- *WhoAm 94*
Rowe, David Winfield 1954- *WhoAmL 94*
Rowe, Donald A. 1937- *WhoAm 94*
Rowe, Donald Edward 1929- *WhAm 10*
Rowe, Donald Francis 1941- *WhoMW 93*
Rowe, Doug(las) *WhoHol 92*
Rowe, Earl *WhoHol 92*
Rowe, Elizabeth (Singer) 1674-1737 *BlmGWL*
Rowe, Evelyn Karla 1943- *WhoFI 94*
Rowe, Frances d1988 *WhoHol 92*
Rowe, G. Steven *WhoAmP 93*
Rowe, Gail Stuart 1936- *WhoWest 94*
Rowe, George Giles 1921- *WhoAm 94*
Rowe, Gilbert Thomas 1942- *WhoScEn 94*
Rowe, Greg *WhoHol 92*
Rowe, Guy 1894-1969 *WhoAmA 93N*
Rowe, Harris 1923- *WhoAmP 93*
Rowe, Harrison Edward 1927- *WhoAm 94, WhoScEn 94*
Rowe, Helen *Who 94*
Rowe, Herbert Joseph 1924- *WhoAm 94*
Rowe, Jack D. 1947- *WhoAmL 94*
Rowe, Jack Field 1927- *WhoAm 94*
Rowe, James A. 1950- *WhoMW 93*
Rowe, James Jefferson 1950- *WhoAmP 93*
Rowe, James W. 1923- *WhoAm 94, WhoFI 94*
Rowe, Jasper C. 1945- *WhoBlA 94*
Rowe, Jay E., Jr. 1947- *WhoScEn 94*
Rowe, Jeremy 1928- *Who 94*
Rowe, Jimmy L. 1932- *WhoBlA 94*
Rowe, John Howland 1918- *WhoAm 94*
Rowe, John Jermyn 1936- *Who 94*
Rowe, John Wallis 1944- *WhoAm 94*
Rowe, John Westel 1924- *WhoAm 94*
Rowe, John William 1945- *WhoAm 94, WhoFI 94*
Rowe, Jonathan Dale 1954- *WhoAmL 94*
Rowe, Joseph Everett 1927- *WhoAm 94, WhoScEn 94*
Rowe, Kathleen M. *WhoFI 94*
Rowe, Kevin S. 1938- *WhoAm 94*
Rowe, Kristin Carter 1965- *WhoAmL 94*
Rowe, Lee Allen 1936- *WhoMW 93*
Rowe, Mae Irene 1927- *WhoMW 93*
Rowe, Marilyn Johnson 1954- *WhoBlA 94*
Rowe, Marjorie Douglas 1912- *WhoWest 94*
Rowe, Mary Sue 1940- *WhoFI 94, WhoWest 94*
Rowe, Matthew John 1966- *WhoFI 94*
Rowe, Max L. 1921- *WhoAm 94*
Rowe, Misty 1950- *WhoHol 92*
Rowe, Nansi Irene 1940- *WhoBlA 94*
Rowe, Nathaniel Hawthorne 1931- *WhoAm 94*
Rowe, Nicholas 1674-1718 *BlmGEL, IntDcT 2*
Rowe, Nicholas 1966- *WhoHol 92*
Rowe, Norbert Edward 1898- *Who 94*
Rowe, Owen John Tressider 1922- *Who 94*
Rowe, Patrick Barton 1939- *Who 94*
Rowe, Peter Grimmond 1945- *WhoAm 94*
Rowe, Peter Noel 1919- *Who 94*
Rowe, Peter Wentworth 1935- *WhoAmL 94*
Rowe, Peter Whitmill 1928- *Who 94*
Rowe, Prentiss d1989 *WhoHol 92*
Rowe, Randall Keith 1954- *WhoFI 94*
Rowe, Reginald M. 1920- *WhoAmA 93*
Rowe, Richard Brian 1933- *Who 94*
Rowe, Richard Edwin 1944- *WhoAmL 94*
Rowe, Richard Holmes 1937- *WhoAm 94*
Rowe, Richard L. 1926- *WhoBlA 94*
Rowe, Richard Lloyd 1926- *WhoAm 94*
Rowe, Richard R. 1933- *WhoAm 94*
Rowe, Robb Wendal 1939- *WhoFI 94*
Rowe, Robert Hetsley 1929- *WhoFI 94, WhoWest 94*
Rowe, Robert Stewart 1920- *Who 94*
Rowe, Roy 1905- *IntMPA 94*
Rowe, Roy Ernest 1929- *Who 94*
Rowe, Stephen Ashford 1953- *WhoAmL 94*
Rowe, Stephen Cooper 1951- *WhoScEn 94*
Rowe, Thomas Dudley, Jr. 1942- *WhoAm 94*
Rowe, Vern d1981 *WhoHol 92*
Rowe, William (Neil) 1942- *WrDr 94*
Rowe, William Davis 1937- *WhoAm 94*
Rowe, William John 1936- *WhoAm 94*
Rowe, William L. S. 1948- *WhoAmL 94*
Rowe, William Leon 1915- *WhoBlA 94*
Rowe, William Westel 1953- *WhoWest 94*
Rowe-Ham, David (Kenneth) 1935- *IntWW 93, Who 94*
Rowell, A. Hoyt, III 1948- *WhoAmL 94*
Rowell, Anthony Aylett 1937- *Who 94*
Rowell, Charles Frederick 1935- *WhoAm 94*
Rowell, Douglas Geoffrey 1943- *WrDr 94*
Rowell, Edward Leonidas 1928- *WhoAmP 93*
Rowell, Edward Morgan 1931- *WhoAm 94, WhoAmP 93*
Rowell, (Douglas) Geoffrey 1943- *Who 94*
Rowell, George 1923- *WrDr 94*
Rowell, James Victor 1939- *WhoAmP 93*
Rowell, John (Joseph) 1916- *Who 94*
Rowell, John Martin 1935- *Who 94*
Rowell, John Thomas 1920- *WhoScEn 94*
Rowell, Katherine Renee 1964- *WhoMW 93*
Rowell, Lester John, Jr. 1932- *WhoFI 94*
Rowell, Margit *WhoAmA 93*
Rowe-Maas, Betty Lu 1925- *WhoFI 94*
Rowen, Carol Lorraine 1934- *WhoFI 94*
Rowen, Harold Charles 1931- *WhoFI 94*
Rowen, Harvey Allen 1943- *WhoFI 94*
Rowen, Henry Stanislaus 1925- *WhoAm 94*
Rowen, Herbert H(arvey) 1916- *WrDr 94*
Rowen, Hobart 1918- *WhoAm 94, WhoFI 94*
Rowen, Marshall *WhoAm 94, WhoWest 94*
Rowen, Robert Bernard, Jr. 1950- *WhoFI 94*
Rowen, Robert G. *WhoAm 94, WhoFI 94*
Rowen, Ruth Halle 1918- *WhoAm 94*
Rowena 1944- *EncSF 93*
Rower, Ann *DrAPF 93*
Rowett, Helen (Graham Quiller) 1915- *WrDr 94*
Rowitz, Louis 1937- *WhoMW 93*
Rowland, Adele d1971 *WhoHol 92*
Rowland, Anne *WhoAmA 93*
Rowland, Arthur Ray 1930- *WhoAm 94, WrDr 94*
Rowland, Benjamin J. R. 1904-1972 *WhoAmA 93N*
Rowland, Christopher Charles 1947- *Who 94*
Rowland, David *Who 94*
Rowland, (John) David 1933- *Who 94*
Rowland, David Jack 1921- *WhoAm 94, WhoFI 94*
Rowland, David Powys 1917- *Who 94*
Rowland, Donald S(ydney) 1928- *EncSF 93*
Rowland, Donald Winslow 1898- *WhAm 10*
Rowland, Doyle Alfred 1938- *WhoAm 94, WhoAmL 94*
Rowland, Elden Hart 1915-1982 *WhoAmA 93N*
Rowland, Esther Edelman 1926- *WhoAm 94*
Rowland, Frank C. 1951- *WhoAmL 94*
Rowland, Frank Sherwood 1927- *EnvEnc, IntWW 93, WhoAm 94, WhoScEn 94, WhoWest 94*
Rowland, Helen *WhoScEn 94*
Rowland, Henry d1984 *WhoHol 92*
Rowland, Herbert Leslie 1925- *WhoAm 94*
Rowland, Howard Ray 1929- *WhoMW 93*
Rowland, Iris 1925- *WrDr 94*
Rowland, Ivan Wendell 1910- *WhoAm 94*
Rowland, J(ohn) R(ussell) 1925- *WrDr 94*
Rowland, J. Roy 1926- *CngDr 93*
Rowland, James (Anthony) 1922- *Who 94*
Rowland, James Anthony 1922- *IntWW 93*
Rowland, James Brian 1946- *WhoMW 93*
Rowland, James H. 1909- *WhoBlA 94*
Rowland, James Richard 1940- *WhoAm 94*
Rowland, James Roy, Jr. 1926- *WhoAmP 93*
Rowland, James Roy Roy 1926- *WhoAm 94*
Rowland, John Arthur 1943- *WhoAm 94, WhoAmL 94*
Rowland, John David 1933- *IntWW 93*
Rowland, John Grosvenor 1957- *WhoAmP 93*
Rowland, John Russell 1925- *IntWW 93*
Rowland, Karen Bailey 1957- *WhoFI 94*
Rowland, Kirk Robin 1960- *WhoFI 94*
Rowland, Landon Hill 1937- *WhoAm 94, WhoFI 94, WhoMW 93*
Rowland, Larry Girard 1946- *WhoFI 94*
Rowland, Lewis Phillip 1925- *WhoAm 94*
Rowland, Peter Kenneth 1938- *WrDr 94*
Rowland, Ralph Thomas 1920- *WhoAm 94*
Rowland, Robert Charles 1946- *WhoScEn 94*
Rowland, Robert Todd 1922- *Who 94*
Rowland, Robin F. 1950- *WrDr 94*
Rowland, Roland W. 1917- *IntWW 93*
Rowland, Ronald Lee 1947- *WhoAm 94, WhoAmL 94*
Rowland, Ronald Wayne 1948- *WhoFI 94*
Rowland, Roy 1902- *IntMPA 94*
Rowland, Ruth Gailey 1922- *WhoWest 94*
Rowland, Steve *WhoHol 92*
Rowland, Susan Blake 1946- *WhoWest 94*
Rowland, Theodore Justin 1927- *WhoAm 94*
Rowland, Thomas William 1948- *WhoFI 94*
Rowland, Walter Speed 1939- *WhoFI 94*
Rowlands, Art d1944 *WhoHol 92*
Rowlands, David *WhoHol 92*
Rowlands, David 1947- *Who 94*
Rowlands, David Thomas 1930- *WhoAm 94*
Rowlands, Edward 1940- *Who 94*
Rowlands, Gena 1934- *IntMPA 94*
Rowlands, Gena 1936- *WhoAm 94, WhoHol 92*
Rowlands, George 1932- *WhoScEn 94*
Rowlands, John (Samuel) 1915- *Who 94*
Rowlands, John Henry Lewis 1947- *Who 94*
Rowlands, John Kendall 1931- *Who 94*
Rowlands, June *WhoAm 94*
Rowlands, Lady *WhoHol 92*
Rowlands, Maldwyn Jones 1918- *Who 94*
Rowlands, Martin *Who 94*
Rowlands, (John) Martin 1925- *Who 94*
Rowlands, Martyn Omar 1923- *Who 94*
Rowlands, Marvin Lloyd, Jr. 1926- *WhoAm 94*
Rowlands, Patsy 1935- *WhoHol 92*
Rowlands, Robert Edward 1936- *WhoAm 94*
Rowlandson, Mary White c. 1636-1678? *BlmGWL*
Rowlenson, Richard Charles 1949- *WhoFI 94*
Rowles, Arlene Beverly 1935- *WhoMW 93*
Rowles, Deirdre Kay 1961- *WhoMW 93*
Rowles, Polly 1914- *WhoHol 92*
Rowlett, Ralph Morgan 1934- *WhoAm 94*
Rowley, Beverley Davies 1941- *WhoAm 94, WhoFI 94*
Rowley, Charles (Robert) 1926- *Who 94*
Rowley, Christopher (B.) 1948- *EncSF 93*
Rowley, Evelyn Fish 1927- *WhoAmP 93*
Rowley, Frank Selby, Jr. 1913- *WhoAm 94*
Rowley, Frederick Allan 1922- *Who 94*
Rowley, Geoffrey Herbert 1935- *WhoFI 94*
Rowley, Geoffrey William 1926- *Who 94*
Rowley, Glenn Harry 1948- *WhoAmL 94*
Rowley, James J. 1908-1992 *AnObit 1992*
Rowley, James J(oseph) 1908-1992 *CurBio 93N*
Rowley, James Robert 1943- *WhoAm 94*
Rowley, Janet Davison 1925- *WhoAm 94*
Rowley, John c. 1668-1728 *DcNaB MP*
Rowley, John Charles 1919- *Who 94*
Rowley, John F. *WhoFI 94*
Rowley, John H. 1917- *IntMPA 94*
Rowley, John Vincent d'Alessio 1907- *Who 94*
Rowley, Joshua c. 1730-1790 *WhAmRev*
Rowley, Joshua Francis 1920- *Who 94*
Rowley, Kathryn S. 1942- *WhoAm 94*
Rowley, Peter 1918- *Who 94*
Rowley, Peter DeWitt 1942- *WhoWest 94*
Rowley, Peter Templeton 1929- *WhoAm 94*
Rowley, (Richard) Trevor 1942- *WrDr 94*
Rowley, William 1585-1637 *BlmGEL*
Rowley, William Dean 1939- *WhoWest 94*
Rowley, William Robert 1943- *WhoAm 94, WhoWest 94*
Rowley, Worth 1916-1988 *WhAm 10*
Rowley-Conwy *Who 94*
Rowley Hill, George Alfred *Who 94*
Rowling, Wallace (Edward) 1927- *Who 94*
Rowling, Wallace Edward 1927- *IntWW 93*
Rowlings, Donald George 1929- *WhoAm 94*
Rowlingson, John Clyde 1948- *WhoAm 94*
Rowlinson, John Shipley 1926- *IntWW 93, Who 94*
Rownd, Robert Harvey 1937- *WhoScEn 94*
Rowney, John Adalbert 1945- *WhoIns 94*
Rowntree, Derek (G. F.) 1936- *WrDr 94*
Rowntree Clifford, Paul *Who 94*
Rowny, Lieut.-Gen. 1917- *IntWW 93*
Rowny, Edward Leon 1917- *WhoAmP 93*
Rowse, A(lfred) L(eslie) 1903- *WrDr 94*
Rowse, Alfred Leslie 1903- *IntWW 93, Who 94*
Rowsell, Edmund Lionel P. *Who 94*
Rowsey, Sharon Easthom 1962- *WhoAmL 94*
Rowson, John Anthony 1930- *Who 94*
Rowson, Richard Cavanagh 1926- *WhoAm 94*
Rowson, Susanna Haswell 1762-1824 *BlmGWL*
Rowthorn, Robert Eric 1939- *Who 94*
Rowton, Cary Blaine 1965- *WhoMW 93*
Roxanne *WhoHol 92*
Roxas, Savina *DrAPF 93*
Roxbee Cox *Who 94*
Roxborough, Mildred 1927- *WhoBlA 94*
Roxburgh, Iain Edge 1943- *Who 94*
Roxburgh, Ian Walter 1939- *Who 94*
Roxburgh, James William 1921- *Who 94*

Roxburgh, John (Charles Young) 1919- Who 94
Roxburghe, Duke of 1954- Who 94
Roxey, Timothy Errol 1950- WhoScEn 94
Roxin, Emilio Oscar 1922- WhoAm 94
Roy, Americus Melvin 1929- WhoBlA 94
Roy, Andrew Donald 1920- Who 94
Roy, Ann Lee 1936- WhoAmP 93
Roy, Archie 1924- EncSF 93
Roy, Archie E. 1924- WrDr 94
Roy, Armand Joseph 1942- WhoAm 94
Roy, Arthur Douglas 1925- Who 94
Roy, Asim 1948- WhoFI 94
Roy, Bill, Jr. 1954- WhoAmP 93
Roy, Bimalendu Narayan WhoScEn 94
Roy, Binota d1978 WhoHol 92
Roy, Catherine Elizabeth 1948- WhoAm 94, WhoWest 94
Roy, Chunilal 1935- WhoAm 94, WhoScEn 94, WhoWest 94
Roy, Claude 1915- IntWW 93
Roy, David P. 1951- WhoFI 94
Roy, David Tod 1933- WhoAm 94
Roy, Derek d1981 WhoHol 92
Roy, Dev Kumar 1951- WhoAsA 94
Roy, Donald Anthony 1965- WhoFI 94
Roy, Elsijane Trimble 1916- WhoAm 94, WhoAmL 94
Roy, Emile Joseph 1920- WhoAmP 93
Roy, Francis Charles 1926- WhoScEn 94
Roy, Gabriel Delvis 1939- WhoScEn 94
Roy, Gabrielle 1909-1983 BlmGWL
Roy, Gloria WhoHol 92
Roy, Harold Edward 1921- WhoFI 94, WhoScEn 94, WhoWest 94
Roy, Harry d1971 WhoHol 92
Roy, Henri A. 1947- WhoFI 94
Roy, Ian 1912- Who 94
Roy, Jacqueline 1954- BlkWr 2, SmATA 74 [port]
Roy, Jahar d1977 WhoHol 92
Roy, James (Henry Barstow) 1922- WrDr 94
Roy, James De Wall 1940- WhoFI 94
Roy, James Stapleton WhoAmP 93
Roy, James Stapleton 1935- WhoAm 94
Roy, Jasper K. WhoBlA 94
Roy, John d1975 WhoHol 92
Roy, John Willie WhoBlA 94
Roy, Jules 1907- IntWW 93
Roy, Karen Mary 1953- WhoScEn 94
Roy, Kenneth Russell 1946- WhoScEn 94
Roy, Melinda WhoAm 94
Roy, P. Norman 1934- WhoAm 94, WhoFI 94
Roy, Patrick 1965- News 94-2 [port], WhoAm 94
Roy, Paul Emile, Jr. 1942- WhoFI 94, WhoMW 93
Roy, Paul Henri 1924- WhoAm 94
Roy, Pierre-Charles 1683-1764 NewGrDO
Roy, Pradip Kumar 1943- WhoAsA 94
Roy, Radha Raman 1921- WhoAm 94
Roy, Ram Mohan 1772-1833 HisWorL [port]
Roy, Ramendra Prasad 1942- WhoWest 94
Roy, Ranjit Kumar 1947- WhoMW 93
Roy, Raymond 1919- WhoWest 94
Roy, Raymond Albert, Jr. 1954- WhoWest 94
Roy, Richard WhoAmP 93
Roy, Richard E. 1939- WhoAm 94, WhoAmL 94
Roy, Richard James 1944- WhoAmL 94
Roy, Rob J. 1933- WhoScEn 94
Roy, Robert Gould 1946- WhoFI 94
Roy, Robert Russell 1957- WhoMW 93
Roy, Robin K. 1959- WhoScEn 94
Roy, Roger P. 1940- WhoAmP 93
Roy, Ronald Aurele 1956- WhoWest 94
Roy, Rustum 1924- WhoAm 94, WhoScEn 94
Roy, Sheila 1948- Who 94
Roy, Stephen Donald 1951- WhoMW 93
Roy, Tuhin Kumar 1923- WhoScEn 94
Roy, William Robert 1926- WhoAmP 93
Royal, H.R.H. The Princess 1950- IntWW 93
Royal, Princess 1950- Who 94R
Royal, A. Richard 1939- WhoAmP 93
Royal, Allan 1944- WhoHol 92
Royal, Ann WhoHol 92
Royal, Brian James EncSF 93
Royal, C. Charles, Sr. WhoBlA 94
Royal, Charles d1955 WhoHol 92
Royal, Dan 1928- WrDr 94
Royal, Darrell K. 1924- WhoAm 94
Royal, James E. 1941- WhoBlA 94
Royal, Richard M. 1935- WhoIns 94
Royal, Richard P. WhoAmA 93
Royal, Rosamond ConAu 140
Royal, Rosamund WrDr 94
Royal, Segolene 1953- WhoWomW 91
Royal, Segolene 1954- IntWW 93
Royal, Selvin Wayne 1941- WhoAm 94
Royal, William Henry 1924- WhoMW 93
Royall, Kenneth Claiborne, Jr. 1918- WhoAmP 93
Royalty, Kenneth M. 1940- WhoAm 94
Royalty, Kenneth Marvin 1940- WhoAmL 94
Royalty, Robert Alan 1966- WhoFI 94
Royalty, Robert Malcolm 1933- WhAm 10
Roy-Arcelin, Nicole WhoWomW 91
Roybal, Dolores E. 1953- WhoHisp 94
Roybal, Edward R. 1916- WhoAm 94, WhoAmP 93, WhoHisp 94
Roybal-Allard, Lucille 1941- CngDr 93, WhoAm 94, WhoAmP 93, WhoHisp 94, WhoWest 94
Roy-Burman, Pradip 1938- WhoAsA 94, WhoWest 94
Royce, Barrie Saunders Hart 1933- WhoAm 94
Royce, Brigham d1939 WhoHol 92
Royce, David Nowill 1920- Who 94
Royce, E.R. EncSF 93
Royce, Ed 1951- CngDr 93
Royce, Edward R. 1951- WhoAm 94, WhoAmP 93, WhoWest 94
Royce, Frederick Henry 1934- WhoAmP 93
Royce, Frosty d1965 WhoHol 92
Royce, H. Charles 1932- WhoAmP 93
Royce, James E. 1914- WrDr 94
Royce, (Roger) John 1944- Who 94
Royce, Josiah 1855-1916 DcAmReB 2, EncEth
Royce, Julian d1946 WhoHol 92
Royce, Kenneth 1920- WrDr 94
Royce, Lionel d1946 WhoHol 92
Royce, Marie Therese Porter 1961- WhoWest 94
Royce, Paul C. 1928- WhoAm 94
Royce, Raymond Watson 1936- WhoAm 94
Royce, Riza d1980 WhoHol 92
Royce, Ruth d1971 WhoHol 92
Royce, Suzanne 1935- WhoAmA 93
Royce, Virginia d1962 WhoHol 92
Royce, William Calvin, III 1948- WhoAm 94
Roychoudhuri, Chandrasekhar 1942- WhoScEn 94
Roycroft, Howard Francis 1930- WhoAm 94
Royde, Frank 1882- WhoHol 92
Roy de Clotte le Barillier, Berthe 1868-1927 BlmGWL
Royden, Christopher (John) 1937- Who 94
Royden, Halsey Lawrence 1928- WhoAm 94
Royds, John Caress 1920- Who 94
Royds, Robert Bruce 1944- WhoScEn 94
Roye, Monica R. Hargrove 1955- WhoBlA 94
Roye, Phillip WhoHol 92
Royer, Alphonse 1803-1875 NewGrDO
Royer, Bill D. 1929- WhoAmP 93
Royer, Charles Theodore 1939- WhoAmP 93
Royer, Clemence 1830-1902 BlmGWL
Royer, David Bruce 1941- WhoMW 93
Royer, David Lee 1950- WhoIns 94
Royer, Donald E. 1949- WhoFI 94
Royer, Harry d1951 WhoHol 92
Royer, Jean 1920- IntWW 93
Royer, Jean Alice 1947- WhoMW 93
Royer, Joseph-Nicolas-Pancrace c. 1705-1755 NewGrDO
Royer, Marilyn Ann 1948- WhoFI 94
Royer, Mona Lee 1944- WhoAmA 93
Royer, Raymond WhoAm 94, WhoFI 94
Royer, Robert Lewis 1928- WhoAm 94
Royer, Ronald Alan 1945- WhoScEn 94
Royer, Theodore Henry 1936- WhoAmP 93
Royer, Thomas Jerry 1943- WhoFI 94
Royko, Mike 1922- WrDr 94
Royko, Mike 1932- WhoAm 94, WhoMW 93
Royle Who 94
Royle, Guinevere Eve 1960- WhoAmL 94
Royle, Roger Michael 1939- Who 94
Royle, Selena d1983 WhoHol 92
Royle, Timothy Lancelot Fanshawe 1931- Who 94
Royle, William d1940 WhoHol 92
Royo Sanchez, Aristides 1940- IntWW 93
Roysam, Badrinath 1961- WhoScEn 94
Royse, John Anthony 1898- WhAm 10
Royse, Mary Kay 1949- WhoAmL 94, WhoMW 93
Royse, Sue Marion 1944- WhoMW 93
Roysher, Hudson (Brisbine) 1911- WhoAmA 93
Royster, Darryl 1954- WhoAm 94, WhoMW 93
Royster, Don M., Sr. 1944- WhoBlA 94
Royster, George Durward, Jr. 1941- WhoAmL 94
Royster, James Edgar 1933- WhoMW 93
Royster, Philip M. WhoBlA 94
Royster, Vermont 1914- WrDr 94
Royster, Vermont Connecticut 1914- IntWW 93, WhoAm 94
Royster, Vivian Hall 1951- WhoBlA 94
Royston, H. James 1951- WhoWest 94
Royston, Ivor 1945- WhoScEn 94
Royston, Richard John 1931- WhoAm 94
Royston, Roy d1976 WhoHol 92
Royton, Verna d1974 WhoHol 92
Rozakis, Gregory d1989 WhoHol 92
Rozanov, Evgeny Grigorevich 1925- IntWW 93
Rozanska, Elektra d1978 WhoHol 92
Rozanski, Stanley Howard 1952- WhoAmL 94
Rozario, Michael Who 94
Rozas, Carlos Luis 1944- WhoHisp 94
Roze, Marie (Hippolyte) 1846-1926 NewGrDO
Roze, Mathieu WhoHol 92
Roze, Uldis 1938- WhoScEn 94
Rozel, Samuel Joseph 1935- WhoAm 94, WhoAmL 94
Rozell, Herbert J. 1931- WhoAmP 93
Rozell, Joseph Gerard 1959- WhoMW 93
Rozell, William Barclay 1943- WhoAmL 94
Rozelle, Lee Theodore 1933- WhoAm 94
Rozelle, Mark Albert 1960- WhoFI 94
Rozelle, Pete ProFbHF [port]
Rozelle, Pete 1926- WhoAm 94
Rozema, Harold Alden 1929- WhoWest 94
Rozen, Jerome George, Jr. 1928- WhoAm 94
Rozen, Yegor Fyodorovich 1800-1860 NewGrDO
Rozenberg, Michael Albert 1949- WhoIns 94
Rozenbergs, John 1948- WhoScEn 94
Rozenfeld, Gregory 1946- WhoScEn 94
Rozenman, Lior 1968- WhoWest 94
Rozenthal, Baron de WhAmRev
Rozes, Simone 1920- IntWW 93
Rozewicz, Tadeusz 1921- ConWorW 93, IntDcT 2, IntWW 93
Rozga, Margaret 1945- WhoMW 93
Rozhdestvensky, Gennadi Nikolaevich 1991- Who 94
Rozhdestvensky, Gennadiy Nikolayevich 1931- IntWW 93
Rozhdestvensky, Gennady (Nikolayevich) 1931- NewGrDO
Rozhdestvensky, Robert Ivanovich 1932- IntWW 93
Rozier, Gilbert Donald 1940- WhoBlA 94
Rozier, Jackson Evander, Jr. 1936- AfrAmG [port]
Rozier, Mike 1961- WhoBlA 94
Rozier, Robert L. WhoAmA 93
Roziner, Felix (Yakovlevich) 1936- ConAu 142
Rozinsky, John Paul 1938- WhoFI 94
Rozkosny, Josef Richard 1833-1913 NewGrDO
Rozman, Gilbert Friedell 1943- WhoAm 94
Rozman, Joseph John 1944- WhoAmA 93
Rozman, Karl Karoly 1945- WhoMW 93
Rozman, Kimberlee Kline 1960- WhoAmL 94
Rozmiarek, Mildred Irene 1917- WhoAmP 93
Rozmus, Karen Janet 1952- WhoMW 93
Rozof, Phyllis Claire 1948- WhoAm 94, WhoAmL 94
Rozov, Viktor Sergeevich 1913- IntWW 93
Rozovsky, Mark Grigorievich 1937- IntWW 93
Rozran, Jack Louis 1939- WhoFI 94, WhoMW 93
Rozsa, Miklos 1907- IntDcF 2-4 [port], IntMPA 94, IntWW 93, WhoAm 94
Rozsnyai, Zoltan Frank 1927-1990 WhAm 10
Rozycki, Ludomir 1884-1953 NewGrDO
Rozzell, Scott Ellis 1949- WhoAm 94, WhoAmL 94
Rozzi (James A.) 1921- WhoAmA 93
R. R. ConAu 42NR
Ru, Wesley 1954- WhoAsA 94
Rua, Milton Juan 1946- WhoAmP 93
Ruan, Ju-Ai 1959- WhoScEn 94
Ruan Chongwu 1933- IntWW 93, WhoPRCh 91 [port]
Ruane, J. Michael WhoAmP 93
Ruane, Joseph Edward 1929- WhoIns 94
Ruane, Thomas D. 1950- WhoAmL 94
Ruano, Araceli 1971- WhoHisp 94
Ruano, Jorge J. 1966- WhoHisp 94
Ruano, Jose WhoHisp 94
Ruano, William J. 1908- WhoAmL 94
Ruan Ruolin WhoPRCh 91
Ruark, Gibbons DrAPF 93
Ruark, Mary Lynn 1948- WhoAmP 93
Ruark, Robert d1965 WhoHol 92
Ruaux, Gillian Doreen 1945- Who 94
Rub, Christian d1956 WhoHol 92
Rub, Louis John 1915- WhoAm 94
Rubach, Peggy 1947- WhoWomW 91
Rubacha, Walter Edward 1948- WhoMW 93
Rubano, Richard Frank 1946- WhoScEn 94
Rubayi, Salah 1942- WhoWest 94
Rubbert, Paul Edward 1937- WhoScEn 94
Rubbia, Carlo 1934- IntWW 93, Who 94, WhoAm 94, WhoScEn 94, WorScD
Rubel, Arthur Joseph 1924- WhoAm 94
Rubel, C. Adrian 1904-1978 WhoAmA 93N
Rubel, Edwin W 1942- WhoScEn 94
Rubeli, Paul E. 1943- WhoFI 94, WhoWest 94
Rubell, Maria WhoHol 92
Rubello, David Jerome 1935- WhoAm 94, WhoAmA 93
Ruben, Alan Miles 1931- WhoAm 94
Ruben, Albert 1918- WhoAmA 93
Ruben, Brent David 1944- WhoAm 94
Ruben, Gary A. 1924- WhoAm 94
Ruben, Ida Gass 1929- WhoAmP 93
Ruben, J. Walter d1941 WhoHol 92
Ruben, Jose d1969 WhoHol 92
Ruben, Joseph HorFD [port]
Ruben, Joseph 1951- IntMPA 94
Ruben, Laurens Norman 1927- WhoScEn 94
Ruben, Lawrence 1926- WhoAm 94
Ruben, Leonard 1921- WhoAm 94
Ruben, Richard S. 1950- WhoAmL 94
Ruben, Richards 1925- WhoAm 94, WhoAmA 93
Ruben, Robert Joel 1933- WhoAm 94, WhoScEn 94
Ruben, Robert Joseph 1923- WhoAm 94
Ruben, William S. EncSF 93
Ruben, William Samuel 1927- WhoAm 94
Rubendall, Howard Lane 1910-1991 WhAm 10
Rubendall, Richard Arthur 1957- WhoScEn 94, WhoWest 94
Rubenfeld, Stanley Irwin 1930- WhoAm 94
Rubens, Alma d1931 WhoHol 92
Rubens, Bernice 1928- BlmGWL, WrDr 94
Rubens, Bernice Ruth Who 94
Rubens, Bernice Ruth 1928- IntWW 93
Rubens, Jeffrey David 1958- WhoFI 94
Rubens, Robert David 1943- WhoScEn 94
Rubens, Sidney Michel 1910- WhoAm 94
Rubens, William Stewart 1927- WhoAm 94
Rubenson, Daniel Leon 1953- WhoFI 94
Rubenstein, Alan 1955- WhoFI 94
Rubenstein, Arthur Harold 1937- WhoAm 94, WhoScEn 94
Rubenstein, Bernard 1937- WhoAm 94
Rubenstein, Bonnie Sue 1961- WhoMW 93
Rubenstein, Carol DrAPF 93
Rubenstein, Edward 1924- IntWW 93, WhoAm 94
Rubenstein, Eli 1949- WhoAmL 94
Rubenstein, Eric Davis 1952- WhoFI 94, WhoMW 93
Rubenstein, Farrell 1930- WhoAm 94
Rubenstein, Harry d1993 NewYTBS 93
Rubenstein, Howard Joseph 1932- WhoAm 94
Rubenstein, Ida d1960 WhoHol 92
Rubenstein, Irwin 1931- WhoMW 93
Rubenstein, James A. 1948- WhoAmL 94
Rubenstein, James Michael 1944- WhoFI 94
Rubenstein, Jerome Max 1927- WhoAm 94
Rubenstein, Joshua Seth 1954- WhoAm 94, WhoAmL 94
Rubenstein, Leonard Samuel 1918- WhoWest 94
Rubenstein, Lewis W. 1908- WhoAmA 93
Rubenstein, Meridel 1948- WhoAmA 93
Rubenstein, Paul D. 1946- WhoAmL 94
Rubenstein, Richard E. 1938- WrDr 94
Rubenstein, Richard Lowell 1924- WhoAm 94, WrDr 94
Rubenstein, Stanley Ellis 1930- WhoAm 94
Rubenstein, Steven Paul 1951- WhoAm 94
Rubeor, Roger Frank 1947- WhoFI 94
Ruberti, Antonio 1927- Who 94
Rubertino, Maria Luisa 1962- BlmGWL
Ruberto, Michael J. 1944- WhoAmL 94
Rubery, Eileen Doris 1943- Who 94
Rubes, Jan WhoHol 92
Rubes, Susan WhoHol 92
Rubey, Tony (George Anton) 1952- WhoAmA 93
Rubia Barcia, Jose 1914- ConAu 41NR
Rubiano-Groot, Alfonso 1921- WhoHisp 94
Rubik, Beverly Anne 1951- WhoScEn 94
Rubik, Erno 1944- IntWW 93
Rubiks, Alfreds Petrovich 1935- IntWW 93
Rubin, Abe 1911-1990 WhAm 10

Ruddick, Nicholas 1952- *ConAu 142*
Ruddick, Stephen Richard 1954- *WhoWest 94*
Ruddick, Steve 1954- *WhoAmP 93*
Rudd-Jones, Derek 1924- *Who 94*
Ruddle, Francis Hugh 1929- *IntWW 93*
Ruddley, John 1912- *WhoAmA 93*
Rudd-Moore, Dorothy 1940- *WhoBlA 94*
Ruddock, Joan Mary 1943- *IntWW 93, Who 94, WhoWomW 91*
Ruddock, John 1897- *WhoHol 92*
Ruddon, Raymond Walter, Jr. 1936- *WhoAm 94*
Ruddy, Albert S. 1934- *IntMPA 94*
Ruddy, Christine Marie 1961- *WhoMW 93*
Ruddy, Frank S. 1937- *WhoAm 94, WhoAmL 94*
Ruddy, Frank Stephen 1937- *WhoAmP 93*
Ruddy, James W. 1949- *WhoAmL 94*
Ruddy, William George 1937- *WhoAmL 94*
Rude, Alfred Lyman 1958- *WhoAmP 93*
Rude, Brian David 1955- *WhoAmP 93, WhoMW 93*
Rude, Chester A. 1895- *WhAm 10*
Rude, George d1993 *NewYTBS 93*
Rude, George F(rederick) E(lliot) 1910-1993 *ConAu 140*
Rude, George Frederic Elliot d1993 *IntWW 93N*
Rude, George Frederick Elliot d1993 *Who 94N*
Rudee, Mervyn Lea 1935- *WhoAm 94, WhoWest 94*
Rudel, Allen Dale 1932- *WhoFI 94*
Rudel, Julius 1921- *NewGrDO, WhoAm 94*
Rudel, Lawrence Lee 1941- *WhoAm 94*
Rudelius, William 1931- *WhoAm 94*
Rudell, Michael I. 1943- *WhoAmL 94*
Rudell, Milton Wesley 1920- *WhoAm 94*
Rudell, Robert Allan 1948- *WhoFI 94*
Rudenko, Bela (Andreyevna) 1933- *NewGrDO*
Rudenko, Yuri Nikolayevitch 1931- *IntWW 93*
Rudenstine, Angelica Zander *WhoAmA 93*
Rudenstine, Neil Leon 1935- *IntWW 93, Who 94, WhoAm 94*
Ruder, Brian 1954- *WhoFI 94*
Ruder, David S. 1929- *WhoAmP 93*
Ruder, David Sturtevant 1929- *WhoAm 94*
Ruder, Lois Jean Rodriguez 1951- *WhoHisp 94*
Ruder, Melvin Harvey 1915- *WhoAm 94, WhoWest 94*
Ruder, William 1921- *WhoAm 94, WhoFI 94*
Ruderman, Armand Peter 1923- *WhoAm 94*
Ruderman, Jerold R. 1943- *WhoAmL 94*
Ruderman, Ronald 1943- *WhoFI 94*
Ruders, Poul 1949- *NewGrDO*
Rudersdorff, Hermine 1822-1882 *NewGrDO*
Rudert, Cynthia Sue 1955- *WhoScEn 94*
Rudge, Alan Walter 1937- *Who 94*
Rudge, William Edwin, IV 1939- *WhoScEn 94, WhoWest 94*
Rudholm, Sten 1918- *IntWW 93*
Rudhyar, Dane d1985 *WhoHol 92*
Rudhyar, Dane 1895- *WhAm 10*
Rudhyar, Dane 1895-1985 *AstEnc*
Rudicel, Chandler Clifton 1905- *WhoAmP 93*
Rudie, Evelyn *IntMPA 94*
Rudie, Evelyn 1947- *WhoHol 92*
Rudin, Alfred 1924- *WhoScEn 94*
Rudin, Anne 1924- *WhoAmP 93, WhoWomW 91*
Rudin, Anne Noto 1924- *WhoAm 94, WhoWest 94*
Rudin, Scott *NewYTBS 93 [port], WhoAm 94*
Rudin, Scott 1958- *IntMPA 94*
Rudin, Toni Richard Perrott 1934- *Who 94*
Ruding, H. O. (Onno) 1939- *IntWW 93*
Ruding, Herman Onno 1939- *WhoAm 94, WhoFI 94*
Rudinger, Joel *DrAPF 93*
Rudini, Gen. 1929- *IntWW 93*
Rudins, Leonids 1928- *WhoFI 94*
Rudinsky, Alexander John 1957- *WhoWest 94*
Rudisill, Barbara Stevenson 1943- *WhoAmL 94*
Rudisill, Richard 1932- *WhoWest 94*
Rudisill, Robert Mack, Jr. 1945- *WhoAm 94, WhoAmL 94*
Rudi Ubeda, Luisa Fernanda 1950- *WhoWomW 91*
Rudkin, David 1936- *BlmGEL*
Rudkin, (James) David 1936- *ConDr 93, IntDcT 2 [port], Who 94, WrDr 94*
Rudkin, Walter Charles 1922- *Who 94*
Rudkin, Yury Dmitrievich 1951- *LngBDD*
Rudland, Margaret Florence 1945- *Who 94*
Rudley, Herbert 1911- *WhoHol 92*
Rudlin, David Alan 1947- *WhoAm 94, WhoAmL 94*
Rudloe, Jack 1943- *WrDr 94*
Rudloff, Hans-Jorg 1940- *Who 94*
Rudloff, William Joseph 1941- *WhoAmL 94*
Rudman, Edward Irving 1937- *WhoFI 94*
Rudman, Herbert Charles 1923- *WhoAm 94*
Rudman, Jeffrey B. 1948- *WhoAm 94, WhoAmL 94*
Rudman, Joan (Combs) 1927- *WhoAmA 93*
Rudman, Mark *DrAPF 93*
Rudman, Michael Edward 1939- *Who 94*
Rudman, Michael P. 1950- *WhoAm 94*
Rudman, Paul L. *WhoAmP 93*
Rudman, Paul Lewis 1935- *WhoAmL 94*
Rudman, Solomon Kal 1930- *WhoAm 94*
Rudman, Warren B. 1930- *WhoAmP 93*
Rudman, Warren Bruce 1930- *IntWW 93, WhoAm 94*
Rudner, Rita 1955- *WhoCom*
Rudner, Rita 1956- *WhoHol 92*
Rudner, Sara 1944- *WhoAm 94*
Rudney, Harry 1918- *WhoAm 94*
Rudnick, Alan A. *WhoAmL 94, WhoFI 94*
Rudnick, Ellen Ava *WhoAm 94*
Rudnick, Irene K. 1929- *WhoAmP 93*
Rudnick, Lawrence 1949- *WhoMW 93*
Rudnick, Marvin Jack 1948- *WhoFI 94*
Rudnick, Paul David 1940- *WhoAm 94*
Rudnick, Rebecca Sophie 1952- *WhoAmL 94, WhoMW 93*
Rudnick, Robert Alan 1948- *WhoAm 94*
Rudnicki, John Walter 1951- *WhoMW 93*
Rudnik, Raphael *DrAPF 93*
Rudnyk, Marian E. 1960- *WhoScEn 94*
Rudo, Milton 1919- *WhoAm 94*
Rudoe, Wulf 1916- *Who 94*
Rudoff, Sheldon 1933- *WhoAm 94*
Rudolf, Anthony 1942- *WrDr 94*
Rudolf, Jacob P. *WhoAmP 93*
Rudolf, Leslie E. 1927-1990 *WhAm 10*
Rudolf, Max 1902- *NewGrDO, WhoAm 94*
Rudolf, Philip Reinhold 1955- *WhoScEn 94*
Rudolf, Robert John 1933- *WhoFI 94*
Rudolf of Habsburg, I 1218-1291 *HisWorL [port]*
Rudolf von Ems c. 1200-c. 1254 *DcLB 138 [port]*
Rudolph, Abraham Morris 1924- *WhoAm 94*
Rudolph, Alan 1943- *IntMPA 94*
Rudolph, Andrew Henry 1943- *WhoScEn 94*
Rudolph, Arnold Jack 1918- *WhoAm 94*
Rudolph, Brian Albert 1961- *WhoScEn 94*
Rudolph, Deborah Ann 1958- *WhoFI 94*
Rudolph, Frederick 1920- *WhoAm 94*
Rudolph, Frederick Byron 1944- *WhoScEn 94*
Rudolph, Frederick William 1929- *WhoAm 94*
Rudolph, Gilbert Lawrence 1946- *WhoAm 94*
Rudolph, Jeffrey Stewart 1942- *WhoScEn 94*
Rudolph, Lavere Christian 1921- *WhoAm 94*
Rudolph, Lee *DrAPF 93*
Rudolph, Lloyd Irving 1927- *WhoAm 94*
Rudolph, Malcolm Rome 1924- *WhoAm 94*
Rudolph, Marshall Skaggs 1965- *WhoAmL 94*
Rudolph, Max Joseph 1961- *WhoMW 93*
Rudolph, Michael c. 1754-c. 1794 *WhAmRev*
Rudolph, Oscar d1991 *WhoHol 92*
Rudolph, Paul Marvin 1918- *IntWW 93*
Rudolph, Ronald Alvin 1949- *WhoFI 94, WhoWest 94*
Rudolph, Susanne Hoeber 1930- *WhoAm 94*
Rudolph, Thomas Keith 1961- *WhoWest 94*
Rudolph, Wallace Morton 1930- *WhoAm 94*
Rudolph, Walter Burnham 1946- *WhoWest 94*
Rudolph, Walter Paul 1937- *WhoWest 94*
Rudolph, Wilma 1940- *AfrAmAl 6*
Rudolph, Wilma Glodean 1940- *WhoBlA 94*
Rudomin, Esther 1930- *WrDr 94*
Rudowski, Witold Janusz 1918- *IntWW 93*
Rudoy, Joshua *WhoHol 92*
Rudquist, Jerry Jacob 1934- *WhoAmA 93*
Rudrum, Alan (William) 1932- *WrDr 94*
Rudstein, David Stewart 1946- *WhoAm 94*
Ru Dusky, Basil Michael 1933- *WhoAm 94*
Rudwall, David Fuller 1953- *WhoAmL 94*
Rudy, C. Guy 1936- *WhoAmP 93*
Rudy, David Robert 1934- *WhoAm 94*
Rudy, Dorothy *DrAPF 93*
Rudy, Elmer Clyde 1931- *WhoAmL 94*
Rudy, Lester Howard 1918- *WhoAm 94*
Rudy, Raymond Bruce, Jr. 1931- *WhoAm 94*
Rudy, Ruth Corman 1938- *WhoAmP 93*
Rudy, Sharon Ruth *WhoAmL 94*
Rudy, Thomas James 1948- *WhoWest 94*
Rudy, Willis 1920- *WhoAm 94, WrDr 94*
Rudyerd, John fl. 1703- *DcNaB MP*
Rudzinski, Kenneth William 1947- *WhoFI 94*
Rudzinski, Witold 1913- *IntWW 93, NewGrDO*
Rudzinski, Zbigniew 1935- *NewGrDO*
Rudzki, Eugeniusz Maciej 1914- *WhoScEn 94*
Rudzki, Robert A. 1953- *WhoFI 94*
Rue, Fabrice Louis 1954- *WhoAmL 94*
Rue, Leonard Lee, III 1926- *WrDr 94*
Rue, Robert Reeve 1948- *WhoFI 94*
Rue, (Elsie) Rosemary 1928- *Who 94*
Rueb, Richard V., Sr. 1939- *WhoAm 94*
Ruebe, Bambi Lynn 1957- *WhoWest 94*
Ruebhausen, Oscar Melick 1912- *WhoAm 94*
Ruebusch, Ronald Raymond 1949- *WhoFI 94*
Rueck, Jon Michael 1940- *WhoAm 94*
Rueckert, Roland Rudyard 1931- *WhoAm 94*
Rued, Dave *WhoAmP 93*
Rueda, Alfonso 1940- *WhoWest 94*
Rueda-Garcia, Ana Isabel 1950- *WhoHisp 94*
Rueden, Henry Anthony 1949- *WhoMW 93*
Ruedenberg, Klaus 1920- *WhoAm 94, WhoScEn 94*
Ruef, John Samuel 1927- *WrDr 94*
Rueff, Margaret Lillian 1922- *WhoAmP 93*
Ruefle, Mary *DrAPF 93*
Rueger, Daniel Scott 1957- *WhoMW 93*
Rueger, Lauren John 1921- *WhoAm 94*
Ruegg, Annelise 1879-1934 *BlmGWL*
Ruegg, Curtis Landon 1962- *WhoWest 94*
Ruegg, Donald George 1924- *WhoAm 94*
Ruegg, Stephen Lawrence 1959- *WhoMW 93, WhoScEn 94*
Ruegger, Philip Theophil, III 1949- *WhoAm 94*
Ruegsegger, Donald Ray, Jr. 1942- *WhoMW 93*
Ruehl, Franklin Robert, Jr. *WhoWest 94*
Ruehl, Mercedes *IntMPA 94, WhoAm 94*
Ruehl, Mercedes 1954- *WhoHol 92*
Ruehlmann, Virginia Juergens 1924- *WhoMW 93*
Ruehmann, Heinz 1902-
See Ruhmann, Heinz 1902- & Ruehmann, Heinz 1902- *WhoHol 92*
Ruehmann, Heinz 1902- *WhoHol 92*
Ruelas, Abraham Antonio 1952- *WhoHisp 94*
Ruell, Patrick 1936- *WrDr 94*
Ruellan, Andre *EncSF 93*
Ruellan, Andree 1905- *WhoAm 94, WhoAmA 93*
Ruelle, David Pierre 1935- *IntWW 93, WhoScEn 94*
Ruello, Samuel Angus 1931- *WhoAm 94*
Rueppel, Merrill Clement 1925- *WhoWest 94*
Rueppell, Gary Edward 1943- *WhoAmL 94*
Ruesch, Janet Carol 1943- *WhoAm 94, WhoAmL 94*
Ruesch, Margaret Ann 1950- *WhoMW 93*
Ruesch, Stephen W. 1951- *WhoWest 94*
Ruesink, Albert William 1940- *WhoAm 94*
Ruetenik, Ted Allen 1949- *WhoFI 94*
Ruether, Rosemary Radford 1936- *IntWW 93, WrDr 94*
Ruetschi, Paul 1925- *WhoScEn 94*
Ruettino, Giovanni Battista *NewGrDO*
Ruetz, Kathleen M. 1955- *WhoMW 93*
Ruf, Harold William, Jr. 1934- *WhoAmL 94, WhoMW 93*
Ruf, Jacob Frederick 1936- *WhoScEn 94*
Rufa, Robert Henry 1943- *WhoAm 94*
Rufe, Redding Kane 1930- *WhoAm 94*
Ruff, Candy *WhoAmP 93*
Ruff, Charles F. C. 1939- *WhoAm 94*
Ruff, Dureen Anne 1931- *WhoMW 93*
Ruff, Edward Joseph 1915- *WhoAmL 94*
Ruff, Frank Miller, Jr. 1949- *WhoAmP 93*
Ruff, Howard Joseph 1930- *WhoAm 94, WhoWest 94*
Ruff, Jamie Carless 1962- *WhoBlA 94*
Ruff, Julius Ralph 1946- *WhoMW 93*
Ruff, Lorraine Marie 1947- *WhoFI 94*
Ruff, Robert Louis 1950- *WhoMW 93, WhoScEn 94*
Ruff, Ronald Armin 1941- *WhoAmP 93*
Ruffalo, Alan Michael 1943- *WhoWest 94*
Ruffelle, Frances 1966- *WhoAm 94*
Ruffer, David Gray 1937- *WhoAm 94*
Ruffer, Michael R. *WhoAm 94, WhoFI 94*
Ruffin, Benjamin F. 1941- *WhoBlA 94*
Ruffin, Edmund 1794-1865 *AmSocL*
Ruffin, George 1834-1886 *AfrAmAl 6*
Ruffin, Herbert 1940- *WhoBlA 94*
Ruffin, James E. 1937- *WhoBlA 94*
Ruffin, Janice E. 1942- *WhoBlA 94*
Ruffin, John 1943- *WhoBlA 94*
Ruffin, John H., Jr. 1934- *WhoBlA 94*
Ruffin, John Walter, Jr. 1941- *WhoBlA 94*
Ruffin, Paul *DrAPF 93*
Ruffin, Richard D. 1924- *WhoBlA 94*
Ruffing, Anne Elizabeth *WhoAm 94, WhoAmA 93*
Ruffini, Attilio 1924- *IntWW 93*
Ruffini, Giovanni d1993 *NewYTBS 93*
Ruffini, Giovanni 1807-1881 *NewGrDO*
Ruffini, James *DrAPF 93*
Ruffini, Richard John 1954- *WhoMW 93*
Ruffini, Sandro d1954 *WhoHol 92*
Ruffini, Stephen Charles 1959- *WhoFI 94*
Ruffins, Reynolds 1930- *WhoBlA 94*
Ruffle, John Frederick 1937- *WhoAm 94*
Ruffle, Mary *Who 94*
Ruffner, Charles Louis 1936- *WhoAmL 94*
Ruffner, Frederick G., Jr. 1926- *WhoAm 94*
Ruffner, Ginny Martin *WhoAm 94*
Ruffner, Ginny Martin 1952- *WhoAmA 93*
Ruffner, Jay Sturgis 1941- *WhoAm 94*
Ruffner, Ray P. 1946- *WhoBlA 94*
Ruffo, Joseph Martin 1941- *WhoAmA 93*
Ruffo, Tito d1953 *WhoHol 92*
Ruffo, Titta 1877-1953 *NewGrDO*
Ruffolo, Giorgio 1926- *IntWW 93*
Ruffolo, Lisa M. *DrAPF 93*
Ruffolo, Paul Gregory 1952- *WhoMW 93*
Ruffus, Stephen *DrAPF 93*
Rufien, Paul Charles 1964- *WhoAmL 94*
Ruflin, Paul Leroy 1954- *WhoAm 94*
Rufner, Richard Kevin 1947- *WhoAmL 94*
Rufolo, Anthony Michael 1948- *WhoWest 94*
Rufus *WhoHol 92*
Rugaber, Walter Feucht, Jr. 1938- *WhoAm 94*
Rugai, Ginger *WhoAmP 93*
Rugambwa, Laurean 1912- *IntWW 93, Who 94*
Ruganda, John 1941- *ConDr 93*
Rugarli, Giampaolo 1932- *IntWW 93*
Rugby, Baron 1951- *Who 94*
Ruge, Daniel August 1917- *WhoAm 94*
Ruge, Michael Helmuth 1962- *WhoFI 94*
Ruge, Neil Marshall 1913- *WhoAm 94, WhoWest 94*
Rugeley, Henry *WhAmRev*
Rugenstein, Robert Wayne 1921- *WhoWest 94*
Ruger, J. Thompson d1993 *NewYTBS 93*
Ruger, William Batterman 1916- *WhoAm 94, WhoFI 94*
Rugeroni, Ian *WhoAm 94*
Rugge, Henry Ferdinand 1936- *WhoAm 94, WhoScEn 94*
Rugge, Hugo Robert 1935- *WhoAm 94, WhoScEn 94*
Rugge, Sue 1941- *WhoWest 94*
Rugge-Price, Charles Keith Napier *Who 94*
Ruggera, Paul Stephen 1944- *WhoScEn 94*
Ruggeri, Robert Edward 1952- *WhoAmL 94*
Ruggeri, Ruggero d1953 *WhoHol 92*
Ruggeri, Zaverio Marcello 1945- *WhoWest 94*
Ruggerio, Dominick J. 1948- *WhoAmP 93*
Ruggero, Mario Alfredo 1943- *WhoMW 93*
Ruggieri, Bernard J. 1926- *WhoAm 94*
Ruggieri, Giovanni Maria fl. c. 1689-1720 *NewGrDO*
Ruggieri, Helen *DrAPF 93*
Ruggiero, Anthony William 1941- *WhoAm 94, WhoFI 94*
Ruggiero, Joseph A. 1943- *WhoAmP 93*
Ruggiero, Laurence J. 1948- *WhoAmA 93*
Ruggiero, Laurence Joseph 1948- *WhoAm 94*
Ruggiero, Matthew John 1932- *WhoAm 94*
Ruggiero, Renato 1930- *IntWW 93*
Ruggiero, Richard S. 1944- *WhoAmP 93*
Ruggiero, Thomas William 1946- *WhoAm 94, WhoAmL 94*
Ruggill, Solomon P. 1906- *WhoAm 94, WhoWest 94*
Ruggles, Carl (Sprague) 1876-1971 *NewGrDO*
Ruggles, Catherine Joan 1953- *WhoWest 94*

Rupp, Daniel Gabriel 1936- WhoFI 94
Rupp, Elaine Helen 1944- WhoMW 93
Rupp, George Erik 1942- NewYTBS 93 [port], WhoAm 94
Rupp, Glenn N. 1944- WhoFI 94
Rupp, James H. 1918- WhoAmP 93
Rupp, James M. 1935- WhoAm 94
Rupp, James M. 1952- ConAu 142
Rupp, Jean Louise 1943- WhoFI 94, WhoWest 94
Rupp, John Norris 1913- WhoAm 94
Rupp, John Peter 1944- WhoAm 94, WhoAmL 94
Rupp, Lee 1938- WhoAmP 93
Rupp, Leila Jane 1950- WhoMW 93
Rupp, Nelson W., Jr. 1949- WhoAmL 94
Rupp, Ralph Russell 1929- WhoAm 94
Rupp, Richard H. 1934- WrDr 94
Rupp, Sheron Adeline 1943- WhoAm 94, WhoAmA 93
Rupp, Sieghardt WhoHol 92
Rupp, William John 1927- WhoAm 94
Ruppar, Peter Geoffrey 1944- WhoAmL 94
Ruppe, Loret Miller 1936- WhoAm 94, WhoAmP 93
Ruppel, David John 1962- WhoMW 93
Ruppel, Dennis G. 1946- WhoAmL 94
Ruppel, Edward Thompson 1925- WhoScEn 94, WhoWest 94
Ruppel, George Robert 1911- WhoAm 94
Ruppel, William J. WhoAmP 93
Ruppenthal, Karl M(axwell) 1917- WrDr 94
Ruppersberg, Allen 1944- WhoAmA 93
Ruppert, Chester EncSF 93
Ruppert, James DrAPF 93
Ruppert, John Lawrence 1953- WhoAm 94, WhoAmL 94
Ruppert, Paul Richard 1958- WhoFI 94
Ruppert, Rupert Earl 1943- WhoAmP 93
Ruppin, Virginia Mildred 1932- WhoMW 93
Ruprecht, G. Steven 1948- WhoAmL 94
Ruprecht, (Josef) Martin c. 1758-1800 NewGrDO
Ruprecht, Mary Margaret 1934- WhoAmP 93
Ruprecht, Thomas G. 1941- WhoIns 94
Rusak, Halina R. WhoAmA 93
Rusan, Otilia Valeria ConWorW 93
Rusanen, Pirjo Maija 1940- WhoWomW 91
Rusaw, Sally Ellen 1939- WhoAm 94
Rusbridge, Brian John 1922- Who 94
Rusbridger, James 1928- WrDr 94
Rusby, Cameron 1926- Who 94
Ruscello, Anthony 1965- WhoScEn 94
Rusch, Hugh Leonard 1902- WhoAm 94
Rusch, Jonathan Jay 1952- WhoAmL 94
Rusch, Kristine Kathryn 1960- EncSF 93
Rusch, Thomas William 1946- WhoAm 94, WhoMW 93
Rusch, William Graham 1937- WhoAm 94
Ruscha, Edward 1937- WhoAm 94
Ruscha, Edward Joseph 1937- IntWW 93, WhoAmA 93
Rusche-Endorf, Cacilie 1873-1939 NewGrDO
Ruscio, Al WhoHol 92
Ruscio, Elizabeth WhoHol 92
Rusconi, Louis Joseph 1926- WhoScEn 94, WhoWest 94
Ruse, Gary Alan 1946- EncSF 93
Ruse, Paul W., Jr. 1943- WhoAmP 93
Ruse, Steven Douglas 1950- WhoAm 94
Rusen, Paul D. 1935- WhoAmP 93
Rush, Aiken P., Jr. 1939- WhoIns 94
Rush, Andrew 1931- WhoAmA 93
Rush, Andrew Wilson 1931- WhoAm 94, WhoWest 94
Rush, Anna Laura 1917- WhoWest 94
Rush, Barbara 1927- IntMPA 94, WhoHol 92
Rush, Benjamin 1745-1813 AmSocL, HisWorL
Rush, Benjamin 1746-1813 AmRev, DcAmReB 2, EncSPD, WhAmRev
Rush, Bobby 1946- CngDr 93, WhoAm 94, WhoAmP 93, WhoBlA 94
Rush, Bobby L. 1946- WhoMW 93
Rush, Brian Paul 1958- WhoAmP 93
Rush, Christopher 1944- WrDr 94
Rush, David 1934- WhoAm 94
Rush, Deborah WhoHol 92
Rush, Deborah 1952- WhoAmA 93
Rush, Domenica Marie 1937- WhoWest 94
Rush, Fletcher Grey, Jr. 1917- WhoAm 94, WhoAmL 94
Rush, Francis Roberts 1916- Who 94
Rush, Fred Williard 1929- WhoWest 94
Rush, Gary Alfred 1935- WhoWest 94
Rush, George fl. c. 1760-1780 NewGrDO
Rush, Herman 1929- IntMPA 94
Rush, Herman E. 1929- WhoAm 94, WhoWest 94
Rush, Hubert Michael 1946- WhoWest 94
Rush, Hugh D. 1926- WhoAmP 93
Rush, J. Richard 1918- WhoMW 93
Rush, Jean C. 1933- WhoAmA 93
Rush, Jeffrey Robert 1950- WhoAm 94, WhoAmL 94
Rush, Jon N. 1935- WhoAmA 93
Rush, Kenneth 1910- IntWW 93, WhoAm 94, WhoAmP 93
Rush, Kenneth G. 1930- WhoAmL 94
Rush, Kent Thomas 1948- WhoAmA 93
Rush, Norman 1933- WhoAm 94
Rush, Patricia WhoMW 93
Rush, Peter 1949- WhoAm 94
Rush, Philip 1908- WrDr 94
Rush, Richard 1930- IntMPA 94
Rush, Richard Henry 1915- WhoAm 94
Rush, Richard P. 1945- WhoAm 94
Rush, Richard R. WhoMW 93
Rush, Sonya C. 1959- WhoBlA 94
Rush, Stephen Kenneth 1942- WhoAmL 94
Rush, Vickie Lynn 1954- WhoMW 93
Rush, William 1919- WhoAmP 93
Rush, William John 1936- WhoAm 94
Rushbrooke, G(eorge) Stanley 1915- Who 94
Rushdie, Salman 1947- BlmGEL [port], News 94-1 [port], WrDr 94
Rushdie, (Ahmed) Salman 1947- EncSF 93, IntWW 93, Who 94
Rushdy, Ahmed 1924- IntWW 93
Rushen, Patrice WhoBlA 94
Rusher, David Lynn 1939- WhoWest 94
Rusher, Del F. 1941- WhoMW 93
Rusher, Derwood H., II 1954- WhoAmL 94
Rusher, William Allen 1923- WhoAm 94, WrDr 94
Rushfelt, Gerald Lloyd 1929- WhoAm 94, WhoAmL 94
Rushford, Antony Redfern Who 94
Rushford, Eloise Johnson WhoFI 94, WhoMW 93
Rushforth, Brenda Lea 1960- WhoWest 94
Rushing, Byron 1942- WhoAmP 93
Rushing, Byron D. 1942- WhoBlA 94
Rushing, Don G. 1948- WhoAmL 94
Rushing, George A. WhoBlA 94
Rushing, Jane Gilmore 1925- WhoAm 94, WrDr 94
Rushing, Jimmy d1972 WhoHol 92
Rushing, Jimmy 1903-1972 AfrAmAl 6
Rushing, Michele Renee 1965- WhoMW 93
Rushing, Roy Eugene 1943- WhoFI 94
Rushmer, Estella Dixie Virginia 1919- WhoWest 94
Rushmer, Robert F(razer) 1914- WrDr 94
Rushmore, Karen WhoHol 92
Rushmore, Stephen 1945- WhoAm 94
Rushnell, Squire Derrick 1938- WhoAm 94
Rushout, John 1769-1859 DcNaB MP
Rushton, Allan Crockett 1939- WhoAmP 93
Rushton, Brian Mandel 1933- WhoAm 94
Rushton, Ian Lawton 1931- Who 94
Rushton, Jared 1974- WhoHol 92
Rushton, Julian (Gordon) 1941- NewGrDO, WrDr 94
Rushton, Robert Archie 1943- WhoAmP 93
Rushton, William 1937- WhoHol 92
Rushton, William (George) 1937- WrDr 94
Rushton, William George 1937- Who 94
Rushton, William James, III 1929- WhoAm 94, WhoFI 94, WhoIns 94
Rushworth, (Frank) Derek 1920- Who 94
Rushworth, Robert Aitken 1924- WhoAm 94
Rusin, Edward A. 1922- WhoAm 94
Rusina, Frederick C. 1943- WhoAmL 94
Rusinek, Michal 1904- IntWW 93
Rusinko, Susan 1922- WrDr 94
Rusk, David Patrick 1940- WhoAmP 93
Rusk, Dean 1909- HisWorL, HisDcKW, IntWW 93, Who 94, WhoAm 94
Rusk, (David) Dean 1909- ConAu 141
Rusk, Howard A. 1901-1989 WhAm 10
Rusk, Jeffrey Ellis 1958- WhoAmL 94
Rusk, Karla Marie 1956- WhoMW 93
Rusk, Robert F. WhoAmP 93
Ruska, Ernst WorInv
Ruska, Ernst d1988 NobelP 91N
Ruskan, Ronald Jan 1951- WhoAmP 93
Ruskey, John A. 1939- WhoAmL 94
Ruskiewicz, Elena Patrice 1966- WhoMW 93
Ruskin, John 1819-1900 BlmGEL
Ruskin, Joseph WhoHol 92
Ruskin, Joseph Richard 1924- WhoAm 94
Ruskin, Lewis J. 1905-1981 WhoAmA 93N
Ruskin, Mary Kathy 1953- WhoWest 94
Ruskin, Shimen d1976 WhoHol 92
Ruslanov, Sviatoslav 1937- WrDr 94
Rusler, Robert WhoHol 92
Rusmisel, Stephen R. 1946- WhoAm 94, WhoAmL 94
Rusnak, Martha Hendrick 1938- WhoMW 93
Rusnell, Joanne D. 1954- WhoAm 94
Ruspoli, Esmeralda WhoHol 92
Russ, Albert J. 1929- WhoAmP 93
Russ, Biff DrAPF 93
Russ, Cary 1948- WhoMW 93
Russ, Charles Paul, III 1944- WhoAmL 94
Russ, Daniel Christopher 1961- WhoWest 94
Russ, Edmond Vincent, Jr. 1944- WhoAm 94, WhoMW 93
Russ, Giannina 1878-1951 NewGrDO
Russ, James Matthias 1929- WhoAmL 94
Russ, Joanna 1937- BlmGWL, EncSF 93, GayLL, WhoAm 94, WrDr 94
Russ, Joseph, IV 1936- WhoAmP 93
Russ, Lavinia 1904-1992 SmATA 74
Russ, Lawrence DrAPF 93
Russ, Michael C. 1944- WhoAmL 94
Russ, Pola d1966 WhoHol 92
Russ, Ronny WhoHol 92
Russ, Stanley 1930- WhoAmP 93
Russ, Tim WhoHol 92
Russ, William WhoHol 92
Russe, Conrad Thomas Campbell 1954- WhoFI 94
Russek, Jorge WhoHol 92
Russek, Rita WhoHol 92
Russek, Trula Wells 1921- WhoAmP 93
Russel, Del 1952- WhoHol 92
Russel, Tony WhoHol 92
Russell Who 94
Russell, Earl 1937- Who 94
Russell, Alan James 1962- WhoScEn 94
Russell, Alan Keith 1932- Who 94
Russell, Albert d1929 WhoHol 92
Russell, Albert d1946 WhoHol 92
Russell, Albert Richard 1915-1989 WhAm 10
Russell, Alexander William 1938- Who 94
Russell, Allan David 1924- WhoAm 94
Russell, Allen Stevenson 1915- WhoAm 94
Russell, Andrew Milo 1948- WhoAm 94
Russell, Andrew Victor Manson 1949- Who 94
Russell, Andy 1920- WhoHol 92
Russell, Angela V. 1943- WhoWest 94
Russell, Angela Veta 1943- WhoAmP 93
Russell, Anna 1911- Who 94
Russell, Anthony John Who 94
Russell, Archibald (Edward) 1904- Who 94
Russell, Archibald Edward 1904- IntWW 93
Russell, Arthur Colin 1906- Who 94
Russell, Barbara Winifred 1910- Who 94
Russell, Bert 1956- WhoAmP 93
Russell, Bertrand (Arthur William) 1872-1970 EncEth, EncSF 93
Russell, Bertrand Arthur William 1872-1970 BlmGEL, WorScD
Russell, Betsy WhoHol 92
Russell, Beverly A. DrAPF 93
Russell, Beverly A. 1947- WhoBlA 94
Russell, Beverly Carradine, Jr. 1947- WhoAmP 93
Russell, Bill 1934- AfrAmAl 6, BasBi, WhoAm 94, WhoBlA 94, WhoWest 94
Russell, Bing WhoHol 92
Russell, Bradley Scott 1963- WhoAmL 94
Russell, Brenda Sue 1958- WhoMW 93
Russell, Brian Fitzgerald 1904- Who 94, WrDr 94
Russell, Brian Henderson 1951- WhoAm 94
Russell, Bruce Alexander 1903-1963 WhoAmA 93N
Russell, Bruce S. 1942- WhoAmL 94
Russell, Byron d1963 WhoHol 92
Russell, C. Edward, Jr. 1942- WhoAmL 94
Russell, Campy (Michael) 1952- WhoBlA 94
Russell, Carol Ann 1943- WhoFI 94, WhoWest 94
Russell, CarolAnn DrAPF 93
Russell, Carolyn WhoAmP 93
Russell, Cazzie 1944- BasBi, WhoBlA 94
Russell, Cecil Anthony Francis 1921- Who 94
Russell, Charles WhoHol 92
Russell, Charles Hinton 1903-1989 WhAm 10
Russell, Charles Ian 1918- Who 94
Russell, Charles Roberts 1914- WhoScEn 94
Russell, Charles S. 1926- WhoAmP 93
Russell, Charles Taze 1852-1916 DcAmReB 2
Russell, Charlie L. 1932- WhoBlA 94
Russell, Christopher Who 94
Russell, (Ronald) Christopher (Gordon) 1940- Who 94
Russell, Christopher Thomas 1943- WhoWest 94
Russell, Chuck IntMPA 94
Russell, Clifford Springer 1938- WhoFI 94
Russell, Connie WhoHol 92
Russell, Conrad (Sebastian Robert) 1937- WrDr 94
Russell, Craig d1990 WhoHol 92
Russell, Craig John 1954- WhoScEn 94
Russell, Cristine Elaine 1953- WhoAm 94
Russell, Dan Chapman 1939- Who 94
Russell, Dan M., Jr. 1913- WhoAm 94, WhoAmL 94
Russell, Dana 1949- WhoWest 94
Russell, David Allison 1935- WhoAm 94
Russell, David E. 1935- WhoAm 94, WhoAmL 94, WhoWest 94
Russell, David Emerson 1922- WhoScEn 94
Russell, David Hamilton Who 94
Russell, David L. 1942- WhoAm 94, WhoAmL 94
Russell, David Lawson 1921- WhoAm 94
Russell, David Sturrock W. Who 94
Russell, David Syme 1916- Who 94, WrDr 94
Russell, David Williams 1945- WhoAmL 94, WhoFI 94, WhoMW 93
Russell, Dian Bishop 1952- WhoBlA 94
Russell, Don d1981 WhoHol 92
Russell, Donald Andrew Frank Moore 1920- Who 94
Russell, Donald Stuart 1906- WhoAm 94, WhoAmL 94, WhoAmP 93
Russell, Dora 1894-1985 BlmGWL
Russell, Dora Isella 1925- BlmGWL
Russell, Doris Mae 1926- WhoAmP 93
Russell, Dorothy Delores 1950- WhoBlA 94
Russell, Edward Augustine 1916- Who 94
Russell, Edward Charles 1938- WhoWest 94
Russell, Edward Thomas 1941- WhoFI 94
Russell, Edward Walter 1904- Who 94
Russell, Edwin Fairman 1914- WhoAm 94
Russell, Edwin John Cumming 1939- Who 94
Russell, Edwin R. 1913- WhoBlA 94
Russell, Eileen Alison Who 94
Russell, Elbert Winslow 1929- WhoScEn 94
Russell, Elizabeth 1916- WhoHol 92
Russell, Elizabeth Cooke (Hoby) 1540-1609 BlmGWL
Russell, Elizabeth Shull WorScD
Russell, Eric Frank 1905-1978 EncSF 93
Russell, Ermea J. 1953- WhoBlA 94
Russell, Ernest 1933- WhoBlA 94
Russell, Evangeline d1966 WhoHol 92
Russell, Evelyn d1976 WhoHol 92
Russell, Evelyn Charles Sackville d1992 Who 94N
Russell, Findlay Ewing 1919- WhoWest 94
Russell, Francia 1938- WhoAm 94, WhoWest 94
Russell, Francis 1910-1989 WhAm 10
Russell, Francis Henry 1904-1989 WhAm 10
Russell, Francis Mark 1927- Who 94
Russell, Frank DrAPF 93
Russell, Frank Eli 1920- WhoAm 94, WhoFI 94, WhoMW 93
Russell, Franklin (Alexander) 1926- WrDr 94
Russell, Fred McFerrin 1906- WhoAm 94
Russell, Gail d1961 WhoHol 92
Russell, Gary 1948- WhoWest 94
Russell, Gary E. 1950- WhoWest 94
Russell, Gay Martin 1933- WhoWest 94
Russell, George 1935- IntWW 93, Who 94
Russell, George A. 1923- WhoBlA 94
Russell, George Albert 1921- WhoAm 94, WhoMW 93
Russell, George Allen 1923- WhoAm 94
Russell, George Alton, Jr. WhoBlA 94
Russell, George Haw 1945- WhoFI 94
Russell, George Michael 1908- Who 94
Russell, George William Erskine 1853-1919 DcNaB MP
Russell, Gerald Francis Morris 1928- Who 94
Russell, Glen Allan 1925- WhoAm 94
Russell, Gordon d1981 WhoHol 92
Russell, Graham R. Who 94
Russell, H. Diane 1936- WhoAm 94
Russell, Harold 1914- WhoHol 92
Russell, Harold Ian Lyle 1934- Who 94
Russell, Harold Louis 1916- WhoAm 94
Russell, Harriet Anne 1941- WhoAmP 93
Russell, Harriet Shaw 1952- WhoMW 93
Russell, Harvey Clarence 1918- WhoBlA 94
Russell, Hattie d1918 WhoHol 92
Russell, Helen Crocker 1896-1966 WhoAmA 93N
Russell, Helen Diane 1936- WhoAmA 93
Russell, Helen Ross 1915- WrDr 94

Russell, Henry 1871-1937 NewGrDO
Russell, Henry George 1941- WhoAm 94, WhoScEn 94
Russell, Henry Norris 1877-1957 WorScD
Russell, Henry Phillip, Jr. 1916- WhoAmP 93
Russell, Herman Jerome 1930- WhoAm 94, WhoBlA 94, WhoFI 94
Russell, Hilary DrAPF 93
Russell, Hollis F. 1953- WhoAmL 94
Russell, "Honey" 1903-1973 BasBi
Russell, Horace L. 1937- AfrAmG [port]
Russell, Howard Lewis DrAPF 93
Russell, Howard Lewis 1962- WrDr 94
Russell, Ian John 1943- Who 94
Russell, Inez Snyder 1951- WhoFI 94
Russell, Iris WhoHol 92
Russell, J. Gordon d1935 WhoHol 92
Russell, J. Shepherd, III 1953- WhoAmL 94
Russell, Jackie WhoHol 92
Russell, James 1936- WrDr 94
Russell, James A., Jr. 1917- WhoBlA 94
Russell, James Alvin, Jr. 1917- WhoAm 94
Russell, James Donald Murray 1934- WhoAm 94
Russell, James Francis Buchanan 1924- Who 94
Russell, James Franklin 1945- WhoAmL 94
Russell, James H. 1943- WhoAm 94
Russell, James Knox 1919- Who 94
Russell, James Paul 1945- WhoFI 94
Russell, James Sargent 1903- IntWW 93, WhoWest 94
Russell, James Webster, Jr. 1921- WhoAm 94
Russell, Jane 1921- IntMPA 94, WhoHol 92
Russell, Jay D. 1950- WhoFI 94
Russell, Jeffrey WhoAmA 93
Russell, Jeffrey Burton 1934- WhoAm 94, WrDr 94
Russell, Jeffrey Scott 1962- WhoScEn 94
Russell, Jeremy (Longmore) 1935- WrDr 94
Russell, John EncSF 93, WhoHol 92
Russell, John d1991 WhoHol 92
Russell, John 1919- IntWW 93, Who 94, WrDr 94
Russell, John, Jr. 1894- WhAm 10
Russell, John Blair 1929- WhoScEn 94
Russell, John David 1928- WhoAm 94
Russell, John Davidson 1946- WhoAmP 93
Russell, John Harry 1926- Who 94
Russell, John Laurel 1916- WhoAmA 93
Russell, John Leonard 1906- WrDr 94
Russell, John Lowell d1937 WhoHol 92
Russell, John Peterson, Jr. 1947- WhoBlA 94
Russell, John Richardson 1951- WhoAmP 93
Russell, John Robert EncSF 93
Russell, John St. Clair, Jr. 1917- WhoAm 94
Russell, John Thomas 1931- WhoAmP 93
Russell, John W. WhoAm 94
Russell, John W. 1923- WhoAmP 93
Russell, John William 1952- WhoFI 94
Russell, Johnny 1933- WhoHol 92
Russell, Joseph 1719-1804 WhAmRev
Russell, Joseph D. 1914- WhoBlA 94
Russell, Joseph J. 1934- WhoBlA 94
Russell, Josette Renee 1964- WhoScEn 94
Russell, Josiah Cox 1900- WhoAm 94
Russell, Joyce Anne Rogers 1920- WhoAm 94
Russell, Joyce M. 1946- WhoAmL 94
Russell, Julie Rapp 1966- WhoMW 93
Russell, Kathryn Louise 1951- WhoMW 93
Russell, Kay A. 1954- WhoBlA 94
Russell, Keith Bradley 1956- WhoBlA 94
Russell, Ken 1927- IntMPA 94, IntWW 93, NewGrDO, Who 94, WhoAm 94, WhoHol 92
Russell, Ken Mark 1956- WhoWest 94
Russell, Kenneth Calvin 1936- WhoAm 94, WhoScEn 94
Russell, Kenneth Victor 1929- WrDr 94
Russell, Kenneth William 1963- WhoScEn 94
Russell, Kimberly 1966- WhoHol 92
Russell, Kurt 1951- ConTFT 11, IntMPA 94, WhoHol 92
Russell, Kurt Von Vogel 1951- WhoAm 94
Russell, Lao d1988 WhAm 10
Russell, Leon W. 1949- WhoBlA 94
Russell, Leonard, Mrs. Who 94
Russell, Leonard Alonzo 1949- WhoBlA 94
Russell, Lewis d1961 WhoHol 92
Russell, Lillian d1922 WhoHol 92
Russell, Lillian 1861-1922 NewGrDO
Russell, Lillian 1942- WhoMW 93
Russell, Louise Bennett 1942- WhoAm 94
Russell, Lucy d1627 BlmGEL
Russell, Lynn Darnell 1937- WhoAm 94
Russell, Mabel d1951 WhoHol 92
Russell, Mark Who 94
Russell, Mark 1932- WhoAm 94, WhoCom
Russell, (Robert) Mark 1929- Who 94
Russell, Marlou 1956- WhoWest 94
Russell, Martin (James) 1934- WrDr 94
Russell, Martin Guthrie 1914- Who 94
Russell, Maurice V. 1923- WhoBlA 94
Russell, Michael Charles 1949- WhoMW 93
Russell, Michael Erwin 1955- WhoMW 93
Russell, Michael Hayden 1948- WhoMW 93
Russell, Michael James 1958- WhoAmL 94, WhoFI 94
Russell, Michele WhoHol 92
Russell, Milicent De'Ance 1950- WhoBlA 94
Russell, Morgan 1886-1953 WhoAmA 93N
Russell, Muir Who 94
Russell, (Alastair) Muir 1949- Who 94
Russell, (Albert) Muir (Galloway) 1925- Who 94
Russell, Newton R. 1927- WhoAmP 93
Russell, Newton Requa 1927- WhoWest 94
Russell, Nipsey 1924- WhoBlA 94, WhoHol 92
Russell, Nipsey 1925- WhoCom
Russell, Norma C. 1937- WhoAmP 93
Russell, Norman H. 1921- WrDr 94
Russell, Osborne c. 1814-1892 WhWE
Russell, Paris Scott, IV 1958- WhoAmL 94
Russell, Patricia T. 1931- WhoAmP 93
Russell, Patrick Who 94
Russell, (Thomas) Patrick 1926- Who 94
Russell, Patrick James 1959- WhoWest 94
Russell, Paul d1979 WhoHol 92
Russell, Paul 1956- WrDr 94
Russell, Paul Edgar 1924- WhoAm 94, WhoWest 94
Russell, Paul Frederick 1948- WhoAm 94
Russell, Paul Lawrence 1947-1991 WhAm 10
Russell, Paul Snowden 1925- WhoAm 94
Russell, Pee Wee d1969 WhoHol 92
Russell, (Irwin) Peter 1921- WrDr 94
Russell, Peter Edward Lionel Russell 1913- IntWW 93, Who 94
Russell, Philip C. 1933- WhoAmA 93
Russell, Philip Welsford Richmond 1919- IntWW 93, Who 94
Russell, R. Dana 1906- WhAm 10
Russell, R. Stephen DrAPF 93
Russell, Ralph Timothy 1948- WhoIns 94
Russell, Ray DrAPF 93
Russell, Ray 1924- WhoAm 94, WrDr 94
Russell, Ray Lamar 1944- WhoScEn 94
Russell, Raymond WhoAmA 93
Russell, Reb d1978 WhoHol 92
Russell, Richard WhoMW 93
Russell, Richard Carl 1949- WhoFI 94
Russell, Richard Doncaster 1929- WhoAm 94
Russell, Richard Harold 1942- WhoAmP 93
Russell, Richard Olney, Jr. 1932- WhoAm 94
Russell, Richard Wayne 1955- WhoWest 94
Russell, Robert WhoHol 92
Russell, Robert Alan 1949- WhoFI 94
Russell, Robert Christopher Hamlyn 1921- Who 94
Russell, Robert Elson, Sr. 1947- WhoAmP 93
Russell, Robert Francis 1952- WhoAmL 94
Russell, Robert Gilmore 1928- WhoAm 94, WhoAmL 94
Russell, Robert Hilton 1927- WhoAm 94
Russell, Robert Leonard 1916- WhoFI 94
Russell, Robert Lloyd 1941- WhoFI 94
Russell, Robert Price 1939- WhoAmA 93
Russell, Robert Pritchard 1945- WhoScEn 94
Russell, Robert T. 1949- WhoAmL 94
Russell, Robert Weldon, III 1946- WhoAmP 93
Russell, Roger 1938- WhoAmP 93
Russell, Roger Wolcott 1914- Who 94, WhoScEn 94
Russell, Ronald 1924- WrDr 94
Russell, Ronald Edward 1948- WhoAmL 94
Russell, Ronald G. 1928- WhoAmP 93
Russell, Rosalind d1976 WhoHol 92
Russell, Rosalind 1907-1976 WhoCom
Russell, Roy 1918- WrDr 94
Russell, Rudolf Rosenfeld 1925- Who 94
Russell, Sam W. 1945- WhoAmP 93
Russell, Samuel Lee 1948- WhoAmL 94
Russell, Sandi Anita 1946- WhoBlA 94
Russell, Sandra DrAPF 93
Russell, Sharman Apt DrAPF 93
Russell, Sharman Apt 1954- ConAu 142
Russell, Shirley 1935- IntDcF 2-4
Russell, Spencer (Thomas) 1923- Who 94
Russell, Spencer Thomas 1923- IntWW 93
Russell, Stanley G., Jr. WhoAm 94
Russell, Stella Pandell 1948- WhoAmA 93
Russell, Stephen Speh 1943- WhoAmL 94
Russell, Tanya WhoHol 92
Russell, Ted McKinnies 1943- WhoScEn 94
Russell, Terence Francis 1931- Who 94
Russell, Terrence 1944- WhoAmL 94
Russell, Theodore 1943- WhoAmL 94
Russell, Theresa 1957- IntMPA 94, WhoHol 92
Russell, Theresa Lynn 1957- WhoAm 94
Russell, Thomas 1920- Who 94
Russell, Thomas Arthur 1953- WhoAmL 94, WhoWest 94
Russell, Thomas S. 1922- WhoAmP 93
Russell, Thomas William Fraser 1934- WhoScEn 94
Russell, Thomas Wright, Jr. 1916- WhoAm 94
Russell, Timothy DrAPF 93
Russell, Tomas Morgan 1934- WhoAm 94, WhoAmL 94, WhoIns 94
Russell, Turner Alan 1944- WhoAm 94, WhoFI 94
Russell, W(illiam) Clark 1844-1911 EncSF 93
Russell, W(illiam) M(oy) S(tratten) 1925- WrDr 94
Russell, Wallace Clayton, Jr. 1928- WhoAmP 93
Russell, Walter Bowman 1871-1963 DcAmReB 2
Russell, Wesley L. 1938- WhoBlA 94
Russell, William DrAPF 93
Russell, William d1929 WhoHol 92
Russell, William 1924- WhoHol 92
Russell, William, Sr. c. 1741-1793 WhAmRev
Russell, William, Jr. 1758-1825 WhAmRev
Russell, William Alexander, Jr. 1946- WhoScEn 94
Russell, William Arthur, Jr. 1947- WhoAmP 93
Russell, William Dean 1938- WhoAmP 93
Russell, William Douglas 1962- WhoFI 94
Russell, William Evans 1949- WhoScEn 94
Russell, William Fletcher, III 1950- WhoAm 94
Russell, William Joseph 1941- WhoAm 94
Russell, William Martin 1947- IntWW 93, Who 94
Russell, William Ray 1939- WhoMW 93
Russell, William Robert 1913- Who 94
Russell, William Steven 1948- WhoAm 94
Russell, Willy 1947- ConDr 93, WrDr 94
Russell Beale, Simon IntWW 93
Russell-Davis, John Darelan 1912- Who 94
Russell-Hunter, William Devigne 1926- WhoAm 94, WhoScEn 94
Russell Of Liverpool, Baron 1952- Who 94
Russell-Scott, R. d1950 WhoHol 92
Russell Taylor, Elisabeth 1930- WrDr 94
Russell-Thomas, Steven Gardner 1943- WhoMW 93
Russell Vick, Arnold Oughtred Who 94
Russell-Wood, Anthony John R. 1939- WhoAm 94
Russen, David EncSF 93
Russert-Given, Jan Lynne 1949- WhoFI 94
Russett, Bruce Martin 1935- WrDr 94
Russett, Cynthia Eagle 1937- WrDr 94
Russhon, Charles J. d1982 WhoHol 92
Russi, Raul 1945- WhoHisp 94
Russiano, John 1942- WhoAm 94
Russianoff, Penelope 1917- WhoHol 92
Russin, Jonathan 1937- WhoAm 94
Russin, Robert I. 1914- WhoAmA 93
Russin, Robert Isaiah 1914- WhoAm 94, WhoWest 94
Russinova, Isabel WhoHol 92
Russman, Richard 1947- WhoAmP 93
Russman, Thomas Anthony 1944- WhoAm 94
Russo, Albert DrAPF 93
Russo, Alexander Peter 1922- WhoAm 94, WhoAmA 93
Russo, Alfred, Jr. 1962- WhoAmP 93
Russo, Alvin Leon 1924- WhoScEn 94, WhoWest 94
Russo, Anne P. DrAPF 93
Russo, Anthony E. 1926- WhoAmP 93
Russo, Anthony Joseph 1953- WhoFI 94
Russo, Anthony Sebastian 1947- WhoFI 94
Russo, Carl L. 1946- WhoAmL 94
Russo, Charline Smith 1950- WhoAm 94
Russo, David C. 1953- WhoAmP 93
Russo, Donna Marie 1963- WhoAmL 94
Russo, Gene C. 1935- WhoAmP 93
Russo, Gianni WhoHol 92
Russo, Gilberto 1948- WhoScEn 94
Russo, Gregory Thomas 1949- WhoAm 94, WhoFI 94
Russo, James 1953- WhoHol 92
Russo, John EncSF 93
Russo, John Duke WhoHol 92
Russo, John Francis 1933- WhoAmP 93
Russo, John Peter 1943- WhoAm 94
Russo, Jose 1942- WhoAm 94
Russo, Joseph Frank 1924- WhoAm 94
Russo, Kathie Regan WhoAmP 93
Russo, Kathleen Marie 1947- WhoAm 94
Russo, Laura 1943- WhoWest 94
Russo, Marius Thomas 1922- WhoAmP 93
Russo, Marty 1944- WhoAmP 93
Russo, Matt WhoHol 92
Russo, Michael WhoHol 92
Russo, Michael John 1960- WhoMW 93
Russo, Michele 1909- WhoAmA 93
Russo, Mike 1947- WhoAmP 93
Russo, Nancy Felipe 1943- WhoHisp 94
Russo, Peter Francis 1932- WhoAm 94
Russo, Rene IntMPA 94, WhoHol 92
Russo, Richard 1949- WrDr 94
Russo, Richard Paul 1954- EncSF 93
Russo, Ronald John 1949- WhoAmL 94
Russo, Rosemary 1951- WhoMW 93
Russo, Roy Lawrence 1935- WhoAm 94
Russo, Roy R. 1936- WhoAmL 94
Russo, Sally Fulton Haley WhoAmA 93
Russo, Salvatore Franklin 1938- WhoWest 94
Russo, Thomas Anthony 1943- WhoAm 94, WhoAmL 94
Russo, Thomas Joseph 1941- WhoAm 94
Russo, Vincent Andrew 1955- WhoFI 94
Russo, Vito 1946-1990 GayLL
Russo, William 1928- NewGrDO
Russo Jervolino, Rosa 1936- IntWW 93
Russoli, Franco 1923-1977 WhoAmA 93N
Russom, James Rayford 1949- WhoWest 94
Russom, Leon WhoHol 92
Russomanno, Herman Joseph 1949- WhoAmL 94
Russon, David 1944- Who 94
Russoniello, Joseph Pascal WhoAm 94
Russotti, Samuel J. d1993 NewYTBS 93
Russwurm, John B. 1799-1851 AfrAmAl 6
Rust, Barbel 1955- WhoWomW 91
Rust, David E. WhoAmA 93
Rust, David Edward 1929- WhoAm 94
Rust, Edward B., Jr. 1950- WhoIns 94
Rust, Edward Barry, Jr. 1950- WhoAm 94, WhoFI 94, WhoMW 93
Rust, Edwin C. 1910- WhoAmA 93
Rust, Friedrich Wilhelm 1739-1796 NewGrDO
Rust, Giacomo 1741-1786 NewGrDO
Rust, Jennifer Lynn 1967- WhoMW 93
Rust, Jo Ellen 1954- WhoMW 93
Rust, Josef 1907- IntWW 93
Rust, Joseph Cutler 1941- WhoAmL 94
Rust, Libby Karen 1951- WhoWest 94
Rust, Lynn Eugene 1952- WhoScEn 94, WhoWest 94
Rust, Marina (Marshall) 1964- ConAu 141
Rust, Mark E. 1957- WhoAmL 94
Rust, Nancy S. 1928- WhoAmP 93
Rust, Nicholas Cregg 1946- WhoWest 94
Rust, Richard 1938- WhoHol 92
Rust, S. Murray, III 1939- WhoFI 94
Rust, William James 1929- WhoAm 94
Rustad, Gerald 1944- WhoAmP 93
Rustad, Norman Eylar 1938- WhoMW 93
Rustagi, Jagdish Sharan 1923- WhoAm 94
Rustagi, Narendra Kumar 1953- WhoFI 94
Rustagi, Ravinder Kumar 1951- WhoAsA 94
Rustam, Mardi Ahmed 1932- WhoFI 94
Rustgi, Moti Lal 1929- WhoAm 94
Rusthoven, Peter James 1951- WhoAm 94, WhoAmL 94
Rustin, Bayard 1910-1987 AfrAmAl 6, AmSocL [port]
Rustin, Dowse Bradwell, III 1950- WhoFI 94
Rustin, Jean 1928- IntWW 93
Rustoff, Michael EncSF 93
Ruston, Donald Allen 1929- WhoAm 94
Ruston, John Harry Gerald Who 94
Rustvold, Katherine Jo 1950- WhoAmA 93
Ruta, Peter Paul 1918- WhoAmA 93
Ruta, Suzanne DrAPF 93
Rutan, Charles Hart d1968 WhoHol 92
Rutan, Douglas Edwin 1949- WhoWest 94
Rutan, Elbert L. 1943- WhoAm 94, WhoScEn 94
Rutan, J. Scott 1940- ConAu 142
Rutan, Richard Glenn 1938- WhoAm 94, WhoWest 94

Ryan, John Michael 1946- *WhoMW 93*
Ryan, John P. *WhoHol 92*
Ryan, John P. 1936- *IntMPA 94*
Ryan, John Thomas, Jr. 1912- *WhoFI 94*
Ryan, John Thomas, III 1943- *WhoAm 94*
Ryan, John William 1929- *WhoAm 94*
Ryan, John William 1937- *WhoAm 94*
Ryan, John William 1957- *WhoAmL 94*
Ryan, John William, Jr. 1940- *WhoAm 94*
Ryan, Jon R. 1947- *WhoFI 94*
Ryan, Joseph 1942- *WhoAm 94, WhoAmL 94*
Ryan, Joseph J. *WhoAmP 93*
Ryan, Joseph Thomas 1913- *WhoAm 94*
Ryan, Joseph W., Jr. 1948- *WhoAm 94, WhoAmL 94*
Ryan, Judith Andre 1936- *WhoAm 94*
Ryan, Kathleen d1985 *WhoHol 92*
Ryan, Kathryn Morgan d1993 *NewYTBS 93*
Ryan, Kathryn Morgan 1925-1993 *ConAu 140*
Ryan, Kay *DrAPF 93*
Ryan, Kenneth Eugene 1936- *WhoFI 94*
Ryan, Kenneth John 1926- *WhoAm 94, WhoScEn 94*
Ryan, Kevin *WhoAmP 93*
Ryan, Kevin Durwood 1961- *WhoFI 94*
Ryan, Laurence *Who 94*
Ryan, Lehan Jerome 1935- *WhoAm 94*
Ryan, Leo Vincent 1927- *WhoAm 94, WhoFI 94, WhoMW 93*
Ryan, Leonard Eames 1930- *WhoAm 94, WhoAmL 94*
Ryan, Linda Marie 1955- *WhoAmL 94*
Ryan, Louis Farthing 1947- *WhoAm 94, WhoAmL 94*
Ryan, M. Paton d1991 *WhAm 10*
Ryan, Madge 1919- *WhoHol 92*
Ryan, Margaret *DrAPF 93*
Ryan, Margaret Anne 1949- *WhoMW 93*
Ryan, Margaret Mary 1925- *WhoAmP 93*
Ryan, Marian Teresa 1954- *WhoAmL 94*
Ryan, Marianne Elizabeth 1964- *WhoAmL 94*
Ryan, Mark Anthony 1964- *WhoMW 93*
Ryan, Mark Stephen 1958- *WhoWest 94*
Ryan, Marleigh Grayer 1930- *WhoAm 94*
Ryan, Marsha Ann 1947- *WhoBlA 94*
Ryan, Mary *WhoHol 92*
Ryan, Mary d1948 *WhoHol 92*
Ryan, Mary A. 1940- *WhoAm 94*
Ryan, Mary Elizabeth *DrAPF 93*
Ryan, Mary Elizabeth 1953- *WhoWest 94*
Ryan, Mary Gene 1953- *WhoWest 94*
Ryan, Mary K. 1950- *WhoAmL 94*
Ryan, Mary Nell H. 1956- *WhoFI 94, WhoMW 93*
Ryan, Mary P(atricia) 1945- *WrDr 94*
Ryan, Matthew J. 1932- *WhoAmP 93*
Ryan, Maurice William 1924- *WhoAmL 94*
Ryan, Meg 1961- *IntMPA 94, IntWW 93, WhoAm 94, WhoHol 92*
Ryan, Meg c. 1962- *News 94-1 [port]*
Ryan, Michael *DrAPF 93*
Ryan, Michael 1951- *WhoFI 94, WhoMW 93*
Ryan, Michael A. 1950- *WhoAmL 94*
Ryan, Michael Beecher 1936- *WhoAm 94*
Ryan, Michael Clifford 1948- *WhoAm 94, WhoAmL 94*
Ryan, Michael E. 1938- *WhoAm 94*
Ryan, Michael J. 1947- *WhoIns 94*
Ryan, Michael Louis 1945- *WhoFI 94, WhoWest 94*
Ryan, Michael M. *WhoHol 92*
Ryan, Mike 1961- *WhoMW 93*
Ryan, Mitch 1934- *WhoHol 92*
Ryan, Mitchell 1928- *IntMPA 94*
Ryan, Nancy d1983 *WhoHol 92*
Ryan, Natasha 1970- *WhoHol 92*
Ryan, Nigel *Who 94*
Ryan, (Christopher) Nigel (John) 1929- *Who 94*
Ryan, Noel 1925- *WhoAm 94*
Ryan, Nolan *NewYTBS 93 [port]*
Ryan, Nolan 1947- *WhoAm 94*
Ryan, Patricia Marie 1960- *WhoFI 94*
Ryan, Patrick G. 1937- *WhoAm 94, WhoFI 94, WhoIns 94*
Ryan, Patrick J. 1938- *WhoAm 94*
Ryan, Patrick John 1937- *WhoFI 94*
Ryan, Patrick Leo 1945- *WhoFI 94*
Ryan, Patrick Michael 1937- *WhoAm 94*
Ryan, Patrick Michael 1944- *WhoAm 94, WhoAmL 94*
Ryan, Patrick Thomas, III 1957- *WhoAmL 94*
Ryan, Paul *WhoHol 92*
Ryan, Paul Phillip 1946- *WhoFI 94*
Ryan, Paula Toomey 1958- *WhoFI 94*
Ryan, Peggy 1924- *WhoHol 92*
Ryan, Peter Allen 1923- *IntWW 93, WrDr 94*
Ryan, Philip J. d1993 *NewYTBS 93*
Ryan, Rachel 1948- *WrDr 94*
Ryan, Ralph James 1931- *WhoWest 94*
Ryan, Randel Edward, Jr. 1940- *WhoWest 94*
Ryan, Ray Darl, Jr. 1945- *WhoAm 94, WhoMW 93*
Ryan, Raymond D. 1922- *WhoAm 94*
Ryan, Reade Haines, Jr. 1937- *WhoAm 94, WhoAmL 94, WhoWest 94*
Ryan, Regina Claire 1938- *WhoAm 94*
Ryan, Richard E. 1950- *WhoAmA 93*
Ryan, Richie 1929- *IntWW 93*
Ryan, Robert d1973 *WhoHol 92*
Ryan, Robert Collins 1953- *WhoAmL 94, WhoMW 93*
Ryan, Robert Davis 1941- *WhoAmL 94*
Ryan, Robert J. d1958 *WhoHol 92*
Ryan, Robert J., Jr. 1939- *WhoAmP 93*
Ryan, Robert Seibert 1922- *WhoAm 94*
Ryan, Robert Thomas 1947- *WhoAmP 93*
Ryan, Robyn Lynne 1953- *WhoAmL 94*
Ryan, Ronald Lee 1948- *WhoMW 93*
Ryan, Roz 1951- *WhoHol 92*
Ryan, Shawn Michael 1954- *WhoFI 94*
Ryan, Sheena Ross 1944- *WhoFI 94*
Ryan, Sheila d1975 *WhoHol 92*
Ryan, Sheila Morag Clark *Who 94*
Ryan, Stephen Anthony 1950- *WhoAmL 94*
Ryan, Stephen Collister 1942- *WhoMW 93*
Ryan, Stephen Joseph, Jr. 1940- *WhoAm 94, WhoScEn 94, WhoWest 94*
Ryan, Steve *WhoHol 92*
Ryan, Steven J. 1953- *WhoAmP 93*
Ryan, Susan Maree 1942- *IntWW 93, WhoWomW 91*
Ryan, Susan Mary 1938- *WhoWest 94*
Ryan, Suzanne Irene 1939- *WhoAm 94, WhoScEn 94*
Ryan, Sylvester D. 1930- *WhoWest 94*
Ryan, Terrance Lee 1947- *WhoAm 94, WhoAmL 94*
Ryan, Theresa Ann Julia 1962- *WhoFI 94*
Ryan, Thomas Anthony 1936- *IntWW 93, Who 94*
Ryan, Thomas F. 1943- *WhoAm 94, WhoAmL 94*
Ryan, Thomas Grady 1949- *WhoAm 94*
Ryan, Thomas J(oseph) 1942- *EncSF 93*
Ryan, Thomas Joseph 1945- *WhoFI 94, WhoMW 93*
Ryan, Thomas P., Jr. 1929- *WhoAmP 93*
Ryan, Thomas Patrick, Jr. 1929- *WhoAm 94*
Ryan, Thomas Timothy, Jr. 1945- *WhoAm 94, WhoAmL 94*
Ryan, Thomas William 1953- *WhoAmL 94*
Ryan, Tim d1956 *WhoHol 92*
Ryan, Timothy William 1962- *WhoScEn 94*
Ryan, Todd Michael 1947- *WhoFI 94*
Ryan, Tom Kreusch 1926- *WhoAm 94*
Ryan, Tubal Claude 1898- *WhAm 10*
Ryan, Una Scully 1941- *WhoMW 93*
Ryan, Vince 1947- *WhoAmP 93*
Ryan, Walter James 1931- *WhoAm 94*
Ryan, William (Michael) 1948- *WrDr 94*
Ryan, William A. 1919- *WhoAmP 93*
Ryan, William Arthur 1954- *WhoMW 93*
Ryan, William B. F. 1939- *WhoScEn 94*
Ryan, William Clark 1951- *WhoAmL 94*
Ryan, William Edward 1936- *WhoAmA 93*
Ryan, William F., Jr. 1951- *WhoAmL 94*
Ryan, William Francis 1925- *WhoAm 94*
Ryan, William Frank 1924- *WhoAm 94, WhoFI 94, WhoMW 93*
Ryan, William J. 1943- *WhoAm 94, WhoFI 94*
Ryan, William Joseph 1932- *WhoAm 94, WhoFI 94*
Ryan, William Joseph 1949- *WhoAmP 93*
Ryan, William M. 1955- *WhoAmP 93*
Ryan, William Matthew 1955- *WhoWest 94*
Ryan, William Murray 1922- *WhoAmP 93*
Ryane, Melody *WhoHol 92*
Ryans, James Lee 1948- *WhoScEn 94*
Ryan-White, Jewell 1943- *WhoBlA 94*
Ryazanov, Eldar Aleksandrovich 1927- *IntWW 93*
Ryba, Jakub (Simon) Jan 1765-1815 *NewGrDO*
Ryba, John J. 1929- *WhoAmP 93*
Rybak, Michael D. 1951- *WhoAmP 93*
Rybak, William C. 1921- *WhoAmP 93*
Rybakov, Anatoliy Naumovich 1911- *IntWW 93*
Rybalka, Michel 1933- *WhoAm 94*
Rybarczyk, Robert L. 1938- *WhoAmP 93*
Rybczynski, Tadeusz Mieczyslaw 1923- *Who 94*
Rybczynski, Witold 1943- *WrDr 94*
Rybczynski, Witold Marian 1943- *WhoAm 94*
Ryberg, Walter Greg 1946- *WhoAmP 93*
Rybot, Doris 1907- *WrDr 94*
Ryburn, Hubert James d1988 *Who 94N*
Ryburn, Samuel McChesney 1914- *WhoAm 94*
Ryce, Donald Theodore 1943- *WhoAmL 94*
Rychecky, Helen Rose 1922- *WhoMW 93*
Rychlak, Joseph F(rank) 1928- *WrDr 94*
Rychlak, Joseph Frank 1928- *WhoAm 94*
Ryckman, Chester d1918 *WhoHol 92*
Ryckman, DeVere Wellington 1924- *WhoAm 94*
Ryckman, Louise 1946- *WhoAmP 93*
Ryckmans, Pierre 1935- *IntWW 93*
Rycroft, Charles 1914- *WrDr 94*
Rycroft, Donald C. 1938- *WhoIns 94*
Rycroft, Donald Cahill 1938- *WhoAm 94*
Rycroft, Michael John 1938- *Who 94*
Rycroft, Richard Newton 1918- *Who 94*
Rycus, Mitchell Julian 1932- *WhoAm 94*
Rydalch, Ann 1935- *WhoAmP 93*
Rydall, Derek *WhoHol 92*
Rydbeck, Bruce Vernon 1948- *WhoScEn 94*
Rydbeck, Olof 1913- *IntWW 93, Who 94*
Ryde, Magnus Olof Waldemar 1956- *WhoWest 94*
Rydeberg, Georg d1983 *WhoHol 92*
Rydell, Amnell Roy 1915- *WhoWest 94*
Rydell, Bobby 1942- *WhoHol 92*
Rydell, Catherine M. 1950- *WhoAmP 93*
Rydell, Charlene B. *WhoAmP 93*
Rydell, Christopher *WhoHol 92*
Rydell, Earl Everett 1944- *WhoScEn 94*
Rydell, Forbes 1923- *WrDr 94*
Rydell, Jack E. 1958- *WhoMW 93*
Rydell, Mark *WhoAm 94*
Rydell, Mark 1934- *IntMPA 94, WhoHol 92*
Rydell, Richard Lewis 1940- *WhoAm 94*
Rydell, Wendell 1927- *WrDr 94*
Rydell, Wendy 1927- *WrDr 94*
Ryden, Hope *WrDr 94*
Ryden, John Graham 1939- *WhoAm 94*
Ryden, Kenneth 1917- *Who 94*
Ryden, Kenneth Glenn 1945- *WhoAmA 93*
Rydenfelt, Sven 1911- *WrDr 94*
Ryder *Who 94*
Ryder, Albert Pinkham 1847-1917 *AmCulL*
Ryder, Alfred 1919- *WhoHol 92*
Ryder, Arthur John 1913- *WrDr 94*
Ryder, Chauncey Foster 1868-1949 *WhoAmA 93N*
Ryder, David R. 1946- *WhoAm 94*
Ryder, Eddie *WhoHol 92*
Ryder, Edward Alexander 1931- *Who 94*
Ryder, Eric Charles 1915- *Who 94*
Ryder, Georgia Atkins 1924- *WhoBlA 94*
Ryder, Hal 1950- *WhoWest 94*
Ryder, Harl Edgar 1938- *WhoAm 94*
Ryder, Henry Clay 1928- *WhoAm 94, WhoMW 93*
Ryder, Jack McBride 1928- *WhoAm 94*
Ryder, James *EncSF 93*
Ryder, Joanne (Rose) 1946- *WrDr 94*
Ryder, John Douglass 1907- *WhoAm 94*
Ryder, John Louis *WhoAmP 93*
Ryder, Jonathan *ConAu 41NR*
Ryder, Jonathan 1927- *WrDr 94*
Ryder, Kenneth, Jr. 1940- *WhoAmP 93*
Ryder, M(ichael) L(awson) 1927- *WrDr 94*
Ryder, Mahler B. 1937- *WhoBlA 94*
Ryder, Mahler Bessinger 1937-1991 *WhoAmA 93N*
Ryder, Malcolm Eliot 1954- *WhoWest 94*
Ryder, Mitch 1945- *ConMus 11 [port]*
Ryder, Oliver Allison 1946- *WhoScEn 94, WhoWest 94*
Ryder, Peter 1942- *Who 94*
Ryder, Peter Hugh Dudley 1913- *Who 94*
Ryder, Richard (Andrew) 1949- *Who 94*
Ryder, Richard Andrew 1949- *IntWW 93*
Ryder, Richard Hood Jack Dudley 1940- *Who 94*
Ryder, Robert Winsor 1946- *WhoScEn 94*
Ryder, Sarah *DrAPF 93*
Ryder, Thom 1938- *WrDr 94*
Ryder, Thomas Michael 1934- *WhoAm 94*
Ryder, Tom 1949- *WhoAmP 93*
Ryder, Virginia Pinkus 1922- *WhoFI 94*
Ryder, Winona 1971- *IntMPA 94, IntWW 93, WhoAm 94, WhoHol 92*
Ryder Of Eaton Hastings, Baron 1916- *IntWW 93, Who 94*
Ryder Of Warsaw, Baroness 1923- *IntWW 93, Who 94, WhoWomW 91*
Rydholm, Nancy Lynn 1958- *WhoMW 93*
Rydholm, Ralph Williams 1937- *WhoAm 94, WhoFI 94*
Rydill, Louis Joseph 1922- *Who 94*
Rydin, Bo 1932- *IntWW 93*
Rydz, John S. 1925- *WhoAm 94*
Rydzel, James A. 1946- *WhoAm 94, WhoAmL 94*
Rye, C. Richard 1935- *IntWW 93*
Rye, David Blake 1943- *WhoAmP 93, WhoWest 94*
Rye, Karl Erik 1952- *WhoFI 94*
Ryecart, Patrick 1952- *WhoHol 92*
Ryen, Louis Arthur 1934- *WhoAmL 94*
Ryen, Richard d1965 *WhoHol 92*
Ryen, Richard Harlan 1933- *WhoWest 94*
Ryerse, William Carlisle 1929- *WhoFI 94*
Ryerson, Alice J. *DrAPF 93*
Ryerson, Ann *WhoHol 92*
Ryerson, Edward L., Jr. 1886-1971 *EncABHB 9 [port]*
Ryerson, Joseph Leslie 1918- *WhoAm 94*
Ryerson, Margery Austin 1886-1989 *WhAm 10*
Ryerson, Mitch *WhoAmA 93*
Ryerson, Paul Sommer 1946- *WhoAm 94, WhoAmL 94*
Ryerson, Sunny Ann 1949- *WhoScEn 94*
Ryerson, Thomas Howard 1951- *WhoAm 94*
Ryerson, Walt d1978 *WhoHol 92*
Ryerson, William Edwin 1936- *WhoAm 94, WhoAmP 93*
Ryga, George 1932-1987 *ConAu 43NR, ConDr 93, IntDcT 2*
Rygiewicz, Paul Thaddeus 1952- *WhoWest 94*
Ryken, Jody Janell 1962- *WhoMW 93*
Ryken, Leland 1942- *WrDr 94*
Ryker, Charles Edwin 1920- *WhoAm 94*
Ryker, Norman J., Jr. 1926- *WhoAm 94, WhoFI 94*
Rykiel, Sonia 1930- *IntWW 93*
Rykwert, Joseph 1926- *Who 94, WhoAm 94, WrDr 94*
Ryland, David Ronald 1945- *WhoAm 94, WhoAmL 94*
Ryland, Greaner Neal 1941- *WhoAm 94*
Ryland, Robert Knight 1873-1951 *WhoAmA 93N*
Ryland, Timothy Richard Godfrey Fetherstonhaugh 1938- *Who 94*
Ryland, Walter H. 1943- *WhoAmL 94*
Rylander, Henry Grady, Jr. 1921- *WhoAm 94, WhoScEn 94*
Rylander, James B., Jr. 1944- *WhoAmL 94*
Rylander, Robert Allan 1947- *WhoWest 94*
Rylands, George Humphrey Wolferstan 1902- *Who 94*
Rylant, Cynthia 1954- *SmATA 76 [port], TwCYAW, WhoAm 94, WrDr 94*
Ryle, Anthony 1927- *WrDr 94*
Ryle, Harold Charles 1925- *WhoFI 94*
Ryle, Joseph Donald 1910- *WhoAm 94*
Ryle, Kenneth Sherriff d1993 *Who 94N*
Ryle, Martin *WorInv*
Ryle, Martin 1918- *WorScD*
Ryle, Michael 1927- *WrDr 94*
Ryle, Michael Thomas 1927- *Who 94*
Ryle, Walter Harrington 1896- *WhAm 10*
Rylee, Robert T., III 1958- *WhoFI 94*
Ryles, Gerald Fay 1936- *WhoAm 94, WhoWest 94*
Ryles, Nancy 1937- *WhoAmP 93*
Ryles, Tim *WhoAmP 93*
Ryles, Tim 1941- *WhoIns 94*
Ryley, J.H. d1922 *WhoHol 92*
Ryll, Frank Maynard, Jr. 1942- *WhoAm 94*
Ryman, Geoff(rey Charles) 1951- *EncSF 93, WrDr 94*
Ryman, John 1930- *Who 94*
Ryman, Ras *EncSF 93*
Ryman, Robert 1930- *WhoAmA 93*
Ryman, Robert Tracy 1930- *WhoAm 94*
Rymar, Julian W. 1919- *WhoFI 94*
Rymer, Judith Marquis 1940- *WhoWest 94*
Rymer, Pamela Ann 1941- *WhoAm 94, WhoAmL 94, WhoAmP 93, WhoWest 94*
Rymer, S. Bradford, Jr. 1915- *WhoAm 94*
Rymer, Thomas 1641-1713 *BlmGEL*
Rymer, Thomas Arrington 1925- *WhoAmP 93*
Rymer, William Zev 1939- *WhoScEn 94*
Rymer-Jones, John Murray 1897- *Who 94*
Rymon, Larry Maring 1934- *WhoScEn 94*
Rymond, Claes Goran 1956- *WhoFI 94*
Ryn, Claes Gosta 1943- *WhoAm 94*
Rynard, Dorothy Ann 1936- *WhoMW 93*
Rynard, Hugh C. *WhoScEn 94*
Rynd, Richard *WhoAmP 93*
Rynear, Nina Cox 1916- *WhoWest 94*
Rynecki, Steven Bernard 1944- *WhoAmL 94*
Ryniker, Bruce Walter Durland 1940- *WhoFI 94, WhoScEn 94, WhoWest 94*
Ryniker, Robert J. 1942- *WhoAmL 94*
Rynkiewicz, Walter Paul 1930- *WhoAmL 94*
Rynn, Debra Lea 1953- *WhoFI 94*
Rynn, Nathan 1923- *WhoAm 94*
Rynne, Etienne Andrew 1932- *IntWW 93*
Ryno, William d1939 *WhoHol 92*
Ryntz, Rose Ann 1957- *WhoMW 93, WhoScEn 94*
Ryom, Heidi 1955- *IntDcB*
Ryon, John Walker, III 1940- *WhoFI 94*

Rypien, David Vincent 1956-
  WhoScEn 94
Rypien, Mark Robert 1962- *WhoAm 94*
Rypka, Eugene Weston 1925-
  WhoWest 94
Ryrie, William (Sinclair) 1928- *Who 94*
Ryrie, William Sinclair 1928- *IntWW 93,*
  WhoFI 94
Rysanek, Leonie 1926- *IntWW 93,*
  NewGrDO, WhoAm 94
Rysavy, Robin Marie 1959- *WhoMW 93*
Ryser, Hugues Jean-Paul 1926-
  WhoAm 94
Ryskamp, Bruce E. 1941- *WhoAm 94*
Ryskamp, Carroll Joseph 1930-
  WhoFI 94, WhoScEn 94
Ryskamp, Charles Andrew 1928-
  WhoAm 94
Ryskamp, Kenneth Lee 1932- *WhoAm 94,*
  WhoAmL 94
Ryskind, Morrie 1895-1985 *IntDcF 2-4*
Ryslinkova, Jana 1951- *WhoWomW 91*
Ryssdal, Rolv Einar 1914- *IntWW 93*
Ryste, Ruth Anlaug 1932- *IntWW 93*
Ryszytiwskyj, William Paul 1952-
  WhoScEn 94
Rytand, David A. 1909-1991 *WhAm 10*
Rytel, Piotr 1884-1970 *NewGrDO*
Rytjkow, Nikolaj d1973 *WhoHol 92*
Rytkheu, Yuriy Sergeyevich 1930-
  IntWW 93
Rytter, Jakob 1932- *IntWW 93*
Ryu, Daisuke 1957- *WhoHol 92*
Ryu, Dewey Doo Young 1936-
  WhoAsA 94, WhoScEn 94
Ryu, Kyoo-Hai Lee 1948- *WhoMW 93,*
  WhoScEn 94
Ryum, Ulla 1937- *BlmGWL*
Ryves, T(homas) E(van) 1895- *EncSF 93*
Ryzhkov, Nikolai Ivanovich 1929-
  IntWW 93, LngBDD
Ryzhov, Yuri Alexeevich 1930- *IntWW 93*
Ryzhov, Yury Petrovich 1930- *LngBDD*
Ryzlak, Maria Teresa 1938- *WhoScEn 94*
Rzepecki, Edward Louis 1921-
  WhoScEn 94
Rzewnicki, Janet 1953- *WhoAmP 93*
Rzeznik, Jozef 1943- *WhoFI 94*
Rzhevsky, Vladimir Vasilevich d1992
  IntWW 93N

S

S, Svend Otto 1916- *WrDr 94*
Sa, Angelo Calmon de 1935- *IntWW 93*
Sa, Luiz Augusto Discher 1944- *WhoScEn 94*
Saa, Yvonne *WhoHol 92*
Saab, Deanne Keltum 1945- *WhoFI 94*
Saad, Henry William 1948- *WhoAm 94, WhoAmL 94*
Saad, Joseph Kanan 1948- *WhoWest 94*
Saad, Margit *WhoHol 92*
Saad, Theodore Shafick 1920- *WhoAm 94*
Saada, Adel Selim 1934- *WhoAm 94*
Saadane, Fabienne Denise 1958- *WhoWest 94*
Saadawi Al, Nawal 1931- *IntWW 93*
Saadeh, Abraham 1955- *WhoWest 94*
Saadian, Javid 1953- *WhoFI 94*
Saafeld, Fred Erich 1935- *WhoAm 94*
Saal, Hubert Daniel 1924- *WhoAm 94*
Saal, Jennifer 1947- *WrDr 94*
Saal, Jocelyn 1947- *WrDr 94*
Saalman, Howard 1928- *WhoAm 94*
Saar, Alison M. 1956- *WhoAmA 93*
Saar, Betye 1926- *AfrAmAl 6, WhoAm 94, WhoAmA 93*
Saar, Betye I. 1926- *WhoBlA 94*
Saar, Frederick Arthur 1946- *WhoWest 94*
Saar, James 1949- *WrDr 94*
Saari, Albin Toivo 1930- *WhoScEn 94, WhoWest 94*
Saari, Carolyn 1939- *ConAu 140*
Saari, Donald Gene 1940- *WhoAm 94*
Saari, John William, Jr. 1937- *WhoAmL 94*
Saari, Kathryn Celeste 1948- *WhoMW 93*
Saari, Leonard Mathew 1938- *WhoAm 94*
Saari, Paula Davis Wilson 1953- *WhoMW 93*
Saari, Peter H. 1951- *WhoAmA 93*
Saari, Russell Edward *WhoWest 94*
Saarinen, Aarne 1913- *IntWW 93*
Saarinen, Arthur William, Jr. 1927- *WhoAm 94*
Saarinen, Eero 1910-1961 *AmCulL, WhoAmA 93N*
Saarinen, Gottlieb Eliel 1873-1950 *AmCulL*
Saarinen, Lilian 1912- *WhoAmA 93*
Saarlas, Maido 1930- *WhoAm 94*
Saask, Aapo 1943- *WhoFI 94*
Saastamoinen, Ulla Riitta 1940- *WhoWomW 91*
Saatchi, Charles 1943- *IntWW 93, Who 94*
Saatchi, Maurice 1946- *IntWW 93, Who 94, WhoAm 94, WhoFI 94*
Saavedra, Alvaro De d1529 *WhWE*
Saavedra, Carlos Raul 1961- *WhoWest 94*
Saavedra, Charles James 1941- *WhoFI 94*
Saavedra, Edgardo 1963- *WhoHisp 94*
Saavedra, Felix W. *WhoHisp 94*
Saavedra, Henry *WhoAmP 93, WhoHisp 94*
Saavedra, José M. 1950- *WhoHisp 94*
Saavedra, Juan M. 1941- *WhoHisp 94*
Saavedra, Juan Ortega 1951- *WhoScEn 94*
Saavedra, Kiki *WhoHisp 94*
Saavedra, Kleber 1940- *WhoHisp 94*
Saavedra, Leonel Orlando 1950- *WhoHisp 94*
Saavedra, Louis 1933- *WhoHisp 94*
Saavedra, Louis E. *WhoAmP 93*

Saavedra, Louis E. 1933- *WhoAm 94, WhoWest 94*
Saavedra, Richard 1954- *WhoHisp 94*
Saavedra, Ro 1952- *WhoWest 94*
Saba, Elias 1932- *IntWW 93*
Saba, Norman Morris 1954- *WhoWest 94*
Saba, Richard 1946- *WhoAmA 93*
Saba, Shoichi 1919- *IntWW 93*
Sabadell, Stewart August 1962- *WhoFI 94*
Sabadini, Bernardo d1718 *NewGrDO*
Sabah, Ali Khalifa al- 1945- *IntWW 93*
Sabah, Jaber al-Ahmad al-Jaber al- 1928- *IntWW 93*
Sabah, Jaber al-Ali al-Salem al- 1928- *IntWW 93*
Sabah, Saad al-Abdullah al-Salem al- 1930- *IntWW 93*
Sabah, Sabah al-Ahmad al-Jaber al- 1929- *IntWW 93*
Sabah, Salim al-Sabah al-Salim al- 1937- *IntWW 93*
Sabah, Saud Nasir al- 1944- *IntWW 93*
Sabanas-Wells, Alvina Olga 1914- *WhoScEn 94*
Sabanos, Michael Paul 1956- *WhoFI 94*
Sabaroff, Rose Epstein 1918- *WhoAm 94*
Sabat, Richard J. 1947- *WhoAm 94*
Sabata, Ashok 1964- *WhoScEn 94*
Sabata, Victor de *NewGrDO*
Sabatell, Henry P. 1937- *WhoFI 94*
Sabatella, Joseph John 1931- *WhoAmA 93*
Sabates, Felix N. *WhoHisp 94*
Sabates, Felix Nabor 1930- *WhoAm 94*
Sabath, Kenneth Michael 1956- *WhoAmL 94*
Sabath, Leon David 1930- *WhoAm 94*
Sabath, Robert Edward 1943- *WhoMW 93*
Sabatier, Jose Manuel 1943- *WhoHisp 94*
Sabatier, Robert 1923- *IntWW 93*
Sabatini, Gabriela 1970- *BuCMET, IntWW 93, WhoAm 94*
Sabatini, John A. 1945- *WhoAmP 93*
Sabatini, Lawrence 1930- *WhoWest 94*
Sabatini, Lawrence John 1919- *Who 94*
Sabatini, Nelson John 1940- *WhoAm 94*
Sabatini, Rafael 1875-1950 *DcNaB MP*
Sabatini, Raphael 1896-1985 *WhoAmA 93N*
Sabatini, Robert N. 1936- *WhoAmP 93*
Sabatini, Steven Thomas 1951- *WhoFI 94*
Sabatini, Vincent Fernando 1942- *WhoAmL 94*
Sabatino, David Matthew 1959- *WhoScEn 94*
Sabatino, Frank C. 1954- *WhoAmL 94*
Sabatino, Nicola c. 1708-1796 *NewGrDO*
Sabatka, Ann M. 1966- *WhoMW 93*
Sabato, Alfred d1956 *WhoHol 92*
Sabato, Antonio *WhoHol 92*
Sabato, Ernesto 1911- *HispLC [port], IntWW 93*
Sabato, Ernesto (R.) 1911- *ConWorW 93*
Sabato, George Frank 1947- *WhoWest 94*
Sabato, Jorge Federico 1938- *IntWW 93*
Sabatova, Anna 1951- *WhoWomW 91*
Sabattani, Aurelio 1912- *IntWW 93*
Sabau, Carmen Sybile 1933- *WhoMW 93*
Sabbagh, Hussein Rashid al- 1938- *IntWW 93*
Sabbah, Michel 1933- *IntWW 93*
Sabbath, Wendy June 1956- *WhoMW 93*

Sabbatini, Giuseppe 1957- *NewGrDO*
Sabben-Clare, Ernest E. d1993 *Who 94N*
Sabben-Clare, James Paley 1941- *Who 94*
Sabel, Bernhard August Maria 1957- *WhoScEn 94*
Sabel, Bradley Kent 1948- *WhoAm 94*
Sabelis, Huibert 1942- *WhoAmA 93*
Sabella, James Carmen 1939- *WhoAm 94*
Sabella, James J. 1951- *WhoAmL 94*
Saberhagen, Bret 1964- *WhoAm 94*
Saberhagen, Fred(erick Thomas) 1930- *EncSF 93*
Saberhagen, Fred (Thomas) 1930- *WrDr 94*
Sabers, Richard Wayne 1938- *WhoAm 94, WhoAmL 94, WhoAmP 93, WhoMW 93*
Sabersky, Rolf Heinrich 1920- *WhoAm 94*
Sabet, Hormoz 1936- *WhoFI 94*
Sabetta, John Carl 1942- *WhoAm 94, WhoAmL 94*
Sabey, John Wayne 1939- *WhoWest 94*
Sabharwal, Chaman Lal 1937- *WhoMW 93*
Sabharwal, Kulbir 1943- *WhoAsA 94*
Sabharwal, Ranjit Singh 1925- *WhoAm 94, WhoWest 94*
Sabhavasu, Pramual 1927- *IntWW 93*
Sabicas d1990 *WhoHol 92*
Sabido, Almeda Alice 1928- *WhoFI 94, WhoScEn 94*
Sabin, Albert 1906-1993 *News 93*
Sabin, Albert B. 1906-1993 *NewYTBS 93 [port]*
Sabin, Albert B(ruce) d1993 *IntWW 93N*
Sabin, Albert B(ruce) 1906-1993 *CurBio 93N*
Sabin, Albert Bruce d1993 *Who 94N*
Sabin, Albert Edward 1906-1993 *WorScD [port]*
Sabin, Arnold Leonard 1926- *WhoAm 94*
Sabin, Arthur Julius 1930- *WhoMW 93*
Sabin, Catherine Jerome d1943 *WhoHol 92*
Sabin, Florence Rena 1871-1953 *WorScD*
Sabin, Howard Westcott 1916- *Who 94*
Sabin, Jack Charles 1921- *WhoFI 94, WhoWest 94*
Sabin, James Thomas 1943- *WhoAm 94*
Sabin, Jeffrey S. 1952- *WhoAmL 94*
Sabin, Marc Leslie 1944- *WhoFI 94*
Sabin, Paul Robert 1943- *Who 94*
Sabin, William Albert 1931- *WhoAm 94*
Sabina, Karel 1813-1877 *NewGrDO*
Sabine, Edward *WorScD*
Sabine, Gordon Arthur 1917- *ConAu 41NR, WhoAm 94*
Sabine, Neil B. 1952- *WhoScEn 94*
Sabine, Neville Warde 1910- *Who 94*
Sabine, Peter Aubrey 1924- *Who 94*
Sabine, Randall Travis 1948- *WhoAmP 93*
Sabine, William Henry Waldo 1903- *WrDr 94*
Sabines, Luis 1917- *WhoHisp 94*
Sabini, John D. *WhoAmP 93*
Sabini, Nicola c. 1675-1705 *NewGrDO*
Sabinson, Harvey Barnett 1924- *WhoAm 94*
Sabio, Christine Monette 1967- *WhoMW 93*
Sabirov, Mukhammat Gallyamovich 1932- *LngBDD*

Sabiston, David Coston, Jr. 1924- *IntWW 93, WhoAm 94, WhoScEn 94*
Sabl, John J. 1951- *WhoAm 94, WhoAmL 94*
Sablan, Jesus Rosario *WhoAmP 93*
Sable, Madeleine de Souvre, Marquise de 1599-1678 *BlmGWL*
Sable, Martin Howard 1924- *WrDr 94*
Sabliere, Marguerite de la 1636-1693 *BlmGWL*
Sablieres, Jean Granouilhet 1627-c. 1700 *NewGrDO*
Sablik, Martin John 1939- *WhoScEn 94*
Sabloff, Jeremy Arac 1944- *WhoAm 94, WhoScEn 94*
Sablon, Germaine d1985 *WhoHol 92*
Sablon, Louette d1970 *WhoHol 92*
Sablow, Rhoda Lillian *WhoAmA 93*
Sabnis, Gajanan M. 1941- *WhoAsA 94*
Sabnis, Suman Trimbak 1935- *WhoAsA 94*
Sabo, Betty Jean 1928- *WhoAmA 93*
Sabo, Dave
  See Bon Jovi *ConMus 10*
Sabo, Martin Olav 1938- *CngDr 93, WhoAm 94, WhoAmP 93, WhoMW 93*
Sabo, Mary Ann 1962- *WhoMW 93*
Sabo, Richard Steven 1934- *WhoAm 94*
Sabo, Walter Richard, Jr. 1952- *WhoAm 94*
Sabol, Joseph Edward 1954- *WhoMW 93*
Sabolcik, Gene 1951- *WhoFI 94*
Sabosik, Patricia Elizabeth 1949- *WhoAm 94, WhoFI 94*
Sabota, Catherine Marie 1949- *WhoScEn 94*
Sabouret, Marie d1960 *WhoHol 92*
Sabouret, Yves Marie Georges 1936- *IntWW 93*
Sabourin, Clemonce 1910-1991 *WhoBlA 94N*
Sabourin, Louis 1935- *IntWW 93*
Sabourin, Paul L. 1943- *WhoMW 93*
Sabournin, Tony *WhoHisp 94*
Sabra, Steven Peter 1951- *WhoAmL 94*
Sabre, Dirk 1922- *WrDr 94*
Sabree, Clarice Salaam 1949- *WhoBlA 94*
Sabrina *WhoHol 92*
Sabry, H. E. Aly 1920-1991 *WhAm 10*
Sabsay, David 1931- *WhoWest 94*
Sabshin, Melvin 1925- *WhoAm 94, WhoScEn 94*
Sabu d1963 *WhoHol 92*
Saburi, Shin d1982 *WhoHol 92*
Saburov, Yevgeny Fedorovich 1947- *IntWW 93*
Saburova, Irina Evgen'evna 1907-1979 *BlmGWL*
Saby, John Sanford 1921- *WhoAm 94*
Sacajawea c. 1784-1812? *WhWE*
Sacanga, Italo 1932- *WhoAmA 93*
Sacasas, Rene 1947- *WhoAmL 94*
Sacastru, Martin *ConAu 43NR, ConWorW 93, RfGShF*
Sacchero, Giacomo d1875 *NewGrDO*
Sacchet, Edward M. 1936- *WhoAm 94*
Sacchetti, Adele Irene 1931- *WhoWest 94*
Sacchetti, Lorenzo 1759-1834? *NewGrDO*
Sacchetto, Rita d1959 *WhoHol 92*
Sacchi, Robert 1941- *WhoHol 92*
Sacchini, Antonio (Maria Gasparo Gioacchino) 1730-1786 *NewGrDO*
Sacco, Frank Vincent 1947- *WhoAm 94*

Sacco, James A. 1935- *WhoAmP 93*
Sacco, John Michael 1952- *WhoFI 94*
Sacco, Russell 1944- *WhoFI 94*
Sacco, Thomas Anthony 1953- *WhoFI 94*
Saccomandi, Vito 1939- *IntWW 93*
Saccomani, Lorenzo 1938- *NewGrDO*
Sacerdote, Manuel Ricardo 1943- *WhoAm 94*
Sacerdote, Peter M. 1937- *WhoAm 94*
Sacha, John F. 1948- *WhoAmL 94*
Sacha, Robert Frank 1946- *WhoAm 94*
Sachan, Dileep Singh 1938- *WhoAsA 94*
Sachar, Abram (Leon) 1899-1993 *CurBio 93N*
Sachar, Abram Leon 1899- *WhoAm 94*
Sachar, Abram Leon 1899-1993 *ConAu 142, NewYTBS 93 [port]*
Sachar, David Bernard 1940- *WhoScEn 94*
Sachar, Emily 1958- *WrDr 94*
Sachar, Howard Morley 1928- *WhoAm 94*
Sachare, Alex Philip 1949- *WhoFI 94*
Sacharow, Stanley 1935- *WhoFI 94, WhoScEn 94*
Sachau, Daniel Arthur 1959- *WhoScEn 94*
Sachdev, Mohindar Singh 1928- *WhoAm 94*
Sachdev, Raj Kumar 1951- *WhoScEn 94*
Sachdev, Ramesh Kumar 1944- *WhoAsA 94*
Sachdev, Ved Parkash 1932- *WhoScEn 94*
Sacher, Charles Philip 1939- *WhoAmL 94*
Sacher, Paul 1906- *IntWW 93*
Sacher, Steven Jay 1942- *WhoAm 94, WhoAmL 94*
Sachetta, Joseph 1958- *WhoFI 94*
Sachitano, Nancy Antoinette 1962- *WhoAmL 94*
Sachs, Alan Arthur 1947- *WhoAm 94*
Sachs, Alan Richard 1944- *WhoAmL 94*
Sachs, Alice *WhoAmP 93*
Sachs, Allan Maxwell 1921-1989 *WhAm 10*
Sachs, Andrew 1930- *WhoHol 92*
Sachs, Clifford Jay 1960- *WhoScEn 94*
Sachs, David 1933- *WhoAm 94*
Sachs, Elizabeth-Ann *DrAPF 93*
Sachs, Harvey M. 1944- *WhoScEn 94*
Sachs, Howard Frederic 1925- *WhoAm 94, WhoAmL 94, WhoMW 93*
Sachs, James H. 1907-1971 *WhoAmA 93N*
Sachs, Jeffrey D. *NewYTBS 93 [port]*
Sachs, Jeffrey D. 1954- *CurBio 93 [port]*
Sachs, Jerry *WhoAm 94*
Sachs, John Peter 1926- *WhoAm 94*
Sachs, Judith 1947- *WrDr 94*
Sachs, Kathleen R. 1951- *WhoFI 94*
Sachs, Kathryn Elizabeth 1932- *WhoMW 93*
Sachs, Leonard d1990 *WhoHol 92*
Sachs, Marilyn (Stickle) 1927- *TwCYAW, WrDr 94*
Sachs, Marilyn Stickle 1927- *WhoAm 94*
Sachs, Martin William 1937- *WhoScEn 94*
Sachs, Mendel 1927- *WrDr 94*
Sachs, Michael Alexander Geddes 1932- *Who 94*
Sachs, Murray 1924- *WrDr 94*
Sachs, Nelly 1891-1970 *BlmGWL*
Sachs, Paul J. 1878-1965 *WhoAmA 93N*
Sachs, Robert Green 1916- *IntWW 93, WhoAm 94*
Sachs, Robert Jay 1948- *WhoAmL 94*
Sachs, Robin 1951- *WhoHol 92*
Sachs, Samuel, II 1935- *WhoAm 94, WhoAmA 93, WhoMW 93*
Sachs, Stephen H. 1934- *WhoAmP 93*
Sachs, Stephen Howard 1934- *WhoAm 94*
Sachs, Stevens Warren 1947- *WhoIns 94*
Sachs, Susan F. *WhoAm 94*
Sachs, Thomas Dudley 1925- *WhoScEn 94*
Sachse, Guenther 1949- *WhoScEn 94*
Sachse, Janice R. 1908- *WhoAmA 93*
Sachse, Peter d1966 *WhoHol 92*
Sachtler, Wolfgang Max Hugo 1924- *WhoAm 94, WhoMW 93, WhoScEn 94*
Sacino, D. F. 1930- *WhoIns 94*
Sack, Burton Marshall 1937- *WhoAm 94*
Sack, Edgar Albert 1930- *WhoAm 94*
Sack, Erna d1972 *WhoHol 92*
Sack, Erna 1898-1972 *NewGrDO*
Sack, Fred David 1947- *WhoMW 93*
Sack, James McDonald, Jr. 1948- *WhoAm 94, WhoMW 93*
Sack, Nathaniel d1966 *WhoHol 92*
Sack, Nathaniel 1941- *WhoAmL 94*
Sack, Robert David 1939- *WhoAm 94*
Sack, Sylvan Hanan 1932- *WhoAm 94, WhoAmL 94*
Sackeim, Harold 1951- *WhoAm 94*
Sackett, Dean Reynolds, III 1963- *WhoAmL 94*
Sackett, Hugh F. 1930- *WhoFI 94*
Sackett, Ross DeForest 1930- *WhoAm 94*
Sackett, William Tecumseh, Jr. 1921- *WhoAm 94*
Sackheim, Robert Lewis 1937- *WhoScEn 94*
Sackheim, William B. 1921- *IntMPA 94*
Sackler, Arthur Brian 1950- *WhoAm 94, WhoAmL 94*
Sackler, Howard 1929-1982 *ConDr 93*
Sackley, Gary David 1950- *WhoAmP 93*
Sacklow, Stewart Irwin 1942- *WhoAm 94*
Sackman, Barbara Mae 1931- *WhoAmP 93*
Sackman, George Lawrence 1933- *WhoScEn 94*
Sackmann, Thomas Fredrick 1952- *WhoFI 94*
Sackner, Marvin Arthur 1932- *WhoAm 94*
Sacko, Soumana *IntWW 93*
Sacks, Albert Martin 1920-1991 *WhAm 10*
Sacks, Bernard Ross 1939- *WhoAmL 94*
Sacks, Beverly & Sacks, Ray *WhoAmA 93*
Sacks, Colin Hamilton 1957- *WhoScEn 94*
Sacks, David Arnold 1940- *WhoAm 94, WhoAmL 94*
Sacks, David G. 1924- *IntWW 93, WhoAm 94*
Sacks, David G. 1950- *WhoAmP 93*
Sacks, David Gregory 1950- *WhoAmL 94*
Sacks, Henry S. 1942- *WhoScEn 94*
Sacks, Herbert Simeon 1926- *WhoAm 94*
Sacks, Ira Stephen 1948- *WhoAm 94, WhoAmL 94*
Sacks, Jonathan 1948- *IntWW 93*
Sacks, Jonathan Henry 1948- *Who 94*
Sacks, Martin *WhoHol 92*
Sacks, Michael 1948- *WhoHol 92*
Sacks, Michael Wm. 1944- *WhoAmL 94*
Sacks, Oliver (Wolf) 1933- *WrDr 94*
Sacks, Oliver Wolf 1933- *IntWW 93, WhoAm 94*
Sacks, Peter *DrAPF 93*
Sacks, Ray
See Sacks, Beverly & Sacks, Ray *WhoAmA 93*
Sacks, Ray *WhoAmA 93*
Sacks, Samuel 1908- *IntMPA 94*
Sacks, Temi J. *WhoAm 94*
Sacksteder, Frederick Henry 1924- *WhoAm 94*
Sacksteder, Thomas M. 1950- *WhoMW 93*
Sackton, Frank Joseph 1912- *WhoAm 94, WhoWest 94*
Sackville *Who 94*
Sackville, Baron 1913- *Who 94*
Sackville, George *WhAmRev*
Sackville, Gordon d1926 *WhoHol 92*
Sackville, Thomas 1536-1608 *BlmGEL, DcLB 132 [port]*
Sackville, Thomas Geoffrey 1950- *Who 94*
Sackville-West *Who 94*
Sackville-West, V(ictoria Mary) 1892-1962 *EncSF 93, GayLL*
Sackville-West, Vita 1892-1962 *BlmGWL*
Sackwood, Mark 1926- *Who 94*
Sacrati, Francesco 1605?-1650 *NewGrDO*
Sada, Federico G. *WhoAm 94, WhoFI 94*
Sadana, Ajit 1947- *WhoAsA 94*
Sadanaga, Ryoichi 1920- *IntWW 93*
Sadasivan, Mahavijayan 1959- *WhoScEn 94*
Sadat, Anwar 1918-1981 *HisWorL [port]*
Sadat, Jihan 1933- *HisWorL*
Sadauki, Pamela *WhoWomW 91*
Sadava, David Eric 1946- *WhoWest 94*
Sa'dawi, Nawal al- 1931- *ConWorW 93*
Sa'dawi, Nawal El 1930- *BlmGWL*
Sadd, John Roswell 1933- *WhoMW 93*
Sadd, William Wheeler 1935- *WhoAm 94*
Saddam Hussein 1937- *IntWW 93*
Saddlemyer, Ann 1932- *WhoAm 94*
Saddlemyer, (Eleanor) Ann 1932- *WrDr 94*
Saddler, Allen 1923- *WrDr 94*
Saddler, Donald Edward 1920- *WhoAm 94*
Saddler, Roderick 1965- *WhoBlA 94*
Saddler, William E. 1915- *WhoBlA 94*
Saddock, Harry G. 1929- *WhoAm 94*
Saddumene, Bernardo fl. 1721-1734 *NewGrDO*
Sade 1958- *WhoHol 92*
Sade 1959- *WhoAm 94*
Sade, Donald Stone 1937- *WhoAm 94*
Sade, Donatien Alphonse, Marquis de 1740-1814 *BlmGEL*
Sade, Donatien-Alphonse-Francois, marquis de 1740-1814 *GuFrLit 2*
Sade, Shuli 1952- *WhoAmA 93*
Sadeghi, Ali 1955- *WhoWest 94*
Sadeghi, Farshid 1956- *WhoScEn 94*
Sadeghi, Nasser 1934- *WhoWest 94*
Sadek, George 1928- *WhoAmA 93*
Sadek, Salah Eldine 1920- *WhoMW 93*
Sadeque, Shahwar 1942- *Who 94*
Sader, Carol H. 1935- *WhoAmP 93*
Sader, Carol Hope 1935- *WhoAm 94*
Sader, Emir 1943- *ConAu 142*
Sader, Neil Steven 1958- *WhoAmL 94, WhoMW 93*
Sader, Robert Mayo 1948- *WhoAmL 94, WhoAmP 93, WhoWest 94*
Sadeur, Jacques c. 1650-1692 *EncSF 93*
Sadi, Marcus Vinicius 1956- *WhoScEn 94*
Sadie, Stanley (John) 1930- *Who 94, WrDr 94*
Sadie, Stanley John 1930- *IntWW 93*
Sadik, Marvin Sherwood 1932- *WhoAm 94, WhoAmA 93*
Sadik, Nafis 1929- *IntWW 93*
Sadilek, Vladimir 1933- *WhoFI 94, WhoWest 94*
Sadjadi, Firooz Ahmadi 1949- *WhoMW 93*
Sadle, Amy Ann Brandon 1940- *WhoAmA 93*
Sadleir, George Forster 1789-1859 *DcNaB MP*
Sadleir, William Kent 1954- *WhoAmP 93*
Sadler, Al 1936- *WhoAmP 93*
Sadler, Alvin Lewis 1925- *WhoMW 93*
Sadler, Amy 1924- *WrDr 94*
Sadler, Arleamon 1947- *WhoAm 94*
Sadler, Barry d1989 *WhoHol 92*
Sadler, Barry 1940-1989 *EncSF 93*
Sadler, Charles d1950 *WhoHol 92*
Sadler, David Gary 1939- *WhoAm 94, WhoFI 94*
Sadler, Dick 1928- *WhoAmP 93*
Sadler, Dick Sherman 1928- *WhoWest 94*
Sadler, Dudley d1951 *WhoHol 92*
Sadler, Eric 1960- *WhoAm 94*
Sadler, Geoffrey Willis 1943- *WrDr 94*
Sadler, Graham Hydrick 1931- *WhoAm 94*
Sadler, Ian d1971 *WhoHol 92*
Sadler, James 1753-1828 *DcNaB MP*
Sadler, James Bertram 1911- *WhoMW 93, WhoScEn 94*
Sadler, Jeff 1943- *WrDr 94*
Sadler, Joan 1927- *Who 94*
Sadler, John 1720-1789 *DcNaB MP*
Sadler, John Peter 1946- *WhoScEn 94*
Sadler, John Stephen 1930- *Who 94*
Sadler, Kenneth Marvin 1949- *WhoBlA 94*
Sadler, Louis Ray 1937- *WhoAmP 93, WhoWest 94*
Sadler, Luther Fuller, Jr. 1942- *WhoAm 94, WhoAmL 94*
Sadler, Mark 1924- *WrDr 94*
Sadler, Paul 1955- *WhoAmP 93*
Sadler, Robert Livingston 1935- *WhoAm 94*
Sadler, Roy H. 1929- *WhoAmP 93*
Sadler, Sallie Inglis 1941- *WhoWest 94*
Sadler, Stuart Ragland 1948- *WhoAmL 94*
Sadler, Theodore R., Jr. 1930- *WhoAm 94*
Sadler, Wilbert L., Jr. *WhoBlA 94*
Sadler, William *WhoHol 92*
Sadler, William Alan, Jr. 1931- *WhoWest 94*
Sadli, Mohammad 1922- *IntWW 93*
Sadlier, George Foster fl. 1819- *WhWE*
Sadlock, Richard Alan 1961- *WhoAmL 94*
Sadlowski, Edward Eugene 1938- *EncABHB 9*
Sado, Keiji d1964 *WhoHol 92*
Sadock, Benjamin James 1933- *WhoAm 94*
Sadoff, Fred E. 1926- *WhoHol 92*
Sadoff, Ira *DrAPF 93*
Sadoff, Robert Leslie 1936- *WhoAm 94*
Sadoul, Jacques 1934- *EncSF 93*
Sadoulet, Bernard 1944- *IntWW 93, WhoScEn 94*
Sadow, Harvey S. 1922- *WhoAm 94, WhoScEn 94*
Sadowski, Anthony James 1938- *WhoAm 94*
Sadowski, Carol (Louise) Johnson 1929- *WhoAmA 93*
Sadowski, George 1950- *WhoWest 94*
Sadowski, Lynda Lee 1947- *WhoMW 93*
Sadowski, Wieslaw 1922- *IntWW 93*
Sadowsky, Edward L. 1929- *WhoAmP 93*
Sadun, Alberto Carlo 1955- *WhoScEn 94*
Sadun, Alfredo Arrigo 1950- *WhoWest 94*
Sadusk, Maureen *WhoHol 92*
Sadusky, Maria Christine 1963- *WhoScEn 94*
Saebo, Magne 1929- *IntWW 93*
Saeden, Erik 1924- *NewGrDO*
Saeed, Mohammad 1948- *WhoMW 93*
Saegert, Ann M. 1953- *WhoAmL 94*
Saegusa, Takeo 1927- *WhoScEn 94*
Saeki, Hiroko Yoda 1936- *WhoAsA 94*
Saeks, Allen Irving 1932- *WhoAm 94, WhoAmL 94*
Saeks, Richard Ephraim 1941- *WhoAm 94*
Saeks, Sumner Marc 1960- *WhoFI 94*
Saemala, Francis Joseph 1944- *IntWW 93*
Saenger, Bruce W. 1943- *WhoIns 94*
Saenger, Bruce Walter 1943- *WhoFI 94*
Saenger, Eugene Lange 1917- *WhoAm 94*
Saenger, Theodore Jerome 1928- *WhoAm 94*
Saenger, Wolfram Heinrich Edmund 1939- *WhoScEn 94*
Saenko, Gennady Vasilevich 1945- *LngBDD*
Saenz, Alonzo A. 1940- *WhoHisp 94*
Saenz, Benito, Jr. 1944- *WhoAmP 93*
Saenz, Carlos Antonio 1951- *WhoFI 94*
Saenz, David R. *WhoHisp 94*
Saenz, Diana Eloise 1949- *WhoHisp 94*
Saenz, Eddie d1971 *WhoHol 92*
Saenz, Gil *DrAPF 93*
Saenz, Gilbert 1941- *WhoHisp 94*
Saenz, Gracie *WhoAmP 93, WhoHisp 94*
Saenz, Jacinto 1940- *WhoHisp 94*
Saenz, Jose Carlos 1938- *WhoHisp 94*
Saenz, Marc B. 1950- *WhoHisp 94*
Saenz, Michael 1925- *WhoHisp 94*
Saenz, P. Alex 1950- *WhoHisp 94*
Saenz, Ramiro 1935- *WhoHisp 94*
Saenz, Richard J. 1954- *WhoHisp 94*
Saenz, Robert 1938- *WhoHisp 94*
Saenz, Rogelio 1958- *WhoHisp 94*
Saenz-Alonso, Mercedes 1917- *BlmGWL*
Saenz De Cosculluela, Javier 1944- *IntWW 93*
Saenz-Garza, Rodolfo 1956- *WhoHisp 94*
Saer, Juan Jose 1937- *ConWorW 93*
Saersibik Istik 1925- *WhoPRCh 91*
Saeta, Philip Max 1931- *WhoAmL 94*
Saether, Ola Magne 1949- *WhoScEn 94*
Saez, Alberto M. 1922- *WhoScEn 94*
Saez, Pedro Justo *WhoHisp 94*
Saez, Pedro P. 1950- *WhoAmL 94*
Saez, Richard 1936- *WhoAm 94*
Safa, Bahram 1941- *WhoFI 94*
Safaai-Jazi, Ahmad 1948- *WhoScEn 94*
Safar, Michal *WhoScEn 94*
Safar, Peter 1924- *WhoScEn 94*
Safarov, Mars Gilyazevich 1937- *LngBDD*
Safars, Berta 1928- *WhoAm 94, WhoScEn 94*
Safdari, Yahya Bhai 1930- *WhoAsA 94*
Safdie, Moshe 1938- *IntWW 93, WhoAm 94, WrDr 94*
Safe, Kenneth Shaw, Jr. 1929- *WhoFI 94*
Safer, Jay Gerald 1946- *WhoAm 94, WhoAmL 94*
Safer, John 1922- *WhoAm 94, WhoAmA 93*
Safer, Morley 1931- *IntMPA 94, WhoAm 94, WrDr 94*
Saferite, Linda Lee 1947- *WhoWest 94*
Saferstein, Harvey I. 1943- *WhoAm 94, WhoAmL 94*
Saff, Donald Jay 1937- *WhoAmA 93*
Saff, Edward Barry 1944- *WhoAm 94, WhoScEn 94*
Saffar, Salman Mohamed al- 1931- *IntWW 93*
Saffeir, Harvey Joseph 1929- *WhoAm 94*
Saffel, E. Frank 1923- *WhoBlA 94*
Saffell, Michael Herbert 1946- *WhoWest 94*
Saffels, Dale Emerson 1921- *WhoAm 94, WhoAmL 94, WhoMW 93*
Saffer, Alfred 1918- *WhoAm 94*
Saffer, Linda Diane 1941- *WhoScEn 94*
Saffer, Morris Barry 1940- *WhoAm 94*
Safferman, Robert Samuel 1932- *WhoAm 94*
Saffioti, Carol Lee *DrAPF 93*
Saffiotti, Umberto 1928- *WhoScEn 94*
Saffir, Herbert Seymour 1917- *WhoAm 94, WhoScEn 94*
Saffle, M. W. 1923- *IntMPA 94*
Saffman, Philip G. 1931- *WhoAm 94*
Saffman, Philip Geoffrey 1931- *Who 94*
Saffo, Mary Beth 1948- *WhoWest 94*
Saffold, Oscar E. 1941- *WhoBlA 94*
Safford, Florence Viray Sunga 1929- *WhoWest 94*
Safford, Robert O. 1934- *WhoIns 94*
Saffran, Bernard 1936- *WhoAm 94, WhoFI 94*
Saffran, Kalman 1947- *WhoAm 94*
Saffran, Murray 1924- *WhoAm 94, WhoMW 93*
Saffron, Morris H. d1993 *NewYTBS 93*
Safian, Gail Robyn 1947- *WhoAm 94*
Safier, Lenore Beryl 1932- *WhoScEn 94*
Safieva, Gulrukhsor 1947- *WhoWomW 91*
Safiol, George E. 1932- *WhoFI 94*
Safir, Andrew Jeffrey 1948- *WhoAm 94*
Safir, Kathlyn Mary 1948- *WhoWest 94*
Safir, Leonard 1921-1992 *ConAu 140*
Safir, Natalie *DrAPF 93*
Safir, Pavittar S. 1936- *WhoIns 94*
Safir, Peter Oliver 1945- *WhoAmL 94*
Safir, Sidney 1923- *IntMPA 94*
Safire, William 1929- *IntWW 93, WhoAm 94, WhoAmP 93, WrDr 94*
Safley, James Robert 1943- *WhoAm 94, WhoAmL 94*

Safley, R. Z. 1946- WhoAmP 93
Safo, Martin Kwasi 1958- WhoScEn 94
Safonov, Michael George 1948- WhoAm 94
Safran, Claire WhoAm 94
Safran, Daniel 1939- WhoWest 94
Safran, Edward Myron 1937- WhoAm 94, WhoFI 94
Safranek, Katherine Ann 1962- WhoMW 93
Safranek, Stephen Joseph 1960- WhoAmL 94
Safron, Robert M. 1945- WhoAmL 94
Sagal, Boris d1981 WhoHol 92
Sagal, Joey WhoHol 92
Sagal, Katey 1955- WhoHol 92
Sagale, Taligalu WhoAmP 93
Sagalkin, Sanford 1942- WhoAm 94
Sagalyn, Lynne B. 1947- WrDr 94
Sagami, Kim WhoAm 94, WhoAsA 94
Sagan, Carl 1934- EncSF 93, WorScD, WrDr 94
Sagan, Carl Edward 1934- IntWW 93, WhoAm 94, WhoScEn 94
Sagan, Dorion 1959- WrDr 94
Sagan, Francoise 1935- BlmGWL, ConWorW 93, IntWW 93, Who 94
Sagan, Gregory Thaddeus 1947- WhoWest 94
Sagan, Hans 1928- WhoAm 94
Sagan, Jean Sanders 1948- WhoAmL 94
Sagan, John 1921- WhoAm 94, WhoFI 94, WhoMW 93
Sagan, Miriam DrAPF 93
Saganic, Livio Michele 1950- WhoAmA 93
Saganov, Vladimir Bizyaevich 1936- LngBDD
Sagansky, Jeff WhoAm 94
Sagansky, Jeff 1953- IntMPA 94
Sagar, Anthony d1973 WhoHol 92
Sagaria, Mary Ann Danowtiz 1947- WhoMW 93
Sagarin, Edward 1913-1986 GayLL
Sagarin, James Leon 1951- WhoMW 93
Sagarra, Eda 1933- IntWW 93
Sagat, Kenneth A. 1943- WhoAmL 94
Sagawa, Shirley Sachi 1961- WhoAm 94, WhoAsA 94
Sagawa, Yoneo 1926- WhoAm 94, WhoAsA 94, WhoWest 94
Sagaye, Gabra Madhen BlkWr 2
Sagdeev, Roald Zinnurovi WhoScEn 94
Sagdeev, Roald Zinnurovich 1932- IntWW 93
Sage, Andrew Gregg Curtin, II 1926- WhoAm 94
Sage, Andrew Patrick, Jr. 1933- WhoAm 94, WhoScEn 94
Sage, Bill B. d1990 WhoAmA 93N
Sage, Byron d1974 WhoHol 92
Sage, Frances d1963 WhoHol 92
Sage, Howard DrAPF 93
Sage, James Timothy 1957- WhoScEn 94
Sage, Kay (Tanguy) 1898-1963 WhoAmA 93N
Sage, Larry Guy 1946- WhoAmL 94
Sage, Lorna 1943- Who 94, WrDr 94
Sage, Robin Dale 1958- WhoAmL 94
Sage, Roderick Duncan 1926- WhoWest 94
Sage, Ronald P., Jr. 1962- WhoAmP 93
Sage, Stephen Paul 1953- Who 94
Sage, Willard d1974 WhoHol 92
Sage, William Matthew 1960- WhoWest 94
Sagebrecht, Marianne 1945- IntMPA 94, WhoHol 92
Sagel, Jim DrAPF 93
Sagendorf, Bud 1915- WhoAm 94
Sagendorph, Robb Hansell 1900-1970 DcLB 137 [port]
Sager, Carole Bayer 1947- WhoAm 94
Sager, Clifford Julius WhoAm 94
Sager, Dennis Merton WhoIns 94
Sager, Donald Allen 1930- WhoIns 94, WhoWest 94
Sager, Donald Jack 1938- WhoAm 94, WhoMW 93
Sager, John William 1946- WhoAm 94, WhoAmL 94
Sager, Jonathan Ward 1954- WhoAmL 94
Sager, Phyllis Kaufman 1945- WhoAmL 94, WhoFI 94
Sager, Richard Benjamin 1944- WhoMW 93
Sager, Roderick Cooper 1923- WhoAm 94
Sager, Ruth 1918- WhoAm 94, WhoScEn 94
Sager, Steven T. 1953- WhoAmP 93
Sager, Steven Travis 1957- WhoAmL 94
Sager, William F. 1918- WhoAm 94
Sagerholm, James Alvin 1927- WhoAm 94
Sagers, Rudolph, Jr. 1955- WhoBlA 94
Saget, Bob WhoAm 94
Saget, Bob 1956- WhoHol 92
Saget, Louis Joseph Edouard 1915- IntWW 93
Sagett, Jan Jeffrey 1943- WhoAm 94, WhoAmL 94
Saggau, David Jon 1964- WhoAmL 94
Saggers, Geoffrey WhoIns 94
Saggese, Alfred E., Jr. 1946- WhoAmP 93
Saggione, Joseph NewGrDO
Saggs, Henry (William Frederick) 1920- WrDr 94
Saghatelian, Susann Marie 1958- WhoWest 94
Sagi-Barba, Emilio 1876-1949 NewGrDO
Saginaw, Rose Blas 1926- WhoFI 94
Sagi-Vela (Barba), Luis 1914- NewGrDO
Saglio, Jean-Francois 1936- IntWW 93
Sagmeister, Edward Frank 1939- WhoWest 94
Sagness, Richard Lee 1937- WhoAm 94
Sago, Paul Edward 1931- WhoAm 94, WhoWest 94
Sagraves, Barbara Darling 1935- WhoAmP 93
Sagraves, Walter Ronald 1934- WhoMW 93
Sagstetter, Karen DrAPF 93
Sagsveen, Murray Gene 1946- WhoAmL 94
Sague, John Elmer 1933- WhoScEn 94
Saguer, Louis 1907- NewGrDO
Sah, Chih-Tang 1932- WhoAsA 94
Sah, Raaj Kumar 1952- WhoFI 94
Saha, Arthur W(illiam) 1923- EncSF 93
Saha, Badal Chandra 1949- WhoMW 93
Saha, Dhanonjoy Chandra 1957- WhoScEn 94
Saha, Gopal Bandhu WhoAsA 94
Saha, Murari Mohan 1947- WhoScEn 94
Sahade, Jorge 1915- IntWW 93
Sahagun, Elena 1963- WhoHol 92
Sahai, Hardeo 1942- WhoAm 94, WhoScEn 94
Sahakian, William S(ahak) 1921- WrDr 94
Sahara, Robert Fumio 1942- WhoWest 94
Sahatjian, Ronald Alexander 1942- WhoScEn 94
Sahgal, Nayantara 1927- BlmGWL, IntWW 93
Sahgal, Nayantara (Pandit) 1927- WrDr 94
Sahgal, Ranjit 1951- WhoFI 94
Sahid, Joseph Robert 1944- WhoAm 94, WhoAmL 94
Sahihi, Ashkan 1963- ConAu 141
Sahinidis, Nikolaos Vasili 1963- WhoMW 93
Sahl, Hans d1993 NewYTBS 93
Sahl, Michael 1934- NewGrDO
Sahl, Mort 1927- WhoCom [port], WhoHol 92
Sahl, Mort(on) Lyon 1927- IntWW 93
Sahl, Morton Lyon 1927- WhoAm 94
Sahlberg, Robert Donald 1926- WhoAm 94
Sahlem, James Robert 1948- WhoAmL 94
Sahler, Helen Gertrude d1950 WhoAmA 93N
Sahlin, Annie Malory 1948- WhoWest 94
Sahlin, Mauritz 1935- IntWW 93
Sahlin, Mona 1957- IntWW 93
Sahlin, Mona Ingeborg 1957- WhoWomW 91
Sahlins, Marshall (David) 1930- WrDr 94
Sahlstrand, James Michael 1936- WhoAmA 93
Sahlstrand, Margaret Ahrens 1939- WhoAmA 93
Sahlstrom, Elmer Bernard 1918- WhoAm 94
Sahner, Todd M. 1949- WhoAmL 94
Sahni, Balraj d1973 WhoHol 92
Sahni, Sham L. 1951- WhoAsA 94
Sahni, Viraht 1944- WhoAsA 94
Sahota, Gian Singh 1924- ConAu 142
Sahota, Gurcharn Singh 1940- WhoFI 94
Sahrbeck, Everett William 1910- WhoAmA 93
Sahu, Kishore d1980 WhoHol 92
Sahu, Ranajit 1961- WhoScEn 94
Sahu, Sunil Kumar 1948- WhoMW 93
Saia, David Joseph 1904- WhoAmP 93
Saia, Jorge WhoAmA 93
Saibold, Hannelore 1943- WhoWomW 91
Saibou, Ali IntWW 93
Saichek, Alan B. 1946- WhoWest 94
Said, Clifford Everett 1937- WhoMW 93
Said, Edward W. 1935- IntWW 93, WhoAm 94, WrDr 94
Said, Faisal bin Ali al- 1927- IntWW 93
Said, Hakim Mohammed 1920- IntWW 93
Said, Hamid M. 1954- WhoWest 94
Said, Kamal E. 1937- WhoFI 94
Said, Seyyid 1791-1856 HisWorL
Saidenberg, Daniel 1906- WhoAmA 93
Saidenberg, Eleanore B. 1911- WhoAmA 93
Saidman, Anne 1952- ConAu 142, SmATA 75 [port]
Saidman, Gary K. 1952- WhoAm 94, WhoAmL 94
Saielli, Roberta Maureen 1964- WhoAmL 94
Saier, Milton H, Jr. 1941- WhoWest 94
Saier, Oskar 1932- IntWW 93
Saif, Abdulla Hassan 1945- IntWW 93
Saif, Mehrdad 1960- WhoScEn 94
Saif Al-Islam, Mohamed al-Badr 1927- IntWW 93
Saifer, Mark Gary Pierce 1938- WhoAm 94, WhoScEn 94
Saifiddinov, Sharofiddin Sanginovich 1929- NewGrDO
Saifudin IntWW 93
Sai-fu-ding WhoPRCh 91
Saigh, Nassir M. Al- 1942- IntWW 93
Saiki, Jessica DrAPF 93
Saiki, Patricia 1930- WhoAm 94, WhoAmP 93, WhoWomW 91
Saiki, Patricia F. 1930- WhoAsA 94
Sail, Lawrence (Richard) 1942- WrDr 94
Sailer, Glenn J. 1938- WhoFI 94
Sailer, Henry Powers 1929- WhoAm 94
Saillon, Alfred 1944- WhoScEn 94
Sailor, Charles WhoHol 92
Sailors, Ken 1922- BasBi
Saima, Atsushi 1923- WhoScEn 94
Saiman, Martin S. 1932- WhoAm 94
Sain, Dan D. 1935- WhoAmP 93
Sain, Michael Kent 1937- WhoAm 94, WhoScEn 94
Sainani, Ram Hariram 1925- WhoFI 94
Sainath, Ramaiyer 1949- WhoScEn 94
Sainctonge, Louise-Genevieve Gillot NewGrDO
Saine, Carroll Lee 1934- WhoAm 94, WhoFI 94
Sainer, Arthur 1924- ConDr 93, WhoAm 94, WrDr 94
Sainer, Leonard 1909- WhAm 10
Saines, Marvin 1942- WhoScEn 94, WhoWest 94
Saini, B(alwant) S(ingh) 1930- WrDr 94
Saini, Gulshan Rai 1924- WhoFI 94
Saini, Vasant Durgadas 1952- WhoScEn 94
Sainju, Mohan Man 1941- IntWW 93
Sainpolis, John WhoHol 92
Sainsbury Who 94
Sainsbury, Baron 1902- Who 94
Sainsbury, Alan John 1902- IntWW 93
Sainsbury, David John 1940- IntWW 93, Who 94
Sainsbury, Edward Hardwicke 1912- Who 94
Sainsbury, Jeffrey Paul 1943- Who 94
Sainsbury, (Richard) Mark 1943- IntWW 93
Sainsbury, Maurice Joseph 1927- WrDr 94
Sainsbury, Robert 1906- Who 94
Sainsbury, Roger Frederick Who 94
Sainsbury, Timothy (Alan Davan) 1932- Who 94
Sainsbury Of Preston Candover, Baron 1927- IntWW 93, Who 94
Sainsbury Of Preston Candover, Lady Who 94
Saint, Andrew (John) 1946- WrDr 94
Saint, Assotto DrAPF 93
Saint, Crosbie Edgerton 1936- WhoAm 94
Saint, Dora Jessie 1913- Who 94
Saint, Eva Marie 1924- IntMPA 94, WhoAm 94, WhoHol 92
Saint, H(arry) F. 1941- EncSF 93
Saint, James Susan 1946- IntMPA 94
Saint, Lawrence 1885-1961 WhoAmA 93N
St. Albans, Archdeacon of Who 94
St. Albans, Bishop of 1929- Who 94
St. Albans, Dean of Who 94
St. Albans, Duke of 1939- Who 94
St. Aldwyn, Earl of 1950- Who 94
St. Alwyn, Harry d1943 WhoHol 92
St. Amand, Joseph 1925- WhoAmA 93
St. Amand, Pierre 1920- WhoAm 94, WhoScEn 94, WhoWest 94
Saint-Amans, Louis Joseph (Claude) 1749-c. 1820 NewGrDO
St. Andre, Richard Joseph 1945- WhoMW 93
St. Andrews, Earl of 1962- Who 94
St. Andrews, B. A. DrAPF 93
St. Andrews, Dunkeld And Dunblane, Bishop of 1925- Who 94
St. Andrews, Dunkeld And Dunblane, Dean of Who 94
St. Andrews And Edinburgh, Archbishop of 1938- Who 94
St. Andrews And Edinburgh, Bishop Auxiliary of Who 94
St. Angel, Michael d1984 WhoHol 92
St. Antoine, Theodore Joseph 1929- WhoAm 94, WhoMW 93
St. Arnold, Dale S. WhoAm 94, WhoMW 93
St. Asaph, Bishop of Who 94
St. Asaph, Dean of Who 94
Saint-Aubin, Ambroise d1780 AmRev
Saint-Aubin, Jeanne Charlotte 1760-1850 NewGrDO
St. Aubin, Susan DrAPF 93
St. Aubin de Teran, Lisa 1953- BlmGWL
St. Aubin de Teran, Lisa Gioconda 1953- IntWW 93
St. Aubyn Who 94
St. Aubyn, (John) Arscott M. Who 94
St. Aubyn, Giles (Rowan) 1925- WrDr 94
St. Aubyn, Rod WhoAmP 93
St. Aubyn, Thomas Edward 1923- Who 94
St. Audrie, Stella d1925 WhoHol 92
St. Boniface, Archbishop of 1926- Who 94
Saint-Chamond, Claire-Marie Mazzarelli 1731- BlmGWL
Saint-Christophle, Mlle de d1682? NewGrDO
St. Clair Who 94
St. Clair, Ana d1976 WhoHol 92
St. Clair, Annetta Elaine 1938- WhoAmP 93
St. Clair, Arthur 1736-1818 AmRev
St. Clair, Arthur 1737-1818 WhAmRev [port]
St. Clair, Bob ProFbHF [port]
St. Clair, Bozo d1976 WhoHol 92
St. Clair, Carl WhoAm 94, WhoWest 94
St. Clair, Donald David 1932- WhoMW 93
St. Clair, Elizabeth WhoHol 92
St. Clair, Giles 1940- WhoFI 94
St. Clair, Hal Kay 1925- WhoAm 94
St. Clair, James Draper 1920- WhoAm 94, WhoAmL 94
St. Clair, James William 1935- WhoAmL 94
St. Clair, Jesse Walton, Jr. 1930- WhoAm 94
St. Clair, Lydia d1970 WhoHol 92
St. Clair, Lydia d1974 WhoHol 92
St. Clair, Mal d1952 WhoHol 92
St. Clair, Malcolm Archibald James 1927- Who 94
St. Clair, Margaret 1911- EncSF 93
St. Clair, Margaret (Neeley) 1911- WrDr 94
St. Clair, Maurice d1970 WhoHol 92
St. Clair, Michael WhoHol 92
St. Clair, Michael 1912- WhoAm 94, WhoAmA 93
St. Clair, Philip DrAPF 93
St. Clair, Rita Erika WhoAm 94
St. Clair, Scott Andrew 1951- WhoAmL 94
St. Clair, Thomas McBryar 1935- WhoAm 94, WhoFI 94
St. Clair, Vernon Garold 1930- WhoWest 94
St. Clair, William 1937- WrDr 94
St. Clair, William Linn 1937- Who 94
St. Clair, Yvonne d1971 WhoHol 92
St. Claire, Erin 1948- WrDr 94
St. Claire, Frank Arthur 1949- WhoAm 94, WhoAmL 94
St. Clair-Erskine Who 94
St. Clair Ford, James (Anson) 1952- Who 94
St. Cloud, Alden DrAPF 93
Saint-Come, Claude Marc 1949- WhoScEn 94
St. Cyr, John Albert, II 1949- WhoMW 93, WhoScEn 94
St. Cyr, Johnny d1966 WhoHol 92
St. Cyr, Lili 1917- WhoHol 92
Saint Cyr, Mona 1934- WhoWomW 91
Saint-Cyr, Renee 1907- WhoHol 92
Saint-Cyran, Jean Duvergier de Hauranne, abbe de 1581-1643 GuFrLit 2
St. Cyres, Viscount 1957- Who 94
St. Davids, Bishop of 1926- Who 94
St. Davids, Dean of Who 94
St. Davids, Viscount 1939- Who 94
St. Denis, Joe d1968 WhoHol 92
St. Denis, Louis Juchereau De 1676-1744 WhWE
Saint-Denis, Michel d1971 WhoHol 92
St. Denis, Paul Andre 1938- WhoAmA 93
St. Denis, Ruth d1968 WhoHol 92
St. Denis, Ruth c. 1878-1968 AmCulL
St. Dennis, Bruce John 1956- WhoScEn 94
St. Dennis, Jerry A. 1942- WhoAm 94, WhoWest 94
Saint-Donat, Bernard Jacques 1946- WhoFI 94
St. Duval, Malila WhoHol 92
St. E. A. of M. and S. GayLL
St. Edmundsbury, Provost of Who 94
St. Edmundsbury And Ipswich, Bishop of 1931- Who 94
Sainte-Johnn, Don 1949- WhoBlA 94
Sainte-Marie, Buffy 1942?- ConMus 11 [port]
Saint-Erne, Nicholas John de 1958- WhoWest 94
St. Etienne, Gregory Michael 1957- WhoBlA 94

Saint-Evremond, Charles de Marquetel de Saint-Denis, Seigneur de 1614-1703 *GuFrLit 2*
Saint-Evremond, Charles de Saint-Denis 1614?-1703 *NewGrDO*
Saint-Exupery, Antoine de 1900-1944 *EncSF 93*
St. Florian, Friedrich Gartler 1932- *WhoAm 94, WhoAmA 93*
Saint-Gaudens, Augustus 1848-1907 *AmCulL*
St. Gaudens, Homer 1879-1958 *WhoAmA 93N*
St. George, Clement 1944- *WhoHol 92*
St. George, David *EncSF 93*
St. George, George (Bligh) 1908- *Who 94*
St. George, John A. d1993 *NewYTBS 93*
St. George, Judith 1931- *WrDr 94*
St. George, Judith Alexander 1931- *WhoAm 94*
St. George, Nicholas James 1939- *WhoAm 94*
St. George, Noel 1948- *WrDr 94*
St. George, William Ross 1924- *WhoAm 94*
Saint-Georges, Chevalier de 1739-1799 *AfrAmAl 6*
Saint-Georges, Joseph Boulogne, Chevalier de c. 1739-1799 *NewGrDO*
Saint-Georges, Jules-Henri Vernoy de 1799-1875 *NewGrDO*
St. Gerard, Michael 1964- *WhoHol 92*
St. Germain, Deanna Marie 1957- *WhoMW 93*
St. Germain, Fernand Joseph *WhoAm 94*
St. Germain, Fernand Joseph 1928- *WhoAmP 93*
St. Germain, Sheryl *DrAPF 93*
St. Germaine, Marie d1984 *WhoHol 92*
St. Germaine, Shirley Ann 1935- *WhoAmP 93*
St. Germans, Bishop Suffragan of 1951- *Who 94*
St. Germans, Earl of 1941- *Who 94*
St. Goar, Edward 1955- *WhoAm 94*
St. Goar, Herbert 1916- *WhoAm 94*
St. Helena, Bishop of 1929- *Who 94*
St. Helens, Baron 1945- *Who 94*
St. Helier, Ivy d1971 *WhoHol 92*
St. Hilaire, Catherine Lillian 1949- *WhoScEn 94*
Saint-Huberty, Mme de 1756-1812 *NewGrDO*
Saint-Jacques, Bernard 1928- *WhoAm 94, WhoWest 94*
Saint-Jacques, Madeleine 1935- *WhoAm 94*
St. Jacques, Raymond d1990 *WhoHol 92*
St. Jacques, Raymond 1930-1990 *WhAm 10*
St. Jacques, Robert H. 1924- *WhoAm 94, WhoFI 94*
St. James, Andrew 1904- *WrDr 94*
St. James, Blakely *EncSF 93*
St. James, Lyn 1947- *WhoAm 94*
Saint James, Susan 1946- *WhoHol 92*
St. James, William d1931 *WhoHol 92*
St. Jean, Catherine Avery 1950- *WhoAm 94*
St. Jean, Garry *WhoAm 94, WhoWest 94*
St. Jean, Guy 1941- *WhoAm 94*
St. Jean, James R. 1952- *WhoAmP 93*
St. Jean, Joseph, Jr. 1923- *WhoAm 94*
St. John *Who 94*
St. John, Adam 1952- *WhoAmA 93*
St. John, Adrian, II 1921- *WhoAm 94*
St. John, Al d1963 *WhoHol 92*
St. John, (Harold) Bernard 1931- *IntWW 93*
St. John, Betta 1929- *WhoHol 92*
St. John, Bill Dean 1931- *WhoAm 94, WhoFI 94*
St. John, Billy Eugene 1932- *WhoAm 94*
St. John, Bob 1937- *WhoAm 94*
St. John, Bruce 1916- *WhoAmA 93N*
St. John, Bruce (Carlisle) 1923- *WrDr 94*
St. John, Charles Virgil 1922- *WhoFI 94, WhoMW 93, WhoScEn 94*
St. John, Christopher 1942- *WhoHol 92*
St. John, David *DrAPF 93*
St. John, David 1918- *WrDr 94*
St. John, Eugene Logan 1947- *WhoWest 94*
Saint John, Gerard J. 1936- *WhoAmL 94*
St. John, Gregory Lynn 1951- *WhoFI 94*
St. John, Henry Sewell, Jr. 1938- *WhoFI 94*
St. John, Howard d1974 *WhoHol 92*
St. John, Howard Chambers *WhoAm 94, WhoAmL 94, WhoFI 94*
St. John, J(ames) Allen 1872-1957 *EncSF 93*
St. John, James Berry, Jr. 1940- *WhoAmL 94*
St. John, Jill 1940- *IntMPA 94, WhoHol 92*
St. John, John 1921- *WhoAm 94*
St. John, Kristoff 1966- *WhoHol 92*
St. John, Leonie 1939- *WrDr 94*
St. John, Lisa 1929- *WrDr 94*
St. John, Marco *WhoHol 92*
St. John, Margaret Kay 1953- *WhoScEn 94*
St. John, Marguerite d1940 *WhoHol 92*
St. John, Michelle *WhoHol 92*
St. John, Nicole *WrDr 94*
St. John, Oliver Beauchamp 1922- *Who 94*
St. John, Patricia Mary 1919- *WrDr 94*
St. John, Patricia Mary 1919-1993 *ConAu 142*
St. John, Paul Marion 1948- *WhoWest 94*
St. John, Philip *ConAu 141, EncSF 93, SmATA 76*
St. John, Philip 1915- *WrDr 94*
St. John, Primus *DrAPF 93*
St. John, Primus 1939- *WhoBlA 94*
St. John, Richard d1977 *WhoHol 92*
St. John, Richard 1933- *WhoAm 94*
St. John, Robert 1902- *WrDr 94*
St. John, Rodney Stephan 1966- *WhoMW 93*
St. John, Roger Ellis Tudor 1911- *Who 94*
St. John, Terry N. 1934- *WhoAmA 93*
St. John, William Saunders 1949- *WhoFI 94*
St. John De La Salle Eno, Brian Peter George 1948- *WhoAm 94*
St. John Of Bletso, Baron 1957- *Who 94*
St. John of Fawsey, Baron 1929- *WrDr 94*
St. John Of Fawsley, Baron 1929- *IntWW 93, Who 94*
St. John Parker, Michael 1941- *Who 94*
St. Johns, Adela Rogers d1988 *WhoHol 92*
St. Johns, Richard R. 1929- *IntMPA 94*
St. John-Stevas *Who 94*
St. Johnston, Colin David 1934- *Who 94*
St. Johnston, Kerry 1931- *Who 94*
St. John Wilson, Colin Alexander *Who 94*
St. Joseph, John Kenneth Sinclair 1912- *IntWW 93, Who 94*
St. Landau, Norman 1925- *WhoAmL 94*
Saint Laurent, Louis S. 1882-1973 *HisDcKW*
Saint-Laurent, Richard E. 1933- *WhoFI 94*
St. Laurent, Roy Thomas 1959- *WhoMW 93*
Saint Laurent, Yves (Henri Donat) 1936- *IntWW 93, Who 94*
St. Lawrence, Joseph Thomas 1913- *WhoAmP 93*
St. Leger *Who 94*
St. Leger, Barry 1737-1789 *WhAmRev*
St. Leo, Leonard d1977 *WhoHol 92*
Saint-Leon, Arthur 1821-1870 *IntDcB [port]*
Saint-Leon, (Charles Victor) Arthur 1821-1870 *NewGrDO*
St. Levan, Baron 1919- *Who 94*
St. Louis, Robert Vincent 1932- *WhoScEn 94*
Saint-Louis, Rudolph Anthony 1951- *WhoBlA 94*
St. Marie, Satenig 1927- *WhoAm 94*
St. Mars, Frank *EncSF 93*
St. Martin, Thomas J. *WhoAmP 93*
St. Mary, Edward Sylvester 1941- *WhoAm 94*
St. Mary, Joseph Jerome 1941- *WhoBlA 94*
St. Maur, Adele d1959 *WhoHol 92*
St. Maur, Kirk *WhoAmA 93*
St. Omer, Garth *WrDr 94*
St. Omer, Garth 1931- *BlkWr 2*
St. Omer, Vincent V. E. 1934- *WhoBlA 94*
St. Onge, Hubert Jules 1946- *WhoMW 93*
Saintonge, Louise-Genevieve Gillot, Dame de 1650-1718 *NewGrDO*
Saintonge, Rolland A. A. C. de *Who 94*
St. Onge, Vivian 1959- *WhoAmP 93*
St. Oswald, Baron 1919- *Who 94*
St. Paul's, Dean of *Who 94*
St. Pe, Gerald J. *WhoFI 94*
St. Peter, Florence *WhoHol 92*
Saint Phalle, Niki de *NewYTBS 93 [port]*
Saint-Phalle, Niki de 1930- *IntWW 93*
St. Pierre, George Roland, Jr. 1930- *WhoAm 94, WhoScEn 94*
St.-Pierre, Jacques 1920- *WhoAm 94*
St. Pierre, Julie *WhoHol 92*
Saint-Pierre, Michael Robert 1947- *WhoFI 94*
Saint-Pierre, Raymond *DrAPF 93*
St. Pierre, Ronald Leslie 1938- *WhoAm 94*
St. Polis, John d1946 *WhoHol 92*
St. Raymond, James V. 1957- *WhoAmP 93*
Saint-Saens, (Charles) Camille 1835-1921 *NewGrDO*
Saintsbury, George Edward Bateman 1845-1933 *BlmGEL*
Saintsbury, H.A. d1939 *WhoHol 92*
Saint-Simon, Claude Henri de Rouroy, Comte de 1760-1825 *WhAmRev*
Saint-Simon, Louis de Rouvroy, duc de 1675-1755 *GuFrLit 2*
Saint-Simon Montblern, Claude Anne, Marquis de 1740-1819 *WhAmRev [port]*
St. Tamara *WhoAmA 93*
Saint Tropez *WhAmRev*
St. Vincent, Viscount 1905- *Who 94*
St. Vincent, Paul 1939- *WrDr 94*
St. Vincent Ferreri *Who 94*
Sainty, Guy Stair 1950- *WhoAm 94*
Sainty, John Christopher 1934- *Who 94*
Sainz, Marco Antonio, Jr. 1962- *WhoAmL 94, WhoHisp 94*
Sainz Garcia, Maria Jesus Amparo 1947- *WhoWomW 91*
Saionji, Kinkazu d1993 *NewYTBS 93*
Saire, David *WhoHol 92*
Sais, Marin d1971 *WhoHol 92*
Sais, Tatjana d1981 *WhoHol 92*
Saisselin, Remy Gilbert 1925- *WhoAm 94*
Saito, Bill 1936- *WhoHol 92*
Saito, Eishiro 1911- *IntWW 93*
Saito, Eizaburo *IntWW 93*
Saito, Frank Kiyoji 1945- *WhoWest 94*
Saito, Gunzi 1945- *IntWW 93*
Saito, Hiroshi 1920- *IntWW 93*
Saito, Isao 1941- *WhoScEn 94*
Saito, Juro 1940- *IntWW 93*
Saito, Kunikichi 1909- *IntWW 93*
Saito, Kunio 1940- *IntWW 93*
Saito, Mitsuru 1952- *WhoScEn 94*
Saito, Nobufusa 1916- *IntWW 93*
Saito, Seiji 1933- *WhoAmA 93, WhoAsA 94*
Saito, Shuzo 1924- *WhoScEn 94*
Saito, Theodore T. 1942- *WhoWest 94*
Saito, Theodore Teruo 1942- *WhoAsA 94*
Saito, Thomas E. 1948- *WhoAsA 94*
Saito, Walter Masao 1929- *WhoAsA 94*
Saito, William Hiroyuki 1971- *WhoWest 94*
Saito, Yoshio 1949- *WhoAsA 94*
Saito, Yoshitaka 1926- *WhoScEn 94*
Saitoh, Tadashi 1940- *WhoScEn 94*
Saitoh, Tamotsu 1938- *WhoScEn 94*
Saitoti, George *IntWW 93*
Saiz, Bernadette Louise 1964- *WhoScEn 94*
Saiz, Enrique 1950- *WhoScEn 94*
Sajadah, Vishwanath *IntWW 93*
Sajak, Pat 1946?- *ConTFT 11, IntMPA 94*
Sajak, Pat 1947- *WhoAm 94*
Sajdak, Bruce T. 1945- *ConAu 142*
Saji, Kiyotaka 1942- *WhoAsA 94*
Sajna, Mike 1950- *ConAu 141*
Sajo, Erno *WhoScEn 94*
Sak, Michael Gerard 1959- *WhoMW 93*
Sakagawa, Richard Masaru 1943- *WhoAsA 94*
Sakaguchi, Genji 1927- *WhoScEn 94*
Sakai, Hiroko 1939- *WhoFI 94*
Sakai, Katsuo 1942- *WhoScEn 94*
Sakai, Kunikazu 1941- *WhoScEn 94*
Sakai, Michael H. 1950- *WhoAsA 94*
Sakai, Peter A. 1954- *WhoAmL 94*
Sakai, Shogo 1948- *WhoScEn 94*
Sakai, Shota 1921- *WhoAmP 93*
Sakai, Toshihiko 1943- *WhoScEn 94*
Sakai, Victoria K. 1943- *WhoAsA 94*
Sakai, Yoshiro 1935- *WhoAm 94*
Sakaki, Hiroyuki 1944- *IntWW 93*
Sakall, S.Z. d1955 *WhoHol 92*
Sakamoto, Arthur, Jr. 1959- *WhoAsA 94*
Sakamoto, Clyde M. 1943- *WhoAm 94*
Sakamoto, Clyde Mitsuru 1943- *WhoAsA 94*
Sakamoto, Ichitaro 1926- *WhoScEn 94*
Sakamoto, Katsuyuki 1938- *WhoAsA 94*
Sakamoto, Lynn *WhoAsA 94*
Sakamoto, Misoji 1923- *IntWW 93*
Sakamoto, Munenori 1936- *WhoScEn 94*
Sakamoto, Norman Lloyd 1947- *WhoWest 94*
Sakamoto, Russell J. 1944- *WhoAmP 93*
Sakamoto, Ryoichi 1952- *IntWW 93*
Sakamoto, Yoshikazu 1927- *WrDr 94*
Sakanashi, Mark Takeshi 1952- *WhoFI 94*
Sakanashi, Matao 1943- *WhoScEn 94*
Sakaoka, Yasue 1933- *WhoAmA 93*
Sakata, Harold d1982 *WhoHol 92*
Sakata, Kimio 1947- *WhoScEn 94*
Sakata, Michita 1916- *IntWW 93*
Sakel, Manfred Joshua 1906-1957 *EncSPD*
Sakellaridis, Theofrastos 1883?-1950 *NewGrDO*
Sakellaropoulos, George Panayotis 1944- *WhoScEn 94*
Saker, Annie d1932 *WhoHol 92*
Saker, James Robert 1945- *WhoMW 93*
Sakers, Don 1958- *EncSF 93*
Sakhare, Vishwa M. 1932- *WhoAsA 94*
Sakharov, Andrei d1989 *NobelP 91N*
Sakharov, Andrei 1921-1989 *HisWorL [port]*
Sakharov, Andrei Dimitriyevich 1921-1989 *WhAm 10*
Saki 1870-1916 *EncSF 93, RfGShF, ShSCr 12 [port]*
Sakievich, Mark John 1956- *WhoAmP 93*
Sakimoto, Philip Jon 1954- *WhoAsA 94*
Sakita, Bunji 1930- *WhoAm 94, WhoAsA 94*
Sakkal, Mamoun 1950- *WhoWest 94*
Sakmann, Bert *WhoScEn 94*
Sakmann, Bert 1942- *NobelP 91 [port], Who 94*
Sakoda, James Minoru 1916- *WhoAsA 94*
Sakol, Jeannie 1928- *WrDr 94*
Sakol, Jonathan H. 1942- *WhoAm 94, WhoAmL 94*
Sakosky, Bartley Allen 1962- *WhoMW 93*
Sakowitz, Robert Tobias 1938- *WhoAm 94*
Saks, Arnold 1931- *WhoAm 94*
Saks, Gene *IntWW 93, WhoAm 94*
Saks, Gene 1921- *IntMPA 94, WhoHol 92*
Saks, Judith-Ann 1943- *WhoAmA 93*
Saks, Matthew *WhoHol 92*
Saks, Michael Jay 1947- *WhoAm 94, WhoAmL 94*
Saks, Mike 1952- *ConAu 140*
Saks, Stephen Howard 1941- *WhoAm 94*
Saksen, Louis Carl 1946- *WhoWest 94*
Sakson, Robert (G.) 1938- *WhoAmA 93*
Sakuma, Thomas Tamotsu 1947- *WhoWest 94*
Sakurada, Yutaka 1933- *WhoScEn 94*
Sakurai, Akira *WhoScEn 94*
Sakurai, Fred Yutaka 1927- *WhoAsA 94*
Sakurai, Jo Mary 1918- *WhoAmA 93*
Sakurai, Kiyoshi 1934- *WhoScEn 94*
Sakurai, Takeo 1938- *WhoScEn 94*
Sakurauchi, Yoshio 1912- *IntWW 93*
Sakuta, Manabu 1947- *WhoScEn 94*
Sakuyama, Shunji 1940- *WhoAmA 93*
Sal, Jack 1954- *WhoAmA 93*
Sala, Anthony Joseph 1948- *WhoFI 94*
Sala, Antonio 1935- *WhoHisp 94*
Sala, Luis Francisco 1919- *WhoAm 94*
Sala, Marius 1932- *IntWW 93*
Sala, Martin Andrew 1957- *WhoScEn 94*
Sala, Nicola 1713-1801 *NewGrDO*
Salaam, Abdul 1929- *WhoBlA 94*
Salaam, Kalamu ya *DrAPF 93*
Salaam, Kalamu ya 1947- *BlkWr 2*
Salaam, Salim A. 1922- *IntWW 93*
Salaam, Sheila Abdus *WhoBlA 94*
Salabert, Maria Teresa 1948- *WhoHisp 94*
Salabounis, Manuel 1935- *WhoMW 93, WhoScEn 94*
Salacrou, Armand 1899-1989 *IntDcT 2*
Salacuse, Jeswald William 1938- *WhoAm 94*
Saladin 1138-1193 *BlmGEL, HisWorL [port]*
Saladin, Emery Frank 1942- *WhoMW 93*
Saladino, Tony 1943- *WhoAmA 93*
Saladrigas, Carlos Augusto 1948- *WhoHisp 94*
Salah, Abdullah A. 1922- *IntWW 93*
Salah, Joseph Elias 1944- *WhoAm 94*
Salaita, George Nicola 1931- *WhoWest 94*
Salakhitdinov, Makhmud 1933- *IntWW 93, WhoScEn 94*
Salam, Abdus 1926- *IntWW 93, Who 94, WhoAm 94, WhoScEn 94, WorScD*
Salam, Debera Jean 1957- *WhoFI 94*
Salam, Saeb 1905- *IntWW 93*
Salama, C. Andre Tewfik 1938- *WhoAm 94*
Salama, Hannu *EncSF 93*
Salaman, Myer Head 1902- *Who 94*
Salamati, Farshid 1949- *WhoFI 94*
Salamon, Julie 1953- *WrDr 94*
Salamon, Linda Bradley 1941- *WhoAm 94*
Salamon, Miklos Dezso Gyorgy 1933- *WhoAm 94, WhoScEn 94, WhoWest 94*
Salamon, Myron Ben 1939- *WhoAm 94, WhoMW 93*
Salamon, Renay 1948- *WhoFI 94*
Salamon, Sonya 1939- *WhoMW 93*
Salamone, Alphonse W. d1993 *NewYTBS 93 [port]*
Salamone, Gary P. 1950- *WhoAm 94*
Salamone, John M. 1947- *WhoAmP 93*
Salamone, Joseph Charles 1939- *WhoAm 94*
Salamone, Nancy A. 1953- *WhoIns 94*
Salamone, Ottavio 1930- *IntWW 93*
Salamone, Philip Joseph 1941- *WhoAm 94*
Salamoni, Francesco c. 1738- *See* Salamoni Family *NewGrDO*
Salamoni, Giuseppe 1710?-1777 *See* Salamoni Family *NewGrDO*
Salamoni, Giuseppe c. 1730-1805? *See* Salamoni Family *NewGrDO*
Salamoni Family *NewGrDO*
Salamoun, Peter V. 1926- *WhoFI 94*
Salamun, Peter Joseph 1919- *WhoMW 93*
Salamun, Tomaz 1941- *ConWorW 93*
Salamy, Farris Najeeb 1929- *WhoAmL 94*

Saland, Linda Carol 1942- WhoWest 94
Saland, Stephanie 1954- WhoAm 94
Saland, Stephen M. 1943- WhoAmP 93
Salane, Thomas Charles 1947- WhoAmL 94
Salanki, Janos 1929- IntWW 93
Salans, Carl Fredric 1933- WhoAm 94
Salans, Lester Barry 1936- WhoAm 94
Salant, Richard d1993 IntMPA 94N
Salant, Richard S. d1993 NewYTBS 93 [port]
Salant, Richard S. 1914- IntMPA 94
Salant, Richard S. 1914-1993 CurBio 93N
Salant, Walter S. 1911- WhoAm 94
Salardino, Michael George 1949- WhoAmP 93
Salari, Francesco 1751-1828 NewGrDO
Salas, Alan R. 1956- WhoHisp 94
Salas, Alejandro WhoHisp 94
Salas, Didio B. 1919- WhoHisp 94
Salas, Floyd DrAPF 93
Salas, Floyd 1931- HispLC [port]
Salas, Floyd Francis 1931- WhoHisp 94
Salas, Francisco Jose WhoHisp 94
Salas, Guillermo, Jr. WhoHisp 94
Salas, Gumecindo 1941- WhoHisp 94
Salas, J. Gustavo WhoHisp 94
Salas, Marcos 1944- WhoHisp 94
Salas, Margaret Laurence 1922- Who 94
Salas, Max E. 1953- WhoHisp 94
Salas, Melodi L. WhoAmP 93
Salas, Michael Lawrence 1950- WhoHisp 94
Salas, Pedro 1957- WhoHisp 94
Salas, Peter 1965- WhoHisp 94
Salas Collantes, Javier 1949- IntWW 93
Salasin, Sal DrAPF 93
Salassi, Otto R. d1993 NewYTBS 93
Salassi, Otto R(ussell) 1939-1993 ConAu 142, SmATA 77
Salassi, Raymond J., Jr. 1940- WhoAmL 94
Salathe, John, Jr. 1928- WhoAm 94
Salatiello, Thomas B. 1945- WhoAmP 93
Salatino, Jim 1949- WhoAmP 93
Salatino, William J. 1956- WhoFI 94, WhoMW 93
Salatka, Charles Alexander 1918- WhoAm 94
Salay, Cindy Rolston 1955- WhoFI 94
Salaz, Mike 1946- WhoAmP 93
Salaz, Mike D. 1946- WhoHisp 94
Salazar, Alan B. 1957- WhoHisp 94
Salazar, Alberto 1958- WhoAm 94, WhoHisp 94
Salazar, Antonio 1889-1970 HisWorL [port]
Salazar, Carmen 1940- WhoHisp 94
Salazar, Cleo 1938- WhoHisp 94
Salazar, David Henry 1942- WhoHisp 94
Salazar, David R. S. WhoHisp 94
Salazar, Debra 1952- WhoFI 94
Salazar, Diego 1945- WhoHisp 94
Salazar, Dolores M. 1945- WhoHisp 94
Salazar, Edward 1944- WhoHisp 94
Salazar, Eliseo M., Jr. 1957- WhoHisp 94
Salazar, Fred James, Jr. 1942- WhoHisp 94
Salazar, George Alberto 1953- WhoHisp 94
Salazar, Gertrude 1936- WhoHisp 94
Salazar, Gilbert R. 1959- WhoHisp 94
Salazar, Guadalupe 1944- WhoHisp 94
Salazar, Guillermo J. 1952- WhoHisp 94
Salazar, Helen Aquila 1944- WhoHisp 94
Salazar, Ismael C. WhoHisp 94
Salazar, Janice 1943- WhoHisp 94
Salazar, John Paul 1943- WhoAmL 94
Salazar, José Francisco 1948- WhoHisp 94
Salazar, Kenneth Vincent 1948- WhoHisp 94
Salazar, L. Yentow 1954- WhoHisp 94
Salazar, Luis Adolfo 1944- WhoHisp 94, WhoWest 94
Salazar, Luis Garcia 1956- WhoHisp 94
Salazar, Lupe Maria 1927- WhoHisp 94
Salazar, Manuel 1887-1950 NewGrDO
Salazar, Maximiliano Wilfredo 1929- WhoHisp 94
Salazar, Michael B. WhoHisp 94
Salazar, Michael E., Sr. 1956- WhoHisp 94
Salazar, Miriam Larios 1962- WhoHisp 94
Salazar, Nick L. WhoAmP 93, WhoHisp 94
Salazar, Rachel DrAPF 93
Salazar, Rachel 1954- WrDr 94
Salazar, Ramiro 1954- WhoAm 94
Salazar, Ramiro S. 1954- WhoHisp 94
Salazar, Raymond Anthony 1947- WhoHisp 94
Salazar, Rudy 1941- WhoHisp 94
Salazar, Steve 1965- WhoHisp 94
Salazar, Terry L. 1954- WhoHisp 94
Salazar, Theresa A. 1955- WhoHisp 94
Salazar, Tony 1959- WhoHisp 94
Salazar, Tony Michael 1952- WhoHisp 94
Salazar, Victor M. WhoHisp 94
Salazar, Walter Roy 1947- WhoHisp 94
Salazar-Carrillo, Jorge 1938- WhoAm 94, WhoFI 94, WhoHisp 94, WhoScEn 94
Salazar Manrique, Roberto 1936- IntWW 93
Salazar Navarro, Hernando 1931- WhoHisp 94
Salbaing, Pierre Alcee 1914- WhoAm 94
Salber, Eva Juliet 1916-1990 WhAm 10
Salce, Luciano d1989 WhoHol 92
Salcedo, Herman Francisco 1958- WhoHisp 94
Salcedo, Hernando 1938- WhoHisp 94
Salcedo, Jorge d1988 WhoHol 92
Salcedo, Jose Jesus 1960- WhoHisp 94
Salcedo, Michael 1961- WhoMW 93
Salcedo, Victor Manuel, Jr. 1952- WhoHisp 94
Salcedo-Bastardo, Jose Luis 1926- IntWW 93
Salch, Steven Charles 1943- WhoAm 94, WhoAmL 94
Salchert, Brian DrAPF 93
Salci, Larry Eugene 1946- WhoAm 94
Salcido, Michael A. d1990 WhoHol 92
Salcido, Richard 1943- WhoHisp 94
Salcido, Silvia Astorga WhoHisp 94
Salcito, Daniel R. 1940- WhoAmP 93
Salcudean, Martha Eva 1934- WhoAm 94, WhoWest 94
Saldamando, Alex WhoHisp 94
Saldamando, George 1950- WhoHisp 94
Saldana, Alfonso Manuel 1960- WhoAmL 94
Saldaña, Andrew Joe 1950- WhoHisp 94
Saldana, Fred, Jr. WhoHisp 94
Saldaña, Johnny 1954- WhoHisp 94
Saldana, Jose M. WhoHisp 94
Saldana, Mariana WhoHisp 94
Saldana, Santiago A., Jr. 1949- WhoHisp 94
Saldana, Theresa 1955- WhoHisp 94, WhoHol 92
Saldana-Luna, Pura 1944- WhoHisp 94
Saldate, Macario, IV 1941- WhoHisp 94
Saldich, Robert Joseph 1933- WhoScEn 94, WhoWest 94
Saldin, Thomas R. 1946- WhoAmL 94, WhoFI 94
Saldívar, José D. 1955- WhoHisp 94
Saldívar, Ramón 1949- WhoHisp 94
Saldivar, Samuel G. 1937- WhoHisp 94
Saldoni (y Remendo), Baltasar 1807-1889 NewGrDO
Sale, Charles d1936 WhoHol 92
Sale, Frances d1969 WhoHol 92
Sale, George Edgar 1941- WhoWest 94
Sale, James Prowant, Jr. 1947- WhoFI 94
Sale, Kirkpatrick 1937- EnvEnc [port], WhoAm 94, WrDr 94
Sale, Llewellyn, III 1942- WhoAm 94, WhoAmL 94
Sale, Marina Evgenevna 1934- LngBDD
Sale, Peter Francis 1941- WhoScEn 94
Sale, Richard d1993 IntMPA 94N, NewYTBS 93
Sale, Richard (Bernard) 1911- WrDr 94
Sale, Richard (Bernard) 1911?-1993 ConAu 140
Sale, Sara Lee 1954- WhoMW 93
Sale, Tom S. 1942- WhoFI 94
Sale, Virginia 1906- WhoHol 92
Sale, William Merritt 1929- WhoAm 94
Salee, Joseph Claude 1960- WhoMW 93
Saleeby, Edward Eli 1927- WhoAmP 93
Saleh, Ali Abdullah 1942- IntWW 93
Saleh, Bahaa E. A. 1944- WhoAm 94
Saleh, David John 1953- WhoAmL 94
Saleh, Dennis DrAPF 93
Saleh, Rachmat 1930- IntWW 93
Salehkhou, Ghassem 1941- IntWW 93
Salek, Mustapha Ould IntWW 93
Salem, Daniel Laurent Manuel 1925- Who 94
Salem, David Andrew 1956- WhoAmL 94
Salem, Donald L. 1938- WhoAmL 94
Salem, Elie 1930- IntWW 93
Salem, George Richard 1953- WhoAm 94, WhoAmP 93
Salem, Ibrahim Ahmed 1932- WhoScEn 94
Salem, Kenneth George 1928- WhoScEn 94
Salem, Peter d1816 WhAmRev
Salem, Sema'an I. 1927- ConAu 142
Salema, Margarida 1954- WhoWomW 91
Salembier, Valerie Birnbaum 1945- WhoAm 94
Salemi, Joseph S. DrAPF 93
Salemi, Marie Anne 1927- WhoAmP 93
Salemme, Antonio 1892- WhoAmA 93
Salemme, Lucia (Autorino) 1919- WhoAmA 93
Salemme, Martha 1912- WhoAmA 93
Salenger, Meredith 1970- WhoHol 92
Salentine, Thomas James 1939- WhoAm 94, WhoFI 94
Saler, John Rudofker 1958- WhoAmP 93
Salerno, Anthony c. 1911-1992 AnObit 1992
Salerno, Charles 1916- WhoAmA 93
Salerno, Enrico Maria WhoHol 92
Salerno, George d1982 WhoHol 92
Salerno, Joseph Michael 1917- WhoWest 94
Salerno, Mary J. 1923- WhoAmP 93
Salerno, Philip Adams 1953- WhoScEn 94
Sales, A. R. 1948- WhoAm 94, WhoFI 94
Sales, Eugenio de Araujo Cardinal 1920- WhoAm 94
Sales, Francois de 1567-1622 GuFrLit 2
Sales, James Bohus 1934- WhoAm 94, WhoAmL 94, WhoFI 94
Sales, Jerry Melvin 1950- WhoMW 93
Sales, (Donald) John 1933- Who 94
Sales, Michel 1928- WhoAm 94
Sales, Pietro Pompeo c. 1729-1797 NewGrDO
Sales, Richard Owen 1948- WhoBlA 94
Sales, Soupy 1926- WhoCom, WhoHol 92
Sales, Walter Lapp 1948- WhoAmL 94
Sales, Walter R. 1927- WhoAmP 93
Salesky, William Jeffrey 1957- WhoFI 94, WhoWest 94
Saless, Fathieh Molaparast 1948- WhoScEn 94
Salesses, John Joseph 1933- WhoAm 94
Salet, Eugene Albert 1911-1992 WhAm 10
Salet, Francis 1909- IntWW 93
Salete, Mademoiselle de fl. 17th cent.- BlmGWL
Salew, John 1897- WhoHol 92
Saleza, Albert 1867-1916 NewGrDO
Salfi, Dominick J. 1937- WhoAmP 93
Salfner, Heinz d1945 WhoHol 92
Salford, Bishop of 1938- Who 94
Salg, George M. 1959- WhoFI 94
Salgado, Annivar 1954- WhoHisp 94
Salgado, Carlos A. 1952- WhoHisp 94
Salgado, José Francisco 1949- WhoHisp 94
Salgado, Juan, III 1956- WhoHisp 94
Salgado, Lissette WhoAm 94
Salgado, Luis J. 1953- WhoHisp 94
Salgado, Maria Antonia 1933- WhoHisp 94
Salgado, Mario A. 1959- WhoHisp 94
Salgado, R. Anthony 1962- WhoAmL 94
Salgado, Ramona Matos WhoHisp 94
Salgado, Sebastiao 1944- News 94-2 [port]
Salgari, Emilio EncSF 93
Salgia, Tansukh J. 1937- WhoMW 93
Salguero Gross, Mercedes Gloria WhoWomW 91
Salhany, Lucie NewYTBS 93 [port]
Salhany, Lucille S. WhoAm 94
Sali, Vlad Naim 1962- WhoScEn 94
Sali, William T. WhoAmP 93
Saliba, Alfred J. 1930- WhoAmP 93
Saliba, Anis Khalil 1933- WhoScEn 94
Saliba, John H. 1938- WhoIns 94
Saliba, Joseph Elias 1955- WhoScEn 94
Saliba, Philip E. 1931- WhoAm 94
Saliba, Van Alexy 1957- WhoFI 94
Salicio, Jose Luis 1954- WhoHisp 94
Salicola, Angiola fl. 1681-1693 NewGrDO
Salieri, Antonio 1750-1825 NewGrDO
Salierno, Donald J. 1949- WhoFI 94
Saliers, Anne Burr 1954- WhoMW 93
Salig, Ronald James 1950- WhoFI 94
Saligman, Harvey 1938- WhoAm 94, WhoFI 94
Salignac, (Eustace) Thomas 1867-1945 NewGrDO
Salih, al-Tayyib 1928- ConWorW 93
Salih, Halil Ibrahim 1939- WhoAm 94
Salii, Ivan Mykolaiovych 1943- LngBDD
Salim, Ali EncSF 93
Salim, Salim Ahmed 1942- IntWW 93
Salimbeni, Felice c. 1712-1751 NewGrDO
Salimei, Marcello 1927- IntWW 93
Salimeno, George Robert 1931- WhoAmP 93
Salin, William Nathan 1931- WhoFI 94
Salinas, Baruj 1935- WhoAmA 93, WhoHisp 94
Salinas, Bobbi WhoHisp 94
Salinas, Emma 1940- WhoHisp 94
Salinas, Harry Roger 1949- WhoHisp 94
Salinas, Homer WhoHisp 94
Salinas, Jone WhoHol 92
Salinas, Jose Maria, Jr. 1941- WhoHisp 94
Salinas, Leonardo 1933- WhoHisp 94
Salinas, Lorina WhoHisp 94
Salinas, Louis H., Jr. 1953- WhoAmL 94
Salinas, Luciano, Jr. 1950- WhoHisp 94
Salinas, Luis 1965- WhoHisp 94
Salinas, Luis Omar 1937- HispLC [port], WhoHisp 94
Salinas, Lupe 1948- WhoHisp 94
Salinas, Maria Elena WhoHisp 94
Salinas, Noe 1924- WhoHisp 94
Salinas, Norberto WhoHisp 94
Salinas, Oscar 1951- WhoHisp 94
Salinas, Pedro 1891-1951 DcLB 134 [port]
Salinas, Raul Francisco 1960- WhoAmL 94
Salinas, Raul G. 1946- WhoHisp 94
Salinas, Ricardo 1960- WhoHisp 94
Salinas, Ruben Longino 1954- WhoHisp 94
Salinas, Rudy 1953- WhoHisp 94
Salinas, Sandra Yvonne 1963- WhoFI 94
Salinas, Sharon Anne 1961- WhoAmL 94
Salinas, Simon 1955- WhoHisp 94, WhoWest 94
Salinas De Gortari, Carlos 1948- IntWW 93, WhoAm 94
Salinas Durón, Mary 1952- WhoHisp 94
Salinas-Ender, Elma T. WhoHisp 94
Salinas Izaguirre, Abel 1930- IntWW 93
Salinas Izaguirre, Saul F. 1932- WhoHisp 94
Saline, Lindon Edgar 1924- WhoAm 94
Saling, Gerald L. WhoAmP 93
Salinger, Diane WhoHol 92
Salinger, J. D. DrAPF 93
Salinger, J(erome) D(avid) 1919- IntWW 93, RfGShF, TwCYAW, WrDr 94
Salinger, Jerome David 1919- Who 94, WhoAm 94
Salinger, Matt 1960- WhoHol 92
Salinger, Pierre (Emil George) 1925- Who 94, WrDr 94
Salinger, Pierre Emil George 1925- IntWW 93, WhoAm 94
Salinger, Robert Meredith 1950- WhoAm 94, WhoAmL 94
Salinger, Ruth Angier 1931- WhoFI 94
Salinger, Sidney Bernerd, Jr. 1933- WhoFI 94
Salinger, Thomas S. 1945- WhoAmL 94
Salinger, Wendy DrAPF 93
Salinsky, Michael H. 1942- WhoAmL 94
Saliola, Frances 1921- WhoFI 94
Salipante, Robert C. WhoIns 94
Salis, Jean Rodolphe de 1901- IntWW 93
Salisachs, Mercedes 1916- BlmGWL
Salisbury, Bishop of 1942- Who 94
Salisbury, Dean of Who 94
Salisbury, Earl of 1591-1668 DcNaB MP
Salisbury, Marquess of 1916- Who 94
Salisbury, Alan Blanchard 1937- WhoFI 94
Salisbury, Alicia Laing 1939- WhoAmP 93, WhoMW 93
Salisbury, David Francis 1947- WhoWest 94
Salisbury, Deale B. WhoAmP 93
Salisbury, Eugene W. 1933- WhoAmL 94
Salisbury, Frank B(oyer) 1926- WrDr 94
Salisbury, Frank Boyer 1926- WhoAm 94
Salisbury, Franklin Cary 1910- WhoAm 94
Salisbury, Graham 1944- SmATA 76 [port]
Salisbury, Harrison E. 1908-1993 NewYTBS 93 [port], WrDr 94N
Salisbury, Harrison E(vans) 1908-1993 ConAu 141, CurBio 93N
Salisbury, Harrison Evans d1993 Who 94N
Salisbury, Harrison Evans 1908- IntWW 93
Salisbury, Jane Jefford 1947- WhoMW 93
Salisbury, Jenny Olivia 1959- WhoMW 93
Salisbury, John Who 94
Salisbury, John 1936- WrDr 94
Salisbury, John Francis 1930- WhoAm 94, WhoAmL 94
Salisbury, John William 1933- WhoScEn 94
Salisbury, Joyce E(llen) 1944- WrDr 94
Salisbury, Kevin Mahon 1935- WhoAm 94
Salisbury, Mike 1942- WrDr 94
Salisbury, Monroe d1935 WhoHol 92
Salisbury, Ralph DrAPF 93
Salisbury, Richard Frank 1926-1989 WhAm 10
Salisbury, Robert Cameron 1943- WhoAm 94, WhoFI 94
Salisbury, Robert G. WhoAmP 93
Salisbury, Robert H(olt) 1930- WrDr 94
Salisbury, Robert Holt 1930- WhoAm 94, WhoMW 93
Salisbury, Tamara Paula 1927- WhoScEn 94
Salisbury, Wayne 1941- WhoAmP 93
Salis-Marschlins, Meta 1855-1929 BlmGWL
Salisse, John Joseph 1926- Who 94
Saliterman, Richard Arlen 1946- WhoAm 94, WhoAmL 94, WhoFI 94, WhoMW 93
Saliu, Ion 1950- WhoScEn 94
Salizzoni, Frank Louis 1938- WhoAm 94, WhoFI 94
Salje, Ekhard Karl Hermann 1946- Who 94
Salk, Jonas E. 1914- WorScD

Salk, Jonas Edward 1914- *IntWW 93, Who 94, WhoAm 94, WhoScEn 94, WhoWest 94*
Salk, Lee 1926-1992 *AnObit 1992, WhAm 10*
Salkey, (Felix) Andrew (Alexander) 1928- *WrDr 94*
Salkin, David 1906- *WhoWest 94*
Salkin, Leo d1993 *NewYTBS 93*
Salkin, Lucien d1977 *WhoHol 92*
Salkin, Patricia E. 1964- *WhoAmL 94*
Salkin, Samuel Joseph 1950- *WhoWest 94*
Salkind, Alexander *IntWW 93*
Salkind, Alexander 1921- *IntMPA 94*
Salkind, Alvin J. 1927- *WhoAm 94, WhoScEn 94*
Salkind, Ilya 1947- *IntMPA 94, IntWW 93*
Salko, Henry S. 1925-1990 *WhAm 10*
Salkow, Sidney 1911- *IntMPA 94*
Sall, Frank M. 1937- *WhoAmP 93*
Sallada, Roland A. 1917- *WhoAmP 93*
Sallade, George Wahr 1922- *WhoAmP 93*
Sallah, Majeed 1920- *WhoFI 94*
Sallah, Ousman Ahmadou 1938- *IntWW 93*
Sallal, Abdullah as- 1917- *IntWW 93*
Sallam, Mohamed Abdulaziz 1933- *IntWW 93*
Sallas, Dennis *WhoHol 92*
Sallay, Tibor 1922- *WhoAmL 94*
Salle, David 1952- *IntWW 93, WhoAm 94, WhoAmA 93*
Salle, Jerome M. 1938- *WhoAm 94*
Salle, Marie 1707-1756 *IntDcB [port], NewGrDO*
Salle, Rene-Robert Cavelier, Sieur De La *WhWE*
Sallee, Don *WhoAmP 93*
Sallee, Mary Lou *WhoAmP 93*
Sallee, Wesley William 1951- *WhoWest 94*
Salleh, M. Nor 1940- *IntWW 93*
Sallen, Ira Bruce 1954- *WhoFI 94*
Sallen, Marvin Seymour 1930- *WhoMW 93*
Saller, Richard Paul 1952- *WhoAm 94*
Saller, Sylvester John 1895- *WhAm 10*
Sallés, Jaime Carlos 1930- *WhoHisp 94*
Sallet, Dirse Wilkis 1936-1992 *WhAm 10*
Salley, John Jones 1926- *WhoAm 94*
Salley, John Thomas 1964- *WhoBlA 94*
Sallick, Lucy Ellen 1937- *WhoAmA 93*
Sallinen, Aulis 1935- *NewGrDO*
Sallinen, Aulis Heikki 1935- *IntWW 93*
Sallinger, Rudolf d1992 *IntWW 93N*
Sallis, James 1944- *EncSF 93, WrDr 94*
Sallis, John C(leveland) 1938- *WrDr 94*
Sallis, Peter 1921- *WhoHol 92*
Sallis, Zoe *WhoHol 92*
Sallmann, Michael Joseph 1961- *WhoMW 93*
Salloum, Salim George 1956- *WhoFI 94*
Sallus, Marc Leonard 1954- *WhoAmL 94*
Salm, Peter 1919-1990 *WhAm 10*
Salman, Carlos 1932- *WhoAmP 93*
Salman, Salah 1936- *IntWW 93*
Salman, Steven L. 1947- *WhoIns 94*
Salman Ibn Abdul Aziz, H.R.H. Prince 1936- *IntWW 93*
Salmans, Charles Gardiner 1945- *WhoAm 94, WhoFI 94*
Salm-Dyck, Constance de 1767-1845 *BlmGWL*
Salmeron, Fernando 1925- *IntWW 93*
Salmhofer, Franz 1900-1975 *NewGrDO*
Salmi, Albert d1990 *WhoHol 92*
Salmi, Ellablanche *DrAPF 93*
Salminen, Matti 1945- *NewGrDO*
Salmirs, Seymour 1928- *WhoScEn 94*
Salmoiraghi, Gian Carlo 1924- *WhoAm 94*
Salmon, Brian Lawson 1917- *IntWW 93, Who 94*
Salmon, Charles B., Jr. *WhoAmP 93*
Salmon, Charles B., Jr. 1938- *WhoAm 94*
Salmon, David Charles 1962- *WhoScEn 94*
Salmon, Denis R. 1951- *WhoAmL 94*
Salmon, E. Dwight d1993 *NewYTBS 93*
Salmon, Edward H. *WhoAmP 93*
Salmon, Fay Tian 1959- *WhoScEn 94*
Salmon, Jaslin Uriah 1942- *WhoBlA 94*
Salmon, John (Hearsey McMillan) 1925- *WrDr 94*
Salmon, John Hearsey McMillan 1925- *WhoAm 94*
Salmon, John Tenison 1910- *IntWW 93*
Salmon, Joseph fl. 1647-1655 *DcNaB MP*
Salmon, Joseph Thaddeus 1927- *WhoAm 94*
Salmon, Karel 1897-1974 *NewGrDO*
Salmon, Louis 1923- *WhoAm 94*
Salmón, Maria Virginia 1954- *WhoHisp 94*
Salmon, Matt 1936- *WhoAmP 93*
Salmon, Matthew James 1958- *WhoWest 94*
Salmon, Merlyn Leigh 1924- *WhoWest 94*
Salmon, Michael John 1936- *Who 94*
Salmon, Nancy (Marion) *Who 94*
Salmon, Raymond Merle 1931- *WhoAmA 93*
Salmon, Robert 1918- *IntWW 93*
Salmón, Roberto Mario 1941- *WhoHisp 94*
Salmon, Russell Owen 1933- *WhoMW 93*
Salmon, Scott d1993 *NewYTBS 93*
Salmon, Stuart Clive 1952- *WhoMW 93*
Salmon, Thomas David 1916- *Who 94*
Salmon, Thomas Noel Desmond Cornwall 1913- *Who 94*
Salmon, Thomas Paul 1932- *WhoAm 94*
Salmon, Vincent 1912- *WhoAm 94*
Salmon, William Alexander 1910- *Who 94*
Salmon, William Cooper 1935- *WhoAm 94, WhoScEn 94*
Salmon, William Irwin 1942- *WhoWest 94*
Salmon Campbell, Joan Mitchell 1938- *WhoBlA 94*
Salmond, Alexander Elliot Anderson 1954- *IntWW 93, Who 94*
Salmond, Jasper 1930- *WhoBlA 94*
Salmond, Mary Anne 1945- *ConAu 142*
Salmonova, Lyda d1968 *WhoHol 92*
Salo, Ann Sexton D. 1947- *WhoAmL 94*
Salo, Harry A. 1944- *WhoFI 94*
Salo, Judith 1948- *WhoAmP 93*
Salolainen, Pertti Edvard 1940- *IntWW 93*
Salom, Roberto 1944- *WhoFI 94*
Salom, Scott Michael 1959- *WhoScEn 94*
Salomon, Darrell Joseph 1939- *WhoAm 94, WhoAmL 94*
Salomon, Frank Loewen 1946- *WhoMW 93*
Salomon, Haym 1740-1785 *AmRev, WhAmRev*
Salomon, Janet Lynn Nowicki 1953- *WhoAm 94*
Salomon, Johann Peter 1745?-1815 *NewGrDO*
Salomon, Joseph-Francois 1649?-1732 *NewGrDO*
Salomon, Kenneth David 1945- *WhoAm 94*
Salomon, Kenneth Harold 1945- *WhoMW 93*
Salomon, Lawrence 1940- *WhoAmA 93*
Salomon, Leon Edward 1936- *WhoAm 94*
Salomon, Mikael *WhoAm 94*
Salomon, Mikael 1945- *IntMPA 94*
Salomon, Phillippe M. 1949- *WhoAmL 94*
Salomon, Richard 1912- *WhoAm 94*
Salomon, Richard Adley 1953- *WhoAm 94, WhoAmL 94*
Salomon, Robert S., Jr. *WhoAm 94, WhoFI 94*
Salomon, Roger Blaine 1928- *WhoAm 94*
Salomon, Servin *WhoHisp 94*
Salomon, (Naphtali) Siegfried 1885-1962 *NewGrDO*
Salomons, David Lionel 1851-1925 *DcNaB MP*
Salomons, Jean-Pierre *IntWW 93*
Salone, Marcus 1949- *WhoBlA 94*
Salonen, Esa-Pekka 1958- *IntWW 93, WhoAm 94, WhoWest 94*
Salonen, Heikki Olavi 1933- *WhoFI 94*
Saloner, Garth 1955- *WhoFI 94*
Salonga, Lea 1971- *WhoAm 94, WhoAsA 94*
Salonia, Antonio Francisco 1927- *IntWW 93*
Salony, John, III 1947- *WhoFI 94*
Saloom, Eugene George 1934- *WhoAmP 93*
Saloom, Joseph A. *WhoAmP 93*
Saloom, Joseph A., III 1948- *WhoAm 94*
Saloom, Kaliste Joseph, Jr. 1918- *WhoAmL 94*
Salop, Archdeacon of *Who 94*
Salop, Arnold 1923- *WhoScEn 94*
Salou, Louis d1948 *WhoHol 92*
Salovey, Peter 1958- *WhoScEn 94*
Salpeter, Alan N. 1947- *WhoAm 94, WhoAmL 94*
Salpeter, Edwin E. 1924- *IntWW 93*
Salpeter, Edwin Ernest 1924- *WhoAm 94, WhoScEn 94*
Salsberg, Arthur Philip 1929- *WhoAm 94*
Salsbury, Roland S., Jr. *WhoAmP 93*
Salsbury, Stephen 1931- *WrDr 94*
Salsbury, Stephen Matthew 1931- *WhoAm 94*
Salsbury, Stuart Marshall 1946- *WhoAmL 94*
Salser, Gregg Alan 1965- *WhoMW 93*
Salsig, Doyen 1923- *WhoWest 94*
Salt *WhoBlA 94*
Salt, George 1903- *Who 94*
Salt, Henry S. 1851-1939 *EnvEnc [port]*
Salt, Henry Shakespear Stephens 1851-1939 *DcNaB MP*
Salt, James Frederick Thomas George 1940- *Who 94*
Salt, Jennifer 1944- *WhoHol 92*
Salt, John 1937- *WhoAmA 93*
Salt, (Thomas) Michael (John) 1946- *Who 94*
Salt, Patrick (Macdonnell) 1932- *Who 94*
Salt, Waldo 1914-1987 *IntDcF 2-4*
Salta, Steven Anthony 1955- *WhoWest 94*
Saltarelli, Eugene A. 1923- *WhoAm 94*
Salten, David George 1913- *WhoAm 94*
Saltenberger, Pamela Guay 1944- *WhoWest 94*
Salter, Douglas Neel 1940- *WhoFI 94*
Salter, Edwin Carroll 1927- *WhoAm 94, WhoMW 93*
Salter, George 1907-1967 *WhoAmA 93N*
Salter, Hans J. 1896- *IntDcF 2-4, IntMPA 94*
Salter, Harry d1928 *WhoHol 92*
Salter, Harry Charles 1918- *Who 94*
Salter, Heidi Lea 1958- *WhoAmL 94*
Salter, Herbert William 1897- *WhAm 10*
Salter, Hugh 1921- *WhoAmP 93*
Salter, Ian George 1943- *Who 94*
Salter, James *DrAPF 93*
Salter, James 1925- *DcLB 130 [port]*
Salter, Joan Moore 1959- *WhoMW 93*
Salter, Joe R. 1943- *WhoAmP 93*
Salter, John Randall 1898-1978 *WhoAmA 93N*
Salter, John Rotherham 1932- *IntWW 93*
Salter, Kevin Thornton 1947- *WhoAmL 94*
Salter, Kwame S. 1946- *WhoBlA 94*
Salter, Lester Herbert 1918- *WhoAm 94*
Salter, Lewis Spencer 1926-1989 *WhAm 10*
Salter, Lionel (Paul) 1914- *NewGrDO*
Salter, Lionel Paul 1914- *IntWW 93*
Salter, Mary D. 1913- *WrDr 94*
Salter, Mary Jo *DrAPF 93*
Salter, Mary Jo 1954- *WrDr 94*
Salter, Patrick Morris, Jr. 1952- *WhoWest 94*
Salter, Richard Mackintire 1940- *WhoAmA 93*
Salter, Robert Bruce 1924- *WhoAm 94*
Salter, Robert Mundhenk, Jr. 1920- *WhoAm 94*
Salter, Roger Franklin 1940- *WhoBlA 94*
Salter, Thelma d1953 *WhoHol 92*
Salter, W. Dean 1941- *WhoAmL 94*
Salters, Richard Stewart 1951- *WhoScEn 94*
Salthouse, Edward Charles 1935- *Who 94*
Salthouse, John *WhoHol 92*
Salthouse, Leonard 1927- *Who 94*
Salthouse, Thomas Newton 1916- *WhoScEn 94*
Saltiel, William David 1895- *WhAm 10*
Saltman, Benjamin *DrAPF 93*
Saltman, Sheldon Arthur 1933- *WhoWest 94*
Saltmarche, Kenneth Charles 1920- *WhoAmA 93*
Saltmarsh, Sara Elizabeth 1956- *WhoAmL 94*
Saltmarsh, Sherman W., Jr. 1929- *WhoAmP 93*
Salton, Albin 1916- *WhoAm 94*
Salton, Gerard 1927- *WhoAm 94*
Salton, Milton Robert James 1921- *Who 94*
Saltonstall, Dudley 1738-1796 *WhAmRev*
Saltonstall, Elizabeth 1900-1990 *WhoAmA 93N*
Saltonstall, George West 1944- *WhoFI 94*
Saltonstall, William Gurdon 1905-1989 *WhAm 10*
Saltonstall, William Lawrence 1927- *WhoAmP 93*
Saltoun, Lady 1930- *Who 94*
Saltoun, Andre Meir 1929- *WhoAm 94*
Saltoun of Abernethy, Lady 1930- *WhoWomW 91*
Saltsman, Donald L. 1933- *WhoAmP 93*
Saltykov, Aleksey Aleksandrovich 1934- *IntWW 93*
Saltykov, Boris Georgevich 1940- *LngBDD*
Saltykov, Boris Georgievich 1940- *IntWW 93, WhoScEn 94*
Saltz, Carole Pogrebin 1949- *WhoAm 94*
Saltz, Howard Joel 1960- *WhoAm 94*
Saltz, Jeffrey S. 1953- *WhoAmL 94*
Saltz, Jerry 1951- *WhoAmA 93*
Saltz, Ralph 1948- *WhoAm 94*
Saltzberg, Bernard 1919-1989 *WhAm 10*
Saltzburg, Stephen Allan 1945- *WhoAm 94, WhoAmL 94*
Saltzer, Jerome Howard 1939- *WhoAm 94*
Saltzman, Arnold Asa 1916- *WhoAm 94*
Saltzman, Arthur M(ichael) 1953- *WrDr 94*
Saltzman, Arthur Michael 1953- *WhoMW 93*
Saltzman, Barry 1931- *WhoAm 94, WhoScEn 94*
Saltzman, Benjamin Nathan 1914- *WhoAm 94*
Saltzman, Charles Eskridge 1903- *IntWW 93, Who 94*
Saltzman, Glenn Alan 1935- *WhoAm 94*
Saltzman, Harry 1915- *IntMPA 94*
Saltzman, Irene Cameron 1927- *WhoFI 94*
Saltzman, Joseph 1939- *WhoAm 94, WhoWest 94*
Saltzman, Marvin 1931- *WhoAmA 93*
Saltzman, Philip 1928- *WhoAm 94*
Saltzman, Robert Michael 1954- *WhoAmL 94*
Saltzman, Robert Paul 1942- *WhoAm 94, WhoFI 94, WhoIns 94, WhoWest 94*
Saltzman, Sidney 1926- *WhoAm 94*
Saltzman, William 1916- *WhoAm 94, WhoAmA 93*
Saltzmann-Stevens, Minnie 1874-1950 *NewGrDO*
Salucio, Ida *BlmGWL*
Saludes-Casado, Esperanza 1934- *WhoHisp 94*
Saluja, Jagdish Kumar 1934- *WhoAsA 94*
Salunkhe, Dattajeerao K. 1925- *WhoAsA 94*
Salusbury-Trelawny, J. B. *Who 94*
Salutin, Rick 1942- *WrDr 94*
Salva, Antonio 1944- *WhoHisp 94*
Salva, Tadeas 1937- *NewGrDO*
Salvador, Andy Padlan 1961- *WhoAmL 94*
Salvador, Armindo Jose Alves Silva 1965- *WhoScEn 94*
Salvador, Fernando 1950- *WhoHisp 94*
Salvador, Francis 1746-1776 *AmRev*
Salvador, Francis 1747-1776 *WhAmRev*
Salvador, Mark Z. 1968- *WhoScEn 94*
Salvador, Matilde 1918- *NewGrDO*
Salvador, Myrna 1956- *WhoHisp 94*
Salvador, Patricia Luisa 1956- *WhoHisp 94*
Salvador, Sal 1925- *WhoAm 94*
Salvador, Tomas *EncSF 93*
Salvadori, Mario 1907- *WhoScEn 94*
Salvadori, Max William 1908-1992 *WrDr 94N*
Salvadori, Tedfilo Alexander 1899- *WhoFI 94*
Salvadori, Vieri R. 1943- *WhoAmA 93*
Salvador Pinheiro, Joao de Deus 1945- *Who 94*
Salvaggio, John Edmond 1933- *WhoAm 94, WhoScEn 94*
Salvai, Maria Maddalena fl. 1716-1731 *NewGrDO*
Salvan, Jacques Léon 1898- *WrDr 94*
Salvan de Saliez le Viguier d'Albi fl. 17th cent.- *BlmGWL*
Salvaneschi, Luigi 1929- *WhoAm 94*
Salvati, Anthony V. 1944- *WhoFI 94*
Salvatici, Nilo 1922- *IntWW 93*
Salvatierra, Richard C. 1920- *WhoHisp 94*
Salvatierra, Richard Caballero 1920- *WhoWest 94*
Salvato, Ersilia 1941- *WhoWomW 91*
Salvatore, Donna Ann 1953- *WhoAm 94*
Salvatore, Frank A. 1922- *WhoAmP 93*
Salvatore, Richard John 1950- *WhoFI 94*
Salvatore, Scott Richard 1960- *WhoScEn 94*
Salvatore, Victor 1885-1965 *WhoAmA 93N*
Salvatori, Celestino c. 1798-1836? *NewGrDO*
Salvatori, Giulia *WhoHol 92*
Salvatori, Renato d1988 *WhoHol 92*
Salvaty, Benjamin Benedict 1940- *WhoAmL 94*
Salvayre, (Gervais Bernard) Gaston 1847-1916 *NewGrDO*
Salvendy, Gavriel 1938- *WhoAm 94*
Salverson, Laura Goodman 1890-1970 *BlmGWL*
Salvesen, Bonnie Forbes 1944- *WhoMW 93*
Salvetti, Carlo 1918- *IntWW 93*
Salvi, Al *WhoAmP 93*
Salvi, Antonio 1664-1724 *NewGrDO*
Salvi, Lorenzo 1810-1879 *NewGrDO*
Salvi, Margherita 1894-1981 *NewGrDO*
Salviat, Catherine *WhoHol 92*
Salvidge, Paul 1946- *Who 94*
Salvini, Alessandro d1955 *WhoHol 92*
Salvini, Giorgio 1920- *WhoScEn 94*
Salvini-Donatelli, Fanny 1815?-1891 *NewGrDO*
Salvio, Robert d1984 *WhoHol 92*
Salvito, Jeannette Hope 1951- *WhoFI 94*
Salvo, Ginger Calhoun 1947- *WhoWest 94*
Salvucci, John T. 1953- *WhoAm 94*
Salway, Thomas c. 1706-1743 *NewGrDO*
Salwen, Michael B(rian) 1954- *ConAu 142*
Salyer, A. Roger 1951- *WhoFI 94*
Salyer, Jerry Lee 1936- *WhoAmL 94*
Salyer, Stephen Lee 1950- *WhoAm 94, WhoFI 94*

Salzarulo-McGuigan, Ann Marie 1958- *WhoWest 94*
Salzburg, Joseph S. 1917- *IntMPA 94*
Salzer, John Michael 1917- *WhoAm 94*
Salzer, Louis William 1918- *WhoMW 93*
Salzinger, Kurt 1929- *WrDr 94*
Salzman, Anne Meyersburg 1928- *WhoWest 94*
Salzman, Arthur George 1929- *WhoAm 94*
Salzman, David Elliot 1943- *WhoAm 94*
Salzman, Diane Lynette 1961- *WhoFI 94*
Salzman, Eric 1933- *NewGrDO*
Salzman, Gary Clyde 1942- *WhoWest 94*
Salzman, Gary Scott 1963- *WhoAmL 94*
Salzman, Herbert 1916-1990 *WhAm 10*
Salzman, Marian 1959- *SmATA 77 [port]*
Salzman, Mark 1959- *WhoHol 92*
Salzman, Mark (Joseph) 1959- *WrDr 94*
Salzman, Pnina 1923- *IntWW 93*
Salzman, Robert Jay 1941- *WhoFI 94*
Salzman, Stanley P. 1931- *WhoAmL 94*
Salzman, Stephen Philip 1937- *WhoAm 94, WhoFI 94*
Salzstein, Richard Alan 1959- *WhoAm 94*
Salzwedel, Richard C. 1941- *WhoIns 94*
Sam, David 1933- *WhoAm 94, WhoAmL 94, WhoWest 94*
Sam, Joseph 1923- *WhoAm 94*
Sama, Vincent Anthony 1957- *WhoAmL 94*
Samachson, Joseph 1906-1980 *EncSF 93*
Samaha, Francis Joseph 1928- *WhoAm 94*
Samalin, Edwin 1935- *WhoAmL 94*
Samalman, Alexander 1904-1956 *EncSF 93*
Samaniego, Pamela Susan 1952- *WhoWest 94*
Samaniego, Ricardo Arturo 1949- *WhoHisp 94*
Samaniego, Robert P. 1952- *WhoHisp 94*
Samaniego, Rose Marie 1951- *WhoHisp 94*
Samaniegos, Ramon *WhoHol 92*
Samanowitz, Ronald Arthur 1944- *WhoAmL 94*
Samanta Roy, Robie Isaac 1968- *WhoScEn 94*
Samara, Noah Azmi 1956- *WhoBlA 94*
Samarakis, Antonis 1919- *IntWW 93*
Samarakoon, Neville Dunbar Mirahawatte 1919- *Who 94*
Samaranayake, Gamini Saratchandra 1955- *WhoScEn 94*
Samaranch, Juan Antonio 1920- *Who 94*
Samaranch Torello, Juan Antonio 1920- *IntWW 93*
Samaras, Andonis 1951- *IntWW 93*
Samaras, Lucas 1936- *WhoAmA 93*
Samaras, Mary Stenning 1928- *WhoWest 94*
Samaras, Nicholas *DrAPF 93*
Samaras, Spyridon (Filiskos) 1861-1917 *NewGrDO*
Samaraweera, Upasiri 1951- *WhoScEn 94*
Samardich, Val 1928- *WhoWest 94*
Samarel, Allen Mark 1951- *WhoMW 93*
Samartini, James Rogers 1935- *WhoAm 94, WhoFI 94*
Sambasivam, Ezhilarasan 1956- *WhoMW 93*
Samberg, Peter 1951- *WhoAmL 94*
Samberson, C. Gene 1934- *WhoAmP 93*
Samblanet, Sean David 1965- *WhoFI 94*
Sambora, Richie c. 1959- *See* Bon Jovi *ConMus 10*
Samborn, James A. 1947- *WhoAmL 94*
Samborn, Randall Arthur 1957- *WhoMW 93*
Sambrell, Aldo *WhoHol 92*
Sambrook, A(rthur) J(ames) 1931- *WrDr 94*
Sambrook, Gordon Hartley 1930- *Who 94*
Sambrook, Joseph Frank 1939- *Who 94*
Sambrot, William (Anthony) 1920- *EncSF 93*
Samburg, Grace (Blanche) *WhoAmA 93*
Samding Dojepamo 1942- *WhoPRCh 91 [port]*
Samek, Edward Lasker 1936- *WhoFI 94*
Samek, Michael Johann 1920- *WhoAm 94*
Samel, Jeffrey 1952- *WhoAmL 94*
Samel, Udo *WhoHol 92*
Samelson, Charles Frederick 1917- *WhoMW 93*
Samelson, Franz 1923- *WhoScEn 94*
Samelson, Lincoln Russell 1926- *WhoAm 94, WhoMW 93*
Samelson, William 1928- *WrDr 94*
Samerjan, George E. 1915- *WhoAmA 93*
Sameroff, Arnold Joshua 1937- *WhoAm 94*
Samet, Andrew Benjamin 1941- *WhoAm 94, WhoAmL 94*
Samet, Andrew James 1957- *WhoAmL 94*
Samet, Jack I. 1940- *WhoAm 94*
Samet, Joseph 1949- *WhoAmL 94*
Samet, Kenneth Alan 1958- *WhoAm 94*
Samet, Marc Krane 1950- *WhoWest 94*
Samford, Karen Elaine 1941- *WhoFI 94*
Samford, Thomas Drake, III 1934- *WhoAm 94*
Samford, Yetta Glenn, Jr. 1923- *WhoAm 94*
Samii, Abdol Hossein 1930- *WhoAm 94, WhoScEn 94*
Samios, Nicholas Peter 1932- *IntWW 93, WhoAm 94, WhoScEn 94*
Samitier, Ricardo 1956- *WhoHisp 94*
Samkange, S.J.T. *BlkWr 2*
Samkange, Stanlake (John Thompson) 1922-1988 *BlkWr 2*
Samkange, Tommie Marie 1932- *WhoBlA 94*
Sammad, Mohamed Abdel 1953- *WhoScEn 94*
Sammak, Paul Joseph 1956- *WhoMW 93*
Samman, George 1946- *WhoAm 94*
Samman, Peter Derrick d1992 *Who 94N*
Sammarco, (Giuseppe) Mario 1868-1930 *NewGrDO*
Sammartini, Giovanni Battista 1700?-1775 *NewGrDO*
Sammartino, Peter 1904-1992 *WhAm 10*
Sammet, Jean E. *WhoAm 94*
Sammet, Rolf 1920- *IntWW 93*
Sammeta, Preethi K. 1953- *WhoFI 94*
Sammis, Richard C. 1948- *WhoAmL 94*
Sammis, S. Fraser 1928- *WhoAm 94*
Sammis, Walter Henry 1896- *WhAm 10*
Sammond, John Stowell 1928- *WhoAm 94*
Sammons, Angela Williams 1959- *WhoAmL 94*
Sammons, Charles A. 1901- *WhAm 10*
Sammons, Charles E. 1944- *WhoAmL 94*
Samms, Emma 1960- *IntMPA 94, WhoHol 92*
Samnick, Norman Kenneth 1940- *WhoAm 94*
Samo, Amando 1948- *WhoWest 94*
Samoff, Joel 1943- *WhoWest 94*
Samoilov, Eughenj *WhoHol 92*
Samoilov, Vladimir Yakovlevich 1924- *IntWW 93*
Samoilova, Tatyana 1934- *WhoHol 92*
Samoilova, Tatyana Yevgeniyevna 1934- *IntWW 93*
Samole, Myron Michael 1943- *WhoAmL 94*
Samolis, Frank Robert 1951- *WhoAm 94, WhoAmL 94*
Samora, Joanne *WhoHisp 94*
Samora, Joseph E., Jr. 1955- *WhoAmP 93, WhoHisp 94*
Samora, Julian 1920- *WhoHisp 94*
Samorek, Alexander Henry 1922- *WhoMW 93, WhoScEn 94*
Samors, Neal S. 1943- *WhoFI 94*
Samosud, Samuil Abramovich 1884-1964 *NewGrDO*
Samour, Carlos M. *WhoScEn 94*
Samowitz, Lee Allan 1953- *WhoAmP 93*
Samp, Edward Joseph, Jr. 1918- *WhoAmL 94*
Sampang, Conrado Carriedo 1952- *WhoAsA 94*
Sampat, Pravin G. 1951- *WhoFI 94*
Sampath, Krishnaswamy 1955- *WhoScEn 94*
Sampedro, Jose *WhoHisp 94*
Sampedro, Jose Luis 1917- *IntWW 93*
Sampedro, Yvette Yrma 1966- *WhoWest 94*
Sampen, Don Ray 1950- *WhoAmL 94*
Samper, Armando 1920- *IntWW 93*
Samper, Felix d1957 *WhoHol 92*
Samper, J. Phillip 1934- *WhoHisp 94*
Samper, Joseph Phillip 1934- *WhoAm 94*
Samphan, Khieu *IntWW 93*
Sampias, Ernest Joseph 1951- *WhoWest 94*
Sampl, Scott Andrew 1956- *WhoWest 94*
Sample, Dan 1956- *WhoMW 93*
Sample, Dorothy E. 1911- *WhoAmP 93*
Sample, Frederick Palmer 1930- *WhoAm 94*
Sample, Herbert Allan 1961- *WhoBlA 94*
Sample, Joe *WhoBlA 94*
Sample, Joseph Scanlon 1923- *WhoAm 94, WhoWest 94*
Sample, Nathaniel Welshire 1918- *WhoAm 94*
Sample, Paul 1896-1974 *WhoAmA 93N*
Sample, Steven Browning 1940- *WhoAm 94, WhoWest 94*
Sample, William Amos 1955- *WhoBlA 94*
Sampler, Philece *WhoHol 92*
Samples, Benjamin Norris 1935- *WhoBlA 94*
Samples, Iris Lynette 1948- *WhoMW 93*
Samples, Jared Lanier 1965- *WhoBlA 94*
Samples, Jerry Wayne 1947- *WhoScEn 94*
Samples, John Wayne 1950- *WhoMW 93*
Samples, Reginald McCartney 1918- *Who 94*
Sampliner, Linda Hodes 1945- *WhoWest 94*
Sampolinski, Anthony Thomas 1926- *WhoAm 94, WhoMW 93*
Samponi, Gioseffo *NewGrDO*
Sampras, Pete 1971- *BuCMET, News 94-1 [port], WhoAm 94*
Sampson, Albert Richard 1938- *WhoBlA 94*
Sampson, Anthony (Terrell Seward) 1926- *IntWW 93, Who 94, WrDr 94*
Sampson, Bryan Dirk *WhoAmL 94, WhoWest 94*
Sampson, Calvin Coolidge 1928- *WhoBlA 94*
Sampson, Charles *NewYTBS 93 [port]*
Sampson, Colin 1929- *Who 94*
Sampson, Daphne Rae 1943- *WhoAm 94*
Sampson, David Synnott 1942- *WhoAmL 94*
Sampson, Deborah 1760-1827 *AmRev, WhAmRev*
Sampson, Donald Ross 1932- *WhoAmL 94*
Sampson, Dorothy Vermelle 1919- *WhoBlA 94*
Sampson, Doug *See* Iron Maiden *ConMus 10*
Sampson, Douglas Andrew 1958- *WhoWest 94*
Sampson, Earldine Robison 1923- *WhoMW 93*
Sampson, Edith 1901-1979 *AfrAmAl 6 [port]*
Sampson, Edward E. 1934- *WrDr 94*
Sampson, Ellanie Sue 1953- *WhoWest 94*
Sampson, Frank 1928- *WhoAmA 93*
Sampson, Geoffrey (Richard) 1944- *WrDr 94*
Sampson, Henry T(homas) 1934- *BlkWr 2*
Sampson, Henry Thomas 1934- *WhoBlA 94*
Sampson, J. Frank 1928- *WhoWest 94*
Sampson, Jerry Wayne 1952- *WhoFI 94*
Sampson, John Eugene 1941- *WhoAm 94*
Sampson, Kelvin *WhoBlA 94*
Sampson, Leonard E. 1918- *IntMPA 94*
Sampson, Lynn Charles 1952- *WhoMW 93*
Sampson, Marva W. 1936- *WhoBlA 94*
Sampson, Michael J. 1944- *WhoWest 94*
Sampson, Patsy Hallock 1932- *WhoAm 94, WhoMW 93*
Sampson, Ralph 1960- *BasBi, WhoBlA 94*
Sampson, Richard Arnim 1927- *WhoWest 94*
Sampson, Richard Thomas 1944- *WhoAm 94, WhoAmL 94*
Sampson, Robert *WhoHol 92*
Sampson, Robert Nash 1921- *WhoMW 93*
Sampson, Robert Neil 1938- *WhoAm 94, WhoScEn 94*
Sampson, Robert R. 1924- *WhoBlA 94*
Sampson, Ronald Alvin 1933- *WhoBlA 94*
Sampson, Ronald Victor 1918- *WrDr 94*
Sampson, Samuel Franklin 1934- *WhoAm 94*
Sampson, Teddy d1970 *WhoHol 92*
Sampson, Thyra Ann 1948- *WhoAmL 94*
Sampson, Tim *WhoHol 92*
Sampson, Will d1987 *WhoHol 92*
Sampson, William Roth 1946- *WhoAm 94, WhoAmL 94, WhoMW 93*
Sampson Gannett, Deborah 1760-1827 *WomPubS*
Sams, Dallas C. 1952- *WhoAmP 93*
Sams, David E., Jr. 1943- *WhoIns 94*
Sams, Eric 1926- *WrDr 94*
Sams, James Farid 1932- *WhoAm 94*
Sams, John Roland 1922- *WhoAm 94*
Sams, Larry Marshall *DrAPF 93*
Sams, Robert Alan 1945- *WhoAm 94*
Samsell, Lewis Patrick 1943- *WhoWest 94*
Samsil, D. M. 1946- *WhoAmL 94*
Samson, Allen Lawrence 1939- *WhoAm 94*
Samson, Alvin 1917- *WhoAm 94*
Samson, Carla Elaine 1951- *WhoMW 93*
Samson, Charles Harold, Jr. 1924- *WhoAm 94*
Samson, Frederick Eugene, Jr. 1918- *WhoAm 94, WhoMW 93, WhoScEn 94*
Samson, Gary David 1948- *WhoAm 94, WhoAmL 94*
Samson, Harvey Gilbert 1947- *WhoAmL 94*
Samson, Ivan d1963 *WhoHol 92*
Samson, Jack 1922- *WrDr 94*
Samson, John G(adsden) 1922- *WrDr 94*
Samson, John Roscoe, Jr. 1948- *WhoScEn 94*
Samson, Peter 1951- *WhoAm 94*
Samson, Richard Max 1946- *WhoAm 94*
Samsonov, Viktor Nikolaevich 1941- *LngBDD*
Samsonowicz, Henryk 1930- *IntWW 93*
Samsova, Galina 1937- *IntDcB [port], Who 94*
Samstad, Lavonne Carrol *WhoAmP 93*
Samstag, Gordon 1906- *WhAm 10, WhoAmA 93N*
Samter, Max 1908- *WhoAm 94*
Samudio, Jeffrey Bryan 1966- *WhoWest 94*
Samudlo, Jeffrey Bryan 1966- *WhoScEn 94, WhoWest 94*
Samuel *Who 94*
Samuel, Viscount 1922- *Who 94*
Samuel, Adolphe(-Abraham) 1824-1898 *NewGrDO*
Samuel, Adrian Christopher Ian 1915- *Who 94*
Samuel, Athanasius Yeshue 1907- *WhoAm 94*
Samuel, Frederick E. 1924- *WhoBlA 94*
Samuel, George 1958- *WhoFI 94, WhoWest 94*
Samuel, Gerhard 1924- *WhoAm 94*
Samuel, Howard David 1924- *WhoAm 94, WhoAmP 93*
Samuel, Jasper H. 1944- *WhoBlA 94*
Samuel, John (Michael Glen) 1944- *Who 94*
Samuel, Juan Milton Romero 1960- *WhoHisp 94*
Samuel, Leopold 1883-1975 *NewGrDO*
Samuel, Lois S. 1925- *WhoBlA 94*
Samuel, Millard Alvin 1904- *WhoFI 94*
Samuel, Minor Booker 1904- *WhoBlA 94*
Samuel, N. K. Peter 1953- *WhoMW 93*
Samuel, Ralph David 1945- *WhoAmL 94*
Samuel, Raphael 1946- *WhoAmL 94*
Samuel, Richard Christopher 1933- *Who 94*
Samuel, Robert Thompson 1944- *WhoMW 93*
Samuelian, Mark George 1963- *WhoFI 94*
Samuel-Rousseau, Marcel (Louis Auguste) 1882-1955 *NewGrDO*
Samuels *Who 94*
Samuels, Abram 1920- *IntMPA 94, WhoAm 94*
Samuels, Allen Robert 1956- *WhoWest 94*
Samuels, Annette Jacqueline 1935- *WhoBlA 94*
Samuels, Barbara Ann 1949- *WhoWest 94*
Samuels, Charlotte 1948- *WhoBlA 94*
Samuels, Cynthia K(alish) 1946- *WrDr 94*
Samuels, Cynthia Kalish 1946- *WhoAm 94*
Samuels, Donald L. 1961- *WhoAmL 94*
Samuels, Dorothy Jane 1951- *WhoAmP 93*
Samuels, Ernest 1903- *ConAu 43NR, WhoAm 94, WrDr 94*
Samuels, Everett Paul 1958- *WhoBlA 94*
Samuels, Gerald 1927- *WhoAmA 93*
Samuels, James E. 1928- *WhoBlA 94*
Samuels, Janet Lee 1953- *WhoAmL 94*
Samuels, John Edward Anthony 1940- *Who 94*
Samuels, John Stockwell, 3rd 1933- *WhoAmA 93*
Samuels, Joseph, Jr. 1949- *WhoWest 94*
Samuels, Lawrence Robert 1946- *WhoAm 94*
Samuels, Leslie B. 1942- *WhoAmL 94*
Samuels, Leslie Eugene 1929- *WhoBlA 94, WhoFI 94*
Samuels, Marcia L. 1937- *WhoBlA 94*
Samuels, Marwyn Stewart 1942- *WhoAm 94*
Samuels, Maurice d1964 *WhoHol 92*
Samuels, Michael Anthony 1939- *WhoAmP 93*
Samuels, Michael Louis 1920- *Who 94*
Samuels, Michele Lauren 1962- *WhoAm 94*
Samuels, Olive Constance 1926- *WhoBlA 94*
Samuels, Peter G. 1949- *WhoAmL 94*
Samuels, Robert J. 1938- *WhoBlA 94*
Samuels, Ronald S. 1941- *WhoBlA 94*
Samuels, Seymour, Jr. 1912-1992 *WhAm 10*
Samuels, Sheldon Wilfred 1929- *WhoAm 94*
Samuels, Sherwin L. 1935- *WhoAm 94*
Samuels, Simon J. *WhoFI 94*
Samuels, Steve 1959- *WhoFI 94*
Samuels, Warren J(oseph) 1933- *WrDr 94*
Samuels, Warren Joseph 1933- *WhoFI 94*
Samuels, Wilfred D. 1947- *WhoBlA 94*
Samuels, William Mason 1929- *WhoAm 94*
Samuelsen, Roy 1933- *WhoAm 94*
Samuelson, Andrew Lief 1938- *WhoScEn 94*
Samuelson, Bengt Ingemar 1934- *IntWW 93*
Samuelson, C. Ransom, II 1946- *WhoAmL 94*
Samuelson, David N(orman) 1939- *EncSF 93*
Samuelson, David W. 1924- *IntMPA 94*
Samuelson, Derrick William 1929- *WhoAm 94*

Samuelson, Donald B. 1932- *WhoAmP 93*
Samuelson, Ellen Banman *WhoAmP 93*
Samuelson, Ellen Banman 1930- *WhoMW 93*
Samuelson, F. A. 1934- *WhoAm 94*
Samuelson, Fred Binder 1925- *WhoAmA 93*
Samuelson, Kenneth Lee 1946- *WhoAmL 94, WhoFI 94*
Samuelson, Marvin Lee 1931- *WhoAm 94*
Samuelson, (Bernard) Michael (Francis) 1917- *Who 94*
Samuelson, Paul 1915- *AmSocL*
Samuelson, Paul A. 1915- *Who 94*
Samuelson, Paul Anthony 1915- *IntWW 93, WhoAm 94, WhoFI 94, WrDr 94*
Samuelson, Paul Steven 1966- *WhoMW 93*
Samuelson, Peter George Wylie 1951- *IntMPA 94*
Samuelson, Robert *WhoAmP 93*
Samuelson, Robert Donald 1929- *WhoScEn 94*
Samuelson, Robert Jacob 1945- *WhoAm 94*
Samuelson, Sydney 1925- *IntMPA 94*
Samuelson, Sydney Wylie 1925- *Who 94*
Samuelson, Sylvia Heller *WhoAm 94*
Samuelson, Wayne Paul 1950- *WhoAmL 94*
Samuelson, William George 1938- *WhoMW 93*
Samuelsson, Bengt Ingemar 1934- *Who 94, WhoAm 94, WhoScEn 94*
Samuelsson, Birgit Marianne 1945- *WhoWomW 91*
Samwell, William 1628-1676 *DcNaB MP*
Samwell-Smith, Paul 1944- *See* Yardbirds, The *ConMus 10*
Samworth, David Chetwode 1935- *Who 94*
Samy Vellu, Dato S. 1936- *IntWW 93*
San, Nguyen Duy 1932- *WhoScEn 94*
Sanabria, Harry Louis 1962- *WhoHisp 94*
Sanabria, Luis Angel 1950- *WhoHisp 94*
Sanabria, Robert 1931- *WhoAmA 93, WhoHisp 94*
Sanabria, Sherry Zvares 1937- *WhoAmA 93*
Sanabria, Tomás V. 1953- *WhoHisp 94*
Sanadi, D. R. 1920- *WhoAsA 94*
San Agustin, Joe Taitano 1930- *WhoAm 94, WhoAmP 93, WhoWest 94*
San Angelo, Ronald S. *WhoAmP 93*
Sananman, Michael Lawrence 1939- *WhoScEn 94*
San Antonio Mendoza, Oscar 1945- *WhoAmP 93*
Sanapia 1895-1968 *EncNAR*
Sanasarian, Harout O. 1929- *WhoAmP 93*
Sanbar, Moshe 1926- *IntWW 93*
San Bento, William, Jr. 1946- *WhoAmP 93*
San Biagio, Pier Luigi 1952- *WhoScEn 94*
Sanborn, Arthur B. 1945- *WhoAmP 93*
Sanborn, B.X. *EncSF 93*
Sanborn, Charles Evan 1919- *WhoScEn 94*
Sanborn, David 1945- *WhoAm 94*
Sanborn, Donald Francis 1959- *WhoWest 94*
Sanborn, Fred d1961 *WhoHol 92*
Sanborn, James *WhoAmA 93*
Sanborn, Joyce d1977 *WhoHol 92*
Sanborn, Margaret 1915- *WrDr 94*
Sanborn, Robert Burns 1929- *WhoIns 94*
Sanborn, Robin *EncSF 93*
Sanbrailo, John A. 1943- *WhoAm 94*
Sancaktar, Erol 1952- *WhoScEn 94*
Sances, Giovanni Felice c. 1600-1679? *NewGrDO*
Sanchez, Adan *WhoHisp 94*
Sanchez, Adolfo Erik 1935- *WhoHisp 94*
Sanchez, Alba 1957- *WhoHisp 94*
Sanchez, Albert 1936- *WhoHisp 94*
Sanchez, Alex A. *WhoHisp 94*
Sanchez, Alicia M. 1946- *WhoHisp 94*
Sanchez, Anna Sinohui 1958- *WhoHisp 94*
Sanchez, Antonio L. 1954- *WhoHisp 94*
Sanchez, Antonio M. 1932- *WhoHisp 94*
Sanchez, Arantxa 1971- *BuCMET*
Sanchez, Arlene Michelle 1966- *WhoHisp 94*
Sanchez, Armand J. 1933- *WhoHisp 94*
Sanchez, Arthur Ronald 1948- *WhoHisp 94*
Sanchez, Arturo E. 1949- *WhoHisp 94*
Sanchez, Beatrice Rivas 1941- *WhoAm 94, WhoAmA 93, WhoMW 93*
Sanchez, Candido Kevin 1938- *WhoHisp 94*
Sanchez, Carlos Alberto 1960- *WhoHisp 94*
Sánchez, Carlos Antonio 1960- *WhoHisp 94*
Sanchez, Carlos J. 1938- *WhoHisp 94*
Sanchez, Carol Lee *BlmGWL [port]*
Sanchez, Cecilia *WhoHisp 94*
Sánchez, Claudio *WhoHisp 94*
Sanchez, Cynthia J. 1962- *WhoHisp 94*
Sanchez, Daniel J. 1964- *WhoHisp 94*
Sanchez, Daniel R. 1936- *WhoHisp 94*
Sanchez, David *WhoHisp 94*
Sanchez, David Alan 1933- *WhoAm 94, WhoHisp 94*
Sanchez, David Joseph, Jr. 1939- *WhoHisp 94*
Sánchez, David Mario 1942- *WhoHisp 94*
Sanchez, Dennis Robert 1956- *WhoWest 94*
Sanchez, Dolores 1936- *WhoHisp 94*
Sánchez, Dolores Camacho Vasquez 1943- *WhoHisp 94*
Sanchez, Don *WhoHisp 94*
Sanchez, Dorothea Yialamas 1960- *WhoScEn 94*
Sanchez, Dorothy L. 1938- *WhoHisp 94*
Sánchez, Edith 1956- *WhoHisp 94*
Sánchez, Edwin 1955- *WhoHisp 94*
Sanchez, Efrain 1949- *WhoHisp 94*
Sánchez, Elba I. 1947- *WhoHisp 94*
Sanchez, Eleazar *WhoHisp 94*
Sanchez, Elena Ruiz 1940- *WhoAmP 93*
Sanchez, Emilio 1965- *BuCMET*
Sanchez, Emily *WhoHisp 94*
Sanchez, Enrique 1932- *WhoHisp 94*
Sanchez, Ernest *WhoHisp 94*
Sanchez, F. H. 1925- *WhoHisp 94*
Sánchez, Fameliza 1940- *WhoHisp 94*
Sanchez, Fausto H. 1953- *WhoHisp 94*
Sánchez, Federico A. 1935- *WhoHisp 94*
Sanchez, Felix *WhoHisp 94*
Sanchez, Felix 1951- *WhoHisp 94*
Sanchez, Fernando Victor 1953- *WhoHisp 94*
Sanchez, Frank William 1953- *WhoHisp 94*
Sanchez, Gabriel Antero, II 1923- *WhoHisp 94*
Sanchez, Gabriel Antonio 1952- *WhoHisp 94*
Sanchez, George L. 1933- *WhoHisp 94*
Sanchez, Gilbert 1938- *WhoAm 94, WhoHisp 94, WhoWest 94*
Sanchez, Gilbert Anthony 1930- *WhoHisp 94*
Sanchez, Gilbert John 1941- *WhoHisp 94*
Sanchez, Gonzalo José 1932- *WhoHisp 94*
Sanchez, Guadalupe 1952- *WhoHisp 94*
Sanchez, Henry Orlando 1937- *WhoHisp 94*
Sanchez, Humberto G. 1947- *WhoHisp 94*
Sanchez, Ignacio Roberto 1965- *WhoHisp 94*
Sanchez, Irma Ann 1961- *WhoHisp 94*
Sanchez, Isaac C. 1941- *WhoHisp 94*
Sanchez, Israel, Jr. 1963- *WhoHisp 94*
Sanchez, James *WhoHisp 94*
Sanchez, Jamie *WhoHol 92*
Sanchez, Javier 1968- *BuCMET*
Sanchez, Javier A. 1960- *WhoHisp 94*
Sanchez, Javier Alberto 1960- *WhoScEn 94*
Sanchez, Jerry 1945- *WhoHisp 94*
Sánchez, Jesús M. 1944- *WhoHisp 94*
Sanchez, Jesus Ramirez 1950- *WhoHisp 94*
Sanchez, Jesusa 1955- *WhoAmP 93*
Sanchez, Joe M. 1933- *WhoHisp 94*
Sanchez, John Charles 1950- *WhoHisp 94*
Sanchez, Jonathan *WhoHisp 94*
Sanchez, Jorge Luis 1956- *WhoHisp 94*
Sanchez, Jose B., Sr. 1940- *WhoHisp 94*
Sanchez, Jose Enrique 1960- *WhoHisp 94*
Sánchez, José Luis 1952- *WhoHisp 94*
Sánchez, José Luis 1955- *WhoHisp 94*
Sanchez, Jose M. 1943- *WhoHisp 94*
Sánchez, José Rámon 1951- *WhoHisp 94*
Sanchez, Joseph M., II 1933- *WhoHisp 94*
Sanchez, Joseph S. 1949- *WhoHisp 94*
Sanchez, Juan 1954- *WhoHisp 94*
Sanchez, Juan Francisco 1928- *WhoHisp 94*
Sanchez, Juan-Manuel 1955- *WhoHisp 94*
Sanchez, Julian Claudio 1938- *WhoHisp 94*
Sanchez, Kathleen 1957- *WhoHisp 94*
Sanchez, Lavinia 1929- *WrDr 94*
Sanchez, Leonard R. 1942- *WhoHisp 94*
Sanchez, Leonedes Monarrize Worthington 1951- *WhoAm 94, WhoFI 94, WhoWest 94*
Sanchez, Leveo V. 1930- *WhoHisp 94*
Sanchez, Lorenzo 1943- *WhoHisp 94, WhoWest 94*
Sanchez, Louis H. 1961- *WhoHisp 94*
Sanchez, Luis 1924- *WhoAmP 93, WhoHisp 94*
Sanchez, Luis Alberto 1900- *IntWW 93*
Sanchez, Luis Humberto 1951- *WhoHisp 94*
Sánchez, Luis Rafael 1936- *WhoHisp 94*
Sanchez, Luis Ruben 1963- *WhoScEn 94*
Sanchez, Lyssil R. 1947- *WhoHisp 94*
Sanchez, Manuel 1947- *WhoAmL 94, WhoHisp 94*
Sanchez, Manuel Tamayo, Jr. 1949- *WhoHisp 94*
Sánchez, Marcos B. 1956- *WhoHisp 94*
Sánchez, Mario Ernesto 1947- *WhoHisp 94*
Sanchez, Marisabel 1963- *WhoHisp 94*
Sanchez, Mark Terrence 1958- *WhoHisp 94*
Sanchez, Marla Rena 1956- *WhoFI 94, WhoHisp 94, WhoWest 94*
Sanchez, Marta *WhoHisp 94*
Sanchez, Martha Alicia 1944- *WhoHisp 94*
Sánchez, Mary B. 1930- *WhoHisp 94*
Sanchez, Mary Lowe (Eliza) 1914- *WhoAmA 93*
Sanchez, Michael S. 1950- *WhoAmP 93*
Sanchez, Michael T. 1961- *WhoHisp 94*
Sanchez, Miguel A. 1945- *WhoHisp 94*
Sanchez, Miguel Angel, Sr. 1933- *WhoHisp 94*
Sanchez, Miguel R. 1950- *WhoHisp 94*
Sanchez, Miguel Ramon 1950- *WhoScEn 94*
Sanchez, Nelson *WhoHisp 94*
Sanchez, Norma R. 1939- *WhoHisp 94*
Sanchez, Osmundo, Jr. 1939- *WhoFI 94*
Sánchez, Pablo Jose 1954- *WhoHisp 94*
Sanchez, Patricia Irene *WhoHisp 94*
Sanchez, Paul *WhoHol 92*
Sanchez, Paul Lester 1949- *WhoAmP 93, WhoHisp 94*
Sanchez, Pedro *WhoHol 92*
Sanchez, Pedro Antonio 1940- *WhoHisp 94*
Sanchez, Pedro Antonio, Jr. 1940- *WhoScEn 94*
Sanchez, Philip A. 1963- *WhoHisp 94*
Sanchez, Phillip Victor 1929- *WhoAmP 93, WhoFI 94, WhoHisp 94*
Sanchez, Poncho 1951- *WhoHisp 94*
Sanchez, Porfirio 1932- *WhoHisp 94*
Sánchez, Rafael 1938- *WhoHisp 94*
Sanchez, Rafael C. 1919- *WhoHisp 94*
Sanchez, Rafael Camilo 1919- *WhoAm 94*
Sanchez, Ramiro 1948- *WhoHisp 94*
Sánchez, Ramón Antonio 1947- *WhoHisp 94*
Sanchez, Ray A. 1940- *WhoHisp 94*
Sanchez, Ray F. 1927- *WhoHisp 94*
Sanchez, Raymond G. 1941- *WhoAmP 93, WhoHisp 94*
Sanchez, Raymond John 1944- *WhoHisp 94*
Sánchez, Raymond L. 1964- *WhoHisp 94*
Sanchez, Ref d1987 *WhoHol 92*
Sanchez, Rey 1967- *WhoHisp 94*
Sanchez, Ricardo *DrAPF 93*
Sánchez, Ricardo 1941- *WhoHisp 94*
Sanchez, Richard *WhoHisp 94*
Sanchez, Richard Correa 1948- *WhoHisp 94*
Sanchez, Richard Ray 1946- *WhoAmP 93, WhoHisp 94*
Sanchez, Rick *WhoHisp 94*
Sanchez, Rick Dante 1940- *WhoHisp 94*
Sanchez, Robert *WhoHisp 94*
Sanchez, Robert Alfred 1938- *WhoHisp 94*
Sanchez, Robert Charles 1956- *WhoHisp 94*
Sanchez, Robert F. 1934- *WhoHisp 94*
Sanchez, Robert Fortune 1934- *WhoAm 94*
Sanchez, Robert Francis 1938- *WhoAm 94, WhoHisp 94*
Sanchez, Robert Michael 1947- *WhoAmL 94*
Sanchez, Robert Mungerro 1953- *WhoHisp 94*
Sánchez, Roberto G. 1922- *WhoHisp 94*
Sanchez, Roberto Luis 1957- *WhoHisp 94*
Sanchez, Roberto R. 1948- *WhoHisp 94*
Sánchez, Rodolfo Balli *WhoHisp 94N*
Sánchez, Rosaura 1941- *WhoHisp 94*
Sanchez, Ross C. 1940- *WhoHisp 94*
Sanchez, Roxanne 1968- *WhoHisp 94*
Sanchez, Rozier Edmond 1931- *WhoHisp 94*
Sanchez, Ruben Dario 1943- *WhoWest 94*
Sanchez, Salvador d1982 *WhoHol 92*
Sanchez, Sergio Arturo 1950- *WhoHisp 94*
Sanchez, Sonia *DrAPF 93*
Sanchez, Sonia 1934- *AfrAmAl 6, BlkWr 2, BlmGWL, WrDr 94*
Sanchez, Sonia Benita 1934- *WhoBlA 94*
Sanchez, Sylvia Bertha 1928- *WhoHisp 94*
Sanchez, Thomas *DrAPF 93*
Sánchez, Thomas 1944- *WhoHisp 94*
Sanchez, Thorvald 1933- *WhoAmA 93*
Sánchez, Trinidad, Jr. *WhoHisp 94*
Sanchez, Victoria E. 1954- *WhoHisp 94*
Sanchez, Victoria Wagner 1934- *WhoAm 94, WhoWest 94*
Sanchez, Vivian Eugenia 1963- *WhoHisp 94*
Sanchez, Walter A. 1958- *WhoHisp 94*
Sanchez, William Q. 1951- *WhoHisp 94*
Sanchez, Yolanda *WhoHisp 94*
Sanchez, Zoraida 1948- *WhoHisp 94*
Sanchez Asiain, Jose Angel 1929- *IntWW 93*
Sanchez-Boudy, Jose 1928- *WhoHisp 94*
Sanchez-Carlo, Maria 1952- *WhoHisp 94*
Sanchez de Cepeda y Ahumada, Teresa *BlmGWL*
Sanchez de Fuentes, Eduardo 1874-1944 *NewGrDO*
Sanchez de la Pena, Salvador Alfonso 1948- *WhoScEn 94*
Sánchez de Sandoval, Oma Erlinda 1939- *WhoHisp 94*
Sanchez Ferrer, Roberto 1927- *NewGrDO*
Sanchez Ferreri, Franco Tulio 1909- *WhoHisp 94*
Sánchez-Grey Alba, Esther 1931- *WhoHisp 94*
Sanchez-H., Jose 1951- *WhoHisp 94, WhoWest 94*
Sanchez Hernandez, Fidel 1917- *IntWW 93*
Sanchez Korrol, Virginia 1936- *WhoHisp 94*
Sanchez-Llaca, Juan 1960- *WhoAm 94*
Sanchez-Longo, Luis P. 1925- *WhoHisp 94*
Sanchez-Lugo, Fermin A. 1947- *WhoHisp 94*
Sanchez-Manjon, Andrés B. 1943- *WhoHisp 94*
Sanchez Munoz, Carlos Eduardo 1957- *WhoScEn 94*
Sanchez-Owens, Yvette Anita 1960- *WhoHisp 94*
Sanchez-Parodi, Milton 1948- *WhoHisp 94*
Sanchez-Perez, Elias 1943- *WhoHisp 94*
Sanchez-Ramos, Juan Ramon 1946- *WhoScEn 94*
Sanchez-Scott, Milcha 1953- *WhoHisp 94*
Sanchez-Scott, Milcha 1955- *ConDr 93*
Sanchez-Sinencio, Edgar 1944- *WhoHisp 94*
Sanchez-Solano, Janie 1951- *WhoHisp 94*
Sanchez Sudon, Fernando 1949- *WhoScEn 94*
Sánchez-Troche, Luis Fernando 1961- *WhoHisp 94*
Sanchez-Vicario, Arantxa 1971- *IntWW 93*
Sanchez-Vilella, Roberto 1913- *IntWW 93*
Sanchez-Villela, Roberto 1913- *WhoAmP 93*
Sánchez-Way, Ruth Dolores 1940- *WhoHisp 94*
Sanchini, Dominick Joseph 1926-1990 *WhAm 10*
Sancho, Fernando d1990 *WhoHol 92*
Sancho, Robert *WhoHisp 94*
Sancho-Rof, Juan 1940- *IntWW 93*
Sanctuary, Gerald Philip 1930- *Who 94*
Sand, David Byron 1946- *WhoAm 94, WhoAmL 94*
Sand, George 1804-1876 *BlmGEL, BlmGWL [port], NinCLC 42 [port]*
Sand, Harvey *WhoAmP 93*
Sand, Inge 1928-1974 *IntDcB*
Sand, Ivan *WhoAmP 93*
Sand, Leonard B. 1928- *WhoAm 94, WhoAmL 94*
Sand, Michael 1940- *WhoScEn 94*
Sand, Michael Patrick 1952- *WhoAmL 94*
Sand, Paul 1941- *WhoHol 92*
Sand, Thomas Charles 1952- *WhoAm 94, WhoAmL 94*
Sanda, Dominique 1948- *WhoHol 92*
Sanda, Dominique 1951- *IntMPA 94*
Sanda, Krista Linnea 1937- *WhoMW 93*
Sandage, Allan Rex 1926- *IntWW 93, WhoAm 94, WhoScEn 94, WhoWest 94*
Sandage, Charles Harold 1902- *WhoAm 94*
Sandage, Elizabeth Anthea 1930- *WhoMW 93*
Sandalls, William Thomas, Jr. 1944- *WhoAm 94*
Sandalow, Terrance 1934- *WhoAm 94, WhoAmL 94*
Sandars, Christopher Thomas 1942- *Who 94*
Sandars, Leibert Jovanovich 1914- *WhoWest 94*
Sandars, Nancy Katharine 1914- *Who 94*
Sandars, Patrick George Henry 1935- *Who 94*
Sandbach, Charlie Bernard 1933- *WhoFI 94*
Sandbach, George Thomas 1946- *WhoAmP 93*
Sandback, Frederick Lane 1943- *WhoAm 94, WhoAmA 93*
Sandback, William Arthur 1945- *WhoAmL 94*

Sandbaek, Ulla Margrethe 1943- WhoWomW 91
Sandbank, Charles Peter 1931- Who 94
Sandbank, Henry 1932- WhoAm 94
Sandbank, Viette DrAPF 93
Sandberg, Adolph Engelbrekt 1898- WhAm 10
Sandberg, Irwin Walter 1934- WhoAm 94
Sandberg, John Steven 1948- WhoAmL 94
Sandberg, Michael (Graham Ruddock) 1927- Who 94
Sandberg, Michael Graham Ruddock 1927- IntWW 93
Sandberg, Robert Alexis 1914- WhoAm 94
Sandberg, Ryne 1959- WhoAm 94, WhoMW 93
Sandberg, Wayne L. WhoAmP 93
Sandberger, Adolf 1864-1943 NewGrDO
Sandblom, (John) Philip 1903- IntWW 93
Sandborg, Verie WhoMW 93
Sandborn, Virgil Alvin 1928- WhoAm 94
Sandbulte, Arend John 1933- WhoFI 94
Sandburg, Carl 1878-1967 AmCulL [port]
Sandburg, Helga 1918- WhoAm 94, WrDr 94
Sand Crane c. 1873-1950 EncNAR
Sande, Barbara 1939- WhoFI 94, WhoWest 94
Sande, John P., III 1949- WhoAmL 94
Sande, Rhoda WhoAmA 93
Sande, Theodore Anton 1933- WhoAm 94
Sande, Walter d1972 WhoHol 92
Sandeen, Ernest DrAPF 93
Sandeen, Roderick Cox 1943- WhoAm 94
Sandefur, J. David 1952- WhoAmP 93
Sandefur, James Tandy 1947- WhoAm 94
Sandefur, Thomas Edwin, Jr. 1939- WhoAm 94
Sandel, Cora 1880-1974 BlmGWL
Sandel, Jerry Wayne 1942- WhoAmP 93
Sandel, Larry W. 1943- WhoAmL 94
Sandell, Richard Arnold 1937- WhoAm 94, WhoFI 94
Sandell, Terence 1948- Who 94
Sandels, Stephen C. 1937- WhoAm 94
Sandelson, Neville Devonshire 1923- Who 94
Sanden, John Howard 1935- WhoAmA 93
Sandenaw, Thomas Arthur, Jr. 1936- WhoAmL 94
Sander, Alfred Dick 1925- WhoWest 94
Sander, Donald Henry 1933- WhoAm 94
Sander, Ellen Jane 1949- WhoWest 94
Sander, Ian WhoHol 92
Sander, Ludwig 1906-1975 WhoAmA 93N
Sander, Malvin Gustav 1946- WhoAm 94
Sander, Michael Arthur 1941- IntWW 93
Sander, Raymond John 1944- WhoAm 94
Sander, Rudolph Charles 1930- WhoFI 94
Sander, Susan Berry 1953- WhoWest 94
Sander, Volkmar 1929- WhoAm 94
Sandercox, Robert Allen 1932- WhoAm 94
Sanderford, Howard 1935- WhoAmP 93
Sanderford, John WhoHol 92
Sandergaard, Theodore Jorgensen 1946- WhoScEn 94
Sanderlin, George 1915- WrDr 94
Sanderlin, James B. 1929- WhoBlA 94
Sanderlin, Owenita 1916- WrDr 94
Sanderling, Kurt 1912- IntWW 93
Sanders, Aaron Perry 1924- WhoAm 94
Sanders, Adelle 1946- WhoWest 94
Sanders, Adrian 1938- WhoWest 94
Sanders, Anita WhoHol 92
Sanders, Anne Kathleen 1955- WhoMW 93
Sanders, Archie, Jr. 1937- WhoBlA 94
Sanders, Augusta Swann 1932- WhoBlA 94, WhoWest 94
Sanders, Barbara A. WhoBlA 94
Sanders, Barry 1968- CurBio 93 [port], WhoAm 94, WhoBlA 94, WhoMW 93
Sanders, Benjamin Elbert 1918-1992 WhAm 10
Sanders, Bernard 1941- CngDr 93, WhoAm 94, WhoAmP 93
Sanders, Brett 1928- WrDr 94
Sanders, Brice Sidney 1930- WhoAm 94
Sanders, Carl Edward 1925- WhoAmP 93
Sanders, Charles A. 1933- WhoFI 94
Sanders, Charles F. 1921- WhoAmP 93
Sanders, Charles Franklin 1931- WhoAm 94
Sanders, Charles Lionel 1936- WhoBlA 94
Sanders, Charlie Eugene 1933- WhoFI 94
Sanders, Chris Allen 1949- WhoMW 93
Sanders, Coyne Steven 1956- ConAu 142
Sanders, Cyril Woods 1912- Who 94
Sanders, Daniel Selvarajah 1928-1989 WhAm 10
Sanders, David 1926- WrDr 94
Sanders, David Clyde 1946- WhoFI 94, WhoWest 94
Sanders, David P. 1949- WhoAm 94, WhoAmL 94
Sanders, Deion Luwynn 1967- WhoAm 94, WhoBlA 94
Sanders, Delbert 1931- WhoBlA 94
Sanders, Donald Neil 1927- IntWW 93, Who 94
Sanders, Dori NewYTBS 93 [port]
Sanders, Dori 1935- WhoBlA 94
Sanders, Dorothy Lucie (McClemans) 1907- WrDr 94
Sanders, Dorsey Addren 1898- WhAm 10
Sanders, Douglas Lee 1946- WhoWest 94
Sanders, E. C. 1920- WhoAmP 93
Sanders, Ed DrAPF 93
Sanders, Ed(ward) 1939- WrDr 94
Sanders, Ed Parish 1937- Who 94
Sanders, Edwin Perry Bartley 1940- WhoAmL 94
Sanders, Ella J. 1947- WhoBlA 94
Sanders, Esther Jeannette 1926- WhoWest 94
Sanders, Evelyn Beatrice 1931- WhoMW 93
Sanders, Frank 1919- WhoAmP 93
Sanders, Franklin D. 1935- WhoAm 94, WhoIns 94
Sanders, Fred Joseph 1928- WhoAm 94
Sanders, Frederick 1923- WhoAm 94
Sanders, Fredric M. 1941- WhoAm 94
Sanders, Gary Glenn 1944- WhoFI 94, WhoMW 93, WhoScEn 94
Sanders, Gary Wayne 1949- WhoAm 94
Sanders, George EncSF 93
Sanders, George d1972 WhoHol 92
Sanders, George L. 1942- WhoBlA 94
Sanders, Georgia Elizabeth 1933- WhoScEn 94
Sanders, Gerald Hollie 1924- WhoAm 94, WhoMW 93
Sanders, Gilbert Otis 1945- WhoScEn 94
Sanders, Glenn Carlos 1949- WhoBlA 94
Sanders, Grant L. 1934- WhoAmP 93
Sanders, Gwendolyn W. 1937- WhoBlA 94
Sanders, Hank 1942- WhoAmP 93, WhoBlA 94
Sanders, Harland d1980 WhoHol 92
Sanders, Harold Barefoot, Jr. 1925- WhoAm 94, WhoAmL 94
Sanders, Henry Marshall 1928- WhoAmP 93
Sanders, Herbert Harvey 1909- WhoAmA 93N
Sanders, Hiram Edmond 1936- WhoMW 93
Sanders, Hobart C. 1929- WhoBlA 94
Sanders, Howard 1941- WhoAm 94
Sanders, Hugh d1966 WhoHol 92
Sanders, Irwin Taylor 1909- WhoAm 94
Sanders, Isaac Warren 1948- WhoBlA 94
Sanders, Jack Ford 1918- WhoAm 94
Sanders, Jack Thomas 1935- WhoAm 94
Sanders, Jacquelyn Seevak 1931- WhoMW 93
Sanders, James Alvin 1927- WhoAm 94, WhoWest 94
Sanders, James Edward 1911- WrDr 94
Sanders, James Grady 1951- WhoScEn 94
Sanders, James Richard 1944- WhoMW 93
Sanders, James William 1929- WhoBlA 94
Sanders, Jay O. WhoHol 92
Sanders, Jay O. 1953- IntMPA 94
Sanders, Jay William 1924- WhoAm 94
Sanders, Jean Marie 1939- WhoFI 94, WhoMW 93
Sanders, Jeremy Thomas 1942- Who 94
Sanders, Jerry 1941- WhoAmP 93
Sanders, Jerry Charles 1942- WhoWest 94
Sanders, John Arnold 1939- WhoAmP 93
Sanders, John Derek 1933- Who 94
Sanders, John Lassiter 1927- WhoAm 94
Sanders, John Leslie Yorath 1929- Who 94
Sanders, John Lyell, Jr. 1924- WhoScEn 94
Sanders, John Moncrief 1936- WhoAm 94
Sanders, John Reynolds M. Who 94
Sanders, John Theodore 1941- WhoAm 94, WhoAmP 93
Sanders, Joop A. 1921- WhoAmA 93
Sanders, Joseph Lee 1940- WhoMW 93
Sanders, Joseph Stanley 1942- WhoAm 94, WhoBlA 94
Sanders, June Ann 1944- WhoAmL 94
Sanders, Kate Emily Tyrrell Who 94
Sanders, Kay Marie 1947- WhoMW 93
Sanders, Keith R. 1939- WhoAm 94, WhoMW 93
Sanders, Larry Joe 1938- WhoAmP 93
Sanders, Larry Philip 1959- WhoFI 94
Sanders, Laura Green 1942- WhoBlA 94
Sanders, Lawrence 1920- EncSF 93, WhoAm 94, WrDr 94
Sanders, Lewis A. WhoFI 94
Sanders, Lina 1937- WhoBlA 94
Sanders, Lou Helen 1951- WhoBlA 94
Sanders, Marc Andrew 1947- WhoScEn 94
Sanders, Mark Steven 1959- WhoWest 94
Sanders, Marlene 1931- WhoAm 94
Sanders, Michael Anthony 1960- WhoBlA 94
Sanders, Michael Kevin 1970- WhoScEn 94
Sanders, Michael Ray Edward 1946- WhoAmL 94
Sanders, Nicholas John 1946- Who 94
Sanders, Pablo Katz 1944- WhoFI 94
Sanders, Paul F. 1927- WhoAmP 93
Sanders, Paul Hampton 1909- WhoAm 94
Sanders, Peter (Basil) 1938- WrDr 94
Sanders, Peter Basil 1938- Who 94
Sanders, Pharoah 1940- WhoAm 94
Sanders, Raymond Adrian 1932- Who 94
Sanders, Reginald Laverne 1967- WhoBlA 94
Sanders, Rhea 1923- WhoAmA 93
Sanders, Rhonda Sheree 1956- WhoBlA 94
Sanders, Richard 1940- WhoHol 92
Sanders, Richard A., Jr. 1963- WhoAmP 93
Sanders, Richard B. 1945- WhoAmP 93
Sanders, Richard Henry 1944- WhoAm 94, WhoAmL 94
Sanders, Richard Kinard 1940- WhoAm 94
Sanders, Richard Louis 1949- WhoAm 94
Sanders, Ricky Wayne 1962- WhoBlA 94
Sanders, Rober LaFayette 1952- WhoBlA 94
Sanders, Robert (Tait) 1925- Who 94
Sanders, Robert B. 1938- WhoBlA 94, WhoScEn 94
Sanders, Robert Martin 1928- WhoAm 94
Sanders, Robert Walter 1952- WhoScEn 94
Sanders, Roger Benedict 1940- Who 94
Sanders, Roger Cobban 1936- WhoAm 94
Sanders, Ronald 1932-1991 WhAm 10
Sanders, Ronald 1948- IntWW 93, Who 94
Sanders, Ronald L. 1946- WhoAmP 93
Sanders, Ronald Robert 1947- WhoFI 94
Sanders, Roy 1937- Who 94
Sanders, Sally Ruth 1952- WhoBlA 94
Sanders, Scott d1956 WhoHol 92
Sanders, Scott Patrick DrAPF 93
Sanders, Scott Russell DrAPF 93
Sanders, Scott Russell 1945- EncSF 93
Sanders, Shepherd WhoHol 92
Sanders, Steve WhoAm 94
Sanders, Steven 1951- WhoAmP 93
Sanders, Steven Gill 1936- WhoAm 94
Sanders, Steven LeRoy 1959- WhoBlA 94
Sanders, Steven Paul 1950- WhoAm 94, WhoAmL 94
Sanders, Teressa Irene 1951- WhoFI 94
Sanders, Terry Barrett 1931- IntMPA 94
Sanders, Thomas James 1957- WhoAmL 94
Sanders, Todd Robert 1964- WhoMW 93
Sanders, Victoria Lynn WhoBlA 94
Sanders, Wallace Wolfred, Jr. 1933- WhoAm 94
Sanders, Walter DrAPF 93
Sanders, Walter Jeremiah, III 1936- WhoAm 94, WhoFI 94, WhoWest 94
Sanders, Wayne R. 1947- WhoAm 94, WhoFI 94
Sanders, Wellford L., Jr. 1945- WhoAmL 94
Sanders, Wendell Rowan 1933- WhoBlA 94
Sanders, Wesley, Jr. 1933- WhoBlA 94
Sanders, Wilfred Leroy, Jr. 1935- WhoAmP 93
Sanders, William Eugene 1933- WhoFI 94
Sanders, William Eugene, Jr. 1934- WhoAm 94
Sanders, William George 1932- WhoAm 94
Sanders, William George 1936- Who 94
Sanders, William Huggins 1922- WhoAmL 94
Sanders, William Mac 1919- WhoBlA 94
Sanders, Winston P. EncSF 93
Sanders, Woodrow Mac 1943- WhoBlA 94
Sanders-Oji, J. Qevin 1962- WhoBlA 94
Sanderson Who 94
Sanderson, Allen WhoAmP 93
Sanderson, Bennett 1893- WhAm 10
Sanderson, (Frank Philip) Bryan d1992 Who 94N
Sanderson, Bryan Kaye 1940- Who 94
Sanderson, Charles Denis 1934- Who 94
Sanderson, Charles Howard 1925- WhoAmA 93
Sanderson, David Alan 1951- WhoFI 94, WhoMW 93
Sanderson, David R. 1933- WhoAm 94, WhoWest 94
Sanderson, Debby P. 1941- WhoAmP 93
Sanderson, Douglas Jay 1953- WhoAm 94, WhoAmL 94
Sanderson, Eric Fenton 1951- Who 94
Sanderson, Frank (Linton) 1933- Who 94
Sanderson, Fred Hugo 1914- WhoAm 94
Sanderson, Gary Warner 1934- WhoAm 94
Sanderson, George Rutherford 1919- Who 94
Sanderson, Glen Charles 1923- WhoScEn 94
Sanderson, Irma 1912- WrDr 94
Sanderson, Ivan T. EncSF 93
Sanderson, James Richard 1925- WhoAm 94
Sanderson, Julia d1975 WhoHol 92
Sanderson, Keith Fred 1932- Who 94
Sanderson, Kent WhoHol 92
Sanderson, Michael David 1943- Who 94
Sanderson, Michael Kelly 1952- WhoAm 94, WhoAmL 94
Sanderson, Peter Oliver 1929- Who 94
Sanderson, Randy Chris 1954- WhoBlA 94
Sanderson, Roy Who 94
Sanderson, Roy 1931- Who 94
Sanderson, (William) Roy 1907- Who 94
Sanderson, Sibyl 1865-1903 NewGrDO
Sanderson, Stewart F(orson) 1924- WrDr 94
Sanderson, Tessa IntWW 93
Sanderson, Warren 1931- WhoAmA 93
Sanderson, William 1948- WhoHol 92
Sanderson, William Fletcher, Jr. 1943- WhoAm 94, WhoAmL 94
Sanderson, William H. 1917- WhoFI 94
Sanderson Of Ayot, Baron Who 94
Sanderson Of Bowden, Baron 1933- Who 94
Sanders-West, Selma D. 1953- WhoBlA 94
Sandeson, William Seymour 1913- WhoAm 94, WhoAmA 93
Sandford, Baron 1920- Who 94
Sandford, Arthur 1941- Who 94
Sandford, Cedric Thomas 1924- Who 94
Sandford, Christopher 1939- WhoHol 92
Sandford, Herbert Henry 1916- Who 94
Sandford, Jeremy Who 94
Sandford, Jeremy 1934- WrDr 94
Sandford, Kenneth Leslie 1915- Who 94
Sandford, Sefton Ronald 1925- Who 94
Sandford, Stanley d1961 WhoHol 92
Sandford Smith, Richard Henry 1909- Who 94
Sandgren, Ernest Nelson 1917- WhoAmA 93
Sandground, Mark Bernard, Sr. 1932- WhoAmA 93
Sandham, William Allan 1952- WhoScEn 94
Sandhu, Bachittar Singh 1935- WhoScEn 94
Sandhu, Jatinder Singh 1961- WhoWest 94
Sandhu, Ranbir Singh 1928- WhoAsA 94
Sandhu, Sarwan Singh 1940- WhoMW 93
Sandhu, Shingara Singh 1932- WhoAsA 94
Sandhurst, Baron 1920- Who 94
Sandi (Meneses), Luis 1905- NewGrDO
Sandidge, Kanita Durice 1947- WhoBlA 94, WhoFI 94
Sandidge, Kent, III 1929- WhoAm 94, WhoAmL 94
Sandifer, Jawn A. 1919- WhoBlA 94
Sandiford, (Lloyd) Erskine 1937- Who 94
Sandiford, Lloyd Erskine 1937- IntWW 93
Sandifur, Cantwell Paul, Sr. 1903- WhoIns 94
Sandilands Who 94
Sandilands, Francis (Edwin Prescott) 1913- Who 94
Sandilands, Francis Edwin Prescott 1913- IntWW 93
Sandison, Alexander 1943- Who 94
Sanditen, Edgar Richard 1920- WhoAm 94
Sanditz, Theodore Bert 1946- WhoMW 93
Sandle, Floyd Leslie 1913- WhoBlA 94
Sandle, Michael Leonard 1936- IntWW 93, Who 94
Sandler, Barbara 1943- WhoAmA 93
Sandler, Benjamin 1957- WhoHisp 94
Sandler, Debbie Rodman 1959- WhoAmL 94
Sandler, Gerald Howard 1934- WhoFI 94
Sandler, Herbert M. 1931- WhoAm 94, WhoFI 94, WhoWest 94
Sandler, Irving (Harry) 1925- WrDr 94
Sandler, Irving Harry 1925- WhoAm 94, WhoAmA 93
Sandler, Jenny WhoAm 94
Sandler, Joan D. 1934- WhoBlA 94
Sandler, Lucy Freeman 1930- WhoAm 94
Sandler, Marion Osher 1930- WhoAm 94, WhoFI 94, WhoWest 94
Sandler, Maurice 1937- WhoWest 94
Sandler, Merton Who 94
Sandler, Merton 1926- WrDr 94
Sandler, Michael David 1946- WhoAm 94, WhoAmL 94

Sandler, Paul Mark 1945- *WhoAmL 94*
Sandler, Philip Stanley 1943- *WhoFI 94*
Sandler, Richard Jay 1947- *WhoAm 94*
Sandler, Robert Michael 1942- *WhoAm 94, WhoFI 94*
Sandler, Ross 1939- *WhoAm 94*
Sandler, Stanley Irving 1940- *WhoAm 94*
Sandler, Thomas R. 1946- *WhoAm 94*
Sandler, Todd Michael 1946- *WhoFI 94*
Sandlin, David Thomas 1956- *WhoAmA 93*
Sandlin, Fred Allen, Jr. 1952- *WhoWest 94*
Sandlin, Joseph Ernest 1919- *WhoAm 94*
Sandlin, Marlon Joe 1953- *WhoWest 94*
Sandlin, Sherry *WhoAmP 93*
Sandlin, Steven Monroe 1935- *WhoFI 94, WhoWest 94*
Sandlin, Tim *DrAPF 93*
Sandlund, Debra *WhoHol 92*
Sandman, Alan 1947- *WhoAmA 93*
Sandman, Dan D. *WhoAmL 94*
Sandman, Irvin Willis 1954- *WhoAmL 94*
Sandman, James Joseph 1951- *WhoAmL 94*
Sandman, Jo 1931- *WhoAmA 93*
Sandman, Peter (Mark) 1945- *WrDr 94*
Sandmeier, Ruedi Beat 1945- *WhoAm 94, WhoScEn 94*
Sandmeyer, Robert Lee 1929- *WhoAm 94*
Sandmo, Agnar 1938- *IntWW 93*
Sandner, John Francis 1941- *WhoAm 94, WhoFI 94*
Sandness, William John 1948- *WhoAmP 93, WhoMW 93*
Sando, Ephriam 1934- *WhoWest 94*
Sando, James Frank 1954- *WhoWest 94*
Sandok, Burton Alan 1937- *WhoAm 94, WhoMW 93*
Sandol, Maynard 1930- *WhoAmA 93*
Sandon, Viscount 1951- *Who 94*
Sandon, J. D. 1938- *WrDr 94*
Sandoni, Pietro Giuseppe 1685-1748 *NewGrDO*
Sandor, Alfred d1983 *WhoHol 92*
Sandor, Ellen Ruth 1942- *WhoMW 93*
Sandor, George Nason 1912- *WhoAm 94, WhoScEn 94*
Sandor, Gyorgy *WhoAm 94*
Sandor, John Abraham *WhoAm 94, WhoWest 94*
Sandor, Richard Laurence 1941- *WhoAm 94*
Sandor, Steve *WhoHol 92*
Sandor, Thomas 1924- *WhoAm 94*
Sandorfy, Camille 1920- *WhoAm 94*
Sandor-Jimenez, Yolanda 1955- *WhoHisp 94*
Sandos, Michael Steven 1951- *WhoHisp 94*
Sandos, Tim *WhoHisp 94*
Sandoungout, Marcel 1927- *IntWW 93*
Sandoval, Alicia Catherine 1943- *WhoHisp 94*
Sandoval, Alphonso J. 1923- *WhoHisp 94*
Sandoval, Andrew M. 1952- *WhoHisp 94*
Sandoval, Antonio Martinez 1941- *WhoHisp 94*
Sandoval, Arturo 1949- *IntWW 93, WhoAm 94, WhoHisp 94*
Sandoval, Chris 1949- *WhoHisp 94*
Sandoval, Dolores S. 1937- *WhoBlA 94*
Sandoval, Don 1966- *WhoHisp 94*
Sandoval, Donald A. 1935- *WhoAmP 93, WhoHisp 94*
Sandoval, Edward C. *WhoAmP 93, WhoHisp 94*
Sandoval, Edward P. 1960- *WhoHisp 94*
Sandoval, Ernie 1948- *WhoHisp 94*
Sandoval, Howard Kenneth 1931- *WhoHisp 94*
Sandoval, James P. *WhoHisp 94*
Sandoval, Jesse Robert 1956- *WhoAmL 94*
Sandoval, Joe G. 1937- *WhoHisp 94*
Sandoval, Joseph *WhoHisp 94*
Sandoval, Marcelo Alex 1960- *WhoHisp 94*
Sandoval, Mary Jane 1951- *WhoHisp 94*
Sandoval, Miguel *WhoHisp 94*
Sandoval, Moises 1930- *WhoHisp 94*
Sandoval, Olivia Medina 1946- *WhoHisp 94*
Sandoval, R. Christoph 1949- *WhoHisp 94*
Sandoval, Raul M. 1957- *WhoHisp 94*
Sandoval, Rik 1952- *WhoAm 94*
Sandoval, Roberto *DrAPF 93*
Sandoval, Rodolpho 1942- *WhoHisp 94*
Sandoval, Rudolph 1929- *WhoHisp 94*
Sandoval, Vanessa Fowler 1967- *WhoWest 94*
Sandoval-Beene, Mercedes 1949- *WhoHisp 94*
Sandow, Eugene d1925 *WhoHol 92*
Sandoz, G(eorge) Ellis 1931- *WrDr 94*
Sandoz, John H. *WhoBlA 94*
Sandoz, Lawrence Broussard, III 1953- *WhoAmL 94*
Sandquist, Elroy C., Jr. 1922- *WhoAmP 93*
Sandquist, Elroy Charles, Jr. 1922- *WhoAm 94*
Sandquist, Gary Marlin 1936- *WhoAm 94, WhoScEn 94, WhoWest 94*
Sandquist, Hans d1935 *WhoHol 92*
Sandrapaty, Ramachandra Rao 1942- *WhoAsA 94*
Sandre, Didier 1946- *IntWW 93*
Sandrelli, Amanda *WhoHol 92*
Sandrelli, Stefania 1946- *WhoHol 92*
Sandrey, Irma *WhoHol 92*
Sandri, Anna-Maria 1930- *WhoHol 92*
Sandri, Francesco fl. 1693-1718 *NewGrDO*
Sandrich, Jay 1932- *IntMPA 94*
Sandrich, Jay H. 1932- *WhoAm 94*
Sandridge, Thomas Glenn 1959- *WhoFI 94*
Sandridge, William Pendleton, Jr. 1934- *WhoAm 94, WhoAmL 94*
Sandrini, Luis d1980 *WhoHol 92*
Sandrock, Adele d1937 *WhoHol 92*
Sandrock, Wilhelmine d1948 *WhoHol 92*
Sandroff, Ronni *DrAPF 93*
Sandrok, Richard William 1943- *WhoAm 94*
Sandroni, Andrew Dennis 1959- *WhoAmL 94*
Sandrow, Hope 1951- *WhoAmA 93*
Sandry, Karla Kay Foreman 1961- *WhoMW 93, WhoScEn 94*
Sands, A. P., III 1945- *WhoAmP 93*
Sands, Billy d1984 *WhoHol 92*
Sands, Comfort 1748-1834 *WhAmRev*
Sands, Darry Gene 1947- *WhoAmL 94*
Sands, Diana d1973 *WhoHol 92*
Sands, Don William 1926- *WhoAm 94, WhoFI 94*
Sands, Donald Edgar 1929- *WhoAm 94*
Sands, Douglas Bruce 1934- *WhoBlA 94*
Sands, Edith Sylvia Abeloff *WhoAm 94*
Sands, Frank Melville 1938- *WhoFI 94*
Sands, George M. 1942- *WhoBlA 94*
Sands, Henry W. 1933- *WhoBlA 94*
Sands, Howard 1942- *WhoScEn 94*
Sands, I. Jay *WhoAm 94*
Sands, Jack 1947- *WhoAmP 93*
Sands, John Eliot 1941- *WhoAm 94*
Sands, John W. 1934- *WhoAm 94*
Sands, Johnny 1927- *WhoHol 92*
Sands, Julian 1957- *WhoHol 92*
Sands, Julian 1958- *IntMPA 94*
Sands, Kathleen M. *ConAu 41NR*
Sands, Kathleen Mullen *ConAu 41NR*
Sands, Lawrence Keith 1955- *WhoWest 94*
Sands, Leslie 1921- *WhoHol 92*
Sands, Martin 1922- *WrDr 94*
Sands, Mary Alice 1941- *WhoBlA 94*
Sands, Matthew Linzee 1919- *WhoAm 94*
Sands, Michael Stephen 1937- *WhoWest 94*
Sands, Robert-John H. 1954- *WhoIns 94*
Sands, Robert O. 1953- *WhoAmL 94*
Sands, Roger Blakemore 1942- *Who 94*
Sands, Rosetta F. *WhoBlA 94*
Sands, Russell Bertram 1940- *WhoWest 94*
Sands, Sharon Louise 1944- *WhoWest 94*
Sands, Thomas Allen 1935- *WhoAm 94*
Sands, Tommy 1936- *WhoHol 92*
Sands, Tommy 1937- *IntMPA 94*
Sands, Velma Ahda *WhoAmL 94*
Sands, William Arthur 1953- *WhoWest 94*
Sandson, John I. 1927- *WhoAm 94*
Sands Smith, David 1943- *Who 94*
Sandstad, Kenneth D. 1946- *WhoAm 94*
Sandstead, Harold Hilton 1932- *WhoAm 94*
Sandstroem, Yvonne L. 1933- *ConAu 140*
Sandstrom, Alice Wilhelmina 1914- *WhoFI 94*
Sandstrom, Dale Vernon 1950- *WhoAmL 94, WhoAmP 93, WhoMW 93*
Sandstrom, Eve K. 1936- *ConAu 141*
Sandstrom, Gunnar Emanuel 1951- *WhoScEn 94*
Sandstrom, Joanne Wulf 1938- *WhoWest 94*
Sandstrom, Mark Roy 1942- *WhoAm 94, WhoAmL 94*
Sandstrom, Robert Edward 1946- *WhoScEn 94, WhoWest 94*
Sandstrum, Steve D. 1953- *WhoScEn 94*
Sandt, John Joseph 1925- *WhoScEn 94*
Sandu, Bogdan Mihai 1968- *WhoScEn 94*
Sandu, Constantine 1943- *WhoFI 94, WhoMW 93, WhoScEn 94*
Sandu, Gabriel 1954- *ConAu 141*
Sandunes, Myro *DrAPF 93*
Sandunova, Elizaveta Semyonovna 1772?-1826 *NewGrDO*
Sandura, Wilson Runyararo 1941- *IntWW 93*
Sandusky, Billy Ray 1945- *WhoAmA 93*
Sandusky, John Thomas, Jr. 1934- *WhoAmP 93*
Sandved, Arthur Olav 1931- *IntWW 93*
Sandven, Lars Arild 1945- *WhoWest 94*
Sandver, Jean Hart 1950- *WhoFI 94*
Sandweg, Gerard K., Jr. 1943- *WhoAmL 94*
Sandweiss, Jack 1930- *WhoAm 94*
Sandweiss, Martha A. 1954- *WhoAm 94*
Sandweiss, Martha A(nn) 1954- *WrDr 94*
Sandweiss, Martha Ann 1954- *WhoAmA 93*
Sandwen, Lee H. 1950- *WhoFI 94*
Sandwich, Earl of *Who 94*
Sandwich, Earl of 1718-1792 *AmRev*
Sandwich, John Montagu, Earl of 1718-1792 *WhAmRev*
Sandwich, Reuben *DrAPF 93*
Sandy, Edward Allen 1958- *WhoScEn 94*
Sandy, Gary 1943- *WhoHol 92*
Sandy, Stephen *DrAPF 93*
Sandy, Stephen 1934- *WhoAm 94, WrDr 94*
Sandy, William Haskell 1929- *WhoAm 94, WhoFI 94*
Sandys, Baron 1931- *Who 94*
Sandys, Julian George Winston 1936- *Who 94*
Sandza, Yvonne Anne 1952- *WhoWest 94*
Sane, Pierre Gabriel 1948- *Who 94*
Sane, Pierre Gabriel Michel 1948- *IntWW 93*
Sanecki, Kay Naylor 1922- *WrDr 94*
Sanejouand, Jean Michel 1934- *IntWW 93*
Sanelli, Gualtiero 1816-1861 *NewGrDO*
Saner, Reg *DrAPF 93*
Saner, Reg(inald Anthony) 1931- *WrDr 94*
Saner, Robert Morton *Who 94*
Sanera, Marge 1911- *WhoMW 93*
Sanes, Joshua Richard 1949- *WhoScEn 94*
Sanes, Scott Adam 1957- *WhoAmL 94*
Saneto, Russell Patrick 1950- *WhoAm 94, WhoScEn 94, WhoWest 94*
Sanetti, Stephen Louis 1949- *WhoAmL 94*
Saneyev, Viktor Daniilovich 1945- *IntWW 93*
Sanfelici, Arthur Hugo 1934- *WhoAm 94*
Sanfelippo, Peter Michael 1938- *WhoAm 94*
San Felix, Marcela de 1605-1688 *BlmGWL*
Sanfield, Steve *DrAPF 93*
Sanfilip, Thomas *DrAPF 93*
Sanfilippo, Jon Walter 1950- *WhoAmL 94, WhoMW 93*
Sanford, Abigail *GayLL*
Sanford, Albert, Jr. d1953 *WhoHol 92*
Sanford, Allan Robert 1927- *WhoWest 94*
Sanford, Annette *DrAPF 93*
Sanford, Annette 1929- *WrDr 94*
Sanford, Bruce W. 1945- *WhoAm 94*
Sanford, Bruce William 1945- *WhoAmL 94*
Sanford, Charles Steadman, Jr. 1936- *IntWW 93, WhoAm 94, WhoFI 94*
Sanford, Christy Sheffield *DrAPF 93*
Sanford, David Boyer 1943- *WhoAm 94*
Sanford, David Hawley 1937- *WhoAm 94*
Sanford, Delores Mae 1931- *WhoMW 93*
Sanford, Elias Benjamin 1843-1932 *DcAmReB 2*
Sanford, Erskine d1969 *WhoHol 92*
Sanford, Frederic Goodman *WhoAm 94*
Sanford, George Robert 1927- *WhoWest 94*
Sanford, Geraldine A. J. *DrAPF 93*
Sanford, Isabel 1917- *IntMPA 94, WhoHol 92*
Sanford, Isabel G. 1917- *WhoBlA 94*
Sanford, Jay Philip 1928- *WhoAm 94*
Sanford, John Elroy *WhAm 10*
Sanford, Kathleen Diane 1952- *WhoWest 94*
Sanford, Leroy Leonard 1934- *WhoWest 94*
Sanford, Loretta Love 1951- *WhoBlA 94*
Sanford, Mark 1953- *WhoBlA 94*
Sanford, Mary Duncan d1993 *NewYTBS 93 [port]*
Sanford, Ralph d1963 *WhoHol 92*
Sanford, Richard D. 1944- *WhoAm 94, WhoFI 94*
Sanford, Ron 1939- *WhoWest 94*
Sanford, Roy Leon 1946- *WhoAm 94*
Sanford, Ruth Eileen 1925- *WhoMW 93*
Sanford, Sarah J. 1949- *WhoAm 94, WhoWest 94*
Sanford, Stanley d1961 *WhoHol 92*
Sanford, Suzanne Langford 1951- *WhoAmL 94*
Sanford, Terry 1917- *IntWW 93, WhoAm 94, WhoAmL 94, WhoAmP 93*
Sanford, Thomas William Louis 1943- *WhoScEn 94*
Sanford, Valerius 1923- *WhoAm 94*
Sanford, Walter Scott 1956- *WhoWest 94*
Sanford, Wilbur Lee 1935- *WhoMW 93*
Sanford, Willard C. 1932- *WhoIns 94*
Sangare, N'Faly 1933- *IntWW 93*
Sanger, Bert d1969 *WhoHol 92*
Sanger, David John 1947- *IntWW 93*
Sanger, Eleanor d1993 *NewYTBS 93*
Sanger, Frederick 1918- *IntWW 93, Who 94, WhoAm 94, WhoScEn 94, WorScD*
Sanger, Gail 1945- *WhoAm 94, WhoAmL 94*
Sanger, Herbert Shelton, Jr. 1936- *WhoAm 94, WhoAmL 94*
Sanger, John 1816-1889 *BlmGEL*
Sanger, John Morton 1943- *WhoAm 94*
Sanger, Margaret 1879-1966 *HisWorL [port]*
Sanger, Margaret Louise Higgins 1883-1966 *AmSocL [port]*
Sanger, Marjory Bartlett 1920- *WrDr 94*
Sanger, Ruth Ann 1918- *IntWW 93, Who 94*
Sanger, Sophy 1881-1950 *DcNaB MP*
Sanger, Stephen W. 1945- *WhoAm 94*
Sanger, Warren J. 1943- *WhoAmL 94*
Sangerman, Harry M. 1941- *WhoAm 94*
Sangerman, Jay J. 1944- *WhoAmL 94*
Sanggyai Yexe *WhoPRCh 91*
Sanghani, Dipti 1964- *WhoFI 94*
Sangheli, Andrei *LngBDD*
San Giacomo, Laura *IntWW 93*
San Giacomo, Laura 1962- *IntMPA 94, WhoHol 92*
Sangiamo, Albert *WhoAmA 93*
Sangiorgio Festa, Maria Luisa 1947- *WhoWomW 91*
Sang Jiejia 1942- *WhoPRCh 91 [port]*
Sangmeister, George E. 1931- *CngDr 93*
Sangmeister, George Edward 1931- *WhoAm 94, WhoAmP 93, WhoMW 93*
Sangree, Walter Hinchman 1926- *WhoAm 94*
Sangrey, Dwight A. 1940- *WhoScEn 94*
Sangster, Alfred d1972 *WhoHol 92*
Sangster, Jimmy 1927- *HorFD, IntDcF 2-4 [port]*
Sangster, John Laing d1993 *Who 94N*
Sangster, Robert Edmund 1936- *IntWW 93, Who 94*
Sang Tong 1923- *WhoPRCh 91*
Sangueli, (Sangeli) Andrey 1944- *IntWW 93*
Sanguineti, Edoardo 1930- *IntWW 93*
Sanguinetti, Eugene F. 1917- *WhoAmA 93*
Sanguinetti, Eugene Frank 1917- *WhoAm 94, WhoWest 94*
Sanguinetti, Julio Maria 1936- *IntWW 93*
Sanguinetty, Jorge A. 1937- *WhoHisp 94*
Sanhueza, Hernan 1935- *WhoAm 94*
Sani, Brahma P. 1937- *WhoAsA 94*
Sani, Robert LeRoy 1935- *WhoAm 94, WhoScEn 94*
Sanipoli, Vittorio 1915- *WhoHol 92*
Sanjian, Avedis K. 1921- *WrDr 94*
Sanjian, Avedis Krikor 1921- *WhoAm 94*
Sanjinés, José H. 1959- *WhoHisp 94*
San Jose, George L. 1956- *WhoHisp 94*
San Juan, E. 1938- *WhoAsA 94*
San Juan, German Moral 1940- *WhoScEn 94*
San Juan, Manuel, Jr. 1920- *WhoIns 94*
San Juan, Olga 1927- *WhoHol 92*
Sanjurjo, Carmen Hilda 1952- *WhoHisp 94*
Sanjust, Filippo 1925- *NewGrDO*
Sank, David Abraham 1962- *WhoFI 94*
Sankar, Subramanian Vaidya 1959- *WhoScEn 94, WhoWest 94*
Sankaran, Aiylam P. 1939- *WhoAsA 94*
Sanker, Donald J. 1960- *WhoAmP 93*
Sankey, Guy Richard 1944- *Who 94*
Sankey, Ira David 1840-1908 *DcAmReB 2*
Sankey, John Anthony 1930- *IntWW 93, Who 94*
Sankey, Vernon Louis 1949- *Who 94*
Sankovich, Joseph Bernard 1944- *WhoWest 94*
Sankovitz, James Leo 1934- *WhoMW 93*
Sankovitz, Richard John 1958- *WhoAmL 94*
Sankowsky, Itzhak 1908- *WhoAmA 93*
Sanks, Charles Randolph, Jr. 1928- *WhoAm 94*
Sanks, Robert Leland 1916- *WhoAm 94, WhoWest 94*
San Mamés, Juan J. 1947- *WhoHisp 94*
San Mao 1943- *BlmGWL*
Sanmartín, Aimeé C. 1960- *WhoHisp 94*
San Martin, Jose de 1778-1850 *HisWorL [port]*
San Martín, Mario Valdés 1934- *WrDr 94*
San Martín, Nancy *WhoHisp 94*
San Martin, Robert L. *WhoAm 94, WhoScEn 94*
Sanmartini, Pietro 1636-1701 *NewGrDO*
San Miguel, Lolita 1934- *WhoHisp 94*

San Miguel, Pedro Luis 1954- *WhoHisp 94*
San Miguel, Richard Hays 1940- *WhoHisp 94*
Sann, Ronald Bruce 1961- *WhoAmL 94*
Sanna, Anna Filippa 1948- *WhoWomW 91*
Sanner, George Elwood 1929- *WhoFI 94, WhoScEn 94*
Sanner, Monty Ray 1953- *WhoWest 94*
Sanner, Robert Charles 1945- *WhoWest 94*
Sanner, Royce N. 1931- *WhoIns 94*
Sanner, Royce Norman 1931- *WhoAm 94, WhoAmL 94, WhoFI 94*
Sannerud, Paul David 1958- *WhoMW 93*
San Nicolas, Henry Deleon *WhoAmP 93*
Sannuti, Peddapullaiah 1941- *WhoAm 94*
Sannwald, William Walter 1940- *WhoAm 94, WhoWest 94*
Sano, Keiji 1920- *WhoScEn 94*
Sano, Kenjiro 1920- *IntWW 93*
Sano, Roy I. *WhoAm 94, WhoWest 94*
Sanocki, Edward John, Jr. 1950- *WhoAmL 94*
San Pedro, Emilio Juan 1964- *WhoHisp 94*
San Pedro, Enrique 1926- *WhoAm 94*
Sanquer, Dagmar Worth d1957 *WhoHol 92*
Sanquirico, Alessandro 1777-1849 *NewGrDO*
Sansaverino, Joseph F. 1937- *WhoAm 94*
Sansberry, Hope d1990 *WhoHol 92*
Sansbury, Cyril Kenneth 1905- *IntWW 93*
Sansbury, (Cyril) Kenneth d1993 *Who 94N*
Sansevero, Michael, Jr. 1952- *WhoAmP 93*
Sansolo, Jack 1943- *WhoAm 94*
Sansom, Andrew William d1992 *Who 94N*
Sansom, Dixie Newton 1948- *WhoAmP 93*
Sansom, Lester A. 1910- *IntMPA 94*
Sansom, Matt Rudiger 1950- *WhoFI 94, WhoWest 94*
Sansom, Peter 1958- *WrDr 94*
Sansom, William 1912-1976 *BlmGEL, ConAu 42NR, DcLB 139 [port], RfGShF*
Sanson, William Hendrix 1926- *WhoAmP 93*
Sanson, Yvonne 1929- *WhoHol 92*
Sansone, Joseph F. 1922- *WhoAmA 93*
Sansone, Robert 1942-1991 *WhAm 10*
Sansone, Rocco Carl 1950- *WhoIns 94*
Sansores, Albert N., Jr. 1950- *WhoHisp 94*
San Soucie, Patricia Molm 1931- *WhoAmA 93*
Sanstead, Wayne Godfrey 1935- *WhoAm 94, WhoAmP 93*
Sansweet, Stephen Jay 1945- *WhoAm 94, WhoWest 94*
Sant, Carmen 1945- *WhoWomW 91*
Sant, John Talbot 1932- *WhoAm 94, WhoFI 94*
Sant, Lorry 1937- *IntWW 93*
Sant, Raymond S. 1937- *WhoAmP 93*
Sant, Thomas 1948- *WrDr 94*
Sant, Thomas D. 1948- *WhoAm 94*
Santa, Donald F., Jr. 1958- *WhoAmP 93*
Santa Anna, Antonio Lopez de 1794-1876 *HisWorL [port]*
Santa Aponte, Jesus *WhoHisp 94*
Santacana, Enrique Oscar 1952- *WhoFI 94*
Santacana, Guido E. 1952- *WhoAm 94*
Santa Clara Gomes, Maria Teresa Doria 1936- *WhoWomW 91*
Santa Cruz, Allan *WhoAmP 93*
Santa-Cruz, Ivan 1930- *WhoHisp 94*
Santa Cruz, Victoria E. 1922- *WhoHisp 94*
Santa-Donato, Frank 1948- *WhoIns 94*
Santaella, Irma Vidal 1924- *WhoHisp 94*
Santamaria, Edward A. *WhoHisp 94*
Santamaria, Henry, Jr. 1948- *WhoHisp 94*
Santamaría, Jaime 1911- *WhoHisp 94*
Santamaría, Mongo 1922- *WhoHisp 94*
Santa Maria, Philip Joseph, III 1945- *WhoAmL 94*
Santa Maria, Zeke Polanco 1942- *WhoHisp 94*
Santamarina, Juan Carlos 1958- *WhoHisp 94*
Santana, Ana V. *WhoHisp 94*
Santana, Anthony *WhoHisp 94*
Santana, Carlos 1947- *WhoAm 94, WhoHisp 94*
Santana, Carlota *WhoHisp 94*
Santana, Elida *WhoHisp 94*
Santana, Ernesto Juan 1949- *WhoHisp 94*
Santana, Jorge Armando 1944- *WhoHisp 94*
Santana, Juan Jose 1942- *WhoHisp 94*
Santana, Manolo 1938- *BuCMET [port]*
Santana, Marie 1951- *WhoHisp 94*
Santana, Pepe 1942- *WhoHisp 94*
Santana, Rafael Francisco 1958- *WhoHisp 94*
Santana, Vasco d1958 *WhoHol 92*
Santana, Victor Manuel, Jr. 1962- *WhoHisp 94*
Santana-Alvarez, Luis F. 1943- *WhoHisp 94*
Santana-Garcia, Mario A. 1956- *WhoScEn 94*
Santanam, Suresh 1959- *WhoScEn 94*
Santander, Teresa 1925- *IntWW 93*
Santangeli, Frank 1934- *WhoAm 94*
Santangelo, George Michael 1956- *WhoScEn 94*
Santangelo, Luke Robert 1957- *WhoAmL 94*
Santangelo, Mario Vincent 1931- *WhoMW 93*
Santaniello, Angelo Gary 1924- *WhoAm 94, WhoAmP 93*
Santapau, Manny 1949- *WhoHisp 94*
Santapoalo, Julie Ann 1958- *WhoMW 93*
Santarelli, Eugene David 1944- *WhoAm 94, WhoWest 94*
Santareno, Bernardo 1920-1980 *IntDcT 2*
Santa Romano, Privitivo d1961 *WhoHol 92*
Santayana, George 1863-1952 *EncEth*
Sante, Sophia (Maria Christina) van 1925- *NewGrDO*
Sante, William Arthur, II 1943- *WhoAm 94*
Santee, Dale William 1953- *WhoAmL 94, WhoFI 94, WhoWest 94*
Santee, Richard Ellis, Jr. 1951- *WhoAmL 94*
Santeiro, Luis 1947- *WhoHisp 94*
Santell, Roberta 1937- *WhoAmP 93*
Santelli, Claude Jean Xavier 1923- *IntWW 93*
Santemma, Jon Noel 1937- *WhoAmL 94*
Santen, Ann Hortenstine 1938- *WhoMW 93*
Santer, Jacques 1937- *IntWW 93*
Santer, Mark *Who 94*
Santer, Mark 1936- *IntWW 93*
Santer, Richard Arthur 1937- *WhoAm 94, WhoMW 93*
Santesson, Hans Stefan 1914-1975 *EncSF 93*
Santez, David Lewis *WhoAmL 94*
Santhanam, Radhika 1959- *WhoAsA 94*
Santhuff, Carol Jean 1946- *WhoMW 93*
Santi, David W. 1949- *WhoAmL 94*
Santi, Jacques d1988 *WhoHol 92*
Santi, Nello 1931- *NewGrDO*
Santi, Peter Alan 1947- *WhoScEn 94*
Santiago, Aida Esther 1957- *WhoHisp 94*
Santiago, Alex 1957- *WhoAmP 93*
Santiago, Alfredo 1953- *WhoHisp 94*
Santiago, Américo *WhoHisp 94*
Santiago, Americo L. *WhoAmP 93*
Santiago, Benito 1965- *WhoHisp 94*
Santiago, Benito Rivera 1965- *WhoAm 94, WhoWest 94*
Santiago, Bonnie 1966- *WhoHisp 94*
Santiago, Cirio H. *HorFD*
Santiago, Dawn Teresa 1959- *WhoWest 94*
Santiago, Edgardo G. 1949- *WhoHisp 94*
Santiago, Elena *BlmGWL*
Santiago, Fabiola 1959- *WhoHisp 94*
Santiago, George 1929- *WhoHisp 94*
Santiago, George L. 1958- *WhoHisp 94*
Santiago, Gloria B. *WhoHisp 94*
Santiago, Henry, Jr. 1960- *WhoHisp 94*
Santiago, Isaura Santiago 1946- *WhoHisp 94*
Santiago, Ismael *WhoHisp 94*
Santiago, Jaime A. *WhoHisp 94*
Santiago, James Severo 1944- *WhoHisp 94*
Santiago, Jorge *WhoHisp 94*
Santiago, Julio A. 1947- *WhoHisp 94*
Santiago, Julio V. 1942- *WhoScEn 94*
Santiago, Julio Victor 1942- *WhoHisp 94*
Santiago, Lorina Yvonne 1966- *WhoHisp 94*
Santiago, Lucy 1948- *WhoHisp 94*
Santiago, Luis Hernandez *WhoAmP 93*
Santiago, Luz M. 1948- *WhoHisp 94*
Santiago, Manuel Antonio 1962- *WhoHisp 94*
Santiago, Maximo, Jr. 1943- *WhoHisp 94*
Santiago, Mayra C. 1952- *WhoHisp 94*
Santiago, Miguel A. *WhoHisp 94*
Santiago, Miguel A. 1953- *WhoAmP 93*
Santiago, Milly 1954- *WhoHisp 94*
Santiago, Nellie *WhoAmP 93*
Santiago, Noel Rivera 1961- *WhoHisp 94*
Santiago, Ramon 1943- *WhoAmA 93*
Santiago, Ramón 1948- *WhoHisp 94*
Santiago, Richard E. 1948- *WhoAmA 93*
Santiago, Roberto 1953- *WhoHisp 94*
Santiago, Roberto 1963- *WhoBlA 94, WhoHisp 94*
Santiago, Rosa Emilia 1935- *WhoHisp 94*
Santiago, Saundra 1957- *WhoHisp 94, WhoHol 92*
Santiago, Soledad *WhoHisp 94*
Santiago, Teresa *WhoHisp 94*
Santiago, Wanda L. 1958- *WhoHisp 94*
Santiago-Avilés, Jorge Juan 1944- *WhoHisp 94*
Santiago-Delpin, Eduardo A. 1941- *WhoHisp 94*
Santiago-Fernandez, Nellie *WhoHisp 94*
Santiago Garcia, Presby 1941- *WhoAmP 93, WhoHisp 94*
Santiago Góñez, Rafael 1955- *WhoHisp 94*
Santiago-Negrón, Salvador 1942- *WhoHisp 94*
Santiago-Rodriguez, Liduvina 1937- *WhoAm 94*
Santiago Vega, Rosa J. 1938- *WhoHisp 94*
Santiesteban, Humberto 1934- *WhoHisp 94*
Santiesteban, Humberto Tati 1934- *WhoAmP 93*
Santillan, Antonio 1936- *WhoFI 94, WhoHisp 94, WhoWest 94*
Santillan, Jose Leopoldo 1957- *WhoWest 94*
Santillanes, Simon Paul 1967- *WhoScEn 94*
Santillano, Sergio Raul 1951- *WhoHisp 94*
Santilli, Alcide 1914- *WhoWest 94*
Santilli, Paul David 1946- *WhoAmP 93*
Santillo, Carl John 1949- *WhoIns 94*
Santina, La *NewGrDO*
Santina, Bruno Della d1968 *WhoHol 92*
Santinello, Cynthia Susan 1961- *WhoAmL 94*
Santini, Anthony David 1948- *WhoMW 93*
Santini, Danilo John 1945- *WhoFI 94, WhoMW 93*
Santini, Gabriele 1886-1964 *NewGrDO*
Santini, James David 1937- *WhoAmP 93*
Santini, John Amedeo 1926- *WhoAm 94*
Santini, Rosemarie *DrAPF 93*
Santini, Vincenzo-Felice 1798?-1836 *NewGrDO*
Santis, Luigi de *NewGrDO*
Santisteban, Carlos 1958- *WhoHisp 94*
Sant Jordi, Rosa de *BlmGWL*
Santley, Charles 1834-1922 *NewGrDO*
Santley, Fred d1953 *WhoHol 92*
Santley, Joseph d1971 *WhoHol 92*
Santlofer, Jonathan 1946- *WhoAmA 93*
Santman, Leon Duane 1930- *WhoAm 94*
Santner, Joseph Stephen 1948- *WhoMW 93*
Santo, El *WhoHol 92*
Santo, Akiko 1942- *IntWW 93, WhoWomW 91*
Santo, Harold Paul 1947- *WhoScEn 94*
Santo, Ronald Joseph 1940- *WhoAm 94, WhoAmL 94*
Santola, Daniel Ralph 1949- *WhoAmL 94*
Santoli, Joseph Ralph 1957- *WhoAmL 94*
Santoliquido, Francesco 1883-1971 *NewGrDO*
Santolucito, Joseph Anthony 1946- *WhoAm 94*
Santomenna, Robert Charles 1934- *WhoAmL 94*
Santomero, Anthony M. 1946- *WhoAm 94, WhoFI 94*
Santomieri, David M. 1945- *WhoIns 94*
Santon, Penny 1916- *WhoHol 92*
Santona, Gloria 1950- *WhoHisp 94*
Santoni, Dante, Jr. 1960- *WhoAmP 93*
Santoni, Reni *WhoHol 92*
Santoni, Ronald Ernest 1931- *WhoAm 94*
Santopietro, Albert Robert 1948- *WhoAmL 94, WhoFI 94*
Santor, Ken *WhoAmP 93*
Santoro, Alex 1936- *WhoFI 94, WhoMW 93, WhoScEn 94*
Santoro, Alfonso L. 1939- *WhoAmP 93*
Santoro, Anthony Richard 1939- *WhoAm 94*
Santoro, Carmelo James 1941- *WhoAm 94, WhoWest 94*
Santoro, Dean d1987 *WhoHol 92*
Santoro, Ferrucio Fontes 1952- *WhoScEn 94*
Santoro, Jack d1980 *WhoHol 92*
Santorum, Richard John 1958- *WhoAmP 93*
Santorum, Rick 1958- *CngDr 93, WhoAm 94*
Santos, Adele Naude *WhoAmA 93*
Santos, Adele Naude 1938- *WhoAm 94*
Santos, Alfred 1940- *WhoAmP 93*
Santos, Alfredo Cruz d1977 *WhoHol 92*
Santos, Bert *WhoHol 92*
Santos, Bienvenido N. *DrAPF 93*
Santos, Corentino Virgilio 1946- *IntWW 93*
Santos, Djalma 1929- *WorESoc*
Santos, Domingo *EncSF 93*
Santos, Edward Dominic 1943- *WhoHisp 94*
Santos, Enos Francis Frank 1933- *WhoWest 94*
Santos, Francisco Rivera 1930- *WhoAmP 93*
Santos, George Wesley 1928- *WhoAm 94*
Santos, Henry J. 1927- *WhoBlA 94*
Santos, Joaquim Felicio Dos *EncSF 93*
Santos, Joe 1931- *WhoHisp 94*
Santos, Joe 1933- *WhoHol 92*
Santos, (Jose Manuel) Joly Braga 1924-1988 *NewGrDO*
Santos, Jose A. 1950- *WhoHisp 94*
Santos, Jose Luis 1962- *WhoAmL 94*
Santos, Julian F. 1936- *WhoHisp 94*
Santos, Leonard Ernest 1946- *WhoAm 94, WhoAmL 94*
Santos, Lizette 1955- *WhoHisp 94*
Santos, Luciano Xavier 1734-1808 *NewGrDO*
Santos, Maria Amelia do Carmo Mota 1952- *WhoWomW 91*
Santos, Mario Alban 1947- *WhoAsA 94*
Santos, Mathies Joseph 1948- *WhoBlA 94*
Santos, Miriam 1956- *WhoHisp 94*
Santos, Nilton 1926- *WorESoc [port]*
Santos, Reydel 1954- *WhoHisp 94*
Santos, Richard *WhoHisp 94*
Santos, Rogelio R. 1943- *WhoHisp 94*
Santos, Rolando Arquiza 1934- *WhoAm 94*
Santos, Ruben M. *WhoHisp 94*
Santos, Rudy Rodriguez 1959- *WhoHisp 94*
Santos, Sherod (A.) 1948- *WrDr 94*
Santos, Tiki d1974 *WhoHol 92*
Santos-Alborna, Gipsy 1965- *WhoHisp 94*
Santos Espinosa, Jesus A. 1958- *WhoHisp 94*
Santos Lopez, Wilfredo *WhoHisp 94*
Santos Oliveira, Joao 1936- *IntWW 93*
Santovenia, Maria de Jesus 1961- *WhoAmL 94*
Santovenia, Nelson Gil 1961- *WhoHisp 94*
Santow, Mona Stephanie 1947- *WhoMW 93*
Santry, Arthur J., Jr. d1993 *NewYTBS 93 [port]*
Santry, Barbara Lea 1948- *WhoFI 94, WhoWest 94*
Santschi, Peter Hans 1943- *WhoAm 94, WhoScEn 94*
Santschi, Tom d1931 *WhoHol 92*
Santti, Gary Allen 1953- *WhoScEn 94*
Santucci, Anthony Charles 1959- *WhoScEn 94*
Santucci, Roberto Giuseppe 1965- *WhoFI 94*
Santuccio, Gianni d1989 *WhoHol 92*
Santulli, Thomas Vincent 1915- *WhoAm 94*
Santunione, Orianna 1934- *NewGrDO*
Santurini, Francesco 1627-1688? *NewGrDO*
Santurini, Francesco fl. 1674-1685 *NewGrDO*
Santy, Jeanne-Lois Marschall 1931- *WhoAmP 93*
San Vincenzo Ferreri, Marquis of 1911- *Who 94*
Sanvitale, Francesca 1929- *BlmGWL*
Sanwick, James Arthur 1951- *WhoFI 94, WhoWest 94*
Sanyour, Michael Louis, Jr. 1930- *WhoAm 94*
San Yu, U. 1919- *IntWW 93*
Sanz, Adolph Nunez 1951- *WhoHisp 94*
Sanz, Eleutherio Llorente 1926- *WhoHisp 94*
Sanz, Ernesto F. 1933- *WhoHisp 94*
Sanz, Kathleen Marie 1955- *WhoWest 94*
Sanz, Luis E. 1943- *WhoHisp 94*
Sanz, Maria 1956- *BlmGWL*
Sanz, Olga E. 1924- *WhoHisp 94*
Sanzara, Rahel 1894-1936 *BlmGWL*
Sanz Gonzalez, Richard *WhoHisp 94*
Sanzo, Anthony Michael 1954- *WhoAm 94*
Sanzogno, Nino 1911-1983 *NewGrDO*
Sao, Maria da Conceicao 1946- *WhoFI 94*
Saobento, Antonio, Jr. *WhoAmP 93*
Saouma, Edouard 1926- *IntWW 93, Who 94*
Sapadin, Linda Alice 1940- *WhoScEn 94*
Sapan, Christine Vogel 1947- *WhoScEn 94*
Saparoff, Peter M. 1942- *WhoAm 94, WhoAmL 94*
Saper, Clifford Baird 1952- *WhoAm 94*
Saper, Jeffrey D. 1948- *WhoAmL 94*
Saper, Vernon P. 1946- *WhoAmL 94*
Sapers, Carl Martin 1932- *WhoAm 94*
Saperstein, Abe 1902-1966 *BasBi*
Saperstein, David 1937- *IntMPA 94, WrDr 94*
Saperstein, David Allan 1937- *WhoAm 94*
Saperstein, Henry G. 1918- *IntMPA 94*

Saperstein, Lee Waldo 1943- *WhoAm 94*
Saperstein, Marc Charles 1953- *WhoAmL 94*
Saperstein, Marc Eli 1944- *WhoAm 94*
Saperstein, Sidney 1923- *WhoWest 94*
Saperston, Howard Truman, Sr. 1899- *WhoAm 94*
Saphier, A. S. 1898- *WhAm 10*
Saphir, Nicholas Peter George 1944- *Who 94*
Saphire, Gary Steven 1952- *WhoScEn 94*
Saphire, Lawrence M. 1931- *WhoAmA 93*
Saphire, Naomi Carrol 1938- *WhoFI 94*
Saphos, Charles Shepherd 1945- *WhoAmL 94*
Sapico, Francisco Lejano 1940- *WhoAm 94*
Sapien, Darryl Rudolph 1950- *WhoAmA 93*
Sapiens, Alexander 1946- *WhoHisp 94*
Sapienza, Anthony Rosario 1917- *WhoScEn 94*
Sapienza, John Thomas 1913- *WhoAm 94*
Sapin, Michel 1952- *IntWW 93*
Sapin, Michel Marie 1952- *Who 94*
Sapinsky, Joseph Charles 1923- *WhoAm 94*
Sapinsley, Lila Manfield 1922- *WhoAmP 93*
Sapir, Richard Ben 1936-1987 *EncSF 93*
Sapiro, Miriam Elizabeth 1960- *WhoAmL 94*
Sapoch, John Crim, Jr. 1937- *WhoWest 94*
Sapoff, Meyer 1927- *WhoFI 94, WhoScEn 94*
Sapolsky, Harvey Morton 1939- *WhoAm 94*
Saponaro, Joseph A. 1939- *WhoAm 94, WhoScEn 94*
Sapontzis, Steve F. 1945- *WhoWest 94*
Saporiti, Teresa 1763-1869 *NewGrDO*
Saporito, Patricia L. 1949- *WhoIns 94*
Saporta, Jack 1927- *WhoMW 93*
Saporta, Marc 1923- *IntWW 93*
Sapos, Mary Ann *WhoAm 94*
Sapp, A. Eugene, Jr. 1933- *WhoAm 94, WhoFI 94*
Sapp, Donald Gene 1927- *WhoAm 94, WhoWest 94*
Sapp, George David 1946- *WhoIns 94*
Sapp, Jo *DrAPF 93*
Sapp, John Raymond 1944- *WhoAm 94, WhoAmL 94*
Sapp, Lauren B. 1945- *WhoBlA 94*
Sapp, Neil Carleton 1939- *WhoFI 94*
Sapp, Richard Jerome 1950- *WhoAmL 94*
Sapp, Roy G. 1928- *WhoWest 94*
Sapp, Walter William 1930- *WhoAm 94, WhoAmL 94, WhoFI 94*
Sapp, William Moore 1963- *WhoFI 94*
Sapp, William Rothwell 1943- *WhoAmA 93*
Sappenfield, Charles Madison 1930- *WhoAm 94*
Sappenfield, Diane Hastings 1940- *WhoFI 94*
Sapper 1888-1937 *EncSF 93*
Sapper, Alan Louis Geoffrey 1931- *Who 94*
Sapper, Eugene Herbert 1929- *WhoHisp 94*
Sappey, Andrew David 1960- *WhoScEn 94*
Sapphire *DrAPF 93*
Sappho fl. 7th cent.BC- *BlmGWL [port]*
Sappho of Lesbos fl. 6th cent.BC- *BlmGEL*
Sappington, Fay d1985 *WhoHol 92*
Sappington, Harriett R. d1980 *WhoHol 92*
Sappington, Lynda Louisa Burton 1950- *WhoMW 93*
Sapritch, Alice d1990 *WhoHol 92*
Sapsamruay, Somchit d1980 *WhoHol 92*
Sapse, Anne-Marie 1939- *WhoScEn 94*
Sapsford, Ralph Neville 1938- *WhoScEn 94*
Sapsowitz, Sidney H. 1936- *WhoAm 94, WhoFI 94, WhoWest 94*
Sara *SmATA 75*
Sara, Mia 1967- *WhoHol 92*
Sara, Mia 1968- *IntMPA 94*
Sarabande, William *EncSF 93*
Sarabasa, Albert Gonzalez, Jr. 1952- *WhoHisp 94*
Sarabhai, Mrinalini 1935- *IntWW 93*
Sarabia, Fermin 1932- *WhoHisp 94*
Sarabia, Guillermo 1937-1985 *NewGrDO*
Sarabia, Horace 1938- *WhoHisp 94*
Sarabia, Louis 1942- *WhoHisp 94*
Sarac, Roger 1928- *EncSF 93*
Saracco, Guillermo Jorge 1964- *WhoScEn 94*
Saraceni, Adelaide 1895- *NewGrDO*
Saraceno, Blues
See Poison *ConMus 11*
Saracinelli, Ferdinando d1640 *NewGrDO*
Saracino, Samuel Francis 1951- *WhoAm 94, WhoAmL 94*
Saraf, Dilip Govind 1942- *WhoScEn 94, WhoWest 94*
Sarafian, Armen 1920-1989 *WhAm 10*
Sarafian, Richard C. 1935- *IntMPA 94*
Sarafoglou, Nikias 1954- *WhoScEn 94*
Sarago, Theo d1970 *WhoHol 92*
Sarah, Duchess of York 1959- *WrDr 94*
Sarah, Peter John 1946- *IntWW 93*
Saraiva, Antonio Jose d1993 *NewYTBS 93*
Saraiva Guerreiro, Ramiro Elysio *IntWW 93*
Sarajcic, Ivo 1915- *Who 94*
Saralegui, Cristina Maria 1948- *WhoHisp 94*
Saramago, Jose (de Sousa) 1922- *ConWorW 93*
Saran, Deo 1955- *WhoFI 94*
Sarandon, Chris 1942- *IntMPA 94, WhoHol 92*
Sarandon, Susan 1946- *IntMPA 94, WhoHol 92*
Sarandon, Susan Abigail 1946- *IntWW 93, WhoAm 94*
Saranow, Mitchell Harris 1945- *WhoMW 93*
Saranti, Galateia 1920- *BlmGWL*
Sarantopoulos, Theodore 1961- *WhoScEn 94*
Saras, James J. 1933- *WhoAm 94, WhoFI 94, WhoWest 94*
Sarasin, Alfred Emanuel 1922- *IntWW 93*
Sarasin, Arsa 1936- *IntWW 93*
Sarasin, Jennifer 1947- *WrDr 94*
Sarasin, Pote 1907- *IntWW 93*
Sarasin, Ronald A. 1934- *WhoAmP 93*
Sarasin, Warren G. 1943- *WhoAmP 93*
Sarasohn, Ira J. *WhoIns 94*
Sarason, Henry 1896-1979 *WhoAmA 93N*
Sarason, Irwin G. 1929- *WhoAm 94*
Sarat, Austin D. 1947- *WhoAm 94*
Sarathy, Partha R. 1942- *WhoAsA 94*
Sarathy, Partha Ragavachari Rangachari 1952- *WhoFI 94, WhoWest 94*
Sarati, Carmen M. 1931- *WhoHisp 94*
Saravanja-Fabris, Neda 1942- *WhoScEn 94*
Saravo, Anne Cobble 1938- *WhoWest 94*
Saravolatz, Louis Donald 1950- *WhoMW 93, WhoScEn 94*
Sarazen, Richard Allen 1933- *WhoAm 94, WhoFI 94*
Sarbach, Donald Victor 1911- *WhoMW 93, WhoScEn 94*
Sarban 1910-1989 *EncSF 93*
Sarbanes, Paul S. 1933- *CngDr 93*
Sarbanes, Paul Spyros 1933- *IntWW 93, WhoAm 94, WhoAmP 93*
Sarbin, Hershel Benjamin 1924- *WhoAm 94*
Sarcey, Martine *WhoHol 92*
Sarchet, Bernard Reginald 1917- *WhoScEn 94*
Sarchi, Bernard 1943- *WhoFI 94*
Sarcletti, Raymond A. 1938- *WhoAmP 93*
Sard, George 1953- *WhoAm 94*
Sardanis, Andreas Sotiris 1931- *IntWW 93*
Sarde, Philippe 1945- *IntDcF 2-4*
Sardeau, Helene 1899-1968 *WhoAmA 93N*
Sardelli, Anna Maria fl. 1649-1659 *NewGrDO*
Sardenberg, Ronaldo Mota 1940- *IntWW 93*
Sardi, Maurice Charles 1935- *WhoFI 94*
Sardi, Peter *WhoHol 92*
Sardina, Adolfo F. 1933- *WhoAm 94*
Sardina, Rafael Herminio 1946- *WhoScEn 94*
Sardinero, Vicente 1937- *NewGrDO*
Sardo, Cosmo d1989 *WhoHol 92*
Sardou, Fernand d1976 *WhoHol 92*
Sardou, Michel *WhoHol 92*
Sardou, Victorien 1831-1908 *IntDcT 2 [port], NewGrDO*
Sarducci, Father Guido 1943- *WhoCom*
Sarduy, Severo 1937- *ConWorW 93*
Sarduy, Severo 1937-1993 *ConAu 142*
Sareeram, Ray Rupchand 1938- *WhoAm 94*
Sarei, Alexis Holyweek 1934- *IntWW 93, Who 94*
Sarell, Richard Iwan Alexander 1909- *Who 94*
Sarell, Roderick (Francis Gisbert) 1913- *Who 94*
Sarellano, Luis Humberto 1947- *WhoHisp 94*
Saret, Alan Daniel 1944- *WhoAmA 93*
Saret, Larry L. 1950- *WhoAmL 94*
Saretsky, Barry G. 1947- *WhoAmL 94*
Sarfati, Alain 1937- *IntWW 93*
Sarfatti, Margherita 1883-1961 *BlmGWL*
Sarfaty, Regina 1932- *NewGrDO*
Sargan, John Denis 1924- *IntWW 93, Who 94*
Sargant, (Henry) Edmund 1906- *Who 94*
Sargant, Ethel *WorScD*
Sargant, Ethel 1863-1918 *DcNaB MP*
Sargant, Naomi Ellen 1933- *Who 94*
Sargeant, Ernest James 1918- *WhoAm 94*
Sargeant, Frank Charles Douglas 1917- *Who 94*
Sargeant, Frank Pilkington *Who 94*
Sargeaunt, Henry Anthony 1907- *Who 94*
Sargent, Alvin *IntDcF 2-4*
Sargent, Alvin 1927- *IntMPA 94*
Sargent, Anne 1923- *WhoHol 92*
Sargent, Ben 1948- *WhoAm 94*
Sargent, Benson Collins 1943- *WhoAm 94*
Sargent, Charles Lee 1937- *WhoFI 94, WhoMW 93*
Sargent, Craig *EncSF 93*
Sargent, David Jasper 1931- *WhoAm 94*
Sargent, Diana Rhea 1939- *WhoWest 94*
Sargent, Dick *Who 94*
Sargent, Dick 1930- *IntMPA 94*
Sargent, Dick 1933- *WhoHol 92*
Sargent, Douglas Robert 1953- *WhoScEn 94*
Sargent, E. N. *DrAPF 93*
Sargent, Ernest Douglas 1931- *WhoAm 94*
Sargent, Harold Eugene 1948- *WhoMW 93*
Sargent, Harry Tompkins 1947- *WhoWest 94*
Sargent, J. McNeil *WhoAmA 93*
Sargent, James Cunningham 1916- *WhoAmL 94*
Sargent, John Allston, Jr. 1937- *WhoAm 94*
Sargent, John E., Jr. 1943- *WhoAmL 94*
Sargent, John Reid 1936- *Who 94*
Sargent, John Richard 1925- *Who 94*
Sargent, John Singer 1856-1925 *AmCulL*
Sargent, John Turner 1924- *IntWW 93, WhoAm 94*
Sargent, Joseph 1925- *IntMPA 94*
Sargent, Joseph Denny 1929- *WhoAm 94*
Sargent, Joseph Dudley 1937- *WhoAm 94*
Sargent, Kenny d1969 *WhoHol 92*
Sargent, Lewis 1904- *WhoHol 92*
Sargent, Liz Elaine 1942- *WhoMW 93*
Sargent, Lyman T(ower) 1940- *WrDr 94*
Sargent, Lyman Tower 1940- *EncSF 93*
Sargent, Malcolm d1967 *WhoHol 92*
Sargent, (Harold) Malcolm (Watts) 1895-1967 *NewGrDO*
Sargent, Margaret Holland 1927- *WhoAmA 93*
Sargent, Maxwell d1949 *WhoHol 92*
Sargent, Maxwell D. 1942- *WhoAmP 93*
Sargent, Murray, III 1941- *WhoWest 94*
Sargent, Noel Boyd 1943- *WhoMW 93*
Sargent, Pamela *DrAPF 93*
Sargent, Pamela 1948- *ConAu 18AS [port], -41NR, EncSF 93, TwCYAW, WhoAm 94, WrDr 94*
Sargent, Pamela Anne 1951- *WhoAmL 94*
Sargent, Richard 1932- *WhoAmA 93*
Sargent, Robert *DrAPF 93*
Sargent, Robert George 1937- *WhoAm 94*
Sargent, Roger William Herbert 1926- *Who 94*
Sargent, Thomas Andrew 1933- *WhoAm 94*
Sargent, Thomas Reece, III 1914- *WhoWest 94*
Sargent, Wallace Leslie William 1935- *IntWW 93, Who 94, WhoAm 94, WhoScEn 94, WhoWest 94*
Sargent, Walter Harriman, II 1958- *WhoAmL 94*
Sargeson, Alan McLeod 1930- *IntWW 93, Who 94*
Sargeson, Frank 1903- *BlmGEL*
Sargeson, Frank 1903-1982 *RfGShF*
Sarginson, Edward William 1919- *Who 94*
Sargon Of Akkad *WhWE*
Sargus, Edmund A., Jr. 1953- *WhoAmL 94*
Sari, Ada 1886-1968 *NewGrDO*
Sarich, Vincent M. 1934- *WhoAm 94*
Saricks, Ambrose 1915- *WhoAm 94, WrDr 94*
Saridis, George Nicholas 1931- *WhoAm 94, WhoScEn 94*
Sarikas, Philip Charles 1960- *WhoWest 94*
Sarin, Harry C. *WhoAsA 94*
Sarin, Vivek Kumar 1967- *WhoMW 93*
Sarinic, Hrvoje *IntWW 93*
Sariraksa, Richard Manith 1963- *WhoFI 94*
Saris, Andrew Jamie 1963- *WhoMW 93*
Saris, John d1646 *WhWE*
Sarjeant, Walter James 1944- *WhoAm 94, WhoScEn 94*
Sark, Seigneur of *Who 94*
Sarkany, Anna Regina 1946- *WhoWest 94*
Sarkany, Zoltan 1948- *WhoWest 94*
Sarkar, Anil Kumar 1912- *WrDr 94*
Sarkar, Dipak Kumar 1950- *WhoWest 94*
Sarkar, Fazlul H. 1952- *WhoAsA 94*
Sarkar, Nitis 1938- *WhoAsA 94*
Sarkar, Santanu Kumar 1942- *WhoAsA 94*
Sarker, Bhaba Ranjan 1949- *WhoAsA 94*
Sarker, Bimal 1939-1993 *WhoAsA 94N*
Sarkis 1909-1977 *WhoAmA 93N*
Sarkis, Anthony Joseph 1964- *WhoAmL 94*
Sarkisian, Cherilyn 1946- *WhoAm 94*
Sarkisian, Jack Reuben 1928- *WhoWest 94*
Sarkisian, Paul 1928- *WhoAmA 93*
Sarkisian, Sos Artashesovich 1929- *IntWW 93*
Sarko, Lynn Lincoln 1956- *WhoAmL 94*
Sarkodie-Mensah, Kwasi 1955- *WhoBlA 94*
Sarkozy de Nagy Bosca, Nicholas Paul Stephane 1955- *IntWW 93*
Sarle, Charles Richard 1944- *WhoAm 94*
Sarles, Lynn Redmon 1930- *WhoWest 94*
Sarley, John G. 1954- *WhoWest 94*
Sarlui, Ed 1925- *IntMPA 94*
Sarma, Gabbita Sundara Rama 1937- *WhoScEn 94*
Sarmiento, Domingo F. 1811-1888 *HisWorL [port]*
Sarmiento, John Carlos 1957- *WhoAmL 94*
Sarmiento, Luis C. 1943- *WhoHisp 94*
Sarmiento, Luis Carlos 1961- *WhoFI 94*
Sarmiento, Luis Carlos, Jr. 1961- *WhoHisp 94*
Sarmiento, Shirley Jean 1946- *WhoBlA 94*
Sarmiento De Biscotti, Luz Socorro 1954- *WhoHisp 94*
Sarmir, Daniel Joseph 1950- *WhoFI 94*
Sarna, John J. 1935- *WhoAmP 93*
Sarna, John Paul 1963- *WhoFI 94*
Sarna, Jonathan D(aniel) 1955- *WrDr 94*
Sarna, Nahum M. 1923- *WrDr 94*
Sarna, Nahum Mattathias 1923- *WhoAm 94*
Sarnat, Bernard George 1912- *WhoAm 94*
Sarnat, Marshall 1929- *WrDr 94*
Sarne, Michael 1939- *WhoHol 92*
Sarnecki, Judith Holland 1944- *WhoMW 93*
Sarnelle, Joseph R. 1951- *WhoAm 94*
Sarner, Alexander d1948 *WhoHol 92*
Sarner, Richard Alan 1955- *WhoAmL 94*
Sarney, Jose 1930- *IntWW 93*
Sarney, Roseana Maciera 1953- *WhoWomW 91*
Sarni, Vincent Anthony 1928- *WhoAm 94, WhoFI 94*
Sarno, Alberto d1987 *WhoHol 92*
Sarno, Hector V. d1953 *WhoHol 92*
Sarno, Janet *WhoHol 92*
Sarno, Maria Erlinda 1944- *WhoAmL 94*
Sarno, Ronald Anthony 1941- *WrDr 94*
Sarnoff, Albert 1925- *WhoAm 94, WhoFI 94*
Sarnoff, Arthur Saron 1912- *WhoAmA 93*
Sarnoff, Dorothy *WhoFI 94, WrDr 94*
Sarnoff, Irving 1922- *WrDr 94*
Sarnoff, Lolo 1916- *WhoAmA 93*
Sarnoff, Robert W. 1918- *IntMPA 94*
Sarnoff, Stanley Jay 1917-1990 *WhAm 10*
Sarnoff, Thomas W. 1927- *IntMPA 94*
Sarnoff, Thomas Warren 1927- *WhoAm 94*
Sarnoff, William 1929- *WhoAm 94*
Sarofim, Adel Fares 1934- *WhoAm 94*
Sarofim, Fayez *NewYTBS 93 [port]*
Sarokin, H. Lee 1928- *WhoAm 94, WhoAmL 94*
Sarony, Leslie d1985 *WhoHol 92*
Saroop, Narindar 1929- *Who 94*
Sarosy, Anne Zvara 1923- *WhoMW 93*
Saro-Wiwa, Ken 1941- *BlkWr 2*
Saro-Wiwa, Ken(ule Beeson) 1941- *ConAu 142*
Saroyan, Aram 1943- *WrDr 94*
Saroyan, Don d1990 *WhoHol 92*
Saroyan, Lucy *WhoHol 92*
Saroyan, William 1908-1981 *ConDr 93, IntDcT 2, RfGShF*
Sarpalius, Bill 1948- *CngDr 93, WhoAmP 93*
Sarpalius, William C. 1948- *WhoAm 94*
Sarpaneva, Timo Tapani 1926- *IntWW 93*
Sarphie, David Francis 1962- *WhoScEn 94*
Sarpkaya, Turgut 1928- *WhoAm 94, WhoScEn 94*
Sarpong, Peter Kwasi 1933- *WhoAm 94*
Sarpy, Leon 1907- *WhoAm 94*
Sarrachini, Gerald d1957 *WhoHol 92*
Sarracino, Cooney 1933- *WhoHisp 94*
Sarracino, Ernest *WhoHol 92*
Sarraute, Nathalie 1900- *ConLC 80 [port], ConWorW 93, IntDcT 2, IntWW 93, Who 94*
Sarraute, Nathalie 1902- *BlmGWL [port]*
Sarrazin, Albertine 1937-1967 *BlmGWL*
Sarrazin, Michael 1940- *IntMPA 94, WhoHol 92*
Sarre, Claude-Alain 1928- *IntWW 93*

Sarre, Massamba 1935- *IntWW 93*
Sarreals, E. Don 1931- *WhoBlA 94*
Sarri, Rosemary Conzemius Alcuin 1926- *WhoMW 93*
Sarris, Andrew George 1928- *WhoAm 94*
Sarris, John 1948- *WhoScEn 94*
Sarro, Domenico Natale 1679-1744 *NewGrDO*
Sarroca, Suzanne 1927- *NewGrDO*
Sarry, Christine 1946- *WhoAm 94*
Sarson, Evelyn Patricia 1937- *WhoAm 94*
Sarson, John Christopher 1935- *WhoAm 94, WhoWest 94*
Sarsony, Robert 1938- *WhoAmA 93*
Sarsten, Gunnar Edward 1937- *WhoAm 94, WhoFI 94*
Sartain, Charles W. 1951- *WhoAmL 94*
Sartain, Gailard *WhoHol 92*
Sartain, James Edward 1941- *WhoAmL 94*
Sarther, Lynette Kay 1947- *WhoMW 93*
Sarti, Giuseppe 1729?-1802 *NewGrDO*
Sartin, Johnny Nelson, Jr. 1960- *WhoBlA 94*
Sarto, Gloria Elizabeth 1929- *WhoAm 94*
Sarto, William Ralph 1948- *WhoMW 93*
Sarton, May *DrAPF 93*
Sarton, May 1912- *BlmGWL, WrDr 94*
Sarton, (Eleanor) May 1912- *GayLL*
Sartor, Anthony Joseph 1943- *WhoAm 94*
Sartor, Daniel Ryan, Jr. 1932- *WhoAm 94, WhoAmL 94*
Sartor, Fabio *WhoHol 92*
Sartore, John Thornton 1946- *WhoAmL 94*
Sartorelli, Alan Clayton 1931- *WhoAm 94, WhoScEn 94*
Sartori, Claudio 1913- *NewGrDO*
Sartori, David Ezio 1962- *WhoScEn 94*
Sartori, Giovanni 1924- *WhoAm 94*
Sartorio, Antonio 1630-1680 *NewGrDO*
Sartorio, Gasparo 1625?-1680 *NewGrDO*
Sartorius, Norman 1935- *IntWW 93*
Sartorius, Peter S. 1947- *WhoAm 94, WhoAmL 94*
Sartory, Thomas J. 1944- *WhoAmL 94*
Sartre, Jean-Paul d1980 *WhoHol 92*
Sartre, Jean-Paul 1905-1980 *BlmGEL, EncEth*
Sartre, Jean-Paul (-Charles-Aymard) 1905-1980 *IntDcT 2 [port], RfGShF*
Sarty, Peter Griffing 1933- *WhoAmP 93*
Sartzetakis, Christos A. 1929- *IntWW 93*
Saru, George 1920- *WhoAmA 93*
Sarum, Archdeacon of *Who 94*
Sarver, Barbara Joan 1940- *WhoAmP 93*
Sarver, Eugene 1943- *WhoAm 94*
Sarwer-Foner, Gerald Jacob 1924- *WhoAm 94, WhoScEn 94*
Saryan, Leon Aram 1948- *WhoMW 93*
Sarychev, Gavriil Andreyevich 1763-1831 *WhWE*
Sary Ieng *IntWW 93*
Sasahara, Arthur Asao 1927- *WhoAm 94, WhoAsA 94*
Sasaki, Betty Gail 1957- *WhoAsA 94*
Sasaki, Chiyo Katano 1925- *WhoAsA 94*
Sasaki, Clarence Takashi 1941- *WhoAm 94*
Sasaki, Dale I. 1948- *WhoAsA 94*
Sasaki, Hideo 1919- *WhoAsA 94*
Sasaki, Man 1926- *IntWW 93*
Sasaki, Masafumi 1929- *WhoScEn 94*
Sasaki, R. A. 1952- *WrDr 94*
Sasaki, Raymond Toshiaki, Jr. 1944- *WhoAsA 94*
Sasaki, Ruth A. 1952- *WhoAsA 94*
Sasaki, Shin-Ichi 1925- *WhoScEn 94*
Sasaki, Shusuke 1956- *WhoScEn 94*
Sasaki, Taizo 1925- *WhoScEn 94*
Sasaki, Tatsuo 1944- *WhoAm 94*
Sasaki, Toshio 1946- *WhoAmA 93*
Sasaki, Wataru 1923- *WhoScEn 94*
Sasaki, Y. Tito 1938- *WhoWest 94*
Sasano, Teiko 1933- *WhoWomW 91*
Sasanow, Terri Feinstein 1952- *WhoAmL 94*
Sasao, Toshiaki 1955- *WhoScEn 94*
Sasayama, Takao 1937- *WhoAm 94*
Sasdi, George P. 1934- *WhoAm 94, WhoFI 94*
Sasdy, Peter 1934- *HorFD*
Sasenick, Joseph Anthony 1940- *WhoAm 94, WhoFI 94*
Saskatchewan, Bishop of 1941- *Who 94*
Saskatoon, Bishop of 1933- *Who 94*
Saslaw, Richard Lawrence 1940- *WhoAmP 93*
Saslaw, Rick d1993 *NewYTBS 93*
Saslow, Helen *DrAPF 93*
Saslow, Michael George 1937- *WhoAmP 93*
Saslow, Richard P. 1947- *WhoAmL 94*
Sasmor, James Cecil 1920- *WhoFI 94*
Sasportas, Howard 1948-1992 *AstEnc*
Sass, Edward d1916 *WhoHol 92*
Sass, James Robertus 1945- *WhoWest 94*
Sass, Martin D. *WhoFI 94*
Sass, Mary Martha *WhoMW 93*
Sass, Sylvia 1951- *NewGrDO*
Sass, Walter John 1943- *WhoMW 93*
Sassa, Shigeru 1935- *WhoAsA 94*
Sassaman, Anne Phillips 1944- *WhoAm 94*
Sassano, Matteo c. 1667-1737 *NewGrDO*
Sassard, Jacqueline 1940- *WhoHol 92*
Sasse, Marie (Constance) 1834-1907 *NewGrDO*
Sasseen, George Thiery 1928- *WhoAm 94, WhoScEn 94*
Sasseen, Robert Francis 1932- *WhoAm 94*
Sassen, Georgia 1949- *WhoScEn 94*
Sassen, Saskia 1947- *WhoHisp 94*
Sasser, Charles W(anye) 1942- *WrDr 94*
Sasser, James R. 1936- *CurBio 93 [port]*
Sasser, James Ralph 1936- *IntWW 93, WhoAm 94, WhoAmP 93*
Sasser, Jim 1936- *CngDr 93*
Sasser, Jonathan Drew 1956- *WhoAmL 94*
Sasser, William David 1962- *WhoFI 94*
Sassi, Gino J. 1922- *WhoAmP 93*
Sassmannshausen, Gunther 1930- *IntWW 93*
Sasso, Cassandra Gay 1946- *WhoAm 94, WhoAmL 94*
Sasso, Eleanor Catherine 1934- *WhoAmP 93*
Sasso, Laurence J., Jr. *DrAPF 93*
Sasso, Roberto A. 1954- *WhoHisp 94*
Sassoli, Dina *WhoHol 92*
Sasson, Michel 1935- *WhoAm 94*
Sassone, Marco 1942- *WhoAmA 93*
Sassoon, Andre Gabriel 1936- *WhoAmL 94*
Sassoon, Catya 1969- *WhoHol 92*
Sassoon, David 1932- *IntWW 93*
Sassoon, Siegfried 1886-1967 *BlmGEL*
Sassoon, Vidal 1928- *IntWW 93, WhoWest 94*
Sassou-Nguesso, Denis 1943- *IntWW 93*
Sassower, Harvey L. 1945- *IntMPA 94*
Sastre (Salvador), Alfonso 1926- *ConWorW 93*
Sastre, Alfonso 1926- *IntDcT 2*
Sastre, Ines *WhoHol 92*
Sastri, Lina *WhoHol 92*
Sastry, Padma Krishnamurthy 1960- *WhoScEn 94*
Sasuta, Daniel Joseph 1952- *WhoMW 93*
Sata, Lindbergh Saburo 1928- *WhoAm 94*
Sata Ineko 1904- *BlmGWL*
Satanowski, Robert 1918- *IntWW 93*
Satarawala, Kershasp Tehmurasp 1916- *IntWW 93*
Satarov, Georgy Aleksandrovich 1947- *LngBDD*
Satchell, Edward William John 1916- *Who 94*
Satchell, Elizabeth *WhoBlA 94*
Satchell, Ernest R. 1941- *WhoBlA 94*
Satcher, David 1941- *WhoBlA 94*
Satcher, Robert Lee, Sr. 1937- *WhoBlA 94*
Satchler, George Raymond 1926- *WhoAm 94*
Satchwill, Charles N. 1947- *WhoMW 93*
Satell, Edward Michael 1936- *WhoFI 94*
Sater, Analya *WhoHisp 94*
Sater, Steven *DrAPF 93*
Sateren, Leland B. 1913- *ConAu 141*
Sateren, Terry 1943- *WhoWest 94*
Satern, Miriam Nella 1951- *WhoMW 93*
Sathe, Sharad Somnath 1940- *WhoAm 94*
Sathe, Vasant P. 1925- *IntWW 93*
Sather, Duane 1944- *WhoAm 94*
Sather, Everett Norman 1935- *WhoMW 93*
Sather, Glen Cameron 1943- *WhoAm 94, WhoWest 94*
Sather, J. Henry 1921- *WhoScEn 94*
Sather, John Henry 1921- *WhoMW 93*
Sather, Larry Douglas 1950- *WhoAmL 94*
Sather, Larry O. *WhoAmP 93*
Sathre, Leroy 1936- *WhoAm 94*
Sathyavagiswaran, Lakshmanan 1949- *WhoAsA 94*
Satie, Erik 1866-1925 *IntDcB*
Satie, Erik (Alfred Leslie) 1866-1925 *NewGrDO*
Satin, Joseph 1920- *WhoAm 94*
Satine, Barry Roy 1951- *WhoAm 94*
Satinover, Jeffrey Burke 1947- *WhoAm 94, WhoFI 94*
Satinskas, Henry Anthony 1936- *WhoAm 94*
Satinsky, Barnett 1947- *WhoAm 94, WhoAmL 94*
Sato, Aiko 1923- *BlmGWL*
Sato, Eunice N. 1921- *WhoAmP 93*
Sato, Eunice Noda 1921- *WhoAm 94*
Sato, Frank Saburo 1929- *WhoAmP 93*
Sato, Frederick Akira 1946- *WhoAsA 94*
Sato, Gary Teruo 1955- *WhoAsA 94*
Sato, Gordon Hisashi 1927- *WhoScEn 94*
Sato, Hiroshi 1918- *WhoAm 94, WhoMW 93, WhoScEn 94*
Sato, Irving Shigeo 1933- *WhoAsA 94, WhoWest 94*
Sato, Kazuo 1927- *IntWW 93*
Sato, Kazuyoshi 1930- *WhoScEn 94*
Sato, Keiko 1959- *WhoAsA 94*
Sato, Koko *IntWW 93*
Sato, Mamoru 1937- *WhoWest 94*
Sato, Masaaki 1941- *WhoAmA 93*
Sato, Masahiko 1955- *WhoAsA 94*
Sato, Megumu 1924- *IntWW 93*
Sato, Michael Kei 1958- *WhoFI 94, WhoWest 94*
Sato, Moriyoshi 1922- *IntWW 93*
Sato, Motoaki 1929- *WhoAm 94, WhoScEn 94*
Sato, Noriaki 1928- *WhoScEn 94*
Sato, Norie 1949- *WhoAmA 93, WhoWest 94*
Sato, Paul Toshio 1932- *WhoAsA 94*
Sato, Reiko d1981 *WhoHol 92*
Sato, Ronald Masahiko 1944- *WhoWest 94*
Sato, Ryuzo 1931- *IntWW 93*
Sato, Shigetada 1940- *WhoAsA 94*
Sato, Sho 1923- *WhAm 10*
Sato, Tadashi 1923- *WhoAm 94, WhoAmA 93, WhoWest 94*
Sato, Takami 1955- *WhoScEn 94*
Sato, Takashi 1927- *IntWW 93*
Sato, Tommy M. 1931- *WhoAsA 94*
Sato, Walter N. 1946- *WhoAsA 94*
Sato, William K. *WhoAsA 94*
Satoh, Yoshiharu 1928- *WhoAm 94*
Satoh Makoto 1943- *IntDcT 2*
Satolli, Francesco 1839-1910 *DcAmReB 2*
Satorius, John Arthur 1946- *WhoAm 94, WhoAmL 94*
Satorsky, Cyril *WhoAmA 93*
Satovsky, Abraham 1907- *WhoAm 94, WhoAmL 94*
Satow, Derek Graham 1923- *Who 94*
Satow, Stuart Alan 1956- *WhoAsA 94*
Satowaki, Joseph Asajiro 1904- *IntWW 93*
Satpathy, Nandini 1931- *IntWW 93*
Satre, Philip Glen 1949- *WhoAm 94, WhoFI 94*
Satre, Rodrick Iverson 1951- *WhoWest 94*
Satriana, Daniel R., Jr. 1954- *WhoAmL 94*
Satrom, Joseph A. *WhoAmP 93*
Satrum, Jerry R. 1933- *WhoAm 94, WhoFI 94*
Sats, Natalya d1993 *NewYTBS 93*
Satsumabayashi, Koko 1940- *WhoScEn 94*
Satsumabayashi, Sadayoshi 1935- *WhoScEn 94*
Sattee, Andrew L. 1920- *WhAm 10*
Satter, Marlene Y. *DrAPF 93*
Satter, Raymond Nathan 1948- *WhoAmL 94*
Satterfield, Ben *DrAPF 93*
Satterfield, Charles *ConAu 141, EncSF 93, SmATA 76*
Satterfield, Charles Nelson 1921- *WhoAm 94*
Satterfield, David E., III 1920- *WhoAmP 93*
Satterfield, Floyd 1945- *WhoBlA 94*
Satterfield, John Edward 1931- *WhoAmA 93*
Satterfield, Pamela Stever 1962- *WhoAmL 94*
Satterfield, Patricia Polson 1942- *WhoBlA 94*
Satterfield, Shelby D. 1945- *WhoAmP 93*
Satterfield, Wade James 1959- *WhoWest 94*
Satterfield-Harris, Rita 1949- *WhoFI 94*
Satterlee, Bruce *WhoHol 92*
Satterlee, Terry Jean 1948- *WhoAmL 94*
Satterly, Jack 1906- *WhoAm 94*
Satterthwaite, Cameron B. 1920- *WhoAm 94*
Satterthwaite, George, II 1935- *WhoFI 94*
Satterthwaite, Helen Foster 1928- *WhoAmP 93*
Satterthwaite, John Richard 1925- *Who 94*
Satterthwaite, Joseph Charles 1900-1990 *WhAm 10*
Satterthwaite, Linton 1897- *WhAm 10*
Satterthwaite, Richard George d1993 *Who 94N*
Satterwhite, Collen Gray d1978 *WhoHol 92*
Satterwhite, Frank Joseph 1942- *WhoBlA 94*
Satterwhite, John H. 1913- *WhoBlA 94*
Satterwhite, Rodney Wayne 1942- *WhoAmL 94*
Satterwhite, Terry Frank 1946- *WhoAmL 94, WhoWest 94*
Satterwhite, William T. 1933- *WhoFI 94*
Sattes, Frederick Lyle 1943- *WhoAmP 93*
Sattianathan, Krupabai 1862-1894 *BlmGWL*
Sattin, Albert 1931- *WhoWest 94*
Sattin, Robert Uman 1948- *WhoAmL 94*
Sattinger, Michael Jack 1943- *WhoFI 94*
Sattler, Bruce W. 1944- *WhoAmL 94*
Sattler, Ernst d1974 *WhoHol 92*
Sattler, Helen Roney 1921-1992 *SmATA 74 [port]*
Sattler, Jill 1947- *WhoAmA 93*
Sattler, Nancy Joan 1950- *WhoMW 93, WhoScEn 94*
Sattler, Robert James 1948- *WhoAmP 93*
Sattler, Rolf 1936- *WhoAm 94*
Satton, Lon(nie) 1926- *WhoHol 92*
Satula, Anthony E., Jr. 1947- *WhoAmL 94*
Satuloff, Barth 1945- *WhoFI 94*
Saturen, Ben 1948- *WhoAmA 93*
Satya Bahin 1944- *WhoWomW 91*
Satyapriya, Coimbatore K. 1949- *WhoAsA 94*
Satyapriya, Combatore Keshavamurthy 1949- *WhoAm 94*
Satz, Janet M. 1933- *WhoAmA 93*
Satz, Louis K. 1927- *WhoAm 94*
Satz, Ludwig d1944 *WhoHol 92*
Satz, Ronald Wayne 1951- *WhoFI 94*
Sauber, Richard A. 1950- *WhoAmL 94*
Sauberlich, Lu d1976 *WhoHol 92*
Sauceda, Dora 1953- *WhoHisp 94*
Sauceda, F. Carolina 1962- *WhoHisp 94*
Sauceda, James Steven 1952- *WhoHisp 94*
Sauceda, Richard 1965- *WhoHisp 94*
Saucedo, Manuel D. V. *WhoHisp 94*
Saucedo, Marcelino 1935- *WhoHisp 94*
Saucedo, Robert 1932- *WhoHisp 94*
Saucedo, Roberto A. 1959- *WhoHisp 94*
Saucedo, Tom 1932- *WhoHisp 94*
Saucedo, Tomas 1954- *WhoHisp 94*
Saucer, George J. 1928- *WhoAm 94*
Saucier, Bonnie L. 1945- *WhoAm 94*
Saucier, Gene D. 1931- *WhoAmP 93*
Saucier Lundy, Karen 1954- *WhoAm 94*
Saud Al-Faisal, H.R.H. Prince 1941- *IntWW 93*
Saude, Linda Koch Robertson 1942- *WhoWest 94*
Sauder, Michael Hockensmith 1948- *WhoFI 94*
Saudi Arabia, King of *IntWW 93*
Sauer, Barry W. 1939- *WhoScEn 94*
Sauer, Christine 1958- *WhoWest 94*
Sauer, David Andrew 1948- *WhoAm 94*
Sauer, Douglas W. 1957- *WhoAmP 93*
Sauer, Elissa Swisher 1935- *WhoAm 94*
Sauer, Gordon C. 1921- *WrDr 94*
Sauer, Gordon Chenoweth 1921- *WhoAm 94, WhoScEn 94*
Sauer, Harold John 1953- *WhoMW 93, WhoScEn 94*
Sauer, Harry John, Jr. 1935- *WhoAm 94, WhoScEn 94*
Sauer, James Edward, Jr. 1934- *WhoAm 94*
Sauer, Jane Gottlieb 1937- *WhoAmA 93*
Sauer, Jonathan Deininger 1918- *WhoAm 94*
Sauer, Kenneth 1931- *WhoAm 94*
Sauer, Louis 1928- *IntWW 93*
Sauer, Michael Richard 1966- *WhoMW 93*
Sauer, Peter William 1946- *WhoMW 93*
Sauer, Richard John 1939- *WhoAm 94*
Sauer, Robert Louis 1925- *WhoFI 94*
Sauer, Russell Fredrick 1955- *WhoAmL 94*
Sauerbrey, Ellen R. 1937- *WhoAmP 93*
Sauerhaft, Stan 1926- *WhoAm 94*
Sauerlander, Willibald 1924- *IntWW 93*
Sauerman, Carl d1924 *WhoHol 92*
Sauers, Isidor 1948- *WhoScEn 94*
Sauers, Joseph d1982 *WhoHol 92*
Sauers, Patricia d1989 *WhoHol 92*
Sauey, William 1927- *WhoMW 93*
Sauey, William R. 1927- *WhoAmP 93*
Saufferer, William Charles *WhoAm 94*
Saufley, William Edward 1956- *WhoAm 94*
Sauget, Henri 1901-1989 *IntDcB*
Saugman, Per Gotfred 1925- *Who 94*
Saugstad, Olaf d1950 *WhoAmA 93N*
Sauguet, Henri 1901-1989 *WhAm 10*
Sauguet, Henri(-Pierre) 1901-1989 *NewGrDO*
Saukerson, Eleanor *WhoAmP 93, WhoMW 93*
Saukkonen, (Veikko Antti) Juhani 1937- *IntWW 93*
Saul, B. Francis, II 1932- *WhoAm 94, WhoFI 94*
Saul, Barbara Ann 1940- *WhoMW 93*
Saul, (Samuel) Berrick 1924- *Who 94*
Saul, Bradley Scott 1960- *WhoFI 94, WhoMW 93*
Saul, Bruce Howard 1956- *WhoAmL 94*
Saul, David John 1950- *WhoIns 94*
Saul, Frank Charles 1910- *WhoAmP 93*
Saul, George Brandon, II 1928- *WhoAm 94*
Saul, Irving Isaac 1929- *WhoAmL 94*

Saul, John Ralston 1947- WrDr 94
Saul, John Woodruff, III 1942- WhoAm 94
Saul, Kenneth Louis 1923- WhoAm 94, WhoFI 94
Saul, Norman Eugene 1932- WhoAm 94
Saul, Oscar 1912- IntMPA 94
Saul, Peter 1934- WhoAm 94, WhoAmA 93
Saul, Ralph Southey 1922- IntWW 93, WhoAm 94, WhoFI 94
Saul, Roger Stephen 1948- WhoWest 94
Saul, William Edward 1934- WhoAm 94, WhoScEn 94
Sauldsberry, Woody 1934- BasBi
Saull, Keith Michael 1927- Who 94
Saulnier, Jacques 1928- IntDcF 2-4 [port]
Saulnier, Jean-Michel 1930- IntWW 93
Sauls, Frederick Inabinette 1934- WhoAmA 93
Sauls, Roger DrAPF 93
Saulsberry, Charles R. 1957- WhoBlA 94, WhoMW 93
Saulson, Harold 1953- WhoAmA 93
Saulter, Gilbert John 1936- WhoBlA 94
Saulter, Paul Reginald 1935- Who 94
Saum, Cliff d1943 WhoHol 92
Saumarez Who 94
Saumarez Smith, Charles Robert 1954- Who 94
Saumier, Andre 1933- WhoAm 94
Saunby, John Brian 1933- WhoAm 94
Saunders, Albert Edward 1919- Who 94
Saunders, Alexander Hall 1941- WhoFI 94
Saunders, Alice d1953 WhoHol 92
Saunders, Andrew Downing 1931- Who 94
Saunders, Ann Loreille 1930- WrDr 94
Saunders, Arlene 1935- NewGrDO, WhoAm 94
Saunders, Aulus Ward 1904-1991 WhoAmA 93N
Saunders, Barbara Ann 1950- WhoBlA 94
Saunders, Barry Collins 1931- WhoScEn 94
Saunders, Basil 1925- Who 94
Saunders, C(icely) M. 1918- WrDr 94
Saunders, Caleb EncSF 93
Saunders, Charles Baskerville, Jr. 1928- WhoAm 94, WhoAmP 93
Saunders, Charles Melvin 1961- WhoMW 93
Saunders, Christopher John 1940- Who 94
Saunders, Christopher Thomas 1907- Who 94
Saunders, Cicely (Mary Strode) 1918- Who 94
Saunders, Clara Rosman d1951 WhoAmA 93N
Saunders, David Alan 1939- WhoAm 94
Saunders, David John 1943- Who 94
Saunders, David Martin St. George 1930- Who 94
Saunders, David William 1936- Who 94
Saunders, Dean P. 1960- WhoAmP 93
Saunders, Derek William 1925- Who 94
Saunders, Dero Ames 1913- WhoAm 94
Saunders, Donald Herbert 1935- WhoAm 94, WhoMW 93
Saunders, Donald Leslie 1935- WhoAm 94
Saunders, Doris E. 1921- WhoBlA 94
Saunders, Doris Evans 1921- WhoAm 94
Saunders, Dorothy Ann 1932- WhoFI 94
Saunders, Duncan Reid 1948- WhoWest 94
Saunders, Edith Dariel Chase 1922- WhoAmA 93
Saunders, Edith Rebecca 1865-1945 DcNaB MP
Saunders, Edward Howard 1926- WhoBlA 94
Saunders, Elijah 1934- WhoBlA 94
Saunders, Elizabeth A. 1948- WhoBlA 94
Saunders, Eric Don 1942- WhoFI 94
Saunders, Eric F. 1947- WhoAmL 94
Saunders, Ernest Walter 1935- IntWW 93, Who 94
Saunders, Ethel 1944- WhoAmP 93
Saunders, Florence d1926 WhoHol 92
Saunders, Frank 1927- WrDr 94
Saunders, Gary Michael 1943- WhoFI 94, WhoMW 93
Saunders, George Lawton, Jr. 1931- WhoAm 94, WhoAmL 94, WhoFI 94, WhoMW 93
Saunders, Gloria d1980 WhoHol 92
Saunders, Grady F. 1938- WhoScEn 94
Saunders, Harold H. 1930- WhoAmP 93
Saunders, Howard N. 1920- WhoAmP 93
Saunders, J. Boyd 1937- WhoAmA 93
Saunders, Jack DrAPF 93
Saunders, Jackie d1954 WhoHol 92
Saunders, Jake 1947- EncSF 93
Saunders, James 1924- WhoWest 94
Saunders, James 1925- Who 94
Saunders, James (A.) 1925- IntDcT 2
Saunders, James A. 1925- ConDr 93, WrDr 94
Saunders, James Harwood 1948- WhoWest 94
Saunders, Jean 1932- WrDr 94
Saunders, Jennifer WhoHol 92
Saunders, Jerry 1953- WhoBlA 94
Saunders, Jimmy d1990 WhoHol 92
Saunders, Jimmy Dale 1948- WhoScEn 94
Saunders, John 1943- WhoAmP 93
Saunders, John (Anthony Holt) 1917- Who 94
Saunders, John Anthony Holt 1917- IntWW 93
Saunders, John D. 1944- WhoAmL 94
Saunders, John Edward, III 1945- WhoBlA 94
Saunders, John Henry Boulton 1949- Who 94
Saunders, John Monk 1897-1940 IntDcF 2-4
Saunders, John Warren, Jr. 1919- WhoScEn 94
Saunders, Joseph Arthur 1926- WhoFI 94
Saunders, Joseph Benjamin, Jr. 1901-1989 WhAm 10
Saunders, Joseph Francis 1950- WhoAm 94
Saunders, Joseph Woodrow 1947- WhoWest 94
Saunders, Judith DrAPF 93
Saunders, Kathryn A. 1920- WhoFI 94
Saunders, Kenneth 1920- Who 94
Saunders, Kenneth D. 1927- WhoAm 94
Saunders, Kenneth Herbert 1915- Who 94
Saunders, Kenneth Paul 1948- WhoBlA 94
Saunders, Larry 1939- WhoAmP 93
Saunders, Lonna Jeanne WhoAmL 94, WhoMW 93
Saunders, Lori 1941- WhoHol 92
Saunders, Lorna D. DrAPF 93
Saunders, Lucille d1919 WhoHol 92
Saunders, Lucille Mae 1930- WhoMW 93
Saunders, Madge d1967 WhoHol 92
Saunders, Margaret Marshall 1861-1947 BlmGWL
Saunders, Mark A. 1946- WhoAmL 94
Saunders, Mary Alice 1938- WhoBlA 94
Saunders, Mary Jane 1943- WhoHol 92
Saunders, Mary Sue 1933- WhoMW 93
Saunders, Mauderie Hancock 1929- WhoBlA 94
Saunders, Meredith Roy 1930- WhoBlA 94
Saunders, Michael WhoHol 92
Saunders, Michael F. 1950- WhoAmL 94
Saunders, Michael Lawrence 1944- Who 94
Saunders, N. Leslie 1936- WhoAmP 93
Saunders, Nancy 1925- WhoHol 92
Saunders, Nellie Peck d1942 WhoHol 92
Saunders, Nelson W. 1949- WhoAmP 93
Saunders, Nicholas 1914- WhoHol 92
Saunders, Owen 1904- IntWW 93
Saunders, Owen (Alfred) 1904- Who 94, WrDr 94
Saunders, Patricia Roper 1945- WhoBlA 94
Saunders, Paul Christopher 1941- WhoAm 94, WhoAmL 94
Saunders, Peter 1911- Who 94
Saunders, Peter Gordon 1940- Who 94
Saunders, Peter Paul 1928- WhoAm 94
Saunders, Phyllis S. 1942- WhoFI 94
Saunders, Raymond 1933- Who 94
Saunders, Raymond Jennings 1934- WhoAm 94, WhoAmA 93
Saunders, Richard 1937- Who 94
Saunders, Richard Henry 1949- WhoAmA 93
Saunders, Richard Peter 1959- WhoAmL 94
Saunders, Richard Wayne 1953- WhoScEn 94
Saunders, Robert Edward 1959- WhoBlA 94
Saunders, Robert M. 1945- WhoAmP 93
Saunders, Robert M. 1959- WhoAmL 94
Saunders, Robert Mallough 1915- WhoAm 94, WhoWest 94
Saunders, Robert Samuel 1951- WhoFI 94
Saunders, Robert William, Sr. 1921- WhoBlA 94
Saunders, Roger Alfred 1929- WhoAm 94
Saunders, Ron 1954- WhoAmP 93
Saunders, Ronald Stephen 1940- WhoWest 94
Saunders, Rubie Agnes 1929- WhoAm 94
Saunders, Russell Joseph 1937- WhoAm 94
Saunders, Sally Love DrAPF 93
Saunders, Sally Love 1940- WhoAm 94
Saunders, Sam Cundiff 1931- WhoAm 94
Saunders, Scott Warren 1948- WhoFI 94
Saunders, Stuart d1988 WhoHol 92
Saunders, Stuart John 1931- IntWW 93
Saunders, Stuart Thomas, Jr. 1941- WhoAm 94
Saunders, Susan Presley 1956- WhoFI 94
Saunders, Terry Rose 1942- WhoAmL 94
Saunders, Theodore D. 1912- WhoBlA 94
Saunders, Thomas Harry 1813-1870 DcNaB MP
Saunders, Thomas Lee 1955- WhoMW 93
Saunders, Vincent E., III 1954- WhoBlA 94
Saunders, Wade 1949- WhoAmA 93
Saunders, Ward Bishop, Jr. 1919- WhoAm 94
Saunders, Wes 1920- WrDr 94
Saunders, Wilfred Leonard 1920- Who 94
Saunders, William 1923- IntMPA 94
Saunders, William Arthur 1930- WhoFI 94
Saunders, William Hundley, Jr. 1926- WhoAm 94, WhoScEn 94
Saunders, William Joseph 1924- WhoBlA 94
Saunders, William Lockwood 1911- WhoAm 94
Saunders-Henderson, Martha M. 1924- WhoBlA 94
Saunders Watson, (Leslie) Michael (Macdonald) 1934- Who 94
Saunier, Mervin Kenneth 1934- WhoFI 94
Saunier-Seite, Alice Louise 1925- IntWW 93
Sauntry, Susan Schaefer 1943- WhoAm 94, WhoAmL 94
Saur, Klaus G. 1941- WhoAm 94
Saur, Klaus Gerhard 1941- IntWW 93
Saura, Carlos 1932- IntMPA 94, IntWW 93
Saura-Calixto, Fulgencio 1946- WhoScEn 94
Saurbier, Scott Alan 1947- WhoAm 94, WhoAmL 94
Saurman, George E. 1926- WhoAmP 93
Sauro, Joan DrAPF 93
Sauro, Joseph Pio 1927- WhoScEn 94
Sause, Samuel H. 1936- WhoWest 94
Sausedo, Patricia WhoHisp 94
Sausedo, Robert A. WhoHisp 94
Sausman, Karen 1945- WhoAm 94, WhoScEn 94
Saussele, Charles William 1933- WhoFI 94
Sausser, Robert Gary 1941- WhoAm 94, WhoWest 94
Saussure, Ferdinand de BlmGWL
Saussure, Ferdinand de 1857-1913 BlmGEL, TwCLC 49 [port]
Sausville, Edward Anthony 1952- WhoScEn 94
Saute, Robert Emile 1929- WhoWest 94
Sauter, Charles Herman WhoAm 94
Sauter, Eric 1948- WrDr 94
Sauter, Franz Fabian 1933- WhoScEn 94
Sauter, John V. 1941- WhoFI 94
Sauter, Van Gordon 1935- WhoAm 94
Sauthier, Claude Joseph 1736-1802 AmRev
Sautter, Christian 1940- IntWW 93
Sautter, Dianne Lee 1949- WhoAm 94
Sautter, Jeannie 1930- WhoAmP 93
Sautter, R. Craig DrAPF 93
Sautter, Richard Daniel 1926- WhoAm 94
Sauvage, Lester Rosaire 1926- WhoScEn 94
Sauvagnargues, Jean Victor 1915- IntWW 93, Who 94
Sauvaigo, Suzanne Liliane Berthe 1930- WhoWomW 91
Sauvain, Philip Arthur 1933- WrDr 94
Sauve, Georges 1925- WhoScEn 94
Sauve, Jacqueline Annmary 1943- WhoMW 93
Sauve, Jeanne d1993 Who 94N
Sauve, Jeanne 1922-1993 CurBio 93N
Sauve, Jeanne (Benoit) d1993 IntWW 93N
Sauve, Maurice 1923-1992 WhAm 10
Sauve, Opal Pittman 1934- WhoAmP 93
Sauveterre, Francois d1775 NewGrDO
Sauvey, Donald Robert 1924- WhoAm 94
Sauvey, Raymond Andrew 1953- WhoAm 94
Sauzier, (Andre) Guy 1910- Who 94
Sauzo, Richard WhoHisp 94
Sava, George EncSF 93
Sava, George 1903- Who 94, WrDr 94
Savage, Alan 1930- WrDr 94
Savage, Albert Walter 1898- Who 94
Savage, Ann 1921- WhoHol 92
Savage, Archie Bernard, Jr. 1929- WhoBlA 94
Savage, Arthur Anthony 1947- WhoMW 93
Savage, Arthur L. 1951- WhoAm 94
Savage, Augusta 1900-1962 AfrAmAl 6, WhoAmA 93N
Savage, Augustus A. 1925- WhoAmP 93, WhoBlA 94
Savage, Ben 1980- WhoHol 92
Savage, Blair deWillis 1941- WhoAm 94
Savage, Blake EncSF 93
Savage, Brad 1965- WhoHol 92
Savage, Charles Francis 1942- WhoAm 94
Savage, Charles William 1933- WhoAmP 93
Savage, David 1929- IntMPA 94
Savage, Deborah 1955- SmATA 76
Savage, Deborah Ellen 1961- WhoScEn 94
Savage, Dennis James 1925- WhoBlA 94
Savage, E. Scott 1947- WhoAmL 94
Savage, Edward Turney 1946- WhoAm 94
Savage, Edward W., Jr. 1933- WhoBlA 94
Savage, Edward Warren, Jr. 1933- WhoAm 94
Savage, Elmer N. WhoAmP 93
Savage, Ernest 1918- WrDr 94
Savage, Ernest (Walter) 1912- Who 94
Savage, Ernest C. 1897- WhAm 10
Savage, Francis Joseph 1943- Who 94
Savage, Frank 1938- WhoBlA 94
Savage, Fred 1976- IntMPA 94, WhoHol 92
Savage, George Roland 1929- WhoMW 93
Savage, Gretchen Susan 1934- WhoFI 94
Savage, Gus 1925- WhoBlA 94
Savage, Henry W(ilson) 1859-1927 NewGrDO
Savage, Horace Christopher 1941- WhoBlA 94
Savage, Ian 1960- WhoFI 94
Savage, J. Diane 1931- WhoMW 93
Savage, James Cathey, III 1947- WhoAm 94, WhoAmL 94
Savage, James Edward, Jr. 1941- WhoBlA 94
Savage, James Francis 1939- WhoAm 94
Savage, James Louis 1941- WhoAmP 93
Savage, Jerry 1936- WhoAmA 93
Savage, John 1949- IntMPA 94, WhoHol 92
Savage, John Edmund 1939- WhoAm 94
Savage, John Paul 1946- WhoMW 93
Savage, John T. 1925- WhoAmP 93
Savage, John William 1951- WhoAmL 94
Savage, Julia S. 1957- WhoAmL 94
Savage, Julian Michele 1956- WhoScEn 94
Savage, Kay Webb 1942- WhoAmL 94, WhoFI 94
Savage, M. Susan WhoAm 94, WhoAmP 93
Savage, Manuel D. 1950- WhoAmL 94
Savage, Mark A. 1922- WhoMW 93
Savage, Martha Frances Walden 1940- WhoAmP 93
Savage, May d1963 WhoHol 92
Savage, Minot Judson 1841-1918 DcAmReB 2
Savage, Naomi 1927- WhoAm 94, WhoAmA 93
Savage, Neve Richard 1944- WhoAm 94
Savage, Patrick Joseph 1944- WhoMW 93
Savage, Peter d1981 WhoHol 92
Savage, Philip Hezekiah 1932- WhoAm 94
Savage, Phillip Erwin 1961- WhoMW 93
Savage, Randall Ernest 1939- WhoAm 94
Savage, Richard 1697?-1743 BlmGEL
Savage, Richard 1917- EncSF 93
Savage, Richard Steven 1953- WhoMW 93
Savage, Richard T. 1939- WhoAm 94, WhoFI 94
Savage, Robert Charles 1937- WhoAmP 93
Savage, Robert Heath 1929- WhoAm 94
Savage, Roger 1941- WhoAmA 93
Savage, Scott David 1954- WhoAm 94
Savage, Sean Joseph 1964- WhoMW 93
Savage, Stephen Michael 1946- WhoAm 94, WhoAmL 94
Savage, Terry Richard 1930- WhoWest 94
Savage, Thomas 1915- WrDr 94
Savage, Thomas Hixon 1928- Who 94, WhoAm 94
Savage, Thomas Joseph 1947- WhoAm 94
Savage, Thomas Yates 1956- WhoAmL 94
Savage, Tom DrAPF 93
Savage, Vernon Thomas 1945- WhoBlA 94
Savage, Wallace Hamilton 1912- WhoAm 94
Savage, Wendy Diane 1935- Who 94
Savage, Whitney Lee 1928- WhoAm 94
Savage, William Who 94
Savage, William 1720-1789 NewGrDO
Savage, (Thomas) William 1937- Who 94
Savage, William Arthur WhoBlA 94
Savage, William Woodrow 1914- WhoAm 94
Savage, Xyla Ruth 1937- WhoAm 94
Savageau, Cheryl DrAPF 93
Savageau, Michael Antonio 1940- WhoAm 94, WhoMW 93

Savagnone, Giuseppe 1902-1984 *NewGrDO*
Savago, Peter J. 1930- *WhoAmP 93*
Saval, Dany 1940- *WhoHol 92*
Savala, Leonard *WhoHisp 94*
Savalas, George d1985 *WhoHol 92*
Savalas, Telly 1922- *WhoHol 92*
Savalas, Telly 1924- *IntMPA 94*
Savalas, Telly (Aristotle) 1926- *IntWW 93*
Savalas, Telly Aristoteles 1926- *WhoAm 94*
Savant, Dean Dominick d1980 *WhoHol 92*
Savant, Doug *WhoHol 92*
Savant, Edward H. 1943- *WhoFI 94*
Savard, (Marie-Emmanuel-)Augustin 1861-1942 *NewGrDO*
Savard, Denis 1961- *WhoAm 94*
Savard, G. S. *WhoScEn 94*
Savard, Serge 1946- *WhoAm 94*
Savarese, Fernando, Signora *Who 94*
Savaria, Louis A. *WhoAmP 93*
Savariego, Samuel *WhoHisp 94*
Savarimuthu, John Gurubatham 1925- *IntWW 93*
Savarin, Julian Jay *EncSF 93*
Savary, Jerome 1942- *IntWW 93, NewGrDO*
Savary, Olga Augusta Maria 1933- *BlmGWL*
Savaryn, Peter 1926- *WhoAm 94*
Savas, Emanuel S. 1931- *WhoAm 94, WhoAmP 93*
Savas, Jo-Ann 1934- *WhoAmA 93*
Savatsky, Bruce Jon 1954- *WhoScEn 94*
Savchenko, Arkadiy Markovich 1936- *IntWW 93*
Savchenko, Vladimir (Ivanovich) 1933- *EncSF 93*
Savedra, Jo Ann 1960- *WhoHisp 94*
Savedra, Ruben 1932- *WhoHisp 94*
Saveker, David Richard 1920- *WhoScEn 94*
Savelev, Viktor Nikolaevich 1948- *LngBDD*
Saveleva, Lyudmila Mikhailovna 1942- *IntWW 93*
Savelkoul, Donald Charles 1917- *WhoAm 94, WhoAmL 94*
Savell, Edward Lupo 1921- *WhoAm 94, WhoAmL 94*
Savelli, Angelo 1911- *WhoAm 94*
Savenor, Betty Carmell 1927- *WhoAmA 93*
Savernake, Viscount 1982- *Who 94*
Savery, Constance Winifred 1897- *WrDr 94*
Savery, Thomas 1650?-1715 *WorInv*
Saveth, Edward Norman 1915- *WhoAm 94*
Saviano, Angelo 1958- *WhoAmP 93*
Saviano, Dennis Michael 1955- *WhoFI 94*
Saviano, Josh *WhoHol 92*
Savic, Michael I. 1967- *WhoScEn 94*
Savic, Pavel 1909- *IntWW 93*
Savic, Sally *DrAPF 93*
Savic, Stanley Dimitrius 1938- *WhoMW 93, WhoScEn 94*
Savich, Sandra Ann 1959- *WhoFI 94*
Savickas, Frank David 1935- *WhoAmP 93*
Savickas, Leslie Michele 1946- *WhoMW 93*
Savicki, William Anthony 1941- *WhoFI 94*
Savic-Rebac, Anica 1892-1953 *BlmGWL*
Savident, John *WhoHol 92*
Savignac, Alida de 1790-1847 *BlmGWL*
Savikas, Victor George 1941- *WhoAm 94, WhoAmL 94*
Savile *Who 94*
Savile, Baron 1919- *Who 94*
Savile, Frank (Mackenzie) *EncSF 93*
Savile, James (Wilson Vincent) 1926- *Who 94*
Savile, Jimmy 1926- *WhoHol 92*
Savill, David Malcolm 1930- *Who 94*
Savill, Kenneth Edward 1906- *Who 94*
Savill, Rosalind Joy 1951- *IntWW 93, Who 94*
Saville, Clive Howard 1943- *Who 94*
Saville, Dudley Albert 1933- *WhoAm 94*
Saville, Gus d1934 *WhoHol 92*
Saville, John 1916- *Who 94*
Saville, Ken *DrAPF 93*
Saville, Ken 1949- *WhoAmA 93*
Saville, Mark (Oliver) 1936- *Who 94*
Saville, Michael Wayne 1962- *WhoScEn 94*
Saville, Ruth d1985 *WhoHol 92*
Saville, Thorndike, Jr. 1925- *WhoAm 94*
Savimbi, Jonas 1934- *IntWW 93, News 94-2 [port]*
Savin, Anatoliy Ivanovich 1920- *IntWW 93*
Savin, Risto 1859-1948 *NewGrDO*
Savin, Ronald Richard 1926- *WhoAm 94, WhoFI 94, WhoScEn 94, WhoWest 94*
Savin, Samuel Marvin 1940- *WhoAm 94*
Savinar, Tad 1950- *WhoAmA 93*
Savinell, Robert F. 1950- *WhoScEn 94*
Saving, Thomas Robert 1933- *WhoFI 94*
Savini, Donato Antonio 1939- *WhoAm 94*
Savini, Tom *IntDcF 2-4, WhoHol 92*
Savinio, Alberto 1891-1952 *NewGrDO*
Savino, Beatriz *WhoHisp 94*
Savino, Thomas Edward 1957- *WhoFI 94*
Savino, William M. 1949- *WhoAm 94*
Savio, Johann Baptist fl. 176-?- *NewGrDO*
Savioni, Mario 1606?-1685 *NewGrDO*
Savir, Etan 1961- *WhoScEn 94*
Saviskas, Judson Peter 1953- *WhoAm 94*
Savit, Carl Hertz 1922- *WhoAm 94*
Savit, Mark Noah 1949- *WhoAmL 94*
Savitskaya, Svetlana Evgenevna 1948- *WhoWomW 91*
Savitsky, Daniel 1921- *WhoAm 94*
Savitt, Dick 1927- *BuCMET*
Savitt, Jan d1948 *WhoHol 92*
Savitt, Lynne *DrAPF 93*
Savitt, Sam *WhoAmA 93, WrDr 94*
Savitt, Steven Lee 1949- *WhoMW 93*
Savitt, Susan Schenkel 1943- *WhoAmL 94*
Savitz, David Barry 1943- *WhoAmL 94*
Savitz, Frieda 1931-1985 *WhoAmA 93N*
Savitz, Harriet May 1933- *TwCYAW*
Savitz, Joseph J. 1922- *WhoAmL 94*
Savitz, Martin Harold 1942- *WhoScEn 94*
Savitz, Maxine Lazarus 1937- *WhoAm 94*
Savitz, Samuel J. 1936- *WhoAm 94, WhoFI 94*
Savitz, Warren Eric 1959- *WhoFI 94*
Savner, David A. 1944- *WhoAm 94, WhoAmL 94*
Savo, Jimmy d1960 *WhoHol 92*
Savo, Jimmy 1896-1960 *WhoCom*
Savoca, Antonio Litterio 1923- *WhoAm 94, WhoFI 94*
Savoca, Susan 1953- *WhoAmL 94*
Savocchio, Joyce *WhoAmP 93*
Savoi, Gaspero fl. 1758-1792 *NewGrDO*
Savoia, Michael Anthony 1955- *WhoFI 94*
Savoie, Blanche d1933 *WhoHol 92*
Savoie, Leonard Norman 1928- *WhoAm 94*
Savolainen, Lea Tuulikki 1946- *WhoWomW 91*
Savona, Michael Richard 1947- *WhoScEn 94, WhoWest 94*
Savonarola, Girolamo 1452-1498 *HisWorL [port]*
Savonarola, Girolamo, Fra 1452-1498 *BlmGEL*
Savonese, Il *NewGrDO*
Savor, Steve 1961- *WhoAmL 94*
Savorgnan, Maria Late fl. 15th cent.- *BlmGWL*
Savory, Hubert Newman 1911- *Who 94*
Savory, Mark 1943- *WhoFI 94*
Savory, Teo *WrDr 94*
Savours, Dale Norman C. *Who 94*
Savova, Galina 1940- *NewGrDO*
Savoy, Bert 1888-1923
See Savoy and Brennan *WhoCom*
Savoy, Chyrl Lenore 1944- *WhoAmA 93*
Savoy, Douglas Eugene 1927- *WhoAm 94*
Savoy, Guy 1953- *IntWW 93*
Savoy, Suzanne Marie 1946- *WhoMW 93*
Savoy, Theresa Ann 1955- *WhoHol 92*
Savoy and Brennan *WhoCom*
Savrann, Richard Allen 1935- *WhoAm 94*
Savrin, Louis 1927- *WhoAm 94*
Savrun, Ender 1953- *WhoFI 94, WhoWest 94*
Savva, Savely L. 1932- *WhoWest 94*
Savvas, Minas *DrAPF 93*
Savvina, Iya Sergeyevna 1936- *IntWW 93*
Sawabini, Nabil George 1951- *WhoAm 94*
Sawabini, Wadi Issa 1917- *WhoAm 94*
Sawachi Hisae 1930- *BlmGWL*
Sawada, Hideo 1934- *WhoScEn 94*
Sawada, Ikune 1936- *WhoAmA 93*
Sawada, Suzanne Roni 1951- *WhoAm 94*
Sawai, Noboru 1931- *WhoAmA 93*
Sawalha, Nadim *WhoHol 92*
Sawallisch, Wolfgang 1923- *IntWW 93, NewGrDO, WhoAm 94*
Sawamatsu, Junko 1948- *BuCMET*
Sawamatsu, Kazuko 1951- *BuCMET*
Sawamura, Kunitaro d1974 *WhoHol 92*
Sawan, Mohamed El-Sayed 1946- *WhoMW 93*
Saward, Ernest Welton 1914-1989 *WhAm 10*
Saward, Michael John 1932- *Who 94*
Sawatari, Takeo 1939- *WhoAsA 94*
Sawatzky, Michael Scott 1956- *WhoFI 94*
Sawaya, George *WhoHol 92*
Sawchuk, Ronald John 1940- *WhoAm 94*
Sawdei, Milan A. 1946- *WhoAmL 94*
Sawdey, Richard Marshall 1943- *WhoAm 94*
Sawdy, Peter Bryan 1931- *IntWW 93, Who 94*
Saweikis, Matthew A. *WhoScEn 94*
Sawelson, Mel 1929- *IntMPA 94*
Sawers, David Richard Hall 1931- *Who 94*
Sawers, Robert John 1955- *Who 94*
Sawh, Lall Ramnath 1951- *WhoScEn 94*
Sawhill, Isabel V(an Devanter) 1937- *WrDr 94*
Sawhill, Isabel Van Devanter 1937- *WhoAm 94*
Sawhill, John Crittenden 1936- *WhoAm 94*
Sawhney, Ajay 1953- *WhoAsA 94*
Sawhney, Gurjeet Singh 1955- *WhoAsA 94*
Sawicki, Joseph, Jr. 1954- *WhoAmP 93*
Sawicki, Thomas 1945- *WhoAm 94*
Sawin, Craig B. 1956- *WhoFI 94*
Sawin, Nancy Churchman 1917- *WhoAm 94*
Sawinski, Vincent John 1925- *WhoAm 94*
Sawiris, Milad Youssef 1922- *WhoAm 94*
Sawitsky, Kitt 1949- *WhoAmL 94*
Sawka, Jan A. 1946- *WhoAmA 93*
Sawko, Felicjan 1937- *Who 94*
Sawlivich, Wayne Bradstreet 1957- *WhoScEn 94*
Saw Maung, Gen. 1928- *IntWW 93*
Sawoski, John Robert 1962- *WhoWest 94*
Sawtell, Stephen M. 1931- *WhoAm 94*
Sawtelle, Edward Stephen 1930- *WhoMW 93*
Sawtelle, William Carter *EncSF 93*
Sawyer, Alan R. 1919- *WhoAmA 93*
Sawyer, Alfred M. 1934- *WhoBlA 94*
Sawyer, Alfred P. 1919- *WhoAmP 93*
Sawyer, Amos *IntWW 93*
Sawyer, Anthony Charles 1939- *Who 94*
Sawyer, Barbara Jo 1948- *WhoAmP 93*
Sawyer, Bonnie Louise 1948- *WhoFI 94*
Sawyer, Broadus Eugene 1921- *WhoBlA 94*
Sawyer, Cameron Friedel 1958- *WhoAmL 94*
Sawyer, Charles Henry 1906- *WhoAmA 93*
Sawyer, Charles Henry 1915- *IntWW 93, WhoAm 94*
Sawyer, Christopher Glenn 1950- *WhoAm 94*
Sawyer, Connie *WhoHol 92*
Sawyer, David c. 1812-1889 *EncNAR*
Sawyer, David Neal 1940- *WhoFI 94, WhoScEn 94*
Sawyer, Diane 1945- *IntMPA 94, WhoAm 94*
Sawyer, (Frederick) Don(ald) 1947- *WrDr 94*
Sawyer, Ed 1926- *WhoAmP 93*
Sawyer, Eugene, Jr. 1934- *WhoAmP 93*
Sawyer, F. Grant 1918- *WhoAmP 93*
Sawyer, Forrest *WhoAm 94*
Sawyer, Forrest Lamar 1932- *WhoAmP 93*
Sawyer, Frank S. *WhoAmP 93*
Sawyer, George Edward 1919- *WhoBlA 94*
Sawyer, Grant 1918- *WhoAmL 94, WhoWest 94*
Sawyer, Harold Murray, Jr. 1946- *WhoAmL 94*
Sawyer, Harold S. 1920- *WhoAmP 93*
Sawyer, Harold Samuel 1920- *WhoAmL 94*
Sawyer, Helen *WhoAmA 93*
Sawyer, Helen Alton *WhoAm 94*
Sawyer, Horace A(dall) 1894- *WhAm 10*
Sawyer, Howard Jerome 1929- *WhoAm 94*
Sawyer, James Lawrence 1947- *WhoScEn 94*
Sawyer, Jim Charles 1939- *WhoMW 93*
Sawyer, Joe d1982 *WhoHol 92*
Sawyer, John *WhoAm 94, WhoMW 93*
Sawyer, John 1919- *WrDr 94*
Sawyer, John Edward 1917- *WhoAm 94*
Sawyer, John R. 1953- *WhoAmA 93*
Sawyer, John S. 1953- *WhoAmL 94*
Sawyer, John Stanley 1916- *Who 94*
Sawyer, Judith Ann 1946- *WhoMW 93*
Sawyer, Kenneth J. 1945- *WhoAmP 93*
Sawyer, Laura d1970 *WhoHol 92*
Sawyer, Lawrence Richard 1953- *WhoAmL 94*
Sawyer, Linda Claire 1944- *WhoScEn 94*
Sawyer, Lynwood *DrAPF 93*
Sawyer, Margo 1958- *WhoAmA 93*
Sawyer, Maria Artemis Papageorge *WhoAmA 93*
Sawyer, Michael Thomas 1958- *WhoAmP 93*
Sawyer, Michael Tom 1958- *WhoHisp 94*
Sawyer, Nancy (Buckingham) 1924- *WrDr 94*
Sawyer, Nelson Baldwin, Jr. 1948- *WhoFI 94*
Sawyer, Pamela Z. *WhoAmP 93*
Sawyer, Philip Ayer d1949 *WhoAmA 93N*
Sawyer, Phyllis Rose 1923- *WhoAmP 93*
Sawyer, Raymond Lee, Jr. 1935- *WhoAm 94, WhoFI 94*
Sawyer, Raymond Terry 1943- *WhoAm 94*
Sawyer, Robert J(ames) 1960- *EncSF 93*
Sawyer, Robert McLaran 1929- *WhoAm 94*
Sawyer, Robert Noel 1946- *WhoIns 94*
Sawyer, Roderick Terrence 1963- *WhoBlA 94*
Sawyer, Roger 1931- *WrDr 94*
Sawyer, Stephen Gilbert 1953- *WhoAmP 93*
Sawyer, Thomas C. 1945- *CngDr 93, WhoAm 94, WhoAmP 93, WhoMW 93*
Sawyer, Thomas Edgar 1932- *WhoFI 94, WhoWest 94*
Sawyer, Thomas William 1933- *WhoAm 94, WhoWest 94*
Sawyer, Warren Allen 1937-1990 *WhAm 10*
Sawyer, Wells M. 1863- *WhoAmA 93N*
Sawyer, Wendell *WhoAmP 93*
Sawyer, Wilbur Henderson 1921- *WhoAm 94*
Sawyer, William 1920- *WhoAmA 93*
Sawyer, William Curtis 1933- *WhoFI 94*
Sawyer, William Dale 1929- *WhoAm 94*
Sawyer, William Gregory 1954- *WhoBlA 94*
Sawyer-Koch, Barbara Jo 1948- *WhoMW 93*
Sawyer-Laucanno, Christopher 1951- *WrDr 94*
Sawyers, Al Baker 1960- *WhoAmL 94*
Sawyers, Elizabeth Joan 1936- *WhoAm 94*
Sawyers, John Lazelle 1925- *WhoAm 94*
Sawyers, June Skinner 1957- *WhoMW 93*
Sawyers, Norma Eileen 1943- *WhoMW 93*
Sawyers, Paul Geoffrey 1959- *WhoFI 94*
Sawyier, Calvin P. 1921- *WhoAm 94*
Sawyier, David R. 1951- *WhoAm 94*
Sawyier, Michael Tod 1948- *WhoAmL 94*
Sawyko, Leon T. 1944- *WhoAmL 94*
Sax, Adolphe 1814-1894 *NewGrDO*
Sax, Boria *DrAPF 93*
Sax, Brian M. *WhoAmL 94*
Sax, Helen Spigel 1915- *WhoAm 94*
Sax, Herbert 1929- *WhoWest 94*
Sax, Joseph L. 1936- *WrDr 94*
Sax, Joseph Lawrence 1936- *WhoAm 94, WhoAmL 94, WhoWest 94*
Sax, Marie *NewGrDO*
Sax, Martin *WhoScEn 94*
Sax, Mary Randolph 1925- *WhoMW 93, WhoScEn 94*
Sax, Paul J. 1944- *WhoAmL 94*
Sax, Richard Alan 1957- *WhoMW 93*
Sax, Robert Edward 1938- *WhoFI 94*
Sax, Stanley Paul 1925- *WhoAm 94*
Saxbe, William B. 1916- *WhoAmP 93*
Saxbe, William Bart 1916- *WhoAm 94*
Saxbee, John Charles 1946- *Who 94*
Saxberg, Borje Osvald 1928- *WhoAm 94*
Saxe, Adrian A. 1943- *WhoAmA 93*
Saxe, Deborah Crandall 1949- *WhoAm 94*
Saxe, Edward A. 1933- *WhoAm 94*
Saxe, Henry 1937- *WhoAmA 93*
Saxe, Jon Sheldon 1936- *WhoAmL 94*
Saxe, Leonard 1947- *WhoAm 94*
Saxe, Steven Louis 1942- *WhoAmL 94*
Saxe, Templar d1935 *WhoHol 92*
Saxena, Amol 1962- *WhoScEn 94, WhoWest 94*
Saxena, Arjun Nath 1932- *WhoScEn 94*
Saxena, Avadh Behari 1960- *WhoWest 94*
Saxena, Brij B. *WhoAm 94, WhoAsA 94*
Saxena, Narendra K. 1936- *WhoWest 94*
Saxena, Renu 1958- *WhoScEn 94*
Saxena, Satish Chandra 1934- *WhoAsA 94, WhoMW 93*
Saxena, Subhash Chandra *WhoAsA 94*
Saxena, Surrendra Kumar 1926- *IntWW 93*
Saxena, Uday 1957- *WhoMW 93*
Saxer, Craig Sandford 1947- *WhoFI 94*
Saxer, Richard Karl 1928- *WhoAm 94, WhoMW 93, WhoScEn 94*
Saxl, Jane Wilhelm 1939- *WhoAmP 93*
Saxl, Richard Hildreth 1948- *WhoAmL 94*
Saxon, Alan 1943- *WrDr 94*
Saxon, Antonia 1947- *WrDr 94*
Saxon, Charles David 1920-1988 *WhoAmA 93N*
Saxon, David Stephen 1920- *Who 94, WhoAm 94*
Saxon, Hugh d1945 *WhoHol 92*
Saxon, John 1934- *WhoHol 92*
Saxon, John 1936- *IntMPA 94*
Saxon, John David 1950- *WhoAm 94, WhoAmL 94*
Saxon, Marie d1941 *WhoHol 92*
Saxon, Mark A. 1949- *WhoAmL 94*
Saxon, Pauline d1949 *WhoHol 92*
Saxon, Peter *EncSF 93*
Saxon, Peter 1940- *WhoAmL 94*
Saxon, Richard *EncSF 93*
Saxon, Vin d1977 *WhoHol 92*
Saxonhouse, Gary Roger 1943- *WhoFI 94*
Saxon-Snell, H. 1889- *WhoHol 92*

Saxton, H. James 1943- *WhoAm 94, WhoAmP 93*
Saxton, James M. 1950- *WhoAmL 94*
Saxton, Jim 1943- *CngDr 93*
Saxton, Josephine (Howard) 1935- *WrDr 94*
Saxton, Josephine (Mary Howard) 1935- *EncSF 93*
Saxton, Judy 1936- *WrDr 94*
Saxton, Mark 1914-1988 *EncSF 93*
Saxton, Richard *AfrAmG*
Saxton, Robert 1953- *NewGrDO*
Saxton, Robert Louis Alfred 1953- *Who 94*
Saxton, Ronald L. 1954- *WhoAmL 94*
Saxton, William Marvin 1927- *WhoAm 94, WhoAmL 94*
Say, Allen 1937- *WhoAsA 94*
Say, Calvin Kwai Yen 1952- *WhoAmP 93*
Say, James Kenneth 1954- *WhoAmL 94*
Say, Marlys Mortensen 1924- *WhoMW 93*
Say, Richard David 1914- *IntWW 93, Who 94*
Sayala, Chhaya 1950- *WhoAsA 94*
Sayala, Dash 1943- *WhoAsA 94*
Sayan, Doug *WhoAmP 93*
Sayano, Reizo Ray 1937- *WhoWest 94*
Sayao, Bidu (de Oliveira) 1902- *NewGrDO*
Sayaphupha, Robert Bouakham 1963- *WhoAsA 94*
Sayari, Hamad Saud al- 1941- *IntWW 93*
Sayas, Conrado Joe 1958- *WhoAmL 94*
Sayatovic, Wayne Peter 1946- *WhoAm 94*
Sayavedra, Leo *WhoHisp 94*
Sayce, Roy Beavan 1920- *Who 94*
Saye, Albert Berry 1912-1989 *WhAm 10*
Saye, Terri Orsini 1955- *WhoAmL 94*
Saye And Sele, Baron 1920- *Who 94*
Sayed, As-Sayed Ali As- 1927- *IntWW 93*
Sayed, Gamal As 1928- *IntWW 93*
Sayed, Mostafa Amr El- 1933- *IntWW 93*
Sayed, Sayed M. 1951- *WhoScEn 94*
Sayeed, (Abul Fatah) Akram 1935- *Who 94*
Sayeed, Jonathan 1948- *Who 94*
Sayenqueraghta d1786 *AmRev*
Sayer, Frank Edward, Jr. 1918- *WhoAmP 93*
Sayer, Guy Mowbray 1924- *Who 94*
Sayer, John Raymond Keer 1931- *Who 94*
Sayer, John Samuel 1917- *WhoScEn 94*
Sayer, Michael 1935- *WhoAm 94*
Sayer, Paul 1938- *WhoWest 94*
Sayer, Paul 1955- *WrDr 94*
Sayer, Philip d1989 *WhoHol 92*
Sayers, Bruce McArthur 1928- *Who 94*
Sayers, Chera Lee 1959- *WhoFI 94*
Sayers, Dorothy L. 1893-1957 *BlmGEL, BlmGWL*
Sayers, Gale *ProFbHF [port]*
Sayers, Gale 1943- *WhoFI 94*
Sayers, Gale E. 1943- *WhoBlA 94*
Sayers, James d1993 *Who 94N*
Sayers, Janet 1945- *WrDr 94*
Sayers, Jo Ann 1918- *WhoHol 92*
Sayers, Martin Peter 1922- *WhoAm 94*
Sayers, Michael Patrick 1940- *Who 94*
Sayers, (Matthew Herbert) Patrick 1908- *Who 94*
Sayers, Peig 1873-1958 *BlmGWL*
Sayers, Valerie *DrAPF 93*
Sayers, Valerie 1952- *WrDr 94*
Sayes, James Ottis 1922- *WhoAm 94*
Sayetta, Thomas Charles 1937- *WhoAm 94*
Saygin, Isilay *WhoWomW 91*
Saygun, Ahmed Adnan 1907-1991 *NewGrDO*
Sayigh, Laela Suad 1963- *WhoScEn 94*
Saykally, Richard James 1947- *WhoAm 94, WhoScEn 94*
Sayle, Alexei *WhoHol 92*
Sayler, Gene *WhoAmP 93*
Sayler, Henry B., Jr. 1921- *WhoAmP 93*
Sayler, J. William 1935- *WhoIns 94*
Sayler, Richard H. 1945- *WhoAm 94*
Sayler, Robert Nelson 1940- *WhoAm 94, WhoAmL 94*
Sayles, Emanuel d1986 *WhoHol 92*
Sayles, Eva 1928- *WhoAmA 93*
Sayles, Francis d1944 *WhoHol 92*
Sayles, George Osborne 1901- *IntWW 93, Who 94*
Sayles, John 1950- *EncSF 93, IntMPA 94, WhoHol 92, WrDr 94*
Sayles, John (Thomas) 1950- *ConAu 41NR*
Sayles, John Thomas 1950- *IntWW 93, WhoAm 94*
Sayles, Leonard Robert 1926- *WhoAm 94*
Sayles, Martin Luther 1957- *WhoWest 94*
Sayles, Richard Alan 1949- *WhoAmL 94*
Sayles, Ronald Lyle 1936- *WhoFI 94, WhoMW 93*
Sayles, Thomas Dyke, Jr. 1932- *WhoAm 94*
Sayles, Tim 1953- *WhoAmP 93*
Saylor, Bruce (Stuart) 1946- *NewGrDO*
Saylor, Charles Horace 1950- *WhoAmL 94*
Saylor, David J. 1945- *WhoAmL 94*
Saylor, H. Clay, III 1960- *WhoFI 94*
Saylor, J(ohn) Galen 1902- *WrDr 94*
Saylor, John Thomas 1931- *WhoAmP 93*
Saylor, Katie *WhoHol 92*
Saylor, Larry James 1948- *WhoAm 94, WhoAmL 94*
Saylor, Mark Julian 1954- *WhoAm 94*
Saylor, Peter M. 1941- *WhoAm 94*
Saylor, Richard Samuel 1926- *WhoWest 94*
Saylor, Shannon 1969- *WhoHol 92*
Saylor, Stanley E. *WhoAmP 93*
Saylor, Stanley Raymond 1916- *WhoAmP 93*
Saylor, Steven 1956- *ConAu 142*
Saylor, Steven Warren 1956- *WhoAm 94*
Saylor, Syd d1962 *WhoHol 92*
Saylors, Jo An 1932- *WhoAmA 93*
Saymanska-Kwiatkowska, Anna *WhoWomW 91*
Saynor, Charles d1979 *WhoHol 92*
Saynor, John 1930- *Who 94*
Sayre, C. Bigelow d1975 *WhoHol 92*
Sayre, David 1924- *WhoAm 94*
Sayre, Edward Charles 1923- *WhoWest 94*
Sayre, Eleanor Axson 1916- *WhoAmA 93*
Sayre, Francis Bowes, Jr. 1915- *WhoAm 94*
Sayre, George Edward 1935- *WhoAm 94*
Sayre, Greg 1957- *WhoAmP 93*
Sayre, Jean Williams *WhoAm 94*
Sayre, Jeffrey d1974 *WhoHol 92*
Sayre, Jeffrey Don 1966- *WhoMW 93*
Sayre, John Marshall 1921- *WhoAm 94, WhoAmL 94, WhoWest 94*
Sayre, Kathleen Pope 1950- *WhoIns 94*
Sayre, Kenneth Malcolm 1928- *WhoAm 94*
Sayre, Larry D. *WhoMW 93*
Sayre, Nancy K. 1955- *WhoWest 94*
Sayre, Patricia Ann White 1958- *WhoMW 93*
Sayre, Ralph Jennings, III 1949- *WhoFI 94*
Sayre, Richard Thomas 1951- *WhoMW 93*
Sayre, Robert Freeman 1933- *WhoAm 94*
Sayre, Robert Marion 1924- *WhoAm 94, WhoAmP 93*
Sayre, Stephen 1736-1818 *WhAmRev*
Sayres, Margaret d1937 *WhoHol 92*
Sayres, William C. d1993 *NewYTBS 93*
Sayres, William C(ortlandt) 1927-1993 *ConAu 140*
Saywell, William George Gabriel 1936- *WhoAm 94*
Sazama, Thomas John 1946- *WhoAmL 94*
Sazegar, Morteza 1933- *WhoAm 94, WhoAmA 93*
Sazer, Gary Neil 1946- *WhoAmL 94*
Sazima, Henry John 1927- *WhoAm 94*
Sbarbaro, John Anthony 1936- *WhoWest 94*
Sbarbaro, Robert Arthur 1933- *WhoAm 94*
Sbarge, Raphael 1964- *WhoHol 92*
Sbarra, Francesco 1611-1668 *NewGrDO*
Sbordon, William G. 1928- *WhoAm 94*
Sbragia, Gary W. 1941- *WhoFI 94*
Sbriglia, Giovanni 1829-1916 *NewGrDO*
Scaasi, Arnold Martin *WhoAm 94*
Scaccetti Fumo, Jane 1954- *WhoFI 94*
Scacchi, Greta *IntWW 93*
Scacchi, Greta 1960- *IntMPA 94, WhoHol 92*
Scacchi, Marco c. 1600-1681? *NewGrDO*
Scaccia, Angelo M. *WhoAmP 93*
Scaccia, Giuseppe fl. 1669-1716 *NewGrDO*
Scaccia, Mario *WhoHol 92*
Scaccia, Mike
See Ministry *ConMus 10*
Scace, William Buell 1905- *WhoFI 94*
Scadding, John Guyett 1907- *Who 94*
Scaduto, Joseph d1943 *WhoHol 92*
Scafe, Judith Arlene 1961- *WhoBlA 94*
Scafe, Lincoln Robert, Jr. 1922- *WhoWest 94*
Scafetta, Joseph, Jr. 1947- *WhoAmL 94*
Scaggs, Boz 1944- *WhoAm 94*
Scaggs, Edward W. 1932- *WhoBlA 94*
Scaggs, Howard Irwin 1921- *WhoAm 94*
Scaglione, Aldo 1925- *WrDr 94*
Scaglione, Aldo Domenico 1925- *WhoAm 94*
Scaglione, Ann *DrAPF 93*
Scaglione, Cecil Frank 1934- *WhoWest 94*
Scaglione, Iris K. 1947- *WhoIns 94*
Scagnelli, John Mark 1951- *WhoAm 94*
Scaia, Mary Julie 1953- *WhoAm 94*
Scaiano, Donald A. 1932- *WhoIns 94*
Scaife, Brendan (Kevin Patrick) 1928- *IntWW 93*
Scairpon, Sharon Cecilia 1946- *WhoScEn 94*
Scala, C. George 1927- *WhoAm 94*
Scala, Gia d1972 *WhoHol 92*
Scala, James 1934- *WhoAm 94*
Scala, Joseph (A.) 1940- *WhoAmA 93*
Scala, Joseph Anthony, Jr. 1940- *WhoAm 94*
Scala, Sinclaire Maximilian 1929- *WhoFI 94*
Scalabrini, Grazia Mellini *NewGrDO*
Scalabrini, Paolo 1713-1803? *NewGrDO*
Scalapino, Douglas James 1933- *WhoAm 94*
Scalapino, Leslie *DrAPF 93*
Scalapino, Leslie 1947- *WrDr 94*
Scalapino, Robert Anthony 1919- *WrDr 94*
Scala-White, Michelle Diane 1968- *WhoWest 94*
Scalberg, Daniel Allen 1952- *WhoWest 94*
Scalchi, Sofia 1850-1922 *NewGrDO*
Scalera, Michael Jose 1933- *WhoHisp 94*
Scales, Alice Marie 1941- *WhoBlA 94*
Scales, Barbara 1926- *ConAu 140*
Scales, Erwin Carlvet 1949- *WhoBlA 94*
Scales, James Ralph 1919- *WhoAm 94*
Scales, Jerome C. 1942- *WhoBlA 94*
Scales, John Tracey 1920- *IntWW 93, Who 94*
Scales, Manderline Elizabeth 1927- *WhoBlA 94*
Scales, Patricia Bowles 1939- *WhoBlA 94*
Scales, Prunella *Who 94*
Scales, Prunella 1932- *WhoHol 92*
Scales, Prunella Margaret Rumney West *IntWW 93*
Scales, Richard Lewis 1928- *WhoFI 94, WhoMW 93*
Scales, Robert L. 1931- *WhoBlA 94*
Scalessa, Donald Francis 1942- *WhoAm 94*
Scales-Trent, Judy 1940- *WhoBlA 94*
Scaletta, Helen Marguerite 1927- *WhoMW 93*
Scaletta, Phillip Jasper 1925- *WhoAmL 94*
Scaletta, Phillip Ralph, III 1949- *WhoAm 94, WhoAmL 94*
Scalettar, Ellen *WhoAmP 93*
Scalfari, Eugenio 1924- *IntWW 93*
Scalfaro, Oscar Luigi 1918- *IntWW 93*
Scali, John Alfred 1918- *WhoAm 94*
Scali, Sam *WhoAm 94*
Scalia, Antonin 1936- *CngDr 93, IntWW 93, Who 94, WhoAm 94, WhoAmL 94, WhoAmP 93*
Scalia, Jack 1950- *WhoHol 92*
Scalia, Toni 1939- *WrDr 94*
Scaling, G. Wilson, II 1938- *WhoAmP 93*
Scaling, George Wilson, II 1938- *WhoAm 94*
Scalise, Frederick Wayne 1954 *WhoWest 94*
Scalise, George Martin 1934- *WhoFI 94*
Scalise, Nicholas Peter 1932- *WhoAmA 93*
Scalise, Osvaldo Hector 1940- *WhoScEn 94*
Scalish, Frank Anthony 1940- *WhoAm 94, WhoFI 94, WhoMW 93*
Scallen, Thomas Kaine 1925- *WhoAm 94, WhoMW 93*
Scalley, John J. 1930- *WhoFI 94*
Scallion, Gerald P. 1953- *WhoAmL 94*
Scally, John Joseph, Jr. 1951- *WhoAm 94, WhoAmL 94*
Scalzi, Carlo fl. 1718-1738 *NewGrDO [port]*
Scamell, Ragnhild 1940- *SmATA 77*
Scammacca, Nat *DrAPF 93*
Scamman, Walter Douglas, Jr. 1941- *WhoAmP 93*
Scammel, Harry Glenn 1948- *WhoAmL 94*
Scammell, Alexander 1744-1781 *AmRev*
Scammell, Alexander 1747-1781 *WhAmRev*
Scammell, William 1939- *WrDr 94*
Scammon, Richard M. 1915- *IntWW 93, WrDr 94*
Scammon, Richard Montgomery 1915- *WhoAm 94, WhoAmP 93*
Scancella, Robert J. 1955- *WhoScEn 94*
Scandalios, John George 1934- *WhoAm 94, WhoScEn 94*
Scandary, E. Jane 1923- *WhoMW 93*
Scandling, William Fredric 1922- *WhoAm 94*
Scandura, Joseph Michael 1932- *WhoAm 94*
Scanlan, Alfred L., Jr. 1950- *WhoAmL 94*
Scanlan, Arthur Brian 1907- *WrDr 94*
Scanlan, Brian James *WhoFI 94*
Scanlan, David M. 1956- *WhoAmP 93*
Scanlan, Dorothy *Who 94*
Scanlan, James Joseph, Jr. 1954- *WhoMW 93*
Scanlan, James Patrick 1927- *WhoAm 94*
Scanlan, John D. *WhoAmP 93*
Scanlan, John Douglas 1927- *WhoAm 94*
Scanlan, John Joseph 1906- *WhoAm 94*
Scanlan, John Oliver 1937- *IntWW 93*
Scanlan, Nelle 1882-1968 *BlmGWL*
Scanlan, Richard Thomas 1928- *WhoAm 94*
Scanlan, Thomas Cleary 1957- *WhoAm 94*
Scanlan, Thomas Joseph 1945- *WhoAm 94*
Scanlan, Thomas Michael 1941- *WhoMW 93*
Scanlin, Cynthia *WhoAmP 93*
Scanlin, Elizabeth *WhoAmL 94*
Scanlin, Steven Fox 1945- *WhoAmP 93*
Scanlon, Baron 1913- *Who 94*
Scanlon, Andrew *WhoScEn 94*
Scanlon, Charles Francis 1935- *WhoAm 94*
Scanlon, Charles Joseph 1915-1990 *WhAm 10*
Scanlon, Deralee Rose 1946- *WhoWest 94*
Scanlon, Edward F. 1918- *WhoAm 94*
Scanlon, Eugene F. 1924- *WhoAmP 93*
Scanlon, Eugene Francis 1947- *WhoAm 94*
Scanlon, Hugh Parr 1913- *IntWW 93*
Scanlon, Jane Cronin 1922- *WhoAm 94*
Scanlon, Joseph 1930- *WhoAmP 93*
Scanlon, Laurie Ann 1961- *WhoFI 94*
Scanlon, Lawrence Joseph 1951- *WhoAmL 94*
Scanlon, Patrick C. 1949- *WhoWest 94*
Scanlon, Patrick Michael 1940- *WhoAm 94, WhoAmL 94*
Scanlon, Peter Redmond 1931- *WhoAm 94, WhoFI 94*
Scanlon, Rosemary 1939- *WhoAm 94*
Scanlon, Terrence Maurice 1939- *WhoAm 94*
Scanlon, Thomas D. 1948- *WhoAmL 94*
Scanlon, Thomas J. 1938- *WhoMW 93*
Scanlon, Thomas Michael 1909- *WhoAm 94*
Scannamusa, Giovanni *NewGrDO*
Scannell, Dale Paul 1929- *WhoAm 94*
Scannell, Frank d1989 *WhoHol 92*
Scannell, Kevin *WhoHol 92*
Scannell, Robert E. 1939- *WhoAm 94, WhoFI 94*
Scannell, Thomas John 1954- *WhoMW 93*
Scannell, Vernon 1922- *IntWW 93, Who 94, WrDr 94*
Scannell, William d1963 *WhoHol 92*
Scannell, William Edward 1934- *WhoFI 94, WhoScEn 94, WhoWest 94*
Scannello, Patrick C. 1936- *WhoAmP 93*
Scantlebury-White, Velma Patricia 1955- *WhoBlA 94*
Scantling, James Grant 1949- *WhoAm 94, WhoAmL 94*
Scapanski, Marilyn Jean 1935- *WhoAmP 93*
Scarabelli, Adelina 1953- *NewGrDO*
Scarabelli, Diamante Maria fl. 1695-1718 *NewGrDO*
Scaramuzzi, Franco 1926- *IntWW 93*
Scarani, Mary-Lou 1928- *WhoAmP 93*
Scarascia-Mugnozza, Carlo 1920- *IntWW 93, Who 94*
Scaratt, David J. 1935- *WhoScEn 94*
Scaravaglione, Concetta Maria 1900-1975 *WhoAmA 93N*
Scarboro, James Eckford 1941- *WhoAmL 94*
Scarborough, Charles Bishop, III 1943- *WhoAm 94*
Scarborough, Charles Davis 1941- *WhoAmP 93*
Scarborough, Charles S. 1933- *WhoBlA 94*
Scarborough, Claude Mood, Jr. 1929- *WhoAm 94*
Scarborough, Frances Songer 1957- *WhoFI 94*
Scarborough, George Edward 1945- *WhoScEn 94*
Scarborough, Hazel Whidden 1922- *WhoAmP 93*
Scarborough, Jon Dale 1935- *WhoAmP 93*
Scarborough, Mark Sheldon 1957- *WhoAmP 93*
Scarborough, Robert Henry, Jr. 1923- *WhoAm 94*
Scarborough, William Kauffman 1933- *WrDr 94*
Scarbrough, Earl of 1932- *Who 94*
Scarbrough, Cleve Knox, Jr. 1939- *WhoAm 94, WhoAmA 93*
Scarbrough, Ernest Earl 1947- *WhoFI 94*
Scarbrough, George Addison *DrAPF 93*
Scarcella, Louis A. 1951- *WhoAmL 94*
Scarcelli, Vincent F. 1914- *WhoAmP 93*
Scard, Dennis Leslie 1943- *Who 94*
Scardellato, Adriano 1955- *WhoScEn 94*
Scardera, Michael Paul 1963- *WhoScEn 94*
Scardino, Albert James 1948- *WhoAm 94*

Scardino, Charles Anthony 1949- *WhoWest 94*
Scardino, Don *IntMPA 94, WhoAm 94*
Scardino, Don 1948- *ConTFT 11, WhoHol 92*
Scardino, Marjorie Morris 1947- *WhoAm 94*
Scardino, Michael Christopher 1948- *WhoAm 94*
Scardon, Paul d1954 *WhoHol 92*
Scarf, Herbert Eli 1930- *IntWW 93, WhoAm 94, WhoFI 94*
Scarf, Maggie 1932- *WrDr 94*
Scarf, Margaret 1932- *WhoAm 94*
Scarface
See Geto Boys, The *ConMus 11*
Scarfe, Alan *WhoHol 92*
Scarfe, Gerald 1936- *Who 94*
Scarfe, Gerald A. 1936- *IntWW 93*
Scarfe, Jane *Who 94*
Scarfe, Wendy (Elizabeth) 1933- *WrDr 94*
Scarff, Edward L. 1930- *WhoAm 94, WhoFI 94*
Scarff, Hope Ann Dyall 1952- *WhoMW 93*
Scarff, William *EncSF 93*
Scargill, Arthur 1938- *IntWW 93, Who 94*
Scargill, David Ian 1935- *WrDr 94*
Scaria, Emil 1838-1886 *NewGrDO*
Scarinci, Donald 1956- *WhoAmL 94*
Scaringi, Michael Joseph 1944- *WhoAmL 94*
Scarl, Ethan Adam 1940- *WhoScEn 94*
Scarlata, Charles Francis 1941- *WhoAmL 94*
Scarlata, Suzanne Frances 1958- *WhoScEn 94*
Scarlatti, (Pietro) Alessandro (Gaspare) 1660-1725
See Scarlatti Family *NewGrDO*
Scarlatti, (Giuseppe) Domenico 1685-1757
See Scarlatti Family *NewGrDO*
Scarlatti, Giuseppe 1718?-1777
See Scarlatti Family *NewGrDO*
Scarlatti Family *NewGrDO*
Scarlett *Who 94*
Scarlett, Bill d1978 *WhoHol 92*
Scarlett, David Edward 1941- *WhoFI 94*
Scarlett, Floyd M. 1906- *WhoAmP 93*
Scarlett, Harold O. *WhoAm 94*
Scarlett, James Harvey Anglin 1924- *Who 94*
Scarlett, John Donald 1923- *WhoAm 94*
Scarlett, John Leopold Campbell 1916- *Who 94*
Scarlett, Kathleen d1978 *WhoHol 92*
Scarlett, William John, III 1936- *WhoFI 94*
Scarman, Baron 1911- *Who 94*
Scarman, Leslie George 1911- *IntWW 93*
Scarminach, Charles Anthony 1944- *WhoAm 94, WhoAmL 94*
Scarne, John 1903- *WhoAm 94*
Scarone, Hector 1898-1968 *WorESoc*
Scarpa, Antonio 1942- *WhoAm 94, WhoScEn 94*
Scarpa, Dorothea 1926- *WhoAmA 93*
Scarpa, Robert Louis 1950- *WhoScEn 94*
Scarpalezos, Spyros-Constantin 1912- *IntWW 93*
Scarpelli, Dante Giovanni 1927- *WhoAm 94*
Scarpelli, Furio 1919-
See Age and Scarpelli *IntDcF 2-4*
Scarpelli, Glenn 1966- *WhoHol 92*
Scarpetti, Lee *WhoAmP 93*
Scarpino, Guy G. *WhoAmP 93*
Scarpino, Pasquale Valentine 1932- *WhoAm 94*
Scarpitta, Salvatore 1919- *WhoAmA 93*
Scarpitti, Frank Roland 1936- *WhoAm 94*
Scarponcini, Paul 1950- *WhoScEn 94*
Scarr, Deryck (Antony) 1939- *WrDr 94*
Scarr, Harry Alan 1934- *WhoAm 94, WhoScEn 94*
Scarr, Sandra Wood 1936- *WhoAm 94, WhoScEn 94*
Scarritt, James Richard 1935- *WhoAm 94*
Scarritt, Richard Winn 1938- *WhoMW 93*
Scarritt, Thomas Varnon 1953- *WhoAm 94*
Scarron, Paul 1610-1660 *GuFrLit 2*
Scarry, Donald Michael 1941- *WhoAmL 94*
Scarry, Huck 1953- *WrDr 94*
Scarry, Mary 1934- *WhoFI 94*
Scarry, Richard 1919- *WrDr 94*
Scarry, Richard (McClure) 1919- *SmATA 75 [port]*
Scarry, Richard McClure 1919- *WhoAm 94*
Scarsdale, Baron 1726-1804 *DcNaB MP*
Scarsdale, Viscount 1924- *Who 94*
Scarth, John Campbell 1924- *WhAm 10*
Scarwid, Diana *IntMPA 94*
Scarwid, Diana 1955- *WhoHol 92*
Scassa, Eugene L. *WhoAmP 93*
Scasta, David Lynn 1949- *WhoScEn 94*
Scatchard, John Percival 1910- *Who 94*
Scatena, Lorraine Borba 1924- *WhoFI 94, WhoWest 94*
Scates, Maxine *DrAPF 93*
Scates, Robert Malcolm 1917- *WhoAmP 93*
Scatia, Giuseppe *NewGrDO*
Scatigna, Louis Gene 1960- *WhoFI 94*
Scattola, Carlo 1878?-1947 *NewGrDO*
Scattolini, Lynn Bertman 1948- *WhoFI 94*
Scaturro, Philip David 1938- *WhoAm 94, WhoFI 94*
Scavella, Michael Duane 1955- *WhoBlA 94*
Scavo, Frank James 1959- *WhoWest 94*
Scavullo, Francesco 1929- *ConAu 43NR, WhoAm 94*
Scazzieri, Roberto 1950- *IntWW 93*
Scearce, Donald E. 1940- *WhoAmL 94*
Scearce, P. Jennings, Jr. *WhoScEn 94*
Scearse, Patricia Dotson 1931- *WhoAm 94*
Scedrov, Andre 1955- *WhoScEn 94*
Scelba, Mario 1901- *WhAm 10*
Scelsi, Joseph S. 1915- *WhoAmP 93*
Scepanski, Jordan Michael 1942- *WhoAm 94*
Sceper, Duane Harold 1946- *WhoAmL 94*
Scerbo, Frank Anthony 1949- *WhoAmL 94*
Scerni, Fred 1948- *WhoAmP 93*
Scerpella, Marino *WhoHisp 94*
Sceve, Maurice 1501?-1564 *GuFrLit 2*
Schaab, Arnold J. 1939- *WhoAmL 94*
Schaack, Philip Anthony 1921- *WhoAm 94*
Schaad, Dee Edwin 1943- *WhoMW 93*
Schaad, H. Ronald *WhoAm 94*
Schaad, Norman Werth 1940- *WhoScEn 94*
Schaaf, Carl Hart 1912- *WhoAm 94*
Schaaf, Johannes 1933- *NewGrDO*
Schaaf, John Urban 1955- *WhoFI 94, WhoScEn 94*
Schaaf, K. C. 1948- *WhoAmL 94*
Schaaf, Milton A. 1911- *WhoAmP 93*
Schaaf, Miv *WhoWest 94*
Schaaf, Robert E. 1935- *WhoIns 94*
Schaafsma, Curtis Forrest 1938- *WhoWest 94*
Schaafsma, David William 1953- *WhoMW 93*
Schaal, Richard 1930- *WhoHol 92*
Schaal, Wendy 1954- *WhoHol 92*
Schaap, James C(alvin) 1948- *ConAu 41NR*
Schaap, James Calvin *DrAPF 93*
Schaap, Richard Jay 1934- *WhoAm 94*
Schaar, Hermann 1909- *WhoFI 94*
Schab, Margo Pollins 1945- *WhoAmA 93*
Schabacker, Betty Barchett 1925- *WhoAmA 93*
Schabarum, Peter F. 1929- *WhoHisp 94*
Schaber, Douglas Craig 1950- *WhoWest 94*
Schaber, Gordon Duane 1927- *WhoAm 94*
Schaberg, Ben Franklin 1916- *WhoWest 94*
Schaberg, Burl Rowland, Jr. 1944- *WhoScEn 94*
Schaberg, John Irvin 1955- *WhoAmL 94*
Schabes, David Allen 1961- *WhoMW 93*
Schable, Robert d1947 *WhoHol 92*
Schabow, John William 1937- *WhoWest 94*
Schabram, Hans 1928- *IntWW 93*
Schach, Paul 1915- *ConAu 142*
Schachar, Henry *WhoAm 94, WhoFI 94*
Schacher, Mario A. 1947- *WhoHisp 94*
Schachman, Howard Kapnek 1918- *IntWW 93, WhoAm 94, WhoWest 94*
Schachner, Nat(haniel) 1895-1955 *EncSF 93*
Schacht, Catherine Ann 1950- *WhoWest 94*
Schacht, Gustave d1943 *WhoHol 92*
Schacht, Henry Brewer 1934- *IntWW 93, WhoAm 94, WhoFI 94, WhoMW 93*
Schacht, Henry Mevis 1916- *WhoAm 94*
Schacht, Jochen Heinrich 1939- *WhoAm 94*
Schacht, Richard 1941- *WrDr 94*
Schacht, Richard Lawrence 1941- *WhoAm 94*
Schacht, Ronald Stuart 1932- *WhoAm 94*
Schacht, Theodor 1748-1823 *NewGrDO*
Schachtel, Barbara Harriet Levin 1921- *WhoScEn 94*
Schachtel, Hyman Judah 1907-1990 *WhAm 10*
Schachter, Barry 1954- *WhoFI 94*
Schachter, Bonnie Lynn 1952- *WhoWest 94*
Schachter, Felice 1964- *WhoHol 92*
Schachter, Gustav 1926- *WhoFI 94*
Schachter, Harry 1933- *WhoAm 94*
Schachter, Hindy Lauer *DrAPF 93*
Schachter, James Robert 1959- *WhoWest 94*
Schachter, Julius 1936- *WhoAm 94*
Schachter, Justine Ranson 1927- *WhoAmA 93*
Schachter, Kenneth W. 1960- *WhoFI 94*
Schachter, Leon d1974 *WhoHol 92*
Schachter, Marvin 1924- *WhoAmP 93*
Schachter, Max 1913- *WhoAm 94*
Schachter, Oscar 1915- *WhoAm 94, WhoAmL 94*
Schachter, Robert Carl 1946- *WhoAmL 94*
Schachter, Sandy Rochelle *DrAPF 93*
Schachter, William David 1942- *WhoAm 94*
Schack, Benedikt (Emanuel) 1758-1826 *NewGrDO*
Schacter, Daniel Lawrence 1952- *WhoAm 94*
Schacter, Janice Lynn 1963- *WhoAmL 94*
Schactman, Barry Robert 1930- *WhoAmA 93*
Schad, Clayton Lewis 1952- *WhoWest 94*
Schad, Theodore MacNeeve 1918- *WhoAm 94, WhoScEn 94*
Schad, Verna J. 1949- *WhoMW 93*
Schade, Fritz d1926 *WhoHol 92*
Schade, George Henry 1936- *WhoWest 94*
Schade, Malcolm Robert 1950- *WhoAm 94, WhoAmL 94*
Schade, Mark Lynn 1959- *WhoScEn 94*
Schade, Rudolf Gottlieb, Jr. 1941- *WhoAmL 94*
Schadewaldt, Hans 1923- *IntWW 93, WhoScEn 94*
Schadle, William James 1932- *WhoAmL 94*
Schadler, Robert A. 1947- *WhoAmP 93*
Schadrack, William Charles, III 1950- *WhoScEn 94*
Schadt, James Phillip 1938- *WhoFI 94*
Schaeberle, Robert M. 1923- *IntWW 93*
Schaechter, Judith 1961- *WhoAmA 93*
Schaechter, Moselio 1928- *WhoAm 94*
Schaedler, Laurie Jean 1955- *WhoAmL 94*
Schaedler, Russell William 1927- *WhoAm 94*
Schaef, Anne Wilson 1934- *WhoWest 94, WrDr 94*
Schaefer, Adolph Oscar, Jr. 1932- *WhoAm 94*
Schaefer, Alan Charles 1952- *WhoAmL 94*
Schaefer, Albert d1942 *WhoHol 92*
Schaefer, Ann d1957 *WhoHol 92*
Schaefer, C. Barry 1939- *WhoAm 94, WhoFI 94*
Schaefer, Carl 1908- *IntMPA 94*
Schaefer, Carl Fellman 1903- *WhoAm 94, WhoAmA 93*
Schaefer, Carl George, Jr. 1962- *WhoScEn 94*
Schaefer, Carl George Lewis *WhoAm 94*
Schaefer, Charles Andrew 1958- *WhoWest 94*
Schaefer, Charles James, III 1926- *WhoAm 94*
Schaefer, Charles R. 1943- *WhoAmL 94*
Schaefer, Dan 1936- *CngDr 93*
Schaefer, Dan L. 1936- *WhoAm 94, WhoAmP 93, WhoWest 94*
Schaefer, David Arnold 1948- *WhoAm 94, WhoAmL 94*
Schaefer, Gail 1938- *WhoAmA 93*
Schaefer, George 1920- *IntMPA 94*
Schaefer, George Louis 1920- *WhoAm 94, WhoWest 94*
Schaefer, Gordon Emory 1932- *WhoAm 94*
Schaefer, Hans-Eckart 1936- *WhoScEn 94*
Schaefer, Hans Michael 1940- *WhoFI 94*
Schaefer, Helene Geraldine 1948- *WhoMW 93*
Schaefer, Henry Frederick, III 1944- *IntWW 93, WhoAm 94*
Schaefer, Howard G. 1945- *WhoAmP 93*
Schaefer, Inge C. 1939- *WhoAmP 93*
Schaefer, Jack Warner 1907-1991 *WhAm 10*
Schaefer, Jacob Wernli 1919- *WhoAm 94*
Schaefer, Jame 1940- *WhoAmP 93*
Schaefer, Jimmie Wayne, Jr. 1951- *WhoAm 94, WhoMW 93*
Schaefer, John A. 1927- *WhoAmP 93*
Schaefer, John Frederick 1943- *WhoAmL 94*
Schaefer, John Paul 1934- *WhoAm 94*
Schaefer, Joseph Albert 1940- *WhoScEn 94*
Schaefer, Joseph Patrick 1958- *WhoFI 94*
Schaefer, Marilyn Louise 1933- *WhoAm 94*
Schaefer, Michael P. 1946- *WhoAmP 93*
Schaefer, Patricia 1930- *WhoMW 93*
Schaefer, Philip Aaron 1941- *WhoAmP 93*
Schaefer, Richard Alan 1943- *WhoWest 94*
Schaefer, Robert E. 1936- *WhoAmP 93*
Schaefer, Robert John 1943- *WhoMW 93*
Schaefer, Robert Wayne 1934- *WhoAm 94*
Schaefer, Roland Michael 1954- *WhoScEn 94*
Schaefer, Ronald H. 1939- *WhoAmA 93*
Schaefer, Russell 1944- *WhoWest 94*
Schaefer, Scott Jay 1948- *WhoAmA 93*
Schaefer, Stephen Scott 1956- *WhoFI 94*
Schaefer, Steven David 1945- *WhoScEn 94*
Schaefer, Ted *DrAPF 93*
Schaefer, Terry W. 1946- *WhoMW 93*
Schaefer, Theodore Peter 1933- *WhoAm 94*
Schaefer, Thomas J. *WhoAm 94, WhoFI 94*
Schaefer, Vincent J. d1993 *NewYTBS 93 [port]*
Schaefer, Vincent J(oseph) 1906-1993 *ConAu 142, CurBio 93N*
Schaefer, W(illiam) Stanley 1907-1989 *WhAm 10*
Schaefer, William D. 1928- *WrDr 94*
Schaefer, William David 1928- *WhoAm 94*
Schaefer, William Donald 1921- *IntWW 93, WhoAm 94, WhoAmP 93*
Schaefer, William G. 1941- *WhoAm 94, WhoAmL 94*
Schaefer, Wilmo d1941 *WhoHol 92*
Schaefers, Wolfgang Friedrich Wilhelm 1930- *IntWW 93*
Schaeffer, Barbara Hamilton 1926- *WhoFI 94*
Schaeffer, Boguslaw 1929- *IntWW 93*
Schaeffer, Charles d1939 *WhoHol 92*
Schaeffer, Edwin Frank, Jr. 1930- *WhoAm 94*
Schaeffer, Frank 1952- *ConAu 140*
Schaeffer, Gary N. 1948- *WhoWest 94*
Schaeffer, Glenn William 1953- *WhoAm 94*
Schaeffer, Kate *WhoAmA 93*
Schaeffer, Leonard David 1945- *WhoWest 94*
Schaeffer, Mark 1956- *ConAu 140*
Schaeffer, Martha J. 1948- *WhoAmA 93*
Schaeffer, Monica Clare 1951- *WhoWest 94*
Schaeffer, Peter Moritz-Friedrich 1930- *WhoWest 94*
Schaeffer, Peter Viktor 1949- *WhoFI 94*
Schaeffer, Pierre 1910- *IntWW 93*
Schaeffer, Rebecca d1989 *WhoHol 92*
Schaeffer, Reiner Horst 1938- *WhoAm 94, WhoWest 94*
Schaeffer, Robert Ollie 1928- *WhoFI 94*
Schaeffer, S(tanley) Allyn 1935- *WhoAmA 93*
Schaeffer, Susan Fromberg *DrAPF 93*
Schaeffer, Susan Fromberg 1941- *WrDr 94*
Schaeffers, Willi d1962 *WhoHol 92*
Schaefgen, Philip P. 1958- *WhoFI 94*
Schaefgen, Susan Marie 1952- *WhoAmL 94*
Schaefler, Leon 1903- *WhoAm 94*
Schaeneman, Lewis G., Jr. 1930- *WhoAm 94, WhoFI 94*
Schaenen, Lee 1925-1993 *NewYTBS 93*
Schaeperkoetter, Jeff W. 1949- *WhoAmP 93*
Schaer, Werner 1940- *WhoAm 94*
Schaerf, Carlo 1935- *WrDr 94*
Schaeter, George A., Jr. *WhoAm 94, WhoFI 94*
Schaetzel, John Robert 1917- *IntWW 93*
Schaetzel Lesko, Wendy 1950- *WrDr 94*
Schafer, Alice Pauline 1899-1980 *WhoAmA 93N*
Schafer, Carl Walter 1936- *WhoAm 94, WhoFI 94*
Schafer, Edward 1946- *WhoAmP 93*
Schafer, Edward Albert, Jr. 1939- *WhoFI 94, WhoScEn 94*
Schafer, Edward Hetzel 1913- *WhAm 10*
Schafer, Edward T. 1946- *WhoAm 94, WhoMW 93*
Schafer, Edwin Thomas 1941- *WhoMW 93*
Schafer, Elizabeth Anne 1960- *WhoFI 94*
Schafer, Gary Lee 1938- *WhoAmP 93*
Schafer, Glenn S. 1949- *WhoIns 94*
Schafer, H. Erle 1938- *WhoAmP 93*
Schafer, James Albert 1948- *WhoAmL 94*
Schafer, Jerry Sanford 1934- *WhoAm 94*
Schafer, John Francis 1921- *WhoAm 94*
Schafer, John H. 1926- *WhoAm 94*
Schafer, John Stephen 1934- *WhoAm 94*
Schafer, Kevin James 1952- *WhoMW 93*
Schafer, Marty 1954- *WhoIns 94*
Schafer, Michael Frederick 1942- *WhoAm 94*
Schafer, Michael Shawn 1954- *WhoMW 93*
Schafer, Natalie d1991 *WhoHol 92*

Schafer, R(aymond) Murray 1933- *NewGrDO*
Schafer, Raymond Murray 1933- *WhoAm 94*
Schafer, Reuben *WhoHol 92*
Schafer, Robert Louis 1937- *WhoAm 94, WhoScEn 94*
Schafer, Rollie Randolph, Jr. 1942- *WhoScEn 94*
Schafer, Ronald William 1938- *WhoAm 94, WhoScEn 94*
Schafer, Stephen G. 1952- *WhoAmL 94*
Schafer, Thomas Wilson 1939- *WhoAm 94*
Schafer, Walter Warren 1919- *WhoScEn 94*
Schafer, William Harry 1936- *WhoFI 94, WhoMW 93*
Schaff, Adam 1913- *IntWW 93*
Schaff, Michael Frederick 1957- *WhoAmL 94*
Schaff, Paula Kay 1945- *WhoFI 94*
Schaff, Philip 1819-1893 *DcAmReB 2*
Schaffel, Hal d1993 *NewYTBS 93*
Schaffel, Lewis *WhoAm 94*
Schaffel, Robert 1944- *IntMPA 94*
Schaffer, Arthur Frederick, Jr. 1931- *WhoWest 94*
Schaffer, Boguslaw 1929- *NewGrDO*
Schaffer, Bruce Alan 1956- *WhoScEn 94*
Schaffer, Claudia Post 1945- *WhoAmA 93*
Schaffer, David Edwin 1929- *WhoFI 94*
Schaffer, David Irving 1935- *WhoAm 94*
Schaffer, Debra S. 1936- *WhoAmA 93*
Schaffer, Diane Maximoff 1946- *WhoAm 94*
Schaffer, Edmund John 1925- *WhoAm 94*
Schaffer, Eric A. 1954- *WhoAmL 94*
Schaffer, Franklin Edwin 1924- *WhoAm 94*
Schaffer, Gregory Lynn 1943- *WhoWest 94*
Schaffer, Harwood David 1944- *WhoMW 93*
Schaffer, Howard B. *WhoAmP 93*
Schaffer, Jack Raymond 1942- *WhoAmP 93*
Schaffer, Jeffrey L. 1952- *WhoAmL 94*
Schaffer, Jeffrey Lee 1958- *WhoWest 94*
Schaffer, Joel Lance 1945- *WhoWest 94*
Schaffer, Lee Ann 1959- *WhoAmL 94*
Schaffer, Marvin Baker 1926- *WhoWest 94*
Schaffer, Peter Keith 1943- *WhoAmL 94*
Schaffer, Priscilla Ann 1941- *WhoScEn 94*
Schaffer, Ray d1993 *NewYTBS 93*
Schaffer, Robert Warren 1962- *WhoAmP 93, WhoWest 94*
Schaffer, Rose d1989 *WhoAmA 93N*
Schaffer, Rose Nussbaum 1923-1989 *WhAm 10*
Schaffer, Seth Andrew 1942- *WhoAmL 94*
Schaffer, Sylvester d1949 *WhoHol 92*
Schaffer, Teresita Currie 1945- *WhoAm 94*
Schaffler, Federico *EncSF 93*
Schaffler, Mitchell Barry 1957- *WhoScEn 94*
Schaffner, Charles Etzel 1919- *WhoAm 94*
Schaffner, Franklin James 1922-1989 *WhAm 10*
Schaffner, George dc. 1795 *WhAmRev*
Schaffner, Harry 1942- *WhoMW 93*
Schaffner, Ingrid L. *WhoAmA 93*
Schaffner, J. Luray *WhoAmA 93*
Schaffner, Joan Elsa 1957- *WhoAmL 94*
Schaffner, John Albert 1937- *WhoMW 93*
Schaffner, Linda Carol 1954- *WhoScEn 94*
Schaffran, Andrew J. 1954- *WhoAmL 94*
Schaffran, Charles Brad 1950- *WhoAmL 94, WhoFI 94*
Schaffstein, Friedrich 1905- *IntWW 93*
Schaffter, Ernest Merill James 1922- *Who 94*
Schafheitlin, Franz d1980 *WhoHol 92*
Schafran, Lynn Hecht 1941- *WhoAmL 94*
Schafrath, Richard P. 1937- *WhoAmP 93*
Schafrick, Frederick Craig 1948- *WhoAmL 94*
Schafrik, Robert Edward 1946- *WhoScEn 94*
Schaible, Grace Berg *WhoAmP 93*
Schaible, Robert Hilton 1931- *WhoScEn 94*
Schaich, William L. 1944- *WhoAm 94*
Schaider, Cynthia Denise 1957- *WhoWest 94*
Schaie, Klaus Warner 1928- *WhoAm 94*
Schain, Eliot *DrAPF 93*
Schairer, George Swift 1913- *IntWW 93, WhoAm 94*
Schake, Lowell Martin 1938- *WhoAm 94*
Schakowsky, Janice 1944- *WhoMW 93*
Schakowsky, Janice D. 1944- *WhoAmP 93*
Schalcosky, S. Richard 1947- *WhoFI 94*
Schaleben, Arville 1907- *WhoAm 94*
Schalestock, Peter Kirk 1967- *WhoWest 94*
Schalk, Franz 1863-1931 *NewGrDO*
Schall, Alvin A. 1944- *CngDr 93, WhoAmP 93*
Schall, Alvin Anthony 1944- *WhoAm 94, WhoAmL 94*
Schall, David John 1946- *WhoMW 93*
Schall, Debra Jean 1952- *WhoMW 93*
Schall, James V(incent) 1928- *ConAu 42NR*
Schallenkamp, Kay 1949- *WhoAm 94*
Schaller, Christopher L. *WhoAm 94*
Schaller, Daryl Richard 1943- *WhoAm 94*
Schaller, Doris Gladys 1915- *WhoMW 93*
Schaller, Francois 1920- *IntWW 93*
Schaller, George B(eals) 1933- *WrDr 94*
Schaller, George Beals 1933- *IntWW 93, WhoAm 94, WhoScEn 94*
Schaller, Gordon A. 1949- *WhoAmL 94*
Schaller, James Patrick 1940- *WhoAmL 94*
Schaller, Jane Green 1934- *WhoAm 94, WhoScEn 94*
Schaller, Joanne Frances 1943- *WhoWest 94*
Schaller, John Walter 1963- *WhoScEn 94*
Schaller, Lyle E(dwin) 1923- *WrDr 94*
Schallert, Donovan H. 1924- *WhoIns 94*
Schallert, Edwin Glenn 1952- *WhoAmL 94*
Schallert, Elsa d1967 *WhoHol 92*
Schallert, James Britton 1948- *WhoIns 94*
Schallert, Thomas Anthony 1952- *WhoFI 94*
Schallert, William 1922- *WhoHol 92*
Schallert, William Joseph 1922- *WhoAm 94*
Schalles, John Frederick 1949- *WhoScEn 94*
Schall Holberg, Britta 1941- *IntWW 93*
Schally, Andrew Victor 1926- *IntWW 93, Who 94, WhoAm 94, WhoScEn 94, WorScD*
Schalon, Charles Lawrence 1941- *WhoMW 93, WhoScEn 94*
Schalow, Gayle Jean 1951- *WhoMW 93*
Schama, Simon 1945- *WhoAm 94*
Schama, Simon (Michael) 1945- *WrDr 94*
Schama, Simon Michael 1945- *IntWW 93*
Schambra, Philip Ellis 1934- *WhoAm 94*
Schamfarber, Richard Carl 1937- *WhoMW 93*
Schanberg, Saul Murray 1933- *WhoAm 94*
Schanberg, Sydney Hillel 1934- *IntWW 93, WhoAm 94*
Schanck, Francis Raber, Jr. 1907-1991 *WhAm 10*
Schanda, Joseph, Sr. 1930- *WhoAmP 93*
Schander, Edwin 1942- *WhoAmL 94, WhoWest 94*
Schander, Mary Lea 1947- *WhoWest 94*
Schang, Frederick C., Jr. 1893- *WhAm 10*
Schank, Roger C(arl) 1946- *WrDr 94*
Schank, Roger Carl 1946- *WhoAm 94*
Schanke, Robert A(nders) 1940- *ConAu 141*
Schanker, Louis 1903-1981 *WhoAmA 93N*
Schankman, Alan Robert 1947- *WhoWest 94*
Schanne, Margrethe 1921- *IntDcB [port]*
Schannep, John Dwight 1934- *WhoAm 94*
Schanstra, Carla Ross 1954- *WhoMW 93*
Schanz, William Z. d1993 *NewYTBS 93*
Schanzel, Dean J. 1942- *WhoAmP 93*
Schanzer, Ros *SmATA 77*
Schanzer, Rosalyn 1942- *SmATA 77 [port]*
Schanzer, Roz *SmATA 77*
Schanzlin, Patricia Roberts 1944- *WhoFI 94*
Schapansky, Elwood Jay 1938- *WhoWest 94*
Schaper, Joseph Raymond 1963- *WhoAmL 94*
Schapera, Isaac 1905- *Who 94*
Schapers, Marina d1981 *WhoHol 92*
Schapery, Richard Allan 1935- *WhoAm 94*
Schapira, Morey Rael 1949- *WhoWest 94*
Schapiro, Arenhold Cohen 1893- *WhAm 10*
Schapiro, Donald 1925- *WhoAm 94*
Schapiro, Herb 1929- *WhoAm 94*
Schapiro, Isabel Margaret *Who 94*
Schapiro, Jerome Bentley 1930- *WhoAm 94, WhoFI 94, WhoScEn 94*
Schapiro, Mary 1955- *WhoAm 94, WhoAmL 94, WhoFI 94*
Schapiro, Meyer 1904- *Who 94, WhoAm 94, WhoAmA 93, WrDr 94*
Schapiro, Miriam 1923- *WhoAm 94, WhoAmA 93*
Schapiro, Morris A. 1903- *WhoAm 94, WhoFI 94*
Schapiro, Ruth Goldman 1926-1991 *WhAm 10*
Schapp, Rebecca Maria 1956- *WhoAm 94, WhoWest 94*
Schappert, Michael James 1955- *WhoAmL 94*
Schapsmeier, Edward Lewis 1927- *WrDr 94*
Schapsmeier, Frederick H(erman) 1927- *WrDr 94*
Schar, Dwight C. 1942- *WhoFI 94*
Schar, Stephen L. 1945- *WhoAmL 94*
Schar, Stuart 1941- *WhoAmA 93*
Schara, Charles Gerard 1952- *WhoAm 94*
Scharansky, Natan 1948- *IntWW 93*
Scharbert, Josef 1919- *WhoAm 94*
Scharf, Aaron 1922-1993 *WrDr 94N*
Scharf, Kenny 1958- *WhoAmA 93*
Scharf, Michael Paul 1963- *WhoAmL 94*
Scharf, Robert Lee 1920- *WhoAmL 94*
Scharf, William 1927- *WhoAm 94, WhoAmA 93*
Scharfenberg, Doris Ann 1917- *WhoAm 94*
Scharfetter, Donald L. 1934- *WhoAm 94*
Scharff, Alex Joseph 1966- *WhoAmL 94*
Scharff, Constance Kramer *WhoAmA 93*
Scharff, Edward E. 1946- *WrDr 94*
Scharff, Herman d1963 *WhoHol 92*
Scharff, Joseph Laurent 1935- *WhoAm 94*
Scharff, Lester d1962 *WhoHol 92*
Scharff, Matthew Daniel 1932- *WhoAm 94, WhoScEn 94*
Scharfman, Scott Phillip 1962- *WhoFI 94*
Scharlatt, Harold 1947- *WhoFI 94*
Scharlemann, Robert Paul 1929- *WhoAm 94*
Scharley, Denise 1918?- *NewGrDO*
Scharoff, Steven Russell 1946- *WhoAmL 94*
Scharp, Anders 1934- *IntWW 93, WhoAm 94, WhoFI 94*
Scharpegge, Ernie d1940 *WhoHol 92*
Scharpf, Francis Robert 1938- *WhoMW 93*
Scharping, Brian Wayne 1966- *WhoScEn 94*
Scharp-Radovic, Carol Ann 1940- *WhoMW 93*
Scharrer, Berta Vogel 1906- *IntWW 93, WhoAm 94, WhoScEn 94*
Schary, Dore 1905-1980 *ConDr 93, IntDcF 2-4*
Schary, Emanuel 1924- *WhoAm 94, WhoAmA 93*
Schary, Saul 1904-1978 *WhoAmA 93N*
Schat, Peter 1935- *NewGrDO*
Schatkin, Sidney Bernhard 1903- *WhoAmL 94*
Schatt, Paul 1945- *WhoAm 94*
Schatten, Gerald Phillip 1949- *WhoMW 93, WhoScEn 94*
Schatten, Kenneth Howard 1944- *WhoScEn 94*
Schattgen, David Allan 1938- *WhoMW 93*
Schattke, Carl David 1962- *WhoMW 93*
Schattner, Jonas Jeffrey 1945- *WhoAmL 94*
Schattschneider, Peter *EncSF 93*
Schatz, Daniel John 1948- *WhoAmL 94*
Schatz, Gottfried 1936- *IntWW 93*
Schatz, Irwin Jacob 1931- *WhoAm 94*
Schatz, Martin 1936- *WhoFI 94*
Schatz, Michael A. *WhoAmP 93*
Schatz, Mona Claire Struhsaker 1950- *WhoWest 94*
Schatz, Philip Ransom 1957- *WhoAmL 94*
Schatz, S. Michael 1921- *WhoAm 94*
Schatz, Steven Mark 1948- *WhoAm 94, WhoAmL 94*
Schatzberg, Alan Frederic 1944- *WhoAm 94*
Schatzberg, Gershon 1955- *WhoFI 94*
Schatzberg, Jerry 1927- *IntMPA 94*
Schatzberg, Jerry Ned 1927- *WhoAm 94*
Schatzel, Robert Mathew 1961- *WhoScEn 94*
Schatzki, George 1933- *WhoAm 94, WhoAmL 94*
Schatzman, Evry 1920- *IntWW 93*
Schatzow, Michael 1949- *WhoAm 94, WhoAmL 94*
Schaub, Fred S. *WhoScEn 94*
Schaub, Harry Carl 1929- *WhoAm 94*
Schaub, James Hamilton 1925- *WhoAm 94*
Schaub, Marilyn McNamara 1928- *WhoAm 94*
Schaub, Mary H(unter) 1943- *ConAu 140*
Schaub, Sherwood Anhder, Jr. 1942- *WhoAm 94, WhoFI 94*
Schaubel, Teresamarie H. 1953- *WhoMW 93*
Schaubert, Daniel Harold 1947- *WhoAm 94*
Schauble, John Eugene 1949- *WhoMW 93*
Schauble, Wolfgang 1942- *IntWW 93, Who 94*
Schaudies, Jesse P., Jr. 1954- *WhoAmL 94*
Schauenberg, Susan Kay 1945- *WhoMW 93*
Schauer, Frederick Franklin 1946- *ConAu 42NR, WhoAm 94*
Schauer, Louis Frank 1928- *WhoAm 94*
Schauer, Nancy Ruth 1950- *WhoAmL 94*
Schauer, Paul Daniel 1944- *WhoAmP 93*
Schauer, Randall Charles 1956- *WhoAmL 94*
Schauer, Thomas Alfred 1927- *WhoFI 94, WhoMW 93*
Schauer, Tone Terjesen 1941- *WhoAmL 94*
Schauer, Wilbert Edward, Jr. 1926- *WhoAm 94*
Schauf, Carolyn Jane 1946- *WhoAmL 94*
Schauf, Debara K. 1948- *WhoAmP 93*
Schauf, Lawrence E. *WhoFI 94*
Schaufele, William Everett, Jr. 1923- *WhoAmP 93*
Schaufuss, Hans Joachim d1941 *WhoHol 92*
Schaufuss, Peter 1949- *IntDcB [port]*
Schaufuss, Peter 1950- *IntWW 93, Who 94, WhoAm 94*
Schauman, Runar d1977 *WhoHol 92*
Schaumann, Ruth 1899-1975 *BlmGWL*
Schaumburg, Donald Roland 1919- *WhoAmA 93*
Schaumburg, Herbert Howard 1932- *WhoAm 94*
Schaumburg-Lever, Gundula Maria 1942- *WhoScEn 94*
Schaunaman, Craig D. *WhoAmP 93*
Schaupp, Joan Pomprowitz 1932- *WhoMW 93*
Schaus, Fred 1925- *BasBi*
Schauss, Alexander George 1948- *WhoScEn 94, WhoWest 94*
Schaut, Joseph William 1928- *WhoAm 94*
Schauwecker, Margaret Liddie 1934- *WhoFI 94*
Schauwecker, Thomas Charles 1953- *WhoMW 93*
Schaw, Walter Alan 1934- *WhoAm 94*
Schawlow, Arthur Leonard 1921- *IntWW 93, Who 94, WhoAm 94, WhoScEn 94, WhoWest 94*
Schayes, Dolph 1928- *BasBi*
Schayk, Toer van *IntDcB*
Schea, Henry Emile, III 1952- *WhoWest 94*
Scheaffer, John E. 1916- *WhoAmP 93*
Schebler, Steven Joseph 1948- *WhoMW 93*
Schech, Marianne 1914- *NewGrDO*
Schechner, Richard 1934- *WhoAm 94*
Schechner-Waagen, Nanette 1806-1860 *NewGrDO*
Schechter, Abel Alan 1907-1989 *WhAm 10*
Schechter, Allen Edward 1935- *WhoAm 94, WhoMW 93*
Schechter, Alvin H. 1933- *WhoAm 94*
Schechter, Clifford 1958- *WhoFI 94*
Schechter, Daniel Philip 1942- *WhoAm 94, WhoAmL 94*
Schechter, Donald Robert 1946- *WhoAmL 94*
Schechter, Martin 1930- *WhoWest 94*
Schechter, Paul J. 1939- *WhoScEn 94*
Schechter, Robert Samuel 1929- *WhoAm 94, WhoScEn 94*
Schechter, Ruth Lisa 1927- *WrDr 94*
Schechter, Solomon 1847-1915 *DcAmReB 2*
Schechter, Stephen Lloyd 1945- *WhoAm 94, WhoFI 94*
Schechter, Sue A. 1952- *WhoAmP 93*
Schechterman, Lawrence 1943- *WhoAmL 94*
Scheck, Frank Foetisch 1923- *WhoAmL 94*
Scheck, Roxane Marsha 1953- *WhoMW 93*
Scheckler, William Edward 1938- *WhoMW 93*
Scheckner, Sy 1924- *WhoAm 94*
Scheckter, Jody David 1950- *IntWW 93*
Schecter, Mary Virginia 1909- *WhoAmP 93*
Schecter, Sandra Jan 1949- *WhoAm 94*
Schecter, Sheldon Dale 1926- *WhoAmP 93*
Schectman, Herbert A. 1930- *WhoAm 94*
Schectman, Stephen Barry 1947- *WhoFI 94*
Schedeen, Anne *WhoHol 92*
Schedler, Gilbert *DrAPF 93*
Schedvin, Carl Boris 1936- *WrDr 94*
Scheeder, Louis 1946- *WhoAm 94*
Scheel, Henry A. d1993 *NewYTBS 93*
Scheel, Mark *DrAPF 93*
Scheel, Nels Earl 1925- *WhoAm 94*
Scheel, Walter 1919- *IntWW 93, Who 94*
Scheele, Carl Wilhelm 1742-1786 *WorScD [port]*

Scheele, Leonard A. d1993 NewYTBS 93 [port]
Scheele, Leonard A(ndrew) 1907-1993 CurBio 93N
Scheele, Paul Drake 1922- WhoAm 94
Scheele, Roy DrAPF 93
Scheele, Roy 1942- WrDr 94
Scheelen, Andre Joannes 1964- WhoScEn 94
Scheeler, Charles 1925- WhoAm 94
Scheeler, James Arthur 1927- WhoAm 94
Scheer, Alan I. 1942- WhoAmL 94
Scheer, Francois 1934- IntWW 93
Scheer, Janet Kathy 1947- WhoWest 94
Scheer, Julian Weisel 1926- WhoAm 94
Scheer, K(arl)-H(erbert) 1928-1991 EncSF 93
Scheer, Lisa N. WhoAmA 93
Scheer, Mark Jeffrey 1962- WhoAmL 94
Scheer, Mark Preston 1959- WhoAmL 94
Scheer, Milton David 1922- WhoAm 94
Scheer, Sherie (Hood) 1940- WhoAmA 93
Scheer, Verlin Harold 1949- WhoIns 94
Scheerbart, Paul EncSF 93
Scheerer, Bobby 1929- WhoHol 92
Scheerer, Paul J. 1945- WhoAm 94, WhoAmL 94
Scheetz, George Henry 1952- WhoMW 93
Scheetz, Henry Franklin, Jr. 1898- WhAm 10
Scheetz, Lawrence R. 1943- WhoAmL 94
Scheetz, Mary JoEllen 1926- WhoAm 94
Scheetz, Terry R. 1941- WhoAmP 93
Scheff, Fritzi d1954 WhoHol 92
Scheff, Fritzi 1879-1954 NewGrDO
Scheffel, Joseph Viktor von 1826-1886 DcLB 129
Scheffer, Dick d1986 WhoHol 92
Scheffer, Robert Paul 1920- WhoMW 93
Scheffer, Victor B(lanchard) 1906- WrDr 94
Schefflein, Susan DrAPF 93
Scheffler, Israel WhoAm 94
Scheffler, Israel 1923- IntWW 93
Scheffler, Lewis Francis 1928- WhoMW 93
Scheffler, Samuel 1951- WhoAm 94
Scheffler, Stuart Jay 1950- WhoAmL 94
Scheffman, David Theodore 1943- WhoAm 94, WhoFI 94
Scheffrin-Falk, Gladys 1928- SmATA 76
Scheftner, Gerold 1937- WhoAm 94
Scheibe, Erhard A.K. 1927- IntWW 93
Scheibe, Karl Edward 1937- WhoAm 94
Scheibel, Arnold Bernard 1923- WhoAm 94, WhoScEn 94
Scheibel, James WhoAmP 93
Scheibel, James 1947- WhoAm 94
Scheibel, Jerry Austin 1950- WhoWest 94
Scheibel, Kenneth Maynard 1920- WhoAm 94
Scheiber, Harry N. 1935- WhoAm 94, WhoAmL 94, WhoWest 94, WrDr 94
Scheiber, Stephen Carl 1938- WhoAm 94
Scheibl, Jerome A. 1930- WhoIns 94
Scheible, Wayne G. 1938- WhoFI 94
Scheich, John F. 1942- WhoAmL 94
Scheid, Linda J. WhoAmP 93
Scheidel, Theodore C., Jr. 1944- WhoAmP 93
Scheidel, Thomas Maynard 1931- WhoAm 94
Scheidemantel, Karl 1859-1923 NewGrDO
Scheidenhelm, Richard Joy 1942- WhoAmL 94
Scheider, Roy 1932- IntMPA 94, IntWW 93
Scheider, Roy 1935- WhoHol 92
Scheider, Roy Richard 1935- WhoAm 94
Scheider, Walt 1930- WhoAmP 93
Scheider, Wilhelm 1928- IntWW 93
Scheidig, Paul A. 1942- WhoWest 94
Scheidl, Theodor 1880-1959 NewGrDO
Scheid-Raymond, Linda Anne 1953- WhoFI 94, WhoWest 94
Scheidt, Francis Matthew 1922- WhoMW 93
Scheidt, Philip Alan 1947- WhoFI 94
Scheidt, Robert vom 1879-1964 NewGrDO
Scheidt, Virgil D. 1928- WhoAmP 93
Scheidt, W. Robert 1942- WhoAm 94
Scheie, Harold Glendon 1909-1990 WhAm 10
Scheier, Libby 1946- WrDr 94
Scheifele, Richard Paul 1934- WhoAm 94
Scheifly, John Edward 1925- WhoAm 94
Scheig, Henry F. WhoIns 94
Scheiman, Eugene R. 1943- WhoAmL 94
Scheimann, Eugene 1897-1993 ConAu 140
Scheimer, Louis 1928- WhoAm 94
Schein, Daniel Bradley 1959- WhoAmL 94
Schein, Eugenie WhoAmA 93
Schein, Harvey L. 1927- WhoAm 94
Schein, Lorraine DrAPF 93
Schein, Philip Samuel 1939- WhoAm 94
Scheinbaum, David 1951- WhoAm 94, WhoWest 94
Scheinbaum, Sandra Lynn 1950- WhoMW 93
Scheinberg, Labe Charles 1925- WhoScEn 94
Scheinberg, Peritz 1920- WhoAm 94
Scheinberg, Steven Eliot 1952- WhoAm 94
Scheindlin, Raymond Paul 1940- WhoAm 94
Scheindlin, Shira A. 1946- WhoAmL 94
Scheiner, Richard Lloyd 1953- WhoFI 94
Scheineson, Irwin Bruce 1955- WhoFI 94
Scheinfeld, James David 1926- WhoAm 94
Scheinholtz, Leonard Louis 1927- WhoAm 94, WhoAmL 94
Scheininger, Lester 1947- WhoAm 94
Scheinkman, Jose Alexandre 1948- WhoAm 94
Scheinman, Andrew 1948- IntMPA 94
Scheinman, Leslie Kass 1953- WhoWest 94
Scheinman, Stanley Bruce 1933- WhoAm 94
Scheirer, George A. 1895-1959 WhoAmA 93N
Scheirman, Lawrence George 1950- WhoFI 94
Scheirman, William Lynn 1921- WhoScEn 94
Scheitlin, Constance Joy 1949- WhoFI 94
Schelar, Virginia Mae 1924- WhoFI 94, WhoScEn 94, WhoWest 94
Schelb, Josef 1894-1977 NewGrDO
Scheld, Robert William 1920- WhoIns 94
Scheld, William Michael 1947- WhoScEn 94
Scheldrup, John M. 1934- WhoAmP 93
Scheler, Brad Eric 1953- WhoAm 94, WhoAmL 94
Scheler, Max (Ferdinand) 1874-1928 EncEth
Scheler, Werner 1923- IntWW 93
Schell, Allan Carter 1934- WhoAm 94, WhoMW 93, WhoScEn 94
Schell, Braxton 1924- WhoAm 94
Schell, Carl 1928- WhoHol 92
Schell, Catherine WhoHol 92
Schell, Eric Franklin 1961- WhoAmL 94
Schell, Farrel Loy 1931- WhoScEn 94, WhoWest 94
Schell, Harry Keely, Jr. 1949- WhoMW 93
Schell, Harry Kent 1950- WhoMW 93
Schell, Homer 1925- WhoAm 94
Schell, James Michael 1949- WhoAmL 94
Schell, James Munson 1944- WhoAm 94
Schell, Jessie DrAPF 93
Schell, Jim 1936- ConAu 142
Schell, John Le Roy 1919- WhAm 10
Schell, Jonathan (Edward) 1943- WrDr 94
Schell, Jozef Stephaan 1935- IntWW 93
Schell, Lois M. 1943- WhoAmP 93
Schell, Maria 1926- IntMPA 94, WhoHol 92
Schell, Maximilian 1930- IntMPA 94, IntWW 93, WhoAm 94, WhoHol 92
Schell, Orville (Hickok) 1940- WrDr 94
Schell, Richard A. 1950- WhoAm 94, WhoAmL 94
Schell, Ronald Perry 1935- WhoAmP 93
Schell, Ronnie 1934- WhoHol 92
Schell, William H. WhoFI 94
Schellen, Nando 1934- WhoMW 93
Schellenberg, August WhoHol 92
Schellenberg, Gerard David 1951- WhoScEn 94
Schellenberg, James A. 1932- WrDr 94
Schellenberg, Joanna WhoHol 92
Schellenberg, Karl Abraham 1931- WhoAm 94
Schellenberger, Robert Earl 1932- WhoAm 94, WhoFI 94
Scheller, Damion 1970- WhoHol 92
Scheller, Erin Linn 1942- WhoWest 94
Scheller, Melanie 1953- SmATA 77
Scheller, Sanford Gregory 1931- WhoFI 94
Schellhaas, Linda Jean 1956- WhoScEn 94
Schellhaas, Robert Wesley 1952- WhoScEn 94
Schellhorn, Edward H. WhoAmP 93
Schellhous, Rosalie Athol 1933- WhoMW 93
Schellin, Robert William 1910-1985 WhoAmA 93N
Schelling, Friedrich Wilhelm Eugen Eberhard von 1906- IntWW 93
Schelling, Friedrich Wilhelm Joseph von 1775-1854 EncEth
Schelling, Gerald Thomas 1941- WhoWest 94
Schelling, Gunther F.K. 1923- IntWW 93
Schelling, John Paul 1924- WhoAm 94
Schelling, Thomas C. 1921- WrDr 94
Schelling, Thomas Crombie 1921- IntWW 93, WhoAm 94, WhoFI 94
Schellinger, James Raymond 1963- WhoWest 94
Schellman, John A. 1924- WhoAm 94, WhoScEn 94
Schellow, Erich WhoHol 92
Schellow, Erich 1915- IntWW 93
Schellpeper, Stan 1934- WhoAmP 93
Schelm, Roger Leonard 1936- WhoAm 94
Schelp, Richard Herbert 1936- WhoAm 94
Schelske, Claire L. 1932- WhoScEn 94
Scheltema, Robert William 1961- WhoScEn 94
Schelwokat, Gunther M. EncSF 93
Scheman, Carol R. WhoAm 94
Schembechler, Bo 1929- WhoAm 94
Schembri, Carmelo 1922- Who 94
Schemel, David Joseph 1951- WhoFI 94
Schemenauer, Robert 1934- WhoAmP 93
Schemenauer, Robert George 1934- WhoMW 93
Schement, Jorge Reina 1948- WhoHisp 94
Schemmel, Rachel Anne 1929- WhoMW 93, WhoScEn 94
Schemmel, Terence Dean 1963- WhoScEn 94, WhoWest 94
Schemnitz, Sanford David 1930- WhoAm 94
Schena, Francesco Paolo 1940- WhoScEn 94
Schenberg, Ivan Irl 1939- WhoAmP 93
Schenck, Andrew Craig 1941- WhoAm 94
Schenck, Aubrey 1908- IntMPA 94
Schenck, Benjamin Robinson 1938- WhoAm 94
Schenck, Earl 1889- WhoHol 92
Schenck, Frederick A. 1928- WhoAm 94, WhoBlA 94
Schenck, Henry Paul 1929- WhoFI 94
Schenck, Hilbert 1926- EncSF 93, WrDr 94
Schenck, Jack Lee 1938- WhoAm 94, WhoScEn 94
Schenck, Joe d1930 WhoHol 92
Schenck, Johannes fl. 16th cent.- EncDeaf
Schenck, Johannes 1660?-1716? NewGrDO
Schenck, Joseph 1878-1961 IntDcF 2-4 [port]
Schenck, Michael U. R. von 1931- IntWW 93
Schenck, Nicholas 1881-1969 IntDcF 2-4
Schenck, William Clinton 1947- WhoAmA 93
Schenck-Hamlin, William Joseph 1947- WhoMW 93
Schendel, Dan Eldon 1934- WhoAm 94
Schendel, Winfried George 1931- WhoWest 94
Schendle, James M. 1944- WhoAmL 94
Schenerman, Mark Allen 1959- WhoScEn 94
Schenk, Alexander Hans 1954- WhoFI 94
Schenk, Anton Franz 1940- WhoMW 93
Schenk, Deborah Huffman 1947- WhoAmL 94
Schenk, George 1934- WhoAm 94, WhoFI 94
Schenk, Johann Baptist 1753-1836 NewGrDO
Schenk, Joseph Bernard 1953- WhoAmA 93
Schenk, Lynn CngDr 93, WhoAm 94, WhoWest 94
Schenk, Lynn 1945- WhoAmP 93
Schenk, Manfred 1930- NewGrDO
Schenk, Otto 1930- NewGrDO
Schenk, Quentin Frederick 1922- WhoAm 94
Schenk, Ray Merlin 1946- WhoWest 94
Schenk, Roy U. 1929- WhoMW 93
Schenk, Worthington George, Jr. 1922- WhoAm 94
Schenkar, Joan M. 1946- ConDr 93
Schenkel, Chris ConTFT 11
Schenkel, Susan 1946- WhoScEn 94
Schenken, Bee d1993 NewYTBS 93
Schenken, Jerald R. 1933- WhoAmP 93
Schenkenberg, Mary Martin 1944- WhoMW 93
Schenkenfelder, John Charles 1952- WhoFI 94
Schenker, Alexander Marian 1924- WhoAm 94
Schenker, Carl Richard, Jr. 1949- WhoAm 94, WhoAmL 94
Schenker, Dona 1947- WrDr 94
Schenker, Eric 1931- WhoAm 94, WhoFI 94
Schenker, Joseph G. 1933- IntWW 93
Schenker, Leo 1922- WhoAm 94
Schenker, Marc Benet 1947- WhoScEn 94, WhoWest 94
Schenker, Steven 1929- WhoAm 94
Schenkkan, Dirk McKenzie 1949- WhoAmL 94
Schenkkan, Robert (Frederic), Jr. 1953- WrDr 94
Schenkkan, Robert Frederic 1953- WhoAm 94
Schenkler, Bernard 1948- WhoAmL 94
Schenkman, John Boris 1936- WhoAm 94
Schenstrom, Carl d1942 WhoHol 92
Schep, Raymond Albert 1946- WhoScEn 94
Schepers, Donald Herbert 1951- WhoMW 93
Schepers, Marlyn Glenn 1933- WhoAmP 93, WhoMW 93
Schepis, Anthony Joseph 1927- WhoAmA 93
Schepisi, Fred 1939- IntMPA 94
Schepisi, Frederic Alan 1939- IntWW 93
Schepp, George Phillip, Jr. 1955- WhoFI 94, WhoWest 94
Scheppach, Raymond Carl, Jr. 1940- WhoAm 94
Scher, Allen Myron 1921- WhoAm 94
Scher, Edward Eric 1958- WhoAmL 94
Scher, Howard Dennis 1945- WhoAm 94, WhoAmL 94
Scher, Irving 1933- WhoAm 94, WhoAmL 94
Scher, Paula Joan 1948- WhoAm 94
Scher, Robert Sander 1934- WhoScEn 94
Scher, Stanley Jules 1929- WhoAm 94
Scher, Steven Paul 1936- WhoAm 94
Scheraga, Harold A. 1921- IntWW 93
Scheraga, Harold Abraham 1921- WhoAm 94, WhoScEn 94
Scherago, Morris 1895- WhAm 10
Scherbakov, Vladimir Ivanovich 1949- IntWW 93
Scherbatow, Kyril d1993 NewYTBS 93
Scherber, Catherine A. 1947- WhoMW 93
Scherber, Herbert Grover 1930- WhoAmA 93
Scherber, Kit Catherine 1947- WhoAmP 93
Scherbring, Dale John 1961- WhoMW 93
Scherchen, Hermann 1891-1966 NewGrDO
Scherdin, Mary Jane Liskovec 1940- WhoMW 93
Schere, Jonathan Lawrence 1938- WhoAm 94
Schere, Leo d1981 WhoHol 92
Schereck, William John 1913- WhoMW 93
Scherer, A. Edward 1942- WhoScEn 94
Scherer, Alfredo Vicente 1903- IntWW 93
Scherer, Anita 1938- WhoMW 93
Scherer, Carol Louise 1943- WhoAmP 93
Scherer, Clarene Mae 1928- WhoMW 93
Scherer, Darvin Jay 1964- WhoMW 93
Scherer, Edward P. 1945- WhoAmL 94
Scherer, Frederic Michael 1932- WhoAm 94, WhoFI 94
Scherer, Gordon Harry 1906-1988 WhAm 10
Scherer, Harold Nicholas, Jr. 1929- WhoAm 94
Scherer, Henri Joseph 1920- WhoAm 94
Scherer, Jacqueline Rita 1931- WhoMW 93
Scherer, Jacques 1912- Who 94
Scherer, John Henry 1954- WhoAmL 94
Scherer, Karla 1937- WhoAm 94, WhoMW 93
Scherer, Lester B(uryl) 1931- WrDr 94
Scherer, Margaret Mary WhoAm 94
Scherer, Paul Joseph 1933- Who 94
Scherer, Peter Julian 1937- IntWW 93
Scherer, Robert Davisson 1929- WhoAm 94
Scherer, Ronald Callaway 1945- WhoWest 94
Scherer, Ross Paul 1922- WhoAm 94
Scherer, Scott 1962- WhoAmP 93
Scherer, Victor Richard 1940- WhoMW 93
Scherer, Wilhelm 1841-1886 DcLB 129 [port]
Scherf, Christopher N. 1950- WhoAm 94
Scherf, Kathleen D. 1960- ConAu 142
Scherff, Avon Marie 1962- WhoMW 93
Schergens, Becky Lou 1940- WhoAm 94
Scherich, Edward Baptiste 1923- WhoAm 94
Scherich, Erwin Thomas 1918- WhoAm 94, WhoFI 94, WhoScEn 94, WhoWest 94
Scherick, Edgar J. 1924- IntMPA 94
Scherl, Donald Jacob WhoAm 94
Scherle, William J. 1923- WhoAmP 93
Scherler, Burl Mark 1950- WhoAmP 93
Schermer, Judith Kahn 1949- WhoAmL 94
Schermer, Lloyd G. 1927- WhoAm 94, WhoMW 93
Schermerhorn, John Watson 1920- WhoAm 94
Schermerhorn, Kenneth Dewitt 1929- WhoAm 94

Schermerhorn, Richard E. 1927- *WhoAmP 93*
Schermerhorn, Sandra Leigh 1944- *WhoAmL 94*
Schermers, Henry G. 1928- *IntWW 93*
Schermers, Henry Gerhard 1928- *Who 94*
Scherpenhuijsen Rom, Willem 1936- *IntWW 93*
Scherpereel, Richard Charles 1931- *WhoAmA 93*
Scherr, Allan Lee 1940- *WhoAm 94*
Scherr, Harry, III 1944- *WhoFI 94*
Scherr, Lawrence 1928- *WhoAm 94, WhoScEn 94*
Scherr, Stephen Arthur 1938- *WhoAmP 93*
Scherrer, Richard Bennington 1947- *WhoAm 94, WhoAmL 94*
Scherrer-Bylund, Paul 1900- *IntWW 93*
Scherson, Isaac David 1952- *WhoWest 94*
Scherson, Yona Talma 1954- *WhoWest 94*
Schersten, H. Donald 1919- *WhoAm 94*
Schertz, Doris Ethel 1938- *WhoMW 93*
Scherzer, Joel *DrAPF 93*
Scherzer, Norman Alan 1939- *WhoScEn 94*
Scherziger, Keith Joseph 1968- *WhoScEn 94*
Schetky, Laurence McDonald 1922- *WhoAm 94*
Scheu, David Robert, Sr. 1944- *WhoAm 94*
Scheu, Friedrich 1942- *WhoWest 94*
Scheu, Leonard 1904- *WhoAmA 93*
Scheuch, Erwin K. 1928- *IntWW 93*
Scheuer, James H. 1920- *WhoAmP 93*
Scheuer, Katherine Dunn 1937- *WhoAm 94*
Scheuer, Paul Josef 1915- *WhoAm 94, WhoScEn 94, WhoWest 94*
Scheuer, Ruth 1952- *WhoAmA 93*
Scheuerman, David Elmer 1967- *WhoMW 93*
Scheuerman, Lisa Marie 1965- *WhoMW 93*
Scheuing, Richard Albert 1927- *WhoScEn 94*
Scheurell, Catherine Anne 1955- *WhoMW 93*
Scheuring, Garry Joseph 1939- *WhoAm 94, WhoFI 94*
Scheurle, Jurgen Karl 1951- *WhoScEn 94*
Scheuzger, Thomas Peter 1960- *WhoScEn 94*
Scheve, May E. 1964- *WhoAmP 93*
Schevill, James *DrAPF 93*
Schevill, James 1920- *IntWW 93*
Schevill, James (Erwin) 1920- *ConDr 93, WrDr 94*
Schevill, James Erwin 1920- *WhoAm 94*
Scheving, Lawrence Einar 1920- *WhoAm 94*
Schewel, Elliot Sidney 1924- *WhoAmP 93*
Schewel, Stanford 1918- *WhoAm 94*
Schexnayder, Brian Edward 1953- *WhoAm 94*
Schexnayder, Charlotte Tillar 1923- *WhoAmP 93*
Schexnayder, Thomas Florent 1933- *WhoAmP 93*
Schexnider, Alvin J. 1945- *WhoBlA 94*
Schey, John Anthony 1922- *WhoAm 94*
Schey, Ralph Edward 1924- *WhoFI 94, WhoMW 93*
Scheyer, Ernst 1900-1985 *WhoAmA 93N*
Scheyer, Lawrence William 1955- *WhoAmL 94*
Scheyer, Richard David 1958- *WhoScEn 94*
Schiaffino, Juan 1925- *WorESoc*
Schiaffino, Rosanna 1940- *WhoHol 92*
Schiaffino, Silvio Stephen 1927- *WhoAm 94*
Schiamberg, Lawrence Barry 1943- *WhoMW 93*
Schiapo, Bambino *WhoAmP 93*
Schiappa, (Anthony) Edward, (Jr.) 1954- *ConAu 141*
Schiassi, Gaetano Maria 1698-1754 *NewGrDO*
Schiavelli, Melvyn David 1942- *WhoAm 94*
Schiavelli, Vincent *WhoHol 92*
Schiavi, Raul Constante 1930- *WhoAm 94, WhoScEn 94*
Schiavina, Laura M. 1917- *WhoAmA 93*
Schiavina, Laura Margaret 1917- *WhoAm 94*
Schiavinato, Giuseppe 1915- *IntWW 93*
Schiavio, Federico 1962- *WhoWest 94*
Schiavo, A. Mary Sterling 1955- *WhoAm 94, WhoFI 94*
Schiavo, Pasco Louis 1937- *WhoAmL 94*
Schiavone, David L. 1943- *WhoAmL 94*
Schiavone, George A. 1930- *WhoAmP 93*
Schiazza, Guido Domenic 1930- *WhoFI 94*
Schibler, Armin 1920-1986 *NewGrDO*
Schicha, Ralph *WhoHol 92*
Schick, Dorothy Wasserman 1930- *WhoAmP 93*
Schick, Edgar Brehob 1934- *WhoAm 94*
Schick, Eleanor 1942- *ConAu 41NR*
Schick, Elliot 1924- *IntMPA 94*
Schick, Frank L(eopold) 1918- *WrDr 94*
Schick, Harold Ralph, III 1955- *WhoWest 94*
Schick, Harry Leon 1927- *WhoAm 94, WhoFI 94*
Schick, Jacob *WorInv*
Schick, Margarete (Luise) 1773-1809 *NewGrDO*
Schick, Paul Walter 1951- *WhoMW 93*
Schick, Thomas Edward 1941- *WhoAm 94*
Schickard, Wilhelm 1592-1635 *WorInv*
Schickel, Richard 1933- *IntWW 93, WhoAm 94*
Schickel, Richard (Warren) 1933- *WrDr 94*
Schickele, Peter 1935- *NewGrDO, WhoAm 94*
Schicker, Johanna 1943- *WhoWomW 91*
Schickman, Mark Isaac 1951- *WhoAmL 94*
Schidlow, Daniel 1947- *WhoScEn 94*
Schidlowsky, Leon 1931- *NewGrDO*
Schiebeler, Daniel 1741-1771 *NewGrDO*
Schieber, Sylvester Joseph 1946- *WhoFI 94*
Schiebler, Gerold Ludwig 1928- *WhoAm 94*
Schiebold, Hans 1938- *WhoAmA 93*
Schied, Peter J. 1944- *WhoFI 94*
Schieder, Joseph Eugene 1908- *WhoAm 94*
Schiefelbein, Kenneth Roland 1943- *WhoAmP 93*
Schiefelbusch, Richard L. 1918- *WhoAm 94*
Schiefer, Alicia C. 1958- *WhoHisp 94*
Schiefer, Johannes *WhoAmA 93N*
Schieferdecker, Ivan E. 1935- *WhoAmA 93*
Schieferdecker, Johann Christian 1679-1732 *NewGrDO*
Schieffelin, Laurie Graham 1941- *WhoAm 94*
Schieffelin, Thomas Lawrence 1936- *WhoFI 94*
Schieffelin, William Jay, III 1922-1989 *WhAm 10*
Schieffer, Bob *IntWW 93, WhoAm 94*
Schieffer, J. Thomas *WhoAm 94*
Schieffer, James Michael 1955- *WhoMW 93*
Schieffer, Rudolf 1947- *IntWW 93*
Schiehlen, Werner Otto 1938- *WhoScEn 94*
Schiel, John Michael 1937- *WhoWest 94*
Schields, Gretchen 1948- *SmATA 75 [port]*
Schields, Vickie Marie 1957- *WhoWest 94*
Schiele, Egon 1890-1918 *ModArCr 4 [port]*
Schiele, James Edwin 1929- *WhoFI 94*
Schiele, Paul Ellsworth, Jr. 1924- *WhoWest 94*
Schiell, Charles Randall 1952- *WhoWest 94*
Schieltz, Donald Eugene 1942- *WhoFI 94*
Schiemann, Konrad Hermann Theodor 1937- *Who 94*
Schier, Donald Stephen 1914- *WhoAm 94*
Schier, Steven Edward 1952- *WhoMW 93*
Schierbeck, Poul (Julius Ouscher) 1888-1949 *NewGrDO*
Schierer, Colleen Kay 1954- *WhoAmL 94*
Schierer, Paul Duane 1954- *WhoAmL 94, WhoWest 94*
Schierholz, Paul Milton 1946- *WhoWest 94*
Schierholz, William Francis, Jr. 1921- *WhoAm 94*
Schierhuber, Agnes 1946- *WhoWomW 91*
Schiering, G. David 1940- *WhoAmL 94*
Schierlman, Dixie Lee 1951- *WhoMW 93*
Schiermeyer, Ruth Corry 1938- *WhoAmP 93*
Schieser, Hans Alois 1931- *WhoAm 94*
Schieske, Alfred d1970 *WhoHol 92*
Schiess, Klaus Joachim 1938- *WhoScEn 94*
Schiessl, Carl John 1959- *WhoAmP 93*
Schiessler, Robert Walter 1918- *WhoAm 94*
Schiesswohl, Cynthia Rae Schlegel 1955- *WhoAmL 94*
Schietinger, James Frederick 1946- *WhoAmA 93*
Schifeling, Barbara Lee 1947- *WhoAmL 94*
Schiff, (Adele M.) 1915- *WhoAmA 93*
Schiff, Adam Bennett 1960- *WhoWest 94*
Schiff, Albert 1893- *WhAm 10*
Schiff, Andras 1953- *IntWW 93, Who 94*
Schiff, April 1957- *WhoAmL 94*
Schiff, David 1945- *NewGrDO*
Schiff, David Tevele 1936- *WhoAm 94*
Schiff, Donald Wilfred 1925- *WhoAm 94*
Schiff, Dorothy 1923-1989 *WhAm 10*
Schiff, Edward H. 1944- *WhoAmL 94*
Schiff, Emile Louis Constant 1918- *IntWW 93*
Schiff, Eric Allan 1950- *WhoScEn 94*
Schiff, Eugene Roger 1937- *WhoAm 94*
Schiff, Gert K. A. 1926-1990 *WhoAmA 93N*
Schiff, Gilbert Martin 1931- *WhoScEn 94*
Schiff, Gunther Hans 1927- *WhoAm 94, WhoAmL 94, WhoWest 94*
Schiff, Harold Irvin 1923- *WhoAm 94*
Schiff, Harris *DrAPF 93*
Schiff, Jayne Nemerow 1945- *WhoFI 94*
Schiff, Jean 1929- *WhoAmA 93*
Schiff, Jerome Arnold 1931- *WhoAm 94*
Schiff, John Jefferson 1916- *WhoAm 94, WhoFI 94, WhoIns 94*
Schiff, Kenneth Edmund 1963- *WhoAmL 94*
Schiff, Laurie 1960- *WhoAmL 94, WhoWest 94*
Schiff, Lonny *WhoAmA 93*
Schiff, Marlene Sandler *WhoFI 94*
Schiff, Martha May 1924- *WhoAmP 93*
Schiff, Martin 1922- *WhoAm 94*
Schiff, Molly Jeanette 1927- *WhoMW 93*
Schiff, Stefan Otto 1930- *WhoAm 94*
Schiff, Steven 1947- *CngDr 93*
Schiff, Steven Harvey 1947- *WhoAm 94, WhoAmP 93, WhoWest 94*
Schiffbauer, William G. 1954- *WhoAmL 94, WhoAmP 93*
Schiffel, Suzanne Driscoll 1946- *WhoMW 93*
Schiffeler, John William 1940- *WhoWest 94*
Schiffer, Claudia 1971- *IntWW 93*
Schiffer, Daniel L. *WhoAm 94, WhoFI 94*
Schiffer, John Paul 1930- *WhoAm 94*
Schiffer, Menahem Max 1911- *IntWW 93*
Schiffer, Michael Brian 1947- *WhoWest 94*
Schiffer, Nancy Jean 1950- *WhoAmL 94*
Schiffman, David M. 1953- *WhoAm 94, WhoAmL 94*
Schiffman, Gerald 1926- *WhoAm 94*
Schiffman, Harold Fosdick 1938- *WhoAm 94*
Schiffman, Joseph Harris 1914- *WhoAm 94*
Schiffman, Louis F. 1927- *WhoFI 94, WhoScEn 94*
Schiffman, Robert S. 1944- *WhoAm 94*
Schiffman, Yale Marvin 1938- *WhoAm 94*
Schiffner, Charles Robert 1948- *WhoScEn 94, WhoWest 94*
Schiffner, Joan Lessing 1944- *WhoWest 94*
Schiffrin, Andre 1935- *IntWW 93, WhoAm 94*
Schiffrin, Milton Julius 1914- *WhoScEn 94, WhoWest 94*
Schifrin, Lalo 1932- *IntDcF 2-4, IntMPA 94, WhoAm 94*
Schifter, Peter Mark d1993 *NewYTBS 93*
Schifter, Richard 1923- *WhoAm 94, WhoAmP 93*
Schifter, Richard Paul 1953- *WhoAmL 94*
Schikaneder, Emanuel (Johann Joseph) 1751-1812 *NewGrDO [port]*
Schikaneder, Karl 1770-1845 *NewGrDO*
Schilbrack, Karen Gail 1949- *WhoWest 94*
Schild, Geoffrey Christopher 1935- *Who 94*
Schild, Kenneth R. 1943- *WhoAmL 94*
Schildberg, Yvonne Marie 1927- *WhoAmP 93*
Schildhause, Sol 1917- *WhoAmL 94*
Schildknecht, Dorothy E. 1943- *WhoAmA 93*
Schildkraut, Joseph d1964 *WhoHol 92*
Schildkraut, Joseph Jacob 1934- *WhoAm 94*
Schildkraut, Rudolph d1930 *WhoHol 92*
Schilffarth, Richard Allen 1931- *WhoAmP 93*
Schilhab, Sian Rose 1963- *WhoAmL 94*
Schiliro, Kelly Ann 1959- *WhoMW 93*
Schill, Gilbert E., Jr. 1946- *WhoAmL 94*
Schillaci, Salvatore 1964- *WorESoc*
Schiller, Alfred George 1918- *WhoAm 94*
Schiller, Arthur A. 1910- *WhoAm 94*
Schiller, Arthur Michael 1930- *WhoAmL 94*
Schiller, Beatrice *WhoAmA 93*
Schiller, Dan(iel T.) 1951- *WrDr 94*
Schiller, Daniel Toby 1951- *WhoWest 94*
Schiller, Danny *WhoHol 92*
Schiller, Donald Charles 1942- *WhoAm 94, WhoAmL 94*
Schiller, Eric M. 1946- *WhoAm 94, WhoAmL 94*
Schiller, Francis 1909- *WhoAm 94*
Schiller, Fred 1924- *IntMPA 94*
Schiller, Frederick 1901- *WhoHol 92*
Schiller, Friedrich 1940- *WhoMW 93*
Schiller, (Johann Christoph) Friedrich von 1759-1805 *EncEth, NewGrDO*
Schiller, (Johnann Christoph) Friedrich von 1759-1805 *IntDcT 2 [port]*
Schiller, Herbert Irving 1919- *WhoAm 94*
Schiller, James Joseph 1933- *WhoAm 94, WhoAmP 93*
Schiller, Jerome Paul 1934- *WhoAm 94*
Schiller, Jerry A. 1932- *WhoAm 94*
Schiller, JoAnn 1949- *ConAu 140*
Schiller, Johannes August 1923- *WhoWest 94*
Schiller, Jonathan David 1946- *WhoAm 94, WhoAmL 94*
Schiller, Karl 1911- *IntWW 93, Who 94*
Schiller, Laurence Dana 1950- *WhoMW 93*
Schiller, Lawrence J. 1936- *IntMPA 94*
Schiller, Lawrence Julian 1936- *WhoAm 94*
Schiller, Norbert d1988 *WhoHol 92*
Schiller, Pieter Jon 1938- *WhoAm 94*
Schiller, William Edward 1909-1990 *WhAm 10*
Schiller, William Richard 1937- *WhoAm 94*
Schillhammer, David *WhoMW 93*
Schilling, Albert Henry 1943- *WhoAm 94*
Schilling, Allan Edward 1935- *WhoFI 94*
Schilling, Arlo Leonard 1924- *WhoAm 94*
Schilling, Dean William 1944- *WhoWest 94*
Schilling, Don Russell 1951- *WhoMW 93*
Schilling, Donald 1935- *WhoMW 93*
Schilling, Edward George 1931- *WhoFI 94*
Schilling, Edwin Carlyle, III 1943- *WhoAmL 94*
Schilling, Franklin Charles, Jr. 1958- *WhoFI 94*
Schilling, Frederick Augustus, Jr. 1931- *WhoScEn 94, WhoWest 94*
Schilling, Gertrud 1949- *WhoWomW 91*
Schilling, Gus d1957 *WhoHol 92*
Schilling, Hartmut 1951- *WhoScEn 94*
Schilling, John Albert 1917- *WhoAm 94*
Schilling, John Michael 1951- *WhoAm 94*
Schilling, Katherine Lee Tracy 1925- *WhoMW 93*
Schilling, Margaret d1976 *WhoHol 92*
Schilling, Marion 1911- *WhoHol 92*
Schilling, Mike *WhoAmP 93*
Schilling, Mona Lee C. 1941- *WhoHisp 94*
Schilling, Ralph Franklin 1921- *WhoAm 94*
Schilling, Richard James 1933- *WhoWest 94*
Schilling, Richard M. 1937- *WhoAm 94, WhoAmL 94*
Schilling, Richard Selwyn Francis 1911- *Who 94*
Schilling, Stephen William 1946- *WhoAmP 93*
Schilling, Vivian *WhoHol 92*
Schilling, William G. *WhoHol 92*
Schilling, William Joseph 1947- *WhoAmL 94*
Schilling, William Richard 1933- *WhoFI 94, WhoScEn 94*
Schillinger, Edwin Joseph 1923- *WhoAm 94*
Schillings, Max von 1868-1933 *NewGrDO*
Schilplin, Yvonne Winter 1946- *WhoMW 93*
Schilpp, Paul A(rthur) 1897- *WrDr 94*
Schilpp, Paul A(rthur) 1897-1993 *ConAu 142*
Schilpp, Paul Arthur 1897- *IntWW 93, WhoAm 94*
Schilsky, Richard Lewis 1950- *WhoAm 94, WhoMW 93*
Schilt, Earl Alfred 1915- *WhoFI 94*
Schiltz, Hugo 1927- *IntWW 93*
Schiltz, John Raymond 1941- *WhoScEn 94*
Schily, Otto 1932- *IntWW 93*
Schimansky, Donya Dobrila *WhoAmA 93*
Schimberg, Armand Bruce 1927- *WhoAm 94*
Schimberg, Barbara Hodes 1941- *WhoMW 93*
Schimberg, Henry Aaron 1933- *WhoAm 94, WhoFI 94*
Schimberg, Lee 1931- *WhoMW 93*
Schimberni, Mario 1923- *IntWW 93*
Schimek, DiAnna R. 1940- *WhoMW 93*
Schimek, Dianna Ruth 1940- *WhoAmP 93*
Schimel, Samuel Jerome 1920- *WhoMW 93*
Schimelpfenig, Clarence William, Jr. 1930- *WhoAm 94*
Schimer, Maria R. *WhoAmL 94*
Schimke, Dennis J. *WhoAmP 93*

Schimke, Robert Tod 1932- *WhoAm 94*
Schimmel, Allan 1940- *WhoAm 94*
Schimmel, Bruce Ian 1951- *WhoAmL 94*
Schimmel, Morry Leon 1927- *WhoMW 93*
Schimmel, Paul Reinhard 1940- *WhoAm 94, WhoScEn 94*
Schimminger, Robin 1947- *WhoAmP 93*
Schimon, Adolf 1820-1887 *NewGrDO*
Schimpf, David Jeffrey 1948- *WhoMW 93*
Schimpf, John Joseph 1949- *WhoAm 94*
Schimpff, Jill Wagner 1945- *WrDr 94*
Schimpff, Stephen Callender 1941- *WhoAm 94*
Schinagl, Erich Friedrich 1932- *WhoAm 94*
Schindel, Cy (Seymore) d1948 *WhoHol 92*
Schindel, Donald Marvin 1932- *WhoAm 94*
Schindel, John 1955- *SmATA 77 [port]*
Schindel, Robert 1944- *NewYTBS 93 [port]*
Schindelmeisser, Louis (Alexander Balthasar) 1811-1864 *NewGrDO*
Schinderle, Robert Frank 1923- *WhoAm 94*
Schindler, Abbott Michael 1950- *WhoWest 94*
Schindler, Albert Isadore 1927- *WhoAm 94*
Schindler, Alexander Moshe 1925- *IntWW 93, WhoAm 94*
Schindler, Devin Sean 1961- *WhoAmL 94*
Schindler, Judith Kay 1941- *WhoMW 93*
Schindler, Keith William 1959- *WhoWest 94*
Schindler, Marvin Samuel 1932- *WhoAm 94*
Schindler, Orville L. *WhoAmP 93*
Schindler, Pesach 1931- *WhoAm 94*
Schindler, Peter David 1931- *WhoAm 94*
Schindler, Povl Christian 1648-1740 *NewGrDO*
Schindler, R. M. 1887-1953 *WhoAmA 93N*
Schindler, S(teven) D. 1952- *SmATA 75*
Schindler, William Stanley 1933- *WhoAm 94*
Schine, G. David 1927- *IntMPA 94*
Schine, Gerard David 1927- *WhoAm 94*
Schine, Jerome Adrian 1926- *WhoFI 94*
Schink, Frank Edward 1922- *WhoAm 94*
Schink, James Harvey 1943- *WhoAm 94, WhoAmL 94*
Schinke, Tad Frederick 1959- *WhoFI 94, WhoMW 93*
Schinkel, Karl Friedrich 1781-1841 *NewGrDO*
Schinske, John Louis 1957- *WhoFI 94*
Schinsky, William Charles 1946- *WhoAmA 93*
Schinto, Jeanne *DrAPF 93*
Schinto, Jeanne 1951- *WrDr 94*
Schinzinger, Roland 1926- *WhoWest 94*
Schiotz, Aksel d1975 *WhoHol 92*
Schiotz, Aksel (Hauch) 1906-1975 *NewGrDO*
Schipa, Carlo d1988 *WhoHol 92*
Schipa, Tito d1965 *WhoHol 92*
Schipa, Tito 1888-1965 *NewGrDO [port]*
Schipke, Roger W. *WhoAm 94, WhoFI 94*
Schippa, Joseph Thomas, Jr. 1957- *WhoScEn 94*
Schippel, Eliana M. 1942- *WhoHisp 94*
Schipper, Anna d1978 *WhoHol 92*
Schipper, Emil (Zacharias) 1882-1957 *NewGrDO*
Schipper, Leon 1928- *WhoScEn 94*
Schipper, Merle Solway *WhoAmA 93*
Schippers, Adair Tune 1939- *WhoAmP 93*
Schippers, David Philip 1929- *WhoAm 94*
Schippers, Thomas 1930-1977 *NewGrDO*
Schira, Cynthia 1934- *WhoAmA 93*
Schira, Francesco 1809-1883 *NewGrDO*
Schirmacher, Kathe 1859-1930 *BlmGWL*
Schirmacher, Peter 1961- *WhoScEn 94*
Schirmacher, Stanley L. 1908- *WhoWest 94*
Schirmbeck, Heinrich 1915- *IntWW 93*
Schirmeister, Charles F. 1929- *WhoAm 94*
Schirmer, Edward Adolph 1901-1989 *WhAm 10*
Schirmer, Henry William 1922- *WhoAm 94*
Schirmer, Howard August, Jr. 1942- *WhoScEn 94*
Schirn, Janet Sugerman *WhoAm 94*
Schirner, Jochen 1939- *IntWW 93*
Schiro-Geist, Chrisann 1946- *WhoMW 93*
Schirr, Gary Richard 1954- *WhoFI 94*
Schirra, Walter Marty, Jr. 1923- *WhoAm 94, WhoScEn 94*
Schirtzinger, Barbara Ann 1959- *WhoMW 93*
Schisgal, Murray *DrAPF 93*
Schisgal, Murray 1926- *WrDr 94*
Schisgal, Murray (Joseph) 1926- *ConDr 93*
Schisgal, Murray Joseph 1926- *WhoAm 94*
Schisler, J(ohn) Harry 1893- *WhAm 10*
Schisler, Kenneth David 1969- *WhoAmP 93*
Schiszik, Keith N. 1948- *WhoAmL 94*
Schiuma, Alfred Luis 1885-1963 *NewGrDO*
Schizer, Zevie Baruch 1928- *WhoAmL 94*
Schjeldahl, Peter *DrAPF 93*
Schjeldahl, Peter 1942- *WhoAmA 93*
Schjelderup, Gerhard (Rosenkrone) 1859-1933 *NewGrDO*
Schklair, Glorya Belgrade 1931- *WhoWest 94*
Schlabach, Leland A. 1931- *WhoScEn 94*
Schlachter, Herbert James 1928- *WhoFI 94*
Schlachter, James Carl 1963- *WhoFI 94*
Schlachter, Roscoe Eugene 1952- *WhoMW 93*
Schlacks, Stephen Mark 1955- *WhoAmL 94*
Schlador, Paul Raymond, Jr. 1934- *WhoFI 94, WhoWest 94*
Schlaefer, Salvador d1993 *NewYTBS 93*
Schlaeger, Wolfgang 1942- *WhoIns 94*
Schlafer, Donald Hughes 1948- *WhoAm 94*
Schlaff, Barbara E. 1950- *WhoAmL 94*
Schlafly, Daniel Lyons, Jr. 1940- *WhoMW 93*
Schlafly, Hubert Joseph, Jr. 1919- *WhoAm 94*
Schlafly, Phyllis Stewart 1924- *AmSocL, WhoAm 94, WhoAmP 93*
Schlag, Edward William 1932- *IntWW 93, WhoScEn 94*
Schlagel, Richard H. 1925- *WhoAm 94*
Schlageter, Robert William 1925- *WhoAm 94, WhoAmA 93*
Schlagintweit, Adolf Von 1829-1857 *WhWE*
Schlagintweit, Hermann Von 1822-1882 *WhWE*
Schlagintweit, Robert Von 1833-1885 *WhWE*
Schlaifer, Charles 1909- *IntMPA 94, WhoAm 94*
Schlaifer, Robert Osher 1914- *WhoAm 94*
Schlaikjer, Jes (Wilhelm) 1897-1982 *WhoAmA 93N*
Schlais, John Henry 1960- *WhoMW 93*
Schlam, Murray J. 1911- *WhoAmA 93*
Schlang, David 1912- *WhoAmL 94, WhoFI 94*
Schlang, Joseph 1911- *IntMPA 94*
Schlanger, Jeff 1937- *WhoAmA 93*
Schlanger, Michael Asher 1943- *WhoAmL 94*
Schlanser, Theresa Dianne 1963- *WhoMW 93*
Schlant, Robert Carl 1929- *WhoAm 94*
Schlapak, Benjamin Rudolph 1937- *WhoWest 94*
Schlarman, Stanley Gerard 1933- *WhoAm 94, WhoMW 93*
Schlather, Mary Agnes 1961- *WhoMW 93*
Schlatter, Charlie 1966- *WhoHol 92*
Schlatter, George 1932- *IntMPA 94*
Schlatter, Konrad 1935- *WhoAm 94, WhoFI 94*
Schlatter, Michael 1716-1790 *DcAmReB 2*
Schlauch, Paul John 1942- *WhoAm 94*
Schlebusch, Alwyn Louis 1917- *IntWW 93*
Schlechter, Peggy Sue 1962- *WhoMW 93*
Schleck, Roth Stephen 1915- *WhoAm 94*
Schlee, Ann 1934- *WrDr 94*
Schlee, Phillip Francis 1950- *WhoMW 93*
Schlee, Walter 1942- *WhoScEn 94*
Schleede, Glenn R. 1933- *WhoAmP 93*
Schleede, Glenn Roy 1933- *WhoAm 94*
Schleeh, Hans Martin 1928- *WhoAmA 93*
Schlef, Earl L. *WhoAmP 93*
Schlegel, Dorothea 1763-1839 *BlmGWL*
Schlegel, Fred Eugene 1941- *WhoAm 94*
Schlegel, John Frederick 1944- *WhoAm 94*
Schlegel, John Peter 1943- *WhoAm 94, WhoWest 94*
Schlegel, Justin J. 1922- *WhoScEn 94*
Schlegel, Paul Lois, Jr. 1927- *WhoWest 94*
Schlegelmilch, Reuben Orville 1916- *WhoScEn 94*
Schlegel-Schelling, Caroline 1763-1809 *BlmGWL*
Schleh, Edward Carl 1915- *WhoWest 94*
Schlei, Norbert Anthony 1929- *WhoAm 94, WhoAmL 94, WhoWest 94*
Schleicher, Nora Elizabeth 1952- *WhoFI 94*
Schleichert, Elizabeth 1945- *SmATA 77 [port]*
Schleiden, Matthias Jacob 1804-1881 *WorScD*
Schleifer, Ronald 1948- *ConAu 43NR*
Schleiger, Robert Carlton *WhoAm 94*
Schleiminger, Gunther 1921- *IntWW 93*
Schlein, Betty Goldman 1931- *WhoAmP 93*
Schlein, Carol Leslie 1955- *WhoAmL 94*
Schlein, Milton Frank 1926- *WhoAmP 93*
Schlein, Miriam *WrDr 94*
Schleman, Margo Mazur 1945- *WhoMW 93*
Schlemm, Anny 1929- *NewGrDO*
Schlemm, Betty Lou 1934- *WhoAmA 93*
Schlemowitz, Abram 1911- *WhoAmA 93*
Schlemper, Elmer Otto 1939- *WhoMW 93*
Schlender, Harold Eugene 1940- *WhoAmP 93*
Schlender, William Elmer 1920- *WhoAm 94*
Schlenk, Fritz 1909- *WhoMW 93*
Schlenker, Edgar Albert 1961- *WhoWest 94*
Schlenker, Robert Alison 1940- *WhoMW 93*
Schlenker, Rudolf 1915- *IntWW 93*
Schlensker, Gary Chris 1950- *WhoAm 94*
Schlereth, Mark 1966- *WhoAm 94*
Schlesinger, Alan R. 1958- *WhoAmP 93*
Schlesinger, Albert Reuben 1941- *WhoAm 94*
Schlesinger, Alexander 1920- *WhoAmP 93*
Schlesinger, Arthur, Jr. 1917- *IntWW 93*
Schlesinger, Arthur (Meier), Jr. 1917- *Who 94, WrDr 94*
Schlesinger, Arthur Meier, Jr. 1917- *AmSocL, WhoAm 94*
Schlesinger, B. Frank 1925- *WhoAm 94*
Schlesinger, Benjamin 1928- *WrDr 94*
Schlesinger, David Harvey 1939- *WhoAm 94*
Schlesinger, Deborah Lee 1937- *WhoWest 94*
Schlesinger, Edward Bruce 1913- *WhoAm 94*
Schlesinger, Harris 1952- *WhoFI 94*
Schlesinger, Harvey Erwin 1940- *WhoAm 94, WhoAmL 94*
Schlesinger, Helmut 1924- *IntWW 93*
Schlesinger, James Rodney 1929- *IntWW 93, WhoAm 94, WhoAmP 93*
Schlesinger, John 1926- *IntMPA 94, WhoHol 92*
Schlesinger, John (Richard) 1926- *NewGrDO*
Schlesinger, John Richard 1926- *IntWW 93, Who 94, WhoAm 94*
Schlesinger, Joseph Abraham 1922- *WhoAm 94*
Schlesinger, Robert Walter 1913- *WhoAm 94*
Schlesinger, Rudolf Berthold 1909- *WhoAm 94, WhoAmL 94, WhoWest 94*
Schlesinger, Sanford Joel 1943- *WhoAm 94, WhoAmL 94, WhoFI 94*
Schlesinger, Stephen Lyons 1940- *WhoAm 94*
Schless, James Murray 1918- *WhoScEn 94*
Schless, Phyllis Ross *WhoAm 94, WhoFI 94*
Schlesselman, M. Lorraine 1926- *WhoMW 93*
Schlesser, Jerleen Ethel 1953- *WhoMW 93*
Schlessinger, Bernard S. 1930- *WhoAm 94*
Schlessinger, Joseph *WhoScEn 94*
Schlessinger, June Hirsch 1933- *WhoMW 93*
Schlett, Mary Lowrey 1938- *WhoAmP 93*
Schlettow, Hans Adelbert (Von) d1945 *WhoHol 92*
Schleusener, Richard August 1926- *WhoAm 94*
Schley, Jim *DrAPF 93*
Schley, Reeve, Jr. d1993 *NewYTBS 93*
Schley, Reeve, III 1936- *WhoAm 94*
Schley, Wayne A. 1940- *WhoAm 94*
Schleyer, Paul von Rague 1930- *IntWW 93, WhoAm 94*
Schleyer, Robert John 1946- *WhoFI 94*
Schlicher, Harlan K. J. 1945- *WhoAmP 93*
Schlicher, John W. 1947- *WhoAmL 94*
Schlicher, Karl Theodore 1905-1989 *WhoAmA 93N*
Schlicht, Jane C. 1958- *WhoAmL 94*
Schlichtemeier-Nutzman, Sue Evelyn 1950- *WhoMW 93*
Schlichting, Diane Marie 1946- *WhoMW 93*
Schlick, Thomas Leroy 1950- *WhoMW 93*
Schlickau, George Hans 1922- *WhoAm 94*
Schlickman, J. Andrew 1952- *WhoAm 94*
Schliebs, Charles Allan 1950- *WhoAm 94, WhoAmL 94*
Schlieker, Janice Elaine Jones 1957- *WhoWest 94*
Schliephake, Dietrich 1930- *IntWW 93*
Schliesmann, John L. 1952- *WhoAmL 94*
Schlifer, Jo Ann T. 1930- *WhoAmP 93*
Schlimpert, Charles Edgar 1945- *WhoAm 94, WhoWest 94*
Schlindwein, James A. 1929- *WhoAm 94, WhoFI 94*
Schlinger, Warren Gleason 1923- *WhoAm 94*
Schlink, Frederick John *WhoScEn 94*
Schlissel, Lois Carter 1950- *WhoAmL 94*
Schlitt, Klaus 1938- *WhoFI 94*
Schlitter, Helga *WhoAmA 93*
Schlitter, Stanley Allen 1950- *WhoAm 94*
Schlitts, Judith Ann 1944- *WhoAmP 93*
Schlobin, Roger C(lark) 1944- *EncSF 93*
Schlobohm, John Carl 1931- *WhoScEn 94*
Schloegel, George Anthony 1940- *WhoAm 94*
Schloemann, Ernst Fritz 1926- *WhoAm 94, WhoScEn 94*
Schloemer, Paul George 1928- *WhoFI 94, WhoMW 93, WhoScEn 94*
Schloerb, Paul Richard 1919- *WhoAm 94*
Schlom, Jeffrey Bert 1942- *WhoScEn 94*
Schlomann, James M. *WhoIns 94*
Schlondorff, Volker 1939- *IntMPA 94, IntWW 93*
Schlosberg, Carl Martin 1936- *WhoAmA 93*
Schlose, William Timothy 1948- *WhoScEn 94, WhoWest 94*
Schloss, Arleen P. 1943- *WhoAmA 93*
Schloss, Danny John 1949- *WhoFI 94*
Schloss, David *DrAPF 93*
Schloss, Ernest Peter 1949- *WhoWest 94*
Schloss, Eugene Mathias, Jr. 1932- *WhoAmL 94*
Schloss, Irving S. 1945- *WhoAmL 94*
Schloss, Nathan 1927- *WhoFI 94, WhoMW 93*
Schloss, Peter Michael *WhoAmL 94*
Schloss, Samuel Leopold, Jr. 1926- *WhoAm 94*
Schloss, Stuart A., Jr. 1947- *WhoAmL 94*
Schlossberg, David L. 1952- *WhoAmL 94*
Schlossberg, Howard Barry 1950- *WhoMW 93*
Schlossberg, Julian 1942- *IntMPA 94*
Schlossberg, Stephen I. 1921- *WhoAm 94*
Schlosser, David Wayne 1958- *WhoMW 93*
Schlosser, Herbert 1929- *WhoScEn 94*
Schlosser, Herbert S. 1926- *IntMPA 94, WhoAm 94*
Schlosser, Imre 1888-1968 *WorESoc*
Schlosser, Max 1835-1916 *NewGrDO*
Schlossman, John Isaac 1931- *WhoAm 94*
Schlossman, Mitchell Lloyd 1935- *WhoScEn 94*
Schlossman, Norman Joseph 1901- *WhAm 10*
Schlossman, Stuart Franklin 1935- *WhoAm 94, WhoScEn 94*
Schlossstein, Steven 1941-1993 *WrDr 94N*
Schlosstein, William Frederic 1963- *WhoFI 94*
Schlotfeldt, Kenneth Walter 1964- *WhoMW 93*
Schlotfeldt, Rozella May 1914- *WhoAm 94*
Schlotterbeck, John Thomas 1948- *WhoMW 93*
Schlotterbeck, Walter Albert 1926- *WhoAm 94*
Schlotterer, William Lee 1955- *WhoMW 93*
Schlotthauer, Julius P. 1937- *WhoAm 94*
Schlueter, David Arnold 1946- *WhoAm 94, WhoAmL 94*
Schlueter, Gerald Francis 1961- *WhoScEn 94*
Schlueter, Irene Selma 1912- *WhoAmP 93*
Schlueter, John William 1943- *WhoFI 94*
Schlueter, Linda Lee 1947- *WhoAm 94, WhoAmL 94*
Schlueter, Michael Anthony 1959- *WhoAmL 94*
Schlueter, Stan 1945- *WhoAmP 93*
Schlumpf, Dennis Lynn 1941- *WhoAmP 93*
Schlumpf, Leon 1925- *IntWW 93*
Schlusnus, Heinrich 1888-1952 *NewGrDO*
Schlusselberg, Martin 1936- *IntMPA 94*
Schluter, Erna 1904-1969 *NewGrDO*
Schluter, Gerald Emil 1942- *WhoFI 94*
Schluter, Peter Mueller 1933- *WhoAm 94, WhoFI 94*
Schluter, Poul Holmskov 1929- *IntWW 93*
Schluter, William E. 1927- *WhoAmP 93*
Schluter-Weiner, Hilma d1956 *WhoHol 92*
Schluttenhofer, Janet Chestelynn 1953- *WhoAm 94*
Schlutter, Lois Cochrane 1953- *WhoMW 93*
Schmalbeck, Richard Louis 1947- *WhoAm 94*
Schmalbrock, Petra 1954- *WhoScEn 94*

Schmale, Allen Lee 1933- *WhoFI 94*
Schmalenbach, Werner 1920- *IntWW 93*
Schmalenberger, Jerry Lew 1934- *WhoAm 94, WhoWest 94*
Schmalensee, Richard Lee 1944- *WhoAm 94*
Schmalfeld, Robert George 1930- *WhoFI 94*
Schmalstieg, William Riegel 1929- *WhoAm 94*
Schmaltz, Roy Edgar 1937- *WhoAmA 93*
Schmaltz, Roy Edgar, Jr. 1937- *WhoWest 94*
Schmalz, Carl (Nelson), Jr. 1926- *WhoAmA 93*
Schmalz, Carl Nelson 1898- *WhAm 10*
Schmalz, Carl Nelson, Jr. 1926- *WhoAm 94*
Schmalz, Gregory David 1952- *WhoWest 94*
Schmalz, Jeffrey d1993 *NewYTBS 93 [port]*
Schmalzer, Victor David 1941- *WhoAm 94, WhoFI 94*
Schmalzried, Marvin Eugene 1924- *WhoAm 94*
Schmalzriedt, Gary 1946- *WhoIns 94*
Schmandt, Henry J. 1918- *WhoRdr 94*
Schmandt, Jurgen 1929- *WhoFI 94*
Schmandt-Besserat, Denise 1933- *ConAu 42NR, WhoAm 94, WhoAmA 93*
Schmaus, Siegfried H. A. 1915- *WhoScEn 94*
Schmeckebier, Laurence E. 1906- *WhoAmA 93N*
Schmedes, Erik 1866-1931 *NewGrDO*
Schmeidler, Blanche J. *WhoAmA 93N*
Schmeidler, Neal Francis 1948- *WhoScEn 94*
Schmeiser, Douglas A. 1934- *WrDr 94*
Schmeits, Alan Joe 1948- *WhoAmL 94*
Schmeling, Gareth 1940- *WhoAm 94*
Schmeling, Helen Margaret 1951- *WhoWest 94*
Schmeling, Max 1905- *WhoHol 92*
Schmell, Eli David 1950- *WhoScEn 94*
Schmeltz, Edward James 1949- *WhoScEn 94*
Schmeltzer, David 1930- *WhoAm 94*
Schmeltzer, Edward 1923- *WhoAm 94*
Schmeltzer, John Charles 1945- *WhoMW 93*
Schmelz, Brenda Lea 1958- *WhoAmL 94*
Schmelzel, John Edwin 1964- *WhoWest 94*
Schmelzer, D. Edwin 1941- *WhoAmL 94*
Schmelzer, Henry Louis Phillip 1943- *WhoAm 94*
Schmelzer, W. K. Norbert 1921- *IntWW 93*
Schmemann, Serge 1945- *WhoAm 94*
Schmenner, Roger William 1947- *WhoFI 94*
Schmerling, Erwin Robert 1929- *WhoAm 94*
Schmerold, Wilfried Lothar 1919- *WhoMW 93*
Schmertmann, John Henry 1928- *WhoAm 94*
Schmertz, Eric Joseph 1925- *WhoAm 94*
Schmertz, Herbert 1930- *WhoAm 94*
Schmertz, Mildred Floyd 1925- *WhoAm 94*
Schmett, Kim D. 1952- *WhoAmP 93, WhoMW 93*
Schmett, Roy Henry 1947- *WhoFI 94*
Schmetterer, Jack Baer 1931- *WhoAm 94, WhoAmL 94*
Schmetterer, Robert Allen 1943- *WhoAm 94*
Schmetzer, Alan David 1946- *WhoMW 93*
Schmetzer, William Montgomery 1924- *WhoScEn 94*
Schmid, Adolf *NewGrDO*
Schmid, Alfred Allan 1935- *WhoMW 93*
Schmid, Anthony Peter 1931- *WhoScEn 94*
Schmid, Charles Ernest 1940- *WhoScEn 94*
Schmid, Frank Richard 1924- *WhoAm 94*
Schmid, George Edward 1932- *WhoAmP 93*
Schmid, Hans Dieter 1939- *WhoScEn 94*
Schmid, Hans Heinrich 1937- *IntWW 93*
Schmid, Harald Heinrich Otto 1935- *WhoScEn 94*
Schmid, Horst A. *WhoWest 94*
Schmid, John 1926- *WrDr 94*
Schmid, John Haviland 1896- *WhAm 10*
Schmid, Karl Neil 1939- *WhoMW 93*
Schmid, Lynette Sue 1958- *WhoMW 93*
Schmid, Peter 1927- *WhoWest 94*
Schmid, Richard Alan 1934- *WhoAmA 93*
Schmid, Richard Jay 1929- *WhoIns 94*
Schmid, Roman G. 1928- *WhoIns 94*
Schmid, Rudi 1922- *IntWW 93, WhoAm 94, WhoFI 94*
Schmid, Rudolf 1942- *WhoWest 94*

Schmid, Thomas Henderson 1943- *WhoMW 93*
Schmid, Wilfried 1943- *WhoAm 94*
Schmid, Wolfgang P(aul) 1929- *IntWW 93*
Schmidbauer, Barbara 1937- *WhoWomW 91*
Schmidbaur, Hubert 1934- *IntWW 93*
Schmidek, Henry Hans-Heinz 1937- *WhoAm 94*
Schmidhauser, John Richard 1922- *WhoAm 94, WhoAmP 93*
Schmidhuber, Peter M. 1931- *IntWW 93*
Schmidhuber, Peter Michael 1931- *Who 94*
Schmidle, Mae S. *WhoAmP 93*
Schmidly, David J. 1943- *WhoScEn 94*
Schmidman, Jo Ann *WhoMW 93*
Schmid-Schoenbein, Geert Wilfried 1948- *WhoScEn 94*
Schmidt, Adolph William 1904- *WhoAm 94*
Schmidt, Alan 1946- *WhoFI 94*
Schmidt, Alan Frederick 1925- *WhoWest 94*
Schmidt, Albert Daniel 1925- *WhoAm 94, WhoMW 93*
Schmidt, Alexander MacKay 1930-1991 *WhAm 10*
Schmidt, Arno (Otto) 1914-1979 *EncSF 93*
Schmidt, Arnold Alfred 1930- *WhoAmA 93*
Schmidt, Arthur Irwin 1927- *WhoMW 93*
Schmidt, Arthur Louis 1927- *WhoAmP 93*
Schmidt, Benno C., Jr. 1942- *IntWW 93*
Schmidt, Benno Charles 1913- *WhoAm 94*
Schmidt, Benno Charles 1942- *Who 94*
Schmidt, Benno Charles, Jr. 1942- *WhoAm 94, WrDr 94*
Schmidt, Berlie Louis 1932- *WhoAm 94*
Schmidt, Betty J. 1938- *WhoFI 94*
Schmidt, Brian Battle 1955- *WhoMW 93*
Schmidt, Bruce 1949- *WhoMW 93*
Schmidt, Carl Walter 1925- *WhoIns 94*
Schmidt, Charles 1939- *WhoAmA 93*
Schmidt, Charles Edward 1951- *WhoAmL 94*
Schmidt, Chauncey Everett 1931- *IntWW 93, WhoAm 94, WhoFI 94*
Schmidt, Christian 1938- *IntWW 93*
Schmidt, Chuck 1947- *WhoAm 94, WhoMW 93*
Schmidt, Claude Henri 1924- *WhoAm 94*
Schmidt, Connie Lu 1949- *WhoWest 94*
Schmidt, Constance Rojko 1954- *WhoScEn 94*
Schmidt, Cyril James 1939- *WhoAm 94*
Schmidt, Dan Raymond 1956- *WhoMW 93*
Schmidt, Daniel Edward, IV 1946- *WhoAmL 94, WhoIns 94*
Schmidt, David Gerard 1961- *WhoMW 93*
Schmidt, David Joseph 1947- *WhoFI 94*
Schmidt, David Kelso 1943- *WhoWest 94*
Schmidt, Debra Jean *WhoMW 93*
Schmidt, Dennis (A.) *EncSF 93*
Schmidt, Dianne Hope 1948- *WhoAmP 93*
Schmidt, Douglas W. 1942- *ConTFT 11*
Schmidt, Earl William 1936- *WhoAmP 93*
Schmidt, Edward Craig 1947- *WhoAm 94, WhoAmL 94*
Schmidt, Edward G. 1942- *WhoMW 93*
Schmidt, Edward William 1946- *WhoAmA 93*
Schmidt, Eric *DrAPF 93*
Schmidt, Eric Emerson 1955- *WhoWest 94*
Schmidt, Frank Broaker 1939- *WhoWest 94*
Schmidt, Franz 1874-1939 *NewGrDO*
Schmidt, Fred 1922- *WhoAm 94*
Schmidt, Fred Henry 1915-1991 *WhAm 10*
Schmidt, Frederick D. 1932- *WhoAmP 93*
Schmidt, Frederick Lee 1937- *WhoAmA 93*
Schmidt, Frederick Louis 1922- *WhoAmA 93*
Schmidt, Frederick Roland 1936- *WhoAmP 93*
Schmidt, Gary David 1957- *WhoMW 93*
Schmidt, Gary J. 1947- *WhoAmP 93*
Schmidt, Gary L. 1942- *WhoAmP 93*
Schmidt, Gene Earl 1942- *WhoAm 94, WhoMW 93*
Schmidt, George 1926- *WhoAm 94*
Schmidt, George Paul 1894-1989 *WhAm 10*
Schmidt, Gerhard 1919- *IntWW 93*
Schmidt, Gerhard 1924- *IntWW 93*
Schmidt, Giovanni (Federico) c. 1775-1840? *NewGrDO*
Schmidt, Glen Riley 1944- *WhoFI 94*
Schmidt, Gregory Lewis 1953- *WhoFI 94*
Schmidt, Gregory M. 1950- *WhoAmL 94*
Schmidt, Gregory Martin 1952- *WhoScEn 94*

Schmidt, Gunter 1913- *WhoMW 93*
Schmidt, Gustav 1816-1882 *NewGrDO*
Schmidt, Harold Robert 1913- *WhAm 10*
Schmidt, Heide 1948- *WhoWomW 91*
Schmidt, Heinrich 1809-1854 *NewGrDO*
Schmidt, Helmut 1918- *IntWW 93*
Schmidt, Helmut H. W. 1918- *Who 94*
Schmidt, Herman J. 1917- *WhoAm 94*
Schmidt, Howard Jerome 1955- *WhoAmP 93*
Schmidt, Jack *WhoHol 92*
Schmidt, Jack 1932- *WhoAm 94*
Schmidt, Jakob Edward 1906- *WhoAm 94, WhoMW 93*
Schmidt, James Craig 1927- *WhoAm 94, WhoFI 94*
Schmidt, James Robert 1932- *WhoScEn 94*
Schmidt, Jane Alcock 1961- *WhoFI 94*
Schmidt, Jeffrey R. 1946- *WhoAmL 94*
Schmidt, Joe *ProFbHF [port]*
Schmidt, Johann Christoph *NewGrDO*
Schmidt, Johann Philipp Samuel 1779-1853 *NewGrDO*
Schmidt, John Edward 1946- *WhoAm 94*
Schmidt, John Edward, III 1960- *WhoAmL 94*
Schmidt, John R. 1943- *WhoAm 94*
Schmidt, John Richard 1924- *WhoAmP 93*
Schmidt, John Richard 1929- *WhoAm 94*
Schmidt, John Thomas 1947- *WhoAmL 94*
Schmidt, John Thomas 1949- *WhoScEn 94*
Schmidt, John Wesley 1917- *WhoAm 94*
Schmidt, Joseph d1942 *WhoHol 92*
Schmidt, Joseph David 1937- *WhoScEn 94, WhoWest 94*
Schmidt, Joseph W. 1946- *WhoAmL 94, WhoFI 94*
Schmidt, Julius 1923- *WhoAm 94, WhoAmA 93*
Schmidt, Karen 1945- *WhoAmP 93*
Schmidt, Karen Anne 1945- *WhoWest 94*
Schmidt, Karen Lee 1953- *WhoFI 94*
Schmidt, Kari Suzanne 1957- *WhoAmL 94*
Schmidt, Karl A. 1947- *WhoAmL 94*
Schmidt, Katherine 1898-1978 *WhoAmA 93N*
Schmidt, Kathleen Marie 1953- *WhoAmL 94, WhoMW 93*
Schmidt, Kenneth Martin 1945- *WhoAm 94, WhoFI 94*
Schmidt, Kenneth Paul 1954- *WhoFI 94*
Schmidt, Kenneth Wilfred 1922- *WhoFI 94*
Schmidt, Kim d1978 *WhoHol 92*
Schmidt, Klaus Dieter 1930- *WhoAm 94*
Schmidt, Klaus Franz 1928- *WhoAm 94*
Schmidt, L. Lee, Jr. 1937- *WhoAm 94*
Schmidt, Lail William, Jr. 1936- *WhoAmL 94, WhoWest 94*
Schmidt, Leigh Eric 1961- *WrDr 94*
Schmidt, Leon Herbert 1909-1989 *WhAm 10*
Schmidt, Lynette 1952- *SmATA 76 [port]*
Schmidt, Lynn Marie Lammer 1951- *WhoMW 93*
Schmidt, Maarten 1929- *IntWW 93, WhoAm 94, WhoScEn 94, WhoWest 94*
Schmidt, Mark Alan 1948- *WhoFI 94*
Schmidt, Marlene *WhoHol 92*
Schmidt, Mary Morris 1926- *WhoAmA 93*
Schmidt, Mary Sylvia 1937- *WhoAm 94*
Schmidt, Michael (Norton) 1947- *WrDr 94*
Schmidt, Michael Edward 1949- *WhoMW 93*
Schmidt, Michael Jack 1949- *WhoAm 94*
Schmidt, Michael R. 1947- *WhoFI 94*
Schmidt, Michael Stephen 1958- *WhoMW 93*
Schmidt, Nancy Ingeborg 1962- *WhoWest 94*
Schmidt, Nancy J. 1936- *WhoAm 94*
Schmidt, Nathaniel 1862-1939 *DcAmReB 2*
Schmidt, Ole 1928- *IntWW 93*
Schmidt, Otto Y. 1891-1956 *WhWE*
Schmidt, Patricia Fain 1941- *WhoWest 94*
Schmidt, Patricia Jean 1941- *WhoMW 93*
Schmidt, Patrick W. 1950- *WhoAmL 94*
Schmidt, Paul Wickham 1948- *WhoAm 94*
Schmidt, Peter *WhoHol 92*
Schmidt, Peter W. 1947- *WhoAmL 94*
Schmidt, R. Jeffrey 1946- *WhoAmL 94*
Schmidt, Randall Bernard 1942- *WhoAmA 93*
Schmidt, Raymond 1944- *WhoAmP 93*
Schmidt, Reinhard O. 1931- *WhoMW 93*
Schmidt, Renate 1943- *WhoWomW 91*
Schmidt, Richard Marlen 1946- *WhoAmP 93*
Schmidt, Richard Marten, Jr. 1924- *WhoAm 94, WhoAmL 94*
Schmidt, Richard R. *WhoAmP 93*

Schmidt, Richard S. 1948- *WhoAm 94, WhoAmL 94*
Schmidt, Robert 1927- *WhoAm 94, WhoMW 93, WhoScEn 94*
Schmidt, Robert Charles, Jr. 1942- *WhoAm 94*
Schmidt, Robert Earl 1948- *WhoAmL 94*
Schmidt, Robert Howard 1954- *WhoWest 94*
Schmidt, Robert Milton 1944- *WhoAm 94, WhoScEn 94*
Schmidt, Roger Phillip 1955- *WhoWest 94*
Schmidt, Ronald G. 1937- *WhoAmP 93*
Schmidt, Rudolph David 1928- *WhoWest 94*
Schmidt, Russel Alan, II 1953- *WhoMW 93*
Schmidt, Ruth Ann 1930- *WhoAm 94*
Schmidt, Samuel 1950- *ConAu 141, WhoHisp 94*
Schmidt, Sandra Jean 1955- *WhoFI 94*
Schmidt, Sherri Jean 1960- *WhoMW 93*
Schmidt, Stanley 1944- *EncSF 93*
Schmidt, Stanley (Albert) 1944- *WrDr 94*
Schmidt, Stanley Albert 1944- *WhoAm 94*
Schmidt, Stefan 1950- *WhoScEn 94*
Schmidt, Stephen C. 1945- *WhoFI 94*
Schmidt, Stephen Christopher 1920- *WhoAm 94, WhoMW 93, WhoScEn 94*
Schmidt, Stephen Robert 1948- *WhoAm 94*
Schmidt, Ted A. 1952- *WhoAm 94, WhoAmL 94*
Schmidt, Terry Lane 1943- *WhoAm 94, WhoWest 94*
Schmidt, Thomas Carson 1930- *WhoAm 94*
Schmidt, Thomas Joseph, Jr. 1945- *WhoAmL 94*
Schmidt, Thomas Mitchell 1956- *WhoMW 93*
Schmidt, Tom *DrAPF 93*
Schmidt, Trudeliese 1934- *NewGrDO*
Schmidt, Valerie A. 1956- *WhoMW 93*
Schmidt, Veronica Jean 1961- *WhoMW 93*
Schmidt, Waldemar Adrian 1941- *WhoWest 94*
Schmidt, Walter Friedrich 1948- *WhoScEn 94*
Schmidt, Walter J. 1923- *WhoScEn 94*
Schmidt, Wayne Walter 1941- *WhoAmL 94, WhoMW 93*
Schmidt, Wendy S. 1959- *WhoFI 94*
Schmidt, Werner P. 1932- *IntWW 93*
Schmidt, Willa *DrAPF 93*
Schmidt, William C. 1938- *WhoAm 94*
Schmidt, William C. 1940- *WhoFI 94, WhoWest 94*
Schmidt, William Joseph 1946- *WhoScEn 94*
Schmidt, Winsor Chase, Jr. 1949- *WhoAmL 94*
Schmidt, Wolf d1977 *WhoHol 92*
Schmidt, Wolf 1937- *IntMPA 94*
Schmidtchen, Rowland H. 1920- *WhoAmP 93*
Schmidt-Clausen, Kurt Hermann 1920- *IntWW 93*
Schmidt-Isserstedt, Hans 1900-1973 *NewGrDO*
Schmidtlein, Mary Virginia 1958- *WhoAmL 94, WhoMW 93*
Schmidtman, Andrew A. 1937- *WhoFI 94*
Schmidtmann, Lucie Ann 1963- *WhoFI 94, WhoScEn 94*
Schmidtmann, Victor Henry 1917- *WhoScEn 94*
Schmidtmer, Christiane 1940- *WhoHol 92*
Schmidt-Monge, Roberto *WhoAm 94, WhoAmL 94*
Schmidt-Nielsen, Bodil Mimi 1918- *WhoAm 94*
Schmidt-Nielsen, Knut 1915- *IntWW 93, WhoAm 94, WrDr 94*
Schmidt-Nielson, Knut 1915- *WhoScEn 94*
Schmidt-Rohr, Ulrich 1926- *IntWW 93*
Schmiechen, Richard 1947-1993 *NewYTBS 93 [port]*
Schmied, Wieland 1929- *IntWW 93*
Schmieder, Carl 1938- *WhoFI 94, WhoWest 94*
Schmieder, Frank Joseph 1941- *WhoAm 94, WhoFI 94*
Schmiedt, Siegfried c. 1756-1799 *NewGrDO*
Schmiege, Marlin John 1947- *WhoFI 94*
Schmiege, Robert 1941- *WhoAm 94, WhoMW 93*
Schmiege, Robert W. 1941- *WhoFI 94*
Schmiegel, Klaus Kurt 1939- *WhoMW 93*
Schmincke, George Thomas 1923- *WhoAmP 93*
Schmit, David E. 1947- *WhoAmL 94*
Schmit, Herman H. 1939- *WhoIns 94*
Schmit, Kenneth William 1935- *WhoFI 94*

Schmit, Lucien Andre, Jr. 1928- *WhoAm 94*
Schmit, Patricia Brady 1943- *WrDr 94*
Schmit, Peter Alan 1963- *WhoAmL 94*
Schmitt, Bernard W. *WhoAm 94*
Schmitt, C. L. 1912- *WhoAmP 93*
Schmitt, Edward E. 1926- *WhoAm 94*
Schmitt, Francis Otto 1903- *IntWW 93, WhoAm 94*
Schmitt, Frederick Adrian 1953- *WhoScEn 94*
Schmitt, Frederick Francis 1951- *WhoMW 93*
Schmitt, George Frederick, Jr. 1939- *WhoAm 94*
Schmitt, George Herbert 1939- *WhoAm 94*
Schmitt, George Joseph 1928- *WhoAm 94*
Schmitt, Gilbert James 1963- *WhoMW 93*
Schmitt, Harrison H. 1935- *IntWW 93*
Schmitt, Harrison Hagan 1935- *WhoAm 94, WhoAmP 93, WhoScEn 94*
Schmitt, Heinz-Josef 1954- *WhoScEn 94*
Schmitt, Jerry 1938- *WhoAmP 93*
Schmitt, Joe 1939- *WhoIns 94*
Schmitt, John Edward 1938- *WhoAm 94*
Schmitt, Karl Michael 1922- *WhoAm 94*
Schmitt, Louis Alfred 1941- *WhoScEn 94*
Schmitt, Margaret Schomburg 1927- *WhoMW 93*
Schmitt, Marilyn Low 1939- *WhoAmA 93, WhoWest 94*
Schmitt, Mark F. 1923- *WhoAm 94, WhoMW 93*
Schmitt, Michael A. *WhoScEn 94*
Schmitt, Neil Martin 1940- *WhoScEn 94*
Schmitt, Patricia Ellen 1950- *WhoMW 93*
Schmitt, Peter *DrAPF 94*
Schmitt, Ralph George 1944- *WhoFI 94*
Schmitt, Richard George 1948- *WhoWest 94*
Schmitt, Roland Walter 1923- *WhoAm 94, WhoFI 94, WhoScEn 94*
Schmitt, Roman Augustine 1925- *WhoWest 94*
Schmitt, Roselyn Josephine 1935- *WhoMW 93*
Schmitt, Ruth Ann 1940- *WhoMW 93*
Schmitt, William Howard 1936- *WhoFI 94, WhoScEn 94*
Schmitt, William Thomas 1954- *WhoFI 94*
Schmitt, Wolfgang Rudolph 1944- *WhoAm 94, WhoMW 93*
Schmittbaur, Joseph Aloys 1718-1809 *NewGrDO*
Schmitter, Charles Harry 1928- *WhoAm 94*
Schmitthoff, Clive Macmillan 1903-1990 *WrDr 94N*
Schmitt-Walter, Karl 1900-1985 *NewGrDO*
Schmitt-Weigand, Adolf 1934- *IntWW 93*
Schmitz, Carl Ludwig 1900-1967 *WhoAmA 93N*
Schmitz, Charles Edison 1919- *WhoWest 94*
Schmitz, David F. 1956- *WrDr 94*
Schmitz, Dennis *DrAPF 93*
Schmitz, Dennis 1937- *WrDr 94*
Schmitz, Dennis Mathew 1937- *WhoAm 94, WhoWest 94*
Schmitz, Dolores Jean 1931- *WhoMW 93*
Schmitz, Edward Henry 1929- *WhoFI 94*
Schmitz, Geraldine *DrAPF 93*
Schmitz, James H(enry) 1911-1981 *EncSF 93*
Schmitz, John Albert 1940- *WhoAm 94*
Schmitz, John Anthony 1955- *WhoFI 94*
Schmitz, John G. 1930- *WhoAmP 93*
Schmitz, John Patrick 1955- *WhoAmL 94*
Schmitz, Judy Neal 1961- *WhoAmL 94*
Schmitz, Marcelle *WhoHol 92*
Schmitz, Mary Virginia 1956- *WhoMW 93*
Schmitz, Ray, III 1949- *WhoMW 93*
Schmitz, Robert Allen 1941- *WhoAm 94*
Schmitz, Robert Joseph 1921- *WhoAmP 93*
Schmitz, Robert Lenzen 1951- *WhoWest 94*
Schmitz, Roger Anthony 1934- *WhoAm 94*
Schmitz, Shirley Gertrude 1927- *WhoMW 93*
Schmitz, Stephen Louis 1953- *WhoFI 94, WhoMW 93*
Schmitz, Sybille d1955 *WhoHol 92*
Schmitz, Vincent Herman 1946- *WhoWest 94*
Schmitz, Wolfgang 1923- *IntWW 93*
Schmitzer, Henrietta d1979 *WhoHol 92*
Schmocker, Kenneth Ernest 1953- *WhoMW 93*
Schmoeller, David *HorFD*
Schmoeller, David 1947- *IntMPA 94*
Schmoke, Kurt 1949- *WhoAm 94*

Schmoke, Kurt L. 1949- *AfrAmAl 6 [port], WhoAmP 94*
Schmoke, Kurt Lidell *WhoBlA 94*
Schmoke, Leroy Joseph, III 1944- *WhoFI 94*
Schmokel, Wolfe W(illiam) 1933- *WrDr 94*
Schmolka, Leo Louis 1939- *WhoAm 94, WhoAmL 94*
Schmoll, Harry F., Jr. 1939- *WhoAm 94, WhoAmL 94*
Schmookler, Andrew Bard 1946- *WrDr 94*
Schmucker, Bruce Owen 1961- *WhoScEn 94*
Schmucker, Martha 1948- *WhoMW 93*
Schmucker, Ruby Elvy Ladrach 1923- *WhoMW 93*
Schmucker, Samuel Simon 1799-1873 *DcAmReB 2*
Schmude, Jurgen 1936- *IntWW 93*
Schmuff, Norman Robert 1952- *WhoScEn 94*
Schmuhl, Robert (Philip) 1948- *WrDr 94*
Schmuhl, Thomas Roeger 1946- *WhoAm 94, WhoAmL 94*
Schmukler, Eli H. 1944- *WhoAmL 94*
Schmults, Edward C. 1931- *WhoAmP 93*
Schmults, Edward Charles 1931- *WhoAm 94, WhoAmL 94, WhoFI 94*
Schmutz, Arthur Walter 1921- *WhoAm 94, WhoWest 94*
Schmutz, Charles Reid 1942- *WhoMW 93*
Schmutz, Dana May 1938- *WhoFI 94*
Schmutz, John F. *WhoAmL 94, WhoFI 94*
Schmutz, Ray S. 1918- *WhoAmP 93*
Schmutzer, Craig Alan 1959- *WhoFI 94*
Schmutzhart, Berthold Josef 1928- *WhoAm 94, WhoWest 94*
Schmutzhart, Slaithong Chengtrakul 1934- *WhoAmA 93*
Schnaar, Ronald Lee 1950- *WhoScEn 94*
Schnabel, Johann Gottfried *EncSF 93*
Schnabel, John Henry 1915- *WhoAm 94*
Schnabel, Julian 1951- *IntWW 93, WhoAm 94, WhoAmA 93*
Schnabel, Karl Ulrich 1909- *WhoAm 94*
Schnabel, Linda Rosanne Westlund 1953- *WhoMW 93*
Schnabel, Robert Victor 1922- *WhoAm 94*
Schnabel, Rockwell Anthony 1936- *WhoAm 94*
Schnabel, Stefan 1912- *WhoHol 92*
Schnabl, Frank Joseph 1927- *WhoAmP 93*
Schnable, George Luther 1927- *WhoScEn 94*
Schnably, Michael B. 1964- *WhoFI 94*
Schnack, Gayle Hemingway Jepson 1926- *WhoFI 94, WhoWest 94*
Schnack, Larry Gene 1937- *WhoAm 94, WhoMW 93*
Schnacke, Kenneth A. 1950- *WhoMW 93*
Schnacke, Robert Howard 1913- *WhoAm 94, WhoWest 94*
Schnackel, John Charles 1955- *WhoMW 93*
Schnackenberg, Roy 1934- *WhoAmA 93*
Schnackenberg, Roy Lee 1934- *WhoAm 94*
Schnadhorst, Francis 1840-1900 *DcNaB MP*
Schnadig, Edgar Louis 1917- *WhoFI 94*
Schnaiberg, Allan 1939- *WhoAm 94*
Schnaitman, William Kenneth 1926- *WhoAm 94*
Schnaitter, Roger Howard 1942- *WhoMW 93*
Schnake, Betty B. 1930- *WhoMW 93*
Schnake, Richard Lane 1957- *WhoAmL 94*
Schnakenberg, Donald G. 1939- *WhoAm 94*
Schnakenberg, Henry 1892-1970 *WhoAmA 93N*
Schnall, Edith Lea 1922- *WhoAm 94, WhoScEn 94*
Schnapf, Abraham 1921- *WhoScEn 94*
Schnapp, Roger Herbert 1946- *WhoAmL 94, WhoFI 94, WhoWest 94*
Schnare, Paul Stewart 1936- *WhoScEn 94*
Schnatterly, Stephen E. 1938- *WhoAm 94*
Schnaut, Gabriele 1953- *NewGrDO*
Schnautz, William Arthur 1938- *WhoFI 94*
Schnebel, Dieter 1930- *NewGrDO*
Schneberg, Willa *DrAPF 93*
Schnebly, Francis David 1926- *WhoWest 94*
Schneck, Gary Alan 1953- *WhoFI 94*
Schneck, Jerome M. 1920- *WhoAm 94, WhoScEn 94*
Schneck, Stuart Austin 1929- *WhoAm 94*
Schneckenburger, Karen Lynne 1949- *WhoFI 94*
Schnee, Charles 1916-1963 *IntDcF 2-4*
Schneebaum, Steven Marc 1948- *WhoAm 94*
Schneebaum, Tobias *DrAPF 93*

Schneebaum, Tobias 1921- *WhoAmA 93, WrDr 94*
Schneeberger, Eveline Elsa 1934- *WhoScEn 94*
Schneegurt, Mark Allen 1962- *WhoScEn 94*
Schneeman, Charles 1912-1972 *EncSF 93*
Schneeman, Elio *DrAPF 93*
Schneeman, Peter *DrAPF 93*
Schneemann, Carolee *DrAPF 93*
Schneemann, Carolee 1939- *WhoAmA 93*
Schneemelcher, Wilhelm 1914- *IntWW 93*
Schneer, Charles H. *EncSF 93*
Schneer, Charles H. 1920- *IntMPA 94*
Schneeweis, Harold Nathan 1938- *WhoWest 94*
Schneewind, Jerome Borges 1930- *WhoAm 94*
Schneibel, Vicki Darlene 1946- *WhoWest 94*
Schneider, Aaron *DrAPF 93*
Schneider, Adam Louis 1956- *WhoFI 94*
Schneider, Alexander 1908-1993 *CurBio 93N, NewYTBS 93 [port]*
Schneider, Allan Frank 1926- *WhoMW 93*
Schneider, Allan Stanford 1940- *WhoAm 94*
Schneider, Anni Christine 1952- *WhoWest 94*
Schneider, Arnold Mark 1945- *WhoWest 94*
Schneider, Arthur 1947- *WhoFI 94, WhoScEn 94*
Schneider, Arthur Paul 1930- *WhoAm 94*
Schneider, Arthur Sanford 1929- *WhoAm 94*
Schneider, B(etty) V(ance) H(umphreys) 1927- *WrDr 94*
Schneider, Barry Charles 1943- *WhoWest 94*
Schneider, Bart *DrAPF 93*
Schneider, Ben Ross, Jr. 1920- *WrDr 94*
Schneider, Benjamin 1938- *WhoAm 94*
Schneider, Bobby Dean 1937- *WhoFI 94*
Schneider, Bruce H. 1949- *WhoAmL 94*
Schneider, Calvin 1924- *WhoScEn 94, WhoWest 94*
Schneider, Carl W. 1932- *WhoAm 94*
Schneider, Charles I. 1923- *WhoAm 94, WhoWest 94*
Schneider, Claudine Cmarada 1947- *WhoAmP 93, WhoWomW 91*
Schneider, Cyril M. 1929- *WhoAm 94*
Schneider, Dan W. 1947- *WhoAm 94*
Schneider, Daniel *WhoHol 92*
Schneider, Daniel Mark 1960- *WhoAmL 94*
Schneider, David Miller 1937- *WhoAm 94, WhoAmL 94*
Schneider, David T. 1922- *WhoAmP 93*
Schneider, David Walter 1942- *WhoAmL 94*
Schneider, Dawn *WhoHol 92*
Schneider, Deena Jo 1950- *WhoAmL 94*
Schneider, Dennis Eugene 1957- *WhoFI 94*
Schneider, Dick *IntMPA 94*
Schneider, Dieter 1935- *IntWW 93*
Schneider, Donald Erik 1965- *WhoWest 94*
Schneider, Donald Frederic 1939- *WhoAm 94*
Schneider, Duane Bernard 1937- *WhoAm 94*
Schneider, Earl Gary 1933- *WhoAmL 94*
Schneider, Edward Lee 1947- *WhoAm 94, WhoWest 94*
Schneider, Edward Lewis 1940- *WhoAm 94, WhoScEn 94, WhoWest 94*
Schneider, Eleonora Frey 1921- *WhoScEn 94*
Schneider, Elisa *SmATA 76*
Schneider, Elisabeth Winterstein 1897- *WhAm 10*
Schneider, Elizabeth Lynn *DrAPF 93*
Schneider, Ellen Shiffrin 1943- *WhoAmL 94*
Schneider, Franz d1993 *NewYTBS 93 [port]*
Schneider, Frederick H. d1991 *WhAm 10*
Schneider, Frederick William, Jr. 1923- *WhoAm 94*
Schneider, Gene W. 1926- *WhoAm 94, WhoFI 94, WhoWest 94*
Schneider, George Alan 1946- *WhoAmL 94*
Schneider, George T. *WhoAm 94*
Schneider, George William 1916- *WhoAm 94*
Schneider, George William 1923- *WhoScEn 94*
Schneider, Gerald Edward 1940- *WhoAm 94*
Schneider, Gregory James 1959- *WhoMW 93*
Schneider, Greta Sara 1954- *WhoFI 94*
Schneider, Gunther d1956 *WhoHol 92*

Schneider, Gustavo Francisco 1960- *WhoHisp 94*
Schneider, Harold Joel 1923- *WhoAm 94*
Schneider, Harold Lawrence 1942- *WhoAmL 94*
Schneider, Harry H., Jr. 1954- *WhoAmL 94*
Schneider, Helen *WhoHol 92*
Schneider, Helen Nancy 1961- *WhoMW 93*
Schneider, Herbert William 1930- *WhoAm 94*
Schneider, Hilde d1961 *WhoHol 92*
Schneider, Hope MacAndrew *WhoFI 94*
Schneider, Hortense (Catherine-Jeanne) 1833-1920 *NewGrDO*
Schneider, Howard 1935- *WhoAm 94*
Schneider, Howard Barry 1955- *WhoWest 94*
Schneider, Howard Stewart 1945- *WhoAm 94*
Schneider, Hubert George, III 1958- *WhoWest 94*
Schneider, Ira 1939- *WhoAmA 93*
Schneider, Jacquelyn Jo 1942- *WhoMW 93*
Schneider, James d1967 *WhoHol 92*
Schneider, James Frederick 1947- *WhoAm 94, WhoAmL 94*
Schneider, James Gordon 1925- *WhoAmP 93*
Schneider, James Joseph 1947- *WhoMW 93*
Schneider, Jan 1933- *WhoAm 94*
Schneider, Janet M. 1950- *WhoAm 94, WhoAmA 93*
Schneider, Janet Marie 1966- *WhoMW 93*
Schneider, Janice Linnea 1938- *WhoFI 94*
Schneider, Jerry Allan 1937- *WhoWest 94*
Schneider, Jo Anne 1919- *WhoAmA 93*
Schneider, JoAnne 1919- *WhoAm 94*
Schneider, John 1954- *IntMPA 94, WhoHol 92*
Schneider, John A. 1926- *IntMPA 94*
Schneider, John Arnold 1926- *WhoAm 94*
Schneider, John David 1948- *WhoMW 93*
Schneider, John Durbin 1937- *WhoAmP 94*
Schneider, John G. 1908?-1964 *EncSF 93*
Schneider, John Hoke 1931- *WhoAm 94*
Schneider, John T. 1945- *WhoAmP 93*
Schneider, John Thomas *WhoAmL 94*
Schneider, Jon D. 1944- *WhoAm 94, WhoAmL 94*
Schneider, Joseph Francis 1932- *WhoWest 94*
Schneider, Judith Lynn 1944- *WhoMW 93*
Schneider, Julie (Saecker) 1944- *WhoAmA 93*
Schneider, Julius 1926- *WhoAmL 94*
Schneider, Karen Bush 1951- *WhoAmL 94*
Schneider, Keith Hilary 1956- *WhoAm 94*
Schneider, Kurt 1887-1967 *EncSPD*
Schneider, Lancelot Raymond A. *Who 94*
Schneider, Lawrence Paul 1938- *WhoAm 94*
Schneider, Laz Levkoff 1939- *WhoAmL 94*
Schneider, Linda Ann 1945- *WhoFI 94*
Schneider, Linda Eve 1954- *WhoAmL 94*
Schneider, Lisa Dawn 1954- *WhoAmA 93*
Schneider, Lloyd Rhynehart 1949- *WhoAmL 94*
Schneider, Magda 1909- *WhoHol 92*
Schneider, Mahlon C. 1939- *WhoAmL 94*
Schneider, Maria 1952- *WhoHol 92*
Schneider, Maria Kristine 1963- *WhoMW 93*
Schneider, Mark *WhoHol 92*
Schneider, Mark 1946- *WhoAm 94*
Schneider, Mark Lewis 1941- *WhoAm 94*
Schneider, Marlin Dale 1942- *WhoAmP 93*
Schneider, Martina *ConAu 142*
Schneider, Marvin Walter 1936- *WhoFI 94*
Schneider, Matthew Roger 1948- *WhoAm 94*
Schneider, Meier *WhoWest 94*
Schneider, Melvin 1914-1990 *WhAm 10*
Schneider, Michael A. 1950- *WhoAmP 93*
Schneider, Michael Joseph 1938- *WhoAm 94*
Schneider, Nell 1940- *WhoFI 94*
Schneider, Nina *DrAPF 93*
Schneider, Noel 1920- *WhoAmA 93*
Schneider, Norman M. 1911- *WhoAm 94*
Schneider, Oscar 1927- *IntWW 93*
Schneider, Pam Horvitz 1951- *WhoAm 94, WhoAmL 94*
Schneider, Pat *DrAPF 93*
Schneider, Paul J. 1944- *WhoAmL 94*
Schneider, Peter, III 1953- *WhoAmP 93*
Schneider, Peter Raymond 1939- *WhoAm 94, WhoFI 94*
Schneider, Phyllis Leah 1947- *WhoAm 94*

Schneider, Raymond Clinton 1920- *WhoAm 94*
Schneider, Richard Alexander 1945- *WhoAmL 94*
Schneider, Richard Clarence 1927- *WhoWest 94*
Schneider, Richard Durbin 1937- *WhoAmA 93*
Schneider, Richard Graham 1930- *WhoAm 94, WhoAmL 94*
Schneider, Richard J. 1936- *WhoAmP 93*
Schneider, Richard Theodore 1927- *WhoAm 94*
Schneider, Richard William 1946- *WhoAm 94*
Schneider, Robert E., II 1939- *WhoAmL 94*
Schneider, Robert Jay 1949- *WhoScEn 94*
Schneider, Robert Jerome 1947- *WhoAm 94, WhoAmL 94*
Schneider, Robert W. 1933- *WrDr 94*
Schneider, Romy d1982 *WhoHol 92*
Schneider, Roy *DrAPF 93*
Schneider, Sanford 1937- *WhoWest 94*
Schneider, Shellie 1932- *WhoAmA 93*
Schneider, Sol 1924- *WhoAm 94*
Schneider, Stephen Henry 1945- *WhoAm 94, WhoScEn 94*
Schneider, Steven Paul 1958- *WhoAmL 94*
Schneider, Thomas Aquinas 1934- *WhoMW 93*
Schneider, Thomas Edwin 1945- *WhoMW 93*
Schneider, Thomas J. 1948- *WhoAmP 93*
Schneider, Thomas Paul 1947- *WhoAmL 94*
Schneider, Thomas Richard 1945- *WhoScEn 94, WhoWest 94*
Schneider, Wesley Clair 1953- *WhoMW 93*
Schneider, Wilfred John, Jr. 1951- *WhoAmL 94*
Schneider, William, Jr. 1941- *WhoAmP 93*
Schneider, William A. 1943- *WhoFI 94*
Schneider, William Charles 1923- *WhoAm 94*
Schneider, William George 1915- *IntWW 93, Who 94, WhoAm 94*
Schneider, William George 1919- *WhoAm 94*
Schneider, William Henry 1934- *WhoAm 94*
Schneider, Willys Hope 1952- *WhoAm 94, WhoAmL 94*
Schneider, Wolf 1953- *WhoAm 94*
Schneider, Wolf-Dieter 1944- *WhoScEn 94*
Schneiderat, Catherine A. 1942- *WhoAmP 93*
Schneider-Criezis, Susan Marie 1953- *WhoMW 93, WhoScEn 94*
Schneiderhan, Wolfgang 1915- *IntWW 93*
Schneiderhan, Wolfgang, Frau *Who 94*
Schneiderman, David Abbott 1947- *WhoAm 94*
Schneiderman, Dorothy 1919- *WhoAmA 93*
Schneiderman, Herbert B. 1945- *WhoMW 93*
Schneiderman, Howard Allen 1927-1990 *WhAm 10*
Schneiderman, Irwin 1923- *WhoAm 94*
Schneiderman, L. J. *DrAPF 93*
Schneiderman, Michael Goodman 1939- *WhoAm 94*
Schneiderman, Richard S. 1948- *WhoAmA 93*
Schneiderman, Richard Steven 1948- *WhoAm 94*
Schneiderman, Rose 1882-1972 *HisWorL [port]*
Schneiderman, Rose 1884-1972 *AmSocL*
Schneiderman, William 1949- *WhoWest 94*
Schneider-Maunoury, Michel 1931- *WhoAm 94, WhoFI 94*
Schneiders, Lolita 1931- *WhoAmP 93, WhoWomW 91*
Schneiders, Sandra Marie 1936- *WhoWest 94*
Schneider-Siemssen, Gunther 1926- *NewGrDO*
Schneidman, Arnold d1993 *NewYTBS 93*
Schneidre, P. *DrAPF 93*
Schneier, Arthur 1930- *WhoAm 94*
Schneier, Donna Frances 1938- *WhoAmA 93*
Schneier, Frederick 1927- *IntMPA 94*
Schneiter, George Malan 1931- *WhoWest 94*
Schnekloth, Hugo 1923- *WhoAmP 93*
Schnell, Carlton Bryce 1932- *WhoAm 94*
Schnell, George Adam 1931- *WhoAm 94, WhoScEn 94*
Schnell, Joseph *WhoAm 94*
Schnell, Lonnie D. 1949- *WhoFI 94*

Schnell, Robert Lee, Jr. 1948- *WhoAm 94, WhoAmL 94, WhoMW 93*
Schnell, Roger Thomas 1936- *WhoFI 94, WhoWest 94*
Schnell, Ruben Enrique 1954- *WhoFI 94*
Schnell, Russell Clifford 1944- *WhoWest 94*
Schnelle, Karl Benjamin, Jr. 1930- *WhoAm 94*
Schneller, Eugene S. 1943- *WhoScEn 94, WhoWest 94*
Schneller, Richard Francis 1922- *WhoAmP 93*
Schnelling, Anthony Hendrik Nehemiah 1947- *WhoAmL 94*
Schneps, Jack 1929- *WhoAm 94*
Schnering, Philip Blessed 1917- *WhoAm 94*
Schnieder, Paul L. 1954- *WhoIns 94*
Schnier, David Christian 1942- *WhoFI 94, WhoMW 93*
Schniewind, Carl O. 1900-1957 *WhoAmA 93N*
Schnipper, Don Martin 1939- *WhoAmL 94*
Schnirman, Alan Joel 1945- *WhoAmL 94*
Schnitker, Jurgen Hinrich 1958- *WhoAmL 94*
Schnittke, Alfred *NewGrDO*
Schnittke, Alfred 1934- *IntWW 93, Who 94*
Schnittmann, Sascha S. 1913- *WhoAmA 93N*
Schnitzer, Arlene 1929- *WhoAmA 93*
Schnitzer, Arlene Director 1929- *WhoWest 94*
Schnitzer, Gary Allen 1942- *WhoWest 94*
Schnitzer, Ignaz 1839-1921 *NewGrDO*
Schnitzer, Klaus A. *WhoAmA 93*
Schnitzer, Martin C(olby) 1925- *WrDr 94*
Schnitzer, Moshe 1921- *IntWW 93*
Schnitzer, Robert C. 1906- *WhoAm 94*
Schnitzlein, Harold Norman 1927- *WhoAm 94*
Schnitzler, Arthur 1862-1931 *IntDcT 2, RfGShF*
Schnitzler, Paul 1936- *WhoScEn 94*
Schnitzler, Robert Neil 1940- *WhoScEn 94*
Schnobrich, Roger William 1929- *WhoAm 94, WhoMW 93*
Schnoebelen, Steven Craig 1957- *WhoMW 93*
Schnoes, Mark Allan 1956- *WhoMW 93*
Schnoll, Howard Manuel 1935- *WhoAm 94, WhoFI 94*
Schnoor, Jerald Lee 1950- *WhoAm 94, WhoMW 93*
Schnorr, Thomas G. 1948- *WhoAmL 94*
Schnorrenberg, John Martin 1931- *WhoAmA 93*
Schnorr von Carolsfeld, Ludwig 1836 1865 *NewGrDO [port]*
Schnose, Linda Mae 1952- *WhoMW 93*
Schnuck, Craig 1948- *WhoAm 94*
Schnucker, Robert Victor 1932- *WhoAm 94, WhoMW 93*
Schnur, Joel Martin *WhoFI 94*
Schnur, Robert Arnold 1938- *WhoAm 94*
Schnur, Steven 1952- *ConAu 140*
Schnurr, Elinore *WhoAmA 93*
Schnyder, Felix d1992 *Who 94N*
Schob, Anthony John 1898- *WhAm 10*
Schober, Charles Coleman, III 1924- *WhoAm 94*
Schober, Gary Michael 1953- *WhoAmL 94*
Schober, John C. 1951- *WhoAmP 93*
Schober, Robert Charles 1940- *WhoScEn 94, WhoWest 94*
Schoberlechner, Franz 1797-1843 *NewGrDO*
Schobesberger, Wolfgang 1960- *WhoFI 94*
Schoby, Barney 1940- *WhoAmP 93*
Schoch, Claude Martin 1955- *WhoAm 94*
Schoch, David Henry 1947- *WhoFI 94*
Schochet, Harvey S. 1948- *WhoAmL 94*
Schochor, Jonathan 1946- *WhoAmL 94*
Schock, Barbara *WhoHol 92*
Schock, Robert Norman 1939- *WhoAm 94*
Schock, Rudolf d1986 *WhoHol 92*
Schock, Rudolf (Johann) 1915-1986 *NewGrDO*
Schock, William Wallace 1923- *WhoScEn 94*
Schockaert, Barbara Ann 1938- *WhoFI 94*
Schockemohle, Alwin 1937- *IntWW 93*
Schocken, Gershom Gustav 1912-1990 *WhAm 10*
Schocken, Joseph L. 1946- *WhoFI 94, WhoAmL 94*
Schodel, Roza 1811-1854 *NewGrDO*
Schoeberle, Stephen Mark 1957- *WhoAmL 94*
Schoeck, Clyde C. 1939- *WhoIns 94*
Schoeck, Othmar 1886-1957 *NewGrDO*

Schoeck, Richard Joseph 1920- *WhoAm 94, WhoMW 93*
Schoeck, V. Jean 1923- *WhoAmP 93*
Schoedinger, David Stanton 1942- *WhoAm 94*
Schoeff, Larry 1946- *WhoScEn 94*
Schoeffel, Jon Michael 1945- *WhoAmL 94*
Schoeffling, Michael *IntMPA 94, WhoHol 92*
Schoeld, Constance Jerrine 1935- *WhoMW 93*
Schoelen, Jill *WhoHol 92*
Schoeler, George Bernard 1961- *WhoScEn 94*
Schoelkopf, Robert J., Jr. 1927-1991 *WhoAmA 93N*
Schoeller, Francois 1934- *IntWW 93*
Schoeller, Franz Joachim Philipp 1926- *IntWW 93*
Schoem, Alan Howard 1946- *WhoAmL 94*
Schoemaker, Maurice 1890-1964 *NewGrDO*
Schoemann, Rudolph Robert 1930- *WhoAmL 94*
Schoemehl, Vincent C., Jr. 1946- *WhoAmP 93*
Schoemehl, Vincent Charles, Jr. 1946- *WhoAm 94, WhoMW 93*
Schoemperlen, Diane 1954- *WrDr 94*
Schoen, Alan Paul 1956- *WhoAmL 94*
Schoen, Allen Harry 1936- *WhoScEn 94*
Schoen, Alvin E., Jr. 1945- *WhoScEn 94*
Schoen, Ann Elizabeth 1961- *WhoFI 94*
Schoen, Arthur Boyer 1923- & Schoen, Arthur Boyer, Mrs. 1915- *WhoAmA 93*
Schoen, Arthur Boyer, Mrs. 1915-
See Schoen, Arthur Boyer 1923- & Schoen, Arthur Boyer, Mrs. 1915- *WhoAmA 93*
Schoen, Arthur Boyer, Mrs. 1915- *WhoAmA 93*
Schoen, Barbara (Taylor) 1924-1993 *ConAu 142*
Schoen, Barbara Taylor d1993 *NewYTBS 93 [port]*
Schoen, Carl Patrick 1947- *WhoMW 93*
Schoen, Charles Judd 1943- *WhoFI 94, WhoMW 93*
Schoen, David Carl 1952- *WhoAmL 94*
Schoen, Eugene 1880-1957 *WhoAmA 93N*
Schoen, Howard Franklin 1946- *WhoScEn 94*
Schoen, LaDonna Faye 1945- *WhoMW 93*
Schoen, Max Howard 1922- *IntWW 93, WhoAm 94*
Schoen, Rem *WhoFI 94*
Schoen, Richard Melvin 1950- *WhoAm 94*
Schoen, Robert Dennis 1960- *WhoScEn 94*
Schoen, Stevan Jay 1944- *WhoAmL 94*
Schoen, William Jack 1935- *WhoAm 94*
Schoenbaum, David Leon 1935- *WhoAm 94*
Schoenbaum, Samuel 1927- *WhoAm 94*
Schoenbeck, Audrey Kay 1949- *WhoMW 93*
Schoenbeck, Paul John 1959- *WhoMW 93*
Schoenberg, Alex d1945 *WhoHol 92*
Schoenberg, Arnold (Franz Walter) 1874-1951 *NewGrDO*
Schoenberg, Arnold Franz Walter 1874-1951 *AmCulL*
Schoenberg, Jeffrey M. 1959- *WhoAmP 93*
Schoenberg, Lawrence Joseph 1932- *WhoAm 94, WhoFI 94*
Schoenberg, Mark George 1947- *WhoAm 94, WhoAmP 93*
Schoenberg, Robert J. 1933- *ConAu 141*
Schoenberger, Charlotte Sally 1917- *WhoAmP 93*
Schoenberger, James Edwin 1947- *WhoAm 94*
Schoenberger, Maralyn Morton 1929- *WhoAmP 93*
Schoenberger, Ronald George 1935- *WhoFI 94*
Schoenbrun, Larry Lynn 1940- *WhoAm 94*
Schoenburg, Bernard Alan 1954- *WhoMW 93*
Schoendienst, Albert Fred 1923- *WhoAm 94*
Schoendoerffer, Pierre 1928- *IntWW 93*
Schoendorf, Judson Raymond 1942- *WhoWest 94*
Schoendorf, Walter John 1927- *WhoAm 94*
Schoene, Kathleen Snyder 1953- *WhoAmL 94, WhoFI 94, WhoMW 93*
Schoener, Ingeborg 1935- & Schoner, Ingeborg 1935- *WhoHol 92*
Schoener, Jason 1919- *WhoAmA 93*
Schoener, Thomas William 1943- *WhoAm 94*
Schoenewolf 1941- *WrDr 94*
Schoenfein, Robert A. 1937- *WhoAm 94, WhoFI 94*
Schoenfeld, Alan Henry 1947- *WhoAm 94*

Schoenfeld, Barbara Braun 1953- *WhoAmL 94*
Schoenfeld, Elinor Randi 1956- *WhoScEn 94*
Schoenfeld, Gary Herman 1962- *WhoWest 94*
Schoenfeld, Hanns-Martin Walter 1928- *WhoAm 94, WhoFI 94*
Schoenfeld, Henry F. 1928- *WhoFI 94*
Schoenfeld, Howard Allen 1948- *WhoAmL 94*
Schoenfeld, Jerry 1951- *WhoAmP 93*
Schoenfeld, Lawrence Jon 1945- *WhoWest 94*
Schoenfeld, Lester 1916- *IntMPA 94*
Schoenfeld, Maxwell Philip 1936- *WrDr 94*
Schoenfeld, Michael P. 1935- *WhoAmL 94*
Schoenfeld, Robert Louis 1920- *WhoScEn 94*
Schoenfeld, Walter Edwin 1930- *WhoAm 94*
Schoenfeldt, Stephanie *DrAPF 93*
Schoenfield, Mae d1977 *WhoHol 92*
Schoenfish, Walter Jean 1961- *WhoMW 93*
Schoengarth, Robert Scott 1949- *WhoWest 94*
Schoenhals, Albrecht d1978 *WhoHol 92*
Schoenhard, William Charles, Jr. 1949- *WhoAm 94, WhoFI 94, WhoMW 93, WhoScEn 94*
Schoenherr, John 1935- *EncSF 93*
Schoenherr, John (Carl) 1935- *WhoAmA 93, WrDr 94*
Schoenherr, John Carl 1935- *WhoAm 94*
Schoenherr, Richard Anthony 1935- *WrDr 94*
Schoeni, Douglas Eugene 1957- *WhoWest 94*
Schoenig, Vincent Werner 1964- *WhoFI 94*
Schoening, Alwina *NewGrDO*
Schoening, Thomas Walter 1948- *WhoMW 93*
Schoenlaub, Fred Edward 1930- *WhoAmL 94*
Schoennauer, Alfred W.W. 1923- *WhoAm 94*
Schoenrock, Tracy Allen 1960- *WhoMW 93*
Schoenstein, Joseph Roy 1957- *WhoWest 94*
Schoenwald, Larry Wayne *WhoAmP 93*
Schoenwetter, Randall R. 1956- *WhoMW 93*
Schoeppe, Hans Juergen 1937- *WhoWest 94*
Schoerwald, Maurice Louis 1920- *WhoFI 94*
Schoeser, Mary 1950- *WrDr 94*
Schoesler, Mark Gerald 1957- *WhoAmP 93, WhoWest 94*
Schoettger, Theodore Leo 1920- *WhoAm 94, WhoWest 94*
Schoette, Frederick John 1939- *WhoMW 93*
Schoettler, Gail Sinton 1943- *WhoAm 94, WhoAmP 93, WhoWest 94*
Schoettler, James Anthony, Jr. 1956- *WhoAmL 94*
Schoettlin, Phillip Andrew 1964- *WhoFI 94*
Schoffer, Nicholas d1992 *IntWW 93N*
Schoffler, Paul 1897-1977 *NewGrDO*
Schofield, Alfred 1913- *Who 94*
Schofield, Alfred Taylor 1846-1929 *EncSF 93*
Schofield, Andrew Noel 1930- *Who 94*
Schofield, Annabel *WhoHol 92*
Schofield, Annette Cecelia 1957- *WhoWest 94*
Schofield, Anthony Wayne 1949- *WhoAmL 94*
Schofield, Bertram 1896- *Who 94*
Schofield, Carey 1955- *WrDr 94*
Schofield, Donald Stewart 1928- *WhoAm 94, WhoFI 94*
Schofield, George H. 1929- *WhoFI 94*
Schofield, Grace Florence 1925- *Who 94*
Schofield, Herbert Spencer, III 1942- *WhoFI 94*
Schofield, Jack H. 1923- *WhoAmP 93*
Schofield, Jack Lund 1923- *WhoAmP 93*
Schofield, James Roy 1953- *WhoWest 94*
Schofield, James W. 1931- *WhoAmP 93*
Schofield, John-David Mercer 1938- *WhoAm 94, WhoMW 93*
Schofield, John Trevor 1938- *WhoAm 94*
Schofield, Johnnie d1955 *WhoHol 92*
Schofield, Keith 1938- *WhoScEn 94*
Schofield, Michael 1919- *WrDr 94*
Schofield, Neill 1946- *Who 94*
Schofield, Nell *WhoHol 92*
Schofield, Paul 1919- *WrDr 94*
Schofield, Robert Edwin 1923- *WhoAm 94*

Schram, Stuart Reynolds 1924- *Who 94*
Schramek, Eric (Emil) von *Who 94*
Schramek, Tomas 1944- *WhoAm 94*
Schramko, Christopher John 1965- *WhoMW 93*
Schramm, Adelaida 1930- *WhoAsA 94*
Schramm, Albert *WhoAmP 93*
Schramm, Bernard Charles, Jr. 1928- *WhoAm 94*
Schramm, Darrell G. H. *DrAPF 93*
Schramm, David *WhoHol 92*
Schramm, David N(orman) 1945- *WrDr 94*
Schramm, David Norman 1945- *WhoAm 94, WhoMW 93, WhoScEn 94*
Schramm, John Clarendon 1908- *WhoAm 94*
Schramm, Karla d1980 *WhoHol 92*
Schramm, Marilyn Jean 1951- *WhoAmL 94*
Schramm, Paul Howard 1933- *WhoAmL 94*
Schramm, Raymond Eugene 1941- *WhoWest 94*
Schramm, Richard *DrAPF 93*
Schramm, Tex *ProFbHF*
Schramm, Texas E. 1920- *WhoAm 94*
Schramm, Willfried 1944- *WhoMW 93*
Schramm, William d1979 *WhoHol 92*
Schrand, Richard Henry 1957- *WhoMW 93*
Schrank, Jeffrey 1944- *WrDr 94*
Schrank, Ralf Gerd 1949- *IntWW 93*
Schraub, J. Jonathan 1951- *WhoAmL 94*
Schrauger, Brian Dale 1955- *WhoFI 94*
Schraut, Kenneth Charles 1913- *WhoAm 94*
Schrauth, William Lawrence 1935- *WhoAm 94*
Schraver, David M. 1945- *WhoAmL 94*
Schreadley, Richard Lee 1931- *WhoAm 94*
Schreck, Harley Carl 1948- *WhoMW 93*
Schreck, Lisa Tanzman 1955- *WhoScEn 94*
Schreck, Max d1936 *WhoHol 92*
Schreck, Michael H. *WhoAmA 93*
Schreck, Richard Michael 1943- *WhoScEn 94*
Schreck, Robert A., Jr. 1952- *WhoAm 94*
Schreckengast, William Owen 1926- *WhoAmL 94*
Schreckenghost, Mary Allyn 1951- *WhoAmL 94*
Schreckengost, Viktor 1906- *WhoAmA 93*
Schrecker, Frederick d1976 *WhoHol 92*
Schreckinger, Sy Edward 1937- *WhoAm 94*
Schrefler, Bernhard Aribo 1942- *WhoScEn 94*
Schreiber *Who 94*
Schreiber, Alan Hickman 1944- *WhoAmL 94*
Schreiber, Alfred Lawrence 1945- *WhoAm 94*
Schreiber, Andrew 1918- *WhoScEn 94, WhoWest 94*
Schreiber, Avery 1935- *WhoHol 92*
  See Also Burns and Schreiber *WhoCom*
Schreiber, Barbara Louise 1915- *WhoMW 93*
Schreiber, Bertram Manuel 1940- *WhoAm 94*
Schreiber, Daniel Nelson 1963- *WhoMW 93*
Schreiber, Edward 1943- *WhoScEn 94, WhoWest 94*
Schreiber, Eileen Sher *WhoAmA 93*
Schreiber, Everett Charles, Jr. 1953- *WhoScEn 94, WhoWest 94*
Schreiber, George Richard 1922- *WhoAm 94*
Schreiber, Georges 1904-1977 *WhoAmA 93N*
Schreiber, Harry, Jr. 1934- *WhoFI 94*
Schreiber, Jan *DrAPF 93*
Schreiber, Jeffrey Lee 1952- *WhoAm 94*
Schreiber, Kurt Gilbert 1946- *WhoAmL 94*
Schreiber, Larry L. 1949- *WhoIns 94*
Schreiber, Le Anne 1945- *ConAu 140*
Schreiber, Lisa Marie 1967- *WhoMW 93*
Schreiber, Lola F. *WhoAmP 93*
Schreiber, Martin 1923- *WhoAmA 93*
Schreiber, Marvin Mandel 1925- *WhoAm 94*
Schreiber, Melvyn Hirsh 1931- *WhoAm 94*
Schreiber, Otto William 1922- *WhoFI 94, WhoWest 94*
Schreiber, Paul Solomon 1941- *WhoAm 94*
Schreiber, Richard Bailey 1942- *WhoAm 94, WhoAmL 94*
Schreiber, Robert John 1950- *WhoScEn 94*
Schreiber, Ron *DrAPF 93*
Schreiber, Roy E. 1941- *ConAu 142*

Schreiber, Roy Stanley 1954- *WhoFI 94*
Schreiber, Sally *WhoHol 92*
Schreiber, Sally Ann 1951- *WhoAm 94*
Schreiber, Scott Bernard 1948- *WhoAmL 94*
Schreiber, Stuart L. 1956- *WhoScEn 94*
Schreiber, William Francis 1925- *WhoAm 94*
Schreiber, William H. 1941- *WhoAmP 93*
Schreibman, Susan *DrAPF 93*
Schreier, Harold *WhoAmP 93*
Schreier, Karen Elizabeth *WhoAmL 94*
Schreier, Leonard 1934- *WhoAm 94*
Schreier, Max N. *WhoAm 94*
Schreier, Peter 1935- *IntWW 93, NewGrDO, WhoAm 94*
Schreiner, Albert William 1926- *WhoAm 94*
Schreiner, Ceinwen Ann 1943- *WhoScEn 94*
Schreiner, Christina Maria *WhoScEn 94*
Schreiner, George E. 1922- *WhoAm 94*
Schreiner, John Christian 1933- *WhoAm 94*
Schreiner, L. D., Jr. 1932- *WhoAmP 93*
Schreiner, Lance D. 1950- *WhoAmL 94*
Schreiner, Olive 1855-1920 *BlmGEL, BlmGWL*
Schreiner, Samuel (Agnew, Jr.) 1921- *WrDr 94*
Schreiner, Warren d1987 *WhoHol 92*
Schreiver, George August d1977 *WhoAmA 93N*
Schreker, Franz 1878-1934 *NewGrDO*
Schremp, Pamela S. 1958- *WhoMW 93*
Schrempf, David William 1942- *WhoAm 94*
Schrempf, Detlef 1963- *WhoAm 94*
Schrempp, Dean 1935- *WhoAmP 93*
Schrempp, Jurgen E. 1944- *IntWW 93*
Schrempp, Warren C. 1919- *WhoAmL 94*
Schrems, Delbert 1941- *WhoAmP 93*
Schrenk, Edward L. 1940- *WhoIns 94*
Schrenk, Edward Lawrence 1940- *WhoFI 94*
Schrenk, Lorenz Philip 1932- *WhoMW 93*
Schrenk, Willi Juergen 1945- *WhoAm 94*
Schrepferman, Richard Lee 1928- *WhoAm 94*
Schrero, Ruth Lieberman *WhoAmA 93*
Schrette, Roland Donald 1929- *WhoAmP 93*
Schretter, Judith Drazen 1947- *WhoAmL 94*
Schreuder, Hein 1951- *WhoScEn 94*
Schreyer, Edward Richard 1935- *IntWW 93, Who 94*
Schreyer, Greta L. 1923- *WhoAmA 93*
Schreyer, Leslie John 1946- *WhoAm 94, WhoAmL 94*
Schreyer, William Allen 1928- *IntWW 93, WhoAm 94, WhoFI 94*
Schriber, Jonathan David 1951 *WhoAm 94*
Schriber, Margrit 1939- *BlmGWL*
Schriber, Thomas Jude 1935- *WhoAm 94*
Schribner, Stanley R., Jr. 1956- *WhoAmP 93*
Schrider, Leo A. 1939- *WhoAm 94*
Schrieffer, John Robert 1931- *IntWW 93, Who 94, WhoAm 94, WhoScEn 94, WorScD*
Schrier, Arnold 1925- *WhoAm 94*
Schrier, Robert William 1936- *WhoAm 94*
Schrier, Stanley Leonard 1929- *WhoAm 94*
Schriesheim, Alan 1930- *WhoAm 94, WhoScEn 94*
Schriever, Bernard Adolph 1910- *WhoAm 94*
Schriever, Fred Martin *WhoAm 94, WhoFI 94*
Schriftman, Ross F. 1952- *WhoAmP 93*
Schrimper, Vernon L. 1933- *WhoAm 94*
Schrimsher, Jerry James 1935- *WhoFI 94*
Schrimsher, Kandace Pearson 1963- *WhoMW 93*
Schriner, Jon Leslie 1937- *WhoAm 94*
Schriver, John T., III 1945- *WhoAm 94, WhoAmL 94*
Schrock, Harold Arthur 1915- *WhoAm 94*
Schrock, John Richard 1946- *WhoMW 93, WhoScEn 94*
Schrock, Joseph Byron 1945- *WhoMW 93*
Schrock, Richard R. 1945- *IntWW 93*
Schrock, Rosalind 1937- *WhoAmP 93*
Schrock, Virgil Edwin 1926- *WhoAm 94*
Schroder, Andrea Ruth Lundeen 1944- *WhoAm 93*
Schroder, Barry Charles 1955- *WhoAmL 94, WhoMW 93*
Schroder, Dieter Karl 1935- *WhoAm 94, WhoWest 94*
Schroder, Ernest Melville d1993 *Who 94N*
Schroder, Ernst *WhoHol 92*
Schroder, Ernst Augustus 1915- *IntWW 93*
Schroder, Gerhard 1921- *IntWW 93*

Schroder, Harald Bertel 1924- *WhoAm 94*
Schroder, Jack Spalding, Jr. 1948- *WhoAm 94, WhoAmL 94*
Schroder, John L., Jr. *WhoScEn 94*
Schroder, Michael H. 1950- *WhoAmL 94*
Schroder, Rick 1970- *IntMPA 94*
Schroder, Rick(y) 1970- *WhoHol 92*
Schroder, Werner Hermann 1914- *IntWW 93*
Schroder-Devrient, Wilhelmine 1804-1860 *NewGrDO [port]*
Schroder-Feinen, Ursula 1936- *NewGrDO*
Schroder-Schrom, Franz Wilhelm d1956 *WhoHol 92*
Schrodinger, Erwin 1887-1961 *WorScD*
Schrodt, George Randolph 1928- *WhoAm 94*
Schroeck, Franklin Emmett, Jr. 1942- *WhoScEn 94*
Schroeck, R. D. 1949- *WhoAmA 93*
Schroeder, Aaron Harold 1926- *WhoAm 94*
Schroeder, Alan 1961- *WrDr 94*
Schroeder, Alfred Christian 1915- *WhoAm 94, WhoScEn 94*
Schroeder, Andreas (Peter) 1946- *WrDr 94*
Schroeder, Arnold Leon 1935- *WhoWest 94*
Schroeder, Barbet 1941- *IntMPA 94, IntWW 93*
Schroeder, Betty Louise 1937- *WhoFI 94*
Schroeder, Bill E. 1942- *WhoAm 94, WhoAmL 94*
Schroeder, Bryce Gregory 1961- *WhoWest 94*
Schroeder, Charles Edgar 1935- *WhoAm 94, WhoFI 94, WhoMW 93*
Schroeder, Charles Henry 1942- *WhoAm 94*
Schroeder, Charles Robbins 1901-1991 *WhAm 10*
Schroeder, Clinton Alan 1930- *WhoAmL 94*
Schroeder, David Harold 1940- *WhoAm 94, WhoFI 94, WhoMW 93, WhoScEn 94*
Schroeder, Donald Perry 1930- *WhoAm 94*
Schroeder, Douglas Robert 1943- *WhoWest 94*
Schroeder, Duane David 1940- *WhoWest 94*
Schroeder, Edison Blake 1935- *WhoWest 94*
Schroeder, Edmund R. 1933- *WhoAm 94*
Schroeder, Edward M. 1940- *WhoMW 93*
Schroeder, Edwin Maher 1937- *WhoAmL 94*
Schroeder, Eric 1904- *WhoAmA 93N*
Schroeder, Fred Erich Harald 1932- *WhoAm 94*
Schroeder, Fred F. 1943- *WhoAmP 93*
Schroeder, Frederick David 1946- *WhoFI 94*
Schroeder, Gary *DrAPF 93*
Schroeder, Gary J. 1944- *WhoAmP 93, WhoWest 94*
Schroeder, George Michael 1957- *WhoAmL 94*
Schroeder, Glenn Burnett 1927- *WhoWest 94*
Schroeder, Glenn C. 1953- *WhoWest 94*
Schroeder, Greta *WhoHol 92*
Schroeder, Hans 1929- *WhoMW 93*
Schroeder, Harold Kenneth, Jr. 1936- *WhoAm 94*
Schroeder, Henry William 1928- *WhoMW 93*
Schroeder, Herman Elbert 1915- *WhoAm 94, WhoScEn 94*
Schroeder, Jack Walter 1925- *WhoFI 94*
Schroeder, James White 1936- *WhoAmL 94*
Schroeder, Jean Darlene 1938- *WhoWest 94*
Schroeder, Jeanne Charlotte *NewGrDO*
Schroeder, John C. 1948- *WhoMW 93*
Schroeder, John H. 1943- *WhoAm 94, WhoMW 93*
Schroeder, John Nicholas 1942- *WhoAmP 93*
Schroeder, John Richard 1951- *WhoAmP 93*
Schroeder, John Speer 1937- *WhoAm 94*
Schroeder, June Ann 1946- *WhoFI 94*
Schroeder, Laverne W. 1933- *WhoAmP 93*
Schroeder, Leila Obier 1925- *WhoAmL 94*
Schroeder, Luella Ruth 1922- *WhoAmP 93*
Schroeder, Manfred Robert 1926- *IntWW 93*
Schroeder, Marcia Fey 1951- *WhoMW 93*
Schroeder, Mark Gerard 1957- *WhoAmP 93*
Schroeder, Mary *WhoAmP 93*
Schroeder, Mary Esther 1947- *WhoWest 94*

Schroeder, Mary M. *WhoAmP 93*
Schroeder, Mary Murphy 1940- *WhoAm 94, WhoAmL 94, WhoWest 94*
Schroeder, Melissa Ann 1953- *WhoAmP 93*
Schroeder, Nicholas John 1955- *WhoMW 93*
Schroeder, Patricia 1940- *CngDr 93, WhoAmP 93, WhoWomW 91*
Schroeder, Patricia Scott 1940- *WhoAm 94, WhoWest 94*
Schroeder, Paul Clemens 1938- *WhoWest 94*
Schroeder, Paul J., Jr. 1947- *WhoAm 94, WhoAmL 94*
Schroeder, Paul W. 1927- *IntWW 93*
Schroeder, Paul W. 1947- *WhoAmL 94*
Schroeder, Peter Allan 1928- *WhoMW 93*
Schroeder, Richard John 1944- *WhoWest 94*
Schroeder, Richard Philip 1951- *WhoScEn 94*
Schroeder, Rita Molthen 1922- *WhoWest 94*
Schroeder, Robert J. 1921- *WhoAm 94*
Schroeder, Robert Louis 1927- *WhoMW 93*
Schroeder, Russell Henry 1954- *WhoFI 94*
Schroeder, Sandra *DrAPF 93*
Schroeder, Stanley Brian 1941- *WhoScEn 94*
Schroeder, Stephan Alan 1948- *WhoMW 93*
Schroeder, Steven Alfred 1939- *IntWW 93, WhoAm 94*
Schroeder, Ted 1921- *BuCMET*
Schroeder, Terry Ralph 1938- *WhoFI 94*
Schroeder, Thomas Martin 1947- *WhoMW 93*
Schroeder, Walter Allen 1954- *WhoAmL 94, WhoFI 94*
Schroeder, Walter G. 1927- *WhoAmP 93*
Schroeder, William Gilbert 1911- *WhoAmP 93*
Schroeder, William John 1944- *WhoAm 94, WhoFI 94*
Schroeder, William P. 1942- *WhoAmL 94*
Schroeder, William R., Jr. 1944- *WhoAmP 93*
Schroeder, William Robert 1941- *WhoWest 94*
Schroeer, Dietrich 1938- *WhoAm 94*
Schroeher, Bruce Charles 1940- *WhoIns 94*
Schroepfer, George John, Jr. 1932- *WhoAm 94, WhoScEn 94*
Schroer, Bernard Jon 1941- *WhoScEn 94*
Schroer, Edmund Armin 1928- *WhoAm 94, WhoFI 94, WhoMW 93*
Schroer, Gene Eldon 1927- *WhoAmL 94*
Schroer, Mary B. *WhoAmP 93*
Schroer, Mary B. 1947- *WhoMW 93*
Schroer, Steven C. 1948- *WhoAmL 94*
Schroeter, Arnold L. 1936- *WhoAm 94*
Schroeter, Dirk Joachim 1949- *WhoScEn 94*
Schroeter, Louis C. 1929- *WhoAm 94, WhoFI 94, WrDr 94*
Schroff, William d1964 *WhoHol 92*
Schroff, William K. 1947- *WhoWest 94*
Schroll, James Robert 1953- *WhoAmP 93*
Schrom, Elizabeth Ann 1941- *WhoMW 93*
Schrom, Gerard Killard 1947- *WhoAm 94*
Schropfer, David Waldron 1939- *WhoFI 94*
Schropp, James Howard 1943- *WhoAm 94, WhoAmL 94*
Schrote, John E. 1936- *WhoAmP 93*
Schrote, John Ellis 1936- *WhoAm 94*
Schroth, Carl-Heinz d1989 *WhoHol 92*
Schroth, Hannelore 1926- *WhoHol 92*
Schroth, Peter William 1946- *WhoAm 94, WhoAmL 94, WhoFI 94*
Schroth, Steven Edward 1965- *WhoFI 94*
Schroth, Thomas Nolan 1920- *WhoAm 94*
Schrott, Janet Ann 1941- *WhoMW 93*
Schrott, Norman 1938- *WhoMW 93*
Schroy, Carter Brett 1947- *WhoWest 94*
Schroy, Jerry Michael 1939- *WhoMW 93*
Schrum, Ruth Anna 1923- *WhoAmP 93*
Schrum, William Roy 1950- *WhoMW 93*
Schrut, Sherry 1928- *WhoAmA 93*
Schryver, Bruce John 1944- *WhoScEn 94, WhoWest 94*
Schryver, Clinton d1954 *WhoHol 92*
Schub, Steven *WhoHol 92*
Schubach, Mark Allen 1918- *WhoAm 94*
Schubaur, Johann Lukas 1749?-1815 *NewGrDO*
Schubel, Jerry Robert 1936- *WhoAm 94, WhoScEn 94*
Schuber, William P. 1947- *WhoAmP 93*
Schubert, Barbara Schuele 1939- *WhoAm 94*
Schubert, Blake H. 1939- *WhoFI 94*
Schubert, Edmund F., Jr. 1936- *WhoIns 94*

Schubert, Esther Virginia 1945-
WhoMW 93
Schubert, Franz (Peter) 1797-1828
NewGrDO
Schubert, Gerald 1939- *WhoScEn 94*
Schubert, Glendon 1918- *WhoAm 94*
Schubert, Guenther Erich 1930-
WhoAm 94, WhoScEn 94
Schubert, Helga 1940- *BlmGWL*
Schubert, Jeffery Scott 1955- *WhoMW 93*
Schubert, Johann Friedrich 1770-1811
NewGrDO
Schubert, John Edward 1912- *WhoAm 94*
Schubert, Karin 1944- *WhoHol 92*
Schubert, Kathryn Ilyne 1941- *WhoFI 94,
WhoMW 93*
Schubert, Marina *WhoHol 92*
Schubert, Richard 1885-1959 *NewGrDO*
Schubert, Richard F. 1936- *IntWW 93*
Schubert, Richard Francis 1936-
WhoAm 94
Schubert, Ronald Hayward 1932-
WhoWest 94
Schubert, Sydney 1928- *Who 94*
Schubert, Thomas L. 1942- *WhoAmL 94*
Schubert, Todd Alan 1968- *WhoWest 94*
Schubert, William Henry 1944-
WhoAm 94, WhoMW 93
Schubert, William Kuenneth 1926-
WhoAm 94, WhoScEn 94
Schubin, Ossip 1854-1934 *BlmGWL*
Schuch, Ernst, Edler von 1846-1914
NewGrDO
Schuchart, John Albert, Jr. 1929-
WhoAm 94, WhoMW 93
Schuch-Proska, Clementine 1850-1932
NewGrDO
Schuchter, Wilhelm 1911-1974 *NewGrDO*
Schuck, Carl Joseph 1915- *WhoAm 94,
WhoAmL 94, WhoWest 94*
Schuck, Ernest F. 1919- *WhoAmP 93*
Schuck, John 1940- *IntMPA 94,
WhoHol 92*
Schuck, Joyce Haber 1937- *WhoWest 94*
Schuck, Marjorie Massey 1921- *WhoFI 94*
Schuck, Peter H. 1940- *WhoAm 94,
WhoAmP 93*
Schuck, Terry Karl 1961- *WhoScEn 94*
Schuck, Thomas Robert 1950-
WhoAm 94, WhoAmL 94
Schuck, William 1951- *WhoAmP 93*
Schucker, Charles 1908- *WhoAmA 93*
Schucking, Levin 1814-1883
DcLB 133 [port]
Schudel, Hansjoerg 1937- *WhoAm 94*
Schudson, Charles B(enjamin) 1950-
WrDr 94
Schudson, Michael 1946- *ConAu 42NR*
Schueffner, Dale Willard 1947-
WhoIns 94
Schuegraf, Klaus Karl 1927- *WhoWest 94*
Schuele, Donald Edward 1934-
WhoAm 94
Schuelein, William M. 1927- *WhoAmP 93*
Schueler, George Frederick 1944-
WhoWest 94
Schueler, Jon Christopher 1955-
WhoWest 94
Schueler, Jon R. 1916-1992
WhoAmA 93N
Schuelka, B. Leora Davis 1931-
WhoMW 93
Schuelke, Constance Patricia 1953-
WhoFI 94
Schueller, John Kenneth 1955- *WhoFI 94*
Schueller, Thomas George 1936-
WhoAm 94
Schueller, Wolfgang Augustus 1934-
WhoAm 94
Schueneman, Arthur Lattz 1943-
WhoMW 93
Schuenke, Donald J. 1929- *WhoIns 94*
Schuenke, Donald John 1929-
WhoAm 94, WhoFI 94
Schuenke, Jeffrey Allen 1956-
WhoWest 94
Schueppert, George Louis 1938-
WhoAm 94, WhoFI 94
Schuerger, Anthony Joseph 1951-
WhoMW 93
Schuerman, John Richard 1938-
WhoAm 94
Schuerman, Norbert Joel 1934-
WhoMW 93
Schuermann, Lisa Ann 1958- *WhoMW 93*
Schuermann, Mark Harry 1946-
WhoScEn 94
Schuessel, Wolfgang 1945- *IntWW 93*
Schuessler, Arthur P., Jr. 1947-
WhoIns 94
Schuessler, Karl Frederick 1915-
WhoAm 94
Schuessler, Morgan McQueen 1935-
WhoFI 94
Schuessler Fiorenza, Elisabeth 1938-
WhoAm 94
Schuett, Opal I. 1913- *WhoAmP 93*
Schuett, Stacey 1960- *SmATA 75 [port]*

Schuette, Bill 1953- *WhoAmP 93*
Schuette, Charles A. 1942- *WhoAmL 94*
Schuette, Keith Edward 1955-
WhoAmP 93
Schuette, Kurt Michael 1962-
WhoWest 94
Schuette, Michael 1937- *WhoAm 94*
Schuette, Oswald Francis 1921-
WhoScEn 94
Schuette, Raymond Lee 1952- *WhoFI 94*
Schuettinger, Robert (Lindsay) 1936-
WrDr 94
Schuetz, Janet Joyce 1964- *WhoMW 93*
Schuetz, John Michael 1947- *WhoFI 94,
WhoWest 94*
Schuetz, Steven Edward 1959- *WhoFI 94*
Schuetzenduebel, Wolfram Gerhard
1932- *WhoAm 94*
Schufftan, Eugen 1940-1977
IntDcF 2-4 [port]
Schug, Kenneth Robert 1924- *WhoAm 94*
Schuh, Frank Joseph 1935- *WhoAm 94*
Schuh, G(eorge) Edward 1930- *WrDr 94*
Schuh, George Edward 1930- *WhoAm 94*
Schuh, Joseph Francis 1963- *WhoMW 93*
Schuh, Martha Schuhmann 1941-
WhoMW 93
Schuh, Merlyn Duane 1945- *WhoScEn 94*
Schuh, Oscar Fritz 1904-1984 *NewGrDO*
Schuh, Sandra Anderson 1947-
WhoScEn 94
Schuh, Willi 1900-1986 *NewGrDO*
Schuhmann, Barbara Lucille 1949-
WhoAmL 94
Schuhmann, Reinhardt, Jr. 1914-
WhoAm 94
Schuk, Linda Lee 1946- *WhoAmL 94*
Schuker, Stephen Alan 1939- *WhoAm 94*
Schuknecht, Harold Frederick 1917-
WhoAm 94
Schul, Bill Dean 1928- *WhoMW 93*
Schulberg, B.P. 1892-1957 *IntDcF 2-4*
Schulberg, Budd *DrAPF 93*
Schulberg, Budd 1914- *IntWW 93,
WhoAm 94*
Schulberg, Budd (Wilson) 1914- *WrDr 94*
Schulberg, Budd Wilson 1914- *IntMPA 94*
Schulberg, Jay William 1939- *WhoAm 94,
WhoFI 94*
Schulberg, June Schilit 1929-
WhoAmL 94
Schulberg, Robin Elise 1950-
WhoAmL 94
Schuldt, Everett Arthur 1938-
WhoWest 94
Schule, Clifford Hamilton 1918-
WhoAmA 93
Schule, Donald Kenneth 1938-
WhoAmA 93
Schuler, Alison Kay 1948- *WhoAmL 94*
Schuler, Jere W. 1934- *WhoAmP 93*
Schuler, John Hamilton 1926-
WhoAmP 93
Schuler, Martin Luke 1958- *WhoScEn 94*
Schuler, Melvin Albert 1924-
WhoAmA 93
Schuler, Mildred Elizabeth 1922-
WhoAmP 93
Schuler, Paul 1931- *WhoAmP 93*
Schuler, Robert Hugo 1926- *WhoAm 94,
WhoScEn 94*
Schuler, Robert L. 1943- *WhoAmP 93*
Schuler, Robert Leo 1943- *WhoMW 93*
Schuler, Ronald Theodore 1940-
WhoScEn 94
Schuler, Ronna Gayle 1954- *WhoMW 93*
Schuler, Ruth Wildes *DrAPF 93*
Schuler, Theodore Anthony 1934-
WhoScEn 94
Schulfer, Roche Edward 1951-
WhoMW 93
Schulhof, Michael Peter 1942-
WhoAm 94, WhoFI 94
Schulhofer, Stephen Joseph 1942-
WhoAm 94, WhoAmL 94
Schulian, John 1945- *WhoAm 94*
Schulke, Herbert Ardis, Jr. 1923-
WhoAm 94
Schulkind, Andy *WhoAmP 93*
Schull, William J. 1922- *WhoScEn 94*
Schuller, Diane Ethel 1943- *WhoScEn 94*
Schuller, Frank *WhoHol 92*
Schuller, Grete *WhoAmA 93N*
Schuller, Gunther 1925- *IntWW 93,
WrDr 94*
Schuller, Gunther (Alexander) 1925-
NewGrDO
Schuller, Gunther Alexander 1925-
WhoAm 94, WhoWest 94
Schuller, Nancy Shelby 1942-
WhoAm 94
Schuller, Robert H(arold) 1926- *WrDr 94*
Schuller, Robert Harold 1926-
WhoWest 94
Schuller, Stephen Arthur 1951-
WhoAmL 94
Schullian, Dorothy May 1906-1989
WhAm 10

Schulman, Alan Michael 1946- *WhoFI 94,
WhoMW 93*
Schulman, Clifford A. 1947- *WhoAm 94,
WhoAmL 94*
Schulman, Elizabeth Weiner 1950-
WhoFI 94, WhoWest 94
Schulman, Grace *DrAPF 93*
Schulman, Grace J. *WhoAm 94*
Schulman, Harold 1930- *WhoAm 94*
Schulman, Helen *DrAPF 93*
Schulman, Irving 1922- *WhoAm 94*
Schulman, Ivan A(lbert) 1931- *WrDr 94*
Schulman, J(oseph) Neil 1953- *EncSF 93*
Schulman, Jacob 1915-1987
WhoAmA 93N
Schulman, John A. 1946- *IntMPA 94*
Schulman, Joseph Daniel 1941-
WhoAm 94
Schulman, Marc Stuart 1955- *WhoFI 94*
Schulman, Marvin 1934- *WhoScEn 94*
Schulman, Michael Adlai 1957-
WhoWest 94
Schulman, Michael Robert 1946-
WhoAm 94
Schulman, Paul Martin 1940- *WhoAm 94,
WhoFI 94*
Schulman, Robert 1924- *WhoAmA 93*
Schulman, Robert S. 1941- *WhoAmL 94*
Schulman, Sandra London 1929-
WhoAm 94
Schulman, Sarah *DrAPF 93*
Schulman, Sarah (Miriam) 1958- *GayLL*
Schulman, Seymour 1926- *WhoWest 94*
Schulman, Sidney 1923- *WhoAm 94*
Schulman, Sydney T. 1938- *WhoHisp 94*
Schulman, Tammy Beth 1960-
WhoMW 93
Schulman, Tom *WhoAm 94*
Schulman, Tom 1951- *WrDr 94*
Schulmann, Horst 1933- *IntWW 93*
Schulner, Lawrence Mayer 1938-
WhoAmL 94, WhoWest 94
Schulsinger, Michael Alan 1952-
WhoMW 93
Schulson, Susan 1941- *WhoAmA 93*
Schulstad, Eugene P. 1944- *WhoMW 93*
Schult, Dain Leslie 1954- *WhoFI 94*
Schult, Thomas Peter 1954- *WhoAmL 94*
Schulte, Anthony Joseph 1954-
WhoMW 93
Schulte, Arthur D. 1906- *WhoAmA 93*
Schulte, Arthur D., Mrs. *WhoAmA 93*
Schulte, Brigitte 1943- *WhoWomW 91*
Schulte, David Michael 1946- *WhoAm 94*
Schulte, Francis B. 1926- *WhoAm 94*
Schulte, Henry Frank 1924- *WhoAm 94*
Schulte, Henry Gustave 1920-
WhoWest 94
Schulte, Jeffrey Lewis 1949- *WhoAm 94,
WhoAmL 94*
Schulte, Josephine Helen 1929-
WhoAm 94
Schulte, Mary Ann 1953- *WhoFI 94*
Schulte, Rainer *DrAPF 93*
Schulte, Stephen Charles 1952-
WhoAm 94, WhoAmL 94
Schulte, Stephen John 1938- *WhoAm 94,
WhoAmL 94*
Schulte, Stephen Thomas 1952-
WhoFI 94
Schulte, William Hobart, III 1962-
WhoWest 94
Schulteis, Joel Robert 1966- *WhoMW 93*
Schulten, Cay Gerhard af 1938-
IntWW 93
Schultenover, David George 1938-
WhoMW 93
Schulter, Eugene C. 1947- *WhoAmP 93*
Schulter-Ellis, Frances Pierce 1923-
WhoAm 94
Schultes, Lorain Medbury 1936-
WhoMW 93
Schultes, Richard Evans 1915-
IntWW 93, WhoAm 94, WhoScEn 94
Schultheis, Patrick Joseph 1964-
WhoWest 94
Schultke, Herbert Ardis, Jr. 1923-
WhoScEn 94
Schultz, Albert Barry 1933- *WhoAm 94,
WhoScEn 94*
Schultz, Andrew Schultz, Jr. 1913-
WhoAm 94
Schultz, Arthur Joseph, Jr. 1918-
WhoAm 94
Schultz, Arthur Warren 1922- *WhoAm 94*
Schultz, Barbara Marie 1943- *WhoFI 94,
WhoMW 93*
Schultz, (Reynolds) Bart(on) 1951-
ConAu 142
Schultz, Bruce Allan *Who 94*
Schultz, Callan Lee 1966- *WhoFI 94,
WhoMW 93*
Schultz, Carl Bruce 1956- *WhoAmL 94*
Schultz, Carl Herbert 1925- *WhoAm 94*
Schultz, Caroline Reel *WhoAmA 93*
Schultz, Caroline Reel 1936- *WhoWest 94*
Schultz, Charles Edward 1951-
WhoMW 93
Schultz, Charles L. 1928- *WhoIns 94*

Schultz, Charles William 1942-
WhoScEn 94
Schultz, Clarence Carven, Jr. 1924-
WhoAm 94
Schultz, Claus *WhoHol 92*
Schultz, Dale Herbert 1948- *WhoScEn 94*
Schultz, Dale W. 1953- *WhoAmP 93,
WhoMW 93*
Schultz, David Harold 1942- *WhoMW 93*
Schultz, Debbie Wasserman 1966-
WhoAmP 93
Schultz, Debora Lynn *WhoMW 93*
Schultz, Dennis Bernard 1946-
WhoAm 94, WhoAmL 94
Schultz, Don Edward 1934- *WhoAm 94*
Schultz, Douglas George 1947-
WhoAm 94, WhoAmA 93
Schultz, Dwight 1947- *IntMPA 94*
Schultz, Dwight 1951- *WhoHol 92*
Schultz, Edward Fred 1947- *WhoFI 94*
Schultz, Eileen Hedy *WhoAm 94*
Schultz, Franklin M. 1917- *WhoAm 94*
Schultz, Frederick Henry 1929-
WhoAm 94
Schultz, G. Robert 1934- *WhoAmL 94*
Schultz, Gerald A. 1934- *WhoMW 93*
Schultz, Gerald Alfred 1941- *WhoFI 94,
WhoScEn 94*
Schultz, Ginger Monica 1965-
WhoMW 93
Schultz, Gordon R. 1945- *WhoAmP 93*
Schultz, Gustav Hobart 1935-
WhoWest 94
Schultz, Harold A. 1907- *WhoAmA 93*
Schultz, Harry d1935 *WhoHol 92*
Schultz, Hyman 1931- *WhoScEn 94*
Schultz, Jason Ramsey 1966-
WhoAmL 94
Schultz, Jeff *WhoHol 92*
Schultz, Jerold Marvin 1935-
WhoScEn 94
Schultz, Jerome Samson 1933-
WhoAm 94
Schultz, Johann Abraham Peter *NewGrDO*
Schultz, John *DrAPF 93*
Schultz, John Bernard 1948- *WhoAmA 93*
Schultz, John Reilly 1963- *WhoFI 94*
Schultz, Jon S. 1941- *WhoAmL 94*
Schultz, Ken A. 1937- *WhoAmP 93*
Schultz, Kirk R. 1956- *WhoScEn 94*
Schultz, Kurt Lee 1946- *WhoAm 94,
WhoAmL 94*
Schultz, Laurence Stuart 1940-
WhoAmL 94
Schultz, Leslie Brown 1936- *WhoFI 94,
WhoWest 94*
Schultz, Linda Jane 1962- *WhoScEn 94*
Schultz, Louis Edwin 1931- *WhoAm 94,
WhoFI 94, WhoMW 93*
Schultz, Louis Michael 1944- *WhoAm 94*
Schultz, Louis W. 1927- *WhoAmP 93*
Schultz, Louis William 1927- *WhoAm 94,
WhoAmL 94, WhoMW 93*
Schultz, Lucy J. 1962- *WhoMW 93*
Schultz, Marilyn Frances 1944-
WhoAmP 93
Schultz, Michael 1938- *IntMPA 94,
WhoAm 94*
Schultz, Michael A. 1938-
ConBlB 6 [port], WhoBlA 94
Schultz, Pamela Anne 1953- *WhoMW 93*
Schultz, Patricia Ann 1946- *WhoFI 94*
Schultz, Paul Neal 1957- *WhoFI 94*
Schultz, Paul Thomas 1962- *WhoFI 94*
Schultz, Per-Olov 1932- *WhoScEn 94*
Schultz, Peter G. *WhoAm 94,
WhoScEn 94*
Schultz, Philip *DrAPF 93*
Schultz, Philip 1945- *WhoAm 94*
Schultz, Philip Fredrick 1957-
WhoAmL 94
Schultz, Philip Stephen 1947-
WhoScEn 94
Schultz, Richard Allen 1939- *WhoAmL 94*
Schultz, Richard Carlton 1927-
WhoAm 94
Schultz, Richard Dale 1929- *WhoAm 94,
WhoMW 93*
Schultz, Richard LeRoy 1950-
WhoMW 93
Schultz, Richard Michael 1942-
WhoScEn 94
Schultz, Richard Otto 1930- *WhoAm 94*
Schultz, Robert Allen 1942- *WhoWest 94*
Schultz, Robert Bernard 1947-
WhoAmL 94
Schultz, Robert J. 1930- *WhoAm 94,
WhoMW 93*
Schultz, Robert Louis 1923- *WhoMW 93*
Schultz, Robert Vernon 1936- *WhoFI 94,
WhoMW 93*
Schultz, Samuel J. 1914- *WrDr 94*
Schultz, Samuel Jacob 1914- *WhoAm 94*
Schultz, Saunders 1927- *WhoAmA 93*
Schultz, Scott Thomas 1957- *WhoAmP 93*
Schultz, Shelly Irene 1953- *WhoFI 94*
Schultz, Stanley George 1931- *WhoAm 94,
WhoScEn 94*

Schultz, Stephen John 1943- *WhoAmL 94*
Schultz, Stephen Warren 1946- *WhoAmA 93*
Schultz, Steven Alan 1953- *WhoIns 94*
Schultz, Susan Martha 1958- *WhoWest 94*
Schultz, Svend S(imon) 1913- *NewGrDO*
Schultz, T. Paul 1940- *WhoAm 94, WhoFI 94*
Schultz, Theodore Edward 1945- *WhoAm 94*
Schultz, Theodore W. 1902- *IntWW 93, Who 94, WrDr 94*
Schultz, Theodore William 1902- *WhoAm 94, WhoFI 94, WhoMW 93*
Schultz, Thomas Robert 1946- *WhoWest 94*
Schultz, Waldemar Herbert 1921- *WhoAmP 93*
Schultz, Warren Robert 1949- *WhoMW 93*
Schultz, William Robert, Jr. 1956- *WhoIns 94*
Schultze, Charles Louis 1924- *IntWW 93, WhoAm 94*
Schultze, Ernst Eugene 1944- *WhoWest 94*
Schulz, Anne Markham 1938- *WhoAmA 93*
Schulz, Bradley Nicholas 1959- *WhoAmL 94*
Schulz, Brian *WhoHol 92*
Schulz, Bruno 1892-1942 *RfGShF, ShSCr 13 [port], TwCLC 51 [port]*
Schulz, Charles (Monroe) 1922- *WrDr 94*
Schulz, Charles Monroe 1922- *IntWW 93, WhoAm 94, WhoAmA 93*
Schulz, Deborah Craft 1949- *WhoMW 93*
Schulz, Debra L. 1956- *WhoMW 93*
Schulz, Eric A. 1948- *WhoMW 93*
Schulz, Ernst (Bernherd) 1896- *WhAm 10*
Schulz, Fritz d1972 *WhoHol 92*
Schulz, Helmut Wilhelm 1912- *WhoScEn 94*
Schulz, James Daniel 1953- *WhoFI 94*
Schulz, Johann Abraham Peter 1747-1800 *NewGrDO*
Schulz, Juergen 1927- *WhoAmA 93*
Schulz, Keith Donald 1938- *WhoAm 94*
Schulz, Kelly Lynn 1962- *WhoMW 93*
Schulz, Ken 1920- *WhoAmA 93*
Schulz, Lawrence A. 1941- *WhoAmL 94*
Schulz, Martin Christian 1963- *WhoMW 93*
Schulz, Max Frederick 1923- *WrDr 94*
Schulz, Michael 1959- *WhoScEn 94*
Schulz, Otto G. 1930- *WhoIns 94*
Schulz, Paul 1911- *WhoScEn 94*
Schulz, Paul C. 1927- *WhoAmP 93*
Schulz, Peter 1930- *IntWW 93*
Schulz, Ralph Richard 1928- *WhoAm 94*
Schulz, Raymond Alexander 1946- *WhoFI 94*
Schulz, Raymond Charles 1942- *WhoMW 93, WhoScEn 94*
Schulz, Richard Burkart 1920- *WhoAm 94*
Schulz, Robert Emil 1929-1978 *WhoAmA 93N*
Schulz, Rockwell Irwin 1929- *WhoAm 94*
Schulz, Royce Henry 1937- *WhoFI 94*
Schulz, Rudolph Walter 1930- *WhoAm 94*
Schulz, Stephen J. 1958- *WhoMW 93*
Schulz, Steven R. 1953- *WhoAmL 94*
Schulz, Thomas Allen 1944- *WhoAmL 94*
Schulz, Walter Kurt 1940- *WhoFI 94*
Schulz, William Frederick 1949- *WhoAm 94*
Schulze, Arthur Robert, Jr. 1931- *WhoAm 94, WhoFI 94*
Schulze, Eric William 1952- *WhoAmL 94*
Schulze, Erwin Emil 1925- *WhoMW 93*
Schulze, Franz 1927- *WhoAmA 93, WrDr 94*
Schulze, Franz, Jr. 1927- *WhoAm 94*
Schulze, Horst *WhoAm 94, WhoFI 94*
Schulze, John 1915- *WhoAmA 93*
Schulze, John B. *WhoAm 94*
Schulze, Keith Alan 1954- *WhoWest 94*
Schulze, Mark Howard 1950- *WhoMW 93*
Schulze, Matthias Michael 1964- *WhoScEn 94*
Schulze, Michael Joseph 1954- *WhoIns 94*
Schulze, Nancy Lark 1942- *WhoAmL 94*
Schulze, Norman Ronnie 1936- *WhoScEn 94*
Schulze, Paul 1934- *WhoAmA 93*
Schulze, Richard Hans 1933- *WhoScEn 94*
Schulze, Richard T. 1929- *WhoAmP 93*
Schulze, Richard Taylor 1929- *WhoAm 94*
Schulze, Richard Wilfred 1937- *WhoAm 94*
Schulze, Robert Currey, Jr. 1942- *WhoWest 94*
Schulze, Robert Oscar 1922- *WhoAm 94*
Schulzinger, Robert David 1945- *WhoWest 94*
Schulzova, Anezka 1868-1905 *NewGrDO*
Schulz-Widmar, Russell Eugene 1944- *WhoAm 94*
Schumacher, Brockman 1924- *WhoBlA 94*
Schumacher, Carl Joseph, Jr. 1926- *WhoAmL 94*
Schumacher, Dale Norman 1942- *WhoFI 94*
Schumacher, E. F. 1911-1977 *ConLC 80 [port]*
Schumacher, Ernst Friedrich 1911-1977 *EnvEnc*
Schumacher, Evelyn A(nn), Sister 1919- *WrDr 94*
Schumacher, Ferdinand Mathias 1939- *WhoMW 93*
Schumacher, Frederick Carl 1911- *WhoAm 94*
Schumacher, Frederick Richmond 1930- *WhoAmL 94, WhoFI 94*
Schumacher, Gebhard Friederich Bernhard 1924- *WhoAm 94*
Schumacher, Hal d1993 *NewYTBS 93*
Schumacher, Harry Ralph 1933- *WhoAm 94, WhoScEn 94*
Schumacher, Harry Richard 1930- *WhoAm 94*
Schumacher, Henry Jerold 1934- *WhoAm 94, WhoWest 94*
Schumacher, Jerry d1975 *WhoHol 92*
Schumacher, Joel 1939- *IntMPA 94*
Schumacher, John Christian 1935- *WhoAm 94*
Schumacher, John N(orbert) 1927- *WrDr 94*
Schumacher, Jon Lee 1937- *WhoAm 94*
Schumacher, Joseph Charles 1911- *WhoAm 94*
Schumacher, Kathleen Miles 1954- *WhoMW 93*
Schumacher, Leon George 1956- *WhoMW 93*
Schumacher, Matthew A. 1942- *WhoAmL 94*
Schumacher, Paul 1951- *WhoAmP 93*
Schumacher, Paul Maynard 1951- *WhoAmL 94*
Schumacher, Richard 1955- *WhoFI 94*
Schumacher, Robert Denison 1933- *WhoAm 94*
Schumacher, Robert Joseph 1929- *WhoFI 94*
Schumacher, Robert Kent 1924- *WhAm 10*
Schumacher, William Jacob 1938- *WhoAm 94*
Schumack, Daniel 1962- *WhoAmL 94*
Schumaker, Clarence Joseph 1936- *WhoAm 94*
Schumaker, Larry Lee 1939- *WhoAm 94*
Schuman, Beatrice *DrAPF 93*
Schuman, Clifford Richard 1913- *WhoAmL 94*
Schuman, Gerald Eugene 1944- *WhoAm 94*
Schuman, Howard 1928- *WhoAm 94*
Schuman, Perry Lee 1930- *WhoAmP 93*
Schuman, Robert Lee 1954- *WhoAmP 93*
Schuman, Stanley 1925- *WhoScEn 94*
Schuman, William 1910-1992 *AnObit 1992, ConMus 10 [port]*
Schuman, William (Howard) 1910-1992 *NewGrDO*
Schuman, William Howard 1910-1992 *WhAm 10*
Schuman, William John, Jr. 1930- *WhoScEn 94*
Schumann, David Robert 1937- *WhoMW 93*
Schumann, Elisabeth 1888-1952 *NewGrDO [port]*
Schumann, Erik *WhoHol 92*
Schumann, Mark Wolfgang 1965- *WhoMW 93*
Schumann, Maurice 1911- *IntWW 93, Who 94*
Schumann, Merritt J. 1928- *WhoAmP 93*
Schumann, Robert (Alexander) 1810-1856 *NewGrDO*
Schumann, Stanley Paul 1954- *WhoScEn 94*
Schumann, Thomas Gerald 1937- *WhoScEn 94*
Schumann, William Frederick 1939- *WhoAm 94*
Schumann, William Henry, III 1950- *WhoAm 94*
Schumann, William Robert 1942- *WhoIns 94*
Schumann-Heink, Ernestine d1936 *WhoHol 92*
Schumann-Heink, Ernestine 1861-1936 *NewGrDO [port]*
Schumann-Heink, Ferdinand d1958 *WhoHol 92*
Schumer, Charles E. 1950- *CngDr 93, WhoAmP 93*
Schumer, Charles Ellis 1950- *WhoAm 94*
Schumer, Douglas Brian 1951- *WhoScEn 94*
Schumer, George Norman 1949- *WhoWest 94*
Schumer, William 1926- *WhoAm 94*
Schumm, Brooke, III 1956- *WhoAmL 94*
Schumm, Hans d1990 *WhoHol 92*
Schumm, Harry d1953 *WhoHol 92*
Schumm, Stanley Alfred 1927- *WhoAm 94*
Schumpeter, Joseph Alois 1883-1950 *AmSocL*
Schumsky, Stanley 1932- *WhoFI 94*
Schundler, Bret Davis 1959- *WhoAm 94, WhoFI 94*
Schundler, Brett 1959- *WhoAmP 93*
Schundler, Lynn Greenfield 1961- *WhoAmL 94*
Schundler, Rudolf d1988 *WhoHol 92*
Schuneman, Calvin W. 1926- *WhoAmP 93*
Schunk, Eric Henry 1955- *WhoAmL 94*
Schunk, Robert 1948- *NewGrDO*
Schunzel, Reinhold d1954 *WhoHol 92*
Schupack, Mark Barry 1931- *WhoAm 94*
Schupak, Leslie Allen 1945- *WhoAm 94, WhoFI 94*
Schuplinsky, Walter 1921-1990 *WhoAmA 93N*
Schupp, James Louis, Jr. 1936- *WhoAmL 94*
Schupp, Keith Lowell 1953- *WhoMW 93*
Schupp, Ronald Irving 1951- *WhoMW 93*
Schupper, John D. 1944- *WhoAmL 94*
Schuppert, Kenneth Matthew, Jr. 1954- *WhoAmL 94*
Schur, Jeffrey 1946- *WhoAm 94*
Schur, Jonathan Andrew 1953- *WhoAmL 94*
Schur, Larry Steven 1952- *WhoMW 93*
Schur, Leon Milton 1923- *WhoAm 94*
Schur, Milton Oscar 1895- *WhAm 10*
Schur, Susan D. 1940- *WhoAmP 93*
Schur, Walter Robert 1914- *WhoScEn 94*
Schur, Willi d1940 *WhoHol 92*
Schure, Alexander 1921- *WhoAm 94*
Schure, Matthew 1948- *WhoAm 94*
Schureman, James 1756-1824 *WhAmRev*
Schurer, Johann Georg c. 1720-1786 *NewGrDO*
Schurle, Robert Ray 1936- *WhoWest 94*
Schurman, Anna Maria van 1607-1678 *BlmGWL*
Schurman, Dennis Wayne 1947- *WhoAmP 93*
Schurman, Donald Glenn 1933- *WhoAm 94*
Schurman, Donald Peter 1947- *WhoAm 94*
Schurman, Joseph Rathborne 1924- *WhoAm 94*
Schurman, Lynn Ann 1956- *WhoMW 93*
Schurmann, Georg Caspar 1672?-1751 *NewGrDO*
Schurmann, Gerard 1924- *WhoWest 94*
Schurmann, Leo 1917- *IntWW 93*
Schurmann, Reiner d1993 *NewYTBS 93*
Schurmeier, L. Jon 1937- *WhoAm 94*
Schurr, Jerry M. 1940- *WhoAmA 93*
Schurrer, Suzanne Barbara 1945- *WhoAm 94*
Schurz, Franklin Dunn, Jr. 1931- *WhoAm 94, WhoFI 94*
Schurz, Scott Clark 1936- *WhoAm 94*
Schuselka, Elfi 1940- *WhoAmA 93*
Schusky, Ernest L. 1931- *WrDr 94*
Schussler, Theodore 1934- *WhoAm 94, WhoAmL 94*
Schuster, Allan D. *WhoAm 94, WhoIns 94*
Schuster, Andrew H. 1950- *WhoAmL 94*
Schuster, Carl 1904- *WhoAmA 93N*
Schuster, Charles Irwin 1945- *WhoMW 93*
Schuster, Charles Roberts 1930- *WhoAm 94*
Schuster, Cita Fletcher 1929- *WhoAmA 93*
Schuster, Donald Gene 1950- *WhoWest 94*
Schuster, Donna Norine 1883-1953 *WhoAmA 93N*
Schuster, Elaine 1947- *WhoAm 94*
Schuster, Eugene Ivan 1936- *WhoAmA 93*
Schuster, Frank Feist 1928- *WhoScEn 94*
Schuster, Franklin Phillip 1895- *WhAm 10*
Schuster, Gary Benjamin 1946- *WhoAm 94*
Schuster, Gary Francis 1942- *WhoAm 94*
Schuster, Hans-Gunter 1918- *IntWW 93*
Schuster, Harold d1986 *WhoHol 92*
Schuster, Ignaz 1779-1835 *NewGrDO*
Schuster, Jack Herman 1937- *WhoWest 94*
Schuster, James *Who 94*
Schuster, (Felix) James (Moncrieff) 1913- *Who 94*
Schuster, James Leo 1912- *Who 94*
Schuster, Joseph 1748-1812 *NewGrDO*
Schuster, Lawrence Joseph 1946- *WhoScEn 94*
Schuster, Max Lincoln 1897- *WhAm 10*
Schuster, Philip Frederick, II 1945- *WhoAmL 94, WhoFI 94, WhoWest 94*
Schuster, Richard Nelson 1941- *WhoWest 94*
Schuster, Robert Parks 1945- *WhoAm 94, WhoAmL 94, WhoWest 94*
Schuster, Seymour 1926- *WhoAm 94*
Schuster, Stephanie Ellen 1952- *WhoFI 94*
Schuster, Stephen Fowler 1943- *WhoAmL 94*
Schuster, Todd Mervyn 1933- *WhoAm 94*
Schusterman, Gerrie Marva 1928- *WhoAmA 93*
Schuth, Katarina 1941- *WhoAm 94*
Schutrumpf, Eckart Ernst 1939- *WhoWest 94*
Schutt, Arthur d1965 *WhoHol 92*
Schutt, Deborah Kay 1953- *WhoMW 93*
Schutt, Jeffry Allen 1959- *WhoScEn 94*
Schutt, Walter Eugene 1917- *WhoMW 93*
Schutta, Henry Szczesny 1928- *WhoAm 94*
Schutte, Charles Frederick 1921-1988 *WhAm 10*
Schutte, Giles W. 1931- *WhoAm 94, WhoFI 94*
Schutte, Henry John 1925- *WhoFI 94*
Schutte, Paul Cameron 1958- *WhoScEn 94*
Schutte, Paula Marion 1941- *WhoFI 94*
Schutte, Richard David 1954- *WhoFI 94*
Schutte, Thomas Frederick 1935- *WhoAmA 93*
Schutter, David John 1945- *WhoMW 93*
Schutting, Jutta 1937- *BlmGWL*
Schutz, Andrea Louise 1948- *WhoBlA 94*
Schutz, Anton 1894-1977 *WhoAmA 93N*
Schutz, Donald Frank 1934- *WhoAm 94*
Schutz, Estelle 1907- *WhoAmA 93*
Schutz, Francoise Jeanne *NewGrDO*
Schutz, Hans 1862-1917 *NewGrDO*
Schutz, Heinrich 1585-1672 *NewGrDO*
Schutz, Helga 1937- *BlmGWL*
Schutz, Herb David 1916- *WhoMW 93*
Schutz, Herbert Dietrich 1922- *WhoAm 94*
Schutz, J(oseph) W(illard) 1912-1984 *EncSF 93*
Schutz, John Adolph 1919- *WhoAm 94, WhoWest 94*
Schutz, Klaus 1926- *IntWW 93*
Schutz, Margaret Bailey 1954- *WhoFI 94*
Schutz, Maurice d1955 *WhoHol 92*
Schutz, Prescott Dietrich 1948-1990 *WhoAmA 93N*
Schutz, Richard Phillip 1951- *WhoAm 94*
Schutz, Susan Jackson 1956- *WhoMW 93*
Schutz, Wallace J. 1908- *WrDr 94*
Schutz, Waltraud 1957- *WhoWomW 91*
Schutz, Will(iam C.) 1925- *WrDr 94*
Schutzeichel, Rudolf 1927- *IntWW 93*
Schutzendorf, Leo 1886-1931 *NewGrDO*
Schutzky, Marilyn Horsley 1936- *WhoWest 94*
Schutzman, Max F. 1946- *WhoAmL 94*
Schutzman, Steven *DrAPF 93*
Schutz-Oldosi, Amalia c. 1800-1839? *NewGrDO*
Schuur, Diane Joan 1953- *WhoAm 94*
Schuur, Robert George 1931- *WhoAm 94, WhoAmL 94*
Schuurman, Anna Maria van 1607-1678 *BlmGWL*
Schuwerk, Robert Paul 1942- *WhoAmL 94*
Schuyler, Cortlandt Van Rensselaer d1993 *NewYTBS 93*
Schuyler, Daniel Merrick 1912- *WhoAm 94, WhoAmL 94, WhoMW 93*
Schuyler, Doris E. *DrAPF 93*
Schuyler, George S(amuel) 1895-1977 *EncSF 93*
Schuyler, George Samuel 1895-1977 *BlkWr 2, ConAu 42NR*
Schuyler, Gregory Alan 1940- *WhoWest 94*
Schuyler, James Marcus 1923-1991 *WhAm 10*
Schuyler, Judy *ConAu 42NR*
Schuyler, Peter R. 1965- *WhoScEn 94*
Schuyler, Philip 1733-1804 *AmRev, WhAmRev [port]*
Schuyler, Philip (Griffin) 1913- *WhoAmA 93N*
Schuyler, Philippa 1932-1969 *AfrAmAl 6 [port]*
Schuyler, Rob Rene 1932- *WhoAmL 94*
Schuyler, Robert Len 1936- *WhoAm 94, WhoFI 94, WhoWest 94*
Schuyler, Ronald G. 1945- *WhoWest 94*
Schuyler, Yost *WhAmRev*
Schvey, Henry I(van) 1948- *WrDr 94*
Schwaab, Richard Lewis 1945- *WhoAm 94, WhoAmL 94*
Schwab, Alice Mae Gwilliam 1938- *WhoWest 94*
Schwab, Arthur James 1946- *WhoAm 94, WhoAmL 94*

Schwerner, Armand *DrAPF 93*
Schwerner, Armand 1927- *WrDr 94*
Schwert, George William, III 1950- *WhoFI 94*
Schwertfeger, Ruth 1941- *WrDr 94*
Schwertly, Harvey Kenneth, Jr. 1941- *WhoScEn 94*
Schwertsik, Kurt 1935- *NewGrDO*
Schwethelm, A. C. 1931- *WhoAmP 93*
Schwezoff, Igor 1904-1982 *IntDcB*
Schwichtenberg, Cathy 1953- *ConAu 142*
Schwichtenberg, Daryl Robert 1929- *WhoWest 94*
Schwickert, Leas George 1919- *WhoMW 93*
Schwidder, Ernst 1931- *WhoAmA 93*
Schwiebert, Mark William 1950- *WhoAmP 93, WhoMW 93*
Schwieger, C. Robert 1936- *WhoAmA 93*
Schwieger, Susan Margaret 1951- *WhoMW 93*
Schwier, Frederick Warren 1923- *WhoAm 94*
Schwier, Priscilla Lamb Guyton 1939- *WhoFI 94*
Schwiering, Conrad 1916- *WhoAmA 93N*
Schwiesow, Ronald Lee 1940- *WhoWest 94*
Schwietz, Roger L. *WhoAm 94, WhoMW 93*
Schwille, Michael Edward 1936- *WhoAmL 94*
Schwimmer, David 1913- *WhoAm 94, WhoScEn 94*
Schwimmer, Rosika 1877-1948 *HisWorL [port]*
Schwind, Bernard Joseph, Jr. 1947- *WhoMW 93*
Schwind, Michael Angelo 1924- *WhoAm 94*
Schwinden, Dore D. 1956- *WhoAmP 93*
Schwinden, Ted 1925- *IntWW 93, WhoAmP 93, WhoWest 94*
Schwing, Charles E. 1929- *WhoAm 94*
Schwing, Frank *WhoHisp 94*
Schwing, Richard Charles 1934- *WhoMW 93*
Schwingendorf, Keith Eugene 1948- *WhoMW 93*
Schwinger, Julian 1918- *Who 94, WhoAm 94, WhoScEn 94, WhoWest 94, WrDr 94*
Schwinger, Julian Seymour 1918- *IntWW 93, WorScD*
Schwinghamer, Robert John 1928- *WhoAm 94*
Schwinkendorf, Kevin Neil 1959- *WhoFI 94*
Schwinn, Donald Edwin 1935- *WhoScEn 94*
Schwinn, Robert James 1930- *WhoAm 94*
Schwister, Jay Edward 1962- *WhoFI 94*
Schwitters, Roy Frederick 1944- *WhoScEn 94*
Schwoch, James 1955- *WhoMW 93*
Schwope, Mary Kathryn 1917- *WhoAmP 93*
Schworer, Philip Joseph 1955- *WhoAmL 94*
Schwortz, Barrie Marshall 1946- *WhoWest 94*
Schwyn, Charles Edward 1932- *WhoAm 94, WhoFI 94, WhoWest 94*
Schwyzer, Robert 1920- *IntWW 93*
Schye, Ted 1948- *WhoAmP 93*
Schygulla, Hanna 1943- *IntMPA 94, IntWW 93, WhoHol 92*
Schyve, Paul Milton 1944- *WhoMW 93*
Sciabica, Vincent Samuel 1959- *WhoFI 94, WhoScEn 94*
Sciacca, Kathleen 1943- *WhoScEn 94*
Sciama, Dennis (William) 1926- *WrDr 94*
Sciama, Dennis William 1926- *IntWW 93, Who 94*
Sciame, Donald Richard 1945- *WhoWest 94*
Sciammarella, Valdo 1924- *NewGrDO*
Sciammas, Jacques Daniel 1956- *WhoFI 94, WhoWest 94*
Sciance, Carroll Thomas 1939- *WhoScEn 94*
Sciarrino, Salvatore 1947- *NewGrDO*
Sciascia, Leonardo 1921-1989 *WhAm 10*
Sciba, JoAnn 1946- *WhoMW 93*
Scibelli, Anthony M. *WhoAmP 93*
Scibetta, Louis P. 1935- *WhoAm 94*
Scibilia, Philip Chester 1940- *WhoFI 94*
Scibor-Rylski, Aleksander 1928-1983 *IntDcF 2-4*
Scicchitano, Carmine David 1962- *WhoFI 94*
Scicluna, Martin Leonard Andrew 1935- *Who 94*
Scieszinski, John Joseph 1953- *WhoAmL 94*
Scieszka, Jon 1954- *WrDr 94*
Scifers, Mark J. 1951- *WhoFI 94*
Scifres, Don R. *WhoAm 94*
Scifres, Donald Ray 1946- *WhoScEn 94*
Sciglimpaglia, Robert Joseph, Jr. 1966- *WhoAmL 94*
Scimone, Claudio 1934- *NewGrDO*
Scindia, Vijaya Raje 1919- *WhoWomW 91*
Scio, Etienne 1766-1796 *NewGrDO*
Scio, Julie-Angelique 1768-1807 *NewGrDO*
Sciocchetti, Paul Vincent 1961- *WhoAmL 94*
Sciolaro, Charles Michael 1958- *WhoWest 94*
Sciolino, Ida d1993 *NewYTBS 93*
Scioly, Anthony Joseph 1950- *WhoScEn 94*
Sciorra, Annabella *WhoHol 92*
Sciorra, Annabella 1964- *IntMPA 94*
Sciortino, Salvatore Anthony 1936- *WhoAmL 94*
Scipio, Beverly Yvette 1951- *WhoMW 93*
Scipio, Howard C. 1921- *WhoAmP 93*
Scipio, Laurence Harold 1942- *WhoBlA 94*
Scipio, Louis Albert, II 1922- *WhoAm 94, WhoScEn 94*
Scipione, Richard Stephen 1937- *WhoAm 94, WhoAmL 94*
Scirica, Anthony J. *WhoAmP 93*
Scirica, Anthony Joseph 1940- *WhoAm 94, WhoAmL 94*
Sciroli, Gregorio 1722-1781 *NewGrDO*
Scisco, Peter Leon 1956- *WhoAm 94*
Scism, Daniel Reed 1936- *WhoAm 94*
Scisson, Sidney E. 1917- *WhAm 10*
Scites, Janice L. 1950- *WhoIns 94*
Scithers, George H(arry) 1929- *EncSF 93*
Scitovsky, Anne A. 1915- *IntWW 93*
Scitovsky, Anne Aickelin 1915- *WhoAm 94*
Sciutti, Graziella 1927- *NewGrDO*
Sciutto, Joseph A. 1906- *WhoWest 94*
Sclar, Charles Bertram 1925- *WhoAm 94*
Sclarow, Marshall Hillel 1930- *WhoWest 94*
Sclater, John G. 1940- *IntWW 93*
Sclater, John George 1940- *Who 94, WhoAm 94, WhoScEn 94*
Sclater, John Richard 1940- *IntWW 93, Who 94*
Sclater-Booth *Who 94*
Sclove, Richard Evan 1953- *WhoScEn 94*
Sclufer, Nicholas George 1919- *WhoFI 94*
Scob, Edith *WhoHol 92*
Scobba, Judy 1944- *WhoMW 93*
Scobey, Brad Preston 1957- *WhoAmL 94*
Scobie, Ilka *DrAPF 93*
Scobie, Kenneth Charles 1938- *Who 94*
Scoble, Christopher Lawrence 1943- *Who 94*
Scoble, (Arthur William) John *Who 94*
Scoby, Donald R. 1931- *WhoMW 93*
Scoby, Gloria *WhoAm 94*
Scofield, Bruce 1948- *AstEnc*
Scofield, Cyrus Ingerson 1843-1921 *DcAmReB 2*
Scofield, David Willson 1957- *WhoAmL 94, WhoWest 94*
Scofield, George W. 1955- *WhoAmL 94*
Scofield, Gordon Lloyd 1925- *WhoAm 94*
Scofield, John 1951- *WhoAm 94*
Scofield, Jonathan 1931- *WrDr 94*
Scofield, Julie Melissa 1958- *WhoAmP 93*
Scofield, Larry Allan 1952- *WhoScEn 94, WhoWest 94*
Scofield, Martin (Paul) 1945- *WrDr 94*
Scofield, Paul 1922- *IntMPA 94, IntWW 93, WhoAm 94, WhoHol 92*
Scofield, (David) Paul 1922- *Who 94*
Scofield, Richard Melbourne 1938- *WhoAm 94*
Scofield, Sandra K. 1947- *WhoAmP 93*
Scofield, Todd Carver 1956- *WhoFI 94*
Scoggin, James Franklin, Jr. 1921- *WhoScEn 94*
Scoggin, Sally A. 1952- *WhoAmL 94*
Scoggins, Donna Ruth 1947- *WhoMW 93*
Scoggins, John 1931- *WhoAmP 93*
Scoggins, Samuel McWhirter 1950- *WhoAm 94, WhoAmL 94*
Scoggins, Tracy 1953- *WhoHol 92*
Scoggins, Tracy 1959- *IntMPA 94*
Scogin, Edward C. 1921- *WhoAmP 93*
Scogin, Robert Erwin 1937- *WhoMW 93*
Scogland, William Lee 1949- *WhoAm 94, WhoAmL 94*
Scognamiglio, Carlo 1944- *IntWW 93*
Scola, Ettore 1931- *IntMPA 94, IntWW 93*
Scola, Ralph Joseph 1943- *WhoAmL 94*
Scolari, Fred 1922- *BasBi*
Scolari, Giuseppe 1720?-1774? *NewGrDO*
Scolari, Peter 1954- *IntMPA 94, WhoHol 92*
Scolaro, Vincent 1958- *WhoAmL 94*
Scoles, Clyde Sheldon 1949- *WhoAm 94, WhoMW 93*
Scoles, Eugene Francis 1921- *WhoAm 94*
Scoles, Giacinto 1935- *WhoScEn 94*
Scoll, Jonathan P. 1943- *WhoAmL 94*
Scollard, Diane Louise 1945- *WhoMW 93*
Scollard, Jeannette Reddish *WhoWest 94*
Scollard, Patrick John 1937- *WhoAm 94*
Scollay, Fred J. 1920- *WhoHol 92*
Scolnick, Edward Mark 1940- *WhoAm 94, WhoFI 94, WhoScEn 94*
Scolnik, Louis *WhoAmP 93*
Sconiers, Daryl Anthony 1958- *WhoBlA 94*
Sconiers, Rose H. *WhoBlA 94*
Scontrino, Antonio 1850-1922 *NewGrDO*
Scooler, Zvee d1985 *WhoHol 92*
Scoon, Paul 1935- *IntWW 93, Who 94*
Scopabirba, Gasparo *NewGrDO*
Scopatz, Stephen David 1957- *WhoMW 93, WhoScEn 94*
Scopaz, John Matthew 1948- *WhoAm 94*
Scoper, Vincent Gradie, Jr. 1933- *WhoAmP 93*
Scopes, Gary Martin 1947- *WhoAm 94*
Scopes, Leonard Arthur 1912- *Who 94*
Scopp, Irwin Walter 1909- *WhoScEn 94*
Scoppettone, Sandra 1936- *Au&Arts 11 [port], ConAu 41NR, GayLL, TwCYAW*
Scora, Rainer Walter 1928- *WhoWest 94*
Scordelis, Alexander Costicas 1923- *WhoAm 94*
Score, Phil d1979 *WhoHol 92*
Scorer, Philip Segar 1916- *Who 94*
Scoresby, William, Sr. 1760-1829 *WhWE*
Scoresby, William, Jr. 1789-1857 *WhWE*
Scorsese, Catherine *WhoHol 92*
Scorsese, Luciano Charles d1993 *NewYTBS 93*
Scorsese, Martin 1942- *AmCulL [port], IntMPA 94, IntWW 93, Who 94, WhoAm 94, WhoHol 92*
Scorsine, John Magnus 1957- *WhoAmL 94, WhoWest 94*
Scorsone, Ernesto 1952- *WhoAmP 93*
Scorsone, Vincent Robert 1935- *WhoFI 94*
Scortia, Thomas N(icholas) 1926-1986 *EncSF 93*
Scorza, Elaine M. 1953- *WhoMW 93*
Scorza, Sylvio Joseph 1923- *WhoAm 94*
Scorza, Thomas J. 1948- *WrDr 94*
Scot, Michael *EncSF 93*
Scot, Reginald c. 1538-1599 *DcLB 136*
Scotford, John Edward 1939- *Who 94*
Scothorne, Raymond John 1920- *Who 94*
Scotland, Jay *ConAu 43NR*
Scotland, Jay 1932- *WrDr 94*
Scott *Who 94*
Scott, Mrs. *NewGrDO*
Scott, A. Hugh 1947- *WhoAm 94*
Scott, A. Timothy 1952- *WhoAm 94*
Scott, Al d1990 *WhoHol 92*
Scott, Alan *WhoHol 92*
Scott, Alan 1947- *EncSF 93*
Scott, Alan 1964- *WhoScEn 94*
Scott, Alan (B.) 1957- *ConAu 141*
Scott, Alan James 1934- *Who 94*
Scott, Alastair Ian 1928- *IntWW 93, Who 94, WhoAm 94*
Scott, Albert J. *WhoAmP 93, WhoBlA 94*
Scott, Albert Nelson 1916- *WhoBlA 94*
Scott, Alex *WhoHol 92*
Scott, Alex 1923- *WhoAmP 93*
Scott, Alexander 1920- *WrDr 94*
Scott, Alexander Brian 1933- *IntWW 93*
Scott, Alexander Robinson 1941- *WhoScEn 94*
Scott, Alexander Whiteford 1904- *Who 94*
Scott, Alfred J. 1913- *WhoBlA 94*
Scott, Alfred James 1913- *WhoAm 94*
Scott, Alice H. *WhoAm 94, WhoBlA 94*
Scott, Allan 1941- *WrDr 94*
Scott, Allan (James Julius) 1952- *EncSF 93*
Scott, Amoret (Tanner) 1930- *WrDr 94*
Scott, Amy Annette Holloway 1916- *WhoMW 93, WhoScEn 94*
Scott, Andrea Kay 1948- *WhoMW 93*
Scott, Andrew 1928- *WhoAm 94, WhoAmL 94*
Scott, Angela Freeman 1967- *WhoScEn 94*
Scott, Anna Marie Porter Wall *WhoMW 93*
Scott, Anna Wall *WhoAmP 93*
Scott, Anne Byrd Firor 1921- *WhoAm 94*
Scott, Anthony (Percy) 1937- *Who 94*
Scott, Anthony Douglas 1933- *Who 94*
Scott, Arden 1938- *WhoAmA 93*
Scott, Arthur Bishop 1938- *WhoBlA 94*
Scott, Arthur Finley 1907- *ConAu 41NR, WrDr 94*
Scott, Artie A. 1946- *WhoBlA 94*
Scott, Aundrea Arthur 1942- *WhoBlA 94*
Scott, Avis *WhoHol 92*
Scott, B. Nibbelink 1944- *WhoAmA 93*
Scott, (Mackay Hugh) Baillie 1865-1945 *DcNaB MP*
Scott, Bainbridge *WhoHol 92*
Scott, Basil Y. 1925- *WhoBlA 94*
Scott, Becky Beckwith 1947- *WhoBlA 94*
Scott, Benjamin 1929- *WhoBlA 94*
Scott, Bernice Green 1945- *WhoAmP 93*
Scott, Bertha 1884-1965 *WhoAmA 93N*
Scott, Beth (Bailey) 1922- *WrDr 94*
Scott, Beverly Angela 1951- *WhoBlA 94*
Scott, Bill 1923- *WrDr 94*
Scott, Bill 1949- *WhoAm 94*
Scott, Bobby Kenneth 1933- *WhoAmP 93*
Scott, Bonnie 1941- *WhoHol 92*
Scott, Bonnie Kime 1944- *ConAu 43NR*
Scott, Boyd Franklin 1911- *WhoAmP 93*
Scott, Bradley Sterling 1948- *WhoFI 94*
Scott, Brenda 1943- *WhoHol 92*
Scott, Brian David 1946- *WhoAmL 94*
Scott, Brian Edward 1936- *WhoIns 94*
Scott, Brough *Who 94*
Scott, (John) Brough 1942- *Who 94*
Scott, Bruce 1947- *WhoHol 92*
Scott, Bruce Douglas 1958- *WhoScEn 94*
Scott, Buck 1929- *WhoAmP 93*
Scott, Byron Antom 1961- *WhoBlA 94*
Scott, C(harles) A(rthur) 1940- *WhoAmA 93*
Scott, C. Waldo 1916- *WhoBlA 94*
Scott, Campbell 1930- *WhoAm 94, WhoAmA 93*
Scott, Campbell 1961- *WhoHol 92*
Scott, Campbell 1962- *IntMPA 94, WhoAm 94*
Scott, Carl Douglas 1937- *WhoScEn 94*
Scott, Carol Della 1950- *WhoAm 94*
Scott, Caroline Georgina Mary 1944- *WhoMW 93*
Scott, Carolyn Marion 1954- *WhoMW 93*
Scott, Carolynne *DrAPF 93*
Scott, Carrie d1928 *WhoHol 92*
Scott, Carstella H. 1928- *WhoBlA 94*
Scott, Catherine Dorothy 1927- *WhoAm 94*
Scott, Catherine Margaret Mary *Who 94*
Scott, Charles 1739-1813 *AmRev, WhAmRev*
Scott, Charles David 1929- *WhoAm 94*
Scott, Charles E. 1940- *WhoBlA 94*
Scott, Charles E. 1949- *WhoBlA 94*
Scott, Charles Edward 1935- *WhoAm 94*
Scott, Charles Frederick 1942- *WhoAmL 94*
Scott, Charles K. 1945- *WhoAmP 93*
Scott, Charles Kennard 1945- *WhoWest 94*
Scott, Charles Lewis 1924- *WhoAm 94*
Scott, Charles R. 1928- *WhoFI 94*
Scott, Charles S. 1932- *WhoIns 94*
Scott, Charles Thomas 1949- *Who 94*
Scott, Charlie 1948- *BasBi*
Scott, Charlotte Hanley 1925- *WhoBlA 94*
Scott, Christopher 1930- *WrDr 94*
Scott, Clifford Alva 1908- *WhoBlA 94*
Scott, Clifton H. 1937- *WhoAmP 93*
Scott, Clyde Eugene 1884-1959 *WhoAmA 93N*
Scott, Colin John Fraser *Who 94*
Scott, Connie *WhoHol 92*
Scott, Connie Lou 1943- *WhoAmP 93*
Scott, Cornealious Socrates, Sr. 1909- *WhoBlA 94*
Scott, Cornelius Adolphus 1908- *WhoBlA 94*
Scott, Cyril d1945 *WhoHol 92*
Scott, Cyril (Meir) 1879-1970 *NewGrDO*
Scott, D. Beck 1931- *WhoAmP 93*
Scott, Dana Stewart 1932- *Who 94*
Scott, Darrel Joseph 1947- *WhoAm 94*
Scott, Dave d1964 *WhoHol 92*
Scott, David *Who 94, WhoHol 92*
Scott, David 1916- *Who 94*
Scott, David 1924- *Who 94*
Scott, David 1947- *WhoAmP 93*
Scott, David (Aubrey) 1919- *Who 94*
Scott, (William) David (Stewart) 1921- *Who 94*
Scott, David Bytovetzski 1919- *WhoAm 94, WhoWest 94*
Scott, David Gidley 1924- *Who 94*
Scott, David Irvin 1947- *WhoWest 94*
Scott, David Knight 1940- *WhoAm 94, WhoScEn 94*
Scott, David L. 1920- *WrDr 94*
Scott, David Lawrence 1956- *WhoScEn 94*
Scott, David McClure 1930- *WhoAm 94*
Scott, David W. *WhoBlA 94*
Scott, David Walter 1947- *WrDr 94*
Scott, David Warren 1950- *WhoAm 94*
Scott, David Winfield 1916- *WhoAmA 93*
Scott, Deborah Ann 1953- *WhoBlA 94*
Scott, Deborah Emont *WhoAm 94, WhoAmA 93*
Scott, Debra Kay 1953- *WhoAmP 93*
Scott, Debralee *WhoHol 92*
Scott, Delbert Lee *WhoAmP 93*
Scott, Dennis (Courtney) 1939-1991 *BlkWr 2*
Scott, Dennis Eugene 1968- *WhoBlA 94*
Scott, DeWitt Alvin, Sr. 1932- *WhoMW 93*
Scott, Dianna Gay 1956- *WhoMW 93*

Scott, Donald *Who 94*
Scott, (William) Donald 1903- *Who 94*
Scott, Donald Allison 1929- *WhoAm 94, WhoAmL 94*
Scott, Donald Fletcher 1930- *WrDr 94*
Scott, Donald L. 1938- *WhoBlA 94*
Scott, Donald Laverne 1938- *AfrAmG [port]*
Scott, Donald Michael 1943- *WhoWest 94*
Scott, Donald Ray 1954- *WhoFI 94*
Scott, Donald Walter 1945- *WhoWest 94*
Scott, Donna *WhoAmP 93*
Scott, Donnell 1947- *WhoBlA 94*
Scott, Donovan *WhoHol 92*
Scott, Douglas Andrew Montagu-Douglas- 1930- *Who 94*
Scott, Douglas Frederick Schumacher 1910- *Who 94*
Scott, Douglas Keith 1941- *Who 94*
Scott, Dred 1795-1858 *AfrAmAl 6*
Scott, Duncan *WhoAmP 93*
Scott, Edward, Jr. 1928- *WhoAmP 93*
Scott, Edward Aloysius 1923- *WhoAmL 94*
Scott, Edward McM. *Who 94*
Scott, Edward Philip 1937- *WhoAm 94, WhoAmP 93*
Scott, Edward Walter *Who 94*
Scott, Edward Walter 1919- *IntWW 93*
Scott, Edward William, Jr. 1938- *WhoAm 94*
Scott, Elinor Mary *Who 94*
Scott, Ella *WhoHol 92*
Scott, Eloise Hale 1932- *WhoAmP 93*
Scott, Elsie L. *WhoBlA 94*
Scott, Esme 1932- *Who 94*
Scott, Eugene Ray 1934- *WhoScEn 94*
Scott, Eva 1926- *WhoAmP 93*
Scott, Evelyn *WhoHol 92*
Scott, Finlay McMillan 1947- *Who 94*
Scott, Forrest Lindsey 1941- *WhoAmL 94*
Scott, Frank *WhoAm 94*
Scott, Frank 1949- *ConAu 141*
Scott, Franklin D. 1901- *WrDr 94*
Scott, Fred 1902- *WhoHol 92*
Scott, Fred William 1915- *WhoAmP 93*
Scott, Freddie, Jr. 1955- *WhoWest 94*
Scott, Frederick Bartlett 1894- *WhAm 10*
Scott, Frederick Isadore, Jr. 1927- *WhoAm 94*
Scott, Frederick T. d1942 *WhoHol 92*
Scott, G. Firth *EncSF 93*
Scott, G. Judson, Jr. 1945- *WhoAmL 94*
Scott, Gail *BlmGWL*
Scott, Gary Kuper 1933- *WhoAm 94*
Scott, Gary Lee 1934- *WhoAmP 93*
Scott, Gary LeRoy 1954- *WhoFI 94*
Scott, Gavin (Duncan) 1950- *WrDr 94*
Scott, Geoffrey *WhoHol 92*
Scott, Geoffrey 1884-1929 *DcNaB MP*
Scott, George C. 1927- *IntMPA 94, WhoHol 92*
Scott, George C(ampbell) 1927- *IntWW 93*
Scott, George Campbell 1927- *WhoAm 94*
Scott, George Ernest 1924- *WhoAm 94*
Scott, George Gallmann 1928- *WhoFI 94*
Scott, George Matthew 1922- *WhoAmP 93*
Scott, George William 1937- *WhoAmP 93*
Scott, Gerald David 1952- *WhoFI 94*
Scott, Gilbert H. 1946- *WhoBlA 94*
Scott, Gloria Dean Randle 1938- *WhoAm 94, WhoBlA 94*
Scott, Gordon 1927- *IntMPA 94, WhoHol 92*
Scott, Gordon Lee 1948- *WhoWest 94*
Scott, Gordon Robert 1936- *WhoFI 94*
Scott, Graham Alexander 1927- *Who 94*
Scott, Gregory Kellam 1943- *WhoAmL 94, WhoWest 94*
Scott, Gregory Kellam Scott *WhoAmP 93*
Scott, Gregory Thomas 1952- *WhoAmL 94*
Scott, Gustavus 1753-1800 *WhAmRev*
Scott, Hal S. 1943- *WhoAm 94, WhoAmL 94*
Scott, Hardiman *Who 94*
Scott, (Peter) Hardiman 1920- *Who 94*
Scott, Harley Earle 1934- *WhoFI 94*
Scott, Harold d1964 *WhoHol 92*
Scott, Harold Bartlett 1917- *WhoAm 94*
Scott, Harold Lee, Jr. 1949- *WhoFI 94*
Scott, Harold Richard 1887-1969 *DcNaB MP*
Scott, Harold Russell, Jr. 1935- *WhoBlA 94*
Scott, Harry d1947 *WhoHol 92*
Scott, Hattie Bell 1945- *WhoBlA 94*
Scott, Hazel d1981 *WhoHol 92*
Scott, Henry d1981 *WhoHol 92*
Scott, Henry E. 1900-1990 *WhoAmA 93N*
Scott, Henry Lawrence 1908- *WhoAm 94*
Scott, Henry William, Jr. 1916- *WhoAm 94*
Scott, Herbert *DrAPF 93*
Scott, Herbert Andrew 1924- *WhoScEn 94*
Scott, Homer Verlyn 1896- *WhAm 10*
Scott, Hosie L. 1943- *WhoBlA 94*
Scott, Howard Winfield, Jr. 1935- *WhoFI 94*
Scott, Hubert R. 1919- *WhoBlA 94*
Scott, Hugh 1900- *WhoAm 94, WhoAmP 93*
Scott, Hugh B. 1949- *WhoBlA 94*
Scott, Hugh J. 1933- *WhoBlA 94*
Scott, I. B. 1930- *WhoAm 94*
Scott, Ian *WhoHol 92*
Scott, Ian Dixon 1909- *Who 94*
Scott, Ian Laurence 1958- *WhoScEn 94*
Scott, Ian Richard 1940- *Who 94*
Scott, Irene Feagin 1912- *CngDr 93, WhoAm 94, WhoAmL 94*
Scott, Isadore Meyer 1912- *WhoAm 94*
Scott, Ivy d1947 *WhoHol 92*
Scott, J. Brian 1963- *WhoWest 94*
Scott, J.M. *EncSF 93*
Scott, Jack Hardiman *Who 94*
Scott, Jacob Reginald 1938- *WhoBlA 94*
Scott, Jacqueline *WhoHol 92*
Scott, James d1964 *WhoHol 92*
Scott, James (Walter) 1924- *Who 94*
Scott, James A. 1942- *WhoAmP 93*
Scott, James Alexander 1931- *Who 94*
Scott, James Alexander 1940- *Who 94*
Scott, James Archibald 1932- *Who 94*
Scott, James C. 1934- *WhoAmP 93*
Scott, James C(ampbell) 1936- *WrDr 94*
Scott, James Craig 1955- *WhoMW 93*
Scott, James F., Sr. 1903- *WhoBlA 94*
Scott, James Henry 1942- *WhoBlA 94*
Scott, James Hunter, Jr. 1945- *WhoFI 94*
Scott, James M. 1934- *WhoIns 94*
Scott, James M. 1938- *WhoAmP 93*
Scott, James Michael 1941- *WhoScEn 94*
Scott, James Noel 1939- *WhoScEn 94*
Scott, James Raymond 1937- *WhoAm 94*
Scott, James Steel 1924- *Who 94*
Scott, James White 1926- *WhoAm 94, WhoMW 93*
Scott, James William 1925- *WhoWest 94*
Scott, Jane 1918- *WrDr 94*
Scott, Jane Ellen 1943- *WhoMW 93*
Scott, Janette 1938- *WhoHol 92*
Scott, Janey *WrDr 94*
Scott, Jay 1949- *WhoAm 94, WrDr 94*
Scott, Jay 1949-1993 *ConAu 142*
Scott, Jean Grant 1940- *Who 94*
Scott, Jean Sampson 1925- *WhoBlA 94*
Scott, Jeremy *EncSF 93*
Scott, Jerry Don 1936- *WhoAm 94, WhoFI 94*
Scott, Jerry Earl 1955- *WhoFI 94*
Scott, Jimmie Dow 1930- *WhoAm 94*
Scott, Jody (Huguelet Wood) 1923- *EncSF 93*
Scott, John *Who 94*
Scott, John 1907- *WhoAmA 93*
Scott, John 1950- *WhoAmA 93*
Scott, (Philip) John 1931- *Who 94*
Scott, (Walter) John 1948- *Who 94*
Scott, John A. 1948- *WrDr 94*
Scott, John Anthony 1916- *WrDr 94*
Scott, John B. 1944- *WhoIns 94*
Scott, John Beldon 1946- *WhoAmA 93*
Scott, John Brooks 1931- *WhoAm 94*
Scott, John Burt 1944- *WhoAm 94, WhoFI 94, WhoMW 93*
Scott, John Carl 1958- *WhoMW 93*
Scott, John Carlyle 1933- *WhoWest 94*
Scott, John Constante 1941- *WhoAm 94*
Scott, John E. *WhoAmP 93*
Scott, John Edward 1920- *WhoAm 94*
Scott, John Edward Smith 1936- *WhoAm 94*
Scott, John F. 1950- *WhoAmP 93*
Scott, John Francis 1944- *WhoWest 94*
Scott, John Fraser 1928- *Who 94*
Scott, John Fredrik 1936- *WhoAmA 93*
Scott, John Gavin 1956- *Who 94*
Scott, John Hamilton 1936- *Who 94*
Scott, John James 1924- *Who 94*
Scott, John Joseph 1950- *WhoFI 94*
Scott, John Lee, Jr. 1953- *WhoAmP 93*
Scott, John Lenard 1921- *WhoAm 94*
Scott, John Morin 1730-1784 *WhAmRev*
Scott, John P. 1933- *WhoAmP 93*
Scott, John P., Jr. 1947- *WhoAmL 94*
Scott, John Paul 1909- *WhoAm 94*
Scott, John Roland 1937- *WhoAmL 94, WhoFI 94*
Scott, John Russell 1951- *WhoAmL 94*
Scott, John Sherman 1937- *WhoBlA 94*
Scott, John T. 1940- *WhoBlA 94*
Scott, John Tarrell 1940- *WhoAmA 93*
Scott, John Walter 1919- *WhoAm 94*
Scott, John William 1935- *WhoAm 94, WhoFI 94*
Scott, John Wyeth 1947- *WhoAmP 93*
Scott, Jonathan 1914- *WhoAmA 93*
Scott, Jonathan 1958- *WrDr 94*
Scott, Jonathan L. 1930- *IntWW 93*
Scott, Jonathan LaVon 1930- *WhoWest 94*
Scott, Joseph M. 1945- *WhoBlA 94*
Scott, Joseph Mitchell, Jr. 1946- *WhoAmL 94*
Scott, Joseph Walter 1935- *WhoBlA 94*
Scott, Joyce 1948- *WhoAmA 93*
Scott, Joyce Alaine 1943- *WhoAm 94*
Scott, Juanita Simons 1936- *WhoBlA 94*
Scott, Judith Ann 1956- *WhoMW 93*
Scott, Judith Sugg 1945- *WhoBlA 94*
Scott, Julius S., Jr. 1925- *WhoBlA 94*
Scott, Karen Bondurant 1946- *WhoMW 93*
Scott, Kathryn Leigh *WhoHol 92*
Scott, Kay d1971 *WhoHol 92*
Scott, Ken d1986 *WhoHol 92*
Scott, Kenneth d1993 *NewYTBS 93*
Scott, Kenneth 1947- *WhoAmL 94*
Scott, Kenneth (Bertram Adam) 1931- *Who 94*
Scott, Kenneth Daniel *WhoAmP 93*
Scott, Kenneth Edmund 1903- *WhoAmP 93*
Scott, Kenneth Elsner 1926- *WhoAm 94*
Scott, Kenneth Eugene 1928- *WhoAm 94*
Scott, Kenneth Farish 1918- *Who 94*
Scott, Kenneth Richard 1934- *WhoBlA 94*
Scott, Kerrigan Davis 1941- *WhoFI 94*
Scott, Kevin *WhoHol 92*
Scott, Kimberly *WhoHol 92*
Scott, Kip *WhoAmP 93*
Scott, Kirk *WhoHol 92*
Scott, Larry B. 1961- *WhoBlA 94, WhoHol 92*
Scott, Larry Jay 1947- *WhoMW 93*
Scott, Larry Marcus 1945- *WhoScEn 94*
Scott, Lary R. 1936- *WhoAm 94*
Scott, Laurence Disraeli *WhoAmL 94*
Scott, Laurence Joseph 1957- *WhoMW 93*
Scott, Lawrence Rowe 1956- *WhoAmL 94*
Scott, Lawrence Vernon 1917- *WhoAm 94*
Scott, Leanne Brooks 1961- *WhoWest 94*
Scott, Lee Allen, Sr. 1940- *WhoFI 94*
Scott, Lee Hansen 1926- *WhoAm 94, WhoFI 94*
Scott, Leland Wakefield 1893- *WhAm 10*
Scott, Leon Leroy 1941- *WhoBlA 94*
Scott, Leonard Lamar 1924- *WhoBlA 94*
Scott, Leonard Lewy, Jr. 1942- *WhoScEn 94*
Scott, Leonard Stephen 1949- *WhoBlA 94*
Scott, Leslie d1969 *WhoHol 92*
Scott, Levan Ralph 1915- *WhoBlA 94*
Scott, Lewis Kelly 1928- *WhoAm 94*
Scott, Lewis Nathanel 1938- *WhoBlA 94*
Scott, Linda *WhoHol 92*
Scott, Linzy, Jr. 1934- *WhoBlA 94*
Scott, Lizabeth 1922- *WhoHol 92*
Scott, Lois 1924- *WhoHol 92*
Scott, Louis Edward 1923- *WhoAm 94*
Scott, Mabel Julienne d1976 *WhoHol 92*
Scott, Malcolm Charles Norman 1951- *Who 94*
Scott, Marc d1981 *WhoHol 92*
Scott, Margaret 1922- *Who 94*
Scott, Margaret Simon 1934- *WhoFI 94*
Scott, Margaretta 1912- *WhoHol 92*
Scott, Marian (Dale) 1906- *WhoAmA 93*
Scott, Marianne Florence 1928- *WhoAm 94*
Scott, Mariette Arguimbau *WhoHisp 94*
Scott, Mark d1960 *WhoHol 92*
Scott, Mark Edward 1955- *WhoFI 94*
Scott, Markie d1958 *WhoHol 92*
Scott, Martha 1914- *WhoHol 92*
Scott, Martha 1916- *IntMPA 94*
Scott, Martha F. 1916- *WhoAmA 93*
Scott, Martha Gene 1935- *WhoAmP 93*
Scott, Marvin Bailey 1944- *WhoBlA 94*
Scott, Marvin Wayne 1952- *WhoBlA 94*
Scott, Mary (Taylor) 1752-1793 *BlmGWL*
Scott, Mary Davies 1944- *WhoAm 94, WhoAmL 94*
Scott, Mary Edith 1888-1979 *BlmGWL*
Scott, Mary Ellen Ann 1949- *WhoScEn 94*
Scott, Mary Francis 1954- *WhoMW 93*
Scott, Mary Shy *WhoBlA 94*
Scott, Matthew Peter 1953- *WhoScEn 94*
Scott, Maurice FitzGerald 1924- *Who 94*
Scott, Melissa *EncSF 93*
Scott, Melody Thomas *WhoHol 92*
Scott, Melvina Brooks 1948- *WhoBlA 94*
Scott, Michael 1923- *IntWW 93, Who 94*
Scott, Michael 1930- *WhoAm 94*
Scott, Michael Dennis 1945- *WhoAm 94, WhoAmL 94, WhoWest 94*
Scott, Michael Frederick 1911- *Who 94*
Scott, Michael Ian Eldon 1941- *Who 94*
Scott, Michael John 1932- *Who 94*
Scott, Michael Lester 1952- *WhoAm 94*
Scott, Michael Ramsey 1956- *WhoAmL 94*
Scott, Michael Timothy 1951- *WhoAm 94, WhoAmL 94*
Scott, Mildred Hope 1926- *WhoMW 93*
Scott, Mimi Koblenz 1940- *WhoAm 94*
Scott, Mona Vaughn *WhoBlA 94*
Scott, Morris Douglas 1945- *WhoWest 94*
Scott, Morris Lee 1927- *WhoAmP 93*
Scott, (Robert James) Munroe 1927- *WrDr 94*
Scott, Murray Leslie 1958- *WhoScEn 94*
Scott, Myrtle 1937- *WhoMW 93*
Scott, Nancy *DrAPF 93*
Scott, Nathan A., Jr. 1925- *WhoBlA 94, WrDr 94*
Scott, Nathan A(lexander) 1925- *BlkWr 2*
Scott, Nathan Alexander, Jr. 1925- *WhoAm 94*
Scott, Nauman S. 1916- *WhoAm 94, WhoAmL 94*
Scott, Nellie Chavarria 1956- *WhoHisp 94*
Scott, Nicholas (Paul) 1933- *Who 94*
Scott, Nigel L. 1940- *WhoBlA 94*
Scott, Norma Joyce 1928- *WhoAmP 93*
Scott, Norman L. 1931- *WhoScEn 94*
Scott, Norman Ross 1918- *WhoMW 93, WhoScEn 94*
Scott, Norman Roy 1936- *WhoAm 94*
Scott, Oliver (Christopher Anderson) 1922- *Who 94*
Scott, Oliver Lester Schreiner 1919- *Who 94*
Scott, Olof Henderson, Jr. 1942- *WhoAm 94*
Scott, Omeria McDonald *WhoAmP 93*
Scott, Orange 1800-1847 *DcAmReB 2*
Scott, Osborne E. 1916- *WhoBlA 94*
Scott, Otis, Sr. 1919- *WhoBlA 94*
Scott, Otis L. 1941- *WhoBlA 94*
Scott, Otto 1918- *WhoWest 94*
Scott, Owen Myers, Jr. 1952- *WhoScEn 94*
Scott, P(aul) H(enderson) 1920- *ConAu 142*
Scott, P. Mars 1953- *WhoAmL 94*
Scott, Pamela Moyers 1961- *WhoScEn 94*
Scott, Patricia *WhoAmP 93*
Scott, Patricia Kaczynski 1964- *WhoFI 94*
Scott, Paul d1944 *WhoHol 92*
Scott, Paul 1920-1978 *BlmGEL*
Scott, Paul Henderson 1920- *Who 94*
Scott, Peg O'Neill *EncSF 93*
Scott, Peggy d1926 *WhoHol 92*
Scott, Peter *Who 94*
Scott, Peter 1935- *IntWW 93*
Scott, Peter 1946- *WrDr 94*
Scott, (Charles) Peter 1917- *Who 94*
Scott, Peter (Markham) 1909-1989 *WhAm 10*
Scott, Peter Bryan 1947- *WhoAmL 94, WhoWest 94*
Scott, Peter Denys John 1935- *Who 94*
Scott, Peter T. *EncSF 93*
Scott, Philip D. 1942- *WhoAmL 94*
Scott, Philip Lawler, Jr. 1948- *WhoMW 93*
Scott, Pippa 1938- *WhoHol 92*
Scott, Portia Alexandria 1943- *WhoBlA 94*
Scott, R. J. *WhoAm 94*
Scott, R. Lee 1943- *WhoBlA 94*
Scott, Rachel Loraine 1954- *WhoBlA 94*
Scott, Ralph C. 1921- *WhoMW 93*
Scott, Ralph Mason 1921- *WhoAm 94*
Scott, Randall Wayne 1945- *WhoAmL 94*
Scott, Randolph d1987 *WhoHol 92*
Scott, Ray 1938- *BasBi*
Scott, Ray Vernon, Jr. 1950- *WhoFI 94*
Scott, Raymond 1909- *WhoHol 92*
Scott, Raymond Gerald 1916- *WhoMW 93*
Scott, Raymond Peter William 1924- *WhoAm 94*
Scott, Rebecca Andrews 1939- *WhoMW 93*
Scott, Richard (Rashleigh Folliott) 1934- *Who 94*
Scott, Richard Allen 1942- *WhoMW 93*
Scott, Richard Eley 1945- *WhoAmP 93, WhoBlA 94*
Scott, Richard Jamieson 1938- *WhoMW 93*
Scott, Richard John Dinwoodie 1939- *Who 94*
Scott, Richard L. *NewYTBS 93 [port]*
Scott, Richard Lynn 1941- *WhoMW 93, WhoScEn 94*
Scott, Richard Philippe 1932- *WhoFI 94*
Scott, Richard Rashleigh 1934- *IntWW 93*
Scott, Richard Walter 1941- *WhoWest 94*
Scott, Richard William 1926- *WhoMW 93*
Scott, Ridley *IntWW 93*
Scott, Ridley 1937- *IntMPA 94*
Scott, Ridley 1939- *EncSF 93, WhoAm 94*
Scott, Robert *WhoHol 92*
Scott, Robert 1913- *Who 94*
Scott, Robert A. *WhoIns 94*
Scott, Robert Allyn 1939- *WhoAm 94, WhoFI 94*
Scott, Robert C. 1947- *CngDr 93*
Scott, Robert Cortez 1947- *WhoAm 94, WhoAmP 93, WhoBlA 94*
Scott, Robert David Hillyer 1944- *Who 94*
Scott, Robert Edmond Gabriel 1920- *Who 94*
Scott, Robert Edward, Jr. 1945- *WhoAm 94, WhoAmL 94*
Scott, Robert Edwin 1944- *WhoAmL 94*

Scott, Robert Falcon 1868-1912 *WhWE*
Scott, Robert Gene 1951- *WhoAmL 94*
Scott, Robert Henry 1833-1916 *DcNaB MP*
Scott, Robert J. 1949- *WhoAmP 93*
Scott, Robert Jerome 1946- *WhoBlA 94*
Scott, Robert L. 1935- *WhoBlA 94*
Scott, Robert Lane 1922- *WhoAm 94*
Scott, Robert Lee 1928- *WhoAm 94*
Scott, Robert Lee, Jr. 1908- *WhoAm 94*
Scott, Robert Montgomery 1929- *WhoAm 94, WhoAmA 93*
Scott, Robin *EncSF 93, Who 94*
Scott, Roderic MacDonald 1916- *WhoAm 94*
Scott, Roger Martin 1944- *Who 94*
Scott, Roger Roy 1935- *WhoAmL 94*
Scott, Roland B. 1909- *WhoBlA 94*
Scott, Roland Boyd 1909- *WhoScEn 94*
Scott, Ronald 1927- *IntWW 93, Who 94*
Scott, Ronald 1947- *WhoAmL 94*
Scott, Ronald Charles 1948- *WhoAmL 94*
Scott, Ronald Fraser 1929- *WhoAm 94*
Scott, Ronald Hubert 1912- *WhoMW 93*
Scott, Ronald McLean 1933- *WhoMW 93*
Scott, RONEY 1910- *WrDr 94*
Scott, Rosie *BlmGWL*
Scott, Roy Vernon 1927- *WrDr 94*
Scott, Ruth 1934- *WhoBlA 94*
Scott, Sam 1940- *WhoAmA 93*
Scott, Samuel 1946- *WhoBlA 94*
Scott, Samuel Francis 1938- *WhoMW 93*
Scott, Sandra Louise 1944- *WhoMW 93*
Scott, Sandy 1943- *WhoAmA 93*
Scott, Sarah (Robinson) 1732-1795 *BlmGWL*
Scott, Sheila d1988 *WhoHol 92*
Scott, Simon *WhoHol 92*
Scott, Sondra *WhoHol 92*
Scott, Spencer W. 1939- *WhoAmP 93*
Scott, Stanley DeForest 1926- *WhoFI 94*
Scott, Stanley S. 1933- *WhoAmP 93*
Scott, Stanley S. 1933-1992 *WhoBlA 94N*
Scott, Stanley VanAken 1943- *WhoWest 94*
Scott, Stephen E. 1948- *ConAu 43NR*
Scott, Stephen Thomas 1931- *WhoAm 94*
Scott, Steven Donald 1941- *WhoAm 94, WhoScEn 94*
Scott, Steven Evans 1961- *WhoMW 93*
Scott, Steven Michael 1952- *WhoFI 94*
Scott, Steven Mike 1955- *WhoScEn 94*
Scott, Stuart Nash 1906-1992 *WhAm 10*
Scott, Susan 1943- *WhoAm 94, WhoAmL 94*
Scott, Terry 1927- *WhoHol 92*
Scott, Theodore R. 1924- *WhoAm 94, WhoAmL 94, WhoMW 93*
Scott, Thomas *WhoAmP 93*
Scott, Thomas 1566?-1635 *DcNaB MP*
Scott, Thomas Clevenger 1936- *WhoAm 94*
Scott, Thomas E. 1943- *WhoAmP 93*
Scott, Thomas Fielding 1807-1867 *DcAmReB 2*
Scott, Thomas Frederick McNair 1901- *Who 94*
Scott, Thomas Jefferson, Jr. 1943- *WhoAm 94, WhoAmL 94*
Scott, Thomas Ryals 1940- *WhoAmP 93*
Scott, Thomas Wright 1948- *WhoAm 94*
Scott, Thora *Who 94*
Scott, Timothy *WhoHol 92*
Scott, Timothy d1988 *WhoHol 92*
Scott, Timothy 1937- *IntWW 93*
Scott, Timothy Van 1942- *WhoBlA 94*
Scott, Tom 1918- *WrDr 94*
Scott, Tom Keck 1931- *WhoAm 94*
Scott, Tony *IntMPA 94, WhoAm 94*
Scott, Tony 1944- *IntWW 93*
Scott, Ulric Carl 1932- *WhoAmP 93*
Scott, Van 1921- *WhoAmP 93*
Scott, Vernell Izora 1948- *WhoAmL 94*
Scott, Veronica J. 1946- *WhoBlA 94*
Scott, Virginia *DrAPF 93*
Scott, W(illiam) G. *Who 94*
Scott, W. Peter *WhoMW 93*
Scott, W. Richard 1932- *IntWW 93*
Scott, Waldron 1929- *WhoAm 94*
Scott, Wallace d1970 *WhoHol 92*
Scott, Walter d1940 *WhoHol 92*
Scott, Walter d1992 *Who 94N*
Scott, Walter 1771-1832 *BlmGEL [port], NewGrDO, RfGShF*
Scott, Walter 1796-1861 *DcAmReB 2*
Scott, Walter 1919- *WhoAmA 93*
Scott, Walter Coke 1919- *WhoAm 94*
Scott, Walter Dill 1931- *WhoAm 94*
Scott, Warwick *EncSF 93, WrDr 94*
Scott, Werner Ferdinand 1957- *WhoBlA 94*
Scott, Whitney *DrAPF 93*
Scott, Willard Herman 1934- *WhoAm 94*
Scott, Willard Philip 1909- *WhoAm 94*
Scott, William (Harvey) *WhoHol 92*
Scott, William Arthur, III 1949- *WhoWest 94*
Scott, William Beverley 1917- *WhoAm 94*
Scott, William Clement, III 1934- *WhoAm 94*
Scott, William Clifford Munro 1903- *Who 94*
Scott, William Coryell 1920- *WhoAm 94, WhoWest 94*
Scott, William Curtiss, Jr. 1934- *WhoFI 94*
Scott, William Dow 1937- *WhoAmP 93*
Scott, William Edd 1944- *WhoBlA 94*
Scott, William Edward 1953- *WhoWest 94*
Scott, William Floyd 1936- *WhoFI 94*
Scott, William Fred 1953- *WhoAm 94*
Scott, William George 1913-1989 *WhAm 10*
Scott, William Henry 1921- *WrDr 94*
Scott, William James, Sr. 1943- *WhoFI 94*
Scott, William L. 1915- *WhoAmP 93*
Scott, William Leonard 1945- *WhoScEn 94*
Scott, William Paul 1928- *WhoAm 94, WhoMW 93*
Scott, William Proctor, III 1946- *WhoAm 94, WhoAmL 94*
Scott, William Richard 1932- *WhoAm 94*
Scott, William Wootton 1930- *Who 94*
Scott, Windie Olivia *WhoBlA 94*
Scott, Winfield 1786-1866 *HisWorL [port]*
Scott, Winifred d1981 *WhoHol 92*
Scott, Zachary d1965 *WhoHol 92*
Scott-Barrett, David (William) 1922- *Who 94*
Scott-Bowden, Logan 1920- *Who 94*
Scott Brown, Denise 1931- *AmCulL, IntWW 93*
Scott-Craven, Arthur d1917 *WhoHol 92*
Scott Duniway, Abigail 1834-1915 *WomPubS*
Scott-Elliot, Aydua Helen 1909- *Who 94*
Scott Elliot, James 1902- *Who 94*
Scott-Ellis *Who 94*
Scott-Gatty, Alexander d1937 *WhoHol 92*
Scott-Gibson, Herbert Nathaniel 1928-1981 *WhoAmA 93N*
Scott-Heron, Gil 1949- *WhoBlA 94*
Scott-Hopkins, James (Sidney Rawdon) 1921- *Who 94*
Scotti, Antonio 1866-1936 *NewGrDO [port]*
Scotti, Frank Anthony 1952- *WhoWest 94*
Scotti, Michael John, Jr. 1938- *WhoAm 94, WhoFI 94*
Scotti, R. A. 1946- *WrDr 94*
Scotti, Tino d1984 *WhoHol 92*
Scotti, Vito 1918- *WhoHol 92*
Scott-Jackson, Lisa Odessa 1960- *WhoBlA 94*
Scott-James, Anne Eleanor 1913- *Who 94*
Scott-Johnson, Roberta Virginia *WhoBlA 94*
Scott-Joynt, Michael Charles *Who 94*
Scott-Malden, (Francis) David (Stephen) 1919- *Who 94*
Scott-Malden, Peter *Who 94*
Scott-Malden, (Charles) Peter 1918- *Who 94*
Scott-Moncrieff, William 1922- *Who 94*
Scott Nichols, Dora Hoeflich 1927- *WhoAmP 93*
Scotto, Renata 1934- *NewGrDO*
Scotto, Renata 1935- *IntWW 93, WhoAm 94*
Scott-Smith, Catharine Mary 1912- *Who 94*
Scott-Thomas, Kristin *IntMPA 94*
Scott-Thomas, Kristin 1960- *WhoHol 92*
Scott-Ware-Brandon, Barbara Ann 1955- *WhoBlA 94*
Scott Whyte, Stuart *Who 94*
Scott-Wilkinson, Sheila *WhoHol 92*
Scott-Williams, Stephanie 1947- *WhoAmP 93*
Scott-Williams, Wendy Lee 1953- *WhoFI 94*
Scott Wright, Margaret 1923- *Who 94*
Scotus, John Duns *EncEth*
Scoular, Angela *WhoHol 92*
Scoular, Florence Isabelle 1897- *WhAm 10*
Scoular, Robert Frank 1942- *WhoAmL 94*
Scouller, (John) Alan 1929- *Who 94*
Scourby, Alexander d1985 *WhoHol 92*
Scourby, Helen *WhoHol 92*
Scourfield, Edward Grismond Beaumont D. *Who 94*
Scouten, William Henry 1942- *WhoAm 94, WhoScEn 94*
Scovel, Al 1939- *WhoAmP 93*
Scovel, Mary Alice 1936- *WhoMW 93*
Scovell, Brian (Souter) 1935- *WrDr 94*
Scovell, E(dith) J(oy) 1907- *WrDr 94*
Scovelli, Gaetano fl. 1767-1792 *NewGrDO*
Scovil, Roger Morris 1929- *WhoAm 94*
Scovil, Samuel Kingston 1923- *WhoAm 94*
Scoville, Herbert, Jr. 1915-1985 *ConAu 43NR*
Scoville, James Griffin 1940- *WhoAm 94, WrDr 94*
Scoville, Jonathan Armstrong 1937- *WhoAmA 93*
Scoville, Laurence McConway, Jr. 1936- *WhoAmL 94*
Scoville, Vernon Eugene, III 1953- *WhoAmP 93*
Scovotti, Jeanette 1936- *NewGrDO*
Scowcroft, Brent 1925- *IntWW 93, WhoAm 94, WhoAmP 93*
Scowcroft, John Major 1924- *WhoWest 94*
Scowen, Eric (Frank) 1910- *Who 94*
Scown, Michael John 1959- *WhoAmL 94*
Scozzie, James Anthony 1943- *WhoScEn 94*
Scrabeck, Jon Gilmen 1938- *WhoMW 93*
Scranage, Clarence, Jr. 1955- *WhoBlA 94*
Scranton, Mary Isabelle 1950- *WhoScEn 94*
Scranton, William Maxwell 1921- *WhoAm 94*
Scranton, William Warren 1917- *IntWW 93, WhoAmP 93*
Scrase-Dickins, Mark Frederick Hakon 1936- *Who 94*
Screech, M(ichael) A(ndrew) 1926- *ConAu 140, WrDr 94*
Screech, Michael Andrew 1926- *IntWW 93, Who 94*
Screen, Pat 1943- *WhoAmP 93*
Screpetis, Dennis 1930- *WhoFI 94, WhoScEn 94*
Screttas, Constantinos George 1933- *WhoScEn 94*
Screwvala, Farrokh Nozer 1939- *WhoFI 94*
Scribe, (Augustin) Eugene 1791-1861 *IntDcT 2 [port], NewGrDO [port]*
Scribner, Allison Kenneth 1898- *WhAm 10*
Scribner, Arthur Gerald, Jr. 1955- *WhoBlA 94*
Scribner, Barbara Colvin 1926- *WhoAm 94*
Scribner, Belding *WorInv*
Scribner, Belding Hibbard 1921- *WhoAm 94*
Scribner, Charles, Jr. 1921- *IntWW 93, WhoAm 94*
Scribner, Charles, III 1951- *WhoAm 94, WhoAmA 93*
Scribner, Dorothy Nesbitt 1938- *WhoWest 94*
Scribner, Fred Clark, Jr. 1908- *WhoAm 94, WhoAmP 93, WhoFI 94*
Scribner, James Bruce 1937- *WhoFI 94, WhoWest 94*
Scribner, Richard Orestes 1936- *WhoAm 94*
Scribner, Ronald Kent 1948- *WhoAm 94*
Scribner, Susan Solomon 1949- *WhoMW 93*
Scribner, Sylvia 1923- *WrDr 94*
Scriggins, Larry Palmer 1936- *WhoAm 94*
Scrimenti, Belinda Jayne 1956- *WhoAmL 94*
Scrimenti, Thomas J. 1960- *WhoAmP 93*
Scrimgeour, G. J. *DrAPF 93*
Scrimgeour, James R. *DrAPF 93*
Scrimger, Joseph Arnold 1924- *WhoScEn 94*
Scrimm, Angus *WhoHol 92*
Scrimshaw, Frank Herbert 1917- *Who 94*
Scrimshaw, George Currie 1925- *WhoWest 94*
Scrimshaw, Nevin Stewart 1918- *IntWW 93, WhoAm 94*
Scripp, John 1943- *WhoAmL 94*
Scripps, Charles Edward 1920- *IntWW 93, WhoAm 94, WhoFI 94, WhoMW 93*
Scripps, Edward Wyllis 1909- *WhoAm 94*
Scripps, John P. 1912-1989 *WhAm 10*
Script, Dee Rossi *DrAPF 93*
Scripter, Frank C. 1918- *WhoFI 94, WhoMW 93*
Scritchfield, Shirley Ann 1947- *WhoMW 93*
Scritsmier, Jerome Lorenzo 1925- *WhoFI 94, WhoWest 94*
Scriven, L. Edward 1931- *WhoAm 94*
Scriven, Pamela 1948- *Who 94*
Scriven, Wilton Maxwell 1924- *Who 94*
Scrivener, Anthony Frank Bertram 1935- *Who 94*
Scrivener, Christiane 1925- *IntWW 93, Who 94, WhoWomW 91*
Scrivener, Michael (Henry) 1948- *WrDr 94*
Scrivener, Ronald Stratford 1919- *Who 94*
Scrivenor, Thomas (Vaisey) 1908- *Who 94*
Scriver, Charles Robert 1930- *IntWW 93, Who 94, WhoAm 94*
Scriver, Robert Macfie 1914- *WhoAm 94, WhoAmA 93, WhoWest 94*
Scrivner, Calla d1981 *WhoHol 92*
Scrivner, James Daniel 1951- *WhoScEn 94*
Scrivner, Thomas William 1948- *WhoAm 94, WhoAmL 94*
Scroggie, Alan Ure Reith 1912- *Who 94*
Scroggins, Daryl *DrAPF 93*
Scroggs, Cedric Annesley 1941- *Who 94*
Scroggs, Debbie Lee 1953- *WhoWest 94*
Scrope, Emanuel 1584-1630 *DcNaB MP*
Scruby, Ronald Victor 1919- *Who 94*
Scrudder, Eugene Owen 1918- *WhoScEn 94*
Scruggs, Allie W. 1927- *WhoBlA 94*
Scruggs, Barbara Lee 1932- *WhoAmP 93*
Scruggs, Booker T., II 1942- *WhoBlA 94*
Scruggs, Charles G. 1923- *WhoAm 94*
Scruggs, Cleorah J. 1948- *WhoBlA 94*
Scruggs, David Wayne 1940- *WhoScEn 94*
Scruggs, Earl Eugene 1924- *WhoAm 94*
Scruggs, Jack Gilbert 1930- *WhoAm 94*
Scruggs, Jimmy d1985 *WhoHol 92*
Scruggs, John Dudley 1911- *WhoAm 94*
Scruggs, Langhorn d1981 *WhoHol 92*
Scruggs, Linda *WhoHol 92*
Scruggs, Otey Matthew 1929- *WhoBlA 94*
Scruggs, Paul C., Jr. 1937- *WhoAmP 93*
Scruggs, Sylvia Ann 1951- *WhoBlA 94*
Scruggs, Yvonne 1933- *WhoBlA 94*
Scrutchions, Benjamin 1926- *WhoBlA 94*
Scruton, Roger 1944- *IntWW 93, WrDr 94*
Scruton, Roger Vernon 1944- *Who 94*
Scrymgeour *Who 94*
Scrymgeour, Lord 1982- *Who 94*
Scrymsour, Ella M. 1888- *EncSF 93*
Scucchi, Robie (Peter), Jr. 1944- *WhoAmA 93*
Scudamore, Margaret d1958 *WhoHol 92*
Scudamore, Peter 1958- *IntWW 93*
Scudamore, Peter Michael 1958- *Who 94*
Scudder, David Benjamin 1923- *WhoWest 94*
Scudder, Edward Wallace, Jr. 1911- *WhoAm 94*
Scudder, Geoffrey George Edgar 1934- *WhoAm 94*
Scudder, Jack Howard 1919- *WhoWest 94*
Scudder, Nathaniel 1733-1781 *WhAmRev*
Scudder, Richard B. 1913- *WhoAm 94*
Scudder, Thayer 1930- *WhoAm 94*
Scudder, Vida Dutton 1861-1954 *DcAmReB 2*
Scuderi, Louis Anthony 1954- *WhoScEn 94*
Scuderi, Salvatore Carmelo 1927- *WhoAmL 94*
Scudery, Georges de 1601-1667 *GuFrLit 2, IntDcT 2*
Scudery, Madeleine de 1607-1701 *BlmGWL*
Scudery, Madeleine de 1608-1701 *GuFrLit 2*
Scudery, Marie-Madeleine du Moncel de Martinval 1627-1711 *BlmGWL*
Scudiere, Debra Hodges 1954- *WhoAmL 94*
Sculfort, Jean-Lou 1944- *WhoScEn 94*
Sculfort, Maurice Charles 1925- *WhoAm 94*
Scull, David Lee 1943- *WhoAmP 93*
Scull, Marie-Louise 1943-1993 *SmATA 77 [port]*
Scullard, Geoffrey Layton 1922- *Who 94*
Sculley, David W. 1946- *WhoAm 94, WhoFI 94*
Sculley, John 1939- *IntWW 93, WhoAm 94, WhoFI 94, WhoWest 94*
Scullin, Frederick James, Jr. 1939- *WhoAm 94, WhoAmL 94*
Scullion, Tsugiko Yamagami 1946- *WhoAm 94*
Scully, Crispian Michael 1945- *Who 94*
Scully, Erik Vincent 1957- *WhoAmL 94*
Scully, Gerald William 1941- *WhoFI 94*
Scully, James *DrAPF 93*
Scully, James (Joseph) 1937- *WrDr 94*
Scully, Joe 1926- *IntMPA 94*
Scully, John C. 1932- *WhoIns 94*
Scully, John Carroll 1932- *WhoAm 94, WhoFI 94*
Scully, John Kenneth 1935- *WhoWest 94*
Scully, John Thomas 1931- *WhoAm 94*
Scully, Joseph C. 1940- *WhoAm 94, WhoFI 94*
Scully, Roger Tehan 1948- *WhoAmL 94, WhoFI 94*
Scully, Samuel Edward 1942- *WhoWest 94*
Scully, Sean *WhoHol 92*
Scully, Sean Paul 1945- *IntWW 93, WhoAm 94*
Scully, Susannah Keith 1921- *WhoAmP 93*
Scully, Vin 1927- *WhoHol 92*
Scully, Vincent 1920- *WrDr 94*
Scully, Vincent Edward 1927- *WhoAm 94*
Scully, William James, Jr. 1939- *WhoAmP 93*

Scully, William Patrick d1981 WhoHol 92
Sculnick, Michael W. WhoAm 94
Scult, Morton Mayer 1932- WhoAmL 94
Sculthorpe, Peter (Joshua) 1929- NewGrDO
Sculthorpe, Peter Joshua 1929- IntWW 93
Scupham, (John) Peter 1933- WrDr 94
Scupin, Raymond Urban 1944- WhoMW 93
Scurlock, Arch Chilton 1920- WhoAm 94
Scuro, Joseph E., Jr. 1948- WhoAmL 94
Scurr, Cyril Frederick 1920- Who 94
Scurry, Fred L. 1942- WhoBlA 94
Scurry, Richardson Gano, Jr. 1938- WhoAm 94
Scurti, Mark Franklin 1963- WhoAmL 94
Scuse, Dennis George 1921- Who 94
Scutt, Der 1934- IntWW 93
Scutt, Robert Carl 1950- WhoAm 94, WhoAmL 94
Scutt, Robin Hugh 1920- Who 94
Scutta, Andreas 1806-1863 NewGrDO
Sczudlo, Paul Allan 1955- WhoAmL 94
Sczudlo, Raymond Stanley 1948- WhoAm 94, WhoAmL 94
Seaberg, Arthur W. 1926- WhoAmP 93
Seaberg, Robert Bertil 1947- WhoMW 93
Seaberg, Steve 1930- WhoAmA 93
Seabolt, James Davidson 1956- WhoFI 94
Seabolt, Richard L. 1949- WhoAmL 94
Seaborg, Glenn 1912- WorScD [port]
Seaborg, Glenn (Theodore) 1912- WrDr 94
Seaborg, Glenn T(heodore) 1912- IntWW 93
Seaborg, Glenn Theodore 1912- Who 94, WhoAm 94, WhoScEn 94, WhoWest 94
Seaborn, Adam EncSF 93
Seaborn, Carol Dean 1947- WhoScEn 94
Seaborn, Katherine M. 1950- WhoAmL 94
Seaborn, Robert Lowder 1911- Who 94
Seabourn, Bert Dail 1931- WhoAmA 93
Seabourn, Connie 1951- WhoAmA 93
Seabright, Idris EncSF 93
Seabright, Idris 1911- WrDr 94
Seabrook, Barry Steven 1966- WhoScEn 94
Seabrook, Bradley Maurice 1928- WhoBlA 94
Seabrook, Geoffrey Leonard 1909- Who 94
Seabrook, Graeme 1939- Who 94
Seabrook, Jeremy 1939- ConDr 93, WrDr 94
Seabrook, John Martin 1917- WhoAm 94
Seabrook, Lawrence B. 1951- WhoAmP 93
Seabrook, Lemuel, III 1952- WhoBlA 94
Seabrook, Robert Childs 1919- WhoIns 94
Seabrook, Robert John 1941- Who 94
Seabrooke, George Alfred 1923- Who 94
Seabrooke, Joseph William, Jr. 1947- WhoFI 94
Seabrooks, Nettie Harris 1934- WhoMW 93
Seabrooks-Edwards, Marilyn S. 1955- WhoBlA 94
Seaburg, Paul Allen 1934- WhoAm 94
Seabury, Forrest d1944 WhoHol 92
Seabury, Paul 1923-1990 WrDr 94N
Seabury, Samuel 1728-1796 WhAmRev
Seabury, Samuel 1729-1796 DcAmReB 2
Seabury, Ynez d1973 WhoHol 92
Seacat, Sondra WhoHol 92
Seacole, Mary 1805-1881 BlmGWL
Seacombe, Dorothy 1905- WhoHol 92
Seacrist, Rudy 1925- WhoAmP 93
Seaden, George 1936- WhoAm 94, WhoScEn 94
Seader, Junior DeVere 1927- WhoAm 94
Seader, Paul Alan 1947- WhoAmL 94
Seadler, Einar Austin 1957- WhoFI 94
Seadler, Stephen Edward 1926- WhoAm 94, WhoFI 94, WhoScEn 94
Seafield, Earl of 1939- Who 94
Seaforth EncSF 93
Seaforth 1848-1933 EncSF 93
Seaforth, Susan 1943- WhoHol 92
Seaga, Edward Philip George 1930- IntWW 93, Who 94
Seagal, Steven 1951- IntMPA 94, WhoAm 94
Seagal, Steven 1952- WhoHol 92
Seager Who 94
Seager, Daniel Albert 1920- WhoAm 94
Seager, Glenn Marvin 1934- WhoMW 93
Seager, Ralph W. DrAPF 93
Seager, Ralph William 1911- WrDr 94
Seager, Ronald Frank 1918- Who 94
Seager, Steven Albert 1958- WhoFI 94
Seager Berry, Thomas Henry 1940- Who 94
Seagle, Edgar Franklin 1924- WhoScEn 94
Seago, James Lynn 1941- WhoScEn 94
Seagram, Lisa WhoHol 92
Seagram, Norman Meredith 1934- WhoAm 94
Seagram, Wilfrid d1938 WhoHol 92
Seagrave, Sterling 1937- WrDr 94
Seagraves, Mary Ann 1939- WhoWest 94
Seagren, Alice 1947- WhoAmP 93
Seagren, Daniel Robert 1927- WhoWest 94
Seagroatt, Conrad Who 94
Seagrove, Jenny IntMPA 94
Seagrove, Jenny 1958- WhoHol 92
Seagull, Barbara WhoHol 92
Seal, Barry Herbert 1937- Who 94
Seal, Elizabeth 1933- WhoHol 92
Seal, James Lee 1945- WhoAmL 94
Seal, John Charles 1950- WhoAm 94, WhoAmP 93
Seal, John S., Jr. 1944- WhoFI 94
Seal, Lorena Faye 1945- WhoFI 94
Seal, Merlin Ireneus 1921- WhoWest 94
Seal, Michael 1930- WhoFI 94, WhoScEn 94
Seal, Peter d1959 WhoHol 92
Seal, Richard Godfrey 1935- Who 94
Seale, Bob 1941- WhoAmP 93
Seale, Bobby 1926- HisWorL [port]
Seale, Bobby 1936- AfrAmAl 6 [port], HisWorL, WhoBlA 94
Seale, D. Mark 1960- WhoFI 94
Seale, Douglas 1913- WhoHol 92
Seale, Douglas (Robert) 1913- Who 94
Seale, James Lawrence, Jr. 1949- WhoScEn 94
Seale, James Richard 1953- WhoFI 94
Seale, Jan Epton DrAPF 93
Seale, John 1942- ConTFT 11
Seale, John Henry 1921- Who 94
Seale, Robert Arthur, Jr. 1942- WhoAmL 94
Seale, Robert L. 1941- WhoAm 94, WhoWest 94
Seale, Robert McMillan 1938- WhoWest 94
Seale, Robert Mills 1942- WhoAmP 93
Seale, Samuel Ricardo 1962- WhoBlA 94
Seale, Stevens WhoAmP 93
Seale, William 1939- WrDr 94
Seale, William Edward 1941- WhoAm 94
Seales, Franklyn d1990 WhoHol 92
Seales, Jerry A. 1961- WhoAmL 94
Seales, Peter Clinton Who 94
Sealey, B. Raphael 1927- WhoAm 94
Sealey, Leonard (George William) 1923- WrDr 94
Sea-Lion 1909- EncSF 93
Seall, Stephen Albert 1940- WhoAm 94
Sealls, Alan Ray WhoBlA 94
Seals, Connie C. 1931- WhoBlA 94
Seals, Dan Wayland 1948- WhoAm 94
Seals, George E. 1942- WhoBlA 94
Seals, Gerald 1953- WhoBlA 94
Seals, Maxine WhoBlA 94
Seals, R. Grant 1932- WhoBlA 94
Seals, Woodrow 1917-1990 WhAm 10
Sealsfield, Charles 1793-1864 DcLB 133 [port]
Sealts, Merton M., Jr. 1915- WrDr 94
Sealts, Merton Miller, Jr. 1915- WhoMW 93
Sealy, Albert H. 1917- WhoAmP 93
Sealy, Albert Henry 1917- WhoAm 94
Sealy, Donald Farrington 1897- WhAm 10
Sealy, I(rwin) Allan 1951- WrDr 94
Sealy, Joan R. 1942- WhoBlA 94
Sealy, Leonard Sedgwick 1930- Who 94
Sealy, Lewis d1931 WhoHol 92
Sealy, Malik 1970- WhoBlA 94
Sealy, Tom 1909-1992 WhAm 10
Seaman, Alfred Barrett 1945- WhoAm 94
Seaman, Alfred Jarvis 1912- WhoAm 94
Seaman, Arlene Anna 1918- WhoWest 94
Seaman, Barbara 1935- WhoAm 94
Seaman, Christopher 1942- IntWW 93, Who 94
Seaman, Daryl Kenneth 1922- WhoAm 94, WhoFI 94
Seaman, Dick Who 94
Seaman, Donald Roy 1925- WhoAm 94
Seaman, Drake F. WhoAmA 93
Seaman, Duncan Campbell 1957- WhoScEn 94
Seaman, Earl d1961 WhoHol 92
Seaman, Edwin Dwight 1934- WhoScEn 94
Seaman, Gerald Roberts 1934- WrDr 94
Seaman, Gilbert Frederick 1912- Who 94
Seaman, Irving, Jr. 1923- WhoAm 94
Seaman, Janet Arlene 1946- WhoAmP 93
Seaman, John Allen 1952- WhoFI 94
Seaman, Keith (Douglas) 1920- Who 94
Seaman, Keith Douglas 1920- IntWW 93
Seaman, Marjorie d1923 WhoHol 92
Seaman, Michael Ray 1951- WhoAm 94, WhoFI 94, WhoWest 94
Seaman, Peggy Jean 1949- WhoAmL 94
Seaman, Peter Wight 1949- WhoFI 94
Seaman, Reginald Jaspar 1923- Who 94
Seaman, Richard Norman 1949- WhoAmL 94
Seaman, Robert Lee 1942- WhoAm 94
Seaman, Roual Duane 1930- WhoFI 94
Seaman, Sylvia Sybil 1910- WrDr 94
Seaman, Tony WhoAm 94
Seaman, William Bernard 1917- WhoAm 94
Seaman, William Casper 1925- WhoAm 94, WhoMW 93
Seaman, William Daniel 1943- WhoScEn 94
Seamans, Beverly Benson 1928- WhoAmA 93
Seamans, David Alvin 1927- WhoWest 94
Seamans, Robert Channing, Jr. 1918- IntWW 93, WhoAm 94, WhoAmP 93
Seamans, Warren Arthur 1935- WhoAm 94
Seamans, William 1925- WhoAm 94
Seamark EncSF 93
Seames, Clarann d1992 WhoAmA 93N
Seammen, Diana Jill 1948- Who 94
Seamon, Hollis Rowan DrAPF 93
Seamons, Quinton Frank 1945- WhoAmL 94
Seams, Francine Swann 1947- WhoBlA 94
Seaquist, Ernest Raymond 1938- WhoAm 94, WhoScEn 94
Sear, Michael 1956- WhoFI 94
Sear, Morey Leonard 1929- WhoAm 94, WhoAmL 94
Sear, Robert J. 1936- WhoIns 94
Sear, Thomas H. 1944- WhoAmL 94
Searby, Daniel MacLeod 1934- WhoFI 94
Searby, Philip James 1924- Who 94
Searby, Richard Henry 1931- Who 94
Searchy, George 1881-1949 See Moran and Mack WhoCom
Searcy, Alan Winn 1925- WhoAm 94
Searcy, Brenita WhoBlA 94
Searcy, James Wendell 1940- WhoAmP 93
Searcy, Jarrell D. Jay 1934- WhoAm 94
Searcy, Mary Glenn 1925- WhoAmP 93
Searcy, Michael John 1954- WhoFI 94
Seare, Nicholas 1925-1992 WrDr 94N
Searelle, (William) Luscombe 1853-1907 NewGrDO
Searight, Patricia Adelaide WhoWest 94
Searing, James Edward 1952- WhoFI 94
Searing, Lee Richard 1948- WhoWest 94
Searing, Marjory Ellen 1945- WhoAm 94
Searl, John Roy Robert 1932- WhoScEn 94
Searle, Eleanor Millard 1926- WhoAm 94
Searle, Elizabeth DrAPF 93
Searle, Graham William 1937- WrDr 94
Searle, Humphrey 1915-1982 NewGrDO
Searle, Jackie 1920- WhoHol 92
Searle, James 1733-1797 WhAmRev
Searle, John 1932- IntWW 93
Searle, John R(ogers) 1932- WrDr 94
Searle, Judith WhoHol 92
Searle, Kamuela d1924 WhoHol 92
Searle, Leonard WhoAm 94, WhoScEn 94
Searle, Malcolm Walter St. Leger 1900- Who 94
Searle, Philip Ford 1924- WhoAm 94
Searle, Rodney N. 1920- WhoAmP 93
Searle, Rodney Newell 1920- WhoAm 94
Searle, Roger Blaine 1953- WhoScEn 94
Searle, Ronald 1920- IntWW 93, WhoAm 94
Searle, Ronald (William Fordham) 1920- WrDr 94
Searle, Ronald William Fordham 1920- Who 94
Searle, Stewart A. 1923- WhoAm 94, WhoFI 94
Searle, Stewart A., III WhoIns 94
Searle, Verna (Ruth) 1919- WrDr 94
Searle, William Louis 1928- WhoAm 94
Searles, A(rthur) Langley 1920- EncSF 93
Searles, Alan Graham 1965- WhoMW 93
Searles, (William) Baird 1934- EncSF 93, WrDr 94
Searles, Charles WhoAmA 93
Searles, Charles 1937- AfrAmAl 6
Searles, Charles R. 1937- WhoBlA 94
Searles, Dewitt Richard 1920- WhoAm 94
Searles, Jerry Lee WhoFI 94, WhoMW 93
Searles, Lynn Marie 1949- WhoMW 93
Searles, Richard Brownlee 1936- WhoAm 94
Searles, Stanley N., Sr. 1919- WhoAmP 93
Searles, Stephen WhoAmA 93
Searls, Donald Turner 1930- WhoScEn 94
Searls, Eileen Haughey 1925- WhoAmL 94
Searls, Frederick Taylor 1912- WhoAm 94
Searls, Hank 1922- EncSF 93, WrDr 94
Searls, Melvin William, Jr. 1935- WhoAm 94
Sears, Allan d1942 WhoHol 92
Sears, Ann WhoHol 92
Sears, Barbara 1917- WhoHol 92
Sears, Bertram E. 1930- WhoBlA 94
Sears, Bradford George 1915- WhoAm 94
Sears, Catherine Marie 1955- WhoScEn 94
Sears, Curtis Thornton, Jr. 1938- WhoAm 94
Sears, David O('Keefe) 1935- WrDr 94
Sears, David O'Keefe 1935- WhoScEn 94
Sears, Dick 1861-1943 BuCMET
Sears, Donald A. DrAPF 93
Sears, Donna Mae 1951- WhoMW 93
Sears, Edward Milner, Jr. 1944- WhoAm 94
Sears, Eleanor d1936 WhoHol 92
Sears, Eleo 1881-1968 BuCMET
Sears, Ernest Robert IntWW 93N
Sears, Ernest Robert 1910-1991 WhAm 10
Sears, Fred F. d1957 WhoHol 92
Sears, Frederick Mark 1952- WhoScEn 94
Sears, George Ames 1926- WhoAm 94, WhoAmL 94
Sears, Heather 1935- WhoHol 92
Sears, Ian WhoHol 92
Sears, Isaac 1730-1786 WhAmRev
Sears, James Donald 1922- WhoWest 94
Sears, Joanne Lewis 1930- WhoAm 94
Sears, John D. 1944- WhoAmP 93
Sears, John Patrick 1940- WhoAm 94, WhoAmP 93
Sears, John Winthrop 1930- WhoAm 94, WhoAmL 94, WhoAmP 93
Sears, Ken 1933- BasBi
Sears, Lowell Edward 1951- WhoWest 94
Sears, Mary Helen WhoAm 94, WhoAmL 94
Sears, Mitchell Martin 1958- WhoMW 93
Sears, Paul B. 1891-1990 EnvEnc
Sears, Peter DrAPF 93
Sears, Raymond Arthur William 1933- Who 94
Sears, Richard W., Jr. 1942- WhoIns 94
Sears, Richard W., Jr. 1943- WhoAmP 93
Sears, Robert Richardson 1908-1989 WhAm 10
Sears, Robert Stephen 1950- WhoAm 94, WhoFI 94
Sears, Rollin George 1950- WhoAm 94
Sears, Samuel Powers, Jr. 1943- WhoAm 94, WhoAmL 94
Sears, Sandra Lee 1952- WhoScEn 94
Sears, Stanton Gray 1950- WhoAmA 93
Sears, Steven Lee 1957- WhoWest 94
Sears, Walter J., III 1948- WhoAmL 94
Sears, William Gray 1910- WhAm 10
Sears, William R. 1928- WhoAmP 93
Sears, William Rees 1913- WhoAm 94, WhoScEn 94
Sears, William Robert 1920- WhoAm 94
Sears, Zelda d1935 WhoHol 92
Sears-Collins, Leah J. WhoAmP 93
Sears-Collins, Leah J. 1955- ConBlB 5 [port], WhoAmL 94
Sears-Collins, Leah Jeanette 1955- WhoBlA 94
Sease, Gene Elwood 1931- WhoAm 94
Sease, John William 1920- WhoAm 94
Seashore, Stanley Emanuel 1915- WhoScEn 94
Seastone, Brian Arthur 1957- WhoWest 94
Seastrand, Andrea WhoAmP 93
Seastrand, James Kent 1929- WhoAmP 93
Seastrom, Dorothy d1930 WhoHol 92
Seastrom, Victor d1960 WhoHol 92
Seaton, Colin Robert 1928- Who 94
Seaton, Edward Lee 1943- WhoAm 94
Seaton, Esta DrAPF 93
Seaton, George Leland 1901- WhoMW 93
Seaton, John Richard 1934- WhoMW 93
Seaton, Maureen DrAPF 93
Seaton, Michael David 1950- WhoFI 94, WhoWest 94
Seaton, Michael John 1923- IntWW 93, Who 94, WhoScEn 94
Seaton, Peter DrAPF 93
Seaton, Richard Melvin 1913- WhoAm 94
Seaton, Robert Finlayson 1930- WhoAm 94
Seaton, Scott d1968 WhoHol 92
Seaton, Shirley Smith WhoBlA 94
Seaton, Vaughn Allen 1928- WhoScEn 94
Seator, Lynette DrAPF 93
Seator, Lynette Hubbard 1929- WhoMW 93
Seats, Peggy Chisolm 1951- WhoFI 94
Seats, Vernon Lavell 1915- WhoMW 93
Seattle, Noah 1786-1866 EnvEnc
Seau, Tiaina, Jr. 1969- WhoAm 94, WhoWest 94
Seaver, Bryan Rondeau 1956- WhoWest 94
Seaver, Esther d1965 WhoAmA 93N
Seaver, James Everett 1918- WhoAm 94
Seaver, Richard Carlton 1922- WhoAm 94
Seaver, Robert Leslie 1937- WhoAmL 94
Seaver, Tom 1944- WhoAm 94
Seavers, Clarence W. 1919- WhoBlA 94
Seavey, Harrison Stedman, Jr. 1952- WhoAmP 93
Seavy, Mary Ethel Ingle 1910- WhoMW 93
Seaward, Colin Hugh 1926- Who 94

Seittelman, Estelle *WhoAm 94*
Seitz, Charles Lewis 1943- *WhoAm 94*
Seitz, Collins Jacques 1914- *WhoAm 94, WhoAmL 94*
Seitz, David Joseph 1962- *WhoMW 93*
Seitz, Dran 1928- & Seitz, Tani 1928- *WhoHol 92*
Seitz, Florian Charles 1926- *WhoMW 93*
Seitz, Frederick 1911- *IntWW 93, WhoAm 94, WhoScEn 94*
Seitz, Gary Francis 1961- *WhoAmL 94*
Seitz, George B. d1944 *WhoHol 92*
Seitz, Harold A. 1938- *WhoFI 94*
Seitz, James Eugene 1927- *WhoMW 93*
Seitz, Janice Ann 1939- *WhoMW 93*
Seitz, Joan Glawe 1949- *WhoAmL 94*
Seitz, John *WhoHol 92*
Seitz, John E. 1930- *WhoAmP 93*
Seitz, John F. 1893-1979 *IntDcF 2-4 [port]*
Seitz, Karen De Raffele 1959- *WhoFI 94*
Seitz, Melvin Christian, Jr. 1939- *WhoMW 93*
Seitz, Nicholas Joseph 1939- *WhoAm 94*
Seitz, Patricia Ann 1946- *WhoAm 94, WhoAmL 94*
Seitz, Raymond G. 1940- *WhoAmP 93*
Seitz, Raymond G. H. 1940- *IntWW 93*
Seitz, Raymond George Hardenbergh 1940- *Who 94, WhoAm 94*
Seitz, Rosalie Fern 1927- *WhoMW 93*
Seitz, Steven Thomas 1947- *WhoMW 93*
Seitz, Tani 1928-
See Seitz, Dran 1928- & Seitz, Tani 1928- *WhoHol 92*
Seitz, Tani 1928- *WhoHol 92*
Seitz, Walter Stanley 1937- *WhoWest 94*
Seitz, Wesley Donald 1940- *WhoAm 94*
Seitz, William Chapin 1914-1974 *WhoAmA 93N*
Seitz, William Rudolf 1943- *WhoScEn 94*
Seitzman, Howard S. 1955- *WhoAmL 94*
Seivers, David *WhoAmP 93*
Seixas, Frank Archibald 1919-1992 *WhAm 10*
Seixas, Gershom Mendes 1746-1816 *WhAmRev*
Seixas, Gershom Mendez 1746-1816 *DcAmReB 2*
Seixas, Vic 1923- *BuCMET*
Seitzinger, Bernd Robert 1956- *WhoScEn 94*
Sejie Kansu Lunzhu Taokai *WhoPRCh 91*
Sejnowski, Terrence Joseph 1947- *WhoScEn 94*
Seka, Ron d1982 *WhoHol 92*
Sekar, M. Chandra 1954- *WhoScEn 94*
Sekar-Rozhansky, Anton Vladislavovich 1863-1952 *NewGrDO*
Sekayumptewa, Loren 1950- *WhoWest 94*
Sekely, Irene d1950 *WhoHol 92*
Sekerak, Deborah Janelle 1966- *WhoMW 93*
Sekeris, Constantine Evangelos 1933- *WhoScEn 94*
Sekerka, Robert Floyd 1937- *WhoAm 94*
Sekers, David Nicholas Oliver 1943- *Who 94*
Sekhar, Chandra 1942- *WhoMW 93*
Sekhon, Jasmeet M. 1937- *WhoMW 93*
Sekhon, Kathleen 1948- *WhoAmP 93*
Sekhonyana, Evaristus Rets'elisitsoe 1937- *IntWW 93*
Seki, Akiro 1943- *WhoAsA 94*
Seki, Hiroharu 1927- *WhoScEn 94*
Seki, Hoken S. 1935- *WhoAm 94*
Sekiguchi, Risa 1962- *WhoAmA 93*
Seki Kowa 1642-1708 *WorScD*
Sekimoto, Tadahiro 1926- *WhoScEn 94*
Sekimura, Toshio 1947- *WhoScEn 94*
Sekine, Masao 1912- *IntWW 93*
Sekioka, Mitsuru 1930- *WhoScEn 94*
Sekitani, Toru 1932- *WhoAm 94, WhoScEn 94*
Sekiya, Gerald Yoshinori 1942- *WhoAmL 94*
Sekiya, Katsutsugu 1938- *IntWW 93*
Sekizawa, Tadashi 1931- *IntWW 93*
Sekka, Johnny 1939- *WhoHol 92*
Sekler, Eduard F(ranz) 1920- *WrDr 94*
Sekler, Eduard Franz 1920- *WhoAm 94*
Sekles, Bernhard 1872-1934 *NewGrDO*
Seko, Masataka 1923- *IntWW 93*
Sekowski, Cynthia Jean 1953- *WhoMW 93*
Sekula, Edward Joseph, Jr. 1937- *WhoAm 94*
Sekuler, Robert William 1939- *WhoAm 94*
Sekulic, Isidora 1877-1958 *BlmGWL*
Sekulovich, Malden 1916- *WhoAm 94*
Sekyi, Henry Van Hien 1928- *Who 94*
Sekyra, Hugo Michael 1941- *WhoScEn 94*
Sela, Michael 1924- *IntWW 93*
Selame, Elinor 1936- *WhoFI 94*
Selander, Arthur F. 1952- *WhoAmL 94*
Selander, Larry 1946- *WhoAm 94, WhoAmL 94*
Selangor, H.R.H. the Sultan of 1926- *IntWW 93*
Selberg, Bruce Paul 1938- *WhoMW 93*
Selberg, Ingrid (Maria) 1950- *WrDr 94*
Selberg, Janice Kay 1953- *WhoAmL 94, WhoMW 93*
Selberherr, Siegfried 1955- *WhoFI 94, WhoScEn 94*
Selbie, Evelyn d1950 *WhoHol 92*
Selbin, Joel 1931- *WhoAm 94*
Selbo, Jule 1954- *ConTFT 11*
Selbo, Ray Gordon 1940- *WhoMW 93*
Selborne, Earl 1940- *IntWW 93*
Selborne, Earl of 1940- *Who 94*
Selbourne, David 1937- *ConDr 93, WrDr 94*
Selbst, Irving d1986 *WhoHol 92*
Selby, Bishop Suffragan of 1938- *Who 94*
Selby, Viscount 1942- *Who 94*
Selby, Barbara Kenaga 1942- *WhoFI 94, WhoMW 93*
Selby, Bettina 1934- *ConAu 41NR*
Selby, Cecily Cannan 1927- *WhoAm 94*
Selby, Cora Norwood 1920- *WhoBlA 94*
Selby, Curt *EncSF 93*
Selby, David 1941- *IntMPA 94, WhoHol 92*
Selby, Elliott 1908- *WrDr 94*
Selby, Frederick Peter 1938- *WhoFI 94*
Selby, Hubert, Jr. *DrAPF 93*
Selby, Hubert, Jr. 1928- *WhoAm 94, WrDr 94*
Selby, Janet S. Groshart 1927- *WhoWest 94*
Selby, Jerome M. 1948- *WhoAm 94, WhoWest 94*
Selby, Kenneth d1992 *Who 94N*
Selby, Leland C. 1944- *WhoAmL 94*
Selby, Myra Consetta 1955- *WhoAmL 94*
Selby, Nicholas 1925- *WhoHol 92*
Selby, Norman d1940 *WhoHol 92*
Selby, Patricia Louise 1944- *WhoAmA 93*
Selby, Peter Stephen Maurice 1941- *Who 94*
Selby, Philip 1948- *IntWW 93*
Selby, Ralph Irving 1930- *WhoBlA 94*
Selby, Ralph Walford 1915- *Who 94*
Selby, Robert Irwin 1943- *WhoMW 93*
Selby, Roger Lowell 1933- *WhoAm 94, WhoAmA 93*
Selby, Roy Clifton, Jr. 1930- *WhoAm 94*
Selby, Sarah d1980 *WhoHol 92*
Selby, Tony 1938- *WhoHol 92*
Selby, William Halford 1902- *Who 94*
Selby Wright, Ronald (William Vernon) *Who 94*
Selcer, David Mark 1943- *WhoAm 94, WhoAmL 94*
Selchow, Roger Hoffman 1911- *WhoAmA 93*
Selck, Hillard Fred 1926- *WhoAmP 93*
Selden, Andrew C. 1947- *WhoAmL 94*
Selden, Bernice *DrAPF 93*
Selden, David Edward 1960- *WhoAmL 94*
Selden, Phoebe Serena 1955- *WhoMW 93*
Selden, Richard Thomas 1922- *WhoAm 94*
Selden, Robert Wentworth 1936- *WhoAm 94*
Selden, William Kirkpatrick 1911- *WhoAm 94*
Selders, Craig Stephen 1953- *WhoFI 94, WhoWest 94*
Selders, Gilbert Vivian 1893- *WhAm 10*
Seldes, George 1890- *WhoAm 94, WrDr 94*
Seldes, Marian *WhoAm 94*
Seldes, Marian 1928- *WhoHol 92*
Seldin, Donald Wayne 1920- *IntWW 93, WhoAm 94*
Seldis, Henry J. 1925-1978 *WhoAmA 93N*
Seldon, Anthony 1953- *WrDr 94*
Seldon, Arthur 1916- *Who 94*
Seldon, Earl W. 1909- *WhoMW 93*
Selecman, Charles E. 1928- *IntWW 93*
Selenica, Eleni *WhoWomW 91*
Seles, Monica 1973- *BuCMET, IntWW 93, WhoAm 94*
Seley, Jason 1919-1983 *WhoAmA 93N*
Seleznev, Gennadiy Nikolaevich 1947- *IntWW 93*
Seleznev, Nikolai Vasilevich 1945- *LngBDD*
Self, Charles Edwin 1934- *WhoAm 94*
Self, Colin Ernest 1941- *IntWW 93*
Self, Edwin F. 1920- *DcLB 137*
Self, Frank Wesley 1949- *WhoBlA 94*
Self, Herschel Clayton 1922- *WhoMW 93*
Self, Hugh Michael 1921- *Who 94*
Self, James Cuthbert 1919- *WhoAm 94*
Self, James Reed 1944- *WhoAm 94*
Self, Madison Allen 1921- *WhoAm 94*
Self, Margaret Callahan d1947 *WhoHol 92*
Self, Peter John Otter 1919- *Who 94*
Self, Sarah Mabel 1924- *WhoAmP 93*
Self, William 1921- *IntMPA 94, WhoHol 92*
Selfe, Robert W. 1943- *WhAm 10*
Selfridge, Barbara *DrAPF 93*
Selfridge, George Dever 1924- *WhoAm 94, WhoMW 93*
Selgas, Alfred Michael 1943- *WhoHisp 94*
Selgas, James W. 1943- *WhoHisp 94*
Selig, Allan H. 1934- *WhoAm 94, WhoMW 93*
Selig, J. Daniel 1938- *WhoAmA 93N*
Selig, Karl-Ludwig 1926- *WhoAm 94*
Selig, Manfred 1909- *WhoAmA 93*
Selig, Manfred, Mrs. *WhoAmA 93*
Selig, Marvin 1923- *WhoFI 94*
Selig, Oury Levy 1924- *WhoFI 94*
Selig, Phyllis Sims 1931- *WhoMW 93, WhoScEn 94*
Selig, Robert William 1910- *IntMPA 94*
Selig, Stephen Fisk 1933- *WhoAmL 94*
Selig, William N. 1864-1948 *IntDcF 2-4*
Seliga, Thomas Anthony 1937- *WhoFI 94*
Seliger, Charles 1926- *WhoAm 94, WhoAmA 93*
Seligman, Charles 1893-1978 *WhoAmA 93N*
Seligman, Daniel 1924- *WhoAm 94*
Seligman, Delice *WhoAmL 94*
Seligman, Henry d1993 *Who 94N*
Seligman, Henry 1909- *IntWW 93*
Seligman, Joel 1950- *WhoMW 93*
Seligman, Madron *Who 94*
Seligman, (Richard) Madron 1918- *Who 94*
Seligman, Peter (Wendel) 1913- *Who 94*
Seligman, Richard Michael 1945- *WhoAm 94, WhoAmL 94*
Seligman, Rudolph Frank 1943- *WhoAm 94*
Seligman, Thomas Knowles 1944- *WhoAm 94, WhoAmA 93, WhoWest 94*
Seligmann, Herbert J. 1891-1984 *WhoAmA 93N*
Seligmann, Kurt 1900-1962 *WhoAmA 93N*
Seligson, Carl H. 1935- *WhoAm 94*
Seligson, Theodore H. 1930- *WhoAm 94*
Selik, Joel Gary 1958- *WhoAmL 94*
Selikoff, Irving John 1915-1992 *WhAm 10*
Selim, I c. 1470-1520 *HisWorL [port]*
Selin, Audrey E. 1952- *WhoAmL 94*
Selin, Ivan *WhoAmP 93*
Selin, Ivan 1937- *WhoAm 94*
Seline, Steven William 1953- *WhoAmL 94*
Seling, Theodore Victor 1928- *WhoWest 94*
Selinger, Benjamin Klaas 1939- *IntWW 93*
Selinger, Jerry Robin 1947- *WhoAmL 94*
Selinger, Patricia Griffiths 1949- *WhoWest 94*
Selinger, Rosemary Celeste Lee 1945- *WhoScEn 94*
Selinsky, Deloris *DrAPF 93*
Selinsky, William J. 1949- *WhoAmL 94*
Selivanov, Valentin Egorovich 1936- *LngBDD*
Selivansky, Dror 1950- *WhoScEn 94*
Seljevold, Peter Jacob 1961- *WhoMW 93*
Selk, George d1967 *WhoHol 92*
Selke, Charles Richard 1947- *WhoAm 94, WhoFI 94*
Selker, Harry Paul *WhoScEn 94*
Selkirk, Earl of 1906- *IntWW 93, Who 94*
Selkirk, Alexander 1676-1721 *BlmGEL, WhWE*
Selkirk, James Kirkwood 1938- *WhoAm 94*
Selkoe, Dennis J. 1943- *WhoAm 94*
Selkowitz, Arthur 1943- *WhoAm 94*
Selkregg, Lidia Lippi 1920- *WhoAmP 93*
Sell, Edward Scott, Jr. 1917- *WhoAm 94*
Sell, Friedrich Leopold 1954- *WhoScEn 94*
Sell, Janie 1941- *WhoHol 92*
Sell, Jeffrey Alan 1952- *WhoScEn 94*
Sell, Jeffrey Zane 1961- *WhoAmL 94*
Sell, Joan Isobel 1936- *WhoFI 94*
Sell, Mary Lou 1943- *WhoHisp 94*
Sell, Nancy Blakeley 1955- *WhoMW 93*
Sell, Robert Emerson 1929- *WhoScEn 94, WhoWest 94*
Sell, Stephen 1941-1989 *WhAm 10*
Sell, Stewart 1935- *WhoScEn 94*
Sell, Warren Edward 1950- *WhoFI 94*
Sell, William David, Jr. 1943- *WhoMW 93*
Sell, William Edward 1923- *WhoAm 94*
Sella, Alvin Conrad 1924- *WhoAmA 93*
Sella, Edward Geoffrey 1958- *WhoFI 94*
Sella, Edward Gerard 1933- *WhoFI 94*
Sella, George John, Jr. 1928- *IntWW 93, WhoAm 94, WhoFI 94, WhoScEn 94*
Sellaeg, Wenche Frogn 1937- *IntWW 93, WhoWomW 91*
Selland, Howard M. 1943- *WhoAm 94, WhoFI 94*
Sellar, George L. 1929- *WhoAmP 93*
Sellars, Elizabeth 1923- *WhoHol 92*
Sellars, Harold Gerard 1953- *WhoBlA 94, WhoFI 94*
Sellars, James (Edward) 1943- *NewGrDO*
Sellars, James Allen 1958- *WhoMW 93*
Sellars, John Ernest 1936- *Who 94*
Sellars, Peter *WhoHol 92*
Sellars, Peter 1957- *IntWW 93, NewGrDO*
Sellars, Wilfrid Stalker 1912- *WhoAm 94*
Selle, Burkhardt Herbert Richard 1938- *WhoScEn 94*
Sellecca, Connie 1955- *IntMPA 94*
Selleck, Margaret 1892- *WhoAmA 93N*
Selleck, Tom 1945- *IntMPA 94, IntWW 93, WhoAm 94, WhoHol 92*
Selleck, Virginia Mildred 1948- *WhoMW 93*
Selleneit, P. Lloyd *WhoAmP 93*
Seller, Robert Herman 1931- *WhoAm 94*
Sellers, Alexandra *WrDr 94*
Sellers, Barbara Jackson 1940- *WhoAm 94, WhoAmL 94*
Sellers, Basil Alfred 1935- *Who 94*
Sellers, Bettie M. *DrAPF 93*
Sellers, Catherine *WhoHol 92*
Sellers, Charles 1887-1935
See Moran and Mack *WhoCom*
Sellers, Donnie R. *WhoAmP 93*
Sellers, Fred Wilson 1942- *WhoAm 94*
Sellers, Geoffrey Bernard 1947- *Who 94*
Sellers, Gregory Jude 1947- *WhoMW 93*
Sellers, James McBrayer 1895- *WhAm 10*
Sellers, John Lewis 1934- *WhoAmA 93*
Sellers, Jonathan Hugh 1949- *WhoFI 94*
Sellers, Lucia Sunhee 1949- *WhoScEn 94*
Sellers, Macklyn Rhett, Jr. 1962- *WhoScEn 94*
Sellers, Margaret Regular 1935- *WhoMW 93*
Sellers, Norman William Malin 1919- *Who 94*
Sellers, Pamela Heflin 1953- *WhoAmL 94*
Sellers, Peter d1980 *WhoHol 92*
Sellers, Peter 1925-1980 *WhoCom [port]*
Sellers, Peter Hoadley 1930- *WhoAm 94*
Sellers, Philip Edward 1937- *Who 94*
Sellers, Richard Morgan 1913-1989 *WhAm 10*
Sellers, Robert Firth 1924- *Who 94*
Sellers, Ronnie *WhoHol 92*
Sellers, Sandra Louise 1944- *WhoMW 93*
Sellers, Theresa Ann 1954- *WhoBlA 94*
Sellers, Thomas J. 1911- *WhoBlA 94*
Sellers, Victoria 1965- *WhoHol 92*
Sellers, Walter G. 1925- *WhoBlA 94*
Sellers, William Freeman 1929- *WhoAmA 93*
Sellert, Wolfgang 1935- *IntWW 93*
Sellick, Phyllis 1911- *IntWW 93*
Sellie, John Martin 1927- *WhoAmP 93*
Sellier, Robert Hugh 1933- *Who 94*
Sellin, Mlle c. 1700-c. 1726 *NewGrDO*
Sellin, David 1930- *WhoAmA 93*
Sellin, Eric 1933- *WhoAm 94, WrDr 94*
Sellin, M. Derek 1968- *WhoScEn 94*
Sellin, Theodore 1928- *WhoAm 94*
Sellinger, James-Robert 1954- *WhoFI 94*
Sellinger, Joseph A. d1993 *NewYTBS 93 [port]*
Sellings, Arthur 1921-1968 *EncSF 93*
Sellitto, Giuseppe 1700-1777 *NewGrDO*
Sellman, Hunton D. 1900-1992 *WrDr 94N*
Sellman, Roger Raymond 1915- *WrDr 94*
Sellmyer, David Julian 1938- *WhoScEn 94*
Sello, Allen Ralph 1939- *WhoAm 94*
Sellon, Charles d1937 *WhoHol 92*
Sellors, Patrick John Holmes 1934- *Who 94*
Sells, Boake Anthony 1937- *WhoAm 94*
Sells, Bruce Howard 1930- *WhoAm 94*
Sells, David (Perronet) 1918- *Who 94*
Sells, Harold E. 1928- *WhoAm 94, WhoFI 94*
Sells, Mamie Earl *WhoBlA 94*
Sellschop, Jacques Pierre Friedrich 1930- *IntWW 93*
Selly, Susan *Who 94*
Selm, Michael Edward 1955- *WhoFI 94*
Selm, Robert Prickett 1923- *WhoMW 93, WhoScEn 94*
Selman, Helen *WhoAmP 93*
Selman, James C. 1942- *WhoAm 94*
Selman, Robyn *DrAPF 93*
Selman, Roland Wooten, III 1941- *WhoAm 94, WhoAmL 94*
Selman, Russell Bertram 1954- *WhoAmL 94*
Selmar, Katherine L. 1956- *WhoWest 94*
Selmeier, Richard James 1943- *WhoAm 94*
Selmer, Knut S. 1924- *IntWW 93*
Selmier, Dean *WhoHol 92*
Selna, James V. 1945- *WhoAmL 94*
Selonke, Irene A. d1981 *WhoAmA 93N*
Selous, Edmund 1857-1934 *DcNaB MP*
Selous, Trista *ConAu 142*

Selover, R. Edwin 1945- WhoAmL 94, WhoFI 94
Selover, William Charlton 1938- WhoWest 94
Selsdon, Baron 1937- Who 94
Selser, Christopher 1950- WhoAmA 93
Selsor, Jonathan 1958- WhoAmP 93
Selsor, Marcia Lorraine 1949- WhoAmA 93
Selsor, Robert James 1960- WhoAmL 94
Selten, Morton d1939 WhoHol 92
Seltenright, Dan Lee 1949- WhoMW 93
Seltser, Raymond 1923- WhoAm 94, WhoScEn 94
Seltz, James Herbert 1948- WhoMW 93
Seltzer, Ada May 1942- WhoAm 94
Seltzer, Bradley Marshall 1953- WhoAm 94
Seltzer, Daniel d1980 WhoHol 92
Seltzer, David 1940- IntMPA 94
Seltzer, H. Jack 1922- WhoAmP 93
Seltzer, Jeffrey Lloyd 1956- WhoAmL 94, WhoFI 94
Seltzer, Joanne DrAPF 93
Seltzer, Joanne Lynn 1946- WhoAmA 93
Seltzer, Leo 1910- WhoAm 94
Seltzer, Leon F(rancis) 1940- WrDr 94
Seltzer, Loretta Mae 1936- WhoMW 93
Seltzer, Martin Stanley 1937- WhoAm 94, WhoAmL 94
Seltzer, Mildred M. 1921- WhoAm 94
Seltzer, Mitchell Sherman 1948- WhoFI 94
Seltzer, Phyllis 1928- WhoAmA 93
Seltzer, Phyllis Estelle 1928- WhoAm 94, WhoMW 93
Seltzer, Richard DrAPF 93
Seltzer, Richard C. 1943- WhoAm 94, WhoAmL 94
Seltzer, Ronald 1931- WhoAm 94
Seltzer, Ronald 1939- WhoMW 93
Seltzer, Ronald Anthony 1935- WhoAm 94
Seltzer, Vicki Lynn 1949- WhoAm 94
Seltzer, Walter 1914- IntMPA 94
Seltzer, Will WhoHol 92
Seltzer, William 1934- WhoAm 94
Selva, Antonio 1824-1889 NewGrDO
Selvadurai, Antony Patrick Sinnappa 1942- WhoAm 94, WhoScEn 94
Selvam, Rathinam Panneer 1955- WhoScEn 94
Selvaratnam, Viswanathan 1934- IntWW 93
Selver, Paul Darryl 1947- WhoAm 94, WhoAmL 94
Selvera, Norma Brito 1947- WhoHisp 94
Selverstone, Bertram d1993 NewYTBS 93
Selvey, Marylin Rose Lundstrom 1954- WhoFI 94, WhoWest 94
Selvidge, Mark F. 1947- WhoAmL 94
Selvig, Forrest Hall 1924- WhoAmA 93
Selvin, Joel 1950 WrDr 94
Selvin, Nancy 1943- WhoAmA 93, WhoWest 94
Selvon, Samu(el Dickson) 1923- BlkWr 2
Selvon, Samuel (Dickson) 1923- WrDr 94
Selvon, Samuel Dickson 1923- Who 94
Selvy, Frank 1932- BasBi
Selwart, Tonio 1896- WhoHol 92
Selway, Martina 1940- SmATA 74 [port]
Selwood, David Henry Deering 1934- Who 94
Selwood, Peter John 1942- WhoFI 94
Selwood, Pierce Taylor 1939- WhoAm 94, WhoAmL 94, WhoFI 94
Selwyn, Archie d1959 WhoHol 92
Selwyn, Donald 1936- WhoAm 94, WhoScEn 94
Selwyn, Edgar d1944 WhoHol 92
Selwyn, Francis 1935- WrDr 94
Selwyn, John Sidney Augustus 1908- Who 94
Selwyn, Ruth d1954 WhoHol 92
Selwynne, Clarissa d1948 WhoHol 92
Selya, Bruce Marshall 1934- WhoAm 94, WhoAmL 94, WhoAmP 93
Selz, Peter 1919- WrDr 94
Selz, Peter H. 1919- WhoAmA 93
Selz, Peter Howard 1919- WhoAm 94, WhoWest 94
Selz, Thalia DrAPF 93
Selzer, Arthur 1911-1991 WhAm 10
Selzer, Charles Louis 1914- WhAm 10
Selzer, Donald W., Jr. 1952- WhoAmL 94
Selzer, Michael David 1947- WhoFI 94
Selzer, Michael Edgar 1943- WhoScEn 94
Selzer, Milton WhoHol 92
Selzer, Richard 1928- CurBio 93 [port]
Selzle, Kurt Ander 1964- WhoMW 93
Selznick, David O. 1902-1965 IntDcF 2-4 [port]
Selznick, Irene Mayer 1907-1990 WhAm 10
Selznick, Stephen Andrew 1941- WhoFI 94
Semaan, Khalil I. H. 1920- WrDr 94
Semadeni, Zbigniew Wladyslaw 1934- WhoScEn 94
Semak, Michael 1934- WhoAmA 93
Semak, Michael William 1934- WhoAm 94
Semans, James Hustead 1910- WhoAmA 93
Semans, Truman Thomas 1926- WhoAm 94
Semansky, Chris DrAPF 93
Semark, Philip Norman 1945- WhoAm 94
Semas, Philip Wayne 1946- WhoAm 94
Semaya, Francine L. 1951- WhoAmL 94
Sembach, Johannes 1881-1944 NewGrDO
Sembene, Ousmane ConWorW 93
Sembler, Charles W., II 1965- WhoAmP 93
Sembler, Mel 1930- WhoAm 94
Sembler, Melvin F. 1930- WhoAmP 93
Sembrich, Marcella 1858-1935 NewGrDO
Semchishen, Orest M. 1932- WhoAmA 93
Semchyshyn, Stefan 1940- WrDr 94
Semega-Janneh, Bocar Ousman 1910- IntWW 93, Who 94
Semegen, Patrick William 1946- WhoAm 94
Semel, Sylvia DrAPF 93
Semel, Terry 1943- IntMPA 94, WhoAm 94, WhoFI 94
Semels, Harry d1946 WhoHol 92
Semelsberger, Kenneth J. 1936- WhoFI 94, WhoMW 93
Semenov IntWW 93
Semenov, Julian ConAu 142
Semenov, Vladimir Magomedovich 1940- IntWW 93, LngBDD
Semenov, Yulian ConAu 142
Semenova, Marina 1908- IntDcB [port]
Semenovich, Joseph DrAPF 93
Semensi, Joseph John 1923- WhoAmP 93
Semento, Lawrence James 1952- WhoAmL 94
Semenyaka, Ludmila 1952- IntDcB [port]
Semenyaka, Lyudmila Ivanova 1952- IntWW 93
Semerad, Roger Dale 1940- WhoAm 94
Semeraro, Michael Archangel, Jr. 1956- WhoScEn 94
Semerdzhiev, Atanas 1924- IntWW 93
Semerjian, Hratch Gregory 1943- WhoAm 94, WhoScEn 94
Seminerio, Anthony S. 1935- WhoAmP 93
Semiramis fl. 800BC- BlmGEL
Semizorova, Nina Lvovna 1956- IntWW 93
Semken, John Douglas 1921- Who 94
Semkow, Jerzy 1928- NewGrDO
Semkow, Jerzy (Georg) 1928- IntWW 93
Semler, Dean ConTFT 11, IntMPA 94
Semler, Jerry D. 1937- WhoAm 94, WhoFI 94, WhoIns 94
Semler, John Emery 1954- WhoMW 93
Semler, Peter 1931- WhoAm 94
Semlyen, Adam 1923- WhoAm 94
Semmel, Bernard 1928- WhoAm 94
Semmel, Joan 1932- WhoAmA 93
Semmel, Paul W. 1939- WhoAmP 93
Semmelweis, Ignaz Philipp 1818-1865 WorScD
Semmence, Adrian Murdoch 1926- Who 94
Semmens, John 1850-1921 EncNAR
Semmer, Robert Clement 1961- WhoWest 94
Semmes, Sally Peterson WhoMW 93
Semmler, Clement William 1914- WrDr 94
Semmler, Lyn WhoHol 92
Semmlow, John Leonard 1942- WhoScEn 94
Semon, Larry d1928 WhoHol 92
Semon, Larry 1889-1928 WhoCom
Semon, Mark David 1950- WhoScEn 94
Semon, Warren Lloyd 1921- WhoAm 94
Semonian, Robert Alexander 1939- WhoAm 94, WhoAmP 93
Semonin, Richard Gerard 1930- WhoAm 94, WhoScEn 94
Semore, Mary Margie 1920- WhoFI 94
Semos, Chris Victor 1936- WhoAmP 93
Semowich, Charles John WhoAmA 93
Sempe, Abel 1912- IntWW 93
Sempe, Jean-Jacques 1932- IntWW 93
Semper, Colin (Douglas) 1938- Who 94
Sempill, Lady 1920- Who 94
Sempill, Master of 1949- Who 94
Semple, Andrew Best 1912- Who 94
Semple, Andrew Greenlees 1934- Who 94
Semple, Cecil Snowdon 1917- WhoAm 94, WhoFI 94
Semple, David Who 94
Semple, (William) David (Crowe) 1933- Who 94
Semple, Jack d1978 WhoHol 92
Semple, James William 1943- WhoAmL 94
Semple, John Laughlin 1940- Who 94
Semple, Lloyd Ashby 1939- WhoAm 94
Semple, Lorenzo, Jr. IntMPA 94
Semple, Stephen John Greenhill 1926- Who 94
Semple-Rowland, Susan Lynn 1955- WhoScEn 94
Sempronia fl. 1st cent.BC- BlmGWL
Semprun, Jorge IntWW 93
Semrod, T. Joseph 1936- WhoAm 94, WhoFI 94
Semrud-Clikeman, Margaret Elaine 1950- WhoWest 94
Semyonov, Julian ConAu 142
Semyonov, Julian 1931-1993 NewYTBS 93
Semyonov, Julian Semenovich 1932- IntWW 93
Semyonov, Pyotr Petrovich 1827-1914 WhWE
Semyonov, Viktor Vladimirovich 1937- IntWW 93
Semyonov, Yulian ConAu 142
Sen, Amartya K(umar) 1933- WrDr 94
Sen, Amartya Kumar 1933- IntWW 93, Who 94
Sen, Arun 1933- WhoAsA 94
Sen, Arun Kumar 1938- WhoAsA 94
Sen, Ashish Kumar 1942- WhoAm 94, WhoAsA 94, WhoMW 93
Sen, B(inay) R(anjan) 1898-1993 CurBio 93N
Sen, Bachoo IntMPA 94
Sen, Binay Ranjan d1993 NewYTBS 93 [port]
Sen, Emma Who 94
Sen, Gautam 1951- WhoAm 94
Sen, Jyotirmoy 1933- WhoScEn 94
Sen, Karabi WhoAsA 94
Sen, Mihir 1947- WhoAsA 94
Sen, Mrinal 1923- IntWW 93
Sen, Pabitra N. 1944- WhoScEn 94
Sen, Pabitra Narayan 1944- WhoAsA 94
Sen, Paresh Chandra 1938- WhoAm 94
Sen, Samar R. 1916- IntWW 93
Sen, Satyendra Nath 1909- IntWW 93, Who 94
Sen, Shri Binay Ranjan d1993 Who 94N
Sen, Tapas K. 1933- WhoAsA 94
Sena, Estevan S. 1945- WhoHisp 94
Sena, Glenda Mary Ann 1964- WhoHisp 94
Sena, John Michael 1950- WhoFI 94
Sena, Kanaga Nitchinga 1944- WhoScEn 94
Senard, Comte Jacques 1919- IntWW 93
Senarens, Luis Philip 1863-1939 EncSF 93
Senatore, Charles Vincent 1954- WhoAmL 94
Senay, Leo Charles, Jr. 1927- WhoMW 93
Senbet, Lemma W. WhoBlA 94
Sendaba, S. M. WhoBlA 94
Sendaba, Sheleme M. 1949- WhoFI 94
Sendak, Maurice 1928- AmCulL, ConTFT 11, WrDr 94
Sendak, Maurice Bernard 1928- IntWW 93, Who 94, WhoAm 94, WhoAmA 93
Sendak, Theodore Lorraine 1918- WhoAmP 93
Sendall, Bernard Charles 1913- Who 94
Sendax, Victor Irven 1930- WhoAm 94, WhoScEn 94
Sender, Jonathan Jerome 1956- WhoAmP 93
Sender, Ramon 1902-1982 HispLC
Sender, Stanton P. 1932- WhoAm 94, WhoAmL 94
Sender Barayon, Ramon 1934- WrDr 94
Senderens, Alain 1939- IntWW 93
Senderling, Jon Townsend WhoAm 94
Senders, Rita Lea 1949- WhoAm 94
Sendlein, Lyle V. A. 1933- WhoAm 94
Sen Dog c. 1966- See Cypress Hill ConMus 11
Sendon, Andres-Rodriguez 1894- WhAm 10
Sendov, Blagovest Hristov 1932- IntWW 93
Sendrey, Albert 1921- IntMPA 94
Sendrovic, Israel 1947- WhoAm 94
Seneca c. 4BC-65AD HisWorL [port]
Seneca, Arlena E. 1919- WhoBlA 94
Seneca, Joe IntMPA 94, WhoHol 92
Seneca, Lucius Annaeus d65AD BlmGEL
Seneca, Lucius Annaeus c. 4BC-65AD EncEth, IntDcT 2 [port]
Senechal, Alice R. 1955- WhoAm 94
Senechal, Michel 1927- NewGrDO
Senechal de Kerkado, Mlle Le NewGrDO
Senefelder, Aloys WorInv
Seneff, Smiley Howard 1925- WhoMW 93
Senegal, Charles 1930- WhoBlA 94
Senegal, Phyllis J. 1930- WhoBlA 94
Seneker, Carl James, II 1942- WhoAmL 94
Seneker, Stanley A. WhoAm 94, WhoFI 94, WhoMW 93
Senensieb, Norbert Louis 1930- WhoWest 94
Sener, Joseph Ward, Jr. 1926- WhoAm 94
Sener, Robert N. H. 1933- WhoIns 94
Senesac, Andrew Frederick 1952- WhoScEn 94
Senese, Donald Joseph 1942- WhoAm 94, WhoAmP 93
Senesi Lombardi, Giovanna 1945- WhoWomW 91
Senesino dc. 1759 NewGrDO
Senesky, George 1922- BasBi
Seney, Joshua 1756-1798 WhAmRev
Senff, Mark D. 1945- WhoAm 94
Seng, Ann Frances 1936- WhoMW 93
Senger-Bettaque, Katherine 1862-1909? NewGrDO
Sengers, Jan Vincent 1931- WhoScEn 94
Senghaas, Dieter 1940- IntWW 93
Senghor, Leopold (Sedar) 1906- ConWorW 93
Senghor, Leopold Sedar 1906- BlkWr 2, HisWorL [port], IntWW 93
Sengpiehl, Paul Marvin 1937- WhoMW 93
Sengqen Lozong Gyaincain 1936- WhoPRCh 91 [port]
Sengstacke, Frederick D. WhoMW 93
Sengstacke, John H. 1912- WhoBlA 94
Sengstacke, John Herman Henry 1912- AfrAmAl 6, WhoAm 94, WhoMW 93
Sengstacke, Whittier Alexander, Sr. 1916- WhoBlA 94
Sengupta, Arjun K. 1937- IntWW 93
Sengupta, Dipak Lal 1931- WhoAm 94, WhoAsA 94
Sengupta, Mritunjoy 1941- WhoScEn 94
Sen Gupta, Ratan 1947- WhoWest 94
Sengupta, Subrata 1948- WhoScEn 94
Senhauser, Donald Albert 1927- WhoAm 94
Senie, Harriet 1943- WhoAmA 93
Senior, Edward (Walters) 1902- Who 94
Senior, Enrique Francisco 1943- WhoAm 94, WhoFI 94
Senior, Gordon Who 94
Senior, (Alan) Gordon 1928- Who 94
Senior, Michael 1940- WrDr 94
Senior, Olive 1943- BlmGWL [port]
Senior, Olive Edith 1934- Who 94
Senior, Richard John Lane 1940- WhoFI 94
Senior, Thomas Bryan A. 1928- WhoAm 94
Senitzky, Israel Ralph 1920- WhoScEn 94
Senkan, Selim M. 1950- WhoScEn 94
Senkayi, Abu Lwanga 1943- WhoScEn 94
Senkbeil, Roger Charles 1946- WhoFI 94
Senkier, Robert Joseph 1916- WhoAm 94
Senkovich, Allen James 1945- WhoMW 93
Senn, Alfred Erich 1932- WrDr 94
Senn, Laurence Vaughn, Jr. 1945- WhoAm 94, WhoAmL 94
Senn, Milton John Edward 1902-1990 WhAm 10
Senn, Peter Richard 1923- WhoFI 94
Senn, Robert Franklin 1945- WhoFI 94
Senna, Ayrton 1960- IntWW 93, Who 94
Sennacherib BlmGEL
Senne, William Ralph 1946- WhoAmP 93
Senner, Robert William 1912- WhoMW 93
Sennet, Charles Joseph 1952- WhoAmL 94
Sennett, Frank Ronald, Jr. 1968- WhoWest 94
Sennett, John DrAPF 93
Sennett, Mack d1960 WhoHol 92
Sennett, Mack 1880-1960 AmCulL [port]
Sennett, Nancy J. 1951- WhoAmL 94
Sennett, Richard 1943- WhoAm 94, WrDr 94
Sennhauser, John d1978 WhoAmA 93N
Senning, Ake 1915- IntWW 93
Senorina de Silva, Isabel c. 1660-1740 BlmGWL
Senour, Maria Nieto 1943- WhoHisp 94
Senoussi, Badreddine 1933- Who 94
Sens, Ginetta NewGrDO
Sens, Mary Ann 1949- WhoScEn 94
Sensabaugh, Mary Elizabeth 1939- WhoFI 94
Senseman, Ronald Sylvester 1912- WhoAm 94
Sensemann, Susan 1949- WhoAmA 93
Sensenbrenner, F. James, Jr. 1943- CngDr 93
Sensenbrenner, F. Joseph, Jr. 1948- WhoAmP 93
Sensenbrenner, Frank James, Jr. 1943- WhoAm 94, WhoAmL 94, WhoAmP 93, WhoMW 93
Sensenbrenner, Maynard E. 1902-1991 WhAm 10
Sensenich, Ila Jeanne 1939- WhoAm 94, WhoAmL 94

Seshadri, Conjeevaram Srirangachari 1932- *Who 94*
Seshadri, Kal S. 1924- *WhoAsA 94*
Seshadri, Rangaswamy 1945- *WhoScEn 94*
Seshan, Kulathu Iyer 1951- *WhoScEn 94*
Seslowsky, Harvey Michael 1942- *WhoFI 94*
Sesonske, Alexander 1921- *WhoAm 94*
Sessa, Todd Raymond 1963- *WhoMW 93*
Sesser, Gary Douglas 1950- *WhoAmL 94*
Sessford, George Minshull 1928- *Who 94*
Sessi, Marianna 1776-1847 *NewGrDO*
Session, Johnny Frank 1949- *WhoBlA 94*
Session, William Terrell 1952- *WhoAmL 94*
Sessions, Almira d1974 *WhoHol 92*
Sessions, James *WhoHol 92*
Sessions, Jefferson Beauregard, III 1946- *WhoAm 94, WhoAmL 94*
Sessions, John *WhoHol 92*
Sessions, John 1953- *Who 94*
Sessions, John O. *WhoAmP 93*
Sessions, Judith Ann 1947- *WhoAm 94*
Sessions, Kathryn L. 1942- *WhoAmP 93*
Sessions, Robert Paul 1926- *WhoAm 94*
Sessions, Roger (Huntington) 1896-1985 *NewGrDO*
Sessions, Roger Huntington 1896-1985 *AmCulL*
Sessions, William S. 1930- *IntWW 93, WhoAmP 93*
Sessions, William Steele 1930- *WhoAm 94, WhoAmL 94*
Sessle, Barry John 1941- *WhoAm 94*
Sessler, Alan D. *WhoMW 93*
Sessler, Albert Louis, Jr. 1925- *WhoAmL 94*
Sessler, Alfred A. 1909-1963 *WhoAmA 93N*
Sessler, Andrew Marienhoff 1928- *WhoAm 94, WhoWest 94*
Sessler, Donna Jean Hotz 1954- *WhoMW 93*
Sessoms, Allen Lee 1946- *WhoAm 94, WhoScEn 94*
Sessoms, Frank Eugene 1947- *WhoBlA 94*
Sessoms, Furmin Douglas 1949- *WhoBlA 94*
Sessoms, Stephanie Thompson 1963- *WhoFI 94*
Sessoms, Stuart McGuire 1921- *WhoAm 94*
Sessoms, Walter Woodrow 1934- *WhoAm 94, WhoFI 94*
Sestak, Jiri Vladimir 1930- *WhoScEn 94*
Sesti, Claire d1990 *WhoHol 92*
Sestina, John E. 1942- *WhoFI 94, WhoMW 93*
Sestini, Giovanna fl. 1772-1791 *NewGrDO*
Sestini, Virgil Andrew 1936- *WhoScEn 94, WhoWest 94*
Sestric, Anthony James 1940- *WhoAmL 94, WhoMW 93*
Setaccioli, Giacomo 1868-1925 *NewGrDO*
Setaro, Nicola c. 1730-c. 1774 *NewGrDO*
Setch, Terry 1936- *IntWW 93*
Setchell, David Lloyd 1937- *IntWW 93*
Setchell, John Stanford, Jr. 1942- *WhoScEn 94*
Setchell, Marcus Edward 1943- *Who 94*
Setchko, Edward Stephen 1926- *WhoWest 94*
Seter, Mordecai 1910- *IntWW 93*
Seteroff, Sviatoslav Steve 1937- *WhoWest 94*
Seth, Arun K. 1953- *WhoAsA 94*
Seth, Oliver 1915- *WhoAm 94, WhoAmL 94, WhoWest 94*
Seth, Philip Doyle 1958- *WhoWest 94*
Seth, Roshan 1942- *WhoHol 92*
Seth, Shyam S. 1943- *WhoAsA 94*
Seth, Vikram *DrAPF 93, NewYTBS 93 [port]*
Seth, Vikram 1952- *IntWW 93, WhoAm 94, WrDr 94*
Sethi, Inder Dev 1935- *WhoFI 94*
Sethi, Ishwar Krishan 1948- *WhoAsA 94*
Sethi, Narendra Kumar 1935- *WrDr 94*
Sethi, Naresh Kumar 1961- *WhoAsA 94*
Sethi, Robbie Clipper *DrAPF 93*
Sethi, Shyam Sunder 1942- *WhoAm 94*
Sethna, Beheruz Nariman 1948- *WhoAm 94*
Sethna, M(inocher) J(ehangirji) 1911- *WrDr 94*
Sethness, Charles Henry, Jr. 1910- *WhoFI 94*
Sethness, Charles Olin 1941- *IntWW 93, WhoAm 94*
Sethuraman, Salem Venkataraman 1935- *WhoScEn 94*
Setlow, Jane Kellock 1919- *WhoAm 94*
Setlow, Neva C. 1940- *WhoAmA 93*
Setlow, Richard Burton 1921- *WhoAm 94, WhoScEn 94*
Seto, Belinda P. 1948- *WhoAsA 94*
Seto, Benjamin S. F. *WhoAsA 94*
Seto, Joseph Tobey 1924- *WhoAm 94, WhoAsA 94, WhoWest 94*
Seto, Robert Mahealani Ming 1936- *WhoAsA 94*
Seto, Thelma G. 1954- *WhoAsA 94*
Seto, Theodore Paul 1951- *WhoAsA 94*
Seto, William Roderick 1954- *WhoAm 94, WhoFI 94*
Seton, Lady *Who 94*
Seton, Anya d1990 *WhAm 10*
Seton, Bruce d1969 *WhoHol 92*
Seton, Charles B. 1910- *WhoAm 94*
Seton, Elizabeth Ann 1774-1821 *HisWorL [port]*
Seton, Elizabeth Ann Bayley 1774-1821 *AmSocL [port], BlmGWL, DcAmReB 2*
Seton, Fenmore Roger 1917- *WhoAm 94*
Seton, Iain (Bruce) 1942- *Who 94*
Seton, Robert (James) 1926- *Who 94*
Seton, Violet d1970 *WhoHol 92*
Setouchi Harumi 1922- *BlmGWL*
Setrakian, Berge 1949- *WhoAm 94, WhoAmL 94*
Setser, Carole Sue 1940- *WhoAm 94*
Setser, Donald Wayne 1935- *WhoAm 94*
Setshogo, Boithoko Moonwa 1941- *Who 94*
Sette, Pietro 1915- *IntWW 93*
Sette, Rural Dean fl. 19th cent.- *EncNAR*
Sette Camara, Jose 1920- *IntWW 93*
Settee, James c. 1809-1902 *EncNAR*
Settee, John R. fl. 19th cent.- *EncNAR*
Setterberg, Carl Georg 1897- *WhoAmA 93N*
Settle, Bill 1937- *WhoAmP 93*
Settle, Eric Lawrence 1961- *WhoAmL 94*
Settle, Frank Alexander, Jr. 1937- *WhoAm 94*
Settle, John R. 1965- *WhoBlA 94*
Settle, Mary Lee 1918- *WhoAm 94, WrDr 94*
Settle, Robert D., Jr. 1948- *WhoAmL 94*
Settle, William Sydnor 1933- *WhoAm 94*
Settlemyer, Claude Harold 1912-1988 *WhAm 10*
Settles, Arthur E. 1947- *WhoIns 94*
Settles, Carl E. 1948- *WhoBlA 94*
Settles, Darryl Stephen 1961- *WhoBlA 94*
Settles, F. Stan, Jr. 1938- *WhoAm 94, WhoFI 94*
Settles, Gary Stuart 1949- *WhoScEn 94*
Settles, Rosetta Hayes 1920- *WhoBlA 94*
Settles, Thomas Edward 1951- *WhoAm 94, WhoAmP 93*
Settles, Trudy Y. 1946- *WhoBlA 94*
Setton, Kenneth M. 1914- *WhoAm 94*
Setton, Ruth Knafo *DrAPF 93*
Setzepfandt, Alvin O. H., II 1924- *WhoAmP 93*
Setzer, Brian 1959- *See* Stray Cats, The *ConMus 11*
Setzer, Gene Willis 1918- *WhoAm 94*
Setzer, Herbert John 1928- *WhoAm 94*
Setzer, Johnsie Julia 1924- *WhoAmP 93*
Setzer, Karen Lee 1944- *WhoWest 94*
Setzer, Kirk *WhoMW 93*
Setzler, Edward Allan 1933- *WhoAm 94, WhoAmL 94*
Setzler, Nikki G. 1945- *WhoAmP 93*
Setzler, William Edward 1926- *WhoAm 94*
Seum, Dan 1940- *WhoAmP 93*
Seume, Johann Gottfried d1810 *WhAmRev*
Seung, Thomas Kaehao 1930- *WhoAm 94*
Seuphor, Michel *ConAu 42NR*
Seurat, Pilar *WhoHol 92*
Seuss, Dr. *SmATA 75, WhAm 10*
Seuss, Dr. 1904-1991 *WrDr 94N*
See Also Geisel, Thedor Seuss 1904-1991 *WhoAmA 93N*
Seuster, Lisa 1942- *WhoWomW 91*
Seva'aetasi, Suitupu *WhoAmP 93*
Sevareid, Arnold Eric d1992 *IntWW 93N*
Sevareid, Eric 1912- *WhoHol 92*
Sevaried, Eric 1912-1992 *AnObit 1992*
Sevario, Joseph A., III 1944- *WhoAmP 93*
Sevcenko, Ihor 1922- *WhoAm 94*
Sevcik, Melanie Jenice 1958- *WhoAm 94*
Seven, Johnny 1930- *WhoHol 92*
Seven, Raymond P. 1921- *WhoMW 93*
Sevening, Dora *WhoHol 92*
Sever, Albert d1953 *WhoHol 92*
Sever, (Eric) John 1943- *Who 94*
Sever, John Louis 1932- *WhoFI 94*
Sever, Lowell Enyeart 1939- *WhoWest 94*
Severac, (Marie-Joseph-Alexandre) Deodat de 1872-1921 *NewGrDO*
Severance, Charles M. 1939- *WhoAmP 93*
Severance, Christopher Churchill 1943- *WhoAm 94*
Severance, Joan 1958- *WhoHol 92*
Severcool, Shirley Jean 1930- *WhoAmP 93*
Severe, John Thomas 1951- *WhoAmL 94*
Severin, Dorothy Virginia Sherman 1942- *Who 94*
Severin, Timothy 1940- *WrDr 94*
Severin, (Giles) Timothy 1940- *IntWW 93, Who 94*
Severine 1855-1929 *BlmGWL*
Severini, Carlo 1793-1828 *NewGrDO*
Severin-Mars, M. d1921 *WhoHol 92*
Severino, Elizabeth Forrest 1945- *WhoFI 94*
Severino, Robert Anthony 1954- *WhoWest 94*
Severinsen, Doc 1927- *WhoAm 94, WhoWest 94*
Severinsen, Hanne 1944- *WhoWomW 91*
Severinsky, Alexander Jacob 1944- *WhoFI 94*
Severn, Billy 1939- *WhoHol 92*
Severn, Christopher 1936- *WhoHol 92*
Severn, Clifford 1926- *WhoHol 92*
Severn, David *Who 94*
Severn, David 1918- *WrDr 94*
Severn, Donald 1931- *WrDr 94*
Severn, Ernest 1935- *WhoHol 92*
Severn, Maida 1902- *WhoHol 92*
Severn, Raymond 1932- *WhoHol 92*
Severn, Roy Thomas 1929- *Who 94*
Severn, Veronica 1922- *WhoHol 92*
Severn, Winston Franklin MacArthur 1943- *WhoHol 92*
Severn, Yvonne 1929- *WhoHol 92*
Severne, John (de Milt) 1925- *Who 94*
Severn Family, The *WhoHol 92*
Severns, Joan Zagar 1929- *WhoAmP 93*
Severns, Penny L. 1952- *WhoAmP 93, WhoMW 93*
Severo, Richard 1932- *WhoAm 94*
Severs, Charles A., III 1942- *WhoAm 94, WhoAmL 94*
Severs, Walter Bruce 1938- *WhoAm 94*
Severson, Elmer D. 1922- *WhoAmP 93*
Severson, Glen Arthur 1949- *WhoAmL 94, WhoMW 93*
Severson, Gregory Dean 1961- *WhoFI 94*
Severson, John Robert 1955- *WhoFI 94*
Severson, Kim Marie 1961- *WhoWest 94*
Severson, Wayne Larson 1921- *WhoMW 93*
Severson, William Conrad 1924- *WhoAmA 93*
Severy, Bruce W. *DrAPF 93*
Severy, Lawrence James 1943- *WhoAm 94*
Sevey, Robert Warren 1927- *WhoWest 94*
Sevier, Ernest Youle 1932- *WhoAm 94, WhoAmL 94*
Sevier, John 1745-1815 *AmRev, WhAmRev*
Sevigne, Marie de Rabutin-Chantal, Marquise de 1626-1696 *BlmGWL, GuFrLit 2*
Sevigny, Maurice Joseph, II 1943- *WhoAmA 93*
Sevik, Maurice 1923- *WhoAm 94*
Sevilla, Carlos A. 1935- *WhoWest 94*
Sevilla, Carlos Arthur 1935- *WhoHisp 94*
Sevilla, Carmen 1930- *WhoHol 92*
Sevilla, Dennis 1958- *WhoHisp 94*
Sevilla, Stanley 1920- *WhoAm 94*
Sevilla-Gardinier, Josefina Zialcita 1931- *WhoMW 93*
Sevillian, Clarence Marvin 1945- *WhoBlA 94*
Sevin, Eugene 1928- *WhoAm 94*
Sevold, Gordon James 1926- *WhoAm 94*
Sevryugin, Nikolai Vasilevich 1939- *LngBDD*
Sevy, Barbara Snetsinger 1926- *WhoAmA 93*
Sevy, Roger Warren 1923- *WhoAm 94*
Sewalk, Kathleen M. *DrAPF 93*
Sewall, Allen D. d1954 *WhoHol 92*
Sewall, Grant d1978 *WhoHol 92*
Sewall, Jonathan 1728-1796 *WhAmRev*
Sewall, Loyall F. 1934- *WhoAmP 93*
Sewall, Lucile d1976 *WhoHol 92*
Sewall, Stephen 1747-1825 *WhAmRev*
Sewall, Tingey Haig 1940- *WhoAm 94*
Seward, Anna 1742-1809 *BlmGWL*
Seward, Anna 1747-1809 *BlmGEL*
Seward, Billie d1982 *WhoHol 92*
Seward, George Chester 1910- *IntWW 93, WhoAm 94, WhoAmL 94, WhoFI 94*
Seward, Guy William 1916- *Who 94*
Seward, James L. *WhoAmP 93*
Seward, Jeffrey James 1953- *WhoAmL 94, WhoFI 94, WhoMW 93*
Seward, John E., Jr. 1943- *WhoIns 94*
Seward, John Edward, Jr. 1943- *WhoFI 94, WhoMW 93*
Seward, John Wesley, Jr. 1948- *WhoFI 94*
Seward, Roland Quincy, Sr. 1917- *WhoAmP 93*
Seward, Russell G. 1920- *WhoAmP 93*
Seward, Steven Le Mar 1946- *WhoMW 93*
Seward, William Henry 1801-1872 *HisWorL [port]*
Seward, William Richard 1922- *Who 94*
Seward, William Ward, Jr. 1913- *WhoAm 94*
Sewards, Colin Frederick 1928- *WhoFI 94*
Sewell, Adrian Clive 1950- *WhoScEn 94*
Sewell, (John) Allan 1915- *Who 94*
Sewell, Anna 1820-1878 *BlmGEL, BlmGWL*
Sewell, Ben Gardner 1911- *WhoAm 94*
Sewell, Beverly Jean 1942- *WhoFI 94*
Sewell, Brocard 1912- *WrDr 94*
Sewell, Cameron Dee 1947- *WhoAmL 94*
Sewell, Charles Haslett 1928- *WhoAm 94*
Sewell, Charles Robertson 1927- *WhoWest 94*
Sewell, Darrel L. 1939- *WhoAmA 93*
Sewell, Darrel Leslie 1939- *WhoAm 94*
Sewell, Dwight A. 1932- *WhoAm 94*
Sewell, Edward C. 1946- *WhoBlA 94*
Sewell, Elizabeth *DrAPF 93*
Sewell, Elizabeth 1815-1906 *BlmGWL*
Sewell, Elizabeth 1919- *WhoAm 94*
Sewell, George 1924- *WhoHol 92*
Sewell, Helen Moore 1897-1957 *WhoAmA 93N*
Sewell, Isiah Obediah 1938- *WhoBlA 94*
Sewell, Jack Vincent 1923- *WhoAmA 93*
Sewell, James Leslie 1903- *WhoAm 94*
Sewell, John Williamson 1935- *WhoAm 94*
Sewell, Joyce Carolyn 1930- *WhoAmP 93*
Sewell, Larry M. 1945- *WhoAmL 94*
Sewell, Leo 1945- *WhoAmA 93*
Sewell, Luther Joseph 1936- *WhoBlA 94*
Sewell, Phyllis Shapiro 1930- *WhoAm 94, WhoFI 94, WhoMW 93*
Sewell, Ralph Byron 1940- *WhoFI 94*
Sewell, Richard George 1942- *WhoAmA 93*
Sewell, Richard Herbert 1931- *WhoAm 94*
Sewell, Richard Hudson 1946- *WhoBlA 94*
Sewell, Robert Terrell, Jr. 1932- *WhoMW 93*
Sewell, Rufus *WhoHol 92*
Sewell, Sandra Serrano *WhoHisp 94*
Sewell, Stephen 1953- *ConDr 93, IntDcT 2, WrDr 94*
Sewell, Steven Edward 1963- *WhoBlA 94*
Sewell, Thomas Robert McKie 1921- *Who 94*
Sewell, Timothy Patrick T. *Who 94*
Sewell, William (Hamilton) 1909- *WrDr 94*
Sewell, William Hamilton 1909- *WhoAm 94*
Sewell, William Hamilton, Jr. 1940- *WhoMW 93*
Sewell, William R. 1926- *WhoWest 94*
Sewell, Winifred 1917- *WhoAm 94*
Sewright, Charles William, Jr. 1946- *WhoFI 94*
Sexauer, Donald Richard *WhoAmA 93*
Sexauer, Roxanne Denise 1952- *WhoWest 94*
Sexton, Adam 1962- *ConAu 142*
Sexton, Amy Manerbino 1957- *WhoScEn 94*
Sexton, Anne 1928-1974 *BlmGWL*
Sexton, Carol Burke 1939- *WhoFI 94*
Sexton, Clarence D., Jr. 1927- *WhoAmP 93*
Sexton, David Farrington 1943- *WhoAm 94*
Sexton, David John 1939- *WhoAm 94*
Sexton, Donald Lee 1932- *WhoAm 94, WhoFI 94*
Sexton, Emily Stryker 1880-1948 *WhoAmA 93N*
Sexton, James Dean 1942- *WhoWest 94*
Sexton, Jo Ann 1933- *WhoMW 93*
Sexton, John (William) 1953- *WhoAmA 93*
Sexton, John Edward 1942- *WhoAm 94, WhoAmL 94*
Sexton, Ken 1949- *WhoAm 94, WhoScEn 94*
Sexton, Kristine Ruth 1951- *WhoMW 93*
Sexton, Landon C. 1941- *WhoAmP 93*
Sexton, Linda Gray 1953- *WrDr 94*
Sexton, (Francis) Michael 1923- *Who 94*
Sexton, Michael Bernard 1958- *WhoAmL 94*
Sexton, Michael James 1965- *WhoAmL 94*
Sexton, Owen James 1926- *WhoAm 94*
Sexton, Patricia Cayo 1924- *ConAu 141*
Sexton, Paul E., Jr. 1946- *WhoAmL 94*
Sexton, Richard 1929- *WhoAm 94*
Sexton, Thomas F. *DrAPF 93*
Sexton, Virginia Staudt 1916- *WrDr 94*
Sexton, Wendell P. *DrAPF 93*
Sexton, William Cottrell 1928- *WhoAm 94*
Sexwale, Tokyo *IntWW 93*
Seybold, Lawrence F. 1897- *WhAm 10*
Seybold, Steven Jon 1959- *WhoWest 94*
Seybolt, George C. d1993 *NewYTBS 93*
Seybou, Ali *IntWW 93*
Seychelles, Bishop of *Who 94*
Seydelmann, Franz 1748-1806 *NewGrDO*
Seyden-Penne, Jacqueline 1930- *WhoScEn 94*
Seydou, Amadou 1928- *IntWW 93*

Seydoux Fornier de Clausonne, Nicolas Pierre 1939- *IntWW 93*
Seyersted, Per *WrDr 94*
Seyfarth, Henry Edward 1908-1991 *WhAm 10*
Seyfert, Howard Bentley, Jr. 1918- *WhoWest 94*
Seyfert, Richard Leopold 1915-1979 *WhoAmA 93N*
Seyferth, Dietmar 1929- *WhoAm 94*
Seyferth, Harold Homer 1922- *WhoWest 94*
Seyferth, Wilfried d1954 *WhoHol 92*
Seyffarth, Linda Jean Wilcox 1948- *WhoFI 94*
Seyffert, J. Robert 1952- *WhoAmA 93*
Seyfried, Ignaz (Xaver), Ritter von 1776-1841 *NewGrDO*
Se-yin-ba-ya-er 1922- *WhoPRCh 91 [port]*
Seyle, Robert Harley 1937- *WhoAmA 93*
Seyler, Abel 1730-1800 *NewGrDO*
Seyler, Athene d1990 *WhoHol 92*
Seyler, (Friederike) Sophie 1738-1789 *NewGrDO*
Seyler, William C. 1921- *WhoFI 94*
Seymore, Stanley 1951- *WhoBlA 94*
Seymour *Who 94*
Seymour, Lord 1982- *Who 94*
Seymour, A. Barry 1942- *WhoMW 93*
Seymour, A(rthur) J(ames) 1914- *BlkWr 2*
Seymour, Alan 1927- *ConDr 93, EncSF 93, WrDr 94*
Seymour, Anne *BlmGWL*
Seymour, Anne d1988 *WhoHol 92*
Seymour, Arthur Hallock 1928- *WhoAm 94*
Seymour, Brian Richard 1944- *WhoAm 94, WhoScEn 94*
Seymour, Carolyn *WhoHol 92*
Seymour, Charles, Jr. 1912-1977 *WhoAmA 93N*
Seymour, Charles Wilfred 1965- *WhoScEn 94*
Seymour, Clarine d1920 *WhoHol 92*
Seymour, Cynthia Maria 1933- *WhoBlA 94*
Seymour, Dan d1993 *IntMPA 94N, NewYTBS 93*
Seymour, Dan 1912- *WhoHol 92*
Seymour, Donald Edward 1946- *WhoAm 94, WhoAmL 94*
Seymour, Ernest Richard 1931-1989 *WhAm 10*
Seymour, Everett Hedden, Jr. 1958- *WhoAmL 94*
Seymour, Frances 1669-1754 *BlmGWL*
Seymour, Francis 1928- *Who 94*
Seymour, Frederick Prescott, Jr. 1924- *WhoScEn 94*
Seymour, Gerald (William Herschel Kean) 1941- *WrDr 94*
Seymour, Harlan Francis 1950- *WhoFI 94, WhoScEn 94*
Seymour, Harry d1967 *WhoHol 92*
Seymour, James Elliott 1943- *WhoMW 93*
Seymour, Jane *BlmGWL*
Seymour, Jane d1956 *WhoHol 92*
Seymour, Jane 1951- *IntMPA 94, WhoAm 94, WhoHol 92*
Seymour, Janet Martha 1957- *WhoScEn 94*
Seymour, Jeffrey Alan 1950- *WhoFI 94, WhoWest 94*
Seymour, John 1937- *WhoAmP 93*
Seymour, John D. d1986 *WhoHol 92*
Seymour, John Herbert 1945- *WhoAm 94*
Seymour, John Laurence 1893-1986 *NewGrDO*
Seymour, Jon *WhoAm 94, WhoFI 94*
Seymour, Laurence Darryl 1935- *WhoBlA 94*
Seymour, Lynn *WhoHol 92*
Seymour, Lynn 1939- *IntDcB [port], IntWW 93, Who 94*
Seymour, Margaret *BlmGWL*
Seymour, Mary Frances 1948- *WhoAmL 94*
Seymour, Mary Powell 1922- *WhoAmP 93*
Seymour, McNeil Vernam 1934- *WhoAm 94, WhoAmL 94*
Seymour, Michael Culme- 1909- *Who 94*
Seymour, Miranda (Jane) 1948- *WrDr 94*
Seymour, Paul 1928- *BasBi*
Seymour, Peter Mark 1948- *WhoWest 94*
Seymour, Phil d1993 *NewYTBS 93*
Seymour, Ralph *WhoHol 92*
Seymour, Raymond Benedict 1912-1991 *WhAm 10*
Seymour, Richard Deming 1955- *WhoMW 93*
Seymour, Richard Kellogg 1930- *WhoAm 94*
Seymour, Richard William 1950- *Who 94*
Seymour, Robert F. 1926- *WhoBlA 94*
Seymour, Ronald Clement 1959- *WhoScEn 94*
Seymour, Stephanie K. *WhoAmP 93*
Seymour, Stephanie Kulp 1940- *WhoAm 94, WhoAmL 94*
Seymour, Sylvia Joan 1937- *WhoMW 93*
Seymour, Thaddeus 1928- *WhoAm 94*
Seymour, William J. *DcAmReB 2*
Seymour, William Joseph 1870-1922 *AfrAmAl 6*
Seymour-Harris, Barbara Laverne 1953- *WhoAmL 94*
Seymour-Smith, Martin 1928- *WrDr 94*
Seynes, Philippe de 1910- *IntWW 93*
Seypidin 1915- *WhoPRCh 91 [port]*
Seypidin Aze 1916- *IntWW 93*
Seyrig, Delphine d1990 *WhoHol 92*
Seys-Llewellyn, John Desmond 1912- *Who 94*
Sezgin, Ismet 1928- *IntWW 93*
Sezgin, Mesut 1948- *WhoScEn 94*
Sezna, John Adam 1944- *WhoMW 93*
Sfar, Rachid 1933- *IntWW 93*
Sfasciotti, Mary L. 1941- *WhoAmL 94*
Sfat, Dina d1989 *WhoHol 92*
Sfekas, Stephen James 1947- *WhoAm 94, WhoAmL 94*
Sferrazza, Peter J. 1945- *WhoAmP 93*
Sferrazza, Peter Joseph 1945- *WhoWest 94*
Sfikas, Peter Michael 1937- *WhoAm 94*
Sfortunato, Joanna 1947- *WhoMW 93*
Sforza, William Thomas 1941- *WhoFI 94*
Sforza-Cesarini, Francesco c. 1772-1816 *NewGrDO*
Sganga, John B. 1931- *WhoAm 94, WhoFI 94*
Sgorlon, Carlo Pietro Antonio 1930- *IntWW 93*
Sgouros, Dimitris 1969- *IntWW 93*
Sgro, Gregory Peter 1961- *WhoMW 93*
Sgro, Joseph Anthony 1937- *WhoAm 94*
Sgroi, Humphrey Joseph 1943- *WhoFI 94*
Sha, Ji-Ping 1957- *WhoAsA 94*
Sha, Shung-tse 1929- *WhoAsA 94*
Sha, William T. 1928- *WhoAsA 94*
Shaaber, Matthias Adam 1897- *WhAm 10*
Shaali, Mohammad Bin Hussain Al- 1950- *IntWW 93*
Shaan, Ron Morgan d1977 *WhoHol 92*
Shaar, H. Erik *WhoAm 94, WhoMW 93*
Shaara, Michael 1929-1988 *EncSF 93*
Sha Bai 1925- *WhoPRCh 91*
Shabaz, John C. 1931- *WhoAm 94, WhoAmL 94, WhoMW 93*
Shabazz, Attallah 1958- *ConBlB 6 [port]*
Shabazz, Betty 1936- *WhoBlA 94*
Shabazz, Kaleem 1947- *WhoBlA 94*
"Shabba-Doo" *WhoHol 92*
Shabbir, Mahnaz Mehdi 1959- *WhoAm 94*
Shabel, Dennis Joseph 1944- *WhoMW 93*
Shabelevsky, Yurek 1911- *IntDcB*
Shaber, David *IntMPA 94*
Sha Boli 1915- *WrDr 94*
Shabunin, Ivan Petrovich 1935- *LngBDD*
Shabushnig, John George 1956- *WhoFI 94*
Shack, John Richard 1940- *WhoMW 93*
Shack, William A. 1923- *WhoBlA 94*
Shack, William Alfred 1923- *IntWW 93, WhoAm 94*
Shack, William Edward, Jr. 1943- *WhoBlA 94*
Shackelford, Barton Warren 1920- *WhoAm 94*
Shackelford, Bud 1918- *WhoAmA 93*
Shackelford, Donald Bruce 1932- *WhoAm 94*
Shackelford, Floyd d1972 *WhoHol 92*
Shackelford, George Franklin 1939- *WhoBlA 94*
Shackelford, George Green 1920- *WhoAm 94*
Shackelford, Ginger Carole Gunn 1946- *WhoAmP 93*
Shackelford, Gordon Lee, Jr. 1948- *WhoWest 94*
Shackelford, Jean A. 1946- *ConAu 43NR*
Shackelford, Jerry F. 1942- *WhoAmL 94*
Shackelford, Jole Richard 1954- *WhoMW 93*
Shackelford, Lottie H. 1941- *WhoBlA 94*
Shackelford, Lottie Holt 1941- *WhoAm 94, WhoAmP 93*
Shackelford, Martin Robert 1947- *WhoMW 93*
Shackelford, Shelby 1899-1987 *WhoAmA 93N*
Shackelford, Ted 1946- *WhoHol 92*
Shackelford, William G., Jr. 1950- *WhoBlA 94*
Shackett, Maryl *DrAPF 93*
Shackett, Ralph E. 1940- *WhoAmP 93*
Shackle, Christopher 1942- *Who 94*
Shackle, George Lennox Sharman 1903-1992 *WrDr 94N*
Shackleford, Covington 1924- *WhoFI 94*
Shackleton, Baron 1911- *Who 94*
Shackleton, C.C. *EncSF 93*
Shackleton, Edward Arthur Alexander 1911- *IntWW 93*
Shackleton, Ernest Henry 1874-1922 *WhWE*
Shackleton, Keith Hope 1923- *Who 94*
Shackleton, Mary Jane 1934- *WhoFI 94, WhoMW 93*
Shackleton, Nicholas John 1937- *Who 94*
Shackleton, Polly *WhoAmP 93*
Shackleton, Robert d1956 *WhoHol 92*
Shackleton, Robert Millner 1909- *IntWW 93, Who 94*
Shackleton Bailey, D. R. *Who 94*
Shackleton, of Burley, Lord 1911- *WrDr 94*
Shacklett, Mary Eberle 1952- *WhoMW 93*
Shacklette, Donna *WhoAmP 93*
Shackley, Douglas John 1938- *WhoFI 94*
Shacklock, Constance 1913- *NewGrDO, Who 94*
Shacks, Samuel James 1939- *WhoScEn 94*
Shacochis, Bob *DrAPF 93*
Shacter, David Mervyn 1941- *WhoAmL 94, WhoWest 94*
Shacter, John 1921- *WhoFI 94, WhoScEn 94*
Shad, John 1923- *WhoAm 94*
Shadaram, Mehdi 1954- *WhoScEn 94*
Shadbolt, Douglas 1925- *WhoAm 94*
Shadbolt, Jack Leonard 1909- *WhoAmA 93*
Shadbolt, Maurice (Francis Richard) 1932- *RfGShF, WrDr 94*
Shaddix, Glenn *WhoHol 92*
Shaddix, James W. 1946- *WhoAmL 94*
Shaddle, Alice 1928- *WhoAmA 93*
Shaddock, Carroll 1940- *WhoAm 94*
Shaddock, Paul Franklin, Sr. 1950- *WhoWest 94*
Shaddock, William Edward, Jr. 1938- *WhoAmL 94*
Shade, Barbara J. 1933- *WhoBlA 94*
Shade, Ellen 1944- *NewGrDO*
Shade, Jamesson d1956 *WhoHol 92*
Shade, Michael William 1954- *WhoFI 94*
Shade, Nancy 1949- *NewGrDO*
Shade, Willard Norman, Jr. 1947- *WhoFI 94*
Shadegg, Stephen 1909- *WhAm 10*
Shader, Richard Irwin 1935- *WhoAm 94*
Shadle, Jackson d1969 *WhoHol 92*
Shadler, Jimmy Arthur 1929- *WhoFI 94*
Shadmehri, Bahram 1952- *WhoWest 94*
Shadoan, George Woodson 1933- *WhoAm 94*
Shadoan, William Lewis 1931- *WhoAmL 94*
Shadrach, Jean H. *WhoAmA 93*
Shadrawy, Bernard Francis, Jr. 1948- *WhoAmL 94*
Shadur, Milton I. 1924- *WhoAm 94, WhoMW 93*
Shadur, Robert H. 1947- *WhoAm 94, WhoAmL 94*
Shadwell, Thomas 1640?-1692 *IntDcT 2 [port]*
Shadwell, Thomas 1642?-1692 *BlmGEL*
Shaeffer, Charles Wayne 1910- *WhoAm 94*
Shaeffer, Charlie Willard, Jr. 1938- *WhoWest 94*
Shaeiwitz, Joseph Alan 1952- *WhoScEn 94*
Shaer, Ali Hassan ash- 1927- *IntWW 93*
Shaeumin, Minaya 1928- *WhoWest 94*
Shaevitz, Jonathon David 1965- *WhoFI 94*
Shaevsky, Mark 1935- *WhoAm 94, WhoAmL 94*
Shafarevich, Igor Rostislavovich 1923- *IntWW 93, LngBDD*
Shafei, Hussein Mahmoud El- 1918- *IntWW 93*
Shafer, Berman Joseph 1927- *WhoScEn 94*
Shafer, Burr d1965 *WhoAmA 93N*
Shafer, Byron Edwin 1947- *Who 94*
Shafer, D. Michael 1953- *WrDr 94*
Shafer, Dallas Eugene 1936- *WhoWest 94*
Shafer, David J. 1965- *WhoAmP 93*
Shafer, Edward G. 1929- *WhoAmP 93*
Shafer, Ernst Smith 1943- *WhoAmP 93*
Shafer, Everett Earl 1925- *WhoAm 94*
Shafer, J. M. 1944- *WhoAm 94*
Shafer, James Albert 1924- *WhoWest 94*
Shafer, John Milton 1951- *WhoFI 94, WhoScEn 94*
Shafer, Joseph Ernest 1903- *WhoAm 94*
Shafer, Jules Alan 1937- *WhoScEn 94*
Shafer, Kent E. 1948- *WhoAmL 94*
Shafer, Kevin Lee 1961- *WhoScEn 94*
Shafer, Marguerite (Phillips) Neuhauser 1888-1976 *WhoAmA 93N*
Shafer, Mollie d1940 *WhoHol 92*
Shafer, Neil 1933- *WrDr 94*
Shafer, Norma R. 1938- *WhoFI 94*
Shafer, Raymond Philip 1917- *WhoAm 94, WhoAmP 93*
Shafer, Robert d1981 *WhoHol 92*
Shafer, Robert (Eugene) 1925- *WrDr 94*
Shafer, Roberta W. Crow 1950- *WhoFI 94*
Shafer, Sam L. 1940- *WhoMW 93*
Shafer, Thomas Edward 1950- *WhoMW 93*
Shaff, Beverly Gerard 1925- *WhoWest 94*
Shaffe, David Bruce 1950- *WhoAmP 93*
Shaffer, Anna *Who 94*
Shaffer, Anthony (Joshua) 1926- *ConDr 93, WrDr 94*
Shaffer, Bernard William 1924- *WhoAm 94*
Shaffer, Charles Alan 1938- *WhoAmL 94*
Shaffer, Charles M., Jr. 1941- *WhoAmL 94*
Shaffer, Clyde H(oover) 1900-1990 *WhAm 10*
Shaffer, Dale Eugene 1929- *WrDr 94*
Shaffer, Dale Lester 1920- *WhoAmP 93*
Shaffer, David 1936- *WhoAm 94*
Shaffer, David H. 1942- *WhoAm 94*
Shaffer, Donald 1928- *WhoAmP 93*
Shaffer, Fern 1944- *WhoAmA 93*
Shaffer, Gail 1948- *WhoWomW 91*
Shaffer, Gail S. 1948- *WhoAm 94, WhoAmP 93*
Shaffer, Gary Morris 1940- *WhoWest 94*
Shaffer, Harriet Ellen 1943- *WhoMW 93*
Shaffer, Harry G. 1919- *WrDr 94*
Shaffer, Heidi Jo 1956- *WhoWest 94*
Shaffer, James Burgess 1945- *WhoAm 94*
Shaffer, Jay Christopher 1947- *WhoAmL 94*
Shaffer, Jerome Arthur 1929- *WhoAm 94, WrDr 94*
Shaffer, Jill 1958- *WhoMW 93, WhoScEn 94*
Shaffer, Jonathan David 1964- *WhoAmL 94*
Shaffer, Jonathan R. 1946- *WhoIns 94*
Shaffer, Kathryn Marsh 1961- *WhoWest 94*
Shaffer, Lee 1939- *BasBi*
Shaffer, Martin 1950- *WhoAmP 93*
Shaffer, Mary Louise 1927- *WhoWest 94*
Shaffer, Michael L. 1945- *WhoMW 93*
Shaffer, Nelson Jay 1951- *WhoFI 94*
Shaffer, Oren George 1942- *WhoFI 94*
Shaffer, Paul 1949- *WhoAm 94*
Shaffer, Paul E. 1926- *WhoAm 94, WhoMW 93*
Shaffer, Peter 1926- *BlmGEL*
Shaffer, Peter (Levin) 1926- *ConDr 93, IntDcT 2, WrDr 94*
Shaffer, Peter Levin 1926- *IntWW 93, Who 94, WhoAm 94*
Shaffer, Raymond C. 1932- *WhoAmP 93*
Shaffer, Richard 1947- *WhoAmA 93*
Shaffer, Richard James 1931- *WhoAm 94, WhoAmL 94, WhoFI 94, WhoWest 94*
Shaffer, Roberta Ivy 1953- *WhoAmL 94*
Shaffer, Roger Lee 1947- *WhoAmP 93*
Shaffer, Rosalind 1949- *WhoAmA 93*
Shaffer, Russell K. 1933- *WhoAm 94*
Shaffer, Sherrill Lynn 1952- *WhoFI 94*
Shaffer, Stephen Carroll 1955- *WhoAmP 93*
Shaffer, Stephen M. 1954- *WhoScEn 94*
Shaffer, Thomas Albert 1933- *WhoWest 94*
Shaffer, Thomas Lindsay 1934- *WhoAm 94*
Shaffer, Tim 1945- *WhoAmP 93*
Shaffer, Wayne Alan 1954- *WhoAmL 94*
Shaffert, Kurt 1929- *WhoAmL 94*
Shaffner, Lillian d1930 *WhoHol 92*
Shaffrey, Ina Theresa 1911- *WhoAmP 93*
Shafie, Haji Mohammed Ghazali 1922- *IntWW 93*
Shafiq, Mohammad Musa 1924- *IntWW 93*
Shafir, Eldar 1959- *WhoScEn 94*
Shafner, R. L. *DrAPF 93*
Shafquat, Sofia 1959- *ConAu 141*
Shafran, Hank 1945- *WhoAm 94*
Shafran, Irving 1944- *WhoAmL 94*
Shafranik, Yury Konstantinovich 1952- *LngBDD*
Shafritz, David Andrew 1940- *WhoAm 94, WhoScEn 94*
Shafroth, Will 1924-1991 *WhAm 10*
Shaft, Grant H. 1962- *WhoAmP 93*
Shafter, Bert *WhoHol 92*
Shaftesbury, Earl of 1671-1713 *EncEth*
Shaftesbury, Earl of 1938- *Who 94*
Shaftesbury, Lord 1621-1683 *BlmGEL*
Shaftesbury, Lord 1671-1713 *BlmGEL*
Shaftesbury, Lord 1801-1885 *BlmGEL*
Shafto, Robert Austin 1935- *WhoAm 94, WhoFI 94*
Shafton, Anthony E. 1941- *WhoAmL 94*
Shagam, Marvin Huckel-Berri *WhoWest 94*
Shagan, Steve 1927- *IntMPA 94, WhoAm 94, WrDr 94*
Shagari, Alhaji Shehu Usman Aliu 1925- *IntWW 93*

Shang Jingcai 1921- WhoPRCh 91 [port]
Shang Ming WhoPRCh 91 [port]
Shango, Shaka Aku DrAPF 93
Shangraw, Clarence Frank 1935- WhoAm 94, WhoAmA 93
Shangraw, Sylvia Chen 1937- WhoAmA 93N
Shang Zhenling WhoPRCh 91
Shang Ziqin 1949- WhoPRCh 91
Shank, Arthur d1966 WhoHol 92
Shank, Charles Vernon 1943- WhoAm 94, WhoScEn 94
Shank, Clare Brown Williams 1909- WhoAm 94
Shank, Clifford Charles 1951- WhoMW 93
Shank, Dale DrAPF 93
Shank, Fred Ross 1940- WhoAm 94, WhoScEn 94
Shank, Gregory Lloyd 1948- WhoWest 94
Shank, Kenneth Earl 1929- WhoFI 94
Shank, Margarethe Erdahl 1910- WrDr 94
Shank, Maurice Edwin 1921- WhoAm 94, WhoWest 94
Shank, Michael H. 1949- WhoMW 93
Shank, Richard Eugene 1932- WhoAmP 93
Shank, Robert Ely 1914- WhoAm 94
Shank, Russell 1925- WhoAm 94, WhoWest 94
Shank, Stephen George 1943- WhoFI 94
Shank, Suzanne Adams 1946- WhoAmL 94
Shank, Theodore 1929- WrDr 94
Shank, Thom Lewis 1953- WhoWest 94
Shank, Warren 1940- WhoMW 93
Shank, Wesley Ivan 1927- WhoAm 94
Shank, William O. 1924- WhoAm 94, WhoAmL 94
Shankar, Arvind Narayan 1956- WhoAmL 94
Shankar, Pandit Ravi 1920- Who 94
Shankar, Ramsewak IntWW 93
Shankar, Ravi 1920- IntDcF 2-4, IntWW 93, WhoHol 92
Shankar, Srinivasan 1950- WhoAsA 94
Shankar, Subramonian WhoAsA 94
Shankar, Vijaya V. WhoScEn 94
Shankara c. 788-820 HisWorL [port]
Shankaranand, B. 1925- IntWW 93
Shankardass, Raghuvansh Kumar Prithvinath 1930 IntWW 93
Shankel, Nancy Ann 1939- WhoMW 93
Shanken, Marvin NewYTBS 93 [port]
Shanker, Albert 1928- WhoAm 94, WhoAmP 93
Shanker, Morris Gerald 1926- WhoAm 94
Shankland, Peter Macfarlane 1901- WrDr 94
Shankland, Richard d1953 WhoHol 92
Shanklin, Douglas Radford 1930- WhoAm 94, WhoScEn 94
Shanklin, Richard Vair, III 1937- WhoAm 94
Shankman, Gary Charles 1950- WhoAmA 93
Shanks, David WhoAm 94
Shanks, Don 1950- WhoHol 92
Shanks, Donald 1940- NewGrDO
Shanks, Duncan Faichney 1937- Who 94
Shanks, Edward (Richard Buxton) 1892-1953 EncSF 93
Shanks, Ernest Pattison 1911- Who 94
Shanks, Eugene B., Jr. WhoAm 94, WhoFI 94
Shanks, Gerald Robert 1942- WhoFI 94
Shanks, Hershel 1930- WhoAm 94, WhoAmL 94
Shanks, Ian Alexander 1948- IntWW 93, Who 94
Shanks, James 1800-1867 DcNaB MP
Shanks, James A. 1912- WhoBlA 94
Shanks, John d1956 WhoHol 92
Shanks, Patricia L. 1940- WhoAmL 94
Shanks, Richard C. 1953- WhoAmL 94
Shanks, Robert Bruce 1950- WhoAm 94
Shanks, Stephen Ray 1956- WhoScEn 94
Shanks, Wilhelmina Byrd 1951- WhoBlA 94
Shanks, William Coleman, Jr. 1917- WhoBlA 94
Shanks, William Ennis, Jr. 1950- WhoAmL 94
Shanley, Bernard Michael 1903-1992 WhAm 10
Shanley, Helen DrAPF 93
Shanley, John Patrick 1950- ConDr 93, IntMPA 94, WrDr 94
Shanley, Robert d1968 WhoHol 92
Shanley, William C., III 1925- WhoFI 94
Shanman, James Alan 1942- WhoAm 94, WhoAmL 94
Shann, Frank Athol 1944- WhoScEn 94
Shannahan, John Henry Kelly 1913- WhoAm 94
Shannahan, William Paul 1934- WhoAmL 94
Shanney, William I. 1925- WhoWest 94
Shanno, David Francis 1938- WhoAm 94
Shannon, Earl of 1924- Who 94
Shannon, Al WhoHol 92
Shannon, Barry Thomas 1952- WhoMW 93
Shannon, Brian G. 1942- WhoAmL 94
Shannon, Charles 1914- WhoAmA 93
Shannon, Charles E. WhoAmP 93
Shannon, Claude Elwood 1916- IntWW 93, WhoAm 94
Shannon, Cora d1957 WhoHol 92
Shannon, Dale, Mrs. d1923 WhoHol 92
Shannon, Dale Lynn 1961- WhoMW 93
Shannon, David Allen 1920- ConAu 43NR
Shannon, David Allen 1920-1991 WhAm 10
Shannon, David Thomas 1933- WhoAm 94, WhoBlA 94
Shannon, David William Francis 1941- Who 94
Shannon, Del 1934-1990 ConMus 10 [port]
Shannon, Donald Hawkins 1923- WhoAm 94
Shannon, Donald Sutherlin 1935- WhoFI 94, WhoMW 93
Shannon, Doris 1924- WrDr 94
Shannon, Edfred L., Jr. 1926- WhoFI 94
Shannon, Edgar Finley, Jr. 1918- WhoAm 94
Shannon, Effie d1954 WhoHol 92
Shannon, Elizabeth d1959 WhoHol 92
Shannon, Ethel d1951 WhoHol 92
Shannon, Frank d1959 WhoHol 92
Shannon, Fred EncSF 93
Shannon, George A. 1918- WhoBlA 94
Shannon, Harry d1964 WhoHol 92
Shannon, Helene Marcella d1990 WhoHol 92
Shannon, Iris Reed WhoAm 94
Shannon, Jack d1968 WhoHol 92
Shannon, James Augustine 1904- IntWW 93
Shannon, James Edward WhoScEn 94
Shannon, James Michael 1952- WhoAmP 93
Shannon, James Patrick 1921- WhoAm 94
Shannon, Jeanne DrAPF 93
Shannon, Joe, Jr. 1940- WhoAmL 94
Shannon, Joel Ingram 1946- WhoAm 94, WhoAmL 94
Shannon, John Kingsley DrAPF 93
Shannon, John Sanford 1931- WhoAm 94, WhoAmL 94
Shannon, John W. 1933- WhoAmP 93
Shannon, John William 1933- WhoAm 94, WhoBlA 94
Shannon, Larry James 1948- WhoScEn 94
Shannon, Lyle William 1920- WhoAm 94
Shannon, Malcolm Lloyd, Jr. 1946- WhoAmL 94
Shannon, Margaret Anne 1945- WhoAm 94, WhoAmL 94
Shannon, Margaret Rita WhoAm 94
Shannon, Marian L. H. 1922- WhoBlA 94
Shannon, Martha Alberter 1958- WhoFI 94
Shannon, Marylin Linfoot 1941- WhoAmP 93
Shannon, Michael Edward 1936- WhoAm 94, WhoFI 94
Shannon, Odessa M. 1928- WhoBlA 94
Shannon, Odessa McKenzie 1928- WhoAmP 93
Shannon, Paul d1990 WhoHol 92
Shannon, Peggy d1941 WhoHol 92
Shannon, Peter Michael, Jr. 1928- WhoAm 94
Shannon, Richard WhoHol 92
Shannon, Richard John 1949- WhoWest 94
Shannon, Richard Stoll, III 1943- WhoWest 94
Shannon, Richard Thomas 1931- IntWW 93
Shannon, Robert F. 1920- WhoBlA 94
Shannon, Robert Rennie 1932- WhoAm 94, WhoScEn 94, WhoWest 94
Shannon, Russell Delbert 1938- WhoFI 94
Shannon, Sabrina Lynn WhoMW 93
Shannon, Stephen Quinby, Jr. WhoAm 94
Shannon, Steve WrDr 94
Shannon, Sylvester Lorenzo 1933- WhoBlA 94
Shannon, Theodore Paul 1944- WhoMW 93
Shannon, Thomas A(nthony) 1940- ConAu 42NR
Shannon, Thomas Alfred 1932- WhoAm 94
Shannon, Thomas F. 1948- WhoWest 94
Shannon, William Norman, III 1937- WhoAm 94, WhoFI 94, WhoMW 93
Shannonhouse, Sandra 1947- WhoAmA 93
Shanok, Michael Elliott 1938- WhoFI 94
Shanor, Clarence Richard 1924- WhoWest 94
Shanor, Donald Read 1927- WhoAm 94
Shanor, Peggy d1935 WhoHol 92
Shansby, John Gary 1937- WhoAm 94, WhoFI 94
Shanstrom, Jack D. 1932- WhoAm 94, WhoAmL 94, WhoWest 94
Shanta, James Anthony WhoHol 92
Shantaram, Vankudre 1901-1990 WhAm 10
Shante c. 1970- ConMus 10 [port]
Shanteau, James 1943- WhoScEn 94
Shantz, Carolyn Uhlinger 1935- WhoMW 93, WhoScEn 94
Shao, Otis Hung-I 1923- WhoAm 94
Shao, Wenjie 1931- WhoScEn 94
Shao Dadi 1938- IntWW 93
Shao En WhoPRCh 91
Shao Fei 1954- WhoPRCh 91
Shao Guifang WhoPRCh 91
Shao Hengqiu 1916- WhoPRCh 91 [port]
Shao Huaze WhoPRCh 91
Shao Maojun WhoPRCh 91 [port]
Shao Ming 1923- WhoPRCh 91 [port]
Shao Qihui 1934- IntWW 93, WhoPRCh 91 [port]
Shao Tianren WhoPRCh 91
Shao Yanxiang 1933- IntWW 93, WhoPRCh 91 [port]
Shao Yu 1910?- WhoPRCh 91
Shao Zhao WhoPRCh 91
Shao Zhenguo 1948- WhoPRCh 91 [port]
Shao Zhuoyuan WhoPRCh 91
Shao Zongming WhoPRCh 91
Shap, Sylvia 1948- WhoAmA 93
Shapar, Howard Kamber 1923- IntWW 93, WhoAmL 94
Shapard, Robert DrAPF 93
Shapcott, Sidney Edward 1920- Who 94
Shapcott, Thomas W(illiam) 1935- WrDr 94
Shapell, Nathan 1922- WhoAm 94, WhoFI 94, WhoWest 94
Shaper, Christopher Thorne 1955- WhoFI 94
Shaper, (Andrew) Gerald 1927- Who 94
Shapere, Dudley 1928- WhoAm 94
Shapero, Esther Geller WhoAmA 93
Shapero, Harris Joel 1930- WhoScEn 94, WhoWest 94
Shapero, James Allen 1943- WhoMW 93
Shapero, Sanford Marvin 1929- WhoScEn 94
Shapero, Theodore A. 1939- WhoAm 94
Shapey, Ralph 1921- WhoAm 94
Shaphren, Susanne DrAPF 93
Shapir, Ol'ga Andreevna 1850-1916 BlmGWL
Shapira, David S. 1942- WhoAm 94
Shapira, Ralph J. 1946- WhoAmL 94
Shapiro, Adrian Michael 1950- WhoAmA 93
Shapiro, Alan Elihu 1942- WhoMW 93
Shapiro, Alan Isaiah 1951- WhoWest 94
Shapiro, Alvin Philip 1920- WhoAm 94
Shapiro, Anita Rae 1941- WhoAmL 94
Shapiro, Arthur Maurice 1946- WhoAm 94
Shapiro, Ascher H(erman) 1916- IntWW 93
Shapiro, Ascher Herman 1916- WhoAm 94
Shapiro, Babe 1937- WhoAm 94, WhoAmA 93
Shapiro, Barbara J(une) 1934- WrDr 94
Shapiro, Barry 1942- WhoFI 94, WhoWest 94
Shapiro, Barry L. 1944- WhoAmL 94
Shapiro, Barry Robert 1947- WhoAm 94
Shapiro, Bennett Michaels 1939- WhoAm 94, WhoScEn 94
Shapiro, Beth Janet 1946- WhoAm 94
Shapiro, Burton Leonard 1934- WhoAm 94
Shapiro, Carl 1955- WhoFI 94
Shapiro, David DrAPF 93
Shapiro, David 1916- WhoAm 94, WhoAmA 93
Shapiro, David 1924- WhoWest 94
Shapiro, David 1944- WhoAmA 93
Shapiro, David 1947- WhoAmA 93
Shapiro, David 1954- WhoIns 94
Shapiro, David (Joel) 1947- WrDr 94
Shapiro, David B. WhoAmP 93
Shapiro, David Israel 1928- WhoAm 94
Shapiro, David L. 1936- WhoAmL 94
Shapiro, David Louis 1932- WhoAm 94
Shapiro, Debbie Lynn WhoAm 94
Shapiro, Dee 1936- WhoAmA 93
Shapiro, Edward Robert 1941- WhoAm 94
Shapiro, Edwin Henry 1938- WhoAmL 94
Shapiro, Edwin Stanley 1931- WhoAmL 94
Shapiro, Eli 1916- IntWW 93, WhoAm 94, WrDr 94
Shapiro, Erin Patria Margaret Who 94
Shapiro, Florence WhoAmP 93
Shapiro, Fred C. d1993 NewYTBS 93
Shapiro, Fred David 1926- WhoAm 94
Shapiro, Fred Louis 1934- WhoAm 94
Shapiro, Fred Richard 1954- WhoAmL 94
Shapiro, Gary Michael 1941- WhoAm 94
Shapiro, Gary Mitchell 1954- WhoFI 94
Shapiro, George Howard 1936- WhoAm 94, WhoAmL 94
Shapiro, George M. 1919- WhoAm 94, WhoAmL 94, WhoFI 94
Shapiro, Gordon M. 1956- WhoAmL 94
Shapiro, Gregg DrAPF 93
Shapiro, Harold Benjamin 1937- WhoAm 94
Shapiro, Harold David 1927- WhoAm 94, WhoAmL 94
Shapiro, Harold T(afler) 1935- WrDr 94
Shapiro, Harold Tafler 1935- IntWW 93, WhoAm 94
Shapiro, Harold Tafler 1936- Who 94
Shapiro, Harry Dean 1940- WhoAm 94
Shapiro, Harry Lionel 1902-1990 WhAm 10
Shapiro, Harry S. DrAPF 93
Shapiro, Harvey DrAPF 93
Shapiro, Harvey 1924- WhoAm 94, WrDr 94
Shapiro, Herbert 1929- WhoMW 93, WrDr 94
Shapiro, Howard 1947- WhoAmL 94
Shapiro, Howard Alan 1932- WhoAm 94
Shapiro, Howard Allan 1930- WhoAm 94
Shapiro, Howard R. 1950- WhoAmL 94
Shapiro, Irving 1927- WhoAmA 93
Shapiro, Irving Saul 1916- WhoAm 94
Shapiro, Irwin I. 1929- IntWW 93
Shapiro, Irwin Ira 1929- WhoAm 94, WhoScEn 94
Shapiro, Isaac 1931- WhoAm 94, WhoAmL 94
Shapiro, Isadore 1916- WhoAm 94, WhoFI 94, WhoScEn 94
Shapiro, Ivan 1928- WhoAm 94
Shapiro, J. Peter 1939- WhoAm 94, WhoAmL 94
Shapiro, James A. 1943- WhoScEn 94
Shapiro, James Edward 1930- WhoAm 94, WhoAmL 94
Shapiro, Jane ConLC 76 [port]
Shapiro, Jeffrey Marc 1965- WhoAmL 94
Shapiro, Jerome Gerson 1924- WhoAm 94
Shapiro, Jerome Herbert 1924- WhoAm 94
Shapiro, Jerome Lee 1932- WhoWest 94
Shapiro, Joan DrAPF 93
Shapiro, Joan Isabelle 1943- WhoFI 94
Shapiro, Joe WhoFI 94
Shapiro, Joel 1941- IntWW 93
Shapiro, Joel (Elias) 1941- WhoAmA 93
Shapiro, Joel Elias 1941- WhoAm 94
Shapiro, Joseph B. 1957- WhoFI 94
Shapiro, Judith R. 1942- WhoAm 94
Shapiro, Karl DrAPF 93
Shapiro, Karl (Jay) 1913- WrDr 94
Shapiro, Karl Jay 1913- AmCulL, IntWW 93, WhoAm 94
Shapiro, Ken 1943- IntMPA 94
Shapiro, Kenneth L. 1936- WhoAmP 93
Shapiro, Kenneth Paul 1946- WhoFI 94
Shapiro, Kimberly Ross 1963- WhoAmL 94
Shapiro, Laurence David 1941- WhoAm 94
Shapiro, Lawrence Bernard 1936- WhoFI 94
Shapiro, Lee Tobey 1943- WhoAm 94
Shapiro, Louis Oren 1948- WhoFI 94
Shapiro, Lucille 1940- WhoAm 94
Shapiro, Lynda P. 1938- WhoScEn 94
Shapiro, Mark d1985 WhoHol 92
Shapiro, Mark Howard 1940- WhoAm 94
Shapiro, Mark L. 1949- WhoAmL 94
Shapiro, Mark Lawrence 1944- WhoAm 94, WhoFI 94
Shapiro, Mark Robert 1950- WhoAmL 94
Shapiro, Marvin Lincoln 1923- WhoAm 94
Shapiro, Marvin S. 1936- WhoAmP 93
Shapiro, Marvin Seymour 1936- WhoAm 94
Shapiro, Maurice Mandel 1915- WhoAm 94, WhoScEn 94
Shapiro, Mel 1935- WhoAm 94
Shapiro, Michael 1942- WhoAm 94
Shapiro, Michael B. 1947- WhoAmL 94
Shapiro, Michael Edward 1949- WhoAm 94, WhoAmA 93
Shapiro, Michael Harold 1949- WhoScEn 94
Shapiro, Michael Henry 1948- WhoAm 94
Shapiro, Michael J. 1951- WhoAmL 94
Shapiro, Milton S. 1913- WhoAmP 93
Shapiro, Milton Stanley 1922- WhoAm 94
Shapiro, Moses 1910-1990 WhAm 10
Shapiro, Murray 1925- WhoScEn 94
Shapiro, Myra DrAPF 93
Shapiro, Myron 1942- WhoAmL 94
Shapiro, Nathan 1915- WhoScEn 94
Shapiro, Neil L. 1947- WhoAmL 94
Shapiro, Neil Robert 1962- WhoAmL 94
Shapiro, Nelson Hirsh 1928- WhoAmL 94

Shapiro, Norma Sondra Levy 1928- *WhoAm 94, WhoAmL 94*
Shapiro, Norman Richard 1930- *WhoAm 94*
Shapiro, Paul E. 1941- *WhoAmL 94*
Shapiro, Perry 1941- *WhoAm 94*
Shapiro, Raymond L. 1934- *WhoAm 94, WhoAmL 94*
Shapiro, Reid Allan 1965- *WhoWest 94*
Shapiro, Richard Charles 1936- *WhoMW 93*
Shapiro, Richard Gerald 1924- *WhoAm 94*
Shapiro, Richard Ray 1945- *WhoFI 94*
Shapiro, Richard Stanley 1925- *WhoAm 94, WhoWest 94*
Shapiro, Robert Alan 1946- *WhoAm 94, WhoFI 94*
Shapiro, Robert Donald 1942- *WhoMW 93*
Shapiro, Robert Eliot 1950- *WhoAmL 94*
Shapiro, Robert Frank 1934- *WhoAm 94, WhoFI 94*
Shapiro, Robert Leslie 1942- *WhoAmL 94*
Shapiro, Robert M. 1945- *WhoFI 94, WhoScEn 94*
Shapiro, Robert W. 1938- *IntMPA 94*
Shapiro, Robert Y. 1953- *ConAu 142*
Shapiro, Ronald Maurice 1943- *WhoAm 94*
Shapiro, Sam 1914- *WhoAm 94*
Shapiro, Samuel Bernard 1909- *WhoAm 94*
Shapiro, Samuel David 1927- *WhoAmP 93*
Shapiro, Sander Wolf 1929- *WhoAm 94*
Shapiro, Sandor Solomon 1933- *WhoScEn 94*
Shapiro, Sandra 1944- *WhoAm 94, WhoAmL 94*
Shapiro, Sidney 1915- *WrDr 94*
Shapiro, Sidney 1931- *WhoAm 94*
Shapiro, Stanley 1925- *WrDr 94*
Shapiro, Stanley 1926-1990 *EncSF 93*
Shapiro, Stanley 1937- *WhoAm 94*
Shapiro, Stanley K. 1956- *WhoAmL 94*
Shapiro, Stephen Michael 1946- *WhoAm 94, WhoAmL 94*
Shapiro, Stephen R. 1934- *WhoAm 94*
Shapiro, Steven *WhoAmL 94*
Shapiro, Steven George 1956- *WhoFI 94*
Shapiro, Stewart 1951- *WhoMW 93*
Shapiro, Stuart Charles 1944- *WhoAm 94*
Shapiro, Sumner 1926- *WhoAm 94*
Shapiro, Susan Jane 1950- *WhoMW 93*
Shapiro, Ted d1980 *WhoHol 92*
Shapiro, Theodore 1923- *WhoScEn 94*
Shapiro, Theodore 1932- *WhoAm 94*
Shapiro, Thomas Guy 1943- *WhoAmL 94*
Shapiro, Victor Lenard 1924- *WhoAm 94*
Shapland, Peter Charles 1923- *Who 94*
Shapland, William (Arthur) 1912- *Who 94*
Shapleigh, Warren McKinney 1920- *IntWW 93*
Shapley, Harlow 1885-1972 *WorScD*
Shapley, John 1890-1969 *WhoAmA 93N*
Shapley, Lloyd Stowell 1923- *IntWW 93, WhoAm 94, WhoWest 94*
Shapley, Robert Martin 1944- *WhoAm 94*
Shapo, Marshall Schambelan 1936- *WhoAm 94*
Shapoff, Stephen H. 1944- *WhoAm 94*
Shaporin, Yury Alexandrovich 1887-1966 *NewGrDO*
Shaposhnikov, Adrian Grigor'yevich 1887-1967 *NewGrDO*
Shaposhnikov, Evgeny Ivanovich 1942- *LngBDD*
Shaposhnikov, Yevgeny Ivanovich 1942- *IntWW 93*
Shapp, Milton J. 1912- *WhoAmP 93*
Shappirio, David Gordon 1930- *WhoAm 94, WhoMW 93, WhoScEn 94*
Shaps, Cyril *WhoHol 92*
Shapses, Paul Mitchel 1958- *WhoAmL 94*
Shapshak, Rene d1985 *WhoAmA 93N*
Sharaf, Mary Waters 1946- *WhoAmL 94*
Sharaff, Irene d1993 *IntMPA 94N, NewYTBS 93 [port]*
Sharaff, Irene 1910- *IntDcF 2-4*
Sharat Chandra, G. S. *DrAPF 93*
Sharat Chandra, G. S. 1938- *WrDr 94*
Sharbaugh, Amandus Harry 1919- *WhoAm 94*
Sharbaugh, Charles T. 1949- *WhoAmL 94*
Sharbaugh, Thomas J. 1952- *WhoAm 94, WhoAmL 94*
Sharbaugh, William James 1914- *WhoScEn 94*
Sharbel, Jean M. *WhoAm 94*
Sharber, Ann Boutwell *WhoFI 94*
Sharber, Jerry W. 1946- *WhoAmP 93*
Sharbutt, Del *WhoHol 92*
Share, Michael *IntMPA 94*
Shareef, Iqbal 1954- *WhoScEn 94*
Sharer, John Daniel 1950- *WhoAm 94*
Sharett, Alan Richard 1943- *WhoAmL 94*
Sharett, Deirdre *DrAPF 93*
Sharf, Donald Jack 1927- *WhoAm 94*
Sharf, Stephan 1920- *WhoAm 94*
Sharfman, Herbert 1909-1992 *WhAm 10*
Sharfstein, Howard F. 1945- *WhoAmL 94*
Sharfstein, Steven Samuel 1942- *WhoAm 94*
Shariat, Hormoz 1955- *WhoWest 94*
Sharick, Merle Dayton, Jr. 1946- *WhoFI 94*
Sharie, Bonnie *WhoHol 92*
Sharier, Dennis Eugene 1952- *WhoMW 93*
Sharif, Mohammad Nawaz 1949- *Who 94*
Sharif, Nawaz 1949- *IntWW 93*
Sharif, Omar 1932- *IntMPA 94, WhoAm 94, WhoHol 92*
Sharif, Omar (Michael Chalhoub) 1932- *IntWW 93*
Sharif, Tarek *WhoHol 92*
Sharif-Emami, Jafar 1910- *IntWW 93, WhoAm 94*
Shariff, Asghar J. 1941- *WhoScEn 94, WhoWest 94*
Sharifi, Iraj Alagha 1938- *WhoScEn 94*
Sharify, Nasser 1925- *WhoAm 94*
Sharir, Abraham 1932- *IntWW 93*
Sharir, Yacov 1940- *WhoAm 94*
Sharistanian, Janet Mae 1943- *WhoMW 93*
Sharits, Dean Paul 1944- *WhoFI 94*
Sharits, Paul 1943-1993 *NewYTBS 93*
Sharits, Paul Jeffrey 1943- *WhoAmA 93*
Shark, Myer Ralph 1913- *WhoAmL 94*
Sharkansky, Ira 1938- *WrDr 94*
Sharkey, Colum John 1931- *Who 94*
Sharkey, Gene Leonard 1939- *WhoFI 94*
Sharkey, Jack 1931-1992 *EncSF 93, WrDr 94N*
Sharkey, Joseph Thomas 1895-1991 *WhAm 10*
Sharkey, Lee *DrAPF 93*
Sharkey, Philip N. *WhoIns 94*
Sharkey, Ray d1993 *IntMPA 94N*
Sharkey, Ray 1952- *WhoHol 92*
Sharkey, Ray 1953-1993 *NewYTBS 93 [port], News 94-1*
Sharkey, Richard David 1957- *WhoWest 94*
Sharkey, Robert Emmett 1942- *WhoAmL 94*
Sharkey, Sailor d1953 *WhoHol 92*
Sharkey, Vincent Joseph 1944- *WhoAm 94*
Sharlach, Jeffrey Roy 1953- *WhoAm 94, WhoFI 94*
Sharland, (Edward) John 1937- *IntWW 93, Who 94*
Sharland, Reginald d1944 *WhoHol 92*
Sharma, Anil F. 1960- *WhoAsA 94*
Sharma, Anthony Francis 1937- *WhoAm 94*
Sharma, Arjun Dutta 1953- *WhoScEn 94, WhoWest 94*
Sharma, Arun 1937- *WhoAsA 94*
Sharma, Arun Kumar 1924- *IntWW 93*
Sharma, Bhu Dev 1938- *WhoAm 94*
Sharma, Bhudev 1938- *WhoAsA 94*
Sharma, Brahama Datta 1931- *WhoScEn 94*
Sharma, Brij Lal 1946- *WhoAsA 94*
Sharma, Deva Datta 1942- *WhoAsA 94*
Sharma, Dwarka Prasad 1933- *IntWW 93*
Sharma, Ghanshyam D. 1931- *WhoAsA 94*
Sharma, Govind Chandra 1944- *WhoAsA 94*
Sharma, Hari Chand 1949- *WhoAsA 94, WhoMW 93*
Sharma, Hari M. 1938- *WhoAsA 94*
Sharma, Jandhyala L. *WhoAsA 94*
Sharma, Kuldeepak Bhardwaj 1956- *WhoScEn 94*
Sharma, M. P. 1947- *WhoAsA 94*
Sharma, Mahendra Kumar 1948- *WhoScEn 94*
Sharma, Minoti 1940- *WhoScEn 94*
Sharma, Mukul Mani 1959- *WhoAsA 94*
Sharma, Mutyam V. 1930- *WhoAsA 94*
Sharma, Onkar Prasad 1937- *WhoAsA 94*
Sharma, Parashu Ram 1946- *WhoAsA 94*
Sharma, Puneet 1967- *WhoAsA 94*
Sharma, Raghubir Prasad 1940- *WhoAsA 94*
Sharma, Ramesh 1953- *WhoAsA 94*
Sharma, Ravindra Nath 1944- *WhoAsA 94*
Sharma, Sanjaya 1962- *WhoWest 94*
Sharma, Santosh Devraj 1934- *WhoAsA 94*
Sharma, Saroj 1945- *WhoAsA 94*
Sharma, Satanand 1948- *WhoAsA 94*
Sharma, Satish 1941- *WhoAsA 94, WhoWest 94*
Sharma, Shanker Dayal 1918- *IntWW 93, Who 94*
Sharma, Shri C. 1945- *WhoAsA 94, WhoFI 94, WhoMW 93*
Sharma, Subhash C. 1951- *WhoAsA 94*
Sharma, Surendra P. 1943- *WhoAsA 94*
Sharma, Surendra Prasad 1943- *WhoWest 94*
Sharma, Sushil Chandra 1956- *WhoAm 94, WhoFI 94*
Sharma, Udhishtra Deva 1928- *WhoAsA 94*
Sharma, Usha Kumari *Who 94*
Sharma, Vinod Kumar 1946- *WhoWest 94*
Sharman, Bill 1926- *BasBi [port]*
Sharman, Colin Morven 1943- *Who 94*
Sharman, Jim *HorFD*
Sharman, Peter William 1924- *Who 94*
Sharman, Richard Lee 1932- *WhoFI 94*
Sharman, William 1926- *WhoAm 94, WhoWest 94*
Sharmat, Marjorie Weinman 1928- *SmATA 74 [port], WrDr 94*
Sharoev, Ioakim Georgevich 1930- *IntWW 93*
Sharon, Ariel 1928- *IntWW 93*
Sharon, Mary B. 1891-1961 *WhoAmA 93N*
Sharon, Michael 1955- *WhoScEn 94*
Sharon, Reva *DrAPF 93*
Sharon, Rose *EncSF 93*
Sharon, Russell 1948- *WhoAmA 93*
Sharon, Timothy Michael 1948- *WhoWest 94*
Sharot, Stephen 1943- *WrDr 94*
Sharp *Who 94*
Sharp, Aaron John 1904- *WhoAm 94*
Sharp, Adrian 1951- *Who 94*
Sharp, Alan *IntMPA 94*
Sharp, Alastair George 1911- *Who 94*
Sharp, Allen 1932- *WhoAm 94, WhoAmL 94, WhoMW 93*
Sharp, Andrew *WhoHol 92*
Sharp, (William Harold) Angus d1993 *Who 94N*
Sharp, Anne 1943- *WhoAmA 93*
Sharp, Anne Catherine 1943- *WhoAm 94*
Sharp, Anthony d1984 *WhoHol 92*
Sharp, Benjamin S. 1944- *WhoAmL 94*
Sharp, Bert Lavon 1926- *WhoAm 94*
Sharp, Bert M. 1933- *WhoAmP 93*
Sharp, Charles David 1960- *WhoFI 94*
Sharp, Charles Louis 1951- *WhoBlA 94*
Sharp, Charles Paul 1942- *WhoScEn 94*
Sharp, Christopher *Who 94*
Sharp, (James) Christopher 1939- *Who 94*
Sharp, Clifford Henry 1922- *WrDr 94*
Sharp, Daniel Asher 1932- *WhoAm 94*
Sharp, David Lee 1952- *WhoWest 94*
Sharp, David Paul 1950- *WhoScEn 94*
Sharp, Dennis 1933- *WrDr 94*
Sharp, Derek Joseph 1925- *Who 94*
Sharp, Dexter Brian 1919- *WhoScEn 94*
Sharp, Don 1921- *IntMPA 94*
Sharp, Don 1922- *HorFD [port]*
Sharp, Donna Valpey 1930- *WhoAmP 93*
Sharp, Doreen Maud 1920- *WrDr 94*
Sharp, Doris Fuller 1924- *WhoAmP 93*
Sharp, Edgar E. 1933- *WhoAm 94, WhoFI 94*
Sharp, Evelyn 1869-1955 *DcNaB MP*
Sharp, Frank W. d1993 *NewYTBS 93 [port]*
Sharp, Frederick (Charles) 1911-1988 *NewGrDO*
Sharp, Gary David 1958- *WhoAmL 94*
Sharp, Gary Duane 1944- *WhoWest 94*
Sharp, George 1919- *Who 94*
Sharp, George Baldwin 1941- *WhoFI 94*
Sharp, George Kendall 1934- *WhoAm 94, WhoAmL 94*
Sharp, Gerald White 1930- *WhoWest 94*
Sharp, Glenn 1938- *WhoMW 93*
Sharp, Granville Maynard 1906- *Who 94*
Sharp, Henry d1964 *WhoHol 92*
Sharp, J. Anthony 1946- *WhoBlA 94*
Sharp, J(ohn) M(ichael) Cartwright 1918- *Who 94*
Sharp, James A., Jr. 1933- *WhoAmP 93*
Sharp, James Alfred 1933- *WhoBlA 94*
Sharp, James Franklin 1938- *WhoAm 94, WhoFI 94*
Sharp, James J. *WhoScEn 94*
Sharp, James Richard 1963- *WhoAmL 94*
Sharp, Jane Ellyn 1934- *WhoAm 94, WhoFI 94, WhoWest 94*
Sharp, Jane Price 1919- *WhoAmP 93*
Sharp, Jean Marie 1945- *WhoBlA 94*
Sharp, Jerrilyn Sue 1957- *WhoMW 93*
Sharp, Joel H., Jr. 1935- *WhoAm 94*
Sharp, John *WhoHol 92*
Sharp, John 1927- *Who 94*
Sharp, John Anderson 1944- *WhoAmP 93*
Sharp, John Malcolm, Jr. 1944- *WhoAm 94, WhoScEn 94*
Sharp, John Spencer 1950- *WhoAmP 93*
Sharp, Karen Tobey 1940- *WhoMW 93*
Sharp, Kenneth (Johnston) 1926- *Who 94*
Sharp, Kerry Lancaster 1949- *WhoWest 94*
Sharp, Kevan Denton 1957- *WhoScEn 94*
Sharp, Larry D. 1944- *WhoAm 94, WhoAmL 94*
Sharp, Lawrence N., Jr. 1959- *WhoBlA 94*
Sharp, Leonard d1958 *WhoHol 92*
Sharp, Lesley *WhoHol 92*
Sharp, Leslie 1936- *Who 94*
Sharp, Lewis Inman 1941- *WhoAmA 93*
Sharp, Louis *WhoScEn 94*
Sharp, M. Rust 1941- *WhoAmL 94*
Sharp, Merrill Kim 1941- *WhoFI 94*
Sharp, Michael Cartwright *Who 94*
Sharp, Milton Reginald 1909- *Who 94*
Sharp, Mitchell William 1911- *Who 94, WhoAm 94*
Sharp, Nikki Annette *WhoAmP 93*
Sharp, Pamela Ann 1950- *WhoWest 94*
Sharp, Patty Ann 1946- *WhoAmP 93*
Sharp, Paul David 1940- *WhoMW 93*
Sharp, Paul Frederick 1918- *WhoAm 94*
Sharp, Peggy Agostino 1950- *WhoWest 94*
Sharp, Philip R. 1942- *CngDr 93, WhoAm 94, WhoAmP 93, WhoMW 93*
Sharp, Phillip Allen 1944- *IntWW 93, WhoAm 94, WhoScEn 94*
Sharp, Ramona d1941 *WhoHol 92*
Sharp, Rex Arthur 1960- *WhoAmL 94*
Sharp, Richard (Lyall) 1915- *Who 94*
Sharp, Richard L. 1947- *WhoAm 94, WhoFI 94*
Sharp, Richard M. 1938- *WhoAmL 94*
Sharp, Robert *EncSF 93*
Sharp, Robert Charles 1907- *Who 94*
Sharp, Robert Charles 1936- *WhoAm 94, WhoFI 94*
Sharp, Robert Joseph 1949- *WhoFI 94*
Sharp, Robert Phillip 1911- *IntWW 93, WhoAm 94, WhoScEn 94, WhoWest 94*
Sharp, Robert Weimer 1917- *WhoAm 94, WhoAmL 94*
Sharp, Robin John Alfred 1935- *Who 94*
Sharp, Ronald Alan 1945- *WhoAm 94*
Sharp, Saundra *DrAPF 93*
Sharp, Saundra 1942- *WhoBlA 94*
Sharp, Stephen R. 1944- *WhoAmP 93*
Sharp, Susan S. 1942- *WhoAmA 93*
Sharp, Susie Marshall 1907- *WhoAmP 93*
Sharp, Thelma Parkinson 1898- *WhAm 10*
Sharp, Thom J. *WhoHol 92*
Sharp, Thomas 1931- *Who 94*
Sharp, Thomas B. 1940- *WhoAmP 93*
Sharp, Thomas Gale 1947- *WhoFI 94*
Sharp, Victoria Lee 1947- *WhoScEn 94*
Sharp, Virginia *DrAPF 93*
Sharp, William 1900-1961 *WhoAmA 93N*
Sharp, William Charles 1953- *WhoScEn 94, WhoWest 94*
Sharp, William James 1958- *WhoAmL 94*
Sharp, William Johnstone 1926- *Who 94*
Sharp, William Lee 1942- *WhoMW 93*
Sharp, William Wheeler 1923- *WhoFI 94, WhoScEn 94*
Sharp, Willoughby 1936- *WhoAmA 93*
Sharp-Bolster, Anita 1900- *WhoHol 92*
Sharpe, Albert 1885- *WhoHol 92*
Sharpe, Audrey Howell 1938- *WhoBlA 94*
Sharpe, (Norman) Blair 1954- *WhoAmA 93*
Sharpe, Brian Sidney 1927- *Who 94*
Sharpe, Calvin William 1945- *WhoBlA 94*
Sharpe, Charles Norval, Jr. 1927- *WhoIns 94*
Sharpe, Charles Ray 1938- *WhoAmP 93*
Sharpe, Charles Richard 1925- *WhoAm 94, WhoFI 94*
Sharpe, Cornelia 1947- *WhoHol 92*
Sharpe, Daniel Roger 1948- *WhoAm 94, WhoAmL 94*
Sharpe, David d1980 *WhoHol 92*
Sharpe, David Thomas 1946- *Who 94*
Sharpe, Donald Edward 1937- *WhoAm 94*
Sharpe, Dorothy Evelyn 1925- *WhoMW 93*
Sharpe, Edith 1894- *WhoHol 92*
Sharpe, Ernest M. 1946- *WhoAmL 94*
Sharpe, Gary Dale 1941- *WhoAmP 93*
Sharpe, Gary L. *WhoAmL 94*
Sharpe, James *WhoAmP 93*
Sharpe, James Shelby 1940- *WhoAmL 94*
Sharpe, Jean Elizabeth *WhoAm 94, WhoAmL 94, WhoFI 94*
Sharpe, John (Henry) 1921- *Who 94*
Sharpe, John Herbert S. *Who 94*
Sharpe, Jon *WrDr 94*
Sharpe, Jon 1927- *WrDr 94*
Sharpe, Judith Louise 1942- *WhoMW 93*
Sharpe, Karen 1934- *WhoHol 92*
Sharpe, Keith Yount 1930- *WhoAm 94*
Sharpe, Kevin 1949- *WrDr 94*
Sharpe, Kevin Michael 1949- *IntWW 93*
Sharpe, Lester d1962 *WhoHol 92*
Sharpe, Louis Kerre 1944- *WhoFI 94*
Sharpe, Lucretia *ConAu 42NR*
Sharpe, Mitchell Raymond 1924- *WhoScEn 94*
Sharpe, Myron E(manuel) 1928- *WrDr 94*
Sharpe, Myron Emanuel 1928- *WhoAm 94*

Sharpe, Peter *DrAPF 93*
Sharpe, Reginald (Taaffe) 1898- *Who 94*
Sharpe, Richard Samuel 1930- *WhoAm 94, WhoFI 94*
Sharpe, Robert Francis 1921- *WhoAm 94*
Sharpe, Rochelle Phyllis 1956- *WhoAm 94*
Sharpe, Roland Leonard 1923- *WhoAm 94, WhoWest 94*
Sharpe, Ronald M. 1940- *WhoBlA 94*
Sharpe, Ronald Martin 1950- *WhoWest 94*
Sharpe, Thomas Ridley 1928- *Who 94*
Sharpe, Tom 1928- *IntWW 93, WrDr 94*
Sharpe, V. Renee 1953- *WhoBlA 94*
Sharpe, Verlos Gene 1924- *WhoAm 94*
Sharpe, Wendell Smith, Jr. 1946- *WhoAm 94, WhoAmL 94*
Sharpe, William 1742-1818 *WhAmRev*
Sharpe, William 1923- *Who 94*
Sharpe, William F. 1934- *NobelP 91 [port]*
Sharpe, William F(orsyth) 1934- *WrDr 94*
Sharpe, William Forsyth 1934- *IntWW 93, Who 94, WhoAm 94, WhoFI 94, WhoWest 94*
Sharpe, William James 1908- *Who 94*
Sharpe, William Norman, Jr. 1938- *WhoAm 94, WhoScEn 94*
Sharpe, William R., Jr. 1928- *WhoAmP 93*
Sharperson, Michael Tyrone 1961- *WhoBlA 94*
Sharpey-Schafer, Edward Albert 1850-1935 *WorScD*
Sharples, Baroness 1923- *Who 94, WhoWomW 91*
Sharples, Christopher John 1947- *Who 94*
Sharples, D. Kent 1943- *WhoAm 94*
Sharples, Florence Elizabeth 1931- *Who 94*
Sharples, Winston Singleton 1932- *WhoFI 94*
Sharpless, Frederick Kingsley 1957- *WhoAmL 94*
Sharpless, K. Barry 1941- *WhoScEn 94*
Sharpless, Richard Kennedy 1911- *WhoAm 94*
Sharpley, Roger Ernest Dion 1928- *Who 94*
Sharp Of Grimsdyke, Baron 1916- *Who 94*
Sharpp, Nancy Charlene *WhoBlA 94*
Sharps, Christian 1811-1874 *WorInv*
Sharpstein, Richard Alan 1950- *WhoAmL 94*
Sharpton, Al *NewYTBS 93 [port]*
Sharpton, Al 1954- *AfrAmAl 6 [port]*
Sharpton, Alfred Charles, Jr. 1954- *WhoBlA 94*
Sharpton, Thomas 1949- *WhoWest 94*
Sharrett, Michael *WhoHol 92*
Sharrieff, Osman Ibn 1935- *WhoBlA 94*
Sharrotta, Angela 1960- *WhoMW 93*
Sharrow, Leonard 1915- *WhoMW 93*
Sharrow, Marilyn Jane *WhoAm 94*
Sharrow, Sheba 1926- *WhoAmA 93*
Shartin, Stacy D. 1949- *WhoAmL 94*
Shartle, Keith Robert *WhoAm 94*
Shartle, Stanley Musgrave 1922- *WhoFI 94, WhoMW 93, WhoScEn 94*
Sharum, Bernard Joseph 1944- *WhoFI 94*
Sharwell, William Gay 1920- *WhoAm 94*
Shashaani, Avideh *WhoFI 94*
Shashaty, Yolanda Victoria 1950- *WhoAmA 93*
Shasteen, Donald Eugene 1928- *WhoAm 94, WhoAmP 93*
Shastid, Jon Barton 1914- *WhoAm 94*
Shastri, Amita 1956- *WhoWest 94*
Shastri, Ranganath Krishna 1951- *WhoMW 93, WhoScEn 94*
Shastry, Shambhu Kadhambiny 1954- *WhoScEn 94*
Shatalin, Stanislav Sergeevich 1934- *LngBDD*
Shatalin, Stanislav Sergeyevich 1934- *IntWW 93*
Shatalin, Yury Vasilevich 1934- *LngBDD*
Shatalow, Vladimir Mihailovich 1917- *WhoAmA 93*
Sha Ting 1905- *WhoPRCh 91 [port]*
Shatkin, Aaron Jeffrey 1934- *IntWW 93, WhoAm 94, WhoScEn 94*
Shatner, Melanie 1964- *WhoHol 92*
Shatner, William 1931- *EncSF 93, IntMPA 94, IntWW 93, WhoAm 94, WhoHol 92*
Shatney, Clayton Henry 1943- *WhoScEn 94, WhoWest 94*
Shatoff, Larry D. 1944- *WhoIns 94*
Shatrov (Marshak), Mikhail Filippovich 1932- *IntWW 93*
Shatskikh, Viktor Mitrofanovich 1959- *LngBDD*
Shatter, Susan Louise 1943- *WhoAmA 93*
Shatto, Ellen Latherow 1946- *WhoScEn 94*
Shatto, Gloria McDermith 1931- *WhoAm 94, WhoFI 94*
Shattock, David John 1936- *Who 94*
Shattock, Gordon 1928- *Who 94*
Shattock, John Swithun Harvey d1993 *Who 94N*
Shattuck, Cathie Ann 1945- *WhoAm 94, WhoAmL 94*
Shattuck, Charles Harlen 1910-1992 *WhAm 10*
Shattuck, Curtis G. 1907- *WhoIns 94*
Shattuck, Daniel Vern 1948- *WhoWest 94*
Shattuck, Douglas E. 1948- *WhoScEn 94*
Shattuck, Ethel d1963 *WhoHol 92*
Shattuck, George Clement 1927- *WhoAm 94, WhoFI 94*
Shattuck, Howard Francis, Jr. 1920- *WhoAmL 94*
Shattuck, Mayo Adams, III 1954- *WhoAm 94, WhoFI 94*
Shattuck, Peter Hamilton 1935- *WhoWest 94*
Shattuck, Ralph Edward 1929- *WhoWest 94*
Shattuck, Roger 1923- *WrDr 94*
Shattuck, Roger W. *DrAPF 93*
Shattuck, Roger Whitney 1923- *WhoAm 94*
Shattuck, Shari *WhoHol 92*
Shattuck, Steven D. 1945- *WhoAmL 94*
Shattuck, Truly d1954 *WhoHol 92*
Shattuck, Ward (Edward) d1948 *WhoHol 92*
Sha Tuo 1926- *WhoPRCh 91 [port]*
Shatz, Marilyn Joyce 1939- *WhoMW 93*
Shatz, Stephen Sidney 1937- *WhoAm 94*
Shatzkin, Leonard 1919- *WhoAm 94*
Shau, Hungyi 1952- *WhoWest 94*
Shaub, Harold Arthur 1915- *WhoAm 94*
Shaud, Grant 1960- *WhoHol 92*
Shaud, John Albert 1933- *WhoAm 94*
Shaudys, Vincent Kirkbride 1927- *WhoAm 94*
Shaughnessy, Baron 1922- *Who 94*
Shaughnessy, Alfred (James) 1916- *WrDr 94*
Shaughnessy, Brian Patrick 1952- *WhoAmL 94*
Shaughnessy, Cheryl Ann 1958- *WhoAm 94*
Shaughnessy, Edward L(awrence) 1932- *WrDr 94*
Shaughnessy, James Michael 1945- *WhoAm 94, WhoAmL 94*
Shaughnessy, John L. 1930- *WhoAmP 93*
Shaughnessy, Marie Kaneko 1924- *WhoFI 94*
Shaughnessy, Mary Alice 1951- *ConAu 141*
Shaughnessy, Michael Joseph 1943- *WhoMW 93*
Shaughnessy, Mickey d1985 *WhoHol 92*
Shaughnessy, Thomas William 1938- *WhoAm 94*
Shaughnessy, Timothy Thomas 1957- *WhoAmP 93*
Shaul, Roger Louis, Jr. 1948- *WhoFI 94*
Shaull, Richard 1919- *WhoAm 94*
Shave, Alan William 1936- *Who 94*
Shave, Kenneth George 1908- *Who 94*
Shavelson, Melville 1917- *IntMPA 94, WhoAm 94*
Shaver, Bob *WhoHol 92*
Shaver, Carl Hutchens 1913- *WhoFI 94*
Shaver, Craig H., III 1956- *WhoAmP 93*
Shaver, Daniel P. 1958- *WhoAmL 94*
Shaver, Helen 1951- *IntMPA 94, WhoHol 92*
Shaver, James L., Jr. 1927- *WhoAmP 93*
Shaver, James Porter 1933- *WhoAm 94*
Shaver, James Robert 1867-1949 *WhoAmA 93N*
Shaver, Jesse Milton 1919- *WhoAm 94*
Shaver, Leslie Robert 1947- *WhoAmP 93*
Shaver, Marc Steven 1963- *WhoScEn 94*
Shaver, Phillip (Robert) 1944- *WrDr 94*
Shaver, Richard S(harpe) 1907-1975 *EncSF 93*
Shavers, Charlie d1971 *WhoHol 92*
Shavishvili, Revaz Leonidovich 1955- *LngBDD*
Shaviv, Eddie 1940- *WhoFI 94*
Shavor, Robert Peter 1938- *WhoAmP 93*
Shaw *Who 94*
Shaw (y Iturralde), Guillermo Fernandez *NewGrDO*
Shaw, Al(bert) d1957 *WhoHol 92*
Shaw, Alan 1930- *WhoAm 94*
Shaw, Alan John 1949- *WhoAm 94*
Shaw, Alan Roger 1938- *WhoAm 94*
Shaw, Alison 1957- *WrDr 94*
Shaw, Alvia A. 1915- *WhoBlA 94*
Shaw, Anabel 1923- *WhoHol 92*
Shaw, Andrew, Jr. 1931- *WhoAm 94*
Shaw, Ann 1921- *WhoBlA 94*
Shaw, Anna Howard 1847-1919 *WomPubS*
Shaw, Anthony d1980 *WhoHol 92*
Shaw, Anthony John 1930- *Who 94*
Shaw, Archie R. *WhoAmP 93*
Shaw, Ardyth M. 1941- *WhoBlA 94*
Shaw, Arnold 1909-1989 *WhAm 10*
Shaw, Arthur Daniel, Jr. 1929- *WhoFI 94*
Shaw, Artie 1910- *WhoAm 94, WhoHol 92*
Shaw, Barclay 1949- *EncSF 93*
Shaw, Barry *Who 94*
Shaw, (Charles) Barry 1923- *Who 94*
Shaw, Barry N. 1940- *WhoAmL 94*
Shaw, Bernard 1940- *AfrAmAl 6 [port], WhoAm 94, WhoBlA 94*
Shaw, (George) Bernard 1856-1950 *NewGrDO*
Shaw, Bernard Leslie 1930- *IntWW 93, Who 94*
Shaw, Bob 1931- *ConAu 41NR, EncSF 93, WrDr 94*
Shaw, Bobbi *WhoHol 92*
Shaw, Booker Thomas 1951- *WhoBlA 94*
Shaw, Brenda *DrAPF 93*
Shaw, Brewster Hopkinson, Jr. 1945- *WhoScEn 94*
Shaw, Brian *EncSF 93*
Shaw, Brian 1919- *WrDr 94*
Shaw, Brian (Piers) 1933- *Who 94*
Shaw, Brian K. 1966- *WhoBlA 94*
Shaw, Bruce Lloyd 1960- *WhoMW 93*
Shaw, Bryan P. H. 1921- *WhoAm 94*
Shaw, Bryce Robert 1930- *WhoScEn 94*
Shaw, Buddy d1976 *WhoHol 92*
Shaw, Bynum *DrAPF 93*
Shaw, Bynum G(illette) 1923- *WrDr 94*
Shaw, C(harles) Thurstan 1914- *Who 94*
Shaw, Carlos Fernandez *NewGrDO*
Shaw, Carlos M. Fernandez *ConAu 140*
Shaw, Carole 1936- *WhoAm 94*
Shaw, (Benjamin) Chandler 1896- *WhAm 10*
Shaw, Charles A. 1944- *WhoBlA 94*
Shaw, Charles Alden 1925- *WhoWest 94*
Shaw, Charles Green 1892-1974 *WhoAmA 93N*
Shaw, Charles Rusanda 1914- *WhoMW 93*
Shaw, Charles Timothy 1934- *Who 94*
Shaw, Colin Don 1928- *Who 94*
Shaw, Courtney Ann 1946- *WhoAmA 93*
Shaw, Curtis E. 1944- *WhoBlA 94*
Shaw, Curtis Mitchell 1944- *WhoBlA 94*
Shaw, Danny G. 1948- *WhoAmL 94*
Shaw, Danny Wayne 1947- *WhoMW 93*
Shaw, David *EncSF 93*
Shaw, David 1936- *Who 94*
Shaw, David Aitken 1924- *Who 94*
Shaw, David Allen 1959- *WhoWest 94*
Shaw, David Lawrence 1950- *Who 94*
Shaw, David Lyle 1943- *WhoAm 94, WhoWest 94*
Shaw, David Paul 1950- *WhoFI 94*
Shaw, David Robert 1950- *WhoMW 93*
Shaw, David T. 1938- *WrDr 94*
Shaw, David Tai-Ko 1938- *WhoAm 94*
Shaw, Dean Alvin 1954- *WhoScEn 94*
Shaw, Denis d1971 *WhoHol 92*
Shaw, Denis Martin 1923- *WhoAm 94*
Shaw, Denise 1949- *WhoBlA 94*
Shaw, Dennis 1936- *Who 94*
Shaw, Dennis Frederick 1924- *Who 94*
Shaw, Dennis Lee 1955- *WhoMW 93*
Shaw, Don Wayne 1937- *WhoAm 94*
Shaw, Donald Edward 1934- *WhoAmA 93*
Shaw, Donald Hardy 1922- *WhoAm 94, WhoAmL 94*
Shaw, Donald Leslie 1930- *WhoAm 94*
Shaw, Doris 1921- *WhoAm 94*
Shaw, Douglas William David 1928- *Who 94*
Shaw, Duncan 1925- *Who 94*
Shaw, E. Clay, Jr. 1939- *CngDr 93, WhoAm 94*
Shaw, Edgar Albert George 1921- *WhoAm 94*
Shaw, Edwin Lawrence 1938- *WhoWest 94*
Shaw, Elizabeth Angela 1946- *Who 94*
Shaw, Elizabeth Orr 1923- *WhoAmL 94*
Shaw, Eloise Laird 1929- *WhoAmP 93*
Shaw, Ernest Carl 1942- *WhoAmA 93*
Shaw, Eugene Clay, Jr. 1939- *WhoAmP 93*
Shaw, Ferdinand 1933- *WhoBlA 94*
Shaw, Fiona 1958- *WhoHol 92*
Shaw, Fred 1919- *WhoAsA 94*
Shaw, Frederick L(incoln) 1928- *EncSF 93*
Shaw, Gavin Brown 1919- *Who 94*
Shaw, Gaylord 1942- *WhoAm 94*
Shaw, Geoffrey Norman 1926- *Who 94*
Shaw, Geoffrey Peter 1944- *Who 94*
Shaw, George Arthur, Jr. 1948- *WhoWest 94*
Shaw, George Bernard 1856-1950 *BlmGEL, EncSF 93, IntDcT 2 [port]*
Shaw, George William 1924- *WhoAmL 94*
Shaw, Giles *Who 94*
Shaw, (John) Giles (Dunkerley) 1931- *Who 94*
Shaw, Glen Byam d1986 *WhoHol 92*
Shaw, Gordon H. 1928- *WhoAm 94*
Shaw, Grace Goodfriend *WhoAm 94, WhoFI 94*
Shaw, H. Reid 1949- *WhoAmL 94*
Shaw, Harold d1926 *WhoHol 92*
Shaw, Harold 1923- *WhoAm 94*
Shaw, Harry Alexander, III 1937- *WhoAm 94, WhoFI 94, WhoMW 93*
Shaw, Helen *WhoHol 92*
Shaw, Helen 1913-1984 *BlmGWL*
Shaw, Henry 1934- *WhoScEn 94*
Shaw, Henry I., Jr. 1926- *WrDr 94*
Shaw, Herbert John 1918- *WhoAm 94*
Shaw, Hester 1586?-1660 *DcNaB MP*
Shaw, Hewitt B., Jr. 1955- *WhoAmL 94*
Shaw, Ian Alexander 1940- *WhoAm 94*
Shaw, Irene 1925- *WrDr 94*
Shaw, Irwin 1934-1984 *ConDr 93*
Shaw, Isabel *WhoAmA 93*
Shaw, Jack d1970 *WhoHol 92*
Shaw, Jack Allen 1939- *WhoAm 94*
Shaw, James 1944- *WhoFI 94*
Shaw, James Headon 1918- *WhoAm 94*
Shaw, James John Sutherland 1912- *Who 94*
Shaw, James William 1940- *WhoWest 94*
Shaw, Janet Beeler *DrAPF 93*
Shaw, Jay Sadler 1897- *WhAm 10*
Shaw, Jeffrey F. 1947- *WhoAmL 94*
Shaw, Jerome 1926- *WhoFI 94*
Shaw, Jerry Michael 1945- *WhoWest 94*
Shaw, Jim 1952- *WhoAmA 93*
Shaw, Joan *DrAPF 93*
Shaw, John *DrAPF 93*
Shaw, John c. 1615-1680 *DcNaB MP*
Shaw, John 1924- *NewGrDO*
Shaw, John Andrew 1957- *WhoScEn 94*
Shaw, John Arthur 1922- *WhoAm 94*
Shaw, John Calman 1932- *Who 94*
Shaw, John Campbell 1949- *Who 94*
Shaw, John Firth 1948- *WhoAm 94, WhoWest 94*
Shaw, John Frederic, Jr. 1944- *WhoAmL 94*
Shaw, John Frederick 1936- *Who 94*
Shaw, John Frederick 1938- *WhoAm 94*
Shaw, John L. 1944- *WhoAmL 94*
Shaw, John Malach 1931- *WhoAm 94, WhoAmL 94*
Shaw, John Michael 1914- *Who 94*
Shaw, John Michael Robert B. *Who 94*
Shaw, John Palmer 1948- *WhoAmA 93*
Shaw, John W. 1951- *WhoAm 94, WhoAmL 94*
Shaw, Johnny Harvey 1938- *WhoScEn 94*
Shaw, Joseph M(inard) 1925- *ConAu 140*
Shaw, Joseph T. 1874-1952 *DcLB 137 [port]*
Shaw, Joseph Winterbotham 1935- *WhoAmA 93*
Shaw, Julius C. 1929- *WhoAm 94, WhoFI 94*
Shaw, Julius Fennell 1942- *WhoBlA 94*
Shaw, Karen 1941- *WhoAmA 93*
Shaw, Keith Moffatt 1944- *WhoScEn 94*
Shaw, Kendall 1924- *WhoAm 94*
Shaw, (George) Kendall 1924- *WhoAmA 93*
Shaw, Kenneth Alan 1939- *WhoAm 94*
Shaw, Kirk Cordell 1944- *WhoAmL 94*
Shaw, L. Edward, Jr. 1944- *WhoAmL 94*
Shaw, Larry Don 1953- *WhoAmP 93*
Shaw, Larry T. 1924-1985 *EncSF 93*
Shaw, Lawrance Neil 1934- *WhoScEn 94*
Shaw, Leander J., Jr. 1930- *WhoAmP 93, WhoBlA 94*
Shaw, Leander Jerry, Jr. 1930- *WhoAm 94, WhoAmL 94*
Shaw, Leonard Glazer 1934- *WhoAm 94*
Shaw, Lewis d1987 *WhoHol 92*
Shaw, Lillie Marie King 1915- *WhoWest 94*
Shaw, Linda *WhoAmP 93*
Shaw, Louise *WhoAmA 93*
Shaw, Margery Wayne Schlamp 1923- *WhoAm 94*
Shaw, Margret 1940- *WrDr 94*
Shaw, Mari Gursky 1947- *WhoAm 94, WhoAmL 94*
Shaw, Mario William 1929- *WhoBlA 94*
Shaw, Mark Howard 1944- *WhoAmL 94, WhoWest 94*
Shaw, Mark Robert 1945- *Who 94*
Shaw, Martin 1945- *WhoHol 92*
Shaw, Martin (Fallas) 1875-1958 *NewGrDO*
Shaw, Martin Andrew 1944- *WhoScEn 94*
Shaw, Martini 1959- *WhoBlA 94*
Shaw, Mary 1814-1876 *NewGrDO*
Shaw, Mary Ann 1937- *WhoScEn 94*
Shaw, Mary Elizabeth 1950- *WhoScEn 94*
Shaw, Mary Louise 1928- *WhoBlA 94*
Shaw, Mary M. 1943- *WhoAm 94*
Shaw, Mary Michal 1933- *Who 94*
Shaw, Mary Todd *WhoAmA 93*
Shaw, Maurice Kenneth 1939- *WhoAm 94, WhoFI 94*

Shaw, Max S. *Who 94*
Shaw, Maxwell d1985 *WhoHol 92*
Shaw, Melvin B. 1940- *WhoBlA 94*
Shaw, Melvin Phillip 1936- *WhoAm 94*
Shaw, Melvin Robert 1948- *WhoMW 93*
Shaw, Michael *Who 94*
Shaw, Michael 1924- *WhoAm 94*
Shaw, (Francis) Michael 1936- *Who 94*
Shaw, Michael (Norman) 1920- *Who 94*
Shaw, Michael Allan 1940- *WhoAm 94, WhoAmL 94, WhoFI 94*
Shaw, Michael Dennis 1949- *WhoBlA 94*
Shaw, Michael H. *WhoAmP 93*
Shaw, Michael Hewitt 1935- *Who 94*
Shaw, Mike 1943- *WhoAmP 93*
Shaw, Milton Clayton 1915- *WhoAm 94, WhoScEn 94*
Shaw, Milton Herbert 1918- *WhoAm 94*
Shaw, Montague d1968 *WhoHol 92*
Shaw, Montgomery Throop 1943- *WhoScEn 94*
Shaw, Morgan Albert 1916- *WhoWest 94*
Shaw, Murray 1908- *WrDr 94*
Shaw, Nancy (Rivard) *WhoAmA 93*
Shaw, Nancy H. 1942- *WhoBlA 94*
Shaw, Nancy Rivard *WhoAm 94*
Shaw, Nathaniel 1735-1782 *WhAmRev*
Shaw, Neil McGowan 1929- *IntWW 93, Who 94, WhoAm 94, WhoFI 94*
Shaw, Neville B. *Who 94*
Shaw, (George) Neville B. *Who 94*
Shaw, Nicholas Glencairn B. *Who 94*
Shaw, Oscar d1967 *WhoHol 92*
Shaw, Paul Jefferson 1951- *WhoAmA 93*
Shaw, Peggy 1958- *WhoAmA 93*
Shaw, Peter *WhoHol 92*
Shaw, Peter Alan 1949- *Who 94*
Shaw, Peter Jack 1924- *Who 94*
Shaw, Randall F. 1931- *WhoAmP 93*
Shaw, Randy Lee 1945- *WhoMW 93*
Shaw, Reesey 1943- *WhoAmA 93*
Shaw, Renata Vitzthum 1926- *WhoAmA 93*
Shaw, Renee Denise 1968- *WhoFI 94*
Shaw, Reta d1982 *WhoHol 92*
Shaw, Richard *DrAPF 93, WhoHol 92*
Shaw, Richard 1941- *WhoAm 94*
Shaw, Richard Blake 1941- *WhoAmA 93*
Shaw, Richard David 1938- *WhoFI 94, WhoMW 93*
Shaw, Richard Gordon 1943- *WhoBlA 94*
Shaw, Richard John Gildroy 1936- *Who 94, WhoFI 94*
Shaw, Richard Leslie 1927- *WhoAm 94*
Shaw, Richard Melvin 1947- *WhoFI 94*
Shaw, Richard Wright 1941- *Who 94*
Shaw, Robert *WhoBlA 94*
Shaw, Robert d1978 *WhoHol 92*
Shaw, Robert 1925- *Who 94*
Shaw, Robert 1937- *WhoAmP 93*
Shaw, Robert (Archibald) 1927-1978 *ConDr 93*
Shaw, Robert Bernard 1934- *WhoAmL 94*
Shaw, Robert Eugene 1933- *WhoMW 93*
Shaw, Robert F. *WhoAmP 93*
Shaw, Robert Fletcher 1910- *WhoAm 94*
Shaw, Robert G. 1924- *WhoAmP 93*
Shaw, Robert Harold 1919- *WhoAm 94*
Shaw, Robert Jennings 1929- *WhoAmP 93*
Shaw, Robert Lawson 1916- *WhoAm 94*
Shaw, Robert Macdonald 1912- *Who 94*
Shaw, Robert T. *WhoFI 94*
Shaw, Robert William, Jr. 1941- *WhoAm 94, WhoFI 94*
Shaw, Ronald Ahrend 1946- *WhoAm 94*
Shaw, Ross Franklin 1930- *WhoWest 94*
Shaw, Roy 1918- *Who 94*
Shaw, Roy Edwin 1925- *Who 94*
Shaw, Run Run 1907- *IntWW 93, Who 94*
Shaw, Russell B(urnham) 1935- *WrDr 94*
Shaw, Russell Burnham 1935- *WhoAm 94*
Shaw, Russell Clyde 1940- *WhoAm 94*
Shaw, Sallye Brown 1941- *WhoAm 94*
Shaw, Samuel 1754-1794 *WhAmRev*
Shaw, Samuel Ervine, II 1933- *WhoAm 94, WhoFI 94*
Shaw, Sandra 1913- *WhoHol 92*
Shaw, Scott 1958- *WhoWest 94*
Shaw, Scott 1964- *WhoAm 94*
Shaw, Scott Richard 1955- *WhoWest 94*
Shaw, Sebastian 1905- *WhoHol 92*
Shaw, Spencer Gilbert 1916- *WhoBlA 94*
Shaw, Stan 1952- *WhoBlA 94, WhoHol 92*
Shaw, Stanford Jay 1930- *WrDr 94*
Shaw, Stanley Miner 1935- *WhoAm 94*
Shaw, Steven Andrew 1946- *WhoAm 94*
Shaw, Steven John 1918- *WhoAm 94*
Shaw, Steven William 1955- *WhoAmL 94*
Shaw, Susan d1978 *WhoHol 92*
Shaw, Susan Damante *WhoHol 92*
Shaw, Suzanne Alix 1945- *WhoWest 94*
Shaw, T. E. *GayLL*
Shaw, Talbert O. *WhoAm 94*
Shaw, Talbert Oscall 1928- *WhoBlA 94*
Shaw, Thomas Douglas 1948- *WhoAm 94*
Shaw, Thomas Gwen 1952- *WhoMW 93*
Shaw, Thurstan *Who 94*
Shaw, Thurstan 1914- *WrDr 94*
Shaw, Tobey Kent 1952- *WhoWest 94*
Shaw, Vance Patrick 1960- *WhoFI 94*
Shaw, Victoria d1988 *WhoHol 92*
Shaw, Walter Rice 1896- *WhAm 10*
Shaw, Wilfred B. 1881- *WhoAmA 93N*
Shaw, William 1924- *WhoFI 94*
Shaw, William 1937- *WhoAmP 93*
Shaw, William Frederick 1920- *WhoAm 94*
Shaw, William Jay 1962- *WhoWest 94*
Shaw, William V. 1933- *Who 94*
Shaw, William Vaughan 1924- *WhoAm 94*
Shaw, William Wei-Lien 1942- *WhoWest 94*
Shaw, Willie G. 1942- *WhoBlA 94*
Shaw, Winifred d1982 *WhoHol 92*
Shaw, Woody Herman 1944-1989 *WhAm 10*
Shawa, Lol Mohammed 1939- *IntWW 93*
Shawan, Aziz *NewGrDO*
Shaw-Cohen, Lori Eve 1959- *WhoAm 94*
Shawcross, Baron 1902- *Who 94*
Shawcross, Hartley William 1902- *IntWW 93*
Shawcross, John T. 1924- *WrDr 94*
Shawcross, Roger Michael 1941- *Who 94*
Shawcross, William 1946- *IntWW 93, WrDr 94*
Shawe-Taylor, Desmond (Christopher) 1907- *IntWW 93, NewGrDO, Who 94*
Shawfield, John Edgar 1940- *WhoFI 94*
Shawhan, Peter Sven 1968- *WhoScEn 94*
Shaw-Jackson, Harold Nicholas 1942- *WhoFI 94*
Shaw-Johnson, Beverly *DrAPF 93*
Shawlee, Joan d1987 *WhoHol 92*
Shawley, John Franklin 1921- *WhoAmP 93*
Shawley, Robert d1990 *WhoHol 92*
Shawn, Dick d1987 *WhoHol 92*
Shawn, Dick 1923-1987 *WhoCom [port]*
Shawn, Edwin Myers 1891-1972 *AmCulL*
Shawn, Frank S. *EncSF 93*
Shawn, Frank S. 1933- *WrDr 94*
Shawn, Michael d1989 *WhoHol 92*
Shawn, Philip d1972 *WhoHol 92*
Shawn, Ted d1972 *WhoHol 92*
Shawn, Wallace *IntWW 93*
Shawn, Wallace 1943- *ConDr 93, IntMPA 94, WhoAm 94, WhoHol 92, WrDr 94*
Shawn, William d1992 *IntWW 93N*
Shawn, William 1907-1992 *AnObit 1992, ConAu 140, DcLB 137 [port], News 93-3, WhAm 10*
Shawnee, Laura Ann 1953- *WhoBlA 94*
Shawstad, Raymond Vernon 1931- *WhoFI 94, WhoMW 93*
Shaw-Stewart, Houston (Mark) 1931- *Who 94*
Shawver, Stanley Walter 1954- *WhoMW 93*
Shawyer, David 1944- *WhoHol 92*
Shaw Yu-Ming 1938- *IntWW 93*
Shawzin, Barry d1968 *WhoHol 92*
Shay, David E. 1962- *WhoAmL 94*
Shay, Dorothy d1978 *WhoHol 92*
Shay, Ed 1947- *WhoAmA 93*
Shay, Edward F. 1944- *WhoAmL 94*
Shay, Edward Griffin 1928- *WhoScEn 94*
Shay, Edward Norman 1929- *WhoAmL 94*
Shay, John E., Jr. 1933- *WhoAm 94*
Shay, Kathleen M. 1952- *WhoAmL 94*
Shay, Lacey *ConAu 41NR*
Shay, Patricia d1966 *WhoHol 92*
Shay, Philipp Wendell 1914- *WhoFI 94*
Shay, Robert Michael 1936- *WhoFI 94*
Shay, Rose Cecilia d1929 *WhoHol 92*
Shay, Roshani Cari 1942- *WhoAm 94, WhoWest 94*
Shay, Stephen Elliott 1951- *WhoAm 94, WhoFI 94*
Shay, Tim *DrAPF 93*
Shaye, Marc K. 1942- *WhoAmL 94*
Shaye, Robert 1939- *IntMPA 94*
Shaye, Robert Kenneth 1939- *WhoAm 94*
Sha Yexin 1939- *WhoPRCh 91 [port]*
Shaykh, Hanan al- 1945- *ConWorW 93*
Shayman, James Alan 1954- *WhoMW 93*
Shayne, Arnie 1929- *WhoAm 94*
Shayne, Konstantin d1974 *WhoHol 92*
Shayne, Neil T. 1932- *WhoAmP 93*
Shayne, Robert *WhoHol 92*
Shayne, Stanley H. *WhoAm 94, WhoAmL 94*
Shayne, Tamara d1983 *WhoHol 92*
Shays, Christopher 1945- *CngDr 93, WhoAm 94, WhoAmP 93*
Shays, Daniel c. 1747-1825 *AmSocL, WhAmRev*
Shays, Rona Joyce 1928- *WhoAmL 94*
Shazly, Saad Mohamed el-Husseiny el- 1922- *IntWW 93*
Shcharansky, Anatoly *IntWW 93*
Shchedrin, Rodion Konstantinovich 1932- *IntWW 93, NewGrDO*
Shchepkina-Kupernik, Tat'iana L'vovna 1874-1952 *BlmGWL*
Shcherbak, Yurii Mykolayovych 1934- *LngBDD*
Shcherbitsky, Vladimir Vailiyevich 1918-1990 *WhAm 10*
Shchukin, Boris d1939 *WhoHol 92*
Shcolnik, Robert Milton 1938- *WhoWest 94*
Shdanoff, Elsa Schreiber d1982 *WhoHol 92*
Shdanoff, George *WhoHol 92*
Shea, Bernard Charles 1929- *WhoFI 94*
Shea, Bird d1924 *WhoHol 92*
Shea, Brian Thomas 1953- *WhoMW 93*
Shea, Cornelius 1863-1920 *EncSF 93*
Shea, Daniel Bartholomew, Jr. 1936- *WhoAm 94*
Shea, Daniel Francis 1937- *WhoMW 93*
Shea, Daniel M. 1944- *WhoAmL 94*
Shea, David John 1947- *WhoMW 93*
Shea, David M. *WhoAmP 93*
Shea, David Michael 1922- *WhoAm 94, WhoAmL 94*
Shea, Dion Warren Joseph 1937- *WhoAm 94*
Shea, Donald F. 1925- *WhoAmP 93*
Shea, Donald Francis 1925- *WhoAm 94, WhoAmL 94*
Shea, Donald Richard 1926- *WhoAm 94*
Shea, Donald William 1936- *WhoAm 94*
Shea, Edward Emmett 1932- *WhoAm 94*
Shea, Edward Fitzgerald, Jr. 1925- *WhoAmL 94*
Shea, Elizabeth Ann 1949- *WhoAmL 94*
Shea, Francis Michael 1905-1989 *WhAm 10*
Shea, Francis Raymond 1913- *WhoAm 94*
Shea, George P., Jr. 1938- *WhoIns 94*
Shea, Gwyn Clarkston 1937- *WhoAmP 93*
Shea, J. Michael 1942- *WhoAmP 93*
Shea, Jack d1970 *WhoHol 92*
Shea, James D. 1919- *WhoAmP 93*
Shea, James L. 1952- *WhoAmL 94*
Shea, James S. 1925- *WhoAmP 93*
Shea, James William 1936- *WhoAm 94*
Shea, Jeremy Charles 1937- *WhoAm 94, WhoAmL 94*
Shea, Joe 1938- *WhoHol 92*
Shea, John 1948- *WhoHol 92*
Shea, John 1949- *IntMPA 94*
Shea, John Edward 1943- *WhoFI 94*
Shea, John Francis 1951- *WhoAmL 94*
Shea, John J. 1938- *WhoFI 94*
Shea, John Leo 1954- *WhoMW 93*
Shea, John Martin, Jr. 1922- *WhoAm 94*
Shea, Joseph William, III 1947- *WhoAmL 94*
Shea, Judith 1948- *WhoAmA 93*
Shea, Kathryn Selleck 1958- *WhoAmL 94*
Shea, Kevin Michael 1951- *WhoAm 94*
Shea, Lance Leonard 1959- *WhoAmL 94*
Shea, Mary E. 1947- *AstEnc*
Shea, Mary Elizabeth Craig 1962- *WhoScEn 94*
Shea, Maura *WhoHol 92*
Shea, Michael 1938- *EncSF 93*
Shea, Michael 1946- *EncSF 93*
Shea, Michael (Sinclair MacAuslan) 1938- *WrDr 94*
Shea, Michael Alan 1946- *WhoWest 94*
Shea, Michael Sinclair MacAuslan 1938- *Who 94*
Shea, Patrick 1908- *WrDr 94*
Shea, Patrick 1948- *WhoAmP 93*
Shea, Patrick William 1955- *WhoFI 94*
Shea, Pegi Deitz 1960- *SmATA 77 [port]*
Shea, Robert (Joseph) 1933- *EncSF 93*
Shea, Robert McConnell 1924- *WhoAm 94*
Shea, Robert Stanton 1928- *WhoFI 94, WhoWest 94*
Shea, Roseanne Marie 1947- *WhoAmL 94*
Shea, Stephen Michael 1926- *WhoAm 94*
Shea, Terrence W. 1941- *WhoIns 94*
Shea, Theodore William 1960- *WhoWest 94*
Shea, Thomas Joseph 1950- *WhoAmP 93*
Shea, Timothy Edward 1953- *WhoMW 93*
Shea, William Alfred 1907-1991 *WhAm 10*
Shea, William Francis 1930- *WhoWest 94*
Shea, William J. d1918 *WhoHol 92*
Shea, William Rene 1937- *WhoAm 94, WhoScEn 94*
Shead, Ken *WhoBlA 94*
Shead, S. Ray 1938- *WhoAmA 93*
Sheafe, Alex *WhoHol 92*
Sheaff, Donald J. 1925- *IntMPA 94*
Sheaffer, Louis d1993 *NewYTBS 93*
Sheaffer, Louis 1912- *WrDr 94*
Sheaffer, Louis 1912-1993 *ConAu 142*
Sheaffer, M.P.A. *DrAPF 93*
Sheaffer, Richard Allen 1950- *WhoWest 94*
Sheafor, Stephen James 1949- *WhoWest 94*
Sheahan, John 1923- *WrDr 94*
Sheahan, John Bernard 1923- *WhoAm 94*
Sheahan, Larry *WhoAmP 93*
Sheahan, Michael F. 1944- *WhoAmP 93*
Sheahan, Michael J. 1950- *WhoAmL 94*
Sheahan, Robert Emmett 1942- *WhoAmL 94*
Sheaks, Barclay *WhoAmA 93*
Shealey, Richard W. *WhoBlA 94*
Shealy, Clyde Norman 1932- *WhoAm 94*
Shealy, David Lee 1944- *WhoAm 94*
Shealy, Miriam Schumpert 1959- *WhoWest 94*
Shealy, Rod R. 1953- *WhoAmP 93*
Shealy, Ryan C. 1923- *WhoAmP 93*
Shealy, William W. 1934- *WhoIns 94*
Shealy, Y. Fulmer 1923- *WhoScEn 94*
Shean, Al d1949 *WhoHol 92*
Shean, Al 1868-1949 *See* Gallagher and Shean *WhoCom*
Shean, Larry d1982 *WhoHol 92*
Shean, Timothy Joseph 1945- *WhoFI 94*
Shear, Kenneth 1945- *WhoAmL 94*
Shear, L. David 1936- *WhoAmL 94*
Shear, Pearl *WhoHol 92*
Shear, S. Sue 1918- *WhoAmP 93*
Shear, Theodore Leslie, Jr. 1938- *WhoAm 94*
Shear, William Albert 1942- *WhoScEn 94*
Shearar, Jeremy Brown 1931- *IntWW 93*
Sheard, Charles, III 1914- *WhoScEn 94*
Sheard, Norma Voorhees *DrAPF 93*
Sheard, Sarah 1953- *ConAu 141*
Sheard, Wendy Stedman 1935- *WhoAmA 93*
Shearer, Beth Jane 1955- *WhoMW 93*
Shearer, Carolyn Juanita 1944- *WhoWest 94*
Shearer, Charles Livingston 1942- *WhoAm 94*
Shearer, Douglas 1899-1971 *IntDcF 2-4 [port]*
Shearer, Georgia Elizabeth 1929- *WhoMW 93*
Shearer, Harry 1941- *WhoHol 92*
Shearer, Harry 1943- *IntMPA 94*
Shearer, Hugh 1926- *WhoAmL 94*
Shearer, Hugh Lawson 1923- *IntWW 93, Who 94*
Shearer, Ian Hamilton *Who 94*
Shearer, Jacqueline d1993 *NewYTBS 93*
Shearer, Janet Sutherland *Who 94*
Shearer, Jill *BlmGWL*
Shearer, Jill 1936- *ConDr 93*
Shearer, John 1926- *Who 94*
Shearer, John Clyde 1928- *WhoAm 94*
Shearer, Lawrence Edward 1946- *WhoMW 93*
Shearer, Linda 1946- *WhoAmA 93*
Shearer, Magnus MacDonald 1924- *Who 94*
Shearer, Marie Kathleen 1959- *WhoMW 93*
Shearer, Mark Smith 1952- *WhoAmP 93*
Shearer, Michael 1951- *WhoAm 94*
Shearer, Moira 1926- *IntDcB [port], Who 94, WhoHol 92*
Shearer, Norma d1983 *WhoHol 92*
Shearer, R. Scott 1949- *WhoAm 94*
Shearer, Rhonda Roland 1954- *WhoAmA 93*
Shearer, Richard Eugene 1919- *WhoAm 94*
Shearer, Ronald Alexander 1932- *WhoAm 94*
Shearer, Sergio 1939- *WhoHisp 94*
Shearer, Thomas Hamilton 1923- *Who 94*
Shearer, Velma Miller 1921- *WhoMW 93*
Shearer, William Kennedy 1931- *WhoAm 94*
Shearer, William T. 1937- *WhoAm 94, WhoScEn 94*
Sheares, Reuben A., II 1933-1992 *WhoBlA 94N*
Shearin, Kimberly Maria 1964- *WhoBlA 94*
Shearing, George 1919- *WhoHol 92*
Shearing, George Albert 1919- *WhoAm 94*
Shearing, Miriam 1935- *WhoAmL 94, WhoAmP 93, WhoWest 94*
Shearing, Renee C. d1987 *WhoHol 92*
Shearlock, David John 1932- *Who 94*
Shearman, Alan *WhoHol 92*
Shearman, Donald Norman 1926- *Who 94*
Shearman, John (Kinder Gowran) 1931- *WrDr 94*
Shearman, John Kinder Gowran 1931- *IntWW 93, Who 94*
Shearn, Edith d1968 *WhoHol 92*
Shearon, Forrest Bedford 1934- *WhoAm 94*
Shearwin, Keith Edward 1965- *WhoScEn 94*
Sheasgreen, Betty 1920- *WhoWest 94*
Shea-Stonum, Marilyn 1947- *WhoAm 94, WhoAmL 94*
Sheath, Robert Gordon 1950- *WhoScEn 94*
Sheats, Marvin Anthony 1958- *WhoBlA 94*

Sheldon, Gilbert Ignatius 1926- WhoMW 93
Sheldon, Glenn DrAPF 93
Sheldon, Harold 1918- Who 94
Sheldon, Harvey M. 1942- WhoAm 94, WhoAmL 94
Sheldon, J. Michael 1951- WhoFI 94
Sheldon, Jack 1931- WhoHol 92
Sheldon, James IntMPA 94
Sheldon, Jerome d1962 WhoHol 92
Sheldon, Jerry d1962 WhoHol 92
Sheldon, John Denby 1941- Who 94
Sheldon, Kathryn d1975 WhoHol 92
Sheldon, Kirk Roy 1958- WhoFI 94
Sheldon, Lee ConAu 41NR
Sheldon, Lee 1917- EncSF 93, WrDr 94
Sheldon, Marion d1944 WhoHol 92
Sheldon, Mark Hebberton 1931- Who 94
Sheldon, Mark Peter 1944- WhoMW 93
Sheldon, Mark Scott 1959- WhoScEn 94, WhoWest 94
Sheldon, Marti Reisman 1961- WhoWest 94
Sheldon, May French 1847-1936 WhWE
Sheldon, Michael Richard 1949- WhoAmL 94
Sheldon, Nancy Way 1944- WhoFI 94
Sheldon, Norman E. 1936- WhoAmP 93
Sheldon, Peter Spafford 1939- WhoAm 94
Sheldon, Raccoona EncSF 93
Sheldon, Richard Robert 1932- WhoAm 94
Sheldon, Robert (Edward) 1923- Who 94
Sheldon, Roy EncSF 93
Sheldon, Roy 1919- WrDr 94
Sheldon, Sidney 1917- IntMPA 94, IntWW 93, WhoAm 94, WrDr 94
Sheldon, Suzanne d1924 WhoHol 92
Sheldon, Terry Edwin 1945- WhoAm 94
Sheldon, Thomas Andrew 1964- WhoWest 94
Sheldon, Thomas Donald 1920- WhoAm 94
Sheldon, Timothy M. 1947- WhoAmP 93
Sheldon, Warren Corydon 1936- WhoWest 94
Sheldon, William Douglas 1941- WhoIns 94
Sheldrick, George Michael 1942- IntWW 93, WhoScEn 94
Shelemay, Kay Kaufman 1948- ConAu 142
Sheleski, Stanley John 1931- WhoFI 94
Shelesnyak, Moses Chaim 1909- WhoAm 94
Shelest, Alla 1919- IntDcB [port]
Sheley, Donald Ray, Jr. 1942- WhoAm 94
Sheley, Lucille Renn 1915- WhoAmP 93
Shelfer, A. Gordon, Jr. 1943- WhAm 10
Shelford, Cornelius William 1908- Who 94
Shelikov, Grigory Ivanovich 1747-1795 WhWE
Shelke, Kantha 1957- WhoScEn 94
Shelkrot, Elliot Louis 1943- WhoAm 94
Shell, Art ProFbHF, WhoAm 94, WhoWest 94
Shell, Art 1946- WhoBlA 94
Shell, Bernard Ray 1925- WhoFI 94
Shell, Billy Joe 1925- WhoAm 94
Shell, Cathy Lynn 1964- WhoFI 94, WhoMW 93
Shell, Debra Mayhew 1949- WhoWest 94
Shell, James Randal 1962- WhoFI 94
Shell, Juanita 1940- WhoBlA 94
Shell, Karl 1938- WhoAm 94, WhoFI 94
Shell, Louis Calvin 1925- WhoAmL 94
Shell, Mary Katherine 1927- WhoAmP 93
Shell, Owen G., Jr. 1936- WhoAm 94, WhoFI 94
Shell, Robert J. 1930- WhoFI 94
Shell, Theodore A. WhoBlA 94
Shell, William H. 1910- WhoBlA 94
Shellan, Ronald A. 1949- WhoAmL 94
Shellard, Michael Francis Linton 1937- Who 94
Shelle, Lori WhoHol 92
Shelledy, James Edwin, III 1942- WhoAm 94
Shellen, Stephen 1958- WhoHol 92
Shellene, Jean Mary 1921- WhoAmP 93
Sheller, John Willard 1950- WhoAm 94, WhoAmL 94
Sheller, Lee A. 1951- WhoAmL 94
Sheller, Patrick Michael 1961- WhoAmL 94
Shelley, Alan John 1931- Who 94
Shelley, Barbara 1933- WhoHol 92
Shelley, Carole 1939- WhoHol 92
Shelley, Carole Augusta 1939- WhoAm 94
Shelley, Charles William Evans d1993 Who 94N
Shelley, Dan 1949- WhoAmP 93
Shelley, David d1989 WhoHol 92
Shelley, Edward Herman, Jr. 1919- WhoAm 94
Shelley, Harry Rowe 1858-1947 NewGrDO
Shelley, Herbert Carl 1947- WhoAm 94
Shelley, Howard Gordon 1950- IntWW 93, Who 94
Shelley, James Edward 1932- Who 94
Shelley, James Herbert 1943- WhoAmL 94
Shelley, James LaMar 1915- WhoAm 94
Shelley, John (Richard) 1943- Who 94
Shelley, John Fletcher 1943- WhoAm 94, WhoAmL 94
Shelley, Joshua d1990 WhoHol 92
Shelley, Mack Clayton, II 1950- WhoMW 93
Shelley, Marlin Carl 1948- WhoWest 94
Shelley, Martha A. DrAPF 93
Shelley, Mary Wollstonecraft 1797-1851 BlmGEL [port], BlmGWL [port], EncSF 93
Shelley, Pat DrAPF 93
Shelley, Percy Bysshe 1792-1822 BlmGEL
Shelley, Robert J. 1941- WhoAmP 93
Shelley, Rulon Gene 1924- IntWW 93
Shelley, Susanne Mary 1928- WhoAmL 94
Shelley, Ursula 1906- Who 94
Shelley, Virgil Dale 1926- WhoMW 93
Shelley, Walter Brown 1917- WhoAm 94
Shellhase, Leslie John 1924- WhoAm 94
Shellhorn, Ruth Patricia 1909- WhoAm 94
Shellman, Eddie J. 1956- WhoAm 94
Shellman, Lee Charles 1937- WhoAmP 93
Shellow, James Myers 1926- WhoAm 94
Shellow, Robert 1929- WhoAm 94
Shelly, Adrienne 1966- WhoHol 92
Shelly, Lisa Maureen 1955- WhoFI 94
Shelly, Norman d1980 WhoHol 92
Shelmire, Bedford 1894- WhAm 10
Shelnutt, Eve DrAPF 93
Shelnutt, Eve 1941- DcLB 130 [port]
Shelnutt, Eve (Brown) 1941- WrDr 94
Shelnutt, Eve Brown 1941- WhoMW 93
Shelor, Earl Dean 1926- WhoAmP 93
Shelow, Hy Rubin Doved 1961- WhoAmL 94
Shelp, Ronald Kent 1941- WhoAm 94, WhoFI 94
Shelton, Abigail WhoHol 92
Shelton, Bob J. 1948- WhoAmL 94
Shelton, Carolyn Zandra 1956- WhoWest 94
Shelton, Charles Alexander 1934- WhoMW 93
Shelton, Charles Bascom, III 1941- WhoFI 94
Shelton, Charles C. 1945- WhoAmL 94
Shelton, Charles E. 1945- WhoBlA 94
Shelton, Charlita Lucille 1958- WhoWest 94
Shelton, Connie d1944 WhoHol 92
Shelton, Cora R. 1925- WhoBlA 94
Shelton, David Howard 1928- WhoAm 94
Shelton, Deborah 1952- WhoHol 92
Shelton, Don d1976 WhoHol 92
Shelton, Dorothy Diehl Rees 1935- WhoAmL 94
Shelton, Gary Richard 1947- WhoAmL 94
Shelton, George .d1971 WhoHol 92
Shelton, Harold Tillman 1941- WhoBlA 94
Shelton, Harvey William 1936- WhoBlA 94
Shelton, J. Elise 1964- WhoAmL 94
Shelton, James d1975 WhoHol 92
Shelton, James Douglas 1939- WhoFI 94
Shelton, Jewell Vennerrie 1928- WhoBlA 94
Shelton, Joanna Reed 1951- WhoAm 94
Shelton, Joel Edward 1928- WhoScEn 94, WhoWest 94
Shelton, John d1972 WhoHol 92
Shelton, John W. 1958- WhoBlA 94
Shelton, Joseph B. 1946- WhoBlA 94
Shelton, Joy 1922- WhoHol 92
Shelton, Karl Mason 1933- WhoAm 94
Shelton, Kevin L. WhoScEn 94
Shelton, Larry Brandon 1934- WhoFI 94
Shelton, Lee Raymond 1927- WhoBlA 94
Shelton, Maria d1954 WhoHol 92
Shelton, Mark L(ogan) 1958- WrDr 94
Shelton, Miles EncSF 93
Shelton, Millicent Beth 1966- WhoBlA 94
Shelton, O. L. 1946- WhoAmP 93, WhoBlA 94, WhoMW 93
Shelton, Peter Arthur 1930- WhoFI 94
Shelton, Peter T. 1951- WhoAmA 93
Shelton, Reid 1924- WhoHol 92
Shelton, Reuben Anderson 1954- WhoBlA 94
Shelton, Richard DrAPF 93
Shelton, Richard 1933- WrDr 94
Shelton, Richard Fottrell 1929- WhoAm 94
Shelton, Robert Arthur 1941- WhoAm 94
Shelton, Robert Charles 1934- WhoWest 94
Shelton, Robert Lee 1939- WhoAmA 93
Shelton, Robert Neal 1948- WhoAm 94
Shelton, Robert Warren 1943- WhoFI 94
Shelton, Ron 1945- IntMPA 94
Shelton, Roy Cresswell, Jr. 1941- WhoBlA 94
Shelton, S. McDowell 1929-1991 WhoBlA 94N
Shelton, Sarah V. 1919- WhoAmP 93
Shelton, Shirley Megan 1934- Who 94
Shelton, Sloane WhoHol 92
Shelton, Sloane 1934- WhoAm 94
Shelton, Stephani WhoAm 94
Shelton, Thomas McKinley 1939- WhoScEn 94
Shelton, Turner Blair 1915- WhoAm 94
Shelton, Ulysses 1917- WhoBlA 94
Shelton, Vern R. 1938- WhoIns 94
Shelton, Violet d1970 WhoHol 92
Shelton, Wayne Vernon 1932- WhoAm 94
Shelton, William (Jeremy Masefield) 1929- Who 94
Shelton, William Chastain 1916- WhoFI 94, WhoScEn 94
Shelton, William E. 1944- IntWW 93
Shelton-Colby, Sally 1944- WhoAmP 93
Sheltra, Carl F. WhoAmP 93
Sheltra, Nancy J. 1948- WhoAmP 93
Shely, Benjamin L. 1933-1990 WhAm 10
Shemchuk, Charles John, Jr. 1945- WhoAmP 93
Shemesh, Haim 1954- ConAu 142
Shemesh, Lorraine R. 1949- WhoAmA 93
Shemie, Bonnie (Jean Brenner) 1949- WrDr 94
Shemin, Barry L. 1942- WhoAm 94
Shemin, David 1911-1991 WhAm 10
Shemyakin, Yevgeniy Ivanovich 1929- IntWW 93
Shen, Benjamin Shih-Ping 1931- WhoAm 94, WhoAsA 94, WhoScEn 94
Shen, Chia Theng 1913- WhoAm 94, WhoAsA 94
Shen, Chung Yu 1921- WhoAsA 94, WhoMW 93
Shen, Gene Giin-Yuan 1957- WhoScEn 94
Shen, Grace Liu 1941- WhoAsA 94
Shen, Hao-Ming 1933- WhoAsA 94
Shen, Hsieh Wen 1931- WhoAm 94, WhoAsA 94, WhoScEn 94, WhoWest 94
Shen, I-Yao 1926- WhoAsA 94
Shen, James C.H. 1909- IntWW 93
Shen, Jerome Tseng Yung 1918- WhoMW 93
Shen, Jun 1959- WhoWest 94
Shen, Kangkang 1958- WhoScEn 94
Shen, Liang Chi 1939- WhoAm 94, WhoAsA 94, WhoScEn 94
Shen, Mason Ming-Sun 1945- WhoScEn 94, WhoWest 94
Shen, Nelson Mu-Ching 1946- WhoAm 94, WhoWest 94
Shen, Samuel Shanpu 1960- WhoWest 94
Shen, Shan-Fu 1921- WhoAsA 94
Shen, Sheldon Shih-Ta 1947- WhoAsA 94
Shen, Tek-Ming 1949- WhoAsA 94
Shen, Theodore Ping 1945- WhoAm 94, WhoFI 94
Shen, Thomas T. 1926- WhoAsA 94
Shen, Tsung Ying 1924- WhoScEn 94
Shen, Wu-Mian 1942- WhoAsA 94
Shen, Xiao-Yan 1963- WhoAsA 94
Shen, Yuan-Yuan 1954- WhoScEn 94
Shen, Yuen-Ron 1935- WhoAsA 94, WhoScEn 94, WhoWest 94
Shen Aiping 1942- WhoPRCh 91 [port]
Shenar, Paul d1989 WhoHol 92
Shen Beizhang WhoPRCh 91 [port]
Shen Congwen 1902-1988 RfGShF
Shen Dali 1938- IntWW 93
Shen Daming WhoPRCh 91
Shen Daren 1928- IntWW 93, WhoPRCh 91 [port]
Shen Derong WhoPRCh 91
Shendrikar, Arun D. 1938- WhoAsA 94
Shenefelt, Philip David 1943- WhoScEn 94
Shenefield, John Hale 1939- WhoAm 94, WhoAmL 94, WhoAmP 93
Shenfield, Barbara (Estelle) Who 94
Sheng, Bright 1955- WhoAsA 94
Sheng, Jack Tse-liang 1929- WhoAmL 94
Sheng, Ping 1946- WhoAsA 94
Sheng, Tony L. 1935- WhoAsA 94
Shengelaia, Eldar Nikolayevich 1933- IntWW 93
Shengelaia, Georgiy Nikolayevich 1937- IntWW 93
Shengelaya, Georgy Nikolaevich 1937- LngBDD
Sheng Huaren WhoPRCh 91
Shengold, Leonard 1925- WrDr 94
Sheng-qin Luo-sang Jian-zan WhoPRCh 91
Sheng Shuren 1929- WhoPRCh 91 [port]
Shenhar, Joram 1940- WhoScEn 94
Shen Hong 1906- WhoPRCh 91 [port]
Shen Hongying WhoPRCh 91
Shenin, Oleg Semonovich 1937- LngBDD
Shenin, Oleg Semyonovich 1937- IntWW 93
Shen Jian 1915- IntWW 93
Shen Jian 1920- WhoPRCh 91 [port]
Shen Jueren 1931- WhoPRCh 91 [port]
Shenk, George H. 1943- WhoAm 94, WhoAmL 94
Shenk, Howard Fred 1939- WhoFI 94
Shenk, John Christian, Jr. 1926- WhoAm 94
Shenk, John Henry 1939- WhoFI 94
Shenk, Richard Lawrence 1940- WhoFI 94, WhoMW 93
Shenk, Sol A. 1911- WhoFI 94
Shenk, Thomas Eugene 1947- WhoAm 94, WhoScEn 94
Shenkarow, Barry WhoAm 94
Shenkarow, Barry L. WhoMW 93
Shen Keqi WhoPRCh 91
Shenker, Israel 1925- WrDr 94
Shenker, Morris Abraham 1907-1989 WhAm 10
Shenkir, William Gary 1938- WhoAm 94
Shenkman, Mark Ronald 1943- WhoFI 94
Shen Lianrui WhoPRCh 91
Shen Maocheng 1934- WhoPRCh 91 [port]
Shennan, Joseph Hugh 1933- IntWW 93, WrDr 94
Shennum, Robert Herman 1922- WhoAm 94
Shenoi, B. A. 1929- WhoAsA 94
Shenon, Philip John 1897- WhAm 10
Shenouda, Anba, III 1923- IntWW 93
Shenouda, George Samaan 1943- WhoScEn 94
Shenoy, Narasimha B. 1949- WhoAsA 94
Shen Panwen WhoPRCh 91
Shen Qiuping 1945- WhoPRCh 91 [port]
Shen Qiuwo 1917- WhoPRCh 91 [port]
Shen Qizhen 1906- WhoPRCh 91 [port]
Shen Ren'gan WhoPRCh 91
Shen Rong 1935- BlmGWL, ConWorW 93, WhoPRCh 91 [port]
Shen Rongjun 1936- WhoPRCh 91 [port]
Shen Runzhang WhoPRCh 91
Shen Shanhong WhoPRCh 91
Shen Shituan WhoPRCh 91
Shenson, Walter IntMPA 94
Shenstone, William 1714-1763 BlmGEL
Shentall, Susan WhoHol 92
Shenton, Clive 1946- Who 94
Shenton, James (Patrick) 1925- WrDr 94
Shen Tong 1968- WrDr 94
Shen Ts'ung-Wen RfGShF
Shen Xiaxi, Haj Iliyas 1921- WhoPRCh 91 [port]
Shen Yifan WhoPRCh 91
Shen Yinluo 1920- IntWW 93, WhoPRCh 91 [port]
Shen Yuan 1916- WhoPRCh 91 [port]
Shen Yun'ao WhoPRCh 91
Shen Yungang 1927- WhoPRCh 91
Shen Zhihuan WhoPRCh 91
Shen Zhu WhoPRCh 91
Shen Zulun 1931- IntWW 93, WhoPRCh 91 [port]
Sheon, Aaron 1937- WhoAm 94, WhoAmA 93
Sheon, Robert Philip 1934- WhoMW 93
Shep, Robert Lee 1933- WhoWest 94
Shepard, A. Courtenay 1939-1991 WhAm 10
Shepard, Aaron 1950- ConAu 142, SmATA 75 [port]
Shepard, Alan B., Jr. 1923- IntWW 93
Shepard, Alan Bartlett, Jr. 1923- WhoAm 94, WhoScEn 94
Shepard, Alice WhoHol 92
Shepard, Allan Guy 1922-1989 WhAm 10
Shepard, Beverly Renee 1959- WhoBlA 94
Shepard, Charles Virgil 1940- WhoFI 94
Shepard, D. C. 1924- WhoAm 94, WhoFI 94, WhoMW 93
Shepard, Donald C. 1953- WhoAmL 94
Shepard, Earl Alden 1932- WhoFI 94, WhoWest 94
Shepard, Elaine WhoHol 92
Shepard, Elaine Elizabeth WhoAm 94
Shepard, Frank Parsons 1895- WhAm 10
Shepard, Geoffrey Carroll 1944- WhoAm 94
Shepard, George Leo 1947- WhoFI 94
Shepard, Giles Richard Carless 1937- Who 94
Shepard, Gregory Mark 1955- WhoIns 94
Shepard, Harold 1897- WhAm 10
Shepard, Huey Percy 1936- WhoBlA 94
Shepard, Iva d1973 WhoHol 92
Shepard, Ivan Albert 1925- WhoFI 94, WhoMW 93
Shepard, J. Neal, Jr. 1947- WhoAmP 93
Shepard, James J. 1931- WhoAm 94
Shepard, Jan WhoHol 92
Shepard, Janie Ray 1954- WhoFI 94
Shepard, Jewel WhoHol 92
Shepard, Joan WhoBlA 94
Shepard, John WhoHol 92

Shepard, Jon Max 1939- WhoAm 94
Shepard, Julian Leigh 1957- WhoAmL 94
Shepard, Kimberly M. 1961- WhoAmP 93
Shepard, Kirk Van, Sr. 1951- WhoMW 93
Shepard, Kyle Mark 1963- WhoWest 94
Shepard, Leslie Alan 1917- WrDr 94
Shepard, Lewis Albert 1945- WhoAmA 93
Shepard, Linda Irene 1945- WhoBlA 94
Shepard, Lois Burke 1938- WhoAmP 93
Shepard, Lucius WrDr 94
Shepard, Lucius 1947- ConAu 141, EncSF 93
Shepard, Maridean Mansfield 1952- WhoWest 94
Shepard, Mark Louis 1949- WhoScEn 94
Shepard, Martin 1934- WrDr 94
Shepard, Michael J. WhoAmL 94
Shepard, Neil DrAPF 93
Shepard, Neil 1951- ConAu 140
Shepard, Paul Howe 1925- WhoAm 94
Shepard, Randall Terry 1946- WhoAm 94, WhoAmL 94, WhoAmP 93, WhoMW 93
Shepard, Ray A. 1940- WhoBlA 94
Shepard, Richmond 1929- WrDr 94
Shepard, Robert Carlton 1933- WhoWest 94
Shepard, Robert M. 1932- WhoAm 94, WhoAmL 94, WhoFI 94
Shepard, Roger Newland 1929- IntWW 93, WhoAm 94
Shepard, Sam 1943- AmCulL [port], ConDr 93, IntDcF 2-4, IntDcT 2, IntMPA 94, IntWW 93, WhoAm 94, WhoHol 92, WrDr 94
Shepard, Samuel, Jr. 1907- WhoBlA 94
Shepard, Stephen Benjamin 1939- WhoAm 94, WhoFI 94
Shepard, Stephen John Richard 1947- WhoAmP 93
Shepard, Thomas Hill 1923- WhoAm 94
Shepard, Thomas Rockwell, Jr. 1918- WhoAm 94
Shepard, Tracy Morgan 1957- WhoIns 94
Shepard, William 1737-1817 WhAmRev
Shepard, William Robert 1943- WhoAmL 94
Shepard, William Seth 1935- WhoAm 94
Shepardson, Jed Phillip 1932- WhoScEn 94
Shepard-Taggart, Gloria Harvey 1932- WhoFI 94
Shephard, Bruce Dennis 1944- WhoScEn 94
Shephard, George Clifford 1915- Who 94
Shephard, Gillian (Patricia) 1940- Who 94
Shephard, Gillian Patricia 1940- IntWW 93, WhoWomW 91
Shephard, Harold Montague 1918- Who 94
Shephard, Roy Jesse 1929- WrDr 94
Shepheard, Joseph Kenneth 1908- Who 94
Shepheard, Peter (Faulkner) 1913- Who 94
Shepheard, Peter Faulkner 1913- IntWW 93
Shepherd, Baron 1918- IntWW 93, Who 94
Shepherd, Alan Arthur 1927- Who 94
Shepherd, Alan J. 1942- WhoAm 94
Shepherd, Allen DrAPF 93
Shepherd, Archie 1922- Who 94
Shepherd, Benjamin A. 1941- WhoBlA 94
Shepherd, Berisford 1917- WhoBlA 94
Shepherd, Burton Hale, Jr. 1956- WhoFI 94
Shepherd, Carl Lee 1952- WhoAm 94
Shepherd, Charles Clinton 1929- WhoFI 94
Shepherd, Charles William Haimes 1917- Who 94
Shepherd, Clark W. 1933- WhoIns 94
Shepherd, Colin 1938- Who 94
Shepherd, Cybill 1950- IntMPA 94, WhoAm 94, WhoHol 92
Shepherd, Daniel Marston 1939- WhoFI 94
Shepherd, David Who 94
Shepherd, (Richard) David 1931- Who 94
Shepherd, David A. 1956- WhoAmL 94
Shepherd, Elizabeth WhoHol 92
Shepherd, Elmira 1959- WhoBlA 94
Shepherd, Elsbeth Weichsel 1952- WhoMW 93
Shepherd, Eric William d1992 Who 94N
Shepherd, Frank Andrew 1946- WhoAm 94, WhoAmL 94
Shepherd, Freeman Daniel 1936- WhoScEn 94
Shepherd, Geoffrey Thomas 1922- Who 94
Shepherd, George Anthony 1931- Who 94
Shepherd, George Buell, Jr. 1943- WhoAmL 94
Shepherd, George W. 1926- WrDr 94
Shepherd, Gregg Reid 1953- WhoWest 94
Shepherd, Greta Dandridge 1930- WhoBlA 94
Shepherd, Helen Parsons 1923- WhoAmA 93
Shepherd, J. Frank 1932- WhoAmP 93
Shepherd, Jack WhoHol 92
Shepherd, Jack 1937- ConAu 43NR
Shepherd, James Rodney 1935- Who 94
Shepherd, Janet Eileen 1950- WhoWest 94
Shepherd, Jean WhoHol 92
Shepherd, Jean 1923- WhoCom
Shepherd, John WhoHol 92
Shepherd, John Alan 1943- Who 94
Shepherd, John C. d1993 NewYTBS 93 [port]
Shepherd, John Calvin 1925- WhoAm 94
Shepherd, John Dodson 1920- Who 94
Shepherd, John Frederic 1954- WhoAmL 94
Shepherd, John Michael 1955- WhoAmL 94
Shepherd, John Thompson 1919- WhoAm 94
Shepherd, Karen CngDr 93
Shepherd, Karen 1940- WhoAm 94, WhoAmP 93, WhoWest 94
Shepherd, Leonard 1872- WhoHol 92
Shepherd, Linda A. 1959- WhoIns 94
Shepherd, Luke fl. 1547-1554 DcLB 136
Shepherd, Malcolm Thomas 1952- WhoBlA 94
Shepherd, Mark, Jr. 1923- WhoAm 94
Shepherd, Mark Richard 1953- WhoAmL 94
Shepherd, Mary Anne 1950- WhoMW 93
Shepherd, Michael ConAu 41NR
Shepherd, Pamela DrAPF 93
Shepherd, Paul H. 1955- WhoAmP 93, WhoWest 94
Shepherd, Paula Virginia 1964- WhoMW 93
Shepherd, Peter (Malcolm) 1916- Who 94
Shepherd, R. F. 1926- WhoWest 94
Shepherd, Reginald 1924- WhoAmA 93
Shepherd, Richard 1927- IntMPA 94
Shepherd, Richard Charles Scrimgeour 1942- Who 94
Shepherd, Robert 1949- WrDr 94
Shepherd, Robert Edward, Jr. 1937- WhoAmL 94
Shepherd, Robert James 1930- WhoAm 94
Shepherd, Robert Patrick 1955- WhoAmL 94
Shepherd, Ronald Francis 1926- Who 94
Shepherd, Roosevelt Eugene 1933- WhoBlA 94
Shepherd, Saundra Dianne 1945- WhAm 10
Shepherd, Saundra Dianne 1945-1992 WhoBlA 94N
Shepherd, Simon WhoHol 92
Shepherd, Stewart Robert 1948- WhoAm 94, WhoAmL 94
Shepherd, Thomas Irvin 1953- WhoFI 94, WhoWest 94
Shepherd, Thomas James 1956- WhoFI 94
Shepherd, Veronika Y. 1947- WhoBlA 94
Shepherd, Walton 1947- WhoAmP 93
Shepherd, William C. 1939- WhoFI 94, WhoWest 94
Shepherd, William Fritz 1943- WhoAmA 93
Shepherd, William H. d1979 WhoHol 92
Shepherd, William Stanley 1918- Who 94
Shepherdson, Charles Philip 1956- WhoMW 93
Shepherdson, John Cedric 1926- Who 94
Shepic, John Anthony 1948- WhoWest 94
Shepich, Steve WhoAmP 93
Shepler, Dwight (Clark) 1905- WhoAmA 93N
Shepler, John Edward 1950- WhoMW 93
Shepley, Hugh 1928- WhoAm 94
Shepley, Michael d1961 WhoHol 92
Shepley, Ruth d1951 WhoHol 92
Shepp, Alan 1935- WhoAmA 93
Shepp, Allan 1928- WhoAm 94
Shepp, Bryan Eugene 1932- WhoAm 94
Shepp, Lawrence Alan 1936- WhoAm 94, WhoScEn 94
Sheppard, Albert Parker, Jr. 1936- WhoAm 94
Sheppard, Allen (John George) 1932- Who 94
Sheppard, Allen John George 1932- IntWW 93
Sheppard, Ben H., Jr. 1943- WhoAmL 94
Sheppard, Bert d1929 WhoHol 92
Sheppard, Berton Scott 1936- WhoAmL 94
Sheppard, Carl Dunkle 1916- WhoAmA 93
Sheppard, Claude-Armand 1935- WhoAm 94
Sheppard, Dalton, Jr. 1936- WhoAmP 93
Sheppard, David Stuart Who 94
Sheppard, David Stuart 1929- IntWW 93, WrDr 94
Sheppard, Delia WhoHol 92
Sheppard, Edward James, IV 1941- WhoAmL 94
Sheppard, Evelyn R. 1958- WhoAmL 94
Sheppard, Francis Henry Wollaston 1921- Who 94
Sheppard, Howard Reece 1926- WhoFI 94, WhoWest 94
Sheppard, Jack W. 1931- WhoAm 94, WhoWest 94
Sheppard, John Craig 1913-1978 WhoAmA 93N
Sheppard, John Tressider 1881-1968 DcNaB MP
Sheppard, John Wilbur 1961- WhoScEn 94
Sheppard, Joseph Sherly 1930- WhoAmA 93
Sheppard, Louis Clarke 1933- WhoAm 94, WhoFI 94, WhoScEn 94
Sheppard, Maurice Raymond 1947- Who 94
Sheppard, Mervyn Cecil ffranck 1905- Who 94
Sheppard, Michael Avery 1960- WhoAmP 93
Sheppard, Morgan WhoHol 92
Sheppard, Nina Akamu WhoAmA 93
Sheppard, Norman 1921- Who 94
Sheppard, Paul Thomas 1963- WhoAmL 94
Sheppard, Peter John 1942- Who 94
Sheppard, Posy 1916- WhoAm 94
Sheppard, Roger Davies 1949- WhoWest 94
Sheppard, Ronald John 1939- WhoBlA 94
Sheppard, Shirley Anne 1914- WhoAmP 93
Sheppard, Stephen 1946- WhoHol 92
Sheppard, Stevenson Royrayson 1945- WhoBlA 94
Sheppard, Thomas Richard 1934- WhoAm 94, WhoAmL 94
Sheppard, William Stevens 1930- WhoAm 94
Sheppard, William Vernon 1941- WhoFI 94, WhoScEn 94
Sheppard-Goerke, Carrol Sahodra 1947- WhoFI 94
Shepperd, Alfred (Joseph) 1925- Who 94
Shepperd, Alfred Joseph 1925- IntWW 93
Shepperd, Frederick Metz 1954- WhoMW 93
Shepperd, James Douglass 1932- WhoAmP 93
Shepperd, John d1983 WhoHol 92
Shepperd, John Ben 1915-1990 WhAm 10
Shepperd, Michael 1927- WrDr 94
Shepperd, Thomas Eugene 1941- WhoFI 94
Shepperson, George Albert 1922- Who 94
Shepperson, Wilbur (Stanley) 1919-1991 WrDr 94N
Shepperson, Wilbur Stanley 1919- WhoAm 94, WhoWest 94
Shepphard, Charles B. 1949- WhoAmP 93
Shepphard, Charles Bernard 1949- WhoBlA 94
Shepro, Richard W. 1953- WhoAm 94
Sheps, Cecil George 1913- IntWW 93, WhoAm 94
Sher, Allan L. 1931- WhoAm 94
Sher, Antony 1949- ConTFT 11, IntWW 93, Who 94, WhoHol 92
Sher, Barbara 1935- WrDr 94
Sher, Barry Nostradamus 1949- WhoFI 94
Sher, Byron 1928- WhoAmP 93
Sher, Byron D. 1928- WhoWest 94
Sher, Elizabeth 1943- WhoAmA 93
Sher, Elizabeth Joy 1958- WhoAmL 94
Sher, Gila ConAu 142
Sher, Joanna Ruth Hollenberg 1933-1992 WhAm 10
Sher, Leopold Zangwill 1953- WhoAm 94, WhoAmL 94
Sher, Louis K. 1914- IntMPA 94
Sher, Michael David 1950- WhoAmL 94
Sher, Patricia R. 1931- WhoAmP 93
Sher, Paul Phillip 1939- WhoAm 94
Sher, Richard Philip 1950- WhoAmL 94
Sher, Rose DrAPF 93
Sher, Samuel Julius 1941- Who 94
Sher, Steven DrAPF 93
Sher, Victor Herman 1947- Who 94
Sherak, Thomas 1945- IntMPA 94
Sherak, Thomas Mitchell 1945- WhoAm 94, WhoFI 94
Sheran, Thomas R. 1945- WhoAmL 94
Sherar, J. William 1930- WhoIns 94
Sherart, Georgia d1929 WhoHol 92
Sheraton, Neil 1914- WrDr 94
Sheraton, Thomas 1751-1806 BlmGEL
Sheratsky, Rodney E(arl) 1933- WrDr 94
Sherbell, Rhoda WhoAm 94, WhoAmA 93
Sherborne, Archdeacon of Who 94
Sherborne, Area Bishop of 1935- Who 94
Sherborne, Montague 1930- Who 94
Sherbourne, Archibald Norbert 1929- WhoAm 94
Sherbourne, Stephen Ashley 1945- Who 94
Sherbrook, Harry J. 1951- WhoAmL 94
Sherbrooke, Archbishop of 1920- Who 94
Sherbrooke, Michael d1957 WhoHol 92
Sherburn, Earl Franklin 1943- WhoWest 94
Sherburne, Donald W. 1929- WrDr 94
Sherburne, Donald Wynne 1929- WhoAm 94
Sherburne, Edward 1616-1702 DcLB 131 [port]
Sherburne, John L. 1923- WhoAmP 93
Sherburne, John Samuel 1757-1830 WhAmRev
Sherburne, Zoa 1912- SmATA 18AS [port]
Sherburne, Zoa (Morin) 1912- EncSF 93, TwCYAW
Sherby, Kathleen Reilly 1947- WhoAmL 94, WhoMW 93
Sherck, Timothy C. 1949- WhoAm 94
Shere, Charles 1935- NewGrDO
Shere, Dennis 1940- WhoAm 94
Sheremet, Cary Mark 1957- WhoMW 93
Sherer, Charles Robert 1895- WhAm 10
Sherer, David Matthew 1943- WhoFI 94
Sherer, Dunham B. 1937- WhoAmL 94
Sherer, Robert Jerome 1927- WhoAmL 94
Sherer, Samuel Ayers 1944- WhoAmL 94
Sheresky, Norman M. 1928- WhoAmL 94
Sherf, Arden Frederick 1916- WhAm 10
Sherf, Harriet N. 1934- WhoWest 94
Sherfesee, John 1948- WhoWest 94
Sherfield, Baron 1904- IntWW 93, Who 94
Shergold, Harold Edward 1936- WhoIns 94
Shergold, Harold Taplin 1915- Who 94
Sherick, Steven Paul 1952- WhoAmL 94
Sheridan, Andrew James, III 1944- WhoScEn 94
Sheridan, Ann d1967 WhoHol 92
Sheridan, Brian David 1949- WhoAmL 94
Sheridan, Bruce Matthew 1959- WhoFI 94
Sheridan, Cecil d1980 WhoHol 92
Sheridan, Cecil Majella 1911- Who 94
Sheridan, Charles Fitzgerald, Jr. 1928- WhoAmL 94
Sheridan, Christopher Frederick 1953- WhoAm 94
Sheridan, Christopher Julian 1943- Who 94
Sheridan, Clara Lou d1967 WhoHol 92
Sheridan, Dan d1963 WhoHol 92
Sheridan, Daniel Joseph 1961- WhoAmL 94
Sheridan, Dinah 1920- WhoHol 92
Sheridan, Frank d1943 WhoHol 92
Sheridan, George d1981 WhoHol 92
Sheridan, George Edward 1915- WhoWest 94
Sheridan, Harriet Waltzer 1925-1992 WhAm 10
Sheridan, Helen Adler WhoAmA 93
Sheridan, James Edward 1922- WhoAm 94
Sheridan, James Leslie 1942- WhoAm 94, WhoFI 94
Sheridan, Jamey WhoHol 92
Sheridan, Jamey 1951- IntMPA 94
Sheridan, Jane ConAu 41NR, WrDr 94
Sheridan, Jim 1949- IntMPA 94
Sheridan, John Brian 1947- WhoAm 94
Sheridan, John Patrick, Jr. 1942- WhoAm 94
Sheridan, Lawrence A. 1919- WhoAmP 93
Sheridan, Lionel Astor 1927- Who 94, WrDr 94
Sheridan, Liz WhoHol 92
Sheridan, Margaret d1982 WhoHol 92
Sheridan, Margaret 1889-1958 NewGrDO
Sheridan, Mark William 1959- WhoMW 93
Sheridan, Michael E. WhoAmP 93
Sheridan, Nicollette 1963- IntMPA 94
Sheridan, Nicollette 1964- WhoHol 92
Sheridan, Patrick Michael 1940- WhoAm 94, WhoFI 94
Sheridan, Peter 1927- Who 94
Sheridan, Philip Henry 1831-1888 HisWorL [port]
Sheridan, Philp Henry 1950- WhoAm 94, WhoScEn 94
Sheridan, Richard Bert 1918- WhoAm 94
Sheridan, Richard Brinsley 1751-1816 BlmGEL, NewGrDO
Sheridan, Richard Brinsley (Butler) 1751-1816 IntDcT 2 [port]
Sheridan, Roderick Gerald 1921- Who 94
Sheridan, Sally Anne WhoAmP 93
Sheridan, Sonia Landy 1925- WhoAm 94, WhoAmA 93
Sheridan, Thomas EncSF 93
Sheridan, Thomas 1938- WrDr 94

Sheridan, William Griffith, Jr. 1941-
WhoAmL 94
Sheridan, William Michael 1956-
WhoFI 94
Sheridan, Wilma Froman 1926-
WhoWest 94
Sherif, S. A. 1952- *WhoScEn 94*
Sheriff, Kenneth Wayne 1942-
WhoMW 93
Sheriff, Linda Lepper 1954- *WhoFI 94*
Sherin, Edwin 1930- *WhoAm 94*
Sherk, George William 1949-
WhoAmL 94
Sherk, Kenneth J. 1933- *WhoAm 94*
Sherk, Warren Arthur 1916- *WhoWest 94*
Sherland, Christopher 1594-1632
DcNaB MP
Sherlaw-Johnson, Robert 1932- *WrDr 94*
Sherline, Harold Albert 1925-
WhoMW 93
Sherlock, Alexander 1922- *IntWW 93,
Who 94*
Sherlock, (Edward) Barry (Orton) 1932-
Who 94
Sherlock, David Christopher 1943-
Who 94
Sherlock, John Michael 1926-
WhoMW 93
Sherlock, Paul V. 1930- *WhoAmP 93*
Sherlock, Philip (Manderson) 1902-
Who 94
Sherlock, Sheila (Patricia Violet) 1918-
Who 94
Sherman, Adah d1942 *WhoHol 92*
Sherman, Alan Theodore 1957-
WhoScEn 94
Sherman, Alfred 1919- *IntWW 93,
Who 94*
Sherman, Allan 1924-1973
WhoCom [port]
Sherman, Arnold 1932- *WrDr 94*
Sherman, Barbara J. 1944- *WhoBlA 94*
Sherman, Barnet 1958- *WhoFI 94*
Sherman, Beatrice Ettinger 1919-
WhoFI 94
Sherman, Bobby 1946- *WhoHol 92*
Sherman, Bradford Winslow 1934-
WhoAmP 93
Sherman, Bradley James 1954-
WhoWest 94
Sherman, Carol *DrAPF 93*
Sherman, Charles Daniel, Jr. 1920-
WhoAm 94
Sherman, Charles Edwin 1934-
WhoAm 94
Sherman, Charlotte Watson 1958-
BlkWr 2
Sherman, Cindy 1954- *IntWW 93,
WhoAm 94, WhoAmA 93*
Sherman, Claire Richter 1930-
WhoAmA 93
Sherman, Connie d1989 *WhoHol 92*
Sherman, David Matthew 1959-
WhoWest 94
Sherman, David Michael 1956-
WhoScEn 94
Sherman, Deborah 1951- *WhoWest 94*
Sherman, Deming Eliot 1943- *WhoAm 94,
WhoAmL 94*
Sherman, Donald H. 1932- *WhoWest 94*
Sherman, Donald Roy 1955- *WhoFI 94*
Sherman, Edward Forrester 1945-
WhoBlA 94
Sherman, Edward Francis 1937-
WhoAm 94
Sherman, Elaine C. 1938- *WhoAm 94,
WhoMW 93*
Sherman, Elliot Mark 1952- *WhoAm 94,
WhoAmL 94*
Sherman, Eric 1947- *WhoWest 94*
Sherman, Eugene Jay 1935- *WhoAm 94,
WhoFI 94*
Sherman, Evelyn d1974 *WhoHol 92*
Sherman, Forrest P. 1896-1951 *HisDcKW*
Sherman, Frances Adams 1934-
WhoWest 94
Sherman, Francis Henry 1918-
WhoAmP 93
Sherman, Frank William 1946-
WhoMW 93
Sherman, Fred d1969 *WhoHol 92*
Sherman, Frederick E. 1944- *WhoAmL 94*
Sherman, Frederick Hood 1947-
WhoAmL 94
Sherman, Gary *HorFD [port]*
Sherman, Gary Bruce 1954- *WhoMW 93*
Sherman, Gary Edward 1949-
WhoAmL 94
Sherman, George M. 1941- *WhoAm 94,
WhoFI 94*
Sherman, Gerald 1938- *WhoWest 94*
Sherman, Geraldine *WhoHol 92*
Sherman, Glenn Terry 1954- *WhoAmL 94*
Sherman, Gordon Rae 1928- *WhoAm 94*
Sherman, Harold M(orrow) 1898-1987
EncSF 93
Sherman, Harris D. 1942- *WhoAmL 94*

Sherman, Hiram d1989 *WhoHol 92*
Sherman, Hiram 1908-1989 *WhAm 10*
Sherman, Howard D. 1961- *WhoFI 94*
Sherman, Ingrid 1919- *WrDr 94*
Sherman, Irwin William 1933-
WhoAm 94
Sherman, James D. 1945- *WhoAmL 94*
Sherman, James Owen 1942-
WhoScEn 94
Sherman, Jeffrey Barry 1948- *WhoAm 94,
WhoFI 94*
Sherman, Jenny *WhoHol 92*
Sherman, Jeremy P. 1951- *WhoAmL 94*
Sherman, Joe *DrAPF 93*
Sherman, Joel Henry *EncSF 93*
Sherman, John *DrAPF 93*
Sherman, John Clinton 1916- *WhoAm 94*
Sherman, John Foord 1919- *WhoAm 94*
Sherman, John K. (Urtz) 1898-1969
WhoAmA 93N
Sherman, Jonathan Goodhue 1907-1989
WhAm 10
Sherman, Jory *DrAPF 93*
Sherman, Joseph Allen 1929-
WhoAmL 94
Sherman, Joseph M. 1926- *WhoAmP 93*
Sherman, Josepha *SmATA 75 [port]*
Sherman, Kenneth 1936- *WhoWest 94*
Sherman, Kerry 1953- *WhoHol 92*
Sherman, Lawrence M. 1940- *WhoAm 94*
Sherman, Lenore (Walton) 1920-
WhoAmA 93
Sherman, Lester Ivan 1936- *WhoAmL 94*
Sherman, Louis *WhoHol 92*
Sherman, Louis Allen 1943- *WhoAm 94,
WhoScEn 94*
Sherman, Lowell d1934 *WhoHol 92*
Sherman, Lynn 1952- *WrDr 94*
Sherman, Malcolm Charles 1931-
WhoWest 94
Sherman, Marion Kyle *WhoAmP 93*
Sherman, Mark A. 1924- *WhoMW 93*
Sherman, Martin 1920- *WhoAm 94*
Sherman, Martin 1938- *ConDr 93,
GayLL, IntDcT 2, WrDr 94*
Sherman, Mary d1980 *WhoHol 92*
Sherman, Mary 1947- *WhoMW 93*
Sherman, Mary Kennedy 1919- *WhoFI 94*
Sherman, Max Ray 1935- *WhoAm 94*
Sherman, Michael *EncSF 93*
Sherman, Michael M. 1945- *WhoAmL 94*
Sherman, Michael S. 1946- *WhoAmL 94*
Sherman, Michael Stuart 1947-
WhoAm 94
Sherman, Milton 1941- *WhoAmL 94*
Sherman, Nancy *DrAPF 93*
Sherman, Norman Mark 1948-
WhoAm 94
Sherman, Orville *WhoHol 92*
Sherman, Paul *WhoHol 92*
Sherman, Paul Jay 1933- *WhoFI 94*
Sherman, Peter Michael *EncSF 93*
Sherman, Randolph S. 1944- *WhoAm 94,
WhoAmL 94*
Sherman, Ransom d1985 *WhoHol 92*
Sherman, Richard Adams 1946-
WhoAmL 94
Sherman, Richard B. 1929- *WrDr 94*
Sherman, Richard H. 1941- *WhoMW 93*
Sherman, Richard M. 1928- *IntMPA 94*
Sherman, Robert *WhoHol 92*
Sherman, Robert 1928- *ConAu 142*
Sherman, Robert 1950- *WhoWest 94*
Sherman, Robert B. 1925- *IntMPA 94*
Sherman, Robert Bernard 1925-
WhoAm 94, WhoWest 94
Sherman, Robert Dewayne 1949-
WhoWest 94
Sherman, Roger *WrDr 94*
Sherman, Roger 1721-1793 *HisWorL,
WhAmRev [port]*
Sherman, Roger 1722-1793 *AmRev*
Sherman, Roger 1930- *WhoAm 94,
WhoFI 94*
Sherman, Roger Talbot 1923- *WhoAm 94*
Sherman, Samuel M. *IntMPA 94*
Sherman, Sarai 1922- *WhoAmA 93*
Sherman, Saul Lawrence 1926-
WhoAm 94
Sherman, Saul S. 1917- *WhoFI 94*
Sherman, Scott Bradley 1954- *WhoFI 94*
Sherman, Signe Lidfeldt 1913- *WhoFI 94,
WhoScEn 94, WhoWest 94*
Sherman, Steve *DrAPF 93*
Sherman, Steve (Barry) 1938- *WrDr 94*
Sherman, Stuart 1945- *ConDr 93*
Sherman, Susan *DrAPF 93*
Sherman, Suzette 1954- *WhoAm 94*
Sherman, Sylvan Robert *WhoHol 92*
Sherman, Thomas D. *WhoAmL 94,
WhoFI 94*
Sherman, Thomas J. 1944- *WhoAmL 94*
Sherman, Thomas Oscar, Jr. 1948-
WhoBlA 94
Sherman, Vincent 1906- *IntMPA 94,
WhoHol 92*
Sherman, Wendy Ruth 1949- *WhoAm 94*
Sherman, William *DrAPF 93*

Sherman, William Courtney 1923-
WhoAm 94
Sherman, William Delano 1942-
WhoAm 94, WhoAmL 94
Sherman, William Farrar 1937-
WhoAmP 93
Sherman, William Michael 1955-
WhoScEn 94
Sherman, William Tecumseh 1820-1891
HisWorL [port]
Sherman, Z. Charlotte *WhoAmA 93*
Sherman, Zelda Charlotte 1924-
WhoWest 94
Sherman-Simpson, Barbara J. 1944-
WhoBlA 94
Shermoen, Richard Eugene 1930-
WhoAm 94
Shern, Stephanie Marie 1948- *WhoAm 94*
Sherow, Don Carl 1949- *WhoBlA 94*
Sherr, Morris Max 1930- *WhoAmL 94*
Sherr, Paul E. 1933- *WhoFI 94*
Sherr, Ronald Norman 1952-
WhoAmA 93
Sherr, Rubby 1913- *WhoScEn 94*
Sherrard, Michael David 1928- *Who 94*
Sherrard, Raymond Henry 1944-
WhoWest 94
Sherrard, Tudor *WhoHol 92*
Sherratt, David John 1945- *Who 94*
Sherratt, Gerald Robert 1931-
WhoAm 94, WhoWest 94
Sherred, T(homas) L. 1915-1985
EncSF 93
Sherrell, Carl 1929-1990 *EncSF 93*
Sherrell, Charles Ronald, II 1936-
WhoBlA 94, WhoHisp 94
Sherrell, Doris d1990 *WhoHol 92*
Sherrell, John Bradford 1951- *WhoAm 94,
WhoAmL 94*
Sherrell, Lori Lyn 1965- *WhoFI 94*
Sherrell, Lynn Margaret 1940-
WhoWest 94
Sherren, Anne Terry 1936- *WhoMW 93,
WhoScEn 94*
Sherrer, Bettina *WhoHol 92*
Sherrer, Charles David 1935- *WhoAm 94*
Sherrer, Gary L. 1948- *WhoAmP 93*
Sherrick, Daniel Nean 1929- *WhoAm 94*
Sherrick, Daniel William 1958-
WhoAmL 94
Sherrick, Rebecca Louise 1953-
WhoMW 93
Sherriff, R. C. 1896-1975 *IntDcF 2-4*
Sherriff, R(obert) C(edric) 1896-1975
ConDr 93, EncSF 93
Sherriffs, Ronald Everett 1934-
WhoAm 94, WhoWest 94
Sherrill, Bradley Marc 1958- *WhoMW 93*
Sherrill, Carlyle 1953- *WhoAmP 93*
Sherrill, Frank Odell 1894- *WhAm 10*
Sherrill, Fred Glover 1894- *WhAm 10*
Sherrill, H. Virgil 1920- *WhoAm 94,
WhoFI 94, WhoMW 93*
Sherrill, Helen Hardwicke 1898-
WhAm 10
Sherrill, Milton Lewis 1949- *WhoAmA 93*
Sherrill, Robert Sommerville 1954-
WhoFI 94
Sherrill, Ronald Nolan 1949-
WhoScEn 94
Sherrill, Thomas Boykin, III 1930-
WhoAm 94, WhoFI 94, WhoMW 93
Sherrill, Tom 1946- *WhoAmP 93*
Sherrill, Vanita Lytle 1945- *WhoBlA 94*
Sherrill, William Henry 1932- *WhoBlA 94*
Sherrill, Wray d1981 *WhoHol 92*
Sherrin, Edward George 1931- *IntWW 93*
Sherrin, Ned 1931- *IntMPA 94, Who 94,
WrDr 94*
Sherrington, Charles Scott 1857-1952
WorScD
Sherrington, David 1941- *IntWW 93,
Who 94*
Sherrington, Terence Brian 1942- *Who 94*
Sherritt, George M. 1927- *WhoIns 94*
Sherrod, Charles M. 1937- *WhoBlA 94*
Sherrod, Charles Melvin 1937-
WhoAmP 93
Sherrod, Ezra Cornell 1950- *WhoBlA 94*
Sherrod, Philip Lawrence 1935-
WhoAmA 93
Sherrod, R. Allen *WhoAmP 93*
Sherrod, Robert Lee 1909- *IntWW 93,
WhoAm 94*
Sherron, Jim K., Jr. 1931- *WhoAmP 93*
Sherrow, Greg Hunter 1953- *WhoWest 94*
Sherry, Arthur Harnett 1908- *WhAm 10*
Sherry, Cameron William 1939-
WhoScEn 94
Sherry, Daniel J. 1950- *WhoAmL 94*
Sherry, George Leon 1924- *WhoAm 94*
Sherry, Henry Ivan 1930- *WhoAm 94*
Sherry, J. Barney d1944 *WhoHol 92*
Sherry, James *DrAPF 93*
Sherry, James (Terence) 1946-
ConAu 41NR
Sherry, Kenneth Edward 1939-
WhoWest 94

Sherry, Norman 1935- *Who 94, WrDr 94*
Sherry, Paul Henry 1933- *WhoAm 94,
WhoMW 93*
Sherry, Robert Joseph 1957- *WhoAmL 94*
Sherry, Sol d1993 *NewYTBS 93 [port]*
Sherry, Sylvia *WrDr 94*
Sherry, Vincent, Mrs. *Who 94*
Sherry, William Grant 1914- *WhoAmA 93*
Shersby, (Julian) Michael 1933- *Who 94*
Shersher, Zinovy 1947- *WhoAmA 93*
Sherston-Baker, Robert (George
Humphrey) 1951- *Who 94*
Shertzer, Bruce Eldon 1928- *WhoAm 94*
Shertzer, Herman d1977 *WhoHol 92*
Sherva, Dennis G. 1942- *WhoAm 94*
Sherval, David Robert 1933- *Who 94*
Shervheim, Lloyd Oliver 1928-
WhoAm 94
Shervington, E. Walter 1906- *WhoBlA 94*
Sherwin, Byron Lee 1946- *WhoMW 93*
Sherwin, Chalmers William 1916-
WhoAm 94
Sherwin, James Terry 1933- *WhoAm 94*
Sherwin, Judith Johnson 1936- *WrDr 94*
Sherwin, Michael Dennis 1939-
WhoAm 94
Sherwin, Roger William 1931-
WhoScEn 94
Sherwin-White, Adrian Nicholas 1911-
Who 94
Sherwood, Bishop Suffragan of 1940-
Who 94
Sherwood, Aaron Wiley 1915- *WhoAm 94*
Sherwood, Allen Joseph 1909-
WhoAm 94, WhoAmL 94, WhoWest 94
Sherwood, (Robert) Antony (Frank) 1923-
Who 94
Sherwood, Arthur Lawrence 1943-
WhoAm 94, WhoAmL 94
Sherwood, Arthur Morley 1939-
WhoAm 94
Sherwood, Arthur W. *WhoHol 92*
Sherwood, Bette Wilson 1920- *WhoAm 94*
Sherwood, Bobby d1981 *WhoHol 92*
Sherwood, C. L. d1941 *WhoHol 92*
Sherwood, David J. 1922- *IntWW 93*
Sherwood, David William 1943-
WhoIns 94
Sherwood, Donald 1897- *WhAm 10*
Sherwood, Frances 1940- *ConLC 81 [port]*
Sherwood, Gale *WhoHol 92*
Sherwood, Henry d1967 *WhoHol 92*
Sherwood, Hugh C. 1928- *WrDr 94*
Sherwood, James *WhoHol 92*
Sherwood, James Blair 1933- *Who 94,
WhoAm 94*
Sherwood, John H(erman Mulso) 1913-
WrDr 94
Sherwood, John Kellogg 1961-
WhoAmL 94
Sherwood, Jonathan *SmATA 74*
Sherwood, Katherine 1952- *WhoAmA 93*
Sherwood, Lawrence Leighton 1954-
WhoWest 94
Sherwood, Leona *WhoAmA 93*
Sherwood, Lillian Anna 1928-
WhoMW 93
Sherwood, Linda Kathleen 1947-
WhoAm 94, WhoAmL 94
Sherwood, Louis 1941- *WhoAm 94*
Sherwood, (Peter) Louis (Michael) 1941-
Who 94
Sherwood, Louis Maier 1937- *WhoAm 94,
WhoFI 94*
Sherwood, Lydia d1989 *WhoHol 92*
Sherwood, Madeleine 1922- *IntMPA 94,
WhoHol 92*
Sherwood, Martha 1775-1851 *BlmGWL*
Sherwood, Martin (Anthony) 1942-
EncSF 93
Sherwood, Morgan Bronson 1929-
WrDr 94
Sherwood, O. Peter 1945- *WhoBlA 94*
Sherwood, Peter Miles Anson 1945-
WhoMW 93
Sherwood, Philip Robert 1949-
WhoAmL 94
Sherwood, Richard E. d1993 *NewYTBS 93*
Sherwood, Robert E. 1896-1955
IntDcF 2-4
Sherwood, Robert E(mmet) 1896-1955
IntDcT 2
Sherwood, Robert Emmet 1896-1955
AmCulL
Sherwood, Robert Lawrence 1953-
WhoMW 93
Sherwood, Robert Petersen 1932-
WhoAm 94, WhoMW 93
Sherwood, Roberta 1912- *WhoHol 92*
Sherwood, Rosina Emmet 1854-1948
WhoAmA 93N
Sherwood, Sherry 1902- *WhoAmA 93N*
Sherwood, Thomas 1934- *Who 94*
Sherwood, Thorne 1910- *WhoAm 94*
Sherwood, Valerie *ConAu 140, WrDr 94*
Sherwood, Wallace Walter 1944-
WhoBlA 94
Sherwood, William d1918 *WhoHol 92*

Sherwood, William Anderson 1875-1951 *WhoAmA 93N*
Sherwood, Yorke d1958 *WhoHol 92*
Sherzan, Gary 1944- *WhoAmP 93*
Sherzer, Harvey Gerald 1944- *WhoAm 94, WhoAmL 94*
She Shiguang *WhoPRCh 91*
Sheshinski, Eytan 1937- *IntWW 93*
Shestack, Alan 1938- *WhoAm 94, WhoAmA 93*
Shestack, Jerome Joseph 1925- *WhoAm 94, WhoAmL 94*
Shestack, Melvin Bernard 1931- *WhoAm 94*
Shestak, Teri Lee 1954- *WhoMW 93*
Shestakov, Sergey Vasiliyevich 1934- *WhoScEn 94*
Shestakova, Tatyana Borisovna 1948- *IntWW 93*
Shestopal, Dawn Angela *Who 94*
Sheth, Ashvin C. 1935- *WhoAsA 94*
Sheth, Atul Chandravadan 1941- *WhoAsA 94, WhoScEn 94*
Sheth, Jagdish Nanchand 1938- *WhoAm 94*
Sheth, Ketankumar Kantilal 1959- *WhoAsA 94*
Sheth, Kishor C. 1943- *WhoAsA 94*
Sheth, Navin D. 1946- *WhoAsA 94*
Sheth, Pranlal 1924- *Who 94*
Sheth, Rajan Indulal 1949- *WhoMW 93*
Shetka, Debra Ann *WhoAmL 94*
Shetler, Stanwyn Gerald 1933- *WhoScEn 94*
Shetreet, Shimon 1946- *IntWW 93*
Shettel, Don Landis, Jr. 1949- *WhoWest 94*
Shetterly, Will *EncSF 93*
Shettles, Landrum Brewer 1909- *WhoAm 94*
Shetty, Anil N. 1952- *WhoAsA 94*
Shetty, Mulki Radhakrishna 1940- *WhoMW 93, WhoScEn 94*
Shetzline, David *DrAPF 93*
Sheu, Bing J. 1955- *WhoAsA 94*
Sheu, Lien-Lung 1959- *WhoAsA 94, WhoScEn 94*
Sheumack, Colin Davies *Who 94*
Shevack, Brett David 1950- *WhoAm 94*
Shevack, Hilda Natalie *WhoFI 94*
Shevardnadze, Eduard *NewYTBS 93 [port]*
Shevardnadze, Eduard Amvrosevich 1928- *LngBDD*
Shevardnadze, Eduard Amvrosiyevich 1928- *IntWW 93, Who 94*
Shevchenko, Arkadiy Nikolayevich 1930- *IntWW 93*
Shevchenko, Sergey Markovich 1952- *WhoScEn 94*
Shevde, Ketan 1943- *WhoAsA 94*
Shevel, Wilbert Lee 1932- *WhoAm 94*
Sheveleva, Yekaterina Vasilyevna 1916- *IntWW 93*
Shevell, Steven King 1950- *WhoMW 93*
Shevick, Steven Karl 1956- *WhoAmP 93*
Shevin, David *DrAPF 93*
Shevin, Frederick Franklin 1921- *WhoMW 93*
Shevin, Maurice L. 1952- *WhoAmL 94*
Shevin, Robert Lewis 1934- *WhoAm 94*
Shevitz, Mark H. 1955- *WhoMW 93*
Shevland, Patrick d1980 *WhoHol 92*
Shew, Rose Jean 1952- *WhoMW 93*
Shew, Rowland *EncSF 93*
Sheward, Richard S. 1944- *WhoAmL 94*
Shewell, Lennington d1978 *WhoHol 92*
Shewmake, Janice Marie 1946- *WhoAmP 93*
Shewmaker, Jack Clifford 1938- *WhoAm 94*
Shewmon, Paul Griffith 1930- *WhoMW 93*
Shewry, Peter Robert 1948- *Who 94*
Sheya *WhoAmA 93*
Sheybal, Vladek 1928- *WhoHol 92*
Sheymov, Victor *NewYTBS 93 [port]*
Sheynis, Viktor Leonidovich 1931- *IntWW 93*
Shi, Zheng 1947- *WhoScEn 94*
Shiach, Allan G. 1941- *WrDr 94*
Shiach, Gordon Iain Wilson 1935- *Who 94*
Shiang, Elaine 1950- *WhoAsA 94*
Shi Anhai *WhoPRCh 91*
Shiao, Daniel Da-Fong 1937- *WhoAsA 94*
Shibaki Yoshiko 1914- *BlmGWL*
Shibano, Takumi 1926- *EncSF 93*
Shi Baoyuan 1937- *WhoPRCh 91 [port]*
Shibata, Akikazu 1935- *WhoScEn 94*
Shibata, Edward Isamu 1942- *WhoAsA 94, WhoMW 93*
Shibata, Erwin Fumio 1950- *WhoScEn 94*
Shibata, Shoji 1927- *WhoAm 94*
Shibayama, Mitsuhiro 1954- *WhoScEn 94*
Shiber, Mary Claire 1960- *WhoScEn 94*
Shibles, Warren 1933- *WrDr 94*
Shibley, Arnold P. 1933- *WhoAmP 93*
Shibley, Gail 1958- *WhoAmP 93*
Shibley, Gertrude *WhoAmA 93*
Shibley, Ralph Edwin, Jr. 1944- *WhoMW 93*
Shibley, Raymond Nadeem 1925- *WhoAm 94*
Shibley, Robert Gordon 1946- *WhoAm 94*
Shibli, Mohammed Abdullah 1952- *WhoFI 94*
Shibutani, Tamotsu 1920- *WrDr 94*
Shibuya, Charlene S. 1956- *WhoFI 94*
Shibuya, Takeshi 1927- *WhoMW 93*
Shi Changxu 1919- *WhoPRCh 91*
Shi Chengxun *WhoPRCh 91*
Shichor, David 1933- *WhoWest 94*
Shick, Bradley Ullin 1956- *WhoFI 94*
Shickle, Paul Eugene 1927- *WhoWest 94*
Shicoff, Neil 1949- *NewGrDO*
Shi Dazhen 1932- *WhoPRCh 91 [port]*
Shide, Don L. *WhoAmP 93*
Shideler, Mary M(cDermott) 1917- *WrDr 94*
Shideler, Ross Patrick 1936- *WhoAm 94*
Shideler, Shirley Ann Williams 1930- *WhoAm 94*
Shiderly, Phyllis J. 1925- *WhoAmP 93*
Shi Dianbang *WhoPRCh 91*
Shiefman, Vicky *DrAPF 93*
Shieh, John Ting-chung 1935- *WhoAm 94, WhoAsA 94*
Shieh, Rong Chung 1933- *WhoAsA 94*
Shieh, Samuel C. *IntWW 93*
Shieh, Tsay-Jiu Brian 1953- *WhoAsA 94*
Shieh, Wun-Ju 1954- *WhoAsA 94*
Shieh, Yuch-Ning 1940- *WhoAsA 94*
Shiekman, Laurence Zeid 1947- *WhoAm 94, WhoAmL 94*
Shiekman, Philip Miner 1925- *WhoAmL 94, WhoFI 94*
Shiel, M(atthew) P(hipps) 1865-1947 *EncSF 93*
Shield, Fred d1974 *WhoHol 92*
Shield, Leslie 1916- *Who 94*
Shield, William 1748-1829 *NewGrDO*
Shields, Alan J. 1944- *WhoAmA 93*
Shields, Allan Edwin 1919- *WhoAm 94*
Shields, Anne Kesler 1932- *WhoAmA 93*
Shields, Arthur d1970 *WhoHol 92*
Shields, Brooke 1965- *IntMPA 94, WhoHol 92*
Shields, Brooke Christa Camille 1965- *IntWW 93, WhoAm 94*
Shields, Carol 1935- *BlmGWL*
Shields, Charles W. 1959- *WhoAmP 93*
Shields, Clarence L., Jr. 1940- *WhoBlA 94*
Shields, Claude A. L. 1954- *WhoAmL 94*
Shields, Cydney Robin 1957- *WhoBlA 94*
Shields, David *DrAPF 93*
Shields, Del Pierce 1933- *WhoBlA 94*
Shields, Elizabeth Lois 1928- *Who 94*
Shields, Ella d1952 *WhoHol 92*
Shields, Esther L. M. *WhoBlA 94*
Shields, Evelyn 1938- *WhoMW 93*
Shields, Frank d1975 *WhoHol 92*
Shields, Frank 1909-1975 *BuCMET*
Shields, Frank Cox 1944- *WhoFI 94*
Shields, Frank Walter 1945- *WhoAmP 93*
Shields, George Benjamin 1959- *WhoMW 93*
Shields, Gregory Alan 1946- *WhoAm 94*
Shields, H. Richard *WhoAm 94*
Shields, Helen d1963 *WhoHol 92*
Shields, Henry, Jr. 1945- *WhoAmL 94*
Shields, J. Todd 1947- *WhoAmL 94*
Shields, Jerry Allen 1937- *WhoAm 94*
Shields, John Charles 1944- *WhoMW 93*
Shields, John H. 1954- *WhoAmP 93*
Shields, John Joseph 1938- *WhoFI 94*
Shields, John Sinclair 1903- *Who 94*
Shields, John Webster d1984 *WhoHol 92*
Shields, John William, Jr. 1937- *WhoAm 94*
Shields, Karen Bethea 1949- *WhoBlA 94*
Shields, Karen Galloway 1949- *WhoBlA 94*
Shields, Landrum Eugene 1927- *WhoBlA 94*
Shields, Laura Aull *WhoFI 94*
Shields, Lawrence Thornton 1935- *WhoAm 94, WhoScEn 94*
Shields, Lora Mangum 1912- *WhoWest 94*
Shields, Loran Donald 1936- *WhoWest 94*
Shields, Margaret 1941- *WhoWomW 91*
Shields, Margaret Kerslake 1941- *IntWW 93*
Shields, Mark *NewYTBS 93 [port]*
Shields, Michael *Who 94*
Shields, (Robert) Michael (Coverdale) 1943- *Who 94*
Shields, Mildred Jean 1935- *WhoAmP 93*
Shields, Neil (Stanley) 1919- *Who 94*
Shields, Nelson T., III d1993 *NewYTBS 93*
Shields, Patrick Thomas, Jr. 1935- *WhoMW 93*
Shields, Paula Blair 1950- *WhoMW 93*
Shields, Perry 1925- *CngDr 93, WhoAm 94, WhoAmL 94*
Shields, Robert 1930- *IntWW 93, Who 94*
Shields, Robert Emmet 1942- *WhoAm 94, WhoAmL 94*
Shields, Robert Francis 1923- *WhoFI 94*
Shields, Robert Lee 1931- *WhoFI 94*
Shields, Roberts *WhoHol 92*
Shields, Stuart *Who 94*
Shields, (Leslie) Stuart 1919- *Who 94*
Shields, Sydney d1960 *WhoHol 92*
Shields, Thomas Charles 1941- *WhoAm 94*
Shields, Thomas Joseph 1959- *WhoFI 94*
Shields, Thomas William 1922- *WhoAm 94*
Shields, Valerie Lynne 1967- *WhoMW 93*
Shields, Varee, Jr. 1935- *WhoBlA 94*
Shields, Vincent O. 1924- *WhoBlA 94*
Shields, Virginia 1937- *WhoAm 94*
Shields, Walter W. 1935- *WhoWest 94*
Shields, William 1943- *WhoAmL 94*
Shields, William A. 1946- *IntMPA 94*
Shields, William Maurice 1937- *WhAm 10*
Shields and Yarnell *WhoHol 92*
Shiell, James Wyllie 1912- *Who 94*
Shiels, George 1886-1949 *IntDcT 2*
Shiely, Albert Raymond, Jr. 1920-1989 *WhAm 10*
Shiely, John Stephen 1952- *WhoAm 94*
Shientag, Florence Perlow *WhoAm 94*
Shier, Daniel Edward 1939- *WhoWest 94*
Shierlaw, Norman Craig 1921- *Who 94*
Shiers, Frank Abram 1920- *WhoAmL 94*
Shi Fangyu *WhoPRCh 91 [port]*
Shiff, Alan Howard William 1934- *WhoAm 94*
Shiff, Richard 1942- *IntMPA 94*
Shiffer, James David 1938- *WhoAm 94, WhoFI 94, WhoWest 94*
Shiffert, Edith *DrAPF 93*
Shifflett, Crandall A(vis) 1938- *WrDr 94*
Shifflett, Lynne Carol *WhoBlA 94*
Shiffman, Bernard 1942- *WhoAm 94*
Shiffman, Max 1914- *WhoWest 94*
Shiffman, Melvin Arthur 1931- *WhoWest 94*
Shiffman, Michael A. 1941- *WhoAmL 94*
Shiffner, Henry David 1930- *Who 94*
Shiffner, John Robert 1941- *Who 94*
Shiflet, W. Marion 1927- *WhoAmP 93*
Shiflett, Betty *DrAPF 93*
Shiflett, Pendleton M., III 1946- *WhoIns 94*
Shifley, Charles W. 1951- *WhoAmL 94*
Shifley, Ralph Louis 1910- *WhoAm 94*
Shi Fong 1942- *WhoAm 94*
Shifrin, Bruce Carl 1947- *WhoWest 94*
Shigehara, Kumiharu 1939- *IntWW 93, Who 94*
Shigemasa, Thomas Ken 1945- *WhoAsA 94*
Shi Geng 1926- *WhoPRCh 91 [port]*
Shigesada, Nanako 1941- *WhoScEn 94*
Shigeta, James 1933- *WhoHol 92*
Shigezawa, Ruth *DrAPF 93*
Shigihara, Patricia *WhoAsA 94*
Shi Guangchang *WhoPRCh 91*
Shih, Arnold Shang-Teh 1943- *WhoAsA 94*
Shih, Benedict Chesang 1935- *WhoWest 94*
Shih, Chia C. 1939- *WhoAsA 94*
Shih, Chia Hsin 1941- *WhoMW 93*
Shih, Chiang 1956- *WhoAsA 94*
Shih, Chilin 1955- *WhoAsA 94*
Shih, Fred F. 1936- *WhoAsA 94*
Shih, Hong 1945- *WhoWest 94*
Shih, Hong-Yee 1957- *WhoAsA 94*
Shih, J. Chung-wen *WhoAm 94*
Shih, Jason Cheng 1942- *WhoAm 94*
Shih, Jason Chia-Hsing 1939- *WhoAm 94, WhoAsA 94*
Shih, Jing-Luen Allen 1961- *WhoScEn 94*
Shih, Joan Fai *WhoAmA 93*
Shih, Joan Fai 1932- *WhoAsA 94*
Shih, John Chau 1939- *WhoAsA 94*
Shih, Ko-Ming 1953- *WhoAsA 94*
Shih, Ming-Che 1953- *WhoAsA 94*
Shih, Philip C. 1943- *WhoAsA 94*
Shih, Stephen Chingyu 1957- *WhoAsA 94*
Shih, Tom I-Ping 1952- *WhoAsA 94*
Shih, Tsung-Ming Anthony 1944- *WhoAsA 94*
Shih, Wei 1933- *WhoAsA 94*
Shihab, Naomi *DrAPF 93*
Shihabi, Samir 1925- *IntWW 93*
Shihata, Ibrahim F. I. 1937- *IntWW 93*
Shihata, Ibrahim Fahmy Ibrahim 1937- *WhoAm 94, WhoAmL 94*
Shih Carducci, Joan Chia-mo 1933- *WhoFI 94*
Shih Chi-Yang 1935- *IntWW 93*
Shi Huan *WhoPRCh 91*
Shi Jian 1924- *WhoPRCh 91 [port]*
Shi Jiuyong 1926- *WhoPRCh 91*
Shi Jun *WhoPRCh 91*
Shikari, Anis Abdullah 1943- *WhoFI 94*
Shikarkhane, Naren Shriram 1954- *WhoScEn 94*
Shikata, Jun-ichi 1926- *WhoScEn 94*
Shikata, Masao 1918- *IntMPA 94*
Shikes, Ralph Edmund 1912-1992 *WrDr 94N*
Shikiar, Richard 1946- *WhoWest 94*
Shikin, Gennadi Serafimovich 1938- *IntWW 93*
Shikler, Aaron 1922- *WhoAm 94, WhoAmA 93*
Shi Laihe 1930- *WhoPRCh 91 [port]*
Shildneck, Barbara Jean 1937- *WhoAm 94*
Shi Lemeng *WhoPRCh 91*
Shilepsky, Arnold Charles 1944- *WhoAm 94*
Shi Liming 1939- *IntWW 93*
Shi Lin *WhoPRCh 91*
Shillato, Robert William 1940- *WhoWest 94*
Shillea, Thomas John 1947- *WhoAmA 93*
Shiller, Helen *WhoAmP 93*
Shiller, Robert J. 1946- *WrDr 94*
Shillestad, John G. 1934- *WhoIns 94*
Shillestad, John Gardner 1934- *WhoAm 94*
Shilling, A. Gary 1937- *WhoAm 94, WhoFI 94*
Shilling, Eric 1920- *NewGrDO*
Shilling, Roy Bryant, Jr. 1931- *WhoAm 94*
Shillingford, Arden *Who 94*
Shillingford, (Romeo) Arden (Coleridge) 1936- *Who 94*
Shillingford, (Romeo) Arden Coleridge 1936- *IntWW 93*
Shillingford, John Parsons 1914- *Who 94*
Shillinglaw, Gordon 1925- *WhoAm 94, WrDr 94*
Shillingsburg, Miriam (Carolyn) Jones 1943- *WrDr 94*
Shillingsburg, Peter LeRoy 1943- *WhoAm 94*
Shillington, (Robert Edward) Graham 1911- *Who 94*
Shillington, Stuart Dennis 1946- *WhoFI 94*
Shillito, Charles Henry 1922- *Who 94*
Shillman, Jeffrey Nathaniel 1945- *WhoAmL 94*
Shillo, Michael *WhoHol 92*
Shiloh, Ailon 1924- *WrDr 94*
Shilov, Aleksandr Maksovich 1943- *IntWW 93*
Shilovsky, Konstantin Stepanovich 1849-1893 *NewGrDO*
Shils, Edward B. 1915- *WhoAm 94*
Shils, Jonathan R. 1946- *WhoAmL 94*
Shilson, Wayne Stuart 1943- *WhoAmA 93*
Shilton, Peter 1949- *IntWW 93, Who 94, WorESoc*
Shilts, Randy *NewYTBS 93 [port]*
Shilts, Randy 1951- *CurBio 93 [port], GayLL, WhoAm 94*
Shilts, Randy c. 1952- *News 93 [port]*
Shim, Eun Sup 1957- *WhoAsA 94*
Shim, Jack V. 1955- *WhoScEn 94*
Shim, Jae K. 1943- *ConAu 142, WhoAsA 94*
Shim, Jae Yong 1939- *WhoMW 93*
Shim, Jung P. 1947- *WhoAsA 94*
Shim, Mike Lee 1956- *WhoWest 94*
Shim, Sang Koo 1942- *WhoFI 94*
Shim, Sang Kyu 1939?-1992 *WhoAsA 94N*
Shim, Sook Chin 1939- *WhoAsA 94*
Shim, Walton Kenn Tsung 1931- *WhoAsA 94*
Shima, John David 1957- *WhoAsA 94*
Shima, Mikiko 1929- *WhoScEn 94*
Shima, Shigenobu 1907- *IntWW 93*
Shimabukuro, Elton Ichio 1950- *WhoWest 94*
Shimada, Katsunori 1922- *WhoAsA 94*
Shimada, Masao 1915- *IntWW 93*
Shimada, Shinji 1952- *WhoScEn 94*
Shimada, Teru *WhoHol 92*
Shimada, Toshiyuki 1951- *WhoAm 94*
Shimada, Yoko *WhoHol 92*
Shimada, Yoshiki 1960- *WhoAsA 94*
Shimahara, Kenzo 1928- *WhoScEn 94*
Shimamoto, Scott Seiya 1960- *WhoAsA 94*
Shimanek, Ronald Wenzel 1945- *WhoScEn 94*
Shimasaki, Hitoshi 1923- *IntWW 93*
Shimazaki, Yasuhisa 1946- *WhoScEn 94*
Shimberg, Steven Jay 1953- *WhoAmL 94*
Shimbo, Masaki 1914- *WhoScEn 94*
Shi Meixin *WhoPRCh 91*
Shi Meiyun *WhoPRCh 91 [port]*
Shimek, Dean Troy 1948- *WhoWest 94*
Shimek, Rosemary Geralyn 1952- *WhoMW 93*
Shimell, William 1952- *NewGrDO*
Shimer, Daniel Lewis 1944- *WhoAm 94, WhoFI 94*
Shimer, Donald Albert 1929- *WhoWest 94*
Shimer, William Allison 1894- *WhAm 10*
Shimer, Zachary 1933- *WhoAm 94*
Shimidzu, Zenzo 1891-1977 *BuCMET*

Shi Min WhoPRCh 91
Shimizu, David WhoAmP 93
Shimizu, Gordon Toshio 1945- WhoAsA 94
Shimizu, Kayoko 1935- WhoWomW 91
Shimizu, Keiichi 1936- WhoFI 94
Shimizu, Nobumichi 1940- WhoAsA 94
Shimizu, Norihiko 1940- WhoFI 94
Shimizu, Osamu 1911-1986 NewGrDO
Shimizu, Scott Edward 1953- WhoAsA 94
Shimizu, Sumiko 1928- WhoWomW 91
Shimizu, Taisuke 1936- WhoAm 94, WhoAsA 94, WhoFI 94, WhoWest 94
Shimizu, Tak 1946- WhoAsA 94
Shimizu, Toru 1947- WhoAsA 94
Shimizu, Yoshiaki 1936- WhoAm 94, WhoAmA 93
Shimkin, Barry E. 1944- WhoAmL 94
Shimkus, Joanna 1943- WhoHol 92
Shimm, Melvin Gerald 1926- WhoAm 94
Shimmin, C. Gary 1945- WhoIns 94
Shimmon, Ross Michael 1942- Who 94
Shimoda, Osamu 1924- WhoAmA 93
Shimoda, Takeso 1907- IntWW 93
Shimoda, Thomas Edward 1952- WhoMW 93
Shimoda, Yuki d1981 WhoHol 92
Shimoji, Sadao 1932- WhoScEn 94
Shimojo, Shin'ichiro 1920- IntWW 93
Shimokihara, Stanley Shigeo 1937- WhoAsA 94
Shimomura, Roger Yutaka 1939- WhoAmA 93
Shimomura, Yukio 1935- WhoAsA 94
Shimoni, Yaacov 1915- ConAu 141
Shimono, Sab WhoHol 92
Shimooka, Russell 1960- WhoAsA 94
Shimotake, Hiroshi 1928- WhoMW 93
Shimoura, James 1953?- WhoAsA 94
Shimp, David Joseph 1945- WhoMW 93
Shimp, Karen Ann 1959- WhoFI 94, WhoMW 93
Shimp, Robert Everett, Jr. 1942- WhoAm 94
Shimp, William Charles 1956- WhoFI 94
Shimpfky, Richard L. WhoWest 94
Shimshak, Stephen J. 1950- WhoAmL 94
Shimura, Takashi d1982 WhoHol 92
Shin, Diane Teruya 1952- WhoFI 94
Shin, Doug Yong 1950- WhoAsA 94
Shin, Ernest Eun-Ho 1935- WhoAsA 94, WhoWest 94
Shin, Hung Sik 1950- WhoAsA 94
Shin, In-Sook Jeong 1949- WhoAsA 94
Shin, Kilman WhoAsA 94
Shin, Kilman 1933- WhoFI 94
Shin, Myung Soo 1930- WhoAsA 94
Shin, Paull H. 1935- WhoAsA 94, WhoWest 94
Shin, SoonMi 1953- WhoAsA 94
Shin, Suk-han 1930- WhoWest 94
Shin, Young WhoAsA 94
Shin, Yung C. 1953- WhoAsA 94
Shina, Sammy Gourgy 1944- WhoScEn 94
Shinaberry, Sterl Franklin 1937- WhoAmL 94
Shinabery, Max Lawrence 1939- WhoAmP 93
Shinagawa, Larry WhoAsA 94
Shinagel, Michael 1934- WhoAm 94, WrDr 94
Shi Nailiang WhoPRCh 91
Shinbach, Bruce D. 1939- IntMPA 94
Shinde, Amrit Rao 1933- IntWW 93
Shindell, Sidney 1923- WhoAm 94
Shinder, Jason (Scott) 1955- WrDr 94
Shindler, Donald A. 1946- WhoAm 94, WhoAmL 94
Shindler, Elaine Rosalie G. 1934- WhoAm 94
Shindler, George (John) 1922- Who 94
Shindler, Michael Charles 1951- WhoAmL 94
Shindo, Eitaro d1977 WhoHol 92
Shine, Bill 1911- WhoHol 92
Shine, David Bruce 1938- WhoAmP 93
Shine, Frances L(ouise) 1927- WrDr 94
Shine, Hugh Dunham 1952- WhoAmP 93
Shine, John L. d1930 WhoHol 92
Shine, Kenneth I. 1935- WhoAm 94, WhoScEn 94
Shine, Neal James 1930- WhoAm 94, WhoMW 93
Shine, Theodis 1931- WhoBlA 94
Shine, Vincent 1962- WhoAmA 93
Shine, Wilfred d1939 WhoHol 92
Shinebourne, Janice 1947- BlmGWL
Shinefield, Henry Robert 1925- IntWW 93, WhoAm 94
Shineman, Edward William, Jr. 1915- WhoAm 94
Shiner, John R. 1943- WhoAmL 94
Shiner, John Stewart 1949- WhoScEn 94
Shiner, Lewis 1950- EncSF 93
Shiner, Ronald d1966 WhoHol 92
Shines, Johnny 1915-1992 AnObit 1992
Shingler, Arthur Lewis 1941- WhoWest 94
Shingler, George Pinckney 1950- WhoAmL 94
Shingler, Helen 1919- WhoHol 92
Shingles, Godfrey Stephen 1939- Who 94
Shingu, Yasuo 1926- IntWW 93
Shinichi, Kano 1952- WrDr 94
Shin Ik-Hi 1894-1956 HisDcKW
Shinkle, John Thomas 1946- WhoAmL 94
Shinkle, Norman Douglas 1950- WhoAmP 93
Shinn, Allen Mayhew 1908- WhoAm 94
Shinn, Allen Mayhew, Jr. 1937- WhoAmL 94
Shinn, Arthur Frederick 1945- WhoMW 93
Shinn, Clinton Wesley 1947- WhoAm 94, WhoAmL 94, WhoFI 94
Shinn, David Hamilton 1940- WhoAm 94
Shinn, Duane K. 1938- WhoWest 94
Shinn, Everett 1876-1953 WhoAmA 93N
Shinn, George WhoAm 94
Shinn, George Latimer 1923- WhoAm 94
Shinn, Michael Robert 1947- WhoAmL 94
Shinn, Paull Hobom 1935- WhoAmP 93
Shinn, Richard Randolph 1918- WhoAm 94
Shinn, Robert C., Jr. 1937- WhoAmP 93
Shinn, William Townsley, Jr. 1936- WhoAm 94
Shinnar, Reuel 1923- WhoAm 94, WhoScEn 94
Shinners, Stanley Marvin 1933- WhoAm 94
Shinnie, Peter Lewis 1915- Who 94
Shinnock, John Barker 1947- WhoAmL 94
Shinoda, Kozo 1926- WhoScEn 94
Shinozaki, Akihiko 1927- IntWW 93
Shinozaki, Toshiko 1918- WhoWomW 91
Shinozuka, Masanobu 1930- WhoAsA 94
Shinpoch, A. N. WhoAmP 93
Shinsato, Francis G. 1951- WhoAsA 94
Shin Sung-Mo 1891-1960 HisDcKW
Shin Tai-Yong 1891-1959 HisDcKW
Shinville, Gerald Terrance 1935- WhoMW 93
Shioiri, Takayuki 1935- WhoScEn 94
Shiokawa, Masajuro 1921- IntWW 93
Shiono Nanao 1937- BlmGWL
Shiota, Takao 1950- WhoWest 94
Shiotsu, Masahiro 1942- WhoScEn 94
Shioya, Suteaki 1945- WhoScEn 94
Shiozaki, Masao 1941- WhoScEn 94
Shiozawa, Dennis Kenji 1949- WhoScEn 94
Shipbaugh, Calvin LeRoy 1958- WhoScEn 94, WhoWest 94
Shipe, Gary Thomas 1960- WhoScEn 94
Shipe, Jamesetta Denise Holmes 1956- WhoBlA 94
Shipkin, Paul M. 1945- WhoScEn 94
Shipkowitz, Nathan L. 1925- WhoScEn 94
Shipler, David K(arr) 1942- WrDr 94
Shipler, David Karr 1942- WhoAm 94
Shipley, Anthony J. 1939- WhoBlA 94
Shipley, David Elliott 1950- WhoAm 94
Shipley, Grant Fredrick 1945- WhoAmL 94
Shipley, James Parish, Jr. 1945- WhoWest 94
Shipley, James R. 1910-1990 WhoAmA 93N
Shipley, James Ross 1910-1990 WhAm 10
Shipley, Jenny WhoWomW 91
Shipley, L. Parks, Jr. 1931- WhoFI 94
Shipley, Lucia Helene 1920- WhoAm 94
Shipley, Roger Douglas 1941- WhoAmA 93
Shipley, Samuel L. 1929- WhoAmP 93
Shipley, Samuel Lynn 1929- WhoAm 94
Shipley, Thomas E., Jr. 1924- WhoFI 94
Shipley, Vergil Alan 1922- WhoAm 94
Shipley, Vivian DrAPF 93
Shipley, Walter Vincent 1935- IntWW 93, WhoAm 94, WhoFI 94
Shipley-Phillips, Jeanette Kay 1954- WhoScEn 94
Shipman, Barry 1912- WhoHol 92
Shipman, Charles William 1924- WhoAm 94
Shipman, David 1932- WrDr 94
Shipman, David Norval 1939- WhoAm 94, WhoMW 93
Shipman, Gwynne WhoHol 92
Shipman, Helen d1986 WhoHol 92
Shipman, Henry Longfellow 1948- WrDr 94
Shipman, James Melton 1939- WhoScEn 94
Shipman, Keith Bryan 1961- WhoWest 94
Shipman, Michael Scott 1963- WhoWest 94
Shipman, Nell d1970 WhoHol 92
Shipman, Nina WhoHol 92
Shipman, Pat 1949- ConAu 141
Shipman, Robert Jack 1933- WhoIns 94
Shipmon, Luther June 1932- WhoBlA 94
Shipow, Mark S. 1954- WhoAmL 94
Shipow, Mark Steven 1954- WhoAmL 94
Shipp, Cherie Gwen 1957- WhoFI 94
Shipp, Dan Shackelford 1946- WhoAmL 94
Shipp, E. R. 1955- WhoBlA 94
Shipp, Howard J., Jr. 1938- WhoBlA 94
Shipp, Joseph Calvin 1927- WhoWest 94
Shipp, Kemmel W., Sr. 1939- WhoAmP 93
Shipp, Maurine Sarah 1913- WhoBlA 94
Shipp, Melvin Douglas 1948- WhoBlA 94
Shipp, Pamela Louise 1947- WhoBlA 94
Shipp, William Weldon 1927- WhoFI 94
Shippee-Larson, Barbara Mett 1927- WhoAmP 93
Shippen, Edward 1729-1806 WhAmRev
Shippen, Nancy BlmGWL
Shippen, William 1736-1808 WhAmRev
Shippen, William, Jr. 1738-1808 AmRev
Shippen, William (the Elder) 1712-1801 WhAmRev
Shipper, Frank Martin 1945- WhoWest 94
Shipper, Todd Jeffrey 1946- WhoWest 94
Shippey, Sandra Lee 1957- WhoAmL 94, WhoFI 94, WhoWest 94
Shippey, T(homas) A(lan) 1943- WrDr 94
Shippey, Tom 1943- EncSF 93
Shippy, John D. WhoBlA 94
Shippy, Larry D. 1946- WhoAmP 93
Shiprack, Robert R. 1950- WhoAmP 93
Shipsey, Ian Peter 1959- WhoMW 93
Shipstad, Roy d1975 WhoHol 92
Shipstead, Patrick E. 1948- WhoAmL 94
Shipton, Harold William 1920- WhoAm 94
Shi Qirong WhoPRCh 91 [port]
Shira, Robert Bruce 1910- WhoAm 94
Shirai, Akiko WhoAmA 93, WhoAsA 94
Shirai, Scott 1942- WhoWest 94
Shirai, Takeshi 1928- WhoScEn 94
Shirai, Yasuto 1961- WhoScEn 94
Shiraishi, Takashi 1921- IntWW 93
Shiraiwa, Kenichi 1928- WhoScEn 94
Shirakawa, George 1939- WhoAsA 94
Shirart, Georgia d1929 WhoHol 92
Shiras, Wilmar H(ouse) 1908-1990 EncSF 93
Shirasawa, Richard Masao 1948- WhoWest 94
Shirayanagi, Peter Seiichi 1928- IntWW 93
Shirbroun, Richard Elmer 1929- WhoAm 94
Shircliff, James Vanderburgh 1938- WhoFI 94
Shire, David 1937- IntMPA 94
Shire, David Lee 1937- WhoAm 94
Shire, Donald Thomas 1930- WhoAm 94
Shire, Harold Raymond 1910- WhoAmL 94, WhoWest 94
Shire, Peter 1947- WhoAmA 93
Shire, Talia 1946- IntMPA 94, WhoHol 92
Shire, Talia Rose 1946- WhoAm 94
Shireff, Jane 1811-1883 NewGrDO
Shirek, John Richard 1926- WhoFI 94
Shirelles, The ConMus 11 [port]
Shireman, Joan Foster 1933- WhoWest 94
Shireman, Joseph Alan 1961- WhoAmP 93
Shireman, Marilyn Jean 1962- WhoMW 93
Shirendev, Badzaryn 1912- IntWW 93
Shirer, William L. 1904-1993 NewYTBS 93 [port]
Shirer, William L(awrence) 1904- WrDr 94
Shirer, William Lawrence 1904- IntWW 93, Who 94, WhoAm 94
Shires, Garald Royse 1941- WhoMW 93
Shires, George Thomas 1925- WhoAm 94, WhoScEn 94
Shires, Sharon Jonelle 1964- WhoMW 93
Shirey, Charles Wyman 1934- WhoFI 94
Shiriashi, Kazuko 1931- IntWW 93
Shirilau, Jeffery Micheal 1953- WhoFI 94, WhoScEn 94, WhoWest 94
Shirilau, Mark Steven 1955- WhoFI 94, WhoScEn 94
Shirinsky, Vasily Petrovich 1901-1965 NewGrDO
Shirk, Helen Z. WhoAmA 93
Shirk, John O. 1943- WhoAmL 94
Shirk, Kevin William 1957- WhoScEn 94
Shirkey, William Dan 1951- WhoFI 94
Shirkhoda, Ali 1945- WhoMW 93
Shirkov, Dmitriy Vasilevich 1928- IntWW 93
Shirky, Sam(uel) B(ryan) 1896- WhAm 10
Shirley Who 94
Shirley, Albert WhoAmP 93
Shirley, Anne d1993 IntMPA 94N, NewYTBS 93 [port]
Shirley, Anne 1918- WhoHol 92
Shirley, Arthur d1925 WhoHol 92
Shirley, Bill d1989 WhoHol 92
Shirley, Bobbie d1970 WhoHol 92
Shirley, Calvin Hylton 1921- WhoBlA 94
Shirley, David A. 1942- WhoAmP 93
Shirley, David Allen 1918-1988 WhAm 10
Shirley, David Andrew 1926- Who 94
Shirley, David Arthur 1934- WhoWest 94
Shirley, Edwin Samuel, Jr. 1922- WhoBlA 94
Shirley, Florence d1967 WhoHol 92
Shirley, Frances Ann 1931- WrDr 94
Shirley, George 1934- AfrAmAl 6, IntWW 93
Shirley, George (Irving) 1934- NewGrDO
Shirley, George Milton, Jr. 1939- WhoFI 94
Shirley, George Pfeiffer 1939- WhoWest 94
Shirley, Glenn Dean 1916- WhoAm 94
Shirley, Graham Edward 1943- WhoAm 94
Shirley, Homer Clifton, Jr. 1953- WhoAm 94
Shirley, James 1596-1666 BlmGEL, IntDcT 2, NewGrDO
Shirley, James Quincy 1942- WhoAmL 94
Shirley, James R. 1951- WhoAmP 93
Shirley, Jasper Clyde 1913- WhoAmP 93
Shirley, Jessie d1918 WhoHol 92
Shirley, John (Patrick) 1953- WrDr 94
Shirley, John (Patrick) 1954- EncSF 93
Shirley, John Jeffery 1955- WhoWest 94
Shirley, John William 1931- WhoAmP 93
Shirley, Landona Hortense 1928- WhoAmP 93
Shirley, Michael James 1941- WhoWest 94
Shirley, Michael Ray 1951- WhoMW 93
Shirley, Peg WhoHol 92
Shirley, Philip Hammond 1912- Who 94
Shirley, Robert Bryce 1951- WhoAmL 94, WhoFI 94, WhoWest 94
Shirley, Robert Clark 1943- WhoWest 94
Shirley, Stephanie Who 94
Shirley, (Vera) Stephanie 1933- Who 94
Shirley, Tom d1962 WhoHol 92
Shirley, Virginia Lee 1936- WhoAm 94, WhoFI 94
Shirley, W. John 1943- WhoAmL 94
Shirley, William McNulty 1949- WhoMW 93
Shirley-Quirk, John 1931- IntWW 93, NewGrDO, WhoAm 94
Shirley-Quirk, John Stanton 1931- Who 94
Shirpser, Clara 1901- WhoAm 94
Shirras, Edward Scott 1937- Who 94
Shirreffs, Gordon Donald 1914- WrDr 94
Shirriff, Catherine WhoHol 92
Shirrod, Terry S. 1946- WhoWest 94
Shirtcliff, Christine Fay WhoAm 94
Shirtcliff, John Delzell 1948- WhoWest 94
Shirts, Randall Brent 1950- WhoWest 94
Shi Ruzhang WhoPRCh 91 [port]
Shirvani, Hamid 1950- WhoAm 94
Shi Shaohua WhoPRCh 91
Shi Shengrong 1919- WhoPRCh 91 [port]
Shishido, Calvin M. 1933- WhoAsA 94, WhoWest 94
Shishido, Fumitake 1960- WhoFI 94, WhoWest 94
Shishim, Francis WhoAmA 93
Shi Shujun WhoPRCh 91 [port]
Shisler, Geoffrey Wayne 1947- WhoIns 94
Shisler, Mary Paul, Sister 1948- WhoMW 93
Shissias, June S. WhoAmP 93
Shissler, Steven Alan 1962- WhoWest 94
Shister, Joseph 1917- WhoAm 94
Shi Tiesheng 1952- WhoPRCh 91 [port]
Shito, Mitsuo 1930- WhoAmP 93
Shiue, Chyng-Yann 1941- WhoMW 93
Shiue, Gong-Huey 1947- WhoScEn 94
Shivanandan, Kandiah 1929- WhoAsA 94
Shivas, Mark IntMPA 94
Shivas, Mark 1938- Who 94
Shive, Philip Augustus 1938- WhoAm 94
Shive, Richard Byron 1933- WhoFI 94, WhoScEn 94
Shively, Daniel Jerome 1924- WhoMW 93
Shively, Elaine Marie 1946- WhoMW 93
Shively, John Adrian 1922- WhoAm 94
Shively, John D. 1947- WhoAmL 94
Shively, John Terry 1943- WhoWest 94
Shively, Russell Alan 1940- WhoWest 94
Shively, William Phillips 1942- WhoAm 94
Shiver, Jube, Jr. 1953- WhoBlA 94
Shivers, Edward Thomas 1939- WhoFI 94
Shivers, Frank R(emer), Jr. 1924- WrDr 94
Shivers, Gary Melville 1945- WhoFI 94
Shivers, Jane 1943- WhoAm 94
Shivers, Jay Sanford 1930- WrDr 94
Shivers, John D., Jr. 1951- WhoAmP 93
Shivers, Louise 1929- WrDr 94
Shivers, P. Derrick 1964- WhoBlA 94
Shivers, S. Michael 1935- WhoBlA 94
Shives, Arnold Edward 1943- WhoAmA 93

Shivler, James Fletcher, Jr. 1918- *WhoAm 94*
Shivpuri, Gopi Krishna 1903-1984 *ConAu 42NR*
Shi Xingmou 1937- *WhoPRCh 91 [port]*
Shi Xiyu *WhoPRCh 91*
Shi Yafeng 1919- *WhoPRCh 91 [port]*
Shi Yuanchun *WhoPRCh 91*
Shi Yuxiao 1933- *WhoPRCh 91 [port]*
Shi Zhanchun *WhoPRCh 91 [port]*
Shi Zhaoqi 1935- *WhoPRCh 91 [port]*
Shi Zhaotang 1909- *WhoPRCh 91 [port]*
Shi Zhongci *WhoPRCh 91*
Shkadov, Ivan Nikolaevich d1991 *IntWW 93N*
Shkapskaia, Mariia Mikhailovna 1891-1952 *BlmGWL*
Shklar, Gerald 1924- *WhoAm 94*
Shklar, Judith Nisse 1928- *WhoAm 94*
Shkolnik, Selwyn 1931- *WhoWest 94*
Shkurkin, Ekaterina Vladimirovna 1955- *WhoWest 94*
Shlaim, Avi 1945- *WrDr 94*
Shlaudeman, Harry Walter 1926- *IntWW 93, WhoAm 94, WhoAmP 93*
Shlian, Deborah Matchar 1948- *WhoScEn 94*
Shlien, Helen S. *WhoAmA 93*
Shlipak, Carole Rolnick 1938- *WhoFI 94*
Shloss, Stephen R. 1947- *WhoFI 94*
S.H.M. *EncSF 93*
Shmaeff, Robert T. 1939- *WhoWest 94*
Shmavonian, Gerald S. 1945- *WhoAm 94*
Shmelev, Nikolai Petrovich 1936- *IntWW 93*
Shmoys, Jerry 1923- *WhoAm 94*
Shmukler, Stanford 1930- *WhoAmL 94*
Shnayerson, Michael 1954- *WrDr 94*
Shnayerson, Robert Beahan 1925- *WhoAm 94*
Shneidman, Edwin S. 1918- *WhoAm 94*
Shneidman, J. Lee 1929- *WhoAm 94, WrDr 94*
Shneidman, N(oah) N(orman) 1924- *WrDr 94*
Shneour, Elie Alexis 1925- *WrDr 94*
Shneour, Elie Alexis 1926- *WhoAm 94, WhoWest 94*
Shnider, Bruce Jay 1950- *WhoAm 94, WhoAmL 94*
Shniderman, Harry Louis 1916- *WhoAm 94*
Shnier, Alan 1928- *WhoAm 94*
Shnitke, Al'fred 1934- *NewGrDO*
Shoaf, John Lester 1950- *WhoAmP 93*
Shoaff, Thomas Mitchell 1941- *WhoAm 94, WhoAmL 94, WhoMW 93*
Shoafstall, Earl Fred 1936- *WhoFI 94, WhoMW 93*
Shoai, Elinor Josephine Kelly 1943- *WhoWest 94*
Shober, Wharton 1926- *WhoAm 94*
Shobert, Erle Irwin, II 1913- *WhoAm 94*
Shoch, David Eugene 1918-1990 *WhAm 10*
Shochat, Avraham 1936- *IntWW 93*
Shock, Maurice 1926- *IntWW 93, Who 94*
Shock, Nathan Wetherill 1906-1989 *WhAm 10*
Shockey, George R., Jr. 1947- *WhoAmL 94*
Shockey, Thomas Edward 1926- *WhoFI 94*
Shockley, Alice Ann 1910- *WhoAmP 93*
Shockley, Alonzo Hilton, Jr. 1920- *WhoBlA 94*
Shockley, Ann Allen *DrAPF 93*
Shockley, Ann Allen 1927- *GayLL, WhoBlA 94, WrDr 94*
Shockley, Carol Frances 1948- *WhoScEn 94*
Shockley, Earl McCoy 1930- *WhoMW 93*
Shockley, Edward Julian 1924- *WhoAm 94*
Shockley, Gary Clark 1957- *WhoAmL 94*
Shockley, Grant S. 1919- *WhoBlA 94*
Shockley, J. B. *WhoAmP 93*
Shockley, James Thomas 1925- *WhoAm 94*
Shockley, Marian d1981 *WhoHol 92*
Shockley, Myrtle 1926- *WhoAmP 93*
Shockley, Thomas Dewey 1923- *WhoAm 94*
Shockley, Thomas Edward 1929- *WhoBlA 94*
Shockley, W. Ray 1924- *WhoAm 94*
Shockley, William d1989 *NobelP 91N*
Shockley, William 1910-1989 *WorInv*
Shockley, William Bradford 1910-1989 *WhAm 10*
Shockley, Woodland Gray 1914-1991 *WhAm 10*
Shockman, Gerald David 1925- *WhoAm 94, WhoScEn 94*
Shockman, Kelly *WhoAmP 93*
Shockro, Michael J. 1942- *WhoAmL 94*
Shoctor, Joseph Harvey 1922- *WhoAm 94, WhoWest 94*
Shoe, Stephen Charles 1935- *WhoWest 94*
Shoecraft, Willard Rendell 1921- *WhoWest 94*
Shoemake, Bransford Hunt 1956- *WhoAmL 94*
Shoemaker, Ann d1978 *WhoHol 92*
Shoemaker, Bill 1931- *WhoAm 94, WhoWest 94*
Shoemaker, Cameron David James 1940- *WhoWest 94*
Shoemaker, Clara Brink 1921- *WhoScEn 94*
Shoemaker, David Powell 1920- *WhoAm 94*
Shoemaker, Don 1912- *WhoAm 94*
Shoemaker, Eleanor Boggs 1935- *WhoAm 94, WhoFI 94*
Shoemaker, Eugene Merle 1928- *IntWW 93, WhoAm 94, WhoScEn 94, WhoWest 94*
Shoemaker, Forrest Hilton, Jr. 1953- *WhoWest 94*
Shoemaker, Frank Crawford 1922- *WhoAm 94*
Shoemaker, Gradus Lawrence 1921- *WhoAm 94*
Shoemaker, Hal Alan 1950- *WhoFI 94*
Shoemaker, Harold Dee 1942- *WhoScEn 94*
Shoemaker, Harold Lloyd 1923- *WhoFI 94, WhoScEn 94, WhoWest 94*
Shoemaker, Helen E. Martin Achor 1915- *WhoMW 93*
Shoemaker, Innis Howe *WhoAm 94*
Shoemaker, Innis Howe 1942- *WhoAmA 93*
Shoemaker, Jack *DrAPF 93*
Shoemaker, James Michael 1960- *WhoMW 93*
Shoemaker, Jeff 1955- *WhoAmP 93*
Shoemaker, Joyce K. *WhoAm 94*
Shoemaker, Lloyd R. 1921- *WrDr 94*
Shoemaker, Lynn *DrAPF 93*
Shoemaker, Marjorie Patterson 1933- *WhoMW 93*
Shoemaker, Michael C. 1945- *WhoAmP 93*
Shoemaker, Patrick Allen 1955- *WhoScEn 94*
Shoemaker, Paul Beck, III 1941- *WhoAm 94*
Shoemaker, Peter 1920- *WhoAmA 93*
Shoemaker, Raleigh A. 1945- *WhoAmL 94*
Shoemaker, Ralph Warren 1941- *WhoWest 94*
Shoemaker, Rebecca Shepherd 1947- *WhoMW 93*
Shoemaker, Richard A. 1951- *WhoAmP 93*
Shoemaker, Robert B(rink) 1956- *ConAu 142*
Shoemaker, Robert C., Jr. 1932- *WhoAmP 93*
Shoemaker, Robert Comly, Jr. 1932- *WhoWest 94*
Shoemaker, Robert G(ardner) 1941- *ConAu 142*
Shoemaker, Robert Morin 1924- *WhoAm 94*
Shoemaker, Robert N. 1925- *WhoAmP 93*
Shoemaker, Robert Shern 1953- *WhoMW 93*
Shoemaker, Sarah 1936- *WrDr 94*
Shoemaker, Scott David 1958- *WhoWest 94*
Shoemaker, Selma Sealey 1923- *WhoAmP 93*
Shoemaker, Sydney 1931- *IntWW 93*
Shoemaker, Sydney S. 1931- *WhoAm 94*
Shoemaker, Vaughn 1902- *WhoAmA 93*
Shoemaker, Vaughn 1902-1991 *WhAm 10*
Shoemaker, Veronica Sapp 1929- *WhoBlA 94*
Shoemaker, William Edward 1945- *WhoAm 94, WhoFI 94*
Shoemaker, Willie 1931- *IntWW 93*
Shoemate, C. Richard 1939- *IntWW 93*
Shoemate, Charles Richard 1939- *WhoAm 94, WhoFI 94*
Shoen, Edward Joseph *WhoAm 94, WhoFI 94*
Shoenberg, David 1911- *IntWW 93, Who 94*
Shoenberger, Allen Edward 1944- *WhoAmL 94*
Shoener, Arthur Lee 1946- *WhoAm 94, WhoFI 94*
Shoener, Jerry J. *WhoAmP 93*
Shoenfelt, Catherine Ruth 1954- *WhoFI 94*
Shoenfelt, Joseph Franklin 1918-1968 *WhoAmA 93N*
Shoesmith, Kathleen A. 1938- *WrDr 94*
Shoesmith, Thomas M. 1954- *WhoAmL 94*
Shoesmith, Thomas P. 1922- *WhoAmP 93*
Shoff, Patricia Ann 1948- *WhoAmL 94*
Shoffner, Clarence L. 1921- *WhoBlA 94*
Shoffner, Garnett Walter 1934- *WhoBlA 94*
Shoffner, James Priest 1928- *WhoBlA 94*
Shogan, Robert *WhoAm 94*
Shoger, Timothy Ross 1959- *WhoMW 93*
Shogo, Watanabe 1915- *IntWW 93*
Shogren, George Henry 1946- *WhoFI 94*
Shogren, Jason Fredrick 1958- *WhoMW 93*
Shohara, Sei 1930- *WhoAsA 94*
Shohet, Albert Jacob 1938- *WhoFI 94*
Shohet, Jeffrey M. 1949- *WhoAmL 94*
Shohet, Juda Leon 1937- *WhoAm 94, WhoMW 93, WhoScEn 94*
Shohet, Stephen Byron 1934- *WhoAm 94*
Shohoji, Takao 1938- *WhoScEn 94*
Shoichi, Ida 1941- *WhoAm 94*
Shoigu, Sergei Kuzhugetovich *LngBDD*
Shoji, Eguchi 1934- *WhoScEn 94*
Shoji, Sadao 1931- *WhoScEn 94*
Shokeir, Mohamed Hassan Kamel 1938- *WhoAm 94, WhoWest 94*
Shokhin, Aleksandr *IntWW 93*
Shokhin, Aleksandr Nikolaevich 1951- *LngBDD*
Shokler, Harry 1896- *WhoAmA 93N*
Sholdar, Mickey 1949- *WhoHol 92*
Sholder, Jack *HorFD*
Sholder, Jason Allen 1944- *WhoScEn 94*
Sholes, Christopher Latham 1819-1890 *WorInv [port]*
Sholes, David 1943- *WhoAmP 93*
Sholes, Ronald W. 1939- *WhoIns 94*
Sholes, Ronald William 1939- *WhoFI 94*
Sholevar, Bahman *DrAPF 93*
Sholin, Terry Michael 1957- *WhoWest 94*
Sholiton, Marilyn Cohen 1935- *WhoMW 93*
Sholl, Betsy *DrAPF 93*
Sholl, Robert Knowlton 1954- *WhoAmL 94*
Shollenberger, Franklin Leroy 1925- *WhoAmP 93*
Sholly, Steven Craig 1953- *WhoWest 94*
Sholomir, Jack d1988 *WhoHol 92*
Sholtis, Joseph Arnold, Jr. 1948- *WhoScEn 94, WhoWest 94*
Sholtis, Robert William 1947- *WhoMW 93*
Shomer, Enid *DrAPF 93*
Shon, Frederick John 1926- *WhoAm 94*
Shon, James T. 1947- *WhoAmP 93*
Shon, Kyo Kwa 1956- *WhoAsA 94*
Shone, John Terence 1935- *Who 94*
Shone, Richard (N.) 1949- *ConAu 141*
Shone, Robert Minshull d1992 *IntWW 93N, Who 94N*
Shone, Ronald 1946- *WrDr 94*
Shonekan, Ernest Adegunle Oladeinde 1936- *IntWW 93*
Shoneman, Charles H. 1947- *WhoAmL 94*
Shonfeld, Edwin Marshall 1936- *WhoWest 94*
Shoning, Don 1915- *WhoAmP 93*
Shonk, Albert Davenport, Jr. 1932- *WhoFI 94, WhoWest 94*
Shono, Senkichi 1913- *IntWW 93*
Shontz, Franklin C(urtis) 1926- *WrDr 94*
Shoob, Marvin H. 1923- *WhoAm 94*
Shook, Ann Jones 1925- *WhoAmL 94*
Shook, Charles David 1939- *WhoMW 93*
Shook, Gene Edwin 1926- *WhoAmL 94*
Shook, Georg 1934- *WhoAmA 93*
Shook, Gerald David 1920- *WhoMW 93*
Shook, James Creighton 1931- *WhoMW 93*
Shook, John York 1952- *WhoMW 93*
Shook, Langley R. 1947- *WhoAm 94*
Shook, Patricia Louise 1919- *WhoBlA 94*
Shook, Robert Louis 1938- *WhoAm 94*
Shook, Winthrop Curtis 1926- *WhoAmP 93*
Shooman, Martin Lawrence 1934- *WhoAm 94*
Shoop, Barry LeRoy 1957- *WhoScEn 94*
Shoop, Glenn Powell 1920- *WhoFI 94*
Shoop, Pamela Susan 1947- *WhoHol 92*
Shoop, Wally 1941- *WhoAmA 93*
Shooster, Frank Mallory 1954- *WhoAmL 94*
Shooter, Eric Manvers 1924- *Who 94, WhoAm 94*
Shooter, James (Charles) 1951- *WrDr 94*
Shooter, Reginald Arthur 1916- *Who 94*
Shooter, Tom 1941- *WhoAmA 93*
Shooting Star d1966 *WhoHol 92*
Shope, Gertrude 1925- *WhoWomW 91*
Shope, Irvin 1900-1977 *WhoAmA 93N*
Shope, Leslie Reed 1894- *WhAm 10*
Shope, Robert Ellis 1929- *WhoScEn 94*
Shopen, Kenneth 1902-1967 *WhoAmA 93N*
Shopiro, Eleanor Marchigiani 1929- *WhoAm 94*
Shopmaker, Michael Louis 1958- *WhoFI 94*
Shopp, George Milton, Jr. 1955- *WhoWest 94*
Shoppee, Charles William 1904- *IntWW 93, Who 94*
Shopshire, James Maynard 1942- *WhoBlA 94*
Shoquist, Mary Lucille 1932- *WhoAmP 93*
Shor, Dan *WhoHol 92*
Shor, Jonathan 1948- *WhoAmL 94*
Shor, Samuel Wendell Williston 1920- *WhoAm 94*
Shorb, Eugene Murray 1920- *WhoAm 94*
Shore, Albert Clarence 1928- *WhoFI 94*
Shore, Anne 1929- *WrDr 94*
Shore, Betty Joyce 1936- *WhoFI 94*
Shore, Caron Dean 1949- *WhoFI 94, WhoMW 93*
Shore, Cindy Brockman 1956- *WhoFI 94*
Shore, David Teignmouth 1928- *Who 94*
Shore, Dinah 1917- *IntMPA 94, WhoHol 92*
Shore, Dinah 1921- *WhoAm 94*
Shore, Elaine *WhoHol 92*
Shore, Elizabeth Catherine 1927- *Who 94*
Shore, Eugene L. 1936- *WhoAmP 93*
Shore, Ferdinand John 1919- *WhoAm 94*
Shore, Herbert 1924- *WhoAm 94*
Shore, Howard *IntMPA 94*
Shore, Howard Leslie 1946- *WhoAm 94*
Shore, Jack 1922- *Who 94*
Shore, James Henry 1940- *WhoAm 94*
Shore, Jane *DrAPF 93*
Shore, John c. 1662-1752 *DcNaB MP*
Shore, Laura Jan *DrAPF 93*
Shore, Lawrence Arthur 1928- *WhoFI 94*
Shore, Mary (Mcgarrity) 1912- *WhoAmA 93*
Shore, Miles Frederick 1929- *WhoAm 94*
Shore, Miles H. 1944- *WhoAmL 94*
Shore, Norman 1914- *WrDr 94*
Shore, Peter (David) 1924- *IntWW 93, Who 94*
Shore, Richard Arnold 1946- *WhoAm 94*
Shore, Roberta 1943- *WhoHol 92*
Shore, Samuel 1924- *WhoAmL 94*
Shore, Stephen 1947- *WhoAm 94, WhoAmA 93*
Shore, Thomas Spencer, Jr. 1939- *WhoAm 94*
Shorell, Irving Daniel 1898- *WhAm 10*
Shorenstein, Walter Herbert 1915- *WhoFI 94*
Shores, Allen Gray 1943- *WhoAmP 93*
Shores, Byron d1957 *WhoHol 92*
Shores, (James) Franklin 1942- *WhoAmA 93*
Shores, Henry Clay 1930- *WhoAmP 93*
Shores, Janie Ledlow 1932- *WhoAmL 94, WhoAmP 93*
Shores, Robert Phelps 1942- *WhoMW 93*
Shorett, Alice Judy 1944- *WhoWest 94*
Shorey, Gregory Day, Jr. 1924- *WhoAmP 93*
Shorin, Vladimir Pavlovich 1939- *LngBDD*
Shorney, George Herbert 1931- *WhoAm 94, WhoFI 94*
Shorney, Margo Kay (Mciver) 1930- *WhoAmA 93*
Shorr, Harriet 1939- *WhoAmA 93*
Shorrock, John Michael 1943- *Who 94*
Shors, Clayton Marion 1925- *WhoAm 94*
Shors, John D. 1937- *WhoAmL 94*
Short *Who 94*
Short, Alexander Campbell 1940- *WhoAm 94, WhoAmL 94*
Short, Alonzo E., Jr. 1939- *AfrAmG [port]*
Short, Antrim d1972 *WhoHol 92*
Short, Bernard David 1935- *Who 94*
Short, Bobby 1924- *WhoBlA 94*
Short, Bobby 1926- *WhoHol 92*
Short, Brian (Michael) 1944- *WrDr 94*
Short, Brian Patrick 1950- *WhoAmL 94, WhoFI 94*
Short, Byron Elliott 1901- *WhoAm 94*
Short, C. Brant 1955- *WhoWest 94*
Short, Cameron 1964- *WhoFI 94*
Short, Clare 1946- *Who 94, WhoWomW 91*
Short, David Gaines 1939- *WhoAm 94*
Short, David Somerset 1918- *Who 94*
Short, De Ronda Miniard 1943- *WhoAmP 93*
Short, Dean Chilton, II 1948- *WhoAmL 94*
Short, Dennis Ray 1954- *WhoScEn 94*
Short, Donald James 1942- *WhoFI 94*
Short, Edward Watson *IntWW 93*
Short, Elizabeth M. 1942- *WhoAm 94, WhoScEn 94*
Short, Eugene Maurice, Jr. 1932- *WhoAmL 94*
Short, Florence d1946 *WhoHol 92*
Short, Frank *DrAPF 93*
Short, George Oscar, III 1957- *WhoFI 94*
Short, George William 1949- *WhoFI 94*
Short, Gertrude d1968 *WhoHol 92*
Short, Harry d1943 *WhoHol 92*

Shugart, Alan F. 1930- *WhoFI 94, WhoWest 94*
Shugart, Cecil Glenn 1930- *WhoAm 94*
Shugart, Herman Henry 1944- *WhoAm 94, WhoScEn 94*
Shugart, Howard Alan 1931- *WhoAm 94*
Shugart, Kenneth Laverne 1925-1985 *WhAm 10*
Shughart, Donald Louis 1926- *WhoAm 94, WhoAmL 94*
Shugrue, Jim *DrAPF 93*
Shugrue, Martin Roger, Jr. 1940- *WhoAm 94, WhoFI 94*
Shugrue, Michael Francis 1934- *WrDr 94*
Shui, Xiaoping 1953- *WhoScEn 94*
Shukat, Charles Philip 1954- *WhoWest 94*
Shukat, Peter Stephen 1945- *WhoAmL 94*
Shuker, Gregory Brown 1932- *WhoAm 94*
Shukhevych, Yurii Romanovych 1936- *LngBDD*
Shukla, Kapil P. 1943- *WhoScEn 94*
Shukla, Mahesh 1927- *WhoScEn 94*
Shukla, Pradip Kantilal 1956- *WhoWest 94*
Shukla, Ravi Kumar 1959- *WhoFI 94*
Shukla, Shivendra D. 1951- *WhoAsA 94*
Shukla, Vidya Charan 1929- *IntWW 93*
Shukman, Harold 1931- *WrDr 94*
Shukman, Solomon 1927- *WhoAmA 93*
Shukry, Ibrahim 1916- *IntWW 93*
Shula, David D. 1959- *WhoAm 94, WhoMW 93*
Shula, Don Francis 1930- *WhoAm 94*
Shula, Robert Joseph 1936- *WhoAm 94*
Shulaw, Richard Allen 1934- *WhoAmL 94*
Shuldham, Molyneux c. 1717-1798 *AmRev, WhAmRev*
Shuldiner, Herbert 1929- *WhoAm 94*
Shuldinger, Herbert 1929- *WrDr 94*
Shuldman, Bennett 1957- *WhoFI 94*
Shulenburger, David Edwin 1945- *WhoFI 94*
Shuler, Ellie Givan, Jr. 1936- *WhoAm 94*
Shuler, G. Philip, III 1944- *WhoAmL 94*
Shuler, Kurt Egon 1922- *WhoAm 94*
Shuler, Michael Louis 1947- *WhoAm 94*
Shuler, Robin Lane 1952- *WhoWest 94*
Shuler, Sally Ann Smith 1934- *WhoWest 94*
Shuler, Thomas H., Jr. 1949- *WhoAmA 93*
Shuler-Donner, Lauren *IntMPA 94*
Shulevitz, Uri 1935- *WhoAm 94*
Shulgasser, Barbara 1954- *WhoAm 94, WhoWest 94*
Shulkin, Anatol 1901-1961 *WhoAmA 93N*
Shulkin, Jerome 1929- *WhoAmL 94*
Shulkin, Martin B. 1944- *WhoAmL 94*
Shull, Carl Edwin 1912- *WhoAmA 93*
Shull, Charles d1986 *WhoHol 92*
Shull, Clifford G. 1915- *WhoAm 94*
Shull, Douglas K. 1943- *WhoAmP 93*
Shull, Harrison 1923- *IntWW 93, WhoAm 94, WhoScEn 94*
Shull, James Marion 1872-1948 *WhoAmA 93N*
Shull, Joe A. 1945- *WhoAmL 94*
Shull, Julian Kenneth, Jr. 1941- *WhoScEn 94*
Shull, Lois Netzley 1917- *WhoMW 93*
Shull, Mary Jean 1923- *WhoMW 93*
Shull, Richard B. 1929- *IntMPA 94, WhoHol 92*
Shull, Richard Bruce 1929- *WhoAm 94*
Shull, William Edgar, Jr. 1947- *WhoAmL 94*
Shulman, Alexandra 1957- *Who 94*
Shulman, Alix Kates *DrAPF 93*
Shulman, Alix Kates 1932- *ConAu 43NR*
Shulman, Arnold 1914- *WhoAm 94*
Shulman, Arthur 1927- *WhoAm 94*
Shulman, Daniel Rees 1944- *WhoAmL 94*
Shulman, David George 1943- *WhoFI 94*
Shulman, Donald L. 1943- *WhoAmL 94*
Shulman, Drusilla Norman *Who 94*
Shulman, Irving 1913- *WrDr 94*
Shulman, Jay A. 1952- *WhoAmL 94*
Shulman, John Gordon 1964- *WhoAmL 94*
Shulman, Lawrence A. 1942- *WhoAmL 94*
Shulman, Lawrence Edward 1919- *IntWW 93, WhoAm 94, WhoScEn 94*
Shulman, Marshall D(arrow) 1916- *WrDr 94*
Shulman, Max *DrAPF 93*
Shulman, Max L. 1908- *WhoAm 94*
Shulman, Max Rees 1945- *WhoAmL 94*
Shulman, Milton *Who 94*
Shulman, Milton 1913- *WrDr 94*
Shulman, Robert Gerson 1924- *IntWW 93, WhoAm 94*
Shulman, Sondra *DrAPF 93*
Shulman, Stanford Taylor 1942- *WhoScEn 94*
Shulman, Stephen Neal 1933- *WhoAm 94*
Shulman, Warren Scott 1942- *WhoAmL 94*
Shulmister, Morris Ross 1940- *WhoAmL 94*
Shultis, Robert Lynn 1924- *WhoAm 94*
Shults, Robert A. 1947- *WhoAmL 94*
Shults, Robert Lee 1936- *WhoFI 94*
Shults, Robert Luther, Jr. 1925- *WhoAm 94*
Shults, Roy L. 1948- *WhoAmL 94*
Shultz, Al *DrAPF 93*
Shultz, C. E. *WhoWest 94*
Shultz, Donald Richard 1930- *WhoAmL 94*
Shultz, Emmet Lavel 1934- *WhoFI 94, WhoWest 94*
Shultz, Erich M. 1953- *WhoAmL 94*
Shultz, Fred Townsend 1923- *WhoWest 94*
Shultz, George P(ratt) 1920- *WrDr 94*
Shultz, George Pratt 1920- *IntWW 93, Who 94, WhoAm 94, WhoAmP 93, WhoFI 94, WhoWest 94*
Shultz, Jack L. 1951- *WhoAmL 94*
Shultz, John David 1939- *WhoAm 94, WhoAmL 94, WhoFI 94*
Shultz, Joseph Randolph 1927- *WhoMW 93*
Shultz, Linda Joyce 1931- *WhoMW 93*
Shultz, Martha Jane 1916- *WhoAm 94*
Shultz, Retha Mills 1914- *WhoMW 93*
Shultz, Richard 1942- *WhoAmP 93*
Shultz, Richard Carl 1927- *WhoAm 94*
Shultz, Silas Harold 1938- *WhoAmL 94, WhoWest 94*
Shultz, Terry Dale 1947- *WhoWest 94*
Shulze, Frederick Bennett 1935- *WhoAm 94*
Shulzke, Margot Seymour *WhoAmA 93*
Shum, Alex C. 1953- *WhoAsA 94*
Shum, William 1957- *WhoAsA 94*
Shumacker, Elizabeth Wight 1912- *WhoAmA 93*
Shumacker, Harris B., Jr. 1908- *WhoAm 94*
Shumadine, Conrad M. 1943- *WhoAmL 94*
Shumake, Glynn *WhoAmP 93*
Shumaker, Anne Williamson 1944- *WhoAmP 93*
Shumaker, Harold Dennis 1946- *WhoAmL 94*
Shumaker, John J. 1929- *WhoAmP 93*
Shumaker, John William 1942- *WhoAm 94*
Shumaker, Peggy *DrAPF 93*
Shumaker, Roger Lee 1950- *WhoAmL 94*
Shumaker, (Charles) Wayne 1910- *WrDr 94*
Shumaker, Wayne Louis, Jr. 1939- *WhoAmL 94*
Shuman, Charles Wilson 1935- *WhoAmP 93*
Shuman, Deanne 1953- *WhoAm 94*
Shuman, Howard E. 1924- *WhoAmP 93*
Shuman, Jerome 1937- *WhoBlA 94*
Shuman, Joseph Duff 1942- *WhoAmL 94*
Shuman, Larry Myers 1944- *WhoAm 94*
Shuman, Marc *WhoAmL 94*
Shuman, Mark Samuel 1936- *WhoAm 94*
Shuman, Mervyn M. 1925- *WhoFI 94*
Shuman, Michael Harrison 1956- *WhoAmL 94*
Shuman, Nicholas Roman 1921- *WhoAm 94*
Shuman, Robert Baird 1929- *WhoAm 94*
Shuman, Roy d1973 *WhoHol 92*
Shuman, Samuel I. 1925- *WrDr 94*
Shuman, Samuel Irving 1925- *WhoAm 94*
Shuman, Stanley S. 1935- *WhoAm 94, WhoFI 94*
Shuman, Thomas Alan 1946- *WhoWest 94*
Shuman, Willard Edward 1943- *WhoIns 94*
Shumate, Charles Albert 1904- *WhoScEn 94, WhoWest 94*
Shumate, Glen 1958- *WhoBlA 94*
Shumate, J. Bernard *WhoIns 94*
Shumate, McKinley, Jr. 1954- *WhoIns 94*
Shumate, Minerva 1949- *WhoMW 93*
Shumate, Paul William, Jr. 1941- *WhoAm 94*
Shumeiko, Vladimir Filippovich 1945- *IntWW 93, LngBDD*
Shumick, Diana Lynn 1951- *WhoScEn 94*
Shumila, Michael John 1947- *WhoScEn 94*
Shumlin, Peter E. 1956- *WhoAmP 93*
Shumov, Vladimir Georgievich 1941- *LngBDD*
Shumpert, Terrance Darnell 1966- *WhoBlA 94*
Shumsky, Zena *ConAu 43NR*
Shumsky, Zena 1926- *WrDr 94*
Shumway, Bettie Sue 1924- *WhoAmP 93*
Shumway, Frank Ritter 1906-1992 *WhAm 10*
Shumway, Jim 1939- *WhoAmP 93*
Shumway, Lee d1959 *WhoHol 92*
Shumway, Lowell 1894- *WhAm 10*
Shumway, Mary *DrAPF 93*
Shumway, Mary Louise 1926- *WhoMW 93*
Shumway, Norman D. 1934- *WhoAm 94, WhoAmP 93, WhoWest 94*
Shumway, Norman Edward 1923- *IntWW 93, WhoScEn 94*
Shumway, Sandra Elisabeth 1952- *WhoScEn 94*
Shumway, Sara J. 1952- *WhoScEn 94*
Shumway, Walter d1965 *WhoHol 92*
Shunk, Thomas H. 1954- *WhoAmL 94*
Shunn, Maxine Faye 1917- *WhoAmP 93*
Shunney, Andrew 1921- *WhoAmA 93N*
Shunpike, Francisco 1920- *WrDr 94*
Shupack, Paul Martin 1940- *WhoAm 94*
Shupe, Lloyd Merle 1918- *WhoScEn 94*
Shupler, Ronald Steven 1954- *WhoScEn 94*
Shupnik, Fred Joseph 1916- *WhoAmP 93*
Shupp, Franklin Richard 1934- *WhoAm 94*
Shupp, Mike 1946- *EncSF 93*
Shur, George Michael 1942- *WhoAmL 94*
Shur, Michael 1942- *WhoAm 94*
Shur, Walter 1929- *WhoAm 94, WhoFI 94, WhoIns 94*
Shurchkov, Igor Olegovich 1950- *LngBDD*
Shurden, Frank David 1940- *WhoAmP 93*
Shurick, Edward Palmes 1912- *WhoAm 94*
Shurin, Aaron *DrAPF 93*
Shurina, Robert David 1957- *WhoScEn 94*
Shurley, Jay Talmadge 1917- *WhoAm 94*
Shurman, Laurence Paul Lyons 1930- *Who 94*
Shurn, Peter Joseph, III 1946- *WhoAmL 94*
Shurpin, Sol 1914- *IntMPA 94*
Shurrager, Phil Sheridan 1907- *WhoAm 94*
Shurtleff, Akiko Aoyagi 1950- *WhoWest 94*
Shurtleff, Leonard Grant 1940- *WhoAm 94, WhoAmP 93*
Shurtleff, Malcolm C. 1922- *WhoAm 94, WhoScEn 94*
Shurtleff, Robert *WhAmRev*
Shurtliff, Marvin Karl 1939- *WhoAm 94*
Shuryak, Edward Vladimirovich 1948- *WhoScEn 94*
Shu Shengyou *WhoPRCh 91*
Shushkevich, Stanislau Stanislavavich 1934- *IntWW 93*
Shushkewich, Kenneth Wayne 1952- *WhoScEn 94*
Shusted, Thomas J. 1926- *WhoAmP 93*
Shuster, Alvin 1930- *WhoAm 94*
Shuster, Bud 1932- *CngDr 93, WhoAmP 93*
Shuster, E. G. 1932- *WhoAm 94*
Shuster, Frank 1916-
 See Wayne and Schuster *WhoCom*
Shuster, Herbert Victor 1924- *WhoAm 94*
Shuster, Joe *EncSF 93*
Shuster, John A. 1939- *WhoFI 94*
Shuster, Joseph 1914-1992 *AnObit 1992*
Shuster, Lewis J. *WhoAm 94*
Shuster, Melvin R. 1946- *WhoAmL 94*
Shuster, Robert G. 1927- *WhoAm 94*
Shusterman, Murray H. 1913- *WhoAm 94*
Shusterman, Nathan 1927- *WhoFI 94*
Shusterman, Neal 1962- *WrDr 94*
Shusterman, Neal Douglas 1962- *WhoAm 94*
Shusterman, Richard (M.) 1949- *WrDr 94*
Shute, Ben E. 1905-1986 *WhoAmA 93N*
Shute, Charles Cameron Donald 1917- *Who 94*
Shute, David 1931- *WhoAmL 94*
Shute, Nevil 1899-1960 *EncSF 93*
Shute, Richard Emil 1938- *WhoAm 94*
Shute, Roberta E. *WhoAmA 93*
Shuteev, Vasily Ivanovich 1949- *LngBDD*
Shuter, Adrienne Joan 1937- *WhoMW 93*
Shuter, Bruce D. 1940- *WhoAm 94*
Shuter, Edward 1728?-1776 *NewGrDO*
Shutiak, James 1932- *WhoAm 94*
Shu Ting 1952- *BlmGWL, IntWW 93, WhoPRCh 91 [port]*
Shutler, Kenneth Eugene 1938- *WhoAm 94, WhoAmL 94, WhoWest 94*
Shutler, Mary Elizabeth 1929- *WhoAm 94*
Shutler, (Ronald) Rex (Barry) 1933- *Who 94*
Shu Tong 1906- *IntWW 93*
Shutt, Bob 1951- *WhoAmP 93*
Shutt, Buffy *IntMPA 94*
Shutt, Edwin Holmes, Jr. 1927- *WhoAm 94*
Shutta, Ethel d1976 *WhoHol 92*
Shutta, Jack d1957 *WhoHol 92*
Shuttee, Anne Katherine 1955- *WhoAmL 94*
Shuttle, Penelope 1947- *BlmGWL*
Shuttle, Penelope (Diane) 1947- *EncSF 93, Who 94, WrDr 94*
Shuttlesworth, Fred L. 1922- *WhoBlA 94*
Shuttleworth, Baron 1948- *Who 94*
Shuttleworth, Anne Margaret 1931- *WhoScEn 94*
Shuttleworth, Joseph 1819-1883 *DcNaB MP*
Shuttleworth, Paul Red *DrAPF 93*
Shutz, Byron Christopher 1928- *WhoAm 94*
Shutz, Byron Theodore 1899-1988 *WhAm 10*
Shvarts, Evgeny (Lvovich) 1896-1958 *IntDcT 2*
Shvyrkov, Vladislav V. 1931- *WhoWest 94*
Shwachman, Ben 1937- *WhoWest 94*
Shwartz, Robert N. 1950- *WhoAm 94*
Shwartz, Ronald Bruce 1953- *WhoAmL 94*
Shwartz, Susan M(artha) 1949- *EncSF 93*
Shwayder, Reva Clamage d1993 *NewYTBS 93*
Shwayder, Sandra *DrAPF 93*
Shwe, Hla 1934- *WhoAsA 94*
Shy, Gus d1945 *WhoHol 92*
Shyer, Charles Richard 1941- *WhoAm 94*
Shyer, John D. 1956- *WhoAmL 94*
Shyllon, Prince E.N. 1943- *WhoAmL 94*
Shyre, Paul 1926-1989 *WhAm 10*
Shyshkin, Viktor Ivanovych 1952- *LngBDD*
Shyy, Wei 1955- *WhoAm 94, WhoScEn 94*
Siad Barre, Mohamed 1921- *IntWW 93*
Siaguru, Anthony 1946- *IntWW 93*
Siale Bileka, Silvestre *IntWW 93*
Sialom, Sedat Sami 1940- *WhoFI 94*
Siamas, John S. 1944- *WhoAmL 94*
Siamis, Janet Neal 1938- *WhoAmA 93*
Siani, Sabrina *WhoHol 92*
Siano, Jerry J. *WhoAm 94*
Siantz, Mary Lou deLeon 1947- *WhoHisp 94*
Siart, William Eric Baxter 1946- *WhoAm 94, WhoFI 94, WhoWest 94*
Sias, John B. 1927- *WhoAm 94*
Siatkowski, Ronald E. 1950- *WhoScEn 94*
Siau, John Finn 1921- *WhoAm 94*
Siavellis, Michael P. 1938- *WhoAmL 94*
Siazon, Domingo L. 1939- *IntWW 93*
Sibal, Nicolas Villadolid 1960- *WhoAsA 94*
Sibbald, John Ristow 1936- *WhoAm 94, WhoFI 94*
Sibbald, Peter Frank Aubrey 1928- *Who 94*
Sibbet, Lorraine Alberta 1939- *WhoMW 93*
Sibbio, Michael Gregory 1955- *WhoWest 94*
Sibble, Edward Matson, Jr. 1951- *WhoAmL 94*
Sibeck, David G. *WhoScEn 94*
Sibelius, Celia d1971 *WhoHol 92*
Sibelius, Jean (Julius Christian) 1865-1957 *NewGrDO*
Sibener, Steven Jay 1954- *WhoMW 93*
Siberell, Anne Hicks *WhoAmA 93*
Siberry, John William Morgan 1913- *Who 94*
Siberry, Michael *WhoHol 92*
Siberry, William Richard 1950- *Who 94*
Sibert, Ernest 1941- *WhoAm 94*
Sibigtroth, Joseph Clarence 1915- *WhoAm 94*
Sibilla d1766 *NewGrDO*
Sibilski, Peter John 1959- *WhoScEn 94*
Sibirskaya, Nadia d1980 *WhoHol 92*
Sibiryakov, Lev (Mikhailovich) 1869-1942 *NewGrDO*
Sibley, Alden Kingsland 1911- *WhoAm 94*
Sibley, Antoinette *WhoHol 92*
Sibley, Antoinette 1939- *IntDcB [port], IntWW 93, Who 94*
Sibley, Celestine 1917- *WhoAm 94*
Sibley, Charles Gald 1917- *WhoAm 94, WhoScEn 94, WorScD*
Sibley, Charles Kenneth 1921- *WhoAmA 93*
Sibley, David Emile 1935- *WhoFI 94*
Sibley, David McAdams 1947- *WhoAmP 93*
Sibley, Dawn Bunnell 1939- *WhoAm 94*
Sibley, Deborah Ellen Thurston 1957- *WhoScEn 94*
Sibley, Horace Holden 1939- *WhoAm 94*
Sibley, Jack Norris 1948- *WhoAmL 94*
Sibley, James Malcolm 1919- *WhoAm 94*
Sibley, Joan d1993 *NewYTBS 93*
Sibley, Lucy d1945 *WhoHol 92*
Sibley, Mark Anderson 1950- *WhoAm 94*
Sibley, Peter E. 1944- *WhoAmL 94*
Sibley, Sylvan Ray 1932- *WhoAmP 93*
Sibley, William Arthur 1932- *WhoAm 94*
Sibley, William Austin 1925- *WhoAm 94*
Sibley, William Hart 1898- *WhAm 10*
Sibley, William Ruck, III 1952- *WhoFI 94*
Sibley, Willis Elbridge 1930- *WhoAm 94*

Sibolski, John Alfred, Jr. 1946- WhoFI 94
Sibomana, Adrien IntWW 93
Siboni, Erik Anthon Valdemar 1828-1892 NewGrDO
Siboni, Giuseppe (Vincenzo Antonio) 1780-1839 NewGrDO
Sibson, Caroline ConAu 141, SmATA 74
Sibson, Francis H(enry) 1899- EncSF 93
Sica 1932- WhoAmA 93
Sica, John 1962- WhoAmL 94
Sica, Richard Vincent 1945- WhoAmL 94
Sicard, Abbe Roch Ambroise Cucurron 1742-1822 EncDeaf
Sicard, Guillermo Rafael 1937- WhoMW 93
Sicard, Raymond Edward 1948- WhoMW 93
Sicari, Joseph R. WhoHol 92
Sicat, Gerardo P. 1935- IntWW 93
Sich, Rupert (Leigh) 1908- Who 94
Sichel, Beatrice Bonne 1934- WhoMW 93
Sichel, Werner 1934- WhoFI 94, WrDr 94
Sicherl, Pavle 1935- WhoAm 94, WhoScEn 94
Sicherman, Carol 1937- WrDr 94
Sicherman, Marvin Allen 1934- WhoAm 94, WhoMW 93
Sichewski, Vernon Roger 1942- WhoScEn 94
Sichko, Vasyl LngBDD
Sichol, Marcia W. 1940- WrDr 94
Siciliani, Francesco 1911- NewGrDO
Siciliano, Enzo 1934- IntWW 93
Siciliano, Rocco C. 1922- WhoAmP 93
Siciliano, Rocco Carmine 1922- WhoAm 94, WhoFI 94
Sick, Gary Gordon 1935- WhoFI 94
Sick, William Norman, Jr. 1935- WhoAm 94, WhoFI 94
Sickel, Joan Sottilare 1941- WhoWest 94
Sickels, Robert Judd 1931- WhoAm 94
Sickels, William Loyd 1936- WhoWest 94
Sickinghe, Jonkheer Feyo Onno Joost 1926- IntWW 93
Sickle, Cody T. 1949- WhoAm 94
Sickler, Michael Allan 1945- WhoAmA 93
Sickles, Carlton R. 1921- WhoAmP 93
Sickman, Jessalee Bane 1905- WhoAmA 93
Sicoli, Dan DrAPF 93
Sicuro, Natale Anthony 1934- WhoAm 94
Sidamon-Eristoff, Anne Phipps 1932- WhoAm 94
Sidamon-Eristoff, Constantine 1930- WhoAm 94, WhoAmL 94
Si Dao, Ruang 1943- BlmGWL
Sidar, Thomas Wilson 1949- WhoFI 94
Sidarevic, Anatol Michailavic 1948- LngBDD
Sidaris, Andy 1932- IntMPA 94
Sidbury, Harold David 1940- WhoBlA 94
Siddal, Elizabeth Eleanor 1829-1862 DcNaB MP
Siddall, Cecil James 1894- WhAm 10
Siddall, Norman 1918- IntWW 93, Who 94
Siddayao, Corazon Morales 1932- WhoScEn 94
Sidd-Champion, Diane WhoAmL 94
Siddeley Who 94
Siddeley, Randle Who 94
Sidders, Patrick Michael 1940- WhoAm 94
Siddhartha c. 563BC-483BC HisWorL [port]
Siddhi Savetsila, Air Chief Marshal 1919- IntWW 93
Siddiky, B. A. 1915- IntWW 93
Siddiqi, M. Raziuddin 1908- IntWW 93
Siddiqi, Obaid 1932- Who 94
Siddiqui, Aamir 1964- WhoMW 93
Siddiqui, Abdul Mannan 1935- IntWW 93
Siddiqui, Aleem Abdul 1948- WhoAsA 94
Siddiqui, Ehtisham Uddin Ahmad 1954- WhoAsA 94
Siddiqui, Faruq Mahmud Anam 1951- WhoAsA 94
Siddiqui, Habib 1953- WhoAsA 94
Siddiqui, Maqbool Ahmad 1941- WhoScEn 94
Siddiqui, Salimuzzaman 1897- Who 94
Siddle, Kenneth 1947- Who 94
Siddon, Thomas Edward 1941- IntWW 93, WhoAm 94
Siddons, Arthur Harold Makins 1911- Who 94
Siddons, Sarah 1755-1831 BlmGEL [port]
Siddoway, Henry Ralph 1905- WhoWest 94
Siddoway, Thane R. 1953- WhoAmP 93
Sidebottom, Edward John 1918- Who 94
Sidel, Ruth WrDr 94
Sidell, Robert Leonard 1930- WhoFI 94
Sidell, Ron Daniel 1941- Who 94
Sidells, Arthur F. 1907- WhoAm 94
Sideman, Eva Stern WhoMW 93
Siden, Franklin 1922- WhoAmA 93
Sidenbladh, Goran 1912- IntWW 93
Sider, Earl Morris 1928- WhoAm 94
Sideris, Alexander 1898-1978 WhoAmA 93N
Siderowicz, Joseph Adam 1953- WhoFI 94
Sides, Charles 1949- WhoAmP 93
Sides, Jack Davis, Jr. 1939- WhoAmL 94
Sides, James Ralph 1936- WhoFI 94
Sides, Julian Earl, Jr. 1925- WhoAmP 93
Sidey, Ernest (Shaw) 1913- Who 94
Sidey, Hugh Swanson 1927- WhoAm 94
Sidey, Thomas Kay Stuart 1908- Who 94
Sidgwick, Henry 1838-1900 EncEth
Sidhu, Gurbachan Singh 1920- IntWW 93
Sidhu, Gurmel Singh 1943- WhoAsA 94, WhoWest 94
Sidhu, Jay S. WhoAm 94, WhoFI 94
Sidhu, Mohan 1950- WhoWest 94
Sidhu, Nancy Dayton 1941- WhoFI 94
Sidhu, Victor S. 1938- WhoFI 94, WhoWest 94
Sidhwa, Bapsi 1938- BlmGWL
Sidi, Jacques Albert 1928- WhoAmP 93
Sidi Baba, Dey Ould 1921- IntWW 93
Sidibe, Sy Oumou Louise WhoWomW 91
Sidi Bombay WhWE
Sidikman, David S. WhoAmP 93
Sidjakov, Nicolas 1924- WhoAm 94
Sidki, Aziz 1920- IntWW 93
Sidle, Roy C. 1948- WhoScEn 94
Sidley, Michael I. 1961- WhoWest 94
Sidlin, Murry 1940- IntWW 93
Sidman, Kenneth Robert 1945- WhoScEn 94
Sidman, Robert John 1943- WhoAm 94, WhoAmL 94
Sidmouth, Viscount 1914- Who 94
Sidnam, William Robert 1934- WhoWest 94
Sidney Who 94
Sidney, Ann WhoHol 92
Sidney, George d1945 WhoHol 92
Sidney, George 1916- IntMPA 94
Sidney, Joan Seliger DrAPF 93
Sidney, Margaret BlmGWL
Sidney, Mary BlmGWL
Sidney, Neilma 1922- WrDr 94
Sidney, Philip 1554-1586 BlmGEL [port]
Sidney, Scott d1928 WhoHol 92
Sidney, Steffi 1937- WhoHol 92
Sidney, Sylvia 1910- IntMPA 94, WhoAm 94, WhoHol 92
Sidney, William Wright 1929- WhoFI 94
Sido, Kevin Richard 1951- WhoAm 94, WhoAmL 94
Sidon, Claudia Marie 1946- WhoMW 93
Sidon, Weslea DrAPF 93
Sidor, David S. 1945- WhoAmL 94
Sidorov, Evgeniy Yurievich 1938- IntWW 93
Sidorov, Evgeny Yurevich 1940- LngBDD
Sidorov, Veniamin Aleksandrovich 1930- IntWW 93
Sidransky, Herschel 1925- WhoAm 94
Sidransky, Ruth 1929- WrDr 94
Sidun, Nancy Marie 1955- WhoMW 93
Sidwell, Martindale 1916- Who 94
Sidwell, Robert William 1937- WhoAm 94
Sidwell, Scott Edward 1950- WhoAmP 93
Sie, Banja T. Who 94
Siebel, Mathias Paul WhoAm 94
Siebel, Richard Allan 1939- WhoAmP 93, WhoMW 93
Sieben, Harry A., Jr. 1943- WhoAmP 93
Sieben, Harry Albert, Jr. 1943- WhoAmL 94
Sieben, Todd 1945- WhoAmP 93
Sieber, Byron Paul 1954- WhoMW 93
Sieber, Ferdinand 1822-1895 NewGrDO
Sieber, Maria WhoHol 92
Sieber, Martin Helmut 1958- WhoMW 93
Sieber, Roy 1923- WhoAmA 93
Siebers, Tobin Anthony 1953- WhoMW 93
Siebert, Bill 1947- WhoAmP 93
Siebert, Calvin D. 1934- WhoAm 94
Siebert, Charles 1938- WhoHol 92
Siebert, Chrisha Louise 1967- WhoMW 93
Siebert, Diane Dolores 1948- WhoAm 94, WhoWest 94
Siebert, Karl Joseph 1945- WhoAm 94, WhoScEn 94
Siebert, Mark Conrad 1955- WhoFI 94
Siebert, Muriel WhoAm 94
Siebert, Sherill 1944- WhoAmL 94
Siebert, Stephanie Ray 1949- WhoFI 94, WhoWest 94
Siebert, William McConway 1925- WhoAm 94
Sieberts, Jan Kristian 1942- WhoWest 94
Siebman, Clyde Moody 1958- WhoAmL 94
Siebner, Herbert 1925- WhoAmA 93
Siebrand, Willem 1932- WhoScEn 94
Sieck, Greg R. 1956- WhoWest 94
Siedlecki, Nancy Therese 1954- WhoMW 93
Siedlecki, Peter DrAPF 93
Siedlecki, Walter Francis, Jr. 1955- WhoMW 93
Siedler, Arthur James 1927- WhoAm 94
Siedow, Jim WhoHol 92
Siedzikowski, Henry Francis 1953- WhoAmL 94
Siefers, Robert George 1945- WhoAm 94, WhoMW 93
Siefert, Diane Lynn 1948- WhoFI 94
Siefert, Richard Carl 1946- WhoAm 94
Siefert-Kazanjian, Donna WhoFI 94
Sieff Who 94
Sieff, David Daniel 1939- Who 94
Sieff, Jeanloup 1933- IntWW 93
Sieff, John Alexander 1923- WhoAm 94
Sieff Of Brimpton, Baron Who 94
Sieff Of Brimpton, Baron 1913- IntWW 93
Siefkin, Randy Richardson 1942- WhoAmP 93
Siefkin, William Charles 1946- WhoFI 94
Sieg, Albert Louis 1930- WhoAm 94
Sieg, Robert Lawrence 1938- WhoAmA 93
Siegal, Allan Marshall 1940- WhoAm 94
Siegal, Burton Lee 1931- WhoAm 94, WhoMW 93, WhoScEn 94
Siegal, Jacob J. 1929- WhoAm 94
Siegal, Joel Davis 1937- WhoAmL 94
Siegal, Marvyn Emanuel 1930- WhoFI 94
Siegal, Rita Goran 1934- WhoAm 94
Siegal, Ronny Jo 1947- WhoAmL 94
Siegan, Bernard Herbert 1924- WhoAm 94, WhoAmL 94
Siegbahn, Kai Manne Borje 1918- IntWW 93, Who 94, WhoScEn 94
Siegel, Abraham J. 1922- WhoFI 94
Siegel, Adrian 1898-1978 WhoAmA 93N
Siegel, Alan Michael 1938- WhoAm 94
Siegel, Allen George 1934- WhoAm 94
Siegel, Arthur 1908- WhoAm 94
Siegel, Arthur Bernard 1932- WhoAmL 94
Siegel, Arthur Herbert 1938- WhoFI 94
Siegel, Barry Alan 1944- WhoMW 93
Siegel, Barry Norman 1929- WhoFI 94
Siegel, Bart Howard 1958- WhoFI 94
Siegel, Benjamin M. 1916-1990 WhAm 10
Siegel, Bernard d1940 WhoHol 92
Siegel, Bernard Louis 1938- WhoAmL 94
Siegel, Bernard S(hepard) 1932- WrDr 94
Siegel, Bernie S. 1932- CurBio 93 [port]
Siegel, Betty Lentz 1931- WhoAm 94
Siegel, Bradd N. 1952- WhoAm 94
Siegel, Bradd Nathan 1952- WhoAmL 94
Siegel, Brock Martin 1947- WhoWest 94
Siegel, Charles 1944- WhoAm 94
Siegel, Cynthia WhoMW 93
Siegel, David Donald 1931- WhoAm 94
Siegel, (Leo) Dink WhoAmA 93
Siegel, Don d1991 WhoHol 92
Siegel, Don 1912-1991 WhAm 10
Siegel, Donald R. WhoAmL 94
Siegel, Edward Charles 1947- WhoMW 93
Siegel, Edward M. 1934- WhoFI 94
Siegel, Fran 1960- WhoAmA 93
Siegel, Frederic Richard 1932- WhoAm 94
Siegel, Gary 1949- WhoAmP 93
Siegel, Gary Howard 1944- WhoFI 94
Siegel, George Henry 1926- WhoAm 94
Siegel, Harold Aryai 1931- WhoAmL 94, WhoFI 94
Siegel, Harvey Robert 1928- WhoMW 93
Siegel, Herbert Bernard 1934- WhoAm 94
Siegel, Herbert Jay 1928- WhoAm 94
Siegel, Howard Jerome 1942- WhoAm 94, WhoAmL 94
Siegel, Ira Theodore 1944- IntWW 93, WhoAm 94
Siegel, Jack Morton 1922- WhoAm 94
Siegel, Jack S. 1946- WhoAm 94, WhoScEn 94
Siegel, Jeffrey Norton 1942- WhoAm 94, WhoAmL 94
Siegel, Jeremy James 1945- WhoFI 94
Siegel, Jerome Richard 1948- WhoAmL 94
Siegel, Jerry 1914- EncSF 93
Siegel, Joan I. DrAPF 93
Siegel, Joel Steven 1943- WhoAm 94
Siegel, Kenneth B. 1951- WhoAmL 94
Siegel, Laurence 1928- WhoAm 94
Siegel, Laurence B. 1954- WhoFI 94
Siegel, Lawrence Iver 1925- WhoFI 94
Siegel, Lloyd H. 1928- WhoAm 94
Siegel, Louis Pendleton 1942- WhoAm 94
Siegel, Marc Monroe 1916- WhoAm 94
Siegel, Mark Alan 1944- WhoAmP 93
Siegel, Mark Jordan 1949- WhoAmL 94
Siegel, Martin 1941-1972 EncSF 93
Siegel, Martin Jay 1942- WhoAm 94, WhoFI 94
Siegel, Marvin 1935- WhoAm 94
Siegel, Melvyn Harry 1944- WhoFI 94
Siegel, Michael Elliot 1942- WhoScEn 94, WhoWest 94
Siegel, Milton P. 1911- IntWW 93, WhoAm 94, WhoFI 94
Siegel, Mo J. 1949- WhoAm 94, WhoFI 94, WhoWest 94
Siegel, Morton Kallos 1924- WhoAm 94
Siegel, Myron E. 1951- WhoAmL 94
Siegel, Nathaniel Harold 1929- WhoAm 94
Siegel, Ned Lawrence 1951- WhoFI 94
Siegel, Neil Barry 1942- WhoAmL 94
Siegel, Paul N. 1916- WrDr 94
Siegel, Richard Allen 1927- WhoFI 94, WhoScEn 94
Siegel, Richard D. 1944- WhoAmL 94
Siegel, Richard David 1939- WhoAm 94
Siegel, Richard Steven 1955- WhoScEn 94
Siegel, Robert DrAPF 93
Siegel, Robert A. d1993 NewYTBS 93
Siegel, Robert Charles 1947- WhoAm 94
Siegel, Robert Gordon 1950- WhoAm 94, WhoAmL 94
Siegel, Robert Ted 1928- WhoAm 94
Siegel, Ruth Willard 1927- WhoAmP 93
Siegel, Samuel 1930- WhoAm 94, WhoFI 94
Siegel, Sheldon C. 1922- WhoAm 94
Siegel, Shirley Jean 1925- WhoWest 94
Siegel, Sid 1927- WhoAm 94
Siegel, Stanley 1935- WhoFI 94
Siegel, Stanley 1941- WhoAm 94, WhoAmL 94
Siegel, Sylvia 1946- WhoAmL 94
Siegel, Thomas Louis 1939- WhoAm 94
Siegelman, Don 1946- WhoAmP 93
Siegelman, Kenneth DrAPF 93
Siegenthaler, Kurt Allen 1962- WhoAmL 94
Sieger, Charles 1944- WhoAm 94
Sieger, Charles Martin 1946- WhoAm 94
Sieger, Edward Regis 1957- WhoScEn 94
Siegert, Barbara Marie 1935- WhoFI 94
Siegert, Cyril Laurence 1923- Who 94
Siegesmund, Richard WhoAmA 93
Siegfried, David Charles 1942- WhoAm 94
Siegfried, Michael George 1946- WhoMW 93
Siegfried, Richard Stephen 1938- WhoAm 94
Siegfried, Robert Edwin 1922- WhoAm 94
Siegfried, William 1925- WhoWest 94
Siegfried, Willis Albert, Jr. 1944- WhoAm 94, WhoAmL 94
Siegl, Theodor d1976 WhoAmA 93N
Sieglaff, Charles Lewis 1927- WhoScEn 94
Siegler, Alan DrAPF 93
Siegler, Howard Matthew 1936- WhoAm 94
Siegler, Mark 1941- WhoAm 94, WhoScEn 94
Siegler, Melody Victoria Stephanie 1948- WhoScEn 94
Siegler, Samuel Lewis, II 1954- WhoAmL 94
Siegler, Thomas Edmund 1934- WhoAm 94
Sieglitz, Frank E. 1944- WhoAmL 94
Sieglitz, Georg 1851-1917 NewGrDO
Siegman, Anthony Edward 1931- WhoAm 94, WhoScEn 94
Siegman, Henry 1930- WhoAm 94
Siegmann, George d1928 WhoHol 92
Siegmeister, Elie 1909-1991 NewGrDO, WhAm 10
Siegmund, Frederick 1930- WhoAmL 94
Siegrist, J. Brent 1952- WhoAmP 93
Siegrist, Lundy 1925-1985 WhoAmA 93N
Siehl, Richard W. 1952- WhoAm 94
Siehr, Gustav 1837-1896 NewGrDO
Siekert, Robert George 1924- WhoAm 94
Siekevitz, Philip 1918- IntWW 93, WhoAm 94
Siekierzynski, Sally J. 1968- WhoMW 93
Siekman, Elizabeth Nancy Ann 1942- WhoMW 93
Siekmann, Donald Charles 1938- WhoAm 94, WhoFI 94
Siekmann, Jorg Hans 1941- WhoScEn 94
Sielicka-Gracka, Maria Teresa WhoWomW 91
Sieloff, Christina Lyne WhoScEn 94
Sieloff, Ronald Bruce 1944- WhoAmP 93
Sieman, Frank WhoHol 92
Siemaszko, Casey 1961- IntMPA 94, WhoHol 92
Siembieda, Matthew John 1945- WhoAm 94, WhoAmL 94
Siemens, Ernst Werner von 1816-1892 WorInv
Siemens, George Robert, Jr. WhoAmP 93
Siemens, Lois Ann WhoWest 94
Siemens, Richard Ernest 1938- WhoWest 94
Siemens, (Karl) Wilhelm 1823-1883 WorInv
Siemer, Deanne C. 1940- WhoAmP 93
Siemer, Deanne Clemence 1940- WhoAm 94, WhoAmL 94
Siemer, Fred Harold 1937- WhoFI 94
Siemer, Paul Jennings 1946- WhoAm 94, WhoFI 94

Siemering, Arthur John 1941- *WhoMW 93*
Siemiatycki, Jack 1946- *WhoAm 94, WhoScEn 94*
Siemon, Joyce Marilyn 1944- *WhoAmL 94*
Siemon-Burgeson, Marilyn M. 1934- *WhoWest 94*
Siemonn, Mabel *NewGrDO*
Siems, Margarethe 1879-1952 *NewGrDO*
Siener, Joseph Frank 1938- *WhoScEn 94*
Siener, William Harold 1945- *WhoAm 94*
Sienkiewicz, Bill 1958- *EncSF 93*
Sienkiewicz, Frank Frederick 1965- *WhoScEn 94*
Sienkiewicz, Henryk (Adam Aleksander Pius) 1846-1916 *RfGShF*
Sienkiewicz-Mercer, Ruth 1950- *WrDr 94*
Siepi, Cesare 1923- *NewGrDO, WhoAm 94, WhoHol 92*
Siepmann, Mary Aline 1912- *IntWW 93, Who 94*
Sieracki, Aloysius Alfred 1929- *WhoMW 93*
Sieracki, Michael Edward 1955- *WhoScEn 94*
Sierakowska, Izabella *WhoWomW 91*
Sierck, Alexander Wentworth 1940- *WhoAmL 94*
Siercks, Randolph LaVerne 1946- *WhoWest 94*
Sierles, Frederick Stephen 1942- *WhoAm 94*
Sieroty, Alan Gerald 1930- *WhoAmP 93*
Sierra, Angel M. 1942- *WhoHisp 94*
Sierra, Antonio M. *WhoHisp 94*
Sierra, Christine Marie 1950- *WhoHisp 94*
Sierra, Diana Myra 1963- *WhoHisp 94*
Sierra, Edward 1956- *WhoMW 93*
Sierra, Gregory *WhoHol 92*
Sierra, Jose Javier 1957- *WhoHisp 94*
Sierra, Joseph Arthur 1953- *WhoHisp 94*
Sierra, Margarita d1963 *WhoHol 92*
Sierra, Miriam Durant 1945- *WhoHisp 94*
Sierra, Paul Alberto 1944- *WhoHisp 94*
Sierra, Paul J. *WhoHisp 94*
Sierra, Rafael Armelio 1949- *WhoHisp 94*
Sierra, Roberto 1953- *NewGrDO*
Sierra, Ruben Angel 1965- *WhoAm 94, WhoBlA 94, WhoHisp 94, WhoWest 94*
Sierra, Selma 1957- *WhoHisp 94*
Sierra, Stella *BlmGWL*
Sierra-Zorita, Radames 1955- *WhoHisp 94*
Siery, Raymond Alexander 1951- *WhoScEn 94*
Sies, Jerry 1941- *WhoAmL 94*
Siess, Alfred Albert, Jr. 1935- *WhoFI 94, WhoScEn 94*
Siess, Chester Paul 1916- *WhoAm 94*
Sietsema, Brian *NewYTBS 93 [port]*
Sietsema, Jelt *WhoAmP 93*
Sietsema, William Kendall 1955- *WhoScEn 94*
Sieu, Benny Lou 1951- *WhoAsA 94*
Sievan, Maurice 1898-1981 *WhoAmA 93N*
Sieveking, Lance 1896-1972 *EncSF 93*
Siever, Raymond 1923- *WhoAm 94, WhoScEn 94*
Sievers, Eric Scott 1957- *WhoBlA 94*
Sievers, Georgia Ann 1924- *WhoAmP 93*
Sievers, Robert H. 1941- *WhoAm 94*
Sievers Wicke, Hugo K. 1903- *IntWW 93*
Sievert, Dorothy Carlton 1946- *WhoMW 93*
Sievert, Frederick J. 1948- *WhoIns 94*
Sievert, Jan *EncSF 93*
Sievert, Ludwig 1887-1966 *NewGrDO*
Sievert, Lynnette Carlson 1957- *WhoScEn 94*
Sieverts, Frank Arne 1933- *WhoAm 94*
Sieverts, Thomas C. W. 1934- *IntWW 93*
Siewers, Christian Nathaniel 1947- *WhoFI 94*
Siewert, Robin Noelle 1956- *WhoFI 94*
Siewiorek, Daniel Paul 1946- *WhoAm 94*
Siface *NewGrDO*
Siferwas, John fl. 1400- *DcNaB MP*
Siffert, Robert Spencer 1918- *WhoAm 94*
Sifford, Benton Alexander, III 1955- *WhoWest 94*
Sifford, Charlie 1922- *WhoBlA 94*
Sifford, Darrell Charles 1931-1992 *WhAm 10*
Sifford, Joyce Wendal 1925- *WhoAmP 93*
Sifft, Josie Marie 1954- *WhoWest 94*
Sifneos, Peter Emanuel 1920- *WhoAm 94*
Sifontes, Jose E. 1926- *WhoHisp 94*
Sifton, Charles Proctor 1935- *WhoAm 94, WhoAmL 94*
Sifton, David Whittier 1940- *WhoAm 94*
Sifton, Patricia Anne 1929- *WhoAm 94*
Sifuentes, Elida *WhoHisp 94*
Sigal, Clancy *DrAPF 93*
Sigal, Clancy 1926- *WrDr 94*
Sigal, Michael Stephen 1942- *WhoAm 94, WhoAmL 94, WhoMW 93*
Sigal, Sanford David 1964- *WhoWest 94*
Sigala, Jerald F. 1945- *WhoHisp 94*
Sigala, Ralph 1942- *WhoHisp 94, WhoWest 94*
Sigala, Stephanie Childs 1947- *WhoAmA 93*
Sigales, Bartomeu 1934- *WhoScEn 94*
Sigall, Harold Fred 1943- *WhoAm 94*
Sigaloff, Eugene d1960 *WhoHol 92*
Sigalos, George Peter 1964- *WhoAm 94*
Sigalow, Steven E. 1950- *WhoAm 94*
Sigaran, Mamerto 1934- *WhoHisp 94*
Sigband, Norman Bruce 1920- *WhoAm 94, WrDr 94*
Sigea, Luisa c. 1531-1560 *BlmGWL*
Sigegyth fl. 8th cent.- *BlmGWL*
Sigel, Marshall Elliot 1941- *WhoAm 94, WhoFI 94*
Sigel, Mola Michael 1920- *WhoAm 94*
Sigel, Steven Michael 1952- *WhoFI 94*
Sigelbaum, Harvey C. 1937- *WhoIns 94*
Sigety, Charles Birge 1952- *WhoFI 94*
Sigety, Charles Edward 1922- *WhoAm 94, WhoFI 94*
Sigfried, Stefan Bertil 1955- *WhoScEn 94*
Siggins, Jack Arthur 1938- *WhoAm 94*
Sigholtz, Sara O'Meara *WhoAm 94*
Sight, Daniel Eugene 1957- *WhoMW 93*
Sights, James Dale 1940- *WhoAmP 93*
Siginer, Dennis A. 1943- *WhoScEn 94*
Sigismondo, Giuseppe 1739-1826 *NewGrDO*
Sigismund, Violet M. *WhoAmA 93*
Siglar, Harold L. 1950- *WhoMW 93*
Sigler, Andrew Clark 1931- *WhoAm 94, WhoFI 94*
Sigler, Hollis 1948- *WhoAmA 93*
Sigler, I. Garland 1932- *WhoBlA 94*
Sigler, Jay Adrian 1933- *WhoAm 94*
Sigler, John William 1946- *WhoWest 94*
Sigler, LeRoy Walter 1926- *WhoAm 94*
Sigler, Paul Benjamin 1934- *WhoAm 94, WhoScEn 94*
Sigler, William Franklin 1909- *WhoAm 94, WhoScEn 94, WhoWest 94*
Siglienti, Sergio 1926- *IntWW 93*
Sigman, Eugene M. 1928- *WhoAm 94*
Sigman, Melvin Monroe 1935- *WhoWest 94*
Sigmier, Charles C. 1898- *WhAm 10*
Sigmon, Joyce Elizabeth 1935- *WhoMW 93*
Sigmon, Robert Leland 1929- *Who 94*
Sigmon, Teresa Jeanne 1956- *WhoAmL 94*
Sigmond, Carol Ann 1951- *WhoAmL 94*
Sigmond, Robert M. 1920- *WhoAm 94*
Sigmund, Diane J. 1943- *WhoAmL 94*
Sigmund, Paul Eugene 1929- *WhoAm 94*
Signer, Gregory Richard 1951- *WhoAmL 94*
Signer, William A. 1949- *WhoAmP 93*
Signor, Philip White 1950- *WhoWest 94*
Signor, Randy Michael *DrAPF 93*
Signorella, Frank 1947- *AstEnc*
Signorelli, Ernest Leonard 1929- *WhoAmL 94*
Signorelli, Joseph 1961- *WhoScEn 94*
Signorelli, Tom *WhoHol 92*
Signoret, Gabriel d1937 *WhoHol 92*
Signoret, Jean *WhoHol 92*
Signoret, Simone d1985 *WhoHol 92*
Signoretti, Rudolph George 1930- *WhoScEn 94*
Signorile, Claudio 1937- *IntWW 93*
Signorile, Vincent Anthony 1959- *WhoAmL 94*
Signorini, Francesca Caccini *NewGrDO*
Signorino, Charles A. 1932- *WhoFI 94*
Signorovitch, Dennis James 1945- *WhoFI 94*
Sigogne, Philippe 1943- *IntWW 93*
Sigourney, Andre R *WrDr 94*
Sigourney, Lydia Huntley 1791-1865 *BlmGWL*
Sigrist, Helmut 1919- *IntWW 93*
Sigua, Tengiz Ippolitovich 1939- *IntWW 93*
Sigueiros, Placido d1946 *WhoHol 92*
Siguenza, Herbert 1959- *WhoHisp 94*
Siguenza, Peter C. *WhoAmP 93*
Siguenza, Peter C., Jr. *WhoAmL 94*
Siguion-Reyna, Leonardo 1921- *WhoAmL 94*
Siguler, George William 1947- *WhoAm 94*
Sigur, Wanda Anne Alexander 1958- *WhoBlA 94*
Sigurd, Jacques d1987 *WhoHol 92*
Sigurdardottir, Johanna 1942- *IntWW 93, WhoWomW 91*
Sigurdsen, Gertrud 1923- *IntWW 93*
Sigurdson, Edwin D. 1942- *WhoFI 94*
Sigurdsson, Haraldur 1939- *WhoAm 94, WhoScEn 94*
Sigurdsson, Jon 1941- *IntWW 93*
Sigurdsson, Niels P. 1926- *IntWW 93, Who 94*
Sigurdsson, Thordur Baldur 1929- *WhoFI 94, WhoScEn 94*
Sigwart, Charles Dallas 1941- *WhoMW 93*
Sigworth, George Fredrick 1956- *WhoAmP 93*
Sigworth, Oliver F(rederic) 1921- *WrDr 94*
Sih, Andrew 1954- *WhoScEn 94*
Sih, Charles John 1933- *WhoMW 93, WhoScEn 94*
Sihag, Ram K. 1950- *WhoAsA 94*
Sihanouk, Norodom *IntWW 93*
Sihanouk, Norodom 1922- *CurBio 93 [port], NewYTBS 93*
Sihler, William Wooding 1937- *WhoAm 94, WhoFI 94*
Siig, Arvi 1938- *IntWW 93*
Siilasvuo, Ensio 1922- *IntWW 93*
Siimes, Jouko 1960- *WhoFI 94*
Siirala, Aarne Johannes 1919- *WrDr 94*
Siirola, Jeffrey John 1945- *WhoScEn 94*
Siitari, David William 1952- *WhoMW 93*
Sijpesteijn, Pieter Johannes 1934- *IntWW 93*
Sijthoff, Hendrik Albert Henri 1915- *IntWW 93*
Sikand, Chander Kumari 1923- *WhoAsA 94*
Siker, Ephraim S. 1926- *WhoAm 94*
Sikes, Alfred C. *WhoAmP 93*
Sikes, C. David
See Boston *ConMus 11*
Sikes, Cynthia 1951- *WhoHol 92*
Sikes, Melvin Patterson 1917- *WhoBlA 94*
Sikes, Robert L. F. 1906- *WhoAm 94*
Sikes, Shirley *DrAPF 93*
Sikivou, Semesa Koroikilai 1917- *IntWW 93*
Sikka, Satish 1945- *WhoWest 94*
Sikkema, Doetze Jakob 1944- *WhoScEn 94*
Sikkema, Ken *WhoAmP 93*
Sikkenga, Diane Elizabeth 1965- *WhoMW 93*
Sikking, James B. 1934- *IntMPA 94*
Sikking, James B. 1935- *WhoHol 92*
Siklos, Csaba 1941- *IntWW 93*
Sikma, Jack 1955- *BasBi*
Sikora, Eugene Stanley 1924- *WhoFI 94*
Sikora, Evelyn Marie 1947- *WhoMW 93*
Sikora, James Robert 1945- *WhoWest 94*
Sikora, John Michael 1953- *WhoFI 94*
Sikora, Karol 1948- *Who 94*
Sikora, Mary Helene 1948- *WhoMW 93*
Sikora, Richard Innes 1927- *WhoAm 94*
Sikora, Suzanne Marie 1952- *WhoMW 93*
Sikorovsky, Eugene Frank 1927- *WhoAm 94, WhoAmL 94, WhoFI 94*
Sikorski, Gerry 1948- *WhoAmP 93*
Sikorski, Wladyslaw 1881-1943 *HisWorL [port]*
Sikorsky, Igor 1889-1972 *WorInv*
Sikoryak, Kim Eugene 1949- *WhoWest 94*
Sikri, Sarv Mittra d1992 *Who 94N*
Silage, Dennis Alex 1946- *WhoScEn 94*
Silagi, Barbara Weibler 1930- *WhoFI 94*
Silagi, Selma 1916- *WhoAm 94*
Silak, Cathy R. 1950- *WhoAmL 94*
Silane, Frank A. 1945- *WhoAmL 94*
Silani, Vincenzo 1952- *WhoScEn 94*
Silao, Ray A. 1967- *WhoAsA 94*
Sila-On, Amaret 1933- *IntWW 93*
Silard, Bela (A.) 1900- *ConAu 140*
Silas, Cecil Jesse 1932- *IntWW 93, WhoAm 94, WhoFI 94*
Silas, James 1949- *BasBi*
Silas, Paul 1943- *BasBi*
Silas, Paul Theron 1943- *WhoBlA 94*
Silas, Richard A. 1938- *WhoIns 94*
Silas-Butler, Jacqueline Ann 1959- *WhoBlA 94*
Silayev, Ivan Stepanovich 1930- *IntWW 93*
Silbajoris, Frank Rimvydas 1926- *WhoAm 94*
Silbaugh, Preston Norwood 1918- *WhoAmL 94*
Silbaugh, Rudy Lamont 1930- *WhoAmP 93, WhoMW 93*
Silber, Diana 1936- *WrDr 94*
Silber, Irwin 1925- *WhoWest 94*
Silber, Joan *DrAPF 93*
Silber, John (Robert) 1926- *WrDr 94*
Silber, John Robert 1926- *IntWW 93, WhoAm 94*
Silber, Mark 1946- *ConAu 43NR*
Silber, Maurice 1922- *WhoAmA 93*
Silber, Nina 1959- *ConAu 140*
Silber, Norman Jules 1945- *WhoAm 94, WhoAmL 94*
Silber, Sherman J(ay) 1941- *WrDr 94*
Silber, Stephen Robert 1944- *Who 94*
Silber, William L. 1942- *WrDr 94*
Silberberg, Donald H. 1934- *WhoAm 94, WhoScEn 94*
Silberberg, Henry J. 1944- *WhoAm 94*
Silberberg, Mary Bickley 1956- *WhoIns 94*
Silberberg, Michael Cousins 1940- *WhoAmL 94*
Silberberg, Rein 1932- *WhoScEn 94*
Silberberg, Richard Howard 1951- *WhoAm 94, WhoAmL 94*
Silberberg, Steven Richard 1956- *WhoScEn 94*
Silberg, Jay Eliot 1941- *WhoAm 94*
Silberg, Nicolas *WhoHol 92*
Silberg, Richard *DrAPF 93*
Silbergeld, Alan Mark 1940- *WhoAmL 94*
Silbergeld, Arthur F. 1942- *WhoAm 94, WhoAmL 94, WhoWest 94*
Silbergeld, Ellen Kovner 1945- *WhoAm 94, WhoScEn 94*
Silberman, Alan Harvey 1940- *WhoAm 94, WhoAmL 94*
Silberman, Arlene *WrDr 94*
Silberman, Arthur 1929- *WhoAmA 93*
Silberman, Charles Eliot 1925- *WhoAm 94, WrDr 94*
Silberman, Curt C. 1908- *WhoAmL 94*
Silberman, H. Lee 1919- *WhoAm 94, WhoFI 94*
Silberman, Irwin Alan 1932- *WhoWest 94*
Silberman, James Henry 1927- *WhoAm 94*
Silberman, Jerome *ConAu 142*
Silberman, John Alan 1951- *WhoAm 94, WhoAmL 94*
Silberman, Laurence Hirsch 1935- *CngDr 93, IntWW 93, WhoAm 94, WhoAmL 94, WhoAmP 93*
Silberman, Leonard J. 1947- *WhoAmL 94*
Silberman, Robert A. S. 1945- *WhoAm 94*
Silberman, Rosalie Gaull 1937- *WhoAm 94, WhoAmP 93, WhoFI 94*
Silbersack, John (Walter) 1954- *EncSF 93*
Silbersack, Mark Louis 1946- *WhoAm 94, WhoAmL 94*
Silberstein, Alan Mark 1947- *WhoAm 94*
Silberstein, David M. 1960- *WhoAmL 94*
Silberstein-Storfer, Muriel Rosoff *WhoAmA 93*
Silberston, (Zangwill) Aubrey 1922- *IntWW 93, Who 94*
Silbert, Amy Foxman 1953- *WhoWest 94*
Silbert, Layle *DrAPF 93*
Silbert, Lisa d1965 *WhoHol 92*
Silbey, Joel Henry 1933- *WhoAm 94*
Silbey, Robert James 1940- *WhoAm 94*
Silbiger, Alexander 1935- *WrDr 94*
Silby, Donald Wayne 1948- *WhoAm 94*
Silcox, Gordon Bruce 1938- *WhoFI 94*
Silcox, Roy W. 1955- *WhoWest 94*
Silecchia, Jerome A. 1941- *WhoScEn 94*
Silen, William 1927- *WhoAm 94*
Silence, Scott 1964- *WhoWest 94*
Silent, William T. 1945- *EncSF 93*
Siler, Brenda Claire 1953- *WhoBlA 94*
Siler, Charles Lewis 1929- *WhoAmP 93*
Siler, Eugene Edward, Jr. 1936- *WhoAm 94, WhoAmL 94, WhoAmP 93*
Siler, Freddie Bush 1956- *WhoBlA 94*
Siler, Joyce B. 1945- *WhoBlA 94*
Siler, Lari Field *DrAPF 93*
Siler, Patrick W. 1939- *WhoAmA 93*
Siler, Todd (Lael) 1953- *WhoAmA 93*
Siler, Walter Orlando, Jr. 1920- *WhoAm 94*
Siler-Khodr, Theresa Marie 1947- *WhoAm 94*
Silesky, Barry *DrAPF 93*
Silesky, Barry 1949- *WrDr 94*
Siles Zuazo, Hernan 1914- *IntWW 93*
Silets, Harvey Marvin 1931- *WhoAm 94, WhoAmL 94, WhoMW 93*
Siletti, Mario d1964 *WhoHol 92*
Siletti, Mario d1991 *WhoHol 92*
Silfen, David M. 1945- *WhoAm 94, WhoFI 94*
Silfugarian, George Martin 1956- *WhoMW 93*
Silfvast, William T. 1937- *WhoAm 94*
Silhavy, Thomas Joseph 1948- *WhoAm 94*
Silins, Andrejs Roberts 1940- *WhoScEn 94*
Silins, Astrida Ilga 1928- *WhoMW 93*
Silins, Ints M. 1942- *WhoAm 94, WhoAmP 93*
Silipigni, Alfredo 1931- *WhoAm 94*
Silja, Anja 1935- *NewGrDO*
Silja, Anja 1940- *IntWW 93*
Siljak, Dragoslav D. 1933- *WhoAm 94*
Silk, Alvin John 1935- *WhoAm 94*
Silk, Bertram Edward 1931- *WhoAm 94*
Silk, David *Who 94*
Silk, (Robert) David *Who 94*
Silk, Dennis (Peter) 1928- *WrDr 94*
Silk, Dennis Raoul Whitehall 1931- *Who 94*
Silk, Eleana S. 1951- *WhoAm 94*
Silk, Frederick C.Z. 1934- *WhoAm 94, WhoFI 94*
Silk, George 1916- *WhoAm 94*
Silk, Gerald 1947- *WrDr 94*
Silk, Joseph (Ivor) 1942- *WrDr 94*
Silk, Leonard S. 1918- *WrDr 94*
Silk, Leonard Solomon 1918- *WhoAm 94*
Silk, Marshall Bruce 1955- *WhoScEn 94, WhoWest 94*

Silverman, Stephen M. 1951- WhoAm 94, WrDr 94
Silverman, Syd 1932- WhoAm 94
Silverman, William 1945- WhoAmL 94
Silverman, Zita 1949- WhoIns 94
Silvern, Charles d1979 WhoHol 92
Silvern, Leonard C(harles) 1919- WrDr 94
Silvern, Leonard Charles 1919- WhoScEn 94, WhoWest 94
Silvernail, Clarke d1930 WhoHol 92
Silvers, David 1949- WhoAm 94
Silvers, Donald Eugene 1929- WhoWest 94
Silvers, E. Randall 1951- WhoWest 94
Silvers, Eileen S. 1948- WhoAm 94, WhoAmL 94
Silvers, Louis WhoHol 92
Silvers, Phil d1985 WhoHol 92
Silvers, Phil 1912-1985 WhoCom
Silvers, Robert Benjamin 1929- WhoAm 94
Silvers, Sid d1976 WhoHol 92
Silvers, Susan WhoHol 92
Silvers, Willys Kent 1929- WhoAm 94
Silvershein, Joel Michael 1961- WhoAmL 94
Silverstein, Alan Jay 1946- WhoScEn 94
Silverstein, Arthur Matthew 1928- WhoAm 94
Silverstein, Barbara Ann 1947- WhoAm 94
Silverstein, Carl Joseph 1928- WhoAmL 94
Silverstein, Charles 1956- WhoAmL 94
Silverstein, Elizabeth Blume 1892-1991 WhAm 10
Silverstein, Elliot 1927- IntMPA 94
Silverstein, Howard Alan 1947- WhoAm 94, WhoFI 94
Silverstein, Ida WhoAmA 93
Silverstein, Ira B. 1947- WhoAmL 94
Silverstein, Jack 1915- WhoAmP 93
Silverstein, Joseph Harry 1932- WhoAm 94, WhoWest 94
Silverstein, Leonard Lewis 1922- WhoAm 94
Silverstein, Louis 1919- WhoAm 94
Silverstein, Martin Elliot 1922- WhoWest 94
Silverstein, Maurice 1912- IntMPA 94
Silverstein, Michael Jay 1955- WhoMW 93
Silverstein, Nathan Milton 1924- WhoAmL 94
Silverstein, Richard WhoAm 94
Silverstein, Robert Alan 1959- SmATA 77 [port]
Silverstein, Robert Selnick 1956- WhoAmL 94
Silverstein, Samuel Charles 1937- WhoAm 94
Silverstein, Seth 1939- WhoScEn 94
Silverstein, Shel(by) 1932- WrDr 94
Silverstein, Shelby 1932- WhoAm 94
Silverstein, Steven David 1966- WhoWest 94
Silverstein, Theodore 1904- WrDr 94
Silverstone, David 1932- WhoAm 94
Silverstone, David Edward 1948- WhoScEn 94
Silverstone, Dorothy d1993 NewYTBS 93
Silverstone, Leon Martin 1939- WhoAm 94
Silverthorn, Robert Sterner, Jr. 1948- WhoAm 94
Silverthorne, Michael James 1941- WhoAm 94
Silverton, Mike DrAPF 93
Silvertooth, Dennis Carl 1957- WhoAmA 93
Silvertooth-Stewart, John 1952- WhoAmP 93
Silverwood, Don d1928 WhoHol 92
Silverwood, Jane 1941- WrDr 94
Silverwood-Cope, Maclachlan Alan Carl d1993 Who 94N
Silvester, Frank ConAu 42NR
Silvester, Frederick John 1933- Who 94
Silvester, John Andrew 1950- WhoWest 94
Silvester, P(eter) P. 1935- WrDr 94
Silvester, Peter (John) 1934- WrDr 94
Silvester, Peter Peet 1935- WhoAm 94
Silvestre, Ami WhoHol 92
Silvestre, Armando WhoHol 92
Silvestri, Antonio Michael 1940- WhoScEn 94
Silvestri, Michael Joseph 1958- WhoFI 94
Silvestri, Philip Salvatore 1944- WhoAmL 94
Silvestri, Stephen Michael 1954- WhoAmL 94
Silvestrini, Achille 1923- IntWW 93
Silvestro, Clement Mario 1924- WhoAm 94
Silvey, Anita Lynne 1947- WhoAm 94
Silvey, Daniel Joseph 1956- WhoFI 94
Silvey, Edward 1937- WhoBlA 94
Silvey, Len 1943- WhoWest 94
Silvey, Ray Newton 1935- WhoMW 93
Silvia, Charles E. WhoAmP 93
Silvia, John David 1960- WhoWest 94
Silvia, John Edwin 1948- WhoFI 94
Silvis, Donn Eugene 1942- WhoWest 94
Silvis, Randall DrAPF 93
Silvis, Randall 1950- WrDr 94
Silvoso, Joseph Anton 1917- WhoAm 94
Silz, Walter 1894- WhAm 10
Sim, Ah Tee 1944- WhoScEn 94
Sim, Alastair d1976 WhoHol 92
Sim, Craig Stephen 1942- WhoAm 94
Sim, Dave 1958- EncSF 93
Sim, Gerald 1925- WhoHol 92
Sim, J. Ronald 1943- WhoAmL 94
Sim, John Cameron 1911-1990 WhAm 10
Sim, John Kim-Chye 1957- WhoAsA 94
Sim, John Mackay d1993 Who 94N
Sim, Katharine Phyllis 1913- WrDr 94
Sim, Richard Guild 1944- WhoFI 94
Sim, Robert Wilson 1944- WhoFI 94
Sim, Sheila 1922- WhoHol 92
Sim, Steven P. 1951- WhoAmL 94
Sima, Edward Donald 1929- WhoFI 94, WhoWest 94
Sima, Oskar d1969 WhoHol 92
Simaan, Marwan A. 1946- WhoAm 94, WhoScEn 94
Simai, Mihaly 1930- IntWW 93
Simak, Clifford D(onald) 1904-1988 EncSF 93
Siman, Jaime Ernesto 1954- WhoWest 94
Simandle, Jerome B. 1949- WhoAm 94, WhoAmL 94
Simandy, Jozsef 1916- NewGrDO
Simanek, Otto d1967 WhoHol 92
Simanek, Vilim 1942- WhoScEn 94
Simatos, Nicholas Jerry 1948- WhoScEn 94
Simatupang, Tahi Bonar 1920- IntWW 93
Si-ma-yi Ai-mai-ti WhoPRCh 91
Simbanaiye, Artemon 1935- IntWW 93
Simbomana, Adrien IntWW 93
Simburg, Earl Joseph 1915- WhoWest 94
Simchak, Matthew Stephen 1947- WhoAm 94
Simches, Seymour Oliver 1919- WhoAm 94
Simckes, Lazare Seymore DrAPF 93
Simcoe, John Graves 1752-1806 AmRev, WhAmRev
Simcox, Carroll E(ugene) 1912- WrDr 94
Simcox, Craig Dennis 1939- WhoAm 94
Simcox, Edwin Jesse 1945- WhoAmP 93
Simcox, Jesse Willard 1915- WhoAmP 93
Simcox, Richard Alfred 1915- Who 94
Sime, Donald Rae 1926- WhoAm 94
Sime, James Thomson 1927- WhoScEn 94
Sime, Mary 1911- WrDr 94
Simek, Vasek WhoHol 92
Simel, Elaine WhoAmA 93
Simenon, Georges 1903-1989 WhAm 10
Simensky, Melvin 1946- WhoAmL 94
Simeon, II 1937- IntWW 93
Simeon, John Edmund Barrington 1911- Who 94
Simeon, John Power Barrington 1929- Who 94
Simeon, Rosa Elena 1943- WhoWomW 91
Simeone, Fiorindo Anthony 1908-1990 WhAm 10
Simeone, Joseph J. 1921- WhoMW 93
Simeone, Reginald Nicola 1927- Who 94
Simeon Negrin, Rosa Elena 1943- IntWW 93, WhoScEn 94
Simeonov, Konstantin Arsen'yevich 1910-1987 NewGrDO
Simeons, Charles Fitzmaurice Creighton 1921- Who 94
Simeral, William Goodrich 1926- WhoAm 94
Simes, Dimitri Konstantin 1947- WhoAm 94
Simes, Stephen Mark 1951- WhoMW 93
Simha, Bharat Kesher 1934- Who 94
Simha, Ettia WhoWomW 91
Simic, Charles DrAPF 93
Simic, Charles 1938- IntWW 93, WhoAm 94, WrDr 94
Simien, Clyde Ray 1960- WhoAmL 94
Simien, Cynthia Regina 1952- WhoAmP 93
Simini, Joseph Peter 1921- WhoWest 94
Siminovitch, Louis 1920- IntWW 93, Who 94, WhoAm 94, WhoScEn 94
Siminski, Kenneth E. d1993 NewYTBS 93
Siminuk, Mark Anthony 1956- WhoWest 94
Simion, Eugen Ioan 1933- IntWW 93
Simionato, Giulietta 1910- NewGrDO
Simionov, Alexandru 1950- WhoAmA 93
Simis, Konstantin 1919- WrDr 94
Simis, Theodore Luckey 1924- WhoAm 94
Simison, Anne Marie 1947- WhoMW 93
Simitiere, Pierre Du WhAmRev
Simitis, Constantine 1936- IntWW 93
Simkanich, John Joseph 1941- WhoAmL 94
Simkin, Morris N. 1941- WhoFI 94
Simkin, Peter Anthony 1935- WhoAm 94
Simkin, Phillips M. 1944- WhoAmA 93
Simkin, Steven 1947- WhoAmL 94
Simkin, Tom 1933- WrDr 94
Simkin, William E. 1907-1992 WhAm 10
Simkins, Charles Anthony Goodall 1912- Who 94
Simkins, George Christopher 1924- WhoBlA 94
Simkins, Jolene Marie 1945- WhoWest 94
Simkins, Leon Jack 1927- WhoAm 94
Simkowitz, Michael Abraham 1938- WhoAm 94
Simmel, Edward Clemens 1932- WhoWest 94
Simmel, Marianne Lenore WhoAm 94
Simmelkjaer, Robert T. WhoBlA 94
Simmen, Rosmarie 1938- WhoWomW 91
Simmer, Karen 1957- WhoMW 93
Simmerman, Jim DrAPF 93
Simmermon, James Everett 1926- WhoAm 94
Simmers, Graeme Maxwell 1935- Who 94
Simmie, James (Martin) 1941- WrDr 94
Simmins, John James 1961- WhoScEn 94
Simmon, Jacqueline A. 1955- WhoAmL 94
Simmon, Vincent Fowler 1943- WhoFI 94
Simmond, Sam d1967 WhoHol 92
Simmonds, Annette d1959 WhoHol 92
Simmonds, James Gordon 1935- WhoAm 94
Simmonds, John 1942- WrDr 94
Simmonds, John Andrew 1939- Who 94
Simmonds, Kennedy Alphonse 1936- IntWW 93, Who 94
Simmonds, Kenneth Royston 1927- Who 94
Simmonds, Martha 1624-1665? DcNaB MP
Simmonds, Posy 1945- Who 94
Simmonds, Richard James 1944- Who 94
Simmonds, Stanley WhoHol 92
Simmonds Ballentine, Rosalie 1949- WhoAmP 93
Simmons, Adele Smith 1941- IntWW 93, WhoAm 94
Simmons, Alan Gerald 1936- Who 94
Simmons, Alan Jay 1924- WhoAm 94
Simmons, Alan John 1950- WhoAm 94
Simmons, Albert Bufort, Jr. 1943- WhoBlA 94
Simmons, Allison Paul 1934- WhoAmP 93
Simmons, Annie Marie 1949- WhoBlA 94
Simmons, Anthony IntMPA 94
Simmons, Barbara Lett 1927- WhoAmP 93
Simmons, Belva Tereshia 1927- WhoBlA 94
Simmons, Betty Jo 1936- WhoFI 94
Simmons, Bill 1941- WhoAm 94
Simmons, Brad Lee 1960- WhoFI 94
Simmons, Bradley Williams 1941- WhoFI 94, WhoWest 94
Simmons, Carroll Day 1896- WhAm 10
Simmons, Cecil Lamar 1946- WhoAmP 93
Simmons, Charles DrAPF 93
Simmons, Charles 1924- WhoAm 94
Simmons, Charles Bedford, Jr. 1956- WhoAmL 94
Simmons, Charles William 1938- WhoBlA 94
Simmons, Clayton Lloyd 1918- WhoBlA 94
Simmons, Cleatous J. 1944- WhoAmL 94
Simmons, Cleda Marie 1927- WhoAmA 93
Simmons, Clinton Craig 1947- WhoFI 94
Simmons, Clyde 1964- WhoAm 94
Simmons, D(avid) R(oy) 1930- WrDr 94
Simmons, Dan 1948- EncSF 93, WrDr 94
Simmons, David 1947- IntWW 93
Simmons, David Norman 1957- WhoAmL 94
Simmons, Donald M. 1935- WhoBlA 94
Simmons, Doreen Anne 1949- WhoAmL 94
Simmons, Earl Melvin 1931- WhoBlA 94
Simmons, Edward Dwyer 1924-1987 WhAm 10
Simmons, Edwin Howard 1921- WhoAm 94
Simmons, Ellamae 1919- WhoBlA 94
Simmons, Elroy, Jr. 1928- WhoAm 94
Simmons, Eric 1920-1981 WhoBlA 94N
Simmons, Eric 1930- Who 94
Simmons, Esmeralda 1950- WhoBlA 94
Simmons, Francis Blair 1930- WhoAm 94
Simmons, Frederick Scott 1925- WhoFI 94
Simmons, Gail Lindsay 1949- WhoAm 94, WhoAmL 94
Simmons, Gary Paul 1941- WhoAmA 93
Simmons, Gene 1949- WhoAm 94, WhoHol 92
Simmons, Geoffrey 1943- EncSF 93
Simmons, George Michael 1943- WhoWest 94
Simmons, Gerald W. 1943- WhoAmL 94
Simmons, Geraldine Crossley 1939- WhoBlA 94
Simmons, Glenn Ballard 1897- WhAm 10
Simmons, Glenn Reuben 1928- WhoFI 94
Simmons, Guy Lintorn 1925- Who 94
Simmons, Hardwick 1940- WhoAm 94, WhoFI 94
Simmons, Harold C. 1931- WhoAm 94, WhoFI 94
Simmons, Harold Lee 1947- WhoBlA 94
Simmons, Harris H. 1954- WhoAm 94, WhoWest 94
Simmons, Harry Dady 1938- WhoScEn 94
Simmons, Howard Ensign, Jr. 1929- WhoScEn 94
Simmons, Howard Koorken 1902- WhoAmL 94
Simmons, Howard L. 1938- WhoBlA 94
Simmons, Isaac Tyrone 1946- WhoBlA 94
Simmons, J. Gerald 1929- WhoAm 94
Simmons, Jack WrDr 94
Simmons, Jack 1915- Who 94
Simmons, James WhoScEn 94
Simmons, James (Stewart Alexander) 1933- WrDr 94
Simmons, James Boyd 1944- WhoFI 94
Simmons, James E. 1927- WhoBlA 94
Simmons, James Richard 1939- WhoBlA 94
Simmons, Jarette 1927- WhoAmP 93
Simmons, Jean 1929- IntMPA 94, IntWW 93, Who 94, WhoAm 94, WhoHol 92
Simmons, Jean Elizabeth Margaret 1914- WhoAm 94
Simmons, Jesse Doyle 1926- WhoAm 94
Simmons, Jim 1916- WhoAmP 93
Simmons, John d1989 WhoHol 92
Simmons, John Barry Eves 1937- Who 94
Simmons, John Derek 1931- WhoAm 94, WhoFI 94
Simmons, John Emmett 1936- WhoBlA 94
Simmons, John Herbert 1938- WhoAmA 93
Simmons, John Kaul 1938- WhoAm 94
Simmons, John Wesley 1918- WhoAm 94
Simmons, Joseph 1923- WhoBlA 94
Simmons, Joseph Jacob, III 1925- WhoAm 94, WhoAmL 94, WhoAmP 93, WhoBlA 94, WhoFI 94
Simmons, Joseph Thomas 1936- WhoAm 94, WhoFI 94, WhoMW 93
Simmons, Joyce Hobson 1947- WhoBlA 94
Simmons, Julie Lutz WhoAmA 93
Simmons, Julius Caesar, Sr. 1925- WhoBlA 94
Simmons, Keith B. 1948- WhoAmL 94
Simmons, Kenneth H. 1933- WhoBlA 94
Simmons, Larry G. 1948- WhoIns 94
Simmons, Laurie 1949- WhoAmA 93
Simmons, Lee Guyton, Jr. 1938- WhoAm 94, WhoScEn 94
Simmons, Lee Howard 1935- WhoAm 94
Simmons, Leonard 1920- WhoBlA 94
Simmons, Lionel J. 1968- WhoBlA 94
Simmons, Marc (Steven) 1937- WrDr 94
Simmons, Marguerite Saffold 1954- WhoFI 94
Simmons, Marilyn Ann 1951- WhoMW 93
Simmons, Marshall Francis 1936- WhoIns 94
Simmons, Marvin Gene 1929- WhoAm 94
Simmons, Mary Jane WhoAmP 93
Simmons, Matty IntMPA 94
Simmons, Maurice Clyde 1957- WhoBlA 94
Simmons, Merle Edwin 1918- WhoAm 94
Simmons, Michael (George) 1937- Who 94
Simmons, Michael Paul 1953- WhoWest 94
Simmons, Miriam Quinn 1928- WhoAmP 93
Simmons, Mollie Lawanna 1962- WhoFI 94
Simmons, Neville Keith 1938- IntWW 93
Simmons, Noel Alexander 1947- WhoWest 94
Simmons, Paul A. 1921- WhoBlA 94
Simmons, Paul Barrett WhoAmP 93
Simmons, Paul Barrett 1942- WhoAm 94
Simmons, Paula Joan 1961- WhoWest 94
Simmons, Percy Slotsky 1906- WhoAmA 93
Simmons, Peter 1931- WhoAm 94, WhoAmL 94
Simmons, Ralph Oliver 1928- WhoMW 93
Simmons, Richard 1918- WhoHol 92
Simmons, Richard D. 1934- IntWW 93
Simmons, Richard De Lacey 1934- WhoAm 94
Simmons, Richard J. 1951- WhoAmL 94
Simmons, Richard Lloyd 1946- WhoFI 94
Simmons, Richard Milton Teagle 1948- WhoAm 94

Simmons, Richard P. 1931- WhoAm 94, WhoFI 94
Simmons, Richard Sheridan 1928-1991 WhAm 10
Simmons, Robert Arthur WhoScEn 94
Simmons, Robert J. 1962- WhoFI 94
Simmons, Robert Malcolm 1938- Who 94
Simmons, Robert Marvin 1959- WhoScEn 94
Simmons, Robert Ruhl 1943- WhoAmP 93
Simmons, Robert Wayne 1946- WhoWest 94
Simmons, Roberta G. 1937-1993 NewYTBS 93
Simmons, Ron WhoBlA 94
Simmons, Roy, Jr. WhoAm 94
Simmons, Roy William 1916- WhoAm 94, WhoFI 94, WhoWest 94
Simmons, Russell WhoBlA 94
Simmons, Russell 1957- WhoAm 94
Simmons, S. Dallas 1940- WhoAm 94, WhoBlA 94
Simmons, Samuel J. 1927- WhoBlA 94
Simmons, Samuel Lee 1929- WhoFI 94
Simmons, Samuel William 1907- WhoScEn 94
Simmons, Sarah R. 1948- WhoAmL 94
Simmons, Shalon Girlee 1966- WhoScEn 94
Simmons, Sheila Anne 1965- WhoBlA 94
Simmons, Sherwin Palmer 1931- WhoAmL 94, WhoFI 94
Simmons, Shirley Davis 1941- WhoBlA 94
Simmons, Shirley J. DrAPF 93
Simmons, Shirley Mae 1931- WhoAmP 93
Simmons, Stanley Clifford 1927- Who 94
Simmons, Susan Annette 1947- WhoFI 94
Simmons, Sylvia J. 1935- WhoBlA 94
Simmons, Ted Conrad 1916- WhoWest 94
Simmons, Ted Lyle 1949- WhoAm 94
Simmons, Thelma M. 1942- WhoBlA 94
Simmons, Tifton 1945- WhoAm 94
Simmons, Vaughan Pippen 1922- WhoAm 94
Simmons, Victor J. 1945- WhoFI 94, WhoWest 94
Simmons, Warren Lee 1937- WhoWest 94
Simmons, William 1884-1949 WhoAmA 93N
Simmons, William 1932- WhoAm 94
Simmons, Willie WhoAmP 93
Simmons, Willie, Jr. 1939- WhoBlA 94
Simmons, Woodrow Jennings 1912- WhoAmP 93
Simmons-Edelstein, Dee 1937- WhoBlA 94
Simms, Albert L. 1931- WhoBlA 94
Simms, Amelia Moss 1954- WhoMW 93
Simms, Arthur Benjamin 1921- WhoAm 94
Simms, Carroll Harris 1924- WhoBlA 94
Simms, Charles Averill 1937- WhoAm 94
Simms, Darrell Dean WhoBlA 94
Simms, David John 1933- IntWW 93
Simms, Eric (Arthur) 1921- WrDr 94
Simms, Garth WhoAmP 93
Simms, Ginny 1916- WhoHol 92
Simms, Hilda 1920- WhoHol 92
Simms, James Edward 1943- WhoBlA 94
Simms, Jeffrey 1947- WhoAmP 93
Simms, John Carson 1952- WhoMW 93, WhoScEn 94
Simms, Larry 1934- WhoHol 92
Simms, Laura DrAPF 93
Simms, Leroy Alanson 1905-1992 WhAm 10
Simms, Margaret Constance 1946- WhoBlA 94
Simms, Maria Ester 1938- WhoFI 94, WhoWest 94
Simms, Maria Kay 1940- WhoWest 94
Simms, Mary Kay 1940- AstEnc
Simms, Mary Margaret 1952- WhoWest 94
Simms, Michael DrAPF 93
Simms, Phillip 1956- WhoAm 94
Simms, Priscilla Clayton 1933- WhoWest 94
Simms, Robert 1761-1843 DcNaB MP
Simms, Robert D. WhoAmP 93
Simms, Robert D. 1926- WhoAmL 94
Simms, Robert H. 1927- WhoBlA 94
Simms, Steven Rodney 1951- WhoWest 94
Simms, Stuart Oswald WhoBlA 94
Simms, W. Timothy 1943- WhoAmP 93
Simms, William 1763-1843 DcNaB MP
Simms, William E. 1944- WhoBlA 94
Simna, John Edward 1947- WhoMW 93
Simnel, Lambert 1477?-1525 BlmGEL
Simo, Ana Maria DrAPF 93
Simo, Ana Maria 1943- BlmGWL
Simo, Isabel-Clara 1943- BlmGWL
Simokaitis, Frank Joseph 1922- WhoAm 94
Simon Who 94
Simon, Viscount 1902- Who 94
Simon, Abe d1969 WhoHol 92
Simon, Albert 1924- WhoAm 94, WhoScEn 94
Simon, Alexander Nathan 1951- WhoAmP 93
Simon, Anton Yulyevich 1850-1916 NewGrDO
Simon, Armando P. 1914- WhoHisp 94
Simon, Art 1945- WhoAmP 93
Simon, Arthur 1930- WrDr 94
Simon, Arthur 1942- WhoAm 94
Simon, Arthur Emil 1895- WhAm 10
Simon, Arthur M. 1945- WhoAmL 94
Simon, Barney 1933- ConDr 93
Simon, Barry 1943- WhoAmL 94
Simon, Barry Philip 1942- WhoAm 94, WhoAmL 94
Simon, Barry S. 1949- WhoAmL 94
Simon, Bernard 1896-1980 WhoAmA 93N
Simon, Bernece Kern 1914- WhoAm 94
Simon, Brian 1915- Who 94
Simon, Bruce T. 1942- WhoAmP 93
Simon, Carl Paul 1945- WhoMW 93
Simon, Carly 1945- WhoAm 94
Simon, Caroline Klein d1993 NewYTBS 93 [port]
Simon, Cathy Jensen 1943- WhoAm 94
Simon, Charlie May 1897- WhAm 10
Simon, Claude 1913- IntWW 93
Simon, Claude (Eugene Henri) 1913- ConWorW 93
Simon, Claude (Henri Eugene) 1913- Who 94
Simon, David 1960- WrDr 94
Simon, David Alan 1967- WhoFI 94
Simon, David Alec Gwyn 1939- IntWW 93, Who 94
Simon, David Harold 1930- WhoAm 94, WhoWest 94
Simon, David L. 1946- WhoAmA 93
Simon, David Robert 1934- WhoAm 94, WhoAmL 94
Simon, Eckehard Peter 1939- WhoAm 94
Simon, Edith 1917- WrDr 94
Simon, Elaine 1944- WhoBlA 94
Simon, Eric Jacob 1924- WhoAm 94
Simon, Eric M. 1892-1978 WhoAmA 93N
Simon, Eric Michael 1959- WhoWest 94
Simon, Erik EncSF 93
Simon, Evelyn 1943- WhoAm 94
Simon, Francois d1982 WhoHol 92
Simon, Frederick Edward 1953- WhoScEn 94
Simon, Gary Leonard 1946- WhoScEn 94
Simon, Gene Lee 1936- WhoMW 93
Simon, Gerald Austin 1927- WhoFI 94, WhoWest 94
Simon, Harold 1930- WhoAm 94
Simon, Helene WhoAmA 93
Simon, Henry Francis 1944- WhoMW 93
Simon, Herbert WhoAm 94, WhoMW 93
Simon, Herbert A. 1916- IntWW 93
Simon, Herbert A(lexander) 1916- Who 94, WrDr 94
Simon, Herbert Alexander 1916- WhoAm 94, WhoFI 94
Simon, Herbert Bernheimer 1927- WhoAmA 93
Simon, Howard 1903-1979 WhoAmA 93N
Simon, Huey Paul 1923- WhoAm 94, WhoAmL 94, WhoFI 94
Simon, Jack Aaron 1919- WhoAm 94
Simon, Jacqueline Albert WhoAm 94
Simon, James F. 1939- WrDr 94
Simon, James Lowell 1944- WhoAm 94, WhoAmL 94
Simon, Jane DrAPF 93
Simon, Jewel Woodard 1911- WhoAmA 93, WhoBlA 94
Simon, Jimmy Louis 1930- WhoAm 94
Simon, Joanna 1940- WhoAm 94
Simon, John Bern 1942- WhoAm 94, WhoAmL 94
Simon, John Gerald 1928- WhoAm 94
Simon, John Ivan 1925- WhoAm 94
Simon, John Michael 1960- WhoAmL 94
Simon, John Oliver DrAPF 93
Simon, John P. 1953- WhoAm 94, WhoAmL 94
Simon, John Roger 1939- WhoAm 94, WhoAmL 94
Simon, John William 1949- WhoAmP 93
Simon, Jonathan Paul 1967- WhoFI 94
Simon, Joseph d1804 WhAmRev
Simon, Joseph Donald 1932- WhoBlA 94
Simon, Joseph Patrick 1932- WhoAm 94
Simon, Josette 1965- WhoHol 92
Simon, Julian L(incoln) 1932- WrDr 94
Simon, Julian Lincoln 1932- WhoAm 94
Simon, Justin Daniel 1947- WhoAm 94, WhoAmL 94
Simon, Karen Jordan 1953- WhoFI 94
Simon, Karen Leslie 1942- WhoAmP 93
Simon, Kate Grobsmith 1912-1990 WhAm 10
Simon, Kathryn Irene 1953- WhoFI 94
Simon, Kenneth Bernard 1953- WhoBlA 94
Simon, Kenneth Mark 1952- WhoAm 94
Simon, Lawrence P., Jr. 1943- WhoAmL 94
Simon, Lee Will 1940- WhoAm 94
Simon, Leonard WhoHol 92
Simon, Leonard Ronald 1936- WhoAmA 93
Simon, Leonard Samuel 1936- WhoAm 94, WhoFI 94
Simon, Lonnie A. 1925- WhoBlA 94
Simon, Lothar 1938- WhoAm 94
Simon, Madeleine Marshall d1993 NewYTBS 93
Simon, Madlen Goldstine 1952- WhoMW 93
Simon, Marc S. 1948- WhoAmL 94
Simon, Marilyn 1941- WhoAmL 94
Simon, Mark 1946- WhoAm 94, WhoFI 94
Simon, Martin Stanley 1926- WhoAm 94
Simon, Martine WhoHol 92
Simon, Marvin Kenneth 1939- WhoAm 94
Simon, Marvin Neil 1927- AmCulL
Simon, Maurya DrAPF 93
Simon, Maya WhoHol 92
Simon, Melvin 1926- IntMPA 94, WhoAm 94, WhoFI 94, WhoMW 93
Simon, Melvin I. 1937- WhoAm 94, WhoScEn 94
Simon, Michael A. 1936- WhoAmA 93, WrDr 94
Simon, Michael Alexander 1936- WhoAm 94
Simon, Michael J. 1947- WhoAmA 93
Simon, Michael Paul 1941- WhoMW 93
Simon, Michael Scott 1954- WhoAmL 94
Simon, Michel d1975 WhoHol 92
Simon, Michele Johanna 1957- WhoScEn 94
Simon, Mordecai 1925- WhoAm 94
Simon, Nancy Ruth 1960- WhoAmL 94
Simon, Neil 1927- IntMPA 94, IntWW 93, Who 94, WhoAm 94, WrDr 94
Simon, (Marvin) Neil 1927- ConDr 93, IntDcT 2 [port]
Simon, Netty D. WhoAmA 93
Simon, Norton 1907- WhoAmA 93
Simon, Norton 1907-1993 NewYTBS 93 [port]
Simon, Norton (Winfred) 1907-1993 CurBio 93N
Simon, Patricia d1993 NewYTBS 93
Simon, Paul 1928- CngDr 93, ConAu 43NR, IntWW 93, WhoAm 94, WhoAmP 93, WhoMW 93
Simon, Paul 1941- IntMPA 94, WhoAm 94
Simon, Paul 1942- IntWW 93, WhoHol 92
Simon, Paul Jerome 1954- WhoMW 93
Simon, Peregrine Charles Hugo 1950- Who 94
Simon, Peter E. WhoAm 94, WhoFI 94
Simon, Peter M. 1950- WhoAmP 93
Simon, Philip Alan 1951- WhoAmL 94
Simon, Ralph 1906- WhoAm 94
Simon, Ralph E. 1930- WhoWest 94
Simon, Raoul Bernard 1893- WhAm 10
Simon, Renee B. 1928- WhoAmP 93
Simon, Richard Alan 1938- WhoIns 94
Simon, Richard Hege 1911- WhoAmL 94, WhoWest 94
Simon, Richard K. 1944- WhoAmL 94
Simon, Richard Louis 1950- WhoWest 94
Simon, Rita J(ames) 1931- WrDr 94
Simon, Rita James 1931- WhoAm 94
Simon, Robert 1930- WrDr 94
Simon, Robert Barry 1952- WhoAmA 93
Simon, Robert F. WhoHol 92
Simon, Robert G. 1927- WhoAm 94
Simon, Robert Michael 1947- WhoMW 93
Simon, Robert Wayne 1947- WhoIns 94
Simon, Robin John Hughes 1947- Who 94
Simon, Roger Who 94
Simon, Roger (Mitchell) 1948- WrDr 94
Simon, Roger L(ichtenberg) 1943- WrDr 94
Simon, Roger Mitchell 1948- WhoAm 94
Simon, Ronald Charles 1951- WhoAm 94
Simon, Ronald I. 1938- WhoAm 94, WhoFI 94, WhoWest 94
Simon, Ronn W. 1963- WhoAmP 93
Simon, Rosalyn McCord 1946- WhoBlA 94
Simon, S. Sylvan d1951 WhoHol 92
Simon, Seymour 1915- WhoAm 94, WhoAmP 93, WhoMW 93
Simon, Seymour 1931- WrDr 94
Simon, Sheldon Weiss 1937- WhoAm 94, WhoWest 94, WrDr 94
Simon, Sidney 1917- WhoAmA 93
Simon, Simone 1910- WhoHol 92
Simon, Simone 1911- IntMPA 94
Simon, Sol d1940 WhoHol 92
Simon, Solomon Henry 1955- WhoScEn 94
Simon, Sophie WhoHol 92
Simon, Stephen G. 1942- WhoAmP 93
Simon, Steven David 1936- WhoWest 94
Simon, Susan Hewitt 1961- WhoAmL 94
Simon, Theodore Ronald 1949- WhoScEn 94
Simon, Ulrich Ernst 1913- Who 94
Simon, Victor 1946- WhoFI 94
Simon, Walter J. 1941- WhoBlA 94
Simon, Wayne Eugene 1928- WhoScEn 94
Simon, William 1929- WhoAm 94
Simon, William Dien 1954- WhoAmP 93
Simon, William E. 1927- WhoAmP 93
Simon, William Edward 1927- IntWW 93, Who 94
Simon, William Leonard 1930- WhoWest 94
Simonaitis, Richard Ambrose 1930- WhoScEn 94
Simonard, Andre d1992 IntWW 93N
Simon Calvo, Irma 1949- WhoWomW 91
Simondi, Michael P. 1944- WhoAmL 94
Simonds, Bruce 1895-1989 WhAm 10
Simonds, Charles Frederick 1945- WhoAmA 93
Simonds, Gordon 1945- WhoAmL 94
Simonds, John Edward 1935- WhoAm 94, WhoWest 94
Simonds, John Ormsbee 1913- WhoAm 94
Simonds, Marshall 1930- WhoAm 94
Simonds, Richard Kimball 1927- WhoFI 94
Simonds, Stephen Paige 1924- WhoAmP 93
Simondsen, Royce Paul 1954- WhoMW 93
Simonds Gooding, Anthony James Joseph 1937- IntWW 93, Who 94
Simone WhoAmA 93
Simone, Albert Joseph 1935- WhoAm 94
Simone, Beverly S. 1946- WhoAm 94, WhoMW 93
Simone, Gail Elisabeth 1944- WhoFI 94
Simone, James Nicholas 1956- WhoScEn 94
Simone, Joseph R. 1949- WhoAm 94, WhoAmL 94
Simone, Kirsten 1934- IntDcB
Simone, Nina 1933- IntWW 93, WhoHol 92
Simone, Nina 1935- ConMus 11 [port]
Simone, Nina 1940- WhoBlA 94
Simone, Peggy 1935- WhoAmP 93
Simone, Philip Anthony 1952- WhoFI 94
Simone, Thomas B. 1942- WhoAm 94
Simoneau, Leopold 1916- NewGrDO
Simoneau, Normand J. 1932- WhoAm 94
Simoneau, Richard WhoAmP 93
Simoneau, Wayne Anthony 1935- WhoAmP 93
Simonelli, Charles Francis 1925- WhoAm 94
Simonelli, Jerry 1952- WhoAmP 93
Simonelli, Michael Tarquin 1946- WhoMW 93
Simonet, Henri Francois 1931- IntWW 93, Who 94
Simonet, John Thomas 1926- WhoAm 94
Simonet, Martine WhoHol 92
Simonet, (Louis Marcel) Pierre 1934- Who 94
Simonet, Sebastian 1898-1948 WhoAmA 93N
Simonett, John E. WhoAmP 93
Simonett, John E. 1924- WhoAmL 94
Simonetta IntWW 93
Simonetta, Richard James 1946- WhoMW 93
Simonetti, Ignazio 1949- WhoScEn 94
Simonetti, Katherine 1965- WhoAmL 94
Simon-Girard, Aime d1950 WhoHol 92
Simon-Girard, Juliette 1859-1954 NewGrDO
Simoni, John Peter 1911- WhoAmA 93
Simoni, Mary Hope 1954- WhoMW 93
Simoni, Renato 1875-1952 NewGrDO
Simonian, John S. WhoAmP 93
Simonian, Judith 1945- WhoAmA 93
Simonian, Simon John 1932- WhoAm 94, WhoScEn 94
Simonides, Constantine B. 1934- WhoAm 94
Simonis, Adrianus J. 1931- IntWW 93
Simonis, Heide 1943- WhoWomW 91
Simonnard, Michel Andre 1933- WhoAm 94
Simonof, Nikolai d1973
See Simonov, Nikolai d1973 & Simonof, Nikolai d1973 WhoHol 92
Simonof, Nikolai d1973 WhoHol 92
Simonoff, Howard Stanley 1933- WhoAmL 94
Simon Of Glaisdale, Baron 1911- IntWW 93, Who 94
Simon Of Wythenshawe, Baron 1913- Who 94
Simonov, Nikolai d1973 & Simonof, Nikolai d1973 WhoHol 92
Simonov, Pavel Vasilyevich 1926- IntWW 93
Simonov, Ruben d1968 WhoHol 92

Simonov, Yevgeniy Rubenovich 1925-
IntWW 93
Simonov, Yuriy Ivanovich 1941-
IntWW 93
Simonov, Yury Ivanovich 1941-
NewGrDO
Simon Peter dc. 63 *HisWorL [port]*
Simons, Albert, Jr. 1918- *WhoAm 94*
Simons, Albert, III 1950- *WhoAm 94,
WhoAmL 94*
Simons, Barbara 1929- *WhoWomW 91*
Simons, Barbara Bluestein 1941-
WhoWest 94
Simons, Barbara M. 1929- *WhoAmL 94*
Simons, Beverley 1938- *ConDr 93,
WrDr 94*
Simons, Beverly 1938- *BlmGWL*
Simons, Charles Earl, Jr. 1916-
WhoAm 94, WhoAmL 94
Simons, David Stuart 1945- *WhoScEn 94*
Simons, Dolph Collins, Jr. 1930-
WhoAm 94
Simons, Elizabeth Reiman 1929-
WhoAm 94
Simons, Elwyn LaVerne 1930- *IntWW 93,
WhoAm 94, WhoScEn 94*
Simons, Eric Ward 1958- *WhoFI 94*
Simons, Gail Derese 1959- *WhoBlA 94*
Simons, Gale Gene 1939- *WhoAm 94,
WhoScEn 94*
Simons, Gordon Donald, Jr. 1938-
WhoAm 94
Simons, Helen 1930- *WhoMW 93*
Simons, Howard 1929-1989 *WhAm 10*
Simons, John H. 1939- *WhoAm 94*
Simons, John Philip 1934- *Who 94*
Simons, Karen Louise 1942- *WhoFI 94*
Simons, Kent Cobb 1935- *WhoFI 94*
Simons, Lawrence Brook 1924-
WhoAm 94, WhoAmP 93
Simons, Leonard Norman Rashall 1904-
WhoAm 94
Simons, Louise *DrAPF 93*
Simons, Louise Bedell 1912-1977
WhoAmA 93N
Simons, Lynn Osborn 1934- *WhoAm 94,
WhoAmP 93, WhoWest 94*
Simons, Marlene J. 1935- *WhoAmP 93,
WhoWest 94*
Simons, Mary Crescenzo *DrAPF 93*
Simons, (Alfred) Murray 1927- *Who 94*
Simons, Priscilla Margaret Smith 1951-
WhoMW 93
Simons, Ray D. 1946- *WhoFI 94*
Simons, Renee V. H. 1949- *WhoBlA 94*
Simons, Richard Andrew 1959-
WhoAmL 94
Simons, Richard D. 1927- *WhoAmP 93*
Simons, Richard Duncan 1927-
WhoAmA 94, WhoAmL 94
Simons, Rita Dandridge *BlkWr 2,
ConAu 141*
Simons, Robert Walter 1945- *WhoWest 94*
Simons, Sharon Kay 1947- *WhoMW 93*
Simons, Stephen 1938- *WhoAm 94,
WhoWest 94*
Simons, Steven Jay 1946- *WhoAm 94*
Simons, Thomas A., Jr. 1946-
WhoAmL 94
Simons, Thomas Cunningham 1928-1988
WhAm 10
Simons, Thomas W. 1938- *WhoAmP 93*
Simons, Thomas W(inston), Jr. 1938-
WrDr 94
Simonsen, Eric A. 1945- *WhoIns 94*
Simonsen, John Charles 1955-
WhoScEn 94
Simonsen, Mario Henrique 1935-
IntWW 93
Simonsen, Martin 1830-1899 *NewGrDO*
Simonsen, Palle 1933- *IntWW 93*
Simonsen, Renee *WhoHol 92*
Simonsen, Robert Alan 1956- *WhoMW 93*
Simonson, Beryl David 1949- *WhoFI 94*
Simonson, David C. 1927- *WhoAm 94*
Simonson, Donna Jeanne 1947- *WhoFI 94*
Simonson, Harold P. 1926- *WrDr 94*
Simonson, Hugh Melvin 1917-1987
WhAm 10
Simonson, John Alexander 1945-
WhoAm 94, WhoFI 94
Simonson, John S. 1947- *WhoAmL 94*
Simonson, Kenneth Wayne, Jr. 1955-
WhoFI 94, WhoWest 94
Simonson, Lee Stuart 1948- *WhoAm 94*
Simonson, Lloyd Grant 1943-
WhoMW 93
Simonson, Margaret *WhoAm 94*
Simonson, Mary Ellen 1949- *WhoAmP 93*
Simonson, Michael 1950- *WhoFI 94,
WhoWest 94*
Simonson, Michael H. 1942- *WhoAmL 94,
WhoWest 94*
Simonson, Miles Kevin 1950-
WhoWest 94
Simonson, Richard D. 1950- *WhoAmP 93*
Simonson, Susan Kay 1946- *WhoWest 94*
Simont, Marc 1915- *WhoAm 94*

Simonton, Ann Josephine 1952-
WhoWest 94
Simonton, Dean Keith 1948- *ConAu 43NR*
Simonton, George Louis 1947-
WhoAmP 93
Simonton, Richard Arnold 1944-
WhoAmL 94, WhoWest 94
Simonton, Robert Bennet 1933-
WhoAm 94
Simonton, Stephanie 1947- *WrDr 94*
Simopoulos, Artemis Panageotis 1933-
WhoAm 94
Simor, Suzanna B. *WhoAmA 93*
Simovic, Laszlo 1957- *WhoMW 93*
Simowitz, Lee H. 1946- *WhoAm 94*
Simper, Frederick 1914- *WhoAmA 93*
Simpers, Glen Richard 1952-
WhoScEn 94
Simpers, Mary P. 1934- *WhoAmP 93*
Simpich, William Morris 1924-
WhoAm 94
Simpkin, Lawrence James 1933-
WhoAm 94
Simpkins, Charles *WhoAm 94*
Simpkins, Cuthbert O. 1925-
WhoAmP 93, WhoBlA 94
Simpkins, J. Edward 1932- *WhoBlA 94*
Simpkins, Kirk Gates 1956- *WhoAmP 93*
Simpkins, Peter G. *WhoScEn 94*
Simpkins, Richard D. 1934- *WhoAmP 93*
Simpkins, Robert David Thomas 1932-
WhoAmP 93
Simpkins, William Joseph 1934-
WhoBlA 94
Simple, Peter *Who 94*
Simplot, John R. 1909- *WhoAm 94,
WhoFI 94, WhoWest 94*
Simplot, Thomas Michael 1961-
WhoWest 94
Simpson, A(lfred) W(illiam) Brian 1931-
WrDr 94
Simpson, Adele 1908- *WhoAm 94*
Simpson, Alan 1914- *IntWW 93, Who 94*
Simpson, Alan 1929- *Who 94*
Simpson, Alan 1937- *Who 94*
Simpson, Alan John 1948- *Who 94*
Simpson, Alan K. 1931- *CngDr 93,
WhoAm 94*
Simpson, Alan Kooi 1931- *IntWW 93,
WhoAm 94, WhoWest 94*
Simpson, Alfred (Henry) 1914- *Who 94*
Simpson, Alfred Moxon 1910- *Who 94*
Simpson, Allan Boyd 1948- *WhoFI 94*
Simpson, Allyson Bilich 1951-
WhoAm 94, WhoAmL 94
Simpson, Amy Marcy 1963- *WhoWest 94*
Simpson, Andrea Lynn 1948- *WhoAm 94,
WhoFI 94, WhoWest 94*
Simpson, Ann Marcoux 1954-
WhoWest 94
Simpson, Anthony Maurice Herbert
1935- *Who 94*
Simpson, Archibald 1790-1847
DcNaB MP
Simpson, Athol John Dundas 1932-
Who 94
Simpson, Beryl B. 1942- *WhoAm 94,
WhoScEn 94*
Simpson, Bob d1989 *WhoHol 92*
Simpson, Brian *Who 94*
Simpson, Brian 1953- *Who 94*
Simpson, (Alfred William) Brian 1931-
IntWW 93, Who 94
Simpson, Bruce Howard 1921- *WhoAm 94*
Simpson, Buster 1942- *WhoAmA 93*
Simpson, C. Dene 1936- *WhoWest 94*
Simpson, Carol Louise 1937- *WhoFI 94*
Simpson, Carole 1940- *AfrAmAl 6 [port],
ConBlB 6 [port], WhoAm 94, WhoBlA 94*
Simpson, Cary Hatcher 1927- *WhoAm 94*
Simpson, Charles Ednam 1929- *Who 94*
Simpson, Charles Herbert 1933-
WhoAm 94
Simpson, Charles R., III 1945-
WhoAm 94, WhoAmL 94
Simpson, Charles Reagan 1921-
WhoAm 94
Simpson, Charles William 1936-
WhoAmP 93
Simpson, Christopher Dale 1941-
WhoFI 94
Simpson, Cortlandt James Woore 1911-
Who 94
Simpson, Craig Evan 1952- *WhoAmL 94*
Simpson, Curtis Chapman, III 1952-
WhoAmL 94
Simpson, Daniel Glenn 1954- *WhoFI 94*
Simpson, Daniel H. 1939- *WhoAm 94,
WhoAmP 93*
Simpson, Daniel Reid 1927- *WhoAm 94,
WhoAmL 94, WhoAmP 93*
Simpson, David 1928- *WhoAmA 93*
Simpson, David 1947- *Who 94*
Simpson, David John 1946- *WhoAm 94*
Simpson, David Penistan 1917- *WrDr 94*
Simpson, David Rae Fisher 1936- *Who 94*
Simpson, David Richard Salisbury 1945-
Who 94

Simpson, David Sackville Bruce 1930-
Who 94
Simpson, David William 1928-
WhoAm 94
Simpson, Dazelle Dean 1924- *WhoBlA 94*
Simpson, Dennis Charles 1931- *Who 94*
Simpson, Dennis Dwayne 1943-
WhoScEn 94
Simpson, Diane Jeannette 1952-
WhoBlA 94
Simpson, Dick 1940- *WrDr 94*
Simpson, Don *WhoAm 94, WhoHol 92*
Simpson, Don 1945- *IntMPA 94*
Simpson, Donnie 1954- *WhoBlA 94*
Simpson, Dorothy 1933- *WrDr 94*
Simpson, Douglas Jackson 1940-
WhoAm 94
Simpson, Duncan Andrew 1956-
WhoAmP 93
Simpson, E. A., Jr. 1935- *WhoAmL 94*
Simpson, E(rvin) P(eter) Y(oung) 1911-
WrDr 94
Simpson, Edward Alexander 1935-
Who 94
Simpson, Edward Hugh 1922- *Who 94*
Simpson, Edward W., Jr. 1916-
WhoAmP 93
Simpson, Elizabeth Ann 1941-
WhoMW 93
Simpson, Esther Eleanor 1919- *Who 94*
Simpson, Fanny d1961 *WhoHol 92*
Simpson, Ffreebairn Liddon 1916-
Who 94
Simpson, Frank d1988 *WhoHol 92*
Simpson, Frank B. 1919- *WhoBlA 94*
Simpson, Frederick James 1922-
WhoAm 94
Simpson, Gail A. *WhoAmA 93*
Simpson, Garry *IntMPA 94*
Simpson, Gene Milton, III 1967-
WhoScEn 94
Simpson, George c. 1792-1860 *WhWE*
Simpson, George 1942- *Who 94*
Simpson, Gordon Russell 1917- *Who 94*
Simpson, Gregory Louis 1958-
WhoBlA 94
Simpson, Helen *WrDr 94*
Simpson, Helen (de Guerry) 1897-1940
EncSF 93
Simpson, Henry Kertan, Jr. 1941-
WhoScEn 94
Simpson, Hilary 1954- *WrDr 94*
Simpson, Howard Matthew 1918-
WhoMW 93
Simpson, Ian 1933- *Who 94*
Simpson, Ian Christopher 1949- *Who 94*
Simpson, Ivan d1951 *WhoHol 92*
Simpson, J. Kirk 1949- *WhoAm 94*
Simpson, Jack Benjamin 1937- *WhoFI 94,
WhoMW 93*
Simpson, Jack Ward 1941- *WhoFI 94*
Simpson, Jacqueline (Mary) 1930-
WrDr 94
Simpson, James (Joseph Trevor) 1908-
Who 94
Simpson, James Alexander 1934- *Who 94*
Simpson, James Arlington 1931-
WhoBlA 94
Simpson, James Carroll 1931-
WhoAmP 93
Simpson, James Charles 1930-
WhoAmP 93
Simpson, James Edward 1933- *WhoAm 94*
Simpson, James Frederick 1936-
WhoAmL 94
Simpson, James Hervey 1813-1883
WhWE
Simpson, James Marlon, Jr. 1952-
WhoAmL 94
Simpson, Joan Ye Vonne 1952- *WhoFI 94*
Simpson, Joanne (Gerould) 1923-
IntWW 93
Simpson, Joanne Malkus 1923-
WhoAm 94, WhoScEn 94
Simpson, Joe Leigh 1943- *WhoAm 94*
Simpson, John *WhoBlA 94*
Simpson, John 1615-1662 *DcNaB MP*
Simpson, John 1957- *WhoAmP 93*
Simpson, John (Cody Fidler) 1944-
ConAu 140, Who 94
Simpson, John E(dwin) 1951- *ConAu 140*
Simpson, John Alexander 1916-
WhoAm 94, WhoScEn 94
Simpson, John Andrew 1953- *Who 94*
Simpson, John Arol 1923- *WhoScEn 94*
Simpson, John Arthur 1933- *Who 94*
Simpson, John Duncan 1937-1989
WhAm 10
Simpson, John Ernest Peter 1942- *Who 94*
Simpson, John Ferguson 1902- *Who 94*
Simpson, John Joseph 1939- *WhoAm 94*
Simpson, John Liddle 1912- *Who 94*
Simpson, John M. 1950- *WhoAmL 94*
Simpson, John Mathes 1948- *WhoAm 94*
Simpson, John Noel 1936- *WhoAm 94*
Simpson, John P. *WhoAmP 93*
Simpson, John Richard 1932-
WhoAmL 94

Simpson, John W. 1922- *WhoAm 94*
Simpson, John Wistar 1914- *WhoAm 94*
Simpson, Joyce Michelle 1959-
WhoBlA 94
Simpson, Juanita H. 1925- *WhoBlA 94*
Simpson, Keith Taylor 1934- *Who 94*
Simpson, Kenneth John 1934- *Who 94*
Simpson, Kenneth W. *DrAPF 93*
Simpson, Lee 1923- *WhoAmA 93*
Simpson, Leland J. 1914- *WhoAmP 93*
Simpson, Lewis P(earson) 1916- *WrDr 94*
Simpson, Lorna 1960- *AfrAmAl 6*
Simpson, Louis *DrAPF 93*
Simpson, Louis (Aston Marantz) 1923-
WrDr 94
Simpson, Louis A. 1936- *WhoAm 94,
WhoFI 94*
Simpson, Louis Allen 1936- *WhoIns 94*
Simpson, Louis Aston Marantz 1923-
IntWW 93, WhoAm 94
Simpson, Lyle Lee 1937- *WhoAmL 94*
Simpson, Malcolm Carter 1929- *Who 94*
Simpson, Marianna Shreve 1949-
WhoAmA 93
Simpson, Marilyn Jean *WhoAmA 93*
Simpson, Marshall 1900-1958
WhoAmA 93N
Simpson, Matt(hew William) 1936-
WrDr 94
Simpson, Matthew 1811-1884
DcAmReB 2
Simpson, Merton D. 1928- *WhoAmA 93*
Simpson, Merton Daniel 1928-
WhoBlA 94
Simpson, Michael 1938- *WhoAm 94,
WhoFI 94*
Simpson, Michael Andrew 1944- *WrDr 94*
Simpson, Michael Frank 1928- *Who 94*
Simpson, Michael K. 1950- *WhoAmP 93*
Simpson, Michael Kevin 1949-
WhoAm 94
Simpson, Michael Marcial 1954-
WhoAm 94
Simpson, Michael Wayne 1959-
WhoAmL 94
Simpson, Mickey d1985 *WhoHol 92*
Simpson, Milward 1897-1993
NewYTBS 93
Simpson, Milward L(ee) 1897-1993
CurBio 93N
Simpson, Mona *DrAPF 93*
Simpson, Mona 1957- *CurBio 93 [port],
WrDr 94*
Simpson, Morag *Who 94*
Simpson, Murray 1921- *WhoAm 94*
Simpson, Myles Alan 1947- *WhoScEn 94*
Simpson, Myrtle Lillias 1931- *WrDr 94*
Simpson, N. F. 1919- *BlmGEL*
Simpson, N(orman) F(rederick) 1919-
ConDr 93, IntDcT 2, WrDr 94
Simpson, Nancy *DrAPF 93*
Simpson, Norman Frederick 1919-
IntWW 93
Simpson, Norvell J. 1931- *WhoBlA 94*
Simpson, O. J. *ProFbHF [port]*
Simpson, O. J. 1947- *AfrAmAl 6,
IntMPA 94, WhoAm 94, WhoBlA 94,
WhoHol 92*
Simpson, Oliver 1924- *Who 94*
Simpson, P. Kelley *WhoAmP 93*
Simpson, Patrick J. 1944- *WhoAmL 94*
Simpson, Paul V. 1952- *WhoAmL 94*
Simpson, Peggy 1913- *WhoHol 92*
Simpson, Peter Kooi 1930- *WhoAmP 93,
WhoWest 94*
Simpson, Peter L. *DrAPF 93*
Simpson, Peter Robert 1936- *Who 94*
Simpson, Portia *WhoWomW 91*
Simpson, R(onald) A(lbert) 1929-
WrDr 94
Simpson, Ralph 1949- *BasBi*
Simpson, Ralph Derek 1949- *WhoBlA 94*
Simpson, Raymond William 1944-
WhoScEn 94
Simpson, Reagan W. 1952- *WhoAmL 94*
Simpson, Reginald d1964 *WhoHol 92*
Simpson, Rennie 1920- *Who 94*
Simpson, Richard Collins 1947-
WhoAmL 94
Simpson, Richard John 1953-
WhoWest 94
Simpson, Richard Lee 1929- *WhoAm 94*
Simpson, Robert 1921- *WrDr 94*
Simpson, Robert 1923- *Who 94*
Simpson, Robert Edward 1917-
WhoAm 94
Simpson, Robert Foster 1928-
WhoAmP 93
Simpson, Robert Glenn 1932- *WhoAm 94*
Simpson, Robert Smith 1906- *WhoAm 94*
Simpson, Robert Watson 1940- *Who 94*
Simpson, Robert Wilfred Levick 1921-
Who 94
Simpson, Robert Wilfrid Levick 1921-
IntWW 93
Simpson, Robin *Who 94*
Simpson, Robin Muschamp Garry 1927-
Who 94

Simpson, Roderick Alexander C. *Who 94*
Simpson, Ronald d1957 *WhoHol 92*
Simpson, Russell d1959 *WhoHol 92*
Simpson, Russell Gordon 1927- *WhoAm 94, WhoAmL 94*
Simpson, Samuel G. 1931- *WhoBlA 94*
Simpson, Scot Matthew 1960- *WhoFI 94*
Simpson, Scott Mitchell 1949- *WhoMW 93*
Simpson, Searcy Lee, Jr. 1947- *WhoAmL 94*
Simpson, (Robert) Smith 1906- *WrDr 94*
Simpson, Stephen Lee 1964- *WhoScEn 94*
Simpson, Stephen Whittington 1945- *WhoBlA 94*
Simpson, Steven Drexell 1953- *WhoAmL 94*
Simpson, Thomas c. 1808-1840 *WhWE*
Simpson, Valerie *WhoBlA 94*
Simpson, Valerie 1948- See Ashford, Nicholas 1943- & Simpson, Valerie 1948- *AfrAmAl 6*
Simpson, Velma Southall 1948- *WhoWest 94*
Simpson, Vi 1946- *WhoAmP 93, WhoMW 93*
Simpson, Vinson Raleigh 1928- *WhoAm 94*
Simpson, Virginia White 1907- *WhoFI 94*
Simpson, Walter 1941- *WhoBlA 94*
Simpson, Warren Carl 1954- *WhoFI 94, WhoWest 94*
Simpson, Willa Jean 1943- *WhoBlA 94*
Simpson, William 1818-1872 *WhoAmA 93N*
Simpson, William (James) 1920- *Who 94*
Simpson, William Arthur 1939- *WhoAm 94, WhoFI 94, WhoIns 94, WhoWest 94*
Simpson, William Brand 1919- *WhoWest 94*
Simpson, William George 1945- *Who 94*
Simpson, William H. 1938- *WhoIns 94*
Simpson, William John, Sr. 1937- *WhoFI 94*
Simpson, William Kelly 1928- *WhoAm 94, WhoAmA 93*
Simpson, William Stewart 1924- *WhoAm 94*
Simpson, William Tilden 1934- *WhoMW 93*
Simpson, Winifred D. 1948- *WhoAmL 94*
Simpson, Zelma Alene 1923- *WhoAm 94*
Simpson-Jones, Peter Trevor 1914- *Who 94*
Simpson-Orlebar, Michael (Keith Orlebar) 1932- *Who 94*
Simpson-Taylor, Dorothy Marie 1944- *WhoBlA 94*
Simpson-Watson, Ora Lee 1943- *WhoBlA 94*
Simrall, Dorothy Van Winkle 1917- *WhoScEn 94*
Simrill, J. Gary 1966- *WhoAmP 93*
Simrin, Harry S. 1945- *WhoScEn 94*
Sims, Adrienne 1952- *WhoBlA 94*
Sims, Andrew Charles Petter 1938- *Who 94*
Sims, August Charles 1948- *WhoAm 94, WhoAmL 94*
Sims, Barbara M. *WhoBlA 94*
Sims, Barbara W. 1940- *WhoAmP 93*
Sims, Bennett Jones 1920- *WhoAm 94*
Sims, Bernard John 1915- *WrDr 94*
Sims, Bill 1932- *WhoAmP 93*
Sims, Billy 1955- *WhoBlA 94*
Sims, Blanche (L.) *SmATA 75*
Sims, Calvin Gene 1963- *WhoBlA 94*
Sims, Carl W. 1941- *WhoBlA 94*
Sims, Charles S. 1950- *WhoAmL 94*
Sims, Christopher Albert 1942- *WhoAm 94*
Sims, Constance Arlette 1940- *WhoBlA 94*
Sims, D(enise) N(atalie) *EncSF 93*
Sims, Diane Marie 1955- *WhoBlA 94*
Sims, Ed 1941- *WhoAmP 93*
Sims, Edward Hackney 1944- *WhoBlA 94*
Sims, Edward Howell 1923- *WhoAm 94*
Sims, Ernest Theodore, Jr. 1932-1988 *WhAm 10*
Sims, Esau, Jr. 1953- *WhoBlA 94*
Sims, Eugene Ralph, Jr. 1920- *WhoFI 94*
Sims, Everett Martin 1920- *WhoAm 94*
Sims, Ezra 1928- *WhoAm 94*
Sims, Genevieve Constance 1947- *WhoBlA 94*
Sims, Geoffrey Donald 1926- *IntWW 93, Who 94*
Sims, George 1923- *WrDr 94*
Sims, George Robert 1847-1922 *DcLB 135 [port], DcNaB MP*
Sims, Glenn Michael d1987 *WhoHol 92*
Sims, Glennis E. 1947- *WhoAmL 94*
Sims, Harold Rudolph 1935- *WhoBlA 94*
Sims, Hunter W., Jr. 1944- *WhoAmL 94*
Sims, Ivor Donald 1912- *WhoAm 94*
Sims, J. Taylor *WhoMW 93*
Sims, James Hylbert 1924- *WhoAm 94*
Sims, James Larry 1936- *WhoAm 94*
Sims, James Micheal 1939- *WhoFI 94*
Sims, Jeffrey Lloyd 1958- *WhoFI 94*
Sims, Jennifer Grace 1958- *WhoFI 94*
Sims, Joan 1930- *IntMPA 94, WhoHol 92*
Sims, Joe 1944- *WhoAm 94, WhoAmL 94*
Sims, John Leonard 1934- *WhoBlA 94*
Sims, John LeRoy 1912- *WhoMW 93*
Sims, John Rogers, Jr. 1924- *WhoAm 94*
Sims, John William 1917- *WhoAm 94*
Sims, Johna Lee 1943- *WhoAmP 93*
Sims, Joseph Kirkland 1950- *WhoAmP 93*
Sims, Joseph William 1937- *WhoBlA 94*
Sims, Julius Rowland 1956- *WhoMW 93*
Sims, Kent Otway 1940- *WhoAm 94*
Sims, Lee d1966 *WhoHol 92*
Sims, Lowery Stokes 1949- *WhoAmA 93, WhoBlA 94*
Sims, Luke E. 1950- *WhoAmL 94*
Sims, Lydia Theresa 1920- *WhoBlA 94*
Sims, Marion D., III 1943- *WhoAm 94, WhoFI 94*
Sims, Mark E. 1955- *WhoAmL 94*
Sims, Melvin Thomas, Jr. 1933- *WhoAmP 93*
Sims, Monica Louie *Who 94*
Sims, Naomi R. 1949- *AfrAmAl 6 [port], WhoBlA 94*
Sims, Norman (Howard) 1948- *WrDr 94*
Sims, Patsy 1938- *WrDr 94*
Sims, Patterson 1947- *WhoAmA 93*
Sims, Paul Kibler 1918- *WhoAm 94, WhoWest 94*
Sims, Pete, Jr. 1924- *WhoBlA 94*
Sims, Peter Andrew 1959- *WhoAmA 93*
Sims, Rebecca Littleton 1957- *WhoAmL 94*
Sims, Richard Lee 1929- *WhoAm 94*
Sims, Richard P. 1941- *WhoAmL 94*
Sims, Riley V. d1993 *NewYTBS 93*
Sims, Ripley Singleton 1907- *WhoBlA 94*
Sims, Robert Barry 1942- *WhoAm 94*
Sims, Robert Bell 1934- *WhoAm 94, WhoAmP 93*
Sims, Robert Carl 1936- *WhoWest 94*
Sims, Robert John 1926- *WhoFI 94*
Sims, Roger Edward 1930- *Who 94*
Sims, Roger Lafe 1941- *WhoWest 94*
Sims, Roger W. 1950- *WhoAmL 94*
Sims, Ronald Cordell 1948- *WhoBlA 94*
Sims, Ruth Leiserson 1920- *WhoAmP 93*
Sims, Sandman *WhoHol 92*
Sims, Sylvia *WhoHol 92*
Sims, Thaddeus Michael 1943- *WhoAmL 94*
Sims, Theophlous Aron, Sr. 1939- *WhoBlA 94*
Sims, Thomas Auburn 1925- *WhoFI 94*
Sims, Victor Dwayne 1959- *WhoAmL 94*
Sims, Warwick *WhoHol 92*
Sims, William 1922- *WhoBlA 94*
Sims, William Dale 1941- *WhoFI 94, WhoIns 94, WhoMW 93*
Sims, William E. 1921- *WhoBlA 94*
Sims, William Riley, Jr. 1938- *WhoAm 94*
Sims, Wilson 1924- *WhoAm 94, WhoAmL 94*
Sims-Davis, Edith R. 1932- *WhoBlA 94*
Simson, Bevlyn A. 1917- *WhoAmA 93*
Simson, Gary Joseph 1950- *WhoAm 94*
Simson, Jo Anne 1936- *WhoAmA 93*
Simson, Michael Ronald Fraser 1913- *Who 94*
Simson, Otto von 1912- *IntWW 93*
Sims-Williams, Nicholas John 1949- *Who 94*
Simton, Chester 1937- *WhoBlA 94*
Simunek, Linda A. *WhoAsA 94*
Simunich, Mary Elizabeth Hedrick *WhoWest 94*
Sin, Jaime L. 1928- *IntWW 93*
Sina, Alejandro 1945- *WhoAmA 93*
Sinacore, Nicole 1969- *WhoFI 94*
Sinagege R. M., Utu *WhoAmP 93*
Sinagra, Anthony Carl 1940- *WhoAmP 93*
Sinagra, Jack G. 1950- *WhoAmP 93*
Sinai, Allen Leo 1939- *WhoAm 94, WhoFI 94, WhoScEn 94*
Sinai, Yakov G. 1935- *WhoScEn 94*
Sinaiko, Arlie 1902- *WhoAmA 93N*
Sinak, David Louis 1953- *WhoAmL 94*
Sinatra, Francis Albert 1915- *AmCulL, Who 94*
Sinatra, Frank 1915- *IntMPA 94, IntWW 93, WhoAm 94, WhoHol 92*
Sinatra, Frank, Jr. 1944- *WhoHol 92*
Sinatra, Frank Raymond 1945- *WhoScEn 94*
Sinatra, Nancy 1940?- *ConTFT 11, WhoHol 92*
Sinay, Hershel David 1938- *WhoAm 94*
Sinay, Joseph 1920- *WhoAm 94*
Sinaz, Guglielmo d1947 *WhoHol 92*
Sinbad 1956- *AfrAmAl 6*
Sinbad 1957- *WhoBlA 94*
Sincerbeaux, Robert Abbott 1913- *WhoAmL 94*
Sincere, Richard E., Jr. 1959- *WhoAmP 93*
Sinclair *Who 94*
Sinclair, Lord 1914- *Who 94*
Sinclair, Master of 1968- *Who 94*
Sinclair, Abiola *DrAPF 93*
Sinclair, Alastair James 1935- *WhoAm 94*
Sinclair, Albert Richard 1940- *WhoScEn 94*
Sinclair, Alexander Riddell 1917- *Who 94*
Sinclair, Andrew 1935- *BlmGEL, IntMPA 94*
Sinclair, Andrew (Annandale) 1935- *EncSF 93, WrDr 94*
Sinclair, Andrew Annandale 1935- *Who 94*
Sinclair, Arthur d1951 *WhoHol 92*
Sinclair, Benito A. 1931- *WhoBlA 94*
Sinclair, Bennie Lee *DrAPF 93*
Sinclair, Betty d1983 *WhoHol 92*
Sinclair, Brett J(ason) 1942- *ConAu 141*
Sinclair, Carolyn Elizabeth Cunningham 1944- *Who 94*
Sinclair, Catherine 1800-1864 *BlmGWL*
Sinclair, Charles James Francis 1948- *Who 94*
Sinclair, Clayton, Jr. 1933- *WhoBlA 94*
Sinclair, Clive (Marles) 1940- *Who 94*
Sinclair, Clive Marles 1940- *IntWW 93*
Sinclair, Daisy 1941- *WhoAm 94*
Sinclair, David Cecil 1915- *Who 94*
Sinclair, Debra Ann 1950- *WhoMW 93*
Sinclair, Duncan Gordon 1933- *WhoAm 94*
Sinclair, Edward d1977 *WhoHol 92*
Sinclair, Ernest Keith 1914- *IntWW 93, Who 94*
Sinclair, Erroll Norman 1909- *Who 94*
Sinclair, Gary Marc 1950- *WhoAmL 94*
Sinclair, George 1912- *WhoAm 94*
Sinclair, George (Evelyn) 1912- *Who 94*
Sinclair, George Brian 1928- *Who 94*
Sinclair, George Michael 1953- *WhoWest 94*
Sinclair, Herbert Joseph 1956- *WhoWest 94*
Sinclair, Horace d1949 *WhoHol 92*
Sinclair, Hugh d1962 *WhoHol 92*
Sinclair, Hugh Francis Paget 1873-1939 *DcNaB MP*
Sinclair, Iain 1943- *ConLC 76 [port], WrDr 94*
Sinclair, Iain (MacGregor) 1943- *EncSF 93*
Sinclair, Ian (McCahon) 1929- *Who 94*
Sinclair, Ian (McTaggart) 1926- *Who 94*
Sinclair, Ian David 1913- *IntWW 93, Who 94*
Sinclair, Ian McCahon 1929- *IntWW 93*
Sinclair, Isabel Lillias *Who 94*
Sinclair, Ivan Earl 1937- *WhoAmP 93*
Sinclair, J. Walter 1953- *WhoAmL 94*
Sinclair, James *ConAu 43NR*
Sinclair, James 1811-1856 *WhWE*
Sinclair, James 1911- *WrDr 94*
Sinclair, Jeff 1958- *SmATA 77 [port]*
Sinclair, Jo 1913- *BlmGWL*
Sinclair, John d1945 *WhoHol 92*
Sinclair, John 1791-1857 *NewGrDO*
Sinclair, John B. 1954- *WhoAmL 94*
Sinclair, John David 1943- *WhoScEn 94*
Sinclair, John Edward 1936- *WhoFI 94*
Sinclair, John Gordon *WhoHol 92*
Sinclair, John McHardy 1933- *Who 94*
Sinclair, John Richley 1935- *WhoAmP 93*
Sinclair, Joseph Samuels 1922- *WhoAm 94*
Sinclair, Joseph Treble, III 1940- *WhoWest 94*
Sinclair, Keith d1993 *Who 94N*
Sinclair, Keith 1922- *WrDr 94*
Sinclair, Keith 1922-1993 *ConAu 142*
Sinclair, Keith Val 1926- *IntWW 93, WrDr 94*
Sinclair, Laurence (Frank) 1908- *Who 94*
Sinclair, Lonnie Ray 1952- *WhoMW 93*
Sinclair, Madge 1938- *IntMPA 94, WhoHol 92*
Sinclair, Madge 1940- *WhoBlA 94*
Sinclair, Marjorie 1913- *WrDr 94*
Sinclair, Mary 1922- *WhoHol 92*
Sinclair, Mary Amelia St Clair 1863-1946 *DcNaB MP*
Sinclair, Maurice Walter *Who 94*
Sinclair, May 1863-1946 *BlmGWL, DcLB 135 [port]*
Sinclair, Michael *EncSF 93, Who 94*
Sinclair, Monica 1925- *NewGrDO*
Sinclair, Olga (Ellen) 1923- *WrDr 94*
Sinclair, Orriette Coiner 1921- *WhoAmP 93*
Sinclair, Patrick 1736-1820 *AmRev*
Sinclair, Patrick (Robert Richard) 1936- *Who 94*
Sinclair, Peter Ross 1934- *Who 94*
Sinclair, Robert (W.) 1939- *WhoAmA 93*
Sinclair, Robert J. *WhoFI 94*
Sinclair, Rolf Malcolm 1929- *WhoAm 94*
Sinclair, Ronald 1924- *WhoHol 92*
Sinclair, Ronald Ormiston 1903- *IntWW 93, Who 94*
Sinclair, Ruth d1984 *WhoHol 92*
Sinclair, Sara Voris 1942- *WhoFI 94, WhoWest 94*
Sinclair, Sonia Elizabeth 1928- *Who 94*
Sinclair, Stephen (Kennedy) 1956- *ConDr 93*
Sinclair, Upton d1968 *WhoHol 92*
Sinclair, Upton (Beall) 1878-1968 *EncSF 93, TwCYAW*
Sinclair, Upton Beall, Jr. 1878-1968 *AmSocL [port]*
Sinclair, Virgil Lee, Jr. 1951- *WhoAm 94, WhoAmL 94*
Sinclair, Warren Keith 1924- *WhoAm 94, WhoScEn 94*
Sinclair, William Donald *WhoWest 94*
Sinclair-Lockhart, Simon (John Edward Francis) 1941- *Who 94*
Sinclair Of Cleeve, Baron 1953- *Who 94*
Sinclair of Freswick, David Boyd A. *Who 94*
Sinclair Oyaneder, Santiago 1927- *IntWW 93*
Sinclair-Stevenson, Christopher Terence 1939- *Who 94*
Sinclitico, Dennis J. 1947- *WhoAmL 94*
Sinco, Victor 1958- *WhoAsA 94*
Sincoff, Michael Z. 1943- *WhoAm 94, WhoFI 94*
Sincoff, Steven Lawrence 1948- *WhoWest 94*
Sindall, Adrian John 1937- *Who 94*
Sindelar, Jody Louise 1951- *WhoFI 94*
Sindelar, Matthias 1903-1939 *WorESoc*
Sindelar, Robert Albert 1943- *WhoScEn 94*
Sindelar, William Francis 1945- *WhoAm 94*
Sindelir, Robert John 1932- *WhoAmA 93*
Sindell, Marion Harwood 1925- *Who 94*
Sinden, Donald 1923- *IntMPA 94, WhoHol 92*
Sinden, Donald (Alfred) 1923- *WrDr 94*
Sinden, Donald Alfred 1923- *IntWW 93, Who 94*
Sinden, Harry 1932- *WhoAm 94*
Sinden, Jeremy 1950- *WhoHol 92*
Sinden, Marc 1954- *WhoHol 92*
Sinder, Mike 1946- *WhoAmL 94, WhoAmP 93, WhoHisp 94*
Sinder, Stuart J. 1942- *WhoAmL 94*
Sinderoff, Rita Joyce 1932- *WhoFI 94*
Sindi, Kamil 1932- *IntWW 93*
Sindici, Gregg C. 1945- *WhoAmL 94*
Sindler, Michael H. 1943- *WhoBlA 94*
Sindler, Robert 1952- *WhoAmP 93*
Sindlinger, Verne E. *WhoMW 93*
Sindoni, Elio 1937- *WhoScEn 94*
Sindoni, John P. 1945- *WhoAmL 94*
Sindoris, Arthur Richard 1943- *WhoScEn 94*
Sindos, Louise King 1930- *WhoBlA 94*
Sindt, Carol Anne Wold 1949- *WhoAmP 93*
Sineath, Timothy Wayne 1940- *WhoAm 94*
Sinegal, James D. 1936- *WhoAm 94, WhoFI 94, WhoWest 94*
Sinel, Norman Mark 1941- *WhoAm 94, WhoAmL 94*
Sines, Brian D. 1962- *WhoMW 93*
Sines, Randy Dwain 1948- *WhoWest 94*
Sines, Raymond E. *WhoAmP 93*
Sinex, Francis Marott 1923- *WhoAm 94*
Sinfelt, John Henry 1931- *IntWW 93, WhoAm 94, WhoScEn 94*
Sing, Fu d1983 *WhoHol 92*
Sing, Lillian K. 1942- *WhoAsA 94*
Sing, Robert Fong 1953- *WhoFI 94*
Sing, William Bender 1947- *WhoAm 94, WhoAmL 94*
Singel, Mark Stephen 1953- *WhoAm 94, WhoAmP 93*
Singer, Adam 1922- *WrDr 94*
Singer, Alexander Theodore 1945- *WhoAmP 93*
Singer, Alfred Ernst 1924- *Who 94*
Singer, Allen Morris 1923- *WhoAm 94*
Singer, Arlene 1948- *WhoAmP 93*
Singer, Armand Edwards 1914- *WhoAm 94*
Singer, Arthur B. 1917-1990 *WhoAmA 93N*
Singer, Arthur Louis, Jr. 1929- *WhoAm 94*
Singer, Aubrey Edward 1927- *Who 94*
Singer, Barry 1942- *WhoAmL 94*
Singer, Benjamin D. 1931- *WrDr 94*
Singer, Beth Ann 1961- *WhoWest 94*
Singer, Burton Herbert 1938- *WhoAm 94, WhoScEn 94*
Singer, Campbell d1976 *WhoHol 92*
Singer, Carl Norman 1916- *WhoFI 94*
Singer, Cecile D. *WhoAm 94, WhoAmP 93*
Singer, Clifford 1955- *WhoAmA 93*
Singer, Clyde J. 1908- *WhoAmA 93*
Singer, Craig 1947- *WhoAm 94*

Singer, Daniel Morris 1930- *WhoAm 94, WhoAmL 94*
Singer, David Michael 1957- *WhoFI 94*
Singer, Davida *DrAPF 93*
Singer, Deborah Louise 1962- *WhoFI 94*
Singer, Donald Ivan 1938- *WhoAm 94*
Singer, Earl Gardner 1930- *WhoWest 94*
Singer, Edward Nathan 1917- *WhoScEn 94*
Singer, Eleanor 1930- *WhoAm 94*
Singer, Elizabeth Wells 1933- *WhoAm 94*
Singer, Elyse Joy 1952- *WhoWest 94*
Singer, Emel 1944- *WhoMW 93*
Singer, Enos Leroy 1943- *WhoBlA 94*
Singer, Esther Forman 1928- *WhoAmA 93*
Singer, Frank J. 1944- *WhoWest 94*
Singer, Frederick Raphael 1939- *WhoAm 94*
Singer, Frieda *DrAPF 93*
Singer, Gary James 1952- *WhoAm 94, WhoAmL 94*
Singer, George 1908-1980 *NewGrDO*
Singer, George Alan 1948- *WhoAm 94*
Singer, Gerald Michael 1920- *WhoAmL 94*
Singer, Harold Samuel 1935- *Who 94*
Singer, Harry Bruce 1921- *Who 94*
Singer, Henry A. 1919- *WhoAm 94*
Singer, Isaac Bashevis d1991 *NobelP 91N*
Singer, Isaac Bashevis 1904-1991 *RfGShF, WhAm 10, WrDr 94N*
Singer, Isaac M. 1811-1875 *WorInv*
Singer, Isadore Manuel 1924- *IntWW 93, WhoAm 94, WhoScEn 94*
Singer, Izzy *WhoHol 92*
Singer, J. David 1925- *WrDr 94*
Singer, Jeffrey Alan 1952- *WhoWest 94*
Singer, Jeffrey Michael 1949- *WhoScEn 94*
Singer, Jerome L(eonard) 1924- *WrDr 94*
Singer, Joel David 1925- *WhoAm 94*
Singer, John 1947- *WhoAmP 93*
Singer, Johnny 1924- *WhoHol 92*
Singer, Josef 1923- *WhoScEn 94*
Singer, Kenneth David 1952- *WhoScEn 94*
Singer, Kurt Deutsch 1911- *WhoAm 94, WhoWest 94*
Singer, Lori 1957- *WhoHol 92*
Singer, Lori 1962- *IntMPA 94*
Singer, Marc *IntMPA 94*
Singer, Marc 1948- *WhoHol 92*
Singer, Marcus George 1926- *WhoAm 94, WrDr 94*
Singer, Marcus Joseph 1914- *WhoMW 93*
Singer, Marilyn 1948- *TwCYAW*
Singer, Marion d1924 *WhoHol 92*
Singer, Markus Morton 1917- *WhoAm 94*
Singer, Maxine 1931- *IntWW 93*
Singer, Maxine Frank 1931- *WhoAm 94, WhoScEn 94*
Singer, Michael 1945- *WhoAmA 93*
Singer, Michael Howard 1941- *WhoAmL 94, WhoWest 94*
Singer, Miriam 1959- *WhoHisp 94*
Singer, Myer Richard 1938- *WhoAmL 94*
Singer, Nancy Barkhouse 1912- *WhoAmA 93*
Singer, Norbert 1931- *Who 94*
Singer, Norman H. 1945- *WhoAm 94, WhoAmL 94*
Singer, Norman Marvin 1940- *WhoMW 93*
Singer, Norman Sol 1937- *WhoMW 93*
Singer, Paul Meyer 1943- *WhoAm 94, WhoAmL 94*
Singer, Peter *Who 94*
Singer, Peter 1937- *WhoScEn 94*
Singer, Peter 1946- *EnvEnc, WrDr 94*
Singer, (Jan) Peter 1944- *Who 94*
Singer, Peter Albert David 1946- *IntWW 93*
Singer, Randy Darrell 1956- *WhoAmL 94*
Singer, Ray (Eleazer) 1916-1992 *ConAu 140*
Singer, Raymond 1948- *WhoHol 92*
Singer, Robert Norman 1936- *WhoAm 94*
Singer, Robert W. 1947- *WhoAmP 93*
Singer, Samuel Benjamin 1895- *WhAm 10*
Singer, Samuel Loewenberg 1911- *WhoAm 94*
Singer, Sandra Manes 1942- *WhoMW 93*
Singer, Sanford Robert 1930- *WhoAm 94, WhoFI 94*
Singer, Sarah *DrAPF 93*
Singer, Sarah Beth 1915- *WhoAm 94, WhoWest 94, WrDr 94*
Singer, Saul Jay 1951- *WhoAmL 94*
Singer, Sherwin Jeffrey 1954- *WhoScEn 94*
Singer, Siegfried Fred 1924- *WhoAm 94*
Singer, Simeon 1848-1906 *DcNaB MP*
Singer, Stanley Thomas, Jr. 1933- *WhoMW 93*
Singer, Stuart H. 1956- *WhoAmL 94*
Singer, T. Thomas 1953- *WhoAmL 94*
Singer, Thomas Eric 1926- *WhoAm 94*
Singer, Thomas Kenyon 1932- *WhoAm 94*
Singer, William Harry 1947- *WhoScEn 94*
Singer-Leone, Mallory Ann 1950- *WhoFI 94*
Singer-Magdoff, Laura Joan Silver 1917- *WhoAm 94*
Singerman, Dona Fatibeno 1939- *WhoMW 93*
Singerman, Paulina d1984 *WhoHol 92*
Singh, Ajaib 1935- *WhoAsA 94*
Singh, Ajaib 1940- *WhoAsA 94*
Singh, Allan 1956- *WhoScEn 94*
Singh, Amarjit 1924- *WhoAm 94, WhoAsA 94*
Singh, Ambuj Kumar 1959- *WhoWest 94*
Singh, Amritjit 1945- *WrDr 94*
Singh, Avtar 1947- *WhoWest 94*
Singh, Baldev 1931- *WhoAmP 93*
Singh, Baldev 1939- *WhoAsA 94*
Singh, Balwant 1934- *WhoAsA 94*
Singh, Bhishma Narain 1933- *IntWW 93*
Singh, Bhogwan d1962 *WhoHol 92*
Singh, Bipin 1918- *IntWW 93*
Singh, Buta 1934- *IntWW 93*
Singh, Devendra Pal 1954- *WhoScEn 94*
Singh, Digvijay Narain *WhoWomW 91*
Singh, Dinesh 1925- *IntWW 93*
Singh, G(han Shyam) 1929- *ConAu 43NR*
Singh, Gajendra 1944- *WhoScEn 94*
Singh, Giani Zail 1916- *IntWW 93, Who 94*
Singh, Gopal 1919- *IntWW 93*
Singh, Gurdial 1934- *WhoAsA 94*
Singh, Harinder 1941- *WhoWest 94*
Singh, Harkishan 1928- *WhoScEn 94*
Singh, Harpal 1941- *WhoAsA 94*
Singh, Jagbir 1940- *WhoAsA 94*
Singh, Jaswant 1937- *WhoScEn 94*
Singh, Kalyan 1932- *IntWW 93*
Singh, Kanwar N. *Who 94*
Singh, Karan 1931- *IntWW 93*
Singh, Khushwant 1915- *IntWW 93, Who 94, WrDr 94*
Singh, Kim 1957- *WhoAsA 94*
Singh, Krishna Deo 1934- *WhoScEn 94*
Singh, Madan Mohan 1933- *WhoAsA 94*
Singh, Madho 1936- *WhoAsA 94*
Singh, Mahendra Pratap 1950- *WhoWest 94*
Singh, Manjit 1956- *WhoFI 94*
Singh, Manmohan 1932- *IntWW 93*
Singh, Manmohan 1940- *WhoMW 93, WhoScEn 94*
Singh, Mota 1930- *Who 94*
Singh, Naresh Pratap 1959- *WhoWest 94*
Singh, Natasha 1964?-1993 *WhoAsA 94N*
Singh, Nirbhay Nand 1952- *WhoScEn 94*
Singh, Pratibha 1929- *WhoWomW 91*
Singh, Preetam 1914- *Who 94*
Singh, Prithipal 1939- *WhoAsA 94*
Singh, Raj Kumar 1949- *WhoMW 93*
Singh, Raj Kumar 1955- *WhoScEn 94*
Singh, Rajendra 1950- *WhoAsA 94, WhoMW 93, WhoScEn 94*
Singh, Rajendra P. 1934- *WhoBlA 94*
Singh, Rakesh Kumar 1952- *WhoScEn 94*
Singh, Ravi *DrAPF 93*
Singh, Reepu Daman 1952- *WhoScEn 94*
Singh, Roy Ranjit *WhoFI 94*
Singh, Sahjendra Narain 1943- *WhoScEn 94*
Singh, Sant P. 1936- *WhoAsA 94*
Singh, Sant Parkash 1936- *WhoMW 93*
Singh, Sarain d1952 *WhoHol 92*
Singh, Sardar Swaran 1907- *IntWW 93, Who 94*
Singh, Sardul 1950- *WhoScEn 94*
Singh, Sharon 1965- *WhoAsA 94*
Singh, Sukhmander 1939- *IntWW 93*
Singh, Surendra Pal 1953- *WhoAsA 94*
Singh, Swayam Prabha 1945- *WhoAm 94*
Singh, Tara 1921- *WhoScEn 94, WhoWest 94*
Singh, Usha *WhoWomW 91*
Singh, Vijay P. 1946- *WhoAsA 94*
Singh, Vijay Pal 1947- *WhoAsA 94*
Singh, Vishwanath Pratap 1931- *IntWW 93, Who 94*
Singha, Nabaghana Shyam 1939- *WhoAsA 94*
Singhal, Avinash Chandra 1941- *WhoAsA 94, WhoScEn 94*
Singhal, Kishore 1944- *WhoAm 94*
Singhal, Radhey Lal 1940- *WhoAm 94*
Singham, Manohar Kularatnam 1950- *WhoMW 93*
Singhania, D.C. 1932- *IntWW 93*
Singhania, Padampat 1905- *Who 94*
Singhasaneh, Suthee 1928- *IntWW 93*
Singhellakis, Panagiotis Nicolaos 1941- *WhoScEn 94*
Singher, Martial 1904-1990 *WhAm 10*
Singher, Martial (Jean-Paul) 1904-1990 *NewGrDO*
Sing Hoo 1908- *WhoAmA 93*
Singhvi, Laxmi Mall 1931- *IntWW 93, Who 94*
Singhvi, Sampat M. 1947- *WhoAsA 94*
Singhvi, Surendra Singh 1942- *WhoAm 94, WhoMW 93*
Single, Richard Wayne, Sr. 1938- *WhoAm 94, WhoAmL 94*
Singlehurst, Dona Geisenheyner 1928- *WhoAm 94, WhoWest 94*
Singletary, Alvin D. 1942- *WhoAmL 94, WhoFI 94*
Singletary, Inez M. *WhoBlA 94*
Singletary, Michael 1958- *WhoAm 94*
Singletary, Michael James 1950- *WhoAmA 93*
Singletary, Michael Willis 1938- *WhoAm 94*
Singletary, Mike 1958- *CurBio 93 [port], WhoBlA 94*
Singletary, Otis Arnold, Jr. 1921- *WhoAm 94*
Singletary, Reggie 1964- *WhoBlA 94*
Singletary, William Hale 1951- *WhoAmP 93*
Singleterry, Gary Lee 1948- *WhoAm 94, WhoFI 94*
Singleton, Alice Faye *WhoWest 94*
Singleton, Barry Neill 1946- *Who 94*
Singleton, Benjamin, Sr. 1943- *WhoBlA 94*
Singleton, Chris 1967- *WhoBlA 94*
Singleton, De Lois Del Jeane *WhoAm 94*
Singleton, Donald Edward 1936- *WhoAm 94*
Singleton, Donna Marie 1960- *WhoFI 94, WhoMW 93*
Singleton, Ernie *WhoBlA 94*
Singleton, Francis Seth 1940- *WhoWest 94*
Singleton, George Monroe 1931- *WhoFI 94*
Singleton, Harold Craig 1950- *WhoWest 94*
Singleton, Harold Douglas 1908- *WhoBlA 94*
Singleton, Harry M. 1949- *WhoAmP 93, WhoBlA 94*
Singleton, Harry Michael 1949- *WhoAm 94*
Singleton, Henry Earl 1916- *WhoFI 94, WhoWest 94*
Singleton, Herbert 1947- *WhoBlA 94*
Singleton, Isaac, Sr. 1928- *WhoBlA 94*
Singleton, James Keith 1939- *WhoAm 94, WhoAmL 94, WhoWest 94*
Singleton, James LeRoy 1944- *WhoBlA 94*
Singleton, James M. 1933- *WhoAmP 93*
Singleton, James Milton 1933- *WhoBlA 94*
Singleton, James Ray 1955- *WhoMW 93*
Singleton, John *WhoAm 94, WhoBlA 94*
Singleton, John 1968- *AfrAmAl 6 [port], BlkWr 2, IntMPA 94*
Singleton, John Virgil, Jr. 1918- *WhoAm 94*
Singleton, Joy Ann 1953- *WhoScEn 94*
Singleton, Kathryn T. 1951- *WhoBlA 94*
Singleton, Kenneth Wayne 1947- *WhoBlA 94*
Singleton, Larry William 1950- *WhoFI 94*
Singleton, Leroy, Sr. 1941- *WhoBlA 94*
Singleton, Mark *WhoHol 92*
Singleton, Marvin Ayers 1939- *WhoAmP 93, WhoMW 93*
Singleton, Norman 1913- *Who 94*
Singleton, Penny 1908- *IntMPA 94, WhoHol 92*
Singleton, Philip Arthur 1914- *WhoAm 94*
Singleton, Robert 1936- *WhoBlA 94*
Singleton, Roger 1942- *Who 94*
Singleton, Samuel Winston 1928- *WhoAm 94*
Singleton, Sara 1940- *WhoFI 94*
Singleton, Valerie 1937- *Who 94*
Singleton, W. James 1949- *WhoAmP 93*
Singleton, William Albert 1946- *WhoMW 93*
Singleton, William Brian 1923- *Who 94*
Singleton, William Dean 1951- *IntWW 93, WhoAm 94, WhoFI 94, WhoWest 94*
Singleton, William Matthew 1924- *WhoBlA 94*
Singleton, Zutty d1975 *WhoHol 92*
Singleton-Wood, Allan James 1933- *WhoAm 94*
Singley, David James 1959- *WhoAmL 94*
Singley, Elijah 1935- *WhoBlA 94*
Singley, John Edward, Jr. 1924- *WhoAm 94*
Singley, Mark Eldridge 1921- *WhoAm 94, WhoScEn 94*
Singley, Yvonne Jean 1947- *WhoBlA 94*
Singmaster, Edwin Henry 1911- *WhoAmP 93*
Singmaster-Hernández, Karen Amalia 1960- *WhoHisp 94*
Singpurwalla, Nozer Darabsha 1939- *WhoAsA 94*
Singreen, Shirley Ann Basile 1941- *WhoAmL 94*
Singsen, Antone G., III 1942- *WhoAmL 94*
Sinha, Baron 1953- *Who 94*
Sinha, Agam Nath 1947- *WhoScEn 94*
Sinha, Akhouri A. 1933- *WhoAsA 94*
Sinha, Alok Kumar 1963- *WhoWest 94*
Sinha, Dipen N. 1951- *WhoAsA 94*
Sinha, Dipendra Kumar 1945- *WhoWest 94*
Sinha, Mahadeva Prasad 1944- *WhoScEn 94*
Sinha, Nirmal K. 1939- *WhoAsA 94*
Sinha, Phulgenda 1924- *WrDr 94*
Sinha, Ramesh Chandra 1934- *WhoAm 94*
Sinha, Ranendra Nath 1930- *WhoMW 93*
Sinha, Rohini Pati 1932- *WhoAm 94*
Sinha, Sarvajit Sahay 1960- *WhoFI 94*
Sinha, Sunil Kumar 1939- *WhoAsA 94*
Sinha, Uday K. 1938- *WhoAsA 94*
Sinha, Yagya Nand 1936- *WhoAsA 94*
Sinharoy, Samar 1940- *WhoScEn 94*
Siniavskii, Andrei *RfGShF*
Siniavskii, Andrei (Donatovich) 1925- *ConWorW 93*
Siniavsky, Andrei *ConWorW 93*
Siniawer, Paul D. 1944- *WhoAmL 94*
Sinicropi, Anthony Vincent 1931- *WhoAm 94*
Sinicropi, Giovanni Andrea 1924- *ConAu 42NR*
Sinicropi, Michael Wilson 1925- *WhoAmP 93*
Sinicropi, Stephen Anthony 1957- *WhoMW 93*
Sinimberghi, Gino 1913- *NewGrDO*
Siniscalco, Gary Richard 1943- *WhoAmL 94*
Sinise, Gary *WhoAm 94*
Sinishta, Gjon 1930- *WhoWest 94*
Sinjohn, John *ConAu 141*
Sink, Charles M. 1951- *WhoAmL 94*
Sink, Charles Stanley 1923- *WhoAm 94*
Sink, John Davis 1934- *WhoAm 94*
Sinkankas, John 1915- *WrDr 94*
Sinker, Michael Roy 1908- *Who 94*
Sinkey, Joseph Francis, Jr. 1944- *WhoFI 94*
Sinkfield, Georganna T. *WhoAmP 93*
Sinkford, Jeanne Craig 1933- *WhoAm 94*
Sinkler, George 1927- *WhoBlA 94*
Sinko, Patrick J. 1959- *WhoScEn 94*
Sinks, John R. 1929- *WhoAmP 93*
Sinn, James Micheal 1950- *WhoMW 93*
Sinnamon, Hercules Vincent 1899- *Who 94*
Sinnard, Elaine (Janice) 1926- *WhoAmA 93*
Sinnatt, Martin Henry 1928- *Who 94*
Sinnema, Elizabeth Jane *WhoFI 94*
Sinnenberg, John Regis 1957- *WhoFI 94*
Sinner, George A. 1928- *WhoAmP 93*
Sinner, George Albert 1928- *IntWW 93, WhoAm 94, WhoMW 93*
Sinnett, James M. 1939- *WhoMW 93*
Sinnett, Peter Frank 1934- *WhoScEn 94*
Sinnett, William McNair 1951- *WhoFI 94*
Sinnette, Calvin Herman 1924- *WhoBlA 94*
Sinnette, Elinor Des Verney 1925- *WrDr 94*
Sinnette, Elinor DesVerney 1925- *WhoBlA 94*
Sinnette, John Townsend, Jr. 1909- *WhoScEn 94, WhoWest 94*
Sinning, Allan Ray 1957- *WhoScEn 94*
Sinninger, Dwight Virgil 1901- *WhoFI 94*
Sinnott, Barbara J. 1933- *WhoAmP 93*
Sinnott, John Patrick 1931- *WhoAmL 94*
Sinnott, Patricia *WhoHol 92*
Sinoel d1949 *WhoHol 92*
Sinon, John Adelbert, Jr. 1956- *WhoScEn 94*
Sinopoli, Carla M. 1956- *ConAu 141*
Sinopoli, Giuseppe 1946- *IntWW 93, NewGrDO, Who 94*
Sinor, Denis 1916- *WhoAm 94, WrDr 94*
Sinor, Howard Earl, Jr. 1949- *WhoAm 94, WhoAmL 94*
Sinoto, Yosihiko H. 1924- *WhoWest 94*
Sinowatz, Fred 1929- *IntWW 93*
Sinrich, Norman 1928- *WhoAm 94*
Sinsabaugh, Art 1924-1983 *WhoAmA 93N*
Sinsheimer, Robert Louis 1920- *IntWW 93, WhoAm 94*
Sinsheimer, Robert Nevin 1955- *WhoFI 94*
Sinsheimer, Warren Jack 1927- *WhoAm 94, WhoAmL 94, WhoFI 94*
Sinsigalli, Andrew Thomas 1967- *WhoWest 94*
Sint, Marjanne 1949- *IntWW 93, WhoWomW 91*
Sinton, Christopher Michael 1946- *WhoScEn 94*
Sinton, Nell (Walter) *WhoAmA 93*

Sinton, William Merz 1925- *WhoWest 94*
Sintz, Edward Francis 1924- *WhoAm 94*
Sintzoff, Michel 1938- *WhoScEn 94*
Sinues y Navarro, Maria del Pilar 1835-1893 *BlmGWL*
Sinyard, David Blair 1956- *WhoFI 94*
Sinyavskaya, Tamara Ilyinichna 1943- *IntWW 93*
Sinyavsky, Andrey (Donatovich) 1925- *EncSF 93*
Sinyavsky, Andrey Donatovich 1925- *IntWW 93*
Siodmak, Curt 1902- *EncSF 93, IntDcF 2-4, IntMPA 94*
Siodmak, Robert d1973 *WhoHol 92*
Sion, Maurice 1928- *WhoAm 94*
Sionil Jose, F(rancisco) 1924- *RfGShF*
Sioris, Gregory Alexander 1957- *WhoAmL 94*
Sioris, Leo James 1952- *WhoMW 93*
Sioui, Richard Henry 1937- *WhoAm 94*
Sipe, Harold David, Jr. 1955- *WhoFI 94*
Sipe, Roger Wayne 1950- *WhoFI 94, WhoMW 93*
Sipes, Bill 1946- *WhoAmP 93*
Sipes, Theodore Lee 1944- *WhoMW 93*
Siphandon, Khamtay 1924- *IntWW 93*
Sipher, Allen James 1927- *WhoAmP 93*
Siphron, Joseph Rider 1933- *WhoAm 94*
Sipila, Helvi Linnea 1915- *IntWW 93*
Sipinen, Arto Kalevi 1936- *IntWW 93*
Sipinen, Seppo Antero 1946- *WhoScEn 94*
Sipiora, Leonard Paul 1934- *WhoAmA 93*
Sipkins, Peter W. 1944- *WhoAmL 94*
Sipkins, Thomas M. 1947- *WhoAmL 94*
Sipley, Nancy E. Young 1929- *WhoMW 93*
Sipolo, Jully 1953- *BlmGWL*
Siporin, Mitchell 1910-1976 *WhoAmA 93N*
Sipos, Charles Andrew 1946- *WhoScEn 94*
Sippel, Heinz 1922- *IntWW 93*
Sippel, William Leroy 1948- *WhoAm 94, WhoAmL 94, WhoMW 93*
Sipperly, Ralph d1928 *WhoHol 92*
Sippo, Arthur Carmine 1953- *WhoMW 93*
Sippy, David Dean 1953- *WhoMW 93*
Sipress, David 1947- *WrDr 94*
Sipress, Morton 1938- *WhoAmP 93*
Siqueira, Jose (de Lima) 1907-1985 *NewGrDO*
Siqueiros, David Alfaro 1896-1974 *WhoAmA 93N*
Siracusa, John 1929- *WhoAmP 93*
Siracuse, Philip L. 1940- *WhoAmL 94*
Siranovich, Stanley Francis 1948- *WhoFI 94*
Sirat, Gabriel Yeshoua 1955- *WhoScEn 94*
Sirat, Rene-Samuel 1930- *IntWW 93*
Siraut, Philippe C. 1961- *WhoScEn 94*
Siravo, Mario Ernest 1947- *WhoFI 94*
Sirc, Ljubo 1920- *WrDr 94*
Sirca, Friderik *NewGrDO*
Sircar, Badal 1925- *ConWorW 93*
Sircar, Ratna 1952- *WhoScEn 94*
Sircar, Rina Schyamcharan 1938- *WhoAsA 94*
Siregar, Melanchton 1913- *IntWW 93*
Siren, Anna-Leena Kaarina 1955- *WhoScEn 94*
Siren, Heikki 1918- *IntWW 93*
Siren, Katri (Kaija) Anna-Maija Helena 1920- *IntWW 93*
Sirena *WhoAmA 93*
Sires, Jonathan 1955- *WhoAmA 93*
Siri, Giuseppe 1906-1989 *WhAm 10*
Siri, Jean Brandenburg 1920- *WhoWest 94*
Siri, William E. 1919- *WhoScEn 94*
Siri, William Emil 1919- *WhoAm 94*
Sirica, Alphonse Eugene 1944- *WhoScEn 94*
Sirica, John 1904-1992 *AnObit 1992*
Sirica, John J. 1952-1992 *WhAm 10*
Sirica, John Joseph d1992 *IntWW 93N*
Sirignano, William Alfonso 1938- *WhoAm 94, WhoScEn 94*
Sirisamphan, Thienchai 1924- *IntWW 93*
Sirisingha, Supa (Luesiri) *BlmGWL*
Sirius, Jean *DrAPF 93*
Sirk, Douglas d1987 *WhoHol 92*
Sirkin, Joel H. 1946- *WhoAm 94, WhoAmL 94*
Sirkin, Michael S. 1947- *WhoAmL 94*
Sirkis, Nancy 1936- *WhoAmA 93*
Sirkis, Robert Lane 1951- *WhoFI 94*
Sirmans, Meredith Franklin 1939- *WhoBlA 94*
Sirmay, Albert *NewGrDO*
Sirna, Anthony Alfred, III 1924- *WhoAm 94*
Sirof, Harriet *DrAPF 93*
Sirof, Harriet 1930- *ConAu 43NR*
Sirois, Allen L. 1950- *SmATA 76 [port]*
Sirois, Gerard 1934- *WhoAm 94*
Sirois, Raymond 1927- *WhoAm 94*
Siroky, Miriam L. 1950- *WhoAmL 94*
Sirola, Bozidar 1889-1956 *NewGrDO*
Sirola, Joseph *WhoHol 92*
Sirola, Orlando 1928- *BuCMET*
Siroonian, Kenneth P. 1952- *WhoFI 94*
Sirota, Ronald Lee 1948- *WhoMW 93*
Sirotkin, Phillip Leonard 1923- *WhoAm 94, WhoWest 94*
Sirowitz, Hal *DrAPF 93*
Sirowitz, Leonard 1932- *WhoAm 94*
Sirpis, Andrew Paul 1944- *WhoFI 94*
Sir Rap-A-Lot
See Geto Boys, The *ConMus 11*
Sirridge, Patrick M. 1949- *WhoAmL 94*
Sirs, William 1920- *Who 94*
Sirtis, Marina 1961- *WhoHol 92*
Sirugo, Sal *WhoAmA 93*
Sis, Raymond Francis 1931- *WhoAm 94*
Sischy, Ingrid B. 1952- *WhoAmA 93*
Sischy, Ingrid Barbara 1952- *WhoAm 94*
Sisco, Elizabeth 1954- *WhoAmA 93*
Sisco, Joseph John 1919- *IntWW 93, WhoAm 94*
Siscoe, George Leonard 1937- *WhoAm 94*
Sisemore, Claudia 1937- *WhoWest 94*
Sisisky, Norman 1927- *CngDr 93, WhoAm 94, WhoAmP 93*
Sisitsky, Alan David 1942- *WhoAmP 93*
Sisk, Albert Fletcher, Jr. 1928- *WhoFI 94*
Sisk, Daniel Arthur 1927- *WhoAm 94*
Sisk, Paul Douglas 1950- *WhoAmL 94*
Sisk, Philip Laurence 1913- *WhoAm 94, WhoAmL 94*
Sisk, Robert J. 1928- *WhoAm 94*
Siska, Richard Stanly 1948- *WhoMW 93*
Siske, Roger Charles 1944- *WhoAm 94, WhoAmL 94, WhoFI 94*
Siskel, Gene 1946- *WhoAm 94, WhoMW 93*
Siskin, Edward Joseph 1941- *WhoAm 94*
Siskind, Aaron 1903-1991 *WhAm 10*
Siskind, Donald Henry 1937- *WhoAm 94*
Siskind, Lawrence Jay 1952- *WhoWest 94*
Siskind, Ralph Walter 1949- *WhoAm 94*
Sisler, George Frederick 1896- *WhAm 10*
Sisler, Harry Hall 1917- *WhoAm 94, WrDr 94*
Sisler, William Philip 1947- *WhoAm 94*
Sisley, Alfred 1839-1899 *DcNaB MP*
Sisley, G. William 1944- *WhoAm 94*
Sisneros, Joe M. 1935- *WhoHisp 94*
Sisneros, Jose *WhoHisp 94*
Sisneros, Michael John 1949- *WhoHisp 94*
Sisneros, Raymond A. 1958- *WhoHisp 94*
Sisney, Ricardo 1939- *WhoBlA 94*
Sisodia, Rajendra Singh 1958- *WhoFI 94*
Sison, Fredilyn 1963- *WhoAsA 94*
Sissel, George Allen 1936- *WhoAm 94, WhoAmL 94, WhoFI 94*
Sisselman, David I. 1955- *WhoAmL 94*
Sissle, Noble d1975 *WhoHol 92*
Sissle, Noble 1889-1975 *AfrAmAl 6*
Sissman, Ben G. 1951- *WhoAmL 94*
Sissom, Evelyn Janelle *WhoAmA 93*
Sissom, John Douglas 1937- *WhoScEn 94*
Sissom, Leighton Esten 1934- *WhoAm 94*
Sisson, C(harles) H(ubert) 1914- *WrDr 94*
Sisson, Charles Hubert 1914- *IntWW 93, Who 94*
Sisson, Donald Benjamin 1932- *WhoFI 94*
Sisson, Everett Arnold 1920- *WhoAm 94, WhoFI 94*
Sisson, George Allen, Sr. 1920- *WhoAm 94*
Sisson, Jack c. 1743-1821 *WhAmRev*
Sisson, Jacqueline D. 1925-1980 *WhoAmA 93N*
Sisson, Jeremiah 1720-1783? *DcNaB MP*
Sisson, Jerry Allan 1956- *WhoAmL 94*
Sisson, John Ross 1926- *WhoWest 94*
Sisson, Jonathan *DrAPF 93*
Sisson, Jonathan 1690?-1747 *DcNaB MP*
Sisson, Laurence P. 1928- *WhoAmA 93*
Sisson, Mary Winifred 1919- *WhoMW 93*
Sisson, Ray L. 1934- *WhoAm 94*
Sisson, Robert F. 1923- *WhoAm 94*
Sisson, Rosemary Anne 1923- *Who 94, WrDr 94*
Sisson, Roy d1993 *Who 94N*
Sisson, Thomas Randolph Clinton 1920- *WhAm 10*
Sisson, Vera d1954 *WhoHol 92*
Sisson, Virginia Evans 1927- *WhoAmP 93*
Sissons, John Gerald Patrick 1945- *Who 94*
Sissons, (Thomas) Michael (Beswick) 1934- *Who 94*
Sissons, Peter George 1942- *IntWW 93, Who 94*
Sissors, Jack Zanville 1919- *WhoMW 93*
Sisto, Elena 1952- *WhoAm 94, WhoAmA 93*
Sisto, Fernando 1924- *WhoAm 94*
Sistrunk, James Dudley 1919- *WhAm 10*
Sistrunk, William Hicks 1937- *WhoAm 94*
Sisulu, Nontsikelelo Albertina *WhoWomW 91*
Sisulu, Nontsikelelo Albertina 1919- *IntWW 93*
Sisulu, Walter Max Ulyate 1912- *IntWW 93*
Sit, Eugene C. 1938- *WhoMW 93*
Sita, Michael John 1953- *WhoMW 93*
Sitarz, Darrell Edwin 1946- *WhoMW 93*
Sitasz, Denise Maria 1960- *WhoMW 93*
Siteman, Alvin Jerome 1928- *WhoAm 94*
Sites, Betsi 1946- *WhoWest 94*
Sites, James Philip 1948- *WhoAmL 94, WhoWest 94*
Sitgreaves, John 1757-1802 *WhAmRev*
Sitgreaves, Lorenzo c. 1811-1888 *WhWE*
Sithole, Ndabaningi 1920- *IntWW 93*
Siti Zaharah Hj Sulaiman, Datuk 1949- *WhoWomW 91*
Sitka, Emil *WhoHol 92*
Sitkovetsky, Dmitry 1954- *IntWW 93*
Sitrick, James Baker 1935- *WhoAm 94*
Sitrick, Michael Steven 1947- *WhoAm 94*
Sitruk, Jo 1944- *IntWW 93*
Sitsky, Larry 1934- *NewGrDO*
Sitta, Eva *WhoHol 92*
Sitter, Concha 1962- *WhoMW 93*
Sitter, John E(dward) 1944- *WrDr 94*
Sitter, John Edward 1944- *WhoAm 94*
Sitter, Willem de 1872-1934 *WorScD*
Sitter, William Hall 1939- *WhoAm 94, WhoFI 94*
Sitterly, Charlotte Moore 1898-1990 *WhAm 10*
Sitterly, Connie Sue 1953- *WhoFI 94*
Sittig, C. Dale 1940- *WhoAmP 93*
Sitting Bull c. 1830-1890 *EncNAR, HisWorL [port]*
Sitting Bull c. 1854-c. 1932 *EncNAR*
Sitting in the Sky d1907 *EncNAR*
Sitton, Claude Fox 1925- *WhoAm 94*
Sitton, Claude Shem 1937- *WhoAmP 93*
Sitton, Fred Monroe 1924-1988 *WhAm 10*
Sitton, Joe 1943- *WhoAmP 93*
Sitton, John M. 1907- *WhoAmA 93*
Sitton, Vivian Smith 1938- *WhoAmP 93*
Sittsamer, Murray J. 1959- *WhoFI 94*
Sitty, Janet L. 1942- *WhoAmP 93*
Situ, Ming 1937- *WhoScEn 94*
Sitwell, Edith 1887-1964 *BlmGEL, BlmGWL*
Sitwell, Francis Gerard 1906- *Who 94*
Sitwell, Osbert 1892-1969 *BlmGEL, EncSF 93*
Sitwell, Peter Sacheverell W. *Who 94*
Sitwell, (Sacheverell) Reresby 1927- *Who 94*
Sitwell, Sacheverell 1897-1988 *BlmGEL*
Sitz, Mark *WhoAmP 93*
Sitzman, Jerry Clayton 1936- *WhoMW 93*
Sitzmann, Thomas George 1944- *WhoAmL 94*
Siu, Nancy 1940- *WhoAsA 94*
Siu, Yum-Tong 1943- *WhoAsA 94*
Sivack, Denis *DrAPF 93*
Sivadas, Iraja 1950- *WhoWest 94*
Sivam, Thangavel Parama 1944- *WhoScEn 94*
Sivan, Amiram 1938- *IntWW 93*
Sivard, Robert Paul 1914-1990 *WhoAmA 93N*
Sivasithamparam, Murgugesu 1923- *IntWW 93*
Sivasubramanian, Kolinjavadi Nagarajan 1945- *WhoScEn 94*
Sivathanu, Yudaya Raju 1962- *WhoScEn 94*
Sive, David 1922- *WhoAm 94*
Sive, Rebecca Anne 1950- *WhoAm 94, WhoMW 93*
Siverd, Robert Joseph 1948- *WhoAmL 94*
Siverio, Manny 1950- *WhoHisp 94*
Sivero, Frank *WhoHol 92*
Siverson, Randolph Martin 1940- *WhoAm 94, WhoWest 94*
Siverson, Susan Jo 1960- *WhoWest 94*
Sivewright, Robert Charles Townsend 1923- *Who 94*
Sivgin, Halil 1950- *IntWW 93*
Sivic, Pavel 1908- *NewGrDO*
Sivick, Robert James 1963- *WhoAmL 94*
Sivie, John Charles 1945- *WhoFI 94*
Sivin, Nathan 1931- *WhoAm 94*
Sivinski, James Anthony 1938- *WhoFI 94*
Sivley, Paul Allen 1958- *WhoAmP 93*
Sivori, Enrique Omar 1935- *WorESoc*
Siward, Richard d1248 *DcNaB MP*
Siwek, Carol A. *WhoAmP 93*
Siwek, Donald Fancher 1954- *WhoScEn 94*
Six, Fred N. 1929- *WhoAm 94, WhoAmL 94, WhoMW 93*
Six, Frederick N. *WhoAmP 93*
Six, James 1730-1793 *DcNaB MP*
Six, Reine Fontaine 1933- *WhoMW 93*
Sixel, Lois Cabalek 1927- *WhoMW 93*
Si Xia *WhoPRCh 91 [port]*
Siy, James Andrew 1967- *WhoAsA 94*
Siyad Barre, Muhammad *IntWW 93*
Siyan, Karanjit Saint Germain Singh 1954- *WhoScEn 94, WhoWest 94*
Sizemore, Barbara A. 1927- *WhoBlA 94*
Sizemore, Barbara Ann 1927- *WhoMW 93*
Sizemore, Carolyn Lee 1945- *WhoScEn 94*
Sizemore, Christine Wick 1945- *WrDr 94*
Sizemore, Frank J., III *WhoAmP 93*
Sizemore, Herman Mason, Jr. 1941- *WhoAm 94, WhoWest 94*
Sizemore, James Middleton, Jr. 1942- *WhoAmP 93*
Sizemore, Nicky Lee 1946- *WhoWest 94*
Sizemore, Robert Carlen 1951- *WhoScEn 94*
Sizemore, Thomas E. 1940- *WhoAmL 94*
Sizemore, Tom *WhoHol 92*
Sizemore, William Christian 1938- *WhoAm 94*
Sizer, Irwin Whiting 1910- *WhoAm 94*
Sizer, John 1938- *Who 94, WrDr 94*
Sizer, Michael Gene 1953- *WhoAmP 93*
Sizer, Phillip Spelman 1926- *WhoAm 94*
Sizer, Theodore R. 1932- *WhoAm 94*
Sizer, Theodore Ryland 1932- *WrDr 94*
Sizer, Thomas R. 1938- *WhoAmL 94*
Sizova, Alla 1939- *IntDcB [port]*
Sizova, Alla Ivanovna 1939- *IntWW 93*
Sjaastad, Anders Christian 1942- *IntWW 93*
Sjadzali, Munawir 1924- *IntWW 93*
Sjoberg, Alf d1980 *WhoHol 92*
Sjoberg, Berndt Olof Harald 1931- *WhoScEn 94*
Sjoberg, Donald *WhoAm 94*
Sjoberg, Gunnar *WhoHol 92*
Sjoen, Kenneth Diomed 1948- *WhoWest 94*
Sjoerdsma, Albert 1924- *WhoAm 94*
Sjogren, Clifford Frank, Jr. 1928- *WhoWest 94*
Sjogren, Donald Ernest 1932- *WhoMW 93*
Sjogren, Sandra Lee 1954- *WhoWest 94*
Sjoholm, Paul Fredric 1961- *WhoWest 94*
Sjolander, Barbara Johnston 1944- *WhoMW 93*
Sjolander, Gary Walfred 1942- *WhoWest 94*
Sjostrand, Arnold d1955 *WhoHol 92*
Sjostrand, Fritiof Stig 1912- *WhoAm 94, WhoScEn 94*
Sjostrom, Joan Sevier 1931- *WhoWest 94*
Sjostrom, Rex William 1930- *WhoWest 94*
Sjostrom, Victor d1960 *WhoHol 92*
Sjulin, R. Paul 1939- *WhoAmP 93*
Skaar, Steven Baard 1953- *WhoScEn 94*
Skadden, Donald Harvey 1925- *WhoAm 94*
Skadden, Nancy Lee Mackey 1939- *WhoAmP 93*
Skaff, Andrew Joseph 1945- *WhoAm 94*
Skaff, George *WhoHol 92*
Skaff, Joseph John 1930- *WhoAm 94*
Skagen, James Colvin 1931- *WhoWest 94*
Skagerberg, Donna Clare 1928- *WhoAmP 93*
Skaggs, Bill 1942- *WhoAmP 93*
Skaggs, David E. 1943- *CngDr 93, WhoAm 94, WhoWest 94*
Skaggs, David Evans 1943- *WhoAmP 93*
Skaggs, Gail E. 1948- *WhoAmL 94*
Skaggs, Jimmie F. *WhoHol 92*
Skaggs, Kathy Cheryl 1956- *WhoAmL 94*
Skaggs, L. Sam 1922- *WhoAm 94, WhoFI 94, WhoWest 94*
Skaggs, Raymond Leo 1933- *WhoAmP 93*
Skaggs, Richard Wayne 1942- *WhoAm 94, WhoScEn 94*
Skaggs, Ricky *WhoAm 94*
Skaggs, Samuel Robert 1936- *WhoWest 94*
Skaggs, Sanford Merle 1939- *WhoAm 94, WhoAmL 94, WhoWest 94*
Skaggs, Wayne Gerard 1929- *WhoAm 94, WhoFI 94*
Skahan, Paul Laurence 1925- *WhoAm 94*
Skak-Nielsen, Niels Verner 1922- *IntWW 93*
Skakun, Mark John, III 1950- *WhoAm 94*
Skal, David J. *EncSF 93*
Skala, Gary Dennis 1946- *WhoMW 93, WhoScEn 94*
Skala, Ivan 1922- *IntWW 93*
Skala, Lilia *WhoHol 92*
Skalagard, Hans 1924- *WhoAmA 93*
Skalagard, Hans Martin 1924- *WhoWest 94*
Skalak, Richard 1923- *WhoAm 94, WhoScEn 94*
Skaldaspillir, Sigfridur 1944- *WrDr 94*
Skalecki, Lisa Marie 1962- *WhoScEn 94*
Skalka, Anna Marie 1938- *WhoScEn 94*
Skalka, Harold Walter 1941- *WhoAm 94, WhoScEn 94*
Skalko, Louise Luchetti 1938- *WhoFI 94*
Skalko, Richard Gallant 1936- *WhoAm 94*

Slater, William John 1927- Who 94
Slatin, Yeffe Kimball 1914-1978 WhoAmA 93N
Slatinaru, Maria 1938- NewGrDO
Slatkes, Leonard J. 1930- WhoAmA 93
Slatkin, Charles E. 1908-1977 WhoAmA 93N
Slatkin, Eric Stuart 1954- WhoAmL 94
Slatkin, Leonard 1944- IntWW 93
Slatkin, Leonard Edward 1944- WhoAm 94, WhoMW 93
Slatkin, Marcia DrAPF 93
Slatkin, Murray 1905- WhoAm 94
Slatkin, Wendy 1950- WhoAmA 93
Slaton, Gwendolyn C. 1945- WhoBlA 94
Slaton, Lewis Roger 1922- WhoAmL 94
Slatopolsky, Eduardo 1934- WhoScEn 94
Slatta, Richard W(ayne) 1947- WrDr 94
Slattery, Charles Wilbur 1937- WhoAm 94
Slattery, David Antony Douglas 1930- Who 94
Slattery, James Charles 1948- WhoAm 94, WhoAmP 93, WhoMW 93
Slattery, James Joseph 1922- WhoAm 94
Slattery, James P. WhoIns 94
Slattery, Jim 1948- CngDr 93
Slattery, Marty 1938- WrDr 94
Slattery, Paul Francis 1940- WhoAm 94
Slattery, Richard X. 1925- WhoHol 92
Slattery, Terrance Lester 1954- WhoMW 93
Slattery, Thomas Edward 1940- WhoAmP 93
Slattery, William Henry 1943- WhoAmL 94
Slatton, Ralph David 1952- WhoAmA 93
Slatyer, Ralph Owen 1929- IntWW 93, Who 94
Slatzer, Robert (Franklin) 1927- WrDr 94
Slatzer, Robert F. WhoHol 92
Slatzer, Robert Franklin 1927- IntMPA 94
Slaughter, Alexander Hoke 1937- WhoAm 94
Slaughter, Audrey Cecelia Who 94
Slaughter, Carole D. 1945- WhoBlA 94
Slaughter, Carolyn 1946- WrDr 94
Slaughter, Edward Ratliff, Jr. 1931- WhoAm 94, WhoAmL 94
Slaughter, Eugene Edward 1909- WrDr 94
Slaughter, Frank G(ill) 1908- WrDr 94
Slaughter, Frank Gill 1908- Who 94, WhoAm 94
Slaughter, Fred L. 1942- WhoBlA 94
Slaughter, Freeman Cluff 1926- WhoScEn 94
Slaughter, Giles David 1937- Who 94
Slaughter, Hazel Burnham 1888-1979 WhoAmA 93N
Slaughter, James Luther, III 1944- WhoMW 93
Slaughter, Joe Keith 1947- WhoMW 93
Slaughter, John Brooks 1934- WhoAm 94, WhoBlA 94, WhoScEn 94, WhoWest 94
Slaughter, John Etta 1929- WhoBlA 94
Slaughter, Louise McIntosh 1929- CngDr 93, WhoAm 94, WhoAmP 93
Slaughter, Lurline Eddy 1919-1991 WhoAmA 93N
Slaughter, M(ary) M(artina) 1940- WrDr 94
Slaughter, Marshall Glenn 1940- WhoAmL 94
Slaughter, Nathaniel G., III 1944- WhoAmL 94
Slaughter, Peter 1928- WhoBlA 94
Slaughter, Robert WhoHol 92
Slaughter, Robert L. 1933- WhoAmP 93
Slaughter, Robert L. 1950- WhoAmP 93
Slaughter, Sgt. WhoHol 92
Slaughter, Tod d1956 WhoHol 92
Slaughter, Vernon L. WhoBlA 94
Slaughter, Webster M. 1964- WhoBlA 94
Slaughter, William Edward, Jr. 1908-1990 WhAm 10
Slaughter, William M. WhoAmP 93
Slaughter-Defoe, Diana T. 1941- WhoBlA 94
Slavens, Thomas Paul 1928- WhoAm 94
Slavenska, Mia WhoHol 92
Slavenska, Mia 1914?- IntDcB [port]
Slavich, Denis Michael 1940- WhoAm 94
Slavick, Lester Irwin 1927- WhoFI 94
Slavick, Susanne Mechtild 1956- WhoAmA 93
Slavik, Donald Harlan 1956- WhoAmL 94
Slavin, Arlene 1942- WhoAm 94, WhoAmA 93
Slavin, Bill 1959- SmATA 76 [port]
Slavin, Craig Steven 1951- WhoMW 93
Slavin, George 1916- IntMPA 94
Slavin, Howard Allan 1941- WhoAmL 94
Slavin, John d1940 WhoHol 92
Slavin, John Jeremiah 1921- WhoAmL 94
Slavin, Jose d1978 WhoHol 92
Slavin, Joseph 1924- WhoAmL 94
Slavin, Joseph Thomas 1958- WhoFI 94
Slavin, Millie WhoHol 92
Slavin, Morris 1913- ConAu 41NR
Slavin, Neal 1941- WhoAm 94, WhoAmA 93
Slavin, Raymond Granam 1930- WhoAm 94
Slavin, Roberta Landau 1929- WhoFI 94
Slavin, Simon 1916- WhoAm 94
Slavina, Mariya 1858-1951 NewGrDO
Slavitt, David (Rytman) 1935- WrDr 94
Slavitt, David R. DrAPF 93
Slavitt, David R(ytman) 1935- ConAu 41NR
Slavitt, David Rytman 1935- IntWW 93
Slavitt, David Walton 1931- WhoAm 94
Slavitt, Earl Benton 1939- WhoAm 94
Slavkin, Harold C. 1938- WhoScEn 94
Slavutin, Debra Claire 1951- WhoFI 94
Slavutin, Lee Jacob 1951- WhoFI 94
Slavutych, Yar 1918- WrDr 94
Slawiatynsky, Marion Michael 1958- WhoScEn 94
Slawinski, Lora Ann, Sister 1952- WhoMW 93
Slawkowski, David John 1950- WhoAm 94, WhoAmL 94
Slawson, John 1898-1989 WhAm 10
Slay, Francis P. 1927- WhoAmP 93
Slayden, James Bragdon 1924- WhoAm 94
Slayer ConMus 10 [port]
Slaymaker, Gene Arthur 1928- WhoAm 94
Slaymaker, H. Olav 1939- WhoAm 94
Slaymaker, Martha 1935- WhoAmA 93
Slayman, Carolyn Walch 1937- WhoAm 94
Slayton, Donald K. 1924-1993 NewYTBS 93 [port]
Slayton, Donald K(ent) 1924-1993 CurBio 93N
Slayton, Frank Marshall 1932- WhoAmP 93
Slayton, Gus 1937- WhoAm 94
Slayton, John Arthur 1918- WhoAm 94
Slayton, John Howard 1955- WhoAmL 94, WhoFI 94
Slayton, Ransom Dunn 1917- WhoScEn 94
Slayton, Richard Courtney 1937- WhoFI 94
Slayton, William Larew 1916- WhoAm 94
Slease, Clyde Harold, III 1944- WhoAmL 94
Sleator, William (Warner, III) 1945- EncSF 93, TwCYAW, WrDr 94
Sleator, William Warner, III WhoAm 94
Slechta, Jiri 1939- WhoScEn 94
Slechta, Robert Frank 1928- WhoAm 94
Sledd, Herbert D. WhoAm 94
Sledd, William Tazwell 1935- WhoMW 93
Sledge, Clement Blount 1930- WhoScEn 94
Sledge, James Scott 1947- WhoAm 94, WhoAmL 94
Sledge, P. Nevin 1921- WhoAmP 93
Sledge, Reginald Leon 1954- WhoFI 94
Sledge, Richard Kitson 1930- Who 94
Slee, Richard EncSF 93
Sleeman, (Stuart) Colin Who 94
Sleeman, Philip d1953 WhoHol 92
Sleep, Wayne 1948- IntWW 93, Who 94, WhoHol 92
Sleeper, Jim 1947- WrDr 94
Sleeper, Martha d1983 WhoHol 92
Sleeper, Ralph William d1993 NewYTBS 93
Sleeper, Ruth 1899-1992 CurBio 93N
Sleep N' Eat d1962 WhoHol 92
Sleet, Moneta, Jr. 1926- AfrAmAl 6, ConBlB 5 [port]
Sleet, Moneta J., Jr. 1926- WhoBlA 94
Sleeth, David Thompson 1957- WhoAmL 94
Sleezer, Paul David 1936- WhoScEn 94
Slegman, Betty Harvey 1922- WhoMW 93
Sleicher, Charles Albert 1924- WhoAm 94
Sleigh, Sylvia WhoAm 94, WhoAmA 93
Sleight, Arthur William 1939- WhoAm 94, WhoWest 94
Sleight, Jessie Adele 1896- WhAm 10
Sleight, Peter 1929- Who 94
Sleight, Richard 1946- Who 94
Sleik, Thomas Scott 1947- WhoAmL 94
Slemmons, Robert Sheldon 1922- WhoFI 94, WhoMW 93, WhoScEn 94
Slemon, Gordon Richard 1924- WhoAm 94, WrDr 94
Slenker, Richard Dreyer, Jr. 1957- WhoFI 94
Sleno, Karen Marie 1969- WhoMW 93
Slentz, Andrew Paul 1961- WhoWest 94
Slepecky, Norma B. 1944- WhoScEn 94
Slepian, David 1923- WhoAm 94
Slepian, Jan(ice B.) 1921- TwCYAW, WrDr 94
Slepian, Paul 1923- WhoAm 94
Slepichev, Oleh Ivanovych 1949- LngBDD
Slepin, Matthew Morgan 1908- WhoAmL 94
Slesar, Henry DrAPF 93
Slesar, Henry 1927- EncSF 93, WrDr 94
Slesiensky, Deloris DrAPF 93
Slesinger, Reuben Emanuel 1916- WhoFI 94
Slesinger, Warren DrAPF 93
Slesinger, Warren 1933- WrDr 94
Slesnick, William Ellis 1925- WhoAm 94
Slessor, Mary Mitchell 1848-1915 DcNaB MP
Slethaug, Gordon E. 1940- ConAu 140
Sletner, Barbara Marie 1939- WhoMW 93
Slettebak, Arne 1925- WhoAm 94
Slettehaugh, Thomas Chester 1925- WhoAmA 93
Sletten, John Robert 1932- WhoAm 94
Slevin, Brian Francis Patrick 1926- Who 94
Slevin, Joseph Raymond 1918- WhoFI 94
Slevin, Margarita H. 1953- WhoWest 94
Slevin, Maurice Louis 1949- Who 94
Slewitzke, Connie Lee 1931- WhoAm 94
Slezak, Leo d1946 WhoHol 92
Slezak, Leo 1873-1946 NewGrDO [port]
Slezak, Margarete d1953 WhoHol 92
Slezak, Walter d1983 WhoHol 92
Slezinger, Josif 1794-1870 NewGrDO
Slichter, Charles Pence 1924- IntWW 93, WhoAm 94, WhoScEn 94
Slichter, William Pence 1922-1990 WhAm 10
Slick, Grace Wing 1939- WhoAm 94
Slick, James Nelson 1901-1979 WhoAmA 93N
Slick, Jonathan BlmGWL
Slicker, Frederick Kent 1943- WhoAmL 94
Slide, Anthony (Clifford) 1944- WrDr 94
Slider, Dorla Dean 1929- WhoAmA 93
Slie, Samuel N. 1925- WhoBlA 94
Sliepcevich, Cedomir M. 1920- WhoAm 94
Slife, Harry WhoAmP 93
Slife, Harry Gene 1923- WhoMW 93
Slifka, Alfred A. 1932- WhoAm 94, WhoFI 94
Slifkin, Lawrence Myer 1925- WhoAm 94
Sliger, Bernard Francis 1924- IntWW 93
Sliger, Rebecca North 1967- WhoScEn 94
Sligh, Clarissa T. 1939- WhoAmA 93
Sligo, Marquess of 1939- Who 94
Sliker, Todd Richard 1936- WhoWest 94
Slim, Viscount 1927- Who 94
Slim, Memphis d1988 WhoHol 92
Slim, Taieb 1919- IntWW 93
Slimmer, Dennis Ray 1947- WhoFI 94
Slimmings, William Kenneth MacLeod 1912- Who 94
Slinde, Elizabeth M. WhoAmP 93
Sliney, James Gilmore, Jr. 1940- WhoMW 93
Sliney, Robert Harold 1957- WhoMW 93
Slinger, William 1917- Who 94
Slingluff, Charles Haines, Jr. 1929- WhoFI 94
Slingluff, Robert Mitchell 1953- WhoFI 94
Slingsby, David WhoHol 92
Slingsby, William Cecil 1849-1929 DcNaB MP
Slinker, David Kent 1952- WhoWest 94
Slinker, John Michael 1952- WhoWest 94
Slipher, Vesto Melvin 1875-1969 WorScD
Slipman, Ronald 1939- WhoFI 94, WhoScEn 94
Slipman, Sue 1949- Who 94
Slipperjack, Ruby 1952- BlmGWL
Slisz, Jozef 1934- IntWW 93
Sliteris, E. Joanne 1942- WhoAmL 94
Sliva, Anatoly Yakovlevich 1940- LngBDD
Slive, Seymour 1920- Who 94, WhoAm 94, WhoAmA 93, WrDr 94
Slivka, David WhoAmA 93
Slivka, Michael Andrew 1955- WhoAmL 94
Sloan, Albert J. H., II 1942- WhoBlA 94
Sloan, Andrew (Kirkpatrick) 1931- Who 94
Sloan, Benjamin DrAPF 93
Sloan, David E. 1923- WhoBlA 94
Sloan, David Edward 1922- WhoAm 94
Sloan, David W. 1937- WhoAmP 93
Sloan, David W. 1941- WhoAm 94, WhoAmL 94
Sloan, Don 1928- ConAu 142
Sloan, Donnie Robert, Jr. 1946- WhoAmL 94
Sloan, Earle Dendy, Jr. 1944- WhoScEn 94, WhoWest 94
Sloan, Edith Barksdale 1940- WhoBlA 94
Sloan, Frank Blaine 1920- WhoAmL 94
Sloan, Frank Keenan 1921- WhoAm 94, WhoAmP 93
Sloan, Greg Brann 1959- WhoMW 93
Sloan, Harold David 1949- WhoScEn 94
Sloan, Herbert Elias 1914- WhoAm 94
Sloan, Hugh Walter, Jr. 1940- WhoAm 94
Sloan, James Park DrAPF 93
Sloan, James Park 1916- WhoAmP 93
Sloan, Jeanette Pasin 1946- WhoAm 94, WhoAmA 93, WhoMW 93
Sloan, Jerry 1942- BasBi, WhoAm 94, WhoWest 94
Sloan, John 1871-1951 WhoAmA 93N
Sloan, John Elliot, Jr. 1936-1991 WhAm 10
Sloan, John R. IntMPA 94
Sloan, Johnny Wade 1949- WhoAm 94
Sloan, Joyce WhoMW 93
Sloan, Kay DrAPF 93
Sloan, L. Lawrence 1947- WhoAm 94, WhoWest 94
Sloan, Lane Everett 1947- WhoAm 94, WhoFI 94
Sloan, Lanny Gene 1945- WhoWest 94
Sloan, Maceo Archibald 1913- WhoBlA 94
Sloan, Maceo Kennedy 1949- WhoAmL 94, WhoBlA 94, WhoFI 94
Sloan, Margaret MacKenzie 1918- WhoWest 94
Sloan, Mark 1957- WhoAmA 93
Sloan, Mary Jean 1927- WhoScEn 94
Sloan, Melanie Togman 1965- WhoAmL 94
Sloan, Michael 1946- WrDr 94
Sloan, Michael Dana 1960- WhoWest 94
Sloan, Michael Dean 1956- WhoMW 93
Sloan, Michael Eugene 1943- WhoFI 94, WhoWest 94
Sloan, Michael Lee 1944- WhoMW 93, WhoScEn 94
Sloan, Norman Alexander 1914- Who 94
Sloan, O. Temple, Jr. 1939- WhoAm 94
Sloan, Pat(rick Alan) 1908-1978 ConAu 43NR
Sloan, Paula Rackoff 1945- WhoScEn 94
Sloan, Philip Roscoe 1939- WhoAmL 94
Sloan, Richard 1935- WhoAm 94, WhoAmA 93
Sloan, Robert David 1957- WhoFI 94
Sloan, Robert Hood, Jr. 1953- WhoFI 94
Sloan, Robert Smullyan 1915- WhoAmA 93
Sloan, Ron WhoHol 92
Sloan, Ronald J. 1932- WhoAmA 93
Sloan, Sheldon Harold 1935- WhoAmP 93
Sloan, Sonia Schorr 1928- WhoAmP 93
Sloan, Stanley 1943- WhoAm 94
Sloan, Stephen 1932- WhoAm 94
Sloan, Stephen 1951- WhoAmP 93
Sloan, Stephen Stehly 1948- WhoFI 94
Sloan, Susan V. 1945- WhoFI 94
Sloan, Tod (Stratton) 1952- ConAu 140
Sloan, Tod Burns 1948- WhoScEn 94
Sloan, Wayne Francis 1950- WhoScEn 94
Sloan, William (Hope) d1933 WhoHol 92
Sloan, William Boyd 1895- WhAm 10
Sloane, Beverly LeBov 1936- WhoAm 94, WhoFI 94, WhoScEn 94, WhoWest 94
Sloane, Bonnie Fiedorek 1944- WhoScEn 94
Sloane, Carl Stuart 1937- WhoAm 94
Sloane, Doreen d1990 WhoHol 92
Sloane, Eric 1910-1985 WhoAmA 93N
Sloane, Everett d1965 WhoHol 92
Sloane, G. Michael WhoIns 94
Sloane, Harvey I. 1936- WhoAmP 93
Sloane, Ian Christopher 1938- Who 94
Sloane, Joseph Curtis 1909- WhoAmA 93
Sloane, Marshall M. 1926- WhoAm 94
Sloane, Neil James Alexander 1939- WhoAm 94
Sloane, Olive d1963 WhoHol 92
Sloane, Peter J(ames) 1942- WrDr 94
Sloane, Peter James 1942- Who 94
Sloane, Phyllis Lester WhoAmA 93
Sloane, Phyllis Lester 1921- WhoMW 93
Sloane, Robert Lindley 1940- WhoAm 94
Sloane, Robert Malcolm 1933- WhoAm 94, WhoWest 94
Sloane, T(homas) O'Conor 1851-1940 EncSF 93
Sloane, Thomas Charles 1922- WhoAm 94
Sloane, Thomas O. 1929- WhoAm 94
Sloane, William M(illigan) 1906-1974 EncSF 93
Sloane, William Martin 1951- WhoAmL 94, WhoAmP 93
Sloat, Barbara Furin 1942- WhoMW 93
Sloat, Richard Joel 1945- WhoAmA 93
Slobodkin, Louis 1903-1975 WhoAmA 93N
Slobodkina, Esphyr 1908- WhoAmA 93, WrDr 94
Slobodskaya, Oda 1888-1970 NewGrDO
Slocomb, Paul D. 1945- WhoAm 94
Slocombe, Douglas 1913- IntDcF 2-4 [port], IntMPA 94
Slocombe, George (Edward) 1894-1963 EncSF 93
Slocombe, Walter Becker 1941- WhoAm 94, WhoAmL 94
Slocum, Barclay 1942- WhoAm 94

Slocum, Brian Donnelly 1947- *WhoFI 94*
Slocum, Cy d1963 *WhoHol 92*
Slocum, Donald Hillman 1930- *WhoFI 94*
Slocum, Donald Warren *WhoAm 94*
Slocum, Frank 1925- *WrDr 94*
Slocum, George Sigman 1940- *WhoFI 94*
Slocum, Henry 1862-1949 *BuCMET*
Slocum, John fl. 1880- *EncNAR*
Slocum, Kirk David 1953- *WhoFI 94*
Slocum, Lester Edwin 1950- *WhoScEn 94*
Slocum, Mary Thompson fl. 1880- *EncNAR*
Slocum, Milton J. d1993 *NewYTBS 93*
Slocum, Milton Jonathan 1905-1993 *ConAu 140*
Slocum, R.C. *WhoAm 94*
Slocum, Rosemarie R. 1948- *WhoFI 94, WhoMW 93*
Sloderbeck, Phillip Eugene 1952- *WhoMW 93*
Sloggett, Jolyon Edward 1933- *Who 94*
Sloggy, John Edward 1952- *WhoFI 94, WhoScEn 94*
Slogoff, Stephen 1942- *WhoAm 94*
Sloman, Albert (Edward) 1921- *Who 94*
Sloman, Albert Edward 1921- *IntWW 93, WrDr 94*
Sloman, (Margaret) Barbara 1925- *Who 94*
Sloman, Edward d1972 *WhoHol 92*
Sloman, Hylda d1961 *WhoHol 92*
Sloman, Joel *DrAPF 93*
Sloman, Marvin Sherk 1925- *WhoAmL 94*
Sloman, Peter 1919- *Who 94*
Slomanson, William Reed 1945- *WhoWest 94*
Slome, Jesse Ronald 1952- *WhoFI 94*
Slomka, Stella Louise 1920- *WhoAm 94*
Slonaker, Norman Dale 1940- *WhoAm 94*
Slonczewski, Joan (Lyn) 1956- *EncSF 93*
Slone, Adolph 1922- *WhoFI 94*
Slone, R. Wayne 1935- *WhoAm 94, WhoFI 94*
Slone, Sandi 1939- *WhoAmA 93*
Slonecker, Charles Edward 1938- *WhoAm 94*
Slonem, Hunt 1951- *WhoAmA 93*
Slonim, Arnold Robert 1926- *WhoAm 94, WhoScEn 94*
Slonim, Ralph Joseph, Jr. 1925- *WhoScEn 94*
Slonim, Reuben 1914- *WrDr 94*
Slonimski, Piotr 1922- *IntWW 93*
Slonimsky, Nicolas 1894- *IntWW 93, WhoAm 94*
Slonimsky, Sergey Mikhailovich 1932- *IntWW 93*
Slonimsky, Sergey Mikhaylovich 1932- *NewGrDO*
Sloniowski, Paul William 1938- *WhoAmL 94*
Slook, George Francis 1946- *WhoAm 94, WhoFI 94*
Slorach, Marie 1951- *NewGrDO*
Slorp, John S. 1936- *WhoAm 94*
Slosar, John Robert 1955- *WhoMW 93*
Slosberg, Mike 1934- *WhoAm 94, WrDr 94*
Slosberg, Samuel Louis 1897- *WhAm 10*
Slosburg-Ackerman, Jill 1948- *WhoAmA 93*
Sloshberg, Leah Phyfer 1937- *WhoAmA 93*
Slosky, Leonard C. 1952- *WhoWest 94*
Slosky, Robert Stanley 1937- *WhoAmL 94*
Sloss *Who 94*
Sloss, Minerva A. 1921- *WhoBlA 94*
Slosser, Paul Dyle 1941- *WhoAmL 94*
Slot, Larry Lee 1947- *WhoScEn 94*
Slot, Peter Maurice Joseph 1932- *Who 94*
Slota, Richard *DrAPF 93*
Slote, A. R. 1935- *IntMPA 94*
Slote, Alfred 1926- *WrDr 94*
Slotin, Ronald David 1963- *WhoAmP 93*
Slotkin, Richard S(idney) 1942- *ConAu 41NR*
Slotkin, Todd James 1953- *WhoFI 94*
Slotnick, Barry Ivan 1939- *WhoAmL 94*
Slotnick, Mortimer H. 1920- *WhoAm 94, WhoAmA 93*
Slott, Nate d1963 *WhoHol 92*
Slott, Phil 1942- *WhoFI 94*
Slouber, James Kirk 1952- *WhoWest 94*
Slough, John Edward 1942- *WhoAmL 94*
Slovacek, Rudolf Edward 1948- *WhoScEn 94*
Slovenko, Ralph 1927- *WrDr 94*
Slover, Archy F. 1920- *WhoWest 94*
Sloves, Marvin 1933- *IntWW 93, WhoAm 94*
Slovic, Stewart Paul 1938- *WhoScEn 94*
Slovik, Thomas Bernard 1946- *WhoMW 93*
Slovikowski, Gerald Jude 1949- *WhoFI 94*
Slovin, Bruce 1935- *WhoAm 94, WhoFI 94*
Slovinec, Joseph George 1958- *WhoMW 93*
Sloviter, Dolores K. *WhoAmP 93*
Sloviter, Dolores Korman 1932- *WhoAm 94, WhoAmL 94*
Sloviter, Henry Allan 1914- *WhoAm 94*
Slovo, Joe 1926- *IntWW 93*
Slowen, Warren Thomas 1943- *WhoAmL 94*
Slowick, Daniel William 1952- *WhoFI 94*
Slowikowski, Mary Kay 1940- *WhoFI 94*
Slowikowski, Synthia Sydnor 1956- *WhoMW 93*
Slowinski, Thomas Frank 1955- *WhoMW 93*
Sloyan, Gerard Stephen 1919- *WhoAm 94*
Sloyan, James *WhoHol 92*
Sloyan, Patrick Joseph 1937- *WhoAm 94*
Sludikoff, Stanley Robert 1935- *WhoAm 94*
Sluiter, Jack 1945- *WhoAmP 93*
Slung, Louis Sheaffer *ConAu 142*
Slusky, Jerry Marvin 1945- *WhoAm 94*
Slusky, Joseph 1942- *WhoAmA 93, WhoWest 94*
Sluss, Stephen Craig 1959- *WhoAmP 93*
Slusser, Eugene Alvin 1922- *WhoFI 94*
Slusser, George Edgar 1939- *EncSF 93*
Slusser, Robert Wyman 1938- *WhoFI 94, WhoWest 94*
Slusser, William Peter 1929- *WhoAm 94, WhoFI 94*
Slutsky, Kenneth Joel 1953- *WhoAm 94, WhoAmL 94*
Slutsky, Leonard Alan 1945- *WhoFI 94*
Slutsky, Lorie Ann 1953- *WhoAm 94*
Sly, Ridge Michael 1933- *WhoAm 94*
Sly, William S. 1932- *WhoScEn 94*
Slye, Leonard Franklin 1911- *WhoAm 94*
Slykhuis, John Timothy 1920- *WhoAm 94*
Slynn Of Hadley, Baron 1930- *IntWW 93, Who 94*
Smaglick, Paul William 1932- *WhoAm 94*
Smaglik, Norman John 1939- *WhoFI 94*
Smagorinsky, Joseph 1924- *WhoAm 94, WhoScEn 94*
Smagula, Cynthia Scott 1943- *WhoScEn 94*
Smailes, George Mason 1916- *Who 94*
Smaldone, Gerald Christopher 1947- *WhoScEn 94*
Smale, John Arthur d1993 *Who 94N*
Smale, John G. 1927- *IntWW 93*
Smale, John Gray 1927- *WhoAm 94, WhoFI 94*
Smale, Stephen 1930- *IntWW 93*
Smales, Fred Benson 1914- *WhoAm 94*
Smalheiser, Harvey 1942- *WhoAm 94*
Smalheiser, Neil Raymond 1954- *WhoMW 93*
Smalkin, Frederic N. *WhoAm 94, WhoAmL 94*
Small, Albert Harrison 1925- *WhoFI 94, WhoScEn 94*
Small, Alden Thomas 1943- *WhoAm 94, WhoAmL 94*
Small, Arthur A., Jr. 1933- *WhoAmP 93*
Small, Austin J. 1894-1929 *EncSF 93*
Small, Bertrice 1937- *WrDr 94*
Small, Bradley Wade 1955- *WhoAmL 94*
Small, Charles John 1919- *IntWW 93*
Small, Clarence Merilton, Jr. 1934- *WhoAmL 94*
Small, David *DrAPF 93*
Small, David Purvis 1930- *Who 94*
Small, Deborah 1948- *WhoAmA 93*
Small, Dick d1972 *WhoHol 92*
Small, Donna *WhoAmP 93*
Small, Edward d1977 *WhoHol 92*
Small, Elaine Luchak 1953- *WhoAm 94, WhoFI 94*
Small, Ernest 1930- *WrDr 94*
Small, Erwin 1924- *WhoAm 94*
Small, George LeRoy 1924- *WhoAm 94*
Small, Henry Gilbert 1941- *WhoAm 94*
Small, Isadore, III 1944- *WhoBlA 94*
Small, Israel G. 1941- *WhoBlA 94*
Small, Jeffrey 1941- *WhoAm 94, WhoAmL 94*
Small, John *Who 94*
Small, (Charles) John 1919- *Who 94*
Small, John H. 1946- *WhoAmL 94*
Small, John Rankin 1933- *Who 94*
Small, Jonathan Andrew 1942- *WhoAm 94, WhoAmL 94*
Small, Jonathan Andrew 1959- *WhoAmL 94*
Small, Kenneth A(lan) 1945- *ConAu 43NR*
Small, Kenneth Alan 1945- *WhoFI 94*
Small, Kenneth Lester 1957- *WhoBlA 94, WhoHisp 94*
Small, Lawrence Farnsworth 1925- *WhoAm 94*
Small, Lawrence Frederick 1934- *WhoWest 94*
Small, Lawrence M. 1942- *WhoAm 94, WhoFI 94*
Small, Lawrence Malcolm 1941- *WhoBlA 94*
Small, Lily B. 1934- *WhoBlA 94*
Small, Marc James 1950- *WhoAmL 94*
Small, Marshall Lee 1927- *WhoAm 94*
Small, Mary Eleanor 1954- *WhoAmP 93*
Small, Marya *WhoHol 92*
Small, Melvin 1939- *WhoAm 94*
Small, Millie 1924- *WhoAmP 93*
Small, Neal *WhoAmP 93*
Small, Neal 1937- *WhoAmA 93*
Small, Neva *WhoHol 92*
Small, Parker Adams, Jr. 1932- *WhoAm 94*
Small, Pearlie Grace H. 1942- *WhoAmP 93*
Small, Peter McMichael 1959- *WhoScEn 94*
Small, Ralph Milton 1917- *WhoAm 94*
Small, Ramsay George 1930- *Who 94*
Small, Richard B. *WhoHol 92*
Small, Richard David 1945- *WhoAm 94*
Small, Richard Donald 1929- *WhoFI 94, WhoMW 93*
Small, Richard F. 1936- *WhoAm 94*
Small, Robert Leonard 1905- *Who 94*
Small, Rosalie A. *WhoAmL 94*
Small, Saul Mouchly 1913- *WhoAm 94*
Small, Stanley Joseph 1946- *WhoBlA 94*
Small, Sydney L. 1941- *WhoBlA 94*
Small, Terry 1942- *ConAu 142, SmATA 75 [port]*
Small, Thomas Randall 1969- *WhoFI 94*
Small, Tony M. 1962- *WhoMW 93*
Small, Torrance 1970- *WhoBlA 94*
Small, Wilfred Thomas 1920- *WhoScEn 94*
Small, William 1940- *WhoBlA 94*
Small, William Andrew 1914- *WhoAm 94*
Small, William Edwin, Jr. 1937- *WhoAm 94*
Small, William Jack 1926- *IntWW 93*
Small Ankle d1888 *EncNAR*
Small-Bodman, Karna *WhoAmP 93*
Smallbone, Graham 1934- *Who 94*
Smallens, Alexander 1888?-1972 *NewGrDO*
Smalley, Arthur Louis, Jr. 1921- *WhoScEn 94*
Smalley, Christopher Joseph 1953- *WhoAm 94*
Smalley, David Allan 1940- *WhoAmA 93*
Smalley, David Vincent 1935- *WhoAm 94*
Smalley, Eugene Byron 1926- *WhoAm 94*
Smalley, I. M. *WhoAmP 93*
Smalley, Janet 1893- *WhoAmA 93N*
Smalley, Kenneth Lee 1930- *WhoFI 94*
Smalley, Paul 1935- *WhoAmP 93, WhoBlA 94*
Smalley, Philips d1939 *WhoHol 92*
Smalley, Richard Errett 1943- *WhoAm 94, WhoScEn 94*
Smalley, Robert M. 1925- *WhoAmP 93*
Smalley, Robert Manning 1925- *WhoAm 94*
Smalley, Stephen Francis 1941- *WhoAmA 93*
Smalley, Stephen S(tewart) 1931- *WrDr 94*
Smalley, Stephen Stewart 1931- *Who 94*
Smalley, Topsy Neher 1943- *WhoWest 94*
Smalley, William Edward 1940- *WhoAm 94, WhoMW 93*
Smalley, William Henry 1943- *WhoAmP 93*
Smallfield, Edward *DrAPF 93*
Smallman, Barry Granger 1924- *Who 94*
Smallman, Beverley N. 1913- *WhoAm 94*
Smallman, Gail Elizabeth 1953- *WhoWest 94*
Smallman, Raymond Edward 1929- *IntWW 93, Who 94*
Smallpeice, Basil d1992 *IntWW 93N*
Smallpeice, Basil 1906-1992 *AnObit 1992*
Smallridge, Peter William 1943- *Who 94*
Smalls, Charley Mae 1943- *WhoBlA 94*
Smalls, Dorothy M. 1920- *WhoBlA 94*
Smalls, Jacquelyn Elaine 1946- *WhoBlA 94*
Smalls, Marcella E. 1946- *WhoBlA 94*
Smalls, O'Neal 1941- *WhoBlA 94*
Smalls, Robert 1839-1915 *AfrAmAl 6 [port]*
Smallwood, Anne Hunter 1922- *Who 94*
Smallwood, Betty 1946- *WhoWest 94*
Smallwood, Denis (Graham) 1918- *Who 94*
Smallwood, Franklin 1927- *WhoAm 94*
Smallwood, Glenn Walter, Jr. 1956- *WhoFI 94, WhoMW 93*
Smallwood, John Frank Monton 1926- *Who 94*
Smallwood, John William 1893- *WhAm 10*
Smallwood, Joseph R(oberts) 1900-1991 *ConAu 43NR*
Smallwood, Joseph Roberts 1900-1991 *WhAm 10*
Smallwood, Osborn Tucker 1911- *WhoBlA 94*
Smallwood, William 1732-1792 *AmRev, WhAmRev*
Smally, Donald Jay 1922- *WhoAm 94*
Smarandache, Florentin *DrAPF 93*
Smarandache, Florentin 1954- *WhoScEn 94, WhoWest 94*
Smardon, Richard Clay 1948- *WhoScEn 94*
Smareglia, Antonio 1854-1929 *NewGrDO*
Smarg, Richard Michael 1952- *WhoFI 94*
Smario, Tom *DrAPF 93*
Smarr, Janet Levarie 1949- *WhoMW 93*
Smarr, Larry Lee 1948- *WhoMW 93, WhoScEn 94*
Smart, Alastair 1922- *WrDr 94*
Smart, Allen Rich, II 1934- *WhoAm 94*
Smart, Andrew 1924- *Who 94*
Smart, Charles Rich 1926- *WhoAm 94*
Smart, Christopher 1722-1771 *BlmGEL*
Smart, Clifton Murray, Jr. 1933- *WhoAm 94*
Smart, David A. 1892-1952 *DcLB 137 [port]*
Smart, David Louis 1941- *WhoAm 94*
Smart, Edward Bernard, Jr. 1949- *WhoBlA 94*
Smart, Edwin *Who 94*
Smart, (Louis) Edwin 1923- *Who 94*
Smart, Elizabeth 1913-1986 *BlmGWL*
Smart, Elnora Sue 1953- *WhoMW 93*
Smart, George (Algernon) 1913- *Who 94*
Smart, Gerald *Who 94*
Smart, (Arthur David) Gerald 1925- *Who 94*
Smart, H. F. d1923 *WhoHol 92*
Smart, Ian Isidore 1944- *BlkWr 2, ConAu 142*
Smart, Irene Balogh 1921- *WhoAmP 93*
Smart, J. Scott d1960 *WhoHol 92*
Smart, Jack *Who 94, WhoHol 92*
Smart, Jack 1920- *Who 94*
Smart, (Raymond) Jack 1917- *Who 94*
Smart, Jackson Wyman, Jr. 1930- *WhoAm 94*
Smart, Jacob Edward 1909- *WhoAm 94*
Smart, Jean 1952- *WhoHol 92*
Smart, Jesse Ray 1939- *WhoAmP 93*
Smart, John d1993 *NewYTBS 93*
Smart, John Jamieson Carswell 1920- *IntWW 93, WrDr 94*
Smart, John W. 1950- *WhoAmP 93*
Smart, Louis Edwin 1923- *IntWW 93*
Smart, Louis Edwin, Jr. 1923- *WhoAm 94*
Smart, Mary-Leigh 1917- *WhoAmA 93*
Smart, Melissa Bedor 1953- *WhoScEn 94*
Smart, Ninian *Who 94*
Smart, (Roderick) Ninian 1927- *IntWW 93, Who 94, WrDr 94*
Smart, Paul M. 1929- *WhoFI 94*
Smart, Peter *Who 94*
Smart, (Alexander Basil) Peter 1932- *IntWW 93, Who 94*
Smart, Rebecca 1979- *WhoHol 92*
Smart, Reginald Piers Alexander de B. *Who 94*
Smart, S(tephen) Bruce, Jr. 1923- *ConAu 142*
Smart, Stephen Bruce, Jr. 1923- *IntWW 93, WhoAm 94*
Smart, Wesley Mitchell 1938- *WhoMW 93*
Smart, William Buckwalter 1922- *WhoAm 94, WhoWest 94*
Smart, William Norman H. *Who 94*
Smart Sanchez, Barbara Ann 1948- *WhoHisp 94*
Smartt, John Madison 1919- *WhoAmL 94*
Smary, Eugene E. 1945- *WhoAmL 94*
Smathers, Frank, Jr. 1909- *WhoAm 94*
Smathers, George Armistead 1913- *WhoAmP 93*
Smathers, James Burton 1935- *WhoAm 94, WhoWest 94*
Smatko, Andrew John 1917- *WhoWest 94*
Smay, Stephen LeRoy 1944- *WhoAmL 94*
Smayling, Lyda Mozella 1923- *WhoMW 93*
Smead, Burton Armstrong, Jr. 1913- *WhoAmL 94*
Smeal, Eleanor *WhoAmP 93*
Smeal, Eleanor Cutri 1939- *WhoAm 94*
Smeal, Paul Lester 1932- *WhoAm 94*
Smeall, James Leathley 1907- *Who 94*
Smeaton, John 1724-1792 *WorInv*
Smectymnuus *BlmGEL*
Smedinghoff, Thomas J. 1951- *WhoAmL 94*
Smedley, Agnes 1892-1950 *BlmGWL*
Smedley, Bernard Ronald 1936- *WhoFI 94*
Smedley, (Frank) Brian 1934- *Who 94*
Smedley, Geoffrey 1927- *IntWW 93, WhoAmA 93*
Smedley, George *Who 94*
Smedley, (Roscoe Relph) George (Boleyne) 1919- *Who 94*
Smedley, Harold 1920- *Who 94*
Smedley, Henry d1932 *WhoHol 92*

Smith, Billy Ray 1944- WhoAmP 93
Smith, Bingo 1946- BasBi
Smith, Bob 1932- WhoBlA 94
Smith, Bobbie Eugene 1933- WhoWest 94
Smith, Bobby Antonia 1949- WhoBlA 94
Smith, Bobby Eugene 1947- WhoAmP 93
Smith, Bobby Ray 1936- WhoFI 94
Smith, Bodrell Joer'dan 1931- WhoScEn 94
Smith, Bonnie Beatrice 1948- WhoFI 94, WhoMW 93
Smith, Bradford S. 1950- WhoAmP 93
Smith, Bradley F. 1931- ConAu 43NR, WrDr 94
Smith, Bradley Youle 1948- WhoAm 94, WhoAmL 94
Smith, Brenda Hensley 1946- WhoAmP 93
Smith, Brent Phillip 1953- WhoAmP 93
Smith, Brian Who 94, WhoHol 92
Smith, Brian 1935- IntWW 93, Who 94
Smith, Brian 1947- Who 94
Smith, Brian (Clive) 1938- WrDr 94
Smith, (Eric) Brian 1933- Who 94
Smith, (Norman) Brian 1928- Who 94
Smith, Brian Arthur Who 94
Smith, Brian David 1953- WhoAmL 94
Smith, Brian Henry 1940- WhoMW 93
Smith, Brian J. 1944- WhoFI 94
Smith, Brian John 1933- Who 94
Smith, Brian Percival 1919- Who 94
Smith, Brian Ray Douglas 1934- WhoAm 94, WhoFI 94
Smith, Brian Richard 1952- WhoScEn 94
Smith, Brian Stanley 1932- Who 94
Smith, Brian W. Who 94
Smith, (Francis) Brian W. Who 94
Smith, Brian William 1938- Who 94
Smith, Brian William 1947- WhoAmL 94, WhoFI 94
Smith, Brice Reynolds, Jr. WhoAm 94, WhoMW 93
Smith, Brooke 1967- WhoHol 92
Smith, Brooke Ellen 1956- WhoAmL 94
Smith, Bruce d1967 WhoHol 92
Smith, Bruce 1963- WhoAm 94
Smith, Bruce Bernard 1963- WhoBlA 94
Smith, Bruce David 1946- WhoAm 94
Smith, Bruce Eugene 1949- WhoAmL 94
Smith, Bruce I. 1934- WhoAmP 93
Smith, Bruce L. R. 1936- ConAu 141
Smith, Bruce Leonard 1946- WhoFI 94
Smith, Bruce Nephi 1934- WhoWest 94
Smith, Bruce Warren 1952- WhoWest 94
Smith, Bryan 1897- WhAm 10
Smith, Bryan Crossley 1925- Who 94
Smith, Bryan Francis, Jr. WhoAmL 94
Smith, Bubba 1945- WhoHol 92
Smith, Bubba 1947- WhoBlA 94
Smith, Bunnie Othanel 1903- WhAm 10
Smith, Byron Owen 1916- WhoAm 94, WhoAmL 94
Smith, C. Aubrey d1948 WhoHol 92
Smith, C. Busby 1924- WrDr 94
Smith, C. D. WhoScEn 94
Smith, C. Kenneth 1918- WhoAm 94
Smith, C. LeMoyne 1934- WhoAm 94
Smith, C. Miles, Jr. 1950- WhoBlA 94
Smith, C. Ross, III 1950- WhoAmL 94
Smith, C(hristopher) U(pham) M(urray) 1930- WrDr 94
Smith, C. W. DrAPF 93
Smith, Caesar WrDr 94
Smith, Calvert H. WhoBlA 94
Smith, Calvin Miles 1924- WhoBlA 94
Smith, Cameron WhoHol 92
Smith, Cameron Mitchell 1935- WrDr 94
Smith, Campbell Sherston d1992 Who 94N
Smith, Capers F., Jr. 1945- WhoIns 94
Smith, Capers Franklin, Jr. 1945- WhoFI 94
Smith, Carl Anthony 1954- WhoWest 94
Smith, Carl B. WhoAmP 93
Smith, Carl Dean, Jr. 1949- WhoFI 94
Smith, Carl Edwin 1906- WhoMW 93
Smith, Carl Michael 1944- WhoAmL 94
Smith, Carl Richard 1933- WhoAm 94
Smith, Carl Thomas 1955- WhoMW 93
Smith, Carl W. 1924- WhoAmP 93
Smith, Carl William 1931- WhoBlA 94
Smith, Carlyle 1939- WhoAmP 93
Smith, Carlyle Shreeve 1915- WhoMW 93
Smith, Carol Babb 1963- WhoWest 94
Smith, Carol Barlow 1945- WhoBlA 94
Smith, Carol J. 1923- WhoBlA 94
Smith, Carol Sturm DrAPF 93
Smith, Carole Dianne 1945- WhoAmL 94
Smith, Carolyn Lee 1942- WhoBlA 94
Smith, Carolyn Polis 1947- WhoFI 94
Smith, Carolyn Williams 1937- WhoAmP 93
Smith, Carroll B. 1936- WhoIns 94
Smith, Carson Eugene 1943- WhoBlA 94
Smith, Carsten 1932- IntWW 93
Smith, Carter Blakemore 1937- WhoWest 94
Smith, Cary 1955- WhoAmA 93
Smith, Catharine Mary S. Who 94
Smith, Catherine Onalee 1966- WhoMW 93
Smith, Cathleen Lynne 1947- WhoWest 94
Smith, Cece 1944- WhoAm 94
Smith, Cecil Alden 1910-1984 WhoAmA 93N
Smith, Cecil Randolph, Jr. 1924- WhoWest 94
Smith, Charlene 1938- WhoMW 93
Smith, Charles d1988 WhoHol 92
Smith, Charles 1914- WhoBlA 94
Smith, Charles 1930- Who 94
Smith, Charles Alphonso 1909- WhoAm 94
Smith, Charles Anthony 1939- WhoWest 94
Smith, Charles B. Who 94
Smith, Charles Bruce 1936- WhoMW 93
Smith, Charles Buchanan 1924- WhoAm 94
Smith, Charles C., Jr. 1946- WhoAmP 93
Smith, Charles Carroll, Jr. 1944- WhoAmP 93
Smith, Charles Conard 1936- WhoWest 94
Smith, Charles Daniel, Jr. 1965- WhoBlA 94
Smith, Charles Edison WhoBlA 94
Smith, Charles Edward 1939- WhoAm 94
Smith, Charles Eugene 1948- WhoAmP 93
Smith, Charles F. 1895- WhAm 10
Smith, Charles F., Jr. 1933- WhoBlA 94
Smith, Charles Francis 1936- WhoWest 94
Smith, Charles H. d1942 WhoHol 92
Smith, Charles Haddon 1926- WhoAm 94
Smith, Charles Hayden 1933- WhoFI 94, WhoScEn 94
Smith, Charles Henry, Jr. 1920- WhoAm 94
Smith, Charles Isaac 1931- WhoAm 94
Smith, Charles James, III 1926- WhoBlA 94
Smith, Charles Kent 1938- WhoAm 94
Smith, Charles Lamont 1956- WhoBlA 94
Smith, Charles Lavester, Jr. 1954- WhoAmP 93
Smith, Charles Lebanon 1938- WhoBlA 94
Smith, Charles Leon 1953- WhoBlA 94
Smith, Charles Lewis 1920- WhoWest 94
Smith, Charles Martin 1953- IntMPA 94
Smith, Charles Martin 1954- WhoHol 92
Smith, Charles Paul 1926- WhoAm 94
Smith, Charles Philip 1926- WhoAmP 93
Smith, Charles Plympton, IV 1954- WhoAmP 93
Smith, Charles R. 1928- WhoAmP 93
Smith, Charles Raymond, Jr. 1948- WhoAm 94, WhoAmL 94
Smith, Charles Richard 1932- WhoFI 94, WhoWest 94
Smith, Charles Robert 1948- WhoScEn 94
Smith, Charles Robert S. Who 94
Smith, Charles Roger 1941- WhoWest 94
Smith, Charles S. 1950- WhoAmP 93
Smith, Charles Thomas 1914- WhoAm 94
Smith, Charles U. WhoBlA 94
Smith, Charles Ullman 1923- WhoAmP 93
Smith, Charles Vinton 1932- WhoWest 94
Smith, Charles W(illiam) (Frederick) 1905-1993 ConAu 142
Smith, Charles W. F. d1993 NewYTBS 93
Smith, Charles Watson 1932- WhoAmP 93
Smith, Charles Wilfred d1971 WhoHol 92
Smith, Charles William 1926- WhoScEn 94
Smith, Charles William 1955- WhoScEn 94
Smith, Charles Wilson, Jr. 1949- WhoAm 94
Smith, Charles Z. 1927- WhoAm 94, WhoAmL 94, WhoAmP 93, WhoWest 94
Smith, Charlie DrAPF 93, WhoAmP 93
Smith, Charlie Calvin 1943- WhoBlA 94
Smith, Charlotte d1928 WhoHol 92
Smith, Cheryl WhoHol 92
Smith, Cheryl K. 1951- WhoAmL 94
Smith, Chester 1930- WhoFI 94, WhoWest 94
Smith, Chester B. 1954- WhoBlA 94
Smith, Chester Horace 1919- WhoAmP 93
Smith, Chester Leo 1922- WhoAm 94
Smith, Chesterfield Harvey 1917- WhoAm 94
Smith, "Chief" Tug d1983 WhoHol 92
Smith, Chris WhoBlA 94
Smith, Chris G. 1970- WhoBlA 94
Smith, Chris Michael 1951- WhoAmL 94
Smith, Christie Parker 1960- WhoScEn 94
Smith, Christopher Allen 1961- WhoFI 94
Smith, Christopher Carlisle 1938- WhoMW 93
Smith, Christopher Culver 1955- WhoWest 94
Smith, Christopher Duncan 1950- WhoWest 94
Smith, Christopher Edward 1958- WhoMW 93
Smith, Christopher H. 1953- CngDr 93
Smith, Christopher Henry 1953- WhoAm 94, WhoAmP 93
Smith, Christopher Hughes 1929- Who 94
Smith, Christopher Robert 1951- Who 94
Smith, Christopher Sydney Winwood 1906- Who 94
Smith, Cindy Thompson 1957- WhoMW 93
Smith, Clarence LeRoy 1941- WhoFI 94
Smith, Clarence O. 1933- WhoAm 94, WhoBlA 94
Smith, Clark Ashton 1893-1961 EncSF 93
Smith, Clark Cavanaugh 1934- WhoWest 94
Smith, Claude C. Who 94
Smith, Claudius d1779 AmRev
Smith, Clay Taylor 1917- WhoWest 94
Smith, Clayton Gordon 1955- WhoFI 94
Smith, Cleveland Emanuel 1924- WhoBlA 94
Smith, Cliff(ord S.) d1937 WhoHol 92
Smith, Clifford Bertram Bruce H. Who 94
Smith, Clifford Lee 1945- WhoAm 94
Smith, Clifford Thorpe 1924- WrDr 94
Smith, Clifford V., Jr. 1931- WhoBlA 94
Smith, Clifford Vaughn, Jr. 1931- WhoAm 94
Smith, Clinton W. 1952- WhoScEn 94
Smith, Clodus Ray 1928- WhoAm 94
Smith, Clyde 1932- WhoAmA 93
Smith, Clyde B. 1926- WhoAmP 93
Smith, Clyde Curry 1929- WhoAm 94, WhoMW 93
Smith, Clyde R. 1933- WhoMW 93
Smith, Colby Arnn 1956- WhoAmL 94
Smith, Colin Who 94
Smith, Colin 1941- Who 94
Smith, (Christopher) Colin 1927- Who 94
Smith, Colin John 1938- Who 94
Smith, Colin Milner 1936- Who 94
Smith, Colin Roderick Who 94
Smith, Colin S. Who 94
Smith, Connie 1941- WhoHol 92
Smith, Conrad P. 1932- WhoBlA 94
Smith, Conrad Warren 1919- WhoBlA 94
Smith, Constance 1928- WhoHol 92
Smith, Cordwainer 1913-1966 EncSF 93
Smith, Corlies Morgan 1929- WhoAm 94
Smith, Cotter 1949- WhoHol 92
Smith, Courtney Charles 1947- WhoIns 94
Smith, Courtney David 1952- WhoFI 94
Smith, Covey Leroy 1942- WhoIns 94
Smith, Craig Alvin 1945- WhoWest 94
Smith, Craig Bennett 1943- WhoAmL 94
Smith, Craig C. 1944- WhoWest 94
Smith, Craig Lindsay 1963- WhoAmL 94
Smith, Craig Malcolm 1952- WhoMW 93
Smith, Craig Richards 1940- WhoAm 94
Smith, Craig Richey 1925- WhoMW 93
Smith, Cullen 1925- WhoAm 94
Smith, Curtis 1932- WhoAmP 93
Smith, Curtis Alfonso, Jr. 1934- WhoMW 93
Smith, Curtis C. 1939- EncSF 93
Smith, Curtis David 1951- WhoAmL 94
Smith, Curtis Johnston 1947- WhoAm 94
Smith, Curtis P. 1916- WhoAmP 93
Smith, Cynthia WhoHol 92
Smith, Cyril d1950 WhoHol 92
Smith, Cyril d1963 WhoHol 92
Smith, Cyril 1928- Who 94
Smith, Cyril James 1930- WhoAm 94
Smith, Cyril Robert d1993 Who 94N
Smith, Cyril Stanley d1992 IntWW 93N
Smith, Cyril Stanley 1925- Who 94
Smith, Cyrus Rowlett 1899-1990 WhAm 10
Smith, D(avid) Alexander 1953- EncSF 93
Smith, D(wight) Moody, Jr. 1931- ConAu 42NR
Smith, D. Paul 1942- WhoMW 93
Smith, D. Richard 1930- WhoMW 93
Smith, DaCosta, Jr. 1917- WhoAm 94, WhoAmL 94
Smith, Dale 1937- WhoAmP 93
Smith, Dale Metz 1928- WhoWest 94
Smith, Dale Wilford 1948- WhoMW 93
Smith, Dalton 1947- WhoAmP 93
Smith, Dan F. WhoFI 94
Smith, Dana Kruse 1957- WhoWest 94
Smith, Dane F., Jr. 1940- WhoAmP 93
Smith, Dane Farnsworth, Jr. 1940- WhoAm 94
Smith, Dane Frederic 1951- WhoFI 94
Smith, Daniel C. 1950- WhoMW 93
Smith, Daniel Clifford 1936- WhoAm 94
Smith, Daniel Edward, III 1960- WhoFI 94
Smith, Daniel H., Jr. 1933- WhoBlA 94
Smith, Daniel Hoyt 1944- WhoWest 94
Smith, Daniel Larsen 1929- WhoMW 93
Smith, Daniel Lynn 1952- WhoAmL 94
Smith, Daniel Montague 1932- WhoScEn 94
Smith, Daniel R. 1934- WhoAm 94, WhoFI 94
Smith, Daniel Walker 1931- WhoMW 93
Smith, Darrell Lee WhoFI 94
Smith, Darrell Wayne 1937- WhoAm 94
Smith, Darryl C. WhoMW 93
Smith, Darryl C. 1966- WhoBlA 94
Smith, Darwin Eatna 1926- IntWW 93
Smith, Darwood K. 1929- WhoHol 92
Smith, Daryl Kent 1942- WhoFI 94
Smith, Datus Clifford, Jr. 1907- WhoAm 94
Smith, Dave DrAPF 93
Smith, Dave 1942- WrDr 94
Smith, David Who 94
Smith, David 1906-1965 WhoAmA 93N
Smith, David 1927- Who 94
Smith, David 1935- Who 94
Smith, David 1939- WhoScEn 94
Smith, David 1951- WhoAmP 93
Smith, (Anthony) David 1938- Who 94
Smith, David (Cecil) 1930- Who 94
Smith, David (Iser) 1933- Who 94
Smith, (Norman John) David 1931- Who 94
Smith, David Allen 1943- WhoWest 94
Smith, David Anthony WhoHol 92
Smith, David Arthur 1938- Who 94
Smith, David Arthur George 1934- Who 94
Smith, David Asher 1946- WhoWest 94
Smith, David Beach 1911-1992 WhAm 10
Smith, David Brookman 1951- WhoAm 94, WhoAmL 94
Smith, David Bruce 1948- WhoAmP 93
Smith, David Buchanan 1936- Who 94
Smith, David Burnell 1941- WhoAmL 94
Smith, David C. Who 94
Smith, David Callaway 1941- WhoAm 94
Smith, David Carr 1944- WhoScEn 94
Smith, David Cecil 1930- IntWW 93
Smith, David Clark 1937- WhoAm 94
Smith, David Clayton 1929- WhoAmP 93
Smith, David Collville 1922- IntWW 93
Smith, David Douglas 1959- WhoAmL 94
Smith, David Douglas R. Who 94
Smith, David Doyle 1956- WhoScEn 94
Smith, David Dury H. Who 94
Smith, David E. 1939- WrDr 94
Smith, David Edmund 1934- WhoAm 94
Smith, David Edward 1939- WhoFI 94
Smith, David Elvin 1939- WhoAm 94, WhoWest 94
Smith, David English 1920- WhoAm 94
Smith, David Eugene 1941- WhoFI 94, WhoWest 94
Smith, David Floyd 1956- WhoScEn 94
Smith, David Gates 1943- WhoFI 94
Smith, David Gerard G. Who 94
Smith, David Gilbert 1926- WhoAm 94
Smith, David-Glen DrAPF 93
Smith, David Grahame G. Who 94
Smith, David H. Who 94
Smith, David Henry 1954- Who 94
Smith, David Huggans 1954- WhoMW 93
Smith, David J. 1942- WhoFI 94
Smith, David James Who 94
Smith, David Jeddie 1942- WhoAm 94
Smith, David John, Jr. 1947- WhoMW 93
Smith, David John Leslie 1938- Who 94
Smith, David Kenneth 1956- WhoWest 94
Smith, David King 1963- WhoWest 94
Smith, David Lawson 1951- WhoWest 94
Smith, David Lee 1939- WhoAm 94
Smith, David Loeffler 1928- WhoAmA 93
Smith, David MacIntyre Bell Armour 1923- Who 94
Smith, David Marshall 1936- WrDr 94
Smith, David Martin 1948- WhoAm 94
Smith, David Martyn 1921- WhoAm 94
Smith, David Matthew 1961- WhoFI 94
Smith, David Michael 1944- WhoFI 94
Smith, David Michael 1949- WhoFI 94
Smith, David Mitchell 1960- WhoScEn 94
Smith, David R. 1940- IntMPA 94
Smith, David R. 1946- WhoBlA 94
Smith, David Roland 1906-1965 AmCulL
Smith, David Rollin 1940- WhoWest 94
Smith, David Ryan 1952- WhoAm 94
Smith, David S. Who 94
Smith, David Shiverick 1918- WhoAm 94
Smith, David Sidney 1963- WhoWest 94
Smith, David Thornton 1935- WhoAm 94
Smith, David Todd 1953- WhoAm 94
Smith, David Waldo Edward 1934- WhoAm 94
Smith, David Wayne 1927- WhoAm 94, WhoWest 94
Smith, David Welton 1942- WhoScEn 94
Smith, Dawn C. F. 1960- WhoBlA 94
Smith, Dean WhoHol 92
Smith, Dean 1925- WhoAm 94
Smith, Dean 1934- BasBi
Smith, Dean Edwards 1931- WhoAm 94
Smith, Dean Orren 1944- WhoMW 93
Smith, Dean Wesley 1950- EncSF 93
Smith, Deane Kingsley, Jr. 1930- WhoScEn 94
Smith, Deborah P. 1951- WhoBlA 94

Smith, DeHaven L. 1928- *WhoBlA 94*
Smith, Deirdre O'Meara 1946- *WhoAmL 94*
Smith, DeLancey Allan 1916- *WhoMW 93*
Smith, Delbert Dudley 1940- *WhoAm 94*
Smith, Delia *Who 94, WrDr 94*
Smith, Delos V., Jr. *WhoHol 92*
Smith, Delos V., Jr. 1906- *WhoMW 93*
Smith, Deming 1920- *WhoAmL 94*
Smith, Denis M. *Who 94*
Smith, Denise Groleau 1951- *WhoFI 94*
Smith, Denise Louise 1957- *WhoAmP 93*
Smith, Dennis 1959- *WhoAm 94, WhoBlA 94, WhoWest 94*
Smith, Dennis Edward 1940- *WhoAm 94*
Smith, Dennis P. 1953- *WhoMW 93*
Smith, Dennis Rae 1961- *WhoBlA 94*
Smith, Dennis W. 1942- *WhoAmP 93*
Smith, Denny 1938- *WhoAmP 93*
Smith, Denver Lester 1946- *WhoBlA 94*
Smith, Derek 1927- *WhoHol 92*
Smith, Derek 1948- *Who 94*
Smith, Derek B. *Who 94*
Smith, Derek Cyril 1927- *Who 94*
Smith, Derek Edward H. *Who 94*
Smith, Derek Ervin 1961- *WhoBlA 94*
Smith, Derek Frank 1929- *Who 94*
Smith, Derek V. *WhoIns 94*
Smith, Derrin Ray 1955- *WhoWest 94*
Smith, Desmond *Who 94*
Smith, (Stanley) Desmond 1931- *Who 94*
Smith, Desmond Milton 1937- *WhoAm 94*
Smith, Dianne Harris 1942- *WhoWest 94*
Smith, Dick 1922- *IntDcF 2-4*
Smith, Dick Martin 1946- *WhoWest 94*
Smith, Dinah Maxwell *WhoAmA 93*
Smith, Dinitia *DrAPF 93*
Smith, Dinitia 1945- *WrDr 94*
Smith, Dodie 1896- *BlmGWL*
Smith, Dodie 1896-1990 *ConDr 93*
Smith, Dolores J. 1936- *WhoBlA 94*
Smith, Dolores Maxine Plunk 1926- *WhoAm 94, WhoMW 93*
Smith, Dolph 1933- *WhoAmA 93*
Smith, Don C. *WhoAmP 93*
Smith, Donald 1922- *NewGrDO*
Smith, Donald Arnold 1931- *WhoAmP 93*
Smith, Donald Arthur 1945- *WhoScEn 94*
Smith, Donald C. 1935- *WhoAmA 93*
Smith, Donald Charles 1910- *Who 94*
Smith, Donald Dean 1946- *WhoScEn 94*
Smith, Donald E. 1930- *WhoWest 94*
Smith, Donald Eugene 1926- *WhoAm 94*
Smith, Donald Eugene 1953- *WhoMW 93*
Smith, Donald Evans 1915- *WhoWest 94*
Smith, Donald Gene 1941- *WhoAm 94*
Smith, Donald Hugh 1932- *WhoBlA 94*
Smith, Donald John 1926- *Who 94*
Smith, Donald Kaye 1932- *WhoAmL 94*
Smith, Donald Kendall 1929- *WhoWest 94*
Smith, Donald L. 1924- *WhoAmP 93*
Smith, Donald Lee 1958- *WhoFI 94*
Smith, Donald Lewis 1943- *WhoFI 94*
Smith, Donald M. 1931- *WhoBlA 94*
Smith, Donald MacKeen 1923- *Who 94*
Smith, Donald Nickerson 1940- *WhoAm 94, WhoMW 93*
Smith, Donald Norbert 1931- *WhoFI 94, WhoScEn 94*
Smith, Donald Ray 1934- *WhoFI 94*
Smith, Donald Richard 1932- *WhoWest 94*
Smith, Donald Roy 1926- *WhoMW 93*
Smith, Donn L. 1915- *WhoAm 94*
Smith, Donna *WhoAmP 93*
Smith, Donna 1954- *WhoAm 94, WhoWest 94*
Smith, Donna Beck 1954- *WhoMW 93*
Smith, Donna Dean 1946- *WhoWest 94*
Smith, Donna Lee 1941- *WhoAmP 93*
Smith, Donnie Louise 1952- *WhoWest 94*
Smith, Doris Buchanan 1934- *SmATA 75 [port], TwCYAW, WrDr 94*
Smith, Dorothy J. 1948- *WhoBlA 94*
Smith, Dorothy Louise White 1939- *WhoBlA 94*
Smith, Dorothy O. 1943- *WhoBlA 94*
Smith, Dorsett David 1937- *WhoWest 94*
Smith, Doug 1969- *WhoBlA 94*
Smith, Douglas *Who 94*
Smith, Douglas (Boucher) 1932- *Who 94*
Smith, Douglas A. 1951- *WhoWest 94*
Smith, Douglas A. 1960- *WhoIns 94*
Smith, Douglas LaRue 1917- *WhoFI 94*
Smith, Douglas Leslie B. *Who 94*
Smith, Douglas Lynn 1963- *WhoWest 94*
Smith, Douglas M. 1942- *WhoBlA 94*
Smith, Douglas Maxwell 1956- *WhoMW 93*
Smith, Douglas Myles 1946- *WhoAmP 93*
Smith, Douglas Omar, Jr. 1935- *WhoAmL 94*
Smith, Douglas Sydney 1929- *WhoAm 94*
Smith, Drew *Who 94*
Smith, (Fraser) Drew 1950- *Who 94*
Smith, Duane A. 1937- *WhoAmP 93*
Smith, Duane Allan 1937- *WhoWest 94, WrDr 94*
Smith, Dudley 1926- *WrDr 94*
Smith, Dudley (Gordon) 1926- *Who 94*
Smith, Dudley Renwick 1937- *WhoAm 94, WhoIns 94*
Smith, Dugal N. *Who 94*
Smith, Dunbar Wallace 1910- *WhoWest 94*
Smith, Dwan *WhoHol 92*
Smith, Dwight Chichester, III 1955- *WhoAmL 94*
Smith, Dwight L. 1918- *WrDr 94*
Smith, Dwight Leon 1946- *WhoFI 94*
Smith, Dwight Morrell 1931- *WhoAm 94*
Smith, Dwight Raymond 1921- *WhoAm 94*
Smith, Dwyane 1961- *WhoMW 93*
Smith, E. Ashley 1946- *WhoAmP 93*
Smith, E. Berry 1926- *WhoFI 94, WhoMW 93*
Smith, E. Brian 1933- *IntWW 93*
Smith, E(ric) D(avid) 1923- *ConAu 41NR*
Smith, E.E. *EncSF 93*
Smith, E(dward) E(lmer) 1890-1965 *EncSF 93*
Smith, E(rnest) Lester d1992 *Who 94N*
Smith, Earl Bradford 1953- *WhoBlA 94*
Smith, Earl E. T. 1926-1991 *WhAm 10*
Smith, Ed H. 1945- *WhoAmP 93*
Smith, Eddie D. 1920- *WhoBlA 94*
Smith, Eddie D., Sr. 1946- *WhoBlA 94*
Smith, Eddie Glenn, Jr. 1926- *WhoBlA 94*
Smith, Eddie Malvin 1943- *WhoAm 94*
Smith, Edgar Benton 1932- *WhoAm 94*
Smith, Edgar E. 1934- *WhoBlA 94*
Smith, Edgar Eugene 1934- *WhoAm 94*
Smith, Edgar James, Jr. 1934- *WhoAm 94, WhoAmL 94*
Smith, Edgar Pichard 1920-1989 *WhAm 10*
Smith, Edith B. 1952- *WhoBlA 94*
Smith, Edward Bruce 1920- *WhoAmP 93*
Smith, Edward Charles 1949- *WhoBlA 94*
Smith, Edward David 1972- *WhoWest 94*
Smith, Edward F. 1950- *WhoAmP 93*
Smith, Edward Herbert 1936- *WhoAm 94*
Smith, Edward John 1927- *WhoScEn 94*
Smith, Edward Joseph 1927- *WhoAmP 93*
Smith, Edward K. 1922- *WhoAm 94*
Smith, (John) Edward (McKenzie) L. *Who 94*
Smith, Edward Lewis, Jr. 1937- *WhoAmP 93*
Smith, Edward Nathaniel, Jr. 1955- *WhoBlA 94*
Smith, Edward Paul, Jr. 1939- *WhoAm 94, WhoAmL 94, WhoFI 94*
Smith, Edward Reaugh 1932- *WhoAm 94*
Smith, Edward Samuel 1919- *CngDr 93, WhoAm 94, WhoAmL 94*
Smith, Edward Walter 1946- *WhoMW 93*
Smith, Edwin David 1938- *WhoScEn 94*
Smith, Edwin Dudley 1936- *WhoAmL 94*
Smith, Edwin Eric 1946- *WhoAm 94, WhoAmL 94*
Smith, Edwin Ide 1924- *WhoAm 94*
Smith, Edwin Milton 1950- *WhoAmL 94, WhoWest 94*
Smith, Edwin O. 1945- *WhoAmP 93*
Smith, Edwin Steeves 1938- *WhoAmP 93*
Smith, Edwin William 1876-1957 *DcNaB MP*
Smith, Eileen S. *Who 94*
Smith, Elaine Campbell *DrAPF 93*
Smith, Elaine Diana 1924- *WhoAm 94*
Smith, Elaine Marie 1947- *WhoBlA 94*
Smith, Elden Leroy 1940- *WhoAm 94, WhoFI 94*
Smith, Eldred Gee 1907- *WhoAm 94*
Smith, Eldred Reid 1931- *WhoAm 94*
Smith, Eleanor Huske 1960- *WhoAmL 94*
Smith, Eleanor Jane 1933- *WhoBlA 94*
Smith, Eleanor Ruth 1932- *WhoFI 94*
Smith, Elias 1769-1846 *DcAmReB 2*
Smith, Elijah 1939- *WhoBlA 94*
Smith, Elise Fiber 1932- *WhoAm 94*
Smith, Elizabeth *WhoHol 92*
Smith, Elizabeth 1776-1806 *DcNaB MP*
Smith, Elizabeth 1943- *WhoAmA 93*
Smith, Elizabeth A(ngele) T(aft) 1958- *WrDr 94*
Smith, Elizabeth Ann 1948- *WhoAmL 94*
Smith, Elizabeth Barker 1930- *WhoMW 93*
Smith, Elizabeth Hull 1956- *WhoFI 94*
Smith, Elizabeth Patience 1949- *WhoAm 94*
Smith, Elizabeth Straubel 1934- *WhoAmP 93*
Smith, Ella 1933- *WrDr 94*
Smith, Ellen Margaret 1950- *WhoMW 93*
Smith, Elliot Steven 1942- *WhoAmA 93*
Smith, Elmer G., Jr. 1957- *WhoBlA 94*
Smith, Elmore 1949- *BasBi*
Smith, Elouise Beard 1920- *WhoFI 94*
Smith, Elsdon Coles 1903- *WrDr 94*
Smith, Elsie Mae 1927- *WhoBlA 94*
Smith, Elton Edward 1915- *WrDr 94*
Smith, Elvie Lawrence 1926- *WhoAm 94*
Smith, Elwin Earl 1922- *WhoAm 94*
Smith, Emil L. 1911- *IntWW 93, WhoAm 94*
Smith, Emily Guthrie 1909-1987 *WhoAmA 93N*
Smith, Emma 1923- *Who 94, WrDr 94*
Smith, Emmitt 1969- *News 94-1 [port]*
Smith, Emmitt J., III 1969- *WhoAm 94, WhoBlA 94*
Smith, Emmitt Mozart 1905- *WhoBlA 94*
Smith, Ephraim Philip 1942- *WhoAm 94*
Smith, Erastus 1787-1837 *EncDeaf*
Smith, Eric Alan 1943- *WhoAm 94*
Smith, Eric Edward 1952- *WhoMW 93*
Smith, Eric John R. *Who 94*
Smith, Eric Norman 1922- *Who 94*
Smith, Eric Parkman 1910- *WhoFI 94*
Smith, Ernest Howard 1931- *WhoBlA 94*
Smith, Ernest John 1919- *WhoAmA 93*
Smith, Ernest Ketcham 1922- *WhoAm 94, WhoScEn 94, WhoWest 94*
Smith, Estella W. *WhoBlA 94*
Smith, Esther Thomas 1939- *WhoScEn 94*
Smith, Estus 1930- *WhoBlA 94*
Smith, Ethel 1921- *WhoHol 92*
Smith, Eual Randall 1947- *WhoScEn 94*
Smith, Eugene *WhoHol 92*
Smith, Eugene 1929- *WhoBlA 94*
Smith, Eugene 1938- *WhoBlA 94*
Smith, Eugene DuBois 1955- *WhoBlA 94*
Smith, Eugene Herbert 1927- *WhoAm 94*
Smith, Eugene Wilson 1930- *WhoAm 94*
Smith, Eunice 1757-1823 *BlmGWL*
Smith, Evan Shreeve 1951- *WhoMW 93*
Smith, Evelyn E. 1927- *EncSF 93*
Smith, Ewart *Who 94*
Smith, (Frank) Ewart 1897- *Who 94*
Smith, Ewart Brian 1938- *WhoWest 94*
Smith, F. Alan 1931- *WhoFI 94*
Smith, F. M. *WhoAmP 93*
Smith, Fern M. 1933- *WhoAm 94, WhoAmL 94, WhoWest 94*
Smith, Fernando Leon Jorge 1954- *WhoHisp 94*
Smith, Ferr *WhoAmP 93*
Smith, Floyd Leslie 1931- *WhoAm 94, WhoFI 94*
Smith, Floyd Rodenback 1913- *WhoAm 94*
Smith, Forrest Harold, Jr. 1944- *WhoMW 93*
Smith, Forrest L. 1945- *WhoAm 94*
Smith, Frances C. *WhoBlA 94*
Smith, Frances Harter Roberts 1945- *WhoAmL 94*
Smith, Frances Kathleen 1913- *WhoAmA 93*
Smith, Francesca *WhoHol 92*
Smith, Francis 1672-1738 *DcNaB MP*
Smith, Francis 1723-1791 *WhAmRev*
Smith, Francis Barrymore 1932- *IntWW 93*
Smith, Francis Graham *IntWW 93*
Smith, Francis Graham- 1923- *Who 94*
Smith, Francis J. *DrAPF 93*
Smith, Francis Pettit *WorInv*
Smith, Francis Taylor 1933- *Who 94*
Smith, Francis Xavier 1960- *WhoFI 94*
Smith, Frank 1910- *WhoBlA 94*
Smith, Frank, Jr. 1942- *WhoAmP 93*
Smith, Frank Anthony 1939- *WhoAmA 93*
Smith, Frank Earl 1931- *WhoAm 94, WhoFI 94, WhoMW 93*
Smith, Frank Edward 1912- *WhoAm 94*
Smith, Frank Junius 1937- *WhoBlA 94*
Smith, Frank Thomas 1948- *IntWW 93, Who 94*
Smith, Frank William G. *Who 94*
Smith, Franklin L. 1943- *WhoAm 94, WhoBlA 94*
Smith, Franklin Sumner, Jr. 1924- *WhoAm 94*
Smith, Fred Dempsey, Jr. 1947- *WhoAmL 94*
Smith, Fred Wesley 1934- *WhoWest 94*
Smith, Freddie Alphonso 1924- *WhoBlA 94*
Smith, Freddye Lee 1938- *WhoFI 94*
Smith, Frederic Newcomb 1925- *WhoAmP 93*
Smith, Frederick Buren 1896- *WhAm 10*
Smith, Frederick Coe 1916- *WhoAm 94*
Smith, Frederick D. 1917- *WhoBlA 94*
Smith, Frederick E(screet) 1922- *WrDr 94*
Smith, Frederick Ellis 1928- *WhoBlA 94*
Smith, Frederick Gerard 1962- *WhoWest 94*
Smith, Frederick Gladstone 1924- *IntWW 93*
Smith, Frederick John Jervis- 1848-1911 *DcNaB MP*
Smith, Frederick Orville, II 1934- *WhoAmP 93*
Smith, Frederick Paul 1951- *WhoAmL 94*
Smith, Frederick Robert, Jr. 1929- *WhoAm 94*
Smith, Frederick Viggers 1912- *Who 94*
Smith, Frederick Wallace 1944- *WhoAm 94, WhoFI 94*
Smith, Frederick Wilson d1944 *WhoHol 92*
Smith, Frederick Winston Furneaux, Earl of Birkenhead 1907-1975 *DcNaB MP*
Smith, Fredrick E. 1935- *WhoBlA 94*
Smith, Freeman Holmes, III 1943- *WhoAmP 93*
Smith, Fronse Wayne, Sr. 1946- *WhoBlA 94*
Smith, G. Albert d1959 *WhoHol 92*
Smith, G. E. Kidder 1913- *WhoAm 94*
Smith, Gardner Watkins 1931- *WhoAm 94*
Smith, Garland M., Jr. 1935- *WhoBlA 94*
Smith, Garland Thomas 1940- *WhoAmL 94*
Smith, Garret 1876?-1954 *EncSF 93*
Smith, Gary 1949- *WhoAmA 93*
Smith, Gary Allen 1932- *WhoMW 93*
Smith, Gary Charles 1952- *WhoAm 94*
Smith, Gary Chester 1938- *WhoScEn 94*
Smith, Gary D. 1941- *WhoMW 93*
Smith, Gary Douglas 1948- *WhoAmA 93, WhoWest 94*
Smith, Gary Howell 1953- *WhoAmL 94*
Smith, Gary Lee 1936- *WhoMW 93*
Smith, Gary Lee 1959- *WhoScEn 94*
Smith, Gary Wayne 1949- *WhoAmL 94*
Smith, Geoffrey Adams 1947- *WhoAm 94, WhoFI 94*
Smith, Geoffrey J. *Who 94*
Smith, Geoffrey M. *Who 94*
Smith, Geoffrey R.W. 1945- *WhoAm 94*
Smith, George 1914- *Who 94*
Smith, George 1919- *Who 94*
Smith, George Bundy *WhoAmP 93*
Smith, George Bundy 1937- *WhoAmL 94, WhoBlA 94*
Smith, George Curtis 1935- *WhoAm 94, WhoAmL 94, WhoMW 93*
Smith, George D. 1870-1920 *DcLB 140 [port]*
Smith, George Drury 1927- *WhoAm 94*
Smith, George Foster 1922- *WhoAm 94*
Smith, George Frederick 1897- *WhAm 10*
Smith, George H(enry) 1922- *EncSF 93, WrDr 94*
Smith, George Hudson *EncSF 93*
Smith, George Iain D. *Who 94*
Smith, George Irving 1927- *WhoWest 94*
Smith, George Larry 1951- *WhoWest 94*
Smith, George Leonard, Jr. 1935- *WhoAm 94*
Smith, George Lester 1951- *WhoAm 94*
Smith, George O(liver) 1911-1981 *EncSF 93*
Smith, George P. *WhoAmP 93*
Smith, George P(atrick), II 1939- *WrDr 94*
Smith, George Patrick, II 1939- *WhoAm 94*
Smith, George S. 1940- *WhoBlA 94*
Smith, George S., Jr. 1948- *WhoAm 94, WhoFI 94*
Smith, George T. 1916- *WhoAmP 93*
Smith, George Thornewell 1916- *WhoAm 94*
Smith, George V. 1926- *WhoBlA 94*
Smith, George V. R. 1937- *WhoIns 94*
Smith, George W. d1947 *WhoHol 92*
Smith, George Walker 1929- *WhoBlA 94*
Smith, George Washington c. 1820-1899 *IntDcB [port]*
Smith, George Wolfram 1932- *WhoAm 94*
Smith, Georgia Floyd 1949- *WhoWest 94*
Smith, Gerald Kendall 1936- *WhoAm 94, WhoAmL 94*
Smith, Gerald Lyman Kenneth 1898-1976 *AmSocL, DcAmReB 2*
Smith, Gerald Oliver d1974 *WhoHol 92*
Smith, Gerald R. 1928- *WhoAmP 93*
Smith, Gerald Stanton 1938- *Who 94*
Smith, Gerald Wayne 1950- *WhoBlA 94*
Smith, Geraldine *WhoHol 92*
Smith, Geraldine T. 1918- *WhoBlA 94*
Smith, Gerard Coad 1914- *IntWW 93, WhoAmP 93*
Smith, Gerard Peter 1935- *WhoAm 94*
Smith, Gerard Thomas C. *Who 94*
Smith, Gerard Vinton 1931- *WhoMW 93*
Smith, Gerrit 1797-1874 *AmSocL*
Smith, Gil Raymond 1952- *WhoMW 93*
Smith, Gilbert *Who 94*
Smith, (Thomas) Gilbert 1937- *Who 94*
Smith, Gina Morton 1966- *WhoAmL 94*
Smith, Glee Sidney, Jr. 1921- *WhoAm 94, WhoAmL 94*
Smith, Glen B. *WhoAm 94, WhoFI 94*
Smith, Glenn A. 1946- *WhoAmL 94*
Smith, Glenn N. 1946- *WhoAmL 94*
Smith, Glenn R. 1945- *WhoBlA 94*
Smith, Glenn Sanborn 1907- *WhoMW 93*
Smith, Glenn Stanley 1945- *WhoAm 94*
Smith, Gloria R. 1934- *WhoBlA 94*

Smith, Godfrey 1926- *Who 94*
Smith, Godfrey Taylor 1935- *WhoAm 94*
Smith, Goff 1916- *WhoAm 94, WhoFI 94*
Smith, Gordon 1919- *WhoAmA 93*
Smith, Gordon 1952- *WhoAmP 93*
Smith, (Raymond) Gordon (Antony) *Who 94*
Smith, Gordon A. 1953- *WhoAmL 94*
Smith, Gordon Allen 1933- *WhoBlA 94*
Smith, Gordon C. 1929- *WhoAm 94, WhoFI 94, WhoWest 94*
Smith, Gordon E. *Who 94*
Smith, Gordon Edward C. *Who 94*
Smith, Gordon Eugene 1953- *WhoWest 94*
Smith, Gordon Henry 1951- *WhoAmP 93*
Smith, Gordon Howell 1915- *WhoAm 94*
Smith, Gordon Laidlaw, Jr. 1926- *WhoAm 94*
Smith, Gordon Mackintosh 1906-1979 *WhoAmA 93N*
Smith, Gordon Paul 1916- *WhoAm 94, WhoWest 94*
Smith, Gordon Ross 1917- *WhoAm 94*
Smith, Gordon Scott 1941- *IntWW 93*
Smith, Gordon Stuart 1928- *WhoWest 94*
Smith, Graham 1942- *WhoAmA 93*
Smith, Grant Gill 1921- *WhoWest 94*
Smith, Grant Warren, II 1941- *WhoAm 94, WhoFI 94*
Smith, Granville L. *WhoBlA 94*
Smith, Granville N. 1927- *WhoBlA 94*
Smith, Greg *WhoAmP 93*
Smith, Greg E. 1963- *WhoHisp 94*
Smith, Gregg Sherwood 1951- *WhoAmA 93*
Smith, Gregory *WhoAmA 93N*
Smith, Gregory 1898- *WhAm 10*
Smith, Gregory 1946- *WhoAmP 93*
Smith, Gregory A. 1947- *WhoAmL 94*
Smith, Gregory Allan 1945- *WhoAm 94, WhoWest 94*
Smith, Gregory Allen 1952- *WhoBlA 94*
Smith, Gregory Allgire 1951- *WhoAm 94*
Smith, Gregory Blake 1951- *ConAu 141, WhoMW 93, WrDr 94*
Smith, Gregory C. 1946- *WhoAmL 94*
Smith, Gregory Dale 1963- *WhoAmL 94*
Smith, Gregory J. 1947- *WhoAmL 94*
Smith, Gregory K. 1951- *WhoAmP 93*
Smith, Gregory Kevin Prillerman 1964- *WhoBlA 94*
Smith, Gregory R. 1944- *WhoAmL 94*
Smith, Gregory Robeson, Sr. 1947- *WhoBlA 94*
Smith, Gregory Stuart 1959- *WhoAmL 94*
Smith, Gregory Warren 1956- *WhoFI 94*
Smith, Gregory White *WhoAm 94*
Smith, Greig Louis 1948- *WhoWest 94*
Smith, Gretchen Kraul 1950- *WhoFI 94*
Smith, Grover Cleveland 1923- *WhoAm 94, WrDr 94*
Smith, "Gunboat" (Edward I.) d1934 *WhoHol 92*
Smith, Guy Lincoln, IV 1949- *WhoAm 94, WhoBlA 94, WhoFI 94*
Smith, Guy W. 1940- *WhoFI 94*
Smith, Gwen Evans 1953- *WhoAmP 93*
Smith, Gwendolyn G. 1945- *WhoBlA 94*
Smith, Gwendolyn Makeda 1961- *WhoWest 94*
Smith, Gwynne P. 1924- *WhoAmP 93*
Smith, H(arry) Allen 1907-1976 *EncSF 93*
Smith, H. Irvin 1934- *WhoFI 94*
Smith, H. Russell 1957- *WhoBlA 94*
Smith, H. Shelton 1893- *WhAm 10*
Smith, H. Zack, Jr. 1924- *WhoAmP 93*
Smith, Hal *WhoHol 92*
Smith, Hal W. 1946- *WhoFI 94*
Smith, Hale 1925- *WhoBlA 94*
Smith, Hallett Darius 1907- *WhoAm 94*
Smith, Hamilton Allen 1923- *WhoWest 94*
Smith, Hamilton O. 1931- *IntWW 93*
Smith, Hamilton Othanel 1931- *Who 94, WhoAm 94, WhoScEn 94*
Smith, Harlan James 1924-1991 *WhAm 10*
Smith, Harmon Lee, Jr. 1930- *WhoAm 94*
Smith, Harold 1933- *WhoAm 94, WhoFI 94*
Smith, Harold Byron, Jr. 1933- *WhoAmP 93*
Smith, Harold Colby 1903- *WhAm 10*
Smith, Harold Douglas 1958- *WhoFI 94*
Smith, Harold Gregory *WhoBlA 94*
Smith, Harold Hill 1910- *WhoAm 94*
Smith, Harry *DrAPF 93*
Smith, Harry d1967 *WhoHol 92*
Smith, Harry 1921- *Who 94*
Smith, Harry B(ache) 1860-1936 *NewGrDO*
Smith, Harry Buchanan, Jr. 1924- *WhoMW 93*
Smith, Harry C. *DrAPF 93*
Smith, Harry James 1932- *WhoScEn 94*
Smith, Harry Mendell, Jr. 1943- *WhoWest 94*
Smith, Harry Vaughn 1929- *WhoMW 93*
Smith, Harry William 1937- *WhoAmA 93*
Smith, Harvey *IntWW 93, Who 94*
Smith, (Robert) Harvey 1938- *IntWW 93, Who 94*
Smith, Harvey Alvin 1932- *WhoAm 94*
Smith, Hassel W., Jr. *WhoAmA 93*
Smith, Hayden, Jr. 1947- *WhoAm 94, WhoAmL 94*
Smith, Heather Kay 1964- *WhoMW 93*
Smith, Heather Lynn 1956- *WhoWest 94*
Smith, Hedrick (Laurence) 1933- *ConAu 41NR, WrDr 94*
Smith, Hedrick Laurence 1933- *WhoAm 94*
Smith, Hedworth Cunningham 1912- *Who 94*
Smith, Helen Dibell 1941- *WhoFI 94*
Smith, Helen Sylvester 1942- *Who 94*
Smith, Helene Sheila Carettnay 1941- *WhoWest 94*
Smith, Heman Bernard 1929- *WhoBlA 94*
Smith, Henry c. 1560-c. 1591 *DcLB 136*
Smith, Henry Charles, III 1931- *WhoAm 94, WhoMW 93, WhoWest 94*
Smith, Henry Clay 1913- *WhoAm 94*
Smith, Henry Holmes 1909-1986 *WhoAmA 93N*
Smith, Henry John Stanley *WorScD*
Smith, Henry O., III 1946- *WhoAm 94*
Smith, Henry P., III 1911- *WhoAmP 93*
Smith, Henry Preserved 1847-1927 *DcAmReB 2*
Smith, Henry R., Jr. 1917- *WhoBlA 94*
Smith, Henry Sidney 1928- *IntWW 93, Who 94*
Smith, Henry Thomas 1937- *WhoBlA 94*
Smith, Herald Leonydus 1909- *WhoBlA 94*
Smith, Herbert Furrer 1938- *WhoAm 94*
Smith, Herbert Leary, Jr. 1923- *WhoAm 94*
Smith, Herman Brunell, Jr. 1927- *WhoBlA 94*
Smith, Herman Talliferrio 1915- *WhoBlA 94*
Smith, Herrick Hayner 1930- *WhoAm 94*
Smith, Hezekiah 1737-1805 *WhAmRev*
Smith, Hilary Cranwell Bowen 1937- *WhoFI 94*
Smith, Hobart Muir 1912- *WrDr 94*
Smith, Hoke LaFollette 1931- *WhoAm 94*
Smith, Holly Saelens 1965- *WhoMW 93*
Smith, Horace 1808-1893 *WorInv*
Smith, Horace Carroll 1922- *WhoAmP 93*
Smith, Howard 1956- *WhoWest 94*
Smith, Howard (Frank Trayton) 1919- *Who 94*
Smith, Howard C. *WhoBlA 94*
Smith, Howard Duane 1941- *WhoScEn 94*
Smith, Howard E., Jr. 1927- *WrDr 94*
Smith, Howard Frank Trayton 1919- *IntWW 93*
Smith, Howard I. d1968 *WhoHol 92*
Smith, Howard K. 1914- *IntMPA 94, WhoHol 92*
Smith, Howard McQueen 1919- *WhoAm 94*
Smith, Howard Richard 1931- *WhoAmL 94*
Smith, Howard Ross 1910- *WhoAmA 93N*
Smith, Howard Ross 1917- *WhoAm 94, WrDr 94*
Smith, Howard Russell 1914- *WhoAm 94, WhoWest 94*
Smith, Howard Wesley 1929- *WhoAm 94*
Smith, Howlett P. 1933- *WhoBlA 94*
Smith, Hueston Merriam 1912- *WhoMW 93*
Smith, Hugh M. 1951- *WhoAm 94*
Smith, Hugh Nilsen 1942- *WhoAmL 94*
Smith, Hulett Carlson 1918- *WhoAmP 93*
Smith, Hy 1934- *IntMPA 94*
Smith, Iain Crichton 1928- *DcLB 139 [port], RfGShF, WrDr 94*
Smith, Iain-Mor L. *Who 94*
Smith, Ian Cormack Palmer 1939- *WhoAm 94, WhoMW 93, WhoScEn 94*
Smith, Ian Douglas 1919- *HisWorL [port], IntWW 93, Who 94*
Smith, Idalia Luna 1956- *WhoHisp 94*
Smith, Irene M. 1910- *WhoAmP 93*
Smith, Irene Patricia *WhoAmP 93*
Smith, Irv 1929- *WhoAmP 93*
Smith, Irvin Aloysious, III 1939- *WhoFI 94*
Smith, Isaac D. 1932- *AfrAmG [port]*
Smith, Isaac Dixon 1932- *WhoBlA 94*
Smith, Isabel Francis 1935- *WhoFI 94*
Smith, Isabelle R. 1924- *WhoBlA 94*
Smith, Ivan Huron 1907- *WhoAm 94*
Smith, Ivor 1926- *IntWW 93*
Smith, Ivor Otterbein 1907- *Who 94*
Smith, Ivor Ramsay 1929- *Who 94*
Smith, J. Alfred, Sr. 1931- *WhoBlA 94*
Smith, J. Brian 1950- *WhoAm 94*
Smith, J. C. 1930- *WhoBlA 94*
Smith, J. Clay, Jr. 1942- *WhoBlA 94*
Smith, J. Harry 1922- *WhoBlA 94*
Smith, J. Kellum, Jr. 1927- *WhoAm 94*
Smith, J. Roland 1933- *WhoAmP 93*
Smith, J. Sebastian d1948 *WhoHol 92*
Smith, J. T. 1955- *WhoBlA 94*
Smith, J. Troy, Jr. 1942- *WhoAmL 94*
Smith, J. W. *WhoMW 93*
Smith, J. Weldon *WhoAmA 93*
Smith, Jack d1989 *WhoHol 92*
Smith, Jack 1928- *IntWW 93, Who 94*
Smith, Jack C. d1944 *WhoHol 92*
Smith, Jack Carl 1928- *WhoAm 94*
Smith, Jack Carter 1943- *WhoWest 94*
Smith, Jack Clifford 1916- *WhoAm 94*
Smith, Jack Donald 1955- *WhoAmP 93*
Smith, Jack Lawrence 1947- *WhoAm 94, WhoAmL 94*
Smith, Jack Lee 1948- *WhoFI 94, WhoWest 94*
Smith, Jack Martin *IntDcF 2-4*
Smith, Jack Prescott 1945- *WhoAm 94*
Smith, Jack Stanley 1916- *Who 94*
Smith, Jacklyn J. 1934- *WhoAmP 93*
Smith, Jaclyn 1947- *IntMPA 94, WhoAm 94, WhoHol 92*
Smith, Jacob Getlar 1898-1958 *WhoAmA 93N*
Smith, Jacqueline Hagan 1954- *WhoScEn 94*
Smith, Jacqueline Sarah 1933-1992 *WhAm 10*
Smith, James *WhoAmP 93*
Smith, James 1713-1806 *WhAmRev*
Smith, James 1737-1812 *WhWE*
Smith, James, Jr. 1932- *WhoBlA 94*
Smith, James A. 1927- *WhoBlA 94*
Smith, James A. 1930- *WhoAm 94*
Smith, James A. 1965- *WhoWest 94*
Smith, James Aikman 1914- *Who 94*
Smith, James Albert 1942- *WhoAmL 94*
Smith, James Alexander 1926- *WhoWest 94*
Smith, James Alfred d1993 *Who 94N*
Smith, James Allen 1959- *WhoAmL 94*
Smith, James Almer, Jr. 1923- *WhoBlA 94*
Smith, James Almer, III 1950- *WhoBlA 94*
Smith, James Andrew Buchan 1906- *Who 94*
Smith, James Archibald Bruce 1929- *Who 94*
Smith, James B., Jr. 1948- *WhoIns 94*
Smith, James Bigelow, Sr. 1908- *WhoScEn 94*
Smith, James Bonner 1950- *WhoAmL 94*
Smith, James Brian 1951- *WhoAmL 94*
Smith, James C. 1937- *WhoIns 94*
Smith, James C. 1940- *WhoAm 94, WhoAmP 93*
Smith, James Cadzow 1927- *Who 94*
Smith, James Copeland 1945- *WhoAm 94, WhoFI 94*
Smith, James Cuthbert 1954- *Who 94*
Smith, James David 1930- *WhoBlA 94*
Smith, James Dean 1955- *WhoWest 94*
Smith, James Dwight 1956- *WhoAmL 94*
Smith, James Edward 1935- *WhoScEn 94*
Smith, James Edward 1946- *WhoAmP 93*
Smith, James Everett Keith 1928- *WhoAm 94*
Smith, James F. 1932- *WhoFI 94*
Smith, James Finley 1938- *WhoAm 94*
Smith, James Forest, Jr. 1929- *WhoAm 94*
Smith, James Forrest 1945- *WhoFI 94*
Smith, James Francis 1936- *WhoAm 94, WhoFI 94*
Smith, James Frank 1942- *WhoAmL 94*
Smith, James Frederick 1944- *WhoFI 94*
Smith, James G. 1933- *WhoAmL 94*
Smith, James Gilbert 1930- *WhoAm 94*
Smith, James Hamilton 1931- *IntWW 93, WhoAm 94, WhoFI 94*
Smith, James Henry 1910-1990 *WhAm 10*
Smith, James Herbert 1947- *IntWW 93*
Smith, James Howard 1947- *WhoFI 94*
Smith, James Ian 1924- *Who 94*
Smith, James Ignatius, III 1931- *WhoAmL 94*
Smith, James John 1914- *WhoAm 94*
Smith, James Kirk 1950- *WhoAm 94, WhoFI 94*
Smith, James L(eslie Clarke) 1936- *WrDr 94*
Smith, James Lanning 1947- *WhoScEn 94*
Smith, James Lawrence 1943- *WhoAm 94, WhoWest 94*
Smith, James Lawrence, III 1960- *WhoAm 94*
Smith, James Louis, III 1943- *WhoAm 94, WhoAmL 94*
Smith, James Michael *WhoAmA 93*
Smith, James Michael 1954- *WhoAmL 94*
Smith, James Morton 1919- *WhoAmA 93*
Smith, James Odell 1953- *WhoBlA 94*
Smith, James Oscar 1928- *WhoAm 94, WhoBlA 94*
Smith, James P. 1950- *WhoAmP 93*
Smith, James Payton 1950- *WhoAm 94*
Smith, James Pembroke 1950- *WhoFI 94*
Smith, James Russell 1931- *WhoBlA 94*
Smith, James Scott 1955- *WhoAmP 93*
Smith, James T. *WhoFI 94*
Smith, James Thomas 1939- *WhoWest 94*
Smith, James Thomas 1947- *WhoFI 94, WhoMW 93*
Smith, James Todd 1968- *WhoAm 94*
Smith, James W., Jr. 1943- *WhoAmL 94*
Smith, James Wilbur, Jr. 1943- *WhoAmL 94*
Smith, James Williams, Jr. 1945- *WhoFI 94*
Smith, Jamie S. 1951- *WhoAmL 94*
Smith, Jan *EncSF 93*
Smith, Jan 1945- *WhoWest 94*
Smith, Jane Farwell *WhoAm 94*
Smith, Jane Schneberger 1928- *WhoMW 93*
Smith, Jane Waller 1946- *WhoFI 94*
Smith, Janet (Hilary) 1940- *Who 94*
Smith, Janet (B.) A. *Who 94*
Smith, Janet Hugie 1945- *WhoAmL 94*
Smith, Janet Maria *WhoBlA 94*
Smith, Janet Sue 1945- *WhoScEn 94*
Smith, Janice Evon 1952- *WhoBlA 94*
Smith, Jared *DrAPF 93*
Smith, Jaune Quick-To-See *WhoAmA 93*
Smith, Jay Lawrence 1954- *WhoFI 94*
Smith, Jay Myrven, Jr. 1932- *WhoWest 94*
Smith, Jay William 1951- *WhoFI 94*
Smith, Jean *WhoScEn 94, WhoWest 94*
Smith, Jean 1940- *WhoAmP 93*
Smith, Jean Chandler 1918- *WhoAm 94*
Smith, Jean Edward 1932- *WrDr 94*
Smith, Jean Kennedy *WhoAm 94, WhoAmP 93*
Smith, Jean M. 1943- *WhoBlA 94*
Smith, Jedediah Strong 1799-1831 *WhWE*
Smith, Jeff 1939- *WrDr 94*
Smith, Jeff(rey Alan) 1958- *WrDr 94*
Smith, Jeff C. *WhoAmP 93*
Smith, Jeff P. 1950- *WhoFI 94*
Smith, Jefferson Verne, Jr. 1925- *WhoAmP 93*
Smith, Jefferson Verne, Jr. 1948- *WhoAmL 94, WhoAmP 93*
Smith, Jeffery Alan 1951- *WhoMW 93*
Smith, Jeffrey Alan 1953- *WhoScEn 94*
Smith, Jeffrey Greenwood 1921- *WhoAm 94*
Smith, Jeffrey Howard 1956- *WhoMW 93*
Smith, Jeffrey J. 1950- *WhoMW 93*
Smith, Jeffrey L. 1939- *WhoAm 94*
Smith, Jeffrey L. 1942- *WhoAmL 94*
Smith, Jeffrey Michael 1947- *WhoAm 94, WhoAmL 94*
Smith, Jeffrey Petit 1947- *WhoAm 94*
Smith, Jeffrey R. 1948- *WhoWest 94*
Smith, Jeffry Alan 1943- *WhoScEn 94, WhoWest 94*
Smith, Jennifer (Mary) 1945- *NewGrDO*
Smith, Jennifer C. 1952- *WhoBlA 94*
Smith, Jeraldine Williams 1946- *WhoBlA 94*
Smith, Jeremy Fox Eric 1928- *Who 94*
Smith, Jeremy James Russell 1947- *Who 94*
Smith, Jeremy Owen 1960- *WhoScEn 94*
Smith, Jerome Hazen 1936- *WhoAm 94*
Smith, Jerry Charles, Jr. 1962- *WhoFI 94*
Smith, Jerry Edwin 1946- *WhoAm 94, WhoAmL 94, WhoAmP 93*
Smith, Jerry L. 1943- *WhoAmP 93*
Smith, Jess d1965 *WhoHol 92*
Smith, Jesse Graham, Jr. 1928- *WhoAm 94*
Smith, Jesse Owens 1942- *WhoBlA 94*
Smith, Jessica 1895- *WhAm 10*
Smith, Jessie 1937- *WrDr 94*
Smith, Jessie Carney *WhoBlA 94*
Smith, Jessie Carney 1930- *BlkWr 2*
Smith, Jessie Mae 1937- *WhoAmP 93*
Smith, Jill Niemczyk 1965- *WhoAmL 94*
Smith, Jimmy 1969- *WhoBlA 94*
Smith, Jo-An 1933- *WhoAmA 93*
Smith, Jo-an Richardson 1933- *WhoWest 94*
Smith, Jo Anne 1930- *WhoAm 94*
Smith, Joachim 1929- *WhoAm 94*
Smith, Joan 1938- *WrDr 94*
Smith, Joan H. *WhoMW 93*
Smith, Joann H. 1934- *WhoAmP 93*
Smith, Joanna Brashaber 1928- *WhoMW 93*
Smith, Joanne Hamlin 1954- *WhoBlA 94*
Smith, Joanne Kaye 1954- *WhoAmP 93*
Smith, Joban Jonathan 1962- *WhoWest 94*
Smith, Jock *Who 94*
Smith, Jock Michael 1948- *WhoBlA 94*
Smith, Joe d1952 *WhoHol 92*
Smith, Joe d1981 *WhoHol 92*
Smith, Joe 1884-1981
See Smith and Dale *WhoCom*
Smith, Joe Dorsey, Jr. 1922- *WhoAm 94*
Smith, Joe Elliott 1938- *WhoBlA 94*
Smith, Joe F. 1918- *WhoAmP 93*
Smith, Joe Lee 1936- *WhoBlA 94*

Smith, Joe Mauk 1916- *WhoAm 94, WhoScEn 94*
Smith, Joey Spauls 1944- *WhoWest 94*
Smith, John c. 1579-1631 *AmSocL*
Smith, John 1580-1631 *HisWorL [port], WhWE [port]*
Smith, John 1825-1910 *DcNaB MP*
Smith, John 1913- *Who 94*
Smith, John 1924- *WrDr 94*
Smith, John 1931- *WhoHol 92*
Smith, John 1938- *IntWW 93, Who 94*
Smith, John (Cyril), Sir 1922- *Who 94*
Smith, John (Lindsay Eric) 1923- *Who 94*
Smith, John (Wilson) 1920- *Who 94*
Smith, John A. 1943- *WhoFI 94*
Smith, John Alfred 1938- *Who 94*
Smith, John Arthur 1937- *WhoBlA 94*
Smith, John Arthur 1941- *WhoAmP 93*
Smith, John B. *WhoBlA 94*
Smith, John Brewster 1937- *WhoAm 94*
Smith, John Bundy 1939- *WhoAm 94*
Smith, John Burnside 1931- *WhoFI 94*
Smith, John Christian B., Jr. 1944- *WhoAmL 94*
Smith, John Christopher 1712-1795 *NewGrDO*
Smith, John Derek 1924- *IntWW 93, Who 94*
Smith, John Drake, Jr. 1950- *WhoAmL 94*
Smith, John Edward 1924- *Who 94*
Smith, John Edward D. *Who 94*
Smith, John Edwin 1921- *WhoAm 94*
Smith, John Edwin 1924-1992 *WhAm 10*
Smith, John F. 1935- *WhoAm 94, WhoFI 94*
Smith, John Francis 1923- *WhoAm 94*
Smith, John Francis, Jr. 1938- *IntWW 93, WhoAm 94, WhoFI 94, WhoMW 93*
Smith, John Francis, III 1941- *WhoAm 94, WhoAmL 94*
Smith, John Frederick 1804?-1890 *DcNaB MP*
Smith, John Frederick 1934- *Who 94*
Smith, John Gelston 1923- *WhoAm 94*
Smith, John H. 1923- *WhoAmP 93*
Smith, John Herbert 1918- *IntWW 93, Who 94*
Smith, John Hilary 1928- *Who 94*
Smith, John Ivor 1927- *WhoAmA 93*
Smith, John J. *WhoAm 94, WhoFI 94*
Smith, John J. 1911- *WhoAm 94*
Smith, John James, Jr. 1936- *WhoScEn 94*
Smith, John Jonah W. *Who 94*
Smith, John Joseph 1911- *WhoAm 94*
Smith, John Joseph 1913- *WhoAm 94*
Smith, John Joseph, Jr. 1942- *WhoFI 94*
Smith, John Julian 1957- *WhoScEn 94*
Smith, John Kenneth N. *Who 94*
Smith, John Kerwin 1926- *WhoWest 94*
Smith, John L., Jr. 1938- *WhoBlA 94*
Smith, John Lee, Jr. 1920- *WhoAm 94*
Smith, John Lewis, Jr. 1912- *WhAm 10*
Smith, John Lewis, III 1941- *WhoAm 94, WhoAmL 94*
Smith, John M. *Who 94*
Smith, John M. 1935- *WhoAm 94*
Smith, John Malcolm 1921- *WhoAm 94*
Smith, John Marvin, III 1947- *WhoScEn 94*
Smith, John Matthew 1936- *WhoAm 94*
Smith, John McNeill, Jr. 1918- *WhoAm 94, WhoAmL 94*
Smith, John Michael 1959- *WhoAmL 94*
Smith, John Mitchell Melvin 1930- *Who 94*
Smith, John P. *Who 94*
Smith, John Paul 1937- *WhoMW 93*
Smith, John Paul 1948- *WhoAmP 93*
Smith, John Paul 1950- *WhoAmP 93*
Smith, John R. 1941- *WhoAmP 93*
Smith, John Raye 1941- *WhoBlA 94*
Smith, John Richard 1931- *WhoFI 94*
Smith, John Robert 1940- *WhoScEn 94*
Smith, John Roger B. *Who 94*
Smith, John Stephen 1938- *WhoScEn 94*
Smith, John Stuart 1943- *WhoAm 94, WhoAmL 94*
Smith, John Thomas 1919- *WhoBlA 94*
Smith, John V., II 1957- *WhoAmL 94*
Smith, John Wallace 1931- *WhoMW 93*
Smith, John William Hugh 1937- *WhoMW 93*
Smith, John William Patrick 1951- *Who 94*
Smith, John Willis 1935- *WhoAm 94*
Smith, Johnston *ConAu 140*
Smith, Jonathan A. *Who 94*
Smith, Jonathan Bayard 1742-1812 *WhAmRev*
Smith, Jonathan Scott 1956- *WhoAmL 94*
Smith, Jonathan Simon Christopher R. *Who 94*
Smith, Jordan *DrAPF 93*
Smith, Jos(eph) A(nthony) 1936- *WhoAmA 93*
Smith, Joscelyn E. 1918- *WhoBlA 94*
Smith, Josef Riley 1926- *WhoAm 94*
Smith, Joseph d1993 *NewYTBS 93 [port]*
Smith, Joseph 1805-1844 *AmSocL [port], DcAmReB 2, HisWorL [port]*
Smith, Joseph (William Grenville) 1930- *Who 94*
Smith, Joseph Benjamin 1928- *WhoAm 94, WhoWest 94*
Smith, Joseph Edward 1925- *WhoBlA 94*
Smith, Joseph Edward 1938- *WhoBlA 94*
Smith, Joseph F. *WhoAmP 93*
Smith, Joseph F. 1945- *WhoBlA 94*
Smith, Joseph Fielding 1838-1918 *DcAmReB 2*
Smith, Joseph Frank 1953- *WhoScEn 94*
Smith, Joseph G. d1993 *NewYTBS 93 [port]*
Smith, Joseph LeConte, Jr. 1929- *WhoAm 94*
Smith, Joseph Lee 1929- *WhoMW 93*
Smith, Joseph Newton, III 1925- *WhoAm 94*
Smith, Joseph P. 1921- *IntMPA 94*
Smith, Joseph Phelan *WhoAm 94*
Smith, Joseph Seton 1925- *WhoAm 94*
Smith, Joseph Victor 1928- *Who 94*
Smith, Josephine Carroll 1884- *WhoAm 94*
Smith, Joshua Hett 1736-1818 *WhAmRev*
Smith, Joshua Isaac 1941- *WhoBlA 94*
Smith, Joshua L. 1934- *WhoBlA 94*
Smith, Juanita Jane 1923- *WhoBlA 94*
Smith, Juanita Smith 1927- *WhoBlA 94*
Smith, Judith Ann 1950- *WhoMW 93*
Smith, Judith Moore 1948- *WhoBlA 94*
Smith, Judson 1880-1962 *WhoAmA 93N*
Smith, Judson Lord 1917- *WhoFI 94*
Smith, Judy Ann 1948- *WhoMW 93*
Smith, Judy Seriale 1953- *WhoAmP 93, WhoBlA 94*
Smith, Jules Louis 1947- *WhoAmL 94*
Smith, Julia (Frances) 1911-1989 *NewGrDO*
Smith, Julia B. 1953- *WhoFI 94, WhoWest 94*
Smith, Julian Cleveland, Jr. 1919- *WhoAm 94, WhoScEn 94*
Smith, Julian Payne 1930- *WhoAm 94*
Smith, Julie 1954- *WrDr 94*
Smith, Julie Leonard 1938- *WhoAmP 93*
Smith, Julious Perry, Jr. 1943- *WhoAmL 94*
Smith, June Burlingame 1935- *WhoAm 94*
Smith, Juney *WhoHol 92*
Smith, Junius *EncSF 93*
Smith, Justin d1986 *WhoHol 92*
Smith, Justin V. 1903- *WhoAmA 93N*
Smith, Justine Townsend 1936- *WhoAm 94*
Smith, K. Clay 1937- *WhoFI 94*
Smith, Karen *WhoHol 92*
Smith, Karen Ann 1958- *WhoMW 93*
Smith, Karen Blonquist 1950- *WhoAmP 93*
Smith, Karen Lynette 1962- *WhoBlA 94*
Smith, Karl Joseph 1943- *WhoWest 94*
Smith, Karleen Stanfield 1958- *WhoFI 94*
Smith, Kate d1986 *WhoHol 92*
Smith, Kathleen Diane 1951- *WhoMW 93*
Smith, Kathleen J(oan) 1929- *WrDr 94*
Smith, Kathleen Tener 1943- *WhoFI 94*
Smith, Kathryn Ann 1955- *WhoMW 93*
Smith, Kathy Ann 1944- *WhoAmP 93, WhoMW 93*
Smith, Katrina Marita 1958- *WhoBlA 94*
Smith, Kay Nolte d1993 *NewYTBS 93*
Smith, Kay Nolte 1932- *ConAu 43NR, WrDr 94*
Smith, Kay Nolte 1932-1993 *ConAu 142*
Smith, Keely 1932- *WhoHol 92*
Smith, Keith *WhoHol 92, WhoMW 93*
Smith, Keith A. 1938- *WhoAm 94, WhoAmA 93*
Smith, Keith Brunton 1960- *WhoScEn 94*
Smith, Keith Dryden, Jr. 1951- *WhoBlA 94*
Smith, Keith Larue 1917- *WhoWest 94*
Smith, Keith Scott 1958- *WhoScEn 94*
Smith, Kelley R. 1946- *WhoAmP 93*
Smith, Ken *DrAPF 93*
Smith, Ken(neth John) 1938- *WrDr 94*
Smith, Kenard Eugene 1946- *WhoMW 93*
Smith, Kenneth d1981 *WhoHol 92*
Smith, Kenneth 1920-1989 *WhAm 10*
Smith, Kenneth Alan 1936- *WhoAm 94*
Smith, Kenneth Blose 1926- *WhoAm 94*
Smith, Kenneth Bryant 1931- *WhoAm 94, WhoBlA 94*
Smith, Kenneth Carless 1932- *WhoAm 94, WhoScEn 94*
Smith, Kenneth Charles, Sr. 1932- *WhoAmP 93*
Smith, Kenneth D., Jr. 1956- *WhoAmP 93*
Smith, Kenneth George 1920- *Who 94*
Smith, Kenneth Graeme Stewart 1918- *Who 94*
Smith, Kenneth James 1948- *WhoWest 94*
Smith, Kenneth L. *WhoAmP 93*
Smith, Kenneth R. 1947- *WhoAmP 93*
Smith, Kenneth W. 1952- *WhoIns 94*
Smith, Kent *EncSF 93*
Smith, Kent d1985 *WhoHol 92*
Smith, Kent Alvin 1943- *WhoAmA 93*
Smith, Kermit A. 1928- *WhoAmP 93*
Smith, Kermit Wayne 1938- *WhoAm 94*
Smith, Kerry Clark 1935- *WhoAm 94*
Smith, Kevin A. 1962- *WhoAmP 93*
Smith, Kevin L. *WhoBlA 94*
Smith, Kim Lee 1941- *WhoAm 94*
Smith, Kingsley Ward 1946- *Who 94*
Smith, Kirk Robert 1947- *WhoWest 94*
Smith, Koert Robert 1943- *WhoMW 93*
Smith, Kurtwood 1942- *IntMPA 94*
Smith, Kurtwood 1943- *WhoHol 92*
Smith, L. Eugene 1921- *WhoAmP 93*
Smith, L. Neil *WrDr 94*
Smith, L. Neil 1946- *EncSF 93*
Smith, La Ron A. *WhoHol 92*
Smith, LaBradford C. 1969- *WhoBlA 94*
Smith, Lacey Baldwin 1922- *WrDr 94*
Smith, Lafayette Kenneth 1947- *WhoBlA 94*
Smith, Lamar 1947- *CngDr 93*
Smith, Lamar Seeligson 1947- *WhoAm 94, WhoAmP 93*
Smith, Lane *IntMPA 94, WhoHol 92*
Smith, Lane 1959- *SmATA 76 [port]*
Smith, Lane Jeffrey 1954- *WhoAm 94, WhoWest 94*
Smith, Langdon G., Jr. 1953- *WhoAmP 93*
Smith, Lanty Lloyd 1942- *WhoAm 94*
Smith, Larkin 1944-1989 *WhAm 10*
Smith, Larry *DrAPF 93*
Smith, Larry E. *WhoAmP 93*
Smith, Larry L. 1950- *WhoAmL 94*
Smith, Larry Steven 1950- *WhoFI 94*
Smith, Larry Van 1947- *WhoAm 94, WhoAmL 94*
Smith, LaSalle, Sr. 1947- *WhoBlA 94*
Smith, Laura *Who 94*
Smith, Laura Whitlock 1931- *WhoAmP 93*
Smith, Laure *EncSF 93*
Smith, Laurel Ann 1955- *WhoMW 93*
Smith, Lauren Ashley 1924- *WhoAmL 94, WhoMW 93*
Smith, Laurence Roger 1939- *WhoFI 94*
Smith, Lawrence A. *WhoAmL 94*
Smith, Lawrence Abner 1921- *WhoScEn 94*
Smith, Lawrence Beall 1909- *WhoAm 94, WhoAmA 93*
Smith, Lawrence Delpre 1905- *Who 94*
Smith, Lawrence F. 1952- *WhoIns 94*
Smith, Lawrence Howard 1942- *WhoWest 94*
Smith, Lawrence J. 1941- *WhoAmP 93*
Smith, Lawrence John, Jr. 1947- *WhoBlA 94*
Smith, Lawrence Joseph *Who 94*
Smith, Lawrence Leighton 1936- *WhoAm 94*
Smith, Lawrence M. C. 1902-1975 *WhoAmA 93N*
Smith, Lawrence Paul 1945- *WhoAmP 93*
Smith, Lawrence R. *DrAPF 93*
Smith, Lawrence R. 1948- *WhoAm 94, WhoAmL 94*
Smith, Lawrence Roger Hines 1941- *Who 94*
Smith, Lawrence Shannon 1943- *WhoAmL 94*
Smith, Lawry 1952- *WhoAmA 93*
Smith, Lawson Wentworth 1947- *WhoAmA 93*
Smith, Le Roi Matthew-Pierre, III 1946- *WhoWest 94*
Smith, Leah Johnson 1943- *WhoFI 94*
Smith, Lee *DrAPF 93*
Smith, Lee Arthur 1957- *WhoAm 94, WhoBlA 94*
Smith, Lee Clark 1942- *WhoFI 94*
Smith, Lee Elton 1937- *WhoAm 94*
Smith, Lee Herman 1935- *WhoAm 94*
Smith, Lee L. 1936- *WhoWest 94*
Smith, Lee Martin 1958- *WhoMW 93*
Smith, Leighton Warren, Jr. 1939- *WhoAm 94*
Smith, Leila Hentzen 1932- *WhoMW 93*
Smith, Leo Emmet 1927- *WhoAmL 94*
Smith, Leo Gilbert 1929- *WhoAm 94*
Smith, Leo Grant 1940- *WhoBlA 94*
Smith, Leon Polk 1906- *WhoAm 94, WhoAmA 93*
Smith, Leonard A. *WhoAmP 93*
Smith, Leonard Bingley 1915- *WhoAm 94*
Smith, Leonard Charles 1921-1990 *WhAm 10*
Smith, Leonard Clinton Geoffrey 1944- *WhoIns 94*
Smith, Leonard L. d1942 *WhoHol 92*
Smith, Leonard Phillip 1960- *WhoBlA 94*
Smith, Leonard R. *WhoHol 92*
Smith, Leora Skolkin *DrAPF 93*
Smith, LeRoi Matthew-Pierre, III 1946- *WhoBlA 94*
Smith, Leroy Harrington, Jr. 1928- *WhoAm 94*
Smith, LeRoy Victor 1933- *WhoBlA 94*
Smith, Leslie (Edward George) 1919- *Who 94*
Smith, Leslie Charles 1918- *Who 94*
Smith, Leslie Edward 1919- *IntWW 93*
Smith, Leslie Roper 1928- *WhoAm 94*
Smith, Lester Martin 1919- *WhoWest 94*
Smith, Lester W. d1993 *NewYTBS 93*
Smith, Leverett Ralph *WhoWest 94*
Smith, Levering 1910- *WhoWest 94*
Smith, Levie David, Jr. 1924- *WhoFI 94*
Smith, Lew d1964 *WhoHol 92*
Smith, Lewis 1957- *WhoHol 92*
Smith, Lewis Dennis 1938- *WhoAm 94*
Smith, Lewis Motter, Jr. 1932- *WhoAm 94*
Smith, Ley S. 1934- *WhoFI 94*
Smith, Lila *WhoBlA 94*
Smith, Lillian 1897-1966 *BlmGWL*
Smith, Linda *WhoAmP 93*
Smith, Linda A. *WhoWest 94*
Smith, Linda Ann *WhoAmP 93*
Smith, Linda Jane 1952- *WhoAmL 94*
Smith, Linda Kridel 1944- *WhoAmL 94*
Smith, Linda Wasmer *DrAPF 93*
Smith, Liz *WhoAm 94, WhoHol 92*
Smith, Liz 1940- *WhoAmP 93*
Smith, Llewellyn Thomas 1944- *Who 94*
Smith, Lloyd 1941- *WhoAm 94*
Smith, Lloyd Barnaby 1945- *Who 94*
Smith, Lloyd Bruce 1920- *IntWW 93*
Smith, Lloyd Hilton 1905- *WhoAm 94, WhoScEn 94*
Smith, Lloyd Muir 1917- *WhoAm 94*
Smith, Lois 1930- *WhoHol 92*
Smith, Lois Ann 1941- *WhoMW 93*
Smith, Lois Arlene 1930- *WhoAm 94*
Smith, Lon A. 1939- *WhoIns 94*
Smith, Lonnie *WhoHol 92*
Smith, Lonnie 1955- *WhoBlA 94*
Smith, Lonnie Max 1944- *WhoAm 94, WhoFI 94*
Smith, Loren Allan 1944- *CngDr 93, WhoAm 94, WhoAmL 94*
Smith, Loring d1981 *WhoHol 92*
Smith, Louis 1934- *WhoScEn 94, WhoWest 94*
Smith, Louis 1939- *WhoBlA 94*
Smith, Louis M., Jr. 1937- *WhoIns 94*
Smith, Louis Milde 1929- *WhoMW 93*
Smith, Lowell *WhoAm 94*
Smith, Lowell Ellsworth 1924- *WhoAmA 93*
Smith, Luther A. 1950- *WhoAmA 93*
Smith, Luther A. 1953- *WhoScEn 94*
Smith, Luther Edward, Jr. 1947- *WhoBlA 94*
Smith, Lyn Wall 1909-1979 *WhoAmA 93N*
Smith, Lynn Howard 1936- *WhoAm 94*
Smith, Lynn Stanford 1951- *WhoBlA 94*
Smith, Lynwood Stephen 1928- *WhoAm 94, WhoWest 94*
Smith, M. Frances 1927- *WhoWest 94*
Smith, Macon Strother 1919- *WhoAm 94*
Smith, Madeline *WhoHol 92*
Smith, Madolyn 1957- *WhoHol 92*
Smith, Maggie 1934- *ConTFT 11, IntMPA 94, Who 94, WhoAm 94, WhoHol 92*
Smith, Maggie Natalie 1934- *IntWW 93*
Smith, Mahlon Brewster 1919- *WhoAm 94*
Smith, Malcolm *WhoHol 92*
Smith, Malcolm Andrew F. *Who 94*
Smith, Malcolm Barry Estes 1939- *WhoAm 94, WhoAmL 94*
Smith, Malcolm Bernard 1923- *WhoAm 94*
Smith, Malcolm Greville 1941- *WhoWest 94*
Smith, Malcolm Norman 1921- *WhoAm 94*
Smith, Malcolm Sommerville 1933- *WhoAm 94*
Smith, Mamie d1946 *WhoHol 92*
Smith, Marc Alan 1962- *WhoAmL 94*
Smith, Marc Kevin 1954- *WhoScEn 94*
Smith, Marcia Jean 1947- *WhoFI 94*
Smith, Margaret *WhoAmP 93*
Smith, Margaret d1960 *WhoHol 92*
Smith, Margaret fl. 1660- *BlmGWL*
Smith, Margaret Chase 1897- *IntWW 93, WhoAmP 93*
Smith, Margaret Hamilton Donald 1915- *WhoAm 94*
Smith, Margo Bradshaw 1950- *WhoWest 94*
Smith, Margot 1918- *Who 94*
Smith, Maria *WhoHol 92*
Smith, Marianne 1948- *WhoWest 94*
Smith, Marie Edmonds 1927- *WhoFI 94, WhoWest 94*
Smith, Marie Evans 1928- *WhoBlA 94*
Smith, Marietta Culbreath 1933- *WhoBlA 94*
Smith, Marilyn Lynne 1944- *WhoFI 94*
Smith, Marilyn Noeltner 1933- *WhoWest 94*

Smith, Marion Edmonds 1926- WhoWest 94
Smith, Marion L. 1901-1991 WhoBlA 94N
Smith, Marion Pafford 1925- WhoAm 94
Smith, Marjorie Alice Walker 1918- WhoMW 93
Smith, Mark DrAPF 93
Smith, Mark d1944 WhoHol 92
Smith, Mark (Richard) 1935- WrDr 94
Smith, Mark Albert 1950- WhoAmL 94
Smith, Mark Barnet 1917- Who 94
Smith, Mark Lee 1957- WhoAm 94, WhoWest 94
Smith, Mark Maurice 1944- WhoMW 93
Smith, Mark Steven 1950- WhoAmL 94
Smith, Mark Warren 1960- WhoFI 94
Smith, Markwick Kern, Jr. 1928- WhoAm 94
Smith, Marlyn Stansbury 1942- WhoBlA 94
Smith, Marschall Imboden 1944- WhoFI 94
Smith, Marshall Savidge 1937- WhoAm 94, WhoWest 94
Smith, Martha WhoHol 92
Smith, Martin ConAu 43NR, EncSF 93
Smith, Martin Bernhard 1930- WhoAm 94, WhoWest 94
Smith, Martin Cruz 1942- ConAu 43NR, IntWW 93, WhoAm 94, WrDr 94
Smith, Martin (William) Cruz 1942- EncSF 93
Smith, Martin Henry 1921- WhoAm 94
Smith, Martin Jay 1934- WhoMW 93, WhoScEn 94
Smith, Martin Jay 1942- WhoAm 94
Smith, Martin Travis WhoAmP 93
Smith, Marvin E. WhoAmP 93
Smith, Marvin Preston 1944- WhoBlA 94
Smith, Marvin Schade 1905- WhoScEn 94
Smith, Mary Alice 1941- WhoAm 94
Smith, Mary Ann WhoAmP 93
Smith, Mary Ann 1938- WhoMW 93
Smith, Mary-Ann Hrivnak 1951- WhoScEn 94
Smith, Mary-Ann Tirone 1944- WrDr 94
Smith, Mary Carter 1919- WhoBlA 94
Smith, Mary Kay Wilhelm 1962- WhoScEn 94
Smith, Mary Levi 1936- WhoBlA 94
Smith, Mary Louise 1914- WhoAm 94, WhoAmP 93
Smith, Mary Lynn 1965- WhoWest 94
Smith, Mary Perkins 1949- WhoFI 94
Smith, Marya Jean 1945- WhoMW 93
Smith, Marzell 1936- WhoBlA 94
Smith, Mason DrAPF 93
Smith, Matthew d1953 WhoHol 92
Smith, Matthew J. 1941- WhoAmP 93
Smith, Matthew Jay 1961- WhoScEn 94
Smith, Maureen McBride 1952- WhoWest 94
Smith, Maurice 1939- IntMPA 94
Smith, Maurice Edward 1919- WhoAm 94
Smith, Maurice George 1915- Who 94
Smith, Maxine A. WhoAmP 93
Smith, Maxine Atkins WhoBlA 94
Smith, Mel 1952- WhoHol 92
Smith, Melancton 1744-1798 WhAmRev
Smith, Melissa Ann 1962- WhoBlA 94
Smith, Melvin WhoAmP 93
Smith, Melvin Kenneth 1952- Who 94
Smith, Melvin Sylvan 1927- WhoFI 94
Smith, Merilyn Roberta 1933- WhoMW 93
Smith, Meriwether 1730-1790 WhAmRev
Smith, Merlin Gale 1928- WhoAm 94
Smith, (Albert) Merriman 1913-1970 CurBio 93N
Smith, Merritt Roe 1940- WhoAm 94
Smith, Michael Who 94
Smith, Michael 1932- IntWW 93, Who 94, WhoScEn 94
Smith, Michael 1935- WrDr 94
Smith, Michael 1940- IntWW 93
Smith, Michael 1942- WrDr 94
Smith, Michael A. 1942- WhoAmA 93
Smith, Michael A. 1949- WhoWest 94
Smith, Michael Alan 1947- WhoFI 94
Smith, Michael Alexis 1944- WhoAm 94
Smith, Michael Anthony 1945- WhoAm 94, WhoMW 93
Smith, Michael C. B. 1955- WhoFI 94
Smith, Michael Edward 1956- WhoAmP 93
Smith, Michael Edward C. Who 94
Smith, Michael Francis 1960- WhoMW 93
Smith, Michael G. d1993 NewYTBS 93
Smith, Michael Garfield d1993 Who 94N
Smith, Michael Gerard A. Who 94
Smith, Michael Howard 1938- WhoAm 94, WhoScEn 94
Smith, Michael James 1945- WhoAm 94
Smith, Michael K. Who 94
Smith, Michael L. 1948- WhoAm 94, WhoFI 94, WhoMW 93
Smith, Michael Lawrence 1958- WhoScEn 94
Smith, Michael Morgan 1948- WhoFI 94, WhoMW 93
Smith, (Anthony) Michael Percival 1924- Who 94
Smith, Michael Peter 1942- WhoAm 94
Smith, Michael Steven 1956- WhoFI 94, WhoScEn 94, WhoWest 94
Smith, Michael T(ownsend) 1935- ConDr 93
Smith, Michael Townsend 1935- WhoAm 94
Smith, Michael W. 1958- ConMus 11 [port]
Smith, Michael Wayne 1951- WhoAm 94
Smith, Michael Willis 1944- WhoAmL 94
Smith, Mike WhoHol 92
Smith, Mildred B. 1935- WhoBlA 94
Smith, Mildred Cassandra WhoScEn 94
Smith, Millard, Jr. 1948- WhoBlA 94
Smith, Milton Curtis 1937- WhoAmL 94
Smith, Milton Ray 1935- WhoAm 94
Smith, Mitchell 1935- WrDr 94
Smith, Miyoshi Delphine 1958- WhoAmL 94
Smith, Moishe 1929- WhoAm 94, WhoAmA 93, WhoWest 94
Smith, Moncrieff Hynson 1917- WhoAm 94
Smith, Monica LaVonne 1966- WhoBlA 94
Smith, Monte 1938- WhoWest 94
Smith, Morgan S. d1993 NewYTBS 93
Smith, Morris Leslie 1933- WhoBlA 94
Smith, Morton 1915- WrDr 94
Smith, Morton 1915-1991 WhAm 10
Smith, Morton Alan 1931- WhoAmL 94
Smith, Morton Howison 1923- WhoAm 94
Smith, Muriel d1985 WhoHol 92
Smith, Murphy D(e Witt) 1920- ConAu 42NR
Smith, Murray Thomas 1939- WhoAm 94, WhoFI 94, WhoMW 93
Smith, Myron D. 1954- WhoFI 94
Smith, Myron John, Jr. 1944- WhoAm 94
Smith, N. Randy 1949- WhoWest 94
Smith, N. Randy 1950- WhoAmP 93
Smith, N(eilson) V(oyne) 1939- WrDr 94
Smith, Nan S(helley) 1952- WhoAmA 93
Smith, Nancy Hohendorf 1943- WhoAm 94, WhoFI 94, WhoMW 93
Smith, Nancy L. 1939- WhoMW 93
Smith, Nancy Weitman 1950- WhoAm 94
Smith, Nathan McKay 1935- WhoAm 94, WhoWest 94
Smith, Nathaniel AfrAmG
Smith, Nathaniel, Jr. WhoBlA 94
Smith, Neal 1920- CngDr 93, WhoAmP 93
Smith, Neal Austin 1919-1989 WhAm 10
Smith, Neal Edward 1920- WhoAm 94, WhoMW 93
Smith, Ned R. WhoAmP 93
Smith, Neil Who 94
Smith, Neil 1966- WhoAm 94, WhoBlA 94, WhoMW 93
Smith, (George) Neil 1936- Who 94
Smith, Neilson Voyne 1939- Who 94
Smith, Nell W. 1929- WhoAmP 93
Smith, Nellie J. 1932- WhoBlA 94
Smith, Nels Jensen 1939- WhoAmP 93
Smith, Neville Vincent 1942- WhoAm 94, WhoScEn 94
Smith, Newman Donald 1936- WhoFI 94
Smith, Nicholas 1934- WhoHol 92
Smith, Nick 1934- CngDr 93, WhoAm 94, WhoMW 93
Smith, Nick H. 1934- WhoAmP 93
Smith, Nico J. 1929- IntWW 93
Smith, Noel Wilson 1933- WhoScEn 94
Smith, Norman Blaine 1927- WhoMW 93
Smith, Norman Brian 1928- IntWW 93
Smith, Norman Clark 1917- WhoAm 94
Smith, Norman Cutler 1915- WhoAm 94
Smith, Norman Edward Mace 1914- WrDr 94
Smith, Norman Frederick 1920- WhoAmP 93
Smith, Norman Henry 1925- IntWW 93
Smith, Norman Jack 1936- Who 94
Smith, Norman Obed 1914- WhoAm 94
Smith, Norman Raymond 1944- WhoBlA 94
Smith, Norman Raymond 1946- WhoAm 94
Smith, Norman T. 1935- WhoAm 94, WhoMW 93
Smith, Norwood WhoHol 92
Smith, Noval Albert, Jr. 1949- WhoScEn 94
Smith, Numa Lamar, Jr. 1915- WhoAm 94
Smith, Oliver 1918- IntDcB, IntWW 93, WhoAm 94
Smith, Oliver P. 1893-1977 HisDcKW
Smith, Ora d1993 NewYTBS 93 [port]
Smith, Orin Robert 1935- IntWW 93, WhoAm 94, WhoFI 94, WhoScEn 94
Smith, Orville Auverne 1927- WhoAm 94
Smith, Oscar d1956 WhoHol 92
Smith, Oscar A., Jr. WhoBlA 94
Smith, Oscar Samuel 1947- WhoFI 94
Smith, Oscar Samuel, Jr. 1929- WhoBlA 94
Smith, Oswald Garrison 1915- WhoBlA 94
Smith, Otis Benton, Jr. 1939- WhoBlA 94
Smith, Otis Fitzgerald 1964- WhoBlA 94
Smith, Otis M. 1922- WhoBlA 94
Smith, Otis Milton 1922- WhoAmP 93
Smith, Otrie 1936- WhoBlA 94
Smith, Otto J. M. 1917- WhoWest 94
Smith, Owen Telfair WhoFI 94
Smith, Ozzie 1954- WhoAm 94, WhoBlA 94, WhoMW 93
Smith, P. R. WhoAmP 93
Smith, Page 1917- WrDr 94
Smith, Pam Burr DrAPF 93
Smith, Pamela C. 1869- BlmGWL
Smith, Parrish c. 1968- See EPMD ConMus 10
Smith, Patricia 1930- WhoHol 92
Smith, Patricia G. 1947- WhoBlA 94
Smith, Patricia J. 1946- WhoMW 93
Smith, Patricia Jacquline 1944- WhoFI 94, WhoWest 94
Smith, Patricia Lahr WhoAmP 93
Smith, Patricia Lynn 1965- WhoFI 94
Smith, Patricia Newell 1943- WhoMW 93
Smith, Patrick D. DrAPF 93
Smith, Patrick Francis 1954- WhoAmL 94
Smith, Patrick J(ohn) 1932- NewGrDO
Smith, Patrick John 1932- WhoAm 94
Smith, Patrick Stephen 1959- WhoAmL 94
Smith, Patti DrAPF 93
Smith, Paul WhoHol 92
Smith, Paul 1935- WhoBlA 94
Smith, Paul Aikin 1934- WhoAmP 93
Smith, Paul Alexander 1949- WhoWest 94
Smith, Paul B. 1946- IntWW 93
Smith, Paul Bernard 1931- WhoBlA 94
Smith, Paul Christian 1950- WhoScEn 94
Smith, Paul E. 1927- WhoAmP 93
Smith, Paul E. 1954- WhoAmL 94
Smith, Paul Frederick 1916- WhoAm 94
Smith, Paul Gerard d1968 WhoHol 92
Smith, Paul Henry 1952- WhoAmP 93
Smith, Paul J. 1931- WhoAmA 93
Smith, Paul John 1945- WhoScEn 94
Smith, Paul Julian 1956- Who 94
Smith, Paul Kimbrell 1895- WhAm 10
Smith, Paul Lester 1935- WhoFI 94
Smith, Paul Letton, Jr. 1932- WhoMW 93, WhoScEn 94
Smith, Paul Louis 1945- WhoMW 93
Smith, Paul M., Jr. 1920- WhoBlA 94
Smith, Paul R. d1993 NewYTBS 93
Smith, Paul S. 1927- WhoAmP 93
Smith, Paul Samuel 1897-1991 WhAm 10
Smith, Paul Thomas 1938- WhoAm 94
Smith, Paul Traylor 1923- WhoAm 94
Smith, Paul Vergon, Jr. 1921- WhoAm 94
Smith, Paula Suzanne 1950- WhoWest 94
Smith, Paulette Wright 1951- WhoMW 93
Smith, Pauline 1882-1959 BlmGWL
Smith, Pauline (Janet) 1882-1959 RfGShF
Smith, Payton 1932- WhoAm 94
Smith, Pearlena W. 1916- WhoBlA 94
Smith, Peggy O'Doniel 1920- WhoScEn 94
Smith, Perry Anderson, III 1934- WhoBlA 94
Smith, Pete d1979 WhoHol 92
Smith, Peter WhoHol 92
Smith, Peter 1924- WhoAm 94
Smith, Peter 1926- Who 94
Smith, Peter 1945- WhoAmP 93
Smith, Peter Alexander Charles 1920- Who 94
Smith, Peter Anthony 1940- Who 94
Smith, Peter Bennett 1934- WhoAm 94, WhoFI 94
Smith, Peter Bruce 1944- Who 94
Smith, Peter Charles Horstead 1940- WrDr 94
Smith, Peter Clarke 1958- WhoAmP 93
Smith, Peter Claudius G. Who 94
Smith, Peter G. 1946- WhoAmL 94
Smith, Peter Garthwaite 1923- WhoAm 94
Smith, Peter Graham 1929- Who 94
Smith, Peter Guy 1950- WhoScEn 94
Smith, Peter J. Who 94
Smith, Peter J. 1931- WrDr 94
Smith, Peter John 1931- WhoAm 94
Smith, Peter John 1936- Who 94
Smith, Peter John 1942- Who 94
Smith, Peter John 1966- WhoAm 94
Smith, Peter Lawrence 1942- WhoAm 94
Smith, Peter Lincoln Chivers 1948- Who 94
Smith, Peter Lloyd 1944- WhoScEn 94
Smith, Peter Vivian Henworth 1928- Who 94
Smith, Peter Walker 1923- WhoAm 94, WhoFI 94
Smith, Peter William Ebblewhite 1937- WhoAm 94
Smith, Peter Wilson 1938- WhoAm 94, WhoMW 93
Smith, Peter Winston 1952- Who 94
Smith, Phil 1952- BasBi
Smith, Philip 1913- Who 94
Smith, Philip Daniel 1933- WhoAm 94
Smith, Philip Edward Lake 1927- WhoAm 94
Smith, Philip G. 1946- WhoAmP 93
Smith, Philip Gene 1928- WhoBlA 94
Smith, Philip George 1911- Who 94
Smith, Philip Hardy 1931- WhoAmP 93
Smith, Philip Jones 1941- WhoAm 94
Smith, Philip Luther 1956- WhoScEn 94
Smith, Philip Meek 1932- WhoAm 94, WhoScEn 94
Smith, Philip S. 1936- WhoFI 94
Smith, Philip Walter 1945- WhoWest 94
Smith, Phillip Dale 1952- WhoWest 94
Smith, Phillip Harden 1936- WhoAmL 94
Smith, Phillip Hartley 1927- WhoAm 94
Smith, Phillip M. 1937- WhoBlA 94
Smith, Phillips Guy 1946- WhoAm 94
Smith, Pierce Reiland 1943- WhoAm 94, WhoFI 94
Smith, Preston Gibson 1941- WhoFI 94
Smith, Priscilla Agnes 1941- WhoHisp 94
Smith, Putter WhoHol 92
Smith, Queenie d1978 WhoHol 92
Smith, Quentin P. 1918- WhoBlA 94
Smith, Quentin Paige, Jr. 1951- WhoBlA 94
Smith, Quentin T. 1937- WhoBlA 94
Smith, R. C. 1795-1832 AstEnc
Smith, R(eginald) D(onald) 1914-1985 ConAu 140
Smith, R. E. DrAPF 93
Smith, R. Evan 1941- WhoAm 94
Smith, R. Gaylord 1951- WhoAmL 94
Smith, R. Gordon 1938- WhoAm 94
Smith, R. Hal 1917- WhoAmP 93
Smith, R(ichard) Selby 1914- Who 94
Smith, R. T. DrAPF 93
Smith, Rachel Norcom 1925- WhoBlA 94
Smith, Rainbeaux WhoHol 92
Smith, Ralph Alexander 1929- WhoAm 94, WhoAmA 93
Smith, Ralph Bernard 1939- WrDr 94
Smith, Ralph Carlisle 1910-1989 WhAm 10
Smith, Ralph Earl 1940- WhoAm 94, WhoScEn 94, WhoWest 94
Smith, Ralph Edward 1953- WhoMW 93
Smith, Ralph Lee 1927- WhoAm 94, WrDr 94
Smith, Ralph O'Hara 1952- WhoBlA 94
Smith, Ralph Wesley, Jr. 1936- WhoAm 94, WhoAmL 94
Smith, Randall 1950- WhoAmL 94
Smith, Randolph Relihan 1944- WhoScEn 94
Smith, Randy 1948- BasBi, WhoAm 94, WhoFI 94
Smith, Rankin M., Jr. 1947- WhoAm 94
Smith, Ray 1936- WhoHol 92
Smith, Ray Fred 1919- IntWW 93
Smith, Ray S., Jr. WhoAmP 93
Smith, Raymond WhoAm 94
Smith, Raymond (Horace) 1917- Who 94
Smith, Raymond Edward 1932- WhoScEn 94, WhoWest 94
Smith, Raymond Lloyd 1917- WhoAm 94
Smith, Raymond Thomas 1925- WhoAm 94
Smith, Raymond Victor 1926- WhoAm 94, WhoWest 94
Smith, Raymond W. 1937- WhoAm 94, WhoFI 94
Smith, Raymond Walter 1942- WhoAmA 93
Smith, Rebecca Beach 1949- WhoAm 94, WhoAmL 94
Smith, Rebecca Lieder 1950- WhoMW 93
Smith, Rebecca Sue 1950- WhoMW 93
Smith, Redbird 1850-1918 EncNAR
Smith, Reed Williams 1949- WhoMW 93
Smith, Reggie 1970- WhoBlA 94
Smith, Reginald Brian Furness 1931- WhoAm 94, WhoScEn 94
Smith, Reginald D. 1918- WhoBlA 94
Smith, Reginald J. WhoAmP 93
Smith, Reginald Keith 1960- WhoBlA 94
Smith, Reid WhoHol 92
Smith, Reuben R., Jr. WhoAmP 93
Smith, Rex 1956- WhoHol 92
Smith, Rex 1957- WhoAmP 93
Smith, Rex William 1952- WhoAm 94
Smith, Richard Who 94
Smith, Richard 1735-1803 WhAmRev
Smith, Richard 1931- IntWW 93
Smith, Richard 1938- WhoAmP 93
Smith, (Walter) Richard 1926- Who 94
Smith, Richard Alan WhoScEn 94

Smith, Richard Alan 1924- *WhoAm 94, WhoFI 94*
Smith, Richard Alfred 1932- *WhoBlA 94*
Smith, Richard Anthony 1939- *WhoFI 94*
Smith, Richard Bowen 1938- *WhoAm 94*
Smith, Richard Carlisle 1930- *WhoAm 94*
Smith, Richard Carlton 1960- *WhoFI 94*
Smith, Richard Clarke 1908- *WhoAmL 94*
Smith, Richard D. 1928- *WhoAm 94, WhoFI 94*
Smith, Richard D. 1954- *WhoFI 94*
Smith, Richard Dale 1949- *WhoScEn 94*
Smith, Richard Donald 1928- *WhoIns 94*
Smith, Richard Emerson 1922- *WhoAm 94*
Smith, Richard Ernest 1935- *WhoAm 94*
Smith, Richard Foster 1934- *WhoWest 94*
Smith, Richard G. 1952- *WhoAmL 94*
Smith, Richard Gideon 1934- *WhoFI 94*
Smith, Richard Grant 1937- *WhoAm 94*
Smith, Richard H. S. *Who 94*
Smith, Richard Harding 1950- *WhoMW 93*
Smith, Richard Harvey 1923- *WhoAmP 93*
Smith, Richard Howard 1927- *WhoAm 94*
Smith, Richard I. 1947- *WhoWest 94*
Smith, Richard John 1934- *IntWW 93, Who 94*
Smith, Richard Joseph 1932- *WhoAm 94*
Smith, Richard Joseph 1944- *ConAu 42NR*
Smith, Richard Joseph 1950- *WhoFI 94*
Smith, Richard Joyce 1903- *WhoAm 94*
Smith, Richard Kenneth 1950- *WhoAm 94*
Smith, Richard Lawrence 1933- *WhoAm 94, WhoWest 94*
Smith, Richard Maybury H. *Who 94*
Smith, Richard Melvyn 1940- *WhoAm 94, WhoScEn 94*
Smith, Richard Michael 1946- *Who 94*
Smith, Richard Mills 1946- *WhoAm 94*
Smith, Richard Muldrow 1939- *WhoAm 94*
Smith, Richard P. *Who 94, WhoAm 94*
Smith, Richard R. V. *Who 94*
Smith, Richard Roy 1954- *WhoMW 93*
Smith, Richard Sydney William 1952- *Who 94*
Smith, Richard Thomas 1925- *WhoAm 94*
Smith, Richard Wendell 1912- *WhoAmL 94*
Smith, Richard Yeadon, III 1943- *WhoFI 94*
Smith, Richey 1933- *WhoAm 94, WhoFI 94*
Smith, Rick *DrAPF 93*
Smith, Rick 1942- *WhoAmP 93*
Smith, Rick A. 1948- *WhoMW 93, WhoScEn 94*
Smith, Robert 1732-1801 *WhAmRev*
Smith, Robert 1937- *WhoBlA 94*
Smith, Robert, Jr. 1951- *WhoBlA 94*
Smith, Robert, III 1939- *WhoAm 94*
Smith, Robert (Courtney) 1927- *Who 94*
Smith, Robert Allen 1936- *WhoFI 94*
Smith, Robert Angus 1817-1884 *EnvEnc*
Smith, Robert B(ache) *NewGrDO*
Smith, Robert Blakeman 1949- *WhoAmL 94*
Smith, Robert Boulware, III 1933- *WhoAm 94*
Smith, Robert Bruce 1920- *WhoAm 94, WhoWest 94*
Smith, Robert Bruce 1937- *WhoAm 94*
Smith, Robert Burns 1929- *WhoAm 94, WhoMW 93*
Smith, Robert C. 1912-1975 *WhoAmA 93N*
Smith, Robert C. 1941- *CngDr 93*
Smith, Robert Carr 1935- *Who 94*
Smith, Robert Charles 1926- *WhoAmA 93*
Smith, Robert Charles 1938- *EncSF 93*
Smith, Robert Charles 1947- *WhoBlA 94*
Smith, Robert Clinton 1941- *IntWW 93, WhoAm 94, WhoAmP 93*
Smith, Robert Courtney 1927- *IntWW 93*
Smith, Robert Drake 1944- *WhoAm 94, WhoFI 94*
Smith, Robert Earl 1923- *WhoAm 94*
Smith, Robert Edward 1943- *WhoBlA 94*
Smith, Robert Ellis 1940- *WhoAmP 93, WrDr 94*
Smith, Robert Elmer 1929- *WhoAmP 93*
Smith, Robert Emmett, Jr. 1937- *WhoMW 93*
Smith, Robert Everett 1936- *WhoAm 94, WhoAmL 94*
Smith, Robert F. 1931- *CngDr 93*
Smith, Robert F., Jr. 1949- *WhoScEn 94*
Smith, Robert Francis 1943- *WhoFI 94, WhoMW 93*
Smith, Robert Freeman 1930- *WhoMW 93*
Smith, Robert Freeman 1931- *WhoAm 94, WhoAmP 93, WhoWest 94*
Smith, Robert G. 1943- *WhoAmL 94*
Smith, Robert G. 1947- *WhoAmL 94, WhoAmP 93*
Smith, Robert G(illen) 1913- *ConAu 42NR*
Smith, Robert H. *WhoBlA 94*
Smith, Robert H. 1951- *WhoAmP 93*
Smith, Robert Hamil 1927- *WhoWest 94*
Smith, Robert Harold 1924- *WhoAm 94*
Smith, Robert Harold 1937- *WhoAmL 94*
Smith, Robert Harvey 1955- *WhoAmL 94*
Smith, Robert Henry 1941- *WhoWest 94*
Smith, Robert Henry Tufrey 1935- *Who 94*
Smith, Robert Hill 1958- *Who 94*
Smith, Robert Houston 1931- *WhoAm 94*
Smith, Robert Howard 1935- *IntWW 93*
Smith, Robert Howard 1958- *WhoMW 93*
Smith, Robert Hughes, Jr. *WhoAm 94*
Smith, Robert James 1944- *WhoAm 94*
Smith, Robert John 1927- *WhoAm 94*
Smith, Robert John, Jr. 1951- *WhoFI 94*
Smith, Robert Johnson 1920- *WhoBlA 94*
Smith, Robert Kimmel 1930- *ConAu 42NR, SmATA 77 [port], WhoAm 94*
Smith, Robert L. *DrAPF 93*
Smith, Robert L. T., Sr. 1902- *WhoBlA 94*
Smith, Robert Lawrence, Sr. 1923- *WhoBlA 94*
Smith, Robert Lee 1921- *WhoAm 94*
Smith, Robert Lee 1923- *WhoAm 94*
Smith, Robert Lee 1939- *WhoAm 94*
Smith, Robert Leo 1925- *WhoAm 94*
Smith, Robert Lewis 1940- *WhoAmA 93*
Smith, Robert Lewis 1950- *WhoAmL 94*
Smith, Robert London 1919- *WhoAm 94, WhoBlA 94, WhoWest 94*
Smith, Robert Louis 1922- *WhoAm 94*
Smith, Robert Luther 1927- *WhoFI 94*
Smith, Robert Martin 1943- *WhoMW 93*
Smith, Robert Mason 1945- *WhoAm 94, WhoFI 94*
Smith, Robert McDavid 1920- *WhoAmL 94*
Smith, Robert McKain 1922- *WhoWest 94*
Smith, Robert McNeil 1932- *WhoAm 94*
Smith, Robert Michael 1940- *WhoFI 94, WhoWest 94*
Smith, Robert Michael 1951- *WhoAmL 94*
Smith, Robert Moors 1912- *WhoAm 94*
Smith, Robert Nathaniel 1944- *WhoAm 94*
Smith, Robert Nelson 1920- *WhoAm 94, WhoAmP 93*
Smith, Robert P., Jr. 1923- *WhoBlA 94*
Smith, Robert Powell 1929- *WhoAm 94*
Smith, Robert Rutherford 1933- *WhoAm 94*
Smith, Robert Samuel 1920- *WhoAm 94*
Smith, Robert Sellers 1931- *WhoAm 94*
Smith, Robert Sherlock 1944- *WhoAmL 94*
Smith, Robert Thornton 1943- *WhoAmL 94*
Smith, Robert Victor 1942- *WhoAm 94, WhoWest 94*
Smith, Robert W. *WhoBlA 94*
Smith, Robert W., Jr. 1918- *WhoBlA 94*
Smith, Robert W(illiam) 1952- *WrDr 94*
Smith, Robert Walter 1937- *WhoAm 94*
Smith, Robert Wesley 1937- *WhoWest 94*
Smith, Robert Weston 1938- *WhoAm 94*
Smith, Robert William 1923- *WhoAm 94*
Smith, Robert William 1951- *WhoWest 94*
Smith, Roberta Ann 1951- *WhoFI 94*
Smith, Roberta Ann Pointer 1944- *WhoMW 93*
Smith, Roberts Angus 1928- *WhoScEn 94*
Smith, Robin Anthony 1943- *Who 94*
Smith, Robin Doyle 1957- *WhoAmL 94*
Smith, Robin Jonathan Norman *Who 94*
Smith, Rodger Field 1941- *WhoFI 94*
Smith, Rodger Hayward *Who 94*
Smith, Rodney *WhoBlA 94*
Smith, Rodney 1860-1947 *DcAmReB 2*
Smith, Rodney Martin 1944- *WhoFI 94*
Smith, Rodney Russell 1946- *WhoFI 94*
Smith, Rodney Wike 1944- *WhoFI 94*
Smith, Roger 1932- *IntMPA 94, WhoHol 92*
Smith, Roger A. 1932- *WhoAmP 93*
Smith, Roger B. 1925- *IntWW 93*
Smith, Roger Bonham 1925- *Who 94, WhoAm 94*
Smith, Roger Dean 1932- *WhoAm 94*
Smith, Roger Guenveur *WhoHol 92*
Smith, Roger John 1939- *Who 94*
Smith, Roger Keith 1962- *WhoFI 94*
Smith, Roger Leroy 1946- *WhoBlA 94*
Smith, Roger Winston 1936- *WhoAm 94*
Smith, Roland 1928- *IntWW 93, Who 94*
Smith, Roland Blair, Jr. 1946- *WhoBlA 94*
Smith, Roland Hedley 1943- *Who 94*
Smith, Ron *DrAPF 93*
Smith, Ron 1915- *Who 94*
Smith, Rona 1944- *WhoFI 94*
Smith, Ronald A. D. *Who 94*
Smith, Ronald Charles 1933- *WhoMW 93*
Smith, Ronald Ehlbert 1947- *WhoAmL 94*
Smith, Ronald Emory 1950- *WhoAm 94*
Smith, Ronald Good 1933- *Who 94*
Smith, Ronald Harland 1935- *WhoMW 93*
Smith, Ronald Lee 1937- *WhoAm 94*
Smith, Ronald Louis 1949- *WhoFI 94, WhoMW 93*
Smith, Ronald Lynn 1940- *WhoAm 94*
Smith, Ronald M. *WhoIns 94*
Smith, Ronald Noel 1946- *WhoMW 93*
Smith, Ronald Scott 1947- *WhoAmL 94*
Smith, Ronald Wayne 1944- *WhoWest 94*
Smith, Ronnie *WhoAmP 93*
Smith, Rosamond 1938- *WrDr 94*
Smith, Rosemary Ann 1932- *Who 94*
Smith, Ross Quentin 1959- *WhoWest 94*
Smith, Ross T. 1952- *WhoIns 94*
Smith, Roulette William 1942- *WhoBlA 94, WhoWest 94*
Smith, Rowena Marcus 1923- *WhoAmA 93*
Smith, Rowland (James) 1938- *ConAu 43NR, WrDr 94*
Smith, Rowland James 1938- *WhoAm 94*
Smith, Roy d1944 *WhoHol 92*
Smith, Roy 1924- *WhoAmP 93*
Smith, Roy David A. *Who 94*
Smith, Roy Edgar 1931- *WhoAmP 93*
Smith, Roy Edward 1940- *WhoScEn 94*
Smith, Roy Philip 1933- *WhoAm 94, WhoAmL 94*
Smith, Royd R. 1932- *WhoAmP 93*
Smith, Ruben A. *WhoAmP 93, WhoHisp 94*
Smith, Rufus Burnett, Jr. 1943- *WhoBlA 94*
Smith, Rufus Grant 1938- *WhoAm 94*
Smith, Rufus Herman 1950- *WhoBlA 94*
Smith, Russell *Who 94*
Smith, (Charles) Russell 1925- *Who 94*
Smith, Russell Bryan 1936- *WhoAmL 94*
Smith, Russell Evans 1908- *WhAm 10*
Smith, Russell Francis 1944- *WhoFI 94*
Smith, Russell Jack 1913- *WhoAm 94*
Smith, Russell L. 1956- *WhoAm 94*
Smith, Russell Lamar 1959- *WhoScEn 94*
Smith, Russell Lynn, Jr. 1919- *WhoWest 94*
Smith, Russell Wesley 1947- *WhoFI 94*
Smith, Ruth Lillian Schluchter 1917- *WhoAm 94*
Smith, Ruth R. 1924- *WhoAmP 93*
Smith, Ruth Reininghaus *WhoAmA 93*
Smith, Sally 1942- *WhoHol 92*
Smith, Sally Bedell 1948- *ConAu 140*
Smith, Sam 1918- *WhoAmA 93*
Smith, Sam 1922- *WhoBlA 94*
Smith, Sam 1948- *ConAu 141*
Smith, Sam Corry 1922- *WhoWest 94*
Smith, Sam J. 1922- *WhoAmP 93*
Smith, Sammie Lee 1967- *WhoBlA 94*
Smith, Sammy *WhoHol 92*
Smith, Samuel 1752-1839 *WhAmRev [port]*
Smith, Samuel 1765-1841 *DcNaB MP*
Smith, Samuel Abbot 1895- *WhAm 10*
Smith, Samuel Boyd 1929- *WhoAm 94*
Smith, Samuel David 1918- *WhoAm 94, WhoWest 94*
Smith, Samuel H. 1955- *WhoAmP 93*
Smith, Samuel Howard 1940- *WhoAm 94, WhoWest 94*
Smith, Samuel Kerr 1952- *WhoFI 94*
Smith, Samuel Stuart 1936- *WhoAmL 94*
Smith, Sandra Jean 1957- *WhoMW 93*
Smith, Sandra Lee 1945- *ConAu 142, SmATA 75 [port]*
Smith, Sarah *BlmGWL*
Smith, Sarah J. *WhoAmP 93*
Smith, Savannah *WhoHol 92*
Smith, Scott A. 1953- *WhoAmL 94*
Smith, Selma Moidel 1919- *WhoAm 94, WhoAmL 94, WhoWest 94*
Smith, Seymour Maslin 1941- *WhoAm 94*
Smith, Shane Dale 1954- *WhoWest 94*
Smith, Sharon d1979 *WhoHol 92*
Smith, Sharon Patricia 1948- *WhoFI 94*
Smith, Shawnee *WhoHol 92*
Smith, Sheldon Harold 1948- *WhoAmL 94*
Smith, Sheldon Stuart 1938- *WhoFI 94*
Smith, Shelley 1912- *WrDr 94*
Smith, Shelley 1952- *WhoHol 92*
Smith, Sherman 1957- *WhoBlA 94*
Smith, Sherri 1943- *WhoAmA 93*
Smith, Sherry L. 1951- *WrDr 94*
Smith, Sherwood Draughon 1925- *WhoAm 94*
Smith, Sherwood Hubbard, Jr. 1934- *WhoAm 94, WhoFI 94*
Smith, Shirley *WhoAmA 93*
Smith, Shirley 1929- *WhoAm 94*
Smith, Shirley LaVerne 1951- *WhoBlA 94*
Smith, Shirley M(ae) 1923- *ConAu 42NR*
Smith, Sid d1928 *WhoHol 92*
Smith, Sidney Oslin, Jr. 1923- *WhoAm 94*
Smith, Sidney Rufus, Jr. 1931- *WhoAm 94*
Smith, Sidney Sharp 1928- *WhoWest 94*
Smith, Sidney Talbert 1954- *WhoMW 93*
Smith, Sidney William 1920- *Who 94*
Smith, Silverheels *WhoHol 92*
Smith, Solly d1933 *WhoHol 92*
Smith, Spencer Bailey 1927- *WhoAm 94*
Smith, Spencer Thomas 1943- *WhoAmL 94*
Smith, Stan 1946- *BuCMET [port]*
Smith, Stan Lee 1947- *WhoScEn 94*
Smith, Stan Vladimir 1946- *WhoAm 94*
Smith, Stanford S. 1923- *WhoAmP 93*
Smith, Stanford Sidney 1923- *WhoAm 94, WhoWest 94*
Smith, Stanley d1974 *WhoHol 92*
Smith, Stanley fl. 1940- *EncNAR*
Smith, Stanley David 1935- *WhoAmL 94*
Smith, Stanley Dean 1951- *WhoWest 94*
Smith, Stanley Frank 1924- *Who 94*
Smith, Stanley G. 1940- *WhoBlA 94*
Smith, Stanley O'Neil, Sr. 1941- *WhoAm 94*
Smith, Stanley Roger 1946- *WhoAm 94*
Smith, Stanton Kinnie, Jr. 1931- *WhoAm 94, WhoFI 94*
Smith, Starita Ann 1949- *WhoBlA 94*
Smith, Stephanie Marie 1955- *WhoWest 94*
Smith, Stephanie Susan 1957- *WhoAmP 93*
Smith, Stephen A. 1950- *WhoAmL 94*
Smith, Stephen Alexander 1957- *WhoAm 94*
Smith, Stephen Arnold 1946- *WhoWest 94*
Smith, Stephen Bradford 1937- *WhoMW 93*
Smith, Stephen Charles 1946- *WhoAmP 93*
Smith, Stephen Charles 1951- *WhoBlA 94*
Smith, Stephen Craig 1965- *WhoAmL 94*
Smith, Stephen Eaton 1943- *WhoAmL 94*
Smith, Stephen F. 1940- *WhoIns 94*
Smith, Stephen Grant 1949- *WhoAm 94*
Smith, Stephen J. 1945- *WhoAmL 94*
Smith, Stephen Kendall 1941- *WhoAm 94, WhoAmL 94*
Smith, Stephen Kevin 1951- *Who 94*
Smith, Stephen Lewis 1951- *WhoFI 94*
Smith, Stephen Robert C. *Who 94*
Smith, Stephen Sinclair 1947- *WhoFI 94*
Smith, Stephen Wayne 1941- *WhoWest 94*
Smith, Steve 1949- *WhoAmP 93*
Smith, Steve Austin 1949- *WhoAmP 93*
Smith, Steve William 1955- *WhoFI 94*
Smith, Steven Cole 1952- *WhoScEn 94*
Smith, Steven D. 1941- *WhoIns 94*
Smith, Steven Delano 1969- *WhoBlA 94*
Smith, Steven F. 1956- *WhoAmP 93*
Smith, Steven George 1951- *WhoFI 94*
Smith, Steven James 1945- *WhoFI 94, WhoIns 94*
Smith, Steven Lee 1952- *WhoAmL 94*
Smith, Steven Phillip *DrAPF 93*
Smith, Steven Ray 1946- *WhoAmL 94*
Smith, Steven Sidney 1946- *WhoAm 94, WhoScEn 94, WhoWest 94*
Smith, Stevie 1902-1971 *BlmGEL, BlmGWL*
Smith, Stewart Edward 1937- *WhoScEn 94*
Smith, Stewart Ranson 1931- *Who 94*
Smith, Stewart Russell 1946- *WhoFI 94*
Smith, Stuart A. 1941- *WhoAm 94*
Smith, Stuart Allan 1955- *WhoMW 93*
Smith, Stuart Brian 1944- *Who 94*
Smith, Stuart Lyon 1938- *WhoAm 94*
Smith, Stuart Robert 1942- *WhoWest 94*
Smith, Stuart Seaborne 1930- *WhoAm 94*
Smith, Sue Frances 1940- *WhoAm 94*
Smith, Sundra Shealey 1948- *WhoBlA 94*
Smith, Susan *WhoAmA 93*
Smith, Susan Bitter 1955- *WhoAmP 93, WhoWest 94*
Smith, Susan Carlton 1923- *WhoAmA 93*
Smith, Susan Finnegan 1954- *WhoScEn 94*
Smith, Susan Kimsey 1947- *WhoAmL 94*
Smith, Susan L. 1959- *WhoBlA 94*
Smith, Swire 1842-1918 *DcNaB MP*
Smith, Sydney d1978 *WhoHol 92*
Smith, Sydney David 1947- *WhoMW 93*
Smith, Sydney Strother, III 1941- *WhoAmP 93*
Smith, Symuel Harold 1922- *WhoBlA 94*
Smith, T. Arthur 1923- *WhoFI 94*
Smith, T(homas) Dan d1993 *Who 94N*
Smith, T(homas) Lynn 1903-1977 *ConAu 42NR*
Smith, Tad Randolph 1928- *WhoAm 94, WhoAmL 94, WhoFI 94*
Smith, Tammeryn M. 1956- *WhoAmL 94*
Smith, Tammy Sue 1961- *WhoMW 93*
Smith, Taylor 1953- *WhoAm 94*

Smits, Jimmy 1955- IntMPA 94, WhoHisp 94, WhoHol 92
Smits, Ronald F. DrAPF 93
Smits, Sonja WhoHol 92
Smitsendonk, Anton G. O. 1928- IntWW 93
Smitten, Richard 1940- WrDr 94
Smittle, Nelson Dean 1934- WhoMW 93
Smoak, David S. 1947- WhoFI 94
Smoak, Karl Randal 1959- WhoScEn 94
Smoak, Lewis Tyson 1944- WhoAmL 94
Smock, Emerson 1922- WhoAmP 93
Smock, Frederick DrAPF 93
Smock, Raymond William 1941- WhoAm 94
Smohalla c. 1815-1895 EncNAR
Smoke, Richard 1944- WhoAm 94
Smoke, Richard Edwin 1945- WhoAmL 94, WhoMW 93
Smoker, Richard E. WhoIns 94
Smokler, Stanley B. 1944- WhoAmA 93
Smoko, Ronald L. WhoAmP 93
Smokovitis, Athanassios A. 1935- WhoScEn 94
Smoktunovsky, Innokenty 1925- WhoHol 92
Smoktunovsky, Innokenty Mikhailovich 1925- IntWW 93
Smol, John Paul 1955- WhoScEn 94
Smola, Cynthia J. 1946- WhoMW 93
Smola, Richard Walrod 1959- WhoMW 93
Smolansky, Oles M. 1930- WhoAm 94
Smolarek, Waldemar 1937- WhoAmA 93
Smolarski, Dennis Chester 1947- WhoWest 94
Smolarz, Roy Barry 1950- WhoAmL 94
Smolderen, Luc Hippolyte Marie 1924- IntWW 93
Smolek, Michael Kevin 1955- WhoScEn 94
Smolen, Cheryl Hosaka 1959- WhoMW 93
Smolen, Donald E. 1923- IntMPA 94
Smolen, James Edward 1949- WhoMW 93
Smolen, Michael H. 1939- WhoFI 94
Smolensky, Eugene 1932- WhoAm 94, WhoWest 94
Smolev, Terence Elliot 1944- WhoAmL 94
Smolik, Mark Andrew 1962- WhoAmL 94
Smolin, Nat 1890-1950 WhoAmA 93N
Smolin, Robert I. 1942- WhoMW 93
Smolin, Ronald Philip 1941- WhoAm 94
Smolinske, Cora Alice 1919- WhoAmP 93
Smolinski, Adam Karol 1910- IntWW 93
Smolinski, Edward Albert 1928- WhoAm 94
Smolinsky, Sidney Joseph 1932- WhoAmL 94
Smolka, James William 1950- WhoWest 94
Smolker, Gary Steven 1945- WhoAmL 94, WhoWest 94
Smolla, Rodney Alan 1953- WhoAm 94
Smollan, David Leslie 1928- WhoFI 94, WhoWest 94
Smollen, Leonard Elliott 1930- WhoFI 94
Smoller, Robert A. 1946- WhoAmL 94
Smollett, Tobias George 1721-1771 BlmGEL [port]
Smollins, John F., Jr. 1940- WhoAmP 93
Smolowitz, Ira Ephraim 1941- WhoAm 94
Smoltz, John Andrew 1967- WhoAm 94
Smoluchowski, Roman 1910- WhoAm 94
Smongeski, Joseph Leon 1914- WhoAmA 93
Smook, Malcolm Andrew 1924- WhoAm 94
Smooke, Michael G. 1945- WhoAmL 94
Smooke, Mitchell David 1951- WhoScEn 94
Smoorenburg, Guido Franciscus 1943- WhoScEn 94
Smoot, Albertha Pearl 1914- WhoBlA 94
Smoot, Carolyn Elizabeth 1945- WhoBlA 94
Smoot, George F. 1945- News 93-3 [port]
Smoot, George Fitzgerald, III 1945- WhoAm 94, WhoScEn 94
Smoot, John Eldon 1960- WhoScEn 94
Smoot, Joseph Grady 1932- WhoMW 93
Smoot, Leon Douglas 1934- WhoAm 94, WhoScEn 94, WhoWest 94
Smoot, Wendell McMeans, Jr. 1921- WhoAm 94, WhoWest 94
Smorada, Robert Francis 1937- WhoFI 94
Smothers, Dick 1939- IntMPA 94, WhoAm 94
See Also Smothers Brothers, The WhoCom
Smothers, Ethel Footman 1944- SmATA 76 [port]
Smothers, Ronald WhoBlA 94
Smothers, Ronald Eric 1946- WhoBlA 94
Smothers, Tom 1937- IntMPA 94, WhoAm 94, WhoHol 92
See Also Smothers Brothers, The WhoCom
Smothers, William Edgar, Jr. 1928- WhoAm 94
Smothers Brothers, The WhoCom [port]
Smotherson, Melvin 1936- WhoBlA 94
Smotrich, David Isadore 1933- WhoAm 94
Smouse, Hervey Russell WhoAm 94, WhoAmL 94
Smout, (Thomas) Christopher 1933- Who 94
Smout, Thomas Christopher 1933- IntWW 93
Smrekar, Karl George, Jr. 1954- WhoFI 94
Smucker, Barbara 1915- BlmGWL
Smucker, Barbara (Claassen) 1915- SmATA 76 [port]
Smucker, Barbara Claassen 1915- WhoAm 94, WrDr 94
Smuckler, Harvey Glasgow 1924- WhoFI 94
Smuckler, Ralph Herbert 1926- WhoAm 94
Smudin, Richard Stanley 1966- WhoWest 94
Smuin, Michael 1938- WhoAm 94
Smukler, Linda DrAPF 93
Smulders, Anthony Peter 1942- WhoAm 94, WhoWest 94
Smulders, Josephine WhoHol 92
Smullen, James Dennis 1916- WhoAm 94
Smullin, Donald Evan 1947- WhoWest 94
Smulski, Stephen John 1955- WhoScEn 94
Smulyan, Jeffrey WhoAm 94
Smurfit, Michael William Joseph IntWW 93
Smurfit, Michael William Joseph 1936- WhoAm 94, WhoFI 94
Smuskiewicz, Ted 1932- WhoAmA 93
Smutny, Jiri 1932- NewGrDO
Smutny, Joan Franklin WhoAm 94
Smuts, Jan Christiaan 1870-1950 HisWorL [port]
Smyche, J. Anthony d1966 WhoHol 92
Smyczek, Thaddeus Martin 1941- WhoFI 94
Smyer, Myrna Ruth 1946- WhoWest 94
Smykowski, James George 1934- WhoAmP 93
Smylie, Michael 1914- WhoAmP 93
Smyllie, J. S. 1955- WrDr 94
Smyly, William Allen, Jr. 1954- WhoAmL 94
Smyntek, John Eugene, Jr. 1950- WhoAm 94
Smyre, Calvin WhoBlA 94
Smyre, Calvin 1948- WhoAmP 93
Smyrl, William H. 1938- WhoScEn 94
Smyrski, Lawrence Anthony 1968- WhoMW 93
Smyrski, Martha Marguerite 1953- WhoAmL 94
Smyser, Adam Albert 1920- WhoAm 94, WhoWest 94
Smyser, C. A. 1949- WhoAmP 93
Smyser, Charles Arvil 1949- WhoWest 94
Smyser, Craig 1951- WhoAmL 94
Smyth, Bernard John 1915- WhoAm 94, WhoWest 94
Smyth, Charles Phelps 1895-1990 WhAm 10
Smyth, Craig Hugh 1915- IntWW 93, WhoAm 94, WhoAmA 93
Smyth, David John 1936- WhoAm 94
Smyth, David Shannon 1943- WhoWest 94
Smyth, Desmond Who 94
Smyth, (Joseph) Desmond 1950- Who 94
Smyth, Donald Morgan 1930- WhoAm 94
Smyth, Donna 1943- BlmGWL
Smyth, Ed 1916- WhoAmA 93
Smyth, Ethel (Mary) 1858-1944 NewGrDO
Smyth, Frederick d1815 WhAmRev
Smyth, Glen Miller 1929- WhoAm 94
Smyth, Harriet Rucker 1926- WrDr 94
Smyth, James Desmond 1917- WrDr 94
Smyth, Joel Douglas 1941- WhoAm 94
Smyth, John Fletcher 1945- Who 94
Smyth, John Jackson 1941- Who 94
Smyth, John McDonnell, III 1915- WhoMW 93
Smyth, John R. 1932- WhoWest 94
Smyth, Joseph Patrick 1933- WhoAm 94
Smyth, Joseph Vincent 1919- WhoAm 94
Smyth, Kelvin Paul 1950- WhoAmP 93
Smyth, Martin Who 94
Smyth, (William) Martin 1931- Who 94
Smyth, Michael 1959- WhoAmP 93
Smyth, Newman 1843-1925 DcAmReB 2
Smyth, Paul DrAPF 93
Smyth, Paul Burton 1949- WhoAmL 94
Smyth, Peter Hayes 1952- WhoAm 94
Smyth, Reginald 1917- Who 94, WhoAm 94
Smyth, Robert Staples Who 94
Smyth, (James) Robert Staples 1926- Who 94
Smyth, Steven Eugene 1956- WhoMW 93
Smyth, Thomas Weyland Bowyer- 1960- Who 94
Smyth, Timothy (John) 1953- Who 94
Smyth, William J. 1949- WrDr 94
Smythe, Clifford Anthony 1938- Who 94
Smythe, Florence d1925 WhoHol 92
Smythe, Marianne Koral 1942- WhoAm 94, WhoFI 94
Smythe, Patricia Rosemary K. Who 94
Smythe, Quentin George Murray 1916- Who 94
Smythe, Reginald Who 94
Smythe, Russell 1949- NewGrDO
Smythe, Sheila Mary 1932- WhoFI 94
Smythe, Tony Who 94
Smythe, Victor N. WhoBlA 94
Smythe, William Rodman 1930- WhoAm 94, WhoScEn 94
Smythe-Haith, Mabel Murphy 1918- WhoAm 94, WhoAmP 93, WhoBlA 94
Smythies, John R(aymond) 1922- WrDr 94
Smythson, Robert 1534?-1614 DcNaB MP
Smyton, James W. 1943- WhoAmL 94
Snader, Jack Ross 1938- WhoAm 94
Snader, Robert Miles 1925- WhoAmL 94
Snagge, John Derrick Mordaunt 1904- Who 94
Snagge, Nancy (Marion) 1906- Who 94
Snaggs, Carmen WhoBlA 94
Snaid, Leon Jeffrey 1946- WhoAmL 94
Snaith, George Robert 1930- Who 94
Snaith, J(ohn) C(ollis) 1876-1936 EncSF 93
Snape, Peter Charles 1942- Who 94
Snape, Royden Eric 1922- Who 94
Snape, Thomas Peter 1925- Who 94
Snape, William John, Jr. 1943- WhoAm 94, WhoWest 94
Snaper, Alvin Allyn 1929- WhoScEn 94
Snapp, Elizabeth 1937- WhoAm 94
Snapp, Roy Baker 1916- WhoAm 94
Snapper, Arthur 1898- WhAm 10
Snapper, Ernst 1913- WhoAm 94, WhoScEn 94
Snare, Carl Lawrence, Jr. 1936- WhoFI 94, WhoWest 94
Snarey, John Robert 1948- WhoScEn 94
Snasdell, Susan Kathleen 1948- WhoWest 94
Snavely, Mark Richard 1963- WhoMW 93
Snavely, Richard Mellinger 1931- WhoAm 94
Snavely, William Brant 1951- WhoMW 93
Snavely, William Pennington 1920- WhoAm 94, WhoFI 94, WhoScEn 94
Snead, George Murrell, Jr. 1922- WhoAm 94
Snead, John D. 1917- WhoBlA 94
Snead, Kathleen Marie 1948- WhoAmL 94
Snead, Michael James 1927- WhoIns 94
Snead, Richard Thomas 1951- WhoAm 94
Snead, Samuel Jackson 1912- IntWW 93, WhoAm 94
Snearly, Sandra Jo 1954- WhoAm 94, WhoMW 93
Sneary, Max Eugene 1930- WhoMW 93, WhoScEn 94
Snedden, Charles Willis 1913-1989 WhAm 10
Snedden, David King 1933- Who 94
Snedden, James Douglas 1925- WhoAm 94
Sneddon, Hutchison Burt 1929- Who 94
Sneddon, Ian Naismith 1919- IntWW 93, Who 94, WrDr 94
Sneddon, Robert 1920- Who 94
Snedeker, James Phyfe 1948- WhoIns 94
Snedeker, John Haggner 1925- WhoAm 94
Snedeker, Robert D. 1943- WhoAm 94
Snedeker, Sedgwick 1909- WhoAmL 94, WhoFI 94
Snediker, David E. 1947- WhoAmL 94
Snedker, Clive John 1947- WhoWest 94
Sneed, James H. 1947- WhoAm 94
Sneed, Joseph Donald 1938- WhoAm 94
Sneed, Joseph Tyree, III 1920- WhoAm 94, WhoAmL 94, WhoWest 94
Sneed, Marie Eleanor Wilkey 1915- WhoMW 93
Sneed, Patricia M. 1922- WhoAmA 93
Sneed, Paula A. 1947- WhoBlA 94
Sneed, Richard Durwood, Jr. 1946- WhoAmL 94
Sneed, William R., III 1949- WhoAmL 94
Sneegas, Stanley Alan 1950- WhoScEn 94
Sneeringer, Stephen Geddes 1949- WhoAmL 94, WhoMW 93
Snegoff, Leonid d1974 WhoHol 92
Snegur, Mircea Ion 1940- LngBDD
Snegur, Mirchea 1940- IntWW 93
Sneider, Martin Karl 1942- WhoFI 94
Snel, Willebrord 1580-1626 WorScD
Snelgrove, Donald George Who 94
Snelgrove, Gordon William WhoAmA 93N
Snelgrove, Rich WhoAmP 93
Snell, Anthony WhoHol 92
Snell, Bruce M., Jr. 1929- WhoAmL 94, WhoAmP 93, WhoMW 93
Snell, Charles 1667-1733 DcNaB MP
Snell, Edmund 1889- EncSF 93
Snell, Eric 1953- WhoAmA 93
Snell, Esmond Emerson 1914- IntWW 93, WhoAm 94
Snell, Fred William 1910- WhoAmP 93
Snell, George Boyd 1907- Who 94
Snell, George Davis 1903- IntWW 93, Who 94, WhoAm 94, WhoScEn 94
Snell, Hilary Fred 1934- WhoAm 94, WhoAmL 94
Snell, Jack Eastlake 1935- WhoAm 94
Snell, James Laurie 1925- WhoAm 94
Snell, Jimmy Gregory 1927- WhoBlA 94
Snell, Joan Yvonne Ervin 1932- WhoBlA 94
Snell, John Nicholas B. Who 94
Snell, John Raymond 1912- WhoAm 94
Snell, Karen Black 1949- WhoScEn 94
Snell, Maeve Who 94
Snell, Michael 1945- ConAu 140
Snell, Ned Colwell 1944- WhoFI 94, WhoWest 94
Snell, Patricia Poldervaart 1943- WhoAm 94
Snell, Peter R. E. 1941- IntMPA 94
Snell, Philip D. 1915- Who 94
Snell, Richard 1930- WhoAm 94, WhoFI 94, WhoWest 94
Snell, Richard S. 1942- WhoAmL 94
Snell, Richard Saxon 1925- WhoAm 94
Snell, Roger Douglas 1956- WhoFI 94
Snell, Thaddeus Stevens, III 1919- WhoAm 94, WhoAmL 94
Snellen, Deborah Sue 1956- WhoFI 94
Snellgrove, Anthony Who 94
Snellgrove, (John) Anthony 1922- Who 94
Snellgrove, David Llewellyn 1920- Who 94
Snellgrove, David Llewelyn 1920- IntWW 93
Snellgrove, Laurence Ernest 1928- WrDr 94
Snelling, Arthur (Wendell) 1914- Who 94
Snelling, Barbara 1928- WhoAm 94
Snelling, Barbara W. WhoAmP 93
Snelling, Charles Darwin 1931- WhoAmP 93
Snelling, George Arthur 1929- WhoAm 94, WhoFI 94
Snelling, Minnette d1945 WhoHol 92
Snelling, Richard Arkwright 1927-1991 WhAm 10
Snelling, William Lee 1931- WhoFI 94
Snelling, William Rodman 1931- WhoFI 94
Snellings, Rolland BlkWr 2
Snelson, Edward Alec Abbott d1992 Who 94N
Snelson, Kenneth D. 1927- WhoAmA 93
Snelson, Kenneth Duane 1927- WhoAm 94
Snetsinger, David Clarence 1930- WhoAm 94
Sneva, Thomas Edsol 1948- WhoAm 94, WhoWest 94
Sniader, David Joseph 1962- WhoMW 93
Snibbe, Richard W. 1916- WhoAm 94
Snider, Clifton DrAPF 93
Snider, Debra Lynn 1959- WhoMW 93
Snider, Donald Lee 1939- WhoAm 94
Snider, Donald Stephen 1943- WhoAmL 94
Snider, Edward Malcolm 1933- WhoAm 94
Snider, George D. 1931- WhoAmP 93
Snider, Gordon Lloyd 1922- WhoAm 94
Snider, Harlan Tanner 1926- WhoAm 94
Snider, Harold Wayne 1923- WhoAm 94
Snider, Howard J. 1929- WhoAmP 93
Snider, James Rhodes 1931- WhoFI 94, WhoScEn 94
Snider, Jay T. WhoAm 94
Snider, Jerome Guy 1950- WhoAm 94
Snider, Jerry W. 1943- WhoAmL 94
Snider, Jim ConAu 141
Snider, John Joseph 1928- WhoAm 94
Snider, Kenneth C. 1946- WhoAmP 93
Snider, L. Britt 1945- WhoAm 94
Snider, Lawrence K. 1938- WhoAm 94, WhoAmL 94
Snider, Marie Anna 1927- WhoMW 93
Snider, Robert F. 1931- WhoAm 94
Snider, Robert Larry 1932- WhoAm 94, WhoFI 94
Snider, Ronald Albert 1948- WhoAmL 94
Sniderman, Allan David 1941- WhoAm 94
Sniderman, Howard Irwin 1953- WhoFI 94
Sniderman, Marvin 1923- WhoScEn 94
Snidow, Gordon E. 1936- WhoAmA 93

Soame, Charles (John) Buckworth-Herne- 1932- Who 94
Soames, Lady 1922- Who 94
Soames, (Arthur) Nicholas (Winston) 1948- Who 94
Soames, Richard 1936- IntMPA 94
Soane, Leslie James 1926- Who 94
Soards, William L. 1942- WhoAmP 93
Soares, Eusebio Lopes 1918- WhoScEn 94
Soares, Joao Clemente Baena 1931- WhoAm 94
Soares, Manuel BlmGWL
Soares, Mario Alberto Nobre Lopes 1924- IntWW 93, Who 94
Soares, Wilfred 1929- WhoAmP 93
Soares Alves, Francisco Jose 1942- IntWW 93
Soares de Mello, Adelino Jose Rodrigues 1931- WhoFI 94
Soaries, Raynes L., Jr. 1924- WhoBlA 94
Soballe, David Michael 1950- WhoScEn 94
Sobchak, Anatoliy Aleksandrovich 1937- IntWW 93
Sobchak, Anatoly Aleksandrovich 1938- LngBDD
Sobchak, Vivian (Carol) 1940- EncSF 93
Sobczak, Darlene Marie 1956- WhoMW 93
Sobczak, Joseph Michael 1932- WhoMW 93
Sobczak, Judy Marie 1949- WhoMW 93
Sobczak, Thomas Victor 1937- WhoFI 94
Sobeck, Greg WhoHol 92
Sobecki, John Francis 1948- WhoAm 94, WhoFI 94
Sobek, Irvin Gene 1934- WhoWest 94
Sobel, Aaron R. 1932- WhoAmL 94
Sobel, Alan 1928- WhoAm 94
Sobel, Barry 1959- WhoHol 92
Sobel, Burton Elias 1937- WhoAm 94
Sobel, Howard Bernard 1929- WhoAm 94
Sobel, Kenneth Mark 1954- WhoScEn 94
Sobel, Larry D. 1951- WhoAm 94
Sobel, Michael A. 1955- WhoAmL 94
Sobel, Walter Howard 1913- WhoAm 94
Sobel, William Lee 1944- WhoMW 93
Sobell, Michael d1993 Who 94N
Sobell, Michael 1892- IntWW 93
Sobelle, Richard E. 1935- WhoAm 94
Sobelsohn, Bernard 1943- WhoAmL 94
Soben, Robert Sidney 1947- WhoScEn 94
Sober, Debra E. 1953- WhoFI 94
Sober, Elliott (Reuben) 1948- WrDr 94
Sober, Phillip 1931- Who 94
Sobering, Geoffrey Simon 1960- WhoScEn 94
Soberon-Ferrer, Horacio 1954- WhoFI 94, WhoHisp 94
Sobers, Austin W. 1914- WhoBlA 94
Sobers, David George 1940- WhoScEn 94
Sobers, Garfield (St. Auburn) 1936- Who 94
Sobers, Garfield St. Auburn 1936- IntWW 93
Sobers, Waynett A., Jr. 1937- WhoBlA 94
Sobery, Julie Sterner 1953- WhoFI 94
Sobey, David F. 1931- WhoFI 94
Sobey, David Frank 1931- WhoAm 94
Sobey, Donald Creighton Rae WhoAm 94
Sobey, Edwin J. C. 1948- WhoAm 94
Sobey, William MacDonald 1927-1989 WhAm 10
Sobhi, Mohamed Ibrahim 1925- IntWW 93, Who 94
Sobhuza, Ngwenyama, II 1899-1982 DcNaB MP
Sobie, Robert Fransis 1955- WhoMW 93
Sobie, Walter Richard 1943- WhoScEn 94
Sobieski, Jaroslaw 1934- WhoAm 94
Sobin, Anthony DrAPF 93
Sobin, Gustaf 1935- WrDr 94
Sobin, Julian M(elvin) 1920- WrDr 94
Sobin, Julian Melvin 1920- WhoAm 94
Sobinov, Leonid Vital'yevich 1872-1934 NewGrDO
Sobkowicz, Hanna Maria 1931- WhoAm 94, WhoMW 93
Soble, James Barry 1942- WhoAm 94
Soble, Mark Richard 1964- WhoAmL 94
Soble, Ron WhoHol 92
Soble, Ron 1932- IntMPA 94
Soble, Stephen M. 1951- WhoAmL 94
Sobol, Bruce J. 1923- WhoScEn 94
Sobol, Donald J. 1924- WrDr 94
Sobol, Harold 1930- WhoAm 94
Sobol, Joshua ConWorW 93
Sobol, Judith Ellen 1946- WhoAm 94, WhoAmA 93
Sobol, Ken 1938- WrDr 94
Sobol, Lawrence Raymond 1950- WhoAm 94, WhoFI 94
Sobol, Louis d1986 WhoHol 92
Sobol, Martin J. 1948- WhoAmL 94
Sobol, Rose 1931- SmATA 76
Sobol, Thomas 1932- WhoAm 94
Sobol, Wlad Theodore 1949- WhoScEn 94
Sobol, Yehoshua 1939- ConWorW 93
Sobolev, Viktor Viktorovich 1915- IntWW 93
Sobolewski, (Johann Friedrich) Eduard 1804-1872 NewGrDO
Sobolewski, Timothy Richard 1951- WhoFI 94
Sobolik, Dennis Merlin 1931- WhoAmP 93
Soboloff, Arnold d1979 WhoHol 92
Sobon, Leon Edward 1934- WhoWest 94
Soboslai, Jan Elizabeth-Smith 1962- WhoFI 94
Soboslay, Dian Jean 1949- WhoMW 93
Sobotka, Ruth d1967 WhoHol 92
Sobottka, Fred Herman 1956- WhoMW 93
Sobti, Krishna 1925- BlmGWL
Soby, James Thrall 1906-1979 WhoAmA 93N
Socarras, Rasciel WhoHisp 94
Socha, Donald Edward 1950- WhoHisp 94
Socha, Douglas David 1960- WhoWest 94
Sochacki, Andrzej 1948- WhoWest 94
Sochalski, Matthew Michael 1947- WhoAmP 93
So Chau, Yim-ping 1927- WhoWomW 91
Sochen, June 1937- ConAu 43NR, WhoAm 94
Sochocki, Timothy D. 1949- WhoAmL 94
Sochynsky, Yaroslav 1946- WhoAmL 94
Socie, Darrell Frederick 1948- WhoAm 94
Socier, Michael James 1957- WhoMW 93
Sockman, Ralph Washington 1889-1970 DcAmReB 2
Sockol, Craig Stewart 1950- WhoFI 94
Sockwell, Oliver R., Jr. 1943- WhoAm 94, WhoBlA 94
Socol, Michael Lee 1949- WhoMW 93
Socol, Sheldon Eleazer 1936- WhoFI 94
Socolofsky, Homer Edward 1922- WrDr 94
Socolofsky, Jon Edward 1946- WhoAm 94
Socolow, Arthur Abraham 1921- WhoAm 94
Socolow, Elizabeth Anne DrAPF 93
Socolow, Robert Harry 1937- WhoAm 94, WhoScEn 94
Socolow, Sanford 1928- WhoFI 94
Socor, Matei 1908-1980 NewGrDO
Socrates 470?BC-399BC BlmGEL, EncEth
Soczek, Joseph Louis, Jr. 1943- WhoFI 94
Soczka, Kevin Martin 1960- WhoAmP 93
Sodal, Ingvar Edmund 1934- WhoAm 94
Sodano, Angelo 1927- Who 94
Sodaro, Edward Richard 1947- WhoScEn 94
Sodberbergh, Steven 1963- IntMPA 94
Sodd, Vincent Joseph 1934- WhoAm 94
Sodders, Judith Townsend 1941- WhoAmP 93
Soddy, Frederick 1877-1956 WorScD
Sodeika, Antanas 1890-1979 NewGrDO
Soden, Dale Edward 1951- WhoWest 94
Soden, Paul Anthony 1944- WhoAm 94, WhoAmL 94
Soden, Richard Allan 1945- WhoAm 94, WhoAmL 94, WhoBlA 94
Soden, Ruth M. 1940- WhoWest 94
Soder, Jon Darwin 1943- WhoFI 94
Soder, Karin A. M. 1928- IntWW 93
Soderberg, Bo Sigfrid 1939- WhoFI 94
Soderberg, David Lawrence 1944- WhoScEn 94
Soderberg, Erik Axel Olof R:son 1926- IntWW 93
Soderberg, Hjalmar 1869-1941 RfGShF
Soderberg, John V. 1945- WhoAmL 94, WhoFI 94
Soderberg, Nancy 1958- WhoAm 94
Soderbergh, Steven 1963- ConTFT 11, IntWW 93
Soderbergh, Steven Andrew 1963- WhoAm 94
Sodergran, Edith 1892-1923 BlmGWL
Soderholm, Lars Gustav 1924- WhAm 10
Soderlind, Sterling Eugene 1926- WhoAm 94
Soderling, Walter d1948 WhoHol 92
Soderquist, Larry Dean 1944- WhoAmL 94
Soderstrom(-Olow), (Anna) Elisabeth 1927- NewGrDO
Soderstrom, Elisabeth Anna 1927- IntWW 93
Soderstrom, Hans Tson 1945- WhoFI 94, WhoScEn 94
Soderstrom, Robert S. 1944- WhoAmL 94
Soderstrom, Rolf Edwin 1932- WhoFI 94
Sodha, Piyush 1958- WhoFI 94
Sodi, Charles c. 1715-1788 NewGrDO
Sodnom, Dumaagiyn 1933- IntWW 93
Sodolski, John 1931- WhoAm 94
Sodor And Man, Bishop of 1932- Who 94
Sodowsky, Roland (E.) 1938- WrDr 94
Sodowsky, Roland E. DrAPF 93
Soebadio, Haryati 1928- WhoWomW 91
Soeberg, Camilla 1966- WhoHol 92
Soedarsono, Nani 1928- IntWW 93
Soederbaum, Kristina 1912- WhoHol 92
Soederstrom, Elisabeth Anna 1927- WhoAm 94
Soedjarwo 1922- IntWW 93
Soeharto, General 1921- Who 94
Soeken, Karen Lynne 1944- WhoScEn 94
Soelberg, Barbara Joyce 1963- WhoWest 94
Soeldner, John Stuart 1932- WhoWest 94
Soelter, Robert R. 1926- WhoAm 94
Soennichsen, Jean Elizabeth 1926- WhoAm 94
Soens, Lawrence D. 1926- WhoAm 94, WhoMW 93
Soergel, Konrad Hermann 1929- WhoAm 94, WhoMW 93
Soet, H. David 1935- WhoAmP 93
Soetanto, Kawan 1951- WhoScEn 94
Soeteber, Ellen 1950- WhoAm 94
Soetebier, Virginia Marie 1930- WhoAmP 93
Sofaer, Abraham d1988 WhoHol 92
Sofaer, Abraham David 1938- IntWW 93, WhoAm 94
Sofer, Anne Hallowell 1937- Who 94
Sofer, Eugene F. 1948- WhoAmP 93
Soffel, Doris 1948- NewGrDO
Soffer, Philip J. 1954- WhoWest 94
Soffer, Sasson 1925- WhoAm 94, WhoAmA 93
Sofia, R. D. 1942- WhoScEn 94
Sofield, Harold Augustus 1900-1987 WhAm 10
Sofin, H. Jonarden S. 1958- WhoWest 94
Sofio, Richard A. 1946- WhoAmP 93
Sofola, Idowu 1934- IntWW 93
Sofola, Zulu 1935- ConDr 93
Sofola, Zulu 1938- BlmGWL [port]
Sofonova, Elena 1956- WhoHol 92
Sofos, Stephany Louise 1954- WhoWest 94
Softly, Barbara (Charmian) 1924- WrDr 94
Softness, Donald Gabriel WhoAm 94
Softness, John 1930- WhoAm 94
Soga, Michio Nishi 1956- WhoFI 94
Sogaard, Poul 1923- IntWW 93
Sogah, Dotsevi Y. 1945- WhoBlA 94
Sogard, Jeffrey W. 1945- WhoAm 94
Sogg, Wilton Sherman 1935- WhoAm 94, WhoAmL 94
Sogi, Francis Y. 1923- WhoAsA 94
Soglin, Paul R. 1945- WhoAm 94, WhoMW 93
Soglin, Paul Richard 1945- WhoAmP 93
Soglo, Nicephore 1934- IntWW 93
Soglow, Otto 1900-1975 WhoAmA 93N
Sogn, Jon Clayton 1961- WhoAmL 94
Sognefest, Peter William 1941- WhoAm 94, WhoFI 94
Sogner, Pasquale 1793-1842 NewGrDO
Sografi, Simeone Antonio 1759-1818 NewGrDO
Soh, Joong Min 1945- WhoAsA 94
Sohahong-Kombet, Jean-Pierre 1935- IntWW 93
Sohaili, Aspi Isfandiar 1966- WhoMW 93, WhoScEn 94
Sohal, Harjit Singh 1944- WhoAsA 94
Sohal, Iqbal Singh 1956- WhoScEn 94
Sohappy, David c. 1921-1991 EncNAR
Sohle, Guy Rose Louis 1956- WhoScEn 94
Sohl, Jerry 1913- EncSF 93, WrDr 94
Sohl, John Franklin 1915- WhoFI 94
Sohlman, Staffan A. R. 1937- IntWW 93
Sohm, Dana Quin WhoAmL 94
Sohmer, Bernard 1929- WhoAm 94
Sohmer, Steve WhoWest 94
Sohmer, Steve 1941- ConTFT 11
Sohmer, Steve 1942- IntMPA 94
Sohmers, Barbara WhoHol 92
Sohn, David Youngwhan 1943- WhoAsA 94
Sohn, Hong Yong 1941- WhoAm 94, WhoAsA 94, WhoScEn 94
Sohn, Louis B(runo) 1914- WrDr 94
Sohn, Louis Bruno 1914- WhoAm 94, WhoAmL 94
Sohn, So Young WhoAsA 94
Sohn, Stephen 1941- WhoFI 94
Sohnen-Moe, Cherie Marilyn 1956- WhoWest 94
Sohnker, Hans d1981 WhoHol 92
Sohn Won-Il 1908-1980 HisDcKW
Sohrabi, Morteza 1945- WhoScEn 94
Soika, Helmut Emil 1941- WhoAm 94, WhoFI 94
Soileau, Curtis Lloyd 1961- WhoAmP 93
Soileau, Jerri H. 1951- WhoAmP 93
Soileau, Kerry Michael 1956- WhoScEn 94
Soileau, Marion Joseph 1944- WhoAm 94
Soiret, Jacques E. 1942- WhoAmL 94
Soisson, Jean-Pierre Henri Robert 1934- IntWW 93
Soja, Eugene Robert 1930- WhoAmP 93
Sojin d1954 WhoHol 92
Sojka, Gary Allan 1940- WhoAm 94
Sojo, Luis 1966- WhoHisp 94
Sokal, Allen Marcel 1946- WhoAm 94, WhoAmL 94
Sokal, Robert Reuven 1926- WhoAm 94
Sokalski, Debra Ann 1959- WhoFI 94
Sokalski, Linda Diane 1948- WhoMW 93
Sokal's'ky, Petro Petrovych 1832-1887 NewGrDO
Sokhanskaia, Nadezhda Stepanovna 1823-1884 BlmGWL
Sokil, Ya 1914- WrDr 94
Sokkappa, Prabhu Marcos 1958- WhoWest 94
Sokler, Bruce Douglas 1949- WhoAm 94, WhoAmL 94
Sokmensuer, Adil 1928- WhoAm 94
Sokol, Christopher Jay 1960- WhoMW 93
Sokol, David Martin 1942- WhoAmA 93
Sokol, Dennis Allen 1945- WhoAm 94, WhoMW 93
Sokol, Jan D. 1952- WhoAmL 94
Sokol, Larry Nides 1946- WhoAmL 94, WhoWest 94
Sokol, Marilyn WhoHol 92
Sokol, Robert James 1941- WhoAm 94
Sokol, Saul 1920- WhoFI 94
Sokol, Sherry Lynn 1960- WhoMW 93
Sokol, Sidney S. 1913-1990 WhAm 10
Sokola, David P. WhoAmP 93
Sokolic, Milenko 1949- WhoScEn 94
Sokolik, Igor 1944- WhoScEn 94
Sokolik, J. Brian 1944- WhoAmL 94
Sokolof, Phil 1922- WhoAm 94
Sokoloff, Alexander Dimitrovitch 1920- WhoWest 94
Sokoloff, Brian S. 1960- WhoAmL 94
Sokoloff, Louis 1921- IntWW 93, WhoAm 94, WhoScEn 94
Sokoloff, Melvin WhAm 10
Sokoloff, Vladimir d1962 WhoHol 92
Sokolov, Aleksandr Vsevolodovich 1943- IntWW 93
Sokolov, Boris Sergeyevich 1914- IntWW 93
Sokolov, Jacque Jenning 1954- WhoWest 94
Sokolov, Raymond DrAPF 93
Sokolov, Richard Saul 1949- WhoAm 94, WhoAmL 94
Sokolov, Sasha 1943- ConWorW 93
Sokolov, Veniamin Sergeevich 1935- LngBDD
Sokolova, Evgenia 1850-1925 IntDcB
Sokolova, Lydia d1974 WhoHol 92
Sokolova, Lydia 1896-1974 IntDcB [port]
Sokolova, Natasha WhoHol 92
Sokolovsky, Mikhail Matveyevich d18th cent.? NewGrDO
Sokolow, Asa D. 1919-1992 WhAm 10
Sokolow, Diane IntMPA 94
Sokolow, Ethel d1970 WhoHol 92
Sokolow, Isobel Folb WhoAmA 93
Sokolow, Lloyd Bruce 1949- WhoAmL 94
Sokolow, Maurice 1911- WhoAm 94
Sokolowaka, Wanda WhoWomW 91
Sokolowski, Chesterlyn 1923- WhoAmP 93
Sokolowski, Krzysztof 1955- EncSF 93
Sokolowski, Linda Robinson 1943- WhoAmA 93
Sokolowski, Megan Kathleen 1964- WhoMW 93
Sokolsky, Andrej Georgiyevich 1950- WhoScEn 94
Sokolsky, Helen Leslie DrAPF 93
Sokolsky, Robert Lawrence 1928- WhoAm 94
Sokoly, Thomas Phillip 1949- WhoMW 93
Sokolyszyn, Aleksander 1914- WrDr 94
Sokomanu, George IntWW 93
Sokorski, Wlodzimierz 1908- IntWW 93
Sola, Michael E., Jr. 1953- WhoHisp 94
Solaita, Levu WhoAmP 93
Solaita, Milovale WhoAmP 93
Solaja, Bogdan Aleksandar 1951- WhoScEn 94
Solan, Miriam DrAPF 93
Solana, Jose L. 1928- WhoHisp 94
Solana Madariaga, Javier 1942- IntWW 93
Solana Madariaga, Luis 1935- IntWW 93
Solana Morales, Fernando IntWW 93
Solana Morales, Fernando 1931- WhoAm 94
Solander, Daniel Carl 1733-1782 WhWE
Solandt, Omond McKillop 1909- IntWW 93
Solanki, Ramniklal Chhaganlal 1931- Who 94
Solano, Carl Anthony 1951- WhoAm 94, WhoAmL 94
Solano, Faustina Venecia 1962- WhoHisp 94
Solano, Henry L. 1950- WhoHisp 94
Solano, Hernando M. 1939- WhoHisp 94
Solano, Juan A. 1950- WhoHisp 94

Soloviev, Yuri 1940-1977 *IntDcB [port]*
Solovitch, Don d1928 *WhoHol 92*
Solovy, Jerold Sherwin 1930- *WhoAm 94*
Solovyev, Gleb Mikhailovich 1928- *IntWW 93*
Solovyev, Nikolay Nikolayevich 1931- *IntWW 93*
Solov'yov, Nikolay Feopemptovich 1846-1916 *NewGrDO*
Solov'yov-Sedoy, Vasily Pavlovich 1907-1979 *NewGrDO*
Solow, Herbert Franklin 1930- *WhoWest 94*
Solow, Lee Howard 1953- *WhoWest 94*
Solow, Robert (Merton) 1924- *WrDr 94*
Solow, Robert A. 1925- *WhoWest 94*
Solow, Robert M. 1924- *NobelP 91 [port]*
Solow, Robert Merton 1924- *IntWW 93, Who 94, WhoAm 94, WhoFI 94*
Solow, Sheldon L. 1950- *WhoAmL 94*
Solow, Steven Paul 1958- *WhoAmL 94*
Soloway, Alan Marc 1955- *WhoAmL 94*
Soloway, Albert Herman 1925- *WhoAm 94*
Soloway, Barry H. 1942- *WhoWest 94*
Soloway, Daniel Mark 1959- *WhoAmL 94*
Soloway, Marilyn Lee 1937- *WhoAmL 94*
Soloway, Reta Burns *WhoAmA 93*
Solowey, Ben 1901-1978 *WhoAmA 93N*
Solski, Bill Peter 1943- *WhoFI 94*
Solt, Andrew W. 1947- *IntMPA 94*
Solt, Leo Frank 1921- *WhoAm 94*
Solt, Mary Ellen *DrAPF 93*
Solt, Mary Ellen 1920- *WrDr 94*
Soltan, Jerzy 1913- *IntWW 93*
Soltanoff, Jack 1915- *WhoScEn 94*
Soltau, Ronald Charles 1944- *WhoScEn 94*
Solterer, Josef 1897-1992 *WhAm 10*
Soltero, Eduardo 1959- *WhoHisp 94*
Soltero, Victor *WhoHisp 94*
Soltero, Victor E. 1938- *WhoAmP 93*
Soltesz, Frank Joseph 1912-1986 *WhoAmA 93N*
Solti, Georg 1912- *IntWW 93, NewGrDO, Who 94, WhoAm 94, WhoMW 93*
Soltis, Jonas F. 1931- *WrDr 94*
Soltis, Robert Alan 1955- *WhoAmL 94*
Soltisiak, Christina Ann 1945- *WhoWest 94*
Soltman, Neil M. 1949- *WhoAm 94, WhoAmL 94*
Soltow, Paul Carl, Jr. 1930- *WhoWest 94*
Soltyk, Grazyna *WhoWomW 91*
Soltys, John Joseph, Jr. 1942- *WhoAm 94, WhoAmL 94*
Soltys, Mieczyslaw 1863-1929 *NewGrDO*
Soltys, Thomas Stanley 1947- *WhoFI 94*
Soltz, Charlene E. *IntMPA 94*
Soltz, Rose Posner d1973 *WhoHol 92*
Solum, Burdette C. *WhoAmP 93*
Solum, James Maurice 1951- *WhoFI 94*
Solursh, Michael 1942- *WhoScEn 94*
Solvay, Ernest 1838-1922 *WorInv*
Solvay, Jacques Ernest 1920- *IntWW 93*
Solveg, Maria *WhoHol 92*
Solway, Carl E. 1935- *WhoAmA 93*
Solwitz, Sharon *DrAPF 93*
Solymar, Laszlo 1930- *Who 94*
Solymosi, Zoltan 1967- *IntWW 93*
Solymossy, Emeric 1948- *WhoWest 94*
Solymosy, Edmond Sigmond Albert 1937- *WhoAm 94*
Solyn, Paul B. *DrAPF 93*
Solzhenitsyn, Aleksandr 1918- *ConLC 78 [port]*
Solzhenitsyn, Aleksandr (Isaevich) 1918- *ConWorW 93, RfGShF*
Solzhenitsyn, Aleksandr I(sayevich) 1918- *WrDr 94*
Solzhenitsyn, Aleksandr Isaevich 1918- *LngBDD*
Solzhenitsyn, Aleksandr Isayevich 1918- *IntWW 93, WhoAm 94*
Solzhenitsyn, Alexander Isayevitch 1918- *Who 94*
Som, Mihir Kumar 1943- *WhoFI 94*
Soma, Mani 1953- *WhoWest 94*
Somack, Jack d1983 *WhoHol 92*
Somadasa, Hettiwatte 1937- *WhoScEn 94*
Somani, Arun K. 1951- *WhoAsA 94*
Somani, Arun Kumar 1951- *WhoScEn 94, WhoWest 94*
Somani, Pitambar 1937- *WhoAsA 94*
Somani, Satu Motilal 1937- *WhoScEn 94*
Somare, Michael (Thomas) 1936- *Who 94*
Somare, Michael Thomas 1936- *IntWW 93*
Somasundaran, Ponisseril 1939- *WhoAm 94, WhoAsA 94, WhoScEn 94*
Somavia, Juan *IntWW 93*
Sombart, Paul C. 1920- *WhoAmP 93*
Somberg, Emilija O. K. 1924- *WhoAmA 93*
Somberg, Herman 1917-1991 *WhoAmA 93N*
Sombert, Claire *WhoHol 92*
Sombrotto, Vincent R. 1923- *WhoAm 94*
Some, Steven Edward 1955- *WhoAmP 93*
Somelofske, Robert Joseph 1947- *WhoIns 94*
Somer, Stanley Jerome 1943- *WhoAmL 94*
Somer, Yanti *WhoHol 92*
Somerfield, Stafford William 1951- *Who 94*
Somerleyton, Baron 1928- *Who 94*
Somero, George Nicholls 1940- *WhoAm 94*
Somers, Baron 1907- *Who 94*
Somers, Anne Ramsay 1913- *WhoAm 94*
Somers, Antoinette Nadezhda 1947- *WhoAm 94*
Somers, Armonia 1918- *BlmGWL*
Somers, Bart *EncSF 93*
Somers, Brett 1927- *WhoHol 92*
Somers, Capt. Fred G. d1970 *WhoHol 92*
Somers, Carin Alma 1934-1990 *WhAm 10*
Somers, Clifford Louis 1940- *WhoAmL 94*
Somers, Edward (Jonathan) 1928- *Who 94*
Somers, Fred Leonard, Jr. 1936- *WhoAmL 94*
Somers, Frederick D(uane) 1942- *WhoAmA 93*
Somers, George Fredrick 1914- *WhoAm 94*
Somers, George Warren 1947- *WhoAmL 94*
Somers, H(arry W.) 1922- *WhoAmA 93*
Somers, Hans Peter 1922- *WhoAm 94*
Somers, Harold Milton 1915- *WhoAm 94*
Somers, Harry (Stuart) 1925- *NewGrDO*
Somers, James Lavaughn 1944- *WhoFI 94*
Somers, Jane 1919- *WrDr 94*
Somers, John A. 1944- *WhoIns 94*
Somers, John Arthur 1944- *WhoAm 94*
Somers, Joseph Moore 1933- *WhoMW 93*
Somers, Julian d1976 *WhoHol 92*
Somers, Linda 1943- *WhoMW 93*
Somers, Paul 1908- *WrDr 94*
Somers, Robert Vance 1937- *WhoAmP 93*
Somers, Suzanne 1915- *WrDr 94*
Somers, Suzanne 1946- *ConTFT 11, IntMPA 94, WhoHol 92*
Somerscales, Thomas Lawrence 1913- *Who 94*
Somers-Clarke, Constance *WhoHol 92*
Somers Cocks, Anna Gwenllian 1950- *Who 94*
Somerset *Who 94*
Somerset, Duke of 1952- *Who 94*
Somerset, Charles Henry 1767-1831 *DcNaB MP*
Somerset, David Henry Fitzroy 1930- *Who 94*
Somerset, Harold Richard 1935- *WhoAm 94, WhoWest 94*
Somerset, Henry Beaufort 1906- *Who 94*
Somerset, Leo L., Jr. 1945- *WhoBlA 94*
Somerset, Margaret Elizabeth 1964- *WhoAmL 94*
Somerset, Pat d1974 *WhoHol 92*
Somerset Fry, Peter George Robin Plantagenet 1931- *Who 94*
Somerset Fry, Plantagenet 1931- *WrDr 94*
Somerset Jones, Eric 1925- *Who 94*
Somerson, Rosanne 1954- *WhoAmA 93*
Somerton, Viscount 1982- *Who 94*
Somervill, Cynthia Belle 1959- *WhoAmL 94*
Somerville, Addison Wimbs 1927- *WhoBlA 94*
Somerville, Christopher Roland 1947- *Who 94*
Somerville, David 1917- *Who 94*
Somerville, Dora B. 1920- *WhoBlA 94*
Somerville, Edith 1858-1949 *BlmGWL, TwCLC 51 [port]*
Somerville, Edith (Anna Oenone) 1858-1949 *RfGShF*
Somerville, Edith OEnone 1858-1949 *DcLB 135*
Somerville, George Arnold 1951- *WhoAmL 94*
Somerville, James Hugh Miller 1922- *WrDr 94*
Somerville, Jane *DrAPF 93*
Somerville, Jane 1933- *Who 94*
Somerville, John Arthur Fownes 1917- *Who 94*
Somerville, John Spenser 1910- *Who 94*
Somerville, Margaret Anne Ganley 1942- *WhoScEn 94*
Somerville, Mary Temple 1952- *WhoAmP 93*
Somerville, Mason Harold 1941- *WhoAm 94*
Somerville, Nicholas *Who 94*
Somerville, (John) Nicholas 1924- *Who 94*
Somerville, Quentin Charles Somerville A. *Who 94*
Somerville, Richard Chapin James 1941- *WhoScEn 94*
Somerville, Robert Alston 1920- *WhoBlA 94*
Somerville, Robert Eugene *WhoAm 94*
Somerville, Romaine Stec 1930- *WhoAm 94, WhoAmA 93*
Somerville, Theodore Elkin 1940- *WhoAmL 94*
Somerville, Thomas David 1915- *Who 94*
Somerville, Walter 1913- *Who 94*
Somerville, William 1675-1742 *BlmGEL*
Somerville, William H. *WhoMW 93*
Somerville and Ross *BlmGWL, RfGShF*
Somerville-Large, Peter 1928- *WrDr 94*
Somes, Daniel E. 1935- *WhoAm 94*
Somes, Grant William 1947- *WhoScEn 94*
Somes, Joan Marie 1952- *WhoMW 93*
Somes, Joseph 1787-1845 *DcNaB MP*
Somes, Michael 1917- *IntDcB [port], WhoHol 92*
Somes, Michael (George) 1917- *Who 94*
Somigli, Domenico 1756-c. 1798 *NewGrDO*
Somigli, Franca 1901-1974 *NewGrDO*
Somilpilp fl. 19th cent.- *EncNAR*
Somit, Albert 1919- *WhoAm 94*
Somjee, Shamoon 1943- *Who 94*
Somjen, George Gustav 1929- *WhoAm 94*
Somlyo, Andrew Paul 1930- *WhoAm 94*
Somlyo, Gyorgy 1920- *IntWW 93*
Somma, Antonio 1809-1864 *NewGrDO*
Somma, Robert 1944- *WhoAmL 94*
Somma, Stephen R. 1961- *WhoAmP 93*
Sommars, Donna Marie 1954- *WhoAmL 94*
Sommars, Julie 1940- *WhoHol 92*
Sommaruga, Cornelio 1932- *IntWW 93, Who 94*
Sommer, Alfred 1942- *WhoAm 94, WhoScEn 94*
Sommer, Alfred Hermann 1909- *WhoScEn 94*
Sommer, Alphonse Adam, Jr. 1924- *WhoAm 94, WhoAmL 94, WhoFI 94*
Sommer, Bert d1990 *WhoHol 92*
Sommer, Elke 1940- *IntMPA 94, IntWW 93, WhoHol 92*
Sommer, Eric Mark 1957- *WhoAmL 94*
Sommer, Frank H., III 1922- *WhoAmA 93*
Sommer, Frederick 1905- *WhoAmA 93*
Sommer, Hans 1837-1922 *NewGrDO*
Sommer, Henry Joseph, III 1952- *WhoScEn 94*
Sommer, Howard Ellsworth 1918- *WhoAm 94*
Sommer, Jeffrey Robert 1958- *WhoAmL 94*
Sommer, Josef 1934- *IntMPA 94, WhoHol 92*
Sommer, Mark 1945- *ConAu 140*
Sommer, Piotr 1948- *ConWorW 93*
Sommer, Robert B. 1947- *WhoAmL 94*
Sommer, Robert George 1959- *WhoAm 94*
Sommer, Robert Riebel, II 1952- *WhoMW 93*
Sommer, Scott 1951-1993 *NewYTBS 93*
Sommer, Theo 1930- *IntWW 93*
Sommer, Wassily 1912-1979 *WhoAmA 93N*
Sommerburg, Miriam d1980 *WhoAmA 93N*
Sommerer, John 1947- *WhoFI 94*
Sommerfeld, Arnold Johannes Wilhelm 1861-1951 *WorScD*
Sommerfeld, David William 1942- *WhoAm 94*
Sommerfeld, Nicholas Ulrich 1926- *WhoAm 94*
Sommerfeld, Raynard Matthias 1933- *WhoAm 94*
Sommerfeldt, John Robert 1933- *WhoAm 94*
Sommerfelt, Soren Christian 1916- *IntWW 93, WhoAm 94*
Sommerfield, Diane *WhoHol 92*
Sommerfield, Thomas A. 1958- *WhoScEn 94*
Sommerhause, Peter M. 1942- *WhoAmL 94*
Sommerlad, Robert Edward 1937- *WhoAm 94*
Sommerman, Kathryn Martha 1915- *WhoScEn 94*
Sommermann, Jeffrey Herbert 1958- *WhoScEn 94*
Sommers, Adele Ann 1955- *WhoScEn 94*
Sommers, Albert Trumbull 1919- *WhoAm 94*
Sommers, Dana Eugene 1953- *WhoMW 93*
Sommers, David Lynn 1949- *WhoMW 93*
Sommers, Duane C. 1932- *WhoAmP 93*
Sommers, Helen Elizabeth 1932- *WhoAmP 93*
Sommers, Herbert Myron 1925- *WhoAm 94*
Sommers, Joanie 1941- *WhoHol 92*
Sommers, Lawrence Melvin 1919- *WhoAm 94*
Sommers, Louise 1948- *WhoAm 94, WhoAmL 94*
Sommers, Mark Richard 1945- *WhoMW 93*
Sommers, Robert Thomas 1926- *WhoAm 94*
Sommers, Shari Catherine 1950- *WhoMW 93*
Sommers, Sheldon Charles 1916- *WhoScEn 94*
Sommers, William Paul 1933- *WhoAm 94*
Sommerschield, William Arthur 1941- *WhoMW 93*
Sommerville, Frank 1952- *WhoAmL 94*
Sommerville, Joseph C. 1926- *WhoBlA 94*
Sommese, Andrew John 1948- *WhoAm 94, WhoMW 93*
Sommese, Lanny Beal 1943- *WhoAmA 93*
Sommi, Debra Lee 1957- *WhoMW 93*
Somnolet, Michel Pierre 1940- *WhoAm 94*
Somogyi, Jozsef d1993 *IntWW 93N*
Somogyi, Laszlo Peter 1931- *WhoFI 94, WhoWest 94*
Somogyl, Erwin George 1912-1990 *WhAm 10*
Somorjai, Gabor Arpad 1935- *IntWW 93, WhoAm 94, WhoScEn 94, WhoWest 94*
Somoza, Joseph *DrAPF 93*
Somoza, Joseph 1940- *WhoHisp 94*
Somoza Debayle, Anastasio 1925-1980 *HisWorL*
Somoza Debayle, Luis 1923-1967 *HisWorL*
Somoza Garcia, Anastasio 1896-1956 *HisWorL [port]*
Sompolski, Timothy Andrew 1952- *WhoFI 94*
Somrock, John Douglas 1942- *WhoFI 94*
Somsky, David Paul 1946- *WhoAmP 93*
Somtow, S.P. 1952- *EncSF 93, WrDr 94*
Son, Ki Sub 1928- *WhoScEn 94*
Son, Trinh Cong *NewYTBS 93 [port]*
Sondak, Arthur 1929- *WhoFI 94*
Sondak, Bradley Wayne 1962- *WhoWest 94*
Sondak, Steven David 1957- *WhoScEn 94*
Sonday, Milton Franklin, Jr. 1939- *WhoAmA 93*
Sonde, Susan *DrAPF 93*
Sonde, Theodore Irwin 1940- *WhoAm 94*
Sondeckis, Saulius 1928- *IntWW 93*
Sonderby, Peter R. 1941- *WhoAm 94, WhoAmL 94*
Sonderby, Susan Pierson 1947- *WhoAm 94, WhoAmL 94, WhoAmP 93*
Sonderegger, Theo Brown 1925- *WhoAm 94, WhoMW 93*
Sondergaard, Gale d1985 *WhoHol 92*
Sondergeld, Donald Ray 1930- *WhoAm 94*
Sonderman, Wilma 1927- *WhoAmP 93*
Sonders, Mark *EncSF 93*
Sonders, Scott *DrAPF 93*
Sonders, Scott 1953- *WrDr 94*
Sondes, Earl 1940- *Who 94*
Sondey, Margaret Ellen 1955- *WhoMW 93*
Sondhaus, Lawrence 1958- *WhoMW 93*
Sondheim, Alan *DrAPF 93*
Sondheim, Stephen 1930- *Au&Arts 11 [port], ConTFT 11, IntMPA 94*
Sondheim, Stephen (Joshua) 1930- *NewGrDO, WrDr 94*
Sondheim, Stephen Joshua 1930- *AmCulL, IntWW 93, Who 94, WhoAm 94*
Sondheimer, Ernst Helmut 1923- *Who 94*
Sondhi, Ranjit 1950- *Who 94*
Sondock, Ruby Kless 1926- *WhoAmL 94*
Sone, Masazumi 1949- *WhoScEn 94*
Sone, Toshio 1935- *WhoAm 94, WhoScEn 94*
Sonea, Sorin I. 1920- *WhoAm 94*
Soned, Warren 1911-1966 *WhoAmA 93N*
Sonego, Ian G. 1954- *WhoAmL 94*
Soneira, Raymond M. 1949- *WhoScEn 94*
Sonenberg, Jack 1925- *WhoAm 94, WhoAmA 93*
Sonenberg, Martin 1920- *WhoAm 94*
Sonenberg, Maya *DrAPF 93*
Sonenberg, Maya 1960- *WrDr 94*
Sonenshein, Nathan 1915- *WhoAm 94*
Sonett, Charles Philip 1924- *WhoAm 94, WhoWest 94*
Sonfield, Robert Leon, Jr. 1931- *WhoAm 94*
Sonfist, Alan 1946- *WhoAm 94, WhoAmA 93*
Song, Cathy *DrAPF 93*
Song, Cathy 1955- *BlmGWL*
Song, Choan-Seng 1929- *WhoAsA 94*
Song, Il-Yeol 1953- *WhoAsA 94*
Song, John D. 1935- *WhoAsA 94*
Song, John S. 1921- *WhoAsA 94*
Song, Joseph M. 1927- *WhoAsA 94*
Song, Limin 1960- *WhoScEn 94*
Song, Ohseop 1954- *WhoScEn 94*
Song, Ralph H. 1926- *WhoAsA 94*
Song, Shin-Min 1951- *WhoAsA 94, WhoMW 93*

Song, Tae-Sung 1941- WhoWest 94
Song, Xiaotong 1934- WhoScEn 94
Song, Xueshu 1955- WhoAsA 94
Song, Yangsoon 1948- WhoAsA 94
Song, Yo Taik 1932- WhoAsA 94
Song, Yong Chol 1959- WhoAsA 94
Songaila, Ringaudas-Bronislovas Igno 1929- IntWW 93
Song Ailing 1890-1973 See Song Sisters HisWorL
Song Bu 1923- WhoPRCh 91 [port]
Song Chaozun WhoPRCh 91
Song Chengzhi 1917- WhoPRCh 91 [port]
Song Chengzhi, Maj.-Gen. 1917- IntWW 93
Song Chunli WhoPRCh 91 [port]
Song Dafan 1930- WhoPRCh 91 [port]
Song Dakang WhoPRCh 91
Song Defu 1946- IntWW 93, WhoPRCh 91 [port]
Song Demin 1930- WhoPRCh 91 [port]
Song Di 1945- WhoPRCh 91
Songer, Mark Anthony 1959- WhoFI 94
Song Fatang WhoPRCh 91
Songgi Ishi WhoPRCh 91
Song Guoqing WhoPRCh 91
Song Hanliang 1934- IntWW 93, WhoPRCh 91 [port]
Song Hong-Zhao 1915- IntWW 93, WhoPRCh 91 [port]
Song Jian 1931- IntWW 93
Song Jian 1932- WhoPRCh 91 [port]
Song Jiwen 1916- IntWW 93, WhoPRCh 91 [port]
Song Keda 1928- WhoPRCh 91 [port]
Song Keda, Lieut.-Gen. 1928- IntWW 93
Song Kun 1929- WhoPRCh 91 [port]
Song Li WhoPRCh 91
Song Meiling 1897- See Song Sisters HisWorL
Song Muwen 1929- WhoPRCh 91 [port]
Song Ong, Roxanne Kay 1953- WhoAmL 94
Song Ping 1917- IntWW 93, WhoPRCh 91 [port]
Song Qingling 1893-1981 See Song Sisters HisWorL
Song Qingwei 1929- WhoPRCh 91 [port]
Song Qingwei, Lieut.-Gen. 1929- IntWW 93
Song Renqiong 1903- IntWW 93
Song Renqiong 1909- WhoPRCh 91 [port]
Song Rufen 1922- WhoPRCh 91 [port]
Song Ruixiang 1939- WhoPRCh 91 [port]
Song Ruyao 1914- WhoPRCh 91 [port]
Song Shilun 1907- WhoPRCh 91 [port]
Song Shixiong 1939- WhoPRCh 91 [port]
Song Shuanglai 1926- WhoPRCh 91 [port]
Song Shuhe WhoPRCh 91
Song Shuhua 1929- WhoPRCh 91 [port]
Song Shusheng 1928- WhoPRCh 91 [port]
Songsiridej, Vanee 1949- WhoMW 93
Song Sisters HisWorL [port]
Songstad, L. Allan, Jr. 1946- WhoAmL 94
Songstad, Sheldon R. WhoAmP 93
Songster, John Hugh 1934- WhoFI 94
Songweaver, Cerin EncSF 93
Song Wenzhi 1919- WhoPRCh 91 [port]
Song Xianzhen 1935- WhoPRCh 91 [port]
Song Xiaoying WhoPRCh 91 [port]
Song Xilian 1907- WhoPRCh 91 [port]
Song Xingchang WhoPRCh 91
Song Yating WhoPRCh 91
Song Yinke 1902- WhoPRCh 91 [port]
Song Yiping 1916- WhoPRCh 91 [port]
Song Zexing 1917- WhoPRCh 91 [port]
Song Zhaosu 1941- WhoPRCh 91 [port]
Song Zhiguang 1916- WhoPRCh 91 [port]
Song Zhiyuan 1930- WhoPRCh 91 [port]
Soni, Narendra 1934- WhoAsA 94
Soniat, Katherine DrAPF 93
Sonju, Norm Arnold 1938- WhoAm 94
Sonka, Steven T. 1948- WhoMW 93
Sonkin, Richard 1949- WhoAmL 94
Sonkkila, Paul WhoHol 92
Sonkowsky, Robert Paul 1931- WhoAm 94
Sonnabend, Joan 1928- WhoAmA 93
Sonnabend, Joseph Adolph 1933- WhoScEn 94
Sonnabend, Roger Philip 1925- WhoAm 94, WhoFI 94
Sonne, Scott W. 1947- WhoAmL 94
Sonneborn, Andrew 1948- WhoAmL 94
Sonneborn, Henry, III 1918- WhoAm 94
Sonneck, Oscar G(eorge) T(heodore) 1873-1928 NewGrDO
Sonnecken, Edwin Herbert 1916- WhoAm 94
Sonnedecker, Glenn Allen 1917- WhoAm 94
Sonneman, Eve 1946- WhoAm 94, WhoAmA 93
Sonnemann, Douglas William 1956- WhoWest 94
Sonnemann, Emmy d1974 WhoHol 92
Sonnemann, Harry 1924- WhoAm 94
Sonnenberg, Ben 1936- WhoAm 94
Sonnenberg, Frances WhoAmA 93
Sonnenberg, Hardy 1939- WhoAm 94
Sonnenburg, William Robert 1952- WhoAmL 94
Sonnenfeld, Albert 1934- WhoWest 94
Sonnenfeld, Jeffrey Alan 1954- WhoFI 94
Sonnenfeld, Marc Jay 1946- WhoAmL 94
Sonnenfeld, Marion 1928- WhoAm 94
Sonnenfeldt, Helmut 1926- IntWW 93, WhoAm 94, WhoAmP 93
Sonnenfeldt, Richard Wolfgang 1923- WhoAm 94
Sonnenschein 1917-1981 WhoAmA 93N
Sonnenschein, Adam 1938- WhoAm 94
Sonnenschein, Allan 1941- WrDr 94
Sonnenschein, Edward, Jr. 1954- WhoAmL 94
Sonnenschein, Hugo Freund 1940- WhoAm 94, WhoFI 94, WhoMW 93
Sonnenschein, Ralph Robert 1923- WhoAm 94
Sonnentag, Richard H. 1940- WhoAm 94
Sonner, David A. 1957- WhoAmL 94
Sonnett, Neal Russell 1942- WhoAmL 94
Sonneveld, Wim d1974 WhoHol 92
Sonnichsen, C(harles) L(eland) 1901-1991 WrDr 94N
Sonnichsen, Charles Leland 1901-1991 WhAm 10
Sonnier, David Joseph 1939- WhoFI 94
Sonnier, Jo-El 1946- ConMus 10 [port]
Sonnier, Keith 1941- WhoAmA 93
Sonnier, Richard Louis, III 1963- WhoFI 94
Sonnino, Carlo Benvenuto 1904- WhoAm 94
Sonnleithner, Joseph von 1766-1835 NewGrDO
Sonntag, Bernard H. 1940- WhoScEn 94
Sonntag, Brian WhoAmP 93
Sonntag, Douglas F. 1926- WhoAmP 93
Sonntag-Wolgast, Cornelie 1942- WhoWomW 91
Sonny & Cher WhoHol 92
Sono Ayako 1931- BlmGWL
Sonogashira, Kenkichi 1931- WhoScEn 94
Sonora, Myrna 1959- WhoHisp 94
Sons, Raymond William 1926- WhoAm 94
Son Sann 1911- IntWW 93
Son Sen 1930- IntWW 93
"Sons Of The Pioneers" WhoHol 92
Sonsteby, Kristi Lee 1958- WhoMW 93, WhoScEn 94
Sonstegaard, Miles Harry 1924- WhoFI 94
Sont, Gerry WhoHol 92
Sontag, Frederick Earl 1924- WhoAm 94, WhoWest 94
Sontag, Frederick H. 1924- WhoAm 94, WhoAmP 93
Sontag, Glennon Christy 1949- WhoFI 94, WhoScEn 94
Sontag, Harvey 1943- WhoFI 94
Sontag, Henriette (Gertrud Walpurgis) 1806-1854 NewGrDO [port]
Sontag, James Mitchell 1939- WhoAm 94
Sontag, Stephanie 1948- WhoAmL 94
Sontag, Susan DrAPF 93, WhoAm 94
Sontag, Susan 1933- IntWW 93, Who 94, WrDr 94
Sontheimer, Harald Wolfgang 1960- WhoScEn 94
Sontheimer, James Albert 1926- WhoFI 94
Sonzogno NewGrDO
Sonzski, William DrAPF 93
Soo, Billy S. 1961- WhoAsA 94
Soo, Chan d1979 WhoHol 92
Soo, Charlie H. 1945- WhoAsA 94
Soo, Jack d1979 WhoHol 92
Soo, Jack 1916-1979 WhoCom
Soo, Shao Lee 1922- WhoAm 94
Sood, Devinder Kumar 1944- WhoAsA 94
Sood, Mohan K. 1941- WhoAsA 94
Sood, Ravinder Singh WhoAsA 94
Soo Hoo, Eric Randolph 1951- WhoAsA 94
Soo Hoo, Karen 1960- WhoAsA 94
SooHoo, Leo, Jr. 1956- WhoAsA 94
Soo Hoo, Richard 1950- WhoAsA 94
Soohoo, Richard Allen 1948- WhoAsA 94
Soo Hoo, William Fong 1948- WhoAsA 94
Soomer, Walter 1878-1955 NewGrDO
Soomro, Akbar Haider 1947- WhoScEn 94
Soomro, Ellahi Bukhsh WhoScEn 94
Soong, Arthur J. 1951- WhoAsA 94
Soong, James Chu-Yul 1942- IntWW 93
Soong Chang-Chih 1916- IntWW 93
Soorholtz, John E. 1930- WhoAmP 93
Soorikian, Diana Tashjian 1928- WhoAmA 93
Soos, R., Jr. DrAPF 93
Soot, Fritz (Wilhelm) 1878-1965 NewGrDO
Sooter, Edward 1934- NewGrDO
Soothill, Keith (Leonard) 1941- WrDr 94
Sooy, C. Darrell 1944- WhoAmL 94
Soper, Baron 1903- IntWW 93, Who 94
Soper, Lord 1903- WrDr 94
Soper, Alexander Coburn 1904-1993 ConAu 140
Soper, Alexander Coburn, III 1904-1993 NewYTBS 93
Soper, Ivan Glen 1951- WhoMW 93
Soper, James Herbert 1916- WhoAm 94
Soper, (Andrew) Laurence 1943- Who 94
Soper, Mark 1954- WhoHol 92
Soper, Quentin Francis 1919- WhoAm 94
Soper, Thomas Sherwood 1947- WhoScEn 94
Soper, Tony 1929- WrDr 94
Sopher, Aaron 1905-1972 WhoAmA 93N
Sopher, Bernhard D. 1879-1949 WhoAmA 93N
Sophia 1630-1714 DcNaB MP
Sophia fl. 1739-1741 BlmGWL
Sophia Dorothea 1666-1726 DcNaB MP
Sophie Elisabeth 1613-1676 NewGrDO
Sophocles c. 496BC-406BC IntDcT 2 [port], NewGrDO
Sophocles 495BC-406BC BlmGEL
Sophusson, Fridrik 1943- IntWW 93
Sopinka, John 1933- WhoAm 94
Sopkin, George 1914- WhoAm 94
Sopko, Michael D. 1939- WhoAm 94
Sopko, Stephen Joseph 1950- WhoScEn 94
Soppelsa, George 1939- WhoAmA 93
Soppelsa, John Joseph 1948- WhoFI 94
Sopper, Dale W. 1941- WhoAmP 93
Sopr, Alois 1913- IntWW 93
Soprani, Luciano 1946- IntWW 93
Sopranos, Orpheus Javaras 1935- WhoAm 94
Sopwith, Charles (Ronald) 1905- Who 94
Sor, (Joseph) Fernando (Macari) 1778-1839 NewGrDO
Sorabji, Richard Rustom Kharsedji 1934- Who 94
Soracco, Reginald John 1946- WhoScEn 94
Sorah, Nelson A. 1946- WhoAmP 93
Sorak, Nancy Beckett 1942- WhoAmL 94
Sorak, Patricia M. 1947- WhoAmP 93
Soral, Agnes WhoHol 92
Soran, Robert L. 1943- WhoFI 94
Sorano, Daniel d1962 WhoHol 92
Sorato, Bruno 1922- IntWW 93
Sorber, Charles Arthur 1939- WhoAm 94
Sorbo, Allen Jon 1953- WhoAm 94, WhoMW 93
Sorby, Donald Lloyd 1933- WhoAm 94, WhoWest 94
Sorby, J. Richard 1911- WhoAmA 93
Sorce, Anthony John 1937- WhoAmA 93
Sorcic, Jim DrAPF 93
Sorci-Thomas, Mary Gay 1956- WhoScEn 94
Sorcsek, Jerome Paul 1949- WhoWest 94
Sordi, Alberto 1919- IntMPA 94, WhoHol 92
Soref, Harold Benjamin d1993 Who 94N
Soreff, Helen WhoAmA 93
Soreff, S. WhoAmA 93
Soreff, Stephen 1931- WhoAmA 93
Soreff, Stephen Mayer 1931- WhoAm 94
Soregaroli, Arthur Earl 1933- WhoScEn 94
Sorel, Cecile d1966 WhoHol 92
Sorel, Charles 1599?-1674 GuFrLit 2
Sorel, Claudette Marguerite WhoAm 94
Sorel, Edward 1929- EncSF 93, WhoAm 94, WhoAmA 93
Sorel, George d1948 WhoHol 92
Sorel, Guy WhoHol 92
Sorel, Jean WhoHol 92
Sorel, Jeanne WhoHol 92
Sorel, Julia 1926- WrDr 94
Sorel, Louise WhoHol 92
Sorel, Nancy Caldwell 1934- WrDr 94
Sorel-Cameron, James (Robert) 1948- WrDr 94
Sorell, Kitty Julia 1937- WhoFI 94
Sorell, Victor Alexander 1944- WhoAmA 93
Sorem, Ronald Keith 1924- WhoWest 94
Soren, Bradley William 1959- WhoFI 94
Soren, David 1946- WhoAm 94, WhoScEn 94, WhoWest 94
Soren, Tabitha L. 1967- WhoAm 94
Sorensen, Alan Robert 1965- WhoMW 93
Sorensen, Albert G. 1932- WhoAmP 93
Sorensen, Allan Chresten 1938- WhoAm 94
Sorensen, Andrew Aaron 1938- WhoAm 94
Sorensen, Anne Elder 1956- WhoMW 93
Sorensen, Bengt Algot 1927- IntWW 93
Sorensen, Bill H. WhoAmP 93
Sorensen, Burton Erhard 1929- WhoAm 94
Sorensen, Carl David 1958- WhoWest 94
Sorensen, Charles W. WhoMW 93
Sorensen, Craig Burg 1946- WhoAmP 93, WhoWest 94
Sorensen, Dean E. WhoAmP 93
Sorensen, Dorothy Allan 1932- WhoWest 94
Sorensen, Elaine Shaw 1949- WhoWest 94
Sorensen, (Kenneth) Eric (Correll) 1942- Who 94
Sorensen, Erik 1944- WhoAm 94
Sorensen, Gillian Martin 1941- WhoAm 94
Sorensen, Harvey R. 1947- WhoAmL 94
Sorensen, Henri 1950- SmATA 77 [port]
Sorensen, Henrik Vittrup 1959- WhoScEn 94
Sorensen, Jacki Faye 1942- WhoAm 94
Sorensen, Jane Forester 1942- WhoFI 94
Sorensen, Jean WhoAmA 93
Sorensen, Jimmy Louis 1927- WhoMW 93
Sorensen, John Hjelmhof 1923-1969 WhoAmA 93N
Sorensen, John Kousgard 1925- IntWW 93
Sorensen, John Noble 1934- WhoScEn 94
Sorensen, Joyce E. 1936- WhoMW 93
Sorensen, Keld 1953- WhoMW 93
Sorensen, Knud 1928- IntWW 93
Sorensen, Leif Boge 1928- WhoAm 94
Sorensen, Linda WhoHol 92
Sorensen, Linda 1945- WhoAmL 94
Sorensen, Mark N. 1948- WhoAmP 93
Sorensen, Mark Wayne 1947- WhoMW 93
Sorensen, Paul WhoHol 92
Sorensen, Peter Alan 1957- WhoFI 94
Sorensen, Raymond Andrew 1931- WhoScEn 94
Sorensen, Robert C. 1923- WhoAm 94, WhoFI 94
Sorensen, Robert Carmine 1952- WhoAmP 93
Sorensen, Robert Holm 1921- WhoAm 94
Sorensen, Roberta Ann 1954- WhoAmP 93
Sorensen, Sally Jo DrAPF 93
Sorensen, Sheila 1947- WhoWest 94
Sorensen, Sheila Anne 1947- WhoAmP 93
Sorensen, Theodore (Chaikin) 1928- WrDr 94
Sorensen, Theodore Chaikin 1928- IntWW 93, WhoAm 94, WhoAmP 93
Sorensen, Thomas Chaikin 1926- WhoAm 94, WrDr 94
Sorensen, Villy 1929- ConWorW 93
Sorensen, Virginia 1912- WhAm 10
Sorensen, Virginia 1912-1991 WrDr 94N
Sorenson, Craig Allen 1954- WhoWest 94
Sorenson, Dean Philip 1939- WhoAmP 93
Sorenson, Herbert 1898- WhAm 10
Sorenson, Liane M. 1947- WhoAmP 93
Sorenson, Lloyd Raymond 1897- WhAm 10
Sorenson, Marc Bruce 1943- WhoWest 94
Sorenson, Ralph Zellar, II 1933- WhoAm 94, WhoFI 94, WhoWest 94
Sorescu, Marin 1936- ConWorW 93, IntWW 93
Sorey, Hilmon S., Jr. 1935- WhoBlA 94
Sorge, Reinhard (Johannes) 1892-1916 IntDcT 2
Sorge, Walter 1931- WhoAmA 93
Sorgen, Michael Steven 1942- WhoAmL 94
Sorgenti, Harold Andrew 1934- WhoAm 94, WhoFI 94
Soria, Humberto Arreola 1949- WhoWest 94
Soria, Marco Raffaello 1945- WhoScEn 94
Soria, Martin Sebastian 1911-1961 WhoAmA 93N
Soria, Paco Martinez WhoHol 92
Sorian, Jack WhoHol 92
Soriano, Enrique Carlos 1922- WhoHisp 94
Soriano, Hugo R. 1936- WhoHisp 94
Soriano, Lee G. 1938- WhoAsA 94
Soriano, Marcel 1942- WhoHisp 94
Soriano Fuertes (y Piqueras), Mariano 1817-1880 NewGrDO
Soriano Jara, Elena 1917- BlmGWL
Sorin, Louis d1961 WhoHol 92
Sorinj, L. T. Who 94
Sorkin, Alan Lowell 1941- WhoAm 94, WhoFI 94
Sorkin, Arleen 1956- WhoHol 92
Sorkin, Barry Gerald 1941- WhoFI 94
Sorkin, Emily WhoAmA 93
Sorkin, Laurence Truman 1942- WhoAm 94, WhoAmL 94
Sorkin, Robert Daniel 1937- WhoScEn 94
Sorley, Charles Hamilton 1895-1915 DcNaB MP
Sorley Walker, Kathrine WrDr 94
Sorman, Steven 1948- WhoAmA 93
Sormani, Charles Robert 1938- WhoAm 94, WhoIns 94

Southgate, Colin *IntWW 93*
Southgate, Colin (Grieve) 1938- *Who 94*
Southgate, David Christopher 1964- *WhoMW 93*
Southgate, Harry Charles 1921- *Who 94*
Southgate, John Eliot 1926- *Who 94*
Southgate, Malcolm John 1933- *Who 94*
Southgate, Minoo S. *WrDr 94*
Southgate, Richard W. 1929- *WhoAm 94*
Southward, Glen Morris 1927- *WhoAm 94*
Southward, Leonard (Bingley) 1905- *Who 94*
Southward, Nigel Ralph 1941- *Who 94*
Southward, Ralph 1908- *Who 94*
Southward, Walter William 1936- *WhoWest 94*
Southwark, Archbishop of 1930- *Who 94*
Southwark, Archdeacon of *Who 94*
Southwark, Auxiliary Bishop in *Who 94*
Southwark, Bishop of 1932- *Who 94*
Southwark, Provost of *Who 94*
Southwell, Bishop of 1934- *Who 94*
Southwell, Provost of *Who 94*
Southwell, Viscount 1930- *Who 94*
Southwell, Carl Erckman 1958- *WhoMW 93*
Southwell, Leonard J. 1924- *WhoAm 94, WhoFI 94*
Southwell, Richard Charles *Who 94*
Southwell, Robert 1561?-1595 *BlmGEL*
Southwell, Roy 1914- *Who 94*
Southwell, Samuel B. *DrAPF 93*
Southwell, William Joseph 1914- *WhoAmA 93*
Southwick, Alpert P. d1929 *WhoHol 92*
Southwick, Arthur Frederick 1924- *WhoAm 94*
Southwick, Charles Henry 1928- *WhoAm 94, WhoScEn 94, WhoWest 94*
Southwick, Christopher Lyn 1956- *WhoMW 93*
Southwick, Dale d1968 *WhoHol 92*
Southwick, Harry Webb 1918- *WhoAm 94*
Southwick, Marcia *DrAPF 93*
Southwick, Paul 1920- *WhoAm 94*
Southwick, Philip Lee 1916-1992 *WhAm 10*
Southwick, Stephen Mark 1956- *WhoWest 94*
Southwold, Stephen *EncSF 93*
Southwood, Horace Gerald 1912- *Who 94*
Southwood, (Thomas) Richard (Edmund) 1931- *Who 94, WrDr 94*
Southwood, (Thomas) Richard Edmund 1931- *IntWW 93*
Southwood, William Frederick Walter 1925- *Who 94*
Southworth, E.D.E.N., Mrs. 1819-1899 *BlmGWL*
Southworth, Frederick 1910- *Who 94*
Southworth, Jean May 1926- *Who 94*
Southworth, Jim O. 1929- *WhoAmP 93*
Southworth, John Franklin, Jr. 1949- *WhoAmL 94*
Southworth, Louis Sweetland, II 1943- *WhoAm 94*
Southworth, Rod Brand 1941- *WhoWest 94*
Southworth, Warren H. 1912- *WrDr 94*
Southworth, William Dixon 1918- *WhoAm 94*
Souto, Javier 1939- *WhoAmP 93*
Souto, Javier D. 1939- *WhoHisp 94*
Souto, Jose A. *WhoHisp 94*
Souto Bachiller, Fernando Alberto 1951- *WhoScEn 94*
Soutou, Jean-Marie Leon 1912- *IntWW 93*
Soutter, Thomas D. 1934- *WhoAm 94, WhoAmL 94, WhoFI 94*
Soutullo (Otero), Reveriano 1884-1932 *NewGrDO*
Souveroff, Vernon William, Jr. 1934- *WhoAm 94*
Souviron, Alvaro 1933- *WhoWest 94*
Souw, Bernard Eng-Kie 1942- *WhoScEn 94*
Souyave, (Louis) Georges 1926- *Who 94*
Souza, Adele de 1761-1836 *BlmGWL*
Souza, Blase Camacho 1918- *WhoWest 94*
Souza, Everett J. 1945- *WhoIns 94*
Souza, Francis Newton 1924- *IntWW 93*
Souza, Marcelo Lopes 1951- *WhoScEn 94*
Souza, Marco Antonio 1951- *WhoScEn 94*
Souza, Ronald Joseph 1936- *WhoAm 94*
Souza, Wade Anthony 1958- *WhoWest 94*
Souza e Silva, Celso de 1924- *Who 94*
Souza Mendes, Paulo Roberto de 1954- *WhoScEn 94*
Souzay, Gerard 1920- *IntWW 93*
Souzay, Gerard 1921- *Who 94*
Souzay, Gerard (Marcel) 1920- *NewGrDO*
Sova, Richard Steven 1946- *WhoMW 93*
Sovatsky, Stuart Charles 1949- *WhoWest 94*
Sovde-Pennell, Barbara Ann 1955- *WhoScEn 94*
Sovern, Clarence d1929 *WhoHol 92*
Sovern, Joan R. d1993 *NewYTBS 93*
Sovern, Michael Ira 1931- *IntWW 93, WhoAm 94, WhoAmL 94*
Sovetky, Jack 1930- *WhoWest 94*
Sovey, William Pierre 1933- *WhoAm 94*
Soviak, Harry 1935- *WhoAmA 93N*
Sovie, Donald E. 1944- *WhoAm 94, WhoAmL 94*
Sovie, Margaret Doe 1934- *WhoAm 94*
Soviero, Diana 1946- *NewGrDO*
Soviero, Diana Barbara 1946- *WhoAm 94*
Sovik, Edward Anders 1918- *WhoAm 94*
Sovinee, Rudy William 1948- *WhoWest 94*
Sovish, Richard Charles 1925- *WhoWest 94*
Sowa, Frank Xavier 1957- *WhoFI 94*
Sowa, Larry 1938- *WhoAmP 93*
Sowa, Paul Edward 1952- *WhoScEn 94*
Sowada, Alphonse Augustus 1933- *WhoAm 94*
Sowande, Bode 1948- *ConDr 93*
Soward, Andrew Michael 1943- *Who 94*
Sowards, George d1975 *WhoHol 92*
Sowards, Paul Michael 1967- *WhoAmP 93*
Sowden, John Percival 1917- *Who 94*
Sowden, Lewis 1905-1974 *EncSF 93*
Sowden, Terence Cubitt 1929- *Who 94*
Sowden, William Carl 1951- *WhoWest 94*
Sowder, Donald Dillard 1937- *WhoScEn 94*
Sowder, Fred Allen 1940- *WhoMW 93*
Sowder, Robert Robertson 1928- *WhoAm 94, WhoScEn 94, WhoWest 94*
Sowell, Ernest Eugene 1950- *WhoAmL 94*
Sowell, James Adolf 1943- *WhoScEn 94*
Sowell, Madison Upshaw 1952- *WhoWest 94*
Sowell, Mike 1948- *WrDr 94*
Sowell, Myzell 1924- *WhoBlA 94*
Sowell, Polly Rollins *WhoAmP 93*
Sowell, Thomas 1930- *BlkWr 2, WhoAm 94, WhoBlA 94, WrDr 94*
Sower, Christopher 1754-1799 *WhAmRev*
Sowers, David Eric 1946- *WhoAmL 94*
Sowers, Edward Eugene 1942- *WhoAmL 94, WhoScEn 94*
Sowers, George Frederick 1921- *WhoAm 94*
Sowers, Jacquelyn J. 1945- *WhoMW 93*
Sowers, Miriam R. 1922- *WhoAmA 93*
Sowers, Miriam Ruth 1922- *WhoWest 94*
Sowers, Wesley H. 1905- *WhoAmP 93*
Sowers, Wesley Hoyt 1905- *WhoAm 94*
Sowers, William Armand 1923- *WhoAm 94*
Sowerwine, Elbert Orla, Jr. 1915- *WhoFI 94, WhoWest 94*
Sow Fall, Aminata *ConWorW 93*
Sow Fall, Aminata 1941- *BlmGWL*
Sowinski, James 1955- *WhoMW 93*
Sowinski, Stanislaus Joseph 1927- *WhoAmA 93, WhoWest 94*
Sowko, Victoria Ann 1969- *WhoMW 93*
Sowle, Donald Edgar 1915- *WhoAm 94*
Sowle, John Steven 1944- *WhoWest 94*
Sowles, Marcia Kay 1950- *WhoAmL 94*
Sowman, Harold Gene 1923- *WhoAm 94*
Sowrey, Frederick (Beresford) 1922- *Who 94*
Sowry, (George Stephen) Clive 1917- *Who 94*
Sox, Harold Carleton, Jr. 1939- *WhoAm 94, WhoScEn 94*
Soydemir, Cetin 1935- *WhoScEn 94*
Soyer, David 1923- *WhoAm 94*
Soyer, Isaac 1902-1981 *WhoAmA 93N*
Soyer, Moses 1899-1974 *WhoAmA 93N*
Soyer, Roger (Julien Jacques) 1939- *NewGrDO*
Soyfer, Valery Nikolayevich 1936- *WhoScEn 94*
Soyinka, Wole 1934- *BlkWr 2, BlmGEL, ConDr 93, IntDcT 2 [port], IntWW 93, Who 94, WrDr 94*
Soyka, Otto *EncSF 93*
Soysa, Warusahennedige Abraham Bastian *Who 94*
Soysal, Sevgi 1936-1976 *BlmGWL*
Soyster, Margaret Blair 1951- *WhoAm 94*
Soza, Michael William 1964- *WhoWest 94*
Soza, William 1936- *WhoHisp 94*
Sozansky, Michael William, Jr. 1949- *WhoAmL 94*
Sozen, Mete Avni 1930- *WhoAm 94*
Sozio, Armando d1966 *WhoAmA 93N*
Spaak, Antoinette 1928- *WhoWomW 91*
Spaak, Catherine 1945- *WhoHol 92*
Spaak, Charles d1975 *WhoHol 92*
Spaak, Charles 1903-1975 *IntDcF 2-4*
Spaan, Willy Josephus 1954- *WhoScEn 94*
Spaar, Lisa Russ *DrAPF 93*
Space, Ace *DrAPF 93*
Space, Arthur d1983 *WhoHol 92*
Space, Theodore Maxwell 1938- *WhoAmL 94, WhoFI 94*
Spacek, Mary Elizabeth (Sissy) 1949- *IntWW 93*
Spacek, Sissy 1949- *IntMPA 94, WhoAm 94, WhoHol 92*
Spacey, John G. d1940 *WhoHol 92*
Spacey, Kevin 1959- *IntMPA 94, WhoAm 94, WhoHol 92*
Spach, John Thom *DrAPF 93*
Spach, Jule Christian 1923- *WhoAm 94*
Spach, Madison Stockton 1926- *WhoAm 94*
Spache, George D. 1909- *WrDr 94*
Spachman, Alan R. 1947- *WhoFI 94*
Spacie, Anne 1945- *WhoMW 93*
Spacie, Keith 1935- *Who 94*
Spackman, Christopher John 1934- *Who 94*
Spackman, David Glendinning 1948- *WhoAm 94, WhoAmL 94*
Spackman, John William Charles 1932- *Who 94*
Spackman, Michael John 1936- *Who 94*
Spackman, Spike d1981 *WhoHol 92*
Spackman, Thomas James 1937- *WhoAm 94*
Spacks, Barry *DrAPF 93*
Spacks, Barry 1931- *WrDr 94*
Spacks, Patricia Meyer 1929- *WhoAm 94, WrDr 94*
Spacu, Petru George 1906- *WhoScEn 94*
Spada, Marianne Rina 1955- *WhoScEn 94*
Spadafora, David Charles 1951- *WhoAm 94*
Spadaro, Charlotte *WhoAmP 93*
Spadaro, Douglas Sebastian 1956- *WhoAm 94*
Spadaro, Odoardo d1965 *WhoHol 92*
Spadaro, Umberto d1981 *WhoHol 92*
Spadavecchia, Antonio Emmanuilovich 1907-1988 *NewGrDO*
Spade, George Lawrence 1945- *WhoScEn 94, WhoWest 94*
Spade, Julie Ann 1958- *WhoMW 93*
Spader, James 1960- *IntMPA 94, WhoAm 94, WhoHol 92*
Spadolini, Giovanni 1925- *IntWW 93*
Spadoro, George A. 1948- *WhoAmP 93*
Spaeder, Roger Campbell 1943- *WhoAm 94, WhoAmL 94*
Spaeh, Winfried Heinrich 1930- *WhoFI 94*
Spaepen, Frans August 1948- *WhoAm 94, WhoScEn 94*
Spaeth, Anthony 1955- *WrDr 94*
Spaeth, Carl Bernhardt 1907-1991 *WhAm 10*
Spaeth, Edmund Benjamin, Jr. 1920- *WhoAm 94, WhoAmL 94*
Spaeth, Eloise O'Mara 1904- *WhoAmA 93*
Spaeth, Gary Lewis 1945- *WhoAmP 93*
Spaeth, George Link 1932- *WhoAm 94*
Spaeth, Joseph Louis 1940- *WhoWest 94*
Spaeth, Karl Henry 1929- *WhoAm 94, WhoFI 94*
Spaeth, Kevin Barry 1950- *WhoAmL 94*
Spaeth, Mary 1938?- *WorInv*
Spaeth, Mary Shepard 1957- *WhoMW 93*
Spaeth, Merrie 1949- *WhoHol 92*
Spaeth, Nicholas 1950- *WhoAmP 93*
Spaeth, Nicholas John 1950- *WhoAm 94, WhoAmL 94, WhoMW 93*
Spaeth, Otto 1897-1966 *WhoAmA 93N*
Spafford, Baby Charlie d1935 *WhoHol 92*
Spafford, Christopher Garnett Howsin 1924- *Who 94*
Spafford, Eugene Howard 1956- *WhoMW 93*
Spafford, George Christopher Howsin 1921- *Who 94*
Spafford, Michael Charles 1935- *WhoAm 94, WhoAmA 93, WhoWest 94*
Spafford, Roswell *DrAPF 93*
Spaght, Monroe E. d1993 *NewYTBS 93 [port], Who 94N*
Spaght, Monroe Edward 1909- *IntWW 93*
Spagna, Arcangelo c. 1632-1726 *NewGrDO*
Spagnardi, Ronald Lee 1943- *WhoAm 94*
Spagnoletto *NewGrDO*
Spagnoletto, Lo *NewGrDO*
Spagnoli, Clementina c. 1735-1778? *NewGrDO*
Spagnolo, Joseph A., Jr. 1943- *WhoAm 94*
Spagnolo, Kathleen Mary 1919- *WhoAmA 93*
Spagnuolo, Filomena d1987 *WhoHol 92*
Spahle, Michael Thomas 1952- *WhoWest 94*
Spahn, Gary Joseph 1949- *WhoAm 94, WhoAmL 94*
Spahn, Gerard Joseph 1938- *WhoWest 94*
Spahn, John Nick 1928- *WhoAmP 93*
Spahn, Mary Attea 1929- *WhoAm 94*
Spahr, Charles Eugene 1913- *IntWW 93*
Spahr, Frederick Thomas 1939- *WhoAm 94*
Spahr, Sidney Louis 1935- *WhoMW 93*
Spaht, Katherine S. 1946- *WhoAmL 94*
Spaight, Richard Dobbs 1758-1802 *WhAmRev*
Spaights, Ernest 1935-1991 *WhoBlA 94N*
Spain, David M. d1993 *NewYTBS 93 [port]*
Spain, Fay d1983 *WhoHol 92*
Spain, Hiram, Jr. 1936- *WhoBlA 94*
Spain, Jack Holland, Jr. 1939- *WhoAm 94*
Spain, James Dorris, Jr. 1929- *WhoAm 94*
Spain, James Earl 1934- *WhoAmP 93*
Spain, James W. 1926- *IntWW 93, WhoAmP 93*
Spain, James William 1926- *WhoAm 94*
Spain, Mark *WhoHol 92*
Spain, Nancy d1964 *WhoHol 92*
Spain, Robert J. 1956- *WhoAmP 93*
Spain, Russell Keith 1944- *WhoWest 94*
Spain, Thomas B. *WhoAmL 94*
Spain, Thomas B. 1928- *WhoAmP 93*
Spainard, Earl d1983 *WhoHol 92*
Spainhour, Kyle 1960- *WhoMW 93*
Spainhour, Tremaine Howard 1924- *WhoAm 94*
Spak, Lorin Mitchell 1941- *WhoAm 94*
Spak, Walter Joseph 1951- *WhoAm 94*
Spake, Karen Jo 1943- *WhoMW 93*
Spake, Ned Bernarr 1933- *WhoAm 94*
Spake, Robert Wright 1923- *WhoScEn 94*
Spakes, Patricia Ann 1948- *WhoWest 94*
Spalatin, Ivo Joseph 1946- *WhoAmP 93*
Spalding, Albert d1953 *WhoHol 92*
Spalding, Andrew Freeman 1951- *WhoAm 94, WhoAmL 94*
Spalding, (Dudley) Brian 1923- *Who 94*
Spalding, Catherine *WhoAmL 94*
Spalding, Catherine Hamilton *WhoAmL 94*
Spalding, D. Brian 1923- *IntWW 93*
Spalding, Eliza Hart 1807-1851 *EncNAR*
Spalding, Elizabeth Ann *WhoMW 93*
Spalding, Frances 1950- *Who 94, WrDr 94*
Spalding, George Robert 1927- *WhoScEn 94*
Spalding, Henry Cannon, Jr. 1938- *WhoFI 94*
Spalding, Henry Harmon 1803-1874 *EncNAR, WhWE*
Spalding, Ian Jaffery L. *Who 94*
Spalding, James Stuart 1934- *WhoAm 94, WhoFI 94*
Spalding, John Lancaster 1840-1916 *DcAmReB 2*
Spalding, John Oliver 1924- *Who 94*
Spalding, John V. 1897- *WhAm 10*
Spalding, Julian 1947- *Who 94*
Spalding, Keith 1913- *WrDr 94*
Spalding, Kenneth Lee 1938- *WhoFI 94*
Spalding, Martin John 1810-1872 *DcAmReB 2*
Spalding, Peter Frederick 1937- *WhoAm 94*
Spalding, Richard Daniel 1948- *WhoFI 94*
Spalding, Ruth *WrDr 94*
Spalding, Thomas James 1948- *WhoFI 94*
Spall, Richard Francis, Jr. 1952 *WhoFI 94*
Spall, Timothy *WhoHol 92*
Spalla, Erminio d1971 *WhoHol 92*
Spallanzani, Lazzaro 1729-1799 *WorScD [port]*
Spallone, Henry J. *WhoAmP 93*
Spalt, Karl Heinz G. 1913- *WrDr 94*
Spalten, Rona *DrAPF 93*
Spaltro, Suree Methmanus 1953- *WhoScEn 94*
Spalty, Edward Robert 1946- *WhoAm 94, WhoAmL 94*
Spalvins, Janis Gunars 1936- *IntWW 93, Who 94*
Spamer, Earle Edward 1952- *WhoScEn 94*
Spampinato, Clemente 1912- *WhoAmA 93*
Span, Robert Steven 1947- *WhoAm 94, WhoAmL 94*
Spanbauer, Tom *ConAu 142, DrAPF 93*
Spanbock, Maurice Samuel 1924- *WhoAmL 94*
Spander, Art 1938- *WhoAm 94*
Spandorf, Lily Gabriella *WhoAmA 93*
Spandorfer, Merle Sue 1934- *WhoAm 94, WhoAmA 93*
Spanel, Harriet *WhoAmP 93*
Spanel, Harriet Rose Albertsen 1939- *WhoWest 94*
Spanfelner, Robert Bruce 1939- *WhoIns 94*
Spang, James Thomas, Jr. 1957- *WhoAmP 93*
Spang, Laurette 1951- *WhoHol 92*
Spangenberg, Augustus Gottlieb 1704-1792 *DcAmReB 2*
Spangenberg, Christa 1928- *IntWW 93*
Spangenberg, Kristin L. 1944- *WhoAmA 93*
Spang-Hanssen, Ebbe 1928- *IntWW 93*
Spangler, Arnold Eugene 1948- *WhoAm 94*
Spangler, Clemmie Dixon, Jr. 1932- *WhoAm 94*
Spangler, David Robert 1940- *WhoAm 94*
Spangler, Jack Leland 1936- *WhoFI 94*

Spangler, Jerry L. 1952- *WhoAmP 93*
Spangler, John Thomas 1953- *WhoAmL 94*
Spangler, Kenneth Lee 1940- *WhoAmL 94*
Spangler, Lorna Carrie 1938- *WhoWest 94*
Spangler, (Maria) Maddalena (Rosalie) 1750-1794 *NewGrDO*
Spangler, Miller Brant 1923- *WhoAm 94, WhoScEn 94*
Spangler, Ronald Leroy 1937- *WhoFI 94*
Spangler, Scott Michael 1938- *WhoAm 94*
Spani, Hina 1896-1969 *NewGrDO*
Spaniardi, Richard J. 1936- *WhoIns 94*
Spanier, Edward Jacob 1937- *WhoFI 94*
Spanier, Francis d1981 *WhoHol 92*
Spanier, Graham Basil 1948- *WhoAm 94, WhoMW 93, WhoScEn 94*
Spanier, Jerome 1930- *WhoWest 94*
Spanier, Muggsy d1967 *WhoHol 92*
Spanier, Muriel *DrAPF 93*
Spanier, Sandra Whipple 1951- *ConAu 141*
Spanier, Suzy Peta *Who 94*
Spaniol, Dennis J. *WhoAmP 93*
Spaniola, Francis Richard 1935- *WhoAmP 93*
Spanke, Timothy Lee 1948- *WhoMW 93*
Spankie, Hugh Oliver 1936- *Who 94*
Spann, Ann Olive 1917- *WhoAmP 93*
Spann, Bettye Jean Patterson 1930- *WhoMW 93*
Spann, George William 1946- *WhoAm 94, WhoFI 94*
Spann, Hyman Dale, Jr. 1935- *WhoMW 93*
Spann, Katharine Doyle *WhoWest 94*
Spann, Keith 1922- *Who 94*
Spann, Laura Nason 1947- *WhoFI 94*
Spann, Noah Atterson, Jr. 1938- *WhoBlA 94*
Spann, Paul Ronald 1943- *WhoBlA 94*
Spann, Ronald Thomas 1949- *WhoAmL 94*
Spann, Stephen Allison 1941- *WhoWest 94*
Spann, Theresa Tieuel 1918- *WhoBlA 94*
Spann, Weldon Oma 1924- *WrDr 94*
Spannaus, Warren Richard 1930- *WhoAmP 93*
Spanner, E(dward) F(rank) 1888- *EncSF 93*
Spanner, Gary Earl 1954- *WhoWest 94*
Spanner, Jack C. 1952- *WhoWest 94*
Spano, August John 1921- *WhoAmP 93*
Spano, Joe 1946- *WhoHol 92*
Spano, Nicholas A. 1953- *WhoAmP 93*
Spano, Vincent 1962- *IntMPA 94, WhoHol 92*
Spanogle, Robert William 1942- *WhoAm 94*
Spanos, Alexander Gus 1923- *WhoAm 94, WhoWest 94*
Spanos, Dean A. 1950- *WhoAm 94*
Spanos, Elias 1948- *WhoFI 94*
Spanos, Harry V. 1926- *WhoAmP 93*
Spanos, James Christopher 1962- *WhoAmL 94*
Spanos, Marcos 1932- *IntWW 93*
Spanos, Pol Dimitrios 1950- *WhoScEn 94*
Spanovich, Milan 1929- *WhoAm 94*
Spanton, (Harry) Merrik 1924- *Who 94*
Spar, Edward Joel 1939- *WhoAm 94*
Spar, Warren Hal 1953- *WhoFI 94*
Sparano, Mark Paul 1964- *WhoFI 94*
Sparano, Vincent Thomas 1934- *WhoAm 94*
Sparberg, Esther B. 1922- *WhoAm 94*
Sparberg, Marshall Stuart 1936- *WhoAm 94*
Sparby, Wallace A. *WhoAmP 93*
Sparer, Malcolm Martin *WhoAm 94*
Sparer, Paul *WhoHol 92*
Sparey, John Raymond 1924- *Who 94*
Sparger, William Harry 1942- *WhoWest 94*
Spargo, Peter Ernest 1937- *IntWW 93*
Spark, Muriel 1918- *BlmGEL [port], BlmGWL, DcLB 139 [port]*
Spark, Muriel (Sarah) *Who 94*
Spark, Muriel (Sarah) 1918- *TwCYAW, WrDr 94*
Spark, Muriel Sarah *IntWW 93, WhoAm 94*
Spark, Victor David 1898-1991 *WhoAmA 93N*
Sparke, Michael c. 1588-1653 *DcNaB MP*
Sparkes, Robert Lyndley 1929- *Who 94*
Sparkman, Brandon Buster 1929- *WhoAm 94*
Sparkman, Gene (Carl), Jr. 1941- *WhoAmA 93*
Sparkman, Robert Satterfield 1912- *WhoAm 94*
Sparkman, Steven Leonard 1947- *WhoAm 94, WhoAmL 94*
Sparkrock, Fred *EncSF 93*
Sparks, Arthur Charles 1914- *Who 94*
Sparks, Bertel Milas 1918- *WhoAm 94*
Sparks, Billy Schley 1923- *WhoAmL 94, WhoFI 94, WhoMW 93*
Sparks, Dana *WhoHol 92*
Sparks, David Emerson 1944- *WhoAm 94*
Sparks, David Glen 1948- *WhoIns 94*
Sparks, David Lee 1931- *WhoFI 94*
Sparks, David Stanley 1922- *WhoAm 94*
Sparks, Edward Franklin 1937- *WhoBlA 94*
Sparks, Ella Warden 1912- *WhoAmP 93*
Sparks, Gary Dean 1959- *WhoAmP 93*
Sparks, Gordon 1935- *WhoAmP 93*
Sparks, Greg Louis 1955- *WhoMW 93*
Sparks, Harry Alan 1953- *WhoMW 93*
Sparks, Harvey Vise, Jr. 1938- *WhoAm 94*
Sparks, Hedley Frederick Davis 1908- *Who 94*
Sparks, Ian Leslie 1943- *Who 94*
Sparks, Irving Alan 1933- *WhoWest 94*
Sparks, Jack Norman 1928- *WhoWest 94*
Sparks, Jessica J. *WhoWest 94*
Sparks, John Edward 1930- *WhoAm 94, WhoAmL 94*
Sparks, John Edwin 1942- *WhoAmA 93*
Sparks, Larry Leon 1940- *WhoScEn 94*
Sparks, Melvin 1921- *WhoMW 93*
Sparks, Merrill 1922- *WhoMW 93*
Sparks, Morgan 1916- *WhoAm 94*
Sparks, Ned d1957 *WhoHol 92*
Sparks, Randy *WhoHol 92*
Sparks, Robert Dean 1932- *WhoAm 94, WhoWest 94*
Sparks, Robert Hermon 1958- *WhoMW 93*
Sparks, Robert Stephen John 1949- *IntWW 93*
Sparks, Robert William 1925- *WhoAm 94, WhoWest 94*
Sparks, Sam 1939- *WhoAm 94, WhoAmL 94*
Sparks, Sherman Paul 1909- *WhoScEn 94*
Sparks, (Robert) Stephen (John) 1949- *Who 94*
Sparks, Thomas E., Jr. 1942- *WhoAm 94, WhoAmL 94*
Sparks, Walter Chappel 1918- *WhoAm 94, WhoWest 94*
Sparks, William Sidney 1951- *WhoScEn 94*
Sparks, Willis Breazeal, III 1934- *WhoAmL 94*
Sparlin, Don Merle 1937- *WhoScEn 94*
Sparlin, W. Michael 1958- *WhoMW 93*
Sparling, James Milton, Jr. 1928- *WhoAmP 93*
Sparling, Mary Christine 1928- *WhoAm 94*
Sparling, Peter David 1951- *WhoAm 94*
Sparr, Daniel Beattie 1931- *WhoAm 94, WhoAmL 94, WhoWest 94*
Sparrazza, Lucille Angela 1954- *WhoFI 94*
Sparrevohn, Frederic Reidtz 1943- *WhoWest 94*
Sparrgrove, Dewain A. 1941- *WhoIns 94*
Sparrman, Anders 1747-1820 *WhWE*
Sparrow, Barbara Jane 1935- *WhoAm 94*
Sparrow, Bryan 1933- *Who 94*
Sparrow, Charles *Who 94*
Sparrow, (Albert) Charles 1925- *Who 94*
Sparrow, Donald *WhoWest 94*
Sparrow, Ephraim Maurice 1928- *WhoAm 94*
Sparrow, Fox *DrAPF 93*
Sparrow, Gregory Brennan 1951- *WhoAmP 93*
Sparrow, Herbert George, III 1936- *WhoAm 94*
Sparrow, John 1933- *Who 94*
Sparrow, Larry Clinton 1947- *WhoMW 93*
Sparrow, Larry J. *WhoAm 94, WhoFI 94, WhoWest 94*
Sparrow, Philip *GayLL*
Sparrow, Rory Darnell 1958- *WhoBlA 94*
Sparrowe, Rollin D. *WhoScEn 94*
Sparshott, Francis (Edward) 1926- *WrDr 94*
Sparshott, Francis Edward 1926- *WhoAm 94*
Sparso, Henning Hempel 1929- *WhoAm 94*
Spartacus, Deutero *EncSF 93*
Spartacus, Tertius *ConAu 42NR*
Spartali, Marie 1843-1927 *DcNaB MP*
Sparv, Camilla 1943- *WhoHol 92*
Spasov, Bozhidar 1949- *NewGrDO*
Spassky, Boris Vasiliyevich 1937- *IntWW 93*
Spataro, Vincent John 1953- *WhoScEn 94*
Spater, Thomas C. 1937- *WhoAmP 93*
Spater-Zimmerman, Susan *WhoScEn 94*
Spates, Frank Harris *WhoAmP 93*
Spath, Gregg Anthony 1952- *WhoAmL 94*
Spath, Lothar 1937- *IntWW 93*
Spatley, James R. d1987 *WhoHol 92*
Spatt, Arthur D. 1925- *WhoAm 94, WhoAmL 94*
Spatt, Robert Edward 1956- *WhoAm 94, WhoAmL 94*
Spatuzza, John George 1925- *WhoAmL 94, WhoMW 93*
Spatz, Jacob William 1909- *WhoWest 94*
Spatz, Kenneth Chris 1940- *WhoScEn 94*
Spatz, Kenneth Christopher, Jr. 1940- *WrDr 94*
Spatz, Lois Settler 1940- *WhoMW 93*
Spatz, Ronald *DrAPF 93*
Spatz, Ronald Marvin 1949- *WhoWest 94*
Spaulding, Aaron Lowery 1943- *WhoBlA 94*
Spaulding, Albert Lee d1992 *WhoBlA 94N*
Spaulding, Daniel Alexander 1963- *WhoFI 94, WhoMW 93*
Spaulding, Daniel W. 1909- *WhoBlA 94*
Spaulding, Frank Henry 1932- *WhoAm 94*
Spaulding, George d1959 *WhoHol 92*
Spaulding, George B. 1952- *WhoAmP 93*
Spaulding, John *DrAPF 93*
Spaulding, John Pierson 1917- *WhoAm 94, WhoFI 94, WhoWest 94*
Spaulding, Josiah A. 1923- *WhoAmP 93*
Spaulding, Kenneth Bridgeforth 1944- *WhoBlA 94*
Spaulding, Kermit R. 1936- *WhoAmP 93*
Spaulding, Lynette Victoria 1954- *WhoBlA 94*
Spaulding, Peter J. 1944- *WhoAmP 93*
Spaulding, Richard W. 1949- *WhoIns 94*
Spaulding, Robert Mark 1929- *WhoAm 94*
Spaulding, Roma Alma 1914- *WhoAmP 93*
Spaulding, Romeo Orlando 1940- *WhoBlA 94*
Spaulding, William *WhoAmP 93*
Spaulding, William Ridley *WhoBlA 94*
Spaulding, William Rowe 1915- *WhoFI 94*
Spaulding, Winston 1939- *IntWW 93*
Spaventa, George 1918-1978 *WhoAmA 93N*
Spaventa, Luigi 1934- *IntWW 93*
Spawforth, David Meredith 1938- *Who 94*
Spaziani, Maria Luisa 1924- *BlmGWL*
Speaight, George 1914- *WrDr 94*
Speaight, Robert d1976 *WhoHol 92*
Speake, Theresa Alvillar 1940- *WhoHisp 94*
Speaker, Edwin Ellis 1928- *WhoScEn 94*
Speaker, Gary David 1948- *WhoWest 94*
Speaker, Ray 1935- *WhoWest 94*
Speaker, Susan Jane 1946- *WhoAmL 94*
Speakes, Larry 1939- *WhoAmP 93*
Speakes, Larry Melvin 1939- *IntWW 93, WhoAm 94*
Speakman, Jeff 1957- *WhoHol 92*
Speakman-Pitt, William 1927- *Who 94*
Speaks, Jerry Mark 1956- *WhoFI 94, WhoWest 94*
Speaks, John Charles, IV 1951- *WhoFI 94*
Spear, Allan Henry 1937- *WhoAm 94, WhoAmP 93, WhoMW 93, WrDr 94*
Spear, Amy M. 1962- *WhoAmP 93*
Spear, Arthur P. 1879-1959 *WhoAmA 93N*
Spear, Barbara L. 1926- *WhoAmP 93*
Spear, Bernard 1919- *WhoHol 92*
Spear, Clay R. 1916- *WhoAmP 93*
Spear, E. Eugene 1938- *WhoBlA 94*
Spear, Harold Cumming 1909- *Who 94*
Spear, Harry d1969 *WhoHol 92*
Spear, Harvey M. 1922- *WhoAm 94*
Spear, Henry Dyke Newcome, Jr. 1935- *WhoAmL 94*
Spear, Hilda D. 1926- *WrDr 94*
Spear, James Hodges 1952- *WhoAmL 94*
Spear, Jean *DrAPF 93*
Spear, Laurinda Hope 1950- *WhoAmA 93*
Spear, Michael David 1941-1990 *WhAm 10*
Spear, Richard Edmund 1940- *WhoAm 94, WhoAmA 93*
Spear, Robert Clinton 1939- *WhoAm 94*
Spear, Robert Steven 1947- *WhoAmL 94*
Spear, Robert W. 1943- *WhoAmP 93*
Spear, Roberta L. *DrAPF 93*
Spear, Traci Lynnette 1964- *WhoMW 93*
Spear, Walter Eric 1921- *IntWW 93, Who 94*
Spear, Wayne, Jr. 1952- *WhoAmP 93*
Speare, Elizabeth George 1908- *TwCYAW, WhoAm 94, WrDr 94*
Spearing, Anthony Colin 1936- *Who 94, WhoAm 94*
Spearing, George David 1927- *Who 94*
Spearing, Nigel John 1930- *Who 94*
Spearly, James Luther 1950- *WhoWest 94*
Spearman, Alexander Young Richard Mainwaring 1969- *Who 94*
Spearman, Clement 1919- *Who 94*
Spearman, James Box 1960- *WhoAmP 93*
Spearman, John L. 1941- *Who 94*
Spearman, Larna Kaye 1945- *WhoBlA 94*
Spearman, Leonard H. O., Sr. 1929- *WhoAm 94, WhoAmP 93*
Spearman, Leonard Hall O'Connell, Sr. 1929- *WhoBlA 94*
Spearman, Maxie Ann 1942- *WhoFI 94*
Spearman, Molly M. *WhoAmP 93*
Spearman, Patsy Cordle 1934- *WhoFI 94*
Spearman, Robert Worthington 1943- *WhoAmL 94, WhoAmP 93*
Spearman, Terence Neil 1948- *WhoScEn 94*
Spearman, Thomas David 1937- *IntWW 93*
Spear-Obermiller, Mary Patricia 1954- *WhoAm 94*
Spears, Alexander White, III 1932- *WhoAm 94*
Spears, Carleton Blaise 1958- *WhoAmL 94*
Spears, Carolyn Lee 1944- *WhoFI 94, WhoWest 94*
Spears, Franklin Scott 1931- *WhoAm 94, WhoAmP 93*
Spears, Gregory Luttrell 1956- *WhoAm 94*
Spears, Harold T., Jr. 1929- *IntMPA 94*
Spears, (Marion) Heather 1934- *WrDr 94*
Spears, Henry Albert, Sr. 1928- *WhoBlA 94*
Spears, Jae *WhoAmP 93*
Spears, Jo Ann Smith 1936- *WhoAmP 93*
Spears, Kenneth George 1943- *WhoMW 93*
Spears, Kenneth Owen, Jr. *WhoAmP 93*
Spears, Larry Jonell 1953- *WhoAmL 94*
Spears, Laura Elizabeth 1953- *WhoMW 93*
Spears, Marian Caddy 1921- *WhoAm 94*
Spears, Melvin Stanley 1927- *WhoAmL 94*
Spears, Monroe K(irk) 1916- *WrDr 94*
Spears, Randall Lynn 1960- *WhoScEn 94*
Spears, Richard W. 1936- *WhoFI 94*
Spears, Robert Fields 1943- *WhoAmL 94*
Spears, Robert Lee 1932- *WhoWest 94*
Spears, Sally 1938- *WhoAm 94*
Spears, Sandra Calvette 1964- *WhoBlA 94*
Spears-Jones, Patricia Kay 1951- *WhoBlA 94*
Speas, Charles Stuart 1944- *WhoFI 94, WhoMW 93*
Speas, Raymond Aaron 1925- *WhoAm 94*
Speas, Robert Dixon 1916- *WhoAm 94, WhoScEn 94, WhoWest 94*
Spease, Joe Lovell 1952- *WhoMW 93*
Spech, Janos 1767-1836 *NewGrDO*
Spech-Salvi, Adelina 1811-1886 *NewGrDO*
Specht, Alice Wilson 1948- *WhoAm 94*
Specht, Eliot David 1959- *WhoScEn 94*
Specht, Gordon Dean 1927- *WhoScEn 94*
Specht, Joseph Phillip, Jr. 1957- *WhoMW 93*
Specht, Kurt Stephen 1956- *WhoFI 94*
Specht, Linda Gayle 1953- *WhoWest 94*
Specht, Lisa 1945- *WhoAmL 94*
Specia, John J., Jr. *WhoHisp 94*
Speciale, Richard 1945- *WhoAm 94, WhoFI 94*
Speck, David George 1945- *WhoAmP 93*
Speck, Francis William 1952- *WhoMW 93*
Speck, Hilda 1916- *WhoMW 93*
Speck, Janice Ann 1954- *WhoMW 93*
Speck, Kenneth Richard 1961- *WhoScEn 94*
Speck, Marvin Luther 1913- *WhoAm 94*
Speck, Robert Charles 1944- *WhoAm 94, WhoWest 94*
Speck, Samuel W., Jr. 1937- *WhoAmP 93*
Speck, Samuel Wallace, Jr. 1937- *WhoAm 94*
Speckman, John Thomas 1945- *WhoIns 94*
Specktor, Frederick 1933- *IntMPA 94*
Specktor, Peggy G. 1940- *WhoAmP 93*
Specter, Arlen 1930- *CngDr 93, IntWW 93, WhoAm 94, WhoAmP 93*
Specter, Howard Alan 1939- *WhoAmL 94*
Specter, Joan *WhoAmP 93*
Specter, Richard Bruce 1952- *WhoAmL 94, WhoWest 94*
Spector, Abraham 1926- *WhoAm 94*
Spector, Albert *DrAPF 93*
Spector, Arthur Jay 1949- *WhoAm 94, WhoAmL 94*
Spector, Buzz 1948- *WhoAmA 93*
Spector, Carlos *WhoHisp 94*
Spector, David M. 1946- *WhoAm 94, WhoAmL 94*
Spector, Donald M. 1954- *WhoAmL 94*
Spector, Earl M. 1939- *WhoFI 94*
Spector, Eleanor Ruth 1943- *WhoAm 94*
Spector, Gershon Jerry 1937- *WhoAm 94*
Spector, Harold Norman 1935- *WhoAm 94*
Spector, Harvey M. 1938- *WhoScEn 94*
Spector, Jack J. 1925- *WhoAmA 93*
Spector, Jack Jerome 1925- *WrDr 94*

Spector, Johanna Lichtenberg *WhoAm 94*
Spector, Jonathan Michael *WhoScEn 94*
Spector, Joseph Robert 1923- *WhoAm 94*
Spector, Leonard S. 1945- *WrDr 94*
Spector, Louis 1918- *WhoAm 94*
Spector, Marshall 1936- *WhoAm 94*
Spector, Martin Wolf 1938- *WhoAm 94, WhoAmL 94, WhoFI 94*
Spector, Melbourne Louis 1918- *WhoAm 94*
Spector, Naomi 1939- *WhoAmA 93*
Spector, Phil 1940- *WhoAm 94, WhoHol 92, WhoWest 94*
Spector, Phillip Louis 1950- *WhoAmL 94*
Spector, Robert D(onald) 1922- *WrDr 94*
Spector, Rose *WhoAmL 94, WhoAmP 93*
Spector, Roy Geoffrey 1931- *Who 94*
Spector, Sherman David 1927- *WrDr 94*
Spector, Stanley 1924- *WhoAm 94*
Spectre, Jay 1929-1992 *WhAm 10*
Spedale, Vincent John 1929- *WhoMW 93*
Spedding, Colin Raymond William 1925- *IntWW 93, Who 94*
Spedding, David Rolland 1943- *Who 94*
Speden, Ian Gordon 1932- *IntWW 93*
Speece, Richard Eugene 1933- *WhoAm 94*
Speece, Wynn Hubler 1917- *WhoMW 93*
Speech c. 1968-
See Arrested Development *News 94-2*
Speechley, Billy 1911- *WhoHol 92*
Speed, Billie Cheney 1927- *WhoAm 94*
Speed, Carol *DrAPF 93, WhoHol 92*
Speed, F(rederick) Maurice 1912- *WrDr 94*
Speed, Frank Warren 1911- *WrDr 94*
Speed, (Ulysses) Grant 1930- *WhoAmA 93*
Speed, James D. *WhoAmP 93*
Speed, James Thomas 1939- *WhoAmP 93*
Speed, John Sackett 1927- *WhoAm 94*
Speed, (Herbert) Keith 1934- *Who 94*
Speed, Martha Ray Matthews 1927- *WhoAmP 93*
Speed, Paul Scott 1957- *WhoMW 93*
Speed, Robert (William Arney) 1905- *Who 94*
Speede-Franklin, Wanda A. 1956- *WhoBlA 94*
Speegle, Paul d1982 *WhoHol 92*
Speegle, Philip Tenney 1938- *WhoFI 94*
Speelman, Cornelis Jacob 1917- *Who 94*
Speelmans, Hermann d1960 *WhoHol 92*
Speer, Albert 1905-1981 *HisWorL*
Speer, Allen Paul, III 1951- *WhoAm 94*
Speer, David Blakeney 1951- *WhoMW 93*
Speer, David James 1927- *WhoAm 94*
Speer, Doris Lynn 1958- *WhoAmL 94*
Speer, Edgar B. 1916-1979 *EncABHB 9 [port]*
Speer, G. William 1940- *WhoAm 94*
Speer, George Scott 1908-1992 *WhAm 10*
Speer, Jack Atkeson 1941- *WhoAm 94*
Speer, James Ramsey 1936- *WhoScEn 94*
Speer, Kathleen A. 1942- *WhoAmP 93*
Speer, Laurel *DrAPF 93*
Speer, Laurel 1940- *WrDr 94*
Speer, Lena Ruth *WhoAmP 93*
Speer, Margaret Marion 1918- *WhoAmP 93*
Speer, Phillip Bradford 1927- *WhoWest 94*
Speer, Richard Lyle 1941- *WhoAm 94, WhoAmL 94*
Speer, Richard Norwood, Jr. 1948- *WhoFI 94*
Speer, Robert Elliott 1867-1947 *DcAmReB 2*
Speer, Roy M. 1932- *WhoAm 94, WhoFI 94*
Speer, William Thomas, Jr. 1936- *WhoAm 94*
Speers, J. Alvin 1930- *WhoWest 94*
Speers, Misako Terui 1962- *WhoFI 94*
Speers, Roland Root, II 1933- *WhoAm 94*
Speers, William Charles 1946- *WhoAmL 94*
Speert, Arnold 1945- *WhoAm 94*
Speght, Rachel 1597- *BlmGWL*
Speice, John Michael 1961- *WhoFI 94*
Speicher, Carl Eugene 1933- *WhoMW 93*
Speicher, Eugene E. 1883-1962 *WhoAmA 93N*
Speicher, Gary Dean 1947- *WhoMW 93*
Speicher, Robert S. 1928- *WhoAmP 93*
Speicher, William Clayton 1937- *WhoFI 94*
Speidel, Carl Caskey 1893- *WhAm 10*
Speidel, David Harold 1938- *WhoAm 94*
Speidel, John Joseph 1937- *WhoAm 94*
Speidel, Richard Eli 1933- *WhoAm 94, WhoAmL 94*
Speier, John L. 1918- *WhoAm 94*
Speier, John Leo, Jr. 1918- *WhoScEn 94*
Speier, K. Jacqueline 1950- *WhoAmP 93*
Speier, Peter Michael 1946- *WhoScEn 94*
Speight, Ceole 1928- *WhoAmP 93*
Speight, Deborah Ann 1962- *WhoFI 94*
Speight, Eva B. 1930- *WhoBlA 94*
Speight, Francis 1896-1989 *WhoAmA 93N*
Speight, Graham (Davies) 1921- *Who 94*
Speight, James Glassford 1940- *WhoAm 94, WhoScEn 94*
Speight, Jerry Brooks 1942- *WhoAmA 93*
Speight, John Blain 1940- *WhoWest 94*
Speight, Johnny 1920- *ConDr 93, Who 94*
Speight, Johnny 1921- *WrDr 94*
Speight, Sarah Blakeslee *WhoAmA 93*
Speight, Velma R. 1932- *WhoBlA 94*
Speights, James Byron, II 1952- *WhoAmP 93*
Speights, John D. 1926- *WhoBlA 94*
Speights, Nathaniel H. 1949- *WhoBlA 94*
Speiginer, Gertha 1917- *WhoBlA 94*
Speir, Betty Smith 1928- *WhoAmP 93*
Speir, Dona *WhoHol 92*
Speir, Jeffrey Alan 1967- *WhoScEn 94*
Speir, Rupert (Malise) 1910- *Who 94*
Speiran, Edward Patrick 1950- *WhoAm 94, WhoAmL 94*
Speirs, Derek James 1933- *WhoAm 94*
Speirs, Graham Hamilton 1927- *Who 94*
Speirs, Robert Frank 1942- *WhoScEn 94*
Speirs, William James McLaren 1924- *Who 94*
Speiser, I. Bruce 1948- *WhoAmL 94*
Speiser, James Warren 1949- *WhoMW 93*
Speiser, Stuart M. 1923- *WhoAmA 93*
Speiser, Theodore Wesley 1934- *WhoWest 94*
Speitel, Gerald Eugene 1930- *WhoAm 94*
Speizer, Mark Adler 1943- *WhoIns 94*
Spejewski, Eugene Henry 1938- *WhoAm 94*
Speke, John Hanning 1827-1864 *WhWE*
Spekreijse, Henk 1940- *IntWW 93*
Spektor, Myron 1949- *WhoFI 94*
Spelfogel, Scott David 1960- *WhoAmL 94*
Speliotis, Theodore C. 1953- *WhoAmP 93*
Spelker, Arnold William 1934- *WhoAm 94*
Spell, George *WhoHol 92*
Spellacy, William Nelson 1934- *WhoScEn 94*
Spellane, Philip Gerard 1955- *WhoAmL 94*
Spellar, John Francis 1947- *Who 94*
Speller, Antony 1929- *Who 94*
Speller, Benjamin Franklin, Jr. 1940- *WhoAm 94*
Speller, Charles K. 1933- *WhoBlA 94*
Speller, Eugene Thurley 1928- *WhoBlA 94*
Speller, J. Finton 1909- *WhoBlA 94*
Speller, Norman Henry 1921- *Who 94*
Spelling, Aaron 1923- *WhoAm 94*
Spelling, Aaron 1928- *IntMPA 94, IntWW 93, WhoHol 92*
Spellman, Alfred B. 1935- *WhoBlA 94*
Spellman, Cathy Cash *WrDr 94*
Spellman, Douglas Toby 1942- *WhoFI 94, WhoWest 94*
Spellman, Ellen B. 1946- *WhoAmL 94*
Spellman, Eugene Paul 1930-1991 *WhAm 10*
Spellman, Francis Joseph 1889-1967 *DcAmReB 2*
Spellman, George Geneser, Sr. 1920- *WhoAm 94, WhoMW 93, WhoScEn 94*
Spellman, Henry Armstrong 1941- *WhoMW 93*
Spellman, John D. 1926- *IntWW 93, WhoAmP 93*
Spellman, John David 1935- *WhoWest 94*
Spellman, John H. 1945- *WhoAm 94*
Spellman, Leora d1945 *WhoHol 92*
Spellman, Martin *WhoHol 92*
Spellman, Oliver B., Jr. 1953- *WhoBlA 94*
Spellman, Robert Edward 1925- *WhoAmP 93*
Spellman, Robert Luther 1937- *WhoMW 93*
Spellman, Steven *WhoAmP 93*
Spellman, Thomas Joseph, Jr. 1938- *WhoAmL 94*
Spellman, W. M. 1956- *ConAu 141*
Spellmire, George W. 1948- *WhoAm 94, WhoAmL 94*
Spellmire, Sandra Marie 1950- *WhoMW 93*
Spelman, Jill Sullivan 1937- *WhoAmA 93*
Spelman, Mark G. 1945- *WhoAmL 94*
Spelman, Sharon *WhoHol 92*
Spelman, Timothy (Mather) 1891-1970 *NewGrDO*
Spelsberg, Thomas Coonan 1940- *WhoAm 94*
Spelson, Nicholas James 1923- *WhoMW 93*
Spelts, Richard John 1939- *WhoAm 94, WhoAmL 94, WhoWest 94*
Speltz, George Henry 1912- *WhoAm 94*
Spelvin, Georgina 1936- *WhoHol 92*
Spence, A. Michael 1943- *WhoAm 94, WhoFI 94, WhoWest 94*
Spence, Alastair Andrew 1936- *Who 94*
Spence, Andrew 1947- *WhoAm 94, WhoAmA 93*
Spence, Bill *ConAu 43NR*
Spence, Bill 1923- *WrDr 94*
Spence, Bruce 1945- *WhoHol 92*
Spence, Catherine Helen 1825-1910 *BlmGWL, EncSF 93*
Spence, Clark Christian 1923- *WhoAm 94*
Spence, Cynthia *SmATA 74*
Spence, Donald Dale 1926- *WhoBlA 94*
Spence, Donald Pond 1926- *WhoScEn 94*
Spence, Douglas Richard 1947- *WhoFI 94*
Spence, Duncan *ConAu 43NR*
Spence, Duncan 1923- *WrDr 94*
Spence, Eleanor 1928- *WrDr 94*
Spence, Eleanor (Rachel) 1928- *TwCYAW*
Spence, Fay Frances 1962- *WhoAmL 94*
Spence, Floyd 1928- *CngDr 93*
Spence, Floyd Davidson 1928- *WhoAm 94, WhoAmP 93*
Spence, Francis John *Who 94*
Spence, Gabriel John 1924- *Who 94*
Spence, Gerald Leonard 1929- *WhoAm 94, WhoAmL 94, WhoWest 94*
Spence, Gerry *NewYTBS 93 [port]*
Spence, Glen Oscar 1927- *WhoAm 94*
Spence, Harry Metcalfe 1905- *WhoAm 94*
Spence, Ian Richard 1938- *Who 94*
Spence, J. A. D. *ConAu 41NR*
Spence, James Robert, Jr. 1936- *WhoAm 94*
Spence, Jonathan D(ermot) 1936- *WrDr 94*
Spence, Jonathan Dermot 1936- *IntWW 93, WhoAm 94*
Spence, Joseph Samuel, Sr. 1950- *WhoBlA 94*
Spence, M. Anne 1944- *WhoAm 94*
Spence, Malcolm Hugh 1934- *Who 94*
Spence, Margaret 1944- *WhoMW 93*
Spence, Michael *DrAPF 93*
Spence, (Frederick) Michael (Alexander) T. *Who 94*
Spence, Paul Herbert 1923- *WhoAm 94*
Spence, Peter 1806-1883 *DcNaB MP*
Spence, Ralph d1949 *WhoHol 92*
Spence, Richard Dee 1925- *WhoAm 94*
Spence, Robert 1933- *Who 94*
Spence, Robert Atwell 1922- *WhoAmL 94*
Spence, Robert Dean 1917- *WhoAm 94*
Spence, Robert Leroy 1931- *WhoAm 94*
Spence, Sandra 1941- *WhoAm 94*
Spence, Stanley Brian 1937- *Who 94*
Spence, Terry R. 1941- *WhoAmP 93*
Spence, William Allen 1942- *WhoAmL 94*
Spence, William John Duncan 1923- *ConAu 43NR, WrDr 94*
Spencer *Who 94*
Spencer, Earl 1924-1992 *AnObit 1992*
Spencer, Earl 1964- *Who 94*
Spencer, Alan Douglas 1920- *Who 94*
Spencer, Alan H. 1937- *WhoIns 94*
Spencer, Alvie Glenn, Jr. 1933- *WhoAmP 93*
Spencer, Anne 1882-1975 *BlkWr 2*
Spencer, Anne Christine 1938- *Who 94*
Spencer, Anthony James Merrill 1929- *IntWW 93, Who 94*
Spencer, Anthony Lawrence 1946- *WhoBlA 94*
Spencer, Bill Raymond 1932- *WhoAm 94*
Spencer, Brenda L. 1951- *WhoBlA 94*
Spencer, Bud *WhoHol 92*
Spencer, Caroline *WhoWest 94*
Spencer, Charles 1920- *WrDr 94*
Spencer, Christopher 1930- *WrDr 94*
Spencer, Clifford Morris 1940- *WhoAmL 94*
Spencer, Colin 1933- *ConDr 93, WrDr 94*
Spencer, Cyril 1924- *Who 94*
Spencer, Cyril Charles 1912- *Who 94*
Spencer, Daniel P. 1948- *WhoIns 94*
Spencer, Danielle *WhoHol 92*
Spencer, Danielle 1965- *WhoHol 92*
Spencer, David d1976 *WhoHol 92*
Spencer, David James 1943- *WhoAm 94, WhoAmL 94*
Spencer, Deirdre Diane 1955- *WhoAmA 93*
Spencer, Derek (Harold) 1936- *Who 94*
Spencer, Donald Andrew 1915- *WhoBlA 94*
Spencer, Donald Clayton 1912- *IntWW 93, WhoAm 94, WhoScEn 94*
Spencer, Donald Spurgeon 1945- *WhoAm 94*
Spencer, Dora (Margaret) 1916- *WrDr 94*
Spencer, Douglas d1960 *WhoHol 92*
Spencer, Douglas Lloyd 1952- *WhoWest 94*
Spencer, Edgar Winston 1931- *WhoScEn 94*
Spencer, Elden A. 1929- *WhoAmP 93*
Spencer, Elihu 1721-1784 *WhAmRev*
Spencer, Elizabeth *DrAPF 93, IntWW 93*
Spencer, Elizabeth 1921- *BlmGWL, WhoAm 94, WrDr 94*
Spencer, Elmore 1969- *WhoBlA 94*
Spencer, Felton LaFrance 1968- *WhoBlA 94*
Spencer, Francis Montgomery James 1943- *WhoScEn 94*
Spencer, Frank dc. 1910 *EncNAR*
Spencer, Fred d1952 *WhoHol 92*
Spencer, Frederick Gilman 1925- *WhoAm 94*
Spencer, George Soule d1949 *WhoHol 92*
Spencer, Harold Edwin 1920- *WhoAmA 93*
Spencer, Harry Chadwick 1905- *WhoAm 94*
Spencer, Harry Irving, Jr. 1925- *WhoAm 94*
Spencer, Henry Benning 1940- *WhoAm 94*
Spencer, Herbert d1983 *WhoHol 92*
Spencer, Herbert d1993 *Who 94N*
Spencer, Herbert 1820-1903 *BlmGEL, EncEth*
Spencer, Herbert 1924- *Who 94*
Spencer, Herbert Ward, III 1945- *WhoWest 94*
Spencer, Howard Dalee 1950- *WhoAmA 93*
Spencer, Hugh 1887-1975 *WhoAmA 93N*
Spencer, Ian James 1916- *Who 94*
Spencer, Isabel Brannon 1940- *WhoAm 94*
Spencer, Isobel *Who 94*
Spencer, Ivan Carlton 1914- *WhoAm 94*
Spencer, James *DrAPF 93*
Spencer, James d1943 *WhoHol 92*
Spencer, James 1947- *Who 94*
Spencer, James Calvin, Sr. 1941- *WhoMW 93*
Spencer, James Owen, Jr. 1937- *WhoAmL 94*
Spencer, James R. *WhoAm 94, WhoAmL 94*
Spencer, Jeffrey Paul 1962- *WhoAmA 93*
Spencer, Joan Moore 1932- *WhoBlA 94*
Spencer, Joanna Miriam 1910- *Who 94*
Spencer, John *WhoHol 92*
Spencer, John 1935- *IntWW 93*
Spencer, John (Barry) 1944- *EncSF 93*
Spencer, John (Walter) 1922- *WrDr 94*
Spencer, John Hedley 1933- *WhoAm 94*
Spencer, John-K Joseph 1938- *WhoFI 94*
Spencer, John Loraine 1923- *Who 94*
Spencer, John Merrill 1919- *WhoAmP 93*
Spencer, John R. 1923- *WhoAmA 93*
Spencer, John Richard 1923- *WhoAm 94*
Spencer, Jonathan Page 1949- *Who 94*
Spencer, Joseph 1714-1789 *WhAmRev*
Spencer, Kelvin Tallent d1993 *Who 94N*
Spencer, Kenneth d1964 *WhoHol 92*
Spencer, Larry Lee 1948- *WhoBlA 94*
Spencer, Laura-Ann 1966- *WhoHisp 94*
Spencer, LaVyrle *WrDr 94*
Spencer, Lee Bowen, Jr. 1943- *WhoAmL 94*
Spencer, Leo 1941- *WhoAmP 93*
Spencer, Leonard G. *EncSF 93*
Spencer, Leontine G. 1882-1964 *WhoAmA 93N*
Spencer, Lewis Douglas 1917- *WhoAm 94*
Spencer, Lewis VanClief 1924- *WhoScEn 94*
Spencer, Lou d1972 *WhoHol 92*
Spencer, Lynne Delanty 1953- *WhoAmL 94*
Spencer, Margaret Beale 1944- *WhoBlA 94*
Spencer, Marian 1905- *WhoHol 92*
Spencer, Marian Alexander 1920- *WhoAmP 93, WhoBlA 94*
Spencer, Marion Wood 1916- *WhoAmP 93*
Spencer, Mark Edward 1954- *WhoMW 93*
Spencer, Mary Eileen 1923- *WhoAm 94*
Spencer, Melvin Joe 1923- *WhoAm 94*
Spencer, Merle Douglas 1963- *WhoMW 93*
Spencer, Michael C. 1951- *WhoAmL 94*
Spencer, Michael Gerald 1947- *Who 94*
Spencer, Michael Gregg 1952- *WhoBlA 94*
Spencer, Miles C. d1955 *WhoHol 92*
Spencer, Milton Harry 1926- *WhoAm 94, WhoMW 93*
Spencer, Neal Raymond 1936- *WhoWest 94*
Spencer, Niles 1893-1952 *WhoAmA 93N*
Spencer, Oscar Alan d1993 *Who 94N*
Spencer, Paul 1932- *WrDr 94*
Spencer, Paul Roger 1941- *WhoWest 94*
Spencer, Penny *WhoHol 92*
Spencer, Peter Simner 1946- *WhoScEn 94*
Spencer, Raine *WrDr 94*
Spencer, Ray Carlos 1957- *WhoAmP 93, WhoFI 94*
Spencer, Richard Paul 1929- *WhoAm 94*
Spencer, Richard R., Jr. 1943- *WhoAmL 94*
Spencer, Richard Rogers 1947- *WhoFI 94*
Spencer, Robert Acheson 1942- *WhoMW 93*
Spencer, Robert C. 1920- *WhoAm 94, WhoWest 94*
Spencer, Robert Edgar 1953- *WhoAmL 94*

Spencer, Robert Wilford 1938- *WhoAm 94, WhoWest 94*
Spencer, Roger Keith 1946- *WhoAm 94, WhoAmL 94*
Spencer, Rosemary Jane 1941- *Who 94*
Spencer, Ross H. 1921- *WrDr 94*
Spencer, Rozelle Jeffery 1936- *WhoBlA 94, WhoMW 93*
Spencer, Samuel 1910- *WhoAm 94*
Spencer, Samuel Burchard 1942- *WhoAmP 93, WhoFI 94*
Spencer, Samuel Reid, Jr. 1919- *WhoAm 94*
Spencer, Sarah Ann 1952- *Who 94*
Spencer, Scott *DrAPF 93, WrDr 94*
Spencer, Scott 1945- *WhoAm 94*
Spencer, Shanita Rene 1960- *WhoBlA 94*
Spencer, Sharon *DrAPF 93*
Spencer, Sharon 1947- *WhoAmP 93*
Spencer, Sharon A. *WhoBlA 94*
Spencer, Shaun Michael 1944- *Who 94*
Spencer, Steven D. 1953- *WhoAm 94*
Spencer, Susan Elizabeth 1954- *WhoAmA 93*
Spencer, Thomas C. 1946- *WhoScEn 94*
Spencer, Thomas Melvin, III 1949- *WhoFI 94*
Spencer, Thomas Newnham Bayley 1948- *Who 94*
Spencer, Thomas Roy 1944- *WhoAmL 94*
Spencer, Tim d1974 *WhoHol 92*
Spencer, Tracie *WhoBlA 94*
Spencer, Tricia Jane 1952- *WhoFI 94*
Spencer, Vaino Hassan 1920- *WhoAm 94*
Spencer, W. E. 1937- *WhoFI 94*
Spencer, Walter d1927 *WhoHol 92*
Spencer, Walter Thomas 1928- *WhoAmL 94*
Spencer, William 1922- *WrDr 94*
Spencer, William Browning 1946- *WrDr 94*
Spencer, William C. 1944- *WhoAmL 94*
Spencer, William Courtney 1919- *WhoAm 94*
Spencer, William Edwin 1926- *WhoFI 94, WhoMW 93*
Spencer, William Franklin, Sr. 1923- *WhoAm 94*
Spencer, William I. 1917- *IntWW 93*
Spencer, William I. 1932- *WhoAmP 93*
Spencer, William Stewart 1949- *WhoScEn 94*
Spencer, Winthrop W. 1897- *WhAm 10*
Spencer-Churchill *Who 94*
Spencer-Churchill, Randolph Frederick Edward 1911-1968 *DcNaB MP*
Spencer-Davidson, Paul Keiner 1957- *WhoWest 94*
Spencer-Green, George Thomas 1946- *WhoScEn 94*
Spencer-Nairn, Robert (Arnold) 1933- *Who 94*
Spencer-Olind, Rebecca 1953- *WhoHisp 94*
Spencer Paterson, Arthur *Who 94*
Spencer-Silver, Peter Hele 1922- *Who 94*
Spencer Smith, David 1934- *Who 94*
Spencer-Smith, John Hamilton 1947- *Who 94*
Spencer Wills *Who 94*
Spender, Dale 1943- *BlmGWL*
Spender, Frederick d1950 *WhoHol 92*
Spender, Percy C. 1897-1985 *HisDcKW*
Spender, Stephen 1909- *BlmGEL, IntWW 93*
Spender, Stephen (Harold) 1909- *GayLL, Who 94, WrDr 94*
Spendiaryan, Alexander (Step'anos Afanas) 1871-1928 *NewGrDO*
Spendlove, Peter Roy 1925- *Who 94*
Spendlove, Rex S. 1926- *WhoWest 94*
Spendlove, Rob *WhoHol 92*
Spengemann, Brian Frank 1942- *WhoFI 94*
Spengler, Dan M. 1941- *WhoAm 94*
Spengler, Joseph John 1902-1991 *WhAm 10*
Spengler, Karen Ann 1952- *WhoFI 94*
Spengler, Kenneth C. *WhoScEn 94*
Spengler, Pierre 1947- *IntMPA 94*
Spengler, Silas 1930- *WhoAm 94*
Spengler, Verne Champney 1932- *WhoMW 93*
Spenner, Gregory Alan 1964- *WhoAmP 93*
Spenny, Louise Virginia 1937- *WhoMW 93*
Speno, Fred Henry 1938- *WhoFI 94*
Spens, Baron 1942- *Who 94*
Spens, Colin Hope 1906- *Who 94*
Spens, John Alexander 1933- *Who 94*
Spenser, Edmund 1552?-1599 *BlmGEL [port], PoeCrit 8 [port]*
Spenser, Ian Daniel 1924- *WhoAm 94*
Spenser, Jeremy 1937- *IntMPA 94, WhoHol 92*
Spensley, Philip Calvert 1920- *Who 94*
Sperakis, Nicholas George 1943- *WhoAm 94, WhoAmA 93*
Sperandio, Glen Joseph 1918- *WhoAm 94*
Sperani, Bruno 1843- *BlmGWL*
Speransky, Nikolay Ivanovich 1877-1952 *NewGrDO*
Sperantzas, Vassilis 1938- *WhoAmA 93*
Speranza *BlmGWL*
Speranza, Giovanni Antonio 1811-1850 *NewGrDO*
Speraz, Beatrice *BlmGWL*
Sperber, Daniel 1930- *WhoAm 94, WhoScEn 94*
Sperber, David Sol 1939- *WhoAmL 94*
Sperber, Irwin *WhoScEn 94*
Sperber, Martin 1931- *WhoAm 94*
Sperber, Matthew Arnold 1938- *WhoFI 94*
Sperber, Milo *WhoHol 92*
Sperber, Wendie Jo 1962- *WhoHol 92*
Sperelakis, Nicholas 1930- *WhoAm 94, WhoScEn 94*
Sperlich, Harold K. 1929- *IntWW 93*
Sperlich, Peter W(erner) 1934- *WrDr 94*
Sperlich, Peter Werner 1934- *IntWW 93*
Sperling, Allan George 1942- *WhoAm 94, WhoAmL 94*
Sperling, Frederick J. 1953- *WhoAmL 94*
Sperling, George *WhoAm 94, WhoScEn 94*
Sperling, George Elmer, Jr. 1915- *WhoAm 94*
Sperling, Godfrey, Jr. 1915- *WhoAm 94*
Sperling, Peter Matthew 1943- *WhoFI 94*
Sperling, Robert Y. 1947- *WhoAm 94, WhoAmL 94*
Spero, Barry Melvin 1937- *WhoAm 94*
Spero, Brian J. *WhoAmP 93*
Spero, Joan Edelman 1944- *WhoAm 94, WhoFI 94*
Spero, Karen Weaver 1943- *WhoFI 94*
Spero, Kathy d1979 *WhoHol 92*
Spero, Keith Erwin 1933- *WhoAmL 94, WhoMW 93*
Spero, Morton Bertram 1920- *WhoAmL 94*
Spero, Nancy 1926- *WhoAmA 93*
Spero, Stanley Leonard 1919- *WhoAm 94, WhoWest 94*
Sperr, Martin 1944- *IntDcT 2*
Sperry, Elmer 1860-1930 *WorInv*
Sperry, James Edward 1936- *WhoMW 93*
Sperry, John Reginald 1924- *Who 94*
Sperry, Michael Winton 1946- *WhoAm 94*
Sperry, Robert 1927- *WhoAmA 93*
Sperry, Roger Wolcott 1913- *IntWW 93, Who 94, WhoAm 94, WhoScEn 94, WhoWest 94*
Sperry, Victoria B. 1943- *WhoWest 94*
Sperry, Warren Myron 1900-1990 *WhAm 10*
Sperryn, Simon George 1946- *Who 94*
Sperti, George Speri 1900-1991 *WhAm 10, WorInv*
Sperzel, Martin d1962 *WhoHol 92*
Speser, Philip Lester 1951- *WhoScEn 94, WhoWest 94*
Spessiva, Olga 1895-1991 *IntDcB [port]*
Spessivtseva, Olga 1895-1991 *IntDcB [port]*
Speth, Gerald Lennus 1934- *WhoFI 94, WhoMW 93*
Speth, James Gustave 1942- *WhoAm 94, WhoScEn 94*
Spetrino, Francesco 1857-1948 *NewGrDO*
Spetrino, Russell John 1926- *WhoAm 94*
Spetzler, Hartmut August Werner 1939- *WhoAm 94*
Spevacek, Joann M. 1935- *WhoAmP 93*
Spevack, Avrom David 1938- *WhoAmL 94*
Spevack, Marvin 1927- *WhoAm 94*
Spevak, Harvey Jay 1964- *WhoFI 94*
Spewack, Bella Cohen 1899-1990 *WhAm 10*
Speyer, Debra Gail 1959- *WhoAmL 94*
Speyer, Nora 1922- *WhoAmA 93*
Speyrer, Jude 1929- *WhoAm 94*
Spezia-Aldighieri, Maria *NewGrDO*
Speziale, A. John 1916- *WhoAm 94*
Speziale, John Albert 1922- *WhoAm 94*
Spezzano, Vincent Edward 1926- *WhoAm 94*
Sphar, Raymond Leslie, Jr. 1934- *WhoAm 94*
Spheeris, Penelope 1945- *ConTFT 11, IntMPA 94, WhoAm 94*
Sphire, Raymond Daniel 1927- *WhoAm 94, WhoMW 93*
Spialter, David C. 1952- *WhoAmL 94*
Spiberg, Philippe Frederic 1957- *WhoScEn 94*
Spicak, Doris Elizabeth 1943- *WhoFI 94*
Spiccia, Joseph George 1957- *WhoMW 93*
Spice, Dennis Dean 1950- *WhoFI 94, WhoMW 93*
Spicer, Carmelita 1946- *WhoBlA 94*
Spicer, Clive Colquhoun 1917- *Who 94*
Spicer, David *DrAPF 93*
Spicer, Eldon M. *WhoAmP 93*
Spicer, Erik John 1926- *WhoAm 94*
Spicer, Holt Vandercook 1928- *WhoAm 94*
Spicer, Jack 1925-1965 *GayLL*
Spicer, James (Wilton) 1925- *Who 94*
Spicer, Janeth Lee 1936- *WhoWest 94*
Spicer, Jean (Doris) Uhl 1935- *WhoAmA 93*
Spicer, John Austin 1930- *WhoFI 94, WhoMW 93, WhoScEn 94*
Spicer, Keith 1934- *WhoAm 94*
Spicer, Kenneth, Sr. 1949- *WhoBlA 94*
Spicer, Michael *Who 94*
Spicer, Michael 1943- *WrDr 94*
Spicer, (William) Michael (Hardy) 1943- *Who 94*
Spicer, Osker, Jr. 1949- *WhoBlA 94*
Spicer, Peter James 1921- *Who 94*
Spicer, Robert J. 1936- *WhoIns 94*
Spicer, Samuel Gary 1942- *WhoAmL 94*
Spicer, Susan Jean 1951- *WhoAmP 93*
Spicer, Warwick Charles Richard 1929- *IntWW 93*
Spicer, William Edward, III 1929- *WhoAm 94*
Spicer-Simpson, Theodore 1871-1959 *WhoAmA 93N*
Spicher, Lawrence Franklin 1949- *WhoFI 94*
Spickernell, Derek Garland 1921- *Who 94*
Spicola, Guy William 1938- *WhoAmP 93*
Spicola, James R. 1930-1991 *WhAm 10*
Spider, Emerson, Sr. fl. 20th cent.- *EncNAR*
Spidle, Craig Alan 1954- *WhoMW 93*
Spiegel, Albert A. 1916- *WhoAmP 93*
Spiegel, Arthur Henry, III 1939- *WhoAm 94*
Spiegel, Barry J. *WhoIns 94*
Spiegel, Bobbie Carol 1940- *WhoAm 94*
Spiegel, Carol Ann 1941- *WhoMW 93*
Spiegel, Francis Herman, Jr. 1935- *WhoAm 94*
Spiegel, H. Jay 1952- *WhoAmL 94*
Spiegel, Hart Hunter 1918- *WhoAm 94, WhoAmL 94*
Spiegel, Henry William 1911- *IntWW 93, WrDr 94*
Spiegel, Herbert 1914- *WhoAm 94, WhoScEn 94*
Spiegel, Jayson Leslie 1959- *WhoAmL 94*
Spiegel, Jerrold Bruce 1949- *WhoAmL 94*
Spiegel, Jerry Allen 1935- *WhoWest 94*
Spiegel, John William 1941- *WhoAm 94*
Spiegel, Larry *IntMPA 94*
Spiegel, Laurie 1945- *WhoAmA 93*
Spiegel, Lawrence Howard 1942- *WhoAm 94*
Spiegel, Linda F. 1953- *WhoAmL 94*
Spiegel, Melvin 1925- *WhoAm 94*
Spiegel, Michael 1937- *WhoFI 94*
Spiegel, Robert Moore 1950- *WhoWest 94*
Spiegel, Ronald John 1942- *WhoScEn 94*
Spiegel, Ronald Stuart 1942- *WhoWest 94*
Spiegel, S. Arthur 1920- *WhoAm 94, WhoAmL 94*
Spiegel, Sam 1903-1985 *IntDcF 2-4 [port]*
Spiegel, Siegmund 1919- *WhoFI 94*
Spiegelberg, Eldora Haskell 1915- *WhoMW 93*
Spiegelberg, Harry Lester 1936- *WhoMW 93*
Spiegelberg, Herbert 1904-1990 *WhAm 10*
Spiegel-Hopkins, Phyllis Marie 1947- *WhoMW 93*
Spiegelman, Art 1948- *ConAu 41NR, ConLC 76 [port], TwCYAW, WhoAm 94*
Spiegelman, Katia *DrAPF 93*
Spiegelman, Lon Howard 1941- *WhoAmA 93*
Spiegelman, Robert Gerald 1928- *WhoAm 94*
Spiegl, Fritz 1926- *Who 94*
Spiek, John Robert, Jr. 1947- *WhoMW 93*
Spiekerman, James Frederick 1933- *WhoAm 94*
Spiel, Hilde 1911-1990 *BlmGWL, WhAm 10*
Spielberg, David 1939- *WhoHol 92*
Spielberg, David C. 1951- *WhoAmL 94*
Spielberg, Peter *DrAPF 93*
Spielberg, Peter 1929- *WrDr 94*
Spielberg, Steven 1947- *EncSF 93, IntMPA 94, IntWW 93, News 93 [port], Who 94, WhoAm 94*
Spielberger, Lawrence 1911- *WhoScEn 94*
Spielhagen, Friedrich 1829-1911 *DcLB 129 [port]*
Spielman, Andrew Ian 1950- *WhoScEn 94*
Spielman, Chris 1965- *WhoAm 94, WhoMW 93*
Spielman, David Vernon 1929- *WhoFI 94*
Spielman, John Russel 1930-1985 *WhAm 10*
Spielman, Kim Morgan 1953- *WhoAmL 94*
Spielvogel, Carl 1928- *IntWW 93, WhoAm 94, WhoFI 94*
Spielvogel, Lawrence George 1938- *WhoFI 94*
Spielvogel, Sidney Meyer 1925- *WhoAm 94*
Spier, Luise Emma 1928- *WhoWest 94*
Spier, Peter (Edward) 1927- *ConAu 41NR*
Spier, Peter Edward 1927- *WhoAm 94, WhoAmA 93*
Spier, Raymond Eric 1938- *WhoScEn 94*
Spierenburg, Pieter (Cornelis) 1948- *WrDr 94*
Spiers, Albert William 1914- *WhoMW 93*
Spiers, Donald (Maurice) 1934- *Who 94*
Spiers, Edward M(ichael) 1947- *ConAu 43NR, WrDr 94*
Spiers, Frederick William d1993 *Who 94N*
Spiers, Graeme Hendry Gordon 1925- *Who 94*
Spiers, Reginald James 1928- *Who 94*
Spiers, Ronald Ian 1925- *IntWW 93, Who 94, WhoAm 94, WhoAmP 93*
Spiers, Walter Lewis 1848-1917 *DcNaB MP*
Spies, Claudio 1925- *WhoAm 94*
Spies, Dennis J. 1941- *WhoAm 94*
Spies, Emerson George 1914-1990 *WhAm 10*
Spies, Frank Stadler 1939- *WhoAmL 94*
Spies, Harold Glen 1934- *WhoWest 94*
Spies, Jacob John 1931- *WhoFI 94, WhoScEn 94*
Spies, Karen Bornemann 1949- *WhoWest 94*
Spies, Leon Fred 1950- *WhoAmL 94*
Spies, Phyllis Bova 1949- *WhoMW 93, WhoScEn 94*
Spiesman, Benjamin Lewis 1961- *WhoScEn 94*
Spiess, Fred Noel 1919- *WhoAm 94*
Spiess, Gary A. *WhoAmL 94*
Spiesser, Jacques *WhoHol 92*
Spiess-Ferris, Eleanor 1941- *WhoAmA 93*
Spies von Bullesheim, Adolf Wilhelm 1929- *IntWW 93*
Spight, Benita Lynn 1963- *WhoBlA 94*
Spigner, Archie 1928- *WhoAmP 93*
Spigner, Clarence 1946- *WhoBlA 94*
Spigner, Donald Wayne 1940- *WhoBlA 94*
Spike, John T(homas) 1951- *ConAu 140*
Spike, Paul *DrAPF 93*
Spiker, Joan E. 1945- *WhoMW 93*
Spiker, Ray d1964 *WhoHol 92*
Spikes, Dolores R. *WhoBlA 94*
Spikes, Jesse J. 1950- *WhoAmL 94*
Spikes, John Jefferson, Sr. 1929- *WhoScEn 94*
Spikes, Warren Nicholas 1951- *WhoFI 94*
Spikings, Barry 1939- *IntMPA 94*
Spikings, Barry Peter 1939- *Who 94, WhoAm 94*
Spikol, Art 1936- *WhoAm 94*
Spilhaus, Athelstan 1911- *WhoAm 94, WrDr 94*
Spilhaus, Athelstan Frederick 1911- *IntWW 93*
Spilhaus, Athelstan Frederick, Jr. 1938- *WhoAm 94, WhoScEn 94*
Spilhaus, Karl Henry 1946- *WhoAm 94*
Spiliotes, Nicholas James 1955- *WhoAmL 94*
Spilka, Mark 1925- *WhoAm 94*
Spilker, Barbara Jo 1938- *WhoAmP 93*
Spillane, John Michael 1956- *WhoAmL 94*
Spillane, Mickey 1918- *WhoAm 94, WhoHol 92, WrDr 94*
Spiller, Dudley P., Jr. 1944- *WhoAmL 94*
Spiller, Eberhard Adolf 1933- *WhoAm 94*
Spiller, Gene Alan 1927- *WhoWest 94*
Spiller, John Anthony Walsh 1942- *Who 94*
Spiller, Pablo Tomas 1951- *WhoFI 94*
Spillers, William Russell 1934- *WhoAm 94*
Spillman, Harry *WhoHol 92*
Spillman, Jane Shadel 1942- *WhoAm 94*
Spilman, James Bruce 1947- *WhoWest 94*
Spilman, Raymond 1911- *WhoAm 94*
Spilman, Richard 1946- *WrDr 94*
Spilman, Richard Allen 1947- *WhoFI 94*
Spilman, Robert Henkel 1927- *WhoAm 94*
Spilman, Timothy Frank 1961- *WhoScEn 94*
Spilsbury, Klinton 1955- *WhoHol 92*
Spina, Anthony *WhoAm 94*
Spina, Anthony Ferdinand 1937- *WhoAmL 94, WhoMW 93*
Spina, Peter A. d1993 *NewYTBS 93*
Spina, Samuel A. 1930- *WhoAmP 93*
Spina, Vincent *DrAPF 93*
Spinazzari, Alessandro fl. 1672-1674 *NewGrDO*
Spindel, Robert Charles 1944- *WhoAm 94, WhoScEn 94, WhoWest 94*
Spindel, William 1922- *WhoAm 94, WhoScEn 94*
Spindler, Dean Ralph 1952- *WhoMW 93*

Spindler, George Dearborn 1920- *WhoAm 94, WhoWest 94, WrDr 94*
Spindler, George S. *WhoAmL 94, WhoFI 94*
Spindler, John Frederick 1929- *WhoAm 94*
Spindler, Michael H. 1942- *WhoAm 94, WhoFI 94, WhoWest 94*
Spindler, Paul 1931- *WhoAm 94*
Spindler, (Franz) Stanislaus 1763-1819 *NewGrDO*
Spindola-Franco, Hugo 1938- *WhoHisp 94*
Spinell, Joe d1989 *WhoHol 92*
Spinell, Mary d1987 *WhoHol 92*
Spinella, Christopher Damian 1960- *WhoWest 94*
Spinella, Joseph John 1946- *WhoFI 94*
Spinella, Stephen *NewYTBS 93, WhoAm 94*
Spinelli, Eileen *DrAPF 93*
Spinelli, Jerry 1941- *Au&Arts 11 [port], TwCYAW, WhoAm 94*
Spinelli, Julio Cesar 1956- *WhoScEn 94*
Spinelli, Nicola 1865-1909 *NewGrDO*
Spinelly d1966 *WhoHol 92*
Spiner, Brent *WhoHol 92*
Spinetti, Victor 1932- *WhoHol 92*
Spinetti, Victor 1933- *IntMPA 94*
Spingarn, Clifford Leroy 1912- *WhoScEn 94*
Spingarn, Joel Elias 1875-1939 *AmSocL*
Spingarn, Lawrence *DrAPF 93*
Spingarn, Lawrence (Perreira) 1917- *WrDr 94*
Spingler, William A. 1941- *WhoAmP 93*
Spinillo, Peter Arsenio 1952- *WhoScEn 94*
Spink, Frank Henry 1935- *WhoAmA 93*
Spink, Ian 1932- *WrDr 94*
Spink, Ian Walter Alfred 1932- *Who 94*
Spink, Reginald 1905- *WrDr 94*
Spink, Reginald (William) 1905- *ConAu 41NR*
Spink, Robert Michael 1948- *Who 94*
Spink, Walter M. 1928- *WhoAmA 93*
Spinka, Harold Matthew, Jr. 1945- *WhoMW 93*
Spinks, James *WhoHol 92*
Spinks, John Lee 1924- *WhoAm 94*
Spinks, Mary Cecilia 1940- *Who 94*
Spinks, Michael 1956- *WhoAm 94, WhoBlA 94*
Spinks, Paul 1922- *WhoAm 94*
Spinn, Marian Rose 1926- *WhoWest 94*
Spinner, Lee Louis 1948- *WhoFI 94, WhoMW 93*
Spinning, Norma Storey 1896- *WhAm 10*
Spinola, Antonio Sebastiao Ribeiro de 1910- *IntWW 93*
Spinosa, Gary Paul 1947- *WhoAmA 93*
Spinoza, Baruch de 1632-1677 *EncEth*
Spinrad, Bernard Israel 1924- *WhoAm 94*
Spinrad, Hyron 1934- *WhoAm 94, WhoScEn 94*
Spinrad, Norman *DrAPF 93*
Spinrad, Norman 1940- *ConAu 19AS [port], WrDr 94*
Spinrad, Norman (Richard) 1940- *EncSF 93*
Spinrad, Robert Joseph 1932- *WhoAm 94, WhoScEn 94, WhoWest 94*
Spinski, Victor 1940- *WhoAmA 93*
Spinweber, Cheryl Lynn 1950- *WhoAm 94, WhoWest 94*
Spiotta, Raymond Herman 1927- *WhoAm 94*
Spiotto, James Ernest 1946- *WhoAm 94, WhoAmL 94*
Spira, Bill 1935- *WhoAmA 93*
Spira, Camilla 1906- *WhoHol 92*
Spira, Julie Margo 1957- *WhoWest 94*
Spira, Melvin 1925- *WhoAm 94*
Spira, Robert Alan 1932- *WhoFI 94*
Spira, Robert Samuel 1927- *WhoWest 94*
Spira, S. Franklin 1924- *WhoFI 94*
Spira, Steven S. 1955- *IntMPA 94*
Spira-Solomon, Darlene Joy 1959- *WhoWest 94*
Spire, Jean-Paul Charles 1942- *WhoMW 93*
Spire, Robert 1925- *WhoAmP 93*
Spirer, Julian Henry 1947- *WhoAmL 94*
Spires, Elizabeth *DrAPF 93*
Spires, Robert Cecil 1936- *WhoAm 94*
Spires, Roberta Lynn 1952- *WhoMW 93*
Spiridakis, Tony 1959- *WhoHol 92*
Spiridonov, Yury Alekseevich 1938- *LngBDD*
Spirin, Aleksandr Sergeyevich 1931- *IntWW 93*
Spirn, Michele Sobel 1943- *WhoAm 94*
Spiro, Benjamin Paul 1917- *WhoAm 94*
Spiro, Herbert (John) 1924- *WrDr 94*
Spiro, Herbert John 1924- *WhoAm 94*
Spiro, Howard Marget 1924- *WhoAm 94*
Spiro, Loida Velazquez *WhoHisp 94*
Spiro, Melford Elliot 1920- *WhoAm 94, WhoScEn 94*
Spiro, Peter *DrAPF 93*
Spiro, Robert Harry, Jr. 1920- *WhoAm 94*
Spiro, Thomas George 1935- *WhoAm 94, WhoScEn 94*
Spiro, Walter Anselm 1923- *WhoAm 94, WhoFI 94*
Spiroiu, Niculae 1936- *IntWW 93*
Spirou, Chris 1942- *WhoAmP 93*
Spirtos, Nicholas George 1950- *WhoWest 94*
Spisak, John Francis 1950- *WhoWest 94*
Spisak, Leslie J. 1944- *WhoAmL 94*
Spitaels, Guy *IntWW 93*
Spital, Hermann Josef Silvester 1925- *IntWW 93*
Spitaleri, Vernon Rosario 1922- *WhoWest 94*
Spitalny, Frank Jay 1929- *WhoIns 94*
Spitalny, Phil d1970 *WhoHol 92*
Spiteri, Lino 1938- *IntWW 93*
Spitler, Clare Blackford 1923- *WhoAmA 93*
Spitler, Larry L. 1943- *WhoAmP 93*
Spitsbergen, Dorothy May 1932- *WhoMW 93*
Spittel, Olaf R. *EncSF 93*
Spitteler, Carl 1845-1924 *DcLB 129 [port]*
Spitz, Arnoldt John 1929- *WhoFI 94*
Spitz, Barbara S. 1926- *WhoAmA 93*
Spitz, Barbara Salomon 1926- *WhoAm 94*
Spitz, Charles Thomas, Jr. 1921- *WhoAm 94*
Spitz, Dan *See* Anthrax *ConMus 11*
Spitz, Erich 1931- *WhoScEn 94*
Spitz, Hugo Max 1927- *WhoAmL 94, WhoFI 94*
Spitz, Jacques 1896-1963 *EncSF 93*
Spitz, James R. 1940- *IntMPA 94*
Spitz, Kathleen Emily *Who 94*
Spitz, Lewis 1939- *Who 94*
Spitz, Lewis William 1922- *WhoAm 94, WhoWest 94, WrDr 94*
Spitz, Seymour James, Jr. 1921- *WhoAm 94*
Spitz, Stephen Andrew 1958- *WhoAmL 94*
Spitzberg, Irving Joseph, Jr. 1942- *WhoAm 94, WhoAmL 94*
Spitze, Robert George Frederick 1922- *WhoAm 94*
Spitzer, Adrian 1927- *WhoAm 94*
Spitzer, Cary Redford 1937- *WhoAm 94*
Spitzer, Hugh D. 1949- *WhoAm 94, WhoAmL 94*
Spitzer, Hugh Davidson 1949- *WhoAmP 93*
Spitzer, Jack J. 1917- *WhoAm 94*
Spitzer, John Brumback 1918- *WhoAm 94*
Spitzer, John J. 1927- *WhoAm 94*
Spitzer, John Ole 1948- *WhoAmP 93*
Spitzer, Laura Claire 1952- *WhoWest 94*
Spitzer, Lyman, (Jr.) 1914- *WrDr 94*
Spitzer, Lyman, Jr. 1914- *IntWW 93, Who 94, WhoAm 94*
Spitzer, Lyman F. 1949- *WhoAmL 94*
Spitzer, Marc L. 1957- *WhoAmP 93*
Spitzer, Marc Lee 1957- *WhoWest 94*
Spitzer, Matthew L. 1929- *WhoWest 94*
Spitzer, Nicholas Canaday 1942- *WhoAm 94*
Spitzer, Nicholas R. 1950- *ConAu 142*
Spitzer, Peter George 1956- *WhoFI 94, WhoWest 94*
Spitzer, Robert Ralph 1922- *WhoAm 94, WhoMW 93*
Spitzer, William George 1927- *WhoAm 94*
Spitzfaden, Paul Riley 1920- *WhoAmP 93*
Spitzli, Donald Hawkes, Jr. 1934- *WhoAmL 94*
Spitzmiller, John C. 1946- *WhoAmL 94*
Spitznagel, Edward Lawrence, Jr. 1941- *WhoMW 93*
Spitznagel, John Keith 1923- *WhoAm 94*
Spiva, Ulysses Van 1931- *WhoBlA 94*
Spivack, Charlotte 1926- *WrDr 94*
Spivack, Gordon Bernard 1929- *WhoAm 94, WhoAmL 94*
Spivack, Henry Archer 1919- *WhoAm 94, WhoFI 94*
Spivack, Herman M. 1927- *WhoScEn 94*
Spivack, Kathleen *DrAPF 93*
Spivack, Kathleen (Romola Drucker) 1938- *WrDr 94*
Spivack, Scott Keith 1963- *WhoAmL 94*
Spivack, Susan Fantl *DrAPF 93*
Spivak, Alice *WhoHol 92*
Spivak, Alvin A. 1927- *WhoAm 94*
Spivak, Charlie d1982 *WhoHol 92*
Spivak, Gayatri Chakravorty 1941- *BlmGWL*
Spivak, Jacque R. 1929- *WhoWest 94*
Spivak, Jonathan M. 1928- *WhoAm 94*
Spivak, Lawrence E. 1900- *DcLB 137 [port], IntMPA 94*
Spivak, Leonard A. 1943- *WhoAm 94, WhoAmL 94*
Spivak, Mira 1934- *WhoWomW 91*
Spivak, Robert Elliot 1936- *WhoFI 94*
Spivakov, Vladimir Teodorovich 1944- *IntWW 93*
Spivakovsky, Tossy 1907- *IntWW 93*
Spivey, Bill 1930- *BasBi*
Spivey, Bruce E. 1934- *WhoAm 94, WhoMW 93*
Spivey, Donald 1948- *WhoBlA 94*
Spivey, Ebbie 1938- *WhoAmP 93*
Spivey, Howard Olin 1931- *WhoScEn 94*
Spivey, Hubert Michael 1948- *WhoAmP 93*
Spivey, Joseph M., III 1935- *WhoAm 94*
Spivey, Lisa 1958- *WhoWest 94*
Spivey, Ted Ray 1927- *WhoAm 94*
Spivey, Victoria d1976 *WhoHol 92*
Spivey, William Ree 1946- *WhoBlA 94*
Spivy d1971 *WhoHol 92*
Spivy, Alexandra Anderson 1942- *WhoAm 94*
Spivy-Anderson, C. Alexandra 1942- *WhoAmA 93*
Spiwak, Jerome 1933- *WhoFI 94*
Spizhenko, Yurii Prokopvych 1950- *LngBDD*
Spizizen, John 1917- *WhoWest 94*
Spizizen, Louise Myers *WhoWest 94*
Spizzirri, John A. 1934- *WhoAmP 93*
Spizzirri, Richard Dominic 1933- *WhoAm 94*
Splain, Francis J., Jr. 1955- *WhoIns 94*
Splaine, James Raymond 1947- *WhoAmP 93*
Splane, Richard Beverley 1916- *WhoAm 94, WhoWest 94*
Splete, Allen Peterjohn 1938- *WhoAm 94*
Spliethoff, William Ludwig 1926- *WhoAm 94*
Splinter, John Paul 1945- *WhoMW 93*
Splinter, William Eldon 1925- *WhoAm 94, WhoScEn 94*
Splitstone, George Dale 1925- *WhoAm 94*
Splitt, David Alan 1945- *WhoAmL 94*
Splittgerber, Fredric Lee 1937- *WhoAm 94*
Splittstoesser, Walter Emil 1937- *WhoAm 94, WhoScEn 94*
Splude, John Wesley 1945- *WhoAm 94*
Spock, Alexander 1929- *WhoAm 94*
Spock, Benjamin 1903- *WhoAmP 93*
Spock, Benjamin (McLane) 1903- *WrDr 94*
Spock, Benjamin McLane 1903- *AmSocL, IntWW 93, Who 94, WhoAm 94, WhoScEn 94*
Spodak, Michael Kenneth 1944- *WhoAm 94*
Spodek, Bernard 1931- *WhoAm 94*
Spodek, Jules L. 1928- *WhoAmP 93*
Spodick, Robert C. 1919- *IntMPA 94*
Spoehr, Alexander 1913- *IntWW 93*
Spoerli, Heinz 1941- *IntDcB [port]*
Spoerry, Vreni 1938- *WhoWomW 91*
Spofford, Harriet Elizabeth Prescott 1835-1921 *BlmGWL*
Spofford, Janice Brogue 1925- *WhoMW 93*
Spofford, Robert Houston 1941- *WhoAm 94, WhoWest 94*
Spofford, Sally 1929- *WhoAmA 93*
Spofford, William B. 1921- *WhoAm 94*
Spohn, Beatrice Evelyn 1907- *WhoAm 94, WhoMW 93*
Spohn, Christine Ann Javer 1950- *WhoMW 93*
Spohn, Clay (Edgar) 1898-1977 *WhoAmA 93N*
Spohn, Daniel Jay 1956- *WhoWest 94*
Spohn, Franz Frederick 1950- *WhoAmA 93*
Spohn, Herbert Emil 1923- *WhoAm 94, WhoScEn 94*
Spohnholz, Ann *WhoAmP 93*
Spohr, Arnold Theodore 1927- *IntWW 93, WhoAm 94*
Spohr, Frederick Stephen 1949- *WhoMW 93*
Spohr, Louis 1784-1859 *NewGrDO*
Spohr, Robert Louis 1935- *WhoAm 94*
Spokane, Robert Bruce 1952- *WhoScEn 94*
Spokes, Ann *Who 94*
Spokes, John Arthur Clayton 1931- *Who 94*
Spokes Symonds, Ann (Hazel) 1925- *Who 94*
Spolan, Harmon Samuel 1935- *WhoAm 94*
Spoll, Michael Jay 1942- *WhoFI 94*
Spollen, John W. 1944- *WhoAm 94, WhoAmL 94*
Spolter, Pari Dokht 1930- *WhoWest 94*
Sponable, Jess M. 1955- *WhoScEn 94*
Sponberg, Raymond Hilding 1914- *WhoFI 94*
Sponenburgh, Mark 1916- *WhoAmA 93*
Spong, Hilda d1955 *WhoHol 92*
Spong, John Shelby 1931- *IntWW 93, WhoAm 94*
Spong, William B., Jr. *WhoAmP 93*
Spong, William Belser, Jr. 1920- *WhoAm 94*
Sponholz, Kuno *WhoHol 92*
Sponsler, George Curtis, III 1927- *WhoAm 94*
Spontini, Gaspare (Luigi Pacifico) 1774-1851 *NewGrDO*
Spoo, James *WhoAmP 93*
Spoon, Alan Gary 1951- *WhoAm 94, WhoFI 94*
Spoon, Elliot A. 1951- *WhoAmL 94*
Spoon, Roy *WhoAmP 93*
Spoonauer, John W. 1948- *WhoIns 94*
Spooner, Cecil d1953 *WhoHol 92*
Spooner, Charles Edward 1932- *WhoAm 94*
Spooner, Charles Michael 1950- *WhoAmP 93*
Spooner, Edna May d1963 *WhoHol 92*
Spooner, Edward Tenney Casswell 1904- *Who 94*
Spooner, Frank 1937- *WhoAmP 93*
Spooner, Frank Clyffurde 1924- *Who 94*
Spooner, James (Douglas) 1932- *Who 94*
Spooner, James Douglas 1932- *IntWW 93*
Spooner, John C. 1950- *WhoBlA 94*
Spooner, Mark Jordan 1945- *WhoAm 94, WhoAmL 94*
Spooner, Richard C. 1945- *WhoBlA 94*
Spooner, Robert Donald 1947- *WhoFI 94*
Spoonhour, James Michael 1946- *WhoAmL 94*
Spoor, James Edward 1936- *WhoWest 94*
Spoor, Leslee Peyton Sherrill 1958- *WhoAmP 93*
Spoor, Richard D. 1944- *WhoAmL 94*
Spoor, William Howard 1923- *WhoAm 94*
Spoorenberg, Erna 1926- *NewGrDO*
Sporborg, Christopher Henry 1939- *IntWW 93, Who 94*
Spore, Keith Kent 1942- *WhoAm 94, WhoMW 93*
Spores, John Michael 1957- *WhoScEn 94*
Spores, Ronald Marvin 1931- *WhoAm 94*
Sporkin, Stanley 1932- *CngDr 93, WhoAm 94, WhoAmL 94*
Sporn, Arthur David 1927- *WhoAm 94*
Sporn, Judith Beryl 1951- *WhoAmL 94*
Sporn, Michael Benjamin 1933- *WhoScEn 94*
Sporn, Stanley Robert 1928- *WhoAm 94*
Spornic, Aneta *WhoWomW 91*
Sportonio, Marc'Antonio c. 1631-c. 1696 *NewGrDO*
Sporus *BlmGEL*
Sposeto, Dominic John 1934- *WhoAmL 94*
Sposito, Garrison 1939- *WhoHisp 94*
Spota, George d1993 *NewYTBS 93*
Spoto, Donald 1941- *WhoAm 94*
Spotswood, Alexander 1676-1740 *WhWE*
Spotswood, Denis 1916- *IntWW 93*
Spotswood, Denis (Frank) 1916- *Who 94*
Spotswood, Robert Keeling 1952- *WhoAm 94, WhoAmL 94*
Spottiswood, James Donald 1934- *Who 94*
Spottiswoode, Roger *IntMPA 94*
Spottsville, Clifford M. 1911- *WhoBlA 94*
Spottswood, Curran Lamar, III 1943- *WhoFI 94*
Spottswood, James d1946 *WhoHol 92*
Spottswood, Paul Gregory 1948- *WhoMW 93*
Spottswood, Stephen Gill 1897-1974 *AfrAmAl 6 [port]*
Spotz, James Donald 1946- *WhoMW 93*
Sprabery, Peggy Peden 1950- *WhoAm 94*
Sprackling, Ian Oliver John 1936- *Who 94*
Sprackling, Michael Thomas 1934- *WrDr 94*
Spradley, Frank Sanford 1946- *WhoBlA 94*
Spradley, Mark Merritt *WhoBlA 94*
Spradlin, G.D. 1920- *IntMPA 94*
Spradlin, G. D. 1926- *WhoHol 92*
Spradlin, Joseph E. 1929- *WhoScEn 94*
Spradlin, Julia Joseph 1951- *WhoMW 93*
Spradlin, Karen Sue 1944- *WhoMW 93*
Spradlin, Timothy Michael 1963- *WhoFI 94*
Spradling, Frank L. 1885-1972 *WhoAmA 93N*
Spradling, Mark Raymond 1956- *WhoAmL 94*
Spradling, Mary Elizabeth Mace *WhoBlA 94*
Sprafkin, Robert Peter 1940- *WhoScEn 94*
Spragens, Thomas Arthur 1917- *WhoAm 94*
Spragg, Howard Eugene 1917-1991 *WhAm 10*
Spraggins, John Robert 1952- *WhoFI 94*
Spraggins, Marianne *WhoBlA 94*
Spraggins, Stewart 1936- *WhoBlA 94*

Spraggins, Thomas Reginald 1930- *WhoAmP 93*
Spraggs, Trevor Owen Keith 1926- *Who 94*
Sprague, Arthur Colby 1895-1991 *WhAm 10*
Sprague, Carter *EncSF 93*
Sprague, Carter 1910- *WrDr 94*
Sprague, Charles Cameron 1916- *WhoAm 94*
Sprague, Dale M. *WhoAmP 93*
Sprague, David Keith 1935- *Who 94*
Sprague, Dewey Dean 1954- *WhoWest 94*
Sprague, Donald Eugene 1955- *WhoMW 93*
Sprague, Edward Auchincloss 1932- *WhoAm 94*
Sprague, George Frederick 1902- *WhoAm 94*
Sprague, Irvine H. 1921- *WhoAmP 93*
Sprague, James Mather 1916- *WhoAm 94*
Sprague, Jo Ann 1931- *WhoAmP 93*
Sprague, John Louis 1930- *WhoAm 94, WhoFI 94*
Sprague, John Reno, Jr. 1941- *WhoAmL 94*
Sprague, Marion Wright 1923- *WhoFI 94*
Sprague, Mark Anderson 1920- *WhoAmA 93*
Sprague, Mary L. *WhoIns 94*
Sprague, Michael James 1940- *WhoAmP 93*
Sprague, Milton Alan 1914-1991 *WhAm 10*
Sprague, Norman Frederick, Jr. 1914- *WhoAm 94, WhoScEn 94*
Sprague, Paul Edward 1933- *WhoAmA 93, WhoMW 93*
Sprague, Peter Julian 1939- *WhoAm 94, WhoFI 94, WhoWest 94*
Sprague, Robert Chapman 1900-1991 *WhAm 10*
Sprague, Robert Joseph 1944- *WhoAmP 93*
Sprague, Roderick, III 1933- *WhoWest 94*
Sprague, Vance Glover, Jr. 1941- *WhoScEn 94*
Sprague, William Wallace, Jr. 1926- *WhoAm 94, WhoFI 94*
Sprague de Camp, L. *DrAPF 93*
Sprague-Smith, Isabelle Dwight 1861-1951 *WhoAmA 93N*
Spraings, Violet Evelyn 1930- *WhoWest 94*
Sprandel, Dennis Steuart 1941- *WhoFI 94, WhoMW 93*
Sprang, Elizabeth *WhoAmA 93*
Sprang, Milton LeRoy 1944- *WhoAm 94, WhoMW 93*
Spranger, Carl-Dieter 1939- *IntWW 93*
Spratlen, Thaddeus H. 1930- *WhoBlA 94*
Spratley, Tom d1987 *WhoHol 92*
Spratt, Brian Geoffrey 1947- *Who 94, WhoScEn 94*
Spratt, Frederick R. 1927- *WhoAmA 93*
Spratt, Greville (Douglas) 1927- *Who 94*
Spratt, Greville Douglas 1927- *IntWW 93*
Spratt, John M., Jr. 1942- *CngDr 93, WhoAmP 93*
Spratt, John McKee, Jr. 1942- *WhoAm 94*
Spratt, Lewis G. *WhoBlA 94*
Spratt, Lewis G. 1921- *WhoAmP 93*
Spraul, Holly Doan 1964- *WhoAmL 94*
Sprauve, Gilbert A. 1937- *WhoBlA 94*
Spray, Elwin L. 1948- *WhoAmP 93*
Spray, Paul 1921- *WhoAm 94, WhoScEn 94*
Spray, Thomas L. 1948- *WhoScEn 94*
Sprayberry, Sheryl McArthur 1947- *WhoMW 93*
Sprayregen, Joel Jay 1934- *WhoAm 94*
Sprayregen, Morris *WhoAmA 93N*
Sprecher, David A. 1930- *WhoAm 94*
Sprecher, Gustav Ewald 1922- *WhoScEn 94*
Sprecher, Peter Leonard, Jr. 1930- *WhoFI 94*
Sprecher, William Gunther 1924- *WhoAm 94*
Spreckley, (John) Nicholas (Teague) 1934- *Who 94*
Spreckley, (John) Nicholas Teague 1934- *IntWW 93*
Spree, Julia E. Burke 1947- *WhoAmP 93*
Spreiregen, Paul (David) 1931- *WrDr 94*
Spreiregen, Paul David 1931- *WhoAm 94*
Spreiter, John Robert 1921- *WhoAm 94*
Sprengel, Helen Jane 1925- *WhoAm 94*
Sprengel, Hermann Johann Philipp 1834-1906 *WorInv*
Sprengnether, Madelon *DrAPF 93*
Sprengnether, Ronald John 1944- *WhoScEn 94*
Sprenkle, Arthur C. *WhoAmP 93*
Sprenkle, Case Middleton 1934- *WhoAm 94*
Sprenkle, David Alan 1953- *WhoFI 94*
Sprent, Janet Irene 1934- *Who 94*
Sprent, John Frederick Adrian 1915- *IntWW 93*
Spreull, James (Spreull Andrew) 1908- *Who 94*
Sprewell, Latrell 1970- *WhoBlA 94*
Spriddell, Peter Henry 1928- *Who 94*
Spriestersbach, Duane Caryl 1916- *WhoAm 94*
Sprigel, Olivier *EncSF 93*
Sprigg, Thomas 1747-1809 *WhAmRev*
Sprigge, Timothy (Lauro Squire) 1932- *WrDr 94*
Sprigge, Timothy Lauro Squire 1932- *IntWW 93, Who 94*
Spriggs, David William 1949- *WhoMW 93*
Spriggs, Elizabeth 1929- *WhoHol 92*
Spriggs, Everett Lee 1930- *WhoAmL 94, WhoWest 94*
Spriggs, G. Max 1925- *WhoBlA 94*
Spriggs, Gaylyn J. 1943- *WhoAmP 93*
Spriggs, Kent 1939- *WhoAmL 94*
Spriggs, Leslie d1990 *Who 94N*
Spriggs, Ray V. 1937- *WhoBlA 94*
Spriggs, Richard Moore 1931- *WhoAm 94, WhoScEn 94*
Sprik, Dale Robert 1937- *WhoAmP 93*
Sprimont, Thomas Eugene 1957- *WhoScEn 94*
Sprincz, Keith Steven 1956- *WhoWest 94*
Spring, Bernard Polmer 1927- *WhoAm 94*
Spring, Carol V. 1947- *WhoMW 93*
Spring, Charles Augustus 1917- *WhoFI 94*
Spring, Dee 1934- *WhoWest 94*
Spring, Frank Stuart 1907- *Who 94*
Spring, Gardiner 1785-1873 *DcAmReB 2*
Spring, Glenn Ernest 1939- *WhoWest 94*
Spring, Helen d1978 *WhoHol 92*
Spring, James J., III 1947- *WhoAmL 94*
Spring, Jeffrey David 1955- *WhoWest 94*
Spring, John Benham 1936- *WhoFI 94*
Spring, Kathleen Marie 1951- *WhoWest 94*
Spring, Michael 1941- *WhoAm 94*
Spring, Molly A. 1963- *WhoMW 93*
Spring, Raymond Lewis 1932- *WhoAm 94*
Spring, Richard 1950- *IntWW 93, Who 94*
Spring, Richard John Grenville 1946- *Who 94*
Spring, S. Stephen, II 1951- *WhoAmL 94*
Spring, Samuel 1747-1819 *WhAmRev*
Spring, Stephen Royston 1945- *WhoAmL 94*
Spring, Wilbur, Jr. 1921- *WhoAmP 93*
Springberg, Gerald Harvey 1933- *WhoFI 94*
Springel, Barry L. 1942- *WhoAm 94, WhoAmL 94*
Springer, Andrea Paulette Ryan 1946- *WhoScEn 94*
Springer, Ashton, Jr. 1930- *WhoBlA 94*
Springer, Carol *WhoAmP 93, WhoWest 94*
Springer, Charles Edward 1928- *WhoAm 94, WhoAmL 94, WhoAmP 93, WhoWest 94*
Springer, David Edward 1952- *WhoAm 94*
Springer, David Edward 1953- *WhoAmP 93*
Springer, Dick 1948- *WhoAmP 93*
Springer, Donald Donner 1938- *WhoFI 94*
Springer, Douglas Hyde 1927- *WhoAm 94*
Springer, Edwin Kent 1912- *WhoAm 94*
Springer, Eric Winston 1929- *WhoBlA 94*
Springer, Felix J. 1946- *WhoAmL 94*
Springer, Finis Louise 1929- *WhoMW 93*
Springer, Floyd Ladean 1922- *WhoWest 94*
Springer, Gary 1954- *WhoHol 92*
Springer, George Chelston 1932- *WhoBlA 94*
Springer, George Stephen 1933- *WhoAm 94, WhoScEn 94, WhoWest 94*
Springer, Gerald William 1943- *WhoWest 94*
Springer, Harry Aaron 1937- *WhoMW 93*
Springer, Haskell Saul 1939- *WhoMW 93*
Springer, Heinrich *WhoAmP 93*
Springer, Hugh (Worrell) 1913- *Who 94*
Springer, Hugh Worrell 1913- *IntWW 93*
Springer, James Berne 1943- *WhoMW 93*
Springer, James vanRoden 1934- *WhoAm 94*
Springer, Jeffrey Alan 1950- *WhoAmL 94*
Springer, Jim *WhoAmP 93*
Springer, John K. 1942- *WhoFI 94*
Springer, John Kelley 1931- *WhoAm 94*
Springer, John Shipman 1916- *WhoAm 94*
Springer, Joseph Gerald 1964- *WhoAmL 94*
Springer, Karl Josef 1935- *WhoAm 94*
Springer, Kenneth N. *WhoAmP 93*
Springer, Konrad Ferdinand 1925- *IntWW 93*
Springer, Lawrence E. 1951- *WhoFI 94*
Springer, Lloyd Livingstone 1930- *WhoBlA 94*
Springer, Michael Louis 1938- *WhoAm 94*
Springer, Nancy *DrAPF 93*
Springer, Nancy 1948- *ConAu 41NR*
Springer, Paul D. *IntMPA 94*
Springer, Paul David 1942- *WhoAm 94, WhoAmL 94, WhoWest 94*
Springer, Randy Raymond 1959- *WhoWest 94*
Springer, Robert Dale 1933- *WhoAm 94*
Springer, Sally Pearl 1947- *WhoWest 94*
Springer, Stanley G. 1927- *WhoAm 94*
Springer, Steven Edward 1948- *WhoAmL 94*
Springer, Thomas 1968- *WhoAmP 93*
Springer, Tobias 1907- *Who 94*
Springer, W. Bruce 1947- *WhoAmL 94*
Springer, Wayne Gilbert 1951- *WhoFI 94*
Springer, William Lee 1909-1992 *WhAm 10*
Springer-Miller, John Holt 1955- *WhoScEn 94*
Springett, Jack Allan 1916- *Who 94*
Springfield, J. *WhoScEn 94*
Springfield, James Francis 1929- *WhoAm 94, WhoFI 94*
Springfield, Rick 1949- *IntMPA 94, WhoHol 92*
Springford, John Frederick Charles 1919- *Who 94*
Springford, Michael 1936- *Who 94*
Springgate, John Patton 1959- *WhoAmL 94*
Springhorn, Carl 1887-1971 *WhoAmA 93N*
Springler, Harry d1953 *WhoHol 92*
Springman, Paul W. 1951- *WhoIns 94*
Springman, Susan Ann 1952- *WhoMW 93*
Springmeyer, Don 1954- *WhoAmL 94*
Spring Rice *Who 94*
Springs, Alice 1923- *IntWW 93*
Springs, Jimmy d1987 *WhoHol 92*
Springs, Lenny F. 1947- *WhoBlA 94*
Springs, Nadia 1952- *WrDr 94*
Springsted, Eric Osmon 1951- *WhoMW 93*
Springsteen, Arthur William 1948- *WhoScEn 94*
Springsteen, Bruce 1949- *IntWW 93, WhoAm 94*
Springsteen, David Folger 1932- *WhoAm 94, WhoFI 94*
Springsteen, George S. d1993 *NewYTBS 93*
Springsteen, Pamela 1962- *WhoHol 92*
Springston, Benjamin N. *WhoAmP 93*
Springstubb, Tricia *DrAPF 93*
Springweiler, Erwin Frederick 1896-1968 *WhoAmA 93N*
Sprinkel, Beryl (Wayne) 1923- *WrDr 94*
Sprinkel, Beryl Wayne 1923- *IntWW 93, WhoAm 94*
Sprinkel, Warren Reed 1922- *WhoAmP 93*
Sprinkle, James Thomas 1943- *WhoScEn 94*
Sprinkle, Patricia Houck 1943- *WrDr 94*
Sprinkle, William Melvin 1945- *WhoScEn 94*
Sprinkle-Hamlin, Sylvia Yvonne 1945- *WhoBlA 94*
Sprinkles, Catherine Childe 1941- *WhoAmL 94*
Sprinson, David Benjamin 1910- *WhoAm 94*
Sprinsteel, Frederick Neil 1940- *WhoMW 93*
Sprinthall, Norman Arthur 1931- *WhoAm 94*
Spritzer, Samuel Lewis 1954- *WhoFI 94*
Spritzer, Shlomo 1953- *WhoFI 94*
Sprizzo, John Emilio 1934- *WhoAm 94, WhoAmL 94*
Sproat, Christopher Townsend 1945- *WhoAmA 93*
Sproat, Iain Mac Donald 1938- *Who 94*
Sproat, John Gerald 1921- *WhoAm 94*
Sproesser, William David, Sr. 1923- *WhoFI 94*
Sproger, Charles Edmund 1933- *WhoAm 94, WhoAmL 94*
Sprole, Frank Arnott 1918- *WhoAm 94*
Sprole, Gregory L. 1947- *WhoFI 94*
Sprot, Aidan Mark 1919- *Who 94*
Sprott, David Arthur 1930- *WhoAm 94*
Sprott, John *WhoAm 94, WhoAmP 93*
Sprott, Richard Lawrence 1940- *WhoAm 94*
Sprotte, Bert d1949 *WhoHol 92*
Sproul, Allan 1896- *WhAm 10*
Sproul, Ann Stephenson 1907- *WhoAmA 93*
Sproul, Curtis Cutter 1948- *WhoAmL 94*
Sproul, Harvey Leonard 1933- *WhoAmL 94, WhoAmP 93*
Sproul, John Allan 1924- *WhoAm 94, WhoFI 94, WhoWest 94*
Sproul, Otis Jennings 1930- *WhoAm 94*
Sproule, Betty Ann 1948- *WhoWest 94*
Sproull, Robert Lamb 1918- *WhoAm 94*
Sproull, Wayne Treber 1906- *WhoScEn 94*
Sprouse, Frederick Scott 1966- *WhoFI 94*
Sprouse, James M. 1923- *WhoAmP 93*
Sprouse, James Marshall 1923- *WhoAm 94, WhoAmL 94*
Sprouse, John Alwyn 1908- *WhoAm 94*
Sprouse, Robert Allen, II 1935- *WhoFI 94, WhoWest 94*
Sprout, Francis Allen 1940- *WhoBlA 94*
Sprow, Frank Barker 1939- *WhoScEn 94*
Sprow, Howard Thomas 1919- *WhoAm 94*
Sprowl, Charles Riggs 1910- *WhoAm 94, WhoAmL 94*
Sprowls, Robert Wayne 1946- *WhoAm 94*
Spruance, Benton 1904-1967 *WhoAmA 93N*
Spruance, Thomas Willing 1947- *WhoAmP 93*
Spruce, Everett Franklin 1908- *WhoAm 94, WhoAmA 93*
Spruce, George W. 1947- *WhoAmP 93*
Spruce, Kenneth L. 1956- *WhoBlA 94*
Spruce, Richard 1817-1893 *WhWE*
Spruch, Larry 1923- *WhoScEn 94*
Sprugel, George, Jr. 1919- *WhoAm 94*
Spruill, Albert Westley 1926- *WhoBlA 94*
Spruill, James Arthur 1937- *WhoBlA 94*
Spruill, Norman Louis 1933- *WhoIns 94*
Spruill, Robert I. 1947- *WhoBlA 94*
Spruill, Steven 1946- *WrDr 94*
Spruill, Steven G(regory) 1946- *EncSF 93*
Spruill, W. Duvall 1946- *WhoAmL 94*
Sprung, Donald W. L. 1934- *WhoAm 94*
Sprunger, Barton T. 1946- *WhoAmL 94*
Sprungl, Katherine Louise 1961- *WhoMW 93*
Spry, Charles Chambers Fowell 1910- *Who 94*
Spry, Christopher John 1946- *Who 94*
Spry, Donald Francis, II 1947- *WhoAmL 94*
Spry, John (Farley) 1910- *Who 94*
Spudich, James A. 1942- *WhoAm 94, WhoWest 94*
Spuehler, Donald Roy 1934- *WhoAm 94*
Spuhl, Tola Manzano 1942- *WhoAmP 93*
Spuhler, James Norman 1917-1992 *WhAm 10*
Spuhler, Willy d1990 *IntWW 93N*
Spulber, Nicolas 1915- *WhoAm 94, WhoFI 94*
Spuller, Thomas M. *WhoIns 94*
Spungin, Joel D. 1937- *WhoFI 94, WhoMW 93*
Spunt, Shepard Armin 1931- *WhoAm 94, WhoFI 94*
Spur, Gunter 1928- *WhoScEn 94*
Spurgeon, Charles Haddon 1834-1892 *BlmGEL*
Spurgeon, Earl E. 1963- *WhoScEn 94*
Spurgeon, Edward Dutcher 1939- *WhoAm 94*
Spurgeon, Leeman Clarence 1924- *WhoAmP 93*
Spurgeon, Nannette SuAnn 1962- *WhoMW 93*
Spurgeon, Peter Lester 1927- *Who 94*
Spurgeon, Roberta Kaye 1938- *WhoAmL 94*
Spurgeon, Sarah 1903-1985 *WhoAmA 93N*
Spurgin, John Edwin 1932- *WhoAmA 93*
Spurlin, Lisa Turner 1962- *WhoScEn 94*
Spurling, Everett Gordon, Jr. 1923- *WhoAm 94*
Spurling, Hilary 1940- *WrDr 94*
Spurling, (Susan) Hilary 1940- *Who 94*
Spurling, John 1936- *ConDr 93, WrDr 94*
Spurling, Norine M. 1930- *WhoAmA 93*
Spurlock, Charles T. 1917- *WhoBlA 94*
Spurlock, Delbert L. 1941- *WhoAmP 93*
Spurlock, Dorothy A. 1956- *WhoBlA 94*
Spurlock, Dorothy Ann 1957- *WhoMW 93*
Spurlock, James B., Jr. 1936- *WhoBlA 94*
Spurlock, Jeanne *WhoBlA 94*
Spurlock, Lallah Jean 1924- *WhoAmP 93*
Spurlock, Langley Augustine 1939- *WhoBlA 94*
Spurlock, LaVerne B. 1930- *WhoBlA 94*
Spurlock, Luther T. 1945- *WhoAmP 93*
Spurlock, Oliver M. 1945- *WhoBlA 94*
Spurlock, Paul Andrew 1960- *WhoScEn 94*
Spurlock, Ted Lee 1938- *WhoAm 94*
Spurlock, William 1945- *WhoAmA 93*
Spurlock-Evans, Karla Jeanne 1949- *WhoBlA 94*
Spurr, Charles Lewis 1913- *WhoAm 94*
Spurr, Daniel 1947- *WhoAm 94*
Spurr, Margaret Anne 1933- *Who 94*
Spurr, Paul Raymond 1957- *WhoScEn 94*
Spurr, Stephen Hopkins 1918-1992 *WhAm 10*
Spurrier, James Joseph 1946- *WhoMW 93*

Spurrier, Peter Brotherton 1942- *Who 94*
Spurrier, Steve *WhoAm 94*
Spurzem, Richard Taliaferro 1960- *WhoFI 94*
Spy, James 1952- *Who 94*
Spyber, John *DrAPF 93*
Spyers-Duran, Peter 1932- *WhoAm 94*
Spyri, Johanna 1827-1901 *BlmGWL*
Spyropoulos, George Yorgo *WhoAmA 93*
Spyropoulos, Jannis 1912- *IntWW 93*
Squadra, John 1932- *WhoAmA 93*
Squadrilli, Alexander E. d1993 *NewYTBS 93 [port]*
Squadron, Howard Maurice 1926- *WhoAm 94*
Squair, George Alexander 1929- *Who 94*
Squanto c. 1580-1622 *WhWE*
Squarcy, Charlotte Van Horne 1947- *WhoAmL 94*
Squazzo, Mildred Katherine *WhoFI 94*
Squibb, Arthur d1680 *DcNaB MP*
Squibb, George Drewry 1906- *Who 94*
Squibb, George S. d1993 *NewYTBS 93*
Squibb, Samuel Dexter 1931- *WhoAm 94, WhoScEn 94*
Squibb, Sandra Hildyard 1943- *WhoMW 93*
Squier, Charles *DrAPF 93*
Squier, Charles LaBarge 1931- *WhoWest 94*
Squier, David Louis 1945- *WhoFI 94*
Squier, Jack Leslie 1927- *WhoAm 94, WhoAmA 93*
Squier, Leslie Hamilton 1917- *WhoAm 94*
Squier, Prudence Ann 1942- *WhoFI 94*
Squier, Robert Dave 1934- *WhoAm 94*
Squiers, Carol 1948- *WhoAmA 93*
Squillace, Alexander Paul 1945- *WhoFI 94*
Squinto, Stephen Paul 1956- *WhoScEn 94*
Squire, Alexander 1917- *WhoAm 94*
Squire, Allan Taft *WhoAmA 93N*
Squire, Anne Marguerite 1920- *WhoAm 94*
Squire, Carole Renee Hutchins 1953- *WhoBlA 94*
Squire, Clifford William 1928- *IntWW 93*
Squire, J.C. *EncSF 93*
Squire, Jack d1938 *WhoHol 92*
Squire, James Robert 1922- *WhoAm 94*
Squire, Judith Maureen 1942- *WhoWest 94*
Squire, Katherine 1903- *WhoHol 92*
Squire, Peter John 1937- *Who 94*
Squire, Peter Ted 1945- *Who 94*
Squire, Rachel Anne 1954- *Who 94*
Squire, Raglan 1912- *Who 94*
Squire, Robin Clifford 1944- *Who 94*
Squire, Ronald d1958 *WhoHol 92*
Squire, Thomas Stuart 1946- *WhoAmL 94*
Squire, Walter Charles 1945- *WhoAmL 94*
Squire, William *Who 94*
Squire, William d1989 *WhoHol 92*
Squire, (Clifford) William 1928- *Who 94*
Squires, Arthur Morton 1916- *WhoAm 94*
Squires, Carolyn 1940- *WhoAmP 93*
Squires, Dale Edward 1950- *WhoFI 94*
Squires, Daniel Joseph 1943- *WhoMW 93*
Squires, Gerald Leopold 1937- *WhoAmA 93*
Squires, James Ralph 1940- *WhoFI 94*
Squires, Jan Ray 1951- *WhoFI 94*
Squires, John Henry 1946- *WhoAm 94, WhoAmL 94*
Squires, Katherine Landey 1959- *WhoFI 94*
Squires, Norma Jean *WhoAmA 93*
Squires, Radcliffe d1993 *NewYTBS 93*
Squires, (James) Radcliffe 1917-1993 *ConAu 140, WrDr 94N*
Squires, Richard Felt 1933- *WhoScEn 94*
Squires, Ron d1993 *NewYTBS 93*
Squires, Scott *WhoAm 94*
Squires, William Allen 1949- *WhoFI 94*
Squires, William Randolph, III 1947- *WhoAm 94, WhoAmL 94*
Squires-Grohe, Linda Lee 1944- *WhoWest 94*
Squyres, Mary Margaret 1950- *WhoAmL 94*
Srager, Leslie 1935- *WhoAm 94*
Sragow, Ellen *WhoAmA 93*
Srb, Adrian Morris 1917- *IntWW 93*
Sreebny, Leo M. 1922- *WhoAm 94*
Sreenan, Patrick Hugh 1959- *WhoFI 94*
Sreenivasan, Katepalli Raju 1947- *WhoAsA 94, WhoScEn 94*
Sreenivasan, Sreenivasa Ranga 1933- *WhoScEn 94*
Sreevalsan, Thazepadath 1935- *WhoAsA 94*
Srere, Benson M. 1928- *WhoAm 94*
Srere, Paul A. 1925- *WhoScEn 94*
Sresty, Guggilam Chalamaiah 1954- *WhoScEn 94*
Sri Delima *BlmGWL*
Sridhara, Channarayapatna Ramakrishna Se 1948- *WhoScEn 94*
Srimongkolkul, Vichai 1958- *WhoMW 93*
Srinivas, Ramachandra 1944- *WhoAsA 94*
Srinivasachari, Samavedam 1926- *WhoScEn 94*
Srinivasan, Gunumakonda Ramaswamiengar *WhoAsA 94*
Srinivasan, Mandayam Paramekanthi 1940- *WhoScEn 94*
Srinivasan, Nagarajan 1964- *WhoMW 93*
Srinivasan, Padmini 1956- *WhoMW 93*
Srinivasan, Ramachandra Srini 1939- *WhoAsA 94*
Srinivasan, Srini 1940- *WhoFI 94*
Srinivasan, Thiru R. 1945- *WhoAsA 94*
Srinivasan, Venkataraman 1944- *WhoAm 94*
Srirama, Malini *WhoAsA 94*
Sriskandan, Kanagaretnam 1930- *Who 94*
Sriskandarajah, Jeganathan 1949- *WhoMW 93*
Srivastava, Chandrika Prasad 1920- *IntWW 93, Who 94*
Srivastava, Hari Mohan 1940- *WhoWest 94*
Srivastava, Kailash Chandra 1947- *WhoScEn 94*
Srivastava, Om P. 1939- *WhoAsA 94*
Srivastava, Om Prakash 1944- *WhoScEn 94*
Srivastava, Prakash Narain 1929- *WhoAsA 94*
Srivastava, Sadanand 1936- *WhoAsA 94*
Srivastava, Satyendra 1935- *ConWorW 93*
Srivatava, Dhanpat Ray *RfGShF*
Sroge, Maxwell Harold 1927- *WhoAm 94*
Sroka, John Walter 1946- *WhoAm 94*
Srole, Leo d1993 *NewYTBS 93*
Sroufe, Evelyn 1945- *WhoAmL 94*
Srull, Lynne Ellen 1952- *WhoMW 93*
Srybnykh, Vyacheslav Mikhailovich 1950- *LngBDD*
Ssekitoleko, Victoria *WhoWomW 91*
Ssemogerere, Paul Kawanga *IntWW 93*
Staab, Heinz A. 1926- *IntWW 93, WhoAm 94, WhoScEn 94*
Staab, Joseph Raymond 1932- *WhoWest 94*
Staab, Michael Joseph 1955- *WhoAmL 94*
Staab, Robert R. 1938- *WhoAmP 93*
Staab, Thomas Eugene 1941- *WhoFI 94*
Staab, Thomas Robert 1942- *WhoAm 94*
Staab, Walter Edward 1933- *WhoAm 94*
Staab, Willodine Leah 1927- *WhoAmP 93*
Staahl, Jim *WhoHol 92*
Staal, Philip Ward 1935- *WhoMW 93*
Staal-Delaunay, Marguerite-Jeanne Cordier de 1684-1750 *BlmGWL*
Staar, Richard F. 1923- *WrDr 94*
Staar, Richard Felix 1923- *WhoAm 94*
Staas, John William 1942- *WhoMW 93*
Staats, Dean Roy 1924- *WhoAm 94*
Staats, Dee Ann 1957- *WhoScEn 94*
Staats, Elmer Boyd 1914- *IntWW 93, WhoAm 94, WhoAmP 93*
Staats, Florence Joan 1940- *WhoBlA 94*
Staats, James Edward 1923- *WhoFI 94*
Staats, Leo 1877-1952 *IntDcB*
Staba, Emil John 1928- *WhoAm 94*
Staback, Edward G. 1937- *WhoAmP 93*
Stabb, William (Walter) 1913- *Who 94*
Stabej, Rudolph John 1952- *WhoMW 93*
Stabenau, James Raymond 1930- *WhoAm 94*
Stabenau, M. Catherine 1948- *WhoScEn 94*
Stabenau, Walter Frank 1942- *WhoScEn 94*
Stabenow, David Lee 1942- *WhoMW 93*
Stabenow, Deborah Ann 1950- *WhoAmP 93, WhoMW 93*
Stabile, Benedict Louis 1927- *WhoAm 94*
Stabile, Dick d1980 *WhoHol 92*
Stabile, Donald Robert 1944- *WhoFI 94*
Stabile, John P. *WhoAmP 93*
Stabile, Mariano 1888-1968 *NewGrDO*
Stabile, Mark Robert 1966- *WhoAmL 94*
Stabinger, Mathias c. 1750-1815 *NewGrDO*
Stabins, Jeff 1959- *WhoAmP 93*
Stabinski, Richard Ernest 1958- *WhoAmL 94*
Stable, (Rondle) Owen (Charles) 1923- *Who 94*
Stableford, Brian M(ichael) 1948- *EncSF 93*
Stableford, Brian M(ichael) 1948-1993 *WrDr 94N*
Stablein, John Joseph, III 1951- *WhoFI 94*
Stablein, Marilyn *DrAPF 93*
Stabler, Arthur Fletcher 1919- *Who 94*
Stabler, Donald Billman 1908- *WhoAm 94*
Stabler, Lewis Vastine, Jr. 1936- *WhoAm 94*
Stabler, Nancy Rae 1946- *WhoMW 93*
Stabler, W. Laird, Jr. 1930- *WhoAmP 93*
Stables, (William) Gordon 1840-1910 *EncSF 93*
Stables, J. Richard 1944- *WhoAmL 94*
Stacey, Bill *WhoHol 92*
Stacey, Carol Ann *WhoIns 94*
Stacey, Carol Horning 1934- *WhoAmP 93*
Stacey, Charles Perry 1906-1989 *WhAm 10*
Stacey, Frank Donald 1929- *IntWW 93*
Stacey, George Alford d1993 *NewYTBS 93 [port]*
Stacey, James Allen 1925- *WhoAmL 94*
Stacey, John Nichol 1920- *Who 94*
Stacey, Judith 1943- *WrDr 94*
Stacey, Kathleen Mary 1951- *WhoAm 94, WhoFI 94*
Stacey, Kathryn *ConAu 141*
Stacey, Lad S. 1926- *WhoAmP 93*
Stacey, Margaret 1922- *Who 94, WrDr 94*
Stacey, Maurice 1907- *IntWW 93, Who 94*
Stacey, Michael Lawrence 1924- *Who 94*
Stacey, Morna Dorothy *Who 94*
Stacey, Nicholas (Anthony Howard) *WrDr 94*
Stacey, Nicolas David 1927- *Who 94*
Stacey, Norma Elaine 1925- *WhoFI 94*
Stacey, Susannah 1926- *WrDr 94*
Stacey, Susannah 1927- *WrDr 94*
Stacey, Thomas Richard 1943- *WhoScEn 94*
Stacey, Tom 1930- *WrDr 94*
Stachacz, John Charles 1952- *WhoAm 94*
Stachel, John Jay 1928- *WhoAm 94, WhoScEn 94*
Stachelberg, Charles G. *WhoAmA 93N*
Stachler, Robert G. 1929- *WhoAm 94*
Stachowiak, David Alan 1957- *WhoMW 93*
Stachowiak, Raymond Charles 1958- *WhoFI 94*
Stachowske, Vicki L. 1952- *WhoAmP 93*
Stachowski, William T. 1949- *WhoAmP 93*
Stacia, Kevin Maurice 1958- *WhoBlA 94*
Stack, Beatriz de Greiff 1939- *WhoAmL 94*
Stack, Brian J. 1959- *WhoAmL 94*
Stack, Charlie Ray 1929- *WhoAmP 93*
Stack, Daniel 1928- *WhoAmL 94*
Stack, Diane Virginia 1958- *WhoFI 94*
Stack, Edward MacGregor 1919- *WrDr 94*
Stack, Edward William 1935- *WhoAm 94*
Stack, Elizabeth 1957- *WhoHol 92*
Stack, Frank Huntington 1937- *WhoAmA 93*
Stack, Gael Z. 1941- *WhoAmA 93*
Stack, Geoffrey Lawrence 1943- *WhoAm 94, WhoFI 94, WhoWest 94*
Stack, George 1932- *WrDr 94*
Stack, George 1946- *Who 94*
Stack, George Joseph *WhoAm 94*
Stack, Gerald Francis 1953- *WhoAmL 94*
Stack, J. William, Jr. 1918- *WhoAm 94*
Stack, Joanne Tunney 1952- *WhoAmL 94*
Stack, John Wallace 1937- *WhoAm 94*
Stack, Kevin J. 1951- *WhoAmL 94*
Stack, Lee Prather 1893- *WhAm 10*
Stack, Maurice Daniel 1917- *WhoAm 94*
Stack, Michael 1941- *WhoAmA 93*
Stack, Neville *Who 94*
Stack, Neville 1928- *Who 94*
Stack, (Thomas) Neville 1919- *Who 94*
Stack, Paul Francis 1946- *WhoAmL 94, WhoMW 93*
Stack, Prunella *Who 94*
Stack, (Ann) Prunella 1914- *Who 94*
Stack, Robert 1919- *IntMPA 94, WhoHol 92*
Stack, Robert Langford 1919- *WhoAm 94*
Stack, Roger *WhoHol 92*
Stack, Stephen A., Jr. 1945- *WhoAm 94, WhoAmL 94*
Stack, Stephen S. 1934- *WhoAm 94, WhoFI 94*
Stackelberg, Olaf Patrick Von 1932- *WhoAm 94*
Stackhouse, Christian Paul 1960- *WhoWest 94*
Stackhouse, Dale E. 1962- *WhoAmL 94*
Stackhouse, David William, Jr. 1926- *WhoMW 93*
Stackhouse, E. Marilyn 1955- *WhoBlA 94*
Stackhouse, Heidi Honegger 1962- *WhoFI 94*
Stackhouse, John Wesley 1940- *WhoFI 94*
Stackhouse, Richard Gilbert 1929- *WhoAm 94*
Stackhouse, Robert 1942- *WhoAmA 93*
Stackhouse, Will, III 1942- *WhoWest 94*
Stackpole, Edouard A. d1993 *NewYTBS 93*
Stackpole, Edouard Alexander 1903-1993 *ConAu 142*
Stackpole, Robert Dauer 1946- *WhoFI 94*
Stacks, William Leon 1928-1991 *WhoAmA 93N*
Stacpoole, H(enry) De Vere 1865-1951 *EncSF 93*
Stacpoole, John Wentworth 1926- *Who 94*
Stacy, Bill Wayne 1938- *WhoAm 94, WhoWest 94*
Stacy, Charles Brecknock 1924- *WhoAm 94*
Stacy, David Harry 1949- *WhoAmL 94*
Stacy, Dennis William 1945- *WhoFI 94, WhoScEn 94*
Stacy, Donald L. 1925- *WhoAmA 93*
Stacy, Gardner W. 1921- *WhoAm 94*
Stacy, Gaylon L. 1934- *WhoAmP 93*
Stacy, James 1936- *WhoHol 92*
Stacy, Jan 1948-1989 *EncSF 93*
Stacy, John Russell 1919- *WhoAmA 93*
Stacy, John Will 1953- *WhoAmP 93*
Stacy, Pheriba 1940- *WhoScEn 94*
Stacy, Richard A. 1942- *WhoAm 94, WhoAmL 94*
Stacy, Roy Lee 1950- *WhoAmL 94*
Stacy, Ryder *EncSF 93*
Stacy, T. Don 1934- *IntWW 93*
Stacy, Theodore 1923- *WhoAmP 93*
Stacy, Thomas Donnie 1934- *WhoAm 94, WhoFI 94, WhoWest 94*
Stacy, Verna Mae 1931- *WhoAmP 93*
Staddon, John Eric Rayner *WhoAm 94, WhoScEn 94*
Stade, Frederica von *NewGrDO*
Stade, George 1933- *WrDr 94*
Stade, George Gustav *WhoAm 94*
Stadel, Renee Ann 1964- *WhoAmL 94*
Stadelman, William Ralph 1919- *WhoAm 94*
Stadelmann, Eduard Joseph 1920- *WhoMW 93*
Stadem, Paul David 1953- *WhoMW 93*
Staden, Berndt von 1919- *IntWW 93*
Staden, Sigmund Theophil 1607?-1655? *NewGrDO*
Stader, Paul *WhoHol 92*
Stading, Sofia Francisca 1763-1837 *NewGrDO*
Stadlbauer, Harald Stefan 1963- *WhoScEn 94*
Stadlen, Lewis J. 1947- *WhoHol 92*
Stadlen, Nicholas Felix 1950- *Who 94*
Stadler, Albert 1923- *WhoAmA 93*
Stadler, Craig Robert 1953- *WhoAm 94, WhoWest 94*
Stadler, Gerald P. 1937- *WhoFI 94*
Stadler, James Robert 1964- *WhoAmL 94*
Stadler, Martin F. 1942- *WhoAm 94*
Stadler, Matthew 1959- *ConAu 140*
Stadler, Maximilian 1748-1833 *NewGrDO*
Stadler, Sara R. 1943- *WhoAmL 94*
Stadler, Sergey Valentinovich 1962- *IntWW 93*
Stadley, Pat Anna May Gough 1918- *WhoWest 94*
Stadlman, Rebecca Murphy 1952- *WhoMW 93*
Stadnyuk, Ivan Fotievich 1920- *IntWW 93*
Stadter, Philip Austin 1936- *WhoAm 94*
Stadtler, Beatrice Horwitz 1921- *WhoAm 94*
Stadtman, Earl R. 1919- *IntWW 93*
Stadtman, Earl Reece 1919- *WhoAm 94, WhoScEn 94*
Stadtman, Thressa Campbell 1920- *IntWW 93, WhoAm 94, WhoScEn 94*
Stadtman, Verne August 1926- *WhoAm 94, WrDr 94*
Stadtmueller, Diana Lynne 1946- *WhoAmP 93*
Stadtmueller, Joseph Peter 1942- *WhoAm 94, WhoAmL 94*
Stadukhin, Mikhail d1666 *WhWE*
Stadum, Tony *WhoAmP 93*
Staebell, Ronald Thomas 1945- *WhoMW 93*
Staebler, Michael B. 1943- *WhoAmL 94*
Staebler, Neil 1905- *WhoAmP 93*
Staehelin, Lucas Andrew 1939- *WhoAm 94, WhoWest 94*
Staehle, Robert L. 1955- *WhoAm 94*
Stael, Germaine Necker de 1766-1817 *BlmGWL*
Stael, Madame de 1766-1817 *HisWorL [port]*
Stael, Viktor d1982 *WhoHol 92*
Staelin, David Hudson 1938- *WhoAm 94*
Staelin, Richard 1939- *WhoAm 94*
Staels-Dompas, Nora 1925- *WhoWomW 91*
Staempfli, Edward 1908- *NewGrDO*
Staempfli, George W. 1910- *WhoAmA 93*
Staes, Beverly N. *WhoBlA 94*
Staff, Frank 1918-1971 *IntDcB [port]*
Staff, Frank William 1908- *WrDr 94*
Staff, Robert James, Jr. 1946- *WhoScEn 94, WhoWest 94*
Staffa, Judy Anne 1960- *WhoScEn 94*
Staffaroni, Robert J. 1952- *WhoAmL 94*
Staffel, Doris 1921- *WhoAmA 93*
Staffel, Rudolf Harry 1911- *WhoAmA 93*

Stark, Graham 1922- *WhoHol 92*
Stark, Gregory Francis 1955- *WhoFI 94*
Stark, Harriet *EncSF 93*
Stark, Jack Gage 1882-1950 *WhoAmA 93N*
Stark, Jack Lee 1934- *WhoAm 94, WhoWest 94*
Stark, Jeffrey G. 1944- *WhoAmL 94*
Stark, Joan Scism 1937- *WhoAm 94, WhoMW 93*
Stark, John 1728-1822 *AmRev, WhAmRev [port]*
Stark, John 1919- *WrDr 94*
Stark, John David 1956- *WhoScEn 94*
Stark, John Edwin 1916- *WhoAm 94*
Stark, Jonathan *WhoHol 92*
Stark, Joshua 1932- *WrDr 94*
Stark, Koo 1956- *WhoHol 92*
Stark, Leighton d1924 *WhoHol 92*
Stark, Linda Robin 1955- *WhoAmL 94*
Stark, Lorraine Antoinette 1967- *WhoAmL 94*
Stark, Mabel d1968 *WhoHol 92*
Stark, Martin Alan 1956- *WhoFI 94*
Stark, Martin J. 1941- *WhoWest 94*
Stark, Maurice Gene 1935- *WhoAm 94*
Stark, Milton Dale 1932- *WhoAm 94, WhoWest 94*
Stark, Nathan J. 1920- *IntWW 93*
Stark, Nathan Julius 1920- *WhoAm 94*
Stark, Norman 1940- *WhoFI 94*
Stark, Patricia Ann 1937- *WhoMW 93*
Stark, Ray *IntMPA 94, WhoAm 94, WhoWest 94*
Stark, Ray c. 1914- *IntDcF 2-4 [port]*
Stark, (Delbert) Raymond 1919- *EncSF 93*
Stark, Richard *EncSF 93*
Stark, Richard 1933- *WrDr 94*
Stark, Richard Boies 1915- *WhoAm 94*
Stark, Richard Clinton 1948- *WhoAm 94, WhoAmL 94*
Stark, Robert 1939- *WhoAmA 93*
Stark, Robert Martin 1930- *WhoAm 94*
Stark, Rohn Taylor 1959- *WhoAm 94, WhoMW 93*
Stark, S. Daniel, Jr. 1953- *WhoFI 94, WhoWest 94*
Stark, Sharon Sheehe *DrAPF 93*
Stark, Shirley J. 1927- *WhoBlA 94*
Stark, Stephen *DrAPF 93*
Stark, Stephen (Edward) 1958- *ConAu 140*
Stark, Steven 1943- *WhoFI 94*
Stark, Susan Allentuck 1955- *WhoAmL 94*
Stark, Temple Cunningham 1946- *WhoIns 94*
Stark, Thomas Michael 1925- *WhoAmL 94*
Stark, Werner 1909- *WrDr 94*
Stark, Werner E. 1921- *WhoFI 94*
Stark, Wilbur 1922- *IntMPA 94*
Stark, William 1770-1813 *DcNaB MP*
Stark-Adamec, Cannie 1945- *WhoAm 94, WhoWest 94*
Starke, Anthony *WhoHol 92*
Starke, Catherine Juanita 1913- *WhoBlA 94*
Starke, Edgar Arlin, Jr. 1936- *WhoAm 94*
Starke, H. F. Gerhard 1916- *IntWW 93*
Starke, Harold E., Jr. 1944- *WhoAmL 94*
Starke, Heinz 1911- *IntWW 93*
Starke, Henderson *EncSF 93*
Starke, Hortensia L. *WhoWomW 91*
Starke, John Erskine 1913- *Who 94*
Starke, Joseph Gabriel 1911- *WrDr 94*
Starke, Pauline d1977 *WhoHol 92*
Starke, Shirley Diana 1950- *WhoMW 93*
Starke, Tod 1961- *WhoHol 92*
Starke, William H. *WhoAmP 93*
Starker, Janos 1924- *IntWW 93, Who 94*
Starkey, Bert d1939 *WhoHol 92*
Starkey, Frank David 1944- *WhoBlA 94*
Starkey, Harry Charles 1925- *WhoWest 94*
Starkey, Joe Warren 1948- *WhoWest 94*
Starkey, John (Philip) 1938- *Who 94*
Starkey, Lawrence Harry 1919- *WhoMW 93*
Starkey, Nelson R., Jr. 1929- *WhoAmP 93*
Starkey, Richard 1940- *IntWW 93, WhoAm 94*
Starkey, Robert Lyman 1899- *WhAm 10*
Starkey, Russell Bruce, Jr. 1942- *WhoFI 94, WhoScEn 94*
Starkey, Thomas c. 1499-1538 *DcLB 132*
Starkman, Betty Provizer 1929- *WhoMW 93*
Starkman, Elaine *DrAPF 93*
Starkman, Gary Lee 1946- *WhoAm 94*
Starkman, Paul Ely 1956- *WhoAmL 94*
Starkoff, Bernard Julius 1917-1991 *WhAm 10*
Starkov, Vladislav Andreyevich 1940- *IntWW 93*
Starks, Doris Nearror 1937- *WhoBlA 94*
Starks, Fred William 1921- *WhoAm 94*
Starks, John *WhoBlA 94*
Starks, Michael Richard 1941- *WhoScEn 94*
Starks, Rick 1948- *WhoBlA 94*
Starks, Robert J. 1945- *WhoAmP 93*
Starks, Robert Terry 1944- *WhoBlA 94*
Starks, William Edward 1965- *WhoFI 94*
Starks, William Oscar 1921- *WhoMW 93*
Starkweather, David 1935- *ConDr 93*
Starkweather, Frederick Thomas 1933- *WhoFI 94, WhoWest 94*
Starkweather, Gary Keith 1938- *WhoScEn 94*
Starkweather, William E. B. 1879-1969 *WhoAmA 93N*
Starkweather, William Henry 1944- *WhoWest 94*
Starkweather-Nelson, Cynthia Louise 1950- *WhoAmA 93*
Starleaf, Dennis Roy 1938- *WhoFI 94*
Starling, Dorothy Mae 1939- *WhoAmP 93*
Starling, Ernest Henry 1866-1922 *WorScD*
Starling, James Lyne 1930- *WhoAm 94*
Starling, John Crawford 1916- *WhoBlA 94*
Starling, Pat 1922- *WhoHol 92*
Starling, Sandra Meira 1944- *WhoWomW 91*
Starling, Thomas *DrAPF 93*
Starlinger, Peter 1931- *IntWW 93*
Starmack, John Robert 1942- *WhoScEn 94*
Starn, Douglas *WhoAmA 93*
Starn, Douglas 1961- *WhoAm 94*
Starn, Mike P. *WhoAmA 93*
Starn, Mike P. 1961- *WhoAm 94*
Starn, Peter 1944- *WhoAm 94, WhoAmL 94*
Starner, Craig Leslie 1934- *WhoFI 94*
Starnes, Earl Maxwell 1926- *WhoAm 94*
Starnes, Edgar Vance 1956- *WhoAmP 93*
Starnes, James Wright 1933- *WhoAmL 94*
Starnes, Paul M. 1934- *WhoAmP 93*
Starnes, R. Leland d1980 *WhoHol 92*
Starnes, Rebecca L. 1941- *WhoAmP 93*
Starnes, Ruth 1929- *WhoAmP 93*
Starnes, William Herbert, Jr. 1934- *WhoAm 94, WhoFI 94, WhoScEn 94*
Starns, Byron E., Jr. 1943- *WhoAmL 94*
Starn Twins 1961- *WhoAmA 93*
Starobinski, Jean 1920- *IntWW 93*
Starodubtsev, Vasily Aleksandrovich 1931- *LngBDD*
Starosolszky, Odon 1931- *WhoScEn 94*
Starovoitova, Galina Vasilevna 1946- *LngBDD*
Starovoytova, Galina Vasilyevna 1946- *IntWW 93*
Starpattern, Rita *WhoAmA 93*
Starr, Allan H. 1944- *WhoAm 94*
Starr, Anne 1929- *WrDr 94*
Starr, Arnold 1932- *WhoAm 94*
Starr, Bart *ProFbHF [port]*
Starr, Bart 1934- *WhoAm 94*
Starr, Bill *EncSF 93*
Starr, Charles 1932- *WhoAmP 93*
Starr, Charles Leonard 1951- *WhoWest 94*
Starr, Chauncey 1912- *WhoAm 94*
Starr, Chester G. 1914- *WhoAm 94, WrDr 94*
Starr, Christopher *WhoHol 92*
Starr, David 1922- *WhoAm 94*
Starr, David 1950- *WhoAm 94*
Starr, David Evan 1962- *WhoAm 94, WhoFI 94, WhoMW 93*
Starr, Donald Robert 1959- *WhoMW 93*
Starr, Ellen Gates 1859-1940 *DcAmReB 2*
Starr, Eugene Carl 1901-1988 *WhAm 10*
Starr, Frances d1973 *WhoHol 92*
Starr, Freddie *WhoHol 92*
Starr, Frederick d1921 *WhoHol 92*
Starr, Frederick Brown 1932- *WhoAm 94, WhoFI 94*
Starr, Gary Eugene 1951- *WhoMW 93*
Starr, Grier Forsythe 1926- *WhoAm 94, WhoWest 94*
Starr, Harold Page 1932- *WhoAmL 94*
Starr, Harvey 1946- *WhoAm 94*
Starr, Henry *ConAu 42NR*
Starr, Henry d1921 *WhoHol 92*
Starr, Isaac 1895-1989 *WhAm 10*
Starr, Isidore 1911- *WhoAm 94, WhoAmL 94*
Starr, Ivar Miles 1950- *WhoAmL 94*
Starr, James Edward 1944- *WhoWest 94*
Starr, James LeRoy 1939- *WhoScEn 94*
Starr, John C. 1939- *WhoAm 94*
Starr, John Carroll, Jr. 1940- *WhoAmP 93*
Starr, John Robert 1927- *WhoAm 94*
Starr, June (O.) *ConAu 140*
Starr, Kate 1912- *WrDr 94*
Starr, Kay 1922- *WhoHol 92*
Starr, Kenneth Winston 1946- *WhoAm 94, WhoAmL 94*
Starr, Leon 1937- *WhoAm 94*
Starr, Luther Wade 1928- *WhoAmL 94*
Starr, M. Gerhard 1963- *WhoMW 93*
Starr, Mark *EncSF 93*
Starr, Martin Kenneth 1927- *WhoAm 94*
Starr, Marvin Blake 1928- *WhoAmL 94*
Starr, Melvin Lee 1922- *WhoWest 94*
Starr, Michael 1948- *WhoAmL 94*
Starr, Mike 1966- *See* Alice in Chains *ConMus 10*
Starr, Miriam Carolyn 1951- *WhoFI 94*
Starr, Paul Elliot 1949- *WhoAm 94*
Starr, Richard Cawthon 1924- *WhoAm 94, WhoScEn 94*
Starr, Richard William 1920- *WhoAm 94*
Starr, Rick 1947- *WhoAm 94, WhoMW 93*
Starr, Ringo 1940- *ConMus 10 [port], IntMPA 94, IntWW 93, WhoAm 94, WhoHol 92*
Starr, Robert A., Jr. 1942- *WhoAmP 93*
Starr, Robert Irving 1932- *WhoWest 94*
Starr, Roland *EncSF 93*
Starr, Ross Marc 1945- *WhoAm 94*
Starr, Stephen Frederick 1940- *WhoAm 94, WhoMW 93*
Starr, Steven Dawson 1944- *WhoAm 94*
Starr, Stuart Howard 1942- *WhoScEn 94*
Starr, Terrell A. 1926- *WhoAmP 93*
Starr, V. Hale 1936- *WhoAm 94*
Starr, Valerie d1967 *WhoHol 92*
Starratt, Patricia Elizabeth 1943- *WhoWest 94*
Starratt, Richard Courtney 1936- *WhoWest 94*
Starrett, Charles d1986 *WhoHol 92*
Starrett, Claude Ennis, Jr. *WhoHol 92*
Starrett, Frederick Kent 1947- *WhoAmL 94*
Starrett, Jack d1989 *WhoHol 92*
Starrett, Jennifer *WhoHol 92*
Starrfield, Sumner Grosby 1940- *WhoAm 94, WhoWest 94*
Starrfield, Susan Lee 1945- *WhoWest 94*
Starrs, Elizabeth Anne 1954- *WhoAmL 94*
Starrs, James Edward 1930- *WhoAmL 94, WhoScEn 94*
Starrs, Mildred *WhoAmA 93N*
Starr-White, Debi 1947- *WhoBlA 94*
Starry, Donn Albert 1925- *WhoAm 94*
Starry, Leo Joseph 1894- *WhAm 10*
Starry, Mary Jane 1918- *WhoAmP 93*
Stars, William Kenneth 1921-1985 *WhoAmA 93N*
Starshak, James L. 1945- *WhoAmL 94*
Startup, Charles Harry 1914- *WhoAm 94*
Startup, Vivian Margaret 1913- *WhoAmP 93*
Startzman, Shirley Kayleen 1946- *WhoMW 93*
Stary, Karen Lynn 1958- *WhoMW 93*
Staryk, Steven S. 1932- *WhoAm 94*
Starzer, Joseph 1726?-1787 *NewGrDO*
Starzer, Michael Ray 1961- *WhoScEn 94*
Starzinger, Vincent Evans 1929- *WhoAm 94*
Starzl, R(oman) F(rederick) 1899-1976 *EncSF 93*
Starzl, Thomas E. 1926- *CurBio 93 [port]*
Starzl, Thomas E(arl) 1926- *ConAu 140*
Starzl, Thomas Earl 1926- *WhoAm 94*
Stasack, Edward Armen 1929- *WhoAm 94, WhoAmA 93*
Stasenko, Richard Edward 1941- *WhoWest 94*
Stasheff, Christopher 1944- *EncSF 93, WrDr 94*
Stasheff, James Dillon 1936- *WhoAm 94*
Stashower, Arthur L. 1930- *WhoWest 94*
Stashower, Daniel (Meyer) 1960- *WrDr 94*
Stashower, Michael David 1926- *WhoAm 94*
Stasi, Bernard 1930- *IntWW 93*
Stasiak, Barbara Castellana 1947- *WhoAmP 93*
Stasik, Andrew J. 1932- *WhoAmA 93*
Stasior, William F. 1941- *WhoScEn 94*
Stasios, James Christos 1948- *WhoFI 94*
Staskun, Benjamin 1925- *WhoScEn 94*
Stasov, Vladimir Vasil'yevich 1824-1906 *NewGrDO*
Stassen, Harold Edward 1907- *Who 94*
Stassen, Hendrik Gerard 1935- *IntWW 93*
Stassen, John Henry 1943- *WhoAm 94, WhoAmL 94*
Stassino, Paul *WhoHol 92*
Stassinopoulos, Arianna 1950- *WrDr 94*
Stassinopoulos, Michael 1905- *IntWW 93*
Stastny, Charles Joseph 1964- *WhoMW 93*
Stastny, John Anton 1921- *WhoFI 94*
Staszesky, Francis Myron 1918- *WhoAm 94*
Stata, Raymond 1934- *WhoFI 94*
Staten, John Edward 1943- *WhoMW 93*
Staten, Marcea Bland 1948- *WhoBlA 94*
Staten, Randolph 1944- *WhoAmP 93*
States, Alan E. 1946- *WhoAmP 93*
States, Bert Olen 1929- *IntWW 93*
States, Jack Sterling 1941- *WhoAm 94*
States, Robert Arthur 1932- *WhoBlA 94*
Statescu, Constantin 1927- *IntWW 93*
Statham, Carl 1950- *WhoBlA 94*
Statham, Norman 1922- *Who 94*
Statham, Stan 1939- *WhoAmP 93*
Stathatos, Stephanos 1922- *Who 94*
Stathis, Georgia *AstEnc*
Stathis, Nicholas John 1924- *WhoAmL 94, WhoFI 94*
Statkowski, Roman 1859-1925 *NewGrDO*
Statler, Betty Jean 1947- *WhoMW 93*
Statler, Charles Daniel 1938- *WhoFI 94*
Statler, Irving Carl 1923- *WhoAm 94, WhoScEn 94, WhoWest 94*
Statler, Oliver 1915- *WrDr 94*
Statler, Oliver Hadley 1915- *WhoAm 94*
Statler, Stuart M. 1943- *WhoAmP 93*
Statler Brothers, The *WhoHol 92*
Statman, Jan B. *WhoAmA 93*
Staton, David Michael 1940- *WhoAmP 93*
Staton, W. Richard 1958- *WhoAmP 93*
Staton, William W. *WhoAmP 93*
Statten, Vargo *EncSF 93*
Statzer, Darrell Eugene, Jr. 1950- *WhoMW 93*
Staub, August William 1931- *WhoAm 94*
Staub, E. Brian 1927- *WhoIns 94*
Staub, Ervin 1938- *WrDr 94*
Staub, John Thomas 1943- *WhoMW 93*
Staub, Ralph d1969 *WhoHol 92*
Staub, W. Arthur 1923- *WhoAm 94*
Staubach, Roger *ProFbHF [port]*
Staubach, Roger Thomas 1942- *WhoAm 94*
Stauber, Joel Vincent 1954- *WhoMW 93*
Stauber, Marilyn Jean 1938- *WhoMW 93*
Stauber-Johnson, Elizabeth Jane 1950- *WhoMW 93*
St-Aubin, Arthur 1930- *WhoAm 94*
Staubinger, Mathias *NewGrDO*
Staubitz, Arthur Frederick 1939- *WhoAm 94, WhoAmL 94, WhoFI 94*
Staublin, Judith Ann 1936- *WhoFI 94*
Staubus, George Joseph 1926- *WhoAm 94*
Staudenmaier, John Michael 1939- *WhoMW 93*
Stauder, William Vincent 1922- *WhoAm 94*
Stauderman, Bruce Ford 1919- *WhoAm 94*
Staudigl, Gisela 1864-1929 *NewGrDO*
Staudigl, Joseph 1850-1916 *NewGrDO*
Staudinger, Hermann *WorScD*
Staudinger, Stephen Stanley 1956- *WhoFI 94*
Staudinger, Ulrich 1935- *IntWW 93*
Staudt, Ronald William 1946- *WhoAmL 94*
Staudte, Diane Elaine 1962- *WhoMW 93*
Stauff, William James 1949- *WhoFI 94*
Stauffenberg, Claus Schenk Graf von 1907-1944 *HisWorL*
Stauffer, Alan C. 1945- *WhoAmP 93*
Stauffer, Charles Henry 1913- *WhoAm 94*
Stauffer, Delmar J. 1944- *WhoAm 94*
Stauffer, Edna Pennypacker 1887-1956 *WhoAmA 93N*
Stauffer, Eric P. 1948- *WhoAmL 94*
Stauffer, Joanne Rogan 1956- *WhoFI 94*
Stauffer, John *WhoAmP 93*
Stauffer, John H. 1928- *WhoAm 94, WhoMW 93*
Stauffer, John Richard 1946- *WhoMW 93*
Stauffer, Larry Allen 1954- *WhoScEn 94*
Stauffer, Peter Wallace 1947- *WhoMW 93*
Stauffer, Richard L. 1932- *WhoAmA 93*
Stauffer, Robert Allen 1920- *WhoAm 94*
Stauffer, Ronald Eugene 1949- *WhoAm 94, WhoAmL 94*
Stauffer, Ronald Jay 1961- *WhoScEn 94*
Stauffer, Sarah Ann 1915- *WhoAm 94, WhoAmP 93*
Stauffer, Stanley Howard 1920- *WhoAm 94, WhoMW 93*
Stauffer, Thomas Bradley 1959- *WhoMW 93*
Stauffer, Thomas George 1932- *WhoAm 94*
Stauffer, Thomas Michael 1941- *WhoAm 94, WhoFI 94*
Stauffer, William Albert 1930- *WhoAm 94*
Staughton, Christopher (Stephen Thomas Jonathan Thayer) 1933- *Who 94*
Staum, Sonja 1959- *WhoAmA 93*
Staum-Kuniej, Sonja 1959- *WhoMW 93*
Staunton, Ann *WhoHol 92*
Staunton, John Joseph Jameson 1911- *WhoMW 93*
Staunton, Marie 1952- *Who 94*
Staunton, Schuyler *EncSF 93*
Stauss, Ima d1976 *WhoHol 92*
Stauter, Susan Ellen 1949- *WhoWest 94*
Stautner, Ernie *ProFbHF [port]*
Stavans, Ilan 1961- *WhoHisp 94*
Stavans, Isaac 1931- *WhoAmA 93*
Stavaridis, Pat(ricia Ann) 1942- *WhoAmA 93*

Steele, Joseph Henry d1980 WhoHol 92
Steele, Joyce Yvonne 1930- WhoBlA 94
Steele, Karen 1934- WhoHol 92
Steele, Karen Kiarsis 1942- WhoAmP 93
Steele, Kathleen F. 1960- WhoAmP 93
Steele, Kathleen Frances 1960- WhoMW 93
Steele, Kenneth Al 1965- WhoMW 93
Steele, Kenneth Franklin, Jr. 1944- WhoAm 94
Steele, Kenneth Walter Lawrence 1914- Who 94
Steele, Kevin D. 1958- WhoWest 94
Steele, Lee WhoHol 92
Steele, Lendell Eugene 1928- WhoAm 94
Steele, Linda EncSF 93
Steele, Lou WhoHol 92
Steele, Marian DrAPF 93
Steele, Marjorie 1930- WhoHol 92
Steele, Mary Q(uintard) 1922- WrDr 94
Steele, Max DrAPF 93
Steele, (Henry) Max(well) 1922- WrDr 94
Steele, Michael Chandos Merrett 1931- Who 94
Steele, Michael Glynn 1955- WhoAmP 93
Steele, Michael W. WhoBlA 94
Steele, Minnie d1949 WhoHol 92
Steele, Morris J. EncSF 93
Steele, Myron Thomas 1945- WhoAmP 93
Steele, Oliver 1928- WhoAm 94
Steele, Oliver Leon 1915- WhoMW 93
Steele, Percy H., Jr. 1920- WhoBlA 94
Steele, Peter 1935- WrDr 94
Steele, Pippa WhoHol 92
Steele, R. David 1931- WrDr 94
Steele, Railey A. 1934- WhoAmP 93
Steele, Ralph J. WhoAmP 93
Steele, Richard 1672-1729 BlmGEL, IntDcT 2
Steele, Richard Allen 1952- WhoMW 93
Steele, Richard Charles 1928- Who 94
Steele, Richard J. 1925- WhoAm 94
Steele, Richard W(illiam) 1934- WrDr 94
Steele, Robert WhoAmP 93
Steele, Robert Edward 1954- WhoIns 94
Steele, Robert Howe 1913- WhoAmP 93
Steele, Robert Michael 1956- WhoAmL 94
Steele, Rodney Redfearn 1930- WhoAm 94, WhoAmL 94
Steele, Ruby L. WhoBlA 94, WhoMW 93
Steele, Rupert Who 94
Steele, (Philip John) Rupert 1920- Who 94
Steele, Shelby 1946- AfrAmAl 6 [port], CurBio 93 [port], WhoAm 94, WhoBlA 94, WrDr 94
Steele, Thomas H. 1948- WhoAmL 94
Steele, Thomas Joseph 1933- WhoWest 94
Steele, Thomas McKnight 1948- WhoAmL 94
Steele, Timothy DrAPF 93
Steele, Timothy (Reid) 1948- WrDr 94
Steele, Tom d1990 WhoHol 92
Steele, Tommy 1936- IntMPA 94, IntWW 93, Who 94, WhoHol 92
Steele, Vernon d1955 WhoHol 92
Steele, Warren Bell 1923- WhoBlA 94
Steele, William d1966 WhoHol 92
Steele, William Arthur 1953- WhoFI 94, WhoWest 94
Steele, William B., III 1950- WhoAmL 94
Steele-Bodger, Alasdair 1924- Who 94
Steele-Bodger, Michael Roland 1925- Who 94
Steele Clapp, Jonathan Charles 1968- WhoScEn 94
Steele-Perkins, Christopher Horace 1947- IntWW 93
Steele-Perkins, Derek (Duncombe) 1908- Who 94
Steelman, David Lloyd 1953- WhoAmP 93
Steelman, Earlene Mae 1927- WhoAmP 93
Steelman, Hosea d1953 WhoHol 92
Steelman, John Robert 1948- WhoMW 93
Steelman, Josie Acosta 1939- WhoHisp 94
Steelman, Robert J(ames) 1914- WrDr 94
Steelman, Sanford Lewis 1922- WhoScEn 94
Steelman, Sara G. 1946- WhoAmP 93
Steen, Anthony David 1939- Who 94
Steen, Carlton Duane 1932- WhoAm 94
Steen, Carol J. 1943- WhoAmA 93
Steen, Charles M. 1943- WhoAmL 94
Steen, David Samuel 1935- WhoWest 94
Steen, Don 1949- WhoAmP 93
Steen, Donald Mariner 1924- WhoAmP 93
Steen, Ellen Rae 1953- WhoFI 94
Steen, Jessica WhoHol 92
Steen, John Francis, Jr. 1954- WhoFI 94
Steen, John Thomas, Jr. 1949- WhoAm 94, WhoAmL 94, WhoFI 94
Steen, Lowell Harrison 1923- WhoAm 94, WhoMW 93
Steen, Melvin Clifford 1907-1992 WhAm 10
Steen, Michael d1983 WhoHol 92
Steen, Norman Frank 1933- WhoAm 94
Steen, Paul Joseph 1932- WhoAm 94, WhoWest 94
Steen, Reiulf 1933- IntWW 93
Steen, Richard Harlan 1949- WhoAmL 94
Steen, Wesley Wilson 1946- WhoAm 94
Steenbergen, Gary Lewis 1959- WhoScEn 94
Steenburgen, Mary 1953- IntMPA 94, WhoAm 94, WhoHol 92
Steene, William 1888-1965 WhoAmA 93N
Steeneck, Lee R. 1948- WhoIns 94
Steenhagen, Robert Lewis 1922- WhoAm 94
Steenland, James Peter 1951- WhoFI 94
Steenrod, Ralston W. 1937- WhoAmL 94
Steensberg, Axel 1906- IntWW 93
Steensgaard, Anthony Harvey 1963- WhoWest 94
Steensgaard, Niels Palle 1932- IntWW 93
Steensland, Ronald Paul 1946- WhoAm 94
Steensma, Andy 1942- WhoAmP 93
Steensma, Robert Charles 1930- WhoAm 94
Steensnaes, Einar 1942- IntWW 93
Steeples, Douglas Wayne 1935- WhoAm 94
Steer, Alfred Gilbert, Jr. 1913- WhoAm 94
Steer, Charles Melvin 1913-1990 WhAm 10
Steer, David 1951- Who 94
Steer, Dulaney Gordon 1956- WhoAmL 94
Steer, John Richard 1949- WhoAmL 94
Steer, John Richardson 1928- Who 94
Steer, Kenneth Arthur 1913- Who 94
Steer, Reginald David 1945- WhoAm 94, WhoAmL 94
Steer, Stanley Charles Who 94
Steer, Wilfred Reed 1926- Who 94
Steer, William Reed Hornby d1993 Who 94N
Steere, Allen Caruthers, Jr. 1943- WhoAm 94
Steere, Clifton WhoHol 92
Steere, Ernest H. L. Who 94
Steere, Peter Kormann 1929- WhoAmL 94
Steere, William Campbell, Jr. 1936- WhoAm 94, WhoFI 94
Steers, Edward 1910- WhoAm 94
Steers, George W. 1941- WhoAmL 94
Steers, Larry d1951 WhoHol 92
Steers, Newton Ivan, Jr. 1917- WhoAm 94, WhoAmP 93
Steers, Thomas c. 1670-1750 DcNaB MP
Steeves, Borden Palmer 1913- WhoAmP 93
Steeves, Doriene Melendy 1937- WhoAmP 93
Steeves, Mark Aaron 1958- WhoAm 94
Stefan, Ross 1934- WhoAmA 93
Stefan, Steve A. 1937- WhoAm 94
Stefan, Verena 1947- BlmGWL
Stefan, Virginia d1964 WhoHol 92
Stefancic, David Russell 1952- WhoMW 93
Stefanek, Margaret Mary 1955- WhoMW 93
Stefanelli, Benito WhoHol 92
Stefanelli, Joe 1921- WhoAmA 93
Stefanelli, Joseph James 1921- WhoAm 94
Stefanescu, I. Stefan 1929- IntWW 93
Stefani, Jan 1746-1829 NewGrDO
Stefani, Jozef 1800-1876 NewGrDO
Stefaniak, Norbert John 1921- WhoAm 94
Stefaniak, Robert C. 1935- WhoAmP 93
Stefanics, Elizabeth T. WhoAmP 93
Stefanides, Christine Marie 1953- WhoFI 94
Stefanides, Steven Arthur 1949- WhoAmP 93
Stefanik, Janet Ruth 1938- WhoMW 93
Stefanile, Felix DrAPF 93
Stefanini, John A. WhoAmP 93
Stefanki, John X. 1920- WhoWest 94
Stefanko, Robert Allen 1943- WhoFI 94
Stefano, Giuseppe di NewGrDO
Stefano, Joseph William 1922- WhoAm 94
Stefano, Ross William 1955- WhoAm 94
Stefanon, Anthony 1949- WhoAmL 94
Stefanopoulos, Constantine 1926- IntWW 93
Stefanov, William Louis 1965- WhoWest 94
Stefanovits, Pal 1920- WhoScEn 94
Stefanschi, Sergiu 1941- WhoAm 94
Stefansson, Vilhjalmur 1879-1962 WhWE [port]
Stefany, William Craig 1954- WhoFI 94
Steffan, Geary WhoHol 92
Steffan, Joseph NewYTBS 93 [port]
Steffan, Wallace Allan 1934- WhoAm 94, WhoScEn 94, WhoWest 94
Steffani, Agostino 1654-1728 NewGrDO
Steffanson, Con EncSF 93
Steffanson, Con 1933- WrDr 94
Steffany, Alo William 1911- WhoAm 94
Steffe, Horst-Otto 1919- IntWW 93
Steffek, Hanny 1927- NewGrDO
Steffel, Martin Henry 1938- WhoAmP 93
Steffen, Alan Leslie 1927- WhoMW 93, WhoScEn 94
Steffen, Christopher J. 1942- WhoAm 94, WhoFI 94
Steffen, Elizabeth Allen WhoMW 93
Steffen, Frederick John 1946- WhoAmP 93
Steffen, Jonathan 1958- WrDr 94
Steffen, Joseph J., Jr. 1957- WhoAmP 93
Steffen, Rey John 1894- WhAm 10
Steffen, Thomas Lee 1930- WhoAmL 94, WhoAmP 93, WhoWest 94
Steffeney-Stark, Sandra Kay 1949- WhoFI 94
Steffens, Bradley 1955- SmATA 77 [port]
Steffens, Dorothy Ruth 1921- WhoAm 94
Steffens, Franz Eugen Aloys 1933- WhoScEn 94
Steffens, John Howard 1941- WhoMW 93
Steffens, John Laundon 1941- WhoAm 94, WhoFI 94
Steffens, Joseph Lincoln, Jr. 1866-1936 AmSocL
Steffens, Karen Lee Miers 1944- WhoMW 93
Steffens, Walter 1934- NewGrDO
Steffensen, Dwight A. 1943- WhoAm 94, WhoFI 94, WhoWest 94
Steffes, Don C. WhoAmP 93
Steffes, Don C. 1930- WhoMW 93
Steffey, Eugene Paul 1942- WhoAm 94, WhoWest 94
Steffey, Lela 1928- WhoWest 94
Steffey, Lela Gardner 1928- WhoAmP 93, WhoWomW 91
Steffey, Richard Dudley 1929- WhoWest 94
Steff-Langston, John Antony 1926- Who 94
Steffler, Alva W. 1934- WhoAmA 93
Stefford, Miriam d1931 WhoHol 92
Steffy, John Richard 1924- WhoAm 94, WhoScEn 94
Stefoff, James Edward 1938- WhoFI 94
Steg, James Louis WhoAmA 93
Steg, James Louis 1922- WhoAm 94
Steg, Leo 1922- WhoAm 94
Stegall, Daniel Richard 1946- WhoAm 94
Stegall, Danny James 1955- WhoFI 94
Stegeman, Charles 1924- WhoAmA 93
Stegeman, Thomas Albert 1948- WhoAmL 94
Stegemeier, Richard Joseph 1928- IntWW 93, WhoAm 94, WhoFI 94, WhoWest 94
Stegenga, David A. 1946- WhoWest 94
Stegenga, James A. 1937- WrDr 94
Stegenga, Preston Jay 1924- WhoAm 94
Steger, C. Donald 1936- WhoBlA 94
Steger, Charles William 1947- WhoAm 94
Steger, Edward Herman 1936- WhoScEn 94
Steger, Evan Evans, III 1937- WhoAm 94
Steger, Herm 1926- WhoAmP 93
Steger, Joseph A. WhoAm 94, WhoMW 93
Steger, Joseph A. 1937- IntWW 93
Steger, Julius d1959 WhoHol 92
Steger, Meritt Homer 1906- WhoAm 94
Steger, Norbert 1944- IntWW 93
Steger, Ralph James 1940- WhoScEn 94
Steger, William Kent 1944- WhoAmL 94
Steger, William Merritt 1920- WhoAm 94, WhoAmL 94, WhoAmP 93
Stegers, Bernice WhoHol 92
Stegert, Scott Raymond 1963- WhoMW 93
Steggle, Terence Harry 1932- Who 94
Steggles, John Charles 1919- WhoAm 94
Stegink, Lewis Dale 1937- WhoScEn 94
Stegmaier, David 1947- WhoAmP 93
Stegman, Charles Alexander 1959- WhoFI 94
Stegman, Patricia 1929- WhoAmA 93
Stegmann, Carl David 1751-1826 NewGrDO
Stegmann, Johannes Augustus 1926- IntWW 93
Stegmann, Thomas Joseph 1946- WhoScEn 94
Stegmayer, Joseph Henry 1951- WhoAm 94
Stegmayer, Matthaus 1771-1820 NewGrDO
Stegmiller, Gary Manuel 1948- WhoMW 93
Stegner, Brice Jon 1963- WhoMW 93
Stegner, Lynn Nadene 1955- WhoFI 94, WhoMW 93
Stegner, Wallace DrAPF 93
Stegner, Wallace 1909-1993 ConLC 81 [port], DcLB Y93N [port], NewYTBS 93 [port]
Stegner, Wallace (Earle) 1909-1993 ConAu 141, CurBio 93N, WrDr 94N
Stegner, Wallace Earle 1909-1993 AmCulL [port]
Stehelin, Dominique Jean Bernard 1943- IntWW 93
Stehle, Adelina 1860-1945 NewGrDO
Stehle, Sophie 1838-1921 NewGrDO
Stehli, Edgar d1973 WhoHol 92
Stehli, Francis Greenough 1924- WhoAm 94
Stehlik, Loren Joe 1946- WhoAmP 93
Stehlin, John Sebastian, Jr. 1923- WhoAm 94, WhoScEn 94
Stehman, Betty Kohls 1952- WhoFI 94
Stehman, John DrAPF 93
Stehr, Frederick William 1932- WhoMW 93
Stehsel, Melvin Louis 1924- WhoAm 94
Steib, James T. 1940- WhoBlA 94
Steibelt, Daniel (Gottlieb) 1765-1823 NewGrDO
Steichen, Edward 1879-1973 AmCulL
Steichen, Edward 1879-1979 WhoAmA 93N
Steichen, Joanna T(aub) 1933- WrDr 94
Steichen, Rene 1942- IntWW 93
Steider, Doris 1924- WhoAmA 93
Steidley, Juan Dwayne 1959- WhoAmP 93
Steidley, Sherry Ann 1944- WhoFI 94
Steier, Rod DrAPF 93
Steiert, Jan N. 1950- WhoAmL 94
Steiert, Robert M. 1953- WhoAmL 94
Steig, Janet Barbara 1938- WhoFI 94
Steig, William 1907- WhoAm 94, WrDr 94
Steigbigel, Roy Theodore 1941- WhoAm 94, WhoScEn 94
Steiger, A(ndrew) J(acob) 1900- EncSF 93
Steiger, Bettie Alexander 1934- WhoFI 94
Steiger, Dale Arlen 1928- WhoFI 94
Steiger, Fred Harold 1929- WhoScEn 94
Steiger, Frederic d1990 WhoAmA 93N
Steiger, Frederic 1905-1990 WhAm 10
Steiger, Gretchen Helene 1960- WhoScEn 94
Steiger, Heidi Schwarzbauer 1953- WhoAm 94, WhoFI 94
Steiger, Janet D. 1939- WhoAmP 93
Steiger, Janet Dempsey 1939- WhoAm 94, WhoFI 94
Steiger, Paul Ernest 1942- WhoAm 94, WhoFI 94
Steiger, Rod 1925- IntMPA 94, IntWW 93, WhoAm 94, WhoHol 92
Steiger, Sam 1929- WhoAmP 93
Steigerwald, Louis John, III 1953- WhoFI 94
Steigerwald, Steven Arthur 1956- WhoAmL 94
Steigerwaldt, Donna Wolf 1929- WhoAm 94
Steighner, Joseph A. 1950- WhoAmP 93
Steigman, Andrew L. 1933- WhoAm 94
Steigman, Gary 1941- WhoMW 93
Steigman, Margot WhoAmA 93
Steigmann, Robert James 1944- WhoAmL 94
Steigmeier, Roger DrAPF 93
Steil, David J. WhoAmP 93
Steil, George Kenneth, Sr. 1924- WhoAm 94, WhoAmL 94
Steilen, James R. 1949- WhoAm 94, WhoAmL 94
Steill, Laurel Lucinda 1940- WhoMW 93
Stein, Agnes DrAPF 93
Stein, Alan L. 1930- WhoFI 94
Stein, Alice P. DrAPF 93
Stein, Allan Mark 1951- WhoAmL 94
Stein, Alvin Maurice 1924- WhoAm 94, WhoAmL 94
Stein, Andrew WhoAmP 93
Stein, Arland Thomas 1938- WhoAm 94
Stein, Arnold 1915- WhoAm 94
Stein, Arnold Bruce 1948- WhoAmL 94
Stein, Arthur Oscar 1932- WhoScEn 94, WhoWest 94
Stein, Aurel 1862-1943 WhWE
Stein, Ben WhoHol 92
Stein, Benjamin J. 1944- WrDr 94
Stein, Bennett Mueller 1931- WhoAm 94
Stein, Bernard 1913- WhoAm 94, WhoFI 94
Stein, Bernard Alvin 1923- WhoAm 94
Stein, Beverly 1947- WhoAmP 93
Stein, Bob WhoAm 94, WhoMW 93
Stein, Bruno 1930- WrDr 94
Stein, Carey M. 1947- WhoAmL 94
Stein, Carl 1943- WhoAm 94
Stein, Carole Ruth 1932- WhoMW 93
Stein, Cassandra Monroe 1944- WhoAmP 93
Stein, Charles DrAPF 93
Stein, Charles 1912- WhoAm 94
Stein, Cheryl Denise 1953- WhoAmL 94

Steinig, Stephen N. *WhoIns 94*
Steinig, Stephen Nelson 1945- *WhoAm 94, WhoFI 94*
Steinitz, Ernst *WorScD*
Steinitz, Hans d1993 *NewYTBS 93*
Steinitz, Kate Trauman 1893- *WhoAmA 93N*
Steinkamp, Fredric *ConTFT 11*
Steinkamp, James Edward 1951- *WhoFI 94*
Steinkamp, James Robert 1954- *WhoMW 93*
Steinkamp, Keith Kendall 1953- *WhoScEn 94*
Steinke, Bettina 1913- *WhoAmA 93*
Steinke, Hans d1971 *WhoHol 92*
Steinke, Kathy R. 1956- *WhoMW 93*
Steinke, Paul Karl Willi 1921-1989 *WhAm 10*
Steinke, Peter 1951- *WhoMW 93*
Steinke, Ronald Joseph 1939- *WhoScEn 94*
Steinke, Russell *DrAPF 93*
Steinkraus, Keith Hartley 1918- *WhoScEn 94*
Steinkraus, Warren Edward 1922-1990 *WhAm 10*
Steinkuhler, Franz 1937- *IntWW 93*
Steinlage, Paul Nicholas 1941- *WhoIns 94*
Steinlauf, Marvin Ira 1938- *WhoFI 94*
Steinle, John Gerard 1916-1990 *WhAm 10*
Steinman, Betty Ann 1939- *WhoWest 94*
Steinman, Charles Hunter 1958- *WhoMW 93*
Steinman, Clayton Marshall 1950- *WhoWest 94*
Steinman, Jerry 1924- *WhoFI 94*
Steinman, John Francis 1916- *WhoWest 94*
Steinman, Lisa Malinowski *DrAPF 93*
Steinman, Lisa Malinowski 1950- *WhoWest 94*
Steinman, Michael 1952- *WrDr 94*
Steinman, Monte 1955- *IntMPA 94*
Steinman, Neal 1942-1993 *NewYTBS 93*
Steinman, Peter Edwin 1948- *WhoAmL 94*
Steinman, Robert Cleeton 1931- *WhoAm 94*
Steinman, Shirley P. 1938- *WhoIns 94*
Steinmann, John Colburn 1941- *WhoScEn 94, WhoWest 94*
Steinmayer, Janet L. *WhoAmL 94*
Steinmetz, Charles Proteus 1865-1923 *WorInv*
Steinmetz, David Curtis 1936- *WhoAm 94*
Steinmetz, Donald W. 1924- *WhoAmP 93*
Steinmetz, Donald Walter 1924- *WhoAmL 94*
Steinmetz, Grace Ernst Titus *WhoAmA 93*
Steinmetz, John Charles 1947- *WhoWest 94*
Steinmetz, Jon David 1940- *WhoMW 93*
Steinmetz, Kaye H. *WhoAmP 93, WhoWomW 91*
Steinmetz, Lawrence Leo 1938- *WrDr 94*
Steinmetz, Leon *WrDr 94*
Steinmetz, Manning Louis, III 1942- *WhoFI 94*
Steinmetz, Paul B. 1928- *EncNAR, WrDr 94*
Steinmetz, Richard *WhoHol 92*
Steinmetz, Richard Bird, Jr. 1929- *WhoAm 94*
Steinmetz, Wayne Edward 1945- *WhoWest 94*
Steinmeyer, Ferdinand *WhAmRev*
Steinmiller, John F. *WhoAm 94, WhoMW 93*
Steinmuller, Angela *EncSF 93*
Steinmuller, Karlheinz *EncSF 93*
Steinnes, Eiliv 1938- *IntWW 93*
Steinrauf, Jean Hamilton 1938- *WhoAm 94*
Steinruck, Charles Francis, Jr. 1908- *WhoAm 94*
Steinrueck, Albert d1929 *WhoHol 92*
Steinsnyder, Jeffrey Neil 1961- *WhoAmL 94*
Steinson, Barbara Jean 1948- *WhoMW 93*
Steinthal, Kenneth L. 1952- *WhoAmL 94*
Steinvall, Kurt Ove 1944- *WhoScEn 94*
Steinwachs, Donald Michael 1946- *WhoScEn 94*
Steinwachs, Ginka 1942- *BlmGWL*
Steinway & Sons 1853- *AmCulL*
Steinworth, Skip 1950- *WhoAmA 93*
Steinwurtzel, Richard A. 1950- *WhoAmL 94*
Steir, Pat 1940- *WhoAmA 93*
Steir, Pat Iris 1940- *WhoAm 94*
Steitz, Joan Argetsinger 1941- *WhoAm 94, WhoScEn 94*
Stekel, Frank Donald 1941- *WhoScEn 94*
Stekoll, Michael Steven 1947- *WhoWest 94*
Stelck, Charles Richard 1917- *WhoAm 94*
Stelfox, Shirley *WhoHol 92*
Stell, H. Kenyon 1910-1990 *WhoAmA 93N*
Stell, Joe M. 1928- *WhoAmP 93*
Stell, Joe M., Jr. 1928- *WhoWest 94*
Stell, John Elwin, Jr. 1954- *WhoAmL 94*
Stell, Philip Michael 1934- *Who 94*
Stell, William Kenyon 1939- *WhoScEn 94*
Stella, Antonietta 1929- *NewGrDO*
Stella, Daniel Francis 1943- *WhoAm 94, WhoAmL 94*
Stella, Frank 1936- *WhoAmA 93*
Stella, Frank D. *WhoAmP 93*
Stella, Frank Dante 1919- *WhoAm 94, WhoMW 93*
Stella, Frank Philip 1936- *AmCulL, WhoAm 94*
Stella, John Anthony 1938- *WhoAm 94*
Stella, Santa fl. 1703-1759 *NewGrDO*
Stella, Valentino John 1946- *WhoScEn 94*
Stella, William J. 1942- *WhoIns 94*
Stellar, Eliot d1993 *NewYTBS 93*
Stellar, Eliot 1919- *WhoAm 94*
Stellato, Louis Eugene 1950- *WhoAmL 94*
Stelle, Kellogg Sheffield 1948- *IntWW 93, WhoScEn 94*
Steller, Arthur Wayne 1947- *WhoAm 94*
Steller, Georg Wilhelm 1709-1746 *WhWE*
Steller, Mitchell Edward 1948- *WhoAm 94*
Stellers, Thomas Joe 1940- *WhoMW 93*
Stelling, James Henry, III 1942- *WhoAmP 93*
Stelling, John Henry Edward 1952- *WhoScEn 94*
Stellini, Salv. John 1939- *Who 94*
Stellman, Leslie Robert 1951- *WhoAm 94*
Stellman, Samuel David 1918- *WhoAm 94*
Stellman, Steven Dale 1945- *WhoScEn 94*
Stellone, Al d1980 *WhoHol 92*
Stellrecht Burns, Kathleen Anne 1959- *WhoScEn 94*
Stellwag, George William 1921- *WhoIns 94*
Stellwagen, Robert Harwood 1941- *WhoAm 94, WhoWest 94*
Stelly, Vic 1941- *WhoAmP 93*
Stelmachowski, Andrzej 1925- *IntWW 93*
Stelmak, Dalton Roy 1941- *WhoFI 94*
Stelson, Arthur Wesley 1955- *WhoScEn 94*
Stelter, Mark Alan 1961- *WhoAmL 94*
Steltzlen, Janelle Hicks 1937- *WhoAmL 94*
Stelzer, Hannes d1945 *WhoHol 92*
Stelzer, Irwin Mark 1932- *WhoFI 94*
Stelzer, John Friedrich 1928- *WhoScEn 94*
Stelzer, Michael Norman 1938- *WhoAmA 93*
Stelzig, Eugene L. *DrAPF 93*
Stelzle, Charles 1869-1941 *DcAmReB 2*
Stelzner, Paul Burke 1935- *WhoFI 94*
Stem, Carl Herbert 1935- *WhoAm 94, WhoFI 94*
Stembler, John H. 1913- *IntMPA 94*
Stembler, William J. 1946- *IntMPA 94*
Stembridge, David Harry 1932- *Who 94*
Stembridge, J. S. d1942 *WhoHol 92*
Stembridge, Vernie Albert 1924- *WhoAm 94*
Stemler, Alan James 1943- *WhoScEn 94*
Stemm, Samuel Mark 1954- *WhoMW 93*
Stemmer, Jay John 1939- *WhoWest 94*
Stemmler, Edward Joseph 1929- *WhoAm 94*
Stempel, Ernest Edward 1916- *WhoAm 94, WhoFI 94, WhoIns 94*
Stempel, Guido Hermann, III 1928- *WhoAm 94*
Stempel, Robert C. 1933- *IntWW 93*
Stemper, Marilyn Miller 1962- *WhoWest 94*
Stemper, William Herman, Jr. *WhoAm 94*
Stemple, Alan Douglas 1963- *WhoScEn 94, WhoWest 94*
Stemple, Donald L. 1930- *WhoAmP 93*
Stempler, Jack Leon 1920- *WhoAm 94*
Sten, Anna d1993 *NewYTBS 93 [port]*
Sten, Anna 1908- *WhoHol 92*
Sten, Johannes Walter 1934- *WhoScEn 94*
Stenback, Par Olav Mikael 1941- *IntWW 93*
Stenberg, Carl Waldamer, III 1943- *WhoAm 94*
Stenberg, Donald B. 1948- *WhoAm 94, WhoAmL 94, WhoAmP 93, WhoMW 93*
Stenbit, John Paul 1940- *WhoAm 94*
Stenborg, Carl 1752-1813 *NewGrDO*
Stenborg, Helen 1925- *WhoHol 92*
Stenchever, Morton Albert 1931- *WhoAm 94*
Stendahl, Allen Jon 1946- *WhoIns 94*
Stendahl, Krister 1921- *WhoAm 94*
Stendahl, Steven James 1955- *WhoScEn 94*
Stender, Charles Frederick 1940- *WhoWest 94*
Stender, John d1993 *NewYTBS 93*
Stender, Laura Lyn 1960- *WhoWest 94*
Stendhal 1783-1842 *NewGrDO*
Stendhal 1788-1842 *BlmGEL*
Stenehjem, Allan *WhoAmP 93*
Stenehjem, Bob *WhoAmP 93*
Stenehjem, Leland Manford 1918- *WhoAm 94*
Stenehjem, Wayne 1953- *WhoAmP 93*
Stenehjem, Wayne Kevin 1953- *WhoMW 93*
Stenerson, Georgiann 1934- *WhoAmP 93*
Stenerud, Jan *ProFbHF*
Stenflo, Jan Olof 1942- *IntWW 93*
Stengel, Casey d1975 *WhoHol 92*
Stengel, Dave 1946- *WhoAmP 93*
Stengel, Eberhard Friedrich Otto 1936- *WhoScEn 94*
Stengel, Richard 1955- *WrDr 94*
Stengel, Robert Frank 1938- *WhoAm 94, WhoScEn 94*
Stengel, Ronald Francis 1947- *WhoAm 94*
Stengele, Harry Everest 1945- *WhoWest 94*
Stenger, James A. 1952- *WhoAm 94*
Stenger, Martin Lane 1949- *WhoWest 94*
Stenger, Vernon Arthur 1908- *WhoMW 93*
Stenger, Victor John 1935- *WhoWest 94*
Stenham, Anthony William Paul 1932- *Who 94*
Stenhammar, (Karl) Wilhelm (Eugen) 1871-1927 *NewGrDO*
Stenholm, Charles W. 1938- *CngDr 93, WhoAm 94, WhoFI 94*
Stenholm, Charles Walter 1938- *WhoAmP 93*
Stenhouse, David 1932- *WrDr 94*
Stenhouse, Evangeline E. 1893- *WhAm 10*
Stenhouse, John Godwyn 1908- *Who 94*
Stenhouse, Nicol 1911- *Who 94*
Stenicka, Charles Edward, III 1929- *WhoMW 93*
Stening, George (Grafton Lees) 1904- *Who 94*
Stening, Yves *WhoHol 92*
Stenius-Kaukonen, Minna Marjatta 1947- *WhoWomW 91*
Stenlake, Rodney Lee 1957- *WhoAmL 94*
Stenlund, Bengt Gustav Verner 1939- *IntWW 93*
Stenmark, Susan *WhoHol 92*
Stennett, W. Clinton 1956- *WhoAmP 93*
Stennett, William Clinton 1956- *WhoWest 94*
Stenning, Arthur d1972 *WhoHol 92*
Stennis, John Cornelius 1901- *IntWW 93, WhoAm 94, WhoAmP 93*
Stennis, John Hampton 1935- *WhoAmP 93*
Stennis, Willie James 1923-1993 *WhoBlA 94N*
Stennis-Williams, Shirley *WhoBlA 94*
Stensland, Linda L. *WhoAmP 93, WhoMW 93*
Stenson, David Edmund 1955- *WhoAmL 94*
Stenson, Robert *WhoAmP 93*
Stenstrom, Michael Knudson 1948- *WhoWest 94*
Stenstrom, Richard Charles 1936- *WhoMW 93*
Stent, Gunther S(iegmund) 1924- *WrDr 94*
Stent, Gunther Siegmund 1924- *IntWW 93, WhoAm 94*
Stent, Madelon Delany 1933- *WhoBlA 94*
Stent, Michelle Dorene 1955- *WhoBlA 94*
Stent, Nicole M. 1960- *WhoBlA 94*
Stent, Theodore R. 1924- *WhoBlA 94*
Stentz, Steven Thomas 1951- *WhoWest 94*
Stenwick, Michael William 1941- *WhoScEn 94*
Stenzel, Alvin Milton 1951- *WhoFI 94*
Stenzel, Kurt Hodgson 1932- *WhoAm 94*
Stenzel, William A. 1923- *WhoAm 94*
Steorts, Nancy Harvey 1936- *WhoAm 94*
Step, Eugene Lee 1929- *WhoAm 94, WhoFI 94, WhoMW 93*
Stepan, Frank Quinn 1937- *WhoAm 94, WhoFI 94*
Stepanchev, Stephen *DrAPF 93*
Stepanchev, Stephen 1915- *WrDr 94*
Stepanek, David Leslie 1929- *WhoFI 94*
Stepanek, Elisabeth *WhoHol 92*
Stepanek, Joseph Edward 1917- *WhoWest 94*
Stepanek, Karel d1980 *WhoHol 92*
Stepaniak, Mark Joseph 1955- *WhoAmL 94*
Stepanian, Ira 1936- *WhoAm 94, WhoFI 94*
Stepanian, Steven Arvid, II 1935- *WhoAmL 94*
Stepaniuk, George N. 1960- *WhoAmL 94*
Stepankov, Valentin Georgevich 1951- *LngBDD*
Stepankov, Valentin Georgievich 1951- *IntWW 93*
Stepanov, Viktor Nikolaevich 1947- *LngBDD*
Stepanova, Mariya Matveyevna 1811?-1903 *NewGrDO*
Stepanova, Yelena Andreyevna 1891-1978 *NewGrDO*
Step'anyan, Haro Levon 1897-1966 *NewGrDO*
Stepashin, Sergei Vadimovich 1952- *LngBDD*
Stephan, Alexander F. 1946- *WhoAm 94*
Stephan, Ann *WhoAmP 93*
Stephan, Bodo 1939- *WhoFI 94*
Stephan, Charles Michael 1949- *WhoAmL 94*
Stephan, Charles Robert 1911- *WhoScEn 94*
Stephan, Daniel Leroy 1947- *WhoAmP 93*
Stephan, Edmund Anton 1911- *WhoAm 94*
Stephan, Egon, Sr. 1933- *WhoAm 94*
Stephan, George Peter 1933- *WhoAm 94*
Stephan, John David 1926- *WhoWest 94*
Stephan, John Jason 1941- *WhoAm 94*
Stephan, Martin 1777-1846 *DcAmReB 2*
Stephan, Robert Downs 1905-1989 *WhAm 10*
Stephan, Robert T. 1933- *WhoAmP 93*
Stephan, Robert Taft 1933- *WhoAm 94, WhoAmL 94, WhoMW 93*
Stephan, Rudi 1887-1915 *NewGrDO*
Stephanedes, Yorgos J. *WhoScEn 94*
Stephanescu, George 1843-1925 *NewGrDO*
Stephani, Christakis 1926- *IntWW 93*
Stephani, Nancy Jean 1955- *WhoMW 93*
Stephanick, Carol Ann 1952- *WhoScEn 94*
Stephanie, Gottlieb 1741-1800 *NewGrDO*
Stephanopoulos, Constantine *IntWW 93*
Stephanopoulos, George R. 1961- *WhoAm 94*
Stephanopoulos, George Robert 1961- *NewYTBS 93 [port], WhoAmP 93*
Stephanopoulos, Gregory 1950- *WhoAm 94, WhoScEn 94*
Stephanson, Loraine Ann 1950- *WhoAmA 93*
Stephany, Jaromir 1930- *WhoAmA 93*
Stephany, Judith Buckley 1944- *WhoAmP 93*
Stephen, Adam c. 1721-1791 *AmRev*
Stephen, Adam c. 1730-1791 *WhAmRev*
Stephen, Barrie Michael Lace *Who 94*
Stephen, David *Who 94*
Stephen, (John) David 1942- *Who 94*
Stephen, Dennis John 1948- *WhoFI 94*
Stephen, Derek Ronald James 1922- *Who 94*
Stephen, Donald Alexander 1935- *WhoAm 94*
Stephen, Edison J. *WhoAmP 93*
Stephen, Felix N. 1925- *BlkWr 2*
Stephen, Francis B. 1916- *WhoAmA 93*
Stephen, George A. d1993 *NewYTBS 93*
Stephen, Harbourne Mackay 1916- *Who 94*
Stephen, Henrietta Hamilton 1925- *Who 94*
Stephen, James Barnett 1925- *WhoAmP 93*
Stephen, John Erle 1918- *WhoAm 94, WhoAmL 94, WhoFI 94*
Stephen, John Low 1912- *Who 94*
Stephen, Leslie 1832-1904 *BlmGEL*
Stephen, Lessel Bruce 1920- *Who 94*
Stephen, Martin *Who 94*
Stephen, Martin 1949- *WrDr 94*
Stephen, (George) Martin 1949- *Who 94*
Stephen, Michael 1942- *Who 94*
Stephen, Michael Anthony 1929- *WhoAm 94*
Stephen, Ninian (Martin) 1923- *Who 94*
Stephen, Ninian Martin 1923- *IntWW 93*
Stephen, Norman McIntyre 1931- *WhoAmP 93*
Stephen, Norman Scott 1941- *WhoIns 94*
Stephen, Patsy *WhoHol 92*
Stephen, Richard Joseph 1945- *WhoMW 93*
Stephen, Rita *Who 94*
Stephen, Robert 1939- *WhoAmP 93*
Stephen, Stainless d1971 *WhoHol 92*
Stephen, Susan 1931- *WhoHol 92*
Stephen, William Procuronoff 1927- *WhoWest 94*
Stephen of Cloyes fl. 1212- *HisWorL*
Stephen of Hungary, I c. 973-1038 *HisWorL*
Stephens, Alan (Archer) 1925- *WrDr 94*
Stephens, Alan J. *WhoAmP 93*
Stephens, Albert Lee, Jr. *WhoAm 94, WhoAmL 94, WhoWest 94*
Stephens, Ann 1931- *WhoHol 92*
Stephens, Ann Sophia 1810-1886 *BlmGWL*

Stephens, Anne 1912- *Who 94*
Stephens, Anthony William 1930- *Who 94*
Stephens, Barbara *WhoHol 92*
Stephens, Barbara Marion 1951- *Who 94*
Stephens, Bart Nelson 1922- *WhoAm 94*
Stephens, Blythe 1936- *WrDr 94*
Stephens, Bobby Gene 1935- *WhoAm 94*
Stephens, Bobby Wayne 1944- *WhoAm 94, WhoFI 94*
Stephens, Booker T. 1944- *WhoAmP 93, WhoBlA 94*
Stephens, Brad 1951- *WhoAm 94*
Stephens, Brenda Wilson 1952- *WhoBlA 94*
Stephens, C. Michael 1949- *WhoFI 94*
Stephens, C. Preston d1993 *NewYTBS 93*
Stephens, Casey 1936- *WrDr 94*
Stephens, Catherine 1794-1882 *NewGrDO*
Stephens, Cedric John 1921- *Who 94*
Stephens, Charles Richard 1938- *WhoBlA 94*
Stephens, Christopher P(eyton) 1943- *EncSF 93*
Stephens, Christopher Wilson T. *Who 94*
Stephens, Curtis 1932- *WhoAmA 93*
Stephens, Cynthia Diane 1951- *WhoBlA 94*
Stephens, Daniel Amos 1955- *WhoWest 94*
Stephens, David Basil 1963- *WhoFI 94, WhoScEn 94*
Stephens, David Bisel 1944- *WhoWest 94*
Stephens, David Pearce 1957- *WhoMW 93*
Stephens, Deborah Lynn 1952- *WhoScEn 94*
Stephens, Delia Marie Lucky 1939- *WhoAmL 94*
Stephens, Deneen Marie 1956- *WhoMW 93*
Stephens, Denny 1932- *WhoAm 94*
Stephens, Donald Joseph 1918- *WhoAm 94*
Stephens, Donald Richards 1938- *WhoAm 94*
Stephens, Doreen Y. 1963- *WhoBlA 94*
Stephens, Dorothy Andrews 1924- *WhoAm 94*
Stephens, Douglas Kimble 1939- *WhoScEn 94*
Stephens, E. Barrie *WhoFI 94*
Stephens, E. Delores B. 1938- *WhoBlA 94*
Stephens, Edward Carl 1924- *WhoAm 94*
Stephens, Elsie Marie 1948- *WhoBlA 94*
Stephens, Elton Bryson 1911- *WhoAm 94, WhoFI 94*
Stephens, F(rank) Douglas 1913- *WrDr 94*
Stephens, Franklin Wilson 1940- *WhoFI 94*
Stephens, Frederick Howard, Jr. 1931- *WhoFI 94*
Stephens, Fredric Milo 1955- *WhoWest 94*
Stephens, G. Douglas 1951- *WhoAmP 93*
Stephens, Gay 1951- *WhoMW 93*
Stephens, George Benjamin Davis 1904- *WhoBlA 94*
Stephens, George Edward, Jr. 1936- *WhoAm 94*
Stephens, George Myers 1930- *WhoFI 94*
Stephens, Gerald D. 1932- *WhoIns 94*
Stephens, Harold 1954- *WhoAmL 94*
Stephens, Harvey d1986 *WhoHol 92*
Stephens, Helen Kay *WhoHol 92*
Stephens, Herbert Malone 1918- *WhoBlA 94*
Stephens, Herman Alvin 1914- *WhoBlA 94*
Stephens, Jack *DrAPF 93*
Stephens, Jack Edward 1923- *WhoScEn 94*
Stephens, Jack Edward, Jr. 1955- *WrDr 94*
Stephens, Jackson Thomas 1923- *WhoAm 94, WhoFI 94*
Stephens, James 1951- *WhoHol 92*
Stephens, James Anthony 1914- *WhoBlA 94*
Stephens, James M. 1946- *WhoAm 94, WhoAmP 93, WhoFI 94*
Stephens, James T. 1939- *WhoAm 94, WhoFI 94*
Stephens, Jane *WhoHol 92*
Stephens, Jay B. 1946- *WhoAm 94*
Stephens, Jeffrey Daniel 1954- *WhoWest 94*
Stephens, Jerry Wayne 1949- *WhoAm 94*
Stephens, Jesse Gordon Skip 1951- *WhoAmL 94*
Stephens, John Allen 1895-1979 *EncABHB 9*
Stephens, John Frank 1949- *WhoAm 94*
Stephens, John Walter 1968- *WhoScEn 94*
Stephens, Juanita K. 1953- *WhoBlA 94*
Stephens, Kathryn Ann 1957- *WhoMW 93*
Stephens, Keith Fielding 1910- *Who 94*
Stephens, Kelli Annette 1964- *WhoMW 93*
Stephens, Kenneth Gilbert 1931- *Who 94*
Stephens, Laraine 1942- *WhoHol 92*
Stephens, Larry Dean 1937- *WhoScEn 94, WhoWest 94*
Stephens, Laurence David, Jr. 1947- *WhoScEn 94*
Stephens, Lawton Evans 1954- *WhoAmP 93*
Stephens, Lee Amiel 1962- *WhoWest 94*
Stephens, Lee B., Jr. 1925- *WhoBlA 94*
Stephens, Lester John, Jr. 1943- *WhoAm 94*
Stephens, Lewis d1978 *WhoHol 92*
Stephens, Louis Cornelius, Jr. 1921- *WhoAm 94*
Stephens, Malcolm George 1937- *Who 94*
Stephens, Maria Carmela 1963- *WhoWest 94*
Stephens, Martha Foster 1961- *WhoAm 94*
Stephens, Martin *Who 94*
Stephens, Martin 1949- *WhoHol 92*
Stephens, (Stephen) Martin 1939- *Who 94*
Stephens, Martin R. 1954- *WhoAmP 93*
Stephens, Meic 1938- *WrDr 94*
Stephens, Michael *DrAPF 93*
Stephens, Michael (Gregory) 1946- *ConAu 43NR*
Stephens, Michael Dean 1942- *WhoAm 94*
Stephens, Michael Jon 1948- *WhoFI 94*
Stephens, Mitchell 1949- *WrDr 94*
Stephens, Nora B. 1931- *WhoAmP 93*
Stephens, Norval Blair, Jr. 1928- *WhoAm 94*
Stephens, Olin James, II 1908- *IntWW 93, WhoAm 94, WhoScEn 94*
Stephens, Paul A. 1921- *WhoBlA 94*
Stephens, Paul Alfred 1921- *WhoMW 93, WhoScEn 94*
Stephens, Paul Andrew, Jr. 1950- *WhoAmL 94*
Stephens, Peter J. 1941- *WhoMW 93*
Stephens, Peter Norman Stuart 1927- *Who 94*
Stephens, Phillip 1940- *WhoWest 94*
Stephens, Phygenau 1923- *WhoBlA 94*
Stephens, Rachel *WhoHol 92*
Stephens, Ray Garrett 1943- *WhoFI 94*
Stephens, Reed 1947- *WrDr 94*
Stephens, Richard Bernard 1934- *WhoAm 94*
Stephens, Richard Merritt 1960- *WhoWest 94*
Stephens, Robert 1909- *Who 94*
Stephens, Robert 1931- *IntMPA 94, IntWW 93, Who 94, WhoHol 92*
Stephens, Robert F. 1927- *WhoAm 94, WhoAmL 94, WhoAmP 93*
Stephens, Robert Floyd 1948- *WhoAm 94*
Stephens, Robert Louis, Jr. 1940- *AfrAmG [port]*
Stephens, Robert Oren 1928- *WrDr 94*
Stephens, Ronald Carlyle 1941- *WhoWest 94*
Stephens, Ronald Earl 1948- *WhoAmP 93*
Stephens, Ronald L. 1933- *WhoAmP 93*
Stephens, Rosemary *DrAPF 93*
Stephens, Shand Scott 1949- *WhoAm 94, WhoAmL 94, WhoWest 94*
Stephens, Sheila *WhoHol 92*
Stephens, Sheryl Lynne 1949- *WhoMW 93, WhoScEn 94*
Stephens, Sidney Dee 1945- *WhoFI 94, WhoScEn 94*
Stephens, Stanley Graham 1929- *WhoAmP 93*
Stephens, Steve Arnold 1945- *WhoMW 93*
Stephens, Stevi *WhoAmP 93*
Stephens, Taylor Lane 1937- *WhoFI 94*
Stephens, Thomas M. 1931- *WrDr 94*
Stephens, Thomas Maron 1931- *WhoAm 94*
Stephens, Thomas Michael 1941- *WhoAmA 93*
Stephens, Thomas Wesley 1950- *WhoScEn 94*
Stephens, Uriah Smith 1821-1882 *AmSocL*
Stephens, Wallace O'Leary 1942- *WhoBlA 94*
Stephens, Warren A. *WhoAm 94, WhoFI 94*
Stephens, William 1932- *WhoAmP 93*
Stephens, William Blakely 1930- *WhoAmA 93*
Stephens, William Edward 1953- *WhoScEn 94*
Stephens, William Haynes 1935- *WhoBlA 94*
Stephens, William Henry 1913- *Who 94*
Stephens, William J. 1906-1982 *EncABHB 9*
Stephens, William Leonard 1929- *WhoAm 94, WhoWest 94*
Stephens, William Mark 1952- *WhoAm 94, WhoFI 94*
Stephens, William Peter 1934- *WrDr 94*
Stephens, William Richard 1932- *WhoAm 94*
Stephens, William Theodore 1922- *WhoAm 94, WhoAmL 94*
Stephens, William Thomas *WhoAm 94, WhoFI 94, WhoWest 94*
Stephens, Willie Oved 1929- *WhoAmP 93*
Stephens, Willis H. 1925- *WhoAmP 93*
Stephens, Wilson (Treeve) 1912- *Who 94*
Stephens, Woodford Cefis 1913- *WhoAm 94*
Stephens-Barr, Patricia Jane 1950- *WhoMW 93*
Stephensen-Payne, Phil 1952- *EncSF 93*
Stephenson, Alan Clements 1944- *WhoAm 94, WhoFI 94*
Stephenson, Allan Anthony 1937- *WhoBlA 94*
Stephenson, Andrew M(ichael) 1946- *EncSF 93, WrDr 94*
Stephenson, Arthur Emmet, Jr. 1945- *WhoAm 94*
Stephenson, Ashley *Who 94*
Stephenson, (Robert) Ashley (Shute) 1927- *Who 94*
Stephenson, Barbera Wertz 1938- *WhoAmL 94, WhoWest 94*
Stephenson, Blair Y. 1947- *WhoFI 94*
Stephenson, Carolyn L. 1945- *WhoBlA 94*
Stephenson, Charles E., III *WhoBlA 94*
Stephenson, Clarence Bruce 1895- *WhAm 10*
Stephenson, Clarine *BlmGWL*
Stephenson, Crocker 1956- *ConAu 142*
Stephenson, Dama F. 1955- *WhoBlA 94*
Stephenson, Diane 1948- *WhoMW 93*
Stephenson, Donald d1993 *Who 94N*
Stephenson, Donald Grier, Jr. 1942- *WhoAm 94*
Stephenson, Donnan 1919- *WhoAm 94*
Stephenson, Dorothy Griffith 1949- *WhoAm 94*
Stephenson, Dorothy Maxine 1925- *WhoMW 93*
Stephenson, Dwight Eugene 1957- *WhoBlA 94*
Stephenson, Edward Thomas 1929- *WhoScEn 94*
Stephenson, Elizabeth Weiss 1927- *WhoAm 94*
Stephenson, Gary Van 1958- *WhoWest 94*
Stephenson, George 1781-1848 *WorInv*
Stephenson, Gordon 1908- *IntWW 93, Who 94*
Stephenson, Gwendolyn W. *WhoMW 93*
Stephenson, Henry d1956 *WhoHol 92*
Stephenson, Henry Shepherd 1905- *Who 94*
Stephenson, Henry Upton 1926- *Who 94*
Stephenson, Herman Howard 1929- *WhoAm 94, WhoFI 94, WhoWest 94*
Stephenson, Howard A. 1950- *WhoAmP 93*
Stephenson, Hugh 1938- *IntWW 93, Who 94*
Stephenson, Hugh Edward, Jr. 1922- *WhoAm 94*
Stephenson, (James) Ian (Love) 1934- *IntWW 93, Who 94*
Stephenson, Irene Hamlen 1923- *WhoFI 94, WhoWest 94*
Stephenson, James d1941 *WhoHol 92*
Stephenson, James Bennett 1916- *WhoAmP 93*
Stephenson, James P. 1943- *WhoAmL 94*
Stephenson, Jan Lynn 1951- *WhoAm 94*
Stephenson, Jim 1932- *Who 94*
Stephenson, John d1963 *WhoHol 92*
Stephenson, John (Frederick Eustace) 1910- *Who 94*
Stephenson, John Aubrey 1929- *Who 94*
Stephenson, John H. 1929- *WhoAmA 93*
Stephenson, John Robin 1931- *Who 94*
Stephenson, Larry Kirk 1944- *WhoWest 94*
Stephenson, Lee Joseph 1953- *WhoWest 94*
Stephenson, Linda Jean 1952- *WhoFI 94*
Stephenson, Linda Sue 1939- *WhoFI 94*
Stephenson, Lynne *Who 94*
Stephenson, Margaret Maud *Who 94*
Stephenson, Mary Johnson 1935- *WhoFI 94*
Stephenson, Mason Williams 1946- *WhoAmL 94*
Stephenson, Michael Murray 1943- *WhoAmL 94, WhoWest 94*
Stephenson, Ned Eldon 1957- *WhoFI 94*
Stephenson, Pamela 1950- *WhoHol 92*
Stephenson, Patrick Hay 1916- *Who 94*
Stephenson, Paul 1937- *Who 94*
Stephenson, Philip Robert 1914- *Who 94*
Stephenson, Richard Allen 1931- *WhoAm 94*
Stephenson, Richard Ismert 1937- *WhoAmL 94*
Stephenson, Robert d1970 *WhoHol 92*
Stephenson, Robert 1803-1859 *WorInv*
Stephenson, Robert Clay 1938- *WhoAm 94*
Stephenson, Robert M. 1948- *WhoAm 94, WhoAmL 94*
Stephenson, Roscoe Bolar, Jr. 1922- *WhoAm 94, WhoAmL 94, WhoAmP 93*
Stephenson, Samuel Edward, Jr. 1926- *WhoAm 94*
Stephenson, Shelby *DrAPF 93*
Stephenson, Stanley 1926- *Who 94*
Stephenson, Stephanie D. 1951- *WhoMW 93*
Stephenson, Susanne G. 1935- *WhoAmA 93*
Stephenson, Tom Birkett 1926- *Who 94*
Stephenson, Tommy 1954- *WhoAmP 93*
Stephenson, Toni Edwards 1945- *WhoAm 94*
Stephenson, William B. 1933- *WhoIns 94*
Stephenson, William Boyd, Jr. 1933- *WhoFI 94*
Stephenson-Costas, Catherine Louise 1965- *WhoMW 93*
Stepin Fetchit *WhoHol 92*
Stepkoski, Robert John 1933- *WhoFI 94*
Stepney, Area Bishop of 1947- *Who 94*
Stepney, Philip Harold Robert 1947- *WhoAm 94, WhoWest 94*
Stepniak, Maria *WhoWomW 91*
Stepnoski, William David 1960- *WhoMW 93*
Steponaitis, Vincas Petras 1953- *WhoAm 94*
Steponkus, William Peter 1935- *WhoAmP 93*
Stepova, Vlasta Anna Marie 1938- *WhoWomW 91*
Stepovich, Michael Leo 1929- *WhoWest 94*
Stepp, Elvin Duane 1948- *WhoMW 93*
Stepp, George Allan, Jr. 1922- *WhoFI 94, WhoWest 94*
Stepp, James Michael 1944- *WhoAm 94*
Stepp, Jeffrey David 1958- *WhoMW 93*
Stepp, Kenneth Stephenson 1947- *WhoAmL 94*
Stepp, Laura Sessions 1951- *WhoAm 94*
Stepp, Marc 1923- *WhoAmP 93, WhoBlA 94*
Stepp, William Edward 1930- *WhoWest 94*
Steppat, Ilse d1969 *WhoHol 92*
Steppat, Leo Ludwig 1910-1964 *WhoAmA 93N*
Stepp Bejarano, Linda Sue 1950- *WhoHisp 94*
Steppe, Cecil H. 1933- *WhoBlA 94*
Steppler, Don 1954- *WhoAmP 93*
Steppler, Howard Alvey 1918- *WhoAm 94*
Steppling, John d1932 *WhoHol 92*
Steppling, John 1951- *ConDr 93*
Steppling, Richard Carew 1935- *WhoAmP 93*
Stept, Sammy d1964 *WhoHol 92*
Stepto, Robert Burns 1945- *WhoBlA 94*
Stepto, Robert Charles 1920- *WhoAm 94, WhoBlA 94*
Steptoe, Lamont Brown 1949- *WhoBlA 94*
Steptoe, Lydia *GayLL*
Steptoe, Mary Lou 1949- *WhoAmL 94*
Steptoe, Philip P., III 1951- *WhoAm 94*
Steptoe, Robert M. *WhoAmP 93*
Steptoe, Robert Mason, Jr. 1943- *WhoAmL 94*
Steptoe, Roosevelt 1934- *WhoBlA 94*
Steptoe, Sonja 1960- *WhoBlA 94*
Steptoe, Thomas Wetherell, Jr. 1951- *WhoAmP 93*
Steranko, James 1938- *EncSF 93*
Sterba, Melanie M. 1957- *WhoAmL 94*
Sterban, Richard Anthony 1943- *WhoAm 94*
Sterbick, Peter Lawrence 1917- *WhoWest 94*
Sterbini, Cesare 1784-1831 *NewGrDO*
Sterck, Gregory Leo 1949- *WhoFI 94*
Stercken, Hans 1923- *IntWW 93*
Sterett, Samuel 1758-1833 *WhAmRev*
Sterge, John Calvin 1931- *WhoFI 94*
Stergios, Peter Doe 1942- *WhoAm 94, WhoAmL 94*
Stergiou, E. James 1949- *WhoIns 94*
Stergiou, Konstantinos 1959- *WhoScEn 94*
Sterke, Jeanette *WhoHol 92*
Sterken, Christiaan (L.) 1946- *ConAu 142*
Sterky, Hakan Karl August 1900- *IntWW 93*
Sterle, Francine *DrAPF 93*
Sterligov, Aleksandr Sergeevich *LngBDD*
Sterling *Who 94*
Sterling, Alexandre *WhoHol 92*
Sterling, Brett *EncSF 93*
Sterling, Bruce 1954- *EncSF 93, WrDr 94*
Sterling, Charles A. 1932- *WhoBlA 94*
Sterling, Claire 1919- *WrDr 94*
Sterling, David Alan 1956- *WhoFI 94*

Sterling, David M. *WhoHol 92*
Sterling, Donald Justus, Jr. 1927- *WhoAm 94, WhoWest 94*
Sterling, Donald T. *WhoAm 94, WhoWest 94*
Sterling, Duane Ray 1938- *WhoMW 93*
Sterling, Duncan, Jr. d1993 *NewYTBS 93*
Sterling, Edward Emanuel 1953- *WhoAmL 94*
Sterling, Edythe d1962 *WhoHol 92*
Sterling, Eric Edward 1949- *WhoAmL 94*
Sterling, Ford d1939 *WhoHol 92*
Sterling, Ford 1889-1939 *WhoCom*
Sterling, Gary C. *DrAPF 93*
Sterling, H. Dwight, Sr. 1944- *WhoBlA 94*
Sterling, Helen *ConAu 43NR*
Sterling, Howard David 1941- *WhoAmL 94*
Sterling, Jan 1921- *WhoHol 92*
Sterling, Jan 1923- *IntMPA 94*
Sterling, Jeffrey Emery 1964- *WhoBlA 94*
Sterling, Jessica 1935- *WrDr 94*
Sterling, Jody T. *DrAPF 93*
Sterling, Keir Brooks 1934- *WhoAm 94*
Sterling, Kenneth 1920- *WhoAm 94*
Sterling, Larry d1958 *WhoHol 92*
Sterling, Leigh Greaser 1959- *WhoFI 94*
Sterling, Merta d1944 *WhoHol 92*
Sterling, Michael John Howard 1946- *IntWW 93, Who 94*
Sterling, Michael Laurence 1956- *WhoAmL 94*
Sterling, Philip *WhoHol 92*
Sterling, Phillip *DrAPF 93*
Sterling, Raymond Leslie 1949- *WhoAm 94, WhoMW 93*
Sterling, Richard d1959 *WhoHol 92*
Sterling, Robert 1917- *IntMPA 94, WhoHol 92*
Sterling, Robert Lee, Jr. 1933- *WhoAm 94, WhoFI 94*
Sterling, Shirley Frampton 1920- *WhoAm 94*
Sterling, Tisha 1944- *WhoHol 92*
Sterling, Vicki Lynn 1953- *WhoAmL 94*
Sterling Of Plaistow, Baron 1934- *IntWW 93, Who 94*
Stermac, Anthony George 1921- *WhoAm 94*
Sterman, Lorraine Taylor 1944- *WhoWest 94*
Stermer, Dugald Robert 1936- *WhoAm 94, WhoAmA 93, WhoWest 94*
Stermer, Raymond Andrew 1924- *WhoScEn 94*
Stern, Alfred E. F. *IntMPA 94*
Stern, Angela Marie 1960- *WhoFI 94*
Stern, Arthur Cecil 1909-1992 *WhAm 10*
Stern, Arthur I. 1950- *WhoAmA 93*
Stern, Arthur Lewis 1911- *WhoAmA 93N*
Stern, Arthur Lewis, Mrs. 1913- *WhoAmA 93N*
Stern, Arthur Paul 1925- *WhoAm 94, WhoFI 94, WhoWest 94*
Stern, Barry Elroy *WhoAm 94*
Stern, Barry H. 1946- *WhoAmP 93*
Stern, Bill d1971 *WhoHol 92*
Stern, Bruce Elliot 1954- *WhoAmL 94*
Stern, C. Elizabeth Espin 1961- *WhoAmL 94*
Stern, Carl Leonard 1937- *WhoAm 94, WhoAmL 94*
Stern, Carl William, Jr. 1946- *WhoMW 93*
Stern, Charles 1920- *WhoAm 94*
Stern, Charles M. 1943- *WhoAm 94, WhoAmL 94*
Stern, Clarence A. 1913- *WrDr 94*
Stern, Daniel *BlmGWL, DrAPF 93*
Stern, Daniel 1928- *WhoAm 94, WrDr 94*
Stern, Daniel 1957- *IntMPA 94, WhoAm 94, WhoHol 92*
Stern, Daniel Alan 1944- *WhoAm 94*
Stern, Daniel Henry 1934- *WhoMW 93*
Stern, Daniel N. 1934- *WrDr 94*
Stern, David 1943- *BasBi*
Stern, David Joel 1942- *WhoAm 94*
Stern, Donald A. 1954- *WhoAmL 94*
Stern, Douglas Donald 1939- *WhoFI 94*
Stern, E. George 1912- *WhoScEn 94*
Stern, Eddie 1917- *IntMPA 94*
Stern, Edward *WhoMW 93*
Stern, Edward Abraham 1930- *WhoAm 94*
Stern, Edward Mayer 1946- *WhoAmL 94*
Stern, Ellen Norman 1927- *WrDr 94*
Stern, Eric Karl 1964- *WhoFI 94*
Stern, Eric Petru 1941- *WhoScEn 94*
Stern, Erik *WhoHol 92*
Stern, Ernest 1928- *WhoAm 94*
Stern, Ernest 1933- *IntWW 93*
Stern, Ezra E. 1908- *IntMPA 94*
Stern, Franc N. 1934- *WhoAmP 93*
Stern, Frank Irvin 1929- *WhoFI 94*
Stern, Fritz 1926- *IntWW 93, WrDr 94*
Stern, Fritz Richard 1926- *WhoAm 94*
Stern, Gail Frieda 1950- *WhoAm 94*
Stern, Gary Edward 1963- *WhoMW 93*
Stern, Geoffrey 1942- *WhoAm 94, WhoAmL 94*
Stern, Geoffrey Adlai 1955- *WhoAm 94*
Stern, Gerald *DrAPF 93*
Stern, Gerald 1925- *WrDr 94*
Stern, Gerald Daniel 1933- *WhoAm 94*
Stern, Gerald Joseph 1925- *WhoAm 94*
Stern, Gerald M. 1937- *WhoAm 94, WhoAmL 94, WhoFI 94*
Stern, Gladys Bertha 1890-1973 *BlmGWL*
Stern, Grace Mary 1925- *WhoAmP 93, WhoMW 93*
Stern, Guy 1922- *WhoAm 94*
Stern, H. Peter *WhoAmA 93*
Stern, Harold Phillip 1922-1977 *WhoAmA 93N*
Stern, Harold S. 1923?-1976 *BlkWr 2*
Stern, Henry Louis 1924- *WhoAm 94*
Stern, Henry Root, Jr. d1993 *NewYTBS 93 [port]*
Stern, Herbert Jay 1936- *WhoAm 94, WhoAmL 94*
Stern, Herbert L. 1915- *WhoAmP 93*
Stern, Howard 1954- *News 93-3 [port]*
Stern, Howard Allan 1954- *WhoAm 94*
Stern, Irene Monat 1932- *WhoAmA 93*
Stern, Isaac 1920- *IntWW 93, Who 94, WhoAm 94, WhoHol 92*
Stern, J(ulius) David 1886-1971 *EncSF 93*
Stern, Jacqueline Lee *ConAu 141*
Stern, Jacques 1932- *IntWW 93*
Stern, James d1993 *NewYTBS 93 [port]*
Stern, James (Andrew) 1904- *WrDr 94*
Stern, James Andrew 1950- *WhoAm 94, WhoFI 94*
Stern, Jan Peter 1926- *WhoAm 94, WhoAmA 93*
Stern, Jay B. 1929- *WrDr 94*
Stern, Jerome H. 1929- *WhoIns 94*
Stern, Jerry A. *WhoAmP 93*
Stern, Joan Naomi 1944- *WhoAm 94, WhoAmL 94*
Stern, John Jules 1955- *WhoAmL 94*
Stern, Joseph A. 1949- *WhoAm 94*
Stern, Joseph Smith, Jr. 1918- *WhoAm 94*
Stern, Joyce Reuben 1935- *WhoAmL 94*
Stern, Judith M. 1951- *ConAu 142, SmATA 75 [port]*
Stern, Karl *BlmGWL*
Stern, Kenneth Mitchel 1950- *WhoFI 94*
Stern, Klaus 1932- *IntWW 93*
Stern, Larry N. 1941- *WhoAmP 93*
Stern, Leo G. 1945- *WhoAm 94*
Stern, Leonard Bernard 1923- *WhoAm 94*
Stern, Leslie Warren 1938- *WhoAm 94, WhoFI 94*
Stern, Lewis Arthur 1934- *WhoAm 94*
Stern, Linda Joy 1941- *Who 94*
Stern, Louis d1941 *WhoHol 92*
Stern, Louis 1945- *WhoAmA 93, WhoWest 94*
Stern, Louis William 1935- *WhoAm 94*
Stern, Louise 1921- *WhoAmA 93*
Stern, Madeleine B. 1912- *DcLB 140 [port], WrDr 94*
See Also Rostenberg, Leona 1908- *DcLB 140*
Stern, Madeleine Bettina 1912- *WhoAm 94*
Stern, Marc Irwin 1944- *WhoAm 94, WhoFI 94, WhoWest 94*
Stern, Marianne 1950- *WhoFI 94*
Stern, Mark David 1945- *WhoAmL 94*
Stern, Martin Oscar 1924- *WhoScEn 94*
Stern, Marvin 1916- *WhoAm 94*
Stern, Marvin 1923- *WhoAm 94*
Stern, Michael 1969- *WhoScEn 94*
Stern, Michael Alan 1954- *WhoAmL 94*
Stern, Michael Charles 1942- *Who 94*
Stern, Michael David 1946- *WhoMW 93*
Stern, Milton 1927- *WhoAm 94*
Stern, Milton H. 1924- *WhAm 10*
Stern, Milton Reid 1918- *WhoWest 94*
Stern, Miroslava d1955 *WhoHol 92*
Stern, Mortimer Phillip 1926- *WhoAm 94*
Stern, Nancy Ann 1944- *WhoAmL 94*
Stern, Neal M. 1951- *WhoIns 94*
Stern, Nicholas Herbert 1946- *Who 94*
Stern, Norissa Cynthia 1947- *WhoMW 93*
Stern, Norman Saul 1938- *WhoFI 94*
Stern, Paul Frederick *EncSF 93*
Stern, Paul George 1938- *WhoAm 94, WhoFI 94*
Stern, Paula 1945- *WhoAm 94, WhoAmP 93*
Stern, Philip M. 1926-1992 *AnObit 1992*
Stern, Philip Maurice 1926-1992 *WhAm 10*
Stern, Phyllis *DrAPF 93*
Stern, Ralph David 1943- *WhoAmL 94*
Stern, Rhoda Helen 1940- *WhoFI 94*
Stern, Richard *DrAPF 93*
Stern, Richard Benjamin 1929- *WhoFI 94*
Stern, Richard David 1936- *WhoAm 94, WhoFI 94*
Stern, Richard G(ustave) 1928- *WrDr 94*
Stern, Richard Gustave 1928- *WhoAm 94*
Stern, Richard James 1922- *WhoAm 94*
Stern, Richard Martin 1915- *WrDr 94*
Stern, Robert A. M. 1939- *WrDr 94*
Stern, Robert Arthur Morton 1939- *IntWW 93*
Stern, Robert D. 1929- *WhoAm 94*
Stern, Robert Louis 1908- *WhoAm 94, WhoAmL 94*
Stern, Robert Morris 1937- *WhoAm 94, WhoScEn 94*
Stern, Robin Lauri 1959- *WhoScEn 94*
Stern, Ronald William 1957- *WhoAmL 94*
Stern, Roslyne Paige 1926- *WhoAm 94*
Stern, Roy Dalton 1943- *WhoMW 93*
Stern, Samuel Alan 1929- *WhoAm 94*
Stern, Sheila (Frances) 1922- *WrDr 94*
Stern, Stanley 1933- *WhoWest 94*
Stern, Stanley B. 1957- *WhoAm 94, WhoFI 94*
Stern, Stephen Jeffrey 1940- *WhoAm 94*
Stern, Stephen L. 1946- *WhoMW 93*
Stern, Steve 1947- *WrDr 94*
Stern, Steven Alan 1943- *WhoFI 94*
Stern, Steven David 1960- *WhoFI 94*
Stern, Steven Neal 1958- *WhoFI 94*
Stern, Stewart 1922- *IntMPA 94*
Stern, Stuart 1935- *WrDr 94*
Stern, Sydney Ladensohn 1947- *WrDr 94*
Stern, T. Noel 1913- *WhoAm 94*
Stern, Theodore 1929- *WhoAm 94*
Stern, Thomas Lee 1920- *WhoMW 93, WhoScEn 94*
Stern, Tom *WhoHol 92*
Stern, Vivien Helen 1941- *Who 94*
Stern, Walter Eugene 1920- *WhoAm 94*
Stern, Walter Eugene 1956- *WhoAmL 94*
Stern, Walter Phillips 1928- *WhoAm 94*
Stern, Wayne Brian 1948- *WhoFI 94*
Stern, Wes 1942- *WhoHol 92*
Stern, William Louis 1926- *WhoAm 94*
Stern, William Samuel 1952- *WhoAmL 94*
Sternbach, Rick 1951- *EncSF 93*
Sternberg, Ben Kollock 1947- *WhoWest 94*
Sternberg, Daniel Arie 1913- *WhoAm 94*
Sternberg, David Edward 1946- *WhoMW 93, WhoScEn 94*
Sternberg, Donna Udin 1951- *WhoAm 94*
Sternberg, Erich Walter 1891-1974 *NewGrDO*
Sternberg, Frances Glazer 1947- *WhoMW 93*
Sternberg, Harry 1904- *WhoAm 94, WhoAmA 93*
Sternberg, Jacques 1923- *EncSF 93*
Sternberg, Josef von 1894-1969 *AmCulL*
Sternberg, Mark Edward 1957- *WhoScEn 94*
Sternberg, Paul 1918- *WhoAm 94*
Sternberg, Paul Edward, Sr. 1934- *WhoAmA 93*
Sternberg, Paul Joseph 1933- *WhoAm 94*
Sternberg, Paul Warren 1956- *WhoScEn 94*
Sternberg, Robert J(effrey) 1949- *WrDr 94*
Sternberg, Rolf Max 1945- *WhoAmL 94*
Sternberg, Seymour 1943- *WhoIns 94*
Sternberg, Sigmund 1921- *Who 94*
Sternberger, Ludwig Amadeus 1921- *WhoAm 94*
Sternberger, Robert S. 1920- *WhoFI 94*
Sternberger, Stephen Jeffrey 1949- *WhoFI 94, WhoMW 93*
Sternburg, Janet *DrAPF 93*
Stern-Chaves, Elidieth I. 1960- *WhoHisp 94*
Sterndale-Bennett, Joan *WhoHol 92*
Sterne, Emma Gelders 1894- *WhAm 10*
Sterne, Hedda 1916- *WhoAmA 93*
Sterne, John Frederick 1956- *WhoMW 93*
Sterne, Joseph Robert Livingston 1928- *WhoAm 94*
Sterne, Laurence 1713-1768 *BlmGEL*
Sterne, Laurence Henry Gordon 1916- *Who 94*
Sterne, Maurice 1878-1957 *WhoAmA 93N*
Sterne, Michael Lyon 1936- *WhoAm 94*
Sterne, Morgan 1926- *WhoHol 92*
Sterne, Richard S(tephen) 1921- *WrDr 94*
Sternecker, Sheila Ann *WhoMW 93*
Sternefeld, Daniel 1905-1986 *NewGrDO*
Sterner, Frank Maurice 1935- *WhoAm 94*
Sterner, Michael Edmund 1928- *WhoAm 94*
Sternfeld, F(rederick) W(illiam) 1914- *NewGrDO*
Sternfeld, Marc Howard 1947- *WhoFI 94*
Sternfeld, Reuben 1924- *IntWW 93*
Sternfels, Lewis Bernard 1933- *WhoWest 94*
Sternglass, Lila M. 1934- *WhoAm 94*
Sterngold, James (S.) 1954- *ConAu 140*
Sternhagen, Frances 1930- *IntMPA 94, WhoAm 94, WhoHol 92*
Sternheim, Carl 1878-1942 *IntDcT 2*
Sternhold, Thomas d1549 *DcLB 132*
Sternlicht, Beno *WhoAm 94*
Sternlicht, Sanford 1931- *WhoAm 94, WrDr 94*
Sternlieb, Cheryl Marcia *WhoScEn 94*
Sternlight, Peter Donn 1928- *WhoAm 94*
Sternman, Joel W. 1943- *WhoAm 94, WhoAmL 94*
Sternroyd, Vincent d1948 *WhoHol 92*
Sterns, Joel Henry 1934- *WhoAm 94, WhoAmL 94*
Sterns, Patricia Margaret 1952- *WhoWest 94*
Sternstein, Allan J. 1948- *WhoAm 94, WhoAmL 94*
Sterrett, Andrew 1924- *WhoMW 93*
Sterrett, Cliff 1883-1964 *WhoAmA 93N*
Sterrett, James Kelley, II 1946- *WhoAm 94, WhoAmL 94*
Sterrett, James Melville 1949- *WhoWest 94*
Sterrett, Malcolm McCurdy Burdett 1942- *WhoAmP 93*
Sterritt, Coleen 1953- *WhoAmA 93*
Stertz, Craig Dee 1961- *WhoMW 93*
Sterzer, Fred 1929- *WhoAm 94*
Stessel, Harry *DrAPF 93*
Stetler, C. Joseph 1917- *WhoAm 94*
Stetler, Charles Edward 1927- *WhoAm 94, WhoWest 94*
Stetler, David J. 1949- *WhoAm 94, WhoAmL 94*
Stetler, David Samuel 1946- *WhoAmP 93*
Stetler, Larry D. 1956- *WhoWest 94*
Stetler, Margaret *DrAPF 93*
Stetler, Russell Dearnley, Jr. 1945- *WhoAm 94*
Stetler, Stephen H. 1949- *WhoAmP 93*
Stetson, Augusta Emma 1842-1928 *DcAmReB 2*
Stetson, Charlotte Perkins *EncSF 93*
Stetson, Daniel Everett 1956- *WhoAm 94, WhoAmA 93*
Stetson, Eugene William, III 1951- *WhoAm 94, WhoFI 94*
Stetson, Jeffrey P. 1948- *WhoBlA 94*
Stetson, John Benjamin Blank 1927- *WhoAm 94*
Stetson, John Charles 1920- *WhoAm 94*
Stetson, Rufus Edwin, Jr. 1922- *WhoAmP 93*
Stetten, DeWitt, Jr. 1909-1990 *WhAm 10*
Stetter, Ib 1917- *IntWW 93*
Stetter, Roger Alan 1947- *WhoAmL 94*
Stettinius, Edward Reilly, Jr. 1900-1949 *EncABHB 9 [port]*
Stettinius, Wallace 1933- *WhoAm 94*
Stettler, Carla Rice 1947- *WhoFI 94*
Stettner, Frank John, III 1969- *WhoFI 94*
Stettner, Irving *DrAPF 93*
Stettner, Louis 1922- *WhoAmA 93*
Stetz, Sylvia Ann 1941- *WhoMW 93*
Steuben, Friedrich Wilhelm von 1730-1794 *AmRev, WhAmRev [port]*
Steuben, Norton Leslie 1936- *WhoAm 94*
Steuer, Richard Marc 1948- *WhoAm 94, WhoAmL 94*
Steuer, Robert B. 1937- *IntMPA 94*
Steuerle, C. Eugene 1946- *WhoAm 94, WhoFI 94*
Steuermann, Salka d1978 *WhoHol 92*
Steuert, Douglas Michael 1948- *WhoAm 94*
Steup, Matthias 1955- *WhoMW 93*
Steussy, Marti 1955- *EncSF 93*
Stevanov, Zoran 1945- *WhoAmA 93*
Stevas *Who 94*
Stevason, John C. 1946- *WhoAm 94, WhoAmL 94*
Steven, Boyd d1967 *WhoHol 92*
Steven, Gary *WhoHol 92*
Steven, James Michael 1938- *WhoAmA 93*
Steven, Stewart 1935- *Who 94*
Steven, Stewart Gustav 1935- *IntWW 93*
Stevenin, Jean-Francois *WhoHol 92*
Stevens *Who 94*
Stevens, Abel 1815-1897 *DcAmReB 2*
Stevens, Alan Douglas 1926- *WhoAm 94*
Stevens, Albert G., Jr. *WhoAmP 93*
Stevens, Alex *DrAPF 93, WhoHol 92*
Stevens, Althea Williams 1931- *WhoBlA 94*
Stevens, Ames 1897- *WhAm 10*
Stevens, Amy Dirks 1965- *WhoWest 94*
Stevens, Andrew 1955- *IntMPA 94, WhoAm 94, WhoHol 92*
Stevens, Andrew Rich 1956- *WhoAmA 93*
Stevens, Andy 1941- *WrDr 94*
Stevens, Anthony John 1926- *Who 94*
Stevens, Art 1935- *WhoAm 94, WhoFI 94*
Stevens, Arthur Wilber, Jr. 1921- *WhoAm 94, WhoWest 94*
Stevens, (John) Austin *WrDr 94*
Stevens, Brenda Joy 1948- *WhoMW 93*
Stevens, Bryna 1924- *WrDr 94*
Stevens, Byron d1964 *WhoHol 92*
Stevens, C. Glenn 1941- *WhoAm 94, WhoAmL 94, WhoMW 93*
Stevens, Carol *WhoHol 92*
Stevens, Caroline Therese 1927- *WhoMW 93*
Stevens, Carolyn Kay Schisler 1934- *WhoAmP 93*
Stevens, Casey *WhoHol 92*

Stevens, Charles d1964 *WhoHol 92*
Stevens, Charles Greville Vincent 1957- *WhoFI 94*
Stevens, Charles Martin 1920- *WhoMW 93*
Stevens, Chester Wayne 1925- *WhoFI 94, WhoMW 93*
Stevens, Christopher 1948- *WrDr 94*
Stevens, Cleveland 1927- *WhoBlA 94*
Stevens, Clifford David 1941- *Who 94*
Stevens, Clyde Benjamin, Jr. 1908- *WhoWest 94*
Stevens, Connie 1938- *IntMPA 94, WhoAm 94, WhoHol 92*
Stevens, Constance *WhoHol 92*
Stevens, Correale F. 1946- *WhoAmP 93*
Stevens, Craig 1918- *IntMPA 94, WhoHol 92*
Stevens, Cy d1974 *WhoHol 92*
Stevens, Dale John 1936- *WhoWest 94*
Stevens, Dale Marlin 1940- *WhoScEn 94*
Stevens, Dan 1950- *WhoAmP 93*
Stevens, Dan J. 1906- *WrDr 94*
Stevens, David 1926- *WhoAm 94*
Stevens, David King 1954- *WhoWest 94*
Stevens, Denis William 1922- *IntWW 93, Who 94*
Stevens, Dennis Max 1944- *WhoFI 94*
Stevens, Dodie 1946- *WhoHol 92*
Stevens, Donald 1941- *WhoScEn 94*
Stevens, Donald King 1920- *WhoScEn 94*
Stevens, Donna Jo 1958- *WhoScEn 94*
Stevens, Doris Loraine 1912- *WhoMW 93*
Stevens, Douglas William 1960- *WhoWest 94*
Stevens, Dwight Marlyn 1933- *WhoAm 94*
Stevens, Ebenezer 1751-1823 *AmRev*
Stevens, Edith M. 1935- *WhoAmL 94*
Stevens, Edmund William 1910-1992 *WhAm 10*
Stevens, Edward 1745-1820 *WhAmRev*
Stevens, Edward Franklin 1940- *WhoWest 94*
Stevens, Edward John, Jr. 1923-1988 *WhAm 10, WhoAmA 93N*
Stevens, Edwin *Who 94*
Stevens, Edwin d1923 *WhoHol 92*
Stevens, (Arthur) Edwin 1905- *Who 94*
Stevens, Eleanor Sandra 1932- *WhoWest 94*
Stevens, Elisabeth *DrAPF 93*
Stevens, Elisabeth Goss 1929- *WhoAm 94*
Stevens, Elizabeth 1950- *WhoScEn 94*
Stevens, Elizabeth Ellen 1943- *WhoWest 94*
Stevens, Elizabeth Goss 1929- *WhoAmA 93*
Stevens, Elliot Leslie 1948- *WhoAm 94*
Stevens, Emily d1928 *WhoHol 92*
Stevens, Evelyn d1938 *WhoHol 92*
Stevens, Fisher 1963- *IntMPA 94, WhoHol 92*
Stevens, Fran *WhoHol 92*
Stevens, Francis 1884-1939? *EncSF 93*
Stevens, Frank Clayton 1921- *WhoFI 94*
Stevens, Frederic Allan 1916- *WhoAmP 93*
Stevens, Frederick George 1869-1946 *EncNAR*
Stevens, Garvin L. *WhoMW 93*
Stevens, Gary *WhoAm 94*
Stevens, George d1975 *WhoHol 92*
Stevens, George 1932- *WhoAmP 93*
Stevens, George, Jr. *WhoHol 92*
Stevens, George, Jr. 1932- *IntMPA 94, WhoAm 94*
Stevens, George Alexander 1923- *WhoWest 94*
Stevens, George Edward, Jr. 1942- *WhoBlA 94*
Stevens, George L. 1932- *WhoBlA 94*
Stevens, George Richard 1932- *WhoAm 94*
Stevens, Gladstone Taylor, Jr. 1930- *WhoAm 94*
Stevens, Gloria Jean 1954- *WhoHisp 94*
Stevens, Graeme Roy 1932- *IntWW 93*
Stevens, Greg *EncSF 93*
Stevens, Greg 1944- *WrDr 94*
Stevens, Handley Michael Gambrell 1941- *Who 94*
Stevens, Harvey *WhoHol 92*
Stevens, Henry 1819-1886 *DcLB 140 [port]*
Stevens, Henry August 1921- *WhoWest 94*
Stevens, Herbert Francis 1948- *WhoAm 94*
Stevens, Herbert Howe 1913- *WhoScEn 94*
Stevens, Holly 1924-1992 *WhAm 10*
Stevens, Inger d1970 *WhoHol 92*
Stevens, J. Paul 1942- *WhoFI 94, WhoMW 93*
Stevens, Jack G. 1937- *WhoAmP 93*
Stevens, Jacquie 1949- *WhoAmA 93*
Stevens, Jadene Felina *DrAPF 93*
Stevens, James Hervey, Jr. 1944- *WhoFI 94, WhoMW 93*
Stevens, James M. 1947- *WhoFI 94*
Stevens, James R(ichard) 1940- *WrDr 94*
Stevens, James Richard 1936- *WhoMW 93*
Stevens, James William 1936- *WhoAm 94*
Stevens, Jane Alden 1952- *WhoAmA 93*
Stevens, Jane M. 1947- *WhoAmA 93*
Stevens, Jean d1981 *WhoHol 92*
Stevens, Jeanette Eileen 1938- *WhoMW 93*
Stevens, Jeannette Eloise 1913- *WhoAmP 93*
Stevens, Jedidiah D. fl. 1830- *EncNAR*
Stevens, Jeff 1954- *WhoMW 93*
Stevens, Jeron Lynn 1942- *WhoAmL 94*
Stevens, Jill Winifred *WhoFI 94*
Stevens, Joan Kelley 1922- *WhoAmP 93*
Stevens, Jocelyn Edward Greville 1932- *IntWW 93, Who 94*
Stevens, John 1715-1792 *WhAmRev*
Stevens, John 1749-1838 *WhAmRev, WorInv*
Stevens, John 1919- *WrDr 94*
Stevens, John (Edgar) 1921- *WrDr 94*
Stevens, John Arthur 1942- *Who 94*
Stevens, John Christopher Courtenay 1955- *Who 94*
Stevens, John Edgar 1921- *IntWW 93, Who 94*
Stevens, John Galen 1943- *WhoAm 94*
Stevens, John Gehret 1941- *WhoScEn 94*
Stevens, John Lawrence 1948- *WhoScEn 94*
Stevens, John Paul 1920- *CngDr 93, IntWW 93, Who 94, WhoAm 94, WhoAmL 94, WhoAmP 93*
Stevens, John Richard 1929- *WhoScEn 94*
Stevens, John Theodore, Sr. 1924- *WhoBlA 94*
Stevens, John Williams 1929- *Who 94*
Stevens, Joseph B., Jr. 1916- *WhoAm 94, WhoFI 94*
Stevens, Joseph Charles 1929- *WhoAm 94*
Stevens, Joseph Edward, Jr. 1928- *WhoAm 94, WhoAmL 94, WhoMW 93*
Stevens, Judy York 1959- *WhoMW 93*
Stevens, Julie *WhoHol 92*
Stevens, K. 1911- *WrDr 94*
Stevens, K. T. 1919- *IntMPA 94, WhoHol 92*
Stevens, Kathleen *WhoAmP 93*
Stevens, Kaye 1933- *WhoHol 92*
Stevens, Kelley Jeane *WhoMW 93*
Stevens, Kenneth Henry 1922- *Who 94*
Stevens, Kenneth Noble 1924- *WhoAm 94, WhoScEn 94*
Stevens, Kenneth William Harry 1922- *Who 94*
Stevens, Kevin Michael 1965- *WhoAm 94*
Stevens, Landers d1940 *WhoHol 92*
Stevens, Laurence (Houghton) 1920- *Who 94*
Stevens, Lawrence Sterne 1886-1960 *EncSF 93*
Stevens, Lawrence Tenny 1896-1972 *WhoAmA 93N*
Stevens, Leith d1970 *WhoHol 92*
Stevens, Leland Robert 1929- *WhoWest 94*
Stevens, Lenore *WhoHol 92*
Stevens, Leota Mae 1921- *WhoMW 93*
Stevens, Leslie 1924- *IntMPA 94*
Stevens, Lewis David 1936- *Who 94*
Stevens, Linda Lee 1942- *WhoAmA 93*
Stevens, Lisa Gay 1952- *WhoMW 93*
Stevens, Lou *DrAPF 93*
Stevens, Lydia Hastings 1918- *WhoAmP 93*
Stevens, Lynn d1950 *WhoHol 92*
Stevens, Marilyn Ruth 1943- *WhoFI 94*
Stevens, Mark 1916- *WhoHol 92*
Stevens, Mark 1922- *IntMPA 94*
Stevens, Mark 1951- *WrDr 94*
Stevens, Mark Gregory 1955- *WhoScEn 94*
Stevens, Mark Whitney 1951- *WhoAm 94*
Stevens, Martin 1927- *WhoAm 94*
Stevens, Martin Brian 1957- *WhoFI 94*
Stevens, Mary Ann *WhoAmP 93*
Stevens, Mary Elizabeth 1955- *WhoScEn 94*
Stevens, Maxwell McDew 1942- *WhoBlA 94*
Stevens, May 1924- *WhoAm 94, WhoAmA 93*
Stevens, Michael Keith 1945- *WhoAmA 93*
Stevens, Milton Lewis, Jr. 1942- *WhoAm 94*
Stevens, Morton d1959 *WhoHol 92*
Stevens, Nancy Williams 1927- *WhoAmP 93*
Stevens, Naomi *WhoHol 92*
Stevens, Neil George 1951- *WhoWest 94*
Stevens, Nelson 1938- *AfrAmAl 6*
Stevens, Nelson L. 1938- *WhoAmA 93*
Stevens, Nettie Maria 1861-1912 *WorScD*
Stevens, Norman d1980 *WhoHol 92*
Stevens, Norman Dennison 1932- *WhoAm 94*
Stevens, Onslow d1977 *WhoHol 92*
Stevens, Oren *WhoHol 92*
Stevens, Patricia 1942- *WhoAmP 93*
Stevens, Patricia Ann 1946- *WhoBlA 94*
Stevens, Paul d1986 *WhoHol 92*
Stevens, Paul Edward 1916- *WhoAm 94*
Stevens, Paul Irving 1915- *WhoAm 94*
Stevens, Perry G. 1931- *WhoIns 94*
Stevens, Peter *EncSF 93*
Stevens, Peter (Stanley) 1927- *WrDr 94*
Stevens, Philip Theodore d1992 *Who 94N*
Stevens, Prescott Allen 1922- *WhoScEn 94*
Stevens, Preston Standish 1896-1989 *WhAm 10*
Stevens, R.L. *EncSF 93*
Stevens, Reatha J. 1931- *WhoBlA 94*
Stevens, Rebecca Sue 1940- *WhoMW 93*
Stevens, Richard P. 1931- *WrDr 94*
Stevens, Richard William 1924- *Who 94*
Stevens, Rise 1913- *NewGrDO, WhoHol 92*
Stevens, Robert d1963 *WhoHol 92*
Stevens, Robert d1981 *WhoHol 92*
Stevens, Robert Bocking 1933- *Who 94, WhoAm 94, WhoWest 94*
Stevens, Robert David 1921- *WhoAm 94*
Stevens, Robert E(llis) 1942- *ConAu 142*
Stevens, Robert Edward 1957- *WhoFI 94, WhoMW 93, WhoScEn 94*
Stevens, Robert Edwin 1927- *WhoAm 94*
Stevens, Robert Jay 1945- *WhoAm 94*
Stevens, Robert Livingston 1787-1856 *WorInv*
Stevens, Robert Tyler *ConAu 43NR*
Stevens, Robert Tyler 1911- *WrDr 94*
Stevens, Rochelle 1966- *WhoBlA 94*
Stevens, Rock *WhoHol 92*
Stevens, Roger Lacey 1910- *WhoAm 94*
Stevens, Roger Seymour 1921- *WhoWest 94*
Stevens, Ron A. 1945- *WhoAm 94*
Stevens, Ronnie 1925- *WhoHol 92*
Stevens, Rosemary (Anne) 1935- *WrDr 94*
Stevens, Rosemary Anne *WhoAm 94*
Stevens, Rosemary Anne 1935- *IntWW 93*
Stevens, Roy W. 1924- *WhoAm 94, WhoFI 94*
Stevens, Ruby *WhAm 10*
Stevens, Ruth Marie 1933- *WhoAmP 93*
Stevens, Shadoe 1947- *WhoHol 92*
Stevens, Shane *DrAPF 93*
Stevens, Shane 1941- *ConAu 43NR*
Stevens, Shane 1951- *WhoAm 94*
Stevens, Sharon A. 1949- *WhoBlA 94*
Stevens, Sinclair McKnight 1927- *IntWW 93, WhoAm 94*
Stevens, Stella 1936- *WhoHol 92*
Stevens, Stella 1937- *IntMPA 94*
Stevens, Stephen Edward *WhoScEn 94, WhoWest 94*
Stevens, Susan Fluhr 1954- *WhoWest 94*
Stevens, Suzanne H. 1938- *WrDr 94*
Stevens, Ted 1923- *CngDr 93*
Stevens, Thaddeus 1792-1868 *HisWorL [port]*
Stevens, Thelma K. 1932- *WhoAmA 93*
Stevens, Theodore Fulton 1923- *IntWW 93, WhoAm 94, WhoAmP 93, WhoWest 94*
Stevens, Thomas d1619 *WhWE*
Stevens, Thomas Charles 1949- *WhoAm 94, WhoAmL 94*
Stevens, Thomas L. 1930- *WhoIns 94*
Stevens, Thomas Lee 1930- *WhoAm 94, WhoAmL 94*
Stevens, Thomas Lorenzo, Jr. 1933- *WhoBlA 94*
Stevens, Thomas Stevens 1900- *Who 94*
Stevens, Timothy John 1940- *Who 94*
Stevens, Timothy John 1946- *Who 94*
Stevens, Timothy S. *WhoBlA 94*
Stevens, Tina Wagner 1957- *WhoMW 93*
Stevens, Tony 1955- *WhoMW 93*
Stevens, Val *WhoAmP 93*
Stevens, Vi d1967 *WhoHol 92*
Stevens, W. Tris *WhoIns 94*
Stevens, Wallace 1879-1955 *AmCulL*
Stevens, Walter Hollis 1927-1980 *WhoAmA 93N*
Stevens, Walter Scott 1962- *WhoWest 94*
Stevens, Warren 1919- *WhoAm 94, WhoHol 92*
Stevens, Warren Sherwood 1941- *WhoBlA 94*
Stevens, Wendell Claire 1931- *WhoAm 94, WhoWest 94*
Stevens, Wendy *DrAPF 93*
Stevens, Wilbur Hunt 1918- *WhoFI 94, WhoWest 94*
Stevens, William Ansel, Sr. 1919- *WhoAmA 93*
Stevens, William Christoper 1921- *WrDr 94*
Stevens, William David 1934- *Who 94*
Stevens, William Dollard 1918- *WhoAm 94*
Stevens, William Frederick, III 1954- *WhoScEn 94*
Stevens, William J. 1940- *WhoAmL 94*
Stevens, William John 1915- *WhoAm 94, WhoFI 94*
Stevens, William Kenneth 1917- *WhoAm 94*
Stevens, William Louis 1932- *WhoMW 93*
Stevens, William Talbert 1952- *WhoFI 94*
Stevens, Yvette Marie 1953- *WhoAm 94*
Stevens-Allen, David Joseph 1925- *WhoWest 94*
Stevens-Arroyo, Antonio M. 1941- *WhoHisp 94*
Stevens Of Ludgate, Baron 1936- *IntWW 93, Who 94*
Stevenson, A. Brockie 1919- *WhoAm 94, WhoAmA 93*
Stevenson, Adlai E. 1900-1965 *HisDcKW*
Stevenson, Adlai E., III 1930- *IntWW 93*
Stevenson, Adlai Ewing, III 1930- *WhoAm 94, WhoAmL 94, WhoAmP 93*
Stevenson, Alan Carruth 1909- *Who 94*
Stevenson, Anne *DrAPF 93, WrDr 94*
Stevenson, Anne 1933- *BlmGEL [port], BlmGWL, WrDr 94*
Stevenson, Ben 1936- *WhoAm 94*
Stevenson, Beulah d1965 *WhoAmA 93N*
Stevenson, Bryan Allen 1959- *WhoAmL 94*
Stevenson, Charles d1943 *WhoHol 92*
Stevenson, Charles A. d1929 *WhoHol 92*
Stevenson, Charles L(eslie) 1908-1979 *EncEth*
Stevenson, Christopher Terence S. *Who 94*
Stevenson, D(orothy) E(mily) 1892-1973 *EncSF 93*
Stevenson, David *Who 94*
Stevenson, David 1942- *WrDr 94*
Stevenson, (Hugh) David 1918- *Who 94*
Stevenson, David John 1948- *Who 94*
Stevenson, Denise L. 1946- *WhoFI 94*
Stevenson, Dennis *Who 94*
Stevenson, Derek Paul 1911- *Who 94*
Stevenson, Donald Lawrence 1934- *WhoMW 93*
Stevenson, Douglas d1934 *WhoHol 92*
Stevenson, Douglas F. 1921- *WhoAm 94*
Stevenson, Dwight Eshelman 1906- *WrDr 94*
Stevenson, Earl, Jr. 1921- *WhoScEn 94*
Stevenson, Elizabeth 1919- *WhoAm 94, WrDr 94*
Stevenson, Eric Van Cortlandt 1926- *WhoAm 94*
Stevenson, Ernest Vail 1922- *WhoAm 94*
Stevenson, Florence *WrDr 94*
Stevenson, Frances Grace 1921- *WhoWest 94*
Stevenson, Frank Earl, II 1955- *WhoAmL 94*
Stevenson, George Franklin 1922- *WhoAm 94*
Stevenson, George Telford 1932- *Who 94*
Stevenson, George William 1938- *Who 94*
Stevenson, Gerald Lee 1937- *WhoFI 94*
Stevenson, Harold 1929- *WhoAmA 93*
Stevenson, Harold William 1924- *WhoAm 94, WhoMW 93, WhoScEn 94*
Stevenson, Henry Dennistoun 1945- *Who 94*
Stevenson, Houseley d1953 *WhoHol 92*
Stevenson, Houseley, Jr. *WhoHol 92*
Stevenson, Howard Higginbotham 1941- *WhoAm 94*
Stevenson, Hugh Alexander 1942- *Who 94*
Stevenson, Ian 1918- *WhoAm 94*
Stevenson, Ian (Pretyman) 1918- *WrDr 94*
Stevenson, J. Ross 1931- *WhoScEn 94*
Stevenson, James 1929- *WrDr 94*
Stevenson, James Lyall 1933- *WhoAm 94*
Stevenson, James Ralph 1949- *WhoScEn 94, WhoWest 94*
Stevenson, James Richard 1937- *WhoAmL 94, WhoWest 94*
Stevenson, Jennifer Anne 1946- *WhoAm 94*
Stevenson, Jim 1937- *Who 94*
Stevenson, Jo Ann C. 1942- *WhoAm 94, WhoAmL 94*
Stevenson, John *EncSF 93*
Stevenson, John 1927- *Who 94*
Stevenson, John (Andrew) 1761-1833 *NewGrDO*
Stevenson, John O'Farrell, Jr. 1947- *WhoScEn 94*
Stevenson, John Reese 1921- *WhoAm 94, WhoAmL 94*
Stevenson, Joseph Aidan 1931- *Who 94*
Stevenson, Juliet *WhoHol 92*
Stevenson, Juliet 1956- *ConTFT 11, IntWW 93*
Stevenson, Justin Jason, III 1941- *WhoAm 94*
Stevenson, Kenneth Lee 1939- *WhoAm 94*
Stevenson, Lillian 1922- *WhoBlA 94*

Stevenson, Madeline D. WhoAmP 93
Stevenson, Margot 1914- WhoHol 92
Stevenson, Mark Joseph Tomlinson 1961- WhoFI 94
Stevenson, Mary d1977 WhoHol 92
Stevenson, McLean 1929- WhoCom, WhoHol 92
Stevenson, Michael Charles 1960- Who 94
Stevenson, Morton Coleman WhoBlA 94
Stevenson, Nancy Backer 1928- WhoAmP 93
Stevenson, Olive 1930- Who 94
Stevenson, Parker 1953- IntMPA 94, WhoHol 92
Stevenson, Philip Davis 1936- WhoAm 94
Stevenson, Ray 1937- WhoFI 94
Stevenson, Richard Gray, III 1958- WhoWest 94
Stevenson, Richard Wilson d1967 WhoHol 92
Stevenson, Robert d1975 WhoHol 92
Stevenson, Robert Benjamin, III 1950- WhoMW 93
Stevenson, Robert Bryce 1926- Who 94
Stevenson, Robert Edwin 1926- WhoAm 94, WhoScEn 94
Stevenson, Robert Francis 1944- WhoMW 93
Stevenson, Robert Louis 1850-1894 DcLB 141 [port], RfGShF
Stevenson, Robert Louis (Balfour) 1850-1894 EncSF 93, TwCYAW
Stevenson, Robert Louis Balfour 1850-1894 BlmGEL [port]
Stevenson, Robert Murrell 1916- WhoAm 94
Stevenson, Robert W. WhoFI 94
Stevenson, Robert Wilfrid 1947- IntWW 93, Who 94
Stevenson, Russell A. 1923- WhoBlA 94
Stevenson, Russell B., Jr. 1941- WhoAm 94, WhoAmL 94
Stevenson, Ruth Carter 1923- WhoAmA 93
Stevenson, Ruth Rolston 1897- WhoAmA 93
Stevenson, Sandra Jean 1949- WhoFI 94
Stevenson, Simpson 1921- Who 94
Stevenson, Thomas Herbert 1951- WhoAmL 94, WhoFI 94, WhoMW 93
Stevenson, Unice Teen 1950- WhoBlA 94
Stevenson, Venetia 1938- WhoHol 92
Stevenson, Vicki Cornell 1955- WhoFI 94
Stevenson, Warren Howard 1938- WhoAm 94, WhoMW 93
Stevenson, Wilf Who 94
Stevenson, William (Henri) 1924- WrDr 94
Stevenson, William Alexander 1934- WhoAm 94
Stevenson, William Booth, II 1952- WhoFI 94
Stevenson, William Henri 1924- ConAu 41NR, WhoAm 94
Stevenson, William John 1949- WhoScEn 94
Stevenson, William Trevor 1921- Who 94
Steventon, Robert Wesley 1948- WhoFI 94
Stever, Donald Winfred 1944- WhoAm 94
Stever, Edward William DrAPF 93
Stever, Horton Guyford 1916- IntWW 93, WhoAm 94, WhoAmP 93, WhoScEn 94
Stever, Margo DrAPF 93
Stevermer, C(aroline) J. 1955- WrDr 94
Steveson, Boyd Donald 1950- WhoAmP 93
Stevie, Richard George 1951- WhoMW 93
Stevin, Simon c. 1548-c. 1620 WorInv, WorScD
Stevovich, Andrew Vlastimir 1948- WhoAmA 93
Steward, Alma Ruth 1935- WhoScEn 94
Steward, Carlos Warren 1950- WhoFI 94
Steward, Cedric John 1931- Who 94
Steward, D. E. DrAPF 93
Steward, Donn Horatio 1921-1986 WhoAmA 93N
Steward, Emanuel 1944- WhoBlA 94
Steward, F(rederick) C(ampion) 1904-1993 ConAu 142
Steward, Frederick Campion 1904- Who 94
Steward, Frederick Campion 1904-1993 NewYTBS 93 [port]
Steward, H. Leighton 1934- WhoAm 94, WhoFI 94
Steward, James Brian 1946- WhoAmL 94
Steward, Lester Howard 1930- WhoWest 94
Steward, Loretta 1918- WhoAmP 93
Steward, Lowell C. 1919- WhoBlA 94
Steward, Maynon d1932 WhoHol 92
Steward, Mollie Aileen 1952- WhoScEn 94
Steward, Samuel M(orris) 1909- GayLL
Steward, Stanley Feargus 1904- Who 94
Steward, Weldon Cecil 1934- WhoAm 94
Stewart Who 94
Stewart, A(gnes) C(harlotte) 1915- WrDr 94
Stewart, Acie David 1943- WhoMW 93
Stewart, Adelle Wright 1922- WhoBlA 94
Stewart, Alan 1917- Who 94
Stewart, Alan (d'Arcy) 1932- Who 94
Stewart, Alan Frederick 1948- WhoScEn 94
Stewart, Alastair (Robin) 1925- Who 94
Stewart, Alastair James 1952- Who 94
Stewart, Alastair Lindsay 1938- Who 94
Stewart, Albert C. WhoBlA 94
Stewart, Albert Clifton 1919- WhoAm 94
Stewart, Albert Elisha 1927- WhoAm 94, WhoMW 93
Stewart, Alec Thompson 1925- WhoAm 94, WhoScEn 94
Stewart, Alexander c. 1740-1794 WhAmRev
Stewart, Alexander Doig 1926- WhoAm 94, WhoFI 94
Stewart, Alexandra 1939- WhoHol 92
Stewart, Allan Who 94
Stewart, (John) Allan 1942- Who 94
Stewart, Allen Warren 1938- WhoAm 94, WhoAmL 94
Stewart, Andrew Struthers 1937- Who 94
Stewart, Angus 1946- Who 94
Stewart, Angus Bynon 1934- WhoWest 94
Stewart, Anita d1961 WhoHol 92
Stewart, Ann Harleman WrDr 94
Stewart, Arlene Jean Golden 1943- WhoScEn 94
Stewart, Arthur 1915- WhoAmA 93
Stewart, Athole d1940 WhoHol 92
Stewart, Barbara D. 1943- WhoIns 94
Stewart, Barbara Elizabeth 1923- WhoAm 94
Stewart, Barbra Houle 1954- WhoMW 93
Stewart, Belynda Pleasants 1946- WhoFI 94
Stewart, Bernard 1950- WhoBlA 94
Stewart, Bernard Francis 1928- WhoMW 93
Stewart, Bert James 1924- WhoAmP 93
Stewart, Bess 1936- WhoBlA 94
Stewart, Betty Bills 1939- WhoMW 93
Stewart, Bill 1941- WhoAmA 93
Stewart, Blanche d1952 WhoHol 92
Stewart, Bob Ray 1940- WhoMW 93
Stewart, Bonnie 1947- WhoAmP 93
Stewart, Brent Kevin 1957- WhoScEn 94
Stewart, Brian John 1945- IntWW 93, Who 94
Stewart, Brian Thomas Webster 1922- Who 94
Stewart, Brice Horace 1911- WhoAmP 93
Stewart, Brittanica 1950- WhoBlA 94
Stewart, Burton Gloyden, Jr. 1933- WhoAm 94
Stewart, Byron 1955- WhoHol 92
Stewart, C. Jean 1947- WhoAmL 94
Stewart, Cameron Leigh 1950- WhoAm 94
Stewart, Campbell Who 94
Stewart, (William Alexander) Campbell 1915- Who 94
Stewart, Carl L. 1936- WhoBlA 94
Stewart, Carleton M. 1921- WhoAm 94
Stewart, Carlyle Veeder, Jr. 1927- WhoAmP 93
Stewart, Catherine Mary 1959- WhoHol 92
Stewart, Charles 1729-1800 WhAmRev
Stewart, Charles Andrew, III 1959- WhoAmL 94
Stewart, Charles Edward, Jr. 1916- WhoAm 94, WhoAmL 94
Stewart, Charles Evan 1952- WhoAm 94, WhoAmL 94, WhoFI 94
Stewart, Charles Franklin, Jr. 1942- WhoWest 94
Stewart, Charles H. 1947- WhoAmP 93
Stewart, Charles J. 1930- WhoBlA 94
Stewart, Charles Leslie 1919- WhoAm 94
Stewart, Charles Vuille 1941- WhoAmL 94
Stewart, Charles Walter 1937- WhoIns 94
Stewart, Charles Wesley, Jr. 1927- WhoAmP 93
Stewart, Christine 1941- WhoWomW 91
Stewart, Clarence P. 1922- WhoAmP 93
Stewart, Colin MacDonald 1922- Who 94
Stewart, Cornelius James, II 1925- WhoAm 94, WhoFI 94
Stewart, Cornelius Van Leuven 1936- WhoAm 94
Stewart, Craig E. 1946- WhoAmL 94
Stewart, Dale Lynn 1954- WhoWest 94
Stewart, Daniel Clark 1947- WhoAmL 94
Stewart, Daniel Kenneth 1925- WrDr 94
Stewart, Daniel Robert 1938- WhoAm 94
Stewart, Danny d1962 WhoHol 92
Stewart, Darneau V. 1928- WhoBlA 94
Stewart, David 1921- WrDr 94
Stewart, David Brodribb d1992 Who 94N
Stewart, David Dickson 1949- WhoMW 93
Stewart, David J. d1966 WhoHol 92
Stewart, David James H. Who 94
Stewart, David Keith 1957- WhoBlA 94
Stewart, David Marshall 1916- WhoAm 94
Stewart, David Pentland 1943- WhoAmL 94
Stewart, David Wayne 1951- WhoFI 94, WhoWest 94
Stewart, Deborah Ruth 1954- WhoAm 94
Stewart, Dick WhoHol 92
Stewart, Don 1935- WhoHol 92
Stewart, Don M. 1937- WhoIns 94
Stewart, Donald d1966 WhoHol 92
Stewart, Donald Charles 1930- WrDr 94
Stewart, Donald Edwin 1926- WhoWest 94
Stewart, Donald H(enderson) 1911- WrDr 94
Stewart, Donald James d1992 IntWW 93N
Stewart, Donald M. 1938- WhoAm 94
Stewart, Donald Mitchell 1938- WhoBlA 94
Stewart, Donald Ogden d1980 WhoHol 92
Stewart, Donald Ogden 1894- WhAm 10
Stewart, Donald Ogden 1894-1980 ConAu 43NR, IntDcF 2-4 [port]
Stewart, Donald W. 1940- WhoAmP 93
Stewart, Donovan 1903- WhoAmP 93
Stewart, Dorothy Nell 1949- WhoBlA 94
Stewart, Dorothy S. WhoAmA 93
Stewart, Douglas (Alexander) 1913-1985 ConDr 93
Stewart, Douglas Day IntMPA 94
Stewart, Dugald 1753-1828 EncEth
Stewart, Duncan E. 1940- WhoAmA 93
Stewart, Duncan James 1939- WhoAm 94, WhoAmL 94
Stewart, Duncan Montgomery 1930- Who 94
Stewart, Edgar Allen 1909- WhoAm 94
Stewart, Edward (Jackson) 1923- Who 94
Stewart, Edward Nicholson 1940- WhoFI 94
Stewart, Eileen d1931 WhoHol 92
Stewart, Eileen Rose 1942- WhoFI 94
Stewart, Elaine 1929- IntMPA 94, WhoHol 92
Stewart, Eleanore WhoHol 92
Stewart, Elizabeth Pierce 1947- WhoBlA 94
Stewart, Ellen Smith 1945- WhoMW 93
Stewart, Emily Jones 1937- WhoBlA 94
Stewart, Etta d1929 WhoHol 92
Stewart, Eugene Lawrence 1920- WhoAm 94, WhoAmL 94, WhoFI 94
Stewart, Evelyn WhoHol 92
Stewart, Ewan WhoHol 92
Stewart, Ewen 1926- Who 94
Stewart, F. Clark 1942- WhoAmA 93
Stewart, Frank DrAPF 93
Stewart, Frank 1946- ConAu 42NR
Stewart, Frank Maurice 1939- WhoAm 94, WhoScEn 94
Stewart, Franklin Randolph 1920- WhoAmL 94
Stewart, Fred d1970 WhoHol 92
Stewart, Fred M(ustard) 1936- WrDr 94
Stewart, Fred Mustard 1936- ConAu 42NR, EncSF 93
Stewart, Fred Ray 1950- WhoWest 94
Stewart, Freddie 1925- WhoHol 92
Stewart, Freddie Mardrell 1943- WhoBlA 94
Stewart, Frederick (Henry) 1916- Who 94
Stewart, Frederick Henry 1916- IntWW 93
Stewart, Frederick Neal 1931- WhoAm 94
Stewart, G. Cope, III 1941- WhoAm 94
Stewart, G. Russell, II 1933- WhoAmP 93
Stewart, Gene d1926 WhoHol 92
Stewart, Geoffrey S. 1951- WhoAm 94, WhoAmL 94
Stewart, George d1945 WhoHol 92
Stewart, George Girdwood 1919- Who 94
Stewart, George R(ippey) 1895-1980 EncSF 93
Stewart, George Ray 1944- WhoAm 94
Stewart, George Russell 1944- Who 94
Stewart, George Taylor 1924- WhoAm 94, WhoFI 94
Stewart, Gilbert Wright 1940- WhoAm 94
Stewart, Gillian Mary 1945- Who 94
Stewart, Glenn W. 1914- WhoAmP 93
Stewart, (George Robert) Gordon 1924- Who 94
Stewart, Gordon Curran 1939- WhoAm 94
Stewart, Gordon Duncan 1958- WhoMW 93
Stewart, Gordon Thallon 1919- Who 94
Stewart, Grace WhoMW 93
Stewart, Grant d1929 WhoHol 92
Stewart, Gregory 1958- WhoBlA 94
Stewart, Guy Harry 1924- WhoAm 94
Stewart, Harold (Frederick) 1916- WrDr 94
Stewart, Harold Brown 1921- WhoAm 94
Stewart, Harold Charles 1906- Who 94
Stewart, Harold Julian 1896- WhAm 10
Stewart, Harold Leroy 1899- WhoAm 94
Stewart, Harold Sanford 1949- WhoFI 94
Stewart, Harris Bates, Jr. 1922- WhoAm 94, WhoScEn 94
Stewart, Harry WhoHol 92
Stewart, Harry A. 1940- WhoAmL 94
Stewart, Henry d1993 NewYTBS 93
Stewart, Homer Joseph 1915- WhoAm 94
Stewart, Horace W. 1910- WhoBlA 94
Stewart, Houston Mark S. Who 94
Stewart, Hugh Charlie Godfray 1897- Who 94
Stewart, Hugh Parker 1934- Who 94
Stewart, I. Daniel 1932- WhoAmP 93
Stewart, Ian George 1923- Who 94
Stewart, Imagene Bigham 1942- WhoBlA 94
Stewart, Inez 1956- WhoHisp 94
Stewart, Irvin 1899-1990 WhAm 10
Stewart, Isaac Daniel, Jr. 1932- WhoAm 94, WhoAmL 94, WhoWest 94
Stewart, Isaac Mitton 1904- WhAm 10
Stewart, J(ohn) Douglas 1934- WhoAmA 93
Stewart, J(ohn) I(nnes) M(ackintosh) 1906- WrDr 94
Stewart, Jack d1966 WhoHol 92
Stewart, Jack 1926- WhoAmA 93
Stewart, Jack M. 1926- WhoFI 94
Stewart, Jackie Who 94
Stewart, James c. 1700-1752 DcNaB MP
Stewart, James 1908- IntMPA 94, WhoHol 92
Stewart, James 1912-1991 WhAm 10
Stewart, James 1951- WhoAmL 94, WhoWest 94
Stewart, James (Douglas) 1925- Who 94
Stewart, James (Maitland) 1908- IntWW 93, Who 94
Stewart, James A., III WhoBlA 94
Stewart, James B. WhoAm 94
Stewart, James B. 1943- WhoAmL 94
Stewart, James Benjamin 1947- WhoBlA 94
Stewart, James Brewer 1940- WhoAm 94
Stewart, James Cecil Campbell 1916- Who 94
Stewart, James E. 1945- WhoAmL 94
Stewart, James Gathings 1942- WhoAm 94, WhoFI 94
Stewart, James H., Jr. 1926- WhoAmP 93
Stewart, James Hamilton, III 1943- WhoAmL 94
Stewart, James Harvey 1939- Who 94
Stewart, James Ian 1928- WhoScEn 94
Stewart, James Joseph Patrick 1946- WhoFI 94
Stewart, James Kevin 1942- WhoAmL 94
Stewart, James L. IntMPA 94
Stewart, James M. 1943- WhoAm 94, WhoFI 94
Stewart, James M. 1946- WhoFI 94, WhoWest 94
Stewart, James Maitland 1908- AmCulL [port], WhoAm 94
Stewart, James Montgomery 1939- WhoAm 94
Stewart, James Robertson 1917- Who 94
Stewart, James Simeon Hamilton 1943- Who 94
Stewart, Jane 1934- WhoScEn 94
Stewart, Janson WhoAmP 93
Stewart, Jarvis Anthony 1914-1981 WhoAmA 93N
Stewart, Jeff 1939- WhoAm 94
Stewart, Jeffrey Bayrd 1952- WhoAmL 94
Stewart, Jewel Hope 1948- WhoBlA 94
Stewart, Joe J. 1938- WhoFI 94
Stewart, Joe William 1928- WhoAmP 93
Stewart, John DrAPF 93
Stewart, John 1787-1823 EncNAR
Stewart, John 1920- WhoHol 92
Stewart, John 1945- WhoAmA 93
Stewart, John 1952- ConAu 142
Stewart, John Alan 1947- WhoAmL 94
Stewart, John Antenen 1920- WhoMW 93
Stewart, John Anthony Benedict 1927- IntWW 93, Who 94
Stewart, John B., Jr. 1930- WhoBlA 94
Stewart, John Cary 1958- WhoMW 93
Stewart, John Craig 1940- Who 94
Stewart, John Daugherty 1915- WhoAm 94
Stewart, John Gilman 1935- WhoAmP 93
Stewart, John Hall 1944- Who 94
Stewart, John Harger 1940- WhoAm 94
Stewart, John Innes Mackintosh 1906- Who 94
Stewart, John Irwin, Jr. 1950- WhoAm 94, WhoAmL 94
Stewart, John Lincoln 1917- WhoAm 94, WhoAmA 93
Stewart, John Morrow 1924- WhoWest 94
Stewart, John Murray 1943- WhoFI 94
Stewart, John O. 1935- WhoBlA 94

Stewart, John Othneil 1933- WhoBlA 94
Stewart, John P. 1945- WhoAmA 93
Stewart, John Spencer 1946- WhoAmL 94
Stewart, John Wray Black 1936- WhoAm 94, WhoWest 94
Stewart, John Young 1939- IntWW 93, Who 94
Stewart, Johnny 1939- WhoHol 92
Stewart, Joseph Grier 1941- WhoAmL 94
Stewart, Joseph Lester 1915- WhoAm 94
Stewart, Joseph M. 1942- WhoBlA 94
Stewart, Joseph Melvin 1942- WhoFI 94
Stewart, Joseph Turner, Jr. 1929- WhoFI 94
Stewart, Judith 1938- WrDr 94
Stewart, Judith A. WhoAmL 94
Stewart, Judith Underwood 1955- WhoAm 94
Stewart, Katherine d1949 WhoHol 92
Stewart, Kay WhoHol 92
Stewart, Kay Lorraine 1962- WhoMW 93
Stewart, Kendall Leuomon 1950- WhoMW 93
Stewart, Kenneth Albert 1925- Who 94
Stewart, Kenneth C. 1939- WhoBlA 94
Stewart, Kenneth Hope 1922- Who 94
Stewart, Kenneth L. 1954- WhoAmL 94
Stewart, Kenneth Ray 1951- WhoScEn 94
Stewart, Kent Kallam 1934- WhoAm 94
Stewart, Kevin James 1928- Who 94
Stewart, Kirk T. 1951- WhoAm 94, WhoFI 94
Stewart, Larry WhoHol 92
Stewart, Larry 1968- WhoBlA 94
Stewart, Larry R. 1948- WhoWest 94
Stewart, Leland Perry 1928- WhoWest 94
Stewart, Leon d1976 WhoHol 92
Stewart, Leslie James 1958- WhoFI 94
Stewart, Loretta A. 1930- WhoBlA 94
Stewart, Lucille Lee d1982 WhoHol 92
Stewart, Lyle Bainbridge 1941- WhoAm 94, WhoAmL 94
Stewart, Mac A. 1942- WhoBlA 94
Stewart, Mae E. 1926- WhoBlA 94
Stewart, Malcolm M. 1920- WhoBlA 94
Stewart, Margaret McBride 1927- WhoAm 94, WhoScEn 94
Stewart, Marianne WhoHol 92
Stewart, Marilyn IntMPA 94
Stewart, Mark Carroll 1947- WhoAm 94
Stewart, Mark Steven 1950- WhoAmL 94
Stewart, Mark Thomas 1948- WhoFI 94
Stewart, Marlene 1949- ConTFT 11
Stewart, Marlene Metzger 1937- WhoFI 94, WhoWest 94
Stewart, Marsha Beach 1952- WhoAm 94, WhoFI 94
Stewart, Martha 1922- WhoHol 92
Stewart, Martha 1941?- CurBio 93 [port]
Stewart, Mary 1916- BlmGWL
Stewart, Mary (Florence Elinor) 1916- TwCYAW, Who 94, WrDr 94
Stewart, Mary Florence Elinor 1916- WhoAm 94
Stewart, Mary Ruth 1929- WhoAmP 93
Stewart, Maurice Evan 1929- Who 94
Stewart, Maxwell Slutz 1900-1990 WhAm 10
Stewart, Mel 1923- WhoHol 92
Stewart, Melbourne George, Jr. 1927- WhoAm 94
Stewart, Melinda Jane 1949- WhoAmL 94
Stewart, Melvin WhoAm 94
Stewart, Melvin Ray 1958- WhoFI 94
Stewart, Michael DrAPF 93
Stewart, Michael 1933- EncSF 93
Stewart, Michael 1945- EncSF 93
Stewart, Michael (James) 1933- WrDr 94
Stewart, Michael (Norman Francis) 1911- Who 94
Stewart, Michael Eugene 1947- WhoAmP 93
Stewart, Michael James 1933- Who 94
Stewart, Michael Jerome 1948- WhoAmL 94
Stewart, Michael Kenneth 1956- WhoScEn 94
Stewart, Michael Leslie 1952- WhoFI 94
Stewart, Michael M. 1947- WhoAmL 94
Stewart, Michael McFadden 1938- WhoFI 94
Stewart, Michael R. 1955- WhoAmL 94
Stewart, Milton Roy 1945- WhoAm 94, WhoAmL 94
Stewart, Moray Who 94
Stewart, (James) Moray 1938- Who 94
Stewart, Muriel (Acadia) 1905- Who 94
Stewart, Murray Baker 1931- WhoAmL 94
Stewart, Nancy Lee 1935- WhoWest 94
Stewart, Nancy Potter 1936- WhoAmP 93
Stewart, Nellie d1931 WhoHol 92
Stewart, Nellie 1858-1931 NewGrDO
Stewart, Nicholas WhoHol 92
Stewart, Nicholas John Cameron 1947- Who 94
Stewart, Nick WhoHol 92
Stewart, Nora Scott 1936- WhoAmP 93
Stewart, Norm 1935- BasBi
Stewart, Norma Lee 1925- WhoWest 94
Stewart, Norman 1947- WhoAmA 93
Stewart, Norman John 1948- WhoAm 94
Stewart, Norman Lawrence 1942- WhoAm 94
Stewart, Norman MacLeod 1934- Who 94
Stewart, Pamela L. 1953- WhoAmL 94
Stewart, Patrice Lafferty 1933- WhoFI 94
Stewart, Patricia Carry 1928- WhoAm 94, WhoFI 94
Stewart, Patrick 1940- IntMPA 94, WhoAm 94, WhoHol 92
Stewart, Paul d1986 WhoHol 92
Stewart, Paul Anthony, II 1952- WhoFI 94, WhoWest 94
Stewart, Paul Arthur 1955- WhoMW 93
Stewart, Paul Leroy 1928- WhoAmA 93
Stewart, Paul Wilbur 1925- WhoBlA 94
Stewart, Paula 1933- WhoHol 92
Stewart, Payne 1957- WhoAm 94
Stewart, Pearl WhoBlA 94
Stewart, Peggy 1923- WhoHol 92
Stewart, Penelope WhoHol 92
Stewart, Peter Beaufort 1923- WhoAm 94
Stewart, Peter G. 1940- WhoAmL 94
Stewart, Porter DrAPF 93
Stewart, Rachel Ann 1943- WhoAmP 93
Stewart, Randall Todd 1960- WhoFI 94
Stewart, Renice Ann 1947- WhoWest 94
Stewart, Rex d1967 WhoHol 92
Stewart, Richard d1939 WhoHol 92
Stewart, Richard Alfred 1945- WhoAm 94, WhoWest 94
Stewart, Richard Allan 1947- WhoScEn 94
Stewart, Richard Burleson 1940- WhoAm 94
Stewart, Richard E. 1933- WhoIns 94
Stewart, Richard Edwin 1933- WhoAm 94
Stewart, Richard Williams 1948- WhoAmL 94
Stewart, Ritson EncSF 93
Stewart, Robert DrAPF 93
Stewart, Robert Alexander 1949- Who 94
Stewart, Robert Andrew 1928- WhoAm 94
Stewart, Robert Christie 1926- Who 94
Stewart, Robert Clarence, Jr. 1936- WhoAm 94
Stewart, Robert Edward 1950- WhoFI 94
Stewart, Robert Forrest, Jr. 1943- WhoAm 94
Stewart, Robert Gordon 1931- WhoAm 94, WhoAmA 93
Stewart, Robert H., III 1925- WhoAm 94
Stewart, Robert Jackson 1958- WhoScEn 94
Stewart, Robert Lee 1942- WhoAm 94, WhoWest 94
Stewart, Robert McLean 1895- WhAm 10
Stewart, Robert W. 1923- IntWW 93
Stewart, Robert William 1923- Who 94, WhoAm 94
Stewart, Robertson (Huntly) 1913- Who 94
Stewart, Robin WhoHol 92
Stewart, Robin Milton 1938- Who 94
Stewart, Rod 1945- IntWW 93
Stewart, Roderick David 1945- WhoAm 94
Stewart, Roger 1920- WhoAmP 93
Stewart, Ron(nie) 1956- ConAu 142
Stewart, Ronald 1941- WhoScEn 94
Stewart, Ronald (Compton) 1903- Who 94
Stewart, Ronald Eugene 1937- WhoAmP 93, WhoMW 93
Stewart, Ronald K. 1948- WhoAmP 93
Stewart, Ronald L. 1936- WhoBlA 94
Stewart, Ronald Patrick 1942- WhoBlA 94
Stewart, Rosemary WrDr 94
Stewart, Ross 1924- WhoAm 94
Stewart, Roy d1933 WhoHol 92
Stewart, Ruth Ann 1942- WhoAm 94, WhoBlA 94
Stewart, S. Jay 1938- IntWW 93
Stewart, Sam WhoHol 92
Stewart, Samuel B. 1908- WhoAm 94
Stewart, Scott Richard 1966- WhoFI 94
Stewart, Sheila L. WhoAmA 93
Stewart, Simon Who 94
Stewart, (John) Simon (Watson) 1955- Who 94
Stewart, Sophie d1977 WhoHol 92
Stewart, Stanley EncSF 93
Stewart, Stanley Toft 1910- Who 94
Stewart, Stephen Malcolm 1914- Who 94
Stewart, Sue Ellen 1955- WhoScEn 94
Stewart, Sue Stern 1942- WhoAm 94, WhoAmL 94
Stewart, Susan Kay 1951- WhoWest 94
Stewart, Suzanne Freda Who 94
Stewart, Terence Patrick 1948- WhoAmL 94
Stewart, Terry Lynn 1943- WhoFI 94
Stewart, Thomas 1928- IntWW 93
Stewart, Thomas (James) 1926- NewGrDO
Stewart, Thomas Clifford 1950- WhoFI 94
Stewart, Thomas Glynn 1949- WhoAmP 93
Stewart, Thomas James, Jr. 1928- WhoAm 94
Stewart, Thomas S. 1954- WhoAmL 94
Stewart, Thomas Ted 1940- WhoMW 93
Stewart, Tom WhoHol 92
Stewart, Trent Anthony 1954- WhoWest 94
Stewart, Trish WhoHol 92
Stewart, Victor Colvin 1921- Who 94
Stewart, Victor F., Jr. 1926- WhoAmP 93
Stewart, W. Douglas 1938- WhoBlA 94
Stewart, Walter c. 1756-1796 AmRev, WhAmRev
Stewart, Walter J. CngDr 93
Stewart, Warren Earl 1924- WhoAm 94
Stewart, Warren Hampton, Sr. 1951- WhoBlA 94
Stewart, Wendell EncSF 93
Stewart, Wesley Holmgreen 1948- WhoAmL 94
Stewart, Will EncSF 93
Stewart, Will 1908- WrDr 94
Stewart, William 1921- Who 94
Stewart, William 1938- WhoAmA 93
Stewart, William A., Jr. 1929- WhoAmP 93
Stewart, William Alexander Campbell 1915- WrDr 94
Stewart, William Arnold 1882-1953 DcNaB MP
Stewart, William D. 1943- WhoAmL 94
Stewart, William D. P. 1935- IntWW 93
Stewart, William Duncan Paterson 1935- Who 94
Stewart, William Elsworth 1928- WhoAmP 93
Stewart, William H. 1935- WhoBlA 94
Stewart, William Ian Who 94
Stewart, William J. 1950- WhoAmP 93
Stewart, William Kenneth, Jr. 1950- WhoScEn 94
Stewart, William O. 1925- WhoAmP 93, WhoBlA 94
Stewart, William R. 1943- WhoAmL 94
Stewart, William Timothy 1965- WhoScEn 94
Stewart, Yvonne WhoHol 92
Stewartby, Baron 1935- Who 94
Stewart-Clark, John 1929- Who 94
Stewart Cox, Arthur George Ernest 1925- Who 94
Stewart-Jones, Richard, Mrs. Who 94
Stewart-Moore, Alexander Wyndham Hume 1915- Who 94
Stewart-Richardson, Simon (Alaisdair) 1947- Who 94
Stewart-Roberts, Phyllida Katharine 1933- Who 94
Stewart-Smith, Christopher Dudley 1941- Who 94
Stewart-Smith, David Cree 1913- Who 94
Stewart-Smith, (Dudley) Geoffrey 1933- Who 94
Stewart-Wilson, Blair Aubyn 1929- Who 94
Steyer, Roy Henry 1918- WhoAm 94, WhoAmL 94, WhoFI 94
Steyn, Daniel Wynand 1923- IntWW 93
Steyn, Jan Hendrik 1928- IntWW 93
Steyn, Johan 1932- Who 94
Steyn, (Stephanus Jacobus) Marais 1914- Who 94
Steyn, S. J. Marais 1914- IntWW 93
Steynovitz, Zamy 1951- WhoAmA 93
Steyrer, Kurt 1920- IntWW 93
Stezoski, Lorise Ann 1963- WhoWest 94
St George, James of c. 1230-1309 DcNaB MP
Stibbard, Peter Jack 1936- Who 94
Stibbe, Austin Jule 1930- WhoMW 93
Stibbe, Philip Godfrey 1921- Who 94
Stibbon, John (James) 1935- Who 94
Stibbs, Douglas Walter Noble 1919- Who 94
Stibel, Gary Marshall 1946- WhoAm 94
Stiber, Alex DrAPF 93
Stibitz, George Robert 1904- WhoAm 94
Stice, James Edward 1928- WhoAm 94
Stich, Carl Joseph, Jr. 1953- WhoAmL 94
Stich, Elizabeth Kottke 1958- WhoMW 93
Stich, Michael 1968- IntWW 93
Stich, Otto 1927- IntWW 93
Stich, Patricia 1940- WhoHol 92
Stich, Sally Simon 1950- WhoWest 94
Stich, Stephen Peter 1943- IntWW 93
Stich-Randall, Teresa 1927- NewGrDO
Sticht, J. Paul 1917- IntWW 93, WhoAm 94
Stick, Alyce Cushing 1944- WhoFI 94, WhoScEn 94
Stick, Thomas Howard Fitchett 1938- WhoFI 94
Stickel, Frederick A. 1921- WhoAm 94, WhoWest 94
Stickel, Frederick George, III 1915- WhoAmL 94
Stickel, Patrick Francis 1950- WhoWest 94
Stickels, Charles Arthur 1933- WhoScEn 94
Sticker, Robert Edward 1922- WhoAmA 93
Stickgold, Bob 1945- EncSF 93
Stickler, Alfons 1910- IntWW 93
Stickler, Daniel Lee 1938- WhoAm 94
Stickler, Fred Charles 1931- WhoAm 94
Stickler, Gunnar Brynolf 1925- WhoAm 94
Stickler, K. Bruce 1946- WhoAm 94, WhoAmL 94
Stickley, Gustav 1858-1942 AmCulL
Stickney, Albert, III 1944- WhoFI 94
Stickney, Benjamin D. 1940- WrDr 94
Stickney, Clifton Howard, Jr. 1932- WhoAmP 93
Stickney, Dorothy 1900- WhoHol 92
Stickney, Janice L. 1941- WhoBlA 94
Stickney, Jessica 1929- WhoAmP 93
Stickney, John DrAPF 93
Stickney, John Moore 1926- WhoAmL 94
Stickney, Phyllis Yvonne WhoBlA 94, WhoHol 92
Stickney, Robert Roy 1941- WhoWest 94
Stickney, William Homer, Jr. 1945- WhoBlA 94
Stidd, Benton Maurice 1936- WhoScEn 94
Stidder, Ted WhoHol 92
Stidham, Shaler, Jr. 1941- WhoAm 94
Stiebel, Eric 1911- WhoAmA 93
Stiebel, Gerald Gustave 1944- WhoAm 94, WhoAmA 93
Stiebel, Penelope Hunter WhoAmA 93
Stieber, Michael Thomas 1943- WhoMW 93
Stiebing, William H(enry), Jr. 1940- ConAu 141
Stiedry, Fritz 1883-1968 NewGrDO
Stief, Louis John 1933- WhoAm 94
Stiefel, D. L. 1945- WhoAmP 93
Stiefel, Frank D. 1944- WhoAmL 94
Stiefel, Milton 1900- WhoHol 92
Stiefel, Sheryl Kay 1958- WhoWest 94
Stiefel, Vernon Leo 1961- WhoScEn 94
Stieffen, Spiros Wallace 1925- WhoAmP 93
Stiefler, Jeffrey E. 1946- WhoAm 94, WhoFI 94
Stiegel, Michael Allen 1946- WhoAmL 94
Stiegelmeyer, Norman Earl 1937- WhoAmA 93N
Stiegemeier, Mary Kathryn 1934- WhoMW 93
Stiegler, Karl Drago 1919- WhoScEn 94
Stiegler, Marc EncSF 93
Stieglitz, Alfred 1864-1946 AmCulL
Stiehl, William D. 1925- WhoAm 94, WhoAmL 94
Stiehm, E. Richard 1933- WhoAm 94
Stiehm, Judith Hicks 1935- WhoAm 94
Stieler, Kurt d1963 WhoHol 92
Stiemer, Siegfried F. WhoScEn 94
Stienmier, Saundra Kay Young 1938- WhoScEn 94
Stierberger, Edward Albert 1933- WhoAmL 94
Stierlin, Helm 1926- WrDr 94
Stiers, David Ogden 1942- IntMPA 94, WhoAm 94, WhoHol 92
Stifel, Frederick Benton 1940- WhoWest 94
Stiff, Hugh Vernon 1916- Who 94
Stiff, John Sterling 1921- WhoAm 94
Stiff, Robert Martin 1931- WhoAm 94
Stiffey, Arthur Van Buren 1918- WhoScEn 94
Stiffle, Dean A. 1945- WhoAmL 94
Stiffler, Jack Justin 1934- WhoAm 94
Stiffler, Kevin Lee 1968- WhoScEn 94
Stiffman, Michael Nathan 1963- WhoMW 93
Stifler, William Curtis, III 1941- WhoAm 94
Stifter, Adalbert 1805-1868 DcLB 133 [port], NinCLC 41 [port], RfGShF
Stiger, R. Barry 1945- WhoAmL 94
Stigler, David Mack 1943- WhoAmL 94
Stigler, Edward A. 1935- WhoAmP 93
Stigler, George d1991 NobelP 91N
Stigler, George J(oseph) 1911-1991 WrDr 94N
Stigler, George Joseph 1911-1991 WhAm 10
Stigler, Stephen Mack 1941- WhoAm 94, WhoScEn 94
Stigliano, Leonard F. 1947- WhoFI 94
Stiglich, Jacob John, Jr. 1938- WhoWest 94
Stiglitz, Joseph E. 1943- WhoAmP 93
Stiglitz, Joseph Eugene 1943- IntWW 93, Who 94, WhoAm 94, WhoFI 94, WhoWest 94
Stiglitz, Martin Richard 1920- WhoScEn 94

Stignani, Ebe d1974 *WhoHol 92*
Stignani, Ebe 1903-1974 *NewGrDO*
Stigwood, Robert 1934- *IntMPA 94*
Stigwood, Robert Colin 1934- *IntWW 93, WhoAm 94*
Stiles, Deborah F. 1947- *WhoAmL 94*
Stiles, Donald Alan 1951- *WhoMW 93*
Stiles, Ezra 1727-1795 *DcAmReB 2, WhAmRev*
Stiles, Helen d1992 *WhoAmA 93N*
Stiles, Jack Elton 1932- *WhoMW 93*
Stiles, James Fleming 1931- *WhoMW 93*
Stiles, John Callender 1927- *WhoScEn 94*
Stiles, Kathleen O'Shea 1956- *WhoWest 94*
Stiles, Kendall Wayne 1960- *WhoFI 94*
Stiles, Mark Wayne 1948- *WhoAmP 93*
Stiles, Martha Bennett *DrAPF 93*
Stiles, Michael *WhoAmL 94*
Stiles, Ned Berry 1932- *WhoAm 94*
Stiles, Phillip John 1934- *WhoAm 94*
Stiles, Thomas Beveridge, II 1940- *WhoAm 94*
Stiles-Murray, Penelope Ann 1962- *WhoFI 94*
Stilgenbauer, Nancy Kieffer 1934- *WhoMW 93*
Stilgoe, Richard Henry Simpson 1943- *Who 94*
Still, Art Barry 1955- *WhoBlA 94*
Still, Bayrd 1906-1992 *WhAm 10*
Still, Charles H. d1961 *WhoHol 92*
Still, Charles Henry 1942- *WhoAm 94, WhoAmL 94*
Still, Clyfford 1904-1981 *WhoAmA 93N*
Still, Edgar 1943- *WrDr 94*
Still, Eugene Fontaine, II 1937- *WhoScEn 94*
Still, Gerald G. 1933- *WhoScEn 94*
Still, Gloria *DrAPF 93*
Still, Harold Henry, Jr. 1925- *WhoFI 94, WhoScEn 94, WhoWest 94*
Still, James *DrAPF 93*
Still, John C., III 1952- *WhoAmP 93*
Still, Lisa Stotsbery 1960- *WhoAmL 94*
Still, Mary Jane 1940- *WhoScEn 94*
Still, Ray 1920- *IntWW 93, WhoAm 94*
Still, Richard (Ralph) 1921-1991 *WrDr 94N*
Still, Robert T. 1954- *WhoAmP 93*
Still, Robin Eugene 1949- *WhoAmP 93*
Still, William 1821-1902 *AmSocL*
Still, William Clark, Jr. 1946- *WhoAm 94*
Still, William Grant 1895-1978 *AfrAmAl 6 [port], NewGrDO*
Still, William N. 1932- *WrDr 94*
Stille, Harry C. 1929- *WhoAmP 93*
Stille, John Kenneth 1930-1989 *WhAm 10*
Stille, Leon E. 1939- *WhoAmP 93*
Stiller, Andrew 1946- *NewGrDO*
Stiller, Ben *WhoHol 92*
Stiller, Brian C(arl) 1942- *ConAu 41NR*
Stiller, Brian Carl 1942- *WhoMW 93*
Stiller, Jennifer Anne 1948- *WhoAm 94, WhoAmL 94*
Stiller, Jerry *WhoAm 94*
Stiller, Jerry 1928- *WhoHol 92*
See Also Stiller and Meara *WhoCom*
Stiller, Mauritz d1928 *WhoHol 92*
Stiller, Nikki *DrAPF 93*
Stiller and Meara *WhoCom*
Stillinger, Frank Henry 1934- *WhoAm 94, WhoScEn 94*
Stillinger, Jack 1931- *WrDr 94*
Stillinger, Jack Clifford 1931- *WhoAm 94*
Stilling-Pedersen, Inger 1929- *WhoWomW 91*
Stillings, Dennis Otto 1942- *WhoScEn 94*
Stillings, Richard Wallace 1928- *WhoAmP 93*
Stillman, Alfred William, Jr. 1942- *WhoFI 94*
Stillman, Andrea L. *WhoAmP 93*
Stillman, Ann Therese 1960- *WhoAmL 94*
Stillman, Anne Walker 1951- *WhoFI 94*
Stillman, Bruce William 1953- *Who 94*
Stillman, Calvin Whitney 1915- *WhoAm 94*
Stillman, Damie 1933- *WhoAmA 93*
Stillman, E. Clark 1907- *WhoAmA 93*
Stillman, Elinor Hadley 1938- *WhoAmL 94*
Stillman, George 1921- *WhoAmA 93*
Stillman, Gerald Israel 1926- *WhoScEn 94*
Stillman, Gregory N. 1948- *WhoAmL 94*
Stillman, John Sterling 1918- *WhoAmP 93*
Stillman, Lucille T. *WhoAmA 93*
Stillman, Marie 1843-1927 *DcNaB MP*
Stillman, Marsha d1962 *WhoHol 92*
Stillman, Michael James 1962- *WhoScEn 94*
Stillman, Michael Randy 1962- *WhoAmL 94*
Stillman, Nina Gidden 1948- *WhoAm 94, WhoAmL 94*
Stillman, Norman A(rthur) 1945- *WrDr 94*
Stillman, Paul O. 1933- *WhoIns 94*
Stillman, Paul Oster 1933- *WhoFI 94*
Stillman, Ralph S. d1993 *NewYTBS 93*
Stillman, Richard J(oseph) 1917- *WrDr 94*
Stillman, Ron *EncSF 93*
Stillman, W. Paul 1897-1989 *WhAm 10*
Stills, Gracie Wiggins *WhoAm 94*
Stills, Stephen 1945- *WhoAm 94*
Stillson, Linda d1977 *WhoHol 92*
Stillwaggon, James George 1920- *WhoFI 94*
Stillwell, George Keith 1918- *WhoAm 94*
Stillwell, James Paul 1931- *WhoAm 94*
Stillwell, Kathleen Ann 1950- *WhoWest 94*
Stillwell, Mary Kathryn *DrAPF 93*
Stilson, Charles B(illings) 1880-1932 *EncSF 93*
Stilson, Walter Leslie 1908- *WhoAm 94, WhoWest 94*
Stilwell, Diane *WhoHol 92*
Stilwell, H. Samuel 1935- *WhoAmP 93*
Stilwell, John Quincy 1933- *WhoAm 94*
Stilwell, Lois Ann 1947- *WhoFI 94*
Stilwell, Martha Ann 1951- *WhoMW 93*
Stilwell, Richard 1942- *NewGrDO*
Stilwell, Richard Dale 1942- *IntWW 93, WhoAm 94*
Stilwell, Richard Giles 1917-1991 *WhAm 10*
Stilwell, Victor E. 1939- *WhoAmL 94*
Stilwell, Wilbur Moore 1908-1974 *WhoAmA 93N*
Stilwill, Belle Jean 1955- *WhoWest 94*
Stimatz, Lawrence G. 1919- *WhoAmP 93*
Stimell, Fredda Toby *WhoAm 94*
Stimley, Leonard David 1946- *WhoFI 94*
Stimmel, Barry 1939- *WhoAm 94*
Stimmel, Darren Clark 1962- *WhoWest 94*
Stimmel, James Russell 1950- *WhoWest 94*
Stimmel, Todd Richard 1954- *WhoAmL 94*
Stimpert, Michael Alan 1944- *WhoAm 94, WhoFI 94*
Stimpson, Catharine Roslyn 1936- *WhoAm 94*
Stimpson, John Hallowell 1926- *WhoAm 94*
Stimson, F.J. *EncSF 93*
Stimson, Frederick Sparks 1919- *WhoAm 94*
Stimson, Henry Lewis 1867-1950 *HisWorL [port]*
Stimson, Judith Nemeth 1942- *WhoAmL 94*
Stimson, Paul Gary 1932- *WhoScEn 94*
Stimson, Robbe Pierce 1948- *WrDr 94*
Stimson, Robert Frederick 1939- *Who 94*
Stimson, Sara 1973- *WhoHol 92*
Stimson, Terry 1943- *WhoAmP 93*
Stinchcomb, Carl J. 1938- *WhoFI 94*
Stinchcomb, Robert G. 1929- *WhoAm 94*
Stinchcomb, Sheri Ann 1964- *WhoMW 93*
Stinchfield, John Edward 1947- *WhoAmL 94, WhoFI 94*
Stinde, John William 1946- *WhoFI 94*
Stine, Charles J. d1934 *WhoHol 92*
Stine, Claire L. 1928- *WhoIns 94*
Stine, Dennis Neal 1952- *WhoAmP 93*
Stine, G(eorge) Harry 1928- *EncSF 93, WrDr 94*
Stine, George Harry 1928- *WhoAm 94, WhoWest 94*
Stine, Gordan Bernard 1924- *WhoAmP 93*
Stine, Hank 1945- *EncSF 93, WrDr 94*
Stine, Jeffrey K. 1953- *WhoScEn 94*
Stine, Jovial Bob *SmATA 76*
Stine, Kevin Jon 1961- *WhoAmL 94*
Stine, R(obert) L(awrence) 1943- *SmATA 76 [port], TwCYAW*
Stine, Timothy D. 1956- *WhoAmP 93*
Stinebaugh, Virgil 1897- *WhAm 10*
Stinehart, Roger Ray 1945- *WhoAm 94, WhoAmL 94*
Stinehart, William, Jr. 1943- *WhoAm 94, WhoAmL 94*
Stiner, Carl Wade 1936- *WhoAm 94*
Stiner, Frederic Matthew, Jr. 1946- *WhoFI 94*
Stines, Fred, Jr. 1925- *WhoAm 94*
Sting *IntWW 93*
Sting 1951- *IntMPA 94, WhoAm 94, WhoHol 92*
Stingel, Donald Eugene 1920- *WhoAm 94*
Stingelin, Valentin 1933- *WhoAm 94*
Stinger, Charles Martin 1949- *WhoAmL 94*
Stingl, Josef 1919- *IntWW 93*
Stingley, Jeff J. 1952- *WhoAmP 93*
Stini, William Arthur 1930- *WhoAm 94, WhoWest 94*
Stinnett, Hester A. 1956- *WhoAmA 93*
Stinnett, Lee Houston 1939- *WhoAm 94*
Stinnett, Mark Allan 1955- *WhoAmL 94*
Stinnett, Mary K. Scott *WhoAmP 93*
Stinnett, Terrance Lloyd 1940- *WhoAmL 94*
Stinnette, Dorothy *WhoHol 92*
Stinsmuehlen-Amend, Susan *WhoAmA 93*
Stinsmuehlen-Amend, Susan 1948- *WhoAmA 93*
Stinson, C. David 1946- *WhoAmL 94*
Stinson, Constance Robinson *WhoBlA 94*
Stinson, David Donnel 1957- *WhoWest 94*
Stinson, David John 1921- *Who 94*
Stinson, Deane Brian 1930- *WhoFI 94*
Stinson, Donald R. 1929- *WhoBlA 94*
Stinson, Edward Brad 1938- *WhoAm 94*
Stinson, George Arthur 1915- *IntWW 93, WhoAm 94*
Stinson, James R. 1952- *WhoAm 94*
Stinson, Jim 1937- *WrDr 94*
Stinson, Joseph McLester 1939- *WhoBlA 94*
Stinson, Karen Hanus 1950- *WhoMW 93*
Stinson, Katherine Anne 1949- *WhoFI 94*
Stinson, Linda 1965- *WhoBlA 94*
Stinson, Michael Roy 1949- *WhoScEn 94*
Stinson, Mortimer d1927 *WhoHol 92*
Stinson, Richard James 1929- *WhoAm 94*
Stinson, Robert Charles 1946- *WhoAm 94, WhoAmL 94*
Stinson, Robert Wayne 1936- *WhoFI 94*
Stinson, Stanley Thomas 1961- *WhoFI 94*
Stinson, Steven Arthur 1946- *WhoAmL 94*
Stinson, Susan *DrAPF 93*
Stinson, Thomas Franklin 1942- *WhoFI 94, WhoMW 93*
Stinson, William W. 1933- *WhoAm 94, WhoFI 94*
Stinton, Colin 1947- *WhoHol 92*
Stinziano, Michael Peter 1944- *WhoAmP 93, WhoMW 93*
Stio, Peter M. 1913- *WhoAmP 93*
Stipano, Daniel P. 1958- *WhoAmL 94*
Stipanovic, Robert Douglas 1939- *WhoScEn 94*
Stipanowich, James William 1959- *WhoFI 94*
Stipe, Edwin, III 1931- *WhoFI 94*
Stipe, Gene 1926- *WhoAmP 93*
Stipe, Michael 1960- *WhoAm 94*
Stipe, Robert Edwin 1928- *WhoAm 94*
Stipher, Karl Joseph 1912-1988 *WhAm 10*
Stipp, John Edgar 1914- *WhoAm 94*
Stirbois, Marie-France 1944- *WhoWomW 91*
Stires, Patrick Wayne 1948- *WhoMW 93*
Stirewalt, Edward Neale 1918- *WhoScEn 94*
Stirewalt, John Newman 1931- *WhoFI 94*
Stiritz, William P. 1934- *WhoAm 94, WhoFI 94, WhoMW 93*
Stirler, Karen Sue 1951- *WhoMW 93*
Stirling, Lord *AmRev, WhAmRev*
Stirling, Alexander (John Dickson) 1926- *Who 94*
Stirling, Angus Duncan Aeneas 1933- *IntWW 93, Who 94*
Stirling, Arthur *TwCYAW*
Stirling, Charles James Matthew 1930- *IntWW 93, Who 94*
Stirling, Dale Alexander 1956- *WhoWest 94*
Stirling, Edward d1948 *WhoHol 92*
Stirling, Edwin Murdoch 1940- *WhoAm 94*
Stirling, Geoffrey William 1925- *WhoAm 94*
Stirling, Ian 1941- *SmATA 77 [port]*
Stirling, James d1992 *IntWW 93N*
Stirling, James 1926-1992 *AnObit 1992, WhAm 10*
Stirling, James Paulman 1941- *WhoAm 94*
Stirling, John Fullarton 1931- *Who 94*
Stirling, Lawrence 1942- *WhoAmP 93*
Stirling, Linda 1921- *WhoHol 92*
Stirling, Michael Grote 1915- *Who 94*
Stirling, Pamela *WhoHol 92*
Stirling, Patrick 1820-1895 *DcNaB MP*
Stirling, S(tephen) M(ichael) 1953- *ConAu 140*
Stirling, S(tephen) M(ichael) 1954- *EncSF 93*
Stirling, Thomas Fluckiger 1955- *WhoWest 94*
Stirling, Thomas Luke, Jr. 1941- *WhoAmL 94*
Stirling-Hamilton, Malcolm William Bruce 1979- *Who 94*
Stirling of Fairburn, Roderick William Kenneth 1932- *Who 94*
Stirling of Garden, James 1930- *Who 94*
Stirm, Eugene Robert 1945- *WhoWest 94*
Stirn, Olivier 1936- *IntWW 93*
Stirnaman, Paul Herbert, Jr. 1944- *WhoAmP 93*
Stirner, Max 1806-1856 *DcLB 129 [port]*
Stirnweis, Shannon 1931- *WhoAmA 93*
Stirrat, Gordon Macmillan 1940- *Who 94*
Stirrat, William Albert 1919- *WhoScEn 94*
Stirratt, Betsy 1958- *WhoAmA 93*
Stirt, Joseph A. 1948- *ConAu 140*
Stish, Thomas B. 1950- *WhoAmP 93*
Stiska, John C. 1942- *WhoAm 94, WhoAmL 94, WhoFI 94*
Stitch, Malcolm Lane 1923-1991 *WhAm 10*
Stites, C. Thomas 1942- *WhoAm 94*
Stites, Francis Noel 1938- *WhoWest 94*
Stites, J. T. 1928- *WhoAmP 93*
Stites, Raymond Sommers 1899-1974 *WhoAmA 93N*
Stites, Susan Kay 1952- *WhoMW 93*
Stith, Antoinette Freeman 1958- *WhoBlA 94*
Stith, Bryant Lamonica 1970- *WhoBlA 94*
Stith, Charles Richard 1949- *WhoBlA 94*
Stith, John E(dward) 1947- *EncSF 93*
Stith, John Stephen 1939- *WhoAm 94*
Stith, Melvin Thomas 1946- *WhoBlA 94*
Stith, Richard Taylor, Jr. 1919- *WhoAm 94*
Stith-Cabranes, Kate 1951- *WhoAmL 94*
Stitley, James Walter, Jr. 1944- *WhoFI 94*
Stitnizky, John Louis 1939- *WhoWest 94*
Stitt, David Tillman 1943- *WhoAm 94*
Stitt, Debra Lynn 1957- *WhoMW 93*
Stitt, Donald K. 1944- *WhoAmP 93*
Stitt, E. Don 1942- *WhoBlA 94*
Stitt, Frederick Hesse 1929- *WhoMW 93*
Stitt, Guy Ames 1957- *WhoWest 94*
Stitt, Kathleen Roberta 1926- *WhoScEn 94*
Stitt, Robert R. 1941- *WhoWest 94*
Stitt, Sonny d1982 *WhoHol 92*
Stitt, Susan (Margaret) 1942- *WhoAmA 93*
Stitt, Thomas Paul, Sr. 1943- *WhoAmL 94*
Stitt, William D. 1913- *WhoWest 94*
Stittich, Eleanor Maryann *WhoWest 94*
Stittsworth, James Dale 1951- *WhoScEn 94*
Stival, Giulio d1953 *WhoHol 92*
Stivale, Charles Joseph 1949- *WhoMW 93*
Stiven, Alan Ernest 1935- *WhoAm 94*
Stiven, James F. 1940- *WhoAmL 94*
Stivender, Donald Lewis 1932- *WhoAm 94, WhoFI 94*
Stivender, Ed 1946- *ConAu 141*
Stivender, Edward David 1933- *WhAm 10*
Stiver, James Frederick 1943- *WhoMW 93, WhoScEn 94*
Stivers, Joan Koch 1921- *WhoAm 94*
Stivers, Joe Alan 1948- *WhoAmP 93*
Stivers, Marshall Lee *WhoScEn 94*
Stivers, Mary 1927- *WhoAmP 93*
Stivers, Theodore Edward 1920- *WhoScEn 94*
Stivers, Thomas Walter 1918- *WhoAmP 93*
Stivers, William Charles 1938- *WhoAm 94, WhoFI 94*
Stivison, David Vaughn 1946- *WhoAmL 94*
Stivison, Ron 1947- *WhoAmP 93*
Stivison, Thomas Homer 1948- *WhoWest 94*
Stix, Thomas Howard 1924- *WhoAm 94*
St John, Ronald Bruce 1943- *ConAu 141*
Stoate, Isabel Dorothy 1927- *Who 94*
Stob, Martin 1926- *WhoAm 94*
Stobaugh, Robert Blair 1927- *WhoAm 94*
Stober, William John, II 1933- *WhoAm 94*
Stober, Wilson Shannon 1940- *WhoAm 94*
Stock, Anita 1938- *WhoMW 93*
Stock, B. E. *DrAPF 93*
Stock, Barbara 1956- *WhoHol 92*
Stock, Carolmarie 1951- *SmATA 75 [port]*
Stock, Francis Edgar 1914- *Who 94*
Stock, Gregg Francis 1925- *WhoAm 94*
Stock, Leon Milo 1930- *WhoAm 94*
Stock, Leroy A., Jr. 1942- *WhoIns 94*
Stock, Nigel d1986 *WhoHol 92*
Stock, Norman *DrAPF 93*
Stock, R(obert) D(ouglas) 1941- *ConAu 43NR*
Stock, Raymond 1913- *Who 94*
Stock, Ronald Wilfred 1950- *WhoWest 94*
Stock, Stuart Chase 1946- *WhoAm 94, WhoAmL 94*
Stock, Timothy Francis 1938- *WhoAmL 94*
Stock, Werner d1972 *WhoHol 92*
Stockanes, Anthony E. *DrAPF 93*
Stockard, James Alfred 1935- *WhoAm 94*
Stockard, Joe Lee 1924- *WhoScEn 94*
Stockard, Robert Thomas 1940- *WhoMW 93*
Stockard, Susan *WhoAm 94*
Stockbridge, Grant *EncSF 93*
Stockbridge, Henry d1952 *WhoHol 92*
Stockburger, Harold E. 1960- *WhoAmP 93*
Stockburger, Jean Dawson 1936- *WhoAmL 94*
Stockdale, Carl d1953 *WhoHol 92*
Stockdale, Eric 1929- *Who 94*
Stockdale, Franklin E. d1950 *WhoHol 92*
Stockdale, Gayle Sue 1955- *WhoFI 94*

Stockdale, James Bond 1923- *WhoAm 94*
Stockdale, John A. D. 1936- *WhoAmA 93*
Stockdale, Mildred Arleen 1947- *WhoMW 93*
Stockdale, Noel *Who 94*
Stockdale, (Arthur) Noel 1920- *Who 94*
Stockdale, Ronald Allen 1934- *WhoFI 94*
Stockdale, Thomas (Minshull) 1940- *Who 94*
Stockenberg, Richard A. 1944- *WhoAmL 94*
Stockenstrom, Wilma 1933- *BlmGWL [port]*
Stocker, Arthur Frederick 1914- *WhoAm 94*
Stocker, Bruce Arnold Dunbar 1917- *Who 94*
Stocker, Harold Le Roy 1929- *WhoFI 94*
Stocker, Helene 1869-1943 *BlmGWL*
Stocker, John (Dexter) 1918- *Who 94*
Stocker, Jule Elias 1906- *WhoAm 94*
Stocker, Kirk W. 1956- *WhoMW 93*
Stocker, Mark (Andrew) 1956- *WrDr 94*
Stocker-Meier, Monika 1948- *WhoWomW 91*
Stocker-Meynert, Dora von 1870-1947 *BlmGWL*
Stockett, Jerry Marvin 1944- *WhoFI 94*
Stockett, Peter McKenzie 1932- *WhoAmP 93*
Stockfield, Betty d1966 *WhoHol 92*
Stockfleth, Maria Katharina c. 1633-1692 *BlmGWL*
Stockglausner, William George 1950- *WhoMW 93*
Stockham, Thomas Greenway, Jr. 1933- *WhoAm 94*
Stockhausen, Karlheinz 1928- *IntWW 93, NewGrDO, Who 94*
Stocking, George Wade, Jr. 1928- *WhoAm 94*
Stocking, George Ward, Jr. 1928- *WhoMW 93*
Stocking, Kathleen 1945- *WrDr 94*
Stocking, Sherl Dee 1945- *WhoWest 94*
Stockland, Alan E. 1938- *WhoWest 94*
Stockley, Cynthia 1872-1936 *BlmGWL*
Stockley, Darleen J. 1943- *WhoMW 93*
Stockley, Grif 1944- *ConAu 140*
Stockley, Jim *WhoAmP 93*
Stockl-Heinefetter, Clara *NewGrDO*
Stockli, Martin Peter 1949- *WhoMW 93*
Stocklin, Alma Katherine 1926- *WhoFI 94*
Stocklin, Franziska 1894-1931 *BlmGWL*
Stockman, Brien David 1961- *WhoAmL 94*
Stockman, David 1879-1951 *NewGrDO*
Stockman, David A(llen) 1946- *WrDr 94*
Stockman, David Allen *WhoAmP 93*
Stockman, David Allen 1946- *IntWW 93, WhoAm 94, WhoFI 94*
Stockman, Gerald R. 1935- *WhoAmP 93*
Stockman, Ida J. 1942- *WhoBlA 94*
Stockmar, Christian Friedrich 1787-1863 *DcNaB MP*
Stockmar, J. Brian 1950- *WhoAm 94*
Stockmar, Ted P. 1921- *WhoAm 94*
Stockmayer, Walter Hugo 1914- *WhoAm 94, WhoScEn 94*
Stockmeyer, Norman Otto, Jr. 1938- *WhoAmL 94*
Stockmeyer, Steven F. 1941- *WhoAmP 93*
Stockport, Bishop Suffragan of 1932- *Who 94*
Stock-Poynton, Amy *WhoHol 92*
Stocks, Eleanor Louise 1943- *WhoBlA 94*
Stocks, Kenneth Duane 1934- *WhoAm 94*
Stocks, Leroy 1923- *WhoAmP 93*
Stocks, Mary Lee 1949- *WhoMW 93*
Stocks, Susan Jennifer 1963- *WhoMW 93*
Stocksdale, Thomas Ray 1952- *WhoFI 94, WhoMW 93*
Stockton, Earl of 1943- *IntWW 93, Who 94*
Stockton, Anderson Berrian 1943- *WhoAm 94, WhoScEn 94, WhoWest 94*
Stockton, Annis Boudinot 1736-1801 *BlmGWL*
Stockton, Barbara Marshall 1923- *WhoBlA 94*
Stockton, Bayard 1930- *WrDr 94*
Stockton, Cecil Eugene 1934- *WhoAmP 93*
Stockton, Clifford, Sr. 1932- *WhoBlA 94*
Stockton, David Knapp 1941- *WhoAm 94, WhoWest 94*
Stockton, Frank R(ichard) 1834-1902 *EncSF 93*
Stockton, John 1962- *BasBi*
Stockton, John Houston 1962- *WhoAm 94*
Stockton, Ralph Madison, Jr. 1927- *WhoAm 94, WhoAmL 94*
Stockton, Richard 1730-1781 *WhAmRev*
Stockton, Richard Lee 1949- *WhoAmL 94*
Stockton, Roderick Alan 1951- *WhoWest 94*
Stockton, Stephen Finch 1947- *WhoFI 94*
Stockton, Thomas B. 1930- *WhoAm 94*
Stockwell, Albert H. 1933- *WhoScEn 94*
Stockwell, Dean 1935- *IntMPA 94*
Stockwell, Dean 1936- *WhoAm 94, WhoHol 92*
Stockwell, Edmund Arthur 1911- *Who 94*
Stockwell, Edward Grant 1933- *WhoMW 93*
Stockwell, Ernest Farnham, Jr. 1923- *WhoAm 94*
Stockwell, Evangelina Ramirez *WhoHisp 94*
Stockwell, Guy 1934- *WhoHol 92*
Stockwell, Harry d1984 *WhoHol 92*
Stockwell, John 1961- *IntMPA 94, WhoHol 92*
Stockwell, Oliver Perkins 1907- *WhoFI 94*
Stockwell, Richard E. 1917- *WhoAm 94*
Stockwell, Robert Paul 1925- *WhoAm 94*
Stockwell, Sherwood Beach 1926- *WhoAm 94*
Stockwell, Winifred d1981 *WhoHol 92*
Stockwin, (James) Arthur (Ainscow) 1935- *WrDr 94*
Stockwin, James Arthur Ainscow 1935- *Who 94*
Stockwood, (Arthur) Mervyn 1913- *IntWW 93, Who 94, WrDr 94*
Stodart *Who 94*
Stodart Of Leaston, Baron 1916- *Who 94*
Stoddard, Alan 1915- *WrDr 94*
Stoddard, Alexandra Hope 1942- *WhoMW 93*
Stoddard, Arthur Grant 1947- *WhoWest 94*
Stoddard, Belle d1950 *WhoHol 92*
Stoddard, Brandon 1937- *IntMPA 94, WhoAm 94*
Stoddard, Donald B. 1951- *WhoIns 94*
Stoddard, Ellwyn R. 1927- *WhoAm 94*
Stoddard, Eugene C. 1927- *WhoAmP 93*
Stoddard, Everett Allen 1951- *WhoMW 93*
Stoddard, Forrest Shaffer 1944- *WhoScEn 94*
Stoddard, George Dinsmore 1897- *WhAm 10*
Stoddard, George Earl 1917- *WhoAm 94*
Stoddard, George Edward 1921- *WhAm 10*
Stoddard, Laurence Ralph, Jr. 1936- *WhoAm 94*
Stoddard, Malcolm 1948- *WhoHol 92*
Stoddard, Nathaniel Clark 1945- *WhoFI 94*
Stoddard, Richard Ethridge 1950- *WhoAm 94*
Stoddard, Robert H. 1928- *WrDr 94*
Stoddard, Roger Eliot 1935- *WhoAm 94*
Stoddard, Solomon 1643-1729 *DcAmReB 2*
Stoddard, Stephen Davidson 1925- *WhoAm 94, WhoAmP 93, WhoWest 94*
Stoddard, William Bert, Jr. 1926- *WhoFI 94*
Stoddart *Who 94*
Stoddart, Anne Elizabeth 1937- *Who 94*
Stoddart, Charles Norman 1948- *Who 94*
Stoddart, Douglas W. *WhoAmP 93*
Stoddart, George Anderson 1933- *WhoAm 94*
Stoddart, John Little 1933- *Who 94*
Stoddart, John Maurice 1938- *Who 94*
Stoddart, Kenneth (Maxwell) 1914- *Who 94*
Stoddart, Michael Craig 1932- *Who 94*
Stoddart Of Swindon, Baron 1926- *Who 94*
Stodder, John Wesley 1923- *WhoFI 94*
Stoddert, Benjamin 1751-1813 *WhAmRev*
Stodghill, Ronald 1939- *WhoBlA 94, WhoMW 93*
Stodghill, William 1940- *WhoBlA 94*
Stodghill, William Wardell 1927- *WhoIns 94*
Stodola, Mark Allen 1949- *WhoAmP 93*
Stoebe, Thomas Gaines 1939- *WhoWest 94*
Stoeckel, Joe d1959 *WhoHol 92*
Stoeckel, Otto d1958 *WhoHol 92*
Stoecker, David Thomas 1939- *WhoAm 94*
Stoeckl, Shelley Joan 1951- *WhoFI 94*
Stoeckle, Thomas Bruce 1955- *WhoMW 93*
Stoefen, Gary E. 1939- *WhoIns 94*
Stoelting, Robert K. 1939- *WhoAm 94*
Stoeltje, Beverly June 1940- *WhoMW 93*
Stoen, J. Thomas 1939- *WhoWest 94*
Stoer, Eric F. 1944- *WhoAm 94, WhoAmL 94*
Stoermer, Eugene Filmore 1934- *WhoMW 93*
Stoermer, Phillip H. 1940- *WhoAmL 94*
Stoermer, Thomas Gregory 1954- *WhoWest 94*
Stoessel, Henry Kurt 1909- *WhoAmA 93N*
Stoessinger, John G. 1927- *WrDr 94*
Stoetzer, Gerald Louis 1914- *WhoAmL 94*
Stoetzner, Eric Woldemar 1901-1990 *WhAm 10*
Stoeveken, Anthony Charles 1938- *WhoAmA 93*
Stoeveken, Christel E. *WhoAmA 93*
Stoever, William Alfred 1939- *WhoFI 94*
Stofer, Kathryn Tamara 1948- *WhoMW 93*
Stoff, Joshua 1958- *WrDr 94*
Stoff, Thomas Patrick 1949- *WhoAmP 93*
Stoffa, James Victor 1942- *WhoAmL 94*
Stoffa, Michael *WhoAmA 93*
Stoffa, Paul L. 1948- *WhoScEn 94*
Stoffel, Klaus Peter 1957- *WhoAmL 94*
Stoffel, Richard Joseph 1953- *WhoMW 93*
Stoffer, Barbara Jean 1946- *WhoScEn 94*
Stoffer, Henry J. *WhoAmP 93*
Stoffer, James Myron, Jr. 1952- *WhoAmL 94*
Stoffer, Sheldon Saul 1940- *WhoMW 93*
Stofferahn, Curtis Warren 1952- *WhoAmP 93*
Stofferahn, Kenneth Darrell 1934- *WhoAmP 93*
Stofferahn, Scott B. 1957- *WhoAmP 93*
Stofferson, Terry Lee 1957- *WhoFI 94*
Stoffle, Carla Joy 1943- *WhoAm 94*
Stofflet, Mary 1942- *WhoAmA 93*
Stoffregen, John Christian, II 1954- *WhoMW 93*
Stoffregen, Philip Eugene 1947- *WhoAmL 94*
Stofft, William A. 1937- *WhoAm 94*
Stogdon, Norman Francis 1909- *Who 94*
Stogel, Leah d1985 *WhoHol 92*
Stogner, Charles A. 1948- *WhoFI 94*
Stogner, Joseph Thomas 1939- *WhoAmP 93*
Stogsdill, Daniel Ray 1957- *WhoAmL 94*
Stohl, Esther A. 1919- *WhoWest 94*
Stohler, Donald Glen 1944- *WhoFI 94*
Stohler, Michael Joe 1956- *WhoMW 93*
Stohlman, Bruce Richard 1949- *WhoMW 93*
Stohlman, Connie Suzanne 1960- *WhoMW 93*
Stohner, Kenneth, Jr. 1950- *WhoAmL 94*
Stohr, Donald J. 1934- *WhoAm 94, WhoAmL 94, WhoMW 93*
Stohr, Erich Charles 1964- *WhoScEn 94*
Stohrer, Philip Charles 1950- *WhoMW 93*
Stoia, Charles J. 1961- *WhoAmL 94*
Stoia, Dennis Vasile 1928- *WhoScEn 94*
Stoia, Viorel G. 1924- *WhoFI 94, WhoMW 93*
Stoianovich, Marcelle *WhoAmA 93*
Stoicheff, Boris Peter 1924- *IntWW 93, Who 94, WhoAm 94*
Stoicheff, James F. 1927- *WhoAmP 93*
Stoichkov, Hristo 1966- *WorESoc*
Stoick, James L. *WhoAmP 93*
Stoikes, Mary Eloise 1960- *WhoMW 93*
Stoizman, Maria Joanna *WhoWomW 91*
Stojadinovic-Srpkinja, Milica 1830-1878 *BlmGWL*
Stojanovic, Petar 1877-1957 *NewGrDO*
Stojanowski, Wiktor J. 1936- *WhoScEn 94*
Stoke, E(dward) G(eorge) 1919- *WrDr 94*
Stokely, Hugh Lawson 1933- *WhoAm 94*
Stoken, Jacqueline Marie 1948- *WhoMW 93*
Stoker, Abraham 1847-1912 *DcNaB MP*
Stoker, Austin *WhoHol 92*
Stoker, Betty Anderson 1927- *WhoAmP 93*
Stoker, Dennis James 1928- *Who 94*
Stoker, H. G. d1966 *WhoHol 92*
Stoker, James Rienewerf 1935- *WhoAm 94*
Stoker, Jeff *WhoAmP 93*
Stoker, Michael (George Parke) 1918- *Who 94*
Stoker, Michael George Parke 1918- *IntWW 93*
Stoker, Richard 1938- *NewGrDO*
Stoker, Warren Cady 1912- *WhoAm 94*
Stokes, Baron 1914- *IntWW 93, Who 94*
Stokes, Adrian Victor 1945- *Who 94*
Stokes, Al(len) d1989 *WhoHol 92*
Stokes, Alistair Michael 1948- *Who 94*
Stokes, Anthony c. 1736-1799 *WhAmRev*
Stokes, Arch Yow 1946- *WhoAmL 94*
Stokes, Arnold Paul 1932- *WhoAm 94*
Stokes, B. R. 1924- *WhoAm 94*
Stokes, Bob *DrAPF 93*
Stokes, Bruce 1948- *WrDr 94*
Stokes, Bunny, Jr. *WhoBlA 94*
Stokes, Carl Burton 1927- *WhoAm 94, WhoAmP 93, WhoBlA 94*
Stokes, Carl Nicholas 1907- *WhoAmL 94*
Stokes, Carolyn Ashe 1925- *WhoBlA 94*
Stokes, Charles Anderson 1915- *WhoScEn 94*
Stokes, Charles Eugene, Jr. 1926- *WhoFI 94*
Stokes, Charles Junius 1922- *WhoAm 94, WhoScEn 94*
Stokes, Daniel M. *DrAPF 93*
Stokes, David Mayhew Allen 1944- *Who 94*
Stokes, Donald Elkinton 1927- *WhoAm 94*
Stokes, Donald Gresham 1914- *WhoAm 94*
Stokes, Donald W. 1947- *WrDr 94*
Stokes, Eric (Norman) 1930- *NewGrDO*
Stokes, Ernest d1964 *WhoHol 92*
Stokes, Gerald Madison 1947- *WhoWest 94*
Stokes, Gerald Virgil 1943- *WhoBlA 94*
Stokes, Harry Michael 1926- *Who 94*
Stokes, James Christopher 1944- *WhoAm 94, WhoAmL 94*
Stokes, James Milton 1938- *WhoAmP 93*
Stokes, James Sewell 1944- *WhoAm 94, WhoAmL 94*
Stokes, John *DrAPF 93*
Stokes, John c. 1610-1665 *DcNaB MP*
Stokes, John (Heydon Romaine) 1917- *Who 94*
Stokes, John Fisher 1912- *Who 94*
Stokes, John Lemacks, II 1908- *WhoAm 94*
Stokes, John W. 1896- *WhAm 10*
Stokes, Johnnie Mae 1941- *WhoBlA 94*
Stokes, Joseph, III 1924-1989 *WhAm 10*
Stokes, Katharine Martin 1906-1989 *WhAm 10*
Stokes, Lillian Gatlin 1942- *WhoBlA 94*
Stokes, Louis 1925- *AfrAmAl 6, CngDr 93, WhoAm 94, WhoAmP 93, WhoBlA 94, WhoMW 93*
Stokes, Louis (Walter) 1941- *WhoAmA 93*
Stokes, Lowell Maurice 1962- *WhoAmL 94*
Stokes, Mack Marion Boyd 1911- *WhoAm 94*
Stokes, Margaret Smith 1950- *WhoBlA 94*
Stokes, Marian 1926- *WhoAmP 93*
Stokes, Maurice 1933- *BasBi*
Stokes, Michael Don 1966- *WhoAmL 94*
Stokes, Olive d1972 *WhoHol 92*
Stokes, Patrick T. 1942- *WhoAm 94, WhoFI 94*
Stokes, Paul Mason 1946- *WhoAm 94, WhoAmL 94*
Stokes, Rembert Edwards 1917- *WhoBlA 94*
Stokes, Robert Allan 1942- *WhoAm 94*
Stokes, Robert Jerome 1942- *WhoAmL 94*
Stokes, Ronald Wayne 1951- *WhoFI 94*
Stokes, Rueben Martine 1957- *WhoBlA 94*
Stokes, Ruth S. 1942- *WhoAmP 93*
Stokes, Sheila Woods 1949- *WhoBlA 94*
Stokes, Simpson *EncSF 93*
Stokes, Sterling J. *WhoBlA 94*
Stokes, Susan B. *WhoAmP 93*
Stokes, Terry *DrAPF 93*
Stokes, Theresa Emma 1943- *WhoFI 94*
Stokes, Thomas Elder, III 1949- *WhoAmL 94*
Stokes, Thomas F. 1948- *WhoIns 94*
Stokes, Thomas Lane, Jr. 1957- *WhoScEn 94*
Stokes, Wanda Bernice 1962- *WhoWest 94*
Stokes, William Lee 1915- *ConAu 42NR, WhoWest 94*
Stokesbury, Leon *DrAPF 93*
Stokes Elias, Janice Elaine 1952- *WhoMW 93*
Stoke-Upon-Trent, Archdeacon of *Who 94*
Stokke, Diane Rees 1951- *WhoAm 94, WhoAmL 94*
Stokowski, Anne K. *WhoAmP 93*
Stokowski, Eugene E. 1921- *WhoAmP 93*
Stokowski, Leopold d1977 *WhoHol 92*
Stokowski, Leopold Anthony 1882-1977 *AmCulL*
Stokstad, Marilyn 1929- *WhoAmA 93*
Stokstad, Marilyn Jane 1929- *WhoAm 94*
Stokvis, Jack Raphael 1944- *WhoAm 94*
Stol, Marten 1940- *IntWW 93*
Stolar, Henry Samuel 1939- *WhoAm 94*
Stolarik, M. Mark 1943- *WhoAm 94*
Stolarski, Edward Joseph, Jr. 1955- *WhoAmL 94*
Stolbach, Gary 1951- *WhoAmL 94*
Stolberg, Ernest Milton 1913- *WhoScEn 94*
Stolberg, Irving J. 1936- *WhoAm 94*
Stolberg, Irving Jules 1936- *WhoAmP 93*
Stolberg, Sheryl Gay 1961- *WhoAm 94*
Stolbov, Bruce *EncSF 93*
Stoldt, Robert James 1925- *WhoAmP 93*
Stolee, Michael Joseph 1930- *WhoMW 93*
Stolen, Rogers Hall 1937- *WhoScEn 94*
Stoler, Louis M. 1954- *WhoAmL 94*
Stoler, Shirley 1929- *WhoHol 92*
Stolgitis, William Charles 1941- *WhoAm 94*
Stolitsa, Liubov' Nikitishna 1884-1934 *BlmGWL*
Stolk, Gloria 1918-1979 *BlmGWL*

Stolker, Richard Samuel 1945- *WhoAmL 94*
Stoll, Berry Vincent, Mrs. 1906- *WhoAmA 93*
Stoll, Charles Buckner 1923- *WhoAm 94*
Stoll, Clifford 1950- *WhoWest 94, WrDr 94*
Stoll, Howard Lester, Jr. 1928- *WhoAm 94*
Stoll, Irma 1929- *WrDr 94*
Stoll, John Henry 1925- *WhoMW 93*
Stoll, John Robert 1950- *WhoAm 94, WhoMW 93*
Stoll, Neal Richard 1948- *WhoAm 94, WhoAmL 94*
Stoll, Peter Alan 1948- *WhoWest 94*
Stoll, Richard Edmund 1927- *WhoAm 94, WhoFI 94*
Stoll, Richard Giles 1946- *WhoAm 94, WhoAmL 94*
Stoll, Rosanna *WhoHisp 94*
Stoll, Steve 1947- *WhoAmP 93*
Stoll, Toni 1922- *WhoAmA 93*
Stoll, Wilhelm 1923- *WhoAm 94*
Stolle, Fred 1938- *BuCMET*
Stolle, Hans Joerg 1935- *WhoMW 93*
Stolle, Kenneth W. 1954- *WhoAmP 93*
Stolle, Philipp 1614-1675 *NewGrDO*
Stollenwerk, John Joseph 1940- *WhoFI 94*
Stoller, Claude 1921- *WhoAm 94*
Stoller, Daniel E. 1945- *WhoAmL 94*
Stoller, Eric Chester 1943- *WhoFI 94*
Stoller, Ezra 1915- *WhoAm 94*
Stoller, John Chapman 1940- *WhoAmA 93*
Stoller, Jonathan White 1954- *WhoFI 94*
Stoller, Robert Jesse 1924-1991 *WhAm 10*
Stollerman, Gene Howard 1920- *WhoAm 94*
Stollerman, Ray 1931- *WhoAm 94*
Stollery, David *WhoHol 92*
Stollery, John Leslie 1930- *Who 94*
Stollery, Robert 1924- *WhoAm 94, WhoScEn 94*
Stolley, Alexander 1922- *WhoAm 94*
Stolley, Paul David 1937- *IntWW 93, WhoAm 94*
Stolley, Richard Brockway 1928- *WhoAm 94*
Stollman, Israel 1923- *WhoAm 94*
Stollnitz, Fred 1939- *WhoScEn 94*
Stollsteimer, John F. 1932- *WhoFI 94*
Stolnitz, Art 1928- *IntMPA 94*
Stolnitz, George Joseph 1920- *WhoAm 94*
Stoloff, Carolyn *DrAPF 93, WhoAmA 93*
Stoloff, Victor 1913- *IntMPA 94*
Stolojan, Theodor 1943- *IntWW 93*
Stolov, Jerry Franklin 1946- *WhoMW 93*
Stolov, Walter Charles 1928- *WhoWest 94*
Stolp, Lauren Elbert 1921- *WhoAm 94*
Stolpe, Daniel Owen 1939- *WhoAmA 93*
Stolpe, Manfred 1936- *IntWW 93*
Stolpe, Marilyn Kathleen 1944- *WhoMW 93*
Stolpen, Spencer *WhoAm 94*
Stolper, Wolfgang Friedrich 1912- *WhoAm 94, WhoFI 94*
Stolpman, Thomas Gerard 1949- *WhoWest 94*
Stolte, Dieter 1934- *IntWW 93*
Stolte, Larry Gene 1945- *WhoMW 93*
Stoltenberg, Cal Dale 1953- *WhoScEn 94*
Stoltenberg, Carl Henry 1924- *WhoWest 94*
Stoltenberg, Curtis Dale 1959- *WhoMW 93*
Stoltenberg, Donald Hugo 1927- *WhoAmA 93*
Stoltenberg, Gerhard 1928- *IntWW 93, Who 94*
Stoltenberg, Thorvald 1931- *IntWW 93*
Stoltman, James Bernard 1935- *WhoMW 93*
Stoltman, Steven John 1962- *WhoMW 93*
Stoltman, Thomas P. 1953- *WhoAmL 94*
Stoltz, Arnold Theodore d1986 *WhoHol 92*
Stoltz, Charles Edward 1936- *WhoMW 93*
Stoltz, Eric 1961- *ConTFT 11, IntMPA 94, WhoAm 94*
Stoltz, Eric 1962- *WhoHol 92*
Stoltz, Joseph Francis 1943- *WhoFI 94*
Stoltz, Merton Philip 1913-1989 *WhAm 10*
Stoltz, Michael Rae 1951- *WhoAmL 94*
Stoltz, Rosine 1815-1903 *NewGrDO*
Stoltzfus, Ben *DrAPF 93*
Stoltzfus, Ben Frank 1927- *WhoWest 94*
Stoltzfus, Ben Frank(lin) 1927- *WrDr 94*
Stoltzfus, J. Lowell *WhoAmP 93*
Stoltzfus, Victor Ezra 1934- *WhoAm 94*
Stoltzman, Richard Leslie 1942- *WhoAm 94*
Stoltzman, William A. 1948- *WhoIns 94*
Stolwijk, Jan Adrianus Jozef 1927- *WhoAm 94*
Stolyarov, Nikolai Sergeevich 1947- *LngBDD*
Stolz, Alan J. 1931- *WhoFI 94*
Stolz, Benjamin Armond 1934- *WhoAm 94*
Stolz, Kathy Lynn 1953- *WhoMW 93*
Stolz, Mary 1920- *TwCYAW*
Stolz, Mary (Slattery) 1920- *ConAu 41NR, WrDr 94*
Stolz, Neil N. 1935- *WhoFI 94*
Stolz, Robert (Elisabeth) 1880-1975 *NewGrDO*
Stolz, Teresa 1834-1902 *NewGrDO*
Stolz, Walter Sargent 1938- *WhoAm 94*
Stolze, Gerhard 1926-1979 *NewGrDO*
Stolze, Lena 1956- *WhoHol 92*
Stolzel, Gottfried Heinrich 1690-1749 *NewGrDO*
Stolzenberg, Edward Alan 1947- *WhoAm 94*
Stolzer, Leo William 1934- *WhoAm 94*
Stolzing, W. di *NewGrDO*
Stolzman, William A. *WhoAmL 94*
Stomer, Raymond S. 1925- *WhoAmP 93*
Stomma, Peter Christopher 1966- *WhoAmL 94*
Stommel, Henry Melson 1920-1990 *WhAm 10*
Stomper, Johnny *WhoHol 92*
Stomps, Walter E., Jr. 1929- *WhoAmA 93*
Stone, Adam *WhoHol 92*
Stone, Alan 1928- *WhoAm 94, WhoFI 94*
Stone, Alan A. 1929- *WhoAmL 94, WrDr 94*
Stone, Alan James 1944- *WhoAm 94*
Stone, Alan Jay 1942- *WhoAm 94, WhoMW 93*
Stone, Alan John 1940- *WhoFI 94*
Stone, Alexander James 1923- *WhoIns 94*
Stone, Alexander Paul 1928- *WhoWest 94*
Stone, Alison J. *DrAPF 93*
Stone, Allan David 1937- *WhoAm 94*
Stone, Alma *DrAPF 93*
Stone, Andrew Grover 1942- *WhoAmL 94, WhoFI 94*
Stone, Andrew L. 1902- *IntMPA 94*
Stone, Andrew Logan 1915- *WhoFI 94*
Stone, Anna B. 1874-1949 *WhoAmA 93N*
Stone, Anthony Charles Peter 1939- *Who 94*
Stone, Arlene *DrAPF 93*
Stone, Arthur d1940 *WhoHol 92*
Stone, Arthur Harold 1916- *WhoAm 94*
Stone, Barbara Suzanne 1951- *WhoMW 93*
Stone, Barton Warren 1772-1844 *DcAmReB 2*
Stone, Beatrice 1900-1962 *WhoAmA 93N*
Stone, Ben Harry 1935- *WhoAmL 94, WhoAmP 93*
Stone, Bernard Leonard 1927- *WhoAmP 93*
Stone, Bertram Allen 1915- *WhoAmL 94*
Stone, Billy d1980 *WhoHol 92*
Stone, Bonnie Carol 1945- *WhoFI 94*
Stone, Bonnie (M.) Domrose 1941- *WrDr 94*
Stone, Brian (Ernest) 1919- *WrDr 94*
Stone, Brinton Harvey 1907- *WhoWest 94*
Stone, Burton J. 1928- *IntMPA 94*
Stone, Carol 1915- *WhoHol 92*
Stone, Carole *DrAPF 93*
Stone, Charles H. *WhoAmP 93*
Stone, Charles Sumner, Jr. 1924- *BlkWr 2*
Stone, Christopher 1925- *WhoHol 92*
Stone, Christopher Dale 1960- *WhoMW 93*
Stone, Chuck *BlkWr 2*
Stone, Chuck 1924- *WhoBlA 94*
Stone, Clifford Fontaine 1894- *WhAm 10*
Stone, Cynthia Hutchinson 1940- *WhoFI 94*
Stone, Daniel M. 1942- *WhoBlA 94*
Stone, Danny *WhoHol 92*
Stone, Danton *WhoHol 92*
Stone, Darlene S. 1953- *WhoFI 94*
Stone, Darrell Edgar 1940- *WhoFI 94*
Stone, David Barnes 1927- *WhoAm 94*
Stone, David Deaderick 1932- *WhoAm 94*
Stone, David Guy 1957- *WhoWest 94*
Stone, David Kendall 1942- *WhoAm 94*
Stone, David Philip 1944- *WhoAm 94, WhoAmL 94*
Stone, David Ulric 1927- *WhoWest 94*
Stone, Dee Wallace 1948- *IntMPA 94*
Stone, Dee Wallace 1949- *WhoHol 92*
Stone, Dennis Alden 1948- *WhoFI 94*
Stone, Dianne S. 1964- *WhoFI 94*
Stone, Dolores June 1939- *WhoBlA 94*
Stone, Don 1929- *WhoAmA 93*
Stone, Donald Crawford 1903- *IntWW 93, WhoAm 94*
Stone, Donald D. 1924- *WhoFI 94, WhoWest 94*
Stone, Donald James 1929- *WhoFI 94*
Stone, Donald Raymond 1938- *WhoAm 94*
Stone, Doris d1981 *WhoHol 92*
Stone, Dorothy d1974 *WhoHol 92*
Stone, Doug 1956- *ConMus 10 [port]*
Stone, Earle Joshua *DrAPF 93*
Stone, Edmund Crispen, III 1942- *WhoAm 94*
Stone, Edward 1702-1768 *DcNaB MP*
Stone, Edward Arthur 1941- *WhoAm 94*
Stone, Edward Carroll 1936- *WhoAm 94, WhoScEn 94, WhoWest 94*
Stone, Edward Durell 1902-1978 *WhoAmA 93N*
Stone, Edward Durell, Jr. 1932- *WhoAm 94*
Stone, Edward Harris, II 1933- *WhoAm 94*
Stone, Edward Herman 1939- *WhoAmL 94*
Stone, Elihu David 1958- *WhoFI 94*
Stone, Elizabeth Wenger 1918- *WhoAm 94*
Stone, Erik J. 1953- *WhoAmL 94*
Stone, Errol Lane 1939- *WhoAmL 94*
Stone, Ethon Leon 1916- *WhoMW 93*
Stone, Evan David Robert 1928- *Who 94*
Stone, Everett Lamar 1954- *WhoFI 94*
Stone, Ezra 1917- *IntMPA 94, WhoHol 92*
Stone, Ezra Chaim 1917- *WhoAm 94*
Stone, F. L. Peter 1935- *WhoAmL 94*
Stone, Ferdinand Fairfax 1908-1989 *WhAm 10*
Stone, Florence d1950 *WhoHol 92*
Stone, Floyd Charles 1945- *WhoMW 93*
Stone, Francis Gordon Albert 1925- *IntWW 93*
Stone, Frank 1947- *WhoAmP 93*
Stone, Frank Bush 1913- *WhoAmL 94*
Stone, Franklin Martin d1990 *WhAm 10*
Stone, Franz Theodore 1907- *WhoAm 94*
Stone, Fred d1959 *WhoHol 92*
Stone, Fred A. 1873-1959 *See* Montgomery and Stone *WhoCom*
Stone, Fred J. 1919- *WhoAmA 93*
Stone, Fred Michael 1943- *WhoAm 94, WhoFI 94*
Stone, Frederick Alistair 1927- *Who 94*
Stone, Ganga *NewYTBS 93 [port]*
Stone, Gene d1947 *WhoHol 92*
Stone, Geoffrey Richard 1946- *WhoAm 94, WhoAmL 94*
Stone, George E. d1967 *WhoHol 92*
Stone, George L. 1934- *WhoIns 94*
Stone, Gerald (Charles) 1932- *WrDr 94*
Stone, Gerald Charles 1932- *Who 94*
Stone, Gerald Paul 1918- *WhoAm 94*
Stone, Gordon *Who 94*
Stone, (Francis) Gordon (Albert) 1925- *Who 94*
Stone, Grace Zaring 1896-1991 *WhAm 10*
Stone, Gregory Michael 1959- *WhoAm 94*
Stone, Gwen 1913- *WhoAmA 93*
Stone, H. Lowell 1936-1984 *WhAm 10*
Stone, Harold Anthony 1949- *WhoBlA 94*
Stone, Harold J. 1917- *WhoHol 92*
Stone, Harold Stuart 1938- *WhoAm 94*
Stone, Harry 1926- *WhoWest 94, WrDr 94*
Stone, Harry Clayton 1944- *WhoMW 93*
Stone, Harry H. 1917- *WhoAm 94*
Stone, Herman, Jr. 1919- *WhoBlA 94*
Stone, Hubert Dean 1924- *WhoAm 94, WhoFI 94*
Stone, I. F. 1907-1989 *WhAm 10*
Stone, Irving 1903-1989 *WhAm 10*
Stone, Irving I. 1909- *WhoAm 94, WhoFI 94*
Stone, Isidor Feinstein 1907-1989 *AmSocL*
Stone, Jack *WhoAm 94*
Stone, Jack I. 1920- *WhoFI 94*
Stone, Jacqueline Marie 1959- *WhoScEn 94*
Stone, James d1969 *WhoHol 92*
Stone, James Howard 1939- *WhoAm 94, WhoFI 94, WhoMW 93*
Stone, James J. 1947- *WhoAm 94*
Stone, James Merrill 1952- *WhoAmL 94*
Stone, James Robert 1948- *WhoAm 94, WhoScEn 94, WhoWest 94*
Stone, James Thomas 1948- *WhoFI 94*
Stone, Janet Marie 1945- *WhoFI 94*
Stone, Jed 1949- *WhoAmL 94*
Stone, Jeffrey *WhoHol 92*
Stone, Jeffrey B. 1942- *WhoAmL 94*
Stone, Jeffrey Ingram 1945- *WhoAmA 93*
Stone, Jennifer *DrAPF 93*
Stone, Jennings Edward 1942- *WhoScEn 94*
Stone, Jeremy 1957- *WhoAmA 93*
Stone, Jeremy Judah 1935- *WhoAm 94*
Stone, Jerry Broadwell 1923- *WhoAmL 94*
Stone, Jerry Duncan 1922- *WhoFI 94*
Stone, Jesse Nealand, Jr. 1924- *WhoBlA 94*
Stone, Jim 1947- *WhoAmA 93*
Stone, Jo Slagle 1925- *WhoFI 94*
Stone, Joan *DrAPF 93*
Stone, Joe Allan 1948- *WhoAm 94, WhoAmP 93, WhoWest 94*
Stone, John *DrAPF 93, WhoHol 92*
Stone, John Franklin 1937- *WhoAmL 94*
Stone, John Helms, Jr. 1927- *WhoWest 94*
Stone, John McWilliams, Jr. 1927- *WhoAm 94*
Stone, John O. 1929- *IntWW 93*
Stone, John S. 1930- *WhoBlA 94*
Stone, John Timothy 1963- *WhoFI 94*
Stone, John Timothy, Jr. 1933- *WhoMW 93*
Stone, Joseph 1920- *WhoAm 94*
Stone, Joseph E. 1926- *WhoAmP 93*
Stone, Julie L. *DrAPF 93*
Stone, Kara Lynn 1929- *WhoBlA 94*
Stone, Ken *DrAPF 93*
Stone, Kice H., Jr. 1941- *WhoAmL 94*
Stone, L. Mark 1957- *WhoFI 94*
Stone, Laurie *DrAPF 93*
Stone, Lawrence *WhoFI 94*
Stone, Lawrence 1919- *IntWW 93, Who 94, WhoAm 94, WrDr 94*
Stone, Lawrence E. *WhoAmP 93*
Stone, Lawrence Maurice 1931- *WhoAm 94*
Stone, Leon 1914- *WhoAm 94*
Stone, Leonard *WhoHol 92*
Stone, Lesley *WrDr 94*
Stone, Leslie F(rances) 1905-c. 1987 *EncSF 93*
Stone, Lewis d1953 *WhoHol 92*
Stone, Lewis Bart 1938- *WhoAm 94*
Stone, Linda D. 1947- *WhoFI 94*
Stone, Lisa Jane 1944- *WhoFI 94, WhoMW 93*
Stone, Lucy 1818-1893 *AmSocL, HisWorL*
Stone, M. Lee 1937- *WhoAmA 93*
Stone, Marcus 1921- *Who 94*
Stone, Margaret N. 1931- *WrDr 94*
Stone, Marguerite Beverley 1916- *WhoAm 94*
Stone, Marianne *IntMPA 94*
Stone, Marianne 1923- *WhoHol 92*
Stone, Mark d1952 *WhoHol 92*
Stone, Mark Wade 1953- *WhoMW 93*
Stone, Martha Barnes 1952- *WhoWest 94*
Stone, Marvin Jules 1937- *WhoAm 94, WhoScEn 94*
Stone, Marvin Lawrence 1924- *WhoAm 94*
Stone, Mary Alice 1940- *WhoFI 94*
Stone, Maxine d1964 *WhoHol 92*
Stone, Merlin (David) 1948- *WrDr 94*
Stone, Merrill Brent 1951- *WhoAm 94*
Stone, Michael David 1953- *WhoScEn 94, WhoWest 94*
Stone, Michael E(dward) 1938- *WrDr 94*
Stone, Michael Kalman 1954- *WhoAmL 94*
Stone, Michael Neil 1953- *WhoFI 94*
Stone, Michael P. W. 1925- *WhoAm 94, WhoAmP 93*
Stone, Michael Paul 1955- *WhoScEn 94*
Stone, Michelle Yvonne 1966- *WhoMW 93*
Stone, Mike *WhoHol 92*
Stone, Milburn d1980 *WhoHol 92*
Stone, Mildred Mary-Anne *WhoMW 93*
Stone, Morris Samuel 1911-1989 *WhAm 10*
Stone, Norman 1941- *IntWW 93, Who 94*
Stone, Norman Michael 1949- *WhoWest 94*
Stone, Norman R., Jr. 1935- *WhoAmP 93*
Stone, Oliver 1946- *IntMPA 94, IntWW 93, WhoAm 94, WhoHol 92*
Stone, Paddy 1924- *WhoHol 92*
Stone, Patrick Philip Dennant 1939- *Who 94*
Stone, Paula 1914- *WhoHol 92*
Stone, Peter 1930- *IntMPA 94, WhoAm 94*
Stone, Peter George 1937- *WhoAm 94, WhoAmL 94*
Stone, Peter J. 1951- *WhoAmL 94*
Stone, Philip 1924- *WhoHol 92*
Stone, Philip M. 1933- *WhoScEn 94*
Stone, Ralph B. 1943- *WhoWest 94*
Stone, Ralph Kenny 1952- *WhoAmP 93*
Stone, Randolph Noel 1946- *WhoAm 94, WhoAmL 94*
Stone, Reese J., Jr. 1945- *WhoFI 94*
Stone, Reese J., Jr. 1947- *WhoBlA 94*
Stone, (John) Richard (Nicholas) 1913- *WrDr 94*
Stone, (John) Richard (Nicholas) 1913-1991 *WhAm 10*
Stone, Richard B. 1928- *WhoAm 94*
Stone, Richard Bernard 1928- *WhoAmP 93*
Stone, Richard E. 1937- *WhoIns 94*
Stone, Richard Frederick 1928- *Who 94*
Stone, Richard James 1945- *WhoAm 94, WhoAmL 94*
Stone, Richard John 1955- *WhoScEn 94*
Stone, Richard Lehman 1916- *WhoWest 94*
Stone, Rob *WhoHol 92*
Stone, Robert *DrAPF 93*
Stone, Robert d1977 *WhoHol 92*
Stone, Robert (Anthony) 1937- *WrDr 94*
Stone, Robert Alan 1935- *WhoAm 94*

Stoterau, H. Peter 1938- *WhoAm 94, WhoAmL 94*
Stothard, Peter 1951- *IntWW 93*
Stothard, Peter Michael 1951- *Who 94*
Stothart, Herbert 1885-1949 *IntDcF 2-4*
Stothers, John B. 1931- *WhoAm 94*
Stotland, Ezra 1924- *WhoAm 94, WrDr 94*
Stotlar, Cynthia Byrd 1953- *WhoMW 93*
Stotler, Alicemarie H. 1942- *WhoAm 94, WhoAmL 94, WhoWest 94*
Stotler, Edith Ann 1946- *WhoFI 94*
Stotler, John Leonard 1938- *WhoAm 94*
Stott, Rt. Hon. Lord 1909- *Who 94*
Stott, Adrian (George Ellingham) 1948- *Who 94*
Stott, Brian 1941- *WhoAm 94, WhoWest 94*
Stott, Deborah 1942- *WhoAmA 93*
Stott, Dorothy (M.) 1958- *WrDr 94*
Stott, Dot 1958- *WrDr 94*
Stott, George Gordon *Who 94*
Stott, Grady Bernell 1921- *WhoAm 94*
Stott, James Charles 1945- *WhoWest 94*
Stott, John Robert Walmsley 1921- *Who 94, WrDr 94*
Stott, Kathryn Linda 1958- *IntWW 93*
Stott, Mary *Who 94*
Stott, (Charlotte) Mary 1907- *Who 94, WrDr 94*
Stott, Mike 1944- *ConDr 93, WrDr 94*
Stott, Peter Frank d1993 *Who 94N*
Stott, Peter Walter 1944- *WhoFI 94, WhoWest 94*
Stott, Richard Keith 1943- *IntWW 93, Who 94*
Stott, Roger 1943- *Who 94*
Stott, Thomas Edward, Jr. 1923- *WhoAm 94*
Stott, William Ross, Jr. 1935- *WhoAm 94*
Stotter, David W. 1904- *WhoAm 94*
Stotter, Harry Shelton 1928- *WhoAm 94*
Stotter, James, II 1929- *WhoWest 94*
Stotter, Lawrence Henry 1929- *WhoAm 94, WhoAmL 94*
Stotter, Mike 1957- *WrDr 94*
Stottlemyer, David Lee 1935- *WhoAm 94*
Stottlemyre, Gary Allen 1948- *WhoAmP 93*
Stotts, Valmon D. 1925- *WhoBlA 94*
Stotz, Carl E. 1910-1992 *AnObit 1992*
Stotzer, Beatriz Olvera 1950- *WhoHisp 94*
Stotzky, Guenther 1931- *WhoScEn 94*
Stoudt, Thomas Henry 1922- *WhoScEn 94*
Stouffer, Daniel Henry, Jr. 1937- *WhoAmA 93, WhoWest 94*
Stouffer, Deborah Marie 1968- *WhoWest 94*
Stouffer, Nancy Kathleen 1951- *WhoFI 94*
Stough, Charles Daniel 1914- *WhoAmL 94, WhoMW 93*
Stough, Charles Senour 1918- *WhoAmP 93*
Stough, Charles Senour 1944- *WhoMW 93*
Stough, Stephen Alan 1950- *WhoFI 94, WhoWest 94*
Stough, William Allen 1949- *WhoFI 94*
Stoughton, Richard Baker 1923-1992 *WhAm 10*
Stoughton, Stephen H. 1944- *WhoAmP 93*
Stoughton-Harris, Anthony Geoffrey 1932- *Who 94*
Stoumen, Lou 1916-1991 *WhoAmA 93N*
Stourton *Who 94*
Stout, Arthur Wendel, III 1949- *WhoAmL 94*
Stout, Carl Frederick 1942- *WhoFI 94*
Stout, Carter Louis 1960- *WhoAmL 94*
Stout, David 1942- *WrDr 94*
Stout, David Ker 1932- *Who 94*
Stout, Dennis Lee 1948- *WhoAm 94, WhoAmP 93, WhoWest 94*
Stout, Donald Everett 1926- *WhoFI 94*
Stout, Edward Irvin 1939- *WhoFI 94, WhoMW 93*
Stout, Frank J. 1926- *WhoAmA 93*
Stout, George Leslie 1897-1978 *WhoAmA 93N*
Stout, Glenn Emanuel 1920- *WhoAm 94, WhoScEn 94*
Stout, Gregory Stansbury 1915- *WhoAm 94*
Stout, Harry S. *WrDr 94*
Stout, J. Barry 1936- *WhoAmP 93*
Stout, James Dudley 1947- *WhoAmL 94*
Stout, James Gerard 1966- *WhoMW 93*
Stout, James Tilman 1942- *WhoWest 94*
Stout, John Willard 1912- *WhoMW 93*
Stout, Joseph A., Jr. 1939- *WrDr 94*
Stout, Juanita Kidd *WhoAmP 93*
Stout, Juanita Kidd 1919- *WhoBlA 94*
Stout, Kenneth Oliver 1929- *WhoAmP 93*
Stout, Koehler Sheridan 1922- *WhoFI 94*
Stout, Larry John 1950- *WhoScEn 94*
Stout, Leatrice Joy 1924- *WhoAmP 93*
Stout, Lowell 1928- *WhoAmL 94, WhoWest 94*
Stout, Maye Alma 1920- *WhoMW 93*
Stout, Paul 1972- *WhoHol 92*
Stout, Phil *WhoAmP 93*
Stout, Philip John 1958- *WhoScEn 94*
Stout, Rex (Todhunter) 1886-1975 *EncSF 93*
Stout, Richard A. 1927- *WhoIns 94*
Stout, Richard Alan 1941- *WhoAm 94*
Stout, Richard Gordon 1934- *WhoAmA 93*
Stout, Robert Joe *DrAPF 93*
Stout, Roger Paul 1956- *WhoWest 94*
Stout, Royal G. d1958 *WhoHol 92*
Stout, Samuel Coredon 1913- *Who 94*
Stout, Shirley Ruth 1926- *WhoAmP 93*
Stout, Thomas Melville 1925- *WhoScEn 94*
Stout, Virgil Loomis 1921- *WhoAm 94*
Stout, William Ferguson 1907- *Who 94*
Stout, William Jewell 1914- *WhoAm 94*
Stoute, Michael Ronald 1945- *Who 94*
Stoutenburg, Jane Sue Williamson 1949- *WhoMW 93*
Stoutes, Katrina Frederick 1962- *WhoMW 93*
Stovall, Allen D. 1937- *WhoAm 94*
Stovall, Audrean 1933- *WhoBlA 94*
Stovall, Dennis Michael 1946- *WhoWest 94*
Stovall, Doris Grace 1934- *WhoMW 93*
Stovall, Floyd 1896- *WhAm 10*
Stovall, Jay 1940- *WhoAmP 93*
Stovall, Jerry 1936- *WhoAm 94*
Stovall, Jerry C. 1936- *WhoIns 94*
Stovall, Luther Mckinley 1937- *WhoAmA 93*
Stovall, Mary Kate 1921- *WhoAmP 93, WhoBlA 94*
Stovall, Melody S. 1952- *WhoBlA 94*
Stovall, Richard L. 1944- *WhoAm 94, WhoMW 93*
Stovall, Robert Henry 1926- *WhoAm 94*
Stovall, Stanley V. 1953- *WhoBlA 94*
Stovall, Thelma Loyace 1919- *WhoAmP 93*
Stove, Betty 1945- *BuCMET*
Stove, David (Charles) 1927- *WrDr 94*
Stove, David Charles 1927- *IntWW 93*
Stover, Carl Frederick 1930- *WhoAm 94*
Stover, Courtney E. *WhoAmP 93*
Stover, David Frank 1941- *WhoAm 94*
Stover, Donald Lewis 1943- *WhoAmA 93*
Stover, Donald Rae 1934- *WhoMW 93, WhoScEn 94*
Stover, Harry M. 1926- *WhoAm 94*
Stover, James Howard 1911- *WhoAm 94*
Stover, Janet d1988 *WhoHol 92*
Stover, John Ford 1912- *WhoAm 94, WrDr 94*
Stover, Kathy A. 1956- *WhoAmL 94*
Stover, Leon (Eugene) 1929- *WrDr 94*
Stover, Leon E(ugene) 1929- *ConAu 43NR, EncSF 93*
Stover, Leon Eugene 1929- *WhoAm 94*
Stover, Mabel Carney *NewYTBS 93 [port]*
Stover, Mark Edward 1955- *WhoFI 94*
Stover, Matthew Joseph 1955- *WhoAm 94*
Stover, Milton Edward 1897- *WhAm 10*
Stover, Phil Sheridan, Jr. 1926- *WhoAm 94*
Stover, Samuel Landis 1930- *WhoScEn 94*
Stover, Stephan Wallace 1946- *WhoMW 93*
Stover, Stephen Leech 1919- *WhoMW 93*
Stover, William Ruffner 1922- *WhoAm 94, WhoFI 94, WhoMW 93*
Stover-McBride, Tama Sue 1957- *WhoWest 94*
Stow, Archdeacon of *Who 94*
Stow, Christopher P. *Who 94*
Stow, John 1525-1605 *DcLB 132 [port]*
Stow, John Montague 1911- *Who 94*
Stow, Ralph Conyers 1916- *Who 94*
Stow, Randolph *Who 94*
Stow, (Julian) Randolph 1935- *EncSF 93, Who 94, WrDr 94*
Stow, Timothy Montague Fenwick 1943- *Who 94*
Stowe, Carol Ann 1951- *WhoMW 93*
Stowe, Charles Robinson Beecher 1949- *WhoAmL 94*
Stowe, David Henry 1910- *WhoAm 94*
Stowe, David Henry, Jr. 1936- *IntWW 93, WhoAm 94, WhoFI 94, WhoMW 93, WhoScEn 94*
Stowe, David Metz 1919- *WhoAm 94, WrDr 94*
Stowe, Harriet Beecher 1811-1896 *BlmGWL*
Stowe, Harriet Elizabeth Beecher 1811-1896 *AmSocL [port], DcAmReB 2*
Stowe, James L. *DrAPF 93*
Stowe, Kenneth (Ronald) 1927- *Who 94*
Stowe, Leland 1899- *IntWW 93, WhoAm 94*
Stowe, Leslie d1949 *WhoHol 92*
Stowe, Madeleine 1958- *IntMPA 94, WhoHisp 94, WhoHol 92*
Stowe, Madeline *WhoAm 94*
Stowe, Noel James 1942- *WhoWest 94*
Stowe, Nonnie 1934- *WhoIns 94*
Stowe, Pauline Malovrh 1927- *WhoMW 93*
Stowe, Robert Allen 1924- *WhoMW 93*
Stowe, Robert Lee, III 1954- *WhoFI 94*
Stowe, William Earl 1923- *WhoMW 93*
Stowe, William Gordon 1925- *WhoAmP 93*
Stowe, William McFerrin 1913-1988 *WhAm 10*
Stowell, C. W. d1940 *WhoHol 92*
Stowell, Christopher R. 1966- *WhoAm 94*
Stowell, Dwight Kenneth, Jr. 1946- *WhoAmP 93*
Stowell, Edward Esty d1993 *NewYTBS 93*
Stowell, Ewell Addison 1922- *WhoMW 93*
Stowell, Geraldine Case 1942- *WhoWest 94*
Stowell, Joseph, III *WhoAm 94*
Stowell, Kent 1939- *WhoAm 94*
Stowell, Larry Joseph 1952- *WhoScEn 94*
Stowell, Linda Rae 1947- *WhoAmP 93*
Stowell, Michael James 1935- *Who 94*
Stowell, Phyllis *DrAPF 93*
Stowell, Richard Brooks 1942- *WhoFI 94*
Stowell, Robert Eugene 1914- *WhoAm 94*
Stowell, Ronald Glenn 1945- *WhoMW 93*
Stowell, Warren 1941- *WhoAmP 93*
Stowell, William d1919 *WhoHol 92*
Stower, Harvey 1944- *WhoAmP 93*
Stowers, Carlton Eugene 1942- *WhoAm 94*
Stowers, Harry E., Jr. *WhoAmP 93*
Stowers, James Evans, Jr. 1924- *WhoAm 94*
Stowers, Mark David 1957- *WhoMW 93*
Stoxen, John Michael 1961- *WhoAmL 94*
Stoy, Philip Joseph 1906- *Who 94*
Stoyanov, Veselin 1902-1969 *NewGrDO*
Stoyer, Mark Alan 1963- *WhoWest 94*
Stoyle, Roger John B. *Who 94*
Stozich, John P. 1927- *WhoAmP 93*
Straach, Mildred Eileen 1928- *WhoAmP 93*
Straatmeyer, Jean Ellen 1938- *WhoWest 94*
Straatsma, Bradley Ralph 1927- *WhoAm 94, WhoScEn 94*
Straayer, Carole Kathleen 1934- *WhoMW 93*
Strabo c. 63BC-c. 21AD *WhWE*
Strabolgi, Baron of England 1914- *Who 94*
Stracciari, Riccardo 1875-1955 *NewGrDO*
Stracey, John (Simon) 1938- *Who 94*
Stracey, Walter Edwin *WhoFI 94*
Strachan, Alan Lockhart Thomson 1946- *Who 94*
Strachan, Alexander William Bruce 1917- *Who 94*
Strachan, Benjamin Leckie 1924- *Who 94*
Strachan, David E. 1947 *WhoAm 94*
Strachan, Donald M. 1923- *WhoAm 94*
Strachan, Douglas Frederick 1933- *Who 94*
Strachan, Douglas Mark Arthur 1946- *Who 94*
Strachan, Gordon R. *WhoHol 92*
Strachan, Graham Robert 1931- *Who 94*
Strachan, Ian Charles 1943- *IntWW 93*
Strachan, J(ohn) George 1910- *WrDr 94*
Strachan, John R. 1916- *WhoBlA 94*
Strachan, Lloyd Calvin, Jr. 1954- *WhoBlA 94*
Strachan, Michael Francis 1919- *Who 94*
Strachan, Nell B. 1941- *WhoAm 94*
Strachan, Richard James 1928- *WhoBlA 94*
Strachan, Valerie Patricia Marie 1940- *Who 94*
Strachan, Walter 1910- *Who 94*
Stracher, Alfred 1930- *WhoAm 94*
Strachey *Who 94*
Strachey, Charles 1934- *Who 94*
Strachey, (Giles) Lytton 1880-1932 *BlmGEL*
Strachey, Rachel Conn 1887-1940 *DcNaB MP*
Strack, Harold Arthur 1923- *WhoAm 94, WhoScEn 94*
Strack, Stephen Naylor 1955- *WhoWest 94*
Straczynski, Joseph Michael 1954- *WhoWest 94*
Strada del Po, Anna Maria fl. 1719-1740 *NewGrDO*
Stradbroke, Earl of 1937- *Who 94*
Stradella, Alessandro 1639-1682 *NewGrDO*
Strader, James David 1940- *WhoAm 94*
Strader, Scott *WhoHol 92*
Strader, Timothy Richards 1956- *WhoAmL 94*
Stradley, Richard Lee *WhoAmL 94*
Stradley, William Jackson 1939- *WhoAm 94*
Stradley, William Lamar 1940- *WhoFI 94*
Stradling, Donald George 1929- *Who 94*
Stradling, Harry 1901-1970 *IntDcF 2-4 [port]*
Stradling, Harry, Jr. 1925- *IntMPA 94*
Stradling, Leslie Edward 1908- *IntWW 93, Who 94, WrDr 94*
Stradner, Rose d1958 *WhoHol 92*
Straede, Christen Andersen 1952- *WhoScEn 94*
Straesser, Joep 1934- *NewGrDO*
Straeter, Jane L. 1919- *WhoFI 94*
Straetz, Robert P. 1921- *WhoAm 94*
Straffon, Ralph Atwood 1928- *WhoAm 94*
Strafford, Earl of 1936- *Who 94*
Strafford, Thomas Wentworth, Earl of 1593-1641 *BlmGEL*
Strafuss, David Louis 1962- *WhoScEn 94*
Stragalas, George, III 1946- *WhoAmP 93*
Stragier, Cynthia Andreas 1957- *WhoScEn 94*
Straham, Clarence Clifford, Jr. 1956- *WhoBlA 94*
Strahan, Aubrey 1852-1928 *DcNaB MP*
Strahan, Bradley R. *DrAPF 93*
Strahan, Jimmie Rose 1942- *WhoScEn 94*
Strahan, Julia Celestine 1938- *WhoFI 94, WhoWest 94*
Strahan, Randall (W.) 1954- *WrDr 94*
Strahilevitz, Meir 1935- *WhoScEn 94*
Strahle, Ronald H. 1921- *WhoAmP 93*
Strahle, Warren Charles 1938- *WhoAm 94, WhoScEn 94*
Strahler, Arthur Newell 1918- *WhoWest 94*
Strahler, Violet Ruth 1918- *WhoMW 93*
Strahm, Samuel Edward 1936- *WhoAm 94*
Straight, Beatrice 1916- *WhoHol 92*
Straight, Beatrice 1918- *IntMPA 94*
Straight, Beatrice Whitney 1918- *WhoAm 94*
Straight, Cathy A. 1963- *WhoBlA 94*
Straight, Clarence d1988 *WhoHol 92*
Straight, Elsie H. *WhoAmA 93*
Straight, Michael (Whitney) 1916- *WrDr 94*
Straight, Richard Coleman 1937- *WhoScEn 94*
Strain, Edward Richard 1925- *WhoMW 93*
Strain, Herbert Arthur, III 1954- *WhoMW 93*
Strain, James Arthur 1944- *WhoAm 94, WhoAmL 94*
Strain, James Ellsworth 1923- *WhoAm 94*
Strain, John Thomas 1939- *WhoWest 94*
Strain, R. H. 1941- *WhoAmP 93*
Strain, Robert W. 1924- *WhoIns 94*
Strain, Terrance James 1958- *WhoMW 93*
Strainer, James Anthony Skip 1968- *WhoMW 93*
Strait, Bradley Justus 1932- *WhoAm 94, WhoScEn 94*
Strait, George 1952- *WhoAm 94*
Strait, George Alfred, Jr. 1945- *WhoBlA 94*
Strait, Jefferson 1953- *WhoScEn 94*
Strait, Lindsy Edward 1955- *WhoWest 94*
Strait, Raymond Earl 1924- *WhoWest 94*
Straiton, Archie Waugh 1907- *WhoAm 94, WhoScEn 94*
Straiton, E(dward) C(ornock) 1917- *ConAu 42NR*
Straiton, Eddie *ConAu 42NR*
Straiton, John S(eal) 1922- *WrDr 94*
Straka, Laszlo Richard 1934- *WhoAm 94, WhoFI 94*
Straka, Michael John 1959- *WhoMW 93*
Straka, William Charles, II 1940- *WhoWest 94*
Strake, George W., Jr. 1935- *WhoAmP 93*
Straker, Bryan John 1929- *Who 94*
Straker, Ivan Charles 1928- *Who 94*
Straker, J(ohn) F(oster) 1904-1987 *WrDr 94N*
Straker, Michael (Ian Bowstead) 1928- *Who 94*
Strakhov, Vladimir Nikolayevich 1932- *WhoScEn 94*
Strakosch, Maurice 1825-1887 *NewGrDO*
Stralem, Donald S. 1903-1976 *WhoAmA 93N*
Stralem, Pierre 1909- *WhoAm 94*
Stralia, Elsa 1881-1945 *NewGrDO*
Straling, Phillip Francis 1933- *WhoAm 94, WhoWest 94*
Stram, Hank Louis 1923- *WhoAm 94*
Stram, Karen D. 1940- *WhoAmP 93*
Stranahan, Robert Paul, Jr. 1929- *WhoAm 94, WhoAmL 94, WhoFI 94*
Stranberg, Wynne Lee 1948- *WhoMW 93*
Strand, Ann S. 1929- *WhoAmP 93*
Strand, Curt Robert 1920- *WhoAm 94*
Strand, David Axel 1935- *WhoAm 94*
Strand, Joe d1982 *WhoHol 92*
Strand, John Gregory 1951- *WhoAmP 93*
Strand, Kaj Aage 1907- *WhoScEn 94*
Strand, Kenneth A(lbert) 1927- *WrDr 94*
Strand, Kenneth T. 1931- *Who 94*

Straw, William Russell 1957-
WhoScEn 94
Strawa, Anthony Walter 1950-
WhoScEn 94, WhoWest 94
Strawberry, Darryl 1962- WhoAm 94,
WhoBlA 94, WhoWest 94
Strawbridge, David R. 1945- WhoAmL 94
Strawbridge, Francis Reeves, III 1937-
WhoFI 94
Strawbridge, Jesse Ronald 1950-
WhoMW 93
Strawbridge, Peter S. 1938- WhoAm 94
Strawbridge, Steven James 1948-
WhoAmL 94
Strawderman, William E. 1941-
WhoScEn 94
Strawhecker, Paul Joseph 1947-
WhoMW 93
Strawn, Aimee Williams 1925-
WhoBlA 94
Strawn, Bernice I. WhoAmA 93
Strawn, Harry Culp 1918- WhoAmP 93
Strawn, Jarrett W. (Jason) 1943-
WhoAmA 93
Strawn, John 1950- WhoWest 94
Strawn, Lois Kathleen Bailey 1954-
WhoMW 93
Strawn, Melvin Nicholas 1929-
WhoAmA 93
Strawn, Oliver Perry, Jr. 1925-
WhoAmP 93
Strawn-Hamilton, Frank 1934-
WhoAm 94
Strawson, Galen John 1952- WrDr 94
Strawson, John Michael 1921- Who 94
Strawson, Peter (Frederick) 1919- Who 94,
WrDr 94
Strawson, Peter Frederick 1919-
IntWW 93
Stray, Christopher 1943- ConAu 142
Stray, Svenn Thorkild 1922- IntWW 93
Stray Cats, The ConMus 11 [port]
Strayer, Frank d1964 WhoHol 92
Strayhorn, Billy 1915-1967 AfrAmAl 6
Strayhorn, Earl Carlton 1948- WhoBlA 94
Strayhorn, Earl E. 1918- WhoBlA 94
Strayhorn, Lloyd WhoBlA 94
Strayhorn, Ralph Nichols, Jr. 1923-
WhoAm 94, WhoAmL 94
Strayton, Robert Gerard 1935-
WhoAm 94
Strazzella, James Anthony 1939-
WhoAmL 94
Strealy, Jerry Lee 1941- WhoWest 94
Stream, Arnold Crager 1918- WhoAm 94
Stream, Jay Wilson 1921- WhoAm 94
Streams, Peter John 1935- Who 94
Strean, Bernard M. 1910- WhoAm 94
Strean, Richard Lockey 1939- WhoFI 94
Strear, Joseph D. 1933- WhoAm 94
Streat, Van, Sr. 1954- WhoAmP 93
Streatfeild, Timothy Stuart Champion
1926- Who 94
Streatfeild-James, John Jocelyn 1929-
Who 94
Streator, Edward James 1930- Who 94,
WhoAm 94
Streator, Edward James, III 1958-
WhoFI 94
Streb, Alan Joseph 1932- WhoAm 94,
WhoScEn 94
Strebig, Randy D. 1963- WhoMW 93
Strecker, David Eugene 1950-
WhoAmL 94
Strecker, Ignatius J. 1917- WhoAm 94,
WhoMW 93
Strecker, Ludwig NewGrDO
Strecker, Robert Edwin 1955-
WhoScEn 94
Streeb, Gordon 1935- WhoAmP 93
Streeb, Gordon Lee 1935- WhoAm 94
Streep, Meryl 1949- IntMPA 94,
IntWW 93, WhoAm 94, WhoHol 92
Streep, Meryl (Mary Louise) 1949-
Who 94
Streeper, Robert William 1951-
WhoScEn 94
Street, Anne A. 1942- WhoBlA 94
Street, Anthony Austin 1926- IntWW 93,
Who 94
Street, Brian Jeffrey 1955- WrDr 94
Street, Dana Morris 1910- WhoAm 94
Street, David d1971 WhoHol 92
Street, David Hargett 1943- WhoAm 94,
WhoFI 94
Street, Douglas Dean 1935- WhoFI 94
Street, Edward Robert 1938-1990
WhAm 10
Street, Erica Catherine 1958- WhoAmL 94
Street, G. S. 1867-1936 DcLB 135 [port]
Street, George 1867- WhoHol 92
Street, Jabez Curry 1906-1989 WhAm 10
Street, John Charles 1930- WhoAm 94
Street, John Edmund Dudley 1918-
Who 94
Street, John F. WhoAmP 93
Street, Julia Montgomery 1898- WrDr 94
Street, Laurence (Whistler) 1926- Who 94

Street, Laurence Whistler 1926-
IntWW 93
Street, Paul Shipley 1948- WhoAmL 94
Street, Peter Ronald 1944- Who 94
Street, Robert 1920- IntWW 93, Who 94
Street, Robert Lynnwood 1934-
WhoAm 94, WhoWest 94
Street, T. Milton 1941- WhoBlA 94
Street, Vivian Sue 1954- WhoBlA 94
Street, William May 1938- WhoFI 94
Streeten, Frank Who 94
Streeten, Paul Patrick 1917- Who 94,
WhoFI 94, WrDr 94
Streeten, Reginald Hawkins 1928- Who 94
Streeter, Alan 1934- WhoAmP 93
Streeter, Anne Paul 1926- WhoAmP 93
Streeter, Bernard A., Jr. 1935-
WhoAmP 93
Streeter, Debra Brister 1956- WhoBlA 94
Streeter, Denise Williams 1962-
WhoBlA 94
Streeter, Elwood James 1930- WhoBlA 94
Streeter, Gary Nicholas 1955- Who 94
Streeter, Henry Schofield 1920-
WhoAm 94
Streeter, Jean M. 1950- WhoAmP 93
Streeter, John Stuart 1920- Who 94
Streeter, John Willis 1947- WhoFI 94,
WhoMW 93, WhoScEn 94
Streeter, Myron Merle 1926- WhoFI 94
Streeter, Richard Edward 1934-
WhoAm 94, WhoMW 93
Streeter, Richard Henry 1943-
WhoAm 94, WhoAmL 94
Streeter, Ruth Cheney 1895- WhAm 10
Streeter, Tal 1934- WhoAm 94,
WhoAmA 93
Streeter, Thomas Winthrop 1883-1965
DcLB 140 [port]
Streeter, Victor John 1940- WhoMW 93
Street-Kidd, Mae WhoBlA 94
Streetman, Ben Garland 1939-
WhoAm 94, WhoScEn 94
Streetman, John William, III 1941-
WhoAm 94, WhoAmA 93, WhoMW 93
Streeton, Terence (George) 1930- Who 94
Streett, Alexander Graham 1939-
WhoAm 94
Streett, Donald Howard 1934- WhoFI 94
Streett, Robert Wells 1938- WhoFI 94
Streett, Tylden Westcott 1922-
WhoAmA 93
Streett, William Bernard 1932-
WhoAm 94
Streff, Clyde E. WhoAmP 93
Streff, Francine K. 1950- WhoAmP 93
Streff, Rodney Joseph 1947- WhoAmP 93
Streff, William Albert, Jr. 1949-
WhoAm 94, WhoAmL 94
Strege, Tim Melvin 1952- WhoFI 94,
WhoWest 94
Strehblow, Hans-Henning Steffen 1939-
WhoScEn 94
Strehle, Glenn Preston 1936- WhoFI 94
Strehler, Giorgio 1921- IntWW 93,
NewGrDO
Strehlow, Roger Albert 1925- WhAm 10
Streibel, Bryce 1922- WhoAmP 93,
WhoMW 93
Streibich, Harold Cecil 1928- WhoAm 94
Streibl, Max 1932- IntWW 93
Streich, Rita 1920-1987 NewGrDO
Streicher, James Franklin 1940-
WhoAm 94, WhoAmL 94
Streicher, Michael Alfred 1921- WhoFI 94
Streichler, Jerry 1929- WhoAm 94
Streicker, James Richard 1944-
WhoAmL 94
Streifer, William 1936-1990 WhAm 10
Streiff, Thomas F. 1958- WhoIns 94
Streinz, James Ray 1955- WhoAmL 94
Streisand, Barbra 1942- IntMPA 94,
WhoHol 92
Streisand, Barbra Joan 1942- IntWW 93,
Who 94, WhoHol 92
Streissler, Erich W. 1933- IntWW 93
Streit, Christopher Michael 1969-
WhoMW 93
Streit, Jeanne Ellen 1953- WhoMW 93
Streitwieser, Andrew, Jr. 1927-
IntWW 93, WhoAm 94, WhoScEn 94,
WhoWest 94, WrDr 94
Strejeck, Donald F. 1957- WhoIns 94
Streletzky, Kathryn D. 1957- WhoFI 94
Strelzer, Martin 1925- WhoAm 94
Strembitsky, Michael Alexander 1935-
WhoWest 94
Stremler, Ferrel G. 1933- WhoAm 94
Strena, Robert Victor 1929- WhoWest 94
Streng, Frederick J. d1993 NewYTBS 93
Streng, Frederick J(ohn) 1933-1993
ConAu 141
Streng, Frederick John 1933- WrDr 94
Streng, William Paul 1937- WhoAm 94
Strenger, George 1906- WhoWest 94
Strenger, Hermann-Josef 1928-
IntWW 93
Strength, Janis Grace 1934- WhoAm 94

Strength, Robert Samuel 1929- WhoFI 94
Strenk, Yasmine Sylvia 1966-
WhoWest 94
Strenski, James B. 1930- WhoAm 94,
WhoFI 94
Strenski, Robert Francis 1947-
WhoAmL 94
Strepponi, Giuseppina 1815-1897
NewGrDO
Stresemann, Gustav 1878-1929
HisWorL [port]
Stresen-Reuter, Frederick Arthur, II
1942- WhoFI 94, WhoScEn 94
Stretch, John Joseph 1935- WhoAm 94
Strete, Craig 1950- WrDr 94
Strete, Craig (Kee) 1950- EncSF 93
Strete, Jane DrAPF 93
Stretton, Ellen d1985 WhoHol 92
Stretton, Eric Hugh Alexander 1916-
Who 94
Stretton, Hesba (Sarah) 1832-1911
BlmGWL
Stretton, Hugh 1924- WrDr 94
Stretton, Peter John 1938- Who 94
Stretton, Ross WhoAm 94
Stretz, Lawrence Albert 1946-
WhoWest 94
Streu, Raymond Oliver 1931- WhoFI 94
Strevey, Guy Donald 1932- WhoMW 93
Strew, Suzanne Claflin 1935- WhoAm 94
Striano, John A. 1942- WhoAm 94
Stribling, Ken 1959- WhoAmP 93
Stribling, Melissa WhoHol 92
Stribling, T.S. EncSF 93
Strichartz, James Leonard 1951-
WhoAmL 94, WhoWest 94
Strick, John, Jr. WhoAmP 93
Strick, Joseph IntWW 93
Strick, Joseph 1923- WhoAm 94
Strick, Philip 1939- EncSF 93
Strick, Robert Charles Gordon 1931-
Who 94
Strick, Wesley IntMPA 94
Stricker, Der c. 1190-c. 1250 DcLB 138
Stricker, Andrew Gerald 1957-
WhoWest 94
Stricker, Augustin Reinhard d1720?
NewGrDO
Stricker, Frank Aloysius 1943-
WhoWest 94
Stricker, Irwin Jesse 1932- WhoFI 94
Stricker, Raphael Becher 1950-
WhoWest 94
Strickland WhoAmA 93
Strickland, Amzie WhoHol 92
Strickland, Anita Maurine 1923-
WhoAm 94
Strickland, Arvah E. 1930- WhoBlA 94
Strickland, Arvarh Eunice 1930-
WhoAm 94
Strickland, Benjamin Vincent Michael
1939- Who 94
Strickland, Bonnie Ruth 1936-
WhoAm 94
Strickland, Brad DrAPF 93
Strickland, Brad 1947- EncSF 93
Strickland, (William) Brad(ley) 1947-
WrDr 94
Strickland, Charles D. 1932- WhoAmP 93
Strickland, Christopher Alan 1957-
WhoScEn 94
Strickland, Clinton Vernal, Jr. 1950-
WhoAm 94, WhoBlA 94
Strickland, Connie WhoHol 92
Strickland, Dorothy S. 1933- WhoBlA 94
Strickland, Frank 1928- Who 94
Strickland, Frederick William, Jr. 1944-
WhoBlA 94
Strickland, Gail IntMPA 94
Strickland, Gail 1946- WhoHol 92
Strickland, George Thomas, Jr. 1934-
WhoAm 94
Strickland, Helen d1938 WhoHol 92
Strickland, Hugh Alfred 1931- WhoAm 94
Strickland, Jeffery 1958- WhoFI 94
Strickland, John S. 1945- WhoAm 94
Strickland, Mabel d1976 WhoHol 92
Strickland, Nancy Kathleen 1949-
WhoAmL 94
Strickland, Nellie B. 1932- WhoAm 94
Strickland, R. James 1930- WhoBlA 94
Strickland, Rennard (James) 1940-
ConAu 43NR
Strickland, Robert Louis 1931-
WhoAm 94, WhoFI 94
Strickland, Robert Ray WhoFI 94
Strickland, Rodney 1966- WhoBlA 94
Strickland, Stephanie DrAPF 93
Strickland, Sylvia Raye 1945-
WhoWest 94
Strickland, Ted 1941- CngDr 93,
WhoAm 94, WhoAmP 93, WhoMW 93
Strickland, Ted L. 1932- WhoAmP 93
Strickland, Thomas J. 1932- WhoAmA 93
Strickland, Thomas Joseph 1932-
WhoAm 94
Strickland, William Jesse 1942-
WhoAm 94, WhoAmL 94

Strickland-Constable, Robert (Frederick)
1903- Who 94
Strickler, Howard Martin 1950-
WhoScEn 94
Strickler, Ivan K. 1921- WhoAm 94,
WhoFI 94, WhoMW 93
Strickler, Joan Carole 1935- WhoMW 93
Strickler, John Rudi 1938- WhoScEn 94
Strickler, Matthew M. 1940- WhoAm 94,
WhoAmL 94
Strickler, Scott Michael 1961-
WhoAmL 94
Strickler, Susan Elizabeth 1952-
WhoAmA 93
Strickley, Robert Gordon 1961-
WhoScEn 94
Stricklin, Al d1986 WhoHol 92
Stricklin, Carl Spencer 1917- WhoFI 94
Stricklin, James 1934- WhoBlA 94
Stricklin, Rebecca Ellen 1954-
WhoMW 93
Stricklyn, Ray 1930- IntMPA 94
Stricklyn, Ray 1933- WhoHol 92
Strickman, Arthur Edwin 1924-
WhoAm 94, WhoFI 94
Strickon, Harvey Alan 1947- WhoAm 94,
WhoAmL 94
Strid, Gail Keys 1953- WhoWest 94
Stride, John 1936- WhoHol 92
Strider, Marjorie Virginia WhoAm 94,
WhoAmA 93
Strider, Maurice William 1913-
WhoBlA 94
Stridiron, Iver A. 1945- WhoAmP 93
Stridsberg, Albert Borden 1929-
WhoFI 94
Strieber, Whitley 1945- EncSF 93
Strieber, (Louis) Whitley 1945-
ConAu 43NR
Strieder, John William 1901- WhoAm 94
Striefsky, Linda A. 1952- WhoAm 94
Striefsky, Linda Ann 1952- WhoAmL 94
Striegel, Andre Michael 1967-
WhoScEn 94
Striegel, Timothy Richard 1967-
WhoMW 93
Striegler, Kurt 1886-1958 NewGrDO
Strienz, Wilhelm 1900-1987 NewGrDO
Striepe, Janice Marie 1947- WhoMW 93
Strier, Karen Barbara 1959- WhoAm 94,
WhoMW 93
Strier, Murray Paul 1923- WhoScEn 94
Striffler, David Frank 1922- WhoAm 94
Striggio, Alessandro 1573?-1630
NewGrDO
Striggles, Matthew C. 1927- WhoAmP 93
Stright, I. Leonard 1916- WhoAm 94
Strike, Donald Peter 1936- WhoScEn 94
Strike, Jeremy 1939- EncSF 93
Striker, Cecil L. 1932- WhoAmA 93
Striker, Cecil Leopold 1932- WhoAm 94
Striker, Gary E. 1934- WhoAm 94
Striker, Joseph d1974 WhoHol 92
Strimbu, Victor, Jr. 1932- WhoAm 94,
WhoAmL 94
Strimpell, Stephen 1941- WhoHol 92
Strinasacchi, Teresa 1768-1830?
NewGrDO
Strindberg, Anita WhoHol 92
Strindberg, August 1849-1912 BlmGEL,
IntDcT 2
Strindberg, (Johan) August 1849-1912
NewGrDO
Strinden, Earl Stanford 1931-
WhoAmP 93
Striner, Herbert Edward 1922- WhoAm 94
String, John F. 1946- WhoAm 94
Stringbean 1915-1973 WhoCom
Stringer, Arthur (John Arbuthnott)
1874-1956 EncSF 93
Stringer, C. Vivian 1948- WhoBlA 94
Stringer, Donald (Edgar) 1930- Who 94
Stringer, Donald Arthur 1922- Who 94
Stringer, Drennon Durwood, Jr. 1954-
WhoMW 93
Stringer, Emerson WhoAmP 93
Stringer, Harold 1944- WhoAmP 93
Stringer, Howard 1942- ConTFT 11,
IntMPA 94, WhoAm 94
Stringer, John 1934- WhoScEn 94
Stringer, Johnny William 1950-
WhoAmP 93
Stringer, Kenneth Dale 1949-
WhoMW 93
Stringer, Mary Evelyn 1921- WhoAm 94,
WhoAmA 93
Stringer, Melvin, Sr. 1927- WhoBlA 94
Stringer, Michael WhoHol 92
Stringer, Moses fl. 1695-1714 DcNaB MP
Stringer, Nelson Howard, Jr. 1948-
WhoBlA 94
Stringer, Pamela Mary 1928- Who 94
Stringer, Samuel 1734-1817 WhAmRev
Stringer, Scott WhoAmP 93
Stringer, Thomas Edward, Sr. 1944-
WhoBlA 94
Stringer, William Jeremy 1944-
WhoWest 94

Stringfellow, David John 1946- WhoFI 94
Stringfellow, Eric DeVaughn 1960- WhoBlA 94
Stringfellow, Gerald B. 1942- WhoAm 94
Stringfellow, John 1799-1883 DcNaB MP
Stringfield, Charles David 1939- WhoAm 94
Stringfield, Hezz, Jr. 1921- WhoAm 94
Stringham, Luther Winters 1915- WhoAm 94
Stringham, Norma 1944- WhoMW 93
Stripling, Hortense M. 1950- WhoHisp 94
Stripling, Luther 1935- WhoBlA 94
Stripp, John E. WhoAmP 93
Strisik, Paul 1918- WhoAm 94, WhoAmA 93
Stritch, C. Donald 1931- WhoAmP 93
Stritch, Elaine 1925- IntWW 93, WhoHol 92
Stritch, Elaine 1926- IntMPA 94, NewYTBS 93 [port]
Strittmatter, Erwin 1912- IntWW 93
Strittmatter, Jere L. 1950- WhoAmP 93
Strittmatter, Peter Albert 1939- WhoAm 94, WhoScEn 94, WhoWest 94
Strizek, Norman Francis 1947- WhoAmL 94
Strizich, William S. 1949- WhoAmP 93
Strnat, Karl Josef 1929-1992 WhAm 10
Strobeck, Charles LeRoy 1928- WhoMW 93
Strobel, David Allen 1942- WhoAm 94, WhoScEn 94, WhoWest 94
Strobel, Kate 1907- IntWW 93
Strobel, Martin Allen 1940- WhoAm 94, WhoAmL 94, WhoFI 94
Strobel, Otto 1895-1953 NewGrDO
Strobel, Pamela B. 1952- WhoAm 94
Strobel, Richard Charles 1963- WhoAmL 94
Strobel, Rudolf Gottfried Karl 1927- WhoMW 93
Strobel, Russ M. 1952- WhoAm 94, WhoAmL 94
Strober, Samuel 1940- WhoAm 94, WhoWest 94
Strobl, Gottlieb Maximilian 1916- IntWW 93
Strobl, K.H. EncSF 93
Strobl, Rudolf 1954- WhoMW 93
Stroblas, Laurie DrAPF 93
Stroble, Larry James 1949- WhoAm 94, WhoAmL 94
Stroble, Robert Eugene 1940- WhoAmP 93
Strock, David Randolph 1944- WhoWest 94
Strock, Herbert L. 1918- IntMPA 94
Strock, Herbert Leonard 1918- WhoAm 94
Strock, James M. 1956- WhoAmP 93
Strock, James Martin 1956- WhoAm 94
Strock, Marcus Henry 1941- WhoAmL 94
Strock, William C. 1942- WhoAm 94, WhoAmL 94
Strode, Joseph Arlin 1946- WhoAmL 94
Strode, Velma McEwen 1919- WhoBlA 94
Strode, William 1562-1637 DcNaB MP
Strode, William Hall, III 1937- WhoAm 94
Strode, Woody 1914- IntMPA 94, WhoHol 92
Strodel, Robert Carl 1930- WhoAm 94
Stroder, Josef d1993 NewYTBS 93
Stroe, Aurel 1932- NewGrDO
Stroesenreuther, George Dale 1954- WhoAm 94, WhoMW 93
Stroessner, Alfredo 1912- IntWW 93
Stroessner, Robert Joseph 1942-1991 WhoAmA 93N
Stroev, Egor Semenovich 1937- LngBDD
Strogatz, Ian A. L. 1948- WhoAmL 94
Stroger, John Herman, Jr. 1929- WhoBlA 94
Stroger, Todd H. WhoAmP 93
Stroh, Charles 1943- WhoAmA 93
Stroh, Oscar Henry 1908- WhoScEn 94
Stroh, Peter Wetherill 1927- WhoFI 94
Stroh, Raymond Eugene 1942- WhoMW 93
Strohbehn, Edward Allen 1952- WhoFI 94
Strohbehn, John Walter 1936- WhoAm 94
Stroheim, Erich von 1885-1957 AmCulL
Strohl, Joseph Allen 1946- WhoAmP 93
Strohm, Paul Holzworth, Jr. 1938- WhoAm 94
Strohm, Raymond William 1924- WhoFI 94
Strohm, Reinhard 1942- NewGrDO, Who 94
Strohm, Richard Louis 1949- WhoAmL 94
Strohmaier, Alan Howard 1942- WhoFI 94
Strohmaier, Thomas Edward 1943- WhoMW 93
Strohmeier, Karl Wilhelm 1957- WhoMW 93

Strohmeier, Tara WhoHol 92
Strohmer, Gerhard Otto 1953- WhoMW 93
Strohmeyer, John 1924- WhoAm 94, WhoWest 94
Strojny, Norman 1943- WhoScEn 94
Stroke, George Wilhelm 1924- WhoFI 94, WhoScEn 94
Stroke, Hinko Henry 1927- WhoAm 94, WhoScEn 94
Strolin, Maryann 1943- WhoIns 94
Stroll, Edson WhoHol 92
Strolle, Jon Martin 1940- WhoWest 94
Stroller, Louis A. 1942- IntMPA 94
Strom, Arthur Van Waters 1946- WhoWest 94
Strom, Bernhard E. 1947- WhoAmP 93
Strom, Dennis R. 1950- WhoAmP 93
Strom, J. Preston, Jr. 1959- WhoAmL 94
Strom, Lyle Elmer 1925- WhoAm 94, WhoAmL 94, WhoMW 93
Strom, Mark Alan 1962- WhoWest 94
Strom, Michael A. 1952- WhoAmL 94
Strom, Milton Gary 1942- WhoAm 94, WhoAmL 94, WhoFI 94
Strom, Robert 1935- WrDr 94
Strom, Shirley Longeteig 1931- WhoAmP 93
Strom, Stephen Eric 1942- WhoScEn 94
Strom, Yale 1957- ConAu 142
Stroman, Cheryl Delores 1956- WhoBlA 94
Stroman, Kenneth 1948- WhoBlA 94
Stromberg, Anne B. WhoAm 94
Stromberg, Arthur Harold 1928- WhoAm 94
Stromberg, Clifford Douglas 1949- WhoAm 94
Stromberg, Hunt 1894-1968 IntDcF 2-4 [port]
Stromberg, Kirk Lester 1937- WhoFI 94
Stromberg, Roland Nelson 1916- WhoAm 94
Stromberg, Ross Ernest 1940- WhoAm 94
Strombom, Mari Diane 1964- WhoWest 94
Strombotne, Mark Lindsey WhoAmL
Strome, Stephen 1945- WhoAm 94, WhoFI 94, WhoMW 93
Stromer, Delwyn Dean 1930- WhoAmP 93
Stromer, Peter Robert 1929- WhoWest 94
Stromholm, Stig Fredrik 1931- IntWW 93
Strominger, Jack L. 1925- IntWW 93
Strominger, Jack Leonard 1925- WhoScEn 94
Stromme, Floyd J. WhoAmP 93
Stromme, Gary L. 1939- WhoAmL 94, WhoWest 94
Strom-Paikin, Joyce Elizabeth 1946- WhoScEn 94
Stromsdorfer, Ayse Gursel 1946- WhoMW 93
Stromsdorfer, Deborah Ann 1961- WhoAmA 93
Stromsodt, Mark L. 1965- WhoMW 93
Stronach, David Brian 1931- Who 94
Stronach, Frank WhoAm 94, WhoFI 94
Strone, Michael Jonathan 1953- WhoAmL 94
Strong, Amanda L. 1935- WhoBlA 94
Strong, Arnold ConTFT 11, WhoHol 92
Strong, Arturo Carrillo 1930- WhoHisp 94
Strong, Augustus Hopkins 1836-1921 DcAmReB 2
Strong, Beatrice Marie 1910- WhoAmP 93
Strong, Beverly Jean WhoAmA 93
Strong, Blondell McDonald 1943- WhoBlA 94
Strong, Brett-Livingstone 1953- WhoAmA 93
Strong, Charles Ralph 1938- WhoAmA 93
Strong, Craig Stephen 1947- WhoBlA 94
Strong, David WhoHol 92
Strong, David F. 1944- IntWW 93, WhoAm 94
Strong, David Malcolm 1913- Who 94
Strong, Debra Kay 1954- WhoWest 94
Strong, Don R. 1939- WhoAmP 93
Strong, Dorothy Swearengen 1934- WhoMW 93
Strong, Douglas Donald 1938- WhoBlA 94
Strong, Edward William 1901-1990 WhAm 10
Strong, Eithne 1923- BlmGWL [port], WrDr 94
Strong, Eugene d1962 WhoHol 92
Strong, Gary Eugene 1944- WhoAm 94, WhoWest 94
Strong, George Gordon, Jr. 1947- WhoAmL 94, WhoFI 94
Strong, George Hotham 1926- WhoFI 94
Strong, George Walter 1937- WhoFI 94
Strong, Helen Francine 1947- WhoBlA 94
Strong, Henry 1923- WhoAm 94
Strong, Herbert E., Jr. 1925- WhoMW 93
Strong, James R. 1921- WhoAmP 93
Strong, Jane DrAPF 93

Strong, Jay d1953 WhoHol 92
Strong, Jedediah 1738-1802 WhAmRev
Strong, Jerome Anton 1947- WhoAmP 93
Strong, John IntMPA 94
Strong, John Anderson 1915- Who 94
Strong, John Clifford 1922- Who 94
Strong, John D. 1936- WhoIns 94
Strong, John David 1936- WhoAm 94, WhoMW 93
Strong, John Donovan 1905-1992 WhAm 10
Strong, John Oliver 1930- WhoWest 94
Strong, John Scott 1956- WhoFI 94
Strong, John William 1935- WhoAm 94
Strong, Jonathan DrAPF 93
Strong, Josiah 1847-1916 DcAmReB 2
Strong, Julia Trevelyan Who 94
Strong, Ken d1979 ProFbHF
Strong, Kent 1948- WhoIns 94
Strong, Lennox GayLL
Strong, Leonard d1980 WhoHol 92
Strong, Leonell C(larence) 1894- WhAm 10
Strong, Leslie 1953- WhoAmA 93
Strong, Liam 1945- Who 94
Strong, Liam (Gerald Porter) 1945- IntWW 93
Strong, Marilyn Terry 1929- WhoWest 94
Strong, Maurice F. 1929- IntWW 93, Who 94
Strong, Maurice Frederick 1929- WhoAm 94, WhoFI 94
Strong, Mayda Nel 1942- WhoWest 94
Strong, Mervyn Stuart 1924- WhoAm 94
Strong, Michael d1980 WhoHol 92
Strong, Otis Reginald, III 1954- WhoBlA 94
Strong, Pamela Kay 1950- WhoWest 94
Strong, Pat 1922- WrDr 94
Strong, Pearl WhoAmP 93
Strong, Peter E. 1930- WhoBlA 94
Strong, Peter Hansen 1952- WhoAm 94
Strong, Porter d1923 WhoHol 92
Strong, Richard Allen 1930- WhoScEn 94
Strong, Robert Campbell 1915- WhoAmP 93
Strong, Robert S. 1949- WhoAm 94
Strong, Roy (Colin) 1935- Who 94, WrDr 94
Strong, Roy Colin 1935- IntWW 93
Strong, Stacie 1965- ConAu 141, SmATA 74 [port]
Strong, Steve d1975 WhoHol 92
Strong, Susan 1870-1946 NewGrDO
Strong, Susan 1927- WrDr 94
Strong, Susan Clancey 1939- WhoFI 94
Strong, Thomas Fremont 1946- WhoWest 94
Strong, Thomas Gorman 1931- WhoAmL 94
Strong, Walter L. WhoBlA 94
Strong, Warren Robert 1933- WhoAm 94
Strong, William L., III 1932- WhoAm 94
Strong, William R. 1943- WhoAmP 93
Stronge, Christopher James 1933- Who 94
Stronge, James Anselan Maxwell 1946- Who 94
Stronge, James Jonathan 1931- WhoFI 94
Strongheart, Nipo d1966 WhoHol 92
Stronghilos, Carol WhoAmA 93
Strongin, Daniel Otto 1951- WhoWest 94
Strongin, Lynn DrAPF 93
Strongin, Theodore 1918- WhoAm 94
Strongi'th'arm EncSF 93
Strong Man of the Pen, The BlkWr 2
Stroock, Daniel Wyler 1940- WhoAm 94
Stroock, Gloria WhoHol 92
Stroock, Mark Edwin, II 1922- WhoAm 94
Stroock, Thomas F. 1925- WhoAmP 93
Stroock, Thomas Frank 1925- WhoAm 94, WhoWest 94
Stroop, William George 1952- WhoAm 94
Strop, Hans Robert 1931- WhoMW 93
Strope, Dora Diaz 1943- WhoHisp 94
Stropp, Robert H., Jr. 1947- WhoAmL 94
Stroppel, Betty Macnair 1927- WhoAmA 93
Strosahl, William 1910- WhoAmA 93
Strosahl, William Austin 1910- WhoAm 94
Stroschein, Sharon Marie 1944- WhoAmP 93, WhoMW 93
Stroscio, Michael Anthony 1949- WhoAm 94
Stross, Jeoffrey Knight 1941- WhoAm 94
Strossen, Nadine WhoWomW 91
Strossen, Nadine 1950- WhoAm 94, WhoAmL 94
Strote, Joel Richard 1939- WhoAm 94
Strother, Bernard WhoHol 92
Strother, Joseph Willis 1933- WhoAmA 93
Strother, Lynn Brehm 1951- WhoWest 94
Strother, Patrick Joseph 1953- WhoFI 94
Strother, Virginia Vaughn 1920- WhoAmA 93
Strothman, James Edward 1939- WhoAm 94
Strothman, Wendy Jo 1950- WhoAm 94

Strothmann, Fred 1880-1958 WhoAmA 93N
Stroud, Albert EncSF 93
Stroud, Clarence d1973 WhoHol 92
Stroud, Claude d1985 WhoHol 92
Stroud, Debra Sue 1954- WhoScEn 94
Stroud, Denise E. 1950- WhoMW 93
Stroud, Derek H. Who 94
Stroud, Don 1937- IntMPA 94, WhoHol 92
Stroud, Dorothy Nancy 1910- Who 94
Stroud, Drew McCord DrAPF 93
Stroud, Duke WhoHol 92
Stroud, Eric Who 94
Stroud, (Charles) Eric 1924- Who 94
Stroud, Ernest Charles Frederick 1931- Who 94
Stroud, Herschel Leon 1930- WhoMW 93
Stroud, Howard Burnett, Sr. 1939- WhoBlA 94
Stroud, James Bart 1897-1989 WhAm 10
Stroud, James Stanley 1915- WhoAm 94
Stroud, Joe Hinton 1936- WhoAm 94
Stroud, John Franklin 1922- WhoScEn 94
Stroud, John Fred, Jr. 1931- WhoAm 94
Stroud, Karen 1956- WhoIns 94
Stroud, Lawrence Lowell 1935- WhoBlA 94
Stroud, Louis Winston 1946- WhoBlA 94
Stroud, Milton WhoBlA 94
Stroud, Peter Anthony 1921- WhoAmA 93
Stroud, Richard Hamilton 1918- WhoAm 94
Stroud, Robert Edward 1934- WhoAm 94, WhoAmL 94
Stroud, Robert Lee, Jr. 1962- WhoWest 94
Stroud, Robert Michael 1942- WhoAm 94
Stroud, Sally Ann WhoHol 92
Stroud, Sally Dawley 1947- WhoScEn 94
Stroudley, William 1833-1889 DcNaB MP
Strouf, Brenda K. 1956- WhoAmP 93
Strougal, Lubomir 1924- IntWW 93
Strougal, Patricia Greganti 1920- WhoAmL 94
Strougo, Robert 1943- WhoAmL 94
Strouhal, Eugen 1931- ConAu 140
Stroup, David Richard 1954- WhoScEn 94
Stroup, Don WhoHol 92
Stroup, Dorothy DrAPF 93
Stroup, Elizabeth Faye 1939- WhoWest 94
Stroup, Herbert 1916- WrDr 94
Stroup, Kala Mays WhoMW 93
Stroup, Richard Lyndell 1943- WhoAm 94, WhoWest 94
Stroup, Robert Lee, II 1941- WhoAmL 94
Stroup, Stanley Stephenson 1944- WhoAm 94, WhoAmL 94
Stroupe, Henry Smith 1914- WhoAm 94
Stroupe, Odes Lawrence, Jr. 1946- WhoAmL 94
Strouse, Charles 1928- ConTFT 11
Strouse, Charles (Louis) 1928- NewGrDO
Strouse, Joseph L. 1955- WhoFI 94
Strouse, Norman H. d1993 NewYTBS 93 [port]
Strouse, Norman H(ulbert) 1906-1993 CurBio 93N
Strout, Barbara E. WhoAmP 93
Strout, Donald A. WhoAmP 93
Strout, Richard Lee 1898-1990 WhAm 10
Strout, Richard Robert 1932- WhoAm 94
Strout, Sewall Cushing, Jr. 1923- WhoAm 94
Strow, Marcia Ann WhoMW 93
Strowger, (Gaston) Jack 1916- Who 94
Stroyan, Ronald Angus Ropner 1924- Who 94
Stroyberg, Annette WhoHol 92
Stroyd, Arthur Heister 1945- WhoAm 94, WhoAmL 94
Strozier, Yvonne Iglehart 1938- WhoBlA 94
Strozzi, Giulio 1583-1652 NewGrDO
Strubbe, John Lewis 1921- WhoAm 94
Strubbe, Thomas Franklin 1937- WhoMW 93
Strubbe, Thomas R. 1940- WhoAm 94
Strubbe, William Burrows 1952- WhoAmL 94
Strubel, Ella Doyle 1940- WhoAm 94
Strubel, Richard Perry 1939- WhoAm 94
Struble, Donald Edward 1942- WhoScEn 94
Struble, Gordon Lee 1937- WhoScEn 94
Struble, Laura May 1957- WhoMW 93
Struble, Leslie Jeanne 1947- WhoScEn 94
Struble, Robert John 1963- WhoFI 94
Struble, Thelma Pauline 1934- WhoMW 93
Struchkova, Raisa 1925- IntDcB [port]
Struchkova, Raisa Stepanovna 1925- IntWW 93
Struck, John Seward 1952- WhoFI 94
Struck, Karin 1947- BlmGWL
Struck, Norma Johansen WhoAmA 93
Struckhoff, Ronald Robert 1947- WhoScEn 94

Struck-Marcell, Curtis 1954- WhoMW 93
Struckmeyer, Fred C., Jr. 1912- WhoAmP 93
Strudler, Robert Jacob 1942- WhoFI 94
Strudwick, Arthur Sidney Ronald 1921- Who 94
Strudwick, John Philip 1914- Who 94
Strudwick, Lindsey H., Sr. 1946- WhoBlA 94
Strudwick, Lindsey Howard 1946- WhoWest 94
Strudwick, Shepperd d1983 WhoHol 92
Strudwick, Warren James 1923- WhoBlA 94
Struebing, Robert Virgil 1919- WhoAm 94
Struecker, Gerhard 1954- WhoScEn 94
Struelens, Michel Maurice Joseph Georges 1928- WhoAm 94
Strugala, Barbara Weber 1954- WhoFI 94
Strugatski, Arkady (Natanovich) 1925-1991 EncSF 93
Strugatski, Boris (Natanovich) 1931- EncSF 93
Strugatsky, Boris Natanovich 1933- IntWW 93
Struggles, John Edward 1913- WhoAm 94
Struhl, Kevin 1952- WhoScEn 94
Struhl, Stanley Frederick 1939- WhoWest 94
Struif, Leo James 1931- WhoAmL 94, WhoMW 93
Struik, Ruth Rebekka 1928- WhoWest 94
Strukoff, Rudolf Stephen 1935- WhoAm 94, WhoMW 93
Strul, Gene M. 1927- WhoFI 94
Strull, Gene 1929- WhoAm 94
Strum, Brian J. 1939- WhoAm 94, WhoFI 94
Strum, Jay Gerson 1938- WhoAm 94, WhoAmL 94
Strum, Lonny Robert 1952- WhoAm 94
Strumingher, Laura Sharon 1945- WhoAm 94
Struminsky, Vladimir Vasiliyevich 1914- IntWW 93
Strungk, Nicolaus Adam 1640?-1700 NewGrDO
Strunk, Herbert Julian 1891- WhoAmA 93N
Strunk, Klaus Albert 1930- IntWW 93
Strunk, Mary Dolores 1912- WhoMW 93
Strunk, Orlo Christopher, Jr. 1925- WhoAm 94
Strupp, David John 1938- WhoAm 94
Strupp, Hans Hermann 1921- WhoAm 94
Strupp, Janet Kaye 1947- WhoMW 93
Struppeck, Jules 1915- WhoAmA 93
Strus, George WhoHol 92
Struss, Karl 1886-1981 IntDcF 2-4
Struthers, Allan Alexander 1964- WhoMW 93
Struthers, Ralph Charles 1933- WhoFI 94, WhoWest 94
Struthers, Sally 1947- IntMPA 94, WhoCom
Struthers, Sally 1948- WhoHol 92
Strutt Who 94
Strutt, John William 1842-1919 WorScD
Strutt, Nigel (Edward) 1916- Who 94
Strutton, Bill 1918- WrDr 94
Strutton, Larry D. 1940- WhoWest 94
Strutz, William A. 1934- WhoAmL 94
Strutzel, Jod Christopher 1947- WhoWest 94
Struve, Guy Miller 1943- WhoAm 94, WhoAmL 94
Struve, William Walter 1936- WhoAmA 93
Struyk, Raymond J(ay) 1944- WrDr 94
Struyk, Robert John 1932- WhoAm 94
Strycker, Steve Lynn 1962- WhoFI 94
Stryer, Lubert 1938- WhoAm 94, WhoScEn 94
Strygler, Bernardo 1959- WhoWest 94
Stryk, Lucien DrAPF 93
Stryk, Lucien 1924- WrDr 94
Stryker, Amy WhoHol 92
Stryker, Christopher d1987 WhoHol 92
Stryker, Daniel EncSF 93
Stryker, Daniel 1946- WrDr 94
Stryker, Dennis James 1958- WhoAmL 94
Stryker, Hal EncSF 93
Stryker, Jack WhoHol 92
Stryker, James William 1940- WhoMW 93
Stryker, Phillip Gene 1941- WhoMW 93
Stryker, Richard Ripley, Jr. 1948- WhoAm 94
Stryker, Steven Charles 1944- WhoAm 94, WhoAmL 94, WhoFI 94
Strzelchik, Vladislav Ignatevich 1921- IntWW 93
Strzelczyk, Robert Edward 1920- WhoMW 93
Strzembosz, Adam Justyn 1930- IntWW 93
Stuart Who 94
Stuart, Viscount 1953- Who 94
Stuart, Alex R. EncSF 93
Stuart, Alex R. 1947- WrDr 94
Stuart, Alexander 1955- WrDr 94
Stuart, Alexander Friedlander 1955- WhoAmL 94
Stuart, Alice Melissa 1957- WhoAmL 94, WhoFI 94
Stuart, Amy WhoHol 92
Stuart, Andrew Christopher 1928- Who 94
Stuart, Antony James Cobham E. Who 94
Stuart, Arabella 1576-1615 BlmGWL
Stuart, Arlen WhoHol 92
Stuart, Barbara WhoHol 92
Stuart, Barbara Gregg 1949- WhoAmL 94
Stuart, Ben R. WhoAm 94, WhoFI 94
Stuart, Binkie 1932- WhoHol 92
Stuart, Brian Michael 1961- WhoWest 94
Stuart, Carole 1941- WhoAm 94
Stuart, Cassie WhoHol 92
Stuart, Charles Edward 1942- WhoScEn 94
Stuart, Charles Rowell d1993 Who 94N
Stuart, Dabney DrAPF 93
Stuart, Dabney 1937- WrDr 94
Stuart, David d1984 WhoAmA 93N
Stuart, David Edward 1945- WhoWest 94
Stuart, Derald Archie 1925- WhoAm 94
Stuart, Don A. EncSF 93
Stuart, Donald d1944 WhoHol 92
Stuart, Donald Alexander 1944- WhoAmA 93
Stuart, Dorothy Mae 1933- WhoWest 94
Stuart, Duncan 1934- Who 94
Stuart, Elsie Sutherland Rast 1931- WhoAmP 93
Stuart, Eugene Page 1927- WhoAmP 93
Stuart, Floyd C. DrAPF 93
Stuart, Francis 1902- IntWW 93, Who 94
Stuart, (Henry) Francis (Montgomery) 1902- EncSF 93, WrDr 94
Stuart, Gary Lester 1939- WhoAmL 94, WhoWest 94
Stuart, Gary Miller 1940- WhoAm 94, WhoFI 94
Stuart, George, Jr. 1946- WhoAmP 93
Stuart, George Hay 1816-1890 DcAmReB 2
Stuart, George Michel 1963- WhoWest 94
Stuart, Gerard William, Jr. 1939- WhoFI 94, WhoWest 94
Stuart, Gil d1977 WhoHol 92
Stuart, Gilbert 1755-1828 WhAmRev
Stuart, Gilbert 1785-1825 AmRev
Stuart, Gilbert Charles 1755-1828 AmCulL
Stuart, Gloria 1910- WhoHol 92
Stuart, Gordon Edgar 1951- WhoMW 93
Stuart, Harold Cutliff 1912- WhoAm 94, WhoAmL 94
Stuart, Herbert Akroyd 1864-1927 DcNaB MP
Stuart, Herbert James 1926- Who 94
Stuart, Ian EncSF 93
Stuart, Ian 1927-1993 WrDr 94N
Stuart, Iris d1936 WhoHol 92
Stuart, Ivan I. WhoBlA 94
Stuart, Jacqueline WhoAmA 93
Stuart, James 1843-1913 DcNaB MP
Stuart, James 1917- WhoAm 94
Stuart, James Beecher d1993 NewYTBS 93
Stuart, James Davies 1941- WhoScEn 94
Stuart, James Donald 1939- WhoMW 93
Stuart, James Fortier 1928- WhoAm 94
Stuart, James Milton 1932-1992 WhAm 10
Stuart, Jane c. 1654-1742 DcNaB MP
Stuart, Jay William 1924- WhoScEn 94
Stuart, Jean d1926 WhoHol 92
Stuart, Jeanne 1908- WhoHol 92
Stuart, Jeb 1833-1864 HisWorL [port]
Stuart, John WhAmRev
Stuart, John d1979 WhoHol 92
Stuart, John c. 1710-1779 WhAmRev
Stuart, John 1718-1779 AmRev
Stuart, John Crichton- 1793-1848 DcNaB MP
Stuart, John M. 1927- WhoFI 94
Stuart, John Malcolm 1946- WhoAmL 94
Stuart, John McDouall 1815-1866 WhWE
Stuart, John McHugh, Jr. 1916- WhoAm 94
Stuart, John Trevor 1929- Who 94
Stuart, Joseph B. Who 94
Stuart, Joseph Martin 1932- WhoAmA 93, WhoMW 93
Stuart, Keith Who 94
Stuart, (James) Keith 1940- Who 94
Stuart, Kenneth (Lamonte) 1920- Who 94
Stuart, Kenneth J. d1993 NewYTBS 93
Stuart, Kenneth James 1905- WhoAm 94, WhoAmA 93
Stuart, Kenneth Lamonte 1920- IntWW 93
Stuart, Laura Jean 1961- WhoFI 94
Stuart, Lawrence David, Jr. 1944- WhoAm 94, WhoAmL 94
Stuart, Leslie d1978 WhoHol 92
Stuart, Lyle 1922- IntWW 93, WhoAm 94
Stuart, Madge 1897- WhoHol 92
Stuart, Marian Elizabeth 1944- Who 94
Stuart, Marjorie Mann 1921- WhoBlA 94
Stuart, Mark M. Who 94
Stuart, Marty 1958- WhoAm 94
Stuart, Mary BlmGWL, WhoAm 94
Stuart, Mary 1929- WhoHol 92
Stuart, Maxine WhoHol 92
Stuart, Michael Francis Harvey 1926- Who 94
Stuart, Michelle 1940- WhoAmA 93
Stuart, Moses 1780-1852 DcAmReB 2
Stuart, Murray Who 94
Stuart, (Charles) Murray 1933- Who 94
Stuart, Nicholas WhoHol 92
Stuart, Nicholas Willoughby 1942- Who 94
Stuart, Nick d1973 WhoHol 92
Stuart, Patrick 1966- WhoHol 92
Stuart, Peter Paul 1945- WhoFI 94
Stuart, Philip 1760-1830 WhAmRev
Stuart, Phillip (Luttrell) 1937- Who 94
Stuart, Ralph d1952 WhoHol 92
Stuart, Raymond Wallace 1941- WhoAmL 94
Stuart, Reginald A. 1948- WhoBlA 94
Stuart, Robert 1785-1848 WhWE
Stuart, Robert 1921- WhoAm 94, WhoFI 94
Stuart, Robert Crampton 1938- WhoAm 94
Stuart, Robert D., Jr. 1916- WhoAmP 93
Stuart, Robert Douglas, Jr. 1916- IntWW 93
Stuart, Sandra Joyce 1950- WhoFI 94, WhoMW 93, WhoScEn 94
Stuart, Sarah Payne 1952- WrDr 94
Stuart, Sidney EncSF 93
Stuart, Sidney 1924- WrDr 94
Stuart, Signe Nelson WhoAmA 93
Stuart, Simeon, Sir d1939 WhoHol 92
Stuart, Simon 1930- WrDr 94
Stuart, W.J. EncSF 93
Stuart, Walker Dabney, III 1937- WhoAm 94
Stuart, Walter Bynum, III 1922- WhoAm 94
Stuart, Walter Bynum, IV 1946- WhoAm 94, WhoAmL 94
Stuart, William Corwin 1920- WhoAm 94, WhoAmL 94, WhoMW 93
Stuart, William Moore 1896- WhAm 10
Stuart, William Roy 1972- WhoWest 94
Stuart-Cole, James d1992 Who 94N
Stuart-Fife, John T. d1981 WhoHol 92
Stuart-Forbes, Charles Edward Who 94
Stuart-Harris, Charles (Herbert) 1909- Who 94
Stuart-Menteth, James Who 94
Stuart-Moore, Michael 1944- Who 94
Stuart Of Findhorn, Viscount 1924- Who 94
Stuart-Paul, Ronald (Ian) 1934- Who 94
Stuart-Shaw, Max 1912- Who 94
Stuart-Smith, James 1919- Who 94
Stuart-Smith, Murray 1927- Who 94
Stuart Taylor, Nicholas (Richard) 1952- Who 94
Stuart-White, Christopher (Stuart) 1933- Who 94
Stuban, Michael L. 1958- WhoAmP 93
Stuban, Ted 1928- WhoAmP 93
Stubbe, JoAnne WhoAm 94, WhoScEn 94
Stubbeman, David WhoAmP 93
Stubberud, Allen Roger 1934- WhoAm 94, WhoScEn 94
Stubbes, Katherine Emmes c. 1571-1590 BlmGWL
Stubbes, Philip 1555?-1611? BlmGEL
Stubbins, Hugh A., Jr. 1912- WhoAm 94
Stubbins, Sara Louise 1947- WhoMW 93
Stubblebine, James Harvey 1920-1987 WhoAmA 93N
Stubblebine, Warren 1917- WhoMW 93
Stubblefield, Frank Milton, Jr. 1935- WhoMW 93
Stubblefield, (Cyril) James 1901- Who 94
Stubblefield, James Bert, Jr. 1934- WhoAm 94
Stubblefield, James Irvin 1953- WhoScEn 94, WhoWest 94
Stubblefield, Jennye Washington 1925- WhoBlA 94
Stubblefield, Joseph Stephen 1947- WhoAmL 94
Stubblefield, Page Kindred 1914- WhoAm 94
Stubblefield, Raymond M. 1945- WhoBlA 94
Stubblefield, Thomas Mason 1922- WhoWest 94
Stubbs, Archie Roy 1910- WhoAmP 93
Stubbs, Daniel, II 1965- WhoBlA 94
Stubbs, Daniel Gaie 1940- WhoWest 94
Stubbs, Genevieve Graffeo 1956- WhoAmL 94
Stubbs, George Winston 1942- WhoBlA 94
Stubbs, Harold K. 1940- WhoBlA 94
Stubbs, Harry d1950 WhoHol 92
Stubbs, Harry Clement 1922- WrDr 94
Stubbs, Imogen 1961- IntMPA 94, WhoHol 92
Stubbs, James (Wilfrid) 1910- Who 94
Stubbs, James Carlton 1924- WhoAm 94
Stubbs, Jan Didra 1937- WhoFI 94, WhoMW 93
Stubbs, Jean 1926- ConAu 43NR, WrDr 94
Stubbs, John F. A. H. Who 94
Stubbs, Judy Hertz 1946- WhoAmP 93
Stubbs, Kendon Lee 1938- WhoAm 94
Stubbs, Levi WhoBlA 94
Stubbs, Levi 1938- See Four Tops, The ConMus 11
Stubbs, Lu 1925- WhoAmA 93
Stubbs, Mark Darwin 1950- WhoAmP 93, WhoWest 94
Stubbs, Michael Wesley 1947- Who 94
Stubbs, Nancy Sheridan 1934- WhoFI 94
Stubbs, Peter Charles 1937- WrDr 94
Stubbs, Randall Arthur 1952- WhoWest 94
Stubbs, Robert G. 1932- WhoAmP 93
Stubbs, Thomas 1926- Who 94
Stubbs, Una 1937- WhoHol 92
Stubbs, W. Terrell WhoAmP 93
Stubbs, William Frederick 1934- Who 94
Stubbs, William Hamilton 1937- Who 94
Stubbs, William Maynard 1926- WhoFI 94
Stuber, Charles William 1931- WhoAm 94, WhoScEn 94
Stublarec, Stephen 1950- WhoAmL 94
Stuck, Haven Laurence 1946- WhoAmL 94
Stuck, Jean-Baptiste 1680-1755 NewGrDO
Stuck, Roger Dean 1924- WhoScEn 94
Stuckeman, Herman Campbell 1914- WhoAm 94
Stucker, Stephen d1986 WhoHol 92
Stuckert, Gregory Kent 1963- WhoScEn 94
Stuckey, John WhoAmP 93
Stuckey, Kent Duane 1957- WhoAmL 94
Stuckey, Scott Sherwood 1956- WhoAm 94
Stuckey, Wayne Keith 1940- WhoWest 94
Stuckey, Williamson Sylvester, Jr. 1935- WhoAmP 93
Stuckgold, Grete 1895-1977 NewGrDO
Stucki, Eugene B. WhoAmP 93
Stucki, Spencer Eugene 1943- WhoAmP 93
Stucklen, Richard 1916- IntWW 93, Who 94
Stuckwisch, Clarence George 1916- WhoAm 94
Stucky, Nathan Paul 1950- WhoMW 93
Stucky, Solomon 1923-1988 ConAu 140
Stucky, Steven Edward 1949- WhoAm 94
Stucley, Hugh (George Coplestone Bampfylde) 1945- Who 94
Studd, Charles Thomas 1860-1931 DcNaB MP
Studd, Edward (Fairfax) 1929- Who 94
Studd, Peter Malden 1916- Who 94
Studdert Kennedy, Geoffrey Anketell 1883-1929 DcNaB MP
Studdert-Kennedy, (William) Gerald 1933- WrDr 94
Studds, Gerry E. 1937- CngDr 93
Studds, Gerry Eastman 1937- WhoAm 94, WhoAmP 93
Stude, Everett Wilson, Jr. 1939- WhoAm 94
Studebaker, Glenn Wayne 1939- WhoMW 93
Studebaker, Irving Glen 1931- WhoWest 94
Studebaker, John Milton 1935- WhoScEn 94
Studebaker, William DrAPF 93
Studeman, William Oliver 1940- WhoAm 94
Studemeister, Paul Alexander 1954- WhoWest 94
Studenikin, Mitrofan Yakovlevich 1923- IntWW 93
Studer, Cheryl 1955- NewGrDO
Studer, Constance E. DrAPF 93
Studer, Ginny 1943- WhoAm 94
Studer, James Edward 1961- WhoScEn 94
Studer, Patricia S. 1942- WhoMW 93
Studer, William Allen 1939- WhoAm 94
Studer, William Joseph 1936- WhoAm 94
Studer, William P. 1941- WhoAmL 94
Studholme, Henry (William) 1958- Who 94
Studier, Frederick William 1936- WhoAm 94, WhoScEn 94
Studley, Helen Ormson 1937- WhoWest 94

Suarez del Otero, Concha 1908- BlmGWL
Suárez-Herrero, Ismael 1949- WhoHisp 94
Suarez Lynch, B. ConAu 43NR, ConWorW 93, RfGShF
Suarez Miramonte, Luis 1935- WorESoc
Suarez-Murias, Marguerite C. 1921- WhoAm 94
Suarez-Quian, Carlos Andrés 1953- WhoHisp 94, WhoScEn 94
Suárez-Rivero, Eliana 1940- WhoHisp 94
Suarez Solis, Sara BlmGWL
Suarez-Villa, Luis 1947- WhoFI 94, WhoHisp 94
Suave, Jeanne 1922-1993 NewYTBS 93
Suazo, Pete 1951- WhoAmP 93
Suba, Antonio Ronquillo 1927- WhoAm 94
Suba, Steven Antonio 1957- WhoScEn 94
Suba, Susanne WhoAmA 93
Subach, James Alan 1948- WhoWest 94
Subadya, Kornelius Tjandra 1958- WhoWest 94
Subak, John Thomas 1929- WhoAm 94, WhoAmL 94
Subak-Sharpe, Gerald Emil 1925- WhoAm 94
Subak-Sharpe, John Herbert 1924- Who 94
Subandrio, Dr. 1914- IntWW 93
Subasic, Christine Ann 1966- WhoScEn 94
Subba Row, Raman 1932- Who 94
Subbaswamy, Kumble Ramarao 1951- WhoAsA 94
Subbulakshmi, Madurai Shanmugavadivu 1916- IntWW 93
Subbuswamy, Muthuswamy 1938- WhoScEn 94
Suber, Fate, Jr. 1954- WhoFI 94
Suber, Martin Gay 1937- WhoAmP 93
Suber, Robin Hall 1952- WhoWest 94
Suber, Tommie Lee 1947- WhoMW 93
Subervi-Vélez, Federico Antonio 1949- WhoHisp 94
Subin, Florence 1935- WhoAmL 94
Su Bingqi WhoPRCh 91
Subira (Puig), Jose 1882-1980 NewGrDO
Subirana, Juan Antonio 1936- WhoScEn 94
Subject, Evelyn d1975 WhoHol 92
Subkowsky, Elizabeth 1949- WhoMW 93
Subler, Alice Ellen 1935- WhoMW 93
Subler, Edward Pierre 1927- WhoAm 94
Sublet, Marie-Josephe 1936- WhoWomW 91
Sublett, Carl C. 1919- WhoAmA 93
Sublett, Carl Cecil 1919- WhoAm 94
Sublett, Charles William, Jr. WhoAmP 93
Sublett, Henry Lee, Jr. 1926- WhoAm 94
Sublett, John W. d1986 WhoHol 92
Sublett, Norma Raedean 1925- WhoAmP 93
Sublette, Walter DrAPF 93
Sublette, William E. WhoAmP 93
Sublette, William Lewis 1799-1845 WhWE
Subligny, Marie-Therese 1666-1735 IntDcB [port]
Subotnick, Morton 1933- WhoAm 94
Subotnick, Morton Leon 1933- IntWW 93
Subraman, Belinda DrAPF 93
Subramani, Suresh 1952- WhoAsA 94
Subramaniam, Chandra Shekar 1952- WhoFI 94
Subramaniam, Chidambaram 1910- IntWW 93, Who 94
Subramaniam, Pramilla N. 1953- WhoAsA 94
Subramaniam, Shivan S. 1949- WhoIns 94
Subramaniam, Shivan Sivaswamy 1949- WhoAm 94
Subramanian, Chelakara Suryanarayanan 1950- WhoScEn 94
Subramanian, Ravanasamudram Venkatachala 1933- WhoWest 94
Subramanian, Sribala 1962- WhoAsA 94
Subramanian, Sundaram 1934- WhoWest 94
Subramanya, Shiva 1933- WhoAsA 94, WhoWest 94
Subramanyan, Kalpathi Ganapathi 1924- IntWW 93
Subroto 1928- IntWW 93
Subryan, Carmen 1944- WhoBlA 94
Subudhi, Manomohan 1946- WhoAsA 94
Su Buqing 1902- IntWW 93, WhoPRCh 91 [port]
Such, Alec Jon c. 1952- See Bon Jovi ConMus 10
Such, Frederick Rudolph Charles 1936- Who 94
Such, Mary Jane 1942- WhoMW 93
Su Changpei 1932- WhoPRCh 91 [port]
Sucharitkul, Sompong 1931- IntWW 93
Sucharitkul, Somtow 1952- WrDr 94
Sucharitkul, Somtow (Papinian) EncSF 93
Sucharow, Lawrence Alan 1949- WhoAmL 94
Suchdolsky, Metod EncSF 93
Suchenek, Marek Andrzej 1949- WhoWest 94
Sucher, Cynthia Clayton Crumb 1943- WhoFI 94
Sucher, Rosa 1849-1927 NewGrDO
Suchet, David WhoHol 92
Suchet, David 1946- Who 94
Suchet, John Aleck 1944- Who 94
Suchlicki, Jaime 1939- WhoHisp 94
Suchocka, Hanna WhoWomW 91
Suchocka, Hanna 1946- IntWW 93, NewYTBS 93 [port]
Suchodolski, Bogdan d1992 IntWW 93N
Suchodolski, Ronald Eugene 1946- WhoAm 94
Suchomel, Jeffrey Raymond 1956- WhoMW 93
Suchon, Eugen 1908- IntWW 93, NewGrDO
Suchora, Daniel Henry 1945- WhoScEn 94
Suchow, Lawrence 1923- WhoScEn 94
Suchting, W. A. 1931- ConAu 142
Suchy, Susanne N. 1945- WhoScEn 94
Suchyta, Casimir John, III 1959- WhoMW 93
Suckewer, Benjamin 1949- WhoAmL 94
Suckiel, Ellen Kappy 1943- WhoAm 94, WhoWest 94
Suckling, Charles W. 1920- IntWW 93
Suckling, Charles Walter 1920- Who 94
Suckling, John 1609-1641 BlmGEL
Suckmann, Erich d1970 WhoHol 92
Suckow, Robert William 1919- WhoMW 93
Sucksdorff, Ake, Mrs. Who 94
Sucksdorff, Arne WhoHol 92
Sucksdorff, Arne Edvard 1917- IntWW 93
Su Cong 1959- WhoPRCh 91 [port]
Sucre, Antonio Jose de 1795-1830 HisWorL [port]
Sucre-Figarella, Jose Francisco 1931- IntWW 93
Suczek, Christopher A. 1942- WhoWest 94
Suda, Stanislav 1865-1931 NewGrDO
Suda, Tatsuya 1953- WhoAsA 94
Suda, Zdenek Ludvik 1920- WrDr 94
Sudak, Howard Stanley 1932- WhoAm 94
Sudan, Ravindra Nath 1931- WhoAm 94, WhoAsA 94, WhoScEn 94
Sudarkasa, Michael Eric Mabogunje 1964- WhoAmL 94, WhoBlA 94
Sudarkasa, Niara 1938- WhoAm 94, WhoBlA 94
Sudarshan, T. S. 1955- WhoAsA 94
Sudarsky, Jerry M. 1918- WhoAm 94, WhoFI 94
Sudbeck, Richard James 1957- WhoWest 94
Sudbery, Rodie 1943- WrDr 94
Sudbury, Archdeacon of Who 94
Sudbury, David Marshall 1945- WhoAm 94
Sudbury, John Dean 1925- WhoAm 94
Sudbury, Leslie G. 1939- WhoBlA 94
Suddaby, Arthur 1919- Who 94
Suddaby, (William) Donald 1900-1964 EncSF 93
Suddards, (Henry) Gaunt d1992 Who 94N
Suddards, Roger Whitley 1930- Who 94
Suddarth, Roscoe Seldon 1935- WhoAmP 93
Sudderth, William H. 1924- WhoBlA 94
Suddick, Patrick Joseph 1923- WhoAm 94
Suddock, Frances Suter Thorson 1914- WhoWest 94
Suddock, Richard Bruce 1962- WhoFI 94
Sudeary, Abdelmuhsin M. Al- 1936- IntWW 93
Sudeley, Baron 1939- Who 94
Suder, Robert Braswell 1945- WhoAmL 94
Sudermann, Hermann 1857-1928 IntDcT 2
Sudhakaran, Gubbi Ramarao 1949- WhoScEn 94
Sudharmono, Gen. 1927- IntWW 93
Sudijono, John Leonard 1966- WhoScEn 94
Sudler, Louis Courtenay 1903- WhoAm 94
Sudlow, Joan d1970 WhoHol 92
Sudlow, Robert N. 1920- WhoAmA 93
Sudman, Susan K. 1949- WhoMW 93
Sudol, Rita A. 1949- WhoHisp 94
Sudol, Walter Edward 1942- WhoAmL 94
Sudomo 1926- IntWW 93
Sudow, Thomas Nisan 1952- WhoMW 93
Sudow, William E. 1945- WhoAmL 94
Sudreau, Pierre Robert 1919- IntWW 93
Suduiko, Ronald Paul 1949- WhoAmP 93
Sudweeks, Walter Bentley 1940- WhoAm 94
Sue, Alan Kwai Keong 1946- WhoAm 94, WhoWest 94
Sue, Lawrence Gene 1939- WhoWest 94
Su'e, Lefao Fuimaono 1930- WhoAmP 93
Suedfeld, Peter 1935- WhoAm 94
Suelflow, August R(obert) 1922- WrDr 94
Suelflow, August Robert 1922- WhoAm 94, WhoMW 93
Suell, Robert May 1917- WhoAmP 93
Sueltenfuss, Elizabeth Anne 1921- WhoAm 94
Suelto, Teem D. 1928- WhoAsA 94
Suelzer, Michael Thomas 1946- WhoMW 93
Suen, Ching Yee 1942- WhoAm 94
Suen, Ching-Yun 1951- WhoAsA 94
Suen, James Yee 1940- WhoAm 94
Suenens, Leo Joseph 1904- Who 94
Suenens, Leo Jozef 1904- IntWW 93
Suenholz, Herman Harry 1924- WhoAm 94
Suenos, Carlos 1952- WhoAmA 93
Suenson-Taylor Who 94
Sueppel, William WhoAmP 93
Suer, Marvin David 1923- WhoAm 94
Suerth, Elizabeth Knittel 1956- WhoMW 93
Sues, Leonard d1971 WhoHol 92
Suess, James Francis 1950- WhoScEn 94
Suessenguth, Walther d1964 WhoHol 92
Suetonius ConAu 140
Suett, Richard 1755-1805 NewGrDO
Suffety, Hamed William, Jr. 1957- WhoAmL 94
Suffian, Tun Mohamed 1917- Who 94
Suffield, Baron 1922- Who 94
Suffield, Frederick Glanville 1920- WhoWest 94
Suffield, (Henry John) Lester 1911- Who 94
Suffling, Mark EncSF 93
Suffolk, Archdeacon of Who 94
Suffolk And Berkshire, Earl of 1935- Who 94
Suffren de Saint-Tropez, Pierre-Andre de 1729-1788 AmRev, WhAmRev
Sufian, Beth Shari 1965- WhoAmL 94
Sufit, Robert Louis 1950- WhoScEn 94
Sufka, Kenneth Joseph 1960- WhoScEn 94
Suflas, Steven William 1951- WhoAmL 94
Sufrin, Barry W. 1948- WhoAmL 94
Sufrin, Mark 1925- SmATA 76
Suga, Hiroshi 1930- WhoScEn 94
Sugai, Kumi 1919- IntWW 93
Su Gang 1920- IntWW 93, WhoPRCh 91 [port]
Sugano, Etsuko 1942- WhoWomW 91
Sugano, Katsuhito 1948- WhoAsA 94
Sugano, Miyoko 1932- WhoAsA 94
Suganuma, Eric Kazuto 1958- WhoWest 94
Sugai, Alan Michael 1947- IntWW 93, Who 94
Sugar, David 1951- WhoAmL 94
Sugar, Jonathan Akiba 1953- WhoMW 93
Sugar, Joseph M. 1922- IntMPA 94
Sugar, Larry 1945- IntMPA 94
Sugar, Paul 1928- WhoAm 94
Sugar, Peter Frigyes 1919- WhoAm 94
Sugar, Robert Joseph 1949- WhoMW 93
Sugarcubes, The ConMus 10 [port]
Sugarman, Alan William 1924- WhoAm 94
Sugarman, Burt IntMPA 94
Sugarman, George 1912- WhoAm 94, WhoAmA 93
Sugarman, Irwin J. 1943- WhoAm 94, WhoAmL 94
Sugarman, Jule M. 1927- WhoAm 94
Sugarman, Jule Meyer 1927- WhoAmP 93
Sugarman, Myron George 1942- WhoAm 94, WhoAmL 94
Sugarman, Nathan 1917-1990 WhAm 10
Sugarman, Paul Ronald 1931- WhoAm 94, WhoAmL 94
Sugarman, Paul William 1947- WhoAm 94, WhoAmL 94
Sugarman, Robert Gary 1939- WhoAm 94, WhoAmL 94
Sugarman, Robert Jay 1938- WhoAm 94
Sugarman, Robert P. 1949- WhoAmL 94
Sugarman, Roger P. 1950- WhoAmL 94
Sugarman, Ronald Samuel 1941- WhoAmL 94
Sugarman, Samuel Louis 1927- WhoAm 94
Sugarman, Suzi Loewenstern 1944- WhoAm 94
Sugawara, Isamu 1949- WhoScEn 94
Sugawara, Sandra Lee 1953- WhoAsA 94
Sugawara, Tamio 1948- WhoScEn 94
Sugden, Arthur 1918- Who 94
Sugden, Francis George 1938- Who 94
Sugden, John Goldthorp 1921- Who 94
Sugden, Richard Lee 1959- WhoMW 93
Sugden, Samuel 1892-1950 DcNaB MP
Sugerman, Abraham Arthur 1929- WhoAm 94, WhoScEn 94
Sugerman, David F. 1959- WhoAmL 94
Sugerman, Lewis Martin 1946- WhoFI 94
Sugerman, Richard Alan 1944- WhoWest 94
Sugg, Aldhelm St. John 1909- Who 94
Sugg, John Logan 1914- WhoAm 94
Sugg, Joyce (Marie) 1926- WrDr 94
Sugg, Margaret Joyce 1929- WhoAmP 93
Sugg, Reed Waller 1952- WhoAmL 94
Sugg, Richard P(eter) 1941- WrDr 94
Sugg, Robert Perkins 1916- WhoAm 94
Suggs, Don 1945- WhoAmA 93
Suggs, Fred Wilson, Jr. 1946- WhoAmL 94
Suggs, Leo H. WhoAm 94, WhoFI 94
Suggs, M(arion) Jack 1924- WrDr 94
Suggs, Marion Jack 1924- WhoAm 94
Suggs, Pat(ricia) Ann 1936- WhoAmA 93
Suggs, Robert Chinelo 1943- WhoBlA 94
Suggs, William Albert 1922- WhoBlA 94
Sughrue, Jack DrAPF 93
Sughrue, Kathryn Eileen WhoAmP 93
Sughrue, Robert Norman 1949- WhoAmL 94
Sugihara, James Masanobu 1918- WhoAsA 94
Sugihara, Jared Genji 1941- WhoAsA 94
Sugihara, Kenzi 1940- WhoAm 94
Sugiki, Shigemi 1936- WhoScEn 94, WhoWest 94
Sugimoto, Yoshio 1939- WrDr 94
Sugimoto Sonoko 1925- BlmGWL
Sugintas, Nora Maria 1956- WhoMW 93
Sugioka, Kenneth 1920- WhoAm 94
Sugioka, Michael Hiroyuki 1948- WhoAsA 94
Sugiura, Binsuke 1911- IntWW 93
Sugiyama, Alan WhoAsA 94
Sugiyama, Kazunori 1950- WhoFI 94, WhoScEn 94
Sugrue, Thomas Joseph 1947- WhoAm 94
Suh, Bernadyn Kim 1940- WhoAsA 94
Suh, Byungse 1941- WhoAsA 94
Suh, Dae-Sook 1931- WhoAsA 94
Suh, Nam Pyo 1936- WhoAm 94, WhoAsA 94
Suh, Yung-Ho 1956- WhoAsA 94
Suhadolnik, Gary C. 1950- WhoAmP 93, WhoMW 93
Suharto, Gen. Who 94
Suharto, Gen. 1921- IntWW 93
Suhartoyo, S. 1926- Who 94
Su He 1925- WhoPRCh 91 [port]
Suhl, Harry 1922- IntWW 93, WhoWest 94
Suhler, John Stuart 1943- WhoAm 94
Suhling, June WhoAmP 93
Su Hongxi WhoPRCh 91
Suhor, Mary Lou 1929- WhoAm 94
Suhoski, Chester A. 1941- WhoAmP 93
Suhowatsky, Stephen Joseph 1939- WhoAm 94
Suhr, Geraldine M. 1960- WhoMW 93
Suhr, J. Nicholas 1942- WhoAmL 94
Suhr, Paul Augustine 1940- WhoAmL 94
Suhrbier, Klaus Rudolf 1930- WhoScEn 94
Suhre, Walter Anthony, Jr. 1933- WhoAm 94, WhoAmL 94
Suhrheinrich, Richard WhoAmP 93
Suhrheinrich, Richard Fred 1936- WhoAm 94, WhoAmL 94, WhoMW 93
Su Hua 1943- WhoPRCh 91
Su Hui fl. 4th cent.- BlmGWL
Sui, Anna 1955?- CurBio 93 [port], WhoAm 94, WhoAsA 94
Suich, Maxwell Victor 1938- IntWW 93
Suinn, Richard M. 1933- WrDr 94
Suinn, Richard Michael 1933- WhoAm 94, WhoWest 94
Sui Qin WhoPRCh 91
Suirdale, Viscount 1952- Who 94
Suit, D. James 1951- WhoScEn 94
Suiter, John William 1926- WhoScEn 94
Suitner, Otmar 1922- IntWW 93, NewGrDO
Suits, Bernard Herbert 1925- WhoAm 94
Suits, Chauncey Guy 1905-1991 WhAm 10
Suits, Daniel Burbidge 1918- WhoAm 94
Suits, Duane D. 1949- WhoFI 94
Suitt, Thomas Howard 1926- WhoFI 94
Sui Yongju 1932- WhoPRCh 91 [port]
Su Jinsan 1906- WhoPRCh 91 [port]
Sujo, Clara Diament WhoAm 94, WhoAmA 93
Suk, Cyril 1967- BuCMET
Suk, Josef 1929- IntWW 93
Suk, Julie DrAPF 93
Suk, Vaclav 1861-1933 NewGrDO
Sukanek, Peter Charles 1947- WhoScEn 94
Sukapatana, Chintara WhoHol 92
Sukarno 1901-1970 HisWorL [port]
Sukenic, Howard David 1961- WhoAmL 94

Sukenick, Lynn *DrAPF 93*
Sukenick, Ronald *DrAPF 93*
Sukenick, Ronald 1932- *WrDr 94*
Sukhanov, Lev Evgenevich 1936- *LngBDD*
Sukhovo-Kobylin, Alexander Vasilievich 1817-1903 *IntDcT 2*
Sukiennik, Leopold Jonah 1936- *WhoFI 94*
Sukis, Lilian 1939- *NewGrDO*
Sukkar, Rafid Antoon 1962- *WhoMW 93*
Suknaski, Andrew, Jr. 1942- *WrDr 94*
Suko, Lonny Ray 1943- *WhoAm 94, WhoAmL 94, WhoWest 94*
Sukov, Richard Joel 1944- *WhoScEn 94, WhoWest 94*
Sukova, Helena 1965- *BuCMET*
Sukova, Vera 1931-1982 *BuCMET*
Sukowa, Barbara 1950- *WhoHol 92*
Sukrija, Ali 1919- *IntWW 93*
Sukselainen, Vieno Johannes 1906- *IntWW 93*
Sulaim, Suliman Abd al aziz as- 1941- *IntWW 93*
Sulcer, Frederick Durham 1932- *WhoAm 94, WhoFI 94*
Sulcer, James R. 1928- *WhoIns 94*
Sulds, Jonathan L. 1950- *WhoAmL 94*
Suleiman, Michael W(adie) 1934- *ConAu 42NR*
Suleiman, Michael Wadie 1934- *WrDr 94*
Suleiman, Susan Rubin 1939- *WrDr 94*
Suleiman The Magnificent 1494?-1566 *HisWorL [port]*
Suleimenov, Olzhas Omarovich 1936- *LngBDD*
Suleimenov, Tuleutai Skakovich 1941- *LngBDD*
Sulek, Stjepan 1914-1986 *NewGrDO*
Sulentic, Daniel McIntyre 1964- *WhoWest 94*
Sulerius, Sara 1953- *WrDr 94*
Suleski, James 1953- *WhoIns 94*
Sulg, Madis 1943- *WhoAm 94*
Sulger, Francis Xavier 1942- *WhoAm 94, WhoAmL 94*
Sulick, Peter, Jr. 1950- *WhoAm 94*
Sulick, Robert John 1947- *WhoFI 94, WhoMW 93*
Sulieman, Jamil *WhoBlA 94*
Sulik, Edwin 1957- *WhoAm 94, WhoFI 94*
Suliman, Douglas Morton 1955- *WhoFI 94*
Sulimirski, Witold Stanislaw 1933- *WhoAm 94*
Sulin, Victor A. *WhoAmP 93*
Suliotis, Elena 1943- *IntWW 93*
Sulivan, Laurence c. 1713-1786 *DcNaB MP*
Sulkin, Howard Allen 1941- *WhoAm 94, WhoMW 93*
Sulkin, Sidney *DrAPF 93*
Sulkin, Sidney 1918- *WhoAm 94*
Sulkin, Stephen David 1944- *WhoScEn 94*
Sulky, Leo d1957 *WhoHol 92*
Sulla, Nancy 1955- *WhoScEn 94*
Sullavan, Margaret d1960 *WhoHol 92*
Sullenbarger, Peggy Ann 1954- *WhoMW 93*
Sullentrup, Michael Gerard 1958- *WhoScEn 94*
Sullerot, Evelyne 1924- *BlmGWL*
Sullins, Robert M. 1926-1991 *WhoAmA 93N*
Sullivan, Adele Woodhouse *WhoAm 94*
Sullivan, (Edward) Alan 1868-1947 *EncSF 93*
Sullivan, Alan L. 1946- *WhoAmL 94*
Sullivan, Alfred A. 1926- *WhoAmL 94*
Sullivan, Allen R. 1941- *WhoBlA 94*
Sullivan, Allen Trousdale 1927- *WhoAm 94*
Sullivan, Alvin D. 1942-1991 *WrDr 94N*
Sullivan, Andrew *IntWW 93, NewYTBS 93 [port]*
Sullivan, Anne Dorothy Hevner 1929- *WhoAmA 93*
Sullivan, Anne Elizabeth 1942- *WhoAm 94*
Sullivan, Arthur (Seymour) 1842-1900 *NewGrDO*
Sullivan, Arthur Forrest 1948- *WhoAmP 93*
Sullivan, Austin Padraic, Jr. 1940- *WhoAm 94, WhoFI 94*
Sullivan, Austin Padraig, Jr. 1940- *WhoMW 93*
Sullivan, Barbara Ann 1933- *WhoAmP 93*
Sullivan, Barbara Boyle 1937- *WhoAm 94*
Sullivan, Barry 1912- *IntMPA 94, WhoHol 92*
Sullivan, Barry 1949- *WhoAm 94, WhoAmL 94*
Sullivan, Barry F. 1930- *IntWW 93*
Sullivan, Barry Michael 1945- *WhoAm 94*
Sullivan, Bernard James 1927- *WhoFI 94, WhoMW 93*
Sullivan, Bill 1942- *WhoAmA 93*
Sullivan, Billy *WhoHol 92*
Sullivan, Billy d1946 *WhoHol 92*
Sullivan, Bolton 1896-1990 *WhAm 10*
Sullivan, Brad *WhoHol 92*
Sullivan, Brenda Ann 1955- *WhoBlA 94*
Sullivan, Brendan 1942- *WhoAmL 94*
Sullivan, Brian d1969 *WhoHol 92*
Sullivan, Brian 1924- *WhoAm 94*
Sullivan, Brian A. 1955- *WhoAmL 94*
Sullivan, Brian L. 1948- *WhoAmL 94*
Sullivan, Brian R. 1945- *ConAu 141*
Sullivan, Brick d1959 *WhoHol 92*
Sullivan, C. Gardner 1886-1965 *IntDcF 2-4*
Sullivan, Carl Rollynn, Jr. 1926- *WhAm 10*
Sullivan, Carley Hayden 1927- *WhoAmP 93*
Sullivan, Caroline Elizabeth 1925- *WhoMW 93*
Sullivan, Charles d1972 *WhoHol 92*
Sullivan, Charles 1933- *WhoAm 94*
Sullivan, Charles, Jr. 1943- *WhoAmL 94*
Sullivan, Charles A. *WhoAm 94, WhoFI 94*
Sullivan, Charles Bernard 1945- *WhoAm 94*
Sullivan, Chuck *DrAPF 93*
Sullivan, Claire Ferguson 1937- *WhoFI 94, WhoWest 94*
Sullivan, Clara K. 1915- *WrDr 94*
Sullivan, Clayton d1931 *WhoHol 92*
Sullivan, Connie Castleberry 1934- *WhoMW 93*
Sullivan, Cornelius J. 1943- *WhoAm 94, WhoAmL 94*
Sullivan, Cornelius Wayne 1943- *WhoAm 94, WhoWest 94*
Sullivan, Dan 1943- *WhoAmP 93*
Sullivan, Dan(iel Joseph) 1935- *WrDr 94*
Sullivan, Dana Joy 1967- *WhoMW 93*
Sullivan, Daniel 1764- *NewGrDO*
Sullivan, Daniel Joseph 1935- *WhoAm 94*
Sullivan, Danny 1950- *WhoAm 94*
Sullivan, David *WhoHol 92*
Sullivan, David Douglas Hooper 1926- *Who 94*
Sullivan, David Edward 1952- *WhoAmL 94, WhoAmP 93*
Sullivan, David Francis 1941- *WhoAmA 93*
Sullivan, Dennis C. 1946- *WhoAmL 94*
Sullivan, Dennis Edward 1894- *WhAm 10*
Sullivan, Dennis F. 1943- *WhoAm 94, WhoFI 94*
Sullivan, Dennis James, Jr. 1932- *WhoFI 94*
Sullivan, Dennis John 1940- *WhoWest 94*
Sullivan, Dennis P. 1941- *IntWW 93*
Sullivan, Dennis W. 1938- *WhoFI 94*
Sullivan, Denton Lee 1947- *WhoMW 93*
Sullivan, Desmond (John) 1920- *Who 94*
Sullivan, Dolores P. 1925- *WhoMW 93*
Sullivan, Don 1938- *WhoHol 92*
Sullivan, Don 1946- *WhoAmP 93*
Sullivan, Donald 1930- *WhoAm 94*
Sullivan, Donald Clifford 1936- *WhoAmP 93*
Sullivan, Donald John 1939- *WhoAm 94*
Sullivan, Ed d1974 *WhoHol 92*
Sullivan, Edmund Wendell 1925- *Who 94*
Sullivan, Edward Christian 1933- *WhoAmP 93*
Sullivan, Edward James 1932- *WhoBlA 94*
Sullivan, Edward Joseph 1915- *WhoFI 94*
Sullivan, Edward Joseph 1945- *WhoAm 94, WhoAmL 94*
Sullivan, Edward L. d1987 *WhoHol 92*
Sullivan, Eleanor Regis 1928-1991 *WhAm 10*
Sullivan, Elliott d1974 *WhoHol 92*
Sullivan, Emmet G. *WhoAmP 93*
Sullivan, Emmet G. 1947- *WhoAmL 94*
Sullivan, Erin 1947- *AstEnc*
Sullivan, Ernest Lee 1952- *WhoBlA 94, WhoMW 93*
Sullivan, Eugene John Joseph 1920- *WhoAm 94*
Sullivan, Eugene Joseph 1943- *WhoAm 94*
Sullivan, Eugene R. 1941- *CngDr 93*
Sullivan, Eugene Raymond 1941- *WhoAm 94, WhoAmL 94*
Sullivan, Evelin 1947- *ConAu 142*
Sullivan, Faith 1933- *WrDr 94*
Sullivan, Frances 1935- *WhoAmP 93*
Sullivan, Frances T. *WhoAmP 93*
Sullivan, Francis Charles 1927- *WhoAm 94*
Sullivan, Francis Edward 1941- *WhoAm 94*
Sullivan, Francis L. d1956 *WhoHol 92*
Sullivan, Francoise 1925- *WhoAmA 93*
Sullivan, Frank, Jr. 1950- *WhoAmL 94*
Sullivan, Frank E. d1993 *NewYTBS 93*
Sullivan, Frank Victor 1931- *WhoAm 94*
Sullivan, Fred d1937 *WhoHol 92*
Sullivan, G. Craig 1940- *WhoAm 94, WhoFI 94, WhoWest 94*
Sullivan, George Anerson *WhoWest 94*
Sullivan, George E(dward) 1927- *WrDr 94*
Sullivan, George Edmund 1932- *WhoAm 94*
Sullivan, George Edward 1927- *WhoAm 94*
Sullivan, George Murray 1922- *WhoAm 94, WhoAmP 93*
Sullivan, Gerald James 1937- *WhoWest 94*
Sullivan, Gordon R. 1937- *WhoAm 94*
Sullivan, Gordon Russell 1937- *WhoAmP 93*
Sullivan, Gregory William 1952- *WhoAmP 93*
Sullivan, Harry Stack 1892-1949 *EncSPD*
Sullivan, Haywood Cooper 1930- *WhoAm 94*
Sullivan, Henry P. 1917- *WhoAmP 93*
Sullivan, Holland Arthur 1945- *WhoFI 94*
Sullivan, Irene A. 1945- *WhoAmL 94*
Sullivan, J. Christopher 1932- *WhoBlA 94*
Sullivan, J. Langdon, Mrs. *WhoAm 94*
Sullivan, Jack, Jr. 1959- *WhoBlA 94, WhoMW 93*
Sullivan, James *DrAPF 93, WhoScEn 94*
Sullivan, James 1744-1808 *WhAmRev*
Sullivan, James Ash 1946- *WhoFI 94*
Sullivan, James Austin 1936- *WhoWest 94*
Sullivan, James E. d1931 *WhoHol 92*
Sullivan, James Francis 1930- *WhoAm 94*
Sullivan, James Gerald 1935- *WhoMW 93*
Sullivan, James Hall 1918- *WhoAm 94*
Sullivan, James Hargrove, Jr. 1962- *WhoScEn 94*
Sullivan, James Jerome 1943- *WhoAmL 94, WhoWest 94*
Sullivan, James Joseph 1922- *WhoFI 94*
Sullivan, James Joseph, Jr. 1955- *WhoAmL 94*
Sullivan, James Kirk 1935- *WhoAm 94, WhoWest 94*
Sullivan, James Lenox 1910- *WhoAm 94*
Sullivan, James Leo 1925- *WhoAm 94, WhoFI 94*
Sullivan, James Michael 1950- *WhoMW 93*
Sullivan, James N. 1937- *WhoAm 94, WhoFI 94, WhoWest 94*
Sullivan, James Stephen 1929- *WhoAm 94, WhoMW 93*
Sullivan, James Thomas 1939- *WhoAm 94*
Sullivan, Jay Michael 1936- *WhoAm 94, WhoScEn 94*
Sullivan, Jean 1923- *WhoHol 92*
Sullivan, Jean 1928- *WhoAmP 93, WhoWomW 91*
Sullivan, Jenny 1946- *WhoHol 92*
Sullivan, Jeremiah *WhoHol 92*
Sullivan, Jeremiah d1993 *NewYTBS 93 [port]*
Sullivan, Jeremiah Stephen 1920- *WhoAm 94*
Sullivan, Jeremy Mirth 1945- *Who 94*
Sullivan, Jerry Stephen 1945- *WhoFI 94*
Sullivan, Jim 1939- *WhoAm 94, WhoAmA 93*
Sullivan, Joan Adele 1962- *WhoAmL 94*
Sullivan, John *WhoHol 92*
Sullivan, John 1740-1795 *AmRev, WhAmRev [port]*
Sullivan, John Fallon, Jr. 1935- *WhoScEn 94*
Sullivan, John Fox 1943- *WhoAm 94*
Sullivan, John James, Jr. 1938- *WhoFI 94*
Sullivan, John Joseph 1920- *WhoAm 94, WhoMW 93*
Sullivan, John L. 1954- *WhoAmL 94*
Sullivan, John Lawrence 1941- *WhoAmP 93*
Sullivan, John Lawrence, III 1943- *WhoScEn 94*
Sullivan, John Louis, Jr. 1928- *WhoAm 94*
Sullivan, John Magruder, II 1959- *WhoFI 94*
Sullivan, John Maurice d1949 *WhoHol 92*
Sullivan, John Patrick d1993 *NewYTBS 93*
Sullivan, John Patrick 1930- *WrDr 94*
Sullivan, John William 1936- *WhoMW 93*
Sullivan, Joseph *WhoHol 92*
Sullivan, Joseph B. 1922- *WhoAm 94*
Sullivan, Joseph C. *WhoAmP 93*
Sullivan, Joseph Patrick 1933- *WhoAm 94, WhoFI 94*
Sullivan, Joseph Peter 1939- *WhoFI 94*
Sullivan, Julia Benitez 1957- *WhoHisp 94*
Sullivan, Katherine McGurk 1949- *WhoAmL 94*
Sullivan, Kathryn Ann 1954- *WhoMW 93*
Sullivan, Kathryn D. 1951- *WhoScEn 94*
Sullivan, Kathryn Jean 1942- *WhoWomW 91*
Sullivan, Kathryn Meara 1942- *WhoFI 94*
Sullivan, Kevin B. 1949- *WhoAmP 93*
Sullivan, Kevin J. 1953- *WhoIns 94*
Sullivan, Kevin Patrick 1953- *WhoAmL 94*
Sullivan, Krispin Nissa 1946- *WhoWest 94*
Sullivan, Larry E. 1944- *WrDr 94*
Sullivan, Laura Patricia 1947- *WhoAm 94, WhoFI 94*
Sullivan, Lawrence Jerome 1953- *WhoScEn 94*
Sullivan, Lawrence Matthew 1937- *WhoAmL 94*
Sullivan, Lee d1981 *WhoHol 92*
Sullivan, Leo Eugene 1918- *WhoAmP 93*
Sullivan, Leon Howard 1922- *AfrAmAl 6, WhoAm 94, WhoBlA 94*
Sullivan, Leonard, Jr. 1925- *WhoAmP 93*
Sullivan, Leonard E. 1934- *WhoAmP 93*
Sullivan, Liam *WhoHol 92*
Sullivan, Linda Ann 1961- *WhoMW 93*
Sullivan, Linda Susan 1952- *WhoAmA 93*
Sullivan, Louis (Graydon) 1951- *WrDr 94*
Sullivan, Louis Henry 1856-1924 *AmCulL*
Sullivan, Louis W. 1933- *AfrAmAl 6 [port], WhoAmP 93*
Sullivan, Louis Wade 1933- *IntWW 93, WhoAm 94, WhoBlA 94, WhoScEn 94*
Sullivan, M(ichael) J(ustin) 1940- *ConAu 142*
Sullivan, Marcia Waite 1950- *WhoAm 94, WhoAmL 94*
Sullivan, Marie Celeste 1929- *WhoAm 94*
Sullivan, Marie Madeline d1991 *WhoHol 92*
Sullivan, Marilyn Bobette 1931- *WhoMW 93*
Sullivan, Martha Adams 1952- *WhoBlA 94*
Sullivan, Mary E. 1932- *WhoAmP 93*
Sullivan, Mary J. 1919- *WhoAmP 93*
Sullivan, Mary M. 1952- *WhoAmP 93*
Sullivan, Mary Rose 1931- *WhoAm 94*
Sullivan, Matthew Barry 1915- *WrDr 94*
Sullivan, Maureen 1954- *WhoAmL 94*
Sullivan, Max William 1909- *WhAm 10*
Sullivan, Maxine d1987 *WhoHol 92*
Sullivan, Michael *Who 94*
Sullivan, (Donovan) Michael 1916- *Who 94, WrDr 94*
Sullivan, Michael D. 1938- *WhoAmP 93*
Sullivan, Michael David 1938- *WhoAm 94, WhoAmL 94*
Sullivan, Michael Evan 1940- *WhoFI 94, WhoWest 94*
Sullivan, Michael Francis 1942- *WhoAmL 94*
Sullivan, Michael Frederick 1940- *Who 94*
Sullivan, Michael J. *WhoAmP 93*
Sullivan, Michael J. 1939- *IntWW 93, WhoAmP 93*
Sullivan, Michael John 1939- *WhoAm 94, WhoWest 94*
Sullivan, Michael John 1957- *WhoWest 94*
Sullivan, Michael Kennedy 1961- *WhoAmL 94*
Sullivan, Michael Maurice 1942- *WhoAmL 94*
Sullivan, Michael Patrick 1933- *WhoAm 94*
Sullivan, Michael Patrick 1934- *WhoAm 94, WhoMW 93*
Sullivan, Michelle Cornejo 1958- *WhoAmL 94*
Sullivan, Mortimer Allen, Jr. 1930- *WhoAm 94, WhoAmL 94*
Sullivan, Nancy *DrAPF 93*
Sullivan, Nancy Jean 1957- *WhoAmL 94*
Sullivan, Neil Maxwell 1942- *WhoFI 94*
Sullivan, Neil Samuel 1942- *WhoScEn 94*
Sullivan, Nicholas G. 1927- *WhoAm 94*
Sullivan, Nicholas Peter 1950- *WhoFI 94*
Sullivan, Pat 1936- *WhoAmP 93*
Sullivan, Patricia Ann 1953- *WhoAmL 94*
Sullivan, Patricia Clare, Sister 1928- *WhoMW 93*
Sullivan, Patricia W. 1936- *WhoFI 94*
Sullivan, Patrick Allen 1932- *WhoWest 94*
Sullivan, Patrick J. 1920- *IntMPA 94*
Sullivan, Paul (Robert) 1951- *WrDr 94*
Sullivan, Paul Andrew 1944- *WhoScEn 94*
Sullivan, Paul Donald 1934- *WhoAmP 93*
Sullivan, Paul John 1943- *WhoMW 93*
Sullivan, Peggy Anne 1929- *WhoAm 94*
Sullivan, Peter D. 1958- *WhoAm 94*
Sullivan, Peter M. 1938- *WhoAmP 93*
Sullivan, Peter Thomas, III 1950- *WhoAmL 94*
Sullivan, R(onald Dee) 1939- *WhoAmA 93*
Sullivan, Richard Arthur 1931- *Who 94*
Sullivan, Richard Cyril 1928- *WhoAm 94*
Sullivan, Richard John 1949- *WhoAm 94*
Sullivan, Richard Joseph 1917- *WhoAmP 93*
Sullivan, Richard Morrissey 1942- *WhoAmL 94*
Sullivan, Robert E(rtel) 1947- *WrDr 94*

Sullivan, Robert Edward 1936-
WhoAm 94, WhoFI 94
Sullivan, Robert Emmet, Jr. 1955-
WhoAmL 94
Sullivan, Robert John 1954- *WhoAmL 94*
Sullivan, Robert Joseph 1940-
WhoAmL 94
Sullivan, Robert Scott 1955- *WhoScEn 94, WhoWest 94*
Sullivan, Rod 1955- *WhoAmL 94*
Sullivan, Roger Charles, Jr. 1946-
WhoFI 94
Sullivan, Roger J. 1928- *WrDr 94*
Sullivan, Roger John 1941- *WhoMW 93*
Sullivan, Roger Winthrop 1929-
WhoAm 94
Sullivan, Ruth Wilkins 1926-
WhoAmA 93
Sullivan, Sarah Louise 1954- *WhoFI 94, WhoMW 93*
Sullivan, Scott A. 1947- *WhoAmA 93*
Sullivan, Sean d1985 *WhoHol 92*
Sullivan, Sean Mei *EncSF 93*
Sullivan, Sean Mei 1913- *WrDr 94*
Sullivan, Selby William 1934- *WhoAm 94*
Sullivan, Sharon Jean 1949- *WhoFI 94*
Sullivan, Shaun S. 1940- *WhoAmL 94*
Sullivan, Sheila (P.) 1927- *EncSF 93*
Sullivan, Stuart Francis 1928- *WhoAm 94, WhoWest 94*
Sullivan, Sue Lynn 1941- *WhoMW 93*
Sullivan, Susan *ConTFT 11*
Sullivan, Teresa Ann 1949- *WhoAm 94*
Sullivan, Thomas Christopher 1937-
WhoAm 94, WhoFI 94
Sullivan, Thomas Eugene 1948-
WhoAmL 94, WhoMW 93
Sullivan, Thomas J. *WhoAmP 93*
Sullivan, Thomas J. 1926- *WhoAmP 93*
Sullivan, Thomas John 1935- *WhoAm 94, WhoFI 94*
Sullivan, Thomas Joseph *WhoAmP 93*
Sullivan, Thomas Michael 1913-1991
WhAm 10
Sullivan, Thomas Patrick 1930-
WhoAm 94
Sullivan, Thomas Patrick 1956-
WhoAmL 94
Sullivan, Thomas Quinn 1933-
WhoAmP 93
Sullivan, Tim(othy Robert) *EncSF 93*
Sullivan, Timothy 1948- *WhoAm 94*
Sullivan, Timothy 1954- *NewGrDO*
Sullivan, Timothy Gerard 1955-
WhoAmP 93
Sullivan, Timothy Jackson 1944-
WhoAm 94, WhoAmL 94
Sullivan, Timothy John, V 1947-
WhoFI 94
Sullivan, Timothy Patrick 1942-
WhoFI 94
Sullivan, Tod 1934- *Who 94*
Sullivan, Tom *WhoHol 92*
Sullivan, Tom d1982 *WhoHol 92*
Sullivan, Vernon *EncSF 93*
Sullivan, Victoria *DrAPF 93*
Sullivan, W. Michael 1953- *WhoAmP 93*
Sullivan, Walter (Laurence) 1924-
WrDr 94
Sullivan, Walter (Seager) 1918- *WrDr 94*
Sullivan, Walter Clay 1933- *WhoFI 94*
Sullivan, Walter Francis 1928- *WhoAm 94*
Sullivan, Walter J. *WhoAmP 93*
Sullivan, Walter Laurence 1924-
WhoAm 94
Sullivan, Walter Seager 1918- *IntWW 93, WhoAm 94*
Sullivan, Whitney Brayton 1922-
WhoWest 94
Sullivan, William Beaumont 1945-
WhoAm 94
Sullivan, William Francis 1950-
WhoAmP 93
Sullivan, William Francis 1952-
WhoAm 94, WhoAmL 94
Sullivan, William H(ealy) 1922- *WrDr 94*
Sullivan, William Hallisey, Jr. 1915-
WhoAm 94
Sullivan, William J. 1937- *WhoAmP 93*
Sullivan, William James 1930-
WhoAm 94, WhoWest 94
Sullivan, William Johnson 1928-
WhoAmP 93
Sullivan, William Litsey 1921-
WhoAmP 93
Sullivan, William M. 1945- *ConAu 43NR*
Sullivan, William R. 1945- *WhoAmP 93*
Sullivan, Winona 1942- *ConAu 141*
Sullivan, Zola Jiles 1921- *WhoBlA 94*
Sullivan-Boyle, Kathleen Marie 1958-
WhoWest 94
Sullivant, William Benton 1940-
WhoAmP 93
Sullo, Fiorentino 1921- *IntWW 93*
Sullo, Joseph Anthony 1921- *WhoAmA 93*
Sulloway, Frank Jones 1947- *WhoAm 94*
Sulltrop, Gordon Donald 1934-
WhoMW 93

Sullwold, Corliss Kay 1946- *WhoMW 93*
Sully, Eva d1990 *WhoHol 92*
Sully, Francois *WhoHol 92*
Sully, Frank d1975 *WhoHol 92*
Sully, Ira Bennett 1947- *WhoAmL 94, WhoMW 93*
Sully, Leonard Thomas George 1909-
Who 94
Sully, Mariette 1874-1940? *NewGrDO*
Sully, Paul 1932- *WrDr 94*
Sulman Al-Khalifa, Isa bin *IntWW 93*
Sulpicia fl. 1st cent.BC- *BlmGWL*
Sulpicia fl. 1st cent.- *BlmGWL*
Sulsona, Michael *WhoHisp 94*
Sulston, John Edward 1942- *IntWW 93, Who 94*
Sult, Jeffery Scot 1956- *WhoFI 94*
Sultan, Altoon 1948- *WhoAmA 93*
Sultan, Donald K. 1951- *WhoAmA 93*
Sultan, Donald Keith 1951- *IntWW 93, WhoAm 94*
Sultan, Fouad 1931- *IntWW 93*
Sultan, Larry A. 1946- *WhoAmA 93*
Sultan, Stanley *DrAPF 93*
Sultan, Stanley 1928- *WrDr 94*
Sultan, Terrie Frances 1952- *WhoAm 94*
Sultana, Donald Edward 1924- *WrDr 94*
Sultan Ibn Abdul Aziz, H.R.H. Prince 1922- *IntWW 93*
Sultan Tanbolatow *WhoPRCh 91 [port]*
Sulter, Maud 1960- *BlmGWL*
Sul-Te-Wan, Mme. d1959 *WhoHol 92*
Sulton, Jacqueline Rhoda 1957-
WhoBlA 94
Sulton, John Dennis 1912- *WhoBlA 94*
Sultzer, Barnet Martin 1929- *WhoScEn 94*
Sulyk, Stephen 1924- *WhoAm 94*
Sulzberger, Arthur Ochs 1926- *IntWW 93, Who 94*
Sulzberger, Arthur Ochs, Sr. 1926-
WhoAm 94, WhoFI 94
Sulzberger, Arthur Ochs, Jr. 1951-
WhoAm 94
Sulzberger, C. L. 1912-1993
NewYTBS 93 [port]
Sulzberger, C(yrus) L(eo, II) 1912-
WrDr 94
Sulzberger, C(yrus) L(eo, II) 1912-1993
ConAu 142, CurBio 93N
Sulzberger, Cyrus Leo 1912- *IntWW 93, WhoAm 94*
Sulzby, James Frederick, Jr. 1905-1988
WhAm 10
Sulzman, Howard Richard 1944-
WhoIns 94
Sum, Grace C. K. *WhoAsA 94*
Sumac, Yma 1922- *WhoHol 92*
Sumanth, David Jonnakoty 1946-
WhoAm 94, WhoFI 94
Sumarno, Ishak 1943- *WhoFI 94*
Sumartojo, Jojok 1937- *WhoAsA 94*
Sumaya, Ciro Valent 1941- *WhoAm 94, WhoHisp 94*
Sumber, Edward Irving 1942-
WhoAmL 94
Sumberg, David Anthony Gerald 1941-
Who 94
Sumberg, John Charles 1949-
WhoAmL 94
Sumichrast, Jozef 1948- *WhoAm 94*
Sumida, Gerald Aquinas 1944-
WhoAm 94, WhoAmL 94, WhoFI 94, WhoWest 94
Sumida, Jon Tetsuro 1949- *WhoAsA 94*
Sumida, Kenneth Dean 1958- *WhoAsA 94*
Sumida, Kevin P.H. 1954- *WhoAmL 94, WhoWest 94*
Sumii, Takao 1936- *WhoAsA 94*
Sumii Sue 1902- *BlmGWL*
Sumisaki, Roy *WhoAsA 94*
Sumita, Satoshi 1916- *IntWW 93*
Sumler-Lewis, Janice L. 1948- *WhoBlA 94*
Sumlin, John Robert 1952- *WhoAmP 93*
Sumlin, William *WhoAmP 93*
Summ, Helmut 1908- *WhoAmA 93*
Summer, Charles Edgar 1923- *WhoAm 94*
Summer, Cree *WhoBlA 94*
Summer, Cree 1969- *WhoHol 92*
Summer, Donna 1948- *IntWW 93, WhoHol 92*
Summer, Donna Andrea 1948-
WhoBlA 94
Summer, (Emily) Eugenia 1923-
WhoAmA 93
Summer, Harry Harmon 1929-
WhoAm 94
Summer, James *WhoHol 92*
Summerall, Pat 1931- *WhoAm 94*
Summerfield, Arthur 1923- *IntWW 93, Who 94*
Summerfield, Eleanor 1921- *WhoHol 92*
Summerfield, George Clark, Jr. 1958-
WhoAmL 94
Summerfield, James Zane 1924-
WhoAmP 93
Summerfield, Joan *WhoHol 92*
Summerfield, John (Crampton) 1920-
Who 94

Summerfield, John Robert 1917-
WhoAm 94
Summerfield, Lin(da Victoria) 1952-
WrDr 94
Summerfield, Martin 1916- *WhoAm 94*
Summerford, Ben Long 1924- *WhoAm 94*
Summerhayes, Colin Peter 1942- *Who 94*
Summerhayes, David Michael 1922-
Who 94
Summerhayes, Gerald Victor 1928-
Who 94
Summerill, John Frederick 1917-
WhoWest 94
Summerland, Augusta *WhoHol 92*
Summerlin, Glenn Wood 1934-
WhoAm 94
Summerour, Darlene Ann 1951-
WhoMW 93
Summerour-Perry, Lisa 1962- *WhoBlA 94*
Summers, Alfred Lawrence, Jr. 1950-
WhoFI 94
Summers, Andy 1942- *WhoAm 94*
Summers, Anita Arrow 1925- *WhoAm 94*
Summers, Ann d1974 *WhoHol 92*
Summers, Anne Fairhurst 1945-
WhoAm 94
Summers, Anne O'Neill 1942- *WhoAm 94*
Summers, Anthony (Bruce) 1942-
WrDr 94
Summers, Anthony J. *DrAPF 93*
Summers, Carol 1925- *WhoAm 94, WhoAmA 93*
Summers, Charles E. *WhoAmP 93*
Summers, Clifford L. 1915- *WhoAmP 93*
Summers, Clyde Wilson 1918- *WhoAm 94*
Summers, D. B. 1928- *WrDr 94*
Summers, David 1941- *WrDr 94*
Summers, David Stewart 1932-
WhoBlA 94
Summers, Dennis *EncSF 93*
Summers, Dennis 1928- *WrDr 94*
Summers, Diana 1922- *WrDr 94*
Summers, Dorothy d1964 *WhoHol 92*
Summers, Dudley Gloyne 1892-1975
WhoAmA 93N
Summers, E. Hardy 1933- *WhoAmL 94*
Summers, Edna White 1919- *WhoBlA 94*
Summers, Edward Lee 1937- *WhoAm 94*
Summers, Essie 1912- *BlmGWL, WrDr 94*
Summers, Felix Roland Brattan *Who 94*
Summers, Frank William 1933-
WhoAm 94
Summers, Gene F. 1936- *WrDr 94*
Summers, Hal 1911- *WrDr 94*
Summers, Hardy 1933- *WhoAm 94, WhoAmP 93*
Summers, Henry Forbes 1911- *Who 94*
Summers, Hope d1979 *WhoHol 92*
Summers, Iris *DrAPF 93*
Summers, James Donald 1955-
WhoScEn 94
Summers, James Irvin 1921- *WhoAm 94*
Summers, Janet Margaret *Who 94*
Summers, Jerry *WhoHol 92*
Summers, John Harold, Jr. 1962-
WhoFI 94
Summers, Jonathan 1946- *NewGrDO*
Summers, Joseph Holmes 1920- *WrDr 94*
Summers, Joseph W. 1930- *WhoBlA 94*
Summers, Judith (Anne) 1953- *WrDr 94*
Summers, Lawrence *IntWW 93*
Summers, Lawrence 1954- *WhoAm 94*
Summers, Leonora d1976 *WhoHol 92*
Summers, Lisa Diane 1957- *WhoAmL 94*
Summers, Lorraine Dey Schaeffer 1946-
WhoAm 94
Summers, Marie Jean 1956- *WhoWest 94*
Summers, Max Duanne 1938- *WhoAm 94, WhoScEn 94*
Summers, Merna 1933- *BlmGWL, WrDr 94*
Summers, Nicholas 1939- *Who 94*
Summers, Retha 1953- *WhoBlA 94*
Summers, Robert 1922- *WhoAm 94, WhoFI 94*
Summers, Rodger 1945- *WhoBlA 94*
Summers, Rowena 1932- *WrDr 94*
Summers, Scott Brooks 1948- *WhoFI 94*
Summers, Shari *WhoHol 92*
Summers, Timothy 1942- *WhoBlA 94*
Summers, William Cofield 1939-
WhoAm 94
Summers, William E., III 1918-
WhoBlA 94
Summers, William E., IV 1943-
WhoBlA 94
Summers, William Lawrence 1942-
WhoAm 94, WhoAmL 94
Summerscale, David Michael 1937-
Who 94
Summerscale, Peter Wayne 1935- *Who 94*
Summersett, James A., III 1957-
WhoAm 94
Summersett, Kenneth George 1922-
WhoMW 93
Summerskill, Shirley Catherine Wynne 1931- *Who 94*

Summerson, Hugo Hawksley Fitzthomas 1950- *Who 94*
Summerson, John 1904-1992 *AnObit 1992*
Summerson, John (Newenham), Sir 1904-1992 *WhAm 94N*
Summerson, John Newenham d1992
IntWW 93N, WhAm 94N
Summerson, John Newenham 1904-1992
WhAm 10
Summerton, Neil William 1942- *Who 94*
Summertree, Katonah *ConAu 42NR*
Summertree, Katonah 1938- *WhoAm 94, WrDr 94*
Summerville, Amelia d1934 *WhoHol 92*
Summerville, George *WhoHol 92*
Summerville, Gregg Thompson 1947-
WhoFI 94
Summerville, James *DrAPF 93*
Summerville, Jane Schneider 1942-
WhoMW 93
Summerville, Katie Mae 1936-
WhoMW 93
Summerville, Slim d1946 *WhoHol 92*
Summey, Steven Michael 1946- *WhoFI 94*
Summit, Paul Eliot 1949- *WhoAmL 94*
Summit, Roger Kent 1930- *WhoAm 94*
Summitt, Gazella Ann 1941- *WhoBlA 94*
Summitt, Robert 1935- *WhoAm 94*
Summitt, Robert Layman 1932-
WhoAm 94
Summitt, Robert Murray 1924-
WhoAm 94, WhoAmL 94
Summlin, Linda Marie 1962- *WhoMW 93*
Summy, Anne Tunis 1912-1986
WhoAmA 93N
Sumner, (Edith) Aurea 1913- *WrDr 94*
Sumner, Bernard 1956-
See New Order ConMus 11
Sumner, Billy Taylor 1923- *WhoAm 94*
Sumner, Charles Allen, II 1945- *WhoFI 94*
Sumner, Christopher John 1939- *Who 94*
Sumner, Daniel Alan 1950- *WhoAm 94, WhoFI 94*
Sumner, David *WhoHol 92*
Sumner, Geoffrey d1989 *WhoHol 92*
Sumner, George 1940- *WhoAmA 93*
Sumner, Gordon, Jr. 1924- *WhoWest 94*
Sumner, Gordon Matthew 1951-
IntWW 93, WhoAm 94
Sumner, (George) Heywood (Maunoir) 1853-1940 *DcNaB MP*
Sumner, Increase 1746-1799 *WhAmRev*
Sumner, James Batcheller 1887-1955
WorScD
Sumner, Jethro c. 1733-1785 *WhAmRev*
Sumner, Jethro 1735-1785 *AmRev*
Sumner, Malcom Edward 1933-
WhoScEn 94
Sumner, Mary Elizabeth 1828-1921
DcNaB MP
Sumner, Norman Leslie, Jr. 1943-
WhoWest 94
Sumner, Peter *WhoHol 92*
Sumner, Rodney William 1950-
WhoWest 94
Sumner, Thomas Barry 1931-
WhoWest 94
Sumner, Thomas Robert 1949-
WhoBlA 94
Sumner, Verlyn d1935 *WhoHol 92*
Sumner, Victor Emmanuel 1929- *Who 94*
Sumner, William Graham 1840-1910
AmSocL
Sumner, William Marvin 1928-
WhoAm 94
Sumners, William Glenn, Jr. 1928-
WhoAmL 94
Sumney, Roland L. 1933- *WhoIns 94*
Sumpter, Dennis Ray 1948- *WhoAmL 94*
Sumpter, Donald *WhoHol 92*
Sumpter, Jerry Lee 1942- *WhoMW 93*
Sumption, Anthony James Chadwick 1919- *Who 94*
Sumption, Jonathan (Philip Chadwick) 1948- *WrDr 94*
Sumption, Jonathan Philip Chadwick 1948- *Who 94*
Sumrall, Amber Coverdale *DrAPF 93*
Sumrall, Lester Frank 1913- *WhoAm 94*
Sumrall, Robert Lavern 1942-
WhoAmP 93
Sumray, Monty 1918- *Who 94*
Sumrell, Gene 1919- *WhoAm 94, WhoFI 94, WhoScEn 94*
Sumsion, Herbert Whitton 1899- *Who 94*
Sumsion, John Walbridge 1928- *Who 94*
Sumter, Thomas 1734-1832 *AmRev, WhAmRev [port]*
Sun, Benedict Ching-San 1934-
WhoScEn 94
Sun, Chang-Tsan 1928- *WhoAsA 94*
Sun, Chih Ree 1923- *WhoAsA 94*
Sun, Cossette Tsung-hung Wu 1937-
WhoAm 94, WhoAmL 94
Sun, Emily M. *WhoFI 94, WhoScEn 94*
Sun, Frank F. 1938- *WhoAsA 94*
Sun, Homer Ko 1961- *WhoScEn 94*

Susann, Jacqueline d1974 *WhoHol 92*
Susann, Jacqueline 1921-1974 *BlmGWL*
Susano, Charles Daniel, Jr. 1936- *WhoAmP 93*
Suschitzky, Peter *IntMPA 94*
Suschitzky, Wolfgang 1912- *IntWW 93*
Su Shaozhi 1923- *IntWW 93, WhoPRCh 91*
Su Shifang *WhoPRCh 91*
Su Shuyang 1938- *WhoPRCh 91 [port]*
Susi, Enrichetta 1941- *WhoScEn 94*
Susie, Sharon Kay 1951- *WhoFI 94*
Suskevic, Stanislau Stanislaujevic 1934- *LngBDD*
Suskiewicz, Halina Elzbieta *WhoWomW 91*
Suskind, Dennis A. 1942- *WhoAm 94*
Suskind, Patrick 1949- *ConWorW 93*
Suskind, Raymond Robert 1913- *WhoAm 94*
Suskind, Sigmund Richard 1926- *WhoAm 94, WhoScEn 94*
Susko, Carol Lynne 1955- *WhoAmL 94*
Suslov, Valdimir Antonovich 1939- *LngBDD*
Susman, Alan Howard 1945- *WhoAmL 94*
Susman, Alan L. *WhoAmP 93*
Susman, Benjamin Mayer 1937- *WhoWest 94*
Susman, Karen Lee 1942- *WhoAmL 94*
Susman, Louis B. 1937- *WhoAmP 93*
Susman, Millard 1934- *WhoAm 94*
Susman, Morton Lee 1934- *WhoAm 94, WhoAmL 94*
Susman, Stephen Daily 1941- *WhoAm 94*
Susman, Thomas Michael 1943- *WhoAm 94, WhoAmL 94, WhoAmP 93*
Susman, Todd *WhoHol 92*
Susman, Tom L. 1959- *WhoAmP 93*
Suson, Daniel Jeffrey 1962- *WhoScEn 94*
Susor, Dorothy Marie Alma Leffel 1922- *WhoMW 93*
Sussan, Sidney Martin 1944- *WhoFI 94*
Sussenguth, Edward Henry 1932- *WhoAm 94*
Sussenguth, Hans 1913- *IntWW 93*
Susser, Mervyn Wilfred 1921- *WhoAm 94*
Sussex, James Neil 1917- *WhoAm 94*
Sussex, Lucy 1957- *EncSF 93*
Susskind, Charles *WhoAm 94*
Susskind, Harriet *DrAPF 93*
Susskind, Herbert 1929- *WhoAm 94*
Susskind, Lawrence Elliott 1947- *WhoAm 94*
Susskind, Teresa Gabriel 1921- *WhoAm 94, WhoWest 94*
Sussman, Alexander Ralph 1946- *WhoAm 94, WhoAmL 94*
Sussman, Arthur 1927- *WhoAmA 93*
Sussman, Barbara J. 1955- *WhoAmA 93*
Sussman, Barry 1934- *WhoAm 94, WrDr 94*
Sussman, Beverly Kall *WhoMW 93*
Sussman, Bonnie K. *WhoAmA 93*
Sussman, Brian Jay 1956- *WhoWest 94*
Sussman, David William 1954- *WhoAmL 94*
Sussman, Deborah Evelyn 1931- *WhoScEn 94*
Sussman, Elizabeth Sacks 1939- *WhoAmA 93*
Sussman, Gary Lawrence 1952- *WhoAmA 93*
Sussman, Gerald 1934- *WhoAm 94*
Sussman, Gerald Jay 1947- *WhoScEn 94*
Sussman, Harold Louis 1955- *WhoWest 94*
Sussman, Harold S. 1958- *WhoFI 94*
Sussman, Henry 1947- *ConAu 43NR*
Sussman, Jill 1954- *WhoAmA 93*
Sussman, Josephine Carr *DrAPF 93*
Sussman, Joshua *WhoHol 92*
Sussman, Karen Ann 1947- *WhoWest 94*
Sussman, Karl Edgar 1929- *WhoScEn 94*
Sussman, Leonard Richard 1920- *WhoAm 94*
Sussman, Mark Richard 1952- *WhoAmL 94*
Sussman, Martin Victor *WhoAm 94*
Sussman, Monica Hilton 1952- *WhoAm 94*
Sussman, Peter Yeger 1941- *WhoWest 94*
Sussman, Richard N. 1908-1971 *WhoAmA 93N*
Sussman, Robert Wald 1941- *WhoMW 93*
Sussman, Steven David 1946- *WhoAm 94, WhoFI 94*
Sussman, Steven Yale 1955- *WhoWest 94*
Sussman, Wendy 1949- *WhoAmA 93*
Sussmann, M. Hal *WhoAmA 93*
Sussmayr, Franz Xaver 1766-1803 *NewGrDO*
Sussmuth, Rita 1937- *IntWW 93, WhoWomW 91*
Sussna, Edward 1926- *WhoAm 94*
Suster, Ronald 1942- *WhoAmP 93*
Susumu, Kamata 1937- *WhoScEn 94*
Suszkowski, Geoffrey John 1940- *WhoMW 93*
Sutardji, Johny Sastra 1960- *WhoWest 94*
Sutch, Herbert d1939 *WhoHol 92*
Sutch, Richard Charles 1942- *WhoFI 94*
Sutcliff, Rosemary 1920- *BlmGWL*
Sutcliff, Rosemary 1920-1992 *TwCYAW, WrDr 94N*
Sutcliffe, Allan 1936- *Who 94*
Sutcliffe, David Miller 1947- *WhoFI 94*
Sutcliffe, Edward Davis 1917- *Who 94*
Sutcliffe, Eric 1909- *WhoAm 94, WhoWest 94*
Sutcliffe, Geoffrey Scott 1912- *Who 94*
Sutcliffe, Halliwell *EncSF 93*
Sutcliffe, James H. 1956- *WhoAm 94*
Sutcliffe, John Harold Vick 1931- *Who 94*
Sutcliffe, Linda 1946- *Who 94*
Sutcliffe, Reginald Cockcroft 1904- *WrDr 94*
Sutcliffe, Richard Joseph 1947- *WhoWest 94*
Suter, Albert Edward 1935- *IntWW 93, WhoAm 94, WhoFI 94*
Suter, Ben 1954- *WhoAmL 94*
Suter, Bruce H. 1921- *WhoIns 94*
Suter, David Winston 1942- *WhoWest 94*
Suter, Eugene Wayne 1949- *WhoFI 94*
Suter, George August 1934- *WhoFI 94*
Suter, Kenneth Harris 1919- *WhoMW 93*
Suter, Michael 1944- *Who 94*
Suter, Sherwood Eugene 1928- *WhoAmA 93*
Suter, Stuart Ross 1941- *WhoAmL 94*
Suter, William Kent 1937- *WhoAm 94, WhoAmL 94*
Sutera, Salvatore Philip 1933- *WhoAm 94*
Sutermeister, Heinrich 1910- *IntWW 93, NewGrDO*
Suthaus, (Heinrich) Ludwig 1906-1971 *NewGrDO*
Sutherland, Countess of 1921- *Who 94, WhoWomW 91*
Sutherland, Duke of 1915- *Who 94*
Sutherland, Hon. Lord 1932- *Who 94*
Sutherland, Alan Roy 1944- *WhoAm 94*
Sutherland, Allan T(homas) 1950- *WrDr 94*
Sutherland, Allen Jennings 1896- *WhAm 10*
Sutherland, Anne d1942 *WhoHol 92*
Sutherland, Anthony (Frederic Arthur) 1916- *Who 94*
Sutherland, Barbara L. 1954- *WhoIns 94*
Sutherland, Bruce *WhoWest 94*
Sutherland, C. A. *WhoScEn 94*
Sutherland, Colin John MacLean 1954- *Who 94*
Sutherland, Dean Alan 1954- *WhoAmP 93*
Sutherland, Dick d1934 *WhoHol 92*
Sutherland, Donald 1934- *WhoHol 92*
Sutherland, Donald 1935- *IntMPA 94, WhoAm 94*
Sutherland, Donald Gray 1929- *WhoAm 94*
Sutherland, Donald James 1931- *WhoAm 94*
Sutherland, Donald McNichol 1935- *IntWW 93*
Sutherland, Doug 1937- *WhoAmP 93*
Sutherland, Earl Christian 1923- *WhoWest 94*
Sutherland, Earl Wilbur, Jr. *WorScD*
Sutherland, Edward d1973 *WhoHol 92*
Sutherland, Efua 1924- *BlmGWL, IntDcT 2*
Sutherland, Efua (Theodora) 1924- *ConDr 93, WrDr 94*
Sutherland, Elizabeth 1926- *WrDr 94*
Sutherland, Esther d1986 *WhoHol 92*
Sutherland, Euan Ross 1943- *Who 94*
Sutherland, Francis A. 1940- *WhoIns 94*
Sutherland, Frank 1945- *WhoAm 94*
Sutherland, Gail Russell 1923- *WhoAm 94*
Sutherland, George Leslie 1922- *WhoAm 94, WhoFI 94, WhoScEn 94*
Sutherland, Ian 1926- *Who 94*
Sutherland, Ian Boyd 1926- *Who 94*
Sutherland, James 1920- *IntWW 93, Who 94*
Sutherland, James (Runcieman) 1900- *Who 94, WrDr 94*
Sutherland, Joan 1926- *IntWW 93, NewGrDO [port], Who 94, WhoAm 94*
Sutherland, Joe Allen 1934- *WhoAm 94*
Sutherland, John d1921 *WhoHol 92*
Sutherland, John 1938- *WrDr 94*
Sutherland, John Alexander Muir 1933- *Who 94*
Sutherland, John Beattie 1932- *WhoAm 94*
Sutherland, John Brewer 1931- *Who 94*
Sutherland, John Bruce, IV 1945- *WhoScEn 94*
Sutherland, John Campbell 1921- *WhoWest 94*
Sutherland, John Clark *WhoScEn 94*
Sutherland, John Menzies 1928- *Who 94*
Sutherland, Kiefer 1964- *WhoHol 92*
Sutherland, Kiefer 1966- *IntMPA 94, WhoAm 94*
Sutherland, Kristine *WhoHol 92*
Sutherland, Lewis Frederick 1952- *WhoFI 94*
Sutherland, Lowell Francis 1939- *WhoAm 94, WhoAmL 94, WhoWest 94*
Sutherland, Malcolm Read, Jr. 1916- *WhoAm 94*
Sutherland, Margaret 1941- *BlmGWL, WrDr 94*
Sutherland, Margaret (Ada) 1897-1984 *NewGrDO*
Sutherland, Marion Schultz *WhoBlA 94*
Sutherland, Maurice 1915- *Who 94*
Sutherland, Muir *Who 94*
Sutherland, Norman Stuart 1927- *IntWW 93, WrDr 94*
Sutherland, Peter D. 1946- *IntWW 93*
Sutherland, Peter Denis 1946- *Who 94*
Sutherland, Ranald Iain *Who 94*
Sutherland, Raymond Carter 1917- *WhoAm 94*
Sutherland, Raymond Elwood 1937- *WhoFI 94*
Sutherland, Richard Earl 1930- *WhoAmP 93*
Sutherland, Robert L. 1916- *WhoAm 94*
Sutherland, Sandy 1902- *WhoAmA 93N*
Sutherland, Stewart Ross 1941- *IntWW 93, Who 94*
Sutherland, Stuart *Who 94*
Sutherland, (Norman) Stuart 1927- *Who 94*
Sutherland, Veronica Evelyn 1939- *Who 94*
Sutherland, Victor d1968 *WhoHol 92*
Sutherland, William (George MacKenzie) 1933- *Who 94*
Sutherland, William Owen Sheppard 1921- *WhoAm 94*
Sutherland, William Paul 1941- *WhoAm 94*
Sutherland-Brown, Malcolm Corsan 1917- *WhoAm 94*
Sutherlin, Wayne *WhoHol 92*
Sutherlund, David Arvid 1929- *WhoAm 94, WhoAmL 94*
Suthers, John William 1951- *WhoAmL 94*
Suthiwart-Narueput, Owart 1926- *Who 94*
Suthren, Victor J. H. 1942- *WhoAm 94*
Sutin, Lawrence 1951- *WrDr 94*
Sutin, Norman *WhoAm 94, WhoScEn 94*
Sutjipto, Suganto 1946- *WhoWest 94*
Sutker, Calvin R. 1923- *WhoAmP 93*
Sutkwewat fl. 19th cent.- *EncNAR*
Sutliff, Kimberly Ann 1964- *WhoScEn 94*
Sutliff, Sandra Anna 1948- *WhoAmL 94*
Sutlin, Vivian *WhoFI 94*
Sutman, Francis Xavier 1927- *WhoAm 94*
Sutnick, Alton Ivan 1928- *WhoAm 94, WhoScEn 94*
Suto, Andras 1927- *ConWorW 93, IntWW 93*
Sutorius, James 1945- *WhoHol 92*
Sutowski, Thor Brian 1945- *WhoAm 94*
Sutphen, Harold Amerman, Jr. 1926- *WhoAm 94*
Sutphen, Robert Ray 1950- *WhoFI 94, WhoScEn 94*
Sutphen, (William Gilbert) Van Tassel 1861-1945 *EncSF 93*
Sutresna, Nana S. 1933- *IntWW 93*
Sutrisno, Tri *IntWW 93*
Sutro, John Alfred 1905- *WhoAm 94*
Sutte, Donald T., Jr. 1933- *WhoAm 94*
Suttell, Paul Allyn 1949- *WhoAmL 94, WhoAmP 93, WhoFI 94*
Suttenfield, Diana 1944- *WhoAmA 93*
Sutter, Barton *DrAPF 93*
Sutter, Brian *WhoAm 94*
Sutter, Carl Clifford 1957- *WhoScEn 94*
Sutter, Carol Jean 1950- *WhoFI 94*
Sutter, Darryl *WhoAm 94, WhoMW 93*
Sutter, Elizabeth Henby 1912- *WhoMW 93*
Sutter, Harvey Mack 1906- *WhoWest 94*
Sutter, James Stewart 1940- *WhoAmA 93*
Sutter, John F. *WhoAmP 93*
Sutter, John Herbert 1928- *WhoAmL 94*
Sutter, Joseph F. 1921- *WhoAm 94, WhoScEn 94, WhoWest 94*
Sutter, Laurence Brenner 1944- *WhoAmL 94*
Sutter, Leslie Strong *WhoAmA 93*
Sutter, Morley Carman 1933- *WhoAm 94*
Sutter, Richard Anthony 1909- *WhoAm 94*
Sutter, William Paul 1924- *WhoAm 94*
Sutterby, Larry Quentin 1950- *WhoScEn 94, WhoWest 94*
Sutterfield, James Ray *WhoAmL 94*
Suttie, (George) Philip Grant- 1938- *Who 94*
Suttill, Margaret Joan *Who 94*
Suttinger, Mary Catherine 1945- *WhoMW 93*
Suttle, Bruce Boehmer 1935- *WhoMW 93*
Suttle, Dorwin Wallace 1906- *WhoAm 94, WhoAmL 94*
Suttle, Harold L. d1993 *NewYTBS 93*
Suttle, Helen Jayson 1925- *WhoAmP 93*
Suttle, Stephen Hungate 1940- *WhoAmL 94*
Suttles, Virginia Grant 1931- *WhoWest 94*
Suttles, William Maurrelle 1920- *WhoAm 94*
Suttman, Paul 1933- *WhoAmA 93*
Suttman, Paul 1933-1993 *NewYTBS 93*
Suttner, Bertha von 1843-1914 *BlmGWL*
Sutton, Alan John 1936- *Who 94*
Sutton, Anne C. 1921- *WhoAmP 93*
Sutton, Anthony Phillip 1953- *WhoAmL 94*
Sutton, Barbara Powderly 1940- *WhoWest 94*
Sutton, Barrett Boulware 1927- *WhoAm 94*
Sutton, Barry Bridge 1937- *Who 94*
Sutton, Berrien Daniel 1926- *WhoAm 94*
Sutton, Brian Dale 1961- *WhoAmL 94*
Sutton, Carol (Lorraine) 1945- *WhoAmA 93*
Sutton, Charles Franklin 1944- *WhoIns 94*
Sutton, Charles Richard 1927- *WhoAm 94*
Sutton, Charyn Diane *WhoBlA 94*
Sutton, Clive (Julian) 1937- *WrDr 94*
Sutton, Clyde A., Sr. 1927- *WhoBlA 94*
Sutton, Colin Bertie John 1938- *Who 94*
Sutton, Dana Ferrin 1942- *WhoAm 94*
Sutton, Daniel 1735-1819 *DcNaB MP*
Sutton, David 1917- *WrDr 94*
Sutton, David John 1944- *WrDr 94*
Sutton, Dianne Floyd 1948- *WhoBlA 94*
Sutton, Dolores *WhoAm 94, WhoHol 92*
Sutton, Dorothy Moseley *DrAPF 93*
Sutton, Dudley 1933- *WhoHol 92*
Sutton, Eddie 193-?- *BasBi*
Sutton, Elbert Lloyd 1956- *WhoFI 94*
Sutton, Elinor Owens 1930- *WhoMW 93*
Sutton, Eve(lyn Mary) 1906- *WrDr 94*
Sutton, Evelyn Mary 1906- *BlmGWL*
Sutton, Francis Xavier 1917- *WhoAm 94*
Sutton, Frank d1974 *WhoHol 92*
Sutton, Frederick (Walter) 1915- *Who 94*
Sutton, Frederick Isler, Jr. 1916- *WhoAm 94, WhoFI 94*
Sutton, Gail Oberholtzer 1953- *WhoMW 93*
Sutton, Gary William 1944- *WhoAmL 94*
Sutton, George Miksch 1898-1982 *WhoAmA 93N*
Sutton, George W. *WhoScEn 94*
Sutton, George Walter 1927- *WhoAm 94*
Sutton, Gertrude L. 1923- *WhoAmP 93*
Sutton, Gloria W. 1952- *WhoBlA 94*
Sutton, Grady 1908- *WhoHol 92*
Sutton, Harry Eldon 1927- *WhoAm 94, WhoScEn 94*
Sutton, Henry *ConAu 41NR, DrAPF 93*
Sutton, Henry 1935- *WrDr 94*
Sutton, Henry V. 1932- *WhoAmP 93*
Sutton, Horace Ashley 1919-1991 *WhAm 10*
Sutton, J. Keith 1951- *WhoAm 94*
Sutton, James Andrew 1934- *WhoAm 94, WhoFI 94*
Sutton, James Carter 1945- *WhoBlA 94*
Sutton, James T. *IntMPA 94*
Sutton, Jane 1950- *WrDr 94*
Sutton, Jean 1917- *EncSF 93*
Sutton, Jeff(erson Howard) 1913-1979 *EncSF 93*
Sutton, John d1963 *WhoHol 92*
Sutton, John (Matthias Dobson) 1932- *Who 94*
Sutton, John Ewing 1950- *WhoAmL 94*
Sutton, John F. 1962- *WhoFI 94*
Sutton, John F., Jr. 1918- *WhoAm 94*
Sutton, John Martin 1922- *WhoFI 94, WhoMW 93*
Sutton, John Paul 1934- *WhoAm 94*
Sutton, John Sydney 1936- *Who 94*
Sutton, Jonathan Stone 1944- *WhoAm 94*
Sutton, Julia *WhoHol 92*
Sutton, Julia Sumberg 1928- *WhoAm 94*
Sutton, Kay d1988 *WhoHol 92*
Sutton, Keith Norman *Who 94*
Sutton, Kelso Furbush 1939- *WhoAm 94*
Sutton, Leonard von Bibra 1914- *WhoAmL 94, WhoAmP 93, WhoFI 94, WhoWest 94*
Sutton, Leslie Ernest d1992 *IntWW 93N, Who 94N*
Sutton, Lorraine J. *DrAPF 93*
Sutton, Lou Nelle *WhoAmP 93*
Sutton, Marcella French 1946- *WhoFI 94, WhoWest 94*
Sutton, Martin Hope 1815-1901 *DcNaB MP*
Sutton, Mary A. 1945- *WhoBlA 94*
Sutton, Michael Scott 1962- *WhoFI 94*
Sutton, Moses 1920- *WhoBlA 94*

Swaney, Cynthia Ann 1959- *WhoMW 93, WhoScEn 94*
Swaney, Thomas Edward 1942- *WhoAm 94, WhoAmL 94*
Swanger, David *DrAPF 93*
Swanger, Sterling Orville 1922- *WhoAm 94*
Swango, William Franklin 1942- *WhoAm 94*
Swanick, Robert V. 1942- *WhoFI 94*
Swanigan, Jesse Calvin 1933- *WhoBlA 94*
Swank, Annette Marie 1953- *WhoScEn 94*
Swank, Arthur Jackson 1896- *WhAm 10*
Swank, Bradd A 1949- *WhoWest 94*
Swank, Emory Coblentz 1922- *WhoAm 94*
Swank, Roy Laver 1909- *WhoAm 94, WhoScEn 94, WhoWest 94*
Swank, Susan Elisabeth Beatty 1957- *WhoMW 93*
Swanke, Albert Homer 1909- *WhoAm 94*
Swankin, David Arnold 1934- *WhoAm 94*
Swann, Arthur M. *WhoAmP 93*
Swann, Benjamin Colin Lewis 1922- *Who 94*
Swann, Bill 1942- *WhoAmL 94*
Swann, Brian *DrAPF 93*
Swann, Brian 1940- *WhoAm 94*
Swann, Donald (Ibrahim) 1923- *ConAu 41NR, WrDr 94*
Swann, Donald Ibrahim 1923- *IntWW 93, Who 94*
Swann, Elaine *WhoHol 92*
Swann, Erwin 1906-1973 *WhoAmA 93N*
Swann, Eugene Merwyn 1934- *WhoBlA 94*
Swann, Frederick Lewis 1931- *WhoAm 94*
Swann, Harold S. 1942- *WhoIns 94*
Swann, Jerre Bailey 1939- *WhoAm 94*
Swann, John 1760-1793 *WhAmRev*
Swann, Julian Dana Nimmo H. *Who 94*
Swann, Larry D. 1952- *WhoAmP 93*
Swann, Lois *DrAPF 93*
Swann, Lynn Curtis 1952- *WhoAm 94, WhoBlA 94*
Swann, Michael (Christopher) 1941- *Who 94*
Swann, Michael M. 1950- *WhoMW 93*
Swann, Michael Meredith 1920-1990 *WhAm 10*
Swann, Robert *WhoHol 92*
Swann, Roberta M. *DrAPF 93*
Swann, Steven Charles 1951- *WhoWest 94*
Swann, Thomas Burnett 1928-1976 *EncSF 93*
Swannell, Nicola Mary *Who 94*
Swansea, Baron 1925- *Who 94*
Swansea, Charleen Whisnant *DrAPF 93*
Swansea and Brecon, Bishop of 1933- *Who 94*
Swansen, Samuel Theodore 1937- *WhoAm 94, WhoAmL 94*
Swanson, Allan Frederick 1929- *WhoMW 93*
Swanson, Arden Wilford 1929- *WhoFI 94*
Swanson, Arnold Arthur 1923- *WhoAm 94*
Swanson, Arthur Dean 1934- *WhoAmL 94*
Swanson, August George 1925- *WhoAm 94*
Swanson, Bernet Steven 1921- *WhoAm 94*
Swanson, Carroll Arthur 1915-1991 *WhAm 10*
Swanson, Charles 1949- *WhoBlA 94*
Swanson, Charles Andrew 1929- *WhoAm 94*
Swanson, Charles Richard 1953- *WhoFI 94*
Swanson, Chip d1978 *WhoHol 92*
Swanson, Darlene Marie Carlson 1925- *WhoMW 93*
Swanson, David Heath 1942- *IntWW 93, WhoAm 94, WhoFI 94, WhoMW 93*
Swanson, David Henry 1930- *WhoAmA 93*
Swanson, David Warren 1932- *WhoAm 94*
Swanson, Deborah Claire 1952- *WhoWest 94*
Swanson, Don Richard 1924- *WhoAm 94*
Swanson, Donald Alan 1938- *WhoAm 94, WhoWest 94*
Swanson, Donald Frederick 1927- *WhoAm 94, WhoMW 93*
Swanson, Edith 1934- *WhoBlA 94*
Swanson, Edwin Archie 1908- *WhoWest 94*
Swanson, Emily 1947- *WhoAmP 93*
Swanson, Ernest Ray 1946- *WhoAm 94*
Swanson, Fern Rose *WhoMW 93*
Swanson, Frank 1917-1990 *WhAm 10*
Swanson, Gary *WhoHol 92*
Swanson, Georgia May 1934- *WhoMW 93*
Swanson, Gladys M. 1926- *WhoAm 94*
Swanson, Gloria d1983 *WhoHol 92*
Swanson, Gloria 1899?-1983 *ConAu 142*
Swanson, Gordon Bell 1944- *WhoFI 94*
Swanson, Guy Edwin 1922- *WhoAm 94*
Swanson, H(arold) N(orling) 1899- *WrDr 94*

Swanson, H(arold) N(orling) 1899-1991 *WhAm 10*
Swanson, Heather (Crichton) 1949- *WrDr 94*
Swanson, Helen Anne 1957- *WhoScEn 94*
Swanson, Howard 1909-1978 *AfrAmAl 6*
Swanson, J. N. 1927- *WhoAmA 93*
Swanson, Jack *WhoHol 92*
Swanson, Jack Lee 1934- *WhoMW 93*
Swanson, James C. 1934- *WhoAmP 93*
Swanson, James T. 1949- *WhoFI 94*
Swanson, Jay Dixon 1933- *WhoAmP 93*
Swanson, Joanne Thatcher 1932- *WhoAmL 94*
Swanson, June 1931- *SmATA 76 [port]*
Swanson, Karin 1942- *WhoFI 94*
Swanson, Kim Lawrence 1945- *WhoAmL 94*
Swanson, Kristy *WhoHol 92*
Swanson, Kristy 1969- *IntMPA 94*
Swanson, Lee Richard 1957- *WhoFI 94, WhoScEn 94, WhoWest 94*
Swanson, Lenard Charles 1937- *WhoAmL 94*
Swanson, Linn McCarthy 1950- *WhoFI 94*
Swanson, Lloyd Oscar 1913- *WhoAm 94*
Swanson, Logan *EncSF 93*
Swanson, Logan 1926- *WrDr 94*
Swanson, Loren Ernest 1923- *WhoWest 94*
Swanson, Mark Todd 1951- *WhoWest 94*
Swanson, Marvin F. 1935- *WhoIns 94*
Swanson, Mary Helen 1926- *WhoAmP 93*
Swanson, Mary Linda 1959- *WhoMW 93*
Swanson, Maureen 1932- *WhoHol 92*
Swanson, Maxine Marie 1927- *WhoAmP 93*
Swanson, Norma Frances 1923- *WhoAm 94*
Swanson, O'Neil D. *WhoBlA 94*
Swanson, Patricia K. 1940- *WhoAm 94*
Swanson, Paul Rubert 1943- *WhoWest 94*
Swanson, Peggy Eubanks 1936- *WhoFI 94*
Swanson, Phillip Dean 1932- *WhoAm 94*
Swanson, Ray V. 1937- *WhoAmA 93*
Swanson, Richard Marvin 1943- *WhoWest 94*
Swanson, Richard William 1934- *WhoAm 94, WhoFI 94, WhoScEn 94, WhoWest 94*
Swanson, Robert A. 1947- *WhoAm 94, WhoFI 94*
Swanson, Robert Draper 1915- *WhoAm 94*
Swanson, Robert Killen 1932- *WhoAm 94, WhoWest 94*
Swanson, Robert Lee 1942- *WhoAmL 94*
Swanson, Robert Martin 1940- *WhoMW 93*
Swanson, Robert Mclean 1920- *WhoMW 93*
Swanson, Robert McLean, Jr. 1949- *WhoMW 93*
Swanson, Robert Paul 1946- *WhoAmL 94*
Swanson, Roy Arthur 1925- *WhoAm 94, WhoMW 93*
Swanson, Roy Joel 1945- *WhoAm 94, WhoAmL 94*
Swanson, Rune E. 1919- *WhoAm 94*
Swanson, Russell Bruce 1941- *WhoAm 94*
Swanson, Steve *DrAPF 93*
Swanson, Steven Clifford 1964- *WhoScEn 94*
Swanson, Susan Marie *DrAPF 93*
Swanson, Sydney Alan Vasey 1931- *Who 94*
Swanson, Thomas Richard 1954- *WhoMW 93*
Swanson, Torre Kolkmeier 1960- *WhoMW 93*
Swanson, Vern Grosvenor 1945- *WhoAmA 93*
Swanson, Victoria Clare Heldman 1949- *WhoAmL 94*
Swanson, Wallace Martin 1941- *WhoAm 94, WhoAmL 94*
Swanson, Warren Lloyd 1933- *WhoAmL 94*
Swanson, Wayne 1951- *WrDr 94*
Swanson, William Russell 1949- *WhoMW 93*
Swanson-Tobias, Joan Ellen 1961- *WhoMW 93*
Swanston, Clarence Eugene 1947- *WhoBlA 94*
Swanton, Ernest William 1907- *Who 94*
Swanton, H. Rae 1918- *WhoAm 94*
Swanton, Susan Irene 1941- *WhoAm 94*
Swanton, Virginia Lee 1933- *WhoMW 93*
Swanwick, Graham Russell 1906- *Who 94*
Swanwick, Helena Maria Lucy 1864-1939 *DcNaB MP*

Swanwick, Michael (Jurgen) 1950- *EncSF 93*
Swanwick, Peter d1968 *WhoHol 92*
Swanz, Donald Joseph 1933- *WhoAmP 93*
Swanzey, Robert Joseph 1935- *WhoAm 94, WhoFI 94*
Swap, Walter Charles 1943- *WhoAmA 93*
Swar Al-Dahab, Gen. *IntWW 93*
Swarbrick, James 1934- *Who 94*
Swarbrick, John Brian, Jr. 1954- *WhoAmL 94*
Sward, Robert *DrAPF 93*
Sward, Robert S. 1933- *WhoAmA 93, WrDr 94*
Sward, Robert Stuart 1933- *WhoWest 94*
Sware, Richard Michael, Jr. 1952- *WhoFI 94*
Swaroop, Anand 1957- *WhoAsA 94*
Swarowsky, Hans 1899-1975 *NewGrDO*
Swart, Karel 1921- *IntWW 93*
Swart, Marvin Dale 1934- *WhoFI 94*
Swart, Robert H. 1946- *WhoAm 94*
Swart, Vernon David, Jr. 1955- *WhoFI 94, WhoAmL 94*
Swartburg, B. Robert 1895-1975 *WhoAmA 93N*
Swarthout, Gladys d1969 *WhoHol 92*
Swarthout, Gladys 1900-1969 *NewGrDO*
Swarthout, Glendon *DrAPF 93*
Swarthout, Glendon 1918-1992 *AnObit 1992, WrDr 94N*
Swarthout, Glendon (Fred) 1918-1992 *TwCYAW*
Swarthout, Glendon Fred 1918-1992 *WhAm 10*
Swarthout, Herbert Marion 1900-1990 *WhAm 10*
Swartley, Willard M(yers) 1936- *ConAu 41NR*
Swartout, Edwin Lester 1949- *WhoAm 94*
Swartout, Glen Martin 1956- *WhoWest 94*
Swarts, Joseph Andrew 1917- *WhoAmP 93*
Swarts, Sara d1949 *WhoHol 92*
Swarts, William *DrAPF 93*
Swartwout, Joseph Rodolph 1925- *WhoAm 94*
Swartz, Benjamin Kinsell, Jr. 1931- *WhoAm 94*
Swartz, Beth Ames 1936- *WhoAmA 93*
Swartz, Charles R. 1944- *WhoAmL 94*
Swartz, Christian LeFevre 1915- *WhoAmL 94*
Swartz, David H. *WhoAmP 93*
Swartz, Donald Everett 1916- *WhoAm 94*
Swartz, Donald Percy 1921- *WhoAm 94*
Swartz, Edward M. 1934- *WhoAmL 94*
Swartz, Edward M(itchell) 1896- *WhAm 10*
Swartz, George Alfred 1928- *Who 94*
Swartz, Jack 1932- *WhoAm 94, WhoMW 93*
Swartz, James Edward 1951- *WhoMW 93*
Swartz, James Franklin, Jr. 1930- *WhoFI 94*
Swartz, James Richard 1942- *WhoFI 94*
Swartz, John L. 1945- *WhoAmL 94*
Swartz, John Michael 1936- *WhoAm 94*
Swartz, Jon David 1934- *WhoAm 94, WrDr 94*
Swartz, Linda 1950- *WhoAmA 93*
Swartz, Malcolm Gilbert 1931- *WhoAm 94*
Swartz, Melvin Jay 1930- *WhoAmL 94*
Swartz, Morton Norman 1923- *WhoAm 94, WhoScEn 94*
Swartz, Paul Frederick 1943- *WhoMW 93*
Swartz, Phillip Scott 1936-1990 *WhoAmA 93N*
Swartz, Ray 1952- *WhoWest 94*
Swartz, Reginald (William Colin) 1911- *Who 94*
Swartz, Reginald William Colin 1911- *IntWW 93*
Swartz, Richard Joel 1942- *WhoWest 94*
Swartz, Roslyn Holt 1940- *WhoWest 94*
Swartz, Seymore Bernard 1923- *WhoMW 93*
Swartz, Stephen Arthur 1941- *WhoAm 94, WhoFI 94*
Swartz, Teresa Anne 1953- *WhoWest 94*
Swartz, Thomas 1946- *WhoAmP 93*
Swartz, William d1978 *WhoHol 92*
Swartz, William John 1934- *IntWW 93, WhoAm 94, WhoMW 93*
Swartzbaugh, Marc L. 1937- *WhoAm 94*
Swartzell, Allen H. 1926- *WhoAm 94*
Swartzendruber, Dale 1925- *WhoAm 94*
Swartzendruber, Douglas Edward 1946- *WhoWest 94*
Swartzlander, Earl Eugene, Jr. 1945- *WhoAm 94, WhoScEn 94, WhoWest 94*
Swartzman, Roslyn 1931- *WhoAmA 93*
Swartzwelder, John Joseph 1949- *WhoWest 94*
Swarup, Govind 1929- *Who 94*
Swarz, Sahl 1912- *WhoAm 94*

Swarzenski, Georg 1876-1957 *WhoAmA 93N*
Swarzman, Herbert George 1937- *WhoFI 94*
Swasey, Elizabeth Jean 1960- *WhoAmL 94*
Swash, Stanley Victor 1896- *Who 94*
Swatek, Frank Edward 1929- *WhoAm 94*
Swaters, Cherie Lynn Butler 1954- *WhoWest 94*
Swatt, Stephen Benton 1944- *WhoWest 94*
Sway, Albert 1913- *WhoAmA 93*
Swayne, Julia d1933 *WhoHol 92*
Swayne, Martin 1884-1953 *EncSF 93*
Swayne, Steven Robert 1957- *WhoBlA 94*
Swaythling, Baron 1928- *IntWW 93, Who 94*
Swaythling, Jean Marcia 1908- *Who 94*
Swayze, Don 1958- *WhoHol 92*
Swayze, John Cameron 1906- *IntMPA 94*
Swayze, John Cameron, Sr. 1906- *WhoAm 94*
Swayze, Patrick 1952- *IntMPA 94, WhoHol 92*
Swayze, Patrick 1954- *IntWW 93, WhoAm 94*
Swazey, E. Michael *WhoAmP 93*
Swazey, Judith Pound 1939- *WhoAm 94*
Swazo 1924-1974 *WhoAmA 93N*
Swe, U Ba 1915- *IntWW 93*
Sweaney, James Leo 1944- *WhoWest 94*
Sweaney, William Douglas 1912- *Who 94*
Swearengen, Jack Clayton, II 1940- *WhoWest 94*
Swearer, Donald K(eeney) 1934- *WrDr 94*
Swearer, Donald Keeney 1934- *WhoAm 94*
Swearer, Howard Robert 1932-1991 *WhAm 10*
Swearer, William B. *WhoAmL 94*
Swearingen, Bert Charles 1936- *WhoAm 94*
Swearingen, David Clarke 1942- *WhoScEn 94*
Swearingen, Edward Hicks 1948- *WhoAmP 93*
Swearingen, George Robert 1923- *WhoAmP 93*
Swearingen, Harold Lyndon 1937- *WhoMW 93*
Swearingen, Jeffrey Van 1959- *WhoMW 93*
Swearingen, John Eldred 1918- *IntWW 93*
Swearingen, Judson Sterling 1907- *WhoAm 94*
Swearingen, Lawson L., Jr. 1944- *WhoAmP 93*
Sweat, Keith *WhoBlA 94*
Sweat, Sheila Diane 1961- *WhoBlA 94*
Sweatman, Willis P. d1930 *WhoHol 92*
Sweatt, A. W. d1944 *WhoHol 92*
Sweazey, George Edgar 1905-1992 *WhAm 10*
Sweda, Edward Leon, Jr. 1955- *WhoAmL 94*
Sweda, Gerald James 1942- *WhoFI 94*
Swedback, James M. 1935- *WhoAm 94, WhoFI 94*
Swedberg, Gertrude Laliah 1933- *WhoWest 94*
Swedberg, Robert Mitchell 1950- *WhoAm 94*
Swedberg, Steven Harold 1964- *WhoWest 94*
Sweden, King of *IntWW 93*
Swedenborg, Emanuel 1688-1722 *BlmGEL*
Swedenborg, Emanuel 1688-1772 *EncSF 93*
Swedlow, Jerold Lindsay 1935-1989 *WhAm 10*
Sweebe, Richard Dale 1951- *WhoAmL 94*
Sweedler, Barry Martin 1937- *WhoAm 94*
Sweeney, Arthur Hamilton, Jr. 1920- *WhoAm 94*
Sweeney, Asher William 1920- *WhoAm 94, WhoAmL 94, WhoAmP 93, WhoMW 93*
Sweeney, Barry 1931- *WrDr 94*
Sweeney, Bob *WhoHol 92*
Sweeney, Bruce L. 1932- *WhoAmP 93*
Sweeney, Bryan Philip 1954- *WhoScEn 94*
Sweeney, Charles Henry 1934- *WhoMW 93*
Sweeney, Christopher Lee 1959- *WhoWest 94*
Sweeney, Clayton Anthony 1931- *WhoAm 94*
Sweeney, D.B. 1961- *IntMPA 94, WhoHol 92*
Sweeney, Daniel Bryan, Jr. 1946- *WhoFI 94, WhoWest 94*
Sweeney, Daniel Thomas 1929- *WhoAm 94*
Sweeney, David Brian 1941- *WhoAm 94*
Sweeney, David McCann 1955- *WhoAmP 93*
Sweeney, Deborah Leah 1945- *WhoFI 94*

Sweeney, Deidre Ann 1953- *WhoAmL 94*
Sweeney, Dennis Joseph 1941- *WhoMW 93*
Sweeney, Dominic *WhoHol 92*
Sweeney, Edward 1947- *WhoAmP 93*
Sweeney, Emily Margaret 1948- *WhoAmL 94*
Sweeney, Francis E. 1934- *WhoAmL 94, WhoAmP 93, WhoMW 93*
Sweeney, Fred d1954 *WhoHol 92*
Sweeney, Fred 1896-1954
See Duffy and Sweeney *WhoCom*
Sweeney, George Bernard 1933- *WhoFI 94*
Sweeney, Gerald H. 1928- *WhoAmP 93*
Sweeney, Henry Whitcomb 1898- *WhAm 10*
Sweeney, J. Gray 1943- *WhoAmA 93*
Sweeney, Jack d1950 *WhoHol 92*
Sweeney, James Aloysius, Jr. 1934- *WhoAmP 93*
Sweeney, James Augustus 1912- *WhoWest 94*
Sweeney, James Lawrence 1951- *WhoIns 94*
Sweeney, James Lee 1930- *WhoFI 94, WhoMW 93*
Sweeney, James Lee 1944- *WhoFI 94*
Sweeney, James Patrick 1952- *WhoAm 94*
Sweeney, James Raymond 1928- *WhoAm 94*
Sweeney, Jerry Kent 1941- *WhoMW 93*
Sweeney, John Albert 1925- *WhoBlA 94*
Sweeney, John E. 1955- *WhoAmP 93*
Sweeney, John Francis 1946- *WhoAmL 94*
Sweeney, Joseph d1963 *WhoHol 92*
Sweeney, Joseph M. 1943- *WhoAmL 94*
Sweeney, Leo 1918- *WrDr 94*
Sweeney, Liam d1985 *WhoHol 92*
Sweeney, Linda Porr 1956- *WhoAmL 94*
Sweeney, Lucy Graham 1946- *WhoScEn 94*
Sweeney, Mark Owen 1942- *WhoAm 94*
Sweeney, Mary Carolyn *WhoFI 94*
Sweeney, Matthew 1952- *WrDr 94*
Sweeney, Michael *WhoAmP 93*
Sweeney, Michael 1950- *WhoWest 94*
Sweeney, Michael J. 1953- *WhoAm 94*
Sweeney, Neal James 1957- *WhoAmL 94*
Sweeney, Nigel Hamilton 1954- *Who 94*
Sweeney, Pamela Alison 1958- *WhoWest 94*
Sweeney, Patrice Ellen 1953- *WhoFI 94*
Sweeney, Patrick A. 1941- *WhoAmP 93*
Sweeney, Phillip P. *DrAPF 93*
Sweeney, Richard James 1944- *WhoAm 94*
Sweeney, Robert 1949- *WhoAmP 93*
Sweeney, Robert Emmet 1931- *WhoAmP 93*
Sweeney, Robert Kevin 1959- *WhoAmL 94*
Sweeney, Robert Murol 1934- *WhoMW 93*
Sweeney, Terrance (Allen) 1945- *ConAu 142*
Sweeney, Terrance Allen 1945- *WhoAm 94*
Sweeney, Thomas Francis 1933- *WhoAmP 93*
Sweeney, Thomas Frederick 1943- *WhoAmL 94*
Sweeney, Thomas John 1936- *WhoAm 94*
Sweeney, Thomas Joseph, Jr. 1923- *WhoAm 94*
Sweeney, Thomas Kevin 1923- *Who 94*
Sweeney, Thomas Leonard 1936- *WhoScEn 94*
Sweeney, Walter Edward 1949- *Who 94*
Sweeney, William Alan 1926- *WhoWest 94*
Sweeney, William R., Jr. *WhoAmP 93*
Sweeny, A. Neil 1951- *WhoFI 94*
Sweeny, Charles David 1936- *WhoScEn 94*
Sweeny, Charlie 1957- *WhoFI 94*
Sweeny, John W., Jr. 1949- *WhoAmL 94*
Sweerts, Cornelis 1669-1742 *NewGrDO*
Sweet, Andrew Arnold 1956- *WhoWest 94*
Sweet, Ann Kielty 1935- *WhoAmP 93*
Sweet, Annette Crain 1957- *WhoMW 93*
Sweet, Arthur 1920- *WhoMW 93*
Sweet, Blanche d1986 *WhoHol 92*
Sweet, Bruce *DrAPF 93*
Sweet, Charles W. 1934- *WhoWest 94*
Sweet, Charles Wheeler 1943- *WhoAm 94, WhoFI 94*
Sweet, Christopher William 1963- *WhoFI 94*
Sweet, Clifford C. 1936- *WhoBlA 94*
Sweet, Cody *WhoAm 94*
Sweet, Darrell 1934- *EncSF 93*
Sweet, David Allen 1950- *WhoFI 94*
Sweet, David Charles 1938- *WhoMW 93*
Sweet, David W. 1948- *WhoAmL 94, WhoAmP 93*
Sweet, Dennis C., III *WhoAmP 93*
Sweet, Dolph d1985 *WhoHol 92*
Sweet, Gary *WhoHol 92*
Sweet, Harry d1933 *WhoHol 92*
Sweet, James M. 1945- *WhoAmL 94*
Sweet, Janice Elaine 1944- *WhoMW 93*
Sweet, Jeffrey 1950- *ConAu 43NR*
Sweet, Joseph John 1914- *WhoAmP 93*
Sweet, Katie 1957- *WhoHol 92*
Sweet, Lewis Taber, Jr. 1932- *WhoAmL 94*
Sweet, Lowell Elwin 1931- *WhoAmL 94, WhoAmP 93, WhoFI 94*
Sweet, Marc Steven 1945- *WhoFI 94*
Sweet, Marion d1978 *WhoHol 92*
Sweet, Mary (French) 1937- *WhoAmA 93*
Sweet, Peter Alan 1921- *Who 94*
Sweet, Philip W. K., Jr. 1927- *WhoMW 93*
Sweet, Rita Genevieve 1959- *WhoScEn 94*
Sweet, Robert Burdette *DrAPF 93*
Sweet, Robert Workman 1922- *WhoAm 94, WhoAmL 94*
Sweet, Roger 1946- *WhoAmA 93*
Sweet, Sheila *WhoHol 92*
Sweet, Shirley Marie 1934- *WhoMW 93*
Sweet, Steve (Steven Mark) 1952- *WhoAmA 93*
Sweet, Stuart J. 1953- *WhoAmP 93*
Sweet, Terrecia W. 1955- *WhoBlA 94*
Sweet, Tom d1967 *WhoHol 92*
Sweet, William Warren 1881-1959 *DcAmReB 2*
Sweetbaum, Henry Alan 1937- *Who 94*
Sweeting, George 1924- *WrDr 94*
Sweeting, William Hart 1909- *Who 94*
Sweetland, Monroe Mark 1910- *WhoAmP 93*
Sweetland, Nancy Rose 1934- *WrDr 94*
Sweetman, Brian Jack 1936- *WhoAm 94*
Sweetman, David 1943- *ConAu 141, WrDr 94*
Sweetman, Doris Dwan 1918- *WhoAmP 93*
Sweetman, Jennifer Joan *Who 94*
Sweetman, John Francis 1930- *Who 94*
Sweetman, John Stuart, Jr. 1939- *WhoMW 93*
Sweetman, Loretta Vinette 1941- *WhoWest 94*
Sweet Medicine *EncNAR*
Sweetnam, (David) Rodney 1927- *Who 94*
Sweetow, Elizabeth Swoope 1947- *WhoWest 94*
Sweets, Ellen Adrienne 1941- *WhoBlA 94*
Sweets, Henry Hayes, III 1949- *WhoAm 94*
Sweetser, Gene G. 1948- *WhoAmP 93*
Sweetser, Susan W. 1958- *WhoAmP 93*
Sweetser, Theodore Higgins 1948- *WhoScEn 94*
Sweetser, Wesley 1919- *WrDr 94*
Sweezy, John W. 1932- *WhoAmP 93*
Sweezy, John William 1932- *WhoMW 93*
Sweezy, Paul Marlor 1910- *WhoAm 94*
Sweig, Michael Terry 1946- *WhoMW 93*
Sweitzer, Charles Leroy 1939- *WhoAmA 93*
Sweitzer, David Eugene 1962- *WhoAmL 94*
Sweitzer, Harry Averil 1943- *WhoAmL 94*
Sweitzer, Kenneth Adair 1928- *WhoFI 94*
Sweitzer, James M. 1947- *WhoIns 94*
Swelgin, James Herman 1942- *WhoWest 94*
Swendiman, Alan Robert 1947- *WhoAmL 94*
Swenka, Arthur John 1937- *WhoAm 94, WhoWest 94*
Swensen, Clifford Henrik, Jr. 1926- *WhoAm 94*
Swensen, Cole *DrAPF 93*
Swensen, Grace Hartman 1931- *WhoMW 93*
Swensen, J(ean) Mary Jeanette Hamilton 1910- *WhoAmA 93*
Swensen, Laird S. 1944- *WhoWest 94*
Swensen, Mary Jean Hamilton 1910- *WhoWest 94*
Swensen, Philip Romney 1943- *WhoWest 94*
Swenson, Alfred d1941 *WhoHol 92*
Swenson, Anne (Beatrice) *WhoAmA 93*
Swenson, Arlen Terry 1947- *WhoFI 94*
Swenson, Betty 1933- *WhoAmP 93*
Swenson, Birger 1895-1990 *WhAm 10*
Swenson, Courtland Sevander 1936- *WhoAm 94*
Swenson, Donald C. 1949- *WhoAm 94*
Swenson, Douglas 1945- *WhoAmP 93*
Swenson, Elizabeth von Fischer 1941- *WhoAmL 94*
Swenson, Eric David 1954- *WhoAmL 94*
Swenson, Eric Pierson 1918- *WhoAm 94*
Swenson, George Warner, Jr. 1922- *WhoAm 94*
Swenson, Harold A. 1927- *WhoAmP 93*
Swenson, Howard William 1901-1960 *WhoAmA 93N*
Swenson, Inga 1933- *WhoHol 92*
Swenson, James Reed 1933- *WhoAm 94*
Swenson, John J. 1942- *WhoAmL 94*
Swenson, Joy A. 1921- *WhoAmP 93*
Swenson, Karen *DrAPF 93*
Swenson, Karen 1936- *WhoAm 94*
Swenson, Karl d1978 *WhoHol 92*
Swenson, Kathleen Susan 1938- *WhoWest 94*
Swenson, Linda *WhoHol 92*
Swenson, Mary Ann *WhoWest 94*
Swenson, May 1913-1989 *BlmGWL, WhAm 10*
Swenson, Orvar 1909- *WhoAm 94*
Swenson, Peggy *EncSF 93*
Swenson, Richard Alan 1948- *WhoMW 93*
Swenson, Ruth Wildman 1924- *WhoMW 93*
Swenson, Severt, Jr. 1940- *WhoAmP 93*
Swenson, Sue Dahl 1953- *WhoMW 93*
Swenson, Swen d1993 *NewYTBS 93*
Swenson, Swen 1934- *WhoHol 92*
Swenson, Ward David 1950- *WhoFI 94*
Swensson, Earl Simcox 1930- *WhoAm 94*
Swensson, Elsie Louise 1922- *WhoAmP 93*
Swerda, Patricia Fine 1916- *WhoWest 94*
Swerdlin, Joyce S. 1949- *WhoAm 94*
Swerdloff, Ileen Pollock 1945- *WhoAmL 94*
Swerdlove, Dorothy Louise 1928- *WhoAm 94*
Swerdlow, Amy 1923- *WhoAm 94*
Swerdlow, Harold 1957- *WhoScEn 94*
Swerdlow, Martin Abraham 1923- *WhoAm 94, WhoScEn 94*
Swerdlow, Tom *WhoHol 92*
Swergold, Marcelle M. 1927- *WhoAmA 93*
Swerling, Jack Bruce 1946- *WhoAmL 94*
Swerling, Jo 1897- *IntDcF 2-4, IntMPA 94*
Swerling, Jo, Jr. 1931- *IntMPA 94*
Swern, Frederic Lee 1947- *WhoScEn 94*
Swetcharnik, Sara Morris 1955- *WhoAmA 93*
Swetcharnik, William Norton 1951- *WhoAmA 93*
Swetland, David Wightman 1916- *WhoMW 93*
Swetlik, William Philip 1950- *WhoMW 93, WhoScEn 94*
Swetlow, Joel *WhoHol 92*
Swetman, Glenn R(obert) 1936- *WrDr 94*
Swetman, Glenn Robert *DrAPF 93*
Swetman, Glenn Robert 1936- *WhoAm 94, WhoFI 94*
Swetnam, Daniel Richard 1957- *WhoAmL 94*
Swetnam, Monte Newton 1936- *WhoAm 94*
Swetnam, Ruth E. Danglade 1940- *WhoMW 93*
Swets, E. Lyall d1930 *WhoHol 92*
Swets, John Arthur 1928- *WhoAm 94, WhoScEn 94*
Swett, Albert Hersey 1923- *WhoAm 94*
Swett, Dale Everett 1937- *WhoWest 94*
Swett, Dana Malcolm 1925- *WhoAmP 93*
Swett, Daniel Robert 1936- *WhoAm 94*
Swett, Dick *WhoAmP 93*
Swett, Dick 1957- *CngDr 93*
Swett, Richard Nelson 1957- *WhoAm 94*
Swett, Robert E. 1928- *WhoIns 94*
Swett, Susan 1962- *WhoScEn 94*
Swette, Robert Francis 1956- *WhoWest 94*
Swetz, Frank J. 1937- *WrDr 94*
Sweven, Godfrey 1846-1935 *EncSF 93*
Swezey, Charles Mason 1935- *WhoAm 94*
Swhier, Claudia Versfelt 1950- *WhoAm 94, WhoAmL 94, WhoMW 93*
Swiatek, Kenneth Robert 1935- *WhoScEn 94*
Swibel, Howard Jay 1950- *WhoAmL 94*
Swibel, Steven Warren 1946- *WhoAm 94, WhoAmL 94*
Swichar, Edward Irving 1940- *WhoAm 94, WhoAmL 94*
Swick, Herbert Morris 1941- *WhoAm 94*
Swick, Linda Ann 1948- *WhoAmA 93*
Swick, Marly 1949- *WrDr 94*
Swickard, Charles d1929 *WhoHol 92*
Swickard, David *DrAPF 93*
Swickard, Joseph d1940 *WhoHol 92*
Swid, Stephen Claar 1940- *WhoAm 94*
Swiden, Ladell Ray 1938- *WhoAm 94, WhoFI 94, WhoMW 93, WhoScEn 94*
Swider, Joseph Charles 1908- *WhoAmP 93*
Swider, Marlene García 1961- *WhoHisp 94*
Swidler, Ann 1944- *WrDr 94*
Swidler, Joseph Charles 1907- *WhoAm 94*
Swiecicki, Marcin 1947- *IntWW 93*
Swiecicki, Peter 1954- *WhoAmL 94*
Swierenga, Robert P. 1935- *WrDr 94*
Swierkiewicz, Akos 1946- *WhoIns 94*
Swieszkowski, Dominick *WhoAmP 93*
Swift, Al 1935- *CngDr 93, WhoAm 94, WhoAmP 93, WhoWest 94*
Swift, Bernie 1922- *WhoAmP 93*
Swift, Bryan 1927- *WrDr 94*
Swift, Calvin Thomas 1937- *WhoAm 94*
Swift, Caroline Jane 1955- *Who 94*
Swift, Clive 1936- *WhoHol 92*
Swift, Clive Walter 1936- *Who 94*
Swift, David 1919- *IntMPA 94*
Swift, David L. 1936- *WhoAm 94*
Swift, David Leslie 1935- *WhoScEn 94*
Swift, Dolores Monica Marcinkevich 1936- *WhoAm 94, WhoMW 93*
Swift, E. Clinton 1945- *WhoFI 94*
Swift, Edward Foster, III 1923- *WhoAm 94*
Swift, Evangeline Wilson 1939- *WhoAm 94*
Swift, Frank Meador 1911- *WhoAm 94*
Swift, Frederic Fay 1907-1989 *WhAm 10*
Swift, Gerald Allan 1964- *WhoScEn 94*
Swift, Graham 1949- *WrDr 94*
Swift, Graham Colin 1949- *IntWW 93, Who 94*
Swift, Harold Augustus 1936- *WhoMW 93*
Swift, Herman *WhAmRev*
Swift, Hewson Hoyt 1920- *IntWW 93*
Swift, Isabel Davidson *WhoAm 94*
Swift, Ivan 1927- *WhoAmP 93*
Swift, Jane Maria 1965- *WhoAmP 93*
Swift, Jay James 1926- *WhoBlA 94*
Swift, Joan *DrAPF 93*
Swift, John Anthony 1940- *Who 94*
Swift, John Francis 1935- *WhoAm 94*
Swift, John Goulding 1955- *WhoAmL 94*
Swift, John Lionel 1947- *WhoScEn 94*
Swift, Jonathan 1667-1745 *BlmGEL [port], EncSF 93*
Swift, Kay 1897-1993 *NewYTBS 93 [port]*
Swift, Kerry Michael 1957- *WhoScEn 94*
Swift, Lela *IntMPA 94*
Swift, Leroy V. 1936- *WhoBlA 94*
Swift, Linda Denise 1965- *WhoBlA 94*
Swift, Lionel 1931- *Who 94*
Swift, Malcolm Robin 1948- *Who 94*
Swift, Mary Grace 1927- *WrDr 94*
Swift, Michael Charles 1921- *Who 94*
Swift, Michael Ronald 1935- *WhoAm 94*
Swift, Reginald Stanley 1914- *Who 94*
Swift, Richard E., Jr. 1951- *WhoAmP 93*
Swift, Richard Gene 1927- *WhoAm 94*
Swift, Richard Newton 1924- *WrDr 94*
Swift, Robert Frederic 1940- *WhoAm 94*
Swift, Robert J. 1948- *WhoAmL 94*
Swift, Robert Walter 1956- *WhoFI 94*
Swift, Stephen Christopher 1954- *WhoAmL 94*
Swift, Stephen J. 1943- *CngDr 93*
Swift, Stephen Jensen 1943- *WhoAm 94, WhoAmL 94*
Swift, Susan 1964- *WhoHol 92*
Swift, Tom 1944- *WhoAmP 93*
Swift, W. Porter 1914- *WrDr 94*
Swift, William Charles 1931- *WhoIns 94*
Swift, William Charles 1961- *WhoAm 94, WhoWest 94*
Swig, Melvin M. d1993 *NewYTBS 93*
Swig, Roselyne Chroman 1930- *WhoAm 94*
Swigart, Lynn S. 1930- *WhoAmA 93*
Swigart, Rob *DrAPF 93*
Swigart, Rob 1941- *EncSF 93*
Swiger, Roy Raymond 1967- *WhoScEn 94*
Swigert, Donna Lee 1939- *WhoFI 94*
Swigert, James Mack 1907- *WhoAm 94, WhoAmL 94*
Swiggart, Carolyn Clay 1958- *WhoAmL 94*
Swigger, B. Keith 1943- *WhoAm 94*
Swiggett, Ernest L. *WhoBlA 94*
Swiggett, Jean Donald 1910- *WhoAmA 93N*
Swihart, Andrew Alan 1954- *WhoMW 93*
Swihart, Fred Jacob 1919- *WhoAmL 94, WhoFI 94, WhoMW 93*
Swihart, H. Gregg 1938- *WhoWest 94*
Swihart, John Marion 1923- *WhoAm 94, WhoWest 94*
Swihart, Lynne Andrews 1961- *WhoFI 94*
Swihart, Thomas L. 1929- *WrDr 94*
Swildens-Rozendaal, Willie 1945- *WhoWomW 91*
Swilky, Jody *DrAPF 93*
Swiller, Randolph Jacob 1946- *WhoScEn 94*
Swilling, Pat 1964- *WhoAm 94, WhoMW 93*
Swillinger, Daniel James 1942- *WhoAmP 93*
Swim, Helen Wilson 1928- *WhoWest 94*
Swimmer c. 1835-1899 *EncNAR [port]*
Swimmer, Brad Howard 1951- *WhoMW 93*
Swinburn, Charles 1942- *WhoAm 94*
Swinburn, Richard (Hull) 1937- *Who 94*
Swinburn, Walter Robert John 1961- *Who 94*
Swinburne, A(lgernon) C(harles) 1837-1909 *GayLL*

Swinburne, Algernon Charles 1837-1909 *BlmGEL, ConAu 140*
Swinburne, Herbert Hillhouse 1912- *WhoAm 94*
Swinburne, Ivan Archie 1908- *Who 94*
Swinburne, James 1858-1958 *WorInv*
Swinburne, Nora 1902- *Who 94, WhoHol 92*
Swinburne, Richard (Granville) 1934- *WrDr 94*
Swinburne, Richard Granville 1934- *Who 94*
Swinburne, Terence Reginald 1936- *Who 94*
Swindal, William G. 1946- *WhoAmL 94*
Swindell, Albin B. 1945- *WhoAmP 93*
Swindell, Archie Calhoun, Jr. 1936- *WhoAm 94*
Swindell, Bertha 1874-1951 *WhoAmA 93N*
Swindell, Warren C. 1934- *WhoBlA 94*
Swindells, David W. 1936- *WhoAm 94*
Swindells, John 1931- *WhoHol 92*
Swindells, Madge *WrDr 94*
Swindells, (George) Michael (Geoffrey) 1930- *Who 94*
Swindells, Robert (Edward) 1939- *TwCYAW, WrDr 94*
Swindells, William, Jr. 1930- *WhoAm 94, WhoFI 94, WhoWest 94*
Swinden, (Thomas) Alan 1915- *Who 94*
Swinden, H. Scott *WhoScEn 94*
Swinderby, William fl. 1382-1392 *DcNaB MP*
Swindin, Norman 1880-1976 *DcNaB MP*
Swindle, Stephen Daniel 1940- *WhoAmL 94*
Swindlehurst, Owen Francis 1928- *Who 94*
Swindler, Daris Ray 1925- *WhoWest 94*
Swindon, Archdeacon of *Who 94*
Swinehart, Frederic Melvin 1939- *WhoScEn 94*
Swinehart, Leonard Robert *WhoAmP 93*
Swinehart, Robert Dane 1937- *WhoFI 94*
Swiner, Connie, III 1959- *WhoBlA 94*
Swinerton, William Arthur 1917- *WhoAm 94, WhoFI 94*
Swiney, Owen 1676-1754 *NewGrDO*
Swinfen, Baron 1938- *Who 94*
Swinford, Ann Elizabeth 1958- *WhoMW 93*
Swinford, David A. 1941- *WhoAmP 93*
Swing, David 1830-1894 *DcAmReB 2*
Swing, Gael Duane 1932-1990 *WhAm 10*
Swing, John Temple 1929- *WhoAm 94*
Swing, Peter Gram 1922- *WhoAm 94*
Swing, William Edwin 1936- *WhoAm 94, WhoWest 94*
Swing, William Lacy 1934- *IntWW 93, WhoAm 94, WhoAmP 93*
Swinger, Hershel Kendell 1939- *WhoBlA 94*
Swingland, Owen Merlin Webb 1919- *Who 94*
Swingle, Donald Morgan 1922- *WhoWest 94*
Swingle, Homer Dale 1916- *WhoScEn 94*
Swingle, Roy Spencer 1944- *WhoWest 94*
Swingler, Bryan Edwin 1924- *Who 94*
Swingler, Raymond John Peter 1933- *Who 94*
Swingley, Sheryl Ann 1951- *WhoMW 93*
Swink, John Lewis 1914-1991 *WhAm 10*
Swink, Laurence Nim 1934- *WhoScEn 94*
Swink, Robert E. 1918- *IntMPA 94*
Swinley, Ion d1937 *WhoHol 92*
Swinley, Margaret Albinia Joanna 1935- *Who 94*
Swinnerton, Edna Huestis d1964 *WhoAmA 93N*
Swinnerton, James 1875-1974 *WhoAmA 93N*
Swinnerton-Dyer, (Henry) Peter (Francis) 1927- *Who 94*
Swinnerton-Dyer, (Henry) Peter Francis 1927- *IntWW 93*
Swinney, Harry Leonard 1939- *WhoAm 94*
Swinney, T. Lewis 1946- *WhoBlA 94*
Swinson, Christopher 1948- *Who 94*
Swinson, Derek Bertram 1938- *WhoWest 94*
Swinson, John (Henry Alan) 1922- *Who 94*
Swint, Joseph Ellis 1952- *WhoScEn 94*
Swinton, Countess of *Who 94*
Swinton, Earl of 1937- *Who 94*
Swinton, David Holmes 1943- *WhoBlA 94*
Swinton, Jeffrey Cheever 1947- *WhoAmL 94*
Swinton, John 1925- *Who 94*
Swinton, Lee Vertis 1922- *WhoBlA 94*
Swinton, Patricia Ann 1954- *WhoBlA 94*
Swinton, Sylvia P. 1909- *WhoBlA 94*
Swinton, Tilda *WhoHol 92*
Swiontek, Steven J. 1954- *WhoAmP 93*
Swire, Adrian (Christopher) 1932- *Who 94*
Swire, John (Anthony) 1927- *Who 94*
Swire, John Kidston 1893-1983 *DcNaB MP*
Swire, Willard 1910-1991 *WhAm 10*
Swirsky, Judith Perlman 1928- *WhoAm 94*
Swirsky, Sherry A. 1951- *WhoAmL 94*
Swiryn, Steven 1947- *WhoMW 93*
Swisher, Charles Duncan 1941- *WhoMW 93*
Swisher, Donald Everett 1921- *WhoFI 94*
Swisher, Joseph Perry 1923- *WhoWest 94*
Swisher Kievet, Penny 1949- *WhoMW 93*
Swiss, Fern *IntMPA 94*
Swiss, Rodney (Geoffrey) 1904- *Who 94*
Swiss, Thomas *DrAPF 93*
Swist, Wally *DrAPF 93*
Swistak, Irena 1964- *WhoFI 94*
Swistock, Edward Elton 1962- *WhoFI 94*
Swiszcz, Paul Gerard 1958- *WhoWest 94*
Swit, Loretta 1937- *WhoAm 94*
Swit, Loretta 1938- *WhoHol 92*
Swit, Loretta 1939- *IntMPA 94*
Switha fl. 8th cent.- *BlmGWL*
Swithin, St. d862 *BlmGEL*
Switlik, John Andrew 1943- *WhoWest 94*
Switzer, Alfalfa 1926-1959 *WhoCom*
Switzer, Barbara 1940- *Who 94*
Switzer, Carl d1959 *WhoHol 92*
Switzer, Clarence Barton, Sr. 1936- *WhoAmP 93*
Switzer, Donald Hugh 1950- *WhoAmL 94*
Switzer, Jon Rex 1937- *WhoFI 94, WhoMW 93, WhoScEn 94*
Switzer, L. Dean 1918- *WhoAmP 93*
Switzer, Lou 1948- *WhoBlA 94*
Switzer, Maurice Harold 1945- *WhoAm 94, WhoMW 93*
Switzer, Robert Earl 1929- *WhoAmL 94, WhoFI 94*
Switzer, Robert Lee 1940- *WhoAm 94*
Switzer, Samuel Thomas 1951- *WhoMW 93*
Switzer, Terence Lee 1957- *WhoScEn 94*
Switzer, Veryl A. 1932- *WhoBlA 94*
Switzer, William Paul 1927- *WhoAm 94*
Swoap, David Bruce 1937- *WhoAm 94, WhoAmP 93*
Swoboda, Donald William 1944- *WhoMW 93*
Swoboda, Lary Joseph 1939- *WhoAmP 93, WhoMW 93*
Swoboda, Peter 1937- *IntWW 93*
Swoboda, Ralph Sande 1948- *WhoAm 94*
Swofford, Donald Anthony 1947- *WhoAm 94*
Swofford, Ken *WhoHol 92*
Swofford, Robert Lee 1949- *WhoAm 94*
Swofford, Stephen Ray 1947- *WhoAmL 94*
Swoger, Harry d1970 *WhoHol 92*
Swolfs, Laurent 1868-1954 *NewGrDO*
Swomley, James Anthony 1929- *WhoAm 94*
Swonger, Alvin Kent 1943- *WhoAm 94*
Swope, Charles Evans 1930- *WhoAm 94*
Swope, Donald Downey 1926- *WhoAm 94*
Swope, Herbert Bayard, Jr. *IntMPA 94*
Swope, Jeffrey Peyton 1945- *WhoAm 94, WhoAmL 94*
Swope, John Franklin 1938- *WhoAm 94, WhoFI 94, WhoIns 94*
Swope, Mary *DrAPF 93*
Swope, Richard McAllister 1940- *WhoAmL 94*
Swope, Robert J. 1936- *WhoScEn 94*
Swope, Topo 1948- *WhoHol 92*
Swope, Tracy Brooks 1952- *WhoHol 92*
Swor, Bert d1943 *WhoHol 92*
Swor, James L. d1954 *WhoHol 92*
Swor, John d1965 *WhoHol 92*
Swor, John 1883-1965
See Moran and Mack *WhoCom*
Sword, Carl Harry 1947- *WhoAmL 94*
Sword, Charles Hege, Jr. 1957- *WhoWest 94*
Sword, Christopher Patrick 1928- *WhoAm 94*
Sword, George c. 1847- *EncNAR*
Sword, John Howe 1915- *Who 94*
Sword, Robert Randolph 1954- *WhoWest 94*
Sword, Wiley 1937- *WrDr 94*
Swords, Gary A. 1947- *WhoIns 94*
Swords, Henry Logan, II 1948- *WhoFI 94*
Swords, Michael Alfred 1965- *WhoMW 93*
Swoyer, Ann Myrtle *WhAm 10*
Swyer, Gerald Isaac Macdonald 1917- *Who 94*
Swygert, H. Patrick 1943- *WhoAm 94*
Swygert, Haywood Patrick 1943- *WhoBlA 94*
Swynnerton, Roger (John Massy) 1911- *Who 94*
Swysgood, Charles 1939- *WhoAmP 93*
Swystun-Rives, Bohdana Alexandra 1925- *WhoScEn 94*
Sy, Antonio Ngo, Jr. 1964- *WhoAsA 94*
Sy, Bon Kiem 1961- *WhoAsA 94*
Sy, Francisco S. 1949- *WhoAsA 94*
Sy, Jose 1944- *WhoAsA 94*
Syal, Jang B. 1948- *WhoFI 94*
Syal, Shanta 1948- *WhoAsA 94*
Syberberg, Hans-Jurgen 1935- *IntWW 93*
Sybesma, Edward D., Jr. 1947- *WhoAmL 94*
Syblik, Detlev Adolf 1943- *WhoScEn 94*
Sydenham, Michael John 1923- *WrDr 94*
Sydenham, Thomas 1624-1689 *WorScD*
Sy Diallo, Mata *WhoWomW 91*
Sydney, Archbishop of 1923- *Who 94*
Sydney, Archbishop of 1931- *Who 94*
Sydney, Assistant Bishop of *Who 94*
Sydney, Aurele d1920 *WhoHol 92*
Sydney, Basil d1968 *WhoHol 92*
Sydney, Bruce d1942 *WhoHol 92*
Sydney, Derek *WhoHol 92*
Sydney, Doris S. 1934- *WhoFI 94*
Sydney, North, Bishop of *Who 94*
Sydney, South, Bishop of *Who 94*
Sydnor, Douglas Bryan 1952- *WhoFI 94*
Sydnor, Earl d1989 *WhoHol 92*
Sydnor, Robert Hadley 1947- *WhoWest 94*
Sydow, Erik von 1912- *IntWW 93*
Sydow, Max von 1929- *IntWW 93*
Sydow, Michael David 1950- *WhoAmL 94*
Syed, Ibrahim Bijli 1939- *WhoScEn 94*
Syed, Karamat A. 1939- *WhoAsA 94*
Syed, Moinuddin 1947- *WhoScEn 94*
Syed Putra Bin Syed Hassan Jamalullail *IntWW 93*
Syeduzzaman, M. 1934- *IntWW 93*
Syer, Warren Bertram 1923- *WhoAm 94*
Syfan, Richard David 1957- *WhoAmL 94*
Syfert, Samuel Ray 1928- *WhoMW 93*
Sygall, Susan E. 1953- *WhoWest 94*
Syke, Cameron John 1957- *WhoAmL 94, WhoWest 94*
Sykee, Gloria *DrAPF 93*
Sykes, Abel B., Jr. 1934- *WhoBlA 94*
Sykes, Alan Larry 1952- *WhoAmP 93*
Sykes, Alfred Geoffrey 1934- *IntWW 93*
Sykes, Arthur Patrick 1906- *Who 94*
Sykes, Bobbi 1943- *BlmGWL*
Sykes, Bonar Hugh Charles 1922- *Who 94*
Sykes, Brenda 1950- *WhoHol 92*
Sykes, Brian Douglas 1943- *WhoAm 94*
Sykes, Dancy Dabbs 1952- *WhoFI 94*
Sykes, David Terrence 1937- *WhoAm 94*
Sykes, Donald Armstrong 1930- *Who 94*
Sykes, Donald Kunkel, Jr. 1956- *WhoMW 93*
Sykes, Edwin Leonard 1914- *Who 94*
Sykes, Eric 1923- *IntMPA 94, WhoHol 92*
Sykes, Gresham M'Cready 1922- *WhoAm 94*
Sykes, James 1725-1792 *WhAmRev*
Sykes, James Thurman 1935- *WhoAmP 93, WhoMW 93*
Sykes, John *Who 94*
Sykes, John (Charles Anthony le Gallais) 1928- *Who 94*
Sykes, (Francis) John (Badcock) 1942- *Who 94*
Sykes, John Bradbury d1993 *Who 94N*
Sykes, John David 1956- *Who 94*
Sykes, Joseph Walter 1915- *Who 94*
Sykes, Keble Watson 1921- *Who 94*
Sykes, Keith *Who 94*
Sykes, (Malcolm) Keith 1925- *Who 94*
Sykes, Kevin Lee 1948- *WhoAmL 94*
Sykes, L. Bonsall 1920- *WhoAmP 93*
Sykes, Lynn R. 1937- *IntWW 93*
Sykes, Lynn Ray 1937- *WhoAm 94*
Sykes, (William) Maltby 1911- *WhoAmA 93*
Sykes, Melvin Julius 1924- *WhoAm 94*
Sykes, Michael *DrAPF 93*
Sykes, Percy Molesworth 1867-1945 *WhWE*
Sykes, Peter 1923- *IntWW 93*
Sykes, Ray *WhoBlA 94*
Sykes, Richard *Who 94*
Sykes, (James) Richard 1934- *Who 94*
Sykes, Richard Brook 1942- *Who 94, WhoScEn 94*
Sykes, Robert A. 1947- *WhoBlA 94*
Sykes, Robert Bruce 1948- *WhoAmL 94, WhoAmP 93*
Sykes, Robert Reed 1952- *WhoAmL 94*
Sykes, Roosevelt d1983 *WhoHol 92*
Sykes, Roy Arnold, Jr. 1948- *WhoWest 94*
Sykes, S(ondra) C(atharine) *EncSF 93*
Sykes, Stephen Whitefield *Who 94*
Sykes, Tatton (Christopher Mark) 1943- *Who 94*
Sykes, Vernon L. 1951- *WhoAmP 93*
Sykes, Vernon Lee 1951- *WhoBlA 94*
Sykes, Weathers York 1927-1990 *WhAm 10*
Sykes, Wilfred 1883-1964 *EncABHB 9*
Sykes, William Richard, Jr. 1948- *WhoBlA 94*
Sykes, William Robert 1840-1917 *DcNaB MP*
Sykora, Barbara Zwach 1941- *WhoAmP 93*
Sykora, Donald D. 1930- *WhoAm 94, WhoFI 94*
Sykora, Harold James 1939- *WhoAm 94*
Sylak, Charles John, Jr. 1950- *WhoFI 94*
Sylbert, Anthea 1939- *IntMPA 94*
Sylbert, Richard 1928- *IntDcF 2-4*
Syler, M. Rene 1963- *WhoBlA 94*
Sylk, Leonard Allen 1941- *WhoFI 94*
Sylla, John Richard 1959- *WhoWest 94*
Sylla, Richard Eugene 1940- *WhoFI 94, WhoScEn 94*
Sylte, Judith Ann Osterberg 1943- *WhoWest 94*
Sylva, Marguerita d1957 *WhoHol 92*
Sylva, Marguerite 1875-1957 *NewGrDO*
Sylvan, Rita M. 1928- *WhoAmA 93*
Sylvani, Gladys d1953 *WhoHol 92*
Sylvanus, Joanne Margaret 1931- *WhoWest 94*
Sylvas, Lionel B. 1940- *WhoBlA 94*
Sylvester, Barbara Thornton 1929- *WhoAmP 93*
Sylvester, Bill *DrAPF 93*
Sylvester, Christopher Urdahl 1929- *WhoAmP 93*
Sylvester, Clara d1941 *WhoHol 92*
Sylvester, (Anthony) David (Bernard) 1924- *Who 94*
Sylvester, Edward Joseph 1942- *WhoWest 94*
Sylvester, George Harold 1907- *Who 94*
Sylvester, George Howard 1927- *WhoAm 94*
Sylvester, Geraldine F. 1931- *WhoAmP 93*
Sylvester, Harold *WhoHol 92*
Sylvester, Harry A. d1993 *NewYTBS 93*
Sylvester, Henry d1961 *WhoHol 92*
Sylvester, Janet *DrAPF 93*
Sylvester, John Vance, IV 1954- *WhoAmL 94*
Sylvester, Joseph Robert 1942- *WhoMW 93*
Sylvester, Lucille 1909- *WhoAmA 93N*
Sylvester, Lynette Marie 1946- *WhoAmP 93*
Sylvester, Melvin R. 1939- *WhoBlA 94*
Sylvester, Morris 1953- *WhoFI 94*
Sylvester, Nancy Katherine 1947- *WhoMW 93*
Sylvester, Odell Howard, Jr. 1924- *WhoBlA 94*
Sylvester, Patrick Joseph *WhoBlA 94*
Sylvester, Philip 1910- *WrDr 94*
Sylvester, Richard Russell 1938- *WhoFI 94*
Sylvester, Terry Lee 1949- *WhoFI 94, WhoMW 93*
Sylvester, William 1922- *WhoHol 92*
Sylvester-Evans, Alun 1918- *Who 94*
Sylvestre, Guy 1918- *WhoAmA 93*
Sylvestre, (Joseph Jean) Guy 1918- *IntWW 93*
Sylvestre, Jean Guy 1918- *WhoAm 94*
Sylvia, Frank J. 1928- *WhoAmP 93*
Sylvia, Gaby d1980 *WhoHol 92*
Sylvie d1970 *WhoHol 92*
Sylvin, Francis 1910- *WrDr 94*
Sym, Igo d1941 *WhoHol 92*
Symanski, Robert Anthony 1946- *WhoAm 94*
Symchych, Janice M. 1951- *WhoAm 94, WhoAmL 94*
Symcox, Geoffrey Walter 1938- *WhoWest 94*
Syme, James 1930- *Who 94*
Syme, (Neville) Ronald 1910- *WrDr 94*
Syme, Sherman Leonard 1932- *WhoAm 94*
Symens, Paul N. *WhoAmP 93*
Symens, Ronald Edwin 1951- *WhoMW 93*
Symeonoglou, Sarantis Miltiadou 1937- *WhoMW 93*
Symes, Clifford E. 1929- *WhoScEn 94*
Symes, Lawrence Richard 1942- *WhoScEn 94*
Symes, (Lilian) Mary 1912- *Who 94*
Symes, R. F. *SmATA 77*
Symington, Donald *WhoHol 92*
Symington, Fife 1945- *WhoAm 94, WhoAmP 93, WhoWest 94*
Symington, James W. 1927- *WhoAmP 93*
Symington, Janey Studt 1928- *WhoMW 93, WhoScEn 94*
Symington, Thomas 1915- *Who 94*
Symmers, William Garth 1910- *WhoAm 94*
Symmers, William St. Clair 1917- *Who 94*
Symmes, Daniel Leslie 1949- *WhoWest 94*
Symmes, John Cleves 1742-1814 *WhAmRev*
Symmes, John Cleves 1780-1829 *EncSF 93*
Symmes, Robert Edward *GayLL*
Symmes, Susanna Livingston fl. 1794-1808 *BlmGWL*

Symmes, William Daniel 1938- *WhoAmL 94*
Symmonds, Algernon Washington 1926- *Who 94*
Symmonds, Richard Earl 1922- *WhoAm 94*
Symmons-Symonolewicz, Konstantin 1909- *WrDr 94*
Symms, Steven D. 1938- *WhoAmP 93*
Symms, Steven Douglas 1938- *IntWW 93*
Symon, Burk d1950 *WhoHol 92*
Symon, Lindsay 1929- *Who 94, WhoAm 94*
Symonds, Ann Hazel S. *Who 94*
Symonds, Augustin d1944 *WhoHol 92*
Symonds, Genevieve Ellen 1931- *WhoAmP 93*
Symonds, James William 1950- *WhoAmL 94*
Symonds, Jane Ursula *Who 94*
Symonds, John *WrDr 94*
Symonds, Matthew John 1953- *Who 94*
Symonds, Norman Leslie 1953- *WhoWest 94*
Symonds, Pamela (Maureen Southey) 1916- *WrDr 94*
Symonds, Paul Southworth 1916- *WhoAm 94*
Symonds, Richard *Who 94*
Symonds, (John) Richard 1918- *WrDr 94*
Symonds, (John) Richard (Charters) 1918- *Who 94*
Symonds, Robert 1926- *WhoHol 92*
Symonds, Ronald Charters 1916- *Who 94*
Symonenko, Valentyn Kostyantynovych 1940- *LngBDD*
Symonik, Daniel Michael 1960- *WhoWest 94*
Symons, A. P. *WhoIns 94*
Symons, Alphonse James Albert 1900-1941 *DcNaB MP*
Symons, Andrew Lyn 1949- *WhoAm 94*
Symons, Carla Cae 1950- *WhoMW 93*
Symons, Christopher John Maurice 1949- *Who 94*
Symons, Edward Leonard, Jr. 1941- *WhoAm 94*
Symons, Elizabeth Conway 1951- *Who 94*
Symons, George Edgar 1903- *WhoScEn 94*
Symons, Geraldine 1909- *WrDr 94*
Symons, Hugh Williams 1927- *WhoFI 94*
Symons, J. Keith 1932- *WhoAm 94*
Symons, James Martin 1931- *WhoAm 94*
Symons, James Martin 1937- *WhoAm 94, WhoWest 94*
Symons, Joyce 1927- *WhoAmP 93*
Symons, Julian (Gustave) 1912- *WrDr 94*
Symons, Julian Gustave 1912- *IntWW 93, Who 94, WhoAm 94*
Symons, Leslie John 1926- *WrDr 94*
Symons, Martyn Christian Raymond 1925- *Who 94*
Symons, Patrick (Jeremy) 1933- *Who 94*
Symons, Patrick Stewart 1925- *IntWW 93, Who 94*
Symons, Robert Henry 1934- *Who 94*
Symons, Robert Spencer 1925- *WhoAm 94, WhoWest 94*
Symons, (H. B.) Scott 1933- *WrDr 94*
Symons, Timothy James McNeil 1951- *WhoAm 94, WhoScEn 94*
Sympson, Tony 1906- *WhoHol 92*
Syms, John Grenville St. George 1913- *Who 94*
Syms, Sylvia 1934- *IntMPA 94, WhoHol 92*
Symuleski, Richard Aloysius 1947- *WhoMW 93*
Synan, Edward A. 1918- *WrDr 94*
Synan, Edward Aloysius, Jr. 1918- *WhoAm 94*
Synan, (Harold) Vinson 1934- *WrDr 94*
Synar, Michael L. 1950- *WhoAmP 93*
Synar, Michael Lynn 1950- *WhoAm 94*
Synar, Mike 1950- *CngDr 93*
Syndergaard, Larry Edward 1936- *WhoMW 93*
Synek, M. 1930- *WhoScEn 94*
Synge, Allen 1930- *ConAu 142*
Synge, Henry Millington 1921- *IntWW 93, Who 94*
Synge, J(ohn) L(yton) 1897- *EncSF 93*
Synge, (Edmund) J(ohn) M(illington) 1871-1909 *ConAu 141, IntDcT 2 [port]*
Synge, John Lighton 1897- *IntWW 93, Who 94*
Synge, John Millington 1871-1909 *BlmGEL, NewGrDO*
Synge, Richard L. M. *WorInv*
Synge, Richard Laurence Millington 1914- *IntWW 93, Who 94, WhoScEn 94*
Synge, Robert Carson 1922- *Who 94*
Synge, Ursula 1930- *WrDr 94*
Synk, James Arthur 1934- *WhoAm 94*
Synnett, Robert John 1958- *WhoFI 94*
Synnot, Anthony (Monckton) 1922- *Who 94*

Synnott, Hilary Nicholas Hugh 1945- *Who 94*
Synnott, Paul A., Jr. 1939- *WhoIns 94*
Synnott, William Raymond 1929- *WhoAm 94, WhoFI 94*
Synodinos, John Anthony 1934- *WhoAm 94*
Synodinou, Anna *WhoWomW 91*
Sypert, George Walter 1941- *WhoAm 94*
Syphax, Burke 1910- *WhoBlA 94*
Syphax, Margarite R. 1923- *WhoBlA 94*
Sypherd, Paul Starr 1936- *WhoAm 94*
Syquia, Enrique 1930- *IntWW 93*
Syquia, Luis Salvador *DrAPF 93*
Syracusa, Anthony 1933- *WhoAmP 93*
Syrdal, Daniel D. 1946- *WhoAmL 94*
Syrett, Barry 1934- *WhoWest 94*
Syrett, Netta 1865-1943 *DcLB 135 [port]*
Syrimis, George 1921- *IntWW 93*
Syring, James John 1942- *WhoWest 94*
Syromiatnikov, Vladimir Sergeevich 1933- *WhoScEn 94*
Syron, Martin Bernard 1936- *WhoFI 94*
Syron, Richard Francis 1943- *WhoAm 94*
Syrop, Konrad 1914- *WrDr 94*
Syrop, Mitchell 1953- *WhoAmA 93*
Syrovatko, Vitaly Grigorevich 1940- *LngBDD*
Syryjczyk, Tadeusz 1948- *IntWW 93*
Syse, Jan P. 1930- *IntWW 93*
Sysonby, Baron 1945- *WhoHol 92*
Sysoyev, Vyacheslav Vyacheslavovich 1937- *IntWW 93*
Systma, Fredric A. 1944- *WhoAmL 94*
Sytek, Donna Page 1944- *WhoAmP 93*
Sytek, John J. 1943- *WhoAmP 93*
Sythes, Percy Arthur 1915- *Who 94*
Sytnyk, Viktor Petrovych 1939- *LngBDD*
Sytsma, Fredric Alan 1944- *WhoAm 94*
Sytsma, Karen L. 1964- *WhoAm 94*
Syvanen, Michael 1943- *WhoScEn 94*
Syverson, Aldrich 1914-1988 *WhAm 10*
Syverson, Dave *WhoAmP 93*
Syvertsen, Edwin Thor, Jr. 1923- *WhoMW 93*
Syvertsen, Ryder *DrAPF 93*
Syvertsen, Ryder (Otto) 1941- *EncSF 93*
Syvertson, Clarence Alfred 1926- *WhoAm 94, WhoWest 94*
Szabad, George Michael 1917- *WhoAm 94*
Szabad, Gyorgy 1924- *IntWW 93*
Szablya, Helen Mary 1934- *WhoWest 94*
Szablya, John Francis 1924- *WhoAm 94*
Szabo, Albert 1925- *WhoAm 94*
Szabo, Alexander, II 1953- *WhoFI 94*
Szabo, August John 1921- *WhoFI 94*
Szabo, Barna Aladar 1935- *WhoAm 94*
Szabo, Daniel 1933- *WhoAm 94, WhoAmP 93*
Szabo, Denis 1929- *ConAu 43NR, IntWW 93, WhoAm 94*
Szabo, Istvan 1938- *IntMPA 94, IntWW 93*
Szabo, Ivan 1934- *IntWW 93*
Szabo, Joseph Clark 1957- *WhoMW 93*
Szabo, Joseph George 1950- *WhoAmA 93*
Szabo, Laszlo *WhoHol 92*
Szabo, Magda 1917- *BlmGWL, IntWW 93*
Szabo, Nicholas 1930- *WhoWest 94*
Szabo, Peter John 1946- *WhoFI 94*
Szabo, Peter Szentmihalyi *EncSF 93*
Szabo, Robert Joseph 1962- *WhoWest 94*
Szabo, Sandor d1966 *WhoHol 92*
Szabo, Stephen Lee 1940- *WhoAmA 93*
Szabo, Violette Reine Elizabeth 1921-1945 *DcNaB MP*
Szabo, Zoltan 1943- *WhoAm 94, WhoWest 94*
Szabolcsi, Miklos 1921- *IntWW 93*
Szajna, Jozef 1922- *IntWW 93*
Szakal, Eva I. 1948- *WhoFI 94*
Szakall, Szdke d1955 *WhoHol 92*
Szal, Grace Rowan 1962- *WhoScEn 94*
Szala, Scott J. 1953- *WhoAm 94*
Szalai, Beatrice Benner 1942- *WhoFI 94*
Szalapski, Judith Raines 1937- *WhoAm 94*
Szalkowski, Charles Conrad 1948- *WhoAm 94, WhoAmL 94*
Szalkowski, Mary Bernadette 1951- *WhoMW 93*
Szaller, James Francis 1945- *WhoAmL 94*
Szamek, Pierre Ervin *WhoAm 94*
Szantho, Enid 1907- *NewGrDO*
Szanto, George 1940- *WhoAm 94*
Szanto, Louis P. 1889-1965 *WhoAmA 93N*
Szanton, Andrew (Emlew) 1963- *ConAu 140*
Szapocznik, José 1947- *WhoHisp 94*
Szarabajka, Keith 1952- *WhoHol 92*
Szarek, Stanislaw Jerzy 1953- *WhoAm 94*
Szarek, Walter Anthony 1938- *WhoAm 94*
Szaro, Judith Salomea 1952- *WhoAm 94*
Szarwark, Ernest John 1951- *WhoAm 94*
Szary, Richard M. *WhoAm 94*
Szasz, Andras Istvan 1947- *WhoScEn 94*
Szasz, Frank V. 1925- *WhoAmA 93*

Szasz, Thomas Stephen 1920- *IntWW 93, WhoAm 94, WhoScEn 94, WrDr 94*
Szaszy, Miraka Petricevich 1921- *Who 94*
Szathmary, Albert d1975 *WhoHol 92*
Szathmary, Sandor *EncSF 93*
Szczarba, Robert Henry 1932- *WhoAm 94*
Szczepanski, Jan 1913- *IntWW 93*
Szczepanski, Slawomir Zbigniew Steven 1948- *WhoAm 94*
Szczepek, John S. 1942- *WhoIns 94*
Szczerba, Victor Bogdan 1966- *WhoWest 94*
Szczesniak, Edward Joseph 1943- *WhoAmP 93*
Szczurek, Thomas Eugene 1957- *WhoMW 93*
Sze, Andrew Wei Tseng 1926- *WhoFI 94*
Sze, Andy Hok-Fan 1951- *WhoAm 94*
Sze, Arthur *DrAPF 93*
Sze, Chia-Ming 1937- *WhoAsA 94*
Sze, Morgan Chuan-Yuan 1917- *WhoAsA 94*
Sze, Paul Y. 1938- *WhoAsA 94*
Szebehely, Victor G. 1921- *WhoAm 94, WhoScEn 94*
Szefler, Stanley James 1948- *WhoAm 94*
Szego, Clara Marian 1916- *WhoAm 94, WhoWest 94*
Szego, Peter A. 1925- *WhoWest 94*
Szekely, Gabor 1944- *IntWW 93*
Szekely, Julian 1934- *WhoScEn 94*
Szekely, Mihaly 1901-1963 *NewGrDO*
Szelc, Dawn Elizabeth Albrecht 1963- *WhoMW 93*
Szeligowski, Tadeusz 1896-1963 *NewGrDO*
Szell, George 1897-1970 *NewGrDO*
Szell, Patrick John 1942- *Who 94*
Szeluto, Apolinary 1884-1966 *NewGrDO*
Szemerenyi, Oswald John Louis 1913- *Who 94*
Szenberg, Michael 1934- *WhoAm 94*
Szentagothai, Janos 1912- *IntWW 93*
Szent-Gyorgyi, Albert 1893-1986 *WorScD*
Szentirmai, George 1928- *WhoAm 94*
Szentpaly, Laszlo Von 1942- *WhoScEn 94*
Szep, Paul Michael 1941- *WhoAm 94*
Szepes, Maria *EncSF 93*
Szer, Wlodzimierz 1924- *WhoAm 94*
Szerejko, James J. 1948- *WhoAmL 94*
Szeremeta-Browar, Taisa Lydia 1957- *WhoMW 93*
Szeri, Andras Z. 1934- *WhoAm 94*
Szerlip, Barbara *DrAPF 93*
Szerlip, William Alan 1949- *WhoFI 94*
Szerszen, Jedrzej Bogumil 1946- *WhoMW 93, WhoScEn 94*
Szesko, Judith Clarann *WhoAmA 93*
Szesko, Lenore Rundle 1933- *WhoAmA 93*
Szeto, Erik K. 1949- *WhoAsA 94*
Szeto, Hung 1936- *WhoFI 94, WhoWest 94*
Szeto, Paul Cheuk-Ching 1940- *WhoWest 94*
Szewczyk, Albin Anthony 1935- *WhoAm 94*
Szewczyk, Martin Joseph 1954- *WhoScEn 94*
Szewczyk, Pawel 1942- *WhoScEn 94*
Szigeti, Cynthia *WhoHol 92*
Szigeti, Joseph d1973 *WhoHol 92*
Szigeti, Michelle Marie 1954- *WhoMW 93*
Szilagyi, Desiderius Emerick 1910- *WhoAm 94*
Szilard, Leo 1898-1964 *EncSF 93, WorInv*
Szilvasy, Linda Markuly 1940- *WhoAmA 93*
Szirmai, Albert 1880-1967 *NewGrDO*
Szirmai, Endre Anreas Franz 1922- *WhoAm 94*
Szirmay, Marta c. 1939- *NewGrDO*
Szirtes, George 1948- *WrDr 94*
Szklenski, Theodore Paul 1959- *WhoScEn 94*
Szladits, Lola Leontin 1923-1990 *WhAm 10*
Szlazak, Anita Christina 1943- *WhoAm 94*
Szletynski, Henryk 1903- *IntWW 93*
Szmagala, Taras G. 1933- *WhoAmP 93*
Szmanda, Charles Raymond *WhoScEn 94*
Szmanda, Lucille Marie 1924- *WhoMW 93*
Sznajderman, Marius S. 1926- *WhoAmA 93*
Szoka, Edmund Casimir 1927- *IntWW 93*
Szoke, John *WhoAmA 93*
Szoke, Joseph Louis 1947- *WhoMW 93*
Szoke, Robert Steven 1950- *WhoMW 93*
Szokolay, Sandor 1931- *IntWW 93, NewGrDO*
Szold, Bernard d1960 *WhoHol 92*
Szold, Harold James 1896- *WhAm 10*
Szold, Henrietta 1860-1945 *DcAmReB 2*
Szollosy, Andras 1921- *IntWW 93*
Szonyi, Erzsebet 1924- *IntWW 93, NewGrDO*

Sztompka, Piotr 1944- *ConAu 141*
Sztrik, Janos 1953- *WhoScEn 94*
Szuch, Clyde Andrew 1930- *WhoAm 94, WhoAmL 94*
Szucs, Andrew Eric 1946- *WhoMW 93*
Szuhaj, Bernard Francis 1942- *WhoScEn 94*
Szukics, James Charles 1957- *WhoScEn 94*
Szulborski, Mary Lou 1957- *WhoAmP 93*
Szulc, Roman Wladyslaw 1935- *WhoScEn 94*
Szulc, Tad 1926- *WhoAm 94, WrDr 94*
Szumigalski, Anne *DrAPF 93*
Szumigalski, Anne 1922- *BlmGWL*
Szuros, Matyas 1933- *IntWW 93*
Szurszewski, Joseph Henry 1940- *WhoAm 94*
Szwajger, Adina B. d1993 *NewYTBS 93 [port]*
Szwajger, Adina Blady 1917- *ConAu 140*
Szwajger, Adina Blady 1917-1993 *ConAu 141*
Szwalbenest, Benedykt Jan 1955- *WhoAmL 94*
Szwarc, Jeannot 1939- *IntMPA 94*
Szwarc, Michael M. 1909- *Who 94, WhoAm 94*
Szybalski, Waclaw 1921- *WhoAm 94*
Szych, Gordon Steve 1961- *WhoFI 94*
Szydlow, Jarl *EncSF 93*
Szydlowski, Mary Vigliante *DrAPF 93*
Szyk, Arthur 1894-1951 *WhoAmA 93N*
Szymanowski, Karol 1882-1937 *NewGrDO*
Szymanski, Barry Walter 1943- *WhoAmL 94*
Szymanski, John James 1960- *WhoScEn 94*
Szymanski, Karen Ann 1952- *WhoAmP 93*
Szymborska, Wislawa 1923- *BlmGWL [port], ConWorW 93, IntWW 93*
Szymoniak, Elaine 1920- *WhoAmP 93*
Szymoniak, Elaine Eisfelder 1920- *WhoMW 93*
Szymonik, Peter Ted 1963- *WhoScEn 94*
Szynaka, Edward M. 1948- *WhoWest 94*
Szyper, Adam *DrAPF 93*

T

T, Mr. *WhoBlA 94*
T, Mr. 1952- *WhoHol 92*
T, Mr. 1953- *IntMPA 94*
Ta, Tai Van 1938- *WhoAmL 94, WhoAsA 94*
Taafe, Alice *WhoHol 92*
Taaffe, James Griffith 1932- *WhoAm 94*
Taagepera, Rein 1933- *WhoAm 94*
Taam, Ronald Everett 1948- *WhoAm 94*
Tabachnick, Anne 1937- *WhoAmA 93*
Tabachnick, Walter Jay 1947- *WhoWest 94*
Tabachnik, Eldred 1943- *Who 94*
Taback, Gary A. 1937- *WhoAmL 94*
Taback, Simms 1932- *WhoAmA 93*
Tabackman, Steven Carl 1950- *WhoAmL 94*
Tabaczynski, Ron *WhoAmP 93*
Tabai, Ieremia T. 1950- *IntWW 93*
Tabak, Chaim 1946- *WhoAmA 93*
Tabakaucoro, Adi Tamari Finau *WhoWomW 91*
Tabakin, Loraine Smith 1940- *WhoAmL 94*
Tabakoff, Boris 1942- *WhoScEn 94*
Tabakov, Oleg Pavlovich 1935- *IntWW 93*
Tabarly, Eric Marcel Guy 1931- *IntWW 93*
Tabascio, Stefano Antonino 1965- *WhoWest 94*
Tabasco, Evangeline *WhoAmA 93*
Tabata, Lyle Mikio 1956- *WhoScEn 94*
Tabata, Yukio 1948- *WhoFI 94, WhoScEn 94*
Tabatabai, M. Ali 1934- *WhoScEn 94*
Tabatoni, Pierre 1923- *IntWW 93*
Tabatznik, Bernard 1927- *WhoAm 94*
Tabau, Robert Louis 1928- *WhoAm 94*
Tabb, Charles Jordan 1955- *WhoAmL 94*
Tabb, William Howard 1951- *WhoWest 94*
Tabba, Mohammad Myassar 1946- *WhoScEn 94*
Tabback, Victor *WhAm 10*
Tabbara, Hani Bahjat 1939- *Who 94*
Tabeev, Fikryat Akhmedzhanovich 1928- *LngBDD*
Tabell, Anthony 1931- *WhoAm 94*
Taben, Stanley 1932- *WhoIns 94*
Tabenkin, Alexander Nathan 1933- *WhoScEn 94*
Taber, Carol A. *WhoAm 94*
Taber, Edward Albert, III 1943- *WhoAm 94, WhoFI 94*
Taber, Eric *WhoAmP 93*
Taber, Margaret Ruth 1935- *WhoAm 94*
Taber, Nancy G. 1946- *WhoMW 93*
Taber, Richard d1957 *WhoHol 92*
Taber, Richard Carl 1950- *WhoAmP 93*
Taber, Robert Clinton 1917- *WhoAm 94*
Taber, Thomas Nelson 1950- *WhoFI 94*
Tabet, Georges Andre d1984 *WhoHol 92*
Tabet, Jean-Claude Marie 1955- *WhoMW 93*
Tabibi, S. Esmail 1945- *WhoScEn 94*
Tabin, Julius 1919- *WhoAm 94*
Tabio, Eduardo Luis 1959- *WhoHisp 94*
Tabiszewski, Edward Kazimierz 1927- *WhoFI 94*
Tabler, Bryan G. 1943- *WhoAm 94, WhoAmL 94*

Tabler, Norman Gardner, Jr. 1944- *WhoAm 94, WhoAmL 94*
Tabler, P. Dempsey d1956 *WhoHol 92*
Tabler, Ronald Dwight 1937- *WhoWest 94*
Tabler, Susan Beidler 1943- *WhoAm 94*
Tabler, William Benjamin 1914- *WhoAm 94, WhoScEn 94*
Tablet, Hilda *ConAu 41NR*
Tabone, Anton 1937- *IntWW 93*
Tabone, Vincent 1913- *IntWW 93, Who 94*
Tabor, David 1913- *IntWW 93, Who 94, WhoScEn 94*
Tabor, David John St. Maur 1922- *Who 94*
Tabor, Edward 1947- *WhoScEn 94*
Tabor, Eric *WhoAmP 93*
Tabor, Hans 1922- *IntWW 93*
Tabor, Joan d1968 *WhoHol 92*
Tabor, John Kaye 1921- *WhoAm 94, WhoAmP 93*
Tabor, John Malcolm 1952- *WhoScEn 94*
Tabor, Langston *WhoBlA 94*
Tabor, Lillie Montague 1933- *WhoBlA 94*
Tabor, Marvin, Jr. 1938- *WhoFI 94*
Tabor, Mary Leeba 1946- *WhoFI 94*
Tabor, Randall Arden 1956- *WhoMW 93*
Tabor, Rose d1925 *WhoHol 92*
Tabor, Roy Thomas 1952- *WhoAmL 94*
Tabor, Sandra LaVonne 1954- *WhoAmL 94*
Tabor, Theodore Emmett 1940- *WhoScEn 94*
Tabor, Virginia S. 1926- *WhoAmA 93*
Taborga de Requena, Lola 1890- *BlmGWL*
Tabori, George 1914- *ConDr 93, WrDr 94*
Tabori, Kristoffer 1952- *WhoHol 92*
Tabori, Paul 1908-1974 *EncSF 93*
Taborn, Jeannette Ann 1926- *WhoMW 93*
Taborn, John Marvin 1935- *WhoBlA 94*
Taborsak, Lynn H. 1943- *WhoAmP 93*
Taborsky, Edward J(oseph) 1910- *WrDr 94*
Tabrisky, Joseph 1931- *WhoWest 94*
Tabrisky, Phyllis Page 1930- *WhoScEn 94*
Tabucchi, Antonio 1943- *ConWorW 93*
Tabuchi, Shoji 1944?- *WhoAsA 94*
Taburianskyi, Leopold Ivanovych 1940- *LngBDD*
Tabuteau, Emily Zack 1943- *WhoMW 93*
Tacca, Ferdinando 1619-1686 *NewGrDO*
Tacchinardi, Nicola 1772-1859 *NewGrDO*
Tacchinardi-Persiani, Fanny 1812-1867 *NewGrDO*
Taccone, Bonnie Krier 1953- *WhoAmL 94*
Tacha, Athena 1936- *WhoAmA 93*
Tacha, Deanell Reece *WhoAmP 93*
Tacha, Deanell Reece 1946- *WhoAm 94, WhoAmL 94, WhoMW 93, WhoWest 94*
Tachi, Ryuichiro 1921- *IntWW 93*
Tachibana, Akitomo 1951- *WhoScEn 94*
Tachibana, Takeshi 1954- *WhoScEn 94*
Tachiwaki, Tokumatsu 1938- *WhoScEn 94*
Tachmindji, Alexander John 1928- *WhoAm 94*
Tachouet, John James 1943- *WhoWest 94*
Tacik, Donald Anthony 1963- *WhoMW 93*
Tacitus, Cornelius 55?-120? *BlmGEL*
Tack, Theresa Rose 1940- *WhoWest 94*

Tackaberry, John Antony 1939- *Who 94*
Tacker, Martha McClelland 1943- *WhoMW 93*
Tacker, Willis Arnold, Jr. 1942- *WhoScEn 94*
Tackett, Gayle Enslow 1956- *WhoMW 93*
Tackett, Natalie Jane *WhoMW 93*
Tacki, Bernadette Susan 1913- *WhoMW 93*
Tackman, Arthur Lester 1916- *WhoWest 94*
Tackney, Stanley *WhoHol 92*
Tackova, Jarmila d1971 *WhoHol 92*
Tacla, Jorge 1958- *WhoAmA 93*
Tacon, Ernest William 1917- *Who 94*
Tacy, Robert E., Jr. 1943- *WhoWest 94*
Tadashi, Okuda 1932- *IntWW 93*
Taddei, Blenda Maria 1946- *WhoWomW 91*
Taddei, Giuseppe *WhoAm 94*
Taddei, Giuseppe 1916- *NewGrDO*
Taddei, Mirian H. 1930- *WhoWest 94*
Taddeo, Angelo A. 1927- *WhoIns 94*
Taddesse, Samuel 1944- *WhoFI 94*
Taddonio, Lee C. *WhoAmP 93*
Tade, George Thomas 1923- *WhoAm 94*
Tadeo, Giorgio 1929- *NewGrDO*
Tadesse, Tesfaye 1943- *IntWW 93*
Tadie, Jean-Yves 1936- *Who 94*
Tadjo, Veronique 1955- *BlmGWL*
Tadlock, R. Jerry 1942- *WhoAm 94*
Tadolini, Eugenia 1809-c. 1851 *NewGrDO*
Tadolini, Giovanni 1789?-1872 *NewGrDO*
Tadros, Tharwat Fouad 1937- *IntWW 93*
Taeger, Ralph 1936- *WhoHol 92*
Taenzer, Jon Charles 1942- *WhoScEn 94*
Taeuber, Conrad 1906- *WhoAm 94*
Tafaro, Stephen Joseph 1951- *WhoAmL 94*
Tafdrup, Pia 1952- *BlmGWL, ConWorW 93*
Tafel, Edgar 1912- *WhoAm 94, WrDr 94*
Tafelski, Michael Dennis 1949- *WhoMW 93*
Taff, Jeffery Lynn 1963- *WhoWest 94*
Taff, Warren Russell 1947- *WhoWest 94*
Taffe, Betty Jo 1942- *WhoAmP 93*
Taffer, Jack J. 1937- *WhoAmP 93*
Taffner, Donald L. *IntMPA 94*
Tafler, Sydney d1979 *WhoHol 92*
Taflove, Allen 1949- *WhoAm 94, WhoScEn 94*
Tafolla, Carmen *DrAPF 93*
Tafolla, Carmen 1951- *WhoHisp 94*
Tafoya, Alfonso d1989 *WhoHol 92*
Tafoya, Arthur N. 1933- *WhoAm 94, WhoWest 94*
Tafoya, Charles P. *WhoHisp 94*
Tafoya, Marcelo H. 1939- *WhoHisp 94*
Taft, Bob 1942- *WhoAm 94, WhoMW 93*
Taft, David Dakin 1938- *WhoAm 94*
Taft, Earl Jay 1931- *WhoAm 94*
Taft, Frances Prindle 1921- *WhoAmA 93*
Taft, John (Thomas) 1950- *WrDr 94*
Taft, John Ailes, Jr. 1927- *WhoAm 94*
Taft, Martin C. 1942- *WhoIns 94*
Taft, Nathaniel Belmont 1919- *WhoAmL 94*
Taft, Peter R. 1936- *WhoAmL 94, WhoWest 94*
Taft, R. Guy 1949- *WhoAmL 94*
Taft, Richard George 1913- *WhoAm 94*
Taft, Robert 1889-1953 *HisWorL [port]*

Taft, Robert 1917- *WhoAmP 93*
Taft, Robert, Jr. d1993 *NewYTBS 93 [port]*
Taft, Robert, Jr. 1917- *IntWW 93, WhoAm 94, WhoAmL 94, WhoMW 93*
Taft, Robert A. 1889-1953 *HisDcKW*
Taft, Robert A., II 1942- *WhoAmP 93*
Taft, Sara d1973 *WhoHol 92*
Taft, Seth Chase 1922- *WhoAm 94, WhoAmL 94*
Taft, Sheldon Ashley 1937- *WhoAm 94*
Taft, Thomas F. *WhoAmP 93*
Taft, William Howard 1857-1930 *HisWorL [port]*
Taft, William Howard 1915- *WhoAm 94*
Taft, William Howard 1945- *Who 94*
Taft, William Howard, IV 1945- *IntWW 93, WhoAmP 93*
Tafti, Hassan Barnaba D. *Who 94*
Tafur, Robert *WhoHol 92*
Tafuri, Nancy 1946- *SmATA 75 [port]*
Tag, Stanley Alan 1962- *WhoMW 93*
Tagala, Isabel Martinez 1930- *WhoFI 94*
Tagaloa, Reupena S. T. *WhoAmP 93*
Tagashira, Gail S. 1948- *WhoAsA 94*
Tagatz, George Elmo 1935- *WhoAm 94*
Tagawa, Cary-Hiroyuki 1950- *WhoAsA 94*
Tagawa, Seiichi 1919- *IntWW 93*
Tager, Jack 1936- *WhoAm 94*
Tager, Marcia *DrAPF 93*
Tagg, Alan 1928- *Who 94*
Taggart, Austin Dale, II 1952- *WhoScEn 94*
Taggart, Ben d1947 *WhoHol 92*
Taggart, Cal S. 1924- *WhoAmP 93*
Taggart, Dennis DeVere 1938- *WhoWest 94*
Taggart, G. Bruce 1942- *WhoScEn 94*
Taggart, Ganson Powers 1918- *WhoAm 94*
Taggart, Hal d1971 *WhoHol 92*
Taggart, James d1949 *WhoHol 92*
Taggart, James Knox 1937- *WhoFI 94*
Taggart, John *DrAPF 93*
Taggart, Kenneth Dale 1935-1989 *WhAm 10*
Taggart, Rita *WhoHol 92*
Taggart, Robert Alexander, Jr. 1946- *WhoFI 94*
Taggart, Sondra 1934- *WhoFI 94, WhoWest 94*
Taggart, Thomas Michael 1937- *WhoAm 94*
Taggart, William Arend 1955- *WhoWest 94*
Taggart, William John 1940- *WhoAmA 93*
Taggie, Benjamin Fredrick 1938- *WhoAm 94*
Tagi-zade-Hajibeyov, Nijazi Zul'fagarovich *NewGrDO*
Tagle, Hilda Gloria 1946- *WhoHisp 94*
Tagliabue, Carlo 1898-1978 *NewGrDO*
Tagliabue, John *DrAPF 93*
Tagliabue, John 1923- *WrDr 94*
Tagliabue, Paul John 1940- *WhoAm 94*
Tagliacozzo, Rhoda S. *DrAPF 93*
Tagliaferri, Lee Gene 1931- *WhoAm 94, WhoFI 94*
Tagliaferro, John Anthony 1944- *WhoAm 94*
Tagliafico, Joseph (Dieudonne) 1821-1900 *NewGrDO*
Tagliavini, Ferruccio 1913- *NewGrDO*

Tagliavini, Franco 1934- NewGrDO
Tagliazucchi, Giampietro fl. 1749-1763 NewGrDO
Taglichsbeck, Thomas 1799-1867 NewGrDO
Taglioni, Filippo 1777-1871 IntDcB, NewGrDO
Taglioni, Marie 1804-1884 IntDcB [port], NewGrDO [port]
Taglioni, Paul 1808-1884 IntDcB
Taglioni, Salvatore 1789-1868 IntDcB
Tago, Ativalu A., Jr. WhoAmP 93
Tagoe, Christopher Cecil 1958- WhoScEn 94
Tagore, Rabindranath 1861-1941 HisWorL [port], IntDcT 2, PoeCrit 8 [port], RfGShF, TwCLC 53 [port]
Tagore, Sharmila WhoHol 92
Taguchi, Tadao WhoFI 94
Taguchi, Yoshitaka 1933- WhoAm 94
Tague, Barry Elwert 1938- WhoAm 94
Tague, Charles Francis 1924- WhoAm 94
Tague, Karl Raymond 1946- WhoAm 94
Tahara, Eiichi 1936- WhoScEn 94
Tahara, Mildred Machiko 1941- WhoAsA 94
Tahedl, Ernestine 1940- WhoAmA 93
Taher, Abdul Hadi 1930- IntWW 93
Taheri, Amir 1942- WrDr 94
Tahiliani, Jamnu H. 1936- WhoAsA 94
Tahiliani, Vasu Hariram 1942- WhoAsA 94
Tahilramani, Sham Atmaram 1945- WhoScEn 94
Tahir, Abe M., Jr. 1931- WhoAmA 93
Tahir, Mary Elizabeth 1933- WhoFI 94
Tahirussawichi c. 1830- EncNAR
Tahkamaa, Taisto Toivo Johannes 1924- IntWW 93
Tahourdin, John Gabriel 1913- Who 94
Tahy, Michael John 1933- WhoMW 93
Tai, C. Stephen 1940- WhoAsA 94
Tai, Chen-To 1915- WhoAm 94, WhoAsA 94
Tai, Dar Fu 1954- WhoScEn 94
Tai, Frank 1955- WhoScEn 94, WhoWest 94
Tai, Hsin-Hsiung 1941- WhoAsA 94
Tai, Jackson Peter 1950- WhoFI 94
Tai, Jane S. 1944- WhoAmA 93
Tai, Julia Chow 1935- WhoAsA 94
Tai, Peter Y. P. 1937- WhoAsA 94
Tai, William P. 1962- WhoAsA 94
Taiber NewGrDO
Taibleson, Mitchell Herbert 1929- WhoAm 94
Taichman, Norton Stanley 1936- WhoScEn 94
Taiganides, E. Paul 1934- WhoScEn 94
Taillard, Willy Francis 1924- IntWW 93
Tailleferre, Germaine (Marcelle) 1892-1983 NewGrDO
Taillibert, Roger Rene 1926- IntWW 93
Taillon, Gus d1953 WhoHol 92
Taillon, Roger de Boucherville 1946- WhoFI 94
Taimuty, Samuel Isaac 1917- WhoScEn 94, WhoWest 94
Tain, Paul Christopher 1950- Who 94
Taina, Anneli Kristiina 1951- WhoWomW 91
Taine, John 1883-1960 EncSF 93
Tainer, Evelina Margherita 1958- WhoFI 94
Tainsh, Tracey WhoHol 92
Taipale, Vappu Tuulikki 1940- IntWW 93
Taira, Frances Snow 1935- WhoMW 93, WhoScEn 94
Taira, Masa Morioka 1923- WhoAmA 93, WhoAsA 94, WhoWest 94
Taira, Toy-Ping Chan 1937- WhoAsA 94
Taishoff, Lawrence Bruce 1933- WhoAm 94
Tait, Alan Anderson 1934- Who 94
Tait, Andrew Wilson 1922- Who 94
Tait, Arthur Gordon 1934- Who 94
Tait, Carleton Drew 1957- WhoScEn 94
Tait, Eric 1945- Who 94
Tait, George Edward 1910- WrDr 94
Tait, Gerald R. 1938- WhoIns 94
Tait, (Allan) Gordon 1921- Who 94
Tait, James (Sharp) 1912- Who 94
Tait, James Francis 1925- IntWW 93, Who 94
Tait, John Charles 1945- WhoAm 94
Tait, John Edwin 1932- WhoAm 94, WhoFI 94
Tait, John Reid 1946- WhoAmL 94, WhoAmP 93, WhoWest 94
Tait, Joseph Edward 1957- WhoWest 94
Tait, Katharine Lamb 1895-1981 WhoAmA 93N
Tait, Michael Logan 1936- Who 94
Tait, Peter 1915- Who 94
Tait, Robert d1950 WhoHol 92
Tait, Robert Ed 1946- WhoAm 94, WhoAmL 94
Tait, Stephen EncSF 93
Tait, Sylvia Agnes Sophia Who 94
Tait, Thomas Frederick 1958- WhoFI 94
Tait, Will(iam) H. 1942- WhoAmA 93
Taitt, Branford Mayhew 1938- IntWW 93
Taitt, David c. 1740-1834 AmRev
Taittinger, Jean 1923- IntWW 93
Tajima, Toshiki 1948- WhoAsA 94
Tajiri, Harvey S. 1944- WhoAmP 93
Tajiri, Shinkichi 1923- WhoAmA 93
Tajo, Italo 1915- NewGrDO
Tajo, Italo 1915-1993 NewYTBS 93 [port]
Tajon, Encarnacion Fontecha 1920- WhoWest 94
TAK Who 94
Taka, Miiko 1932- WhoHol 92
Takach, Eileen Therese 1946- WhoMW 93
Takach, Mary H. WhoAmA 93
Takach, Peter Edward 1954- WhoScEn 94
Takacs, Eva 1779-1845 BlmGWL
Takacs, James Eric 1935- WhoWest 94
Takacs, Tibor 1954- HorFD [port]
Takacs-Nagy, Gabor 1956- IntWW 93
Takada, Minoru d1977 WhoHol 92
Takagaki, Tasuku 1928- IntWW 93
Takagi, Dana Y. 1954- ConAu 141, WhoAsA 94
Takagi, Hideaki 1950- WhoScEn 94
Takagi, Norio 1947- WhoAsA 94
Takagi, Shigeru 1956- WhoScEn 94
Takagi, Shinji 1953- WhoScEn 94
Takagi Nobuko 1946- BlmGWL
Takahara, Sumiko IntWW 93
Takahashi, Gen. 1924- IntWW 93
Takahashi, Abraham Tomio 1939- WhoAsA 94
Takahashi, Brian Toshio 1954- WhoWest 94
Takahashi, Fumiaki 1950- WhoMW 93, WhoScEn 94
Takahashi, Hiroyasu 1945- WhoWest 94
Takahashi, Iichiro 1922- WhoScEn 94
Takahashi, Joseph S. 1951- WhoAsA 94
Takahashi, Joseph Shigehiro 1951- WhoMW 93
Takahashi, Kazuko 1935- WhoScEn 94
Takahashi, Keiichi 1931- WhoScEn 94
Takahashi, Ken M. 1959- WhoAsA 94
Takahashi, Kozo 1948- WhoAsA 94
Takahashi, Lorey K. 1953- WhoAsA 94
Takahashi, Masato 1933- WhoAsA 94
Takahashi, Masayuki 1942- WhoScEn 94
Takahashi, Patrick Kenji 1940- WhoAm 94
Takahashi, Rita WhoAsA 94
Takahashi, Taro 1930- WhoAsA 94
Takahashi, Tsutomu 1949- WhoScEn 94
Takahashi Takako 1932- BlmGWL
Takai, Ronald T(oshiyuki) 1939- WrDr 94
Takaki, Melvin Hiroyuki WhoAmP 93
Takaki, Ronald 1939- WhoAsA 94
Takaki, Ryuji 1940- WhoScEn 94
Takakoshi, William K. WhoAsA 94
Takakura, Ken WhoHol 92
Takal, Peter 1905- WhoAm 94, WhoAmA 93
Takamatsu, Shin 1948- IntWW 93
Takami, David A. 1957- WhoAsA 94
Takami, Hideki 1943- WhoAsA 94
Takamine, Dwight Y. 1953- WhoAmP 93
Takamori, Akio 1950- WhoAmA 93
Takamura, Jeanette Chiyoko 1947- WhoWest 94
Takano, Mark A 1961- WhoWest 94
Takano, Mark Allan 1960- WhoAsA 94
Takano, Masaharu 1935- WhoAm 94, WhoAsA 94
Takao, Hama 1931- WhoScEn 94
Takasaki, Etsuji 1929- WhoAm 94, WhoScEn 94
Takasaki, Richard Sadaji 1918- WhoAsA 94
Takasaki, Ted Akira 1957- WhoFI 94
Takasaki, William Yoshi Tsugu 1939- WhoAsA 94
Takasaki, Yoshitaka 1938- WhoScEn 94
Takasaki, Yuko 1948- WhoWomW 91
Takashima, Hideo 1919- WhoAmL 94
Takashima, Shiro 1923- WhoAsA 94
Takashima, Shizuye Violet 1928- WhoAmA 93
Takashio, Masachika 1946- WhoScEn 94
Takasugi, Nao WhoAmP 93
Takasugi, Nao 1922- WhoAm 94, WhoAsA 94, WhoWest 94
Takasugi, Robert M. 1930- WhoAsA 94
Takasugi, Robert Mitsuhiro 1930- WhoAm 94, WhoAmL 94, WhoWest 94
Takata, Kevin Kenji 1956- WhoWest 94
Takata, Nobu 1938- WhoWest 94
Takata, Saburo 1913- NewGrDO
Takata, Sayoko 1937- WhoWest 94
Takata, Susan Reiko 1953- WhoMW 93
Takatori, Osamu 1929- IntWW 93
Takayama, Akira WhoAm 94, WhoFI 94
Takayama, Akira 1932- WhoAsA 94
Takayama, Gregg 1952- WhoAsA 94
Takayama, Linda Chu 1948- WhoWest 94
Takeda, Harunori 1948- WhoScEn 94
Takeda, Kimiko 1964- WhoAmL 94
Takeda, Masaaki 1942- WhoMW 93
Takeda, Timothy Scott 1956- WhoWest 94
Takeda, Yasuhiko 1927- WhoAsA 94
Takeda, Yasuhiro 1940- WhoScEn 94
Takeda, Yoshiyuki 1933- WhoScEn 94
Takeda, Yutaka 1914- IntWW 93
Takei, George 1937- EncSF 93, IntMPA 94
Takei, George 1939- WhoHol 92
Takei, George Hosato 1937- WhoAsA 94
Takei, Richard 1947- WhoAsA 94
Takei, Toshihisa 1931- WhoScEn 94, WhoWest 94
Takekawa, Thomas Tsuyoshi 1933- WhoAsA 94
Takemi, Taro 1904- IntWW 93
Takemine, Jokichi 1854-1922 WorScD
Takemitsu, Toru 1930- IntDcF 2-4
Takemori, Akira Eddie 1929- WhoAsA 94
Takemoto, Henry Tadaaki 1930- WhoAmA 93
Takemoto, Kiichi 1930- WhoScEn 94
Takemoto Mink, Patsy 1927- WhoWomW 91
Takemura, Yasuko 1933- WhoWomW 91
Takenaka, Heizo 1951- ConAu 142
Takenaka, Makoto B. WhoAsA 94
Takenaka, Tadashi 1946- WhoScEn 94
Takenishi Hiroko 1929- BlmGWL
Takeoka, Shinji 1963- WhoScEn 94
Takeoka, Tsuneyuki 1944- WhoScEn 94
Takes, Peter Arthur 1957- WhoMW 93, WhoScEn 94
Takes Gun, Frank fl. 20th cent.- EncNAR
Takeshima, Yoichi 1952- WhoScEn 94
Takeshita, Chieko 1958- WhoAmL 94
Takeshita, Kenichi 1957- WhoAsA 94
Takeshita, Noboru 1924- IntWW 93
Takeuchi, Esther Kiyomi 1941- WhoAsA 94
Takeuchi, Hajime Jim 1941- WhoWest 94
Takeuchi, Kenji 1934- WhoAsA 94
Takeuchi, Kenneth James 1953- WhoAsA 94
Takeuchi, Shokoh Akira 1920- WhoAm 94
Takeuchi, Sylvia Fujie 1939- WhoWest 94
Takeuchi, Takao 1945- WhoScEn 94
Takhtadzhyan, Armen Leonovich 1910- WhoScEn 94
Takhtajan, Armen Leonovich 1910- IntWW 93
Takhvelidze, Albert 1930- IntWW 93
Takiguchi, Masako 1932- WhoAsA 94
Takimoto, Hideyo Henry 1928- WhoAsA 94
Takimoto, Mabel Yayoko WhoAsA 94
Takino, Masuichi 1904- WhoScEn 94
Takis, Nicholas 1903-1965 WhoAmA 93N
Takitani, Henry T. 1924- WhoAmP 93
Takiura, Mitsuru 1939- WhoWest 94
Takizawa, Akira 1927- WhoScEn 94
Takla, Laila WhoWomW 91
Takla, Philippe 1915- IntWW 93
Takle, Darien WhoHol 92
Takle, Roberta Piper 1940- WhoAmP 93
Tako, Gabriella 9999- WhoWest 94
Tako, Masakuni 1947- WhoScEn 94
Takriti, Saddam Hussein IntWW 93
Taksa, Patti Silliman 1950- WhoAmL 94
Taktakishvili, Otar Vasil'yevich 1924-1989 NewGrDO
Taktakishvili, Shalva Mikhailovich 1900-1965 NewGrDO
Takumi, Roy M. 1952- WhoAmP 93, WhoAsA 94
Takumi, Roy Mitsuo 1952- WhoWest 94
Takushi, Robert WhoAmP 93
Takyi, Isaac Kwame WhoFI 94
Tal, Jacob 1945- WhoScEn 94
Tal, Josef 1910- NewGrDO
Talaba, L. 1943- WhoAmA 93
Talafous, Joseph John 1929- WhoAmL 94
Talal, Marilynn DrAPF 93
Talalay, Paul 1923- WhoAm 94
Talal Ibn Abdul Aziz, H.R.H. Prince 1934- IntWW 93
Talamantes, Florence 1931- WhoHisp 94
Talamantes, Frank 1943- WhoHisp 94
Talamantes, Frank J. 1943- WhoScEn 94
Talamantez, Connie Juarez 1947- WhoHisp 94
Talan, David B. 1948- WhoAmP 93
Talarico, Maria Theresa 1960- WhoMW 93
Talarico, Ross DrAPF 93
Talarzyk, W. Wayne 1940- WrDr 94
Talat Pasha 1874-1920 HisWorL
Talavera, Ismael 1943- WhoHisp 94
Talavera, Sandra 1956- WhoHisp 94
Talazac, Jean-Alexandre 1851-1896 NewGrDO
Talazac, Odette d1948 WhoHol 92
Talbert, Bill 1918- BuCMET
Talbert, Hamilton Bowen, Jr. 1929- WhoAmP 93
Talbert, Hugh Mathis 1937- WhoAmL 94
Talbert, James Denis 1947- WhoFI 94
Talbert, James Lewis 1931- WhoAm 94
Talbert, LaVonda 1963- WhoMW 93
Talbert, Luther Marcus 1926- WhoAm 94
Talbert, Marc 1953- WrDr 94
Talbert, Melvin George 1934- WhoAm 94, WhoBlA 94, WhoWest 94
Talbert, Richard Harrison 1957- WhoAmA 93
Talbert, Ted WhoBlA 94
Talbert, Willard Lindley, Jr. 1932- WhoWest 94
Talbot, Alfred Kenneth, Jr. 1916- WhoBlA 94
Talbot, Bernard 1937- WhoAm 94, WhoScEn 94
Talbot, Brud d1986 WhoHol 92
Talbot, Bryan EncSF 93
Talbot, David Arlington Roberts, Sr. 1916- WhoBlA 94
Talbot, Dennis Edmund Blaquiere 1908- Who 94
Talbot, Donald Roy 1931- WhoAm 94
Talbot, Earl d1914 WhoHol 92
Talbot, Emile Joseph 1941- WhoAm 94
Talbot, FitzRoy Who 94
Talbot, (Arthur Allison) FitzRoy 1909- Who 94
Talbot, Frank Hamilton 1930- IntWW 93, WhoAm 94, WhoScEn 94
Talbot, George 1816-1886 DcNaB MP
Talbot, Gerald E. 1931- WhoAmP 93
Talbot, Gerald Edgerton 1931- WhoBlA 94
Talbot, Godfrey Walker 1908- IntWW 93, Who 94, WrDr 94
Talbot, Harry 1888- WhoHol 92
Talbot, Helen WhoHol 92
Talbot, Hilary Gwynne 1912- Who 94
Talbot, Howard Chase, Jr. 1925- WhoAm 94
Talbot, James Edward 1947- WhoWest 94
Talbot, James Patterson, Sr. 1950- WhoBlA 94
Talbot, James Thomas 1935- WhoAm 94
Talbot, Jarold Dean 1907- WhoAmA 93
Talbot, John 1645-1727 DcAmReB 2
Talbot, John, Earl of Shrewsbury 1791-1852 DcNaB MP
Talbot, John Dudley 1953- WhoMW 93
Talbot, Jonathan 1939- WhoAmA 93
Talbot, Lawrence EncSF 93
Talbot, Lee Merriam 1930- WhoAm 94
Talbot, Lyle 1902- IntMPA 94
Talbot, Lyle 1904- WhoHol 92
Talbot, Mary (Irene) 1922- Who 94
Talbot, Matthew J. 1937- WhoAm 94
Talbot, Maurice John 1912- Who 94
Talbot, Michael 1953- WrDr 94
Talbot, Michael Owen 1943- Who 94
Talbot, Nita 1930- WhoHol 92
Talbot, Norman Clare 1936- WrDr 94
Talbot, Pamela 1946- WhoAm 94
Talbot, Patrick James 1948- WhoWest 94
Talbot, Patrick John 1946- Who 94
Talbot, Phillips 1915- WhoAm 94
Talbot, Prue WhoAm 94
Talbot, Richard Burritt 1933- WhoAm 94
Talbot, Richard Joseph 1932- WhoAm 94
Talbot, Richard Michael Arthur Chetwynd d1993 Who 94N
Talbot, Silas 1751-1813 WhAmRev [port]
Talbot, Slim d1973 WhoHol 92
Talbot, Theodore A. 1923- WhoBlA 94
Talbot, Timothy Ralph 1916- WhAm 10
Talbot, William (H. M.) 1918-1980 WhoAmA 93N
Talbot, William Henry Fox 1800-1877 WorInv
Talbot Of Malahide, Baron 1931- Who 94
Talbott, Ben Johnson, Jr. 1940- WhoAmL 94
Talbott, Dorothy Adams 1928- WhoWest 94
Talbott, Frank, III 1929- WhoAm 94
Talbott, George Harold 1894- WhAm 10
Talbott, George Robert 1925- WhoScEn 94, WhoWest 94
Talbott, Gloria 1931- WhoHol 92
Talbott, John Harold 1902-1990 WhAm 10
Talbott, Jonathan L. 1952- WhoWest 94
Talbott, Joseph B. 1933- WhoAmP 93
Talbott, Karen Lee 1947- WhoMW 93
Talbott, Michael WhoHol 92
Talbott, Philip Melville 1896- WhAm 10
Talbott, Strobe 1946- ConAu 42NR, WrDr 94
Talbott, William Bruce 1949- WhoAmP 93
Talboys, Brian (Edward) 1921- Who 94
Talboys, Brian Edward 1921- IntWW 93
Talburt, John Randolph 1945- WhoScEn 94
Talcott, Gigi WhoAmP 93

Talcott, Wesley Conrad 1938- *WhoMW 93*
Talcott, William *DrAPF 93*
Taleb, Yusef Sabri Abu 1929- *IntWW 93*
Talebi, Nahid 1954- *WhoWest 94*
Talegalli, Alberto d1961 *WhoHol 92*
Talel, Eva Coben 1948- *WhoAmL 94*
Talent, James M. 1956- *CngDr 93, WhoAm 94, WhoAmP 93, WhoMW 93*
Talese, Gay 1932- *WhoAm 94, WrDr 94*
Talese, Joseph F. d1993 *NewYTBS 93 [port]*
Talese, Nan Ahearn 1933- *WhoAm 94*
Talesnick, Alan Lee 1945- *WhoAmL 94*
Talesnick, Stanley 1927- *WhoAmL 94*
Taleyarkhan, Homi J. H. 1917- *IntWW 93*
Talhelm, Daniel Roderick 1941- *WhoFI 94*
Talhouni, Bahjat 1913- *IntWW 93*
Talia, Jorge Eduardo 1944- *WhoMW 93*
Taliaferro, Addison 1936- *WhoBlA 94*
Taliaferro, Benjamin 1750-1821 *WhAmRev*
Taliaferro, Bruce Owen 1947- *WhoAmL 94*
Taliaferro, Cecil R. 1942- *WhoBlA 94*
Taliaferro, Edith d1958 *WhoHol 92*
Taliaferro, George 1927- *WhoBlA 94*
Taliaferro, Hal *WhoHol 92*
Taliaferro, Henry Beauford, Jr. 1932- *WhoAmL 94*
Taliaferro, Mabel d1979 *WhoHol 92*
Taliaferro, Mark, Jr. 1942- *WhoAmL 94*
Taliaferro, Nettie Howard 1944- *WhoBlA 94*
Taliaferro, Paul Anthony 1934- *WhoAmP 93*
Taliaferro, Philip, III 1937- *WhoAmL 94*
Taliaferro, Robert 1945- *WhoWest 94*
Taliaferro, Viola J. 1928- *WhoBlA 94*
Taliaferro, Yvon Rochelle 1957- *WhoWest 94*
Talib, Imran *EncSF 93*
Talib, Naji 1917- *IntWW 93*
Talich, Vaclav 1883-1961 *NewGrDO*
Taliesin fl. 6th cent.BC- *BlmGEL*
Talifero, Gerald 1950- *SmATA 75 [port]*
Talimcioglu, Nazmi Mete 1961- *WhoScEn 94*
Talingdan, Arsenio Preza 1930- *WhoAm 94*
Talintyre, Douglas George 1932- *Who 94*
Talisman, Mark Elliott 1941- *WhoAmP 93*
Talkington, Deborah Frances 1954- *WhoScEn 94*
Talkington, Robert Van 1929- *WhoAm 94, WhoAmP 93*
Tall, Aminata *WhoWomW 91*
Tall, Booker T. 1928- *WhoBlA 94*
Tall, Deborah *DrAPF 93*
Tall, Franklin David 1944- *WhoAm 94*
Tall, Stephen 1908-1981 *EncSF 93*
Tallackson, Harvey Dean 1925- *WhoAmP 93*
Tallackson, Jeffrey Stephen 1943- *WhoAm 94*
Tallal, Paula 1947- *WhoScEn 94*
Tallamy, Bertram Dalley 1901-1989 *WhAm 10*
Tallant, David, Jr. 1931- *WhoAm 94, WhoAmL 94*
Tallas, Jim 1937- *WhoAmP 93*
Tallawy, Mervat 1937- *IntWW 93*
Tallboys, Richard Gilbert 1931- *IntWW 93, Who 94*
Tallchief, Maria 1925- *IntDcB [port], WhoAm 94, WhoHol 92*
Tallchief, Marjorie 1926- *IntDcB*
Tallchief, Marjorie 1927- *IntWW 93, WhoHol 92*
Talleda, Miguel L. 1919- *WhoHisp 94*
Tallemant des Reaux, Gedeon 1619-1692 *GuFrLit 2*
Tallent, Elizabeth *DrAPF 93*
Tallent, Elizabeth 1954- *DcLB 130 [port]*
Tallent, Marc Andrew 1954- *WhoScEn 94*
Tallent, Norman 1921- *WhoScEn 94, WrDr 94*
Tallent, Stephen Edison 1937- *WhoAm 94*
Tallent, Timothy N. *WhoAmP 93*
Tallent, William Hugh 1928- *WhoAm 94*
Taller, Joe Anthony 1933- *WhoAmP 93*
Tallerico, Thomas Joseph 1946- *WhoAmL 94*
Tallett, Elizabeth Edith 1949- *WhoAm 94*
Talleur, John Joseph 1925- *WhoAm 94*
Talley, Bonnie Eileen 1928- *WhoMW 93*
Talley, Brian Chandler 1955- *WhoMW 93*
Talley, Carol Lee 1937- *WhoAm 94*
Talley, Charles Richmond 1925- *WhoAm 94*
Talley, Clarence, Sr. 1951- *WhoBlA 94*
Talley, Claude Alvin, Jr. 1927- *WhoFI 94*
Talley, Curtiss J. 1939- *WhoBlA 94*
Talley, Dan R. 1951- *WhoAmA 93*
Talley, Darryl Victor 1960- *WhoAm 94, WhoBlA 94*
Talley, Dennis R. 1947- *WhoMW 93*
Talley, Denver 1938- *WhoAmP 93*
Talley, James Edward 1940- *WhoBlA 94*
Talley, John Stephen 1930- *WhoBlA 94*
Talley, Kevin David 1951- *WhoAmP 93*
Talley, Madelon DeVoe 1932- *WhoAm 94*
Talley, Marion 1906- *WhoHol 92*
Talley, Marion 1907-1983 *NewGrDO*
Talley, Martha Ann 1941- *WhoWest 94*
Talley, Michael Frank, Sr. 1945- *WhoBlA 94*
Talley, Richard Bates 1947- *WhoAmL 94*
Talley, Robert Cochran 1936- *WhoAm 94*
Talley, Robert Morrell 1924- *WhoAm 94*
Talley, Truman Macdonald 1925- *WhoAm 94*
Talley, Warren Dennis Rick 1934- *WhoAm 94, WhoWest 94*
Talley, William Giles, Jr. 1939- *WhoAm 94, WhoFI 94*
Talley-Ronsholdt, Deanna Jean 1945- *WhoMW 93*
Tallichet, Leon Edgar 1925- *WhoAm 94*
Tallichet, Margaret d1991 *WhoHol 92*
Tallier, Armand d1958 *WhoHol 92*
Talling, John Francis 1929- *IntWW 93, Who 94*
Tallis, Robyn *ConAu 142, SmATA 75*
Tallmadge, Benjamin 1754-1835 *WhAmRev [port]*
Tallmadge, Diane Joyce 1934- *WhoWest 94*
Tallmadge, Guy Kasten 1932- *WhoWest 94*
Tallman, Frank d1978 *WhoHol 92*
Tallman, Johanna Eleonore 1914- *WhoAm 94, WhoWest 94*
Tallman, Lori A. 1964- *WhoAmL 94*
Tallman, Peleg 1764-1840 *WhAmRev*
Tallman, Richard C. 1953- *WhoAm 94, WhoAmL 94*
Tallman, Robert Hall 1915- *WhoMW 93*
Tallman, Samuel Vose 1947- *WhoFI 94*
Tallman, Thomas Abel 1951- *WhoIns 94*
Tallmer, Margot 1925- *WhoAm 94*
TallMountain, Mary *DrAPF 93*
Tallo, Jozef *EncSF 93*
Tallon, James R., Jr. 1941- *WhoAmP 93*
Tallon, Joseph Charles 1949- *WhoWest 94*
Tallon, Robert M., Jr. 1946- *WhoAmP 93*
Tally, Brett Richard 1963- *WhoWest 94*
Tally, Lura Self 1921- *WhoAmP 93*
Tally, Ted 1952- *ConDr 93, WrDr 94*
Talma, Louise 1906- *NewGrDO*
Talma, Louise J. 1906- *WhoAm 94*
Talmadge, Constance d1973 *WhoHol 92*
Talmadge, Margaret d1933 *WhoHol 92*
Talmadge, Mary Christine 1940- *WhoAm 94*
Talmadge, Natalie d1969 *WhoHol 92*
Talmadge, Norma d1957 *WhoHol 92*
Talmadge, Philip A. 1952- *WhoAmP 93*
Talmadge, Quilla *WhoAmP 93*
Talmadge, Richard d1981 *WhoHol 92*
Talmadge, Wooddall Wells 1958- *WhoAmL 94, WhoWest 94*
Talmage, Anne 1920- *WrDr 94*
Talmage, David Wilson 1919- *WhoAm 94, WhoScEn 94*
Talmage, John H. *WhoFI 94*
Talmage, Kenneth Kellogg 1946- *WhoWest 94*
Talmage, Thomas DeWitt 1832-1902 *DcAmReB 2*
Talman, William d1968 *WhoHol 92*
Talmi, Igal 1925- *IntWW 93*
Talmi, Yoav 1943- *WhoAm 94, WhoWest 94*
Talomie, Frank G., Sr. 1921- *WhoAmP 93*
Talon, Marianne Goedert 1958- *WhoAmL 94*
Talon, Neil S. 1950- *WhoMW 93*
Talton, Alix *WhoHol 92*
Talton, Chester Lovelle 1941- *WhoAm 94, WhoWest 94*
Talton, Robert E. 1945- *WhoAmP 93*
Talu, Naim 1919- *IntWW 93*
Talucci, Samuel James 1929- *WhoAm 94*
Talun, Walter d1980 *WhoHol 92*
Talvela, Martti (Olavi) 1935-1989 *NewGrDO*
Talvela, Martti Olavi 1935-1989 *WhAm 10*
Talvi, Ilkka Ilari 1948- *WhoAm 94*
Talvj 1797-1870 *DcLB 133 [port]*
Talwani, Manik 1933- *WhoAm 94, WhoAsA 94, WhoScEn 94*
Talyzin, Nikolai Vladimirovich 1929- *WhAm 10*
Tam, Alfred Yat-Cheung 1953- *WhoScEn 94*
Tam, Christopher Kwong-Wah 1939- *WhoAsA 94*
Tam, Eric Tak-Keung 1962- *WhoAsA 94*
Tam, Francis Man Kei 1938- *WhoAsA 94*
Tam, Henry 1965- *WhoAsA 94*
Tam, James Pingkwan 1947- *WhoAsA 94*
Tam, Leo 1955- *WhoAsA 94*
Tam, Maria Wai-chu 1945- *WhoWomW 91*
Tam, Reuben 1916-1991 *WhAm 10*
Tam, Reuben 1916-1992 *WhoAmA 93N*
Tam, Richard Y. 1953- *WhoMW 93*
Tam, Rod 1953- *WhoAmP 93, WhoWest 94*
Tam, Roland Fook Seng 1946- *WhoWest 94*
Tam, Sang William 1953- *WhoAsA 94*
Tam, Simon M. W. 1960- *WhoAsA 94*
Tam, Thomas Kwai-Sang 1942- *WhoAsA 94*
Tam, Tommy Tit-Kwan 1951- *WhoFI 94*
Tamagnini, Giulio 1921- *IntWW 93*
Tamagno, Francesco 1850-1905 *NewGrDO [port]*
Tamaki, Jeanne Keiko 1954- *WhoAsA 94*
Tamames Gomez, Ramon 1933- *IntWW 93*
Tamara d1943 *WhoHol 92*
Tamarelli, Alan Wayne 1941- *WhoAm 94*
Tamarez, Tom d1963 *WhoHol 92*
Tamariz, Joaquin 1950- *WhoScEn 94*
Tamaro, George John 1937- *WhoFI 94*
Tamaron, Marques de 1941- *IntWW 93*
Tamashiro, Thomas Koyei 1926- *WhoScEn 94*
Tamaye, Elaine E. 1952- *WhoScEn 94*
Tamayo, Carlos T. *WhoHisp 94*
Tamayo, Charles, Jr. 1951- *WhoHisp 94*
Tamayo, Fernando M. 1942- *WhoHisp 94*
Tamayo, James Anthony 1949- *WhoHisp 94*
Tamayo, Mario Alejandro *WhoHisp 94*
Tamayo, Rufino 1899-1991 *WhoAmA 93N*
Tamba, Tetsuro *WhoHol 92*
Tambasco, Anthony J(oseph) 1939- *ConAu 41NR*
Tamberg, Eino 1930- *NewGrDO*
Tamberlani, Carlo d1980 *WhoHol 92*
Tamberlik, Enrico 1820-1889 *NewGrDO*
Tamberrino, Frank Michael 1955- *WhoFI 94*
Tambiah, Stanley Jeyarajah 1929- *WhoAm 94*
Tamblin, Pamela Joy 1926- *Who 94*
Tamblyn, Eddie d1957 *WhoHol 92*
Tamblyn, Russ 1934- *WhoHol 92*
Tamblyn, Russ 1935- *IntMPA 94*
Tambo, Oliver d1993 *IntWW 93N*
Tambo, Oliver 1917-1993 *CurBio 93N*
Tambo, Oliver R. 1917-1993 *NewYTBS 93 [port]*
Tambor, Jeffrey *WhoHol 92*
Tambor, Jeffrey 1944- *IntMPA 94, WhoAm 94*
Tamborello, Steven L. 1949- *WhoMW 93*
Tambrino, Paul August *WhoMW 93*
Tambs, Lewis Arthur 1927- *WhoAm 94, WhoAmP 93*
Tamburine, Jean Helen 1930- *WhoAmA 93*
Tamburini, Antonio 1800-1876 *NewGrDO [port]*
Tamburini, Joseph Urban 1951- *WhoWest 94*
Tamburino, Louis Anthony 1936- *WhoMW 93*
Tamburro, Wendell Biddle 1916- *WhoAmP 93*
Tambuzi, Jitu *DrAPF 93*
Tamby, Marie Cassese 1925- *WhoAmP 93*
Tame, William Charles 1909- *Who 94*
Tamerlane 1336-1405 *HisWorL [port]*
Tamerlis, Zoe *WhoHol 92*
Tames, Richard Lawrence 1946- *WrDr 94*
Tamez, Eloisa G. 1935- *WhoHisp 94*
Tamez, George N. *WhoHisp 94*
Tamez, Gilberto A. 1951- *WhoHisp 94*
Tamez, Israel 1946- *WhoHisp 94*
Tamez, Jesse 1957- *WhoHisp 94*
Tamhane, Ajit C. 1946- *WhoAsA 94*
Tamimi, Nasser Taher 1951- *WhoScEn 94*
Tamin, Azaibi 1959- *WhoScEn 94*
Tamir, Theodor 1927- *WhoAm 94, WhoScEn 94*
Tamiroff, Akim d1972 *WhoHol 92*
Tamiya, Jiro d1978 *WhoHol 92*
Tamke, George William 1947- *WhoFI 94*
Tamke, Thomas Gregg 1952- *WhoMW 93*
Tamkin, Curtis Sloane 1936- *WhoFI 94, WhoWest 94*
Tamkin, S. Jerome 1926- *WhoAm 94*
Tamm, Ditlev 1946- *IntWW 93*
Tamm, Eleanor Ruth 1921- *WhoMW 93*
Tamm, Igor 1922- *IntWW 93, WhoAm 94, WhoScEn 94*
Tamm, Mary *WhoHol 92*
Tamm, Peter 1928- *IntWW 93*
Tammadge, Alan Richard 1921- *Who 94*
Tammadge, Kathleen Donovan 1965- *WhoAmL 94*
Tammany, Albert Squire, III 1946- *WhoFI 94, WhoWest 94*
Tammaro, Antonio J. *WhoAmP 93*
Tammelleo, A. David 1935- *WhoAmL 94*
Tammen, James F. 1925- *WhoScEn 94*
Tammeus, William David 1945- *WhoAm 94*
Tamminga, Frederick W(illiam) 1934- *WrDr 94*
Tammuz, Binyamin *EncSF 93*
Tamor, Stephen 1925- *WhoScEn 94*
Tamposi, Elizabeth Marian 1955- *WhoAmP 93*
Tamrat, Befecadu 1947- *WhoScEn 94*
Tamres, Milton 1922- *WhoAm 94*
Tams, Arthur W. 1848-1927 *NewGrDO*
Tams, Thomas Walter 1921- *WhoScEn 94*
Tamu 1951- *WhoHol 92*
Tamulonis, Frank Louis, Jr. 1946- *WhoAmL 94*
Tamulski, James J. 1947- *WhoAmL 94*
Tamuno, Tekena Nitonye 1932- *Who 94*
Tamura, Cary Kaoru 1944- *WhoWest 94*
Tamura, Hajime 1924- *IntWW 93*
Tamura, Imao 1923- *WhoScEn 94*
Tamura, Neal Noboru 1953- *WhoWest 94*
Tamvakis, Haralampos 1969- *WhoMW 93*
Tam Wong, Rosanna Yick-ming 1952- *WhoWomW 91*
Tamworth, Viscount 1952- *Who 94*
Tan, Amy *DrAPF 93*
Tan, Amy 1952- *BlmGWL, SmATA 75 [port], TwCYAW, WrDr 94*
Tan, Amy Ruth 1952- *WhoAm 94, WhoAsA 94*
Tan, Arjun 1943- *WhoAm 94*
Tan, Barrie 1953- *WhoAsA 94*
Tan, Boen Hie 1926- *WhoScEn 94*
Tan, Chai Tiam 1943- *WhoScEn 94*
Tan, Cheng Imm 1958- *WhoAsA 94*
Tan, Cheng-Pheng 1953- *WhoAsA 94*
Tan, Chin An 1961- *WhoAsA 94*
Tan, Chor Weng 1936- *WhoAsA 94*
Tan, Colleen Woo 1923- *WhoAsA 94*
Tan, Eng Meng 1926- *WhoAm 94*
Tan, Eric Tuanlee 1945- *WhoAsA 94*
Tan, Henry S. I. 1932- *WhoAsA 94*
Tan, Hui Qian 1948- *WhoMW 93*
Tan, Jack Sim Eddy 1958- *WhoAsA 94*
Tan, John K. 1934- *WhoFI 94, WhoScEn 94*
Tan, Kim Howard 1926- *WhoAsA 94*
Tan, Kim Leong 1936- *WhoScEn 94*
Tan, Kok Tin 1958- *WhoScEn 94*
Tan, Lawrence W. 1964- *WhoAsA 94*
Tan, Li-Su Lin 1956- *WhoFI 94*
Tan, Mary 1929- *WhoAsA 94*
Tan, Nady 1936- *WhoAsA 94*
Tan, S. Y. 1946- *WhoAsA 94*
Tan, Sinforosa G. 1943- *WhoAsA 94*
Tan, Teresa 1948- *WhoWest 94*
Tan, Tjiauw-Ling 1935- *WhoAsA 94, WhoScEn 94*
Tan, Wai-Yuan 1934- *WhoAsA 94*
Tan, William Lew 1949- *WhoAm 94, WhoWest 94*
Tan, Yoke San 1955- *WhoScEn 94*
Tan, Zoe *WhoAsA 94*
Tana, Akira 1952- *WhoAsA 94*
Tana, Patti *DrAPF 93*
Tana, Phongpan 1946- *WhoAsA 94*
Tanabe, Charles Y. 1951- *WhoAmL 94*
Tanabe, George Joji, Jr. 1943- *WhoAsA 94*
Tanabe, Makoto 1922- *IntWW 93*
Tanabe, Yo 1950- *WhoScEn 94*
Tanabe Seiko 1928- *BlmGWL*
Tanabu, Masami *IntWW 93*
Tanacredi, John Thomas 1947- *WhoScEn 94*
Tanada, Takuma 1919- *WhoAsA 94*
Tanaka, Beatrice 1932- *SmATA 76 [port]*
Tanaka, Eddy Sei 1934- *WhoAsA 94*
Tanaka, Gary Alan Shinichi 1954- *WhoAsA 94*
Tanaka, James Junji 1940- *WhoAsA 94*
Tanaka, Jeannie E. 1942- *WhoAmL 94, WhoWest 94*
Tanaka, Jeffrey Scott 1958-1992 *WhAm 10*
Tanaka, John 1924- *WhoAsA 94*
Tanaka, John Augustus 1955- *WhoWest 94*
Tanaka, Joseph S. 1941- *WhoAmP 93*
Tanaka, Kakuei 1918- *IntWW 93*
Tanaka, Kakuei 1918-1993 *NewYTBS 93 [port]*
Tanaka, Kinuyo d1977 *WhoHol 92*
Tanaka, Kouichi Robert 1926- *WhoAm 94, WhoAsA 94*
Tanaka, Leila Chiyako 1954- *WhoAmL 94*
Tanaka, Nobuyoshi 1934- *WhoScEn 94*
Tanaka, Richard I. 1928- *WhoAm 94, WhoAsA 94, WhoScEn 94*
Tanaka, Richard Koichi, Jr. 1931- *WhoWest 94*
Tanaka, S. Ken 1951- *WhoAsA 94*
Tanaka, Shoji d1918 *WhoHol 92*
Tanaka, Shun-Ichi 1926- *IntWW 93*
Tanaka, Tatsuo 1910- *IntWW 93*
Tanaka, Thomas Victor Camacho 1940- *WhoAmP 93*

Tanaka, Toshijiro 1944- WhoScEn 94
Tanaka, Ty Skip 1952- WhoAsA 94
Tanaka, Wayne D. 1950- WhoAsA 94
Tanaka, Yoshiki EncSF 93
Tanarro, Fernando Manuel 1933- WhoFI 94
Tanasie, Petre 1927- IntWW 93
Tanburn, Jennifer Jephcott 1929- Who 94
Tancig, Peter 1944- WhoScEn 94
Tanck, James Robert 1944- WhoFI 94
Tancock, John (Leon) 1942- WrDr 94
Tancock, John Leon 1942- WhoAmA 93
Tancred, H. L. Who 94
Tancredi, James J. 1954- WhoAmL 94
Tancredi, Laurence Richard 1940- WhoAm 94, WhoAmL 94
Tandler, Bernard 1933- WhoAm 94
Tandon, Anand 1949- WhoAsA 94
Tandon, Don Ashoka 1944- WhoFI 94, WhoScEn 94
Tandon, Rajiv 1944- WhoAsA 94
Tandon, Rajiv 1956- WhoMW 93, WhoScEn 94
Tan Dongsheng WhoPRCh 91
Tan Dun 1957- IntWW 93, WhoPRCh 91 [port]
Tandy, Charles C. WhoAmP 93
Tandy, Jessica 1909- IntMPA 94, IntWW 93, Who 94, WhoAm 94, WhoHol 92
Tandy, Mark WhoHol 92
Tandy, Mary B. WhoBlA 94
Tandy, Valerie d1965 WhoHol 92
Taneff, Thomas N. 1961- WhoAmL 94
Ta-Ne-Haddle fl. 19th cent.- EncNAR
Taneja, Arun K. 1947- WhoWest 94
Tanen, Ned 1931- IntMPA 94
Tanenbaum, Allan Jay 1946- WhoAmL 94
Tanenbaum, Andrew Stuart 1944- WhoScEn 94
Tanenbaum, Basil Samuel 1934- WhoAm 94, WhoWest 94
Tanenbaum, Bernard Jerome, Jr. 1934- WhoAm 94
Tanenbaum, Gerald Stephen 1945- WhoAmL 94, WhoFI 94
Tanenbaum, Jay Harvey 1933- WhoAmL 94
Tanenbaum, Jeffrey L. 1952- WhoAmL 94
Tanenbaum, Marc 1925-1992 AnObit 1992
Tanenbaum, Marc Harris 1943- WhoWest 94
Tanenbaum, Marc Herman 1925-1992 WhAm 10
Tanenbaum, Robert Earl 1936- WhoWest 94
Tanenbaum, William Alan 1954- WhoAmL 94
Tanenolee fl. 19th cent.- EncNAR
Taney, J. Charles WhoAm 94
Taneyev, Sergey Ivanovich 1856-1915 NewGrDO
Tanfield, Jennifer Bridget 1941- Who 94
Tanford, Charles 1921- IntWW 93
Tan Fuyun WhoPRCh 91
Tang, Alex Ying Ho 1960- WhoAsA 94
Tang, America 1955- WhoAsA 94
Tang, Andrew Hing-Yee 1936- WhoAsA 94
Tang, Anthony Matthew 1924- WhAm 10
Tang, Assumpta 1934- WhoAsA 94
Tang, Bishop Dominic 1908- IntWW 93
Tang, Chao 1958- WhoScEn 94
Tang, Charles Chau Ching 1948- WhoAsA 94
Tang, Chik-Kwun 1941- WhoAsA 94
Tang, Chung Liang 1934- WhoAsA 94
Tang, Chung-Shih 1938- WhoAsA 94
Tang, Dah-Lain Almon 1955- WhoScEn 94
Tang, David Kwong-Yu 1953- WhoAsA 94
Tang, Deborah Canada 1947- WhoBlA 94
Tang, Eugenia C. G. WhoAsA 94
Tang, Frank d1968 WhoHol 92
Tang, Ignatius Ning-Bang 1933- WhoScEn 94
Tang, Jianxin 1952- WhoAsA 94
Tang, Jicheng 1960- WhoMW 93
Tang, Jinke 1961- WhoScEn 94
Tang, John C. 1960- WhoWest 94
Tang, Julie Mong-See 1949- WhoAsA 94
Tang, Kin Ling 1936- WhoAsA 94
Tang, Klairon Kit-ling WhoAsA 94
Tang, Kunikyo 1966- WhoWest 94
Tang, Kwei 1953- WhoAsA 94
Tang, Lillian Y. D. 1923- WhoAsA 94
Tang, Mark Giakhy 1956- WhoAsA 94
Tang, Ming-Je 1953- WhoAsA 94
Tang, Pan-Pan 1942- IntWW 93
Tang, Pascal Biloa 1937- IntWW 93
Tang, Paul Chi Lung 1944- WhoAsA 94
Tang, Pui Fun Louisa 1956- WhoScEn 94
Tang, Qing 1964- WhoScEn 94
Tang, Raili Kaarina 1950- IntWW 93
Tang, Roger Y. W. 1947- WhoAsA 94
Tang, Roger Yin Wu 1947- WhoFI 94
Tang, Sherman 1936- WhoAsA 94
Tang, Thomas WhoAmP 93
Tang, Thomas 1922- WhoAm 94, WhoAmL 94, WhoAsA 94, WhoWest 94
Tang, Thomas Li-Ping 1949- WhoAsA 94
Tang, Thomas Tze-Tung 1920- WhoAsA 94
Tang, Tom 1946- WhoFI 94, WhoWest 94
Tang, Victor K. T. 1929- WhoAsA 94
Tang, Wallace T. Y. WhoAsA 94
Tang, Wen 1921- WhoAsA 94
Tang, Wilson Hon-chung 1943- WhoAm 94, WhoAsA 94
Tang, Wing Tsang 1958- WhoWest 94
Tang, Yi-Noo 1938- WhoAsA 94
Tang, Yingchan Edwin 1953- WhoAsA 94
Tang, You-Zhi 1959- WhoScEn 94
Tang, Yu 1954- WhoScEn 94
Tang, Yu-Sun 1922- WhoAsA 94
Tang Aoqing 1915- IntWW 93, WhoPRCh 91 [port]
Tan Gaosheng 1916- WhoPRCh 91 [port]
Tangaroa, Tangaroa 1921- IntWW 93, Who 94
Tangarone, Bruce Steven 1961- WhoScEn 94
Tang Bangxing WhoPRCh 91 [port]
Tang Bingda WhoPRCh 91
Tangco, Ambrosio Flores 1912- WhoScEn 94
Tang Dacheng WhoPRCh 91
Tang Dequan 1915- WhoPRCh 91 [port]
Tang Dingyuan 1920- WhoPRCh 91 [port]
Tange, Arthur (Harold) 1914- Who 94
Tange, Kenzo 1913- IntWW 93
Tangen, Lyn 1945- WhoAmL 94
Tanger, Susanna 1942- WhoAmA 93
Tang Fuquan WhoPRCh 91
Tang Gengyao WhoPRCh 91 [port]
Tang Guangcai 1929- WhoPRCh 91 [port]
Tang Guizhang 1901- WhoPRCh 91 [port]
Tang Hongguang 1921- WhoPRCh 91 [port]
Tang Houzhi WhoPRCh 91
Tang Ke 1918- IntWW 93, WhoPRCh 91 [port]
Tangler, James Louis 1940- WhoScEn 94
Tang Longbin WhoPRCh 91
Tang Min WhoPRCh 91 [port]
Tang Min 1954- BlmGWL
Tang Mingzhao 1910- WhoPRCh 91
Tang Muhai WhoPRCh 91
Tang Muli 1947- WhoPRCh 91
Tangney, Eugene Michael 1928- WhoAm 94
Tang Nianci WhoPRCh 91
Tango, Egisto 1873-1951 NewGrDO
Tangora, Martin Charles 1936- WhoMW 93
Tang Peisong 1903- WhoPRCh 91 [port]
Tang Peisung 1903- IntWW 93
Tang Pingwu WhoPRCh 91
Tangredi, Vincent 1950- WhoAmA 93
Tangretti, Thomas A. 1946- WhoAmP 93
Tang Shichu 1950?- WhoPRCh 91 [port]
Tang Shubei WhoPRCh 91
Tang Tao 1913- WhoPRCh 91 [port]
Tanguay, Anita Walburga 1936- WhoFI 94
Tanguay, Eva d1947 WhoHol 92
Tanguay, Eva 1878-1947 WhoCom
Tanguma, Baldemar WhoHisp 94
Tanguy, Charles Reed 1921- WhoAm 94
Tanguy, Nicole Renee 1950- WhoAmL 94
Tanguy, Yves 1900-1955 WhoAmA 93N
Tang Wensheng WhoPRCh 91 [port]
Tang Xianzu 1550-1616 IntDcT 2
Tang Xiaowei 1931- IntWW 93
Tang Xingbo WhoPRCh 91
Tang Yijie 1927- WhoPRCh 91 [port]
Tang Yonggui WhoPRCh 91
Tang Youqi 1920- WhoPRCh 91 [port]
Tang Yuanbing 1909- WhoPRCh 91 [port]
Tang Yun 1910- WhoPRCh 91 [port]
Tang Zhaoyou WhoPRCh 91 [port]
Tang Zhe 1905- WhoPRCh 91 [port]
Tang Zhenxu 1911- WhoPRCh 91 [port]
Tang Zhisong 1925- IntWW 93
Tang Zhongwen 1930- IntWW 93, WhoPRCh 91 [port]
Tanham, George Kilpatrick 1922- WhoAm 94, WrDr 94
Tan Haosheng 1915- WhoPRCh 91
Tan Haosheng 1916- IntWW 93
Tani, Shohei 1942- WhoAm 94, WhoScEn 94
Tani, Yoko WhoHol 92
Tanick, Marshall Howard 1947- WhoAmL 94
Tanigawa, Kanzo IntWW 93, WhoScEn 94
Taniguchi, Alan Y. 1922- WhoAsA 94
Taniguchi, Brian T. 1951- WhoAmP 93
Taniguchi, Izumi 1926- WhoWest 94
Taniguchi, Makoto 1930- IntWW 93
Taniguchi, Raymond Masayuki 1934- WhoAm 94, WhoWest 94
Taniguchi, Richard Ryuzo 1913- WhoFI 94
Taniguchi, Robert Iwao 1945- WhoAsA 94
Taniguchi, Tokuso 1915- WhoAm 94, WhoScEn 94, WhoWest 94
Tanikawa, Kazuo 1930- IntWW 93
Tanimoto, George 1926- WhoAm 94, WhoWest 94
Tanimoto, Steven Larry 1949- WhoWest 94
Tanimura, Hiroshi 1916- IntWW 93
Tanis, James Robert 1928- WhoAm 94
Tanis, John Jacob 1926- WhoAm 94, WhoFI 94
Tanis, Norman Earl 1929- WhoAm 94
Taniuchi, Kiyoshi 1926- WhoScEn 94
Taniuk, Les Stepanovich 1938- LngBDD
Tanizaki Jun'ichiro 1886-1965 RfGShF
Tan Jiazhen 1909- IntWW 93, WhoPRCh 91 [port]
Tank, Himat G. 1951- WhoWest 94
Tanke, Thomas John 1944- WhoWest 94
Tankelevich, Roman Lvovich 1941- WhoScEn 94, WhoWest 94
Tan Keng Yam, Tony 1940- IntWW 93
Tankersley, Dan WhoAmP 93
Tankersley, Robert K. 1927- IntMPA 94
Tankerville, Earl of 1956- Who 94
Tankin, Richard Samuel 1924- WhoAm 94
Tanksley, Ann 1934- WhoAmA 93
Tanlaw, Baron 1934- Who 94
Tanler, Ronald F. WhoFI 94
Tan Liangde 1966- WhoPRCh 91 [port]
Tann, Daniel J. 1960- WhoBlA 94
Tann, Jennifer 1939- WrDr 94
Tannahill, Reay 1929- WrDr 94
Tannan, Ashok 1942- WhoAsA 94
Tannebaum, Samuel Hugo 1933- WhoFI 94
Tannehill, Cynthia Louise 1953- WhoMW 93
Tannehill, John C. 1943- WhoAm 94
Tannehill, Myrtle d1977 WhoHol 92
Tannehill, Robert Cooper 1934- WhoMW 93
Tannen, Beatrice d1960 WhoHol 92
Tannen, Charles d1981 WhoHol 92
Tannen, Deborah Frances 1945- WhoAm 94
Tannen, Julius d1965 WhoHol 92
Tannen, Leonard Phillip 1959- WhoFI 94
Tannen, Ricki Lewis 1952- WhoAmL 94
Tannen, Stephen Daniel 1946- WhoFI 94
Tannen, Steve WhoHol 92
Tannen, William d1976 WhoHol 92
Tannenbaum, Abe Alan 1922- WhoMW 93
Tannenbaum, Barbara Lee 1952- WhoAmA 93
Tannenbaum, Bernice Salpeter WhoAm 94
Tannenbaum, Ira L. 1941- WhoAmL 94
Tannenbaum, John O. 1946- WhoAm 94, WhoAmL 94
Tannenbaum, Judith DrAPF 93
Tannenbaum, Judith E. 1944- WhoAmA 93
Tannenbaum, Steven Robert 1937- WhoAm 94
Tannenberg, Dieter E. A. 1932- WhoAm 94, WhoFI 94, WhoMW 93
Tannenwald, Leslie Keiter 1949- WhoAm 94
Tannenwald, Peter 1943- WhoAm 94, WhoAmL 94
Tannenwald, Theodore, Jr. 1916- CngDr 93, WhoAm 94, WhoAmL 94
Tanner, Alain 1933- IntWW 93
Tanner, Allan Bruce 1950- WhoMW 93
Tanner, Benjamin Tucker 1835-1923 DcAmReB 2
Tanner, Beverly Francine 1932- WhoFI 94
Tanner, Brian Michael 1941- Who 94
Tanner, Champ Bean 1920- WhAm 10
Tanner, Clay WhoHol 92
Tanner, Craig Richard 1949- WhoScEn 94
Tanner, Daniel 1926- WhoAm 94
Tanner, David Allen 1958- WhoFI 94
Tanner, David Burnham 1945- WhoScEn 94
Tanner, David Earl 1948- WhoWest 94
Tanner, David Williamson 1930- Who 94
Tanner, Dee Boshard 1913- WhoAmL 94, WhoWest 94
Tanner, Douglas Alan 1953- WhoAm 94
Tanner, Douglas Howard 1935- WhoAmP 93
Tanner, Fred d1982 WhoHol 92
Tanner, Gloria Geraldine 1935- WhoAmP 93
Tanner, Gloria Travis 1935- WhoBlA 94
Tanner, Gordon WhoHol 92
Tanner, Harold 1932- WhoAm 94
Tanner, Hazel Marie 1946- WhoMW 93
Tanner, Helen Hornbeck 1916- WhoAm 94
Tanner, Henry Ossawa 1859-1937 AfrAmAl 6, ModArCr 4 [port], WhoAmA 93N
Tanner, Jack E. 1919- WhoBlA 94
Tanner, Jack Edward 1919- WhoWest 94
Tanner, Jacqui Dian 1946- WhoFI 94
Tanner, James L. 1941- WhoAmA 93
Tanner, James W., Jr. 1936- WhoBlA 94
Tanner, Jane 1946- SmATA 74 [port]
Tanner, Jimmie Eugene 1933- WhoAm 94
Tanner, Joanne Elizabeth 1944- WhoScEn 94
Tanner, Joe D. WhoAmP 93
Tanner, John DrAPF 93
Tanner, John (Ian) 1927- WrDr 94
Tanner, John Douglas, Jr. 1943- WhoWest 94
Tanner, John Ian 1927- Who 94
Tanner, John S. 1944- CngDr 93, WhoAm 94, WhoAmP 93
Tanner, John W. 1923- Who 94
Tanner, Jordan 1931- WhoAmP 93
Tanner, Laurel Nan 1929- WhoAm 94
Tanner, Lynn 1953- WhoWest 94
Tanner, Marion d1986 WhoHol 92
Tanner, Mary Elizabeth 1938- Who 94
Tanner, Meg Who 94
Tanner, Paul Antony 1935- Who 94
Tanner, Richard Dean 1952- WhoWest 94
Tanner, Roger Ian 1933- IntWW 93
Tanner, Ron DrAPF 93
Tanner, Stephen L. 1938- WrDr 94
Tanner, Terence A(rthur) 1948- WrDr 94
Tanner, Tony 1932- WhoHol 92
Tanner, Tony 1935- WrDr 94
Tanner, Walter Rhett 1938- WhoAm 94
Tanner, Warren 1942- WhoAmA 93N
Tanner, William Coats, Jr. 1920- WhoWest 94
Tannery, Jean-Paul 1911- IntWW 93
Tannian, Francis Xavier 1933- WhoAm 94
Tanno, Ronald Louis 1937- WhoWest 94
Tannous, Afif I. 1905- IntWW 93
Tannura, Nicholas Donald 1960- WhoAm 94
Tanny, Mark d1975 WhoHol 92
Tanous, James Joseph 1947- WhoAmL 94
Tanous, Michael Allan 1939- WhoWest 94
Tanous, Peter Joseph 1938- WhoFI 94
Tanouye, Marian Natsuko 1965- WhoWest 94
Tanouye, Mark Allen 1950- WhoAsA 94
Tan Qilong 1912- WhoPRCh 91 [port]
Tan Qinglian 1938- WhoPRCh 91 [port]
Tan Qixiang d1992 IntWW 93N
Tansel, Ibrahim Nur 1956- WhoScEn 94
Tanselle, G(eorge) Thomas 1934- WrDr 94
Tanselle, George Thomas 1934- WhoAm 94
Tansey, Emma d1942 WhoHol 92
Tansey, Iva Lee Marie 1930- WhoAmP 93
Tansey, Michael Richard 1943- WhoMW 93
Tansey, Robert d1951 WhoHol 92
Tan Shanhe WhoPRCh 91 [port]
Tan Shaowen d1993 IntWW 93N
Tan Shaowen 1929- WhoPRCh 91 [port]
Tansik, Linda Stiles 1942- WhoFI 94
Tansill, Donald Bender 1896- WhAm 10
Tansill, Frederick Joseph 1948- WhoAm 94, WhoAmL 94
Tansill, Frederick Riker 1914- WhoAm 94
Tanski, Adam 1946- IntWW 93
Tansman, Alexandre 1897-1986 NewGrDO
Tansor, Robert Henry 1935- WhoAm 94
Tant, Martin Ray 1953- WhoScEn 94
Tantala, Albert Martin 1938- WhoScEn 94
Tanter, Raymond 1938- WhoBlA 94
Tantillo, Charles Robert 1936- WhoMW 93
Tantillo, John 1951- WhoFI 94
Tan Tiwu 1902- WhoPRCh 91 [port]
Tan Wenrui 1922- WhoPRCh 91 [port]
Tan Xingju WhoPRCh 91
Tany, Luke de d1282 DcNaB MP
Tan Yizhi WhoPRCh 91
Tan Youlin WhoPRCh 91 [port]
Tan Youlin, Maj.-Gen. 1916- IntWW 93
Tan Yunhe 1922- WhoPRCh 91
Tanzania, Archbishop of 1932- Who 94
Tanzer, Andrew Ethan 1958- WhoScEn 94
Tanzer, Jed Samuel 1947- WhoAmL 94, WhoFI 94
Tanzer, Lester 1929- WhoAm 94
Tan Zhigang WhoPRCh 91
Tan Zhigeng WhoPRCh 91
Tan Zhuzhou 1936- WhoPRCh 91 [port]
Tanzmann, Virginia Ward 1945- WhoWest 94
Tao, Kar-Ling James 1941- WhoScEn 94
Tao, Mariano 1938- WhoScEn 94
Tao, Rongjia 1947- WhoScEn 94
Tao, Stephen G. 1963- WhoAsA 94
Tao, Yong-Xin 1954- WhoScEn 94
Tao Aiying 1931- WhoPRCh 91 [port]
Tao Benyi WhoPRCh 91
Tao Dayong 1918- IntWW 93, WhoPRCh 91 [port]

Tasker, Steven Jay 1962- *WhoAm 94*
Tasker, Thomas R. 1944- *WhoAmL 94*
Taskier, Paul R. 1955- *WhoAmL 94*
Taskin, (Emile-)Alexandre 1853-1897 *NewGrDO*
Tasma *BlmGWL*
Tasman, Abel Janszoon c. 1603-1659 *WhWE*
Tasman, William S. 1929- *WhoAm 94*
Tasmania, Bishop of 1930- *Who 94*
Tassani, Sally Marie 1948- *WhoMW 93*
Tasse, M. Jeanne *WhoAmA 93*
Tasse, Marie Jeanne 1925- *WhoMW 93*
Tasse, Roger 1931- *WhoAm 94*
Tasse, Yvon Roma 1910- *WhoScEn 94*
Tassell-Getman, Terri Louanne 1956- *WhoAmL 94, WhoMW 93*
Tassi, Niccolo fl. 1763-1781 *NewGrDO*
Tassian, George J. 1929- *WhoMW 93*
Tassie, Robert V. *WhoBlA 94*
Tassin, Leslie Paul, Sr. 1946- *WhoAmP 93*
Tassinari, Pia (Domenica) 1903- *NewGrDO*
Tasso, Torquato 1544-1595 *BlmGEL, IntDcT 2, NewGrDO*
Tassone, Bruce Anthony 1960- *WhoFI 94, WhoScEn 94*
Tassone, Gelsomina 1944- *WhoFI 94*
Tast, Alan Herbert 1961- *WhoMW 93*
Tastu, Amable 1798-1885 *BlmGWL*
Taswell, Harold Langmead Taylor *IntWW 93N*
Taswell, Howard Filmore 1928- *WhoAm 94*
Tata, Giovanni 1954- *WhoWest 94*
Tata, J. R. D. 1904-1993 *NewYTBS 93 [port]*
Tata, Jamshed Rustom 1930- *IntWW 93, Who 94*
Tata, Jehangir Ratanji Dadabhoy 1904- *IntWW 93*
Tata, Paul M., Sr. d1962 *WhoHol 92*
Tata, Prakasam Bala Surya 1936- *WhoMW 93*
Tata, Ratan 1937- *IntWW 93*
Tata, Robert 1930- *WhoAmP 93*
Tata, Sam Bejan 1911- *WhoAmA 93*
Tatangelo, Aldo 1913- *WhoAmP 93, WhoHisp 94*
Tatar, John Joseph 1951- *WhoScEn 94*
Tatarian, Hrach Roger 1916- *WhoAm 94*
Tatarinov, Leonid Petrovich 1926- *IntWW 93, WhoScEn 94*
Tatarskii, Valerian Il'ich 1929- *WhoWest 94*
Tate, Adolphus, Jr. 1942- *WhoBlA 94*
Tate, Albert, Jr. 1920- *WhoAmP 93*
Tate, Blair 1952- *WhoAmA 93*
Tate, Brett Andre 1963- *WhoBlA 94*
Tate, Charles Montgomery c. 1853-1933 *EncNAR*
Tate, Cullen d1947 *WhoHol 92*
Tate, David Kirk 1939- *WhoBlA 94*
Tate, David Orey 1935- *WhoAmP 93*
Tate, Eleanora E *DrAPF 93*
Tate, Eleanora E(laine) 1948- *BlkWr 2, ConAu 43NR, TwCYAW*
Tate, Eleanora Elaine 1948- *WhoBlA 94*
Tate, Ellalice *BlmGWL, ConAu 140, SmATA 74*
Tate, Ellalice 1906-1993 *WrDr 94N*
Tate, Eula Booker 1948- *WhoBlA 94*
Tate, Fran M. 1929- *WhoFI 94*
Tate, Francis Herbert 1913- *Who 94*
Tate, Frederick George 1925- *WhoAm 94*
Tate, Gayle Blair 1944- *WhoAmA 93*
Tate, Geraldine Williams 1954- *WhoFI 94*
Tate, Grady B. 1932- *WhoBlA 94*
Tate, Hardy Hagen *WhoAmP 93*
Tate, Harold Simmons, Jr. 1930- *WhoAm 94*
Tate, Harry d1940 *WhoHol 92*
Tate, Henry 1902- *Who 94*
Tate, Herbert Holmes, Jr. 1953- *WhoBlA 94*
Tate, Horace Edward 1922- *WhoAmP 93, WhoBlA 94*
Tate, James *DrAPF 93*
Tate, James (Vincent) 1943- *WrDr 94*
Tate, James A. 1927- *WhoBlA 94*
Tate, James Solomon, Jr. 1954- *WhoAmL 94*
Tate, James Vincent 1943- *WhoAm 94*
Tate, Jeffrey 1943- *NewGrDO*
Tate, Jeffrey L. 1957- *WhoScEn 94*
Tate, Jeffrey Philip 1943- *IntWW 93, Who 94*
Tate, Jerry Allen 1956- *WhoWest 94*
Tate, Joan 1922- *WrDr 94*
Tate, Joan C. 1946- *WhoAmP 93*
Tate, John d1979 *WhoHol 92*
Tate, John Edward 1930- *WhoScEn 94*
Tate, John Orley Allen 1899-1979 *AmCulL*
Tate, Lars Jamel 1966- *WhoBlA 94*
Tate, Lenore Artie 1952- *WhoBlA 94*
Tate, Loretta Hitchings 1936- *WhoAmP 93*
Tate, Mable Leigh 1947- *WhoAmP 93*
Tate, Maggie *NewGrDO*
Tate, Manford Ben 1916- *WhoScEn 94*
Tate, Margaret Townsend 1934- *WhoAmP 93*
Tate, Matthew 1940- *WhoBlA 94*
Tate, Maurice William 1895-1956 *DcNaB MP*
Tate, Merze 1905- *WhoBlA 94*
Tate, Michael J. 1954- *WhoAmP 93*
Tate, Michael Lynn 1947- *WhoMW 93*
Tate, Nahum 1652-1715 *BlmGEL, IntDcT 2, NewGrDO*
Tate, Nick *WhoHol 92*
Tate, Peter *EncSF 93, WrDr 94*
Tate, Phil *WhoAmP 93*
Tate, Phil 1946- *WhoAmP 93*
Tate, Ralph Richards, Jr. 1941- *WhoAmP 93*
Tate, Randy *WhoAmP 93*
Tate, Reginald d1955 *WhoHol 92*
Tate, Robert Brian 1921- *IntWW 93, Who 94*
Tate, Robin *EncSF 93*
Tate, Saxon *Who 94*
Tate, (Henry) Saxon 1931- *Who 94*
Tate, Sharon d1969 *WhoHol 92*
Tate, Sheila Burke 1942- *WhoAm 94, WhoFI 94*
Tate, Sherman E. 1945- *WhoBlA 94*
Tate, Steven Gary 1954- *WhoAmL 94*
Tate, Stonewall Shepherd 1917- *WhoAm 94, WhoAmL 94*
Tate, Thaddeus Wilbur, Jr. 1924- *WhoAm 94*
Tate, Troy Dale 1963- *WhoMW 93*
Tate, Valencia Faye 1956- *WhoBlA 94*
Tate, Willis McDonald 1911-1989 *WhAm 10*
Tateishi, Yoshiharu 1946- *WhoWest 94*
Tatel, David Stephen 1942- *WhoAm 94, WhoAmL 94*
Tatelbaum, Linda *DrAPF 93*
Tatelman, Milton J. d1993 *NewYTBS 93*
Tatem, Moira (Phillips) 1928- *WrDr 94*
Tatem, Patricia Ann 1946- *WhoBlA 94*
Tateoka, Reid 1954- *WhoAmL 94*
Tatera, James Frank 1946- *WhoScEn 94*
Tateyama, Ichiro 1952- *WhoScEn 94*
Tatgenhorst, Robert 1918- *WhoAm 94*
Tatham, David Everard 1939- *IntWW 93, Who 94*
Tatham, David Frederic 1932- *WhoAm 94, WhoAmA 93*
Tatham, Francis Hugh Currer 1916- *Who 94*
Tatham, Gregory Arthur 1953- *WhoWest 94*
Tati, Jacques d1982 *WhoHol 92*
Tati, Jacques 1908-1982 *WhoCom*
Tatibouet, Andre Stephan 1941- *WhoAm 94, WhoFI 94*
Tatibouet, Jane B. *WhoAmP 93*
Tatina, Robert Edward 1942- *WhoScEn 94*
Tatishvili, Tsisana Bezhanovna 1939- *IntWW 93*
Tatistcheff, Peter Alexis 1938- *WhoAmA 93*
Tatkon-Coker, Andrea Laura 1954- *WhoMW 93*
Tatlock, Anne M. 1939- *WhoAm 94, WhoFI 94*
Tatlow, John Colin 1923- *Who 94*
Tatlow, Richard Henry, III d1993 *NewYTBS 93*
Tatman, Edward J. 1949- *WhoMW 93*
Tatman, Richard Wakefield 1943- *WhoMW 93*
Tatman, Robin Reich 1959- *WhoWest 94*
Tatnall, George Jacob 1923- *WhoScEn 94*
Tatom, Absalom 1742-1802 *WhAmRev*
Tatom, John Anthony 1945- *WhoFI 94*
Taton, (Andre) Rene 1915- *IntWW 93*
Tatooles, Constantine John 1936- *WhoAm 94*
Tatossian, Armand 1948- *WhoAmA 93*
Tatrai, Vilmos 1912- *IntWW 93*
Tatro, Rene P. 1953- *WhoAmL 94*
Tatro, Ronald Edward 1943- *WhoAmA 93*
Tatsumi, Sotoo 1923- *IntWW 93*
Tatta, John Louis 1920- *WhoAm 94, WhoFI 94*
Tattenbach-Yglesias, Christian 1924- *IntWW 93*
Tattermuschova, Helena 1933- *NewGrDO*
Tattersall, Geoffrey Frank 1947- *Who 94*
Tattersall, (Honor) Jill 1931- *WrDr 94*
Tatti, Benedict Michael 1917- *WhoAmA 93*
Tatton Brown, William Eden 1910- *Who 94*
Tatum, Art d1956 *WhoHol 92*
Tatum, Art 1909-1956 *AfrAmAl 6*
Tatum, Arthur, Jr. 1910-1956 *AmCulL*
Tatum, Buck d1941 *WhoHol 92*
Tatum, Carol Evora 1943- *WhoBlA 94*
Tatum, Donn B. d1993 *IntMPA 94N, NewYTBS 93*
Tatum, Edward Lawrie 1909-1975 *WorScD*
Tatum, Ellyna d1986 *WhoHol 92*
Tatum, Ezra Carl, Jr. 1926- *WhoAmP 93*
Tatum, Franklin M., III 1946- *WhoAmL 94*
Tatum, Goose 1917- *BasBi*
Tatum, Grace Martinez 1960- *WhoHisp 94*
Tatum, James Bernard 1925- *WhoAmP 93*
Tatum, Jerry *WhoBlA 94*
Tatum, Jesse Seaton 1952- *WhoMW 93*
Tatum, Marianne *WhoHol 92*
Tatum, Mildred Carthan 1940- *WhoBlA 94*
Tatum, Omar Lee 1926- *WhoFI 94*
Tatum, Rita 1948- *WhoAm 94*
Tatum, Ronald Winston 1935- *WhoWest 94*
Tatum, Thomas Deskins 1946- *WhoWest 94*
Tatum, Wilbert A. 1933- *WhoBlA 94*
Tatus, Ronald Peter 1944- *WhoWest 94*
Tatyrek, Alfred Frank 1930- *WhoAm 94, WhoScEn 94*
Tau, Mari Suzanne 1964- *WhoFI 94*
Taub, Abraham 1901-1990 *WhAm 10*
Taub, Abraham Haskel 1911- *WhoWest 94*
Taub, Eli Irwin 1938- *WhoAmL 94*
Taub, Jesse 1923- *WhoFI 94*
Taub, Jesse J. 1927- *WhoAm 94*
Taub, Richard Paul 1937- *WhoAm 94*
Taub, Robert Allan 1923- *WhoAm 94*
Taub, Sam d1979 *WhoHol 92*
Taub, Shmuel Duvid 1947- *WhoAmL 94*
Taub, Theodore Calvin 1935- *WhoAmL 94*
Taube *NewGrDO*
Taube, Adam A.S. 1932- *WhoScEn 94*
Taube, Henry 1915- *IntWW 93, Who 94, WhoAm 94, WhoScEn 94, WhoWest 94*
Taube, Mathias d1934 *WhoHol 92*
Taube, Myron *DrAPF 93*
Taube, Nicholas 1944- *WhoIns 94*
Taube, Robert d1964 *WhoHol 92*
Taube, Robert Roy 1936- *WhoMW 93*
Taube, Sven-Bertil *WhoHol 92*
Taubenfeld, Harry Samuel 1929- *WhoAmL 94*
Tauber, Alfred Imre 1947- *WhoAm 94*
Tauber, Joel David 1935- *WhoAm 94*
Tauber, Maria Anna fl. 1777-1779 *NewGrDO*
Tauber, Mark J. 1949- *WhoAm 94, WhoAmL 94*
Tauber, Orner J., Jr. 1914- *WhoFI 94*
Tauber, Richard d1948 *WhoHol 92*
Tauber, Richard 1891-1948 *DcNaB MP, NewGrDO*
Tauber, Ronald Steven 1944- *WhoAm 94*
Tauberova, Maria 1911- *NewGrDO*
Taubert, Frederick Wayne 1933- *WhoFI 94*
Taubert, Lyall Warren 1920- *WhoAmP 93*
Taubert, (Carl Gottfried) Wilhelm 1811-1891 *NewGrDO*
Taubes, Clifford H. *WhoScEn 94*
Taubes, Frederic 1900-1981 *WhoAmA 93N*
Taubes, Timothy Evan 1955- *WhoAmA 93*
Taubin, Michael J. 1950- *WhoAmL 94*
Taubitz, Fredricka 1944- *WhoAm 94, WhoFI 94*
Taubman, A. Alfred 1925- *CurBio 93 [port], IntWW 93, WhoAm 94*
Taubman, Bruce 1947- *ConAu 141*
Taubman, (Hyman) Howard 1907- *IntWW 93*
Taubman, Jane A. 1942- *WrDr 94*
Taubman, Martin Arnold 1940- *WhoAm 94*
Taubman, Paul James 1939- *WhoAm 94*
Taubman, William Chase 1941- *WhoAm 94*
Tauc, Jan 1922- *WhoAm 94, WhoScEn 94*
Tauch, Waldine Amanda 1892-1986 *WhoAmA 93N*
Taucher, Curt 1885-1945 *NewGrDO*
Tauchert, Theodore Richmond *WhoAm 94*
Tauck, David Lawrence 1956- *WhoWest 94*
Tauer, Paul E. *WhoAmP 93*
Tauer, Paul E. 1935- *WhoWest 94*
Taufa'ahau, Tupou, IV 1918- *IntWW 93*
Taufen, Paul Michael 1952- *WhoWest 94*
Taukalo, (David) Dawea 1920- *Who 94*
Tauke, Thomas J. 1950- *WhoAmP 93*
Taulbee, Frances Laverne 1937- *WhoAmP 93*
Taulbert, Clifton L(emoure) 1945- *BlkWr 2*
Taulbert, Clifton LeMoure 1945- *WhoBlA 94*
Taunton, Archdeacon of *Who 94*
Taunton, Bishop Suffragan of 1943- *Who 94*
Taunton, Eric 1921- *WrDr 94*
Taunton, Harold Dean 1953- *WhoWest 94*
Taura, Richard Bill 1953- *WhoAsA 94*
Taurel, Sidney Afriat 1949- *WhoFI 94*
Taurman, John David 1946- *WhoAmL 94*
Tauro, Joseph Louis 1931- *WhoAm 94, WhoAmL 94*
Taurog, Norman d1981 *WhoHol 92*
Taus, Josef 1933- *IntWW 93*
Taus, Robert Leo 1938- *WhoFI 94*
Tauschek, Terrence Alan 1948- *WhoAm 94, WhoWest 94*
Tauscher, John Walter 1929- *WhoAm 94*
Tausend, Fredric Cutner 1933- *WhoAm 94, WhoAmL 94*
Tausig, Michael Robert 1948- *WhoWest 94*
Tausky, Vilem 1910- *Who 94*
Taussig, Eric Alfred 1944- *WhoFI 94*
Taussig, Helen Brooke 1898-1986 *WorScD*
Taussig, Joseph Knefler, Jr. 1920- *WhoAm 94*
Taussig, Peter Richard 1930- *WhoMW 93*
Taussig, Robert Trimble 1938- *WhoWest 94*
Tautenhayn, Ernst 1873-1944 *NewGrDO*
Tautolo, Agaoleatu Charlie *WhoAmP 93*
Tauzin, W. J. 1943- *CngDr 93, WhoAmP 93*
Tauzin, Wilbert J., II 1943- *WhoAm 94*
Tavaglione, David 1930- *WhoScEn 94*
Tavaiqia, Josaia (Nasorowale) 1930- *Who 94*
Tavakolian, Bahram Mehdi 1945- *WhoMW 93*
Tavallali, Jalal Chaicar 1964- *WhoAmL 94*
Tavano, Frank 1962- *WhoScEn 94*
Ta Van Tai 1938- *WrDr 94*
Tavard, Georges Henri 1922- *IntWW 93*
Tavare, Andrew Kenneth 1918- *Who 94*
Tavare, John 1920- *Who 94*
Tavares, Arthur d1954 *WhoHol 92*
Tavares, Braulio 1950- *EncSF 93*
Tavares, Dennis Joseph 1951- *WhoWest 94*
Tavares, Hannibal Manuel 1919- *WhoAmP 93*
Tavares, Joseph 1945- *WhoFI 94*
Tavares, Paul J. 1952- *WhoAmP 93*
Tavares, Salette 1922- *BlmGWL*
Tavarez, José Luis 1968- *WhoHisp 94*
Taveggia, Thomas Charles 1943- *WhoAm 94, WhoWest 94*
Tavegia, James A. *WhoAmP 93*
Tavel, James Wilson 1945- *WhoAmL 94*
Tavel, Mark Kivey 1945- *WhoAm 94*
Tavel, Morton Allen 1939- *WhoAm 94*
Tavel, Ronald *DrAPF 93*
Tavel, Ronald 1941- *ConDr 93, WrDr 94*
Tavenas, Francois 1942- *WhoAm 94*
Tavener, John 1944- *IntWW 93, Who 94*
Tavener, John (Kenneth) 1944- *NewGrDO*
Tavenner, Frank Lee 1948- *WhoWest 94*
Tavenner, Patricia *WhoAmA 93*
Taveras, Juan Manuel 1919- *WhoAm 94*
Taverna, Rodney Elward 1947- *WhoWest 94*
Tavernas-Guzman, Juan Aristides 1936- *IntWW 93*
Taverne, Dick 1928- *Who 94, WrDr 94*
Taverner, Sonia 1936- *IntWW 93*
Tavernier, Bertrand 1941- *IntMPA 94*
Tavernier, Bertrand Rene Maurice 1941- *IntWW 93*
Taviani, Paolo 1931- *IntWW 93*
Taviani, Paolo 1931- & Taviani, Vittorio 1929- *IntMPA 94*
Taviani, Paolo Emilio 1912- *IntWW 93*
Taviani, Vittorio 1929- *IntMPA 94, IntWW 93*
Taviani, Vittorio 1929- *See* Taviani, Paolo 1931- & Taviani, Vittorio 1929- *IntMPA 94*
Tavibo c. 1835-c. 1915 *EncNAR*
Taviss, Patricia Ann 1955- *WhoMW 93*
Tavistock, Marquess of 1940- *Who 94*
Tavlin, Michael John 1946- *WhoMW 93*
Tavora, Concha *WhoHol 92*
Tavoularis, Dean 1932- *IntDcF 2-4 [port]*
T'avrizyan, Mik'ayel Arsen 1907-1957 *NewGrDO*
Taw, Dudley Joseph 1916- *WhoAm 94*
Tawa, Nicholas E. 1923- *WrDr 94*
Tawara, Takashi *IntWW 93*
Tawata, Shinkichi 1949- *WhoScEn 94*
Tawfiq Al-Hakim 1898-1987 *IntDcT 2*
Tawil, Soha *NewYTBS 93 [port]*
Tawney, Lenore *WhoAmA 93*
Tawshunsky, Alan Neal 1954- *WhoAmL 94*
Tax, Meredith *DrAPF 93*
Tax, Sol 1907- *IntWW 93*

Taxell, (Lars Evald) Christoffer 1948- IntWW 93
Taxer, Eric John 1963- WhoWest 94
Taxier, Arthur WhoHol 92
Taxter, Michael J. 1950- WhoIns 94
Tay, Roger Yew-Siow 1958- WhoScEn 94
Taya, Maawiya Ould Sid'Ahmed 1943- IntWW 93
Tayari, Kabili 1950- WhoBlA 94
Tayback, Vic d1990 WhAm 10, WhoHol 92
Tayler, Alan Breach 1931- Who 94
Tayler, Harold Clive 1932- Who 94
Tayler, Irene WrDr 94
Taylor Who 94
Taylor, Lady 1914- Who 94
Taylor, Adam David 1917- WhoFI 94
Taylor, Al d1947 WhoHol 92
Taylor, Al C. 1948- WhoAmA 93
Taylor, Alan Who 94
Taylor, (Robert) Alan 1944- Who 94
Taylor, Alan Broughton 1939- Who 94
Taylor, Alan Henry 1954- WhoScEn 94
Taylor, Alan John Percivale 1906-1990 WhAm 10
Taylor, Albert d1940 WhoHol 92
Taylor, Albert, Jr. 1957- WhoBlA 94
Taylor, Alexander DrAPF 93
Taylor, Alfred Hendricks, Jr. 1930- WhoAm 94
Taylor, Alfred Wayne 1946- WhoMW 93
Taylor, Allan (Macnab) 1919- Who 94
Taylor, Allan Bert 1948- WhoAm 94, WhoAmL 94
Taylor, Allan Richard 1932- IntWW 93, WhoAm 94, WhoFI 94
Taylor, Allan Ross 1931- WhoAm 94
Taylor, Allegra 1940- WrDr 94
Taylor, Allen Jeffry 1943- WhoAmP 93
Taylor, Alma d1974 WhoHol 92
Taylor, Almina 1933- WhoBlA 94
Taylor, Alphonse 1937- WhoAmP 93
Taylor, Anderson WhoBlA 94
Taylor, Andre Jerome 1946- WhoBlA 94
Taylor, Andrew (John Robert) 1951- WrDr 94
Taylor, Andrew (McDonald) 1940- WrDr 94
Taylor, Andrew Christopher 1960- WhoScEn 94
Taylor, Andrew James 1902- Who 94
Taylor, Andy d1948 WhoHol 92
Taylor, Ann Who 94
Taylor, Ann 1782-1866 BlmGEL, BlmGWL
Taylor, Ann 1941- WhoAmA 93
Taylor, Ann 1947- WhoWomW 91
Taylor, (Winifred) Ann 1947- Who 94
Taylor, Ann Louise 1937- WhoFI 94
Taylor, Ann R. DrAPF 93
Taylor, Ann Siegrist 1953- WhoMW 93
Taylor, Anna Diggs 1932- WhoAm 94, WhoAmL 94, WhoBlA 94, WhoMW 93
Taylor, Anna Heyward 1879-1956 WhoAmA 93N
Taylor, Anne 1934- ConAu 140
Taylor, Annie Royle 1855-1907? WhWE
Taylor, Arlene M. J. 1955- WhoBlA 94
Taylor, Arnold H. 1929- WhoBlA 94
Taylor, Arnold Joseph 1911- IntWW 93, Who 94
Taylor, Arthur Duane 1920- WhoBlA 94
Taylor, Arthur John d1992 Who 94N
Taylor, Arthur Robert 1935- IntWW 93, Who 94, WhoAm 94
Taylor, Arthur Ronald 1921- Who 94
Taylor, Austin Starke, Jr. 1922- WhoAmP 93
Taylor, B. Eldon 1945- WhoWest 94
Taylor, Barry E. 1948- WhoAmL 94
Taylor, Barry Llewellyn 1937- WhoScEn 94, WhoWest 94
Taylor, Barry Norman 1936- WhoAm 94
Taylor, Benjamin 1947- WhoAm 94
Taylor, Bernard C. 1948- WhoBlA 94
Taylor, Bernard David 1935- IntWW 93, Who 94
Taylor, Bernard J., II 1925- WhoAm 94
Taylor, Beverly (White) 1947- WrDr 94
Taylor, Bill 1926- WhoAmA 93
Taylor, Billy d1930 WhoHol 92
Taylor, Billy 1921- AfrAmAl 6
Taylor, Bobby Joe 1943- WhoAmP 93
Taylor, Brenda Carol 1956- WhoMW 93, WhoScEn 94
Taylor, Brenda L. 1949- WhoBlA 94
Taylor, Brian DrAPF 93
Taylor, Brian David 1954- WhoWest 94
Taylor, Brian Hyde 1931- Who 94
Taylor, Brian William 1933- Who 94
Taylor, Brian William 1942- WhoAm 94
Taylor, Brie 1923- WhoAmA 93
Taylor, Bruce DrAPF 93
Taylor, Buck 1938- WhoHol 92
Taylor, Byron Keith 1955- WhoMW 93
Taylor, C(larence) J(ohn) 1893- WhAm 10
Taylor, Calvin Lee 1946- WhoMW 93
Taylor, Carl Ernest 1916- IntWW 93, WhoAm 94
Taylor, Carl Larsen 1937- WhoAmL 94
Taylor, Carole Jan Hudson 1949- WhoFI 94
Taylor, Carole Lillian WhoBlA 94
Taylor, Carolyn WhoAmP 93
Taylor, Carroll Stribling 1944- WhoAmL 94
Taylor, Carson William 1942- WhoAm 94
Taylor, Casper R., Jr. 1934- WhoAmP 93
Taylor, Cassandra W. 1951- WhoBlA 94
Taylor, Cavan 1935- Who 94
Taylor, Cecil 1929- AfrAmAl 6
Taylor, Cecil P(hilip) 1929-1981 ConDr 93
Taylor, Cecil Percival 1933- WhoAm 94
Taylor, Celianna I. WhoAm 94, WhoMW 93, WhoScEn 94
Taylor, Charity Who 94
Taylor, Charles IntWW 93
Taylor, Charles 1931- IntWW 93
Taylor, Charles 1941- WhoAmP 93
Taylor, Charles, Jr. 1929- WhoAmP 93
Taylor, Charles (Alfred) 1922- WrDr 94
Taylor, Charles Avon WhoBlA 94
Taylor, Charles E. 1944- WhoBlA 94
Taylor, Charles Edward 1931- WhoBlA 94
Taylor, Charles H. 1941- CngDr 93, WhoAm 94
Taylor, Charles Henry 1928- WhoAm 94
Taylor, Charles Margrave 1931- Who 94
Taylor, Charles Richard 1939- WhoAm 94
Taylor, Charles Russell, Jr. 1948- WhoAmL 94
Taylor, Charles Senn 1948- WhoMW 93
Taylor, Charley ProFbHF [port]
Taylor, Charley R. 1942- WhoBlA 94
Taylor, Christopher Andrew 1947- WhoAm 94, WhoFI 94
Taylor, Christopher Lenard 1923- WhoBlA 94
Taylor, Clarence B. 1937- WhoBlA 94
Taylor, Clarice 1927- WhoHol 92
Taylor, Claude I. 1925- WhoAm 94, WhoFI 94
Taylor, Clayton Charles 1952- WhoAm 94, WhoFI 94
Taylor, Cledie Collins 1926- WhoBlA 94
Taylor, Clifford 1941- Who 94
Taylor, Clifford Curtis 1895- WhAm 10
Taylor, Clifford Woodworth 1942- WhoAmL 94
Taylor, Clyde Calvin, Jr. 1936- WhoAm 94
Taylor, Clyde D. 1937- WhoAmP 93
Taylor, Colin Campbell d1938 WhoHol 92
Taylor, Comer L., Jr. 1949- WhoBlA 94
Taylor, Conciere DrAPF 93
Taylor, Constance Lidsay 1907- WrDr 94
Taylor, Cora 1928- WhoBlA 94
Taylor, Cordy 1925- WhoAmP 93
Taylor, Craig P. 1957- WhoAmP 93
Taylor, Cyril 1935- WhoAm 94
Taylor, Cyril (Julian Hebden) 1935- Who 94
Taylor, D. Lansing 1946- WhoScEn 94
Taylor, Daisy Curry 1948- WhoBlA 94
Taylor, Dale B. 1939- WhoBlA 94
Taylor, Dale L. 1959- WhoMW 93
Taylor, Dalmas A. 1933- WhoBlA 94
Taylor, Dalmas Arnold 1933- WhoAm 94
Taylor, Daniel A. 1942- WhoAmL 94
Taylor, Daniel Brumhall Cochrane 1921- Who 94
Taylor, Daniel Jennings 1941- WhoMW 93
Taylor, Darl Coder 1913- WhoAm 94
Taylor, David (Conrad) 1934- WrDr 94
Taylor, David Afton 1949- WhoAmL 94
Taylor, David Brooke 1942- WhoAm 94, WhoAmL 94
Taylor, David George 1929- WhoAm 94
Taylor, David George Pendleton 1933- Who 94
Taylor, David John 1947- Who 94
Taylor, David Kerr 1928- WhoFI 94
Taylor, David Lowell 1964- WhoMW 93
Taylor, David Michael 1954- WhoMW 93
Taylor, David Richard, III 1949- WhoBlA 94
Taylor, David Vassar 1945- WhoBlA 94
Taylor, David Wyatt Aiken 1925- WhoAm 94
Taylor, Davidson 1907-1979 WhoAmA 93N
Taylor, Dean Perron 1947- WhoScEn 94
Taylor, Deems d1966 WhoHol 92
Taylor, (Joseph) Deems 1885-1966 NewGrDO
Taylor, DeForrest Walker 1933- WhoBlA 94
Taylor, Delores WhoHol 92
Taylor, Delores 1939- IntMPA 94
Taylor, (Edmund) Dennis 1940- ConAu 43NR
Taylor, Dennis Del 1946- WhoMW 93
Taylor, Dennis Howard 1944- WhoAmL 94, WhoFI 94
Taylor, Derek 1930- Who 94
Taylor, Dermot Brownrigg 1915- WhoAm 94
Taylor, Desmond S. Who 94
Taylor, Domini 1929- WrDr 94
Taylor, Don 1920- IntMPA 94, WhoHol 92
Taylor, Don Lee 1932- WhoAmP 93
Taylor, Donald 1927- WhoFI 94
Taylor, Donald Arthur 1923- WhoAm 94
Taylor, Donald Fulton, Sr. 1932- WhoBlA 94
Taylor, Donald R. 1949- WhoAmL 94
Taylor, Donna Bloyd 1958- WhoMW 93
Taylor, Doris d1986 WhoHol 92
Taylor, Doris Denice 1955- WhoMW 93
Taylor, Dorothy Harris 1931- WhoFI 94
Taylor, Douglas Floyd 1942- WhoScEn 94
Taylor, Douglas Hugh Charles 1938- Who 94
Taylor, Douglas Sterling 1956- WhoWest 94
Taylor, Dub 1909- WhoHol 92
Taylor, Eartha Lynn 1957- WhoBlA 94
Taylor, Eddie Milton 1945- WhoWest 94
Taylor, Edmund Frederick 1960- WhoFI 94
Taylor, Edna Jane 1934- WhoFI 94, WhoWest 94
Taylor, Edward Curtis 1923- WhoAm 94, WhoScEn 94
Taylor, Edward Macmillan 1937- Who 94
Taylor, Edward McKinley, Jr. 1928- WhoAmL 94
Taylor, Edward Plunket 1901-1989 WhAm 10
Taylor, Edward Stewart 1911- WhoAm 94
Taylor, Edward Walter 1926- WhoBlA 94
Taylor, Edward William, Jr. 1961- WhoMW 93
Taylor, Edwin William 1929- Who 94
Taylor, Elaine WhoHol 92
Taylor, Eldon Donivan 1929- WhoAm 94
Taylor, Eleanor Ross DrAPF 93
Taylor, Elinor Z. 1921- WhoAmP 93
Taylor, Elisabeth (D.) 1931- WrDr 94
Taylor, Elisabeth Coler 1942- WhoMW 93
Taylor, Elizabeth 1912-1975 BlmGWL [port], DcLB 139 [port]
Taylor, Elizabeth 1932- IntMPA 94, IntWW 93, News 93-3 [port], WhoAm 94, WhoHol 92
Taylor, Elizabeth (Rosemond) 1932- Who 94
Taylor, Elizabeth Atwood 1936- ConAu 142
Taylor, Elizabeth Jane 1941- WhoFI 94
Taylor, Ellis Clarence, Sr. 1931- WhoBlA 94
Taylor, Eloise d1987 WhoHol 92
Taylor, Emily 1860-1952 WhoAmA 93N
Taylor, Eric 1931- Who 94
Taylor, Eric Charles 1962- WhoBlA 94
Taylor, Eric Scollick 1918- Who 94
Taylor, Eric W. 1909- Who 94
Taylor, Ernest G., Jr. 1945- WhoAmL 94
Taylor, Ernest Norman, Jr. 1953- WhoBlA 94
Taylor, Ernest Richard d1993 Who 94N
Taylor, Estelle d1958 WhoHol 92
Taylor, Estelle Wormley 1924- WhoAm 94, WhoBlA 94
Taylor, Eugene Donaldson 1922- WhoBlA 94
Taylor, Eva Marietta WhoMW 93
Taylor, Felicia Michelle 1960- WhoBlA 94
Taylor, Ferris d1961 WhoHol 92
Taylor, Finley L. 1945- WhoAmL 94
Taylor, Florietta Mae 1931- WhoAmP 93
Taylor, Floye d1957 WhoHol 92
Taylor, Forrest d1965 WhoHol 92
Taylor, Foster Jay 1923- WhoAm 94
Taylor, Francis Henry 1903-1957 WhoAmA 93N
Taylor, Frank Who 94, WrDr 94
Taylor, Frank 1915- Who 94
Taylor, Frank A. 1953- WhoAmL 94
Taylor, Frank C. 1946- WhoIns 94
Taylor, Frank Henry 1907- Who 94
Taylor, Frank Henry 1932- Who 94
Taylor, Fred WhoAmP 93
Taylor, Fred 1925- BasBi
Taylor, Fred J(ames) 1919- WrDr 94
Taylor, Fred Monroe 1901-1988 WhAm 10
Taylor, Frederick Bourchier 1906- WhoAmA 93N
Taylor, Frederick William, Jr. 1933- WhoAmL 94
Taylor, Fredric William 1944- Who 94
Taylor, Frieda D. 1936- WhoIns 94
Taylor, Gardner C. 1918- AfrAmAl 6
Taylor, Gary Eugene 1953- WhoAmP 93
Taylor, Gary L. 1938- WhoAm 94, WhoAmL 94, WhoWest 94
Taylor, Gary Matthew 1949- WhoMW 93
Taylor, Gary S. 1943- WhoAmP 93
Taylor, Gayland Wayne 1958- WhoBlA 94
Taylor, Gaylon Don 1960- WhoScEn 94
Taylor, Gene 1928- WhoAmP 93
Taylor, Gene 1953- CngDr 93, WhoAm 94
Taylor, Geoffrey H. Who 94
Taylor, Geoffrey William 1927- Who 94
Taylor, George d1939 WhoHol 92
Taylor, George d1970 WhoHol 92
Taylor, George 1716-1781 WhAmRev
Taylor, George 1904- IntWW 93, Who 94
Taylor, George Allen 1906- WhoAm 94, WhoWest 94
Taylor, George Braxton 1860-1942 DcAmReB 2
Taylor, George Frederick 1928- WhoAm 94, WhoWest 94
Taylor, George Kimbrough, Jr. 1939- WhoAm 94
Taylor, George Malcolm, III 1953- WhoAmL 94
Taylor, George Simpson 1940- WhoFI 94
Taylor, Gerard William 1920- Who 94
Taylor, Gilbert Leon 1937- WhoBlA 94
Taylor, Glenhall E. 1925- WhoAm 94
Taylor, Gloria Jean WhoBlA 94
Taylor, Godfrey Who 94
Taylor, (Arthur) Godfrey 1925- Who 94
Taylor, Gordon DrAPF 93
Taylor, Gordon 1944- Who 94
Taylor, Gordon William 1928- Who 94
Taylor, Grace Martin WhoAmA 93
Taylor, Graham 1944- Who 94
Taylor, Grant WhoHol 92
Taylor, Gregory WhoAm 94
Taylor, Greville Laughton 1902- Who 94
Taylor, Grigor WhoHol 92
Taylor, Guy Watson 1919- WhoAm 94
Taylor, H. Baldwin 1920- WrDr 94
Taylor, Harlin R. 1948- WhoAmP 93
Taylor, Harold d1993 NewYTBS 93 [port]
Taylor, Harold 1914-1993 ConAu 140
Taylor, Harold (Alexander) 1914-1993 CurBio 93N
Taylor, Harold Allen, Jr. 1936- WhoAm 94, WhoFI 94
Taylor, Harold Joseph d1993 Who 94N
Taylor, Harold Leon 1946- WhoBlA 94
Taylor, Harold McCarter 1907- IntWW 93, Who 94
Taylor, Harriet Hardy 1807-1858 DcNaB MP
Taylor, Harry Danner 1944- WhoFI 94
Taylor, Harry George 1918- WhoAmA 93
Taylor, Harry Grant 1908- WhoAmP 93
Taylor, Harry William 1925- WhoAm 94
Taylor, Helen 1947- WrDr 94
Taylor, Henry DrAPF 93
Taylor, Henry d1969 WhoHol 92
Taylor, Henry 1942- WrDr 94
Taylor, Henry F. WhoBlA 94
Taylor, Henry George 1904- Who 94
Taylor, Henry L. 1933- WhoScEn 94
Taylor, Henry Louis, Jr. 1943- WhoBlA 94
Taylor, Henry Marshall 1932- WhoBlA 94
Taylor, Henry Milton 1903- IntWW 93, Who 94
Taylor, Henry Splawn 1942- WhoAm 94
Taylor, Herbert Cecil, Jr. 1924- WhAm 10
Taylor, Herbert Charles 1948- WhoBlA 94
Taylor, Herman Daniel 1937- WhoBlA 94
Taylor, Hermon 1905- Who 94
Taylor, Holland 1944- WhoHol 92
Taylor, Howard WhoHol 92
Taylor, Howard F. 1939- WhoBlA 94
Taylor, Howard Francis 1939- WhoAm 94
Taylor, (James) Hudson 1832-1905 DcNaB MP
Taylor, Hugh Holloway 1941- WhoAmA 93
Taylor, Hugh Pettingill, Jr. 1932- WhoAm 94, WhoScEn 94
Taylor, Hugh Ringland 1947- WhoScEn 94
Taylor, Humphrey John Fausitt 1934- WhoAm 94
Taylor, Humphrey Vincent Who 94
Taylor, Hycel B. 1936- WhoBlA 94
Taylor, Ian Colin 1945- Who 94
Taylor, Ian Galbraith 1924- Who 94
Taylor, Ira Mooney 1935- WhoAmA 93
Taylor, Iris WhoBlA 94
Taylor, Irving 1912- WhoFI 94, WhoScEn 94, WhoWest 94
Taylor, Ivor Ralph 1927- Who 94
Taylor, J(ames) Herbert 1916- IntWW 93
Taylor, J. Paul WhoAmP 93, WhoHisp 94
Taylor, J.R. 1950- WhoMW 93
Taylor, J. Thomas, III 1947- WhoWest 94
Taylor, Jack WhoHol 92
Taylor, Jack d1932 WhoHol 92
Taylor, Jack 1935- WhoAmP 93
Taylor, Jack Alvin, Jr. 1949- WhoBlA 94
Taylor, Jack J. WhoAmP 93
Taylor, Jackie 1935- WhoAmP 93
Taylor, Jackie Lynn WhoHol 92
Taylor, James DrAPF 93
Taylor, James 1902- IntWW 93, Who 94

Taylor, James 1922- *WhoBlA 94*
Taylor, James 1948- *WhoHol 92*
Taylor, James, Jr. 1942- *WhoAm 94*
Taylor, James A. 1949- *WhoAmL 94*
Taylor, James Barton 1938- *WhoFI 94, WhoWest 94*
Taylor, James Bennett 1943- *WhoFI 94*
Taylor, James Boyd 1919- *WhoFI 94*
Taylor, James C. 1930- *WhoBlA 94*
Taylor, James Coleridge 1922- *WhoBlA 94*
Taylor, James David 1947- *WhoAm 94*
Taylor, James E. *WhoAmL 94, WhoFI 94*
Taylor, James Elton 1947- *WhoBlA 94*
Taylor, James F., Jr. 1944- *WhoFI 94*
Taylor, James Francis 1951- *WhoFI 94*
Taylor, James Gavin 1932- *WhoWest 94*
Taylor, James Harry, II 1951- *WhoMW 93*
Taylor, James Herbert 1916- *WhoAm 94, WhoScEn 94*
Taylor, James Howard 1947- *WhoAm 94*
Taylor, James Hutchings 1930- *WhoAm 94, WhoScEn 94*
Taylor, James Idol 1939- *WhoFI 94*
Taylor, James Joseph 1929- *WhoAmL 94*
Taylor, James Kenneth 1929- *WhoScEn 94*
Taylor, James L. *WhoIns 94*
Taylor, James Marion, II 1926- *WhoFI 94*
Taylor, James Marshall 1929- *WhoFI 94*
Taylor, James Sturdevant 1895- *WhAm 10*
Taylor, James Vernon 1948- *WhoAm 94*
Taylor, James Walter 1933- *WhoAm 94, WhoFI 94, WhoWest 94*
Taylor, Jane 1783-1824 *BlmGEL, BlmGWL*
Taylor, Jane Lundeen 1935- *WhoMW 93*
Taylor, Janelle (Diane Williams) 1944- *ConAu 43NR, WrDr 94*
Taylor, Janelle Diane Williams 1944- *WhoAm 94*
Taylor, Janet R. 1941- *WhoAmA 93*
Taylor, Janice A. 1954- *WhoBlA 94*
Taylor, Jasper G., III 1951- *WhoAmL 94*
Taylor, Jayne 1948- *WrDr 94*
Taylor, Jean (Elizabeth) 1916- *Who 94*
Taylor, Jeannine *WhoHol 92*
Taylor, Jeff *WhoMW 93*
Taylor, Jeffery Charles 1957- *WhoBlA 94*
Taylor, Jennifer (Evelyn) 1935- *WrDr 94*
Taylor, Jeremy 1613-1667 *BlmGEL*
Taylor, Jeremy John Fox 1952- *WhoFI 94*
Taylor, Jerome 1940- *WhoBlA 94*
Taylor, Jerry Duncan 1938- *WhoAm 94*
Taylor, Jesse Elliott, Jr. *WhoBlA 94*
Taylor, Jessie *Who 94*
Taylor, (Margaret) Jessie 1924- *Who 94*
Taylor, Jim *ProFbHF [port]*
Taylor, Jimmie Wilkes 1934- *WhoAm 94*
Taylor, Joan 1925- *WhoHol 92*
Taylor, Job, III 1942- *WhoAm 94, WhoAmL 94*
Taylor, Jocelyn Mary 1931- *WhoAm 94, WhoMW 93*
Taylor, Joe Clinton 1942- *WhoAm 94, WhoAmL 94*
Taylor, Joe T., III 1943- *WhoAmL 94*
Taylor, Joel Sanford 1942- *WhoAm 94, WhoAmL 94*
Taylor, John c. 1580-1653 *BlmGEL*
Taylor, John 1955- *WhoAmP 93*
Taylor, John (Gerald) 1931- *WrDr 94*
Taylor, John (Laverack) 1937- *WrDr 94*
Taylor, John (of Caroline) 1753-1824 *WhAmRev*
Taylor, John (Williams) 1897-1983 *WhoAmA 93N*
Taylor, John Alfred *DrAPF 93*
Taylor, John Ansel 1942- *WhoMW 93*
Taylor, John Barrington d1993 *Who 94N*
Taylor, John Bernard *Who 94*
Taylor, John Bernard 1929- *IntWW 93*
Taylor, John Bryan 1928- *IntWW 93, Who 94*
Taylor, John C. 1925- *WhoAmP 93*
Taylor, John C. E. 1902-1985 *WhoAmA 93N*
Taylor, John Charles 1931- *Who 94*
Taylor, John Chestnut, III 1928- *WhoAm 94*
Taylor, John Clayton 1930- *IntWW 93, Who 94*
Taylor, John D. *Who 94*
Taylor, John David 1937- *Who 94*
Taylor, John Felton, II 1925- *WhoWest 94*
Taylor, John Frank, II 1939- *WhoAmL 94*
Taylor, John Frederick 1944- *WhoWest 94*
Taylor, John Gerald 1931- *Who 94*
Taylor, John H. *Who 94*
Taylor, John Jackson Jay 1931- *WhoAm 94*
Taylor, John Joseph 1922- *WhoAm 94, WhoScEn 94*
Taylor, John L. *WhoAm 94*
Taylor, John L. 1947- *WhoBlA 94*
Taylor, John Lang 1924- *Who 94*
Taylor, John Lloyd 1935- *WhoAmA 93N*
Taylor, John Lockhart 1927- *WhoAm 94, WhoWest 94*
Taylor, John Mark 1941- *Who 94*
Taylor, John Mitchell *Who 94*
Taylor, John O'Mara 1953- *WhoWest 94*
Taylor, John R. 1946- *WhoAmP 93*
Taylor, John Read, Jr. 1943- *WhoFI 94*
Taylor, John Richard 1952- *WhoMW 93*
Taylor, John Robert 1951- *WrDr 94*
Taylor, John Russell 1935- *IntMPA 94, IntWW 93, Who 94, WrDr 94*
Taylor, John-Stephen Adolfino 1954- *WhoMW 93*
Taylor, John Vernon 1914- *Who 94, WrDr 94*
Taylor, John Wilkinson 1906- *WhoAm 94*
Taylor, John William Ransom 1922- *Who 94, WrDr 94*
Taylor, Jolynn 1948- *WhoWest 94*
Taylor, Jon Guerry 1939- *WhoScEn 94*
Taylor, Jonathan Francis 1935- *Who 94, WhoAm 94*
Taylor, Joseph B. 1927- *WhoAmP 93*
Taylor, Joseph Christopher 1959- *WhoScEn 94*
Taylor, Joseph Hooton, Jr. 1941- *WhoAm 94, WhoScEn 94*
Taylor, Joseph Richard 1907- *WhoAmA 93*
Taylor, Joseph T. 1913- *WhoBlA 94*
Taylor, Josephine d1964 *WhoHol 92*
Taylor, Josh *WhoHol 92*
Taylor, Joshua Charles 1917-1981 *WhoAmA 93N*
Taylor, Joyce *WhoHol 92*
Taylor, Judith Ann 1944- *WhoWest 94*
Taylor, Judy 1932- *Who 94*
Taylor, Julia d1976 *WhoHol 92*
Taylor, Julia W. *WhoAm 94, WhoFI 94*
Taylor, Julia W. 1936- *WhoBlA 94*
Taylor, Julian Howard 1943- *WhoFI 94*
Taylor, Julius H. 1914- *WhoBlA 94*
Taylor, June Laffoon 1921- *WhoAmP 93*
Taylor, Keith *EncSF 93, WhoHol 92*
Taylor, Keith Breden 1924- *Who 94, WhoAm 94*
Taylor, Keith Henry 1938- *Who 94*
Taylor, Ken 1922- *IntWW 93*
Taylor, Kenard Lyle, Jr. 1943- *WhoMW 93*
Taylor, Kendall Frances *WhoAmA 93*
Taylor, Kendrick Jay 1914- *WhoWest 94*
Taylor, Kenneth 1921- *Who 94*
Taylor, Kenneth Douglas 1942- *WhoFI 94, WhoScEn 94*
Taylor, Kenneth Doyle 1949- *WhoBlA 94*
Taylor, Kenneth Grant 1936- *WhoAm 94*
Taylor, Kenneth John 1929- *Who 94*
Taylor, Kenneth John W. 1939- *WhoAm 94*
Taylor, Kenneth MacDonald 1947- *Who 94*
Taylor, Kenneth Matthew *WhoBlA 94*
Taylor, Kenneth Nathaniel 1917- *WhoAm 94*
Taylor, Kenneth William 1953- *WhoFI 94*
Taylor, Kent *DrAPF 93*
Taylor, Kent d1987 *WhoHol 92*
Taylor, Kent Douglas 1952- *WhoScEn 94*
Taylor, Kim *Who 94*
Taylor, Kimberly Hayes 1962- *WhoBlA 94*
Taylor, Kimberly Kaye 1960- *WhoMW 93*
Taylor, Kit *WhoHol 92*
Taylor, Koko *WhoMW 93*
Taylor, Koko 1935- *ConMus 10 [port]*
Taylor, Kristin Clark 1959- *WhoAm 94*
Taylor, La Jean 1944- *WhoAmP 93*
Taylor, Lance, Sr. d1984 *WhoHol 92*
Taylor, Lance Jerome 1940- *IntWW 93, WhoAm 94*
Taylor, Larry *WhoHol 92*
Taylor, Larry Arthur 1951- *WhoWest 94*
Taylor, Laura Marie *WhoScEn 94*
Taylor, Lauren-Marie *WhoHol 92*
Taylor, Laurette d1946 *WhoHol 92*
Taylor, Laurie *DrAPF 93, Who 94*
Taylor, Lawrence 1959- *WhoAm 94*
Taylor, Lawrence Julius 1959- *WhoBlA 94*
Taylor, Lawrence Palmer 1940- *WhoAm 94*
Taylor, Lawrence Stanton 1959- *WhoScEn 94*
Taylor, Lee Roger, Jr. 1944- *WhoWest 94*
Taylor, Leigh Herbert 1941- *WhoAm 94*
Taylor, Leland Alan 1945- *WhoScEn 94*
Taylor, Leland Harris, Jr. 1958- *WhoScEn 94*
Taylor, Len Clive 1922- *Who 94*
Taylor, Leon Eric Manners 1917- *Who 94*
Taylor, Leonard Stuart 1928- *WhoAm 94*
Taylor, Leonard Wayne 1946- *WhoBlA 94*
Taylor, Lesli Ann 1953- *WhoScEn 94*
Taylor, Leslie George 1922- *WhoWest 94*
Taylor, Lester D. 1938- *WrDr 94*
Taylor, Lester Dean 1938- *WhoFI 94*
Taylor, Levola *WhoAmP 93*
Taylor, Lili 1967- *IntMPA 94, WhoHol 92*
Taylor, Linda Rathbun 1946- *WhoFI 94*
Taylor, Linda Suzanna, Sister 1947- *WhoBlA 94*
Taylor, Lindajean Thorton 1942- *WhoWest 94*
Taylor, Lindsay David, Jr. 1945- *WhoAm 94*
Taylor, Lisa 1933-1991 *WhAm 10, WhoAmA 93N*
Taylor, Liz McNeill 1931- *WrDr 94*
Taylor, Liza Pennywitt 1955- *ConAu 140*
Taylor, Louis Henry 1944- *WhoWest 94*
Taylor, Luther L., Jr. 1949- *WhoAmP 93*
Taylor, Lyle Dewey 1934- *WhoAm 94*
Taylor, Lyle H. 1936- *WhoScEn 94*
Taylor, Lynn Jennings 1953- *WhoAmL 94*
Taylor, Malcolm *Who 94*
Taylor, Malcolm 1960- *WhoBlA 94*
Taylor, Marcella B. *DrAPF 93*
Taylor, Marcella Bernadette 1933- *WhoMW 93*
Taylor, Marcia *WhoHol 92*
Taylor, Maretta M. 1935- *WhoAmP 93*
Taylor, Margaret 1917- *WhoBlA 94*
Taylor, Margaret Condon *DrAPF 93*
Taylor, Margaret Wischmeyer 1920- *WhoMW 93*
Taylor, Marian Alecia 1961- *WhoMW 93*
Taylor, Marie de Porres 1947- *WhoBlA 94*
Taylor, Marilyn *DrAPF 93*
Taylor, Marion Sayle d1942 *WhoHol 92*
Taylor, Mark 1927- *WhoAm 94*
Taylor, Mark Alan 1955- *WhoMW 93*
Taylor, Mark Christopher 1958- *Who 94*
Taylor, Mark Douglas 1951- *WhoAm 94*
Taylor, Mark Edward 1953- *WhoAmP 93*
Taylor, Mark Fletcher 1957- *WhoAmP 93*
Taylor, Mark Jesse 1957- *WhoScEn 94*
Taylor, Mark L. *WhoHol 92*
Taylor, Marshall W. 1878-1932 *AfrAmAl 6*
Taylor, Martha 1941- *WhoBlA 94*
Taylor, Martin Gibbeson 1935- *Who 94*
Taylor, Mary Cazort *WhoAmA 93*
Taylor, Mary Elizabeth 1933- *WhoFI 94, WhoWest 94*
Taylor, Mary Kay 1954- *WhoMW 93*
Taylor, Matthew Owen John 1963- *Who 94*
Taylor, Maureen Denise 1948- *WhoMW 93*
Taylor, Maurice *Who 94*
Taylor, Maurice Clifton 1950- *WhoBlA 94*
Taylor, Maxwell D. 1901-1987 *HisDcKW*
Taylor, Meldrick *WhoAm 94*
Taylor, Mertz Anderson, Jr. 1927- *WhoAmP 93*
Taylor, Mervyn 1931- *IntWW 93*
Taylor, Meshach *IntMPA 94, WhoAm 94, WhoBlA 94*
Taylor, Meshach 1947- *WhoHol 92*
Taylor, Michael 1958- *WhoBlA 94*
Taylor, Michael (Estes) 1944- *WhoAmA 93*
Taylor, Michael Alan 1940- *WhoAm 94*
Taylor, Michael Byron d1987 *WhoHol 92*
Taylor, Michael Earl 1952- *WhoAmP 93*
Taylor, Michael Hugh 1936- *IntWW 93, Who 94*
Taylor, Michael J(oseph) 1924- *WrDr 94*
Taylor, Michael James 1941- *WhoWest 94*
Taylor, Michael Leslie 1954- *WhoAmL 94*
Taylor, Michael Loeb 1947- *WhoBlA 94*
Taylor, Michele F. 1946- *WhoAmA 93*
Taylor, Michelle M. 1945- *WhoFI 94*
Taylor, Mike Allen 1949- *WhoScEn 94*
Taylor, Mildred D. 1943- *BlkWr 2, TwCYAW, WhoBlA 94, WrDr 94*
Taylor, Mildred E. Crosby 1919- *WhoBlA 94*
Taylor, Mildred Juanita 1947- *WhoFI 94*
Taylor, Miles Edward 1964- *WhoBlA 94*
Taylor, Millard Benjamin 1913- *WhoAm 94*
Taylor, Milton William 1931- *WhoMW 93*
Taylor, Minna 1947- *WhoWest 94*
Taylor, Morris Anthony 1922- *WhoMW 93, WhoScEn 94*
Taylor, Myron C. 1874-1958 *EncABHB 9 [port]*
Taylor, Nathalee Britton 1941- *WhoFI 94*
Taylor, Nathaniel William 1786-1858 *DcAmReB 2*
Taylor, Neville 1930- *Who 94*
Taylor, Nevin J. 1966- *WhoWest 94*
Taylor, Nicholas George Frederick 1917- *Who 94*
Taylor, Nicholas Richard S. *Who 94*
Taylor, Noah *WhoHol 92*
Taylor, Noel C. 1924- *WhoAmP 93, WhoBlA 94*
Taylor, Norman Eugene 1948- *WhoBlA 94*
Taylor, Norman Floyd 1932- *WhoAm 94*
Taylor, Norman William 1923- *WhoAm 94*
Taylor, Octavia G. 1925- *WhoBlA 94*
Taylor, Orlando L. 1936- *WhoBlA 94*
Taylor, Overton Hume 1897- *WhAm 10*
Taylor, P(hilip) A. M. 1920- *WrDr 94*
Taylor, Patricia E. 1942- *WhoBlA 94*
Taylor, Patricia Elsie 1929- *WhoScEn 94*
Taylor, Patricia Tate 1954- *WhoBlA 94*
Taylor, Paul *NewYTBS 93 [port]*
Taylor, Paul 1930- *IntDcB [port], WhoAm 94*
Taylor, Paul 1958-1992 *WhoAmA 93N*
Taylor, Paul Albert 1943- *WhoAm 94*
Taylor, Paul Allen 1952- *WhoScEn 94*
Taylor, Paul B. 1930- *IntWW 93*
Taylor, Paul Belville, Jr. 1930- *AmCulL*
Taylor, Paul Bradford 1955- *WhoAm 94*
Taylor, Paul D. 1939- *WhoAmP 93*
Taylor, Paul David 1937- *WhoBlA 94*
Taylor, Paul Duane, Jr. 1969- *WhoScEn 94*
Taylor, Pauline J. 1911- *WhoBlA 94*
Taylor, Perry Lee, Jr. 1948- *WhoAmL 94*
Taylor, Peter *DrAPF 93*
Taylor, Peter 1924- *Who 94*
Taylor, Peter (Hillsman) 1917- *RfGShF*
Taylor, Peter (Hillsman) 1919- *WrDr 94*
Taylor, Peter John Whittaker 1939- *Who 94*
Taylor, Peter Matthew Hillsman 1917- *WhoAm 94*
Taylor, Peter van Voorhees 1934- *WhoWest 94*
Taylor, Peter William Edward 1917- *Who 94*
Taylor, Peyton Troy, Jr. 1941- *WhoAm 94*
Taylor, Philip 1954- *See* Motorhead *ConMus 10*
Taylor, Philip Harley, Jr. 1959- *WhoWest 94*
Taylor, Philip Liddon 1937- *WhoAm 94*
Taylor, Philippe Arthur 1937- *Who 94*
Taylor, Phyllis Mary Constance 1926- *Who 94*
Taylor, Prentiss (Hottel) 1907-1991 *WhoAmA 93N*
Taylor, Prentiss Hottel 1907-1991 *WhAm 10*
Taylor, Preston M., Jr. 1933- *AfrAmG [port]*
Taylor, Prince Albert, Jr. 1907- *WhoBlA 94*
Taylor, Priscilla G. 1931- *WhoAmP 93*
Taylor, Quintard, Jr. 1948- *WhoAm 94, WhoBlA 94*
Taylor, Ralph d1993 *NewYTBS 93*
Taylor, Ralph Arthur, Jr. 1948- *WhoAm 94, WhoAmL 94*
Taylor, Ralph Orien, Jr. 1919- *WhoMW 93*
Taylor, Ramona Garrett 1930- *WhoAm 94*
Taylor, Randall William 1948- *WhoMW 93*
Taylor, Randy Steven 1951- *WhoScEn 94*
Taylor, Ray 1923- *WhoMW 93*
Taylor, Ray Allen 1923- *WhoAmP 93*
Taylor, Ray Counsel 1926- *WhoAmP 93*
Taylor, Rayner 1747-1825 *NewGrDO*
Taylor, Reese Hale, Jr. 1928- *WhoAm 94, WhoAmP 93*
Taylor, Regina *WhoAm 94*
Taylor, Reginald Redall, Jr. 1939- *WhoBlA 94*
Taylor, Ren *WhoAmP 93*
Taylor, Rene Claude 1916- *WhoAmA 93*
Taylor, Renee 1933- *WhoHol 92*
Taylor, Renee 1935- *IntMPA 94*
Taylor, Richard *DrAPF 93, WhoHol 92*
Taylor, Richard 1919- *WhoAm 94*
Taylor, Richard Charles 1942- *WhoAmL 94*
Taylor, Richard E. 1929- *NobelP 91 [port]*
Taylor, Richard Edward 1929- *IntWW 93, Who 94, WhoAm 94, WhoScEn 94, WhoWest 94*
Taylor, Richard Fred, Jr. 1933- *WhoAm 94, WhoAmL 94*
Taylor, Richard Keith 1949- *WhoWest 94*
Taylor, Richard L. 1944- *WhoBlA 94*
Taylor, Richard Lee 1954- *WhoAmL 94*
Taylor, Richard Powell 1928- *WhoAm 94, WhoAmL 94*
Taylor, Richard Smith 1941- *WhoAmL 94*
Taylor, Richard Stuart 1942- *WhoMW 93*
Taylor, Richard Trelore 1917- *WhoAm 94*
Taylor, Richard William 1926- *WhoAm 94*
Taylor, Richard William 1945- *WhoAmL 94*
Taylor, Richard Wirth 1923- *WhoAm 94*
Taylor, Rip 1930- *WhoHol 92*
Taylor, Rip 1934- *WhoCom*
Taylor, Robert d1969 *WhoHol 92*
Taylor, Robert 1925- *WhoAmA 93*
Taylor, Robert, III 1946- *WhoBlA 94*
Taylor, Robert Bonds 1939- *WhoScEn 94*
Taylor, Robert Brown 1936- *WhoAm 94, WhoWest 94*
Taylor, Robert Carruthers 1939- *Who 94*
Taylor, Robert Charles 1963- *WhoFI 94*
Taylor, Robert Cooper 1917- *WhoMW 93*

Taylor, Robert Derek 1961- WhoBlA 94
Taylor, Robert Earlington, Jr. 1937- WhoBlA 94
Taylor, Robert Homer 1922- WhoMW 93
Taylor, Robert James 1943- WhoFI 94, WhoMW 93
Taylor, Robert Lee 1943- WhoMW 93
Taylor, Robert Lee 1944- WhoAm 94
Taylor, Robert Lee 1947- WhoAmL 94
Taylor, Robert Lewis 1912- EncSF 93, WrDr 94
Taylor, Robert Lewis 1939- WhoAm 94
Taylor, Robert Love 1914- WhoAmL 94
Taylor, Robert Love, Jr. DrAPF 93
Taylor, Robert Martin, Jr. 1941- WhoMW 93
Taylor, Robert Morgan 1941- WhoAm 94
Taylor, Robert P. 1939- WhoAm 94, WhoAmL 94
Taylor, Robert Richardson d1993 Who 94N
Taylor, Robert Selby 1909- IntWW 93, Who 94
Taylor, Robert Sundling 1925- WhoAm 94
Taylor, Robert Thomas 1933- Who 94
Taylor, Robert William 1929- WhoAm 94
Taylor, Robert William 1932- WhoAm 94
Taylor, Robin L. 1943- WhoAmP 93
Taylor, Rockie 1945- WhoBlA 94
Taylor, Rod 1929- WhoHol 92
Taylor, Rod 1930- IntMPA 94
Taylor, Roger Conant 1931- WhoAm 94
Taylor, Roger Lee 1941- WhoAm 94, WhoAmL 94
Taylor, Roger Miles Whitworth 1944- Who 94
Taylor, Ronald Who 94
Taylor, (Robert) Ronald 1916- Who 94
Taylor, Ronald A. 1948- WhoBlA 94
Taylor, Ronald B. 1930- ConAu 142
Taylor, Ronald E. 1962- WhoWest 94
Taylor, Ronald George 1935- Who 94
Taylor, Ronald Lee 1943- WhoFI 94, WhoMW 93
Taylor, Ronald Lewis 1938- WhoFI 94
Taylor, Ronald Lewis 1942- WhoBlA 94
Taylor, Ronald Oliver 1931- Who 94
Taylor, Ronald Russell 1945- WhoScEn 94
Taylor, Ronald Wentworth 1932- Who 94
Taylor, Ronnie 1924- IntMPA 94
Taylor, Rose Perrin 1916- WhoWest 94
Taylor, Rosemary WhoAmA 93
Taylor, Roslyn Donny 1941- WhoWest 94
Taylor, Roy Lewis 1932- WhoAm 94, WhoMW 93, WhoScEn 94
Taylor, Roy Marcellus 1925- WhoBlA 94
Taylor, Rush W., Jr. 1934- WhoAmP 93
Taylor, Russell Benton 1925- WhoMW 93
Taylor, Ruth d1984 WhoHol 92
Taylor, Ruth Anne 1961- WhoWest 94
Taylor, Ruth Sloan 1918- WhoBlA 94
Taylor, S. Martin WhoBlA 94
Taylor, Samuel 1912- WrDr 94
Taylor, Samuel Albert 1912- WhoAm 94
Taylor, Samuel Coleridge NewGrDO
Taylor, Samuel James 1929- WhoAm 94, WhoScEn 94
Taylor, Samuel S. WhoAmP 93
Taylor, Samuel Wayne 1935- WhoAmL 94
Taylor, Sandra Elaine 1946- WhoBlA 94
Taylor, Sandra Ortiz 1936- WhoAmA 93
Taylor, Scott Douglas 1954- WhoWest 94
Taylor, Scott Maxfield 1953- WhoFI 94
Taylor, Scott Morris 1957- WhoBlA 94
Taylor, Scott Thomas 1950- WhoScEn 94
Taylor, Seldon Duane 1915- WhoAmP 93
Taylor, Selina WhoWomW 91
Taylor, Selwyn Francis 1913- Who 94
Taylor, Sharen Rae McCall 1946- WhoMW 93
Taylor, Sherrill Wightman 1924- WhoAm 94
Taylor, Sinthy E. 1947- WhoBlA 94
Taylor, Slats d1978 WhoHol 92
Taylor, Stephen 1948- WrDr 94
Taylor, Stephen Dewitt 1945- WhoAm 94, WhoFI 94
Taylor, Stephen K. 1946- WhoAmL 94
Taylor, Stephen Lee 1947- WhoAmL 94, WhoAmP 93
Taylor, Stephen P. d1993 NewYTBS 93
Taylor, Sterling R. 1942- WhoBlA 94
Taylor, Steve Henry 1947- WhoAm 94
Taylor, Steve Lloyd 1946- WhoScEn 94
Taylor, Steven Bruce 1954- WhoWest 94
Taylor, Steven C. 1956- WhoAmP 93
Taylor, Steven Lloyd 1948- WhoBlA 94
Taylor, Stratton 1956- WhoAmP 93
Taylor, Stuart A. 1936- WhoBlA 94
Taylor, Stuart Ross 1925- IntWW 93
Taylor, Stuart Symington 1913- WhoAm 94
Taylor, Sue Ann Perkins 1935- WhoMW 93
Taylor, Susan 1946- AfrAmAl 6 [port]
Taylor, Susan L. 1946- WhoBlA 94
Taylor, T(homas) F(ish), Rev 1913- WrDr 94
Taylor, T. Raber 1910- WhoAmL 94, WhoWest 94
Taylor, Teddy Who 94
Taylor, Telford 1908- WhoAm 94, WrDr 94
Taylor, Teresa Marie 1949- WhoFI 94
Taylor, Thad, Jr. 1937- WhoBlA 94
Taylor, Theodore DrAPF 93
Taylor, Theodore 1921- ChlLR 30 [port], TwCYAW, WrDr 94
Taylor, Theodore Brewster 1925- WhoAm 94
Taylor, Theodore D. 1930- WhoBlA 94
Taylor, Theodore Langhans 1921- WhoAm 94
Taylor, Theodore Roosevelt WhoBlA 94
Taylor, Theophilus Mills 1909-1989 WhAm 10
Taylor, Thomas Alexander, III 1930- WhoAm 94
Taylor, Thomas Alfred 1942- WhoIns 94
Taylor, Thomas Daniel 1957- WhoWest 94
Taylor, Thomas Hewitt, Jr. 1935- WhoAm 94
Taylor, Thomas Hudson, Jr. 1920- WhoFI 94
Taylor, Thomas Roger 1945- WhoMW 93
Taylor, Thomas William 1943- WhoAm 94, WhoAmL 94
Taylor, Thomas William 1951- WhoMW 93
Taylor, Timothy Alan 1958- WhoMW 93
Taylor, Timothy Davies 1945- WhoWest 94
Taylor, Timothy Henry 1918- WhoAmP 93
Taylor, Timothy Kiven 1944- WhoWest 94
Taylor, Timothy Merritt 1931- WhoBlA 94
Taylor, Tom 1817-1880 IntDcT 2
Taylor, Tommie W. 1929- WhoBlA 94
Taylor, Tommy W. 1944- WhoAmL 94
Taylor, Tony 1935- WhoHisp 94
Taylor, Trotti Truman WhoHol 92
Taylor, Valerie d1988 WhoHol 92
Taylor, Valerie Charmayne 1962- WhoBlA 94
Taylor, Vaughan Edward 1947- WhoAmL 94
Taylor, Vaughn d1983 WhoHol 92
Taylor, Vernon Anthony 1946- WhoBlA 94
Taylor, Veronica C. 1941- WhoBlA 94
Taylor, Victoria Currie 1949- WhoFI 94
Taylor, Victoria Ferrara 1960- WhoMW 93
Taylor, Virginia S. WhoAm 94, WhoAmL 94
Taylor, Vivian A. 1924- WhoBlA 94
Taylor, Vivian Lorraine 1948- WhoBlA 94
Taylor, Volney 1939- WhoFI 94
Taylor, W. O. 1932- WhoAmP 93
Taylor, Wadsworth d1981 WhoHol 92
Taylor, Wally WhoHol 92
Taylor, Walter Harold 1905- WrDr 94
Taylor, Walter L. d1971 WhoHol 92
Taylor, Walter Lewis 1964- WhoAmL 94
Taylor, Walter Reynell 1928- Who 94
Taylor, Walter Scott 1916- WhoBlA 94
Taylor, Walter Wallace 1925- WhoAmL 94, WhoWest 94
Taylor, Walton Perry, III 1936- WhoAmP 93
Taylor, Washington Theophilus 1931- WhoScEn 94
Taylor, Watson Robbins, Jr. 1956- WhoFI 94
Taylor, Wayne WhoHol 92
Taylor, Wayne Fletcher 1943- WhoAm 94, WhoAmL 94
Taylor, Wayne Michael 1945- WhoWest 94
Taylor, Welford Dunaway 1938- WrDr 94
Taylor, Welton Ivan 1919- WhoBlA 94
Taylor, Wendy Ann 1945- IntWW 93, Who 94
Taylor, Wesley Alan 1958- WhoFI 94
Taylor, Wilda WhoHol 92
Taylor, Wilford, Jr. 1950- WhoBlA 94
Taylor, William d1992 WhAm 10
Taylor, William c. 1753-1825 NewGrDO
Taylor, William 1930- IntWW 93, Who 94
Taylor, William 1938- WrDr 94
Taylor, William 1947- Who 94
Taylor, William Al 1928- WhoAmL 94, WhoWest 94
Taylor, William Bernard 1930- Who 94
Taylor, William Brockenbrough 1925- WhoScEn 94
Taylor, William Brooks, II 1910- WhoAm 94
Taylor, William C. 1959- ConAu 142
Taylor, William D. 1946- WhoAmL 94
Taylor, William Desmond d1922 WhoHol 92
Taylor, William E. DrAPF 93
Taylor, William Edward 1921- WhoBlA 94
Taylor, William Edward 1949- WhoAmL 94
Taylor, William Edward Michael 1944- Who 94
Taylor, William Ernest 1856-1927 DcNaB MP
Taylor, William Glenn 1942- WhoBlA 94
Taylor, William Henry, Sr. 1931- WhoBlA 94
Taylor, William Horace 1908- Who 94
Taylor, William James 1944- Who 94
Taylor, William James 1948- WhoAm 94, WhoAmL 94
Taylor, William Jape 1924- WhoAm 94
Taylor, William Jesse, Jr. 1933- WhoAm 94
Taylor, William L. 1931- WhoBlA 94
Taylor, William Leroy 1931- WhoMW 93
Taylor, William Logan 1947- WhoScEn 94
Taylor, William M. 1923- WhoAmP 93
Taylor, William M., Jr. WhoAm 94
Taylor, William Malcolm 1933- WhoWest 94
Taylor, William McCaughey 1926- Who 94
Taylor, William Osgood 1932- WhoAm 94, WhoFI 94
Taylor, William Randolph 1895-1990 WhAm 10
Taylor, William Robert 1950- WhoMW 93
Taylor, William Robert 1954- WhoFI 94
Taylor, William Rodney E. Who 94
Taylor, William Romayne 1926- WhoAmP 93
Taylor, William Woodruff, III 1944- WhoAmL 94
Taylor, Willie Marvin 1955- WhoBlA 94
Taylor, Willis H(orr), Jr. 1894- WhAm 10
Taylor, Wilson H. WhoAm 94, WhoFI 94
Taylor, Wilton d1925 WhoHol 92
Taylor, Zachary 1784-1850 HisWorL [port]
Taylor, Zack WhoHol 92
Taylor, Zack 1964- WhoWest 94
Taylor-Archer, Mordean 1947- WhoBlA 94
Taylor-Gooby, Peter 1947- ConAu 41NR
Taylor-Grigsby, Queenie Delores 1948- WhoWest 94
Taylor-Hunt, Mary Bernis Buchanan 1904- WhoWest 94
Taylor-Little, Carol 1941- WhoAmP 93
Taylor Of Blackburn, Baron 1929- Who 94
Taylor of Gosforth, Baron 1930- IntWW 93, Who 94
Taylor Of Gryfe, Baron 1912- Who 94
Taylor Of Hadfield, Baron 1905- Who 94
Taylor-Smith, Jean WhoHol 92
Taylorson, John Brown 1931- Who 94
Taylor Thompson, John Derek 1927- Who 94
Taylor-Young, Leigh 1944- WhoHol 92
Taylor-Young, Leigh 1945- IntMPA 94
Taylour Who 94
Taymor, Betty 1921- WhoAmP 93
Tayon, Jeffrey Earl 1963- WhoMW 93
Tayoun, James J. 1930 WhoAmP 93
Taysom, Wayne Pendelton 1925- WhoAmA 93
Tazabekov, Marat Kasymbekovich 1958- LngBDD
Tazawa, Kichiro 1918- IntWW 93
Tazdait, Djida 1957- WhoWomW 91
Tazewell, Charles 1900-1972 SmATA 74
Tazewell, Henry 1753-1799 WhAmRev
Tazieff, Haroun 1914- IntWW 93
Tazoi, Norma WhoAsA 94
Tazzioli-David, Denise 1952- WhoMW 93
Tchaikovsky, Alexander Vladimirovich NewGrDO
Tchaikovsky, Modest Il'yich 1850-1916 NewGrDO
Tchaikovsky, Petr 1840-1893 IntDcB
Tchaikovsky, Pyotr Il'yich 1840-1893 NewGrDO
Tchakalian, Sam 1929- WhoAmA 93
Tchekhov, Anton IntDcT 2
Tchekova, Olga WhoHol 92
Tchelitchev, Pavel 1898-1957 IntDcB
Tchelitchew, Pavel 1898-1957 IntDcB
Tchen, John Kuo Wei 1951- WhoAsA 94
Tcherepnin, Alexander (Nikolayevich) 1899-1977 NewGrDO
Tcherepnin, Nikolay (Nikolayevich) 1873-1945 NewGrDO
Tcherina, Ludmila 1924- IntDcB [port], IntWW 93
Tcherina, Ludmilla 1925- WhoHol 92
Tcherkassky, Alexis d1980 WhoHol 92
Tcherkassky, Marianna 1952- IntDcB [port]
Tcherkassky, Marianna Alexsavena 1952- WhoAm 94
Tchernicheva, Lubov 1890-1976 IntDcB [port]
Tchetchet, Tatiana WhoAmA 93
Tchobanoglous, George 1935- WhoAm 94
Tchoryk, Robert Charles 1956- WhoFI 94
Tchudi, Stephen N. 1942- TwCYAW
Tchukhatjian, Tigran 1837-1898 NewGrDO
Teachout, Noreen Ruth 1939- WhoMW 93
Teachout, Steven Douglas 1939- WhoMW 93
Teachout, Terry 1956- WrDr 94
Teachout, Walter Floyd 1957- WhoWest 94
Tead, Phil d1974 WhoHol 92
Teaford, Jane 1935- WhoAmP 93
Teaford, Norman Baker 1944- WhoScEn 94
Teaford, Stephen D. 1945- WhoAmL 94
Teagan, John Gerard 1947- WhoAm 94
Teagarden, George 1943- WhoAmP 93
Teagarden, Jack d1964 WhoHol 92
Teagarden, Jack 1905-1964 ConMus 10 [port]
Teagle, Terry Michael 1960- WhoBlA 94
Teague, Anthony 1940- WhoHol 92
Teague, Barry Elvin 1944- WhoAm 94
Teague, Bernice Rita 1957- WhoFI 94
Teague, Bert F. 1917- WhoAmP 93
Teague, Bob BlkWr 2
Teague, Bob 1946- WhoAmP 93
Teague, Donald 1897-1991 WhAm 10, WhoAmA 93N
Teague, Edgar Clayton 1941- WhoScEn 94
Teague, Edward, III WhoAmP 93
Teague, Edward H. WhoAmA 93
Teague, George M. 1945- WhoAmL 94
Teague, Gladys Peters 1921- WhoBlA 94
Teague, Guy d1970 WhoHol 92
Teague, Hyman Faris 1916- WhoAm 94
Teague, Larry Gene 1954- WhoAm 94
Teague, Lavette Cox, Jr. 1934- WhoWest 94
Teague, Lewis 1941- HorFD, IntMPA 94
Teague, Marjorie 1935- WhoWomW 91
Teague, Mark (Christopher) 1963- WrDr 94
Teague, Marshall WhoHol 92
Teague, Patrick Leigh 1951- WhoAmL 94
Teague, Peyton Clark 1915- WhoAm 94
Teague, Randal Cornell, Sr. 1944- WhoAm 94, WhoAmL 94, WhoAmP 93
Teague, Robert 1929- BlkWr 2, WhoBlA 94
Teague, Sam Fuller 1918- WhoAm 94
Teague, Sharon B. 1952- WhoAmP 93
Teague, Thomas Morse 1924- WhoAmP 93
Teague, Walter Dorwin 1884-1960 WhoAmA 93N
Teague, Wayne 1927- WhoAm 94
Teakle, Neil William 1949- WhoScEn 94
Teal, Edwin Earl 1914- WhoScEn 94
Teal, Ella S. 1947- WhoBlA 94
Teal, G. Donn 1932- WrDr 94
Teal, Gilbert Earle 1912- WhoScEn 94
Teal, Gilbert Earle, II 1959- WhoAmL 94
Teal, Gordon Kidd 1907- WhoAm 94
Teal, Ray d1976 WhoHol 92
Tealdi, Giovanna Maria 1942- WhoWomW 91
Teale, Nellie Imogene Donovan d1993 NewYTBS 93
Teale, Owen WhoHol 92
Teaman, Richard Alan 1960- WhoFI 94, WhoWest 94
Teamer, Charles C. 1933- WhoBlA 94
Teaney, Carol Ruth 1950- WhoAmL 94, WhoMW 93
Teannaki, Teatao IntWW 93
Tear, Robert 1939- IntWW 93, NewGrDO, Who 94
Teare, Andrew Hubert 1942- Who 94
Teare, Ethel d1959 WhoHol 92
Teare, Iwan Dale 1931- WhoAm 94
Teare, John James 1924- WhoBlA 94
Teare, John Richard, Jr. 1954- WhoAmL 94, WhoFI 94
Teare, Nigel John Martin 1952- Who 94
Teare, Wallace Gleed 1907- WhAm 10
Tearle, Conway d1938 WhoHol 92
Tearle, Godfrey d1953 WhoHol 92
Tearle, John L. 1917- ConAu 140
Tearney, Michael Gautier 1942- WhoFI 94
Tearney, Russell James 1938- WhoBlA 94
Teasdale, Joseph Patrick 1936- WhoAmP 93
Teasdale, Kenneth Fulbright 1934- WhoAm 94, WhoAmL 94
Teasdale, Sara 1884-1933 BlmGWL, GayLL

Teasdale, Thomas Hennings 1933- *WhoAm 94*
Teasdale, Verree d1987 *WhoHol 92*
Tease, James Edward 1939- *WhoAm 94*
Teasley, Anna Delores 1949- *WhoFI 94*
Teasley, Larkin 1936- *WhoBlA 94, WhoFI 94, WhoIns 94*
Teasley, Marie R. *WhoBlA 94*
Te Atairangikaahu, Arikinui 1931- *Who 94*
Teater, Dorothy Seath 1931- *WhoAmP 93*
Teates, Charles David 1936- *WhoAm 94*
Te Awekotoku, Ngahuia *BlmGWL*
Tebaldi, Renata 1922- *IntWW 93, NewGrDO, Who 94, WhoAm 94, WhoHol 92*
Tebay, James Elwood 1930- *WhoAm 94*
Tebbel, John 1912- *WhoAm 94*
Tebben, Craig Brian 1957- *WhoMW 93*
Tebben, Sharon Lee 1943- *WhoMW 93*
Tebbit, Baron 1931- *Who 94*
Tebbit, Donald (Claude) 1920- *Who 94*
Tebbit, Donald Claude 1920- *IntWW 93*
Tebbit, Norman Beresford 1931- *IntWW 93*
Tebble, Norman 1924- *Who 94*
Tebedo, Maryanne 1936- *WhoAmP 93, WhoWest 94*
Tebelius, Mark Alan 1953- *WhoAmL 94*
Tebo, Julian Drenner 1903-1991 *WhAm 10*
Teboul, Albert 1936- *WhoFI 94*
Tebrinke, Kevin Richard 1958- *WhoScEn 94*
Tecayehuatzin, Victor Saucedo 1937- *WhoHisp 94*
Tecco, Romuald Gilbert Louis Joseph 1941- *WhoAm 94*
Teclaff, Ludwik Andrzej 1918- *WhoAm 94, WhoAmL 94*
Tecson, Joseph A. 1928- *WhoAmP 93*
Tecumseh c. 1768-1813 *HisWorL [port]*
Teczar, Steven W. 1948- *WhoAmA 93*
Tedards, Jack H., Jr. 1945- *WhoAmL 94*
Tedder, Baron 1926- *Who 94*
Tedder, John Michael 1926- *IntWW 93*
Tedder, Joseph G. 1962- *WhoAmP 93*
Tedeschi, Giovanni c. 1715-1787? *NewGrDO*
Tedeschi, Henry 1930- *WhoScEn 94*
Tedeschi, James Theodore, Jr. 1928- *WhoAm 94*
Tedeschi, John Alfred 1931- *WhoAm 94*
Tedeschi, Linda L. 1948- *WhoAmL 94*
Tedesco, Bruce Grey 1947- *WhoMW 93*
Tedesco, Fortunata 1826-1866 *NewGrDO*
Tedesco, Francis Joseph 1944- *WhoAm 94*
Tedesco, Frank 1936- *WhoAmP 93*
Tedesco, Frank A. d1993 *NewYTBS 93*
Tedesco, Paolo *WhoHol 92*
Tedesco, Susan Mary 1954- *WhoMW 93*
Tedesco Tato, Giglia 1926- *WhoWomW 91*
Tedesko, Anton 1903- *WhoAm 94*
Tedford, Charles Franklin 1928- *WhoWest 94*
Tedford, David John 1931- *Who 94*
Tedford, Jack Nowlan, III 1943- *WhoAmP 93, WhoFI 94, WhoWest 94*
Tedford, John Roy, Jr. 1936- *WhoAmP 93*
Tedford, William G. *EncSF 93*
Tedford, William Howard, Jr. 1936- *WhoAm 94*
Tedisco, James Nicholas 1950- *WhoAmP 93*
Tedlock, Dennis 1939- *WhoAm 94, WhoScEn 94*
Tedmarsh, William J. d1937 *WhoHol 92*
Tedone, David A. 1953- *WrDr 94*
Tedro, Henrietta d1948 *WhoHol 92*
Tedros, Theodore Zaki 1910- *WhoAm 94*
Tedrow, Irene 1907- *WhoHol 92*
Tedrow, John C. F. 1917- *ConAu 142*
Tedrow, John Charles Fremont 1917- *WhoAm 94*
Tedstrom, Peter Finley 1959- *WhoFI 94*
Tee, Master 1966- *WhoBlA 94*
Tee, Richard d1993 *NewYTBS 93*
Teece, David John 1948- *WhoAm 94, WhoScEn 94*
Teed, Nancy Elizabeth 1949- *WhoWomW 91*
Teegarden, Kenneth Leroy 1921- *WhoAm 94*
Teege, Joachim d1969 *WhoHol 92*
Teegen, Evelyn I. 1931- *WhoAmP 93*
Teeguarden, Dennis Earl 1931- *WhoAm 94*
Teekah, George Anthony 1948- *WhoBlA 94*
Teel, Dale 1925- *WhoAm 94*
Teel, Ward 1924- *WhoAmP 93*
Teele, Arthur E., Jr. 1946- *WhoAmP 93*
Teele, Arthur Earle, Jr. 1946- *WhoBlA 94*
Teele, Thurston Ferdinand 1934- *WhoFI 94*
Teeley, Peter *WhoAm 94*
Teeley, Peter Barry 1940- *WhoAmP 93*
Teelock, Boodhun 1922- *Who 94*
Teem, John McCorkle 1925- *WhoAm 94*
Teem, Paul Lloyd, Jr. 1948- *WhoAm 94, WhoFI 94*
Teepen, Thomas Henry 1935- *WhoAm 94*
Teeple, Fiona Diane 1943- *WhoAm 94*
Teeple, Richard Duane 1942- *WhoAm 94, WhoAmL 94*
Teer, Barbara Ann 1937- *WhoBlA 94*
Teer, Kees 1925- *IntWW 93*
Teerlinc, Levina 1510?-1576 *DcNaB MP*
Teerlink, Joseph Leland 1935- *WhoFI 94, WhoWest 94*
Teerlink, Richard Francis 1936- *WhoAm 94, WhoFI 94*
Tees, Richard Chisholm 1940- *WhoAm 94*
Teesdale, Edmund Brinsley 1915- *Who 94*
Teeter, Bradley Warren 1959- *WhoMW 93*
Teeter, Dwight Leland, Jr. 1935- *WhoAm 94*
Teeter, Karl van Duyn 1929- *WhoAm 94*
Teeter, Lorna Madsen 1948- *WhoWest 94*
Teeter, Rob R. 1957- *WhoWest 94*
Teeters, Clarence 1933- *WhoWest 94*
Teeters, Nancy Hays 1930- *WhoAm 94, WhoAmP 93, WhoFI 94*
Teets, Charles Edward 1947- *WhoFI 94*
Teets, John William 1933- *IntWW 93, WhoAm 94, WhoFI 94, WhoWest 94*
Teets, Stacey A. 1968- *WhoMW 93*
Teeuwissen, Pieter 1966- *WhoBlA 94*
Tee-Van, Helen Damrosch 1893-1976 *WhoAmA 93N*
Teevan, Richard Collier 1919- *WhoAm 94*
Teevans, James William 1963- *WhoAmL 94*
Tefet, Charles Eugene 1874- *WhoAmA 93N*
Teffi 1872-1952 *BlmGWL*
Tefft, Elden Cecil 1919- *WhoAmA 93*
Tefft, Melvin 1932- *WhoAm 94*
Tefkin, Blair Ashleigh *WhoHol 92*
Tegelaar-Boonacker, Haty 1930- *WhoWomW 91*
Tegeler, Dorothy 1950- *WhoWest 94*
Tegenkamp, Gary Elton 1946- *WhoAmL 94*
Tegeris, Andrew Stanley 1929- *WhoAm 94*
Tegfeldt, Jennifer Ann 1956- *WhoAmL 94*
Teglasi, Hedwig *WhoScEn 94*
Tegner, Ian Nicol 1933- *Who 94*
Tegtmeier, Ronald Eugene 1943- *WhoScEn 94, WhoWest 94*
Tegtmeyer, Rene Desloge 1934- *WhoAmL 94*
Tehan, Arline Boucher 1930- *WrDr 94*
Tehan, John Bashir 1948- *WhoAm 94, WhoAmL 94*
Tehan, Robert Emmet, Jr. 1931- *WhoAmL 94*
Tehan, Timothy P. 1952- *WhoAmL 94*
Te Heuheu, Hepi (Hoani) 1919- *Who 94*
Tehorenhaegnon fl. 17th cent.- *EncNAR*
Tei, Takuri 1924- *WhoMW 93*
Tei Abal, Sir 1932- *Who 94*
Teiber *NewGrDO*
Teich, Albert, Jr. 1929- *WhoAmP 93*
Teich, Malvin Carl 1939- *IntWW 93, WhoAm 94, WhoScEn 94*
Teicher, Morton Irving 1920- *WhoAm 94*
Teichert, Curt 1905- *WhoAm 94*
Teichgraeber, Richard D. 1941- *WhoFI 94*
Teichman, Mary Melinda 1954- *WhoAmA 93*
Teichman, Sabina d1983 *WhoAmA 93N*
Teichmann, Katjia *WhoHol 92*
Teichner, Lester 1944- *WhoAm 94*
Teicholz, Bruce B. d1993 *NewYTBS 93 [port]*
Teicholz, Paul M. 1937- *WhoScEn 94*
Teichrob, Carol 1939- *WhoWest 94*
Teig, Marlowe Gilman 1938- *WhoFI 94*
Teig, Robert L. *WhoAmL 94*
Teigen, Curtis Duane 1963- *WhoMW 93*
Teiger, David 1929- *WhoAm 94*
Teilhet, Raoul Edward 1933- *WhoAmP 93*
Teilhet-Fisk, Jehanne Hildegarde 1939- *WhoAmA 93*
Teillon, L. Pierre, Jr. 1943- *WhoAmL 94*
Teiman, Richard B. 1938- *WhoAm 94*
Teish, Luisah 1948- *BlkWr 2, ConAu 141*
Teissedre de Fleury, Francois Louis, Marquis de 1749- *WhAmRev*
Teitel, Jeffrey Hale 1943- *WhoAmL 94*
Teitel, Nathan *DrAPF 93*
Teitel, Simon 1928- *WhoAm 94*
Teitelbaum, Harry 1930- *WhoAm 94*
Teitelbaum, Irving 1939- *WhoAm 94*
Teitelbaum, Leonard 1931- *WhoAmP 93*
Teitelbaum, Philip 1928- *IntWW 93, WhoAm 94*
Teitelbaum, Sheldon 1955- *EncSF 93*
Teitelbaum, Steven Lazarus 1938- *WhoAm 94*
Teitelbaum, Steven Usher 1945- *WhoAmL 94*
Teitell, Conrad Laurence 1932- *WhoAm 94*
Teitelman, Jill *DrAPF 93*
Teitelman, Robert 1954- *WrDr 94*
Teitsma, Albert 1943- *WhoScEn 94*
Teitz, Jeffrey Jonathan 1953- *WhoAmP 93*
Teitz, Michael B. 1935- *WhoAm 94*
Teiwes, Helga 1930- *ConAu 140*
Teixeira, Antonio 1707-1770 *NewGrDO*
Teixeira, Pedro De 1575-1640 *WhWE*
Teixeira, Virgilio 1917- *WhoHol 92*
Teixeira da Cruz, Antonio 1935- *WhoScEn 94*
Teixier, Annie Mireille J. 1937- *WhoScEn 94*
Tejada, Celia 1958- *WhoHisp 94*
Tejada, Daniel M. *WhoHisp 94*
Tejada, Marquis de *IntWW 93*
Tejan-Sie, Banja 1917- *Who 94*
Tejeda, Frank 1945- *WhoAm 94*
Tejeda, Frank M. 1945- *CngDr 93, WhoAmP 93, WhoHisp 94*
Tejeda, Rennie *WhoHisp 94*
Tejeda, Robert *WhoHisp 94*
Tejidor, Estela Maria 1956- *WhoHisp 94*
Tejidor, Roberto A. 1942- *WhoHisp 94*
Te Kaat, Erich Heinz 1937- *IntWW 93*
Tekakwitha, Catherine 1656?-1680 *DcAmReB 2*
Tekakwitha, Kateri 1656-1680 *EncNAR*
Te Kanawa, Kiri 1944- *IntWW 93, NewGrDO, WhoAm 94*
Te Kanawa, Kiri (Janette) 1944- *Who 94*
Tekelioglu, Meral 1936- *WhoScEn 94*
Tekippe, Rudy Joseph 1943- *WhoScEn 94*
Tekkanat, Bora 1953- *WhoScEn 94*
Teklits, Joseph Anthony 1952- *WhoAmL 94*
Telaak, Bill d1963 *WhoHol 92*
Telberg, Val 1910- *WhoAmA 93*
Telegdi, Valentine L. 1922- *IntWW 93*
Telegdi, Valentine Louis 1922- *WhoScEn 94*
Telegen, Arthur G. 1947- *WhoAmL 94*
Telek, Leona G. Lee 1931- *WhoAmP 93*
Teleki, Blanka 1806-1862 *BlmGWL*
Teleki, Samuel 1845-1916 *WhWE*
Telemann, Georg Philipp 1681-1767 *NewGrDO*
Telemaque, Eleanor Wong *DrAPF 93*
Telepas, George Peter 1935- *WhoAmL 94*
Teles, Ligia Fagundes 1923- *BlmGWL*
Telesca, Francis Eugene 1921- *WhoAm 94*
Telesca, Michael Anthony 1929- *WhoAm 94, WhoAmL 94*
Telesco, Paula Jean 1956- *WhoMW 93*
Telesetsky, Walter 1938- *WhoScEn 94*
Telesilla *BlmGWL*
Teletzke, Gerald Howard 1928- *WhoScEn 94*
Televantos, John Yiannakis 1952- *WhoFI 94, WhoScEn 94*
Telewski, Frank William 1955 *WhoAm 94*
Telfair, Edward 1735-1807 *WhAmRev*
Telfer, Richard Greenwell 1922- *WhoWest 94*
Telfer, Robert Gilmour Jamieson 1928- *Who 94*
Telford, Barry B. 1946- *WhoAmP 93*
Telford, Ira Rockwood 1907- *WhoAm 94*
Telford, Robert 1915- *Who 94*
Telford, Robert Lee 1899-1989 *WhAm 10*
Telford, Thomas 1757-1834 *WorInv*
Telford Beasley, John 1929- *Who 94*
Telgarsky, Rastislav Jozef 1943- *WhoWest 94*
Telinde, Richard Wesley 1894-1989 *WhAm 10*
Tell, A. Charles 1937- *WhoAm 94, WhoAmL 94*
Tell, Alma d1937 *WhoHol 92*
Tell, M. David 1936- *WhoAmL 94*
Tell, Olive d1951 *WhoHol 92*
Tell, William Kirn, Jr. 1934- *WhoAm 94, WhoFI 94*
Tella, Guido Jose Mario di 1931- *IntWW 93*
Tella, Luigi 1939- *WhoFI 94*
Telle, Jack Martin 1962- *WhoAmP 93*
Telleen, John Martin 1922- *WhoAm 94*
Telleen, Steven Louis 1947- *WhoWest 94*
Tellefsen, Gerald 1938- *WhoAm 94*
Tellegen, Lou d1934 *WhoHol 92*
Tellegen, Mike d1970 *WhoHol 92*
Tellem, Susan Mary 1945- *WhoAm 94, WhoWest 94*
Tellenbach, Gerd 1903- *IntWW 93*
Tellep, Daniel Michael 1931- *IntWW 93, WhoAm 94, WhoFI 94, WhoScEn 94, WhoWest 94*
Teller 1948- See Penn and Teller *WhoHol 92*
Teller, Aaron Joseph 1921- *WhoAm 94*
Teller, Al *WhoBlA 94*
Teller, Alvin Norman 1944- *WhoAm 94*
Teller, David Norton 1936- *WhoAm 94*
Teller, Douglas H. 1933- *WhoAmA 93*
Teller, Edward 1908- *IntWW 93, Who 94, WhoAm 94, WhoScEn 94, WorInv [port]*
Teller, Gayl *DrAPF 93*
Teller, Harriet 1949- *WhoMW 93*
Teller, Ira 1940- *IntMPA 94*
Teller, Jane (Simon) *WhoAmA 93N*
Teller, Neville 1931- *WrDr 94*
Teller, Ray 1948- See Penn and Teller *WhoCom*
Teller, Richard E. 1949- *WhoAm 94*
Teller, Walter d1993 *NewYTBS 93*
Teller, Walter (Magnes) 1910-1993 *ConAu 140*
Teller, Walter Magnes 1910- *WrDr 94*
Telles, Cynthia Ann *WhoHisp 94*
Telles, Lygia Fagundes 1924- *ConWorW 93, RfGShF*
Telles, Rick *WhoHol 92*
Telles, Rick David 1962- *WhoHisp 94*
Tellez, Gabriel *IntDcT 2*
Tellez, George Henry 1951- *WhoScEn 94*
Tellez, Gorki C. *WhoHisp 94*
Tellez, Isabelle Ogaz 1924- *WhoHisp 94*
Tellez, Laura E. 1955- *WhoHisp 94*
Tellez, Louis *WhoHisp 94*
Tellier, Henri 1918- *WhoAm 94*
Tellier, Paul M. 1939- *WhoAm 94, WhoFI 94*
Tellier, Richard Davis 1942- *WhoAm 94*
Telling, Edward Riggs 1919- *WhoAm 94*
Tellinghuisen, Roger *WhoAmP 93*
Tello, Alfonso Sanchez d1979 *WhoHol 92*
Tello, Manuel 1935- *Who 94*
Tello, Oldemar 1959- *WhoHisp 94*
Tello, Rafael 1872-1946 *NewGrDO*
Telmer, Frederick Harold 1937- *IntWW 93, WhoAm 94*
Telow, John 1914- *WhoAmP 93*
Telpner, Joel Stephan 1956- *WhoAmL 94*
Telser, Lester G(reenspan) 1931- *WrDr 94*
Telson, Stanley Alan 1957- *WhoWest 94*
Teltschik, Horst 1940- *IntWW 93*
Telva, Marian 1897-1962 *NewGrDO*
Tem, Steve Rasnic *DrAPF 93*
Temaat, Scott 1965- *WhoMW 93*
Tema-Lyn, Laurie 1951- *WhoAm 94*
Temam, Roger M. 1940- *WhoScEn 94*
Temanel, Billy Estoque 1958- *WhoScEn 94*
Tembo, John Zenas Ungapake 1932- *IntWW 93*
Temerlin, Leiner 1928- *IntWW 93*
Temerlin, Liener 1928- *WhoAm 94, WhoFI 94*
Temes, Clifford Lawrence 1930- *WhoScEn 94*
Temes, Gabor Charles 1929- *WhoAm 94, WhoWest 94*
Temes, Mort 1928- *WhoAmA 93*
Temeyer, Todd John 1963- *WhoMW 93*
Temin, Howard M. 1934- *IntWW 93*
Temin, Howard M(artin) 1934- *Who 94*
Temin, Howard Martin 1934- *WhoAm 94, WhoMW 93, WhoScEn 94, WorScD*
Temin, Michael Lehman 1933- *WhoAm 94*
Temin, Peter 1937- *WrDr 94*
Temirkanov, Yuri 1938- *Who 94*
Temirkanov, Yuriy Khatuyevich 1938- *IntWW 93*
Temirkanov, Yury 1938- *NewGrDO*
Temkin, Charles B., Jr. 1948- *WhoAmL 94*
Temkin, Harvey Leon 1952- *WhoAm 94*
Temkin, Jennifer 1948- *Who 94*
Temkin, Robert Harvey 1943- *WhoAm 94, WhoFI 94*
Temko, Allan 1924- *WrDr 94*
Temko, Allan Bernard 1924- *WhoAm 94, WhoWest 94*
Temko, Edward James 1952- *Who 94*
Temko, Stanley Leonard 1920- *WhoAm 94*
Temlitz, Sylvia 1947- *WhoMW 93*
Temmer, Stephen Francis 1928-1992 *WhAm 10*
Tempany, Myles McDermott 1924- *Who 94*
Tempel, Jean C. *WhoAm 94, WhoFI 94*
Tempel, Jean Curtin 1943- *WhoFI 94*
Tempel, Thomas Robert 1939- *WhoAm 94*
Tempelis, Constantine Harry 1927- *WhoAm 94*
Tempelman, Jerry Henry 1962- *WhoFI 94*
Tempelman, Steven Carlos 1967- *WhoWest 94*
Temperley, H. N. V. *WhoScEn 94*
Temperley, (Harold) Neville (Vazeille) 1915- *WrDr 94*
Temperley, Nicholas 1932- *WrDr 94*
Temperley, Nicholas (Mark) 1932- *NewGrDO*
Tempero, Kenneth Floyd 1939- *WhoAm 94, WhoScEn 94*
Tempest, Drake S. 1953- *WhoAmL 94*
Tempest, Gerard Francis 1918- *WhoAmA 93*

Tempest, Harrison F. WhoAm 94, WhoFI 94
Tempest, Marie d1942 WhoHol 92
Tempest, Marie (Susan) 1864-1942 NewGrDO
Tempest, Peter Rob 1962- WhoWest 94
Tempest, Richard B. 1935- WhoAmP 93
Tempest, Rick 1950- WhoAmP 93
Tempest, Sarah 1907- WrDr 94
Tempest, Tom d1955 WhoHol 92
Tempest, Victor 1915- WrDr 94
Temple (Black), Shirley Jane 1928- IntMPA 94
Temple, Alan Harrison 1896- WhAm 10
Temple, Anthony Dominic Afamado 1945- Who 94
Temple, Byron 1933- WhoAmA 93
Temple, Dan 1916- WrDr 94
Temple, Donald 1933- WhoAm 94, WhoMW 93
Temple, Donald Edward 1946- WhoFI 94
Temple, Donald Melvin 1953- WhoBlA 94
Temple, Douglas 1919- WhoAmL 94
Temple, Edward Stanley 1927- WhoBlA 94
Temple, Frederick Stephen 1916- Who 94
Temple, George d1992 IntWW 93N
Temple, George Frederick 1933- Who 94
Temple, Herbert 1919- WhoBlA 94
Temple, James Frederick, II 1944- WhoWest 94
Temple, John (Meredith) 1910- Who 94
Temple, John Anthony 1942- WhoMW 93
Temple, Joseph George, Jr. 1929- IntWW 93, WhoAm 94, WhoFI 94
Temple, Judy Ann 1962- WhoMW 93
Temple, Larry Eugene 1935- WhoAm 94
Temple, Lee Brett 1956- WhoFI 94, WhoScEn 94
Temple, Lewis 1800-1854 AfrAmAl 6, WorInv
Temple, Nancy Anne 1964- WhoAmL 94
Temple, Nigel (Hal Longdale) 1926- WrDr 94
Temple, Oney D. WhoBlA 94
Temple, Philip 1939- WrDr 94
Temple, Phillip Aaron 1940- WhoAm 94
Temple, Rawden (John Afamado) 1908- Who 94
Temple, Reginald Robert 1922- Who 94
Temple, Richard 1847-1912 NewGrDO
Temple, Richard Anthony Purbeck 1913- Who 94
Temple, Riley Keene 1949- WhoAm 94
Temple, Robert 1941- WhoAm 94
Temple, Robert (Kyle Grenville) 1945- WrDr 94
Temple, Robert Winfield 1934- WhoFI 94
Temple, Robin EncSF 93
Temple, Ronald J. 1940- WhoBlA 94
Temple, Sanderson Who 94
Temple, (Ernest) Sanderson 1921- Who 94
Temple, Shirley IntWW 93
Temple, Shirley 1928- WhoHol 92
Temple, Victor Bevis Afoumado 1941- Who 94
Temple, Wayne C(alhoun) 1924- WrDr 94
Temple, Wayne Calhoun 1924- WhoAm 94
Temple, Wick 1937- WhoAm 94
Temple, William 1628-1699 BlmGEL
Temple, William F(rederick) 1914-1989 EncSF 93
Temple, William Harvey Ernest 1931- WhoAmP 93
Temple-Gore-Langton Who 94
Templeman, Baron 1920- Who 94
Templeman, John Alden 1945- WhoWest 94
Templeman, Michael 1943- Who 94
Templeman, Sydney William 1920- IntWW 93
Temple-Morris, Peter 1938- Who 94
Temple Of Stowe, Earl 1924- Who 94
Templer, Donald Irvin 1938- WhoScEn 94
Templer, James Robert 1936- Who 94
Temples, Dent Larkin, Jr. 1946- WhoAm 94, WhoFI 94
Templeton, Alan Robert 1947- WhoAm 94
Templeton, Alec d1963 WhoHol 92
Templeton, (Alexander) Allan 1946- Who 94
Templeton, Barbara Ann 1954- WhoMW 93
Templeton, Carson Howard 1917- WhoAm 94
Templeton, Darwin Herbert 1922- Who 94
Templeton, Edith 1916- Who 94, WrDr 94
Templeton, Fay d1939 WhoHol 92
Templeton, Fiona DrAPF 93
Templeton, Garry Lewis 1956- WhoBlA 94
Templeton, George d1980 WhoHol 92
Templeton, George Earl 1931- WhoAm 94
Templeton, George Earl, II 1931- WhoScEn 94
Templeton, Hugh Campbell 1929- IntWW 93
Templeton, Ian Malcolm 1929- WhoAm 94
Templeton, John 1802-1886 NewGrDO
Templeton, John (Marks) 1912- Who 94
Templeton, John M. 1912- IntWW 93
Templeton, John Marks 1912- WhoAm 94
Templeton, John Marks, Jr. 1940- WhoScEn 94
Templeton, Nancy Valentine Smyth 1952- WhoScEn 94
Templeton, Robert Clark 1929-1991 WhoAmA 93N
Templeton, Robert Earl 1931- WhoAm 94
Templeton-Cotill, John Atrill 1920- Who 94
Templeton Olive d1979 WhoHol 92
Temple-Troya, José Carlos 1947- WhoHisp 94
Templin, Donald C. 1945- WhoAmL 94
Templin, John Alton 1927- WhoWest 94
Templin, John Leon, Jr. 1940- WhoAm 94, WhoFI 94
Templin, Kathleen Ann 1947- WhoWest 94
Templin, Kenneth Elwood 1927- WhoAm 94
Templin, Mildred Clara 1913- WhoMW 93
Templin, Thomas David 1965- WhoMW 93
Temsamani, Jamal 1960- WhoScEn 94
Tena, Patricia Beatrice 1963- WhoHisp 94
Tenaglia, Antonio Francesco c. 1610-c. 1661 NewGrDO
Tenaglio, Francis Xavier 1949- WhoAmP 93
ten Bensel, Robert William 1936- WhoMW 93
Ten Berge, H.C. ConWorW 93
Ten Boeck, Abraham 1734-1810 WhAmRev
Ten Broeke, Jan 1930- WhoAmA 93
TenBrook, Donald M. 1932- WhoMW 93
Tenbrook, Harry d1960 WhoHol 92
Tenby, Viscount 1927- Who 94
Ten Cate, Arnold Richard 1933- WhoAm 94
Tench, David Edward 1929- Who 94
Tench, William Henry 1921- Who 94
Tencin, Claudine-Alexandrine Guerin de 1685-1749 BlmGWL
Tencza, Thomas Michael 1932- WhoScEn 94
Tenczar, Alan J. 1956- WhoMW 93
Tendler, David 1938- WhoAm 94
Tendler, Mark d1990 WhoHol 92
Tenducci, Giusto Ferdinando c. 1735-1790 NewGrDO
Tenenbaum, Bernard Hirsh 1954- WhoFI 94
Tenenbaum, Irving 1908- WhoAmL 94
Tenenbaum, Louis 1922- WhoAm 94
Tenenbaum, Michael 1913- WhoAm 94
Tenenbaum, Michael 1914- EncABHB 9
Tenenbaum, Samuel Jay 1943- WhoAmP 93
Tenenholtz, Elihu d1971 WhoHol 92
Tener, John E. 1938- WhoAmL 94
Tener, Robert L. DrAPF 93
Tener, William Terrence 1941- WhoWest 94
Tenes, Diana Rodriguez 1957- WhoHisp 94
Ten Eyck, Alicia Rose 1959- WhoFI 94
Ten Eyck, Catryna 1931- WhoAmA 93
Ten Eyck, Lillian d1966 WhoHol 92
Teng, Anthony Yung-yuan 1939- WhoAsA 94
Teng, Chung-Chu 1955- WhoScEn 94
Teng, Henry Shao-lin 1947- WhoAsA 94
Teng, Hsi Ching 1919- WhoAsA 94
Teng, Lee Chang-Li 1926- WhoAsA 94
Teng, Mabel Sik Mei 1953- WhoAsA 94
Teng, Mao-Hua 1958- WhoScEn 94
Teng, Philip Chin Huei 1922- WhoAm 94
Teng, Tsuchi Paul 1939- WhoAsA 94
Tengbom, Anders 1911- IntWW 93
Tenggren, Gustav Adolf 1896-1970 WhoAmA 93N
Teng Hua 1910-1980 HisDcKW
Tengi, Frank R. 1920- WhoAm 94, WhoAmL 94
Teng Jinxian WhoPRCh 91 [port]
Tengroth, Mirra WhoAmA 93
Teng Shaozhi WhoPRCh 91
Teng Teng 1930- WhoPRCh 91 [port]
Teng Wenji WhoPRCh 91 [port]
Ten Haken, Richard Ervin 1934- WhoFI 94
TenHoeve, Thomas 1935- WhoMW 93
Ten Holt, Friso 1921- IntWW 93
Tenhouse, Art 1950- WhoAmP 93
Ten Hoven, James Alan 1951- WhoMW 93
Tenhula, John 1951- WrDr 94
Teniente, Richard WhoHisp 94
Teninga, Walter Henry 1928- WhoAm 94, WhoFI 94, WhoMW 93
Tenison Who 94
Ten Kate, Peter Cornelius 1948- WhoScEn 94
Tenn, William 1919- WrDr 94
Tenn, William 1920- EncSF 93
Tennant Who 94
Tennant, Anthony (John) 1930- Who 94
Tennant, Anthony John 1930- IntWW 93
Tennant, Bernard 1930- Who 94
Tennant, Charles WorInv
Tennant, Donna Kay 1949- WhoAmA 93
Tennant, Dorothy d1942 WhoHol 92
Tennant, Emma 1937- BlmGEL, BlmGWL
Tennant, Emma 1943- Who 94
Tennant, Emma (Christina) 1937- EncSF 93, WrDr 94
Tennant, Emma Christina 1937- IntWW 93, Who 94
Tennant, Francis K. 1954- WhoAmL 94
Tennant, George Bill 1948- WhoAmP 93
Tennant, Harry 1917- Who 94
Tennant, Hazel M. Bennett 1907- WhoMW 93
Tennant, Howard Edward 1941- WhoWest 94
Tennant, Iain (Mark) 1919- Who 94
Tennant, John Randall 1940- WhoAm 94
Tennant, Kylie 1912-1988 BlmGWL
Tennant, Melvin, II 1959- WhoBlA 94
Tennant, Michael Trenchard 1941- Who 94
Tennant, Peter (Frank Dalrymple) 1910- Who 94, WrDr 94
Tennant, Peter Frank Dalrymple 1910- IntWW 93
Tennant, Robert Hamilton 1954- WhoAmL 94
Tennant, Samuel McKibben 1928- WhoFI 94
Tennant, Smithson 1761-1815 WorScD
Tennant, Thomas Michael 1948- WhoAm 94
Tennant, Veronica 1947- IntDcB [port], WhoAm 94
Tennant, Victoria 1950- WhoHol 92
Tennant, Victoria 1953- IntMPA 94
Tennant of Balfluig, Mark Iain 1932- Who 94
Tennberg, Jean-Marc d1971 WhoHol 92
Tennefos, Jens 1930- WhoAmP 93
Tennekes, Hendrik 1936- IntWW 93
Tennekoon, Victor 1914- Who 94
Tennen, Ken 1949- WhoWest 94
Tennenbaum, Michael Ernest 1935- WhoAm 94, WhoFI 94
Tennenbaum, Silvia DrAPF 93
Tennent, Gilbert 1703-1764 DcAmReB 2
Tennent, Michael D. 1948- WhoAm 94
Tennent, Valentine Leslie 1919- WhoFI 94, WhoWest 94
Tennent, William 1673-1746 DcAmReB 2
Tenner, David Mark 1959- WhoAmL 94
Tenneshaw, S.M. EncSF 93
Tennessen, Robert J. 1939- WhoAmP 93
Tennessen, Robert Joseph 1939- WhoAmL 94
Tennet, Elizabeth WhoWomW 91
Tenney, Anne WhoHol 92
Tenney, Boyd 1915- WhoAmP 93
Tenney, Charles Henry 1911- WhoAm 94, WhoAmL 94
Tenney, Dudley Bradstreet 1918- WhoAm 94
Tenney, Edward Jewett, II 1924- WhoAmL 94
Tenney, Irene 1941- WhoHisp 94
Tenney, Kevin S. HorFD
Tenney, Leon Walter 1949- WhoScEn 94
Tenney, Robert Carl 1950- WhoAmL 94
Tenney, Robert Nelson 1942- WhoWest 94
Tenney, Ruth Dawn 1940- WhoMW 93
Tenney, Stephen Marsh 1922- WhoAm 94, WhoScEn 94
Tenney, Tabitha Gilman 1762-1837 BlmGWL
Tenney, William Frank 1946- WhoAm 94, WhoWest 94
Tenniel, John 1820-1914 SmATA 74 [port]
Tennis, Stephen M. 1942- WhoAmL 94
Tennison, Don 1950- WhoWest 94
Tennison, William Ray, Jr. 1941- WhoFI 94, WhoWest 94
Tenno, Jeanne Hiroko 1960- WhoWest 94
Tennon, Julius WhoHol 92
Tennstedt, Klaus 1926- IntWW 93, NewGrDO, Who 94, WhoAm 94
Tenny, Edward Millard 1941- WhoWest 94
Tennyson, Baron 1920- Who 94
Tennyson, Alfred 1809-1892 BlmGEL [port]
Tennyson, G(eorg) B(ernhard) 1930- WrDr 94
Tennyson, Georg Bernhard 1930- WhoAm 94, WhoWest 94
Tennyson, Gladys d1983 WhoHol 92
Tennyson, Joseph Alan 1958- WhoMW 93
Tennyson, Mary Maureen 1955- WhoAmL 94
Tennyson, Peter Joseph 1946- WhoAm 94
Tennyson, Roderick C. 1937- WhoScEn 94
Tennyson, Wilmat 1927- WhoAm 94, WhoFI 94
Tennyson-d'Eyncourt, Mark (Gervais) 1967- Who 94
Tenopir, Lawrence 1950- WhoAmP 93
Tenopyr, Mary Louise Welsh 1929- WhoScEn 94
Tenor, Randall Benson 1946- WhoAmL 94
Tenorio, Froilan C. WhoAmP 93
Tenorio, Manoel Fernando da Mota 1957- WhoScEn 94
Tenorio, Pedro A. WhoAmP 93
Tenorio, Pedro P. 1934- WhoAmP 93
Tenorio, Pedro Pangelinan 1934- WhoAm 94
Tenorio, Rafael Alberto 1960- WhoMW 93
Tenorio, Victor 1937- WhoWest 94
Tenpas, Kathleen M. DrAPF 93
Tenskwatawa 1768?-1837 DcAmReB 2, HisWorL [port]
Tenskwatawa 1775-1836 EncNAR [port]
Tenuta, Jean Louise 1958- WhoMW 93
Tenuta, Judy 1951- WhoCom [port]
Tenuta, Luigia 1954- WhoAmL 94
Tenzel, Richard Ruvin 1929- WhoAm 94
Tenzer, Herbert d1993 NewYTBS 93 [port]
Tenzer, Jonathan A., Mrs. 1940- WhoAmA 93
Tenzin Gyatso 1935- Who 94
Teo, Kim-See 1948- WhoFI 94
Teo, (Fiatau) Penitala 1911- Who 94
Teodorescu, George 1947- WhoScEn 94
Teodorescu, Ion d1985 WhoHol 92
Teodorini, Elena 1857-1926 NewGrDO
Teodoru, Constantin Valeriu 1915-1991 WhAm 10
Teodosio, Alexander Ernest 1924- WhoAmP 93
Teotochi-Albrizzi, Isabella 1760-1836 BlmGWL
Tepe, Ann Silcott 1946- WhoMW 93
Tepedino, Francis Joseph 1937- WhoAm 94
Teper, Douglas Clark 1958- WhoAmP 93
Tephly, Thomas Robert 1936- WhoAm 94
Teplitz, Jerry V. 1947- WhoFI 94
Teplitzky, Philip Herman 1949- WhoScEn 94
Teplova, Nadezhda Sergeevna 1814-1848 BlmGWL
Teplow, Theodore Herzl 1928- WhoAm 94
Teply, Mark Lawrence 1942- WhoMW 93
Tepper, Allan 1947- WhoFI 94
Tepper, Arthur Lewis 1935- WhoAmL 94
Tepper, Lynn Marsha 1946- WhoAm 94
Tepper, Michael Howard 1941- WhoAm 94
Tepper, Natalie Arras 1895-1950 WhoAmA 93N
Tepper, Robert Joseph 1920- WhoWest 94
Tepper, Roberta Marie 1961- WhoMW 93
Tepper, Sheri S. 1929- EncSF 93
Tepper, William WhoHol 92
Terabe, Shigeru 1940- WhoScEn 94
Terabust, Elisabetta 1946- IntDcB [port]
Terada, Yoshinaga 1919- WhoScEn 94
Terai, Tsunemasa 1949- WhoAm 94
Teraji, Thomas Shuichi 1919- WhoAsA 94
Terakedis, John, Jr. 1945- WhoAmL 94
Teralandur, Parthasarathy Krishnaswamy 1956- WhoScEn 94
Teramoto, Yoshitsugu 1931- WhoAsA 94
Teran, Alfredo J. 1953- WhoHisp 94
Teran, Ana Enriqueta 1919- BlmGWL
Teran, Heriberto DrAPF 93
Teran, Miguel A., Sr. 1941- WhoHisp 94
Teran, Timothy Eric Alba 1956- WhoAm 94
Terao, Katsuo 1943- WhoMW 93
Terao, Toshio 1930- WhoScEn 94
Teraoka, Iwao 1958- WhoScEn 94
Teraoka, Masami 1936- WhoAmA 93
Ter-Arutunian, Rouben 1920-1992 AnObit 1992, CurBio 93N
Teras, Kapteeni EncSF 93
Terasawa, Mititaka 1937- WhoScEn 94
Terasawa, Yoshio IntWW 93
Teraskiewicz, Edward Arnold 1946- WhoFI 94
Terasmae, Jaan 1926- WhoAm 94
Terayama Shuji 1935-1983 IntDcT 2
Ter Beek, Relus 1944- IntWW 93
Terbizan, Donna Jean 1953- WhoMW 93
Terborg, Margitta 1941- WhoWomW 91
Terborgh, Bert 1945- WhoAm 94
Terborg-Penn, Rosalyn M. 1941- WhoBlA 94
Terc, Alexander WhoHisp 94
Terc, Miguel Angel, Jr. 1968- WhoHisp 94

Terc, Sigrid Roslyn 1962- *WhoHisp 94*
Terechow, Wladislaw Petrowich 1933- *IntWW 93*
Teregeyo, Aña S. *WhoAmP 93*
Terekhova, Margarita Borisovna 1942- *IntWW 93*
Terence c. 194BC-159BC *IntDcT 2*
Terence 190?BC-159?BC *BlmGEL*
Terence, Susan *DrAPF 93*
Terenius, Lars Yngve 1940- *IntWW 93*
Terenzio, Joseph Vincent 1918- *WhoAm 94*
Terenzio, Peter Bernard 1916- *WhoAm 94*
Terenzio, Pio-Carlo 1921- *IntWW 93*
Teresa, Mother 1910- *IntWW 93, Who 94*
Teresa de Avila, Santa 1515-1582 *BlmGWL*
Teresah 1877-1964 *BlmGWL*
Teresa of Avila 1515-1582 *HisWorL [port]*
Teresa of Calcutta, Mother 1910- *HisWorL [port]*
Tereshchenko, Sergei Aleksandrovich 1951- *LngBDD*
Tereshchenko, Sergey Alexandrovich 1961- *IntWW 93*
Tereshkova, Valentina N. *Who 94*
Tereshkova, Valentina Vladimirovna 1937- *IntWW 93*
Teresi, Joseph 1941- *WhoAm 94, WhoWest 94*
Teresi, Tom Perry 1943- *WhoMW 93*
Teret, Stephen Paul 1945- *WhoAm 94*
Terezakis, Terry Nicholas 1961- *WhoScEn 94*
Terfel, Bryn 1965- *NewGrDO*
Tergit, Gabrielle 1894-1982 *BlmGWL*
ter Haar, Roger Eduard Lound 1952- *Who 94*
Terhes, Joyce Lyons 1940- *WhoAmP 93*
terHorst, Jerald Franklin 1922- *WhoAm 94*
Terhune, Jane Howell 1932- *WhoAmL 94*
Terhune, Max d1973 *WhoHol 92*
Terhune, Robert William 1926- *WhoScEn 94*
Terjung, Werner Heinrich 1931- *WhoAm 94*
Terkel, Studs 1912- *WhoAm 94, WhoHol 92, WhoMW 93*
Terkel, Studs (Louis) 1912- *WrDr 94*
Terkel, Studs Louis 1912- *IntWW 93*
Terkel, Susan Neiburg 1948- *WhoAm 94*
Terken, John 1912- *WhoAmA 93*
ter Keurs, Henk E. D. J. 1942- *WhoAm 94*
Terkhorn, Henry K. 1930- *WhoAm 94*
Terkla, Louis Gabriel 1925- *WhoAm 94*
Terlaje, David Salas 1937- *WhoAmP 93*
Terlecki, Tymon Tadeusz J(ulian) 1905- *WrDr 94*
Terlesky, John *WhoHol 92*
Terlezki, Stefan 1927- *Who 94*
Terlizzi, James Vincent, Jr. 1940- *WhoScEn 94*
Terlizzi, Raymond Thomas 1935- *WhoAm 94*
Terlouw, Jan-Cornelis 1931- *IntWW 93*
Terman, Douglas 1933- *WrDr 94*
Terman, Lewis Madison 1935- *WhoAm 94*
Termes, (Dick A.) 1941- *WhoAmA 93*
Termine, John David 1938- *WhoMW 93*
Termini, Christine 1947- *WhoAmA 93*
Termini, Roseann Bridget 1953- *WhoAm 94, WhoAmL 94*
Ternant, Jean Baptiste Charles de 1751-1816 *AmRev*
Ternay, Charles Louis d'Arsac 1722-1780 *WhAmRev*
Ternberg, Jessie Lamoin 1924- *WhoAm 94*
Ternes, Alan Paul 1931- *WhoAm 94*
Ternes, Donavon Peter 1959- *WhoWest 94*
Ternina, Milka 1863-1941 *NewGrDO [port]*
Terninko, Margaret B. 1936- *WhoAmP 93*
Ternus, Jean Ann 1944- *WhoMW 93*
Ternyik, Stephen 1960- *WhoScEn 94*
Tero, Lawrence 1952- *WhoBlA 94*
Terp, Dana George 1953- *WhoMW 93*
Terp, Thomas Thomsen 1947- *WhoAm 94, WhoAmL 94*
Terpening, Virginia Ann 1917- *WhoMW 93*
Ter-Petrosyan, Levon Akopovich 1945- *IntWW 93*
Terpin, Michael James 1957- *WhoWest 94*
Ter-Pogossian, Michel Mathew 1925- *WhoScEn 94*
Terpstra, Erica G. 1943- *WhoWomW 91*
Terpstra, Vern 1927- *WhoAm 94, WrDr 94*
Terr, Al d1967 *WhoHol 92*
Terr, Lenore (C.) 1936- *WrDr 94*
Terra, Dale Edward 1948- *WhoWest 94*
Terra, Daniel J. 1911- *WhoAmA 93*
Terra, Daniel James 1911- *WhoAm 94, WhoAmP 93*
Terra, Jean M. 1931- *WhoAmP 93*
Terracciano, Anthony Patrick 1938- *WhoAm 94, WhoFI 94*
Terrace, Herbert S. 1936- *WrDr 94*
Terrace, Herbert S(ydney) 1936- *ConAu 43NR*
Terracina, Roy David 1946- *WhoAm 94*
Terradas, Jaume 1943- *WhoScEn 94*
Terradellas, Domenech Miguel Bernabe 1713?-1751 *NewGrDO*
Terrades, (Giovanni) Antonio fl. 1755-1792 *NewGrDO*
Terragno, Paul James 1938- *WhoAm 94*
Terragno, Rodolfo H. 1945- *IntWW 93*
Terrail, Patrick Andre 1942- *WhoWest 94*
Terraine, John Alfred 1921- *IntWW 93, Who 94, WrDr 94*
Terranova, Dan *WhoHol 92*
Terranova, Dino d1969 *WhoHol 92*
Terranova, Elaine *DrAPF 93*
Terranova, Patricia Helen 1952- *WhoWest 94*
Terranova, Paul 1919- *WhoFI 94*
Terras, Victor 1921- *WhoAm 94*
Terrassa, Juan A. 1948- *WhoIns 94*
Terrasse, Claude (Antoine) 1867-1923 *NewGrDO*
Terrazas, Bill 1953- *WhoHisp 94*
Terrazas, Jack C. 1932- *WhoHisp 94*
Terrazas, Johnnie Almaguer 1947- *WhoHisp 94*
Terrazas, Paul Edward 1947- *WhoWest 94*
Terrazas, Ronald 1948- *WhoHisp 94*
Terreault, R. Charles 1935- *WhoAm 94*
Terrebonne, Annie Marie 1932- *WhoScEn 94*
Terrel, Ronald Lee 1936- *WhoAm 94*
Terrell, A. John 1927- *WhoWest 94*
Terrell, Allen McKay, Jr. 1943- *WhoAmL 94*
Terrell, Catherine Milligan 1944- *WhoBlA 94*
Terrell, Charles William 1927- *WhoAm 94*
Terrell, Dorothy 1945- *WhoBlA 94*
Terrell, Ethel 1926- *WhoBlA 94*
Terrell, Francis 1944- *WhoBlA 94*
Terrell, Francis D'Arcy 1940- *WhoBlA 94*
Terrell, Frederick *WhoBlA 94*
Terrell, G. Irvin 1946- *WhoAm 94, WhoAmL 94*
Terrell, Henry Matthew 1940- *WhoBlA 94*
Terrell, Howard Bruce 1952- *WhoWest 94*
Terrell, J. Anthony 1943- *WhoAm 94, WhoAmL 94*
Terrell, James 1923- *WhoAm 94*
Terrell, James Edward 1948- *WhoAmP 93*
Terrell, John L. 1930- *WhoBlA 94*
Terrell, Ken d1966 *WhoHol 92*
Terrell, Lawrence P. 1948- *WhoWest 94*
Terrell, Mable Jean 1936- *WhoBlA 94*
Terrell, Mary Ann 1944- *WhoBlA 94*
Terrell, Mary Lou 1934- *WhoAmP 93*
Terrell, Melvin C. 1949- *WhoBlA 94*
Terrell, Norman Edwards 1933- *WhoAm 94*
Terrell, Pat 1968- *WhoBlA 94*
Terrell, Reginald V. 1959- *WhoBlA 94*
Terrell, Richard Warren 1946- *WhoBlA 94*
Terrell, Robert E. 1943- *WhoBlA 94*
Terrell, Robert H. 1857-1915 *AfrAmAl 6*
Terrell, Robert L. 1943- *WhoBlA 94*
Terrell, Rose Elizabeth, Sister 1940- *WhoMW 93*
Terrell, Stanley E. 1949- *WhoBlA 94*
Terrell, Stephen *Who 94*
Terrell, William Glenn 1920- *WhoAm 94, WhoScEn 94, WhoWest 94*
Terrenoire, Louis 1908-1992 *AnObit 1992*
Terreros, Guillermo 1922- *WhoHisp 94*
Terrick, Richard James 1936- *WhoAmP 93*
Terrie, Philip Gibson 1948- *WhoMW 93*
Terrien, George Blaise 1941- *WhoAm 94*
Terrill, Albert Lee 1937- *WhoAmP 93*
Terrill, Clair Elman 1910- *WhoAm 94*
Terrill, Ivan Dale 1936- *WhoMW 93*
Terrill, John A. 1951- *WhoAmL 94*
Terrill, Karen Stapleton 1939- *WhoWest 94*
Terrill, Kathryn *DrAPF 93*
Terrill, Richard C. *DrAPF 93*
Terrill, Robert Carl 1927- *WhoAm 94*
Terrill, Ross Gladwin *WhoAm 94*
Terrill, W. H. Tyrone, Jr. 1953- *WhoBlA 94*
Terrington, Baron 1915- *Who 94*
Terris, Albert 1916- *WhoAmA 93*
Terris, Bruce Jerome 1933- *WhoAmL 94*
Terris, Malcolm *WhoHol 92*
Terris, Milton 1915- *WhoAm 94*
Terris, Norma d1989 *WhoHol 92*
Terris, Susan *DrAPF 93*
Terris, Susan 1937- *SmATA 77 [port], WrDr 94*
Terris, Susan 1944- *WhoScEn 94*
Terris, Virginia R. *DrAPF 93*
Terris, William 1937- *WhoFI 94*
Terriss, Ellaline d1971 *WhoHol 92*
Terriss, Tom d1964 *WhoHol 92*
Terrizzi, Frank William 1943- *WhoFI 94*
Terry, Adeline Helen 1931- *WhoBlA 94*
Terry, Alice d1987 *WhoHol 92*
Terry, Angela Owen 1941- *WhoBlA 94*
Terry, Becky Faye 1959- *WhoScEn 94*
Terry, Bob 1936- *WhoBlA 94*
Terry, Bobby Sweede 1943- *WhoMW 93*
Terry, C. V. 1908- *WrDr 94*
Terry, Charles C. 1934- *WhoBlA 94*
Terry, Charles James 1949- *WhoScEn 94*
Terry, Christopher Bryant 1953- *WhoFI 94*
Terry, Clark 1920- *WhoAm 94, WhoBlA 94*
Terry, Clifford Lewis 1937- *WhoAm 94*
Terry, Colin George 1943- *Who 94*
Terry, Conrad Martin 1947- *WhoFI 94*
Terry, Dale Randolph 1947- *WhoWest 94*
Terry, Darrell Merle 1933- *WhoWest 94*
Terry, Don d1988 *WhoHol 92*
Terry, Duncan Niles 1909-1989 *WhoAmA 93N*
Terry, Eleanor Foster 1942- *WhoMW 93*
Terry, Eli 1772-1852 *WorInv*
Terry, Ellen d1928 *WhoHol 92*
Terry, Ethel Grey d1931 *WhoHol 92*
Terry, F. Davis, Jr. 1954- *WhoAm 94*
Terry, Frank Jeffrey *WhoWest 94*
Terry, Frank W. 1919- *WhoBlA 94*
Terry, Fred d1933 *WhoHol 92*
Terry, Frederick Arthur, Jr. 1932- *WhoAm 94*
Terry, Garland Benjamin 1927- *WhoBlA 94*
Terry, Gary A. 1935- *WhoAm 94*
Terry, George (Walter Roberts) 1921- *Who 94*
Terry, Harriet Eleanor 1912- *WhoAmP 93*
Terry, Harry 1887- *WhoHol 92*
Terry, Hazel d1974 *WhoHol 92*
Terry, Hilda 1914- *WhoAmA 93*
Terry, James Joseph, Jr. 1952- *WhoAm 94*
Terry, Jay Dean 1931- *WhoAmL 94*
Terry, Joan R. 1953- *WhoMW 93*
Terry, John *WhoHol 92*
Terry, John 1913- *IntMPA 94*
Terry, John A. 1933- *WhoAmP 93*
Terry, John Alfred 1933- *WhoAm 94, WhoAmL 94*
Terry, John Elliott 1913- *Who 94*
Terry, John Hart 1924- *WhoAm 94, WhoAmL 94, WhoAmP 93*
Terry, John Joseph 1937- *WhoAm 94*
Terry, John Quinlan 1937- *IntWW 93*
Terry, John Timothy 1933- *WhoAm 94*
Terry, Joseph Ray, Jr. 1938- *WhoAmL 94*
Terry, Joshua 1825- *EncNAR*
Terry, Kay Adell 1939- *WhoFI 94*
Terry, Leon Cass 1940- *WhoAm 94, WhoMW 93*
Terry, Lucy 1730 1821 *AfrAmAl 6, BlmGWL*
Terry, Marshall Northway, Jr. 1931- *WhoAm 94*
Terry, Marvin Lee 1950- *WhoBlA 94*
Terry, Mary Sue 1947- *WhoAmP 93, WhoWomW 91*
Terry, Megan *DrAPF 93*
Terry, Megan 1932- *ConAu 43NR, ConDr 93, IntDcT 2, WhoAm 94, WrDr 94*
Terry, Michael Edward Stanley I. *Who 94*
Terry, Nigel 1945- *WhoHol 92*
Terry, Paul 1887-1971 *IntDcF 2-4*
Terry, Paul Edward 1954- *WhoMW 93*
Terry, Peter (David George) 1926- *Who 94*
Terry, Peter Anthony 1952- *WhoAm 94*
Terry, Peyton Huber 1923- *WhoAmP 93*
Terry, Philip Alexander 1960- *WhoFI 94*
Terry, Phillip 1907- *WhoHol 92*
Terry, Preston H., III 1958- *WhoAmP 93*
Terry, Quinlan *Who 94*
Terry, (John) Quinlan 1937- *Who 94*
Terry, Richard d1967 *WhoHol 92*
Terry, Richard d1987 *WhoHol 92*
Terry, Richard Allan 1920- *WhoAm 94*
Terry, Richard Edward 1937- *WhoAm 94, WhoMW 93*
Terry, Richard Frank 1949- *WhoWest 94*
Terry, Richmond Bohler 1934- *WhoAm 94, WhoFI 94*
Terry, Robert d1980 *WhoHol 92*
Terry, Robert Davis 1924- *WhoAm 94, WhoScEn 94, WhoWest 94*
Terry, Robert J. 1943- *WhoHisp 94*
Terry, Robert Wayne 1949- *WhoFI 94*
Terry, Ronald Anderson 1930- *WhoAm 94, WhoFI 94*
Terry, Roy 1944- *WhoBlA 94*
Terry, Ruth 1920- *WhoHol 92*
Terry, Saralee *ConAu 41NR*
Terry, Saunders 1911- *WhoBlA 94*
Terry, Sheila d1957 *WhoHol 92*
Terry, Shirley Reeves 1938- *WhoAmP 93*
Terry, Sonny d1986 *WhoHol 92*
Terry, Steven Spencer 1942- *WhoWest 94*
Terry, Stuart Lee 1942- *WhoScEn 94*
Terry, Tex d1985 *WhoHol 92*
Terry, Thomas Edward 1937- *WhoAm 94*
Terry, Walter *WhoHol 92*
Terry, Ward Edgar, Jr. 1943- *WhoAmL 94*
Terry, William 1914- *WhoHol 92*
Terry-Thomas d1990 *WhoHol 92*
Terry-Thomas 1911-1990 *WhoCom [port]*
Terschan, Frank Robert 1949- *WhoAmL 94, WhoMW 93*
Tersigni, Anthony 1949- *WhoAm 94*
Tersol, Teresa Anne 1951- *WhoAmP 93*
Terson, Peter 1932- *ConDr 93, WrDr 94*
Terteryan, Avet Ruben 1929- *NewGrDO*
Terts, Abram *ConWorW 93*
Terts, Abram 1925- *RfGShF*
Tertz, Abram *ConWorW 93, EncSF 93*
Teruel, Javier G. *WhoHisp 94*
Terveen, John Victor 1914- *WhoAmP 93*
Ter Veld, Elske 1944- *WhoWomW 91*
Tervo, James M. 1947- *WhoAmL 94*
Tervo, Timo Martti 1950- *WhoScEn 94*
Terwilleger, George E. *WhoAmP 93*
Terwilliger, Cynthia Lou 1955- *WhoWest 94*
Terwilliger, George James, III 1950- *WhoAm 94*
Terwilliger, Herbert Lee 1914- *WhAm 10*
Terwilliger, Joseph Douglas 1965- *WhoScEn 94*
Terwilliger, Robert Barden 1956- *WhoWest 94*
Terwilliger, Robert Elwin 1917-1991 *WhAm 10*
Terwilliger, Roy W. 1937- *WhoAmP 93*
Terzian, James Richard 1961- *WhoFI 94, WhoWest 94*
Terzian, Karnig Yervant 1928- *WhoFI 94, WhoScEn 94*
Terzian, Yervant 1939- *WhoAm 94*
Terziani, Eugenio 1824-1889 *NewGrDO*
Terziani, Pietro 1765-1831 *NewGrDO*
Terzic, Branko Dusan 1947- *WhoAmP 93*
Terzich, Michael Irving 1951- *WhoWest 94*
Terzich, Robert M., Sr. 1935- *WhoAmP 93*
Terzieff, Laurent 1935- *WhoHol 92*
Tesar, Delbert 1935- *WhoAm 94, WhoScEn 94*
Tesar, Milo Benjamin 1920- *WhoAm 94*
Tesarek, Dennis George 1935- *WhoFI 94*
Tesauro, Giuseppe 1942- *IntWW 93*
Tesch, Emmanuel Camille Georges Victor 1920- *IntWW 93*
Tesch, Lorraine Barbara 1948- *WhoAm 94*
Teschemacher, Margarete 1903-1959 *NewGrDO*
Teschner, Douglass Paul 1949- *WhoAmP 93*
Teschner, Richard Rewa 1908- *WhoAm 94*
Teselle, Eugene 1931- *WrDr 94*
Tesfagiorgis, Freida 1946- *WhoAmA 93*
Tesh, John *WhoAm 94*
Tesh, John 1953?- *ConTFT 11*
Tesh, Robert Mathieson 1922- *Who 94*
Teshighara, Hiroshi 1927- *IntWW 93*
Teshima, Yazaemon d1978 *WhoHol 92*
Teshoian, Nishan 1941- *WhoAm 94*
Tesi (Tramontini), Vittoria 1700-1775 *NewGrDO [port]*
Tesich, Nadja *DrAPF 93*
Tesich, Steve 1942- *IntMPA 94, WhoAm 94, WrDr 94*
Tesich, Steve 1943- *ConDr 93*
Teske, Edmund Rudolph 1911- *WhoAmA 93*
Teske, Eldor Martin 1933- *WhoMW 93*
Teske, Richard Glenn 1930- *WhoMW 93*
Teske, Richard Henry 1939- *WhoAm 94, WhoScEn 94*
Tesky, Adeline Margaret c. 1850-1924 *BlmGWL*
Tesla, Nikola 1856-1943 *WorInv [port]*
Tesler, Brian 1929- *IntMPA 94, Who 94*
Tesler, Jack d1976 *WhoHol 92*
Tesler, Lawrence Gordon 1945- *WhoFI 94, WhoWest 94*
Tesler, Marc Stanley 1945- *WhoFI 94*
Teslik, W. Randolph 1949- *WhoAmL 94*
Tesluk, Nicholas George 1948- *WhoWest 94*
Tesmer, Louise Marie 1942- *WhoAmP 93*
Tesoriero, Americo Miguel 1899-1977 *WorESoc*
Tess(arolo), Giulia 1889-1976 *NewGrDO*
Tess, Roy William Henry 1915- *WhoScEn 94, WhoWest 94*
Tessema, Tesfaye 1951- *WhoBlA 94*
Tessendorf, K(enneth) C(harles) 1925- *ConAu 142, SmATA 75 [port]*
Tessier, Frank Andrew 1954- *WhoAmL 94*
Tessier, Jean-Michel 1941- *WhoAm 94*
Tessier, Mark A. 1959- *WhoScEn 94*
Tessier, Robert d1990 *WhoHol 92*

Theilade, Nini 1916- *WhoHol 92*
Theile, Burkhard 1940- *WhoScEn 94*
Theile, Johann 1646-1724 *NewGrDO*
Theilen, Gordon Henry 1928- *WhoWest 94*
Theiler, Mary Alice 1949- *WhoAmL 94*
Theis, Adolf 1933- *IntWW 93*
Theis, Bernard Regis 1957- *WhoFI 94*
Theis, Don Layne 1954- *WhoMW 93*
Theis, Francis William 1920- *WhoAm 94*
Theis, Frank Gordon 1911- *WhoAm 94, WhoAmL 94, WhoMW 93*
Theis, Henry Ericsson 1933- *WhoFI 94*
Theis, James F. 1924- *WhoIns 94*
Theis, Joan C. 1948- *WhoWest 94*
Theis, Kathryn Claire 1952- *WhoAmL 94*
Theis, Paul Anthony 1923- *WhoAmP 93*
Theis, Peter Frank 1937- *WhoMW 93*
Theis, Steven Thomas 1959- *WhoFI 94*
Theis, William Harold 1945- *WhoAmL 94*
Theisen, Edwin Mathew 1930- *WhoFI 94*
Theisen, George I. 1926- *WhoFI 94*
Theisen, Janine Anne 1953- *WhoFI 94*
Theisen, Marissa Roche 1952- *WhoWest 94*
Theismann, Joseph Robert 1949- *WhoAm 94*
Theiss, Brooke d'Auvergne 1970- *WhoHol 92*
Theiss, Douglas Joe 1954- *WhoMW 93*
Theissen, Gerd 1943- *ConAu 41NR*
Theisz, Erwin Jan 1924- *WhoScEn 94*
Thel, Steve Scott 1954- *WhoAmL 94*
Thelen, Bruce Cyril 1951- *WhoAm 94, WhoAmL 94*
Thelen, Daniel Gerard 1958- *WhoMW 93*
Thelen, David P(aul) 1939- *WrDr 94*
Thelen, Jodi 1962- *WhoHol 92*
Thelen, John F. 1949- *WhoIns 94*
Thelen, Max, Jr. 1919- *WhoAm 94*
Thelen, Trisha Ann 1960- *WhoAmP 93*
Thelin, Valfred P. 1934- *WhoAmA 93*
Thellusson *Who 94*
Thelwell, Michael (Miles) 1939- *BlkWr 2*
Thelwell, Michael M. *WhoBlA 94*
Thelwell, Norman 1923- *Who 94*
Themelis, Nickolas John *WhoAm 94*
Themerson, Stefan 1910-1988 *EncSF 93*
Themstrup, Bendt *WhoIns 94*
Thenappan, Vis 1941- *WhoFI 94*
Thenard, Louis Jacques 1777-1857 *WorScD*
Thenen, Shirley Warnock 1935- *WhoMW 93, WhoScEn 94*
Thenhaus, Paulette Ann 1948- *WhoAmA 93*
Theno, Daniel O'Connell 1947- *WhoAmP 93*
Theobald, David A. 1950- *WhoFI 94*
Theobald, Edward Robert 1947- *WhoAmL 94, WhoFI 94, WhoMW 93*
Theobald, George Peter 1931- *Who 94*
Theobald, Gillian Lee 1944- *WhoAmA 93*
Theobald, H. Rupert 1930- *WhoAmL 94*
Theobald, Jurgen Peter 1933- *WhoScEn 94*
Theobald, Michael Paul 1949- *WhoWest 94*
Theobald, Robert 1929- *EncSF 93, WrDr 94*
Theobald, Thomas C. 1937- *IntWW 93*
Theobald, Thomas Charles 1937- *WhoAm 94, WhoFI 94, WhoMW 93*
Theobalde *NewGrDO*
Theocharis, Reghinos D. 1929- *IntWW 93*
Theocharous, Gregory 1929- *Who 94*
Theocritus fl. 3rd cent.BC- *BlmGEL*
Theodora c. 500-548 *HisWorL [port]*
Theodorakis, Mikis 1925- *IntDcF 2-4, IntMPA 94, IntWW 93*
Theodore, Brother *WhoHol 92*
Theodore, Mlle 1760-1796 *IntDcB*
Theodore, Ares Nicholas 1933- *WhoMW 93, WhoScEn 94*
Theodore, Carla *DrAPF 93*
Theodore, Eustace D. 1941- *WhoAm 94*
Theodore, Katherine d1980 *WhoHol 92*
Theodore, Keith Felix 1948- *WhoBlA 94*
Theodore, Nick Andrew 1928- *WhoAm 94, WhoAmP 93*
Theodore, Philip A. 1953- *WhoAmL 94*
Theodore, Samuel S. 1952- *WhoFI 94*
Theodore, Yvonne M. 1939- *WhoBlA 94*
Theodorescu, Radu Amza Serban 1933- *WhoAm 94*
Theodorou, Jerry 1959- *WhoFI 94*
Theodosius, His Beatitude Metropolitan 1933- *WhoAm 94*
Theodosius, Metropolitan *WhoAm 94*
Theofiles, George 1947- *WhoAmA 93*
Theoharis, Lakis Efstathios 1952- *WhoFI 94*
Theologitis, John Michael 1956- *WhoFI 94*
Theon, John Speridon 1934- *WhoAm 94*
Theophile de Viau *GuFrLit 2*
Theophrastus fl. 4th cent.BC- *BlmGEL*
Theoret, France 1942- *BlmGWL*
Theos, Jerry Nicholas 1957- *WhoAmL 94*
Theos, Nick *WhoAmP 93*
Theremin, Leon d1993 *NewYTBS 93 [port]*
Theriac, Errol Gene 1948- *WhoMW 93*
Theriault, Raynold 1936- *WhoAmP 93*
Theriault, Romeo J. 1923- *WhoAmP 93*
Theriault, Yves 1915-1983 *ConLC 79 [port]*
Therion, Master *GayLL*
Theriot, Mitchell R. 1963- *WhoAmP 93*
Theriot, Sam, Sr. 1914- *WhoAmP 93*
Theriot, Sam H., Jr. 1954- *WhoAmP 93*
Theriot, Steve Joseph 1946- *WhoAmP 93*
Therkildsen, Mark B. 1959- *WhoMW 93*
Thermenos, Nicholas 1939- *WhoFI 94*
Thern, Karoly 1817-1886 *NewGrDO*
Thernstrom, Stephan Albert 1934- *WhoAm 94*
Theroigne de Mericourt, Anne-Joseph d1817 *BlmGWL*
Theron, Johan 1924- *ConAu 140*
Theros, Elias George 1919- *WhoAm 94*
Theroux, Alexander (Louis) 1939- *WrDr 94*
Theroux, Alexander Louis *DrAPF 93*
Theroux, Carol 1930- *WhoAmA 93*
Theroux, Eugene 1938- *WhoAm 94, WhoAmL 94*
Theroux, Joseph (Peter) 1953- *WrDr 94*
Theroux, Paul 1941- *WrDr 94*
Theroux, Paul (Edward) 1941- *EncSF 93*
Theroux, Paul Edward 1941- *IntWW 93, Who 94, WhoAm 94*
Theroux, Peter (Christopher Sebastian) 1956- *WrDr 94*
Theroux, Peter Christopher Sebastian 1956- *WhoWest 94*
Theroux, Steven Joseph 1961- *WhoScEn 94*
Therriault, Gene 1960- *WhoAmP 93*
Therrien, Francois Xavier, Jr. 1928- *WhoFI 94*
Therrien, Valerie Monica 1951- *WhoAmP 93*
Thesen, Arne 1943- *WhoAm 94*
Thesen, Hjalmar Peter 1925- *WrDr 94*
Thesen, Sharon 1946- *BlmGWL, WrDr 94*
Thesiger *Who 94*
Thesiger, Ernest d1961 *WhoHol 92*
Thesiger, Roderic Miles Doughty 1915- *Who 94*
Thesiger, Wilfred 1910- *IntWW 93*
Thesiger, Wilfred (Patrick) 1910- *WrDr 94*
Thesiger, Wilfred Patrick 1910- *Who 94*
Thesman, Jean *SmATA 74 [port]*
Thespis fl. 6th cent.BC- *BlmGEL*
Thetford, Bishop Suffragan of 1935- *Who 94*
The Tjong Khing 1933- *SmATA 76 [port]*
Theuer, Charles Philip 1963- *WhoScEn 94*
Theuer, Paul John 1936- *WhoFI 94*
Theumer, Herbert A. 1939- *WhoMW 93*
Theunissen, Gerald 1933- *WhoAmP 93*
Theurer, Byron W. 1939- *WhoWest 94*
Theurer, Jessop Clair 1928- *WhoMW 93*
Theus, Lucius 1922- *AfrAmG [port], WhoBlA 94*
Theus, Reggie 1957- *BasBi, WhoBlA 94*
Theut, Clarence Peter 1938- *WhoAm 94*
Thevenard, Gabriel-Vincent 1669-1741 *NewGrDO*
Thevoz, Michel 1936- *WrDr 94*
Thewlis, David *WhoHol 92*
Thews, Gerhard 1926- *IntWW 93, WhoScEn 94*
Thews, Verl Jasper 1923- *WhoAmP 93*
Theydon, John *EncSF 93*
Theys, Paul Bernard 1955- *WhoMW 93*
Thiagarajan, Sivasailam 1938- *WhoMW 93*
Thiam, Awa *BlmGWL*
Thiam, Habib 1933- *IntWW 93*
Thian, Robert Peter 1943- *Who 94*
Thiandoum, Hyacinthe 1921- *IntWW 93*
Thibau, Jacques Henri 1928- *IntWW 93*
Thibaudeau, May Murphy 1908- *WhoMW 93, WrDr 94*
Thibaudeau, Pat *WhoAmP 93*
Thibault, Chuck L. 1956- *WhoFI 94*
Thibault, Jean-Marc *WhoHol 92*
Thibault, Joseph Laurent 1944- *WhoAm 94, WhoFI 94*
Thibault, Mireille *WhoHol 92*
Thibault, Timothy John 1956- *WhoAmL 94*
Thibaut, Charest deLauzon, Jr. 1922- *WhAm 10*
Thibaut, Richard L. 1968- *WhoWest 94*
Thibeau, Jack *DrAPF 93, WhoHol 92*
Thibeault, Dale Wilkins 1938- *WhoAm 94*
Thibeault, George Walter 1941- *WhoAmL 94, WhoFI 94*
Thibeault, Robert Allen 1948- *WhoAmP 93*
Thibeault, Thomas Francis 1953- *WhoMW 93*
Thibert, Patrick A. 1943- *WhoAmA 93*
Thibert, Roger Joseph 1929- *WhoAm 94*
Thibo, Gary Lynn 1945- *WhoMW 93*
Thibodeau, Gary A. 1938- *WhoAm 94, WhoMW 93*
Thibodeau, Thomas Raymond 1942- *WhoAmL 94*
Thibodeaux, Donald 1937- *WhoAmP 93*
Thibodeaux, James Marvin 1930- *WhoAmP 93*
Thibodeaux, Mary Shepherd 1945- *WhoBlA 94*
Thibodeaux, Sylvia Marie 1937- *WhoBlA 94*
Thicke, Alan *WhoAm 94*
Thicke, Alan 1947- *WhoHol 92*
Thickins, Graeme Richard 1946- *WhoMW 93*
Thicksten, Edward F. 1947- *WhoAmP 93*
Thiebaud, Jim *WhoHol 92*
Thiebaud, Wayne 1920- *IntWW 93*
Thiebaud, (Morton) Wayne 1920- *WhoAmA 93*
Thiebaut, William, Jr. 1947- *WhoAmP 93*
Thiebauth, Bruce Edward 1947- *WhoFI 94, WhoMW 93*
Thiede, Brian Earle 1955- *WhoMW 93*
Thiede, Janet Lynn 1958- *WhoMW 93*
Thiede, Paul Martin 1947- *WhoAmP 93*
Thiede, Richard Wesley 1936- *WhoMW 93*
Thieffry, Patrick Edmond 1955- *WhoAmL 94*
Thiel, Barbara Vogel 1953- *WhoMW 93*
Thiel, Daniel Joseph 1963- *WhoScEn 94*
Thiel, Frank Anthony 1928- *WhoIns 94*
Thiel, Karl *WhAmRev*
Thiel, Philip 1920- *WhoAm 94*
Thiel, Robert James 1958- *WhoFI 94*
Thiel, Ruth Eleanor 1930- *WhoMW 93*
Thiel, Thelma King 1926- *WhoAm 94*
Thiel, Thomas Joseph 1928- *WhoFI 94, WhoScEn 94*
Thiele, Colin (Milton) 1920- *TwCYAW, WrDr 94*
Thiele, Herbert William Albert 1953- *WhoAmL 94*
Thiele, Hertha *WhoHol 92*
Thiele, Howard Nellis, Jr. 1930- *WhoAm 94*
Thiele, Leslie Kathleen 1952- *WhoAmL 94*
Thiele, Norma Jean 1930- *WhoMW 93*
Thiele, Paul Frederick 1914- *WhoAm 94*
Thiele, Terry Vernon 1954- *WhoAmL 94*
Thiele, Wilhelm J. d1975 *WhoHol 92*
Thiele, William E. 1942- *WhoIns 94*
Thiele, William Edward 1942- *WhoAm 94, WhoFI 94*
Thielen, Cynthia *WhoAmP 93, WhoWest 94*
Thielen, Greg Glen 1940- *WhoAmA 93*
Thielen, Joseph Edward 1949- *WhoAmL 94*
Thielman, Dorothy Elizabeth 1937- *WhoFI 94*
Thielsch, Helmut John 1922- *WhoAm 94*
Thieman, Alice Anne 1941- *WhoMW 93*
Thieman, Frederick W. *WhoAmL 94*
Thiemann, Bernd 1943- *IntWW 93*
Thiemann, Charles Lee 1937- *WhoAm 94, WhoFI 94*
Thiemann, Ronald Frank 1946- *WhoAm 94*
Thieme, Steven P. 1970- *WhoMW 93*
Thiemele, Amoakon-Edjampan 1941- *IntWW 93*
Thienemann, Rolf Arthur, Jr. 1931- *WhoMW 93*
Thienes, Clinton Hobart 1896- *WhAm 10*
Thier, Samuel Osiah 1937- *IntWW 93, WhoAm 94*
Thierauf, Richard James 1933- *WrDr 94*
Thiering, Barbara (Elizabeth) 1930- *ConAu 140*
Thieriot, Richard Tobin 1942- *WhoAm 94, WhoWest 94*
Thierolf, Richard Burton, Jr. 1948- *WhoAmL 94, WhoWest 94*
Thierry, John Adams 1913- *WhoAm 94*
Thierry, Marthe d1979 *WhoHol 92*
Thierry, Robert Charles 1938- *WhoScEn 94*
Thiers, Eugene Andres 1941- *WhoHisp 94, WhoScEn 94, WhoWest 94*
Thies, Austin Cole 1921- *WhoAm 94*
Thies, Charles Herman 1940- *WhoAmA 93*
Thies, David Charles 1955- *WhoAmL 94*
Thies, John d1993 *NewYTBS 93*
Thies, Richard B. 1943- *WhoAm 94*
Thies, Richard Brian 1943- *WhoAmL 94*
Thiesen, Gregory Alan 1958- *WhoWest 94*
Thiesenhusen, William Charles 1936- *WhoAm 94*
Thiess, Kenneth Charles 1952- *WhoAmL 94*
Thiess, Leslie Charles d1992 *Who 94N*
Thiess, Manuela *WhoHol 92*
Thiess, Ursula 1924- *WhoHol 92*
Thiessen, Dan *WhoAmP 93*
Thiessen, Delbert Duane 1932- *WhoAm 94*
Thiessen, Gordon George 1938- *WhoAm 94*
Thiessen, J. Grant *EncSF 93*
Thieu, Nguyen Van *IntWW 93*
Thiewes, Rachelle R. 1952- *WhoAmA 93*
Thigpen, Alton Hill 1927- *WhoAm 94*
Thigpen, Calvin Herritage 1924- *WhoBlA 94*
Thigpen, Edmund Leonard 1930- *WhoBlA 94*
Thigpen, Helen d1966 *WhoHol 92*
Thigpen, Lynne *IntMPA 94, WhoBlA 94, WhoHol 92*
Thigpen, Neal Dorsey 1939- *WhoAmP 93*
Thigpen, Rich 1966- *WhoWest 94*
Thigpen, Richard Elton, Jr. 1930- *WhoAm 94, WhoAmL 94*
Thigpen, Robert Thomas 1963- *WhoAm 94*
Thigpen, William Henry 1928-1989 *WhAm 10*
Thiher, O. Allen 1941- *WhoMW 93*
Thijssen, Felix *EncSF 93*
Thill, Georges d1984 *WhoHol 92*
Thill, Georges 1897-1984 *NewGrDO*
Thillon, Sophie Anne 1819-1903 *NewGrDO*
Thimann, Kenneth Vivian 1904- *IntWW 93, Who 94, WhoAm 94, WrDr 94*
Thimayya, Kadendera Subayya 1906-1965 *HisDcKW*
Thimig, Helene d1974 *WhoHol 92*
Thimig, Hermann d1982 *WhoHol 92*
Thimig, Hugo *WhoHol 92*
Thimonnier, Barthelemy *WorInv*
Thimont, Bernard Maurice 1920- *Who 94*
Thin, U. Tun *IntWW 93*
Thind, Gurdarshan S. 1940- *WhoScEn 94*
Thinnes, Roy 1938- *IntMPA 94, WhoHol 92*
Thio, Alan PooAn 1931- *WhoScEn 94*
Thiong'o, Ngugi Wa 1938- *WrDr 94*
Third, Richard Henry McPhail 1927- *Who 94*
Thirkell, Angela 1890-1961 *BlmGWL [port]*
Thirkell, Angela (Margaret) 1890-1961 *ConAu 140*
Thirkettle, (William) Ellis 1904- *Who 94*
Thirkield, Rob d1986 *WhoHol 92*
Thirlwall, George Edwin 1924- *Who 94*
Thiroux d'Arconville, Marie Genevieve-Charlotte Darlus 1721?-1804 *BlmGWL*
Thirring, Walter E. 1927- *IntWW 93*
Thirsk, (Irene) Joan 1922- *IntWW 93, Who 94, WrDr 94*
Thiruvathukal, Kris V. 1925- *WhoAsA 94*
Thiry, Marcel *EncSF 93*
Thiry, Paul 1904- *WhoAm 94, WhoScEn 94*
Thiry, Paul (Albert) 1904- *WhoAmA 93*
Thiselton, Anthony Charles 1937- *Who 94*
Thissell, Charles William 1931- *WhoAmL 94, WhoWest 94*
Thissell, James Dennis 1935- *WhoWest 94*
Thisted, Ronald Aaron 1951- *WhoMW 93*
Thistel, Cynthia Grelle 1955- *WhoWest 94*
Thistle, Dale *WhoAmP 93*
Thistlethwaite, Frank 1915- *Who 94*
Thistlethwaite, Mark Edward 1948- *WhoAmA 93*
Thiusen, Ismar 1836-1909 *EncSF 93*
Tho, Le Duc *IntWW 93*
Thobe, Urban Albert 1935- *WhoMW 93*
Thoday, John Marion 1916- *Who 94*
Thode, Edward Frederick 1921- *WhoAm 94*
Thode, Henry George 1910- *IntWW 93, Who 94, WhoScEn 94*
Thode, Jeffrey Alan 1962- *WhoFI 94*
Thody, Henry d1977 *WhoHol 92*
Thody, Philip (Malcolm Waller) 1928- *WrDr 94*
Thody, Philip Malcolm Waller 1928- *Who 94*
Thoelen, Frank Thomas 1948- *WhoFI 94*
Thoen, Doris Rae 1925- *WhoAmP 93*
Thoennes, Karl Evald, III 1962- *WhoWest 94*
Thoft, Bob 1929- *WhoAmP 93*
Thogmartin, Clyde Orville 1940- *WhoMW 93*
Thola, Kathleen Alma 1936- *WhoMW 93*
Tholborn, Brett Lewis 1957- *WhoWest 94*
Thole, Karel 1914- *EncSF 93*
Tholen, Lawrence Arthur 1938- *WhoFI 94*
Tholen, Steven Wayne 1950- *WhoFI 94*
Tholey, Paul Nikolaus 1937- *WhoScEn 94*

Tholfsen, Trygve R(ainone) 1924- *WrDr 94*
Thollander, Earl 1922- *WhoAmA 93*
Thom, Alexander 1894-1985 *DcNaB MP*
Thom, Arleen Kaye 1957- *WhoScEn 94*
Thom, Douglas Andrew 1939- *WhoAm 94*
Thom, James Alexander *DrAPF 93*
Thom, James Alexander 1933- *WrDr 94*
Thom, Joseph M. 1919- *WhoAm 94*
Thom, Kenneth Cadwallader 1922- *Who 94*
Thom, Norman d1931 *WhoHol 92*
Thom, Richard David 1944- *WhoAm 94*
Thom, Ronald James 1923- *WhAm 10*
Thoma, Carl Dee 1948- *WhoAm 94*
Thoma, Klaus Dieter 1945- *WhoAmL 94*
Thoma, Kurt Michael 1946- *WhoFI 94*
Thoma, Maria *WhoWomW 91*
Thoma, Michael d1982 *WhoHol 92*
Thoma, Therese *NewGrDO*
Thomacini, Jean-Pierre *WhoHol 92*
Thomadakis, Panagiotis Evangelos 1941- *WhoScEn 94*
Thomadsen, Bruce Robert 1948- *WhoMW 93*
Thomae, Betty Kennedy 1920- *WrDr 94*
Thomae, Mary Joan Pangborn 1958- *WhoMW 93*
Thomajan, Robert 1941- *WhoAm 94*
Thoman, Henry Nixon 1957- *WhoAm 94*
Thoman, John Everett 1925- *WhoFI 94, WhoWest 94*
Thoman, Mark 1935- *WhoAm 94*
Thoman, Mark Edward 1936- *WhoAm 94, WhoMW 93*
Thomann, Gary Calvin 1942- *WhoScEn 94*
Thomas *Who 94*
Thomas fl. c. 1170- *BlmGEL*
Thomas, Abdelnour Simon 1913- *WhoScEn 94*
Thomas, Abigail *DrAPF 93*
Thomas, Adrian Tregerthen 1947- *Who 94*
Thomas, Adrian Wesley 1939- *WhoScEn 94*
Thomas, Adrienne 1897-1980 *BlmGWL*
Thomas, Al d1976 *WhoHol 92*
Thomas, Alan *Who 94*
Thomas, Alan 1923- *WhoFI 94, WhoMW 93*
Thomas, (John) Alan 1943- *Who 94*
Thomas, Alan Gradon 1911- *WrDr 94*
Thomas, Alan Richard 1942- *WhoAm 94*
Thomas, Albert, Jr. 1958- *WhoMW 93*
Thomas, Alfred Robert 1927- *WhoAmP 93*
Thomas, Alfred Victor 1929- *WhoAmP 93*
Thomas, Allen Lloyd 1939- *WhoAm 94*
Thomas, Alma W. 1891-1978 *AfrAmAl 6*
Thomas, Alma Woodsey 1891-1978 *WhoAmA 93N*
Thomas, Alston Havard Rees 1925- *Who 94*
Thomas, Alvin 1951- *WhoBlA 94*
Thomas, Ambler Reginald 1913- *Who 94*
Thomas, (Charles Louis) Ambroise 1811-1896 *NewGrDO*
Thomas, Andre Jean 1905- *IntWW 93*
Thomas, Aneurin Morgan 1921- *Who 94*
Thomas, Ann d1989 *WhoHol 92*
Thomas, Ann Freda 1951- *WhoAmL 94*
Thomas, Ann Van Wynen 1919- *WhoAm 94*
Thomas, Archibald Johns, III 1952- *WhoAmL 94*
Thomas, Arthur E. *WhoBlA 94*
Thomas, Arthur Goring 1850-1892 *NewGrDO*
Thomas, Arthur Lafayette, III 1960- *WhoBlA 94*
Thomas, Arthur Lawrence 1931- *WhoAm 94*
Thomas, Arthur Lawrence 1952- *WhoMW 93*
Thomas, Audrey 1935- *RfGShF*
Thomas, Audrey (Grace) 1935- *WrDr 94*
Thomas, Audrey G. 1935- *ConAu 19AS [port]*
Thomas, Audrey Grace 1935- *BlmGWL*
Thomas, Audria Acty 1954- *WhoBlA 94*
Thomas, B. J. 1942- *WhoHol 92*
Thomas, Bailey Alfred *WhoFI 94*
Thomas, Barbara Singer 1946- *WhoAm 94*
Thomas, Barry D. 1963- *WhoAmL 94*
Thomas, Benjamin 1910- *WhoBlA 94*
Thomas, Benjamin, Jr. 1961- *WhoBlA 94*
Thomas, Bertram 1892-1950 *WhWE*
Thomas, Beth Eileen Wood 1916- *WhoAm 94*
Thomas, Betty 1947- *WhoHol 92*
Thomas, Betty 1948- *IntMPA 94*
Thomas, Bide Lakin 1935- *WhoMW 93*
Thomas, Bill 1941- *CngDr 93*
Thomas, Billie 1931-1980 *AfrAmAl 6*
Thomas, Billy d1980 *WhoHol 92*
Thomas, Billy Joe 1942- *WhoAm 94*
Thomas, Billy Marshall 1940- *WhoAm 94*
Thomas, Blair *WhoBlA 94*
Thomas, Blanche d1977 *WhoHol 92*
Thomas, Blythe J. 1933- *WhoAmP 93*
Thomas, Brian C. *WhoAmP 93*
Thomas, Brian Chester 1939- *WhoWest 94*
Thomas, Brinley *Who 94*
Thomas, Broderick 1967- *WhoBlA 94*
Thomas, Brooks 1931- *WhoAm 94*
Thomas, Bruce *WrDr 94*
Thomas, Bruce Robert 1938- *WhoMW 93*
Thomas, Buckwheat 1931-1980 *WhoCom*
Thomas, Byron 1902-1978 *WhoAmA 93N*
Thomas, C. David 1946- *WhoAmA 93*
Thomas, Calvert 1916- *WhoAm 94*
Thomas, Calvin Lewis 1960- *WhoBlA 94*
Thomas, Caren D. 1950- *WhoAm 94, WhoAmL 94*
Thomas, Carl Alan 1924- *WhoBlA 94*
Thomas, Carl D. 1950- *WhoBlA 94*
Thomas, Carmen 1968- *WhoHol 92*
Thomas, Carol M. 1930- *WhoBlA 94*
Thomas, Catherine Anne 1954- *WhoMW 93*
Thomas, Cedric Marshall 1930- *Who 94*
Thomas, Charles *Who 94*
Thomas, Charles, Jr. 1948- *WhoAmP 93*
Thomas, (Antony) Charles 1928- *Who 94, WrDr 94*
Thomas, Charles Allen, Jr. 1927- *WhoAm 94, WhoScEn 94*
Thomas, Charles Carlisle, Jr. 1925- *WhoWest 94*
Thomas, Charles Carroll 1930- *WhoFI 94*
Thomas, Charles Columbus *DrAPF 93*
Thomas, Charles Columbus 1940- *WhoBlA 94*
Thomas, Charles Edward 1927- *Who 94*
Thomas, Charles Edwin 1949- *WhoScEn 94*
Thomas, Charles F. *WhoAm 94*
Thomas, Charles H. 1934- *WhoAmP 93*
Thomas, Charles Howard, II 1934- *WhoAm 94*
Thomas, Charles Richard 1933- *WhoBlA 94*
Thomas, Charles W. 1940- *WhoBlA 94*
Thomas, Charles William, II 1926-1990 *WhAm 10, WhoBlA 94N*
Thomas, Chauncey 1822-1898 *EncSF 93*
Thomas, Cheryl Schroeder 1949- *WhoAmL 94*
Thomas, Christine *WhoHol 92*
Thomas, Christopher Robert 1948- *WhoFI 94*
Thomas, Christopher Sydney 1950- *Who 94*
Thomas, Christopher Yancey, III 1923- *WhoAm 94, WhoMW 93*
Thomas, Clara 1919- *BlmGWL*
Thomas, Clara McCandless 1919- *WhoAm 94, WrDr 94*
Thomas, Clarence *AfrAmAl 6 [port], IntWW 93, NewYTBS 93 [port]*
Thomas, Clarence 1948- *AfrAmAl 6 [port], CngDr 93, WhoAm 94, WhoAmL 94, WhoAmP 93, WhoBlA 94, WhoFI 94*
Thomas, Claude Roderick 1943- *WhoBlA 94*
Thomas, Claudewell Sidney 1932- *WhoAm 94, WhoWest 94*
Thomas, Colin Agnew 1921- *Who 94*
Thomas, Colin Gordon, Jr. 1918- *WhoAm 94*
Thomas, Craig 1933- *CngDr 93, WhoAm 94, WhoAmP 93, WhoWest 94*
Thomas, Craig 1942- *WrDr 94*
Thomas, Craig (David) 1942- *EncSF 93*
Thomas, Craig Eugene 1958- *WhoMW 93*
Thomas, Cynthia Elizabeth 1958- *WhoMW 93*
Thomas, Cynthia Gail 1956- *WhoMW 93*
Thomas, D. Kelly, Jr. 1952- *WhoAmP 93*
Thomas, D. M. 1935- *BlmGEL*
Thomas, D(onald) M(ichael) 1935- *EncSF 93, WrDr 94*
Thomas, D(avid) O(swald) 1924- *ConAu 41NR*
Thomas, Dale E. 1947- *WhoAm 94*
Thomas, Damien *WhoHol 92*
Thomas, Dan 1929- *EncSF 93*
Thomas, Dana Jane 1966- *WhoFI 94*
Thomas, Daniel C. d1993 *NewYTBS 93*
Thomas, Daniel Foley 1950- *WhoAm 94, WhoFI 94*
Thomas, Danny d1991 *WhoHol 92*
Thomas, Danny 1912?-1991 *ConTFT 11, WhoCom*
Thomas, Danny 1914-1991 *WhAm 10*
Thomas, Danny Ray 1949- *WhoAmP 93*
Thomas, Darrell Denman 1931- *WhoAm 94, WhoAmL 94, WhoWest 94*
Thomas, Darwin LaMar 1933- *WhoAm 94*
Thomas, Dave 1948- *WhoHol 92*
Thomas, David d1981 *WhoHol 92*
Thomas, David 1931- *Who 94, WrDr 94*
Thomas, David 1942- *Who 94*
Thomas, David 1943- *IntWW 93, NewGrDO*
Thomas, David 1945- *WhoAmP 93*
Thomas, David 1949- *WhoAmP 93*
Thomas, David, III 1946- *WhoAmL 94*
Thomas, David Albert 1944- *WhoAmL 94*
Thomas, David Ansell 1917- *WhoAm 94, WhoFI 94*
Thomas, David Arthur 1925- *WrDr 94*
Thomas, David Bowen 1931- *Who 94*
Thomas, David Burton 1943- *WhoScEn 94*
Thomas, David Churchill 1933- *Who 94*
Thomas, David Emrys 1935- *Who 94*
Thomas, David H(urst) 1945- *WrDr 94*
Thomas, David Hamilton Pryce 1922- *Who 94*
Thomas, David Hurst 1945- *WhoAm 94*
Thomas, David John 1924- *WhoAmL 94*
Thomas, David L., Jr. 1949- *WhoAmL 94*
Thomas, David Lloyd 1942- *WhoFI 94*
Thomas, David Monro 1915- *Who 94*
Thomas, David Owen 1926- *Who 94*
Thomas, David Phillip 1918- *WhoAm 94*
Thomas, David Robert 1954- *WhoFI 94*
Thomas, David St. John 1929- *WrDr 94*
Thomas, David Stanley 1946- *WhoWest 94*
Thomas, David Wayne 1951- *WhoScEn 94*
Thomas, David William Penrose 1959- *Who 94*
Thomas, Davis 1928- *WhoAm 94*
Thomas, Debi 1967- *WhoAm 94, WhoBlA 94*
Thomas, Deborah Barrett 1966- *WhoFI 94*
Thomas, Denis 1922- *WrDr 94*
Thomas, Denise *DrAPF 93*
Thomas, Dennis Dee 1954- *WhoAmL 94*
Thomas, Dennis R. *WhoIns 94*
Thomas, Derek (Morison David) 1929- *Who 94*
Thomas, Derek John 1934- *Who 94*
Thomas, Derek Morison David 1929- *IntWW 93*
Thomas, Derek Wilfrid 1952- *WhoFI 94*
Thomas, Deroy C. 1926- *IntWW 93, WhoAm 94*
Thomas, Derrick Vincent 1967- *WhoBlA 94*
Thomas, Dewayne 1954- *WhoAmP 93*
Thomas, Dewi Alun 1917- *Who 94*
Thomas, Donald Charles 1935- *WhoAm 94*
Thomas, Donald Earl, Jr. 1951- *WhoAm 94*
Thomas, Donald Martin *Who 94*
Thomas, Donald Michael 1935- *IntWW 93, Who 94*
Thomas, Donna Johns 1945- *WhoMW 93*
Thomas, Donnall *Who 94*
Thomas, (Edward) Donnall 1920- *Who 94*
Thomas, Dorothy Lois 1927- *WhoAmP 93*
Thomas, Douglas L. 1945- *WhoBlA 94*
Thomas, Dudley Breckinridge 1933- *WhoAm 94*
Thomas, Dudley Lloyd 1946- *Who 94*
Thomas, Dudley Scott 1896- *WhAm 10*
Thomas, Duke Winston 1937- *WhoAm 94*
Thomas, Duncan Campbell 1945- *WhoScEn 94*
Thomas, Dylan 1914-1953 *DcLB 139 [port]*
Thomas, Dylan (Marlais) 1914-1953 *RfGShF*
Thomas, Dylan Marlais 1914-1953 *BlmGEL*
Thomas, E. Donnall 1920- *NobelP 91 [port]*
Thomas, E. J. 1951- *WhoAmP 93*
Thomas, Earl *WhoBlA 94*
Thomas, Earle Frederick 1925- *WhoBlA 94*
Thomas, Edgar Albert 1940- *WhoFI 94*
Thomas, Edith Matilda 1854-1925 *BlmGWL*
Thomas, Edith Peete 1940- *WhoBlA 94*
Thomas, Edmund Barrington 1929- *WrDr 94*
Thomas, Edna d1974 *WhoHol 92*
Thomas, Edward d1943 *WhoHol 92*
Thomas, Edward Donnall 1920- *WhoAm 94, WhoScEn 94, WhoWest 94*
Thomas, Edward Francis, Jr. 1937- *WhoAm 94*
Thomas, Edward P. 1920- *WhoBlA 94*
Thomas, Edward St. Clair 1934- *WhoAm 94, WhoMW 93*
Thomas, Edwin L. *WhoScEn 94*
Thomas, Elaine Freeman 1923- *WhoAmA 93*
Thomas, Elean 1947- *BlmGWL*
Thomas, Elizabeth *Who 94*
Thomas, (Mary) Elizabeth 1935- *Who 94*
Thomas, Elizabeth Gray 1924- *WhoAmP 93*
Thomas, Elizabeth Marjorie 1919- *Who 94*
Thomas, Elwood L. *WhoAmP 93*
Thomas, Elwood Lauren 1930- *WhoAmL 94, WhoMW 93*
Thomas, Emyr 1920- *Who 94*
Thomas, Eric Jason 1964- *WhoBlA 94*
Thomas, Erma Lee 1928- *WhoBlA 94*
Thomas, Eryl Stephen 1910- *Who 94*
Thomas, Esther Merlene 1945- *WhoWest 94*
Thomas, Ethel Colvin Nichols 1913- *WhoWest 94*
Thomas, Eula Wiley 1948- *WhoBlA 94*
Thomas, Eunice S. *WhoBlA 94*
Thomas, Everette Earl 1935- *WhoAmL 94*
Thomas, F. Richard *DrAPF 93*
Thomas, Faye Evelyn J. 1933- *WhoMW 93*
Thomas, Francena B. 1936- *WhoBlA 94*
Thomas, Frances 1943- *WrDr 94*
Thomas, Francis Darrell 1928- *WhoFI 94*
Thomas, Francis Thornton 1939- *WhoAm 94*
Thomas, Frank *Who 94*
Thomas, Frank, Jr. 1948- *WhoAm 94*
Thomas, (John) Frank (Phillips) 1920- *Who 94*
Thomas, Frank Edward 1968- *WhoAm 94, WhoBlA 94, WhoMW 93*
Thomas, Frank Joseph 1930- *WhoWest 94*
Thomas, Frank M. d1989 *WhoHol 92*
Thomas, Frank M., Jr. 1947- *WhoAm 94, WhoAmL 94*
Thomas, Frankie 1921- *WhoHol 92*
Thomas, Frankie Taylor 1922- *WhoBlA 94*
Thomas, Franklin 1934- *IntWW 93*
Thomas, Franklin A. 1934- *ConBlB 5 [port], WhoBlA 94*
Thomas, Franklin Augustine 1934- *Who 94, WhoAm 94*
Thomas, Franklin F. 1913-1992 *WrDr 94N*
Thomas, Franklin Whitaker 1925- *WhoBlA 94*
Thomas, Fred *WhoBlA 94*
Thomas, Fred 1958- *WhoAmP 93*
Thomas, Frederick Bradley 1949- *WhoAm 94*
Thomas, Frederick William 1906- *Who 94*
Thomas, G.K. *EncSF 93*
Thomas, Gareth *WhoHol 92*
Thomas, Gareth 1932- *IntWW 93, WhoScEn 94, WhoWest 94*
Thomas, Garland Leon 1920- *WhoScEn 94*
Thomas, Garnett Jett 1920- *WhoFI 94*
Thomas, Garth Johnson 1916- *WhoAm 94*
Thomas, Gary L. 1937- *WhoAm 94*
Thomas, Gary Lynn 1942- *WhoAm 94, WhoFI 94*
Thomas, Gary Marshall 1943- *WhoFI 94*
Thomas, Geoffrey C. *WhoAm 94, WhoFI 94*
Thomas, Geoffrey L. 1944- *WhoAmL 94*
Thomas, George *IntWW 93*
Thomas, Georgie A. 1943- *WhoAmP 93*
Thomas, Gerald 1920- *IntMPA 94*
Thomas, Gerald Eustis 1929- *AfrAmG [port], WhoBlA 94*
Thomas, Gladys Roberts *WhoAm 94*
Thomas, Gloria V. *WhoBlA 94*
Thomas, Gordon 1933- *WrDr 94*
Thomas, Graham Stuart 1909- *ConAu 41NR, Who 94, WrDr 94*
Thomas, Greg Hamilton 1959- *WhoMW 93, WhoScEn 94*
Thomas, Gregg Darrow 1951- *WhoAmL 94*
Thomas, Gregory Matthew 1960- *WhoFI 94*
Thomas, Gretchen d1964 *WhoHol 92*
Thomas, Gus d1926 *WhoHol 92*
Thomas, Gwendolyn Jeanne 1922- *WhoWest 94*
Thomas, Gwyn 1913-1981 *ConDr 93*
Thomas, Gwyn Edward Ward *Who 94*
Thomas, H. Reynolds 1927-1991 *WhoAmA 93N*
Thomas, Harold Allen, Jr. 1913- *WhoAm 94*
Thomas, Harold William 1941- *WhoScEn 94*
Thomas, Harry E. 1920- *IntMPA 94*
Thomas, Harry L. *WhoAmP 93*
Thomas, Harry Lee 1919- *WhoBlA 94*
Thomas, Harvey *Who 94*
Thomas, (John) Harvey (Noake) 1939- *Who 94*
Thomas, Harvey Gantenbein 1923- *WhoMW 93*
Thomas, (John) Harvey Noake 1939- *IntWW 93*
Thomas, Hayward 1921- *WhoWest 94*
Thomas, Heather 1957- *WhoHol 92*
Thomas, Helen 1920- *CurBio 93 [port], WhoAmP 93*
Thomas, Helen (Doane) *WhoAmA 93*
Thomas, Helen A. 1920- *WhoAm 94*
Thomas, Henri 1912- *IntWW 93*

Thomas, Henry 1971- *IntMPA 94, WhoHol 92*
Thomas, Henry Evans, IV 1937- *WhoAmP 93*
Thomas, Henry Lee, Jr. 1965- *WhoAm 94, WhoMW 93*
Thomas, Henry Noel 1955- *WhoFI 94*
Thomas, Herman Edward 1941- *WhoBlA 94*
Thomas, Howard Christopher 1945- *Who 94*
Thomas, Howard Johnston 1926- *WhoAmP 93*
Thomas, Howard Paul 1942- *WhoAm 94, WhoWest 94*
Thomas, Howell Moore 1906- *WhoAmP 93*
Thomas, Hugh *Who 94, WhoHol 92*
Thomas, Hugh d1981 *WhoHol 92*
Thomas, Hugh 1931- *WrDr 94*
Thomas, Hugh Owen 1834-1891 *DcNaB MP*
Thomas, Ian d1993 *NewYTBS 93*
Thomas, Ian Leslie Maurice 1937- *WhoAm 94*
Thomas, Irving 1966- *WhoBlA 94*
Thomas, Isaac Daniel, Jr. 1939- *WhoBlA 94*
Thomas, Isaiah 1749-1831 *WhAmRev*
Thomas, Isiah 1961- *BasBi*
Thomas, Isiah Lord, III 1961- *WhoAm 94, WhoBlA 94, WhoMW 93*
Thomas, Ivor 1905- *WrDr 94*
Thomas, Ivor Bulmer 1905- *IntWW 93*
Thomas, J. Earl 1918- *WhoAm 94*
Thomas, Jack c. 1850- *EncNAR*
Thomas, Jack E. *WhoFI 94*
Thomas, Jack H. 1941- *WhoAm 94, WhoFI 94*
Thomas, Jack Ward 1934- *WhoScEn 94, WhoWest 94*
Thomas, Jacqueline Marie 1952- *WhoBlA 94*
Thomas, Jacquelyn Small 1938- *WhoBlA 94*
Thomas, James *DrAPF 93*
Thomas, James (Son) 1926-1993 *NewYTBS 93 [port]*
Thomas, James Bert, Jr. 1935- *WhoAm 94*
Thomas, James Brown 1922- *WhoIns 94*
Thomas, James Edward, Jr. 1950- *WhoFI 94*
Thomas, James Gladwyn 1901-1990 *WhAm 10*
Thomas, James Gordon 1946- *WhoWest 94*
Thomas, James Henry, III 1960- *WhoWest 94*
Thomas, James Joseph, II 1951- *WhoAmL 94*
Thomas, James L. 1946- *WhoBlA 94*
Thomas, James Lou[illegible] 1943- *WhoAmP 93*
Thomas, James Lyle 1946- *WhoAmP 93*
Thomas, James O., Jr. 1930- *WhoBlA 94*
Thomas, James Raymond 1947- *WhoFI 94*
Thomas, James Ritter, Jr. 1950- *WhoFI 94*
Thomas, James Russell, Jr. 1941- *WhoAm 94*
Thomas, James Samuel 1919- *WhoBlA 94*
Thomas, James Talbert, IV 1951- *WhoAmL 94*
Thomas, James William 1949- *WhoAmL 94, WhoMW 93*
Thomas, Jameson d1939 *WhoHol 92*
Thomas, Janet Marie *WhoFI 94*
Thomas, Janice Morrell 1946- *WhoBlA 94*
Thomas, Janice Norine Ragon 1930- *WhoMW 93*
Thomas, Janis P. 1954- *WhoBlA 94*
Thomas, Jay *WhoHol 92*
Thomas, Jay 1948- *IntMPA 94*
Thomas, Jean-Jacques Robert 1948- *WhoAm 94*
Thomas, Jean Olwen 1942- *IntWW 93, Who 94*
Thomas, Jeanette Mae 1946- *WhoFI 94, WhoWest 94*
Thomas, Jeffery Michael 1955- *WhoFI 94*
Thomas, Jeffrey Arthur 1964- *WhoMW 93*
Thomas, Jeffrey Scott 1960- *WhoAmL 94*
Thomas, Jenkin 1938- *Who 94*
Thomas, Jeremiah Lindsay, III 1946- *WhoAmL 94*
Thomas, Jeremy *IntWW 93*
Thomas, Jeremy 1949- *IntMPA 94*
Thomas, Jeremy (Cashel) 1931- *IntWW 93, Who 94*
Thomas, Jeremy Jack 1949- *Who 94*
Thomas, Jerold Ray 1966- *WhoMW 93*
Thomas, Jerry Aroe *WhoAmP 93*
Thomas, Jerry Arthur 1942- *WhoMW 93, WhoScEn 94*
Thomas, Jess 1927- *WhoAm 94*
Thomas, Jess 1927-1993 *NewYTBS 93 [port]*
Thomas, Jess (Floyd) 1927- *NewGrDO*
Thomas, Jewel M. *WhoBlA 94*
Thomas, Jim *WhoAm 94, WhoBlA 94, WhoWest 94*
Thomas, Jimmy Lynn 1941- *WhoAm 94, WhoFI 94*
Thomas, Jo *WhoHisp 94*
Thomas, Joab Langston 1933- *WhoAm 94, WhoScEn 94*
Thomas, Joan McHenry Bates 1928- *WhoBlA 94*
Thomas, Joe Carroll 1931- *WhoAm 94*
Thomas, John 1724-1776 *AmRev, WhAmRev*
Thomas, John 1922- *WhoBlA 94*
Thomas, John 1927- *WhoAmA 93*
Thomas, John 1941- *WhoBlA 94*
Thomas, John 1946- *WhoMW 93*
Thomas, John Alva 1940- *WhoMW 93*
Thomas, John Anthony Griffiths 1943- *Who 94*
Thomas, John C. 1944- *WhoAmL 94*
Thomas, John Charles d1960 *WhoHol 92*
Thomas, John Charles 1891-1960 *NewGrDO*
Thomas, John Charles 1950- *WhoAm 94, WhoAmL 94, WhoAmP 93, WhoMW 93*
Thomas, John Cox, Jr. 1927- *WhoAm 94*
Thomas, John David 1931- *Who 94*
Thomas, John David 1951- *WhoMW 93*
Thomas, John David Ronald 1926- *IntWW 93*
Thomas, John Davidson 1961- *WhoAmL 94*
Thomas, John Earl 1943- *WhoAm 94*
Thomas, John Edward 1947- *WhoAm 94*
Thomas, John Edwin 1931- *WhoAm 94*
Thomas, John F. 1947- *WhoAmL 94*
Thomas, John Henderson, III 1950- *WhoBlA 94*
Thomas, John Hollie 1922- *WhoAmP 93*
Thomas, John Howard 1941- *WhoAm 94*
Thomas, John J. 1923- *WhoAmP 93*
Thomas, John James Absalom 1908- *Who 94*
Thomas, John Kerry 1934- *WhoAm 94, WhoScEn 94*
Thomas, John Melvin 1933- *WhoAm 94, WhoScEn 94*
Thomas, John Meurig 1932- *IntWW 93, Who 94, WhoScEn 94*
Thomas, John Paul 1940- *WhoAm 94*
Thomas, John Richard 1921- *WhoAm 94*
Thomas, John Thieme 1935- *WhoAm 94*
Thomas, John Wesley 1932- *WhoBlA 94*
Thomas, John William 1937- *WhoAm 94*
Thomas, Johnny B. 1953- *WhoBlA 94*
Thomas, Jon Roger 1946- *WhoAm 94*
Thomas, Jorge A. 1946- *WhoHisp 94*
Thomas, Joseph d1986 *WhoHol 92*
Thomas, Joseph Allan 1929- *WhoAm 94, WhoAmL 94*
Thomas, Joseph Edward 1955- *WhoAmL 94*
Thomas, Joseph Edward, Jr. 1950- *WhoBlA 94*
Thomas, Joseph Fleshman 1915- *WhoAm 94*
Thomas, Joseph H. 1933- *WhoBlA 94*
Thomas, Joseph H. 1940- *WhoAmP 93*
Thomas, Joseph R. 1935- *WhoFI 94*
Thomas, Joseph W. 1940- *WhoBlA 94*
Thomas, Joseph Winand 1940- *WhoAmL 94*
Thomas, Joyce Carol *DrAPF 93*
Thomas, Joyce Carol 1938- *Au&Arts 12 [port], BlkWr 2, TwCYAW, WhoBlA 94*
Thomas, Juanita Ware 1923- *WhoBlA 94*
Thomas, Kalin Normoet 1961- *WhoBlA 94*
Thomas, Karen P. 1957- *WhoAm 94*
Thomas, Kathleen K. 1940- *WhoAmA 93*
Thomas, Keith (Vivian) 1933- *Who 94, WrDr 94*
Thomas, Keith Henry Westcott 1923- *Who 94*
Thomas, Keith Vern 1946- *WhoWest 94*
Thomas, Keith Vivian 1933- *IntWW 93*
Thomas, Kendall 1957- *WhoBlA 94*
Thomas, Kenneth Glyndwr 1944- *WhoAm 94*
Thomas, Kenneth Rowland 1927- *Who 94*
Thomas, Kenneth Wayne 1939- *WhoMW 93*
Thomas, Kent Swenson 1955- *WhoWest 94*
Thomas, Kurt 1956- *WhoHol 92*
Thomas, L. E. 1925- *WhoAmP 93*
Thomas, Lancelot 1930- *Who 94*
Thomas, Larry D. *DrAPF 93*
Thomas, Larry W. 1943- *WhoAmA 93*
Thomas, Latta R., Sr. 1927- *WhoBlA 94*
Thomas, Laura Marlene 1936- *WhoWest 94*
Thomas, Lawrason Dale 1934- *WhoFI 94*
Thomas, Lawrence Eldon 1942- *WhoAm 94*
Thomas, Lee Daniel 1951- *WhoAmL 94*
Thomas, Lee M. 1944- *EnvEnc*
Thomas, Leo 1947- *WhoFI 94*
Thomas, Leo J. 1936- *WhoAm 94, WhoScEn 94*
Thomas, Leona Marlene 1933- *WhoMW 93, WhoScEn 94*
Thomas, Leroy, Sr. 1923- *WhoBlA 94*
Thomas, Leslie d1967 *WhoHol 92*
Thomas, Leslie (John) 1931- *WrDr 94*
Thomas, Leslie John 1931- *Who 94*
Thomas, Lewis 1913- *IntWW 93, WhoAm 94, WrDr 94*
Thomas, Lewis 1913-1993 *NewYTBS 93 [port]*
Thomas, Lewis Edward 1913- *WhoMW 93*
Thomas, Lewis Jones, Jr. 1930- *WhoAm 94, WhoScEn 94*
Thomas, Lillie 1950- *WhoBlA 94*
Thomas, Linda Craig 1944- *WhoAmP 93*
Thomas, Lindsay 1943- *WhoAmP 93*
Thomas, Liz A. 1946- *WhoBlA 94*
Thomas, Llewellyn Hilleth d1992 *IntWW 93N*
Thomas, Lloyd A. 1922- *WhoBlA 94*
Thomas, Lloyd Brewster 1941- *WhoFI 94, WhoMW 93*
Thomas, Lorenzo *DrAPF 93*
Thomas, Louis Godfrey Lee 1896- *WhAm 10*
Thomas, Louphenia *WhoAmP 93*
Thomas, Louphenia 1918- *WhoBlA 94*
Thomas, Lowell d1981 *WhoHol 92*
Thomas, Lowell, Jr. 1923- *WhoAm 94, WhoAmP 93, WhoWest 94*
Thomas, Lowell Jackson 1892-1981 *AmSocL*
Thomas, Lowell Shumway, Jr. 1931- *WhoAmL 94*
Thomas, Lucia Theodosia 1917- *WhoBlA 94*
Thomas, Lucille Cole 1921- *WhoBlA 94*
Thomas, Lucille Pauline 1935- *WhoAmP 93*
Thomas, Luther Daniel 1946- *WhoAmL 94*
Thomas, Lydia Waters 1944- *WhoAm 94, WhoBlA 94*
Thomas, Mable *WhoAmP 93*
Thomas, Mable 1957- *WhoBlA 94*
Thomas, Madoline d1989 *WhoHol 92*
Thomas, Maldwyn *Who 94*
Thomas, (John) Maldwyn 1918- *Who 94*
Thomas, Margaret 1916- *Who 94*
Thomas, Margaret Jean 1943- *WhoAm 94*
Thomas, Marion May 1935- *WhoMW 93*
Thomas, Mark 1941- *WhoHol 92*
Thomas, Mark Stanton 1931- *WhoAm 94*
Thomas, Mark Stanton 1952- *WhoAmL 94*
Thomas, Marla Renee 1956- *WhoBlA 94, WhoFI 94*
Thomas, Marlin S. 1933- *WhoAmP 93*
Thomas, Marlin Uluess 1942- *WhoScEn 94*
Thomas, Marlo 1938- *IntMPA 94, WhoHol 92*
Thomas, Marlo 1943- *WhoAm 94*
Thomas, Martin 1913-1985 *EncSF 93*
Thomas, Martin 1937- *Who 94*
Thomas, Martin Lewis H. 1935- *WhoScEn 94*
Thomas, Marvette Jeraldine 1953- *WhoBlA 94*
Thomas, Mary A. 1933- *WhoBlA 94*
Thomas, Mary Leath 1905-1959 *WhoAmA 93N*
Thomas, Matt d1981 *WhoHol 92*
Thomas, Maurice McKenzie 1943- *WhoBlA 94*
Thomas, Maxine F. 1947- *WhoBlA 94*
Thomas, Maxine Freddie 1947- *WhoAmP 93*
Thomas, Maxine Suzanne 1948- *WhoBlA 94*
Thomas, Maxwell McNee 1926- *Who 94*
Thomas, Melody 1956- *WhoHol 92*
Thomas, Merrill Patrick 1932- *WhoWest 94*
Thomas, Merritt L. 1926- *WhoAmP 93*
Thomas, Michael *Who 94*
Thomas, (Godfrey) Michael (David) 1925- *Who 94*
Thomas, (William) Michael (Marsh) 1930- *Who 94*
Thomas, Michael Allen 1947- *WhoFI 94*
Thomas, Michael David 1933- *Who 94*
Thomas, Michael Eugene 1951- *WhoScEn 94*
Thomas, Michael John Glyn 1938- *Who 94*
Thomas, Michael Stuart 1944- *Who 94*
Thomas, Michael T. *Who 94*
Thomas, Michael Tilson 1944- *NewGrDO, WhoAm 94*
Thomas, Mitchell, Jr. 1936- *WhoAm 94*
Thomas, Mitchell, Jr. 1952- *WhoBlA 94*
Thomas, Monica Maria Primus 1954- *WhoBlA 94*
Thomas, N. Charles 1929- *WhoBlA 94*
Thomas, Nadine *WhoAmP 93*
Thomas, Nathaniel 1957- *WhoBlA 94*
Thomas, Ned Albert 1943- *WhoMW 93*
Thomas, Neville *Who 94*
Thomas, (Robert) Neville 1936- *Who 94*
Thomas, Nicholas (Jeremy) 1960- *WrDr 94*
Thomas, Nida E. 1914- *WhoBlA 94*
Thomas, Nina M. 1957- *WhoBlA 94*
Thomas, Noreen Carol 1935- *WhoAmP 93*
Thomas, Norman 1921- *Who 94*
Thomas, Norman Carl 1932- *WhoMW 93*
Thomas, Norman Matoon 1884-1968 *DcAmReB 2*
Thomas, Olive d1920 *WhoHol 92*
Thomas, Olivia Smith 1956- *WhoBlA 94*
Thomas, Ora P. 1935- *WhoBlA 94*
Thomas, Orville C. 1915- *WhoAm 94*
Thomas, Owen Clark 1922- *WhoAm 94*
Thomas, Pamela Adrienne 1940- *WhoMW 93*
Thomas, Pamella D. 1947- *WhoBlA 94*
Thomas, Pat Franklin 1933- *WhoAmP 93*
Thomas, Patricia Anne 1940- *Who 94*
Thomas, Patricia Grafton 1921- *WhoMW 93*
Thomas, Patricia O'Flynn 1940-1991 *WhoBlA 94N*
Thomas, Patrick Arnold 1956- *WhoBlA 94*
Thomas, Patrick Herbert 1942- *WhoAm 94, WhoFI 94*
Thomas, Paul *GayLL*
Thomas, Paul 1908- *WrDr 94*
Thomas, Paul Denis 1935- *WhoWest 94*
Thomas, Paul Emery 1927- *WhoAm 94*
Thomas, Paul Irving 1906- *WhoAm 94*
Thomas, Paul Massenna, Jr. 1935- *WhoWest 94*
Thomas, Paula H. *WhoAmP 93*
Thomas, Payne Edward Lloyd 1919- *WhoAm 94*
Thomas, Peter *DrAPF 93, WhoHol 92*
Thomas, Peter 1946- *WhoScEn 94*
Thomas, Peter M. 1950- *WhoAm 94*
Thomas, Peter Marsden 1958- *WhoFI 94*
Thomas, Philip Edward 1878-1917 *BlmGEL*
Thomas, Philip Michael 1949- *IntMPA 94, WhoBlA 94, WhoHol 92*
Thomas, Philip S. 1946- *WhoBlA 94*
Thomas, Philip Stanley 1928- *WhoAm 94, WhoFI 94*
Thomas, Phillip Charles 1942- *Who 94*
Thomas, Piri 1928- *WhoHisp 94*
Thomas, Powys d1977 *WhoHol 92*
Thomas, Priscilla D. 1934- *WhoBlA 94*
Thomas, Quentin Jeremy 1944- *Who 94*
Thomas, R. David 1932- *WhoAm 94, WhoFI 94*
Thomas, R. Lar 1958- *WhoAmL 94*
Thomas, R. P. 1932- *WhoAmP 93*
Thomas, R. S. 1913- *BlmGEL*
Thomas, R(onald) S(tuart) 1913- *WrDr 94*
Thomas, Rachel *WhoHol 92*
Thomas, Ralph 1896- *WhAm 10*
Thomas, Ralph 1915- *IntMPA 94*
Thomas, Ralph Albert 1954- *WhoBlA 94*
Thomas, Ralph Charles, III 1949- *WhoBlA 94*
Thomas, Ralph Dane 1951- *WhoAmL 94*
Thomas, Ralph Philip *Who 94*
Thomas, Ralph Upton 1942- *WhoFI 94*
Thomas, Raymond Jean 1923- *WhoScEn 94*
Thomas, Regina O'Brien 1948- *WhoAm 94*
Thomas, Reginald 1928- *Who 94*
Thomas, Reginald Maurice 1964- *WhoBlA 94*
Thomas, Rene Francois 1929- *IntWW 93*
Thomas, Reno Henry 1922- *WhoAmP 93*
Thomas, Rhonda Churchill 1947- *WhoAmL 94*
Thomas, Rhonda Churchill 1948- *WhoAm 94*
Thomas, Ricardo D'Wayne 1966- *WhoFI 94*
Thomas, Richard *Who 94*
Thomas, Richard 1938- *Who 94*
Thomas, Richard 1941- *WhoAm 94*
Thomas, Richard 1951- *IntMPA 94, WhoAm 94, WhoHol 92*
Thomas, (Anthony) Richard 1939- *Who 94*
Thomas, (William) Richard (Scott) 1932- *Who 94*
Thomas, Richard Dean 1947- *WhoScEn 94*
Thomas, Richard Denison 1933- *WhoMW 93*
Thomas, Richard Glyndwr, Jr. 1932- *WhoAmP 93*
Thomas, Richard Irwin 1944- *WhoAmL 94*
Thomas, Richard James 1949- *Who 94*

Thomas, Richard Lee 1931- *IntWW 93, WhoAm 94, WhoFI 94, WhoMW 93*
Thomas, Richard Stephen 1949- *WhoFI 94, WhoMW 93*
Thomas, Richard V. 1932- *WhoAmP 93*
Thomas, Richard Van 1932- *WhoAm 94, WhoAmL 94, WhoWest 94*
Thomas, Richards Christopher 1942- *WhoFI 94*
Thomas, Ritchie Tucker 1936- *WhoAm 94*
Thomas, Robert (Evan) 1901- *Who 94*
Thomas, Robert Allen 1946- *WhoAm 94*
Thomas, Robert C(harles) 1925-1993 *ConAu 141*
Thomas, Robert Charles 1932- *WhoBlA 94*
Thomas, Robert Chester 1924-1987 *WhoAmA 93N*
Thomas, Robert Dean 1933- *WhoAm 94*
Thomas, Robert Eggleston 1914- *WhoAm 94*
Thomas, Robert Francis 1952- *WhoFI 94*
Thomas, Robert G. 1943- *IntMPA 94*
Thomas, Robert Glenn 1926- *WhoScEn 94*
Thomas, Robert J. 1922- *IntMPA 94*
Thomas, Robert J. 1950- *WhoAmP 93*
Thomas, Robert Joseph 1922- *WhoAm 94, WhoWest 94*
Thomas, Robert Knoll 1933- *WhoFI 94*
Thomas, Robert L. 1941- *WhoFI 94*
Thomas, Robert Lancefield 1909- *WhoWest 94*
Thomas, Robert Lee 1938- *WhoFI 94*
Thomas, Robert Leighton 1938- *WhoScEn 94*
Thomas, Robert Lewis 1944- *WhoBlA 94*
Thomas, Robert Michael 1954- *WhoMW 93*
Thomas, Robert Morton, Jr. 1941- *WhoAm 94*
Thomas, Robert Murray 1921- *WhoAm 94*
Thomas, Robert P. 1941- *WhoAmP 93*
Thomas, Robert Paige 1941- *WhoAmL 94*
Thomas, Robert Ray 1926- *WhoFI 94*
Thomas, Robert Walton 1935- *WhoAm 94*
Thomas, Robert Wilburn 1937- *WhoAm 94*
Thomas, Robin *WhoHol 92*
Thomas, Roderick 1939- *WhoBlA 94*
Thomas, Rodney Lamar 1965- *WhoBlA 94*
Thomas, Roger Christopher 1939- *Who 94*
Thomas, Roger Gareth 1925- *Who 94*
Thomas, Roger Humphrey 1942- *Who 94*
Thomas, Roger John Laugharne 1947- *Who 94*
Thomas, Roger Kent 1953- *WhoMW 93*
Thomas, Roger Lloyd 1919- *Who 94*
Thomas, Roger Meriwether 1930- *WhoAm 94*
Thomas, Roger Parry 1951- *WhoWest 94*
Thomas, Roger R. *Who 94*
Thomas, Roger Warren 1937- *WhoAm 94*
Thomas, Ronald F. 1944- *WhoBlA 94*
Thomas, Ronald Richard 1929- *Who 94*
Thomas, Ronald Stuart 1913- *IntWW 93, Who 94*
Thomas, Rosalind 1959- *WrDr 94*
Thomas, Rosanne Daryl *DrAPF 93*
Thomas, Rosie 1947- *WrDr 94*
Thomas, Ross 1926- *WrDr 94*
Thomas, Ross Elmore 1926- *WhoAm 94*
Thomas, Roy L. 1938- *WhoBlA 94*
Thomas, Roydon Urquhart 1936- *Who 94*
Thomas, Russell Alvin 1939- *WhoFI 94*
Thomas, Ruth Jeanne 1950- *WhoAmL 94*
Thomas, S. Bernard 1921- *WhoAm 94*
Thomas, Sam B. *WhoAmP 93*
Thomas, Samuel 1943- *WhoBlA 94*
Thomas, Samuel 1945- *WhoAmP 93*
Thomas, Sarah Harding 1954- *WhoAmL 94*
Thomas, Scott *WhoHol 92*
Thomas, Scott E. 1953- *WhoAm 94, WhoAmP 93*
Thomas, Seth Richard 1941- *WhoMW 93*
Thomas, Shailer 1936- *WhoMW 93*
Thomas, Sharon *WhoHol 92*
Thomas, Sherri Booker *WhoBlA 94*
Thomas, Shirley *WhoAm 94*
Thomas, Sidney 1915- *WhoAm 94*
Thomas, Sidney Gilchrist 1850-1885 *WorInv*
Thomas, Sirr Daniel 1933- *WhoBlA 94*
Thomas, Spencer *WhoBlA 94*
Thomas, Stanley *WhoFI 94*
Thomas, Stanley B., Jr. 1942- *WhoBlA 94*
Thomas, Steffen Wolfgang 1906-1990 *WhoAmA 93N*
Thomas, Stephanie Grace 1964-
Thomas, Stephen Clair 1952- *WhoAm 94, WhoMW 93*
Thomas, Stephen Douglas 1954- *WhoWest 94*

Thomas, Stephen Paul 1938- *WhoAm 94, WhoAmL 94*
Thomas, Stephen Richard 1938- *WhoMW 93*
Thomas, Steve D. 1951- *WhoWest 94*
Thomas, Steven Joseph 1952- *WhoScEn 94*
Thomas, Stuart Denis 1938- *WhoAm 94*
Thomas, Suzanne Ward 1954- *WhoMW 93*
Thomas, Swinton (Barclay) 1931- *Who 94*
Thomas, Sylvia Ann 1947- *WhoWest 94*
Thomas, Tamara B. *WhoAmA 93*
Thomas, Ted 1920- *WrDr 94*
Thomas, Telfer Lawson 1932- *WhoScEn 94*
Thomas, Terence 1966- *WhoBlA 94*
Thomas, Teresa Ann 1939- *WhoWest 94*
Thomas, Terra Leatherberry 1947- *WhoBlA 94*
Thomas, Thalia Ann Marie 1935- *WhoAmA 93*
Thomas, Theodore (Christian Friedrich) 1835-1905 *NewGrDO*
Thomas, Theodore L. 1920- *EncSF 93*
Thomas, Thomas A. 1919- *WhoAm 94*
Thomas, Thomas Darrah 1932- *WhoAm 94*
Thomas, Thomas T(hurston) 1948- *EncSF 93*
Thomas, Thresia K. 1952- *WhoScEn 94*
Thomas, Thurman 1966- *WhoAm 94*
Thomas, Thurman L. 1966- *WhoBlA 94*
Thomas, Timothy 1962- *WhoFI 94*
Thomas, Tobias Adam 1963- *WhoFI 94*
Thomas, Tom 1932- *WhoFI 94*
Thomas, Tommy 1949- *WhoAmP 93*
Thomas, Towyna d1988 *WhoHol 92*
Thomas, Trevor d1993 *Who 94N*
Thomas, Trudelle Helen 1952- *WhoMW 93*
Thomas, Vaughan 1934- *WrDr 94*
Thomas, Verneda Estella 1936- *WhoWest 94*
Thomas, Vickie *WhoHol 92*
Thomas, Victoria 1934- *WrDr 94*
Thomas, Vincent Robert 1963- *WhoFI 94*
Thomas, Violeta de los Angeles 1949- *WhoFI 94, WhoWest 94*
Thomas, Virginia M. *WhoAmP 93*
Thomas, Vonnie *DrAPF 93*
Thomas, W. Curtis 1948- *WhoAmP 93, WhoBlA 94*
Thomas, W. Dennis 1943- *WhoAm 94, WhoAmP 93*
Thomas, Waddell Robert 1909- *WhoBlA 94*
Thomas, Wade Hamilton, Sr. 1922- *WhoBlA 94*
Thomas, Walter Babington 1919- *Who 94*
Thomas, Walter Gable, Jr. 1953- *WhoMW 93*
Thomas, Warren Hafford 1933- *WhoAm 94*
Thomas, Wayne Lee 1945- *WhoAm 94, WhoAmL 94*
Thomas, Wilbon 1921- *WhoBlA 94*
Thomas, Wilbur C. 1916- *WhoBlA 94*
Thomas, Wilbur Gene 1946- *WhoAm 94*
Thomas, William d1948 *WhoHol 92*
Thomas, William 1935- *WhoBlA 94*
Thomas, William Bruce 1926- *WhoAm 94, WhoFI 94*
Thomas, William Christopher 1939- *WhoBlA 94*
Thomas, William David 1941- *Who 94*
Thomas, William Elwood 1932- *WhoWest 94*
Thomas, William Esmant, Jr. 1958- *WhoWest 94*
Thomas, William Fremlyn Cotter 1935- *Who 94*
Thomas, William Geraint 1931- *WhoWest 94*
Thomas, William Griffith 1939- *WhoAm 94*
Thomas, William Henry, III 1949- *WhoAmL 94*
Thomas, William James Cooper 1919- *Who 94*
Thomas, William Jordison 1927- *Who 94*
Thomas, William Kernahan 1911- *WhoAm 94, WhoAmL 94*
Thomas, William L. 1938- *WhoBlA 94*
Thomas, William LeRoy 1920- *WhoAm 94*
Thomas, William M. 1941- *WhoAmP 93*
Thomas, William Marshall 1941- *WhoAm 94, WhoWest 94*
Thomas, William P. 1937- *WhoAmP 93*
Thomas, William Scott 1949- *WhoAm 94, WhoAmL 94, WhoWest 94*
Thomas, Willie c. 1869- *EncNAR*
Thomas, Wyndham 1924- *Who 94*
Thomas, Yvonne *WhoAmA 93*
Thomas, Yvonne 1904- *WhoHol 92*
Thomas Aquinas, Saint *AstEnc*

Thomas Aquinas, Saint 1225?-1274 *EncCrD*
Thomas Becket *BlmGEL*
Thomas-Bowlding, Harold Clifton 1941- *WhoBlA 94*
Thomas-Carter, Jean Cooper 1924- *WhoBlA 94*
Thomasch, Roger Paul 1942- *WhoAm 94, WhoAmL 94*
Thomasen, Ole 1934- *IntWW 93*
Thomasen, Ole 1934- *IntWW 93*
Thomashefsky, Boris d1939 *WhoHol 92*
Thomashefsky, Howard *WhoHol 92*
Thomasin von Zerclaere c. 1186-c. 1259 *DcLB 138*
Thomasius, Christian 1655-1728 *EncEth*
Thomas King, McCubbin, Jr. 1925- *WhoScEn 94*
Thomasma, Timothy Dale 1954- *WhoMW 93*
Thomas Of Gwydir, Baron 1920- *Who 94*
Thomas of Hales fl. 1250- *BlmGEL*
Thomas Of Swynnerton, Baron 1931- *IntWW 93, Who 94*
Thomas of York c. 1220- *DcNaB MP*
Thomason, Byron 1941- *WhoAmP 93*
Thomason, C. Jo 1937- *WhoWest 94*
Thomason, Douglas Naaman 1949- *WhoAmL 94, WhoWest 94*
Thomason, George Frederick 1927- *Who 94*
Thomason, Jacqueline 1954- *WhoAmL 94*
Thomason, Larry 1948- *WhoAmP 93*
Thomason, Michael Vincent 1942- *WhoAmA 93*
Thomason, Nola Faye 1957- *WhoMW 93*
Thomason, Pamela Jean 1956- *WhoAmL 94*
Thomason, Phillip Brian 1949- *WhoWest 94*
Thomason, Robert 1947- *WhoAmP 93*
Thomason, (Kenneth) Roy 1944- *Who 94*
Thomason, Tom William 1934- *WhoAmA 93*
Thomason, William Edison, III 1965- *WhoFI 94*
Thomas-Orr, Betty Jo 1937- *WhoWest 94*
Thomas-Richards, Jose Rodolfo 1944- *WhoBlA 94*
Thomas-Richardson, Valerie Jean 1947- *WhoBlA 94*
Thomassen, Petter 1941- *IntWW 93*
Thomasson, Dan King 1933- *WhoAm 94*
Thomasson, George Orin 1937- *WhoWest 94*
Thomasson, Patsy *WhoAm 94*
Thomas Topp, Margaret Ann 1951- *WhoMW 93*
Thomas-Williams, Gloria M. 1938- *WhoBlA 94*
Thomborson, Clark David 1954- *WhoScEn 94*
Thombre, Melanie Susan 1953- *WhoMW 93*
Thome, Dennis Wesley 1939- *WhoAmL 94*
Thome, Francis 1850-1909 *NewGrDO*
Thome, Karin 1943- *WhoHol 92*
Thomerson, Tim *WhoHol 92*
Thomet, Dennis Paul 1954- *WhoMW 93*
Thomey, Tedd 1920- *WrDr 94*
Thomi, Lois Joy 1927- *WhoMW 93*
Thominet, Maurice J. 1928- *WhoAm 94*
Thomlinson, Ralph 1925- *WhoAm 94*
Thomlison, Ray J. 1943- *WhoAm 94, WhoWest 94*
Thomlison, Terry Dean 1945- *WhoAm 94*
Thommen, Edward d1977 *WhoHol 92*
Thomopoulos, Anthony D. 1938- *IntMPA 94*
Thomopulos, Gregs G. 1942- *WhoAm 94, WhoMW 93*
Thom Oxford, Julia Rae 1958- *WhoWest 94*
Thompas, George Henry, Jr. 1941- *WhoBlA 94*
Thompkins, Toney d1988 *WhoHol 92*
Thompkins, William Tilton, Jr. 1946- *WhoFI 94*
Thompsen, Joyce Ann 1946- *WhoMW 93*
Thompson *Who 94*
Thompson, Mrs. *NewGrDO*
Thompson, Aaron A. 1930- *WhoBlA 94*
Thompson, Al d1960 *WhoHol 92*
Thompson, Alan 1920- *Who 94*
Thompson, Alan 1927- *WhoAmP 93*
Thompson, Alan Eric 1924- *IntWW 93, Who 94*
Thompson, Albert N. *WhoBlA 94*
Thompson, Albert W., Sr. 1922- *WhoBlA 94*
Thompson, Alden Lloyd 1943- *WhoAm 94*
Thompson, Alexis W. 1850-1923 *EncABHB 9 [port]*
Thompson, Allan Robert 1932- *WhoScEn 94*
Thompson, Allen Joseph 1937- *WhoFI 94*
Thompson, Almose Alphonse 1942- *WhoAm 94*

Thompson, Almose Alphonse, II 1942- *WhoBlA 94*
Thompson, Alvin 1939- *WhoAmP 93*
Thompson, Alvin Brent 1947- *WhoMW 93*
Thompson, Alvin J. 1924- *WhoBlA 94*
Thompson, Andrea *WhoHol 92*
Thompson, Andrew Ernest 1947- *WhoScEn 94*
Thompson, Ann Marie 1956- *WhoScEn 94*
Thompson, Anna Blanche 1914- *WhoWest 94*
Thompson, Anne Elise 1934- *WhoAm 94, WhoAmL 94, WhoBlA 94*
Thompson, Anne Marie 1920- *WhoWest 94*
Thompson, Annie Figueroa 1941- *WhoAm 94, WhoHisp 94*
Thompson, Annie Laura 1937- *WhoWest 94*
Thompson, Ansel Frederick, Jr. 1941- *WhoAm 94, WhoFI 94*
Thompson, Anthony Arthur Richard 1932- *Who 94*
Thompson, Anthony Q. 1967- *WhoBlA 94*
Thompson, Anthony Richard 1931- *WhoAm 94*
Thompson, Anthony Wayne 1940- *WhoAm 94*
Thompson, Arlene Rita 1933- *WhoWest 94*
Thompson, Arnold R. 1935- *WhoAmP 93*
Thompson, Arnold Wilbur 1926- *WhoFI 94*
Thompson, Art, III 1955- *WhoBlA 94*
Thompson, Arthur, Sr. d1950 *WhoHol 92*
Thompson, Aubrey Gordon D. *Who 94*
Thompson, Aylmer Henry 1922- *WhoWest 94*
Thompson, Barbara *DrAPF 93*
Thompson, Barbara Storck 1924- *WhoAm 94*
Thompson, Beatrice *WhoAmP 93*
Thompson, Beatrice R. 1934- *WhoBlA 94*
Thompson, Ben Warren 1945- *WhoAmL 94*
Thompson, Benjamin *WorScD*
Thompson, Benjamin 1753-1814 *AmRev, WhAmRev, WorInv*
Thompson, Benjamin 1918- *WhoScEn 94*
Thompson, Benjamin Franklin 1947- *WhoBlA 94*
Thompson, Bennie *WhoAm 94*
Thompson, Bennie 1948- *CngDr 93, WhoAmP 93*
Thompson, Bennie G. *WhoAm 94*
Thompson, Bennie G. 1948- *WhoBlA 94*
Thompson, Bert Allen 1930- *WhoAm 94*
Thompson, Bert Martin 1928- *WhoIns 94*
Thompson, Bertha Boya 1917- *WhoMW 93*
Thompson, Bette Mae 1939- *WhoBlA 94*
Thompson, Betty E. Taylor 1943- *WhoBlA 94*
Thompson, Betty Jane 1923- *WhoWest 94*
Thompson, Betty Lou 1939- *WhoBlA 94*
Thompson, Bill d1971 *WhoHol 92*
Thompson, Bill M. 1932- *WhoAm 94, WhoFI 94*
Thompson, Bjorn J. 1934- *WhoAm 94, WhoFI 94*
Thompson, Bob d1966 *WhoAmA 93N*
Thompson, Bob 1937-1966 *AfrAmAl 6*
Thompson, Bobby E. 1937- *WhoAmP 93, WhoBlA 94*
Thompson, Bonnie Ransa 1940- *WhoWest 94*
Thompson, Boyd 1921- *WhoAm 94, WhoWest 94*
Thompson, Bradbury 1911- *WhoAm 94, WhoAmA 93*
Thompson, Bradley Merrill 1961- *WhoMW 93*
Thompson, Brenda Smith 1948- *WhoBlA 94*
Thompson, Bretran *WhoAmP 93*
Thompson, Brian *WhoHol 92*
Thompson, Brian John 1932- *WhoAm 94*
Thompson, Brian Seymour 1932- *WhoMW 93*
Thompson, Bruce 1949- *WhoAmP 93*
Thompson, Bruce Edward, Jr. 1949- *WhoAm 94*
Thompson, Bruce Rutherford 1911-1992 *WhAm 10*
Thompson, Bruce Stewart 1944- *WhoFI 94*
Thompson, Butch 1943- *WhoMW 93*
Thompson, C. Nicholas 1954- *WhoAmL 94*
Thompson, C. W. Sydnor 1924- *WhoAmP 93*
Thompson, Calvin A. *WhoAmP 93*
Thompson, Cappy *WhoAmA 93*
Thompson, Carilton Frederick 1924- *WhoAmL 94*
Thompson, Carl Eugene 1953- *WhoBlA 94*
Thompson, Carl William 1914- *WhoAmP 93*

Thompson, Carla Jo Horn 1951-
WhoScEn 94
Thompson, Carlos d1990 WhoHol 92
Thompson, Carol Belita 1951- WhoBlA 94
Thompson, Carol Lewis 1918- WhoAm 94
Thompson, Caroline 1956- ConTFT 11
Thompson, Carolyn A. 1957- WhoAmP 93
Thompson, Carolyn Stallings 1949-
WhoAmL 94
Thompson, Carolyn Wynelle 1939-
WhoMW 93
Thompson, Carson R. 1939- WhoAm 94
Thompson, Cecil, Sr. 1930- WhoBlA 94
Thompson, Charlcie White 1932-
WhoAmP 93
Thompson, Charles Allister 1922- Who 94
Thompson, Charles Curtis 1953-
WhoWest 94
Thompson, Charles Edward 1929-
WhoFI 94
Thompson, Charles H. 1945- WhoBlA 94
Thompson, Charles Lemuel 1839-1924
DcAmReB 2
Thompson, Charles Murray 1942-
WhoAm 94
Thompson, Charles Norman 1922-
Who 94
Thompson, Charles Russell 1938-
WhoMW 93
Thompson, Cheryl Mae 1951- WhoFI 94,
WhoMW 93
Thompson, China ConAu 43NR
Thompson, Christopher WhoHol 92
Thompson, Christopher (Peile) 1944-
Who 94
Thompson, Christopher John 1964-
WhoWest 94
Thompson, Christopher Noel 1932-
Who 94
Thompson, Christopher Ronald 1927-
Who 94
Thompson, Cindy Ann WhoHol 92
Thompson, Clarence Miles, Jr. 1929-
WhoAm 94
Thompson, Clarissa J. 1930- WhoBlA 94
Thompson, Clark David 1954-
WhoScEn 94
Thompson, Claudia G(reig) 1953-
ConAu 142
Thompson, Clayton Howard 1939-
WhoWest 94
Thompson, Cleon F., Jr. WhoAm 94
Thompson, Cleon Franklyn, Jr. 1931-
WhoBlA 94
Thompson, Cliff F. 1934- WhoAm 94
Thompson, Clifton C. 1939- WhoAm 94
Thompson, Clive Hepworth 1937- Who 94
Thompson, Colin Edward 1919- Who 94
Thompson, Consuelo Connie WhoAmP 93
Thompson, Courtney Ralph 1955-
WhoFI 94
Thompson, Craig 1969- WhoBlA 94
Thompson, Craig Chris 1950-
WhoAmL 94
Thompson, Craig Snover 1932-
WhoAm 94, WhoFI 94, WhoWest 94
Thompson, Dale E. WhoAmP 93
Thompson, Dale Moore 1897- WhAm 10
Thompson, Daley (Francis Morgan) 1958-
IntWW 93
Thompson, Daniel Emerson 1947-
WhoFI 94, WhoWest 94
Thompson, Daniel Joseph WhoBlA 94
Thompson, Danny L. 1951- WhoAmP 93
Thompson, Darrell 1967- WhoBlA 94
Thompson, David d1957 WhoHol 92
Thompson, David 1770-1857 WhWE
Thompson, David 1954- BasBi
Thompson, David Alfred 1929-
WhoAm 94, WhoScEn 94
Thompson, David Allen 1941-
WhoAm 94, WhoFI 94
Thompson, David B. WhoAm 94
Thompson, David Brian 1936- Who 94
Thompson, David Charles, Sr. 1942-
WhoWest 94
Thompson, David Duvall 1922-
WhoAm 94
Thompson, David Elbridge WhoAmA 93
Thompson, David Jerome 1937-
WhoAm 94
Thompson, David L. 1938- WhoAmP 93
Thompson, David M. 1946- WhoHisp 94
Thompson, David O. 1954- WhoBlA 94
Thompson, David Paige 1943-
WhoAmP 93
Thompson, David R. WhoAmP 93
Thompson, David Ralph 1959-
WhoWest 94
Thompson, David Renwick WhoAm 94,
WhoAmL 94, WhoWest 94
Thompson, David Richard 1916- Who 94
Thompson, David Robin Bibby 1946-
Who 94
Thompson, David Russell 1944-
WhoScEn 94
Thompson, David Walker 1954-
WhoScEn 94

Thompson, David William 1914-
WhoAm 94
Thompson, David Wyler 1965- WhoFI 94
Thompson, Deborah Maria 1958-
WhoBlA 94
Thompson, DeHaven Leslie 1939-
WhoBlA 94
Thompson, Dennis Cameron 1914-
Who 94
Thompson, Dennis Frank 1940-
WhoAm 94
Thompson, Dennis Peters 1937-
WhoAm 94, WhoWest 94
Thompson, Dennis Ray 1950-
WhoMW 93
Thompson, Donald 1928- ConAu 140
Thompson, Donald 1931- Who 94
Thompson, Donald Charles 1930-
WhoAm 94
Thompson, Donald Henry 1911- Who 94
Thompson, Donald Mizelle 1963-
WhoAmL 94
Thompson, Donald Roy 1936-
WhoAmA 93
Thompson, Donna Kay WhoAmP 93
Thompson, Donnell 1958- WhoBlA 94
Thompson, Donnis Hazel 1933-
WhoBlA 94
Thompson, Dora Jean 1929- WhoAm 94
Thompson, Dorothy 1894-1961 AmSocL
Thompson, Dorothy (Katherine) 1923-
ConAu 142
Thompson, Dorothy Burr 1900-
WhoAmA 93
Thompson, Dorothy Denise 1953-
WhoMW 93
Thompson, Douglas Evan 1947-
WhoAm 94, WhoWest 94
Thompson, Douglas Maison 1929-
WhoAm 94
Thompson, Duane d1970 WhoHol 92
Thompson, Dwight Alan 1955-
WhoWest 94
Thompson, E. P. 1924-1993 NewYTBS 93
Thompson, E(dward) P(almer) 1924-
EncSF 93, WrDr 94
Thompson, E(rnest) V(ictor) 1931-
WrDr 94
Thompson, Earl Albert 1938- WhoAm 94
Thompson, Edgar Joseph WhoWest 94
Thompson, Edward EncSF 93
Thompson, Edward (Hugh Dudley) 1907-
Who 94
Thompson, Edward Arthur 1914- Who 94
Thompson, Edward Hugh Dudley 1907-
IntWW 93
Thompson, Edward Ivins Brad 1933-
WhoAm 94
Thompson, Edward K., III 1958-
WhoAmP 93
Thompson, Edward K(ramer) 1907-
IntWW 93
Thompson, Edward Kramer 1907-
WhoAm 94
Thompson, Edward Palmer d1993
Who 94N
Thompson, Edward Thorwald 1928-
WhoAm 94
Thompson, Edwin A. WhoBlA 94
Thompson, Elbert Orson 1910-
WhoScEn 94, WhoWest 94
Thompson, Eldon Dale 1934- WhoAm 94
Thompson, Elizabeth WhoHol 92
Thompson, Elizabeth M. 1952-
WhoAmL 94
Thompson, Elwood Nelson 1913-
WhoMW 93
Thompson, Emma NewYTBS 93 [port],
WhoHol 92
Thompson, Emma 1959?- ConTFT 11,
IntMPA 94, IntWW 93, Who 94,
WhoAm 94
Thompson, Era Bell 1905-1986 BlkWr 2
Thompson, Eric 1929- WhoHol 92
Thompson, Eric John 1934- Who 94
Thompson, Eric R. 1941- WhoBlA 94
Thompson, Eric Thomas 1962-
WhoMW 93
Thompson, Ernest Thorne d1992
WhoAmA 93N
Thompson, Ernest Thorne 1897-1992
WhAm 10
Thompson, Ernest Thorne, Jr. 1928-
WhoAmA 93
Thompson, Ernest Trice 1894- WhAm 10
Thompson, Eugene Edward 1938-
WhoBlA 94
Thompson, Eugene George 1948-
WhoIns 94
Thompson, Evan WhoHol 92
Thompson, Flora Jane 1876-1947
DcNaB MP
Thompson, Florence P. d1966 WhoHol 92
Thompson, Floyd 1914- WhoBlA 94
Thompson, Floyd Henry 1951-
WhoWest 94
Thompson, Francesca 1932- WhoBlA 94
Thompson, Francis 1859-1907 BlmGEL

Thompson, Francis C. 1941- WhoAmP 93
Thompson, Francis George 1931-
WrDr 94
Thompson, Francis Michael Longstreth
1925- IntWW 93, Who 94
Thompson, Francis Neal 1940- WhoFI 94
Thompson, Frank 1927- WhoBlA 94
Thompson, Frank Derek 1939- Who 94
Thompson, Frank Joseph 1944-
WhoAm 94
Thompson, Frank L. 1903- WhoBlA 94
Thompson, Frank William 1928-
WhoBlA 94
Thompson, Fred Clayton 1928-
WhoAm 94
Thompson, Fred Dalton 1943- WhoHol 92
Thompson, Frederick d1925 WhoHol 92
Thompson, Frederick 1904-1956
WhoAmA 93N
Thompson, Frederick William 1914-
Who 94
Thompson, French F., Jr. 1953-
WhoBlA 94
Thompson, G. Robert 1924- WhoAmP 93
Thompson, Garfield W. 1916-
WhoAmP 93
Thompson, Garland Lee 1943-
WhoBlA 94
Thompson, Gary DrAPF 93
Thompson, Gayle Ann-Spencer 1956-
WhoBlA 94
Thompson, Geneva Florence 1915-
WhoMW 93
Thompson, Geoffrey Hewlett Who 94
Thompson, George d1929 WhoHol 92
Thompson, George Albert 1919-
WhoAm 94, WhoScEn 94, WhoWest 94
Thompson, George Ellsworth 1945-
WhoMW 93
Thompson, George H. 1928- Who 94
Thompson, George Howard 1930-
WhoMW 93
Thompson, George Lee 1933- WhoAm 94,
WhoFI 94
Thompson, George Louis 1913-1981
WhoAmA 93N
Thompson, George Richard 1930-
WhoMW 93
Thompson, Gerald E. 1947- WhoAm 94
Thompson, Gerald Everett 1924-
WhoFI 94
Thompson, Gerald Francis Michael
Perronet 1910- Who 94
Thompson, Gerald Luther 1923-
WhoAm 94
Thompson, Gerald Raymond 1939-
WhoAmP 93
Thompson, Geraldine WhoBlA 94
Thompson, Geraldine Jean 1931-
WhoMW 93
Thompson, Gilbert (Williamson) 1930-
Who 94
Thompson, Glenn Judean 1936-
WhoAm 94
Thompson, Glenn Michael 1946-
WhoWest 94
Thompson, Gloria Crawford 1942-
WhoBlA 94
Thompson, Godfrey Who 94
Thompson, (William) Godfrey 1921-
Who 94
Thompson, Godfrey James M. Who 94
Thompson, Gordon, Jr. 1929- WhoAm 94,
WhoAmL 94, WhoWest 94
Thompson, Gordon William 1940-
WhoAm 94
Thompson, Greg Alan 1955- WhoWest 94
Thompson, Gregg James 1964-
WhoAmP 93
Thompson, Gregory Lee 1946- WhoFI 94
Thompson, Guy Bryan 1940- WhoAm 94
Thompson, Guy Thomas 1942-
WhoScEn 94
Thompson, H. Bradford 1927-
WhoScEn 94
Thompson, H. Brian 1939- WhoScEn 94
Thompson, Hal d1966 WhoHol 92
Thompson, Harold Fong 1943-
WhoBlA 94
Thompson, Harold Lee 1945-
WhoAmL 94, WhoMW 93
Thompson, Harold Lindsay 1929-
IntWW 93
Thompson, Haydn Ashley 1965-
WhoScEn 94
Thompson, Herbert, Jr. WhoMW 93
Thompson, Herbert, Jr. 1968- WhoAm 94
Thompson, Herbert Ernest 1923-
WhoWest 94
Thompson, Herbert Stanley 1932-
WhoAm 94
Thompson, Herman G. WhoBlA 94
Thompson, Hewlett Who 94
Thompson, Hilarie 1949- WhoHol 92
Thompson, Hilton Lond 1927-
WhoBlA 94
Thompson, Hobson, Jr. 1931- WhoBlA 94
Thompson, Holly DrAPF 93

Thompson, Homer Armstrong 1906-
IntWW 93
Thompson, Howard Who 94
Thompson, (James) Howard 1942-
Who 94
Thompson, Howard Doyle 1934-
WhoScEn 94
Thompson, Howard Elliott 1934-
WhoAm 94
Thompson, Hugh WhoHol 92
Thompson, Hugh, Jr. 1928- WhoFI 94
Thompson, Hugh (Leslie Owen) 1931-
Who 94
Thompson, Hugh Lee 1934- WhoAm 94,
WhoMW 93
Thompson, Hunter S(tockton) 1939-
WrDr 94
Thompson, Hunter Stockton 1937-
WhoAm 94
Thompson, Hunter Stockton 1939-
AmSocL
Thompson, Ian Bently 1936- WrDr 94
Thompson, Ike 1915- WhoAmP 93
Thompson, Imogene A. 1927- WhoBlA 94
Thompson, Isaiah 1915- WhoBlA 94
Thompson, J. Andy 1943- WhoAm 94
Thompson, J. Lee 1914- IntMPA 94
Thompson, J(ay) Lee 1914- IntWW 93
Thompson, Jack 1940- IntMPA 94,
WhoHol 92
Thompson, Jack 1946- WhoAmA 93
Thompson, Jack Edward 1924-
WhoAm 94
Thompson, Jacqueline Anne 1948-
WhoFI 94
Thompson, Jacqueline Kay 1950-
WhoAmP 93
Thompson, Jacqueline Kay 1954-
WhoMW 93
Thompson, James 1932- WrDr 94
Thompson, James Alexander, Jr. 1945-
WhoAmL 94
Thompson, James Burleigh, Jr. 1921-
IntWW 93, WhoAm 94
Thompson, James Charles 1928-
WhoAm 94
Thompson, James Clark 1939-
WhoAm 94, WhoFI 94
Thompson, James Craig 1933- Who 94
Thompson, James David 1945-
WhoAm 94, WhoFI 94
Thompson, James Harold 1927-
WhoAm 94, WhoAmL 94, WhoWest 94
Thompson, James Howard 1934-
WhoAm 94
Thompson, James Kenneth 1926-
WhoMW 93
Thompson, James Kent 1951-
WhoMW 93
Thompson, James Kirk 1953- WhoAm 94,
WhoFI 94, WhoWest 94
Thompson, James Lawton Who 94
Thompson, James Myers ConAu 140
Thompson, James R. 1936- IntWW 93
Thompson, James R. 1961- WhoAmL 94
Thompson, James R., Jr. 1936-
WhoAmP 93
Thompson, James Richard 1933-
WhoFI 94
Thompson, James Robert, Jr. 1936-
WhoAm 94, WhoScEn 94
Thompson, James W. 1943- WhoBlA 94
Thompson, James W., Jr. 1948-
WhoMW 93
Thompson, James William 1936-
WhoAmL 94, WhoWest 94
Thompson, James William 1939-
WhoAm 94, WhoFI 94
Thompson, Janet 1941- Who 94
Thompson, Jay Alan 1948- WhoAmL 94
Thompson, Jean DrAPF 93
Thompson, Jean 1950- WrDr 94
Thompson, Jean Danforth 1933-
WhoAmA 93
Thompson, Jean Marie 1962- WhoMW 93
Thompson, Jean Tanner 1929- WhoAm 94
Thompson, Jeanie DrAPF 93
Thompson, Jeff Who 94, WhoHol 92
Thompson, Jeffrey Douglas 1949-
WhoMW 93
Thompson, Jeffrey Earl 1955- WhoBlA 94
Thompson, Jere William 1932-
WhoAm 94
Thompson, Jesse Eldon 1919- WhoAm 94
Thompson, Jesse Jackson 1919-
WhoWest 94
Thompson, Jesse M. 1946- WhoBlA 94
Thompson, Jim d1977 WhoHol 92
Thompson, Jim (Myers) 1906-1977?
ConAu 140
Thompson, Jimmy WhoHol 92
Thompson, Joan Kathryn 1956-
WhoMW 93
Thompson, Joanna DrAPF 93
Thompson, Joe Floyd 1939- WhoScEn 94
Thompson, Joe L. 1938- WhoAmP 93
Thompson, John 1907- WhoAm 94
Thompson, John 1922- IntWW 93

Thompson, John 1928- *Who 94*
Thompson, John 1941- *BasBi, WhoAm 94*
Thompson, John 1945- *Who 94*
Thompson, John A. *DrAPF 93*
Thompson, John Alan 1926- *Who 94*
Thompson, John Andrew 1907- *WhoBlA 94*
Thompson, John Andrew 1953- *WhoMW 93*
Thompson, John Brian 1928- *Who 94*
Thompson, John Daniel 1927- *WhoAm 94*
Thompson, John Derek T. *Who 94*
Thompson, John Douglas 1934- *WhoAm 94*
Thompson, John Eveleigh 1941- *WhoScEn 94*
Thompson, John Griggs 1932- *Who 94*
Thompson, John Handby 1929- *Who 94*
Thompson, John Henry 1933- *WhoAm 94, WhoMW 93*
Thompson, John James 1942- *WhoScEn 94*
Thompson, John Jeffrey 1938- *Who 94*
Thompson, John Keith Lumley 1923- *Who 94*
Thompson, John Leonard C. *Who 94*
Thompson, John Lester, III 1926- *WhoAm 94, WhoWest 94*
Thompson, John Lewis 1956- *WhoFI 94*
Thompson, John Marlow 1914- *Who 94*
Thompson, John Michael Anthony 1941- *Who 94*
Thompson, John Michael Tutill 1937- *Who 94*
Thompson, John Mortimer 1951- *WhoAmL 94*
Thompson, John N. 1951- *WhoScEn 94*
Thompson, John Reed 1948- *WhoAm 94*
Thompson, John Robert, Jr. 1941- *WhoBlA 94*
Thompson, John Taliaferro *WorInv*
Thompson, John Theodore 1917- *WhoAm 94*
Thompson, John W. *WhoAmP 93*
Thompson, John Walter 1945- *WhoMW 93*
Thompson, John Wesley 1939- *WhoBlA 94*
Thompson, John William 1945- *whoAm 94, WhoWest 94*
Thompson, John William McWean 1920- *Who 94*
Thompson, John Yelverton 1909- *Who 94*
Thompson, Johnnie 1930- *WhoBlA 94*
Thompson, Joseph Allan 1906- *WhoBlA 94*
Thompson, Joseph Earl, Sr. *WhoBlA 94*
Thompson, Joseph Isaac 1922- *WhoBlA 94*
Thompson, Joseph P. 1937- *WhoFI 94*
Thompson, Joseph Warren 1950- *WhoMW 93*
Thompson, Josie 1949- *WhoWest 94*
Thompson, Joyce (Marie) 1948- *EncSF 93*
Thompson, Joyce Lurine 1931- *WhoMW 93*
Thompson, Judith 1954- *ConDr 93*
Thompson, Judith Kastrup 1933- *WhoWest 94*
Thompson, Judith Kay 1940- *WhoAmA 93*
Thompson, Julian *Who 94*
Thompson, (Rupert) Julian (de la Mare) 1941- *IntWW 93, Who 94*
Thompson, Julian Howard Atherden 1934- *Who 94*
Thompson, Julian O. *Who 94*
Thompson, Juliet H. d1956 *WhoAmA 93N*
Thompson, Julius Eric *DrAPF 93*
Thompson, Juul Harold 1945- *WhoAmL 94, WhoFI 94*
Thompson, Karen Ann 1955- *WhoBlA 94*
Thompson, Katherine Genevieve 1945- *WhoAmL 94*
Thompson, Kay 1912- *WhoHol 92*
Thompson, Keith Bruce 1932- *Who 94*
Thompson, Kenneth Lyle 1951- *WhoAm 94, WhoAmL 94*
Thompson, Kenneth N. 1937- *WhoAmP 93*
Thompson, Kenneth W(infred) 1921- *WrDr 94*
Thompson, Kenneth Webster 1907- *WhoAmA 93*
Thompson, Kenneth Winfred 1921- *WhoAm 94*
Thompson, Kevin Odis 1961- *WhoMW 93*
Thompson, Kim 1956- *WhoBlA 94*
Thompson, La Salle 1961- *WhoBlA 94*
Thompson, Lancelot C. A. 1925- *WhoAm 94*
Thompson, Larry Angelo 1944- *WhoAm 94*
Thompson, Larry Clark 1935- *WhoMW 93*
Thompson, Larry D. 1945- *WhoBlA 94*
Thompson, Larry Dean 1945- *WhoAm 94, WhoAmL 94*

Thompson, Larry Flack 1944- *WhoAm 94, WhoScEn 94*
Thompson, Larry James 1960- *WhoAmL 94*
Thompson, Larry Joseph 1955- *WhoScEn 94*
Thompson, Laurence Graham 1920- *WrDr 94*
Thompson, Lauretta Peterson *WhoBlA 94*
Thompson, LaVerne Elizabeth Thomas 1945- *WhoMW 93*
Thompson, Lawrence Franklin, Jr. 1941- *WhoAm 94, WhoScEn 94*
Thompson, Lawrence Hyde 1943- *WhoAm 94*
Thompson, Lawrence L. 1945- *WhoAmL 94*
Thompson, Lea 1961- *IntMPA 94, WhoHol 92*
Thompson, Lee Bennett 1902- *WhoAm 94, WhoAmL 94, WhoFI 94*
Thompson, Leigh Lassiter 1960- *WhoScEn 94*
Thompson, Leonard Allen 1927- *WhoFI 94, WhoMW 93*
Thompson, Leonard Monteath 1916- *WrDr 94*
Thompson, LeRoy, Jr. 1913- *WhoAm 94, WhoFI 94, WhoScEn 94*
Thompson, Leroy B. 1921- *WhoBlA 94*
Thompson, Leslie Melvin 1936- *WhoAm 94*
Thompson, Leslie P. 1880-1963 *WhoAmA 93N*
Thompson, Lillian Hurlburt 1947- *WhoFI 94*
Thompson, Linda Jo 1953- *WhoBlA 94, WhoFI 94*
Thompson, Linda Lou 1945- *WhoAmL 94*
Thompson, Lindsay Hamilton Simpson 1923- *Who 94*
Thompson, Lindsay Taylor 1955- *WhoWest 94*
Thompson, Lionel *Who 94*
Thompson, (Thomas) Lionel (Tennyson) 1921- *Who 94*
Thompson, Litchfield O'Brien 1937- *WhoBlA 94*
Thompson, Lloyd Earl 1934- *WhoBlA 94*
Thompson, Lockwood 1901- *WhoAmA 93*
Thompson, Lohren Matthew 1926- *WhoAm 94, WhoFI 94, WhoWest 94*
Thompson, Lois Jean Heidke Ore 1933- *WhoAm 94, WhoScEn 94, WhoWest 94*
Thompson, Lola May 1931- *WhoMW 93*
Thompson, Lonnie Joseph 1961- *WhoFI 94, WhoMW 93*
Thompson, Loran Tyson 1947- *WhoAmL 94*
Thompson, Loren P. *WhoAmP 93*
Thompson, Loring Moore 1918- *WhoAm 94*
Thompson, Louis Milton 1914- *WhoAm 94*
Thompson, Lowell Dennis 1947- *WhoBlA 94*
Thompson, Luther Howard 1934- *WhoFI 94*
Thompson, Lyle Eugene 1956- *WhoScEn 94, WhoWest 94*
Thompson, Lynn P. 1922- *WhoAmA 93*
Thompson, M. Karen 1947- *WhoAmL 94*
Thompson, M. T., Jr. 1951- *WhoBlA 94*
Thompson, Mack A. 1922- *WhoAmP 93*
Thompson, Mack Eugene 1921- *WhoAm 94*
Thompson, Malcolm Barton 1916- *WhoAmA 93*
Thompson, Malcolm Francis 1921- *WhoScEn 94, WhoWest 94*
Thompson, Marcus Aurelius 1946- *WhoBlA 94*
Thompson, Marcus L. 1940- *WhoAmL 94*
Thompson, Margaret d1969 *WhoHol 92*
Thompson, Margaret M. 1921- *WhoAm 94*
Thompson, Marjorie *WhoWomW 91*
Thompson, Marjorie Ellis 1957- *Who 94*
Thompson, Mark *Who 94*
Thompson, Mark 1952- *ConAu 142*
Thompson, (Owen) Mark 1957- *Who 94*
Thompson, Mark Alan 1957- *WhoScEn 94*
Thompson, Mark Bradbury 1943- *WhoFI 94*
Thompson, Mark Duaine 1956- *WhoWest 94*
Thompson, Mark L. *WhoAmA 93*
Thompson, Mark Randolph 1955- *WhoBlA 94*
Thompson, Mark Wesley 1960- *WhoFI 94*
Thompson, Marshall 1925- *WhoHol 92*
Thompson, Martha Ellen 1947- *WhoWest 94*
Thompson, Martin Christian 1938- *WhoAm 94*
Thompson, Marttie L. 1930- *WhoBlA 94*
Thompson, Mary L. 1938- *WhoAmP 93*
Thompson, Maurice 1604-1676 *DcNaB MP*

Thompson, Mavis Sarah 1927- *WhoBlA 94*
Thompson, Maxine Leak 1938- *WhoWest 94*
Thompson, McKim *Who 94*
Thompson, (Ian) McKim 1938- *Who 94*
Thompson, Mervyn (Garfield) 1936-1992 *ConDr 93, WrDr 94N*
Thompson, Michael (Warwick) 1931- *Who 94*
Thompson, Michael Alan 1964- *WhoMW 93*
Thompson, Michael Greenwood 1940- *WhoAmL 94*
Thompson, Michael Harry Rex 1931- *Who 94*
Thompson, Michael Jacques 1936- *Who 94*
Thompson, Michael John 1944- *WhoWest 94*
Thompson, Michael Warwick 1931- *IntWW 93*
Thompson, Mike *WhoAmP 93*
Thompson, Mike 1942- *WhoAmP 93*
Thompson, Milt 1959- *WhoBlA 94*
Thompson, Milton O. 1926-1993 *NewYTBS 93 [port]*
Thompson, Milton Orville 1926- *WhoScEn 94*
Thompson, Molly d1928 *WhoHol 92*
Thompson, Morley Punshon 1927- *WhoAm 94*
Thompson, Morris Lee 1946- *WhoAm 94*
Thompson, Mozelle Willmont 1954- *WhoAmL 94*
Thompson, Mychal 1955- *BasBi*
Thompson, Myron H. *WhoAm 94, WhoAmL 94, WhoBlA 94*
Thompson, N. David 1934- *WhoAm 94, WhoIns 94*
Thompson, Nancy Kunkle 1941- *WhoAmA 93*
Thompson, Natalie A. 1960- *WhoMW 93*
Thompson, Neil 1929- *WrDr 94*
Thompson, Neil Bruce 1941- *WhoWest 94*
Thompson, Nick d1980 *WhoHol 92*
Thompson, Nicolas de la Mare 1928- *Who 94*
Thompson, Noel Brentnall Watson 1932- *Who 94*
Thompson, Norman Sinclair 1920- *Who 94*
Thompson, Norman Winslow 1932- *WhoAm 94*
Thompson, Oliver Frederic d1993 *Who 94N*
Thompson, Oswald 1926- *WhoBlA 94*
Thompson, Patrick *Who 94, WhoHol 92*
Thompson, (Hugh) Patrick 1935- *Who 94*
Thompson, Patrick Alan 1949- *WhoAmL 94*
Thompson, Paul (Anthony) 1939- *Who 94*
Thompson, Paul Bryan 1924- *WhAm 10*
Thompson, Paul DeVries 1939- *WhoFI 94*
Thompson, Paul Harold 1938- *WhoAm 94, WhoWest 94*
Thompson, Paul Michael 1935- *WhoAm 94*
Thompson, Paul Richard 1935- *Who 94*
Thompson, Peggy Caryl 1949- *WhoAm 94, WhoMW 93*
Thompson, Peter *Who 94*
Thompson, Peter 1922- *WhoHol 92*
Thompson, Peter (Anthony) 1928- *Who 94*
Thompson, (John) Peter (Stuart) 1925- *Who 94*
Thompson, Peter John 1937- *Who 94*
Thompson, Peter Kenneth James 1937- *Who 94*
Thompson, Peter Rule 1943- *WhoAmL 94*
Thompson, Peter Russell 1921- *WhoFI 94*
Thompson, Philip Andrew 1928- *WhoAm 94*
Thompson, Philip Blinn 1954- *WhoMW 93*
Thompson, Philip Mason 1942- *WhoWest 94*
Thompson, Phyllis Hoge *DrAPF 93*
Thompson, Portia Wilson 1944- *WhoBlA 94*
Thompson, Pratt *Who 94*
Thompson, (William) Pratt 1933- *Who 94*
Thompson, Priscilla Angelena 1951- *WhoBlA 94*
Thompson, R. M. *WhoAmP 93*
Thompson, Rahmona Ann 1953- *WhoScEn 94*
Thompson, Ralph Gordon 1934- *WhoAm 94, WhoAmL 94*
Thompson, Ralph Newell 1918- *WhoAm 94*
Thompson, Randall 1899-1984 *NewGrDO*
Thompson, Ray d1927 *WhoHol 92*
Thompson, Ray A. 1953- *WhoHisp 94*
Thompson, Ray Anthony 1953- *WhoFI 94*
Thompson, Raymond 1925- *Who 94*
Thompson, Raymond Edward 1936- *WhoAmL 94*

Thompson, Rebecca *DrAPF 93*
Thompson, Regina *WhoBlA 94*
Thompson, Reginald Aubrey 1905- *Who 94*
Thompson, Rena 1950- *WhoAmA 93*
Thompson, Renold Durant 1926- *WhoAm 94*
Thompson, Rex 1942- *WhoHol 92*
Thompson, Richard (Hilton Marler) 1912- *Who 94*
Thompson, Richard A. 1934- *WhoAmP 93*
Thompson, Richard C. *WhoAm 94*
Thompson, Richard Craig 1945- *WhoAmA 93*
Thompson, Richard Dickson 1955- *WhoWest 94*
Thompson, Richard E., Jr. 1939- *WhoAmA 93*
Thompson, Richard Earl, Sr. 1914-1991 *WhoAmA 93N*
Thompson, Richard Edward 1946- *WhoScEn 94*
Thompson, Richard Ellis 1935- *WhoBlA 94*
Thompson, Richard Frederick 1930- *WhoAm 94*
Thompson, Richard Leon 1944- *WhoAm 94, WhoAmL 94*
Thompson, Richard Paul Hepworth 1940- *Who 94*
Thompson, Richard Stephen 1931- *WhoAm 94*
Thompson, Richard Treadwell 1944- *WhoFI 94*
Thompson, Richard Victor, Jr. 1951- *WhoFI 94*
Thompson, Rita Marie 1930- *WhoWest 94*
Thompson, Riving Benard, Jr. 1948- *WhoFI 94*
Thompson, Robert d1984 *WhoHol 92*
Thompson, Robert (Grainger Ker) 1916-1992 *WrDr 94N*
Thompson, Robert A. 1943- *WhoAmL 94*
Thompson, Robert Allan 1937- *WhoScEn 94*
Thompson, Robert Bruce 1920- *WrDr 94*
Thompson, Robert Campbell 1938- *WhoScEn 94*
Thompson, Robert Charles 1936- *WhoAmA 93*
Thompson, Robert Charles 1942- *WhoAm 94, WhoAmL 94, WhoWest 94*
Thompson, Robert Douglas 1944- *WhoMW 93*
Thompson, Robert Elliott 1921- *WhoAm 94*
Thompson, Robert Eugene 1942- *WhoFI 94*
Thompson, Robert Farris 1932- *WhoBlA 94, WrDr 94*
Thompson, Robert Henry Stewart 1912- *IntWW 93, Who 94*
Thompson, Robert James 1953- *WhoFI 94*
Thompson, Robert James 1962- *WhoScEn 94*
Thompson, Robert L., Jr. 1944- *WhoAm 94*
Thompson, Robert Lee 1945- *WhoAm 94*
Thompson, Robert M. 1927- *WhoAmP 93*
Thompson, Robert M. 1932- *WhoIns 94*
Thompson, Robert McBroom 1928- *WhoAm 94*
Thompson, Robert Norman 1914- *IntWW 93, WrDr 94*
Thompson, Robert Randall 1962- *WhoAm 94, WhoWest 94*
Thompson, Robert S. 1940- *WhoAmP 93*
Thompson, Robert Thomas 1930- *WhoAm 94, WhoAmL 94*
Thompson, Robert W. 1919- *WhoScEn 94*
Thompson, Roderick M. 1955- *WhoAmL 94*
Thompson, Roger Craig 1941- *WhoWest 94*
Thompson, Roger Francis 1933- *WrDr 94*
Thompson, Roland 1950- *WhoMW 93*
Thompson, Ronald Edward 1931- *WhoAm 94, WhoAmL 94, WhoWest 94*
Thompson, Ronald M. 1951- *WhoAmP 93*
Thompson, Ronald MacKinnon 1916- *WhoWest 94*
Thompson, Ronelle Kay Hildebrandt 1954- *WhoMW 93*
Thompson, Rosie L. 1950- *WhoBlA 94*
Thompson, Ross *WhoHol 92*
Thompson, Ross d1972 *WhoHol 92*
Thompson, Roy H(erbert) 1894- *WhAm 10*
Thompson, Roy Lloyd 1927- *WhoMW 93*
Thompson, Roy S., Jr. 1917- *WhoIns 94*
Thompson, Rufus E. 1943- *WhoAm 94, WhoAmL 94*
Thompson, Russell Glenwood 1929- *WhoAm 94*
Thompson, Ryan Orlando 1967- *WhoBlA 94*
Thompson, Sada 1929- *IntMPA 94, WhoHol 92*

Thompson, Sally Ann 1943- *WhoMW 93*
Thompson, Sally Engstrom 1940-
WhoAm 94, WhoAmP 93, WhoMW 93
Thompson, Sandra *DrAPF 93*
Thompson, Sandra Ann *WhoBlA 94*
Thompson, Sandra S. *DrAPF 93*
Thompson, Sarah Sue 1948- *WhoBlA 94*
Thompson, Scott Gallatin 1944-
WhoIns 94
Thompson, Scott Stanley 1957- *WhoFI 94*
Thompson, Senfronia 1939- *WhoAmP 93*
Thompson, Seth Charles 1927-
WhoMW 93
Thompson, Sharon *DrAPF 93,
WhoAmP 93*
Thompson, Shaun Richard 1951-
WhoAmL 94
Thompson, Sheila Roseann 1961-
WhoMW 93
Thompson, Sheldon Lee 1938- *WhoAm 94*
Thompson, Sheree Louisee 1959-
WhoMW 93
Thompson, Sherman Lee 1934-
WhoWest 94
Thompson, Sherwood 1928- *WhoBlA 94*
Thompson, (Humphrey) Simon M.
Who 94
Thompson, Stanley *Who 94*
Thompson, (Reginald) Stanley 1899-
Who 94
Thompson, Stephen *WhoBlA 94*
Thompson, Stephen Arthur 1934-
WhoAm 94, WhoScEn 94
Thompson, Stephen Burk 1946- *WhoFI 94*
Thompson, Stephen Lynn 1953-
WhoAmL 94
Thompson, Stephen Mark 1947-
WhoWest 94
Thompson, Steve 1950- *WhoAmP 93*
Thompson, Steve Delwyn 1935-
WhoAmP 93
Thompson, Steven M. 1949- *WhoFI 94*
Thompson, Steven Thomas 1960-
WhoMW 93
Thompson, Sue Ann 1941- *WhoMW 93*
Thompson, Sue Ellen *DrAPF 93*
Thompson, Susan (Ayers) 1946- *WrDr 94*
Thompson, Susan Jane 1950- *WhoMW 93*
Thompson, Sylvia A. Davis *WhoAmP 93*
Thompson, Sylvia Moore 1937-
WhoBlA 94
Thompson, Tamara 1935- *WhoAmA 93*
Thompson, Tawana Sadiela 1957-
WhoBlA 94
Thompson, Taylor 1919- *WhoBlA 94*
Thompson, Terence William 1952-
WhoAmL 94, WhoFI 94, WhoWest 94
Thompson, Terri Ann 1968- *WhoFI 94*
Thompson, Terry Howard, Sr. 1946-
WhoFI 94
Thompson, Terry Kevin 1961-
WhoMW 93
Thompson, Theodis 1944- *WhoBlA 94*
Thompson, Theodore Kvale 1944-
WhoAm 94
Thompson, Theodore Robert 1943-
WhoAm 94
Thompson, Thomas 1739-1809 *AmRev*
Thompson, Thomas 1913-1993 *WrDr 94N*
Thompson, Thomas Adrian 1944-
WhoMW 93
Thompson, Thomas Henry 1924-
WhoAm 94
Thompson, Thomas Keith 1938-
WhoAmP 93
Thompson, Thomas Martin 1943-
WhoAm 94, WhoAmL 94
Thompson, Thomas Michael 1943-
WhoWest 94
Thompson, Thomas Nolan 1949-
WhoAmP 93
Thompson, Thomas Sanford 1916-
WhoAm 94
Thompson, Thomas Scott 1956-
WhoFI 94
Thompson, Timothy Howard 1955-
WhoWest 94
Thompson, Tina Lewis Chryar 1929-
WhoFI 94, WhoWest 94
Thompson, Tommy George 1941-
*IntWW 93, WhoAm 94, WhoAmP 93,
WhoMW 93*
Thompson, Travis 1937- *WhoScEn 94*
Thompson, Tyler 1915- *Who 94*
Thompson, Ulu d1957 *WhoHol 92*
Thompson, Vance 1863-1925 *EncSF 93*
Thompson, Verdine Mae 1941- *WhoAm 94*
Thompson, Verla Darlene 1932-
WhoAmP 93
Thompson, Vern *WhoAmP 93*
Thompson, Vernon 1943- *WhoAmP 93*
Thompson, Vernon Cecil 1905- *Who 94*
Thompson, Victor Alexander 1912-
WhoAm 94
Thompson, Victor Montgomery, Jr. 1924-
WhoAm 94
Thompson, Victoria *WhoHol 92*

Thompson, Virginia Lou 1928-
WhoWest 94
Thompson, Vivian L. 1911- *WrDr 94*
Thompson, W. Randolph 1946-
WhoAmL 94
Thompson, W. Reid 1924- *WhoFI 94*
Thompson, Wade Francis Bruce 1940-
WhoAm 94
Thompson, Wade Marshall 1959-
WhoWest 94
Thompson, Wade S. 1946- *WhoAmA 93*
Thompson, Walker d1922 *WhoHol 92*
Thompson, Walter 1946- *WhoHol 92*
Thompson, Walter Whitcomb 1882-1948
WhoAmA 93N
Thompson, Warren S. 1929- *WhoScEn 94*
Thompson, Webster T. 1954- *WhoMW 93*
Thompson, Wesley Duncan 1926-
WhoAm 94
Thompson, Willard Lee, Jr. *WhoAmP 93*
Thompson, Willard Scott 1942-
WhoAmP 93
Thompson, William 1727-1796 *WhAmRev*
Thompson, William 1736-1781 *AmRev,
WhAmRev*
Thompson, William, Jr. 1936- *WhoAm 94*
Thompson, William B. 1949- *WhoAmL 94*
Thompson, William B(ernard) 1914-
WrDr 94
Thompson, William B. D. *WhoBlA 94*
Thompson, William Bell 1922- *Who 94*
Thompson, William Benbow, Jr. 1923-
WhoAm 94, WhoScEn 94, WhoWest 94
Thompson, William Cannon, Jr. 1938-
WhoAm 94, WhoFI 94
Thompson, William Charles 1954-
WhoAmL 94, WhoScEn 94, WhoWest 94
Thompson, William Coleridge 1924-
WhoBlA 94
Thompson, William David 1921-
WhoAm 94, WhoFI 94
Thompson, William David 1929-
WhoAm 94, WrDr 94
Thompson, William Dean 1950-
WhoAmP 93
Thompson, William Dennison, Jr. 1920-
WhoWest 94
Thompson, William Edward 1948-
WhoAmP 93
Thompson, William Grant 1925-
WhoAm 94
Thompson, William H. d1923 *WhoHol 92*
Thompson, William H. d1945 *WhoHol 92*
Thompson, William Henry 1933-
WhoBlA 94
Thompson, William Irwin 1938-
WhoAm 94, WrDr 94
Thompson, William Joseph 1926-
WhoAmA 93
Thompson, William L. 1951- *WhoBlA 94*
Thompson, William Moreau 1943-
WhoAm 94
Thompson, William N. 1940- *WrDr 94*
Thompson, William Neil 1920-
WhoAm 94
Thompson, William Paul, Jr. 1934-
WhoWest 94
Thompson, William Reid 1924-
WhoAm 94
Thompson, William S. 1914- *WhoBlA 94*
Thompson, William Scott 1930-
WhoAmL 94
Thompson, William Stansbury 1963-
WhoBlA 94
Thompson, William Taliaferro, Jr. 1913-
WhoAm 94
Thompson, Willie Edward 1940-
WhoBlA 94
Thompson, Willoughby Harry 1919-
Who 94
Thompson, Wilmer Leigh 1938-
WhoAm 94
Thompson, Winfred Lee 1945- *WhoAm 94*
Thompson, Winston 1940- *IntWW 93*
Thompson, Winston Edna 1933-
WhoBlA 94
Thompson, Wynelle Doggett 1914-
WhoAm 94
Thompson-Clemmons, Olga Unita 1928-
WhoBlA 94
Thompson-Cope, Nancy L. 1948-
WhoAmP 93
Thompson Hancock, P(ercy) E(llis)
Who 94
Thompson-McCausland, Benedict Maurice
Perronet 1938- *Who 94*
Thompson-Moore, Ann 1949- *WhoBlA 94*
Thoms, Bonnie Anne 1952- *WhoWest 94*
Thoms, David Moore 1948- *WhoAmL 94,
WhoMW 93*
Thoms, Donald H. 1948- *WhoBlA 94*
Thoms, Jeannine Aumond *WhoAmL 94*
Thomsen, Allen Leroy 1942- *WhoMW 93*
Thomsen, Charles Burton 1932-
WhoAm 94
Thomsen, Donald Laurence, Jr. 1921-
WhoAm 94
Thomsen, Ib 1925- *IntWW 93*

Thomsen, John Stearns 1921-
WhoAmP 93
Thomsen, Michael Bernard 1952-
WhoWest 94
Thomsen, Nancy Lee *WhoWest 94*
Thomsen, Niels Jorgen 1930- *IntWW 93*
Thomsen, Pamela Dee 1948- *WhoMW 93*
Thomsen, Thomas Richard 1935-
WhoAm 94
Thomson *Who 94*
Thomson, Adam 1926- *IntWW 93,
Who 94*
Thomson, Andrew James 1940- *Who 94*
Thomson, Archie d1981 *WhoHol 92*
Thomson, Basil Henry, Jr. 1945-
WhoAmL 94
Thomson, Beatrix d1986 *WhoHol 92*
Thomson, Brian 1946- *NewGrDO*
Thomson, Brian Edward 1946- *IntWW 93*
Thomson, Brian Harold 1918- *Who 94*
Thomson, Carl L. 1913- *WhoAmA 93*
Thomson, Charles 1729-1824
WhAmRev [port]
Thomson, Charles LeRoy 1924-
WhoWest 94
Thomson, Charles Wyville 1830-1882
WhWE
Thomson, Colin (H) 1949- *WhoAmA 93*
Thomson, Cynthia Ann 1957-
WhoScEn 94
Thomson, D(aisy) H(icks) 1918- *WrDr 94*
Thomson, Dale Cairns 1923- *WhoAm 94*
Thomson, David *Who 94*
Thomson, David 1912-1970 *DcNaB MP*
Thomson, David 1941- *EncSF 93*
Thomson, (Frederick Douglas) David
1940- *Who 94*
Thomson, David Kinnear d1992
Who 94N
Thomson, David Paget 1931- *Who 94*
Thomson, David Phillips 1942- *Who 94*
Thomson, David Spence 1915- *IntWW 93,
Who 94*
Thomson, Derick S(mith) 1921- *WrDr 94*
Thomson, Derick Smith 1921- *Who 94*
Thomson, Dorothy Lampen 1904-
WhoFI 94
Thomson, Duncan 1934- *Who 94*
Thomson, Edward 1919- *WrDr 94*
Thomson, Elihu 1853-1937 *WorInv*
Thomson, Evan (Rees Whitaker) 1919-
Who 94
Thomson, Francis Paul 1914- *Who 94,
WrDr 94*
Thomson, Fred d1928 *WhoHol 92*
Thomson, Garry 1925- *Who 94*
Thomson, George Henry 1924- *WrDr 94*
Thomson, George Malcolm 1899- *Who 94,
WrDr 94*
Thomson, George Ronald 1959-
WhoAm 94, WhoAmL 94
Thomson, Gerald Edmund 1932-
WhoAm 94, WhoRlA 94
Thomson, Gordon 1945- *WhoHol 92*
Thomson, Grace Marie 1932-
WhoScEn 94, WhoWest 94
Thomson, Harry J., Jr. 1928- *WhoAmP 93*
Thomson, Helen *WhoHol 92*
Thomson, Ian *Who 94*
Thomson, Ian Mackenzie 1926- *Who 94*
Thomson, James 1700-1748 *BlmGEL*
Thomson, James 1834-1882 *BlmGEL*
Thomson, James Adolph 1924-
WhoMW 93
Thomson, James Alan 1945- *WhoAm 94,
WhoWest 94*
Thomson, James Claude, Jr. 1931-
WhoAmP 93
Thomson, James Leonard 1905- *Who 94*
Thomson, James McIlhany 1924-
WhoAmP 93
Thomson, James Miln 1921- *WrDr 94*
Thomson, John *Who 94*
Thomson, John 1805-1841 *NewGrDO*
Thomson, John 1908- *IntWW 93, Who 94*
Thomson, John (Adam) 1927- *Who 94*
Thomson, (Charles) John 1941- *Who 94*
Thomson, John A(idan) F(rancis) 1934-
WrDr 94
Thomson, John Adam 1927- *IntWW 93*
Thomson, John Alan 1950- *WhoAm 94*
Thomson, John Ansel Armstrong 1911-
WhoScEn 94, WhoRlA 94
Thomson, John C. *WhoIns 94*
Thomson, John Rankin 1935-
WhoWest 94
Thomson, John Sutherland 1920- *Who 94*
Thomson, John Wanamaker 1928-
WhoFI 94, WhoMW 93
Thomson, Joseph 1858-1895 *WhWE*
Thomson, Joseph John 1856-1940
WorScD [port]
Thomson, Joseph McGeachy 1948-
Who 94
Thomson, June 1930- *WrDr 94*
Thomson, Keith Stewart 1938- *WhoAm 94*
Thomson, Kenneth d1967 *WhoHol 92*

Thomson, Kenneth James 1936-
WhoFI 94
Thomson, Kenneth R. 1923- *WhoFI 94*
Thomson, Kim *WhoHol 92*
Thomson, Leonard S. 1911- *WhoAmP 93*
Thomson, Malcolm George 1950- *Who 94*
Thomson, Mark 1739-1803 *WhAmRev*
Thomson, Mark (Wilfrid Home) 1939-
Who 94
Thomson, Maurice 1604-1676 *DcNaB MP*
Thomson, Maynard F. 1944- *WhoAm 94,
WhoAmL 94*
Thomson, N. R. *WhoScEn 94*
Thomson, Nigel Ernest Drummond 1926-
Who 94
Thomson, Pat 1939- *SmATA 77*
Thomson, Paul C. 1955- *WhoIns 94*
Thomson, Paul van Kuykendall 1916-
WhoAm 94
Thomson, Peter (William) 1938- *WrDr 94*
Thomson, Peter Alexander Bremner
1938- *IntWW 93, Who 94*
Thomson, Peter William 1929- *IntWW 93*
Thomson, R. H. *WhoHol 92*
Thomson, Richard Harvey 1959-
WhoFI 94
Thomson, Richard Murray 1933-
IntWW 93, WhoAm 94, WhoFI 94
Thomson, Robert 1921- *WrDr 94*
Thomson, Robert George 1949-
WhoWest 94
Thomson, Robert Howard Garry *Who 94*
Thomson, Robert James 1927-
WhoAm 94, WhoFI 94
Thomson, Robert John Stewart 1922-
Who 94
Thomson, Robert Norman 1935- *Who 94*
Thomson, Robert Stephen 1955-
WhoAm 94
Thomson, Robert William 1822-1873
WorInv
Thomson, Robert William 1934-
WhoAm 94
Thomson, Sharon *DrAPF 93*
Thomson, Shirley Lavinia 1930-
WhoAm 94, WhoMW 93
Thomson, Sophia Antoinette 1923-
WhoMW 93
Thomson, Stuart McGuire, Jr. 1945-
WhoScEn 94
Thomson, Thomas (James) 1923- *Who 94*
Thomson, Thomas Harold 1935-
IntWW 93
Thomson, Thomas Harold 1935-1992
WhAm 10
Thomson, Thomas James 1923-
IntWW 93
Thomson, Thyra Godfrey 1916-
WhoAm 94, WhoWest 94
Thomson, Virgil 1896-1989 *IntDcF 2-4,
WhAm 10*
Thomson, Virgil (Garnett) 1896-1989
NewGrDO
Thomson, William 1824-1907 *WorInv,
WorScD*
Thomson, William 1927- *ConAu 141*
Thomson, William Barry 1952-
WhoAm 94, WhoFI 94
Thomson, William Cran 1926- *IntWW 93*
Thomson, William E., Jr. *WhoAmP 93*
Thomson, William Hills 1942- *WhoFI 94*
Thomson, William Oliver 1925- *Who 94*
Thomson, William R. *IntWW 93*
Thomson Of Fleet, Baron 1923-
IntWW 93, Who 94
Thomson Of Monifieth, Baron 1921-
IntWW 93, Who 94
Thon, Melanie Rae 1957- *WrDr 94*
Thon, William 1906- *WhoAm 94,
WhoAmA 93*
Thondavadi, Nandu N. 1954- *WhoFI 94*
Thone, Charles *WhoAmP 93*
Thone, Charles 1924- *IntWW 93*
Thonemann, Peter Clive 1917- *IntWW 93,
Who 94*
Thong, Phing 1963- *WhoFI 94*
Thong, Tran 1951- *WhoAm 94,
WhoWest 94*
Thonnard, Ernst 1898- *WhoScEn 94*
't Hooft, Gerardus 1946- *IntWW 93*
Thor, Jerome *WhoHol 92*
Thor, Larry d1976 *WhoHol 92*
Thor, Linda M. 1950- *WhoWest 94*
Thor, Peter K. 1954- *WhoFI 94*
Thor, Terry *EncSF 93*
Thorarensen, Oddur C.S. 1925-
WhoScEn 94
Thorbeck, Thomas George 1945-
WhoAm 94, WhoAmL 94
Thorbecke, Erik 1929- *WhoAm 94*
Thorborg, Kerstin 1896-1970 *NewGrDO*
Thorburn, Andrew 1934- *Who 94*
Thorburn, Carolyn Coles 1941-
WhoBlA 94
Thorburn, Clifford Charles Devlin 1948-
IntWW 93
Thorburn, David 1940- *WhoAm 94*

Thorburn, James Alexander 1923- *WhoAm 94*
Thorburn, John Thomas, III 1920- *WhoScEn 94*
Thorburn, June d1967 *WhoHol 92*
Thorburn, Wayne J. 1944- *WhoAmP 93*
Thordarson, Agnar 1917- *ConWorW 93*
Thordarson, William 1929- *WhoWest 94*
Thordsen, Kelly d1978 *WhoHol 92*
Thoreau, Henry David 1817-1862 *AmCulL, AmSocL [port], EncEth, EnvEnc [port]*
Thorelli, Hans B. 1921- *WrDr 94*
Thorelli, Hans Birger *WhoFI 94*
Thoren-Peden, Deborah Suzanne 1958- *WhoAmL 94, WhoWest 94*
Thorens, Justin Pierre 1931- *IntWW 93*
Thoresen, Asa Clifford 1930- *WhoAm 94*
Thoresen, Jean Helen 1944- *WhoAmL 94*
Thorfinnson, A. Rodney 1934- *WhoAm 94*
Thorgeirsson, Gudmundur 1946- *WhoScEn 94*
Thorgeirsson, Snorri Sveinn 1941- *WhoScEn 94*
Thorgren, Richard Lee 1949- *WhoAmL 94*
Thorington, John M., Jr. 1943- *WhoAm 94, WhoFI 94*
Thorley, Charles Graham 1914- *Who 94*
Thorley, Simon Joe 1950- *Who 94*
Thorley, Victor *WhoHol 92*
Thorman, Richard *DrAPF 93*
Thorn, Arline Roush 1946- *WhoAm 94*
Thorn, Brian Earl 1955- *WhoFI 94*
Thorn, Donald Childress 1929- *WhoFI 94*
Thorn, E. Gaston 1928- *Who 94*
Thorn, Garvin Beaty 1956- *WhoAmP 93*
Thorn, Gaston 1928- *IntWW 93*
Thorn, George Widmer 1906- *IntWW 93, WhoAm 94*
Thorn, James Douglas 1959- *WhoScEn 94*
Thorn, John d1935 *WhoHol 92*
Thorn, John (Samuel) 1911- *Who 94*
Thorn, John Leonard 1925- *Who 94*
Thorn, John Thomas 1945- *WhoAm 94, WhoAmL 94*
Thorn, Niels Anker 1924- *IntWW 93*
Thorn, Richard Gordon, Jr. 1936- *WhoFI 94*
Thorn, Robert Jerome 1914- *WhoScEn 94*
Thorn, Robert Nicol 1924- *WhAm 10*
Thorn, Roger Eric 1948- *Who 94*
Thorn, Rosemary Kost 1954- *WhoAm 94*
Thorn, Terence H. 1946- *WhoFI 94*
Thornberry, Betty Jane 1946- *WhoAmP 93*
Thornberry, Homer 1909- *WhoAm 94*
Thornberry, Terence Patrick 1945- *WhoAm 94*
Thornberry, William Homer 1909- *WhoAmL 94, WhoAmP 93*
Thornbrugh, C. Michael 1959- *WhoAmP 93*
Thornburg, Dick 1904-1990 *WhAm 10*
Thornburg, Frederick Fletcher 1940- *WhoAm 94*
Thornburg, Lacy H. 1929- *WhoAmP 93*
Thornburg, Lacy Herman 1929- *WhoAm 94, WhoAmL 94*
Thornburg, Newton *DrAPF 93*
Thornburgh, Dick 1932- *IntWW 93, WhoAm 94, WhoAmL 94*
Thornburgh, Richard Edward 1952- *WhoAm 94, WhoFI 94*
Thornburgh, Richard L. 1932- *WhoAmP 93*
Thornburgh, Richard Lewis 1932- *Who 94*
Thornbury, Charlotte R. 1920- *WhoAmP 93*
Thornbury, John Rousseau 1929- *WhoAm 94*
Thornbury, William Mitchell 1944- *WhoAmL 94, WhoWest 94*
Thornby, Robert T. d1953 *WhoHol 92*
Thorndal, John LaFleur 1936- *WhoAmL 94, WhoWest 94*
Thorndal, Nancy Herbison 1930- *WhoMW 93*
Thorndike, Edward Harmon 1934- *WhoAm 94*
Thorndike, Edward Lee 1874-1949 *AmSocL*
Thorndike, John *DrAPF 93*
Thorndike, John 1942- *WrDr 94*
Thorndike, John Lowell 1926- *WhoAm 94*
Thorndike, Joseph J(acobs, Jr.) 1913- *WrDr 94*
Thorndike, Joseph Jacobs, Jr. 1913- *WhoAm 94*
Thorndike, Oliver d1954 *WhoHol 92*
Thorndike, Richard King 1913- *WhoAm 94*
Thorndike, Robert Ladd 1910-1990 *WhAm 10*
Thorndike, Robert Mann 1943- *WhoScEn 94*
Thorndike, Russell d1972 *WhoHol 92*
Thorndike, Sybil d1976 *WhoHol 92*
Thorndike, William Downie, Jr. 1953- *WhoFI 94*
Thorndyke, Helen Louise 1905- *WrDr 94*
Thorndyke, Lloyd Milton 1927- *WhoAm 94*
Thorndyke, Lucyle d1935 *WhoHol 92*
Thorne, Angela *WhoHol 92*
Thorne, Benjamin 1922- *Who 94*
Thorne, Cecil Michael 1929- *WhoBlA 94*
Thorne, Charles Hugh 1923- *WhoAm 94*
Thorne, Christopher (Guy) 1934-1992 *WrDr 94N*
Thorne, David (Calthrop) 1933- *Who 94*
Thorne, David W. 1945- *WhoAmL 94*
Thorne, Dyanne *WhoHol 92*
Thorne, Edward Courtney 1923- *Who 94*
Thorne, Francis 1922- *WhoAm 94*
Thorne, Frank A., Sr. d1953 *WhoHol 92*
Thorne, Geoffrey *WhoHol 92*
Thorne, George d1922 *WhoHol 92*
Thorne, Guy 1874-1923 *EncSF 93*
Thorne, Ian *EncSF 93*
Thorne, Jerrold Lewis 1929- *WhoAmP 93*
Thorne, John (H.) 1943- *WrDr 94*
Thorne, John Carl 1943- *WhoMW 93*
Thorne, John Reinecke 1926- *WhoAm 94*
Thorne, John Watson, III 1934- *WhoAm 94*
Thorne, Kip Stephen 1940- *IntWW 93, WhoAm 94, WhoScEn 94, WhoWest 94*
Thorne, Mike 1940- *WhoAmP 93*
Thorne, Neil Gordon 1932- *Who 94*
Thorne, Nellie d1960 *WhoHol 92*
Thorne, Nicholas Christian Kruuse 1953- *WhoAm 94*
Thorne, Nicola *WrDr 94*
Thorne, Oakleigh Blakeman 1932- *WhoAm 94, WhoFI 94*
Thorne, Peter (Francis) 1914- *Who 94*
Thorne, Richard d1957 *WhoHol 92*
Thorne, Richard Mansergh 1942- *WhoAm 94*
Thorne, Robert d1965 *WhoHol 92*
Thorne, Robert 1954- *WhoAmL 94*
Thorne, Robin Horton John 1917- *Who 94*
Thorne, Sabina *DrAPF 93*
Thorne, Stanley George 1918- *Who 94*
Thorne, W. L. d1948 *WhoHol 92*
Thornell, Jack Randolph 1939- *WhoAm 94*
Thornell, Richard Paul 1936- *WhoAmL 94, WhoBlA 94*
Thornely, Gervase Michael Cobham 1918- *Who 94*
Thorner, Michael Oliver 1945- *WhoAm 94*
Thorner, Peter 1943- *WhoAm 94, WhoFI 94*
Thorne-Smith, Courtney 1967- *WhoHol 92*
Thorne-Thomsen, Ruth T. 1943- *WhoAmA 93*
Thorne-Thomsen, Thomas 1949- *WhoAm 94*
Thorneycroft, Baron 1909- *Who 94*
Thorneycroft, (George Edward) Peter 1909- *IntWW 93*
Thorngate, John Hill 1935- *WhoWest 94*
Thornhill, Adrine Virginia 1945- *WhoBlA 94*
Thornhill, Andrew Robert 1943- *Who 94*
Thornhill, Arthur Horace, Jr. 1924- *IntWW 93, WhoAm 94*
Thornhill, Claude d1965 *WhoHol 92*
Thornhill, Edmund Basil 1898- *Who 94*
Thornhill, Georgia L. 1925- *WhoBlA 94*
Thornhill, Herbert Louis *WhoBlA 94*
Thornhill, James 1675?-1734 *NewGrDO*
Thornhill, Jan 1955- *SmATA 77 [port]*
Thornhill, Paula Georgia 1958- *WhoMW 93*
Thornhill, Robert Gordon, Jr. 1948- *WhoAmL 94*
Thorning-Petersen, Rudolph 1927- *Who 94*
Thorning Petersen, Rudolph Anton 1927- *IntWW 93*
Thornley, Wendy Ann 1948- *WhoAmA 93*
Thornlow, Carolyn 1954- *WhoAmL 94*
Thorns, John Cyril, Jr. 1926- *WhoAmA 93*
Thorns, Odail, Jr. 1943- *WhoBlA 94*
Thornsjo, Douglas Fredric 1927- *WhoWest 94*
Thornton, Abraham c. 1793-1860 *DcNaB MP*
Thornton, Alan *WhoFI 94*
Thornton, Alice 1626-1707 *DcNaB MP*
Thornton, Allan Charles 1949- *Who 94*
Thornton, Andre 1949- *WhoBlA 94*
Thornton, Anthony Christopher Lawrence 1947- *Who 94*
Thornton, Barry F. 1947- *WhoAmL 94*
Thornton, Bruce H. 1936- *WhoIns 94*
Thornton, Cameron Mitchell 1954- *WhoFI 94*
Thornton, Charles Victor 1915- *WhoAm 94*
Thornton, Charles Victor 1942- *WhoAmL 94*
Thornton, Clarence Gould 1925- *WhoAm 94*
Thornton, Clifford E. 1936- *WhoBlA 94*
Thornton, Clinton L. 1907- *WhoBlA 94*
Thornton, Clive Edward Ian 1929- *IntWW 93, Who 94*
Thornton, Colleen Bridget 1948- *WhoMW 93*
Thornton, Cora Ann Barringer 1941- *WhoBlA 94*
Thornton, Cornelius *WhoBlA 94*
Thornton, D. McCarty 1947- *WhoAmL 94*
Thornton, D. Whitney, II 1946- *WhoAm 94*
Thornton, Dean Dickson 1929- *WhoAm 94, WhoFI 94, WhoWest 94*
Thornton, Don Ray *DrAPF 93*
Thornton, Dozier W. 1928- *WhoBlA 94*
Thornton, Earl Arthur 1936- *WhoScEn 94*
Thornton, Edmund B. 1930- *WhoMW 93*
Thornton, Edmund Braxton 1930- *WhoAmP 93*
Thornton, Edna 1875-1964 *NewGrDO*
Thornton, Edward Lawrence 1951- *WhoAmL 94*
Thornton, Frank 1921- *WhoHol 92*
Thornton, George Morriss d1989 *WhoHol 92*
Thornton, Gladys d1964 *WhoHol 92*
Thornton, Hall *EncSF 93*
Thornton, Helen Ann Elizabeth *Who 94*
Thornton, Henry 1750-1818 *DcNaB MP*
Thornton, Ivan Tyrone 1961- *WhoBlA 94*
Thornton, J. Duke 1944- *WhoWest 94*
Thornton, J. Edward 1907- *WhoAm 94*
Thornton, J. Ronald 1939- *WhoFI 94, WhoScEn 94*
Thornton, Jack Edward Clive 1915- *Who 94*
Thornton, Jack Nelson 1932- *WhoAm 94, WhoWest 94*
Thornton, Jackie C. 1960- *WhoBlA 94*
Thornton, James Francis, III 1959- *WhoAmL 94*
Thornton, James Ivan, Jr. 1944- *WhoAm 94*
Thornton, James Scott 1941- *WhoWest 94*
Thornton, Jimmy 1932- *WhoAmP 93*
Thornton, John C. 1940- *WhoBlA 94*
Thornton, John Henry 1930- *Who 94*
Thornton, John Leonard 1913 *WrDr 94*
Thornton, John S., IV *WhoWest 94*
Thornton, John T. 1937- *WhoAm 94*
Thornton, John Vincent 1924- *WhoAm 94*
Thornton, John W., Sr. 1928- *WhoAmL 94*
Thornton, John William 1921-1992 *WhAm 10*
Thornton, Joseph Scott 1936- *WhoAm 94, WhoFI 94, WhoScEn 94*
Thornton, Kathryn C. 1952- *WhoScEn 94*
Thornton, Kevin 1969- *WhoBlA 94*
Thornton, Larry Lee 1937- *WhoAm 94*
Thornton, Laurie Anne 1962- *WhoWest 94*
Thornton, Lawrence 1937- *WrDr 94*
Thornton, Leland Wilbur 1933- *WhoMW 93*
Thornton, Leo Maze 1922- *WhoWest 94*
Thornton, Leonard (Whitmore) 1916- *Who 94*
Thornton, Leslie Eileen 1953- *WhoWest 94*
Thornton, M. Robert 1951- *WhoAmL 94*
Thornton, Malcolm *Who 94*
Thornton, (George) Malcolm 1939- *Who 94*
Thornton, Margaret *NewGrDO*
Thornton, Mark 1960- *ConAu 141*
Thornton, Matthew 1714-1803 *WhAmRev*
Thornton, Maurice 1930- *WhoBlA 94*
Thornton, Michael 1941- *WrDr 94*
Thornton, Neil Ross 1950- *Who 94*
Thornton, Osie M. 1939- *WhoBlA 94*
Thornton, Peter (Eustace) 1917- *Who 94*
Thornton, Peter (Kai) 1925- *ConAu 43NR*
Thornton, Peter Brittin 1949- *WhoScEn 94*
Thornton, Peter Kai 1925- *Who 94*
Thornton, Peter Ribblesdale 1946- *Who 94*
Thornton, Ray 1928- *CngDr 93, WhoAm 94, WhoAmP 93*
Thornton, Richard d1936 *WhoHol 92*
Thornton, Richard 1776-1865 *DcNaB MP*
Thornton, Richard Eustace 1922- *Who 94*
Thornton, Richard Samuel 1934- *WhoAmA 93*
Thornton, Robert A., Jr. 1948- *WhoAmP 93*
Thornton, Robert James, Sr. 1943- *WhoFI 94*
Thornton, Robert John 1919- *Who 94*
Thornton, Robert Ribblesdale 1913- *Who 94*
Thornton, Sally *Who 94*
Thornton, Sandi Tokoa 1953- *WhoAm 94*
Thornton, Sigrid *WhoHol 92*
Thornton, Spencer P. 1929- *WhoAm 94*
Thornton, Stafford Earl 1934- *WhoScEn 94*
Thornton, Sydney d1980 *WhoHol 92*
Thornton, Theodore Kean 1949- *WhoAm 94, WhoFI 94*
Thornton, Thomas Elton 1924- *WhoScEn 94*
Thornton, Thomas Noel 1950- *WhoAm 94*
Thornton, Timothy R. 1949- *WhoAmL 94*
Thornton, Valerie Genestra Marion d1991 *IntWW 93N*
Thornton, W. B. *ConAu 41NR*
Thornton, Wayne Allen 1952- *WhoWest 94*
Thornton, Wayne T. 1958- *WhoBlA 94*
Thornton, William Dickson 1930- *Who 94*
Thornton, William E. *WhoAmP 93*
Thornton, William James, Jr. 1919- *WhoAm 94*
Thornton, William Joseph 1930- *WhoAmP 93*
Thornton, Willie James, Jr. 1954- *WhoBlA 94*
Thornton, Winfred Lamotte 1923- *WhoAm 94, WhoFI 94*
Thornton-Sherwood, Madeleine *WhoHol 92*
Thornwell, James Henley 1812-1862 *DcAmReB 2*
Thornycroft, Ann 1944- *WhoAmA 93*
Thorogood, Alfreda 1942- *Who 94*
Thorogood, Bernard George 1927- *IntWW 93, Who 94*
Thorogood, Kenneth Alfred Charles 1924- *IntWW 93, Who 94*
Thorold, Anthony (Henry) 1903- *Who 94*
Thoroughgood, John c. 1595-1675 *DcNaB MP*
Thoroughgood, Myles *WhoHol 92*
Thorp, Benjamin A., III 1938- *WhoAm 94, WhoFI 94*
Thorp, David 1945- *Who 94*
Thorp, David Oliver 1932- *WhoAmP 93*
Thorp, Earl Norwell d1951 *WhoAmA 93N*
Thorp, Edward Oakley 1932- *WhoFI 94, WhoWest 94*
Thorp, Emmy Lou 1931- *WhoMW 93*
Thorp, Grace Fish 1923- *WhoMW 93*
Thorp, James Alan 1953- *WhoMW 93*
Thorp, James Harrison, III 1948- *WhoScEn 94*
Thorp, James Shelby 1937- *WhoAm 94*
Thorp, Jeremy Walter 1941- *Who 94*
Thorp, Mitchell Leon 1910- *WhoAmP 93*
Thorp, Roderick 1936- *WrDr 94*
Thorp, Roderick Mayne, Jr. 1936- *WhoWest 94*
Thorp, Ruth d1971 *WhoHol 92*
Thorp, Sarah Maur *WhoHol 92*
Thorp, Willard Long 1899-1992 *WhAm 10*
Thorp, Williard L. 1899-1992 *AnObit 1992*
Thorpe, Adrian Charles 1942- *Who 94*
Thorpe, Anthony Geoffrey Younghusband 1941- *Who 94*
Thorpe, Betsy Tucker 1956- *WhoFI 94*
Thorpe, Brian Russell 1929- *Who 94*
Thorpe, Calvin E. 1938- *WhoWest 94*
Thorpe, Douglas L. 1937- *WhoAmL 94*
Thorpe, Earl Howard 1936- *WhoBlA 94*
Thorpe, Elwood *WhoAmP 93*
Thorpe, Fred d1899 *EncSF 93*
Thorpe, Gary Stephen 1951- *WhoWest 94*
Thorpe, George d1961 *WhoHol 92*
Thorpe, Herbert Clifton 1923- *WhoBlA 94*
Thorpe, Hilda (Shapiro) 1919- *WhoAmA 93*
Thorpe, Jack Victor 1949- *WhoScEn 94*
Thorpe, James 1915- *IntWW 93, WhoAm 94, WhoWest 94, WrDr 94*
Thorpe, James, III 1942- *WhoAm 94*
Thorpe, James Alfred 1929- *WhoAm 94, WhoFI 94, WhoWest 94*
Thorpe, James George 1951- *WhoAmA 93*
Thorpe, (John) Jeremy 1929- *IntWW 93, Who 94*
Thorpe, Jim d1953 *ProFbHF, WhoHol 92*
Thorpe, Josephine Horsley 1943- *WhoBlA 94*
Thorpe, Judith Kathleen 1951- *WhoWest 94*
Thorpe, Kay *WrDr 94*
Thorpe, Kenneth Earl 1956- *WhoAm 94*
Thorpe, Leon Ferber 1940- *WhoFI 94*
Thorpe, Marjorie 1941- *IntWW 93*
Thorpe, Mathew Alexander 1938- *Who 94*
Thorpe, Merle, Jr. 1917- *WhoAm 94*
Thorpe, Nigel James 1945- *Who 94*
Thorpe, Norman Ralph 1934- *WhoAmL 94*
Thorpe, Otis 1962- *WhoBlA 94*
Thorpe, Otis Henry 1962- *WhoAm 94*
Thorpe, Otis L. 1953- *WhoBlA 94*
Thorpe, Phillip Andrew 1954- *Who 94*
Thorpe, R. Wayne 1954- *WhoAmL 94*

Thorpe, Richard d1991 *WhoHol 92*
Thorpe, Richard 1896-1991 *ConTFT 11*
Thorpe, Stephen Austen *Who 94*
Thorpe, Stephen J. *DrAPF 93*
Thorpe, Sylvia 1926- *WrDr 94*
Thorpe, Trebor *EncSF 93*
Thorpe, Trebor 1935- *WrDr 94*
Thorpe, Wesley Lee 1926- *WhoBlA 94*
Thorpe-Bates, Peggy d1989 *WhoHol 92*
Thorpe Davie, Cedric 1913-1983 *NewGrDO*
Thorpe-Tracey, Stephen Frederick 1929- *Who 94*
Thorsen, James Hugh 1943- *WhoWest 94*
Thorsen, Jon Joseph 1959- *WhoMW 93*
Thorsen, Madge S. 1949- *WhoAmL 94*
Thorsen, Nancy Dain 1944- *WhoFI 94, WhoWest 94*
Thorsen, Richard Darrell 1928- *WhoFI 94*
Thorsland, Edgar, Jr. 1942- *WhoMW 93*
Thorsness, Leo K. 1932- *WhoAmP 93*
Thorson, Alice R. 1953- *WhoAmA 93*
Thorson, James Alden 1946- *WhoScEn 94*
Thorson, James Donald 1933- *WhoAmP 93*
Thorson, James Llewellyn 1934- *WhoAm 94, WhoWest 94*
Thorson, John Martin, Jr. 1929- *WhoAm 94*
Thorson, Lee A. 1949- *WhoAm 94, WhoAmL 94*
Thorson, Linda 1947- *WhoHol 92*
Thorson, Marcelyn Marie 1927- *WhoAm 94*
Thorson, Oswald Hagen 1912- *WhoAm 94*
Thorson, Russell d1982 *WhoHol 92*
Thorson, Steven Greg 1948- *WhoAmL 94*
Thorson, Stuart J. 1946- *WhoAm 94*
Thorson, Thomas Bertel 1917- *WhoAm 94*
Thorsteinsson, Raymond 1921- *WhoAm 94*
Thorstenberg, Laurence 1925- *WhoAm 94*
Thorstenson, Verne E. *WhoAmP 93*
Thorton, Alice 1626-1707 *BlmGWL*
Thorup, Alvin Robert 1952- *WhoAmL 94*
Thorup, James Tat 1930- *WhoMW 93*
Thorup, Kirsten 1942- *BlmGWL, ConWorW 93*
Thorup, Richard Maxwell 1930- *WhoScEn 94*
Thorvald Ericsson *WhWE*
Thor Vilhjalmsson *ConWorW 93*
Thottungal, Francis John 1968- *WhoMW 93*
Thottupuram, Kurian Cherian *WhoMW 93*
Thouless, David James 1934- *IntWW 93, Who 94, WhoAm 94, WhoScEn 94*
Thouron, John (Rupert Hunt) 1908- *Who 94*
Thovson, Brett Lorin 1960- *WhoScEn 94*
Thow, George Bruce 1930- *WhoAm 94*
Thoyer, Judith Reinhardt 1940- *WhoAm 94*
Thraen-Fisher, Annette Christine 1959- *WhoWest 94*
Thrailkill, Daniel B. 1957- *WhoAmL 94*
Thrailkill, Larry T. 1946- *WhoAmL 94*
Thrale, Hester Lynch 1741-1821 *BlmGEL*
Thrale, Hester Lynch Piozzi *BlmGWL*
Thrall, Arthur 1926- *WhoAmA 93*
Thrall, Arthur Alvin 1926- *WhoAm 94*
Thrall, Donald Stuart 1918- *WhoAm 94*
Thrall, Grant Ian 1947- *WhoFI 94*
Thrall, Robert McDowell 1914- *WhoAm 94*
Thrane, Hans Erik 1918- *IntWW 93*
Thrane, Loanne R. 1933- *WhoAmP 93*
Thrane, Waldemar 1790-1828 *NewGrDO*
Thrash, Edsel E. 1925- *WhoAm 94*
Thrash, Patricia Ann 1929- *WhoAm 94*
Thrash, Purvis James, Sr. 1927- *WhoAm 94*
Thrasher, Hugh *WhoAm 94, WhoFI 94*
Thrasher, John 1943- *WhoAmP 93*
Thrasher, Penelope Ann 1954- *WhoMW 93*
Thrasher, Peter Adam 1923- *WrDr 94*
Thrasher, Rose Marie 1948- *WhoMW 93*
Thrasher, William Edward 1950- *WhoBlA 94*
Threadgall, Colin 1941- *SmATA 77 [port]*
Threat, N.E. 1944- *WhoWest 94*
Threatt, Robert 1928- *WhoBlA 94*
Threatt, Sedale Eugene 1961- *WhoBlA 94*
Threefoot, Sam Abraham 1921- *WhoAm 94*
Three Marias, The *BlmGWL [port]*
Three Stooges, The *WhoCom [port]*
Threet, Jack Curtis 1928- *WhoAm 94*
Threlfall, David *WhoHol 92*
Threlfall, David 1953- *Who 94*
Threlfall, John Brooks 1920- *WhoAmP 93*
Threlfall, Richard Ian 1920- *Who 94*
Threlfall, Robert Gorden 1952- *WhoFI 94*
Threlkeld, Dale 1944- *WhoAmA 93*
Threlkeld, Richard D. 1937- *WhoAmP 93*
Threlkeld, Richard Davis 1937- *WhoAm 94*
Threlkeld, Steven Wayne 1956- *WhoWest 94*
Threlkeld-Wesaw, Sallie Easley 1934- *WhoWest 94*
Thribb, E. J. 1940- *WrDr 94*
Thring, Frank *WhoHol 92*
Thring, George Arthur 1903- *Who 94*
Thring, M(eredith) W(ooldridge) 1915- *WrDr 94*
Thring, Meredith Wooldridge 1915- *Who 94*
Thro, William Eugene 1963- *WhoAmL 94*
Throckmorton, Anthony (John Benedict) 1916- *Who 94*
Throckmorton, Clare McLaren *Who 94*
Throckmorton, George c. 1489-1552 *DcNaB MP*
Throckmorton, Joan Helen 1931- *WhoAm 94*
Throckmorton, John 1946- *WhoAm 94*
Throckmorton, Peter Eugene 1927- *WhoMW 93*
Throckmorton, Rex Denton 1941- *WhoWest 94*
Throckmorton, William Robert, Sr. 1923- *WhoAm 94*
Throdahl, Monte Corden 1919- *WhoAm 94*
Throne, Dale Homer 1942- *WhoAmP 93*
Throndson, Edward Warner 1938- *WhoFI 94*
Throne, James Edward 1954- *WhoScEn 94*
Throne, Malachi *WhoHol 92*
Throner, Guy Charles, Jr. 1919- *WhoAm 94*
Throop, Tom H. 1947- *WhoAmP 93*
Thropay, John Paul 1949- *WhoWest 94*
Thrope, B. Michael 1944- *WhoAmL 94*
Thrower, Charles S. 1920- *WhoBlA 94*
Thrower, Ellen *WhoAm 94*
Thrower, Ellen E. 1947- *WhoIns 94*
Thrower, F. Mitchell, III 1968- *WhoFI 94*
Thrower, Julius A. 1917- *WhoBlA 94*
Thrower, Julius B. 1938- *WhoBlA 94*
Thrower, Keith James 1941- *WhoScEn 94*
Thrower, Lee Tobin 1954- *WhoMW 93*
Thrower, Norman Joseph William 1919- *WhoAm 94*
Thrower, Randolph William 1913- *WhoAm 94*
Thrun, Richard William 1941- *WhoMW 93*
Thrush, Brian Arthur 1928- *IntWW 93, Who 94*
Thruston, Charles Mynn 1738-1812 *WhAmRev*
Thubron, Colin Gerald Dryden 1939- *IntWW 93, Who 94, WrDr 94*
Thucydides fl. 5th cent.BC-4th cent.BC *BlmGEL*
Thue-Hansen, Vidar 1944- *WhoScEn 94*
Thuering, George Lewis 1919- *WhoAm 94*
Thuerk, Kathleen Kearins 1933- *WhoMW 93*
Thuesen, Gerald Jorgen 1938- *WhoAm 94*
Thueson, David Orel 1947- *WhoWest 94*
Thuilier, Raymond d1993 *NewYTBS 93*
Thuille, Ludwig 1861-1907 *NewGrDO*
Thuillier, Leslie de Malapert 1905- *Who 94*
Thuillier, Luc *WhoHol 92*
Thuillier, Richard Howard 1936- *WhoScEn 94*
Thulean, Donald Myron 1929- *WhoAm 94*
Thulean, Richard Howard 1943- *WhoMW 93*
Thulin, Adelaide Ann 1925- *WhoMW 93*
Thulin, Ingrid 1929- *IntMPA 94, IntWW 93, WhoHol 92*
Thulin, Lars Uno 1939- *WhoFI 94*
Thulin, Walter Willis 1929- *WhoAm 94*
Thullen, Manfred 1938- *WhoHisp 94*
Thum, Marcella 1924- *WrDr 94*
Thum, Robert B. 1945- *WhoAmL 94*
Thumann, Albert 1942- *WhoAm 94*
Thumma, Samuel Anderson 1962- *WhoAmL 94, WhoFI 94*
Thums, Charles William 1945- *WhoAm 94, WhoFI 94, WhoScEn 94, WhoWest 94*
Thuna, Leonora 1929- *IntMPA 94*
Thunborg, Anders 1934- *IntWW 93*
Thunder, Spencer K 1939- *WhoWest 94*
Thundercloud, John d1987 *WhoHol 92*
Thunholm, Lars-Erik 1914- *IntWW 93*
Thunhorst, Wade Allen 1956- *WhoAmL 94*
Thuning-Robinson, Claire 1945- *WhoScEn 94*
Thunman, Nils Ronald 1932- *WhoAm 94*
Thurau, Klaus Walther Christian 1928- *IntWW 93*
Thurber, Clarence Egbert 1921-1988 *WhAm 10*
Thurber, Cleveland 1896-1987 *WhAm 10*
Thurber, Cleveland, Jr. 1925- *WhoAm 94, WhoAmL 94, WhoFI 94*
Thurber, Cooper Campbell 1944- *WhoAmL 94*
Thurber, Davis Peabody 1925- *WhoAm 94*
Thurber, Donald MacDonald Dickinson 1918- *WhoAm 94*
Thurber, James (Grover) 1894-1961 *RfGShF*
Thurber, James Grover 1894-1961 *AmCulL*
Thurber, John Alexander 1939- *WhoAm 94*
Thurber, Mary Frances 1957- *WhoAmL 94*
Thurber, Peter Palms 1928- *WhoAm 94*
Thurber, Robert Eugene 1932- *WhoAm 94*
Thurburn, Gwynneth Loveday d1993 *Who 94N*
Thurlbeck, William Michael 1929- *WhoAm 94*
Thurley, Jon (Mark) *ConAu 42NR*
Thurlow, Baron 1912- *IntWW 93, Who 94*
Thurlow, David (Michael) 1932- *WrDr 94*
Thurlow, Fearn Cutler 1924-1982 *WhoAmA 93N*
Thurm, Gil 1947- *WhoFI 94*
Thurm, Ulrich 1931- *WhoScEn 94*
Thurm, William Henry 1906- *WhoAmP 93*
Thurmaier, Mary Jean 1931- *WhoAmP 93*
Thurman, Alfonzo 1946- *WhoBlA 94*
Thurman, Allen George 1933- *WhoWest 94*
Thurman, Andrew Edward 1954- *WhoAmL 94*
Thurman, Bill *WhoHol 92*
Thurman, Christa Charlotte Mayer 1934- *WhoAmA 93*
Thurman, Frances Ashton 1919- *WhoBlA 94*
Thurman, Gary Montez, Jr. 1964- *WhoBlA 94*
Thurman, Harold Lane 1934- *WhoMW 93*
Thurman, Howard 1899-1981 *AfrAmAl 6 [port]*
Thurman, Howard 1900-1981 *DcAmReB 2*
Thurman, Judith *DrAPF 93*
Thurman, Karen 1951- *WhoAm 94, WhoAmP 93*
Thurman, Karen L. 1951- *CngDr 93*
Thurman, Kathryn Anne 1964- *WhoAmL 94*
Thurman, Marjorie Ellen *WhoBlA 94*
Thurman, Mark (Gordon Ian) 1948- *WrDr 94*
Thurman, Mary d1925 *WhoHol 92*
Thurman, Maxwell R. 1931- *WhoAm 94*
Thurman, Pamela Jumper 1947- *WhoScEn 94*
Thurman, Panna 1954- *WhoMW 93*
Thurman, Ralph Holloway 1949- *WhoAm 94, WhoFI 94*
Thurman, Randy 1954- *WhoAmP 93*
Thurman, Sam Wesley 1961- *WhoWest 94*
Thurman, Samuel David 1913- *WhoAm 94*
Thurman, Uma 1970- *IntMPA 94, News 94-2 [port], WhoHol 92*
Thurman, William Gentry 1928- *WhoAm 94, WhoScEn 94*
Thurmer, Robert 1953- *WhoAmA 93*
Thurmon, Jack Jewel 1944- *WhoFI 94*
Thurmon, Theodore Francis 1937- *WhoAm 94*
Thurmond, George Murat 1930- *WhoAmL 94*
Thurmond, Michael L. *WhoAmP 93*
Thurmond, Nancy Moore 1946- *WrDr 94*
Thurmond, Nate 1941- *BasBi, WhoBlA 94*
Thurmond, Strom 1902- *CngDr 93, IntWW 93, WhoAm 94, WhoAmP 93*
Thurnham, Peter Giles 1938- *Who 94*
Thurow, Lester (Carl) 1938- *WrDr 94*
Thurow, Lester Carl 1938- *WhoAm 94, WhoFI 94*
Thursby, David d1977 *WhoHol 92*
Thursby, Mary Taylor 1911- *WhoAmP 93*
Thurso, Viscount 1922- *Who 94*
Thurston, A. Donald 1925- *WhoAmP 93*
Thurston, Alice Janet 1916- *WhoAm 94*
Thurston, Bill 1930- *WhoAmP 93*
Thurston, Carol d1969 *WhoHol 92*
Thurston, Charles d1940 *WhoHol 92*
Thurston, Charles Sparks 1934- *WhoBlA 94*
Thurston, Charles Wheeler 1958- *WhoFI 94*
Thurston, Donald Allen 1930- *WhoAm 94*
Thurston, Fred Stone 1931- *WhoFI 94*
Thurston, George Butte 1924- *WhoAm 94*
Thurston, Harry d1955 *WhoHol 92*
Thurston, Jacqueline Beverly 1939- *WhoAmA 93*
Thurston, Morris Ashcroft 1943- *WhoAm 94, WhoAmL 94*
Thurston, Paul E. 1938- *WhoBlA 94*
Thurston, Ralph Lloyd 1952- *WhoWest 94*
Thurston, Rob Jenkins 1957- *WhoFI 94*
Thurston, Robert (Donald) 1936- *EncSF 93, WrDr 94*
Thurston, Ted *WhoHol 92*
Thurston, Thea *Who 94*
Thurston, William A. 1944- *WhoBlA 94*
Thurston, William Paul 1946- *WhoAm 94*
Thurston, William Richardson 1920- *WhoFI 94, WhoScEn 94, WhoWest 94*
Thurswell, Gerald Elliott 1944- *WhoAmL 94, WhoMW 93*
Thursz, Daniel 1929- *WhoAm 94*
Thutmose, III c. 1500BC-1436BC *HisWorL [port]*
Thwaite, Ann (Barbara) 1932- *WrDr 94*
Thwaite, Ann (Barbara Harrop) 1932- *ConAu 41NR*
Thwaite, Ann Barbara 1932- *Who 94*
Thwaite, Anthony (Simon) 1930- *ConAu 41NR, WrDr 94*
Thwaite, Anthony Simon 1930- *Who 94*
Thwaites, Bryan 1923- *Who 94*
Thwaites, Charles Winstanley 1904- *WhoAmA 93*
Thwaites, Jacqueline Ann 1931- *Who 94*
Thwaites, Ronald 1946- *Who 94*
Thwaites, Roy 1931- *Who 94*
Thwing, Kirby R. 1918- *WhoAmP 93*
Thyateira And Great Britain, Archbishop of *Who 94*
Thyden, James Eskel 1939- *WhoWest 94*
Thyen, Herbert Edward 1912- *WhoFI 94*
Thyen, James C. 1943- *WhoFI 94*
Thyen, John T. *WhoFI 94*
Thyen, Ronald J. 1937- *WhoFI 94*
Thygesen, Jacob Christoffer 1901- *IntWW 93*
Thyne, Malcolm Tod 1942- *Who 94*
Thynn *Who 94*
Thynn, Alexander *Who 94*
Thynn, Alexander (George) 1932- *WrDr 94*
Thynne, John Corelli James 1931- *Who 94*
Thynne, Thomas *WhAmRev*
Thyssen, Francois fl. 162-?- *WhWE*
Thyssen, Greta *WhoHol 92*
Thyssen-Bornemisza, Hans Heinrich 1921- *WhoAm 94*
Thyssen-Bornemisza De Kaszon, Hans Heinrich 1921- *IntWW 93, Who 94*
Tiahrt, Todd *WhoAmP 93*
Tiahrt, W. Todd 1951- *WhoMW 93*
Tian Bao 1917- *WhoPRCh 91 [port]*
Tian Chengping 1945- *WhoPRCh 91 [port]*
Tian Congming 1943- *WhoPRCh 91 [port]*
Tian Ding *WhoPRCh 91*
Tian Fengshan *WhoPRCh 91*
Tian Fu *WhoPRCh 91*
Tian Fuda *WhoPRCh 91 [port]*
Tian Futing *WhoPRCh 91*
Tiangco, Eddie Eugenio 1941- *WhoAsA 94*
Tian Guangtao 1921- *WhoPRCh 91 [port]*
Tian Jin *WhoPRCh 91*
Tian Jiyun 1929- *IntWW 93, WhoPRCh 91 [port]*
Tian Maijiu 1940- *WhoPRCh 91 [port]*
Tian Min 1927- *WhoPRCh 91 [port]*
Tian Rukang *WhoPRCh 91*
Tian Shiguang 1916- *WhoPRCh 91 [port]*
Tian Xueyuan *WhoPRCh 91*
Tian Yimin *WhoPRCh 91*
Tian Ying 1924- *WhoPRCh 91 [port]*
Tian Yinong *WhoPRCh 91 [port]*
Tian Yuan 1954- *WhoPRCh 91 [port]*
Tian Yumei 1965- *WhoPRCh 91 [port]*
Tian Zengpei 1930- *IntWW 93, WhoPRCh 91 [port]*
Tian Zhaowu 1927- *IntWW 93, WhoPRCh 91 [port]*
Tian Zhuangzhuang *WhoPRCh 91*
Tiarks, Henry Frederic 1900- *Who 94*
Tiawit fl. 19th cent.- *EncNAR*
Tiazza, Dario d1974 *WhoHol 92*
Tibaldi, Giuseppe (Luigi) 1729-c. 1790 *NewGrDO*
Tibber, Anthony Harris 1926- *Who 94*
Tibber, Robert 1929- *WrDr 94*
Tibber, Rosemary 1929- *WrDr 94*
Tibbets, Robin Frank 1924- *WhoAm 94, WhoWest 94*
Tibbett, Lawrence d1960 *WhoHol 92*
Tibbett, Lawrence 1896-1960 *NewGrDO*
Tibbetts, Fred W. 1928- *WhoFI 94*
Tibbetts, Gary George 1939- *WhoMW 93*
Tibbetts, Orlando L. 1919- *WrDr 94*
Tibbetts, Pamela Lee *WhoMW 93*
Tibbits, David (Stanley) 1911- *Who 94*
Tibbitts, Samuel John 1924- *WhoAm 94, WhoFI 94, WhoWest 94*
Tibbitts, Theodore William 1929- *WhoAm 94*
Tibble, Douglas Clair 1952- *WhoAm 94*

Tillinghast, Charles Carpenter, III 1936- *WhoAm 94*
Tillinghast, David *DrAPF 93*
Tillinghast, David Rollhaus 1930- *WhoAm 94*
Tillinghast, John Avery 1927- *WhoAm 94*
Tillinghast, Richard *DrAPF 93*
Tillinghast, Richard 1940- *WrDr 94*
Tillion, Clem Vincent 1925- *WhoAmP 93*
Tillis, Frederick C. 1930- *WhoBlA 94*
Tillis, Mel *WhoHol 92*
Tillis, Melvin 1932- *WhoAm 94*
Tillis, Pam 1957- *WhoAm 94*
Tillman, Barrett 1948- *WrDr 94*
Tillman, Caroline Elizabeth 1927- *WhoMW 93*
Tillman, Cedric *WhoBlA 94*
Tillman, Christine L. 1952- *WhoBlA 94*
Tillman, Dorothy 1948- *WhoAmP 93*
Tillman, E. C. 1926- *WhoAmP 93*
Tillman, Henry Barrett 1948- *WhoWest 94*
Tillman, Jacqueline 1944- *WhoHisp 94*
Tillman, Joseph Nathaniel 1926- *WhoBlA 94, WhoWest 94*
Tillman, Lauralee Agnes 1951- *WhoFI 94*
Tillman, Lawyer James, Jr. 1966- *WhoBlA 94*
Tillman, Lillian G. 1934- *WhoBlA 94*
Tillman, Mary A. T. 1935- *WhoBlA 94*
Tillman, Massie Monroe 1937- *WhoAmL 94*
Tillman, Mayre Lutha 1928- *WhoAmP 93*
Tillman, Michael Gerard 1951- *WhoAmL 94*
Tillman, Murray Howell 1940- *WhoAm 94*
Tillman, Myron Edgar 1932- *WhoAmP 93*
Tillman, Patricia Ann *WhoAmA 93*
Tillman, Paula Sellars 1949- *WhoBlA 94*
Tillman, Robert John 1948- *WhoMW 93*
Tillman, Rollie, Jr. 1933- *WhoAm 94*
Tillman, Talmadge Calvin, Jr. 1925- *WhoBlA 94*
Tillman, Wheeler Mellette 1941- *WhoAmP 93*
Tillmon-Mallory, Bobbi 1952- *WhoAmL 94*
Tillon, Charles 1897-1993 *NewYTBS 93 [port]*
Tillotson, Carolyn *WhoAmP 93*
Tillotson, David F. 1943- *WhoAmL 94*
Tillotson, Dwight Keith 1951- *WhoScEn 94*
Tillotson, Frank Lee 1941- *WhoAm 94*
Tillotson, Henry Michael 1928- *Who 94*
Tillotson, John Robert *WhoHol 92*
Tillotson, Johnny 1939- *WhoHol 92*
Tillotson, Kathleen Mary 1906- *Who 94*
Tillsley, Bramwell Harold 1931- *Who 94*
Tillson, John Bradford, Jr. 1944- *WhoAm 94, WhoMW 93*
Tilly, Anne Petersen 1915- *WhoAmP 93*
Tilly, Earl F. 1934- *WhoAmP 93*
Tilly, Jennifer 1962- *WhoHol 92*
Tilly, Meg 1960- *IntMPA 94, WhoHol 92*
Tilly, Nancy McFadden *DrAPF 93*
Tillyard, Aelfrida (Catherine Wetenhall) 1883- *EncSF 93*
Tilman, Charles Austin, III 1954- *WhoMW 93*
Tilman, Fred *WhoAmP 93*
Tilman, George David 1949- *WhoMW 93*
Tilmon, James A. 1934- *WhoBlA 94*
Tilms, Richard A. *EncSF 93*
Tilney, Charles Edward 1909- *Who 94*
Tilney, Edmund c. 1536-1610 *DcLB 136 [port]*
Tilney, Guinevere 1916- *Who 94*
Tilney, John (Dudley Robert Tarleton) 1907- *Who 94*
Tilney, William *WhoAmP 93*
Tilney, William Stephen 1939- *WhoAm 94*
Tilotilo, Faoa *WhoAmP 93*
Tilson, Donald Heath, Jr. 1930- *WhoWest 94*
Tilson, Dorothy Ruth 1918- *WhoFI 94, WhoScEn 94*
Tilson, Hugh Hanna 1940- *WhoAm 94*
Tilson, John Quillin 1911- *WhoAm 94, WhoAmL 94*
Tilson, Joseph 1928- *IntWW 93*
Tilson, Joseph Charles 1928- *Who 94*
Tilson, Robert Ray 1932- *WhoFI 94*
Tilson Thomas, Michael 1944- *IntWW 93, Who 94*
Tilsworth, Timothy 1939- *WhoAm 94, WhoWest 94*
Tiltman, John Hessell 1894-1982 *DcNaB MP*
Tilton, Charlene 1958- *WhoHol 92*
Tilton, David Lloyd 1926- *WhoAm 94, WhoFI 94*
Tilton, Edwin Booth d1926 *WhoHol 92*
Tilton, Elmira F. 1950- *WhoAmP 93*
Tilton, George Robert 1923- *WhoAm 94, WhoWest 94*
Tilton, James 1745-1822 *AmRev, WhAmRev*
Tilton, James Charles 1953- *WhoScEn 94*
Tilton, James Floyd 1937- *WhoAm 94*
Tilton, James Joseph 1942- *WhoScEn 94*
Tilton, John Elvin 1939- *WhoAm 94*
Tilton, Martha *WhoHol 92*
Tilton, Richard N. 1944- *WhoAmL 94*
Tilton, Robert Daymond 1964- *WhoScEn 94*
Tilton, Robert Eugene 1930- *WhoAmP 93*
Tilton, Ronald William 1944- *WhoWest 94*
Tilton, Samuel O. 1944- *WhoAmL 94*
Tilton, Webster, Jr. 1922- *WhoFI 94*
Tilvern, Alan *WhoHol 92*
Tily, Stephen Bromley, III 1937- *WhoFI 94*
Timakata, Fred 1936- *IntWW 93*
Timar, Tibor 1953- *WhoScEn 94*
Timasheff, Serge Nicholas 1926- *WhoScEn 94*
Timberg, Herman d1952 *WhoHol 92*
Timberg, Herman, Jr. *WhoHol 92*
Timberg, Sigmund 1911- *WhoAm 94, WhoAmL 94*
Timberlake, Charles Edward 1935- *WhoAm 94*
Timberlake, Constance Hector *WhoBlA 94*
Timberlake, Herman Leslie Patterson 1914- *Who 94*
Timberlake, John Paul 1950- *WhoBlA 94*
Timberlake, Marshall 1939- *WhoAmL 94*
Timberlake, Richard Henry, Jr. 1922- *WrDr 94*
Timberlake, Stephen Grant 1958- *WhoFI 94*
Timbers, Stephen Bryan 1944- *WhoAm 94, WhoFI 94*
Timbers, William Homer 1915- *WhoAm 94, WhoAmL 94*
Timblin, Lloyd O., Jr. 1927- *WhoWest 94*
Timblin, Slim d1962 *WhoHol 92*
Timbrell, Clayton Carey 1921-1988 *WhAm 10*
Timbury, Morag Crichton 1930- *Who 94*
Times, Betty J. 1939- *WhoBlA 94*
Times, Betty Jean 1939- *WhoAmP 93*
Times, Misbrew Louise 1950- *WhoAmP 93*
Timinski, Robert *WhoFI 94*
Timken, W. Robert, Jr. 1938- *WhoAm 94, WhoFI 94*
Timlett, Peter Valentine 1933- *EncSF 93*
Timlin, James Clifford 1927- *WhoAm 94*
Timlin, William M(itcheson) 1892-1943 *EncSF 93*
Timm, Albert Leonard 1929- *WhoFI 94*
Timm, Deborah A. 1953- *WhoMW 93*
Timm, Gary Everett 1943- *WhoScEn 94*
Timm, Helga 1924- *WhoWomW 91*
Timm, Jerry Roger 1942- *WhoWest 94*
Timm, Kent Edward 1958- *WhoMW 93*
Timm, Laurance Milo 1949- *WhoAm 94*
Timm, Mike *WhoAmP 93*
Timm, Robert Dale 1921- *WhoAmP 93*
Timm, Robert Merle 1949- *WhoWest 94*
Timm, Roger K. 1947- *WhoAmL 94*
Timm, Terry L. 1948- *WhoIns 94*
Timm, Terry Lee 1948- *WhoFI 94*
Timm, Walter Clement 1931- *WhoScEn 94*
Timmas, Osvald 1919- *WhoAmA 93*
Timmer, Barbara 1946- *WhoAm 94, WhoAmL 94*
Timmer, Charles Peter 1941- *WhoAm 94*
Timmer, David Hart 1953- *WhoFI 94, WhoScEn 94*
Timmer, J.D. 1933- *IntWW 93*
Timmer, John L. *WhoAmP 93*
Timmer, Stephen Blaine 1962- *WhoAmL 94*
Timmer, Steven Alan 1966- *WhoMW 93*
Timmerhaus, Klaus Dieter 1924- *WhoAm 94, WhoWest 94*
Timmerman, Dora Mae 1931- *WhoMW 93*
Timmerman, Kenneth R. 1953- *ConAu 141*
Timmerman, Leon Bernard 1924- *WhoFI 94*
Timmerman, Robert Wilson 1944- *WhoFI 94, WhoScEn 94*
Timmins, Cali *WhoHol 92*
Timmins, Edward Patrick 1955- *WhoAmL 94*
Timmins, James Donald 1955- *WhoWest 94*
Timmins, John Bradford 1932- *Who 94*
Timmins, Michael Joseph 1952- *WhoFI 94*
Timmins, Richard Haseltine 1924- *WhoMW 93*
Timmins, William Joseph, Jr. 1917- *WhoAmP 93*
Timmons, Bonita Terry 1963- *WhoBlA 94*
Timmons, Charles McDonald 1926- *WhoIns 94*
Timmons, Charles McDonald, Jr. 1950- *WhoIns 94*
Timmons, Deborah Denise 1961- *WhoBlA 94*
Timmons, Earl L. 1937- *WhoFI 94*
Timmons, Edwin O'Neal 1928- *WhoAm 94*
Timmons, Gerald Dean 1931- *WhoAm 94*
Timmons, Jay Warner 1962- *WhoAmP 93*
Timmons, Jimmy Hodge *WhoAmP 93*
Timmons, Joanne d1962 *WhoHol 92*
Timmons, Joseph Dean 1948- *WhoAm 94*
Timmons, Kyle W. 1960- *WhoAmP 93*
Timmons, Peter John 1954- *WhoAmL 94*
Timmons, Richard Brendan 1938- *WhoAm 94*
Timmons, Robert G. 1938- *WhoWest 94*
Timmons, Sharon L. 1949- *WhoMW 93*
Timmons, William Edward 1924- *WhoAmL 94*
Timmons, William Evan 1930- *WhoAm 94, WhoAmP 93*
Timmons, William Milton 1933- *WhoAm 94, WhoWest 94*
Timmons, William R., Jr. 1924- *WhoIns 94*
Timmons, William Richardson, III 1951- *WhoIns 94*
Timmreck, Thomas C. 1946- *WhoAm 94, WhoWest 94*
Timms, A. Jackson 1938- *WhoAm 94*
Timms, Cecil 1911- *Who 94*
Timms, Eugene Dale 1932- *WhoAmP 93, WhoWest 94*
Timms, George Boorne 1910- *Who 94*
Timms, Kathleen 1943- *WrDr 94*
Timms, Leonard Joseph, Jr. 1936- *WhoAm 94, WhoFI 94*
Timms, Noel Walter 1927- *Who 94*
Timms, Peter Rowland 1942- *WhoAm 94, WhoAmA 93*
Timms, Vera Kate 1944- *Who 94*
Timofeev, Lev Mikhailovich 1936- *LngBDD*
Timofeyeva, Nina 1935- *IntDcB [port]*
Timofeyeva, Nina Vladimirovna 1935- *IntWW 93*
Timon fl. 5th cent.BC- *BlmGEL*
Timoney, Peter Joseph 1941- *WhoAm 94*
Timothy *WhoMW 93*
Timothy 1930- *WhoAm 94*
Timothy, Christopher 1940- *WhoHol 92*
Timothy, David H. 1928- *WhoAm 94*
Timothy, Grover *WhoAmA 93*
Timothy, Raymond Joseph 1932- *WhoAm 94*
Timothy, Robert Keller 1918- *WhoAm 94*
Timour, John Arnold 1926- *WhoAm 94*
Timoxena fl. 2nd cent.- *BlmGWL*
Timpanaro, Philip Anthony 1947- *WhoFI 94*
Timpane, Philip Michael 1934- *WhoAm 94*
Timpanelli, Gioia *DrAPF 93*
Timpano, Anne *WhoAmA 93*
Timpe, Michael Wayne 1951- *WhoMW 93*
Timperlake, Edward Thomas 1946- *WhoAm 94, WhoAmP 93*
Timperley, Rosemary Kenyon 1920- *WrDr 94*
Timpson, John Harry Robert 1928- *Who 94*
Timrava 1867-1951 *BlmGWL*
Tims, John William c. 1858-1945 *EncNAR*
Tims, Michael (David) 1931- *Who 94*
Tims, Michael Wayne *WhoAmA 93*
Timson, Penelope Anne Constance *Who 94*
Tin, Bo 1936- *WhoAsA 94*
Tin, Kam Chung 1943- *WhoScEn 94*
Tina, Turner 1939- *ConBlB 6 [port]*
Tinaglia, Anthony Carmen 1953- *WhoMW 93*
Tinajero, Josefina Villamil 1949- *WhoHisp 94*
Tinayre, Marcelle 1877-1948 *BlmGWL*
Tinbergen, Jan 1903- *IntWW 93, Who 94, WhoAm 94, WhoFI 94*
Tinbergen, Niko d1988 *NobelP 91N*
Tincher, Fay d1983 *WhoHol 92*
Tincher, Wendell Laverne 1936- *WhoAmP 93*
Tincrowder, Leo Queequeg *EncSF 93*
Tindal, D. Leslie 1928- *WhoAmP 93*
Tindal, Ralph Lawrence 1940- *WhoAm 94, WhoWest 94*
Tindal-Carill-Worsley, Geoffrey Nicolas Ernest 1908- *Who 94*
Tindale, Gordon Anthony 1938- *Who 94*
Tindale, Lawrence Victor Dolman 1921- *IntWW 93, Who 94*
Tindale, Patricia Randall 1926- *Who 94*
Tindall, Frederick Cryer 1900- *Who 94*
Tindall, George Brown 1921- *WhoAm 94*
Tindall, George Taylor 1928- *WhoAm 94*
Tindall, Gillian (Elizabeth) 1938- *WrDr 94*
Tindall, Gillian Elizabeth 1938- *Who 94*
Tindall, James *WhoAmP 93*
Tindall, James Robert 1945- *WhoMW 93*
Tindall, Kenneth (Thomas) 1937- *ConAu 42NR*
Tindall, Loren d1973 *WhoHol 92*
Tindall, Robert Emmett 1934- *WhoWest 94*
Tindall, Victor Ronald 1928- *Who 94*
Tindell, Harry J. *WhoAmP 93*
Tindell, Jeffrey W. 1949- *WhoAmL 94*
Tindell, Runyon Howard 1933- *WhoScEn 94*
Tindemans, Leo 1922- *IntWW 93, Who 94*
Tinder, John Daniel 1950- *WhoAm 94, WhoAmL 94*
Tinder, Thomas Grant 1967- *WhoMW 93*
Tindle, David 1932- *IntWW 93, Who 94*
Tindle, Ray Stanley 1926- *Who 94*
Tine, Jacques Wilfrid Jean Francis 1914- *IntWW 93*
Tine, Michael P. 1945- *WhoAm 94*
Ting, Albert Chia 1950- *WhoAm 94*
Ting, Benjamin Shiu-Ming 1950- *WhoWest 94*
Ting, Chen-Hanson 1939- *WhoScEn 94*
Ting, Jan C. 1948- *WhoAsA 94*
Ting, Joseph K. 1950- *WhoAsA 94*
Ting, Lee Hsia 1923- *WhoAsA 94*
Ting, Paul Cheng Tung 1936- *WhoScEn 94*
Ting, Robert Yen-Ying 1942- *WhoAsA 94, WhoScEn 94*
Ting, Samuel C. C. 1936- *WhoAsA 94*
Ting, Samuel Chao Chung 1936- *IntWW 93, Who 94, WhoAm 94, WhoScEn 94, WorScD [port]*
Ting, Sandra 1960- *WhoAsA 94*
Ting, Shih-Fan 1917- *WhoAsA 94*
Ting, T. C. 1935- *WhoAsA 94*
Ting, Thomas Chi Tsai 1933- *WhoAsA 94*
Ting, Walasse 1929- *WhoAmA 93*
Ting, Ying Ji 1927- *WhoAsA 94*
Tingay, Lance 1915-1990 *BuCMET*
Ting Cang-Kim, Donna Marie 1957- *WhoAsA 94*
Tingelstad, Jon Bunde 1935- *WhoAm 94*
Tinghitella, Stephen 1915- *WhoAm 94*
Tingle, Aubrey James 1943- *WhoAm 94*
Tingle, James O'Malley 1928- *WhoAm 94*
Tingle, Lawrence May 1947- *WhoBlA 94*
Tingley, Floyd Warren 1933- *WhoAm 94*
Tingley, Walter Watson 1946- *WhoWest 94*
Ting Mao 1913- *WhoPRCh 91 [port]*
Ting Shoa Kuang 1939- *WhoAmA 93*
Tinguely, Jean 1925-1991 *ModArCr 4 [port]*
Tinguely, Jean 1960-1991 *WhAm 10*
Tingwell, Charles 1917- *WhoHol 92*
Tinic, Seha Mehmet 1941- *WhoAm 94*
Tinitali, Soa P. *WhoAmP 93*
Tinjum, Larry Ervin 1947- *WhoAmP 93*
Tinker, Carol Wicks 1920- *WhoAmP 93*
Tinker, Chauncey Brewster 1876-1963 *DcLB 140 [port]*
Tinker, Grant A. 1926- *IntMPA 94, WhoAm 94*
Tinker, Harold Burnham 1939- *WhoAm 94, WhoScEn 94*
Tinker, Hugh (Russell) 1921- *WrDr 94*
Tinker, Hugh Russell 1921- *Who 94*
Tinker, Jack 1936- *Who 94*
Tinker, Jack 1938- *WrDr 94*
Tinker, Mark 1951?- *ConTFT 11*
Tinker, Mark Christian 1951- *WhoWest 94*
Tinker, Peter Allmond 1956- *WhoWest 94*
Tinker, Philip Bernard Hague 1930- *Who 94*
Tinkham, Michael 1928- *IntWW 93, WhoAm 94*
Tinkham, Thomas W. 1944- *WhoAm 94, WhoAmL 94*
Tinkle, F. Lorain 1913- *WhoAmL 94*
Tinkler, Barrie Keith 1935- *WhoAmA 93*
Tinkler, Jack Donald 1936- *WhoAm 94*
Tinkler, Nancy Emily 1948- *WhoWest 94*
Tinling, Marion (Rose) 1904- *ConAu 142*
Tinling, Ted 1910-1990 *BuCMET*
Tinn, James 1922- *Who 94*
Tinne, Alexandrine Pieternella Francoise 1835-1869 *WhWE*
Tinner, Franziska Paula 1944- *WhoMW 93*
Tinnerello, Mike 1944- *WhoAmP 93*
Tinnerino, Natale Francis 1939- *WhoScEn 94*
Tinney, Frank d1940 *WhoHol 92*
Tinnin, Thomas Peck 1948- *WhoWest 94*
Tinning, George Campbell 1910- *WhoAmA 93*
Tinniswood, Maurice Owen 1919- *Who 94*
Tinniswood, Peter 1936- *ConAu 43NR, WrDr 94*
Tinoco, Ignacio, Jr. 1930- *WhoAm 94, WhoScEn 94*

Tinoco, Patricia Ann 1950- WhoMW 93
Tinsley, Adrian 1937- WhoAm 94
Tinsley, Barry 1942- WhoAmA 93
Tinsley, Charles Henry 1914- Who 94
Tinsley, Diane Johnson 1944- WhoMW 93
Tinsley, Eleanor 1926- WhoAmP 93
Tinsley, Ernest John d1992 IntWW 93N
Tinsley, Ernest John 1919- WrDr 94
Tinsley, Fred Leland, Jr. 1944- WhoAmP 93, WhoBlA 94
Tinsley, Jackson Bennett 1934- WhoAm 94
Tinsley, Lee Owen 1969- WhoBlA 94
Tinsley, Lyn D. WhoAmP 93
Tinsley, Mary WhoAmP 93
Tinsley, Pauline (Cecilia) 1928- NewGrDO
Tinsley, Walton Eugene 1921- WhoAm 94
Tinsley-Williams, Alberta 1954- WhoBlA 94
Tinsman, Maggie 1936- WhoAmP 93, WhoWomW 91
Tinson, Susan (Myfanwy) 1943- Who 94
Tinstman, Dale Clinton 1919- WhoAm 94
Tintarev, Kyril 1956- WhoWest 94
Tinti, Gabriele WhoHol 92
Tintner, Georg (Bernhard) 1917- NewGrDO
Tinto, Joseph Vincent 1957- WhoScEn 94
Tintori, John Joseph 1963- WhoMW 93
Tiny, Tim 1927- WhoHol 92
Tió, Adrián Ricardo 1951- WhoHisp 94
Tio, Kek-Kiong 1960- WhoScEn 94
Tiomkin, Dimitri 1899-1979 IntDcF 2-4 [port]
Tiphaigne De La Roche, C(harles) F(rancois) 1729-1774 EncSF 93
Tipirneni, Tirumala Rao 1948- WhoScEn 94
Tipka, Donald Allan 1941- WhoMW 93
Tipp, Karen Lynn Wagner 1947- WhoMW 93, WhoScEn 94
Tipper, Harry, III 1949- WhoFI 94
Tippet, Anthony (Sanders) 1928- Who 94
Tippet, Clark d1992 WhAm 10
Tippet, Clark 1954-1992 AnObit 1992
Tippets, Dennis W. 1938- WhoAmP 93
Tippets, Dennis Wilcock 1938- WhoAm 94
Tippets, John H. 1952- WhoAmP 93
Tippett, Andre Bernard 1959- WhoBlA 94
Tippett, James Royall, Jr. 1909- WhoAmL 94
Tippett, Michael (Kemp) 1905- NewGrDO, Who 94
Tippett, Michael Kemp 1905- IntWW 93
Tippett, Willis Paul, Jr. 1932- IntWW 93, WhoAm 94
Tippette, Giles 1936- WrDr 94
Tippetts, Rutherford Berriman 1913- Who 94
Tippin, Aaron 1958- WhoAm 94
Tipping, Harry A. 1944- WhoAmL 94
Tipping, Simon Patrick 1949- Who 94
Tipping, William Malcolm 1931- WhoAm 94, WhoFI 94
Tippins, Bedell A. 1948- WhoAm 94, WhoAmL 94
Tippins, Timothy Michael 1949- WhoAmL 94
Tippit, Hassel 1897- WhAm 10
Tippit, John Harlow 1916- WhoAm 94
Tippit, Mike WhoHol 92
Tippit, Wayne WhoHol 92
Tipple, H. D. WhoAm 94, WhoFI 94
Tippler, John 1929- Who 94
Tippner, Norman Albert 1943- WhoWest 94
Tippo, Oswald 1911- WhoAm 94
Tipps, Maynard E. 1946- WhoAmL 94
Tipps, Paul 1936- WhoAmP 93
Tipps, Tina Jean 1962- WhoFI 94
Tippur, Hareesh V. 1958- WhoScEn 94
Tippy, Alan Clay 1953- WhoWest 94
Tipsword, Jean Ann 1961- WhoMW 93
Tipsword, Rolland Fortner 1925- WhoAmP 93
Tipton, Carl William 1935- WhoAm 94
Tipton, Clyde Raymond, Jr. 1921- WhoAm 94
Tipton, Dale Leo 1930- WhoBlA 94
Tipton, Daniel L. WhoMW 93
Tipton, Darrell Lee 1948- WhoAmP 93
Tipton, David 1934- WrDr 94
Tipton, E. Linwood 1934- WhoAm 94
Tipton, Elden C. 1918- WhoAmP 93
Tipton, Elizabeth Howse 1925- WhoBlA 94
Tipton, Gary Lee 1941- WhoFI 94, WhoWest 94
Tipton, Glenn
See Judas Priest ConMus 10
Tipton, Harry B. 1927- WhoAmP 93
Tipton, Harry Basil, Jr. 1927- WhoWest 94
Tipton, Ian Charles 1937- WrDr 94
Tipton, James Alva 1931- WhoMW 93
Tipton, James Ceamon 1938- WhoWest 94
Tipton, Jennifer 1937- WhoAm 94
Tipton, John J. 1946- WhoAm 94
Tipton, Jon Paul 1934- WhoMW 93, WhoScEn 94
Tipton, Kenneth Warren 1932- WhoScEn 94
Tipton, Paul S. WhoAm 94
Tipton, Thomas Wesley 1952- WhoScEn 94
Tipton, Toni Hamilton 1959- WhoBlA 94
Tipton, Whitney Hord WhoAm 94, WhoFI 94
Tiptree, James, Jr. 1915-1987 EncSF 93
Tirado, Daniel Ramon 1949- WhoHisp 94
Tirado, Isabel A. 1947- WhoHisp 94
Tirado, Olga Luz 1960- WhoHisp 94
Tirado, Rafael Caro WhoAmP 93
Tirado, Romualdo d1963 WhoHol 92
Tirado Delgado, Cirilo 1938- WhoHisp 94
Tirakis, Judith Angelina 1938- WhoAm 94
Tirana, Bardyl Rifat 1937- WhoAm 94, WhoAmP 93
Tiras, Herbert Gerald 1924- WhoScEn 94
Tirella, Eduardo d1966 WhoHol 92
Tirelli, Teresa d1989 WhoHol 92
Tiria, Kumari Sushila 1956- WhoWomW 91
Tiriac, Ion NewYTBS 93 [port]
Tiriac, Ion 1939- BuCMET
Tirikatene-Sullivan, Tini Whetu Marama 1932- IntWW 93
Tirikatene-Sullivan, Whetu 1932- WhoWomW 91
Tirimo, Martino 1942- IntWW 93
Tirino, Philip Joseph 1940- WhoFI 94
Tirkel, Anatol Zygmunt 1949- WhoScEn 94
Tiroff, James d1975 WhoHol 92
Tirpak, Thomas Michael 1966- WhoMW 93
Tirpitz, Alfred von 1894-1930 HisWorL [port]
Tirre, William Charles 1952- WhoScEn 94
Tirrell, Elvin Drew 1931- WhoAmP 93
Tirrell, John Albert 1934- WhoAm 94
Tirres, Richard Raymond 1950- WhoHisp 94
Tirro, Frank Pascale 1935- WhoAm 94
Tirso de Molina 1580?-1648 IntDcT 2
Tirvengadum, Harry (Krishnan) 1933- Who 94
Tiryakian, Edward Ashod 1929- WhoAm 94
Tisch, James S. 1953- WhoFI 94
Tisch, Laurence A. 1923- IntMPA 94
Tisch, Laurence Alan 1923- IntWW 93, WhoAm 94, WhoFI 94
Tisch, Preston Robert 1926- IntMPA 94, WhoAm 94, WhoFI 94
Tisch, Ronald Irwin 1944- WhoAm 94
Tisch, Steve 1949- IntMPA 94
Tischauser, Leslie Vincent 1942- WhoMW 93
Tischendorf, John Allen 1929- WhoWest 94
Tischfield, Jay Arnold 1946- WhoMW 93
Tischler, David William 1935- WhoWest 94
Tischler, Gary Lowell 1935- WhoAm 94, WhoWest 94
Tischler, Hans 1915- WrDr 94
Tischler, Herbert 1924- WhoAm 94
Tischler, John E. 1934- WhoAm 94
Tischler, Lewis Paul 1947- WhoFI 94
Tischler, Ronald B. 1944- WhoAmL 94
Tischler, Victor 1890-1951 WhoAmA 93N
Tischman, Michael Bernard 1937- WhoAm 94
Tisdale, Celes 1941- WhoBlA 94
Tisdale, Charles H., Jr. 1947- WhoAmL 94
Tisdale, Douglas Michael 1949- WhoAmL 94, WhoWest 94
Tisdale, Franklin M. d1947 WhoHol 92
Tisdale, Henry Nehemiah 1944- WhoBlA 94
Tisdale, Herbert Clifford 1928- WhoBlA 94
Tisdale, Jeffrey Alan 1949- WhoAmL 94, WhoFI 94
Tisdale, John R. 1946- WhoAmL 94
Tisdale, Patrick David WhoScEn 94
Tisdale, Sallie 1957- ConAu 142
Tisdale, Stuart Williams 1928- WhoAm 94, WhoMW 93
Tisdale, Wayman Lawrence 1964- WhoBlA 94
Tisdel, Darlene LuElla 1929- WhoMW 93
Tisdell, Clement Allan 1939- WrDr 94
Tise, George Francis, II 1937- WhoWest 94
Tise, Larry Edward 1942- WhoAm 94
Tisei, Richard R. WhoAmP 93
Tiselius, Arne Wilhelm Kaurin 1902-1971 WorScD
Tish, Kelly WhoWomW 91
Tishchenko, Boris Ivanovich 1939- IntWW 93
Tisher, Sharon S. 1951- WhoAm 94
Tishk, Alan Jay 1949- WhoAm 94, WhoMW 93
Tishler, Gillian 1958- Who 94
Tishler, Max 1906-1989 WhAm 10
Tishman, Jack A. d1966 WhoAmA 93N
Tishman, Robert V. 1916- WhoAm 94, WhoFI 94
Tisinger, Catherine Anne 1936- WhoAm 94
Tisma, Aleksandar 1924- ConWorW 93
Tison, Ben 1930- WhoAmP 93
Tison, David Lawrence 1952- WhoScEn 94
Tison-Braun, Micheline Lucie 1913- WhoAm 94
Tisopulos, Laki T. 1959- WhoWest 94
Tiss, George John 1925- WhoWest 94
Tisse, Edward 1897-1961 IntDcF 2-4 [port]
Tisser, Clifford Roy 1946- WhoScEn 94
Tisser, Doron Moshe 1955- WhoWest 94
Tissier, Jean d1973 WhoHol 92
Tissot, Alice d1971 WhoHol 92
Titan, Earl EncSF 93
Titarenko, Mikhail Leonidovich 1934- IntWW 93
Titche, Leon 1939- WhoMW 93
Titchell, John 1926- Who 94
Titchener, Alan Ronald 1934- Who 94
Titchener, (John) Lanham (Bradbury) 1912- Who 94
Titchener, Louise 1941- WrDr 94
Titchener-Barrett, Dennis (Charles) Who 94
Titcomb, Bonnie L. WhoAmP 93
Titcomb, Caldwell 1926- WhoAm 94
Titcomb, John Blake 1940- WhoMW 93
Titcomb, Woodbury Cole 1923- WhoAm 94
Tite, Michael Stanley 1938- Who 94
Titelbaum, Daniel E. 1946- WhoAmL 94
Titen, Andrew Barry 1950- WhoFI 94
Titford, Donald George 1925- Who 94
Titheradge, Dion d1934 WhoHol 92
Titheradge, Madge d1961 WhoHol 92
Titheridge, John Edward 1932- IntWW 93
Titheridge, Roger Noel 1928- Who 94
Titherington, Mary 1927- WhoAmP 93
Titialii, Jacinta Eleina 1955- WhoAmL 94
Titiens, Therese NewGrDO
Titl, Antonin Emil (Frantisek Seraf) 1809-1882 NewGrDO
Titland, Martin Nils 1938- WhoAm 94
Title, Gail Migdal 1946- WhoAmL 94
Title, Peter Stephen 1950- WhoAmL 94
Titlebaum, Richard Theodore 1939- WhoMW 93
Titley, Gary 1950- Who 94
Titley, Jane 1940- Who 94
Titley, Larry J. 1943- WhoAm 94, WhoAmL 94
Titley, Robert L. 1947- WhoAmL 94
Titlow, Frank Graham 1943- WhoFI 94
Titlow, Larry Wayne 1945- WhoAm 94
Titman, John (Edward Powis) 1926- Who 94
Titmuss, Phyllis d1946 WhoHol 92
Tito, Marshal 1892-1980 HisWorL [port]
Titone, Vito J. 1929- WhoAmP 93
Titone, Vito Joseph 1929- WhoAm 94, WhoAmL 94
Titov, Alexey Nikolayevich 1769-1827 NewGrDO
Titov, Herman Stepanovich 1935- IntWW 93
Titov, Konstantin Alekseevich 1944- LngBDD
Titov, Sergey Nikolayevich 1770-1825 NewGrDO
Titov, Vladimir Georgievich 1947- IntWW 93
Titov, Yuriy Evlampievich 1935- IntWW 93
Tits, Jacques Leon 1930- IntWW 93
Titta, Ruffo Cafiero NewGrDO
Tittle, Carole Jean 1959- WhoMW 93
Tittle, David O. 1942- WhoAmL 94
Tittle, Ernest Fremont 1885-1949 DcAmReB 2
Tittle, Y. A. ProFbHF
Tittler, Jonathan (Paul) 1945- ConAu 43NR
Tittman, Jay 1922- WhoScEn 94
Tittmann, Bernhard Rainer 1935- WhoAm 94
Tittsworth, Clayton Magness 1920- WhoAmL 94
Titus, Alan 1945- NewGrDO
Titus, Alice Cestandina 1950- WhoAmP 93
Titus, Bruce E. 1942- WhoAmL 94
Titus, Curtis Vest 1933- WhoAmL 94
Titus, David Kenneth 1947- WhoMW 93
Titus, Douglas Jules, Jr. 1950- WhoAmL 94
Titus, Dudley Seymour 1929- WhoMW 93
Titus, Edward Depue 1931- WhoWest 94
Titus, Eve 1922- WrDr 94
Titus, Jack L. 1926- WhoAm 94
Titus, Jon Alan 1955- WhoAmL 94, WhoWest 94
Titus, LeRoy Robert 1938- WhoBlA 94
Titus, Lydia Yeamans d1929 WhoHol 92
Titus, Myer L. WhoBlA 94
Titus, Roger Warren 1941- WhoAm 94
Titus, Stacey P. 1965- WhoFI 94
Titus, Theo, III WhoAmP 93
Titus-Dillon, Pauline Y. 1938- WhoBlA 94
Titze, Ingo Roland 1941- WhoAm 94
Tiu, Nicolae 1948- LngBDD
Tiunov, Oleg Ivanovich 1937- LngBDD
Tiverton, Viscount Who 94
Tivin, Paul J. 1945- WhoFI 94
Tiwari, Narayan Datt 1925- IntWW 93, Who 94
Tiwari, Subhash Ramadhar 1949- WhoScEn 94
Tixier, Claude 1913- IntWW 93
Tizard, Barbara 1926- Who 94
Tizard, Catherine (Anne) 1931- IntWW 93, Who 94
Tizard, Catherine Anne 1931- WhoWomW 91
Tizard, (John) Peter (Mills) 1916- Who 94
Tizard, Robert James 1924- IntWW 93, Who 94
Tizzio, Thomas R. 1938- WhoIns 94
Tizzio, Thomas Ralph 1938- WhoAm 94, WhoFI 94
Tjeknavorian, Loris-Zare 1937- IntWW 93
Tjoelker, Michael Lyle 1954- WhoWest 94
Tjoflat, Gerald Bard 1929- WhoAm 94, WhoAmL 94, WhoAmP 93
Tjosvold, Dean 1948- ConAu 142
Tkach, Robert William 1954- WhoScEn 94
Tkachenko, Evgeny Victorovich 1935- LngBDD
Tkachuk, Vasyl Mykhailovych 1933- LngBDD
Tlachac, Norbert James 1932- WhoMW 93
Tlali, Miriam 1933- BlmGWL [port]
Tlalka, Jacek 1937- WhoAm 94
Tlass, Mustapha el- 1932- IntWW 93
Tleuzh, Adam Khuseinovich 1951- LngBDD
Tlou, Thomas 1932- IntWW 93
Tlusty, Jay Richard 1955- WhoAmP 93
Toadvin-Bester, Josephine Vesella 1926- WhoMW 93
Toadvine, JoAnne Elizabeth 1933- WhoWest 94
Toal, Christopher Anthony 1953- WhoWest 94
Toal, James Francis 1932- WhoAm 94
Toal, Jean Hoefer 1943- WhoAm 94, WhoAmL 94, WhoAmP 93
Toale, Thomas Edward 1953- WhoAm 94
Toba, Hachiro Harold 1932- WhoAsA 94
Toback, Frederick Gary 1941- WhoMW 93
Toback, James WhoHol 92
Toback, James 1944- IntMPA 94
Tobar, Lea Martinez 1942- WhoHisp 94
Tobar Zaldumbide, Carlos 1912- IntWW 93
Tobback, Louis 1938- IntWW 93
Tobe, Christopher Bayless 1962- WhoFI 94
Tobe, Stephen Solomon 1944- WhoAm 94, WhoScEn 94
Tober, Lester Victor 1916- WhoAm 94
Tober, Mark Robert 1959- WhoFI 94
Tober, Stephen Lloyd 1949- WhoAm 94, WhoAmL 94
Tobert, Jonathan Andrew 1945- WhoScEn 94
Tobet, Stuart Allen 1956- WhoScEn 94
Tobey, Alton S. 1914- WhoAmA 93
Tobey, Alton Stanley 1914- WhoAm 94
Tobey, Beatrice d1993 NewYTBS 93
Tobey, Bette Marie 1959- WhoFI 94
Tobey, Carl Wadsworth 1923- WhoAm 94
Tobey, Joel N. 1929- WhoIns 94
Tobey, Kenneth 1919- WhoHol 92
Tobey, Mark 1890-1976 WhoAmA 93N
Tobia, Blaise Joseph 1953- WhoAmA 93
Tobia, Ronald Lawrence 1944- WhoAmL 94
Tobia, Sergio B. 1939- WhoIns 94
Tobia, Stephen Francis, Jr. 1955- WhoAm 94
Tobias, Abraham Joel 1913- WhoAmA 93
Tobias, Andrew P. 1947- WrDr 94
Tobias, Andrew Previn 1947- WhoAm 94
Tobias, Arthur DrAPF 93
Tobias, Charles H. 1945- WhoAmL 94

Tobias, Charles Harrison, Jr. 1921- WhoAm 94
Tobias, Charles William 1920- WhoAm 94
Tobias, Christopher Ord 1962- WhoWest 94
Tobias, Cynthia Lee 1945- WhoWest 94
Tobias, Geoffrey S. 1948- WhoAmL 94
Tobias, George d1980 WhoHol 92
Tobias, John Jacob 1925- WrDr 94
Tobias, Julius 1915- WhoAm 94, WhoAmA 93
Tobias, Michael (Charles) 1951- ConAu 140
Tobias, Oliver 1947- WhoHol 92
Tobias, Paul Henry 1930- WhoAm 94, WhoAmL 94
Tobias, Phillip Vallentine 1925- IntWW 93
Tobias, Randall L. 1942- WhoAm 94, WhoFI 94
Tobias, Randolf A. 1940- WhoBlA 94
Tobias, Richard 1952- WhoAmA 93
Tobias, Richard C. 1925- WrDr 94
Tobias, Robert M., Jr. 1954- WhoHisp 94
Tobias, Robert Max 1943- WhoAm 94, WhoAmL 94
Tobias, Robert Paul 1933- WhoAmA 93
Tobias, Thomas J. 1906-1970 WhoAmA 93N
Tobiassen, Thomas Johan 1931- WhoAmP 93
Tobiasz, Robert Brian 1945- WhoAm 94, WhoFI 94
Tobin, A. Stephen WhoAmP 93
Tobin, Arthur H. 1930- WhoAmP 93
Tobin, Bentley 1924- WhoAm 94
Tobin, Bruce Howard 1955- WhoAmL 94
Tobin, Calvin Jay 1927- WhoAm 94, WhoMW 93, WhoScEn 94
Tobin, Christopher Ward 1957- WhoMW 93
Tobin, Craig Daniel 1954- WhoAmL 94
Tobin, Dan d1982 WhoHol 92
Tobin, David L. 1928- WhoAmL 94
Tobin, Dennis Michael 1948- WhoAmL 94
Tobin, Genevieve 1901- WhoHol 92
Tobin, Helen McLane WhoMW 93
Tobin, Ilona Lines 1943- WhoMW 93
Tobin, Jack Norman 1941- WhoAmP 93
Tobin, James 1918- IntWW 93, Who 94, WhoAm 94, WhoFI 94, WrDr 94
Tobin, James Michael 1948- WhoAm 94, WhoAmL 94, WhoWest 94
Tobin, James Robert 1944- WhoAm 94, WhoFI 94
Tobin, John Everard 1923- WhoAm 94
Tobin, John Joseph 1934- WhoFI 94
Tobin, Katherine Colleen 1950- WhoWest 94
Tobin, Keith Milman 1961- WhoMW 93
Tobin, Kiefer A. 1937- WhoWest 94
Tobin, Lee 1954- WhoMW 93
Tobin, Mary Ann WhoAmP 93
Tobin, Michael Alan 1952- WhoMW 93
Tobin, Michael Edward 1926- WhoAm 94
Tobin, Michele 1961- WhoHol 92
Tobin, Nancy 1943- WhoAmA 93
Tobin, Patricia L. 1943- WhoBlA 94
Tobin, Richard J. 1934- WhoAm 94
Tobin, Richard Willis, II 1953- WhoAmL 94
Tobin, Robert Manford, Jr. 1958- WhoWest 94
Tobin, Saul 1928- WhoWest 94
Tobin, Sheldon S(idney) 1931- WrDr 94
Tobin, Steven Michael 1940- WhoFI 94
Tobin, Thomas F. 1929- WhoAm 94
Tobin, Thomas M. 1943- WhoIns 94
Tobin, Timothy Bruce 1956- WhoWest 94
Tobin, William Joseph 1927- WhoWest 94
Tobin, William Thomas 1931- WhoAm 94, WhoFI 94
Tobis, Jerome Sanford 1915- WhoAm 94
Tobisman, Stuart Paul 1942- WhoAm 94, WhoAmL 94
Tobkin, Christine Anderson 1952- WhoAm 94
Tobkin, Vincent Henry 1951- WhoWest 94
Tobler, D. Lee 1933- WhoAm 94, WhoFI 94
Tobler, Waldo Rudolph 1930- WhoAm 94
Tobolowsky, Stephen WhoHol 92
Tobolowsky, Stephen 1951- IntMPA 94
Tobon, Hector 1934- WhoHisp 94
Toburen, Karen Ruth 1945- WhoMW 93
Toburen, Larry Howard 1940- WhoWest 94
Toburen, Lawrence Richter 1915- WhoAm 94
Toby, Jackson 1925- WhoAm 94
Toby, Jerry 1963- WhoAmP 93
Toby, Ronald Paul 1942- WhoMW 93
Toby, William, Jr. 1934- WhoBlA 94
Toca, Jesse 1958- WhoHisp 94
Tocci, Ronald C. 1941- WhoAmP 93
Tocco, James 1943- WhoAm 94
Toch, Ernst 1887-1964 NewGrDO
Toch, Henry 1923- WrDr 94
Tochi, Brian 1959- WhoHol 92
Tocino Biscarolasaga, Isabel 1949- WhoWomW 91
Tock, Joseph 1954- WhoAmL 94
Tocklin, Adrian Martha 1951- WhoAm 94, WhoFI 94, WhoIns 94
Tockman, Ronald Chester 1945- WhoFI 94
Toczek, Nick 1950- WrDr 94
Toczynski, Janet Marie 1953- WhoMW 93
Toczyska, Stefania 1943- NewGrDO
Tod, G. Robert 1939- WhoAm 94
Tod, John Hunter H. Who 94
Tod, Jonathan James Richard 1939- Who 94
Tod, Osma Gallinger d1983 WhoAmA 93N
Toda, Harold Keiji 1925- WhoAsA 94
Toda, Jusho 1928-1987 IntDcF 2-4
Toda, Kunio 1915- NewGrDO
Todaro, George Joseph 1937- WhoScEn 94
Todaro, James Alan WhoMW 93
Todd, Baron 1907- Who 94
Todd, A. W. WhoAmP 93
Todd, Alastair 1920- Who 94
Todd, Alexander Robertus 1907- IntWW 93, WhoAm 94, WhoScEn 94, WorScD
Todd, Anderson 1921- WhoAm 94
Todd, Andrew Stewart 1926- Who 94
Todd, Ann d1993 IntMPA 94N, NewYTBS 93 [port], Who 94N
Todd, Ann 1909- WhoHol 92
Todd, Arthur Ruric, III 1942- WhoAmP 93
Todd, Beth Ann 1959- WhoScEn 94
Todd, Beverly WhoBlA 94, WhoHol 92
Todd, Beverly 1946- IntMPA 94
Todd, Bob 1921- WhoHol 92
Todd, Bosworth Moss, Jr. 1930- WhoFI 94
Todd, Brent W. 1948- WhoAmL 94
Todd, Bruce WhoAm 94
Todd, Bruce M. WhoAmP 93
Todd, Charles Byron 1934- WhoFI 94
Todd, Charles Irwin 1956- WhoFI 94
Todd, Charles O. 1915- WhoBlA 94
Todd, Cynthia Jean 1951- WhoBlA 94
Todd, David Carl 1936- WhoAm 94
Todd, David Fenton Michie 1915- WhoAm 94
Todd, David Franza 1952- WhoWest 94
Todd, Donald Frederick WhoScEn 94
Todd, Doug 1929- WhoAmP 93
Todd, Flake 1917- WhoAmP 93
Todd, Garfield Who 94
Todd, (Reginald Stephen) Garfield 1908- IntWW 93, Who 94
Todd, Gary Owen 1966- WhoAmL 94
Todd, Gayle Louise 1956- WhoMW 93
Todd, Glenn William 1927- WhoAm 94
Todd, Harold Wade 1938- WhoAm 94, WhoWest 94
Todd, Harry d1935 WhoHol 92
Todd, Harry Williams 1922- WhoAm 94, WhoFI 94
Todd, Howell Wayne WhoMW 93
Todd, Ian (Pelham) 1921- Who 94
Todd, J. C. DrAPF 93
Todd, J. C. 1943- WhoAm 94
Todd, J. R., Jr. 1943- WhoAmP 93
Todd, James d1968 WhoHol 92
Todd, James Averill, Jr. 1928- WhoAm 94, WhoFI 94
Todd, James Dale 1943- WhoAm 94, WhoAmL 94
Todd, James Gilbert 1937- WhoWest 94
Todd, James S. 1931- WhoScEn 94
Todd, James Stiles 1931- WhoAm 94
Todd, Janet Margaret 1942- Who 94
Todd, Jeffrey Warren 1949- WhoMW 93
Todd, JoAnn Byrne DrAPF 93
Todd, Joe Thomas 1940- WhoAmP 93
Todd, John 1911- WhoAm 94
Todd, John Arthur 1908- Who 94
Todd, John Dickerson, Jr. 1912- WhoAm 94
Todd, John Francis James 1937- Who 94
Todd, John Joseph 1927- WhoAm 94
Todd, John M. 1918-1993 NewYTBS 93
Todd, John M(urray) 1918- WrDr 94
Todd, John M(urray) 1918-1993 ConAu 141
Todd, John Rawling 1929- Who 94
Todd, Jon William 1959- WhoMW 93
Todd, Judith 1936- WhoWest 94
Todd, Judith F. 1946- WhoAmL 94
Todd, Kathryn Doi 1942- WhoAsA 94
Todd, Kenneth S., Jr. 1936- WhoAm 94
Todd, Kevin J. 1963- WhoMW 93
Todd, Lisa 1948- WhoHol 92
Todd, Lola WhoHol 92
Todd, Louise 1954- WrDr 94
Todd, Malcolm 1939- Who 94
Todd, Malcolm Clifford 1913- WhoAm 94
Todd, Margaret Blake 1962- WhoAmL 94
Todd, Mary Ludwig 1947- WhoMW 93
Todd, Mary Williamson Spottiswoode 1909- Who 94
Todd, Matthew Dean 1958- WhoWest 94
Todd, Melvin R. 1933- WhoBlA 94
Todd, Michael Cullen 1935- WhoAmA 93
Todd, Mike 1947- WhoAmP 93
Todd, Mike 1953- WhoAmP 93
Todd, Olivier 1929- IntWW 93
Todd, Orlando 1958- WhoBlA 94
Todd, Paul 1944- WrDr 94
Todd, Paul Harold, Jr. 1921- WhoAmP 93
Todd, Paul Wilson 1936- WhoWest 94
Todd, Richard 1919- IntMPA 94, Who 94, WhoHol 92
Todd, Richard Andrew Palethorpe 1919- IntWW 93
Todd, Richard Henry 1906- WhoScEn 94
Todd, Roger Harold 1928- WhoScEn 94
Todd, Ron WhoAmP 93, WhoIns 94
Todd, Ronald 1927- IntWW 93, Who 94
Todd, Ronald Gary 1946- WhoAm 94
Todd, Rufo Wesley d1958 WhoHol 92
Todd, Russell WhoHol 92
Todd, Ruthven 1914-1978 EncSF 93
Todd, Stephen Max 1941- WhoAmL 94
Todd, Terry Ray 1947- WhoScEn 94
Todd, Thelma d1935 WhoHol 92
Todd, Thelma 1905-1935 WhoCom
Todd, Thomas Abbott 1928- WhoAm 94
Todd, Thomas N. 1938- WhoBlA 94
Todd, Thomas W. 1927- WhoAmP 93
Todd, Troy W. 1929- WhoFI 94
Todd, Virgil Holcomb 1921- WhoAm 94
Todd, Wesley Mark 1946- WhoMW 93
Todd, William Burton 1919- WhoAm 94
Todd, William Judson 1928- WhoAmP 93
Todd, William Michael 1952- WhoAm 94
Todd, William S. 1940- WhoBlA 94
Todd, Zane Grey 1924- WhoAm 94, WhoMW 93, WhoScEn 94
Todd Copley, Judith Ann 1950- WhoAm 94
Todd of Trumpington 1907- WhoScEn 94
Todd of Trumpington, Baron 1907- WhoAm 94
Todea, Rockling 1942- WhoWest 94
Todesca, La NewGrDO
Todeschi, Joseph L. 1935- WhoWest 94
Todhunter, Carl Eugene 1966- WhoMW 93
Todhunter, John Anthony 1949- WhoAmP 93
Todi, Luisa (Rosa) 1753-1833 NewGrDO [port]
Todisco, Nunzio c. 1942- NewGrDO
Todman, Howard 1920- IntMPA 94
Todman, Jureen Francis 1935- WhoBlA 94
Todman, Terence A. 1926- WhoAm 94, WhoAmP 93, WhoBlA 94
Todo, Satoru 1947- WhoAsA 94
Todorov, Stanko 1920- IntWW 93
Todorov, Tzvetan 1939- EncSF 93
Todorovic, Radmilo Antonije 1927- WhoAm 94
Todreas, Neil Emmanuel 1935- WhoAm 94
Todsen, Thomas Kamp 1918- WhoWest 94
Todt, Malcolm S. 1945- WhoAm 94
Toedt, Dell Charles, III 1954- WhoAmL 94
Toedt, Elizabeth Mary 1957- WhoWest 94
Toedtman, James Smith 1941- WhoAm 94
Toedtman, John Kumler 1943- WhoMW 93
Toegemann, Alfred C. 1928- WhoIns 94
Toekes, Barna 1923- WhoScEn 94
Toelle, Richard Alan 1949- WhoWest 94
Toenies, Brenda Marie 1969- WhoMW 93
Toeniskoetter, Richard Henry 1931- WhoMW 93
Toennies, Jan Peter 1930- IntWW 93
Toensing, Victoria 1941- WhoAm 94, WhoAmL 94
Toensmeier, Arthur M. 1942- WhoAmL 94
Toepfer, Robert Adolph 1920- WhoAm 94
Toepke, Utz Peter 1940- WhoAm 94, WhoAmL 94
Toeplitz, Jerzy 1909- IntWW 93
Toeppe, William Joseph, Jr. 1931- WhoScEn 94, WhoWest 94
Toerner, David Paul 1963- WhoMW 93
Toevs, Alden Louis 1949- WhoAm 94
Toews, Daryl 1949- WhoAmP 93
Tofel, Jennings 1892-1959 WhoAmA 93N
Tofel, Richard Jeffrey 1957- WhoFI 94
Toffan, Michael Jay 1956- WhoMW 93
Toffel, Alvin Eugene 1935- WhoAm 94
Toffler, Alvin 1928- EncSF 93, WhoAm 94, WrDr 94
Toffolo, Adrian Titian 1944- Who 94
Tofias, Allan 1930- WhoFI 94
Tofolo, David Michael 1965- WhoFI 94
Toft, Anthony Douglas 1944- Who 94
Toft, (Eric) John 1933- WrDr 94
Toft, Jurgen Herbert 1943- WhoScEn 94
Toft, Martin John, III 1936- WhoAm 94
Toft, Richard Paul 1936- WhoAm 94
Tofte, Arthur R. 1902-1980 EncSF 93
Toftner, Richard Orville 1935- WhoAm 94, WhoFI 94, WhoMW 93
Toftness, Cecil Gillman 1920- WhoAmL 94, WhoFI 94, WhoWest 94
Tofts, Catherine c. 1685-1756 NewGrDO
Togafau, Malaetasi WhoAmP 93
Toganivalu, Josua Brown 1930- Who 94
Togerson, John Dennis 1939- WhoFI 94, WhoScEn 94, WhoWest 94
Toglhofer, Wolfgang 1959- WhoScEn 94
Toglia, Thomas Vincent 1954- WhoWest 94
Tognarelli, Richard Lee 1949- WhoMW 93
Tognazzi, Rick WhoHol 92
Tognazzi, Ugo d1990 WhoHol 92
Togni, Camillo 1922- NewGrDO
Tognino, John Nicholas 1938- WhoAm 94
Tognoli, Carlo 1938- IntWW 93
Togo, Yukiyasu 1924- WhoWest 94
Toguchi, Charles Teruo 1941- WhoAm 94, WhoWest 94
Toguchi, Tamako 1937- WhoWomW 91
Toh Chin Chye 1921- IntWW 93, Who 94
Tohill, Jim Barnette 1947- WhoAmL 94
To Huu 1920- IntWW 93
Toibin, Colm 1955- ConAu 142
Toibin, Niall WhoHol 92
Toida, Saburo IntWW 93
Toigo, Daniel Joseph 1912-1992 WhoAmA 93N
Toi-Kai-Rakan fl. 115-?- WhWE
Toirac, Alfredo Rafael 1918- WhoHisp 94
Toirac, Margarita WhoHisp 94
Toirac, Seth Thomas 1951- WhoMW 93
Toivanen, Paavo Uuras 1937- WhoScEn 94
Toivo, Andimba Toivo ja 1924- IntWW 93
Toivonen, Hannu Tapio 1952- WhoScEn 94
Tojo Hideki 1884-1948 HisWorL [port]
Tokach, Richard M. WhoAmP 93
Tokar, Bette Lewis 1935- WhoFI 94
Tokar, Daniel 1937- WhoWest 94
Tokar, Edward Thomas 1947- WhoAm 94, WhoFI 94
Tokar, Gloria Joyce 1941- WhoAmP 93
Tokar, John Michael 1951- WhoScEn 94
Tokar, Louis John 1923- WhoWest 94
Tokarczyk, Michelle M. DrAPF 93
Tokareva, Viktoriia Samoilovna 1937- BlmGWL
Tokars, Fredric William 1953- WhoAmL 94
Tokasz, Paul 1946- WhoAmP 93
Tokaty, Grigori Alexandrovich Who 94
Tokatyan, Armand 1894-1960 NewGrDO
Tokayer, Ira Daniel 1957- WhoAmL 94
Tokei, Ferenc 1930- IntWW 93
Toker, Franklin 1944- WhoAmA 93
Toker, Franklin K. 1944- WhoAm 94
Tokerud, Robert Eugene 1936- WhoScEn 94
Tokes, Laszlo 1952- IntWW 93
Tokheim, Robert Edward 1936- WhoScEn 94, WhoWest 94
Tokioka, Franklin M. 1936- WhoIns 94
Tokioka, Franklin Makoto 1936- WhoFI 94
Toklas, Alice B(abette) 1877-1967 GayLL
Tokley, Joanna Nutter WhoBlA 94
Tokmakoff, George 1928- WhoWest 94
Tokody, Ilona IntWW 93
Tokody, Ilona 1953- NewGrDO
Tokofsky, Jerry H. 1936- IntMPA 94
Tokofsky, Jerry Herbert 1936- WhoAm 94, WhoWest 94
Tokoly, Mary Andree 1940- WhoScEn 94
Tokombayeva, Aysulu Asanbekovna 1947- IntWW 93
Tokuda, Marilyn WhoHol 92
Tokuda, Wendy 1950- WhoAsA 94
Tokue, Ikuo 1947- WhoScEn 94
Tokugawa Ieyasu 1542-1616 HisWorL [port]
Tokun, Ralph 1952- WhoBlA 94
Tokunaga, Howard Taira 1957- WhoAsA 94
Tokunaga, Katsumi 1923- WhoAsA 94
Tokuuke, Terrance Katsuki 1954- WhoAsA 94
Tol, Peter J. 1935- WhoIns 94
Tolan, David J. 1927- WhoAmL 94, WhoFI 94
Tolan, David Joseph 1933- WhoAm 94, WhoFI 94
Tolan, James Francis 1934- WhoAm 94
Tolan, Kathleen WhoHol 92
Tolan, Michael 1925- WhoHol 92
Tolan, Robert Warren 1960- WhoMW 93, WhoScEn 94
Tolan, Stephanie S. DrAPF 93

Toland, Gregg 1904-1948 *IntDcF 2-4 [port]*
Toland, John (Willard) 1912- *WrDr 94*
Toland, John Robert 1944- *WhoMW 93*
Toland, John Willard 1912- *WhoAm 94*
Tolar, Carroll T. 1929- *WhoFI 94*
Tolba, Mostafa Kamal 1922- *IntWW 93*
Tolbert, Anthony James, III 1932- *WhoMW 93*
Tolbert, Berlinda *WhoHol 92*
Tolbert, Bert Mills 1921- *WhoAm 94*
Tolbert, Bruce Edward 1948- *WhoBlA 94*
Tolbert, Charles Madden 1922- *WhoAm 94*
Tolbert, Edward T. 1929- *WhoBlA 94*
Tolbert, Herman Andre 1948- *WhoBlA 94*
Tolbert, Jacquelyn C. 1947- *WhoBlA 94*
Tolbert, James R., III 1935- *WhoAm 94*
Tolbert, John W., Jr. 1905- *WhoBlA 94*
Tolbert, Lawrence J. 1914- *WhoBlA 94*
Tolbert, Nathan Edward 1919- *WhoAm 94, WhoMW 93*
Tolbert, Odie Henderson, Jr. 1939- *WhoBlA 94*
Tolbert, Roger M. 1952- *WhoAm 94, WhoAmL 94*
Tolbert, Sharon Renee 1945- *WhoBlA 94*
Tolbert, Tommy *WhoAmP 93*
Tolbert, Tony Lewis 1967- *WhoBlA 94*
Tolchin, Edward Jay 1954- *WhoAmL 94*
Tolchin, Martin 1928- *WhoAm 94*
Tolchin, Susan J(ane) 1941- *ConAu 141*
Tolden, Verna L. 1935- *WhoAmP 93*
Toldra, Eduardo 1895-1962 *NewGrDO*
Toledano, Ralph de 1916- *WhoAm 94, WrDr 94*
Toledo, Angel D. *WhoHisp 94*
Toledo, Angeles 1958- *WhoAmA 93*
Toledo, Christopher L. 1960- *WhoHisp 94*
Toledo, Elizabeth Anne 1962- *WhoHisp 94*
Toledo, Evaristo Miguel 1935- *WhoHisp 94*
Toledo, Francisco 1940- *WhoAmA 93*
Toledo, Lawrence Ralph 1941- *WhoHisp 94*
Toledo, Robert Anthony 1942- *WhoHisp 94*
Toledo Feria, Freya M. 1960- *WhoHisp 94*
Toledo-Pereyra, Luis Horacio 1943- *WhoAm 94, WhoMW 93, WhoScEn 94*
Tolefree, Bryce Hugh 1962- *WhoAmL 94*
Tolentino, Casimiro Urbano 1949- *WhoAm 94, WhoWest 94*
Tolentino, Shirley A. 1943- *WhoBlA 94*
Tolentino, Virginia Cantor 1940- *WhoAsA 94*
Toler *Who 94*
Toler, Burl Abron 1928- *WhoBlA 94*
Toler, David Arthur Hodges 1920- *Who 94*
Toler, Hooper d1922 *WhoHol 92*
Toler, James C. 1936- *WhoScEn 94*
Toler, James Larkin 1935- *WhoAm 94*
Toler, Sidney d1947 *WhoHol 92*
Toles, Alvin 1963- *WhoBlA 94*
Toles, Edward Bernard 1909- *WhoAm 94, WhoAmL 94, WhoBlA 94*
Toles, Elwin Bonds 1916- *WhoAmP 93*
Toles, James LaFayette, Jr. 1933- *WhoBlA 94*
Toles, Thomas Gregory 1951- *WhoAm 94*
Tolete-Velcek, Francisca Agatep 1943- *WhoScEn 94*
Tolgesy, Victor 1928-1980 *WhoAmA 93N*
Tolhurst, John Gordon 1943- *Who 94*
Toliver, Harold Earl 1932- *WhoWest 94*
Toliver, Harold Eugene, Jr. 1944- *WhoBlA 94*
Toliver, Lee 1921- *WhoScEn 94, WhoWest 94*
Toliver, Raymond Frederick 1914- *WrDr 94*
Toliver, Richard T. 1930- *WhoAmP 93*
Toliver, Virginia F. 1948- *WhoBlA 94*
Tolkan, James *WhoHol 92*
Tolkan, James 1931- *IntMPA 94*
Tolkien, J. R. R. 1892-1973 *BlmGEL*
Tolkien, J(ohn) R(onald) R(euel) 1892-1973 *EncSF 93, TwCYAW*
Tolkin, Michael 1950- *IntMPA 94*
Tolksdorf, Gary Douglas 1958- *WhoMW 93*
Toll, Barbara Elizabeth 1945- *WhoAmA 93*
Toll, Bruce Elliot 1943- *WhoAm 94*
Toll, Charles Hulbert 1931- *WhoWest 94*
Toll, Daniel Roger 1927- *WhoAm 94, WhoFI 94*
Toll, Eduard Von 1858-1902 *WhWE*
Toll, Eric Jay 1951- *WhoWest 94*
Toll, Jack Benjamin 1925- *WhoAm 94*
Toll, John Sampson 1923- *WhoAm 94, WhoScEn 94*
Toll, Maynard Joy 1906-1988 *WhAm 10*
Toll, Maynard Joy, Jr. 1942- *WhoAm 94, WhoFI 94*
Toll, Perry Mark 1945- *WhoAm 94, WhoAmL 94*
Toll, Robert Charles 1938- *WrDr 94*
Toll, Robert Irwin 1940- *WhoAm 94*
Toll, Seymour I. 1925- *WhoAmL 94*
Toll, Sheldon Samuel 1940- *WhoAm 94, WhoAmL 94*
Tollaire, August d1959 *WhoHol 92*
Tollaksen, Brent S. 1966- *WhoMW 93*
Tollaksen, Peter Russell 1942- *WhoMW 93*
Tollakson, Rick Joel 1953- *WhoFI 94, WhoMW 93*
Toll-Crossman, Jacqueline Joy 1947- *WhoMW 93*
Tolle, Donald James 1918- *WhoAm 94*
Tolle, Glen Conrad 1939- *WhoScEn 94*
Tollefsen, Gerald Elmer 1942- *WhoScEn 94*
Tollefson, Ben 1927- *WhoAmP 93*
Tollefson, Ben C. 1927- *WhoMW 93*
Tollefson, Gordon Val 1942- *WhoAmL 94*
Tollefson, John Oliver 1937-1991 *WhAm 10*
Tollemache, Baron 1939- *Who 94*
Tollemache, Lyonel (Humphry John) 1931- *Who 94*
Tollen, Otz d1965 *WhoHol 92*
Tollenaere, Lawrence Robert 1922- *WhoAm 94, WhoFI 94, WhoWest 94*
Tollens, Salomon Rondon *WhoAmP 93*
Toller, Ernst 1893-1939 *IntDcT 2 [port]*
Toller, William Robert 1930- *WhoAm 94, WhoFI 94*
Tollerud, Jim *DrAPF 93*
Tolles, Bryant Franklin, Jr. 1939- *WhoAm 94, WhoAmA 93*
Tolles, Martha 1921- *SmATA 76 [port]*
Tolleson, Frederic LeRoy 1932- *WhoFI 94*
Tolleson, James E. 1906- *WhoAmP 93*
Tollestrup, Alvin Virgil 1924- *WhoAm 94, WhoScEn 94*
Tollett, Brenda Lynne 1963- *WhoAmL 94*
Tollett, Charles Albert, Sr. *WhoBlA 94*
Tollett, Leland Edward 1937- *WhoFI 94*
Tolley, Aubrey Granville 1924- *WhoAm 94*
Tolley, Edward Donald 1950- *WhoAmL 94*
Tolley, George 1925- *Who 94*
Tolley, James Little 1930- *WhoAm 94*
Tolley, Jerry Russell 1942- *WhoAm 94*
Tolley, John Stewart 1953- *WhoWest 94*
Tolley, Leslie John 1913- *Who 94*
Tolley, William Pearson 1900- *WhoAm 94*
Tollison, Grady Franklin, Jr. 1937- *WhoAmP 93*
Tolliver, Charles 1942- *WhoBlA 94*
Tolliver, David Joseph 1951- *WhoMW 93*
Tolliver, Don L. 1938- *WhoAm 94*
Tolliver, Dorothy Olivia *WhoMW 93*
Tolliver, Gerald Arthur 1935- *WhoScEn 94*
Tolliver, James David, Jr. 1938- *WhoWest 94*
Tolliver, Joel 1946- *WhoBlA 94*
Tolliver, Kevin Paul 1951- *WhoMW 93*
Tolliver, Lennie-Marie P. 1928- *WhoBlA 94*
Tolliver, Ned, Jr. 1943- *WhoBlA 94*
Tolliver, Richard Lamar 1945- *WhoBlA 94*
Tolliver, Ruby C. *DrAPF 93*
Tolliver, Stanley Eugene, Sr. 1925- *WhoBlA 94*
Tolliver, Steve *EncSF 93*
Tolliver, Thomas C., Jr. 1950- *WhoBlA 94*
Tolliver-Palma, Calvin Eugene 1950- *WhoWest 94*
Tollner, Ernest William 1949- *WhoScEn 94*
Tolmach, Jane Louise 1921- *WhoAmP 93*
Tolman, Gareth W. 1938- *WhoIns 94*
Tolman, Leland Locke 1908-1991 *WhAm 10*
Tolman, Richard Robins 1937- *WhoWest 94*
Tolman, Steven Kay 1946- *WhoAmL 94*
Tolman, Suzanne Nelson 1931- *WhoMW 93*
Tolman, Warren E. 1959- *WhoAmP 93*
Tolmie, Donald McEachern 1928- *WhoAm 94*
Tolmie, Kenneth Donald 1941- *WhoAm 94, WhoAmA 93*
Tolnaes, Gunnar d1940 *WhoHol 92*
Tolo, Marilu 1943- *WhoHol 92*
Toloa, Letuli 1930- *WhoAmP 93*
Tololo, Alkan *Who 94*
Tolonen, Risto Markus 1965- *WhoScEn 94*
Tolor, Alexander 1928- *WhoAm 94*
Tolpadi, Anil Kumar 1960- *WhoScEn 94*
Tolpin, Richard William 1943- *WhoAmP 93*
Tolpo, Carolyn Lee 1940- *WhoAmA 93*
Tolpo, Carolyn Lee Mary 1940- *WhoWest 94*
Tolpo, Vincent Carl 1950- *WhoAmA 93, WhoWest 94*
Tol Saut *IntWW 93*
Tolsky, Susan 1943- *WhoHol 92*
Tolsma, Dennis Dwayne 1939- *WhoAm 94*
Tolson, Jay 1948- *ConAu 141*
Tolson, Jay Henry 1935- *WhoAm 94*
Tolson, Jennifer Gale 1955- *WhoAmL 94*
Tolson, John J. 1948- *WhoAm 94*
Tolson, Jon Hart 1939- *WhoWest 94*
Tolstaia, Tatiana (Nikitinichna) 1951- *ConWorW 93, RfGShF*
Tolstaia, Tat'iana Mikhailovna 1951- *BlmGWL*
Tolstaya, Tatyana *ConWorW 93*
Tolstoi, Lev 1828-1910 *RfGShF*
Tolstoy, Alexandra L(vovna) 1884-1979 *ConAu 42NR*
Tolstoy, Alexei 1882-1945 *EncSF 93*
Tolstoy, Alexei Konstantinovich 1817-1875 *IntDcT 2*
Tolstoy, Dimitry 1912- *Who 94*
Tolstoy, Leo 1828-1910 *IntDcT 2*
Tolstoy, Leo Nikolaevitch 1828-1910 *BlmGEL*
Tolstoy, Lev Nikolayevich 1828-1910 *NewGrDO*
Tolstoy, Maria d1993 *NewYTBS 93*
Toltz, Steven David 1958- *WhoAmL 94*
Tom, Angelo C. 1956- *WhoAsA 94*
Tom, C. Y. 1907- *IntMPA 94*
Tom, Clarence Yung Chen 1927- *WhoWest 94*
Tom, Creighton Harvey 1944- *WhoWest 94*
Tom, Franklin 1941- *WhoAmL 94*
Tom, James Robert 1939- *WhoFI 94*
Tom, Lauren *WhoHol 92*
Tom, Lawrence 1950- *WhoWest 94*
Tom, Leland B. 1932- *WhoAsA 94*
Tom, Melvin Gee Lim 1950- *WhoAsA 94*
Tom, Ping 1935- *WhoAsA 94*
Tom, Terrance W. H. 1948- *WhoAmP 93*
Tom, Willard Ken 1952- *WhoAmL 94*
Toma, David 1933- *ConAu 42NR*
Toma, Joseph S. 1930- *WhoScEn 94*
Toma, Kyle Takeyoshi 1953- *WhoWest 94*
Tomac, Steven W. 1953- *WhoAmP 93, WhoMW 93*
Tomack, David d1977 *WhoHol 92*
Tomack, Sid d1962 *WhoHol 92*
Tomaino, Joseph Carmine 1948- *WhoMW 93*
Tomaino, Michael Thomas 1937- *WhoAm 94*
Tomalin, Claire 1933- *IntWW 93, Who 94, WrDr 94*
Tomalin, Ruth *WrDr 94*
Toman, Henry Edward 1944- *WhoAmP 93*
Toman, Mary Ann 1954- *WhoAm 94*
Toman, Michael Allen 1954- *WhoFI 94*
Toman, Michael J. *WhoIns 94*
Toman, Stephen E. *WhoFI 94*
Toman-Cubbage, Cheryl Ann 1956- *WhoAmL 94*
Tomar, Richard Thomas 1945- *WhoAmL 94*
Tomar, Russell Herman 1937- *WhoAm 94*
Tomarchio, Ludivoci d1947 *WhoHol 92*
Tomas, Harry A. 1945- *WhoHisp 94*
Tomas, Jerold F. V. *WhoAm 94*
Tomasch, Mark Robert 1947- *WhoMW 93*
Tomaschewsky, Michaela Maria 1947- *WhoMW 93*
Tomaschke, John Edward 1949- *WhoWest 94*
Tomasek, Frantisek d1992 *IntWW 93N*
Tomasek, Frantisek 1899-1992 *WhAm 10*
Tomasek, Frantisek, Cardinal 1899-1992 *AnObit 1992*
Tomasek, Robert Dennis 1928- *WhoAm 94*
Tomasek, Vaclav Jan Krtitel 1774-1850 *NewGrDO*
Tomaselli, Julius Louis 1928-1984 *WhAm 10*
Tomaselli, Kevin James 1957- *WhoWest 94*
Tomash, Erwin 1921- *WhoAm 94*
Tomashefsky, Clark Steven 1950- *WhoAmL 94*
Tomashevich, George Vid 1927- *WrDr 94*
Tomasi, Giovanni Battista fl. c. 1656-1692 *NewGrDO*
Tomasi, Henri 1901-1971 *NewGrDO*
Tomasi, Thomas B. 1927- *WhoAm 94, WhoScEn 94*
Tomasiak, James W. 1960- *WhoFI 94*
Tomasini, Roberto Jorge 1929- *IntWW 93*
Tomasini, Wallace J. 1926- *WhoAmA 93*
Tomasini, Wallace John 1926- *WhoAm 94*
Tomason, Bruce A. 1947- *WhoFI 94*
Tomasovic, Stephen Peter 1947- *WhoScEn 94*
Tomassi, Craig Arthur 1951- *WhoAmL 94*
Tomassi, Louie 1923- *WhoAmP 93*
Tomassini, Joanne Elizabeth 1952- *WhoScEn 94*
Tomassini, Lawrence Anthony 1945- *WhoAm 94, WhoFI 94*
Tomasson, Helgi 1942- *IntDcB [port], WhoAm 94, WhoWest 94*
Tomasson, Tomas Armann 1929- *IntWW 93*
Tomasson, Verna Safran *DrAPF 93*
Tomassoni, David 1952- *WhoAmP 93*
Tomassoni, David Joseph 1952- *WhoMW 93*
Tomasulo, Virginia Merrills 1919- *WhoAm 94*
Tomaszewicz, Elizabeth Eleonora 1946- *WhoMW 93*
Tomaszewski, Henryk 1919- *IntWW 93*
Tomaszewski, Marian Edna 1935- *WhoAmP 93*
Tomaszewski, Mary Lou 1938- *WhoMW 93*
Tomaszkiewicz, Francis Xavier 1946- *WhoMW 93, WhoScEn 94*
Tomazi, George Donald 1935- *WhoMW 93, WhoScEn 94*
Tomazinis, Anthony Rodoflos 1929- *WhoAm 94*
Tomba, Alberto 1966- *CurBio 93 [port]*
Tombach, Ivar Harald 1941- *WhoWest 94*
Tombaugh, Clyde William 1906- *IntWW 93, WhoAm 94, WhoScEn 94*
Tombaugh, Wayne H. 1910- *WhoAmP 93*
Tombes, Andrew d1976 *WhoHol 92*
Tombes, Averett Snead 1932- *WhoWest 94*
Tomblin, Earl Ray 1952- *WhoAmP 93*
Tomblinson, James Edmond 1927- *WhoAm 94*
Tombrello, Thomas Anthony, Jr. 1936- *WhoAm 94, WhoWest 94*
Tombros, Peter George 1942- *WhoAm 94*
Tombs, Baron 1924- *Who 94*
Tombs, Francis Leonard 1924- *IntWW 93*
Tomchuk, Marjorie 1933- *WhoAmA 93*
Tomcik, Andrew Michael 1938- *WhoAmA 93*
Tomei, Marisa *WhoHol 92*
Tomei, Marisa 1964- *IntMPA 94, WhoAm 94*
Tomek, Laura Lindemann 1940- *WhoMW 93*
Tomek, William Goodrich 1932- *WhoAm 94, WhoScEn 94*
Tomelty, Frances *WhoHol 92*
Tomelty, Joseph 1910- *WhoHol 92*
Tomeo, James Francis 1958- *WhoFI 94*
Tomeo, Thomas P. 1911- *WhoAmP 93*
Tomeoni, Irene 1763-1830 *NewGrDO*
Tomeoni, Pellegrino c. 1729-1816? *NewGrDO*
Tomes, Henry, Jr. 1932- *WhoBlA 94*
Tomeu, Enrique J. *WhoHisp 94*
Tomey, Ingrid 1943- *SmATA 77 [port]*
Tomfohrde, Mitchell Gerald 1962- *WhoMW 93*
Tomhave, Beverly Korstad 1947- *WhoMW 93*
Tomich, Lillian 1935- *WhoAmL 94, WhoFI 94, WhoWest 94*
Tomicich, Helen Espinoza 1944- *WhoHisp 94*
Tominaga, Brenda Elaine 1958- *WhoWest 94*
Tominaga, Lynn S. *WhoAmP 93*
Tominomori, Eiji 1928- *IntWW 93*
Tominova, Zdena 1941- *WhoWomW 91*
Tomioka Taeko 1937- *BlmGWL*
Tomita, Etsuji 1942- *WhoScEn 94*
Tomita, Tadanori 1945- *WhoMW 93*
Tomita, Tamlyn *WhoHol 92*
Tomita, Tamlyn Naomi *WhoAsA 94*
Tomita, Vincent Sadao 1957- *WhoWest 94*
Tomiyasu, Kiyo 1919- *WhoAm 94*
Tomizuka, Masayoshi 1946- *WhoScEn 94, WhoWest 94*
Tomjanovich, Rudolph 1948- *WhoAm 94*
Tomjanovich, Rudy 1948- *BasBi*
Tomkiel, Judith Irene 1949- *WhoFI 94, WhoWest 94*
Tomkins, Allyson Jones 1954- *WhoWest 94*
Tomkins, Calvin 1925- *WhoAm 94, WhoAmA 93, WrDr 94*
Tomkins, Edward Emile 1915- *Who 94*
Tomkins, Frank Sargent 1915- *WhoAm 94*
Tomkins, Jasper 1946- *WrDr 94*
Tomkins, Oliver Stratford d1992 *IntWW 93N, Who 94N*
Tomkins, Oliver Stratford 1908-1992 *WrDr 94N*
Tomkins, Silvan Solomon 1911-1991 *WhAm 10*
Tomkiw, Lydia *DrAPF 93*
Tomko, George Peter 1936- *WhoAmA 93*
Tomko, Jozef 1924- *IntWW 93*
Tomkowit, Thaddeus Walter 1918-1989 *WhAm 10*

Tomkys, (W.) Roger 1937- *IntWW 93*
Tomkys, (William) Roger 1937- *Who 94*
Tomlan, Gwynne *WhoHol 92*
Tomlin, Bradley Walker 1899-1953 *WhoAmA 93N*
Tomlin, Josephine D. 1952- *WhoBlA 94*
Tomlin, Lily 1939- *IntMPA 94, WhoAm 94, WhoCom [port], WhoHol 92*
Tomlin, Pinky d1987 *WhoHol 92*
Tomlins, Jason *WhoHol 92*
Tomlinson, Alexander Cooper 1922- *WhoAm 94*
Tomlinson, Ambrose Jessup 1865-1943 *DcAmReB 2*
Tomlinson, Bernard (Evans) 1920- *Who 94*
Tomlinson, Bill *WhoAmP 93*
Tomlinson, Bruce Lloyd 1950- *WhoScEn 94*
Tomlinson, Charles *Who 94*
Tomlinson, Charles 1927- *BlmGEL*
Tomlinson, (Alfred) Charles 1927- *Who 94, WrDr 94*
Tomlinson, Charles Matthew 1922- *WhoMW 93*
Tomlinson, Charles Wesley, Jr. 1947- *WhoAm 94*
Tomlinson, David 1917- *WhoHol 92*
Tomlinson, David (Cecil MacAlister) 1917- *Who 94*
Tomlinson, David L. 1929- *WhoAmP 93*
Tomlinson, Frank S. 1912- *HisDcKW*
Tomlinson, G. Richard 1942- *WhoScEn 94*
Tomlinson, Gary Earl 1951- *WhoMW 93, WhoScEn 94*
Tomlinson, George Herbert 1912- *WhoAm 94*
Tomlinson, Gus 1933- *WhoAm 94*
Tomlinson, Harry 1943- *WrDr 94*
Tomlinson, Herbert Weston 1930- *WhoAmL 94*
Tomlinson, J. Richard 1930- *WhoAm 94*
Tomlinson, James Francis 1925- *WhoAm 94*
Tomlinson, James Lawrence 1935- *WhoMW 93*
Tomlinson, Jerry Lanning 1944- *WhoWest 94*
Tomlinson, John 1946- *IntWW 93, NewGrDO, Who 94*
Tomlinson, John Edward 1939- *Who 94*
Tomlinson, John Michael 1949- *WhoFI 94*
Tomlinson, John Race Godfrey 1932- *Who 94*
Tomlinson, Joseph Bradley 1944- *WhoFI 94*
Tomlinson, Joseph Ernest 1939- *WhoAm 94*
Tomlinson, Mel Alexander 1954- *IntWW 93, WhoBlA 94*
Tomlinson, Michael James 1958- *WhoFI 94*
Tomlinson, Michael John 1929- *Who 94*
Tomlinson, Michael John 1942- *Who 94*
Tomlinson, Milton Ambrose 1906- *WhoAm 94*
Tomlinson, Randolph R. 1920- *WhoBlA 94*
Tomlinson, Rawdon *DrAPF 93*
Tomlinson, Richard Allan 1932- *Who 94*
Tomlinson, Robert *WhoAmP 93*
Tomlinson, Robert 1938- *WhoBlA 94*
Tomlinson, Robert Eugene 1931- *WhoWest 94*
Tomlinson, Robert M. 1945- *WhoAmP 93*
Tomlinson, Roger W. *WhoScEn 94*
Tomlinson, Sally 1936- *Who 94*
Tomlinson, Stanley *Who 94*
Tomlinson, (Frank) Stanley 1912- *Who 94*
Tomlinson, Stephen Miles 1952- *Who 94*
Tomlinson, Thomas King 1934- *WhoScEn 94*
Tomlinson, Warren Leon 1930- *WhoAm 94, WhoAmL 94*
Tomlinson, William Holmes 1922- *WhoAm 94, WhoFI 94*
Tomlinson, William M. 1948- *WhoAmL 94*
Tomlinson-Keasey, Carol Ann 1942- *WhoAm 94, WhoWest 94*
Tomlinson-Tarantino, Patricia Ann 1952- *WhoMW 93*
Tomljanovich, Esther *WhoAmP 93*
Tomljanovich, Esther M. 1931- *WhoAmL 94, WhoMW 93*
Tommasini, Vincenzo 1878-1950 *NewGrDO*
Tommeraasen, Miles 1923- *WhoAm 94*
Tomoeda, Cheryl Kuniko 1958- *WhoWest 94*
Tomomatsu, Hideo 1929- *WhoAsA 94*
Tomonaga, Sin-itiro 1906-1979 *WorScD*
Tomos 1932- *IntWW 93*
Tomos 1936- *WhoPRCh 91 [port]*
Tomowa-Sintow, Anna 1941- *NewGrDO*
Tomowa-Sintow, Anna 1943- *IntWW 93*
Tompa, Gary Steven 1958- *WhoScEn 94*
Tompkins, Alan 1907- *WhoAmA 93*
Tompkins, Angel 1943- *WhoHol 92*
Tompkins, Arthur Wilson 1895- *WhAm 10*
Tompkins, Betty (I) 1945- *WhoAmA 93*
Tompkins, Christopher Wilson 1949- *WhoAmL 94*
Tompkins, Curtis Johnston 1942- *WhoAm 94, WhoMW 93*
Tompkins, Daniel D. *WhoAm 94*
Tompkins, Daniel Nelson 1928- *WhoWest 94*
Tompkins, Daniel Reuben 1931- *WhoAm 94*
Tompkins, Donald Robert 1941- *WhoFI 94*
Tompkins, Eileen J. 1933- *WhoAmP 93*
Tompkins, Frederick Clifford 1910- *Who 94*
Tompkins, James Arthur 1946- *WhoAm 94*
Tompkins, James Francis 1948- *WhoMW 93*
Tompkins, Joan *WhoHol 92*
Tompkins, Joseph Buford, Jr. 1950- *WhoAm 94, WhoAmL 94*
Tompkins, Laurie 1950- *WhoScEn 94*
Tompkins, Michael 1955- *WhoAmA 93*
Tompkins, Rachel Victoria 1951- *WhoMW 93*
Tompkins, Raymond Edgar 1934- *WhoAmL 94*
Tompkins, (Granville) Richard (Francis) d1992 *Who 94N*
Tompkins, Robert George 1923- *WhoAm 94*
Tompkins, Ronald K. 1934- *WhoAm 94*
Tompkins, Susie *WhoAm 94*
Tompkins, Thomas Jay 1959- *WhoAmL 94*
Tompkins, William Finley 1913-1989 *WhAm 10*
Tompsett, Michael Francis 1939- *WhoAm 94*
Tompsett, William C. 1948- *WhoAm 94*
Tompson, Marian Leonard 1929- *WhoAm 94*
Toms, Billy Leroy 1944- *WhoFI 94*
Toms, Carl 1927- *Who 94*
Toms, Edward Ernest 1920- *Who 94*
Toms, Michael Anthony 1940- *WhoWest 94*
Toms, Robert Lee 1935- *WhoAm 94*
Tomsett, Alan Jeffrey 1922- *Who 94*
Tomsett, Janet Moffat 1943- *WhoAmL 94, WhoMW 93*
Tomsic, Vida 1913- *WhoWomW 91*
Tomsky, Judy 1959- *WhoWest 94*
Tomsovic, Edward Joseph 1922- *WhoAm 94*
Toms-Robinson, Dolores C. 1926- *WhoBlA 94*
Tomur Dawamat 1927- *IntWW 93*
Tomur Dawamat 1928- *WhoPRCh 91 [port]*
Ton, Dao-Rong 1940- *WhoScEn 94*
Ton, L. Eugene *WhoMW 93*
Tonagawa, Susumu 1939- *WorScD*
Tonai, Rosalyn *WhoAsA 94*
Tonarelli, Lorenzo fl. 1747-1771 *NewGrDO*
Tonay, Veronica Katherine 1960- *WhoWest 94*
Tonbridge, Archdeacon of *Who 94*
Tonbridge, Bishop Suffragan of 1943- *Who 94*
Toncic-Sorinj, Lujo 1915- *IntWW 93, Who 94*
Tonda, Joseph John 1940- *WhoFI 94*
Tondel, Lawrence Chapman 1946- *WhoAm 94, WhoAmL 94*
Tondel, Lyman Mark, Jr. 1912- *WhoAmL 94*
Tondering, Claus 1953- *WhoScEn 94*
Tondeur, Philippe Maurice 1932- *WhoAm 94*
Tone, Franchot d1968 *WhoHol 92*
Tone, Jeffrey R. 1953- *WhoAm 94, WhoAmL 94*
Tone, Kenneth Edward 1930- *WhoAm 94*
Tone, Michael P. 1949- *WhoAmL 94*
Tone, Philip Willis 1923- *WhoAm 94*
Tone, Yasunao *DrAPF 93*
Tonegawa, Susumu 1939- *IntWW 93, NobelP 91 [port], Who 94, WhoAm 94, WhoAsA 94, WhoScEn 94*
Tonelli, Edith Ann 1949- *WhoAmA 93*
Tonello-Stuart, Enrica Maria *WhoAm 94, WhoWest 94*
Tonelson, Jack Martin 1930- *WhoAm 94*
Toner, Frank J. 1930- *WhoAm 94*
Toner, Mike 1944- *WhoAm 94*
Toner, Tom *WhoHol 92*
Toner, Walter Joseph, Jr. 1921- *WhoScEn 94*
Toney, Adam 1938- *WhoAmP 93*
Toney, Andrew 1957- *WhoBlA 94*
Toney, Anthony 1913- *WhoAm 94, WhoAmA 93*
Toney, Anthony 1962- *WhoBlA 94*
Toney, Edna Amadon d1993 *NewYTBS 93*
Toney, Jim d1973 *WhoHol 92*
Toney, Robert L. 1934- *AfrAmG [port], WhoAm 94*
Toney, Steven L. 1946- *WhoAmL 94, WhoMW 93*
Tong, Alex Wai Ming 1952- *WhoAsA 94*
Tong, Alvin H. 1939- *WhoAsA 94*
Tong, Benjamin 1966- *WhoAsA 94*
Tong, Benjamin Robert *WhoAsA 94*
Tong, Dalton Arlington 1950- *WhoBlA 94*
Tong, Douglas L. 1955- *WhoAsA 94*
Tong, Franklin Fuk-Kay 1956- *WhoAsA 94*
Tong, Gary S. 1942- *WrDr 94*
Tong, Hing 1922- *WhoAm 94*
Tong, Jacqueline 1951- *WhoHol 92*
Tong, Jennie S. 1952- *WhoAsA 94*
Tong, Kam d1969 *WhoHol 92*
Tong, Larry Wingloon 1962- *WhoWest 94*
Tong, Lik Kuen 1935- *WhoAsA 94*
Tong, Mary Powderly 1924- *WhoScEn 94*
Tong, Raymond 1922- *WrDr 94*
Tong, Richard Dare 1930- *WhoWest 94*
Tong, Sammee d1964 *WhoHol 92*
Tong, Siu Wing 1950- *WhoWest 94*
Tong, Sun-De 1950- *WhoAsA 94*
Tong, Ts'ing H. 1923- *WhoAsA 94*
Tong, Wen-How 1949- *WhoAsA 94*
Tong, Yit Chow 1948- *WhoScEn 94*
Tonga, King of *IntWW 93*
Tonga, King of 1918- *Who 94*
Tong Changyin *WhoPRCh 91*
Tong Dalin *WhoPRCh 91 [port]*
Tonge, Brian Lawrence 1933- *Who 94*
Tonge, David Theophilus 1930- *Who 94*
Tonge, Fred 1875- *WhoHol 92*
Tonge, H. Assheton d1927 *WhoHol 92*
Tonge, Philip d1959 *WhoHol 92*
Tonge, Roger 1946-1981 *WhoHol 92*
Tong Enzheng *EncSF 93*
Tong Enzheng 1935- *WhoPRCh 91 [port]*
Tonggar Losang Chilai 1927- *WhoPRCh 91*
Tong Guorong 1931- *WhoPRCh 91 [port]*
Tong Hui 1963- *WhoPRCh 91 [port]*
Tongue, Carole 1955- *Who 94, WhoWomW 91*
Tongue, Paul Graham 1932- *WhoAm 94, WhoFI 94*
Tongue, Thomas Healy 1943- *WhoAmL 94*
Tongue, William Walter 1915- *WhoAm 94*
Tong Zenggong *WhoPRCh 91*
Tong Zengyin 1934- *WhoPRCh 91 [port]*
Tonick, Illene 1951- *WhoWest 94*
Tonina, La *NewGrDO*
Tonini, Leon Richard 1931- *WhoWest 94*
Tonino, Robert Henry 1944- *WhoFI 94*
Tonjes, Marian Jeannette Benton 1929- *WhoAm 94, WhoWest 94*
Tonkel, J. Rock 1937- *WhoAm 94*
Tonkin, David Oliver 1929- *IntWW 93, Who 94*
Tonkin, Derek 1929- *Who 94*
Tonkin, Elizabeth 1934- *ConAu 140*
Tonkin, Humphrey Richard 1939- *WhoAm 94*
Tonkin, Leo Sampson 1937- *WhoAm 94*
Tonkin, Peter Francis 1950- *WrDr 94*
Tonkin, William G. 1943- *WhoAmL 94*
Tonko, Paul D. 1949- *WhoAmP 93*
Tonkovich, Dan Richard 1946- *WhoAmP 93*
Tonks, Angela *EncSF 93*
Tonks, Robert Stanley *WhoAm 94*
Tonkyn, Richard George 1927- *WhoAm 94*
Tonn, Bruce Edward 1955- *WhoScEn 94*
Tonn, David Michael 1961- *WhoFI 94*
Tonn, Elverne Meryl 1929- *WhoWest 94*
Tonn, Robert James 1927- *WhoMW 93, WhoScEn 94*
Tonndorf, Juergen 1914-1989 *WhAm 10*
Tonos Florenzan, Fernando 1956- *WhoAmP 93*
Tonti, Henri De c. 1650-1704 *WhWE*
Tontz, Jay Logan 1938- *WhoAm 94, WhoWest 94*
Tontz, Robert L. 1917- *WhoAm 94*
Tonucci, Vincent J. *WhoAmP 93*
Tonyn, Patrick *AmRev*
Tonyn, Patrick 1725-1804 *WhAmRev*
Tonypandy, Viscount 1909- *IntWW 93, Who 94*
Too, Danny 1958- *WhoWest 94*
Tooher, Meave Marie 1959- *WhoAmL 94*
Toohey, Brian Frederick 1944- *WhoAm 94, WhoAmL 94*
Toohey, Cynthia 1934- *WhoAmP 93*
Toohey, Daniel Weaver 1940- *WhoAm 94, WhoFI 94*
Toohey, Edward Joseph 1930- *WhoFI 94*
Toohey, James Kevin 1944- *WhoAm 94, WhoAmL 94*
Toohey, Joyce 1917- *Who 94*
Toohey, Michael Weaver 1941- *WhoMW 93*
Toohey, Philip S. 1943- *WhoAmL 94*
Toohig, Michael Francis 1924- *WhoFI 94*
Toohig, Timothy E. 1928- *WhoScEn 94*
Toohulhulsote c. 1810-1877 *EncNAR*
Took, John Michael Exton 1926- *Who 94*
Took, Steve Peregrine 1949-1980 *See* T. Rex *ConMus 11*
Tooker, Carl E. 1947- *WhoAm 94, WhoFI 94*
Tooker, Gary Lamarr 1939- *WhoAm 94, WhoMW 93*
Tooker, George 1920- *WhoAm 94, WhoAmA 93*
Tooker, Richard (Presley) 1902-1988 *EncSF 93*
Tooker, William H. d1936 *WhoHol 92*
Tookes, James Nelson 1934- *WhoFI 94*
Tookey, Marcia Hickman 1932- *WhoAmP 93*
Tookey, Richard William 1934- *Who 94*
Tookey, Robert C. 1925- *WhoIns 94*
Tookey, Robert Clarence 1925- *WhoWest 94*
Toolan, Brian Paul 1950- *WhoAm 94*
Toolan, Robert Emmet 1925- *WhoFI 94*
Toole, Allan H. 1920- *WhoAm 94*
Toole, Clyde Rowland, Jr. 1933- *WhoWest 94*
Toole, David George 1942- *WhoAm 94*
Toole, Edward Charles, Jr. 1937- *WhoAmL 94*
Toole, Floyd Edward 1938- *WhoWest 94*
Toole, Howard 1949- *WhoAmL 94, WhoAmP 93, WhoWest 94*
Toole, James Francis 1925- *WhoAm 94, WhoScEn 94*
Toole, Joan Trimble 1923- *WhoWest 94*
Toole, John Harper 1941- *WhoAmL 94*
Toole, Lee K. 1936- *WhoFI 94*
Toole, William Walter 1959- *WhoAmL 94*
Tooley, Charles Frederick 1947- *WhoAmP 93*
Tooley, John 1924- *IntWW 93, NewGrDO, Who 94*
Tooley, Keith David 1960- *WhoAmL 94*
Tooley, Linda Faye 1942- *WhoMW 93*
Tooley, William Lander 1934- *WhoFI 94, WhoWest 94*
Toolson, Andy *WhoBlA 94*
Toomajian, William Martin 1943- *WhoAm 94, WhoAmL 94, WhoMW 93*
Toombs, Alfred (Gerald) 1912- *EncSF 93*
Toombs, Charles Phillip 1952- *WhoBlA 94*
Toombs, Eugene Martin, III 1941- *WhoMW 93*
Toombs, Kenneth Eldridge 1928- *WhoAm 94*
Toombs, Robert *EncSF 93*
Toombs, Robert d1993 *NewYTBS 93*
Toombs, Russ William 1951- *WhoScEn 94*
Toomer, Clarence 1952- *WhoBlA 94*
Toomer, Jean 1894-1967 *AfrAmAl 6, ConBlB 6 [port], PoeCrit 7, RfGShF*
Toomer, Vann Alma Rosalee *WhoBlA 94*
Toomey, Daniel 1938- *WhoAmP 93*
Toomey, John Christopher 1964- *WhoMW 93*
Toomey, Kathryn 1942- *WhoAmP 93*
Toomey, Ralph 1918- *Who 94*
Toomey, Regis 1902- *WhoHol 92*
Toomey, Robert E., Jr. 1945- *EncSF 93*
Toomey, Thomas Murray 1923- *WhoAm 94*
Toomey, Timothy J., Jr. *WhoAmP 93*
Toomey, William Shenberger 1935- *WhoFI 94, WhoMW 93*
Toomin, Louis A. 1935- *WhoAmP 93*
Toomin, Louis Allen 1935- *WhoWest 94*
Toomre, Alar 1937- *WhoScEn 94*
Toomy, Joseph F. 1948- *WhoAmP 93*
Toon, Al Lee, Jr. 1963- *WhoBlA 94*
Toon, Leonard Eugene 1932- *WhoWest 94*
Toon, Malcolm 1916- *IntWW 93, WhoAm 94, WhoAmP 93*
Toone, Elam Cooksey, Jr. 1908- *WhoAm 94*
Toone, Geoffrey 1910- *WhoHol 92*
Toones, Fred d1962 *WhoHol 92*
Toor, Bruce A. 1934- *WhoAmL 94*
Toor, Helen Mary 1956- *WhoAmL 94*
Toor, Herbert Lawrence 1927- *WhoAm 94*
Toot, Joseph F., Jr. 1935- *WhoAm 94, WhoFI 94, WhoMW 93*
Toote, Gloria E. A. *WhoAm 94*
Toote, Gloria E. A. 1931- *WhoBlA 94*
Tooth, Geoffrey Cuthbert 1908- *Who 94*
Tooth, (Hugh) John L. *Who 94*
Toothman, John William 1954- *WhoAmL 94*
Top, Don *WhoAmP 93*
Top, Franklin Henry, Jr. 1936- *WhoAm 94, WhoScEn 94*

Topa, Edward F. 1941- *WhoIns 94*
Topal, Michael David 1945- *WhoScEn 94*
Topaz, David Ethan 1967- *WhoWest 94*
Topazio, Virgil William 1915- *WhoAm 94*
Topchevsky, Morris 1899- *WhoAmA 93N*
Topcheyev, Yuriy Ivanovich 1920- *IntWW 93*
Tope, Dwight Harold 1918- *WhoFI 94, WhoWest 94*
Tope, Graham Norman 1943- *Who 94*
Tope, James Owen 1955- *WhoMW 93*
Tope, Trimbak Krishna 1914- *IntWW 93*
Topel, David Glen 1937- *WhoAm 94, WhoScEn 94*
Topel, David Louis 1953- *WhoAmL 94*
Topelius, Kathleen E. 1948- *WhoAm 94*
Toperzer, Thomas Raymond 1939- *WhoAm 94, WhoAmA 93*
Topete Stonefield, Liz 1955- *WhoHisp 94*
Topey, Ishmael Aloysius 1926- *WhoMW 93*
Topey, Lester d1920 *WhoHol 92*
Topfer, Klaus 1938- *IntWW 93*
Topfer, Morton Louis 1936- *WhoAm 94*
Topham, Anthony 1947-
See Yardbirds, The *ConMus 10*
Topham, Douglas William *WhoWest 94*
Topham, Lawrence Garth 1914- *Who 94*
Topik, Steven Curtis 1949- *WhoWest 94*
Topinka, Judy Baar 1944- *WhoAmP 93*
Topitzes, Nicholas James *WhoMW 93*
Topjon, Ann Johnson 1940- *WhoWest 94*
Topkis, Jay 1924- *WhoAmL 94*
Topley, Keith *Who 94*
Topley, (William) Keith 1936- *Who 94*
Topley, Kenneth Wallis Joseph 1922- *Who 94*
Toplikar, John M. *WhoAmP 93*
Topliss, Harry, Jr. 1923- *WhoAm 94*
Toplitz, George Nathan 1936- *WhoAmL 94*
Topol 1935- *IntMPA 94, WhoHol 92*
Topol, Allan Jerry 1941- *WhoAm 94*
Topol, Chaim 1935- *IntWW 93*
Topol, Clive M. 1949- *WhoAm 94*
Topol, Eric Jeffrey 1954- *WhoAm 94*
Topol, Josef 1935- *IntDcT 2*
Topol, Robert Martin 1925- *WhoAm 94, WhoAmA 93*
Topol, Robin April Levitt *WhoAmL 94*
Topolski, Feliks 1907-1989 *WhAm 10*
Toporov, Vladimir Alekseevich 1946- *IntWW 93*
Toporov, Vladimir Mikhailovich 1946- *LngBDD*
Toporov, Vladimir Nikolayevich 1928- *IntWW 93*
Topp, Alphonso Axel, Jr. 1920- *WhoWest 94*
Topp, Elizabeth Murphy 1957- *WhoMW 93*
Topp, George Clarke 1937- *WhoAm 94*
Topp, Roger Leslie 1923- *Who 94*
Toppan, Clara Anna Raab 1910- *WhoFI 94*
Toppel, Bert Jack 1926- *WhoScEn 94*
Toppel, Harold H. 1924- *WhoFI 94*
Toppel, Milton 1919- *WhoAm 94*
Toppen, Timothy Robert 1955- *WhoMW 93*
Topper, Burt *WhoHol 92*
Topper, David R. 1943- *WhoAmA 93*
Topper, Hertha 1924- *NewGrDO*
Topper, Tim *WhoHol 92*
Toppin, Edgar Allan 1928- *WhoBlA 94*
Topping, Frank 1937- *Who 94*
Topping, James 1879-1949 *WhoAmA 93N*
Topping, James 1904- *Who 94*
Topping, John A. 1860-1934 *EncABHB 9*
Topping, Norman Hawkins 1908- *WhoAm 94*
Topping, Peter 1916- *WhoAm 94*
Topping, Robert Joe 1936- *WhoAmP 93*
Topping, Seymour 1921- *WhoAm 94*
Topuzes, Thomas 1947- *WhoHisp 94*
Tor, Michael *WhoHol 92*
Toradze, David Alexandrovich 1922-1983 *NewGrDO*
Torain, Tony William 1954- *WhoBlA 94*
Toraldo Di Francia, Giuliano 1916- *IntWW 93*
Toran, Anthony 1939- *WhoBlA 94*
Toran, Daniel James 1948- *WhoAm 94, WhoFI 94*
Toran, Kay Dean 1943- *WhoBlA 94*
Toraño, Francisco José 1944- *WhoHisp 94*
Toraño-Pantin, Maria Elena 1938- *WhoHisp 94*
Toranzos, Gary Antonio 1958- *WhoScEn 94*
Toraya, Margarita F. 1940- *WhoHisp 94*
Torbert, Clement Clay, Jr. 1929- *WhoAm 94, WhoAmP 93*
Torbert, Donald Robert 1910-1985 *WhoAmA 93N*
Torbert, Meg Birch 1912- *WhoWest 94*
Torbert, Preston M. 1943- *WhoAm 94*
Torbert, Stephanie Birch 1945- *WhoAmA 93*
Torbert, William C. 1935- *WhoAmP 93*
Torbet, John Randolph 1943- *WhoAmL 94*
Torbet, Walter 1933- *WhoWest 94*
Torbett, Gary Burl 1942- *WhoFI 94*
Torchinsky, Alberto 1944- *WhoHisp 94*
Torcivia, Benedict J., Sr. 1929- *WhoAm 94*
Torcoletti, Enzo 1943- *WhoAmA 93*
Tordesillas, Jesus d1973 *WhoHol 92*
Tordoff, Baron 1928- *Who 94*
Tordoff, Harrison Bruce 1923- *WhoAm 94*
Torell, John Raymond, III 1939- *WhoAm 94, WhoFI 94*
Torelli, Giacomo 1608-1678 *NewGrDO*
Torem, Charles d1993 *NewYTBS 93*
Toren, Brian Keith 1935- *WhoMW 93*
Toren, Mark 1950- *WhoFI 94*
Toren, Marta d1957 *WhoHol 92*
Toren, Robert 1915- *WhoWest 94*
Torena, Juan *WhoHol 92*
Torf, Lois Beurman 1926- *WhoAmA 93*
Torg, Joseph Steven 1934- *WhoAm 94*
Torga, Miguel *ConAu 141*
Torga, Miguel 1907- *ConWorW 93, RfGShF*
Torgelson, David Jon 1960- *WhoMW 93*
Torgersen, Eric *DrAPF 93*
Torgersen, Torwald Harold 1929- *WhoAm 94*
Torgerson, Jim *WhoAmP 93*
Torgerson, John W. 1950- *WhoAmP 93*
Torgerson, Larry Keith 1935- *WhoAmL 94, WhoFI 94, WhoMW 93*
Torgerson, Les 1946- *WhoAmL 94*
Torgerson, Richard Warren 1956- *WhoFI 94*
Torgeson, Roy d1991 *EncSF 93*
Torget, Arne O. 1916- *WhoScEn 94, WhoWest 94*
Torgoff, Irving d1993 *NewYTBS 93*
Torgow, Eugene N. 1925- *WhoAm 94, WhoFI 94*
Tori, Motoo 1948- *WhoScEn 94*
Torian, Edward Torrence 1933- *WhoBlA 94*
Toribara, Taft Yutaka 1917- *WhoAm 94*
Toriello, Helga Valdmanis 1952- *WhoMW 93*
Toriello, John Michael 1952- *WhoAmL 94*
Torigian, Puzant Crossley 1922- *WhoFI 94, WhoScEn 94*
Torii, Shuko 1930- *WhoScEn 94*
Torii, Sigeru 1932- *WhoScEn 94*
Torii, Tetsuya 1918- *WhoScEn 94*
Torino, James Anthony 1965- *WhoFI 94*
Torino, Thomas Michael 1947- *WhoFI 94*
Tork, Peter 1942- *WhoHol 92*
Torkanowsky, Werner 1926-1992 *WhAm 10*
Torkelson, Gwen Ellen 1952- *WhoFI 94*
Torkelson, Lucile Emma 1915- *WhoMW 93*
Torkelson, Rita Katherine 1943- *WhoMW 93*
Torkildsen, Peter 1958- *WhoAm 94*
Torkildsen, Peter G. 1958- *CngDr 93*
Torkildsen, Peter Gerard 1958- *WhoAmP 93*
Torkildson, Raymond Maynard 1917- *WhoAmL 94, WhoAmP 93*
Torklep, Lynlee 1942- *WhoWest 94*
Torlakson, James Daniel 1951- *WhoAmA 93*
Torlen, Michael Arnold 1940- *WhoAmA 93*
Torlesse, Arthur David 1902- *Who 94*
Torley, John Frederic 1911- *WhoAm 94*
Tormala, Pertti 1945- *IntWW 93*
Tormanen, Calvin Douglas 1946- *WhoMW 93*
Torme, Mel 1925- *IntMPA 94, WhoHol 92*
Torme, Melvin 1925- *WhoAm 94*
Tormey, Douglass Cole 1938- *WhoAm 94*
Tormey, James Roland, Jr. 1935- *WhoAmL 94*
Tormey, Terrence O'Brien 1954- *WhoFI 94*
Tormis, Velio 1930- *NewGrDO*
Torn, Jerry 1933- *WhoAmA 93*
Torn, Rip 1931- *IntMPA 94, WhoAm 94, WhoHol 92*
Tornabene, Russell C. 1923- *WhoAm 94*
Tornabene, Thomas Guy 1937- *WhoAm 94*
Tornade, Pierre *WhoHol 92*
Tornaes, Laurits 1936- *IntWW 93*
Tornaritis, Criton George 1902- *Who 94*
Tornatore, Giuseppe 1956- *IntWW 93*
Tornatore, Joe *WhoHol 92*
Torneden, Connie Jean 1955- *WhoMW 93*
Torneden, Roger Lee 1944- *WhoFI 94*
Tornek, Anna d1985 *WhoHol 92*
Tornek, J. K. d1974 *WhoHol 92*
Tornek, Terry E. 1945- *WhoAm 94*
Tornes, Virginia L. 1923- *WhoMW 93*
Tornetta, Frank Joseph 1916- *WhoScEn 94*
Torney, Thomas William 1915- *Who 94*
Tornheim, Norman 1942- *WhoAmA 93*
Torno, Laurent Jean, Jr. 1936- *WhoScEn 94*
Tornquist, Claudia W. 1952- *WhoAm 94*
Tornqvist, Kerttu Annikki 1942- *WhoWomW 91*
Tornstrom, Robert Ernest 1946- *WhoAmL 94*
Tornudd, Klaus 1931- *IntWW 93*
Toro, Carlos Hans 1943- *WhoHisp 94*
Toro, Eugenio E. 1937- *WhoHisp 94*
Toro, Eusebio *WhoHisp 94*
Toro, Joe *WhoHisp 94*
Toro, Manuel A. 1937- *WhoHisp 94*
Toro, Severo Colberg *WhoAmP 93*
ToRobert, Henry Thomas 1942- *IntWW 93, Who 94*
Torok, John Anthony, III 1952- *WhoMW 93*
Torok, Margaret Louise 1922- *WhoAm 94, WhoFI 94*
Torok, Raymond Patrick 1946- *WhoMW 93*
Torok, Sophie *BlmGWL*
Toron, Caryl R. 1958- *WhoHisp 94*
Toronto, Archbishop of 1930- *Who 94*
Toronto, Bishop of 1937- *Who 94*
Toronto, Bishop Suffragan of *Who 94*
Toronto, Ellen Leslie Kaylor 1944- *WhoMW 93*
Toro-Ventura, Gilbert 1956- *WhoHisp 94*
Torp, Niels A. 1940- *IntWW 93*
Torpey, Richard *WhoAmP 93*
Torpey, Richard I. 1931- *WhoAmL 94*
Torpey, Scott Raymond 1955- *WhoAmL 94*
Torphichen, Lord 1946- *Who 94*
Torquemada, Tomas de 1420-1498 *BlmGEL*
Torr, Ann M. 1935- *WhoAmP 93*
Torr, Franklin G. 1930- *WhoAmP 93*
Torr, Ralph 1931- *WhoAmP 93*
Torrado, Alberto M. *WhoHisp 94*
Torrance, Ellis Paul 1915- *WhoAm 94, WhoScEn 94*
Torrance, James Bruce 1923- *Who 94*
Torrance, Lee 1920- *WrDr 94*
Torrance, Thomas Forsyth 1913- *IntWW 93, Who 94, WrDr 94*
Torrando, Francisco *WhoHisp 94*
Torras, Mary R. 1927- *WhoAmP 93*
Torre, Bennett Patrick 1962- *WhoScEn 94*
Torre, Carlos 1951- *WhoHisp 94*
Torre, Douglas Paul 1919- *WhoAm 94*
Torre, Elias R. 1932- *WhoHisp 94*
Torre, Joseph Paul 1940- *WhoAm 94, WhoMW 93*
Torre, Malcolm *BlmGWL*
Torreano, John Francis 1941- *WhoAmA 93*
Torregian, Sotere *DrAPF 93*
Torregrosa, Hector Luis, Jr. 1957- *WhoMW 93*
Torregrosa, Tomas Lopez 1868-1913 *NewGrDO*
Torregrossa, Joseph Anthony 1944- *WhoAm 94, WhoAmL 94*
Torrejon y Velasco, Tomas de 1644?-1728 *NewGrDO*
Torrelio Villa, Celso 1933- *IntWW 93*
Torrence, David d1951 *WhoHol 92*
Torrence, Ernest d1933 *WhoHol 92*
Torrence, Gwen *WhoBlA 94*
Torrence, Howard H. 1903-1990 *WhAm 10*
Torrence, Jacquelyn Seals 1944- *WhoBlA 94*
Torrence, Richard 1936- *WhoAm 94*
Torrence, Samuel Lee 1940- *WhoFI 94*
Torrens, Pip *WhoHol 92*
Torrens-Spence, (Frederick) Michael (Alexander) 1914- *Who 94*
Torrent, Ana *WhoHol 92*
Torrent, Karen E. 1959- *WhoAmL 94*
Torrenzano, Richard *WhoAm 94*
Torres, Adeline *WhoHisp 94*
Torres, Andres A. 1943- *WhoHisp 94*
Torres, Angel *IntWW 93*
Torres, Antonio 1956- *WhoScEn 94*
Torres, Antonio 1957- *WhoHisp 94*
Torres, Art *WhoWest 94*
Torres, Art 1946- *WhoAmP 93, WhoHisp 94*
Torres, Arturo D. *WhoHisp 94*
Torres, Arturo G. *WhoHisp 94*
Torres, Arturo Lopez 1948- *WhoAmL 94, WhoHisp 94*
Torres, Baldomero Chapa 1935- *WhoHisp 94*
Torres, Carlos Alberto 1950- *WhoWest 94*
Torres, Celia Margaret 1936- *WhoHisp 94*
Torres, Cynthia Ann 1958- *WhoFI 94*
Torres, David 1934- *WhoAm 94, WhoHisp 94*
Torres, David 1956- *WhoHisp 94*
Torres, David P., Jr. *WhoHisp 94*
Torres, Diana Cristina 1956- *WhoHisp 94*
Torres, Donald d1986 *WhoHol 92*
Torres, Durbal, Jr. 1944- *WhoHisp 94*
Torres, Edmundo S., Jr. 1938- *WhoHisp 94*
Torres, Eduardo Jose 1961- *WhoHisp 94*
Torres, Edward, IV 1966- *WhoHisp 94*
Torres, Edwin *WhoHisp 94*
Torres, Edwin 1947- *WhoHisp 94*
Torres, Eileen *WhoHisp 94*
Torres, Eligio 1958- *WhoMW 93*
Torres, Eliseo S. 1945- *WhoHisp 94*
Torres, Elizabeth 1947- *WhoHisp 94*
Torres, Ernest C. 1941- *WhoAm 94, WhoAmL 94, WhoHisp 94*
Torres, Ernesto Cesar 1950- *WhoHisp 94*
Torres, Estanislao Tudela *WhoAmP 93*
Torres, Esteban Edward 1930- *CngDr 93, WhoAm 94, WhoAmP 93, WhoHisp 94, WhoWest 94*
Torres, Esther Aida 1949- *WhoHisp 94*
Torres, Fernando 1924- *WhoHisp 94*
Torres, Francesc 1948- *WhoAmA 93*
Torres, Frank 1928- *WhoHisp 94*
Torres, Frederico M. *WhoHisp 94*
Torres, Gerald 1952- *WhoHisp 94*
Torres, Gladys 1938- *WhoHisp 94*
Torres, Gloria Ann 1957- *WhoHisp 94*
Torres, Guido Adolfo 1938- *WhoScEn 94*
Torres, Guillermo M. *WhoHisp 94*
Torres, Hector c. 1954-
See Bon Jovi *ConMus 10*
Torres, Horacio 1924-1976 *WhoAmA 93N*
Torres, Isidore B. 1947- *WhoHisp 94*
Torres, Israel 1934- *WhoScEn 94*
Torres, Ivan Lincoln 1948- *WhoHisp 94*
Torres, J. Antonio 1949- *WhoHisp 94*
Torres, Jake *WhoHisp 94*
Torres, Jess G. *WhoHisp 94*
Torres, Jesús *WhoHisp 94*
Torres, Jesus U. 1927- *WhoAmP 93*
Torres, Joe H. *WhoHisp 94*
Torres, John R. 1959- *WhoHisp 94*
Torres, Jose *WhoHisp 94*
Torres, Jose Antonio 1952- *WhoHisp 94*
Torres, José B. 1946- *WhoHisp 94*
Torres, Jose E. *WhoHisp 94*
Torres, José Luis 1936- *WhoHisp 94*
Torres, José Manuel 1935- *WhoHisp 94*
Torres, Joseph James 1950- *WhoHisp 94*
Torres, Joseph L. 1927- *WhoHisp 94*
Torres, Juan Carlos 1948- *WhoHisp 94*
Torres, Juan E. Lopez *WhoAmP 93*
Torres, Juan S. *WhoAmP 93*
Torres, Julio *WhoHisp 94*
Torres, Lady A. 1948- *WhoHisp 94*
Torres, Lawrence Arthur 1960- *WhoHisp 94*
Torres, Lawrence E. 1927- *WhoHisp 94*
Torres, Lawrence J. 1946- *WhoHisp 94*
Torres, Leida I. 1949- *WhoHisp 94*
Torres, Leo *WhoHisp 94*
Torres, Leonard 1926- *WhoHisp 94*
Torres, Leyda Luz 1955- *WhoHisp 94*
Torres, Linda Marie *WhoHisp 94*
Torres, Lissette Diaz *WhoAmP 93*
Torres, Liz 1947- *WhoHol 92*
Torres, Lou C. 1950- *WhoHisp 94*
Torres, Luis 1943- *WhoHisp 94*
Torres, Luis A. 1922- *WhoHisp 94*
Torres, Luis A., Jr. *WhoHisp 94*
Torres, Luis Ruben 1950- *WhoHisp 94*
Torres, Luis Vaez De fl. 160-?- *WhWE*
Torres, Magdalena 1930- *WhoHisp 94*
Torres, Magdalena 1944- *WhoHisp 94*
Torres, Manuel 1963- *WhoScEn 94*
Torres, Margarita M. 1955- *WhoHisp 94*
Torres, Maria de los Angeles 1955- *WhoHisp 94*
Torres, Marta Carmen 1954- *WhoHisp 94*
Torres, Martin R. 1943- *WhoHisp 94*
Torres, Maximino deJesus 1932- *WhoHisp 94*
Torres, Mayé 1960- *WhoHisp 94*
Torres, Michael Alfonso 1956- *WhoWest 94*
Torres, Milton J. 1931- *WhoHisp 94*
Torres, Myrna A. 1941- *WhoHisp 94*
Torres, Nancy P. 1953- *WhoHisp 94*
Torres, Néstor *WhoHisp 94*
Torres, Noe Acosta 1956- *WhoHisp 94*
Torres, Omar 1945- *WhoHisp 94*
Torres, Oscar *WhoHisp 94*
Torres, Oscar L., Sr. *WhoHisp 94*
Torres, Oscar Modesto, Jr. 1945- *WhoHisp 94*
Torres, Ovidio L. 1962- *WhoHisp 94*
Torres, Paul 1952- *WhoHisp 94*
Torres, Rafael *WhoHisp 94*
Torres, Ramon Hernan, Jr. 1953- *WhoHisp 94*
Torres, Raquel d1987 *WhoHol 92*
Torres, Raymond 1957- *WhoHisp 94*
Torres, Refugio R. 1925- *WhoHisp 94*
Torres, Reinaldo E. 1935- *WhoHisp 94*
Torres, Rene 1943- *WhoFI 94*
Torres, Ricardo, Jr. *WhoHisp 94*
Torres, Ricardo A. *WhoHisp 94*

Torres, Richard Fielding 1947- *WhoFI 94*
Torres, Richard R. 1961- *WhoHisp 94*
Torres, Rigo Romualdo 1963- *WhoScEn 94*
Torres, Rita A. 1951- *WhoHisp 94*
Torres, Robert Anthony 1948- *WhoHisp 94*
Torres, Robert John 1963- *WhoHisp 94*
Torres, Rodolfo 1925- *WhoHisp 94*
Torres, Rosario *WhoHisp 94*
Torres, Roy Arthur 1961- *WhoAmL 94*
Torres, Sally *WhoHisp 94*
Torres, Salvio 1932- *WhoHisp 94*
Torres, Sara 1942- *WhoHisp 94*
Torres, Sixto E. 1944- *WhoHisp 94*
Torres, Tereska *DrAPF 93*
Torres, Veronica Imelda 1965- *WhoHisp 94*
Torres, Victor M. 1928- *WhoHisp 94*
Torres, Xiomara *WhoHisp 94*
Torres, Xohana 1931- *BlmGWL*
Torres, Zaida Hernandez *WhoAmP 93*
Torres-Aybar, Francisco G. 1934- *WhoHisp 94*
Torres-Aybar, Francisco Gualberto 1934- *WhoScEn 94*
Torres-Bauza, Luis José 1951- *WhoHisp 94*
Torres Bernardez, Santiago 1929- *IntWW 93*
Torrescano, Adolfo Jimenez 1937- *WhoFI 94*
Torres-Comas, Hortensia M. 1949- *WhoHisp 94*
Torresella, Fanny 1856-1914 *NewGrDO*
Torres-Figueroa, Saul 1948- *WhoHisp 94*
Torres-Geary, Miriam Beatriz 1956- *WhoHisp 94*
Torres-Gil, Fernando M. 1948- *WhoHisp 94*
Torres-Guzmán, María E. 1951- *WhoHisp 94*
Torres-Horwitt, C. Aída *WhoHisp 94*
Torres-James, Alicia 1943- *WhoAmP 93*
Torres-Labawld, Jose D. 1932- *WhoHisp 94*
Torres-Labawld, Jose Dimas 1932- *WhoFI 94*
Torres-Lemir, Carlos 1939- *WhoHisp 94*
Torres Marques, Helena de Melo 1941- *WhoWomW 91*
Torres Medina, Emilio 1934- *WhoScEn 94*
Torres-Meléndez, Elaine 1957- *WhoHisp 94*
Torres Moore, Dominga *WhoHisp 94*
Torres-Olivencia, Noel R. 1966- *WhoScEn 94*
Torres Oliver, Juan Fremiot 1925- *WhoAm 94*
Torres Pohl, Elizabeth *WhoHisp 94*
Torres Quiles, Herbert 1930- *WhoHisp 94*
Torres Reyes, Emilio 1935- *WhoHisp 94*
Torres-Rioseco, Arture 1897- *WhAm 10*
Torres Rivera, Lina M. 1953- *WhoHisp 94*
Torres-Rivera, Rebeca 1931- *WhoHisp 94*
Torres-Santiago, José Manuel 1940- *WhoHisp 94*
Torres-Santos, Raymond 1958- *WhoHisp 94*
Torres-Trujillo, Mayé Carmela 1960- *WhoHisp 94*
Torres-Vélez, Félix L. 1939- *WhoHisp 94*
Torres Yribar, Wilfredo 1933- *IntWW 93*
Torres y Torres Lara, Carlos *IntWW 93*
Torrey, Claudia Olivia 1958- *WhoAmL 94*
Torrey, David Leonard 1931- *WhoAm 94*
Torrey, Ella King *WhoAmA 93*
Torrey, Henry Cutler 1911- *WhoScEn 94*
Torrey, James D. 1940- *WhoWest 94*
Torrey, Reuben Archer 1856-1928 *DcAmReB 2*
Torrey, Richard Frank 1926- *WhoAm 94*
Torrey, Roger 1938- *WhoHol 92*
Torrey, Rubye Prigmore 1926- *WhoBlA 94*
Torrez, Adolfo Jose, Jr. 1948- *WhoHisp 94*
Torrez, Ervin E. 1935- *WhoHisp 94*
Torrez, Fernando M. 1944- *WhoHisp 94*
Torrez, Jerry A. 1943- *WhoHisp 94*
Torrez, Mariano A. 1939- *WhoAmP 93, WhoHisp 94*
Torrez, Naomi E. 1939- *WhoWest 94*
Torrez, Robert J. 1949- *WhoHisp 94*
Torrezao, Guiomar 1844-1898 *BlmGWL*
Torri, Anna Maria fl. 1684-1708 *NewGrDO*
Torri, Pietro c. 1650-1737 *NewGrDO*
Torriani, Aimee d1963 *WhoHol 92*
Torriani, Maria Antonietta *BlmGWL*
Torriani-Gorini, Annamaria 1918- *WhoAm 94*
Torribio, John H. *WhoHisp 94*
Torricelli, Evangelista 1608-1647 *WorInv [port], WorScD [port]*
Torricelli, Robert G. 1951- *CngDr 93, WhoAm 94, WhoAmP 93*
Torrieri, Don Joseph 1942- *WhoScEn 94*
Torrington, Viscount 1743-1813 *DcNaB MP*
Torrington, Viscount 1943- *Who 94*
Torrison, William Rahr 1945- *WhoMW 93*
Torro, Pel *EncSF 93*
Torro, Pel 1935- *WrDr 94*
Torroja Menendez, Jose Maria 1916- *IntWW 93*
Torru, John Egon 1963- *WhoWest 94*
Torru, Katharine Lucas 1964- *WhoWest 94*
Torruco, Miguel d1956 *WhoHol 92*
Torruella, Juan E. 1960- *WhoHisp 94*
Torruella, Juan R. *WhoAmP 93*
Torruella, Juan R. 1933- *WhoAm 94, WhoAmL 94, WhoHisp 94*
Torruella, Radamés A. 1940- *WhoHisp 94*
Torry, Alvin c. 1798- *EncNAR*
Torshen, Jerome Harold 1929- *WhoAmL 94, WhoFI 94, WhoMW 93*
Torsney, Cheryl B. 1955- *WrDr 94*
Torstendahl, Rolf 1936- *IntWW 93*
Tortarolo, Joann Mary 1948- *WhoAmP 93*
Tortelier, Paul 1914-1990 *WhAm 10*
Tortelier, Yan Pascal 1947- *IntWW 93, Who 94*
Torten, Michael 1935- *WhoWest 94*
Tortolero, Carlos *WhoHisp 94*
Tortora, Robert D. 1946- *WhoScEn 94*
Tortorella, Albert James 1942- *WhoAm 94*
Tortoriello, Robert Laurence 1950- *WhoAm 94*
Torumtay, Necip 1926- *IntWW 93*
Torvay, Jose d1973 *WhoHol 92*
Tory, Avraham 1909- *ConAu 140*
Tory, Geofroy (William) 1912- *Who 94*
Tory, John A. *WhoAm 94, WhoFI 94*
Torz, Richard J. 1956- *WhoFI 94*
Tosar, Hector A. 1923- *IntWW 93*
Tosatti, Barbara Maria 1891-1934 *BlmGWL*
Tosatti, Vieri 1920- *NewGrDO*
Toscan, Richard Eric 1941- *WhoWest 94*
Toscan du Plantier, Daniel 1941- *IntWW 93*
Toscanini, Arturo d1957 *WhoHol 92*
Toscanini, Arturo 1867-1957 *AmCulL, NewGrDO*
Toscano, (Dolores A.) *WhoAmA 93*
Toscano, James Vincent 1937- *WhoAm 94*
Toscano, Linda Laursen 1951- *WhoFI 94*
Toscano, Maria Guadalupe 1965- *WhoHisp 94*
Toscano, Norman *WhoHisp 94*
Toscano, Oscar Ernesto 1951- *WhoAmL 94*
Toscano, Patrick Peter, Jr. 1960- *WhoAmL 94*
Toscano, Peter Ralph 1920- *WhoMW 93*
Toscano, Sebastian J. 1955- *WhoHisp 94*
Toscano, William Michael 1945- *WhoFI 94*
Tosch, Gilbert B. 1939- *WhoIns 94*
Toschik, Larry 1922- *WhoAmA 93*
Toseland, Ronald James 1933- *Who 94*
Tosh, Nancy Peckham 1932- *WhoAm 94*
Tosh, Robert Lowell 1944- *WhoAmP 93*
Tosi, Adelaide c. 1800-1859 *NewGrDO*
Tosi, Giuseppe Felice fl. 1677-1693 *NewGrDO*
Tosi, Oscar I. 1929- *WhoAm 94*
Tosi, Pier Francesco 1654-1732 *NewGrDO*
Tosk, Jeffrey Morton 1951- *WhoScEn 94*
Toso, Otello d1966 *WhoHol 92*
Tosovsky, Josef 1950- *IntWW 93*
Tossi Brutti, Graziella 1938- *WhoWomW 91*
Tosta, Timothy A. 1948- *WhoAmL 94*
Tostado, Maria Elena 1940- *WhoHisp 94*
Tostao 1947- *WorESoc [port]*
Tosteson, Heather *DrAPF 93*
Tostevin, Lola Lemire 1937- *BlmGWL*
Tosti, (Francesco) Paolo 1846-1916 *DcNaB MP*
Tostrud, Daniel David 1964- *WhoAmL 94*
Totaro, Rosemarie 1933- *WhoAmP 93*
Totaro, Samuel C., Jr. 1947- *WhoAmL 94*
Totenberg, Nina 1944- *WhoAm 94*
Totenberg, Roman 1911- *WhoAm 94*
Toter, Kimberly Mrowiec 1956- *WhoMW 93*
Toth, Aladar 1898-1968 *NewGrDO*
Toth, Alan 1944- *WhoFI 94*
Toth, Carl 1947- *WhoAmA 93*
Toth, Danny Andrew 1946- *WhoScEn 94*
Toth, David Clay 1952- *WhoFI 94*
Toth, Elizabeth Levay *WhoWest 94*
Toth, Georgina Gy 1932- *WhoAmA 93*
Toth, James Joseph 1956- *WhoScEn 94*
Toth, James Michael 1943- *WhoScEn 94*
Toth, Joseph Michael, Jr. 1935- *WhoWest 94*
Toth, Judith Coggeshall 1937- *WhoAmP 93*
Toth, Julius 1935- *IntWW 93*
Toth, Karoly Charles 1954- *WhoScEn 94*
Toth, Laura Anne 1949- *WhoMW 93*
Toth, Louis McKenna 1941- *WhoScEn 94*
Toth, Robert Charles 1928- *WhoAm 94*
Toth, Stephen Michael 1946- *WhoFI 94*
Toth, Susan Allen *DrAPF 93*
Tothacer, Austin Joseph, Jr. 1955- *WhoAmL 94*
To'Thova', Katarina 1940- *IntWW 93*
Totino, Louis J. 1933- *WhoAm 94*
Totis, Giuseppe Domenico de *NewGrDO*
Totlis, Gust John 1939- *WhoAm 94, WhoMW 93*
Totman, Patrick Steven 1944- *WhoAm 94, WhoFI 94*
Totnes, Archdeacon of *Who 94*
Toto d1967 *WhoHol 92*
Toto, Billie d1928 *WhoHol 92*
Toto The Clown d1938 *WhoHol 92*
Totten, Arthur Irving, Jr. 1906- *WhoScEn 94*
Totten, Bernice E. 1921- *WhoBlA 94*
Totten, Caroline *DrAPF 93*
Totten, Donald Lee 1933- *WhoAmP 93*
Totten, Gary Allen 1949- *WhoScEn 94*
Totten, George Oakley, III 1922- *WhoAm 94, WhoWest 94*
Totten, Herman Lavon 1938- *WhoBlA 94*
Totten, Joseph Byron d1946 *WhoHol 92*
Totten, Randolph Fowler 1943- *WhoAm 94, WhoAmL 94*
Totten, Venita Laverne 1963- *WhoScEn 94*
Tottenham *Who 94*
Tottenham, Merle *WhoHol 92*
Tottenham, Terry Oliver 1944- *WhoAm 94, WhoAmL 94*
Totter, Audrey 1918- *IntMPA 94, WhoHol 92*
Totter, John Randolph 1914- *WhoAm 94*
Totterman, Richard Evert Bjornson 1926- *IntWW 93, Who 94*
Tottie, Thomas 1930- *IntWW 93*
Tottle, Charles Ronald 1920- *Who 94, WrDr 94*
Tottola, Andrea Leone d1831 *NewGrDO*
Tottress, Richard Edward 1917- *WhoBlA 94*
Totz, Sue Rosene 1954- *WhoMW 93*
Tou, Julius T. 1926- *WhoScEn 94*
Toubert, Pierre Marcel Paul 1932- *IntWW 93*
Toubes, Norbert *WhoHisp 94*
Toubon, Jacques 1941- *IntWW 93*
Touby, Kathleen Anita 1943- *WhoAmL 94*
Touby, Michael Brian 1966- *WhoFI 94*
Touch, Arthur Gerald 1911- *Who 94*
Touchberry, Robert Walton 1921- *WhoWest 94*
Touche, Anthony (George) 1927- *Who 94*
Touche, Rodney (Gordon) 1928- *Who 94*
Touchet, Donovan Bernard 1949- *WhoFI 94*
Touchstone, John E. 1939- *WhoBlA 94*
Touchy, Deborah K. P. 1957- *WhoAmL 94*
Touffaire, Pierre Julien 1933- *WhoScEn 94*
Tougas, Gerard Raymond 1921- *IntWW 93*
Tougas, Roger L. *WhoAmP 93*
Touger, David 1959- *WhoAmL 94*
Touhey, Maura Abeln 1955- *WhoAmL 94*
Touhill, Blanche Marie 1931- *WhoAm 94, WhoMW 93*
Touhill, C. Joseph 1938- *WhoScEn 94*
Touhy, John P. 1919- *WhoAmP 93*
Toukonen, Eric Lee 1953- *WhoMW 93*
Toulemon, Robert 1927- *IntWW 93*
Toulis, Vasilios (Apostolos) 1931- *WhoAmA 93*
Toulmin, John Kelvin 1941- *Who 94*
Toulmin, Priestley, III 1930- *WhoAm 94*
Toulmin, Stephen E(delston) 1922- *WrDr 94*
Toulmin, Stephen Edelston 1922- *Who 94, WhoAm 94*
Toulouse, Gerard 1939- *IntWW 93*
Toulouse, Robert Bartell 1918- *WhoAm 94*
Toulout, Jean d1962 *WhoHol 92*
Toulson, Roger Grenfell 1946- *Who 94*
Toulson, Shirley 1924- *WrDr 94*
Toumanova, Tamara 1917- *WhoHol 92*
Toumanova, Tamara 1919- *IntDcB [port]*
Toumey, Hubert John *WhoAm 94*
Toumpas, John N. 1901- *IntWW 93*
Toupin, Harold Ovid 1927- *WhoAm 94*
Toupin, Jacques *NewGrDO*
Toupin, L. David 1955- *WhoAmL 94*
Tour, Robert Louis 1918- *WhoWest 94*
Touraine, Alain Louis Jules Francois 1925- *IntWW 93*
Toural, Amelia 1949- *WhoIns 94*
Tourangeau, Huguette 1938- *NewGrDO*
Toure, Amadou Toumani *IntWW 93*
Toure, Askia Muhammad Abu Bakr el 1938- *BlkWr 2*
Toure, Kwame 1941- *WhoBlA 94*
Toure, Mamoudou 1928- *IntWW 93*
Toure, Mohamed Ali 1949- *WhoFI 94*
Toure, Sekou 1922-1984 *ConBlB 6 [port]*
Toure, Yonoussi 1941- *IntWW 93*
Tourel, Jennie d1973 *WhoHol 92*
Tourel, Jennie 1900-1973 *NewGrDO*
Touret, Jacques Leon Robert 1936- *IntWW 93*
Tourevski, Mark 1952- *ConAu 142*
Tourgee, Albion Winegar 1838-1905 *AmSocL*
Tourgeman, Eli A. 1945- *WhoHisp 94*
Tourino, Ralph Gene 1941- *WhoAm 94*
Tourlentes, Thomas Theodore 1922- *WhoAm 94*
Tournas, Methodios 1946- *WhoAm 94*
Tournemire, Charles (Arnould) 1870-1939 *NewGrDO*
Tourneur, Cyril 1575?-1626 *BlmGEL, IntDcT 2*
Tourneur, Jacques d1977 *WhoHol 92*
Tourneur, Jacques 1904-1977 *HorFD [port]*
Tourneur, Maurice d1961 *WhoHol 92*
Tournier, Michel 1924- *IntWW 93*
Tournier, Michel (Edouard) 1924- *ConWorW 93, GayLL*
Tournillon, Nicholas Brady 1933- *WhoAm 94*
Tours, Hugh Berthold 1910- *WrDr 94*
Tourtellotte, Charles Dee 1931- *WhoAm 94*
Tourtillott, Eleanor Alice 1909- *WhoMW 93, WhoScEn 94*
Tousard, A. Louis de 1749-1817 *WhAmRev*
Tousard, Anne Louis de 1749-1817 *AmRev*
Tous de Torres, Luz M. 1944- *WhoFI 94*
Tousey, Frank *EncSF 93*
Tousey, Richard 1908- *IntWW 93, WhoAm 94, WhoScEn 94*
Tousignant, Claude 1932- *IntWW 93, WhoAmA 93*
Tousley, Russell Frederick 1938- *WhoAmL 94, WhoWest 94*
Toussaint, Allen 1938- *ConMus 11 [port]*
Toussaint, Allen Richard 1938- *WhoAm 94*
Toussaint, Donald Raymond 1952- *WhoFI 94*
Toussaint, Rose-Marie 1956- *WhoBlA 94*
Toussant, Lorraine *WhoHol 92*
Tousson, Maurice *WhoFI 94*
Touster, Saul 1925- *WhoAm 94*
Tout, Herbert 1904- *Who 94*
Toutain, Roland d1977 *WhoHol 92*
Touyz, Stephen William 1950- *WhoScEn 94*
Touzalin, Robert *EncSF 93*
Tovar, Carole L. 1940- *WhoWest 94*
Tovar, Dave R. 1967- *WhoHisp 94*
Tovar, Humberto Toby 1911- *WhoHisp 94*
Tovar, Irene F. 1938- *WhoAmP 93*
Tovar, Lorenzo 1942- *WhoHisp 94*
Tovar, Lupita 1911- *WhoHol 92*
Tovar, Nicholas Mario 1960- *WhoWest 94*
Tovar, Pedro De fl. 154-?- *WhWE*
Tovatt, Patrick *WhoHol 92*
Tove, Samuel B. 1921- *WhoScEn 94*
Tovell, Laurence 1919- *Who 94*
Tover, May d1949 *WhoHol 92*
Tovey, Brian (John Maynard) 1926- *Who 94*
Tovey, George d1982 *WhoHol 92*
Tovey, Joseph 1938- *WhoFI 94*
Tovey, Roberta *WhoHol 92*
Tovey, Weldon Reynolds 1938- *WhoWest 94*
Tovish, Harold 1921- *WhoAm 94, WhoAmA 93*
Tovolgyi, Titusz *EncSF 93*
Tovue, Ronald 1933- *Who 94*
Tow, Bruce Lincoln 1952- *WhoWest 94*
Tow, Leonard 1928- *WhoAm 94, WhoFI 94*
Tow, Theow Huang 1945- *WhoAm 94*
Towb, Harry 1925- *WhoHol 92*
Towbin, Abraham Robert 1935- *WhoAm 94, WhoFI 94*
Towbin, Belmont d1993 *NewYTBS 93*
Towe, Peter Milburn 1922- *IntWW 93*
Towe, Thomas Edward 1937- *WhoAmP 93, WhoWest 94*
Toweett, Taaitta 1925- *IntWW 93*
Towell, Linda Ladd 1948- *WhoAmL 94*
Towell, Timothy L. 1934- *WhoAmP 93*
Towell, William Earnest 1916- *WhoAm 94*
Tower, Alton G., Jr. 1927- *WhoScEn 94*
Tower, Horace Linwood, III 1932- *WhoAm 94, WhoFI 94*
Tower, Joan Peabody 1938- *WhoAm 94*
Tower, John Goodwin 1925-1991 *WhAm 10*
Tower, Lee William 1946- *WhoAmL 94*
Tower, Philip Thomas 1917- *Who 94*

Tracy, Lee d1968 WhoHol 92
Tracy, Lois Bartlett 1901- WhoAmA 93
Tracy, Lorna 1934- WrDr 94
Tracy, Louis 1863-1928 EncSF 93
Tracy, Martin Booth 1940- WhoMW 93
Tracy, Michael 1943- WhoAmA 93
Tracy, Michael Alec 1932- WrDr 94
Tracy, Michael Cameron 1952- WhoAm 94
Tracy, Mona Innes 1892-1959 BlmGWL
Tracy, Nathaniel 1751-1796 WhAmRev
Tracy, (John) Nicholas 1944- ConAu 141
Tracy, Philip R. 1942- WhoFI 94
Tracy, Richard H. C. WhoAmP 93
Tracy, Robert Edward 1928- WhoAm 94
Tracy, Robert H. 1948- WhoAmA 93
Tracy, Roger Wahlquist 1938- WhoAmP 93
Tracy, Russell Peter 1949- WhoScEn 94
Tracy, Spencer d1967 WhoHol 92
Tracy, Stephen Victor 1941- WhoAm 94
Tracy, Steve d1986 WhoHol 92
Tracy, Susan M. WhoAmP 93
Tracy, Thomas Kit 1938- WhoAm 94
Tracy, Thomas Miles 1936- WhoAm 94
Tracy, Walter Valentine 1914- Who 94
Tracy, William d1967 WhoHol 92
Tracy, William Allan 1940- WhoAmP 93
Tracy, William B. 1943- WhoIns 94
Trader, George Henry d1951 WhoHol 92
Trader, Harriet Peat 1922- WhoBlA 94
Trader, Joseph Edgar 1946- WhoAm 94, WhoMW 93
Trader, Rhonda Sue 1950- WhoMW 93
Traeger, Charles Henry, III 1942- WhoAm 94
Traeger, Donna Jean 1956- WhoScEn 94
Traeger, John Andrew 1921- WhoAmP 93
Traeger, Kim d1987 WhoHol 92
Traeger, Richard K. 1932- WhoWest 94
Traeger, Rick d1987 WhoHol 92
Traetta, Tommaso (Michele Francesco Saverio) 1727-1779 NewGrDO
Trafford, Abigail 1940- WhoAm 94
Trafford, Ian Colton 1928- Who 94
Trafford, Robert Ward 1951- WhoAm 94, WhoAmL 94
Traficant, James A., Jr. 1941- CngDr 93, WhoAm 94, WhoAmP 93, WhoMW 93
Traficante, Michael Anthony 1939- WhoAmP 93
Trafis, Gerald Anthony 1950- WhoFI 94
Trafton, Barbara M. 1949- WhoAmP 93
Trafton, E. Joan 1930- WhoMW 93
Trafton, George d1971 ProFbHF
Trafton, Herbert d1979 WhoHol 92
Trafton, Richard L. WhoAmP 93
Trafton, Stephen J. 1946- WhoAm 94, WhoFI 94, WhoWest 94
Trager, Gary Alan 1950- WhoScEn 94
Trager, Neil C. WhoAmA 93
Trager, Philip 1935- WhoAm 94, WhoAmA 93
Trager, Russell Harlan 1945- WhoWest 94
Trager, William 1910- IntWW 93, WhoAm 94
Tragos, William George 1934- WhoAm 94
Trahair, John Rosewarne 1921- Who 94
Trahan, Barry G. 1954- WhoAmP 93
Trahan, Margaret Fritchey 1934- WhoFI 94
Trahern, Charles Garrett 1953- WhoScEn 94
Trahern, George Eugene 1936- WhoAmP 93, WhoWest 94
Trahern, Joseph Baxter, Jr. 1937- WhoAm 94
Traherne, Cennydd (George) 1910- Who 94
Traherne, Thomas 1637?-1674 DcLB 131, DcNaB MP
Traherne, Thomas c. 1638-1674 BlmGEL
Traicoff, Ellen Braden WhoMW 93, WhoScEn 94
Traicoff, George 1932- WhoAm 94
Traicoff, Sandra M. 1944- WhoAm 94
Trail, George Arthur, III 1936- WhoAm 94, WhoAmP 93
Trailescu, Cornel 1926- NewGrDO
Traill, Alan 1935- IntWW 93
Traill, Alan Towers 1935- Who 94
Traill, Catherine Parr 1802-1899 BlmGWL
Traill, David Angus 1942- WhoWest 94
Train, Arthur (Cheney) 1875-1945 EncSF 93
Train, Christopher John 1932- Who 94
Train, David 1919- Who 94
Train, Harry Depue, II 1927- WhoAm 94
Train, Jack d1966 WhoHol 92
Train, John 1928- WhoAm 94
Train, Oswald 1915-1988 EncSF 93
Train, Russell E. 1920- EnvEnc
Train, Russell Errol 1920- IntWW 93, WhoAm 94
Traina, Albert Salvatore 1927- WhoAm 94
Traina, Jeffrey Francis 1956- WhoMW 93
Traina, Paul Joseph 1934- WhoScEn 94
Traina, Richard Paul 1937- WhoAm 94
Trainer, James Edward 1895- WhAm 10
Trainor, Bernard Edmund 1928- WhoAm 94
Trainor, Charles Warren 1945- WhoAmL 94
Trainor, Howard Allen 1943- WhoAm 94
Trainor, John Felix 1921- WhoMW 93
Trainor, Joseph Sidney 1919- WhoAmP 93
Trainor, Leonard d1940 WhoHol 92
Trainor, Paul Vincent 1948- WhoScEn 94
Trainor, Richard M. 1942- WhoFI 94
Traisman, Howard Sevin 1923- WhoAm 94
Traisman, Kenneth Neil 1958- WhoAmL 94
Traister, Robert Edwin 1937- WhoAm 94
Trajan c. 53-117 HisWorL [port]
Trajetta, Tommaso NewGrDO
Trakas, Demetrius Alexander 1932- WhoMW 93
Trakas, Deno DrAPF 93
Trakas, George 1944- WhoAmA 93
Trakis, Louis 1927- WhoAmA 93
Tralins, S(andor) Robert 1926- EncSF 93
Trambitsky, Viktor Nikolayevich 1895-1970 NewGrDO
Trambley, Estela Portillo 1936- WhoHisp 94
Trambukis, William J. 1926- IntMPA 94
Trame, Theresa Marie 1947- WhoMW 93
Tramel d1948 WhoHol 92
Tramiel, Jack 1928- WhoFI 94
Tramiel, Kenneth Ray, Sr. 1946- WhoBlA 94
Tramiel, Sam 1950- WhoFI 94
Trammel, Kevin Gene 1957- WhoFI 94
Trammell, Herbert Eugene 1927- WhoAm 94
Trammell, Martin Gil 1959- WhoWest 94
Trammell, Robert Dewitt 1945- WhoAmP 93
Trammell, Wilbur WhoBlA 94
Trammell, William Rivers 1926- WhoBlA 94
Trammer, Monte Irvin 1951- WhoBlA 94, WhoFI 94
Tramontano, John Patrick, Jr. 1941- WhoFI 94
Tramontine, John O. 1932- WhoAm 94
Tramontozzi, Louis Robert 1958- WhoScEn 94
Tramuto, James Arnold 1948- WhoFI 94
Tran, Dean 1948- WhoScEn 94
Tran, Dorothy N. 1957- WhoAsA 94
Tran, Hong-Y Thi 1959- WhoAsA 94
Tran, Huyen Lam 1946- WhoAsA 94
Tran, Johan-Chanh Minh 1958- WhoScEn 94
Tran, John Kim-Son Tan 1945- WhoScEn 94
Tran, La Dinh 1956- WhoAsA 94
Tran, Loc Binh 1946- WhoAsA 94
Tran, Loi Huu 1939- WhoAsA 94
Tran, Long Trieu 1956- WhoAsA 94, WhoFI 94, WhoScEn 94
Tran, Myluong Thi WhoAsA 94
Tran, Nang Tri 1948- WhoMW 93, WhoScEn 94
Tran, Nghia T. 1963- WhoWest 94
Tran, Nhut Van 1935- WhoAsA 94
Tran, Phuoc Huu 1939- WhoAsA 94
Tran, Phuoc Xuan 1945- WhoScEn 94
Tran, Qui-Phiet 1937- WhoAsA 94
Tran, Thang Nhut 1941- WhoAsA 94
Tran, Thinh Quy 1954?- WhoAsA 94
Tran, Thomas 1968- WhoAsA 94
Tran, Thuan Van 1948- WhoAsA 94
Tran, Toan Vu 1956- WhoScEn 94
Tran, Tri Duc 1963- WhoScEn 94
Tran, Tri K. 1960- WhoAsA 94
Tran, Tuyet-Nhung T. 1948- WhoAsA 94
Tranchell, Peter (Andrew) 1922- NewGrDO
Tran-Cong, Ton 1953- WhoScEn 94
Trandel, Richard Samuel 1937- WhoAm 94
Tranelli, Deborah WhoHol 92
Tranfaglia, Christina Marie 1962- WhoMW 93
Trang, Kien 1933- WhoWest 94
Trani, Eugene Paul 1939- WhoAm 94
Tranin, Amy Strauss 1959- WhoMW 93
Trank, Douglas Monty 1944- WhoAm 94
Trank, Lynn Edgar 1918- WhoAmA 93
Tranmire, Baron 1903- Who 94
Tran Nam Trung IntWW 93
Tranquada, Robert Ernest 1930- WhoAm 94, WhoWest 94
Transtromer, Tomas (Gosta) 1931- ConWorW 93
Transue, Brooke Mullen 1942- WhoMW 93
Transue, Pamela Jean 1950- WhoWest 94
Trant, Douglas Allen 1951- WhoAmL 94
Trant, Gerald Ion 1928- IntWW 93
Trant, Richard (Brooking) 1928- Who 94
Tran Tam Tinh, Rev. 1929- IntWW 93
Tranter, Jack C. 1946- WhoAmL 94
Tranter, John (Ernest) 1943- WrDr 94
Tranter, John Clement 1909- WrDr 94
Tranter, Nigel (Godwin) 1909- WrDr 94
Tranter, Nigel Godwin 1909- Who 94
Tranter, Terence Michael 1944- WhoAmP 93
Trantham, Roy Munsten WhoAmP 93
Tran Thien Khiem, Gen. 1925- IntWW 93
Trantino, Joseph Peter 1924- WhoAmP 93
Trantino, Tommy DrAPF 93
Trantoul, Antonin 1887-1966 NewGrDO
Tran Van Huong 1903- IntWW 93
Tran Van Tra, Gen. 1918- IntWW 93
Tran-Viet, Tu 1949- WhoScEn 94
Traore, Amadou Toumani IntWW 93
Traore, Diara IntWW 93
Traore, Mohamed 1940- IntWW 93
Traore, Moussa 1936- IntWW 93
Trap, Jennifer Josephine 1951- WhoMW 93
Trapani, Catherine 1952- WhoMW 93, WhoScEn 94
Trapani, Kevin A. WhoIns 94
Trapani, Ralph James 1952- WhoWest 94
Trapasso, Lorraine 1950- WhoFI 94
Trapeznikov, Vadim Aleksandrovich 1905- IntWW 93
Traphagen, Ethel 1882-1963 WhoAmA 93N
Trapido, Barbara 1941- WrDr 94
Trapier, Paul 1749-1778 WhAmRev
Trapier, Pierre Pinckney Alston 1897-1957 WhoAmA 93N
Trapikas, Bruno Peter 1951- WhoMW 93
Trapnel, Anna fl. 1642-1660 DcNaB MP
Trapnel, Anna fl. 165-?- BlmGWL
Trapnell, Barry Maurice Waller 1924- Who 94
Trapnell, Britt WhoIns 94
Trapnell, Joan P. 1946- WhoIns 94
Trapnell, John Arthur 1913- Who 94
Trapolin, Frank Winter 1913- WhoFI 94
Trapp, Donald W. 1946- WhoBlA 94
Trapp, Ellen Simpson 1920- WhoBlA 94
Trapp, Eric Joseph d1993 Who 94N
Trapp, Frank Anderson 1922- WhoAm 94, WhoAmA 93
Trapp, Gerald Bernard 1932- WhoWest 94
Trapp, Howard 1934- WhoAmP 93
Trapp, James M. 1934- WhoAm 94
Trapp, Joseph Burney 1925- IntWW 93, Who 94
Trapp, Leslie Combs 1954- WhoAmP 93
Trapp, Wendell H. 1949- WhoAmL 94
Trapp-Dukes, Rosa Lee 1942- WhoBlA 94
Trappe, James Martin 1931- WhoAm 94
Trapp-Fleenor, Kathryn Anne 1957- WhoMW 93
Trappier, Arthur Shives 1937- WhoBlA 94
Traprock, Walter E. 1877-1946 EncSF 93
Trasatti, Sergio 1937- WhoScEn 94
Trasenster, Michael Augustus Tulk 1923- Who 94
Trask, Grover C. WhoAmL 94
Trask, James L. 1932- WhoIns 94
Trask, Linda Ann 1956- WhoWest 94
Trask, Raiford Graham, Sr. d1993 NewYTBS 93
Trask, Robert Chauncey Riley 1939- WhoWest 94
Trask, Tallman Harlow, III 1947- WhoWest 94
Trask, Wayland d1918 WhoHol 92
Traske, Mary fl. 1660- BlmGWL
Trasler, Gordon Blair 1929- Who 94, WrDr 94
Trasobares, Cesar 1949- WhoAmA 93
Traster, David Madison 1955- WhoAmL 94
Trasviña, John D. 1958- WhoHisp 94
Tratner, Alan Arthur 1947- WhoFI 94, WhoWest 94
Tratt, David Michael 1955- WhoWest 94
Trattner, Walter I. 1936- WrDr 94
Traub, Charles H. 1945- WhoAmA 93
Traub, George James 1942- WhoAmP 93
Traub, Joseph Frederick 1932- WhoAm 94
Traub, Judy 1940- WhoAmP 93
Traub, Paul 1952- WhoAmL 94
Traub, Peter 1935- WhoScEn 94
Traub, Peter Pearson, Jr. 1956- WhoAmL 94
Traub, Richard Kenneth 1950- WhoAm 94, WhoAmL 94
Traub, Robert Tyler 1965- WhoAmL 94
Traubel, Helen d1972 WhoHol 92
Traubel, Helen (Francesca) 1899-1972 NewGrDO
Traubert, Michael 1957- WhoAmP 93
Traubmann, Sophie 1867-1951 NewGrDO
Traudt, Mary B. 1930- WhoMW 93
Trauerman, Margy Ann WhoAmA 93
Trauger, Donald Byron 1920- WhoAm 94
Traugh, Jolinda Ann WhoAm 94
Traughber, Charles M. 1943- WhoBlA 94
Traugott, Elizabeth Closs 1939- WhoAm 94
Traum, Jerome S. 1935- WhoAm 94
Trauner, Alexandre 1906- IntDcF 2-4
Trauner, Sergio 1934- IntWW 93
Traurig, Robert Henry 1925- WhoAm 94
Trausch, Paul Joseph 1941- WhoAm 94
Trausch, Thomas V. 1943- WhoAmA 93
Trauscht, Donald C. 1933- WhoAm 94, WhoFI 94, WhoMW 93
Trause, Paul Karl 1948- WhoAmP 93
Trautenberg, David Herbert 1958- WhoWest 94
Trautenberg, Gerald Anthony 1935- WhoAm 94
Trauth, Joseph Louis, Jr. 1945- WhoAmL 94
Trautlein, Donald Henry 1926- IntWW 93
Trautman, Andrzej 1933- IntWW 93
Trautman, Donald W. 1936- WhoAm 94
Trautman, Harold N. WhoAmP 93
Trautman, Herman Louis 1911- WhoAmL 94
Trautman, Leo C., Jr. 1954- WhoWest 94
Trautman, William E. 1938- WhoFI 94
Trautman, William Ellsworth 1940- WhoAm 94
Trautmann, Catherine 1951- WhoWomW 91
Trautmann, Frederic 1936- WrDr 94
Trautmann, Thomas R(oger) 1940- WrDr 94
Trautmann, Thomas Roger 1940- WhoAm 94
Trautwein, George William 1927- WhoAm 94
Travaglini, Raymond 1928- WhoMW 93
Travaglini, Robert E. WhoAmP 93
Travaglino, Joseph A., Jr. 1941- WhoAmP 93
Travalena, Fred 1942- WhoHol 92
Travanti, Daniel J. 1940- IntMPA 94, WhoHol 92
Travanti, Daniel John WhoAm 94
Travanti, Leon Emidio 1936- WhoAmA 93
Travell, Janet G. 1901- IntWW 93
Traveller, Bruce Frank 1955- WhoWest 94
Travelstead, Chester Coleman 1911- WhoAm 94
Traven, Kevin Charles 1959- WhoScEn 94
Traver, Courtland Lee 1935- WhoAm 94, WhoAmL 94
Traver, Donald 1957- WhoAmA 93
Traver, Harry J. 1947- WhoFI 94
Traver, Noel Allen 1959- WhoMW 93
Traver, Peggy Cox 1935- WhoAmP 93
Traver, Robert ConAu 42NR, WhAm 10
Traver, Robert 1903-1991 WrDr 94N
Travers, Basil Holmes 1919- Who 94, WrDr 94
Travers, Ben 1886-1980 BlmGEL, ConDr 93
Travers, Ben(jamin) 1886-1980 IntDcT 2 [port]
Travers, Bill 1922- IntMPA 94, WhoHol 92
Travers, Brendan d1992 Who 94N
Travers, Celia d1975 WhoHol 92
Travers, Gwyneth Mabel 1911-1982 WhoAmA 93N
Travers, Henry d1965 WhoHol 92
Travers, Judith Lynnette 1950- WhoFI 94, WhoWest 94
Travers, Kenneth 1908- WrDr 94
Travers, Linden 1913- WhoHol 92
Travers, Nat d1958 WhoHol 92
Travers, Oliver S., Jr. 1926- WhoAm 94, WhoFI 94
Travers, P(amela) L(yndon) 1906- WrDr 94
Travers, Richard d1935 WhoHol 92
Travers, Susan WhoHol 92
Travers, Thomas (a Beckett) 1902- Who 94
Travers, Tony d1959 WhoHol 92
Travers, Victor d1948 WhoHol 92
Traverse, Alfred 1925- WhoAm 94
Traverse, Jean d1947 WhoHol 92
Traverse, Madlaine d1964 WhoHol 92
Traverse-Healy, Thomas Hector 1923- Who 94
Traversi, Derek A(ntona) 1912- WrDr 94
Traverso, Peggy Bosworth 1938- WhoWest 94
Travers-Smith, Brian John 1931- WhoAmA 93
Travia, Anthony J., Sr. d1993 NewYTBS 93
Travilla ConTFT 11
Travilla, William 1920-1990 ConTFT 11
Travinski, Marilyn L. 1947- WhoAmP 93
Travis, Aaron ConAu 142
Travis, Alex 1908- WrDr 94
Travis, Alexander B. 1930- WhoBlA 94
Travis, Alice 1943- WhoAmP 93
Travis, Andrew David 1944- WhoAm 94
Travis, Benjamin WhoBlA 94

Travis, Bernie d1984 *WhoHol 92*
Travis, Charles William d1917 *WhoHol 92*
Travis, David B. 1948- *WhoAm 94, WhoAmA 93*
Travis, David M. 1948- *WhoAmP 93*
Travis, Della Mary 1941- *WhoMW 93*
Travis, Dempsey J. 1920- *WhoBlA 94, WrDr 94*
Travis, Dempsey Jerome 1920- *WhoAm 94*
Travis, Dennis M. 1944- *WhoAm 94*
Travis, Elizabeth (Frances Chandler) 1920- *WrDr 94*
Travis, Forrest 1938- *WhoFI 94*
Travis, Frederick F. 1942- *WrDr 94*
Travis, Geraldine 1931- *WhoBlA 94*
Travis, Geraldine Washington 1931- *WhoAmP 93*
Travis, Harry J. 1954- *WhoMW 93*
Travis, Jack 1952- *ConAu 141, WhoBlA 94*
Travis, Jill Helene 1948- *WhoFI 94*
Travis, Joe Lane 1931- *WhoAmP 93*
Travis, John D. 1940- *WhoAmP 93*
Travis, John Richard 1942- *WhoWest 94*
Travis, June 1914- *WhoHol 92*
Travis, Kathryne Hail 1894-1972 *WhoAmA 93N*
Travis, Lawrence Allan 1942- *WhoFI 94, WhoMW 93*
Travis, Marlene O. *WhoFI 94, WhoMW 93*
Travis, Martin Bice 1917- *WhoAm 94*
Travis, Merle d1983 *WhoHol 92*
Travis, Myron 1963- *WhoBlA 94*
Travis, Nancy 1961- *ConTFT 11, IntMPA 94, WhoHol 92*
Travis, Olin (Herman) 1888-1975 *WhoAmA 93N*
Travis, Paul Nicholas 1949- *WhoWest 94*
Travis, Philip 1940- *WhoAmP 93*
Travis, Randy 1959- *WhoHol 92*
Travis, Randy Bruce 1959- *WhoAm 94*
Travis, Richard d1989 *WhoHol 92*
Travis, Roy 1922- *WhoWest 94*
Travis, Roy (Elihu) 1922- *NewGrDO*
Travis, Stacey *WhoHol 92*
Travis, Susan Kathryn 1940- *WhoFI 94*
Travis, Vance Kenneth 1926- *WhoAm 94*
Travisano, Frank Peter 1921- *WhoFI 94*
Travis Copess, Joyce Marie 1947- *WhoFI 94*
Travkin, Nikolai Ilich 1946- *LngBDD*
Travkin, Nikolai Ilyich 1946- *IntWW 93*
Travolta, Ellen *WhoHol 92*
Travolta, Helen d1978 *WhoHol 92*
Travolta, Joey 1952- *WhoHol 92*
Travolta, John 1954- *IntMPA 94, IntWW 93, WhoAm 94, WhoHol 92*
Travsky, Amber Long 1955- *WhoWest 94*
Trawick, Buckner Beasley 1914- *WrDr 94*
Trawick, Lafayette James, Jr. 1965- *WhoScEn 94*
Trawick, Leonard *DrAPF 93*
Trawick, Leonard Moses 1933- *WhoAm 94*
Traxel, Josef 1916-1975 *NewGrDO*
Traxler, Bob 1931- *WhoAmP 93*
Traxler, Gabrielle 1942- *WhoWomW 91*
Traxler, Patricia *DrAPF 93*
Traxler, Vieri 1928- *IntWW 93*
Traxler, William Byrd 1912- *WhoAm 94, WhoAmL 94*
Traxler, William Byrd, Jr. 1948- *WhoAm 94, WhoAmL 94*
Traylor, Angelika 1942- *WhoAmA 93*
Traylor, Claire 1931- *WhoAmP 93*
Traylor, Claire Guthrie 1931- *WhoWest 94*
Traylor, Eleanor W. *WhoBlA 94*
Traylor, Horace Jerome 1931- *WhoBlA 94*
Traylor, Jack R., Sr. 1922- *WhoAmP 93*
Traylor, Joan Sadler *WhoAm 94*
Traylor, Kenneth Noel 1932- *WhoMW 93*
Traylor, Lee Clyde 1932- *WhoAmP 93*
Traylor, Orba Forest 1910- *WhoAm 94, WhoFI 94*
Traylor, Rudolph A. 1918-1992 *WhoBlA 94N*
Traylor, William d1989 *WhoHol 92*
Traylor, William Robert 1921- *WhoWest 94*
Traynham, James Gibson 1925- *WhoAm 94*
Traynor, Harry Sheehy 1911- *WhoAm 94*
Traynor, J. Michael 1934- *WhoAm 94, WhoAmL 94*
Traynor, John F. d1955 *WhoHol 92*
Traynor, John T. *WhoAmP 93*
Traynor, John Thomas, Jr. 1955- *WhoMW 93*
Traystman, Ellen Susan 1961- *WhoAmL 94*
Traywick, Flo Crisman Neher 1924- *WhoAmP 93, WhoWomW 91*
Treach c. 1971- *See* Naughty by Nature *ConMus 11*
Treacher, Arthur d1975 *WhoHol 92*
Treacher, John (Devereux) 1924- *Who 94*
Treacy, Colman Maurice 1949- *Who 94*
Treacy, David Matthew 1953- *WhoFI 94*
Treacy, Edward Thomas 1941- *WhoAmP 93*
Treacy, Emerson d1967 *WhoHol 92*
Treacy, Gerald Bernard 1951- *WhoAmL 94*
Treacy, Jane Friedlander 1939- *WhoMW 93*
Treacy, Thomas Bernard 1928- *WhoAmL 94*
Treacy, Vincent Edward 1942- *WhoAmL 94*
Treadgold, Donald Warren 1922- *WhoAm 94, WrDr 94*
Treadgold, Hazel Rhona 1936- *Who 94*
Treadgold, John David 1931- *Who 94*
Treadgold, Mary 1910- *WrDr 94*
Treadgold, Sydney William 1933- *Who 94*
Treadway, Barbara Elaine 1963- *WhoMW 93*
Treadway, Charlotte d1963 *WhoHol 92*
Treadway, Douglas Morse 1942- *WhoAm 94, WhoMW 93*
Treadway, Frank DeWitt 1941- *WhoWest 94*
Treadway, James Curran 1943- *WhoAm 94, WhoAmL 94, WhoFI 94*
Treadway, Jessica *DrAPF 93*
Treadway, John David 1950- *WhoAm 94*
Treadway, Joseph L. 1947- *WhoAmP 93*
Treadway, Richard Fowle 1913- *WhoAmP 93*
Treadway, Stephen Joseph 1947- *WhoAm 94, WhoFI 94*
Treadwell, Carleton Raymond 1911-1989 *WhAm 10*
Treadwell, Charles James 1920- *Who 94*
Treadwell, David Merrill 1940- *WhoBlA 94*
Treadwell, Fay Rene Lavern 1935- *WhoBlA 94*
Treadwell, Grace 1893- *WhAm 10*
Treadwell, Hugh Wilson 1921- *WhoAm 94*
Treadwell, Kenneth Myron 1923- *WhoScEn 94*
Treadwell, Laura d1960 *WhoHol 92*
Treadwell, Robert D., Sr. 1933- *WhoAmP 93*
Treakle, James Edward, Jr. 1946- *WhoAmL 94*
Treanor, Charles Edward 1924- *WhoAm 94*
Treanor, Gerard Francis, Jr. 1943- *WhoAm 94, WhoAmL 94*
Treanor, Walter John 1922- *WhoWest 94*
Treas, Jack Hanson 1929- *WhoFI 94*
Treas, Judith Kay 1947- *WhoAm 94*
Treas, Terri 1956- *WhoHol 92*
Trease, Geoffrey *Who 94*
Trease, (Robert) Geoffrey 1909- *TwCYAW, Who 94, WrDr 94*
Treaster, Richard A. 1932- *WhoAmA 93*
Treaster, Steven D. 1951- *WhoAmL 94*
Treasure, John Albert Penberthy 1924- *Who 94, WhoAm 94*
Treat, Jessica *DrAPF 93*
Treat, John Elting 1946- *WhoAm 94, WhoWest 94*
Treat, Lawrence 1903- *WhoAm 94, WrDr 94*
Treat, Sharon Anglin *WhoAmP 93*
Treat, Thomas Frank 1937- *WhoAm 94*
Trebek, Alex 1940- *WhoAm 94*
Trebelli, Zelia 1838-1892 *NewGrDO*
Treber, Brian David 1961- *WhoMW 93*
Trebilcott, James Joseph 1917- *WhoAm 94*
Trebing, Connie Louanne 1955- *WhoFI 94*
Trebing, David Martin 1961- *WhoFI 94*
Treble, Frederick Christopher 1916- *WhoScEn 94*
Trebor, Robert *EncSF 93, WhoHol 92*
Trecate, Luigi Ferrari *NewGrDO*
Trechera, Rafael Marin *EncSF 93*
Trechsel, Gail Andrews 1953- *WhoAmA 93*
Trechsel, Stefan 1937- *IntWW 93*
Treckelo, Richard M. 1926- *WhoAm 94*
Trecker, Stanley Matthew 1944- *WhoAmA 93*
Trede, Michael 1928- *IntWW 93*
Tredennick, Dorothy W. 1914- *WhoAmA 93*
Tredgold, Nye 1909- *WrDr 94*
Tredinnick, David Arthur Stephen 1950- *Who 94*
Tredway, John Thomas 1935- *WhoAm 94, WhoMW 93*
Tree, Ann Maria 1801-1862 *NewGrDO*
Tree, David 1915- *WhoHol 92*
Tree, David Alan 1959- *WhoScEn 94*
Tree, David L. *WhoAm 94*
Tree, Dorothy 1909- *WhoHol 92*
Tree, Herbert Beerbohm d1917 *WhoHol 92*
Tree, Herbert Beerbohm 1853-1917 *BlmGEL*
Tree, Lady d1937 *WhoHol 92*
Tree, Marietta Peabody d1991 *WhAm 10*
Tree, Michael 1934- *WhoAm 94*
Tree, Viola d1938 *WhoHol 92*
Treece, Henry 1911-1966 *TwCYAW*
Treece, James Lyle 1925- *WhoWest 94*
Treece, John W. 1952- *WhoAm 94, WhoAmL 94*
Treece, Joseph Charles 1934- *WhoWest 94*
Treece, Kenneth James 1961- *WhoAmL 94*
Treen, David Conner 1928- *IntWW 93, WhoAmL 94, WhoAmP 93*
Treen, Mary d1989 *WhoHol 92*
Trees, Candice D. 1953- *WhoBlA 94*
Trees, Clyde C. 1885-1960 *WhoAmA 93N*
Trees, John Simmons 1932- *WhoAm 94*
Trees, Merle Jay 1944- *WhoFI 94*
Trees, William Jeff 1959- *WhoMW 93*
Treese, William R. 1932- *WhoAmA 93*
Trefethen, Florence *DrAPF 93*
Trefethen, Lloyd MacGregor 1919- *WhoScEn 94*
Trefeu (de Treval), Etienne (Victor) 1821-1903 *NewGrDO*
Treffert, Darold A(llen) 1933- *WrDr 94*
Treffert, Darold Allen 1933- *WhoAm 94*
Treffry, Joseph Thomas 1782-1850 *DcNaB MP*
Trefgarne, Baron 1941- *Who 94*
Trefil, James 1938- *WrDr 94*
Trefil, James S. 1938- *WhoAm 94*
Trefilova, Vera 1875-1943 *IntDcB [port]*
Trefny, John Ulric 1942- *WhoWest 94*
Trefousse, Hans Louis 1921- *WrDr 94*
Trefry, Richard Greenleaf 1924- *WhoAmP 93*
Trefts, Albert S. 1929- *WhoMW 93, WhoScEn 94*
Trefusis *Who 94*
Trefusis, Violet 1894-1972 *BlmGWL*
Trefzger, Richard Charles 1948- *WhoMW 93*
Tregarthen Jenkin, Ian Evers *Who 94*
Tregde, LorraineC. 1928- *WhoAm 94*
Tregear, Mary 1924- *Who 94*
Tregenza, Norman Hughson 1937- *WhoFI 94*
Treger, Harvey 1924- *WhoMW 93*
Treger, Mark Alan 1938- *WhoWest 94*
Tregidgo, Philip Sillince 1926-1992 *WrDr 94N*
Treglio, James Ronald 1946- *WhoWest 94*
Treglown, Jeremy Dickinson 1946- *IntWW 93, Who 94*
Trego, Walter *ConAu 142*
Tregoe, Benjamin Bainbridge 1927- *WhoFI 94*
Tregoe, William d1989 *WhoHol 92*
Tregoning, Joseph E. 1941- *WhoAmP 93*
Tregurtha, Paul Richard 1935- *WhoAm 94*
Trehane, (Walter) Richard 1913- *Who 94*
Trehearne, Elizabeth 1942- *WrDr 94*
Treherne, Katie Thamer 1955- *SmATA 76*
Trehero, John c. 1883-1985 *EncNAR*
Trehub, Arnold 1923- *ConAu 140*
Treiber, Eleanore d1988 *WhoHol 92*
Treibich, S(teven) J(ohn) 1936-1972 *EncSF 93*
Treibitz, C. Howard 1950- *WhoFI 94*
Treichel, Bruce Alan 1953- *WhoMW 93*
Treichl, Heinrich 1913- *IntWW 93*
Treichler, Harvey Albert 1927- *WhoFI 94*
Treichler, Ray 1907- *WhoScEn 94*
Treiger, Irwin Louis 1934- *WhoAm 94, WhoAmL 94, WhoWest 94*
Treigle, Norman 1927-1975 *NewGrDO*
Treiki, Ali A. 1938- *IntWW 93*
Treil, Laurent *WhoHol 92*
Treiman, David Murray 1940- *WhoScEn 94*
Treiman, Joyce Wahl 1922-1991 *WhAm 10, WhoAmA 93N*
Treiman, Sam Bard 1925- *IntWW 93, WhoAm 94, WhoScEn 94*
Treinavicz, Kathryn Mary 1957- *WhoFI 94, WhoMW 93*
Treinen, Sylvester William 1917- *WhoAm 94, WhoWest 94*
Treister, George Marvin 1923- *WhoAm 94*
Treister, Kenneth 1930- *WhoAm 94, WhoAmA 93*
Treitel, G(ünter) H(einz) 1928- *WrDr 94*
Treitel, Guenter Heinz 1928- *IntWW 93, Who 94*
Treitel, Margot *DrAPF 93*
Treitschke, Georg Friedrich 1776-1842 *NewGrDO*
Trejo, Arnulfo Duenes 1922- *WhoHisp 94*
Trejo, Constantino *WhoHisp 94*
Trejo, Jose Humberto 1942- *WhoHisp 94*
Trejo, Leonard Joseph 1955- *WhoScEn 94*
Trejo, Maggie *WhoHisp 94*
Trejo-Meehan, Tamiye M. *WhoHisp 94*
Trejos Fernandez, Jose Joaquin 1916- *IntWW 93*
Trekel-Burckhardt, Ute 1939- *NewGrDO*
Trela, D. J. 1958- *WhoMW 93*
Trelawney, Richard Arthur 1936- *WhoAm 94*
Trelawny, John Barry Salusbury- 1934- *Who 94*
Trelease, Allen William 1928- *WhoAm 94*
Trelease, Stephen Waldo 1934- *WhoFI 94*
Treleaven, Phillips Albert 1928- *WhoAm 94*
Trelfa, Richard T. 1918- *WhoAmP 93*
Trelfa, Richard Thomas 1918- *WhoAm 94*
Trelford, Donald Gilchrist 1937- *IntWW 93, Who 94*
Trelka, Janice Margaret Nace 1944- *WhoMW 93*
Trelles Montes, Oscar 1904- *IntWW 93*
Trello, Fred A. 1929- *WhoAmP 93*
Tremain, Alan 1935- *WhoAm 94*
Tremain, Barbara d1982 *WhoHol 92*
Tremain, Rose 1943- *BlmGWL, IntWW 93, Who 94, WrDr 94*
Tremaine, F(rederick) Orlin 1899-1956 *EncSF 93*
Tremaine, Frances Elizabeth d1980 *WhoHol 92*
Tremaine, Jennie 1936- *WrDr 94*
Tremaine, Nelson *EncSF 93*
Tremaine, Scott Duncan 1950- *WhoAm 94, WhoScEn 94*
Tremayne, Bertram William, Jr. 1914- *WhoAm 94*
Tremayne, Les 1913- *IntMPA 94, WhoHol 92*
Tremblay, Andre Gabriel 1937- *WhoAm 94*
Tremblay, Bill *DrAPF 93*
Tremblay, Gail *DrAPF 93*
Tremblay, Johanne-Marie *WhoHol 92*
Tremblay, Laurier Joseph, Jr. 1955- *WhoWest 94*
Tremblay, Marc-Adelard 1922- *IntWW 93, Who 94, WhoAm 94*
Tremblay, Michel 1942- *ConWorW 93, GayLL, IntDcT 2, IntWW 93*
Tremblay, Rodrigue 1939- *WhoAm 94*
Trembly, Cristy 1958- *WhoWest 94*
Trembly, Dennis Michael 1947- *WhoAm 94, WhoWest 94*
Tremens, Del *SmATA 76*
Tremens, Del 1951- *WrDr 94*
Tremier, Wilbert M. 1911- *WhoIns 94*
Treml, Vladimir Guy 1929- *WhoAm 94, WhoFI 94*
Tremlett, Anthony Frank 1937- *Who 94*
Tremlett, David Rex 1945- *IntWW 93*
Tremlett, George (William) 1939- *ConAu 142*
Tremlett, George William 1939- *Who 94*
Trémols, Guillermo Antonio 1937- *WhoHisp 94*
Tremper, Edward Payson 1898- *WhAm 10*
Trenaman, John *WhoHol 92*
Trenaman, Nancy Kathleen 1919- *Who 94*
Trenary, Michael 1956- *WhoMW 93, WhoScEn 94*
Trenberth, Kevin Edward 1944- *WhoAm 94, WhoWest 94*
Trench *Who 94*
Trench, John 1932- *Who 94*
Trench, John (Chenevix) 1920- *WrDr 94*
Trench, Peter (Edward) 1918- *Who 94*
Trench, Richard 1949- *WrDr 94*
Trench, William Frederick 1931- *WhoAm 94, WhoScEn 94*
Trenchard, Viscount 1951- *Who 94*
Trenchard, Peter Thomas 1938- *WhoMW 93*
Trenchard, Warren Charles 1944- *WhoWest 94*
Trencher, Gary Joseph 1964- *WhoScEn 94*
Trend, Michael (St. John) 1952- *Who 94*
Trendall, Arthur Dale 1909- *Who 94, WrDr 94*
Trendt, Timothy Lee 1965- *WhoMW 93*
Treneff, Craig Paul 1952- *WhoMW 93*
Trenerry, Walter N. 1917- *WrDr 94*
Trenet, Charles 1913- *WhoHol 92*
Trengganu, H.R.H. The Sultan of 1930- *IntWW 93*
Trengove, Alan Thomas 1929- *WrDr 94*
Trengrove, Kim *WhoHol 92*
Trenhaile, John Stevens 1949- *WrDr 94*
Trenholme, Helen d1962 *WhoHol 92*
Trenier, Claude 1920- *WhoHol 92*
Trenier, Cliff d1983 *WhoHol 92*
Trenker, Luis d1990 *WhoHol 92*
Trennel, Lawrence William 1955- *WhoMW 93*
Trennepohl, Gary Lee 1946- *WhoAm 94, WhoFI 94*
Trennert, Robert Anthony, Jr. 1937- *WhoWest 94*

Trenoweth, Roy Wilbur 1942- WhoWest 94
Trense, Sharon 1939- WhoAmP 93
Trent, Bertram J. 1918- WhoAmP 93
Trent, Charles H. WhoAmP 93
Trent, Darrell M. 1938- WhoAm 94, WhoAmP 93
Trent, Debra Renee 1954- WhoAmP 93
Trent, Gary Charles 1947- WhoMW 93
Trent, Jack d1961 WhoHol 92
Trent, James E. 1936- WhoBlA 94
Trent, Jay Lester 1940- WhoBlA 94
Trent, John d1966 WhoHol 92
Trent, John Spencer 1950- WhoBlA 94
Trent, John Thomas, Jr. 1954- WhoAmL 94
Trent, Judith M. 1939- WhoAmP 93
Trent, Lee d1988 WhoHol 92
Trent, Marcia M. 1948- WhoBlA 94
Trent, Olaf EncSF 93
Trent, Olaf 1935- WrDr 94
Trent, Richard Darrell 1925- WhoBlA 94
Trent, Richard O. 1920- WhoIns 94
Trent, Richard Owen 1920- WhoFI 94
Trent, Robert 1936- WhoAmP 93
Trent, Robert Harold 1933- WhoAm 94
Trent, Sheila d1954 WhoHol 92
Trent, Wendell Campbell 1940- WhoAm 94
Trent, William Bret, Jr. 1947- WhoAmP 93
Trent, William J., Jr. d1993 NewYTBS 93 [port]
Trent, William Johnson, Jr. 1910- WhoBlA 94
Trentham, Barbara 1945- WhoHol 92
Trentham, David R. 1938- IntWW 93
Trentham, David Rostron 1938- Who 94
Trentham, Gary Lynn 1939- WhoAmA 93
Trenti, Mme. NewGrDO
Trentini, Emma 1885-1959 NewGrDO
Trentman, Rose WhoHisp 94
Trentmann, Janet Holt 1951- WhoMW 93
Trento, Vittorio c. 1761-1833 NewGrDO
Trenton, Gail 1938- WrDr 94
Trenton, Patricia Jean WhoAmA 93
Trenz, Erika 1947- WhoWomW 91
Trepod, Gary A. 1944- WhoAmL 94
Trepp, Leo 1913- WrDr 94
Trepper, Myron 1943- WhoAmL 94
Treppler, Irene 1926- WhoWomW 91
Treppler, Irene E. 1926- WhoAmP 93
Treppler, Irene Esther 1926- WhoMW 93
Trepte, Paul 1954- Who 94
Treptow, Gunther (Otto Walther) 1907-1981 NewGrDO
Tresaguet, Pierre 1716-1796 WorInv
Trescott, Harold Charles 1938- WhoIns 94
Trescott, Jacqueline Elaine 1947- WhoBlA 94
Trescott, Robert Lyman 1945- WhoAmL 94
Trescott, Sara Lou 1954- WhoScEn 94
Trescowthick, Donald (Henry) 1930- Who 94
Tresidder, Argus John 1907- WrDr 94
Tresidder, Gerald Charles 1912- Who 94
Tresidder, Stephen John 1949- WhoAmL 94
Tresilian, Liz ConAu 42NR
Treskoff, Olga d1938 WhoHol 92
Tresnowski, Bernard Richard 1932- WhoAm 94, WhoFI 94
Tress, Ronald Charles 1915- Who 94
Tresselt, Alvin 1916- ChlLR 30 [port], WrDr 94
Tressillian, Richard WrDr 94
Tressler, Otto d1965 WhoHol 92
Trestman, Frank D. 1934- WhoAm 94
Tresvant, John Bernard 1938- WhoBlA 94
Treswell, Ralph c. 1540-1616? DcNaB MP
Tretbar, Harold Carl 1931- WhoWest 94
Tretheway, James Andrew WhoFI 94
Trethowan, William (Henry) 1917- Who 94
Trethowan, William (Kenneth Illtyd) 1907- WrDr 94
Tretler, Donald C. 1936- WhoIns 94
Tretnik, Daniel George 1948- WhoFI 94
Tretschok, Dale Deege 1941- WhoAmL 94
Tretter, James Ray 1933- WhoAm 94, WhoScEn 94
Tretter, Robert Charles 1956- WhoFI 94, WhoMW 93
Tretyakov, Sergei (Mikhailovich) 1892-1937? IntDcT 2 [port]
Tretyakov, Valery Stepanovich 1941- LngBDD
Treu, Daniel Gottlob 1695-1749 NewGrDO
Treu, James William 1959- WhoMW 93
Treuer, Robert 1926- WhoMW 93
Treuherz, Julian Benjamin 1947- Who 94
Treuhold, Robert Charles 1957- WhoAmL 94
Treumann, Louis 1872-1942 NewGrDO
Treumann, Paul d1951 WhoHol 92
Treumann, William Borgen 1916- WhoAm 94
Treurnicht, Andries P. 1921-1993 NewYTBS 93 [port]
Treurnicht, Andries Petrus d1993 IntWW 93N
Treutelaar, Barbara WhoHol 92
Trevanian 1925-1992 WrDr 94N
Trevarthen, Hal P. EncSF 93
Trevarthen, Noel WhoHol 92
Trevathan, Robert E 1925- WrDr 94
Trevelyan, Dennis John 1929- Who 94
Trevelyan, George (Lowthian) 1906- Who 94
Trevelyan, Hilda d1959 WhoHol 92
Trevelyan, (Adye) Mary Who 94
Trevelyan, Norman Irving 1915- Who 94
Trevelyan, Percy 1928- WrDr 94
Trevelyan, Raleigh 1923- WrDr 94
Trevelyan, Una d1948 WhoHol 92
Trevelyan Oman, Julia Who 94
Trevena, John EncSF 93
Trever, John Cecil 1915- WrDr 94
Treves, Frederick WhoHol 92
Treves, Jean-Francois 1930- WhoScEn 94
Treves, Ralph 1906- WrDr 94N
Treves, Samuel Blain 1925- WhoAm 94, WhoMW 93
Treves, Vanni Emanuele 1940- Who 94
Trevethin, Baron Who 94
Trevethin, Baron 1880-1971 DcNaB MP
Trevett, Kenneth Parkhurst 1947- WhoAmL 94
Trevett, Peter George 1947- Who 94
Trevett, Thomas Neil 1942- WhoAmL 94
Trevey, Robert Frank 1945- WhoAmL 94
Treville, Roger WhoHol 92
Trevillian, Wallace Dabney 1918- WhoAm 94
Treviño, A. L. WhoHisp 94
Treviño, Alberto Faustino 1931- WhoHisp 94
Trevino, Alex 1957- WhoHisp 94
Treviño, Anthony 1950- WhoHisp 94
Trevino, Carlos 1944- WhoHisp 94
Trevino, Carlos R. 1938- WhoHisp 94
Treviño, Daniel Louis 1943- WhoHisp 94
Treviño, Fernando Manuel 1949- WhoHisp 94
Trevino, Genie 1954- WhoHisp 94
Treviño, Gilbert Timothy 1944- WhoHisp 94
Trevino, Jesse WhoHisp 94
Treviño, Jesse 1947- WhoHisp 94
Treviño, Jesús Salvador 1946- WhoHisp 94
Trevino, Jose Adan 1932- WhoHisp 94
Trevino, Julian G. 1947- WhoHisp 94
Trevino, Laramie M. 1953- WhoHisp 94
Treviño, Lee 1939- WhoHisp 94
Trevino, Lee Buck 1939- IntWW 93, WhoAm 94
Trevino, Maria del Carmel 1951- WhoHisp 94
Trevino, Mario 1952- WhoHisp 94
Treviño, Miguel Angel 1958- WhoHisp 94
Trevino, Rafael Maria, Sr. 1932- WhoHisp 94
Trevino, Rene Agustine 1963- WhoAmP 93
Treviño, Richard, Jr. 1957- WhoHisp 94
Trevino, Rosa Ena 1939- WhoHisp 94
Trevino, Samuel Francisco 1936- WhoHisp 94
Treviño, T. Oscar, Jr. 1955- WhoHisp 94
Trevino, Teresa Roque 1960- WhoHisp 94
Trevis, Diane Ellen 1947- Who 94
Trevisan, Maurizio 1952- WhoScEn 94
Trevithick, Richard 1771-1833 WorInv
Trevithick, Ronald James 1944- WhoFI 94, WhoWest 94
Trevor, Baron 1928- Who 94
Trevor, Alexander Bruen 1945- WhoAm 94
Trevor, Ann d1970 WhoHol 92
Trevor, Austin d1978 WhoHol 92
Trevor, Bronson 1910- WhoAm 94, WhoFI 94
Trevor, Claire 1909- WhoHol 92
Trevor, Claire 1910- IntMPA 94
Trevor, Elleston Who 94, WrDr 94
Trevor, Elleston 1920- EncSF 93
Trevor, Hugh d1933 WhoHol 92
Trevor, John 1855-1930 DcNaB MP
Trevor, Kenneth Rowland Swetenham 1914- Who 94
Trevor, Kirk David Niell 1952- WhoAm 94
Trevor, Leigh Barry 1934- WhoAm 94, WhoAmL 94
Trevor, Meriol 1919- Who 94
Trevor, (Lucy) Meriol 1919- EncSF 93, WrDr 94
Trevor, Norman d1929 WhoHol 92
Trevor, Spencer d1945 WhoHol 92
Trevor, William 1928- ConDr 93, DcLB 139 [port], IntWW 93, RfGShF, Who 94, WrDr 94
Trevor Cox, Horace Brimson Who 94
Trevor-Roper Who 94
Trevor-Roper, Hugh (Redwald) 1914- WrDr 94
Trevor-Roper, Hugh Redwald IntWW 93
Trevor-Roper, Patrick (Dacre) 1916- WrDr 94
Trevor-Roper, Patrick Dacre 1916- Who 94
Trevorrow, Linda Baker 1947- WhoMW 93
Trew, Antony (Francis) 1906- WrDr 94
Trew, Francis Sidney Edward 1931- IntWW 93, Who 94
Trew, Peter John Edward 1932- Who 94
Trewby, (George Francis) Allan 1917- Who 94
Trewhella, Raymond Matthew 1935- WhoFI 94
T. Rex ConMus 11 [port]
Trexler, Charles B. 1916- IntMPA 94
Trexler, Edgar Ray 1937- WhoAm 94
Trexler, Lee Hill d1957 WhoHol 92
Trexler, Vernon Lee 1948- WhoWest 94
Trexler, Wynn Ridenhour 1941- WhoAmL 94
Treybig, Edwina Hall 1949- WhoFI 94
Treybig, James G. 1940- WhoFI 94, WhoScEn 94, WhoWest 94
Treynor, Jack Lawrence 1930- WhoAm 94
Treyz, Joseph Henry 1926- WhoAm 94
Treyz, Russell 1940- WrDr 94
Trezek, George James 1937- WhoAm 94
Trezevant, John Gray 1923-1991 WhAm 10
Trezise, Percy (James) 1923- WrDr 94
Trezise, Philip Harold 1912- WhoAm 94
Trezza, Alphonse F(iore) 1920- ConAu 42NR
Trezza, Alphonse Fiore 1920- WhoAm 94
Tri, William Franklin 1955- WhoAmL 94
Triaca, Alberto Jorge 1941- IntWW 93
Trial, Antoine 1737-1795 See Trial Family NewGrDO
Trial, Armand-Emmanuel 1771-1803 See Trial Family NewGrDO
Trial, Jean-Claude 1732-1771 See Trial Family NewGrDO
Trial Family NewGrDO
Triana, Estrella WhoHisp 94
Triana, Jose 1931- IntDcT 2
Triano, Anthony Thomas 1928- WhoAmA 93
Triano, Nicholas Patrick, III 1960- WhoAmL 94
Triant, Thanos Michael 1946- WhoWest 94
Triantafillopoulos, Nick George 1955- WhoMW 93
Triantafyllides, Michalakis Antoniou 1927- IntWW 93
Trias, Jose Enrique 1944- WhoAm 94
Trias-Monge, Jose 1920- WhoAm 94
Tribbitt, Sherman W. WhoAmP 93
Tribble, Alan Charles 1961- WhoScEn 94
Tribble, Edwin 1907-1986 ConAu 142
Tribble, Huerta Cassius 1939- WhoBlA 94
Tribble, Israel, Jr. 1940- WhoBlA 94
Tribble, Keith WhoBlA 94
Tribble, Richard Walter 1948- WhoFI 94, WhoWest 94
Tribe, Geoffrey Reuben 1924- Who 94
Tribe, Glenn Owen 1934- WhoFI 94
Tribe, Ivan M. 1940- WhoMW 93
Tribe, Laurence H(enry) 1941- WrDr 94
Tribe, Laurence Henry 1941- IntWW 93, WhoAm 94, WhoAmL 94
Tribe, Raymond Haydn 1908- Who 94
Tribett, A. E. Gene 1928- WhoAmP 93
Tribken, Craig L. WhoAmP 93
Trible, Paul Seward 1946- IntWW 93
Trible, Paul Seward, Jr. 1946- WhoAmP 93
Tribler, Willis R. 1934- WhoIns 94
Tribou, Denis-Francois c. 1695-1761 NewGrDO
Triboulet, Raymond 1906- IntWW 93
Tribus, Myron 1921- WhoAm 94, WrDr 94
Tricarico, Giuseppe 1623-1697 NewGrDO
Tricarico, Nicolo fl. 1685-1727 NewGrDO [port]
Tricart, Jean Leon Francois 1920- IntWW 93
Trice, Jessie Collins 1929- WhoBlA 94
Trice, Juniper Yates 1921- WhoBlA 94
Trice, Luther William 1910- WhoBlA 94
Trice, Ron WhoHol 92
Trice, Ronald Wayne 1940- WhoAm 94
Trice, William B. 1924- WhoBlA 94
Trice, William Henry 1933- WhoAm 94, WhoScEn 94
Trich, Leo J., Jr. 1951- WhoAmP 93
Triche, Arthur, Jr. 1961- WhoBlA 94
Triche, Warren J., Jr. 1949- WhoAmP 93
Trick, Roger Lee 1950- WhoWest 94
Trick, Timothy Noel 1939- WhoAm 94
Trickel, Neal Edward 1954- WhoMW 93, WhoScEn 94
Trickel, William, Jr. 1937- WhoFI 94
Tricker, Robert Ian 1933- Who 94
Trickett, Jon Hedley 1950- Who 94
Trickett, Joyce 1915- WrDr 94
Trickett, (Mabel) Rachel 1923- Who 94, WrDr 94
Trickett, Vicki 1940- WhoHol 92
Trickey, Edward Lorden 1920- Who 94
Trickey, Samuel Baldwin 1940- WhoScEn 94
Trickler, Sally Jo 1948- WhoMW 93
Tricoles, Gus Peter 1931- WhoAm 94, WhoWest 94
Tricoli, Carlo d1966 WhoHol 92
Tricoli, James Vincent 1953- WhoScEn 94
Tricoli, John Joseph 1950- WhoFI 94
Tridente, Giuseppe 1939- WhoScEn 94
Tridle, David R. 1950- WhoAm 94
Triebensee, Josef 1772-1846 NewGrDO
Triebwasser, Sol 1921- WhoAm 94
Trieff, Selina 1934- WhoAmA 93
Triegel, Elly Kirsten 1947- WhoScEn 94
Trien, Jay William 1940- WhoFI 94
Trienens, Howard Joseph 1923- WhoAm 94
Trier, Jerry Steven 1933- WhoAm 94
Trier, Peter Eugene 1919- IntWW 93, Who 94
Trier, William C., Jr. 1949- WhoAmL 94
Trier, William Cronin 1922- WhoWest 94
Trier Morch, Dea 1941- BlmGWL, ConWorW 93
Triesault, Ivan d1980 WhoHol 92
Triesman, David Maxim 1943- Who 94
Triest, Frank d1987 WhoHol 92
Trieste, Leopoldo WhoHol 92
Trietsch, Ken d1987 WhoHol 92
Trietsch, Paul d1980 WhoHol 92
Trieweiler, Terry N. 1948- WhoAmP 93
Trieweiler, Terry Nicholas 1948- WhoAm 94, WhoAmL 94, WhoWest 94
Triffin, Nicholas 1942- WhoAm 94, WhoAmL 94
Triffin, Robert d1993 IntWW 93N
Triffin, Robert 1911- WrDr 94
Triffin, Robert 1911-1993 ConAu 140, NewYTBS 93 [port]
Trifon, Harriette WhoAmA 93N
Trifonidis, Beverly Ann 1947- WhoAm 94, WhoWest 94
Triftshauser, Werner 1938- WhoScEn 94
Trigano, Gilbert 1920- IntWW 93
Triger, David Ronald d1993 Who 94N
Trigere, Pauline 1912- WhoAm 94
Trigg, Beth Anne 1964- WhoMW 93
Trigg, Clifton Thomas 1932- WhoScEn 94
Trigg, Donald Clark 1949- WhoAmL 94
Trigg, Paul Reginald, Jr. 1913- WhoAm 94
Trigg, Roger Hugh 1941- WhoAm 94
Trigger, Bruce Graham 1937- WhoAm 94, WrDr 94
Trigger, Ian WhoHol 92
Trigger, Ian James Campbell 1943- Who 94
Trigger, Kenneth James 1910- WhoScEn 94
Triggiani, Leonard Vincent 1930- WhoAm 94, WhoMW 93
Triggiani, Roberto 1942- WhoAm 94
Triggle, David John 1935- WhoAm 94
Triggs, Michael Lynn 1953- WhoAmP 93
Triggs, Vincent L. 1948- WhoAmP 93
Triggs, William Michael 1937- WhoWest 94
Trigiano, Lucien Lewis 1926- WhoWest 94
Trigiano, Robert Nicholas 1953- WhoScEn 94
Trigoboff, Daniel Howard 1953- WhoScEn 94
Trigo Boix, Luis Felipe 1951- WhoHisp 94
Trigona, Alex Sceberras 1950- IntWW 93
Trigueiro, Ronald Dean 1959- WhoWest 94
Trigueros, Raul C. 1944- WhoHisp 94
Trikaminas, Peter A. 1943- WhoIns 94
Trikilis, Emmanuel Mitchell 1916- WhoAm 94
Trikonis, Gus IntMPA 94, WhoHol 92
Triller, Armand d1939 WhoHol 92
Trillin, Calvin DrAPF 93
Trillin, Calvin (Marshall) 1935- WrDr 94
Trillin, Calvin Marshall 1935- WhoAm 94
Trilling, Diana 1905- WhoAm 94, WrDr 94
Trilling, Donald R. 1928- WhoAm 94
Trilling, George Henry 1930- WhoAm 94
Trilling, Helen Regina 1950- WhoAm 94
Trilling, Leon 1924- WhoAm 94, WhoScEn 94
Trillo, Manny 1950- WhoHisp 94
Trim, Claude Albert 1935- WhoAmP 93
Trim, Cynthia Mary 1947- WhoAm 94
Trim, John H. 1931- WhoBlA 94
Trimarchi, Domenico 1940- NewGrDO

Trimas, Marvin 1934- *WhoMW 93*
Trimble, Barbara Margaret 1921- *WrDr 94*
Trimble, Bernard Henry 1930- *WhoFI 94*
Trimble, Cesar *WhoHisp 94*
Trimble, David *Who 94*
Trimble, (William) David 1944- *Who 94*
Trimble, George S. d1925 *WhoHol 92*
Trimble, George Simpson 1915- *WhoAm 94*
Trimble, Gilbert Kohler 1898- *WhAm 10*
Trimble, Jacquelyn *EncSF 93*
Trimble, James T., Jr. 1931- *WhoAm 94*
Trimble, James T., Jr. 1932- *WhoAmL 94*
Trimble, Jenifer *Who 94*
Trimble, John Leonard 1944- *WhoScEn 94*
Trimble, Larry d1954 *WhoHol 92*
Trimble, Louis (Preston) 1917-1988 *EncSF 93*
Trimble, Marian Alice Eddy 1933- *WhoAm 94*
Trimble, Paul Joseph 1930- *WhoAm 94, WhoAmL 94, WhoFI 94*
Trimble, Phillip R. 1937- *WhoAmP 93*
Trimble, Phillip Richard 1937- *WhoAmL 94*
Trimble, Preston Albert 1930- *WhoAm 94*
Trimble, Richard Douglas 1962- *WhoWest 94*
Trimble, Roy Harvey 1955- *WhoAmP 93*
Trimble, Stanley Wayne 1940- *WhoWest 94*
Trimble, Steve 1942- *WhoAmP 93*
Trimble, Thomas James 1931- *WhoAm 94, WhoAmL 94, WhoFI 94, WhoWest 94*
Trimble, Todd Bradford 1962- *WhoFI 94*
Trimble, Tony P. *WhoAmP 93*
Trimble, Vance Henry 1913- *WhoAm 94*
Trimble, William Cattell, Jr. 1935- *WhoAm 94*
Trimboli, Steven Richard 1918- *WhoAmP 93*
Trimiar, J. Sinclair 1933- *WhoBlA 94*
Trimino, Carmen *WhoHisp 94*
Trimlestown, Baron 1928- *Who 94*
Trimm, Adon 1895-1959 *WhoAmA 93N*
Trimm, H. Wayne 1922- *WhoAmA 93*
Trimmer, Brenda Kay 1955- *WhoScEn 94*
Trimmer, Eric J(ames) 1923- *WrDr 94*
Trimmer, Harold Sharp, Jr. 1938- *WhoAm 94*
Trimmer, J. Kevin 1952- *WhoAmL 94*
Trimmer, Joseph F(rancis) 1941- *ConAu 42NR*
Trimmer, Joyce *WhoAm 94*
Trimmier, Charles Stephen, Jr. 1943- *WhoAmL 94*
Trimmier, Roscoe, Jr. 1944- *WhoAm 94, WhoAmL 94*
Trimmingham, Ernest d1942 *WhoHol 92*
Trimpe, Michael Anthony 1958- *WhoScEn 94*
Trincere, Li 1959- *WhoAmA 93*
Trinchera, Pietro 1702-1755 *NewGrDO*
Trinder, Frederick William 1930- *Who 94*
Trinder, Rachel Bandele 1955- *WhoAmL 94*
Trinder, Tommy d1989 *WhoHol 92*
Trine, Ralph Waldo 1866-1958 *DcAmReB 2*
Tringale, Anthony Rosario 1942- *WhoFI 94*
Tringale, Paul Michael 1964- *WhoMW 93*
Tringali, Joseph 1960- *WhoFI 94*
Tringham, Neal *EncSF 93*
Trinh, Eugene *WhoAsA 94*
Trinh, Hoang Huy 1958- *WhoAsA 94*
Trinh, Nam Ky 1961- *WhoAsA 94*
Trinh, Xuan Lang 1927- *IntWW 93*
Trinidad, David *DrAPF 93*
Trinidad, Ruben *WhoHisp 94*
Trinkaus, Charles 1911- *WrDr 94*
Trinkaus, Erik 1948- *ConAu 140*
Trinkaus, John Philip 1918- *WhoAm 94*
Trinkley, Karla *WhoAmA 93*
Trinks, Hauke Gerhard 1943- *WhoScEn 94*
Trinnaman, John E. 1942- *WhoAmL 94*
Trinque, Andrea Marie 1964- *WhoFI 94*
Trintignant, Jean-Louis 1930- *IntMPA 94, WhoHol 92*
Trintignant, Jean-Louis (Xavier) 1930- *IntWW 93*
Trintignant, Marie 1961- *WhoHol 92*
Trintignant, Vincent 1975- *WhoHol 92*
Trio, Edward Alan 1952- *WhoAmL 94*
Triola, Anne *WhoHol 92*
Triolet, Elsa 1897-1970 *BlmGWL*
Triolo, Audrey d1993 *NewYTBS 93*
Triolo, Peter 1927- *WhoAm 94*
Triolo, Peter T. 1951- *WhoMW 93*
Triona, James Paul 1953- *WhoAmL 94*
Tripathi, Gorakh Nath Ram 1944- *WhoAsA 94*
Tripathi, Ramesh Chandra 1936- *WhoAm 94, WhoAsA 94*
Tripathi, Satish Chandra 1956- *WhoAsA 94*
Tripathi, Satish K. 1951- *WhoAsA 94*
Tripathi, Uma Prasad 1945- *WhoFI 94*
Tripathi, Vijai Kumar 1942- *WhoAsA 94*
Tripathy, Deoki N. 1933- *WhoAsA 94*
Triplehorn, Charles A. 1927- *WhoAm 94*
Triplehorn, Charles A(lbert) 1927- *WrDr 94*
Triplehorn, Don Murray 1934- *WhoWest 94*
Triplett, Arlene 1942- *WhoAmP 93*
Triplett, Arlene Ann 1942- *WhoAm 94*
Triplett, Douglas Arnold 1943- *WhoMW 93*
Triplett, Douglas Edward 1954- *WhoMW 93*
Triplett, Kelly B. *WhoScEn 94*
Triplett, Raymond Francis 1921- *WhoWest 94*
Triplett, Rick Donald 1954- *WhoAmL 94*
Triplett, Timothy Wayne 1954- *WhoAmL 94*
Triplett, Tom *WhoAmP 93*
Triplett, William Carryl 1915- *WhoScEn 94*
Tripodi, Louis Anthony 1931- *WhoAm 94, WhoFI 94*
Tripodi, Thomas Charles 1932- *ConAu 141*
Tripodi, Tom *ConAu 141*
Tripodi, Tony 1932- *WrDr 94*
Tripp, David Richard 1946- *WhoAm 94, WhoAmL 94*
Tripp, Frederick Gerald 1936- *WhoFI 94*
Tripp, Gilbert Allen, Jr. 1943- *WhoAm 94*
Tripp, Herbert Alan 1948- *WhoScEn 94*
Tripp, Howard George 1927- *Who 94*
Tripp, James d1981 *WhoHol 92*
Tripp, Jan Peter 1945- *WhoAmA 93*
Tripp, Karen 1923-1993 *ConAu 141*
Tripp, Leonard Lee 1941- *WhoScEn 94, WhoWest 94*
Tripp, Lucius Charles 1942- *WhoBlA 94*
Tripp, Luke Samuel 1941- *WhoBlA 94*
Tripp, Miles (Barton) 1923- *WrDr 94*
Tripp, Minot Weld, Jr. 1939- *WhoAmP 93*
Tripp, Norman Densmore 1938- *WhoAmL 94*
Tripp, Paul *WhoHol 92*
Tripp, (John) Peter 1921- *IntWW 93, Who 94*
Tripp, Raymond Plummer, Jr. 1932- *WhoWest 94*
Tripp, Susan Gerwe 1945- *WhoAmA 93*
Tripp, Thomas Neal 1942- *WhoAmL 94, WhoFI 94, WhoMW 93*
Trippe, Charles White 1935- *WhoFI 94*
Trippe, Kenneth Alvin Battershill 1933- *WhoAm 94*
Trippi, Charley *ProFbHF*
Trippier, David (Austin) 1946- *Who 94*
Tripplehorn, Jeanne 1963- *WhoAm 94*
Tripucka, Kelly 1959- *BasBi*
Triscari, Joseph 1945- *WhoScEn 94*
Trischan, Glenn Martin 1951- *WhoMW 93*
Trischetta, Elaine Anne 1951- *WhoFI 94*
Trisco, Robert Frederick 1929- *WhoAm 94*
Triska, Bradley Frank 1950- *WhoWest 94*
Triska, Jan Francis 1922- *WhoAm 94, WhoWest 94*
Trisko, Kenneth P. d1982 *WhoHol 92*
Trissel, James Nevin 1930- *WhoAmA 93*
Tristan, Andrew R. 1936- *WhoHisp 94*
Tristan, Dorothy 1942- *WhoHol 92*
Tristan, Flora 1803-1844 *BlmGWL*
Tristan L'Hermite 1601?-1655 *GuFrLit 2*
Tristao, Nuno fl. 144-?- *WhWE*
Tristram *GayLL*
Tritsch, Jerre A. 1951- *WhoAmL 94*
Tritt, Clyde Edward 1920- *WhoAm 94*
Tritt, Travis 1963- *WhoAm 94*
Tritten, James John 1945- *WhoWest 94*
Tritter, Richard Paul 1945- *WhoAm 94*
Trittin, Dennis John 1954- *WhoFI 94*
Tritto, Giacomo (Domenico Mario Antonio Pasquale Giusepp 1733-1824 *NewGrDO*
Tritton, Alan George 1931- *Who 94*
Tritton, Anthony (John Ernest) 1927- *Who 94*
Tritton, (Elizabeth) Clare 1935- *Who 94*
Trivedi, Jay Sanjay 1961- *WhoScEn 94*
Trivedi, Kishor S. 1946- *WhoAsA 94*
Trivedi, Mohan Manubhai 1953- *WhoAsA 94*
Trivedi, Nayan B. 1947- *WhoAsA 94*
Trivedi, Nayana Mohan 1959- *WhoAsA 94*
Trivedi, Ram Krishna 1921- *IntWW 93*
Trivedi-Doctor, Minakshi Dipak 1956- *WhoAsA 94*
Trivelpiece, Alvin William 1931- *WhoAm 94, WhoAmP 93, WhoScEn 94*
Trivelpiece, Laurel *DrAPF 93*
Trivelpiece, Laurel 1926- *WrDr 94*
Trivigno, Pat 1922- *WhoAmA 93*
Trivison, Donna Rae 1951- *WhoMW 93*
Trivisonno, Nicholas Louis 1947- *WhoFI 94*
Triviz, Rita Marilyn 1947- *WhoAmP 93*
Trkula, David 1927- *WhoScEn 94*
Trnecek, Hanus 1858-1914 *NewGrDO*
Trnka, Jiri 1912-1969 *IntDcF 2-4*
Trnka, Zdenek 1943- *WhoWest 94*
Troan, Gordon Trygve 1960- *WhoFI 94, WhoWest 94*
Troberman, Richard Jonathan 1946- *WhoAmL 94*
Trocano, Russell Peter 1963- *WhoAmL 94*
Troccoli, Antonio Americo 1925- *IntWW 93*
Trochak, Stephanie Ellen 1953- *WhoWest 94*
Troche, E. Gunter 1909-1971 *WhoAmA 93N*
Troche, Pedro Juan, Jr. 1963- *WhoHisp 94*
Trocki, Linda Katherine 1952- *WhoScEn 94, WhoWest 94*
Trodden, Stephen 1939- *WhoAm 94*
Troedsson, Ingegerd 1929- *WhoWomW 91*
Troell, Jan 1931- *IntMPA 94*
Troelstra, Arne 1935- *WhoAm 94*
Troen, Philip 1925- *WhoAm 94*
Troester, Carl Augustus, Jr. 1916- *WhoAm 94*
Troester, Gerald Dale 1931- *WhoMW 93*
Trofimuk, Andrey Alekseyevich 1911- *IntWW 93*
Trog, Ronald Francis 1960- *WhoMW 93*
Trogan, Nicholas Richard, III 1943- *WhoAmL 94*
Trogdon, Dewey Leonard, Jr. 1932- *WhoAm 94, WhoFI 94*
Trohan, Walter 1903- *WhoAm 94*
Troiani, Douglas M. 1976- *WhoAmP 93*
Troidl, Richard John 1944- *WhoAm 94*
Troilo, Arthur, III 1953- *WhoAmL 94*
Troise, Joseph Louis 1942- *WhoWest 94*
Troisgros, Pierre Emile Rene 1928- *IntWW 93*
Troisi, Massimo *WhoHol 92*
Trojan, Judith 1947- *WrDr 94*
Trojan, Vaclav 1907-1983 *NewGrDO*
Trolander, Hardy Wilcox 1921- *WhoAm 94*
Trolinger, James Davis 1940- *WhoAm 94*
Troll, Ralph 1932- *WhoMW 93*
Troll-Borostyani, Irma von 1847-1912 *BlmGWL*
Troller, Fred 1930- *WhoAm 94*
Trolley, Leonard *WhoHol 92*
Trollinger, Robert M. 1959- *WhoFI 94*
Trollope, Andrew David Hedderwick 1948- *Who 94*
Trollope, Anthony 1815-1882 *BlmGEL [port], EncSF 93, RfGShF*
Trollope, Anthony (Simon) 1945- *Who 94*
Trollope, Frances 1779-1863 *BlmGWL*
Trollope, Frances 1780-1863 *BlmGEL*
Trollope, Joanna 1943- *IntWW 93, Who 94, WrDr 94*
Trombino, Roger A. 1939- *WhoAm 94*
Trombley, Joseph Edward 1935- *WhoFI 94*
Trombley, Michael Jerome 1933- *WhoAmL 94*
Trombley, Peter G. 1948- *WhoAmP 93*
Trombley, William Holden 1929- *WhoAm 94, WhoWest 94*
Trombly, Rick A. 1957- *WhoAmP 93*
Trombold, Walter Stevenson 1910- *WhoMW 93*
Trommeter, Edgar Joseph 1949- *WhoAm 94*
Tronc, Nicolas *WhoHol 92*
Troncale, Frank Thomas 1941- *WhoAmA 93*
Troncelliti, Manrico d1993 *NewYTBS 93*
Troncoso, Theodore Thomas 1949- *WhoFI 94*
Trone, Donald Burnell 1954- *WhoFI 94, WhoWest 94*
Tron Family *NewGrDO*
Tronsarelli, Ottavio d1646 *NewGrDO*
Tronson de Coudray, Philippe Charles 1738-1777 *WhAmRev*
Troobnick, Gene 1926- *WhoHol 92*
Trooboff, Peter Dennis 1942- *WhoAm 94, WhoAmL 94*
Trooien, Todd Philip 1960- *WhoMW 93*
Trook, Jackie Lee 1942- *WhoAm 94*
Troop, Walter Michael *WhoAmL 94*
Trop, Sandra *WhoAmA 93*
Trop, Timothy Neil 1953- *WhoAmL 94*
Tropper, Joshua 1955- *WhoAmL 94, WhoWest 94*
Trosclair, Carlton James 1939- *WhoAmL 94*
Trosino, Vincent Joseph 1940- *WhoAm 94*
Troska, J.M. *EncSF 93*
Troske, L. A. 1931- *WhoAm 94, WhoIns 94*
Trosko, James Edward 1938- *WhoMW 93*
Trosky, Helene Roth *WhoAmA 93*
Tross, Jonathan Edward Simon 1949- *Who 94*
Trost, Barry Martin 1941- *IntWW 93, WhoAm 94, WhoScEn 94, WhoWest 94*
Trost, Carlisle Albert Herman 1930- *WhoAm 94*
Trost, Eileen Bannon 1951- *WhoAm 94, WhoAmL 94*
Trost, J. Ronald 1932- *WhoAm 94*
Trost, Johann Baptist Matthaus fl. 1714-1726 *NewGrDO*
Trost, Martha Ann 1951- *WhoWest 94*
Trost, Phoebe Scherr 1921- *WhoAmP 93*
Trostel, David H. 1946- *WhoFI 94*
Trostel, Michael Frederick 1931- *WhoAm 94*
Trosten, Leonard Morse 1932- *WhoAm 94*
Trostle, Mary Pat 1951- *WhoAm 94*
Trostorff, Ander Peter 1951- *WhoAm 94, WhoAmL 94*
Troszel, Wilhelm 1823-1887 *NewGrDO*
Trotman, Alexander J. *NewYTBS 93 [port]*
Trotman, Alexander J. 1933- *WhoFI 94*
Trotman, Alexander James 1933- *WhoMW 93*
Trotman, Bob 1947- *WhoAmA 93*
Trotman, Jack *WrDr 94*
Trotman, Richard Edward 1942- *WhoBlA 94*
Trotman-Dickenson, Aubrey (Fiennes) 1926- *Who 94*
Trotman-Dickenson, Aubrey Fiennes 1926- *IntWW 93, WrDr 94*
Trotsky, Leon d1940 *WhoHol 92*
Trotsky, Leon 1879-1940 *HisWorL [port]*
Trott, Helen 1936- *WhoAmA 93*
Trott, James Jenkins 1800-1868 *EncNAR*
Trott, Keith Dennis 1952- *WhoScEn 94*
Trott, Sabert Scott, II 1941- *WhoAm 94*
Trott, Stephen S. 1939- *WhoAmP 93*
Trott, Stephen Spangler 1939- *WhoAm 94, WhoAmL 94, WhoWest 94*
Trotta, Frank P. 1955- *WhoAmP 93*
Trotta, Frank Paul, Jr. 1955- *WhoAmL 94*
Trotta, George Benedict 1930- *WhoIns 94*
Trotter (Cockburn), Catherine 1679-1749 *BlmGWL*
Trotter, Andrew Leon 1949- *WhoBlA 94*
Trotter, Decatur W. 1932- *WhoAmP 93*
Trotter, Decatur Wayne 1932- *WhoBlA 94*
Trotter, Donne E. 1950- *WhoAmP 93, WhoMW 93*
Trotter, Frederick Thomas 1926- *WhoWest 94*
Trotter, Haynie Seay 1931- *WhoAm 94*
Trotter, Ide Peebles 1932- *WhoFI 94*
Trotter, John Scott d1975 *WhoHol 92*
Trotter, Kate *WhoHol 92*
Trotter, Mary Frances *WhoAmL 94*
Trotter, Neville Guthrie 1932- *Who 94*
Trotter, Richard Clayton 1950- *WhoAmL 94*
Trotter, Ronald (Ramsay) 1927- *Who 94*
Trotter, Ronald Ramsay 1927- *IntWW 93*
Trotter, Ruth M. 1920- *WhoAmP 93*
Trotter, Teddy Norman *WhoAmP 93*
Trotter, Thomas Andrew 1957- *Who 94*
Trotter, Thomas Robert 1949- *WhoAm 94, WhoAmL 94*
Trotter, William Monroe 1872-1934 *AfrAmAl 6*
Trotter, William Perry 1919- *WhoAmP 93*
Trotter, William R., (Jr.) 1943- *ConAu 141*
Trotti, Lamar 1900-1952 *IntDcF 2-4*
Trotti, Lisa Onorato 1960- *WhoScEn 94*
Trottier, Bryan John 1956- *WhoAm 94*
Trottier, Paul Norman 1953- *WhoMW 93*
Trottman, Alphonso 1936- *WhoBlA 94*
Trottman, Charles Henry 1934- *WhoBlA 94*
Trotula fl. 15th cent.- *BlmGWL*
Trotzig, Birgitta 1929- *BlmGWL*
Trotzky, Howard M. 1940- *WhoAmP 93*
Troubetzkoy, Eugene Serge 1931- *WhoScEn 94*
Troubridge, Thomas (Richard) 1955- *Who 94*
Troughton, David 1950- *WhoHol 92*
Troughton, Henry Lionel 1914- *Who 94*
Troughton, Patrick d1987 *WhoHol 92*
Troughton, Peter 1943- *Who 94*
Trouillon-Lacombe, Louis *NewGrDO*
Troum, Mark Stephan 1958- *WhoAmL 94*
Trouncer, Cecil d1953 *WhoHol 92*
Trouncer, Ruth *WhoHol 92*
Trounson, Ronald Charles 1926- *Who 94*
Troup, Alistair Mewburn 1927- *Who 94*
Troup, Anthony *Who 94*
Troup, (John) Anthony (Rose) 1921- *Who 94*
Troup, Bobby 1918- *WhoHol 92*
Troup, Elliott Vanbrugh 1938- *WhoBlA 94*
Troup, Malcolm Graham 1918- *WhoWest 94*
Troup, Robert 1757-1832 *WhAmRev*
Troup, Thomas James 1923- *WhoAm 94*

Troupe, Charles Quincy 1936- *WhoAmP 93, WhoBlA 94*
Troupe, Marilyn Kay 1945- *WhoBlA 94*
Troupe, Quincy *DrAPF 93*
Troupe, Quincy (Thomas, Jr.) 1943- *BlkWr 2, ConAu 43NR*
Troupe, Quincy Thomas, Jr. 1943- *WhoBlA 94*
Troupe, Terry Lee 1947- *WhoAm 94*
Troupe, Tom *WhoHol 92*
Troupe-Frye, Betty Jean 1935- *WhoBlA 94*
Troupin, Teri Lynn 1955- *WhoMW 93*
Troupis, James Roberts 1953- *WhoAm 94*
Trousdale, Elmer Bernard 1931- *WhoAm 94*
Trout, Barbara Ann 1927- *WhoAmP 93*
Trout, Calvin Daniel 1946- *WhoMW 93*
Trout, Charles Hathaway 1935- *WhoAm 94*
Trout, Francis d1950 *WhoHol 92*
Trout, Jerome Joseph 1943- *WhoMW 93*
Trout, Kilgore *DrAPF 93, EncSF 93*
Trout, Kilgore 1918- *WrDr 94*
Trout, Linda Copple 1951- *WhoAmL 94, WhoWest 94*
Trout, Maurice Elmore 1917- *WhoAm 94*
Trout, Monroe, Jr. *NewYTBS 93 [port]*
Trout, Monroe Eugene 1931- *WhoAm 94, WhoScEn 94, WhoWest 94*
Trout, Nelson W. 1920- *WhoBlA 94*
Trout, Robert J(ay) 1947- *ConAu 142*
Trout, Robert Vernal 1949- *WhoAmL 94*
Trout, Roscoe Marshall, Jr. 1944- *WhoFI 94, WhoWest 94*
Trout, Thomas James 1949- *WhoScEn 94*
Troutbeck, John 1832-1899 *NewGrDO*
Troutman, Arenda 1957- *WhoAmP 93*
Troutman, Charles H., III 1944- *WhoAmP 93*
Troutman, Conaught M. 1955- *WhoIns 94*
Troutman, Courtland Warren 1929- *WhoAm 94*
Troutman, E. Mac 1915- *WhoAm 94, WhoAmL 94*
Troutman, Holmes Russell 1933- *WhoAmL 94*
Troutman, Porter Lee, Jr. 1943- *WhoBlA 94*
Troutman, Ronald R. 1940- *WhoAm 94*
Troutman, William Wilson 1954- *WhoFI 94*
Troutt, Timothy Ray 1950- *WhoScEn 94*
Troutt Goldbeck, Tiffany Shirese *WhoMW 93*
Troutwine, Gayle Leone 1952- *WhoAmL 94*
Trova, Ernest Tino 1927- *WhoAm 94, WhoAmA 93*
Trover, Ellen Lloyd 1947- *WhoAmL 94, WhoWest 94*
Trovoada, Miguel Anjos da Cunha Lisboa *IntWW 93*
Trow, Clifford Wayne 1929- *WhoAmP 93*
Trow, JD 1945- *WhoWest 94*
Trow, William d1973 *WhoHol 92*
Trowbridge, Alexander B., Jr. 1929- *IntWW 93*
Trowbridge, Alexander Buel, Jr. 1929- *WhoAm 94, WhoFI 94*
Trowbridge, Amelia Ann 1945- *WhoFI 94*
Trowbridge, C. Robertson 1932- *WhoAm 94, WhoAmP 93*
Trowbridge, Calvin D. 1898- *WhAm 10*
Trowbridge, Calvin Durand, Jr. 1934- *WhoAm 94*
Trowbridge, Charles d1967 *WhoHol 92*
Trowbridge, Edmund 1709-1793 *WhAmRev*
Trowbridge, Edward K. 1928- *WhoIns 94*
Trowbridge, Edward Kenneth 1928- *WhoAm 94*
Trowbridge, George William Job 1911- *Who 94*
Trowbridge, John F. 1924- *WhoAmP 93*
Trowbridge, John Parks 1947- *WhoFI 94, WhoScEn 94*
Trowbridge, Martin Edward O'Keeffe 1925- *Who 94*
Trowbridge, Richard (John) 1920- *IntWW 93, Who 94*
Trowbridge, Thomas, Jr. 1938- *WhoAm 94, WhoFI 94, WhoWest 94*
Trowbridge, William *DrAPF 93*
Trowell, Brian (Lewis) 1931- *NewGrDO*
Trowell, Brian Lewis 1931- *Who 94*
Troxel, John Milton 1960- *WhoWest 94*
Troxel, Oliver Leonard, Jr. 1919- *WhoAmP 93*
Troxell, Raymond Robert, Jr. 1932- *WhoAm 94*
Troxil, Thomas Robert 1966- *WhoFI 94*
Troxler, David W. 1952- *WhoAmP 93*
Troy, Anthony Francis 1941- *WhoAm 94*
Troy, B. Theodore 1932- *WhoAm 94*
Troy, Brian J. 1943- *WhoAmL 94*
Troy, Daniel Patrick 1948- *WhoAmP 93*
Troy, Elinor d1949 *WhoHol 92*
Troy, Hannah d1993 *NewYTBS 93 [port]*
Troy, Hector *WhoHol 92*
Troy, Helen d1942 *WhoHol 92*
Troy, Henry P. 1943- *WhoFI 94*
Troy, Joseph Freed 1938- *WhoAm 94*
Troy, Katherine *WrDr 94*
Troy, Louise *WhoHol 92*
Troy, Marleen Abbie 1957- *WhoScEn 94*
Troy, Matthew William 1951- *WhoAmP 93*
Troy, Richard Hershey 1937- *WhoAmL 94*
Troy, Robert Sweeney, Sr. 1949- *WhoAmL 94*
Troy, Ronald William 1943- *WhoMW 93*
Troy, Sidney Z. d1978 *WhoHol 92*
Troy, Thomas Charles 1930- *WhoAmL 94*
Troy, Una 1910- *WrDr 94*
Troy, Vincent d1976 *WhoHol 92*
Troya, Ilion 1947- *WhoHisp 94*
Troyanos, Tatiana 1938- *NewGrDO, WhoAm 94*
Troyanos, Tatiana 1938-1993 *CurBio 93N, NewYTBS 93 [port]*
Troyanovich, Steve *DrAPF 93*
Troyanovsky, Oleg Aleksandrovich 1919- *IntWW 93*
Troyat, Henri 1911- *IntWW 93, Who 94*
Troyer, Alvah Forrest 1929- *WhoAm 94, WhoFI 94, WhoScEn 94*
Troyer, Deryl Lee 1947- *WhoMW 93, WhoScEn 94*
Troyer, John Robert 1928- *WhoAm 94*
Troyer, Judith Portia 1969- *WhoMW 93*
Troyer, Thomas Alfred 1933- *WhoAm 94*
Trozzolo, Anthony Marion 1930- *WhoAm 94, WhoMW 93, WhoScEn 94*
Trpis, Milan 1930- *WhoAm 94, WhoScEn 94*
Truan, Carlos F. 1935- *WhoHisp 94*
Truan, Carlos Flores 1935- *WhoAmP 93*
Truax, Dennis Dale 1953- *WhoScEn 94*
Truax, Donald Robert 1927- *WhoWest 94*
Truax, John d1969 *WhoHol 92*
Truax, Maude d1939 *WhoHol 92*
Truban, William A. 1924- *WhoAmP 93*
Trubeck, William Lewis 1946- *WhoFI 94*
Trubek, Josephine Susan 1942- *WhoAm 94*
Trubensee, Josef *NewGrDO*
Trubin, John 1917- *WhoAm 94*
Trubitt, Hayden Jay 1953- *WhoAmL 94*
Trubner, Henry 1920- *WhoAmA 93, WhoWest 94*
Trubshaw, (Ernest) Brian 1924- *Who 94*
Trubshawe, Michael 1905- *WhoHol 92*
Truby, Betsy Kirby 1926- *WhoAmA 93*
Truby, John Louis 1933- *WhoAm 94*
Trucano, Michael 1945- *WhoAm 94, WhoAmL 94*
Truce, William Everett 1917- *WhoAm 94*
Truck, Fred *DrAPF 93*
Trucksis, Theresa A. 1924- *WhoMW 93*
Trudeau, Arthur Gilbert 1902-1991 *WhAm 10*
Trudeau, Deanna Dallolio 1963- *WhoWest 94*
Trudeau, Garry (B) 1948- *WrDr 94*
Trudeau, Garry B. 1948- *IntWW 93, WhoAm 94, WhoAmA 93*
Trudeau, Margaret 1949- *WhoHol 92*
Trudeau, Noah Andre 1949- *WrDr 94*
Trudeau, Patricia Margaret 1931- *WhoWest 94*
Trudeau, Pierre Elliott 1919- *IntWW 93, Who 94, WhoAm 94, WhoAmL 94*
Trudeau, Stephanie Erin Dutchess 1957- *WhoAmL 94*
Trudeau, Terry Murray 1934- *WhoAmP 93*
Trudeau, Yves 1930- *WhoAmA 93*
Trudel, John Davis 1942- *WhoWest 94*
Trudel, Marc J. *WhoAm 94*
Trudel, Mary Renee *WhoAm 94*
Trudel, Michel 1944- *WhoScEn 94*
Trudell, Dennis *DrAPF 93*
Trudgill, Peter John 1943- *Who 94*
True, Bess d1947 *WhoHol 92*
True, David 1942- *WhoAmA 93*
True, Diemer D. 1946- *WhoWest 94*
True, Diemer Durland 1946- *WhoAmP 93*
True, Edward Keene 1915- *WhoAm 94*
True, Fred Lewis, Jr. 1923- *WhoAmP 93*
True, Gary Edward 1954- *WhoAmL 94*
True, Harry G. *WhoAmP 93*
True, Henry Alfonso, Jr. 1915- *WhoAm 94, WhoWest 94*
True, Katie *WhoAmP 93*
True, Leland Beyer 1921- *WhoWest 94*
True, Raymond Stephen 1934- *WhoMW 93*
True, Richard Brownell 1943- *WhoWest 94*
True, Roy Joe 1938- *WhoAm 94, WhoAmL 94*
True, S. M., Jr. *WhoIns 94*
True, Virgil 1925- *WhoWest 94*
True, Wendell Cleon 1934- *WhoAm 94*
True, William Herndon 1938- *WhoAm 94*
True, William Wadsworth 1925- *WhoWest 94*
Trueblood, Alan Stubbs 1917- *WhoAm 94*
Trueblood, David Elton 1900- *WhoAm 94*
Trueblood, Emily Herrick 1942- *WhoAmA 93*
Trueblood, Harry Albert, Jr. 1925- *WhoAm 94, WhoFI 94, WhoWest 94*
Trueblood, Jo Ann Rita 1934- *WhoAmP 93*
Trueblood, Mark 1948- *WhoScEn 94*
Trueblood, Paul G(raham) 1905- *WrDr 94*
Trueblood, Paul Graham 1905- *WhoAm 94, WhoWest 94*
Trueblood, Vera J. 1962- *WhoBlA 94*
Trueheart, Harry Parker, III 1944- *WhoAm 94, WhoAmL 94*
Trueheart, William E. 1942- *WhoAm 94, WhoBlA 94*
Truell, James H. 1947- *WhoAmP 93*
Truelove, David James 1957- *WhoAmL 94*
Trueman, Chrysostom *EncSF 93*
Trueman, Edwin Royden 1922- *Who 94*
Trueman, Frederick Sewards 1931- *Who 94*
Trueman, Paula 1907- *WhoHol 92*
Trueman, Walter 1928- *WhoAm 94*
Trueman, William Peter Main 1934- *WhoAm 94*
Truemper, John James, Jr. 1924- *WhoAm 94*
Truesdale, C. W. *DrAPF 93*
Truesdale, Gerald Lynn 1949- *WhoScEn 94*
Truesdale, Howard d1941 *WhoHol 92*
Truesdale, John Cushman 1921- *WhoAm 94, WhoAmP 93*
Truesdale, William Thomas 1963- *WhoMW 93*
Truesdell, Carolyn Gilmour 1939- *WhoAmL 94*
Truesdell, Clifford Ambrose, III 1919- *WhoAm 94*
Truesdell, Fred C. d1929 *WhoHol 92*
Truesdell, George Frederick d1937 *WhoHol 92*
Truesdell, Timothy L. 1951- *WhoFI 94*
Truesdell, Wesley Edwin 1927- *WhoAm 94*
Truett, George Washington 1867-1944 *DcAmReB 2*
Truett, Harold Joseph, III 1946- *WhoAmL 94, WhoWest 94*
Truett, Lila Flory 1947- *WhoAm 94, WhoFI 94*
Truettner, William H. *WhoAmA 93*
Truex, Dorothy Adine 1915- *WhoAm 94*
Truex, Duane Philip, III *WhoAmA 93*
Truex, Ernest d1973 *WhoHol 92*
Truex, George Robert, Jr. 1924-1988 *WhAm 10*
Truex, Philip *WhoHol 92*
Truex, Van Day 1904- *WhoAmA 93N*
Trufant, William von Phul 1922- *WhoFI 94*
Truffaut, Francois d1984 *WhoHol 92*
Truffaut, Michelle 1942- *WhoWest 94*
Truglia, Christel *WhoAmP 93*
Truhaut, Rene Charles 1909- *IntWW 93*
Truhlar, Donald Gene 1944- *WhoAm 94, WhoScEn 94*
Truhlar, Doris Broaddus 1946- *WhoAmL 94*
Truhlsen, Stanley Marshall 1920- *WhoAm 94*
Truinet, Charles-Louis-Etienne *NewGrDO*
Truitt, Anne 1921- *WrDr 94*
Truitt, Anne (Dean) 1921- *ConAu 142, WhoAmA 93*
Truitt, Anne Dean 1921- *WhoAm 94*
Truitt, Duane Jay 1954- *WhoFI 94*
Truitt, Kenneth Ray 1945- *WhoFI 94*
Truitt, Mary M. *DrAPF 93*
Truitt, Max O'Rell, Jr. 1931- *WhoAm 94*
Truitt, Phyllis Lynn 1945- *WhoMW 93*
Truitt, Richard Hunt 1932- *WhoAm 94*
Truitt, Robert Lindell 1946- *WhoMW 93*
Truitt, Robert Ralph, Jr. 1948- *WhoAmL 94*
Truitt, Thomas Hulen 1935- *WhoAm 94*
Truitt, Victoria Mize 1949- *WhoFI 94*
Truitt, Wesley Byron 1939- *WhoWest 94*
Truitte, James F. *WhoBlA 94*
Trujillo, Anna Marie 1945- *WhoAmP 93*
Trujillo, Anthony J. 1933- *WhoHisp 94*
Trujillo, Armida Manuela 1937- *WhoHisp 94*
Trujillo, Arnold Paul 1951- *WhoHisp 94*
Trujillo, Augustine 1940- *WhoHisp 94*
Trujillo, C. B. 1932- *WhoAmP 93*
Trujillo, Camilla 1956- *WhoHisp 94*
Trujillo, Candelario, Jr. 1932- *WhoHisp 94*
Trujillo, Carlos Alberto 1957- *WhoHisp 94*
Trujillo, Eddie A. *WhoHisp 94*
Trujillo, Edward M. 1947- *WhoHisp 94*
Trujillo, Ingrid 1955- *WhoHisp 94*
Trujillo, J. B. *WhoHisp 94*
Trujillo, J. Frank 1907- *WhoAmP 93*
Trujillo, Jacobo Eduardo 1940- *WhoHisp 94*
Trujillo, Jake Antonio 1944- *WhoHisp 94*
Trujillo, Jimmy E. 1948- *WhoHisp 94*
Trujillo, Joe Anthony 1937- *WhoHisp 94*
Trujillo, Joe D. 1940- *WhoHisp 94*
Trujillo, John J. *WhoHisp 94*
Trujillo, Joseph Ben 1947- *WhoWest 94*
Trujillo, Juan 1940- *WhoAmP 93*
Trujillo, Julian 1956- *WhoHisp 94*
Trujillo, Keith Arnold 1956- *WhoScEn 94*
Trujillo, Larry E. *WhoHisp 94*
Trujillo, Larry E., Sr. 1940- *WhoAmP 93*
Trujillo, Laurence Michael 1955- *WhoHisp 94*
Trujillo, Linda K. *DrAPF 93*
Trujillo, Lionel Gil *WhoHisp 94*
Trujillo, Lorenzo d1962 *WhoHol 92*
Trujillo, Lorenzo A. 1951- *WhoWest 94*
Trujillo, Lori Sue 1958- *WhoWest 94*
Trujillo, Luis *WhoHisp 94*
Trujillo, Marc Allen *WhoHisp 94*
Trujillo, Marisela Carrasco 1947- *WhoHisp 94*
Trujillo, Michael Joseph 1939- *WhoHisp 94*
Trujillo, Mike A. 1926- *WhoHisp 94*
Trujillo, Paul Edward *DrAPF 93*
Trujillo, Phillip M., Sr. 1921- *WhoHisp 94*
Trujillo, Rafael 1891-1961 *HisWorL [port]*
Trujillo, Roberto Gabriel 1951- *WhoHisp 94*
Trujillo, Rudolpho Andres 1939- *WhoHisp 94*
Trujillo, Solomon D. 1951- *WhoHisp 94*
Trujillo, Stephen Michael 1932- *WhoWest 94*
Trujillo, Virginia Marie 1948- *WhoHisp 94*
Trujillo, William Andrew 1946- *WhoHisp 94*
Trujillo Maestas, Abby 1949- *WhoHisp 94*
Trujillo Molina, Hector Bienvenido 1908- *IntWW 93*
Trukenbrod, William Sellery 1939- *WhoAm 94*
Trull, Francine Sue 1950- *WhoAm 94*
Trulock, Paul H. *WhoAmP 93*
Truluck, Ben d1987 *WhoHol 92*
TruLuck, James Paul, Jr. 1933- *WhoScEn 94*
Truluck, Ray Mason 1943- *WhoFI 94*
Truly, Richard H. 1937- *IntWW 93, WhoScEn 94*
Truman, Bennett S. 1962- *WhoAmP 93*
Truman, Dan
See Diamond Rio *ConMus 11*
Truman, Harry S 1884-1972 *HisWorL [port]*
Truman, Harry S. 1884-1973 *HisDcKW*
Truman, Margaret 1924- *WhoAm 94, WrDr 94*
Truman, Peter D. 1935- *WhoAmP 93*
Truman, Ralph d1977 *WhoHol 92*
Truman, Ruth 1931- *WrDr 94*
Trumble, Beverly (Jane) *WhoAmA 93*
Trumble, Robert Jasper 1943- *WhoWest 94*
Trumble, Robert Roy 1940- *WhoAm 94*
Trumbo, Dalton d1976 *WhoHol 92*
Trumbo, Dalton 1905-1976 *IntDcF 2-4, TwCYAW*
Trumbo, George William 1926- *WhoBlA 94*
Trumbo, Malfourd W. 1954- *WhoAmP 93*
Trumbull, Benjamin 1735-1820 *WhAmRev*
Trumbull, Douglas *WhoAm 94*
Trumbull, Douglas 1942- *IntDcF 2-4, IntMPA 94*
Trumbull, John 1750-1831 *WhAmRev [port]*
Trumbull, John 1756-1843 *AmRev, WhAmRev*
Trumbull, Jonathan 1710-1785 *AmRev*
Trumbull, Jonathan (the Elder) 1710-1785 *WhAmRev [port]*
Trumbull, Jonathan (the Younger) 1740-1809 *WhAmRev*
Trumbull, Joseph 1738-1778 *AmRev, WhAmRev*
Trumbull, Richard 1916- *WhoAm 94*
Trumbull, Stephen Michael 1954- *WhoFI 94*
Trumbull, Walter Henry, Jr. 1959- *WhoWest 94*
Trumka, Richard Louis 1949- *IntWW 93*
Trump, Benjamin Franklin 1932- *WhoAm 94*
Trump, Charles S., IV 1960- *WhoAmP 93*
Trump, Darryl Dwayne 1955- *WhoMW 93*
Trump, Donald 1946- *WhoHol 92, WrDr 94*

Trump, Donald John 1946- *IntWW 93, WhoAm 94, WhoFI 94*
Trump, Ivana M. 1949- *ConAu 140*
Trump, Joyce Kathleen 1932- *WhoMW 93*
Trumpington, Baroness *Who 94*
Trumpington, Baroness 1922- *WhoWomW 91*
Trumpler, Paul Robert 1914-1990 *WhAm 10*
Trumpy, D. Rudolf 1921- *IntWW 93*
Trundle, Winfield Scott 1939- *WhoAm 94*
Trundlett, Helen B. *ConAu 41NR*
Trundy, Natalie 1940- *WhoHol 92*
Truninger, Lauren L. 1918- *WhoAmP 93*
Trunk, Gary 1941- *WhoWest 94*
Trunnell, Thomas Newton 1942- *WhoScEn 94*
Trunnelle, Mabel d1981 *WhoHol 92*
Trunzo, Caesar 1926- *WhoAmP 93*
Trunzo, Robert Nicholas 1956- *WhoMW 93*
Trunzo, Thomas Harold, Jr. 1948- *WhoAmL 94*
Truong, Hoa Phu 1953- *WhoAmL 94*
Truong, Jeff Van 1959- *WhoFI 94*
Truong, Thoi Van 1952- *WhoFI 94*
Truong Nhu Tang 1923- *IntWW 93*
Truong Thi, Hoa-Dien 1923- *WhoAsA 94*
Trupp, Barbara Lee 1950- *WhoAmA 93*
Trupp, Robin Jean 1953- *WhoMW 93*
Truppi, Danny d1970 *WhoHol 92*
Truran, James Wellington, Jr. 1940- *WhoAm 94, WhoMW 93*
Truran, William R. 1951- *WhoFI 94, WhoScEn 94*
Truro, Bishop of 1932- *Who 94*
Truro, Dean of *Who 94*
Truscott, George (James Irving) 1929- *Who 94*
Truscott, Gerry *EncSF 93*
Truscott, Robert Blake *DrAPF 93*
Trusel, Lisa *WhoHol 92*
Trusheim, H. Edwin 1927- *WhoFI 94*
Truskowski, John Budd 1945- *WhoAm 94, WhoAmL 94, WhoMW 93*
Truslow, Sara *WhoHol 92*
Trussell, Charles Tait 1925- *WhoAm 94*
Trussell, Donna *DrAPF 93*
Trussell, Robert Rhodes *WhoWest 94*
Trust, Ronald Irving 1947- *WhoScEn 94*
Trusta, H. *BlmGWL*
Trustman, Benjamin Arthur 1902- *WhoAm 94*
Trustman, Susan 1939- *WhoHol 92*
Trustram Eve *Who 94*
Trusty, John Ray 1955- *WhoFI 94*
Trusty, Roy Lee 1924- *WhoAm 94*
Trusty, Thomas F. 1931- *WhoIns 94*
Truswell, (Arthur) Stewart 1928- *Who 94*
Truta, Marianne Patricia 1951- *WhoAm 94, WhoWest 94*
Truteau, Jean-Baptiste 1748-1827 *WhWE*
Truth, Sojourner c. 1797-1883 *AfrAmAl 6 [port], AmSocL [port], BlmGWL, DcAmReB 2, HisWorL [port], WomPubS*
Truthan, Charles Edwin 1955- *WhoMW 93, WhoScEn 94*
Trutt, William J. 1937- *WhoIns 94*
Trutter, John Thomas 1920- *WhoAm 94, WhoFI 94, WhoMW 93*
Trutty-Coohill, Patricia *WhoAmA 93*
Truxal, John Groff 1924- *WhoAm 94, WhoScEn 94*
Truxton, James Harold 1952- *WhoFI 94*
Truxtun, Thomas 1755-1822 *WhAmRev*
Tryban, Esther Elizabeth 1958- *WhoAmL 94*
Tryber, Thomas Anthony, Jr. 1943- *WhoFI 94, WhoMW 93*
Trybus, Raymond J. 1944- *WhoWest 94*
Trygstad, Lawrence Benson 1937- *WhoAm 94*
Tryman, Mfanya Donald 1948- *WhoBlA 94*
Tryon, Baron 1940- *Who 94*
Tryon, Glenn d1970 *WhoHol 92*
Tryon, John Griggs 1920- *WhoScEn 94*
Tryon, Thomas 1926-1991 *WhAm 10*
Tryon, Tom 1926-1991 *WhoHol 92*
Tryon, William 1729-1788 *AmRev*
Tryon, William 1729-1798 *WhAmRev*
Tryon-Wilson, Charles Edward 1909- *Who 94*
Trypanis, C(onstantine) A(thanasius) 1909-1993 *ConAu 140*
Trypanis, Constantine Athanasius d1993 *IntWW 93N, Who 94N*
Tryphe *GayLL*
Trytek, Linda Faye 1947- *WhoScEn 94*
Trythall, Anthony John 1927- *Who 94*
Trythall, Harry Gilbert 1930- *WhoAm 94*
Trzebiatowski, Gregory L. 1937- *WhoAm 94*
Trzeciakowski, Witold Mieczyslaw 1926- *IntWW 93*
Trzetrzelewska, Basia *WhoAm 94*
Trznadel, Frank Dwight, Jr. 1942- *WhoAm 94*
Trzyna, Thomas Nicholas 1946- *WhoWest 94*
Tsaban, Yair 1930- *IntWW 93*
Tsai, Betty L. *WhoAsA 94*
Tsai, Bilin Paula 1949- *WhoAsA 94*
Tsai, Bor-sheng 1950- *WhoAsA 94*
Tsai, Chester 1935- *WhoAsA 94*
Tsai, Chi-Tay 1956- *WhoScEn 94*
Tsai, Chia-Yin 1937- *WhoAsA 94, WhoMW 93*
Tsai, Chon-Kwo 1955- *WhoAsA 94*
Tsai, Chuang Chuang 1950- *WhoAsA 94*
Tsai, Frank Y. 1934- *WhoAsA 94*
Tsai, Gerald 1928- *IntWW 93*
Tsai, Gow-Jen 1955- *WhoAsA 94*
Tsai, Hsiao Hsia *WhoAmA 93*
Tsai, James H. 1934- *WhoAsA 94*
Tsai, Jeffrey J. P. *WhoAsA 94*
Tsai, Jen-San 1943- *WhoAsA 94*
Tsai, Jir-Shiong *WhoAsA 94*
Tsai, Kuei-wu 1941- *WhoAsA 94*
Tsai, Lin 1922- *WhoAsA 94*
Tsai, Lung-Wen 1945- *WhoAsA 94*
Tsai, Mark F. 1950- *WhoAsA 94*
Tsai, Mavis 1954- *WhoScEn 94*
Tsai, Michael Ming-Ping 1939- *WhoAsA 94, WhoWest 94*
Tsai, Ming-Daw 1950- *WhoAsA 94*
Tsai, Stanley 1950- *WhoAsA 94*
Tsai, Stephen Wei-Lun 1929- *WhoAsA 94*
Tsai, Theodore F. 1948- *WhoAsA 94*
Tsai, Ti-Dao 1936- *WhoMW 93, WhoScEn 94*
Tsai, Tom Chunghu 1948- *WhoScEn 94*
Tsai, Wen-Ying 1928- *WhoAm 94, WhoAmA 93, WhoScEn 94*
Tsai, Wilman 1960- *WhoWest 94*
Tsai Cheng-wen 1915- *HisDcKW*
Tsakas, Spyros Christos 1941- *WhoScEn 94*
Tsalaky, Teresa 1959- *WhoWest 94*
Tsaloumas, Dimitris 1921- *WrDr 94*
Tsamis, Donna Robin 1957- *WhoAmL 94*
Tsan, Min-Fu 1942- *WhoAsA 94*
Tsang, Bion Yu-Ting 1967- *WhoAsA 94*
Tsang, Charles C. 1965- *WhoFI 94*
Tsang, Chit-Sang 1952- *WhoWest 94*
Tsang, Chiu *WhoAsA 94*
Tsang, Dean Zensh 1952 *WhoAsA 94*
Tsang, James Chen-Hsiang 1946- *WhoScEn 94*
Tsang, Sai Ki *WhoWest 94*
Tsang, Wai Lin 1951- *WhoAsA 94*
Tsao, Chich-Hsing Alex 1953- *WhoWest 94*
Tsao, Francis Hsiang-Chian 1936- *WhoAsA 94*
Tsao, George T. 1931- *WhoAsA 94*
Tsao, John Chur 1952- *WhoScEn 94*
Tsao, Nai-Kuan 1939- *WhoMW 93*
Ts'ao Yu *ConWorW 93, IntDcT 2*
Tsapatsaris, Nicholas 1965- *WhoScEn 94*
Tsapogas, Makis J. 1926- *WhoAm 94*
Tsarapkin, Semyon K. 1906-1984 *HisDcKW*
Tsaroukis 1910- *IntWW 93*
Tsatsaronis, George 1949- *WhoScEn 94*
Tsay, Ruey Shiong 1951- *WhoMW 93*
Tschachbasov, Nahum 1899-1984 *WhoAmA 93N*
Tschacher, Darell Ray 1945- *WhoFI 94*
Tschantz, Bruce Allen 1938- *WhoAm 94*
Tschepe, Kurt d1967 *WhoHol 92*
Tscherny, George 1924- *WhoAm 94*
Tscherter, Steven Alan 1946- *WhoFI 94*
Tschetter, Paul 1905- *WhoAmP 93*
Tscheuschner, Ralf Dietrich 1956- *WhoScEn 94*
Tschiemer, Robert Steven 1954- *WhoAmL 94*
Tschinkel, Sheila Lerner 1940- *WhoAm 94, WhoFI 94*
Tschoepe, Thomas 1915- *WhoAm 94*
Tschopp, Theodore Martin 1937- *WhoFI 94*
Tschudi, Hans-Peter 1913- *IntWW 93*
Tschudi, Johann Jakob Von 1818-1889 *WhWE*
Tschudi-Madsen, Stephan 1923- *IntWW 93*
Tse, Charles Jack-Ching 1952- *WhoAsA 94*
Tse, Edmund Sze-Wing 1938- *WhoAm 94, WhoFI 94*
Tse, Francis Lai-Sing 1952- *WhoAsA 94*
Tse, Harley Yau-Shuin 1947- *WhoAsA 94*
Tse, John Yung Dong 1924- *WhoAsA 94*
Tse, Ming-Kai 1953- *WhoAsA 94*
Tse, Po Yin 1959- *WhoScEn 94*
Tse, Sau P. 1964- *WhoAsA 94*
Tse, Stephen 1938- *WhoAmA 93, WhoAsA 94*
Tse, Stephen Yung Nien 1931- *WhoAm 94, WhoFI 94*
Tsebrikova, Mariia Konstantinovna 1835-1917 *BlmGWL*
Tseckares, Charles Nicholas 1936- *WhoAm 94*
Tsedasheev, Gurodarma Tsedashievich 1948- *LngBDD*
Tsedenbal, Yumjaagiyn 1916-1991 *WhAm 10*
Tse Dinh, Yuk-Ching 1956- *WhoAsA 94*
Tsegaye, Gabre-Medhin *BlkWr 2*
Tsegaye Gabre-Medhin 1936- *ConDr 93*
Tsekanovskii, Eduard Ruvimovich 1937- *WhoScEn 94*
Tselikis, Gregory A. 1942- *WhoAmL 94*
Tselkov, Oleg 1934- *IntWW 93*
Tselos, Dimitri Theodore 1900- *WhoAmA 93*
Tsen, May F. 1933- *WhoAsA 94*
Tsen, Meng Chi 1934- *WhoAsA 94*
Tseng, Beatrice Shan-Yi 1966- *WhoAsA 94*
Tseng, Chia-Jeng 1949- *WhoScEn 94*
Tseng, Christopher Kuo-Hou 1946- *WhoScEn 94*
Tseng, Howard Shih Chang 1935- *WhoFI 94*
Tseng, Hsiung Scott 1948- *WhoMW 93, WhoScEn 94*
Tseng, Huan-Chi Chris 1957- *WhoAsA 94*
Tseng, James H. W. *WhoAsA 94*
Tseng, Leon F. 1937- *WhoAsA 94*
Tseng, Louisa 1944- *WhoAsA 94*
Tseng, Mou-sien 1936- *WhoAsA 94*
Tseng, Muna Siu-Chuk 1953- *WhoAsA 94*
Tseng, Rose Y. L. 1943- *WhoAsA 94*
Tseng, S. C. 1935- *WhoAsA 94*
Tseng, Tien-Jiunn 1938- *WhoScEn 94*
Tseng, Wan Chi 1952- *WhoAsA 94*
Tseng Chengkui *IntWW 93*
Tseng Kwang-Shun 1924- *IntWW 93*
Tseng Yu-Ho 1924- *WhoAmA 93*
Tsenoglou, Christos 1954- *WhoScEn 94*
Tsering, Dago 1941- *IntWW 93*
Tsevat, Matitiahu 1913- *WhoMW 93*
Tshering, Ugyen 1954- *IntWW 93*
Tshisekedi, Etienne *IntWW 93*
Tshombe, Moise 1917-1969 *HisWorL [port]*
Tsi, Paul 1921- *WhoMW 93*
Tsiang, H. T. d1971 *WhoHol 92*
Tsiang, Kenneth Weng-Heng 1933- *WhoFI 94*
Tsiang, S. C. 1918-1993 *NewYTBS 93*
Tsiang Ting-Fu 1895-1965 *HisDcKW*
Tsiapera, Maria 1935- *WhoAm 94*
Tsien, Roger Yonchien 1952- *WhoScEn 94*
Tsikotski, Yevgeny Karlovich *NewGrDO*
Tsin, Andrew Tsang Cheung 1950- *WhoScEn 94*
Tsina, Richard Vasil 1941- *WhoAm 94*
Tsintsadze, Sulkhan Fyodorovich 1925- *NewGrDO*
Tsiolkovsky, Konstantin 1857-1935 *WorInv*
Tsiolkovsky, Konstantin (Eduardovich) 1857-1935 *EncSF 93*
Tsiongas, K. Nicholas 1952- *WhoAmP 93*
Tsipis, Kosta Michael 1934- *WhoAm 94*
Tsiros, John Andreas 1963- *WhoWest 94*
Tsiros, William 1944- *WhoAmP 93*
Tsirpanlis, Constantine N. 1935- *WhoAm 94*
Tsividis, Yannis P. 1946- *WhoAm 94*
Tso, Hola fl. 1940-1956 *EncNAR*
Tso, Joseph 1924- *WhoAmL 94*
Tso, L. Hilary 1961- *WhoAsA 94*
Ts'o, Paul On-Pong 1929- *WhoAm 94, WhoAsA 94*
Tso, Thomasze Chung Mou 1949- *WhoFI 94*
Tso, Tien Chioh 1917- *WhoAm 94, WhoAsA 94*
Tsohatzopoulos, Apostolos Athanasios 1939- *IntWW 93*
Tsoi, Viktor d1990 *WhoHol 92*
Tsolov, Tano 1918- *IntWW 93*
Ts'ong, Fou *Who 94*
Tsong, Tian Yow 1934- *WhoMW 93*
Tsongas, Paul E. 1941- *IntWW 93, WhoAmP 93*
Tsongas, Paul Efthemios 1941- *WhoAm 94*
Tsonis, Panagiotis Antonios 1953- *WhoScEn 94*
Tsopel, Corinna 1944- *WhoHol 92*
Tsosie, Leonard *WhoAmP 93*
Tsosie, William Ben-Begay, Jr. 1961- *WhoWest 94*
Tsotetsi, Michael Nkhahle 1938- *IntWW 93*
Tsou, Tang 1918- *WhoAm 94*
Tsoucalas, Nicholas 1926- *CngDr 93, WhoAm 94, WhoAmL 94*
Tsouderou, Virginia 1924- *WhoWomW 91*
Tsougarakis, George Antonios 1961- *WhoAmL 94*
Tsoulfanidis, Nicholas 1938- *WhoAm 94*
Tsovolas, Dimitris 1942- *IntWW 93*
Tsu, Irene 1943- *WhoHol 92*
Tsuang, Ming T. 1931- *WhoAsA 94*
Tsuang, Ming Tso 1931- *WhoAm 94*
Tsubaki, Andrew Takahisa 1931- *WhoAm 94*
Tsuburaya, Eiji *EncSF 93*
Tsuburaya, Eiji 1901-1970 *IntDcF 2-4*
Tsuchida, Eishun 1930- *WhoScEn 94*
Tsuchiya, Yutaka 1942- *WhoScEn 94*
Tsuda, Kyosuke 1907- *WhoScEn 94*
Tsuda, Takao 1940- *WhoScEn 94*
Tsuei, Y. G. 1932- *WhoAsA 94*
Tsuge, Shin 1939- *WhoScEn 94*
Tsuha, Wallace K., Jr. 1943- *WhoAsA 94*
Tsuha, Wallace Koichi 1914- *WhoAsA 94*
Tsui, Annie *WhoAsA 94*
Tsui, Cheryl Wai-Kuen 1962- *WhoAsA 94*
Tsui, Chia-Chi 1953- *WhoScEn 94*
Tsui, Daniel Chee 1939- *WhoAsA 94*
Tsui, Kitty *DrAPF 93*
Tsui, Lap-Chee 1950- *IntWW 93, Who 94, WhoAm 94*
Tsui, Pauline Woo 1920- *WhoAsA 94*
Tsui, Susan Lee 1938- *WhoAsA 94*
Tsuji, Haruo 1933- *WhoScEn 94*
Tsuji, Kiyoshi 1931- *WhoAsA 94*
Tsuji, Moriya 1958- *WhoScEn 94*
Tsuka, Kohei (Bong Woon) 1948- *IntWW 93*
Tsukahira, Toshio George 1915- *WhoAsA 94*
Tsukamoto, Jack Toru 1931- *WhoAsA 94*
Tsukamoto, Mary Tsuruko 1915- *WhoAsA 94*
Tsukamoto, Raynum K. d1974 *WhoHol 92*
Tsukasa, Kimura 1935- *WhoAm 94*
Tsukiji, Richard Isao 1946- *WhoWest 94*
Tsukuno, Paul 1951?- *WhoAsA 94*
Tsumura Setsuko 1928- *BlmGWL*
Tsuneishi, Warren Michio 1921- *WhoAsA 94*
Tsunoda Fusako 1914- *BlmGWL*
Tsur, Yaakov 1906- *IntWW 93*
Tsurtani, Taketsugu 1935- *WhoAm 94*
Tsuruta, Yutaka 1936- *WhoScEn 94*
Tsurya Nanboku, IV *IntDcT 2*
Tsusaka, Jun 1961- *WhoAsA 94*
Tsushima Yuko 1947- *BlmGWL [port], ConWorW 93, RJGShF*
Tsusue, Akio 1928- *WhoScEn 94*
Tsutakawa, Edward Masao 1921- *WhoFI 94, WhoWest 94*
Tsutakawa, George 1910- *WhoAmA 93, WhoAsA 94*
Tsutakawa, Gerard K. 1947- *WhoAsA 94*
Tsutakawa, Mayumi 1949- *WhoWest 94*
Tsutani, Motohiro 1935- *WhoFI 94*
Tsutras, Frank Gus 1929- *WhoAmP 93*
Tsutsui, James Haruo, Jr. 1952- *WhoAsA 94*
Tsutsui, Yasutaka *EncSF 93*
Tsutsumi, Yoshiaki *IntWW 93*
Tsvetaeva, Marina Ivanovna 1892-1941 *BlmGWL*
Tsvetkov, Aleksey 1947- *IntWW 93*
Tsvett, Mikhail *WorInv*
Tsztoo, David Fong 1952- *WhoScEn 94*
Tu, Charles W. 1951- *WhoAsA 94*
Tu, Charles Wuching 1951- *WhoScEn 94*
Tu, Ching-I 1935- *WhoAsA 94*
Tu, Elsie 1913- *WhoWomW 91*
Tu, Harold Kai 1948- *WhoAsA 94*
Tu, King-Ning 1937- *WhoScEn 94*
Tu, Samson W. 1954- *WhoAsA 94*
Tu, Shengru 1950- *WhoAsA 94*
Tu, Shiao-Chun 1943- *WhoAsA 94*
Tu, Shu-chen H. *WhoAsA 94*
Tu, Wei-Ming 1940- *WhoAm 94*
Tuam, Archbishop of 1933- *Who 94*
Tuam, Killala And Achonry, Bishop of 1945- *Who 94*
Tuan, Debbie Fu-tai 1930- *WhoAsA 94*
Tuan, San Fu 1932- *WhoAm 94, WhoAsA 94*
Tubalkain, Toomas 1950- *WhoMW 93*
Tubb, Barry 1963- *IntMPA 94, WhoHol 92*
Tubb, E(dwin) C(harles) 1919- *EncSF 93, WrDr 94*
Tubb, Ernest d1984 *WhoHol 92*
Tubb, James Clarence *WhoAm 94*
Tubbesing, Debbie Brletic 1954- *WhoWest 94*
Tubbs, Bill d1953 *WhoHol 92*
Tubbs, David Eugene 1948- *WhoScEn 94*
Tubbs, Edward Lane 1920- *WhoFI 94*
Tubbs, Helen d1986 *WhoHol 92*
Tubbs, Oswald Sydney 1908- *Who 94*
Tubbs, Ralph 1912- *Who 94*
Tubbs, Tallant 1897- *WhAm 10*
Tubbs, W. A. *WhoAmP 93*
Tubbs, William Reid, Jr. 1950- *WhoWest 94*
Tubby, Josiah Thomas 1875-1958 *WhoAmA 93N*
Tubby, Roger Wellington 1910-1991 *WhAm 10*
Tubesing, Richard Lee 1937- *WhoAm 94*

Tubin, Eduard 1905-1982 *NewGrDO*
Tubis, Seymour 1919- *WhoAmA 93*
Tubman, Harriet c. 1820-1913 *AmSocL, HisWorL [port]*
Tubman, Harriet (Ross) 1820-1913 *AfrAmAl 6 [port]*
Tubman, Robert Colden 1939- *IntWW 93*
Tubman, William Charles 1932- *WhoAm 94, WhoAmL 94, WhoWest 94*
Tubman, William Willis, Jr. 1947- *WhoAmP 93*
Tubman, Winston A. 1941- *IntWW 93*
Tuburan, Isidra Bombeo 1955- *WhoScEn 94*
Tubylov, Valentin Kuzmich 1935- *LngBDD*
Tucceri, Vincent Anthony 1953- *WhoAmL 94*
Tucci, Daniel Patrick 1943- *WhoAm 94, WhoFI 94*
Tucci, Gabriella 1929- *NewGrDO*
Tucci, James Vincent 1939- *WhoScEn 94*
Tucci, Maria 1941- *WhoHol 92*
Tucci, Mark A. 1950- *WhoAm 94*
Tucci, Niccolo *DrAPF 93*
Tucci, Niccolo 1908- *WrDr 94*
Tucci, Stanley *WhoHol 92*
Tuccille, Jerome 1937- *WrDr 94*
Tuccio, Sam Anthony 1939- *WhoFI 94, WhoScEn 94, WhoWest 94*
Tucek, Jan c. 1743-1783 *NewGrDO*
Tucek, Vincenc (Tomas Vaclav) 1773-1821 *NewGrDO*
Tuchfarber, Charles Orrin 1946- *WhoMW 93*
Tuchi, Ben Joseph 1936- *WhoFI 94*
Tuchman, Gaye 1943- *WrDr 94*
Tuchman, Kenneth I. *WhoAm 94, WhoFI 94*
Tuchman, Maurice 1936- *WhoAmA 93*
Tuchman, Maurice Simon 1936- *WhoAm 94*
Tuchman, Phyllis 1947- *WhoAmA 93*
Tuchmann, Robert 1946- *WhoAm 94, WhoAmL 94*
Tucholke, Christel-Anthony 1941- *WhoAmA 93*
Tuck, Anthony *Who 94*
Tuck, (John) Anthony 1940- *Who 94*
Tuck, Bruce (Adolph Reginald) 1926- *Who 94*
Tuck, Clarence Edward Henry 1925- *Who 94*
Tuck, Denise Deringer 1943- *WhoAmP 93*
Tuck, Doletta Sue 1966- *WhoAmL 94*
Tuck, Donald H(enry) 1922- *EncSF 93*
Tuck, Edward Hallam 1927- *WhoAm 94*
Tuck, Grayson Edwin 1927- *WhoAm 94*
Tuck, John Chatfield 1945- *WhoAm 94*
Tuck, John Philip 1911- *Who 94*
Tuck, Michael Ray 1941- *WhoWest 94*
Tuck, Norman Victor 1945- *WhoAmA 93*
Tuck, Ronald Humphrey 1921- *Who 94*
Tuck, Russell R., Jr. 1934- *WhoAm 94, WhoWest 94*
Tucker, Alan Curtiss 1943- *WhoAm 94*
Tucker, Alan David 1936- *WhoAm 94*
Tucker, Allan 1921-1992 *WhAm 10*
Tucker, Allen Brown, Jr. 1942- *WhoAm 94*
Tucker, Anne W(ilkes) 1945- *WrDr 94*
Tucker, Anne Wilkes 1945- *WhoAm 94, WhoAmA 93*
Tucker, Anthony 1924- *WrDr 94*
Tucker, Anthony 1957- *WhoBlA 94*
Tucker, Beverly Sowers 1936- *WhoMW 93, WhoScEn 94*
Tucker, Bil 1943- *WhoWest 94*
Tucker, Billy J. 1934- *WhoBlA 94*
Tucker, Bob *EncSF 93*
Tucker, Bowen Hayward 1938- *WhoAmL 94, WhoFI 94, WhoMW 93*
Tucker, Brian George 1922- *Who 94*
Tucker, C. DeLores 1927- *WhoBlA 94*
Tucker, Carolyn Sue 1939- *WhoAmP 93*
Tucker, Carroll M. 1927- *WhoIns 94*
Tucker, Charles Clement 1913- *WhoAmA 93*
Tucker, Charles Cyril 1942- *WhoWest 94*
Tucker, Charles Leroy, III 1953- *WhoMW 93*
Tucker, Charles William 1953- *WhoAmL 94*
Tucker, Clarence T. 1940- *WhoBlA 94*
Tucker, Clive Fenemore 1944- *Who 94*
Tucker, Connie 1956- *WhoWest 94*
Tucker, Curtis (Dee) 1939-1992 *WhoAmA 93N*
Tucker, Curtis R., Jr. 1954- *WhoAmP 93*
Tucker, Cynthia Anne 1955- *WhoAm 94, WhoBlA 94*
Tucker, Cynthia Delores 1927- *WhoAmP 93*
Tucker, Cynthia Grant 1941- *WrDr 94*
Tucker, David *WhoAm 94*
Tucker, David Winans 1944- *WhoAmL 94*
Tucker, Dennis Carl 1945- *WhoMW 93*
Tucker, Don Eugene 1928- *WhoAm 94*
Tucker, Donald 1938- *WhoAmP 93, WhoBlA 94*
Tucker, Donald Frederick 1946- *WhoAmP 93*
Tucker, Donna Frances 1958- *WhoMW 93*
Tucker, Dorothy M. 1942- *WhoBlA 94*
Tucker, Edward William 1908- *Who 94*
Tucker, Elizabeth Mary 1936- *Who 94*
Tucker, Eric M. 1950- *WhoBlA 94*
Tucker, Eric Merle 1954- *WhoFI 94*
Tucker, Ethel d1926 *WhoHol 92*
Tucker, Forrest d1986 *WhoHol 92*
Tucker, Francis Carlile 1915- *WhoMW 93*
Tucker, Frederick Thomas 1940- *WhoAm 94, WhoFI 94*
Tucker, Gardiner Luttrell 1925- *WhoAm 94*
Tucker, Garland Scott, III 1947- *WhoFI 94*
Tucker, Gary Jay 1934- *WhoAm 94*
Tucker, George *EncSF 93*
Tucker, George Loane d1921 *WhoHol 92*
Tucker, George Maxwell, Sr. 1950- *WhoFI 94*
Tucker, Geraldine Coleman 1952- *WhoBlA 94*
Tucker, Geraldine Jenkins 1948- *WhoBlA 94*
Tucker, Gordon Locke 1932- *WhoWest 94*
Tucker, H. Richard 1936- *WhoAm 94*
Tucker, Hal Beall 1928- *WhoAm 94, WhoFI 94*
Tucker, Harland d1949 *WhoHol 92*
Tucker, Helen 1926- *WrDr 94*
Tucker, Herbert E., Jr. 1915- *WhoBlA 94*
Tucker, Herbert Harold 1925- *Who 94*
Tucker, Hubert E. 1931- *WhoFI 94*
Tucker, (Allan) James 1929- *WrDr 94*
Tucker, James B. *EncSF 93*
Tucker, James Elliott 1914- *WhoAmL 94*
Tucker, James Ewing 1930- *WhoAmA 93*
Tucker, James F. 1924- *WhoBlA 94*
Tucker, James Howard 1950- *WhoFI 94*
Tucker, Jerry 1926- *WhoHol 92*
Tucker, Jim Guy 1943- *IntWW 93*
Tucker, Jim Guy, Jr. 1943- *WhoAm 94, WhoAmP 93*
Tucker, Jo-Von 1937- *WhoFI 94*
Tucker, Joel Lawrence 1932- *WhoWest 94*
Tucker, John d1922 *WhoHol 92*
Tucker, John B. 1937- *WhoAmP 93*
Tucker, John Bartholomew *WhoHol 92*
Tucker, John Edward 1955- *WhoFI 94*
Tucker, John Joseph 1940- *WhoFI 94*
Tucker, John Pierce, Jr. 1943- *WhoAmL 94*
Tucker, John W., Jr. 1950- *WhoAmP 93*
Tucker, Karen 1952- *WhoBlA 94*
Tucker, Katherine Louise 1955- *WhoScEn 94*
Tucker, Larry *WhoHol 92*
Tucker, Laurey Dan 1936- *WhoAm 94*
Tucker, Leatrice Yvonne *WhoAmA 93*
Tucker, Lem 1938-1991 *AfrAmAl 6 [port], WhAm 10*
Tucker, Leota Marie 1944- *WhoBlA 94*
Tucker, Link *ConAu 42NR*
Tucker, Lorenzo d1986 *WhoHol 92*
Tucker, Louis Leonard 1927- *WhoAm 94*
Tucker, M. Belinda 1949- *WhoBlA 94*
Tucker, Marcia 1940- *WhoAmA 93*
Tucker, Marcus O., Jr. 1934- *WhoBlA 94*
Tucker, Marcus Othello 1934- *WhoAm 94, WhoAmL 94, WhoWest 94*
Tucker, Martin *DrAPF 93, Who 94*
Tucker, Martin 1928- *WrDr 94*
Tucker, (Henry John) Martin 1930- *Who 94*
Tucker, Mary 1936- *WhoAmP 93*
Tucker, Melville 1916- *IntMPA 94, WhoWest 94*
Tucker, Memye Curtis *DrAPF 93*
Tucker, Michael 1944- *IntMPA 94, WhoAm 94*
Tucker, Michael 1945- *WhoHol 92*
Tucker, Michael Kevin 1957- *WhoBlA 94*
Tucker, Michael Thomas 1946- *WhoFI 94*
Tucker, Morrison Graham 1911- *WhoAm 94*
Tucker, Norma Jean 1932- *WhoBlA 94*
Tucker, Norman 1910-1978 *NewGrDO*
Tucker, Norman Dave 1945- *WhoAmL 94*
Tucker, O. Ruth *WhoBlA 94*
Tucker, Orrin 1911- *WhoHol 92*
Tucker, Paul, Jr. 1943- *WhoBlA 94*
Tucker, Paul William 1921- *WhoAm 94*
Tucker, Peri 1911- *WhoAmA 93*
Tucker, Peter Louis 1927- *Who 94*
Tucker, Randolph Wadsworth 1949- *WhoAm 94, WhoScEn 94*
Tucker, Ray Moss *WhoFI 94*
Tucker, Richard d1942 *WhoHol 92*
Tucker, Richard 1913-1975 *NewGrDO*
Tucker, Richard (Howard) 1930- *Who 94*
Tucker, Richard Douglas 1962- *WhoScEn 94*
Tucker, Richard Howard 1960- *WhoFI 94*
Tucker, Richard Lee 1935- *WhoAm 94, WhoScEn 94*
Tucker, Richard Lee 1940- *WhoAm 94*
Tucker, Robert Arnold 1941- *WhoScEn 94*
Tucker, Robert B. *WhoAmP 93*
Tucker, Robert C 1918- *WrDr 94*
Tucker, Robert Dennard 1933- *WhoAm 94*
Tucker, Robert Ely 1947- *WhoFI 94*
Tucker, Robert Keith 1936- *WhoScEn 94*
Tucker, Robert L. 1929- *WhoBlA 94*
Tucker, Robert S. 1921- *WhoAmP 93*
Tucker, Robert W(arren) 1924- *WrDr 94*
Tucker, Robin Florence 1955- *WhoWest 94*
Tucker, Rodney Stuart 1948- *WhoScEn 94*
Tucker, Ronald Leslie 1946- *WhoFI 94*
Tucker, Roy Anthony 1951- *WhoScEn 94, WhoWest 94*
Tucker, Samuel 1747-1833 *AmRev, WhAmRev*
Tucker, Samuel Joseph 1930- *WhoBlA 94*
Tucker, Sheilah L. Wheeler 1951- *WhoBlA 94*
Tucker, Sheridan Gregory 1950- *WhoMW 93*
Tucker, Shirleen 1941- *WhoAmP 93*
Tucker, Shirley Lois Cotter 1927- *WhoAm 94, WhoScEn 94*
Tucker, Sophie d1966 *WhoHol 92*
Tucker, Sophie 1884-1966 *WhoCom*
Tucker, Stefan Franklin 1938- *WhoAm 94*
Tucker, Steven Barry 1946- *WhoWest 94*
Tucker, Susan (Norris) 1950- *WrDr 94*
Tucker, Susan C. *WhoAmP 93*
Tucker, Susan Martin *WhoWest 94*
Tucker, Tanya 1958- *WhoHol 92*
Tucker, Tanya Denise 1958- *WhoAm 94*
Tucker, Thomas James 1929- *WhoAm 94*
Tucker, Thomas Randall 1931- *WhoFI 94, WhoMW 93*
Tucker, Thomas Tudor 1745-1828 *WhAmRev*
Tucker, Tim 1944- *WhoAmP 93*
Tucker, Tommy d1989 *WhoHol 92*
Tucker, Trent 1959- *BasBi, WhoBlA 94*
Tucker, Walter R., III 1957- *CngDr 93*
Tucker, Walter Rayford 1924- *WhoAmP 93*
Tucker, Walter Rayford, III 1957- *WhoAm 94, WhoWest 94*
Tucker, Walter Rayford, III 1958- *WhoBlA 94*
Tucker, Watson Billopp 1940- *WhoAm 94, WhoAmL 94*
Tucker, Wilbur Carey 1943- *WhoBlA 94*
Tucker, William E. 1937- *WhoAmL 94, WhoFI 94*
Tucker, William Edward 1932- *WhoAm 94, WrDr 94*
Tucker, William Edward 1935- *WhoAmP 93*
Tucker, William G. 1935- *WhoAmA 93*
Tucker, William Gene 1942- *WhoScEn 94*
Tucker, William Jewett 1839-1926 *DcAmReB 2*
Tucker, William Philip 1932- *WhoAm 94, WhoAmL 94*
Tucker, William Thomas, III 1942- *WhoMW 93*
Tucker, William Vincent 1934- *WhoAm 94*
Tucker, Willis Carleton 1907- *WhoAm 94*
Tucker, (Arthur) Wilson 1914- *EncSF 93, WrDr 94*
Tucker-Allen, Sallie 1936- *WhoBlA 94*
Tuckerman, David R. 1946- *IntMPA 94*
Tuckerman, Jane Bayard 1947- *WhoAmA 93*
Tuckerman, Joseph 1778-1840 *DcAmReB 2*
Tuckett, LeRoy E. 1932- *WhoBlA 94*
Tuckett, Rhona Bennett 1947- *WhoAm 94, WhoFI 94*
Tuckey, Andrew Marmaduke Lane 1943- *Who 94*
Tuckey, Simon (Lane) 1941- *Who 94*
Tuckman, Bruce Wayne 1938- *WhoAm 94, WrDr 94*
Tuckman, Frederick Augustus 1922- *Who 94*
Tuckman, Howard Paul 1941- *WhoAm 94*
Tuckson, Reed V. *WhoScEn 94*
Tuckwell, Barry Emmanuel 1931- *IntWW 93, Who 94, WhoAm 94*
Tucs, Marty 1950- *WhoMW 93*
Tuculescu, Constantin 1947- *WhoFI 94*
Tudao Doje 1942- *WhoPRCh 91 [port]*
Tudball, Peter Colum 1933- *Who 94*
Tuddenham, William Marvin 1924- *WhoWest 94*
Tudela, Benjamin Of *WhWE*
Tudhope, David Hamilton 1921- *Who 94*
Tudhope, James Mackenzie 1927- *Who 94*
Tudjman, Franjo 1922- *IntWW 93*
Tudman, Cathi Graves 1953- *WhoWest 94*
Tudor, Andrew Frank 1942- *WrDr 94*
Tudor, Antony 1908?-1987 *IntDcB [port]*
Tudor, Christine 1951- *WhoHol 92*
Tudor, Elizabeth *BlmGWL*
Tudor, Gregory Scott 1965- *WhoScEn 94*
Tudor, Hal B. 1945- *WhoAm 94, WhoAmL 94*
Tudor, James Cameron 1919- *IntWW 93, Who 94*
Tudor, (Richard) John 1930- *Who 94*
Tudor, John Julian 1945- *WhoScEn 94*
Tudor, Mary *BlmGWL*
Tudor, Mary Louise Drummond 1937- *WhoWest 94*
Tudor, Rosamond 1878-1949 *WhoAmA 93N*
Tudor, Stephen H. *DrAPF 93*
Tudor, Tasha 1915- *WrDr 94*
Tudoran, Ionel 1913- *NewGrDO*
Tudor Evans, Haydn 1920- *Who 94*
Tudorica, Adrian 1940- *WhoMW 93*
Tudryn, Joyce Marie 1959- *WhoAm 94*
Tudway Quilter, David C. *Who 94*
Tudy Jackson, Janice 1945- *WhoBlA 94*
Tuegel, Michele B. 1952- *WhoAmA 93*
Tuell, Jack Marvin 1923- *WhoAm 94, WhoWest 94*
Tuemmler, William Bruce 1927-1989 *WhAm 10*
Tueni, Ghassan 1926- *IntWW 93*
Tueni, Nadia 1935-1983 *BlmGWL*
Tuepker, Max C. 1953- *WhoAmL 94*
Tuerbayier 1931- *WhoPRCh 91 [port]*
Tuerff, James Rodrick 1941- *WhoAm 94, WhoFI 94, WhoIns 94*
Tuerk, Fred James 1922- *WhoAmP 93*
Tuerk, Richard Carl 1941- *WhoAm 94*
Tufarelli, Nicola 1923- *IntWW 93*
Tufariello, Joseph James 1935- *WhoAm 94*
Tufaro, Richard Chase 1944- *WhoAm 94*
Tu Fengjun *WhoPRCh 91*
Tuffin, Marquis de la Rouerie *WhAmRev*
Tuffin, Alan David 1933- *Who 94*
Tuffin, Paul Jonathan 1927- *WhoBlA 94*
Tufon, Chris 1959- *WhoBlA 94*
Tuft, Mark L. 1943- *WhoAmL 94*
Tuft, Mary Ann 1934- *WhoAm 94*
Tufte, Edward Rolf 1942- *WhoAm 94*
Tufte, Erling Arden 1946- *WhoScEn 94*
Tufte, Marilyn Jean 1939- *WhoMW 93*
Tufte, Obert Norman 1932- *WhoAm 94*
Tufton *Who 94*
Tufts, David Albert, Jr. 1945- *WhoAm 94, WhoFI 94*
Tufts, Donald Winston 1933- *WhoAm 94*
Tufts, Eleanor M. d1991 *WhoAmA 93N*
Tufts, Eleanor May 1927-1991 *WhAm 10*
Tufts, J. Arthur 1921- *WhoAmP 93*
Tufts, Robert L. *WhoAmP 93*
Tufts, Sonny d1970 *WhoHol 92*
Tufty, Barbara 1923- *WrDr 94*
Tufty, Harold Guilford 1922- *WhoAm 94*
Tugcu, Nejat 1945- *WhoFI 94*
Tugendhat, Baron 1937- *Who 94*
Tugendhat, Christopher (Samuel) 1937- *WrDr 94*
Tugendhat, Christopher Samuel 1937- *IntWW 93*
Tugendhat, Julia 1941- *WrDr 94*
Tugendhat, Michael George 1944- *Who 94*
Tuggle, Chester Timothy 1954- *WhoFI 94*
Tuggle, Dorie C. 1944- *WhoBlA 94*
Tuggle, Dorothy V. 1935- *WhoBlA 94*
Tuggle, Francis Douglas 1943- *WhoAm 94, WhoFI 94*
Tuggle, Jessie Lloyd 1965- *WhoBlA 94*
Tuggle, Mike *DrAPF 93*
Tuggle, Reginald 1947- *WhoBlA 94*
Tuggle, Richard 1948- *IntMPA 94*
Tugman, Pat 1941- *WhoAmP 93*
"Tugo" d1952 *WhoHol 92*
Tu Guangchi 1920- *WhoPRCh 91 [port]*
Tu Guangzhi 1920- *IntWW 93*
Tu Guowei *WhoPRCh 91*
Tugwell, John 1940- *WhoAm 94, WhoFI 94*
Tugwell, Maurice A. J 1925- *WrDr 94*
Tuia, Tuana'itau F. *WhoAmP 93*
Tu'ipelahake, Fatafehi 1922- *IntWW 93*
Tu'ipelehake, Fatafehi 1922- *Who 94*
Tuipine, Soliai F. 1938- *WhoAmP 93*
Tuita, Mariano (Kelesimalefo) 1932- *Who 94*
Tuita, Siosaia Aleamotu'a Laufilitonga Tuita 1920- *IntWW 93*
Tuite, Christopher (Hugh) 1949- *Who 94*
Tuite, John Francis 1927-1991 *WhAm 10*
Tuitt, Jane Eliza 1908- *WhoBlA 94*
Tuivaga, Timoci (Uluiburotu) 1931- *IntWW 93, Who 94*
Tuke, Anthony (Favill) 1920- *Who 94*
Tuke, Anthony Favill 1920- *IntWW 93*
Tuke, Robert Dudley 1947- *WhoAmL 94*
Tuke, Seymour Charles 1903- *Who 94*
Tukey, Harold Bradford, Jr. 1934- *WhoAm 94, WhoScEn 94, WhoWest 94*

Turnage, Jean A. 1926- WhoAm 94, WhoAmL 94, WhoAmP 93, WhoWest 94
Turnage, Joe Clayton 1945- WhoWest 94
Turnage, Mark-Anthony 1960- NewGrDO, Who 94
Turnage, Thomas K. 1923- WhoAmP 93
Turnage-Ferber, Jacqueline Kay 1965- WhoMW 93
Turnbaugh, Douglas Blair 1934- WhoAm 94
Turnbaugh, Hank WhoAmP 93
Turnbaugh, Roy Carroll 1945- WhoAm 94
Turnberg, Leslie Arnold 1934- Who 94
Turnbull, Adam Michael Gordon 1935- WhoAm 94
Turnbull, Andrew 1945- Who 94
Turnbull, Ann Patterson 1947- WhoAm 94
Turnbull, Betty 1924- WhoAmA 93
Turnbull, Charles Vincent 1933- WhoAm 94
Turnbull, Charles Wesley 1935- WhoBlA 94
Turnbull, Colin M(acmillan) 1924- WrDr 94
Turnbull, David 1915- WhoAm 94
Turnbull, David Charles 1944- Who 94
Turnbull, Douglas Taylor 1895- WhAm 10
Turnbull, Fred Gerdes 1931- WhoAm 94
Turnbull, Gael 1928- BlmGEL
Turnbull, Gael (Lundin) 1928- WrDr 94
Turnbull, George WhAmRev
Turnbull, George Henry d1992 IntWW 93N, Who 94N
Turnbull, Gordon Keith 1935- WhoAm 94, WhoFI 94, WhoScEn 94
Turnbull, Grace Hill 1880-1976 WhoAmA 93N
Turnbull, H. Rutherford, III 1937- WhoAmL 94
Turnbull, Horace Hollins 1949- WhoBlA 94
Turnbull, James B. 1906-1976 WhoAmA 93N
Turnbull, Jeffrey Alan 1934- Who 94
Turnbull, John d1956 WhoHol 92
Turnbull, John Cameron 1923- WhoAm 94
Turnbull, John Neil 1940- WhoAm 94
Turnbull, Lucy WhoAmA 93
Turnbull, Lyle E. J. L. 1928- IntWW 93
Turnbull, Malcolm Bligh 1954- IntWW 93, Who 94
Turnbull, Margaret Hathaway 1946- WhoAm 94
Turnbull, Michael Who 94
Turnbull, (Anthony) Michael (Arnold) Who 94
Turnbull, Miles Watson 1929- WhoWest 94
Turnbull, Peter (John) 1950- WrDr 94
Turnbull, Reginald March 1907- Who 94
Turnbull, Renaldo Antonio 1963- WhoBlA 94
Turnbull, Richard (Gordon) 1909- Who 94
Turnbull, Robert Scott 1929- WhoAm 94
Turnbull, Stanley d1924 WhoHol 92
Turnbull, Stephen (Richard) 1948- WrDr 94
Turnbull, Walter J. 1944- WhoBlA 94
Turnbull, William 1922- IntWW 93
Turnbull, William, Jr. 1935- IntWW 93, WhoAm 94
Turnell, Roy L. 1947- WhoAmL 94
Turner Who 94
Turner, A. Richard 1932- WhoAmA 93
Turner, Alan 1943- WhoAmA 93
Turner, Alan B. Who 94
Turner, Alan Todd 1959- WhoWest 94
Turner, Alberta T. DrAPF 93
Turner, Alexander (Kingcome) d1993 Who 94N
Turner, Alexander (Kingcome) 1901- WrDr 94
Turner, Allen H. 1923- WhoBlA 94
Turner, Almon Richard 1932- WhoAm 94
Turner, Amédée (Edward) 1929- WrDr 94
Turner, Amedee Edward 1929- Who 94
Turner, Ann (Warren) 1945- SmATA 77
Turner, Annie Uribe 1958- WhoHisp 94
Turner, Anthony Peter Francis 1950- WhoScEn 94
Turner, Antony Hubert Michael 1930- Who 94
Turner, (Charles) Arthur 1940- WhoAmA 93
Turner, Arthur Campbell 1918- WhoAm 94
Turner, Arthur Edward 1931- WhoAm 94
Turner, Arthur L. 1950- WhoAmP 93
Turner, B. L., II 1945- ConAu 142
Turner, Bailey W. 1932- WhoBlA 94
Turner, Barbara WhoHol 92
Turner, Bennie WhoBlA 94
Turner, Bennie L. WhoAmP 93
Turner, Betty WhoAmP 93, WhoWomW 91
Turner, Big Joe d1985 WhoHol 92
Turner, Billie B. 1930- WhoAm 94, WhoFI 94
Turner, Billie Lee 1925- WhoAm 94, WhoScEn 94
Turner, Bob 1934- WhoAmP 93
Turner, Bonese Collins WhoAmA 93, WhoWest 94
Turner, Bonnie 1932- ConAu 142, SmATA 75 [port]
Turner, Bowditch d1933 WhoHol 92
Turner, Brenda Kaye 1948- WhoAmP 93
Turner, Brian (Lindsay) 1944- WrDr 94
Turner, Bridget 1939- WhoHol 92
Turner, Bruce (Malcolm) 1922- WrDr 94
Turner, Bruce Backman 1941- WhoAmA 93
Turner, Bryan S. 1945- WrDr 94
Turner, Cal, Sr. WhoFI 94
Turner, Cameron Archer 1915- Who 94
Turner, Carl Jeane 1933- WhoFI 94, WhoScEn 94
Turner, Carmen Elizabeth d1992 WhoBlA 94N
Turner, Castellano Blanchet 1938- WhoBlA 94
Turner, Cathy WhoAm 94
Turner, Cedric Edward 1926- Who 94
Turner, Charles Carre 1944- WhoAm 94, WhoAmL 94
Turner, Charles Hall 1961- WhoMW 93
Turner, Charles Robert 1910-1991 WhoBlA 94N
Turner, Charles Robert 1943- WhoFI 94
Turner, Charles Wayland 1916- WhoAmP 93
Turner, Charlie Guilford 1944- WhoFI 94
Turner, Christopher Gilbert 1929- Who 94
Turner, Christopher John 1933- Who 94
Turner, Claire Denise Yarbrough 1956- WhoAmL 94
Turner, Claramae WhoHol 92
Turner, Claramae 1920- NewGrDO
Turner, Clifford 1913- IntMPA 94
Turner, Clyde ProFbHF
Turner, Clyde T. 1937- WhoFI 94
Turner, Colin Francis 1930- Who 94
Turner, Colin William 1933- Who 94
Turner, Colin William Carstairs 1922- Who 94
Turner, Daniel Stoughton 1917- WhoWest 94
Turner, Darwin T 1931- WrDr 94
Turner, Darwin Theodore Troy 1931-1991 WhAm 10
Turner, David 1927-1990 ConDr 93
Turner, David 1948- WhoAmA 93
Turner, David Andrew 1947- Who 94
Turner, David Eldridge 1947- WhoAmL 94
Turner, David Reuben 1915- WhoAm 94
Turner, David Warren 1927- Who 94
Turner, Dean Edson 1927- WhoWest 94
Turner, Debbie 1957- WhoHol 92
Turner, Dennis 1942- Who 94
Turner, Diane Young 1950- WhoBlA 94
Turner, Donald Frank 1921- WhoAm 94
Turner, Donald R. 1938- WhoIns 94
Turner, Donald William 1925- Who 94
Turner, Doris 1930- WhoBlA 94
Turner, Doris J. WhoBlA 94
Turner, Douglas Clark 1961- WhoWest 94
Turner, Dudley Russell Flower 1916- Who 94
Turner, E. Deane 1928- WhoAm 94
Turner, E(rnest) S(ackville) 1909- WrDr 94
Turner, Eardley d1929 WhoHol 92
Turner, Eddie William 1931- WhoBlA 94
Turner, Edgar EncSF 93
Turner, Edna WhoBlA 94
Turner, Edward L. WhoBlA 94
Turner, Elizabeth Adams Noble 1931- WhoAm 94
Turner, Elmyra G. 1928- WhoBlA 94
Turner, Emanuel A. d1941 WhoHol 92
Turner, Ernest John Donaldson 1914- Who 94
Turner, Ervin 1948- WhoBlA 94
Turner, Ethel 1872-1958 BlmGWL
Turner, Eugene 1934- WhoBlA 94
Turner, Eugene Andrew 1928- WhoAm 94
Turner, Eva 1892-1990 NewGrDO [port]
Turner, Evan Hopkins 1927- WhoAm 94, WhoAmA 93, WhoMW 93
Turner, Evelyn Evon 1954- WhoBlA 94
Turner, F. A. d1923 WhoHol 92
Turner, Florence d1946 WhoHol 92
Turner, Florence Frances 1926- WhoWest 94
Turner, Floyd, Jr. 1966- WhoBlA 94
Turner, Frances Bernadette 1903- WhoMW 93
Turner, Frank WhoHol 92
Turner, Frank De Launy d1957 WhoHol 92
Turner, Frank Miller 1944- WhoAm 94
Turner, Franklin Delton 1933- WhoAm 94
Turner, Franklin James 1960- WhoBlA 94
Turner, Fred L. 1933- WhoFI 94
Turner, Fred Lamar 1949- WhoFI 94
Turner, Frederick DrAPF 93
Turner, Frederick 1943- EncSF 93
Turner, Frederick 1946- IntMPA 94
Turner, Frederick C 1938- WrDr 94
Turner, Frederick Clair 1938- WhoFI 94
Turner, Frederick Jackson 1861-1932 AmSocL [port]
Turner, G. W. 1923- WhoAmP 93
Turner, Garth 1949- WhoAm 94
Turner, Geneva 1949- WhoBlA 94
Turner, Geoffrey Martin 1934- Who 94
Turner, Geoffrey Whitney 1948- WhoWest 94
Turner, George d1947 WhoHol 92
Turner, George d1968 WhoHol 92
Turner, George 1935- IntWW 93
Turner, George (Reginald) 1916- EncSF 93, WrDr 94
Turner, George Pearce 1915- WhoAm 94
Turner, George R. 1944- WhoBlA 94
Turner, George Timothy WhoBlA 94
Turner, George William 1921- IntWW 93, WrDr 94
Turner, Gerald Henry 1942- WhoAmP 93
Turner, Gerald Phillip 1930- WhoAm 94
Turner, Glennette Tilley 1933- WrDr 94
Turner, Graham Michael 1955- WhoAm 94
Turner, Gregory Alan 1959- WhoMW 93
Turner, Grenville 1936- IntWW 93, Who 94
Turner, Guthrie Lewis, Jr. 1930- AfrAmG [port]
Turner, Gwenda 1947- ConAu 42NR
Turner, Gwendolyn Yvonne 1951- WhoMW 93
Turner, H. Lee 1927- WhoAmL 94
Turner, Hal Wesley 1932- WhoWest 94
Turner, Harold 1909-1962 IntDcB [port]
Turner, Harold Edward 1921- WhoAm 94
Turner, Harold Walter 1911- WrDr 94
Turner, Harriet French d1967 WhoAmA 93N
Turner, Harry Edward 1927- WhoAm 94, WhoAmP 93
Turner, Harry Edward 1935- Who 94
Turner, Harry Glenn 1951- WhoBlA 94
Turner, Harry Woodruff 1939- WhoAm 94
Turner, Henry A., Jr. 1919- WhoAm 94
Turner, Henry A(ndrew, Jr.) 1919- WrDr 94
Turner, Henry Brown 1936- WhoAm 94, WhoFI 94
Turner, Henry Ernest William 1907- Who 94
Turner, Henry McNeal 1834-1915 AfrAmAl 6, DcAmReB 2
Turner, Henry McNeal 1843-1915 ConBlB 5 [port]
Turner, Herbert Arthur (Frederick) 1919- Who 94, WrDr 94
Turner, Herbert Branch 1926- WhoWest 94
Turner, Hester Hill 1917- WhoAm 94
Turner, Howard Sinclair 1911- WhoAm 94
Turner, Hugh Joseph, Jr. 1945- WhoAm 94, WhoAmL 94
Turner, Hugh Wason 1923- Who 94
Turner, Ike 1931- WhoHol 92
Turner, Isiah 1945- WhoBlA 94
Turner, J. E. WhoAmP 93
Turner, Jack Henry 1934- WhoFI 94
Turner, James Crewdson 1946- WhoMW 93
Turner, James Edward, Jr. 1942- WhoWest 94
Turner, James Harry 1953- WhoAmL 94
Turner, James Johnson 1935- Who 94
Turner, James P. WhoAmP 93
Turner, James P. 1930- WhoAm 94, WhoAmL 94
Turner, James Reginald 1934- WhoAmP 93
Turner, James T. 1938- CngDr 93
Turner, James Thomas 1938- WhoAm 94, WhoAmL 94
Turner, James Thomas, Sr. 1933- WhoAmA 93
Turner, Janet E. 1914-1988 WhoAmA 93N
Turner, Janet Sullivan 1935- WhoAmA 93
Turner, Janine 1962- IntMPA 94
Turner, Janine 1963- WhoAm 94, WhoHol 92
Turner, Jean Taylor 1943- WhoBlA 94
Turner, Jerome 1942- WhoAm 94, WhoAmL 94
Turner, Jerry E. 1944- WhoAmL 94
Turner, Jesse H., Jr. WhoBlA 94
Turner, Jim 1946- WhoAmP 93
Turner, Joanna Elizabeth 1923- Who 94
Turner, Joe d1990 WhoHol 92
Turner, Joe Lynn
See Deep Purple ConMus 11
Turner, Joey Robert 1968- WhoFI 94
Turner, John 1932- WhoHol 92
Turner, John 1946- Who 94
Turner, John A., Jr. 1948- WhoBlA 94
Turner, John Andrew 1949- WhoFI 94, WhoScEn 94
Turner, John B. 1922- WhoBlA 94
Turner, John Barrimore 1942- WhoBlA 94
Turner, John Christopher 1928- WrDr 94
Turner, John Derfel 1928- Who 94
Turner, John Douglas 1938- WhoMW 93
Turner, John Frayn 1923- WrDr 94
Turner, John Freeland 1942- WhoAmP 93, WhoScEn 94, WhoWest 94
Turner, John G. 1939- WhoIns 94
Turner, John Gosney 1939- WhoAm 94, WhoFI 94
Turner, John Napier 1929- IntWW 93, Who 94, WhoAm 94
Turner, John Sidney, Jr. 1930- WhoAm 94, WhoScEn 94
Turner, John Stewart 1930- Who 94
Turner, John Turnage 1929- Who 94
Turner, Johnnie Rodgers 1940- WhoBlA 94
Turner, Jon Anthony 1936- WhoFI 94
Turner, Joseph 1892-1973 WhoAmA 93N
Turner, Joseph Ellis 1939- AfrAmG [port], WhoBlA 94
Turner, Judith Estelle WhoAmA 93
Turner, Judy 1936- WrDr 94
Turner, Justin George 1898- WhAm 10
Turner, Justin Leroy 1915- WhoFI 94
Turner, Karen Elaine 1953- WhoMW 93
Turner, Katharine Charlotte 1910- WrDr 94
Turner, Kathleen 1954- IntMPA 94, IntWW 93, WhoAm 94, WhoHol 92
Turner, Keena 1958- WhoBlA 94
Turner, Kenneth L., Sr. 1934- WhoAmP 93
Turner, Kermit DrAPF 93
Turner, Kim Smith 1959- WhoBlA 94
Turner, La Ferria Maria 1962- WhoFI 94
Turner, Lana 1920- WhoAm 94
Turner, Lana 1921- IntMPA 94, WhoHol 92
Turner, Lana 1950- WhoBlA 94
Turner, Larry 1939- WhoAmP 93
Turner, Leaf 1943- WhoScEn 94
Turner, Lee S., Jr. 1926- WhoAm 94
Turner, Leslie M. 1957- WhoAmP 93
Turner, Lester Nathan 1933- WhoAmL 94
Turner, Lillian Erna 1918- WhoWest 94
Turner, Linda Darnell 1947- WhoBlA 94
Turner, Lisa Phillips 1951- WhoAm 94, WhoFI 94
Turner, Lloyd Charles 1938- Who 94
Turner, Louis Edouard 1939- WhoBlA 94
Turner, Louis Mark 1942- WrDr 94
Turner, Loyce Warren 1927- WhoAmP 93
Turner, Loyd Leonard 1917- WhoAm 94
Turner, Lucille Ellen 1956- WhoAmL 94
Turner, Lynne Alison 1941- WhoAm 94
Turner, M. Annette 1953- WhoBlA 94
Turner, Maidel d1953 WhoHol 92
Turner, Malcolm Elijah 1929- WhoScEn 94
Turner, Malcolm Elijah, Jr. 1929- WhoAm 94
Turner, Marcellus 1963- WhoBlA 94
Turner, Marcus Jared 1966- WhoBlA 94
Turner, Margot d1993 Who 94N
Turner, Marguerite Rose 1920- WhoAmP 93
Turner, Mark Anthony 1951- WhoBlA 94
Turner, Marshall Chittenden, Jr. 1941- WhoAm 94, WhoWest 94
Turner, Marta Dawn 1954- WhoAm 94
Turner, Martin d1957 WhoHol 92
Turner, Martin 1948- ConAu 142
Turner, Marvin Wentz 1959- WhoBlA 94
Turner, Mary 1926- WrDr 94
Turner, Mary Lee 1945- WhoAm 94, WhoFI 94
Turner, Mary Louise 1954- WhoFI 94
Turner, Mason E., Jr. 1942- WhoAmL 94
Turner, Maureen Barbara 1936- WhoWest 94
Turner, Maurice T., Jr. d1993 NewYTBS 93 [port]
Turner, Melvin Duval 1949- WhoBlA 94
Turner, Merfyn 1915-1991 WrDr 94N
Turner, Michael 1921- WhoHol 92
Turner, Michael (John) 1931- Who 94
Turner, Michael Griswold 1925- WhoAm 94
Turner, Michael Ralph 1929- Who 94
Turner, Michael Seth 1948- WhoWest 94
Turner, Michael Wallace 1960- WhoWest 94
Turner, Mikoel 1950- WhoBlA 94
Turner, Mortimer Darling 1920- WhoWest 94
Turner, Moses 1938- WhoBlA 94
Turner, Nancy J. 1947- ConAu 142
Turner, Nancy Kay 1947- WhoWest 94

Tysall, John Robert 1938- *WhoAm 94*
Tysdahl, Bjuorn Johan 1933- *WrDr 94*
Tysdal, Lauris Lloyd 1949- *WhoAmP 93*
Tyser, Patricia Ellen 1952- *WhoAmA 93*
Tysiac, Lawrence Leon 1953- *WhoFI 94*
Tysinger, James W. 1921- *WhoAmP 93*
Tysl, Gloria Jeanne 1931- *WhoMW 93*
Tysoe, John Sidney 1932- *Who 94*
Tyson, Alan Walker 1926- *IntWW 93,*
   Who 94
Tyson, Alma Learetta 1951- *WhoAmL 94*
Tyson, Bertrand Oliver 1931- *WhoBlA 94*
Tyson, Cathy 1966- *WhoHol 92*
Tyson, Cicely *WhoAm 94*
Tyson, Cicely 1933- *AfrAmAl 6,*
   IntMPA 94, WhoBlA 94, WhoHol 92
Tyson, Clay, Jr. d1976 *WhoHol 92*
Tyson, Cleveland Allen 1946- *WhoBlA 94*
Tyson, Don *NewYTBS 93 [port]*
Tyson, Donald John 1930- *WhoAm 94,*
   WhoFI 94
Tyson, H. Michael 1938- *WhoAm 94*
Tyson, Harry James 1945- *WhoAm 94,*
   WhoFI 94
Tyson, Harvey Wood 1928- *IntWW 93*
Tyson, J(ohn) Aubrey 1870-1930
   EncSF 93
Tyson, John, II 1958- *WhoFI 94*
Tyson, John C. 1951- *WhoAm 94,*
   WhoBlA 94
Tyson, John D., Jr. 1937- *WhoFI 94*
Tyson, John David, Jr. 1937- *WhoMW 93*
Tyson, John Marsh 1953- *WhoAmL 94*
Tyson, Joseph B. 1928- *WrDr 94*
Tyson, Joseph B., Jr. 1949- *WhoAmL 94*
Tyson, Kenneth Robert Thomas 1936-
   WhoAm 94
Tyson, Kirk W. M. 1952- *WhoAm 94*
Tyson, Laura D'Andrea *IntWW 93,*
   WhoAmP 93
Tyson, Laura D'Andrea 1947-
   NewYTBS 93 [port], News 94-1 [port]
Tyson, Laura D'Andrea 1948- *WhoAm 94,*
   WhoFI 94
Tyson, Lorena E. 1933- *WhoBlA 94*
Tyson, Mary 1909- *WhoAmA 93*
Tyson, Mike 1966- *WhoBlA 94*
Tyson, Mike G. 1966- *IntWW 93*
Tyson, Monica Elizabeth 1927- *Who 94*
Tyson, Patti Birge 1939- *WhoAmP 93*
Tyson, Remer (Hoyt) 1934- *WrDr 94*
Tyson, Richard 1961- *WhoHol 92*
Tyson, Robert Carroll 1905-1974
   EncABHB 9 [port]
Tyson, Sean Michael 1961- *WhoWest 94*
Tyson, Victor E., Jr. d1993 *NewYTBS 93*
Tysseland, Terry Lawrence 1941-
   WhoWest 94
Tyszkiewicz, Robert Edward 1948-
   WhoWest 94
Tyszkiewicz, Zygmunt Jan Ansgary 1934-
   IntWW 93
Tytanic, Christopher Alan 1961-
   WhoAmL 94
Tytell, John 1939- *WhoAm 94*
Tytell, Louis 1913- *WhoAmA 93*
Tytler, Christian Helen F. *Who 94*
Tytler, Linda Jean 1947- *WhoAmP 93,*
   WhoWest 94
Tytus, John Butler 1875-1944 *EncABHB 9*
Tyulkin, Viktor Arkadevich 1951-
   LngBDD
Tyus, E. Leroy 1916- *WhoAmP 93*
Tyus, Wyomia 1945- *WhoBlA 94*
Tyzack, Margaret *WhoAm 94*
Tyzack, Margaret 1933- *WhoHol 92*
Tyzack, Margaret Maud 1931- *Who 94*
Tyzack, Michael 1933- *WhoAmA 93*
Tzagournis, Manuel *WhoAm 94,*
   WhoScEn 94
Tzavella-Evjen, Hara 1936- *WhoWest 94*
Tzelniker, Meier 1894- *WhoHol 92*
Tzeng, Kenneth Kai-Ming 1937-
   WhoAsA 94
Tzimas, Nicholas Achilles 1928-
   WhoAm 94
Tzimeas, John d1978 *WhoHol 92*
Tzitsikas, Helene 1926- *WhoMW 93*
Tzomes, Chancellor Alfonso 1944-
   WhoBlA 94
Tzveych, Biserka *NewGrDO*

U

Uatioa, Mere 1924- *Who 94*
Uba, George R. *WhoAsA 94*
Uba, Jude Ebere 1960- *WhoAm 94*
Ubaidullaeva, Reno Akhatovna *WhoWomW 91*
Uban, Stephen Alan 1950- *WhoScEn 94*
Ubans, Juris K. 1938- *WhoAmA 93*
Ubarry, Grizel 1953- *WhoHisp 94*
Ubarry, Hechtor *WhoHol 92*
Ubbelohde, Carl William 1924- *WhoMW 94*
Ubee, Sydney Richard 1903- *Who 94*
Ubell, Donald Paul 1945- *WhoAm 94*
Ubell, Earl 1926- *WhoAm 94*
Ubell, Robert Neil 1938- *WhoAm 94*
Uber, Christian Friedrich Hermann 1781-1822 *NewGrDO*
Uber, Ralph Leroy 1920- *WhoWest 94*
Uberall, Herbert Michael Stefan 1931- *WhoAm 94*
Uberoi, Mahinder Singh 1924- *WhoAm 94, WhoWest 94*
Uberstine, Mitchell Neil 1956- *WhoWest 94*
Ubhayakar, Shivadev K. 1946- *WhoAsA 94*
Ubinger, John W. 1949- *WhoAm 94*
Ubleis, Heinrich 1933- *IntWW 93*
Ubogy, Jo 1940- *WhoAmA 93*
Ubozhko, Lev Grigorevich 1933- *LngBDD*
Ubriaco, Robert David, Jr. 1956- *WhoMW 93*
Ubuka, Toshihiko 1934- *WhoAm 94, WhoScEn 94*
Ubukata, Taiji 1916- *IntWW 93*
Uccello, Vincenza Agatha *WhoAmA 93*
Uccello, Vincenza Agatha 1921- *WhoAm 94*
Ucelli, Loretta M. 1954- *WhoAm 94*
Uchida, Deborah Knowlton *WhoWest 94*
Uchida, Hideo 1919- *WhoScEn 94*
Uchida, Irene Ayako 1917- *WhoAm 94*
Uchida, Mitsuko 1948- *IntWW 93*
Uchida, Richard Noboru 1929- *WhoAsA 94*
Uchida, Yoshihiro *WhoAsA 94*
Uchida, Yoshiko *DrAPF 93*
Uchida, Yoshiko 1921-1992 *AnObit 1992, WhoAsA 94N, WrDr 94N*
Uchima, Ansei 1921- *WhoAmA 93*
Uchima, Toshiko *WhoAmA 93*
Uchimoto, Dennis D. 1945- *WhoAsA 94*
Uchimoto, Dennis Den 1945- *WhoMW 93*
Uchimoto, Eijiro 1955- *WhoWest 94*
Uchimoto, William Warren 1955- *WhoAsA 94*
Uchimura, Bruce Jiro 1959- *WhoAsA 94*
Uchitelle, Louis 1932- *WhoAm 94, WhoFI 94*
Uchiyama, Shoichi 1927- *WhoScEn 94*
Uchtenhagen-Brunner, Lilian 1928- *WhoWomW 91*
Uchupi, Elazar 1928- *WhoScEn 94*
Ucko, Barbara 1945- *WrDr 94*
Ucko, David Alan 1948- *WhoAm 94, WhoFI 94, WhoMW 93*
Uda, Hatsuo d1981 *WhoHol 92*
Uda, Robert Takeo 1942- *WhoAsA 94, WhoScEn 94*
Udall, Calvin Hunt 1923- *WhoAm 94*
Udall, Morris 1922- *IntWW 93*
Udall, Morris King 1922- *WhoAm 94, WhoAmP 93, WhoWest 94*

Udall, Nicholas 1504-1556 *IntDcT 2*
Udall, Nicholas 1505-1556 *BlmGEL*
Udall, Stewart Lee 1920- *IntWW 93, NewYTBS 93 [port]*
Udall, Thomas 1948- *WhoAmL 94*
Udall, Tom 1948- *WhoAm 94, WhoAmP 93, WhoWest 94*
Udani, Kanak H. 1936- *WhoAsA 94*
Udavchak, Richard M. 1933- *WhoIns 94*
Udbye, Martin Andreas 1820-1889 *NewGrDO*
Udcoff, George Joseph 1946- *WhoAm 94*
ud-Din, Khair- 1921- *Who 94*
Uddin, Waheed 1949- *WhoScEn 94*
Ude, Wayne *DrAPF 93*
Ude, Wayne 1946- *WrDr 94*
Udeinya, Iroka Joseph 1953- *WhoScEn 94*
Udelhofen, John Henry 1931- *WhoMW 93*
Udell, Jon Gerald 1935- *WhoFI 94*
Udell, Richard 1932- *WhoAm 94, WhoAmL 94*
Udenfriend, Sidney 1918- *IntWW 93, WhoAm 94*
Udet, Ernst d1941 *WhoHol 92*
Udevitz, Norman 1929- *WhoAm 94*
Udinotti, Agnese 1940- *WhoAmA 93*
Udler, Dmitry 1954- *WhoScEn 94*
Udoma, (Egbert) Udo 1917- *IntWW 93, Who 94*
Udry, J. Richard 1928- *WrDr 94*
Udry, Janice (May) 1928- *WrDr 94*
Udvardy, John Warren *WhoAmA 93*
Udvardy, Miklos Dezso Ferenc 1919- *WhoScEn 94*
Udvardy, Tibor d1981 *WhoHol 92*
Udvarhelyi, George Bela 1920- *WhoAm 94*
Udwadia, Firdaus Erach 1947- *WhoAm 94, WhoFI 94, WhoScEn 94, WhoWest 94*
Udy, Claudia *WhoHol 92*
Udy, Helene *WhoHol 92*
Ueberroth, John 1943- *WhoFI 94*
Ueberroth, John A. 1944- *WhoAm 94, WhoWest 94*
Ueberroth, Peter 1937- *IntWW 93*
Uebleis, Andreas Michael 1963- *WhoScEn 94*
Uecker, Bob 1935- *WhoAm 94, WhoHol 92*
Ueda, Clarence Tad 1942- *WhoAsA 94*
Ueda, Einosuke 1933- *WhoScEn 94*
Ueda, Issaku 1924- *WhoWest 94*
Ueda, Makoto 1931- *WrDr 94*
Uehlein, Edward Carl, Jr. 1941- *WhoAm 94*
Uehling, Barbara S. 1932- *IntWW 93*
Uehling, Barbara Staner 1932- *WhoAm 94, WhoWest 94*
Uehling, Gordon Alexander, Jr. 1939- *WhoFI 94*
Uehling, Rick 1953- *WhoAmP 93*
Uehlinger, John Clark 1929- *WhoAm 94*
Ueki, Shigeaki 1935- *IntWW 93*
Ueland, Arnulf, Jr. 1920- *WhoAmP 93*
Ueland, Sigurd, Jr. 1937- *WhoAm 94*
Uelsmann, Jerry 1934- *WhoAmA 93*
Uelsmann, Jerry Norman 1934- *WhoAm 94*
Uematsu, Kunihiko 1931- *IntWW 93*
Uematsu, Yoshiaki 1957- *WhoFI 94*
Uemoto, Karen *WhoAsA 94*

Uemura, Joseph Norio 1926- *WhoAsA 94*
Ueng, Charles En-Shiuh 1930- *WhoAsA 94*
Ueno, Taichi 1924- *IntWW 93*
Ueno, Takemi 1966- *WhoAsA 94*
Ueoka, Meyer Masato 1920- *WhoAsA 94*
Uerlings, James Robert 1950- *WhoWest 94*
Uezono, Yasuhito 1959- *WhoWest 94*
Ufema, John William 1946- *WhoFI 94*
Uff, John Francis 1942- *Who 94*
Uffelman, Malcolm Rucj 1935- *WhoAm 94*
Uffen, Kenneth James 1925- *IntWW 93, Who 94*
Uffen, Robert James 1923- *IntWW 93, WhoAm 94*
Uffner, Michael S. 1945- *WhoFI 94*
Ufford, Charles Wilbur, Jr. 1931- *WhoAm 94, WhoAmL 94*
Ufholz, Philip John 1947- *WhoAmP 93*
Ulfimtsev, Pyotr Yakovlevich 1931- *WhoScEn 94*
Ugalde, Delphine 1829-1910 *NewGrDO*
Uganda, Archbishop of 1927- *Who 94*
Ugarte, Floro M(eliton) 1884-1975 *NewGrDO*
Ugarte, Jose M. 1941- *WhoHisp 94*
Ugelow, Albert Jay 1950- *WhoFI 94*
Ugent, Alvin Ronald 1929- *WhoAmL 94*
Ugent, Donald 1933- *ConAu 141*
Uggams, Leslie 1943- *AfrAmAl 6 [port], IntMPA 94, WhoAm 94, WhoBlA 94, WhoHol 92*
Uggerud, Ward Lee 1949- *WhoMW 93*
Ugglas, Margaretha af 1939- *IntWW 93*
Ughetta, William C. 1954- *WhoAm 94, WhoAmL 94, WhoFI 94*
Ughetta, William Casper 1933- *WhoAm 94*
Ughi, Uto 1944- *IntWW 93*
Uglow, Alan 1941- *WhoAmA 93*
Uglow, Euan 1932- *IntWW 93*
Uglum, John Richard 1909- *WhoAmP 93*
Ugolyn, Victor 1947- *WhoFI 94*
Ugresic, Dubravka 1949- *BlmGWL [port], ConWorW 93*
Ugrin, Bela 1928- *WhoAm 94*
Ugrin, Emese *WhoWomW 91*
Ugwu, David Egbo 1950- *WhoAm 94, WhoFI 94, WhoMW 93*
Ugwu, Martin Cornelius 1956- *WhoScEn 94*
Uhde, George Irvin 1912- *WhoAm 94, WhoScEn 94*
Uhde, Hermann 1914-1965 *NewGrDO*
Uhde, Larry Jackson 1939- *WhoWest 94*
Uhde, Milan 1936- *IntWW 93*
Uher, D. R. 1937- *WhoAmP 93*
Uher, Lorna 1948- *WrDr 94*
Uherka, David Jerome 1938- *WhoMW 93*
Uhl, Alfred 1909-1992 *NewGrDO*
Uhl, Charles Harrison 1918- *WhoScEn 94*
Uhl, Fritz 1928- *NewGrDO*
Uhl, Joseph Andrew 1906- *WhoFI 94*
Uhl, Petr 1941- *IntWW 93*
Uhl, Philip Edward 1949- *WhoWest 94*
U Hla Maung 1932- *Who 94*
Uhlaner, Julius Earl 1917- *WhoWest 94*
Uhlenbeck, Karen Keskulla 1942- *WhoAm 94, WhoScEn 94*
Uhlenhuth, Eberhard Henry 1927- *WhoAm 94*

Uhler, Ruth Pershing 1898- *WhoAmA 93N*
Uhler, Walter Charles 1948- *WhoFI 94*
Uhley, Patricia d1988 *WhoHol 92*
Uhlig, Herbert H. d1993 *NewYTBS 93*
Uhlig, Theodor 1822-1853 *NewGrDO*
Uhlir, Arthur, Jr. 1926- *WhoAm 94*
Uhlmann, Wesley Carl 1935- *WhoAmP 93*
Uhlmann, Frederick Godfrey 1929- *WhoAm 94*
Uhlmann, Richard Frederick 1898-1989 *WhAm 10*
Uhm, Dan 1964- *WhoScEn 94*
Uhm, Jay Yun 1964- *WhoWest 94*
Uhnak, Dorothy 1933- *WrDr 94*
Uhran, Nancy McCleskey 1953- *WhoFI 94*
Uhrhammer, Douglas John 1950- *WhoMW 93*
Uhrich, Richard Beckley 1932- *WhoAm 94, WhoWest 94*
Uhrig, John Allan 1928- *IntWW 93*
Uhrig, Robert Eugene 1928- *WhoAm 94*
Uhrman, Celia 1927- *WhoAmA 93*
Uhrman, Esther 1921- *WhoAmA 93*
Uhry, Alfred 1936- *ConDr 93, WrDr 94*
Uhry, Alfred Fox 1936- *WhoAm 94*
Uicker, James Leo 1943- *WhoFI 94*
Uicker, Theresa A. 1962- *WhoMW 93*
Uijtdehaage, Sebastian Hendricus J. 1959- *WhoScEn 94*
Uipi, Phil H. 1949- *WhoAmP 93*
Uitti, Karl David 1933- *WhoAm 94*
Ujfalussy, Jozsef 1920- *IntWW 93*
Ukegbu, John Nwachukwu 1958- *WhoAmL 94*
Ukeles, Mierle Laderman *WhoAmA 93*
Ukishima, Daniel S. *WhoAmL 94*
Ukropina, James Robert 1937- *WhoAm 94, WhoWest 94*
Uku, Eustace Oris, Sr. 1947- *WhoBlA 94*
Ulabarro, José Antonio, Jr. 1933- *WhoHisp 94*
Ulaby, Fawwaz Tayssir 1943- *WhoAm 94, WhoScEn 94*
Ulacia, Richard 1963- *WhoHol 92*
Ulack, Richard 1942- *ConAu 140*
Ulakovich, Ronald Stephen 1942- *WhoFI 94, WhoMW 93*
Ulam, Adam B. 1922- *WhoAm 94*
Ulam, Adam Bruno 1922- *WrDr 94*
Ulam, Francoise 1918- *WhoWest 94*
Ulan, Martin Sylvester 1912- *WhoScEn 94*
Ulanmulun *WhoPRCh 91*
Ulanov, Barry 1918- *WhoAm 94*
Ulanova, Galina 1910- *IntDcB [port]*
Ulanova, Galina 1912- *WhoHol 92*
Ulanova, Galina Sergeyevna 1910- *IntWW 93, Who 94*
Ulasi, Adaora Lily *BlmGWL*
Ulbrecht, Jaromir Josef 1928- *WhoAm 94*
Ulbrich, Maximilian 1743-1814 *NewGrDO*
Ulbrich, John 1926- *WhoAm 94*
Ulbricht, Walter 1893-1973 *HisWorL [port]*
Ulchaker, Stanley Louis 1938- *WhoAm 94, WhoFI 94*
Ulerich, William Keener 1910- *WhoAm 94*
Ulett, George Andrew 1918- *WhoMW 93*
Ulevich, Neal Hirsh 1946- *WhoAm 94*

Ulf, Franklin Edgar 1931- *WhoFI 94*
Ulfelder, Howard 1911-1990 *WhAm 10*
Ulfelt, Leonora Christine 1621-1698 *BlmGWL*
Ulfung, Ragnar (Sigurd) 1927- *NewGrDO*
Uliana, Joseph M. 1965- *WhoAmP 93*
Ulibarri, Ernie B. *WhoHisp 94*
Ulibarri, John E. 1939- *WhoHisp 94*
Ulibarri, John Elias 1939- *WhoAmP 93*
Ulibarri, Sabine R. 1919- *WhoHisp 94*
Ulibarri, Sabine R(eyes) 1919- *RfGShF*
Ulibarrí, Yvonne 1956- *WhoHisp 94*
Ulichny, Barbara Lynn 1947- *WhoAmP 93*
Ulicki, Mary Jo 1952- *WhoFI 94*
Ulin, David L. *DrAPF 93*
Ulisse, Peter J. *DrAPF 93*
Ulizio, B. George 1889-1969 *DcLB 140 [port]*
Ullah, M. Rifat 1957- *WhoAsA 94*
Ullberg, Kent 1945- *WhoAmA 93*
Ullberg, Kent Jean 1945- *WhoAm 94*
Ullendorff, Edward 1920- *IntWW 93, Who 94, WrDr 94*
Ullestad, Merwin Allan 1949- *WhoFI 94*
Ullian, Joseph Silbert 1930- *WhoAm 94*
Ulliman, Joseph James 1935- *WhoWest 94*
Ullman, Bernard 1817?-1885 *NewGrDO*
Ullman, Edwin Fisher 1930- *WhoAm 94, WhoScEn 94*
Ullman, Frank Gordon 1926- *WhoAm 94, WhoMW 93*
Ullman, Frederic, Jr. d1948 *WhoHol 92*
Ullman, George W., Mrs. *WhoAmA 93*
Ullman, Greta d1972 *WhoHol 92*
Ullman, Harold P. 1899- *WhoAmA 93N*
Ullman, Jane F. 1908- *WhoAmA 93*
Ullman, Jeffrey David 1942- *WhoAm 94, WhoWest 94*
Ullman, Joan Connelly 1929- *WhoAm 94*
Ullman, Joseph Leonard 1923- *WhoMW 93*
Ullman, Karl Scott 1965- *WhoFI 94*
Ullman, Leo Solomon 1939- *WhoAm 94*
Ullman, Leslie *DrAPF 93*
Ullman, Louis Jay 1931- *WhoAm 94*
Ullman, Myron E., III *NewYTBS 93 [port]*
Ullman, Myron Edward, III 1946- *WhoAm 94, WhoFI 94*
Ullman, Patricia 1953- *WhoWest 94*
Ullman, Richard Henry 1933- *WhoAm 94*
Ullman, Samuel C. 1943- *WhoAmL 94*
Ullman, Tracey 1959- *IntMPA 94, IntWW 93, WhoAm 94, WhoCom, WhoHol 92*
Ullmann, Edward Hans 1967- *WhoScEn 94*
Ullmann, John E(manuel) 1923- *WrDr 94*
Ullmann, Linn 1967- *WhoHol 92*
Ullmann, Liv 1938- *WhoAm 94, WhoHol 92*
Ullmann, Liv 1939- *IntMPA 94*
Ullmann, Liv (Johanne) 1938- *Who 94*
Ullmann, Liv Johanne 1938- *IntWW 93*
Ullmann, Regina 1884-1961 *BlmGWL*
Ullmann, Viktor 1898-1944 *NewGrDO*
Ullo, J. Chris 1928- *WhoAmP 93*
Ulloa, Derby Leonel 1944- *WhoHisp 94*
Ulloa, Eunice *WhoHisp 94*
Ulloa, Franciso De dc. 1540 *WhWE*
Ulloa, Justo C. 1942- *WhoHisp 94*
Ulloa, Justo Celso 1942- *WhoAm 94*
Ulloa, Sergio E. 1955- *WhoHisp 94*
Ulloa Elias, Manuel d1992 *IntWW 93N*
Ullom, Lawrence Charles, Jr. 1964- *WhoScEn 94*
Ullrich, Bruce Edward 1946- *WhoFI 94*
Ullrich, Dennis L. 1947- *WhoWest 94*
Ullrich, Donald William, Jr. 1952- *WhoAmL 94*
Ullrich, John Frederick 1940- *WhoAm 94*
Ullrich, Robert Albert 1939- *WhoAm 94*
Ullstein, Augustus Rupert Patrick Anthony 1947- *Who 94*
Ullsten, Ola 1931- *IntWW 93*
Ullstrom, L. Berwyn 1919-1989 *WhAm 10*
Ullswater, Viscount 1942- *Who 94*
Ulman, Craig Hawkins 1951- *WhoAm 94*
Ulman, Ernst d1977 *WhoHol 92*
Ulman, Louis Jay 1946- *WhoAm 94*
Ulman, Roman Witold 1942- *WhoAmP 93*
Ulmar, Geraldine 1862-1932 *NewGrDO*
Ulmer, Alfred Conrad 1916- *WhoAm 94*
Ulmer, Anna d1928 *WhoHol 92*
Ulmer, Anne Close 1940- *WhoMW 93*
Ulmer, Daniel C., Jr. *WhoAm 94, WhoFI 94*
Ulmer, Daniel P. 1950- *WhoAmP 93*
Ulmer, Edgar G. 1904-1972 *HorFD [port]*
Ulmer, Eldon Robert 1918- *WhoAmP 93*
Ulmer, Frances Ann *WhoWomW 91*
Ulmer, Frances Ann 1947- *WhoAmP 93*
Ulmer, Friedrich d1952 *WhoHol 92*
Ulmer, Georges d1989 *WhoHol 92*
Ulmer, Gregory L(eland) 1944- *WrDr 94*
Ulmer, Melville Jack 1911- *WhoAm 94, WhoFI 94*
Ulmer, Melville Paul 1943- *WhoAm 94*
Ulmer, Shirley Sidney 1923- *WhoAm 94*
Ulmer, Walter F., Jr. 1929- *WhoAm 94*
Ulp, Clifford McCormick 1885-1957 *WhoAmA 93N*
Ulreich, Nura Woodson d1950 *WhoAmA 93N*
Ulrey, William B. 1961- *WhoAmP 93*
Ulric, Lenore d1970 *WhoHol 92*
Ulrich, Alfred Daniel, III 1961- *WhoScEn 94*
Ulrich, Celeste 1924- *WhoWest 94*
Ulrich, David Alan 1950- *WhoAmA 93*
Ulrich, Delmont Marion 1919- *WhoWest 94*
Ulrich, Diane Lynne 1950- *WhoAmP 93*
Ulrich, Edward Huber 1897- *WhAm 10*
Ulrich, Edwin Abel 1897- *WhoAmA 93*
Ulrich, Einer 1896- *BuCMET*
Ulrich, Gertrude Willems 1927- *WhoAmP 93*
Ulrich, Jeannette *WhoHisp 94*
Ulrich, John August 1915- *WhoScEn 94*
Ulrich, John Ross Gerald 1929- *WhoScEn 94*
Ulrich, Jorgen 1935- *BuCMET*
Ulrich, Joyce Louise 1956- *WhoFI 94*
Ulrich, Laurel Thatcher 1938- *ConAu 142, WhoAm 94*
Ulrich, Max Marsh 1925- *WhoAm 94*
Ulrich, Paul Graham 1938- *WhoAm 94, WhoAmL 94, WhoFI 94, WhoWest 94*
Ulrich, Peter Henry 1922- *WhoAm 94*
Ulrich, Richard Kevin 1955- *WhoAm 94*
Ulrich, Richard William 1950- *WhoAm 94, WhoFI 94*
Ulrich, Robert 1933- *WhoAmP 93*
Ulrich, Robert Gardner 1935- *WhoAm 94, WhoAmL 94, WhoFI 94*
Ulrich, Robert Gene 1941- *WhoAm 94*
Ulrich, Shirley Irene 1926- *WhoAmP 93*
Ulrich, Theodore Albert 1943- *WhoAm 94, WhoAmL 94*
Ulrich, Torben 1928- *BuCMET*
Ulrich, Walter Otto 1927- *Who 94*
Ulrich, Werner 1931- *WhoAm 94*
Ulrich, Werner Richard 1941- *WhoFI 94*
Ulrichsen, Wilhelm 1924- *IntWW 93*
Ulrich-Vogtlin, Ursula 1947- *WhoWomW 91*
Ulrich von Liechtenstein c. 1200-c. 1275 *DcLB 138*
Ulrich von Zatzikhoven 1194?-1214? *DcLB 138 [port]*
Ulsenheimer, Dean 1941- *WhoMW 93*
Ulseth, George Walter 1918- *WhoIns 94*
Ulshen, Martin Howard 1944- *WhoScEn 94*
Ulster, Earl of 1974- *Who 94*
Ultan, Lloyd 1938- *WhoAm 94*
Ultmann, John Ernest 1925- *WhoAm 94*
Ultra Violet 1934- *WhoAmA 93, WhoHol 92*
Ulug, Batuhan 1967 *WhoMW 93*
Ulum, Jennifer Lynn 1957- *WhoWest 94*
Ulusu, Bulent 1923- *IntWW 93*
Ulvang, John 1929- *WhoAmP 93*
Ulveling, Roger Alan 1943- *WhoWest 94*
Ulvila, Jacob Walter 1950- *WhoFI 94*
Ulyanov, Mikhail Aleksandrovich 1927- *IntWW 93*
Umali, Filemon J. 1925- *WhoAsA 94*
Uman, Martin Allan 1936- *WhoAm 94*
Umans, Alvin Robert 1927- *WhoAm 94*
Umansky, Michael M. 1941- *WhoAmL 94*
Umarji, Sanjay Govind 1960- *WhoMW 93*
Umbach, Eberle *DrAPF 93*
Umbach, Lawrence Cutler 1932- *WhoFI 94*
Umba Di Lutete 1939- *IntWW 93*
Umba Kyamitala 1937- *IntWW 93*
Umbaugh, Scott E. 1957- *WhoMW 93*
UmBayemake Joachim, Linda 1953- *WhoBlA 94*
Umberg, Thomas John 1955- *WhoAmL 94, WhoWest 94*
Umberg, Tom 1955- *WhoAmP 93*
Umbreit, Wayne William 1913- *WhoAm 94*
Umeda, Zenji 1913- *IntWW 93*
Umeki, Miyoshi 1929- *WhoHol 92*
Umeki, Shigenobu 1951- *WhoScEn 94*
Umezawa, Ado 1962- *WhoMW 93*
Umezawa, Hiroomi 1924- *WhoAm 94, WhoWest 94*
Umholtz, Clyde Allan 1947- *WhoFI 94*
Umidi Sala, Neida Maria 1948- *WhoWomW 91*
Umland, Pauline Sawyer 1903- *WhoWest 94*
Umland, Samuel Joseph 1954- *WhoMW 93*
Umlauf, Charles 1911- *WhoAmA 93*
Umlauf, Ignaz 1746-1796 *NewGrDO*
Umlauf, Karl A. 1939- *WhoAmA 93*
Umlauf, Lynn (Charlotte) 1942- *WhoAmA 93*
Umlauf, Michael 1781-1842 *NewGrDO*
Ummel, Stephen L. 1941- *WhoMW 93*
Ummer, James Walter 1945- *WhoAmL 94*
Umminger, Bruce Lynn 1941- *WhoAm 94, WhoScEn 94*
Umm Nizar (Salma al-Mala'ika) 1908-1953 *BlmGWL*
Umolu, Mary Harden 1927- *WhoBlA 94*
Umolu, Sheila Andrea 1966- *WhoBlA 94*
Umphress, David Ashley 1955- *WhoMW 93*
Umpierre, Gustavo 1931- *WhoHisp 94*
Umpierre, Luz Maria 1947- *WhoHisp 94*
Umpierre-Herrera, Luzma 1947- *WhoHisp 94*
Umpierre-Suarez, Enrique 1941- *WhoHisp 94*
Umpleby, Stuart Anspach 1944- *WhoScEn 94*
Umri, Hassan *IntWW 93*
Umrigar, Dara Nariman 1953- *WhoScEn 94*
Umscheid, Christina-Ma *DrAPF 93*
Umscheid, Ludwig Joseph 1937- *WhoScEn 94*
Umstadter, Karl Robert 1970- *WhoScEn 94*
Umstattd, Elizabeth Coles 1933- *WhoAmP 93*
Umstattd, James Greenleaf 1896- *WhAm 10*
Un, Howard Ho-Wei 1938- *WhoAsA 94*
Unada 1927- *WrDr 94*
Unaeze, Felix Eme 1952- *WhoBlA 94*
Unakar, Nalin Jayantilal 1935- *WhoAm 94, WhoAsA 94*
Unamuno (y Jugo), Miguel de 1864-1936 *RfGShF*
Unamuno, Miguel de 1864-1936 *HispLC [port]*
Unanue, Frank *WhoHisp 94*
Unanue, Joseph *WhoAm 94, WhoFI 94*
Unanue, Joseph A. 1926- *WhoHisp 94*
Unanue, Joseph F. 1957- *WhoHisp 94*
Unanue, Mary Ann 1959- *WhoHisp 94*
Unbehaun, Rick D. 1949- *WhoAmP 93*
Unckel, Per *IntWW 93, WhoScEn 94*
Uncle Shelby 1932- *WrDr 94*
Underberg, Alan J. 1929- *WhoAm 94*
Underberg, Mark Alan 1955- *WhoAm 94, WhoAmL 94*
Undercofler, Jonas Clayton 1940- *WhoAm 94, WhoAmL 94*
Underdown, David Edward 1925- *WhoAm 94*
Underdown, Edward 1908- *WhoHol 92*
Underdown, Emma Dankoski 1960- *WhoMW 93*
Underheim, Gregg 1950- *WhoAmP 93*
Underhill, Baron d1993 *Who 94N*
Underhill, Anne Barbara 1920- *WhoAm 94*
Underhill, Cave 1634-1710? *BlmGEL*
Underhill, Charles 1936- *WrDr 94*
Underhill, David Stuart 1960- *WhoAmL 94*
Underhill, Geoff d1978 *WhoHol 92*
Underhill, Henry Reginall d1993 *NewYTBS 93*
Underhill, Herbert Stuart 1914- *Who 94*
Underhill, Jacob Berry, III 1926- *WhoAm 94*
Underhill, John d1941 *WhoHol 92*
Underhill, Karen Jean 1960- *WhoWest 94*
Underhill, Linn B. *WhoAmA 93*
Underhill, Nicholas Edward 1952- *Who 94*
Underhill, Robert Alan 1944- *WhoMW 93, WhoScEn 94*
Underhill, William 1933- *WhoAmA 93*
Underland-Rosow, Vicki Louise 1947- *WhoMW 93*
Underweiser, Irwin Philip 1929- *WhoAm 94, WhoFI 94*
Underwood, Arthur C. *WhoBlA 94*
Underwood, Arthur Louis, Jr. 1924- *WhoAm 94, WhoScEn 94*
Underwood, Bernard Edward 1925- *WhoAm 94*
Underwood, Blair *WhoAm 94*
Underwood, Blair 1964- *IntMPA 94, WhoBlA 94, WhoHol 92*
Underwood, Cecil H. 1922- *IntWW 93, WhoAm 94*
Underwood, Cecil Harland 1922- *WhoAmP 93*
Underwood, Darlene Joyce 1949- *WhoMW 93*
Underwood, Edwin Hill, Sr. 1920- *WhoAmL 94*
Underwood, Elisabeth (Kendall) 1896-1976 *WhoAmA 93N*
Underwood, Evelyn Notman 1898-1983 *WhoAmA 93N*
Underwood, Frances d1961 *WhoHol 92*
Underwood, Franklin d1940 *WhoHol 92*
Underwood, Frankye Harper 1953- *WhoBlA 94*
Underwood, Frederick Dexter 1954- *WhoMW 93*
Underwood, George Alfred 1924- *WhoScEn 94*
Underwood, Glenn 1917- *WhoAmP 93*
Underwood, H. John 1947- *WhoAmP 93*
Underwood, Harry Burnham, II 1943- *WhoAm 94*
Underwood, James 1938- *WhoBlA 94*
Underwood, James H. 1946- *WhoAmP 93*
Underwood, James Martin 1909- *WhoAm 94*
Underwood, Jane Hainline Hammons 1931- *WhoAm 94*
Underwood, Jay D. *WhoHol 92*
Underwood, John Morris *Who 94*
Underwood, Joseph M., Jr. 1947- *WhoBlA 94*
Underwood, Lawrence d1939 *WhoHol 92*
Underwood, Leonard I. *WhoAmP 93*
Underwood, Loyal d1966 *WhoHol 92*
Underwood, Maude Esther 1930- *WhoBlA 94*
Underwood, Michael *ConAu 140*
Underwood, Michael 1916- *WrDr 94*
Underwood, Nancy Sue 1960- *WhoMW 93*
Underwood, Patricia Ruth 1939- *WhoAm 94*
Underwood, Paul 1940- *WhoFI 94*
Underwood, Paul Benjamin 1934- *WhoAm 94*
Underwood, Peter 1923- *WrDr 94*
Underwood, Ralph Edward 1947- *WhoWest 94*
Underwood, Ralph T. *WhoAmP 93*
Underwood, Ray *WhoHol 92*
Underwood, Richard Allan 1933- *WhoAm 94*
Underwood, Robert A. 1948- *CngDr 93*
Underwood, Robert Anacletus 1948- *WhoAmP 93, WhoAsA 94*
Underwood, Robert Donovan 1956- *WhoAmP 93*
Underwood, Robert Leigh 1944- *WhoFI 94, WhoMW 93*
Underwood, Roger Hasting 1935- *WhoAmL 94*
Underwood, Ron 1953- *IntMPA 94*
Underwood, Steven Clark 1960- *WhoAm 94, WhoWest 94*
Underwood, Thomas Woodbrook 1930- *WhoWest 94*
Underwood, Tim (Edward) 1948- *EncSF 93*
Underwood, Troy Jervis 1932- *WhoMW 93*
Underwood, Vernon O., Jr. 1940- *WhoFI 94*
Undlin, Charles Thomas 1928- *WhoAm 94, WhoMW 93*
Undset, Sigrid 1882-1949 *BlmGWL*
Unerman, Sandra Diane 1950- *Who 94*
Ungar, Eric Edward 1926- *WhoAm 94*
Ungar, Irwin Allan 1934- *WhoAm 94*
Ungar, Klara *WhoWomW 91*
Ungar, Lois *DrAPF 93*
Ungar, Manya Shayon 1928- *WhoAm 94*
Ungar, Robert Arthur 1955- *WhoAmL 94*
Ungar, Sanford J 1945- *WrDr 94*
Ungarelli, Rosa fl. 1709-1732 *NewGrDO*
Ungaretti, Richard Anthony 1942- *WhoAmL 94*
Ungaro, Emanuel Matteotti 1933- *IntWW 93*
Ungaro, Joan 1951- *WhoFI 94*
Ungaro, Joseph Michael 1930- *WhoAm 94*
Ungaro, Patrick J. 1941- *WhoAmP 93*
Ungaro-Benages, Ursula 1951- *WhoAm 94, WhoAmL 94*
Ungeheuer, Frederick d1993 *NewYTBS 93*
Ungeheuer, Gunther d1989 *WhoHol 92*
Unger, Anthony B. 1940- *IntMPA 94*
Unger, Arlene Klein 1952- *WhoWest 94*
Unger, Barbara *DrAPF 93*
Unger, Bertil d1990 *WhoHol 92*
Unger, David *DrAPF 93*
Unger, David 1950- *WhoHisp 94*
Unger, Deborah *WhoHol 92*
Unger, Donald Charles, Jr. 1949- *WhoWest 94*
Unger, Douglas 1952- *WrDr 94*
Unger, Elizabeth Ann 1939- *WhoMW 93*
Unger, Felix 1946- *IntWW 93*
Unger, Georg 1837-1887 *NewGrDO*
Unger, George D. 1924- *WhoBlA 94*
Unger, Gerhard 1916- *NewGrDO*
Unger, Gilbert Samuel 1925- *WhoMW 93*
Unger, Harlow G. 1931- *ConAu 142, SmATA 75 [port]*
Unger, Howard Albert 1944- *WhoAm 94*
Unger, Irwin 1927- *WhoAm 94*
Unger, Israel 1938- *WhoScEn 94*
Unger, John Thomas 1951- *WhoAmL 94*
Unger, Joseph Edward 1957- *WhoMW 93*
Unger, Karoline 1803-1877 *NewGrDO*
Unger, Kurt 1922- *IntMPA 94*
Unger, Lenore 1929- *WhoWest 94*

Unger, Leonard 1917- *WhoAmP 93*
Unger, Mary Ann 1945- *WhoAmA 93*
Unger, Michael 1945- *WhoAmL 94*
Unger, Michael Ronald 1943- *IntWW 93, Who 94*
Unger, Paul A. 1914- *WhoAm 94, WhoMW 93*
Unger, Paul Temple 1942- *WhoFI 94*
Unger, Paul Walter 1931- *WhoAm 94*
Unger, Peter K(enneth) 1942- *WrDr 94*
Unger, Peter Kenneth 1942- *WhoAm 94*
Unger, Peter Van Buren 1957- *WhoAmL 94*
Unger, Richard Allan 1948- *WhoWest 94*
Unger, Richard Mahlon 1945- *WhoAmL 94*
Unger, Richard Watson 1942- *WhoAm 94*
Unger, Ronald E. *WhoHisp 94*
Unger, Ronald Lawrence 1930- *WhoAm 94, WhoAmL 94*
Unger, Sonja Franz 1921- *WhoFI 94*
Unger, Stephen A. 1946- *IntMPA 94*
Unger, Stephen Herbert 1931- *WhoAm 94*
Unger, Sydney Elliott 1947- *WhoAmL 94*
Ungerer, Miriam 1929- *WrDr 94*
Ungerer, Tomi 1931- *Who 94*
Ungerer, Werner 1927- *IntWW 93*
Unger-Hamilton, Clive (Wolfgang) 1942- *ConAu 42NR*
Ungerleider, Linda Salsman 1941- *WhoMW 93*
Ungerman, Kimball Reid 1957- *WhoFI 94, WhoWest 94*
Ungers, Leslie Joseph 1951- *WhoScEn 94*
Ungers, Oswald M. 1926- *WhoAm 94*
Ungers, Oswald Mathias 1926- *IntWW 93*
Unglesby, Lewis O. 1949- *WhoAmL 94*
Unhjem, Michael B. 1953- *WhoAmP 93*
Unhjem, Michael Bruce 1953- *WhoMW 93*
Uniacke, Charles Allyn 1945- *WhoMW 93*
Unis, Richard L. 1928- *WhoAm 94, WhoAmL 94, WhoAmP 93, WhoWest 94*
Unitas, Johnny *ProFbHF [port]*
Unithan, Dolly 1940- *WhoAmA 93*
Unklesbay, Athel Glyde 1914- *WhoAm 94*
Unkovic, David 1954- *WhoAmL 94*
Unkovic, John Clark 1943- *WhoAmL 94*
Unno, Juza *EncSF 93*
Uno, Anne Quan 1942 *WhoAsA 94*
Uno, Hideo 1929- *WhoAsA 94*
Uno, Osamu 1917- *IntWW 93*
Uno, Sosuke 1922- *IntWW 93*
Uno Chiyo 1897- *BlmGWL*
Unpingco, Antonio Reyes 1942- *WhoAmP 93, WhoWest 94*
Unpingco, John Walter Sablan 1950- *WhoAm 94, WhoAmL 94*
Unruh, James Arlen 1941- *WhoAm 94, WhoFI 94*
Unruh, Joanna M. 1931- *WhoAmP 93*
Unruh, Paula 1929- *WhoAmP 93*
Unruh, Philip W. 1950- *WhoAmL 94, WhoAmP 93*
Unruh, Terry Lee 1947- *WhoAmL 94*
Unruh, Trude 1925- *WhoWomW 91*
Unruh, William G. 1945- *WhoAm 94*
Unseld, Siegfried 1924- *IntWW 93*
Unseld, Wes 1946- *BasBi, WhoBlA 94*
Unseld, Westley Sissel 1946- *WhoAm 94*
Unsell, Lloyd Neal 1922- *WhoAm 94*
Unser, Al 1939- *WhoAm 94, WhoWest 94*
Unser, Alfred, Jr. 1962- *WhoAm 94*
Unser, Bobby 1934- *WhoAm 94, WhoWest 94*
Unsoeld, Jolene 1931- *CngDr 93, WhoAm 94, WhoAmP 93, WhoWest 94, WhoWomW 91*
Unsworth, Barrie John 1934- *IntWW 93*
Unsworth, Barry 1930- *ConLC 76 [port], IntWW 93*
Unsworth, Barry (Forster) 1930- *WrDr 94*
Unsworth, Barry Forster 1930- *Who 94*
Unsworth, Edgar (Ignatius Godfrey) 1906- *Who 94*
Unsworth, Geoffrey 1914-1978 *IntDcF 2-4 [port]*
Unsworth, Richard Preston 1927- *WhoAm 94*
Untener, Kenneth E. 1937- *WhoAm 94, WhoMW 93*
Unterberger, Betty Miller *WrDr 94*
Unterberger, Betty Miller 1923- *WhoAm 94*
Unterborn, Lee Robert 1951- *WhoAmL 94*
Unterkircher, Hans d1971 *WhoHol 92*
Unterkoefler, Ernest L. 1917- *WhoAm 94*
Unterman, Eugene Rex 1953- *WhoMW 93*
Unterman, Ira Nathan 1964- *WhoWest 94*
Unterman, Thomas Edward 1944- *WhoAmL 94*
Untermann, Jurgen 1928- *IntWW 93*
Untermeyer, Charles G. 1946- *WhoAm 94*
Untermeyer, Charles Graves 1946- *WhoAmP 93*
Unterreiner, Bernard *WhoIns 94*
Unterreiner, C. Martin 1940- *WhoFI 94*
Unterseher, Chris Christian 1943- *WhoAmA 93*
Unthank, G. Wix 1923- *WhoAm 94, WhoAmL 94*
Unthank, Tessa *WhoAm 94*
Unton, Theodore Francis 1944- *WhoFI 94*
Unver, Erdal Ali 1953- *WhoScEn 94*
Unverzagt, George William, Jr. 1931- *WhoMW 93*
Unwin, Brian *Who 94*
Unwin, (James) Brian 1935- *IntWW 93, Who 94*
Unwin, Christopher Philip 1917- *Who 94*
Unwin, David (Storr) 1918- *WrDr 94*
Unwin, David Storr 1918- *Who 94*
Unwin, Eric Geoffrey 1942- *Who 94*
Unwin, Kenneth 1926- *Who 94*
Unwin, (Peter) Nigel (Tripp) 1942- *Who 94*
Unwin, Nora Spicer d1982 *WhoAmA 93N*
Unwin, Peter William 1932- *IntWW 93, Who 94*
Unwin, Rayner (Stephens) 1925- *WrDr 94*
Unwin, Rayner Stephens 1925- *Who 94*
Unwin, Stanley *WhoHol 92*
Unwin, Stephen Dale 1956- *WhoMW 93*
Unz, Richard Frederick 1935- *WhoAm 94*
Unzer, Johanne Charlotte 1725-1782 *BlmGWL*
Unzicker, Katerina Dawn 1965- *WhoWest 94*
Unzueta, Manuel 1949- *WhoHisp 94*
Unzueta, Silvia M. 1948- *WhoHisp 94*
Uoka, Satele M. *WhoAmP 93*
Uosukainen, Riitta Maria 1942- *WhoWomW 91*
Uotila, Urho Antti Kalevi 1923- *WhoAm 94*
Upadhyay, Jitendra Mohanlal 1931- *WhoMW 93*
Upadhyay, Shailendra Kumar 1929- *IntWW 93*
Upadhyay, Yogendra Nath 1938- *WhoScEn 94*
Upadhyaya, Shrinivasa Kumbhashi 1950- *WhoAm 94*
Upadrashta, Kameswara Rao *WhoFI 94*
Upatnieks, Juris 1936- *WhoAm 94*
Upbin, Hal Jay 1939- *WhoAm 94*
Upbin, Shari *WhoAm 94*
Upcher, Peter d1963 *WhoHol 92*
Upchurch, Avery C. *WhoAm 94, WhoAmP 93*
Upchurch, Hamilton D. 1925- *WhoAmP 93*
Upchurch, Michael *DrAPF 93*
Upchurch, Samuel E., Jr. 1952- *WhoAm 94*
Upchurch, Tracy W. 1956- *WhoAmP 93*
Updegraft, Kenneth E., Jr. 1946- *WhoAm 94, WhoAmL 94*
Updike, Helen Hill 1941- *WhoAm 94*
Updike, John *DrAPF 93*
Updike, John 1932- *ShSCr 13 [port]*
Updike, John (Hoyer) 1932- *EncSF 93, RfGShF, WrDr 94*
Updike, John Hoyer 1932- *AmCulL, IntWW 93, Who 94, WhoAm 94*
Updike, Margaret Rachel 1947- *WhoAmP 93*
Upgren, Arthur Reinhold, Jr. 1933- *WhoAm 94*
Upham, Charles Hazlitt 1908- *Who 94*
Upham, Chester R., Jr. 1925- *WhoAmP 93*
Upham, Steadman 1949- *WhoWest 94*
Uphoff, Evelyn M. 1918- *WhoAmP 93*
Uphoff, James Kent 1937- *WhoAm 94*
Uphoff, John Vincent 1965- *WhoScEn 94*
Uphoff, Joseph 1955- *WhoWest 94*
Uphoff, Louise Joan 1947- *WhoAmP 93*
Uphus, Sylvester Bernard 1927- *WhoAmP 93*
Upjohn, E. Gifford d1993 *NewYTBS 93*
Upjohn, Everard Miller 1903-1978 *WhoAmA 93N*
Upjohn, Gordon Farleigh 1912- *Who 94*
Upjohn, Richard 1802-1878 *AmCulL*
Uplegger, Francis fl. 1919-1939 *EncNAR*
Uppman, Jean Seward 1922- *WrDr 94*
Uppman, Theodor 1920- *NewGrDO, WhoAm 94*
Upponi, Ashwin Dattatraya 1961- *WhoFI 94*
Upright, Diane W. *WhoAmA 93*
Upright, Diane Warner *WhoAm 94*
Upshaw, Dawn 1960- *NewGrDO, WhoAm 94*
Upshaw, Gene *ProFbHF [port]*
Upshaw, Gene 1945- *WhoAm 94, WhoBlA 94*
Upshaw, Harry Stephan 1926- *WhoAm 94*
Upshaw, Mary J. 1951- *WhoMW 93*
Upshaw, Sam, Jr. 1964- *WhoBlA 94*
Upshaw, Timothy Alan 1958- *WhoScEn 94*
Upshaw, Willie Clay 1957- *WhoBlA 94*
Upson, Donald V. 1934- *WhoAm 94*
Upson, Jeannine Martin 1942- *WhoAmP 93*
Upson, Stuart Barnard 1925- *WhoAm 94, WhoFI 94*
Upson, Thomas F. 1941- *WhoAmP 93*
Uptegrove, Deane 1896- *WhAm 10*
Upton, Arthur Canfield 1923- *IntWW 93, WhoAm 94, WhoScEn 94*
Upton, Barbara A. 1921- *WhoAmP 93*
Upton, Bertha 1849-1912 *DcLB 141*
Upton, Charles *DrAPF 93*
Upton, E. H. 1924- *WhoBlA 94*
Upton, Florence K. 1873-1922 *DcLB 141 [port]*
Upton, Frances d1975 *WhoHol 92*
Upton, Fred 1953- *CngDr 93*
Upton, Fred Stephen 1953- *WhoAmP 93*
Upton, Frederick Stephen 1953- *WhoAm 94, WhoMW 93*
Upton, Helen M. d1993 *NewYTBS 93*
Upton, Howard B., Jr. 1922- *WhoAm 94*
Upton, James Nathan 1948- *WhoWest 94*
Upton, John David 1932- *WhoAmA 93*
Upton, Lee *DrAPF 93*
Upton, Mark *EncSF 93*
Upton, Martin 1933- *WrDr 94*
Upton, Morgan *WhoHol 92*
Upton, Richard F. 1914- *WhoAm 94*
Upton, Richard Thomas *WhoAmA 93*
Upton, Richard Thomas 1931- *WhoAm 94*
Upton, Robert *DrAPF 93*
Upward, Allen 1863-1926 *EncSF 93*
Upward, Edward 1903- *BlmGEL*
Upward, Edward (Falaise) 1903- *WrDr 94*
Upward, Janet *Who 94*
'Uraib dc. 899 *BlmGWL*
Urakami, Hiroko 1937- *ConAu 140*
Uram, Gerald Robert 1941- *WhoAmL 94*
Uram, Lauren Michelle 1957- *WhoAmA 93*
Uranga, Jose N. 1946- *WhoHisp 94*
Uranga, Victor Manuel 1942- *WhoHisp 94*
Uranga McKane, Steven 1952- *WhoHisp 94*
Urano, Muneyasu 1936- *WhoAsA 94*
Urbach, Ephraim Elimelech 1912-1991 *WhAm 10*
Urbach, Frederick 1922- *WhoAm 94*
Urbach, Frederick Lewis 1938- *WhoAm 94*
Urbach, Gerald P. 1943- *WhoAmL 94*
Urbain, Robert 1930- *IntWW 93*
Urbaitis, Elena *WhoAmA 93*
Urban, II c. 1042-1099 *HisWorL [port]*
Urban, Albert 1909-1959 *WhoAmA 93N*
Urban, Andrew Robert 1949- *WhoAm 94*
Urban, Carlyle Woodrow 1914- *WhoAm 94*
Urban, Cathleen Andrea 1947- *WhoFI 94, WhoScEn 94*
Urban, Dorothy d1961 *WhoHol 92*
Urban, Frank Henry 1930- *WhoAmP 93, WhoMW 93*
Urban, Frank M. 1953- *WhoHisp 94*
Urban, Gilbert William 1928- *WhoAm 94*
Urban, Henry Zeller 1920- *WhoAm 94*
Urban, Horst W. 1936- *IntWW 93*
Urban, James Arthur 1927- *WhoAm 94*
Urban, Jerome Andrew 1914-1991 *WhAm 10*
Urban, Jerzy 1933- *IntWW 93*
Urban, Josef 1872-1933 *NewGrDO*
Urban, Lee Donald 1946- *WhoAmL 94*
Urban, Marek Wojciech 1952- *WhoScEn 94*
Urban, Michael John, Jr. 1951- *WhoAmP 93*
Urban, Milan, Jr. 1966- *WhoFI 94*
Urban, Reva 1925-1987 *WhoAmA 93N*
Urban, Sharon Kay *WhoMW 93*
Urban, Thomas Francis, II 1963- *WhoAmL 94*
Urban, Thomas N. 1934- *WhoAm 94, WhoFI 94, WhoMW 93*
Urban, Vladimir T. 1952- *WhoAmA 93*
Urbanec, Bartolomej 1918-1983 *NewGrDO*
Urbanek, Karel 1941- *IntWW 93*
Urbanek, Zdenek 1917- *ConAu 140*
Urbani, Valentino *NewGrDO*
Urbaniak, James Randolph 1936- *WhoAm 94*
Urbano, Maryann *WhoHol 92*
Urbanowicz, Anna *WhoWomW 91*
Urbanowski, Frank 1936- *WhoAm 94*
Urbanowski, John Richard 1947- *WhoFI 94*
Urbanski, Douglas James 1957- *WhoWest 94*
Urbantke, Hugh Edmund 1922- *WhoAm 94*
Urbigkit, Walter C., Jr. 1927- *WhoAmP 93*
Urbik, Jerome Anthony 1929- *WhoFI 94*
Urbina, Eduardo 1948- *WhoHisp 94*
Urbina, Jeffrey Alan 1955- *WhoHisp 94*
Urbina, Leonidas Diaz *WhoAmP 93*
Urbina, Manuel, II 1939- *WhoHisp 94*
Urbina, Nicasio 1958- *WhoHisp 94*
Urbina, Ricardo Manuel 1946- *WhoHisp 94*
Urbina, Susana P. 1946- *WhoHisp 94*
Urbina de Breen, Marlene Victoria 1958- *WhoHisp 94*
Urbizu, William 1950- *WhoHisp 94*
Urbom, Donna Lynne 1951- *WhoAmL 94, WhoMW 93*
Urbom, Warren Keith 1925- *WhoAm 94, WhoAmL 94, WhoMW 93*
Urbont, Harry d1987 *WhoHol 92*
Urbzaska, Botenna *WhoWomW 91*
Urch, Elizabeth 1921- *WrDr 94*
Urch, George T. 1959- *WhoAmP 93*
Urcia, Ingeborg 1934- *WhoWest 94*
Urciolo, John Raphael, II 1947- *WhoFI 94*
Urciuoli, J. Arthur 1937- *WhoAm 94, WhoFI 94*
Urdan, Jennifer Anne 1959- *WhoFI 94*
Urdaneta, Andres De 1508-1568 *WhWE*
Urdaneta, Luis Fernando 1936- *WhoHisp 94*
Urdaneta, María-Luisa 1931- *WhoHisp 94*
Urdang, Alexandra 1956- *WhoAm 94*
Urdang, Constance (Henriette) 1922- *WrDr 94*
Urdang, Laurence 1927- *WhoAm 94*
Urdiales, Richard, Sr. 1946- *WhoHisp 94*
Urdy, Charles E. 1933- *WhoBlA 94*
Urdy, Charles Eugene 1933- *WhoAmP 93*
Ure, David 1951- *WhoAmP 93*
Ure, James Mathie 1925- *Who 94*
Ure, Jean 1943- *TwCYAW, WrDr 94*
Ure, John (Burns) 1931- *Who 94, WrDr 94*
Ure, John Burns 1931- *IntWW 93*
Ure, Mary d1975 *WhoHol 92*
Urecal, Minerva d1966 *WhoHol 92*
Urello, Donald Richard 1934- *WhoMW 93*
Uren, Thomas 1921- *IntWW 93*
Ureña, Luis Francisco 1948- *WhoHisp 94*
Urena-Alexiades, Jose Luis 1949- *WhoScEn 94, WhoWest 94*
Ureneck, Louis Adam 1950- *WhoAm 94*
Uresti, Gilberto *WhoHisp 94*
Uretsky, Jack Leon 1924- *WhoMW 93*
Urey, Harold Clayton 1893-1981 *WorScD*
Urfe, Honore d' 1568?-1625 *GuFrLit 2*
Urgenson, Lawrence A. *WhoAmL 94*
Urgo, Steven David 1965- *WhoAmL 94*
Urhausen, James Nicholas 1943- *WhoFI 94, WhoMW 93*
Uri, George Wolfsohn 1920- *WhoAm 94, WhoWest 94*
Uri, Pierre 1911-1992 *AnObit 1992*
Uri, Pierre Emmanuel d1992 *IntWW 93N*
Uria, Alvin Patrick 1952- *WhoHisp 94*
Uria, Miguel 1937- *WhoHisp 94*
Uria, Peter Monico 1946- *WhoHisp 94*
Uriarte-Otheguy, Francisco Javier 1968- *WhoHisp 94*
Urias, Carmen Carrasco 1966- *WhoHisp 94*
Urias, Rodolfo 1957- *WhoHisp 94*
Urias-Islas, Martha Alicia 1960- *WhoHisp 94*
Uribe, Alberto Ramiro 1957- *WhoHisp 94*
Uribe, Charles 1937- *WhoHisp 94*
Uribe, Ernest G. 1935- *WhoHisp 94*
Uribe, Ernesto 1937- *WhoHisp 94*
Uribe, George D., II 1968- *WhoHisp 94*
Uribe, Hector 1946- *WhoAmP 93*
Uribe, Hector R. 1946- *WhoHisp 94*
Uribe, Javier Miguel 1941- *WhoFI 94*
Uribe, Javier R. *WhoHisp 94*
Uribe, John 1937- *WhoHisp 94*
Uribe, John William 1949- *WhoHisp 94*
Uribe, José Alta 1959- *WhoHisp 94*
Uricchio, Michael Anthony 1953- *WhoAmL 94*
Urich, Robert 1946- *IntMPA 94, WhoHol 92*
Urich, Robert 1947- *WhoAm 94*
Uricheck-Holzapfel, Maryanne 1960- *WhoScEn 94*
Urick, Kevin *DrAPF 93*
Urie, (John) Dunlop 1915- *Who 94*
Urie, John James 1920- *WhoAm 94*
Urion, Melinda S. 1953- *WhoIns 94*
Urion, Melinda Sue 1953- *WhoAm 94, WhoFI 94*
Urioste, Frank J. *WhoAm 94*
Uris, Leon 1924- *WhoAm 94*
Uris, Leon (Marcus) 1924- *WrDr 94*
Uris, Leon Marcus 1924- *IntWW 93*
Urisko, Richard Francis Xavier 1957- *WhoAmL 94*
Urist, Marshall Raymond 1914- *WhoAm 94, WhoScEn 94*
Urista, Juan 1957- *WhoWest 94*
Urista, Moctezuma S. 1931- *WhoHisp 94*
Urista-Heredia, Alberto 1947- *WhoHisp 94*
Urista-Heredia, Alberto Baltazar 1947- *WhoAm 94*

V

Va, Moananu 1937- *WhoAmP 93*
Vaa, Aslaug 1889-1967 *BlmGWL*
Vaadia, Boaz 1951- *WhoAmA 93*
Vaal, Joseph John, Jr. 1947- *WhoMW 93*
Vaca, Alvar Nunez Cabeza De *WhWE*
Vaca, Nicolas Corona 1943- *WhoHisp 94*
Vaca, Santiago Mauricio 1960- *WhoHisp 94*
Vacala, Gregory George 1958- *WhoAmL 94*
Vacariou, Nicolae 1943- *IntWW 93*
Vacca, Charles Martin, Jr. 1955- *WhoAmL 94*
Vacca, John Joseph, Jr. 1922- *WhoAm 94*
Vacca, Roberto *EncSF 93*
Vaccai, Nicola 1790-1848 *NewGrDO*
Vaccarelli, Marie C. 1948- *WhoAmL 94*
Vaccarella, Anthony T. d1993 *NewYTBS 93 [port]*
Vaccarino, Robin 1928- *WhoAmA 93*
Vaccaro, Brenda 1939- *IntMPA 94, WhoAm 94, WhoHol 92*
Vaccaro, Charles G. 1940- *WhoAm 94, WhoAmA 94*
Vaccaro, Christopher Mark 1959- *WhoAmL 94*
Vaccaro, Frank d1948 *WhoHol 92*
Vaccaro, Louis Charles 1930- *WhoAm 94*
Vaccaro, Luella Grace 1934- *WhoAmA 93*
Vaccaro, Nick Dante 1931- *WhoAmA 93*
Vaccaro, Patrick Frank *WhoAmA 93*
Vaccaro, Ralph Francis 1919- *WhoAm 94*
Vaccaro, Richard Francis 1949- *WhoFI 94*
Vacchi, Fabio 1949- *NewGrDO*
Vacek, Milos 1928- *NewGrDO*
Vacek, Miroslav 1935- *IntWW 93*
Vache, Warren *WhoHol 92*
Vachher, Prehlad Singh 1933- *WhoScEn 94*
Vachon, Jean d1989 *WhoHol 92*
Vachon, Jean-Roch *WhoAmA 94, WhoFI 94*
Vachon, Louis-Albert 1912- *IntWW 93, Who 94*
Vachon, Marilyn Ann 1924- *WhoAm 94*
Vachon, Pierre 1731-1803 *NewGrDO*
Vachon, Reginald Irenee 1937- *WhoFI 94*
Vachon, Rogatien Rosaire 1945- *WhoAm 94, WhoWest 94*
Vachon, Russell Bertrand 1945- *WhoAm 94*
Vachon, Serge Jean 1939- *WhoAm 94*
Vachss, Andrew H(enry) 1942- *WrDr 94*
Vachss, Andrew Henry 1942- *WhoAmL 94*
Vacic, Aleksandar M. 1936- *IntWW 93*
Vacik, James Paul 1931- *WhoAm 94*
Vacio, Natividad *WhoHol 92*
Vacketta, Carl Lee 1941- *WhoAm 94*
Vactor, Alma Kane 1925- *WhoWest 94*
Vaculik, Ludvik 1926- *ConWorW 93*
Vad, Poul 1927- *ConAu 142*
Vadalabene, Sam Martin 1914- *WhoAmP 93*
Vade, Jean-Joseph 1719-1757 *NewGrDO*
Vaden, Christopher Scott 1956- *WhoAmL 94*
Vaden, Frank Samuel, III 1934- *WhoAmL 94*
Vadia, Rafael 1950- *WhoAmA 93*
Vadim, Annette *WhoHol 92*
Vadim, Christian 1962- *WhoHol 92*
Vadim, Roger 1928- *IntMPA 94, WhoHol 92*

Vadim, Roger (Plemiannikov) 1928- *IntWW 93*
Vadis, Dan d1987 *WhoHol 92*
Vadkerti-Gavornikova, Lydia 1932- *BlmGWL*
Vadlamudi, Sri Krishna 1927- *WhoAsA 94*
Vadnais, Alfred William 1935- *WhoAm 94*
Vadre, Leslie *EncSF 93*
Vaduva, Leontina 1962- *IntWW 93*
Vaea, Baron, of Houma *IntWW 93*
Vaea, Baron of Houma 1921- *Who 94*
Vaela'a, Tuilefano *WhoAmP 93*
Vaes, Robert 1919- *IntWW 93, Who 94*
Vaez, Gustave 1812-1862 *NewGrDO*
Vafeades, Peter 1957- *WhoScEn 94*
Vafiades, Markos 1906-1992 *AnObit 1992*
Vafidis, Matthew P. 1956- *WhoAmL 94*
Vafopoulou, Xanthe 1949- *WhoScEn 94*
Vaganova, Agrippina 1879-1951 *IntDcB*
Vagelos, Pindaros Roy 1929- *IntWW 93, WhoAm 94, WhoFI 94*
Vaget, Hans Rudolf 1938- *WhoAm 94*
Vaggalis, Katherine Lynn 1957- *WhoAmL 94*
Vagis, Polygnotis 1894-1965 *WhoAmA 93N*
Vagley, Robert Everett 1940- *WhoAm 94*
Vagliano, Alexander Marino 1927- *WhoAm 94*
Vaglio-Laurin, Roberto 1929- *WhoAm 94*
Vagnieres, Robert Charles, Jr. 1954- *WhoMW 93*
Vagnorius, Gediminas 1957- *IntWW 93*
Vagnozzi, Aldo 1925- *WhoAmP 93*
Vago, Constant 1921- *IntWW 93*
Vago, Pierre 1910- *IntWW 93*
Vagts, Detlev Frederick 1929- *WhoAm 94, WhoAmL 94*
Vague, Jean Marie 1911- *WhoAm 94, WhoScEn 94*
Vague, Vera d1974 *WhoHol 92*
Vahabzadeh, Farzaneh 1951- *WhoScEn 94*
Vahanian, Gabriel 1927- *WrDr 94*
Vahaviolos, Sotirios John 1946- *WhoAm 94, WhoScEn 94*
Vahdat, Nader 1947- *WhoAm 94*
Vahey, David William 1944- *WhoScEn 94*
Vahi, Tiit 1947- *IntWW 93*
Vahlenkamp, Virgil Leeroy, Jr. 1958- *WhoAmL 94*
Vahsholtz, Robert John 1935- *WhoAm 94*
Vai, Marjorie Theresa 1947- *WhoAm 94*
Vaid, Jyotsna *WhoAsA 94*
Vaidehi 1945- *BlmGWL*
Vaidhyanathan, Vishnampet S. 1933- *WhoAsA 94*
Vaidya, Kirit Rameshchandra 1937- *WhoAsA 94, WhoScEn 94*
Vail, Alfred 1807-1859 *WorInv*
Vail, Amanda *BlkWr 2*
Vail, Bambi Lynn 1955- *WhoMW 93*
Vail, Charles Daniel 1936- *WhoAm 94*
Vail, Charles Rowe 1915- *WhoAm 94*
Vail, David Lynn 1953- *WhoWest 94*
Vail, Desire *DrAPF 93*
Vail, Iris Jennings 1928- *WhoMW 93*
Vail, Joane Rand 1928- *WhoAmP 93*
Vail, Laurence 1857-1968 *WhoAmA 93N*
Vail, Lester d1959 *WhoHol 92*
Vail, Luki Styskal 1937- *WhoFI 94, WhoWest 94*

Vail, Mary Barbara 1956- *WhoWest 94*
Vail, Myrtle d1978 *WhoHol 92*
Vail, Olive d1951 *WhoHol 92*
Vail, Peter Robbins 1930- *WhoScEn 94*
Vail, Thomas Van Husen 1926- *WhoMW 93*
Vail, Van Horn 1934- *WhoAm 94*
Vailas, Arthur C. *WhoScEn 94*
Vaile, Robert Brainard, Jr. 1907- *WhoWest 94*
Vaillancourt, Armand 1929- *WhoAmA 93*
Vaillancourt, Daniel Gilbert 1947- *WhoAm 94*
Vaillancourt, Jean-Guy 1937- *WhoAm 94*
Vaillant, Janet G. 1937- *WrDr 94*
Vaillaud, Michel L. 1931- *IntWW 93*
Vaillaud, Pierre 1935- *IntWW 93*
Vailliencourt, William J., Jr. 1961- *WhoAmL 94*
Vainio, Pirkko 1957- *SmATA 76 [port]*
Vainio, Vesa Veikko 1942- *IntWW 93*
Vainisi, Jerome Robert 1941- *WhoMW 93*
Vainonen, Vasily 1901-1964 *IntDcB*
Vainshtein, Boris Konstantinovich 1921- *IntWW 93*
Vainstein, Rose 1920- *WhoAm 94*
Vaira, Peter Francis 1937- *WhoAm 94, WhoAmL 94*
Vairo, Robert John 1930- *WhoAm 94*
Vaisey, David George 1935- *IntWW 93, Who 94*
Vaishnava, Prem Prakash 1942- *WhoScEn 94*
Vaishnavi, Vijay Kumar 1948- *WhoAm 94*
Vaisman, Meyer 1960- *WhoAmA 93*
Vaitukaitis, Judith Louise 1940- *WhoAm 94, WhoScEn 94*
Vaivads, Sandra N. 1959- *WhoFI 94*
Vaizey, Lady 1938- *Who 94*
Vaizey, Marina (Alandra) 1938- *WrDr 94*
Vajda, Ernest 1887-1954 *IntDcF 2-4*
Vajda, Gyorgy 1927- *IntWW 93, WhoScEn 94*
Vajda, James, Jr. 1947- *WhoAmP 93*
Vajeeprasee Thongsak, Thomas 1935- *WhoFI 94*
Vajk, Hugo 1928- *WhoAm 94*
Vajna, Andrew 1944- *IntMPA 94*
Vajna, Andy *WhoAm 94*
Vajpayee, Atal Bihari 1926- *IntWW 93, Who 94*
Vakakis, Alexander F. 1961- *WhoScEn 94*
Vakalis, Ignatios Efstratios 1960- *WhoMW 93*
Vakalo, Eleni 1921- *BlmGWL*
Vakalo, Emmanuel-George 1946- *WhoMW 93, WhoScEn 94*
Vakerics, Thomas Vincent 1944- *WhoAmL 94*
Vakhromeyev, Kryil Varfolomeyevich *IntWW 93*
Vakil, Jayshree 1957- *WhoWest 94*
Vakili-Mirzamani, Jalaleddin 1943- *WhoWest 94*
Vakirtzis, Adamantios Montos 1964- *WhoScEn 94*
Vakula, Alex Benjamin 1961- *WhoAmL 94*
Vaky, Viron Peter 1925- *WhoAm 94*
Vala, Katri 1901-1944 *BlmGWL*
Vala, Robert 1930- *WhoWest 94*
Valadao, Maria Bahia Peixoto 1931- *WhoWomW 91*

Valade, Alan Michael 1952- *WhoAm 94*
Valadez, Bernadette Dolores 1963- *WhoHisp 94*
Valadez, Gustavo 1952- *WhoHisp 94*
Valadez, John 1951- *WhoAmA 93*
Valadez, John Robert 1944- *WhoHisp 94*
Valadez, Lando X. *WhoAmP 93*
Valadez, Ray Michael 1947- *WhoHisp 94*
Valadez, Robert Allen 1960- *WhoAmL 94*
Valadez, Stanley David 1924-1994 *WhoHisp 94N*
Valadez-Ortiz, Gustavo Rosenber 1943- *WhoHisp 94*
Valadie, Dominique *WhoHol 92*
Valan, Merlyn O. 1926- *WhoAmP 93*
Valance, Marsha Jeanne 1946- *WhoMW 93*
Valandra, Paul *WhoAmP 93*
Valandrey, Charlotte 1968- *WhoHol 92*
Valaskovic, David William 1961- *WhoMW 93*
Valberg, Birgitta *WhoHol 92*
Valberg, Leslie Stephen 1930- *WhoAm 94, WhoScEn 94*
Valbergh, Ivan 1766-1819 *IntDcB*
Valberkh, Ivan 1766-1819 *IntDcB*
Valbrun, Marjory 1963- *WhoBlA 94*
Valbuena-Briones, Angel Julian 1928- *WhoAm 94*
Valcarcel, Marta Iris 1931- *WhoAm 94*
Valcavado, Beatus Of *WhWE*
Valcavi, Umberto 1928- *WhoScEn 94*
Valcourt, Bernard 1952- *IntWW 93, WhoAm 94, WhoScEn 94*
Valdar, Colin Gordon 1918- *Who 94*
Valdata, Patricia 1952- *WhoScEn 94*
Valdemarin, Livio 1944- *WhoScEn 94*
Valdengo, Giuseppe 1914- *NewGrDO*
Valderrama, Alexander Stanley 1964- *WhoMW 93*
Valderrama, David M. 1933- *WhoAmP 93*
Valderrama, David Mercado 1933- *WhoAsA 94*
Valdés, Albert Charles 1907- *WhoHisp 94*
Valdés, Alberto 1946- *WhoHisp 94*
Valdes, Berardo A. 1943- *WhoHisp 94*
Valdes, Carlos L. 1951- *WhoAmP 93*
Valdés, Carlos Leonardo 1951- *WhoHisp 94*
Valdés, Dario 1938- *WhoHisp 94*
Valdes, Frank A, Jr. 1931- *WhoHisp 94*
Valdes, Gilberto *WhoHisp 94*
Valdes, Hector Jose, Sr. 1930- *WhoHisp 94*
Valdes, James John 1951- *WhoHisp 94*
Valdes, Jorge E. 1940- *WhoHisp 94*
Valdés, Jorge Nelson 1942- *WhoHisp 94*
Valdés, Juan José 1953- *WhoHisp 94*
Valdes, Karen W. 1945- *WhoAmA 93*
Valdes, Laura *WhoBlA 94*
Valdés, M. Isabel 1949- *WhoHisp 94*
Valdés, Mario J. 1934- *WrDr 94*
Valdes, Maximiano *WhoAm 94, WhoHisp 94*
Valdes, Miguel A. 1943- *WhoAm 94*
Valdes, Pedro H. 1945- *WhoBlA 94*
Valdes, Pedro Hilario, Jr. 1945- *WhoHisp 94*
Valdes, Petra G. *WhoHisp 94*
Valdes, Teresa A. 1938- *WhoHisp 94*
Valdes, Victor A., Sr. 1936- *WhoHisp 94*
Valdes-Dapena, Marie Agnes 1921- *WhoAm 94*

1155

Valli, Frankie 1927- *WhoHol 92*
Valli, Frankie 1937- *ConMus 10 [port], WhoAm 94*
Valli, June d1993 *NewYTBS 93*
Valli, Romolo d1980 *WhoHol 92*
Valli, Valli d1927 *WhoHol 92*
Valli, Virginia d1968 *WhoHol 92*
Valliant, John Peden 1947- *WhoAmP 93*
Vallier, Helene *WhoHol 92*
Vallila, Marja R. 1950- *WhoAmA 93*
Valli Muthusamy *WhoWomW 91*
Vallin, Ninon 1886-1961 *NewGrDO*
Vallin, Rick d1977 *WhoHol 92*
Vallings, George (Montague Francis) 1932- *Who 94*
Vallis, Michael Anthony 1929- *Who 94*
Vallis, Val(entine Thomas) 1916- *WrDr 94*
Vallon, Michael d1973 *WhoHol 92*
Vallone, Peter F. *WhoHisp 94*
Vallone, Peter F. 1934- *WhoAmP 93*
Vallone, Raf 1916- *IntMPA 94, WhoHol 92*
Vallone, Ralph, Jr. 1947- *WhoAmL 94*
Vallort, Ronald Peter 1942- *WhoScEn 94*
Valls, Nicolas J. 1964- *WhoHisp 94*
Valls, Oriol Tomas 1947- *WhoMW 93*
Valmon, Andrew Orlando 1965- *WhoBlA 94*
Valmonte, Arnel Elvambuena 1965- *WhoAsA 94*
Valner, Rudy 1960- *WhoWest 94*
Valois, Ninette de *IntDcB, Who 94*
Valois, Robert Arthur 1938- *WhoAmL 94*
Valois, Roger 1928- *WhoAmP 93*
Valone, Keith Emerson 1953- *WhoWest 94*
Valor, Joaquin, Jr. 1944- *WhoHisp 94*
Valori, Bice d1980 *WhoHol 92*
Valoski, Michael Peter 1951- *WhoScEn 94*
Valot, Daniel L. 1944- *WhoAm 94, WhoFI 94, WhoWest 94*
Valpreda, Mark David 1964- *WhoWest 94*
Valrand, Carlos Bruno 1943- *WhoScEn 94*
Valsangiacomo, Oreste Victor, Sr. 1919- *WhoAmP 93*
Valsaraj, Kalliat Thazhathuveetil 1957- *WhoScEn 94*
Valsini, Frencasco *NewGrDO*
Valticos, Nicholas 1918- *IntWW 93*
Valtman, Edmund 1914- *WhoAmA 93*
Valukas, Anton Ronald 1943- *WhoAm 94, WhoAmL 94*
Valvano, Jim d1993 *NewYTBS 93 [port]*
Valverde (y Sanjuan), Joaquin 1875-1918 *NewGrDO*
Valverde, Joaquin 1846-1910 *NewGrDO*
Valverde, Joe A. 1935- *WhoHisp 94*
Valverde, Leonard A. 1943- *WhoHisp 94, WhoWest 94*
Valverde, Rawley *WhoHol 92*
Valverde, Rodrigo Alberto 1952- *WhoHisp 94*
Valverde, Sylvia Ann 1956- *WhoHisp 94*
Vambery, Armin 1832-1913 *WhWE*
Vammen, James Oliver 1932- *WhoMW 93*
Vamos, George A. 1912- *WhoScEn 94*
Vamos, Tibor 1926- *IntWW 93*
Vampilov, Alexander 1937-1972 *IntDcT 2*
Vampira 1921- *WhoHol 92*
Vamplew, Wray 1943- *WrDr 94*
Vamvounaki, Maro 1948- *BlmGWL*
Van, Billy d1973 *WhoHol 92*
Van, Billy B. d1950 *WhoHol 92*
Van, Bobby d1980 *WhoHol 92*
Van, Connie d1961 *WhoHol 92*
Van, Frankie d1978 *WhoHol 92*
Van, George Paul 1940- *WhoAm 94*
Van, Gus d1968 *WhoHol 92*
Van, Peter 1936- *WhoAm 94, WhoAmL 94, WhoFI 94*
Van, Thanhtan C. 1961- *WhoAsA 94*
Van, Vester L., Jr. 1941- *WhoBlA 94*
Van, Wally d1974 *WhoHol 92*
Van Aalten, Jacques 1907- *WhoAmA 93*
Van Aanhold, Michael John 1964- *WhoFI 94*
Van Aardenne, Gijs M. C. 1930- *IntWW 93*
Van Ackeren, Maurice Edward 1911- *WhoAm 94, WhoMW 93*
Van Aerschot, Octave d1977 *WhoHol 92*
Van Agt, Andries A. M. *IntWW 93*
Van Aken, William Russell 1912- *WhoAmP 93*
Van Alen, Jimmy 1902-1991 *BuCMET*
Van Allan, Richard 1935- *IntWW 93, NewGrDO, Who 94*
Van Allburg, Chris 1949- *WrDr 94*
Van Allen, James 1914- *WorInv [port], WorScD*
Van Allen, James Alfred 1914- *IntWW 93, Who 94, WhoAm 94, WhoScEn 94*
VanAllen, Morton Curtis 1950- *WhoBlA 94*
Van Allen, William Kent 1914- *WhoAm 94, WhoAmL 94*
Van Allman, Don Thomas 1932- *WhoMW 93*
Van Allsburg, Chris 1949- *WhoAm 94*
Van Alstine, John Richard 1952- *WhoAmA 93*
Van Alstyne, Judith Sturges 1934- *WhoAm 94*
Van Alstyne, Vance Brownell 1924- *WhoFI 94*
Van Alstyne, W. Scott, Jr. 1922- *WhoAm 94*
Van Alstyne, William Warner 1934- *WhoAm 94*
Van Altena, William Foster 1939- *WhoAm 94*
Van Ammelrooy, Willeke 1944- *WhoHol 92*
Vanamo, Jorma Jaakko 1913- *IntWW 93*
Van Amringe, John Howard 1932- *WhoWest 94*
Van Amson, George Louis 1952- *WhoBlA 94*
Van Andel, Betty Jean 1921- *WhoMW 93*
Van Andel, Jay 1924- *WhoAm 94, WhoFI 94, WhoMW 93*
van Andel, Katharine Bridget *Who 94*
Van Andel, Nan 1953- *WhoFI 94*
Van Antwerp, Albert d1946 *WhoHol 92*
Van Antwerp, Jack 1963- *WhoMW 93*
Van Antwerp, James C., Jr. 1923- *WhoAmP 93*
Van Antwerp, Rosemary Dirkie 1946- *WhoAmL 94, WhoFI 94*
Van Antwerpen, Franklin Stuart 1941- *WhoAm 94, WhoAmL 94*
Van Antwerpen, Regina Lane 1939- *WhoFI 94, WhoMW 93*
Van Ark, Joan *WhoAm 94*
Van Ark, Joan 1943- *IntMPA 94*
Van Ark, Joan 1944- *WhoHol 92*
Van Arkel, Jo Beth 1958- *WhoMW 93*
van Arnam, Dave 1935- *EncSF 93*
Van Arsdale, Catherine Eva 1917- *WhoAmP 93*
Van Arsdale, Curtis Ray 1947- *WhoMW 93*
Van Arsdale, Dick 1943- *BasBi, WhoAm 94, WhoWest 94*
Van Arsdale, James W. 1926- *WhoAmP 93*
Van Arsdale, Tom 1943- *BasBi*
Van Arsdales, The *BasBi*
Van Arsdall, Robert Armes 1925- *WhoAm 94*
Van Arsdel, Eugene Parr 1925- *WhoScEn 94*
Van Arsdel, Paul Parr, Jr. 1926- *WhoAm 94, WhoWest 94*
Van Arsdel, Rosemary T(horstenson) 1926- *ConAu 43NR*
Van Arsdel, William Campbell, III 1920- *WhoScEn 94*
Van Arsdell, Madelene 1918- *WhoAmP 93*
Van Arsdell, Paul Marion 1905- *WhoAm 94*
Van Arsdol, Maurice Donald, Jr. 1928- *WhoAm 94, WhoWest 94*
Van Artsdalen, Donald West 1919- *WhoAm 94, WhoAmL 94*
Van Artsdalen, Ervin Robert 1913- *WhoAm 94*
Vanasek, Robert Edward 1949- *WhoAmP 93*
Van Asperen, Morris Earl 1943- *WhoAm 94, WhoFI 94, WhoWest 94*
Van Assche, Frans Jan Maurits 1948- *WhoScEn 94*
Vanasse, Albert J. 1918- *WhoAmP 93*
Vanasse, Louis Raymond 1931- *WhoAmA 93*
Vanatta, Chester B. 1935- *WhoAm 94*
Van Atta, David Murray 1944- *WhoAm 94, WhoAmL 94*
Vanatta, John Crothers, III 1919- *WhoAm 94*
VanAtta, Merry Janice 1938- *WhoWest 94*
Van Atta, Shelley Gay 1956- *WhoWest 94*
Van Auken, Barbara Sandberg 1946- *WhoAmL 94, WhoMW 93*
Van Auken, Robert Danforth 1915- *WhoFI 94*
Van Auker, C. K. d1938 *WhoHol 92*
Van Ausdall, Robert Loren 1920- *WhoMW 93*
Van Baak, Anthony Edward 1949- *WhoFI 94*
Van Balen, Gary Lee 1954- *WhoFI 94*
Van Basten, Marco 1964- *WorESoc*
Van Bebber, George Thomas 1931- *WhoAm 94, WhoAmL 94, WhoMW 93*
Van Beck, Todd W. 1952- *WhoFI 94*
Van Beek, Dianne Margaret 1946- *WhoMW 93*
Van Beek, Gus Willard 1922- *WhoAm 94*
Van Beers, Stanley d1961 *WhoHol 92*
van Belle, Gerald 1936- *WhoWest 94*
Van Bellinghen, Carolyn *WhoHol 92*
van Bellinghen, Jean-Paul 1925- *Who 94*
Van Bennekom, Pieter *WhoAm 94, WhoFI 94*
Van Bergen, Lewis *WhoHol 92*
Van Biene, Auguste d1913 *WhoHol 92*
Vanbiesbrouck, John 1963- *WhoAm 94*
Van Blaricom, Margaret Elena 1964- *WhoWest 94*
Van Bokkelen, William Requa 1946- *WhoAm 94*
Van Booven, Judy Lee 1952- *WhoFI 94, WhoMW 93, WhoScEn 94*
Van Borssum, John Bernard 1947- *WhoWest 94*
Van Bortel, Howard Martin 1930- *WhoFI 94*
Van Boven, D. Lauris 1919- *WhoAmP 93*
Van Boven, H. Lee 1939- *WhoAmL 94*
Van Boxtel, Diane Lynn 1952- *WhoFI 94*
van Brabant, Jozef M(artin) 1942- *ConAu 141*
Van Breda Kolff, Butch 1924- *BasBi*
Van-Breemen, Bertram 1919- *WhoMW 93*
VanBremen, Lee 1938- *WhoAm 94, WhoMW 93*
Van Brocklin, Norm d1983 *ProFbHF [port]*
VanBrode, Derrick Brent, IV 1940- *WhoAm 94*
Van Broekhoven, Rollin Adrian 1940- *WhoAmL 94*
van Bruchem, Jan 1929- *WhoAm 94*
Van Bruggen, Ariena Hendrika Cornelia 1949- *WhoScEn 94*
Vanbrugh, Irene d1949 *WhoHol 92*
Vanbrugh, John 1664-1726 *BlmGEL, IntDcT 2, NewGrDO*
Vanbrugh, Violet d1942 *WhoHol 92*
Van Brunt, Albert Daniel 1920- *WhoAm 94*
Van Brunt, Edmund Ewing 1926- *WhoWest 94*
Van Brunt, Lloyd *DrAPF 93*
Van Brunt, Marcia Adele 1937- *WhoMW 93*
Van Brunt, Philip G. 1935- *WhoAmA 93*
Van Bruwaene, Susi Marie 1964- *WhoWest 94*
Van Buhler, Robert Allan 1944- *WhoWest 94*
Van Bulck, Hendrikus Eugenius 1950- *WhoFI 94*
Van Buren, A. H. d1965 *WhoHol 92*
Van Buren, Abigail 1918- *WhoAm 94*
VanBuren, Cynthia Way 1955- *WhoAmL 94*
Van Buren, David S. *DrAPF 93*
Van Buren, Erik M. 1966- *WhoFI 94*
Van Buren, Mabel d1947 *WhoHol 92*
Van Buren, Phyllis Eileen 1947- *WhoMW 93*
Van Buren, Raeburn 1891-1987 *WhAm 10, WhoAmA 93N*
Van Buren, Steve *ProFbHF [port]*
Van Buren, William Benjamin, III 1922- *WhoAm 94*
Van Buren, William Ralph, III 1956- *WhoAmL 94*
Van Burkleo, Bill Ben 1942- *WhoScEn 94*
Van Buskirk, Abraham *WhAmRev*
Van Caenegem, Raoul Charles Joseph 1927- *Who 94*
Van Camp, Brian Ralph 1940- *WhoAm 94, WhoAmL 94*
Van Camp, Bruce Alan 1958- *WhoMW 93*
Van Camp, Donald Ray, Jr. 1970- *WhoMW 93*
Van Camp, Mike 1941- *WhoAmP 93*
Van Campen, Darrell Robert 1935- *WhoScEn 94*
van Campen, Karl *EncSF 93*
Van Campen, Stephen Bernard 1941- *WhoAm 94, WhoFI 94*
Vancas, Mark Francis 1947- *WhoWest 94*
Van Caspel, Venita Walker *WhoAm 94*
Vance, Andrew Peter 1925- *WhoAm 94, WhoAmL 94*
Vance, Bernard Wayne 1947- *WhoAm 94*
Vance, Blake *WhoWest 94*
Vance, Bridgid Rowan 1952- *WhoAmP 93*
Vance, Carl D. 1945- *WhoMW 93*
Vance, Carol Stoner 1933- *WhoAm 94*
Vance, Carrie Temple 1944- *WhoWest 94*
Vance, Charles Elijah, III 1938- *WhoWest 94*
Vance, Charles Fogle, Jr. 1924- *WhoAm 94*
Vance, Charles Ivan 1929- *Who 94*
Vance, Christopher M. 1962- *WhoAmP 93*
Vance, Courtney B. 1959- *WhoHol 92*
Vance, Cyrus Roberts 1917- *IntWW 93, Who 94, WhoAm 94, WhoAmP 93*
Vance, Danitra *WhoHol 92*
Vance, David Alvin 1948- *WhoFI 94*
Vance, Dennis 1924- *WhoHol 92*
Vance, Dennis Edward 1942- *WhoAm 94*
Vance, Don Kelvin 1935- *WhoAm 94*
Vance, Edward Flavus 1929- *WhoAm 94*
Vance, Edward Odell 1937- *WhoMW 93*
Vance, Elbridge Putnam 1915- *WhoAm 94*
Vance, Estil A. 1938- *WhoAmP 93*
Vance, Estil August, Jr. 1938- *WhoAmL 94*
Vance, George 1936- *WhoAmP 93*
Vance, Gerald *EncSF 93*
Vance, Howard Grant 1915- *WhoAmP 93*
Vance, Irvin E. 1928- *WhoBlA 94*
Vance, Jack 1916- *EncSF 93, WrDr 94*
Vance, James 1930- *WhoAm 94*
Vance, Joan Emily Jackson 1925- *WhoMW 93*
Vance, John Holbrook 1916- *WrDr 94*
Vance, Kenneth E. 1917- *WhoAm 94*
Vance, Kenny *WhoHol 92*
Vance, Lawrence N. 1949- *WhoBlA 94*
Vance, Lee 1907- *WhoAm 94*
Vance, Leigh 1922- *IntMPA 94*
Vance, Lucile d1974 *WhoHol 92*
Vance, Lynn Margaret 1952- *WhoFI 94*
Vance, Michael C. 1951- *WhoAmP 93*
Vance, Michael Charles 1951- *WhoAmL 94, WhoMW 93*
Vance, Morag L. *WhoAmP 93*
Vance, Patricia H. 1936- *WhoAmP 93*
Vance, Richard *DrAPF 93*
Vance, Robert Mercer 1916- *WhoAm 94, WhoFI 94*
Vance, Robert Patrick 1948- *WhoAm 94, WhoAmL 94*
Vance, Robert Smith 1931- *WhoAmP 93*
Vance, Robert Smith 1931-1989 *WhAm 10*
Vance, Ronald *DrAPF 93*
Vance, Roy Carroll *WhoAmP 93*
Vance, Roy N. 1921- *WhoAmP 93*
Vance, Sheldon Baird 1917- *WhoAm 94, WhoAmP 93*
Vance, Stanley Charles 1915- *WhoAm 94*
Vance, Steve 1952- *EncSF 93*
Vance, Tommie Rowan 1929- *WhoBlA 94*
Vance, Vera R. 1908- *WhoBlA 94*
Vance, Verne Widney, Jr. 1932- *WhoAm 94*
Vance, Virginia d1942 *WhoHol 92*
Vance, Vivian d1979 *WhoHol 92*
Vance, Vivian 1912-1979 *WhoCom*
Vance, William J., Sr. 1923- *WhoBlA 94*
Vance, William L. 1932- *WhoMW 93*
Vance, William L(ynn) 1934- *WrDr 94*
Vance, Zinna Barth 1917- *WhoAm 94*
Vance Siebrasse, Kathy Ann 1954- *WhoMW 93*
Vanchiasong, Siong Koua 1944- *WhoAsA 94*
Van Citters, Robert L. 1926- *IntWW 93*
Van Citters, Robert Lee 1926- *WhoWest 94*
Vancko, Robert Michael 1942- *WhoMW 93*
VanCleave, Janice 1942- *ConAu 142, SmATA 75 [port]*
Van Cleave, Peter 1927- *WhoMW 93*
Van Cleave, William Robert 1935- *WhoAm 94*
Van Cleef, Jabez Lindsay 1948- *WhoScEn 94*
Van Cleef, Lee d1989 *WhoHol 92*
Van Cleef, Lee 1925-1989 *WhAm 10*
Van Cleef, Robert Edward 1946- *WhoWest 94*
Van Cleve, Bruce C. 1960- *WhoMW 93*
Van Cleve, Edith d1985 *WhoHol 92*
Van Cleve, John Vickrey 1947- *WhoAm 94*
Van Cleve, Ruth Gill 1925- *WhoAm 94, WhoAmP 93*
Van Cleve, William Moore 1929- *WhoAm 94*
Vanco, John L. 1945- *WhoAm 94*
Vanco, John Leroy 1945- *WhoAmA 93*
Van Cortland, Jan d1928 *WhoHol 92*
Van Cortlandt, Philip 1749-1831 *WhAmRev*
Van Cortlandt, Pierre 1721-1814 *WhAmRev*
Van Cott, Harold Porter 1925- *WhoScEn 94*
Van Cott, Jeffrey Mark 1945- *WhoWest 94*
Vancouver, Archbishop of 1928- *Who 94*
Vancouver, George 1757-1798 *WhWE*
Vancrum, Robert J. 1946- *WhoAmP 93*
Vancrum, Robert James 1946- *WhoMW 93*
Van-Culin, Samuel 1930- *IntWW 93, Who 94, WhoAm 94*
Vancura, Arnost c. 1750-1802 *NewGrDO*
Van Cura, Joyce Bennett 1944- *WhoMW 93*
Vancura, Sandra Lee 1958- *WhoMW 93*
Vandal, Steven Offerdal 1948- *WhoWest 94*
van Dam, Heiman 1920- *WhoAm 94*
Van Dam, Jose 1940- *IntWW 93, NewGrDO*
Vandam, Leroy David 1914- *WhoScEn 94*

Van Deven, Louis Francis 1919-
WhoMW 93
Van De Ven, Monique 1952- *WhoHol 92*
Vandevender, Barbara Jewell 1929-
WhoMW 93
Van Devender, J. Pace 1947- *WhoScEn 94*
Vandevender, Robert Lee, II 1958-
WhoFI 94, WhoMW 93, WhoScEn 94
Van Deventer, Pieter Gabriel 1945-
WhoAm 94
Vandever, Michael *WhoHol 92*
Vandever, Rhonda Toews 1964-
WhoMW 93
Vandever, William Dirk 1949-
WhoAm 94, WhoAmL 94
Van Devere, Trish 1943- *WhoHol 92*
Van Devere, Trish 1945- *IntMPA 94*
Van de Vyver, Mary Francilene 1941-
WhoAm 94
Van de Walle, Chris Gilbert 1959-
WhoScEn 94
VandeWalle, Don Michael 1955-
WhoMW 93
VandeWalle, Don Micheal 1955-
WhoFI 94
VandeWalle, Gerald Wayne 1933-
*WhoAm 94, WhoAmL 94, WhoAmP 93,
WhoMW 93*
Van de Water, Margaret Smith 1919-
WhoAmP 93
Van De Water, Thomas Roger 1939-
WhoScEn 94
Vandeweghe, Ernie 1927- *BasBi*
Vandeweghe, Kiki 1958- *BasBi*
Van De Weghe, Raymond Francis 1934-
WhoFI 94
Van De Wetering, Janwillem 1931-
WrDr 94
Van de Wetering, John Edward 1927-
WhoAm 94
Van de Workeen, Priscilla Townsend
1946- *WhoFI 94*
Vandiford, Douglas Aaron 1947-
WhoAmP 93
Van Dijk, Cornelis Pieter 1931-
IntWW 93
Van Dijk, Ko d1978 *WhoHol 92*
Van Dijk, Petrus 1943- *IntWW 93*
Van Dine, Harold Forster, Jr. 1930-
WhoAm 94
Van Dine, Vance 1925- *WhoAm 94*
Vandis, Titos *WhoHol 92*
Van Dishoect, Edwine *WhoScEn 94*
Vandiver, Frank Everson 1925- *WrDr 94*
Vandiver, Pamela Bowren 1946-
WhoScEn 94
Vandiver, Robert Sanford 1937-
WhoWest 94
Vandivier, Blair Robert 1955-
WhoAmL 94
Vandivier, Richard White 1932-
WhoAm 94, WhoAmL 94
Vandivier, Robert E. 1928- *WhoFI 94*
Vando, Gloria *DrAPF 93, WhoHisp 94*
Van Domelen, John E(mory) 1935-
WrDr 94
Van Domelen, John Francis 1942-
WhoAm 94
Van Dommelen, Caroline d1957
WhoHol 92
Van Dommelen, David B. 1929-
WhoAm 94, WhoAmA 93
Van Dommelen, Jan d1942 *WhoHol 92*
van Dongen 1920- *EncSF 93*
Van Dongen, Frits d1975 *WhoHol 92*
Van Dongen, Helen 1909- *IntDcF 2-4*
Vandore, Peter Kerr 1943- *Who 94*
Van Doren, Charles 1926- *WhoAm 94*
Van Doren, Dorothy d1993 *NewYTBS 93*
Van Doren, Dorothy Graffe 1896-
WhAm 10
Van Doren, Dorothy Graffe 1896-1993
ConAu 141
Van Doren, Harold Livingston 1896-1957
WhoAmA 93N
Van Doren, Mamie 1931- *WhoHol 92*
Van Doren, Mamie 1933- *IntMPA 94*
Van Dorn, Harold Archer 1896- *WhAm 10*
Van Dorn, Peter Douglas 1941-
WhoFI 94, WhoWest 94
Van Dover, Donald 1932- *WhoMW 93*
Vandover, Samuel Taylor 1942-
WhoAm 94
Van Dreel, Mary Lou E. 1935-
WhoAmP 93
Van Dreelen, John 1922- *WhoHol 92*
Van Dreser, Merton Lawrence 1929-
WhoAm 94
Van Dresser, William 1871-1950
WhoAmA 93N
Vandross, Luther *IntWW 93, WhoAm 94*
Vandross, Luther 1951- *AfrAmAl 6*
Vandross, Luther R. 1951- *WhoBlA 94*
Van Druten, John (William) 1901-1957
IntDcT 2 [port]
Van Duinwyk, George Paul 1941-
WhoAmA 93
Van Dunem, Fernando *IntWW 93*

Van Durme, Jef *NewGrDO*
Van Dusen, Albert 1916- *IntWW 93*
Van Dusen, Albert Clarence 1915-
WhoAm 94
Van Dusen, Ann Brenton 1919-
WhoWest 94
Van Dusen, Francis Lund d1993
NewYTBS 93
Van Dusen, Gerald Charles 1946-
WhoMW 93
Van Dusen, Granville *WhoHol 92*
Van Dusen, Harold Alan, Jr. 1922-
WhoScEn 94
Van Dusen, Henry Pitney 1897-1975
DcAmReB 2
Van Dusen, James 1952- *WhoScEn 94*
Van Dusen, Lani Marie 1960-
WhoScEn 94
Van Dusen, Richard Campbell 1925-1991
WhAm 10
Van Duyn, Mona *DrAPF 93*
Van Duyn, Mona 1921- *IntWW 93,
WrDr 94*
Van Duyn, Mona Jane 1921- *WhoAm 94*
Van Duyne, Leroy 1923- *WhoAmP 93*
Van Dyck, Ernest (Marie Hubert)
1861-1923 *NewGrDO*
van Dyck, Nicholas Booraem 1933-
WhoAm 94
Van Dyck, Wendy *WhoAm 94*
Van Dyk, Frederick Theodore 1934-
WhoAm 94
Van Dyk, Jere 1945- *WrDr 94*
Van Dyk, Michael Anthony 1950-
WhoScEn 94
Vandyk, Neville David 1923- *Who 94*
Van Dyk, Robert 1953- *WhoScEn 94*
Van Dyke, Annette Joy 1943- *WhoMW 93*
Van Dyke, Clifford Craig 1929-
WhoAm 94
Van Dyke, Conny *WhoHol 92*
Van Dyke, Dan Ross 1950- *WhoAmP 93*
Van Dyke, Daniel Trostle 1946-
WhoFI 94
Van Dyke, David 1949- *WhoWest 94*
Van Dyke, Dick 1925- *IntMPA 94,
WhoAm 94, WhoCom [port], WhoHol 92*
Van Dyke, Earl 1930-1992 *WhoBlA 94N*
Van Dyke, Elinor Floyd 1929-
WhoAmP 93
Van Dyke, Henry 1852-1933 *DcAmReB 2*
Van Dyke, Henry 1928- *WhoBlA 94,
WrDr 94*
van Dyke, Jacob 1933- *WhoScEn 94*
Van Dyke, Jerry *WhoAm 94*
Van Dyke, Jerry 1931- *WhoCom,
WhoHol 92*
Van Dyke, Michael J. 1948- *WhoAmL 94*
Van Dyke, Milton Denman 1922-
WhoAm 94
Van Dyke, Nicolas 1738-1789 *WhAmRev*
Van Dyke, Robert Lowell 1922-
WhoAmP 93
Van Dyke, Thomas Wesley 1938-
WhoAm 94
Van Dyke, Truman d1984 *WhoHol 92*
Van Dyke, Vernon B. 1912- *WrDr 94*
Van Dyke, W. S. d1943 *WhoHol 92*
Van Dyke-Cooper, Anny Marion 1928-
WhoFI 94
Van Dyken, Lambertus Peter 1910-
WhoAmP 93
Van Dyken, Roger Lee 1945- *WhoAmP 93*
Vandyne, Bruce Dewitt 1932-
WhoScEn 94
van Dyne, Edith *EncSF 93*
Van Dyne, Michele Miley 1959-
WhoMW 93
Vane *Who 94*
Vane, Alida 1899-1969 *NewGrDO*
Vane, Bret 1925- *WrDr 94*
Vane, Denton d1940 *WhoHol 92*
Vane, John (Robert) 1927- *Who 94*
Vane, John Robert 1927- *IntWW 93,
WhoAm 94, WhoScEn 94*
Vane, Myrtle d1932 *WhoHol 92*
Vane, Sylvia Brakke 1918- *WhoWest 94*
Vane, Terence G., Jr. 1942- *WhoAm 94,
WhoFI 94*
VanEaton, Earl Neal 1940- *WhoAm 94*
Vaneck, Pierre *WhoHol 92*
Vanecko, Robert Michael 1935-
WhoAm 94
Van Eeckhout, Gerald Duane 1940-
WhoFI 94, WhoWest 94
Van Eekelen, Willem Frederik 1931-
IntWW 93
Van Eenenaam, Jeffrey Alan 1957-
WhoMW 93
Vanegas, Guillermo J. *WhoHisp 94*
Vanegas, Horacio 1939- *WhoScEn 94*
Vanegas, Jorge Alberto 1956- *WhoHisp 94*
Vanek, Gary M. 1940- *WhoAmP 93*
Vanek, Jaroslav 1930- *WhoAm 94*
Vanel, Charles d1989 *WhoHol 92*
Van Emburgh, Joanne 1953- *WhoAm 94*
Van Engelen, Debra Lynn 1952-
WhoScEn 94

Van Engen, Thomas Lee 1953-
WhoAmP 93
Van Eron, Kevin J. 1957- *WhoIns 94,
WhoMW 93*
Van Es, Andree C. 1953- *WhoWomW 91*
Van Eseltine, William Parker 1924-
WhoAm 94
Vaness, Carol *NewYTBS 93 [port]*
Vaness, Carol 1952- *NewGrDO,
WhoAm 94*
Van Ess, Connie *WhoHol 92*
Vaness, Margaret Helen 1919-
WhoAmA 93
Vanessa *BlmGEL*
Van Essen, W(illiam) 1910- *WrDr 94*
Vane-Tempest-Stewart *Who 94*
Van Etten, Peter Walbridge 1946-
WhoFI 94
Van Evera, Richard Kepler 1948-
WhoAmL 94
Van Everen, Brooks 1934- *WhoWest 94*
Van Ewijk, Casper 1953- *ConAu 140*
van Eyck, Aldo Ernest 1918- *Who 94*
Van Eyck, Peter d1969 *WhoHol 92*
Van Eysinga, Frans W. 1940- *WhoAm 94*
Van Eyssen, John 1925- *WhoHol 92*
Van Fleet, George Allan 1953-
WhoAm 94, WhoAmL 94
Van Fleet, James A. 1892- *HisDcKW*
Van Fleet, James A. 1892-1992
AnObit 1992
Van Fleet, Jo 1919- *IntMPA 94,
WhoHol 92*
Van Fleet, Julia Mae 1955- *WhoWest 94*
Van Fleet, William Mabry 1915-
WhoWest 94
Van Flein, Thomas Vincent 1963-
WhoAmL 94
Van Fossan, Robert Virgil 1926-1989
WhAm 10
Van Fossen, Larry Jack 1937- *WhoAm 94*
van Fraassen, Bas C. 1941- *WrDr 94*
Van Fraassen, Bastiaan Cornelis 1941-
IntWW 93
Van Geel, Tyll R. 1940- *WhoAm 94*
van Geert, Paul 1950- *WrDr 94*
Vangelis & Vangelis Papathanassiou
IntWW 93
Vangelis 1943- *IntMPA 94*
Vangelis 1943- *IntDcF 2-4*
Vangelis Papathanassiou
   See Vangelis & Vangelis Papathanassiou
IntWW 93
Vangelisti, Paul *DrAPF 93*
Van Genuchten, Martinus Theodorus
1945- *WhoAm 94*
Vanger, Milton Isadore 1925- *WhoAm 94*
Van Gerpen, Edward E. *WhoAmP 93*
Van Gerven, Walter M. 1935- *IntWW 93*
van Gestel, Allan 1935- *WhoAm 94,
WhoAmL 94*
Van Geyt, Henri Louis 1947-
WhoScEn 94
Van Gilder, Derek Robert 1950-
WhoAmL 94, WhoFI 94
Van Gilder, John Corley 1935- *WhoAm 94*
Van Gilse, Jan *NewGrDO*
Van Gilst, Bass 1911- *WhoAmP 93*
Van Ginkel, Blanche Lemco *WhoAmA 93*
van Ginkel, Blanche Lemco 1923-
WhoAm 94
Van Ginkel, James Carol 1954-
WhoMW 93
Van Ginneken, Jaap 1943- *ConAu 142*
Van Gorden, Heron A. 1926- *WhoAmP 93*
Van Gorder, John Frederic 1943-
WhoAmL 94, WhoFI 94
Van Gorkom, Jerome William 1917-
WhoAm 94
Van Gorp, Gary Wayne 1953- *WhoFI 94*
Van Graafeiland, Ellsworth Alfred 1915-
WhoAm 94, WhoAmL 94
Van Graafeiland, Gary P. *WhoAmL 94*
Van Grack, Steven 1948- *WhoAmP 93*
van Greenaway, Peter 1929-1988
EncSF 93
Van Grit, William 1937- *WhoWest 94*
Van Grunsven, Paul Robert 1961-
WhoAmL 94
Vangsaae, Mona 1920-1983 *IntDcB [port]*
Van Gundy, Gregory Frank 1945-
WhoAm 94, WhoAmL 94
Van Gundy, James Justin 1939-
WhoAm 94
Van Gundy, Seymour Dean 1931-
WhoAm 94, WhoScEn 94
Van Haaften, Julia 1946- *WhoAmA 93*
Van Haden, Anders d1936 *WhoHol 92*
Van Halen, Eddie 1957- *WhoAm 94*
Van Halm, Renee 1949- *WhoAmA 93*
Van Hamel, Martine 1945- *IntDcB [port]*
VanHandel, Ralph Anthony 1919-
WhoAm 94, WhoMW 93
Van Haren, W. Michael 1948-
WhoAmL 94
Van Harlingen, Jean (Ann) 1947-
WhoAmA 93

VanHarn, Gordon Lee 1935- *WhoAm 94*
Van Hassel, Henry John 1933-
WhoAm 94, WhoWest 94
van Hasselt, Marc 1924- *Who 94*
Van Hauer, Robert 1910- *WhoAm 94*
Van Hecke, Gerald Raymond 1939-
WhoWest 94
Van Hecke, Jim, Jr. 1947- *WhoAmP 93*
Van Hecke, Mark August 1959-
WhoMW 93
Van Heemskerck Pillis-Duvekot, Sari
1940- *WhoWomW 91*
Van Heerden, Neil Peter 1939- *IntWW 93*
Van Heijst, Jakob 1936- *WhoAm 94*
Van Heller, Macus 1928- *WhoFI 94*
Van Hemeldonck, Marijke 1931-
WhoWomW 91
Van Hemert, Judy 1947- *WhoFI 94*
Van Hemmen, Hendrik Fokko 1960-
WhoScEn 94
van Hengel, Maarten 1927- *WhoAm 94,
WhoFI 94*
van Hengel, Maarten R. 1953- *WhoFI 94*
Van Hentenryck, Kevin *WhoHol 92*
van Herck, Paul 1939- *EncSF 93*
van Herk, Aritha 1954- *BlmGWL [port]*
van Herp, Jacques *EncSF 93*
Van Heusen, James 1913-1990 *WhAm 10*
Van Heusen, Jimmy 1913-1990
ConTFT 11
van Heusen, John M., Jr. d1993
NewYTBS 93
Van Heyde, J. Stephen 1943- *WhoAm 94,
WhoAmL 94*
Van Heyningen, Roger Steven 1927-
WhoAm 94
VanHilst, Lucas 1920- *WhoWest 94*
Van Hoecke, Robert George 1962-
WhoFI 94
Van Hoesen, Beth 1926- *WhoAmA 93*
Van Hoesen, Beth Marie 1926-
WhoAm 94
Van Hoeven, L. C., Jr. 1936- *WhoAm 94*
van Hoften, James Dougal Adrianus
1944- *WhoAm 94, WhoScEn 94*
Van Holde, Kensal Edward 1928-
WhoAm 94
VanHole, William Remi 1948-
WhoAm 94
van Holk, Freder *EncSF 93*
Vanhollen, Christopher, Jr. 1959-
WhoAmP 93
Van Hoof, Jef *NewGrDO*
Van Hooff, Jan A. R. A. M. 1936-
IntWW 93
Van Hook, David H. 1923-1986
WhoAmA 93N
Van Hook, George Ellis, Jr. 1948-
WhoBlA 94
Van Hook, Warren Kenneth 1920-
WhoBlA 94
Van Hool, Roger 1940- *WhoHol 92*
Van Hoomissen, George Albert 1930-
*WhoAm 94, WhoAmL 94, WhoAmP 93,
WhoWest 94*
Van Hoose, Pamela Hoffman 1958-
WhoMW 93
Van Hoosier, Gerald Leonard 1934-
WhoScEn 94
Van Hooven, Eckart 1925- *IntWW 93*
Van Horn, Catherine Ann 1954-
WhoAmL 94
Van Horn, Dana Carl 1950- *WhoAmA 93*
Van Horn, Darren John 1966- *WhoFI 94*
Van Horn, Jimmy d1966 *WhoHol 92*
Van Horn, John Kenneth 1948-
WhoMW 93
Van Horn, Lecia Joseph 1963- *WhoAm 94*
Van Horn, Louis George 1958-
WhoMW 93
Van Horn, Mary Renee 1940-
WhoScEn 94
Van Horn, Phyllis Marcia 1943-
WhoWest 94
Van Horn, Rebecca Ann 1957-
WhoMW 93
Van Horn, Richard Linley 1932-
WhoAm 94
Van Horn, Verne Hile, III 1938-
WhoFI 94
Van Horne, Edward K(elsey) 1898-
WhAm 10
Van Horne, Emile d1967 *WhoHol 92*
Van Horne, James Carter 1935-
WhoAm 94
van Horne, Jon W. 1945- *WhoAm 94*
Van Horne, R. Richard 1931- *WhoAm 94*
Van Horne, Terry Eugene 1946-
WhoAmP 93
Van Horssen, Arden Darrell 1917-
WhoWest 94
Van Horssen, Charles Arden 1944-
WhoWest 94
Van House, Nancy Anita 1950-
WhoAm 94
Van Housen, Thomas Corwin, III 1927-
WhoMW 93
Van Houten, David J. 1955- *WhoAsA 94*

Varn, Richard James 1958- *WhoMW 93*
Varnado, Arthur 1932- *WhoBlA 94*
Varnam, Ivor 1922- *Who 94*
Varnay, Astrid (Ibolyka Maria) 1918- *NewGrDO*
Varnay Jones, Theodora 1942- *WhoAmA 93*
Varnedoe, Heeth, III 1937- *WhoFI 94*
Varnedoe, John Kirk Train 1946- *WhoAm 94, WhoAmA 93*
Varnelis, Kazys 1917- *WhoAmA 93*
Varner, Barton Douglas 1920- *WhoAm 94*
Varner, Charleen LaVerne McClanahan 1931- *WhoAm 94, WhoFI 94, WhoMW 93*
Varner, Chilton Davis 1943- *WhoAm 94, WhoAmL 94*
Varner, David Eugene 1937- *WhoAm 94*
Varner, Helen Dickey 1946- *WhoAm 94*
Varner, Henry, Jr. 1931- *WhoAmP 93*
Varner, James, Sr. 1934- *WhoBlA 94*
Varner, Jeannette J(ohnson) 1909- *WrDr 94*
Varner, Jewell C. 1918- *WhoBlA 94*
Varner, John 1906- *WhoAmP 93*
Varner, Joseph Elmer 1921- *WhoAm 94, WhoMW 93, WhoScEn 94*
Varner, Nellie M. 1935- *WhoBlA 94*
Varner, Robert Bernard 1930- *WhoMW 93*
Varner, Robert Edward 1921- *WhoAm 94*
Varner, Robert Lee, Sr. 1932- *WhoBlA 94*
Varner, Scott G. 1962- *WhoAmP 93*
Varner, Sterling Verl 1919- *WhoAm 94, WhoFI 94*
Varnerin, Lawrence John 1923- *WhoAm 94*
Varnes, David Joseph 1919- *WhoWest 94*
Varney, Bernard Keith 1919- *WhoWest 94*
Varney, Carleton Bates, Jr. 1937- *WhoAm 94*
Varney, Edwin 1944- *WhoAmA 93*
Varney, Jim 1949- *ConTFT 11, IntMPA 94, WhoHol 92*
Varney, Kevin William 1962- *WhoMW 93*
Varney, Louis 1844-1908 *NewGrDO*
Varney, Peter Justin 1942- *WhoWest 94*
Varney, Reg 1922- *WhoHol 92*
Varney, Robert Nathan 1910- *WhoScEn 94, WhoWest 94*
Varnhagen, Melvin Jay 1944- *WhoFI 94, WhoScEn 94*
Varnhagen, Rahel Antonie Friederike 1771-1833 *BlmGWL*
Varno, Roland 1908- *WhoHol 92*
Varnum, Charles Henry 1933- *WhoAmP 93*
Varnum, James Mitchell 1748-1789 *WhAmRev*
Varnum, James William 1940- *WhoAm 94*
Varnum, Joseph Bradley 1750-1821 *WhAmRev*
Varon, Dan 1935- *WhoScEn 94*
Varona, Daniel Robert 1944- *WhoAmL 94*
Varona, Jose Luciano 1930- *NewGrDO*
Varonin, Yury Mikhailovich 1939- *LngBDD*
Varpasuo, Paivi Paula Annikki 1945- *WhoWomW 91*
Varrenti, Adam, Jr. 1949- *WhoFI 94*
Varriale, Wanda (Stella) 1927- *WhoAmA 93*
Varro, Barbara Joan 1938- *WhoAm 94*
Varrone, Angelo Robert 1947- *WhoAm 94*
Varrone, John M. *WhoAmP 93*
Vars, Addison Foster, III 1945- *WhoAmL 94*
Vars, Gordon Forrest 1923- *WhoAm 94*
Varsanyi-Nagy, Maria 1942- *WhoScEn 94*
Varshavsky, Alexander Jacob 1946- *WhoScEn 94*
Varshni, Yatendra Pal 1932- *WhoAm 94*
Varsi, Diane d1992 *IntMPA 94N*
Varsi, Diane 1938- *WhoHol 92*
Varsi, Diane 1938-1992 *AnObit 1992*
Vartan, Sylvie 1945- *WhoHol 92*
Vartanian, Aram 1922- *WhoAm 94*
Vartanian, Elsie 1930- *WhoAmP 93, WhoWomW 91*
Vartanian, Elsie Virginia 1930- *WhoAm 94*
Vartanian, Michael G. 1948- *WhoAm 94*
Vartanian, Michael Gary 1948- *WhoAmL 94*
Vartanian, Thomas P. 1949- *WhoAmL 94*
Varte, Rosy *WhoHol 92*
Varthema, Ludovico Di c. 1470-1511? *WhWE*
Vartio, Marj-Liisa 1924-1966 *BlmGWL*
Varty, Keith 1952- *IntWW 93*
Varvak, Mark 1939- *WhoScEn 94*
Varvaro, Gloria d1976 *WhoHol 92*
Varvaro, James Glen 1959- *WhoMW 93*
Varvik, Dagfinn 1924- *IntWW 93*
Varviso, Silvio 1924- *NewGrDO*
Vary, James Patrick 1943- *WhoMW 93, WhoScEn 94*
Varzally, Michael Alan 1947- *WhoAm 94*
Vasa, (Velizar Mihich) 1933- *WhoAmA 93*
Vasa, Rohitkumar Bhupatrai 1947- *WhoMW 93, WhoScEn 94*
Vasak, David Jiri Jan 1951- *WhoScEn 94*
Vasalis, M. 1909- *BlmGWL*
Vasallo, Pedro E. *WhoHisp 94*
Vasan, Srini Varadarajan 1956- *WhoAsA 94*
Vasarely, Victor 1908- *IntWW 93*
Vasary, Tamas 1933- *IntWW 93, Who 94*
Vascellaro, Frank John 1942- *WhoFI 94*
Vasconcellos, John 1932- *WhoAmP 93, WhoHisp 94*
Vasconcellos, Josefina Alys Hermes de *Who 94*
Vasconcelos, Carolina Michaelis de 1851-1925 *BlmGWL*
Vas Dias, Robert 1931- *WrDr 94*
Vasek, Marisha *WhoHol 92*
Vasek, Richard Jim 1935- *WhoAm 94*
Vasey, Bill 1939- *WhoAmP 93*
Vasey, Daniel Eugene 1942- *WhoMW 93*
Vasey, Jon Albert 1957- *WhoAmL 94*
Vasey, William Joseph 1939- *WhoWest 94*
Vasholz, Lothar A. 1930- *WhoAm 94, WhoFI 94*
Vasil, Art *WhoHol 92*
Vasil, Raj Kumar 1931- *WrDr 94*
Vasilakis, Andrew D. 1943- *WhoScEn 94*
Vasile, Gennaro James 1946- *WhoAm 94*
Vasilenko, Sergey Nikiforovich 1872-1956 *NewGrDO*
Vasilev, Dmitry Dmitrievich 1945- *LngBDD*
Vasilev, Steven Anatol 1954- *WhoWest 94*
Vasiliades, John 1945- *WhoScEn 94*
Vasilieff, Nicholas 1892-1970 *WhoAmA 93N*
Vasiliev, Vladimir 1940- *IntDcB [port]*
Vasiliu, Emanuel 1929- *IntWW 93*
Vasils, Albert 1915- *WhoAmA 93N*
Vasilyev, Anatoli Aleksandrovich 1942- *IntWW 93*
Vasilyev, Boris Lvovich 1924- *IntWW 93*
Vasilyev, Ivan Afanasivevich 1924- *IntWW 93*
Vasilyev, Vladimir 1828-1900 *NewGrDO*
Vasilyev, Vladimir Viktorovich 1940- *IntWW 93*
Vasilyeva, Larisa Nikolayevna 1935- *IntWW 93*
Vasios, James Albert 1950- *WhoAmL 94*
Vaslef, Irene 1934- *WhoAm 94*
Vaslef, Nicholas P. 1930- *WhoAm 94*
Vasoli, Pietro fl. 1812-1814 *NewGrDO*
Vasova, Alta *EncSF 93*
Vasquez, Alfred (Joseph) 1923- *Who 94*
Vasquez, Arturo *WhoHisp 94*
Vasquez, Cesar Luis 1935- *WhoHisp 94*
Vasquez, Fernando, Sr. 1955- *WhoHisp 94*
Vasquez, Florentino John 1957- *WhoHisp 94*
Vasquez, Floyd Estevan, II 1963- *WhoHisp 94*
Vasquez, Gabriel Marcus 1960- *WhoHisp 94*
Vasquez, Gaddi 1955- *WhoWest 94*
Vasquez, Gaddi Holguin 1955- *WhoHisp 94*
Vasquez, Gilbert Reynaldo 1939- *WhoHisp 94*
Vasquez, Hector Rey 1952- *WhoHisp 94*
Vasquez, Ilda G. 1944- *WhoHisp 94*
Vasquez, Irene Sosa 1950- *WhoHisp 94*
Vasquez, James Alan 1932- *WhoHisp 94*
Vasquez, Jeffery 1956- *WhoHisp 94*
Vasquez, Jose, Jr. 1950- *WhoHisp 94*
Vasquez, Joseph Anthony, Jr. 1950- *WhoHisp 94*
Vasquez, Joseph B. *WhoBlA 94, WhoHisp 94*
Vasquez, Joseph J. 1927- *WhoHisp 94*
Vásquez, Juan *WhoHisp 94*
Vasquez, Juanita Sylvia 1919- *WhoHisp 94*
Vasquez, Lee 1945- *WhoHisp 94*
Vasquez, Lois 1942- *WhoHisp 94*
Vasquez, Louis 1798-1868 *WhWE*
Vasquez, Manuel Daniel 1959- *WhoHisp 94*
Vásquez, Martha *WhoHisp 94*
Vasquez, Nick Antonio 1951- *WhoWest 94*
Vasquez, Paul 1952- *WhoAmP 93, WhoHisp 94*
Vasquez, Philip Daniel 1955- *WhoHisp 94*
Vasquez, Raul 1954- *WhoHisp 94*
Vasquez, Raul Herrera, Jr. 1949- *WhoHisp 94*
Vasquez, Richard *DrAPF 93*
Vásquez, Richard 1928- *WhoHisp 94*
Vasquez, Robert J. 1931- *WhoHisp 94*
Vasquez, Roberta *WhoHol 92*
Vasquez, Rodolfo Anthony 1954- *WhoScEn 94*
Vasquez, William Leroy 1944- *WhoAm 94, WhoFI 94*
Vásquez-Ajmac, Luis Alfredo 1961- *WhoHisp 94*
Vasquez Nava, Maria Elena *WhoWomW 91*
Vass, Joan 1925- *WhoAm 94*
Vassa, Gustavus c. 1745-c. 1801 *AfrAmAl 6 [port]*
Vassalli, Giuliano 1915- *IntWW 93*
Vassalli, Shorty 1948- *WhoWest 94*
Vassallo, Edward E. 1943- *WhoAmL 94*
Vassallo, Efrain David 1928- *WhoHisp 94*
Vassallo, John A. 1937- *WhoAmL 94*
Vassanji, M(oyez) G. 1950- *WrDr 94*
Vassar, John Dixie, Jr. 1953- *WhoFI 94*
Vassar, Queenie d1960 *WhoHol 92*
Vassar-Smith, Richard Rathborne 1909- *Who 94*
Vassberg, David E(rland) 1936- *WrDr 94*
Vassberg, David Erland 1936- *WhoAm 94*
Vassell, Gregory S. 1921- *WhoAm 94*
Vasseur, Leon (Felix Augustin Joseph) 1844-1917 *NewGrDO*
Vassi, Patricia M. 1957- *WhoFI 94*
Vassil, Pamela 1943- *WhoAm 94*
Vassilas, Anastasios Eugene 1949- *WhoFI 94*
Vassiliou, George 1931- *Who 94*
Vassiliou, George Vassos 1931- *IntWW 93*
Vassilopoulos, Dimitri *WhoHol 92*
Vassilopoulou-Sellin, Rena *WhoScEn 94*
Vasson, Pierre *NewGrDO*
Vassy, David Leon, Jr. *WhoScEn 94*
Vasta, Bruno Morreale 1933- *WhoAm 94*
Vasta, Edward 1928- *WrDr 94*
Vastine, J. Robert, Jr. 1937- *WhoAmP 93*
Vasu, Bangalore Seshachalam *WhoWest 94*
Vasudeva *DrAPF 93*
Vasudevan, Asuri Krishnaswami 1943- *WhoScEn 94*
Vasudevan, Ramaswami 1947- *WhoWest 94*
Vasylyshyn, Andrii Volodymyrovych 1933- *LngBDD*
Vater, Charles J. 1950- *WhoAmL 94*
Vater, Regina 1943- *WhoAmA 93*
Vathsal, Srinivasan 1947- *WhoScEn 94*
Vatikiotis, P(anayiotis) J 1928- *WrDr 94*
Vatikiotis, Panayiotis Jerasimos 1928- *IntWW 93*
Vatolin, Nikolay Anatolevich 1926- *IntWW 93*
Vatter, Harold Goodhue 1910- *WhoFI 94, WhoWest 94*
Vatter, Paul August 1924- *WhoAm 94*
Vatterott-Grogan, Jeanne Marie 1957- *WhoAmL 94*
Vattier, Robert d1982 *WhoHol 92*
Vatz, Olga 1954- *WhoWest 94*
Vaucanson, Jacques de 1709-1782 *WorInv*
Vaucher, Andrea R. 1949- *ConAu 142*
Vauchez, Andre Michel 1938- *IntWW 93*
Vaucorbeil, Auguste Emmanuel 1821-1884 *NewGrDO*
Vaudry, J. William, Jr. 1941- *WhoAmL 94*
Vaughan *Who 94*
Vaughan, Viscount 1945- *Who 94*
Vaughan, Alden T(rue) 1929- *WrDr 94*
Vaughan, Benjamin Noel Young 1917- *Who 94*
Vaughan, Bernard Joseph 1955- *WhoAmL 94*
Vaughan, C. Porter, III 1945- *WhoAmL 94*
Vaughan, Clifford James 1934- *WhoFI 94*
Vaughan, David Arthur John 1938- *IntWW 93, Who 94*
Vaughan, David John 1924- *WhoFI 94, WhoMW 93*
Vaughan, David Lisle 1922-1990 *WhAm 10*
Vaughan, Denis (Edward) 1926- *NewGrDO*
Vaughan, Dennis Ralsten, Jr. 1941- *WhoAmL 94, WhoFI 94*
Vaughan, Donald Ray 1952- *WhoAmL 94*
Vaughan, Dorothy d1955 *WhoHol 92*
Vaughan, Edgar *Who 94*
Vaughan, (George) Edgar 1907- *IntWW 93, Who 94*
Vaughan, Edwin Darracott, Jr. 1939- *WhoAm 94*
Vaughan, Elizabeth *Who 94*
Vaughan, Elizabeth 1937- *NewGrDO*
Vaughan, Elizabeth Crownhart 1929- *WhoWest 94*
Vaughan, Emmett John 1934- *WhoAm 94*
Vaughan, Eugene H. 1933- *WhoAm 94*
Vaughan, Frankie 1928- *WhoHol 92*
Vaughan, Gerald R. 1957- *WhoBlA 94*
Vaughan, Gerard (Folliott) 1923- *Who 94*
Vaughan, Gillian *WhoHol 92*
Vaughan, Gordon Lamar 1952- *WhoAmL 94*
Vaughan, Gregory Neil 1951- *WhoMW 93*
Vaughan, Harold Amos 1933- *WhoMW 93*
Vaughan, Henry 1621-1695 *DcLB 131*
Vaughan, Henry 1622-1695 *BlmGEL*
Vaughan, Herbert Wiley 1920- *WhoAm 94, WhoAmL 94, WhoFI 94*
Vaughan, Jack 1961- *WhoAmP 93*
Vaughan, Jack M. 1947- *WhoAmL 94*
Vaughan, James Arthur, Jr. 1914- *WhoWest 94*
Vaughan, James Edward 1943- *WhoBlA 94*
Vaughan, Janet Maria d1993 *IntWW 93N, Who 94N*
Vaughan, John d1795 *WhAmRev*
Vaughan, John c. 1731-1795 *AmRev*
Vaughan, John 1799-1868 *DcNaB MP*
Vaughan, John Charles, III 1934- *WhoAm 94*
Vaughan, John Nolen 1941- *WhoMW 93*
Vaughan, John Thomas 1932- *WhoAm 94*
Vaughan, John Thomas 1959- *WhoScEn 94*
Vaughan, Joseph Lee 1905- *WhoAm 94*
Vaughan, Joseph Lee, Jr. 1942- *WhoAm 94*
Vaughan, Joseph Robert 1916- *WhoAm 94*
Vaughan, Keith W. 1950- *WhoAmL 94*
Vaughan, Kirk William 1943- *WhoAm 94*
Vaughan, Leslie Clifford 1927- *Who 94*
Vaughan, Luva D. 1932- *WhoMW 93*
Vaughan, Margaret Evelyn 1948- *WhoScEn 94*
Vaughan, Martha 1926- *WhoAm 94, WhoScEn 94*
Vaughan, Martin *WhoHol 92*
Vaughan, Michael B. 1954- *WhoWest 94*
Vaughan, Mimi C. R. *WhoHisp 94*
Vaughan, Norman 1927- *WhoHol 92*
Vaughan, Odie Frank 1936- *WhoAm 94*
Vaughan, Olive Elizabeth 1925- *WhoFI 94*
Vaughan, Otha H., Jr. 1929- *WhoScEn 94*
Vaughan, Paris *WhoHol 92*
Vaughan, Patrick Joseph 1929- *WhoAmP 93*
Vaughan, Peter 1923- *WhoHol 92*
Vaughan, Peter Rolfe 1935- *Who 94*
Vaughan, Peter St. George *Who 94*
Vaughan, Richard Alaric 1965- *WhoWest 94*
Vaughan, Richard Allen 1946- *WhoFI 94*
Vaughan, Richard Patrick 1919- *WrDr 94*
Vaughan, Robert Alan 1953- *WhoAmP 93*
Vaughan, Robert Charles 1945- *Who 94*
Vaughan, Roger 1944- *Who 94*
Vaughan, Roger Davison 1923- *Who 94*
Vaughan, Samuel Snell 1928- *WhoAm 94*
Vaughan, Sarah d1990 *WhoHol 92*
Vaughan, Sarah 1924-1990 *AfrAmAl 6*
Vaughan, Sarah Lois 1924-1990 *WhAm 10*
Vaughan, Skeeter d1989 *WhoHol 92*
Vaughan, Stephen Owens 1961- *WhoScEn 94*
Vaughan, Stevie Ray *WhoHol 92*
Vaughan, Stuart M., Jr. 1945- *WhoAmL 94*
Vaughan, Thomas 1621-1666 *DcLB 131*
Vaughan, Thomas James Gregory 1924- *WhoAm 94*
Vaughan, Warren Taylor, Jr. 1920- *WhoWest 94*
Vaughan, Wayland Edward 1934- *WhoFI 94*
Vaughan, William Addison 1935-1989 *WhAm 10*
Vaughan, William Randal 1912- *Who 94*
Vaughan, William Walton 1930- *WhoAm 94*
Vaughan, Worth Edward 1936- *WhoAm 94*
Vaughan-Jackson, Oliver James 1907- *Who 94*
Vaughan-Kroeker, Nadine 1947- *WhoScEn 94*
Vaughan-Morgan *Who 94*
Vaughan Williams, Ralph 1872-1958 *NewGrDO*
Vaughan Williams, Ursula 1911- *WrDr 94*
Vaughn, Adamae d1943 *WhoHol 92*
Vaughn, Alberta 1906- *WhoHol 92*
Vaughn, Alvin 1939- *WhoBlA 94*
Vaughn, Arkell M. 1895- *WhAm 10*
Vaughn, Audrey Smith 1958- *WhoBlA 94*
Vaughn, Charles L. 1919- *WhoAmP 93*
Vaughn, Charles Melvin 1915- *WhoAm 94*
Vaughn, Clarence B. 1928- *WhoBlA 94*
Vaughn, Clarence Roland, Jr. 1921- *WhoAmP 93*
Vaughn, Danny Mack 1948- *WhoWest 94*
Vaughn, Donald Charles 1936- *WhoAm 94*
Vaughn, Eddie Michael 1956- *WhoScEn 94*
Vaughn, Edward 1934- *WhoAmP 93*
Vaughn, Elbert Hardy 1946- *WhoFI 94*
Vaughn, Eleanor 1922- *WhoFI 94*
Vaughn, Eleanor L. 1922- *WhoAmP 93*

Vaughn, Eugenia Marchelle Washington 1957- *WhoBlA 94*
Vaughn, Fred D. 1920- *WhoAmP 93*
Vaughn, Gregory Lamont 1965- *WhoAm 94, WhoBlA 94*
Vaughn, H. George, Jr. 1939- *WhoAmP 93*
Vaughn, Hilda d1957 *WhoHol 92*
Vaughn, Jackie, III *WhoAmP 93, WhoMW 93*
Vaughn, Jackie, III 1939- *WhoBlA 94*
Vaughn, Jacqueline Barbara 1935- *WhoBlA 94*
Vaughn, James English, Jr. 1939- *WhoWest 94*
Vaughn, James Michael 1939- *WhoFI 94, WhoMW 93*
Vaughn, James T. 1925- *WhoAmP 93*
Vaughn, Jimmy Lee *WhoHol 92*
Vaughn, John Rolland 1938- *WhoAm 94*
Vaughn, John Vernon 1909- *WhoAm 94*
Vaughn, Karen Iversen 1944- *WhoAm 94*
Vaughn, Lewis 1950- *ConAu 41NR*
Vaughn, Lewis R. 1934- *WhoAmP 93*
Vaughn, Lisa Dawn 1961- *WhoMW 93*
Vaughn, Mary Kathryn 1949- *WhoBlA 94*
Vaughn, Mo 1967- *WhoBlA 94*
Vaughn, Ned *WhoHol 92*
Vaughn, Nora Belle 1914- *WhoBlA 94*
Vaughn, Norman 1932- *WhoWest 94*
Vaughn, Percy Joseph, Jr. 1932- *WhoBlA 94*
Vaughn, Phyllis d1977 *WhoHol 92*
Vaughn, Raymond L., Jr. 1948- *WhoAmP 93*
Vaughn, Robert 1932- *IntMPA 94, WhoAm 94, WhoHol 92*
Vaughn, Robert Lockard 1922- *WhoAm 94*
Vaughn, Rufus Mahlon 1924- *WhoAm 94*
Vaughn, Sammy *WhoHol 92*
Vaughn, Vivian d1966 *WhoHol 92*
Vaughn, William d1946 *WhoHol 92*
Vaughn, William John 1931- *WhoFI 94*
Vaughn, William Preston 1933- *WhoAm 94*
Vaughn, William Samuel, III 1955- *WhoBlA 94*
Vaughn, William Smith 1930- *WhoBlA 94*
Vaughn, William Weaver 1930- *WhoAm 94*
Vaughns, Fred L. 1923- *WhoBlA 94*
Vaught, Cheryl Annette 1959- *WhoAmL 94*
Vaught, Douglas Stephen 1951- *WhoAmP 93*
Vaught, Elmer Richard 1928- *WhoAmP 93*
Vaught, John M. 1947- *WhoAmL 94*
Vaught, Loy Stephon 1967- *WhoBlA 94*
Vaught, Richard Loren 1933- *WhoMW 93, WhoScEn 94*
Vaught, Wilma L. 1930- *WhoAm 94*
Vaught-Alexander, Karen 1951- *WhoWest 94*
Vaughters-Johnson, Cecilie A. 1953- *WhoBlA 94*
Vaupen, Burton 1930- *WhoAm 94, WhoFI 94*
Vauquelin, Louis Nicolas 1763-1829 *WorScD*
Vause, Edwin Hamilton 1923- *WhoAm 94*
Vause, L(aurence) Mikel 1952- *ConAu 140*
Vautour, Roland Rene 1929- *WhoAm 94*
Vautrin, Jean 1933- *IntWW 93*
Vauvenargues, Luc de Clapiers, marquis de 1715-1747 *GuFrLit 2*
Vaux, Lord 1509-1556 *DcLB 132 [port]*
Vaux, Dora Louise 1922- *WhoWest 94*
Vaux, Henry James 1912- *WhoAm 94, WhoScEn 94, WhoWest 94*
Vaux, Nicholas Francis 1936- *Who 94*
Vaux, Richard 1940- *WhoAmA 93*
Vaux, Sandra Marie *WhoAmA 93*
Vaux Of Harrowden, Baron 1915- *Who 94*
Vauzelle, Michel Marie 1944- *IntWW 93*
Vava, R. J. *WhoAmL 94*
Vavala, Domenic Anthony 1925- *WhoAm 94*
Vavasour, Geoffrey William 1914- *Who 94*
Vavasour, Mervin 1819-1866 *WhWE*
Vaverka, Anton d1937 *WhoHol 92*
Vavitch, Michael d1930 *WhoHol 92*
Vavoulis, George J. 1911- *WhoAmP 93*
Vavra, Otakar 1911- *IntWW 93*
Vawter, Donald 1920- *WhoWest 94*
Vawter, Jay 1934- *WhoFI 94*
Vawter, Mary H. Murray 1871- *WhoAmA 93N*
Vawter, Robert Roy, Jr. 1943- *WhoAm 94, WhoAmL 94*
Vawter, Ron 1948- *WhoHol 92*
Vawter, William Snyder 1931- *WhoScEn 94*
Vax, Michael Norman 1942- *WhoWest 94*
Vayda, Andrew P. 1931- *WrDr 94*
Vayhinger, John Monroe 1916- *WhoAm 94*
Vaynberg, Moisey Samuilovich 1919- *NewGrDO*
Vaynman, Semyon 1949- *WhoScEn 94*
Vayo, David Joseph 1957- *WhoAm 94, WhoMW 93*
Vayos, Daphne Renee 1962- *WhoAmL 94*
Vayrynen, Paavo Matti 1946- *IntWW 93*
Vayssade, Marie-Claude 1936- *WhoWomW 91*
Vaz, (Nigel) Keith (Anthony Standish) 1956- *Who 94*
Vaz, Nuno Artur 1951- *WhoMW 93, WhoScEn 94*
Vaz Dias, Selma d1977 *WhoHol 92*
Vazem, Ekaterina 1848-1937 *IntDcB*
Vaz Ferreira, Maria Eugenia 1875-1924 *BlmGWL*
Vazgen, I 1908- *IntWW 93*
Vázquez, Albert 1947- *WhoHisp 94*
Vazquez, Angel Antonio 1949- *WhoHisp 94*
Vazquez, Angela M. 1940- *WhoHisp 94*
Vazquez, Anna T. 1918- *WhoHisp 94*
Vazquez, Arturo, Jr. 1956- *WhoHisp 94*
Vazquez, Eddie Zavala *WhoAmP 93*
Vazquez, Edna 1952- *WhoHisp 94*
Vazquez, Eloy 1935- *WhoHisp 94*
Vazquez, Emil C. 1947- *WhoHisp 94*
Vazquez, Gilbert Falcon 1952- *WhoAm 94, WhoAmL 94*
Vazquez, J. Michael *WhoHisp 94*
Vazquez, Jaime 1949- *WhoHisp 94*
Vazquez, John David 1935- *WhoHisp 94*
Vazquez, Jorge Alberto 1943- *IntWW 93*
Vazquez, Jose 1895-1961 *NewGrDO*
Vazquez, Jose Luis Lopez *WhoHol 92*
Vázquez, Juan M. 1949- *WhoHisp 94*
Vazquez, Martha Elisa 1954- *WhoHisp 94*
Vazquez, Olga *WhoHisp 94*
Vazquez, Paul 1933- *WhoAmA 93*
Vazquez, Raul A. 1939- *WhoHisp 94*
Vazquez, Rebecca C. 1957- *WhoHisp 94*
Vazquez, Robert C. 1955- *WhoHisp 94*
Vazquez, Roberto 1923- *WhoHisp 94*
Vazquez, Siro 1910-1990 *WhAm 10*
Vazquez-Bauza, Juan Jose 1956- *WhoHisp 94*
Vazquez Correa, Beraldo Antonio 1946- *WhoWest 94*
Vazquez Montalban, Manuel 1939- *DcLB 134 [port]*
Vázquez Pérez, Amalia 1956- *WhoHisp 94*
Vazquez-Quintana, Enrique 1937- *WhoAmP 93*
Vázquez-Raña, Mario 1932- *WhoHisp 94*
Vazquez Richard, Juan 1949- *WhoHisp 94*
Vazsonyi, Andrew 1916- *WhoAm 94*
Vazzana, Patricia Anne 1947- *WhoFI 94*
Vazzoler, Elsa d1989 *WhoHol 92*
Véa, Alfredo, Jr. *WhoHisp 94*
Vea, Katena *WhoHol 92*
Veach, Darrell Alves 1928- *WhoMW 93*
Veach, Robert Raymond, Jr. 1950- *WhoAm 94, WhoAmL 94*
Veal, Donald Lyle 1931- *WhoWest 94*
Veal, Howard Richard 1942- *WhoBlA 94*
Veal, John Bartholomew 1909- *Who 94*
Veal, Rex R. 1956- *WhoAmL 94*
Veal, William Thomas, Jr. 1939- *WhoWest 94*
Veal, Yvonnecris Smith 1936- *WhoBlA 94*
Veale, Alan (John Ralph) 1920- *Who 94*
Veale, Alan John Ralph 1920- *IntWW 93*
Veale, Tinkham, II 1914- *WhoAm 94*
Veals, Craig Elliott 1955- *WhoBlA 94*
Veasey, E. Norman 1933- *WhoAmP 93*
Veasey, Eugene Norman 1933- *WhoAmL 94*
Veasey, Jack *DrAPF 93*
Veasey, Josephine 1930- *IntWW 93, NewGrDO, Who 94*
Veasey, William d1956 *WhoHol 92*
Veatch, J. William, III 1946- *WhoAmL 94*
Veatch, Jean Louise Corty 1932- *WhoMW 93*
Veatch, Marcus Robert 1953- *WhoFI 94*
Veatch, Robert Marlin 1939- *WhoAm 94, WhoScEn 94*
Veazey, Monty Mobley 1954- *WhoAmP 93*
Veazey, Richard Edward 1941- *WhoMW 93*
Veazey, Sidney Edwin 1937- *WhoFI 94*
Veazie, Carol d1984 *WhoHol 92*
Veblen, John Elvidge 1944- *WhoAmL 94*
Veblen, Thomas Clayton 1929- *WhoAm 94, WhoFI 94*
Veblen, Thorstein Bunde 1857-1929 *AmSocL*
Veburg, Ronald Neil 1930- *WhoMW 93*
Vecchiarelli, Panfilo Guido 1937- *WhoAm 94*
Vecchio, Gary John 1953- *WhoAmP 93*
Vecchio, Raymond 1933- *WhoAmP 93*
Vecchio, Robert Peter 1950- *WhoAm 94, WhoMW 93*
Vecchione, Frank Joseph 1935- *WhoAm 94*
Vecci, Raymond Joseph 1943- *WhoAm 94, WhoFI 94, WhoWest 94*
Vecellio, Anthony Mario *WhoMW 93*
Vecellio, Leo Arthur, Jr. 1946- *WhoAm 94, WhoFI 94*
Vecheslova, Tatyana 1910-1991 *IntDcB [port]*
Veciana-Suarez, Ana 1956- *WhoHisp 94*
Vecla, Djemma *NewGrDO*
Vecoli, Rudolph John 1927- *WhoAm 94, WhoMW 93*
Vecsei, Eva Hollo 1930- *IntWW 93*
Vecsey, Esther Barbara 1944- *WhoAmA 93*
Vecsey, George Spencer 1939- *WhoAm 94*
Vedamuthu, Ebenezer Rajkumar 1932- *WhoAsA 94*
Vedder, Byron Charles 1910- *WhoAm 94*
Vedder, Eddie 1965- *See* Pearl Jam *News 94-2*
Vedder, Richard Kent 1940- *WhoFI 94*
Vedder, William H. d1961 *WhoHol 92*
Vedel, Georges 1910- *IntWW 93*
Veder, Slava J. *WhoAm 94*
Vedernikov, Alexander (Filippovich) 1927- *NewGrDO*
Vedernikov, Nikolai Trofimovich 1934- *LngBDD*
Vedral, Joyce L(auretta) 1943- *ConAu 41NR*
Vedros, Chris Nicholas 1930- *WhoMW 93*
Vedros, Neylan Anthony 1929- *WhoAm 94*
Vedung, Evert Oskar 1938- *WhoScEn 94*
Vedvig, Helen Harriet 1920- *WhoMW 93*
Vedvik, Jerry Donald 1936- *WhoWest 94*
Vee, Bobby 1943- *WhoHol 92*
Vee, Steven Howard 1947- *WhoMW 93*
Veeck, Bill d1986 *WhoHol 92*
Veeder, Peter Greig 1941- *WhoAmL 94*
Veeder, Van Vechten 1948- *Who 94*
Veenendaal, Cornelia *DrAPF 93*
Veenhuis, Eugene H. 1944- *WhoAmL 94*
Veening, Hans 1931- *WhoScEn 94*
Veenker, Claude Harold 1919- *WhoAm 94*
Veenstra, Harvey Dean 1969- *WhoMW 93*
Veeraraghavan, Dharmaraj Tharuvai 1965- *WhoScEn 94*
Veerhoff, Carlos 1926- *NewGrDO*
Veerkamp, Patrick Burke 1943- *WhoAmA 93*
Veesart, Janet Lyle 1961- *WhoWest 94*
Vega, Adrian Miguel, Jr. 1948- *WhoHisp 94*
Vega, Alberto Leon 1947- *WhoHisp 94*
Vega, Ana Lydia 1946- *BlmGWL, ConWorW 93*
Vega, Anthony 1919- *WhoHisp 94*
Vega, Arturo 1958- *WhoHisp 94*
Vega, Benjamin Urbizo 1916- *WhoAmL 94, WhoWest 94*
Vega, Carlos A. 1953- *WhoHisp 94*
Vega, Dora Celsa 1971- *WhoHisp 94*
Vega, Ed *DrAPF 93*
Vega, Ed 1936- *WhoHisp 94*
Vega, Edward 1938- *WhoAmA 93*
Vega, Felix Lope de *NewGrDO*
Vega, Flavio 1943- *WhoHisp 94, WhoMW 93*
Vega, Francisco *WhoHisp 94*
Vega, Frank J. *WhoHisp 94, WhoMW 93*
Vega, Isela 1940- *WhoHol 92*
Vega, J. William 1931- *WhoAm 94*
Vega, Janine Pommy *DrAPF 93*
Vega, Jose Guadalupe 1953- *WhoWest 94*
Vega, Juan Ramón 1931- *WhoHisp 94*
Vega, Lazaro Nava, III 1960- *WhoHisp 94*
Vega, Lope de 1562-1635 *LitC 23 [port]*
Vega, Manuel 1929- *WhoHisp 94*
Vega, Mariano, Jr. 1949- *WhoHisp 94*
Vega, Marylois Purdy 1914- *WhoAm 94*
Vega, Matias Alfonso 1952- *WhoAm 94*
Vega, Paul *WhoHisp 94*
Vega, Rafael 1925- *WhoHisp 94*
Vega, Rafael Evaristo 1934- *WhoHisp 94*
Vega, Ralph, Jr. 1953- *WhoHisp 94*
Vega, Rene L. *WhoHisp 94*
Vega, Rosa Elia 1952- *WhoHisp 94*
Vega, Rosa Martin 1948- *WhoAmL 94*
Vega, Rufino A. *WhoHisp 94*
Vega, Santos Carbajal 1931- *WhoHisp 94*
Vega, Steve 1949- *WhoMW 93*
Vega, Suzanne 1959- *WhoAm 94*
Vega, Valorie *WhoHisp 94*
Vega, William M. *WhoHisp 94*
Vega, Yvonne *WhoHisp 94*
Vega Carpio, Lope (Felix) de 1562-1635 *IntDcT 2 [port]*
Vega De Seoane Azpilicueta, Javier 1947- *IntWW 93*
Vega-García, Edna Rosa 1950- *WhoHisp 94*
Vega Jacome, Rafael 1944- *WhoHisp 94*
Vega Trejos, Guillermo 1927- *Who 94*
Vega Yunqué, Edgardo 1936- *WhoHisp 94*
Vegeres, Joseph d1977 *WhoHol 92*
Vegh, Claudine 1934- *ConAu 142*
Veghte, Robert Illingworth 1952- *WhoAm 94*
Vegh Villegas, Alejandro 1928- *IntWW 93*
Veglia, Ambrose Joachim 1917- *WhoFI 94*
Vehar, August Randall 1950- *WhoAmP 93*
Vehar, Gordon Allen 1948- *WhoWest 94*
Veichtner, Franz Adam 1741-1822 *NewGrDO*
Veidenheimer, Malcolm Charles 1928- *WhoAm 94*
Veidt, Conrad d1943 *WhoHol 92*
Veierod, Tove 1940- *WhoWomW 91*
Veiga, Jose Augusto Ferreira 1838-1903 *NewGrDO*
Veigel, Jon Michael 1938- *WhoScEn 94*
Veil, Simone 1927- *IntWW 93*
Veil, Simone Annie 1927- *Who 94, WhoWomW 91*
Veillard, Eric *WhoHol 92*
Veiller, Anthony d1965 *WhoHol 92*
Veiller, Anthony 1903-1965 *IntDcF 2-4*
Veilleux, Gerard 1942- *WhoAm 94, WhoFI 94*
Veilleux, Marcel Paul 1956- *WhoAmP 93*
Veinott, Cyril George 1905- *WhoAm 94*
Veis, Jaroslav *EncSF 93*
Veit, Fritz 1907- *WhoAm 94, WhoMW 93*
Veit, Lawrence A. 1938- *WhoFI 94*
Veit, Werner 1929- *WhoMW 93*
Veit, William Arthur 1947- *WhoFI 94, WhoWest 94*
Veitch, Boyer Lewis 1930- *WhoFI 94*
Veitch, Stephen William 1927- *WhoAm 94*
Veitch, Tom *DrAPF 93*
Veitch, William A. 1925- *WhoAmP 93*
Veith, Ilza 1915- *WhoAm 94*
Veith, Mary Roth 1931- *WhoFI 94*
Veith, Michael 1944- *WhoScEn 94*
Veith, Paul Eric 1965- *WhoAmL 94*
Veith, Richard Lee 1940- *WhoAm 94*
Veith, Robert Woody 1952- *WhoScEn 94*
Veizer, Jan 1941- *WhoAm 94, WhoScEn 94*
Veizer, Keith *DrAPF 93*
Vejar, Harry J. d1968 *WhoHol 92*
Vejar, Rudolph Lawrence 1933- *WhoHisp 94*
Vejdelek, Cestmir *EncSF 93*
Vejzovic, Dunja 1943- *NewGrDO*
Vekich, Max M., Jr. 1954- *WhoAmP 93*
Vekroff, Perry d1937 *WhoHol 92*
Veksler, Vladmir Iosifovich 1907-1966 *WorInv*
Vela, David *WhoAmL 94*
Vela, Emilio Lamar 1939- *WhoHisp 94*
Vela, Filemon B. 1935- *WhoAm 94, WhoAmL 94, WhoHisp 94*
Vela, Gerard Roland 1927- *WhoHisp 94*
Vela, Librada D. 1953- *WhoHisp 94*
Vela, Noelia 1949- *WhoHisp 94*
Vela, Ricardo Rene 1956- *WhoHisp 94*
Vela, Rosie 1954- *WhoHol 92*
Vela, San Juanita Rosario 1947- *WhoHisp 94*
Vela-Creixell, Mary I. 1938- *WhoHisp 94*
Velaer, Charles Alfred 1932- *WhoMW 93*
Velagaleti, Ranga Rao 1946- *WhoScEn 94*
Velarde, Anita Renee 1966- *WhoHisp 94*
Velarde, Carlos E. 1929- *WhoHisp 94*
Velarde, Kukuli 1962- *WhoHisp 94*
Velarde, Linda Marie *WhoHisp 94*
Velarde, Luis Alfonso, Jr. 1936- *WhoHisp 94*
Velarde, Randy 1962- *WhoHisp 94*
Velardo, Joseph Thomas 1923- *WhoAm 94, WhoMW 93, WhoScEn 94, WrDr 94*
Velasco, Agustin C. *WhoHisp 94*
Velasco, Alfredo Frank 1944- *WhoHisp 94*
Velasco, Bernardo P. 1949- *WhoHisp 94*
Velasco, Conchita *WhoHol 92*
Velasco, Eugenio 1944- *WhoAm 94*
Velasco, Frank E. 1948- *WhoHisp 94*
Velasco, James 1919- *WhoScEn 94*
Velasco, Jerry *WhoHol 92*
Velasco, Jerry G. *WhoHisp 94*
Velasco, Julio Humberto Cruz 1950- *WhoWest 94*
Velasco, Ralph E., Jr. 1926- *WhoHisp 94*
Velasco, Raymond Lester 1951- *WhoHisp 94*
Velasco, Tomas 1962- *WhoHisp 94*
Velasco Negueruela, Arturo 1944- *WhoScEn 94*
Velasquez, Angelo *WhoHisp 94*
Velasquez, Arthur Raymond 1938- *WhoHisp 94*
Velasquez, Baldemar 1947- *WhoHisp 94*
Velasquez, Benito J. 1956- *WhoHisp 94*
Velasquez, Carlos 1948- *WhoHisp 94*
Velasquez, Diego De c. 1460-1524 *WhWE*
Velasquez, Edward Bustos 1946- *WhoHisp 94*

Verdi, David Joseph 1956- *WhoAm 94*
Verdi, Francis M. d1952 *WhoHol 92*
Verdi, Giuseppe (Fortunino Francesco) 1813-1901 *NewGrDO [port]*
Verdi, Joe d1957 *WhoHol 92*
Verdi, Nejat Hasan 1913- *WhoFI 94*
Verdi, Philip Paul 1940- *WhoAm 94*
Verdier, Marie fl. 1675-1680 *NewGrDO*
Verdier, Philippe Maurice 1912- *WhoAm 94*
Verdier, Quentin Roosevelt 1921- *WhoFI 94, WhoMW 93*
Verdin, Clarence 1963- *WhoBlA 94*
Verdon, Brent d1989 *WhoHol 92*
Verdon, Daniel Robert 1962- *WhoMW 93*
Verdon, Gwen 1925- *IntMPA 94, WhoAm 94, WhoHol 92*
Verdone, Carlo *WhoHol 92*
Verdonk, Edward Dennis 1961- *WhoScEn 94*
Verdon-Smith, (William) Reginald d1992 *IntWW 93N*
Verdoorn, Robert James 1934- *WhoIns 94*
Verdoorn, Sid 1939- *WhoAm 94*
verDorn, Bethea (Stewart) 1952- *SmATA 76*
Verducci, John d1977 *WhoHol 92*
Verducci, Joseph Stephen 1947- *WhoMW 93*
Verdugo, Elena 1925- *WhoHol 92*
Verdugo, Fidel 1935- *WhoHisp 94*
Verdugo, Jane M. 1944- *WhoWest 94*
Verduin, Jacob 1913- *WhoAm 94*
Verduin, John Richard, Jr. 1931- *WrDr 94*
Verduzco, J. Jorge *WhoHisp 94*
Verdy, Violette 1933- *IntDcB [port]*
Vere, Anne Cecil de 1556-1588 *BlmGWL*
Verebelyi, Ernest Raymond 1947- *WhoMW 93*
Verebes, Erno d1971 *WhoHol 92*
Vered, Ruth 1940- *WhoAm 94*
Vereen, Ben 1946- *IntMPA 94, WhoAm 94, WhoHol 92*
Vereen, Ben Augustus 1946- *AfrAmAl 6, WhoBlA 94*
Vereen, Dixie Diane 1957- *WhoBlA 94*
Vereen, Michael L. 1965- *WhoBlA 94*
Vereen, Nathaniel 1924- *WhoBlA 94*
Vereen, Robert Charles 1924- *WhoAm 94*
Vereen, William Coachman, Jr. 1913- *WhoAm 94*
Vereen, William Jerome 1940- *WhoAm 94, WhoFI 94*
Vereen-Gordon, Mary Alice 1950- *WhoBlA 94*
Vere-Hodge, Michael John Davy 1946- *Who 94*
Vere-Jones, David 1936- *IntWW 93*
Vereker *Who 94*
Vereker, John Michael Medlicott 1944- *Who 94*
Vereker, Peter William Medlicott 1939- *Who 94*
Vereketis, Constantin Kimon 1908- *WhoFI 94*
Verendrye, Louis Joseph Gaultier De La 1717-1761 *WhWE*
Verendrye, Pierre Gaultier De Varennes Et De La 1685-1749 *WhWE*
Verenes, John Chris 1956- *WhoAmP 93*
Veretti, Antonio 1900-1978 *NewGrDO*
Verey, David John 1950- *Who 94*
Verey, Michael John 1912- *IntWW 93, Who 94*
Verey, Rev. C. *GayLL*
Verey, Rosemary 1918- *WrDr 94*
Vereysky, Orest Georgievich 1915- *IntWW 93*
Verga, Giovanni 1840-1922 *NewGrDO, RfGShF*
Vergara, Alfonso Ignacio 1931- *WhoHisp 94*
Vergara, Isabel R. 1951- *WhoHisp 94*
Vergara, Lautaro Jorge 1916-1992 *WhoHisp 94N*
Vergara, Rosalyn Patrice 1952- *WhoAmP 93*
Vergara-Vives, Alfonso 1931- *WhoHisp 94*
Vergari, Carl Anthony 1921- *WhoAmL 94*
Verga Sheggi, Annamaria 1929- *WhoScEn 94*
Verge, Pierre 1936- *IntWW 93, WhoAm 94*
Vergennes, Charles Gravier 1717-1787 *AmRev*
Vergennes, Charles Gravier, Comte de 1719-1787 *WhAmRev [port]*
Verger, Jean Baptiste Antoine de 1762-1851 *WhAmRev*
Verger, Morris David 1915- *WhoAm 94*
Vergere, Michael George 1952- *WhoMW 93*
Vergeront, Susan B. 1945- *WhoAmP 93*
Vergeront, Susan Bowers 1945- *WhoMW 93*
Verges, Jacques 1925- *IntWW 93*
Verghese, Thadikkal Paul *IntWW 93*
Vergiels, John M. 1937- *WhoAmP 93*
Vergil, Polydore *BlmGEL*
Vergil, Polydore c. 1470-1555 *DcLB 132 [port]*
Vergin, Timothy Lynn 1962- *WhoFI 94, WhoMW 93*
Vergne-Marini, Pedro Juan 1942- *WhoAm 94*
Vergnet, Edmond(-Alphonse) 1850-1904 *NewGrDO*
Verhaegen, Georges 1937- *IntWW 93*
Ver Hagen, Jan Karol 1937- *WhoAm 94, WhoFI 94*
Verhalen, Robert Donald 1935- *WhoAm 94*
Verhesen, Anna Maria Hubertina 1932- *WhoMW 93*
Verhey, James Norman 1941- *WhoAm 94*
Verhey, Joseph William 1928- *WhoWest 94*
Verheyen, Egon 1936- *WhoAm 94*
Verheyen, Marcel Mathieu 1951- *WhoScEn 94*
Verheyen, Pierre Emmanuel c. 1750-1819 *NewGrDO*
Ver Hoef, Lisa Carol 1963- *WhoMW 93*
Verhoef, Martin 1945- *WhoAmL 94*
Verhoeven, Paul 1938- *IntMPA 94, IntWW 93, WhoAm 94*
Verhofstadt, Guy *IntWW 93*
Verhoogen, John 1912- *WhoAm 94*
Verhulsdonk, Roswitha 1927- *WhoWomW 91*
Verich, Demetrio 1932- *WhoAmP 93*
Verich, Michael Gregory 1953- *WhoAmP 93*
Verigan, Terrence 1948- *WhoFI 94*
Verillon, Francis Charles 1944- *WhoScEn 94*
Vering, John Albert 1951- *WhoAm 94, WhoAmL 94*
Verink, Ellis Daniel, Jr. 1920- *WhoAm 94*
Verity, Anthony Courtenay Froude 1939- *Who 94*
Verity, C. William 1917- *EncABHB 9 [port]*
Verity, Calvin William, Jr. 1917- *IntWW 93*
Verity, George Luther 1914- *WhoAm 94*
Verity, George Matthew 1865-1942 *EncABHB 9 [port]*
Verity, Hedley 1905-1943 *DcNaB MP*
Verity, Maurice Anthony 1931- *WhoAm 94*
Verivakis, Elevtherios 1935- *IntWW 93*
Verkamp, John *WhoAmP 93*
Verkamp, John 1940- *WhoWest 94*
Verkauf-Verlon, Willy Andre 1917- *IntWW 93*
Verkler, Richard Lee 1936- *WhoAm 94*
Verlag, Cora 1937- *WrDr 94*
Verlander, Paul Jeffrey 1963- *WhoAmL 94*
Verleger, Philip King 1918- *WhoAm 94*
Verley, Bernard 1939- *WhoHol 92*
Verley, Renaud *WhoHol 92*
Verlier, Karine *WhoHol 92*
Verlinden, (Jean) Charles (Alphonse) 1907- *IntWW 93*
Verma, Ajay 1962?- *WhoAsA 94*
Verma, Ajit K. 1944- *WhoAsA 94*
Verma, Anil K. 1958- *WhoAsA 94*
Verma, Dhani Ram 1929- *WhoAsA 94*
Verma, Dhirendra 1961- *WhoScEn 94*
Verma, Ghasi Ram 1927- *WhoAm 94*
Verma, Krishnanand 1946- *WhoMW 93*
Verma, Nirmal *ConWorW 93*
Verma, Ram Sagar 1946- *WhoAsA 94, WhoScEn 94*
Verma, Usha 1933- *WhoWomW 91*
Verma, Veena 1941- *WhoWomW 91*
Vermaas, Susan Kim 1964- *WhoWest 94*
Vermaas, Willem Frederik Johan 1959- *WhoWest 94*
Vermeer, Marianne 1957- *WhoMW 93*
Vermeer, Mark Ellis 1949- *WhoFI 94, WhoScEn 94*
Vermeer, Maureen Dorothy 1945- *WhoFI 94*
Vermeersch, Jef 1928- *NewGrDO*
Vermes, Geza 1924- *Who 94, WrDr 94*
Vermette, Raymond Edward 1942- *WhoAm 94*
Vermeule, Cornelius Clarkson, III 1925- *WhoAm 94, WhoAmA 93*
Vermeule, Emily Dickinson Townsend 1928- *Who 94, WrDr 94*
Vermeule, Emily Townsend 1928- *WhoAm 94*
Vermeulen, Cornelius W. 1912-1991 *WhAm 10*
Vermillion, John F. *WhoAmP 93*
Vermillion, Lois Jeanne 1945- *WhoAmL 94*
Vermilya, Dale Nelson 1959- *WhoFI 94*
Vermilye, Peter Hoagland 1920- *WhoAm 94*
Vermilyea, Harold d1958 *WhoHol 92*
Vermoyal, Paul d1925 *WhoHol 92*
Vermylen, Paul Anthony, Jr. 1946- *WhoAm 94*
Vern, David *EncSF 93*
Verna, Anna C. *WhoAmP 93*
Verna, Donna Joyce 1951- *WhoWest 94*
Vernac, Denise d1984 *WhoHol 92*
Vernarelli, Michael Joseph 1948- *WhoFI 94, WhoScEn 94*
Vernay, Annie d1941 *WhoHol 92*
Vernberg, Frank John 1925- *WhoAm 94, WhoScEn 94*
Verne, Jules 1828-1905 *TwCLC 52 [port]*
Verne, Jules (Gabriel) 1828-1905 *EncSF 93*
Verne, Kaaren d1967 *WhoHol 92*
Verne, Maxine H. 1955- *WhoIns 94*
Verne, Michel *EncSF 93*
Vernejoul, Robert d1992 *IntWW 93N*
Vernekar, Anandu Devarao 1932- *WhoAsA 94*
Verner, Elizabeth O'Neill 1883-1979 *WhoAmA 93N*
Verner, Hans *WhoHol 92*
Verner, James Melton 1915- *WhoAm 94*
Vernerder, Gloria Jean 1930- *WhoMW 93*
Vernette, Tevaite *WhoHol 92*
Verneuil, Henri 1920- *IntWW 93*
Verney *Who 94*
Verney, Douglas (Vernon) 1924- *WrDr 94*
Verney, Guy d1970 *WhoHol 92*
Verney, John d1993 *Who 94N*
Verney, John 1913- *WrDr 94*
Verney, John 1913-1993 *ConAu 140, SmATA 75*
Verney, Lawrence (John) 1924- *Who 94*
Verney, Michael Palmer 1923- *WrDr 94*
Verney, Peter (Vivian Lloyd) 1930- *WrDr 94*
Verney, Ralph (Bruce) 1915- *Who 94*
Verney, Sebastian *Who 94*
Verney, (John) Sebastian 1948- *Who 94*
Verney, Stephen Edmund 1919- *Who 94, WrDr 94*
Verni, Andrea c. 1765-1822 *NewGrDO*
Vernick, Arnold Sander 1933- *WhoScEn 94*
Vernier, Pierre *WhoHol 92*
Vernier, Pierre-Francois 1736-1780 *WhAmRev*
Vernier, Richard 1929- *WhoAm 94*
Verniero, Joan Evans 1937- *WhoWest 94*
Vernier-Palliez, Bernard Maurice Alexandre 1918- *IntWW 93, Who 94*
Vernikos, Joan 1934- *WhoScEn 94*
Verno, Jerry d1975 *WhoHol 92*
Vernon *Who 94*
Vernon 1948- *WhoAmA 93*
Vernon, Baron 1923- *Who 94*
Vernon, Mrs. *NewGrDO*
Vernon, Anne 1924- *IntMPA 94*
Vernon, Anne 1925- *WhoHol 92*
Vernon, Bobby d1939 *WhoHol 92*
Vernon, Carl Atlee, Jr. 1926- *WhoAm 94*
Vernon, Charles A. 1956- *WhoAmL 94*
Vernon, Christie Dougherty 1929- *WhoAmP 93*
Vernon, Darryl Mitchell 1956- *WhoAmL 94*
Vernon, David Bowater 1926- *Who 94*
Vernon, David Harvey 1925- *WhoAmL 94*
Vernon, David Paul 1948- *WhoWest 94*
Vernon, Dorothy d1970 *WhoHol 92*
Vernon, Easton D. 1934- *WhoBlA 94*
Vernon, Francine M. 1939- *WhoBlA 94*
Vernon, Glenn 1923- *WhoHol 92*
Vernon, Harvey *WhoHol 92*
Vernon, Howard *WhoHol 92*
Vernon, Isabel d1930 *WhoHol 92*
Vernon, Jack Allen 1922- *WhoScEn 94*
Vernon, Jackie d1987 *WhoHol 92*
Vernon, Jackie 1928-1987 *WhoCom*
Vernon, James 1910- *IntWW 93, Who 94*
Vernon, James William 1915- *Who 94*
Vernon, John *DrAPF 93*
Vernon, John 1932- *IntMPA 94, WhoHol 92*
Vernon, Joseph c. 1737-1782 *NewGrDO*
Vernon, Kate *WhoHol 92*
Vernon, Kenneth Robert 1923- *Who 94*
Vernon, Larry Skip *WhoAmP 93*
Vernon, Lillian 1927- *WhoAm 94, WhoFI 94*
Vernon, Lou d1971 *WhoHol 92*
Vernon, Magdalen Dorothea 1901- *WrDr 94*
Vernon, Michael *Who 94*
Vernon, (William) Michael 1926- *IntWW 93, Who 94*
Vernon, Nell d1959 *WhoHol 92*
Vernon, Nigel (John Douglas) 1924- *Who 94*
Vernon, Raymond 1913- *IntWW 93, WhoAm 94, WhoFI 94, WrDr 94*
Vernon, Richard 1925- *WhoHol 92*
Vernon, Robert Brian 1954- *WhoWest 94*
Vernon, Roger Lee 1924- *EncSF 93*
Vernon, Shirley Jane 1930- *WhoAm 94*
Vernon, Sidney 1906- *WhoScEn 94*
Vernon, Virginia Lee 1931- *WhoAmP 93*
Vernon, Wally d1970 *WhoHol 92*
Vernon, Weston, III 1931- *WhoAm 94*
Vernon, William Bradford 1951- *WhoAmP 93*
Vernon-Chesley, Michele Joanne 1962- *WhoBlA 94*
Vernoy de Saint-Georges, Jules-Henri *NewGrDO*
Verocai, Giovanni c. 1700-1745 *NewGrDO*
Veroli, Giacomo c. 1730-c. 1797 *NewGrDO*
Veron, Earl Ernest 1922-1990 *WhAm 10*
Veron, J. Michael 1950- *WhoAmL 94*
Veron, Louis 1798-1867 *NewGrDO*
Verona, Bartolomeo 1744-1813 *NewGrDO*
Verona, Michael Ross *WhoHol 92*
Verona, Paula 1950- *WhoAmA 93*
Verona, Stephen 1940- *IntMPA 94*
Veronda, Raymond Joseph, II 1946- *WhoWest 94*
Veronelli, Ernesto 1938- *NewGrDO*
Veronesi, Umberto 1925- *WhoFI 94*
Veronica, Christina *WhoHol 92*
Veronis, Peter 1923- *WhoAm 94*
Verosta, Stephan Eduard 1909- *IntWW 93*
Verostko, Roman Joseph 1929- *WhoAmA 93*
Verosub, Kenneth Lee 1944- *WhoAm 94, WhoWest 94*
Verot, Jean-Pierre Augustin Marcellin 1805-1876 *DcAmReB 2*
Verplaetse, Alfons Remi Emiel 1930- *IntWW 93*
Verplanck, William Samuel 1916- *WhoAm 94*
Verr, Harry Coe 1937- *WrDr 94*
Verrall, John (Weedon) 1908- *NewGrDO*
Verrant, Jane Frances 1936- *WhoMW 93*
Verrazano, Giovanni Da 1485-1528 *WhWE*
Verrecchia, Alfred J. 1943- *WhoAm 94, WhoFI 94*
Verrell, Cec *WhoHol 92*
Verret, Douglas Peter 1947- *WhoScEn 94*
Verret, John Cyril 1945- *WhoAm 94*
Verrett, Joyce M. 1932- *WhoBlA 94*
Verrett, Shirley 1931- *IntWW 93, NewGrDO*
Verrett, Shirley 1933- *AfrAmAl 6 [port], WhoHol 92*
Verrill, A(lpheus) Hyatt 1871-1954 *EncSF 93*
Verrill, Charles Owen, Jr. 1937- *WhoAm 94, WhoAmL 94, WhoFI 94*
Verrill, Chester Roland 1912- *WhoAmP 93*
Verrill, F. Glenn 1923- *WhoAm 94*
Verrill, Harold Everett 1893- *WhAm 10*
Verrillo, Ronald Thomas 1927- *WhoScEn 94*
Verrone, Patric Miller 1959- *WhoAm 94, WhoAmL 94, WhoWest 94*
Verrue, Betty d1962 *WhoHol 92*
Verry, William Robert 1933- *WhoScEn 94, WhoWest 94*
Versace, Gianni 1946- *CurBio 93 [port], IntWW 93, WhoAm 94*
Versaggi, Joseph Angelo 1961- *WhoAm 94*
Verschoor, Curtis Carl 1931- *WhoAm 94*
Verschuur, Gerrit L(aurens) 1937- *ConAu 142*
Versfelt, David Scott 1951- *WhoAm 94, WhoAmL 94*
Vershbow, Arthur Emmanuel 1922- *WhoAm 94*
Versi, Ibrahim Yusuf 1957- *WhoFI 94*
Versic, Ronald James 1942- *WhoMW 93*
Versini, Marie 1939- *WhoHol 92*
Versins, Pierre 1923- *EncSF 93*
Versnel, Machteld Maria 1940- *WhoWomW 91*
Versois, Odile d1980 *WhoHol 92*
Ver Steeg, Clarence Lester 1922- *WhoAm 94, WhoMW 93*
Ver Steeg, Donna Lorraine Frank 1929- *WhoWest 94*
Ver Steeg, Eugene Duane 1942- *WhoAmP 93*
Verstovsky, Alexey Nikolayevich 1799-1862 *NewGrDO*
Verstraete, Marc 1925- *IntWW 93*
Verstraete, Mary Clare 1960- *WhoScEn 94*
Vert (y Carbonell), Juan 1890-1931 *NewGrDO*
Vertefeuille, Albert Benoit 1933- *WhoAmP 93*
Vertes, Marcel 1895-1961 *WhoAmA 93N*
Vertetis, Maria C. 1958- *WhoFI 94*
Vertreace, Martha M. *DrAPF 93*
Vertreace, Martha M. 1945- *BlkWr 2*
Vertreace, Martha Modena 1945- *WhoBlA 94*

Vertreace, Walter Charles 1947- *WhoBlA 94*
Verts, Lita Jeanne 1935- *WhoWest 94*
Vertua Gentile, Anna 1850-1927 *BlmGWL*
Vertue, William c. 1465-1527 *DcNaB MP*
Verulam, Earl of 1951- *Who 94*
Verushka 1941- *WhoHol 92*
Verval, Alain 1906- *WrDr 94*
Verville, Elizabeth Giavani 1940- *WhoAm 94*
Ver Vynck-Potter, Virginia Mary 1940- *WhoMW 93*
Verwey, Timothy Andrew 1964- *WhoScEn 94*
Ver Wiebe, Richard Chrisler 1931- *WhoMW 93*
Verwoerd, Hendrik 1901-1966 *HisWorL [port]*
Verwoerdt, Adriaan 1927- *WhoAm 94*
Verwolf, Nick Steven 1946- *WhoAmL 94*
Verwolf, William Joseph 1943- *WhoWest 94*
Veryan, Patricia 1923- *WrDr 94*
Verykivs'ky, Mykhaylo 1896-1962 *NewGrDO*
Verzar, Christine B. 1940- *WhoAmA 93*
Verzar, Christine Beatrice 1940- *WhoMW 93*
Verzone, Ronald D. 1947- *WhoFI 94*
Verzyl, June Carol 1928- *WhoAmA 93*
Verzyl, Kenneth H. 1922-1987 *WhoAmA 93N*
Vesaas, Halldis Moren 1907- *BlmGWL, ConWorW 93*
Vesak, Norbert Franklin 1936-1990 *WhAm 10*
Vesalius, Andreas 1514-1564 *WorScD*
Vescovi, Selvi 1930- *WhoFI 94, WhoMW 93*
Veselits, Charles Francis 1930- *WhoFI 94*
Veselitskaia, Lidiia Ivanovna 1857-1936 *BlmGWL*
Veselkova-Kil'shtet, Mariia Grigor'evna 1861-1931 *BlmGWL*
Veselsky, Ernst Eugen 1932- *IntWW 93*
Vesely, Alexander 1926- *WhoAm 94, WhoFI 94*
Vesely, Charles Steven 1953- *WhoWest 94*
Vesely, Karel 1921- *WhoScEn 94*
Vesen'ev, Iv. *BlmGWL*
Veseth, Michael 1949- *WrDr 94*
Vesey *Who 94*
Vesey, Denmark 1767-1822 *AfrAmAl 6*
Vesey, Elizabeth 1715-1791 *BlmGWL*
Vesey, Godfrey (Norman Agmondisham) 1923- *WrDr 94*
Vesey, Henry *Who 94*
Vesey, (Nathaniel) Henry (Peniston) 1901- *Who 94*
Vesey, Paul 1917- *WrDr 94*
Veski, Erik 1952- *WhoAmL 94*
Vesna, Victoria 1959- *WhoAmA 93*
Ve Sota, Bruno d1976 *WhoHol 92*
Vespa, John Vernon 1963- *WhoMW 93*
Vespa, Ned Angelo 1942- *WhoAm 94*
Vespaget, Josephine M. 1946- *WhoWomW 91*
Vesper, Karl H(amptom) 1932- *WrDr 94*
Vesper, Karl Hampton 1932- *WhoAm 94*
Vesper, Rose *WhoAmP 93*
Vespucci, Amerigo 1451-1512 *WhWE [port]*
Vesque von Puttlingen, Johann 1803-1883 *NewGrDO*
Vesser, Carolyn *EncSF 93*
Vessey, John W., Jr. 1922- *IntWW 93*
Vessey, Martin Paterson 1936- *Who 94*
Vessiliadou, Georgia d1980 *WhoHol 92*
Vessot, Robert Frederick Charles 1930- *WhoAm 94*
Vessup, Aaron Anthony 1947- *WhoBlA 94*
Vest, Ben 1940- *WhoAmP 93*
Vest, Charles Marstiller 1941- *IntWW 93, Who 94, WhoAm 94, WhoScEn 94*
Vest, Donald Seymour, Sr. 1930- *WhoBlA 94*
Vest, Frank Harris, Jr. 1936- *WhoAm 94*
Vest, G. Waverly, Jr. 1947- *WhoAmL 94*
Vest, George Graham 1930- *WhoAm 94*
Vest, George S. 1918- *WhoAmP 93*
Vest, George Southall 1918- *WhoAm 94*
Vest, Hilda Freeman 1933- *WhoBlA 94*
Vest, Hyrum Grant, Jr. 1935- *WhoAm 94*
Vest, John P. W. d1993 *NewYTBS 93*
Vest, Marvin Lewis 1906- *WhoAm 94*
Vest, Robert Wilson 1930- *WhoAm 94*
Vestal, David 1924- *WhoAmA 93*
Vestal, John Harrison 1951- *WhoAmL 94*
Vestal, Josephine Burnet 1949- *WhoAm 94, WhoAmL 94*
Vestal, Lowell Alan 1934- *WhoAmP 93*
Vestal, Lucian LaRoe 1925- *WhoAm 94*
Vestal, Tommy Ray 1939- *WhoAmL 94, WhoScEn 94*
Vester, Terry Y. 1955- *WhoBlA 94*
Vestey, Baron 1941- *Who 94*
Vestey, (John) Derek 1914- *Who 94*
Vestey, Edmund Hoyle 1932- *IntWW 93, Who 94*
Vestly, Anne-Cath 1920- *BlmGWL*
Vestly, Anne-Cath(arina) 1920- *ConAu 41NR*
Vestmar, Brigel Johannes Ahlmann 1937- *WhoScEn 94*
Vestoff, Virginia d1982 *WhoHol 92*
Vestris, Auguste 1760-1842 *IntDcB [port]*
Vestris, Gaetano 1729-1808 *IntDcB [port]*
Vestris, Lucia Elizabeth 1797-1856 *NewGrDO [port]*
Vestry, Art d1976 *WhoHol 92*
Vet, T. V. *ConAu 42NR*
Vetch, Thomas *EncSF 93*
Vetchinsky, Alex d1980 *IntDcF 2-4*
Vetere, Richard *DrAPF 93*
Vetlesen, Vesla 1939- *IntWW 93*
Veto, Janine M. *DrAPF 93*
Vetog, Edwin Joseph 1921- *WhoAm 94*
Vetra, Mariss 1901-1965 *NewGrDO*
Vetri, Victoria 1944- *WhoHol 92*
Vetro, James Paul 1960- *WhoScEn 94*
Vette, David Edward 1946- *WhoWest 94*
Vetter, Betty McGee 1924- *WhoAm 94*
Vetter, Herbert 1920- *WhoAm 94*
Vetter, James George, Jr. 1934- *WhoAm 94, WhoAmL 94*
Vetter, James L. 1933- *WhoAm 94*
Vetter, Mary Margaret 1945- *WhoFI 94*
Vetter, Pamela Jane 1948- *WhoMW 93*
Vetter, Richard 1928- *IntMPA 94*
Vetter, Richard James 1943- *WhoMW 93*
Vetter, Robert Norman 1951- *WhoFI 94*
Vetterli, Doris Arlene 1941- *WhoWest 94*
Vettori, Paul Marion 1944- *WhoAmL 94*
Veverka, Donald John 1935- *WhoAmL 94*
Vevers, Tabitha 1957- *WhoAmA 93*
Vevers, Tony 1926- *WhoAmA 93*
Vevier, Charles 1924- *WhoAm 94*
Vey, Deborah Lynn 1966- *WhoMW 93*
Veydt, Gerald Raymond 1953- *WhoFI 94*
Veysberg, Yuliya Lazarevna 1880-1942 *NewGrDO*
Veysey, Arthur (Ernest) 1914- *WrDr 94*
Veysey, Arthur Ernest 1914- *WhoAm 94*
Veytia, Albert Charles 1958- *WhoHisp 94*
Veytía, Edgar Bertolo 1953- *WhoHisp 94*
Vezeridis, Michael Panagiotis 1943- *WhoScEn 94*
Vezey, Al 1949- *WhoAmP 93*
Vezina, George Robert 1935- *WhoAm 94*
Vezina, Joseph 1849-1924 *NewGrDO*
Vezina, Monique *IntWW 93, WhoAm 94, WhoScEn 94*
Vezina, Monique 1935- *WhoWomW 91*
Veziroglu, Turhan Nejat 1924- *WhoAm 94, WhoScEn 94*
VeZolles, Janet Lee 1953- *WhoWest 94*
Vezys, Gintautas 1926- *WhoAmA 93*
Vezzani, Cesare 1886-1951 *NewGrDO*
Via, Clarence Wilson 1914- *WhoWest 94*
Via, Dennis Martin 1952- *WhoIns 94*
Via, Thomas Henry 1959- *WhoBlA 94*
Vial, Kenneth Harold 1912- *Who 94*
Vial, Pedro c. 1746-1814 *WhWE*
Vialacki, Ales Viktaravic 1962- *LngBDD*
Vialar, Paul 1898- *IntWW 93*
Viale, Agostinho c. 1620-1667 *WhWE*
Vialle, Karen *WhoAm 94, WhoAmP 93, WhoWest 94*
Viamonte, Manuel, Jr. 1930- *WhoHisp 94*
Vian, Boris 1920-1959 *EncSF 93, IntDcT 2*
Vian, Orfeo 1924-1989 *WhoAmA 93N*
Viana, Thomas Arnold 1951- *WhoScEn 94*
Vianco, Paul Thomas 1957- *WhoScEn 94*
Vianesi, Auguste Charles Leonard Francois 1837-1908 *NewGrDO*
Viani, James L. 1932- *WhoAm 94*
Viano, David Charles 1946- *WhoAm 94*
Viardot, (Michelle Ferdinande) Pauline 1821-1910 *NewGrDO*
Viar-Holt, Dixie Fae 1936- *WhoWest 94*
Viart, Guy Pascal 1957- *WhoFI 94*
Viau, Theophile de 1590-1626 *GuFrLit 2*
Viault, Birdsall Scrymser 1932- *WhoAm 94*
Viavant, Christopher Robin 1956- *WhoFI 94*
Vibart, Henry d1939 *WhoHol 92*
Vibe, Kjeld 1927- *IntWW 93*
Vic and Sade *WhoCom*
Vicary, Douglas Reginald 1916- *Who 94*
Viccellio, Henry, Jr. *WhoAm 94*
Viccellio, Nancy Blair 1914- *WhoAmL 94*
Vice, Charles Loren 1921- *WhoScEn 94, WhoWest 94*
Vice, David G. *WhoAm 94, WhoFI 94*
Vice, LaVonna Lee 1952- *WhoAmL 94*
Vice, Lisa *DrAPF 93*
Vicens, Antonia 1942- *BlmGWL*
Vicens, Enrique 1926- *WhoAmP 93*
Vicens, Guillermo Juan 1948- *WhoHisp 94*
Vicente, Esteban 1903- *WhoAmA 93*
Vicente, Gil c. 1465-c. 1536 *IntDcT 2*
Vicente, José Alberto 1954- *WhoHisp 94*
Vicente, Paula c. 1600-1660 *BlmGWL*
Vicente, Ralph A. 1946- *WhoHisp 94*
Viceps, Karlis David 1956- *WhoScEn 94*
Vician, Roy A. 1941- *WhoMW 93*
Vicino, Frank Leo 1935- *WhoWest 94*
Vicious, Sid d1979 *WhoHol 92*
Vick, Arnold Oughtred Russell 1933- *Who 94*
Vick, (Francis) Arthur 1911- *IntWW 93, Who 94*
Vick, Austin Lafayette 1929- *WhoScEn 94*
Vick, Connie R. 1947- *WhoAmA 93*
Vick, Gina Marie 1968- *WhoWest 94*
Vick, Graham 1953- *NewGrDO*
Vick, James Albert 1945- *WhoAm 94*
Vick, John 1933- *WhoScEn 94*
Vick, Kathleen 1938- *WhoWomW 91*
Vick, Kathleen M. 1938- *WhoAmP 93*
Vick, Marie 1922- *WhoAm 94, WhoScEn 94*
Vick, Paul Ashton 1945- *WhoAm 94*
Vick, Richard (William) 1917- *Who 94*
Vicker, Ray 1917- *WhoAm 94, WhoWest 94*
Vickerman, Anastasia Lynn 1963- *WhoMW 93*
Vickerman, Barb *WhoAmP 93*
Vickerman, Jim 1931- *WhoAmP 93*
Vickerman, Keith 1933- *Who 94, WhoScEn 94*
Vickerman, Sara Elizabeth 1949- *WhoWest 94*
Vickers, Baroness *Who 94, WhoWomW 91*
Vickers, Al *EncSF 93*
Vickers, Alexandra d1979 *WhoHol 92*
Vickers, Amy *WhoScEn 94*
Vickers, Billy Jack 1957- *WhoWest 94*
Vickers, Claude L. *WhoAmP 93*
Vickers, Deanna 1940- *WhoAmP 93, WhoWomW 91*
Vickers, Dolores Ehlin 1935- *WhoAmP 93*
Vickers, Eric 1921- *Who 94*
Vickers, Eric Erfan 1953- *WhoBlA 94*
Vickers, Holly Ann 1957- *WhoFI 94*
Vickers, James Hudson 1930- *WhoAm 94, WhoScEn 94*
Vickers, James Oswald Noel 1916- *Who 94*
Vickers, John Stuart 1958- *IntWW 93, Who 94*
Vickers, Jon 1926- *IntWW 93, Who 94*
Vickers, Jon(athan Stewart) 1926- *NewGrDO [port]*
Vickers, Martha d1971 *WhoHol 92*
Vickers, Michael Douglas Allen 1929- *Who 94*
Vickers, Michael Edwin *Who 94*
Vickers, Richard (Maurice Hilton) 1928- *Who 94*
Vickers, Robert Arthur 1918- *WhoWest 94*
Vickers, Roger Henry 1945- *Who 94*
Vickers, Roger Spencer 1937- *WhoAm 94*
Vickers, Russ(ell Geron) 1923- *WhoAmA 93*
Vickers, Thomas Douglas 1916- *Who 94*
Vickers, Thomas Joseph 1939- *WhoAm 94*
Vickers, Tom 1936- *WhoAmP 93*
Vickers, Tony 1932- *Who 94*
Vickers, Yvette *WhoHol 92*
Vickerstaff, Robert Percy 1935- *WhoIns 94*
Vickery, Ann Morgan 1944- *WhoAm 94*
Vickery, Brian Campbell 1918- *Who 94*
Vickery, Byrdean Eyvonne Hughes 1928- *WhoWest 94*
Vickery, Charles Bridgeman 1913- *WhoAmA 93*
Vickery, Eugene Livingstone 1913- *WhoMW 93, WhoScEn 94*
Vickery, Glenn Wheeler 1938- *WhoAmL 94*
Vickery, James d1979 *WhoHol 92*
Vickery, James A. 1931- *WhoIns 94*
Vickery, Katherine 1898- *WhAm 10*
Vickery, Melba 1925- *WhoWest 94*
Vickery, Millie Margaret 1920- *WhoMW 93*
Vickery, Raymond Ezekiel, Jr. 1942- *WhoAm 94, WhoAmL 94, WhoAmP 93*
Vickery, Robert Craig 1958- *WhoFI 94*
Vickery, Trammell Eugene 1932- *WhoAm 94*
Vickery, William *WhoMW 93*
Vickrey, Jene *WhoAmP 93*
Vickrey, Robert Edward, Jr. 1912- *WhoFI 94*
Vickrey, Robert Remsen 1926- *WhoAm 94, WhoAmA 93*
Vickrey, William Spencer 1914- *WhoAm 94, WhoFI 94*
Vick-Williams, Marian Lee *WhoBlA 94*
Vico, Diana fl. 1707-1726 *NewGrDO*
Victor, A. Paul 1938- *WhoAm 94*
Victor, Andrew Crost 1934- *WhoScEn 94*
Victor, Barbara 1946- *ConAu 141*
Victor, Charles d1965 *WhoHol 92*
Victor, Charles B. 1935-1987 *WrDr 94N*
Victor, Daniel D(avid) 1944- *ConAu 140*
Victor, Dee d1983 *WhoHol 92*
Victor, Ed 1939- *Who 94*
Victor, Edward 1914- *WrDr 94*
Victor, Henry d1945 *WhoHol 92*
Victor, James *WhoHol 92*
Victor, James 1939- *IntMPA 94, WhoWest 94*
Victor, Katherine 1928- *WhoHol 92*
Victor, Martin 1913-1990 *WhAm 10*
Victor, Mary O'Neill 1924- *WhoAmA 93*
Victor, Michael Gary 1945- *WhoAmL 94*
Victor, Paul-Emile 1907- *IntWW 93*
Victor, Richard Steven 1949- *WhoAmL 94*
Victor, Robert Eugene 1929- *WhoAm 94*
Victor, William Weir 1924- *WhoAm 94*
Victor Emmanuel, II 1820-1878 *HisWorL [port]*
Victoria *BlmGEL*
Victoria 1819-1901 *HisWorL [port]*
Victoria, Queen 1819-1901 *BlmGWL*
Victoria, Francisco D. 1955- *WhoHisp 94*
Victoria, Vesta d1951 *WhoHol 92*
Victorin, His Eminence The Most Reverend 1912- *WhoAm 94*
Victorin, Steven Robert 1961- *WhoFI 94*
Victors, Alexis Peter 1937- *WhoWest 94*
Victorson, Michael Bruce 1954- *WhoAmL 94*
Victory, Gerard 1921- *NewGrDO*
Vicuña, Cecilia 1948- *WhoHisp 94*
Vicuna, Francisco O. *Who 94*
Vicuña, Patricio Ricardo 1953- *WhoHisp 94*
Vida, Stephen Robert 1951- *WhoScEn 94*
Vidacovich, Irvine d1966 *WhoHol 92*
Vidaillet, Humberto José 1927- *WhoHisp 94*
Vidal, Adriana *WhoHisp 94*
Vidal, Alexander Thomas Emeric 1792-1863 *DcNaB MP*
Vidal, Avis Carlotta 1945- *WhoHisp 94*
Vidal, Dagmar Lund 1917- *WhoAmP 93*
Vidal, Eduardo R. 1957- *WhoAmL 94, WhoHisp 94*
Vidal, Federico S. 1920- *WhoHisp 94*
Vidal, Francisco Fernandez 1946- *WhoAmA 93*
Vidal, Gore *DrAPF 93*
Vidal, Gore 1925- *AmCulL [port], ConDr 93, EncSF 93, IntWW 93, Who 94, WhoAm 94, WrDr 94*
Vidal, (Eugene Luther) Gore 1925- *GayLL*
Vidal, Hahn 1919- *WhoAmA 93*
Vidal, Henri d1959 *WhoHol 92*
Vidal, James Emeric 1945- *WhoAmP 93*
Vidal, Judith C. 1942- *WhoHisp 94*
Vidal, Mary Theresa 1815-1869 *BlmGWL*
Vidal, Paul (Antonin) 1863-1931 *NewGrDO*
Vidal, Ricardo 1931- *IntWW 93*
Vidal, Ulises *WhoHisp 94*
Vidalin, Robert d1989 *WhoHol 92*
Vidan, Walter Charles 1947- *WhoMW 93*
Vidaurri, Alfredo Garcia 1930- *WhoHisp 94*
Vidaver, Anne Marie 1938- *WhoMW 93*
Vidaver, Doris *DrAPF 93*
Videla, Jorge Rafael 1925- *IntWW 93*
Viderman, Linda Jean 1957- *WhoAmL 94, WhoFI 94*
Vidger, Leonard Perry 1920- *WrDr 94*
Vidic, Branislav 1934- *WhoScEn 94*
Vidic, Dobrivoje 1918- *Who 94*
Vidler, Alexander Roper 1899-1991 *WrDr 94N*
Vidler, Steven *WhoHol 92*
Vidmar, James A., Jr. 1954- *WhoAmL 94*
Vidoli, Vivian Ann 1941- *WhoWest 94*
Vidor, Florence d1977 *WhoHol 92*
Vidor, John *WhoHol 92*
Vidor, King d1982 *WhoHol 92*
Vidosic, Tihomil 1902-1973 *NewGrDO*
Vidov, Oleg 1947- *WhoHol 92*
Vidovic, Christopher M. 1963- *WhoAmL 94*
Vidovich, Danko Victor 1958- *WhoScEn 94*
Vidricksen, Ben E. 1927- *WhoAmP 93*
Vidricksen, Ben Eugene 1927- *WhoMW 93*
Vidt, Karl John 1955- *WhoWest 94*
Vidueira, Joe R. 1963- *WhoHisp 94*
Vidulich, Joseph Peter 1956- *WhoAmL 94*
Vie, Florence d1939 *WhoHol 92*
Vie, Richard Carl 1937- *WhoAm 94, WhoFI 94*
Viebig, Clara 1860-1952 *BlmGWL*
Viegas, Kenneth Dell 1931- *WhoHisp 94*
Viehland, Larry Alan 1947- *WhoMW 93*
Vieillard-Baron, Bertrand Louis 1940- *WhoScEn 94*
Vieira, Asia 1982- *WhoHol 92*
Vieira, Joao Bernardo 1939- *IntWW 93*
Vieira, Maruja 1922- *BlmGWL*

Vieira, Vasco Rocha 1940- IntWW 93
Viele, Arnaud Cornelius c. 1620-1700 WhWE
Viele, George Brookins 1932- WhoAm 94
Vielehr, William Ralph 1945- WhoAmA 93
Vieler, Geoffrey Herbert 1910- Who 94
Vielhaber, Lawrence Michael 1952- WhoMW 93
Viener, John D. 1939- WhoAm 94, WhoAmL 94, WhoFI 94
Vienken, Joerg Hans 1948- WhoScEn 94
Vienna, La NewGrDO
Vienna, Anthony M. 1943- WhoAmL 94
Vienot, Marc 1928- IntWW 93
Viera, Antonio Torres 1962- WhoHisp 94
Viera, Charles David 1950- WhoAmA 93
Viera, Jackelyn WhoHisp 94
Viera, James Joseph 1940- WhoAm 94
Viera, John Joseph 1932- WhoAm 94
Viera, Pedro WhoHisp 94
Viera, Ricardo 1945- WhoAmA 93
Viera-Martinez, Angel 1915- WhoAmP 93
Vierck, Charles John, Jr. 1936- WhoAm 94
Viereck, George S(ylvester) 1884-1962 EncSF 93
Viereck, Peter DrAPF 93
Viereck, Peter 1916- IntWW 93, WhoAm 94
Viereck, Peter (Robert Edwin) 1916- WrDr 94
Vieregg, Robert Todd 1934- WhoAm 94, WhoAmL 94
Vierheller, Todd 1958- WhoWest 94
Vierling, John Moore 1945- WhoWest 94
Viermetz, Kurt F. 1939- WhoAm 94, WhoFI 94
Vierny, Sacha 1919- IntDcF 2-4
Vierra, Frank Huey 1946- WhoScEn 94
Viertel, Deborah Kerr Who 94
Viertel, Joseph DrAPF 93
Viertel, Joseph 1915- WrDr 94
Viertel, Salka d1978 WhoHol 92
Vierthaler, Bonnie WhoAmA 93
Vieru, Anatol 1926- IntWW 93, NewGrDO
Vieselmeyer, Ron R. 1941- WhoAmP 93
Viessman, Warren, Jr. 1930- WhoAm 94, WhoScEn 94
Viest, Ivan Miroslav 1922- WhoAm 94
Viesulas, Romas 1918- WhoAmA 93N
Viet-Chau, Nguyen Duc 1935- WhoAsA 94
Viete, Francois 1540-1603 WorScD
Vieth, G. Duane 1923- WhoAm 94
Vieth, Paul Herman 1895- WhAm 10
Vieth, Wolf Randolph 1934- WhoAm 94
Vietor, Harold Duane 1931- WhoAm 94, WhoAmL 94, WhoMW 93
Viets, Hermann 1943- WhoAm 94, WhoMW 93
Viets, Richard N. 1930- WhoAmP 93
Viets, Robert O. 1943- WhoAm 94, WhoFI 94, WhoMW 93
Vieuille, Felix 1872-1953 NewGrDO
Vieweg, Bruce Wayne 1947- WhoMW 93
Viezer, Timothy Wayne 1959- WhoFI 94, WhoScEn 94
Vig, Baldev Krishan 1935- WhoWest 94
Vig, Vernon Edward 1937- WhoAm 94
Vigano, Onorato (Rinaldo Giuseppe Maria) 1739-1811 NewGrDO
Vigano, Renata 1900-1976 BlmGWL
Vigano, Salvatore 1769-1821 IntDcB [port]
Vigarani, Carlo 1623-1713 NewGrDO
Vigarani, Gaspare 1586?-c. 1663 NewGrDO
Vigard, Kristen WhoHol 92
Vigars, Della Who 94
Vigars, Robert Lewis 1923- Who 94
Vigdor, James Scott 1953- WhoFI 94
Vigdor, Martin George 1939- WhoScEn 94
Vigen, Kathryn L. Voss 1934- WhoMW 93
Vigfusson, Johannes Orn 1945- WhoScEn 94
Viggers, Peter John 1938- Who 94
Viggers, Robert Frederick 1923- WhoScEn 94
Viggiano, Paul M. 1943- WhoAmP 93
Vigier, Francois Claude Denis 1931- WhoAm 94
Vigil, Allan R. 1947- WhoHisp 94
Vigil, Andres Abelino 1935- WhoHisp 94
Vigil, Arthur Margarito 1942- WhoHisp 94
Vigil, Bernadette 1955- WhoHisp 94
Vigil, Charles S. 1912- WhoAm 94, WhoAmL 94, WhoWest 94
Vigil, Daniel A. 1947- WhoHisp 94
Vigil, Daniel Agustin 1947- WhoAmL 94, WhoWest 94
Vigil, David Anthony 1930- WhoHisp 94
Vigil, David Charles 1944- WhoWest 94
Vigil, Dolores 1938- WhoHisp 94
Vigil, Edward Francis 1964- WhoWest 94
Vigil, Evangelina BlmGWL
Vigil, James Diego 1938- WhoHisp 94, WrDr 94
Vigil, John Carlos 1939- WhoHisp 94
Vigil, John Jess 1952- WhoHisp 94
Vigil, Kathleen Rolfe 1964- WhoMW 93
Vigil, Maria Azucena 1935- WhoHisp 94
Vigil, Maurilio Eutimio 1941- WhoHisp 94, WhoWest 94
Vigil, Neddy Augustin 1939- WhoHisp 94
Vigil, Patrick Richard, Jr. 1954- WhoHisp 94
Vigil, Ralph H. 1932- WhoHisp 94
Vigil, Richard Martin, Sr. 1928- WhoHisp 94
Vigil, Robert 1953- WhoAmP 93
Vigil, Robert E. 1953- WhoHisp 94
Vigil, Samuel F. WhoAmP 93
Vigil, Samuel F., Jr. WhoHisp 94
Vigil, Veloy Joseph 1931- WhoAmA 93, WhoHisp 94
Vigilante, Joseph Louis 1925- WhoAm 94
Vigil-Giron, Rebecca 1954- WhoAmP 93
Vigil-Girón, Rebecca D. 1954- WhoHisp 94
Vigil-Perez, Angie WhoHisp 94
Vigil-Piñón, Evangelina 1949- WhoHisp 94
Vigler, Mildred Sceiford 1914- WhoScEn 94
Vigliante, Mary DrAPF 93
Vigliante, Mary 1946- EncSF 93
Viglione, Eugene Lawrence 1931- WhoWest 94
Viglione-Borghese, Domenico 1877-1957 NewGrDO
Vigliotti, Anthony Joseph 1942- WhoAmP 93
Vigliotti, Louis John 1957- WhoFI 94
Vigmo, Josef 1922- WhoScEn 94
Vignal, Pascale WhoHol 92
Vignal, Renaud 1943- IntWW 93
Vignas, Francesco NewGrDO
Vignati, Giuseppe d1768 NewGrDO
Vignau, Nicolas De fl. 160-?- WhWE
Vigneau, Robert A. 1920- WhoAmP 93
Vignelli, Massimo 1931- WhoAm 94
Vigneri, Joseph William 1956- WhoAmL 94
Vignes, Michelle Marie WhoAmA 93
Vignola, Andrew Michael, Sr. 1938- WhoFI 94
Vignola, Giuseppe 1662-1712 NewGrDO
Vignola, Joseph C. 1949- WhoAmP 93
Vignola, Robert d1953 WhoHol 92
Vignoles, Mark 1957- WhoWest 94
Vignoles, Roger Hutton 1945- Who 94
Vignolo, Biagio Nickolas, Jr. 1947- WhoAm 94
Vignon, Jean-Paul WhoHol 92
Vignone, Ronald John 1941- WhoAm 94
Vigny, Alfred (Victor) de 1797-1863 IntDcT 2
Vigo, Benny Richard 1933- WhoHisp 94
Vigoda, Abe 1921- WhoAm 94, WhoCom
Vigoda, Abe 1922- WhoHol 92
Vigoda, David DrAPF 93
Vigran, Herb(ert) d1986 WhoHol 92
Vigran, Stanley Louis 1926- WhoFI 94
Vigtel, Gudmund 1925- WhoAm 94, WhoAmA 93
Vigue, James F. 1949- WhoFI 94
Viguerie, Richard Art 1933- IntWW 93
Viharo, Robert WhoHol 92
Vihstadt, Robert Francis 1941- WhoWest 94
Viidikas, Vicki 1948- BlmGWL
Vijayabhaskar, Rajagopal Coimbatore 1966- WhoScEn 94
Vijayendran, Bhima R. 1941- WhoAsA 94
Vijh, Ashok Kumar 1938- WhoAm 94, WhoScEn 94
Vijil, Alfonso Jose 1956- WhoHisp 94
Vijit, Supinit IntWW 93
Vijitha-Kumara, Kanaka Hewage 1953- WhoMW 93
Vijverberg, Wim Petrus Maria 1955- WhoFI 94
Vik, Anne 1933- IntWW 93
Vik, Anne Petrea 1933- WhoWomW 91
Vik, Bjorg 1935- BlmGWL
Vik, Bjorg (Turid) 1935- ConWorW 93, RfGShF
Vik, Roland Kristian 1932- WhoMW 93
Viken, Linda Lea M. 1945- WhoAmP 93
Vikis-Freibergs, Vaira 1937- WhoAm 94
Viklund, William Edwin 1940- WhoAm 94
Vikram, Chandra Shekhar 1950- WhoAsA 94
Vikstrom, John Edvin 1931- IntWW 93
Viktil, Martin 1944- WhoScEn 94
Viktorov, Valeryan Nikolaevich 1951- LngBDD
Vikulov, Vladimir Ivanovich 1946- IntWW 93
Vila, Adis Maria 1953- WhoAm 94, WhoHisp 94
Vila, Bob 1946- WhoHisp 94
Vila, Raul Ivan 1954- WhoHisp 94
Vila, Robert Joseph 1946- WhoAm 94
Vila, Sabra De Shon d1917 WhoHol 92
Viladecans, Joan-Pere 1948- IntWW 93
Viladesau, Richard R., Jr. 1944- WhoHisp 94
Vilandre, Paul Connell 1942- WhoFI 94
Vilaplana, Jose M. 1927- WhoHisp 94
Vilaplana, Victor A. 1946- WhoAmL 94
Vilar, Jean d1971 WhoHol 92
Vilar, Jose Teodoro 1836-1905 NewGrDO
Vilardell, Francisco 1926- IntWW 93
Vilardi, Agnes Francine 1918- WhoWest 94
Vilarino, Idea 1920- BlmGWL
Vilarino Pintos, Daria 1928- IntWW 93
Vila Ruiz, Joaquin A. 1959- WhoHisp 94
Vilas, Guillermo 1952- BuCMET
Vilas, Santiago 1931- WhoHisp 94
Vilato, Roberto 1952- WhoHisp 94
Vilbert, Henri WhoHol 92
Vil'boa, Konstantin Petrovich 1817-1882 NewGrDO
Vilcek, Jan Tomas 1933- WhoAm 94, WhoScEn 94
Vilche, Jorge Roberto 1946- WhoScEn 94
Vilches-O'Bourke, Octavio Augusto 1923- WhoFI 94
Vilchez, Blanca Rosa 1957- WhoHisp 94
Vilda, Maria NewGrDO
Vile, Maurice John Crawley 1927- Who 94
Vilers, Vania WhoHol 92
Vilgalys, Patricia Welzel 1957- WhoWest 94
Vilhjalmsson, Thor 1925- ConWorW 93
Vilhjalmsson, Thor 1930- IntWW 93
Vilim, John Robert 1922- WhoMW 93
Vilim, Nancy Catherine 1952- WhoFI 94
Vilione, Michael C. 1954- WhoMW 93
Viljoen, Gerrit van Niekerk 1926- IntWW 93
Viljoen, Hendrik Christo 1937- IntWW 93
Viljoen, Henri Pieter 1932- IntWW 93
Viljoen, Lettie 1948- BlmGWL
Viljoen, Marais 1915- IntWW 93, Who 94
Vilker, Vincent Lee 1943- WhoAm 94
Vilkitis, James Richard WhoWest 94
Villa, Alvaro J. 1940- WhoHisp 94
Villa, Carlos WhoAmA 93
Villa, Carlos Cesar 1941- WhoHisp 94
Villa, Claudio d1987 WhoHol 92
Villa, Daniel Joseph 1956 WhoHisp 94
Villa, David WhoHisp 94
Villa, Edmond Roland 1929- WhoFI 94
Villa, Fernando Luis 1956- WhoHisp 94
Villa, Francisco 1878-1923 HisWorL [port]
Villa, John Joseph 1917- WhoHisp 94
Villa, John Kazar 1948- WhoAmL 94, WhoFI 94
Villa, Jose Garcia 1914- IntWW 93
Villa, Juan Francisco 1941- WhoHisp 94
Villa, Mario 1956- WhoAmA 93
Villa, Raul Manuel 1940- WhoHisp 94
Villa, Roberto Riccardo 1961- WhoScEn 94
Villa, Theodore B. 1936- WhoAmA 93
Villablanca, Jaime Rolando 1929- WhoAm 94
Villacampa Méndez, Alcides Antonio 1952- WhoHisp 94
Villacres, Gerardo 1945- WhoHisp 94
Villafaña, Allan Francis 1961- WhoHisp 94
Villafaña, Manuel A. 1940- WhoHisp 94
Villafaña, Theodore 1936- WhoHisp 94
Villafañe, Juan, Jr. 1951- WhoHisp 94
Villafane, Robert 1941- WhoHisp 94
Villafranca, Joseph J. 1944- WhoAm 94, WhoScEn 94
Villafranchi, Giovanni Cosimo NewGrDO
Villafuerte, Lisa Marie 1966- WhoHisp 94
Village People WhoHol 92
Villaggio, Paolo WhoHol 92
Villa-Gilbert, Mariana (Soledad Magdelena) 1937- WrDr 94
Villagomez, Ramon Garrido 1949- WhoAmL 94
Villagomez, Thomas Pangelinan WhoAmP 93
Villagrán, Gilbert J. 1948- WhoHisp 94
Villagran De Leon, Francisco 1954- IntWW 93
Villagran Rodriguez, Dolores 1954- WhoHisp 94
Villain, Claude Edouard Louis Etienne 1935- IntWW 93
Villaire, William Louis 1967- WhoScEn 94
Villa-Komaroff, Lydia 1947- WhoHisp 94
Villalba, Jovito 1908- IntWW 93
Villa-Lobos, Heitor 1887-1959 NewGrDO
Villalobos, J. Alex 1963- WhoAmP 93
Villalobos, Ruben L., Jr. 1946- WhoHisp 94
Villalobos Padilla, Francisco 1921- WhoAm 94
Villalon, Dalisay Manuel 1941- WhoMW 93
Villalon, Manuel F. 1944- WhoHisp 94
Villalón, Pedro Augusto 1925- WhoHisp 94
Villalpando, Alberto 1949- WhoHisp 94
Villalpando, Catalina Vasquez 1940- WhoHisp 94
Villalpando, David 1958- WhoHol 92
Villalpando, Jesse M. 1959- WhoHisp 94
Villalpando, Jesse Michael 1959- WhoAmP 93
Villamanan, Manuel WhoHisp 94
Villamarin, Juan A. 1939- WhoHisp 94
Villamil, Jose Antonio 1946- WhoHisp 94
Villamil, Lydia I. 1951- WhoHisp 94
Villamil, Richard James 1942- WhoAm 94
Villamor, Catherine WhoHisp 94
Villamor, Enrique 1961- WhoHisp 94
Villane, Anthony M., Jr. WhoAmP 93
Villani, Antonio fl. 1744-1767 NewGrDO
Villani, Daniel Dexter 1947- WhoScEn 94
Villani, Jim DrAPF 93
Villani, Joseph Trigg 1961- WhoWest 94
Villanis, Angelo 1821-1865 NewGrDO
Villani Zamora, Mario A. 1939- WhoHisp 94
Villano, Peter F. WhoAmP 93
Villanova, Melissa Hope 1922- WhoAm 94
Villanueva, Alma DrAPF 93
Villanueva, Alma Luz 1944- WhoHisp 94
Villanueva, Chris WhoAsA 94
Villanueva, Daniel D. WhoHisp 94
Villanueva, Edward Anthony 1946- WhoHisp 94
Villanueva, Hector 1964- WhoHisp 94
Villanueva, José A. WhoHisp 94
Villanueva, José Antonio WhoHisp 94
Villanueva, Marianne Del Rosario 1958- WhoAsA 94
Villanueva, Miguel Ramon, Sr. 1936- WhoHisp 94
Villanueva, Ricardo WhoHisp 94
Villanueva, Tino DrAPF 93
Villanueva, Tino 1941- WhoHisp 94
Villanueva, Tomas Ayala 1941- WhoHisp 94
Villanueva, Victor, Jr. 1948- WhoHisp 94
Villanueva, Vincent C. 1943- WhoHisp 94
Villapalos-Salas, Gustavo 1949- IntWW 93
Villapiano, John A. 1951- WhoAmP 93
Villar, Arturo Ignacio 1933- WhoHisp 94
Villar, Isabel Elsa 1948- WhoHisp 94
Villar, Juan C. 1960- WhoHisp 94
Villar, Ramon F. WhoAmL 94
Villard, Fanny Garrison 1844-1928 AmSocL
Villard, Frank d1980 WhoHol 92
Villard, Juliette d1971 WhoHol 92
Villard, Oswald Garrison 1872-1949 AmSocL
Villard, Tom WhoHol 92
Villareal, Dewey R. 1926- WhoAm 94
Villa-Real, Olivia Canchela 1948- WhoAsA 94
Villareal, Patricia 1951- WhoAmL 94
Villaret, Joao d1961 WhoHol 92
Villarini, Pedro 1933- WhoHisp 94
Villarino, Maria de 1905- BlmGWL
Villaronga, Raul Gabriel 1938- WhoHisp 94
Villar-Palasi, Carlos 1928- WhoAm 94
Villarreal, Alfred William 1957- WhoHisp 94
Villarreal, Anita Mary 1914- WhoHisp 94
Villarreal, Carlos Castaneda 1924- WhoAm 94, WhoScEn 94
Villarreal, David 1958- WhoHisp 94
Villarreal, Fernando M. 1956- WhoHisp 94
Villarreal, G. Claude 1930- WhoHisp 94
Villarreal, Homer Anthony 1952- WhoHisp 94
Villarreal, Homero Atenogenes 1946- WhoAm 94
Villarreal, Humberto 1940- WhoHisp 94
Villarreal, Joaquin WhoHisp 94
Villarreal, Jose Antonio 1924- HispLC [port], WrDr 94
Villarreal, Jose Rolando WhoHisp 94
Villarreal, Julio d1958 WhoHol 92
Villarreal, Lorenzo 1951- WhoHisp 94
Villarreal, Luis Mario WhoHisp 94
Villarreal, Martha Ellen 1942- WhoHisp 94
Villarreal, Melecio Mercado, Jr. 1924- WhoHisp 94
Villarreal, Mike WhoHisp 94
Villarreal, Mike A., Sr. 1933- WhoHisp 94
Villarreal, Norma 1955- WhoHisp 94
Villarreal, Osiel, Jr. 1968- WhoHisp 94
Villarreal, Pedro Corona 1964- WhoHisp 94
Villarreal, Raul, Sr. 1904- WhoHisp 94
Villarreal, Rita 1931- WhoHisp 94
Villarreal, Robert P. 1951- WhoHisp 94

Villarreal, Roberto E. *WhoHisp 94*
Villarreal, Romeo Manuel 1936- *WhoHisp 94*
Villarreal, Rosalva 1957- *WhoHisp 94*
Villarreal, Santos Solis, Jr. 1936- *WhoHisp 94*
Villarreal, Servando Jose 1939- *WhoHisp 94*
Villarrubia, Jan *DrAPF 93*
Villarrubia, John Steven 1957- *WhoScEn 94*
Villars, Felix Marc Hermann 1921- *WhoAm 94*
Villarta, Angeles 1942- *BlmGWL*
Villar y Ortiz De Urdia, Francisco 1945- *IntWW 93*
Villas Boas, Claudio 1916- *IntWW 93*
Villas-Boas, Jose Manuel P. de 1931- *IntWW 93*
Villas Boas, Orlando 1914- *IntWW 93*
Villasenor, Victor Edmundo *DrAPF 93*
Villaseñor, Victor Edmundo 1940- *WhoHisp 94*
Villasoto, Dolores Cruz 1937- *WhoAmP 93*
Villasuso, Raul, Jr. 1965- *WhoHisp 94*
Villate, Gaspar 1851-1891 *NewGrDO*
Villati, Leopoldo de 1701-1752 *NewGrDO*
Villatoro, Carlos d1963 *WhoHol 92*
Villavaso, Stephen Donald 1949- *WhoAm 94, WhoAmL 94*
Villaverde, Roberto 1945- *WhoHisp 94, WhoScEn 94*
Villavicencio, Ana 1962- *WhoWest 94*
Villavicencio, Armando *WhoHisp 94*
Villa-Vicencio, Charles 1942- *IntWW 93*
Villax, Ivan Emeric 1925- *WhoScEn 94*
Villchur, Edgar 1917- *WhoScEn 94*
Villebois, Konstantin Petrovich *NewGrDO*
Villechaize, Herve d1993 *IntMPA 94N, NewYTBS 93 [port]*
Villechaize, Herve 1943- *IntMPA 94, WhoHol 92*
Villechaize, Herve c. 1943-1993 *News 94-1*
Villedieu, Madame de *BlmGWL [port]*
Villee, Claude Alvin, Jr. 1917- *WhoAm 94*
Villegas, Carmen Milagros 1954- *WhoHisp 94*
Villegas, Daniel John 1950- *WhoHisp 94*
Villegas, Emilio 1943- *WhoHisp 94*
Villegas, J. Frank *WhoHisp 94*
Villegas, Joaquin 1946- *WhoHisp 94*
Villegas, Joel 1965- *WhoHisp 94*
Villegas, Kathryn Thompson 1907- *WhoAmP 93*
Villegas, Lucio d1968 *WhoHol 92*
Villegas, Patricia Soule-Perfect de 1922- *WhoHisp 94*
Villegas, Richard Junipero 1938- *WhoWest 94*
Villegas De Clercamp, Eric Auguste Marc Ghislain de 1924- *IntWW 93*
Villella, Edward 1936- *ConAu 140, IntDcB [port], IntWW 93, WhoHol 92*
Villella, Edward Joseph 1936- *WhoAm 94*
Villella, Gary Allen 1947- *WhoWest 94*
Villemejane, Bernard de 1930- *IntWW 93*
Villena, Isabel de 1430-1490 *BlmGWL*
Villena, Luis Antonio de 1951- *DcLB 134 [port]*
Villeneuve, Donald Avila 1930- *WhoAm 94, WhoWest 94*
Villeneuve, Gabrielle-Suzanne Barbot Gallon de d1755 *BlmGWL*
Villeret, Jacques *WhoHol 92*
Villers, Philippe 1935- *WhoAm 94*
Villeta-Trigo, Juan Altagracia 1952- *WhoFI 94*
Villforth, John Carl 1930- *WhoAm 94*
Villhard, Victor Joseph 1957- *WhoWest 94*
Villi, Olga d1989 *WhoHol 92*
Villiers *Who 94*
Villiers, Viscount 1948- *Who 94*
Villiers, Charles Nigel 1941- *Who 94*
Villiers, James 1930- *WhoHol 92*
Villiers, Kenneth 1912- *WhoHol 92*
Villiers, Mavis d1976 *WhoHol 92*
Villiers de l'Isle-Adam 1838-1889 *ShSCr 14 [port]*
Villiers De L'Isle-Adam, (Jean-Marie-Mathias-Philippe-Auguste, Comte de) 1840-1889 *EncSF 93*
Villiers de L'Isle-Adam, (Jean-Marie Mathias Philippe) Auguste (Comte) de 1838-1889 *RfGShF*
Villifranchi, Giovanni Cosimo 1646-1699 *NewGrDO*
Villines, Floyd G. *WhoAmP 93*
Villinger, Hermine 1849-1917 *BlmGWL*
Villinski, Paul 1960- *WhoAmA 93*
Villodas, Jack *WhoHisp 94*
Villon, Vladimar 1905-1976 *WhoAmA 93N*
Villoresi, Pamela *WhoHol 92*
Villum, Kjartan *ConWorW 93*
Villwock, Jeffrey Carlton 1954- *WhoFI 94*
Villwock, Kenneth James 1953- *WhoFI 94*
Vilnrotter, Victor Alpar 1944- *WhoWest 94*
Vilott, Rhondi *EncSF 93*
Vilsack, Tom *WhoAmP 93*
Vilter, Richard William 1911- *WhoAm 94*
Viltz, Edward Gerald 1947- *WhoBlA 94*
Vilzak, Anatole 1896- *IntDcB [port]*
Vimmerstedt, John Paul 1931- *WhoMW 93*
Vimond, Paul Marcel 1922- *IntWW 93*
Vimont, Jacques Pierre 1911- *IntWW 93*
Vimont, Richard Elgin 1936- *WhoAmL 94*
Vinaccesi, Benedetto c. 1666-1719 *NewGrDO*
Vinar, Benjamin 1935- *WhoAmL 94*
Vinas, Francisco 1863-1933 *NewGrDO*
Vinaver, Michel 1927- *ConWorW 93, IntDcT 2*
Vinay, Ramon 1912- *NewGrDO*
Vince, Clinton Andrew 1949- *WhoAm 94, WhoAmL 94*
Vince, George R. 1946- *WhoAmL 94*
Vince, Pruitt Taylor *WhoHol 92*
Vince, Robert E. 1930- *WhoAmP 93*
Vincenot, Louis d1967 *WhoHol 92*
Vincent, Alex *WhoHol 92*
Vincent, Allen d1979 *WhoHol 92*
Vincent, Andrew 1951- *ConAu 141*
Vincent, Anthony Lionel 1933- *Who 94*
Vincent, Brian Dale 1956- *WhoAmL 94*
Vincent, Bruce Havird 1947- *WhoFI 94*
Vincent, Charles 1933- *WhoBlA 94*
Vincent, Charles Eagar, Jr. 1940- *WhoAm 94*
Vincent, Clare 1935- *WhoAmA 93*
Vincent, Daniel Paul 1939- *WhoBlA 94*
Vincent, David Ridgely 1941- *WhoAm 94, WhoFI 94, WhoWest 94*
Vincent, Douglas 1916- *Who 94*
Vincent, Dwight Harold 1930- *WhoAmP 93*
Vincent, Edward 1920- *WhoAm 94*
Vincent, Edward 1934- *WhoAmP 93, WhoBlA 94, WhoWest 94*
Vincent, Ewart Albert 1919- *Who 94*
Vincent, Fay 1938- *WhoAm 94*
Vincent, Francis C. 1925- *WhoAmP 93*
Vincent, Francis T., Jr. 1938- *IntMPA 94*
Vincent, Francis Thomas, Jr. 1938- *IntWW 93, WhoAm 94*
Vincent, Frank *WhoHol 92*
Vincent, Frank Arthur 1948- *WhoMW 93*
Vincent, Frederick Michael 1948- *WhoScEn 94*
Vincent, Gene d1971 *WhoHol 92*
Vincent, George H. 1957- *WhoAmL 94*
Vincent, Hal Wellman 1927- *WhoAm 94*
Vincent, Harl 1893-1968 *EncSF 93*
Vincent, Helen *WhoAm 94*
Vincent, Helene *WhoHol 92*
Vincent, Henry 1862-1935 *AmSocL*
Vincent, Irvin James 1932- *Who 94*
Vincent, Irving H. 1934- *WhoBlA 94*
Vincent, Isabella 1735-1802 *NewGrDO*
Vincent, Ivor Francis Sutherland 1916- *Who 94*
Vincent, James d1957 *WhoHol 92*
Vincent, James Louis 1939- *WhoAm 94, WhoFI 94, WhoScEn 94*
Vincent, Jan-Michael 1945- *IntMPA 94, WhoHol 92*
Vincent, Jay Fletcher 1959- *WhoBlA 94*
Vincent, Jean-Pierre 1942- *IntWW 93*
Vincent, John (Russell) 1937- *WrDr 94*
Vincent, John C. 1942- *WhoAmP 93*
Vincent, John James 1929- *IntWW 93, Who 94, WrDr 94*
Vincent, John Joseph 1907- *Who 94*
Vincent, John Russell 1937- *IntWW 93, Who 94*
Vincent, June 1920- *WhoHol 92*
Vincent, Katharine 1918- *IntMPA 94*
Vincent, Larry d1975 *WhoHol 92*
Vincent, Larry R. 1941- *WhoAmP 93*
Vincent, Leonard Grange 1916- *Who 94*
Vincent, Lloyd Drexell 1924- *WhoAm 94*
Vincent, Marcus Alan 1956- *WhoWest 94*
Vincent, Marjorie Judith 1964- *WhoBlA 94*
Vincent, Mark Kent 1959- *WhoAmL 94, WhoWest 94*
Vincent, Norman Fuller 1930- *WhoAm 94*
Vincent, Norman L. 1933- *WhoAm 94*
Vincent, Olatunde Olabode 1925- *IntWW 93*
Vincent, Pierre 1955- *WhoAm 94*
Vincent, Richard (Frederick) 1931- *IntWW 93, Who 94*
Vincent, Robbie d1968 *WhoHol 92*
Vincent, Robert Carr 1930- *WhoAmP 93*
Vincent, Robert David 1942- *WhoAmP 93*
Vincent, Romo d1989 *WhoHol 92*
Vincent, Ruth 1878-1955 *NewGrDO*
Vincent, Sailor d1966 *WhoHol 92*
Vincent, Sam 1963- *WhoBlA 94*
Vincent, Scott Garrison 1958- *WhoFI 94*
Vincent, Stephen *DrAPF 93*
Vincent, Susan Gailey 1957- *WhoIns 94*
Vincent, Thomas James 1934- *WhoAm 94*
Vincent, Timothy Allen 1953- *WhoMW 93*
Vincent, Tony 1946- *WhoAm 94*
Vincent, Val D. 1948- *WhoAmP 93*
Vincent, Virginia *WhoHol 92*
Vincent, William (Percy Maxwell) 1945- *Who 94*
Vincent, William Ellsworth 1936- *WhoAm 94*
Vincent, Yves *WhoHol 92*
Vincent Brown, Kenneth *Who 94*
Vincent-Daviss, Diana d1993 *NewYTBS 93*
Vincenti, Sheldon Arnold 1938- *WhoAmL 94, WhoWest 94*
Vincenti, Walter Guido 1917- *WhoAm 94*
Vinci, John Nicholas 1937- *WhoAm 94*
Vinci, Leonardo c. 1696-1730 *NewGrDO*
Vinci, Leonardo da *WorInv*
Vinck, William Charles 1947- *WhoMW 93*
Vincze, L. Stephan 1957- *WhoAmL 94*
Vincze, Paul 1907- *Who 94*
Vinde, Pierre L. V. 1931- *IntWW 93*
Vine, Allyn Collins 1914- *WhoAm 94*
Vine, Barbara *BlmGWL*
Vine, Barbara 1930- *WrDr 94*
Vine, Billy d1958 *WhoHol 92*
Vine, Frederick John 1939- *Who 94*
Vine, John M. 1944- *WhoAmL 94*
Vine, Leo 1930- *WhoAmL 94*
Vine, Phyllis 1945- *WrDr 94*
Vine, Roy 1923- *Who 94*
Vine, (Roland) Stephen 1910- *Who 94*
Vineburgh, James Hollander 1943- *WhoAm 94*
Vinella, Ray 1933- *WhoAmA 93*
Vinelott, John (Evelyn) 1923- *Who 94*
Vinen, William Frank 1930- *Who 94*
Viner, Frank Lincoln 1937- *WhoAmA 93*
Viner, Mark William 1961- *WhoScEn 94*
Viner, Michael 1945- *IntMPA 94*
Viner, Monique Sylvaine 1926- *Who 94*
Vines, Bill *WhoAmP 93*
Vines, Charles Jerry 1937- *WhoAm 94*
Vines, David Anthony 1949- *IntWW 93, Who 94*
Vines, Doyle Ray 1947- *WhoWest 94*
Vines, Ellsworth 1911- *BuCMET [port]*
Vines, Eric Victor 1929- *Who 94*
Vines, Henry Ellsworth, III 1950- *WhoFI 94*
Vines, Pamela Lynn Dyson 1955- *WhoMW 93*
Vines, William (Joshua) 1916- *Who 94*
Vines, William Joshua 1916- *IntWW 93*
Viney, Anne Margaret 1926- *Who 94*
Viney, Elliott (Merriam) 1913- *Who 94*
Viney, John Alvin 1932- *WhoWest 94*
Vineyard, Susan Kay 1938- *WhoMW 93*
Vineyard, Timothy J. 1946- *WhoAmL 94*
Vinezeano, Frederick Carmen 1961- *WhoMW 93*
Ving, Lee *WhoHol 92*
Vinge, Joan (Carol) D(ennison) *TwCYAW*
Vinge, Joan (Carol) D(ennison) 1948- *EncSF 93, WrDr 94*
Vinge, Vernor (Steffen) 1944- *EncSF 93, WrDr 94*
Vingo, James Ray 1938- *WhoAm 94*
Vingoe, Francis James 1931- *WhoScEn 94*
Vinich, John Paul 1950- *WhoAmP 93*
Vinick, Fredric James 1947- *WhoScEn 94*
Vinicoff, Eric *EncSF 93*
Vinik, Hymie Ronald 1932- *WhoAm 94*
Vinik, Jeffrey *WhoAm 94, WhoFI 94*
Vining, Cronin Beals 1957- *WhoScEn 94*
Vining, Elizabeth Gray 1902- *TwCYAW, WhoAm 94, WrDr 94*
Vining, John 1758-1802 *WhAmRev*
Vining, John Kendall 1953- *WhoMW 93*
Vining, Joseph 1938- *WhoAm 94*
Vining, Robert Luke, Jr. 1931- *WhoAm 94, WhoAmL 94*
Vining, Rowena Adelaide 1921- *Who 94*
Vinitz, Jack d1978 *WhoHol 92*
Vinkemulder, H. Yvonne 1930- *WhoAmL 94*
Vinken, Pierre 1927- *IntWW 93*
Vinklar, Josef *WhoHol 92*
Vinnie c. 1971-
See Naughty by Nature *ConMus 11*
Vinocur, M. Richard 1934- *WhoAm 94*
Vinocur, Paul David 1948- *WhoAmL 94*
Vinogradov, Oleg 1937- *IntDcB [port]*
Vinogradov, Oleg Mikhailovich 1937- *IntWW 93*
Vinogradov, Vladimir Alekseyevich 1921- *IntWW 93*
Vinokur, Roman Yudkovich 1948- *WhoScEn 94*
Vinokurov, Evgeny Mikhailovich d1993 *IntWW 93N*
Vinovich, Steve *WhoHol 92*
Vinroot, Richard A. 1941- *WhoAmP 93*
Vinroot, Richard Allen 1941- *WhoAm 94*
Vinson, Baron 1931- *Who 94*
Vinson, Arlone Ann 1920- *WhoAmP 93*
Vinson, Bernard L. 1919- *WhoFI 94*
Vinson, C. Roger 1940- *WhoAm 94, WhoAmL 94*
Vinson, Chuck Rallen 1956- *WhoBlA 94*
Vinson, Gary d1984 *WhoHol 92*
Vinson, Helen 1907- *WhoHol 92*
Vinson, James Spangler 1941- *WhoAm 94, WhoMW 93*
Vinson, Jan d1981 *WhoHol 92*
Vinson, John William 1955- *WhoWest 94*
Vinson, Julius Ceasar 1926- *WhoBlA 94*
Vinson, Kathryn 1911- *WrDr 94*
Vinson, Laurence Duncan, Jr. 1947- *WhoAm 94*
Vinson, Rosalind Rowena 1962- *WhoBlA 94*
Vinson, William T. *WhoAm 94, WhoAmL 94, WhoFI 94*
Vint, Alan *WhoHol 92*
Vint, Bill *WhoHol 92*
Vint, Jesse *WhoHol 92*
Vint, Muriel Mosconi *WhoWest 94*
Vint, Robert James 1934- *WhoWest 94*
Vinter, Michael *EncSF 93*
Vinter, Peter *Who 94*
Vinter, (Frederick Robert) Peter 1914- *Who 94*
Vinton, Alfred Merton 1938- *Who 94*
Vinton, Alice Helen 1942- *WhoWest 94*
Vinton, Arthur d1963 *WhoHol 92*
Vinton, Bobby *WhoAm 94*
Vinton, Bobby 1935- *WhoHol 92*
Vinton, Horace d1930 *WhoHol 92*
Vinton, Will *IntDcF 2-4*
Vinyard, John Wesley 1945- *WhoFI 94*
Vinyard, Robert Austin 1945- *WhoAmP 93*
Vinz, Frank Louis 1932- *WhoScEn 94*
Vinz, Mark *DrAPF 93*
Vinzant, Janet Coble 1954- *WhoWest 94*
Vinzing, Ute 1936- *NewGrDO*
Viola, Bill 1951- *WhoAmA 93*
Viola, Frank John, Jr. 1960- *WhoAm 94*
Viola, Herman Joseph 1938- *WhoAm 94*
Viola, Lynne 1955- *WrDr 94*
Viola, Roberto Eduardo 1924- *IntWW 93*
Violante, Joseph Anthony 1950- *WhoAmL 94*
Violante, Lawrence Joseph 1924- *WhoFI 94, WhoWest 94*
Violet, Arlene 1943- *WhoAmP 93*
Violet, Woodrow Wilson, Jr. 1937- *WhoScEn 94, WhoWest 94*
Violette, Carol Ann 1956- *WhoScEn 94*
Violette, Elmer H. 1921- *WhoAmP 93*
Violette, Glenn Phillip 1950- *WhoScEn 94, WhoWest 94*
Violette, Paul Elmer 1955- *WhoAmP 93*
Violi, Paul *DrAPF 93*
Violinsky, Sol d1963 *WhoHol 92*
Viollet, Paul 1919- *IntWW 93*
Viornery, Pascal Andre 1954- *WhoFI 94*
Viorst, Judith 1931- *WrDr 94*
Viorst, Judith Stahl 1931- *WhoAm 94*
Viorst, Milton 1930- *WhoAm 94, WrDr 94*
Viot, Jacques Edmond 1921- *IntWW 93, Who 94*
Viot, Pierre 1925- *IntWW 93*
Viotti, Gino d1951 *WhoHol 92*
Viozzi, Giulio 1912-1984 *NewGrDO*
Vipond, William Richard 1963- *WhoAmL 94*
Vipulanandan, Cumaraswamy 1956- *WhoScEn 94*
Vique, Marc J. *WhoAmP 93*
Viramontes, Helena Maria 1954- *BlmGWL*
Viramontes, Julio Cesar *WhoHisp 94*
Virani, Nazmudin Gulamhusein 1948- *Who 94*
Virata, Cesar Enrique 1930- *IntWW 93*
Virchow, Rudolf Carl 1821-1902 *WorScD*
Virden, Peter Lowber, Jr. 1963- *WhoFI 94*
Virelli, Louis James, Jr. 1948- *WhoAmL 94*
Viren, John Joseph 1949- *WhoWest 94*
Viren, Lasse 1949- *IntWW 93*
Viret, Margaret Mary 1913- *WhoAmA 93*
Virga, Vincent *DrAPF 93*
Virgil 70BC-19BC *BlmGEL, NewGrDO*
Virgil, Ozzie 1933- *WhoHisp 94*
Virgil, Ozzie 1956- *WhoHisp 94*
Virgil, Robert L. *WhoFI 94*
Virgil, Scott Christopher 1965- *WhoScEn 94*
Virgil-Giron, Rebecca 1954- *WhoWomW 91*
Virgin, Keith Watson 1962- *WhoAmL 94*
Virgin Queen *BlmGEL*
Virgo, John Michael 1943- *WhoAm 94, WhoMW 93*
Virgo, Julie Anne Carroll 1944- *WhoAm 94*
Virgo, Katherine Sue 1959- *WhoMW 93*
Virgo, Peter *WhoHol 92*
Virgo, Peter, Jr. *WhoHol 92*
Virgona, Hank 1929- *WhoAmA 93*

Vogel, Charles-Louis-Adolphe 1808-1892 NewGrDO
Vogel, Charles Stimmel 1932- WhoAm 94
Vogel, Christian 1933- IntWW 93
Vogel, Daniel Girard 1963- WhoAmL 94
Vogel, David Jay 1947- WhoAm 94
Vogel, Donald S. 1917- WhoAmA 93
Vogel, Donald Stanley 1917- ConAu 141, WhoAm 94
Vogel, Edwin Chester 1883-1973 WhoAmA 93N
Vogel, Eleanore d1973 WhoHol 92
Vogel, Eric Leslie 1955- WhoWest 94
Vogel, Eugene L. 1931- WhoAm 94
Vogel, Eugenio Emilio 1946- WhoScEn 94
Vogel, Ezra F. 1930- WhoAm 94, WrDr 94
Vogel, Frank Edward 1949- WhoAmL 94
Vogel, Frederick John 1943- WhoAm 94
Vogel, Gerhard Hans 1927- WhoScEn 94
Vogel, H. Victoria WhoScEn 94
Vogel, Hans 1914- WrDr 94
Vogel, Hans-Jochen 1926- IntWW 93, Who 94
Vogel, Henry d1925 WhoHol 92
Vogel, Henry Elliott 1925- WhoAm 94
Vogel, Henry James 1920- WhoAm 94
Vogel, Herbert, Mr. 1922- & Dorothy, Vogel, Mrs. 1935- WhoAmA 93
Vogel, Howard H. 1949- WhoAm 94
Vogel, Howard Stanley 1934- WhoAmL 94, WhoFI 94
Vogel, Johann Christoph 1756?-1788 NewGrDO
Vogel, Johann Heinrich c. 1670-1726? NewGrDO
Vogel, John Arnold 1962- WhoWest 94
Vogel, John Henry 1944- WhoAm 94, WhoAmL 94, WhoFI 94
Vogel, John Walter 1948- WhoAmL 94
Vogel, Joseph 1911- WhoAmA 93
Vogel, Joseph Otto 1936- WhoAm 94
Vogel, Julius 1835-1899 EncSF 93
Vogel, Julius 1924- WhoAm 94
Vogel, Klaas Anko 1961- WhoFI 94
Vogel, Mitch 1956- WhoHol 92
Vogel, Nelson J., Jr. 1946- WhoAm 94, WhoAmL 94
Vogel, Orville Alvin 1907-1991 WhAm 10
Vogel, Paula 1951- ConLC 76 [port]
Vogel, Paula (Anne) 1951- ConDr 93
Vogel, Peter d1979 WhoHol 92
Vogel, Randy 1953- WhoAmP 93
Vogel, Randy Charles 1953- WhoWest 94
Vogel, Robert 1918- WhoAm 94
Vogel, Robert Lee 1934- WhoAm 94
Vogel, Roberta Burrage 1938- WhoBlA 94
Vogel, Ronald Bruce 1934- WhoScEn 94
Vogel, Rudolf d1967 WhoHol 92
Vogel, Rudolf 1918- IntWW 93
Vogel, Sarah WhoAmP 93
Vogel, Scott Alan 1953- WhoFI 94
Vogel, Steve 1946- WrDr 94
Vogel, Susan Mullin WhoAm 94
Vogel, Vickie Lynn 1951- WhoMW 93
Vogel, Victoria Rachel 1960- WhoAmL 94
Vogel, Werner Paul 1923- WhoFI 94
Vogel, William Alan 1951- WhoFI 94
Vogel, Wolfgang NewYTBS 93 [port]
Vogelaar, Carl Bengemin 1925- WhoWest 94
Vogeley, Clyde Eicher, Jr. 1917- WhoScEn 94
Vogelman, Joseph Herbert 1920- WhoAm 94, WhoFI 94
Vogelman, Lawrence Allen 1949- WhoAmL 94
Vogelpoel, Pauline Who 94
Vogels, Hanns Arnt 1926- IntWW 93
Vogelsang, Arthur DrAPF 93
Vogelsang, Gunter 1920- IntWW 93
Vogelstein, Bert WhoScEn 94
Vogelstrom, Fritz 1882-1963 NewGrDO
Vogelzang, Jeanne Marie 1950- WhoMW 93
Vogelzang, Nicholas John 1949- WhoMW 93
Vogh, James EncSF 93
Vogl, Adolf 1873-1961 NewGrDO
Vogl, Anna Katharina 1967- WhoScEn 94
Vogl, Don George 1929- WhoAmA 93
Vogl, Heinrich 1845-1900 NewGrDO
Vogl, Johann Michael 1768-1840 NewGrDO
Vogl, Otto 1927- WhoAm 94, WhoScEn 94
Vogl, Therese 1845-1921 NewGrDO
Vogler, Charles C. 1931- WhoAmP 93
Vogler, Frederick Wright 1931- WhoAm 94
Vogler, Georg Joseph 1749-1814 NewGrDO
Vogler, James R. 1952- WhoAm 94
Vogler, James Waylan 1948- WhoWest 94
Vogler, Karl Michael WhoHol 92
Vogler, Kevin Paul 1957- WhoWest 94
Vogler, Rudiger WhoHol 92
Vogler, Walter d1955 WhoHol 92
Vognild, Larry L. 1932- WhoAmP 93, WhoWest 94
Vogt, Carl W. WhoAmP 93
Vogt, Carl-Willi d1968 WhoHol 92
Vogt, Carl William 1936- WhoAm 94
Vogt, Diana J. 1952- WhoAmL 94
Vogt, Erich Wolfgang 1929- WhoAm 94, WhoScEn 94
Vogt, Evon Zartman, Jr. 1918- WhoAm 94
Vogt, Evon Zartman, III 1946- WhoFI 94, WhoWest 94
Vogt, Hans 1911- NewGrDO
Vogt, Hersleb 1912- IntWW 93
Vogt, John Henry 1918- WhoAm 94
Vogt, John W. 1936- WhoAmP 93
Vogt, Martha Diane 1952- WhoAmL 94
Vogt, Marthe Louise 1903- IntWW 93, Who 94
Vogt, Peter K. 1932- IntWW 93
Vogt, Peter W. 1949- WhoAmL 94
Vogt, Rochus Eugen 1929- WhoAm 94, WhoFI 94, WhoScEn 94, WhoWest 94
Vogt, William 1902-1968 EnvEnc
Vogten, Arnold Jozef Maria 1943- WhoMW 93
Vogt Lorentzen, Fredrik 1946- IntWW 93
Vogue, Robert WhoAmP 93
Vohra, Indu 1951- WhoAsA 94
Vohra, Ranbir WhoAsA 94
Vohra, Ranbir 1928- WhoAm 94
Vohra, Saroj Kumar 1947- WhoFI 94
Vohs, Cheree Rae 1963- WhoMW 93
Vohs, James Arthur 1928- IntWW 93, WhoAm 94
Vohs, Joan 1931- WhoHol 92
Voice, Jack Wilson, Jr. 1945- WhoWest 94
Voight, David K. 1941- WhoAmP 93
Voight, Elizabeth Anne 1944- WhoAmL 94
Voight, Jerry D. 1937- WhoAm 94
Voight, Jon 1938- IntMPA 94, IntWW 93, WhoAm 94, WhoHol 92
Voight, Nancy Lee 1945- WhoMW 93
Voigt, Cynthia 1942- TwCYAW, WhoAm 94, WrDr 94
Voigt, Donald Bernard 1947- WhoWest 94
Voigt, Ellen Bryant DrAPF 93
Voigt, Ellen Bryant 1943- WrDr 94
Voigt, Gale E. 1936- WhoAmP 93
Voigt, Hans-Dieter 1941- WhoScEn 94
Voigt, Hans-Heinrich 1921- IntWW 93
Voigt, John Jacob 1942- WhoFI 94
Voigt, Milton 1924- WhoWest 94, WrDr 94
Voigt, Paul Warren 1940- WhoAm 94
Voigt, Richard 1946- WhoAm 94
Voigt, Robert G. 1939- WhoScEn 94
Voigt, Scott Kenneth 1964- WhoWest 94
Voigt, Steven Russell 1952- WhoAmL 94
Voigt, Walter C. 1939- WhoWest 94
Voigt-Diederichs, Helene 1875-1961 BlmGWL
Voigtman, Edward George, Jr. 1949- WhoScEn 94
Voilquin, Suzanne 1801-1877 BlmGWL
Voinea, Radu 1923- IntWW 93
Voinov, Yury Nikolaevich 1931- LngBDD
Voinovich, George V. 1936- WhoAm 94, WhoAmP 93, WhoMW 93
Voinovich, Victor Steven, Sr. 1946- WhoMW 93
Voinovich, Vladimir (Nikolaevich) 1932- ConWorW 93, EncSF 93
Voisin-Lestringant, Emmanuelle Marie 1956- WhoScEn 94
Voiskunsky, Evgeny (L'Vovich) 1922- EncSF 93
Voit, Franz Johann, Jr. 1932- WhoFI 94
Voit, Karl von 1831-1908 WorScD
Voitle, Robert (Brown) 1919- WrDr 94
Voitle, Robert Allen 1938- WhoAm 94
Voiture, Vincent 1597-1648 GuFrLit 2
Vojak, Bruce Arthur 1955- WhoMW 93
Vojcak, Edward Daniel 1960- WhoScEn 94
Vojta, George J. 1935- WhoAm 94, WhoFI 94
Vojta, Paul Alan 1957- WhoScEn 94, WhoWest 94
Vojtech, Richard Joseph 1959- WhoScEn 94
Voke, Richard A. WhoAmP 93
Vokes, Harry d1922 WhoHol 92
Vokes, May d1957 WhoHol 92
Voketaitis, Arnold 1932- NewGrDO
Voketaitis, Arnold Mathew 1930- WhoAm 94
Vokins, Joan d1690 BlmGWL
Vokits, Bonnie Jean 1947- WhoMW 93
Voland, Herb d1981 WhoHol 92
Volanek, Antonin (Josef Alois) 1761-1817 NewGrDO
Volarich, David Thomas 1951- WhoMW 93
Volarich, Maria Anna 1963- WhoFI 94
Volberg, Herman William 1925- WhoScEn 94, WhoWest 94
Volborth, Alexis 1924- WhoWest 94
Volcker, Paul A. 1927- IntWW 93, Who 94, WhoAm 94, WhoAmP 93, WhoFI 94
Volckhausen, William Alexander 1937- WhoAm 94
Volckmann, David Boyd 1942- WhoWest 94
Volckmann, Peter Terrel 1941- WhoWest 94
Voldman, Steven Howard 1957- WhoFI 94, WhoScEn 94
Volente, Deo ConAu 142
Volentine, Debora Franklin 1962- WhoFI 94
Volentine, Kenneth Lee 1941- WhoAmP 93
Volentine, Richard J., Jr. 1955- WhoAmL 94
Volesky, Ron James 1954- WhoAmP 93
Volgenau, Douglas 1937- WhoAm 94
Volger, Hendrik Cornelis 1932- IntWW 93, Who 94
Volgy, Thomas John 1946- WhoAm 94, WhoWest 94
Volgy, Tom WhoAmP 93
Volicer, Ladislav 1935- WhoAm 94
Volid, Ruth WhoAmA 93
Volin, John Joseph 1956- WhoAmL 94
Volinin, Alexandre 1882-1955 IntDcB [port]
Volinine, Alexandre 1882-1955 IntDcB [port]
Voliva, Sharon Lee Grossman 1944- WhoMW 93
Volk, Cecilia Ann 1956- WhoMW 93
Volk, Claudia Jean 1947- WhoFI 94
Volk, David Joseph 1960- WhoAmL 94
Volk, David Lawrence 1947- WhoAmP 93
Volk, Eugene John 1931- WhoIns 94
Volk, Harry J. 1905- WhoAm 94
Volk, Jan WhoAm 94
Volk, John A. 1915- WhoAmP 93
Volk, Kenneth H. 1922- WhoAm 94, WhoAmL 94
Volk, Norman Hans 1935- WhoFI 94
Volk, Patricia DrAPF 93
Volk, Patricia 1943- IntWW 93
Volk, Patricia (Gay) 1943- ConAu 140
Volk, Robert Harkins 1932- WhoFI 94, WhoWest 94
Volk, Stephen Richard 1936- WhoAm 94
Volkan, Kevin 1958- WhoWest 94
Volkenstein, Mikhail Vladimirovich d1992 IntWW 93N
Volker, Dale M. 1940- WhoAmP 93
Volker, Franz 1899-1965 NewGrDO
Volker, Joseph Francis 1913-1989 WhAm 10
Volker, Todd David 1963- WhoMW 93
Volkerding, Laura 1939- WhoAmA 93
Volkers, Burton Jay 1957- WhoMW 93
Volkersz, Willem 1939- WhoAmA 93
Volkert, Franz (Joseph) 1778-1845 NewGrDO
Volkert, Michael Rudolf 1949- WhoScEn 94
Volkhardt, John Malcolm 1917- WhoAm 94
Volkholz, Sybille 1944- WhoWomW 91
Volkie, Ralph d1987 WhoHol 92
Volkin, Hilda Appel 1933- WhoAmA 93
Volkland, Gregory Erle 1945- WhoMW 93
Volkman, Alvin 1926- WhoScEn 94
Volkman, Beatrice Kramer 1940- WhoAm 94
Volkman, David J. 1945- WhoScEn 94
Volkman, Ernest 1940- WrDr 94
Volkman, Ivan d1972 WhoHol 92
Volkmann, Daniel George, Jr. 1924- WhoAm 94
Volkmann, Frances Cooper 1935- WhoAm 94
Volkmar, Leon 1879-1959 WhoAmA 93N
Volkmer, Harold L. 1931- CngDr 93, WhoAm 94, WhoAmP 93, WhoMW 93
Volkoff, George Michael 1914- WhoAm 94
Volkogonov, Dmitri Antonovich 1928- IntWW 93
Volkogonov, Dmitry Antonovich 1928- LngBDD
Volkov, Nikolai WhoHol 92
Volkov, Nikolai Mikhailovich 1951- LngBDD
Volkov, Vyacheslav Vasilevich LngBDD
Volkova, Bronislava DrAPF 93
Volkova, Vera 1904-1975 IntDcB
Voll, John Obert 1936- WhoAm 94
Voll, Michael John 1950- WhoAmP 93
Vollack, Anthony F. WhoAmP 93
Vollack, Anthony F. 1929- WhoAmL 94, WhoWest 94
Vollen, Robert Jay 1940- WhoAm 94
Vollenweider, Richard 1922- EnvEnc
Vollenweider, Richard Albert 1922- WhoAm 94
Vollero, Richard 1938- WhoAmL 94
Vollerthun, Georg 1876-1945 NewGrDO
Vollhardt, Kurt Peter Christian 1946- WhoAm 94, WhoWest 94
Vollman, James William 1952- WhoMW 93
Vollmann, William T. 1959- EncSF 93, WrDr 94
Vollmar, John Raymond 1929- WhoAm 94
Vollmer, Denise Kay 1957- WhoMW 93
Vollmer, Howard Robert 1930- WhoMW 93
Vollmer, James 1924- WhoAm 94
Vollmer, Richard Wade 1926- WhoAm 94, WhoAmL 94
Vollmer, Ruth d1982 WhoAmA 93N
Vollrath, Lutz Ernst Wolf 1936- Who 94
Vollum, Robert Boone 1933- WhoFI 94
Volman, David Herschel 1916- WhoAm 94
Volmer, Nancy Kay 1960- WhoWest 94
Volney, Taylor 1939- WhoAm 94
Volny, Zdenek EncSF 93
Volodin, Alexander 1919- IntDcT 2
Volonte, Gian Maria 1933- IntMPA 94, WhoHol 92
Volontir, Mikhai 1934- IntWW 93
Voloshin, Alex d1960 WhoHol 92
Volp, Patricia Marie 1950- WhoMW 93
Volpe, Angelo Anthony 1938- WhoAm 94
Volpe, Edmond Loris 1922- WhoAm 94
Volpe, Erminio Peter 1927- WhoAm 94, WhoScEn 94
Volpe, Frederick d1932 WhoHol 92
Volpe, Giovanni Battista c. 1620-c. 1691 NewGrDO
Volpe, Joseph WhoAm 94
Volpe, Joseph John 1938- WhoAm 94
Volpe, Loretta Ann 1954- WhoAm 94
Volpe, Peter Anthony 1936- WhoAm 94
Volpe, Ralph Pasquale 1936- WhoFI 94
Volpe, Richard Gerard 1950- WhoWest 94
Volpe, Robert 1926- WhoAm 94, WhoScEn 94
Volpe, Robert 1942- WhoAmA 93
Volpe, Thomas J. 1935- WhoAm 94
Volpe, Vernon L(ewis) 1955- WrDr 94
Volpert, Mary Katherine 1959- WhoMW 93
Volpert, Richard Sidney 1935- WhoAm 94, WhoWest 94
Volpi, Walter Mark 1946- WhoAm 94, WhoAmL 94
Volpicelli, Frederick Gabriel 1946- WhoScEn 94
Volpicelli, Stephen L. 1945- WhoAm 94
Volpin, Aleksandr Sergeyevich (Esenin-) 1924- IntWW 93
Volponi, Paolo 1924- ConWorW 93
Volsky, Arkadiy Ivanovich 1932- IntWW 93
Volsky, Arkady Ivanovich 1932- LngBDD
Volsky, Viktor Vatslavovich 1921- IntWW 93
Volstad, John WhoHol 92
Volta, Alessandro 1745-1827 WorInv, WorScD [port]
Voltaire 1694-1778 BlmGEL, EncSF 93, GuFrLit 2, IntDcT 2, NewGrDO, ShSCr 12 [port]
Voltaire (Francois Marie Arouet de) 1694-1778 EncEth
Volter, Philippe WhoHol 92
Voltmer, Michael Dale 1952- WhoScEn 94
Voltura, Gerald Anthony 1965- WhoWest 94
Voltz, Sterling Ernest 1921- WhoScEn 94
Voluck, Allan S. WhoFI 94
Voluse, Charles Rodger, III 1943- WhoAm 94
Volz, Charles Harvie, Jr. 1925- WhoAm 94
Volz, Jim 1953- WhoWest 94
Volz, Marlin Milton 1917- WhoAm 94
Volz, Nedra WhoHol 92
Volz, William Harry 1946- WhoAm 94
Volzke, Doris Matilda 1921- WhoAmP 93
Vomacka, Boleslav 1887-1965 NewGrDO
vom Baur, Francis Trowbridge 1908- WhoAm 94
Vomhof, Daniel William 1938- WhoWest 94
Von Alemann, Mechthild 1937- WhoWomW 91
Von Alten, Ferdinand d1933 WhoHol 92
Von Ambesser, Axel d1988 WhoHol 92
Vonarburg, Elisabeth 1947- EncSF 93
Von Aroldingen, Karin 1941- IntDcB [port]
von Arx, Dolph William 1934- WhoAm 94, WhoFI 94
von Baeyer, Hans Christian 1938- ConAu 41NR
Von Barghan, Barbara 1949- WhoAmA 93
Von Baudissin, Wolf 1907- IntWW 93
Von Beckh, Harald J. 1917- IntWW 93
Von Behren, Linda Marie 1948- WhoMW 93

Von Berg, Robert Lee 1918- *WhoScEn 94*
Von Bergen Wessels, Pennie Lea 1949-
WhoAmP 93
Von Berne, Eva d1930? *WhoHol 92*
von Bernuth, Carl W. *WhoAm 94,*
WhoAmL 94, WhoFI 94
von Bernuth, Robert Dean 1946-
WhoMW 93, WhoScEn 94
von Bittenfeld *Who 94*
Von Block, Bela d1962 *WhoHol 92*
Von Blondel, Sacy d1983 *WhoHol 92*
von Brandenstein, Patrizia *ConTFT 11,*
WhoAm 94
von Braun, Wernher *WorInv*
von Brecht, Forrest Godfrey 1913-
WhoFI 94
Von Brincken, Wilhelm d1946
WhoHol 92
von Brock, A. Raymond 1922- *WhoAm 94*
Von Bulow, Andreas 1937- *IntWW 93*
von Bulow, Michael 1960- *WhoFI 94*
Vonch, David Lee 1931- *WhoFI 94*
von Clemm, Michael 1935- *Who 94,*
WhoAm 94, WhoFI 94
von Cramm, Gottfried 1909-1976
BuCMET
von Dalin, Olof *EncSF 93*
von Daniken, Erich 1935- *EncSF 93*
von dem Bussche, Axel d1993
NewYTBS 93
Von Der Dunk, Hermann Walther 1928-
IntWW 93
Von Der Golz, Jan *WhoAmA 93*
VonderHaar, William Purcell 1930-
WhoAm 94
Vonderheid, Arda Elizabeth 1925-
WhoAm 94
von der Heyden, Karl Mueller Ingolf
1936- *WhoAm 94, WhoFI 94*
von der Heydt, James Arnold 1919-
WhoAm 94
Von Der Lancken, Frank 1872-1950
WhoAmA 93N
Vonderohe, Alan Paul 1947- *WhoAm 94*
von Destinon, Mark Alan 1956-
WhoWest 94
Von Diossy, Arthur d1940 *WhoHol 92*
Von Dohlen, Lenny 1958- *WhoHol 92*
Von Dohlen, Tim 1943- *WhoAmP 93*
Von Dohnanyi, Christoph 1929-
IntWW 93, WhoAm 94, WhoMW 93
Von Dohnanyi, Klaus 1928- *IntWW 93*
Vondra, Lawrence Steven 1963-
WhoScEn 94
Vondra, Vladimir 1930- *IntWW 93*
Vondrak, Robert Richard 1949-
WhoWest 94
Vondrasek, Frank Charles, Jr. 1928-
WhoAm 94
Von Drehle, Ramon Arnold 1930-
WhoAm 94
Vondruska, Eloise Marie 1950-
WhoMW 93
Von Eckardt, Wolf 1918- *WhoAm 94*
Voneida, Jane Diane 1944- *WhoMW 93*
von Eiff, Theodore William 1942-
WhoAm 94
von Elbe, Joachim 1902- *WrDr 94*
Von Eltz, Theodore d1964 *WhoHol 92*
Von Ende, Carl H. 1942- *WhoAm 94,*
WhoAmL 94
Von Eschen, Robert Leroy 1936-
WhoScEn 94
Vonesh, Raymond James 1916-1991
WhAm 10
Von Eye, Rochelle Kay 1949- *WhoMW 93*
von Ferstel, Marilou McCarthy 1937-
WhoAm 94
Von Fischer, George Herman 1935-
WhoScEn 94
von Fraunhofer-Kosinski, Katherina
WhoAm 94
von Frisch, Karl (Ritter) *ConAu 42NR*
Von Fuehrer, Ottmar F. d1967
WhoAmA 93N
von Fuerer-Haimendorf, Christoph 1909-
WrDr 94
von Furstenberg, Betsy 1931- *WhoAm 94*
von Furstenberg, Betsy 1935- *WhoHol 92*
Von Furstenberg, Diane
NewYTBS 93 [port]
von Furstenberg, Diane 1946-
News 94-2 [port]
Von Furstenberg, Diane Simone Michelle
1946- *WhoAm 94*
von Furstenberg, George Michael 1941-
WhoAm 94
Von Gersdorf, Frederich Johann, Jr.
d1951 *WhoHol 92*
Von Gierke, Henning Edgar 1917-
WhoAm 94
Von Glahn, Gerhard Ernst 1911- *WrDr 94*
Von Glahn, Keith G. 1952- *WhoAm 94,*
WhoAmL 94
Von Goeler, Eberhard 1930- *WhoScEn 94*
Von Gremp, Jim 1949- *WhoAmP 93*
von Grimmelshausen, Johann Jakob
Christoffel *EncSF 93*

Vongsay, Kithong 1937- *IntWW 93*
von Guericke, Otto *WorInv, WorScD*
von Gunden, Kenneth 1946- *EncSF 93*
Vo Nguyen Giap, Gen. 1912- *IntWW 93*
von Haartman, Harry Ulf 1942-
WhoWest 94
von Hanstein, Otfried *EncSF 93*
von Harbou, Thea 1888-1954 *EncSF 93,*
IntDcF 2-4 [port]
von Harz, James Lyons 1915- *WhoAm 94,*
WhoFI 94
von Hase, Karl-Gunther 1917- *Who 94*
Von Hassel, George A. 1929- *WhoIns 94*
von Helmburg, Roger Lyle 1931-
WhoMW 93, WhoScEn 94
von Helmholtz, Hermann *WorScD*
Von Hernried, Paul *WhoHol 92*
Von Hernried Ritter Von
Wasel-Waldingau, Paul Georg Julius
WhAm 10
Von Herzen, Richard Pierre 1930-
WhoAm 94
Von Hilsheimer, George Edwin, III 1934-
WhoScEn 94
Von Hippel, Arthur Robert 1898-
WhAm 10
Von Hippel, Frank Niels 1937-
WhoAm 94, WhoScEn 94
von Hippel, Peter Hans 1931- *WhoAm 94,*
WhoWest 94
Von Hirschberg, C. F. G. 1926- *IntWW 93*
von Hoffman, Nicholas 1929- *WhoAm 94,*
WrDr 94
Von Holden, Martin Harvey 1942-
WhoAm 94
Von Jost, Alexander 1889-1968
WhoAmA 93N
Vonk, Hans 1942- *NewGrDO*
von Kalinowski, Julian Onesime 1916-
WhoAm 94, WhoAmL 94, WhoFI 94,
WhoWest 94
Von Kaminsky, Elaine Isabelle 1963-
WhoFI 94, WhoWest 94
von Kann, Clifton Ferdinand 1915-
WhoAm 94
von Kappelhoff, Doris 1924- *WhoAm 94*
Von Karajan, Herbert d1989 *WhoHol 92*
Von Karajan, Herbert 1908-1989
WhAm 10
von Kehl, Inge 1933- *WhoScEn 94*
von Khuon, Ernst *EncSF 93*
Von Klaussen, Ronald *WhoHol 92*
von Klemperer, Klemens 1916-
WhoAm 94
Von Klitzing, Klaus 1943- *IntWW 93,*
Who 94
von Knorring, Henrik Johan 1943-
WhoAm 94
Von Koczian, Johanna 1933- *WhoHol 92*
Von Kotzebue, August *IntDcT 2*
von Krenner, Walther G. 1940-
WhoWest 94
von Kunheim, Eberhard 1928- *Who 94*
von Kutzleben, Siegfried Edwin 1920-
WhoScEn 94
von Lang, Frederick William 1929-
WhoMW 93
Von Laue, Theodore H 1916- *WrDr 94*
Von Laue, Theodore Herman 1916-
WhoAm 94
Von Ledebur, Leopold d1955 *WhoHol 92*
Von Leer, Hunter *WhoHol 92*
von Leyden, Wolfgang (Marius) 1911-
WrDr 94
von Linsowe, Marina Dorothy 1952-
WhoFI 94, WhoScEn 94
Von Losberg, Les *DrAPF 93*
Von Losberg, Lester Charles, Jr. 1947-
WhoFI 94
Von Losch, Maria Magdalena *WhAm 10*
von Mallinckrodt, Georg Wilhelm 1930-
Who 94
von Meduna *EncSPD*
von Mehren, Arthur Taylor 1922-
WhoAm 94, WrDr 94
von Mehren, George M. 1950-
WhoAm 94, WhoAmL 94
von Mehren, Robert Brandt 1922-
WhoAm 94
von Mering, Otto Oswald 1922-
WhoAm 94
Von Meyerinck, Hubert d1971
WhoHol 92
von Minckwitz, Bernhard 1944-
WhoAm 94
Von Minden, Merle *WhoAmP 93*
Von Minden, Milton Charles, Jr. 1936-
WhoWest 94
Von Mohr, Stephen Joseph, III 1947-
WhoAm 94
von Moltke, Helmuth James 1907-1945
ConAu 140
Vonn, Veola *WhoHol 92*
Von Nagy, Kaethe 1909- *WhoHol 92*
Vonnegut, Kurt *DrAPF 93*
Vonnegut, Kurt, Jr. 1922- *AmCulL,*
ConDr 93, EncSF 93, IntWW 93,

TwCYAW, Who 94, WhoAm 94,
WhoHol 92, WrDr 94
von Neumann, John *WorInv, WorScD*
von Neupauer, Joseph Ritter *EncSF 93*
Von Noe, Margarethe Schell *WhoHol 92*
von Ohain, Hans Joachim 1911-
WhoAm 94
von Ohain, Hans Joachim P. 1911-
WhoScEn 94
Von Otter, Anne Sofie 1955- *IntWW 93,*
Who 94
von Pagenhardt, Robert 1923-
WhoWest 94
Von Palen, Anna d1939 *WhoHol 92*
Von Palleske, Heidi *WhoHol 92*
Von Passenheim, John Burr 1964-
WhoAmL 94, WhoWest 94
Von Raab, William 1942- *WhoAmP 93*
von Rachen, Kurt *EncSF 93*
Von Reichbauer, Peter *WhoAmP 93*
von Reichbauer, Peter Graves 1944-
WhoWest 94
Von Reinhold, Calvin 1927- *WhoHol 92*
von Reitzenstein, Hans-Joachim Freiherr
Who 94
von Rhein, John Richard 1945-
WhoAm 94
Von Riesemann, Walter Arthur 1930-
WhoWest 94
Von Riesen, Daniel D. 1943- *WhoScEn 94*
Von Ringelheim, Paul Helmut *WhoAm 94,*
WhoAmA 93
Von Ritzau, Erik d1936 *WhoHol 92*
Von Roenn, Kelvin Alexander 1949-
WhoMW 93
Von Rosen, Elsa Marianne 1924- *IntDcB*
Von Rothkirch, Edward 1919- *IntMPA 94*
Von Rotz, Richard Alan 1956- *WhoFI 94*
Von Rydingsvard, Ursula 1942-
WhoAmA 93
von Sadovszky, Otto Joseph 1925-
WhoAm 94
von Schack, Wesley W. 1944- *WhoAm 94,*
WhoFI 94
VonSchimmelmann, Ronald Harold
1940- *WhoFI 94*
Von Schlabrendorff, Fabian Gotthard
Herbert 1944- *IntWW 93*
Von Schlegell, David 1920-1992
WhAm 10, WhoAmA 93N
Von Schletton, Hans Adalbert *WhoHol 92*
Von Schmidt, Eric 1931- *WhoAmA 93*
Von Schoultz, Solveig *ConWorW 93*
von Schramek, Eric (Emil) 1921- *Who 94*
von Schubert, Andreas 1922- *WhoFI 94*
von Schuller-Goetzburg, Viktorin Wolfgan
1924- *WhoScEn 94*
von Segesser, Ludwig Karl 1952-
WhoScEn 94
von Seldeneck, Judith Metcalfe 1940-
WhoAm 94, WhoFI 94
Von Seyffertitz, Gustav d1943 *WhoHol 92*
von Siemens, Ernst Werner *WorInv*
Vonsovskiy, Sergey Vasiliyevich 1910-
IntWW 93
von Sprecher, Andreas 1951- *WhoScEn 94*
Von Stade, Frederica 1945- *IntWW 93,*
NewGrDO [port], WhoAm 94
Von Stroh, Gordon E. 1943- *WhoFI 94*
Von Stroheim, Erich d1957 *WhoHol 92*
Von Stroheim, Erich, Jr. d1968
WhoHol 92
von Studnitz, Gilbert Alfred 1950-
WhoWest 94
Von Sydow, Max 1929- *IntMPA 94,*
WhoAm 94, WhoHol 92
Von Taaffe-Rossmann, Cosima T. 1944-
WhoScEn 94
Von Tersch, Frances Knight 1963-
WhoScEn 94
Von Tersch, Lawrence Wayne 1923-
WhoAm 94
Von Thellmann, Erika d1988 *WhoHol 92*
von Tilsit, Heidemarie 1944- *WhoWest 94*
Von Tilzer, Harry d1946 *WhoHol 92*
von Trojan, Kurt 1937- *EncSF 93*
Von Trotta, Margarethe 1942- *IntMPA 94,*
IntWW 93
von Tungeln, George Robert 1931-
WhoAm 94
Von Viczay, Marika Ilona 1935-
WhoScEn 94
von Voss, Julius *EncSF 93*
Von Wagenheim, Gustav d1975
WhoHol 92
Von Wald, Larry M. 1944- *WhoAmL 94*
Von Wald, Richard B. *WhoFI 94*
von Waldow, Arnd N. 1957- *WhoAmL 94*

von Wechmar, Rudiger 1923- *Who 94*
Von Weise, Wenda Fraker 1941-
WhoAmA 93N
von Weizsacker, Carl-Friedrich 1912-
Who 94
von Weizsacker, Ernst Ulrich 1939-
WhoScEn 94
Von Weizsacker, Richard 1920- *Who 94*
Von Wicht, John 1888-1970
WhoAmA 93N
Von Wiegand, Charmion 1898-1983
WhoAmA 93N
von Wilpert, Gero 1933- *IntWW 93*
von Winckler, Beverly Ann Purnell 1935-
WhoFI 94
Von Winkle, William Anton 1928-
WhoScEn 94
von Winterfeldt, (Hans) Dominik 1937-
Who 94
Von Winterstein, Eduard d1961
WhoHol 92
Von Zell, Harry d1981 *WhoHol 92*
von Zeppelin, Ferdinand *WorInv*
Von Zerneck, Danielle 1965- *WhoHol 92*
Von Zerneck, Frank 1940- *IntMPA 94*
von Zerneck, Frank Ernest 1940-
WhoAm 94
Von Zerneck, Peter 1908- *WhoHol 92*
Von Zur Muehien, Peter 1939-
WhoAmA 93
Von Zur Muehlen, Bernis Susan 1942-
WhoAmA 93
Von Zur Muhlen, Alexander Meinhard
1936- *WhoScEn 94*
von Zweck, Dina *DrAPF 93*
Voo, Liming M. 1959- *WhoScEn 94*
Vook, Frederick Ludwig 1931- *WhoAm 94*
Vook, Frederick Werner 1966-
WhoScEn 94
Voorhees, Donald Edward 1926-
WhoAm 94
Voorhees, Donald Shirley 1916-1989
WhAm 10
Voorhees, Enders McClumpha 1891-1980
EncABHB 9 [port]
Voorhees, Frank Ray 1935- *WhoScEn 94*
Voorhees, Harold J., Sr. *WhoAmP 93*
Voorhees, James Dayton, Jr. 1917-
WhoAm 94
Voorhees, John H. 1936- *AfrAmG [port]*
Voorhees, John Henry 1936- *WhoAm 94,*
WhoBlA 94
Voorhees, John Schenck 1923- *WhoAm 94*
Voorhees, Josephine Palmer 1894-
WhAm 10
Voorhees, Lee R., Jr. 1937- *WhoAm 94*
Voorhees, Lorraine Isobel 1947-
WhoWest 94
Voorhees, Richard Lesley 1941-
WhoAm 94, WhoAmL 94
Voorhees, Vernon W., II 1942- *WhoIns 94*
Voorhies, E. Gregory 1952- *WhoAm 94*
Voorn, John Cornell 1944- *WhoAmL 94*
Voorn, Randall Jay 1946- *WhoMW 93*
Voorsanger, Bartholomew 1937-
WhoAm 94, WhoAmA 93
Voortman, John J. 1931- *WhoAm 94*
Voos, Paula Beth 1949- *WhoFI 94*
Voos, William John 1930- *WhoAm 94,*
WhoAmA 93
Voots, Terry Lynne 1956- *WhoScEn 94*
Vora, Ashok 1947- *WhoAm 94, WhoFI 94*
Vora, Manhar Morarji 1948- *WhoScEn 94*
Vora, Manu Kishandas 1945-
WhoScEn 94
Vora, Motilal 1928- *IntWW 93*
Vora, Narendra Mohanlal 1947-
WhoAsA 93
Vora, Pramathesh S. 1946- *WhoAsA 93*
Voran, Joel Bruce 1952- *WhoAmL 94*
Vorbrich, Lynn Karl 1939- *WhoAm 94,*
WhoFI 94
Vorbrueggen, Helmut Ferdinand 1930-
WhoScEn 94
Vorburger, Theodore Vincent 1944-
WhoScEn 94
Vorder-Bruegge, Frederick Mark, Jr.
1953- *WhoAmL 94*
Vorderbruggen, Alan Joseph 1963-
WhoMW 93
Vore, Ronald Eugene 1950- *WhoWest 94*
Vorenberg, Alan R. 1951- *WhoWest 94*
Vorenberg, James 1928- *WhoAm 94,*
WhoAmL 94
Vorfolomeev, Vladimir Petrovich 1934-
LngBDD
Vorhauer, Delia Villegas 1940-
WhoHisp 94
Vorhees, Francine Barbara 1956-
WhoWest 94
Vorhies, Carl Brad 1949- *WhoWest 94*
Vorhies, Jack McKim 1923- *WhoMW 93*
Vorhies, John R(oyal Harris) 1920-
EncSF 93
Vorhies, Mahlon Wesley 1937-
WhoAm 94, WhoScEn 94
Vorholt, Jeffrey Joseph 1953- *WhoAm 94,*
WhoAmL 94, WhoFI 94

Vories, Dennis Lynn 1952- *WhoWest 94*
Vories, Eugene Capps 1923- *WhoAmP 93*
Voris, Anna Maybelle 1920-1989 *WhAm 10*
Voris, David Woodrow 1951- *WhoFI 94*
Voris, Mark 1907-1974 *WhoAmA 93N*
Voris, William 1924- *WhoAm 94, WhoFI 94, WhoWest 94*
Vorkapich, Slavko 1895-1976 *IntDcF 2-4*
Vorlova, Slava 1894-1973 *NewGrDO*
Vorndam, Paul Eric 1947- *WhoScEn 94*
Vornholt, John *EncSF 93*
Vornle von Haagenfels, John P. 1958- *WhoFI 94*
Vorobev, Andrei Ivanovich 1928- *LngBDD*
Vorobev, Eduard Arkadevich 1938- *LngBDD*
Vorobev, Vasily Vasilevich 1946- *LngBDD*
Vorobyov, Ivan Alekseyevich 1921- *IntWW 93*
Vorob'yova, Anna Yakovlevna *NewGrDO*
Voronkov, Mikhail Grigorevich 1921- *IntWW 93*
Voronov, Avenir Arkadyevich d1992 *IntWW 93N*
Vorontsov, Yuli Mikhailovich 1929- *LngBDD*
Vorontsov, Yuliy Mikhailovich 1929- *IntWW 93*
Voros, Gerald John 1930- *WhoAm 94*
Vorotnikov, Vitaliy Ivanovich 1926- *IntWW 93*
Vorpagel, Wilbur Charles 1926- *WhoWest 94*
Vorres, Karl Spyros 1927- *WhoMW 93*
Vorsanger, Fred S. 1928- *WhoAm 94*
Vorse, Mary Marvin Heaton 1874-1966 *AmSocL*
Vorster, Balthazar Johannes 1915-1983 *HisWorL [port]*
Vorster, Gordon d1988 *WhoHol 92*
Vorster, Gordon 1924- *WrDr 94*
Vorva, Jerry *WhoAmP 93*
Vorwerk, E. Charlsie 1934- *WhoAmA 93*
Vorys, Arthur I. 1923- *WhoIns 94*
Vorys, Arthur Isaiah 1923- *WhoAm 94, WhoAmL 94*
Vorys, John Carpenter 1953- *WhoAmL 94, WhoMW 93*
Vos, Frank 1919- *WhoAm 94*
Vos, Geoffrey Charles 1955- *Who 94*
Vos, Geoffrey Michael 1927- *Who 94*
Vos, Hubert Daniel 1933- *WhoAm 94, WhoFI 94*
Vos, Morris 1944- *WhoAm 94*
Vosbeck, Robert Randall 1930- *WhoAm 94*
Vosburgh, Alfred d1958 *WhoHol 92*
Vosburgh, David *WhoHol 92*
Vosburgh, Frederick George 1904- *WhoAm 94*
Vosburgh, Harold d1926 *WhoHol 92*
Voscherau, Henning 1941- *IntWW 93*
Vose, Harry L. 1927- *WhoAmP 93*
Vose, Joseph 1738-1816 *WhAmRev*
Vose, Robert C. 1873-1965 *WhoAmA 93N*
Vose, Robert Churchill, Jr. 1911- *WhoAm 94, WhoAmA 93*
Voshell, Robert J. 1933- *WhoAmP 93*
Voskovec, George d1981 *WhoHol 92*
Voskuhl, Sean 1966- *WhoAmP 93*
Vosler, Deborah 1957- *WhoAm 94*
Vosper, F. Kent 1921- *WhoAmP 93*
Vosper, Frank d1937 *WhoHol 92*
Vosper, John d1954 *WhoHol 92*
Vosper, Robert Gordon 1913- *WhoAm 94, WhoFI 94*
Voss, Anne Coble 1946- *WhoMW 93*
Voss, Barry Vaughan 1952- *WhoAmL 94*
Voss, Carl Hermann 1910- *WhoAm 94*
Voss, Dawn 1957- *WhoMW 93*
Voss, Edward William, Jr. 1933- *WhoAm 94*
Voss, Frank d1917 *WhoHol 92*
Voss, Gordon Owen 1938- *WhoAmP 93*
Voss, Jack Donald 1921- *WhoAm 94, WhoFI 94*
Voss, James Frederick 1930- *WhoAm 94*
Voss, James Leo 1934- *WhoAm 94*
Voss, James Milton d1993 *NewYTBS 93*
Voss, Jerrold Richard 1932- *WhoAm 94, WhoMW 93*
Voss, John 1917- *WhoAm 94*
Voss, Jurgen 1936- *WhoScEn 94*
Voss, Omer Gerald 1916- *WhoAm 94*
Voss, Paul Joseph 1943- *WhoScEn 94*
Voss, Regis Dale 1931- *WhoAm 94, WhoMW 93*
Voss, Steven Ronald 1962- *WhoScEn 94*
Voss, Terence J. 1942- *WhoScEn 94*
Voss, Werner 1949- *WhoScEn 94*
Voss, Werner Konrad Karl 1935- *WhoScEn 94*
Voss, William Charles 1937- *WhoAm 94, WhoFI 94*
Voss, William R. 1951- *WhoAm 94, WhoFI 94*

Vossberg, Arthur Edmund, III 1951- *WhoAmL 94*
Vossel, Richard Alan 1953- *WhoScEn 94*
Vossler, John Albert 1925- *WhoScEn 94*
Vossoughi, Shapour 1945- *WhoMW 93, WhoScEn 94*
Vostrak, Zbynek 1920-1985 *NewGrDO*
Votava, Cari Lynn 1957- *WhoAmL 94*
Votava, Thomas Anthony 1925- *WhoMW 93*
Votaw, Carmen Delgado *WhoHisp 94*
Votaw, Charles Lesley 1929- *WhoAm 94*
Votaw, Dow 1920- *WrDr 94*
Voth, Alden H. 1926- *WhoWest 94*
Voth, Andrew C. 1947- *WhoWest 94*
Votolato, Arthur Nicholas, Jr. 1930- *WhoAm 94, WhoAmL 94*
Votre, Kenneth Alan 1960- *WhoAmL 94*
Votrian, Peter *WhoHol 92*
Votto, Antonino 1896-1985 *NewGrDO*
Vought, Franklin Kipling 1965- *WhoScEn 94*
Voulkos, Peter 1924- *WhoAm 94, WhoAmA 93, WhoWest 94*
Voultsos-Vourtzis, Pericles 1910- *WhoAm 94*
Vounas, Ronald R. 1936- *WhoIns 94*
Vourvoulias, Joyce Bush *WhoAmA 93*
Voute, William Joseph 1938-1992 *WhAm 10*
Voutilainen, Erkki Juhani 1946- *WhoWest 94*
Voutilainen, Pertti Juhani 1940- *IntWW 93*
Voutsas, Alexander Matthew *WhoFI 94*
Voutsas, Apostolos Theoharis 1966- *WhoScEn 94*
Voutsinas, Andreas *WhoHol 92*
Vovakis, Lewis Harry 1934- *WhoAmL 94*
Vovan, Ba 1952- *WhoAm 94*
Vo Van Kiet 1922- *IntWW 93*
Vovchok, Marko 1834-1907 *BlmGWL*
Vowell, Jack C. 1927- *WhoAmP 93*
Vowell, Julia Ann 1960- *WhoMW 93*
Vowles, Paul Foster 1919- *Who 94*
Vowles, Richard Beckman 1917- *WhoAm 94*
Voyager, Alyn 1950- *WhoFI 94*
Voyagis, Yorgo *WhoHol 92*
Voydat, Linda Lory 1957- *WhoAmL 94*
Voyer, Giovanni 1901-1976 *NewGrDO*
Voyiadjis, George Zino 1946- *WhoScEn 94*
Voykhansky, I. Grigory 1966- *WhoMW 93*
Voynovich, Vladimir Nikolayevich 1932- *IntWW 93*
Voysest, Oswaldo 1933- *WhoScEn 94*
Voysey, Reginald George d1993 *Who 94N*
Vozenilek, Helen S. 1958- *ConAu 140*
Voznesenskaia, Iuliia Nikolaevna 1940- *BlmGWL*
Voznesenskii, Andrei (Andreevich) 1933- *ConWorW 93*
Voznesensky, Andrei *ConWorW 93*
Voznesensky, Andrey Andreyevich 1933- *IntWW 93*
Voznyak, Vasily Yakovlevich 1944- *LngBDD*
Vraalsen, Tom Eric 1936- *IntWW 93*
Vrable, John Bernard 1929- *WhoFI 94*
Vrablik, Edward Robert 1932- *WhoAm 94*
Vrachas, Constantinos Aghisilaou 1931- *WhoScEn 94*
Vradelis, James Theodore 1956- *WhoAmL 94*
Vradenburg, George, III *WhoAm 94, WhoFI 94*
Vrakas, Daniel P. *WhoAmP 93*
Vrakatitsis, Zoe 1919- *WhoAmP 93*
Vrana, Barbara Brown 1955- *WhoAm 94*
Vrana, Verlon Kenneth 1925- *WhoAm 94, WhoMW 93*
Vrancken, Robert Danloy 1936- *WhoAm 94*
Vrandecic-Dwyer, Aurelia Marie 1950- *WhoHisp 94*
Vranesic, John Ralph 1948- *WhoAmL 94*
Vranicar, Gregory Leonard 1950- *WhoAmL 94*
Vranicar, Matthew Gerald 1964- *WhoMW 93*
Vranicky, Pavel *NewGrDO*
Vranish, Luise Shelley 1914- *WhoAmP 93*
Vranitzky, Franz 1937- *IntWW 93*
Vratil, John Logan 1945- *WhoAmL 94*
Vratil, Kathryn Hoefer 1949- *WhoAm 94, WhoAmL 94, WhoMW 93*
Vratusa, Anton 1915- *IntWW 93*
Vrbancic, John Emerick 1955- *WhoMW 93*
Vrchlicky, Jaroslav 1853-1912 *NewGrDO*
Vrdolyak, Edward Robert 1937- *WhoAmP 93*
Vredeling, Hendrikus 1924- *Who 94*
Vredeling, Henk 1924- *IntWW 93*
Vredenbregt, Jeffrey Carl 1953- *WhoMW 93*

Vredenburg, Dwight Charles 1914- *WhoFI 94*
Vredevoe, Donna Lou 1938- *WhoAm 94*
Vree, Roger Allen 1943- *WhoAm 94*
Vreeken, Johannes 1929- *IntWW 93*
Vreeland, Diana Dalziel 1924-1989 *WhAm 10*
Vreeland, Frederick *WhoAmP 93*
Vreeland, James P., Jr. 1910- *WhoAmP 93*
Vreeland, Robert Wilder 1923- *WhoScEn 94, WhoWest 94*
Vreeland, Russell Glenn 1960- *WhoFI 94*
Vreeland, Ruth Marianne 1935- *WhoAmP 93*
Vreeland, Susan *DrAPF 93*
Vreeland, Thomas Reed 1925- *WhoAm 94*
Vrentas, Christine Mary 1953- *WhoScEn 94*
Vreuls, Diane *DrAPF 93*
Vreuls, Victor (Jean Leonard) 1876-1944 *NewGrDO*
Vreven, Alfred 1937- *IntWW 93*
Vrhovcak, Ivanka 1933- *WhoWomW 91*
Vrhovec, Josip 1926- *IntWW 93*
Vriends, Brian *WhoHol 92*
Vries, Egbert de 1901- *IntWW 93*
Vries, Hugo de 1848-1935 *WorScD*
Vriesman, Robert John 1953- *WhoWest 94*
Vrigny, Roger 1920- *IntWW 93*
Vrijenhoek, Robert Charles 1946- *WhoScEn 94*
Vroman, Barbara *DrAPF 93*
Vroman, Barbara Fitz 1933- *WhoMW 93*
Vroman, Georgine Marie 1921- *WhoScEn 94*
Vroman, Margaret Ellan 1955- *WhoAmL 94*
Vroom, Frederick d1942 *WhoHol 92*
Vroom, Victor H 1932- *WrDr 94*
Vroom, Victor Harold 1932- *WhoAm 94*
Vroon, Peter R. *WhoAmP 93*
Vroons, Frans 1911- *NewGrDO*
Vrtiska, Floyd P. 1926- *WhoAmP 93*
Vryonis, Speros, Jr. 1928- *WhoAm 94*
Vu, Bien Quang 1951- *WhoScEn 94*
Vu, Cung 1951- *WhoScEn 94*
Vu, Jean-Pierre 1934- *WhoFI 94*
Vu, Joseph 1952- *WhoAsA 94*
Vu, Liem T. 1964- *WhoAsA 94*
Vu, Quang 1931- *WhoAsA 94*
Vu-An, Eric *WhoHol 92*
Vuataz, Roger 1898-1988 *NewGrDO*
Vucanovich, Barbara 1921- *WhoWomW 91*
Vucanovich, Barbara F. 1921- *CngDr 93, WhoAmP 93*
Vucanovich, Barbara Farrell 1921- *WhoAm 94, WhoWest 94*
Vuchetich, Patrick J. 1952- *WhoAmL 94*
Vuckovich, Dragomir Michael 1927- *WhoAm 94*
Vuich, Rose Ann *WhoAmP 93*
Vuillemenot, Fred A 1890-1952 *WhoAmA 93N*
Vuillemin, Jules Marie Etienne 1920- *IntWW 93*
Vuillequez, Jean 1911-1991 *WhAm 10*
Vuilleumier, Francois 1938- *WhoAm 94*
Vuitch, Milan M. 1915-1993 *NewYTBS 93*
Vuitton, Henry-Louis 1911- *WhoAm 94*
Vukasin, John P., Jr. d1993 *NewYTBS 93*
Vukasin, John Peter, Jr. 1928- *WhoAm 94, WhoWest 94*
Vukasovich, Mark Samuel 1927- *WhoMW 93*
Vukelic, James Morris 1950- *WhoAmL 94*
Vukotic, Dusan 1927- *IntDcF 2-4*
Vukovic, Drago Vuko 1934- *WhoFI 94, WhoScEn 94*
Vukovich, Joseph John 1945- *WhoAmP 93*
Vukovich, Robert Anthony 1943- *WhoAm 94*
Vukovich, Thomas Walter 1952- *WhoMW 93*
Vuksic, Nelly 1938- *WhoHisp 94*
Vuksta, Michael Joseph 1926- *WhoWest 94*
Vuletic, Zivko 1923- *WrDr 94*
Vulevich, Edward, Jr. 1933- *WhoAmL 94*
Vulgamore, Melvin L. 1935- *WhoAm 94, WhoMW 93*
Vulis, Dimitri Lvovich 1964- *WhoScEn 94*
Vulk, Raymond Paul, Sr. 1943- *WhoAmP 93*
Vulliamy, Shirley *Who 94*
Vullo, Maria Therese 1963- *WhoAmL 94*
Vulpetti, Giovanni 1945- *WhoScEn 94*
Vulpius, Christian August 1762-1827 *NewGrDO*
Vumbaco, Brenda J. 1941- *WhoFI 94*
Vunibobo, Berenado 1932- *IntWW 93*
Vuolo, Tito d1962 *WhoHol 92*
Vuong Van Bac 1927- *IntWW 93*
Vuono, Carl E. 1934- *IntWW 93, WhoAm 94*
Vuorilehto, Simo 1930- *IntWW 93*

Vuorinen Ruppi, Sakari Antero 1948- *WhoScEn 94*
Vuoristo, Osmo Jalmari 1929- *IntWW 93*
Vurek, Ruth Kathryn 1932- *WhoAmP 93*
Vurich, John David 1946- *WhoWest 94*
Vurobaravu, Nikenike 1951- *IntWW 93*
Vuskovic, Leposava 1941- *WhoScEn 94*
Vu Van Mau 1914- *IntWW 93*
Vuyk, Beb (Elizabeth) 1905-1991 *BlmGWL*
Vyain, Jenny Anne 1957- *WhoMW 93*
Vyas, Gaurang Rajnikant 1955- *WhoAsA 94*
Vyas, Girish N. 1933- *WhoAsA 94*
Vyas, Girish Narmadashankar 1933- *WhoAm 94*
Vyas, Premila Hariprasad 1928- *WhoAsA 94*
Vyas, Udaykumar Dayalal 1940- *WhoAsA 94*
Vyborny, Carl Joseph 1950- *WhoMW 93*
Vye, Murvyn d1976 *WhoHol 92*
Vyhlidal, Sandra 1947- *WhoMW 93*
Vykukal, Eugene Lawrence 1929- *WhoAm 94*
Vynalek, Michael Thomas 1953- *WhoMW 93*
Vyncke, Kris Douglas 1954- *WhoMW 93*
Vyner, Margaret 1915- *WhoHol 92*
Vyroubova, Nina 1921- *IntDcB [port]*
Vyshinsky, Andrei Y. 1883-1954 *HisDcKW*
Vysotsky, Evgeny Vasilevich 1947- *LngBDD*
Vysotsky, Vladimir d1980 *WhoHol 92*
Vytal, James Alfred 1936- *WhoFI 94*
Vyvyan, Jennifer (Brigit) 1925-1974 *NewGrDO*
Vyvyan, John (Stanley) 1916- *Who 94*
Vyzas, Vincas Mark 1963- *WhoAmL 94*

W

Waack, Richard Eugene 1923-
WhoAmP 93
Waage, Frederick O. *DrAPF 93*
Waage, Mervin Bernard 1944-
WhoAmL 94
Waagenaar, Sam 1908- *WrDr 94*
Waak, Richard Walter 1946- *WhoAmL 94*
Waaland, Irving Theodore 1927-
WhoAm 94, WhoScEn 94
Waaland, James Brearley, II 1953-
WhoAmA 93
Waaler, Bjarne Arentz 1925- *IntWW 93,
WhoScEn 94*
Waalkes, Konrad Lothar d1981
WhoHol 92
Waalkes, Michael Phillip 1953-
WhoScEn 94
Waals, Johannes Diderik van der
1837-1923 *WorScD*
Waanders, Gerald L. 1944- *WhoWest 94*
Waano-Gano, Joe 1906-1982
WhoAmA 93N
Waara, Maria Esther 1930- *WhoMW 93*
Waard, Elly de 1940- *BlmGWL*
Waart, Edo de *NewGrDO*
Waas, Julie Rebecca Reby 1961-
WhoAmL 94
Waas, Norman Murray 1961-
WhoAmL 94
Waban c. 1604-c. 1676 *EncNAR*
Waber, Bernard 1924- *WrDr 94*
Wabler, Robert Charles, II 1948-
WhoAm 94, WhoScEn 94
Wabokieshiek c. 1794-1841 *EncNAR*
Wace c. 1100-c. 1175 *BlmGEL*
Wachal, Robert Stanley 1929- *WhoAm 94*
Wachbrit, Jill Barrett 1955- *WhoFI 94,
WhoWest 94*
Wachenfeld, William Thomas 1926-
WhoAm 94
Wachman, Harold Yehuda 1927-
WhoAm 94
Wachman, Marvin 1917- *WhoAm 94*
Wachmann, Ion Andrei 1807-1863
NewGrDO
Wachner, Linda Joy 1946- *WhoAm 94,
WhoFI 94, WhoWest 94*
Wacholder, Ben Zion 1924- *WhoMW 93*
Wachowski, Theodore John 1907-
WhoMW 93
Wachs, Ethel 1923- *WhoAmA 93*
Wachs, Joel *WhoAmP 93*
Wachs, Kate Mary *WhoAm 94*
Wachs, Martin 1941- *WhoAm 94*
Wachsler, Robert Alan 1934- *WhoAm 94*
Wachsman, Harvey Frederick 1936-
WhoAm 94, WhoAmL 94, WhoScEn 94
Wachsmuth, Robert William 1942-
WhoAmL 94
Wachspress, Melvin Harold 1926-
WhoScEn 94
Wachsteter, George 1911- *WhoAmA 93*
Wachtel, Alan Larry 1947- *WhoWest 94*
Wachtel, Chuck *DrAPF 93*
Wachtel, David Edward 1962- *WhoAm 94*
Wachtel, Eleanor 1947- *WrDr 94*
Wachtel, Eli 1951- *WhoWest 94*
Wachtel, Harry H. 1917- *WhoAm 94*
Wachtel, Joel Gordon 1935- *WhoMW 93*
Wachtel, Norman Jay 1941- *WhoAm 94,
WhoAmL 94*
Wachtel, Paul Spencer 1947- *WrDr 94*
Wachtel, Theodor 1823-1893 *NewGrDO*

Wachtell, Roger Bruce 1959- *WhoWest 94*
Wachtell, Thomas 1928- *WhoFI 94,
WhoWest 94*
Wachter, Johann Michael 1794-1853
NewGrDO
Wachter, Oralee (Roberts) 1935- *WrDr 94*
Wachtler, Sol 1930- *WhoAm 94*
Wachtman, Lynn R. *WhoAmP 93*
Wachtmeister, Wilhelm H. F. 1923-
WhoAm 94
Wachtmeister, Wilhelm Hans Frederik
1923- *IntWW 93*
Waciuma, Charity *BlmGWL*
Wack, Edward W. *WhoHol 92*
Wack, Thomas E. 1944- *WhoAm 94,
WhoAmL 94*
Wackenhut, George Russell 1919-
WhoAm 94, WhoFI 94
Wackenhut, Richard Russell 1947-
WhoAm 94, WhoFI 94
Wacker, Frederick Glade, Jr. 1918-
WhoAm 94, WhoFI 94
Wacker, John Frederick 1954-
WhoWest 94
Wacker, Margaret Morrissey 1951-
WhoFI 94
Wacker, Warren Ernest Clyde 1924-
WhoAm 94, WhoScEn 94
Wackerle, Carl Michael 1956-
WhoMW 93
Wackerle, Frederick William 1939-
WhoAm 94, WhoFI 94
Wackerlin, Tess Rose 1956- *WhoMW 93*
Wackernagel, Wilhelm 1806-1869
DcLB 133 [port]
Wada, Akiyoshi 1929- *WhoScEn 94*
Wada, Debra Sadako 1962- *WhoAsA 94*
Wada, Eitaro 1939- *WhoScEn 94*
Wada, Emi 1937- *IntWW 93*
Wada, Harry Nobuyoshi 1919-
WhoAm 94
Wada, Henry Garrett 1948- *WhoWest 94*
Wada, Patricia *WhoAsA 94*
Wada, Sadami Chris 1932- *WhoAm 94*
Wada, Toshimasa Francis 1945-
WhoAsA 94
Wadati, Kiyoo 1902- *IntWW 93*
Waddell, Alexander (Nicol Anton) 1913-
Who 94
Waddell, Alfred Moore, Jr. 1939-
WhoAm 94
Waddell, Charles Lindy 1932-
WhoAmP 93
Waddell, David Garrett 1941-
WhoScEn 94
Waddell, Dix K. 1933- *WhoFI 94*
Waddell, Gary *WhoHol 92*
Waddell, Gary Evans 1950- *WhoAmP 93*
Waddell, Gordon Herbert 1937-
IntWW 93, Who 94
Waddell, Harry Lee 1912- *WhoAm 94*
Waddell, James (Henderson) 1914-
Who 94
Waddell, James Madison, Jr. 1922-
WhoAmP 93
Waddell, John Comer 1937- *WhoFI 94*
Waddell, John Henry 1921- *WhoAmA 93*
Waddell, Martin 1941- *ChlLR 31 [port],
WrDr 94*
Waddell, Mathis Theron, Jr. 1941-
WhoAmP 93
Waddell, Mildred Zent 1939- *WhoMW 93*

Waddell, Oliver W. 1930- *WhoAm 94,
WhoFI 94*
Waddell, Perry 1964- *WhoWest 94*
Waddell, Phillip Dean 1948- *WhoAmL 94*
Waddell, Richard H. d1974
WhoAmA 93N
Waddell, Richard W. *WhoAmP 93*
Waddell, Robert P. 1948- *WhoAmP 93*
Waddell, Rolanda Wilson 1961-
WhoFI 94
Waddell, Ruchadina LaDesiree 1965-
WhoBlA 94
Waddell, St. John 1896- *WhAm 10*
Waddell, Theodore 1941- *WhoAmA 93*
Waddell, Theodore R. 1934- *WhoBlA 94*
Waddell, William Angus 1924- *Who 94*
Waddell, William Joseph 1929-
WhoAm 94
Waddell, William Robert 1940-
WhoAm 94
Wadden, Christopher David 1959-
WhoFI 94
Wadden, Richard Albert 1936-
WhoAm 94, WhoScEn 94
Wadden, Thomas Antony 1952-
WhoAm 94, WhoScEn 94
Waddilove, Lewis Edgar 1914- *Who 94*
Waddingham, John Alfred 1915-
WhoAm 94, WhoAmA 93, WhoWest 94
Waddington, Baron 1929- *Who 94*
Waddington, David 1929- *IntWW 93*
Waddington, David James 1932- *Who 94,
WhoScEn 94*
Waddington, Gary Lee 1944- *WhoWest 94*
Waddington, Gerald Eugene 1909-
Who 94
Waddington, Henry Richard 1939-
WhoFI 94
Waddington, John Albert Henry 1910-
Who 94
Waddington, Leslie 1934- *Who 94*
Waddington, Leslie 1936- *IntWW 93*
Waddington, Miriam 1917- *BlmGWL,
WrDr 94*
Waddington, Patrick d1987 *WhoHol 92*
Waddington, Raymond B(ruce) 1935-
WrDr 94
Waddington, Raymond Bruce, Jr. 1935-
WhoAm 94, WhoWest 94
Waddington, Robert Murray 1927-
Who 94
Waddington-Feather, John Joseph 1933-
WrDr 94
Waddle, John Frederick 1927- *WhoAm 94*
Waddle, Ted W. 1928- *WhoAmP 93*
Waddles, Charleszetta Lina 1912-
WhoBlA 94
Waddles, George Wesley, Sr. 1948-
WhoBlA 94
Waddoups, Michael Grant 1948-
WhoAmP 93
Wadds, Jean Casselman 1920- *IntWW 93,
Who 94, WhoAm 94*
Waddy, Arthur Robert 1943- *WhoBlA 94*
Waddy, Charis 1909- *WrDr 94*
Waddy, Edward d1968 *WhoHol 92*
Waddy, Lawrence Heber 1914- *Who 94,
WrDr 94*
Waddy, Walter James 1929- *WhoBlA 94*
Wade, Achille Melvin 1943- *WhoBlA 94*
Wade, Adam 1935- *WhoHol 92*
Wade, Alan 1916- *WrDr 94*

Wade, (Douglas) Ashton (Lofft) 1898-
Who 94
Wade, Barry K. d1993 *NewYTBS 93*
Wade, Ben Frank 1935- *WhoAm 94*
Wade, Beryl Elaine 1956- *WhoBlA 94*
Wade, Bessie d1966 *WhoHol 92*
Wade, Bill 1928- *WrDr 94*
Wade, Brent James 1959- *WhoBlA 94*
Wade, Bruce L. 1951- *WhoBlA 94*
Wade, Casey, Jr. 1930- *WhoBlA 94*
Wade, Charles *WhoAmP 93*
Wade, Donald L. 1934- *WhoIns 94*
Wade, Edmond D. 1941- *WhoAmL 94*
Wade, Edwin Lee 1932- *WhoAm 94,
WhoAmL 94*
Wade, Emmett Cleve 1944- *WhoAmL 94*
Wade, Eugene Henry-Peter 1954-
WhoBlA 94
Wade, George Edward 1853-1933
DcNaB MP
Wade, George Joseph 1938- *WhoAm 94,
WhoAmL 94*
Wade, Gerald James 1942- *WhoWest 94*
Wade, Glen 1921- *WhoAm 94*
Wade, Greta Evona 1897- *WhoAmP 93*
Wade, Hardon McDonald, Jr. 1933-
WhoFI 94
Wade, Jack Warren, Jr. 1948- *WrDr 94*
Wade, Jacqueline E. 1940- *WhoBlA 94*
Wade, James Alan 1950- *WhoAmL 94*
Wade, James Michael 1943- *WhoAm 94*
Wade, James Nathaniel 1933- *WhoBlA 94*
Wade, James O'Shea 1940- *WhoAm 94*
Wade, James Paul, Jr. 1930- *WhoAmP 93*
Wade, James William 1964- *WhoScEn 94*
Wade, Jamie A. 1948- *WhoAmL 94*
Wade, Jane 1925- *WhoAmA 93*
Wade, Jarrel Blake 1943- *WhoAm 94*
Wade, Jeffrey Lee 1946- *WhoAmL 94*
Wade, Jeffrey Louis 1964- *WhoAmL 94*
Wade, Jennifer 1936- *WrDr 94*
Wade, Jerry Bovender 1959- *WhoFI 94*
Wade, John d1949 *WhoHol 92*
Wade, John H., II 1959- *WhoWest 94*
Wade, John Stevens *DrAPF 93*
Wade, John William 1925-1991 *WhAm 10*
Wade, Joseph Augustine c. 1801-1845
NewGrDO
Wade, Joseph Downey 1938- *WhoBlA 94*
Wade, Joseph Frederick 1919- *Who 94*
Wade, Joyce K. 1949- *WhoBlA 94*
Wade, Judy Lee 1939- *WhoBlA 94*
Wade, Kenneth 1932- *IntWW 93, Who 94*
Wade, Kevin 1954- *WhoHol 92*
Wade, Kim Marie 1957- *WhoBlA 94*
Wade, Lyndon Anthony 1934-
WhoBlA 94
Wade, Mark Lloyd 9157- *WhoWest 94*
Wade, Martha Georgie 1939-
WhoWest 94
Wade, Mason 1913- *WrDr 94*
Wade, Michael John 1949- *WhoScEn 94*
Wade, Michael Robert Alexander 1945-
WhoFI 94
Wade, Michael Stephen 1948-
WhoWest 94
Wade, Mildred Moncrief 1926-
WhoBlA 94
Wade, Nicholas Michael Landon 1942-
WhoAm 94
Wade, Norma Adams *WhoBlA 94*
Wade, Owen Lyndon 1921- *Who 94*
Wade, Patrick John 1941- *WhoWest 94*

Wade, R(obert) Hunter 1916- *Who 94*
Wade, Rene 1961- *WhoMW 93*
Wade, Richard Lawrence 1938- *Who 94*
Wade, Robert 1920- *WrDr 94*
Wade, Robert Glenn 1933- *WhoFI 94, WhoScEn 94*
Wade, Robert Hirsch Beard 1916- *WhoAm 94, WhoAmP 93*
Wade, Robert Paul 1936- *WhoAm 94*
Wade, Robert Schrope 1943- *WhoAmA 93*
Wade, Rodger Grant 1945- *WhoFI 94, WhoScEn 94, WhoWest 94*
Wade, Ronald Eustace 1905- *Who 94*
Wade, Russell 1917- *WhoHol 92*
Wade, Ruthven (Lowry) 1920- *Who 94*
Wade, Sidney 1951- *WrDr 94*
Wade, Stacy Lynn 1965- *WhoScEn 94*
Wade, Susan Kaye 1956- *WhoMW 93*
Wade, Suzanne 1938- *WhoFI 94*
Wade, Terence (L. B.) 1930- *ConAu 141*
Wade, Terry Lee 1947- *WhoAmL 94*
Wade, Thomas Edward 1943- *WhoAm 94, WhoFI 94, WhoScEn 94*
Wade, Tom W. *EncSF 93*
Wade, Tommy *NewYTBS 93 [port]*
Wade, Virginia 1945- *BuCMET*
Wade, (Sarah) Virginia 1945- *IntWW 93, Who 94, WrDr 94*
Wade, William *Who 94*
Wade, (Henry) William (Rawson) 1918- *IntWW 93, Who 94*
Wade, (Henry) William (Rawson), Sir 1918- *WrDr 94*
Wade, William Allen 1953- *WhoFI 94*
Wade, William C., Jr. 1943- *WhoBlA 94*
Wade, William Carl 1934- *WhoBlA 94*
Wade, William Edward, Jr. 1942- *WhoFI 94*
Wade, William James 1941- *WhoAmL 94*
Wade-Gayles, Gloria Jean *BlkWr 2, ConAu 142, WhoBlA 94*
Wade-Gery, Robert (Lucian) 1929- *IntWW 93, Who 94*
Waden, Fletcher Nathaniel, Jr. 1928- *WhoBlA 94*
Wade Of Chorlton, Baron 1932- *Who 94*
Wadewitz, Werner Karl 1912- *WhoMW 93*
Wadey, Brian Leu 1941- *WhoScEn 94*
Wadey, Victor *EncSF 93*
Wadhams, Golden d1929 *WhoHol 92*
Wadhams, Peter 1948- *Who 94*
Wadhams, Richard Ivory 1955- *WhoAmP 93*
Wadia, Maneck S 1931- *WrDr 94*
Wadia, Maneck Sorabji 1931- *WhoWest 94*
Wadkins, Lanny 1949- *WhoAm 94*
Wadkins, Mack Loyd 1937- *WhoAmP 93*
Wadkins, Peter Charles, Sr. 1954- *WhoFI 94*
Wadleigh, Michael 1941- *IntMPA 94*
Wadler, Arnold L. 1943- *WhoAm 94*
Wadley, M. Richard *WhoAm 94, WhoFI 94, WhoWest 94*
Wadlington, W. M. 1944- *WhoFI 94, WhoWest 94*
Wadlington, Walter James 1931- *WhoAm 94, WhoScEn 94*
Wadlington, Warwick Paul 1938- *WhoAm 94*
Wadlow, Joan Krueger 1932- *WhoAm 94, WhoWest 94*
Wadlow, R. Clark 1946- *WhoAm 94, WhoAmL 94*
Wadman, William Wood, III 1936- *WhoFI 94, WhoScEn 94, WhoWest 94*
Wadso, B. Ingemar 1930- *WhoScEn 94*
Wadsworth, Charles William 1929- *WhoAm 94*
Wadsworth, Dyer Seymour 1936- *WhoAm 94*
Wadsworth, Frank Whittemore 1919- *WhoAm 94*
Wadsworth, Ginger 1945- *WrDr 94*
Wadsworth, Harold Wayne 1930- *WhoAm 94, WhoAmL 94*
Wadsworth, Henry d1974 *WhoHol 92*
Wadsworth, Herbert Robinson, Jr. 1931- *WhoAmP 93*
Wadsworth, Homer Clark 1913- *WhoAm 94*
Wadsworth, James 1730-1817 *WhAmRev*
Wadsworth, James Marshall 1939- *WhoAm 94*
Wadsworth, James Patrick 1940- *Who 94*
Wadsworth, Jeremiah 1743-1804 *AmRev, WhAmRev*
Wadsworth, Karen O. 1945- *WhoAmP 93*
Wadsworth, Peleg 1748-1829 *WhAmRev*
Wadsworth, Phyllis Marie *EncSF 93*
Wadsworth, Robert David 1942- *WhoAm 94, WhoFI 94*
Wadsworth, Stephen 1953- *NewGrDO*
Wadsworth, William d1950 *WhoHol 92*
Wadzinski, Henry Teofil 1938- *WhoScEn 94*
Waechter, Arthur Joseph, Jr. 1913- *WhoAm 94, WhoAmL 94*
Waechter, Eberhard 1929-1992 *NewGrDO*
Waehner, Ralph Livingston 1935- *WhoAm 94*
Waelbroeck, Jean Louis 1927- *IntWW 93*
Waelde, Lawrence Richard 1951- *WhoScEn 94*
Waelput, Hendrik 1845-1885 *NewGrDO*
Waelsch, Salome G. 1907- *IntWW 93*
Waelsch, Salome Gluecksohn 1907- *WhoAm 94, WhoScEn 94*
Waelti-Walters, Jennifer (Rose) 1942- *WrDr 94*
Waesche, Richard Henley Woodward 1930- *WhoScEn 94*
Waetjen, Herman Charles 1929- *WhoAm 94, WhoWest 94*
Waetjen, Walter Bernhard 1920- *WhoAm 94*
Wafer, Lela 1940- *WhoMW 93*
Wafford, Daniel Eugene 1950- *WhoFI 94*
Wagaman, Karen Lee 1959- *WhoMW 93*
Wagar, Harvey D., III 1951- *WhoAmL 94*
Wagar, Joseph Boyanton 1949- *WhoFI 94*
Wagar, Kenneth Eugene 1956- *WhoWest 94*
Wagar, Nelson William, III 1954- *WhoAmL 94*
Wagar, W(alter) Warren 1932- *EncSF 93*
Wagemaker, David Isaac 1949- *WhoFI 94*
Wageman, Don H(enry) 1894- *WhAm 10*
Wageman, Thomas J. *WhoWest 94*
Wagenaar, Johan 1862-1941 *NewGrDO*
Wagener, Donna Lynn 1959- *WhoFI 94, WhoMW 93*
Wagener, Hobart D. 1921- *WhoAm 94*
Wagener, James Wilbur 1930- *WhoAm 94*
Wagenhals, Walter Lincoln 1934- *WhoWest 94*
Wagenheim, Charles d1979 *WhoHol 92*
Wagenius, Jean 1941- *WhoMW 93*
Wagenius, Jean D. 1941- *WhoAmP 93*
Wagenknecht, Edward 1900- *WhoAm 94, WrDr 94*
Wagenknecht, Walter Chappell 1947- *WhoScEn 94*
Wagenman, Barton Lee 1942- *WhoAmL 94*
Wagensberg, Jorge 1948- *WhoScEn 94*
Wagenseil, Georg Christoph 1715-1777 *NewGrDO*
Wager, Anthony 1933- *WhoHol 92*
Wager, Jerry William 1937- *WhoWest 94*
Wager, Lisa Klein 1959- *WhoAmL 94*
Wager, Michael 1925- *WhoHol 92*
Wager, Walter Herman 1924- *WhoAm 94*
Wager, Willis Joseph 1911-1991 *WhAm 10*
Wagers, Gardner D. 1948- *WhoAmL 94*
Wagers, Robert Shelby 1943- *WhoAm 94*
Wagers, William Delbert, Jr. 1949- *WhoScEn 94*
Wages, Robert Coleman 1963- *WhoFI 94*
Waggener, Richard *WhoAmP 93*
Waggener, Ronald Edgar 1926- *WhoAm 94*
Waggener, Susan Lee 1951- *WhoAm 94, WhoAmL 94, WhoWest 94*
Waggener, Theryn Lee 1941- *WhoWest 94*
Waggner, George 1894-1984 *HorFD [port]*
Waggoner, Barbara Ashton 1920- *WhoMW 93*
Waggoner, Daniel 1952- *WhoAmL 94*
Waggoner, Daniel LeRoy 1934- *WhoMW 93*
Waggoner, David Carl 1953- *WhoWest 94*
Waggoner, Doris Evon 1940- *WhoMW 93*
Waggoner, James Clyde 1946- *WhoAm 94, WhoAmL 94, WhoWest 94*
Waggoner, James Norman 1925- *WhoAm 94*
Waggoner, James Thomas, Jr. 1937- *WhoAmP 93*
Waggoner, James Virgil 1927- *WhoAm 94, WhoFI 94*
Waggoner, Jane Byrn 1921- *WhoAmP 93*
Waggoner, John Edward 1959- *WhoScEn 94*
Waggoner, Kenneth L. 1948- *WhoAmL 94*
Waggoner, Laine Morais 1933- *WhoWest 94*
Waggoner, Lawrence William 1937- *WhoAm 94*
Waggoner, Lee Reynolds 1940- *WhoScEn 94*
Waggoner, Leland Tate 1916- *WhoAm 94*
Waggoner, Linda Suzette 1947- *WhoWest 94*
Waggoner, Lyle 1935- *IntMPA 94, WhoHol 92*
Waggoner, Paul Edward 1923- *IntWW 93, WhoAm 94*
Waggoner, Raymond Walter 1901- *WhoAm 94*
Waggoner, Samuel Lee 1930- *WhoFI 94*
Waggoner, Susan Marie 1952- *WhoMW 93, WhoScEn 94*
Waggoner, William Johnson 1928- *WhoAmL 94*
Wagle, Susan 1953- *WhoAmP 93*
Wagley, Charles Walter 1913- *WhAm 10*
Wagman, Christine Bernadette 1966- *WhoMW 93*
Wagman, David S. 1951- *WhoFI 94*
Wagman, Frederick Herbert 1912- *WhoAm 94*
Wagman, Gerald Howard 1926- *WhoAm 94, WhoScEn 94*
Wagman, Morton 1925- *ConAu 141*
Wagman, Robert John 1942- *WhoAm 94*
Wagner, A. Keith 1953- *WhoAmP 93*
Wagner, Alan Cyril 1931- *WhoAm 94*
Wagner, Alfred Lawrence 1915- *WhoAmP 93*
Wagner, Allan Ray 1934- *WhoAm 94*
Wagner, Alvin Louis, Jr. 1939- *WhoAm 94*
Wagner, Ann Dorothy 1950- *WhoFI 94*
Wagner, Anneliese *DrAPF 93*
Wagner, Annice M. *WhoAmL 94, WhoAmP 93*
Wagner, Anthony (Richard) 1908- *Who 94, WrDr 94*
Wagner, Anthony Richard 1908- *ConAu 42NR, IntWW 93*
Wagner, Arthur 1923- *WhoAm 94*
Wagner, Arthur Ward, Jr. 1930- *WhoAm 94, WhoAmL 94*
Wagner, Aubrey Joseph 1912-1990 *WhAm 10*
Wagner, Augustus F., Jr. 1941- *WhoAmL 94*
Wagner, Ben Henry 1926- *WhoFI 94*
Wagner, Bernhard Rupert 1951- *WhoScEn 94*
Wagner, Betty Valiree 1923- *WhoAm 94*
Wagner, Blanche Collet 1873- *WhoAmA 93N*
Wagner, Brett Alan 1959- *WhoMW 93*
Wagner, Brian Allen 1958- *WhoMW 93*
Wagner, Bruce 1954- *ConAu 140*
Wagner, Bruce Jeffrey 1960- *WhoAmL 94*
Wagner, Bruce Stanley 1943- *WhoAm 94*
Wagner, Burton Allan 1941- *WhoAm 94*
Wagner, C. L., Jr. 1944- *WhoAmL 94*
Wagner, C. Peter 1930- *WhoWest 94*
Wagner, Carruth John 1916- *WhoAm 94, WhoScEn 94, WhoWest 94*
Wagner, Catherine 1953- *WhoAmA 93*
Wagner, Catherine Feeley 1929- *WhoMW 93*
Wagner, Charles Alan 1948- *WhoMW 93*
Wagner, Charles H. *WhoAmA 93*
Wagner, Charles Leonard 1925- *WhoAm 94*
Wagner, Christel Eva *WhoFI 94*
Wagner, Christian Joergen 1960- *WhoFI 94, WhoWest 94*
Wagner, Christian Nikolaus Johann 1927- *WhoAm 94, WhoWest 94*
Wagner, Christina Breuer 1954- *WhoAm 94, WhoFI 94*
Wagner, Chuck *WhoHol 92*
Wagner, Curtis Lee, Jr. 1928- *WhoAm 94, WhoAmL 94*
Wagner, D. William 1943- *WhoAm 94, WhoAmL 94*
Wagner, Daniel Frederick 1961- *WhoAmL 94*
Wagner, Daniel John 1943- *WhoMW 93*
Wagner, David Bruce 1952- *WhoAmP 93*
Wagner, David H. 1926- *WhoBlA 94*
Wagner, David J. *WhoAmA 93*
Wagner, David J. 1952- *WhoWest 94*
Wagner, David James 1946- *WhoWest 94*
Wagner, Dennis P. 1953- *WhoAm 94*
Wagner, Diane 1959- *WrDr 94*
Wagner, Donald Arthur 1963- *WhoFI 94*
Wagner, Donald Bert 1930- *WhoAm 94*
Wagner, Donald Edward 1942- *WhoMW 93*
Wagner, Dorothy Marie 1924-1990 *WhAm 10*
Wagner, Douglas Edward 1952- *WhoAmL 94*
Wagner, Douglas T. 1954- *WhoAmP 93, WhoWest 94*
Wagner, Douglas Walker Ellyson 1938- *WhoAm 94*
Wagner, Durrett 1929- *WhoAm 94*
Wagner, Ed *WhoHol 92*
Wagner, Edward Frederick, Jr. 1938- *WhoFI 94*
Wagner, Edward Kurt 1936- *WhoAm 94*
Wagner, Elin Matilda Elisabeth 1882-1949 *BlmGWL*
Wagner, Eliot *DrAPF 93*
Wagner, Ellen Deutsch 1952- *WhoFI 94*
Wagner, Elsa d1975 *WhoHol 92*
Wagner, Emilie C. 1910- *WhoAmP 93*
Wagner, Emmett d1977 *WhoHol 92*
Wagner, Falk (Oskar Paul Alfred) 1939- *IntWW 93*
Wagner, Frank W. 1955- *WhoAmP 93*
Wagner, Fred W. 1940- *WhoMW 93*
Wagner, Frederic A. 1938- *WhoAmP 93*
Wagner, Frederick Balthas, Jr. 1916- *WhoAm 94*
Wagner, Frederick Reese 1928- *WhoAm 94*
Wagner, Frederick William 1933- *WhoAm 94*
Wagner, Fritz Arno 1891-1958 *IntDcF 2-4*
Wagner, George Francis Adolf 1941- *WhoAm 94*
Wagner, George O. *WhoAmP 93*
Wagner, Gerrit Abram 1916- *Who 94*
Wagner, Gilbert Keith 1929- *WhoIns 94*
Wagner, Gillian (Mary Millicent) 1927- *ConAu 141*
Wagner, Gillian Mary Millicent 1927- *Who 94*
Wagner, Gladys Noble 1907- *WhoAmA 93N*
Wagner, Glenn Norman 1946- *WhoScEn 94*
Wagner, Gordon Parsons 1915-1987 *WhoAmA 93N*
Wagner, Harold A. 1935- *WhoAm 94, WhoFI 94*
Wagner, Harvey Alan 1941- *WhoFI 94*
Wagner, Harvey Arthur 1905- *WhoAm 94*
Wagner, Heinz Georg 1928- *IntWW 93*
Wagner, Helen Adeene 1931- *WhoMW 93*
Wagner, Henri Paul 1960- *WhoScEn 94*
Wagner, Henry Carrh, III 1942- *WhoAm 94*
Wagner, Henry George 1917- *WhoAm 94*
Wagner, Henry Nicholas, Jr. 1927- *WhoAm 94, WhoScEn 94*
Wagner, Henry R. 1862-1957 *DcLB 140 [port]*
Wagner, Hunter Owen, Jr. 1930- *WhoAmP 93*
Wagner, Jack d1965 *WhoHol 92*
Wagner, James Arthur 1945- *WhoAm 94*
Wagner, James Peyton 1939- *WhoAmL 94*
Wagner, Jane 1935- *ConAu 42NR, IntMPA 94*
Wagner, Jean 1924- *Who 94*
Wagner, Jenny *WrDr 94*
Wagner, Joan A. 1935- *WhoAmP 93*
Wagner, Joel H. *WhoScEn 94*
Wagner, Johanna 1826-1894 *See* Wagner family *NewGrDO*
Wagner, John Garnet 1921- *WhoAm 94*
Wagner, John Julius 1949- *WhoAm 94*
Wagner, John Kyle *WhoWest 94*
Wagner, John Leo 1954- *WhoAm 94, WhoAmL 94*
Wagner, John Philip 1940- *WhoScEn 94*
Wagner, John Victor 1947- *WhoIns 94*
Wagner, Joseph Crider 1907- *WhoMW 93*
Wagner, Joseph Edward 1938- *WhoAm 94, WhoScEn 94*
Wagner, Joseph F. *WhoAmP 93*
Wagner, Judith Buck 1943- *WhoAm 94, WhoFI 94, WhoWest 94*
Wagner, Julia Anne 1924- *WhoAm 94*
Wagner, Karel, Jr. 1931- *WhoScEn 94*
Wagner, Karen E. 1952- *WhoAmL 94*
Wagner, Karl Jacob 1772-1822 *NewGrDO*
Wagner, Katie 1964- *WhoHol 92*
Wagner, Kenneth Larkin 1960- *WhoAmL 94*
Wagner, Kenneth Lynn 1956- *WhoAmL 94*
Wagner, Kimberly A. 1962- *WhoMW 93*
Wagner, Lee d1993 *NewYTBS 93*
Wagner, Leon *WhoHol 92*
Wagner, Leslie 1943- *Who 94*
Wagner, Lester Thomas 1942- *WhoAmL 94*
Wagner, Lindsay 1949- *IntMPA 94, WhoHol 92*
Wagner, Lindsay J. 1949- *WhoAm 94*
Wagner, Lou *WhoHol 92*
Wagner, Louis Carson, Jr. 1932- *WhoAm 94*
Wagner, Lowell J. 1939- *WhoFI 94*
Wagner, Lynn Edward 1941- *WhoAmL 94, WhoFI 94*
Wagner, Marcia Claire 1943- *WhoMW 93*
Wagner, Marie 1883-1975 *BuCMET*
Wagner, Mark Anthony 1958- *WhoMW 93*
Wagner, Marvin 1919- *WhoMW 93, WhoScEn 94*
Wagner, Mary Ann 1947- *WhoMW 93*
Wagner, Mary Anthony 1916- *WhoMW 93*
Wagner, Mary Emma 1927- *WhoScEn 94*
Wagner, Mary Kathryn 1932- *WhoAmP 93, WhoMW 93*
Wagner, Mary M. 1946- *WhoAm 94*
Wagner, Maryfrances *DrAPF 93*
Wagner, Max d1975 *WhoHol 92*
Wagner, Max Michael 1949- *WhoScEn 94*
Wagner, Merrill 1935- *WhoAmA 93*
Wagner, Michael D. 1948- *WhoIns 94*
Wagner, Michael D. 1957- *WhoAmP 93*
Wagner, Michael Dean 1962- *WhoMW 93*

Wagner, Michael Dickman 1957-
WhoMW 93
Wagner, Michael Grafton 1935-
WhoFI 94
Wagner, Michael J. 1941- *WhoAmP 93*
Wagner, Mike d1987 *WhoHol 92*
Wagner, Milt *WhoBlA 94*
Wagner, Nancy Hughes 1943-
WhoAmP 93
Wagner, Nancy Jo 1946- *WhoMW 93*
Wagner, Norman Ernest 1935-
WhoAm 94, WhoWest 94
Wagner, Norman Joseph, III 1962-
WhoScEn 94
Wagner, Orvin Edson 1930- *WhoWest 94*
Wagner, Patricia H. 1936- *WhoAm 94,
WhoAmL 94*
Wagner, Paul Dean 1937- *WhoMW 93*
Wagner, Peter Ewing 1929- *WhoAm 94*
Wagner, Peter Henry 1956- *WhoFI 94*
Wagner, Phil *DrAPF 93*
Wagner, Philip Marshall 1904- *IntWW 93*
Wagner, Philip Warren 1950-
WhoAmL 94
Wagner, R. Thomas, Jr. 1955-
WhoAmP 93
Wagner, Ray David 1924- *WhoWest 94*
Wagner, Ray(mond) David 1924-
ConAu 41NR
Wagner, Raymond James 1925-
IntMPA 94
Wagner, Raymond Thomas, Jr. 1959-
WhoAmL 94
Wagner, Richard 1813-1883
DcLB 129 [port]
Wagner, Richard 1927- *WhoAm 94,
WhoWest 94*
Wagner, (Wilhelm) Richard 1813-1883
See Wagner family *NewGrDO*
Wagner, Richard Charles 1931-
WhoIns 94
Wagner, Richard Elliott 1932-
WhoWest 94
Wagner, Richard Ellis 1923- *WhoAmA 93*
Wagner, Richard Eric 1951- *WhoAm 94,
WhoFI 94*
Wagner, Richard Lorraine, Jr. 1936-
WhoAmP 93
Wagner, Robert 1930- *IntMPA 94,
IntWW 93, WhoAm 94, WhoHol 92*
Wagner, Robert Earl 1921- *WhoAm 94*
Wagner, Robert F. 1910-1991 *WhAm 10*
Wagner, Robert F. 1942- *WhoAmL 94*
Wagner, Robert F., Jr. 1944-1993
NewYTBS 93 [port]
Wagner, Robert Roderick 1923-
WhoAm 94
Wagner, Robert Todd 1932- *WhoAm 94,
WhoMW 93*
Wagner, Robert Wayne 1956- *WhoFI 94*
Wagner, Robin 1933- *ConTFT 11*
Wagner, Robin Samuel Anton 1933-
WhoAm 94
Wagner, Rod 1948- *WhoAm 94*
Wagner, Roman Frank 1927- *WhoFI 94*
Wagner, Ronald E. 1944- *WhoAmL 94*
Wagner, Roy 1938- *WhoAm 94*
Wagner, Rudolph Fred 1921- *WrDr 94*
Wagner, Sharon Blythe 1936- *WrDr 94*
Wagner, Sheldon Leon 1929-
WhoWest 94
Wagner, (Helferich) Siegfried (Richard)
1869-1930
See Wagner family *NewGrDO*
Wagner, Sigurd *WhoAm 94*
Wagner, Stephen Anthony 1953-
WhoAm 94
Wagner, Stephen Carroll 1951- *WhoFI 94*
Wagner, Stephen Evon 1951- *WhoIns 94*
Wagner, Sterling Robacker 1904-
WhoFI 94
Wagner, Steve 1949- *WhoWest 94*
Wagner, Sue Ellen 1940- *WhoAm 94,
WhoAmP 93, WhoWest 94,
WhoWomW 91*
Wagner, Susan Jane *WhoFI 94*
Wagner, Theodore Franklin 1921-
WhoAmP 93
Wagner, Thomas Alfred 1953-
WhoScEn 94
Wagner, Thomas Edward 1937-
WhoMW 93
Wagner, Thomas Edward 1944-
WhoAm 94, WhoAmL 94
Wagner, Thomas John 1938- *WhoAm 94*
Wagner, Thomas Joseph 1939-
WhoAm 94, WhoAmL 94, WhoFI 94
Wagner, Thomas Patrick 1952-
WhoAmL 94
Wagner, Todd Gladden 1964-
WhoMW 93
Wagner, Vallerie Denise 1959-
WhoBlA 94
Wagner, Vernon E. 1926- *WhoAmP 93*
Wagner, Victoria 1898- *WhAm 10*
Wagner, Wanda Faye 1956- *WhoMW 93*
Wagner, Warren Herbert, Jr. 1920-
WhoAm 94, WhoScEn 94

Wagner, Wayne 1946- *WhoAmP 93*
Wagner, Wenceslas J. 1917- *WrDr 94*
Wagner, Wende *WhoHol 92*
Wagner, Wieland (Adolf Gottfried)
1917-1966
See Wagner family *NewGrDO*
Wagner, William d1964 *WhoHol 92*
Wagner, William Bradley 1949-
WhoAm 94, WhoAmL 94
Wagner, William Burdette 1941-
WhoAm 94
Wagner, William Charles 1932-
WhoAm 94, WhoMW 93
Wagner, William Douglas 1953-
WhoMW 93
Wagner, William Gerard 1936-
WhoAm 94, WhoWest 94
Wagner, William Michael 1949-
WhoScEn 94
Wagner, William Robert 1959-
WhoAmL 94
Wagner, William Thomas 1950-
WhoFI 94
Wagner, Wolfgang 1919- *IntWW 93*
Wagner, Wolfgang (Manfred Martin)
1919-
See Wagner family *NewGrDO*
Wagner family *NewGrDO [port]*
Wagner-Jacobsen, Carolyn Frieda 1945-
WhoMW 93
Wagner-Mann, Colette Carol 1952-
WhoMW 93
Wagner-Martin, Linda C. 1936- *WrDr 94*
Wagner-Regeny, Rudolf 1903-1969
NewGrDO
Wagner Tizon, Allan 1942- *IntWW 93*
Wagner-Westbrook, Bonnie Joan 1953-
WhoFI 94
Wagner Williams, Carol Ann 1950-
WhoMW 93
Wagnon, Joan 1940- *WhoMW 93*
Wagnon, Joan Davis 1940- *WhoAmP 93*
Wagnon, William Odell, Jr. 1939-
WhoAm 94
Wagoner, Dan 1932- *IntWW 93*
Wagoner, David *DrAPF 93*
Wagoner, David (Russell) 1926- *WrDr 94*
Wagoner, David Everett 1928-
WhoAm 94, WhoAmL 94, WhoWest 94
Wagoner, David Russell 1926- *IntWW 93,
WhoAm 94*
Wagoner, J. Robert 1938- *WhoBlA 94*
Wagoner, Porter 1927- *WhoAm 94,
WhoHol 92*
Wagoner, Ralph Howard 1938-
WhoAm 94, WhoMW 93
Wagoner, Robert B. 1928- *WhoAmA 93*
Wagoner, Robert Vernon 1938-
WhoAm 94, WhoScEn 94
Wagoner, Thomas Frank 1952-
WhoWest 94
Wagoner, Thomas Patrick 1958-
WhoFI 94
Wagoner, William Douglas 1947-
WhoMW 93
Wagoner, William Hampton 1927-
WhoAm 94
Wagonseller, James Myrl 1920-
WhoAm 94
Wagschal, Kathleen 1947- *WhoWest 94*
Wagstaff, Christopher John Harold 1936-
Who 94
Wagstaff, David St. John Rivers 1930-
Who 94
Wagstaff, Edward Malise Wynter 1930-
Who 94
Wagstaff, Joan Kay 1951- *WhoFI 94*
Wagstaff, Lee Stillman 1944-
WhoWest 94
Wagstaff, Robert Hall 1941- *WhoAmL 94*
Wagstaff, Samuel Standfield, Jr. 1945-
WhoMW 93
Wagstaff, Thomas Walton 1946-
WhoAmL 94
Wagstaffe, Elsie 1899- *WhoHol 92*
Wah, Fred(erick James) 1939- *ConAu 141*
Wahba, Grace *WhoAm 94*
Wahbi, Youssef d1983 *WhoHol 92*
Wahdan, Josephine Barrios 1937-
WhoHisp 94
Waheed, Desmond Zakee 1962-
WhoMW 93
Wahi, Prem Nath 1908- *IntWW 93*
Wahl, Edward Thomas 1957-
WhoAmL 94
Wahl, Floyd Michael 1931- *WhoWest 94*
Wahl, Howard Wayne 1935- *WhoAm 94*
Wahl, J. Phillip *WhoMW 93*
Wahl, Jacques Henri 1932- *IntWW 93*
Wahl, Jan 1933- *WrDr 94*
Wahl, Jan Boyer 1933- *WhoAm 94*
Wahl, Jonathan Michael 1945-
WhoAm 94
Wahl, Ken 1953- *IntMPA 94*
Wahl, Ken 1957- *WhoHol 92*
Wahl, Martha Stoessel 1916- *WhoScEn 94*
Wahl, Paul 1922- *WhoAm 94*
Wahl, Robert H. 1920- *WhoAmL 94*

Wahl, Rosalie E. *WhoAmP 93*
Wahl, Rosalie E. 1924- *WhoAm 94,
WhoAmL 94, WhoMW 93*
Wahl, Walter Dare d1974 *WhoHol 92*
Wahl, William Bryan 1963- *WhoFI 94*
Wahl, William Joseph, Jr. 1947-
WhoFI 94
Wahlberg, Allen Henry 1933- *WhoAm 94,
WhoFI 94*
Wahlberg, Kenneth Roger 1922-1988
WhAm 10
Wahlberg, Philip Lawrence 1924-
WhoAm 94
Wahle, F. Keith *DrAPF 93*
Wahlen, Bruce Edward 1947-
WhoWest 94
Wahlen, Edwin Alfred 1919- *WhoAm 94,
WhoAmL 94*
Wahler, Harry Joe 1919- *WhoWest 94*
Wahling, Jon B. 1938- *WhoAmA 93*
Wahlke, John Charles 1917- *WhoAm 94,
WhoWest 94*
Wahlman, James Spencer 1943-
WhoMW 93
Wahlman, Maude Southwell *WhoAmA 93*
Wahlmann, Theodore Raymond 1934-
WhoMW 93
Wahloo, Per 1926-1975 *EncSF 93*
Wahlquist, Andrew F. 1940- *WhoAmP 93*
Wahlquist, Jack R. 1933- *WhoIns 94*
Wahls, Myron H. 1931- *WhoAmP 93,
WhoMW 93*
Wahls, Myron Hastings 1931- *WhoBlA 94*
Wahlsten, Rudy Earl 1949- *WhoMW 93*
Wahlstrom, Harold Eugene 1947-
WhoWest 94
Wahlstrom, Jarl Holger 1918- *IntWW 93,
Who 94*
Wahlstrom, Norman O. *WhoAmP 93*
Wahoske, Michael James 1953-
WhoAm 94, WhoAmL 94
Wai, Samuel Siu Ming 1953- *WhoAm 94*
Waiapu, Bishop of 1936- *Who 94*
Waiaru, Amos Stanley *Who 94*
Waiaru, Amos Stanley 1944- *WhoAm 94*
Waid, Jim 1942- *WhoAmA 93*
Waide, (Edward) Bevan 1936- *Who 94*
Waide, Jacqueline Ann 1938-
WhoWest 94
Waidelich, Charles J. 1929- *IntWW 93*
Waidelich, Donald Long 1915-
WhoScEn 94
Waidson, Herbert Morgan 1916- *WrDr 94*
Waif Wander *BlmGWL*
Waigel, Theodor 1939- *IntWW 93,
Who 94*
Waiguchu, Muruku 1937- *WhoBlA 94*
Waihee, John D., III 1946- *WhoAmP 93*
Waihee, John David 1946- *WhoAsA 94*
Waihee, John David, III 1946- *IntWW 93,
WhoAm 94, WhoWest 94*
Wailand, Adele Rosen 1949- *WhoFI 94*
Wailand, George 1947- *WhoAm 94,
WhoAmL 94*
Wailer, Bunny 1947- *ConMus 11 [port]*
Wailes, Rodney Duane 1956-
WhoWest 94
Wailes, William George 1954-
WhoAmL 94
Wain, Christopher Henry, Jr. 1951-
WhoWest 94
Wain, John 1925- *BlmGEL [port],
DcLB 139 [port]*
Wain, John (Barrington) 1925- *WrDr 94*
Wain, John Barrington 1925- *IntWW 93,
Who 94*
Wain, (Ralph) Louis 1911- *Who 94*
Wain, Ralph Louis 1911- *IntWW 93*
Waina, Richard Baird 1939- *WhoWest 94*
Wainberg, Alan 1937- *WhoAm 94*
Wainberg, Robert Howard 1953-
WhoScEn 94
Waine, Colin 1936- *Who 94*
Waine, John *Who 94*
Wainer, Lee d1979 *WhoHol 92*
Wainer, Stanley Allen 1926- *WhoWest 94*
Wainerdi, Richard Elliott 1931-
WhoAm 94
Wainess, Marcia Watson 1949-
WhoFI 94, WhoWest 94
Wainio, Mark Ernest 1953- *WhoFI 94,
WhoWest 94*
Waininpaa, John William 1946-
WhoScEn 94, WhoWest 94
Wainman, Barbara Walden 1956-
WhoAmP 93
Wainright, Carol *DrAPF 93*
Wainright, Sam Chapman 1954-
WhoScEn 94
Wainscott, James Lawrence 1957-
WhoFI 94
Wainscott, Jeffrey Mize 1946-
WhoAmP 93
Wainscott, Ronald H(arold) 1948-
WrDr 94
Waintroob, Andrea Ruth 1952-
WhoAm 94

Wainwright, A(lfred) 1907-1991
ConAu 140
Wainwright, Carroll Livingston, Jr. 1925-
WhoAm 94
Wainwright, Cheryl Lee *WhoFI 94*
Wainwright, Edwin 1908- *Who 94*
Wainwright, Geoffrey 1939- *WrDr 94*
Wainwright, Geoffrey John 1937- *Who 94*
Wainwright, Gloria Bessie 1950-
WhoBlA 94
Wainwright, Gordon Ray 1937- *WrDr 94*
Wainwright, Hilary 1949- *WrDr 94*
Wainwright, Hope d1972 *WhoHol 92*
Wainwright, James 1938- *WhoHol 92*
Wainwright, Jeffrey 1944- *ConAu 142,
WrDr 94*
Wainwright, John 1921- *WrDr 94*
Wainwright, Loudon, III 1946-
ConMus 11 [port], WhoHol 92
Wainwright, Marie d1923 *WhoHol 92*
Wainwright, Oliver O'Connell 1936-
WhoBlA 94
Wainwright, Paul Edward Blech 1917-
WhoAm 94
Wainwright, Richard Scurrah 1918-
Who 94
Wainwright, Robert Barry 1935-
WhoAmA 93
Wainwright, Sam 1924- *Who 94*
Wainwright, Stephen A. 1931-
WhoAm 94, WhoScEn 94
Wainwright, William 1947- *WhoAmP 93*
Wainwright, William Judson 1935-
WhoMW 93
Waisanen, Gail Sue 1954- *WhoFI 94*
Waisbrot, Ann M. *WhoAmA 93*
Wais de Badgen, Irene Rut 1957-
WhoScEn 94
Waismann, Friedrich 1896-1959
DcNaB MP
Wait, Barbara Ellen *WhoAmP 93*
Wait, Carol Grace Cox 1942- *WhoAm 94*
Wait, Charles Valentine 1951- *WhoFI 94*
Wait, James Richard 1924- *WhoAm 94,
WhoScEn 94*
Wait, Mark W. 1947- *WhoWest 94*
Wait, Ronald A. 1944- *WhoAmP 93*
Wait, Samuel Charles, Jr. 1932-
WhoAm 94
Waite, Charles d1951 *WhoHol 92*
Waite, Charles Morrison 1932-
WhoAm 94
Waite, Conrad W. 1938- *WhoAmP 93*
Waite, Constance Mason 1952- *WhoFI 94*
Waite, Daniel Elmer 1926- *WhoAm 94*
Waite, Darvin Danny *WhoFI 94,
WhoMW 93*
Waite, Dennis Vernon 1938- *WhoAm 94*
Waite, Ellen Jane 1951- *WhoAm 94*
Waite, Genevieve 1949- *WhoHol 92*
Waite, Gerald Donald 1952- *WhoAmL 94*
Waite, James LeRoy 1940- *WhoMW 93*
Waite, John (Douglas) 1932- *Who 94*
Waite, John Lapp 1939- *WhoAm 94*
Waite, Larry Michael 1946- *WhoFI 94*
Waite, Lawrence Wesley 1951-
WhoMW 93, WhoScEn 94
Waite, Malcolm d1949 *WhoHol 92*
Waite, Marguerite Frances 1938-
WhoAm 94
Waite, Norma Lillia 1950- *WhoBlA 94*
Waite, Norman, Jr. 1936- *WhoAm 94*
Waite, Perry D. 1943- *WhoAmP 93*
Waite, Peter (Busby) 1922- *WrDr 94*
Waite, Ralph 1928- *WhoHol 92*
Waite, Ralph 1929- *IntMPA 94,
WhoAm 94*
Waite, Ric *IntMPA 94*
Waite, Robert Allan 1949- *WhoMW 93*
Waite, Robert George Leeson 1919-
WhoAm 94
Waite, Ruth Irene 1957- *WhoMW 93*
Waite, Stephen Holden 1936- *WhoAm 94*
Waite, Terence Hardy 1939- *IntWW 93,
Who 94*
Waiter, Serge-Albert 1930- *WhoAm 94*
Waiters, Gail Elenoria 1954- *WhoBlA 94*
Waiters, Granville S. 1961- *WhoBlA 94*
Waiters, Lloyd Winferd, Jr. 1948-
WhoBlA 94
Waites, Candy Y. 1943- *WhoAmP 93*
Waites, Elizabeth Angeline 1939-
WhoMW 93
Waites, Thomas G. 1954- *WhoHol 92*
Waites-Howard, Shirley Jean 1948-
WhoBlA 94
Waith, Eldridge 1918- *WhoBlA 94*
Waits, John A. 1947- *WhoAm 94*
Waits, Thomas Alan 1949- *WhoAm 94*
Waits, Tom *NewYTBS 93 [port]*
Waits, Tom 1949- *IntMPA 94,
WhoHol 92*
Waits-Abraham, Va Lita F. 1947-
WhoBlA 94
Waitt, Ted *WhoAm 94, WhoFI 94,
WhoMW 93*
Waitzkin, Howard 1945- *ConAu 141*

Waitzkin, Howard Bruce 1945- *WhoAm 94*
Waitzkin, Stella *WhoAmA 93*
Waiyaki, Munyua 1926- *IntWW 93*
Wajcman, Judy 1950- *ConAu 140*
Wajda, Andrze J. 1926- *IntMPA 94*
Wajda, Andrzej 1926- *IntWW 93, Who 94*
Wajda, Caroline *WhoHol 92*
Wajenberg, Arnold Sherman 1929- *WhoAm 94*
Wajer, Ronald Edward 1943- *WhoAm 94, WhoMW 93*
Wajert, Sean Peter 1960- *WhoAmL 94*
Wajnert, Thomas C. 1943- *WhoAm 94, WhoFI 94*
Wakabayashi, Ron 1944- *WhoAsA 94*
Wakamatsu, Don 1962?- *WhoAsA 94*
Wake, David Burton 1936- *WhoAm 94, WhoScEn 94, WhoWest 94*
Wake, Hereward 1916- *Who 94*
Wake, Marvalee Hendricks 1939- *WhoAm 94, WhoWest 94*
Waked, Robert Jean 1957- *WhoScEn 94*
Wakefield, Bishop of 1942- *Who 94*
Wakefield, Provost of *Who 94*
Wakefield, Anne *WhoHol 92*
Wakefield, Benton McMillin, Jr. 1920- *WhoAm 94, WhoFI 94*
Wakefield, Dan *DrAPF 93*
Wakefield, Dan 1932- *WhoAm 94, WrDr 94*
Wakefield, Derek John 1922- *Who 94*
Wakefield, Duggie d1951 *WhoHol 92*
Wakefield, Florence d1943 *WhoHol 92*
Wakefield, Gordon Stevens 1921- *Who 94*
Wakefield, Greg *WhoAmP 93*
Wakefield, Henry de c. 1335-1395 *DcNaB MP*
Wakefield, Howard 1936- *WhoWest 94*
Wakefield, Hugh d1971 *WhoHol 92*
Wakefield, Humphry *Who 94*
Wakefield, (Edward) Humphry (Tyrrell) 1936- *Who 94*
Wakefield, J. Alvin 1938- *WhoBlA 94*
Wakefield, John 1936- *NewGrDO*
Wakefield, Juana Rosella 1955- *WhoMW 93*
Wakefield, Norman (Edward) 1929- *Who 94*
Wakefield, Oliver d1956 *WhoHol 92*
Wakefield, Peter (George Arthur) 1922- *Who 94*
Wakefield, Peter George Arthur 1922- *IntWW 93*
Wakefield, Richard Alan 1947- *WhoAm 94*
Wakefield, Richard Colin 1947- *WhoFI 94*
Wakefield, Stanley Craig 1950- *WhoAmL 94*
Wakefield, Stephen Alan 1940- *WhoAm 94, WhoAmL 94*
Wakefield, Wesley Halpenny 1929- *WhoAm 94*
Wakefield, William Barry 1930- *Who 94*
Wakefield Master, The *IntDcT 2*
Wakeford, Geoffrey Michael Montgomery 1937- *Who 94*
Wakeford, Richard (Gordon) 1922- *Who 94*
Wakeham, Baron 1932- *Who 94*
Wakeham, Deborah 1955- *WhoHol 92*
Wakeham, Helmut Richard Rae 1916- *WhoAm 94*
Wakeham, John 1932- *IntWW 93*
Wakehurst, Baron 1925- *Who 94*
Wakehurst, Dowager Lady 1899- *Who 94*
Wakeley, John (Cecil Nicholson) 1926- *Who 94*
Wakelin, James Henry, Jr. 1911- *WhoAmP 93*
Wakelin, James Henry, Jr. 1911-1990 *WhAm 10*
Wakeling, John Denis 1918- *Who 94*
Wakeling, Richard Keith Arthur 1946- *Who 94*
Wakely, Jimmy d1982 *WhoHol 92*
Wakely, Leonard John Dean 1909- *Who 94*
Wakelyn, Phillip Jeffrey 1940- *WhoScEn 94*
Wakeman, Edward Offley Bertram 1934- *Who 94*
Wakeman, Evans 1937- *WrDr 94*
Wakeman, Fred Joseph 1928- *WhoAm 94*
Wakeman, Frederic Evans, Jr. 1937- *WhoAm 94, WrDr 94*
Wakeman, Rick 1949- *WhoAm 94*
Wakeman, Thomas George 1945- *WhoScEn 94*
Wakerley, Richard MacLennon 1942- *Who 94*
Wakham, Bernard Brock 1964- *WhoWest 94*
Wakhevitch, Georges 1907-1984 *IntDcF 2-4, NewGrDO*
Wakil, Abdul 1945- *IntWW 93*
Wakil, Salih Jawad 1927- *WhoAm 94*
Wakimura, Yoshitaro 1900- *WhoScEn 94*
Wakin, Malham M. 1931- *WhoWest 94*
Wa Kinyatti, Maina 1944- *WrDr 94*
Wakley, Bertram Joseph 1917- *Who 94*
Wakley, James Turner 1921- *WhoAm 94*
Waknine, Samuel 1959- *WhoScEn 94*
Wakoff, Robert 1925- *WhoScEn 94*
Wakosi, Diane 1937- *BlmGWL*
Wakoski, Diane *DrAPF 93*
Wakoski, Diane 1937- *WhoAm 94, WrDr 94*
Waks, Jay Warren 1946- *WhoAm 94, WhoAmL 94*
Waksberg, Naomi 1947- *WhoAmA 93*
Waksman, Byron Halsted 1919- *WhoAm 94*
Waksman, Selman Abraham 1888-1973 *WorScD*
Waksman, Ted Stewart 1949- *WhoAm 94*
Walasek, Otto Frank 1919- *WhoWest 94*
Walaszek, Edward Joseph 1927- *WhoAm 94*
Walba, David Mark 1949- *WhoWest 94*
Walbank, F(rank) W(illiam) 1909- *ConAu 142*
Walbank, Frank William 1909- *Who 94, WrDr 94*
Walberg, Garry 1923- *WhoHol 92*
Walberg, Herbert John 1937- *WhoAm 94*
Walberg, Keith Allen 1962- *WhoMW 93*
Walberg, Timothy Lee 1951- *WhoAmP 93*
Walbert, Florence Catherine 1929- *WhoMW 93*
Walbey, Theodosia Emma Draher 1950- *WhoBlA 94*
Walborsky, Harry M. 1923- *WhoAm 94*
Walbrandt, Charles D. 1938- *WhoFI 94*
Walbridge, John Tuthill, Jr. 1925- *WhoAmP 93*
Walbridge, Stephen Edward 1948- *WhoFI 94*
Walbridge, Willard Eugene 1913- *WhoAm 94*
Walbrook, Anton d1967 *WhoHol 92*
Walbrook, Louise 1916- *WrDr 94*
Walburg, Gerald 1936- *WhoAmA 93*
Walburg, Judith Ann 1948- *WhoBlA 94*
Walburn, John Clifford 1945- *WhoMW 93*
Walburn, Raymond d1969 *WhoHol 92*
Walby, Christine Mary 1940- *Who 94*
Walcamp, Marie d1936 *WhoHol 92*
Walch, John Leo 1918- *WhoAmA 93*
Walch, John MacArthur Dunsmore 1926- *WhoAmP 93*
Walch, Marianne 1957- *WhoScEn 94*
Walch, Peter Sanborn 1940- *WhoAm 94, WhoWest 94*
Walch, Timothy George 1947- *WhoMW 93*
Walch, W. Stanley 1934- *WhoAm 94*
Walcher, Alan Ernest 1949- *WhoAm 94, WhoAmL 94*
Walcott, Arthur 1857- *WhoHol 92*
Walcott, Charles 1934- *WhoAm 94*
Walcott, Derek *DrAPF 93, IntWW 93*
Walcott, Derek 1930- *BlmGEL, ConBlB 5 [port], ConLC 76 [port]*
Walcott, Derek (Alton) 1930- *BlkWr 2, ConDr 93, IntDcT 2 [port], WrDr 94*
Walcott, Derek Alton 1930- *WhoAm 94*
Walcott, Gregory 1932- *WhoHol 92*
Walcott, Richard Irving 1933- *Who 94*
Walczak, Zbigniew Kazimierz 1932- *WhoScEn 94*
Wald, A. G. *NewGrDO*
Wald, Bernard Joseph 1932- *WhoAm 94, WhoAmL 94, WhoFI 94*
Wald, Bruce Lewis 1946- *WhoAmL 94, WhoMW 93*
Wald, Carol 1935- *WhoAmA 93*
Wald, Diane *DrAPF 93*
Wald, Donna Gene 1947- *WhoAm 94*
Wald, Francine Joy Weintraub 1938- *WhoScEn 94*
Wald, Francis John 1935- *WhoAmP 93*
Wald, George 1906- *IntWW 93, Who 94, WhoAm 94, WhoScEn 94, WorScD*
Wald, Jane *WhoHol 92*
Wald, Jeff Sommers 1944- *WhoAm 94*
Wald, Jerry 1911-1962 *IntDcF 2-4*
Wald, Lillian D. 1867-1940 *AmSocL [port], HisWorL [port]*
Wald, Malvin 1917- *IntMPA 94*
Wald, Martin 1934- *WhoAm 94*
Wald, Mary S. 1943- *WhoFI 94*
Wald, Michael H. 1953- *WhoAmL 94*
Wald, Michael Leonard 1951- *WhoFI 94*
Wald, Nicholas John 1944- *Who 94*
Wald, Niel 1925- *WhoAm 94*
Wald, Palmer B. 1930-1988 *WhoAmA 93N*
Wald, Patricia M. 1928- *WhoAmP 93*
Wald, Patricia McGowan 1928- *CngDr 93, IntWW 93, WhoAm 94, WhoAmL 94*
Wald, Richard C. *IntWW 93*
Wald, Richard C. 1931- *IntMPA 94*
Wald, Robert Gray 1963- *WhoWest 94*
Wald, Robert Lewis 1926- *WhoAmL 94*
Wald, Sylvia *WhoAmA 93*
Wald, Sylvia 1915- *WhoAm 94*
Walda, John D. 1950- *WhoAmL 94*
Waldau, Gustav d1958 *WhoHol 92*
Waldauer, Charles 1935- *WhoFI 94*
Waldbauer, Gilbert Peter 1928- *WhoAm 94*
Waldbaum, Maxim Howard 1942- *WhoAmL 94*
Waldbrunn, Ernst d1977 *WhoHol 92*
Walde, David Bruce 1960- *WhoFI 94*
Walde, Thomas 1949- *IntWW 93*
Waldeck, Gary Cranston 1943- *WhoWest 94*
Waldeck, John Walter, Jr. 1949- *WhoAm 94, WhoAmL 94, WhoFI 94, WhoMW 93*
Waldecker, Thomas Raymond 1950- *WhoMW 93*
Waldegrave, Earl 1905- *Who 94*
Waldegrave, William 1946- *IntWW 93*
Waldegrave, William (Arthur) 1946- *Who 94*
Waldemar, IV c. 1320-1375 *HisWorL*
Waldemar, Richard d1947 *WhoHol 92*
Waldemar, Shirley Elise 1944- *WhoFI 94*
Walden, Amelia Elizabeth *TwCYAW, WhoAm 94*
Walden, Barbara 1936- *WhoBlA 94*
Walden, Ben Parrish 1931- *WhoWest 94*
Walden, (Alastair) Brian 1932- *IntWW 93, Who 94*
Walden, Daniel 1922- *WhoAm 94*
Walden, Edith M. *DrAPF 93*
Walden, Emerson Coleman 1923- *WhoBlA 94*
Walden, Emory Earl 1898- *WhAm 10*
Walden, George Gordon Harvey 1939- *Who 94*
Walden, Graham Howard *Who 94*
Walden, Greg 1957- *WhoAmP 93*
Walden, Herbert Richard Charles 1926- *Who 94*
Walden, James Lee 1955- *WhoWest 94*
Walden, James William 1936- *WhoAm 94, WhoFI 94, WhoMW 93*
Walden, Martha d1988 *WhoHol 92*
Walden, Narada Michael 1952- *WhoBlA 94*
Walden, Omi Gail 1945- *WhoScEn 94*
Walden, Philip Michael 1940- *WhoAm 94*
Walden, Robert 1943- *WhoAm 94, WhoHol 92*
Walden, Robert Edison 1920- *WhoBlA 94*
Walden, Robert Thomas 1939- *WhoScEn 94*
Walden, Ron William 1947- *WhoAmL 94*
Walden, Stanley Eugene 1932- *WhoAm 94*
Walden, Sylvia *WhoHol 92*
Walden, Thurman L. 1926- *WhoAmP 93*
Walden, W.G. 1951?- *ConTFT 11*
Walden, W. Thomas 1950- *WhoScEn 94*
Walden, William *DrAPF 93*
Waldenstrom, Jan Gosta 1906- *IntWW 93*
Walder, Edwin James 1921- *Who 94*
Walder, Ernest *WhoHol 92*
Walder, Joseph 1908- *WhoAm 94*
Walder, Ruth Christabel 1906- *Who 94*
Waldera, Gerald Joseph 1931- *WhoAmP 93*
Waldera, Wayne Eugene 1930- *WhoAm 94, WhoMW 93*
Waldeyer, John Thomas, Jr. 1948- *WhoAmP 93*
Waldeyer-Hartz, Wilhelm von 1836-1921 *WorScD*
Waldfogel, LaRue Verl 1926- *WhoScEn 94*
Waldfogel, Morton Sumner 1922- *WhoAm 94*
Waldhauer, Fred Donald 1927- *WhoAm 94, WhoWest 94*
Waldhausen, John Anton 1929- *WhoAm 94*
Waldhauser, Cathy Howard 1949- *WhoAm 94*
Waldheim, Kurt 1918- *IntWW 93, Who 94*
Waldherr, Kris 1963- *SmATA 76 [port]*
Waldholtz, Joseph P. 1963- *WhoAmP 93*
Waldis, Otto d1974 *WhoHol 92*
Waldman, Anne *DrAPF 93*
Waldman, Anne 1945- *WrDr 94*
Waldman, Anne Lesley 1945- *WhoAm 94*
Waldman, Bart 1948- *WhoAm 94, WhoAmL 94*
Waldman, Harvey *WhoHol 92*
Waldman, Jay Carl 1944- *WhoAm 94, WhoAmL 94*
Waldman, Jerald Paul 1946- *WhoWest 94*
Waldman, Jules Lloyd 1912-1990 *WhAm 10*
Waldman, Mel *DrAPF 93*
Waldman, Paul 1936- *WhoAmA 93*
Waldman, Robert Hart 1938- *WhoAm 94*
Waldman, Saul Joseph 1931- *WhoMW 93*
Waldman, Suzyn *NewYTBS 93 [port]*
Waldman, Walter d1993 *IntMPA 94N*
Waldmann, Herman 1945- *Who 94*
Waldmann, Maria 1842-1920 *NewGrDO*
Waldmann, Raymond John 1938- *WhoAmP 93*
Waldmann, Thomas Alexander 1930- *WhoAm 94, WhoScEn 94*
Waldmeir, Peter Nielsen 1931- *WhoAm 94*
Waldmeir, Peter William 1953- *WhoAm 94, WhoAmL 94*
Waldmuller, Lizzi d1945 *WhoHol 92*
Waldner-Haugrud, Lisa Kay 1963- *WhoMW 93*
Waldo, Anna Lee 1925- *WrDr 94*
Waldo, Burton Corlett 1920- *WhoAmL 94, WhoWest 94*
Waldo, Carol Dunn *WhoBlA 94*
Waldo, Dwight 1913- *WhoAm 94*
Waldo, James Chandler 1948- *WhoAmL 94*
Waldo, Janet 1918- *WhoHol 92*
Waldo, Jeffrey Ralph 1956- *WhoAmL 94*
Waldo, Robert Leland 1923- *WhoAm 94*
Waldon, Alton R., Jr. 1936- *WhoAmP 93*
Waldon, Alton Ronald, Jr. 1936- *WhoBlA 94*
Waldon, Lori Annette 1961- *WhoBlA 94*
Waldon, Marja Parker 1939- *WhoMW 93*
Waldorf, Eugene 1936- *WhoAmP 93*
Waldorf, Geraldine Polack 1942- *WhoAmL 94*
Waldow, Stephen Michael 1959- *WhoScEn 94*
Waldram, Scott G. 1951- *WhoWest 94*
Waldrep, Kenneth *WhoAmP 93*
Waldrep, Robert L., Jr. *WhoAmP 93*
Waldridge, Harold d1957 *WhoHol 92*
Waldron, Acie Chandler 1930- *WhoAm 94*
Waldron, Andrew d1932 *WhoHol 92*
Waldron, Arthur (Nelson) 1948- *WrDr 94*
Waldron, Charles d1946 *WhoHol 92*
Waldron, Charles, Jr. d1952 *WhoHol 92*
Waldron, Ellis Leigh 1915- *WhoAm 94*
Waldron, Jack d1967 *WhoHol 92*
Waldron, James Mackeilar 1909-1974 *WhoAmA 93N*
Waldron, James Thomas, Jr. 1945- *WhoAm 94, WhoAmL 94*
Waldron, John Graham Claverhouse 1909- *Who 94*
Waldron, Kenneth John 1943- *WhoMW 93, WhoScEn 94*
Waldron, Kenneth Lynn 1941- *WhoAmL 94*
Waldron, May *WhoHol 92*
Waldron, Orval Hubert 1918- *WhoAmP 93*
Waldron, Steve 1946- *WhoAmP 93*
Waldron-Ramsey, Waldo Emerson 1930- *Who 94*
Waldrop, Bernard Keith 1932- *WhoAm 94*
Waldrop, Dave C., Jr. 1943- *WhoAmP 93*
Waldrop, Francis Neil 1926- *WhoAm 94*
Waldrop, Gerald Wayne 1942- *WhoAmP 93*
Waldrop, Gideon William 1919- *WhoAm 94*
Waldrop, Howard 1946- *ConAu 41NR, EncSF 93, WrDr 94*
Waldrop, Isaac Merit, Jr. 1933- *WhoAmP 93*
Waldrop, Keith *DrAPF 93*
Waldrop, Richard E. 1952- *WhoFI 94*
Waldrop, Rosmarie *DrAPF 93*
Waldrup, Charles E. 1925- *WhoAmP 93*
Waldschmidt, Paul Edward 1920- *WhoAm 94, WhoWest 94*
Waldseemuller, Martin c. 1470-c. 1522 *WhWE*
Waldstein, Arne *WhoAmP 93*
Waldstein, Edith Josefine 1951- *WhoMW 93*
Waldstein, Sheldon Saul 1924- *WhoAm 94*
Walecki, Wojciech Jan 1964- *WhoScEn 94*
Walen, Harry Leonard 1915- *WhoAm 94*
Walen, James Robert 1947- *WhoWest 94*
Walendowski, George Jerry 1947- *WhoFI 94*
Walenga, Jeanine Marie 1955- *WhoMW 93*
Wales, Archbishop of 1934- *Who 94*
Wales, H.R.H. The Prince of 1948- *IntWW 93*
Wales, H.R.H. The Princess of 1961- *IntWW 93*
Wales, Prince of 1948- *Who 94R*
Wales, Daphne Beatrice 1917- *Who 94*
Wales, Ethel d1952 *WhoHol 92*
Wales, Gwynne Huntington 1933- *WhoAm 94*
Wales, H. Elliot 1930- *WhoAmL 94*
Wales, Harold Webster 1928- *WhoAm 94*
Wales, Hugh Gregory 1910- *WhoAm 94, WhoWest 94*

Wales, M. Elizabeth 1932- *WhoMW 93*
Wales, Nym 1907- *WrDr 94*
Wales, Richard Bert 1952- *WhoWest 94*
Wales, Robert 1923- *WrDr 94*
Wales, Ross Elliot 1947- *WhoAm 94, WhoAmL 94*
Wales, Wally d1980 *WhoHol 92*
Wales, Walter D. 1933- *WhoAm 94*
Walesa, Lech 1943- *IntWW 93, Who 94, WhoHol 92*
Waletzky, Cecelia Grobla *WhoAmA 93*
Waletzky, Tsirl *WhoAmA 93*
Waley, Daniel Philip 1921- *Who 94*
Waley, Felix *Who 94*
Waley, (Andrew) Felix 1926- *Who 94*
Waley-Cohen, Joyce Constance Ina 1920- *Who 94*
Waley-Cohen, Stephen (Harry) 1946- *Who 94*
Walfish, Benjamin H. 1925- *WhoAm 94*
Walford, A(lbert) J(ohn) 1906- *WrDr 94*
Walford, Christopher Rupert 1935- *Who 94*
Walford, Diana Marion 1944- *Who 94*
Walford, E. John 1945- *WhoAmA 93*
Walford, John Howard 1927- *Who 94*
Walford, John Thomas 1933- *Who 94*
Walford, Lucy 1845-1915 *BlmGWL*
Walfred, Hugo Anderson 1925- *WhoAm 94*
Walgran, Craig Chance 1953- *WhoFI 94*
Walgreen, Charles Rudolph, III 1935- *WhoAm 94, WhoFI 94, WhoMW 93*
Walgren, Doug 1940- *WhoAmP 93*
Walgren, Gordon Lee 1933- *WhoAmP 93*
Walgren, Paul Castleton 1922- *WhoAmP 93*
Walhain, Michael Octave Marie Louis 1915- *IntWW 93*
Walhout, Justine Simon 1930- *WhoMW 93*
Wali, Kameshwar 1927- *WhoAm 94*
Wali, Mohan Kishen 1937- *WhoAm 94, WhoMW 93, WhoScEn 94*
Walia, Harjeet Rosie 1950- *WhoAsA 94*
Walia, Jasjit Singh 1934- *WhoAsA 94*
Walia, Satish Kumar 1951- *WhoScEn 94*
Walicki, Andrzej Stanislaw 1930- *WhoAm 94*
Waligora, James 1954- *WhoFI 94*
Waligorski, Ewaryst 1937- *IntWW 93*
Walinska, Anna 1916- *WhoAmA 93*
Walinski, Nicholas Joseph 1920- *WhoAm 94*
Walinsky, Louis Joseph 1908- *WhoAm 94*
Walinsky, Paul 1940- *WhoScEn 94*
Waliser, Beverly Kay 1956- *WhoMW 93*
Walize, Reuben Thompson, III 1950- *WhoFI 94, WhoScEn 94, WhoWest 94*
Walk, George 1949- *WhoAmP 93*
Walk, Richard David 1920- *WhoAm 94*
Walk, Ronald Douglas 1943- *WhoAm 94, WhoFI 94*
Walke, David Michael 1954- *WhoAm 94, WhoFI 94*
Walke, Raymond J. 1936- *WhoIns 94*
Walken, Christopher 1943- *IntMPA 94, IntWW 93, WhoAm 94, WhoHol 92*
Walken, Ken 1937- *WhoHol 92*
Walkenbach, Ronald Joseph 1948- *WhoScEn 94*
Walkenhorst, Phillip Lloyd 1939- *WhoMW 93*
Walkenhorst, Walter Ted 1948- *WhoAmL 94*
Walker *Who 94*
Walker, A. Harris 1935- *WhoAmL 94*
Walker, A. Maceo 1909- *WhoIns 94*
Walker, A. Maceo, Sr. 1909- *WhoBlA 94*
Walker, Alan 1911- *IntWW 93, Who 94, WrDr 94*
Walker, Albert L. 1945- *WhoBlA 94*
Walker, Albertina 1929- *WhoBlA 94*
Walker, Alexander 1930- *ConAu 142, Who 94, WrDr 94*
Walker, Alexander E. 1887-1960? *EncABHB 9 [port]*
Walker, Alfred John 1954- *WhoFI 94*
Walker, Alfred L., Jr. 1935- *WhoAmP 93*
Walker, Alice *DrAPF 93*
Walker, Alice 1944- *AfrAmAl 6 [port], BlmGWL [port], EncSF 93, WrDr 94*
Walker, Alice (Malsenior) 1944- *BlkWr 2, RfGShF, TwCYAW*
Walker, Alice Davis 1931- *WhoFI 94*
Walker, Alice Malsenior 1944- *IntWW 93, WhoAm 94, WhoBlA 94*
Walker, Allan (Grierson) 1907- *Who 94*
Walker, Allene Marsha 1953- *WhoBlA 94*
Walker, Ally *WhoHol 92*
Walker, Angus Henry 1935- *Who 94*
Walker, Ann B. 1923- *WhoBlA 94*
Walker, Ann Yvonne 1954- *WhoAmL 94*
Walker, Anne Collins 1939- *ConAu 141*
Walker, Annie Mae 1913- *WhoBlA 94*
Walker, Antoinette d1970 *WhoHol 92*
Walker, Antony (Kenneth Frederick) 1934- *Who 94*
Walker, Arman Kennis 1957- *WhoBlA 94*
Walker, Arnetia *WhoHol 92*
Walker, Arthur B. C. 1901- *WhoBlA 94*
Walker, Arthur Carleton 1943- *WhoFI 94*
Walker, Arthur Geoffrey 1909- *Who 94*
Walker, Aurora d1964 *WhoHol 92*
Walker, Baldwin Patrick 1924- *Who 94*
Walker, Barbara Ann 1960- *WhoFI 94*
Walker, Barth Powell 1914- *WhoFI 94*
Walker, Ben d1924 *WhoHol 92*
Walker, Benjamin 1753-1818 *WhAmRev*
Walker, Benjamin 1923- *WrDr 94*
Walker, Berta *WhoAmA 93*
Walker, Betsy Ellen 1953- *WhoAm 94*
Walker, Betty d1982 *WhoHol 92*
Walker, Betty A. *ConAu 140*
Walker, Betty Jean *WhoAmP 93*
Walker, Betty Stevens 1944- *WhoBlA 94*
Walker, Bill *Who 94, WhoHol 92*
Walker, Billy Kenneth 1946- *WhoAm 94, WhoFI 94*
Walker, Bobby *Who 94*
Walker, Brent Taylor 1963- *WhoAmP 93*
Walker, Brian *DrAPF 93*
Walker, Brian Wilson 1930- *Who 94*
Walker, Bruce d1973 *WhoHol 92*
Walker, Bruce Edward 1926- *WhoAm 94, WhoMW 93, WhoScEn 94*
Walker, Bruce Howard 1946- *WhoWest 94*
Walker, Bruce J. *WhoAmP 93*
Walker, Burton Leith 1927- *WhoWest 94*
Walker, C. Eugene 1939- *WhoAm 94*
Walker, C. J. 1867-1919 *AfrAmAl 6*
Walker, Carl 1934- *Who 94*
Walker, Carl, Jr. 1924- *WhoBlA 94*
Walker, Carol Ann 1937- *WhoFI 94*
Walker, Carolyn *WhoBlA 94*
Walker, Carolyn Louise 1947- *WhoWest 94*
Walker, Catherine *IntWW 93*
Walker, Catherine Marguerite Marie-Therese *Who 94*
Walker, Cecil *Who 94*
Walker, (Alfred) Cecil 1924- *Who 94*
Walker, Charles 1945- *WhoBlA 94*
Walker, Charles A. *WhoBlA 94*
Walker, Charles A. 1935-1992 *WhAm 10*
Walker, Charles Allen 1914- *WhoAm 94*
Walker, Charles B. 1939- *WhoAm 94, WhoFI 94*
Walker, Charles Douglas 1915- *WhoBlA 94*
Walker, Charles E. 1935- *WhoBlA 94*
Walker, Charles Edward, Jr. 1951- *WhoBlA 94*
Walker, Charles H. 1951- *WhoBlA 94*
Walker, Charles Henri 1951- *WhoAmL 94*
Walker, Charles Montgomery 1915- *WhoAm 94*
Walker, Charles Norman 1923- *WhoAm 94*
Walker, Charles R., III 1930- *WhoAm 94*
Walker, Charles Ray 1927- *WhoAmP 93*
Walker, Charles Urmston 1931- *WhoAm 94*
Walker, Charles W. 1947- *WhoAmP 93*
Walker, Charlotte d1958 *WhoHol 92*
Walker, Charlotte Zoe *DrAPF 93*
Walker, Charls E. 1923- *Who 94*
Walker, Charls Edward 1923- *IntWW 93, WhoAm 94, WhoAmP 93*
Walker, Cheryl d1971 *WhoHol 92*
Walker, Chester 1940- *WhoBlA 94*
Walker, Chet 1940- *BasBi*
Walker, Chico 1957- *WhoBlA 94*
Walker, Chris *WhoBlA 94*
Walker, Chris L. 1957- *WhoIns 94*
Walker, Christy d1918 *WhoHol 92*
Walker, Cindy Lee 1952- *WhoBlA 94*
Walker, Clarence Wesley 1931- *WhoAm 94, WhoAmL 94*
Walker, Claud L. 1934- *WhoAmP 93*
Walker, Claude 1934- *WhoBlA 94*
Walker, Clint 1927- *IntMPA 94, WhoHol 92*
Walker, Colin (John Shedlock) 1934- *Who 94*
Walker, Cora T. 1926- *WhoBlA 94*
Walker, Coyd McConnell 1942- *WhoMW 93*
Walker, Craig J. 1962- *WhoBlA 94*
Walker, Craig Michael 1947- *WhoAm 94, WhoAmL 94*
Walker, Cynthia Bush 1956- *WhoBlA 94*
Walker, Cynthia Mary 1954- *WhoAmL 94*
Walker, Dale Rush 1943- *WhoAm 94*
Walker, Daniel Jay 1960- *WhoScEn 94*
Walker, Daniel Joshua, Jr. 1915- *WhoAmL 94*
Walker, Darcy Lynn 1949- *WhoAm 94*
Walker, Darrell 1961- *WhoBlA 94*
Walker, David d1976 *WhoHol 92*
Walker, David 1934- *NewGrDO*
Walker, David (Alan) 1939- *Who 94*
Walker, David (Harry) 1911-1992 *EncSF 93, WrDr 94N*
Walker, David (Maxwell) 1920- *WrDr 94*
Walker, David Alan 1928- *IntWW 93, Who 94*
Walker, David Alan 1939- *IntWW 93*
Walker, David Alan 1941- *WhoAm 94*
Walker, David Bradstreet 1927- *WhoAm 94*
Walker, David Bruce 1934- *IntWW 93, Who 94*
Walker, David Bruce 1943- *WhoFI 94*
Walker, David C. *DrAPF 93*
Walker, David Critchlow 1940- *Who 94*
Walker, David H. 1925- *WhoAmP 93*
Walker, David Harry 1911-1992 *AnObit 1992, WhAm 10*
Walker, David Maxwell 1920- *IntWW 93, Who 94*
Walker, David Michael 1951- *WhoAm 94, WhoFI 94*
Walker, David T. 1941- *WhoWest 94*
Walker, David Wild 1941- *WhoAm 94*
Walker, Dean Everest 1898- *WhAm 10*
Walker, Debra May 1956- *WhoMW 93*
Walker, Dennis Eugene 1961- *WhoMW 93*
Walker, Dennis William, III 1948- *WhoFI 94*
Walker, Derek William Rothwell 1924- *Who 94*
Walker, Derrick N. 1967- *WhoBlA 94*
Walker, Deward E(dgar), Jr. 1935- *ConAu 43NR*
Walker, Deward Edgar, Jr. 1935- *WhoAm 94, WhoWest 94*
Walker, Doak *ProFbHF [port]*
Walker, Donald 1928- *Who 94*
Walker, Donald Ezzell 1921- *WhoAm 94*
Walker, Donald Robert, Jr. 1955- *WhoMW 93*
Walker, Donna Henry 1954- *WhoFI 94*
Walker, Donna Jeanne 1953- *WhoFI 94*
Walker, Doreen 1920- *WrDr 94*
Walker, Dorothea Bernice 1906- *WhoBlA 94*
Walker, Doug *WhoAmP 93*
Walker, Douglas F. 1937- *WhoBlA 94*
Walker, Duard Lee 1921- *WhoAm 94*
Walker, Duncan Edward 1942- *WhoWest 94*
Walker, Duncan Moore Henry 1956- *WhoScEn 94*
Walker, E. Cardon 1916- *IntMPA 94*
Walker, E. Jerry 1918- *WhoWest 94*
Walker, Earl E. 1921- *WhoAm 94, WhoScEn 94*
Walker, Edward Bullock, III 1922- *IntWW 93*
Walker, Edward D. 1946- *WhoAmA 93*
Walker, Edward Keith, Jr. 1933- *WhoAm 94*
Walker, Edward S., Jr. *WhoAmP 93*
Walker, Edward S., Jr. 1940- *WhoAm 94*
Walker, Edwin A. 1909-1993 *NewYTBS 93 [port]*
Walker, Edwin Hockaday, IV 1932- *WhoMW 93*
Walker, Edwin L. 1956- *WhoBlA 94*
Walker, Edyth 1867?-1950 *NewGrDO*
Walker, Elizabeth 1947- *WhoHol 92*
Walker, Elizabeth Jane 1936- *WhoAmP 93*
Walker, Elizabeth Virginia 1947- *WhoWest 94*
Walker, Eljana M. du Vall 1924- *WhoWest 94*
Walker, Elkanah 1805-1877 *EncNAR*
Walker, Ellen W. *WhoAmP 93*
Walker, Elva Mae Dawson 1914- *WhoMW 93*
Walker, Eric Arthur 1910- *WhoAm 94*
Walker, Ernest L. 1941- *WhoBlA 94*
Walker, Ernest Winfield 1917- *WhoAm 94*
Walker, Ernestein 1926- *WhoBlA 94*
Walker, Esper Lafayette, Jr. 1930- *WhoScEn 94*
Walker, Ethel Pitts 1943- *WhoBlA 94*
Walker, Eugene Allen 1963- *WhoAmL 94*
Walker, Eugene Henry 1925- *WhoBlA 94*
Walker, Eugene Kevin 1951- *WhoBlA 94*
Walker, Eugene P. *WhoAmP 93*
Walker, Eugene Wilson 1919- *WhoAmP 93*
Walker, Evelyn *WhoAm 94, WhoFI 94*
Walker, Everett d1968 *WhoAmA 93N*
Walker, F. Ann 1940- *WhoAm 94*
Walker, Felix Carr, Jr. 1949- *WhoBlA 94*
Walker, Fiona 1944- *WhoHol 92*
Walker, Floyd Lee 1919- *WhoAm 94*
Walker, Frances 1924- *WhoBlA 94*
Walker, Frances Morine 1931- *WhoMW 93*
Walker, Francis Joseph 1922- *WhoAmL 94, WhoFI 94, WhoWest 94*
Walker, Frank Banghart 1931- *WhoAm 94, WhoMW 93, WhoScEn 94*
Walker, Frank Dilling 1934- *WhoAm 94*
Walker, Fred Elmer 1931- *WhoAm 94*
Walker, Frederick 1934- *Who 94*
Walker, Freeman, III 1965- *WhoBlA 94*
Walker, G. Edward 1942- *WhoBlA 94*
Walker, Gary S. 1947- *WhoBlA 94*
Walker, Gay Hunner Parsons 1939- *WhoAm 94*
Walker, Gayle Jean 1947- *WhoMW 93*
Walker, Geoffrey de Q(uincey) 1940- *WrDr 94*
Walker, George 1922- *AfrAmAl 6*
Walker, George Alfred 1929- *IntWW 93, Who 94*
Walker, George Allen 1929- *WhoAm 94*
Walker, George Edward 1940- *WhoBlA 94*
Walker, George F. 1947- *ConAu 43NR, WrDr 94*
Walker, George F(rederick) 1947- *ConDr 93, IntDcT 2*
Walker, George Herbert, III 1931- *WhoAm 94, WhoFI 94*
Walker, George Kontz 1938- *WhoAm 94, WhoAmL 94*
Walker, George Moore 1952- *WhoAmL 94*
Walker, George P. L. 1926- *IntWW 93*
Walker, George Patrick Leonard 1926- *Who 94*
Walker, George Raymond 1936- *WhoBlA 94*
Walker, George Robert 1915- *WhoIns 94*
Walker, George T. 1922- *WhoBlA 94*
Walker, George Theophilus, Jr. 1922- *WhoAm 94*
Walker, George W. *WhoMW 93*
Walker, George Walton, III 1964- *WhoAmL 94*
Walker, Gerald *DrAPF 93*
Walker, Gerald T. 1940- *WhoIns 94*
Walker, Gervas (George) 1920- *Who 94*
Walker, Gordon Arthur Hunter 1936- *WhoAm 94*
Walker, Gordon Davies 1944- *WhoAm 94*
Walker, Gordon T. 1942- *WhoAm 94, WhoAmL 94*
Walker, Graham Charles 1948- *WhoScEn 94*
Walker, Grover Pulliam 1941- *WhoBlA 94*
Walker, H. Jay, III 1947- *WhoAmP 93*
Walker, H. Lawson 1949- *WhoAm 94*
Walker, Hal d1972 *WhoHol 92*
Walker, Hal Wilson 1929- *WhoAmP 93*
Walker, Harold 1927- *Who 94*
Walker, Harold (Berners) 1932- *Who 94*
Walker, Harold Blake 1904- *WhoAm 94*
Walker, Harold Osmonde 1928- *WhoAm 94*
Walker, Harrell Lynn 1945- *WhoScEn 94*
Walker, Harry *Who 94*
Walker, Harry 1920- *WrDr 94*
Walker, Harry Grey 1924- *WhoAm 94, WhoAmP 93*
Walker, Helen d1968 *WhoHol 92*
Walker, Henry Babcock, Jr. 1885-1966 *WhoAmA 93N*
Walker, Henry Gilbert 1947- *WhoAm 94*
Walker, Henry Lawson, II 1949- *WhoAmP 93*
Walker, Herbert Ashcombe 1868-1949 *DcNaB MP*
Walker, Herbert Brooks 1927- *WhoAmA 93*
Walker, Herbert John 1919- *IntWW 93*
Walker, Herbert Leslie, Jr. 1918- *WhoAm 94*
Walker, Herbert Samuel 1924- *IntWW 93*
Walker, Herschel 1962- *WhoAm 94, WhoBlA 94*
Walker, Herschel Carey *WhoAmA 93N*
Walker, Homer Franklin 1943- *WhoWest 94*
Walker, Howard Ernest 1944- *WhoAm 94, WhoAmL 94*
Walker, Howard K. 1935- *WhoAmP 93*
Walker, Howard Kent 1935- *WhoBlA 94*
Walker, Howard Painter 1932- *WhoAmL 94*
Walker, Hudson D. 1907-1976 *WhoAmA 93N*
Walker, Hugh 1941- *EncSF 93*
Walker, Hugh (Ronald) 1925- *Who 94*
Walker, Irving Edward 1952- *WhoAm 94, WhoAmL 94*
Walker, J. 1932- *WrDr 94*
Walker, J. Wilbur 1912- *WhoBlA 94*
Walker, Jack D. 1922- *WhoAmP 93*
Walker, James 1916- *Who 94*
Walker, James 1926- *WhoBlA 94*
Walker, James (Graham) 1913- *Who 94*
Walker, James A. 1949- *WhoIns 94*
Walker, James Adams 1921-1987 *WhoAmA 93N*
Walker, James Bernard 1946- *Who 94*
Walker, James Calvin 1951- *WhoFI 94, WhoScEn 94*
Walker, James Elliot Cabot 1926- *WhoAm 94*
Walker, James Findlay 1916- *Who 94*
Walker, James George 1958- *WhoFI 94*

Walker, James Heron 1914- *Who 94*
Walker, James Kenneth 1936- *WhoAm 94*
Walker, James R. 1849-1926 *EncNAR*
Walker, James Roderick 1946- *WhoWest 94*
Walker, James Ronald 1947- *WhoAmP 93*
Walker, James Roy 1937- *WhoAm 94*
Walker, James Silas 1933- *WhoAm 94, WhoMW 93*
Walker, James William, Jr. 1927- *WhoAm 94*
Walker, James Zell, II 1932- *WhoBlA 94*
Walker, Jean Kindy 1933- *WhoAmP 93*
Walker, Jeanne Murray *DrAPF 93*
Walker, Jennie Louise 1962- *WhoFI 94*
Walker, Jerald Carter 1938- *WhoAm 94*
Walker, Jerry Euclid 1932- *WhoBlA 94*
Walker, Jerry Quenten 1953- *WhoWest 94*
Walker, Jewel Lee 1950- *WhoMW 93*
Walker, Jill Marie 1955- *WhoWest 94*
Walker, Jimmie *WhoHol 92*
Walker, Jimmie 1945- *WhoBlA 94*
Walker, Jimmie 1947- *WhoBlA 94*
Walker, Jimmie 1949- *WhoCom*
Walker, Jimmie Kent 1940- *WhoMW 93, WhoScEn 94*
Walker, Jimmy 1944- *BasBi*
Walker, Joe 1934- *WhoBlA 94*
Walker, John 1906- *IntWW 93, Who 94*
Walker, John 1929- *Who 94*
Walker, John (Robert) 1936- *Who 94*
Walker, John Andrew 1939- *WhoAm 94*
Walker, John Charles 1893- *IntWW 93*
Walker, John David 1924- *Who 94*
Walker, John Denley 1921- *WhoAm 94*
Walker, John E. 1938- *WhoIns 94*
Walker, John Eric A. *Who 94*
Walker, John Leslie 1933- *WhoBlA 94*
Walker, John Letham 1946- *WhoAmP 93*
Walker, John Lockwood 1952- *WhoAm 94*
Walker, John M., Jr. 1940- *WhoAmP 93*
Walker, John Malcolm 1930- *Who 94*
Walker, John Mercer, Jr. 1940- *WhoAm 94, WhoAmL 94*
Walker, John Michael 1942- *WhoFI 94, WhoScEn 94*
Walker, John Neal 1930- *WhoAm 94, WhoScEn 94*
Walker, John Patrick 1956- *WhoMW 93*
Walker, John Scott 1944- *WhoScEn 94*
Walker, John Sumpter, Jr. 1921- *WhoAm 94, WhoAmL 94, WhoFI 94, WhoWest 94*
Walker, John Thomas 1925- *WhAm 10*
Walker, John William 1938- *WhoWest 94*
Walker, Johnnie d1949 *WhoHol 92*
Walker, Jonathan Alan 1958- *WhoMW 93*
Walker, Jonathan Lee 1948- *WhoAmL 94, WhoMW 93*
Walker, Joseph 1922- *WhoAm 94*
Walker, Joseph A. 1935- *ConDr 93, WrDr 94*
Walker, Joseph B. 1892-1985 *IntDcF 2-4 [port]*
Walker, Joseph Brent 1946- *WhoAmL 94*
Walker, Joseph G. *WhoAmP 93*
Walker, Joseph Hillary, Jr. 1919- *WhoAmL 94*
Walker, Joseph Reddeford 1798-1876 *WhWE*
Walker, Joseph Robert 1942- *WhoWest 94*
Walker, Joseph Vincent 1947- *WhoAm 94, WhoAmL 94*
Walker, Joseph Wylie 1948- *WhoAmP 93*
Walker, Joyce *WhoHol 92*
Walker, Joyce Marie 1948- *WhoWest 94*
Walker, Julian Fortay 1929- *Who 94*
Walker, Julian Guy Hudsmith 1936- *Who 94*
Walker, June d1966 *WhoHol 92*
Walker, Junior *WhoHol 92*
Walker, Kasey *WhoHol 92*
Walker, Kath *BlmGWL*
Walker, Kath 1920- *BlmGEL*
Walker, Kathryn *IntMPA 94, WhoHol 92*
Walker, Keith Allen 1948- *WhoWest 94*
Walker, Kenneth 1964- *WhoBlA 94*
Walker, Kenneth Henry 1940- *WhoAm 94*
Walker, Kenneth Joseph 1948- *WhoAmL 94*
Walker, Kenneth R. 1930- *WhoBlA 94*
Walker, Kenneth R. 1951- *WhoBlA 94*
Walker, Kenneth Roland 1928- *WrDr 94*
Walker, Kent 1944- *WhoAm 94*
Walker, Kent Arthur 1954- *WhoWest 94*
Walker, Kerry *WhoHol 92*
Walker, Kerry L. 1955- *WhoWest 94*
Walker, Kevin Patrick 1966- *WhoWest 94*
Walker, Kim *WhoHol 92*
Walker, Kim Bishton 1955- *WhoAm 94*
Walker, Kimberly J. 1954- *WhoAmL 94*
Walker, L. Mark 1957- *WhoAmL 94*
Walker, Laneuville V. 1947- *WhoBlA 94*
Walker, Lannon *WhoAmP 93*
Walker, Lannon 1936- *WhoAm 94*
Walker, Larry *WhoBlA 94*
Walker, Larry 1935- *WhoAmA 93*
Walker, Larry 1952- *WhoAmA 93*
Walker, Larry C. 1942- *WhoAmP 93*
Walker, Larry M. 1935- *WhoBlA 94*
Walker, Larry Vaughn 1939- *WhoBlA 94*
Walker, Laura d1951 *WhoHol 92*
Walker, Lawrence Arthur 1956- *WhoFI 94*
Walker, Lawrence D. 1948- *WhoAmL 94*
Walker, Lawrence Daniel 1928- *WhoAmP 93*
Walker, Lawrence Reddeford 1951- *WhoScEn 94*
Walker, Lee H. 1938- *WhoBlA 94*
Walker, Leila Stephanie 1979- *WhoWest 94*
Walker, Leland Jasper 1923- *WhoAm 94, WhoWest 94*
Walker, Leonard, Jr. 1961- *WhoFI 94*
Walker, LeRoy 1918- *WhoAm 94*
Walker, LeRoy Tashreau 1918- *WhoBlA 94*
Walker, Lewis 1936- *WhoBlA 94*
Walker, Lillian d1975 *WhoHol 92*
Walker, Linda *Who 94*
Walker, Linda Ann 1956- *WhoFI 94, WhoWest 94*
Walker, Lisa M. 1961- *WhoAmP 93*
Walker, Lisa Marie 1961- *WhoFI 94*
Walker, Liza *WhoHol 92*
Walker, Lois S. *WhoAmP 93*
Walker, Lois V. *DrAPF 93*
Walker, Loren Haines 1936- *WhoAm 94*
Walker, Lou *WhoHol 92*
Walker, Lucius *WhoBlA 94*
Walker, Lucius, Jr. 1930- *WhoBlA 94*
Walker, Lucy 1907- *WrDr 94*
Walker, Lula Aquillia 1955- *WhoBlA 94*
Walker, Lydia Le Baron 1869-1958 *WhoAmA 93N*
Walker, Lyn Gammill 1950- *WhoAmL 94*
Walker, Lynn Jones *WhoBlA 94*
Walker, M. Lucius, Jr. 1936- *WhoAm 94, WhoBlA 94*
Walker, Maggie Lena 1867-1934 *AfrAmAl 6 [port]*
Walker, Malcolm Conrad 1946- *Who 94*
Walker, Mallory 1939- *WhoAm 94, WhoFI 94*
Walker, Mallory Elton 1935- *WhoAm 94*
Walker, Manuel Lorenzo 1930- *WhoBlA 94*
Walker, Marcy *WhoHol 92*
Walker, Margaret *DrAPF 93*
Walker, Margaret 1915- *BlmGWL*
Walker, Margaret (Abigail) 1915- *BlkWr 2, WrDr 94*
Walker, Margaret Abigail 1915- *AfrAmAl 6 [port], WhoBlA 94*
Walker, Maria Latanya 1957- *WhoBlA 94*
Walker, Marie-Louise *WhoHol 92*
Walker, Marie Sheehy 1952- *WhoAmA 93*
Walker, Mark A. 1941- *WhoAm 94, WhoAmL 94*
Walker, Mark Lamont 1952- *WhoBlA 94*
Walker, Mark Steven 1952- *WhoAmA 93*
Walker, Martha Yeager 1940- *WhoAmP 93*
Walker, Martin d1955 *WhoHol 92*
Walker, Martin Dean 1932- *WhoAm 94, WhoFI 94, WhoMW 93*
Walker, Mary Alexander *DrAPF 93*
Walker, Mary Alice 1941- *WhoBlA 94*
Walker, Mary Ann 1953- *WhoAm 94, WhoAmL 94*
Walker, Mary Carolyn 1938- *WhoAmA 93*
Walker, Mary L. 1948- *WhoAm 94, WhoAmP 93*
Walker, Mary L. 1951- *WhoBlA 94*
Walker, Maurice Edward 1937- *WhoBlA 94*
Walker, Max 1924- *WrDr 94*
Walker, May 1943- *WhoBlA 94*
Walker, Melford Whitfield, Jr. 1958- *WhoBlA 94*
Walker, Melinda Sue *WhoMW 93*
Walker, Melvin E., Jr. 1946- *WhoBlA 94*
Walker, Michael *Who 94*
Walker, Michael 1931- *Who 94*
Walker, Michael 1941- *WhoHol 92*
Walker, (Charles) Michael 1916- *Who 94*
Walker, Michael Charles, Sr. 1940- *WhoFI 94*
Walker, Michael Claude 1940- *WhoAm 94, WhoFI 94, WhoMW 93*
Walker, Michael John 1946- *WhoFI 94, WhoWest 94*
Walker, Michael John Dawson 1944- *Who 94*
Walker, Michael Leolin F. *Who 94*
Walker, Mike 1949- *WhoAmP 93*
Walker, Miles Rawstron 1940- *IntWW 93, Who 94*
Walker, Moira Kaye 1940- *WhoWest 94*
Walker, Mort 1923- *WhoAm 94, WhoAmA 93*
Walker, Moses Andre 1929- *WhoBlA 94*
Walker, Moses L. 1940- *WhoBlA 94*
Walker, Nancy 1921-1992 *WhoCom*
Walker, Nancy 1922- *WhoHol 92*
Walker, Nancy 1922-1992 *AnObit 1992, ConTFT 11, WhAm 10*
Walker, Nancy A. 1942- *WrDr 94*
Walker, Nancy Eileen 1951- *WhoFI 94*
Walker, Nathan Belt 1952- *WhoAmP 93*
Walker, Nella d1971 *WhoHol 92*
Walker, Nigel (David) 1917- *WrDr 94*
Walker, Nigel David 1917- *Who 94*
Walker, Noel John 1948- *Who 94*
Walker, Norman 1907-1963 *NewGrDO*
Walker, Olene S. 1930- *WhoAm 94, WhoAmP 93, WhoWest 94*
Walker, Oliver M. 1898- *WhAm 10*
Walker, Pamela *DrAPF 93*
Walker, Patricia *WhoHol 92*
Walker, Patricia Kathleen Randall *Who 94*
Walker, Patricia Lillian 1943- *WhoFI 94*
Walker, Patrick (Jeremy) 1932- *Who 94*
Walker, Paul d1993 *NewYTBS 93*
Walker, Paul 1921- *EncSF 93*
Walker, Paul Crawford 1940- *Who 94*
Walker, Paul David 1934- *WhoMW 93*
Walker, Paul Dean 1937- *WhoFI 94*
Walker, Paul Francis 1932- *Who 94*
Walker, Paul R. 1945- *WhoAmL 94*
Walker, Pauline Ann *Who 94*
Walker, Peter *WhoHol 92*
Walker, Peter 1938- *HorFD*
Walker, Peter Knight 1919- *Who 94*
Walker, Peter Martin Brabazon 1922- *Who 94*
Walker, Philip (Doolittle) 1924- *WrDr 94*
Walker, Philip Chamberlain, II 1944- *WhoAm 94, WhoMW 93*
Walker, Philip Gordon 1912- *Who 94*
Walker, Philip Henry Conyers 1926- *Who 94*
Walker, Philip Smith 1933- *WhoAm 94, WhoAmL 94*
Walker, Polly *WhoHol 92*
Walker, Priscilla Bowman 1949- *WhoWest 94*
Walker, Ralph Clifford 1938- *WhoAm 94*
Walker, Ray d1980 *WhoHol 92*
Walker, Raymond Augustus 1943- *Who 94*
Walker, Raymond Charles 1925- *WhoAm 94*
Walker, Raymond Francis 1914- *WhoFI 94, WhoWest 94*
Walker, Raymond James 1943- *Who 94*
Walker, Raymond John 1942- *WhoScEn 94*
Walker, Richard 1942- *Who 94*
Walker, Richard, Jr. 1948- *WhoScEn 94*
Walker, Richard (John) 1952- *WrDr 94*
Walker, Richard Adolph 1951- *WhoAmL 94, WhoFI 94*
Walker, Richard Allen 1935- *WhoWest 94*
Walker, Richard Alwyne F. *Who 94*
Walker, Richard Bruce 1948- *WhoAmP 93*
Walker, Richard David 1932- *WhoFI 94*
Walker, Richard Frank 1924- *WhoAm 94*
Walker, Richard Harold 1928- *WhoAm 94*
Walker, Richard Henry 1943- *WhoFI 94*
Walker, Richard John Boileau 1916- *Who 94*
Walker, Richard K. 1948- *WhoAm 94*
Walker, Richard L. *WhoAmP 93*
Walker, Richard Louis 1922- *WhoAm 94*
Walker, Richard Philip 1958- *WhoAmL 94*
Walker, Robert d1951 *WhoHol 92*
Walker, Robert d1954 *WhoHol 92*
Walker, Robert 1801-1865 *DcNaB MP*
Walker, Robert 1924- *Who 94*
Walker, Robert 1938- *Who 94*
Walker, Robert 1940- *WhoHol 92*
Walker, Robert 1943- *WhoAmL 94*
Walker, Robert Dixon, III 1936- *WhoAm 94*
Walker, Robert E. *WhoAmP 93*
Walker, Robert Harris 1924- *WhoAm 94*
Walker, Robert Hugh 1935- *WhoAm 94*
Walker, Robert J. 1940- *WhoAmL 94*
Walker, Robert Lewis 1950- *WhoAmL 94*
Walker, Robert Mowbray 1929- *IntWW 93, WhoAm 94, WhoScEn 94*
Walker, Robert S. 1942- *CngDr 93*
Walker, Robert Scott 1913- *Who 94*
Walker, Robert Shackford 1945- *WhoAmL 94*
Walker, Robert Smith 1942- *WhoAm 94, WhoAmP 93*
Walker, Robert Wyman 1933- *WhoScEn 94*
Walker, Roger Antony Martineau- 1940- *Who 94*
Walker, Roger Geoffrey 1939- *WhoAm 94, WhoScEn 94*
Walker, Ron E. 1947- *WhoAmP 93*
Walker, Ronald *IntWW 93*
Walker, Ronald C. *WhoAm 94, WhoFI 94*
Walker, Ronald Edward 1935- *WhoAm 94*
Walker, Ronald F. 1938- *WhoAm 94, WhoFI 94, WhoIns 94, WhoMW 93*
Walker, Ronald Hugh 1937- *WhoAm 94*
Walker, Ronald Jack 1940- *Who 94*
Walker, Ronald Plezz 1953- *WhoBlA 94*
Walker, Rosalee Taylor 1929- *WhoAmP 93*
Walker, Rose d1951 *WhoHol 92*
Walker, Roy *Who 94*
Walker, (Christopher) Roy 1934- *Who 94*
Walker, Russell *WhoAmP 93*
Walker, Sally Barbara 1921- *WhoAm 94, WhoFI 94*
Walker, Sally C. *WhoWest 94*
Walker, Sally W. 1929- *WhoAmP 93*
Walker, Samuel E. 1942- *WrDr 94*
Walker, Samuel R. d1993 *NewYTBS 93 [port]*
Walker, Samuel Sloan, Jr. 1926-1992 *WhAm 10*
Walker, Sandra 1946- *WhoAm 94*
Walker, Sandra Lynne 1968- *WhoMW 93*
Walker, Sandra Venezia 1949- *WhoBlA 94*
Walker, Sarah *WhoHol 92*
Walker, Sarah 1943- *NewGrDO*
Walker, Sarah Breedlove 1867-1919 *WorInv*
Walker, Sarah Elizabeth Royle *IntWW 93, Who 94*
Walker, Scott *WhoHol 92*
Walker, Sharon Leslie 1958- *WhoWest 94*
Walker, Sheila Mosley 1917- *Who 94*
Walker, Sheila Suzanne 1944- *WhoBlA 94*
Walker, Sherry 1960- *WhoAmP 93*
Walker, Solomon W., II *WhoBlA 94*
Walker, Sonia 1937- *WhoBlA 94*
Walker, Sonja Caprice 1964- *WhoAmL 94*
Walker, Stanley Clay 1923- *WhoAmP 93*
Walker, Stanley Kenneth 1916- *Who 94*
Walker, Stanley M. 1942- *WhoBlA 94*
Walker, Stella Archer *WrDr 94*
Walker, Stephen (Francis) 1941- *WrDr 94*
Walker, Sterling Wilson 1912- *WhoBlA 94*
Walker, Steven Anderson 1957- *WhoWest 94*
Walker, Stuart d1941 *WhoHol 92*
Walker, Stuart Andrew 1963- *WhoFI 94*
Walker, Sue *DrAPF 93*
Walker, Susan Armour d1993 *Who 94N*
Walker, Syd d1945 *WhoHol 92*
Walker, Sydney 1921- *WhoHol 92*
Walker, Sydney, III 1931- *WhoScEn 94*
Walker, Tanya Rosetta 1953- *WhoBlA 94*
Walker, Ted *DrAPF 93*
Walker, Ted 1934- *WrDr 94*
Walker, Tennyson A. 1927- *WhoAm 94*
Walker, Terence William 1935- *Who 94*
Walker, Theodore Delbert 1933- *WhoAm 94*
Walker, Theresa Lynn 1960- *WhoMW 93*
Walker, Thomas 1698-1744 *NewGrDO*
Walker, Thomas 1715-1794 *WhAmRev, WhWE*
Walker, Thomas 1945- *WhoMW 93*
Walker, Thomas Cole 1929- *WhoFI 94*
Walker, Thomas F. 1916- *WhoAmP 93*
Walker, Thomas G. d1993 *NewYTBS 93*
Walker, Thomas L. 1948- *WhoBlA 94*
Walker, Thomas Overington 1933- *Who 94*
Walker, Thomas W(illiam) 1940- *ConAu 142*
Walker, Thomas William 1916- *Who 94*
Walker, Timmothy James 1961- *WhoMW 93*
Walker, Timothy Blake 1940- *WhoAm 94, WhoAmL 94*
Walker, Timothy Edward 1946- *Who 94*
Walker, Timothy Edward Hanson 1945- *Who 94*
Walker, Timothy John 1948- *WhoScEn 94*
Walker, Valaida Smith *WhoBlA 94*
Walker, Vaughn R. 1944- *WhoAm 94, WhoAmL 94, WhoWest 94*
Walker, Victoria Patricia Ann *Who 94*
Walker, Virgil Wayne 1925- *WhoAmP 93*
Walker, Virginia *WhoBlA 94*
Walker, Virginia d1946 *WhoHol 92*
Walker, Waldo Sylvester 1931- *WhoAm 94*
Walker, Wally d1975 *WhoHol 92*
Walker, Walter d1947 *WhoHol 92*
Walker, Walter (Colyear) 1912- *Who 94*
Walker, Walter (Herbert, III) 1949- *ConAu 42NR*
Walker, Walter Basil Scarlett 1915- *Who 94*
Walker, Walter Herbert, III 1949- *WhoAmL 94*
Walker, Walter Lorenzo 1935- *WhoBlA 94*
Walker, Walter Wayne 1938- *WhoFI 94*

Walker, Walter Willard 1911- *WhoFI 94, WhoMW 93*
Walker, Walton H. 1899-1950 *HisDcKW*
Walker, Warren Christopher 1965- *WhoMW 93*
Walker, Warren Stanley 1921- *WhoAm 94*
Walker, Wayne 1966- *WhoBlA 94*
Walker, Wendell P. 1930- *WhoBlA 94*
Walker, Wendy *DrAPF 93*
Walker, Wendy (Alison) 1951- *WrDr 94*
Walker, Wendy Joy 1949- *WhoAm 94*
Walker, Wendy K. 1961- *WhoFI 94*
Walker, Wendy Lauren 1960- *WhoAmP 93*
Walker, Wesley Darcel 1955- *WhoBlA 94*
Walker, Wesley M. 1915- *WhoAm 94*
Walker, Whimsical d1934 *WhoHol 92*
Walker, Wilbert A. 1910- *EncABHB 9*
Walker, Wilbur P. 1936- *WhoBlA 94*
Walker, Willard Brewer 1926- *WhoAm 94*
Walker, William 1824-1860 *HisWorL [port]*
Walker, William 1960- *WhoAmP 93*
Walker, William Bond 1930- *WhoAm 94, WhoAmA 93*
Walker, William Connoll 1929- *Who 94*
Walker, William Easton 1945- *WhoAm 94*
Walker, William Edward 1946- *WhoMW 93*
Walker, William G. *WhoAmP 93*
Walker, William George 1928- *WrDr 94*
Walker, William Harold 1915- *WhoBlA 94*
Walker, William Laurens 1937- *WhoAm 94*
Walker, William MacLelland 1933- *Who 94*
Walker, William Paul, Jr. 1940- *WhoBlA 94*
Walker, William Ray 1923- *WhoAm 94*
Walker, William Ross 1934- *WhoAm 94*
Walker, William Sonny 1933- *WhoBlA 94*
Walker, William Tidd, Jr. 1931- *WhoAm 94*
Walker, Willie F. 1942- *WhoBlA 94*
Walker, Willie M. 1929- *WhoBlA 94*
Walker, Willie Mark 1929- *WhoMW 93*
Walker, Williston 1860-1922 *DcAmReB 2*
Walker, Winston Wakefield, Jr. 1943- *WhoAm 94, WhoFI 94*
Walker, Woodrow Wilson 1919- *WhoAmL 94*
Walker, Woodson DuBois 1950- *WhoBlA 94*
Walker, Wyatt Tee 1929- *WhoBlA 94*
Walker, Zena 1934- *WhoHol 92*
Walker-Daniels, Kimberly Kayne 1958- *WhoFI 94*
Walker-Haworth, John Liegh 1944- *Who 94*
Walker-Johnson, Geneva Marie 1944- *WhoBlA 94*
Walker Of Worcester, Baron 1932- *IntWW 93, Who 94*
Walker-Okeover, Peter (Ralph Leopold) 1947- *Who 94*
Walker-Shaw, Patricia 1939- *WhoBlA 94*
Walker-Smith, Angelique Keturah 1958- *WhoAm 94, WhoBlA 94*
Walker-Smith, (John) Jonah 1939- *Who 94*
Walker-Taylor, Yvonne *WhoBlA 94*
Walker-Thoth, Daphne LaVera 1954- *WhoBlA 94*
Walker-Williams, Hope Denise 1952- *WhoBlA 94*
Walkey, Frederick P. 1922- *WhoAmA 93*
Walkey, John R. 1938- *WhoAm 94*
Walkham, Walter *EncSF 93*
Walkine, Herbert Cleveland 1929- *Who 94*
Walkingstick, Kay 1935- *WhoAmA 93*
Walklet, John James, Jr. 1922- *WhoAm 94*
Walkley, Barbara Ann 1945- *WhoAm 94*
Walkov, Perry 1951- *WhoWest 94*
Walkovik, Donald C. 1948- *WhoAmL 94*
Walkowiak, Diane Kaye 1958- *WhoAmP 93*
Walkowiak, Vincent Steven 1946- *WhoAm 94, WhoAmL 94*
Walkowicz, Chris 1943- *WrDr 94*
Walkowitz, Abraham 1880-1965 *WhoAmA 93N*
Walkowitz, Daniel J. 1942- *WhoAm 94*
Walks-Alone, Kuuks d1938 *WhoHol 92*
Walkup, Bruce 1914- *WhoAm 94*
Walkup, Charlotte Lloyd 1910- *WhoAmL 94*
Walkup, Homer Allen 1917- *WhoAmL 94*
Walkup, John Frank 1941- *WhoAm 94*
Walkup, Mary Roe 1924- *WhoAmP 93*
Walkwitz, Jon Jeffrey 1949- *WhoWest 94*
Wall, Alfreda *Who 94*
Wall, Allen J. 1945- *WhoAmL 94*
Wall, (Alice) Anne 1928- *Who 94*
Wall, Barron Stephen 1951- *WhoIns 94*
Wall, Bennett Harrison 1914- *WhoAm 94*
Wall, Betty Jane 1936- *WhoFI 94*
Wall, Brian 1931- *IntWW 93, WhoAmA 93*
Wall, Brian Arthur 1931- *WhoAm 94*
Wall, Brian Owen 1933- *Who 94*
Wall, Brian Raymond 1940- *WhoFI 94, WhoScEn 94, WhoWest 94*
Wall, Bruce C. 1954- *WhoAmA 93*
Wall, Bruce Michael 1951- *WhoAmL 94*
Wall, Carroll Edward 1942- *WhoAm 94*
Wall, Charles Terence Clegg 1936- *IntWW 93, Who 94*
Wall, Clarence Vinson 1947- *WhoAmP 93*
Wall, Dave d1938 *WhoHol 92*
Wall, David 1946- *IntDcB [port]*
Wall, David (Richard) 1946- *Who 94*
Wall, Donald Arthur 1946- *WhoAm 94, WhoAmL 94*
Wall, Douglas Foster 1965- *WhoMW 93*
Wall, Edward Millard 1929- *WhoFI 94*
Wall, Eric St. Quintin 1915- *Who 94*
Wall, Erving Henry, Jr. 1934- *WhoAmP 93*
Wall, Ethan 1939- *WrDr 94*
Wall, F. L., III 1947- *WhoAmA 93*
Wall, Francis Joseph 1927- *WhoWest 94*
Wall, Frank A. 1949- *IntWW 93*
Wall, Fred Graham 1934- *WhoAm 94*
Wall, Frederick Theodore 1912- *IntWW 93, WhoAm 94, WhoScEn 94*
Wall, G.A. *EncSF 93*
Wall, Gerald Aloysius d1992 *Who 94N*
Wall, Geraldine d1970 *WhoHol 92*
Wall, Howard Elden 1929- *WhoAm 94*
Wall, Jacqueline Remondet 1958- *WhoScEn 94*
Wall, James Edward 1947- *WhoAm 94*
Wall, James M(cKendree) 1928- *WrDr 94*
Wall, James McKendree 1928- *WhoAm 94, WhoAmP 93*
Wall, Janet G. 1949- *WhoAmP 93*
Wall, Jean Marie 1936- *WhoAmL 94*
Wall, Jerry Leon 1942- *WhoAm 94*
Wall, Joe Layton 1939- *WhoAm 94*
Wall, John Antony 1930- *Who 94*
Wall, John Edward 1946- *WhoAmL 94*
Wall, John F. 1913- *WhoAmP 93*
Wall, Joseph Frazier 1920- *WhoAm 94, WhoMW 93, WrDr 94*
Wall, Kenneth E., Jr. 1944- *WhoAmL 94*
Wall, Lloyd L. 1936- *WhoWest 94*
Wall, M. Danny *WhoAm 94*
Wall, Margaret V. 1895-1958 *WhoAmA 93N*
Wall, Mark Emanuel 1937- *WhoFI 94*
Wall, Mark Henry 1932- *WhoWest 94*
Wall, Mary Sprague 1916- *WhoAmP 93*
Wall, Max d1990 *WhoHol 92*
Wall, Michael 1950- *WhoMW 93*
Wall, Michael, Mrs. *Who 94*
Wall, Nicholas (Peter Rathbone) 1945- *Who 94*
Wall, O. Edward 1934- *WhoAm 94*
Wall, Patrick (Henry Bligh) 1916- *Who 94, WrDr 94*
Wall, Patrick David 1925- *IntWW 93, Who 94*
Wall, Peter K. 1953- *WhoFI 94*
Wall, Ralph Alan 1932- *WhoAmA 93*
Wall, Randall B. 1943- *WhoAmL 94*
Wall, Rhonda 1956- *WhoAmA 93*
Wall, Robert *WhoHol 92*
Wall, Robert (William) 1929- *Who 94*
Wall, Robert Anthony, Jr. 1945- *WhoAmL 94*
Wall, Robert Emmet 1937- *WhoAm 94*
Wall, Robert F. 1952- *WhoAm 94*
Wall, Robert H. 1928- *WhoIns 94*
Wall, Robert Lee, Jr. 1936- *WhoAmP 93*
Wall, Robert Percival Walter 1927- *Who 94*
Wall, Robert Seth 1958- *WhoWest 94*
Wall, Robert Wilson, Jr. 1916- *WhoAm 94*
Wall, Ronald Rae 1941- *WhoMW 93*
Wall, Sidney Smith Roderick Jr. 1942- *WhoFI 94*
Wall, Sonja Eloise 1938- *WhoFI 94, WhoScEn 94, WhoWest 94*
Wall, Stephen *Who 94*
Wall, (John) Stephen 1947- *Who 94*
Wall, Stephen D. 1948- *ConAu 140*
Wall, Stephen James 1947- *WhoAm 94*
Wall, Steven S. 1946- *WhoAmL 94*
Wall, Sue 1950- *WhoAmA 93*
Wall, T. Michael 1952- *WhoAmL 94*
Wall, Thomas Ulrich 1944- *WhoWest 94*
Wall, William Douglas 1913- *Who 94*
Wall, William E. 1928- *WhoWest 94*
Wall, William John 1946- *WhoFI 94*
Wallace *Who 94*
Wallace, Albert Frederick 1921- *Who 94*
Wallace, Alfred Russel 1823-1913 *WhWE [port], WorScD*
Wallace, Andrew Grover 1935- *WhoAm 94*
Wallace, Anthony F. C. 1923- *IntWW 93*
Wallace, Anthony Francis Clarke 1923- *WhoAm 94*
Wallace, Arnold D., Sr. 1932- *WhoBlA 94*
Wallace, Arthur 1919- *WhoAm 94*
Wallace, Arthur, Jr. 1939- *WhoAm 94, WhoBlA 94, WhoFI 94*
Wallace, Barbara d1976 *WhoHol 92*
Wallace, Barbara Brooks *SmATA 17AS [port], WrDr 94*
Wallace, Beryl d1948 *WhoHol 92*
Wallace, Betty Louise Dollar 1935- *WhoMW 93*
Wallace, Bill 1956- *WhoAmP 93*
Wallace, Bonnie Ann 1951- *WhoScEn 94*
Wallace, Brenda Anne 1941- *WhoAmP 93*
Wallace, Bronwen 1945-1989 *BlmGWL*
Wallace, Bruce *DrAPF 93*
Wallace, Bruce 1920- *IntWW 93, WrDr 94*
Wallace, Bruce McClain, Jr. 1931- *WhoAmL 94*
Wallace, C. Everett 1951- *WhoBlA 94*
Wallace, Charles lee 1960- *WhoFI 94*
Wallace, Charles Leslie 1945- *WhoBlA 94*
Wallace, Charles William 1926- *Who 94*
Wallace, Christopher 1947- *WhoAm 94*
Wallace, Clarence 1894- *WhAm 10*
Wallace, Claudette J. *WhoBlA 94*
Wallace, Clifford Noble, III 1947- *WhoAm 94*
Wallace, Danny *WhoAmP 93*
Wallace, David *WhoHol 92*
Wallace, David Alexander 1917- *WhoAm 94*
Wallace, David Foster *DrAPF 93*
Wallace, David Foster 1962- *WrDr 94*
Wallace, David James 1945- *IntWW 93, Who 94*
Wallace, David P. 1945- *WhoAmL 94*
Wallace, Dee *WhoHol 92*
Wallace, Derrick D. 1953- *WhoBlA 94*
Wallace, DeWitt 1889-1981 *DcLB 137 [port]*
Wallace, Don, Jr. 1932- *WhoAm 94, WhoAmL 94*
Wallace, Donald John, III 1941- *WhoScEn 94*
Wallace, Donald Querk 1931- *WhoAm 94*
Wallace, Doreen 1897- *EncSF 93*
Wallace, Dwane L. 1911-1989 *WhAm 10*
Wallace, Edgar d1932 *WhoHol 92*
Wallace, Edgar 1875-1932 *EncSF 93*
Wallace, Elaine Wendy 1949- *WhoAmL 94*
Wallace, Elizabeth S. *WhoAmA 93*
Wallace, Ethel Lee d1956 *WhoHol 92*
Wallace, F. Blake 1933- *WhoFI 94, WhoScEn 94*
Wallace, F(loyd) L. *EncSF 93, WrDr 94*
Wallace, Fleming *Who 94*
Wallace, (James) Fleming 1931- *Who 94*
Wallace, Frank d1966 *WhoHol 92*
Wallace, Franklin Sherwood 1927- *WhoAmL 94, WhoMW 93*
Wallace, Frederick E. 1893-1958 *WhoAmA 93N*
Wallace, Gael Lynn 1941- *WhoAmA 93*
Wallace, George *DrAPF 93*
Wallace, George d1960 *WhoHol 92*
Wallace, George 1917- *WhoHol 92*
Wallace, George C., Jr. 1951- *WhoAmP 93*
Wallace, George Corley 1919- *IntWW 93, WhoAm 94, WhoAmP 93*
Wallace, George Karren 1958- *WhoWest 94*
Wallace, Harold Gene 1945- *WhoBlA 94*
Wallace, Harold James, Jr. 1930- *WhoAm 94*
Wallace, Harold Lew 1932- *WhoAm 94*
Wallace, Harry Leland 1927- *WhoAm 94*
Wallace, Hedger *WhoHol 92*
Wallace, Helen 1946- *IntWW 93*
Wallace, Helen Margaret 1913- *WhoWest 94*
Wallace, Helen Winfree-Peyton 1927- *WhoBlA 94*
Wallace, Henry Jared, Jr. 1943- *WhoAmL 94*
Wallace, Herbert Norman 1937- *WhoAmL 94*
Wallace, Herbert William 1930- *WhoAm 94*
Wallace, Homer L. 1941- *WhoBlA 94*
Wallace, Ian 1912- *EncSF 93, WrDr 94*
Wallace, Ian 1919- *IntWW 93*
Wallace, Ian 1950- *WrDr 94*
Wallace, Ian (Bryce) 1919- *NewGrDO*
Wallace, Ian (James) 1916- *Who 94*
Wallace, Ian Alexander 1917- *Who 94*
Wallace, Ian Bryce 1919- *Who 94*
Wallace, Ian Norman Duncan 1922- *Who 94*
Wallace, Inez d1966 *WhoHol 92*
Wallace, Irving 1916-1990 *WhAm 10*
Wallace, Ivan Harold Nutt 1935- *Who 94*
Wallace, J. Clifford 1928- *WhoAm 94, WhoAmL 94, WhoAmP 93, WhoWest 94*
Wallace, Jack *WhoHol 92*
Wallace, (Dorothy) Jacqueline H. *Who 94*
Wallace, James *EncSF 93*
Wallace, James 1731-1803 *WhAmRev*
Wallace, James 1928- *WrDr 94*
Wallace, James H., Jr. 1942- *WhoAmP 93*
Wallace, James Harold, Jr. 1941- *WhoAm 94, WhoAmL 94*
Wallace, James Jr. 1932- *WhoScEn 94*
Wallace, James P. 1928- *WhoAmL 94*
Wallace, James Price 1928- *WhoAmP 93*
Wallace, James Robert 1954- *Who 94*
Wallace, James Wendell 1930- *WhoAm 94, WhoWest 94*
Wallace, Jane House 1926- *WhoScEn 94*
Wallace, Jane Young 1933- *WhoAm 94*
Wallace, Jean d1990 *WhoHol 92*
Wallace, Jeannette O. 1934- *WhoAmP 93*
Wallace, Jeannette Owens 1934- *WhoWest 94*
Wallace, Jeffrey J. 1946- *WhoBlA 94*
Wallace, Jesse Wyatt 1925- *WhoAm 94, WhoFI 94*
Wallace, Joan S. 1930- *WhoAmP 93, WhoScEn 94*
Wallace, Joel Keith 1933- *WhoWest 94*
Wallace, John d1946 *WhoHol 92*
Wallace, John 1929- *WhoAmA 93*
Wallace, John Craig 1954- *WhoMW 93*
Wallace, John Duncan 1933- *WhoAm 94*
Wallace, John E., Jr. 1942- *WhoBlA 94*
Wallace, John Edwin 1913- *WhoAm 94*
Wallace, John H. 1926- *WhoMW 93*
Wallace, John H., Jr. 1906- *WhAm 10*
Wallace, John Howard 1925-1991 *WhoBlA 94N*
Wallace, John Joseph 1947- *WhoWest 94*
Wallace, John Lawrence 1956- *WhoScEn 94*
Wallace, John Loys 1941- *WhoAm 94*
Wallace, John M. d1993 *NewYTBS 93*
Wallace, John Malcolm 1928- *WrDr 94*
Wallace, John Malcolm Agnew 1928- *Who 94*
Wallace, John McChrystal 1893-1989 *WhAm 10*
Wallace, John Michael 1940- *WhoAm 94, WhoScEn 94*
Wallace, John Williamson 1949- *Who 94*
Wallace, Joseph Fletcher, Jr. 1921- *WhoBlA 94*
Wallace, Judy *WhoHol 92*
Wallace, Karen Smyley 1943- *WhoBlA 94*
Wallace, Keith M. 1956- *WhoAmL 94*
Wallace, Kendrick T. 1945- *WhoAmL 94*
Wallace, Kenneth Alan 1938- *WhoWest 94*
Wallace, Kenneth Donald 1918- *WhoAm 94*
Wallace, Kenneth William 1945- *WhoAmA 93*
Wallace, King *EncSF 93*
Wallace, L. Kirk 1948- *WhoAmL 94*
Wallace, Laura V. d1943 *WhoHol 92*
Wallace, Lawrence James 1913- *Who 94*
Wallace, Lee 1930- *WhoHol 92*
Wallace, Leigh Allen, Jr. 1927- *WhoAm 94, WhoWest 94*
Wallace, Lila Acheson 1889-1984 *DcLB 137 [port]*
Wallace, Lila Norma *WhoAmA 93*
Wallace, Linda M. 1941- *WhoAmP 93*
Wallace, Lou Ella 1936- *WhoAmP 93*
Wallace, Louise Chapman d1962 *WhoHol 92*
Wallace, Louise Margaret 1942- *WhoMW 93, WhoScEn 94*
Wallace, Mack 1929- *WhoAmP 93*
Wallace, Malcolm Charles Robarts 1947- *Who 94*
Wallace, Malcolm Vincent Timothy 1915- *WhoAm 94*
Wallace, Marc Charles 1957- *WhoWest 94*
Wallace, Marcia 1942- *WhoHol 92*
Wallace, Marjorie Shiona *Who 94*
Wallace, Mark Allen 1953- *WhoAm 94*
Wallace, Martha Redfield 1927-1989 *WhAm 10*
Wallace, Mary Elaine *WhoAm 94*
Wallace, Matthew Walker 1924- *WhoWest 94*
Wallace, Maude d1952 *WhoHol 92*
Wallace, May d1938 *WhoHol 92*
Wallace, Mike 1918- *IntMPA 94, WhoAm 94*
Wallace, Milton d1956 *WhoHol 92*
Wallace, Milton De'Nard 1957- *WhoBlA 94*
Wallace, Minor Gordon, Jr. 1936- *WhoFI 94*
Wallace, Morgan d1953 *WhoHol 92*
Wallace, Nancy Diane 1958- *WhoWest 94*
Wallace, Nellie d1948 *WhoHol 92*
Wallace, Nora Ann 1951- *WhoAmL 94*
Wallace, Patricia Jean 1945- *WhoWest 94*
Wallace, Patty A. 1957- *WhoAmA 93*
Wallace, Paul 1938- *WhoHol 92*

Wallace, Paul Harvey 1944- *WhoAmL 94, WhoWest 94*
Wallace, Paul Starett, Jr. 1941- *WhoBlA 94*
Wallace, Peggy Mason 1948- *WhoBlA 94*
Wallace, Peter Rudy 1954- *WhoAmP 93*
Wallace, Philip Russell 1915- *WhoAm 94*
Wallace, Phyllis A. *WhoBlA 94*
Wallace, Phyllis A. d1993 *NewYTBS 93 [port]*
Wallace, R. Byron 1945- *WhoAm 94, WhoAmL 94*
Wallace, R. H., Jr. 1943- *WhoAmL 94*
Wallace, Raeh Brown 1944- *WhoAmL 94*
Wallace, Ralph Howes 1916- *WhoAm 94*
Wallace, Ralph Ray, III 1949- *WhoAmP 93*
Wallace, Randy 1954- *WhoFI 94*
Wallace, Ratch *WhoHol 92*
Wallace, Regina d1978 *WhoHol 92*
Wallace, Reginald James 1919- *Who 94*
Wallace, Renee C. *WhoBlA 94*
Wallace, Richard 1957- *WhoAm 94*
Wallace, Richard Alexander 1946- *Who 94*
Wallace, Richard Christopher, Jr. 1931- *WhoAm 94*
Wallace, Richard Harris, Jr. 1944- *WhoAmP 93*
Wallace, Richard K. 1947- *WhoAm 94*
Wallace, Richard Otho 1948- *WhoFI 94*
Wallace, Richard Warner 1929- *WhoBlA 94*
Wallace, Richard William 1933- *WhoAmA 93*
Wallace, Ritchie Ray 1955- *WhoBlA 94*
Wallace, Roanne 1949- *WhoFI 94*
Wallace, Robert *DrAPF 93*
Wallace, Robert 1905- *WrDr 94*
Wallace, Robert 1911- *Who 94*
Wallace, Robert Ardell 1938- *WhoWest 94*
Wallace, Robert Bruce 1931- *WhoAm 94*
Wallace, Robert Bruce 1944- *WhoAm 94*
Wallace, Robert Dan 1923- *WhoAmA 93*
Wallace, Robert Earl 1916- *WhoAm 94, WhoScEn 94, WhoWest 94*
Wallace, Robert Eugene, Jr. 1956- *WhoBlA 94, WhoScEn 94*
Wallace, Robert Glenn 1926- *WhoAm 94*
Wallace, Robert Luther, II 1949- *WhoMW 93, WhoScEn 94*
Wallace, Robert M. 1947- *ConAu 141*
Wallace, Ronald *DrAPF 93*
Wallace, Ronald (William) 1945- *ConAu 42NR*
Wallace, Ronald E. 1947- *WhoFI 94*
Wallace, Ronald Wilfred 1941- *WhoBlA 94*
Wallace, Rowena *WhoHol 92*
Wallace, Royce *WhoHol 92*
Wallace, Samuel Taylor 1943- *WhoAm 94, WhoMW 93*
Wallace, Sharon Ann 1946- *WhoMW 93*
Wallace, Soni 1931- *WhoAmA 93*
Wallace, Spencer Miller, Jr. 1923- *WhoAm 94*
Wallace, Steven Charles 1953- *WhoAmL 94*
Wallace, Sylvia *WrDr 94*
Wallace, Ted 1948- *WhoFI 94*
Wallace, Terry Charles, Sr. 1933- *WhoScEn 94*
Wallace, Terry Charles, Jr. 1956- *WhoScEn 94*
Wallace, Terry S. *DrAPF 93*
Wallace, Theodore Calvin 1941- *WhoAmP 93*
Wallace, Thomas A. 1949- *WhoIns 94*
Wallace, Thomas Christopher 1933- *WhoAm 94*
Wallace, Thomas D. 1929- *WhoAmP 93*
Wallace, Thomas Henry d1932 *WhoHol 92*
Wallace, Thomas Patrick 1935- *WhoAm 94, WhoMW 93*
Wallace, Thomas Robert 1954- *WhoAm 94*
Wallace, Victor L., II 1938- *WhoAm 94, WhoAmL 94*
Wallace, (William) Vincent 1812-1865 *NewGrDO*
Wallace, W. Lawrence 1949- *WhoAmP 93*
Wallace, Walter C. 1924- *WhoAm 94*
Wallace, Walter Ian James 1905- *Who 94*
Wallace, Walter L. 1927- *WhoAm 94*
Wallace, Walter Wilkinson 1923- *IntWW 93, Who 94*
Wallace, Wayne Charles 1967- *WhoMW 93*
Wallace, Wellesley Theodore Octavius 1938- *Who 94*
Wallace, William *WhoHol 92*
Wallace, William 1270?-1305 *BlmGEL*
Wallace, William, III 1926- *WhoAm 94*
Wallace, William Alan 1935- *WhoAm 94*
Wallace, William Arthur, Jr. 1942- *WhoWest 94*
Wallace, William Augustine 1918- *WhoAm 94*
Wallace, William C. 1941- *WhoAm 94*
Wallace, William Edward 1917- *WhoAm 94*
Wallace, William Frank, Jr. 1940- *WhoHisp 94*
Wallace, William Hall 1933- *WhoAm 94*
Wallace, William James Lord 1908- *WhoBlA 94*
Wallace, William John Lawrence 1941- *Who 94*
Wallace, William Laurie 1934- *WhoFI 94*
Wallace, William Ray 1923- *WhoAm 94, WhoFI 94*
Wallace, William Wales 1959- *WhoWest 94*
Wallace, Wilton Lawrence 1949- *WhoAm 94*
Wallace-Crabbe, Christopher (Keith) 1934- *WrDr 94*
Wallace-Crabbe, Christopher Keith 1934- *IntWW 93*
Wallace-Martinez, Elvia 1948- *WhoHisp 94*
Wallace Of Campsie, Baron 1915- *Who 94*
Wallace Of Coslany, Baron 1906- *Who 94*
Wallach, Alan 1942- *WhoAmA 93*
Wallach, Allan Henry 1927- *WhoAm 94*
Wallach, Anne Jackson *WhoAm 94*
Wallach, Barbara Price 1946- *WhoMW 93*
Wallach, Edward Eliot 1933- *WhoAm 94*
Wallach, Eli 1915- *IntMPA 94, IntWW 93, WhoAm 94, WhoHol 92*
Wallach, Eric Jean 1947- *WhoAm 94, WhoAmL 94*
Wallach, Erica 1922- *WrDr 94*
Wallach, George 1918- *IntMPA 94*
Wallach, Hans 1904- *WhoAm 94*
Wallach, Ira 1913- *WhoAm 94, WrDr 94*
Wallach, Ira David 1909- *WhoAm 94*
Wallach, Jason Jonathan 1957- *WhoFI 94*
Wallach, John Paul 1943- *WhoAm 94*
Wallach, John Sidney 1939- *WhoAm 94, WhoMW 93*
Wallach, Lance H. 1950- *WhoFI 94*
Wallach, Lew *WhoHol 92*
Wallach, Mark Irwin 1949- *WhoAm 94, WhoAmL 94*
Wallach, Maud Barger 1870-1954 *BuCMET*
Wallach, Paul 1925- *WhoFI 94, WhoWest 94*
Wallach, Paul Geoffry 1947- *WhoAm 94*
Wallach, Philip Charles 1912- *WhoAm 94*
Wallach, Robert Charles 1935- *WhoAm 94*
Wallach, Robert P. *WhoAmP 93*
Wallach, Roberta 1955- *WhoHol 92*
Wallach, Stephen Martin 1942- *WhoFI 94*
Wallach, Yonah 1944-1985 *BlmGWL*
Wallada bint al-Mustakfi dc. 1091 *BlmGWL*
Wallance, Gregory J. 1948- *WhoAm 94, WhoAmL 94*
Wallberg, Heinz 1923- *NewGrDO*
Walleen, Hans Axel 1902-1978 *WhoAmA 93N*
Walleigh, Robert Shuler 1915- *WhoAm 94*
Wallek-Walewski, Boleslaw 1885-1944 *NewGrDO*
Wallem, Daniel Ray 1961- *WhoScEn 94*
Wallen, Burr 1941- *WhoAmA 93N*
Wallen, Ella Kathleen 1914- *Who 94*
Wallen, Martha Louise 1946- *WhoMW 93*
Wallen, Richard Lee 1953- *WhoMW 93*
Wallen, Vera S. 1941- *WhoAm 94*
Wallenberg, Peter 1926- *IntWW 93, Who 94*
Wallenborn, Janice Rae 1938- *WhoAm 94*
Wallender, Michael Todd 1950- *WhoAm 94, WhoAmL 94, WhoFI 94*
Wallenfang, Ronald L. 1943- *WhoAmL 94*
Wallenstein, Albrecht von 1583-1634 *HisWorL [port]*
Wallenstein, Barry *DrAPF 93*
Wallenstein, James Harry 1942- *WhoAm 94, WhoAmL 94*
Wallenstein, John S. 1950- *WhoAmL 94*
Waller, Aaron Bret 1935- *WhoAmA 93*
Waller, Aaron Bret, III 1935- *WhoAm 94*
Waller, Anne d1662 *BlmGWL*
Waller, Arlou Gill 1922- *WhoMW 93*
Waller, Augustus Desire 1856-1922 *DcNaB MP*
Waller, Calvin Agustine Hoffman 1937- *AfrAmG [port]*
Waller, Cheryl Lynn Gary 1955- *WhoWest 94*
Waller, David 1920- *WhoHol 92*
Waller, Donald Macgregor 1951- *WhoMW 93*
Waller, Eddy d1977 *WhoHol 92*
Waller, Edmund 1606-1687 *BlmGEL*
Waller, Edward Martin, Jr. 1942- *WhoAmL 94*
Waller, Ellis J. 1896- *WhAm 10*
Waller, Eunice McLean 1921- *WhoBlA 94*
Waller, Fats d1943 *WhoHol 92*
Waller, Gary Fredric 1944- *WhoAm 94*
Waller, Gary Peter Anthony 1945- *Who 94*
Waller, George (Stanley) 1911- *Who 94*
Waller, George Macgregor 1919- *WhoAm 94, WrDr 94*
Waller, Harold Myron 1940- *WhoAm 94*
Waller, Irene Ellen 1928- *WrDr 94*
Waller, J. Michael 1959- *WhoAmL 94*
Waller, James Edward, Jr. 1961- *WhoScEn 94*
Waller, Jane (Ashton) 1944- *WrDr 94*
Waller, John James 1924- *WhoAmL 94, WhoWest 94*
Waller, John Louis 1944- *WhoAm 94, WhoScEn 94*
Waller, John Oscar 1916- *WhoAm 94*
Waller, John Stanier 1917- *Who 94*
Waller, John Stevens 1924- *Who 94*
Waller, Juanita Ann 1958- *WhoBlA 94*
Waller, Keith *Who 94*
Waller, (John) Keith 1914- *Who 94*
Waller, Larry 1947- *WhoBlA 94*
Waller, Larry Gene 1948- *WhoWest 94*
Waller, Leslie 1923- *WrDr 94*
Waller, Lewis d1915 *WhoHol 92*
Waller, Louis E. 1928- *WhoBlA 94*
Waller, Mark *Who 94*
Waller, (George) Mark 1940- *Who 94*
Waller, Niels Gordon 1957- *WhoScEn 94*
Waller, Paul Pressley, Jr. 1924- *WhoAmL 94*
Waller, Peter William 1926- *WhoWest 94*
Waller, Ray Albert 1937- *WhoWest 94*
Waller, Reggie *WhoBlA 94*
Waller, Rhoda *DrAPF 93*
Waller, Robert Morris 1944- *WhoMW 93*
Waller, Robert Rex 1937- *WhoAm 94, WhoMW 93*
Waller, Robert William 1934- *Who 94*
Waller, Samuel Carpenter 1918- *WhoAmP 93*
Waller, Susan 1948- *WhoAmA 93*
Waller, Thomas 1904-1943 *AfrAmAl 6 [port]*
Waller, Wallet d1951 *WhoHol 92*
Waller, Wilhelmine Kirby 1914- *WhoAm 94*
Waller, William L. 1926- *WhoAmP 93*
Wallerstedt-Wehrle, JoAnna Katherine 1944- *WhoAm 94*
Wallerstein, Bruce Lee 1943- *WhoWest 94*
Wallerstein, David B. d1993 *NewYTBS 93*
Wallerstein, George 1930- *WhoAm 94*
Wallerstein, Harry d1993 *NewYTBS 93*
Wallerstein, Leibert Benet 1922- *WhoAm 94, WhoFI 94, WhoScEn 94*
Wallerstein, Ralph O. 1922- *IntWW 93*
Wallerstein, Ralph Oliver 1922- *WhoAm 94, WhoWest 94*
Wallerstein, Robert Solomon 1921- *WhoAm 94, WhoScEn 94, WhoWest 94*
Wallerstein, Rose d1961 *WhoHol 92*
Wallestad, Philip Weston 1922- *WhoFI 94, WhoMW 93*
Wallette, Alonzo Vandolph 1940- *WhoBlA 94*
Walley, Bryon S. *EncSF 93*
Walley, Byron 1951- *WhoAm 94*
Walley, Deborah 1941- *WhoHol 92*
Walley, Francis 1918- *Who 94*
Walley, Joan Lorraine 1949- *Who 94, WhoWomW 91*
Walley, John 1906- *Who 94*
Walley, Keith Henry 1928- *Who 94*
Walley, Page Blakeslee 1957- *WhoAmP 93*
Wallfesh, Henry Maurice 1937- *WhoAm 94*
Wallgren, Gunn d1983 *WhoHol 92*
Wallgren, Pernilla *WhoHol 92*
Wallhauser, George M. d1993 *NewYTBS 93*
Wallich, George Charles 1815-1899 *DcNaB MP*
Wallick, Ernest Herron 1928- *WhoBlA 94*
Wallick, Robert Daniel 1926- *WhoAm 94*
Wallin, Amos *ConAu 42NR*
Wallin, Angie *WhoWest 94*
Wallin, Bengt Gunnar 1936- *WhoScEn 94*
Wallin, David Ernest 1955- *WhoFI 94*
Wallin, Franklin Whittelsey 1925- *WhoAm 94*
Wallin, Jack Robb 1915- *WhoAm 94*
Wallin, James Peter 1958- *WhoAmL 94*
Wallin, Kenneth E. 1930- *WhoAmP 93*
Wallin, Lawrence Bier 1944- *WhoAmA 93*
Wallin, Leland Dean 1942- *WhoAmA 93*
Wallin, Luke 1943- *WrDr 94*
Wallin, Norman Elroy 1914- *WhoAmP 93*
Wallin, Winston Roger 1926- *WhoAm 94*
Walling, Cheves (Thomson) 1916- *IntWW 93*
Walling, Cheves Thomson 1916- *WhoAm 94, WhoScEn 94*
Walling, Effie B. d1961 *WhoHol 92*
Walling, Esther Kolb 1940- *WhoAmP 93*
Walling, Margaret S. 1924- *WhoAmP 93*
Walling, Robert H. 1927- *WhoAmP 93*
Walling, Roy d1964 *WhoHol 92*
Walling, Will R. d1932 *WhoHol 92*
Walling, William (Herbert) 1926- *EncSF 93*
Walling, William English 1877-1936 *AmSocL*
Walling, Willis Ray *WhoAmP 93*
Wallinger, Karl 1957- *ConMus 11 [port]*
Wallinger, Melvin Bruce 1945- *WhoAmL 94*
Wallingford, Anne 1949- *WhoMW 93*
Wallingford, John Rufus 1940- *WhoAm 94*
Wallingford, Lee 1947- *ConAu 142*
Wallington, George 1923-1993 *NewYTBS 93*
Wallington, Jeremy Francis 1935- *Who 94*
Wallington, Jimmy d1972 *WhoHol 92*
Wallins, Roger Peyton 1941- *WhoWest 94*
Wallis, B. *EncSF 93*
Wallis, Barnes 1887-1979 *WorInv*
Wallis, Ben Alton, Jr. 1936- *WhoAmL 94*
Wallis, Bertram d1952 *WhoHol 92*
Wallis, Carlton Lamar 1915- *WhoAm 94*
Wallis, Catherine Louise 1938- *WhoWest 94*
Wallis, Dave 1917- *EncSF 93*
Wallis, Diana Lynn 1946- *WhoAm 94*
Wallis, Dick 1931- *WhoAmP 93*
Wallis, Diz 1949- *SmATA 77 [port]*
Wallis, Donald Wills 1950- *WhoAm 94*
Wallis, Doyle R. 1940- *WhoAmP 93*
Wallis, Edmund Arthur 1939- *Who 94*
Wallis, Elizabeth Susan 1953- *WhoMW 93*
Wallis, Eric G. 1950- *WhoAmL 94*
Wallis, Franklin F. 1944- *WhoAmL 94*
Wallis, Frederick Alfred John E. *Who 94*
Wallis, G(eraldine June) McDonald 1925- *EncSF 93*
Wallis, George C. 1871-1956 *EncSF 93*
Wallis, Graham Blair 1936- *WhoAm 94*
Wallis, Hal B. 1899-1986 *IntDcF 2-4*
Wallis, Henry 1830-1916 *DcNaB MP*
Wallis, Jeffrey Joseph 1923- *Who 94*
Wallis, John 1616-1703 *WorScD*
Wallis, Kay F. 1944- *WhoAmP 93*
Wallis, Larry *See* Motorhead *ConMus 10*
Wallis, Lloyd Randall 1954- *WhoMW 93*
Wallis, Michael Van 1961- *WhoMW 93*
Wallis, Olney Gray 1940- *WhoAmL 94*
Wallis, Peter (Gordon) 1935- *Who 94*
Wallis, Peter Ralph 1924- *Who 94*
Wallis, Peter Spencer 1945- *Who 94*
Wallis, Richard Fisher 1924- *WhoAm 94*
Wallis, Robert Joe 1938- *WhoScEn 94*
Wallis, Robert Ray 1927- *WhoAm 94*
Wallis, Samuel d1798 *WhAmRev*
Wallis, Samuel 1728-1795 *WhWE*
Wallis, Shani 1941- *WhoHol 92*
Wallis, Victor Harry 1922- *Who 94*
Wallis, W. Allen 1912- *WhoAmP 93*
Wallis, Walter Denis 1941- *WhoMW 93*
Wallis, Wendy S. 1948- *WhoFI 94*
Wallis, William *DrAPF 93*
Wallis, Wilson Allen 1912- *WhoAm 94, WhoFI 94, WhoScEn 94*
Walliser, Otto Heinrich 1928- *IntWW 93*
Wallis-Jones, Ewan Perrins 1913- *Who 94*
Wallis-King, Colin Sainthill 1926- *Who 94*
Wallison, Frieda K. 1943- *WhoAm 94, WhoAmL 94*
Wallison, Peter J. 1941- *WhoAm 94*
Wallman, Charles James 1924- *WhoFI 94, WhoMW 93*
Wallman, Charles Stephen 1953- *WhoFI 94*
Wallman, David Thees 1949- *WhoFI 94, WhoIns 94*
Wallman, George 1917- *WhoAm 94*
Wallman, Steven Mark Harte 1953- *WhoAm 94*
Wallman, Walter 1932- *IntWW 93*
Wallmann, Jeffrey Miner 1941- *WhoWest 94*
Wallmann, Margarita 1904-1992 *NewGrDO*
Wallmeyer, Dick 1931- *WrDr 94*
Wallmeyer, Richard 1931- *WrDr 94*
Wallnau, Larry Brownstein 1949- *WhoScEn 94*
Wallner, Franz 1937- *WhoScEn 94*
Wallner, Mary Jane 1946- *WhoAmP 93*
Wallner, Peter M. 1949- *WhoIns 94*
Wallnofer, Adolf 1854-1946 *NewGrDO*
Walloch, Esther Coto 1938- *WhoHisp 94*
Wallock, Edwin N. d1951 *WhoHol 92*
Wallop *Who 94*
Wallop, Douglass *DrAPF 93*
Wallop, Malcolm 1933- *CngDr 93, IntWW 93, WhoAm 94, WhoAmP 93, WhoWest 94*

Wallot, Jean-Pierre 1935- *IntWW 93, WhoAm 94, WhoMW 93*
Walloughby, Lee Davis 1952- *WrDr 94*
Wallower, Lucille 1910- *WrDr 94*
Wallraff, Barbara Jean 1953- *WhoAm 94, WhoFI 94*
Wallrock, John 1922- *Who 94*
Walls, Betty L. Webb 1932- *WhoMW 93*
Walls, Betty Lou 1930- *WhoAmP 93*
Walls, Carmage 1908- *WhoAm 94*
Walls, Daniel Frank 1942- *IntWW 93, Who 94*
Walls, David Stuart 1941- *WhoWest 94*
Walls, Doyle Wesley *DrAPF 93*
Walls, Dwayne Estes 1932- *WhoAm 94*
Walls, Eldred Wright 1912- *Who 94*
Walls, Forest Wesley 1939- *WhoAm 94*
Walls, Fredric T. 1935- *WhoBlA 94*
Walls, Gary Bruce 1952- *WhoMW 93*
Walls, Geoffrey Nowell 1945- *Who 94*
Walls, George Hilton, Jr. 1942- *AfrAmG [port], WhoBlA 94*
Walls, George Rodney 1945- *WhoAm 94, WhoAmL 94*
Walls, Glen Alan *WhoMW 93*
Walls, Greg
  See Anthrax *ConMus 11*
Walls, Ian G 1922- *WrDr 94*
Walls, John William 1927- *WhoMW 93*
Walls, Johnnie E., Jr. *WhoAmP 93*
Walls, Louise A. M. *WhoFI 94*
Walls, Martha Ann Williams 1927- *WhoAm 94*
Walls, Melvin 1948- *WhoBlA 94*
Walls, (George) Peter 1926- *IntWW 93*
Walls, Roland Charles 1917- *Who 94*
Walls, Stephen Roderick 1947- *Who 94*
Walls, Thomas Francis 1947- *WhoFI 94*
Walls, Tom d1949 *WhoHol 92*
Walls, William Jacob 1885-1975 *DcAmReB 2*
Wallschleger, Charles H. 1920- *WhoAmP 93*
Wallstrom, Margot *WhoWomW 91*
Wallstrom, Margot 1954- *IntWW 93*
Wallstrom, Wesley Donald 1929- *WhoFI 94, WhoWest 94*
Wallwork, Craig Raymond 1951- *WhoFI 94*
Wallwork, John 1946- *Who 94*
Wallwork, John Sackfield 1918- *Who 94*
Wallwork, William Wilson, III 1961- *WhoFI 94*
Wallworth, Cyril 1916- *Who 94*
Wally, Gus d1966 *WhoHol 92*
Wally, Walter Edward 1929- *WhoFI 94*
Wallyn, Robert Henry 1945- *WhoWest 94*
Walman, Jerome 1937- *WhoAm 94*
Walman, Thomas H. 1943- *WhoAmP 93*
Walmer, Edwin Fitch 1930- *WhoAm 94*
Walmer, James L. 1948- *WhoAmL 94*
Walmsley, Arnold Robert 1912- *Who 94*
Walmsley, Brian 1936- *Who 94*
Walmsley, David George 1938- *IntWW 93*
Walmsley, Francis Joseph 1926- *Who 94*
Walmsley, Jon 1956- *WhoHol 92*
Walmsley, Nigel Norman 1942- *Who 94*
Walmsley, Peter James 1929- *Who 94*
Walmsley, Peter Newton 1936- *WhoFI 94*
Walmsley, Robert 1906- *Who 94*
Walmsley, Robert 1941- *Who 94*
Walmsley, Robert Miller, Jr. 1946- *WhoAmL 94*
Walmsley, William Aubrey 1923- *WhoAmA 93*
Walner, Robert Joel 1946- *WhoAm 94, WhoAmL 94, WhoMW 93*
Walper, Cicely d1981 *WhoHol 92*
Walpin, Gerald 1931- *WhoAm 94, WhoAmL 94*
Walpole, Baron 1938- *Who 94*
Walpole, Horace 1717-1797 *BlmGEL*
Walpole, Hugh d1941 *WhoHol 92*
Walpole, Robert 1676-1745 *BlmGEL, HisWorL [port]*
Walpurgis *NewGrDO*
Walrad, Charlene Chuck 1946- *WhoWest 94*
Walrad, Paul Alfred 1947- *WhoAm 94*
Walrath, Harry Rienzi 1926- *WhoWest 94*
Walrath, Patricia A. 1941- *WhoAmP 93*
Walravens, Philip Alfred 1939- *WhoWest 94*
Walrod, David James 1946- *WhoAm 94*
Walschot, Leopold Gustave 1936- *WhoScEn 94*
Walser, David 1923- *Who 94*
Walser, Mackenzie 1924- *WhoAm 94*
Walser, Martin 1927- *ConWorW 93, IntDcT 2, IntWW 93*
Walser, Randal Louis 1949- *WhoWest 94*
Walsh, Alan 1916- *IntWW 93, Who 94*
Walsh, Alan John 1947- *WhoMW 93*
Walsh, Annmarie Hauck 1938- *WhoAm 94*
Walsh, Anthony F. 1942- *WhoAmL 94*
Walsh, Arthur *WhoHol 92*
Walsh, Arthur Stephen 1926- *IntWW 93, Who 94*
Walsh, Bernard Lawrence, Jr. 1932- *WhoWest 94*
Walsh, Blanche d1915 *WhoHol 92*
Walsh, Bonita A. 1952- *WhoFI 94*
Walsh, Brian 1935- *Who 94*
Walsh, Brian Joseph 1959- *WhoAmL 94*
Walsh, Chad *DrAPF 93*
Walsh, Chad 1914-1991 *WrDr 94N*
Walsh, Charles Hunter *WhoHol 92*
Walsh, Charles J. 1942- *WhoAmL 94*
Walsh, Charles Richard 1939- *WhoAm 94, WhoFI 94*
Walsh, Cheryl L. 1956- *WhoMW 93*
Walsh, Christine 1954- *IntDcB [port]*
Walsh, Christopher Thomas 1944- *WhoScEn 94*
Walsh, Clune Joseph, Jr. 1928- *WhoMW 93*
Walsh, Colin Stephen 1955- *Who 94*
Walsh, Cornelius Stephen 1907- *WhoAm 94*
Walsh, Daniel B. 1935- *WhoAmP 93*
Walsh, Daniel Francis 1937- *WhoAm 94, WhoWest 94*
Walsh, Daniel Stephen 1941- *WhoScEn 94*
Walsh, David Graves 1943- *WhoAm 94, WhoAmL 94*
Walsh, Delano B. 1945- *WhoBlA 94*
Walsh, Denny Jay 1935- *WhoAm 94, WhoWest 94*
Walsh, Dermot 1924- *ConTFT 11, WhoHol 92*
Walsh, Dermot Francis d1992 *Who 94N*
Walsh, Don 1931- *IntWW 93, WhoAm 94*
Walsh, Donald F. *WhoIns 94*
Walsh, Donald Peter 1930- *WhoAmL 94, WhoFI 94*
Walsh, Donnie *WhoAm 94*
Walsh, Dylan 1963- *WhoHol 92*
Walsh, Edward *WhoHol 92*
Walsh, Edward Joseph 1932- *WhoAm 94, WhoWest 94*
Walsh, Edward M. 1939- *IntWW 93*
Walsh, Edward Patrick 1937- *WhoAm 94*
Walsh, Everald J. 1938- *WhoBlA 94*
Walsh, F. Howard 1913- *WhoAm 94*
Walsh, Frank d1932 *WhoHol 92*
Walsh, Frederick Rall, Jr. 1952- *WhoFI 94*
Walsh, Gary Eugene 1949- *WhoAm 94, WhoAmL 94*
Walsh, Geoffrey 1909- *Who 94*
Walsh, Geoffrey David Jeremy *Who 94*
Walsh, George d1981 *WhoHol 92*
Walsh, George William 1923- *WhoAm 94*
Walsh, George William 1931- *WhoAm 94*
Walsh, Gerry 1951- *WhoAmP 93*
Walsh, Graham Robert 1989- *Who 94*
Walsh, Gregory Sheehan 1955- *WhoScEn 94*
Walsh, Henry George 1939- *Who 94*
Walsh, J(ames) M(organ) 1897-1952 *EncSF 93*
Walsh, J(ohn) Michael 1953- *WhoAmA 93*
Walsh, J. T. *IntMPA 94, WhoHol 92*
Walsh, James 1954- *WhoAmA 93*
Walsh, James Augustine 1906-1991 *WhAm 10*
Walsh, James Hamilton 1947- *WhoAm 94, WhoAmL 94*
Walsh, James Jerome 1924- *WhoAm 94*
Walsh, James Joseph 1930- *WhoAm 94, WhoAmL 94*
Walsh, James Mark 1909- *Who 94*
Walsh, James Michael 1947- *WhoFI 94*
Walsh, James Patrick 1944- *WhoAm 94*
Walsh, James Patrick 1953- *WhoMW 93*
Walsh, James Patrick, Jr. 1910- *WhoAm 94, WhoFI 94, WhoMW 93*
Walsh, James Peter, Jr. 1940- *WhoAmL 94*
Walsh, James T. 1947- *CngDr 93, WhoAmP 93*
Walsh, James Thomas 1947- *WhoAm 94*
Walsh, Jane Ellen McCann 1941- *WhoScEn 94*
Walsh, Janet Barbara 1939- *WhoAmA 93*
Walsh, Jason Todd 1963- *WhoFI 94*
Walsh, Jeremiah Edward, Jr. 1937- *WhoAm 94*
Walsh, Jerome Leo 1932- *WhoAmP 93*
Walsh, Jerome Mikel 1952- *WhoAmP 93*
Walsh, Jill P. *Who 94*
Walsh, Joanne Elizabeth 1942- *WhoMW 93*
Walsh, Joe 1943- *IntWW 93*
Walsh, Joey 1938- *WhoHol 92*
Walsh, John 1937- *Who 94, WhoAm 94, WhoAmA 93*
Walsh, John (Patrick) *WrDr 94*
Walsh, John (Patrick) 1911- *Who 94*
Walsh, John Breffni 1927- *WhoAm 94*
Walsh, John Bronson 1927- *WhoAmL 94, WhoFI 94*
Walsh, John Charles 1924- *WhoAm 94*
Walsh, John E., Jr. 1927- *WhoAm 94*
Walsh, John Harley 1938- *WhoScEn 94*
Walsh, John Henry Martin 1953- *Who 94*
Walsh, John James d1992 *Who 94N*
Walsh, John Joseph d1993 *NewYTBS 93*
Walsh, John Joseph 1924- *WhoAm 94*
Walsh, John Joseph 1943- *WhoFI 94, WhoMW 93*
Walsh, John P. *Who 94*
Walsh, Joseph A., Jr. 1949- *WhoAm 94*
Walsh, Joseph B. *WhoAmP 93*
Walsh, Joseph Fidler 1947- *WhoAm 94*
Walsh, Joseph Leo, III 1954- *WhoAmL 94*
Walsh, Joseph Michael 1943- *WhoAm 94*
Walsh, Joseph T. *WhoAmP 93*
Walsh, Joseph Thomas 1930- *WhoAm 94, WhoAmL 94*
Walsh, Joseph William 1941- *WhoAmP 93*
Walsh, Joy *DrAPF 93*
Walsh, Julia Montgomery 1923- *WhoAm 94, WhoFI 94*
Walsh, Katherine H. 1944- *WhoAmP 93*
Walsh, Katherine Herald 1944- *WhoMW 93*
Walsh, Kay 1914- *WhoHol 92*
Walsh, Kenneth *WhoHol 92*
Walsh, Kenneth Albert 1922- *WhoScEn 94*
Walsh, Kenneth Andrew 1931- *WhoWest 94*
Walsh, Kevin A. 1950- *WhoAm 94*
Walsh, Kevin J. 1949- *WhoAmL 94*
Walsh, Larry Donald 1956- *WhoWest 94*
Walsh, Lawrence *NewYTBS 93 [port]*
Walsh, Lawrence Edward 1912- *IntWW 93, WhoAm 94, WhoAmL 94*
Walsh, Leo Marcellus 1931- *WhoAm 94*
Walsh, Loren Melford 1927- *WhoAm 94*
Walsh, M. Emmet 1935- *IntMPA 94, WhoHol 92*
Walsh, Marcus 1947- *ConAu 41NR*
Walsh, Margaret Mary 1920- *WhoAmP 93*
Walsh, Maria Elena 1930- *BlmGWL*
Walsh, Marian C. *WhoAmP 93*
Walsh, Marie Therese 1935- *WhoAm 94*
Walsh, Martin R. 1952- *WhoAm 94, WhoFI 94*
Walsh, Mason 1912- *WhoAm 94, WhoWest 94*
Walsh, Maurice David, Jr. 1924- *WhoAm 94*
Walsh, Michael F. 1946 *WhoIns 94*
Walsh, Michael Francis 1947- *WhoWest 94*
Walsh, Michael Francis 1956- *WhoAm 94*
Walsh, Michael H. 1942- *IntWW 93*
Walsh, Michael Harries 1942- *WhoAm 94, WhoFI 94*
Walsh, Michael J. 1932- *WhoAm 94*
Walsh, Michael John Hatley 1927- *Who 94*
Walsh, Michael Patrick 1956- *WhoAmP 93*
Walsh, Michael Patrick 1961- *WhoWest 94*
Walsh, Michael S. 1951- *WhoAmL 94*
Walsh, Michael Samuel 1946- *WhoMW 93*
Walsh, Michael Thomas 1943- *Who 94*
Walsh, Milton O'Neal 1941- *WhoAmL 94*
Walsh, Nan d1978 *WhoHol 92*
Walsh, Noel Perrings 1919- *Who 94*
Walsh, (Mary) Noelle 1954- *Who 94*
Walsh, P(atrick) G(erard) 1923- *WrDr 94*
Walsh, Patricia Ruth *WhoAmA 93*
Walsh, Patrick Craig 1938- *WhoAm 94*
Walsh, Patrick Joseph *Who 94*
Walsh, Percy d1952 *WhoHol 92*
Walsh, Peter Alexander 1935- *IntWW 93*
Walsh, Peter Joseph 1929- *WhoAm 94*
Walsh, Philip Cornelius 1921- *WhoAm 94*
Walsh, Philip J. 1945- *WhoAmL 94*
Walsh, Philip Joseph, III 1951- *WhoAm 94*
Walsh, Ralph Edward 1923- *WhoAmP 93*
Walsh, Raoul d1980 *WhoHol 92*
Walsh, Richard A. *WhoAmP 93*
Walsh, Richard George 1930- *WhoAm 94*
Walsh, Richard Michael 1958- *WhoAmL 94*
Walsh, Robert Anthony 1938- *WhoAmL 94, WhoWest 94*
Walsh, Robert Charles 1938- *WhoFI 94*
Walsh, Robert Lawrence 1933- *WhoAmP 93*
Walsh, Robert R. 1939- *WhoAmP 93*
Walsh, Roberta Annette 1938- *WhoWest 94*
Walsh, Robin 1940- *Who 94*
Walsh, Rodger John 1924- *WhoAm 94*
Walsh, Ruth Elizabeth 1919- *WhoAmP 93*
Walsh, Scott Wesley 1947- *WhoScEn 94*
Walsh, Sean Patrick 1950- *WhoAmP 93*
Walsh, Semmes Guest 1926- *WhoAm 94*
Walsh, Sheila 1928- *WrDr 94*
Walsh, Stephen 1942- *WrDr 94*
Walsh, Sydney 1961- *WhoHol 92*
Walsh, T(homas) J(oseph) 1911-1988 *NewGrDO*
Walsh, Terrence Merlyn 1942- *WhoAm 94*
Walsh, Thomas Blake 1959- *WhoFI 94*
Walsh, Thomas Charles 1940- *WhoAm 94*
Walsh, Thomas G. 1942- *WhoIns 94*
Walsh, Thomas Gerard 1942- *WhoAm 94, WhoFI 94*
Walsh, Thomas H. d1925 *WhoHol 92*
Walsh, Thomas J. 1960- *WhoAmP 93, WhoMW 93*
Walsh, Thomas James, Jr. 1947- *WhoAmL 94*
Walsh, Thomas John, Sr. 1927- *WhoAmL 94*
Walsh, Thomas Joseph 1931- *WhoAm 94, WhoScEn 94*
Walsh, Thomas Joseph 1952- *WhoScEn 94*
Walsh, Thomas M. 1948- *WhoAmL 94*
Walsh, Thomas P. *WhoAmP 93*
Walsh, Timothy John 1952- *WhoWest 94*
Walsh, Timothy Maurice 1950- *WhoFI 94*
Walsh, Tom 1937- *WhoAmP 93*
Walsh, W. Terence 1943- *WhoAm 94, WhoAmL 94*
Walsh, Walter J. 1929- *WhoIns 94*
Walsh, William *WhoHol 92*
Walsh, William d1921 *WhoHol 92*
Walsh, William 1663-1708 *BlmGEL*
Walsh, William 1916- *Who 94, WrDr 94*
Walsh, William 1931- *WhoAm 94, WhoWest 94*
Walsh, William Albert 1933- *WhoAm 94*
Walsh, William Arthur, Jr. 1949- *WhoAm 94, WhoAmL 94*
Walsh, William Charles 1948- *WhoAmL 94*
Walsh, William D. 1924- *WhoAmP 93*
Walsh, William Desmond 1930- *WhoAm 94, WhoFI 94*
Walsh, William J. *DrAPF 93*
Walsh, William Joseph 1841-1921 *DcNaB MP*
Walsh, William Joseph, Jr. 1942- *WhoIns 94*
Walsh, William L., Jr. 1941- *WhoAmL 94*
Walsham, John Scarlett Warren d1992 *Who 94N*
Walsham, Timothy (John) 1939- *Who 94*
Walsh-Atkins, Leonard Brian 1915- *Who 94*
Walshe, Brian Francis 1958- *WhoScEn 94*
Walshe, Dolores 1949- *BlmGWL*
Walshe, Peter (Aubrey) 1934- *WrDr 94*
Walshe, R(obert) D(aniel) 1923- *WrDr 94*
Walsh-Gorski, Kathleen Anne 1963- *WhoMW 93*
Walsh-McGehee, Martha Bosse *WhoFI 94, WhoScEn 94*
Walsingham, Baron 1925- *Who 94*
Walske, Max Carl, Jr. 1922- *WhoAm 94, WhoWest 94*
Walsmith, Charles Rodger 1926- *WhoWest 94*
Walson, John, Sr. d1993 *NewYTBS 93*
Walstad, William Bathurst 1949- *WhoFI 94*
Walston, Claude Ellsworth 1926- *WhoAm 94*
Walston, Lola Inge 1943- *WhoMW 93*
Walston, Ray 1917- *WhoHol 92*
Walston, Ray 1918- *IntMPA 94*
Walston, Ray 1924- *WhoAm 94*
Walston, Rick Lyle Josh 1954- *WhoWest 94*
Walston, Roderick Eugene 1935- *WhoAm 94, WhoWest 94*
Walston, Woodrow William 1918- *WhoBlA 94*
Walstrom, Julie Carter 1956- *WhoAmP 93*
Walsworth, Ronald Lee 1935- *WhoAm 94*
Walt, Alexander Jeffrey 1923- *WhoAm 94*
Walt, Deon van der 1958- *NewGrDO*
Walt, Dick K. 1935- *WhoAm 94*
Walt, Harold Richard 1923- *WhoAm 94*
Walt, Lewis William 1913-1989 *WhAm 10*
Walt, Martin 1926- *WhoAm 94*
Walt, Stephen Martin 1955- *WhoMW 93*
Waltemath, Joan 1953- *WhoAmA 93*
Walter, Alan Stuart 1945- *WhoMW 93*
Walter, Ann Lynn 1946- *WhoMW 93*
Walter, Bert Mathew 1915- *WhoWest 94*
Walter, Bruce Alexander 1922- *WhoWest 94*
Walter, Bruno d1962 *WhoHol 92*
Walter, Bruno 1876-1962 *NewGrDO*
Walter, Clark E. 1946- *WhoAmL 94*
Walter, David 1949- *WhoFI 94*
Walter, David Keith 1944- *WhoAmP 93*
Walter, Donald Ellsworth 1936- *WhoAm 94, WhoAmL 94*
Walter, Douglas Hanson 1941- *WhoAm 94*
Walter, Elizabeth *WrDr 94*

Walter, Elizabeth Mitchell 1936- *WhoAmA 93*
Walter, Eugene d1941 *WhoHol 92*
Walter, Frank Sherman 1926- *WhoAm 94*
Walter, Frederick John 1944- *WhoWest 94*
Walter, Fritz 1920- *WorESoc*
Walter, Glenn Alan 1934- *WhoAmP 93*
Walter, (William) Grey 1910-1977 *DcNaB MP*
Walter, Gustav 1834-1910 *NewGrDO*
Walter, Harold (Edward) 1920- *Who 94*
Walter, Harold Edward 1920- *IntWW 93*
Walter, Harriet *WhoHol 92*
Walter, (Johann) Ignaz 1755-1822 *NewGrDO*
Walter, Ingo 1940- *WhoAm 94, WhoFI 94*
Walter, J. Jackson 1940- *WhoAm 94*
Walter, James Frederic 1956- *WhoScEn 94*
Walter, James Lloyd 1946- *WhoWest 94*
Walter, James Smiley 1946- *WhoMW 93*
Walter, Jerry d1979 *WhoHol 92*
Walter, Jessica 1940- *WhoHol 92*
Walter, Jessica 1944- *IntMPA 94*
Walter, John 1948- *WrDr 94*
Walter, John C. 1933- *WhoBlA 94*
Walter, John Robert 1947- *WhoAm 94, WhoFI 94*
Walter, Kenneth Burwood 1918- *Who 94*
Walter, Martha 1875-1976 *WhoAmA 93N*
Walter, Martin Edward 1945- *WhoAm 94*
Walter, Mary Lou 1939- *WhoAmP 93*
Walter, May E. *WhoAmA 93*
Walter, Melinda Kay 1957- *WhoFI 94*
Walter, Michael Charles 1956- *WhoAmL 94, WhoWest 94*
Walter, Michael David 1960- *WhoBlA 94*
Walter, Michele Ann 1954- *WhoFI 94*
Walter, Mildred Pitts *WhoBlA 94*
Walter, Mildred Pitts d1992 *WrDr 94N*
Walter, Mildred Pitts 1922- *BlkWr 2, TwCYAW*
Walter, Nancy 1939- *ConDr 93*
Walter, Neil Douglas 1942- *Who 94*
Walter, Norbert 1944- *IntWW 93*
Walter, Otto L. 1907- *WhoAmL 94*
Walter, Paul 1930- *WhoAmL 94*
Walter, Paul F. 1935- *WhoAmA 93*
Walter, Paul Hermann Lawrence 1934- *WhoAm 94, WhoScEn 94*
Walter, Priscilla Anne 1943- *WhoAm 94*
Walter, Ralph Bruno 1935- *WhoFI 94*
Walter, Ralph Collins, III 1946- *WhoMW 93*
Walter, Richard Lawrence 1933- *WhoAm 94*
Walter, Rita *WhoHol 92*
Walter, Robert D. 1945- *WhoAm 94, WhoFI 94*
Walter, Robert Irving 1920- *WhoAm 94*
Walter, Ronald Anderson 1949- *WhoAmP 93*
Walter, Ruedi d1990 *WhoHol 92*
Walter, Sandra K. 1942- *WhoAmP 93*
Walter, Silja 1919- *BlmGWL*
Walter, Tracey *IntMPA 94, WhoHol 92*
Walter, Virginia Lee 1937- *WhoAm 94*
Walter, W(illiam) Grey 1910-1977 *EncSF 93*
Walter, Wilfrid d1958 *WhoHol 92*
Walter, William Arnold, Jr. 1922- *WhoAm 94*
Walter, William F. 1904-1977 *WhoAmA 93N*
Walter, Wilmer d1941 *WhoHol 92*
Walter de Exonia c. 1220-1280 *DcNaB MP*
Walter de Hopton c. 1235-1296 *DcNaB MP*
Walter-Ellis, Desmond 1914- *WhoHol 92*
Walter-Robinson, Carol Sue 1942- *WhoWest 94*
Walters, Alan (Arthur) 1926- *Who 94*
Walters, Alan Arthur 1926- *IntWW 93, WrDr 94*
Walters, Alan Stanley 1941- *WhoAm 94*
Walters, Anna Lee *DrAPF 93*
Walters, Arthur M. 1918- *WhoBlA 94*
Walters, Barbara 1931- *IntMPA 94, IntWW 93, WhoAm 94*
Walters, Bill Peter 1943- *WhoAmP 93*
Walters, Billie 1927- *WhoAmA 93*
Walters, Casey *WhoHol 92*
Walters, Charles d1982 *WhoHol 92*
Walters, Charles Lee 1945- *WhoMW 93*
Walters, Christopher Kent 1942- *WhoAm 94, WhoAmL 94*
Walters, Curla Sybil 1929- *WhoBlA 94*
Walters, D. Eric 1951- *WhoMW 93, WhoScEn 94*
Walters, Daniel Lee 1959- *WhoFI 94*
Walters, David 1951- *WhoAm 94, WhoAmP 93*
Walters, David C. 1940- *WhoIns 94*
Walters, David McLean 1917- *WhoAm 94*
Walters, David R. 1961- *WhoFI 94*
Walters, David W. 1965- *WhoFI 94*
Walters, Dennis 1928- *Who 94*
Walters, Dennis George 1945- *WhoFI 94*
Walters, Dennis H. 1950- *WhoAmL 94*
Walters, Derrick *Who 94*
Walters, (Rhys) Derrick (Chamberlain) 1932- *Who 94*
Walters, Donald 1925- *Who 94*
Walters, Donald E. 1934-1990 *WhAm 10*
Walters, Dorothy d1934 *WhoHol 92*
Walters, Eric 1937- *WhoWest 94*
Walters, Eric G. 1952- *WhoFI 94*
Walters, Ernest 1927- *WhoAmA 93*
Walters, Everett 1915- *WhoAm 94*
Walters, Farah M. 1945- *WhoAm 94, WhoMW 93*
Walters, George O. 1930- *WhoAmL 94*
Walters, George W., Mrs. d1916 *WhoHol 92*
Walters, Geraint Gwynn 1910- *Who 94*
Walters, Glen Robert 1943- *WhoAm 94*
Walters, Gomer Winston 1937- *WhoAmL 94*
Walters, Gordon *EncSF 93*
Walters, Hal d1941 *WhoHol 92*
Walters, Harry N. 1936- *WhoAm 94*
Walters, Henry 1848-1931 *DcLB 140 [port]*
Walters, Hubert Everett 1933- *WhoBlA 94*
Walters, Hugh 1910- *EncSF 93*
Walters, Hugh 1910-1993 *WrDr 94N*
Walters, Hugh 1939- *WhoHol 92*
Walters, Jack d1944 *WhoHol 92*
Walters, Jefferson Brooks 1922- *WhoAm 94, WhoMW 93*
Walters, Jess 1908- *NewGrDO*
Walters, Jesse Raymond, Jr. 1938- *WhoWest 94*
Walters, Joe Aldrich 1920- *WhoMW 93*
Walters, John Alexander 1938- *WhoFI 94*
Walters, John Beauchamp 1903- *WrDr 94*
Walters, John Linton 1924- *WhoScEn 94*
Walters, John Sherwood 1917- *WhoAm 94*
Walters, John William Townshend 1926- *Who 94*
Walters, Johnnie McKeiver 1919- *WhoAm 94*
Walters, Jonathan Kirschner 1949- *WhoAmL 94*
Walters, Joyce Dora *Who 94*
Walters, Judith Richmond 1944- *WhoAm 94*
Walters, Julie 1949- *WhoHol 92*
Walters, Julie 1950- *IntMPA 94, IntWW 93, Who 94*
Walters, Kenn David 1957- *WhoFI 94, WhoScEn 94*
Walters, Kenneth 1934- *Who 94*
Walters, Kenneth D. 1941- *WrDr 94*
Walters, Lauri *WhoHol 92*
Walters, Lawrence M. 1950- *WhoFI 94*
Walters, Linda Jane 1961- *WhoWest 94*
Walters, Lori Antionette 1967- *WhoScEn 94*
Walters, Marrian d1990 *WhoHol 92*
Walters, Marten Doig 1953- *WhoScEn 94*
Walters, Mary C. 1922- *WhoAmP 93*
Walters, Mary Dawson 1923- *WhoBlA 94*
Walters, Max *Who 94*
Walters, Merri d1984 *WhoHol 92*
Walters, Michael Quentin 1927- *Who 94*
Walters, Milton James 1942- *WhoAm 94, WhoFI 94*
Walters, Nancy Lu 1938- *WhoMW 93*
Walters, Peter (Ingram) 1931- *Who 94*
Walters, Peter (Hugh Bennetts) Ensor 1912- *Who 94*
Walters, Peter Ernest 1913- *Who 94*
Walters, Peter Ingram 1931- *IntWW 93*
Walters, Phyllis Kobel 1939- *WhoAmP 93*
Walters, Raymond, Jr. 1912- *WhoAm 94*
Walters, Raymond L. 1943- *WhoWest 94*
Walters, Rebecca Russell Yarborough 1951- *WhoFI 94*
Walters, Rita 1930- *WhoAmP 93*
Walters, Robert Dean 1935- *WhoMW 93*
Walters, Robert Philip 1962- *WhoAmL 94*
Walters, Robert Stephen 1941- *WhoFI 94*
Walters, Roger (Talbot) 1917- *Who 94*
Walters, Roger Talbot 1917- *IntWW 93*
Walters, Ronald *BlkWr 2*
Walters, Ronald 1938- *WhoBlA 94*
Walters, Ronald Arlen 1940- *WhoWest 94*
Walters, Ronald Neal 1950- *WhoAmP 93*
Walters, Ronald Ogden 1939- *WhoAm 94*
Walters, S(tuart) Max 1920- *Who 94*
Walters, Selene *WhoHol 92*
Walters, Shirley 1925- *WhoWomW 91*
Walters, Stacey Ann 1957- *WhoWest 94*
Walters, Stephen Scott 1945- *WhoAm 94, WhoAmL 94*
Walters, Sumner J. 1916- *WhoAmL 94*
Walters, Susan 1963- *WhoHol 92*
Walters, Sylvia Solochek 1938- *WhoAmA 93, WhoWest 94*
Walters, Thomas N. *DrAPF 93*
Walters, Thorley 1913- *WhoHol 92*
Walters, Timothy Carl 1955- *WhoWest 94*
Walters, Tom Frederick 1931- *WhoMW 93*
Walters, Tracy Wayne 1963- *WhoScEn 94*
Walters, Tyler *WhoAm 94*
Walters, Vernon A. 1917- *WhoAmP 93*
Walters, Vernon Anthony 1917- *IntWW 93, WhoAm 94*
Walters, Waltman 1895-1988 *WhAm 10*
Walters, Warren W. 1932- *WhoBlA 94*
Walters, Wilfred Nelson, Jr. 1942- *WhoAm 94*
Walters, William LeRoy 1932- *WhoAm 94*
Walters, William Owen 1952- *WhoAmP 93*
Walters, William Peter 1943- *WhoAmL 94*
Walters, William Place 1943- *WhoScEn 94*
Waltershausen, Hermann Wolfgang (Sartorius) 1882-1954 *NewGrDO*
Walterspiel, Otto Heinrich 1927- *IntWW 93*
Walthall, Anna Mae d1950 *WhoHol 92*
Walthall, Daniel Eugene 1956- *WhoWest 94*
Walthall, Henry B. d1936 *WhoHol 92*
Walthall, Hugh *DrAPF 93*
Walthall, Lee Wade 1953- *WhoAm 94*
Waltham, Tony (A. C.) 1942- *WrDr 94*
Walther, Barbara Ann Lane 1952- *WhoAmL 94*
Walther, Carl Ferdinand Wilhelm 1811-1887 *DcAmReB 2*
Walther, Carolina *NewGrDO*
Walther, Charles Marion, Jr. 1935- *WhoAmP 93*
Walther, Daniel 1940- *EncSF 93*
Walther, Eric H(arry) 1960- *ConAu 140*
Walther, Gretchen *WhoHol 92*
Walther, Herbert 1935- *IntWW 93, WhoScEn 94*
Walther, Joseph Edward 1912- *WhoAm 94, WhoScEn 94*
Walther, Paul 1927- *BasBi*
Walther, Roger Kenneth 1949- *WhoFI 94*
Walther, Zerita 1927- *WhoAmL 94*
Walther von der Vogelweide c. 1170-c. 1230 *DcLB 138 [port]*
Walti, Randal Fred 1939- *WhoAm 94, WhoWest 94*
Waltman, Alfred A. *WhoAmP 93*
Waltman, Bob 1933- *WhoAmP 93*
Waltman, William Dewitt, III 1946- *WhoFI 94*
Waltmann, Harry Franklin 1871-1951 *WhoAmA 93N*
Waltner, Beverly Ruland *WhoAmA 93*
Waltner, John Randolph 1938- *WhoFI 94, WhoMW 93*
Waltner, Richard Hege 1931- *WhoWest 94*
Walton *Who 94*
Walton, Alan 1932- *WhoScEn 94*
Walton, Alan George 1936- *WhoAm 94*
Walton, Alvin Earl 1964- *WhoBlA 94*
Walton, Anthony John 1934- *WhoAm 94*
Walton, Anthony Michael 1925- *Who 94*
Walton, Anthony Scott 1965- *WhoBlA 94*
Walton, Arthur Halsall 1916- *Who 94*
Walton, Bill 1952- *BasBi [port], WhoAm 94*
Walton, Booker T., Jr. 1950- *WhoFI 94*
Walton, Brian 1947- *WhoAm 94, WhoWest 94*
Walton, Bryce 1918-1988 *EncSF 93*
Walton, Cedar Anthony 1901- *WhoBlA 94*
Walton, Charles D. 1948- *WhoAmP 93*
Walton, Charles Michael 1941- *WhoAm 94, WhoScEn 94*
Walton, Charlie 1947- *WhoAmP 93*
Walton, Clarence 1915- *WhoAm 94*
Walton, Clifford Wayne 1954- *WhoMW 93*
Walton, Clyde Francis 1946- *WhoWest 94*
Walton, Corinne Hemeter 1925- *WhoAm 94*
Walton, Craig 1934- *WhoWest 94*
Walton, Deborah Gail 1950- *WhoWest 94*
Walton, Denise Marie 1966- *WhoAmL 94*
Walton, DeWitt T., Jr. 1937- *WhoBlA 94*
Walton, Donald William *WhoAmA 93*
Walton, Douglas d1961 *WhoHol 92*
Walton, Edmund Lewis, Jr. 1936- *WhoAmL 94, WhoAmP 93*
Walton, Edward D. *WhoBlA 94*
Walton, Elbert Arthur, Jr. 1942- *WhoAmP 93, WhoBlA 94*
Walton, Emma 1962- *WhoHol 92*
Walton, Ernest T. S. 1903- *WorInv*
Walton, Ernest Thomas Sinton 1903- *IntWW 93, Who 94, WhoScEn 94, WorScD*
Walton, Flavia Batteau 1947- *WhoBlA 94*
Walton, Florence d1981 *WhoHol 92*
Walton, Frank Emulous 1909- *WhoAm 94, WhoWest 94*
Walton, Fred *HorFD [port]*
Walton, Fred d1936 *WhoHol 92*
Walton, Geoffrey Elmer 1934- *Who 94*
Walton, George c. 1741-1804 *WhAmRev*
Walton, George 1750-1804 *AmRev*
Walton, George D. 1932- *WhoAmP 93*
Walton, Gerald Wayne 1934- *WhoAm 94*
Walton, Gladys d1993 *NewYTBS 93 [port]*
Walton, Gladys 1904- *WhoHol 92*
Walton, Guy E. 1935- *WhoAmA 93*
Walton, Hanes, Jr. 1942- *WhoBlA 94*
Walton, Harold Frederic 1912- *WhoScEn 94*
Walton, Harold Vincent 1921- *WhoAm 94*
Walton, Harriett J. 1933- *WhoBlA 94*
Walton, Harry A., Jr. 1918- *WhoAmA 93*
Walton, Henry John 1924- *IntWW 93, WrDr 94*
Walton, Herbert C. d1954 *WhoHol 92*
Walton, Izaac 1593-1683 *BlmGEL*
Walton, James 1911- *WrDr 94*
Walton, James Donald 1952- *WhoBlA 94*
Walton, James Edward 1944- *WhoBlA 94*
Walton, James M. 1930- *WhoAm 94*
Walton, James Madison 1926- *WhoBlA 94*
Walton, James Meade 1947- *WhoWest 94*
Walton, Jeffrey Howard 1958- *WhoScEn 94*
Walton, Jerome O'Terrell 1965- *WhoBlA 94*
Walton, Jess *WhoHol 92*
Walton, Joan 1939- *WhoAm 94*
Walton, John *WhoHol 92*
Walton, John 1738-1783 *WhAmRev*
Walton, John (Nicholas) 1922- *WrDr 94*
Walton, John H. 1939- *WhoIns 94*
Walton, John Robert 1904- *Who 94*
Walton, John Wayne 1947- *WhoAmL 94*
Walton, John William Scott 1925- *Who 94*
Walton, Jon David 1942- *WhoAm 94, WhoAmL 94*
Walton, Jonathan Taylor 1930- *WhoAm 94, WhoFI 94, WhoMW 93*
Walton, Kathleen Endres 1961- *WhoAm 94*
Walton, Kendall L(ewis) 1939- *WrDr 94*
Walton, Kimberly Ann 1965- *WhoScEn 94*
Walton, Lludloo Charles 1950- *WhoBlA 94*
Walton, M. Douglas 1942- *WhoAmA 93*
Walton, Marion 1899- *WhoAmA 93*
Walton, Matt Savage 1915- *WhoAm 94*
Walton, Meredith 1936- *WhoAm 94*
Walton, Mildred Lee 1926- *WhoBlA 94*
Walton, Morgan Lauck, III 1932- *WhoAm 94*
Walton, Ortiz (Montaigne) 1933- *WrDr 94*
Walton, Ortiz Montaigne *WhoAm 94, WhoBlA 94*
Walton, Ralph Ervin 1903- *WhoWest 94*
Walton, Ralph Gerald 1942- *WhoMW 93*
Walton, Reggie Barnett 1949- *WhoBlA 94*
Walton, Richard Eugene 1931- *WhoAm 94*
Walton, Richard J(ohn) 1928- *WrDr 94*
Walton, Richard K. 1931- *WhoAmP 93*
Walton, Richard R. d1993 *NewYTBS 93 [port]*
Walton, Richmond Lee 1923- *WhoMW 93*
Walton, Robert Owen 1927- *WhoAm 94, WhoMW 93*
Walton, Robert Prentiss 1938- *WhoAmL 94*
Walton, Rodney Earl 1947- *WhoAm 94*
Walton, Roger Alan 1941- *WhoAm 94, WhoWest 94*
Walton, Roland J. *WhoBlA 94*
Walton, Ronald Linn 1955- *WhoWest 94*
Walton, S. Robson 1945- *WhoAm 94, WhoFI 94, WhoWest 94*
Walton, Sam 1918-1992 *AnObit 1992*
Walton, Sam Moore 1920-1992 *WhAm 10*
Walton, Stanley Anthony, III 1939- *WhoAm 94, WhoAmL 94*
Walton, Steven L. 1945- *WhoWest 94*
Walton, Thomas Bardeen 1896- *WhAm 10*
Walton, Thomas Cody 1956- *WhoScEn 94*
Walton, Tracy Matthew, Jr. 1930- *WhoBlA 94*
Walton, Vera d1965 *WhoHol 92*
Walton, Wesley Scott 1938- *WhoAm 94*
Walton, William 1902-1983 *IntDcF 2-4*
Walton, William (Turner) 1902-1983 *NewGrDO*
Walton, William Harris, Jr. *WhoFI 94*
Walton, William Robert 1949- *WhoFI 94*
Walton, William Stephen 1933- *Who 94*
Walton Of Detchant, Baron 1922- *IntWW 93, Who 94*
Waltrip, Darrell Lee 1947- *WhoAm 94*
Waltrip, Mather K. 1960- *WhoWest 94*
Waltrip, Robert 1924- *WhoBlA 94*
Waltrip, Robert L. 1931- *WhoFI 94*
Walts, Lou Eugene 1932- *WhoWest 94*

Wangchuck, Sonam Chhoden 1953- *WhoWomW 91*
Wang Chuguang 1934- *WhoPRCh 91 [port]*
Wangchuk, Jigme Singye 1955- *IntWW 93*
Wang Congwu 1905- *WhoPRCh 91 [port]*
Wang Daguan 1917- *WhoPRCh 91 [port]*
Wang Daheng 1915- *WhoPRCh 91 [port]*
Wang Daohan 1915- *WhoPRCh 91 [port]*
Wang Daoyi 1925- *WhoPRCh 91 [port]*
Wang Dapeng 1954- *WhoPRCh 91 [port]*
Wang Datong 1937- *WhoPRCh 91*
Wang Debao 1918- *WhoPRCh 91 [port]*
Wang Degong *WhoPRCh 91*
Wang Deyan 1931- *IntWW 93, WhoPRCh 91*
Wang Deyi *WhoPRCh 91*
Wang Deying 1931- *WhoPRCh 91 [port]*
Wang Dezhao 1902- *IntWW 93*
Wang Dezhao 1905- *WhoPRCh 91*
Wang Dianzuo *WhoPRCh 91*
Wang Dingjiong *WhoPRCh 91*
Wang Donghai 1938- *IntWW 93*
Wang Dongxing 1916- *IntWW 93, WhoPRCh 91 [port]*
Wangel, Hedwig d1961 *WhoHol 92*
Wang Enmao 1912- *WhoPRCh 91 [port]*
Wanger, Oliver Winston 1940- *WhoAm 94, WhoAmL 94, WhoWest 94*
Wanger, Walter 1894-1968 *IntDcF 2-4*
Wangerin, Walter, Jr. 1944- *TwCYAW*
Wang Fang 1920- *IntWW 93, WhoPRCh 91 [port]*
Wang Fei *WhoPRCh 91*
Wang Feng 1910- *WhoPRCh 91 [port]*
Wang Feng 1931- *WhoPRCh 91 [port]*
Wang Fosong *WhoPRCh 91 [port]*
Wang Fuli 1949- *WhoPRCh 91 [port]*
Wang Furu *WhoPRCh 91*
Wang Fuzhi 1923- *WhoPRCh 91 [port]*
Wang Fuzhi, Maj.-Gen. 1923- *IntWW 93*
Wang Fuzhou 1931- *IntWW 93, WhoPRCh 91 [port]*
Wang Ganchang 1907- *IntWW 93, WhoPRCh 91 [port]*
Wang Ganghua *WhoPRCh 91*
Wang Genzhong 1903- *WhoPRCh 91 [port]*
Wang Geyi 1896- *WhoPRCh 91 [port]*
Wang Guangmei 1921- *IntWW 93, WhoPRCh 91 [port]*
Wang Guangxi *WhoPRCh 91*
Wang Guangxi 1930- *WhoPRCh 91 [port]*
Wang Guangying 1919- *IntWW 93, WhoPRCh 91 [port]*
Wang Guangyu 1919- *IntWW 93, WhoPRCh 91 [port]*
Wang Guangzhong 1921- *IntWW 93, WhoPRCh 91 [port]*
Wang Guixin *WhoPRCh 91 [port]*
Wang Gungwu 1930- *IntWW 93, Who 94*
Wang Guobeng *WhoPRCh 91*
Wang Guoquan c. 1916- *WhoPRCh 91 [port]*
Wang Hai 1925- *WhoPRCh 91 [port]*
Wang Hai, Gen. 1925- *IntWW 93*
Wang Hairong 1938- *WhoPRCh 91 [port]*
Wang Haiyan 1929- *WhoPRCh 91 [port]*
Wang Hanbin 1925- *IntWW 93*
Wang Hanbin 1927- *WhoPRCh 91 [port]*
Wang Hanjie 1917- *WhoPRCh 91 [port]*
Wang Hanzhang 1930- *WhoPRCh 91 [port]*
Wang Hao 1930- *WhoPRCh 91 [port]*
Wang Haowei 1940- *WhoPRCh 91 [port]*
Wang Heshou 1908- *WhoPRCh 91 [port]*
Wang Hongwen d1992 *IntWW 93N*
Wang Hongzhen 1916- *WhoPRCh 91 [port]*
Wang Houde 1933- *WhoPRCh 91 [port]*
Wang Houli *WhoPRCh 91*
Wang Hu *WhoPRCh 91*
Wang Huaiqing 1944- *WhoPRCh 91*
Wang Huaiyuan *WhoPRCh 91*
Wang Huanzhen *WhoPRCh 91*
Wang Hui *WhoPRCh 91*
Wang Huide *WhoPRCh 91*
Wang Huique 1936- *WhoPRCh 91*
Wang Jiafu *WhoPRCh 91 [port]*
Wang Jiahua *WhoPRCh 91*
Wang Jiaji *WhoPRCh 91*
Wang Jialiu 1929- *WhoPRCh 91 [port], WhoWomW 91*
Wang Jian 1915- *WhoPRCh 91 [port]*
Wang Jianbang *WhoPRCh 91*
Wang Jianhua *WhoPRCh 91*
Wang Jianli *WhoPRCh 91*
Wang Jianshi *WhoPRCh 91*
Wang Jianshuang 1936- *WhoPRCh 91 [port]*
Wang Jianxing *WhoPRCh 91*
Wang Jiaohua 1900- *WhoPRCh 91*
Wang Jiaqi *WhoPRCh 91*
Wang Jiaxin 1957- *WhoPRCh 91*
Wang Jida 1935- *IntWW 93, WhoPRCh 91*
Wang Jingbo *WhoPRCh 91*
Wang Jingshi *WhoPRCh 91*
Wang Jinling 1917- *WhoPRCh 91 [port]*
Wang Jinqing *WhoPRCh 91*
Wang Jintang *WhoPRCh 91*
Wang Jinxi *WhoPRCh 91*
Wang Jinyuan 1940- *WhoPRCh 91*
Wang Jiuan *WhoPRCh 91 [port]*
Wang Julu 1945- *WhoPRCh 91 [port]*
Wang Jun *WhoPRCh 91 [port]*
Wang Jun 1934- *WhoPRCh 91 [port]*
Wang Juzhen *WhoPRCh 91 [port]*
Wang Kangle 1908?- *WhoPRCh 91 [port]*
Wang Kefen 1927- *IntWW 93*
Wang Keping 1949- *WhoPRCh 91*
Wang Kewen *WhoPRCh 91*
Wang Keying *WhoPRCh 91*
Wang Kuang 1917- *WhoPRCh 91 [port]*
Wang Kun *WhoPRCh 91 [port]*
Wang Lanxi *WhoPRCh 91*
Wang Lei 1914- *WhoPRCh 91*
Wang Lequan *WhoPRCh 91*
Wangler, Mark Adrian 1955- *WhoMW 93*
Wangler, William C. 1929- *WhoIns 94*
Wangler, William Clarence 1929- *WhoAm 94, WhoFI 94*
Wang Li *WhoPRCh 91*
Wang Lianzheng 1930- *IntWW 93, WhoPRCh 91 [port]*
Wang Libin 1930- *WhoPRCh 91 [port]*
Wang Lin *WhoPRCh 91*
Wang Liusheng 1912- *WhoPRCh 91*
Wang Liwei *WhoPRCh 91*
Wang Lizhi 1921- *WhoPRCh 91 [port]*
Wang Luguang *WhoPRCh 91*
Wang Luming 1920- *WhoPRCh 91 [port]*
Wang Luolin *WhoPRCh 91*
Wang Maolin 1934- *WhoPRCh 91 [port]*
Wang Maolin 1935- *IntWW 93*
Wang Meng 1920- *WhoPRCh 91 [port]*
Wang Meng 1934- *ConWorW 93, IntWW 93, WhoPRCh 91 [port]*
Wang Min 1929- *WhoPRCh 91 [port]*
Wang Mingda 1935- *WhoPRCh 91 [port]*
Wang Mingzhe *WhoPRCh 91*
Wang Nai 1927- *WhoPRCh 91 [port]*
Wang Ning 1923- *WhoPRCh 91 [port]*
Wang Nongsheng *WhoPRCh 91*
Wangomen fl. 176-?-179-? *EncNAR*
Wang Peide *WhoPRCh 91*
Wang Peizhou *WhoPRCh 91 [port]*
Wang Ping 1907- *WhoPRCh 91 [port]*
Wang Ping 1917- *WhoPRCh 91 [port]*
Wang Ping 1955- *WhoPRCh 91 [port]*
Wang Pingshan 1926- *WhoPRCh 91 [port]*
Wang Pinqing 1930- *WhoPRCh 91 [port]*
Wang Qi 1926- *WhoPRCh 91*
Wang Qian 1917- *WhoPRCh 91*
Wang Qiang *BlmGWL*
Wang Qianghua *WhoPRCh 91*
Wang Qiaozhang 1915- *WhoPRCh 91*
Wang Qidong 1921- *WhoPRCh 91 [port]*
Wang Qihao *WhoPRCh 91*
Wang Qingcheng 1928- *WhoPRCh 91*
Wang Qingsheng 1932- *WhoPRCh 91 [port]*
Wang Qingshu *WhoPRCh 91*
Wang Qishan *WhoPRCh 91*
Wang Qun 1926- *IntWW 93, WhoPRCh 91 [port]*
Wang Rensheng *WhoPRCh 91*
Wang Renzhi 1933- *IntWW 93, WhoPRCh 91 [port]*
Wang Renzhong 1917- *WhoPRCh 91 [port]*
Wang Rongzhen 1931- *WhoPRCh 91 [port]*
Wang Rui *WhoPRCh 91*
Wang Ruilin 1929- *WhoPRCh 91 [port]*
Wang Ruilin, Lieut.-Gen. 1929- *IntWW 93*
Wang Ruisheng 1928- *WhoPRCh 91 [port]*
Wang Rulin 1932- *WhoPRCh 91 [port]*
Wang Runsheng 1919- *WhoPRCh 91 [port]*
Wang Runzi 1946- *WhoPRCh 91*
Wang Ruoshui *WhoPRCh 91*
Wang Senhao 1932- *IntWW 93*
Wang Senhao 1933- *WhoPRCh 91 [port]*
Wangsgard, Chris Prince 1941- *WhoAmL 94*
Wangsgard, Robert Louis 1915- *WhoAm 94*
Wang Shaoyan 1904- *WhoPRCh 91 [port]*
Wang Shenyin 1915- *WhoPRCh 91 [port]*
Wang Sheyun 1934- *WhoPRCh 91 [port]*
Wang Shi *WhoPRCh 91*
Wang Shichao 1921- *WhoPRCh 91 [port]*
Wang Shigu *WhoPRCh 91*
Wang Shijun 1927- *WhoPRCh 91 [port]*
Wang Shirong *WhoPRCh 91*
Wang Shitai 1909- *WhoPRCh 91*
Wang Shouchu *WhoPRCh 91*
Wang Shoudao 1906- *WhoPRCh 91 [port]*
Wang Shouguan 1923- *IntWW 93, WhoPRCh 91*
Wang Shoumao *WhoPRCh 91*
Wang Shouqiang *WhoPRCh 91*
Wang Shouren *WhoPRCh 91*
Wang Shouting *WhoPRCh 91*
Wang Shouwu 1919- *WhoPRCh 91*
Wang Shu *WhoPRCh 91 [port]*
Wang Shuangxi 1936- *WhoPRCh 91 [port]*
Wang Shufang 1930- *WhoPRCh 91 [port]*
Wang Shuhui 1912- *WhoPRCh 91 [port]*
Wang Shuming 1933- *WhoPRCh 91 [port]*
Wang Shurong *WhoPRCh 91*
Wang Shusan *WhoPRCh 91*
Wang Shuwen *WhoPRCh 91*
Wang Shuxian *WhoPRCh 91 [port]*
Wangsness, Wayne Roger 1941- *WhoMW 93*
Wang Songda 1935- *WhoPRCh 91 [port]*
Wang Taizhi 1934- *WhoPRCh 91*
Wang Tao 1931- *IntWW 93*
Wang Tao 1932- *WhoPRCh 91 [port]*
Wang Tian-Ren 1939- *IntWW 93*
Wang Tieya *WhoPRCh 91*
Wang Tingchen 1935- *WhoPRCh 91*
Wang Tingdong 1923- *WhoPRCh 91 [port]*
Wang Tongyi *WhoPRCh 91 [port]*
Wangui, wa Goro *BlmGWL*
Wan Guoquan 1919- *WhoPRCh 91 [port]*
Wang Wei 1919- *WhoPRCh 91 [port]*
Wang Weibao 1942- *WhoPRCh 91 [port]*
Wang Weicheng 1929- *IntWW 93, WhoPRCh 91 [port]*
Wang Weixin 1938- *WhoPRCh 91*
Wang Wendong *WhoPRCh 91*
Wang Wenfang 1938- *WhoPRCh 91 [port]*
Wang Wenfeng *WhoPRCh 91*
Wang Wenli *WhoPRCh 91*
Wang Wenqian *WhoPRCh 91*
Wang Wenqing *WhoPRCh 91*
Wang Wenshi 1921- *IntWW 93, WhoPRCh 91*
Wang Wenyuan 1931- *WhoPRCh 91 [port]*
Wang Wenzhe *WhoPRCh 91*
Wang Xi *WhoPRCh 91 [port]*
Wang Xianghao *WhoPRCh 91*
Wang Xiangtian 1930- *WhoPRCh 91 [port]*
Wang Xianjin 1930- *WhoPRCh 91 [port]*
Wang Xiaodong 1970- *WhoPRCh 91*
Wang Xiaofeng 1944- *WhoPRCh 91*
Wang Xiaoguang 1924- *IntWW 93, WhoPRCh 91 [port]*
Wang Xiaoxian *WhoPRCh 91*
Wang Xiaoying 1947- *BlmGWL*
Wang Xibin *WhoPRCh 91*
Wang Xijue 1929- *WhoPRCh 91 [port]*
Wang Xingda *WhoPRCh 91*
Wang Xintian *WhoPRCh 91*
Wang Xiulin *WhoPRCh 91*
Wang Xiuting 1965- *WhoPRCh 91 [port]*
Wang Xueming, Francis 1909- *WhoPRCh 91*
Wang Xuezhen 1926- *IntWW 93*
Wang Xuezhen 1927- *WhoPRCh 91*
Wang Xugong *WhoPRCh 91*
Wang Yachen 1930- *WhoPRCh 91*
Wang Yahui 1930- *WhoPRCh 91*
Wang Yamin *WhoPRCh 91*
Wang Yan *WhoPRCh 91*
Wang Yanchang *WhoPRCh 91*
Wang Yang-Ming 1472-1529 *EncEth*
Wang Yanli 1913- *WhoPRCh 91 [port]*
Wang Yanling 1964- *WhoPRCh 91 [port]*
Wang Yanmou *WhoPRCh 91*
Wang Yanxin 1929- *WhoPRCh 91 [port]*
Wang Yanyan *WhoPRCh 91 [port]*
Wang Yaolun 1917- *WhoPRCh 91 [port]*
Wang Yaoting *WhoPRCh 91 [port]*
Wang Yaping 1956- *WhoPRCh 91 [port]*
Wang Yaxiang *WhoPRCh 91*
Wang Yidi 1929- *WhoPRCh 91*
Wang Yingchun 1942- *WhoPRCh 91 [port]*
Wang Yingfan *WhoPRCh 91*
Wang Yinglai 1907- *IntWW 93*
Wang Yinglai 1910- *WhoPRCh 91 [port]*
Wang Yiping *WhoPRCh 91*
Wang Yishi 1926- *WhoPRCh 91 [port]*
Wang Yongxing 1925- *WhoPRCh 91 [port]*
Wang Youfen *WhoPRCh 91*
Wang Youhan *WhoPRCh 91*
Wang Youhui 1934- *WhoPRCh 91 [port]*
Wang Youping 1910- *WhoPRCh 91*
Wang You-Tsao 1925- *IntWW 93*
Wang Yu 1931- *WhoPRCh 91*
Wang Yuan *WhoPRCh 91*
Wang Yuan 1930- *IntWW 93*
Wang Yuanjian 1929- *WhoPRCh 91*
Wang Yuefeng 1930- *IntWW 93, WhoPRCh 91 [port]*
Wang Yumin 1921- *WhoPRCh 91 [port]*
Wang Yun *WhoPRCh 91 [port]*
Wang Yung-Ching 1917- *IntWW 93*
Wang Yunkun *WhoPRCh 91*
Wang Yuqing 1911- *WhoPRCh 91 [port]*
Wang Yusheng *WhoPRCh 91*
Wang Yusheng 1927- *WhoPRCh 91 [port]*
Wang Yuzhao 1926- *WhoPRCh 91 [port]*
Wang Zemin 1921- *WhoPRCh 91 [port]*
Wang Zengjing 1933- *WhoPRCh 91 [port]*
Wang Zengqi 1920- *IntWW 93, WhoPRCh 91 [port]*
Wang Zenong 1907- *WhoPRCh 91 [port]*
Wang Zhanchang 1927- *WhoPRCh 91 [port]*
Wang Zhanxiang *WhoPRCh 91*
Wang Zhanyi 1930- *WhoPRCh 91 [port]*
Wang Zhao 1923- *WhoPRCh 91*
Wang Zhaoguo 1941- *IntWW 93, WhoPRCh 91 [port]*
Wang Zhaohua *WhoPRCh 91*
Wang Zhaojun fl. 1st cent.BC- *BlmGWL*
Wang Zhen d1993 *IntWW 93N*
Wang Zhen 1908- *WhoPRCh 91 [port]*
Wang Zhen 1908-1993 *NewYTBS 93*
Wang Zhengguang *WhoPRCh 91*
Wang Zhenjiang *WhoPRCh 91*
Wang Zhenjiang 1925- *WhoPRCh 91 [port]*
Wang Zhenxi *WhoPRCh 91 [port]*
Wang Zhenying *WhoPRCh 91*
Wang Zhijiang *WhoPRCh 91*
Wang Zhiren 1929- *WhoPRCh 91*
Wang Zhiwu *WhoPRCh 91*
Wang Zhixi *WhoPRCh 91*
Wang Zhong *WhoPRCh 91*
Wang Zhongfang 1921- *IntWW 93, WhoPRCh 91*
Wang Zhongfu 1942- *WhoPRCh 91*
Wang Zhonglu 1930- *WhoPRCh 91 [port]*
Wang Zhongqi *WhoPRCh 91*
Wang Zhongshu 1925- *ConAu 41NR, IntWW 93*
Wang Zhongyu 1933- *IntWW 93, WhoPRCh 91 [port]*
Wang Zhou 1930- *WhoPRCh 91*
Wang Zhuoru 1911- *WhoPRCh 91*
Wang Zigang *WhoPRCh 91*
Wang Zikun 1929- *IntWW 93*
Wang Ziwu 1936- *WhoPRCh 91 [port]*
Wang Ziye *WhoPRCh 91*
Wang Zongchun 1935- *WhoPRCh 91 [port]*
Wang Zongfa *WhoPRCh 91*
Wang Zuoliang *WhoPRCh 91*
Wang Zuwu 1929- *WhoPRCh 91 [port]*
Wang Zuxun *WhoPRCh 91*
Wan Haifeng 1920- *WhoPRCh 91 [port]*
Wan Haifeng, Gen. 1920- *IntWW 93*
Wani, Mansukhlal Chhaganlal 1925- *WhoAsA 94*
Wani, Silvanus 1916- *Who 94*
Waniek, Marilyn Nelson *DrAPF 93*
Wan Jiabao *ConWorW 93, IntDcT 2*
Wan Jianzhong 1917- *WhoPRCh 91 [port]*
Wank, Gerald Sidney 1925- *WhoAm 94*
Wank, Neil N. 1944- *WhoWest 94*
Wankat, Phillip Charles 1944- *WhoAm 94*
Wanke, Ronald Lee 1941- *WhoAm 94, WhoAmL 94*
Wankel, Felix *WorInv*
Wanlass, Stanley Glen 1941- *WhoAmA 93*
Wanless, Derek 1947- *IntWW 93, Who 94*
Wan Li 1916- *IntWW 93, WhoPRCh 91 [port]*
Wan Liangshi *WhoPRCh 91*
Wann, David L. *DrAPF 93*
Wann, Laymond Doyle 1924- *WhoScEn 94*
Wannamethee, Phan 1924- *Who 94*
Wannenmacher, Philip 1960- *WhoAmP 93*
Wanner, F. Walton 1914- *WhoAmP 93*
Wanner, Hughes *WhoHol 92*
Wanner, Irene *DrAPF 93*
Wanniski, Jude 1936- *WrDr 94*
Wannstedt, David Raymond 1952- *WhoAm 94, WhoMW 93*
Wan Runnan 1946- *WhoPRCh 91 [port]*
Wansel, Dexter Gilman 1950- *WhoBlA 94*
Wan Shaofen 1930- *IntWW 93, WhoPRCh 91 [port]*
Wan Shaofen 1931- *WhoWomW 91*
Wanstall, Charles Gray 1912- *Who 94*
Wanstreet, Diane Elaine 1954- *WhoMW 93*
Wan-Tatah, Victor Fon 1949- *WhoMW 93*
Wantland, William Charles 1934- *WhoAm 94, WhoMW 93*
Wanton, Eva C. 1935- *WhoBlA 94*
Wantuch, Peter S. 1952- *WhoFI 94*
Wan Yongxiang *WhoPRCh 91*
Wanzek, Terry *WhoAmP 93*
Wanzenried, David E. 1948- *WhoAmP 93*
Wanzer, Arthur d1949 *WhoHol 92*
Wanzer, Bobby 1925- *BasBi*
Wanzer, Mary Kathryn 1942- *WhoScEn 94*
Wapiennik, Carl Francis 1926- *WhoAm 94*
Waples, Eric Snowden 1944- *WhoWest 94*
Wapner, Seymour 1917- *WhoAm 94*
Wapnewski, Peter 1922- *IntWW 93*
Wappis, Elisabeth 1952- *WhoWomW 91*
Wapshott, Nicholas (Henry) 1952- *WrDr 94*

Wapshott, Nicholas Henry 1952- *Who 94*
Warady, Joel David 1956- *WhoFI 94, WhoMW 93*
Warakomski, Alphonse Walter Joseph, Jr. 1943- *WhoMW 93*
Waram, Percy d1961 *WhoHol 92*
Waran, David Anthony 1957- *WhoWest 94*
Waranch, Seeman *WhoIns 94*
Waranius-Vass, Rosalie Jean 1938- *WhoMW 93*
Warashina, M. Patricia *WhoAmA 93*
Warashina, M. Patricia 1940- *WhoAsA 94*
Warbeck, David *WhoHol 92*
Warbeck, Perkin 1474-1499 *BlmGEL*
Warble, Ralph Vernon 1934- *WhoMW 93*
Warburg, Eric Max 1900-1990 *WhAm 10*
Warburg, Otto Heinrich 1883-1970 *WorScD*
Warburg, Stephanie Wenner 1941- *WhoAmA 93*
Warburg, Wilma Shannon d1993 *NewYTBS 93*
Warburton, Alfred Arthur 1913- *Who 94*
Warburton, Anne (Marion) 1927- *Who 94*
Warburton, Anne Marion 1927- *IntWW 93*
Warburton, Charles d1952 *WhoHol 92*
Warburton, David 1942- *Who 94*
Warburton, Geoffrey Barratt 1924- *Who 94*
Warburton, Irvine d1982 *WhoHol 92*
Warburton, Ivor William 1946- *Who 94*
Warburton, Jacqueline Williams 1930- *WhoAmP 93*
Warburton, John d1981 *WhoHol 92*
Warburton, John Kenneth 1932- *Who 94*
Warburton, N. Calvin, Jr. 1910- *WhoAmP 93*
Warburton, Patrick *WhoHol 92*
Warburton, Peter Egerton 1813-1889 *WhWE*
Warburton, Ralph Joseph 1935- *WhoAm 94, WhoFI 94, WhoScEn 94*
Warburton, Richard John 1935- *WhoFI 94*
Warburton, Richard Maurice 1928- *Who 94*
Warch, George W. 1912- *WhoIns 94*
Warch, Richard 1939- *WhoAm 94, WhoMW 93*
Warchol, Mark Francis Andrew 1954- *WhoScEn 94*
Warcup, Edmund 1627-1712 *DcNaB MP*
Ward *Who 94*
Ward, Alan Gordon 1914- *Who 94*
Ward, Alan Hylton 1938- *Who 94*
Ward, Alan J 1937- *WrDr 94*
Ward, Alan S. 1931- *WhoAm 94*
Ward, Albert d1956 *WhoHol 92*
Ward, Albert A. 1929- *WhoBlA 94*
Ward, Albert Eugene 1940- *WhoWest 94*
Ward, Albert M. 1929- *WhoBlA 94*
Ward, Alex 1944- *WhoAm 94*
Ward, Aline Hollopeter 1898- *WhoAmP 93*
Ward, Amelita *WhoHol 92*
Ward, Anita Bolanos 1964- *WhoAmL 94*
Ward, Ann DeVoe 1930- *WhoWest 94*
Ward, Ann Sarita 1923- *Who 94*
Ward, Anna Elizabeth 1952- *WhoBlA 94*
Ward, Anthony John 1931- *WhoAmL 94*
Ward, Arnette S. 1937- *WhoBlA 94*
Ward, Artemus 1727-1800 *AmRev, WhAmRev*
Ward, Arthur (Hugh) 1906- *Who 94*
Ward, Arthur Frederick 1912- *Who 94*
Ward, Barbara M. 1946- *WhoMW 93*
Ward, Beatrice d1964 *WhoHol 92*
Ward, Benjamin 1926- *WhoBlA 94*
Ward, Bethea 1924- *WhoAm 94*
Ward, Bonnie Jean 1947- *WhoWest 94*
Ward, Brendan *WhoHol 92*
Ward, Burke Thomas 1947- *WhoFI 94*
Ward, Burt 1945- *IntMPA 94, WhoHol 92*
Ward, Calvin E. 1955- *WhoBlA 94*
Ward, Calvin Edouard 1925- *WhoBlA 94*
Ward, Carl Edward 1948- *WhoAm 94, WhoWest 94*
Ward, Carol Buhner 1947- *WhoMW 93*
Ward, Carole Geneva 1943- *WhoBlA 94*
Ward, Carrie Clark d1926 *WhoHol 92*
Ward, Cecil 1929- *Who 94*
Ward, Chance d1949 *WhoHol 92*
Ward, Charles d1986 *WhoHol 92*
Ward, Charles Daniel 1935- *WhoAmL 94*
Ward, Charles Leslie 1916- *Who 94*
Ward, Charles Raymond 1949- *WhoScEn 94*
Ward, Charles Richard 1940- *WhoAm 94*
Ward, Charlotte 1936- *WrDr 94*
Ward, Chester Lawrence 1932- *WhoAm 94*
Ward, Christopher *WrDr 94*
Ward, Christopher John 1942- *Who 94*
Ward, Christopher John Ferguson 1942- *Who 94*
Ward, Clara d1973 *WhoHol 92*
Ward, Conley, Jr. 1947- *WhoAmP 93*
Ward, Daniel 1934- *WhoBlA 94*
Ward, Daniel P. 1918- *WhoAmP 93*
Ward, Daniel Patrick 1918- *WhoAm 94, WhoMW 93*
Ward, Daniel Thomas 1942- *WhoAm 94*
Ward, David d1945 *WhoHol 92*
Ward, David 1922-1983 *NewGrDO*
Ward, David 1937- *Who 94*
Ward, David 1938- *WrDr 94*
Ward, David Allen 1933- *WhoAm 94*
Ward, David Conisbee 1933- *Who 94*
Ward, David S. 1947- *IntMPA 94*
Ward, David Schad 1947- *WhoAm 94*
Ward, David W. 1953- *WhoAmP 93*
Ward, Dean Morris 1925- *WhoMW 93*
Ward, Denitta Dawn 1963- *WhoAmL 94*
Ward, Dennis Joseph 1949- *WhoAm 94, WhoAmL 94*
Ward, Derek William 1956- *WhoScEn 94*
Ward, Diane *DrAPF 93*
Ward, Diane Korosy 1939- *WhoAmL 94, WhoFI 94, WhoWest 94*
Ward, Donald Albert 1920- *Who 94*
Ward, Donald Butler 1919- *WhoAm 94*
Ward, Doris Margaret 1932- *WhoBlA 94*
Ward, Douglas Turner *WhoHol 92*
Ward, Douglas Turner 1930- *ConDr 93, WhoBlA 94, WrDr 94*
Ward, Duane 1964- *WhoAm 94*
Ward, E.D. *EncSF 93*
Ward, Edith Miller 1911- *WhoMW 93*
Ward, Edmund Fisher *Who 94*
Ward, Edward 1667-1731 *BlmGEL*
Ward, Edwin James Greenfield 1919- *Who 94*
Ward, Elaine 1929- *WhoAmA 93*
Ward, Elizabeth Honor 1926- *WrDr 94*
Ward, Erica Anne 1950- *WhoAm 94, WhoAmL 94*
Ward, Evelyn Svec d1989 *WhoAmA 93N*
Ward, Everett Blair 1958- *WhoAmP 93, WhoBlA 94*
Ward, Fannie d1952 *WhoHol 92*
Ward, Felker *WhoBlA 94*
Ward, Fleming d1962 *WhoHol 92*
Ward, Frances Marie 1964- *WhoBlA 94*
Ward, Frank Dixon *Who 94*
Ward, Fred 1942- *WhoHol 92*
Ward, Fred 1943- *IntMPA 94, WhoAm 94*
Ward, Gary Lamell 1953- *WhoBlA 94*
Ward, Gene 1943- *WhoAmP 93*
Ward, Geoffrey C(hampion) 1940- *ConAu 141, WrDr 94*
Ward, Geoffrey Champion 1940- *WhoAm 94*
Ward, George Frank, Jr. 1945- *WhoAm 94*
Ward, George Truman 1927- *WhoFI 94*
Ward, Hap, Sr. d1944 *WhoHol 92*
Ward, Hap, Jr. d1940 *WhoHol 92*
Ward, Harriet 1808-c. 1860 *BlmGWL*
Ward, Harry Frederick 1873-1966 *DcAmReB 2*
Ward, Harry Merrill 1929- *WrDr 94*
Ward, Harry Pfeffer 1933- *WhoAm 94*
Ward, Haskell G. 1940- *WhoBlA 94*
Ward, Helene Statfeld 1938- *WhoAmP 93*
Ward, Henry 1913?- *EncSF 93*
Ward, Herbert D(ickinson) 1861-1932 *EncSF 93*
Ward, Hiley Henry 1929- *WhoAm 94*
Ward, Hiram Hamilton 1923- *WhoAm 94, WhoAmL 94*
Ward, Holcombe 1878-1967 *BuCMET*
Ward, Horace T. 1927- *WhoBlA 94*
Ward, Horace Taliaferro 1927- *WhoAm 94, WhoAmL 94*
Ward, Hubert 1931- *Who 94*
Ward, Humphry, Mrs. 1851-1920 *BlmGEL, BlmGWL*
Ward, Ian Macmillan 1928- *IntWW 93, Who 94*
Ward, Ivor William 1916- *Who 94*
Ward, J. Basil 1893- *WhAm 10*
Ward, Jack D. 1952- *WhoAmL 94*
Ward, James *WhoHol 92*
Ward, James Alto, III 1951- *WhoFI 94*
Ward, James Dale 1959- *WhoBlA 94*
Ward, James David 1935- *WhoWest 94*
Ward, James Frank 1938- *WhoMW 93*
Ward, James Hubert 1937- *WhoWest 94*
Ward, James Vernon 1940- *WhoScEn 94, WhoWest 94*
Ward, Jasper Dudley, III 1921- *WhoAm 94*
Ward, Jay 1955- *WhoAmP 93*
Ward, Jeffrey Blair, Sr. 1951- *WhoFI 94*
Ward, Jennifer C. 1944- *WhoAm 94, WhoAmP 93*
Ward, Jerome d1954 *WhoHol 92*
Ward, Jerry W. *DrAPF 93*
Ward, Jerry Washington, Jr. 1943- *WhoBlA 94*
Ward, Joan Gaye *WhoScEn 94*
Ward, Joe Henry, Jr. 1930- *WhoAmL 94*
Ward, John *Who 94, WhoAmP 93*
Ward, (Christopher) John (William) 1942- *Who 94*
Ward, John Aloysius *Who 94*
Ward, John Aloysius 1929- *IntWW 93*
Ward, John Carlton, Jr. 1893- *WhAm 10*
Ward, John Clive 1924- *Who 94*
Ward, John Devereux 1925- *Who 94*
Ward, John J. 1920- *WhoWest 94*
Ward, John Lawrence 1938- *WhoAmA 93*
Ward, John Mark 1951- *WhoFI 94*
Ward, John Milton 1917- *WhoAm 94*
Ward, John Orson 1942- *WhoAm 94, WhoFI 94*
Ward, John Robert 1923- *WhoAm 94, WhoWest 94*
Ward, John Stanton 1917- *IntWW 93, Who 94*
Ward, John Wesley 1925- *WhoAm 94, WhoScEn 94*
Ward, John William 1929- *WhoWest 94*
Ward, John X. 1926- *WhoAmP 93*
Ward, Jonas 1939- *WrDr 94*
Ward, Jonathan *WhoHol 92*
Ward, Joseph Haggitt 1926- *Who 94*
Ward, Joseph James Laffey 1946- *Who 94*
Ward, Joseph Marshall 1922- *WhoAmA 93*
Ward, Joseph Simeon 1925- *WhoAm 94*
Ward, Judy Kitchen 1940- *WhoFI 94*
Ward, Katheryn Hope 1941- *WhoMW 93*
Ward, Kathleen W. 1928- *WhoAmP 93*
Ward, Kathrin Clare d1938 *WhoHol 92*
Ward, Keith *Who 94*
Ward, (John Stephen) Keith 1938- *Who 94, WrDr 94*
Ward, Kelly *WhoHol 92*
Ward, Ken 1949- *WrDr 94*
Ward, Kenton Craig 1954- *WhoMW 93*
Ward, Kurt Christian 1959- *WhoFI 94*
Ward, Kyle 1902- *WhoMW 93*
Ward, Larry d1985 *WhoHol 92*
Ward, Laura Suzanne 1956- *WhoWest 94*
Ward, Lauriston 1883-1960 *WhoAmA 93N*
Ward, Lenwood E. *WhoBlA 94*
Ward, Leon d1927 *WhoHol 92*
Ward, Leslie Allyson 1946- *WhoAm 94*
Ward, Lester Lowe, Jr. 1930- *WhoAm 94, WhoAmL 94, WhoWest 94*
Ward, Lew O. 1930- *WhoAmP 93*
Ward, Lewis Edes 1925- *WhoWest 94*
Ward, Linda Gayle 1954- *WhoAmP 93*
Ward, Llewellyn Orcutt, III 1930- *WhoAm 94, WhoFI 94, WhoScEn 94*
Ward, Lorene Howelton 1927- *WhoBlA 94*
Ward, Louis Emmerson 1918- *WhoAm 94*
Ward, Louis Larrick 1919- *WhoAm 94*
Ward, Lowell Sanford 1949- *WhoWest 94*
Ward, Lucille d1952 *WhoHol 92*
Ward, Lyle Edward 1922- *WhoAmA 93*
Ward, Lyman *WhoHol 92*
Ward, Lynd (Kendall) 1905-1985 *WhoAmA 93N*
Ward, Mackenzie 1903- *WhoHol 92*
Ward, Malcolm Beverley 1931- *Who 94*
Ward, Malcolm Stanley 1951- *Who 94*
Ward, Marc A. 1957- *WhoMW 93*
Ward, Marcia Balmut 1946- *WhoMW 93*
Ward, Maria Frances 1949- *WhoFI 94, WhoMW 93*
Ward, Marie d1982 *WhoHol 92*
Ward, Marilyn Kay 1961- *WhoMW 93*
Ward, Marion Haggard 1924- *WhoAm 94*
Ward, Marvin 1914- *WhoAmP 93*
Ward, Marvin K. 1950- *WhoAmP 93*
Ward, Melvin Fitzgerald, Sr. 1918- *WhoBlA 94*
Ward, Michael 1915- *WhoHol 92*
Ward, (William) Michael 1957- *WhoAmA 93*
Ward, Michael D. 1951- *WhoAmP 93*
Ward, Michael Dunn 1954- *WhoMW 93*
Ward, Michael George 1951- *WhoWest 94*
Ward, Michael Jackson 1931- *Who 94*
Ward, Michael James 1959- *WhoMW 93*
Ward, Michael John 1931- *Who 94*
Ward, Michael Phelps 1925- *IntWW 93, Who 94*
Ward, Milton Hawkins 1932- *WhoAm 94, WhoFI 94, WhoScEn 94, WhoWest 94*
Ward, Myra d1990 *WhoHol 92*
Ward, Nicholas Donnell 1941- *WhoAmL 94, WhoFI 94*
Ward, Nolan F. 1945- *WhoBlA 94*
Ward, Norman 1918- *WhAm 10, WrDr 94*
Ward, Olivia Tucker *WhoHol 92*
Ward, P. Michael 1949- *WhoAmL 94*
Ward, Patricia Spain 1931- *WhoMW 93*
Ward, Patrick *WhoHol 92*
Ward, Paul Bruce 1937- *WhoAmL 94*
Ward, Paul Hutchins 1928- *WhoAm 94, WhoWest 94*
Ward, Paul Jerald 1949- *WhoAmL 94, WhoWest 94*
Ward, Paul William 1893- *WhAm 10*
Ward, Peggy d1960 *WhoHol 92*
Ward, Penelope Dudley d1982 *WhoHol 92*
Ward, Perry W. *WhoBlA 94*
Ward, (William) Peter 1943- *WrDr 94*
Ward, Peter Alexander 1930- *Who 94*
Ward, Peter Allan 1934- *WhoAm 94*
Ward, Philip 1938- *WrDr 94*
Ward, Philip (John Newling) 1924- *Who 94*
Ward, Philip J. 1949- *WhoAmL 94*
Ward, Phillip A. 1927- *WhoAmA 93N*
Ward, Polly 1908- *WhoHol 92*
Ward, Rachel 1957- *IntMPA 94*
Ward, Rachel 1958- *WhoHol 92*
Ward, Ralph Gerard 1933- *WrDr 94*
Ward, Reginald *Who 94*
Ward, (Albert Joseph) Reginald 1927- *Who 94*
Ward, Reginald George 1942- *Who 94*
Ward, Richard d1979 *WhoHol 92*
Ward, Richard C. 1937- *WhoAm 94*
Ward, Richard Compton 1941- *WhoMW 93*
Ward, Richard Eugene 1931- *WhoMW 93*
Ward, Richard Hurley 1939- *WhoMW 93*
Ward, Richard Jan 1947- *WhoAmP 93*
Ward, Richard Joseph 1921- *WhoAm 94*
Ward, Richard Paul 1942- *WhoAm 94, WhoAmL 94*
Ward, Richard S. 1940- *WhoAmL 94*
Ward, Richard Storer 1920- *WhoAm 94*
Ward, Richard Vance, Jr. 1929- *WhoAm 94*
Ward, Robert 1917- *WhoAm 94*
Ward, Robert (Eugene) 1917- *NewGrDO*
Ward, Robert Allen 1940- *WhoFI 94*
Ward, Robert Allen, Jr. 1937- *WhoFI 94*
Ward, Robert D. 1940- *WhoAmP 93*
Ward, Robert Edward 1916- *WhoAm 94, WhoWest 94*
Ward, Robert Joseph 1926- *WhoAm 94*
Ward, Robert Lee 1948- *WhoScEn 94*
Ward, Robert M. 1943- *WhoAmL 94*
Ward, Robert M. 1952- *WhoAmP 93*
Ward, Robert R. *DrAPF 93*
Ward, Robert William 1935- *Who 94*
Ward, Robertson, Jr. 1922- *WhoAm 94*
Ward, Robin *WhoHol 92*
Ward, Robin William 1931- *Who 94*
Ward, Rodman, Jr. 1934- *WhoAm 94*
Ward, Roger Coursen 1922- *WhoAm 94*
Ward, Roger Wilson 1944- *WhoWest 94*
Ward, Ronald d1978 *WhoHol 92*
Ward, Ronald R. 1947- *WhoBlA 94*
Ward, Roscoe d1956 *WhoHol 92*
Ward, Roscoe Fredrick 1930- *WhoAm 94*
Ward, Roy Livingstone 1925- *Who 94*
Ward, Russel (Braddock) 1914- *WrDr 94*
Ward, Sam d1952 *WhoHol 92*
Ward, Samuel 1725-1776 *WhAmRev*
Ward, Samuel, Jr. 1756-1832 *WhAmRev*
Ward, Sandra L. 1963- *WhoBlA 94*
Ward, Sandy *WhoHol 92*
Ward, Sela *WhoHol 92*
Ward, Sharon Lynne 1942- *WhoMW 93*
Ward, Shelby Dean 1938- *WhoAmP 93*
Ward, Sherman Carl, III 1958- *WhoMW 93*
Ward, Simon 1941- *IntMPA 94, IntWW 93, WhoHol 92*
Ward, Simon B. *Who 94*
Ward, Solly d1942 *WhoHol 92*
Ward, Sophie 1965- *WhoHol 92*
Ward, Stephen Beecher 1955- *WhoWest 94*
Ward, Stephen William 1955- *WhoAmL 94*
Ward, Suzanne Mary 1956- *WhoMW 93*
Ward, Sylvan Donald 1909- *WhoAm 94*
Ward, T. John 1943- *WhoAmL 94*
Ward, Taylor Dudley 1956- *WhoAmL 94*
Ward, Thomas Jerome 1936- *WhoAm 94*
Ward, Thomas Joseph 1950- *WhoFI 94*
Ward, Thomas Leon 1930- *WhoAm 94*
Ward, Thomas Monroe 1952- *WhoAmL 94*
Ward, Thomas Morgan 1935- *WhoAmP 93*
Ward, Thomas William 1918- *Who 94*
Ward, Todd Pope 1938- *WhoMW 93*
Ward, Tony *WhoHol 92*
Ward, Trevor *WhoHol 92*
Ward, Vernon Graves 1928- *WhoMW 93*
Ward, Victoria d1957 *WhoHol 92*
Ward, Vincent 1956- *IntMPA 94, IntWW 93*
Ward, Viola d1978 *WhoHol 92*
Ward, Virginia Lee 1944- *WhoMW 93*
Ward, Wallace Dixon 1924- *WhoAm 94*
Ward, Wally *WhoHol 92*
Ward, Walter 1911- *WhoAmP 93*
Ward, Walter Chalmers 1930- *WhoAmL 94*
Ward, Walter L., Jr. *WhoAmP 93*
Ward, Walter L., Jr. 1943- *WhoBlA 94*
Ward, Wanda Elaine 1954- *WhoScEn 94*
Ward, Warwick d1967 *WhoHol 92*
Ward, William Alan H. *Who 94*
Ward, William Alec 1928- *Who 94*
Ward, William Binnington 1917- *WhoAm 94*

Ward, William E. *WhoAm 94, WhoAmP 93*
Ward, William Edward 1922- *WhoAmA 93, WhoMW 93*
Ward, William Ernest Frank 1900- *Who 94*
Ward, William Francis 1951- *WhoAmL 94*
Ward, William Francis, Jr. 1928- *WhoAm 94*
Ward, William Kenneth 1918- *Who 94*
Ward, William L. 1936- *WhoIns 94*
Ward, William Reed 1918- *WhoAm 94*
Ward, William Wade 1953- *WhoScEn 94*
Ward, Yvette Hennig 1910- *WhoAm 94*
Ward, Zana Rogers 1915- *WhoBlA 94*
Wardale, Geoffrey (Charles) 1919- *Who 94*
Ward-Booth, John Antony 1927- *Who 94*
Ward-Brooks, Joyce Renee 1952- *WhoBlA 94*
Warde, Anthony d1975 *WhoHol 92*
Warde, Ernest C. d1923 *WhoHol 92*
Warde, Frances 1810-1884 *DcAmReB 2*
Warde, Frederick d1935 *WhoHol 92*
Warde, Harlan d1980 *WhoHol 92*
Warde, John Robins 1920- *Who 94*
Warde, Willie d1943 *WhoHol 92*
Wardeberg, George E. 1935- *IntWW 93*
Wardell, Charles Willard Bennett, III 1945- *WhoAm 94, WhoFI 94*
Wardell, Gareth Lodwig 1944- *Who 94*
Wardell, Jay Howard 1943- *WhoMW 93*
Wardell, Joe Russell, Jr. 1929- *WhoAm 94*
Wardell, Paula Louise 1952- *WhoMW 93*
Wardell, Phyl(lis Robinson) 1909- *WrDr 94*
Wardell, William Wilkinson 1823-1899 *DcNaB MP*
Warden, Gail Lee 1938- *WhoAm 94*
Warden, Gary George 1951- *WhoScEn 94*
Warden, Gary Russell 1950- *WhoFI 94*
Warden, George W. 1944- *WhoBlA 94*
Warden, Glenn Donald 1943- *WhoScEn 94*
Warden, Herbert Edgar 1920- *WhoAm 94*
Warden, Jack 1920- *IntMPA 94, WhoAm 94, WhoHol 92*
Warden, John L. 1941- *WhoAm 94, WhoAmL 94*
Warden, John Peter 1942- *WhoWest 94*
Warden, Lawrence A. *WhoAmP 93*
Warden, Lewis Christopher 1913- *WrDr 94*
Warden, Margaret Smith 1917- *WhoAmP 93*
Warden, May d1978 *WhoHol 92*
Warden, Philip S. 1943- *WhoAmL 94*
Warden, Richard Dana 1931- *WhoAm 94*
Warden, Rob 1940- *ConAu 142*
Warden, Robert Martin 1953- *WhoWest 94*
Warder, Ann Head c. 1758-1829 *BlmGWL*
Warder, John Morgan 1927- *WhoBlA 94*
Warder, Richard Currey, Jr. 1936- *WhoAm 94*
Warder, William 1920- *WhoAmA 93*
Ward-Hagen, Stacey Lea 1959- *WhoWest 94*
Wardhana, Ali 1928- *IntWW 93*
Wardhaugh, Ronald 1932- *WrDr 94*
Ward Howe, Julia 1819-1910 *WomPubS*
Wardington, Baron 1924- *Who 94*
Ward-Jackson, (Audrey) Muriel 1914- *Who 94*
Ward-Jones, Norman Arthur 1922- *Who 94*
Wardlaw, Alvia Jean 1947- *WhoBlA 94*
Wardlaw, Alvin Holmes 1925- *WhoBlA 94*
Wardlaw, Donna Eileen 1950- *WhoAmL 94*
Wardlaw, Frank Harper, Jr. 1913-1989 *WhAm 10*
Wardlaw, George Melvin 1927- *WhoAmA 93*
Wardlaw, Henry (John) 1930- *Who 94*
Wardlaw, Jack 1907- *WhoIns 94*
Wardlaw, McKinley, Jr. 1927- *WhoBlA 94*
Wardle, Charles Frederick 1939- *Who 94*
Wardle, David 1930- *WrDr 94*
Wardle, (John) Irving 1929- *Who 94, WrDr 94*
Wardle, Thomas (Edward Jewell) 1912- *Who 94*
Wardlow, Floyd H., Jr. 1921- *WhoAmP 93*
Wardman, Gordon 1948- *WrDr 94*
Ward-McLemore, Ethel 1908- *WhoScEn 94*
Wardner, Rich *WhoAmP 93*
Wardroper, John Edmund 1923- *WrDr 94*
Wardropper, Bruce Wear 1919- *WhoAm 94*
Wardropper, Ian Bruce 1951- *WhoAm 94*
Wardrup, Leo C., Jr. 1936- *WhoAmP 93*
Ward-Shaw, Sheila Theresa 1951- *WhoWest 94*
Ward-Steinman, David 1936- *WhoAm 94, WhoWest 94*
Ward-Thomas, Evelyn *Who 94*
Ward Thomas, Gwyn Edward 1923- *Who 94*
Wardwell, Allen 1935- *WhoAm 94, WhoAmA 93*
Wardwell, Geoffrey d1955 *WhoHol 92*
Wardwell, James Charles 1952- *WhoScEn 94*
Wardwell, Nathaniel Philips 1943- *WhoAmL 94*
Wardyga, Alan Stephen 1955- *WhoFI 94*
Ware, Andre T. 1968- *WhoBlA 94*
Ware, Anna *Who 94*
Ware, Barbara Ann 1955- *WhoBlA 94*
Ware, Benjamin Ray 1946- *WhoScEn 94*
Ware, Brendan John 1932- *WhoAm 94*
Ware, Carl 1943- *WhoBlA 94, WhoFI 94*
Ware, Charles Jerome 1948- *WhoBlA 94*
Ware, Clyde 1934- *WhoWest 94*
Ware, Cyril George 1922- *Who 94*
Ware, D. Clifton 1937- *WhoAm 94*
Ware, Deano Carlos 1968- *WhoMW 93*
Ware, Derek *WhoHol 92*
Ware, Donald R. 1949- *WhoAmL 94*
Ware, Dyahanne 1958- *WhoBlA 94*
Ware, Edwin Oswald, III 1927- *WhoAmP 93*
Ware, Eliot B. 1908- *WhoAmP 93*
Ware, George Henry 1924- *WhoMW 93*
Ware, Gilbert 1933- *WhoBlA 94*
Ware, Helen d1939 *WhoHol 92*
Ware, Henry Neill, Jr. 1954- *WhoAmL 94*
Ware, Herta *WhoHol 92*
Ware, Irene Johnson 1935- *WhoBlA 94*
Ware, J. Lowell 1928-1991 *WhoBlA 94N*
Ware, James Edman 1937- *WhoWest 94*
Ware, James Edwin 1925- *WhoAm 94*
Ware, James T. 1926- *WhoFI 94*
Ware, James W. 1946- *WhoAm 94, WhoAmL 94, WhoWest 94*
Ware, Jane (O.) 1936- *WrDr 94*
Ware, Jean 1914- *WrDr 94*
Ware, Jennifer Peyton 1955- *WhoAm 94*
Ware, John David 1947- *WhoFI 94*
Ware, John H., III 1908- *WhoAmP 93*
Ware, John Thomas, III 1931- *WhoAmL 94*
Ware, Juanita Glee 1923- *WhoBlA 94*
Ware, Kallistos (Timothy Richard) 1934- *WrDr 94*
Ware, Lawrence Leslie, Jr. 1920- *WhoScEn 94*
Ware, Linda 1923- *WhoHol 92*
Ware, Marcus John 1904- *WhoAm 94*
Ware, Martin 1915- *Who 94*
Ware, Michael John 1932- *Who 94*
Ware, Midge *WhoHol 92*
Ware, Mitchell 1933- *WhoAm 94*
Ware, Omego John Clinton, Jr. 1928- *WhoBlA 94*
Ware, Patricia J. *DrAPF 93*
Ware, Paul F., Jr. 1944- *WhoAmL 94*
Ware, R. David 1954- *WhoBlA 94*
Ware, Richard Anderson 1919- *WhoAm 94*
Ware, Robert 1958- *WhoFI 94*
Ware, Thaddeus Van 1935- *WhoAm 94*
Ware, Wallace 1922- *WrDr 94*
Ware, Walter d1936 *WhoHol 92*
Ware, William L. 1934- *WhoBlA 94*
Ware, Willis Howard 1920- *WhoAm 94, WhoWest 94*
Warehall, William Donald 1942- *WhoAm 94, WhoAmA 93, WhoWest 94*
Wareham, Alton L. 1920- *WhoBlA 94*
Wareham, Franklin Dee 1933- *WhoFI 94*
Wareham, James Lyman 1939- *WhoAm 94, WhoFI 94*
Wareham, Levada E. 1921- *WhoAmP 93*
Wareham, Raymond Noble 1948- *WhoAm 94, WhoFI 94*
Wareham, Ronald James 1944- *WhoFI 94*
Wareing, Lesley 1913- *WhoHol 92*
Wareing, Philip Frank 1914- *Who 94*
Wareing, Robert Nelson 1930- *Who 94*
Wareing, Thomas Hightower 1953- *WhoMW 93*
Waren, Allan David 1935- *WhoMW 93*
Waren, Jack L. 1936- *WhoFI 94*
Waren, Stanley A. 1919- *WhoAm 94*
Warf, J. H. 1904- *WhoAmP 93*
Warfel, Christopher George 1958- *WhoScEn 94*
Warfel, John Hiatt 1916- *WhoScEn 94*
Warfield, Benjamin Breckinridge 1851-1921 *DcAmReB 2*
Warfield, Chris *WhoHol 92*
Warfield, (A.) Gallatin 1946- *ConAu 140*
Warfield, Gerald Alexander 1940- *WhoAm 94*
Warfield, Guy W. 1955- *WhoAmL 94*
Warfield, Irene d1961 *WhoHol 92*
Warfield, Janet Ellen 1944- *WhoMW 93*
Warfield, John Nelson 1925- *WhoAm 94*
Warfield, Marcia 1955- *WhoCom*
Warfield, Marjorie d1991 *WhoHol 92*
Warfield, Marlene *WhoHol 92*
Warfield, Marsha 1955- *WhoBlA 94, WhoHol 92*
Warfield, Paul *ProFbHF [port]*
Warfield, Paul D. 1942- *WhoBlA 94*
Warfield, Robert N. 1948- *WhoBlA 94*
Warfield, Sandra 1929- *NewGrDO*
Warfield, Ted Robert 1942- *WhoMW 93*
Warfield, William 1920- *NewGrDO, WhoHol 92*
Warfield, William C. 1920- *AfrAmAl 6 [port], WhoBlA 94*
Warfield, William Caesar 1920- *WhoAm 94*
Warfield-Coppock, Nsenga Patricia 1949- *WhoBlA 94*
Warford, Malcolm Lyle 1942- *WhoAm 94*
Warford, Stuart Leighton 1950- *WhoAm 94*
Warga, Jack 1922- *WhoAm 94*
Wargo, Tom 1943- *WhoAm 94*
Warhaftig, Solomon L. 1938- *WhoAm 94*
Warham, John 1919- *WrDr 94*
Warhol, Andy d1987 *WhoHol 92*
Warhol, Andy 1928-1987 *AmCulL [port], Au&Arts 12 [port], ModArCr 4 [port]*
Warhol, Robyn R. 1955- *WrDr 94*
Warhover, Stephen Hunt 1944- *WhoFI 94*
Warhurst, Alan 1927- *Who 94*
Warhurst, William R. 1955- *WhoAmL 94*
Warhus, Mark Ellerton 1951- *WhoMW 93*
Warin, F. Joseph 1950- *WhoAmL 94*
Warin, Roger E. 1945- *WhoAm 94, WhoAmL 94*
Waring, Derek 1930- *WhoHol 92*
Waring, Eloise Botts 1920- *WhoAmP 93*
Waring, Fred d1984 *WhoHol 92*
Waring, Herbert d1932 *WhoHol 92*
Waring, (Alfred) Holburt 1933- *Who 94*
Waring, John Alfred 1913- *WhoScEn 94*
Waring, Laura Wheeler d1949 *WhoAmA 93N*
Waring, Laura Wheeler 1887-1948 *AfrAmAl 6*
Waring, Mary d1964 *WhoHol 92*
Waring, Richard *DrAPF 93*
Waring, Richard d1993 *NewYTBS 93*
Waring, Richard 1911- *WhoHol 92*
Waring, Todd *WhoHol 92*
Waring, Virginia 1915- *WhoFI 94*
Waring, Walter Weyler 1917- *WhoAm 94*
Waring, William Winburn 1923- *WhoAm 94*
Warioba, Joseph Sinde 1940- *IntWW 93*
Waris, Klaus 1914- *IntWW 93*
Waris, Michael, Jr. 1921- *WhoAm 94, WhoAmL 94*
Waris, Richard Marion 1954- *WhoAmL 94*
Wark, John Charles 1959- *WhoWest 94*
Wark, Robert Rodger 1924- *WhoAm 94, WhoAmA 93*
Wark, Steve *WhoAmP 93*
Wark, Thomas Edison 1934- *WhoAm 94*
Warkany, Josef 1902-1992 *WhAm 10*
Warke, Robert Alexander *Who 94*
Warkenthien, Gene E. *WhoAmP 93*
Warkomski, Theodore Robert 1924- *WhoAmP 93*
Warkov, Esther 1941- *WhoAmA 93*
Warland, Allen *EncSF 93*
Warland, Betsy 1946- *BlmGWL*
Warlick, Robert Patterson 1924- *WhoAm 94*
Warlick, Roger Kinney 1930- *WhoAm 94*
Warlitner, Todd Jeffrey 1962- *WhoFI 94*
Warlock, Billy *WhoHol 92*
Warltire, John 1738?-1810 *DcNaB MP*
Warlum, Michael Frank *DrAPF 93*
Warm, Hermann 1889-1976 *IntDcF 2-4*
Warmack, Kevin Lavon 1956- *WhoBlA 94, WhoFI 94*
Warman, Daniel Reid 1947- *WhoAmL 94*
Warman, Oliver Byrne 1932- *Who 94*
Warman, Raymond E. 1948- *WhoAmL 94*
Warmbold, Theodore Fredrick, II 1943-1990 *WhAm 10*
Warmbrod, Catharine Phelps 1929- *WhoMW 93*
Warmbrod, James Robert 1929- *WhoAm 94*
Warmenhoven, Daniel John 1950- *WhoAm 94*
Warmer, Richard Craig 1936- *WhoAm 94, WhoAmL 94*
Warmington, Marshall George Clitheroe 1910- *Who 94*
Warmington, S. J. d1941 *WhoHol 92*
Warmington, William Allan 1922- *WrDr 94*
Warmly, Leon 1941- *WhoBlA 94*
Warmond, Ellen 1930- *BlmGWL*
Warn, Emily *DrAPF 93*
Warnas, Joseph John 1933- *WhoWest 94*
Warnath, Maxine Ammer 1928- *WhoWest 94*
Warne, Antony M. *Who 94*
Warne, (Ernest) John (David) 1926- *Who 94*
Warne, Ronson Joseph 1930- *WhoScEn 94*
Warne, William Elmo 1905- *WhoAm 94, WhoFI 94, WhoScEn 94, WhoWest 94*
Warnecke, Gordon *WhoHol 92*
Warnecke, Michael O. 1941- *WhoAm 94, WhoAmL 94*
Warneke, Heinz 1895-1983 *WhoAmA 93N*
Warneke, Michael Steven 1959- *WhoFI 94*
Warnemunde, Bradley Lee 1933- *WhoAm 94*
Warner, Alan (John) 1912- *WrDr 94*
Warner, Alex *WhoAmP 93*
Warner, Anna Bartlett 1827-1915 *BlmGWL*
Warner, Anne Elizabeth 1940- *Who 94*
Warner, Astrid *WhoHol 92*
Warner, Barbara Ann 1941- *WhoAmP 93*
Warner, Barry Gregory 1955- *WhoAm 94, WhoScEn 94*
Warner, Bennie D. 1935- *IntWW 93*
Warner, Bradford Arnold 1910- *WhoAm 94*
Warner, Brian 1939- *IntWW 93*
Warner, Cecil d1924 *WhoHol 92*
Warner, Cecil Randolph, Jr. 1929- *WhoAm 94*
Warner, Charles Collins 1942- *WhoAm 94, WhoAmL 94*
Warner, Clarence E. 1938- *WhoAmP 93*
Warner, Colin Bertram 1935- *WhoAm 94*
Warner, Curt 1961- *WhoBlA 94*
Warner, Dale J. 1929- *WhoAmP 93*
Warner, Daniel 1946- *ConAu 141*
Warner, Darrell G. *WhoAm 94, WhoFI 94*
Warner, David 1941- *IntMPA 94, IntWW 93, WhoHol 92*
Warner, David Ross, Jr. 1943- *WhoAm 94*
Warner, Deborah 1959- *ConTFT 11, IntWW 93, Who 94*
Warner, Denis Ashton 1917- *IntWW 93*
Warner, Dennis Allan 1940- *WhoAm 94*
Warner, Don Lee 1934- *WhoAm 94*
Warner, Dorothy Marie 1922- *WhoAmP 93*
Warner, Douglas Alexander, III 1946- *WhoAm 94, WhoFI 94*
Warner, Douglas Warfield 1930- *WhoAmA 93*
Warner, E. John 1942- *WhoFI 94*
Warner, E. Parry 1945- *WhoAmL 94*
Warner, Edward (Redston) 1911- *Who 94*
Warner, Edward L. 1939- *WhoBlA 94*
Warner, Edward Waide, Jr. 1951- *WhoAm 94*
Warner, Everett Longley 1877-1963 *WhoAmA 93N*
Warner, Francis 1937- *WrDr 94*
Warner, Francis (Robert Le Plastrier) 1937- *Who 94*
Warner, Frank Shrake 1940- *WhoAmL 94, WhoWest 94*
Warner, Fred Archibald 1918- *IntWW 93*
Warner, Frederick (Edward) 1910- *Who 94*
Warner, Frederick Archibald 1918- *Who 94*
Warner, Frederick Edward 1910- *IntWW 93*
Warner, George Blackburn, Jr. 1951- *WhoAmP 93*
Warner, Gerald Chierici 1931- *Who 94*
Warner, Graeme Christopher 1948- *Who 94*
Warner, H. B. d1958 *WhoHol 92*
Warner, Harold Clay, Jr. 1939- *WhoAm 94*
Warner, Harry (Backer), Jr. 1922- *EncSF 93*
Warner, Harry Hathaway 1935- *WhoAm 94*
Warner, Henry *Who 94*
Warner, (Edward Courtenay) Henry 1951- *Who 94*
Warner, Herbert Kelii, Jr. 1943- *WhoAmA 93*
Warner, Irving *DrAPF 93*
Warner, Isaiah H. 1916- *WhoBlA 94*
Warner, Ivan 1919- *WhoBlA 94*
Warner, J(ohn) F. 1929- *ConAu 142, SmATA 75*
Warner, Jack d1929 *WhoHol 92*
Warner, Jack d1981 *WhoHol 92*
Warner, Jack, Jr. 1916- *IntMPA 94, WhoAm 94*
Warner, Jack L. d1978 *WhoHol 92*
Warner, Jack L. 1892-1978 *IntDcF 2-4 [port]*
Warner, James B. d1924 *WhoHol 92*
Warner, James John 1942- *WhoMW 93*
Warner, Janet Claire 1964- *WhoScEn 94*
Warner, Jean-Pierre Frank Eugene 1924- *Who 94*
Warner, Jerome 1927- *WhoAmP 93*

Warrender *Who 94*
Warrender, Harold d1953 *WhoHol 92*
Warrender, Robin Hugh 1927- *Who 94*
Warren Evans, (John) Roger 1935- *Who 94*
Warren-Lazenberry, Lillian Frances 1928- *WhoAmP 93*
Warren-Smith, Neil 1930-1981 *NewGrDO*
Warrenton, Lule d1932 *WhoHol 92*
Warrick, Alan Everett 1953- *WhoBlA 94*
Warrick, Bryan Anthony 1959- *WhoBlA 94*
Warrick, James Craig 1938- *WhoAm 94*
Warrick, Mary Lelane 1940- *WhoWest 94*
Warrick, Mildred Lorine 1917- *WhoWest 94*
Warrick, Pamela Dianne 1958- *WhoMW 93*
Warrick, Patricia S(cott) 1925- *EncSF 93*
Warrick, Ruth 1915- *WhoHol 92*
Warrick, Ruth 1916- *IntMPA 94*
Warrick-Crisman, Jeri Everett *WhoBlA 94*
Warrilow, David *WhoHol 92*
Warriner, Frederic Freeman 1916-1992 *WhAm 10*
Warriner, Joseph B. 1934- *WhoIns 94*
Warriner, Laura B. 1943- *WhoAmA 93*
Warrington, Archdeacon of *Who 94*
Warrington, Bishop Suffragan of 1928- *Who 94*
Warrington, Ann d1934 *WhoHol 92*
Warrington, Clayton Linwood, Jr. 1936- *WhoAm 94*
Warrington, Elizabeth Kerr *IntWW 93, Who 94*
Warrington, George d1968 *WhoHol 92*
Warrington, John Wesley 1914- *WhoAm 94*
Warrington, John Wesley, Jr. 1957- *WhoMW 93*
Warrington, Robert O'Neil, Jr. 1945- *WhoScEn 94*
Warrington, Willard Glade 1920- *WhoAm 94*
Warrington-Betts, Leah 1932- *WhoWomW 91*
Warsawer, Harold Newton *WhoAm 94*
Warschausky, Judith Sue 1957- *WhoMW 93*
Warschaw, Carmen H. 1917- *WhoAmP 93*
Warsh, Jeff 1960- *WhoAmP 93*
Warsh, Lewis *DrAPF 93*
Warsh, Lewis 1944- *WrDr 94*
Warshafsky, Ted M. 1926- *WhoAmL 94*
Warshauer, Irene Conrad 1942- *WhoAm 94*
Warshauer, Jacques 1915- *WhoWest 94*
Warshavsky, Suzanne May 1944- *WhoAmL 94*
Warshaw, Allen Charles 1948- *WhoAm 94, WhoAmL 94*
Warshaw, Andrew Louis 1939- *WhoAm 94*
Warshaw, Elaine N. 1924- *WhoAmA 93*
Warshaw, Howard 1920- *WhoAmA 93N*
Warshaw, Joseph Bennett 1936- *WhoAm 94*
Warshaw, Larry 1936- *WhoAmA 93*
Warshaw, Leon J. 1917- *WhoAm 94*
Warshaw, Martin Richard 1924- *WhoAm 94*
Warshaw, Michael Thomas 1950- *WhoAmL 94*
Warshaw, Stanley Irving 1931- *WhoAm 94*
Warshaw, Stephen Isaac 1939- *WhoScEn 94*
Warshaw-Freedman, Sandra 1943- *WhoWomW 91*
Warshawski, Morrie *DrAPF 93*
Warshawsky, Abel George 1884-1962 *WhoAmA 93N*
Warshawsky, Arnold Stephen 1946- *WhoWest 94*
Warshawsky, Isidore 1911- *WhoMW 93*
Warshawsky, Ruth *WhoHol 92*
Warshofsky, David *WhoHol 92*
Warsinske, Norman George 1929- *WhoAmA 93*
Warson, Toby Gene 1937- *WhoFI 94*
Warsop, John Charles 1927- *Who 94*
Wartel, Pierre Francois 1806-1882 *NewGrDO*
Wartels, Nat 1902-1990 *WhAm 10*
Warter, Carlos 1947- *WhoWest 94*
Warters, D(ennis) N(oel) 1896- *WhAm 10*
Warters, William d1953 *WhoHol 92*
Warth, James Arthur 1942- *WhoScEn 94*
Warth, Robert Douglas 1921- *WhoAm 94*
Warthen, Harry Justice, III 1939- *WhoAm 94, WhoAmL 94*
Warthen, John Edward 1922- *WhoFI 94*
Warther, Richard Owen 1954- *WhoFI 94*
Warthin, Thomas Angell 1909- *WhoAm 94*
Wartick, Ronald D. 1942- *WhoIns 94*
Wartman, Carl Henry 1952- *WhoAmL 94*
Wartnaby, John 1926- *Who 94*

Wartner, Paul Dennis 1939- *WhoAmP 93*
Wartofsky, (William) Victor 1931- *WrDr 94*
Warton, Joseph 1722-1800 *BlmGEL*
Warton, Thomas 1728-1790 *BlmGEL*
Wartski, Maureen (Ann) Crane 1940- *TwCYAW*
Waruk, Kona *BlkWr 2*
Warwick *Who 94*
Warwick, Archdeacon of *Who 94*
Warwick, Bishop Suffragan of 1937- *Who 94*
Warwick, Earl of 1934- *Who 94*
Warwick, Diana 1945- *Who 94*
Warwick, Dionne 1940- *WhoBlA 94*
Warwick, Dionne 1941- *IntWW 93, WhoAm 94*
Warwick, Ethel d1951 *WhoHol 92*
Warwick, Hannah Cambell Grant *Who 94*
Warwick, John d1972 *WhoHol 92*
Warwick, Richard 1945- *WhoHol 92*
Warwick, Robert d1964 *WhoHol 92*
Warwick, Robert Franklin 1936- *WhoAmP 93*
Warwick, Roger 1912- *WrDr 94*
Warwick, Thomas J. 1932- *WhoAmP 93*
Warwick, Warren J. 1928- *WhoScEn 94*
Warwick, William Eldon 1912- *Who 94*
Warwicke, Dionne 1941- *WhoHol 92*
Wasan, Darsh T. 1938- *WhoAsA 94*
Wasan, Darsh Tilakchand 1938- *WhoAm 94*
Wasbauer, Marius Sheridan 1928- *WhoWest 94*
Wasbrough, Matthew 1753-1781 *DcNaB MP*
Wasch, Allan Denzel 1962- *WhoScEn 94*
Wascher, Aribert d1961 *WhoHol 92*
Waschon, Pierre *NewGrDO*
Wasden, Jed W. 1919- *WhoAmP 93*
Wasden, Wiley Anderson, III 1959- *WhoAmL 94*
Wasden, Winifred Sawaya 1938- *WhoWest 94*
Wasem, Penny Lou 1964- *WhoFI 94*
Waser, Maria 1878-1939 *BlmGWL*
Waser, Peter Gaudenz 1918- *IntWW 93*
Wasey, Jane 1912- *WhoAmA 93N*
Wasfi, Sadiq Hassan 1936- *WhoAm 94*
Wasfie, Tarik Jawad 1946- *WhoMW 93, WhoScEn 94*
Wash, Glenn Edward 1931- *WhoBlA 94*
Wash, Martha 1954- *WhoBlA 94*
Washak, Ronald Victor 1948- *WhoMW 93*
Washbourne, Mona d1988 *WhoHol 92*
Washbrook, John(ny) 1944- *WhoHol 92*
Washburn, Alice d1929 *WhoHol 92*
Washburn, Anne Burton 1950- *WhoAmL 94*
Washburn, Arthur Lawrence, Jr. 1935- *WhoAmL 94*
Washburn, Barbara *WhoScEn 94*
Washburn, Beverly *WhoHol 92*
Washburn, Bryant d1963 *WhoHol 92*
Washburn, Bryant, Jr. d1960 *WhoHol 92*
Washburn, Cadwallader 1866-1965 *WhoAmA 93N*
Washburn, Cephas 1793-1860 *EncNAR*
Washburn, David Thacher 1930- *WhoAm 94*
Washburn, Deric *IntMPA 94*
Washburn, Donald Arthur 1944- *WhoAm 94, WhoFI 94*
Washburn, Frank Murray 1926- *WhoWest 94*
Washburn, Gordon Bailey 1904- *WhoAmA 93N*
Washburn, H. Bradford, Jr. 1910- *WhoScEn 94*
Washburn, Harriet Louise 1946- *WhoMW 93*
Washburn, Henry Bradford, Jr. 1910- *WhoAm 94*
Washburn, Jack 1927- *WhoHol 92*
Washburn, Jerry Martin 1943- *WhoFI 94*
Washburn, Joan T. 1929- *WhoAmA 93*
Washburn, John H. d1917 *WhoHol 92*
Washburn, John James 1956- *WhoAmL 94*
Washburn, John Rosser 1943- *WhoFI 94*
Washburn, L(ivia) J(ane) 1957- *WrDr 94*
Washburn, Lawrence Robert 1941- *WhoWest 94*
Washburn, Louese B. 1875-1959 *WhoAmA 93N*
Washburn, Paul 1911-1989 *WhAm 10*
Washburn, Peter Lloyd 1943- *WhoWest 94*
Washburn, Richard R. *WhoHol 92*
Washburn, Robert Brooks 1928- *WhoAm 94*
Washburn, Robert Charles 1944- *WhoFI 94*
Washburn, Robert Charles 1944- *WhoFI 94*
Washburn, Stan 1943- *WhoAm 94, WhoAmA 93*
Washburn, Stewart Alexander 1923- *WhoFI 94*

Washburn, Thomas Dale 1947- *WhoFI 94*
Washburn, Watty 1894-1973 *BuCMET*
Washburn, Wilcomb Edward 1925- *WhoAm 94*
Washbush, Thomas Charles 1957- *WhoMW 93*
Washington, Mrs. fl. 1890- *EncNAR*
Washington, Allen Reed *WhoScEn 94*
Washington, Arna D. 1927- *WhoBlA 94*
Washington, Arthur, Jr. 1922- *WhoBlA 94*
Washington, Arthur Clover 1939- *WhoBlA 94*
Washington, Ava F. 1949- *WhoBlA 94*
Washington, Ben James, Jr. 1946- *WhoBlA 94*
Washington, Bennetta B. 1918- *WhoBlA 94*
Washington, Bennetta Bullock 1918-1991 *WhAm 10*
Washington, Betty Lois 1948- *WhoBlA 94*
Washington, Blue d1970 *WhoHol 92*
Washington, Booker T. 1856-1915 *HisWorL [port]*
Washington, Booker Taliaferro 1856-1915 *AfrAmAl 6 [port], AmSocL [port], DcAmReB 2*
Washington, Bushrod 1762-1829 *WhAmRev*
Washington, C. Clifford *WhoBlA 94*
Washington, Carl Douglas 1943- *WhoBlA 94*
Washington, Charles Edward 1933- *WhoWest 94*
Washington, Charles Joseph 1938- *WhoWest 94*
Washington, Claudell 1954- *WhoBlA 94*
Washington, Consuela M. 1948- *WhoBlA 94*
Washington, Craig A. 1941- *CngDr 93, WhoAm 94, WhoBlA 94*
Washington, Craig Anthony 1941- *WhoAmP 93*
Washington, Dante Deneen 1970- *WhoBlA 94*
Washington, Darryl McKenzie 1948- *WhoBlA 94*
Washington, David Earl 1962- *WhoScEn 94*
Washington, David Warren 1949- *WhoBlA 94*
Washington, Denzel 1954- *AfrAmAl 6 [port], IntMPA 94, IntWW 93, WhoAm 94, WhoBlA 94, WhoHol 92*
Washington, Dinah d1963 *WhoHol 92*
Washington, Dinah 1924-1963 *AfrAmAl 6*
Washington, Dino *WhoHol 92*
Washington, Earl Melvin 1939- *WhoBlA 94*
Washington, Earl S. *WhoBlA 94*
Washington, Earl Stanley 1944- *WhoWest 94*
Washington, Earlene 1951- *WhoBlA 94*
Washington, Edith May Faulkner 1933- *WhoBlA 94*
Washington, Edward 1936- *WhoBlA 94*
Washington, Edward, Jr. 1931- *WhoBlA 94*
Washington, Eli H. 1962- *WhoBlA 94*
Washington, Elmer L. 1935- *WhoBlA 94*
Washington, Emery, Sr. 1935- *WhoBlA 94*
Washington, Eric T. 1953- *WhoAmP 93*
Washington, Floyd, Jr. 1943- *WhoBlA 94, WhoMW 93*
Washington, Ford Lee d1955 *WhoHol 92*
Washington, Fredi 1903- *WhoHol 92*
Washington, George 1732-1799 *AmRev, BlmGEL, HisWorL [port], WhAmRev [port]*
Washington, Gladys J. 1931- *WhoBlA 94*
Washington, Grover, Jr. 1943- *WhoAm 94, WhoBlA 94*
Washington, Harold 1922-1987 *AfrAmAl 6 [port], ConBlB 6 [port]*
Washington, Henry L. 1922- *WhoBlA 94*
Washington, Herman A., Jr. 1935- *WhoBlA 94*
Washington, Isaiah Edward 1908- *WhoBlA 94*
Washington, Jacquelin Edwards 1931- *WhoBlA 94*
Washington, Jacquelyn M. 1965- *WhoBlA 94*
Washington, James A. 1950- *WhoBlA 94*
Washington, James A., Jr. 1915- *WhoAmP 93*
Washington, James Edward 1927- *WhoBlA 94*
Washington, James Lee 1948- *WhoBlA 94*
Washington, James Melvin 1948- *WhoBlA 94*
Washington, James W., Jr. *WhoAmA 93, WhoBlA 94*
Washington, James Winston, Jr. 1909- *WhoAm 94, WhoWest 94*
Washington, Jerry 1940- *WhoAmP 93*
Washington, Jesse d1919 *WhoHol 92*
Washington, Joe c. 1875- *EncNAR*

Washington, Joe Dan 1953- *WhoBlA 94*
Washington, John Calvin, III 1950- *WhoBlA 94*
Washington, John Michael George 1948- *WhoFI 94*
Washington, John William 1921- *WhoBlA 94*
Washington, Johnnie M. 1936- *WhoBlA 94*
Washington, Joseph R., Jr. 1930- *WhoBlA 94, WrDr 94*
Washington, Josie B. 1943- *WhoBlA 94*
Washington, Keith *WhoBlA 94*
Washington, Kenneth S. 1922- *WhoBlA 94*
Washington, Kenny d1971 *WhoHol 92*
Washington, Kermit 1951- *WhoBlA 94*
Washington, Leroy 1925- *WhoBlA 94*
Washington, Lester Renez 1954- *WhoBlA 94*
Washington, Linda Phaire 1948- *WhoBlA 94*
Washington, Lionel 1960- *WhoBlA 94*
Washington, Luisa 1946- *WhoBlA 94*
Washington, MaliVai *WhoBlA 94*
Washington, MaliVai 1969- *WhoAm 94*
Washington, Marian *WhoBlA 94*
Washington, Martha Custis 1732-1802 *WhAmRev [port]*
Washington, Martha Dandridge Custis 1731-1802 *AmRev*
Washington, Mary Helen 1941- *BlkWr 2, WhoBlA 94*
Washington, Mary Parks *WhoBlA 94*
Washington, McKinley, Jr. 1936- *WhoAmP 93*
Washington, Michael Harlan 1950- *WhoBlA 94*
Washington, Nancy Ann 1938- *WhoBlA 94*
Washington, Napoleon, Jr. 1948- *WhoFI 94, WhoWest 94*
Washington, Nat Willis 1914- *WhoAmP 93*
Washington, Nereida C. 1965- *WhoHisp 94*
Washington, Oscar D. 1912- *WhoBlA 94*
Washington, Paul M. 1921- *WhoBlA 94*
Washington, Reginald Louis 1949- *WhoAm 94, WhoScEn 94, WhoWest 94*
Washington, Robert Benjamin, Jr. 1942- *WhoAmP 93, WhoBlA 94*
Washington, Robert E. *WhoAmP 93*
Washington, Robert E. 1936- *WhoBlA 94*
Washington, Robert Orlanda 1935- *WhoAm 94, WhoBlA 94*
Washington, Ronald 1952- *WhoBlA 94*
Washington, Roosevelt, Jr. 1932- *WhoBlA 94*
Washington, Rudy 1951- *WhoBlA 94*
Washington, Samuel T. 1901- *WhoBlA 94*
Washington, Sandra Beatrice 1946- *WhoBlA 94*
Washington, Sarah M. 1942- *WhoBlA 94*
Washington, Shelley Lynne 1954- *WhoAm 94*
Washington, Sherry Ann 1956- *WhoBlA 94*
Washington, Shirley *WhoHol 92*
Washington, Thomas 1937- *WhoBlA 94*
Washington, U. L. 1953- *WhoBlA 94*
Washington, Valdemar Luther 1952- *WhoBlA 94*
Washington, Valora 1953- *WhoAm 94*
Washington, Vernon d1988 *WhoHol 92*
Washington, Von Hugo, Sr. 1943- *WhoBlA 94*
Washington, Walter 1923- *WhoAm 94, WhoBlA 94*
Washington, Walter E. 1915- *IntWW 93, WhoBlA 94*
Washington, Warren Morton 1936- *WhoAm 94, WhoBlA 94*
Washington, William *WhoBlA 94*
Washington, William 1752-1810 *WhAmRev [port]*
Washington, William 1853-1936 *EncNAR*
Washington, William Augustine 1752-1810 *AmRev*
Washington, William Montell 1939- *WhoBlA 94*
Washington, Wilma J. 1949- *WhoMW 93*
Washington-Walls, Shirley 1962- *WhoBlA 94*
Washlow, Robert Jacob 1944- *WhoAmL 94*
Washow, Paula Burnette 1948- *WhoFI 94*
Wasick, Mary Ann 1946- *WhoMW 93*
Wasicsko, Nicolas C. 1959- *WhoAmP 93*
Wasiele, Harry W., Jr. 1926- *WhoAm 94*
Wasik, John Francis 1957- *WhoAm 94*
Wasilewska, Ewa 1958- *WhoWest 94*
Wasilewski, Vincent Thomas 1922- *WhoAm 94*
Wasiluk, Scott Allen 1958- *WhoMW 93*
Wasim Akram 1966- *IntWW 93*
Wasinger, David 1963- *WhoAmL 94*
Wasinger, Kristi Lynn 1967- *WhoMW 93*

Wasinger, Thomas Michael 1951- *WhoAmP 93*
Wasiolek, Edward 1924- *WhoAm 94, WhoMW 93, WrDr 94*
Wasiteck *EncNAR*
Waska, Ronald Jerome 1942- *WhoAmL 94*
Waskel, Shirley Ann 1935- *WhoMW 93*
Waskell, Lucy Ann 1942- *WhoWest 94*
Wasko, Stephen Gerard 1959- *WhoFI 94*
Wasko-Flood, Sandra Jean 1943- *WhoAmA 93*
Waskow, Arthur Ocean 1933- *WhoAm 94*
Waskowski, Ted 1950- *WhoAmL 94*
Wasmund, Suzanne 1936- *WhoMW 93*
Wasmuth, Carl Erwin 1916- *WhoAm 94*
Wason, Sandys c. 1870- *EncSF 93*
Wasowski, Andrzej 1924-1993 *NewYTBS 93*
Waspi, Kevin Glenn 1954- *WhoFI 94*
Wass, Douglas (William Gretton) 1923- *Who 94*
Wass, Douglas William Gretton 1923- *IntWW 93*
Wass, Hannelore Lina 1926- *WhoAm 94*
Wass, Paul 1925- *WhoAmP 93*
Wass, Ted *WhoHol 92*
Wass, Wallace Milton 1929- *WhoAm 94*
Wassell, Loren W. 1948- *WhoMW 93*
Wassell, Stephen Robert 1963- *WhoScEn 94*
Wassem, Rebecca *WhoHol 92*
Wassenaar, Carolyn Mae 1951- *WhoMW 93*
Wassenberg, Shirley Mae 1927- *WhoAmP 93*
Wasser, Henry 1919- *WhoAm 94*
Wasser, Joseph 1920- *WhoAmP 93*
Wasser, M. Elizabeth 1952- *WhoMW 93*
Wasserburg, Gerald Joseph 1927- *IntWW 93, WhoAm 94, WhoScEn 94, WhoWest 94*
Wasserlein, John Henry 1941- *WhoAm 94, WhoFI 94*
Wasserman, Abby Lois 1945- *WhoMW 93*
Wasserman, Albert 1920- *WhoAmA 93*
Wasserman, Albert 1921- *WhoAm 94*
Wasserman, Arnold Saul 1934- *WhoAm 94*
Wasserman, Barry Lee 1935- *WhoAm 94*
Wasserman, Bert W. *WhoAm 94, WhoFI 94*
Wasserman, Bruce Arlen 1954- *WhoWest 94*
Wasserman, Burton 1929- *WhoAmA 93*
Wasserman, Cary (Robert) 1939- *WhoAmA 93*
Wasserman, Dale 1917- *IntMPA 94, WhoAm 94, WrDr 94*
Wasserman, Diana 1947- *WhoHisp 94*
Wasserman, Edel 1932- *WhoAm 94*
Wasserman, Edward Arnold 1946- *WhoAm 94*
Wasserman, Edward M. 1928- *WhoMW 93*
Wasserman, Eric 1944- *WhoMW 93*
Wasserman, Fumiko Hachiya 1947- *WhoAsA 94*
Wasserman, Gerald Steward 1937- *WhoScEn 94*
Wasserman, Gordon Joshua 1938- *Who 94*
Wasserman, Harry Hershal 1920- *WhoScEn 94*
Wasserman, Irving N. 1921- *WhoWest 94*
Wasserman, Jack 1921- *WhoAmA 93*
Wasserman, James Donald 1952- *WhoWest 94*
Wasserman, Jeffrey 1946- *WhoAmA 93*
Wasserman, Julia B. *WhoAmP 93*
Wasserman, Karen Boling 1944- *WhoScEn 94*
Wasserman, Lew 1913- *IntMPA 94*
Wasserman, Lew R. 1913- *IntWW 93, WhoAm 94, WhoFI 94, WhoWest 94*
Wasserman, Louis Robert 1910- *WhoAm 94*
Wasserman, Mark Daniel 1964- *WhoWest 94*
Wasserman, Martin Allan 1941- *WhoAm 94*
Wasserman, Muriel 1935- *WhoAmA 93*
Wasserman, Paul 1924- *WhoAm 94, WrDr 94*
Wasserman, Richard Leo 1948- *WhoAm 94, WhoAmL 94*
Wasserman, Robert Harold 1926- *IntWW 93, WhoAm 94, WhoScEn 94*
Wasserman, Robert Zachary 1947- *WhoWest 94*
Wasserman, Rosanne *DrAPF 93*
Wasserman, Stanley 1951- *WhoMW 93, WhoScEn 94*
Wasserman, Stephen Ira 1942- *WhoAm 94*
Wasserman, William Phillip 1945- *WhoAm 94, WhoAmL 94*
Wasserstein, Abraham 1921- *Who 94*
Wasserstein, Bernard Mano Julius 1948- *WhoAm 94*
Wasserstein, Bruce 1947- *IntWW 93, WhoAm 94*
Wasserstein, Jeffrey Alan 1958- *WhoFI 94*
Wasserstein, Wendy *WrDr 94*
Wasserstein, Wendy 1950- *BlmGWL, ConDr 93, DramC 4 [port], IntWW 93, WhoAm 94*
Wasshausen, Dieter Carl 1938- *WhoAm 94*
Wassil, Aly *WhoHol 92*
Wassink, Darwin 1934- *WhoFI 94*
Wassmer, Robert William 1961- *WhoFI 94, WhoMW 93*
Wassmo, Herbjorg 1942- *BlmGWL*
Wassner, Steven Joel 1946- *WhoAm 94*
Wasson, Alexander Verner 1896- *WhAm 10*
Wasson, Barbara Hickam 1918- *WhoMW 93*
Wasson, Christina 1964- *WhoMW 93*
Wasson, Craig 1954- *IntMPA 94, WhoHol 92*
Wasson, Douglas 1927- *WhoWest 94*
Wasson, James Walter 1951- *WhoWest 94*
Wasson, Richard Lee 1932- *WhoMW 93*
Wasson, Richard O. *WhoAmP 93*
Wassung, Eric Todd 1963- *WhoMW 93*
Wastberg, Per (Erik) 1933- *ConWorW 93*
Wastell, Cyril Gordon 1916- *Who 94*
Wastell, John fl. 1485-c. 1515 *DcNaB MP*
Wastie, Winston Victor 1900- *Who 94*
Wasylik, Kenneth Edward 1957- *WhoMW 93*
Wasylkowski, Steve Eugene 1941- *WhoMW 93*
Wasylyk, Peter N. 1957- *WhoAmP 93*
Wat, James Kam-Choi 1949- *WhoWest 94*
Watai, Madge S. 1927- *WhoAsA 94*
Watanabe, August Masaru 1941- *WhoAm 94*
Watanabe, Bunzo 1907- *IntWW 93*
Watanabe, Clyde Kazuto 1953- *WhoAsA 94*
Watanabe, Corinne Kaoru Amemiya 1950- *WhoWest 94*
Watanabe, Eric Katsuji 1951- *WhoFI 94, WhoWest 94*
Watanabe, Fumio *WhoHol 92*
Watanabe, Gedde *IntMPA 94*
Watanabe, Gedde 1955- *WhoHol 92*
Watanabe, Hideo *IntWW 93*
Watanabe, Hiroshi 1951- *WhoWest 94*
Watanabe, Hirosuko *WhoFI 94*
Watanabe, Jeffrey Noboru 1943- *WhoWest 94*
Watanabe, John Mamoru 1952- *WhoAsA 94*
Watanabe, Kouichi 1942- *WhoAm 94, WhoFI 94, WhoScEn 94*
Watanabe, Kozo *IntWW 93*
Watanabe, Kyoichi Aloysius 1935- *WhoScEn 94*
Watanabe, Larry Geo 1950- *WhoWest 94*
Watanabe, Mamoru 1933- *WhoAm 94*
Watanabe, Mark David 1955- *WhoMW 93*
Watanabe, Mark Hisashi 1953- *WhoAsA 94*
Watanabe, Michio 1923- *IntWW 93*
Watanabe, Mike 1946- *WhoAsA 94*
Watanabe, Misako *WhoHol 92*
Watanabe, Neil T. 1954- *WhoFI 94*
Watanabe, Osamu Richard 1960- *WhoAmL 94*
Watanabe, Paul Yashihiko 1951- *WhoAsA 94*
Watanabe, Richard Megumi 1962- *WhoScEn 94, WhoWest 94*
Watanabe, Robert 1926?-1992 *WhoAsA 94N*
Watanabe, Roy Noboru 1947- *WhoAmL 94*
Watanabe, Ruth Taiko 1916- *WhoAm 94*
Watanabe, Suwako 1959- *WhoAsA 94*
Watanabe, Takeji 1913- *IntWW 93*
Watanabe, Toshiharu 1924- *WhoScEn 94*
Watanabe, Walter Yukiaki 1924- *WhoWest 94*
Watanabe, Yoko 1953- *NewGrDO*
Watanabe, Yoshihito 1953- *WhoScEn 94*
Watanabe, Youji 1923- *IntWW 93*
Watanabe, Yuki 1952- *WhoAsA 94*
Watanakunakorn, Chatrchai 1935- *WhoMW 93*
Watanuki, Tamisuke 1927- *IntWW 93*
Watari, Sugiichiro 1925- *IntWW 93*
Wataru, Weston Yasuo 1957- *WhoFI 94*
Watchetaker, George Smith d1993 *NewYTBS 93*
Watchman, Leo C. *WhoAmP 93*
Watchorn, C. L. F. 1945- *WhoIns 94*
Watchorn, William Ernest 1943- *WhoAm 94*
Watel, Meg M. 1960- *WhoFI 94*
Water, Silas *EncSF 93*
Waterborg, Jakob Harm 1948- *WhoScEn 94*
Waterbury, Jackson DeWitt 1937- *WhoFI 94, WhoMW 93*
Waterbury, Ruth d1982 *WhoHol 92*
Waterer, Louis Phillipp 1939- *WhoWest 94*
Waterfield, Bob d1983 *ProFbHF*
Waterfield, Giles Adrian 1949- *Who 94*
Waterfield, Harry Lee, II 1943- *WhoIns 94*
Waterfield, John Percival 1921- *Who 94*
Waterfield, Michael Derek 1941- *Who 94*
Waterfield, Richard A. 1939- *WhoAmP 93*
Waterford, Earl of 1791-1852 *DcNaB MP*
Waterford, Marquess of 1933- *Who 94*
Waterhouse, Charles Howard 1924- *WhoAmA 93*
Waterhouse, David Martin 1937- *Who 94*
Waterhouse, Douglas Frew 1916- *IntWW 93, Who 94*
Waterhouse, Frederick Harry 1932- *Who 94*
Waterhouse, John William 1957- *WhoFI 94*
Waterhouse, Keith 1929- *IntMPA 94*
Waterhouse, Keith (Spencer) 1929- *ConDr 93, WrDr 94*
Waterhouse, Keith Spencer 1929- *IntWW 93, Who 94*
Waterhouse, Olga 1917- *WhoAmP 93*
Waterhouse, Rachel (Elizabeth) 1923- *Who 94*
Waterhouse, Ronald (Gough) 1926- *Who 94*
Waterhouse, Russell Rutledge 1928- *WhoAmA 93*
Waterhouse, Stephen Lee 1943- *WhoFI 94*
Waterloo, Claudia 1952- *WhoAm 94*
Waterloo, Stanley 1846-1913 *EncSF 93*
Waterlow, Anthony John 1938- *Who 94*
Waterlow, Christopher Rupert 1959- *Who 94*
Waterlow, (James) Gerard 1939- *Who 94*
Waterlow, John Conrad 1916- *IntWW 93, Who 94*
Waterman, Andrew (John) 1940- *WrDr 94*
Waterman, Cary *DrAPF 93*
Waterman, Cecily A. 1949- *WhoAmL 94*
Waterman, Charles K. *DrAPF 93*
Waterman, Daniel 1927- *WhoAm 94, WhoScEn 94*
Waterman, David F. 1949- *WhoAmL 94*
Waterman, Denis 1948- *WhoHol 92*
Waterman, Donald Calvin 1928-1979 *WhoAmA 93N*
Waterman, Emma Caroline 1931- *WhoWest 94*
Waterman, Fanny 1920- *Who 94*
Waterman, Homer D. 1915- *WhoBlA 94*
Waterman, Ida d1941 *WhoHol 92*
Waterman, Lewis E. *WorInv*
Waterman, Lori 1914- *WhoWest 94*
Waterman, Merton C. *WhoAmP 93*
Waterman, Michael Spencer 1942- *WhoAm 94*
Waterman, Mignon Redfield 1944- *WhoAmP 93, WhoFI 94*
Waterman, Peter Lewis 1955- *WhoMW 93*
Waterman, Robert A. 1954- *WhoAmL 94*
Waterman, Thelma M. 1937- *WhoBlA 94*
Waterman, Thomas Chadbourne 1937- *WhoAm 94*
Waterman, Willard 1914- *WhoHol 92*
Waterman, William, Jr. 1937- *WhoAmL 94*
Waterpark, Baron 1926- *Who 94*
Waters, Aaron Clement 1905-1991 *WhAm 10*
Waters, Andre 1962- *WhoBlA 94*
Waters, Betty Lou 1943- *WhoAm 94*
Waters, Brenda Joyce 1950- *WhoBlA 94*
Waters, Bunny *WhoHol 92*
Waters, Catherine C. *ConAu 141*
Waters, Charles H., Jr. 1941- *WhoAmL 94*
Waters, Chocolate *DrAPF 93*
Waters, Crystal *WhoBlA 94*
Waters, Daniel 1731-1816 *WhAmRev*
Waters, David H. 1951- *WhoAmL 94*
Waters, David Rogers 1932- *WhoAm 94*
Waters, David Watkin 1911- *Who 94, WrDr 94*
Waters, Dean A. 1936- *WhoScEn 94*
Waters, Donald Eugene 1941- *WhoMW 93*
Waters, Donald Henry 1937- *Who 94, WhoFI 94*
Waters, Donald Joseph 1952- *WhoAm 94*
Waters, Donovan W. 1928- *WhoAm 94*
Waters, Doris d1978 *WhoHol 92*
Waters, Edward Neighbor 1906-1991 *WhAm 10*
Waters, Elizabeth Hannah d1993 *NewYTBS 93*
Waters, Ellen Maureen 1938- *WhoMW 93*
Waters, Elsie d1990 *WhoHol 92*
Waters, Ethel d1977 *WhoHol 92*
Waters, Ethel 1895-1977 *ConMus 11 [port]*
Waters, Ethel 1900-1977 *AfrAmAl 6*
Waters, Frank *DrAPF 93*
Waters, Frank, Mrs. *Who 94*
Waters, Frank (Joseph) 1902- *WrDr 94*
Waters, Garth Rodney 1944- *Who 94*
Waters, George d1923 *EncNAR*
Waters, George Bausch 1920- *WhoAm 94*
Waters, George Fite 1894-1961 *WhoAmA 93N*
Waters, George Gary 1928- *WhoWest 94*
Waters, Gwendolyn 1954- *WhoMW 93*
Waters, H. Franklin 1932- *WhoAm 94, WhoAmL 94*
Waters, Harry N. 1936- *WhoAmP 93*
Waters, Henrietta E. 1927- *WhoBlA 94*
Waters, Herbert (Ogden) 1903- *WhoAmA 93*
Waters, J. Kevin 1933- *WhoWest 94*
Waters, Jack 1954- *WhoAmA 93*
Waters, James d1985 *WhoHol 92*
Waters, James Larry 1953- *WhoAmP 93*
Waters, James Lipscomb 1930- *WhoAm 94*
Waters, James Logan 1925- *WhoAm 94*
Waters, Jan 1937- *WhoHol 92*
Waters, Jennifer Nash 1951- *WhoAm 94, WhoAmL 94*
Waters, Jerry B. 1933- *WhoAmP 93*
Waters, John *Who 94, WhoHol 92*
Waters, John 1946- *IntMPA 94, WhoAm 94, WrDr 94*
Waters, (Charles) John 1935- *Who 94*
Waters, John B. 1929- *WhoAm 94, WhoAmL 94, WhoFI 94*
Waters, John F(rederick) 1930- *WrDr 94*
Waters, John W. 1936- *WhoBlA 94*
Waters, Joseph Michael d1993 *NewYTBS 93*
Waters, Kathleen Frances 1940- *WhoWest 94*
Waters, Laughlin Edward 1914- *WhoAmL 94, WhoWest 94*
Waters, Linda Julene 1941- *WhoWest 94*
Waters, M. Bruce 1950- *WhoWest 94*
Waters, Martin Vincent 1917- *WhoBlA 94*
Waters, Maxine *WhoAmP 93, WhoBlA 94, WhoWomW 91*
Waters, Maxine 1938- *AfrAmAl 6 [port], CngDr 93, WhoAm 94, WhoWest 94*
Waters, Michael *DrAPF 93*
Waters, Michael Cooper 1942- *WhoAm 94*
Waters, Michael Robert 1955- *WhoFI 94*
Waters, Mira *WhoHol 92*
Waters, Montague 1917- *Who 94*
Waters, Muddy d1983 *WhoHol 92*
Waters, Muddy 1915-1983 *AfrAmAl 6*
Waters, Neville R., III 1957- *WhoBlA 94*
Waters, Norman S. 1925- *WhoAmP 93*
Waters, Paul Eugene, Jr. 1959- *WhoBlA 94*
Waters, Richard 1926- *WhoAm 94*
Waters, Robert Allen 1955- *WhoAmP 93*
Waters, Robert George 1948- *WhoScEn 94*
Waters, Roger 1947- *WhoAm 94*
Waters, Rollie Odell 1942- *WhoFI 94*
Waters, Russell 1908- *WhoHol 92*
Waters, Stephen Russell 1954- *WhoAmP 93, WhoMW 93*
Waters, Steven A. 1949- *WhoAmL 94*
Waters, Sylvia *WhoAm 94*
Waters, Sylvia Ann 1949- *WhoBlA 94*
Waters, T(homas) A. 1938- *EncSF 93*
Waters, Tara *DrAPF 93*
Waters, Thomas Alfred 1940- *WhoAmP 93*
Waters, Timothy J. 1943- *WhoAm 94, WhoAmL 94*
Waters, Tony 1958- *ConAu 142, SmATA 75 [port]*
Waters, Wayne Arthur 1929- *WhoMW 93*
Waters, Will Estel 1931- *WhoScEn 94*
Waters, William David 1924- *WhoBlA 94*
Waters, William Ernest 1928- *WhoFI 94*
Waters, William Francis 1932- *WhoFI 94*
Waters, William Frederick 1943- *WhoScEn 94*
Waters, William L. 1941- *WhoBlA 94*
Waters, Willie Anthony 1951- *WhoAm 94*
Waters, Wimbley, Jr. 1943- *WhoBlA 94*
Waterson, James *WhoHol 92*
Waterson, Nigel Christopher 1950- *Who 94*
Waterston, Charles Dewar 1925- *Who 94*
Waterston, Harry Clement 1909- *WhoAmA 93*
Waterston, John James 1811-1883 *DcNaB MP*
Waterston, Sam 1940- *IntMPA 94, WhoHol 92*
Waterston, Samuel Atkinson 1940- *WhoAm 94*
Waterston, William King 1937- *WhoAm 94*

Waterstone, David George Stuart 1935- *Who 94*
Waterstone, Timothy John Stewart 1939- *IntWW 93*
Waterstone, Timothy John Stuart 1939- *Who 94*
Waterstreet, Ken 1940- *WhoAmA 93*
Waterton, Eric 1943- *WhoAm 94*
Waterton, William Arthur 1916- *Who 94*
Waterworth, Alan William 1931- *Who 94*
Wates, Christopher (Stephen) 1939- *Who 94*
Wates, Michael Edward 1935- *Who 94*
Watford, Charles Lamar *WhoAmP 93*
Watford, Glen Alan 1957- *WhoWest 94*
Watford, Gwen 1927- *WhoHol 92*
Watford, Jeanette Patterson 1928- *WhoAmP 93*
Watford, Tyrone Michael 1949- *WhoMW 93*
Wathall, Bettie Geraldine *WhoAmA 93*
Wathelet, Melchior 1949- *IntWW 93*
Wathen, Daniel E. 1939- *WhoAmP 93*
Wathen, Daniel Everett 1939- *WhoAm 94, WhoAmL 94*
Wathen, Julian Philip Gerard 1923- *Who 94*
Wathen, Richard 1917- *WrDr 94*
Wathen, Richard B. 1917- *WhoAmP 93*
Wathen, Richard W. d1993 *NewYTBS 93*
Wathne, Carl Norman 1930- *WhoAm 94*
Watia, Tarmo 1938- *WhoAmA 93, WhoWest 94*
Watiker, Albert David, Jr. 1938- *WhoBlA 94*
Watkin, (Christopher) Aelred (Paul) 1918- *Who 94*
Watkin, David 1925- *IntDcF 2-4, IntMPA 94, WhoAm 94*
Watkin, David John 1941- *Who 94*
Watkin, Pierre d1960 *WhoHol 92*
Watkin, Virginia Guild 1925- *WhoAm 94*
Watkins, Alan (Rhun) 1933- *Who 94, WrDr 94*
Watkins, Alan Keith 1938- *IntWW 93, Who 94*
Watkins, Ann Esther 1949- *WhoWest 94*
Watkins, Aretha La Anna 1930- *WhoBlA 94*
Watkins, Benjamin Wilston 1922- *WhoBlA 94*
Watkins, Birge Swift 1949- *WhoAm 94*
Watkins, Brian 1933- *IntWW 93, Who 94*
Watkins, Carlene 1952- *WhoHol 92*
Watkins, Carlton Gunter 1919- *WhoAm 94*
Watkins, Carolyn A. 1934- *WhoMW 93*
Watkins, Charles B., Jr. 1942- *WhoBlA 94*
Watkins, Charles Booker, Sr. 1913- *WhoBlA 94*
Watkins, Charles Booker, Jr. 1942- *WhoAm 94, WhoScEn 94*
Watkins, Charles Eugene, Jr. 1930- *WhAm 10*
Watkins, Charles Morgan 1954- *WhoAmL 94*
Watkins, Charles Reynolds 1951- *WhoFI 94, WhoScEn 94, WhoWest 94*
Watkins, Cheryl Denise 1963- *WhoAm 94*
Watkins, Christopher Andrew 1958- *WhoAmL 94*
Watkins, Dane *WhoAmP 93*
Watkins, David 1941- *WhoAm 94*
Watkins, David John 1925- *Who 94*
Watkins, Dean Allen 1922- *WhoAm 94*
Watkins, Edwin Arthur d1881 *EncNAR*
Watkins, Eileen Frances 1950- *WhoAmA 93*
Watkins, Evan Paul 1946- *WhoWest 94*
Watkins, Felix Scott 1946- *WhoFI 94*
Watkins, Floyd C 1920- *WrDr 94*
Watkins, Franklin Chenault 1894-1972 *WhoAmA 93N*
Watkins, Frederick D. 1915- *WhoIns 94*
Watkins, G. Gail 1951- *WhoAm 94*
Watkins, Gary *WhoHol 92*
Watkins, Gary L. 1946- *WhoAmP 93*
Watkins, George Daniels 1924- *WhoAm 94*
Watkins, George M. 1935- *WhoScEn 94*
Watkins, Gerrold 1939- *WrDr 94*
Watkins, Gino 1907-1932 *WhWE*
Watkins, Gloria 1955?- *BlkWr 2*
Watkins, Gloria Elizabeth 1950- *WhoBlA 94*
Watkins, Gordon Derek 1929- *Who 94*
Watkins, Gordon R. *DrAPF 93*
Watkins, Grath 1922- *IntMPA 94*
Watkins, Guy Hansard 1933- *Who 94*
Watkins, Hannah Bowman 1924- *WhoBlA 94*
Watkins, Harold D., Sr. 1933- *WhoBlA 94*
Watkins, Harold Robert 1928- *WhoMW 93*
Watkins, Hays Thomas 1926- *WhoAm 94, WhoFI 94*
Watkins, Izear Carl 1926- *WhoBlA 94*
Watkins, James D. 1927- *WhoAmP 93*
Watkins, James Darnell 1949- *WhoBlA 94*
Watkins, James David 1927- *IntWW 93, WhoScEn 94*
Watkins, James Louis *WhoHol 92*
Watkins, Jane *DrAPF 93*
Watkins, Jay B. 1948- *WhoBlA 94*
Watkins, Jeffrey Clifton 1929- *Who 94*
Watkins, Jerry D. 1939- *WhoBlA 94*
Watkins, Jerry West 1931- *WhoAm 94, WhoFI 94*
Watkins, Jim 1944- *WhoHol 92*
Watkins, John Chester Anderson 1912- *WhoAm 94*
Watkins, John Chewning 1947- *WhoAmP 93*
Watkins, John Cumming, Jr. 1935- *WhoAm 94*
Watkins, John Francis 1925- *WhoAm 94*
Watkins, John Goodrich 1913- *WhoAm 94, WhoWest 94, WrDr 94*
Watkins, John M., Jr. 1942- *WhoBlA 94*
Watkins, John Marcella, Jr. 1942- *AfrAmG [port]*
Watkins, John W., Jr. 1938- *WhoIns 94*
Watkins, Joseph Philip 1953- *WhoBlA 94*
Watkins, Juanita *WhoAmP 93*
Watkins, Juanita 1939- *WhoBlA 94*
Watkins, Juanita E. *WhoAmP 93*
Watkins, Judith Ann 1942- *WhoWest 94*
Watkins, Kay Orville 1932- *WhoWest 94*
Watkins, Lenice J. 1933- *WhoBlA 94*
Watkins, Levi 1911- *WhoBlA 94*
Watkins, Levi, Jr. 1944- *WhoBlA 94*
Watkins, Lewis 1945- *WhoAmA 93*
Watkins, Linda d1976 *WhoHol 92*
Watkins, Lloyd Irion 1928- *WhoAm 94*
Watkins, Lottie Heywood *WhoAmP 93, WhoBlA 94*
Watkins, Lou Rogers 1942- *WhoAmP 93*
Watkins, Mary Frances 1925- *WhoBlA 94*
Watkins, Michael James 1945- *WhoMW 93*
Watkins, Michael Thomas 1954- *WhoBlA 94*
Watkins, Mose 1940- *WhoBlA 94*
Watkins, Mozelle Ellis 1924- *WhoBlA 94*
Watkins, Paul 1964- *WrDr 94*
Watkins, Peter *WhoHol 92*
Watkins, Peter 1935- *EncSF 93*
Watkins, Peter Rodney 1931- *Who 94*
Watkins, Price I. 1925- *WhoBlA 94*
Watkins, Ragland Tolk 1948- *WhoAmA 93*
Watkins, Raymond *AfrAmG*
Watkins, Robert Charles 1927- *WhoBlA 94*
Watkins, Rolanda Rowe 1956- *WhoBlA 94*
Watkins, Ronald 1904- *WrDr 94*
Watkins, Ronald J(oseph) 1945- *WrDr 94*
Watkins, Rufus Nathaniel 1963- *WhoWest 94*
Watkins, Stephen Edward 1922- *WhoAm 94*
Watkins, Susan Gail 1962- *WhoAmL 94*
Watkins, Sylvestre C., Sr. 1911- *WhoBlA 94*
Watkins, Tasker 1918- *Who 94*
Watkins, Ted 1923- *WhoBlA 94*
Watkins, Thomas, Jr. *WhoBlA 94*
Watkins, Thomas Frederick 1914- *Who 94*
Watkins, Thomas W. 1955- *WhoAmP 93*
Watkins, Toney Davis d1986 *WhoHol 92*
Watkins, Walter C., Jr. 1946- *WhoBlA 94*
Watkins, Warren Hyde 1953- *WhoFI 94*
Watkins, Wesley Lee 1953- *WhoFI 94*
Watkins, Wesley Wade 1938- *WhoAmP 93*
Watkins, Wiliam John 1942- *WrDr 94*
Watkins, William, Jr. 1932- *WhoBlA 94, WhoFI 94*
Watkins, William Henry 1929- *WhoScEn 94*
Watkins, William Howard, Jr. 1941- *WhoAmP 93*
Watkins, William John *DrAPF 93*
Watkins, William Jon 1942- *EncSF 93*
Watkins, William Law 1910- *WhoAm 94*
Watkins, William Shepard 1950- *WhoWest 94*
Watkins, Winifred May 1924- *IntWW 93, Who 94*
Watkins, Wynfred C. 1946- *WhoBlA 94*
Watkins-Cannon, Gloria Ann 1952- *WhoBlA 94*
Watkinson, Viscount 1910- *Who 94*
Watkinson, Carolyn 1949- *NewGrDO*
Watkinson, Harold Arthur 1910- *IntWW 93*
Watkinson, John Taylor 1941- *Who 94*
Watkinson, Patricia Grieve 1946- *WhoAm 94, WhoAmA 93, WhoWest 94*
Watkinson, Thomas G. 1931- *WhoAmP 93*
Watkinson, W. Grant 1941- *WhoWest 94*
Watkins-Pitchford, John 1912- *Who 94*
Watkin Williams, Peter 1911- *Who 94*
Watkiss, David Keith 1924- *WhoAmL 94*
Watley, Jody 1960- *WhoBlA 94*
Watley, Margaret Ann 1925- *WhoBlA 94*
Watling, (David) Brian 1935- *Who 94*
Watling, Jack 1923- *WhoHol 92*
Watlington, Arturo, Jr. 1953- *WhoAmP 93*
Watlington, Janet Berecia 1938- *WhoBlA 94*
Watlington, John Francis, Jr. 1911- *WhoAm 94*
Watlington, Mario A. 1917- *WhoAmP 93, WhoBlA 94*
Watlington, Sarah Jane 1938- *WhoMW 93*
Watmough, David 1926- *WrDr 94*
Watmough, David (Arthur) 1926- *GayLL*
Watne, Gene M. *WhoAmP 93*
Watniss, Wendy 1943- *WhoAmA 93*
Watring, Watson Glenn 1936- *WhoAm 94, WhoWest 94*
Watrous, James Scales 1908- *ConAu 141, WhoAmA 93*
Watrous, Philip Jordan 1933- *WhoFI 94*
Watrous, William Russell 1939- *WhoAm 94*
Watsky, Matthew 1957- *WhoAmL 94*
Watson *Who 94*
Watson, Adam *Who 94*
Watson, (John Hugh) Adam 1914- *Who 94*
Watson, Adele d1933 *WhoHol 92*
Watson, Alan *Who 94*
Watson, Alan 1933- *WrDr 94*
Watson, Alan Albert 1929- *Who 94*
Watson, Alan Andrew 1938- *Who 94*
Watson, Alan Eugene *WhoIns 94*
Watson, Alan George *Who 94*
Watson, Alan John 1941- *Who 94*
Watson, Albert MacKenzie 1942- *WhoAm 94*
Watson, Alberta *WhoHol 92*
Watson, Aldren A. 1917- *WhoAmA 93*
Watson, Alexander F. 1939- *WhoAmP 93*
Watson, Alexander Fletcher 1939- *IntWW 93, WhoAm 94*
Watson, Alfred Nelson 1910-1988 *WhAm 10*
Watson, Allan John, III 1951- *WhoFI 94*
Watson, Amy Zakrzewski 1965- *SmATA 76*
Watson, Andrew *Who 94*
Watson, (James) Andrew 1937- *Who 94*
Watson, Andrew Linton 1927- *Who 94*
Watson, Andrew Samuel 1920- *WhoAm 94, WhoAmL 94*
Watson, Anne 1945- *WhoBlA 94*
Watson, Anthony Gerard 1955- *Who 94*
Watson, Anthony Heriot 1912- *Who 94*
Watson, Antony Edward Douglas 1945- *Who 94*
Watson, Arthur Christopher 1927- *IntWW 93, Who 94*
Watson, Arthur Dennis 1950- *WhoAm 94, WhoAmP 93*
Watson, Ben d1968 *WhoHol 92*
Watson, Ben 1955- *WhoBlA 94*
Watson, Ben Charles 1944- *WhoAm 94*
Watson, Bernard C. 1928- *WhoBlA 94*
Watson, Bernard Charles *WhoAm 94*
Watson, Betty Collier 1946- *WhoBlA 94*
Watson, Beverly A. 1935- *WhoAmP 93*
Watson, Billy *EncSF 93*
Watson, Billy d1945 *WhoHol 92*
Watson, Billy 1924- *WhoHol 92*
Watson, Billy 1938- *WhoAm 94*
Watson, Bobby d1965 *WhoHol 92*
Watson, Bobs 1930- *WhoHol 92*
Watson, Brian Hoyt 1962- *WhoWest 94*
Watson, Bruce 1928- *IntWW 93*
Watson, Bruce (Dunstan) 1928- *Who 94*
Watson, Carol Kay 1949- *WhoAmP 93*
Watson, Carole M. 1944- *WhoBlA 94*
Watson, Catherine Elaine 1944- *WhoAm 94*
Watson, Caven d1953 *WhoHol 92*
Watson, Celia *DrAPF 93*
Watson, Charles Irwin 1926- *WhoAmP 93*
Watson, Cheryl Ann 1955- *WhoMW 93*
Watson, Claire 1927-1986 *NewGrDO*
Watson, Clarissa H. *WhoAmA 93*
Watson, Cletus Claude 1938- *WhoBlA 94*
Watson, Clifford D. 1946- *WhoBlA 94*
Watson, Clyde 1947- *WrDr 94*
Watson, Clyniece Lois 1948- *WhoBlA 94*
Watson, Constance A. 1951- *WhoBlA 94*
Watson, Coy d1968 *WhoHol 92*
Watson, Coy, Jr. 1912- *WhoHol 92*
Watson, Craig *DrAPF 93*
Watson, D. Rahim *DrAPF 93*
Watson, Daniel 1938- *WhoBlA 94*
Watson, Darliene Keeney 1929- *WhoAmA 93*
Watson, David Bruce 1955- *WhoMW 93*
Watson, David Colquitt 1936- *WhoFI 94, WhoScEn 94, WhoWest 94*
Watson, David John 1949- *Who 94*
Watson, David Leon 1952- *WhoAmP 93*
Watson, David Leslie 1955- *WhoFI 94*
Watson, David Raymond 1933- *WhoScEn 94*
Watson, Debbie *WhoHol 92*
Watson, Deborah L. 1953- *WhoMW 93*
Watson, Delmar 1927- *WhoHol 92*
Watson, Denise Sander 1960- *WhoFI 94, WhoMW 93*
Watson, Dennis Rahiim 1953- *WhoBlA 94*
Watson, Dennis Wallace 1914- *WhoAm 94*
Watson, Denton L. 1935- *WhoBlA 94*
Watson, Dexter G. *WhoAmP 93*
Watson, Diane Edith 1933- *WhoAmP 93, WhoBlA 94, WhoWest 94*
Watson, Doc 1923- *WhoAm 94*
Watson, Donald Charles 1945- *WhoScEn 94*
Watson, Donald Ralph 1937- *WhoAm 94*
Watson, Douglas C. d1993 *NewYTBS 93*
Watson, Douglass d1989 *WhoHol 92*
Watson, Duncan *Who 94*
Watson, Duncan (Amos) 1926- *Who 94*
Watson, (Noel) Duncan 1915- *Who 94*
Watson, Ed 1943- *WhoAmP 93*
Watson, Ed Raymond 1920- *WhoAmP 93*
Watson, Edward L. 1934- *WhoFI 94*
Watson, Elizabeth Marion 1949- *WhoAm 94*
Watson, Ellen I. 1948- *WhoAm 94*
Watson, Eugenia Baskerville 1919- *WhoBlA 94*
Watson, Fanny d1970 *WhoHol 92*
Watson, Felicia 1962- *WhoMW 93*
Watson, Forrest Albert 1951- *WhoAmL 94, WhoFI 94*
Watson, Francis John Bagott d1992 *IntWW 93N*
Watson, Frank Burton, Jr. 1921- *WhoAmL 94*
Watson, Frank Charles 1945- *WhoAmP 93*
Watson, Frank M. d1946 *WhoHol 92*
Watson, Fred 1927- *ConDr 93*
Watson, Fred D. 1919- *WhoBlA 94*
Watson, Garry *WhoHol 92*
Watson, Gary L. *WhoAm 94*
Watson, Gavin *Who 94*
Watson, (Angus) Gavin 1944- *Who 94*
Watson, Genevieve 1950- *WhoBlA 94*
Watson, George (Grimes) 1927- *ConAu 42NR, WrDr 94*
Watson, George Henry, Jr. 1936- *WhoAm 94*
Watson, George William 1926- *WhoAm 94, WhoAmL 94*
Watson, George William 1947- *WhoFI 94*
Watson, Georgette 1943- *WhoBlA 94*
Watson, Georgianna 1949- *WhoAm 94*
Watson, Gerald Walter 1934- *Who 94*
Watson, Geraldine G. *WhoAmP 93*
Watson, Gladys 1926- *WhoAmP 93*
Watson, Glenn Robert 1917- *WhoAmL 94*
Watson, Gloria *WhoHol 92*
Watson, Golda Gladis d1979 *WhoHol 92*
Watson, H.B. Marriott *EncSF 93*
Watson, Harlan Leroy 1944- *WhoAm 94*
Watson, Harold *WhoAmP 93*
Watson, Harold George 1931- *WhoAm 94, WhoWest 94*
Watson, Harry 1922- *WhoHol 92*
Watson, Harry B. d1930 *WhoHol 92*
Watson, Helen Gray 1915- *WrDr 94*
Watson, Helen Richter 1926- *WhoAmA 93*
Watson, Henrietta d1964 *WhoHol 92*
Watson, Henry 1910- *Who 94*
Watson, Henry Crocker Marriott *EncSF 93*
Watson, Herman Doc 1931- *WhoBlA 94*
Watson, Hildegarde Lasell d1976 *WhoAmA 93N*
Watson, Howard N(oel) 1929- *WhoAmA 93*
Watson, Ian 1943- *EncSF 93, WrDr 94*
Watson, Irmatean Yelling 1940- *WhoAmP 93*
Watson, Ivory d1969 *WhoHol 92*
Watson, J(ohn) R(ichard) 1934- *WrDr 94*
Watson, J. Warren 1923- *WhoBlA 94*
Watson, Jack 1921- *WhoHol 92*
Watson, Jack Crozier 1928- *WhoAm 94, WhoAmL 94, WhoAmP 93*
Watson, Jack H., Jr. 1938- *WhoAm 94*
Watson, James 1936- *WrDr 94*
Watson, James A., Jr. *WhoHol 92*
Watson, James D(ewey) 1928- *WrDr 94*
Watson, James Dewey 1928- *IntWW 93, Who 94, WhoAm 94, WhoScEn 94, WorScD*
Watson, James Edwin 1952- *WhoScEn 94*
Watson, James Kay Graham 1936- *IntWW 93, Who 94*
Watson, James Kenneth 1935- *Who 94*
Watson, James L. 1922- *CngDr 93, WhoBlA 94*
Watson, James Lopez 1922- *WhoAm 94, WhoAmL 94*

Watson, James Patrick 1936- *Who 94*
Watson, Jean 1934- *BlmGWL*
Watson, Jean 1936- *ConAu 41NR*
Watson, Jean Louise 1943- *WhoMW 93*
Watson, Jeanette Marie 1931- *WhoWest 94*
Watson, Jeffrey John Seagrief 1939- *Who 94*
Watson, Jerome Richard 1938- *WhoAm 94*
Watson, Jerry Carroll 1943- *WhoFI 94*
Watson, Jesse Paul 1896- *WhAm 10*
Watson, Jim Albert 1939- *WhoAm 94, WhoAmL 94*
Watson, Joann Nichols 1951- *WhoBlA 94*
Watson, John 1914- *Who 94*
Watson, John Allen 1946- *WhoAm 94, WhoAmL 94*
Watson, John C. 1932- *WhoIns 94*
Watson, John Calier, III 1955- *WhoFI 94*
Watson, John Cecil 1932- *WhoMW 93*
Watson, John Dewey 1941- *WhoAmL 94*
Watson, John Edward 1949- *WhoFI 94, WhoWest 94*
Watson, John Forbes I. *Who 94*
Watson, John Francis 1962- *WhoWest 94*
Watson, John Grenville Bernard 1943- *Who 94*
Watson, John King, Jr. 1926- *WhoAm 94*
Watson, John Lawrence, III 1932- *WhoAm 94, WhoFI 94*
Watson, John Michael 1945- *WhoFI 94*
Watson, John Michael 1956- *WhoFI 94*
Watson, John R. 1922- *WhoAm 94*
Watson, John S. 1924- *WhoAmP 93*
Watson, John T. d1992 *Who 94N*
Watson, John W. Tadwell 1748-1826 *WhAmRev*
Watson, Joseph d1942 *WhoHol 92*
Watson, Joseph W. 1940- *WhoBlA 94*
Watson, Joy Lynn 1969- *WhoMW 93*
Watson, Joyce Ann 1946- *WhoMW 93*
Watson, Joyce Margaret 1922- *WhoScEn 94*
Watson, Juanita 1923- *WhoBlA 94*
Watson, Judy *EncSF 93*
Watson, Julian 1918- *WhoAm 94*
Watson, Justice d1962 *WhoHol 92*
Watson, Katharine Johnson 1942- *WhoAm 94, WhoAmA 93*
Watson, Keith Stuart 1942- *WhoAmL 94*
Watson, Kenneth Frederick 1942- *WhoWest 94*
Watson, Kenneth Jerome 1959- *WhoMW 93*
Watson, Kenneth Marshall 1921- *IntWW 93, WhoAm 94, WhoWest 94*
Watson, Kitty d1967 *WhoHol 92*
Watson, Lawrence *DrAPF 93*
Watson, Lee Ann 1952- *WhoAm 94, WhoAmL 94*
Watson, Leonidas 1910- *WhoBlA 94*
Watson, Lillian 1947- *NewGrDO*
Watson, Linda Hanson 1941- *WhoAmP 93*
Watson, Louise *WhoHol 92*
Watson, Lucile d1962 *WhoHol 92*
Watson, Lyall 1939- *IntWW 93, WrDr 94*
Watson, Lyndon Lee 1960- *WhoWest 94*
Watson, Lynn *DrAPF 93*
Watson, Madale *WhoAmP 93*
Watson, Maelissa R. M. 1945- *WhoAmL 94*
Watson, Margaret d1940 *WhoHol 92*
Watson, Margaret Elizabeth 1917- *WhoAmP 93*
Watson, Mark Henry 1938- *WhoAmL 94*
Watson, Mary Ann 1944- *WhoWest 94*
Watson, Mary Anne *WhoAmA 93*
Watson, Mary Ellen 1931- *WhoFI 94, WhoScEn 94, WhoWest 94*
Watson, Maud 1864-1946 *BuCMET*
Watson, Michael Goodall 1949- *Who 94*
Watson, Michael M. *Who 94*
Watson, (Leslie) Michael (Macdonald) S. *Who 94*
Watson, Mildred L. 1923- *WhoBlA 94*
Watson, Mills 1940- *WhoHol 92*
Watson, Milton H. 1927- *WhoBlA 94*
Watson, Milton Russell 1934- *WhoWest 94*
Watson, Minor d1965 *WhoHol 92*
Watson, Moray 1928- *WhoHol 92*
Watson, Nancy Dingman *DrAPF 93*
Watson, Newton Frank 1923- *Who 94*
Watson, Odest Jefferson, Sr. 1924- *WhoBlA 94*
Watson, Oliver Lee, III 1938- *WhoWest 94*
Watson, Patty Jo 1932- *WhoAm 94*
Watson, Paula D. 1945- *WhoAm 94*
Watson, Percy Willis 1951- *WhoAmP 93*
Watson, Perry 1950- *WhoBlA 94*
Watson, Perry, III 1951- *WhoBlA 94*
Watson, Peter 1944- *Who 94*
Watson, Peter Robert 1936- *Who 94*
Watson, Philip (Alexander) 1919- *Who 94*
Watson, Ralph Phillip 1958- *WhoAmP 93*
Watson, Raymond Coke, Jr. 1926- *WhoScEn 94*
Watson, Raymond Leslie 1926- *WhoAm 94, WhoFI 94*
Watson, Reginald Gordon Harry 1928- *Who 94*
Watson, Richard *DrAPF 93*
Watson, Richard Allan 1931- *WhoAm 94*
Watson, Richard (Eagleson Gordon) Burges 1930- *Who 94*
Watson, Richard Charles Challinor 1923- *Who 94*
Watson, Richard F. *EncSF 93*
Watson, Richard H. 1941- *WhoWest 94*
Watson, Richard Thomas 1933- *WhoMW 93*
Watson, Robert *DrAPF 93, WhoAmP 93*
Watson, Robert (Winthrop) 1925- *WrDr 94*
Watson, Robert A. 1960- *WhoAmP 93*
Watson, Robert Barden 1914- *WhoScEn 94*
Watson, Robert C. 1947- *WhoBlA 94*
Watson, Robert Francis 1936- *WhoAmL 94*
Watson, Robert James 1954- *WhoAmP 93*
Watson, Robert James 1955- *WhoAmL 94*
Watson, Robert Joe 1934- *WhoAm 94*
Watson, Robert Jose 1946- *WhoBlA 94*
Watson, Robert K. 1932- *WhoIns 94*
Watson, Robert Marion 1914- *WhoAmP 93*
Watson, Robert Ogle 1934- *WhoAmP 93*
Watson, Robert R. 1944- *WhoAm 94*
Watson, Robert Tanner 1922- *WhoAm 94, WhoScEn 94*
Watson, Robert Winthrop 1925- *WhoAm 94*
Watson, Roberta Casper 1949- *WhoAmL 94*
Watson, Roberta Conwell *WhoBlA 94*
Watson, Roderick 1943- *WrDr 94*
Watson, Roderick Anthony d1993 *Who 94N*
Watson, Ronald G. 1941- *WhoAmA 93*
Watson, Ronald Raymond 1957- *WhoMW 93*
Watson, Roslyn Marie 1949- *WhoFI 94*
Watson, Ross 1934- *WhoAmA 93*
Watson, Roy d1937 *WhoHol 92*
Watson, Roy H., Jr. 1937- *WhoAmP 93*
Watson, Roy William 1926- *Who 94*
Watson, Sally (Lou) 1924- *TwCYAW*
Watson, Sharon Gitin 1943- *WhoAm 94, WhoWest 94*
Watson, Sheila 1909- *BlmGWL*
Watson, Solomon B., IV 1944- *WhoBlA 94*
Watson, Solomon Brown, IV 1944- *WhoAm 94, WhoAmL 94*
Watson, Stanley Ellis 1957- *WhoFI 94*
Watson, Stephen E. *WhoFI 94*
Watson, Stephen Roger 1943- *Who 94*
Watson, Sterl Arthur, Jr. 1942- *WhoAm 94*
Watson, Sterling *DrAPF 93*
Watson, Steven 1947- *WrDr 94*
Watson, Steven Edward 1952- *WhoScEn 94*
Watson, Stewart *Who 94*
Watson, (Daniel) Stewart 1911- *Who 94*
Watson, Stewart Charles 1922- *WhoAm 94, WhoFI 94*
Watson, Stuart *Who 94*
Watson, (Henry) Stuart (Ramsay) 1922- *Who 94*
Watson, Stuart Lansing 1948- *WhoScEn 94*
Watson, Susan *DrAPF 93*
Watson, Sylvia 1938- *WhoAmP 93*
Watson, Theresa Lawhorn 1945- *WhoBlA 94*
Watson, Thomas 1545?-1592 *DcLB 132*
Watson, Thomas Allan, Jr. 1950- *WhoFI 94*
Watson, Thomas Campbell 1931- *WhoAm 94*
Watson, Thomas Frederick 1906- *Who 94*
Watson, Thomas J. *WorInv*
Watson, Thomas J., Jr. 1914- *IntWW 93, WhoAm 94*
Watson, Thomas Philip 1933- *WhoAmP 93*
Watson, Thomas Roger 1951- *WhoAmL 94*
Watson, Thomas S., Jr. *WhoBlA 94*
Watson, Thomas Sellers, Jr. *WhoFI 94*
Watson, Thomas Sturges 1949- *IntWW 93, WhoAm 94*
Watson, Thomas Yirrell 1906- *Who 94*
Watson, Tom *WhoHol 92*
Watson, Vernaline 1942- *WhoBlA 94*
Watson, Vernee *WhoHol 92*
Watson, Victor Hugo 1928- *Who 94*
Watson, Vivian *WhoHol 92*
Watson, W. Robert 1943- *WhoAm 94, WhoFI 94*
Watson, Wendy (McLeod) 1942- *SmATA 74*
Watson, Wilbur H. 1938- *WhoBlA 94*
Watson, William *WhoHol 92*
Watson, William 1917- *IntWW 93, Who 94*
Watson, William A. J. 1933- *WhoAm 94*
Watson, William Albert 1930- *Who 94*
Watson, William Alexander Jardine 1933- *Who 94*
Watson, William D. 1943- *WhoAm 94, WhoAmL 94*
Watson, William Downing, Jr. 1938- *WhoFI 94*
Watson, William Edward 1936- *WhoAmP 93*
Watson, William Randy 1950- *WhoWest 94*
Watson, Wylie d1966 *WhoHol 92*
Watson-Brodnax, Shirley Jean *WhoWest 94*
Watson Children, The *WhoHol 92*
Watson-Watt, Robert 1892-1973 *WorInv*
Watson-Wentworth, Charles *WhAmRev*
Watt *Who 94*
Watt, Alfred Ian 1934- *Who 94*
Watt, Andrew 1909- *Who 94*
Watt, Charles Vance 1934- *WhoFI 94*
Watt, Charlotte Joanne *Who 94*
Watt, David Harrington 1957- *ConAu 141*
Watt, Dean Day 1917- *WhoAm 94*
Watt, Diana Lynn 1956- *WhoWest 94*
Watt, Donald Cameron *Who 94*
Watt, Douglas 1914- *WhoAm 94*
Watt, Dwight, Jr. 1955- *WhoScEn 94*
Watt, Garland Wedderick 1932- *WhoBlA 94*
Watt, Graham Wend 1926- *WhoAmP 93*
Watt, Hamish 1925- *Who 94*
Watt, Ian (Pierre) 1917- *WrDr 94*
Watt, Ian Pierre 1917- *WhoAm 94*
Watt, James 1736-1819 *BlmGEL, WorInv [port]*
Watt, James 1914- *Who 94*
Watt, James Gaius 1938- *EnvEnc, IntWW 93, WhoAm 94, WhoAmP 93*
Watt, James H. *Who 94*
Watt, James L. 1944- *WhoAmP 93*
Watt, James Park 1948- *IntWW 93*
Watt, James Wilfrid 1951- *Who 94*
Watt, Jeffrey Xavier 1961- *WhoMW 93, WhoScEn 94*
Watt, John 1948- *WhoAmP 93*
Watt, John Gillies McArthur 1949- *Who 94*
Watt, John H. 1927- *WhoAm 94*
Watt, Joseph M. *WhoAmP 93*
Watt, Joseph Michael *WhoAmL 94*
Watt, Kenneth Edmund Ferguson 1929- *WhoAm 94*
Watt, Martin Dalen 1964- *WhoFI 94*
Watt, Marty *WhoHol 92*
Watt, Melvin 1945- *CngDr 93*
Watt, Melvin L. 1945- *WhoAm 94, WhoAmP 93, WhoBlA 94*
Watt, Mike c. 1958- See fIREHOSE *ConMus 11*
Watt, Norman Ramsay 1928- *WhoScEn 94*
Watt, Randal Lynn 1952- *WhoMW 93*
Watt, Robert 1923- *Who 94*
Watt, Robert Douglas 1945- *WhoAm 94*
Watt, Ronald William 1943- *WhoAm 94, WhoFI 94*
Watt, Stan *WhoHol 92*
Watt, Stuart George 1934- *WhoAm 94, WhoFI 94*
Watt, W(illiam) Montgomery 1909- *Who 94, WrDr 94*
Watt, William George 1934- *WhoIns 94*
Watt, William Joseph 1925- *WhoAm 94*
Watt, William Lee 1959- *WhoAmP 93*
Watt, William Smith 1913- *Who 94*
Watt, William Stewart 1937- *WhoScEn 94*
Wattel, Harold Louis 1921- *WhoAm 94, WhoFI 94*
Watten, Barrett *DrAPF 93*
Wattenberg, Albert 1917- *WhoAm 94*
Wattenberg, Ben J 1933- *WrDr 94*
Wattenberg, David E. 1940- *WhoAmP 93*
Wattenberg, Martin P(aul) 1956- *ConAu 142*
Wattenmaker, Richard J. 1941- *WhoAmA 93*
Wattenmaker, Richard Joel 1941- *WhoAm 94*
Watters, Belva *WhoAmP 93*
Watters, Cynthia Ellen 1944- *WhoFI 94*
Watters, David George 1945- *Who 94*
Watters, Edward McLain, III 1943- *WhoAm 94, WhoAmL 94*
Watters, Linda A. 1953- *WhoBlA 94*
Watters, Richard Campbell 1947- *WhoAmL 94*
Watters, Richard Donald 1951- *WhoAmL 94*
Watters, Robert James 1946- *WhoWest 94*
Watters, Russell Francis 1952- *WhoAmL 94*
Watters, Thomas Robert 1955- *WhoScEn 94*
Watterson, Bill 1958- *WhoAm 94, WrDr 94*
Watterson, Joyce Grande 1937- *WhoMW 93*
Watterson, Thomas Batchelor 1938- *WhoMW 93*
Watt-Evans, Lawrence 1954- *EncSF 93, SmATA 75 [port]*
Watteyne, Kevin Kyle 1957- *WhoFI 94*
Wattis, Richard d1975 *WhoHol 92*
Wattles, Jeffrey Hamilton 1945- *WhoMW 93*
Wattles, Joshua *WhoFI 94*
Wattles, Joshua S. 1951- *IntMPA 94*
Wattleton, Alyce Faye 1943- *AmSocL, WhoAm 94, WhoBlA 94*
Wattleton, Faye 1943- *WhoBlA 94*
Wattley, Graham Richard 1930- *Who 94*
Wattley, Ralph P. d1993 *NewYTBS 93*
Wattley, Thomas Jefferson 1953- *WhoBlA 94*
Wattman, Malcolm Peter 1941- *WhoAm 94*
Watton, James Augustus 1915- *Who 94*
Watts, Alan (James) 1925- *WrDr 94*
Watts, Alan Wilson 1915-1973 *DcAmReB 2*
Watts, Andre 1946- *AfrAmAl 6 [port], WhoAm 94, WhoBlA 94*
Watts, Anne Wimbush 1943- *WhoBlA 94*
Watts, Anthony Brian 1945- *Who 94*
Watts, Anthony John 1942- *WrDr 94*
Watts, Arthur (Desmond) 1931- *Who 94*
Watts, Arthur Desmond 1931- *IntWW 93*
Watts, Barbara Gayle 1946- *WhoAm 94*
Watts, Barbara Karen 1954- *WhoWest 94*
Watts, Barry Allen 1943- *WhoWest 94*
Watts, Beverly L. 1948- *WhoBlA 94*
Watts, Bob 1930- *WhoAmP 93*
Watts, Carl Augustus 1935- *WhoBlA 94*
Watts, Charles d1966 *WhoHol 92*
Watts, Charles d1968 *WhoHol 92*
Watts, Charles DeWitt 1917- *WhoAm 94, WhoBlA 94*
Watts, Charles Henry, II 1926- *WhoAm 94*
Watts, Charlie 1944- *WhoAmP 93*
Watts, Claudius Elmer, III 1936- *WhoAm 94*
Watts, Cynthia Gay 1962- *WhoAmL 94, WhoWest 94*
Watts, Daniel Thomas 1916- *WhoAm 94*
Watts, Dave Henry 1932- *WhoAm 94, WhoFI 94*
Watts, David Eide 1921- *WhoAm 94*
Watts, Dey Wadsworth 1923- *WhoAm 94, WhoAmL 94, WhoMW 93*
Watts, Dodo d1990 *WhoHol 92*
Watts, Donald Walter 1934- *IntWW 93, Who 94*
Watts, Dorothy Burt (Trout) 1892-1977 *WhoAmA 93N*
Watts, Edward 1940- *Who 94*
Watts, Elizabeth d1967 *WhoHol 92*
Watts, Emily Stipes 1936- *WhoAm 94*
Watts, Ernest Francis 1937- *WhoAm 94*
Watts, Eugene J. 1942- *WhoAmP 93*
Watts, Frederick, Jr. 1929- *WhoBlA 94*
Watts, George d1942 *WhoHol 92*
Watts, Glenn Ellis 1920- *WhoAm 94, WhoAmP 93*
Watts, Grady d1986 *WhoHol 92*
Watts, Guy Leland 1941- *WhoAmP 93*
Watts, Gwendolyn *WhoHol 92*
Watts, Harold H. 1906- *WrDr 94*
Watts, Harold Ross 1944- *WhoAm 94*
Watts, Harold Wesley 1932- *WhoAm 94*
Watts, Heather 1953- *IntDcB [port], WhoAm 94*
Watts, Helen (Josephine) 1927- *NewGrDO*
Watts, Helen Caswell 1958- *WhoScEn 94*
Watts, Helen Josephine 1927- *IntWW 93, Who 94*
Watts, Helen L. Hoke 1903-1990 *ConAu 43NR*
Watts, Helena Roselle 1921- *WhoScEn 94*
Watts, Henry Miller, Jr. 1904- *WhoAm 94*
Watts, Isaac 1674-1748 *BlmGEL*
Watts, J. C. 1957- *WhoAmP 93*
Watts, J. C., Jr. 1957- *WhoBlA 94*
Watts, James Harrison 1951- *WhoWest 94*
Watts, James Lawrence 1949- *WhoFI 94, WhoWest 94*
Watts, Jeanne *WhoHol 92*
Watts, Jeffrey Alan 1950- *WhoWest 94*
Watts, John Arthur 1947- *Who 94*
Watts, John Cadman 1913- *Who 94*
Watts, John E. 1936- *WhoBlA 94*
Watts, John Francis 1926- *Who 94, WrDr 94*
Watts, John McCleave 1933- *WhoAm 94*

Watts, John Peter Barry Condliffe 1930-
Who 94
Watts, John Ransford 1930- WhoMW 93
Watts, Kenneth Michael 1964-
WhoScEn 94
Watts, Leroy, Jr. d1990 WhoHol 92
Watts, Lucile WhoBlA 94
Watts, Malcolm L. 1937- WhoScEn 94
Watts, Malcolm Stuart McNeal 1915-
WhoAm 94
Watts, Marvin Lee 1932- WhoAmP 93,
WhoScEn 94
Watts, May Petrea Theilgaard 1893-
WhAm 10
Watts, Michael Arthur 1955-
WhoScEn 94
Watts, Nigel 1957- WrDr 94
Watts, Olin E(thredge) 1899- WhAm 10
Watts, Oliver Edward 1939- WhoAm 94,
WhoWest 94
Watts, Otto O(live) 1893- WhAm 10
Watts, Patricia L. 1949- WhoBlA 94
Watts, Patsy Jeanne 1943- WhoFI 94,
WhoWest 94
Watts, Peggy d1966 WhoHol 92
Watts, Queenie d1980 WhoHol 92
Watts, Quincy WhoAm 94
Watts, Quincy Duswan 1970- WhoBlA 94
Watts, R. Michael 1951- WhoAmA 93
Watts, Rachel Mary Who 94
Watts, Ridley, Jr. 1956- WhoMW 93
Watts, Robert Allan 1936- WhoMW 93
Watts, Roberta Ogletree 1939-
WhoBlA 94
Watts, Ronald George d1993 Who 94N
Watts, Ronald Lester 1934- WhoAm 94
Watts, Roy d1993 IntWW 93N, Who 94N
Watts, Stephen Hurt, II 1947- WhoAm 94,
WhoAmL 94
Watts, Steven Richard 1955- WhoAmL 94
Watts, Susan Elizabeth 1952-
WhoAmL 94
Watts, Susanna 1768-1842 DcNaB MP
Watts, Thomas D(ale) 1941- ConAu 41NR
Watts, Thomas Rowland 1917- Who 94
Watts, Timothy 1957- ConAu 141
Watts, Victor Brian 1927- Who 94
Watts, Victor Lewis 1955- WhoBlA 94
Watts, Vivian E. 1940- WhoAmP 93
Watts, William Arthur 1930- IntWW 93,
Who 94
Watts, William David 1938- WhoFI 94
Watts, William Edward 1952- WhoAm 94
Watts, Wilsonya Richardson WhoBlA 94
Wattson, Robert Kean 1922- WhoScEn 94
Watz, Martin Charles 1938- WhoFI 94
Wauchope, Keith Leveret 1941-
WhoAmP 93
Wauchope, Roger (Hamilton) Don- 1938-
Who 94
Waud, Christopher Denis George Pierre
1928- Who 94
Waud, Roger Neil 1938- WhoAm 94
Wauer, Roland Horst 1934- WhoScEn 94
Waufle, Alan Duane 1951- WhoAmA 93
Waugh, Auberon (Alexander) 1939-
WrDr 94
Waugh, Auberon Alexander 1939-
IntWW 93, Who 94
Waugh, Charles G(ordon) 1943- EncSF 93
Waugh, Coulton 1896-1973
WhoAmA 93N
Waugh, Debra Riggin DrAPF 93
Waugh, Dorothy WrDr 94
Waugh, Douglas Oliver William 1918-
WhoAm 94
Waugh, Eric Alexander 1933- Who 94
Waugh, Evelyn 1903-1966
BlmGEL [port], EncSF 93
Waugh, Evelyn (Arthur St. John)
1903-1966 GayLL, RfGShF
Waugh, Frederick Vail 1898- WhAm 10
Waugh, Hillary (Baldwin) 1920- WrDr 94
Waugh, John David 1932- WhoAm 94
Waugh, John Stewart 1929- IntWW 93,
WhoAm 94, WhoScEn 94
Waugh, Judith Ritchie 1939- WhoBlA 94
Waugh, Michael L. WhoAmP 93
Waugh, Richard W. 1943- WhoIns 94
Waugh, Sidney B. 1904-1963
WhoAmA 93N
Waugh, Theodore Rogers 1926-
WhoAm 94
Waugh, William Howard 1925-
WhoScEn 94
Waugh, William Kansas, III 1943-
WhoAmL 94
Waugh McCulloch, Catharine 1862-1945
WomPubS
Wauhop, Iles W. 1934- WhoIns 94
Wauls, Inez La Mar 1924- WhoBlA 94
Wauquier, Albert 1940- WhoMW 93
Wauters, Shirley Stapleton 1936-
WhoWest 94
Wautier, Jean Luc 1942- WhoScEn 94
Waverley, Viscount 1949- Who 94
Waverly, Frances d1984 WhoHol 92
Wawerka, Anton WhoHol 92

Wawrzyn, Ronald M. 1945- WhoAm 94,
WhoAmL 94
Wawrzyniak, Stephen David 1949-
WhoFI 94
Wawzonek, Stanley 1914-1988 WhAm 10
Wax, Bernard 1930- WhoAm 94
Wax, Edward L. 1937- WhoAm 94
Wax, George Louis 1928- WhoAmL 94,
WhoFI 94
Wax, John M. 1948- WhoAmA 93
Wax, Morton Dennis 1932- IntMPA 94
Wax, Murray L 1922- WrDr 94
Wax, Nadine Virginia 1927- WhoFI 94,
WhoMW 93
Wax, William Edward 1956- WhoAm 94
Waxenberg, Alan M. 1935- WhoAm 94
Waxlax, Lorne R. 1933- WhoFI 94
Waxler, Beverly Jean 1949- WhoMW 93
Waxler, Robert Phillip 1944- WhoAm 94
Waxman, Al 1935- WhoHol 92
Waxman, David 1918- WhoAm 94
Waxman, Franz 1906-1967
IntDcF 2-4 [port]
Waxman, Henry A. 1939- CngDr 93
Waxman, Henry Arnold 1939-
WhoAm 94, WhoAmP 93, WhoWest 94
Waxman, Herbert J. DrAPF 93
Waxman, M. D. d1931 WhoHol 92
Waxman, Margery Hope 1942-
WhoAm 94
Waxman, Ronald 1933- WhoAm 94,
WhoScEn 94
Waxman, Seth Paul 1951- WhoAmL 94
Waxman, Sheldon Robert 1941-
WhoAmL 94
Waxman, Stanley WhoHol 92
Waxman, Stephen George 1945-
WhoAm 94
Waxse, David John 1945- WhoAm 94,
WhoAmL 94, WhoMW 93
Waxter, Thomas, Jr. 1934- WhoAmP 93
Way, Alva Otis 1929- IntWW 93
Way, Ann WhoHol 92
Way, Anthony Gerald 1920- Who 94
Way, Carol Jane 1940- WhoFI 94
Way, Curtis J. 1935- WhoBlA 94
Way, Edward Leong 1916- WhoAm 94,
WhoWest 94
Way, Eileen WhoHol 92
Way, Gary Darryl 1958- WhoBlA 94
Way, Greg 1950- WhoWest 94
Way, Jacob Edson, III 1947- WhoAm 94,
WhoWest 94
Way, James Leong 1926- WhoAm 94
Way, Kenneth L. 1939- WhoAm 94,
WhoFI 94
Way, Margaret WrDr 94
Way, Peter 1936- EncSF 93
Way, Peter (Howard) 1936- WrDr 94
Way, Peter T. 1936- WhoAmP 93
Way, Richard 1914- IntWW 93
Way, Richard (George Kitchener) 1914-
Who 94
Way, Steven H. 1950- WhoWest 94
Way, Walter Lee 1931- WhoAm 94
Wayans, Damon WhoBlA 94
Wayans, Damon 1960- IntMPA 94,
WhoHol 92
Wayans, Damon 1961- WhoAm 94
Wayans, Keenan Ivory 1958-
AfrAmAl 6 [port], Au&Arts 11 [port]
Wayans, Keenen Ivory WhoBlA 94
Wayans, Keenen Ivory 1958?- BlkWr 2,
ConAu 140, IntMPA 94, WhoAm 94,
WhoHol 92
Wayborn, Kristina 1954- WhoHol 92
Wayburn, Edgar 1906- WhoWest 94
Wayburn, Laurie Andrea 1954-
WhoScEn 94
Wayburn, Ned d1942 WhoHol 92
Wayburn, Peggy 1917- WhoWest 94
Waycoff, Leon WhoHol 92
Wayditch, Gabriel von 1888-1969
NewGrDO
Waydo, George J. 1943- WhoFI 94
Waye, Jerome Victor 1953- WhoAmL 94
Waygood, Ernest Roy 1918- WhoAm 94
Wayland, Francis 1796-1865 DcAmReB 2
Wayland, James Harold 1909-
WhoAm 94, WhoMW 93, WhoScEn 94
Wayland, Len IntMPA 94
Wayland, Marilyn Ticknor 1949-
WhoMW 93, WhoScEn 94
Wayland, Newton Hart 1940- WhoAm 94
Wayland, Russell Gibson, Jr. 1913-
WhoAm 94, WhoScEn 94
Wayland, Sarah Catherine 1963-
WhoScEn 94
Wayland, Sharon Morris 1951-
WhoAmL 94
Wayland, William Francis 1935-
WhoFI 94
Wayland-Smith, Robert Dean 1943-
WhoAm 94
Waylett, Thomas Robert 1941-
WhoAm 94
Wayman, Clarence Marvin 1930-
WhoAm 94

Wayman, David Anthony 1950-
WhoMW 93
Wayman, Morris 1915- WhoAm 94
Wayman, Patrick Arthur 1927-
IntWW 93, WhoScEn 94
Wayman, Tom 1945- WrDr 94
Wayman, Tony Russell 1929- EncSF 93
Wayman, Vivienne 1926- WrDr 94
Waymer, David d1993
NewYTBS 93 [port]
Waymer, David Benjamin, Jr. 1958-1993
WhoBlA 94N
Waymire, David Dean 1956- WhoMW 93
Waymouth, Charity 1915- Who 94
Waymouth, John Francis 1926-
WhoAm 94
Wayne, Anthony 1745-1796 AmRev,
HisWorL [port], WhAmRev [port]
Wayne, Bernie d1993 NewYTBS 93
Wayne, Carol d1985 WhoHol 92
Wayne, Charles S. 1914- WhoFI 94
Wayne, David 1914- IntMPA 94,
WhoHol 92
Wayne, David Alan 1946- WhoWest 94
Wayne, Donald 1930- WrDr 94
Wayne, Elsie Eleanore 1932- WhoAm 94
Wayne, Frances d1978 WhoHol 92
Wayne, Fredd WhoHol 92
Wayne, George Howard, Sr. 1938-
WhoBlA 94
Wayne, Jane Ellen 1936- ConAu 42NR
Wayne, Jane O. DrAPF 93
Wayne, Jim 1948- WhoAmP 93
Wayne, Joel IntMPA 94
Wayne, John d1979 WhoHol 92
Wayne, John Ethan 1962- WhoHol 92
Wayne, Johnny 1918-1990
See Wayne and Schuster WhoCom
Wayne, Joseph 1906- WrDr 94
Wayne, Joseph T. 1956- WhoMW 93
Wayne, June WhoAmA 93
Wayne, Justine Washington 1945-
WhoBlA 94
Wayne, Keith WhoHol 92
Wayne, Ken WhoHol 92
Wayne, Kyra Petrovskaya 1918-
WhoWest 94
Wayne, Lawrence Gershon 1926-
WhoScEn 94
Wayne, Lloyd WhoHol 92
Wayne, Lowell Grant 1918- WhoAm 94,
WhoWest 94
Wayne, M. Howard 1948- WhoWest 94
Wayne, Mabel d1978 WhoHol 92
Wayne, Marvin Alan 1943- WhoWest 94
Wayne, Michael A. 1934- IntMPA 94
Wayne, Naunton d1970 WhoHol 92
Wayne, Nina 1943- WhoHol 92
Wayne, Patricia WhoHol 92
Wayne, Patrick 1939- IntMPA 94,
WhoHol 92
Wayne, Richard d1958 WhoHol 92
Wayne, Robert d1946 WhoHol 92
Wayne, Robert Andrew 1938-
WhoAmL 94
Wayne, Robert Jonathan 1951-
WhoAmL 94
Wayne, Thomas Francis 1954- WhoFI 94
Wayne and Schuster WhoCom
Waynes, Kathleen Yanes 1920-
WhoBlA 94
Waynewood, Freeman Lee 1942-
WhoBlA 94
Waysdorf, Richard Hillard 1953-
WhoAmL 94
Wayt, Gard Russell 1938- WhoAmP 93
Wayt, Michael Allen 1963- WhoWest 94
Wayte, Alan 1936- WhoAm 94
Waytula, Anthony J. 1944- WhoMW 93
Waywell, Geoffrey Bryan 1944- Who 94
Waz, Joseph Walter, Jr. 1953-
WhoAmL 94
Wazneh, Leila Hussein 1957-
WhoScEn 94
Wazontek, Stella Catherine 1961-
WhoScEn 94
Wazzan, Ahmed Rassem Frank 1935-
WhoAm 94
Wazzan, Chafiq al- 1925- IntWW 93
Wead, Rodney Sam 1935- WhoBlA 94
Wead, William Badertscher 1940-
WhoAm 94
Weadock, Daniel Peter 1939- WhoFI 94
Weady, Louis Stanley Charles-Marie
1940- WhoAmP 93
Weaire, Denis Lawrence 1942- IntWW 93
Weakland, Kevin L. 1963- IntMPA 94
Weakland, Rembert G. 1927- WhoAm 94,
WhoMW 93
Weakley, Donald Irving, Sr. 1936-
WhoAmP 93
Weaks, Mary Louise 1961- WhoMW 93,
WrDr 94
Weale, Anne WrDr 94
Weale, Mary Jo 1924- WhoAmA 93
Weales, Gerald 1925- WrDr 94
Weamys, Anna BlmGWL
Weare, Meshech 1713-1786 WhAmRev

Weare, Shane 1936- WhoAmA 93
Weare, Trevor John 1943- Who 94
Wearing, J. P. ConAu 41NR
Wearly, William Levi 1915- WhoAm 94,
WhoWest 94
Wearn, Wilson Cannon 1919- WhoAm 94
Wearne, Alan 1948- WrDr 94
Wearsch, Daniel Charles 1937-
WhoMW 93
Weart, Spencer R(ichard) 1942- WrDr 94
Weary, A. C. WhoHol 92
Weary, Dolphus 1946- WhoBlA 94
Weary, Lawrence Clifton 1928-
WhoAmP 93
Weary, Ogdred 1925- WrDr 94
Weary, Peyton Edwin 1930- WhoAm 94
Weather, Leonard, Jr. 1944- WhoBlA 94
Weatherall, David (John) 1933- Who 94
Weatherall, David John 1933- IntWW 93
Weatherall, James (Lamb) 1936-
IntWW 93, Who 94
Weatherall, Miles 1920- Who 94
Weatherbee, Artemus Edwin 1918-
WhoAm 94
Weatherbee, Carl 1916- WhoMW 93,
WhoScEn 94
Weatherbee, Charles 1926-
See Jones, Dexter 1926- WhoAmA 93N
Weatherbee, Donald Emery 1932-
WhoAm 94
Weatherbee, Ellen Gene Elliott 1939-
WhoMW 93
Weatherby, Gregg DrAPF 93
Weatherford, Alan Mann 1932-
WhoWest 94
Weatherford, Catherine J. WhoAmP 93
Weatherford, George Edward 1932-
WhoMW 93, WhoScEn 94
Weatherford, Willis Duke, Jr. 1916-
WhoAm 94
Weatherhead, A(ndrew) Kingsley 1923-
WrDr 94
Weatherhead, Albert John, III 1925-
WhoMW 93
Weatherhead, Alexander Stewart 1931-
Who 94
Weatherhead, Andrew Kingsley 1923-
WhoWest 94
Weatherhead, Chris WhoHol 92
Weatherhead, James Leslie 1931-
IntWW 93, Who 94
Weatherhead, Leslie R. 1956-
WhoAmL 94, WhoWest 94
Weatherill, Baron 1920- Who 94
Weatherill, (Bruce) Bernard 1920-
IntWW 93
Weatherill, John Frederick William 1932-
WhoAm 94
Weatherill, Nigel Peter 1954-
WhoScEn 94
Weatherington-Rice, Julie Bishop Paynter
1948- WhoMW 93
Weatherley, Paul Egerton 1917-
IntWW 93, Who 94
Weatherly, John Hugh 1924- WhoAmP 93
Weatherly, Julie Jennings 1961-
WhoAmL 94
Weatherly, Robert Stone, Jr. 1929-
WhoAm 94
Weatherly, Shawn WhoHol 92
Weathers, Carl 1947- WhoBlA 94
Weathers, Carl 1948- IntMPA 94,
WhoHol 92
Weathers, Clarence 1962- WhoBlA 94
Weathers, J. Leroy 1936- WhoBlA 94
Weathers, K. Russell 1942- WhoAm 94,
WhoMW 93
Weathers, Margaret A. 1922- WhoBlA 94
Weathers, Milledge Wright 1926-
WhoFI 94
Weathers, Philip 1908- WrDr 94
Weathers, Warren Russell 1947-
WhoWest 94
Weathersby, George Byron 1944-
WhoAm 94
Weathersby, Joseph Brewster 1929-
WhoBlA 94
Weathersby, Qevin Q. 1962- WhoBlA 94
Weathersby, Tom WhoAmP 93
Weatherspoon, Clarence 1970-
WhoBlA 94
Weatherspoon, Jimmy Lee 1947-
WhoBlA 94
Weatherspoon, Keith Earl 1949-
WhoBlA 94
Weatherston, (William) Alastair (Paterson)
1935- Who 94
Weatherston, George Douglas, Jr. 1952-
WhoFI 94
Weatherstone, Dennis 1930- IntWW 93,
Who 94, WhoAm 94, WhoFI 94
Weatherstone, James W. 1925- WhoIns 94
Weatherstone, Robert Bruce 1926-
Who 94
Weatherup, Roy Garfield 1947-
WhoAm 94, WhoAmL 94, WhoWest 94
Weatherwax, David Allen 1956-
WhoAmL 94

Webber, Richard Blackstone, II 1956- *WhoAmL 94*
Webber, Richard John 1948- *WhoAm 94*
Webber, Robert d1989 *WhoHol 92*
Webber, Robert 1953-1989 *WhAm 10*
Webber, Rolland Lloyd 1932- *WhoAmP 93*
Webber, Ross A 1934- *WrDr 94*
Webber, Roy Seymour 1933- *Who 94*
Webber, Sabra J. 1945- *ConAu 141*
Webber, Thomas Charles 1947- *WhoAmP 93*
Webber, Walter E. 1943- *WhoAmL 94*
Webber, William Alexander 1934- *WhoAm 94, WhoWest 94*
Webber, William Stuart 1942- *WhoBlA 94*
Webeck, Alfred Stanley 1913- *WhoMW 93*
Weber, Alban 1915- *WhoAmL 94*
Weber, Albert Jacob 1919- *WhoAmA 93*
Weber, Alfons 1927- *WhoAm 94, WhoScEn 94*
Weber, Alfred Herman 1906- *WhoAm 94*
Weber, Alois Hughes 1910- *WhoWest 94*
Weber, Aloysia *NewGrDO*
Weber, Andre *WhoHol 92*
Weber, Arnold R. 1929- *WhoAm 94, WhoMW 93*
Weber, Arthur 1926- *WhoAm 94*
Weber, Arthur Phineas 1920- *WhoScEn 94*
Weber, Barbara M. 1945- *WhoFI 94*
Weber, Beate 1943- *WhoWomW 91*
Weber, Bernhard Anselm 1764-1821 *NewGrDO*
Weber, Bertram Anton 1898-1989 *WhAm 10*
Weber, Brom 1917- *WhoAm 94, WrDr 94*
Weber, Bruce 1946- *IntWW 93*
Weber, Carl Maria (Friedrich Ernst) von 1786-1826 *NewGrDO*
Weber, Charlene Lydia 1943- *WhoWest 94*
Weber, Charles 1947- *WhoMW 93*
Weber, Charles Alan 1951- *WhoFI 94*
Weber, Charles Edward 1930- *WhoAm 94*
Weber, Charles Walter 1931- *WhoAm 94*
Weber, Charles Walton 1943- *WhoScEn 94*
Weber, Charles William 1946- *WhoAmP 93*
Weber, Christine Ann 1968- *WhoMW 93*
Weber, Daniel 1942- *WhoBlA 94*
Weber, Daniel E. 1940- *WhoAm 94*
Weber, Darrell Jack 1933- *WhoWest 94*
Weber, David *EncSF 93*
Weber, David Alexander 1939- *WhoScEn 94*
Weber, David Carter 1924- *WhoAm 94*
Weber, David Frederick 1939- *WhoScEn 94*
Weber, David Joseph 1940- *WrDr 94*
Weber, David Joseph 1962- *WhoScEn 94*
Weber, David Paul 1933- *WhoIns 94*
Weber, Delbert Dean 1932- *WhoMW 93*
Weber, Dennis Paul 1952- *WhoAmP 93, WhoWest 94*
Weber, (Edmund) Derek (Craig) 1921- *Who 94*
Weber, Diane 1953- *WhoFI 94, WhoMW 93*
Weber, Diane Theresa 1965- *WhoAmL 94*
Weber, Donald Charles 1958- *WhoScEn 94*
Weber, Dorothy Jo 1951- *WhoWest 94*
Weber, Dwight Edward 1951- *WhoFI 94*
Weber, (Franz)Edmund (Kaspar Johann Nepomuk Joseph Mari 1766-1828 *NewGrDO*
Weber, Edward F. 1931- *WhoAmP 93*
Weber, Eicke Richard 1949- *WhoScEn 94, WhoWest 94*
Weber, Elizabeth *DrAPF 93*
Weber, Ernst 1901- *WhoAm 94*
Weber, Eugen 1925- *WhoAm 94, WhoWest 94, WrDr 94*
Weber, Fred J. 1919- *WhoAm 94, WhoAmL 94, WhoAmP 93, WhoWest 94*
Weber, Frederic 1939- *WhoAm 94*
Weber, Frederick Theodore 1883-1956 *WhoAmA 93N*
Weber, Fredric Alan 1948- *WhoAm 94, WhoAmL 94*
Weber, Gail L. 1955- *WhoAmL 94*
Weber, Georg Franz 1962- *WhoScEn 94*
Weber, George 1922- *WhoAm 94, WhoScEn 94*
Weber, George Richard 1929- *WhoAm 94, WhoFI 94, WhoWest 94*
Weber, Gerald Joseph 1914- *WhoAmL 94*
Weber, Gloria 1933- *WhoAmP 93*
Weber, Gloria Richie *WhoMW 93*
Weber, Hans Jurgen 1939- *WhoAm 94*
Weber, Harm Allen 1926- *WhoAm 94*
Weber, Harold 1959- *WhoFI 94*
Weber, Henry George 1900-1991 *WhAm 10*
Weber, Herman Jacob 1927- *WhoAm 94, WhoAmL 94, WhoMW 93*
Weber, Hugo 1918-1971 *WhoAmA 93N*
Weber, Idelle *WhoAmA 93*
Weber, Jacques *WhoHol 92*
Weber, James Edward 1957- *WhoMW 93*
Weber, James Stuart 1947- *WhoFI 94*
Weber, Jan *WhoAmA 93*
Weber, Janet M. 1936- *WhoAm 94*
Weber, Jean M. 1933- *WhoAmA 93*
Weber, Jean MacPhail 1933- *WhoAm 94*
Weber, Jeffrey L. 1952- *WhoFI 94*
Weber, Jeffrey William 1953- *WhoMW 93*
Weber, Jerome Charles 1938- *WhoAm 94*
Weber, Joe d1942 *WhoHol 92*
Weber, Joe 1867-1942 *See* Weber and Fields *WhoCom*
Weber, Joe 1945- *ConAu 141*
Weber, John 1932- *WhoAmA 93*
Weber, John Bertram 1930- *WhoMW 93, WhoScEn 94*
Weber, John H. 1799-1859 *WhWE*
Weber, John Pitman 1942- *WhoAmA 93*
Weber, John Walter 1959- *WhoAmL 94*
Weber, Jonna d1977 *WhoHol 92*
Weber, Joseph H. 1930- *WhoAm 94*
Weber, Joseph James 1942- *WhoWest 94*
Weber, Joseph Miroslav 1854-1906 *NewGrDO*
Weber, Josepha *NewGrDO*
Weber, Julian L. 1929- *WhoAm 94*
Weber, Karen *WhoAmA 93*
Weber, Karl d1990 *WhoHol 92*
Weber, Karl William 1953- *WhoAm 94*
Weber, Kathy Kaufman 1961- *WhoMW 93*
Weber, Kenneth 1936- *WhoAmL 94*
Weber, Lavern John 1933- *WhoAm 94, WhoScEn 94*
Weber, Lawrence Kirkwood, Jr. 1930- *WhoFI 94*
Weber, Leo L. 1929- *WhoAm 94*
Weber, Linda Diane 1948- *WhoMW 93*
Weber, Lois d1939 *WhoHol 92*
Weber, Lowell Wyckoff 1923- *WhoScEn 94*
Weber, Ludwig 1899-1974 *NewGrDO [port]*
Weber, Marc *DrAPF 93*
Weber, Margaret Laura Jane 1933- *WhoMW 93*
Weber, Mary E. 1948- *WhoAmL 94*
Weber, Mary Suzanne 1953- *WhoWest 94*
Weber, Mary Virginia 1927- *WhoAmP 93*
Weber, Max 1864-1920 *EncEth*
Weber, Max 1881-1961 *WhoAmA 93N*
Weber, Max O. 1929- *WhoAm 94*
Weber, Merrill Evan 1956- *WhoAmL 94*
Weber, Michael Howard 1960- *WhoScEn 94*
Weber, Michael Willard 1944- *WhoMW 93*
Weber, Milan George 1908- *WhoFI 94, WhoMW 93*
Weber, Monika 1943- *WhoWomW 91*
Weber, Morton M. 1922- *WhoAm 94*
Weber, Nancy Walker 1936- *WhoAm 94*
Weber, Owen 1946- *WhoAm 94*
Weber, Philip Joseph 1909- *WhoAm 94*
Weber, R. B. *DrAPF 93*
Weber, Ralph E 1926- *WrDr 94*
Weber, Rex d1918 *WhoHol 92*
Weber, Richard 1941- *WhoFI 94*
Weber, Robert Carl 1950- *WhoAm 94, WhoAmL 94*
Weber, Robert F. 1950- *WhoAm 94*
Weber, Robert George 1939- *WhoAm 94*
Weber, Robert Maxwell 1924- *WhoAm 94*
Weber, Robert R. 1925- *WhoAmP 93*
Weber, Ronald 1934- *ConAu 43NR*
Weber, Ronald Gilbert 1916- *WhoAm 94*
Weber, Samuel 1926- *WhoAm 94*
Weber, Shirley Nash 1948- *WhoBlA 94*
Weber, Stephen Lewis 1942- *WhoAm 94*
Weber, Steven *WhoHol 92*
Weber, Steven Louis 1958- *WhoFI 94*
Weber, Susan 1941- *WhoAm 94*
Weber, Sybilla Mittell 1892-1957 *WhoAmA 93N*
Weber, Thomas Alan 1949- *WhoWest 94*
Weber, Thomas Andrew 1944- *WhoAm 94*
Weber, Thomas William 1930- *WhoAm 94, WhoScEn 94*
Weber, Vin 1952- *WhoAmP 93*
Weber, Walter Jacob, Jr. 1934- *WhoAm 94*
Weber, Wendell William 1925- *WhoAm 94*
Weber, Wilford Alexander 1939- *WhoAm 94*
Weber, Wilhelm K. 1939- *WhoWest 94*
Weber, William P. 1940- *WhoAm 94, WhoFI 94*
Weber, William Palmer 1940- *WhoWest 94*
Weber, William Philip, Jr. 1957- *WhoMW 93*
Weber, Winnie P. *WhoAmP 93*
Weber and Fields *WhoCom*
Weberman, Ben 1923- *WhoAm 94*
Weberpal, Michael Andrew 1951- *WhoAmL 94*
Webley, John d1971 *WhoHol 92*
Webley, Paul Anthony 1961- *WhoScEn 94*
Weblin, Harold 1930- *Who 94*
Webster, Aen Walker 1957- *WhoAmP 93*
Webster, Al *WhoHol 92*
Webster, Alan Brunskill 1918- *Who 94, WrDr 94*
Webster, Albert Knickerbocker 1937- *WhoAm 94*
Webster, Alec 1934- *Who 94*
Webster, Alexander James 1925- *WhoScEn 94*
Webster, Archibald Wilson 1897- *WhAm 10*
Webster, Augusta 1837-1894 *BlmGWL*
Webster, Ben d1947 *WhoHol 92*
Webster, Ben 1909-1973 *AfrAmAl 6*
Webster, Bennett Addison 1923- *WhoAmP 93*
Webster, Bethuel Matthew 1900-1989 *WhAm 10*
Webster, Bryan Courtney 1931- *Who 94*
Webster, Burnice Hoyle 1910-1991 *WhAm 10*
Webster, Byron *WhoHol 92*
Webster, Carl M. 1956- *WhoIns 94*
Webster, Carrie Lee 1966- *WhoAmP 93*
Webster, Cecil Ray 1954- *WhoBlA 94*
Webster, Charles *Who 94*
Webster, Charles 1936- *IntWW 93, WhoBlA 94*
Webster, Charles M. *WhoAmP 93*
Webster, Charles S. d1983 *WhoHol 92*
Webster, Cyril Charles 1909- *Who 94*
Webster, Daniel 1782-1852 *HisWorL [port]*
Webster, Daniel 1949- *WhoAmP 93*
Webster, Daniel Robert 1945- *WhoAm 94*
Webster, David 1931- *Who 94*
Webster, David (Lumsden) 1903-1971 *NewGrDO*
Webster, David A. 1948- *WhoAm 94*
Webster, David Arthur 1937- *WhoAm 94*
Webster, David MacLaren 1937- *Who 94*
Webster, Derek Adrian 1927- *Who 94*
Webster, DeWitt T., Jr. 1932- *WhoBlA 94*
Webster, Donald Everett 1901- *WhoWest 94*
Webster, Douglas Peter 1957- *WhoMW 93*
Webster, Edgar Lewis 1941- *WhoAm 94*
Webster, Edward William 1922- *WhoAm 94, WhoScEn 94*
Webster, Elroy *WhoAm 94, WhoFI 94*
Webster, Ernest 1923- *WrDr 94*
Webster, F(rederick) A(nnesley) M(itchell) 1886- *EncSF 93*
Webster, Frederick Elmer, Jr. 1937- *WhoAm 94*
Webster, Gary Dean 1934- *WhoWest 94*
Webster, George 1797-1864 *DcNaB MP*
Webster, George Drury 1921- *WhoAm 94, WhoAmL 94, WhoFI 94*
Webster, H. T. 1885-1952 *WhoAmA 93N*
Webster, Henry deForest 1927- *WhoAm 94, WhoScEn 94*
Webster, Henry George 1917- *Who 94*
Webster, Hugh d1986 *WhoHol 92*
Webster, Ian Stevenson 1925- *Who 94*
Webster, Isabel Gates 1931- *WhoBlA 94*
Webster, James c. 1743-1781 *WhAmRev*
Webster, James 1942- *NewGrDO*
Webster, James Carmody 1938- *WhoAmP 93*
Webster, James Douglas 1940- *WhoAmP 93*
Webster, James Randolph, Jr. 1931- *WhoAm 94*
Webster, Jan 1924- *WrDr 94*
Webster, Janice Helen 1944- *Who 94*
Webster, Jean 1876-1916 *BlmGWL*
Webster, Jeffery Norman 1954- *WhoScEn 94*
Webster, Jeffrey Leon 1941- *WhoMW 93*
Webster, Jerry Lynn 1950- *WhoAmP 93*
Webster, John 1578-1632 *BlmGEL*
Webster, John 1579?-c. 1634 *IntDcT 2*
Webster, John (Morrison) 1932- *Who 94*
Webster, John Alexander R. *Who 94*
Webster, John Chas 1944- *WhoWest 94*
Webster, John E., Jr. 1938- *WhoAmP 93*
Webster, John Goodwin 1932- *WhoAm 94, WhoScEn 94*
Webster, John Kimball 1934- *WhoAm 94, WhoFI 94*
Webster, John Kingsley Ohl, II 1950- *WhoFI 94, WhoWest 94*
Webster, John Lawrence Harvey 1913- *Who 94*
Webster, John M. 1936- *WhoWest 94*
Webster, John Robert 1916- *WhoScEn 94*
Webster, John Roger 1926- *Who 94*
Webster, John Rouse d1993 *NewYTBS 93*
Webster, John W., III 1961- *WhoBlA 94*
Webster, Keith Edward 1935- *Who 94*
Webster, Larry 1930- *WhoAmA 93*
Webster, Larry Russell 1930- *WhoAm 94*
Webster, Lee Sydney 1963- *WhoFI 94*
Webster, Leonard Irell 1965- *WhoBlA 94*
Webster, Lesley Douglass 1949- *WhoBlA 94*
Webster, Leslie Tillotson, Jr. 1926- *WhoAm 94*
Webster, Lillian d1920 *WhoHol 92*
Webster, Lois Shand 1929- *WhoFI 94, WhoScEn 94*
Webster, Lonnie 1922- *WhoBlA 94*
Webster, Lucile *WhoHol 92*
Webster, Margaret Clamser 1930- *WhoFI 94*
Webster, Marvin Nathaniel 1952- *WhoBlA 94*
Webster, Mary Clark 1947- *WhoAmP 93*
Webster, Mary Morison 1894-1980 *BlmGWL*
Webster, Melville Jay, III 1944- *WhoMW 93*
Webster, Merlyn Hugh, Jr. 1946- *WhoScEn 94, WhoWest 94*
Webster, Michael *Who 94*
Webster, (Richard) Michael (Otley) 1942- *Who 94*
Webster, Michael George Thomas 1920- *Who 94*
Webster, Michael Jay 1963- *WhoFI 94*
Webster, Niambi Dyanne *WhoBlA 94*
Webster, Noah 1758-1843 *AmSocL*
Webster, Noah 1928- *WrDr 94*
Webster, Norman Eric 1941- *WhoAm 94*
Webster, Norman William 1920- *WrDr 94*
Webster, Owen Wright 1929- *WhoScEn 94*
Webster, Paige Virginia Roberson 1962- *WhoMW 93*
Webster, Patrick 1928- *Who 94*
Webster, Peter (Edlin) 1924- *Who 94*
Webster, Peter Bridgman 1941- *WhoAmL 94*
Webster, Peter David 1949- *WhoAmL 94*
Webster, R.A. 1933- *IntMPA 94*
Webster, Ralph Terrence 1922- *WhoWest 94*
Webster, Raymond Earl 1948- *WhoScEn 94*
Webster, Reginald Howard 1910-1990 *WhAm 10*
Webster, Rex 1918-1989 *WhAm 10*
Webster, Robert David 1938- *WhoAm 94*
Webster, Robert Gordon 1932- *Who 94*
Webster, Robert Kenly 1933- *WhoAm 94*
Webster, Robert Louis 1959- *WhoFI 94*
Webster, Robert N. *EncSF 93*
Webster, Robin Welander 1956- *WhoWest 94*
Webster, Ronald Arthur 1938- *WhoAmP 93*
Webster, Ronald B. 1942- *WhoAm 94*
Webster, Ronald D. 1949- *WhoFI 94*
Webster, Sally 1938- *ConAu 140*
Webster, Sally (Sara B.) 1938- *WhoAmA 93*
Webster, Sharon B. 1937- *WhoFI 94*
Webster, Stanley B. 1929- *WhoAmP 93*
Webster, Stephen W. 1943- *WhoAmP 93*
Webster, Stokely 1912- *WhoAmA 93*
Webster, Susan Jean 1946- *WhoMW 93*
Webster, Theodore *WhoBlA 94*
Webster, Thomas Glenn 1924- *WhoAm 94*
Webster, William H. 1924- *WhoAmP 93*
Webster, William H. 1946- *WhoBlA 94*
Webster, William Hedgcock 1924- *IntWW 93, WhoAm 94*
Webster, William L. *WhoAmP 93*
Webster, Winston Roosevelt 1943- *WhoBlA 94*
Wechmar, Rudiger Baron Von 1923- *IntWW 93*
Wechsberg, Manfred Ingo 1940- *WhoScEn 94*
Wechsler, Herman J. 1904-1976 *WhoAmA 93N*
Wechsler, Alfred Elliot 1934- *WhoAm 94, WhoFI 94*
Wechsler, Arnold L. 1943- *WhoFI 94*
Wechsler, Henry 1932- *WhoAm 94*
Wechsler, Herbert 1909- *WhoAm 94*
Wechsler, Judith Glatzer 1940- *ConAu 42NR, WhoAm 94, WhoAmA 93*
Wechsler, Mary Heyrman 1948- *WhoAmL 94, WhoWest 94*
Wechsler, Max d1993 *NewYTBS 93*
Wechsler, Raymond Henry 1945- *WhoAm 94, WhoFI 94*
Wechsler, Sergio 1944- *WhoMW 93*
Wechsler, Susan 1943- *WhoAmA 93*
Wecht, Cyril H. 1931- *WhoAmP 93*
Wechter, Angela Pirolli 1937- *WhoAmP 93*
Wechter, Clari Ann 1953- *WhoFI 94, WhoMW 93*

Wechter, Ira Martin 1947- WhoFI 94
Wechter, Norman Robert 1926- WhoMW 93
Wechter, Vivienne Thaul DrAPF 93, WhoAm 94, WhoAmA 93
Wechter, William Julius 1932- WhoWest 94
Weck, Edward Alexander 1952- WhoFI 94
Weck, Kristin Willa 1959- WhoFI 94, WhoMW 93
Weckel, Arthur R. d1993 NewYTBS 93
Wecker, Denese 1931- WhoWest 94
Wecker, Walter Andre 1895- WhAm 10
Weckerlin, Jean-Baptiste (Theodore) 1821-1910 NewGrDO
Weckesser, Ernest Prosper, Jr. 1933- WhoAm 94
Weckmann-Munoz, Luis 1923- IntWW 93
Weckstein, Richard Selig 1924- WhoAm 94
Weclew, Robert George 1911- WhoAm 94
Weclew, Victor T. 1916- WhoAm 94
Wedd, George Morton 1930- Who 94
Wedde, Ian 1946- WrDr 94
Weddell, James 1787-1834 WhWE
Wedderburn Who 94
Wedderburn, Alexander 1733-1805 WhAmRev
Wedderburn, Andrew John Alexander O. Who 94
Wedderburn, Dorothy Enid Cole 1925- Who 94
Wedderburn Of Charlton, Baron 1927- IntWW 93, Who 94
Wedderspoon, Alexander Gillan 1931- Who 94
Weddig, Lee John 1935- WhoAm 94
Weddige, Emil A. 1907- WhoAmA 93
Weddige, Emil Albert 1907- WhoMW 93
Wedding, Charles Randolph 1934- WhoAm 94
Wedding, Walter Joseph 1952- WhoAmA 93
Weddington, Elaine 1963- WhoBlA 94
Weddington, Rachel Thomas 1917- WhoBlA 94
Weddington, Sarah Ragle 1945- WhoAm 94, WhoAmL 94, WhoAmP 93
Weddington, Wayne P., Jr. 1936- WhoBlA 94
Weddington, Wilburn Harold, Sr. 1924- WhoBlA 94
Weddle, Judith Ann 1944- WhoWest 94
Weddle, Rebecca Rae 1942- WhoMW 93
Weddle, Stephen Shields 1938- WhoAm 94
Wedeen, Marvin Meyer 1926- WhoAm 94
Wedega, Alice 1905- Who 94
Wedekind, Erika 1869-1944 NewGrDO
Wedekind, (Benjamin) Frank(lin) 1864-1918 IntDcT 2 [port], NewGrDO
Wedel, Cynthia Clark 1908-1986 DcAmReB 2
Wedel, Janine (R.) 1957- WrDr 94
Wedel, John Mark 1953- WhoAmP 93
Wedel, Millie Redmond 1939- WhoWest 94
Wedel, Paul George 1927- WhoAm 94
Wedel, Victor James 1950- WhoMW 93
Wedel, Waldo Rudolph 1908- WhoAm 94
Wedell, Eberhard George 1927- WrDr 94
Wedell, (Eberhard Arthur Otto) George 1927- Who 94
Wedemeier, Robert Gorham 1942- WhoFI 94, WhoWest 94
Wedemeyer, Albert Coady 1897-1989 WhAm 10
Wedemeyer, Erich Hans 1927- WhoScEn 94
Wedemeyer, Herman 1924- WhoHol 92
Wedepohl, Leonhard M. 1933- WhoAm 94, WhoScEn 94
Weder, Erwin Henry 1904-1992 WhAm 10
Wedge, Dorothy Ann 1935- WhoAm 94
Wedge, Jimmy Joe 1942- WhoAmP 93
Wedge, Scott William 1961- WhoFI 94
Wedge, Thomas Willim 1943- WhoMW 93
Wedgelock, Colin EncSF 93
Wedgeworth, Ann WhoAm 94
Wedgeworth, Ann 1934- WhoHol 92
Wedgeworth, Ann 1935- IntMPA 94
Wedgeworth, Robert 1937- WhoAm 94
Wedgeworth, Robert, Jr. 1937- WhoBlA 94
Wedgle, Richard Jay 1951- WhoAmL 94
Wedgwood BlmGEL
Wedgwood, Baron 1954- Who 94
Wedgwood, C(icely) V(eronica) 1910- WrDr 94
Wedgwood, John Alleyne 1920- Who 94
Wedgwood, Josiah 1730-1795 BlmGEL
Wedgwood, (Hugo) Martin 1933- Who 94
Wedgwood, Ruth WhoAmL 94
Wedgwood, Thomas 1771-1805 BlmGEL
Wedgwood, Veronica Who 94
Wedgwood, (Cicely) Veronica 1910- IntWW 93, Who 94
Wedin, Bernard d1948 WhoHol 92
Wedlock, Eldon Dyment, Jr. 1942- WhoAmL 94
Wedner, H. James 1941- WhoMW 93
Wedoff, Robert John 1963- WhoMW 93
Wedow, David Walter 1953- WhoFI 94
Wedow, Rudy 1906-1965 WhoAmA 93N
Weeber, Gretchen WhoAmA 93N
Wee Chong Jin 1917- IntWW 93, Who 94
Weed, Edward Reilly 1940- WhoFI 94
Weed, Frederic Augustus 1918- WhoWest 94
Weed, Herbert M. 1921-1989 WhAm 10
Weed, Ithamar Dryden 1914- WhoAm 94
Weed, Maurice James 1912- WhoAm 94
Weed, Ronald De Vern 1931- WhoScEn 94, WhoWest 94
Weed, Ronald Leaming 1942- WhoMW 93
Weede, James Russell 1945- WhoMW 93
Weede, Robert 1903-1972 NewGrDO
Weeden, Craig DrAPF 93
Weeden, Norman Dexter 1898- WhAm 10
Weeden, Timothy L. 1951- WhoAmP 93, WhoMW 93
Weeding, Cecil 1934- WhoAmP 93
Weedman, Kenneth Russell 1939- WhoAmA 93
Weedn, Trish Throckmorton 1950- WhoAmP 93
Weedon, Alan Charles 1951- WhoAm 94
Weedon, Basil Charles Leicester 1923- IntWW 93, Who 94
Weedon, Chris 1952- BlmGWL
Weedon, Dudley William 1920- Who 94
Weedon, George 1734-1793 AmRev, WhAmRev
Weege, William WhoAmA 93
Weekes, Ambrose Walter Marcus 1919- Who 94
Weekes, Mark K. Who 94
Weekes, Martin Edward 1933- WhoBlA 94
Weekes, Philip Gordon 1920- Who 94
Weekes, Shirley Marie 1917- WhoAmA 93
Weekes, Trevor C. 1940- WhoScEn 94
Wee Kim Wee 1915- IntWW 93, Who 94
Weekley, Frederick Clay, Jr. 1939- WhoAm 94
Weekley, Gene Rolland, Jr. 1940- WhoFI 94
Weekley, George McClellan, II 1948- WhoFI 94
Weekley, Ian (George) 1933- EncSF 93
Weekley, Richard J. DrAPF 93
Weekly, James Keith 1933- WhoAm 94
Weekly, John William 1931- WhoAm 94, WhoFI 94, WhoMW 93
Weeks, Alan 1948- WhoHol 92
Weeks, Alan Frederick 1923- Who 94
Weeks, Albert Loren 1923- WhoAm 94
Weeks, Anson d1969 WhoHol 92
Weeks, Arthur Andrew 1914- WhoAm 94, WhoAmL 94
Weeks, Barbara 1913- WhoHol 92
Weeks, Brigitte 1943- WhoAm 94
Weeks, Charles Carson 1914-1991 WhAm 10
Weeks, Daniel J. DrAPF 93
Weeks, David Frank 1926- WhoAm 94
Weeks, David I. 1916- WhoIns 94
Weeks, David Jamison 1950- WhoScEn 94
Weeks, Deborah Redd 1947- WhoBlA 94
Weeks, Dennis Alan 1943- WhoWest 94
Weeks, Donna Joyce 1953- WhoAmL 94
Weeks, Dorothy Mae 1924- WhoWest 94
Weeks, Edward Augustus 1898-1989 WhAm 10
Weeks, Edward Augustus, Jr. 1898-1989 DcLB 137 [port]
Weeks, Edward F. (Ted) WhoAmA 93
Weeks, Francis William 1916- WhoAm 94
Weeks, Gary Lynn 1936- WhoAm 94, WhoFI 94
Weeks, James (Darrell Northrup) 1922- WhoAmA 93
Weeks, James Page 1946- WhoMW 93
Weeks, James W. 1937- WhoAmP 93
Weeks, Janet H. WhoAmP 93
Weeks, Janet Healy 1932- WhoAmL 94
Weeks, Jeffrey 1945- GayLL, WrDr 94
Weeks, Jimmie Ray WhoHol 92
Weeks, John David 1943- WhoAm 94, WhoScEn 94
Weeks, John F. 1932- WhoAmP 93
Weeks, John F. 1941- ConAu 141
Weeks, John Henry 1938- Who 94
Weeks, John Randel, IV 1927- WhoScEn 94
Weeks, John Robert 1944- WhoAm 94
Weeks, Joseph Preble 1937- WhoAmP 93
Weeks, Julie Rae 1957- WhoFI 94
Weeks, Leo Rosco 1903-1977 WhoAmA 93N
Weeks, Lloyd F. 1932- WhoAmP 93
Weeks, M. J. 1942- WhoFI 94, WhoMW 93
Weeks, Marcia Gail 1938- WhoAmP 93
Weeks, Marion d1968 WhoHol 92
Weeks, Morris T., Jr. d1993 NewYTBS 93
Weeks, Oliver Douglas 1896- WhAm 10
Weeks, Paul Martin 1932- WhoAm 94
Weeks, Ramona Martinez DrAPF 93
Weeks, Ranny d1979 WhoHol 92
Weeks, Renee Jones 1948- WhoBlA 94
Weeks, Richard Ralph 1932- WhoAm 94
Weeks, Robert Andrew 1924- WhoAm 94
Weeks, Robert Earl 1925- WhoMW 93
Weeks, Robert Lewis DrAPF 93
Weeks, Roland, Jr. 1936- WhoAm 94
Weeks, Sherry Lee Cranford 1944- WhoAm 94
Weeks, Steven Wiley 1950- WhoAm 94, WhoAmL 94
Weeks, Thomas J. 1941- WhoScEn 94
Weeks, Walter d1961 WhoHol 92
Weeks, Walter LeRoy 1923- WhoAm 94
Weeks, Wilford Frank 1929- WhoAm 94, WhoWest 94
Weeks-Calander, Susan K. 1955- WhoMW 93
Weems, Carrie Mae WhoAmA 93
Weems, Carrie Mae 1953- AfrAmAl 6
Weems, Damon Louis 1946- WhoAmL 94
Weems, Debbie d1978 WhoHol 92
Weems, Frank Taylor 1924- WhAm 10
Weems, John Edward 1924- WrDr 94
Weems, Katharine Lane 1899-1989 WhAm 10
Weems, Katherine Lane 1899- WhoAmA 93N
Weems, Luther B. 1944- WhoBlA 94
Weems, Robert Cicero 1910- WhoAm 94
Weems, Ted d1963 WhoHol 92
Weems, Vernon Eugene, Jr. 1948- WhoBlA 94
Weeple, Edward John 1945- Who 94
Weeramantry, Christopher Gregory 1926- IntWW 93
Weergang, Alida 1941- WhoAmP 93
Weerth, Georg 1822-1856 DcLB 129 [port]
Weertman, Johannes 1925- WhoAm 94, WhoScEn 94
Weertman, Julia Randall 1926- WhoAm 94
Weerts, Richard Kenneth 1928- WhoMW 93
Weese, Benjamin Horace 1929- WhoAm 94
Weese, Cynthia Rogers 1940- WhoAm 94
Weese, Donald B. 1946- WhoAmP 93
Weese, Harry M. 1915- IntWW 93
Weese, Harry Mohr 1915- WhoAm 94
Weese, Norris Keith 1939- WhoWest 94
Weese, Samuel H. 1935- WhoAm 94, WhoIns 94
Weesner, Betty Jean 1926- WhoMW 93
Weesner, Lowell Michael 1949- WhoWest 94
Weetch, Kenneth Thomas 1933- Who 94
Wefald, Jon 1937- WhoMW 93
Wefald, Robert Ovrom 1942- WhoAmP 93
Wefler, Wilson Daniel 1927- WhoMW 93
Weg, Frank A. 1927- WhoIns 94
Weg, John Gerard 1934- WhoAm 94, WhoMW 93, WhoScEn 94
Wege, Peter M. WhoAm 94, WhoFI 94
Wegelin, Christof (Andreas) 1911- WrDr 94
Wegeman, Alvin Paul, Jr. 1964- WhoWest 94
Wegener, Alfred L. 1880-1930 WorScD
Wegener, Alfred Lothar 1880-1930 WhWE
Wegener, Beverly Joan 1956- WhoFI 94
Wegener, Mark Douglas 1948- WhoAm 94
Wegener, Paul d1948 WhoHol 92
Wegenke, Gary 1938- WhoMW 93
Wegge, Leon Louis Francois 1933- WhoAm 94, WhoWest 94
Weggeland, Ted WhoAmP 93
Wegher, Pearl Ella 1911- WhoWest 94
Weghorst, Dwight Edward 1948- WhoMW 93
Wegloski, Daniel Joseph 1949-1988 WhAm 10
Weglyn, Michi Nishiura 1926- WhoAsA 94
Wegman, Harold Hugh 1916- WhoAm 94
Wegman, Myron Ezra 1908- WhoAm 94
Wegman, Steven Michael 1953- WhoMW 93
Wegman, William 1943- WhoAmA 93
Wegman, William George 1943- WhoAm 94
Wegman, William Leo 1938- WhoAmL 94, WhoMW 93
Wegmann, Cynthia Anne 1949- WhoAmL 94
Wegmann, George J. 1901- WhoIns 94
Wegmann, M. K. 1948- WhoAmA 93
Wegmann, Robert Gene 1938- WhoAm 94
Wegner, Dale Dean, Jr. 1957- WhoMW 93
Wegner, Gary Alan 1944- WhoAm 94, WhoScEn 94
Wegner, Helmuth Adalbert 1917- WhoAm 94
Wegner, James Darwin 1955- WhoAmL 94
Wegner, Judith Welch 1950- WhoAmL 94
Wegner, Karl Heinrich 1930- WhoAm 94
Wegner, Konstanze 1938- WhoWomW 91
Wegner, Nadene R. 1950- WhoAmA 93
Wegner, Robert E. DrAPF 93
Wegner, Samuel Joseph 1952- WhoAm 94
Wegner, Steven Gaird 1958- WhoAmL 94
Wegrzyn, Malgorzata WhoWomW 91
Wegscheid, Darril 1944- WhoAmP 93
Wegst, Audrey V. 1934- WhoScEn 94
Wegst, Walter Frederick, Jr. 1934- WhoWest 94
Weguelin, Thomas 1885- WhoHol 92
Weh, Allen Edward 1942- WhoWest 94
Wehage, Rodger John 1949- WhoAmP 93
Wehde, Albert Edward 1935- WhoAmL 94
Wehde, Roger Allan 1951- WhoMW 93
Weheba, Abdulsalam Mohamad 1930- WhoScEn 94
Wehen, Joy DeWeese 1936- WrDr 94
Wehle, John Louis 1916- WhoAm 94
Wehling, Bob d1983 WhoHol 92
Wehling, Fred Lowell 1963- WhoWest 94
Wehling, Robert Louis 1938- WhoAm 94, WhoMW 93
Wehling, Thomas Matthew 1951- WhoMW 93
Wehmeier, Helge H. WhoAm 94, WhoFI 94, WhoScEn 94
Wehmer, Sally Bell 1934- WhoMW 93
Wehmeyer, Josephine Mont 1916- WhoHisp 94
Wehmeyer, Keith Reynolds 1959- WhoMW 93
Wehmeyer, Victor William 1904- WhoAmP 93
Wehmhoefer, Jerry L. 1945- WhoMW 93
Wehmhoefer, Richard Allen 1951- WhoAmL 94, WhoWest 94
Wehner, Alfred Peter 1926- WhoAm 94, WhoWest 94
Wehner, Dwight Lynn 1947- WhoMW 93
Wehner, Edward Adam WhoFI 94
Wehner, Henry Otto, III 1942- WhoScEn 94
Wehner, Patricia 1956- WhoMW 93
Wehofer, Steven Robert 1962- WhoMW 93
Wehr, Paul Adam 1914-1973 WhoAmA 93N
Wehr, Wesley Conrad 1929- WhoAmA 93
Wehrbein, Roger R. 1938- WhoAmP 93
Wehrbein, Roger Ralph 1938- WhoMW 93
Wehrbein, William Mead 1948- WhoMW 93
Wehrberger, Klaus Herbert 1959- WhoScEn 94
Wehrer, Charles Siecke 1914- WhoAm 94
Wehring, Bernard William 1937- WhoAm 94, WhoScEn 94
Wehrle, Leroy Snyder 1932- WhoAm 94
Wehrle, Martha Gaines 1925- WhoAm 94, WhoAmP 93
Wehrli, Jonathan Allen 1962- WhoFI 94
Wehrli, Werner 1892-1944 NewGrDO
Wehrly, Joseph Malachi 1915- WhoWest 94
Wehrstein, Karen EncSF 93
Wehrwein, Austin Carl 1916- WhoMW 93
Wei, Anthony Yueh-shan 1933- WhoAsA 94
Wei, Benjamin Min 1930- WhoAm 94, WhoAsA 94
Wei, Chao Hui 1956- WhoAsA 94
Wei, Gaoyuan 1961- WhoScEn 94
Wei, I-Yuan 1940- WhoScEn 94
Wei, James 1930- WhoAm 94, WhoAsA 94, WhoScEn 94
Wei, Jen Yu 1938- WhoWest 94
Wei, Kuo-Yen 1953- WhoAsA 94
Wei, Lester Yeehow 1944- WhoMW 93
Wei, Musheng 1948- WhoScEn 94
Wei, Robert 1939- WhoAsA 94
Wei, Robert Peh-Ying 1931- WhoScEn 94
Wei, Susanna 1946- WhoAsA 94
Wei, Victor Keh 1954- WhoScEn 94
Wei, Wei 1952- WhoAsA 94
Wei, Wei-Zen 1951- WhoAsA 94
Wei, William 1948- WhoAsA 94
Wei, William L. 1960- WhoMW 93
Wei, William Wu-Shyong 1940- WhoAsA 94
Wei, Yau-Huei 1952- WhoScEn 94
Wei, Yen 1957- WhoAsA 94
Weiant, William Morrow 1938- WhoAm 94, WhoFI 94
Wei Baowen WhoPRCh 91
Weibel, Gladys Helen 1921- WhoAmP 93

Weibel, Thomas Michael 1951- *WhoAmL 94*
Weibell, Fred John 1927- *WhoWest 94*
Weible, Robert A. 1953- *WhoAm 94*
Weich, Ronald H. 1959- *WhoAmL 94*
Wei Chengdong 1928- *WhoPRCh 91 [port]*
Weichert, Dieter Horst 1932- *WhoAm 94, WhoScEn 94*
Weichsel, Elizabeth *NewGrDO*
Weichselbaum, Ralph R. *WhoScEn 94*
Wei Chunshu 1922- *IntWW 93, WhoPRCh 91 [port]*
Weick, Fred E. d1993 *NewYTBS 93 [port]*
Weicker, Jack Edward 1924- *WhoMW 93*
Weicker, Lowell P., Jr. 1931- *CurBio 93 [port]*
Weicker, Lowell Palmer, Jr. 1931- *IntWW 93, WhoAm 94, WhoAmP 93*
Weickhardt, George Geoffrey 1944- *WhoAm 94, WhoAmL 94*
Weida, George Albert F. 1936- *WhoWest 94*
Weida, Lewis Dixon 1924- *WhoFI 94*
Weida, William J. 1942- *WrDr 94*
Weide, William Wolfe 1923- *WhoAm 94, WhoFI 94, WhoWest 94*
Weidemann, Celia Jean 1942- *WhoAm 94*
Weidemann, Friedrich 1871-1919 *NewGrDO*
Weidemeyer, Carleton Lloyd 1933- *WhoAmL 94, WhoFI 94*
Weidenaar, Dennis Jay 1936- *WhoAm 94, WhoFI 94*
Weidenaar, Reynold Henry 1915-1985 *WhoAmA 93N*
Weidenbaum, Murray 1927- *WrDr 94*
Weidenbaum, Murray Lew 1927- *IntWW 93, Who 94, WhoAm 94, WhoAmP 93, WhoFI 94*
Weidenfeld, Baron 1919- *IntWW 93, Who 94*
Weidenfeld, Edward Lee 1943- *WhoAm 94*
Weidenfeld, Werner 1947- *IntWW 93*
Weidenfeller, Anne Marie 1965- *WhoAmL 94*
Weidenhamer, Jeffrey David 1957- *WhoMW 93*
Weidenhofer, Neal 1940- *WhoWest 94*
Weidensaul, Thomas Craig 1939- *WhoAm 94*
Weidenthal, Maurice David 1925- *WhoAm 94*
Weider, John Richard 1946- *WhoAmL 94*
Wei Desen *WhoPRCh 91*
Weidinger, Christine *IntWW 93*
Weidinger, Christine 1946- *NewGrDO*
Weidler, Virginia d1968 *WhoHol 92*
Weidlinger, Paul 1914- *IntWW 93, WhoAm 94*
Weidman, Carole Louise 1955- *WhoAmL 94*
Weidman, Charles d1975 *WhoHol 92*
Weidman, Dick 1940- *WhoAmP 93*
Weidman, Harold D. 1929- *WhoAmP 93*
Weidman, Hazel Hitson 1923- *WhoAm 94*
Weidman, Jeffrey 1945- *WhoAmA 93, WhoMW 93*
Weidman, Jerome *DrAPF 93*
Weidman, Jerome 1913- *ConDr 93, WhoAm 94, WrDr 94*
Weidman, Richard 1942- *WhoAmL 94*
Weidmann, Josef 1742-1810 *NewGrDO*
Weidmann, Paul 1747-1810 *NewGrDO*
Weidner, Charles Kenneth 1904- *WhAm 10*
Weidner, Donald J. 1945- *WhoScEn 94*
Weidner, Edward William 1921- *WhoAm 94*
Weidner, M. Robert, III 1956- *WhoMW 93*
Weidner, Marilyn Kemp 1928- *WhoAmA 93*
Weidner, Marilyn Susan 1960- *WhoMW 93*
Weidner, Marvin Detweiler 1911- *WhoAmP 93*
Weidner, Mary Elizabeth 1950- *WhoAmA 93*
Weidner, Richard Tilghman 1921- *WhoAm 94*
Weidner, Ronald Dale 1954- *WhoMW 93*
Weidner, Roswell Theodore 1911- *WhoAm 94, WhoAmA 93*
Wei Dong *WhoPRCh 91*
Weidt, Lucie c.1880-1940 *NewGrDO*
Weier, T. Elliott 1903-1991 *WhAm 10*
Weierstall, Richard Paul 1942- *WhoAm 94*
Weierstrass, Karl *WorScD*
Wei Fuhai 1930- *WhoPRCh 91 [port]*
Wei Fulin *WhoPRCh 91*
Weigall, Peter Raymond 1922- *Who 94*
Weigand, Herbert Michael 1951- *WhoAmA 93*
'Veigand, James Gary 1935- *WhoAm 94*
·igand, Jan Christine 1952- *hoMW 93*
Weigand, Richard G. 1938- *WhoAmP 93*
Weigand, Tory Andrew 1960- *WhoAmL 94*
Weigand, William Keith 1937- *WhoAm 94, WhoWest 94*
Weigel, Gustave 1906-1964 *DcAmReB 2*
Weigel, Helene d1971 *WhoHol 92*
Weigel, Henry Donald 1964- *WhoScEn 94*
Weigel, John J. 1932- *WhoAm 94, WhoAmL 94*
Weigel, Keith W. *WhoAmP 93*
Weigel, Lucinda Mae 1965- *WhoMW 93*
Weigel, Maure Leo 1951- *WhoMW 93*
Weigel, Ollie J. 1922- *WhoMW 93, WhoScEn 94*
Weigel, Paul d1951 *WhoHol 92*
Weigel, Paul Henry 1946- *WhoAm 94, WhoScEn 94*
Weigel, Rainer R. 1933- *WhoAm 94*
Weigel, Stanley Alexander 1905- *WhoAm 94, WhoWest 94*
Weigel, Teri *WhoHol 92*
Weigel, Tom *DrAPF 93*
Weigel, William Frederick 1923-1990 *WhAm 10*
Weigel, William H. 1949- *WhoAmL 94*
Weigend, Guido Gustav 1920- *WhoAm 94, WhoWest 94*
Weiger, John George 1933- *WhoAm 94*
Weigert, Andrew Joseph 1934- *WhoMW 93*
Weigh, Brian 1926- *Who 94*
Weighardt, Paul 1897- *WhAm 10*
Weighell, Sidney 1922- *Who 94*
Weighill, Robert Harold George 1920- *Who 94*
Weight, Carel Victor Morlais 1908- *IntWW 93, Who 94*
Weight, George Dale 1934- *WhoAm 94, WhoFI 94, WhoWest 94*
Weight, Michael Anthony 1940- *WhoAmL 94*
Weightman, Donald Sharp 1949- *WhoAmL 94*
Weightman, Judy Mae 1941- *WhoAmL 94, WhoWest 94*
Weigl, Bruce *DrAPF 93*
Weigl, Etta Ruth *DrAPF 93*
Weigl, Joseph 1766-1846 *NewGrDO*
Weigl, Thaddaus 1776-1844 *NewGrDO*
Weigle, Luther Allan 1880-1976 *DcAmReB 2*
Weigle, Rebecca A. 1953- *WhoMW 93*
Weigle, Robert Edward 1927- *WhoScEn 94*
Weigle, William Oliver 1927- *WhoAm 94, WhoWest 94*
Weigmann, Hans-Dietrich H. 1930- *WhoScEn 94*
Weigner, Brent James 1949- *WhoWest 94*
Weih, Rolf d1969 *WhoHol 92*
Weihaupt, John George 1930- *WhoAm 94, WhoWest 94*
Weihe, Clifton Meyer 1916- *WhoWest 94*
Weihing, John 1921- *WhoAmP 93*
Weihing, John Lawson 1921 *WhoMW 93*
Weihrich, Heinz *WhoAm 94*
Weihs, Daniel 1942- *WhoScEn 94*
Weihs, Erika 1917- *WhoAmA 93*
Wei Jiankun *WhoPRCh 91*
Wei Jianxing 1931- *IntWW 93, WhoPRCh 91 [port]*
Wei Jinshan 1927- *WhoPRCh 91 [port]*
Wei Jinshan, Vice-Adm. 1927- *IntWW 93*
Wei Jixin 1950- *WhoPRCh 91 [port]*
Wei Jizhong *WhoPRCh 91*
Wei Junjie *WhoPRCh 91*
Wei Junyi 1917- *BlmGWL, WhoPRCh 91 [port]*
Weik, Thomas Wilbur 1942- *WhoFI 94*
Weikart, David Powell 1931- *WhoAm 94, WhoMW 93*
Weikel, Malcolm Keith 1938- *WhoMW 93*
Weikert, Jerard Lee 1929- *WhoMW 93*
Weikl, Bernd 1942- *IntWW 93, NewGrDO*
Weiksner, Sandra S. 1945- *WhoAm 94, WhoAmL 94*
Weil, Andrew (Thomas) 1942- *ConAu 43NR*
Weil, Cass Sargent 1946- *WhoAmL 94*
Weil, Daniel Wilkus 1940- *WhoAmL 94*
Weil, Donald Wallace 1923- *WhoAm 94*
Weil, Edward David 1928- *WhoScEn 94*
Weil, Ernst *WhoAm 94, WhoFI 94*
Weil, Frank A. 1931- *WhoAm 94*
Weil, Fred B. 1942- *WhoAmL 94*
Weil, Gilbert Harry 1912- *WhoAm 94*
Weil, Harold G. 1942- *WhoAmP 93*
Weil, Harry d1974 *WhoHol 92*
Weil, Herman 1905- *WhoAm 94*
Weil, Hermann 1876-1949 *NewGrDO*
Weil, Irwin 1928- *WhoAm 94*
Weil, James L. *DrAPF 93*
Weil, Jeffrey George 1951- *WhoAm 94, WhoAmL 94*
Weil, Jerry *WhoAm 94*
Weil, Jiri 1900-1959 *ConAu 141*
Weil, John Albert 1952- *WhoAmL 94*
Weil, John Ashley 1929- *WhoAm 94*
Weil, John David 1947- *WhoAm 94*
Weil, John William 1928- *WhoAm 94*
Weil, Kurt Hermann 1895- *WhAm 10*
Weil, Leon Jerome 1927- *WhoAm 94, WhoAmP 93*
Weil, Leonard 1922- *WhoAm 94*
Weil, Lisl *WhoAmA 93*
Weil, Louis Arthur, Jr. 1905- *WhoAm 94*
Weil, Louis Arthur, III 1941- *WhoAm 94*
Weil, Max Harry 1927- *WhoAm 94, WhoScEn 94*
Weil, Michael Scott 1955- *WhoMW 93*
Weil, Myron 1918- *WhoAm 94*
Weil, Paul P. 1936- *WhoAm 94, WhoAmL 94*
Weil, Peter Henry 1933- *WhoAm 94*
Weil, Raymond 1923- *IntWW 93*
Weil, Raymond Richard 1948- *WhoAm 94*
Weil, Robert E. *WhoHol 92*
Weil, Robert Irving 1922- *WhoAmL 94, WhoWest 94*
Weil, Robert L. 1932- *WhoBlA 94*
Weil, Rolf Alfred 1921- *WhoAm 94, WhoMW 93*
Weil, Roman Lee 1940- *WhoAm 94*
Weil, Sidney, Jr. 1926- *WhoAmP 93*
Weil, Simone 1909-1943 *BlmGWL, EncEth*
Weil, Stephen E. 1928- *WhoAmA 93*
Weil, Stephen Edward 1928- *WhoAm 94*
Weil, Steven Mark 1949- *WhoWest 94*
Weil, Suzanne S. Fern 1933- *WhoWest 94*
Weil, Thomas Alexander 1930- *WhoAm 94*
Weil, Thomas P. 1932- *WhoAm 94*
Weiland, Charles Hankes 1921- *WhoAm 94*
Weiland, Galen Franklin *WhoAmP 93*
Weiland, Peter Lawrence 1956- *WhoScEn 94*
Weiland, Stephen Cass 1948- *WhoAm 94, WhoAmL 94*
Weiland, William H. 1944- *WhoAmL 94*
Weilbacher, William Manning 1928- *WhoAm 94*
Weiler, Barbara 1946- *WhoWomW 91*
Weiler, Barbara Brandt 1937- *WhoMW 93*
Weiler, Caroline Susan 1949- *WhoWest 94*
Weiler, Dennis Edward 1952- *WhoWest 94*
Weiler, Dorothy Esser 1914- *WhoWest 94*
Weiler, Gerald E. 1928- *IntMPA 94*
Weiler, Jeffry Louis 1942- *WhoAm 94, WhoAmL 94, WhoMW 93*
Weiler, Joseph Ashby 1946- *WhoAm 94*
Weiler, Joseph Flack 1943- *WhoAmA 93*
Weiler, Kurt Walter 1943- *WhoScEn 94*
Weiler, Melody M. 1947- *WhoAmA 93*
Weiler, Michael Reid 1954- *WhoIns 94*
Weiler, Paul Cronin 1939- *WhoScEn 94*
Weiler, Robert Alan 1945- *WhoMW 93*
Weiler, Scott Michael 1952- *WhoFI 94, WhoMW 93*
Weiler, Terence Gerard 1919- *Who 94*
Weilerstein, Sadie Rose 1894-1993 *ConAu 141, SmATA 75*
Weilert, Matthew Edward 1961- *WhoWest 94*
Weilert, Ronald Lee 1948- *WhoFI 94, WhoMW 93*
Weiling, Franz Joseph Bernard 1909- *WhoScEn 94*
Weill, Claudia 1947- *IntMPA 94*
Weill, Erna *WhoAmA 93*
Weill, Georges Gustave 1926- *WhoAm 94*
Weill, Hans 1933- *WhoAm 94, WhoScEn 94*
Weill, Harry, Sr. 1916- *WhoAmL 94*
Weill, Kurt (Julian) 1900-1950 *NewGrDO [port]*
Weill, Kurt Julian 1900-1950 *AmCulL*
Weill, Michel Alexandre D. *Who 94*
Weill, Richard L. 1943- *WhoAmL 94*
Weill, Samuel, Jr. 1916- *WhoAm 94, WhoFI 94, WhoWest 94*
Weill, Sandy *NewYTBS 93 [port]*
Weill, Sanford I. 1933- *IntWW 93, WhoAm 94, WhoFI 94*
Weiller, David Barry 1957- *WhoWest 94*
Weiller, Paul Annik 1933- *WhoFI 94*
Weiller, Paul-Louis 1893- *IntWW 93*
Wei Longxiang 1912- *WhoPRCh 91 [port]*
Weiman, Mark Bernard 1950- *WhoWest 94*
Weimar, Robert Alden 1950- *WhoScEn 94*
Weimer, Douglas Reid 1953- *WhoAmL 94*
Weimer, Ferne Lauraine 1950- *WhoMW 93*
Weimer, Franklin E. *WhoAmP 93*
Weimer, Maryellen 1947- *WrDr 94*
Weimer, Paul Kessler 1914- *WhoAm 94, WhoScEn 94*
Weimer, Peter Dwight 1938- *WhoAmL 94, WhoFI 94*
Weimer, Richard Paul 1947- *WhoFI 94*
Weimer, Robert Jay 1926- *WhoAm 94*
Weimers, Leigh Albert 1935- *WhoWest 94*
Wei Minghai 1921- *WhoPRCh 91 [port]*
Wei Mingyi *WhoPRCh 91*
Wei Mingyi 1924- *IntWW 93*
Wein, Alan Jerome 1941- *WhoAm 94, WhoScEn 94*
Wein, Albert W. 1915-1991 *WhoAmA 93N*
Wein, Bibi *DrAPF 93*
Wein, Howard J. 1950- *WhoAmL 94*
Weinacht, Richard Jay 1931- *WhoScEn 94*
Weinbach, Arthur Frederic 1943- *WhoFI 94*
Weinbach, Lawrence Allen 1940- *WhoAm 94, WhoFI 94*
Weinbaum, Jean 1926- *WhoAmA 93*
Weinbaum, Stanley G(rauman) 1902-1935 *EncSF 93*
Weinberg, Alvin M. 1915- *IntWW 93*
Weinberg, Alvin Martin 1915- *WhoAm 94, WhoScEn 94*
Weinberg, Barbara Bickerstaffe 1936- *WhoAmP 93*
Weinberg, Bella Rebecca 1912- *WhoAmA 93*
Weinberg, D. Mark 1952- *WhoWest 94*
Weinberg, David B. 1952- *WhoAm 94*
Weinberg, Edward 1918- *WhoAm 94*
Weinberg, Edward Brill 1945- *WhoAmL 94*
Weinberg, Elaine Joseph 1929- *WhoAmP 93*
Weinberg, Elbert 1928- *WhoAmA 93*
Weinberg, Elbert 1928-1991 *WhAm 10*
Weinberg, Ephraim 1938- *WhoAmA 93*
Weinberg, Eugene David 1922- *WhoAm 94*
Weinberg, Felix Jiri 1928- *IntWW 93, Who 94*
Weinberg, Florence M(ay) 1933- *WrDr 94*
Weinberg, Gerhard Ludwig 1928- *WhoAm 94*
Weinberg, Gus d1952 *WhoHol 92*
Weinberg, H. Barbara *WhoAmA 93, WrDr 94*
Weinberg, H. Barbara 1942- *WhoAm 94*
Weinberg, Harry Bernard 1913- *WhoAm 94*
Weinberg, Harvey A. 1937- *WhoAm 94*
Weinberg, Herschel Mayer 1927- *WhoAm 94*
Weinberg, Horst D. 1928- *WhoWest 94*
Weinberg, Ira Jay 1959- *WhoWest 94*
Weinberg, Irwin Robert 1928- *WhoAm 94*
Weinberg, Jeffrey J. 1948- *WhoAm 94, WhoAmL 94*
Weinberg, Joanna *WhoHol 92*
Weinberg, John Lee 1941- *WhoAm 94, WhoAmL 94, WhoWest 94*
Weinberg, John Livingston 1925- *WhoAm 94, WhoFI 94*
Weinberg, Kerry *WrDr 94*
Weinberg, Kristina Anna 1954- *WhoFI 94*
Weinberg, Leonard Burton 1939- *WhoAm 94*
Weinberg, Lila Shaffer *WhoAm 94*
Weinberg, Loretta 1935- *WhoAmP 93*
Weinberg, Louis 1918- *WhoAmA 93N*
Weinberg, Louise *WhoAm 94*
Weinberg, Mark (Aubrey) 1931- *Who 94*
Weinberg, Martin Herbert 1923- *WhoAm 94*
Weinberg, Meyer 1920- *WhoAm 94, WrDr 94*
Weinberg, Michael, Jr. 1925- *WhoAm 94*
Weinberg, Milton, Jr. 1924- *WhoMW 93*
Weinberg, Moisey Samuilovich *NewGrDO*
Weinberg, Norman Louis 1936- *WhoAm 94*
Weinberg, Robert A. 1942- *IntWW 93*
Weinberg, Robert Allan 1942- *WhoAm 94, WhoScEn 94*
Weinberg, Robert E(dward) 1946- *EncSF 93*
Weinberg, Robert Jay 1953- *WhoAmL 94*
Weinberg, Robert L. 1947- *WhoMW 93*
Weinberg, Robert Leonard 1923- *WhoAm 94, WhoAmL 94*
Weinberg, Robert Lester 1931- *WhoAm 94*
Weinberg, Robert Stephen 1945- *WhoAm 94*
Weinberg, Samuel 1926- *WhoScEn 94*
Weinberg, Sanford Israel 1948- *WhoAmL 94*
Weinberg, Steve 1948- *ConAu 142*
Weinberg, Steven 1933- *IntWW 93, Who 94, WhoAm 94, WhoScEn 94, WorScD, WrDr 94*
Weinberg, Steven Marc 1952- *WhoAmL 94*
Weinberg, Susan C. *DrAPF 93*

Weir, Alexander Fortune Rose 1928- *Who 94*
Weir, Andrew John 1919- *Who 94*
Weir, Bob 1947- *SmATA 76 [port]*
Weir, Cecil James Mullo 1897- *Who 94*
Weir, D. Robert *WhoScEn 94*
Weir, David Bruce *Who 94*
Weir, David Thomas Henderson 1939- *Who 94*
Weir, Don Clair 1912- *WhoAm 94*
Weir, Edward Kenneth 1943- *WhoMW 93, WhoScEn 94*
Weir, Ernest Tener 1875-1957 *EncABHB 9 [port]*
Weir, Felix Fowler 1884-1978 *AfrAmAl 6*
Weir, Gillian Constance 1941- *IntWW 93, Who 94*
Weir, Gordon Bruce 1919- *WhAm 10*
Weir, Gregg *WhoHol 92*
Weir, Jane d1937 *WhoHol 92*
Weir, Jim Dale 1956- *WhoWest 94*
Weir, John Arnold 1916- *WhoMW 93*
Weir, John Keeley 1947- *WhoAmL 94*
Weir, Judith 1954- *IntWW 93, NewGrDO, Who 94*
Weir, Julian Paul 1923- *WhoAmP 93*
Weir, Kenneth Wynn 1930- *WhoAm 94*
Weir, La Vada *WrDr 94*
Weir, Maurice Dean 1939- *WhoWest 94*
Weir, Michael (Scott) 1925- *Who 94*
Weir, Michael H. 1924- *WhoAmP 93*
Weir, Michael Ross 1942- *WhoWest 94*
Weir, Molly 1920- *WhoHol 92, WrDr 94*
Weir, Morton Webster 1934- *WhoAm 94, WhoMW 93*
Weir, Paul Joseph 1923- *WhoAm 94*
Weir, Peter 1944- *IntMPA 94*
Weir, Peter Frank 1933- *WhoAm 94*
Weir, Peter Lindsay 1944- *IntWW 93, Who 94, WhoAm 94*
Weir, Reginald 1911-1987 *BuCMET*
Weir, Richard Stanton 1933- *Who 94*
Weir, Robert H. 1922- *WhoAmL 94*
Weir, Robert McColloch 1933- *WhoAm 94*
Weir, Robin d1993 *NewYTBS 93*
Weir, Roderick (Bignell) 1927- *Who 94*
Weir, Ronald Blackwood 1944- *WrDr 94*
Weir, Rosemary 1905- *WrDr 94*
Weir, Stephen James 1940- *WhoAm 94*
Weir, Stephen Lynn 1949- *WhoAm 94*
Weir, Stuart Peter 1938- *IntWW 93, Who 94*
Weir, Thomas Charles 1933- *WhoAm 94, WhoFI 94*
Weir, Wendy 1949- *SmATA 76 [port]*
Weir, William C., III 1937- *WhoAm 94*
Weirich, C. Geoffrey 1957- *WhoAmL 94*
Weirich, Paul Robert 1946- *WhoMW 93*
Weirick, William Newton 1952- *WhoFI 94*
Wei Rongjue *WhoPRCh 91*
Weis, Darlene Marie 1937- *WhoAmP 93*
Weis, Don 1922- *IntMPA 94*
Weis, Eberhard 1925- *IntWW 93*
Weis, Joseph Francis, Jr. 1923- *WhoAm 94, WhoAmL 94*
Weis, Karel 1862-1944 *NewGrDO*
Weis, Konrad Max 1928- *WhoAm 94*
Weis, Laura Visser 1961- *WhoAmL 94*
Weis, R. *DrAPF 93*
Weis, Serge 1960- *WhoScEn 94*
Weis, Sigfried 1916- *WhoFI 94*
Weisbaum, Earl 1930- *WhoAmL 94*
Weisbaum, Richard Bruce 1936- *WhoWest 94*
Weisbecker, Clement *WhoAmA 93N*
Weisberg, Bernard 1925- *WhoAm 94, WhoAmL 94*
Weisberg, D. Kelly 1949- *WhoAmL 94*
Weisberg, David Charles 1938- *WhoAmL 94*
Weisberg, Gabriel P. 1942- *WhoAmA 93*
Weisberg, Herbert Frank 1941- *WhoAm 94*
Weisberg, Jonathan Mark 1943- *WhoAm 94*
Weisberg, Joseph 1937- *WrDr 94*
Weisberg, Leonard R. 1929- *WhoAm 94, WhoFI 94, WhoMW 93*
Weisberg, Morris L. 1921- *WhoAm 94*
Weisberg, Ruth Ellen 1942- *WhoAmA 93*
Weisberg, Seymour William 1910- *WhoMW 93*
Weisberger, Barbara 1926- *WhoAm 94*
Weisberger, Joseph R. 1920- *WhoAmP 93*
Weisberger, Joseph Robert 1920- *WhoAm 94, WhoAmL 94*
Weisbin, Charles Richard 1944- *WhoScEn 94*
Weisblat, David Irwin 1916-1990 *WhAm 10*
Weisbrod, Burton A. 1931- *IntWW 93*
Weisbrod, Burton Allen 1931- *WhoAm 94*
Weisbrod, Carl Barry 1944- *WhoAmL 94*
Weisbrod, John Andre 1949- *WhoFI 94*
Weisbrod, Ken 1957- *WhoFI 94, WhoWest 94*
Weisbrod, Mark Edward 1954- *WhoWest 94*
Weisbrod, Rita Roffers 1933- *WhoMW 93*
Weisbrot, Robert (S.) 1951- *WrDr 94*
Weisbuch, Robert Alan 1946- *WhoAm 94*
Weisburd, Steven I. 1949- *WhoAmL 94*
Weisburger, Elizabeth Kreiser 1924- *WhoAm 94*
Weisburger, John Hans 1921- *WhoAm 94*
Weise, Charles Martin 1926- *WhoAm 94*
Weise, Frank Earl, III 1944- *WhoAm 94, WhoFI 94*
Weise, Joan Carolyn 1939- *WhoFI 94*
Weise, Richard Henry 1935- *WhoAm 94, WhoAmL 94, WhoFI 94*
Weise, Robert Lewis 1945- *WhoAmP 93*
Weise, Theodore Lewis 1944- *WhoFI 94*
Weisel, Deborah Delp d1951 *WhoAmA 93N*
Weisel, George Ferdinand 1915- *WhoScEn 94*
Weisenberg, Harvey 1933- *WhoAmP 93*
Weisenberger, Richard 1938- *WhoAmP 93*
Weisenburger, Randall 1959- *WhoAm 94, WhoFI 94*
Weisenburger, Theodore Maurice 1930- *WhoAmL 94, WhoWest 94*
Weisend, Martha B. 1931- *WhoAmP 93*
Weisengoff, Paul Edmund 1932- *WhoAmP 93*
Weisenreder, Kurt Richard 1951- *WhoFI 94*
Weisenthal, Bruce Paul 1957- *WhoMW 93*
Weiser, Conrad 1696-1760 *WhWE*
Weiser, Dan 1933- *WhoAmP 93*
Weiser, Frank Alan 1953- *WhoAmL 94, WhoFI 94, WhoWest 94*
Weiser, Grete d1970 *WhoHol 92*
Weiser, Mark David 1952- *WhoAm 94, WhoWest 94*
Weiser, Martin Jay 1943- *WhoAmL 94*
Weiser, Norman Sidney d1993 *NewYTBS 93*
Weiser, Norman Sidney 1919- *WhoAm 94, WhoFI 94*
Weiser, Paul David 1936- *WhoAm 94*
Weiser, Ralph Raphael 1925- *WhoAm 94*
Weiser, Sherwood Manuel 1931- *WhoAm 94, WhoFI 94*
Weiser, Terry Lee 1954- *WhoAmL 94*
Weiser, William Elwood 1954- *WhoAmP 93*
Weisfeld, Sheldon 1946- *WhoAmL 94*
Weisfeld, Steven Adrian 1965- *WhoAmL 94*
Weisfeldt, Myron Lee 1940- *WhoAm 94*
Weisgall, Hugo (David) 1912- *NewGrDO*
Weisgall, Hugo David 1912- *WhoAm 94*
Weisgall, Jonathan Michael 1949- *WhoAmL 94*
Weisgerber, David Wendelin 1938- *WhoAm 94*
Weisgerber, Edward Victor 1952- *WhoAm 94*
Weisgerber, John Sylvester 1940- *WhoWest 94*
Weisgerber, William Denny 1930- *WhoAmP 93*
Weishaus, Joel *DrAPF 93*
Wei Shili *EncSF 93*
Weisinger, Mort(imer) 1915-1978 *EncSF 93*
Wei Siqi 1922- *WhoPRCh 91 [port]*
Weiskittel, Ralph Joseph 1924- *WhoAm 94*
Weiskopf, William Harvard 1938- *WhoFI 94, WhoWest 94*
Weiskrantz, Lawrence 1926- *IntWW 93, Who 94*
Weisleder, Stanley 1933- *WhoIns 94*
Weisman, Ann E. *DrAPF 93*
Weisman, Brent Richards 1952- *ConAu 142*
Weisman, Gary Andrew 1951- *WhoMW 93*
Weisman, Harlan Frederick 1952- *WhoFI 94*
Weisman, Herbert Neal 1940- *WhoMW 93*
Weisman, Irving 1918- *WhoAm 94*
Weisman, James Lewis 1938- *WhoAmL 94*
Weisman, Joel 1928- *WhoAm 94, WhoScEn 94*
Weisman, John 1942- *WhoAm 94*
Weisman, Lorenzo David 1945- *WhoAm 94, WhoFI 94*
Weisman, Malcolm *Who 94*
Weisman, Martin Jerome 1930- *WhoWest 94*
Weisman, Paul Howard 1957- *WhoAmL 94*
Weisman, Richard Scott 1956- *WhoAmL 94*
Weisman, Robert Evans 1950- *WhoWest 94*
Weisman, Robin *WhoHol 92*
Weismann, Donald L 1914- *WrDr 94*
Weismann, Donald Leroy 1914- *WhoAm 94, WhoAmA 93*
Weismann, Julius 1879-1950 *NewGrDO*
Weismantel, Gregory Nelson 1940- *WhoAm 94, WhoFI 94, WhoMW 93*
Weismeyer, Richard Wayne 1943- *WhoWest 94*
Weismiller, Edward Ronald 1915- *WhoAm 94*
Weisner, Joan R. 1950- *WhoAmP 93*
Weisner, Kenneth *DrAPF 93*
Weisner, Maurice Franklin 1917- *WhoAm 94*
Weiss, Alan 1946- *WhoAm 94*
Weiss, Allan Joseph 1932- *WhoAm 94*
Weiss, Althea McNish *Who 94*
Weiss, Alvin Harvey 1928- *WhoAm 94*
Weiss, Andre 1952- *WhoAm 94*
Weiss, Andrew Murray 1947- *WhoFI 94*
Weiss, Armand Berl 1931- *WhoAm 94, WhoFI 94, WhoScEn 94*
Weiss, Arnold Hans 1924- *WhoAmL 94*
Weiss, Arnold M. 1933- *WhoAmP 93*
Weiss, Arthur Eric 1960- *WhoFI 94*
Weiss, Benton Herbert 1942- *WhoMW 93*
Weiss, Bernard 1943- *WhoFI 94, WhoWest 94*
Weiss, Bretta Lydia 1925- *WhoAm 94*
Weiss, Brian 1945- *WhoAmL 94, WhoFI 94*
Weiss, Charles Andrew 1942- *WhoAm 94, WhoAmL 94*
Weiss, Charles Manuel 1918- *WhoAm 94*
Weiss, Charles Stanard 1952- *WhoAm 94*
Weiss, Christopher John 1952- *WhoAmL 94*
Weiss, Courtney Ross 1960- *WhoFI 94*
Weiss, David 1928- *WhoAm 94*
Weiss, David Raymond 1948- *WhoAm 94*
Weiss, Debra S. 1953- *WhoMW 93*
Weiss, Denis Anthony 1942- *WhoMW 93*
Weiss, Dick J. 1946- *WhoAmA 93*
Weiss, Donald Logan 1926- *WhoAm 94*
Weiss, Donald Richard 1943- *WhoWest 94*
Weiss, Dudley Albert 1912- *WhAm 10*
Weiss, Earle Burton 1932- *WhoAm 94*
Weiss, Ed, Jr. *WhoBlA 94*
Weiss, Edward Abraham 1931- *WhoAmL 94*
Weiss, Egon Arthur 1919- *WhoAm 94*
Weiss, Ellen Covner 1947- *WhoAmL 94*
Weiss, Elliott B. 1946- *WhoAmL 94*
Weiss, Ellyn Renee 1947- *WhoAm 94, WhoAmL 94*
Weiss, Eric Robert 1958- *WhoAmL 94*
Weiss, Ethel d1979 *WhoHol 92*
Weiss, Eva 1919- *WhoAmP 93*
Weiss, Gail Ellen 1946- *WhoAm 94*
Weiss, George Arthur 1921- *WhoScEn 94*
Weiss, George C. 1946- *WhoAm 94*
Weiss, George Herbert 1930- *WhoScEn 94*
Weiss, Gerhard Hans 1926- *WhoAm 94*
Weiss, Gerson 1939- *WhoAm 94*
Weiss, Harlan Lee 1941- *WhoAmL 94*
Weiss, Harvey 1922- *SmATA 76 [port], WhoAmA 93*
Weiss, Herbert Klemm 1917- *WhoAm 94, WhoFI 94, WhoScEn 94, WhoWest 94*
Weiss, Howard A. *WhoAm 94*
Weiss, Ira Francis 1909- *WhoAm 94*
Weiss, Irving *DrAPF 93*
Weiss, Irving Norman 1937- *WhoFI 94*
Weiss, J. Claude 1941- *AstEnc*
Weiss, Jack Meyar 1947- *WhoAmL 94*
Weiss, James Michael 1946- *WhoAm 94, WhoFI 94*
Weiss, James Moses Aaron 1921- *WhoAm 94*
Weiss, James Robert 1949- *WhoAm 94*
Weiss, Jan *EncSF 93*
Weiss, Jason Lee *DrAPF 93*
Weiss, Jay Michael 1941- *WhoAm 94*
Weiss, Jerome Nathan 1959- *WhoAmA 93*
Weiss, Jerome Paul 1934- *WhoAm 94*
Weiss, John Joseph 1941- *WhoAmA 93*
Weiss, John Roger 1944- *Who 94*
Weiss, Jonathan Mark 1960- *WhoAmL 94*
Weiss, Joseph 1913- *WhoScEn 94*
Weiss, Joseph Henry, Jr. 1943- *WhoAmP 93*
Weiss, Joseph Joel 1931- *WhoAm 94*
Weiss, Joseph John 1895- *WhAm 10*
Weiss, Joyce Lacey 1941- *WhoBlA 94*
Weiss, Judith Kelner 1950- *WhoAmL 94*
Weiss, Karel *NewGrDO*
Weiss, Keith Douglas 1951- *WhoFI 94*
Weiss, Kenneth Andrew 1951- *WhoAm 94, WhoAmL 94*
Weiss, Laurence S. 1919- *WhoAmP 93*
Weiss, Lawrence N. 1942- *WhoAmL 94*
Weiss, Lawrence Robert 1937- *WhAm 10*
Weiss, Lee 1928- *WhoAmA 93*
Weiss, Leo Abraham 1918-1991 *WhAm 10*
Weiss, Leonard 1934- *WhoAm 94*
Weiss, Lionel Edward 1927- *WhoAm 94*
Weiss, Lisa Ann 1958- *WhoAmL 94*
Weiss, Loren Elliot 1947- *WhoWest 94*
Weiss, Lucinda 1950- *WhoMW 93*
Weiss, Manuel Martin 1952- *WhoAmL 94*
Weiss, Mareda Ruth 1941- *WhoMW 93*
Weiss, Mark *DrAPF 93*
Weiss, Mark Anschel 1937- *WhoAm 94*
Weiss, Mark Lawrence 1945- *WhoAm 94*
Weiss, Martin E. 1926- *WhoMW 93*
Weiss, Martin Harvey 1939- *WhoAm 94, WhoWest 94*
Weiss, Marvin 1929- *WhoAm 94, WhoAmL 94*
Weiss, Max Tibor 1922- *WhoScEn 94*
Weiss, Michael *ConAu 141, WhoHol 92*
Weiss, Michael James 1941- *WhoScEn 94*
Weiss, Mikal Marcus 1956- *WhoAmL 94*
Weiss, Mike 1942- *ConAu 141*
Weiss, Milton 1912- *WhoAmA 93*
Weiss, Morry 1940- *WhoAm 94, WhoFI 94*
Weiss, Murray John 1922- *WhoWest 94*
Weiss, Myrna Grace 1939- *WhoAm 94*
Weiss, Myron 1894- *WhAm 10*
Weiss, Nigel Oscar 1936- *Who 94*
Weiss, Norm A. 1935- *WhoWest 94*
Weiss, Norman Louis 1951- *WhoWest 94*
Weiss, Paul 1901- *WhoAm 94, WrDr 94*
Weiss, Paul Alfred 1898-1989 *WhAm 10*
Weiss, Paul Thomas 1944- *WhoAm 94*
Weiss, Peter (Ulrich) 1916-1982 *IntDcT 2*
Weiss, Peter H. 1956- *WhoWest 94*
Weiss, Philip David 1934- *WhoAmL 94*
Weiss, Rachel 1954- *WhoAmA 93*
Weiss, Randall Dunn 1946- *WhoFI 94*
Weiss, Raymond L. 1930- *ConAu 142*
Weiss, Raymond Lee 1955- *WhAm 10*
Weiss, Regis John 1949- *WhoWest 94*
Weiss, Renee Karol 1923- *WhoAm 94*
Weiss, Rhett Louis 1961- *WhoAmL 94, WhoFI 94*
Weiss, Richard 1954- *WhoAmL 94*
Weiss, Richard Gerald 1942- *WhoScEn 94*
Weiss, Richard Louis 1944- *WhoWest 94*
Weiss, Rita S. 1935- *WhoFI 94*
Weiss, Robert Alan 1950- *WhoAm 94*
Weiss, Robert Anthony 1940- *Who 94*
Weiss, Robert Benjamin 1948- *WhoAm 94, WhoAmL 94*
Weiss, Robert Francis 1924- *WhoAm 94*
Weiss, Robert Franklin 1946- *WhoScEn 94*
Weiss, Robert Jerome 1917- *WhoAm 94*
Weiss, Robert M. 1936- *WhoAm 94, WhoScEn 94*
Weiss, Robert Michael 1940- *WhoScEn 94*
Weiss, Robert Orr 1926- *WhoAm 94*
Weiss, Robert Stephen 1946- *WhoAm 94, WhoFI 94, WhoWest 94*
Weiss, Roger Douglas 1951- *WhoAm 94*
Weiss, Roger William 1930- *WhAm 10*
Weiss, Ronald Phillip 1947- *WhoAmL 94*
Weiss, Ronald Whitman 1939- *WhoAm 94*
Weiss, Rudolf John 1958- *WhoAmP 93*
weiss, ruth *DrAPF 93*
Weiss, S. Shirley 1932- *WhoAmP 93*
Weiss, Samuel Abraham 1923- *WhoScEn 94*
Weiss, Sanford *DrAPF 93*
Weiss, Sanford Ronald 1931- *WhoWest 94*
Weiss, Scott Jeffrey 1968- *WhoScEn 94*
Weiss, Shirley F. 1921- *WhoAm 94, WhoFI 94*
Weiss, Sigmund *DrAPF 93*
Weiss, Stanley Alan 1926- *WhoAm 94, WhoScEn 94*
Weiss, Stanley C. 1929- *WhoAm 94*
Weiss, Steinberg 1942- *WhoWomW 91*
Weiss, Stephen Henry 1935- *WhoFI 94*
Weiss, Stephen Joel 1938- *WhoAm 94*
Weiss, Steven Alan 1944- *IntMPA 94*
Weiss, Susan Christine 1944- *WhoMW 93*
Weiss, Susan Ellen 1951- *WhoMW 93*
Weiss, Suzanne Terry 1946- *WhoAmL 94*
Weiss, Ted 1927-1992 *AnObit 1992*
Weiss, Theodore *DrAPF 93*
Weiss, Theodore (Russell) 1916- *WrDr 94*
Weiss, Theodore Russell 1916- *WhoAm 94*
Weiss, Theodore S. 1927-1992 *WhAm 10*
Weiss, Thomas Edward 1916- *WhoAm 94*
Weiss, Thomas Fischer 1934- *WhoAm 94*
Weiss, Thomas G. 1946- *ConAu 142*
Weiss, Ulrich 1936- *IntWW 93*
Weiss, Volker 1930- *WhoAm 94*
Weiss, Walter Stanley 1929- *WhoAm 94*
Weiss, William Hans 1952- *WhoWest 94*
Weiss, William Lee 1929- *WhoAm 94, WhoFI 94, WhoMW 93*
Weiss, Winfried (Ferdinand) 1937-1991 *ConAu 140*
Weissbach, Herbert 1932- *WhoAm 94*

Weissbard, David Raymond 1940-
WhoAm 94
Weissbard, Samuel Held 1947-
WhoAm 94, WhoAmL 94
Weissberg, Eliot Mitchel 1958- *WhoFI 94*
Weissberg, Yuliya Lazarevna *NewGrDO*
Weiss Bizzoco, Richard Lawrence 1940-
WhoWest 94
Weissbluth, Mitchel 1915-1990 *WhAm 10*
Weissbort, Daniel 1935- *WrDr 94*
Weissbrodt, David Samuel 1944-
WhoAmL 94
Weissbuch, Oscar d1948 *WhoAmA 93N*
Weissburg, Edward d1950 *WhoHol 92*
Weisse, Christian Felix 1726-1804
NewGrDO
Weisse, Hanni d1967 *WhoHol 92*
Weissenbach, John Alfred 1955-
WhoAmL 94
Weissenberg, Alexis 1929- *IntWW 93*
Weissenberger, Harry George 1928-
WhoAmL 94
Weissenborn, Sheridan Kendall 1948-
WhoAmL 94
Weissenburger, Fred Elmer *WhoMW 93*
Weissenburger, Jason Ticknor 1932-
WhoMW 93
Weisser, Henry George 1935-
WhoWest 94
Weissfeld, Joachim Alexander 1927-
WhoAm 94
Weissheimer, Wendelin 1838-1910
NewGrDO
Weissinger, Charles Hyde, Jr. 1950-
WhoAmP 93
Weissinger, Thomas, Sr. 1951-
WhoBlA 94
Weisskopf, Bernard 1929- *WhoAm 94*
Weisskopf, Thomas E. 1940- *WrDr 94*
Weisskopf, Victor Frederick 1908-
Who 94, WhoAm 94, WhoScEn 94
Weissler, Gerhard Ludwig 1918-1989
WhAm 10
Weissler, Robert Charles 1954-
WhoAmL 94
Weissman, Barry Leigh 1948-
WhoAmL 94
Weissman, Bessie d1978 *WhoHol 92*
Weissman, Dora d1974 *WhoHol 92*
Weissman, Eugene Yehuda 1931-
WhoAm 94
Weissman, Gail Kuhn *WhoAm 94*
Weissman, Jack 1921- *WhoAm 94*
Weissman, Jerrold 1936- *WhoWest 94*
Weissman, Julian Paul 1943- *WhoAmA 93*
Weissman, Michael Lewis 1934-
WhoAm 94
Weissman, Murray *IntMPA 94*
Weissman, Norman 1925- *WhoAm 94*
Weissman, Paul Marshall 1931-
WhoAm 94
Weissman, Robert Allen 1950-
WhoAmL 94
Weissman, Robert Evan 1940-
WhoAm 94, WhoFI 94
Weissman, Seymour J. 1931- *IntMPA 94*
Weissman, Walter 1946- *WhoAmA 93*
Weissman, William R. 1940- *WhoAm 94,
WhoAmL 94*
Weissmann, August Friedrich Leopold
1834-1914 *WorScD*
Weissmann, David *DrAPF 93*
Weissmann, Eric Albert Hale 1964-
WhoFI 94
Weissmann, Gerald 1930- *WhoAm 94*
Weissmann, Heidi Seitelblum 1951-
WhoAm 94, WhoScEn 94
Weissmann, Paul Martin 1964-
WhoAmP 93, WhoWest 94
Weissmann, Paul Thomas 1948-
WhoWest 94
Weissmuller, Alberto Augusto 1927-
Who 94
Weissmuller, Johnny d1984 *WhoHol 92*
Weissmuller, Johnny, Jr. *WhoHol 92*
Weissmuller, Peter d1969 *WhoHol 92*
Weisstein, Ulrich W(erner) 1925-
WrDr 94
Weisstein, Ulrich Werner 1925-
WhoAm 94
Weisstub, David N(orman) 1944-
WrDr 94
Weisstuch, Donald N. 1935- *WhoFI 94*
Weiss-Wunder, Linda Teresa 1960-
WhoScEn 94
Weist, Dwight *WhoHol 92*
Weist, Dwight 1910- *WrDr 94*
Weist, Dwight Wilson 1910-1991
WhAm 10
Weist, William Bernard 1938-
WhoAmL 94
Weiswasser, Stephen Anthony 1940-
WhoAm 94, WhoAmL 94
Weisweiler, Peter 1945- *WhoScEn 94*
Weisz, Adrian 1949- *WhoAm 94*
Weisz, George 1951- *WhoAmP 93*
Weisz, Michael Jay 1957- *WhoAmL 94*

Weisz, Paul Burg 1919- *WhoAm 94,
WhoScEn 94*
Weisz, Peter R. 1953- *WhoAmL 94*
Weisz, Reuben R. 1946- *WhoScEn 94*
Weisz, Richard Lee 1951- *WhoAmL 94*
Weisz, Rita Lanyce 1951- *WhoMW 93*
Weisz, William Julius 1927- *WhoAm 94,
WhoFI 94*
Weiszhaar, Gerald Francis 1943-
WhoMW 93
Weitbrecht, Robert H. 1920-1983
EncDeaf
Weithas, William Vincent 1929-
WhoAm 94
Weithers, John G. 1933- *WhoFI 94,
WhoMW 93*
Weithman, Allan Stephen 1953-
WhoScEn 94
Weithorn, Stanley Stephen 1924-
WhoAm 94
Weitkamp, Fredrick John 1927-
WhoAmL 94, WhoWest 94
Weitkamp, William George 1934-
WhoAm 94
Weitling, Wilhelm 1808-1871
DcLB 129 [port]
Weitnauer, John Carson 1952-
WhoAmL 94
Weitz, Bernard George Felix 1919-
Who 94
Weitz, David Allan 1944- *WhoMW 93*
Weitz, Frederick William 1929-
WhoAm 94
Weitz, John 1923- *WhoAm 94*
Weitz, Raanan 1913- *IntWW 93*
Weitz, Sue Dee 1948- *WhoWest 94*
Weitz, Wallace Roger 1949- *WhoMW 93*
Weitze, William Frederick 1960-
WhoWest 94
Weitzel, John Anthony 1945- *WhoFI 94*
Weitzel, John Patterson 1923- *WhoAm 94*
Weitzel, John Quinn 1928- *WhoWest 94*
Weitzel, Marilyn Lee 1946- *WhoMW 93*
Weitzel, William Conrad, Jr. 1935-
WhoAm 94
Weitzen, Edward H. d1991 *WhAm 10*
Weitzenhoffer, A. Max 1939- *WhoAmA 93*
Weitzenhoffer, Aaron Max, Jr. 1939-
WhoFI 94
Weitzer, Bernard 1929- *WhoAm 94*
Weitzman, Allan Harvey 1949-
WhoAmL 94
Weitzman, Arthur Joshua 1933-
WhoAm 94
Weitzman, Bruce H. 1951- *WhoAm 94,
WhoAmL 94*
Weitzman, Linda Sue 1959- *WhoAmL 94*
Weitzman, Marc Herschel 1950-
WhoAmL 94, WhoWest 94
Weitzman, Peter 1926- *Who 94*
Weitzman, Robert Harold 1937-
WhoAm 94
Weitzman, Sarah Brown *DrAPF 93*
Weitzman, Stanley Howard 1927-
WhoScEn 94
Weitzmann, Carl Joseph 1955-
WhoScEn 94
Weitzmann, Kurt d1993 *NewYTBS 93*
Weitzmann, Kurt 1904- *WhoAmA 93*
Weitzmann, Kurt 1904-1993 *ConAu 141*
Weitzner, David 1938- *IntMPA 94*
Weitzner, Harold 1933- *WhoAm 94*
Wei Wei 1920- *IntWW 93,
WhoPRCh 91 [port]*
Wei Xigen *WhoPRCh 91*
Wei Youhai *WhoPRCh 91*
Wei Yu 1940- *WhoPRCh 91 [port]*
Wei Yuming 1924- *WhoPRCh 91 [port]*
Wei Yung 1937- *IntWW 93*
Wei Yunyu 1931- *WhoPRCh 91 [port]*
Wei Zhangping 1920- *WhoPRCh 91 [port]*
Wei Zixi 1915- *WhoPRCh 91 [port]*
Weizman, Ezer 1924- *IntWW 93, Who 94*
Weizman, Savine Gross 1929- *WrDr 94*
Weizmann, Chaim 1874-1952
HisWorL [port]
Weizsacker, Carl Friedrich 1912-
IntWW 93
Weizsacker, Richard von 1920-
IntWW 93
Wejchert, Andrzej 1937- *WhoFI 94*
Wejcman, Linda 1939- *WhoAmP 93*
Wekenborg, Connie Louise 1959-
WhoMW 93
Wekesser, Carol A. 1963-
SmATA 76 [port]
Wekezer, Jerzy Wladyslaw 1946-
WhoWest 94
Weksler, Babette Barbash 1937-
WhoScEn 94
Wekwerth, Manfred 1929- *IntWW 93*
Welander, David Charles St. Vincent
1925- *Who 94*
Welber, David Alan 1949- *WhoAm 94,
WhoFI 94*
Welber, Irwin 1924- *WhoScEn 94*
Welborn, Briney 1948- *WhoAmP 93*

Welborn, Caryl Bartelman 1951-
WhoAm 94
Welborn, Helen 1956- *WhoWest 94*
Welborn, Jesse Floyd 1870-1945
EncABHB 9
Welborn, John Alva *WhoAmP 93*
Welborn, John Alva 1932- *WhoMW 93*
Welborn, Reich Lee 1945- *WhoAmL 94,
WhoFI 94*
Welborn, Sarah 1943- *WhoMW 93*
Welborne, John Howard 1947-
WhoAmL 94
Welbourn, Richard Burkewood 1919-
Who 94
Welburn, Edward T. 1950- *AfrAmAl 6*
Welburn, Edward Thomas, Jr. 1950-
WhoBlA 94
Welburn, Ron *DrAPF 93*
Welburn, Ronald Garfield 1944-
WhoBlA 94
Welby, Bruno *Who 94*
Welby, (Richard) Bruno (Gregory) 1928-
Who 94
Welby, Philip *EncSF 93*
Welby-Everard, Christopher Earle 1909-
Who 94
Welch, Agnes 1924- *WhoAmP 93*
Welch, Amanda (Jane) 1945-
SmATA 75 [port]
Welch, Ann Courtenay 1917- *WrDr 94*
Welch, Anthony Edward d1993 *Who 94N*
Welch, Archie W., Jr. 1940- *WhoAmP 93*
Welch, Arnold Demerritt 1908-
WhoAm 94
Welch, Ashley James 1933- *WhoAm 94,
WhoScEn 94*
Welch, Ashton Everett 1942- *WhoAmP 93*
Welch, Betty Jo 1934-1988 *WhAm 10*
Welch, Betty Leonora 1961- *WhoFI 94,
WhoWest 94*
Welch, Billy d1980 *WhoHol 92*
Welch, Bo *ConTFT 11, WhoAm 94*
Welch, Bob 1956- *WhoAm 94,
WhoWest 94*
Welch, Brent Ballinger 1960- *WhoWest 94*
Welch, Byron Eugene 1928- *WhoAm 94*
Welch, Carol Ann 1938- *WhoAm 94*
Welch, Charles C. *WhoHol 92*
Welch, Charles D. 1948- *WhoAmA 93*
Welch, Charles David 1953- *WhoAm 94*
Welch, Charles R. 1928- *WhoAmP 93*
Welch, Claude Emerson 1906- *WhoAm 94*
Welch, Claude Emerson, Jr. 1939-
WhoAm 94
Welch, Claude Raymond 1922-
WhoAm 94, WhoWest 94
Welch, Colin *Who 94*
Welch, (James) Colin (Ross) 1924-
Who 94
Welch, David 1933- *Who 94*
Welch, David 1950- *WrDr 94*
Welch, David A. 1940- *WhoAmP 93*
Welch, David C. *WhoFI 94*
Welch, David Tyrone 1927- *WhoAmP 93*
Welch, David William 1941-
WhoAmL 94, WhoMW 93
Welch, (Maurice) Denton 1915-1948
DcNaB MP, GayLL
Welch, Don *DrAPF 93*
Welch, Don(ovan LeRoy) 1932-
ConAu 43NR
Welch, Earl Ellis 1901-1990 *WhAm 10*
Welch, Eddie d1963 *WhoHol 92*
Welch, Edward Kenneth, II 1955-
WhoAmL 94
Welch, Edward L. 1928- *WhoBlA 94*
Welch, Edward Lawrence C. *Who 94*
Welch, Edward P. 1950- *WhoAmL 94*
Welch, Edwin Hugh 1944- *WhoAm 94*
Welch, Eleanor Barnes d1981 *WhoHol 92*
Welch, Elisabeth 1908- *WhoHol 92*
Welch, Garry Lee 1948- *WhoWest 94*
Welch, Garth 1936- *IntDcB*
Welch, Garth Larry 1937- *WhoAm 94,
WhoWest 94*
Welch, Gary Lee 1946- *WhoWest 94*
Welch, George Osman 1948- *WhoScEn 94*
Welch, Glenn Charles 1948- *WhoFI 94*
Welch, Harry d1973 *WhoHol 92*
Welch, Harry Scoville 1923- *WhoAm 94*
Welch, Harvey, Jr. 1932- *WhoBlA 94*
Welch, Jack 1935- *News 93-3 [port]*
Welch, James *DrAPF 93*
Welch, James d1917 *WhoHol 92*
Welch, James d1949 *WhoHol 92*
Welch, James 1940- *ConAu 42NR,
WrDr 94*
Welch, James A. *WhoFI 94*
Welch, James Monroe 1916- *WhAm 10*
Welch, James S. *WhoAm 94*
Welch, James Wymore 1928-
WhoAmA 93
Welch, Jennifer *DrAPF 93*
Welch, Jerry 1963- *WhoFI 94*
Welch, Jesse Roy 1949- *WhoBlA 94*
Welch, Joe d1918 *WhoHol 92*
Welch, Joe Ben 1940- *WhoAm 94*
Welch, John (Reader) 1933- *Who 94*

Welch, John Francis, Jr. 1935- *IntWW 93,
WhoAm 94, WhoFI 94*
Welch, John K. *Who 94*
Welch, John L. 1929- *WhoBlA 94*
Welch, Joseph Daniel 1952- *WhoAmL 94*
Welch, Joseph F. 1934- *WhoFI 94*
Welch, Joseph N. d1960 *WhoHol 92*
Welch, K. M. A. *WhoAm 94*
Welch, Katherine d1953 *WhoHol 92*
Welch, Kathleen E(thel) 1951- *WrDr 94*
Welch, L(uderne) Edgar 1855- *EncSF 93*
Welch, Lawrence Andrew, Jr. 1961-
WhoAmL 94
Welch, Leslie d1980 *WhoHol 92*
Welch, Lew d1952 *WhoHol 92*
Welch, Linda Ogden 1958- *WhoAm 94,
WhoFI 94*
Welch, Livingston 1901-1976
WhoAmA 93N
Welch, Lloyd Richard 1927- *WhoAm 94,
WhoWest 94*
Welch, Lois Rieser *WhoMW 93*
Welch, Louie 1918- *WhoAm 94,
WhoAmP 93*
Welch, Louise *WhoHol 92*
Welch, Mabel R. d1959 *WhoAmA 93N*
Welch, Margaret *WhoHol 92*
Welch, Margaret Miller 1937- *WhoFI 94*
Welch, Mark Joseph 1960- *WhoAmL 94*
Welch, Martin E., III 1948- *WhoAm 94,
WhoFI 94*
Welch, Mary d1958 *WhoHol 92*
Welch, Matt *WhoAmP 93*
Welch, Michael John 1939- *WhoAm 94*
Welch, Michael Joseph 1956-
WhoAmL 94
Welch, Neal William 1908- *WhoAm 94*
Welch, Nelson *WhoHol 92*
Welch, Neville *Who 94*
Welch, (William) Neville 1906- *Who 94*
Welch, Niles d1976 *WhoHol 92*
Welch, Noble 1930- *WhoFI 94*
Welch, Olga Michele 1948- *WhoBlA 94*
Welch, Oliver Wendell 1930- *WhoFI 94*
Welch, Patricia L. 1953- *WhoAmP 93*
Welch, Patrick Daniel 1948- *WhoAmP 93*
Welch, Patrick James 1944- *WhoFI 94*
Welch, Peter 1947- *WhoAmP 93*
Welch, Philip Burland 1931- *WhoScEn 94*
Welch, Phyllis *WhoHol 92*
Welch, Raquel 1940- *IntMPA 94,
IntWW 93, WhoAm 94, WhoHisp 94,
WhoHol 92*
Welch, Richard Edwin, Jr. 1924-1989
WhAm 10
Welch, Richard Enlow 1895- *WhAm 10*
Welch, Robert Bond 1927- *WhoAm 94*
Welch, Robert G. 1915- *WhoAmA 93N*
Welch, Robert G., Mrs. *WhoAmA 93*
Welch, Robert Morrow, Jr. 1927-
WhoAm 94
Welch, Robert Radford 1929- *Who 94*
Welch, Robert T. 1958- *WhoAmP 93*
Welch, Robert Thomas 1958-
WhoMW 93
Welch, Robert Winfield 1961-
WhoMW 93
Welch, Roger 1946- *WhoAmA 93*
Welch, Ronald J. 1945- *WhoAm 94*
Welch, Ross Maynard 1943- *WhoAm 94*
Welch, Rowland *EncSF 93*
Welch, Sandy *WhoHol 92*
Welch, Stephen Anthony 1942-
WhoAm 94
Welch, Stuart Cary 1928- *WhoAmA 93*
Welch, Tahnee 1962- *WhoHol 92*
Welch, Theodore Franklyn 1933-
WhoAm 94
Welch, Thomas Andrew 1936- *WhoAm 94*
Welch, Thomas Patrick 1947-
WhoAmP 93
Welch, Timothy LeRoy 1935-
WhoWest 94
Welch, Walter Scott, III 1939-
WhoAmL 94
Welch, William Henry 1929- *WhoAm 94*
Welch, William John 1934- *WhoAm 94,
WhoScEn 94, WhoWest 94*
Welch, Winfred Bruce 1918- *WhoBlA 94*
Welcher, Ronnie Dean 1946-
WhoScEn 94
Welcher, Rosalind 1922- *WrDr 94*
Welchert, Steven Joseph 1956-
WhoWest 94
Welchhance, Brenda Sue 1959-
WhoMW 93
Welchman, Harry d1966 *WhoHol 92*
Welch-Wedding, Cindy Anne 1962-
WhoMW 93
Welckle, John Edwin 1935- *WhoMW 93*
Welcome, John 1914- *WrDr 94*
Weld, Jonathan Minot 1941- *WhoAm 94,
WhoAmL 94*
Weld, Roger Bowen 1953- *WhoWest 94*
Weld, Theodore Dwight 1803-1895
AmSocL, DcAmReB 2
Weld, Tuesday 1943- *IntMPA 94,
WhoHol 92*

Weld, Tuesday Ker 1943- IntWW 93, WhoAm 94
Weld, William F. WhoAmP 93
Weld, William F. 1945- CurBio 93 [port]
Weld, William Floyd 1945- IntWW 93, WhoAm 94, WhoAmL 94
Welden, Arthur Luna 1927- WhoAm 94
Welden, Ben 1901- WhoHol 92
Welden, Daniel W. 1941- WhoAmA 93
Weld Forester Who 94
Weldon, Ann WhoHol 92
Weldon, Anthony (William) 1947- Who 94
Weldon, Barbara Maltby WhoAmA 93
Weldon, Barbara Maltby 1931- WhoWest 94
Weldon, Charles WhoHol 92
Weldon, Curt 1947- CngDr 93
Weldon, David Black 1925- WhoAm 94
Weldon, Duncan Clark 1941- Who 94
Weldon, Fay 1931- BlmGEL, BlmGWL, EncSF 93, IntWW 93, Who 94, WrDr 94
Weldon, Jasper d1968 WhoHol 92
Weldon, Jeffrey Alan 1963- WhoAmP 93, WhoFI 94
Weldon, Jessie d1925 WhoHol 92
Weldon, Joan 1933- WhoHol 92
Weldon, John 1676-1736 NewGrDO
Weldon, Norman Ross 1934- WhoAm 94, WhoFI 94
Weldon, Onah Conway 1926- WhoBlA 94
Weldon, Ramon N. 1932- WhoBlA 94
Weldon, Robert William 1934- WhoIns 94
Weldon, Theodore Tefft, Jr. 1932- WhoMW 93
Weldon, Tim WhoHol 92
Weldon, Virginia Verral 1935- IntWW 93
Weldon, Wayne Curtis 1947- WhoAm 94, WhoAmP 93
Weldon, William Forrest 1945- WhoAm 94, WhoScEn 94
Weldon, William Kimberly 1921- WhoAmP 93
Weldon-Linne, C. Michael 1953- WhoMW 93
Weldy, Curtis D. 1964- WhoFI 94
Weldy, Tina Dawn 1955- WhoMW 93
Weldy, Virgil Millard, Jr. 1948- WhoFI 94
Weleminsky, Judith Ruth 1950- Who 94
Welfare, Simon 1946- WrDr 94
Welfer, Thomas, Jr. 1936- WhoAm 94, WhoFI 94
Welford, Dallas d1946 WhoHol 92
Welford, Jay Lawrence 1957- WhoAmL 94
Welford, Nancy 1904- WhoHol 92
Welford, Sue 1942- ConAu 142, SmATA 75 [port]
Welge, Donald Edward 1935- WhoAm 94
Welge, Jack Herman, Jr. 1951- WhoAmL 94
Welikson, Jeffrey Alan 1957- WhoAm 94, WhoAmL 94
Welin, Walter 1908- WhoAm 94, WhoFI 94
Welinsky, Howard S. 1949- WhoAmP 93
Welish, Marjorie DrAPF 93
Welitsch, Ljuba 1913- NewGrDO
Welk, Lawrence 1903-1992 AnObit 1992
Welker, Edward Philip 1932- WhoFI 94
Welker, Frank WhoHol 92
Welker, Ray WhoAmP 93
Welker, Wallace Irving 1926- WhoAm 94
Welker, William S. 1951- WhoMW 93
Welkey, Joseph John 1947- WhoFI 94
Welkowitz, Joan WhoAm 94
Welkowitz, Walter 1926- WhoAm 94
Well, Gordon Lee 1937- WhoAmP 93
Well, Gunther Wilhelm van 1922- IntWW 93
Welland, Colin 1934- IntWW 93, Who 94
Welland, Colin 1944- WhoHol 92
Wellbeloved, James 1926- Who 94
Wellborn, Charles Ivey 1941- WhoAm 94
Wellborn, J(eanette) D(arleen) 1943- WhoAmA 93
Wellby, Roger Stanley 1906- Who 94
Welle, Alan W. 1945- WhoAmP 93
Wellek, Rene 1903- IntWW 93, WrDr 94
Wellen, Edward (Paul) 1919- EncSF 93
Wellen, Robert Howard 1946- WhoAm 94, WhoAmL 94
Weller, Albert Hermann 1922- IntWW 93
Weller, Allen Stuart 1907- WhoAmA 93
Weller, Andrew Michael WhoFI 94
Weller, Augustus Bookstaver 1894- WhAm 10
Weller, Charles David 1944- WhoAmL 94
Weller, Charles Weston 1948- WhoMW 93
Weller, Don Mighell 1937- WhoAmA 93
Weller, Donald Douglas 1945- WhoWest 94
Weller, Edwin Estabrook 1909-1991 WhAm 10
Weller, Frank Harlow, Jr. 1938- WhoAm 94
Weller, Gerald C. WhoAmP 93
Weller, Gunter Ernst 1934- WhoAm 94, WhoWest 94
Weller, Harold Leighton 1941- WhoWest 94
Weller, Janet Louise 1953- WhoAm 94
Weller, John Sidney 1928-1981 WhoAmA 93N
Weller, Karen Anne 1948- WhoMW 93
Weller, Laurie June 1953- WhoAmA 93
Weller, Louis Stevan 1949- WhoAmL 94, WhoWest 94
Weller, Malcolm Philip Isadore 1935- IntWW 93
Weller, Mary Louise WhoHol 92
Weller, Michael 1942- ConDr 93, WhoAm 94, WrDr 94
Weller, Paul 1912- WhoAmA 93
Weller, Peter 1947- IntMPA 94, WhoAm 94, WhoHol 92
Weller, Philip Douglas 1948- WhoAmL 94
Weller, Ralph Albert 1921- WhoAm 94
Weller, Robert G. WhoHisp 94
Weller, Robert Norman 1939- WhoAm 94, WhoFI 94
Weller, Robert R. 1946- WhoAmL 94
Weller, Ronald Alan 1948- WhoMW 93
Weller, Sheila DrAPF 93
Weller, Sol William 1918- WhoAm 94, WhoScEn 94
Weller, Thomas 1915- WorScD
Weller, Thomas Huckle 1915- IntWW 93, Who 94, WhoAm 94, WhoScEn 94
Weller, Tom WhoAm 94
Weller, Walter 1939- IntWW 93, NewGrDO, Who 94
Wellershoff, Dieter 1925- IntWW 93
Wellershoff, Dieter 1933- IntWW 93
Welles, Beatrice WhoHol 92
Welles, Edward Randolph 1907-1991 WhAm 10
Welles, Elizabeth 1930- WrDr 94
Welles, George Orson 1915-1985 AmCulL
Welles, George William, III 1940- WhoMW 93
Welles, Gwen d1993 NewYTBS 93 [port]
Welles, Gwen 1949- WhoHol 92
Welles, James Bell, Jr. 1918- WhoAm 94
Welles, Jesse WhoHol 92
Welles, John Galt 1925- WhoAm 94, WhoWest 94
Welles, Mel WhoHol 92
Welles, Melinda Fassett 1943- WhoAm 94, WhoWest 94
Welles, Melvin J. WhoAm 94
Welles, Meri d1973 WhoHol 92
Welles, Orson EncSF 93
Welles, Orson d1985 WhoHol 92
Welles, Orson 1915-1985 ConLC 80 [port]
Welles, Rebecca WhoHol 92
Welles, Samuel P(aul) 1907- WrDr 94
Welles, Virginia 1925- WhoHol 92
Wellesley Who 94
Wellesley, Alfred 1875- WhoHol 92
Wellesley, Arthur 1769-1852 HisWorL [port]
Wellesley, Charles d1946 WhoHol 92
Wellesley, Julian Valerian 1933- Who 94
Wellesley, Kenneth 1911- WrDr 94
Wellesley, Marie d1927 WhoHol 92
Wellesley, Richard 1760-1842 HisWorL [port]
Wellesz, Egon (Joseph) 1885-1974 NewGrDO
Wellford, Harry Walker 1924- WhoAm 94, WhoAmL 94
Wellford, Hill B., Jr. 1942- WhoAm 94, WhoAmL 94
Wellford, W. Harrison 1940- WhoAmP 93
Wellhausen, John William 1953- WhoFI 94
Wellin, Keith Sears 1926- WhoAm 94
Welling, James 1951- WhoAmA 93
Welling, Larry Wayne 1940- WhoScEn 94
Wellings, David Gordon 1940- Who 94
Wellings, Jack (Alfred) 1917- Who 94
Wellings, Victor Gordon 1919- Who 94
Wellington, Archbishop of 1930- Who 94
Wellington, Bishop of Who 94
Wellington, Duke of 1915- Who 94
Wellington, Arthur Wellesley, Duke of 1769-1852 BlmGEL
Wellington, Babe d1954 WhoHol 92
Wellington, Carol Strong 1948- WhoAmL 94
Wellington, Duke 1896-1987 WhoAmA 93N
Wellington, Harry Hillel 1926- WhoAm 94
Wellington, John Sessions 1921- WhoAm 94
Wellington, John Stanley 1916- WhoAm 94
Wellington, Judith Lynn 1947- WhoAm 94
Wellington, Monica 1957- WrDr 94
Wellington, Peter Scott 1919- Who 94
Wellington, Ralph Glenn 1946- WhoAm 94, WhoAmL 94
Wellington, Robert Hall 1922- WhoAm 94, WhoMW 93
Wellington, Robert John 1954- WhoWest 94
Wellington, Sheila Wacks 1932- WhoAm 94
Wellington, William George 1920- WhoAm 94
Wellisch, William Jeremiah 1938- WhoWest 94
Wellish, Corinne Suzane 1946- WhoMW 93
Welliver, Albertus Delmar 1934- WhoAm 94, WhoFI 94
Welliver, Charles Harold 1945- WhoAm 94
Welliver, Neil G. 1929- WhoAmA 93
Welliver, Warren Dee 1920- WhoAm 94, WhoAmP 93, WhoMW 93
Wellman, Carl Pierce 1926- WhoAm 94, WrDr 94
Wellman, Donald DrAPF 93
Wellman, Gerald Edwin, Jr. 1948- WhoMW 93
Wellman, Howard 1944- WhoAmP 93
Wellman, James WhoHol 92
Wellman, Mac DrAPF 93
Wellman, Mac 1945- ConDr 93
Wellman, Manly Wade 1903-1986 EncSF 93
Wellman, Michael Davis 1946- WhoMW 93
Wellman, Richard Vance 1922- WhoAm 94
Wellman, Thomas Adams 1958- WhoFI 94
Wellman, Thomas Peter 1932- WhoAmL 94
Wellman, Wendell WhoHol 92
Wellman, William d1975 WhoHol 92
Wellman, William, Jr. 1937- WhoHol 92
Wellner, James Alton 1953- WhoAmL 94
Wellner, Jon August 1945- WhoAm 94
Wellner, Marcel Nahum 1930- WhoAm 94
Wellner, Robert Brian 1948- WhoScEn 94
Wellnitz, Craig Otto 1946- WhoAmL 94
Wellon, Robert G. 1948- WhoAmL 94
Wells, Archdeacon of Who 94
Wells, Dean of Who 94
Wells (Barnett), Ida Bell 1862-1931 BlmGWL
Wells, Alan Arthur Who 94
Wells, Angus 1943- EncSF 93
Wells, Anne Jones 1939- WhoMW 93
Wells, Arthur Stanton 1931- WhoAm 94, WhoFI 94
Wells, Barbara Jones 1939- WhoBlA 94
Wells, Basil (Eugene) 1912- EncSF 93
Wells, Benjamin Gladney 1943- WhoAm 94, WhoAmL 94
Wells, Betty Childs 1926- WhoAmA 93
Wells, Betty Ellen 1957- WhoMW 93
Wells, Betty Ruth 1927- WhoMW 93
Wells, Billy Gene WhoBlA 94
Wells, Bobby Ray 1956- WhoBlA 94
Wells, Bombardier Billy d1967 WhoHol 92
Wells, Bowen 1935- Who 94
Wells, Brigid Who 94
Wells, (Jennifer) Brigid (Ellen) 1928- Who 94
Wells, Cady 1904-1954 WhoAmA 93N
Wells, Card Ovrey 1897- WhAm 10
Wells, Carmel WhoAmP 93
Wells, Carol Menthe WhoWest 94
Wells, Carol Menthe 1942- WhoAmA 93
Wells, Carole 1943- WhoHol 92
Wells, Carole C. 1943- WhoAmP 93
Wells, Charles B. d1924 WhoHol 92
Wells, Charles Chauncey 1944- WhoMW 93
Wells, Charles Donald 1946- WhoAmP 93
Wells, Charles Maltby 1908- Who 94
Wells, Charles William 1934- WhoAm 94, WhoFI 94
Wells, Christine 1948- WhoAm 94
Wells, Christopher Brian 1948- WhoAm 94
Wells, Chuck WhoHol 92
Wells, Claudia WhoHol 92
Wells, Clayton E. 1937- WhoAmP 93
Wells, Clyde Kirby 1937- Who 94, WhoAm 94
Wells, Damon, Jr. 1937- WhoAm 94, WhoFI 94
Wells, Daniel Ruth 1921- WhoAm 94
Wells, Danny WhoHol 92
Wells, David Arthur 1941- Who 94
Wells, David Charles 1958- WhoMW 93
Wells, David George 1941- Who 94
Wells, David John 1949- WhoFI 94, WhoScEn 94
Wells, David Nelson 1960- WhoFI 94
Wells, Dawn WhoHol 92
Wells, Deering d1961 WhoHol 92
Wells, Dewey Wallace 1929- WhoAm 94, WhoAmL 94
Wells, Dicky d1985 WhoHol 92
Wells, Donald Eugene 1940- WhoAm 94
Wells, Donna Frances 1948- WhoFI 94, WhoWest 94
Wells, Doreen 1937- IntDcB [port]
Wells, Doreen Patricia Who 94
Wells, Dwight Allen 1925- WhoAmP 93
Wells, Elaine L. WhoAmP 93
Wells, Elaine Louise 1951- WhoMW 93
Wells, Elmer Eugene 1939- WhoBlA 94
Wells, Everett Clayton, Jr. 1954- WhoAm 94, WhoFI 94
Wells, Frances Jean 1937- WhoFI 94
Wells, Frank G. 1932- IntMPA 94, WhoAm 94, WhoFI 94, WhoWest 94
Wells, Gabriel 1862-1946 DcLB 140 [port]
Wells, Gary Ray 1938- WhoFI 94
Wells, Gary Wayne 1953- WhoMW 93
Wells, George Albert 1926- Who 94
Wells, George Douglas 1935- WhoFI 94
Wells, Guy Jackson 1930- WhoAmP 93
Wells, H. G. d1946 WhoHol 92
Wells, H. G. 1866-1946 BlmGEL [port]
Wells, H(erbert) G(eorge) 1866-1946 EncSF 93, RfGShF, TwCYAW
Wells, Helena c. 1760-c. 1809 BlmGWL
Wells, Henry E. 1915- WhoAmP 93
Wells, Herbert James d1993 Who 94N
Wells, Herman B. 1902- IntWW 93, WhoAm 94
Wells, Herschel James 1924- WhoAm 94, WhoMW 93, WhoScEn 94
Wells, Horace WorScD
Wells, Hoyt Mellor 1926- WhoAm 94, WhoFI 94
Wells, Hubert George EncSF 93
Wells, Huey Thomas, Jr. 1950- WhoAmL 94
Wells, Ima Lee WhoAmP 93
Wells, Ingeborg WhoHol 92
Wells, Ira J. K., Jr. 1934- WhoBlA 94
Wells, J. C. WhoHol 92
Wells, Jack Dennis 1928- Who 94
Wells, Jacqueline WhoHol 92
Wells, James A. 1933- WhoBlA 94
Wells, James Dale 1928- WhoAmP 93
Wells, James David, Jr. 1969- WhoScEn 94
Wells, James Douglas 1953- WhoScEn 94
Wells, James Lesesne 1902- WhoBlA 94
Wells, James Wayne 1941- WhoWest 94
Wells, Jane Frances 1944- WhoMW 93
Wells, Jeffrey M. 1948- WhoAmP 93
Wells, Jerome Covell 1936- WhoFI 94
Wells, Jerrold WhoHol 92
Wells, Joel Freeman 1930- WhoAm 94, WrDr 94
Wells, Joel Reaves, Jr. 1928-1991 WhAm 10
Wells, John 1936- WhoHol 92
Wells, John (Campbell) 1936- WrDr 94
Wells, John (Julius) 1925- Who 94
Wells, John Campbell 1936- Who 94
Wells, John Christopher 1939- Who 94
Wells, John Jay EncSF 93
Wells, John Marcum 1956- WhoAm 94
Wells, John Marvin 1918- WhoAmP 93
Wells, John West 1907- IntWW 93
Wells, Jon Barrett 1937- WhoFI 94, WhoScEn 94, WhoWest 94
Wells, Jonathan WhoAmP 93
Wells, Joseph M(erton) 1922-1991 WhAm 10
Wells, Judee Ann 1951- WhoAm 94
Wells, Kim Bradford 1949- WhoAmP 93
Wells, Kitty 1919- WhoAm 94
Wells, L. M. d1923 WhoHol 92
Wells, Leonard Nathaniel David, Jr. 1914- WhoAm 94
Wells, Linda A. 1958- WhoAm 94
Wells, Linda Ivy 1948- WhoBlA 94
Wells, Lionelle Dudley 1921- WhoScEn 94
Wells, Lloyd C. A. 1924- WhoBlA 94
Wells, Lu 1915- WhoWest 94
Wells, Lynton 1940- WhoAmA 93
Wells, Mac 1925- WhoAmA 93
Wells, Malcolm Henry Weston 1927- Who 94
Wells, Margaret d1989 WhoHol 92
Wells, Marie d1949 WhoHol 92
Wells, Marion WhoHol 92
Wells, Mark WhoIns 94
Wells, Mark Alan 1960- WhoWest 94
Wells, Martha 1964- ConAu 142
Wells, Martin John 1928- WrDr 94
Wells, Mary 1943-1992 AfrAmAl 6, AnObit 1992
Wells, Mary Esther 1943-1992 WhoBlA 94N
Wells, Max WhoAmP 93
Wells, May d1941 WhoHol 92
Wells, Melissa F. WhoAmP 93
Wells, Melissa Foelsch 1932- WhoAm 94
Wells, Merle William 1918- WhoAm 94, WhoWest 94
Wells, Michael A. 1953- WhoAmP 93

Wells, Michael Gordon 1955- WhoMW 93
Wells, Oris Vernon 1903-1986 WhAm 10
Wells, Patricia 1946- WrDr 94
Wells, Patricia Bennett 1935- WhoWest 94
Wells, Patrick Harrington 1926- WhoWest 94
Wells, Patrick Roland 1931- WhoBlA 94
Wells, Payton R. 1933- WhoBlA 94
Wells, Peter Boyd, Jr. 1915-1992 WhAm 10
Wells, Peter F., Sr. 1943- WhoAmP 93
Wells, Peter Frederick 1918- WrDr 94
Wells, Peter Nathaniel 1938- WhoAmL 94
Wells, Peter Scoville 1938- WhoFI 94
Wells, Petrie Bowen Who 94
Wells, R. Michael 1949- WhoAmP 93
Wells, Ray(mond) d1941 WhoHol 92
Wells, Richard Burton 1940- Who 94
Wells, Richard H. 1940- WhoAm 94, WhoFI 94
Wells, Rick WhoHol 92
Wells, Robert 1929- EncSF 93
Wells, Robert Alfred 1942- WhoAmL 94
Wells, Robert Benjamin, Jr. 1947- WhoBlA 94
Wells, Robert Lewis 1952- WhoWest 94
Wells, Robert Steven 1951- WhoAm 94
Wells, Roderick John 1936- Who 94
Wells, Roger 1947- WrDr 94
Wells, Roger Stanley 1949- WhoWest 94
Wells, Rona Lee 1950- WhoFI 94
Wells, Ronald Alfred 1920- Who 94
Wells, Ronnie EncSF 93
Wells, Rosemary 1943- TwCYAW, WrDr 94
Wells, Rufus Michael Grant 1947- IntWW 93
Wells, Samuel Alonzo, Jr. 1936- WhoAm 94
Wells, Samuel Jay 1924- WhoAmP 93
Wells, Sheilah WhoHol 92
Wells, Stanley, Mrs. Who 94
Wells, Stanley (William) 1930- WrDr 94
Wells, Stanley William 1930- Who 94
Wells, Steve C. 1944- WhoAmP 93
Wells, Steve Carroll 1944- WhoFI 94
Wells, Ted d1947 WhoHol 92
Wells, Theodora (Westmont) 1926- WrDr 94
Wells, Thomas (Winchester) 1916- WhoAmA 93
Wells, Thomas B. 1945- CngDr 93, WhoAm 94, WhoAmL 94
Wells, Thomas Leonard 1930- Who 94
Wells, Thomas Umfrey 1927- Who 94
Wells, Tobias 1923- WrDr 94
Wells, Tracy WhoHol 92
Wells, Van L. 1941- WhoIns 94
Wells, Vernon WhoHol 92
Wells, Veronica WhoHol 92
Wells, Victor Hugh, Jr. 1924- WhoAm 94
Wells, Walter 1937- WrDr 94
Wells, William DrAPF 93
Wells, William Henry Weston 1940- Who 94
Wells, William K. d1956 WhoHol 92
Wells Barnett, Ida 1862-1931 HisWorL [port]
Wells Barnett, Ida B. 1862-1931 WomPubS
Wells-Barnett, Ida Bell 1862-1931 AmSocL [port]
Wells-Davis, Margie Elaine 1944- WhoBlA 94
Wells-Henderson, Ronald John 1934- WhoFI 94
Wells-Mamlet, Daphne 1934- WhoWest 94
Wells-Merrick, Lorraine Roberta 1938- WhoBlA 94
Wells-Prines, Vesta Lynn 1950- WhoMW 93
Wells-Schooley, Jane 1949- WhoAmP 93
Wellsted, James d1836 WhWE
Wellstone, Paul 1944- WhoAm 94, WhoMW 93
Wellstone, Paul D. 1944- CngDr 93, CurBio 93 [port]
Wellstone, Paul David 1944- WhoAmP 93
Wellwarth, George E 1932- WrDr 94
Welmaker, Forrest Nolan 1925- WhoAmL 94
Welman, Douglas Pole 1902- Who 94
Welmon, Vernis M. 1951- WhoBlA 94
Welna, Cecilia 1927- WhoAm 94
Welnetz, David Charles 1947- WhoAm 94, WhoFI 94
Welpott, Jack Warren 1923- WhoAm 94, WhoAmA 93
Wels, Richard Hoffman 1913-1990 WhAm 10
Welsby, John Kay 1938- Who 94
Welsby, Norman 1939- NewGrDO
Welsby, Paul Antony 1920- Who 94
Welsch, Glenn Albert 1915- WhoAm 94
Welsch, James Lester 1917- WhoWest 94
Welsch, Joseph P. 1928- WhoAmP 93
Welser-Most, Franz 1960- IntWW 93
Welsh, Alexander 1933- WrDr 94
Welsh, Alfred John 1947- WhoAmL 94
Welsh, Andrew Paton 1944- Who 94
Welsh, Brian Richard 1958- WhoAmL 94
Welsh, Dominic Who 94
Welsh, (James Anthony) Dominic 1938- Who 94
Welsh, Donald Emory 1943- WhoAm 94
Welsh, Edward Cristy 1909-1990 WhAm 10
Welsh, Elizabeth Ann 1960- WhoScEn 94
Welsh, Frank (Reeson) 1931- WrDr 94
Welsh, Frank Reeson 1931- Who 94
Welsh, Freddie d1982 WhoHol 92
Welsh, H. Ronald 1950- WhoAmL 94
Welsh, Harry d1957 WhoHol 92
Welsh, James Neal 1942- WhoFI 94
Welsh, Jane 1905- WhoHol 92
Welsh, Jeffrey P. 1956- WhoIns 94
Welsh, John d1985 WhoHol 92
Welsh, John Beresford, Jr. 1940- WhoAmL 94
Welsh, John Robert 1924- WhoMW 93
Welsh, Joseph John 1955- WhoAmP 93
Welsh, Kenneth WhoHol 92
Welsh, Margaret WhoHol 92
Welsh, Mary McAnaw 1920- WhoWest 94
Welsh, Matthew Empson 1912- WhoAm 94, WhoAmP 93
Welsh, Michael Collins 1926- Who 94
Welsh, Michael John 1942- Who 94
Welsh, Michael John 1947- WhoMW 93
Welsh, Moray Meston 1947- IntWW 93
Welsh, Patrick T. 1950- WhoAmP 93
Welsh, Peter Corbett 1926- WhoAm 94
Welsh, Peter Miles 1930- Who 94
Welsh, Ronald Arthur 1926- WhoAm 94
Welsh, Ronnie d1993 NewYTBS 93
Welsh, Thomas c. 1780-1848 NewGrDO
Welsh, Thomas J. 1921- WhoAm 94
Welsh, William DrAPF 93
Welsh, William d1946 WhoHol 92
Welsh, William Brownlee 1924- WhoAmP 93
Welsh, William F., II WhoFI 94
Welshans, Merle Talmadge 1918- WhoMW 93
Welshimer, Gwen WhoAmP 93
Welshimer, Gwen R. 1935- WhoMW 93
Welsing, Frances Cress 1935- BlkWr 2, ConAu 142, ConBlB 5 [port], WhoBlA 94
Welt, Henry 1946- WhoAmL 94
Weltchek, Robert Jay 1955- WhoAmL 94
Welte, Noreen McNamara 1946- WhoMW 93
Welter, Cole H. 1952- WhoAmA 93
Welter, Darrell Robert 1964- WhoMW 93
Welter, Jerry WhoAmP 93
Welter, Lee Orrin 1943- WhoScEn 94
Welter, Rush (Eastman) 1923- WrDr 94
Welter, Vanessa Marie 1960- WhoMW 93
Welter, William Michael 1946- WhoAm 94
Welting, Ruth 1949- NewGrDO
Welting, Ruth Lynn 1948- IntWW 93
Weltman, David Lee 1933- WhoAm 94
Weltman, Joel Kenneth 1933- WhoScEn 94
Weltner, Charles Longstreet 1927-1992 WhAm 10
Welton, Alice Gordon Guilfoy 1948- WhoMW 93
Welton, Charles Ephraim 1947- WhoAmL 94, WhoWest 94
Welton, James Arthur 1921- WhoFI 94
Welton, Kathleen Ann 1956- WhoAm 94
Welton, Michael Peter 1957- WhoWest 94
Welton, Robert Breen 1938- WhoAm 94
Welty, Eudora DrAPF 93, Who 94, WhoAm 94
Welty, Eudora 1909- BlmGWL, IntWW 93, WrDr 94
Welty, Eudora (Alice) 1909- RfGShF
Welty, Eudora Alice 1909- AmCulL [port]
Welty, James R. 1933- WhoScEn 94
Welty, John D. 1944- IntWW 93
Welty, John Donald 1944- WhoAm 94
Welty, John Rider 1948- WhoAmL 94
Welty, Kenneth Harry 1933- WhoScEn 94
Welty, Richard Edward 1942- WhoAmP 93
Weltzheimer, Marie Kash WhoAmA 93
Welu, James A. 1943- WhoAm 94
Welvaert, Dennis M. 1948- WhoFI 94
Welz, Stephen Gary 1950- WhoAmL 94
Welzig, Werner 1935- WhoScEn 94
Wempe, Jack 1934- WhoAmP 93
Wemple, Clark Cullings 1927- WhoAmP 93
Wemple, William 1912- WhoAm 94
Wemyss, Earl of 1912- Who 94
Wemyss, Martin La Touche 1927- Who 94
Wen, Cheng Paul 1933- WhoScEn 94
Wen, Eric Lewis 1953- Who 94
Wen, Lisa 1953- WhoMW 93
Wen, Shih-Liang WhoAm 94, WhoAsA 94
Wen, Wen-Yang 1931- WhoAsA 94
Wenaas, Eric Paul 1942- WhoWest 94
Wenawine, Bruce Harley 1949- WhoAmA 93
Wenban-Smith, Nigel Who 94
Wenban-Smith, (William) Nigel 1936- Who 94
Wenban-Smith, William 1908- Who 94
Wen Biqiu WhoPRCh 91
Wences, Senor WhoHol 92
Wences, Senor 1912- WhoCom
Wenceslas 907-929 HisWorL [port]
Wen Chi WhoPRCh 91
Wenck, William Ariste 1947- WhoAmP 93, WhoFI 94
Wenckus, James R. 1941- WhoIns 94
Wend, David VanVranken 1923- WhoMW 93
Wendeborn, Richard Donald WhoAm 94
Wendel, John Fredric 1936- WhoAmL 94
Wendel, Lara WhoHol 92
Wendel, Martin 1944- WhoAm 94, WhoAmL 94
Wendel, Richard Frederick 1930- WhoAm 94
Wendel, Thomas Michael 1936- WhoAm 94
Wendel, William Hall 1914-1990 WhAm 10
Wendelburg, Allan 1954- WhoAmL 94
Wendelessen EncSF 93
Wendell, Barbara Taylor 1920- WhoMW 93
Wendell, Howard d1975 WhoHol 92
Wendell, Julia DrAPF 93
Wendell, Leilah DrAPF 93
Wendell, Steven John NewYTBS 93 [port]
Wendelstedt, Harry Hunter, Jr. 1938- WhoAm 94
Wenden, Henry Edward 1916-1991 WhAm 10
Wender, Ira Tensard 1927- WhoAm 94
Wender, Paul Herbert 1934- WhoWest 94
Wender, Phyllis Bellows 1934- WhoAm 94
Wenders, Wim WhoHol 92
Wenders, Wim 1945- IntMPA 94, IntWW 93
Wendholt, Norman William 1958- WhoScEn 94
Wendkos, Paul 1926- IntMPA 94
Wendlandt, John Charles 1960- WhoWest 94
Wendleton, Patricia Ann 1942- WhoAmP 93
Wendling, Dorothea 1736-1811 NewGrDO
Wendling, Elisabeth (Augusta) 1746-1786 NewGrDO
Wendling, Elizabeth Louise 1949- WhoFI 94
Wendling, Louis Charles 1951- WhoFI 94
Wendorf, Denver Fred, Jr. 1924- WhoAm 94
Wendorf, Hulen Dee 1916- WhoAm 94
Wendorf, Richard Harold 1948- WhoAm 94
Wendorff, Laiola d1966 WhoHol 92
Wendrow, Sylvia Diann WhoMW 93
Wendt, Albert 1939- IntWW 93, RfGShF, WrDr 94
Wendt, Allen WhoAm 94, WhoAmP 93
Wendt, Charles William 1931- WhoAm 94
Wendt, E. Allan 1935- WhoAm 94
Wendt, Elizabeth Warczak 1931- WhoMW 93
Wendt, Gary Carl 1942- WhoAm 94, WhoFI 94
Wendt, George 1948- IntMPA 94
Wendt, George 1949- WhoHol 92
Wendt, George Robert WhoAm 94
Wendt, Hans Werner 1923- WhoAm 94, WhoMW 93, WhoScEn 94
Wendt, Henry 1933- IntWW 93, Who 94
Wendt, Henry, III 1933- WhoAm 94, WhoFI 94
Wendt, Hildegard WhoHol 92
Wendt, Ingrid DrAPF 93
Wendt, John Arthur Frederic, Jr. WhoAmL 94
Wendt, Lloyd 1908- WhoAm 94
Wendt, Michael James 1948- WhoWest 94
Wendt, Richard K. 1932- WhoIns 94
Wendt, Richard Kurt 1932- WhoAm 94
Wendt, Robin Glover 1941- Who 94
Wendt, Steven William 1948- WhoFI 94, WhoWest 94
Wendt, Thomas Gene 1951- WhoFI 94, WhoMW 93
Wendte, Ron 1948- WhoAmP 93
Wener, Mark Howard 1949- WhoWest 94
Weng, Armin George 1897- WhAm 10
Weng, Peter A. 1939-1992 WhoBlA 94N
Weng, Will d1993 NewYTBS 93 [port]
Weng, Wu-Tsung 1944- WhoAsA 94
Wengenroth, Stow 1906-1978 WhoAmA 93N
Wenger, Antoine 1919- IntWW 93
Wenger, Bruce Edward 1948- WhoAmA 93
Wenger, Derrick Eliot 1961- WhoFI 94
Wenger, Eugene Edward 1928- WhoMW 93
Wenger, Fredrick W. 1943- WhoAmP 93
Wenger, J(ohn) C(hristian) 1910- WrDr 94
Wenger, Jane (B.) 1944- WhoAmA 93
Wenger, Joann Helen 1943- WhoMW 93
Wenger, John Christian 1910- WhoAm 94
Wenger, Larry Bruce 1941- WhoAm 94, WhoAmL 94
Wenger, Lisa 1858-1941 BlmGWL
Wenger, Luke Huber 1939- WhoAm 94
Wenger, Muriel 1915-1989 WhoAmA 93N
Wenger, Noah W. 1934- WhoAmP 93
Wenger, Sigmund 1910- WhoAmA 93
Wengerd, Sherman Alexander 1915- WhoAm 94, WhoScEn 94, WhoWest 94
Wengert, Eugene Mark 1942- WhoMW 93
Wengert, Norman Irving 1916- WhoAm 94
Wenglowski, Gary Martin 1942- WhoAm 94
Wengraf, Hans WhoHol 92
Wengraf, John d1974 WhoHol 92
Wengronowitz, Ann Marie 1958- WhoFI 94
Wengrovitz, Judith 1931- WhoAmA 93
Wen Guoqing WhoPRCh 91
Wenham, Brian George 1937- Who 94
Wenham, Jane WhoHol 92
Wenig, Cathleen Newlove 1958- WhoMW 93
Wenig, Harold George 1924- WhoFI 94
Wenig, Lynn S. 1953- WhoFI 94
Weninger, Howard L. 1904- WhoAmP 93
Wen Jiabao 1942- IntWW 93, WhoPRCh 91 [port]
Wen Jiasi 1905- WhoPRCh 91 [port]
Wen Jieruo 1927- BlmGWL
Wen Jing WhoPRCh 91 [port]
Wen Jingyi WhoPRCh 91
Wen Junru WhoPRCh 91
Wenk, Edward, Jr. 1920- WhoAm 94
Wen Kegang WhoPRCh 91
Wenkel, Ortrun 1942- NewGrDO
Wenker, Judith Ann 1944- WhoAmL 94
Wenker, Paul F. 1942- WhoAmL 94
Wenkert, Daniel 1956- WhoWest 94
Wenkoff, Spas 1928- NewGrDO
Wenley, Archibald Gibson 1898-1962 WhoAmA 93N
Wen Li 1933- WhoPRCh 91 [port]
Wenman, Henry d1953 WhoHol 92
Wenman, Thomas Lee 1950- WhoFI 94
Wen Minsheng 1916- WhoPRCh 91 [port]
Wennberg, Samuel Robert 1958- WhoFI 94
Wenner, Bruce Richard 1938- WhoMW 93
Wenner, Charles Roderick 1947- WhoAm 94, WhoAmL 94
Wenner, Edward James, III 1956- WhoScEn 94
Wenner, Gene Charles 1931- WhoAm 94
Wenner, Herbert Allan 1912- WhoAm 94
Wenner, Jann WhoHol 92
Wenner, Jann Simon 1946- WhoAm 94
Wenner, Kate DrAPF 93
Wenner, Michael Alfred 1921- Who 94
Wenner, Paul Francis 1947- WhoWest 94
Wenner, Seymour J. d1993 NewYTBS 93
Wennerstrom, Arthur John 1935- WhoScEn 94
Wennerstrom, Mary H(annah) 1939- WrDr 94
Wennlund, Larry 1941- WhoAmP 93
Wen Qiang WhoPRCh 91 [port]
Wenrich, John William 1937- WhoAm 94
Wenrich, Karen Jane 1947- WhoWest 94
Wenrich, Percy d1952 WhoHol 92
Wen Shengchang WhoPRCh 91 [port]
Wen Shizhen 1940- WhoPRCh 91 [port]
Wensinger, Arthur Stevens 1926- WhoAm 94
Wensley, William Charles d1984 WhoAmA 93N
Wenstrom, Frank Augustus 1903- WhoAmP 93
Wenstrom, Gene R. 1946- WhoAmP 93
Wenstrup, H. Daniel 1934- WhoFI 94, WhoMW 93
Went, David 1947- IntWW 93
Went, John Stewart 1944- Who 94
Wenthe, P. K. 1937- WhoIns 94
Wenthold, James Robert 1943- WhoMW 93
Wentler, Esther Ruth 1914- WhoMW 93
Wentley, Richard Taylor 1930- WhoAm 94, WhoAmL 94
Wentrup, Curt 1942- WhoScEn 94
Wents, Doris Roberta 1944- WhoScEn 94
Wentscher, Dora 1883-1964 BlmGWL
Wentworth, Alberta M. WhoAmP 93
Wentworth, Andrew Stowell 1938- WhoMW 93

Wentworth, Anne fl. 1676- BlmGWL
Wentworth, Jack Roberts 1928- WhoAm 94, WhoFI 94
Wentworth, Janet 1957- WhoAmA 93
Wentworth, Jason David 1966- WhoAmP 93
Wentworth, Jeff 1940- WhoAmP 93
Wentworth, John 1737-1820 WhAmRev
Wentworth, John, Jr. 1745-1787 WhAmRev
Wentworth, Malinda Ann Nachman WhoFI 94
Wentworth, Martha d1974 WhoHol 92
Wentworth, Maurice Frank Gerard 1908- Who 94
Wentworth, Murray Jackson 1927- WhoAm 94, WhoAmA 93
Wentworth, Paul d1793 WhAmRev
Wentworth, Richard Leigh 1930- WhoAm 94
Wentworth, Robert EncSF 93
Wentworth, Stephen d1935 WhoHol 92
Wentworth, Stephen 1943- Who 94
Wentworth, Theodore Sumner 1938- WhoAmL 94, WhoWest 94
Wentz, Billy Melvin, Jr. 1953- WhoAm 94
Wentz, Howard Beck, Jr. 1930- WhoAm 94, WhoFI 94
Wentz, Janet Marie 1937- WhoAmP 93, WhoWomW 91
Wentz, Jeffrey Lee 1956- WhoWest 94
Wentz, Sidney Frederick 1932- WhoAm 94
Wentz, Walter John 1928- WhoAm 94
Wentzel, Jacob Johannes Greyling 1925- IntWW 93
Wentzel, Karen Lynn 1949- WhoMW 93
Wentzler, Nancy Anne 1951- WhoFI 94
Wentzler, Thomas H. 1947- WhoScEn 94
Wen Xiaoyu 1938- BlmGWL
Wen Xiushan 1922- WhoPRCh 91 [port]
Wenzel, Arthur A. d1961 WhoHol 92
Wenzel, Arthur J. WhoHol 92
Wenzel, Carol Marion Nagler 1936- WhoWest 94
Wenzel, David J. 1945- WhoAmP 93
Wenzel, Donald Charles, Jr. 1959- WhoMW 93
Wenzel, Doris Replogle 1940- WhoMW 93
Wenzel, Elizabeth Marie 1954- WhoWest 94
Wenzel, Fred William 1916- WhoAm 94, WhoFI 94
Wenzel, James Gottlieb 1926- WhoAm 94
Wenzel, Joan Ellen WhoAmA 93
Wenzel, Lee Bey 1930-1990 WhAm 10
Wenzel, Leonard Andrew 1923- WhoAm 94
Wenzel, Sandra Lee Ann 1940- WhoMW 93
Wenzel, Stephen G. 1946- WhoAmP 93
Wenzig, Josef 1807-1875 NewGrDO
Wenzler, Edward William 1954- WhoMW 93
Wenzler, William Paul 1929- WhoAm 94
Wepener, Willem Jacobus 1927- IntWW 93
Wepman, Barry Jay 1944- WhoScEn 94
Weppner, Robert Stephens 1936- WhoAm 94
Weprin, Saul 1927- WhoAmP 93
Werba, Gabriel 1930- WhoAm 94
Werbach, Melvyn Roy 1940- WhoScEn 94, WhoWest 94
Werber, Stephen Jay 1940- WhoAm 94, WhoAmL 94
Werbiseck, Gisela d1956 WhoHol 92
Werblow, Joan Louise 1939- WhoFI 94
Werbner, Eliot DrAPF 93
Werbos, Paul John 1947- WhoScEn 94
Werbow, Stanley Newman 1922- WhoAm 94
Werckmeister, O(tto) K(arl) 1934- ConAu 140
Werckmeister, Otto Karl 1934- WhoAm 94
Werder, Felix 1922- NewGrDO
Werder, Mark Robert 1949- WhoAmL 94
Were, Miriam 1940- BlmGWL
Werfel, Alma 1879-1962 BlmGWL
Werfel, Franz 1890-1945 EncSF 93, NewGrDO
Werfel, Gina S. 1951- WhoAmA 93
Werger, Art(hur Lawrence) 1955- WhoAmA 93
Werger, Marinus Johannes Antonius 1944- IntWW 93
Werger, Paul Myron 1931- WhoMW 93
Werich, Jan d1980 WhoHol 92
Werkema, Steven John 1956- WhoMW 93
Werkheiser, Steven Lawrence 1945- WhoWest 94
Werkhoven, Theunis 1922- WhoAmP 93
Werking, Richard Hume 1943- WhoAm 94
Werkman, Nick 1942- BasBi
Werkman, Sidney Lee 1927- WhoAm 94
Werle, Barbara WhoHol 92
Werle, Lars Johan 1926- NewGrDO
Werlein, Ewing, Jr. 1936- WhoAm 94, WhoAmL 94
Werling, Donn Paul 1945- WhoAm 94
Werlock, Abby Holmes Potter 1942- WhoMW 93
Werman, David Sanford 1922- WhoAm 94
Werman, Thomas Ehrlich 1945- WhoAm 94
Werme, Judith Georgette 1950- WhoAm 94
Wermers, Donald Joseph 1934- WhoMW 93
Wermers, Mary Ann 1946- WhoWest 94
Wermerskirchen, Mark G. 1962- WhoAmL 94
Wermiel, Jared Sam 1949- WhoScEn 94
Wermiel, Stephen Jacques 1950- WhoAmL 94
Wermuth, Mary Louella 1943- WhoMW 93
Wermuth, Michael Anthony 1946- WhoAmP 93
Wermuth, Paul Charles 1925- WhoAm 94
Wernecke, Heinz 1922- WhoFI 94, WhoMW 93
Werner, (Charles George) 1909- WhoAmA 93
Werner, Alfred 1866-1919 WorScD
Werner, Alfred 1911-1979 WhoAmA 93N
Werner, Alfred Emil Anthony 1911- Who 94
Werner, Alice 1859-1935 DcNaB MP
Werner, Andrew Joseph 1936- WhoScEn 94
Werner, Anthony Matthias 1894- WhAm 10
Werner, Arnold 1938- WhoMW 93
Werner, Barry Leonard 1944- WhoWest 94
Werner, Beverly Kay 1951- WhoMW 93
Werner, Burton Kready 1933- WhoFI 94, WhoIns 94
Werner, Cecelia Marie 1955- WhoMW 93
Werner, Charles George 1909- WhoAm 94
Werner, Christian Thor 1916- WhoMW 93
Werner, Clarence L. 1937- WhoAm 94, WhoFI 94, WhoMW 93
Werner, David Charles 1938- WhoMW 93
Werner, Donald (Lewis) 1929- WhoAmA 93
Werner, E. Louis, Jr. WhoAmL 94, WhoWest 94
Werner, Elmer Louis, Jr. 1927- WhoIns 94
Werner, Frank David 1922- WhoScEn 94
Werner, Frank Robert 1936- WhoAmA 93
Werner, Gerhard 1921- WhoAm 94
Werner, Glenn Allen 1955- WhoMW 93
Werner, Gloria S. 1940- WhoAm 94, WhoWest 94
Werner, Hans 1946- WrDr 94
Werner, Helene Rose 1946- WhoMW 93
Werner, Helmut 1936- IntWW 93
Werner, Howard 1951- WhoAmA 93
Werner, Joanne Loucille 1940- WhoFI 94
Werner, John Ellis 1932- WhoAm 94
Werner, Joseph 1925- WhoFI 94
Werner, Joseph Granberry 1940- WhoAm 94, WhoAmL 94
Werner, Karl Ferdinand 1924- IntWW 93
Werner, Mario 1931- WhoAm 94
Werner, Mark Henry 1954- WhoScEn 94
Werner, Marlin Spike 1927- WhoWest 94
Werner, (Robert) Mort 1916-1990 WhAm 10
Werner, Nancy Darlington 1942- WhoMW 93
Werner, Nat 1907-1991 WhoAmA 93N
Werner, Oskar d1984 WhoHol 92
Werner, Peter 1947- IntMPA 94
Werner, Pierre 1913- IntWW 93
Werner, Ralph 1935- WhoAmL 94
Werner, Richard Allen 1936- WhoWest 94
Werner, Richard Budd 1931- WhoAm 94
Werner, Richard Vincent 1948- WhoAm 94
Werner, Robert J. 1950- WhoAmL 94
Werner, Robert Joseph 1932- WhoAm 94
Werner, Robert L. 1913- WhoAm 94, WhoAmL 94
Werner, Roger Harry 1950- WhoWest 94
Werner, Roger Livingston, Jr. 1950- WhoAm 94
Werner, Ronald Louis 1924- Who 94
Werner, Roy Anthony 1944- WhoScEn 94, WhoWest 94
Werner, Sandra Lee 1938- WhoAmP 93
Werner, Seth Mitchell 1954- WhoAm 94
Werner, Sidney Charles 1909- WhoAm 94
Werner, Stuart Lloyd 1932- WhoFI 94
Werner, Thomas Lee 1945- WhoAm 94
Werner, Tom WhoAm 94, WhoWest 94
Werner-Jacobsen, Emmy Elisabeth 1929- WhoAm 94
Werner Vaughn, Salle WhoAmA 93
Werness, Hope B. 1943- WhoAmA 93
Wernette, Ronald Cole, Jr. 1960- WhoAmL 94
Wernham, Richard Bruce 1906- Who 94
Wernher der Gartenaere fl. c. 1265-1280 DcLB 138
Wernick, Andrew (Lee) 1945- ConAu 142
Wernick, Jack Harry 1923- WhoAm 94
Wernick, Justin 1936- WhoScEn 94
Wernick, Richard Frank 1934- WhoAm 94
Wernicke, Herbert 1946- NewGrDO
Wernicke, Otto d1965 WhoHol 92
Werper, Barton EncSF 93
Werrenrath, Reinald d1953 WhoHol 92
Werries, E. Dean 1929- WhoAm 94, WhoFI 94
Werris, Snag d1987 WhoHol 92
Wersba, Barbara 1932- TwCYAW, WrDr 94
Werson, James Byrd 1916- WhoAm 94
Werstler, Richard Emerson 1927- WhoAm 94
Wert, Charles Allen 1919- WhoAm 94, WhoMW 93, WhoScEn 94
Wert, Doris Lee 1959- WhoFI 94
Wert, James Junior 1933- WhoAm 94
Wert, James William 1946- WhoAm 94, WhoFI 94
Wert, Jonathan (Maxwell, Jr.) 1939- WrDr 94
Wert, Jonathan Maxwell, II 1939- WhoAm 94
Wert, Lucille Mathena 1919- WhoAm 94
Wert, Ned Oliver 1936- WhoAmA 93
Wert, Robert Clifton 1944- WhoAmL 94
Wertel, Joan Ellen 1951- WhoFI 94
Wertenbaker, Lael Tucker 1909- WrDr 94
Wertenbaker, Timberlake BlmGWL [port], IntWW 93, WrDr 94
Wertenbaker, (Lael Louisiana) Timberlake ConDr 93, IntDcT 2
Wertenberger, Steven Bruce 1953- WhoScEn 94
Werth, Andrew M. 1934- WhoAm 94
Werth, Susan 1948- WhoAm 94, WhoAmL 94
Werthan, Jeffrey Michael 1954- WhoAmL 94
Wertheim, Bill DrAPF 93
Wertheim, James Scott 1960- WhoAmL 94
Wertheim, Maurice, Mrs. d1974 WhoAmA 93N
Wertheim, Mitzi Mallina WhoAm 94
Wertheim, Robert Halley 1922- WhoAm 94
Wertheim, Sally Harris 1931- WhoAm 94
Wertheimer, David Eliot 1955- WhoScEn 94
Wertheimer, Franc 1927- WhoAm 94
Wertheimer, Fred WhoAmP 93
Wertheimer, Fredric Michael 1939- WhoAm 94
Wertheimer, James Louis 1944- WhoAm 94, WhoFI 94
Wertheimer, Richard Frederick, II 1943- WhoFI 94
Wertheimer, Richard James 1936- WhoAm 94
Wertheimer, Robert E. 1928- WhoFI 94
Wertheimer, Robert I. 1945- WhoAmL 94
Wertheimer, Sydney Bernard 1914- WhoAm 94
Wertheimer, Thomas 1938- IntMPA 94
Werthen, Hans Lennart Oscar 1919- IntWW 93
Werther, Ellen Ruth 1954- WhoAmL 94
Wertime, Richard DrAPF 93
Wertimer, Ned WhoHol 92
Wertimer, Sidney 1920- WhoAm 94
Wertkin, Gerard Charles 1940- WhoAm 94
Wertmuller, Lina 1928- IntMPA 94, IntWW 93
Wertmuller, Massimo WhoHol 92
Werts, Merrill Harmon 1922- WhoAmP 93, WhoMW 93
Wertsch, Paul Anthony 1943- WhoFI 94
Wertsman, Vladimir Filip 1929- WhoAm 94
Wertz, Andrew Walter, Sr. 1928- WhoBlA 94
Wertz, Barry L. 1942- WhoAmL 94
Wertz, Clarence d1935 WhoHol 92
Wertz, Glenda M. 1959- WhoFI 94
Wertz, Harvey Joe 1936- WhoWest 94
Wertz, Jack Lowell 1931- WhoAmP 93
Wertz, James Claude, Jr. 1931- WhoMW 93
Wertz, John Alan 1945- WhoMW 93
Wertz, Kenneth Dean 1946- WhoAm 94
Wertz, Robert Charles 1932- WhoAmP 93
Wertz, Spencer K. 1941- WhoAm 94
Wery, Carl d1975 WhoHol 92
Werzberger, Alan 1954- WhoAm 94, WhoScEn 94
Wesaw, George fl. 20th cent.- EncNAR
Wesaw, Tom fl. 20th cent.- EncNAR
Wesberry, James Pickett, Jr. 1934- WhoAm 94
Wesbury, Stuart Arnold, Jr. 1933- WhoAm 94, WhoFI 94
Wesche, Percival A. 1912- WhoAmP 93
Weschke, Karl Martin 1925- IntWW 93
Weschler, Anita WhoAm 94, WhoAmA 93
Weschler, Lawrence 1952- WrDr 94
Weschler, Lawrence Michael 1952- WhoAm 94
Wescoat, Kyle Burley 1951- WhoFI 94
Wescoatt, Rusty d1962 WhoHol 92
Wescoe, William Clarke 1920- WhoAm 94
Wescott, Paul 1904-1970 WhoAmA 93N
Wescott, Roger Williams 1925- WhoAm 94, WhoScEn 94
Wescourt, Gordon WhoHol 92
Weseli, Roger William 1932- WhoAm 94, WhoMW 93
Wesely, Don 1954- WhoAmP 93
Wesely, Donald Raymond 1954- WhoMW 93
Wesely, Edwin Joseph 1929- WhoAm 94
Wesemael, Francois WhoScEn 94
Wesemann, Wolfgang 1931- WhoScEn 94
Wesemeyer, Craig Herman 1965- WhoMW 93
Wesenberg, John Herman 1927- WhoAm 94
Wesener, Barbara Ann 1948- WhoMW 93
Wesierska, George, Mrs. Who 94
Wesil, Dennis 1915- Who 94
Weske, Brian WhoHol 92
Weske, J. Victor d1960 WhoHol 92
Wesker, Arnold 1932- BlmGEL, ConDr 93, IntDcT 2, IntWW 93, Who 94, WrDr 94
Weslager, Clinton Alfred 1909- WhoAm 94
Wesler, Oscar 1921- WhoAm 94
Wesley, Barbara Ann 1930- WhoBlA 94
Wesley, Charles 1707-1788 BlmGEL
Wesley, Clarence E. 1940- WhoBlA 94
Wesley, Clemon Herbert, Jr. 1936- WhoBlA 94
Wesley, Dean Edward 1937- WhoMW 93
Wesley, Elizabeth 1918- WrDr 94
Wesley, Gloria Walker 1928-1993 WhoBlA 94N
Wesley, Herman Eugene, III 1961- WhoBlA 94
Wesley, Irene Varelas 1943- WhoScEn 94
Wesley, James Paul 1921- WhoScEn 94
Wesley, James Wyatt, Jr. 1933- WhoAm 94
Wesley, John 1703-1791 BlmGEL, HisWorL [port]
Wesley, John 1928- WhoAmA 93
Wesley, John Mercer 1928- WhoAm 94
Wesley, John Milton DrAPF 93
Wesley, Mary IntWW 93, Who 94
Wesley, Mary 1912- WrDr 94
Wesley, Nathaniel, Jr. 1943- WhoBlA 94
Wesley, Richard (Errol) 1945- ConDr 93, WrDr 94
Wesley, Richard C. 1949- WhoAmP 93
Wesley, Richard Errol 1945- WhoBlA 94
Wesley, Stephen Burton 1949- WhoFI 94, WhoScEn 94
Wesley, Stephen Harrison 1961- WhoFI 94
Wesley, Virginia Anne 1951- WhoWest 94
Wesling, Donald Truman 1939- WhoAm 94
Weslock, Shelley Lee 1962- WhoMW 93
Wesnick, Richard James 1938- WhoAm 94, WhoWest 94
Wesolow, Adam 1923- WhoAm 94
Wesolowski, David Jude 1954- WhoScEn 94
Wesolowski, Leonard Vincent 1927- WhoFI 94
Wesolowski, Sigmund Adam d1993 NewYTBS 93 [port]
Wess, Julius WhoScEn 94
Wesse, David Joseph 1951- WhoFI 94, WhoMW 93
Wessel, Dennis James 1949- WhoMW 93
Wessel, Dick d1965 WhoHol 92
Wessel, Fred W. 1946- WhoAmA 93
Wessel, Harold Cosby 1916-1989 WhAm 10
Wessel, Helen S. WrDr 94
Wessel, Henry 1942- WhoAm 94, WhoAmA 93
Wessel, James Kenneth 1939- WhoScEn 94
Wessel, Jeanette Driver 1942- WhoAmP 93
Wessel, Johan Hermann EncSF 93
Wessel, Milton R. 1923-1991 WhAm 10
Wessel, Morris Arthur 1917- WhoScEn 94
Wessel, Nancy Kathryn 1935- WhoAmP 93
Wessel, Paul 1959- WhoScEn 94
Wessel, Peter 1952- WhoAmL 94
Wessel, Robert Leslie 1912- Who 94

Wessel, Thomas Mark 1956- *WhoFI 94*
Wessel, William Roy 1937- *WhoWest 94*
Wesselhoeft, Eleanor d1945 *WhoHol 92*
Wesselhoft, Charles William 1950- *WhoAmL 94*
Wesselink, David Duwayne 1942- *WhoAm 94, WhoFI 94*
Wessells, Norman Keith 1932- *WhoScEn 94*
Wesselmann, Glenn Allen 1932- *WhoMW 93*
Wesselmann, Tom 1931- *IntWW 93, WhoAmA 93*
Wessels, Charles Henry 1940- *WhoAmP 93*
Wessels, Daniel L. 1953- *WhoAmL 94*
Wessels, Glenn Anthony 1895-1982 *WhoAmA 93N*
Wessels, Izak Frederick 1948- *WhoWest 94*
Wessels, Leon 1946- *IntWW 93*
Wessels, Wolfgang 1948- *IntWW 93*
Wesselski, Clarence J. *WhoScEn 94*
Wessely, Carl Bernhard 1768-1826 *NewGrDO*
Wessely, Paula 1908- *WhoHol 92*
Wessendorf Knau, Suana Le 1953- *WhoMW 93*
Wesser, Yvonne D. 1935- *WhoAmA 93*
Wessex, Martyn *EncSF 93*
Wessinger, W. David 1924- *WhoAm 94*
Wessinger, William David 1951- *WhoScEn 94*
Wessjohann, Ludger Aloisius 1961- *WhoScEn 94*
Wessler, Melvin Dean 1932- *WhoFI 94, WhoWest 94*
Wessler, Richard Lee 1936- *WhoAm 94*
Wessler, Stanford 1917- *WhoAm 94*
Wessling, Donald Moore 1936- *WhoAm 94*
Wessling, Francis Christopher 1939- *WhoAm 94*
Wessling, Gregory Jay 1951- *WhoFI 94*
Wessling, Robert Bruce 1937- *WhoAm 94*
Wessman, Henry C. 1937- *WhoAmP 93*
Wessman, Joan Feeney 1950- *WhoMW 93*
Wessner, Deborah Marie 1950- *WhoFI 94*
Wessner, Kenneth Thomas 1922- *WhoFI 94*
Wesso, H.W. 1894- *EncSF 93*
Wessolowski, Hans Waldemar *EncSF 93*
Wesson, C. W. 1924- *WhoAmP 93*
Wesson, Cleo 1924- *WhoBlA 94*
Wesson, Daniel Baird 1825-1906 *WorInv*
Wesson, Dick d1979 *WhoHol 92*
Wesson, Eileen *WhoHol 92*
Wesson, Gene d1975 *WhoHol 92*
Wesson, Kenneth Alan 1948- *WhoBlA 94*
Wesson, Robert G. 1920-1991 *WhAm 10, WrDr 94N*
Wesson, William Simpson 1929- *WhoAm 94*
West *Who 94*
West, Adam 1929- *IntMPA 94, WhoHol 92*
West, Anthony 1914-1987 *EncSF 93*
West, Anthony C. 1910- *WrDr 94*
West, Arleigh Burton 1910- *WhoAm 94*
West, Arnold Sumner 1922- *WhoAm 94*
West, Arthur James, II 1927- *WhoAm 94*
West, Barbara *WhoHol 92*
West, Basil d1934 *WhoHol 92*
West, Ben, Jr. 1941- *WhoAmP 93*
West, Benjamin 1738-1820 *AmCulL*
West, Bernard 1931- *WhoAm 94*
West, Bernie 1918- *WhoHol 92*
West, Billie d1951 *WhoHol 92*
West, Billie d1967 *WhoHol 92*
West, Billy d1975 *WhoHol 92*
West, Billy 1892-1975 *WhoCom*
West, Billy Gene 1946- *WhoWest 94*
West, Bob 1931- *WhoAm 94*
West, Bradley Craig 1963- *WhoAmL 94*
West, Brian John 1935- *Who 94*
West, Brooks d1984 *WhoHol 92*
West, Buster d1966 *WhoHol 92*
West, Byron Kenneth 1933- *WhoAm 94, WhoFI 94*
West, Carol Catherine 1944- *WhoAmL 94*
West, Charles d1943 *WhoHol 92*
West, Charles Converse 1921- *WhoAm 94*
West, Charles David 1937- *WhoScEn 94*
West, Charles P. 1921- *WhoAmP 93*
West, Charles Patrick 1952- *WhoAm 94*
West, Charles W. 1898- *WhAm 10*
West, Christopher John 1941- *Who 94*
West, Christopher O. 1915-1981 *WhoBlA 94N*
West, Christopher Read 1950- *WhoAm 94, WhoAmL 94*
West, Christopher Robin 1944- *Who 94*
West, Christopher Wayne 1961- *WhoWest 94*
West, Clara Faye Johnson 1923- *WhoAmA 93*
West, Clark Darwin 1918- *WhoAm 94*
West, Colin 1951- *WrDr 94*
West, Cornel 1953- *ConBlB 5 [port], CurBio 93 [port], News 94-2 [port], WhoBlA 94*
West, D(onald) J(ames) 1924- *ConAu 42NR*
West, Dale Reed 1954- *WhoWest 94*
West, Daniel Alan 1955- *WhoFI 94*
West, Daniel Jones, Jr. 1949- *WhoAm 94*
West, David Arthur James 1927- *Who 94*
West, David Lee 1937- *WhoAmL 94*
West, David Thomson 1923- *Who 94*
West, David William 1937- *WhoAmP 93*
West, Delno Cloyde, Jr. 1936- *WhoWest 94*
West, Delouris Jeanne 1943- *WhoFI 94*
West, Dennis Paul 1944- *WhoScEn 94*
West, Dobson 1946- *WhoAmL 94*
West, Donald James 1924- *Who 94, WrDr 94*
West, Donald V. 1930- *WhoAm 94*
West, Dorothy 1905- *WrDr 94*
West, Dorothy 1907- *BlkWr 2, WhoBlA 94*
West, Dorothy 1912- *BlmGWL*
West, Dottie d1991 *WhAm 10*
West, Dottie 1932-1991 *WhoHol 92*
West, Doug 1967- *WhoBlA 94*
West, Douglas Brent 1953- *WhoMW 93*
West, E. Gordon 1933- *WhoAmA 93*
West, Earl M. 1912- *WhoBlA 94*
West, Earle Huddleston 1955- *WhoScEn 94*
West, Edna d1963 *WhoHol 92*
West, Edward Alan 1928- *WhoFI 94, WhoWest 94*
West, Edward Mark 1923- *IntWW 93, Who 94*
West, Edward Nason 1909-1990 *WhAm 10*
West, Edward Staunton 1896- *WhAm 10*
West, Elizabeth fl. 18th cent.- *BlmGWL*
West, Emery Joseph 1940- *WhoFI 94*
West, Emily J. 1810-1899 *EncNAR*
West, Ewan (D.) 1960- *ConAu 142*
West, Felton 1926- *WhoAm 94*
West, Ford d1936 *WhoHol 92*
West, Fowler Claude 1940- *WhoAmP 93*
West, Francis Horner 1909- *Who 94*
West, Francis James 1927- *IntWW 93, WrDr 94*
West, Frederic Hadleigh, Jr. 1956- *WhoFI 94*
West, Gail Berry 1942- *WhoAm 94*
West, Gary Richard 1954- *WhoAmL 94*
West, Gayle Dianne 1944- *WhoAmP 93*
West, George d1963 *WhoHol 92*
West, George 1936- *WhoAmP 93*
West, George Arthur Alston-Roberts- 1937- *Who 94*
West, George Ferdinand, Jr. 1940- *WhoBlA 94*
West, George M. 1923- *WhoAmP 93*
West, Gerald Ivan 1937- *WhoBlA 94*
West, Glenn D. 1953- *WhoAmL 94*
West, Glenn Edward 1944- *WhoAm 94, WhoFI 94*
West, Gus Knox 1961- *WhoHisp 94*
West, H. E. *WhoHol 92*
West, Harold Dadford 1904- *WhoBlA 94*
West, Harold Dadford 1962- *WhoMW 93*
West, Henry d1936 *WhoHol 92*
West, Henry St. Barbe d1935 *WhoHol 92*
West, Henry William 1917- *Who 94*
West, Herbert Buell 1916-1990 *WhAm 10*
West, Herbert Lee, Jr. 1947- *WhoBlA 94*
West, Howard Norton 1919- *WhoAm 94*
West, Hugh Brian 1939- *WhoMW 93*
West, Hugh Sterling 1930- *WhoFI 94, WhoWest 94*
West, Isabel d1942 *WhoHol 92*
West, J. A. d1928 *WhoHol 92*
West, J. Robinson 1946- *WhoAm 94, WhoAmP 93*
West, Jack Henry 1934- *WhoScEn 94, WhoWest 94*
West, Jade Christine 1950- *WhoAmP 93*
West, James E. 1951- *WhoAmP 93*
West, James Harold 1926- *WhoAm 94, WhoFI 94*
West, James Joe 1936- *WhoWest 94*
West, James Joseph 1945- *WhoAm 94*
West, James L(emuel) W(ills, III) 1946- *WrDr 94*
West, Jay 1951- *WhoAmP 93*
West, Jean *DrAPF 93*
West, Jerry 1938- *BasBi [port]*
West, Jerry Alan 1938- *WhoAm 94, WhoWest 94*
West, (Mary) Jessamyn 1902-1984 *EncSF 93, TwCYAW*
West, John 1778-1845 *EncNAR*
West, John A. 1940- *WhoAmL 94*
West, John Andrew 1942- *WhoBlA 94*
West, John Anthony *DrAPF 93*
West, John Burnard 1928- *WhoAm 94, WhoWest 94*
West, John C. 1922- *IntWW 93*
West, John Carl 1922- *WhoAmP 93*
West, John Clifford 1922- *Who 94*
West, John Dunham 1906-1989 *WhAm 10*
West, John Foster *DrAPF 93*
West, John Frederick 1929- *WrDr 94*
West, John G(ilbert) 1941- *ConAu 142*
West, John Gregory 1947- *WhoAmP 93*
West, John H., III 1942- *WhoAm 94, WhoAmL 94*
West, John L. 1944- *WhoAmL 94*
West, John Merle 1920- *WhoAm 94*
West, John Raymond 1931- *WhoBlA 94*
West, John S. d1944 *WhoHol 92*
West, John Thomas 1924- *WhoScEn 94*
West, Johnny Carl 1951- *WhoScEn 94*
West, Joseph D. 1949- *WhoAmL 94*
West, Joseph King 1929- *WhoAmL 94, WhoBlA 94*
West, Judi *WhoHol 92*
West, Karen *WhoHol 92*
West, Kathleene *DrAPF 93*
West, Keith H. 1948- *WhoAmL 94*
West, Kenneth 1930- *Who 94*
West, Kenneth Edward 1963- *WhoAmL 94*
West, Lee Roy 1929- *WhoAm 94, WhoAmL 94*
West, Lloyd Albert 1944- *WhoWest 94*
West, Lockwood d1989 *WhoHol 92*
West, Lois Jean 1939- *WhoMW 93*
West, Louis Jolyon 1924- *WhoAm 94, WhoWest 94*
West, M. Holland 1952- *WhoAmL 94*
West, Madge d1985 *WhoHol 92*
West, Mae d1980 *WhoHol 92*
West, Mae 1892-1980 *AmCulL*
West, Mae 1893-1980 *WhoCom [port]*
West, Marc Peter d1983 *WhoHol 92*
West, Marcella Polite *WhoBlA 94*
West, Marcellus 1913- *WhoBlA 94*
West, Marianne V. 1951- *WhoMW 93*
West, Mark Andre 1960- *WhoBlA 94*
West, Mark David 1964- *WhoScEn 94*
West, Mark Johnson 1954- *WhoFI 94*
West, Martin *WhoHol 92*
West, Martin Litchfield 1937- *IntWW 93, Who 94*
West, Marvin Leon 1934- *WhoAm 94*
West, Matt 1958- *WhoHol 92*
West, Maxine Marilyn 1945- *WhoMW 93*
West, Michael *DrAPF 93*
West, Michael Alan 1938- *WhoAm 94, WhoMW 93*
West, Michael Charles B. *Who 94*
West, Michael Howard 1952- *WhoScEn 94*
West, Michael M. A. R. 1905-1978 *HisDcKW*
West, Michelle Lynne 1961- *WhoAm 94*
West, Millard Farrar, Jr. 1910- *WhoAm 94*
West, Morris (Langlo) 1916- *EncSF 93, IntWW 93, Who 94, WrDr 94*
West, Morris Langlo 1916- *WhoAm 94*
West, Myrna Louise 1941- *WhoMW 93*
West, Natalie E. 1947- *WhoAmL 94*
West, Nigel *Who 94*
West, Norman 1935- *Who 94*
West, Norman Ariel 1928- *WhoAmL 94*
West, Olive d1943 *WhoHol 92*
West, Owen *EncSF 93, TwCYAW*
West, Owen 1945- *WrDr 94*
West, Pamela 1945- *EncSF 93*
West, Pamela Marshall 1956- *WhoAmL 94*
West, Pat d1944 *WhoHol 92*
West, Paul *DrAPF 93*
West, Paul 1930- *WrDr 94*
West, Paul Noden 1930- *WhoAm 94*
West, Pennerton d1965 *WhoAmA 93N*
West, Peter 1920- *Who 94*
West, Peter 1953- *WhoAmA 93*
West, Pheoris 1950- *WhoBlA 94*
West, Philip William 1913- *WhoAm 94, WhoScEn 94*
West, Pilar Ramirez 1935- *WhoHisp 94*
West, Prunella Margaret Rumney *Who 94*
West, Ralph Leland 1915- *WhoAm 94*
West, Ralph W., Jr. *WhoAm 94, WhoWest 94*
West, Rebecca d1983 *WhoHol 92*
West, Rebecca 1892-1983 *BlmGWL [port]*
West, Rexford Leon 1938- *WhoAm 94*
West, Rhea Horace, Jr. 1920-1990 *WhAm 10*
West, Richard G. 1926- *IntWW 93*
West, Richard Gilbert 1926- *Who 94*
West, Richard John 1939- *Who 94*
West, Richard Luther 1925- *WhoAm 94*
West, Richard Paul 1947- *WhoWest 94*
West, Richard Rollin 1938- *WhoAm 94*
West, Richard Vincent 1934- *WhoAm 94, WhoAmA 93*
West, Rita Ann d1986 *WhoHol 92*
West, Robert Cooper 1913- *WhoAm 94*
West, Robert Culbertson 1928- *WhoAm 94, WhoMW 93, WhoScEn 94*
West, Robert Hunter 1907- *WhAm 10*
West, Robert Lewis 1951- *WhoFI 94*
West, Robert MacLellan 1942- *WhoAm 94, WhoScEn 94*
West, Robert Sumner 1935- *WhoWest 94*
West, Robert V., Jr. 1921- *WhoAmP 93*
West, Robert Van Osdell, Jr. 1921- *WhoAm 94, WhoFI 94*
West, Roberta Bertha 1904- *WhoMW 93*
West, Roger Seiker, III 1949- *WhoFI 94*
West, Ronald D. 1952- *WhoAmL 94*
West, Ronald David 1954- *WhoMW 93*
West, Roy A. 1930- *WhoAmP 93*
West, Royce 1952- *WhoAmP 93*
West, Royce Barry 1952- *WhoBlA 94*
West, Ruth Tinsley 1945- *WhoAm 94, WhoAmL 94*
West, Sally Jo 1951- *WhoMW 93*
West, Samuel *WhoHol 92*
West, Samuel 1731-1807 *WhAmRev*
West, Samuel Edward 1938- *WhoFI 94*
West, Sarah Jane 1963- *WhoMW 93*
West, Shelby Jay 1938- *WhoFI 94, WhoWest 94*
West, Stephanie Roberta 1937- *Who 94*
West, Stephen Allan 1935- *WhoAm 94*
West, Stephen Kingsbury 1928- *WhoAm 94*
West, Stephen Owen 1946- *WhoAm 94*
West, Stephen Robert 1931- *WhoAmP 93*
West, Stewart John 1934- *IntWW 93*
West, Tamsin *WhoHol 92*
West, Terence Douglas 1948- *WhoFI 94*
West, Thomas d1932 *WhoHol 92*
West, Thomas A. *DrAPF 93*
West, Thomas Lowell, Jr. 1937- *WhoFI 94*
West, Thomas Meade 1940- *WhoAm 94, WhoFI 94, WhoMW 93*
West, Thomas Moore 1940- *WhoWest 94*
West, Thomas Patrick 1953- *WhoMW 93*
West, Thomas Summers 1927- *Who 94*
West, Timothy 1934- *IntMPA 94, WhoHol 92*
West, Timothy Lancaster 1934- *IntWW 93, Who 94*
West, Togo Dennis, Jr. 1942- *WhoAm 94, WhoBlA 94, WhoFI 94*
West, Tony d1923 *WhoHol 92*
West, Tony 1937- *WhoAm 94, WhoAmP 93, WhoWest 94*
West, Vikki Lynn 1948- *WhoWest 94*
West, Virginia M. *WhoAmA 93*
West, W. C. d1918 *WhoHol 92*
West, W. Richard 1912- *WhoAmA 93*
West, Wallace (George) 1900-1980 *EncSF 93*
West, Wally *WhoHol 92*
West, Weldon Wallace 1921- *WhoWest 94*
West, Will d1922 *WhoHol 92*
West, William Beverley, III 1922- *WhoAm 94*
West, William Dixon 1901- *Who 94*
West, William H. d1915 *WhoHol 92*
West, William Lionel 1923- *WhoBlA 94*
West, William M. 1948- *WhoWest 94*
West, William Ward 1963- *WhoScEn 94*
Westall, Robert d1993 *NewYTBS 93*
Westall, Robert 1929-1993 *Au&Arts 12 [port], WrDr 94N*
Westall, Robert (Atkinson) 1929- *EncSF 93*
Westall, Robert (Atkinson) 1929-1993 *ConAu 141, SmATA 75, TwCYAW*
Westall, Robert Atkinson d1993 *Who 94N*
Westall, William 1781-1850 *WhWE*
Westall, William (Bury) 1835-1903 *EncSF 93*
Westapal, Adrian Ely 1935- *WhoFI 94*
Westbay, Charles Duane 1930- *WhoFI 94*
Westberg, Helen Groff 1917- *WhoAmP 93*
Westberg, John Augustin 1931- *WhoAmL 94*
Westberg, Robert Myers 1932- *WhoAm 94*
Westberry, Billy Murry 1926- *WhoAm 94*
Westblom, T. Ulf 1951- *WhoMW 93*
Westbo, Leonard Archibald, Jr. 1931- *WhoWest 94*
Westbrook, April Lynn 1942- *WhoAmP 93*
Westbrook, Edward J. 1952- *WhoAmL 94*
Westbrook, Elouise *WhoBlA 94*
Westbrook, Eric Ernest 1915- *Who 94*
Westbrook, Franklin Solomon 1958- *WhoBlA 94*
Westbrook, Fred Emerson 1916- *WhoScEn 94*
Westbrook, Gilson Howard 1947- *WhoBlA 94*
Westbrook, James Edwin 1934- *WhoAm 94*
Westbrook, Joel Whitsitt, III 1916- *WhoAm 94, WhoAmL 94*
Westbrook, John d1989 *WhoHol 92*
Westbrook, Joseph W., III 1919- *WhoBlA 94*

Westbrook, Michael John David 1936-
Who 94
Westbrook, Neil (Gowanloch) 1917-
Who 94
Westbrook, Patrick Alan De Lujan 1924-
WhAm 10
Westbrook, Paul 1939- *WhoFI 94*
Westbrook, Perry D *WrDr 94*
Westbrook, Roger 1941- *IntWW 93,
Who 94*
Westbrook, Scott C., III 1939-1991
WhoBlA 94N
Westbrook, Susan Elizabeth 1939-
WhoScEn 94
Westbrooks, Alphonso 1934- *WhoMW 93*
Westbrooks, Logan H. 1937- *WhoBlA 94*
Westbury, Baron 1922- *Who 94*
Westbury, Gerald 1927- *Who 94*
Westby, Steven A. 1954- *WhoAmL 94*
Westby, Timothy Scott 1957-
WhoScEn 94
Westcoat, Rusty d1987 *WhoHol 92*
Westcott, Brian John 1957- *WhoFI 94,
WhoWest 94*
Westcott, Frederick John 1866-1941
DcNaB MP
Westcott, George Lamar 1894- *WhAm 10*
Westcott, Gordon d1935 *WhoHol 92*
Westcott, Helen 1928- *WhoHol 92*
Westcott, Helen 1929- *IntMPA 94*
Westcott, Jan (Vlachos) 1912- *WrDr 94*
Westcott, John Hugh 1920- *IntWW 93,
Who 94*
Westcott, John McMahon, Jr. 1944-
WhoAm 94, WhoAmL 94
Westcott, Netta d1953 *WhoHol 92*
Westcott, Walker d1978 *WhoHol 92*
Westcott Jones, Kenneth 1921- *WrDr 94*
West Cumberland, Archdeacon of *Who 94*
West-Eberhard, Mary Jane 1941-
WhoAm 94
Westenbarger, Don Edward 1928-
WhoFI 94, WhoMW 93
Westendorf, Gayl A. 1950- *WhoAmL 94*
Westendorf, Wolfhart 1924- *IntWW 93*
Westenfelder, Christof 1942- *WhoWest 94*
Westenfelder, Grant Orville 1940-
WhoMW 93
Westenholtz, Ernst Carl Ludwig
1694-1753 *NewGrDO*
Westenra *Who 94*
Wester, Barbara Ann 1966- *WhoAm 94*
Wester, John R. 1946- *WhoAmL 94*
Wester, Keith Albert 1940- *WhoAm 94,
WhoWest 94*
Wester, Richard Clark 1945- *WhoBlA 94*
Westerbeck, Daniel J. 1944- *WhoMW 93*
Westerbeck, David F. 1945- *WhoIns 94*
Westerbeck, Gregory Joseph 1952-
WhoMW 93
Westerbeck, Kenneth Edward 1919-
WhoAm 94
Westerberg, Arthur William 1938-
WhoAm 94
Westerberg, Bengt 1943- *IntWW 93*
Westerberg, Kurt Hagen 1950-
WhoMW 93
Westerberg, Per 1951- *IntWW 93*
Westerberg, Thomas Bates 1930-
WhoFI 94
Westerberg, Verne Edward 1931-
WhoAm 94
Westerberg, Victor John 1912-
WhoAmP 93
Westerdahl, John Brian 1954-
WhoAm 94, WhoScEn 94, WhoWest 94
Westerfield, H(olt) Bradford 1928-
WrDr 94
Westerfield, Hargis *DrAPF 93*
Westerfield, Holt Bradford 1928-
WhoAm 94
Westerfield, James d1971 *WhoHol 92*
Westerfield, Louis 1949- *WhoBlA 94*
Westerfield, Nancy G. *DrAPF 93*
Westerfield, Putney 1930- *IntWW 93,
WhoAm 94, WhoFI 94*
Westergaard, John (Harald) 1927-
ConAu 43NR
Westergaard, Peter (Talbot) 1931-
NewGrDO
Westergaard, Peter Talbot 1931-
WhoAm 94
Westergard, Mark S. 1955- *WhoAmL 94*
Westerhaus, Douglas Bernard 1951-
WhoAmL 94
Westerhoff, Harold E. 1915- *WhoAm 94*
Westerhoff, John Henry, III 1933-
WhoAm 94
Westerholm, Leo Lyder 1922-
WhoAmP 93
Westerhout, Gart 1927- *WhoAm 94,
WhoScEn 94*
Westerhout, Nicola van 1857-1898
NewGrDO
Westerling, Karel 1929- *WhoAm 94*
Westerlund, Bengt Elis 1921- *IntWW 93*
Westerlund, Catrin d1982 *WhoHol 92*

Westerlund Roosen, Mia 1942-
WhoAmA 93
Westerman, (Wilfred) Alan 1913-
IntWW 93, Who 94
Westerman, Arnold Rodman 1938-
WhoAm 94
Westerman, Floyd *WhoHol 92*
Westerman, Gayl Shaw 1939- *WhoAm 94,
WhoAmL 94*
Westerman, Percy F. *EncSF 93*
Westerman, Peter F. 1942- *WhoMW 93*
Westerman, Philip William 1945-
WhoMW 93, WhoScEn 94
Westerman, Susan S. 1943- *WhoAm 94*
Westerman, Sylvia Hewitt *WhoAm 94*
Westermann, David 1920- *WhoAm 94*
Westermann, H. C. 1922- *WhoAmA 93*
Westermann, Horace Clifford 1922-
WhoAm 94
Westermann, Horace Clifford 1922-1981
WhoAmA 93N
Westermarck, Edward (Alexander)
1862-1939 *EncEth*
Westermeier, John Thomas, Jr. 1941-
WhoAmL 94
Westermeier, Paul d1972 *WhoHol 92*
Western, Arthur Boyd, Jr. 1944-
WhoScEn 94
Western, Ethel *NewGrDO*
Western, Mark 1937- *WrDr 94*
Western, T. S. d1931 *WhoHol 92*
Westerterp, Theodorus Engelbertus (Tjerk)
1930- *IntWW 93*
Westerton, Frank H. d1923 *WhoHol 92*
Westervelt, James 1946- *WhoIns 94*
Westervelt, James Joseph 1946-
WhoAm 94, WhoFI 94
Westervelt, Jane McQuaid 1927-
WhoAmP 93
Westervelt, Robert F. 1928- *WhoAmA 93*
Westfahl, Bernard James 1947-
WhoAmL 94
Westfall, Bernard G. 1941- *WhoAm 94*
Westfall, Carol D. 1938- *WhoAmA 93*
Westfall, Carroll William 1937-
WhoAm 94
Westfall, John Edward 1938-
WhoWest 94
Westfall, Linda Louise 1954-
WhoScEn 94
Westfall, Morris Gene 1939- *WhoAmP 93*
Westfall, Richard Merrill 1956-
WhoWest 94
Westfall, Richard S(amuel) 1924-
WrDr 94
Westfall, Richard Samuel 1924-
WhoAm 94
Westfall, Stephen Donald 1953-
WhoFI 94
Westfall, Stephen V. R. 1953-
WhoAmA 93
Westgaard, Thomas Paul 1939-
WhoAmP 93
West Ham, Archdeacon of *Who 94*
Westheimer, David *DrAPF 93*
Westheimer, David 1917- *WrDr 94*
Westheimer, David Kaplan 1917-
WhoAm 94
Westheimer, Frank Henry 1912-
IntWW 93, WhoAm 94, WhoScEn 94
Westheimer, Gerald 1924- *Who 94,
WhoAm 94, WhoWest 94*
Westheimer, Ruth 1928- *WhoHol 92*
Westheimer, (Karola) Ruth 1928-
WrDr 94
Westheimer, Ruth Siegel *WhoAm 94*
Westheimer, Ruth Welling 1922-
WhoAm 94
Westhoff, Dennis Charles 1942-
WhoAm 94
Westin, Alan Furman 1929- *WhoAm 94*
Westin, David Lawrence 1952-
WhoAmL 94
Westin, Robert H. 1946- *WhoAmA 93*
Westin, Robert Lee 1932- *WhoWest 94*
West Indies, Archbishop of 1928- *Who 94*
Westine, Lezlee Hiegel 1960- *WhoWest 94*
Westinghouse, George 1846-1914 *WorInv*
Westlake, Donald E 1933- *WrDr 94*
Westlake, Donald E(dwin Edmund)
1933- *EncSF 93*
Westlake, Donald Edwin 1933-
WhoAm 94
Westlake, Michael 1942- *EncSF 93*
Westlake, Paul Edward, Jr. 1952-
WhoMW 93
Westlake, Peter Alan Grant 1919- *Who 94*
Westlake, Robert Elmer, Sr. 1918-
WhoAm 94
Westlake, Vernon L. 1921- *WhoAmP 93*
Westley, Helen d1942 *WhoHol 92*
Westley, John d1948 *WhoHol 92*
Westley, John Richard 1939- *WhoAm 94,
WhoFI 94*
Westlin, Bertil 1911- *WhoFI 94*
Westling, Hakan 1928- *IntWW 93*
Westling, Jon 1942- *WhoAm 94*

Westling, Louise (Hutchings) 1942-
WrDr 94
Westling, Louise Hutchings 1942-
WhoWest 94
Westlock, Jeannine Marie 1959-
WhoMW 93, WhoScEn 94
Westlund, Harry E. 1941- *WhoAmA 93*
Westly, Steven Paul 1956- *WhoAmP 93,
WhoWest 94*
Westmacott, Richard 1941- *ConAu 141*
Westmacott, Richard Kelso 1934- *Who 94*
Westman, Carl Edward 1943- *WhoAm 94,
WhoAmL 94*
Westman, Jack Conrad 1927- *WhoAm 94*
Westman, John Albert 1938- *WhoFI 94*
Westman, Nydia d1970 *WhoHol 92*
Westman, Patricia Ann 1941-
WhoAmP 93
Westman, Richard A. 1959- *WhoAmP 93*
Westman, Robert Allan 1926-
WhoMW 93
Westman, Theodore, Jr. d1927
WhoHol 92
Westman, Wesley Charles 1936-
WhoScEn 94
Westmark, Stephen Harold 1949-
WhoMW 93
Westmeath, Earl of 1928- *Who 94*
Westmeyer, Mark Paul 1962- *WhoMW 93*
Westminster, Archbishop of 1923-
Who 94
Westminster, Auxiliary Bishop of *Who 94*
Westminster, Dean of *Who 94*
Westminster, Duke 1951- *IntWW 93*
Westminster, Duke of 1951- *Who 94*
Westminster, Ayn 1938- *WrDr 94*
Westminster, Edward of d1265
DcNaB MP
Westmore, Bud 1918- *IntDcF 2-4 [port]
See Also* Westmore Family, The
IntDcF 2-4
Westmore, Ern 1904-1968 *IntDcF 2-4
See Also* Westmore Family, The
IntDcF 2-4
Westmore, Frank 1923-1985 *IntDcF 2-4
See Also* Westmore Family, The
IntDcF 2-4
Westmore, George 1879-1931 *IntDcF 2-4
See Also* Westmore Family, The
IntDcF 2-4
Westmore, Michael George 1938-
WhoAm 94
Westmore, Mont 1902-1940 *IntDcF 2-4
See Also* Westmore Family, The
IntDcF 2-4
Westmore, Perc d1970 *WhoHol 92*
Westmore, Perc 1904-1970 *IntDcF 2-4
See Also* Westmore Family, The
IntDcF 2-4
Westmore, Richard Louis, IV 1956-
WhoMW 93
Westmore, Wally 1906-1973 *IntDcF 2-4
See Also* Westmore Family, The
IntDcF 2-4
Westmore Family, The *IntDcF 2-4 [port]*
Westmoreland, James *WhoHol 92*
Westmoreland, Jim 1937- *WhoAmP 93*
Westmoreland, Keith *WhoAmP 93*
Westmoreland, Kent Ewing 1949-
WhoAm 94, WhoAmL 94
Westmoreland, Lynn A. 1950-
WhoAmP 93
Westmoreland, Norma Jane 1936-
WhoAmP 93
Westmoreland, Reginald Conway 1926-
WhoAm 94
Westmoreland, Samuel Douglas 1944-
WhoBlA 94
Westmoreland, William Childs 1914-
IntWW 93
Westmorland, Earl of d1993 *Who 94N*
Westmorland, Earl of 1924- *IntWW 93*
Westmorland, Earl of 1951- *Who 94*
Westmorland And Furness, Archdeacon
of *Who 94*
Westoff, Charles F 1927- *WrDr 94*
Westoff, Charles Francis 1927-
WhoAm 94
Westoll, James 1918- *Who 94*
Westoll, Thomas Stanley 1912- *Who 94*
Weston, Allen 1905- *WrDr 94*
Weston, Arthur Walter 1914 *WhoAm 94*
Weston, Bert d1936 *WhoHol 92*
Weston, Bertram John 1907- *Who 94*
Weston, Brad *WhoHol 92*
Weston, Brett 1911-1993 *NewYTBS 93*
Weston, (Theodore) Brett 1911-1993
CurBio 93N
Weston, Bryan Henry 1930- *Who 94*
Weston, Burns H. 1933- *WrDr 94*
Weston, Cecil d1945 *WhoHol 92*
Weston, Cecil d1976 *WhoHol 92*
Weston, Celia *WhoHol 92*
Weston, Charles Arthur Winfield 1922-
Who 94
Weston, Christopher John 1937- *Who 94*
Weston, Cole 1951- *WrDr 94*

Weston, Corinne Comstock 1919-
WrDr 94
Weston, David 1938- *WhoHol 92*
Weston, David Wilfrid Valentine 1937-
Who 94
Weston, Deirdre Denise 1964-
WhoWest 94
Weston, Dick *WhoHol 92*
Weston, Donna Jean 1950- *WhoFI 94*
Weston, Doris d1960 *WhoHol 92*
Weston, Eddie 1925- *WhoHol 92*
Weston, Edward 1925- *WhoWest 94*
Weston, Edward Henry 1886-1958
AmCulL
Weston, Frances 1954- *WhoAmP 93*
Weston, Frank Valentine 1935- *Who 94*
Weston, Galen *Who 94*
Weston, Garfield Howard 1927-
IntWW 93, Who 94
Weston, Geoffrey Harold 1920- *Who 94*
Weston, George 1880-1965 *EncSF 93*
Weston, Harold 1894-1972 *WhoAmA 93N*
Weston, Jack 1915- *WhoHol 92*
Weston, Jack 1924- *IntMPA 94*
Weston, Jay 1929- *IntMPA 94*
Weston, Jeff *WhoHol 92*
Weston, Jessie Edith 1867-1944 *BlmGWL*
Weston, Joe d1972 *WhoHol 92*
Weston, John *Who 94*
Weston, (Philip) John 1938- *IntWW 93,
Who 94*
Weston, John Carruthers *Who 94*
Weston, John Frederick 1916-
WhoAm 94, WhoFI 94
Weston, John Pix 1920- *Who 94*
Weston, John William 1915- *Who 94*
Weston, Josh S. 1928- *WhoAm 94,
WhoFI 94*
Weston, Kath 1958- *WhoWest 94*
Weston, Kim *WhoHol 92*
Weston, Larry Carlton 1948- *WhoBlA 94*
Weston, Leslie *WhoHol 92*
Weston, M. Moran, II 1910- *WhoBlA 94,
WhoFI 94*
Weston, Maggie d1926 *WhoHol 92*
Weston, Margaret (Kate) 1926- *Who 94*
Weston, Mark *WhoHol 92*
Weston, Martin V. 1947- *WhoBlA 94*
Weston, Michael (Charles Swift) 1937-
Who 94
Weston, Michael C. 1938- *WhoAmL 94*
Weston, Michael Charles Swift 1937-
IntWW 93
Weston, Paul *WhoAm 94*
Weston, Peter 1944- *EncSF 93*
Weston, Phyllis Jean 1921- *WhoMW 93*
Weston, R. Timothy 1947- *WhoAm 94,
WhoAmP 93*
Weston, Randy 1926- *WhoAm 94*
Weston, Randy 1958- *WhoAmP 93*
Weston, Roger Lance 1943- *WhoAm 94,
WhoFI 94*
Weston, Roy Francis 1911- *WhoAm 94*
Weston, Ruth d1955 *WhoHol 92*
Weston, Sharon 1956- *WhoAmP 93,
WhoBlA 94*
Weston, Susan 1943- *WrDr 94*
Weston, Susan (Brown) 1943- *EncSF 93*
Weston, Susan B. *DrAPF 93*
Weston, Theodore Brett 1911-
WhoAm 94, WhoWest 94
Weston, W(illard) Galen 1940- *Who 94*
Weston, Willard Galen 1940- *WhoAm 94,
WhoFI 94*
Weston, William 1926- *WrDr 94*
Weston, William Lee 1938- *WhoAm 94*
Weston, William R. 1947- *WhoIns 94*
Westover, Samuel Lee 1955- *WhoAm 94,
WhoWest 94*
Westover, Winifred d1978 *WhoHol 92*
Westphal, Andrew Jonathan 1961-
WhoScEn 94
Westphal, Everett August 1914-1988
WhAm 10
Westphal, Heinz 1924- *IntWW 93*
Westphal, Hugo Louis, III 1953-
WhoMW 93
Westphal, James Phillip 1961-
WhoAmL 94
Westphal, Klaus Wilhelm 1939-
WhoScEn 94
Westphal, Leonard Wyrick 1946-
WhoAm 94, WhoMW 93
Westphal, Marjorie Lord 1940-
WhoAmL 94
Westphal, Paul 1950- *BasBi, WhoAm 94,
WhoWest 94*
Westphal-Cantrell, Deborah Louise
WhoMW 93
Westphalen, Mary Lynne 1943-
WhoMW 93
Westra, Vincent Castelli 1952-
WhoAmL 94
Westray, Kenneth Maurice 1952-
WhoBlA 94
Westreich, Natalie Jean-Grodnik 1936-
WhoMW 93
Westrup, Jack Allan 1904-1975 *NewGrDO*

West-Russell, David (Sturrock) 1921- *Who 94*
Westwater, Angela King 1942- *WhoAmA 93*
Westwater, Heather 1968- *WhoWest 94*
Westwater, James William 1919- *WhoAm 94*
Westwell, Alan Reynolds 1940- *Who 94*
Westwood, Baron 1944- *Who 94*
Westwood, Albert Ronald Clifton 1932- *WhoAm 94*
Westwood, Gordon 1919- *WrDr 94*
Westwood, Gwen 1915- *WrDr 94*
Westwood, James Nicholson 1944- *WhoAm 94, WhoAmL 94*
Westwood, Jean Miles 1923- *WhoAmP 93*
Westwood, John Norton 1931- *WrDr 94*
Westwood, Melvin Neil 1923- *WhoAm 94*
Westwood, Vivienne *IntWW 93*
Westwood, William John *Who 94*
Wetanson, Burt *EncSF 93*
Wetenhall, John 1957- *WrDr 94*
Wetere, Koro Tainui 1935- *IntWW 93*
Wetesnik, Kim Marie 1958- *WhoAm 94*
Wetherald, Agnes Ethelwyn 1857-1940 *BlmGWL*
Wetherald, Dawn Margaret 1963- *WhoMW 93*
Wetherall, Frances d1923 *WhoHol 92*
Wetherby, Lawrence Winchester 1908- *WhoAmP 93*
Wethered, Joyce 1901- *Who 94*
Wethered, Julian Frank Baldwin 1929- *Who 94*
Wetherell, Alan Marmaduke 1932- *Who 94*
Wetherell, Claire 1919- *WhoAmP 93, WhoWest 94*
Wetherell, Elizabeth *BlmGWL*
Wetherell, Gordon Geoffrey 1948- *Who 94*
Wetherell, M. A. d1939 *WhoHol 92*
Wetherell, Michael E. 1945- *WhoWest 94*
Wetherell, Michael Edward 1945- *WhoAmP 93*
Wetherell, Thomas Kent 1945- *WhoAmP 93*
Wetherell, Virginia 1943- *WhoHol 92*
Wetherell, W. D. *DrAPF 93*
Wetherill, Eikins 1919- *WhoAm 94*
Wetherill, George West 1925- *IntWW 93, WhoAm 94, WhoScEn 94*
Wetherington, C Barry 1940- *WhoAm 94*
Wetherington, Tom Lee 1926- *WhoAmP 93*
Wethey, Harold Edwin 1902-1984 *WhoAmA 93N*
Wethington, Charles T., Jr. *WhoAm 94*
Wethington, John Abner, Jr. 1921- *WhoAm 94*
Wethington, Norbert Anthony 1943- *WhoMW 93*
Wethington, Wilma Zella 1918- *WhoAmA 93*
Wethington-Hadley, Wilma Zella *WhoAmA 93*
Wethli, Mark 1949- *WhoAmA 93*
Wetlaufer, Donald Burton 1925- *WhoAm 94, WhoScEn 94*
Wetmore, Claude H(azeltine) 1862-1944 *EncSF 93*
Wetmore, Frank Orton, II 1929-1989 *WhAm 10*
Wetmore, Gordon 1938- *WhoAmA 93*
Wetmore, Joan d1989 *WhoHol 92*
Wetmore, Michael H. 1949- *WhoAmL 94*
Wetmore, Robert D. 1930- *WhoAmP 93*
Wetmore, Thomas Trask, III 1925- *WhoAm 94*
Wetmore, William *DrAPF 93*
Wetsch, John Robert 1959- *WhoScEn 94*
Wetsch, Peggy A. *WhoWest 94*
Wetstein, Gary M. *WhoAm 94, WhoFI 94*
Wettach, George Edward 1940- *WhoWest 94*
Wettach, Thomas C. 1941- *WhoAmL 94*
Wettack, F. Sheldon *WhoAm 94*
Wettaw, John 1939- *WhoAmP 93*
Wette, Adelheid 1858-1916 *NewGrDO*
Wette, Eduard Wilhelm 1925- *WhoScEn 94*
Wettenhall, Roger L. 1931- *WrDr 94*
Wetter, Edward 1919- *WhoAm 94*
Wetter, Friedrich 1928- *IntWW 93*
Wetter, Jack 1943- *WhoWest 94*
Wetter, Melvin G. 1929- *WhoAmP 93*
Wetterau, Theodore C. 1927- *WhoAm 94, WhoFI 94*
Wettergreen, Richard A. 1943- *WhoIns 94*
Wettergren, Gertrud 1897- *NewGrDO*
Wetters, Howard *WhoAmP 93*
Wettig, Patricia *WhoAm 94*
Wettig, Patricia 1951- *IntMPA 94, WhoHol 92*
Wetton, Philip Henry Davan 1937- *Who 94*
Wettstein, Diter von 1929- *IntWW 93*
Wetz, Richard 1875-1935 *NewGrDO*
Wetzel, Carroll Robbins 1906- *WhoAm 94*
Wetzel, Cherie Lalaine Rivers 1930- *WhoAm 94*
Wetzel, Damian 1931- *WhoAm 94*
Wetzel, Dave 1942- *Who 94*
Wetzel, Don 1945- *WhoFI 94*
Wetzel, Donald Truman 1937- *WhoMW 93*
Wetzel, Edward Thomas 1937- *WhoFI 94*
Wetzel, Heinz 1935- *WhoAm 94*
Wetzel, John H. 1942- *WhoMW 93*
Wetzel, John Paul 1963- *WhoScEn 94*
Wetzel, Karen J. 1953- *WhoMW 93*
Wetzel, Karl Joseph 1937- *WhoWest 94*
Wetzel, Kim Donald 1954- *WhoFI 94*
Wetzel, Margaret Lou 1922- *WhoAmP 93*
Wetzel, Robert George 1936- *WhoAm 94*
Wetzel, Stephen Peter 1959- *WhoFI 94*
Wetzler, James Warren 1947- *WhoAm 94*
Wetzler, Monte Edwin 1936- *WhoAm 94*
Wetzler, Sandra Sue 1947- *WhoAmL 94*
Wever, Ned d1984 *WhoHol 92*
Wevers, John William 1919- *WhoAm 94*
Wewer, William Paul 1947- *WhoAmL 94*
Wexberg, Marcia J. 1953- *WhoAmL 94, WhoMW 93*
Wexelbaum, Michael 1946- *WhoAmL 94*
Wexler, Anne 1930- *WhoAm 94, WhoAmP 93*
Wexler, Claire Thyra *WhoAmA 93*
Wexler, David Mark 1938- *WhoAmL 94*
Wexler, Evelyn *DrAPF 93*
Wexler, George 1925- *WhoAmA 93*
Wexler, Ginia Davis 1923- *WhoAm 94*
Wexler, Haskell 1922- *WhoAm 94*
Wexler, Haskell 1926- *IntDcF 2-4, IntMPA 94*
Wexler, Herbert I. 1916- *WhoAm 94*
Wexler, Howard B. 1951- *WhoIns 94*
Wexler, Jacqueline Grennan 1926- *WhoAm 94*
Wexler, Jerome Leroy 1923- *WhoAmA 93*
Wexler, Jerrold 1924-1992 *WhAm 10*
Wexler, Jerry 1917- *ConAu 142*
Wexler, Jodi 1945- *WhoHol 92*
Wexler, Judie Gaffin 1945- *WhoWest 94*
Wexler, Lee Edward 1951- *WhoAmA 93*
Wexler, Leonard D. 1924- *WhoAm 94, WhoAmL 94*
Wexler, Max Mendel 1946-1989 *WhAm 10*
Wexler, Paul d1979 *WhoHol 92*
Wexler, Peter John 1936- *WhoAm 94*
Wexler, Philip *DrAPF 93*
Wexler, Raymond P. 1942- *WhoAm 94*
Wexler, Richard 1953- *WrDr 94*
Wexler, Richard Lewis 1941- *WhoAm 94*
Wexler, Robert 1961- *WhoAmP 93*
Wexler, Yale 1930- *WhoHol 92*
Wexler-Johnson, Eileen Lugar 1915- *WhoAmP 93*
Wexman, Virginia Wright 1941- *WhoMW 93*
Wexner, Leslie Herbert 1937- *WhoAm 94, WhoFI 94, WhoMW 93*
Wexton, Jane Leslie 1943- *WhoAmL 94*
Wey, Jong Shinn 1944- *WhoScEn 94*
Weyand, Frederick Carlton 1916- *IntWW 93, WhoAm 94, WhoWest 94*
Weyand, Ronald *WhoHol 92*
Weyand, Ruth 1912-1989 *WhAm 10*
Weyandt, Gregory M. 1949- *WhoAmL 94*
Weyant, John Peter 1947- *WhoScEn 94*
Wey Cooke, Sharon Kay 1954- *WhoMW 93*
Weyel, Gudrun 1927- *WhoWomW 91*
Weyenberg, Donald Richard 1930- *WhoAm 94, WhoFI 94, WhoScEn 94*
Weyenberg, Thomas Richard 1962- *WhoMW 93*
Weyerhaeuser, George Hunt 1926- *IntWW 93, WhoAm 94, WhoFI 94, WhoWest 94*
Weyers, Marius *WhoHol 92*
Weyforth, Mimi 1944- *WhoAm 94*
Weyforth Dawson, Mary Ann 1944- *WhoAmP 93*
Weygand, Leroy Charles 1926- *WhoFI 94, WhoWest 94*
Weygand, Robert 1948- *WhoAmP 93*
Weygand, Robert A. 1948- *WhoAm 94*
Weyhe, Arthur *WhoAmA 93*
Weyher, Harry Frederick 1921- *WhoAm 94*
Weyher, Harry Frederick, III 1956- *WhoAm 94*
Weyhing, Ed *DrAPF 93*
Weyhrich, Joseph H. 1942- *WhoAmL 94*
Weyland, Joseph 1943- *Who 94*
Weyland, Louis Frederick 1894- *WhAm 10*
Weyland, Otto P. 1902-1979 *HisDcKW*
Weyler, Kenneth L. 1941- *WhoAmP 93*
Weyler, Walter Eugen, Jr. 1963- *WhoScEn 94*
Weyman, Mark 1947- *WhoWest 94*
Weyman, Stanley J. 1855-1928 *DcLB 141*
Weymann, Gert 1919- *IntWW 93*
Weymann, Ray J. 1934- *WhoScEn 94*
Weymann, Thomas F. 1950- *WhoAmL 94*
Weymar, F. Helmut 1936- *WhoAm 94*
Weymes, John Barnard 1927- *Who 94*
Weymouth, Viscount 1974- *Who 94*
Weymouth, George fl. 160-?- *WhWE*
Weymouth, Norman E. *WhoAmP 93*
Weymouth, Thomas Thynne 1734-1796 *WhAmRev*
Weyna, Terry Marie 1956- *WhoAmL 94*
Weynen, Wolfgang 1913- *IntWW 93*
Weynerowski, Hanna *WhoAmA 93*
Weyprecht, Karl 1838-1881 *WhWE*
Weyr, Thomas 1927- *ConAu 142*
Weyrauch, Paul Turney 1941- *WhoAm 94*
Weyrauch, Walter Otto 1919- *WhoAm 94*
Weyrens, Jerry P. 1932- *WhoAmP 93*
Weyrich, James Henry 1944- *WhoAmP 93*
Weyrich, Paul Michael 1942- *WhoAm 94*
Weyse, Christoph Ernst Friedrich 1774-1842 *NewGrDO*
Whaddon, Baron 1927- *Who 94*
Whale, Arthur Richard 1923- *WhoAm 94*
Whale, James 1889-1957 *HorFD [port]*
Whale, John (Hilary) 1931- *WrDr 94*
Whale, John Hilary 1931- *Who 94*
Whale, John Seldon 1896- *Who 94*
Whalen, Barbara Rhoads 1960- *WhoScEn 94*
Whalen, Brian B. 1939- *WhoMW 93*
Whalen, Charles William, Jr. 1920- *WhoAm 94*
Whalen, Geoffrey Henry 1936- *Who 94*
Whalen, George Edwin 1919- *WhoAmP 93*
Whalen, Harold d1940 *WhoHol 92*
Whalen, James Joseph 1927- *WhoAm 94*
Whalen, James Michael 1946- *WhoAm 94, WhoAmL 94*
Whalen, Jerome Demaris 1943- *WhoAm 94*
Whalen, John Sydney 1934- *WhoAm 94*
Whalen, Joseph R. *WhoAmP 93*
Whalen, Laurence J. 1944- *WhoAm 94, WhoAmL 94*
Whalen, Lawrence J. 1944- *CngDr 93*
Whalen, Lucille 1925- *WhoAm 94*
Whalen, Margaret Cavanagh 1913- *WhoWest 94*
Whalen, Martin J. 1940- *WhoAmL 94, WhoFI 94*
Whalen, Michael d1974 *WhoHol 92*
Whalen, Michael S. 1954- *WhoAmL 94*
Whalen, Michelle O. 1964- *WhoWest 94*
Whalen, Paul Lewellin *WhoAmL 94*
Whalen, Philip *DrAPF 93*
Whalen, Philip (Glenn) 1923- *WrDr 94*
Whalen, Philip Glenn 1923- *WhoAm 94*
Whalen, Raymond Anthony 1948- *WhoMW 93*
Whalen, Richard James 1935- *WhoAm 94, WrDr 94*
Whalen, Robert J. 1953- *WhoAmL 94*
Whalen, Thomas Earl 1938- *WhoAm 94, WhoScEn 94, WhoWest 94*
Whalen, Thomas J. 1945- *WhoAmL 94*
Whalen, Thomas Michael, III 1934- *WhoAmP 93*
Whalen, Timothy J. 1956- *WhoAmP 93*
Whalen, Tom *DrAPF 93*
Whalen, Vermel M. *WhoAmP 93*
Whalen, Wayne W. 1939- *WhoAm 94*
Whalen-Bennett, Laura Lynn 1963- *WhoMW 93*
Whaley, Bert D. d1973 *WhoHol 92*
Whaley, Charles Edward 1928- *WhoWest 94*
Whaley, Charles H., IV 1958- *WhoBlA 94*
Whaley, Charles Henry, IV 1958- *WhoFI 94*
Whaley, Douglas John 1943- *WhoAmL 94*
Whaley, Foster 1920- *WhoAmP 93*
Whaley, Frances Budd d1966 *WhoHol 92*
Whaley, Frank 1962- *WhoHol 92*
Whaley, Frank 1963- *IntMPA 94*
Whaley, George *WhoHol 92*
Whaley, James E. 1942- *WhoAmL 94*
Whaley, John Alexander 1940- *WhoAm 94*
Whaley, Joseph S. 1933- *WhoBlA 94*
Whaley, Kimberly Kay 1959- *WhoAmL 94*
Whaley, Mary H. *WhoBlA 94*
Whaley, Max Weldon 1947- *WhoScEn 94*
Whaley, Randall McVay 1915-1989 *WhAm 10*
Whaley, Storm Hammond 1916- *WhoAm 94*
Whaley, Wayne Edward 1949- *WhoBlA 94*
Whalley, Edward 1925- *WhoAm 94*
Whalley, Jeffrey 1942- *Who 94*
Whalley, John Mayson 1932- *Who 94*
Whalley, Joyce Irene *WrDr 94*
Whalley, Lawrence Reginald 1943- *WhoFI 94*
Whalley, Lawrence Robert 1943- *WhoWest 94*
Whalley, Michael D. 1953- *WhoAmP 93*
Whalley, Peter 1946- *WrDr 94*
Whalley, Richard Carlton 1922- *Who 94*
Whalley, William Basil 1916- *Who 94*
Whalley, William Leonard 1930- *Who 94*
Whalley-Kilmer, Joanne 1963- *WhoHol 92*
Whalley-Kilmer, Joanne 1964- *IntMPA 94, IntWW 93*
Whallon, Evan Arthur, Jr. 1923- *WhoAm 94*
Whallon, William 1928- *WhoAm 94*
Whalum, Kenneth Twigg 1934- *WhoBlA 94*
Wham, David Buffington *DrAPF 93*
Wham, Dorothy Stonecipher 1925- *WhoAmP 93, WhoWest 94*
Wham, George Sims 1920- *WhoAm 94*
Wham, Robert S. 1926- *WhoAmP 93*
Wham, William Neil 1934- *WhoAm 94*
Whang, Benjamin 1937- *WhoAsA 94*
Whang, Kyu-Young 1951- *WhoScEn 94*
Whang, Robert 1928- *WhoAsA 94*
Whang, Seungjin 1952- *WhoAsA 94*
Whang, Sukoo Jack 1934- *WhoAsA 94*
Whang, Sung H. 1936- *WhoScEn 94*
Whang, Un-Young 1954- *WhoAsA 94, WhoMW 93*
Whang, Yun Chow 1931- *WhoAm 94*
Whang, Yun Chow 1933- *WhoAsA 94*
Whangbo, Myung-Hwan 1945- *WhoAsA 94*
Whaples, Robert MacDonald 1961- *WhoFI 94*
Wharncliffe, Earl of 1953- *Who 94*
Wharton, Baroness 1934- *Who 94*
Wharton, A. C., Jr. 1944- *WhoBlA 94*
Wharton, Annabel Jane *WhoAmA 93*
Wharton, Anne 1659-1685 *BlmGWL*
Wharton, Betsy Freeman 1950- *WhoAmP 93*
Wharton, Beverly Ann 1953- *WhoAm 94*
Wharton, Blaze Douglas 1956- *WhoAmP 93, WhoWest 94*
Wharton, Carol Forbes 1907-1958 *WhoAmA 93N*
Wharton, Charles Benjamin 1926- *WhoAm 94*
Wharton, Charles Ellis 1943- *WhoAmL 94, WhoWest 94*
Wharton, Clifton R., Jr. 1926- *AfrAmAl 6 [port], IntWW 93, WhoAmP 93, WhoBlA 94*
Wharton, Clifton Reginald, Jr. 1926- *WhoAm 94, WhoFI 94*
Wharton, Clyde Wilson *WhoAmP 93*
Wharton, Danny Carroll 1947- *WhoScEn 94*
Wharton, David W. 1951- *WhoAmA 93, WhoWest 94*
Wharton, Dolores D. 1927- *WhoBlA 94*
Wharton, Edith 1862-1937 *AmCulL, BlmGWL [port], RfGShF, TwCLC 53 [port]*
Wharton, Ferdinand D., Jr. *WhoBlA 94*
Wharton, Goodwin 1653-1704 *DcNaB MP*
Wharton, J. David 1943- *WhoAmL 94*
Wharton, James Pearce 1893-1963 *WhoAmA 93N*
Wharton, John Martin *Who 94*
Wharton, John Michael 1944- *WhoAmL 94*
Wharton, Lennard 1933- *WhoAm 94*
Wharton, Margaret Agnes 1943- *WhoAmA 93*
Wharton, Michael Bernard 1913- *Who 94*
Wharton, Milton S. 1946- *WhoBlA 94*
Wharton, Ralph Nathaniel 1932- *WhoScEn 94*
Wharton, Samuel 1732-1800 *WhAmRev*
Wharton, Thomas Heard, Jr. 1930- *WhoAm 94, WhoAmL 94*
Wharton, Thomas William 1943- *WhoScEn 94, WhoWest 94*
Wharton, Tilford Girard 1904-1992 *WhAm 10*
Wharton, Tom Michael 1950- *WhoWest 94*
Wharton, William 1925- *WrDr 94*
Wharton, William 1926- *EncSF 93*
Wharton, William Polk *WhoScEn 94*
Wharton Boyd, Linda F. 1956- *WhoBlA 94*
Whatcoat, Richard 1736-1806 *DcAmReB 2*
Whatley, Alfred Thielen 1922- *WhoWest 94*
Whatley, Booker Tillman 1915- *WhoBlA 94*
Whatley, Ennis 1962- *WhoBlA 94*
Whatley, Frederick Robert 1924- *IntWW 93, Who 94*
Whatley, Harriette Williford 1918- *WhoAmP 93*
Whatley, Jacqueline Beltram 1944- *WhoAmL 94*

Whatley, James Frederick 1947- *WhoMW 93*
Whatley, Liem 1962- *WhoHol 92*
Whatley, Wallace *DrAPF 93*
Whatley, William Henry Potts 1922- *Who 94*
Whatley, William Wayne 1958- *WhoAmL 94*
Whatmore, A. R. d1960 *WhoHol 92*
Whatmough, J. Jeremy T. 1934- *WhoAm 94*
Whatmough, Michael Anthony 1950- *Who 94*
Wheadon, Richard Anthony 1933- *Who 94*
Whealey, Lois Deimel 1932- *WhoMW 93*
Whealon, John Francis 1921-1991 *WhAm 10*
Whealon, Robert F. 1934- *WhoIns 94*
Whealton, John H. 1943- *WhoScEn 94*
Wheare, Thomas David 1944- *Who 94*
Wheat, Alan 1951- *CngDr 93, WhoAmP 93, WhoBlA 94*
Wheat, Alan Dupree 1951- *WhoAm 94, WhoMW 93*
Wheat, Charles Donald Edmund 1937- *Who 94*
Wheat, (Marcus) Ed(ward, Jr.) 1926- *ConAu 42NR*
Wheat, Francis Millspaugh 1921- *WhoAm 94*
Wheat, George Anthony 1944- *WhoAmL 94*
Wheat, James Weldon, Jr. 1948- *WhoBlA 94*
Wheat, Joe Ben 1916- *WhoAm 94*
Wheat, Joe Franklin 1939- *WhoAmL 94*
Wheat, John Nixon 1952- *WhoAmL 94*
Wheat, Julie Yager 1930- *WhoAmP 93*
Wheat, Lawrence d1963 *WhoHol 92*
Wheat, Maxwell Corydon, Jr. *DrAPF 93*
Wheat, Myron William, Jr. 1924- *WhoScEn 94*
Wheat, Willis James 1926- *WhoAm 94*
Wheatcroft, Adeline Stanhope d1935 *WhoHol 92*
Wheatcroft, Geoffrey 1945- *WrDr 94*
Wheatcroft, John *DrAPF 93*
Wheatcroft, John Stewart 1925- *WrDr 94*
Wheatcroft, Stanhope d1966 *WhoHol 92*
Wheatcroft, Stephen Frederick 1921- *Who 94*
Wheathill, Elizabeth *BlmGWL*
Wheatland, David Pingree d1993 *NewYTBS 93*
Wheatland, Richard, II 1923- *WhoAm 94*
Wheatland, Stephen 1897- *WhAm 10*
Wheatley, Alan d1991 *WhoHol 92*
Wheatley, Alan Edward 1938- *Who 94*
Wheatley, Anthony 1933- *Who 94*
Wheatley, Arthur 1931- *Who 94*
Wheatley, Dennis (Yeats) 1897-1977 *EncSF 93*
Wheatley, Derek Peter Francis 1925- *Who 94*
Wheatley, Ford Harry, IV 1953 *WhoAmL 94, WhoWest 94*
Wheatley, Gary Francis 1937- *WhoFI 94*
Wheatley, Jean George 1936- *WhoWest 94*
Wheatley, John Derek 1927- *Who 94*
Wheatley, John Francis 1941- *Who 94*
Wheatley, Melvin Ernest, Jr. 1915- *WhoAm 94*
Wheatley, Myron Daniel 1953- *WhoAmL 94*
Wheatley, Nadia 1949- *BlmGWL*
Wheatley, Paul Charles 1938- *Who 94*
Wheatley, Phillis 1753-1784 *AfrAmAl 6, BlmGEL, BlmGWL, WhAmRev*
Wheatley, Robert Ray, III 1934- *WhoFI 94*
Wheatley, Stanley Harold 1934- *WhoWest 94*
Wheatley, William Arthur 1944- *WhoFI 94*
Wheatley, William Ogden, Jr. 1944- *WhoAm 94*
Wheaton, Alice Alshuler 1920- *WhoFI 94, WhoWest 94*
Wheaton, Amy *WhoHol 92*
Wheaton, David 1969- *WhoAm 94*
Wheaton, David Harry 1930- *Who 94*
Wheaton, David Joe 1940- *WhoAm 94*
Wheaton, Harry James 1941- *WhoWest 94*
Wheaton, Janice C. 1943- *WhoBlA 94*
Wheaton, O. Andrew 1964- *WhoAmL 94*
Wheaton, Perry Lee 1942- *WhoAm 94*
Wheaton, Thelma Kirkpatrick 1907- *WhoBlA 94*
Wheaton, Wil 1972- *IntMPA 94*
Wheaton, Wil 1973- *WhoHol 92*
Wheatstone, Charles 1802-1875 *WorInv*
Whedon, Aida Anthony 1915- *WhoAmA 93*
Whedon, George Donald 1915- *WhoAm 94*
Whedon, Margaret Brunssen *WhoAm 94*
Whedon, Ralph Gibbs 1949- *WhoAm 94*
Wheel, Pat d1986 *WhoHol 92*
Wheelan, Belle Louise 1951- *WhoBlA 94*
Wheelan, Richelieu Edward 1945- *WhoAmL 94*
Wheeldon, John Murray 1929- *IntWW 93*
Wheeler, Albert Harold 1915- *WhoBlA 94*
Wheeler, Albin Gray 1958- *WhoAm 94*
Wheeler, Annemarie Ruth 1959- *WhoScEn 94*
Wheeler, Anthony *Who 94*
Wheeler, (Harry) Anthony 1919- *IntWW 93, Who 94*
Wheeler, Anthony Clyde 1953- *WhoFI 94*
Wheeler, Arthur Walter 1927- *Who 94*
Wheeler, Arthur William Edge 1930- *Who 94*
Wheeler, Benita Louise 1939- *WhoWest 94*
Wheeler, Bert d1968 *WhoHol 92*
Wheeler, Bert 1895-1968
See Wheeler and Woolsey *WhoCom*
Wheeler, Beth M. *WhoAmP 93*
Wheeler, Betty McNeal 1932- *WhoBlA 94*
Wheeler, Bruce 1948- *WhoHisp 94*
Wheeler, Burritt d1957 *WhoHol 92*
Wheeler, Burton M. 1927- *WhoAm 94*
Wheeler, C. Herbert 1915- *WhoAm 94*
Wheeler, Carl 1932- *WhoScEn 94*
Wheeler, Charles (Cornelius-) 1923- *Who 94*
Wheeler, (Selwyn) Charles (Cornelius-) *Who 94*
Wheeler, Charles B. 1926- *WhoAmP 93*
Wheeler, Charles Bertan 1926- *WhoAm 94*
Wheeler, Clarence Joseph, Jr. 1917- *WhoScEn 94*
Wheeler, Clayton Eugene, Jr. 1917- *WhoAm 94*
Wheeler, Cyril d1971 *WhoHol 92*
Wheeler, Daniel Scott 1947- *WhoAm 94*
Wheeler, David John 1927- *Who 94*
Wheeler, David K. 1959- *WhoAmP 93*
Wheeler, David Laurie 1934- *WhoAm 94*
Wheeler, David Wayne 1952- *WhoFI 94*
Wheeler, Dennis K. 1947- *WhoAmL 94*
Wheeler, Donald Craig 1959- *WhoWest 94*
Wheeler, Donald Keith 1960- *WhoFI 94, WhoScEn 94*
Wheeler, Douglas Paul 1942- *WhoAm 94*
Wheeler, Ed *WhoHol 92*
Wheeler, Ed Ray 1947- *WhoAm 94*
Wheeler, Edward Kendall 1913- *WhoAm 94*
Wheeler, Ellen *WhoHol 92*
Wheeler, Elton Samuel 1943- *WhoFI 94*
Wheeler, Emma B. 1916- *WhoAmP 93*
Wheeler, Frank Basil 1937- *Who 94*
Wheeler, Frederick (Henry) 1914- *Who 94*
Wheeler, Fredric Robert, II 1946- *WhoMW 93*
Wheeler, Gena *WhoHol 92*
Wheeler, George Charles 1923- *WhoFI 94, WhoScEn 94*
Wheeler, George Lawrence 1944- *WhoScEn 94*
Wheeler, George Montague 1842-1905 *WhWE*
Wheeler, George William 1924- *WhoAm 94*
Wheeler, Gerridee Stenehjem 1927- *WhoAmP 93*
Wheeler, Gordon *Who 94*
Wheeler, (William) Gordon 1910- *Who 94*
Wheeler, Harold Alden 1903- *WhoAm 94, WhoScEn 94*
Wheeler, Harold Austin, Sr. 1925- *WhoAmL 94*
Wheeler, Harold H. 1929- *WhoAmP 93, WhoMW 93*
Wheeler, (John) Harvey 1918-1988? *EncSF 93*
Wheeler, Helen Rippier *WhoWest 94, WrDr 94*
Wheeler, Henry Clark 1916- *WhoAm 94*
Wheeler, Hewitt Brownell 1929- *WhoAm 94*
Wheeler, Hugh (Callingham) 1912-1987 *ConDr 93*
Wheeler, Hugh Callingham 1912-1987 *NewGrDO*
Wheeler, Ira *WhoHol 92*
Wheeler, Jack Cox 1939- *WhoAm 94*
Wheeler, James Julian 1921- *WhoAmL 94*
Wheeler, James Richard 1925- *WhoWest 94*
Wheeler, Jesse Harrison, Jr. 1918- *WhoFI 94, WhoMW 93*
Wheeler, Jimmy d1973 *WhoHol 92*
Wheeler, John *WhoHol 92*
Wheeler, John (Daniel) 1940- *Who 94*
Wheeler, John (Hieron) 1905- *Who 94*
Wheeler, John Archibald 1911- *IntWW 93, WhoAm 94, WrDr 94*
Wheeler, John Craig 1943- *WhoAm 94, WhoScEn 94*
Wheeler, John D. 1940- *WhoAm 94*
Wheeler, John Harvey 1918- *WhoAm 94*
Wheeler, John Hervey 1908- *WhoBlA 94*
Wheeler, John Oliver 1924- *WhoAm 94*
Wheeler, John Watson 1938- *WhoAm 94, WhoAmL 94*
Wheeler, John William d1991 *WhAm 10*
Wheeler, Jos Ridley 1927- *WhoWest 94*
Wheeler, Joseph J. 1947- *WhoAmL 94*
Wheeler, Katherine Wells 1940- *WhoAm 94, WhoAmP 93*
Wheeler, Kenneth (Henry) 1912- *Who 94*
Wheeler, Kenneth Theodore, Sr. 1911- *WhoAmP 93*
Wheeler, Ladd 1937- *WhoAm 94*
Wheeler, Larry Richard 1940- *WhoFI 94, WhoWest 94*
Wheeler, Laura Marie 1956- *WhoMW 93*
Wheeler, Leonard 1901- *WhoAm 94*
Wheeler, Leslie William Frederick 1930- *Who 94*
Wheeler, Lloyd G. 1907- *WhoBlA 94*
Wheeler, Lois 1920- *WhoHol 92*
Wheeler, Lyle 1905-1990 *IntDcF 2-4*
Wheeler, Malcolm Edward 1944- *WhoAm 94*
Wheeler, Margaret *WhoHol 92*
Wheeler, Mark 1943- *WhoAmA 93*
Wheeler, Mark Lowell Batchelder 1937- *WhoAmL 94*
Wheeler, Marshall Ralph 1917- *WhoAm 94*
Wheeler, Mary *WhoAmA 93*
Wheeler, Mercy fl. 1733- *BlmGWL*
Wheeler, Michael R. 1952- *WhoAmP 93*
Wheeler, Michael Terence 1966- *WhoFI 94*
Wheeler, Neal *WhoHol 92*
Wheeler, Neil *Who 94*
Wheeler, (Henry) Neil (George) 1917- *Who 94*
Wheeler, Nita d1980 *WhoHol 92*
Wheeler, Norman Edgar 1940- *WhoFI 94*
Wheeler, Orson Shorey 1902- *WhoAmA 93N*
Wheeler, Orville Eugene 1932- *WhoAm 94*
Wheeler, Otis Bullard 1921- *WhoAm 94*
Wheeler, Paul Leonard 1926- *WhoMW 93*
Wheeler, Penny Estes 1943- *WrDr 94*
Wheeler, Porter King 1940- *WhoFI 94*
Wheeler, Primus, Jr. 1950- *WhoBlA 94*
Wheeler, Raymond Louis 1945- *WhoAm 94, WhoAmL 94*
Wheeler, Richard Henry Littleton 1906- *Who 94*
Wheeler, Richard Kenneth 1934- *WhoAm 94, WhoAmL 94*
Wheeler, Richard S. 1935- *WrDr 94*
Wheeler, Richard Warren 1929- *WhoAm 94*
Wheeler, Robert Hobert 1945 *WhoAm 94, WhoAmL 94*
Wheeler, Robert L. 1940- *WhoAmP 93*
Wheeler, Roger Neil 1941- *Who 94*
Wheeler, Ron 1954- *WrDr 94*
Wheeler, Ronald G. 1946- *WhoAmP 93*
Wheeler, Russell Charles 1897- *WhAm 10*
Wheeler, Sam d1989 *WhoHol 92*
Wheeler, Samuel Crane, Jr. 1913- *WhoMW 93*
Wheeler, Scott *EncSF 93*
Wheeler, Shirley Y. 1935- *WhoBlA 94*
Wheeler, Steven M. 1949- *WhoAmL 94*
Wheeler, Susan *DrAPF 93*
Wheeler, Susie Weems 1917- *WhoBlA 94*
Wheeler, Sylvia *DrAPF 93*
Wheeler, Teresa d1975 *WhoHol 92*
Wheeler, Thaddeus James 1948- *WhoBlA 94*
Wheeler, Theodore Stanley 1931- *WhoBlA 94*
Wheeler, Thomas Beardsley 1936- *WhoAm 94, WhoFI 94*
Wheeler, Thomas Clay *WhoAmP 93*
Wheeler, Thomas Edgar 1946- *WhoAm 94*
Wheeler, Thomas Gerald *EncSF 93*
Wheeler, Thomas Jay 1951- *WhoScEn 94*
Wheeler, Walter Hall 1923-1989 *WhAm 10*
Wheeler, Warren Gage, Jr. 1921- *WhoAm 94*
Wheeler, Wayne Bidwell 1869-1927 *DcAmReB 2*
Wheeler, Wayne Cable 1938- *WhoWest 94*
Wheeler, Wesley Dreer 1933- *WhoScEn 94*
Wheeler, William Crawford 1914- *WhoScEn 94*
Wheeler, William Henry 1907- *Who 94*
Wheeler, William R., Jr. 1961- *WhoAmP 93*
Wheeler, William Thornton 1911- *WhoAm 94*
Wheeler, Wilmot Fitch, Jr. 1923- *WhoAm 94*
Wheeler and Woolsey *WhoCom*
Wheeler-Bennett, Richard Clement 1927- *Who 94*
Wheeler-Booth, Michael Addison John 1934- *Who 94*
Wheeler-Nicholson, Dana *WhoHol 92*
Wheeler-Nicholson, Malcolm 1890-1968 *EncSF 93*
Wheelock, Arthur Kingsland, Jr. 1943- *WhoAmA 93*
Wheelock, Charles C. d1948 *WhoHol 92*
Wheelock, Eleazar 1711-1779 *DcAmReB 2, EncNAR*
Wheelock, John 1754-1817 *WhAmRev*
Wheelock, Kenneth Steven 1943- *WhoScEn 94*
Wheelock, Larry Arthur 1938- *WhoMW 93*
Wheelock, Major William, Jr. 1936- *WhoAm 94*
Wheelock, Morgan Dix, Jr. 1938- *WhoAm 94*
Wheelock, Scott A. 1967- *WhoScEn 94*
Wheelock, Warren F. 1880-1960 *WhoAmA 93N*
Wheelon, Albert Dewell 1929- *WhoAm 94, WhoScEn 94, WhoWest 94*
Wheelwright, Betty Coon *DrAPF 93*
Wheelwright, Edward Lawrence 1921- *WrDr 94*
Wheelwright, John T. *EncSF 93*
Wheelwright, Joseph Storer 1948- *WhoAmA 93*
Wheelwright, Julie (Diana) 1960- *WrDr 94*
Wheelwright, Steven C. 1943- *WhoAm 94*
Wheen, Natalie Kathleen 1947- *Who 94*
Whelahan, Yvette Ann 1943- *WhoScEn 94*
Whelan, Albert d1961 *WhoHol 92*
Whelan, Alison *WhoHol 92*
Whelan, Arleen 1918- *WhoHol 92*
Whelan, Charles Duplessis, III 1956- *WhoAmL 94*
Whelan, Christopher John 1958- *WhoMW 93*
Whelan, Donald Joseph 1934- *WhoMW 93*
Whelan, Elizabeth Ann Murphy 1943- *WhoAm 94, WhoScEn 94*
Whelan, Eugene 1924- *IntWW 93*
Whelan, Gloria *DrAPF 93*
Whelan, James Michael 1925- *WhoWest 94*
Whelan, Jannice Karen 1952- *WhoAmP 93*
Whelan, John Theodore 1961- *WhoAmL 94*
Whelan, John William 1922- *WhoAm 94*
Whelan, Joseph L. 1917- *WhoAm 94, WhoScEn 94*
Whelan, Joseph Leo 1917 *WhoMW 93*
Whelan, Joseph Michael 1954- *WhoFI 94*
Whelan, Karen M.L. 1947- *WhoFI 94*
Whelan, Michael 1950- *EncSF 93*
Whelan, Michael George 1947- *Who 94*
Whelan, Michael John 1931- *IntWW 93, Who 94*
Whelan, Noel 1940- *IntWW 93*
Whelan, Peter 1931- *ConDr 93*
Whelan, Ralph W. d1993 *NewYTBS 93*
Whelan, Richard J. 1931- *WhoAm 94*
Whelan, Richard Vincent, Jr. 1933- *WhoAm 94*
Whelan, Robert Louis 1912- *WhoAm 94, WhoWest 94*
Whelan, Roger Michael 1936- *WhoAm 94, WhoAmL 94*
Whelan, Ron d1965 *WhoHol 92*
Whelan, Sidney Smith, Jr. 1929- *WhoAm 94*
Whelan, Stephen Thomas 1947- *WhoAm 94, WhoAmL 94*
Whelan, Tensie 1960- *ConAu 141*
Whelan, Terence Leonard 1936- *Who 94*
Whelan, Tim d1957 *WhoHol 92*
Whelan, Wendy *WhoAm 94*
Whelan, William Anthony 1921- *WhoAm 94, WhoWest 94*
Whelan, William Joseph 1924- *Who 94, WhoAm 94*
Whelar, Lanois Mardi d1918 *WhoHol 92*
Whelchel, Lisa 1963- *WhoHol 92*
Whelchel, Sandra Jane 1944- *WhoWest 94*
Wheldon, Juliet Louise 1950- *Who 94*
Whelehan, David D. 1942- *WhoFI 94, WhoIns 94*
Whelehan, Patricia Elizabeth 1947- *WhoAm 94*
Whelen, Andrew Christian 1959- *WhoScEn 94*
Whelen, Christopher 1927- *NewGrDO*
Whelen, Jill 1966- *WhoHol 92*
Wheler, Edward (Woodford) 1920- *Who 94*
Whelihan, James Bruce 1942- *WhoFI 94*

Whelley, John Gerard, Jr. 1948- *WhoAmL 94*
Whellock, John Graham 1947- *WhoWest 94*
Whelon, Charles Patrick Clavell 1930- *Who 94*
Whelpley, Dennis Porter 1951- *WhoAm 94, WhoAmL 94*
Whelton, Clark *DrAPF 93*
Whent, Gerald Arthur 1927- *Who 94*
Wherrett, Richard Bruce 1940- *IntWW 93*
Wherry, Daniel d1955 *WhoHol 92*
Wherry, Edward John, Jr. 1942- *WhoAmL 94*
Wherry, Nancy Jeanne 1938- *WhoMW 93*
Wherry, Timothy Lee 1948- *WhoAm 94*
Whetsell, Jonathan Wayne 1968- *WhoFI 94*
Whetstone, Anthony John 1927- *Who 94*
Whetstone, George 1550-1587 *BlmGEL, DcLB 136*
Whetstone, (Norman) Keith 1930- *Who 94*
Whetstone, Raymond David 1949- *WhoAm 94*
Whetten, John Theodore 1935- *WhoAm 94, WhoWest 94*
Whetten, Lawrence Lester 1932- *WhoAm 94*
Whetzel, Robert William 1960- *WhoAmL 94*
Wheway, Albert James 1922- *Who 94*
Whewell, Charles Smalley 1912- *Who 94*
Whewell, William 1794-1866 *EncEth*
Whichard, Willis Padgett 1940- *WhoAm 94, WhoAmL 94, WhoAmP 93*
Whicher, Peter George 1929- *Who 94*
Whicker, Alan (Donald) 1925- *WrDr 94*
Whicker, Alan Donald 1925- *IntWW 93, Who 94*
Whicker, Floyd Ward 1937- *WhoScEn 94*
Whidden, Stanley John 1947- *WhoAm 94*
Whiddon, Carol Price 1947- *WhoAm 94, WhoWest 94*
Whiddon, Frederick Palmer 1930- *WhoAm 94*
Whiffen, Blanche d1936 *WhoHol 92*
Whiffen, David Hardy *Who 94*
Whiffen, David Hardy 1922- *IntWW 93*
Whiffen, James Douglass 1931- *WhoAm 94*
Whigham, D. Keith 1938- *WhoMW 93*
Whigham, Mark Anthony 1959- *WhoFI 94, WhoScEn 94*
Whigham, Thomas Edmondson 1952- *WhAm 10*
Whikehart, John R. 1947- *WhoAmP 93*
Whilden, Walter Burleson 1938- *WhoFI 94*
Whildin, Eileen Bachman 1955- *WhoAmP 93*
Whiley, Manning 1915- *WhoHol 92*
Whinery, Michael Albert 1951- *WhoScEn 94*
Whinfield, John Rex 1901-1966 *DcNaB MP, WorInv*
Whinnery, Barbara *WhoHol 92*
Whinnery, James Elliott 1946- *WhoAm 94*
Whinnery, John Roy 1916- *IntWW 93, WhoAm 94, WhoScEn 94, WhoWest 94*
Whinney, Michael Humphrey Dickens 1930- *Who 94*
Whinston, Arthur Lewis 1925- *WhoAm 94*
Whiplash, Montana d1977 *WhoHol 92*
Whipper, Leigh d1975 *WhoHol 92*
Whipper, Lucille Simmons 1928- *WhoAmP 93, WhoBlA 94*
Whipple, Abraham 1733-1819 *AmRev, WhAmRev*
Whipple, Amiel Weeks 1816-1863 *WhWE*
Whipple, Andrew Powell 1949- *WhoMW 93, WhoScEn 94*
Whipple, Barbara d1989 *WhoAmA 93N*
Whipple, Barbara 1921-1989 *WhAm 10*
Whipple, Blaine 1930- *WhoAmP 93*
Whipple, Dean 1938- *WhoAm 94, WhoAmL 94, WhoMW 93*
Whipple, Douglas P. 1953- *WhoAmL 94*
Whipple, Douglas R. 1953- *WhoAmL 94, WhoWest 94*
Whipple, Enez Mary *WhoAmA 93*
Whipple, Fred Lawrence 1906- *IntWW 93, Who 94, WhoAm 94*
Whipple, George Stephenson 1950- *WhoWest 94*
Whipple, Harry *WhoMW 93*
Whipple, Henry Benjamin 1822-1901 *DcAmReB 2, EncNAR*
Whipple, Janice U. *WhoIns 94*
Whipple, Kenneth 1934- *WhoFI 94*
Whipple, Prince *WhAmRev*
Whipple, Prince 1700?-1797 *AfrAmAl 6*
Whipple, Taggart 1912-1992 *WhAm 10*
Whipple, V. Thayne, II 1964- *WhoWest 94*
Whipple, Walter Leighton 1940- *WhoWest 94*
Whipple, William 1730-1785 *AmRev, WhAmRev*
Whipple, William Perry 1913- *WhoMW 93*
Whippman, Michael Lewis 1938- *Who 94*
Whipps, Edward Franklin 1936- *WhoAm 94, WhoAmL 94, WhoMW 93*
Whipps, Mary N. 1945- *WhoBlA 94*
Whisenand, James Dudley 1947- *WhoAm 94, WhoFI 94*
Whisenhunt, Carolyn Sue 1954- *WhoAmL 94*
Whisenhunt, Donald Wayne 1938- *WhoAm 94, WhoWest 94*
Whisenhunt, Livia L. 1958- *WhoFI 94*
Whisenton, Andre C. 1944- *WhoBlA 94*
Whishaw, Anthony 1930- *IntWW 93*
Whishaw, Anthony Popham Law 1930- *Who 94*
Whishaw, Charles (Percival Law) 1909- *Who 94*
Whisher, Bradley Edward 1954- *WhoFI 94*
Whisker, James Biser 1939- *WhoAmP 93*
Whisler, James Steven 1954- *WhoAm 94, WhoFI 94*
Whisler, Kenneth Eugene 1937- *WhoMW 93*
Whisler, Kirk 1951- *WhoWest 94*
Whisler, Walter William 1934- *WhoAm 94*
Whisman, Linda Anne 1954- *WhoAmL 94*
Whisnant, Charleen *DrAPF 93*
Whisnant, Jack Page 1924- *WhoAm 94*
Whistler, Alwyne Michael Webster 1909- *Who 94*
Whistler, Edna d1934 *WhoHol 92*
Whistler, James Abbott McNeill 1834-1903 *AmCulL*
Whistler, Kathryn Anne 1948- *WhoAmL 94*
Whistler, Laurence 1912- *IntWW 93, Who 94, WrDr 94*
Whistler, Margaret d1939 *WhoHol 92*
Whistler, Philip A. 1952- *WhoAmL 94*
Whistler, Roy Lester 1912- *WhoAm 94, WhoFI 94, WhoScEn 94*
Whiston, Brian James 1961- *WhoMW 93*
Whiston, Peter Rice 1912- *Who 94*
Whiston, Richard Michael 1944- *WhoAmL 94, WhoFI 94*
Whitacre, Diane Louise 1953- *WhoFI 94*
Whitacre, Duane A. 1960- *WhoMW 93*
Whitacre, Edward E., Jr. *IntWW 93*
Whitacre, Edward E., Jr. 1941- *WhoAm 94, WhoFI 94*
Whitacre, John 1953- *WhoWest 94*
Whitacre, Vernon C. *WhoAmP 93*
Whitacre, Wendell Britt 1927- *WhoWest 94*
Whitaker, Albert Duncan 1932- *WhoAm 94, WhoAmL 94*
Whitaker, Alexander 1585-1617 *DcAmReB 2*
Whitaker, Arthur L. 1921- *WhoBlA 94*
Whitaker, Audie Dale 1949- *WhoMW 93*
Whitaker, Ben(jamin Charles George) 1934- *WrDr 94*
Whitaker, Benjamin Charles George 1934- *Who 94*
Whitaker, Bruce D. 1948- *WhoWest 94*
Whitaker, Bruce Ezell 1921- *WhoAm 94*
Whitaker, Charles *WhoMW 93*
Whitaker, Charles d1960 *WhoHol 92*
Whitaker, Charles Larimore 1943- *WhoAm 94*
Whitaker, Clem, Jr. 1922- *WhoAm 94*
Whitaker, Damon 1972- *WhoHol 92*
Whitaker, David Haddon 1931- *Who 94*
Whitaker, Donald L. 1931- *WhoAmP 93*
Whitaker, Eileen Monaghan 1911- *WhoAm 94, WhoAmA 93*
Whitaker, Forest 1961- *IntMPA 94, WhoAm 94, WhoBlA 94, WhoHol 92*
Whitaker, Fred Maynard 1925- *WhoWest 94*
Whitaker, Frederic 1891-1980 *WhoAmA 93N*
Whitaker, Gilbert R(iley), Jr. 1931- *WrDr 94*
Whitaker, Gilbert Riley, Jr. 1931- *WhoAm 94, WhoFI 94*
Whitaker, Glenn Virgil 1947- *WhoAmL 94*
Whitaker, Henry Philip 1921-1989 *WhAm 10*
Whitaker, James Herbert Ingham 1925- *Who 94*
Whitaker, James R. 1946- *WhoAmL 94*
Whitaker, Jeffrey David 1956- *WhoMW 93*
Whitaker, John Barclay 1939- *WhoAmP 93*
Whitaker, John King 1933- *WhoAm 94*
Whitaker, John Ogden, Jr. 1935- *WhoMW 93*
Whitaker, Johnny 1959- *WhoHol 92*
Whitaker, Lawrence c. 1579-1654 *DcNaB MP*
Whitaker, Louis Rodman 1957- *WhoBlA 94*
Whitaker, Meade 1919- *CngDr 93, WhoAm 94*
Whitaker, Mical Rozier 1941- *WhoBlA 94*
Whitaker, Morris Duane 1940- *WhoWest 94*
Whitaker, Pernell *WhoAm 94*
Whitaker, Robert C. 1941- *WhoIns 94*
Whitaker, Rod 1925-1992 *WrDr 94N*
Whitaker, Rupert Edward David 1963- *WhoWest 94*
Whitaker, Sheila 1936- *Who 94*
Whitaker, Shirley Ann 1955- *WhoFI 94*
Whitaker, Susanne Kanis 1947- *WhoAm 94*
Whitaker, Thomas Kenneth 1916- *IntWW 93, Who 94*
Whitaker, Thomas Russell 1925- *WhoAm 94*
Whitaker, Von Frances *WhoBlA 94*
Whitaker, Wayne Orson 1960- *WhoFI 94, WhoWest 94*
Whitaker, Willard H. 1912- *WhoBlA 94*
Whitaker, William 1943- *WhoAmA 93*
Whitbeck, Frank d1963 *WhoHol 92*
Whitbread, Fatima 1961- *IntWW 93*
Whitbread, Samuel Charles 1937- *IntWW 93, Who 94*
Whitbread, Thomas *DrAPF 93*
Whitbread, Thomas Bacon 1931- *WhoAm 94*
Whitbread, William Henry 1900- *Who 94*
Whitburn, Gerald 1944- *WhoAm 94, WhoMW 93*
Whitburn, Merrill Duane 1938- *WhoAm 94*
Whitby, Bishop Suffragan of 1934- *Who 94*
Whitby, Arthur d1922 *WhoHol 92*
Whitby, Charles Harley 1926- *Who 94*
Whitby, Gwynne d1984 *WhoHol 92*
Whitby, Joy 1930- *Who 94*
Whitby, Lionel Gordon 1926- *Who 94*
Whitby, Owen *WhoIns 94*
Whitby, Sharon 1935- *WrDr 94*
Whitcher, Alice *DrAPF 93*
Whitcher, Frances Miriam Berry c. 1814-1852 *BlmGWL*
Whitcomb, Barry d1928 *WhoHol 92*
Whitcomb, Benjamin Bradford, Jr. 1908- *WhoAm 94*
Whitcomb, Donald Dooley 1946- *WhoAm 94*
Whitcomb, Edgar Doud 1917- *WhoAmP 93*
Whitcomb, Harold Craig 1939- *WhoWest 94*
Whitcomb, James Hall 1940- *WhoScEn 94*
Whitcomb, John 1713-1783 *WhAmRev*
Whitcomb, John C(lement) 1924- *WrDr 94*
Whitcomb, Kay 1921- *WhoAmA 93*
Whitcomb, Noel 1918- *WrDr 94*
Whitcomb, Noel 1918?-1993 *ConAu 141*
Whitcomb, Richard Travis 1921- *WhoAm 94*
Whitcomb, Robert Fay Wright 1896- *WhAm 10*
Whitcomb, Skip 1946- *WhoAmA 93*
Whitcomb, Stanley R. 1944- *WhoWest 94*
Whitcomb, Therese Truitt 1930- *WhoAmA 93*
Whitcomb, Thomas Grant 1962- *WhoMW 93*
Whitcomb, Walter E. *WhoAmP 93*
Whitcraft, Edward C. R. 1914- *WhoAm 94*
Whitcraft, Elizabeth *WhoHol 92*
Whitcraft, James Richard, Jr. 1947- *WhoMW 93*
White *Who 94*
White, Baroness 1909- *IntWW 93, Who 94, WhoWomW 91*
White, Adrian Michael Stephen 1940- *WhoAm 94*
White, Adrian N. S. *Who 94*
White, Aidan Patrick 1951- *Who 94*
White, Alan *WhoHol 92*
White, Alan 1930- *Who 94*
White, Alan Richard 1922- *WrDr 94*
White, Albert d1991 *WhoAmA 93N*
White, Albert J. 1933- *WhoAm 94, WhoFI 94*
White, Alfred d1972 *WhoHol 92*
White, Alfred Benard 1956- *WhoMW 93*
White, Alfred Kenneth, Jr. 1929- *WhoAmL 94*
White, Alice d1983 *WhoHol 92*
White, Alice Virginia 1946- *WhoFI 94*
White, Allan *WhoAmP 93*
White, Allan 1950- *WhoMW 93*
White, Allen Mark 1959- *WhoWest 94*
White, Alma Bridwell 1862-1946 *DcAmReB 2*
White, Alvin, Jr. *WhoBlA 94*
White, Alvin Swauger 1918- *WhoAm 94*
White, Amos, IV *WhoAmA 93*
White, Andrew *WhoHol 92*
White, Andrew 1579-1656 *DcAmReB 2, EncNAR*
White, Andrew Stewart 1941- *WhoIns 94*
White, Anne Underwood 1919-1989 *WhAm 10*
White, Anthony Charles Gunn 1955- *WhoBlA 94*
White, Antonia 1889-1930 *BlmGWL [port]*
White, Ared 1881-1941 *EncSF 93*
White, Arthur Clinton 1925- *WhoAm 94*
White, Arthur W., Jr. 1943- *WhoBlA 94*
White, Artis Andre 1926- *WhoBlA 94*
White, Augustus A., III 1936- *WhoBlA 94*
White, Augustus Aaron, III 1936- *WhoAm 94*
White, B. J. 1946- *WhoAmA 93*
White, Bailey *NewYTBS 93 [port]*
White, Bailey 1950- *ConAu 141*
White, Barbara 1924- *WhoHol 92*
White, Barbara Ann 1942- *WhoWest 94*
White, Barbara Ehrlich 1936- *WrDr 94*
White, Barbara Williams 1943- *WhoBlA 94*
White, Barrington Raymond 1934- *Who 94*
White, Barry 1944- *WhoBlA 94, WhoHol 92*
White, Barry A. 1948- *WhoAm 94*
White, Barry Bennett 1943- *WhoAm 94, WhoAmL 94*
White, Beatrice Lockhart 1906- *WhoWest 94*
White, Benjamin Ballard, Jr. 1927- *WhoAmL 94*
White, Benjamin H., Jr. *WhoAmL 94*
White, Benjamin Taylor 1946- *WhoAm 94, WhoAmL 94*
White, Bernie *WhoHol 92*
White, Bertram Milton 1923- *WhoFI 94, WhoScEn 94*
White, Betty 1922- *WhoAm 94, WhoCom, WhoHol 92*
White, Betty 1924- *IntMPA 94*
White, Beverly Anita 1960- *WhoBlA 94*
White, Beverly Jean 1928- *WhoAmP 93*
White, Bill d1933 *WhoHol 92*
White, Bill 1934- *AfrAmAl 6 [port], WhoBlA 94*
White, Billy Ray 1936- *WhoBlA 94*
White, Bonnie Yvonne 1940- *WhoWest 94*
White, Booker Taliaferro 1907- *WhoBlA 94*
White, Bren Douglas 1957- *WhoFI 94*
White, Brenda Black *DrAPF 93*
White, Brent William 1948- *WhoAmL 94*
White, Brian George 1944- *WhoWest 94*
White, Brian William 1934- *WhoWest 94*
White, Brittan Romeo 1936- *WhoWest 94*
White, Bruce Emerson, Jr. 1961- *WhoFI 94*
White, Bruce Hilding 1933- *WhoAmA 93*
White, Bryan Oliver 1929- *Who 94*
White, Buel 1941- *WhoAmL 94*
White, Burton Leonard 1929- *WhoAm 94*
White, Byron R. 1917- *WhoAm 94, WhoAmL 94, WhoAmP 93*
White, Byron R(aymond) 1917- *Who 94*
White, Byron Raymond 1917- *CngDr 93*
White, C. Dale 1925- *WhoAm 94*
White, C. Thomas 1928- *WhoAmL 94, WhoAmP 93*
White, Callan *WhoHol 92*
White, Calvin John 1948- *WhoAm 94*
White, Carol 1943- *WhoHol 92*
White, Carol Ita *WhoHol 92*
White, Carolina d1961 *WhoHol 92*
White, Caroline 1935- *WhoAmP 93*
White, Carolinne 1955- *ConAu 142*
White, Carolyn *DrAPF 93*
White, Carter Hixson 1916- *WhoFI 94*
White, Catharine Boswell 1958- *WhoMW 93*
White, Catherine Kilmurray 1930- *WhoAmP 93*
White, Cecil Ray 1937- *WhoWest 94*
White, Cedina Miran Kim 1963- *WhoAsA 94*
White, Cedric Masey 1898- *Who 94*
White, Celestino, Sr. 1945- *WhoAmP 93*
White, Chandler T. 1894- *WhAm 10*
White, Charles 1918-1979 *AfrAmAl 6*
White, Charles 1920- *WhoHol 92*
White, Charles Albert, Jr. 1922- *WhoAm 94*
White, Charles Douglas 1956- *WhoFI 94*
White, Charles M. 1891-1977 *EncABHB 9 [port]*
White, Charles R. 1937- *WhoBlA 94*
White, Charles Richard 1937- *WhoAm 94*
White, Charles Wilbert 1918-1979 *WhoAmA 93N*
White, Chrissie d1989 *WhoHol 92*
White, Christian S. 1943- *WhoAm 94*
White, Christine *WhoHol 92*

White, Christine Larkin 1946- WhoBlA 94
White, Christopher c. 1650-1695 DcNaB MP
White, Christopher (John) 1930- WrDr 94
White, Christopher (Robert Meadows) 1940- Who 94
White, Christopher John 1930- IntWW 93, Who 94
White, Christopher Minot 1951- WhoFI 94
White, Christopher Stuart Stuart- Who 94
White, Christopher W. 1964- WhoMW 93
White, Clair Fox 1949- WhoAmL 94
White, Claire Nicolas DrAPF 93
White, Clara Jo 1927- WhoFI 94
White, Clarence Cameron 1880-1960 AfrAmAl 6, NewGrDO
White, Clarence Dean 1946- WhoBlA 94
White, Clarice Mary 1947- WhoWest 94
White, Claude Esley 1949- WhoBlA 94
White, Clayton Cecil 1942- WhoBlA 94
White, Cloid 1952- WhoFI 94
White, Clovis Leland 1953- WhoBlA 94
White, Constance Burnham 1954- WhoWest 94
White, Cordon d1943 WhoHol 92
White, Craig Mitchell 1952- WhoAm 94
White, Craig William 1944- WhoIns 94
White, D. Richard 1947- WhoBlA 94
White, Damon L. 1934- WhoBlA 94
White, Dan d1980 WhoHol 92
White, Daniel Bowman 1948- WhoAmL 94
White, Daniel Eugene 1950- WhoAmL 94
White, Danny Levius 1956- WhoWest 94
White, David d1990 WhoHol 92
White, David Alan 1956- WhoFI 94
White, David Alan, Jr. 1942- WhoFI 94
White, David Calvin 1922- WhoAm 94
White, David Cleaveland 1929- WhoScEn 94
White, David D. 1901-1992 WhoBlA 94N
White, David Harry 1929- Who 94
White, David Hywel 1931- WhoAm 94
White, David J. 1946- WhoAmL 94
White, David L. 1947- WhoAmL 94
White, David Michael 1951- WhoMW 93
White, David Olds 1921- WhoWest 94
White, David P. WhoFI 94
White, David Stuart 1944- WhoFI 94
White, David Thomas 1931- Who 94
White, DeAnna H. 1959- WhoWest 94
White, Deborah WhoAmA 93
White, Deidre R. 1958- WhoBlA 94
White, Dennis J. 1947- WhoAm 94, WhoAmL 94
White, Derek Leslie 1933- Who 94
White, Devon Markes 1962- WhoAm 94, WhoBlA 94
White, De'voreaux WhoHol 92
White, Dewey Anderson, Jr. 1923- WhoAmP 93
White, Dezra 1941- WhoBlA 94
White, Dick d1993 NewYTBS 93
White, Dick Goldsmith d1993 Who 94N
White, Dirk Bradford 1955- WhoMW 93
White, Diz WhoHol 92
White, Don(ald Edwin) 1933- NewGrDO
White, Don Lee WhoBlA 94
White, Don William 1942- WhoFI 94, WhoWest 94
White, Donald F. 1908- WhoBlA 94
White, Donald Harvey 1931- WhoAm 94, WhoWest 94
White, Donald J. 1938- WhoIns 94
White, Donald L. 1949- WhoAmP 93
White, Donald R., Jr. 1949- WhoBlA 94
White, Donald Richard, Jr. 1953- WhoMW 93
White, Doris Anne 1924- WhoAm 94
White, Doris Gnauck 1926- WhoScEn 94
White, Doug WhoAmP 93
White, Douglas James, Jr. 1934- WhoAm 94
White, Douglas R. 1942- WhoWest 94
White, Earl Harvey 1934- WhoBlA 94
White, Ed Pearson 1911- WhoBlA 94
White, Edgar B. d1978 WhoHol 92
White, Edgar Nkosi 1947- ConDr 93
White, Edmund DrAPF 93
White, Edmund 1940- IntWW 93, WrDr 94
White, Edmund (Valentine, III) 1940- GayLL
White, Edmund Valentine 1940- WhoAm 94
White, Edward Alfred 1934- WhoAmL 94
White, Edward Allen 1928- WhoWest 94
White, Edward Clarence, Jr. 1956- WhoBlA 94
White, Edward George 1923- Who 94
White, Edward Gibson, II 1954- WhoAmL 94
White, Edward Hurley, III 1930- WhoAmL 94
White, Edward M 1933- WrDr 94
White, Edward Stanislaus 1961- WhoAmL 94
White, Elijah 1806-1879 EncNAR
White, Elizabeth Flad 1954- WhoWest 94
White, Elizabeth Moffat d1993 NewYTBS 93
White, Ella Flowers 1941- WhoBlA 94
White, Ellen E(merson) TwCYAW
White, Ellen Gould Harmon 1827-1915 DcAmReB 2
White, Elwyn Brooks 1899-1985 WhAm 10
White, Emil Henry 1926- WhoScEn 94
White, Eric Walter 1905-1985 NewGrDO
White, Ernest G. 1946- WhoBlA 94
White, Erskine Norman, Jr. 1924- WhoAm 94
White, Eugene 1963- WhoAmP 93
White, Eugene B. d1966 WhoAmA 93N
White, Eugene James 1928- WhoAm 94
White, Eugene M. 1937- WhoAmP 93
White, Eugene Michael 1950- WhoFI 94
White, Eugene R. WhoFI 94
White, Eugene Thomas, III 1956- WhoScEn 94
White, Eugene Vaden 1924- WhoScEn 94
White, F. Clifton d1993 NewYTBS 93 [port]
White, F(rederick) Clifton 1918-1993 ConAu 140
White, Frances d1969 WhoHol 92
White, Francis Edward 1915- WhoAm 94
White, Frank d1893 EncNAR
White, Frank 1932- IntWW 93
White, Frank, Jr. 1950- WhoBlA 94
White, Frank D. 1933- WhoAmP 93
White, Frank John 1927- Who 94
White, Frank M. WhoScEn 94
White, Frank N. 1963- WhoAmL 94
White, Frank Paul WhoAmP 93
White, Frank Richard 1939- Who 94
White, Frankie Walton 1945- WhoBlA 94
White, Franklin 1943- WhoAmA 93
White, Franklin Morse 1920- WhAm 10
White, Fred(erick) M(errick) 1859- EncSF 93
White, Fred Rollin, Jr. 1913- WhoAm 94
White, Frederic Paul, Jr. 1948- WhoBlA 94
White, Frederick Andrew 1918- WhoAm 94
White, Frederick William George 1905- IntWW 93, Who 94
White, Fredrick John 1952- WhoMW 93
White, Gail DrAPF 93
White, Garland Anthony 1932- WhoBlA 94
White, Gary WhoAmP 93
White, Gary Conner 1937- WhoWest 94
White, Gary L. 1932- WhoAm 94, WhoFI 94
White, Gary Leon 1932- WhoBlA 94
White, Gayle Clay 1944- WhoWest 94
White, George d1968 WhoHol 92
White, George 1934- WhoBlA 94
White, George (Stanley James) 1948- Who 94
White, George A. 1941- WhoIns 94
White, George Alan 1932- Who 94
White, George C. 1919- WhoIns 94
White, George Cooke 1935- WhoAm 94
White, George Edward 1941- WhoAm 94, WhoScEn 94
White, George Gregory 1953- WhoBlA 94
White, George H. EncSF 93
White, George Malcolm 1920- WhoAm 94
White, George W. 1931- WhoAm 94, WhoAmL 94, WhoBlA 94, WhoMW 93
White, George Wendell, Jr. 1915- WhoAmL 94
White, Gerald Andrew 1934- WhoAm 94
White, Gerald Taylor 1913-1989 WhAm 10
White, Gilbert 1720-1793 BlmGEL, EnvEnc
White, Gilbert Anthony 1916- Who 94
White, Gilbert F(owler) 1911- IntWW 93
White, Gilbert Fowler 1911- WhoAm 94
White, Gillian Mary 1936- WrDr 94
White, Gloria Alice 1949- WhoMW 93
White, Gloria Waters 1934- WhoBlA 94
White, Gordon Eliot 1933- WhoAm 94
White, Gordon Lindsay 1923- WhoAm 94, WhoFI 94
White, Granville C. 1927- WhoBlA 94
White, Gregory Durr, Mrs. 1908- WhoBlA 94
White, Guy Kendall 1925- IntWW 93
White, H. Blair 1927- WhoAm 94
White, H. Melton 1924-1991 WhoBlA 94N
White, Halbert Lynn, Jr. 1950- WhoFI 94
White, Harlow F. 1941- WhoAm 94, WhoFI 94, WhoWest 94
White, Harold (Leslie) d1992 Who 94N
White, Harold Clare 1919- Who 94
White, Harold Clark Mitchelle 1948- WhoBlA 94
White, Harold Corley d1993 NewYTBS 93
White, Harold F. 1920- WhoAm 94, WhoAmL 94
White, Harold Leslie d1992 IntWW 93N
White, Harold R. 1936- WhoFI 94
White, Harold Rogers 1923- WhoBlA 94
White, Harold Tredway, III 1947- WhoAm 94, WhoFI 94
White, Harry Edward, Jr. 1939- WhoAm 94
White, Harry Keith 1946- WhoAmP 93
White, Henry 1732-1786 WhAmRev
White, Henry Arthur Dalrymple D. Who 94
White, Herbert Spencer 1927- WhoAm 94
White, Howard Ashley 1913-1991 WhAm 10
White, Huey d1938 WhoHol 92
White, Hugh Vernon, Jr. 1933- WhoAm 94
White, Hugo (Moresby) 1939- Who 94
White, Ian Who 94
White, Ida Margaret 1924- WhoBlA 94
White, Irving d1944 WhoHol 92
White, Isaac Davis 1901-1990 WhAm 10
White, Ivon W. DrAPF 93
White, J. Fisher d1945 WhoHol 92
White, J. V. 1925- WhoIns 94
White, Jack d1942 WhoHol 92
White, Jack 1935- WhoAmP 93
White, Jack E. 1946- WhoBlA 94
White, Jack Raymond 1936- WhoAmL 94
White, Jacqueline 1922- WhoHol 92
White, Jaleel WhoBlA 94
White, James Who 94
White, James 1913- Who 94
White, James 1928- EncSF 93, WrDr 94
White, James 1937- Who 94
White, James Allen 1948- WhoFI 94
White, James Arthur 1933- WhoAm 94
White, James Ashton V. Who 94
White, James Barr 1941- WhoAm 94
White, James Boyd 1938- WhoAm 94
White, James David 1942- WhoIns 94
White, James David 1964- WhoBlA 94
White, James E. WhoAmP 93
White, James Edward 1918- WhoAm 94, WhoWest 94
White, James Floyd 1932- WrDr 94
White, James George 1929- WhoAm 94
White, James Howard 1930- WhoAmP 93
White, James Louis, Jr. 1949- WhoBlA 94
White, James M., III 1938- WhoAmL 94
White, James P. DrAPF 93
White, James P(atrick) 1940- ConAu 42NR
White, James Patrick 1931- WhoAm 94
White, James Richard 1948- WhoAm 94, WhoAmL 94
White, James Richard 1950- WhoAmA 93
White, James S. 1930- WhoBlA 94
White, James Spratt, IV 1941- WhoFI 94
White, James Wilson 1926- WhoAmP 93
White, Jane 1922- WhoHol 92
White, Jane 1934-1985 EncSF 93
White, Jane See 1950- WhoWest 94
White, Janice G. 1938- WhoBlA 94
White, Javier A. 1945- WhoBlA 94
White, Jay P. DrAPF 93
White, Jean Tillinghast 1934- WhoAmP 93
White, Jeanne Ann 1931- WhoWest 94
White, Jeffrey Lee 1957- WhoAm 94
White, Jeffrey Louis 1945- WhoAm 94, WhoFI 94
White, Jeffrey M. 1948- WhoAmL 94
White, Jeffrey Paul 1955- WhoAmL 94, WhoMW 93
White, Jere Lee 1954- WhoAmP 93
White, Jerry Allen 1937- WhoAm 94
White, Jerry S. 1946- WrDr 94
White, Jesse 1918- WhoHol 92
White, Jesse 1920- IntMPA 94
White, Jesse C., Jr. 1934- WhoAmP 93, WhoBlA 94
White, Jesse Marc WhoAm 94
White, Jesse Wathen 1955- WhoFI 94
White, Jill Carolyn 1934- WhoAmL 94
White, Jim 1935- WhoAmP 93
White, Jo Jo 1946- BasBi [port], WhoBlA 94
White, Joan 1909- WhoHol 92
White, Joe Lloyd 1921- WhoAm 94, WhoMW 93
White, John EncSF 93, WhoAmP 93
White, John fl. 158-?-159-? WhWE
White, John 1936- NewGrDO
White, John 1937- WhoAmP 93
White, John, Jr. 1930- WhoFI 94
White, John (Charles) 1911- Who 94
White, John (Sylvester) 1919- ConDr 93, WrDr 94
White, John (Woolmer) 1947- Who 94
White, John Aaron, Jr. 1943- WhoAmL 94
White, John Abiathar 1948- WhoAm 94, WhoWest 94
White, John Arnold 1933- WhoAm 94
White, John Austin 1942- Who 94
White, John Austin, Jr. 1939- WhoAm 94, WhoScEn 94
White, John C. 1945- WhoWest 94
White, John Charles 1939- WhoAm 94
White, John Clinton 1942- WhoBlA 94
White, John Coyle 1924- WhoAmP 93
White, John David 1931- WhoAm 94
White, John David 1948- WhoAm 94
White, John Edward (Clement Twarowski) 1924- WrDr 94
White, John Edward Clement Twarowski 1924- Who 94
White, John F. 1924- WhoBlA 94
White, John Francis 1929- WhoAm 94
White, John Henry 1945- WhoMW 93
White, John Hoxland, Jr. 1933- ConAu 42NR
White, John Joseph, III 1948- WhoAmL 94
White, John Kenneth 1952- WrDr 94
White, John L. 1930- WhoAmP 93
White, John Lee 1962- WhoBlA 94
White, John Lindsey 1930- WhoAm 94
White, John M. 1926- WhoAmP 93
White, John M. 1937- WhoAmA 93
White, John Michael 1938- WhoAm 94
White, John Sampson 1916- Who 94
White, John Sidney, Jr. 1930- WhoAmL 94
White, John Simon 1910- WhoAm 94
White, John Sylvester d1988 WhoHol 92
White, John Wesley, Jr. 1933- WhoAm 94
White, John William 1937- Who 94
White, John Wythe 1945- WhoWest 94
White, Johnstone d1969 WhoHol 92
White, Jon Manchip DrAPF 93
White, Jon Manchip 1924- WrDr 94
White, Joseph B. 1959- WhoAm 94
White, Joseph Charles 1922- WhoAm 94
White, Joseph Lee 1951- WhoMW 93
White, Joseph Mallie, Jr. 1921- WhoAm 94
White, Joseph W. 1941- WhoMW 93
White, Josh d1969 WhoHol 92
White, Juanita M. 1912- WhoAmP 93
White, Jude Gilliam 1947- ConAu 41NR
White, Judith Ann O'Radnik 1943- WhoMW 93
White, Jules J. d1984 WhoHol 92
White, Julian Eugene, Jr. 1932- WhoWest 94
White, June Joyce 1949- WhoBlA 94
White, Kande 1950- WhoMW 93
White, Karen J. 1943- WhoAmA 93
White, Karen Malina WhoHol 92
White, Karl Raymond 1950- WhoWest 94
White, Karyn WhoBlA 94
White, Kate WhoAm 94
White, Katherine Patricia 1948- WhoAmL 94, WhoFI 94
White, Kathleen Merritt 1921- WhoWest 94
White, Katie Kinnard 1932- WhoBlA 94
White, Keith Merrill 1951-1991 WhAm 10
White, Kenneth 1936- WrDr 94
White, Kenneth James 1948- Who 94, WhoAmL 94
White, Kenneth R. 1929- WhoMW 93
White, Kenneth William 1947- WhoScEn 94
White, Kermit Earle 1917- WhoBlA 94
White, Kerr Lachlan 1917- WhoAm 94
White, Kevin Hagan 1929- WhoAmP 93
White, Larry J. 1947- WhoAmL 94
White, Larry Keith 1948- WhoScEn 94
White, Laurens Park 1925- WhoWest 94
White, Lawrence Gilbert 1963- WhoAmP 93
White, Lawrence J. 1943- WhoAm 94, WrDr 94
White, Lawrence John 1915- Who 94
White, Lawrence Todd 1953- WhoMW 93
White, Lee d1949 WhoHol 92
White, Lee Calvin 1923- WhoAm 94
White, Leo d1948 WhoHol 92
White, Leo, Jr. 1957- WhoBlA 94
White, Leonard IntMPA 94, WhoHol 92
White, Lester WhoAmP 93
White, Linda 1964- WhoMW 93
White, Linda Diane 1952- WhoAm 94, WhoAmL 94
White, Linnea Carol WhoMW 93
White, Lionel 1905- WrDr 94
White, Lloyd Michael 1949- WhoAm 94
White, Lola DrAPF 93
White, Loray Betty 1934- WhoWest 94
White, Lorenzo Maurice 1966- WhoBlA 94
White, Lowell E., Jr. 1928- WhoAm 94
White, Lowell Smiley 1897- WhAm 10
White, Luther D. 1937- WhoBlA 94
White, Luther J. 1936- WhoBlA 94
White, Luther Wesley 1923- WhoAm 94
White, Lynette Michele 1950- WhoWest 94
White, Lynn Townsend, Jr. 1907-1987 EnvEnc
White, Lynton (Stuart) 1916- Who 94

White, Mabel *WhoBlA 94*
White, Madge d1978 *WhoHol 92*
White, Major C. 1926- *WhoBlA 94*
White, Margarette Paulyne Morgan 1934- *WhoBlA 94*
White, Margit Triska 1932- *WhoFI 94*
White, Margita Eklund 1937- *WhoAm 94*
White, Marjorie d1935 *WhoHol 92*
White, Mark Arlington 1958- *WhoFI 94*
White, Mark Arvid *DrAPF 93*
White, Mark W., Jr. *WhoAmP 93*
White, Mark Wells, Jr. 1940- *IntWW 93*
White, Marsha *DrAPF 93*
White, Martin *Who 94*
White, (Edward) Martin (Everatt) 1938- *Who 94*
White, Martin Andrew C. *Who 94*
White, Martin Christopher 1943- *WhoAm 94*
White, Martin Spencer 1944- *Who 94*
White, Mary Jane *DrAPF 93*
White, Mary Jo *WhoAmL 94*
White, Mary Louise 1933- *WhoFI 94*
White, Matthew 1941- *WhoWest 94*
White, Maude Adams 1916- *WhoWest 94*
White, Melvyn Lee 1941- *WhoBlA 94*
White, Merit Penniman 1908- *WhoAm 94*
White, Merry (I.) 1941- *ConAu 141*
White, Michael Bernknopf 1942- *WhoFI 94*
White, Michael Charles 1945- *Who 94*
White, Michael D. 1947- *WhoFI 94*
White, Michael D. 1948- *WhoIns 94*
White, Michael Dennis 1952- *WhoFI 94*
White, Michael Elias 1958- *WhoScEn 94*
White, Michael Ernest 1958- *WhoMW 93, WhoScEn 94*
White, Michael K. 1938- *WhoIns 94*
White, Michael N. 1953- *WhoAmL 94*
White, Michael R. 1951- *ConBlB 5 [port], WhoAmP 93*
White, Michael Reed 1951- *WhoAm 94, WhoBlA 94, WhoMW 93*
White, Michael Simon 1936- *IntWW 93, Who 94*
White, Milton *DrAPF 93*
White, Minor 1908-1976 *WhoAmA 93N*
White, Morgan Wilson 1945- *WhoWest 94*
White, Morton (Gabriel) 1917- *WrDr 94*
White, Morton Gabriel 1917- *WhoAm 94*
White, Myrna *WhoHol 92*
White, Nan E. 1931- *WhoBlA 94*
White, Nancy Margaret 1938- *WhoAmP 93*
White, Nathan Emmett, Jr. 1941- *WhoAmP 93*
White, Nathaniel *WhoHol 92*
White, Nathaniel B. 1914- *WhoBlA 94*
White, Nathaniel Miller 1941- *WhoWest 94*
White, Neal J. 1951- *WhoAm 94, WhoAmL 94*
White, Neville Helme 1931- *Who 94*
White, Nicholas J. 1945- *WhoFI 94*
White, Norman A. 1922- *IntWW 93*
White, Norman Arthur 1922- *Who 94, WhoFI 94, WhoScEn 94*
White, Norman Lee 1955- *WhoFI 94*
White, Norman Triplett 1938- *WhoAmA 93*
White, Norval Crawford 1926- *WhoAm 94*
White, O. C. 1932-1992 *WhoBlA 94N*
White, Pamela Janice 1952- *WhoAm 94, WhoAmL 94*
White, Patricia *WhoHol 92*
White, Patricia (Ann) 1937- *ConAu 43NR*
White, Patricia Holmes 1948- *WhoAmP 93*
White, Patrick d1990 *NobelP 91N*
White, Patrick 1912-1990 *BlmGEL [port], WhAm 10*
White, Patrick (Victor Martindale) 1912-1990 *ConAu 43NR, ConDr 93, GayLL, IntDcT 2 [port], RfGShF*
White, Paul Christopher 1947- *WhoBlA 94*
White, Paul Dunbar 1917- *WhoAm 94, WhoAmL 94, WhoMW 93*
White, Paul R. 1930- *WhoAmP 93*
White, Paul Richard, Sr. 1950- *WhoAmL 94*
White, Pearl d1938 *WhoHol 92*
White, Perry James 1944- *WhoWest 94*
White, Perry Merrill, Jr. 1925- *WhoAm 94*
White, Peter *WhoHol 92*
White, Peter 1919- *Who 94*
White, Peter Richard 1942- *Who 94*
White, Peter Sawyer 1938- *WhoAmP 93*
White, Philip Butler 1935- *WhoAm 94, WhoAmA 93*
White, Phillip, III 1956- *WhoBlA 94*
White, Phillips 1729-1811 *WhAmRev*
White, Phyllis Dorothy James 1920- *ConAu 43NR*
White, Polly Sears 1931- *WhoMW 93*
White, Quincy 1933- *WhoAmP 93*
White, Quitman, Jr. 1945- *WhoBlA 94*
White, R. Meadows d1973 *WhoHol 92*
White, R. Quincy 1933- *WhoAm 94, WhoFI 94*
White, Ralph 1921- *WhoAmA 93*
White, Ralph Dallas 1919- *WhoAm 94*
White, Ralph David 1931- *WhoAm 94*
White, Ralph L. 1930- *WhoBlA 94*
White, Ralph Paul 1926- *WhoAm 94*
White, Randy 1967- *WhoBlA 94*
White, Ray Lewis 1941- *WhoMW 93, WrDr 94*
White, Ray William, Jr. 1941- *WhoMW 93*
White, Raymond d1934 *WhoHol 92*
White, Raymond Burton 1943- *WhoFI 94*
White, Raymond Edwin, Jr. 1933- *WhoWest 94*
White, Raymond P. 1937- *IntWW 93*
White, Raymond Petrie, Jr. 1937- *WhoAm 94*
White, Raymond Rodney, Sr. 1953- *WhoBlA 94*
White, Raymond Walter Ralph 1923- *IntWW 93, Who 94*
White, Reggie 1961- *ConBlB 6 [port], News 93 [port], WhoAm 94, WhoMW 93*
White, Reggie 1970- *WhoBlA 94*
White, Reginald (Ernest Oscar) 1914- *WrDr 94*
White, Reginald Howard 1961- *WhoBlA 94*
White, Reginald Wesley 1951- *WhoMW 93*
White, Renee Allyn 1945- *WhoAmL 94*
White, Rex Harding, Jr. 1932- *WhoAmL 94*
White, Richard 1942- *WhoAmP 93*
White, Richard 1949- *WhoAmP 93*
White, Richard Booth 1930- *WhoAm 94*
White, Richard C. 1941- *WhoBlA 94*
White, Richard Clarence 1933- *WhoAm 94, WhoAmL 94*
White, Richard Crawford 1923- *WhoAmP 93*
White, Richard David 1953- *WhoAm 94, WhoFI 94*
White, Richard H. 1950- *WhoBlA 94*
White, Richard Hamilton Hayden 1939- *Who 94*
White, Richard L. 1939- *WhoFI 94*
White, Richard Manning 1930- *WhoAm 94*
White, Richard N. 1949- *WhoIns 94*
White, Richard Norman 1933- *WhoAm 94*
White, Richard Stanton, Jr. 1934- *WhoAm 94*
White, Richard Taylor 1908- *Who 94*
White, Richard Thomas 1945- *WhoBlA 94*
White, Richard W(eddington), Jr. 1936- *ConAu 142*
White, Robb 1909- *TwCYAW, WhoAm 94*
White, Robert (Winthrop) 1921- *WhoAmA 93*
White, Robert Allan 1934- *WhoAm 94*
White, Robert Edward 1917- *WhoAm 94*
White, Robert Edward 1926- *WhoAmP 93*
White, Robert F. 1912- *WhoAm 94*
White, Robert Gordon 1938- *WhoWest 94*
White, Robert I. 1908-1990 *WhAm 10*
White, Robert J. 1926- *WhoAm 94*
White, Robert James 1923- *IntWW 93*
White, Robert James 1927- *WhoAm 94, WhoMW 93*
White, Robert James 1958- *WhoFI 94*
White, Robert Joel 1946- *WhoAm 94, WhoAmL 94, WhoFI 94*
White, Robert L. 1916- *WhoBlA 94*
White, Robert L. G., Jr. 1941- *WhoFI 94*
White, Robert Lee 1927- *WhoAm 94, WhoWest 94*
White, Robert Lee 1928- *WrDr 94*
White, Robert M., II 1915- *IntWW 93, WhoAm 94*
White, Robert Marshall 1938- *WhoAm 94, WhoScEn 94*
White, Robert Mayer 1923- *IntWW 93, WhoAm 94*
White, Robert Miles Ford 1928- *WhoFI 94*
White, Robert Milton 1948- *WhoWest 94*
White, Robert Rankin 1942- *WhoWest 94*
White, Robert Roy 1916- *WhoAm 94*
White, Robert Stephen 1920- *WhoAm 94, WhoScEn 94, WhoWest 94*
White, Robert Stephen 1952- *Who 94*
White, Robert Wellington, Jr. 1940- *WhoAmP 93*
White, Robert Winslow 1934- *WhoAm 94*
White, Robin *DrAPF 93*
White, Robin Bernard G. *Who 94*
White, Robin Shepard 1950- *WhoWest 94*
White, Roderick Macleod 1928- *WhoAm 94*
White, Roger 1950- *Who 94*
White, Roger Bruce 1947- *WhoWest 94*
White, Roger Lowrey 1928- *Who 94*
White, Roland Charles, Jr. 1952- *WhoFI 94*
White, Romaine Lubs 1961- *WhoAmL 94*
White, Ron *WhoHol 92*
White, Ronald Leon 1930- *WhoAm 94, WhoFI 94*
White, Ronnie L. *WhoAmP 93*
White, Rory Wilbur 1959- *WhoBlA 94*
White, Roy B. 1926- *IntMPA 94*
White, Roy Bernard *WhoAm 94, WhoFI 94*
White, Russell Lynn 1950- *WhoWest 94*
White, Russell Neil 1958- *WhoWest 94*
White, Ruth d1969 *WhoHol 92*
White, Ruth 1911- *WhoAmA 93*
White, Ruth Lillian 1924- *WhoAm 94*
White, Ruth Margaret 1922- *WhoWest 94*
White, Ruth O'Brien 1909- *WhoAm 94*
White, Ryan 1971-1990 *ConAu 141*
White, Sammy d1960 *WhoHol 92*
White, Sandra LaVelle 1941- *WhoBlA 94*
White, Scott A., Sr. 1909- *WhoBlA 94*
White, Scott Ray 1963- *WhoScEn 94*
White, Sharon Brown 1963- *WhoBlA 94*
White, Sheila 1950- *WhoHol 92*
White, Slappy *WhoHol 92*
White, Stanford 1853-1906 *AmCulL*
White, Stanhope 1913- *WrDr 94*
White, Stanley Archibald 1931- *WhoAm 94, WhoWest 94*
White, Stephen d1993 *NewYTBS 93*
White, Stephen (Leonard) 1945- *WrDr 94*
White, Stephen Emery 1957- *WhoMW 93*
White, Stephen Fraser 1922- *Who 94*
White, Stephen Halley 1940- *WhoAm 94*
White, Stephen Tracy 1947- *WhoAmP 93*
White, Steve *EncSF 93*
White, Steven F. *DrAPF 93*
White, Steven Gregory 1957- *WhoAmL 94*
White, Stewart Edward 1873-1946 *EncSF 93*
White, Stuart James 1944- *WhoAmA 93*
White, Susan Chrysler 1954- *WhoAmA 93*
White, Susan Page 1961- *WhoAmL 94*
White, Susie Mae 1914- *WhoScEn 94*
White, Sylvia Kay 1955- *WhoBlA 94*
White, T(erence) H(anbury) 1906-1964 *EncSF 93, TwCYAW*
White, Ted 1938- *EncSF 93, WrDr 94*
White, Terence de Vere 1912- *Who 94*
White, (Herbert) Terence de Vere 1912- *WrDr 94*
White, Terence Hanbury 1906-1964 *DcNaB MP*
White, Terence Philip 1932- *Who 94*
White, Terrence Harold 1943- *IntWW 93, WhoAm 94*
White, Terry R. 1940- *WhoAm 94, WhoMW 93*
White, Terry Wayne 1952- *WhoAm 94*
White, Thelma 1910- *WhoHol 92*
White, Thomas *WhoAmP 93*
White, Thomas 1943- *WhoAm 94*
White, Thomas Anthony B. *Who 94*
White, Thomas Astley Woollaston 1904- *Who 94*
White, Thomas David *WhoScEn 94*
White, Thomas David, II 1946- *WhoFI 94*
White, Thomas Edward 1933- *WhoAm 94*
White, Thomas Edward 1936- *WhoAm 94*
White, Thomas Eugene 1950- *WhoMW 93*
White, Thomas Lester 1903- *WhoMW 93*
White, Thomas Owen 1940- *WhoAmL 94*
White, Thomas P. 1950- *WhoAmP 93*
White, Thomas S. 1949- *WhoAmL 94*
White, Thomas Stuart 1947- *WhoAm 94*
White, Thomas Stuart, Jr. 1943- *WhoFI 94*
White, Tim 1952- *EncSF 93*
White, Timothy Jerome 1961- *WhoMW 93*
White, Timothy Oliver 1948- *WhoAm 94*
White, Timothy Thomas Anthony 1952- *WhoAm 94*
White, Tom *Who 94*
White, Tom Willingham 1943- *WhoFI 94*
White, Tommie Lee 1944- *WhoBlA 94*
White, Tony L. *WhoAm 94, WhoFI 94*
White, Travis Gordon 1942- *WhoAmL 94*
White, Valerie d1975 *WhoHol 92*
White, Van Freeman 1924- *WhoBlA 94*
White, Vanna 1957- *WhoHol 92*
White, Vanna Marie 1957- *WhoHisp 94*
White, Vicki Lee 1960- *WhoMW 93*
White, Virginia 1939- *WhoScEn 94*
White, Virginia Lou 1932- *WhoAmP 93*
White, W. Christopher 1951- *WhoAm 94*
White, W. Paul 1945- *WhoAmP 93*
White, Walter *WhoHol 92*
White, Walter Francis 1893-1955 *AmSocL*
White, Walter Hiawatha, Jr. 1954- *WhoAmL 94*
White, Walter L. d1963 *WhoAmA 93N*
White, Walter Preston, Jr. 1923- *WhoAm 94, WhoAmL 94*
White, Ward d1987 *WhoHol 92*
White, Ward Allen, III 1938- *WhoAmL 94*
White, Warren Wurtele 1932- *WhoAm 94, WhoFI 94*
White, Wendell F. 1939- *WhoBlA 94*
White, Wendy S. 1950- *WhoAmL 94*
White, Will Walter, III 1930- *WhoAm 94*
White, Willard 1946- *NewGrDO*
White, Willard Wentworth 1946- *IntWW 93, Who 94*
White, William 1748-1836 *DcAmReB 2*
White, William 1910- *WrDr 94*
White, William 1928- *WhoAm 94, WhoScEn 94*
White, William, Jr. 1934- *WrDr 94*
White, William Allen 1868-1944 *AmSocL*
White, William Arthur 1916- *WhoAm 94, WhoMW 93, WhoScEn 94*
White, William Blaine 1934- *WhoAm 94, WhoScEn 94*
White, William Dekova 1934- *WhoAm 94*
White, William E. 1934- *WhoBlA 94*
White, William Fredrick 1948- *WhoAm 94*
White, William H. 1932- *WhoBlA 94*
White, William Hale 1831-1913 *BlmGEL*
White, William Hedges 1948- *WhoFI 94*
White, William Henry 1924-1989 *WhAm 10*
White, William J. 1926- *WhoBlA 94*
White, William J. 1935- *WhoBlA 94*
White, William James 1938- *IntWW 93, WhoAm 94, WhoFI 94, WhoMW 93*
White, William Joseph 1942- *WhoHisp 94*
White, William Kelvin Kennedy 1930- *Who 94*
White, William Luther 1931- *WrDr 94*
White, William M. *DrAPF 93*
White, William Nelson 1938- *WhoAmL 94*
White, William North 1925- *WhoAm 94*
White, William Roy 1943- *WhoAm 94*
White, William Samuel 1937- *WhoAm 94*
White, William T., III 1947- *WhoBlA 94*
White, Willis Sheridan, Jr. 1926- *WhoAm 94, WhoMW 93*
White, Willmon Lee 1932- *WhoAm 94, WhoMW 93*
White, Winifred Demarest *WhAm 10*
White, Winifred Viaria 1953- *WhoBlA 94*
White, Woodie W *WhoAm 94, WhoBlA 94*
White, Yolanda Simmons 1955- *WhoBlA 94*
Whiteaker, Raymond Eads 1928- *WhoAmL 94*
Whitebird, J. *DrAPF 93*
Whitebrook, Robert Ballard 1917- *WhAm 10*
White Buffalo Man, Frank d1977 *WhoHol 92*
White Bull c. 1837-1921 *EncNAR*
White Colt 1853-1936 *EncNAR*
Whitecuff, Benjamin *WhAmRev*
Whited, Charles 1929- *ConAu 141*
Whited, Frances Patricia 1958- *WhoMW 93*
White Eyes d1778 *AmRev*
White Eyes c. 1730-1778 *WhAmRev*
Whitefield, Axel O. d1944 *WhoHol 92*
Whitefield, Billie Buntin 1921- *WhoAmP 93*
Whitefield, George 1714-1770 *DcAmReB 2*
Whitefoord, Caleb 1734-1810 *WhAmRev*
Whiteford, Andrew Hunter 1913- *WhoAm 94*
Whiteford, John P. d1962 *WhoHol 92*
Whiteford, Wynne N(oel) 1915- *EncSF 93*
Whitehall, Wayne *WhoHol 92*
Whitehead, Alfred North 1861-1947 *WorScD*
Whitehead, Barbara Elaine 1947- *WhoFI 94*
Whitehead, Barry 1910- *WhAm 10*
Whitehead, Burgess d1993 *NewYTBS 93*
Whitehead, Charles A. 1935- *WhoAmP 93*
Whitehead, Christopher Cleo 1954- *WhoWest 94*
Whitehead, David (Henry) 1958- *WrDr 94*
Whitehead, David Barry 1946- *WhoAmL 94, WhoWest 94*
Whitehead, David William 1946- *WhoBlA 94*
Whitehead, E. Douglas 1939- *WhoAm 94*
Whitehead, Eddie L. 1944- *WhoBlA 94*
Whitehead, Edward Anthony 1933- *Who 94*
Whitehead, Edwin 1919-1992 *AnObit 1992*
Whitehead, Frances 1953- *WhoAmA 93*
Whitehead, Frank 1916- *WrDr 94*
Whitehead, Frank Ernest 1930- *Who 94*
Whitehead, Geoffrey 1939- *WhoHol 92*

Whitehead, Geoffrey Michael 1921- *WrDr 94*
Whitehead, (Garnet) George (Archie) 1916- *Who 94*
Whitehead, George Sydney 1915- *Who 94*
Whitehead, George William 1918- *IntWW 93*
Whitehead, Gillian 1941- *NewGrDO*
Whitehead, Godfrey Oliver 1941- *Who 94*
Whitehead, Graham Wright *Who 94*
Whitehead, Howard Murr 1950- *WhoFI 94*
Whitehead, J. Rennie *WhoAm 94*
Whitehead, James *DrAPF 93*
Whitehead, James 1936- *WrDr 94*
Whitehead, James Fred, III 1946- *WhoAmL 94*
Whitehead, James Madison 1929- *WhoAmL 94*
Whitehead, James Ray 1949- *WhoAm 94, WhoMW 93*
Whitehead, James S. 1948- *WhoAm 94, WhoAmL 94*
Whitehead, James T., Jr. 1934- *AfrAmG [port], WhoBlA 94*
Whitehead, Janet 1958- *WrDr 94*
Whitehead, John d1962 *WhoHol 92*
Whitehead, John (Stainton) 1932- *Who 94*
Whitehead, John C. 1939- *WhoAm 94*
Whitehead, John C. 1946- *WhoAmL 94*
Whitehead, John Cunningham 1922- *WhoAm 94*
Whitehead, John Ernest Michael 1920- *IntWW 93, Who 94*
Whitehead, John Jed 1945- *WhoAm 94*
Whitehead, John L., Jr. 1924- *WhoBlA 94*
Whitehead, John Stainton 1932- *IntWW 93*
Whitehead, John Wayne 1946- *WhoAmL 94, WhoFI 94*
Whitehead, Kate 1960- *WrDr 94*
Whitehead, Kenneth Dean 1930- *WhoAm 94*
Whitehead, Martha *WhoAmP 93*
Whitehead, Marvin Delbert 1917- *WhoAm 94*
Whitehead, Mary Elizabeth 1922- *WhoAmP 93*
Whitehead, Matthew Jackson 1908-1990 *WhAm 10*
Whitehead, Michael Anthony 1935- *WhoAm 94*
Whitehead, Nelson Peter 1960- *WhoScEn 94*
Whitehead, O. Z. *WhoHol 92*
Whitehead, Paxton *WhoHol 92*
Whitehead, Phillip 1937- *Who 94*
Whitehead, Richard Lee 1927- *WhoAm 94, WhoIns 94*
Whitehead, Robert 1916- *WhoAm 94*
Whitehead, Roger George 1933- *Who 94*
Whitehead, Rowland (John Rathbone) 1930- *Who 94*
Whitehead, Samuel Lyman 1937- *WhoAmP 93*
Whitehead, Steven Wyckoff 1943- *WhoMW 93*
Whitehead, Ted *Who 94*
Whitehead, Ted 1933- *ConDr 93, WrDr 94*
Whitehead, Thomas Patterson 1923- *Who 94*
Whitehead, Wayne William, Sr. 1940- *WhoFI 94*
Whitehead, Wiley Leon, Jr. 1943- *WhoAmP 93*
Whitehead, William C. 1955- *WhoFI 94*
Whitehill, Clarence (Eugene) 1871-1932 *NewGrDO*
Whitehill, Clifford Lane 1931- *WhoAm 94, WhoAmL 94, WhoFI 94, WhoHisp 94*
Whitehill, David Barnard 1945- *WhoAmL 94*
Whitehill, James Arthur 1959- *WhoAmL 94, WhoWest 94*
Whitehill, Walter Muir 1905-1978 *WhoAmA 93N*
Whitehorn, John Clare 1894- *WhAm 10*
Whitehorn, John Roland Malcolm 1924- *Who 94*
Whitehorn, Katharine (Elizabeth) *WrDr 94*
Whitehorn, Katharine Elizabeth *Who 94*
Whitehorn, Kenneth Lee 1947- *WhoMW 93*
Whitehorne, Donald 1955- *WhoFI 94*
Whitehouse, Alton Winslow, Jr. 1927- *WhoAm 94*
Whitehouse, Anne *DrAPF 93*
Whitehouse, Charles Sheldon 1921- *WhoAmP 93*
Whitehouse, David (Bryn) 1941- *WrDr 94*
Whitehouse, David Bryn 1941- *Who 94*
Whitehouse, David Rae Beckwith 1945- *Who 94*
Whitehouse, David Rempfer 1929- *WhoAm 94*
Whitehouse, Fred Waite 1926- *WhoAm 94*
Whitehouse, George Edward, Jr. 1929- *WhoMW 93*
Whitehouse, Jack Pendleton 1924- *WhoFI 94, WhoWest 94*
Whitehouse, John Harlan, Jr. 1951- *WhoMW 93*
Whitehouse, Mary 1910- *Who 94*
Whitehouse, Sheldon 1955- *WhoAmL 94*
Whitehouse, Walter Alexander 1915- *Who 94, WrDr 94*
White-Hunt, Keith 1950- *WhoFI 94, WhoWest 94*
Whitehurst, Brooks Morris 1930- *WhoAm 94, WhoScEn 94*
Whitehurst, Charles Bernard, Sr. 1938- *WhoBlA 94*
Whitehurst, Daniel Keenan 1948- *WhoAmP 93*
Whitehurst, George William 1925- *WhoAmP 93*
Whitehurst, Harry Bernard 1922- *WhoAm 94, WhoWest 94*
White-Hurst, John Marshall 1942- *WhoAmL 94*
Whitehurst, William Wilfred, Jr. 1937- *WhoAm 94, WhoFI 94*
Whiteker, Roy Archie 1927- *WhoAm 94*
Whitelaw, Viscount 1918- *Who 94*
Whitelaw, Barret d1947 *WhoHol 92*
Whitelaw, Billie 1932- *IntMPA 94, IntWW 93, Who 94, WhoHol 92*
Whitelaw, Brian William 1954- *WhoAmL 94*
Whitelaw, David Peter 1935- *WhoWest 94*
Whitelaw, James Hunter 1936- *Who 94*
Whitelaw, Nancy 1933- *SmATA 76 [port]*
Whitelaw, Robert I. 1945- *WhoAmL 94*
Whitelaw Of Penrith, Viscount 1918- *IntWW 93*
Whitelegge, (Benjamin) Arthur 1852-1933 *DcNaB MP*
Whiteley *Who 94*
Whiteley, Anne Fullerton 1954- *WhoAmL 94*
Whiteley, Arkie *WhoHol 92*
Whiteley, Benjamin R. 1929- *WhoIns 94*
Whiteley, Benjamin Robert 1929- *WhoAm 94, WhoWest 94*
Whiteley, Frank Grice 1931- *WhoFI 94*
Whiteley, Gerald Abson 1915- *Who 94*
Whiteley, Hugo Baldwin H. *Who 94*
Whiteley, James Morris 1927- *WhoScEn 94*
Whiteley, Jon 1945- *WhoHol 92*
Whiteley, Kent 1946- *WhoAmL 94*
Whiteley, Norman Franklin, Jr. 1940- *WhoFI 94*
Whiteley, Peter (John Frederick) 1920- *Who 94*
Whiteley, Robert Claude, Jr. 1957- *WhoAm 94*
Whiteley, Samuel Lloyd 1913- *Who 94*
Whiteley, Sandra Marie 1943- *WhoAm 94*
Whiteley, William Richard, Sr. 1940-1990 *WhAm 10*
Whitelock, Richard Lawrence 1930- *WhoAmP 93*
Whitely, Donald Harrison 1955- *WhoBlA 94*
Whitely, James Lowell 1936- *WhoFI 94*
Whiteman, (David) Bruce 1952- *WrDr 94*
Whiteman, Donna L. 1948- *WhoAmP 93*
Whiteman, Douglas E. 1961- *WhoAm 94*
Whiteman, Edward Russell 1938- *WhoAmA 93*
Whiteman, Elizabeth Anne Osborn 1918- *Who 94*
Whiteman, Frank *WhoHol 92*
Whiteman, Gilbert Lee 1931- *WhoFI 94*
Whiteman, Herbert Wells, Jr. 1936- *WhoBlA 94*
Whiteman, Horace Clifton 1925- *WhoAm 94*
Whiteman, John Robert 1938- *Who 94*
Whiteman, Joseph David 1933- *WhoAm 94, WhoAmL 94*
Whiteman, (Joseph Hilary) Michael 1906- *WrDr 94*
Whiteman, Paul d1967 *WhoHol 92*
Whiteman, Paul Samuel 1890-1967 *AmCulL*
Whiteman, Peter George 1942- *Who 94*
Whiteman, Richard Frank 1925- *WhoAm 94*
Whiteman, Roberta Hill *DrAPF 93*
Whiteman, Rodney David Carter 1940- *Who 94*
Whiteman, Wayne Edward 1957- *WhoScEn 94*
Whitemore, Hugh 1936- *IntMPA 94*
Whitemore, Hugh (John) 1936- *ConDr 93, WrDr 94*
Whitemore, Hugh John 1936- *Who 94*
Whiten, Colette 1945- *WhoAmA 93*
Whiten, Mark Anthony 1966- *WhoBlA 94*
Whiten, Tim 1941- *WhoAmA 93*
Whitener, Basil Lee 1915-1989 *WhAm 10*
Whitener, Paul A. W. 1911-1959 *WhoAmA 93N*
Whitener, Philip Charles 1920- *WhoScEn 94, WhoWest 94*
Whitener, Scott Douglas 1950- *WhoAm 94*
Whitener, Tommie Wayne 1942- *WhoAmL 94*
Whitener, William Garnett 1951- *WhoAm 94*
Whiteoak, John Edward Harrison 1947- *Who 94*
White Of Hull, Baron 1923- *Who 94*
White-Parson, Willar F. 1945- *WhoBlA 94*
Whitescarver, Olin Dravo 1936- *WhoWest 94*
Whitesell, Dale Edward 1925- *WhoAm 94*
Whitesell, Faris Daniel 1895- *WhAm 10*
Whitesell, John D. 1942- *WhoAmA 93*
Whitesell, John Edwin 1938- *WhoAm 94*
Whiteshield, Harvey 1867- *EncNAR*
Whiteside, Carol Gordon 1942- *WhoAm 94, WhoAmP 93, WhoWest 94*
Whiteside, Dale 1930- *WhoAmP 93*
Whiteside, Daniel Fowler 1931- *WhoAm 94*
Whiteside, Derek Thomas 1932- *Who 94*
Whiteside, Ernestyne E. *WhoBlA 94*
Whiteside, John 1679-1729 *DcNaB MP*
Whiteside, Larry W. 1937- *WhoBlA 94*
Whiteside, Lowell Stanley 1946- *WhoWest 94*
Whiteside, Theresa Listowski 1939- *WhoScEn 94*
Whiteside, Walker d1942 *WhoHol 92*
Whiteside, William Albert, II 1925- *WhoAmA 93*
Whiteside, William Anthony, Jr. 1929- *WhoAm 94*
Whitesides, George McClelland 1939- *WhoAm 94, WhoScEn 94*
Whitesides, Lawson Ewing 1910- *WhoFI 94, WhoMW 93*
Whitespear, Greg d1956 *WhoHol 92*
Whitest, Beverly Joyce 1951- *WhoBlA 94*
Whitestone, Herbert William 1920- *WhoAmP 93*
White-Thomson, Ian Hugh 1904- *Who 94*
White-Thomson, Ian Leonard 1936- *WhoAm 94, WhoWest 94*
White Thunder c. 1763-1838 *EncNAR*
White Thunder, Joanne L. 1956- *WhoMW 93*
White-Vondran, Mary Ellen 1938- *WhoWest 94*
White-Ware, Grace Elizabeth 1921- *WhoBlA 94*
White Wolf, E. Bruce 1945- *WhoAmL 94*
Whitfield *Who 94*
Whitfield, Adrian 1937- *Who 94*
Whitfield, Alan 1939- *Who 94*
Whitfield, Anne *WhoHol 92*
Whitfield, Charles Richard 1927- *Who 94*
Whitfield, David 1940- *WhoAm 94*
Whitfield, Frances Smith 1946- *WhoAmP 93*
Whitfield, Gary Hugh 1951- *WhoScEn 94*
Whitfield, George (Joshua Newbold) 1909- *WrDr 94*
Whitfield, George Joshua Newbold 1909- *Who 94*
Whitfield, Glen Smith 1947- *WhoWest 94*
Whitfield, Graham Frank 1942- *WhoScEn 94*
Whitfield, Harley A. 1930- *WhoIns 94*
Whitfield, Jack Duane 1928- *WhoAm 94*
Whitfield, Jeri Lynn 1950- *WhoAmL 94*
Whitfield, John 1941- *Who 94*
Whitfield, John Flett 1922- *Who 94*
Whitfield, John Humphreys 1906- *Who 94, WrDr 94*
Whitfield, John Lester, Jr. 1951- *WhoAmL 94*
Whitfield, June *WhoHol 92*
Whitfield, June Rosemary 1925- *Who 94*
Whitfield, Lynn *WhoBlA 94, WhoHol 92*
Whitfield, Lynn 1954?- *ConTFT 11*
Whitfield, Michael 1940- *Who 94*
Whitfield, Roderick 1937- *Who 94*
Whitfield, Sarah 1942- *ConAu 141*
Whitfield, Smoki d1967 *WhoHol 92*
Whitfield, Stephen Thomas 1966- *WhoFI 94*
Whitfield, Terry Bertland 1953- *WhoBlA 94*
Whitfield, Thomas d1992 *WhoBlA 94N*
Whitfield, Timberly N. 1966- *WhoBlA 94*
Whitfield, Vantile E. 1930- *WhoBlA 94*
Whitfield, Walter d1966 *WhoHol 92*
Whitfield, William *Who 94*
Whitfield Lewis, Herbert John *Who 94*
Whitford, Annabelle d1961 *WhoHol 92*
Whitford, George V. 1914- *WhoIns 94*
Whitford, John (Norman Keates) 1913- *Who 94*
Whitford, Joseph P. 1950- *WhoAm 94, WhoAmL 94*
Whitford, Peter *WhoHol 92*
Whitford, Philip Clason 1951- *WhoScEn 94*
Whitgift, John c. 1533-1604 *DcLB 132 [port]*
Whitham, Frank d1993 *NewYTBS 93*
Whitham, Gerald Beresford 1927- *IntWW 93, Who 94, WhoAm 94*
Whitham, Kenneth 1927- *WhoAm 94*
Whitin, Harry T. d1993 *NewYTBS 93*
Whitin, Richard Courtney, Jr. 1921- *WhoAm 94*
Whiting, Alan 1946- *Who 94*
Whiting, Albert Nathaniel 1917- *WhoAm 94, WhoBlA 94*
Whiting, Allen Suess 1926- *WhoAm 94, WhoWest 94*
Whiting, Arthur Milton 1928- *WhoWest 94*
Whiting, Barbara 1931- *WhoHol 92*
Whiting, Barbara E. 1936- *WhoBlA 94*
Whiting, Charlotte d1974 *WhoHol 92*
Whiting, Emanuel *WhoBlA 94*
Whiting, Fred C. *WhoAmP 93*
Whiting, George d1943 *WhoHol 92*
Whiting, Gordon *WhoHol 92*
Whiting, Henry H. *WhoAm 94, WhoAmL 94*
Whiting, Henry H. 1923- *WhoAmP 93*
Whiting, Hugh Richard 1945- *WhoAm 94, WhoAmL 94*
Whiting, Jack d1961 *WhoHol 92*
Whiting, James Vincent 1926- *WhoWest 94*
Whiting, John 1917-1963 *BlmGEL*
Whiting, John (Robert) 1917-1963 *IntDcT 2*
Whiting, John Randolph 1914- *WhoAm 94*
Whiting, Kelly Reid 1958- *WhoMW 93*
Whiting, Leonard 1950- *WhoHol 92*
Whiting, Leroy 1938- *WhoBlA 94*
Whiting, Lynn Gary 1944- *WhoWest 94*
Whiting, Margaret *WhoHol 92*
Whiting, Margaret 1924- *WhoHol 92*
Whiting, Maybelle Stevens 1925- *WhoBlA 94*
Whiting, Napoleon d1984 *WhoHol 92*
Whiting, Nathan *DrAPF 93*
Whiting, Pamela Jane 1958- *WhoWest 94*
Whiting, Peter Graham 1930- *Who 94*
Whiting, Phil d1956 *WhoHol 92*
Whiting, Richard *WhoHol 92*
Whiting, Richard Albert 1922- *WhoAm 94, WhoAmL 94*
Whiting, Richard Brooke 1947- *WhoAm 94*
Whiting, Robert 1942- *WrDr 94*
Whiting, Robert L. *WhoAmP 93*
Whiting, Stephen Clyde 1952- *WhoAmL 94*
Whiting, Thomas J. 1923- *WhoBlA 94*
Whiting, Van Robert, Jr. 1950- *WhoWest 94*
Whiting, Willie *WhoBlA 94*
Whitlam, (Edward) Gough 1916- *IntWW 93, Who 94, WrDr 94*
Whitlam, Michael Richard 1947- *Who 94*
Whitlam, Nicholas Richard 1945- *Who 94*
Whitley, Arthur Francis 1927- *WhoAm 94*
Whitley, Chester Buchan 1950- *WhoMW 93*
Whitley, Crane d1957 *WhoHol 92*
Whitley, David Scott 1953- *WhoHisp 94, WhoWest 94*
Whitley, Douglas Best 1928- *WhoAmP 93*
Whitley, Ebb K., Jr. 1934- *WhoAmP 93*
Whitley, Elizabeth Young 1915- *Who 94*
Whitley, George *EncSF 93*
Whitley, Joe d1980 *WhoHol 92*
Whitley, Joe Dally 1950- *WhoAm 94, WhoAmL 94*
Whitley, John (Rene) 1905- *Who 94*
Whitley, John Reginald 1926- *Who 94*
Whitley, Joseph Efird 1931-1989 *WhAm 10*
Whitley, Nancy O'Neil 1932- *WhoAm 94*
Whitley, Oliver John 1912- *Who 94*
Whitley, R. Joyce 1930- *WhoBlA 94*
Whitley, Ray d1979 *WhoHol 92*
Whitley, William N. 1934- *WhoBlA 94*
Whitling, Townsend d1952 *WhoHol 92*
Whitlock, Albert 1915-1982 *IntDcF 2-4*
Whitlock, Bennett Clarke, Jr. 1927- *WhoAm 94*
Whitlock, C. William 1942- *WhoAm 94*
Whitlock, Charlene Ann 1962- *WhoMW 93*
Whitlock, Charles Preston 1919- *WhoAm 94*
Whitlock, David C. 1935- *WhoAm 94*
Whitlock, David Wesley 1962- *WhoAmP 93*
Whitlock, Denise Lucille 1959- *WhoFI 94*
Whitlock, Don E. 1929- *WhoAmP 93*
Whitlock, Edward Madison, Jr. 1933- *WhoScEn 94*
Whitlock, Foster Brand 1914-1991 *WhAm 10*

Whitlock, Fred Henry 1936- *WhoBlA 94*
Whitlock, Gaylord Purcell 1917- *WhoWest 94*
Whitlock, Irene M. 1933- *WhoAmP 93*
Whitlock, James C., Jr. 1939- *WhoAmP 93*
Whitlock, John Joseph 1935- *WhoAm 94, WhoAmA 93*
Whitlock, John L. 1946- *WhoAm 94, WhoAmL 94*
Whitlock, John Merrill 1955- *WhoAmL 94*
Whitlock, Laura Alice 1959- *WhoScEn 94*
Whitlock, Lloyd d1966 *WhoHol 92*
Whitlock, Louis M. *WhoAmP 93*
Whitlock, Luder Gradick, Jr. 1940- *WhoAm 94*
Whitlock, McDonald Lee 1943- *WhoMW 93*
Whitlock, Orion *WhoIns 94*
Whitlock, Ralph 1914- *WrDr 94*
Whitlock, William Abel 1929- *WhoAm 94*
Whitlock, William Charles 1918- *Who 94*
Whitlock, Willie Walker 1925- *WhoAmP 93*
Whitlon, Donna Sue 1952- *WhoScEn 94*
Whitlow, Barbara Wheeler 1939- *WhoBlA 94*
Whitlow, Jill *WhoHol 92*
Whitlow, Tony E. 1933- *WhoAmP 93*
Whitlow, Woodrow, Jr. 1952- *WhoBlA 94*
Whitmal, Nathaniel 1937- *WhoBlA 94*
Whitman, Alexander H., Jr. 1944- *WhoScEn 94*
Whitman, Alice *SmATA 76*
Whitman, Andrew Franklin 1938- *WhoMW 93*
Whitman, Ann C. d1991 *WhAm 10*
Whitman, Betsey Sellner 1938- *WhoAm 94*
Whitman, Bradford F. 1945- *WhoAm 94, WhoAmL 94*
Whitman, Bruce Nairn 1933- *WhoAm 94*
Whitman, Dale Alan 1939- *WhoAm 94*
Whitman, David E. 1942- *WhoAmP 93*
Whitman, Ernest d1954 *WhoHol 92*
Whitman, Estelle d1970 *WhoHol 92*
Whitman, Frederic Bennett 1898- *WhAm 10*
Whitman, Gayne d1958 *WhoHol 92*
Whitman, Gerald John 1943- *WhoAm 94*
Whitman, James Thomas 1940- *WhoWest 94*
Whitman, Jules Isidore 1923- *WhoAm 94*
Whitman, Kari *WhoHol 92*
Whitman, Kenneth Jay 1947- *WhoAm 94, WhoWest 94*
Whitman, Kip *WhoHol 92*
Whitman, Mal 1877-1932 *BuCMET*
Whitman, Manuel S. 1937- *WhoFI 94*
Whitman, Mara Arden 1964- *WhoAmL 94*
Whitman, Marcus 1802-1847 *DcAmReB 2, EncNAR, WhWE*
Whitman, Marina von Neumann 1935- *IntWW 93, WhoFI 94*
Whitman, Marland Hamilton, Jr. 1947- *WhoAm 94, WhoAmL 94*
Whitman, Narcissa Prentiss 1808-1847 *DcAmReB 2, EncNAR*
Whitman, Reginald Norman 1909- *WhoAm 94*
Whitman, Robert 1936- *WhoAm 94*
Whitman, Robert Leslie 1933- *WhoMW 93*
Whitman, Robert Van Duyne 1928- *WhoAm 94*
Whitman, Russell Wilson 1940- *WhoAm 94, WhoAmL 94*
Whitman, Ruth *DrAPF 93*
Whitman, Ruth 1922- *WhoAm 94, WrDr 94*
Whitman, Sarah Helen Power 1803-1878 *BlmGWL*
Whitman, Stuart 1928- *IntMPA 94*
Whitman, Stuart 1928- *WhoHol 92*
Whitman, Walt d1928 *WhoHol 92*
Whitman, Walt 1819-1892 *AmCulL [port]*
Whitman, William *DrAPF 93, WhoHol 92*
Whitman, William Joseph 1963- *WhoMW 93*
Whitmer, Frederick Lee 1947- *WhoAm 94, WhoAmL 94*
Whitmer, Leslie Gay 1941- *WhoAmL 94*
Whitmer, Melvin Howard 1928- *WhoMW 93*
Whitmer, Robert V. 1923- *WhoAmP 93*
Whitmire, Bryant Andrew, Jr. 1946- *WhoAmL 94*
Whitmire, John Harris 1949- *WhoAmP 93*
Whitmire, Kathryn Jean 1946- *WhoAmP 93, WhoWomW 91*
Whitmire, Melburn G. 1939- *WhoAm 94*
Whitmire, Virginia d1981 *WhoHol 92*
Whitmont, Andrew Douglas 1947- *WhoWest 94*
Whitmore, Beatrice Eileen 1935- *WhoFI 94*
Whitmore, Charles 1945- *WhoBlA 94*

Whitmore, Charles Horace 1914- *WhoAm 94*
Whitmore, Chris 1921- *WrDr 94*
Whitmore, Clive (Anthony) 1935- *Who 94*
Whitmore, Darrell 1968- *WhoBlA 94*
Whitmore, Deborah Harkins 1953- *WhoFI 94*
Whitmore, Donald Clark 1932- *WhoWest 94*
Whitmore, Edward Hugh 1926-1992 *WhAm 10*
Whitmore, George *DrAPF 93*
Whitmore, George Merle, Jr. 1928- *WhoAm 94, WhoFI 94*
Whitmore, James 1921- *IntMPA 94, WhoHol 92*
Whitmore, James, Jr. *WhoHol 92*
Whitmore, James Allen 1921- *WhoAm 94*
Whitmore, John (Henry Douglas) 1937- *Who 94*
Whitmore, John Rogers 1933- *WhoAm 94, WhoFI 94*
Whitmore, Jon Scott 1945- *WhoAm 94*
Whitmore, Kay Rex 1932- *IntWW 93, WhoAm 94, WhoFI 94*
Whitmore, Lori K. 1958- *WhoAmP 93*
Whitmore, Menandra Sabina 1936- *WhoHisp 94*
Whitmore, R. Peter *WhoAmP 93*
Whitmore, Raymond Leslie 1920- *WrDr 94*
Whitmore, Sharp 1918- *WhoAm 94*
Whitmore, Susan H. d1993 *NewYTBS 93*
Whitmore, William Francis 1917- *WhoAm 94, WhoWest 94*
Whitmyer, Robert Wayne 1957- *WhoMW 93, WhoScEn 94*
Whitmyer, Russell Eliot 1915- *WhoAm 94*
Whitnah, Donald Robert 1925- *WrDr 94*
Whitner, Donna K. 1951- *WhoBlA 94*
Whitner, Jane Marvin 1935- *WhoScEn 94, WhoWest 94*
Whitney, A. James 1943- *WhoAmP 93*
Whitney, Barbara d1993 *NewYTBS 93*
Whitney, Barry Lyn 1947- *WhoAm 94*
Whitney, Carol Marie 1946- *WhoFI 94*
Whitney, Ce Ce *WhoHol 92*
Whitney, Charles Allen 1929- *WhoAm 94*
Whitney, Charles E. 1903-1977 *WhoAmA 93N*
Whitney, Charlotte Armide 1923- *WhoAmA 93N*
Whitney, Claire d1969 *WhoHol 92*
Whitney, Constance Clein *WhoWest 94*
Whitney, Cornelius Vanderbilt 1899-1992 *AnObit 1992, WhAm 10*
Whitney, Courtney 1897-1969 *HisDcKW*
Whitney, Daniel DeWayne 1937- *WhoWest 94*
Whitney, David Clay 1937- *WhoAm 94, WhoWest 94*
Whitney, Edgar Albert 1891- *WhoAmA 93N*
Whitney, Edward Bonner 1945- *WhoAm 94, WhoFI 94*
Whitney, Eleanore 1914- *WhoHol 92*
Whitney, Eli 1765-1825 *WorInv*
Whitney, Enoch Jonathan 1945- *WhoAmL 94*
Whitney, Fred 1956- *WhoAm 94*
Whitney, Geoffrey 1552?-1601 *DcLB 136*
Whitney, Glayde Dennis 1939- *WhoScEn 94*
Whitney, Grace Ann 1945- *WhoFI 94*
Whitney, Grace Lee 1930- *WhoHol 92*
Whitney, Gwin Richard 1932- *WhoMW 93*
Whitney, Harvey Brent 1949- *WhoFI 94*
Whitney, Hassler 1907-1989 *WhAm 10*
Whitney, Isabel Lydia d1962 *WhoAmA 93N*
Whitney, Isabella fl. 1566-1573 *DcLB 136*
Whitney, Isabella fl. 1567-1573 *BlmGWL*
Whitney, J. D. *DrAPF 93*
Whitney, Jane 1941- *WhoWest 94*
Whitney, John d1985 *WhoHol 92*
Whitney, John Adair 1932- *WhoAmP 93*
Whitney, John Clarence 1915- *WhoAm 94, WhoAmL 94*
Whitney, John Franklin 1953- *WhoAmL 94*
Whitney, John Freeman, Jr. 1944- *WhoAmP 93*
Whitney, John Hay 1904-1982 *WhoAmA 93N*
Whitney, John Norton Braithwaite 1930- *IntWW 93, Who 94*
Whitney, Jon R. 1944- *WhoFI 94, WhoWest 94*
Whitney, Larry Gene 1946- *WhoAmL 94*
Whitney, Malika Lee 1946- *WrDr 94*
Whitney, Maynard Merle 1931- *WhoAmA 93*
Whitney, Mike *WhoHol 92*
Whitney, Patrick Foster 1951- *WhoAm 94*
Whitney, Peter d1972 *WhoHol 92*
Whitney, Philip Richardson 1878- *WhoAmA 93N*

Whitney, Phyllis A(yame) 1903- *TwCYAW, WrDr 94*
Whitney, Phyllis Ayame 1903- *WhoAm 94*
Whitney, Raymond William 1930- *Who 94*
Whitney, Renee d1971 *WhoHol 92*
Whitney, Richard Buckner 1948- *WhoAm 94, WhoAmL 94*
Whitney, Richard Wheeler 1946- *WhoAmA 93*
Whitney, Robert 1911- *WhoHol 92*
Whitney, Robert, II d1969 *WhoHol 92*
Whitney, Robert A., Jr. 1935- *WhoAm 94, WhoScEn 94*
Whitney, Robert Avery 1912- *WhoAm 94*
Whitney, Robert James 1926- *WhoAmP 93*
Whitney, Robert Michael 1949- *WhoAm 94*
Whitney, Rosalyn L. 1950- *WhoBlA 94*
Whitney, Ruth Reinke 1928- *WhoAm 94*
Whitney, Stewart Bowman 1938- *WhoFI 94*
Whitney, Virginia Koogler 1927- *WhoAmP 93*
Whitney, W. Monty 1945- *WhoBlA 94*
Whitney, Wendy d1978 *WhoHol 92*
Whitney, William Chowning 1920- *WhoAm 94*
Whitney, William Elliot, Jr. 1933- *WhoAm 94*
Whitney, William Gordon 1922- *WhoFI 94*
Whitney, William Kuebler 1921-1985 *WhAm 10, WhoAmA 93N*
Whitney, William Percy, II 1940- *WhoScEn 94*
Whitney-Welles, Darla 1949- *WhoAmP 93*
Whitrow, Benjamin *WhoHol 92*
Whitsel, Richard Harry 1931- *WhoAm 94, WhoScEn 94, WhoWest 94*
Whitsel, Robert Malcolm 1929- *WhoIns 94, WhoMW 93*
Whitsell, Doris Benner 1923- *WhoMW 93*
Whitsell, Helen Jo 1938- *WhoAm 94*
Whitsey, Fred 1919- *Who 94*
Whitsitt, Michael Eugene 1947- *WhoAm 94*
Whitsitt, Robert James 1956- *WhoAm 94, WhoWest 94*
Whitson 1941- *WhoAmA 93*
Whitson, Angie *WhoAmA 93*
Whitson, David Frederick 1956- *WhoMW 93*
Whitson, Frank d1946 *WhoHol 92*
Whitson, James Norfleet, Jr. 1935- *WhoAm 94*
Whitson, Keith Roderick 1943- *Who 94*
Whitson, Lish 1942- *WhoAmL 94*
Whitson, Robert Edd 1942- *WhoFI 94*
Whitson, Thomas Jackson 1930- *Who 94*
Whitson, Zane C., Jr. 1933- *WhoAmP 93*
Whitsun-Jones, Paul d1974 *WhoHol 92*
Whitt, David V. 1935- *WhoIns 94*
Whitt, Dixie Dailey 1939- *WhoMW 93*
Whitt, Dwight Reginald 1949- *WhoBlA 94*
Whitt, Gregory Sidney 1938- *WhoAm 94*
Whitt, Karen Denise 1954- *WhoAmL 94*
Whitt, Laurie Anne *DrAPF 93*
Whitt, Mary White 1916- *WhoAmP 93*
Whitt, Michael D. 1952- *WhoAmP 93*
Whitt, Richard Ernest 1944- *WhoAm 94*
Whitt, Thomas Richard 1937- *WhoFI 94*
Whittaker, Alfred Heacock 1894- *WhAm 10*
Whittaker, Alun Howard 1946- *WhoWest 94*
Whittaker, Bill Douglas 1943- *WhoAm 94*
Whittaker, C(harles) R(ichard) 1929- *WrDr 94*
Whittaker, David 1933- *Who 94*
Whittaker, David Michael 1959- *WhoWest 94*
Whittaker, Geoffrey Owen 1932- *Who 94*
Whittaker, George 1918- *WhoAmP 93*
Whittaker, Jeanne Evans 1934- *WhoAm 94*
Whittaker, Marion Alma *WhoAmL 94*
Whittaker, Mary Frances 1926- *WhoFI 94*
Whittaker, Nigel 1948- *Who 94*
Whittaker, Patricia DiMaggio 1952- *WhoAm 94*
Whittaker, Peter Anthony 1939- *WhoScEn 94*
Whittaker, Robert 1939- *WhoAmP 93*
Whittaker, Sharon Elaine 1952- *WhoBlA 94*
Whittaker, Sheelagh Dillon 1947- *WhoAm 94*
Whittaker, Stanley Henry 1935- *Who 94*
Whittaker, Terry McKinley 1950- *WhoBlA 94*
Whittall, (Harold) Astley 1925- *Who 94*
Whittall, Michael Charlton 1926- *Who 94*
Whittam, Ronald 1925- *IntWW 93, Who 94*

Whittam Smith, Andreas 1937- *IntWW 93, Who 94*
Whitted, Earl, Jr. 1931- *WhoBlA 94*
Whitted, Glend O. 1926- *WhoAmP 93*
Whitted, Vincent LeRoy 1945- *WhoMW 93*
Whittell, James Michael Scott 1939- *Who 94*
Whittell, Josephine d1961 *WhoHol 92*
Whittelsey, Stuart Gordon, Jr. 1929-1992 *WhAm 10*
Whittemore, Anne Marie 1946- *WhoAm 94*
Whittemore, Colin Trengove 1942- *Who 94*
Whittemore, Donald Osgood 1944- *WhoMW 93*
Whittemore, Edward Reed, II 1919- *WhoAm 94*
Whittemore, Ernest William 1916- *Who 94*
Whittemore, Frank N. *WhoAmP 93*
Whittemore, Helen Simpson *WhoAmA 93N*
Whittemore, James A. 1914- *WhoAmP 93*
Whittemore, Laurence Frederick 1929- *WhoAm 94, WhoFI 94*
Whittemore, Marjorie Maas 1947- *WhoFI 94, WhoMW 93*
Whittemore, Paul Baxter 1948- *WhoScEn 94*
Whittemore, Reed *DrAPF 93*
Whittemore, (Edward) Reed, (Jr.) 1919- *WrDr 94*
Whittemore, Robert Clifton 1921-1988 *WhAm 10*
Whitten, Barbara Judith 1941- *WhoMW 93*
Whitten, Benjamin C. 1923- *WhoBlA 94*
Whitten, Bertwell Kneeland 1941- *WhoAm 94*
Whitten, Bobby Lee 1930- *WhoAmP 93*
Whitten, C. G. 1925- *WhoAmL 94*
Whitten, Charles Alexander, Jr. 1940- *WhoAm 94*
Whitten, Charles Arthur 1909- *WhoScEn 94*
Whitten, Charles F. 1922- *WhoBlA 94*
Whitten, David George 1938- *WhoAm 94, WhoScEn 94*
Whitten, David Owen 1940- *WhoFI 94*
Whitten, Dolphus, Jr. 1916- *WhoAm 94*
Whitten, Eloise Culmer 1929- *WhoRlA 94*
Whitten, Eric Harold Timothy 1927- *WhoAm 94*
Whitten, Jamie L. *CngDr 93*
Whitten, Jamie L. 1910- *WhoBlA 94*
Whitten, Jamie Lloyd 1910- *WhoAm 94, WhoAmP 93*
Whitten, Jerry Lynn 1937- *WhoAm 94, WhoScEn 94*
Whitten, Larry 1938- *WhoAmP 93*
Whitten, Leslie Hunter, Jr. 1928- *WhoAm 94, WrDr 94*
Whitten, Marguerite d1990 *WhoHol 92*
Whitten, Mary Ella 1933- *WhoFI 94*
Whitten, Norman E., Jr. 1937- *WrDr 94*
Whitten, Thomas P. 1937- *WhoBlA 94*
Whittengton, Robert E. *WhoAmP 93*
Whitteridge, David 1912- *IntWW 93, Who 94*
Whitteridge, Gordon (Coligny) 1908- *Who 94*
Whitters, James Payton, III 1939- *WhoAm 94, WhoAmL 94*
Whittick, Richard James 1912- *Who 94*
Whittier, Frederick Charles 1939- *WhoMW 93*
Whittier, John Greenleaf 1807-1892 *AmCulL*
Whittier, Monte Ray 1955- *WhoAmL 94*
Whittier, Sarajane 1912-1991 *WhAm 10*
Whittingdale, John Flasby Lawrance 1959- *Who 94*
Whittingham, Charles Arthur 1930- *WhoAm 94*
Whittingham, Charles Edward 1913- *WhoAm 94*
Whittingham, Charles Percival 1922- *Who 94, WrDr 94*
Whittingham, Harry Edward, Jr. 1918- *WhoAm 94*
Whittingham, Michael Stanley 1941- *WhoScEn 94*
Whittinghill, Dick 1913- *WhoHol 92*
Whittington, Bernard Wiley 1920- *WhoAm 94*
Whittington, Floyd Leon 1909- *WhoAmP 93*
Whittington, Gene *WhoHol 92*
Whittington, Geoffrey 1938- *ConAu 42NR, Who 94, WrDr 94*
Whittington, Harrison DeWayne 1931- *WhoBlA 94*
Whittington, Harry Benjamin 1915-1989 *WhAm 10*
Whittington, Harry Blackmore 1916- *Who 94*

Whittington, Horace Greeley 1929- WhoWest 94
Whittington, Jeremiah 1946- WhoWest 94
Whittington, John P. 1947- WhoAmL 94
Whittington, Jon Hammon 1938- WhoAmA 93
Whittington, Joseph Basil 1921- Who 94
Whittington, Margery d1957 WhoHol 92
Whittington, Mary K(athrine) 1941- SmATA 75 [port]
Whittington, Peter 1936- WrDr 94
Whittington, Richard d1423 BlmGEL
Whittington, Robert Bruce 1927- WhoAm 94
Whittington, Stuart Gordon 1942- WhoAm 94
Whittington, Thomas Alan 1916- Who 94
Whittington, Verle Glenn 1929-1988 WhAm 10
Whittington-Egan, Richard 1924- ConAu 42NR
Whittington-Smith, Marianne Christine Who 94
Whittle, Alfred J., Jr. d1993 NewYTBS 93
Whittle, Charles Edward, Jr. 1931- WhoAm 94
Whittle, Christopher 1947- WhoAm 94
Whittle, Frank 1907- IntWW 93, Who 94, WhoScEn 94, WorInv [port]
Whittle, Gail Harding 1920- WhoAmP 93
Whittle, John J. 1936- WhoIns 94
Whittle, John Joseph 1936- WhoAm 94
Whittle, Kenneth Francis 1922- Who 94
Whittle, Peter 1927- IntWW 93, Who 94, WrDr 94
Whittle, Philip Rodger 1943- WhoScEn 94
Whittle, Stephen Charles 1945- Who 94
Whittle, Tyler 1927- WrDr 94
Whittle, William Arthur 1946- WhoAmP 93
Whittlesey, Charles W. d1940 WhoHol 92
Whittlesey, Dennis J. 1942- WhoAmL 94
Whittlesey, Eunice Baird WhoAmP 93
Whittlesey, Faith Ryan 1939- WhoAmP 93
Whittlesey, John Williams 1917- WhoAmL 94
Whittome, (Leslie) Alan 1926- Who 94
Whittome, Irene F. 1942- WhoAmA 93
Whitton, Cuthbert Henry 1905- Who 94
Whitton, Kenneth S(tuart) 1925- WrDr 94
Whitton, Margaret 1952- WhoHol 92
Whitton, Peter William 1925- Who 94
Whittuck, Gerald Saumarez 1912- Who 94
Whitty, Jim 1931- WhoAmP 93
Whitty, John Lawrence 1943- Who 94
Whitty, May d1948 WhoHol 92
Whitwam, Barry WhoHol 92
Whitwam, David Ray 1942- WhoAm 94, WhoFI 94, WhoMW 93
Whitwam, Derek Firth 1932- Who 94
Whitwell, Stephen John 1920- Who 94
Whitwer, Glen Sterling, Jr. 1944- WhoFI 94
Whitworth, Claudia Alexander 1927- WhoBlA 94
Whitworth, David Timothy 1954- WhoAmL 94
Whitworth, Douglas Neil 1965- WhoMW 93
Whitworth, E. Leo, Jr. WhoBlA 94
Whitworth, F. Dixon, Jr. 1944- WhoAm 94
Whitworth, Francis John 1925- Who 94
Whitworth, Frank 1910- Who 94
Whitworth, H. Philip, Jr. 1947- WhoAmL 94
Whitworth, Hall Baker 1919- WhoAm 94
Whitworth, Hugh Hope Aston 1914- Who 94
Whitworth, John 1945- WrDr 94
Whitworth, John Harvey, Jr. 1933- WhoAm 94
Whitworth, John McKelvie 1942- WrDr 94
Whitworth, Joseph 1803-1887 WorInv
Whitworth, Kathrynne Ann 1939- WhoAm 94
Whitworth, Peggy W. 1939- WhoWest 94
Whitworth, Reginald Henry 1916- Who 94
Whitworth, Rex 1916- WrDr 94
Whitworth, William A. 1937- WhoAm 94
Whitworth-Jones, Anthony 1945- Who 94
Whone, Herbert 1925- WrDr 94
Whorf, David WhoHol 92
Whorf, John 1903-1959 WhoAmA 93N
Whorf, Richard d1966 WhoHol 92
Whoriskey, Robert Donald 1929- WhoAm 94
Whorton, Charles, Jr. 1924- WhoAmP 93
Whorton, M. Donald 1943- WhoAm 94
Whorton, M. Donald 1946- ConAu 43NR
Whyatt, Frances DrAPF 93
Whybrew, Edward Graham 1938- Who 94
Whybrow, Christopher John 1942- Who 94
Whybrow, John William 1947- Who 94
Whybrow, Peter Charles 1939- WhoAm 94
Whyland, Christopher Mark 1965- WhoAmL 94
Whyman, Deborah 1958- WhoAmP 93
Whynott, Robert Donald 1945- WhoAmP 93
Whytal, Russ d1930 WhoHol 92
Whytal, Russ, Mrs. d1946 WhoHol 92
Whyte, Andrew A(dams) EncSF 93
Whyte, Anne Veronica 1942- WhoAm 94
Whyte, Archie James 1936- WhoIns 94
Whyte, Bruce Lincoln 1941- WhoAmA 93, WhoFI 94
Whyte, Donn WhoHol 92
Whyte, Garrett 1915- WhoBlA 94
Whyte, George Kenneth, Jr. 1936- WhoAm 94
Whyte, Hartzell J. 1927- WhoBlA 94
Whyte, Helena Mary 1948- WhoWest 94
Whyte, James Aitken 1920- Who 94
Whyte, James Primrose, Jr. 1921- WhoAm 94
Whyte, John Stuart 1923- Who 94
Whyte, Martin King 1942- WhoAm 94
Whyte, Patrick WhoHol 92
Whyte, Raymond A. 1923- WhoAmA 93
Whyte, Ronald M. 1942- WhoAm 94, WhoAmL 94, WhoWest 94
Whyte, Stuart Scott Who 94
Whyte, (John) Stuart Scott 1926- Who 94
Whyte, Violet BlmGWL
Whyte, William Foote 1914- WhoAm 94
Whyte, William Hollingsworth 1917- IntWW 93, WhoAm 94
Whyte-Banks, Hila Jane 1949- WhoWest 94
Wiacek, Raymond J. 1950- WhoAmL 94
Wiackley, Mildred DrAPF 93
Wiant, Allen John 1924- WhoAmP 93
Wiant, Sarah Kirsten 1946- WhoAmL 94
Wiard, Stephen Lee WhoAmP 93
Wiata, Inia te NewGrDO
Wiatr, Christopher L. 1948- WhoScEn 94
Wiatr, Jeanne Malecki 1952- WhoMW 93
Wiatrak, Loretta M. 1966- WhoMW 93
Wiazemsky, Anne 1947- WhoHol 92
Wibaux, Fernand 1921- IntWW 93
Wibbenmeyer, Carl Thomas 1959- WhoAmL 94
Wibberley, Gerald Percy 1915- Who 94
Wibberley, Leonard (Patrick O'Connor) 1915-1983 EncSF 93
Wibble, Anne 1943- IntWW 93
Wibble, Anne Marie 1943- WhoWomW 91
Wiberg, Donald Martin 1936- WhoAm 94
Wiberg, Kenneth Berle 1927- IntWW 93, WhoScEn 94
Wiberg, V. Demont 1937- WhoAmP 93
Wiberley, Stephen Edward 1919- WhoAm 94
Wible, Charles Stephen 1937- WhoAmP 93
Wible, Connie WhoAmP 93
Wible, Connie 1943- WhoMW 93
Wible, Mary Grace WhoAmA 93
Wiblin, Derek John 1933- Who 94
Wiblin, Jo Ann 1944- WhoFI 94
Wiblishauser, Elmer Hubert 1910- WhAm 10
Wiborg, James Hooker 1924- WhoFI 94, WhoWest 94
Wice, Paul Clinton 1944- WhoMW 93
Wich, Donald Anthony, Jr. 1947- WhoAmL 94
Wich, Gunther 1928- NewGrDO
Wicha, Max S. 1949- WhoScEn 94
Wichern, Dean William 1942- WhoAm 94
Wichlenski, John Joseph 1943- WhoFI 94
Wichterle, Otto 1913- IntWW 93
Wick, Bruno WhoHol 92
Wick, Carolyn Brown 1958- WhoMW 93
Wick, Carter 1924- WrDr 94
Wick, Charles Z. 1917- IntWW 93
Wick, Donald Paul 1962- WhoMW 93
Wick, Gian Carlo 1909-1992 WhAm 10
Wick, Hal Gerard 1944- WhoAmP 93
Wick, Hilton 1920- WhoAmP 93
Wick, Hilton Addison 1920- WhoAm 94
Wick, James Eugene 1947- WhoWest 94
Wick, James Joseph 1960- WhoWest 94
Wick, Lawrence Scott 1945- WhoAmL 94
Wick, Margaret 1942- WhoAm 94
Wick, Raymond Victor 1940- WhoWest 94
Wick, Robert Thomas 1927- WhoAm 94
Wick, William David 1949- WhoAm 94, WhoAmL 94
Wickberg, Erik E. 1904- IntWW 93, Who 94
Wickbom, Sten 1931- IntWW 93
Wickens, Alan Herbert 1929- Who 94
Wickens, Aryness Joy 1901-1991 WhAm 10
Wickens, Paul L. 1946- WhoAmL 94
Wickens, Peter Charles 1912- WrDr 94
Wickens, William George 1905- WhoAmL 94
Wicker, Allan Wert 1941- WhoWest 94
Wicker, Brian John 1929- WrDr 94
Wicker, David Bryan 1965- WhoAmL 94
Wicker, Dennis A. 1951- WhoAm 94
Wicker, Dennis A. 1952- WhoAmP 93
Wicker, Elmus Rogers 1926- WhoFI 94, WhoMW 93
Wicker, Henry Sindos 1928- WhoBlA 94
Wicker, J. J., II 1950- WhoAmL 94
Wicker, James Caldwell 1895- WhAm 10
Wicker, Nina A. DrAPF 93
Wicker, Robert A. 1944- WhoAmL 94
Wicker, Roger Frederick 1951- WhoAmP 93
Wicker, Thomas Carey, Jr. 1923- WhoAmL 94
Wicker, Thomas Grey 1926- IntWW 93, WhoAm 94
Wicker, Tom 1926- WrDr 94
Wicker, Veronica DiCarlo WhoAm 94, WhoAmL 94
Wicker, William Walter 1930- WhoAm 94
Wickersham, Kirk 1943- WhoAmL 94
Wickersham, William R. 1948- WhoAmP 93
Wickerson, John (Michael) 1937- Who 94
Wickert, Erwin 1915- IntWW 93
Wickert, Frederic Robinson 1912- WhoMW 93
Wickert, Max A. DrAPF 93
Wickes, Charles G. Who 94
Wickes, George 1698-1761 DcNaB MP
Wickes, George 1923- WhoAm 94, WhoWest 94
Wickes, Lambert c. 1735-1777 WhAmRev
Wickes, Lambert 1742-1777 AmRev
Wickes, Mary IntMPA 94, WhoAm 94, WhoWest 94
Wickes, Mary 1912- WhoHol 92
Wickes, Richard Paul 1948- WhoAm 94, WhoAmL 94
Wickes, William Castles 1946- WhoWest 94
Wickesberg, Albert Klumb 1921- WhoAm 94
Wickfield, Eric Nelson 1953- WhoFI 94
Wickham, Anna 1884-1947 BlmGWL
Wickham, Daphne Elizabeth 1946- Who 94
Wickham, David 1944- ConAu 141
Wickham, DeWayne 1946- WhoBlA 94
Wickham, Edward Ralph 1911- Who 94, WrDr 94
Wickham, Glynne (William Gladstone) 1922- WrDr 94
Wickham, Glynne William Gladstone 1922- Who 94
Wickham, Henry Alexander 1846-1928 WhWE
Wickham, Jeffrey WhoHol 92
Wickham, John Adams, Jr. 1928- WhoAm 94, WhoAmP 93
Wickham, John Ewart Alfred 1927- Who 94
Wickham, Kenneth Gregory 1913- WhoAm 94
Wickham, Marvin Gary 1942- WhoScEn 94
Wickham, Tony d1948 WhoHol 92
Wickham, William Rayley 1926- Who 94
Wickham-St. Germain, Margaret Edna 1956- WhoMW 93, WhoScEn 94
Wicki, Bernhard 1919- WhoHol 92
Wicki, Dieter 1931- WhoFI 94
Wicki-Fink, Agnes 1919- IntWW 93
Wickins, David Allen 1920- Who 94
Wickiser, Ralph Lewanda 1910- WhoAm 94, WhoAmA 93
Wickizer, Cindy Louise 1946- WhoWest 94
Wickizer, Mary Alice 1938- WhoAm 94, WhoWest 94
Wickland, Diane Elizbeth 1951- WhoScEn 94
Wickland, Larry d1938 WhoHol 92
Wicklander, Edward A. 1952- WhoAmA 93
Wicklein, John Frederick 1924- WhoAm 94
Wickliff, Aloysius M , Sr. 1921- WhoBlA 94
Wickliffe, Jerry L. 1941- WhoAm 94, WhoAmL 94
Wicklund, David Wayne 1949- WhoAmL 94
Wicklund, Millie Mae DrAPF 93
Wickman, Herbert Hollis 1936- WhoScEn 94
Wickman, John Edward 1929- WhoAm 94, WhoMW 93
Wickman, Krister 1924- IntWW 93
Wickman, Lance B. 1940- WhoAmL 94
Wickman, Paul Everett 1912- WhoAm 94, WhoWest 94
Wickramanayake, Godage Bandula 1953- WhoScEn 94
Wickramasinghe, Nalin Chandra 1939- IntWW 93, Who 94, WrDr 94
Wickreme, A. S. K. Who 94
Wickremesinghe, Walter Gerald 1897- Who 94
Wicks, Alan 1948- WhoAmL 94
Wicks, Allan 1923- Who 94
Wicks, David Vaughan 1918- Who 94
Wicks, Eugene Claude 1931- WhoAm 94, WhoAmA 93
Wicks, Frank Eugene 1939- WhoScEn 94
Wicks, Geoffrey Leonard 1934- Who 94
Wicks, Harry Oliver, III 1931- WhoFI 94
Wicks, James (Albert) 1910- Who 94
Wicks, John Harold 1963- WhoFI 94
Wicks, John R. 1937- WhoAm 94
Wicks, Malcolm Hunt 1947- Who 94
Wicks, Mark EncSF 93
Wicks, Moye, III 1932- WhoScEn 94
Wicks, Nigel (Leonard) 1940- Who 94
Wicks, Nigel Leonard 1940- IntWW 93
Wicks, Ralph Edwin 1921- Who 94
Wicks, Sidney 1949- BasBi
Wicks, Wesley D. 1936- WhoAm 94
Wicks, William Withington 1923- WhoAm 94
Wickser, John Philip 1922- WhoAm 94
Wickstead, Cyril 1922- Who 94
Wickstrand, Owen Conrad 1936- WhoWest 94
Wickstrom, Carl Webster 1944- WhoScEn 94
Wickstrom, Karl Youngert 1935- WhoAm 94
Wickstrom, Lois DrAPF 93
Wickwire, James D., Jr. WhoIns 94
Wickwire, Jon M. 1944- WhoAmL 94
Wickwire, Patricia Joanne Nellor WhoScEn 94, WhoWest 94
Wicomb, Zoe 1948- BlmGWL
Widaman, Gregory Alan 1955- WhoFI 94, WhoWest 94
Widdas, Wilfred Faraday 1916- Who 94
Widdecombe, Ann Noreen 1947- Who 94, WhoWomW 91
Widdecombe, James Murray 1910- Who 94
Widdecombe, Wallace d1969 WhoHol 92
Widdel, John Earl, Jr. 1936- WhoAm 94, WhoAmL 94
Widder, Charles Joseph 1941- WhoIns 94
Widder, Patricia A. 1953- WhoWest 94
Widder, Willard Graves 1924- WhoAm 94
Widdicombe, David Graham 1924- Who 94
Widdicombe, Richard Palmer 1941- WhoAm 94
Widdoes, Kathleen 1939- WhoHol 92
Widdoes, Lawrence Lewis 1932- WhoAm 94
Widdop, Walter 1892-1949 NewGrDO
Widdows, Charles Who 94
Widdows, (Stanley) Charles 1909- Who 94
Widdows, Roland Hewlett 1921- Who 94
Widdowson, Elsie May 1906- Who 94
Widdowson, Henry George 1935- Who 94
Widdrington, Peter Nigel Tinling 1930- IntWW 93, WhoAm 94, WhoFI 94
Widdup, Malcolm 1920- Who 94
Wideburg, Norman Earl 1933- WhoScEn 94
Wideman, Gilder LeVaugh 1927- WhoScEn 94
Wideman, John Edgar 1941- BlkWr 2, ConAu 42NR, ConBlB 5 [port], WhoAm 94, WhoBlA 94, WrDr 94
Widener, Bill A. 1939- WhoAmP 93
Widener, Bruce E. 1948- WhoAmP 93
Widener, Edward Ladd 1926- WhoMW 93
Widener, H. Emory, Jr. 1923- WhoAmP 93
Widener, Harry Elkins 1885-1912 DcLB 140 [port]
Widener, Herbert Lloyd 1941- WhAm 10
Widener, Hiram Emory, Jr. 1923- WhoAm 94, WhoAmL 94
Widener, James Curtis 1943- WhoAm 94
Widener, Warren H. 1938- WhoAmP 93
Widener, Warren Hamilton 1938- WhoBlA 94
Widengren, Ulf Nils Joel 1931-1987 WhAm 10
Widera, G. E. O. 1938- WhoAm 94
Widerberg, Bo 1930- IntWW 93
Widershien, Marc DrAPF 93
Wides, Burton V. 1941- WhoAmL 94
Widger, Rodric Alan 1952- WhoAmL 94
Widger, Stanley W., Jr. 1950- WhoAmL 94
Widgery, Jan DrAPF 93
Widgery, William c. 1753-1822 WhAmRev
Widgoff, Mildred 1924- WhoAm 94
Widin, Gregory Peter 1952- WhoMW 93
Widing, Lawrence Carl 1964- WhoMW 93
Widiss, Alan I. 1938- WhoAm 94
Widlowski, Larry R. 1939- WhoIns 94
Widlund, Olof Bertil 1938- WhoAm 94

Wiggins, David 1933- *IntWW 93, Who 94, WrDr 94*
Wiggins, Dewayne Lee 1949- *WhoFI 94*
Wiggins, Edith Mayfield 1942- *WhoBlA 94*
Wiggins, Edward A. 1933- *WhoAmP 93*
Wiggins, Gary *WhoAmP 93*
Wiggins, George I. *WhoAmP 93*
Wiggins, Glenn B. 1927- *WhoScEn 94*
Wiggins, Guy A. 1920- *WhoAmA 93*
Wiggins, Guy C. 1883-1962 *WhoAmA 93N*
Wiggins, Harry *WhoAmP 93*
Wiggins, Harry 1934- *WhoMW 93*
Wiggins, James Bryan 1935- *WhoAm 94*
Wiggins, James Russell 1903- *IntWW 93, WhoAm 94, WrDr 94*
Wiggins, John *Who 94*
Wiggins, (Anthony) John 1938- *Who 94*
Wiggins, Joseph L. 1944- *WhoBlA 94*
Wiggins, K. Douglas 1959- *WhoAmA 93*
Wiggins, Kip Acker 1950- *WhoAm 94*
Wiggins, Larry Don 1949- *WhoAmP 93*
Wiggins, Leslie 1936- *WhoBlA 94*
Wiggins, Lillian Cooper 1932- *WhoBlA 94*
Wiggins, Marianne 1947- *WrDr 94*
Wiggins, Maxwell Lester 1915- *Who 94*
Wiggins, Mitchell 1959- *WhoBlA 94*
Wiggins, Myra Albert 1869-1956 *WhoAmA 93N*
Wiggins, Nancy Bowen 1948- *WhoFI 94*
Wiggins, Norman Adrian 1924- *WhoAm 94, WhoAmL 94*
Wiggins, Paul R. 1955- *WhoBlA 94*
Wiggins, Roger C. 1945- *WhoScEn 94*
Wiggins, Samuel Paul 1919- *WhoAm 94*
Wiggins, Tudi 1935- *WhoHol 92*
Wiggins, Walton Wray 1924-1992 *WhoAmA 93N*
Wiggins, William H., Jr. 1934- *WhoBlA 94*
Wiggins-Durgin, Maud Ann 1925- *WhoAmP 93*
Wigginton, Eugene H. 1935- *WhoAm 94*
Wigglesworth, David Cunningham 1927- *WhoWest 94*
Wigglesworth, Frank 1918- *NewGrDO*
Wigglesworth, Gordon Hardy 1920- *Who 94*
Wigglesworth, Vincent (Brian) 1899- *IntWW 93, Who 94*
Wigglesworth, William Robert Brian 1937- *Who 94*
Wiggs, David Harold, Jr. 1947- *WhoFI 94*
Wiggs, Eugene Overbey 1928- *WhoAm 94*
Wiggs, Jonathan Louis 1952- *WhoBlA 94*
Wiggs, P. David 1942- *WhoWest 94*
Wight, Darlene 1926- *WhoMW 93*
Wight, Doris T. *DrAPF 93*
Wight, Frederick S. 1902-1986 *WhoAmA 93N*
Wight, James Alfred 1916- *Who 94, WhoAm 94*
Wight, Lawrence John *WhoFI 94, WhoMW 93*
Wight, M. Arnold, Jr. *WhoAmP 93*
Wight, Nancy Elizabeth 1947- *WhoWest 94*
Wight, Randy Lee 1951- *WhoWest 94*
Wight, Richard J. 1949- *WhoAmL 94*
Wight, Robin 1944- *Who 94*
Wightman, Alec 1951- *WhoAm 94, WhoAmL 94*
Wightman, Ann 1958- *WhoAmL 94*
Wightman, Arthur Strong 1922- *IntWW 93, WhoAm 94, WhoScEn 94*
Wightman, Charlotte Kunkel 1954- *WhoAmL 94*
Wightman, Hazel Hotchkiss 1886-1974 *BuCMET*
Wightman, Jim 1957- *WhoMW 93*
Wightman, Robert *WhoHol 92*
Wightman, Thomas Valentine 1921- *WhoWest 94*
Wightman, William David 1939- *Who 94*
Wightwick, Charles Christopher Brooke 1931- *Who 94*
Wigington, Ronald Lee 1932- *WhoAm 94*
Wigler, Andrew Jeffrey 1965- *WhoAmL 94*
Wigler, Michael 1947- *WhoAm 94*
Wigler, Michael H. 1947- *WhoScEn 94*
Wigley, Dafydd 1943- *IntWW 93, Who 94*
Wigley, Richard Ellis 1918- *WhoAmP 93*
Wigmore, Barrie Atherton 1941- *WhoAm 94*
Wigmore, James Arthur Joseph 1928- *Who 94*
Wigmore, John Grant 1928- *WhoAm 94*
Wigmore, William Mark 1961- *WhoAmL 94*
Wignall, T(revor) C. 1883-1958 *EncSF 93*
Wignarajah, Kanapathipillai 1944- *WhoScEn 94, WhoWest 94*
Wigner, Eugene P(aul) 1902- *Who 94*
Wigner, Eugene Paul 1902- *IntWW 93, WhoAm 94, WhoScEn 94*
Wigoder, Baron 1921- *Who 94*
Wigodner, Byron I. 1952- *WhoMW 93*
Wigram, Baron 1915- *Who 94*
Wigram, Clifford Woolmore 1911- *Who 94*
Wigram, Derek Roland 1908- *Who 94*
Wigsten, Paul Bradley, Jr. 1947- *WhoFI 94*
Wigton, Paul Norton 1932- *WhoAm 94*
Wigzell, Hans 1938- *IntWW 93*
Wihby, Linda S. 1951- *WhoAmP 93*
Wihtol, Arn S. 1944- *IntMPA 94*
Wiig, Elisabeth Hemmersam 1935- *WhoAm 94*
Wiig, Howard Calvert 1940- *WhoWest 94*
Wiig, Karl Martin 1934- *WhoScEn 94*
Wiik, Bjorn H. *WhoScEn 94*
Wiin-Nielsen, Aksel Christopher 1924- *Who 94, WhoAm 94*
Wiin-Nielsen, Aksel Christopher 1929- *IntWW 93*
Wiitala, Stephen John 1942- *WhoAmP 93*
Wiitasalo, Shirley 1949- *WhoAmA 93*
Wijaya, Andi 1936- *WhoScEn 94*
Wijenaike, Punyakanthi 1935- *BlmGWL*
Wijeratne, Ranjan 1931- *WhAm 10*
Wijesekera, Nandadeva 1908- *IntWW 93*
Wijesundera, Vishaka 1962- *WhoScEn 94*
Wijetunge, D.B. 1922- *IntWW 93*
Wijewardane, Nissanka 1926- *IntWW 93*
Wijeysundera, Nihal Ekanayake 1943- *WhoScEn 94*
Wik, Jean Marie 1938- *WhoMW 93*
Wikander, Lawrence Einar 1915- *WhoAm 94*
Wikarski, Nancy Susan 1954- *WhoFI 94, WhoMW 93, WhoScEn 94*
Wike, Edward L. 1922- *WrDr 94*
Wikenhauser, Charles Joseph 1948- *WhoAm 94, WhoMW 93*
Wiker, Steven Forrester 1952- *WhoScEn 94, WhoWest 94*
Wiklund, K. Lars C. 1943- *WhoScEn 94*
Wikman, Georg Karl 1943- *WhoScEn 94*
Wikmanson, Johan 1753-1800 *NewGrDO*
Wikoff, Virgil Cornwell 1927- *WhoAmP 93*
Wiksten, Barry Frank 1935- *WhoAm 94*
Wikstrom, Francis M. 1949- *WhoAmL 94*
Wikstrom, Jan-Erik 1932- *IntWW 93*
Wiktor, Peter Jan 1956- *WhoScEn 94*
Wiktorowicz, John Edward 1949- *WhoScEn 94*
Wiland, Harry Alan 1944- *WhoAm 94*
Wilander, Mats *IntWW 93*
Wilander, Mats 1964- *BuCMET [port]*
Wilatsi fl. 19th cent.- *EncNAR*
Wilbanks, Jan Joseph 1928- *WhoAm 94*
Wilbanks, Wesley Gerald 1941- *WhoFI 94*
Wilbarger, Edward Stanley 1931- *WhoWest 94*
Wilbekin, Harvey E. 1926- *WhoBlA 94*
Wilber, Bernard 1924- *WhoAmP 93*
Wilber, Charles Grady 1916- *WhoAm 94, WhoWest 94*
Wilber, Charles K. 1935- *WrDr 94*
Wilber, Clare Marie 1928- *WhoWest 94*
Wilber, Cynthia J. 1951- *ConAu 140*
Wilber, Donald Newton 1907- *WrDr 94*
Wilber, Elinor F. *WhoAmP 93*
Wilber, Ida Belinda 1956- *WhoBlA 94*
Wilber, John Franklin 1935- *WhoScEn 94*
Wilber, John James 1967- *WhoWest 94*
Wilber, Laura Ann 1934- *WhoAm 94*
Wilber, Margie Robinson *WhoBlA 94*
Wilber, Robert Edwin 1932- *WhoAm 94*
Wilber, Shirley d1987 *WhoHol 92*
Wilberforce, Baron 1907- *IntWW 93, Who 94*
Wilberforce, William 1759-1833 *BlmGEL*
Wilberforce, William John Antony 1930- *Who 94*
Wilberg, Richard Willard 1948- *WhoFI 94*
Wilbert, Dennis P. 1948- *WhoAmL 94*
Wilbert, Lawrence J. *WhoAmP 93*
Wilbert, Robert John 1929- *WhoAmA 93*
Wilbon, Joan Marie 1949- *WhoBlA 94*
Wilborn, Letta Grace Smith 1936- *WhoBlA 94*
Wilborn, W. Stephen 1947- *WhoAmP 93*
Wilborn, Woody Stephen 1947- *WhoAmL 94*
Wilbourn, Gordon Gene 1933- *WhoAm 94, WhoFI 94*
Wilbraham *Who 94*
Wilbraham, John *EncSF 93*
Wilbraham, John Harry George 1944- *IntWW 93*
Wilbraham, Richard B. *Who 94*
Wilbrandt, Adolf von 1837-1911 *DcLB 129 [port]*
Wilbun, Marcus 1921- *WhAm 10*
Wilbun, Shepperson A. 1924-1991 *WhoBlA 94N*
Wilbur, Brayton, Jr. 1935- *WhoAm 94*
Wilbur, Claude Glenn 1956- *WhoWest 94*
Wilbur, Crane d1973 *WhoHol 92*
Wilbur, E. Packer 1936- *WhoAm 94*
Wilbur, George Craig 1946- *WhoAmP 93*
Wilbur, George P. 1942- *WhoHol 92*
Wilbur, James B(enjamin), III 1924- *ConAu 41NR*
Wilbur, James Benjamin, III 1924- *WhoAm 94*
Wilbur, James H. 1811-1887 *EncNAR*
Wilbur, Karl Milton 1912- *WhoAm 94, WhoScEn 94*
Wilbur, Kirby Allen 1953- *WhoAmP 93*
Wilbur, Lawrence Nelson 1897-1988 *WhoAmA 93N*
Wilbur, Leslie Clifford 1924- *WhoAm 94*
Wilbur, Leslie Eugene 1924- *WhoWest 94*
Wilbur, Lyman Dwight 1900- *WhoAm 94*
Wilbur, Paul James 1937- *WhoScEn 94, WhoWest 94*
Wilbur, Richard *DrAPF 93*
Wilbur, Richard (Purdy) 1921- *IntWW 93, WrDr 94*
Wilbur, Richard Purdy 1921- *WhoAm 94*
Wilbur, Richard Sloan 1924- *IntWW 93, WhoAm 94*
Wilbur, Robert Lynch 1925- *WhoScEn 94*
Wilburn, Isaac Earphette 1932- *WhoBlA 94*
Wilburn, Jerry *WhoAmP 93*
Wilburn, Marion Turner 1946- *WhoAm 94*
Wilburn, Mary Nelson 1932- *WhoAmL 94*
Wilburn, Victor H. 1931- *WhoBlA 94*
Wilby, Basil Leslie 1930- *ConAu 41NR, WrDr 94*
Wilby, James *IntWW 93*
Wilby, James 1958- *IntMPA 94, WhoHol 92*
Wilby, Maurice, Mrs. d1939 *WhoHol 92*
Wilby, William Langfitt 1944- *WhoFI 94*
Wilcher, Ina Florence 1936- *WhoAmP 93*
Wilcher, LaJuana Sue 1954- *WhoAm 94, WhoAmL 94*
Wilcher, Larry Keith 1950- *WhoAm 94*
Wilchins, Howard Martin 1945- *WhoAmL 94*
Wilchins, Sidney A. 1940- *WhoScEn 94*
Wilck, Carl Thomas 1933- *WhoWest 94*
Wilckens, Ulrich 1928- *IntWW 93*
Wilcock, Christopher Camplin 1939- *Who 94*
Wilcock, Donald Frederick 1913- *WhoAm 94*
Wilcock, James William 1917- *WhoAm 94*
Wilcock, William Leslie 1922- *Who 94*
Wilcox, Albert Frederick 1909- *Who 94*
Wilcox, Alfred H. 1943- *WhoAmL 94*
Wilcox, Benson Reid 1932- *WhoAm 94*
Wilcox, Beverly Joan 1940- *WhoMW 93*
Wilcox, Brett E. 1953- *WhoWest 94*
Wilcox, Bruce Gordon 1947- *WhoAm 94*
Wilcox, Calvin Hayden 1924- *WhoWest 94*
Wilcox, Charles Julian 1930- *WhoAm 94, WhoScEn 94*
Wilcox, Collin 1924- *WrDr 94*
Wilcox, Collin 1935- *WhoHol 92*
Wilcox, Collin M. 1924- *WhoAm 94*
Wilcox, David Eric 1939- *WhoAm 94, WhoFI 94*
Wilcox, David John Reed 1939- *Who 94*
Wilcox, David Peter *Who 94*
Wilcox, David Robert 1944- *WhoWest 94*
Wilcox, Debra Kay 1955- *WhoAmL 94*
Wilcox, Dennis Lee 1941- *WhoWest 94*
Wilcox, Desmond John 1931- *Who 94*
Wilcox, Dina Lynn 1947- *WhoAmL 94*
Wilcox, Don 1905- *EncSF 93*
Wilcox, Donald Alan 1951- *WhoAmL 94, WhoMW 93*
Wilcox, Douglas Abel 1949- *WhoMW 93*
Wilcox, Earl V. *WhoAmP 93, WhoHisp 94*
Wilcox, Elizabeth Harrison 1935- *WhoAmP 93*
Wilcox, Esther Louise *Who 94*
Wilcox, Evlyn *WhoAmP 93, WhoWest 94*
Wilcox, Frank d1974 *WhoHol 92*
Wilcox, Fred T. 1935- *WhoWest 94*
Wilcox, Gordon Cumnock 1934- *WhoAmA 93*
Wilcox, Gordon W. 1943- *WhoAmL 94*
Wilcox, Harlow d1960 *WhoHol 92*
Wilcox, Harold Edgar 1940- *WhoWest 94*
Wilcox, Harry Hammond 1918- *WhoAm 94*
Wilcox, Harry Wilbur, Jr. 1925- *WhoAm 94*
Wilcox, Harvey John 1937- *WhoAm 94, WhoAmL 94*
Wilcox, Helen (Elizabeth) 1955- *WrDr 94*
Wilcox, Janice Horde 1940- *WhoBlA 94*
Wilcox, Jeffrey Merrill 1963- *WhoFI 94, WhoMW 93*
Wilcox, John Caven 1942- *WhoAm 94*
Wilcox, John Chapman 1943- *WhoMW 93*
Wilcox, John W. 1945- *WhoAmL 94*
Wilcox, Jon P. 1936- *WhoAmL 94, WhoMW 93*
Wilcox, Judith Ann *Who 94*
Wilcox, Judith Lynne 1938- *WhoMW 93*
Wilcox, Kenneth Parmelee 1948- *WhoFI 94*
Wilcox, Laird (M.) 1942- *ConAu 140*
Wilcox, Laird Maurice 1942- *WhoMW 93*
Wilcox, Larry 1948- *WhoHol 92*
Wilcox, Lee Roy 1912- *WhoMW 93*
Wilcox, Lisa *WhoHol 92*
Wilcox, Lucia *WhoAmA 93N*
Wilcox, Lynn E. 1935- *WhoWest 94*
Wilcox, Mark Dean 1952- *WhoAm 94, WhoAmL 94, WhoMW 93*
Wilcox, Mark M. 1951- *WhoAmL 94*
Wilcox, Marsha Ann 1956- *WhoFI 94*
Wilcox, Mary *WhoHol 92*
Wilcox, Mary Rose 1949- *WhoAmP 93, WhoHisp 94*
Wilcox, Maud 1923- *WhoAm 94*
Wilcox, Michael Wing 1941- *WhoAm 94*
Wilcox, Patricia *DrAPF 93*
Wilcox, Paul Horne 1950- *WhoScEn 94*
Wilcox, Paul Stewart 1948- *WhoAmP 93*
Wilcox, Philip C. 1937- *WhoAm 94*
Wilcox, Preston 1923- *WhoBlA 94*
Wilcox, Ralph 1950- *WhoHol 92*
Wilcox, Rano Roger 1946- *WhoScEn 94*
Wilcox, Rhoda Davis 1918- *WhoWest 94*
Wilcox, Richard Cecil 1959- *WhoFI 94, WhoScEn 94*
Wilcox, Richard Guy 1961- *WhoMW 93*
Wilcox, Richard Hoag 1927- *WhoScEn 94*
Wilcox, Robert d1955 *WhoHol 92*
Wilcox, Roger Clark 1934- *WhoScEn 94*
Wilcox, Ronald *EncSF 93*
Wilcox, Ronald Bruce 1934- *WhoAm 94*
Wilcox, Ruth 1889-1958 *WhoAmA 93N*
Wilcox, Shannon *WhoHol 92*
Wilcox, Sheila Maureen 1965- *WhoMW 93*
Wilcox, Silas d1945 *WhoHol 92*
Wilcox, Stephen F. 1951- *ConAu 141*
Wilcox, Steven Alan 1955- *WhoAmL 94*
Wilcox, Susan Schmittzehe 1962- *WhoMW 93*
Wilcox, Tara Leigh 1966- *WhoAmL 94*
Wilcox, Thomas Robert d1993 *NewYTBS 93 [port]*
Wilcox, Thomas Robert, III 1958- *WhoAmL 94*
Wilcox, Timothy James 1949- *WhoWest 94*
Wilcox, Walter James, Sr. 1949- *WhoAmP 93*
Wilcox, Walter Mark 1954- *WhoScEn 94*
Wilcox, Wayne F. 1950- *WhoScEn 94*
Wilcox, Winton Wilfred, Jr. 1945- *WhoWest 94*
Wilcoxen, Joan Heeren 1948- *WhoFI 94*
Wilcoxon, Henry d1984 *WhoHol 92*
Wilczak, Thomas Patrick 1954- *WhoAmL 94*
Wilczek, Elmar Ulrich 1948- *WhoScEn 94*
Wilczek, Frank Anthony 1951- *WhoAm 94, WhoScEn 94*
Wilczek, John Franklin 1929- *WhoWest 94*
Wilczek, Otto Vincent 1944- *WhoMW 93*
Wilczek, Robert Joseph 1944- *WhoAm 94*
Wilczynska, Zofia *WhoWomW 91*
Wilczynski, Janusz S. 1929- *WhoAm 94*
Wilczynski, Ryszard Leslaw 1949- *WhoScEn 94*
Wild, Christopher *WhoHol 92*
Wild, David 1930- *Who 94*
Wild, David Humphrey 1927- *Who 94*
Wild, Dirk Jonathan 1967- *WhoFI 94*
Wild, Earl 1915- *IntWW 93*
Wild, Franz 1791-1860 *NewGrDO*
Wild, Gerald Percy 1908- *Who 94*
Wild, Hans Jochen 1935- *WhoScEn 94*
Wild, Heidi Karin 1948- *WhoFI 94*
Wild, Jack 1952- *WhoHol 92*
Wild, John Julian 1914- *WhoAm 94*
Wild, John Paul 1923- *IntWW 93*
Wild, John Vernon 1915- *Who 94*
Wild, Nelson Hopkins 1933- *WhoAm 94, WhoAmL 94*
Wild, Paul *Who 94*
Wild, (John) Paul 1923- *Who 94*
Wild, Peter *DrAPF 93*
Wild, Peter 1940- *WrDr 94*
Wild, Raymond 1940- *Who 94*
Wild, Richard P. 1947- *WhoAm 94, WhoAmL 94*
Wild, Robert 1932- *Who 94*
Wild, Robert Arnold 1946- *WhoFI 94*
Wild, Robert Lee 1921- *WhoAm 94*
Wild, Robert Warren 1942- *WhoAm 94, WhoAmL 94*
Wild, Stephen Kent 1948- *WhoFI 94*
Wild, Victor Allyn 1946- *WhoAmL 94*
Wild, Warren H., Jr. 1948- *WhoAmL 94*
Wildasin, David Earl 1950- *WhoFI 94, WhoMW 93*
Wildau, Karen 1946- *WhoAmL 94*
Wildavsky, Aaron d1993 *NewYTBS 93 [port]*

Wilkens, Leonard R. 1937- *WhoBlA 94*
Wilkens, Leonard Randolph, Jr. 1937- *WhoAm 94*
Wilkens, Robert Allen 1929- *WhoAm 94, WhoMW 93*
Wilkens, William W. 1923- *WhoFI 94*
Wilker, Gertrud 1924-1984 *BlmGWL*
Wilker, P. Jay 1944- *WhoAmL 94*
Wilkerson, Bill d1966 *WhoHol 92*
Wilkerson, Charles Edward 1921- *WhoAm 94*
Wilkerson, Charles W. 1916- *WhoAmP 93*
Wilkerson, Curtis 1926- *WhoAmP 93*
Wilkerson, Dianne *WhoAmP 93, WhoBlA 94*
Wilkerson, Dick 1943- *WhoAmP 93*
Wilkerson, Doxey A. d1993 *NewYTBS 93 [port]*
Wilkerson, Guy d1971 *WhoHol 92*
Wilkerson, Isabel A. *WhoBlA 94*
Wilkerson, James Neill 1939- *WhoAmL 94*
Wilkerson, Jerry F. 1945- *WhoAmP 93*
Wilkerson, John Lee 1945- *WhoFI 94*
Wilkerson, Kenneth L. *WhoFI 94*
Wilkerson, Margaret Buford 1938- *WhoBlA 94*
Wilkerson, Marjorie JoAnn Madar 1930- *WhoFI 94*
Wilkerson, Michael *DrAPF 93*
Wilkerson, Pinkie Carolyn 1948- *WhoAmP 93*
Wilkerson, Timothy L. 1962- *WhoMW 93*
Wilkerson, Walter D., Jr. 1930- *WhoAmP 93*
Wilkerson, William Avery 1938- *WhoAmP 93*
Wilkerson, William Edward, Jr. 1946- *WhoScEn 94*
Wilkerson, William Holton 1947- *WhoAm 94, WhoFI 94*
Wilkes, Angela Biggs 1952- *WhoMW 93*
Wilkes, Brent Ames 1952- *WhoAm 94, WhoFI 94*
Wilkes, Charles 1798-1877 *WhWE*
Wilkes, Delano Angus 1935- *WhoMW 93*
Wilkes, Donna 1961- *WhoHol 92*
Wilkes, Eric 1920- *Who 94*
Wilkes, Helen Barbour *WhoAmP 93*
Wilkes, Jamaal 1953- *BasBi [port]*
Wilkes, Jamaal (Keith) 1953- *WhoBlA 94*
Wilkes, Jennifer Ruth 1960- *WhoWest 94*
Wilkes, John 1725-1797 *AmRev*
Wilkes, John 1727-1797 *BlmGEL, WhAmRev [port]*
Wilkes, John Joseph 1936- *Who 94*
Wilkes, Joseph Allen 1919- *WhoAm 94*
Wilkes, Lorna M. 1943- *WhoAmP 93*
Wilkes, Mattie d1927 *WhoHol 92*
Wilkes, Maurice Vicent 1913- *IntWW 93*
Wilkes, Maurice Vincent 1913- *Who 94*
Wilkes, Michael (John) 1940- *Who 94*
Wilkes, Michael Jocelyn James P. *Who 94*
Wilkes, Paul 1938- *ConAu 42NR*
Wilkes, Penny Ferançe 1946- *WhoWest 94*
Wilkes, Reggie Wayman 1956- *WhoBlA 94*
Wilkes, Richard Geoffrey 1928- *Who 94*
Wilkes, Robert Lee 1942- *WhoWest 94*
Wilkes, Shelby R. 1950- *WhoBlA 94*
Wilkes, Timothy C. 1948- *WhoAmP 93*
Wilkes, William R. 1902- *WhoBlA 94*
Wilkes-Gibbs, Deanna Lynn 1955- *WhoScEn 94*
Wilkey, Malcolm Richard 1918- *WhoAm 94*
Wilkey, Mary 1940- *WhoMW 93*
Wilkie, Alan Fraser 1947- *Who 94*
Wilkie, Donald Walter 1931- *WhoAm 94, WhoWest 94*
Wilkie, Douglas Robert 1922- *IntWW 93, Who 94*
Wilkie, Earl Augustus T. 1930- *WhoBlA 94*
Wilkie, Gerry L. *WhoAmP 93*
Wilkie, John 1904-1991 *WhAm 10*
Wilkie, John Frederick 1951- *WhoFI 94*
Wilkie, Leighton Allyn d1993 *NewYTBS 93*
Wilkie, Margery Michelle 1958- *WhoWest 94*
Wilkie, Nancy Clausen 1942- *WhoMW 93*
Wilkie, Valleau, Jr. 1923- *WhoAm 94*
Wilkin, Eugene Welch 1923- *WhoWest 94*
Wilkin, (Frederick) John 1916- *Who 94*
Wilkin, Karen *WhoAmA 93*
Wilkin, Richard Edwin 1930- *WhoAm 94*
Wilkin, Ruth Warren 1918- *WhoAmP 93*
Wilkins, Allen Henry 1934- *WhoBlA 94*
Wilkins, Arthur Norman 1925- *WhoMW 93*
Wilkins, Barratt 1943- *WhoAm 94*
Wilkins, Betty 1922- *WhoBlA 94*
Wilkins, Burleigh Taylor 1932- *WhoAm 94*
Wilkins, C. Howard, Jr. 1938- *WhoAmP 93*
Wilkins, Caroline Hanke 1937- *WhoAm 94, WhoAmP 93, WhoWest 94*
Wilkins, Charles L. 1938- *WhoAm 94, WhoWest 94*
Wilkins, Charles O. 1938- *WhoBlA 94*
Wilkins, Christopher Putnam 1957- *WhoAm 94, WhoWest 94*
Wilkins, Cornelius Kendall 1938- *WhoScEn 94*
Wilkins, Daniel R. *WhoScEn 94*
Wilkins, David Brian *WhoBlA 94*
Wilkins, David George 1939- *WhoAm 94, WhoAmA 93*
Wilkins, David Horton 1946- *WhoAmP 93*
Wilkins, Dominique 1960- *WhoAm 94*
Wilkins, Dominique (Jacques) 1960- *WhoBlA 94*
Wilkins, Earle Wayne, Jr. 1919- *WhoAm 94*
Wilkins, Eddie Lee 1962- *WhoBlA 94*
Wilkins, Ervin W. 1919- *WhoBlA 94*
Wilkins, Floyd, Jr. 1925- *WhoAm 94*
Wilkins, Gary Clifton 1963- *WhoBlA 94*
Wilkins, George Hubert 1888-1958 *WhWE*
Wilkins, Gerald Bernard 1963- *WhoBlA 94*
Wilkins, Graham John 1924- *IntWW 93, Who 94*
Wilkins, Henry, III 1930- *WhoBlA 94*
Wilkins, Herbert P. 1930- *WhoAmP 93*
Wilkins, Herbert Priestly 1942- *WhoBlA 94*
Wilkins, Herbert Putnam 1930- *WhoAm 94, WhoAmL 94*
Wilkins, J. Ernest, Jr. 1923- *WhoAm 94*
Wilkins, James Raymond 1928- *WhAm 10*
Wilkins, Jeremy *WhoHol 92*
Wilkins, Jerry Lynn 1936- *WhoAmL 94, WhoFI 94*
Wilkins, John 1614-1672 *EncSF 93*
Wilkins, John Anthony Francis 1936- *Who 94*
Wilkins, John Warren 1936- *WhoAm 94*
Wilkins, Josetta E. 1932- *WhoAmP 93*
Wilkins, Josetta Edwards 1932- *WhoBlA 94*
Wilkins, June d1972 *WhoHol 92*
Wilkins, Kay H. 1940- *WhoAmL 94, WhoWest 94*
Wilkins, Kenneth C. 1952- *WhoBlA 94*
Wilkins, Leona B. 1922- *WhoBlA 94*
Wilkins, Linda Ann 1951- *WhoMW 93*
Wilkins, Lucy Lee 1934- *WhoAmP 93*
Wilkins, Malcolm Barrett 1933- *Who 94*
Wilkins, Maurice Hugh Frederick 1916- *IntWW 93, Who 94, WhoScEn 94, WorScD*
Wilkins, Michael (Compton Lockwood) 1933- *Who 94*
Wilkins, Michael Gray 1938- *WhoWest 94*
Wilkins, Michael Ion 1948 *WhoAmL 94*
Wilkins, Michael S. *WhoAmP 93*
Wilkins, Nancy 1932- *Who 94*
Wilkins, Ormsby *WhoAm 94*
Wilkins, Philip Charles 1913- *WhoAm 94, WhoAmL 94, WhoWest 94*
Wilkins, Richard Gundersen 1952- *WhoWest 94*
Wilkins, Rillastine Roberta 1932- *WhoBlA 94*
Wilkins, Rita Denise 1951- *WhoAm 94, WhoFI 94*
Wilkins, Robert Henry 1934- *WhoAm 94*
Wilkins, Robert Pearce 1933- *WhoAm 94*
Wilkins, Roger Carson 1906- *WhoAm 94*
Wilkins, Roger L. 1928- *WhoBlA 94*
Wilkins, Roger Wood 1932- *WhoBlA 94*
Wilkins, Roy 1901-1981 *AfrAmAl 6, AmSocL [port], HisWorL [port]*
Wilkins, S. Vance, Jr. 1936- *WhoAmP 93*
Wilkins, Sondra Ann 1938- *WhoMW 93*
Wilkins, Susan *DrAPF 93*
Wilkins, Thomas A. 1930- *WhoBlA 94*
Wilkins, Thomas Alphonso 1956- *WhoBlA 94*
Wilkins, Tracy Dale 1943- *WhoAm 94, WhoScEn 94*
Wilkins, (William) Vaughan 1890-1959 *EncSF 93*
Wilkins, W. Gary 1945- *WhoHisp 94*
Wilkins, Warren Edward 1937- *WhoFI 94*
Wilkins, William S. 1942- *WhoFI 94*
Wilkins, William W., Jr. 1942- *WhoAmP 93*
Wilkins, William Walter, Jr. 1942- *WhoAm 94, WhoAmL 94*
Wilkins, Willie T. 1929- *WhoBlA 94*
Wilkinson *Who 94*
Wilkinson, Alan Bassindale 1931- *Who 94*
Wilkinson, Albert Mims, Jr. 1925- *WhoAm 94*
Wilkinson, Alec 1952- *WrDr 94*
Wilkinson, Alexander Birrell 1932- *Who 94*
Wilkinson, Allan Harrison 1947- *WhoFI 94*
Wilkinson, Andrew Wood 1914- *Who 94*
Wilkinson, Anne 1910-1961 *BlmGWL*
Wilkinson, Bonaro *ConAu 142*
Wilkinson, Brenda 1946- *BlkWr 2, TwCYAW, WhoBlA 94*
Wilkinson, Brian James 1946- *WhoMW 93*
Wilkinson, Bruce W. 1944- *WhoAm 94, WhoFI 94*
Wilkinson, (J.) Burke 1913- *WrDr 94*
Wilkinson, Carol Lynn *DrAPF 93*
Wilkinson, Charles Brock 1922-1992 *WhoBlA 94N*
Wilkinson, Charles McNulty 1962- *WhoWest 94*
Wilkinson, Christopher 1941- *ConDr 93*
Wilkinson, Christopher David Wicks 1940- *Who 94*
Wilkinson, Christopher Foster 1938- *WhoAm 94*
Wilkinson, Christopher Richard 1941- *Who 94*
Wilkinson, Clifford Steven 1953- *WhoScEn 94*
Wilkinson, Clive Victor 1938- *Who 94*
Wilkinson, Connie Marie 1965- *WhoMW 93*
Wilkinson, D. G. B. *Who 94*
Wilkinson, David Anthony 1947- *Who 94*
Wilkinson, David Lawrence 1936- *WhoAm 94, WhoWest 94*
Wilkinson, David Lloyd 1937- *Who 94*
Wilkinson, David Lowell 1933- *WhoMW 93*
Wilkinson, David Todd 1935- *WhoAm 94*
Wilkinson, Debbie Kay 1966- *WhoMW 93*
Wilkinson, Denys (Haigh) 1922- *Who 94, WrDr 94*
Wilkinson, Denys Haigh 1922- *IntWW 93*
Wilkinson, Donald Charles 1936- *WhoBlA 94*
Wilkinson, Donald McLean, Jr. 1938- *WhoFI 94*
Wilkinson, Doris Yvonne *WhoBlA 94*
Wilkinson, Doris Yvonne 1936- *WhoAm 94*
Wilkinson, E. G., Jr. *WhoAm 94*
Wilkinson, Edward Anderson, Jr. 1933- *WhoAm 94*
Wilkinson, Eliza Yonge fl. 1779-1782 *BlmGWL*
Wilkinson, Elizabeth Mary 1909- *Who 94*
Wilkinson, Eugene Parks 1918- *WhoAm 94, WhoWest 94*
Wilkinson, Frank Smith, Jr. 1939- *WhoIns 94*
Wilkinson, Frederick D., Jr. 1921- *WhoBlA 94*
Wilkinson, Geoffrey d1955 *WhoHol 92*
Wilkinson, Geoffrey 1921- *IntWW 93, Who 94, WhoAm 94, WhoScEn 94*
Wilkinson, Geoffrey Crichton 1926- *Who 94*
Wilkinson, Gerald Stewart 1955- *WhoScEn 94*
Wilkinson, Graham 1947- *Who 94*
Wilkinson, Harold Arthur 1935- *WhoAm 94*
Wilkinson, Harry J. 1937- *WhoFI 94*
Wilkinson, Heather Carol *Who 94*
Wilkinson, Hei Sook 1947- *WhoMW 93*
Wilkinson, Iris *BlmGWL*
Wilkinson, J. Harvie, III *WhoAmP 93*
Wilkinson, J. Richard 1944- *WhoAmL 94*
Wilkinson, James 1757-1825 *AmRev, WhAmRev*
Wilkinson, James Allan 1945- *WhoAmL 94*
Wilkinson, James Harvie, III 1944- *WhoAm 94, WhoAmL 94*
Wilkinson, James Wellington 1935- *WhoBlA 94*
Wilkinson, Janet Worman 1944- *WhoFI 94*
Wilkinson, Jeffrey David 1958- *WhoMW 93*
Wilkinson, Jeffrey Vernon 1930- *Who 94*
Wilkinson, Jeffrey Wade 1966- *WhoWest 94*
Wilkinson, Jemima 1752-1819 *DcAmReB 2, WhAmRev*
Wilkinson, John 1728-1808 *WorInv*
Wilkinson, John 1913-1973 *WhoAmA 93N*
Wilkinson, John (Donald) 1929- *ConAu 42NR, WrDr 94*
Wilkinson, John Arbuthnot Du Cane 1940- *Who 94*
Wilkinson, John Burke 1913- *WhoAm 94*
Wilkinson, John Francis 1926- *Who 94*
Wilkinson, John Frederick 1897- *IntWW 93, Who 94*
Wilkinson, John Hart 1940- *WhoAm 94, WhoAmL 94*
Wilkinson, Joseph C. 1955- *WhoAmL 94*
Wilkinson, June *WhoHol 92*
Wilkinson, Kate d1993 *NewYTBS 93*
Wilkinson, Keith Howard 1948- *Who 94*
Wilkinson, Kenneth Herbert 1928- *WhoAm 94*
Wilkinson, Laura 1957- *WhoWest 94*
Wilkinson, Leon Guy 1928- *Who 94*
Wilkinson, Louise Cherry 1948- *WhoAm 94*
Wilkinson, Marie L. 1910- *WhoBlA 94*
Wilkinson, Marilyn Jo 1943- *WhoMW 93*
Wilkinson, Michael Kennerly 1921- *WhoAm 94*
Wilkinson, Milton James 1937- *WhoAm 94*
Wilkinson, Nicholas John 1941- *Who 94*
Wilkinson, Nigel Vivian Marshall 1949- *Who 94*
Wilkinson, Paul 1937- *IntWW 93, Who 94, WrDr 94*
Wilkinson, Peter (Allix) 1914- *Who 94*
Wilkinson, Peter Barr 1924-1989 *WhAm 10*
Wilkinson, Peter Maurice 1941- *WhoScEn 94*
Wilkinson, Philip (William) 1927- *Who 94*
Wilkinson, Philip William 1927- *IntWW 93*
Wilkinson, R. L. *WhoScEn 94*
Wilkinson, Raymond M., Jr. 1943- *WhoBlA 94*
Wilkinson, Raymond Stewart 1919- *Who 94*
Wilkinson, Richard D. 1952- *WhoAmL 94*
Wilkinson, Richard Denys 1946- *Who 94*
Wilkinson, Richard Francis, Jr. 1944- *WhoFI 94*
Wilkinson, Richard K. 1957- *WhoAmL 94*
Wilkinson, Robert Eugene 1926- *WhoAm 94*
Wilkinson, Robert Purdy 1933- *Who 94*
Wilkinson, Robert Shaw, Jr. 1928- *WhoBlA 94*
Wilkinson, Robert Steven 1955- *WhoBlA 94*
Wilkinson, Ronald Eugene 1945- *WhoScEn 94*
Wilkinson, Ronald Sterne 1934- *WhoScEn 94*
Wilkinson, Rosemary C. *DrAPF 93*
Wilkinson, Rosemary C(halloner) 1924- *ConAu 42NR*
Wilkinson, Rosemary Regina Challoner 1924- *WhoWest 94*
Wilkinson, Rosemond *NewGrDO*
Wilkinson, Sheppard Field *WhoBlA 94*
Wilkinson, Stanley Ralph 1931- *WhoAm 94*
Wilkinson, Sylvia *DrAPF 93*
Wilkinson, Sylvia J 1940- *WrDr 94*
Wilkinson, Tim 1912- *WrDr 94*
Wilkinson, Todd Thomas 1959- *WhoScEn 94*
Wilkinson, Tom *WhoHol 92*
Wilkinson, Wallace G. 1941- *IntWW 93, WhoAmP 93*
Wilkinson, (Arthur) Warren, Jr. 1945- *WrDr 94*
Wilkinson, Warren Scripps 1920- *WhoAm 94, WhoFI 94*
Wilkinson, William (Henry Nairn) 1932- *Who 94*
Wilkinson, William Kunkel 1959- *WhoScEn 94*
Wilkinson, William Lionel 1931- *Who 94*
Wilkinson, William Scott 1895-1989 *WhAm 10*
Wilkinson, William Sherwood 1933- *WhoAm 94*
Wilkinson, Winifred 1922- *WrDr 94*
Wilkinson-Latham, Robert John 1943- *WrDr 94*
Wilkniss, Peter E. 1934- *WhoAm 94, WhoScEn 94*
Wilkomirska, Wanda 1929- *IntWW 93*
Wilkow, Clifton Jack *WhoMW 93*
Wilkowski, Joseph Stephen 1952- *WhoMW 93*
Wilks, Alan Delbert 1943- *WhoScEn 94*
Wilks, Dick Lloyd 1923- *WhAm 10*
Wilks, Gertrude 1927- *WhoBlA 94*
Wilks, Ivor Gordon Hughes 1928- *WhoAm 94*
Wilks, Jay F. 1938- *WhoAmL 94*
Wilks, Jean Ruth Fraser 1917- *Who 94*
Wilks, Jim *Who 94*
Wilks, Larry Dean 1955- *WhoAmL 94, WhoAmP 93*
Wilks, Ralph Kenneth, Jr. 1956- *WhoMW 93*
Wilks, Robert 1665?-1732 *BlmGEL*
Wilks, Ronald 1930- *WhoScEn 94*
Wilks, Stanley David 1920- *Who 94*
Will, Clifford M(artin) 1946- *WrDr 94*
Will, Clifford Martin 1946- *WhoAm 94, WhoMW 93*

Williams, Bransby d1961 *WhoHol 92*
Williams, Brenda Joan 1965- *WhoMW 93*
Williams, Brian Carroll 1951- *WhoAmP 93*
Williams, Brian Carson 1969- *WhoBlA 94*
Williams, Brian David 1960- *WhAm 10*
Williams, Brian James 1959- *WhoScEn 94*
Williams, Brian O'Neal 1969- *WhoBlA 94*
Williams, Bronwyn 1930- *WrDr 94*
Williams, Brook *WhoHol 92*
Williams, Brown F 1940- *WhoAm 94*
Williams, Bruce 1934- *WhoAmP 93*
Williams, Bruce (Rodda) 1919- *IntWW 93, Who 94*
Williams, Bruce E. 1931- *WhoBlA 94*
Williams, Bruce Livingston 1945- *WhoFI 94*
Williams, Bruce Rodda 1919- *WrDr 94*
Williams, Bruce Warren 1948- *WhoScEn 94*
Williams, Buck 1960- *BasBi, WhoAm 94, WhoBlA 94, WhoWest 94*
Williams, Bunnis Curtis 1939- *WhoAmP 93*
Williams, C. Arthur, Jr. 1924- *WrDr 94*
Williams, C(hristopher) J(ohn) F(ardo) 1930- *WrDr 94*
Williams, C. Jay d1945 *WhoHol 92*
Williams, C. K. *DrAPF 93*
Williams, C(harles) K(enneth) 1936- *WrDr 94*
Williams, Calvin 1946- *WhoMW 93*
Williams, Calvin John, Jr. 1967- *WhoBlA 94*
Williams, Camilla *WhoAm 94, WhoBlA 94*
Williams, Camilla 1922- *NewGrDO*
Williams, Cara 1925- *IntMPA 94, WhoHol 92*
Williams, Carl Chanson 1937- *WhoAm 94*
Williams, Carl E., Sr. *WhoAm 94*
Williams, Carl Harwell 1915- *WhoAm 94*
Williams, Carl Michael 1928- *WhoAmP 93*
Williams, Carl W. 1927- *IntMPA 94*
Williams, Carletta Celeste 1956- *WhoBlA 94*
Williams, Carlon 1966- *WhoFI 94*
Williams, Carlton Hinkle 1914- *WhoAm 94*
Williams, Carlton Ray, Jr. 1957- *WhoBlA 94*
Williams, Carmen Lourdes 1953- *WhoHisp 94*
Williams, Carol *WhoHol 92*
Williams, Caroline *WhoHol 92*
Williams, Carolyn Chandler 1947- *WhoBlA 94*
Williams, Carolyn Delores 1954- *WhoWest 94*
Williams, Carolyn Ruth Armstrong 1944- *WhoBlA 94*
Williams, Carrington 1919- *WhoAmP 93*
Williams, Carroll Burns, Jr. 1929- *WhoBlA 94*
Williams, Carroll Milton 1916-1991 *WhAm 10*
Williams, Casey 1947- *WhoAmA 93*
Williams, Cassandra Faye 1948- *WhoBlA 94*
Williams, Catherine G. 1914- *WhoBlA 94*
Williams, Catrin Mary 1922- *Who 94*
Williams, Cecil *WhoBlA 94*
Williams, Cecil Beaumont 1926- *Who 94*
Williams, Chancellor 1905- *BlkWr 2, ConAu 142*
Williams, Charlene J. 1949- *WhoBlA 94*
Williams, Charles d1958 *WhoHol 92*
Williams, Charles d1985 *WhoHol 92*
Williams, Charles 1886-1945 *EncSF 93*
Williams, Charles 1939- *WhoAmP 93*
Williams, Charles Bernard 1925- *Who 94*
Williams, Charles C. 1939- *WhoBlA 94*
Williams, Charles David 1935- *WhoAm 94*
Williams, Charles E., III 1946- *WhoBlA 94*
Williams, Charles Finn, II 1954- *WhoFI 94*
Williams, Charles Fred 1943- *WhoAm 94*
Williams, Charles Frederick 1924- *WhoBlA 94*
Williams, Charles J., Sr. 1942- *WhoBlA 94*
Williams, Charles Judson 1930- *WhoAmL 94*
Williams, Charles Kenneth 1936- *WhoAm 94*
Williams, Charles Laval, Jr. 1916- *WhoAm 94*
Williams, Charles Lester, Jr. 1931- *WhoMW 93*
Williams, Charles Marvin 1917- *WhoAm 94*
Williams, Charles Mason, Jr. 1960- *WhoBlA 94*
Williams, Charles Murray 1931- *WhoAm 94, WhoFI 94, WhoScEn 94*
Williams, Charles Nolan 1946- *WhoAmL 94*
Williams, Charles Oliver, Jr. 1939- *WhoScEn 94*
Williams, Charles Richard 1948- *WhoBlA 94*
Williams, Charles Terrence 1946- *WhoAmL 94*
Williams, Charles Thomas 1916- *WhoBlA 94*
Williams, Charles Thomas 1941- *WhoBlA 94*
Williams, Charles Van 1944- *WhoAmP 93*
Williams, Charles Wesley *WhoAm 94*
Williams, Charles Wilmot 1916- *WhoScEn 94*
Williams, Charlie G. *WhoAmP 93*
Williams, Charlotte Leola 1928- *WhoBlA 94*
Williams, Cheryl L. 1954- *WhoBlA 94*
Williams, Chester Arthur *WhoBlA 94*
Williams, Chester Arthur, Jr. 1924- *WhoAm 94*
Williams, Chester Lee 1944- *WhoAmA 93, WhoBlA 94*
Williams, Christian 1943- *WrDr 94*
Williams, Christopher *Who 94*
Williams, Cindy 1947- *IntMPA 94, WhoHol 92*
Williams, Clara d1928 *WhoHol 92*
Williams, Clarence 1945- *WhoBlA 94*
Williams, Clarence, III 1939- *WhoHol 92*
Williams, Clarence Donald, II 1939- *WhoFI 94*
Williams, Clarence Earl, Jr. 1950- *WhoBlA 94*
Williams, Clarence G. 1938- *WhoBlA 94*
Williams, Clarence R. 1941- *WhoIns 94*
Williams, Clarice Leona 1936- *WhoBlA 94*
Williams, Clark d1989 *WhoHol 92*
Williams, Clark D. *WhoAmP 93*
Williams, Claudette *WrDr 94*
Williams, Clay Rule 1935- *WhoAmL 94, WhoMW 93*
Williams, Clayton Richard 1920- *WhoBlA 94*
Williams, Clifford 1926- *Who 94*
Williams, Clifford Glyn 1928- *WrDr 94*
Williams, Clyde 1939- *WhoBlA 94*
Williams, Clyde E., Jr. 1919- *WhoAm 94, WhoMW 93*
Williams, Clyde Elmer 1893- *WhAm 10*
Williams, Colin *Who 94*
Williams, Colin Hartley 1938- *Who 94*
Williams, Cora d1927 *WhoHol 92*
Williams, Corey 1970- *WhoBlA 94*
Williams, Craig Lamar 1952- *WhoAmL 94*
Williams, Curt Alan 1953- *WhoScEn 94*
Williams, Cynda 1966- *WhoHol 92*
Williams, Cynthia Althea 1968- *WhoFI 94*
Williams, Cynthia Lee 1957- *WhoAmA 93*
Williams, Cynthia Marie 1954- *WhoBlA 94*
Williams, Dafydd Wyn J. *Who 94*
Williams, Damon S. *WhoScEn 94*
Williams, Dan 1947- *WhoAmP 93*
Williams, Daniel *DrAPF 93*
Williams, Daniel Charles 1935- *IntWW 93*
Williams, Daniel Edwin 1933- *WhoBlA 94*
Williams, Daniel Everett 1962- *WhoAmL 94*
Williams, Daniel Hale 1856-1931 *AfrAmAl 6 [port]*
Williams, Daniel Hale 1858-1931 *WorInv*
Williams, Daniel Louis 1926- *WhoBlA 94*
Williams, Daniel Salu 1942- *WhoBlA 94*
Williams, Danny 1949- *WhoAmP 93*
Williams, Darleen Dorothy 1938- *WhoWest 94*
Williams, Darryl Marlowe 1938- *WhoAm 94*
Williams, Dave Harrell 1932- *WhoAm 94, WhoAmA 93, WhoFI 94*
Williams, David d1984 *WhoHol 92*
Williams, David 1754-1831 *WhAmRev*
Williams, David 1921- *IntWW 93, Who 94*
Williams, David 1926- *WrDr 94*
Williams, David 1934- *IntWW 93*
Williams, David 1938- *Who 94*
Williams, David (Glyndwr Tudor) 1930- *Who 94*
Williams, David Allan 1949- *WhoMW 93, WhoScEn 94*
Williams, David Apthorp 1911- *Who 94*
Williams, David Arthur 1953- *WhoAm 94, WhoMW 93*
Williams, David Barry 1931- *Who 94*
Williams, David Benton 1920- *WhoAm 94*
Williams, David Bernard 1949- *WhoScEn 94*
Williams, David Carlton 1912- *Who 94*
Williams, David Charles 1945- *WhoAmL 94*
Williams, David Claverly 1917- *Who 94*
Williams, David Fulton 1926- *WhoAm 94*
Williams, David George 1939- *WhoBlA 94*
Williams, David Glyndwr Tudor 1930- *IntWW 93*
Williams, David Gurth 1930- *WhoFI 94*
Williams, David Howard 1945- *WhoAm 94, WhoAmL 94*
Williams, David Howard 1950- *WhoAmL 94*
Williams, David Innes 1919- *Who 94*
Williams, David Iorwerth 1913- *Who 94*
Williams, David John 1914- *Who 94*
Williams, David John 1941- *Who 94*
Williams, David Jon 1944- *WhoAmA 93*
Williams, David Keith 1965- *WhoFI 94*
Williams, David L. 1953- *WhoAmP 93*
Williams, David Lee 1947- *WhAm 10*
Williams, David Lincoln 1937- *Who 94*
Williams, David Michael 1936- *WhoFI 94, WhoWest 94*
Williams, David Oliver 1926- *Who 94*
Williams, David Owen 1937- *WhoAm 94*
Williams, David Owen C. *Who 94*
Williams, David Perry 1934- *WhoAm 94, WhoFI 94*
Williams, David Raymond 1941- *Who 94*
Williams, David Rogerson, Jr. 1921- *WhoAm 94*
Williams, David Russell 1932- *WhoAm 94*
Williams, David S., Jr. 1945- *WhoBlA 94*
Williams, David Vandergrift 1943- *WhoScEn 94*
Williams, David W. 1910- *WhoBlA 94*
Williams, David Wakelin 1913- *Who 94*
Williams, David Welford 1910- *WhoAm 94, WhoAmL 94, WhoWest 94*
Williams, Deborah Ann 1951- *WhoBlA 94*
Williams, Deborah Brown 1957- *WhoBlA 94*
Williams, Deleta *WhoAmP 93*
Williams, Delwyn *Who 94*
Williams, (David John) Delwyn 1938- *Who 94*
Williams, Delwyn Charles 1936- *WhoAm 94*
Williams, Deniece 1951- *WhoBlA 94*
Williams, Denis (Joseph Ivan) 1923- *BlkWr 2, ConAu 41NR*
Williams, Denise 1950- *WhoMW 93*
Williams, Dennis 1957- *WhoBlA 94*
Williams, Dennis B. 1943- *WhoIns 94*
Williams, Dennis Thomas 1925- *WhoScEn 94*
Williams, Dennis Vaughn 1946- *WhoAmL 94*
Williams, Denys (Ambrose) 1929- *Who 94*
Williams, Denys Ambrose 1929- *IntWW 93*
Williams, Derek 1908- *WhoHol 92*
Williams, Derek, Jr. 1958- *WhoWest 94*
Williams, Derek Alfred H. *Who 94*
Williams, Derrick *Who 94*
Williams, (Richard) Derrick 1926 *Who 94*
Williams, Dewey Gene 1925- *WhoAm 94*
Williams, Dewitt 1919- *WhoAmP 93*
Williams, Diahn *WhoHol 92*
Williams, Diane Dorothy 1948- *WhoAmP 93*
Williams, Diane Wray 1938- *WhoAmP 93*
Williams, Dick 1891-1968 *BuCMET [port]*
Williams, Dick Anthony 1938- *WhoBlA 94, WhoHol 92*
Williams, Dillwyn *Who 94*
Williams, (Edward) Dillwyn 1929- *Who 94*
Williams, Doiran George 1926- *Who 94*
Williams, Dolores Louise 1937- *WhoFI 94*
Williams, Donald *WhoBlA 94*
Williams, Donald C. 1939- *WhoAmP 93*
Williams, Donald Clyde 1939- *WhoAm 94*
Williams, Donald E., Jr. *WhoAmP 93*
Williams, Donald Eugene 1929- *WhoBlA 94*
Williams, Donald H. 1936- *WhoBlA 94*
Williams, Donald Herbert 1936- *WhoAm 94*
Williams, Donald John 1933- *WhoAm 94, WhoScEn 94*
Williams, Donald Mark 1954- *Who 94*
Williams, Donald Maxey 1959- *WhoAm 94*
Williams, Donald Shand 1930- *WhoAm 94*
Williams, Donald Spencer 1939- *WhoWest 94*
Williams, Donald Victor 1936- *WhoWest 94*
Williams, Donna Lee H. 1960- *WhoAmP 93*
Williams, Donnie *WhoHol 92*
Williams, Doris Carson 1949- *WhoAmP 93*
Williams, Dorothy Daniel 1938- *WhoBlA 94*
Williams, Dorothy P. 1938- *WhoBlA 94*
Williams, Doug Lee 1955- *WhoBlA 94*
Williams, Douglas d1968 *WhoHol 92*
Williams, Douglas 1912- *WhoFI 94, WhoWest 94*
Williams, Douglas 1917- *Who 94*
Williams, Douglas Allan 1938- *WhoWest 94*
Williams, Douglas H. 1948- *WhoAm 94, WhoAmL 94*
Williams, Douglas Lloyd 1957- *WhoFI 94*
Williams, Doyle Z. 1939- *WhoAm 94*
Williams, Drew Davis 1935- *WhoAm 94*
Williams, Dudley Howard 1937- *IntWW 93, Who 94*
Williams, E. Faye 1941- *WhoBlA 94*
Williams, E. Thomas, Jr. 1937- *WhoBlA 94*
Williams, E. Virginia 1914-1984 *IntDcB*
Williams, Earl 1938- *WhoBlA 94*
Williams, Earl, Jr. 1935- *WhoBlA 94*
Williams, Earl Duane 1929- *WhoFI 94*
Williams, Earl George 1945- *WhoScEn 94*
Williams, Earl West 1928- *WhoBlA 94*
Williams, Earle d1927 *WhoHol 92*
Williams, Earle Carter 1929- *WhoAm 94*
Williams, Ed E., III 1948- *WhoAmL 94, WhoAmP 93*
Williams, Eddie, Sr. *WhoBlA 94*
Williams, Eddie Nathan 1932- *WhoAm 94, WhoBlA 94*
Williams, Eddie R. 1925- *WhoAmP 93*
Williams, Eddie R. 1945- *WhoScEn 94*
Williams, Eddie R., Jr., Dr. 1945- *WhoBlA 94*
Williams, Edgar (Trevor) 1912- *Who 94*
Williams, Edgar Gene 1922- *WhoAm 94*
Williams, Edgar Purell 1918- *WhoWest 94*
Williams, Edna C. 1933- *WhoBlA 94*
Williams, Edna Doris 1908- *WhoMW 93*
Williams, Edson Poe 1923- *WhoAm 94, WhoMW 93*
Williams, Edward (Stratten) 1921- *Who 94*
Williams, Edward Alexander Wilmot 1910- *Who 94*
Williams, Edward David 1932- *WhoAm 94, WhoFI 94*
Williams, Edward Earl, Jr. 1945- *WhoAm 94, WhoFI 94*
Williams, Edward Ellis 1938- *WhoBlA 94*
Williams, Edward F. *DrAPF 93*
Williams, Edward Foster, III 1935- *WhoAmP 93, WhoScEn 94*
Williams, Edward G. *DrAPF 93*
Williams, Edward Gilman 1926- *WhoAm 94*
Williams, Edward Joseph 1942- *WhoAm 94, WhoBlA 94*
Williams, Edward K. 1870- *WhoAmA 93N*
Williams, Edward M. 1933- *WhoBlA 94*
Williams, Edward Stanley 1924- *Who 94*
Williams, Edward Taylor 1911- *Who 94*
Williams, Edward Vinson 1935- *WhoAm 94*
Williams, Edwin William 1912- *WhoAm 94*
Williams, Edy 1942- *WhoHol 92*
Williams, Elaine *WhoHol 92*
Williams, Elaine d1947 *WhoHol 92*
Williams, Eleanor Joyce 1936- *WhoMW 93*
Williams, Eleazar 1788-1858 *EncNAR*
Williams, Elizabeth *IntWW 93*
Williams, Elizabeth 1943- *Who 94*
Williams, Elizabeth Evenson 1940- *WhoMW 93*
Williams, Ellis 1931- *WhoBlA 94*
Williams, Elmo 1913- *IntMPA 94*
Williams, Elynor A. 1946- *WhoBlA 94*
Williams, Emlyn *IntDcT 2*
Williams, Emlyn d1987 *WhoHol 92*
Williams, (George) Emlyn 1905-1987 *ConDr 93*
Williams, Emmett *DrAPF 93*
Williams, Emmett 1925- *WrDr 94*
Williams, Emory 1911- *WhoAm 94*
Williams, Enoch H. 1927- *WhoAmP 93, WhoBlA 94*
Williams, Eric (Eustace) 1911-1981 *BlkWr 2*
Williams, Eric C(yril) 1918- *EncSF 93*
Williams, Erma Brooks 1957- *WhoMW 93*
Williams, Ernest, 2nd *WhoHol 92*
Williams, Ernest Curran 1944- *WhoWest 94*
Williams, Ernest Donald, Jr. 1949- *WhoBlA 94*
Williams, Ernest Edward 1914- *WhoAm 94*
Williams, Ernest Going 1915- *WhoAm 94, WhoFI 94*
Williams, Ernest W. *WhoAmL 94*
Williams, Ernest William, Jr. 1916- *WhoAm 94*
Williams, Ernest Y. d1990 *WhAm 10*
Williams, Ernest Y. 1900- *WhoBlA 94*

Williams, Ernie d1986 *WhoHol 92*
Williams, Esther 1921- *WhoHol 92*
Williams, Esther 1923- *IntMPA 94*
Williams, Ethel Jean 1922- *WhoBlA 94*
Williams, Ethel Langley *WhoBlA 94*
Williams, Euphemia G. 1938- *WhoBlA 94*
Williams, Evan James 1903-1945
DcNaB MP
Williams, Evelyn Faithfull M. *Who 94*
Williams, Everett Belvin 1932-
WhoBlA 94
Williams, Faith *DrAPF 93*
Williams, Felton Carl 1946- *WhoBlA 94*
Williams, Forman Arthur 1934-
WhoAm 94, WhoScEn 94, WhoWest 94
Williams, Frances *WhoHol 92*
Williams, Frances d1959 *WhoHol 92*
Williams, Francis (John Watkin) 1905-
Who 94
Williams, Francis Julian 1927- *Who 94*
Williams, Francis Leon 1918-
WhoScEn 94
Williams, Francis Owen Garbett 1942-
Who 94
Williams, Frank 1903-1970 *EncSF 93*
Williams, Frank 1931- *WhoHol 92*
Williams, Frank Denry Clement 1913-
Who 94
Williams, Frank J. 1938- *WhoBlA 94*
Williams, Frank J. 1940- *WhoAmL 94,
WhoFI 94*
Williams, Frank James, Jr. 1938-
WhoAm 94
Williams, Franklin d1993 *NewYTBS 93*
Williams, Franklin Hall 1917-1990
WhAm 10
Williams, Franklin John 1940-
WhoAmA 93
Williams, Fred *WhoHol 92*
Williams, Fred d1924 *WhoHol 92*
Williams, Fred 1935- *WhoAmP 93*
Williams, Fred A. 1938- *WhoIns 94*
Williams, Fred C. 1922- *WhoBlA 94*
Williams, Fred J. d1942 *WhoHol 92*
Williams, Freddye H. 1917- *WhoAmP 93*
Williams, Freddye Harper 1917-
WhoBlA 94
Williams, Frederic Allen 1898-1958
WhoAmA 93N
Williams, Frederick 1922- *WhoAm 94*
Williams, Frederick (Dowell) 1933-
WrDr 94
Williams, Frederick Ballard 1871-1956
WhoAmA 93N
Williams, Frederick Boyd 1939-
WhoBlA 94
Williams, Frederick Daniel Crawford
1943- *WhoBlA 94*
Williams, Frederick Wallace 1939-
WhoScEn 94
Williams, Freeman 1956- *BasBi*
Williams, Gail Susan 1951- *WhoMW 93*
Williams, Gareth Howel 1925- *Who 94*
Williams, Gareth Lloyd 1935- *Who 94*
Williams, Gareth R. *Who 94*
Williams, Garth (Montgomery) 1912-
WrDr 94
Williams, Garth Montgomery 1912-
WhoAm 94
Williams, Gary *DrAPF 93*
Williams, Gary Don 1946- *WhoAmP 93*
Williams, Gary Murray 1940- *WhoAm 94,
WhoScEn 94*
Williams, Gary Randall 1946-
WhoAmL 94
Williams, Gayle Terese Taylor 1964-
WhoBlA 94
Williams, Geline Bowman *WhoAmP 93*
Williams, Gene *WhoHol 92*
Williams, Geoffrey Guy 1930- *Who 94*
Williams, George d1936 *WhoHol 92*
Williams, George 1919- *WhoAmP 93*
Williams, George A. 1942- *WhoMW 93*
Williams, George Arthur 1925-
WhoBlA 94
Williams, George B. d1931 *WhoHol 92*
Williams, George Christopher 1926-
WhoAm 94, WhoScEn 94
Williams, George Earnest 1923-
WhoAm 94
Williams, George Howard 1918-
WhoAm 94, WhoAmL 94
Williams, George Huntston 1914-
WhoAm 94
Williams, George L., Sr. 1929- *WhoBlA 94*
Williams, George Melville 1930-
WhoAm 94
Williams, George Mervyn 1918- *Who 94*
Williams, George Rainey 1926-
WhoAm 94
Williams, George W., III 1946-
WhoBlA 94
Williams, George Walton 1922-
WhoAm 94
Williams, Georgianna M. 1938-
WhoBlA 94
Williams, Gerald 1963- *WhoBlA 94*
Williams, Gerald Lee 1941- *WhoMW 93*

Williams, Gerhild S. 1942- *WhoMW 93*
Williams, Gertie Boothe *WhoAm 94*
Williams, Gex 1952- *WhoAmP 93*
Williams, Gil *DrAPF 93*
Williams, Gilbert Anthony 1951-
WhoFI 94
Williams, Gilbert Thomas 1956-
WhoMW 93
Williams, Glanmor 1920- *IntWW 93,
Who 94*
Williams, Glanville (Llewelyn) 1911-
WrDr 94
Williams, Glanville Llewelyn 1911-
IntWW 93, Who 94
Williams, Glen Garfield 1923- *Who 94*
Williams, Glen Morgan 1920- *WhoAm 94*
Williams, Glenn Carber 1914-1991
WhAm 10
Williams, Gloria *WhoHol 92*
Williams, Gloria Louise 1949-
WhoMW 93
Williams, Glynn Anthony 1939- *Who 94*
Williams, Gordon 1934- *WrDr 94*
Williams, Gordon (MacLean) 1934-
EncSF 93
Williams, Gordon Bretnell 1929-
WhoAm 94
Williams, Gordon Harold 1937-
WhoAm 94
Williams, Gordon Oliver 1925-
WhoAmP 93
Williams, Gordon Roland 1914-
WhoAm 94
Williams, Grace (Mary) 1906-1977
NewGrDO
Williams, Grady Carter 1939- *WhoBlA 94*
Williams, Graeme *Who 94*
Williams, (George Haigh) Graeme 1935-
Who 94
Williams, Graham Charles 1937- *Who 94*
Williams, Gregg 1959- *WhoAmL 94*
Williams, Gregory Howard 1943-
WhoAm 94, WhoBlA 94
Williams, Gregory M. *WhoBlA 94*
Williams, Guinn d1962 *WhoHol 92*
Williams, Gus 1953- *BasBi, WhoBlA 94*
Williams, Guthrie J. 1914- *WhoBlA 94*
Williams, Guy d1989 *WhoHol 92*
Williams, Guy R(ichard Owen) 1920-
WrDr 94
Williams, Gwen d1962 *WhoHol 92*
Williams, H. Harold 1923- *WhoAmL 94*
Williams, H. Randolph 1942- *WhoAm 94*
Williams, Hal *WhoBlA 94*
Williams, Hal 1938- *WhoHol 92*
Williams, Hank d1953 *WhoHol 92*
Williams, Hank, Jr. 1949- *WhoAm 94,
WhoHol 92*
Williams, Harcourt d1957 *WhoHol 92*
Williams, Hardy 1931- *WhoAmP 93,
WhoBlA 94*
Williams, Harmon d1977 *WhoHol 92*
Williams, Harold 1934- *WhoAm 94*
Williams, Harold Anthony 1916-
WhoAm 94
Williams, Harold Cleophas 1943-
WhoBlA 94
Williams, Harold Edward 1949-
WhoBlA 94
Williams, Harold Guy L. *Who 94*
Williams, Harold Louis 1924- *WhoBlA 94*
Williams, Harold Marvin 1928-
WhoAm 94
Williams, Harold McNeal 1932-
WhAm 10
Williams, Harold Roger 1935- *WhoAm 94*
Williams, Harri Llwyd H. *Who 94*
Williams, Harriette F. 1930- *WhoBlA 94*
Williams, Harrison Arlington, Jr. 1919-
IntWW 93
Williams, Harry Abbott 1919- *Who 94*
Williams, Harry Edward 1925-
WhoWest 94
Williams, Harry Leverne 1916-
WhoAm 94
Williams, Harvey *WhoBlA 94*
Williams, Harvey Dean 1930-
AfrAmG [port]
Williams, Harvey Joseph 1941-
WhoBlA 94
Williams, Harvey Lavance 1967-
WhoBlA 94
Williams, Hattie d1942 *WhoHol 92*
Williams, Hayward J. 1944- *WhoBlA 94*
Williams, Hazel Browne *WhoBlA 94*
Williams, Heathcote 1941- *ConDr 93,
WrDr 94*
Williams, Heather 1955- *WhoScEn 94*
Williams, Helen 1948- *SmATA 77 [port]*
Williams, Helen B. 1916- *WhoBlA 94*
Williams, Helen Cora 1931- *WhoAmP 93*
Williams, Helen Elizabeth 1933-
WhoBlA 94
Williams, Helen Elizabeth Webber 1938-
Who 94
Williams, Helen Margaret 1947-
WhoFI 94

Williams, Helen Maria 1762-1827
BlmGWL
Williams, Henry 1923- *WhoBlA 94*
Williams, Henry Eugene 1950-
WhoAmL 94
Williams, Henry Leslie 1919- *Who 94*
Williams, Henry P. 1941- *WhoBlA 94*
Williams, Henry R. 1937- *WhoBlA 94*
Williams, Henry Rudolph 1919-
WhoFI 94
Williams, Henry S. 1929- *WhoBlA 94*
Williams, Henry Stratton 1929-
WhoAm 94, WhoWest 94
Williams, Henry Thomas 1932-
WhoAm 94
Williams, Henry Ward, Jr. 1930-
WhoAmL 94
Williams, Herb d1936 *WhoHol 92*
Williams, Herb E. 1946- *WhoBlA 94*
Williams, Herb L. 1958- *WhoBlA 94*
Williams, Herbert (Lloyd) 1932- *WrDr 94*
Williams, Herbert C. 1930- *WhoBlA 94*
Williams, Herbert Hoover 1929-1990
WhAm 10
Williams, Herbert Lee 1932- *WhoBlA 94*
Williams, Herbert Russell 1945-
WhoWest 94
Williams, Herberta Cassidy d1981
WhoHol 92
Williams, Herman 1943- *WhoBlA 94*
Williams, Herman Michael 1965-
WhoBlA 94
Williams, Hermann Warner, Jr.
1908-1975 *WhoAmA 93N*
Williams, Hibbard Earl 1932- *WhoAm 94,
WhoWest 94*
Williams, Hilary a'Beckett E. *Who 94*
Williams, Hilda Yvonne 1946-
WhoBlA 94
Williams, Hiram Draper 1917-
WhoAm 94, WhoAmA 93
Williams, Hiram Hank 1923-1953
AmCulL
Williams, Holland Huffman 1951-
WhoFI 94
Williams, Homer LaVaughan 1925-
WhoBlA 94
Williams, Hooper Anderson, Jr. 1918-
WhoFI 94
Williams, Hope d1990 *WhoHol 92*
Williams, Hope Denise 1952-
WhoMW 93
Williams, Hosea L. 1926- *WhoBlA 94*
Williams, Hosea Lorenzo 1926-
WhoAmP 93
Williams, Howard Copeland 1921-
WhoBlA 94
Williams, Howard L(loyd) 1950-
ConAu 41NR
Williams, Howard Russell 1915-
WhoAm 94, WhoWest 94
Williams, Howard Vernon 1951-
WhoWest 94
Williams, Howard Walter 1937-
WhoWest 94
Williams, Hubert 1939- *WhoBlA 94*
Williams, Hubert Glyn 1912- *Who 94*
Williams, Hugh d1969 *WhoHol 92*
Williams, Hugh Alexander, Jr. 1926-
WhoAm 94, WhoFI 94, WhoScEn 94
Williams, Hugh Hermes 1945-
WhoBlA 94
Williams, Hugh Steadman 1935- *WrDr 94*
Williams, Hugo 1942- *WrDr 94*
Williams, Hugo Mordaunt 1942- *Who 94*
Williams, Hulen Brown 1920- *WhoAm 94*
Williams, Ian Malcolm Gordon 1914-
Who 94
Williams, Idaherma *WhoAmA 93*
Williams, Ioan M(iles) 1941- *WrDr 94*
Williams, Iola 1936- *WhoBlA 94*
Williams, Ira Joseph 1926- *WhoBlA 94*
Williams, Ira Lee 1930- *WhoBlA 94*
Williams, Irene d1970 *WhoHol 92*
Williams, Irving Laurence 1935-
WhoScEn 94
Williams, Israel 1709-1788 *WhAmRev*
Williams, J. Bedell 1923-1991
WhoBlA 94N
Williams, J. Bryan 1947- *WhoAm 94,
WhoAmL 94*
Williams, J. D. 1942- *WhoAmP 93*
Williams, J. Marshall 1930- *WhoAmP 93*
Williams, J. R. 1930- *WrDr 94*
Williams, J. Vernon 1921- *WhoAm 94,
WhoAmL 94*
Williams, J.X. *EncSF 93*
Williams, Jack *WhoHol 92*
Williams, Jack Kenny 1920- *IntWW 93*
Williams, Jack Marvin 1938- *WhoAm 94,
WhoScEn 94*
Williams, Jack Raymond 1923-
WhoMW 93, WhoScEn 94
Williams, James 1934- *WhoBlA 94*
Williams, James Alexander 1929-
WhoAm 94
Williams, James Arthur 1932- *WhoAm 94*
Williams, James Arthur 1939- *WhoBlA 94*

Williams, James B. 1945- *WhoAm 94,
WhoFI 94*
Williams, James B., Jr. 1930- *WhoAmP 93*
Williams, James Bryan 1933- *WhoAm 94,
WhoFI 94*
Williams, James Case 1938- *WhoAm 94*
Williams, James Clayton, Jr. 1947-
WhoFI 94
Williams, James DeBois 1926-
WhoBlA 94
Williams, James E. *WhoAm 94*
Williams, James E., Jr. 1936- *WhoBlA 94*
Williams, James Edward 1943-
WhoBlA 94
Williams, James Edward 1955-
WhoBlA 94
Williams, James Eugene, Jr. 1927-
WhoAm 94
Williams, James Franklin, II 1944-
WhoAm 94
Williams, James Gordon 1938- *Who 94*
Williams, James H., Jr. 1941- *WhoBlA 94*
Williams, James Hiawatha 1945-
WhoBlA 94
Williams, James Howard 1947- *WhoFI 94*
Williams, James Kelley 1934- *WhoAm 94,
WhoFI 94*
Williams, James Kendrick *WhoAm 94*
Williams, James Lee 1941- *WhoAm 94*
Williams, James McSpadden 1952-
WhoMW 93
Williams, James Melvin 1910-
WhoAmP 93
Williams, James Oliver 1936-
WhoAmP 93
Williams, James Orrin 1937- *WhoAm 94*
Williams, James P., Jr. 1944- *WhoAm 94*
Williams, James Page 1951- *WhoAmL 94*
Williams, James R. 1933- *WhoBlA 94*
Williams, James Richard 1932-
WhoFI 94, WhoScEn 94
Williams, James Samuel, Jr. 1943-
WhoScEn 94
Williams, James Talbot 1942-
WhoAmL 94
Williams, James Thomas 1933-
WhoBlA 94
Williams, James W. 1942- *WhoAmL 94*
Williams, Jamye Coleman 1918-
WhoBlA 94
Williams, Jane *DrAPF 93*
Williams, Jane E. 1947- *WhoBlA 94*
Williams, Janice Bostic 1934-
WhoAmP 93
Williams, Janice E. 1954- *WhoAmA 93*
Williams, Janice L. 1938- *WhoBlA 94*
Williams, Jarvis Eric 1965- *WhoBlA 94*
Williams, Jason *WhoHol 92*
Williams, Jason Harold 1944- *WhoBlA 94*
Williams, Jay d1978 *WhoHol 92*
Williams, Jayson 1968- *WhoBlA 94*
Williams, Jean Carolyn 1956- *WhoBlA 94*
Williams, Jean Perkins 1951- *WhoBlA 94*
Williams, Jeanette K. 1917- *WhoAmP 93*
Williams, Jeanette Marie 1942-
WhoBlA 94
Williams, Jeanne 1930- *WrDr 94*
Williams, (Edward) Jeffery 1920- *WrDr 94*
Williams, Jeffrey d1938 *WhoHol 92*
Williams, Jeffrey Clarke 1940-
WhoWest 94
Williams, Jeffrey Keith Benjamin 1957-
WhoFI 94
Williams, Jeffrey Lee 1958- *WhoFI 94*
Williams, Jeffrey Thomas 1952-
WhoWest 94
Williams, Jerald Arthur 1942-
WhoWest 94
Williams, Jerome D. 1947- *WhoBlA 94*
Williams, Jerre S. d1993 *NewYTBS 93*
Williams, Jerre Stockton 1916-
WhoAm 94
Williams, Jesse 1922- *WhoBlA 94*
Williams, Jesse T., Sr. 1940- *WhoBlA 94*
Williams, Jester C. 1924- *WhoBlA 94*
Williams, Jewel L. 1937- *WhoBlA 94*
Williams, Jimmie Lewis 1953-
WhoScEn 94
Williams, Jimmy *WhoHol 92*
Williams, Jo Beth 1953- *IntMPA 94*
Williams, Joan *DrAPF 93*
Williams, Joanne Louise 1949-
WhoBlA 94
Williams, Joanne Molitor 1935-
WhoMW 93
Williams, JoBeth 1949- *WhoHol 92*
Williams, Joe 1918- *ConBlB 5 [port],
ConMus 11 [port], WhoAm 94,
WhoBlA 94, WhoHol 92*
Williams, Joe H. 1937- *WhoBlA 94*
Williams, Joe Lee d1982 *WhoHol 92*
Williams, John *DrAPF 93*
Williams, John d1983 *WhoHol 92*
Williams, John 1731-1799 *WhAmRev*
Williams, John 1752-1806 *WhAmRev*
Williams, John 1922- *WrDr 94*
Williams, John 1932- *IntDcF 2-4,
IntMPA 94*

Williams, John 1941- IntWW 93, Who 94
Williams, John 1962- WhoBlA 94
Williams, John (Robert) 1922- Who 94
Williams, John A. DrAPF 93
Williams, John A. 1925- WhoAm 94
Williams, John A. 1950- WhoAm 94
Williams, John A(lfred) 1925- BlkWr 2, EncSF 93, WrDr 94
Williams, John Albert 1941- WhoMW 93
Williams, John Alden 1928- WhoAmA 93
Williams, John Alfred 1925- WhoBlA 94
Williams, John Andrew 1941- WhoAm 94
Williams, John B. 1945- WhoAmP 93
Williams, John Berry 1939- WrDr 94
Williams, John Brindley 1919- WhoWest 94
Williams, John Brinley 1927- Who 94
Williams, John Carl 1952- WhAm 10
Williams, John Charles 1912- Who 94
Williams, John Charles 1938- Who 94
Williams, John Cobb 1930- WhoAm 94
Williams, John Cornelius 1903- WhoAm 94
Williams, John Earl 1948- WhoBlA 94
Williams, John Edward 1946- WhoAm 94
Williams, John Edwin 1928- WhoAm 94
Williams, John Eirwyn F. Who 94
Williams, John Ellis Caerwyn 1912- IntWW 93, Who 94
Williams, John Eryl Hall 1921- Who 94
Williams, John Foster 1743-1814 WhAmRev
Williams, John Franklin 1959- WhoMW 93
Williams, John Griffith 1944- Who 94
Williams, John H. 1934- WhoBlA 94
Williams, John Hartley 1942- WrDr 94
Williams, John Henry 1948- WhoBlA 94
Williams, John Herbert 1919- Who 94
Williams, John Horter 1918- WhoAm 94
Williams, John Howard WhoFI 94, WhoScEn 94
Williams, John J. d1918 WhoHol 92
Williams, John James, Jr. 1949- WhoFI 94, WhoWest 94
Williams, John L. 1937- WhoBlA 94
Williams, John L. 1964- WhoBlA 94
Williams, John Leighton 1941- Who 94
Williams, John Louis 1948- WhoMW 93
Williams, John Lyle 1944- WhoWest 94
Williams, John M(eredith) 1926- Who 94
Williams, John Melville 1931- Who 94
Williams, John Noctor 1931- Who 94
Williams, John Pattison, Jr. 1941- WhoAm 94
Williams, John Pershing 1919- WhoWest 94
Williams, John Peter Rhys 1949- IntWW 93, Who 94
Williams, John Philip 1947- WhoAmL 94
Williams, John R. 1937- WhoBlA 94
Williams, John Raymond, Jr. 1958- WhoFI 94
Williams, John Richard 1909- WhoAmP 93
Williams, John Robert 1922- IntWW 93
Williams, John Rodman 1918- WhoAm 94
Williams, John Sam 1966- WhoBlA 94
Williams, John Steven Meurig 1948- WhoWest 94
Williams, John Stuart 1920- WrDr 94
Williams, John T. 1932- IntWW 93
Williams, John Taylor 1938- WhoAm 94
Williams, John Thomas 1931- WhoAmP 93
Williams, John Tilman 1925- WhoAm 94
Williams, John Towner 1932- Who 94, WhoAm 94
Williams, John Troy 1924- WhoMW 93
Williams, John Tudno 1938- Who 94
Williams, John Waldo 1911- WhoBlA 94
Williams, John Walter Olding 1936- WhoWest 94
Williams, John Wesley 1928- WhoAm 94, WhoAmA 93
Williams, John Woodbridge 1950-1992 WhAm 10
Williams, Johnny Wayne 1946- WhoBlA 94
Williams, Jon EncSF 93
Williams, Jonathan DrAPF 93, WhoHol 92
Williams, Jonathan 1750-1815 WhAmRev
Williams, Jonathan (Chamberlain) 1929- WrDr 94
Williams, Jonathan R. Who 94
Williams, Joseph B. 1921- WhoBlA 94
Williams, Joseph Barbour 1945- WhoBlA 94
Williams, Joseph Dalton 1926- IntWW 93, WhoAm 94, WhoFI 94
Williams, Joseph David 1954- WhoFI 94
Williams, Joseph Henry 1931- WhoBlA 94
Williams, Joseph Hill 1933- WhoAm 94, WhoFI 94
Williams, Joseph Lanier 1921- WhoFI 94
Williams, Joseph Lee 1945- WhoBlA 94
Williams, Joseph R. 1918- WhoBlA 94
Williams, Joseph R. 1931- WhoAm 94
Williams, Joseph Rulon 1904- WhoAmP 93
Williams, Joseph Theodore 1937- WhoAm 94
Williams, Joseph Thuman 1950- WhoAmL 94
Williams, Josephine d1937 WhoHol 92
Williams, Josephine P. 1921- WhoAmP 93
Williams, Joslyn N. 1940- WhoAmP 93
Williams, Joy DrAPF 93
Williams, Joy 1944- WrDr 94
Williams, Joyce WhoHol 92
Williams, Joyce Bernice 1958- WhoMW 93
Williams, Juan 1954- BlkWr 2
Williams, Juanita Hingst 1922- WhAm 10
Williams, Juanita Terry WhoAmP 93
Williams, Judi Who 94
Williams, Judith L. 1948- WhoAm 94
Williams, Judith Renee 1968- WhoScEn 94
Williams, Julia d1936 WhoHol 92
Williams, Julia Brook WhoAmL 94
Williams, Julia Tochie 1887-1948 WhoAmA 93N
Williams, Julie Belle 1950- WhoMW 93
Williams, Julie Ford 1948- WhoAm 94
Williams, June Vanleer WrDr 94
Williams, Junius W. 1943- WhoBlA 94
Williams, Justin W. 1942- WhoAm 94
Williams, Karen 1950- WhoWomW 91
Williams, Karen Hastie 1944- WhoAm 94, WhoAmL 94, WhoBlA 94
Williams, Karen J. WhoAmP 93
Williams, Karen Johnson 1951- WhoAmL 94
Williams, Karen Lynn 1952- WrDr 94
Williams, Karen R. 1950- WhoAmP 93
Williams, Karen Renee 1954- WhoBlA 94
Williams, Karl Morgan 1958- WhoScEn 94
Williams, Kate WhoHol 92
Williams, Katherine d1982 WhoHol 92
Williams, Katherine 1941- WhoBlA 94
Williams, Kathi WhoAmP 93
Williams, Kathlyn d1960 WhoHol 92
Williams, Kathy Ann 1963- WhoBlA 94
Williams, Kay d1983 WhoHol 92
Williams, Keith David 1956- WhoBlA 94
Williams, Keith Edward 1958- WhoWest 94
Williams, Keith Shaw 1905-1951 WhoAmA 93N
Williams, Kellie Shanygne 1976- WhoHol 92
Williams, Kenneth d1988 WhoHol 92
Williams, Kenneth Eugene 1955- WhoFI 94, WhoMW 93
Williams, Kenneth Herbert 1945- WhoBlA 94
Williams, Kenneth James 1924- WhoWest 94
Williams, Kenneth Ogden 1924- WhoAmP 93
Williams, Kenneth Raynor 1912-1989 WhAm 10
Williams, Kenneth Scott 1955- WhoAm 94, WhoFI 94
Williams, Kenny WhoHol 92
Williams, Kenny Ray 1969- WhoBlA 94
Williams, Kent WhoHol 92
Williams, Kevin A. 1956- WhoBlA 94
Williams, Kimmika L(yvette Hawes) 1959- BlkWr 2
Williams, Kimmika L.H. DrAPF 93
Williams, Kimmika L. H. 1959- WhoBlA 94
Williams, Kingsley Who 94
Williams, (John Bucknall) Kingsley 1927- Who 94
Williams, Kneely WhoBlA 94
Williams, Knox 1928- WhoWest 94
Williams, Kourt Durell 1962- WhoScEn 94
Williams, Kyffin Who 94
Williams, (John) Kyffin 1918- IntWW 93, Who 94
Williams, L. Colene 1921- WhoBlA 94
Williams, Lafayette W. 1937- WhoBlA 94
Williams, Langbourne Meade 1903- WhoAm 94
Williams, Larry d1980 WhoHol 92
Williams, Larry Bill 1945- WhoAm 94
Williams, Larry C. 1931- WhoBlA 94
Williams, Larry Emmett 1936- WhoAm 94, WhoFI 94, WhoMW 93
Williams, Larry McClease 1955- WhoWest 94
Williams, Larry O. WhoHol 92
Williams, Larry Richard 1942- WhoWest 94
Williams, Larry Ritchie 1935- WhoFI 94
Williams, LaShina Brigette 1957- WhoBlA 94
Williams, Laura WhoHol 92
Williams, Lavinia d1989 WhoHol 92
Williams, Lawrence Craig 1956- WhoFI 94
Williams, Lawrence Soper 1917- WhoAm 94
Williams, Lea E. 1947- WhoBlA 94
Williams, Lea Everard 1924- WhoAm 94
Williams, Leamon D. 1935- WhoFI 94
Williams, Leamon Dale 1935- WhoAm 94
Williams, Lee 1925- WhoAmP 93
Williams, Lee R. 1936- WhoBlA 94
Williams, Leon L. WhoAmP 93
Williams, Leon Lawson 1922- WhoBlA 94
Williams, Leona Rae 1928- WhoWest 94
Williams, Leonard 1919- Who 94
Williams, Leonard, Sr. 1945- WhoBlA 94
Williams, Leonard Edmund Henry 1919- Who 94
Williams, Leonard Todd, Jr. 1947- WhoAm 94
Williams, Leroy Joseph 1937- WhoBlA 94
Williams, Leslie Who 94
Williams, (John) Leslie 1913- Who 94
Williams, Leslie Arthur 1909- Who 94
Williams, Leslie J. 1947- WhoBlA 94
Williams, Leslie Pearce 1927- WhoAm 94
Williams, Lewis Frederick 1938- WhoAmL 94, WhoWest 94
Williams, Lewis W., II 1918-1990 WhoAmA 93N
Williams, Lillian C. 1924- WhoBlA 94
Williams, Linda Bergendahl 1946- WhoFI 94
Williams, Linda Turner 1941- WhoWest 94
Williams, Lloyd L. 1944- WhoBlA 94
Williams, Londell 1939- WhoBlA 94
Williams, Lonnie Ray 1954- WhoBlA 94
Williams, Lorece P. 1927- WhoBlA 94
Williams, Loretta Dodson 1936- WhoFI 94
Williams, Lottie d1962 WhoHol 92
Williams, Lottie Mae 1931- WhoBlA 94
Williams, Louis Alvin 1931- AfrAmG
Williams, Louis Booth 1916- WhoFI 94
Williams, Louis Clair, Jr. 1940- WhoAm 94
Williams, Louis Gressett 1913- WhoAm 94
Williams, Louis Nathaniel 1929- WhoBlA 94
Williams, Louis Stanton 1919- WhoAm 94
Williams, Louise Bernice 1937- WhoBlA 94
Williams, Louise Taylor 1921- WhoMW 93
Williams, Lowell Craig 1947- WhoAm 94, WhoFI 94
Williams, Lu 1947- WhoBlA 94
Williams, Lucinda NewYTBS 93 [port]
Williams, Lucinda c. 1953- ConMus 10 [port]
Williams, Lucretia Murphy 1941- WhoBlA 94
Williams, Luther Steward 1940- WhoAm 94, WhoScEn 94
Williams, Lyman Neil, Jr. 1936- WhoAm 94, WhoAmL 94
Williams, Lyn Who 94
Williams, Lynda Eileen 1953- WhoMW 93
Williams, Lynn Roy 1945- WhoMW 93
Williams, Lynn Russell 1924- IntWW 93, WhoAm 94, WhoFI 94
Williams, Lynne WhoHol 92
Williams, M(artin) A(nthony) J(ames) 1941- ConAu 141
Williams, M. Wright 1949- WhoScEn 94
Williams, Maceo Merton 1939- WhoBlA 94
Williams, Mack d1965 WhoHol 92
Williams, Mack Geoffrey Denis 1939- IntWW 93
Williams, Malcolm d1937 WhoHol 92
Williams, Malcolm Demosthenes 1909- WhoBlA 94
Williams, Malcolm Demosthenes 1909-1991 WhAm 10
Williams, Malvin A. 1942- WhoBlA 94
Williams, Marc H. 1952- WhoWest 94
Williams, Marcus Doyle 1952- WhoAmL 94, WhoBlA 94
Williams, Margaret WhoAm 94
Williams, Margaret Ann 1954- NewYTBS 93 [port]
Williams, Margaret Estelean Kemp 1948- WhoAmL 94
Williams, Margo E. 1947- WhoBlA 94
Williams, Marie d1967 WhoHol 92
Williams, Marie B. 1926- WhoAmP 93
Williams, Marilyn WhoAmP 93
Williams, Marion Lester 1933- WhoWest 94
Williams, Mark Allen 1959- WhoMW 93
Williams, Mark Alvin 1935- WhoWest 94
Williams, Mark Colburn 1963- WhoAmL 94
Williams, Mark Edward 1950- WhoScEn 94
Williams, Mark Kendall 1959- WhoAmL 94
Williams, Marsha Kay 1963- WhoScEn 94
Williams, Marsha Rhea 1948- WhoScEn 94
Williams, Marshall Burns 1912- WhoAmP 93
Williams, Marshall Henry, Jr. 1924- WhoAm 94
Williams, Martha Ethelyn 1934- WhoAm 94
Williams, Martha Jane Shipe 1935- WhoAm 94
Williams, Martha S. 1921- WhoBlA 94
Williams, Martha Spring 1951- WhoAm 94
Williams, Martin 1924-1992 AnObit 1992
Williams, Martin John 1941- Who 94
Williams, Martin Tudor 1924-1992 WhAm 10
Williams, Marvin 1944- WhoFI 94
Williams, Marvin Justine 1958- WhoAmL 94
Williams, Mary 1943- WhoIns 94
Williams, Mary Alice Baldwin 1928- WhoMW 93
Williams, Mary Ann Sheridan 1945-1992 WhoBlA 94N
Williams, Mary Beatrice 1938- WhoAmP 93
Williams, Mary DEnnen WhoWest 94
Williams, Mary Lou 1910-1981 AfrAmAl 6
Williams, Mary Lou Newman 1918- WhoAm 94
Williams, Mary Pearl 1928- WhoAm 94
Williams, Marylou Lord Study WhoAmA 93
Williams, Matt 1965- WhoAm 94, WhoWest 94
Williams, Matthew Albert 1929- WhoBlA 94
Williams, Mattie Pearl 1951- WhoFI 94
Williams, Maureen DrAPF 93
Williams, Maurice 1952- WhoScEn 94
Williams, Maurice Jacoutot 1920- IntWW 93, WhoAm 94
Williams, Max Who 94
Williams, (William) Max (Harries) 1926- Who 94
Williams, Max Lea, Jr. 1922- WhoAm 94, WhoScEn 94
Williams, Maxine Eleanor 1940- WhoMW 93
Williams, McCullough, Jr. 1927- WhoBlA 94
Williams, McDonald 1917- WhoBlA 94
Williams, Melba Ruth WhoAmP 93
Williams, Melissa 1951- WhoAmA 93
Williams, Melvin 1944- WhoBlA 94
Williams, Melvin D. 1933- WhoBlA 94
Williams, Melvin Donald 1933- WhoMW 93
Williams, Melvin Walker 1939- WhoBlA 94
Williams, Merrell W. 1950- WhoFI 94
Williams, Michael 1935- Who 94, WhoHol 92, WrDr 94
Williams, Michael Alan 1948- WhoMW 93
Williams, Michael Anthony 1932- WhoAm 94
Williams, Michael Dale 1947- WhoIns 94
Williams, Michael Edward 1955- WhoAmL 94
Williams, Michael I. 1955- WhoMW 93
Williams, Michael Joseph 1942- Who 94
Williams, Michael Lamar 1947- WhoFI 94
Williams, Michael Leonard 1935- IntWW 93, Who 94
Williams, Michael Lindsay 1940- EncSF 93
Williams, Michael Lodwig 1948- Who 94
Williams, Michael Maurice Rudolph 1935- Who 94
Williams, Michael O. Who 94
Williams, Michael Roy 1946- WhoAm 94, WhoFI 94
Williams, Micheal Douglas 1966- WhoBlA 94
Williams, Micheal R. 1955- WhoAmP 93
Williams, Miller DrAPF 93
Williams, Miller 1930- WhoAm 94, WrDr 94
Williams, Milton 1936- WhoBlA 94
Williams, Milton Lawrence 1932- WhoAm 94, WhoBlA 94
Williams, Molly d1967 WhoHol 92
Williams, Montel WhoBlA 94
Williams, Morgan Lewis 1948- WhoScEn 94
Williams, Morgan Lloyd 1935- WhoAm 94
Williams, Morris O. WhoBlA 94
Williams, Moses, Sr. 1932- WhoBlA 94
Williams, Murat Willis 1914- WhoAm 94
Williams, Myra Nicol 1941- WhoAm 94
Williams, Myrna T. 1929- WhoAmP 93

Williams, N. Thomas 1933- WhoFI 94
Williams, Nancy Ann 1962- WhoMW 93
Williams, Nancy Ellen Webb WhoBlA 94, WhoWest 94
Williams, Nancy Ondrovik 1952- WhoAmL 94
Williams, Naomi B. 1942- WhoBlA 94
Williams, Naomi Fisher 1913-1992 WhoBlA 94N
Williams, Napoleon 1919- WhoBlA 94
Williams, Neil WhoAmA 93N
Williams, Nelson Garrett 1926- WhoAmL 94
Williams, Nicholas James Donald 1925- IntWW 93, Who 94
Williams, Nicholas John S. Who 94
Williams, Nick (Van) Boddie 1906-1992 EncSF 93
Williams, Nigel 1948- ConDr 93, WrDr 94
Williams, Nigel Christopher Ransome 1937- IntWW 93, Who 94
Williams, Noel Ignace B. Who 94
Williams, Nolan Eugene 1957- WhoFI 94
Williams, Norman DrAPF 93, Who 94
Williams, Norman 1915- WhoAm 94, WhoAmL 94
Williams, (Reginald) Norman 1917- Who 94
Williams, Norman Dale 1924- WhoAm 94
Williams, Norris Gerald 1948- WhoBlA 94
Williams, Norris Hagan, Jr. 1943- WhoScEn 94
Williams, Novella Stewart 1927- WhoAmP 93, WhoBlA 94
Williams, Numan Arthur 1928- WhoFI 94
Williams, O. S. 1921- WorInv
Williams, O. T. d1976 WhoHol 92
Williams, Oliver Alan, Jr. 1948- WhoScEn 94
Williams, Omer S. J. 1940- WhoAm 94
Williams, Ora 1926- WhoBlA 94
Williams, Ora P. 1935- WhoBlA 94
Williams, Oscar IntMPA 94
Williams, Osmond 1914- Who 94
Williams, Otho Holland 1749-1794 AmRev, WhAmRev [port]
Williams, Otis (C.) 1941- WrDr 94
Williams, Otis P. WhoBlA 94
Williams, Owen Lenn 1914- Who 94
Williams, Pamela Diane 1950- WhoAmL 94
Williams, Parham Henry, Jr. 1931- WhoAm 94, WhoAmL 94
Williams, Pat 1937- CngDr 93, WhoAm 94, WhoAmP 93, WhoWest 94
Williams, Pat Ward 1948- WhoAmA 93
Williams, Pater WhoHol 92
Williams, Patricia Anne 1943- WhoBlA 94
Williams, Patricia Anne Johnson 1944- WhoMW 93
Williams, Patricia Hill 1939- WhoBlA 94
Williams, Patricia R. 1943- WhoBlA 94
Williams, Patrick WhoHol 92
Williams, Patrick Moody 1939- WhoAm 94
Williams, Patrick Nehemiah 1928- WhoAmP 93, WhoBlA 94
Williams, Paul WhoHol 92
Williams, Paul 1929- WhoBlA 94
Williams, Paul 1940- IntMPA 94, WhoHol 92
Williams, Paul 1943- IntMPA 94
Williams, Paul (Steven) 1948- EncSF 93
Williams, Paul Alan 1934- WhoAmA 93
Williams, Paul Glyn 1922- Who 94
Williams, Paul H. Who 94
Williams, Paul Hamilton 1940- WhoAm 94
Williams, Paul L. 1953- WhoAmP 93
Williams, Paul Michael 1939- WhoMW 93
Williams, Paul O(sborne) 1935- EncSF 93, WrDr 94
Williams, Paul Osborne DrAPF 93
Williams, Paul Randall 1934- Who 94
Williams, Paul Revere 1894-1980 AfrAmAl 6
Williams, Paul Robert 1937- WhoMW 93
Williams, Paul Whitcomb 1903- WhoAmL 94
Williams, Pearl 1914-1991 WhoCom
Williams, Peggy Ryan 1947- WhoAm 94
Williams, Pelham C. WhoBlA 94
Williams, Penny Baldwin 1937- WhoAmP 93
Williams, Penry Herbert 1925- Who 94
Williams, Percy Don 1922- WhoAm 94, WhoAmL 94
Williams, Pete 1913- WrDr 94
Williams, Peter Charles 1949- WhoScEn 94
Williams, Peter F. Who 94
Williams, Peter H. Who 94
Williams, Peter Keegan 1938- Who 94
Williams, Peter Lancelot 1914- Who 94
Williams, Peter Maclellan 1931- WhoScEn 94
Williams, Peter Michael 1945- Who 94
Williams, Peter Orchard 1925- IntWW 93, Who 94
Williams, Peter W. Who 94
Williams, Peter Whitridge 1936- WhoAm 94
Williams, Peyton, Jr. 1942- WhoBlA 94
Williams, Philip Who 94
Williams, (Robert) Philip (Nathaniel) 1950- Who 94
Williams, Philip B. 1922- WhoBlA 94
Williams, Philip Copelain 1917- WhoMW 93, WhoScEn 94
Williams, Philip F. C. 1956- WhoWest 94
Williams, Phillip L. WhoFI 94
Williams, Phillip Stephen 1949- WhoAm 94
Williams, Phyllis Cutforth 1917- WhoAm 94, WhoWest 94
Williams, Preston N. 1926- WhoBlA 94
Williams, Preston Noah 1926- WhoAm 94
Williams, Quentin Christopher 1964- WhoScEn 94
Williams, Quinn Patrick 1949- WhoAm 94, WhoAmL 94, WhoWest 94
Williams, R. J. WhoHol 92
Williams, Raleigh R. WhoBlA 94
Williams, Ralph Chester, Jr. 1928- WhoAm 94
Williams, Ralph Watson, Jr. 1933- WhoAm 94
Williams, Randolph 1944- WhoBlA 94
Williams, Randy Lee 1949- WhoAmL 94
Williams, Ray 1954- BasBi
Williams, Raymond 1921-1987 BlmGEL
Williams, Raymond (Brady) 1935- WrDr 94
Williams, Raymond (Henry) 1921-1988 EncSF 93
Williams, Raymond Crawford 1924- WhoAm 94
Williams, Raymond Lester 1926- WhoAmA 93
Williams, Raymond Lloyd 1927- Who 94
Williams, Reba White 1936- WhoAmA 93
Williams, Rebecca Lynn 1959- WhoAmL 94
Williams, Redford Brown 1940- WhoAm 94, WhoScEn 94
Williams, Reg Arthur 1944- WhoMW 93
Williams, Reggie 1954- WhoBlA 94
Williams, Reggie 1964- WhoBlA 94
Williams, Regina E. DrAPF 93
Williams, Regina Vloyn-Kinchen 1947- WhoBlA 94
Williams, Reginald Clark 1950- WhoBlA 94
Williams, Reginald T. 1945- WhoBlA 94
Williams, Rex WhoHol 92
Williams, Rex Enoch 1925- WhoMW 93
Williams, Rhys d1969 WhoHol 92
Williams, Rhys 1929- WhoAm 94
Williams, Richard 1933- IntDcF 2-4 [port], IntMPA 94
Williams, Richard, Jr. 1933- WhoBlA 94
Williams, Richard, Jr. 1947- WhoScEn 94
Williams, Richard Clarence 1923- WhoAm 94
Williams, Richard Donald 1926- WhoAm 94
Williams, Richard Dwayne 1944- WhoAm 94
Williams, Richard E., Jr. 1962- WhoBlA 94
Williams, Richard Eaton 1930- WhAm 10
Williams, Richard Edmund 1933- IntWW 93
Williams, Richard Eldon 1934- WhoAmA 93
Williams, Richard F. 1941- WhoIns 94
Williams, Richard Hall 1926- Who 94
Williams, Richard Hirschfeld 1929- WhoAm 94
Williams, Richard James 1942- WhoFI 94
Williams, Richard Lee, II 1959- WhoBlA 94
Williams, Richard Lenwood 1931- WhoBlA 94
Williams, Richard Leroy 1923- WhoAm 94, WhoAmL 94
Williams, Richard Lippincott 1910-1989 WhAm 10
Williams, Richard Llewellyn 1929- WhoAm 94
Williams, Richard Lucas, III 1940- WhoAm 94
Williams, Richard Pascal, Jr. 1939- WhoWest 94
Williams, Richard Thomas 1945- WhoAm 94, WhoAmL 94, WhoFI 94
Williams, Richard W. 1949- WhoMW 93
Williams, Richmond Dean 1925- WhoAm 94
Williams, Robb 1962- WhoWest 94
Williams, Robert d1896 EncNAR
Williams, Robert d1931 WhoHol 92
Williams, Robert (Evan Owen) 1916- Who 94
Williams, Robert B. d1978 WhoHol 92
Williams, Robert B. 1921- WhoIns 94
Williams, Robert B. 1943- WhoBlA 94
Williams, Robert C. 1930- WhoAm 94, WhoFI 94
Williams, Robert Carlton 1948- WhoScEn 94
Williams, Robert Chadwell 1938- WhoAm 94
Williams, Robert Cody 1948- WhoIns 94
Williams, Robert D. 1931- WhoBlA 94
Williams, Robert D., Sr. 1916- WhoBlA 94
Williams, Robert Dana 1939- WhoAmL 94
Williams, Robert E. 1934- WhoIns 94
Williams, Robert H. WhoScEn 94
Williams, Robert H. 1938- WhoBlA 94
Williams, Robert Henry 1946- WhoFI 94, WhoScEn 94
Williams, Robert Hope, Jr. 1910-1991 WhAm 10
Williams, Robert Hughes 1941- Who 94
Williams, Robert Jene 1931- WhoAm 94, WhoAmL 94
Williams, Robert Joseph Paton 1926- IntWW 93, Who 94
Williams, Robert K. WhoAmP 93
Williams, Robert L. 1930- WhoBlA 94
Williams, Robert Lee 1933- WhoBlA 94
Williams, Robert Lee 1936- WhoBlA 94
Williams, Robert Lee, Jr. 1955- WhoBlA 94
Williams, Robert Leon 1922- WhoAm 94
Williams, Robert Luther 1923- WhoAm 94
Williams, Robert Lyle 1942- WhoAm 94
Williams, Robert Martin 1913- WhoAm 94
Williams, Robert Martin 1919- IntWW 93, Who 94
Williams, Robert Michael 1946- WhoFI 94
Williams, Robert Michael 1949- WhoFI 94
Williams, Robert Moore 1907-1977 EncSF 93
Williams, Robert Pete d1980 WhoHol 92
Williams, Robert R. d1993 NewYTBS 93
Williams, Robert Runnels WorScD
Williams, Robert Stone 1952- WhoWest 94
Williams, Robert Van 1923- WhoMW 93
Williams, Robert W. 1922- WhoBlA 94
Williams, Robert Walter 1920- WhoAm 94
Williams, Robert Wilmot 1943- WhoWest 94
Williams, Roberta Magdalene 1927- WhoAmP 93
Williams, Robin Who 94
Williams, Robin 1951- IntMPA 94, IntWW 93, WhoAm 94
Williams, Robin 1952- WhoCom [port], WhoHol 92
Williams, Robin (Philip) 1928- Who 94
Williams, Robin Guy 1930- Who 94
Williams, Robin L. 1961- WhoAmP 93
Williams, Robin Murphy, Jr. 1914- IntWW 93, WhoAm 94
Williams, Robin Patricia 1953- WhoWest 94
Williams, Rodney Elliott 1928- WhoBlA 94
Williams, Roger WhoBlA 94, WhoMW 93
Williams, Roger c. 1603-1682? EncNAR
Williams, Roger 1603-1683 AmSocL, DcAmReB 2
Williams, Roger c. 1603-1688 HisWorL [port]
Williams, Roger 1924- WhoAm 94
Williams, Roger 1926- IntMPA 94
Williams, Roger 1942- Who 94
Williams, Roger Courtland 1944- WhoAmL 94
Williams, Roger Lawrence 1923- WhoAm 94
Williams, Roger Stanley 1931- IntWW 93, Who 94
Williams, Roger Stewart 1941- WhoAm 94
Williams, Roger Wright 1918- WhoAm 94
Williams, Roland 1910- WrDr 94
Williams, Ron Robert 1944- WhoBlA 94
Williams, Ronald Boal, Jr. 1938- WhoFI 94
Williams, Ronald Charles 1948- WhoBlA 94
Williams, Ronald David 1944- WhoFI 94, WhoScEn 94, WhoWest 94
Williams, Ronald Doherty 1927- WhoAmL 94
Williams, Ronald Eugene 1941- WhoFI 94
Williams, Ronald L. 1935- WhoAm 94
Williams, Ronald Lee 1936- WhoWest 94
Williams, Ronald Lee 1949- WhoBlA 94
Williams, Ronald Millward 1922- Who 94
Williams, Ronald Oscar 1940- WhoFI 94, WhoScEn 94, WhoWest 94
Williams, Ronald Paul 1947- WhoAm 94, WhoAmL 94
Williams, Ronald Wesley 1946- WhoBlA 94
Williams, Ronald William 1926- Who 94
Williams, Rosa B. 1933- WhoBlA 94
Williams, Rosalie WhoHol 92
Williams, Rose 1949- WhoMW 93
Williams, Ross Arnold 1953- WhoMW 93
Williams, Rowan Douglas Who 94
Williams, Roy WhoAm 94
Williams, Roy 1934- Who 94
Williams, Roy Nolan, Jr. 1941- WhoAmP 93
Williams, Ruby Mai 1904- WhoBlA 94
Williams, Ruby Ora 1926- WhoWest 94
Williams, Rudy V. WhoBlA 94
Williams, Runette Flowers 1945- WhoBlA 94
Williams, Russ DrAPF 93
Williams, Russell, II 1952- WhoAm 94, WhoBlA 94
Williams, Ruth J. WhoWest 94
Williams, Ruth Lee 1944- WhoWest 94
Williams, Ruthann Evege 1945- WhoBlA 94
Williams, S. Linn 1946- WhoAm 94
Williams, St. Claire Nathaniel 1949- WhoAmP 93
Williams, Sam 1934- WhoAmP 93
Williams, Samm-Art 1946- WhoBlA 94
Williams, Samuel Lewis 1934- Who 94
Williams, Samuel Riley 1895- WhAm 10
Williams, Sandra K. 1954- WhoBlA 94
Williams, Sandra Roberts 1940- WhoBlA 94
Williams, Scott WhoBlA 94
Williams, Scott A. 1958- WhoFI 94
Williams, Scott Joseph 1967- WhoMW 93
Williams, Scott W. 1943- WhoBlA 94
Williams, Sharon Mae 1945- WhoMW 93
Williams, Shawnell 1962- WhoBlA 94
Williams, Shelton Cross 1940- WhoAmL 94
Williams, Sherda Kaye 1954- WhoMW 93
Williams, Sherley Anne DrAPF 93
Williams, Sherley Anne 1944- BlkWr 2, WhoBlA 94
Williams, Sherman 1961- WhoBlA 94
Williams, Sheron 1955- SmATA 77
Williams, Shirley BlkWr 2
Williams, Shirley Jean Oostenbroek 1931- WhoMW 93
Williams, Shirley Yvonne WhoBlA 94
Williams, Sidmond Carl 1943- WhoFI 94
Williams, Sidney B., Jr. 1935- WhoBlA 94
Williams, Simon 1943- WrDr 94
Williams, Simon 1946- WhoHol 92
Williams, Snowden J. 1959- WhoBlA 94
Williams, Spencer d1969 WhoHol 92
Williams, Spencer M. 1922- WhoAm 94, WhoAmL 94, WhoHol 92
Williams, Spice WhoHol 92
Williams, Stanley 1925- WhoAm 94
Williams, Stanley Alan 1934- WhoAm 94
Williams, Stanley Clark 1939- WhoWest 94
Williams, Stanley King 1948- WhoBlA 94
Williams, Starks J. 1921- WhoBlA 94
Williams, Stephanie E. WhoHol 92
Williams, Stephen 1926- IntWW 93, WhoAm 94
Williams, Stephen Edward 1951- WhoAmL 94
Williams, Stephen F. 1936- CngDr 93, WhoAmP 93
Williams, Stephen Fain 1936- WhoAm 94, WhoAmL 94
Williams, Stephen Joseph 1948- WhoWest 94
Williams, Stephen T. 1956- WhoAmP 93
Williams, Sterling B., Jr. 1941- WhoBlA 94
Williams, Steve 1952- WhoIns 94
Williams, Steven WhoHol 92
Williams, Steven Lindsey 1956- WhoFI 94
Williams, Steven Orville 1951- WhoAmP 93
Williams, Stuart Konradd 1952- WhoWest 94
Williams, Stuart Mendenhall 1936- WhoWest 94
Williams, Sue M. 1942- WhoFI 94, WhoWest 94
Williams, Susan 1960- ConAu 141
Williams, Susan Eileen 1952- WhoFI 94, WhoWest 94
Williams, Susan Elizabeth 1942- Who 94
Williams, Susan Eva 1915- Who 94
Williams, Susan Longley WhoAmL 94
Williams, Sydney Who 94
Williams, (Henry) Sydney 1920- Who 94
Williams, Sylvia H. 1936- WhoAmA 93
Williams, Sylvia Hill 1936- WhoAm 94
Williams, Sylvia J. 1939- WhoBlA 94

Williams, T. Owen *EncSF 93*
Williams, T. Raymond 1940- *WhoAm 94*
Williams, Tad *EncSF 93*
Williams, Tamara *WhoHol 92*
Williams, Ted 1918- *WhoAm 94*
Williams, Temple Weatherly, Jr. 1934- *WhoAm 94*
Williams, Tennessee 1911-1983 *ConDr 93, DramC 4 [port], GayLL, IntDcT 2 [port]*
Williams, Terri L. 1958- *WhoBlA 94*
Williams, Terrie Michelle 1954- *WhoBlA 94*
Williams, Terry 1952- *WhoBlA 94*
Williams, Terry Lee 1950- *WhoAmP 93*
Williams, Tex d1985 *WhoHol 92*
Williams, Theartrice 1934- *WhoBlA 94*
Williams, Thelda *WhoAmP 93*
Williams, Theodore Earle 1920- *WhoAm 94, WhoFI 94, WhoWest 94*
Williams, Theodore Joseph 1923- *WhoAm 94*
Williams, Theodore Joseph, Jr. 1947- *WhoAmL 94*
Williams, Theodore P. 1933- *WhoScEn 94*
Williams, Theodore R. 1931- *WhoBlA 94*
Williams, Theopolis Charles 1956- *WhoBlA 94*
Williams, Thomas 1737-1802 *DcNaB MP*
Williams, Thomas 1950- *WhoAm 94*
Williams, Thomas (Alonzo) 1926-1990 *WhAm 10*
Williams, Thomas Allen 1959- *WhoBlA 94*
Williams, Thomas Allison 1936- *WhoAm 94*
Williams, Thomas Arthur 1943- *WhoAmL 94*
Williams, Thomas Eifion Hopkins 1923- *Who 94*
Williams, Thomas Eugene 1936- *WhoScEn 94*
Williams, Thomas Ffrancon 1928- *WhoAm 94*
Williams, Thomas Franklin 1921- *WhoAm 94, WhoScEn 94*
Williams, Thomas Hewett 1936- *WhoMW 93*
Williams, Thomas J. 1948- *WhoIns 94*
Williams, Thomas James 1963- *WhoWest 94*
Williams, Thomas Joseph 1951- *WhoWest 94*
Williams, Thomas Lanier *GayLL*
Williams, Thomas Lanier 1911-1983 *AmCulL [port]*
Williams, Thomas Pedworth 1910- *WhoBlA 94*
Williams, Thomas Rhys 1928- *WhoScEn 94*
Williams, Thomas Stafford *Who 94*
Williams, Thomas Stafford 1930- *IntWW 93*
Williams, Thomas T. 1925- *WhoAmP 93*
Williams, Thurmon *WhoFI 94*
Williams, Timothy John 1966- *WhoFI 94*
Williams, Timothy Shaler 1928- *WhoAm 94*
Williams, Tom d1928 *WhoHol 92*
Williams, Tom 1902- *NewGrDO*
Williams, Tommy Joe 1951- *WhoAmL 94*
Williams, Tommye Joyce 1930- *WhoBlA 94*
Williams, Tonda 1949- *WhoFI 94*
Williams, Tony d1992 *WhoBlA 94N*
Williams, Tony 1945- *WhoAm 94*
Williams, Treat 1951- *WhoAm 94*
Williams, Treat 1952- *IntMPA 94, WhoHol 92*
Williams, Trevor *Who 94*
Williams, (Albert) Trevor 1938- *Who 94*
Williams, Trevor Illtyd 1921- *Who 94, WrDr 94*
Williams, Trevor Wilson 1954- *WhoScEn 94*
Williams, Tyrell Clay 1949- *WhoWest 94*
Williams, Ulysses Jean 1947- *WhoBlA 94*
Williams, Valerie Jeanne 1961- *WhoMW 93*
Williams, Van 1934- *WhoHol 92*
Williams, Vanessa *WhoBlA 94*
Williams, Vanessa 1963- *ConMus 10 [port], WhoAm 94, WhoHol 92*
Williams, Vaughan *Who 94*
Williams, (James) Vaughan 1912- *Who 94*
Williams, Vaughn Charles 1945- *WhoAm 94, WhoAmL 94*
Williams, Vera B. 1927- *WrDr 94*
Williams, Vergil Lewis 1935- *WhoAm 94*
Williams, Vernice Louise 1934- *WhoBlA 94*
Williams, Vernon L. *WhoAmP 93*
Williams, Veronica Ann 1956- *WhoFI 94*
Williams, Vesta *WhoBlA 94*
Williams, Virginia Walker *WhoBlA 94*
Williams, W. Bill, Jr. 1939- *WhoBlA 94*

Williams, W. Clyde *WhoAm 94, WhoBlA 94*
Williams, W. Donald 1936- *WhoBlA 94*
Williams, W. Gene 1928- *WhoAm 94*
Williams, W. Vail 1940- *WhoMW 93*
Williams, Wade Allen 1960- *WhoAmP 93*
Williams, Wade Hampton, III 1942- *WhoMW 93*
Williams, Walker Richard, Jr. 1928- *WhoBlA 94, WhoMW 93*
Williams, Wallace C. *WhoBlA 94*
Williams, Walt *WhoHol 92*
Williams, Walt Ander 1970- *WhoBlA 94*
Williams, Walter *WhoHol 92*
Williams, Walter d1940 *WhoHol 92*
Williams, Walter 1932- *WhoWest 94*
Williams, Walter 1939- *WhoBlA 94*
Williams, Walter Baker 1921- *WhoAm 94, WhoWest 94*
Williams, Walter Bernard 1942- *WhoFI 94*
Williams, Walter E(dward) 1936- *WrDr 94*
Williams, Walter Fred 1929- *IntWW 93, WhoAm 94, WhoFI 94*
Williams, Walter Gordon Mason 1923- *Who 94*
Williams, Walter Harrison 1941- *WhoWest 94*
Williams, Walter Jackson, Jr. 1925- *WhoAm 94*
Williams, Walter Jon 1953- *EncSF 93*
Williams, Walter Joseph 1918- *WhoAm 94*
Williams, Walter W. *WhoAm 94, WhoFI 94*
Williams, Walter Waylon 1933- *WhoAm 94*
Williams, Warner 1903-1982 *WhoAmA 93N*
Williams, Warren Gamiel 1948- *WhoWest 94*
Williams, Warren Grey 1962- *WhoFI 94*
Williams, Wayne Allan 1964- *WhoBlA 94*
Williams, Wayne Darnell 1967- *WhoBlA 94*
Williams, Wayne De Armond 1914- *WhoAm 94*
Williams, Wayne Francis 1937- *WhoAmA 93*
Williams, Wayne Scott 1949- *WhoFI 94*
Williams, Wayne Warren 1963- *WhoAmL 94*
Williams, Wendell P. 1950- *WhoAmP 93*
Williams, Wendy O. *WhoHol 92*
Williams, Wesley S., Jr. 1942- *WhoBlA 94*
Williams, Wesley Samuel, Jr. 1942- *WhoAm 94, WhoAmL 94*
Williams, Wheeler 1897-1972 *WhoAmA 93N*
Williams, Wilbert 1924- *WhoBlA 94*
Williams, Wilbert Edd 1948- *WhoBlA 94*
Williams, Wilbert Lee 1938- *WhoBlA 94*
Williams, William d1942 *WhoHol 92*
Williams, William 1731-1811 *WhAmRev*
Williams, William fl. 183-?-184-? *WhWE*
Williams, William, Jr. 1939- *WhoBlA 94*
Williams, William Appleman 1921-1990 *WhAm 10*
Williams, William Arnold 1922- *WhoAm 94, WhoWest 94*
Williams, William Carlos 1883-1963 *AmCulL, PoeCrit 7 [port], RfGShF*
Williams, William Clyde, Dr. 1949- *WhoAm 94*
Williams, William Corey 1937- *WhoAm 94, WhoWest 94*
Williams, William David 1917- *Who 94*
Williams, William Earle 1950- *WhoAmA 93*
Williams, William Harrison 1924- *WhoAm 94*
Williams, William Henry, II 1931- *WhoFI 94*
Williams, William J. 1935- *WhoBlA 94*
Williams, William John 1928- *IntWW 93*
Williams, William John 1943- *WhoMW 93*
Williams, William John, Jr. 1937- *WhoAm 94*
Williams, William Joseph 1915- *WhoFI 94, WhoIns 94*
Williams, William Joseph 1926- *WhoAm 94*
Williams, William K. 1943- *WhoAmP 93*
Williams, William Kinsey 1942- *WhoFI 94*
Williams, William Lane 1914- *WhoAm 94*
Williams, William Orville 1940- *WhoAm 94*
Williams, William Paul 1948- *WhoAmP 93*
Williams, William Ralston 1910- *WhoAm 94*
Williams, William Sherley 1787-1849 *WhWE*
Williams, William T. 1942- *AfrAmAl 6 [port]*

Williams, William Thomas 1913- *Who 94*
Williams, William Thomas 1942- *WhoAm 94, WhoAmA 93, WhoBlA 94*
Williams, William Thomas, Jr. 1908-1989 *WhAm 10*
Williams, William Trevor 1925- *Who 94*
Williams, Willie 1943- *WhoAm 94, WhoWest 94*
Williams, Willie 1947- *WhoBlA 94*
Williams, Willie, Jr. *WhoBlA 94*
Williams, Willie, Jr. 1947- *WhoAm 94*
Williams, Willie Elbert 1927- *WhoBlA 94*
Williams, Willie J. *DrAPF 93*
Williams, Willie J. 1949- *WhoBlA 94*
Williams, Willie L. 1943- *WhoBlA 94*
Williams, Willie LaVern 1940- *WhoBlA 94*
Williams, Willie S. 1932- *WhoBlA 94*
Williams, Willis Ray 1937- *WhoWest 94*
Williams, Winston *WhoBlA 94*
Williams, Winton Hugh 1920- *WhoFI 94, WhoScEn 94*
Williams, Wyatt Clifford 1921- *WhoBlA 94*
Williams, Wyn Lewis 1951- *Who 94*
Williams, Yarborough, Jr. 1950- *WhoBlA 94*
Williams, Yarborough Burwell, Jr. 1928- *WhoBlA 94*
Williams, Yvonne Carter 1932- *WhoBlA 94*
Williams, Yvonne LaVerne 1938- *WhoBlA 94*
Williams, Yvonne Lovat 1920- *Who 94*
Williams, Zack d1958 *WhoHol 92*
Williams-Ashman, Howard Guy 1925- *WhoAm 94, WhoScEn 94*
Williams Boyd, Sheila Anne 1951- *WhoBlA 94*
Williams Brothers, The *WhoHol 92*
Williams-Bulkeley, Richard (Thomas) 1939- *Who 94*
Williams-Daly, Angelia Evette 1960- *WhoFI 94*
Williams Davis, Edith G. 1958- *WhoBlA 94*
Williams-Dovi, Joanna 1953- *WhoBlA 94*
Williams-Garcia, Rita *TwCYAW*
Williams-Garner, Debra 1957- *WhoBlA 94*
Williams-Green, Joyce F. 1948- *WhoBlA 94*
Williams-Harris, Diane Beatrice 1949- *WhoBlA 94*
Williams-Jones, Michael 1947- *IntMPA 94*
Williams-Myers, Albert J. 1939- *WhoBlA 94*
Williams Of Crosby, Baroness 1930- *IntWW 93, Who 94*
Williams Of Elvel, Baron 1933- *IntWW 93, Who 94*
Williams Of Mostyn, Baron 1941- *Who 94*
Williamson *WhoAm 94*
Williamson, Mrs. *NewGrDO*
Williamson, Ada C. 1883-1958 *WhoAmA 93N*
Williamson, Alan (Bacher) 1944- *WrDr 94*
Williamson, Alan Bacher 1944- *WhoAm 94*
Williamson, Alistair *WhoHol 92*
Williamson, Andrew c. 1730-1786 *AmRev, WhAmRev*
Williamson, Andrew George 1948- *Who 94*
Williamson, Arline Trudy 1948- *WhoMW 93*
Williamson, Bill Logan 1938- *WhoAmL 94*
Williamson, Brian *Who 94*
Williamson, (Robert) Brian 1945- *Who 94*
Williamson, Carl Augustus 1950- *WhoFI 94*
Williamson, Carl Vance 1955- *WhoBlA 94*
Williamson, Carlton 1958- *WhoBlA 94*
Williamson, Charles Joseph 1945- *WhoAmL 94*
Williamson, Clara McDonald d1976 *WhoAmA 93N*
Williamson, Clarence Kelly 1924- *WhoAm 94*
Williamson, Coy Colbert, Jr. 1936- *WhoBlA 94*
Williamson, Craig *DrAPF 93*
Williamson, David (Geoffrey) 1927- *WrDr 94*
Williamson, David (Keith) 1942- *ConAu 41NR, ConDr 93, IntDcT 2, WrDr 94*
Williamson, David F. 1934- *IntWW 93*
Williamson, David Francis 1934- *Who 94*
Williamson, David Keith 1942- *IntWW 93*
Williamson, David Theodore Nelson d1992 *IntWW 93N*
Williamson, Don *WhoAm 94, WhoWest 94*

Williamson, Donald Ray 1943- *WhoAm 94*
Williamson, Doug 1944- *WrDr 94*
Williamson, Douglas Franklin, Jr. 1930- *WhoAm 94*
Williamson, Douglas Mark 1951- *WhoAmL 94*
Williamson, Edward Hughes 1947- *WhoFI 94*
Williamson, Edward L. *WhoScEn 94*
Williamson, Edwin Dargan 1939- *WhoAm 94, WhoAmL 94*
Williamson, Edwin Lee 1947- *WhoWest 94*
Williamson, Elizabeth Ann 1963- *WhoMW 93*
Williamson, Ernest Lavone 1924- *WhoAm 94*
Williamson, Ethel W. 1947- *WhoBlA 94*
Williamson, Faye Denise 1958- *WhoMW 93*
Williamson, Fletcher Phillips 1923- *WhoAm 94, WhoFI 94*
Williamson, Frank Edger 1917- *Who 94*
Williamson, Fred 1937- *IntMPA 94*
Williamson, Fred 1938- *WhoHol 92*
Williamson, Frederick Beasley, III 1918- *WhoAm 94*
Williamson, G. Malcolm 1939- *IntWW 93*
Williamson, George Arthur 1938- *WhoAmP 93*
Williamson, George Beauchamp 1946- *WhoAmP 93*
Williamson, George Franklin 1897- *WhAm 10*
Williamson, Gilbert P. 1937- *IntWW 93*
Williamson, Gilbert Pemberton 1937- *WhoAm 94, WhoFI 94*
Williamson, Glenn Robert 1962- *WhoMW 93*
Williamson, Handy, Jr. 1945- *WhoAm 94, WhoBlA 94*
Williamson, Harold E. 1930- *WhoMW 93*
Williamson, Harry 1911-1992 *AnObit 1992*
Williamson, Harwood Danford 1932- *WhoFI 94*
Williamson, Hazel Eleanor 1947- *Who 94*
Williamson, Henry Gaston, Jr. 1947- *WhoAm 94, WhoFI 94*
Williamson, Henry M. *WhoBlA 94*
Williamson, Herbert Clarke, III 1948- *WhoFI 94*
Williamson, Hugh 1735-1819 *WhAmRev*
Williamson, Hugh Godfrey Maturin 1947- *Who 94*
Williamson, J. N. *DrAPF 93*
Williamson, Jack 1908- *EncSF 93, WhoAm 94, WhoWest 94, WrDr 94*
Williamson, James *WhoHol 92*
Williamson, James 1842-1930 *DcNaB MP*
Williamson, James 1920- *Who 94*
Williamson, James Allen 1951- *WhoAmP 93*
Williamson, James Larry 1952- *WhoAmP 93*
Williamson, Jason H. 1926- *WhoAmA 93*
Williamson, Jo Ann 1951- *WhoMW 93, WhoScEn 94*
Williamson, Joel 1930- *WrDr 94*
Williamson, Joel V. 1945- *WhoAm 94*
Williamson, John 1937- *IntWW 93*
Williamson, John Craig 1935- *WhoWest 94*
Williamson, John Maurice 1938- *WhoMW 93*
Williamson, John Michael 1962- *WhoFI 94*
Williamson, John P. 1835-1917 *EncNAR*
Williamson, John Pritchard 1922- *WhoAm 94, WhoWest 94*
Williamson, John Steven 1958- *WhoScEn 94*
Williamson, John Thomas, Sr. 1925- *WhoFI 94*
Williamson, Johnny H. 1934- *WhoIns 94*
Williamson, Julie Ann Stulce 1944- *WhoAmL 94*
Williamson, Karen Elizabeth 1947- *WhoBlA 94*
Williamson, Karl Allen 1951- *WhoMW 93*
Williamson, Kate *WhoHol 92*
Williamson, Keith (Alec) 1928- *IntWW 93, Who 94*
Williamson, Kenneth Lee 1934- *WhoScEn 94*
Williamson, Kenneth Robert 1929- *WhoWest 94*
Williamson, Laird 1937- *WhoAm 94*
Williamson, Larry C. 1930- *WhoAmP 93*
Williamson, Linda Jean M. 1952- *WhoAmP 93*
Williamson, Liz *WhoAm 94*
Williamson, Lowell James 1923- *WhoWest 94*
Williamson, Malcolm *Who 94*
Williamson, Malcolm (Benjamin Graham Christopher) 1931- *NewGrDO*

Williamson, (George) Malcolm 1939- *Who 94*
Williamson, Malcolm Benjamin Graham 1931- *IntWW 93*
Williamson, Malcolm Benjamin Graham Christopher 1931- *Who 94*
Williamson, Marianne 1952- *ConAu 141, CurBio 93 [port]*
Williamson, Marilyn Lammert 1927- *WhoAm 94*
Williamson, Marjorie *Who 94*
Williamson, (Elsie) Marjorie 1913- *Who 94*
Williamson, Maurice Alan 1946- *WhoWest 94*
Williamson, Michael George 1951- *WhoAmL 94*
Williamson, Michael Joe 1944- *WhoFI 94, WhoMW 93*
Williamson, Michael Roy 1944- *WhoMW 93*
Williamson, Mykel T. *WhoHol 92*
Williamson, Myrna Hennrich 1937- *WhoAm 94*
Williamson, Neil Robert 1940- *WhoWest 94*
Williamson, Neil Seymour, III 1935- *WhoWest 94*
Williamson, Nicholas Frederick Hedworth 1937- *Who 94*
Williamson, Nicol *WhoHol 92*
Williamson, Nicol 1938- *IntMPA 94, IntWW 93, Who 94*
Williamson, Nigel 1954- *Who 94*
Williamson, Oliver Eaton 1932- *WhoAm 94, WhoWest 94*
Williamson, Patricia Mary 1952- *WhoFI 94*
Williamson, Patrick 1929- *IntMPA 94*
Williamson, Paul Alan 1947- *WhoMW 93*
Williamson, Peter David 1944- *WhoAm 94, WhoAmL 94*
Williamson, Peter Roger 1942- *Who 94*
Williamson, Richard 1935- *WrDr 94*
Williamson, Richard Arthur 1930- *WhoWest 94*
Williamson, Richard Arthur 1932- *Who 94*
Williamson, Richard Cardinal 1939- *WhoAm 94*
Williamson, Richard Duane 1948- *WhoAmP 93*
Williamson, Richard F. 1952- *WhoAmP 93*
Williamson, Richard Hall 1940- *WhoAm 94*
Williamson, Richard Salisbury 1949- *WhoAm 94*
Williamson, Robert d1949 *WhoHol 92*
Williamson, Robert 1938- *Who 94*
Williamson, Robert C(lifford) 1916- *WrDr 94*
Williamson, Robert Charles 1925- *WhoAm 94, WhoFI 94*
Williamson, Robert Elmore 1937- *WhoAm 94*
Williamson, Robert Emmett 1937- *WhoWest 94*
Williamson, Robert Kerr *Who 94*
Williamson, Robert Webster 1942- *WhoFI 94*
Williamson, Robin *DrAPF 93*
Williamson, Robin d1935 *WhoHol 92*
Williamson, Robin (Duncan Harry) 1943- *WrDr 94*
Williamson, Robin Charles Noel 1942- *Who 94*
Williamson, Ronald Edwin 1941- *WhoScEn 94*
Williamson, Ronald Thomas 1948- *WhoAmL 94*
Williamson, Roy *Who 94*
Williamson, Sam 1910- *WhoAm 94*
Williamson, Samuel Chris 1946- *WhoScEn 94*
Williamson, Samuel P. 1949- *WhoBlA 94*
Williamson, Samuel Perkins 1949- *WhoScEn 94*
Williamson, Samuel R. 1943- *WhoBlA 94*
Williamson, Samuel Ruthven, Jr. 1935- *WhoAm 94*
Williamson, Stephen 1948- *Who 94*
Williamson, Thomas Arnold 1939- *WhoAm 94, WhoFI 94*
Williamson, Thomas Daniel 1959- *WhoMW 93*
Williamson, Thomas Garnett 1934- *WhoAm 94, WhoScEn 94*
Williamson, Thomas S. 1800-1879 *EncNAR*
Williamson, Thomas Samuel, Jr. 1946- *WhoAm 94, WhoAmL 94, WhoFI 94*
Williamson, Thomas W., Jr. 1950- *WhoAmL 94*
Williamson, Timothy A. 1962- *WhoAmP 93*
Williamson, Timothy Lamment 1957- *WhoAmL 94*
Williamson, Tommy Lee 1940- *WhoMW 93*
Williamson, Vikki Lyn 1956- *WhoFI 94, WhoMW 93*
Williamson, Walter Robert 1921- *WhoAmP 93*
Williamson, Warren Pyatt, Jr. 1900- *WhoAm 94*
Williamson, William E. 1927- *WhoAmP 93*
Williamson, William Floyd, Jr. 1924- *WhoAm 94*
Williamson, William Paul, Jr. 1929- *WhoAm 94*
Williamson-Ige, Dorothy Kay 1950- *WhoBlA 94*
Williams-Stanton, Sonya Denise 1963- *WhoBlA 94*
Williams-Wynn, (David) Watkin 1940- *Who 94*
Williams-Wynne, John Francis 1908- *Who 94*
William the Conqueror c. 1027-1087 *HisWorL [port]*
William the Conqueror, I fl. 1066-1087 *BlmGEL*
William the Englishman fl. 1180- *DcNaB MP*
William the Silent 1533-1584 *HisWorL [port]*
Willian, Clyde Franklin 1930- *WhoAm 94*
Willich, (Walter) Martin (Philipp) 1945- *IntWW 93*
Willie, Charles Vert 1927- *WhoAm 94, WhoBlA 94*
Willie, Louis J. 1923- *WhoBlA 94*
Willie D. *See* Geto Boys, The *ConMus 11*
Willier, Russell 1947- *EncNAR*
Williford, Cynthia W. 1917- *WhoBlA 94*
Williford, Donald Bratton 1936- *WhoAm 94*
Williford, Hollis R. 1940- *WhoAmA 93*
Williford, John Frederic, Jr. 1938- *WhoScEn 94*
Williford, Richard Allen 1934- *WhoScEn 94*
Williford, Robert Marion 1937- *WhoScEn 94*
Williford, Stanley O. 1942- *WhoBlA 94*
Willig, Karl Victor 1944- *WhoAm 94, WhoFI 94, WhoWest 94*
Willig, Robert Daniel 1947- *WhoAm 94, WhoAmL 94*
Willihnganz, Paul Waddell 1937- *WhoFI 94*
Williman, Sara Jane 1933- *WhoMW 93*
Willimon, William Henry 1946- *WhoAm 94*
Willing, David Nicholas 1945- *WhoMW 93*
Willing, Foy d1978 *WhoHol 92*
Willing, James *AmRev*
Willing, James Richard 1958- *WhoWest 94*
Willing, Katherine McConahay *WhoAmP 93*
Willing, Maria Paula Figueiroa *Who 94*
Willing, Thomas 1731-1821 *WhAmRev*
Willingham, Allan King 1941- *WhoMW 93*
Willingham, Ben Hill 1914-1991 *WhAm 10*
Willingham, Calder *DrAPF 93*
Willingham, Calder (Barnard, Jr.) 1922- *EncSF 93*
Willingham, Calder (Baynard, Jr.) 1922- *WrDr 94*
Willingham, Clark Suttles 1944- *WhoAm 94, WhoAmL 94*
Willingham, Edward Bacon, Jr. 1934- *WhoAm 94*
Willingham, Harry G. d1943 *WhoHol 92*
Willingham, Noble *WhoHol 92*
Willingham, Thomas W. 1945- *WhoIns 94*
Willingham, Voncile 1935- *WhoBlA 94*
Willingham, Warren Willcox 1930- *WhoAm 94, WhoScEn 94*
Willink, Charles (William) 1929- *Who 94*
Willink, Mathilde d1977 *WhoHol 92*
Williquette, Gerald F. 1940- *WhoIns 94*
Willis, Baron d1992 *IntWW 93N, Who 94N*
Willis, Andrew 1938- *WhoBlA 94*
Willis, Ann *WhoHol 92*
Willis, Austin *WhoHol 92*
Willis, Barbara Florence 1932- *WhoAmA 93*
Willis, Bill *ProFbHF [port]*
Willis, Bruce 1955- *IntMPA 94, WhoHol 92*
Willis, Bruce Donald 1941- *WhoAm 94*
Willis, Bruce Walter 1955- *IntWW 93, WhoAm 94*
Willis, Cecil B. *WhoBlA 94*
Willis, Charles *EncSF 93*
Willis, Charles F., Jr. d1993 *NewYTBS 93*
Willis, Charles L. 1926- *WhoBlA 94*
Willis, Charles Reginald 1906- *Who 94*
Willis, Clayton 1933- *WhoAm 94, WhoFI 94*
Willis, Clifford Leon 1913- *WhoScEn 94, WhoWest 94*
Willis, Connie 1945- *EncSF 93, WrDr 94*
Willis, Craig Dean 1935- *WhoAm 94*
Willis, Cynthia Elaine 1955- *WhoMW 93*
Willis, Dave d1973 *WhoHol 92*
Willis, David Edwin 1926- *WhoAm 94*
Willis, David Lee 1927- *WhoAm 94*
Willis, David Leon 1959- *WhoAmL 94*
Willis, David Paul 1956- *WhoScEn 94*
Willis, Dawn Louise 1959- *WhoAmL 94, WhoWest 94*
Willis, Donald J. 1962- *WhoScEn 94*
Willis, Douglas Alan 1963- *WhoMW 93*
Willis, Doyle 1908- *WhoAmP 93*
Willis, Ed 1923- *WhoAmP 93*
Willis, Edgar E(rnest) 1913- *WrDr 94*
Willis, Elizabeth Bayley *WhoAmA 93*
Willis, Eric (Archibald) 1922- *Who 94*
Willis, Eric Archibald 1922- *IntWW 93*
Willis, Everett Irving 1908- *WhoAm 94*
Willis, Frank B. 1947- *WhoBlA 94*
Willis, Frank Edward 1939- *WhoAm 94*
Willis, Frank Roy 1930- *WhoAm 94*
Willis, Frank William 1947- *Who 94*
Willis, Franklin Knight 1942- *WhoAm 94*
Willis, Frederic L. 1937- *WhoBlA 94*
Willis, Gary K. 1946- *WhoFI 94*
Willis, Gaspard *Who 94*
Willis, (Robert William) Gaspard 1905- *Who 94*
Willis, George Clark 1938- *WhoWest 94*
Willis, George Edmund 1920- *WhoFI 94*
Willis, George Edward 1932- *WhoAm 94*
Willis, George Henry 1941- *WhoAm 94*
Willis, Gerald 1940- *WhoAmP 93*
Willis, Gladys January 1944- *WhoBlA 94*
Willis, Gordon *IntMPA 94, WhoAm 94*
Willis, Gordon 1931- *IntDcF 2-4*
Willis, Grover Cleveland 1933- *WhoAmP 93*
Willis, Guye Henry, Jr. 1937- *WhoScEn 94*
Willis, Harold Wendt, Sr. 1927- *WhoWest 94*
Willis, Irene *DrAPF 93*
Willis, Isaac 1940- *WhoBlA 94, WhoScEn 94*
Willis, Jack B. 1946- *WhoAmP 93*
Willis, James *Who 94*
Willis, (Guido) James 1923- *Who 94*
Willis, James Alfred 1925- *IntWW 93*
Willis, Jay Stewart 1940- *WhoAmA 93*
Willis, Jeffrey Lynn 1951- *WhoAmL 94*
Willis, Jeffrey Scott 1962- *WhoScEn 94*
Willis, Jerome *WhoHol 92*
Willis, Jill Michelle 1952- *WhoBlA 94*
Willis, Jimmy Roy 1942- *WhoWest 94*
Willis, John (Frederick) 1937- *Who 94*
Willis, John A(lvin) 1916- *WrDr 94*
Willis, John Alvin 1916- *WhoAm 94*
Willis, John Brooke 1906- *Who 94*
Willis, John Brooker 1926- *Who 94*
Willis, John Edward 1946- *Who 94*
Willis, John Fristoe 1910- *WhoAm 94*
Willis, John Patrick 1947- *WhoFI 94*
Willis, John Randolph 1929- *WhoAm 94*
Willis, John Raymond 1940- *Who 94*
Willis, John Trueman 1918- *Who 94*
Willis, Joseph Robert McKenzie 1909- *Who 94*
Willis, Judith H. 1935- *WhoScEn 94*
Willis, Kathi Grant 1959- *WhoBlA 94*
Willis, Kenneth Henry George *Who 94*
Willis, Kevin Alvin 1962- *WhoAm 94*
Willis, Kevin Andre 1962- *WhoBlA 94*
Willis, Larryann C. 1947- *WhoAmP 93*
Willis, Lawrence Jack 1948- *WhoScEn 94*
Willis, Leo d1952 *WhoHol 92*
Willis, Levy E. *WhoBlA 94*
Willis, Matt d1989 *WhoHol 92*
Willis, Maud *EncSF 93*
Willis, Meredith Sue *DrAPF 93*
Willis, Miechelle Orchid 1954- *WhoBlA 94*
Willis, Nell Elaine 1940- *WhoWest 94*
Willis, Norma Byers 1931- *WhoAmP 93*
Willis, Norman 1903- *WhoHol 92*
Willis, Norman David 1933- *IntWW 93, Who 94*
Willis, Patricia Ann 1957- *WhoFI 94*
Willis, Paul *DrAPF 93*
Willis, Paul Allen 1941- *WhoAm 94*
Willis, Ralph 1938- *IntWW 93, Who 94*
Willis, Ralph Houston 1942- *WhoScEn 94*
Willis, Raymond Edson 1930- *WhoAm 94*
Willis, Rebecca Lynn 1947- *WhoScEn 94*
Willis, Richard d1945 *WhoHol 92*
Willis, Robert Addison 1949- *WhoMW 93*
Willis, Robert Andrew 1947- *Who 94*
Willis, Robert E. 1922- *WhoAmA 93N*
Willis, Roberta Berk 1951- *WhoAmP 93*
Willis, Roger Blenkiron 1906- *Who 94*
Willis, Ronald James 1939- *WhoFI 94*
Willis, Rose W. 1939- *WhoBlA 94*
Willis, Selene Lowe 1958- *WhoScEn 94, WhoWest 94*
Willis, Sharon White 1964- *WhoScEn 94*
Willis, Shelby Kenneth 1924- *WhoScEn 94*
Willis, Sidney F. 1930- *WhoAmA 93*
Willis, Stephen Murrell 1929- *Who 94*
Willis, Susan *WhoHol 92*
Willis, Ted 1918- *ConDr 93*
Willis, Ted 1918-1992 *AnObit 1992, ConAu 140, ConTFT 11, WrDr 94N*
Willis, Thornton 1936- *WhoAmA 93*
Willis, Thornton Wilson 1936- *WhoAm 94*
Willis, Val 1946- *WrDr 94*
Willis, Walt *EncSF 93*
Willis, Wesley Robert 1941- *WhoAm 94*
Willis, William Darrell, Jr. 1934- *WhoAm 94, WhoScEn 94*
Willis, William Ervin 1926- *WhoAm 94*
Willis, William Harold, Jr. 1927- *WhoAm 94, WhoFI 94*
Willis, William Henry 1951- *WhoAm 94*
Willis, William Henry, Jr. 1940- *WhoAmA 93*
Willis, William Pascal 1910- *WhoAmP 93*
Willis, William Scott 1921- *WhoAm 94*
Williscroft, Dagmar Christine 1940- *WhoAmP 93*
Williscroft, Robert Grover 1942- *WhoAmP 93*
Willison, David (John) 1919- *Who 94*
Willison, James E. 1925- *WhoAmP 93*
Willison, John (Alexander) 1914- *Who 94*
Willison, Mildred Lucille 1921- *WhoAmP 93*
Willison, Sue Kindred 1926- *WhoAmP 93*
Willison, Walter 1947- *WhoHol 92*
Willis-Smith, Nancy Marie 1964- *WhoMW 93*
Willits, Lon Kedric 1939- *WhoWest 94*
Willke, Thomas Aloys 1932- *WhoAm 94*
Willkie, Wendell Lewis 1951- *WhoAmP 93*
Willkie, Wendell Lewis, II 1951- *WhoAm 94, WhoAmL 94*
Willkomm, Ernst 1810-1886 *DcLB 133 [port]*
Willliams, Heathcote 1941- *WrDr 94*
Willm, Pierre-Richard d1983 *WhoHol 92*
Willman, John 1949- *Who 94*
Willman, John Norman 1915- *WhoAm 94, WhoFI 94*
Willman, Lee A. *WhoIns 94*
Willman, Noel d1988 *WhoHol 92*
Willman, Philip Louis 1953- *WhoAmL 94*
Willman, Vallee Louis 1925- *WhoAm 94, WhoMW 93*
Willmann, (Maria Anna Magdalena) Caroline 1796-c. 1860 *NewGrDO*
Willmarth, Mary Sue 1963- *WhoWest 94*
Willmarth, William Walter 1924- *WhoAm 94*
Willmer, Catherine *WhoHol 92*
Willmer, Edward Nevill 1902- *WrDr 94*
Willmer, John Franklin 1930- *Who 94*
Willmer, Nevill *Who 94*
Willmer, (Edward) Nevill 1902- *Who 94*
Willmore, (Albert) Peter 1930- *Who 94*
Willmore, Robert Louis 1955- *WhoAm 94*
Willmot, Donald Gilpin 1916- *WhoAm 94*
Willmott, Dennis James 1932- *Who 94*
Willmott, Edward George 1936- *Who 94*
Willmott, John Charles 1922- *Who 94*
Willmott, Peter 1923- *Who 94, WrDr 94*
Willmott, Peter Sherman 1937- *WhoFI 94*
Willms, Andre *WhoHol 92*
Willms, Arthur Henry 1939- *WhoFI 94*
Willms, Dirk Albert 1935- *WhoFI 94*
Willms, John 1927- *WhoMW 93*
Willms, Richard Scott 1957- *WhoWest 94*
Willner, A(lfred) M(aria) 1859-1929 *NewGrDO*
Willner, Alan Eli 1962- *WhoScEn 94*
Willner, Ann Ruth 1924- *WhoAm 94*
Willner, Dorothy 1927- *WhoAm 94*
Willner, Dorothy 1927-1993 *ConAu 140*
Willner, Eugene Burton 1934- *WhoFI 94*
Willner, Hal c. 1948- *ConMus 10 [port]*
Willner, Jay R. 1924- *WhoFI 94*
Willner, Larry Elliott 1932- *WhoFI 94*
Willner, Robert Franklin 1942- *WhoAm 94*
Willoch, Kare Isaachsen 1928- *IntWW 93*
Willochra, Bishop of 1940- *Who 94*
Willock, Colin (Dennistoun) 1919- *WrDr 94*
Willock, Dave d1990 *WhoHol 92*
Willock, Marcelle Monica 1938- *WhoAm 94, WhoBlA 94*
Willock, William Charles, Jr. 1952- *WhoAmL 94*
Willocks, Robert Max 1924- *WhoAm 94*

Willott, Brian *Who 94*
Willott, (William) Brian 1940- *IntWW 93, Who 94*
Willoughby *Who 94*
Willoughby, Alfred 1898- *WhAm 10*
Willoughby, Bruce Edward 1948- *WhoMW 93*
Willoughby, Bruce Nicholas 1942- *WhoAmL 94*
Willoughby, Carroll Vernon 1913- *WhoAm 94*
Willoughby, Charles A. 1892-1972 *HisDcKW*
Willoughby, Christopher R. 1938- *IntWW 93*
Willoughby, Christopher Ronald 1938- *WhoAm 94*
Willoughby, Clarice E. 1934- *WhoBlA 94*
Willoughby, David Albert 1931- *Who 94*
Willoughby, David Charles 1940- *WhoMW 93*
Willoughby, Gerald *WhoAmP 93*
Willoughby, Harvey William 1946- *WhoAm 94*
Willoughby, Hugh c. 1500-1554 *WhWE*
Willoughby, Hugh 1916- *WrDr 94*
Willoughby, James Russell 1928- *WhoWest 94*
Willoughby, Jane Baker *WhoAmA 93*
Willoughby, John Wallace 1932- *WhoAm 94*
Willoughby, Joyce Carol 1939- *WhoAmP 93*
Willoughby, Kenneth James 1922- *Who 94*
Willoughby, Lee Davis 1910- *WrDr 94*
Willoughby, Lee Davis 1924- *WrDr 94*
Willoughby, Lewis d1968 *WhoHol 92*
Willoughby, Noel Vincent *Who 94*
Willoughby, Robin Kay *DrAPF 93*
Willoughby, Rodney Erwin 1925- *WhoAm 94*
Willoughby, Roger James 1939- *Who 94*
Willoughby, Stephen Schuyler 1932- *WhoAm 94*
Willoughby, Stuart Carroll 1951- *WhoFI 94, WhoWest 94*
Willoughby, Susan Melita 1925- *WhoBlA 94*
Willoughby, William, II 1933- *WhoScEn 94*
Willoughby, William Franklin, II 1936- *WhoAm 94*
Willoughby, Winston Churchill 1907- *WhoBlA 94*
Willoughby De Broke, Baron 1938- *Who 94*
Willoughby De Eresby, Baroness 1934- *Who 94*
Willow, Shannon 1940- *WrDr 94*
Willows, Arthur Owen Dennis 1941- *WhoScEn 94*
Willrich, Emzy James 1959- *WhoBlA 94*
Willrich, Mason 1933- *WrDr 94*
Willrich, Rudolph *WhoHol 92*
Wills *Who 94*
Wills, Alfred J(ohn) 1927- *WrDr 94*
Wills, Arthur William 1926- *Who 94*
Wills, Bart Francis 1955- *WhoMW 93*
Wills, Beverly d1963 *WhoHol 92*
Wills, Bob d1975 *WhoHol 92*
Wills, Bob, Jr. *WhoHol 92*
Wills, Brember d1948 *WhoHol 92*
Wills, Brian Alan 1927- *Who 94*
Wills, Charles Francis 1914- *WhoAm 94*
Wills, Chill d1978 *WhoHol 92*
Wills, Christopher 1938- *WrDr 94*
Wills, Colin Spencer 1937- *Who 94*
Wills, Cornelia 1953- *WhoBlA 94*
Wills, David *Who 94*
Wills, (Hugh) David (Hamilton) 1917- *Who 94*
Wills, David Wood 1942- *WhoAm 94*
Wills, Dean Robert 1933- *IntWW 93, Who 94*
Wills, Drusilla d1951 *WhoHol 92*
Wills, Duane Arthur 1939- *WhoAm 94*
Wills, Fingal O'Flahertie
See Wilde, Oscar 1854-1900 *NewGrDO*
Wills, Garry 1934- *AmSocL, WhoAm 94, WhoMW 93, WrDr 94*
Wills, Helen *Who 94*
Wills, Henry *WhoHol 92*
Wills, J. Robert 1940- *WhoAm 94, WhoWest 94*
Wills, James Willard 1933- *WhoBlA 94*
Wills, John Vernon 1928- *Who 94*
Wills, Katherine Vasilios 1957- *WhoMW 93*
Wills, Lou d1968 *WhoHol 92*
Wills, Maury *WhoHol 92*
Wills, Michael *WhoHol 92*
Wills, Michael Ralph 1931- *WhoAm 94*
Wills, Nat d1917 *WhoHol 92*
Wills, Nicholas Kenneth Spencer 1941- *Who 94*
Wills, Norma *WhoHol 92*
Wills, Penelope Hornschemeier 1952- *WhoWest 94*
Wills, Peter Gordon Bethune 1931- *Who 94*
Wills, Robert Hamilton 1926- *WhoAm 94, WhoMW 93*
Wills, Seton *Who 94*
Wills, (David) Seton 1939- *Who 94*
Wills, Sheila *WhoHol 92*
Wills, Tom 1937- *WhoAmP 93*
Wills, Walter d1967 *WhoHol 92*
Wills, Walter J 1915- *WrDr 94*
Wills, Walter Joe 1915- *WhoAm 94, WhoFI 94*
Wills, William John 1834-1861 *WhWE*
Wills, William Ridley, II 1934- *WhoAm 94*
Willse, James Patrick 1944- *WhoAm 94*
Willson, Alan Neil, Jr. 1939- *WhoAm 94*
Willson, Douglas James d1993 *Who 94N*
Willson, Francis Michael Glenn 1924- *IntWW 93*
Willson, (Francis Michael) Glenn 1924- *Who 94*
Willson, James Douglas 1915- *WhoAm 94*
Willson, John Harrison, III 1959- *WhoWest 94*
Willson, John Michael 1931- *Who 94*
Willson, John Michael 1940- *WhoAm 94*
Willson, Margaret (Bosshardt) Pace 1919- *WhoAmA 93*
Willson, Marion Elaine 1939- *WhAm 10*
Willson, Mary F. 1938- *WhoAm 94*
Willson, Prentiss, Jr. 1943- *WhoAm 94, WhoAmL 94*
Willson, Robert 1912- *WhoAmA 93*
Willson, Robert Frank, Jr. 1939- *WhoMW 93*
Willson, Steven Robert 1949- *WhoAm 94*
Willson, Warrack G. *WhoScEn 94*
Willstatter, Alfred 1925- *WhoWest 94*
Willstatter, Richard 1872-1942 *WorScD*
Willumsen, Dorrit *EncSF 93*
Willumsen, Dorrit 1940- *BlmGWL*
Willy *GayLL*
Willy, Colette *GayLL*
Willy, Edgar d1980 *WhoHol 92*
Willy, John G. 1942- *WhoAmP 93*
Willy, Margaret (Elizabeth) 1919- *WrDr 94*
Willy, Thomas Ralph 1943- *WhoAmL 94, WhoMW 93*
Willyoung, David Mac Cleggan 1924- *WhoAm 94*
Willys, Richard c. 1615-1690 *DcNaB MP*
Wilman, Derry Edward Vincent 1946- *WhoScEn 94*
Wilmarth, Gary Russell 1947- *WhoFI 94*
Wilmarth, Mary Ann 1960- *WhoWest 94*
Wilmarth, Richard *DrAPF 93*
Wilmer, Clive 1945- *WrDr 94*
Wilmer, Dale 1920- *WrDr 94*
Wilmer, Douglas 1920- *WhoHol 92*
Wilmer-Brown, Maisie d1973 *WhoHol 92*
Wilmerding, Harold Pratt 1937- *WhoAm 94*
Wilmerding, John 1938- *WhoAm 94, WhoAmA 93, WrDr 94*
Wilmers, Robert George 1934- *WhoAm 94, WhoFI 94*
Wilmeth, Don B(urton) 1939- *ConAu 41NR*
Wilmeth, Ernest, II 1952- *WhoAmA 93*
Wilmington, Joseph (Robert) 1932- *Who 94*
Wilmore, Douglas Wayne 1938- *WhoScEn 94*
Wilmore, Gayraud S(tephen), Jr. 1921- *WrDr 94*
Wilmore, Gayraud Stephen 1921- *WhoBlA 94*
Wilmore, Lillian A. 1943- *WhoAmL 94*
Wilmot, David 1943- *Who 94*
Wilmot, David Winston 1944- *WhoBlA 94*
Wilmot, Henry Robert 1967- *Who 94*
Wilmot, Irvin Gorsage 1922- *WhoAm 94*
Wilmot, John 1647-1680 *BlmGEL*
Wilmot, John Assheton E. *Who 94*
Wilmot, Robb *Who 94*
Wilmot, Robert William 1945- *Who 94*
Wilmot, Ronan *WhoHol 92*
Wilmoth, Wade Franklin 1934- *WhoAmP 93*
Wilmoth, William David 1950- *WhoAmL 94*
Wilmot-Sitwell, Peter Sacheverell 1935- *Who 94*
Wilmott, Peter Graham 1947- *Who 94*
Wilmouth, Robert K. 1928- *WhoAm 94, WhoFI 94*
Wilms, Dorothee 1929- *IntWW 93, WhoWomW 91*
Wilms, Ronald Edward 1949- *WhoMW 93*
Wilmshurst, John Barry 1936- *Who 94*
Wilmshurst, Michael Joseph 1934- *Who 94*
Wilms-Kegel, Heike 1952- *WhoWomW 91*
Wilmut, Charles Gordon 1947- *WhoScEn 94*
Wilner, Alvin Gustav 1940- *WhoAm 94*
Wilner, Eleanor *DrAPF 93*
Wilner, Freeman Marvin 1926- *WhoMW 93, WhoScEn 94*
Wilner, Morton Harrison 1908- *WhoAm 94, WhoAmL 94*
Wilner, Paul Andrew 1950- *WhoAm 94*
Wilner, Thomas Bernard 1944- *WhoAm 94*
Wiloch, Thomas *DrAPF 93*
Wiloughby, Cass 1932- *WrDr 94*
Wilsdon, Thomas Arthur 1942- *WhoScEn 94*
Wilsey, Jay d1961 *WhoHol 92*
Wilsey, John 1939- *IntWW 93*
Wilsey, John (Finlay Willasey) 1939- *Who 94*
Wilsey, Philip Arthur 1958- *WhoMW 93, WhoScEn 94*
Wilsford, David 1956- *ConAu 140*
Wilshin, Sunday 1905-1991 *WhoHol 92*
Wilshire, Brian 1937- *WhoScEn 94*
Wilshire, David 1943- *Who 94*
Wilske, Kenneth Ray 1935- *WhoAm 94*
Wilsker, Ira lee 1950- *WhoFI 94*
Wilson *Who 94*
Wilson, Baron 1915- *Who 94*
Wilson, A(lfred) Jeyaratnam 1928- *WrDr 94*
Wilson, A. N. 1950- *CurBio 93 [port]*
Wilson, A(ndrew) N 1950- *WrDr 94*
Wilson, Abraham 1922- *WhoAmL 94*
Wilson, Addison Joe Graves 1947- *WhoAmP 93*
Wilson, Ajita d1987 *WhoHol 92*
Wilson, Al d1932 *WhoHol 92*
Wilson, Alan (Herries) 1906- *Who 94*
Wilson, Alan Fenn 1919- *WhoWest 94*
Wilson, Alan Geoffrey 1939- *IntWW 93, Who 94*
Wilson, Alan Herries 1906- *IntWW 93*
Wilson, Alan Martin 1940- *Who 94*
Wilson, Alastair James Drysdale 1946- *Who 94*
Wilson, Albert Eugene 1927- *WhoAm 94*
Wilson, Alex *WhoHol 92*
Wilson, Alexander 1921- *IntWW 93, Who 94*
Wilson, Alexander Erwin, Jr. 1910- *WhoAm 94*
Wilson, Alexander Galbraith 1924- *IntWW 93*
Wilson, Alexander Thornton 1955- *WhoScEn 94*
Wilson, Alexandra *WhoHol 92*
Wilson, Alice d1944 *WhoHol 92*
Wilson, Alice Hornbuckle 1909- *WhoMW 93*
Wilson, Allan Byron 1948- *WhoAm 94, WhoFI 94*
Wilson, Allan Charles 1934-1991 *WhAm 10*
Wilson, Allyn 1943- *WhoWest 94*
Wilson, Alma *WhoAm 94, WhoAmL 94, WhoAmP 93*
Wilson, Almon Chapman 1924- *WhoAm 94*
Wilson, Alva L. 1922- *WhoBlA 94*
Wilson, Andrew *Who 94*
Wilson, Andrew 1923- *WrDr 94*
Wilson, (Ronald) Andrew (Fellowes) 1941- *Who 94*
Wilson, Andrew James *Who 94*
Wilson, Andrew James Ayjay 1926- *WhoWest 94*
Wilson, Andrew N. 1950- *IntWW 93, Who 94*
Wilson, Andrew Thomas 1926- *Who 94*
Wilson, Angela Dickinson 1962- *WhoMW 93*
Wilson, Angus 1913-1991 *BlmGEL, DcLB 139 [port], WhAm 10*
Wilson, Angus (Frank Johnstone) 1913- *RfGShF*
Wilson, Angus (Frank Johnstone) 1913-1991 *EncSF 93*
Wilson, Ann Dustin 1950- *WhoWest 94*
Wilson, Anna 1954- *EncSF 93*
Wilson, Anne Gawthrop 1949- *WhoAmA 93*
Wilson, Anne Glenny 1848-1930 *BlmGWL*
Wilson, Anthony 1928- *IntWW 93, Who 94*
Wilson, Anthony Joseph 1937- *Who 94*
Wilson, Anthony Keith 1939- *Who 94*
Wilson, Anthony Vincent 1936- *WhoAm 94*
Wilson, April 1948- *WhoMW 93*
Wilson, Arnold Jesse 1941- *WhoWest 94*
Wilson, Arthur Gillespie *Who 94N*
Wilson, Arthur James Cochran 1914- *Who 94, WrDr 94*
Wilson, August 1945- *AfrAmAl 6 [port], BlkWr 2, ConAu 42NR, ConDr 93, IntDcT 2 [port], IntWW 93, WhoAm 94, WhoBlA 94, WrDr 94*
Wilson, Austin *DrAPF 93*
Wilson, Austin Peter 1938- *Who 94*
Wilson, Barbara *DrAPF 93*
Wilson, Barbara 1933- *WrDr 94*
Wilson, Barbara 1951- *BlmGWL*
Wilson, Barbara (Ellen) 1950- *GayLL*
Wilson, Barbara Jean 1940- *WhoBlA 94*
Wilson, Barbara Ker 1929- *WrDr 94*
Wilson, Barbara Louise 1952- *WhoWest 94*
Wilson, Barry (Nigel) 1936- *Who 94*
Wilson, Barry H. 1948- *WhoFI 94*
Wilson, Barry William 1931- *WhoAm 94*
Wilson, Basil Wrigley 1909- *WhoAm 94*
Wilson, Ben d1930 *WhoHol 92*
Wilson, Ben 1913- *WhoAmA 93*
Wilson, Benjamin Calvin 1947- *WhoMW 93*
Wilson, Bertha 1923- *WhoAm 94*
Wilson, Betty M. 1947- *WhoIns 94*
Wilson, Betty May 1947- *WhoAm 94, WhoFI 94*
Wilson, Bill *WhoBlA 94*
Wilson, Blair Aubyn S. *Who 94*
Wilson, Blenda J. 1941- *WhoBlA 94*
Wilson, Blenda Jacqueline 1941- *WhoAm 94, WhoWest 94*
Wilson, Bobby d1933 *WhoHol 92*
Wilson, Bobby L. 1942- *WhoBlA 94*
Wilson, Brandon Laine 1953- *WhoAm 94, WhoWest 94*
Wilson, Brian David Henderson 1948- *Who 94*
Wilson, Brian Douglas 1942- *WhoAm 94*
Wilson, Brian G. 1930- *IntWW 93*
Wilson, Brian Graham 1930- *Who 94*
Wilson, Brian Harvey 1915- *Who 94*
Wilson, Brian William John Gregg 1937- *Who 94*
Wilson, Bruce Allen 1961- *WhoAmL 94*
Wilson, Bruce Brighton 1936- *WhoAm 94, WhoAmL 94, WhoFI 94*
Wilson, Bruce Everett 1955- *WhoWest 94*
Wilson, Bruce G. 1949- *WhoAm 94, WhoAmL 94*
Wilson, Bruce Nord 1954- *WhoScEn 94*
Wilson, Bruce Winston *Who 94*
Wilson, Bryan R. 1926- *WrDr 94*
Wilson, Bryan R(onald) 1926- *ConAu 41NR*
Wilson, Bryan Ronald 1926- *Who 94*
Wilson, Burton S. d1956 *WhoHol 92*
Wilson, Buster d1980 *WhoHol 92*
Wilson, C. Daniel, Jr. 1941- *WhoAm 94*
Wilson, C. Nick 1942- *WhoAm 94*
Wilson, Cal *WhoHol 92*
Wilson, Calvin T. 1928- *WhoBlA 94*
Wilson, Carey d1962 *WhoHol 92*
Wilson, Carey 1889-1962 *IntDcF 2-4*
Wilson, Carl Arthur 1947- *WhoFI 94, WhoWest 94*
Wilson, Carl L. 1921- *WhoBlA 94*
Wilson, Carl Robert 1940- *WhoScEn 94*
Wilson, Carl Weldon, Jr. 1933- *WhoFI 94*
Wilson, Carletta 1951- *BlkWr 2, ConAu 141*
Wilson, Carlos Guillermo 1941- *WhoHisp 94, WhoWest 94*
Wilson, Carole Winston 1943- *WhoAmL 94*
Wilson, Carrie Lois 1944- *WhoAmA 93*
Wilson, Carroll Lloyd 1937- *WhoBlA 94*
Wilson, Carter 1941- *WrDr 94*
Wilson, Catherine c. 1936- *NewGrDO*
Wilson, Catherine 1951- *WrDr 94*
Wilson, Catherine Mary 1945- *Who 94*
Wilson, Cecilia Rosezetta, Sister 1955- *WhoMW 93*
Wilson, Charles d1948 *WhoHol 92*
Wilson, Charles 1931- *NewGrDO*
Wilson, Charles 1933- *CngDr 93, WhoAm 94*
Wilson, Charles 1935- *IntWW 93*
Wilson, Charles (P.) 1939- *WrDr 94*
Wilson, Charles B. 1929- *WhoScEn 94*
Wilson, Charles Banks 1918- *WhoAm 94, WhoAmA 93*
Wilson, Charles E. 1886-1972 *HisDcKW*
Wilson, Charles Edward 1937- *WhoAm 94*
Wilson, Charles Edward T. *Who 94*
Wilson, Charles F. 1925-1992 *WhoBlA 94N*
Wilson, Charles Glen 1948- *WhoAm 94*
Wilson, Charles H. 1937- *WhoAmA 93*
Wilson, Charles Harrison 1941- *WhoFI 94*
Wilson, Charles Haynes 1909- *IntWW 93, Who 94*
Wilson, Charles Lee, Sr. 1941- *WhoBlA 94*
Wilson, Charles Martin 1935- *Who 94*
Wilson, Charles N. 1933- *WhoAmP 93*
Wilson, Charles Reginald 1904- *WhoAm 94*
Wilson, Charles Stanley, Jr. 1952- *WhoBlA 94*

Wilson, Charles Steven 1940- WhoAmL 94
Wilson, Charles Thomas 1941- WhoFI 94
Wilson, Charles Thomas Rees 1869-1959 WorInv
Wilson, Charles Vincent 1949- WhoMW 93
Wilson, Charles Z., Jr. 1929- WhoBlA 94
Wilson, Charles Zachary, Jr. 1929- WhoAm 94, WhoWest 94
Wilson, Cheryl-Ann WhoHol 92
Wilson, Chris WhoHol 92
Wilson, Christian Paul 1958- WhoWest 94
Wilson, Christina Mosher 1954- WhoAmP 93
Wilson, Christine 1930- WrDr 94
Wilson, Christopher Maynard 1928- Who 94
Wilson, Christopher T. 1961- WhoScEn 94
Wilson, Clarence A. 1943- WhoBlA 94
Wilson, Clarence H. d1941 WhoHol 92
Wilson, Clarence Ivan 1927- WhoAm 94
Wilson, Clarence Northon 1920- WhoBlA 94
Wilson, Clarence S., Jr. 1945- WhoAmA 93, WhoBlA 94
Wilson, Clarence Sylvester, Jr. 1945- WhoAmL 94, WhoMW 93
Wilson, Claude WhoHol 92
Wilson, Claude Raymond, Jr. 1933- WhoAm 94, WhoAmL 94
Wilson, Cleo Francine 1943- WhoBlA 94
Wilson, Clifford 1906- Who 94
Wilson, Clive Hebden 1940- Who 94
Wilson, Colin 1931- BlmGEL
Wilson, Colin (Henry) 1931- EncSF 93, WrDr 94
Wilson, Colin Alexander St. John 1922- IntWW 93, Who 94
Wilson, Colin Henry 1931- IntWW 93, Who 94, WhoAm 94
Wilson, Connie WhoAmP 93
Wilson, Connie Ann Corcoran 1945- WhoMW 93
Wilson, Connie Drake 1953- WhoBlA 94
Wilson, Constance Marilyn 1937- WhoMW 93
Wilson, Curtis Sprague 1958- WhoFI 94
Wilson, Cynthia Lindsay 1945- WhoAmA 93
Wilson, Dale Owen, Jr. 1955- WhoWest 94
Wilson, Dale William, Jr. 1956- WhoScEn 94
Wilson, Dana WhoHol 92
Wilson, Daniel Crowell 1946- WhoAmL 94
Wilson, Daniel Donald 1958- WhoFI 94
Wilson, Danton Thomas 1958- WhoBlA 94
Wilson, Dare Who 94
Wilson, (Ronald) Dare 1919- Who 94
Wilson, Darrell Glenn 1939- WhoMW 93
Wilson, Darryl Cedric 1961- WhoAm 94, WhoAmL 94
Wilson, David Who 94, WhoHol 92
Wilson, David 1928- Who 94
Wilson, David 1954- WhoBlA 94
Wilson, (Anthony) David 1927- ConAu 43NR
Wilson, (Christopher) David 1916- Who 94
Wilson, David (Mackenzie) 1931- Who 94
Wilson, David Allen 1926- WhoWest 94
Wilson, David Clifford 1942- WhoScEn 94
Wilson, David Clive IntWW 93
Wilson, David Eugene 1940- WhoWest 94
Wilson, David Henry 1937- WrDr 94
Wilson, David Lee 1941- WhoWest 94
Wilson, David Louis 1943- WhoScEn 94
Wilson, David M(ackenzie) 1931- WrDr 94
Wilson, David Mackenzie 1931- IntWW 93
Wilson, David Philip 1909- WhoAmA 93
Wilson, David S(cofield) 1931- WrDr 94
Wilson, David William 1941- Who 94
Wilson, David William 1958- WhoAmL 94
Wilson, Deborah Throop 1951- WhoWest 94
Wilson, Delano Dee 1934- WhoAm 94
Wilson, Delbert Ray 1926- WhoAm 94, WhoMW 93
Wilson, Demond WhoBlA 94
Wilson, Demond 1946- WhoHol 92
Wilson, Dennis d1983 WhoHol 92
Wilson, Derek Edward 1943- WhoScEn 94
Wilson, Des 1941- Who 94, WrDr 94
Wilson, Diana d1937 WhoHol 92
Wilson, Diane Doerge 1948- WhoFI 94
Wilson, Dianne Carol 1951- WhoMW 93
Wilson, Dick WhoHol 92
Wilson, Don d1982 WhoHol 92
Wilson, Don Whitman 1942- WhoAm 94, WhoAmP 93
Wilson, Donald Who 94
Wilson, (Robert) Donald 1922- Who 94
Wilson, Donald Edward 1936- WhoAm 94, WhoScEn 94
Wilson, Donald Eugene, Jr. 1948- WhoFI 94
Wilson, Donald Grey 1917- WhoAm 94
Wilson, Donald K., Jr. 1935- WhoIns 94
Wilson, Donald M. 1925- IntWW 93
Wilson, Donald Malcolm 1925- WhoAm 94
Wilson, Donald P. WhoBlA 94
Wilson, Donald Ray 1962- WhoAmP 93
Wilson, Donald Wallin 1938- WhoAm 94, WhoMW 93
Wilson, Donella Joyce 1951- WhoBlA 94
Wilson, Dooley d1953 WhoHol 92
Wilson, Doric 1939- ConDr 93, GayLL, WrDr 94
Wilson, Doris Evelyn 1947- WhoMW 93
Wilson, Dorothy 1909- WhoHol 92
Wilson, Dorothy Clarke 1904- WhoAm 94, WrDr 94
Wilson, Douglas Downes 1947- WhoAmL 94
Wilson, Douglas Fenn 1953- WhoAmA 93
Wilson, Douglas Larone 1940- WhoFI 94
Wilson, Douglas Lawson 1935- WhoAm 94
Wilson, Duane Isaac 1920- WhoMW 93
Wilson, Dwight Liston 1931- WhoAm 94
Wilson, E(dgar) Bright d1992 IntWW 93N
Wilson, Earl d1987 WhoHol 92
Wilson, Earl, Jr. 1932- WhoBlA 94
Wilson, Earl Lawrence 1923- WhoBlA 94
Wilson, Earl M. 1939- WhoAmP 93
Wilson, Earl Ray 1939- WhoFI 94
Wilson, Ed d1975 WhoHol 92
Wilson, Ed 1925- WhoBlA 94
Wilson, Edgar Hunter 1923-1990 WhAm 10
Wilson, Edith d1981 WhoHol 92
Wilson, Edith N. 1938- WhoBlA 94
Wilson, Edmund 1895-1972 AmCulL
Wilson, Edmund Beecher 1856-1939 WorScD
Wilson, Edna (Mae) d1960 WhoHol 92
Wilson, Edward Adrian 1872-1912 WhWE
Wilson, Edward Converse, Jr. 1928- WhoAm 94
Wilson, Edward Dotson 1954- WhoWest 94
Wilson, Edward Francis 1844-1915 EncNAR
Wilson, Edward G. d1993 NewYTBS 93 [port]
Wilson, Edward Hamilton, Jr. 1951- WhoAmP 93
Wilson, Edward N. 1925- WhoAmA 93
Wilson, Edward Nathan 1941- WhoAm 94
Wilson, Edward O(sborne) 1929- WrDr 94
Wilson, Edward Osborne 1929- EnvEnc [port], IntWW 93, WhoAm 94, WhoScEn 94
Wilson, Edwin Graves WhoAm 94
Wilson, Edwin H. d1993 NewYTBS 93
Wilson, Edwina Allison 1961- WhoAmL 94
Wilson, Effingham 1785-1868 DcNaB MP
Wilson, Eleanor WhoHol 92
Wilson, Elizabeth 1925- IntMPA 94, WhoHol 92
Wilson, Elizabeth 1936- WrDr 94
Wilson, Elizabeth 1941- WhoWomW 91
Wilson, Elizabeth Ann 1941- WhoAmP 93
Wilson, Elizabeth Karsian 1931- WhoAmP 93
Wilson, Elsie Jane d1965 WhoHol 92
Wilson, Emily Herring DrAPF 93
Wilson, Emily Marie 1951- WhoWest 94
Wilson, Eric DrAPF 93
Wilson, Eric Charles Twelves 1912- Who 94
Wilson, Eric Randall 1964- WhoWest 94
Wilson, Ernest 1925- WhoBlA 94
Wilson, Ernest 1936- WhoBlA 94
Wilson, Ernest Henry 1876-1930 DcNaB MP
Wilson, Ernest Staton, Jr. 1927- WhoAm 94
Wilson, Ervin McDonald 1928- WhoWest 94
Wilson, Esther Marie 1932- WhoAmP 93
Wilson, Ethel 1888-1980 BlmGWL
Wilson, Eugene Rolland 1938- WhoAm 94
Wilson, Eugene T. 1924- WhoAmP 93
Wilson, Evan Carter 1953- WhoAmA 93
Wilson, Evan Roy 1943- WhoMW 93
Wilson, Ewen Maclellan 1944- WhoAm 94, WhoFI 94
Wilson, F. Leon 1953- WhoBlA 94
Wilson, F(rancis) Paul 1946- EncSF 93, WrDr 94
Wilson, Flip 1933- AfrAmAl 6 [port], IntMPA 94, WhoAm 94, WhoCom [port], WhoHol 92
Wilson, Flip (Clerow) 1933- WhoBlA 94
Wilson, Floyd Edward, Jr. 1935- WhoBlA 94
Wilson, Frances Engle 1922- WrDr 94
Wilson, Francis d1935 WhoHol 92
Wilson, Francis Paul 1946- WhoAm 94
Wilson, Frank WhoHol 92
Wilson, Frank d1956 WhoHol 92
Wilson, Frank Douglas 1928- WhoWest 94
Wilson, Frank Edward 1940- WhoBlA 94
Wilson, Frank Elmore 1909- WhoAm 94
Wilson, Frank Fredrick, III 1936- WhoBlA 94
Wilson, Frank Henry 1935- WhoScEn 94
Wilson, Frank Richard 1920- Who 94
Wilson, Franklin Leondus, III 1941- WhoAm 94
Wilson, Fred 1954- WhoAmA 93
Wilson, Fred Eugene 1943- WhoAmL 94
Wilson, Frederic Sandford 1944- WhoFI 94
Wilson, Frederick A. 1946- WhoBlA 94
Wilson, Frederick Allen 1937- WhoAm 94
Wilson, Gahan 1930- WhoAm 94
Wilson, Gary D. DrAPF 93
Wilson, Gary Dean 1943- WhoAm 94, WhoAmL 94
Wilson, Gary L. WhoAm 94, WhoFI 94
Wilson, Geoffrey 1929- Who 94
Wilson, (Brian) Geoffrey 1920- WrDr 94
Wilson, Geoffrey Alan 1934- Who 94
Wilson, Geoffrey Hazlitt 1929- IntWW 93, Who 94
Wilson, Geoffrey Masterman 1910- Who 94
Wilson, Geoffrey Studholme 1913- Who 94
Wilson, George Who 94
Wilson, George d1954 WhoHol 92
Wilson, George 1631-1711 DcNaB MP
Wilson, (William) George 1921- Who 94
Wilson, George G. 1929- WhoBlA 94
Wilson, George Lewis 1930-1987 WhoAmA 93N
Wilson, George McConnell 1913- WhoMW 93
Wilson, George Patton 1943- WhoFI 94
Wilson, George Peter 1939- WhoScEn 94
Wilson, George Pritchard Harvey 1918 Who 94
Wilson, George Simpson, III 1932- WhoAmL 94
Wilson, George Washington 1823-1893 DcNaB MP
Wilson, George Wharton 1923- WhoAm 94
Wilson, George Wilton 1928- WhoAm 94, WrDr 94
Wilson, Georges WhoHol 92
Wilson, Georges 1921- IntWW 93
Wilson, Gerald Alan 1951- WhoWest 94
Wilson, Gerald Einar 1922- WhoAm 94
Wilson, Gerald Robertson 1939- Who 94
Wilson, Gerald Stanley 1918- WhoBlA 94
Wilson, Gilbert 1908- Who 94
Wilson, Gillian Brenda Who 94
Wilson, Gina 1943- WrDr 94
Wilson, Glen Parten 1922- WhoAm 94
Wilson, Glenn 1929- WhoAm 94
Wilson, Glenn Ashby 1918- WhoAmP 93
Wilson, Gordon IntWW 93, Who 94
Wilson, (Robert) Gordon 1938- IntWW 93, Who 94
Wilson, Gordon Russel 1947- WhoWest 94
Wilson, Gordon Wallace 1926- Who 94
Wilson, Graeme McDonald d1992 Who 94N
Wilson, Graham Alastair 1949- WhoFI 94
Wilson, Graham McGregor 1944- WhoAm 94
Wilson, Grant Paul, Jr. 1943- WhoBlA 94
Wilson, Greer Dawson 1943- WhoBlA 94
Wilson, Gregory S. 1954- WhoIns 94
Wilson, Gregory Scott 1960- WhoMW 93
Wilson, (John) Grosvenor 1866- EncSF 93
Wilson, Grover Cleveland, Jr. 1922-1987 WhAm 10
Wilson, Guy Murray 1950- Who 94
Wilson, Hal d1933 WhoHol 92
Wilson, Hamline Cassard, Jr. 1937- WhoFI 94
Wilson, Harold 1916- HisWorL [port], WrDr 94
Wilson, Harold 1931- Who 94
Wilson, (James) Harold IntWW 93
Wilson, Harold Arthur Cooper B. Who 94
Wilson, Harold Frederick 1922- WhoAm 94
Wilson, Harold Mark 1959- WhoScEn 94
Wilson, Harold Wray 1938- WhoMW 93
Wilson, Harriet E. BlmGWL
Wilson, Harriett C(harlotte) 1916- WrDr 94
Wilson, Harrison B. 1928- WhoBlA 94
Wilson, Harry Who 94
Wilson, Harry d1978 WhoHol 92
Wilson, Harry Burgoyme 1917- WhoAm 94
Wilson, Harry Cochrane 1945- WhoAm 94
Wilson, Harry L. 1942- WhoAm 94, WhoAmL 94
Wilson, Hazel Forrow Simmons 1927- WhoBlA 94
Wilson, Helen 1884-1974 WhoAmA 93N
Wilson, Helen Frances 1921- WhoAmP 93
Wilson, Helen Louise 1921- WhoAmP 93
Wilson, Helen Marie 1930- WhoWest 94
Wilson, Helen Tolson WhoBlA 94
Wilson, Helena WhoAmA 93
Wilson, Helene d1981 WhoHol 92
Wilson, Henry, Jr. 1938- WhoBlA 94
Wilson, Henry Arthur, Jr. 1939- WhoFI 94, WhoMW 93
Wilson, Henry Braithwaite 1911- Who 94
Wilson, Henry Wallace 1923- Who 94
Wilson, Herschel Manuel 1930- WhoAm 94, WhoWest 94
Wilson, Hugh 1943- IntMPA 94
Wilson, Hugh A. 1940- WhoBlA 94
Wilson, Hugh Mal 1930- WhoAmL 94, WhoAmP 93
Wilson, Hugh Shannon 1926- WhoAm 94
Wilson, Hugh Steven 1947- WhoAm 94, WhoAmL 94
Wilson, Hughlyne Perkins 1931- WhoBlA 94
Wilson, Ian 1901- WhoHol 92
Wilson, Ian D. Who 94
Wilson, Ian E. 1943- WhoAm 94
Wilson, Ian Holroyde 1925- WhoFI 94
Wilson, Ian Matthew 1926- Who 94
Wilson, Ian Robert 1929- WhoAm 94
Wilson, Ilona WhoHol 92
Wilson, Irene K. DrAPF 93
Wilson, J. Arbuthnot EncSF 93
Wilson, J.R. 1949- WhoWest 94
Wilson, J. Ray 1937- WhoBlA 94
Wilson, J(ohn) Tuzo 1908-1993 ConAu 141, CurBio 93N
Wilson, J. Tylee 1931- WhoAm 94
Wilson, Jack EncNAR
Wilson, Jack d1966 WhoHol 92
Wilson, Jack 1926- WhoAmP 93
Wilson, Jack 1933- WhoAm 94, WhoScEn 94
Wilson, Jack Fredrick 1920- WhoAm 94
Wilson, Jack Martin 1945- WhoAm 94
Wilson, Jackie 1934-1984 AfrAmAl 6 [port]
Wilson, Jacqueline (Aitken) 1945- WrDr 94
Wilson, Jacqueline Prophet 1949- WhoBlA 94
Wilson, James Who 94
Wilson, James 1742-1798 WhAmRev
Wilson, James 1922- NewGrDO, Who 94
Wilson, (Alexander) James 1921- Who 94
Wilson, James (William Douglas) 1990- Who 94
Wilson, James Alan 1951- WhoMW 93
Wilson, James Barker 1926- WhoAmL 94
Wilson, James Boyd 1942- WhAm 10
Wilson, James Charles, Jr. 1947- WhoAmL 94
Wilson, James Davis 1937- WhoBlA 94
Wilson, James Edward 1914- WhAm 10
Wilson, James Edward 1930- WhoAm 94
Wilson, James Eldon 1948- WhoAmL 94
Wilson, James Eric 1970- WhoMW 93
Wilson, James Ernest 1915- WhoAm 94, WhoWest 94
Wilson, James Erwin 1940- WhoMW 93
Wilson, James Gregory 1950- WhoAmP 93
Wilson, James Hargrove, Jr. 1920- WhoAm 94, WhoAmL 94
Wilson, James John 1933- WhoFI 94
Wilson, James Lawrence 1936- WhoAm 94, WhoFI 94
Wilson, James Lee 1920- WhoAm 94, WhoScEn 94
Wilson, James lee 1947- WhoMW 93
Wilson, James Maxwell Glover 1913- Who 94
Wilson, James Michael 1958- WhoFI 94
Wilson, James Milton, III 1934- WhoAm 94
Wilson, James Newman 1927- WhoAm 94
Wilson, James Noel 1919- Who 94
Wilson, James Paris 1907- WhoBlA 94
Wilson, James Quinn WhoAm 94
Wilson, James Quinn 1931- WrDr 94
Wilson, James Ray 1930- WhoFI 94, WhoMW 93
Wilson, James Richard 1953- WhoScEn 94
Wilson, James Rigg 1941- WhoAm 94

Wilson, James Robert 1927- *WhoAm 94, WhoWest 94*
Wilson, James Robert 1948- *WhoWest 94*
Wilson, James Rodney 1937- *WhoMW 93*
Wilson, James Stewart 1909- *Who 94*
Wilson, James William 1928- *WhoAm 94, WhoAmL 94, WhoFI 94*
Wilson, Jane 1924- *WhoAm 94, WhoAmA 93*
Wilson, Janet Lynn 1959- *WhoMW 93*
Wilson, Janice d1982 *WhoHol 92*
Wilson, Janie Menchaca 1936- *WhoAm 94, WhoHisp 94*
Wilson, Janis *WhoHol 92*
Wilson, Jay D. 1947- *WhoWest 94*
Wilson, Jean Donald 1932- *IntWW 93, WhoAm 94*
Wilson, Jean L. 1928- *WhoAmP 93*
Wilson, Jean S. *WhoAmA 93*
Wilson, Jean Spann 1929- *WhAm 10*
Wilson, Jeanette Kurtz 1929- *WhoWest 94*
Wilson, Jeanna *WhoHol 92*
Wilson, Jeannie *WhoHol 92*
Wilson, Jeffrey Dale 1955- *WhoAmL 94*
Wilson, Jeffrey R. *WhoBlA 94*
Wilson, Jeril B. 1938- *WhoAmP 93*
Wilson, Jimmie L. *WhoBlA 94*
Wilson, Jimmie L. 1945- *WhoAmP 93*
Wilson, Jimmy L. *WhoBlA 94*
Wilson, Joan Hoff 1937- *WrDr 94*
Wilson, Joe *Who 94*
Wilson, Joe L. 1946- *WhoAmP 93*
Wilson, Joe Mack 1919- *WhoAmP 93*
Wilson, John 1785-1854 *BlmGEL*
Wilson, John 1800-1849 *NewGrDO*
Wilson, John c. 1840-1901 *EncNAR*
Wilson, John 1922- *AfrAmAl 6, WhoAm 94, WhoAmA 93, WhoBlA 94*
Wilson, John (Boyd) 1928- *WrDr 94*
Wilson, John (Foster) 1919- *Who 94, WrDr 94*
Wilson, John A. 1943-1993 *WhoBlA 94N*
Wilson, John Alan 1917-1991 *WhAm 10*
Wilson, John Anthony 1938- *WhoScEn 94*
Wilson, John B. 1959- *WhoFI 94*
Wilson, John Benedict 1959- *WhoAm 94*
Wilson, John Burgess 1917- *WrDr 94*
Wilson, John Cowles 1921- *WhoAm 94*
Wilson, John D. 1931- *WhoAm 94*
Wilson, John David 1934- *WhoAmA 93*
Wilson, John Donald 1913- *WhoAm 94*
Wilson, John E. 1932- *WhoBlA 94*
Wilson, John Eric 1919- *WhoAm 94, WhoScEn 94*
Wilson, John Fletcher 1923- *WhAm 10*
Wilson, John Foster 1919- *IntWW 93*
Wilson, John Francis 1937- *WhoWest 94*
Wilson, John Gardiner 1913- *Who 94*
Wilson, John Graham 1911- *Who 94*
Wilson, John Grover 1945- *WhoFI 94*
Wilson, John Hewitt 1924- *Who 94*
Wilson, John Hill Tucker 1934- *WhoAm 94*
Wilson, John James 1927- *WhoAm 94, WhoAmL 94, WhoWest 94*
Wilson, John James 1932- *Who 94*
Wilson, John Kenneth 1953- *WhoScEn 94*
Wilson, John Lewis 1943- *WhoAm 94, WhoWest 94*
Wilson, John Martindale d1993 *Who 94N*
Wilson, John Michael 1946- *WhoIns 94*
Wilson, John Morgan 1942- *WhoAmL 94*
Wilson, John Murray 1926- *Who 94*
Wilson, John Oliver 1938- *WhoAm 94*
Wilson, John P. 1923- *IntWW 93*
Wilson, John Page 1922- *WhoFI 94*
Wilson, John Pasley 1933- *WhoWest 94*
Wilson, John Richard Meredith 1944- *WhoWest 94*
Wilson, John Ross 1920- *WhoAm 94*
Wilson, John Samuel 1916- *WhoAm 94*
Wilson, John Spark d1993 *Who 94N*
Wilson, John Stuart Gladstone 1916- *Who 94, WrDr 94*
Wilson, John T., Jr. 1924- *WhoBlA 94*
Wilson, John Truesdell 1898- *WhAm 10*
Wilson, John Tuzo d1993 *IntWW 93N*
Wilson, John Tuzo 1908-1993 *NewYTBS 93 [port]*
Wilson, John Veitch D. *Who 94*
Wilson, John W. 1928- *WhoBlA 94*
Wilson, John Warley 1936- *Who 94*
Wilson, John Warwick 1937- *Who 94*
Wilson, Johnnie Edward 1944- *AfrAmG [port]*
Wilson, Johnniece Marshall 1944- *ConAu 142, SmATA 75 [port]*
Wilson, Johnny Leaverne 1954- *WhoBlA 94*
Wilson, Jon 1955- *WhoBlA 94*
Wilson, Jon Louis 1946- *WhoAmL 94*
Wilson, Jon Stephen 1935- *WhoWest 94*
Wilson, Jonathan Charles, Jr. 1949- *WhoBlA 94*
Wilson, Joseph *DrAPF 93*
Wilson, Joseph Albert 1922- *Who 94*
Wilson, Joseph Charles 1952- *WhoWest 94*
Wilson, Joseph Charles, IV *WhoAmP 93*
Wilson, Joseph Charles, IV 1949- *WhoAm 94*
Wilson, Joseph F. 1951- *WhoBlA 94*
Wilson, Joseph Henry, Jr. 1966- *WhoBlA 94*
Wilson, Joseph Lopez 1960- *WhoAmL 94*
Wilson, Joseph Morris, III 1945- *WhoAmL 94*
Wilson, Josephine d1990 *WhoHol 92*
Wilson, Josephine Evadna *WhoAmP 93*
Wilson, Josephine Frances 1937- *WhoWest 94*
Wilson, Joy Johnson 1954- *WhoBlA 94*
Wilson, Judy *WhoHol 92*
Wilson, Judy Vantrease 1939- *WhoAm 94*
Wilson, Julie 1924- *WhoHol 92*
Wilson, Julie Joyce 1962- *WhoFI 94*
Wilson, June 1925- *WrDr 94*
Wilson, June 1946- *WhoAmA 93*
Wilson, Justin Potter 1945- *WhoAmL 94*
Wilson, Karen Lee 1949- *WhoAmA 93*
Wilson, Karen Lee 1949- *WhoAm 94, WhoMW 93*
Wilson, Karen LeRohl 1950- *WhoAmL 94*
Wilson, Kathy Kay 1961- *WhoFI 94, WhoMW 93*
Wilson, Kay E. *WhoAmA 93*
Wilson, Keith *DrAPF 93*
Wilson, Keith 1927- *WrDr 94*
Wilson, Keith Crookston 1953- *WhoScEn 94*
Wilson, Keith O. 1925- *WhoAmP 93*
Wilson, Ken d1993 *NewYTBS 93*
Wilson, Kenneth Geddes 1936- *IntWW 93, Who 94, WhoAm 94, WhoMW 93, WhoScEn 94*
Wilson, Kenneth Jay 1944- *WhoAm 94*
Wilson, Kevin J. *WhoHol 92*
Wilson, "Kid" Wesley d1958 *WhoHol 92*
Wilson, Kim Robin 1959- *WhoMW 93*
Wilson, Kimberly Jo 1963- *WhoFI 94*
Wilson, Kirk George 1951- *WhoAm 94, WhoWest 94*
Wilson, Kirk Stephen 1950- *WhoMW 93*
Wilson, Kristin Marie 1947- *WhoWest 94*
Wilson, Lambert 1959- *WhoHol 92*
Wilson, Lance Henry 1948- *WhoAmP 93, WhoBlA 94*
Wilson, Lanford 1937- *WhoAm 94, WrDr 94*
Wilson, Lanford (Eugene) 1937- *ConDr 93, GayLL, IntDcT 2*
Wilson, Larry *ProFbHF [port]*
Wilson, Lauren Ross 1936- *WhoAm 94*
Wilson, Laval S. 1935- *WhoBlA 94*
Wilson, Lawrence Alexander 1935- *WhoFI 94*
Wilson, Lawrence C. 1932- *WhoBlA 94*
Wilson, Lawrence E., III 1951- *WhoBlA 94*
Wilson, Lawrence Frank 1938- *WhoAm 94*
Wilson, Lee Britt 1960- *WhoScEn 94*
Wilson, Leigh Allison *DrAPF 93*
Wilson, Leland Earl 1925- *WhoFI 94*
Wilson, Lennox Norwood 1932- *WhoAm 94*
Wilson, Leon E., Jr. 1945- *WhoBlA 94*
Wilson, Leonard D. 1933- *WhoBlA 94*
Wilson, Leonard Gilchrist 1928- *WhoAm 94*
Wilson, Leonard Richard 1906- *WhoScEn 94*
Wilson, Leroy 1928- *WhoAm 94*
Wilson, Leroy, Jr. 1939- *WhoBlA 94*
Wilson, Leroy, III 1951- *WhoBlA 94*
Wilson, Leslie 1941- *WhoAm 94*
Wilson, Leslie William 1918- *Who 94*
Wilson, Lester d1993 *NewYTBS 93*
Wilson, Lester Arnauld, III 1948- *WhoAmL 94*
Wilson, LeVon Edward 1954- *WhoAmL 94*
Wilson, Lewis Lansing 1932- *WhoAmP 93, WhoFI 94*
Wilson, Linda A. 1943- *WhoAmL 94*
Wilson, Linda S. 1936- *IntWW 93*
Wilson, Linda Smith 1936- *WhoAm 94*
Wilson, Lionel J. 1915- *WhoBlA 94*
Wilson, Lloyd Lee 1947- *WhoAm 94*
Wilson, Logan 1907-1990 *WhAm 10*
Wilson, Lois d1988 *WhoHol 92*
Wilson, Lois (M.) 1927- *WrDr 94*
Wilson, Lois M. 1927- *WhoAm 94*
Wilson, Lois Mayfield 1924- *WhoWest 94*
Wilson, Lois Miriam 1927- *IntWW 93*
Wilson, Lorraine M. 1931- *WhoMW 93*
Wilson, Louis Hugh 1920- *IntWW 93*
Wilson, Lucy Jean 1938- *WhoAm 94*
Wilson, Lucy R. 1930- *WhoBlA 94*
Wilson, Lynn Anthony 1939- *Who 94*
Wilson, Lynton Ronald 1940- *WhoAm 94, WhoFI 94*
Wilson, M. Sue 1949- *WhoAmL 94*
Wilson, Madelaine Majette 1920- *WhoBlA 94*
Wilson, Malcolm 1914- *WhoAm 94*
Wilson, Malcolm Campbell 1942- *WhoAm 94, WhoFI 94*
Wilson, Malin 1947- *WhoAmA 93*
Wilson, Mannie L. *WhoBlA 94*
Wilson, Marc F. 1941- *WhoAmA 93*
Wilson, Marc Fraser 1941- *WhoAm 94, WhoMW 93*
Wilson, Marcus 1968- *WhoBlA 94*
Wilson, Margaret Bush 1919- *WhoAm 94, WhoBlA 94*
Wilson, Margaret Dauler 1939- *WhoAm 94*
Wilson, Margaret F. 1932- *WhoBlA 94*
Wilson, Margaret Mary 1950- *WhoMW 93*
Wilson, Margaret Sullivan 1924- *WhoAmP 93*
Wilson, Margery d1986 *WhoHol 92*
Wilson, Margot Lois 1957- *WhoAm 94*
Wilson, Marie d1972 *WhoHol 92*
Wilson, Marily Sharronn 1942- *WhoFI 94*
Wilson, Marjorie Price *WhoAm 94*
Wilson, Mark K. 1943- *WhoAmL 94*
Wilson, Mark Kent 1947- *WhoScEn 94*
Wilson, Markly 1947- *WhoBlA 94*
Wilson, Martha *DrAPF 93*
Wilson, Mary 1930- *WrDr 94*
Wilson, Mary 1944- *AfrAmAl 6*
Wilson, Mary Catherine 1962- *WhoMW 93*
Wilson, Mary Elizabeth 1942- *WhoScEn 94*
Wilson, Mary Louise *WhoHol 92*
Wilson, Mary Louise 1940- *WhoAm 94*
Wilson, Mary Louise Owens 1934- *WhoMW 93*
Wilson, Mathew John Anthony 1935- *Who 94*
Wilson, Mathew Kent 1920- *WhoAm 94*
Wilson, Matthew Frederick 1956- *WhoAm 94, WhoWest 94*
Wilson, Melissa Anne 1968- *WhoAmA 93*
Wilson, Melvin Nathaniel 1948- *WhoScEn 94*
Wilson, Michael *WhoBlA 94*
Wilson, Michael 1914-1978 *IntDcF 2-4*
Wilson, Michael 1942- *WhoBlA 94, WhoMW 93*
Wilson, Michael Alan 1947- *WhoFI 94*
Wilson, Michael Anthony 1936- *Who 94*
Wilson, Michael Bruce 1943- *WhoAmL 94, WhoWest 94*
Wilson, Michael E. 1951- *WhoAmL 94*
Wilson, Michael Gregg 1942- *WhoWest 94*
Wilson, Michael Holcombe 1937- *IntWW 93*
Wilson, Michael Joseph 1953- *WhoFI 94*
Wilson, Michael K. 1944- *WhoAmP 93*
Wilson, Michael Moureau 1952- *WhoAmL 94*
Wilson, Michael Summer 1943- *Who 94*
Wilson, Michelle *WhoHol 92*
Wilson, Miles *DrAPF 93*
Wilson, Millard K. d1933 *WhoHol 92*
Wilson, Millie 1948- *WhoAmA 93*
Wilson, Milner Bradley, III 1933- *WhoAm 94*
Wilson, Milton 1915- *WhoBlA 94*
Wilson, Minter Lowther, Jr. 1925- *WhoAm 94*
Wilson, Miriam Geisendorfer 1922- *WhoAm 94*
Wilson, Monti Robert 1945- *WhoMW 93*
Wilson, Mookie (William Hayward) 1956- *WhoBlA 94*
Wilson, Muriel *Who 94*
Wilson, (Katherine) Muriel (Irwin) 1920- *Who 94*
Wilson, Myron Robert, Jr. 1932- *WhoAm 94, WhoScEn 94, WhoWest 94*
Wilson, Nahum Thomas, IV 1953- *WhAm 10*
Wilson, Nancy 1931- *WhoHol 92*
Wilson, Nancy 1937- *WhoAm 94, WhoBlA 94*
Wilson, Natarsha Juliet 1961- *WhoBlA 94*
Wilson, Ned *WhoHol 92*
Wilson, Neil *WhoHol 92*
Wilson, Neil 1944- *WrDr 94*
Wilson, Neil 1956- *NewGrDO*
Wilson, Nelson 1945- *WhoAm 94*
Wilson, Nicholas (Allan Roy) 1945- *Who 94*
Wilson, Nicholas Jon 1947- *WhoAmA 93*
Wilson, Nick 1942- *WhoAmP 93*
Wilson, Nigel Guy 1935- *IntWW 93, Who 94*
Wilson, Nixon Albert 1930- *WhoMW 93*
Wilson, Norma Clark 1946- *WhoMW 93*
Wilson, Norma F. 1940- *WhoHisp 94*
Wilson, Norma June 1940- *WhoBlA 94*
Wilson, Norman George d1992 *Who 94N*
Wilson, Norman Ward 1948- *WhoIns 94*
Wilson, Olin C. 1909- *IntWW 93*
Wilson, Olin Chaddock 1909- *WhoAm 94*
Wilson, Olivia Hodge d1976 *WhoHol 92*
Wilson, Olly W. 1937- *AfrAmAl 6, WhoBlA 94*
Wilson, Ora Brown 1937- *WhoBlA 94*
Wilson, Orme 1885-1966 *WhoAmA 93N*
Wilson, Owen Meredith, Jr. 1939- *WhoAm 94*
Wilson, Pat(ricia Elsie) 1910- *WrDr 94*
Wilson, Patricia A. 1948- *WhoBlA 94*
Wilson, Patricia I. 1940- *WhoBlA 94*
Wilson, Patricia Jane 1946- *WhoAm 94*
Wilson, Patricia Jervis 1951- *WhoBlA 94*
Wilson, Patricia Marie 1942- *WhoMW 93*
Wilson, Patrick Elliott 1934- *WhoIns 94*
Wilson, Patrick Michael Ernest David McN. *Who 94*
Wilson, Paul C., Jr. *WhoAm 94*
Wilson, Paul Edwin 1913- *WhoAm 94*
Wilson, Paul Hastings *DrAPF 93*
Wilson, Paul Holliday, Jr. 1942- *WhoAm 94, WhoAmL 94*
Wilson, Paul Lowell 1951- *WhoAmL 94*
Wilson, Paul Wayne 1933- *WhoFI 94*
Wilson, Paul Wayne 1958- *WhoFI 94*
Wilson, Peggy Ann 1945- *WhoAmP 93*
Wilson, Peggy Mayfield Dunlap 1927- *WhoAmP 93*
Wilson, Pete 1933- *IntWW 93, WhoAm 94, WhoAmP 93, WhoWest 94*
Wilson, Peter Michael 1948- *WhoFI 94*
Wilson, Peter Northcote 1928- *Who 94*
Wilson, Peter Scott 1955- *WhoAmL 94*
Wilson, Peter Sinclair 1958- *WhoFI 94*
Wilson, Philip Alexander P. *Who 94*
Wilson, Philip Duncan, Jr. 1920- *WhoAm 94*
Wilson, Phillip (John) 1922- *WrDr 94*
Wilson, Phyllis Starr 1928- *WhAm 10*
Wilson, Porterfield 1933- *WhAm 10*
Wilson, Prince E. *WhoBlA 94*
Wilson, Quentin Charles 1955- *WhoAmP 93*
Wilson, Quintin Campbell 1913- *Who 94*
Wilson, R. Dale 1949- *WhoAm 94*
Wilson, R. Merinda D. 1952- *WhoAm 94*
Wilson, Ralph Edwin 1921- *WhoAm 94*
Wilson, Ralph L. 1934- *WhoBlA 94*
Wilson, Ramon B. 1922- *WhoAm 94*
Wilson, Ramona C. *DrAPF 93*
Wilson, Randolph Preston 1945- *WhoMW 93*
Wilson, Ray F. 1926- *WhoBlA 94*
Wilson, Raymond 1925- *Who 94*
Wilson, Raymond Clark 1915- *WhoAm 94*
Wilson, Raymond Gale 1932- *WhoMW 93*
Wilson, Rebecca Sue 1950- *WhoMW 93*
Wilson, Reginald (Holmes) 1905- *Who 94*
Wilson, Rhys Thaddeus 1955- *WhoAmL 94, WhoFI 94*
Wilson, Richard 1920-1987 *EncSF 93*
Wilson, Richard 1926- *WhoScEn 94*
Wilson, Richard 1936- *WhoHol 92*
Wilson, Richard Allan 1927- *WhoAm 94*
Wilson, Richard Anderson 1933- *WhoMW 93*
Wilson, Richard Brian 1944- *WhoAmA 93*
Wilson, Richard Christian 1921- *WhoAm 94*
Wilson, Richard Cushman 1953- *WhoAmP 93*
Wilson, Richard Dale 1933- *WhoFI 94*
Wilson, Richard Edward 1941- *WhoAm 94*
Wilson, Richard Harold 1930- *WhoAm 94*
Wilson, Richard Middlewood 1908- *Who 94*
Wilson, Richard Randolph 1950- *WhoAmL 94, WhoWest 94*
Wilson, Richard Thomas James 1942- *Who 94*
Wilson, Richard Voorhees 1951- *WhoFI 94*
Wilson, Rickey Lee 1954- *WhoMW 93*
Wilson, Rita *WhoHol 92*
Wilson, Rita P. 1946- *WhoBlA 94*
Wilson, Robert *WhoAmA 93, WhoFI 94*
Wilson, Robert 1927- *IntWW 93, Who 94*
Wilson, Robert 1941- *NewGrDO*
Wilson, Robert, Jr. 1955- *WhoAmP 93*
Wilson, Robert Alan 1949- *WhoAmA 93*
Wilson, Robert Albert 1936- *WhoFI 94*
Wilson, Robert Allen 1936- *WhoAm 94*
Wilson, Robert Anton 1932- *EncSF 93, WrDr 94*
Wilson, Robert Burton 1936- *WhoAm 94*
Wilson, Robert Bynum 1943- *WhoAmL 94*
Wilson, Robert Byron 1936- *WhoMW 93*
Wilson, Robert Charles 1953- *EncSF 93*
Wilson, Robert Charles, Jr. 1953- *WhoMW 93*
Wilson, Robert Dale 1952- *WhoAmP 93*
Wilson, Robert E. 1943- *WhoAmL 94*
Wilson, Robert Foster 1926- *WhoAmL 94, WhoMW 93*

Winarski, Daniel James 1948- *WhoWest 94*
Winawer, Sidney Jerome 1931- *WhoAm 94*
Winberg, Claes Ulrik 1925- *WhAm 10*
Winberg, (Sven) Hakan 1931- *IntWW 93*
Winbergh, Gosta 1943- *NewGrDO*
Winberry, Phillip B. 1944- *WhoAmL 94*
Winbigler, Paul Hobert 1943- *WhoMW 93*
Winbish, Doug
See Living Colour *News 93-3*
Winborn, Marsha (Lynn) 1947- *SmATA 75 [port]*
Winborn, Terry Lee 1950- *WhoAm 94, WhoAmL 94*
Winborne, George E. 1937- *WhoAmP 93*
Winburn, B. J. 1918- *WhoBlA 94*
Winburn, Gene Mack 1937- *WhoAmL 94*
Winburn, John T. 1942- *WhoAmL 94*
Winbush, Clarence, Jr. 1948- *WhoBlA 94*
Wincek, Mark D. 1950- *WhoAm 94*
Wincer, Simon *IntMPA 94*
Wince-Smith, Deborah L. *WhoAm 94*
Winch, David Monk 1933- *WhoAm 94*
Winch, Donald Norman 1935- *IntWW 93, Who 94*
Winch, Peter (Guy) 1926- *WrDr 94*
Winch, Peter Guy 1926- *IntWW 93*
Winch, Terence *DrAPF 93*
Winchell, Paul 1922- *WhoHol 92*
Winchell, Paul 1924- *IntMPA 94*
Winchell, Robert Allen 1945- *WhoWest 94*
Winchell, Roderick d1968 *WhoHol 92*
Winchell, Walter d1972 *WhoHol 92*
Winchell, William Olin 1933- *WhoAmL 94, WhoFI 94, WhoScEn 94*
Winchester, Archdeacon of *Who 94*
Winchester, Bishop of 1926- *Who 94*
Winchester, Dean of *Who 94*
Winchester, Marquess of 1941- *Who 94*
Winchester, Albert McCombs 1908- *WhoAm 94*
Winchester, Alice 1907- *WhoAmA 93*
Winchester, Arna-Maria *WhoHol 92*
Winchester, Barbara d1968 *WhoHol 92*
Winchester, Elhanan 1751-1797 *DcAmReB 2*
Winchester, Ian Sinclair 1931- *Who 94*
Winchester, Jack *ConAu 43NR*
Winchester, Jack 1936- *WrDr 94*
Winchester, James 1752-1826 *WhAmRev*
Winchester, Kennard *WhoBlA 94*
Winchester, Lyman Gene 1935- *WhoAmP 93*
Winchester, Robert C. 1945- *WhoAmP 93*
Winchester, Simon 1944- *WrDr 94*
Winchester, Warren Howey 1932- *WhoFI 94*
Winchilsea, Earl of 1936- *Who 94*
Winchilsea, Anne Finch, Countess of 1661-1720 *BlmGEL*
Winckles, Kenneth 1918- *Who 94*
Wincor, Michael Z. 1946- *WhoAm 94, WhoScEn 94, WhoWest 94*
Wincott, Jeff 1956- *WhoHol 92*
Wincott, Michael *WhoHol 92*
Wincup, G. Kim 1944- *WhoAm 94*
Wind, Barry 1942- *ConAu 140*
Wind, Herbert Hamilton, Jr. 1915- *WhoAmP 93*
Wind, Herbert Warren 1916- *WhoAm 94*
Wind, Yoram Jerry 1938- *WhoAm 94*
Winde, Beatrice *WhoHol 92*
Windebank, Anthony J. *WhoMW 93*
Windeknecht, Margaret Brake 1936- *WhoAmA 93*
Windelen, Heinrich 1921- *IntWW 93*
Windeler, Leon A. 1910- *WhoAmP 93*
Windell, Violet Bruner 1943- *WhoAmA 93*
Windels, Paul, Jr. 1921- *WhoAm 94, WhoAmL 94, WhoFI 94*
Winder, Alfred M. *WhoBlA 94*
Winder, Barbara *DrAPF 93*
Winder, Clarence Leland 1921- *WhoAm 94*
Winder, David Kent 1932- *WhoAm 94, WhoAmL 94, WhoWest 94*
Winder, Levin 1757-1819 *WhAmRev*
Winder, Robert James 1959- *Who 94*
Winder, Robert Owen 1934- *WhoAm 94*
Winder, Sammy 1959- *WhoBlA 94*
Windes, James Dudley 1937- *WhoScEn 94*
Windeyer, Brian (Wellingham) 1904- *Who 94*
Windeyer, Brian Wellingham 1904- *IntWW 93*
Windfeldt, Tom A. 1949- *WhoFI 94*
Windfohr, Robert Fralry 1894- *WhAm 10*
Windgassen, Wolfgang 1914-1974 *NewGrDO [port]*
Windhager, Erich Ernst 1928- *WhoAm 94, WhoScEn 94*
Windham, Donald 1920- *WrDr 94*
Windham, Douglas M(acArthur) 1943- *ConAu 43NR*
Windham, Edward James 1950- *WhoWest 94*
Windham, John Franklin 1948- *WhoAmL 94*
Windham, Revish 1940- *WhoBlA 94*
Windham, Thomas *WhoAm 94*
Windham, William Ashe Dymoke 1926- *Who 94*
Windham, William Russell S. *Who 94*
Windhausen, Rodolfo A. 1944- *WhoHisp 94*
Windheim, Marek d1960 *WhoHol 92*
Windhorst, Fritz H. 1935- *WhoAmP 93*
Windhorst, John William, Jr. 1940- *WhoAm 94*
Windhorst, Steve 1957- *WhoAmP 93*
Winding, Victor 1929- *WhoHol 92*
Windingstad, Harold Oliver, Jr. 1929- *WhoAmP 93*
Windisch, Cheryl Lee 1946- *WhoMW 93*
Windlaus, Adolf Otto Reinhold *WorScD*
Windle, Alan Hardwick 1942- *Who 94*
Windle, John Mark *WhoAmP 93*
Windle, John Taylor 1901- *WhAm 10*
Windle, Terence Leslie William 1926- *Who 94*
Windler, Donald Richard 1940- *WhoScEn 94*
Windlesham, Baron 1932- *IntWW 93, Who 94*
Windley, Walter H., III *WhoAmP 93*
Windling, Terri 1958- *EncSF 93*
Windman, Arnold Lewis 1926- *WhoAm 94*
Windmuller, John Philip 1923- *WhoAm 94*
Windom, Michael Young 1954- *WhoFI 94*
Windom, Robert Neal, Jr. 1947- *WhoWest 94*
Windom, Steve *WhoAmP 93*
Windom, William 1923- *IntMPA 94, WhoAm 94, WhoHol 92*
Windrich, Elaine 1921- *WrDr 94*
Windrow, Martin C(live) 1944- *WrDr 94*
Windsor, Dean of *Who 94*
Windsor, Viscount 1951- *Who 94*
Windsor, Barbara 1937- *WhoHol 92*
Windsor, Claire d1972 *WhoHol 92*
Windsor, Frank 1927- *WhoHol 92*
Windsor, James Thomas, Jr. 1924- *WhoAm 94*
Windsor, Laurence Charles, Jr. 1935- *WhoAm 94*
Windsor, Marie 1922- *IntMPA 94*
Windsor, Marie 1924- *WhoHol 92*
Windsor, Patricia 1938- *ConAu 42NR, WhoAm 94, WrDr 94*
Windsor, Patricia (Frances) 1938- *TwCYAW*
Windsor, Romy *WhoHol 92*
Windsor, Ted Bacon 1924- *WhoScEn 94*
Windsor-Clive *Who 94*
Windust, Irene *WhoHol 92*
Wine, Dick 1944- *WrDr 94*
Wine, Donald Arthur 1922- *WhoAm 94, WhoAmL 94*
Wine, L. Mark 1945- *WhoAm 94*
Wine, Mark Philip 1949- *WhoAm 94, WhoAmL 94*
Wine, Sherwin Theodore 1928- *WhoAm 94*
Wineapple, Brenda 1949- *WrDr 94*
Wine-Banks, Jill Susan 1943- *WhoAm 94, WhoMW 93*
Wineberg, Howard 1955- *WhoWest 94*
Wineberry, Jesse *WhoAmP 93*
Winebrenner, Susan Kay 1939- *WhoMW 93*
Winecoff, David Fleming 1939- *WhoWest 94*
Winegar, Albert Lee 1931- *WhoAm 94*
Winegarten, Jonathan Isaac 1944- *Who 94*
Winegarten, Renee 1922- *WrDr 94*
Wineglass, Henry 1938- *WhoBlA 94*
Winegrad, Albert Irvin 1926- *WhoScEn 94*
Winegrad, Gerald William 1944- *WhoAmP 93*
Wineinger, Barbara Ann 1941- *WhoMW 93*
Wineke, Joseph Steven 1957- *WhoAmP 93*
Wineland, David J. *WhoScEn 94*
Wineland, Fred L. 1926- *IntMPA 94, WhoAmP 93*
Wineman, Alan Stuart 1937- *WhoAm 94*
Winemiller, James D. 1944- *WhoMW 93*
Winer, Deborah Grace 1961- *WrDr 94*
Winer, Donald Arthur 1927- *WhoAmA 93*
Winer, Edward L. 1943- *WhoAmL 94*
Winer, Gregory John 1958- *WhoFI 94*
Winer, Helene 1936- *WhoAmA 93*
Winer, Jerome Allen 1938- *WhoMW 93*
Winer, Ward Otis 1936- *WhoAm 94*
Winer, Warren James 1946- *WhoMW 93*
Wines, James N. 1932- *WhoAmA 93*
Wines, Lawrence Eugene 1957- *WhoAmL 94, WhoAmP 93, WhoMW 93*
Winesanker, Michael Max 1913-1989 *WhAm 10*
Winetrout, Kenneth 1912- *WrDr 94*
Winett, Samuel Joseph 1934- *WhoAm 94*
Winfield, Arnold F. 1926- *WhoBlA 94*
Winfield, Dave 1951- *ConBlB 5 [port]*
Winfield, David Mark 1951- *WhoAm 94, WhoBlA 94, WhoMW 93*
Winfield, Elayne Hunt 1925- *WhoBlA 94*
Winfield, Florence F. 1926- *WhoBlA 94*
Winfield, George Lee 1943- *WhoBlA 94*
Winfield, Graham 1931- *Who 94*
Winfield, James Eros 1944- *WhoBlA 94*
Winfield, Joan d1978 *WhoHol 92*
Winfield, John Buckner 1942- *WhoAm 94, WhoScEn 94*
Winfield, Julia *SmATA 77*
Winfield, Linda Fitzgerald 1948- *WhoBlA 94*
Winfield, Novalyn L. 1950- *WhoAm 94, WhoAmL 94*
Winfield, Paul 1940- *IntMPA 94, WhoHol 92*
Winfield, Paul 1941- *AfrAmAl 6*
Winfield, Paul Edward 1941- *WhoAm 94, WhoBlA 94*
Winfield, Peter Stevens 1927- *Who 94*
Winfield, Rodney M. 1925- *WhoAmA 93*
Winfield, Susan Rebecca Holmes 1948- *WhoBlA 94*
Winfield, Thalia Beatrice 1924- *WhoBlA 94*
Winfield, Thomas J. 1963- *WhoAmP 93*
Winfield, William T. 1944- *WhoBlA 94*
Winfree, Arthur Taylor 1942- *WhoAm 94, WhoScEn 94*
Winfrey, Angela Rosette 1959- *WhoMW 93*
Winfrey, Audrey Theresa *WhoBlA 94*
Winfrey, Carey Wells 1941- *WhoAm 94*
Winfrey, Charles Everett 1935- *WhoBlA 94*
Winfrey, Diana Lee 1955- *WhoAmL 94*
Winfrey, Frank Lee 1952- *WhoFI 94*
Winfrey, John Crawford 1935- *WhoAm 94*
Winfrey, Marion Lee 1932- *WhoAm 94*
Winfrey, Oprah 1954- *AfrAmAl 6 [port], IntMPA 94, IntWW 93, WhoAm 94, WhoBlA 94, WhoHol 92, WhoMW 93*
Wing, Ada Schick 1896- *WhoAmP 93*
Wing, Adrien Katherine 1956- *WhoAmL 94*
Wing, Anna *WhoHol 92*
Wing, Betsy 1936- *ConAu 140*
Wing, Charmeen Hah-Ming 1958- *WhoAsA 94*
Wing, Dan d1969 *WhoHol 92*
Wing, David Allan 1948- *WhoAm 94*
Wing, Elizabeth Nelson *ConAu 140*
Wing, Elizabeth Schwarz 1932- *WhoAm 94*
Wing, Francis William 1941- *WhoAmP 93*
Wing, Frank *WhoHisp 94*
Wing, George Milton 1923- *WhoWest 94*
Wing, Gloria A. 1931- *WhoAmP 93*
Wing, James 1929- *WhoAsA 94*
Wing, James C., Jr. 1956- *WhoAmL 94*
Wing, James David 1943- *WhoAmL 94*
Wing, James Erwin 1958- *WhoFI 94*
Wing, Jeannette M. *WhoAsA 94*
Wing, John Adams 1935- *WhoFI 94*
Wing, John K. 1923- *WrDr 94*
Wing, John Kenneth 1923- *Who 94*
Wing, John Russell 1937- *WhoAm 94, WhoAmL 94*
Wing, Linda Peterson 1941- *WhoAmP 93*
Wing, Martin Richard 1954- *WhoAmL 94*
Wing, Pat 1914- *WhoHol 92*
Wing, Robert Farquhar 1939- *WhoMW 93*
Wing, Roger 1945- *WhoWest 94*
Wing, Susan 1947- *WhoAmL 94*
Wing, Theodore W., II 1948- *WhoBlA 94*
Wing, Thomas 1929- *WhoScEn 94*
Wing, Toby 1916- *WhoHol 92*
Wing, Ward d1945 *WhoHol 92*
Wingard, George Frank 1935- *WhoAmP 93*
Wingate, Arline (Hollander) *WhoAmA 93*
Wingate, Charles Douglas 1953- *WhoAmL 94*
Wingate, David Aaron 1921- *WhoAm 94*
Wingate, Edwin Henry 1932- *WhoAm 94*
Wingate, George B. 1941- *WhoAmA 93*
Wingate, Henry Taylor, Jr. 1929- *WhoAm 94*
Wingate, Henry Travillion 1947- *WhoAm 94, WhoAmL 94*
Wingate, Jay D. 1921- *WhoAmP 93*
Wingate, John (Allan) 1920- *WrDr 94*
Wingate, Livingston L. 1915- *WhoBlA 94*
Wingate, Lydia *WhoMW 93*
Wingate, Marcel Edward 1923- *WhoWest 94*
Wingate, Miles (Buckley) 1923- *Who 94*
Wingate, Paine *WhAmRev*
Wingate, Phillip Jerome 1913- *WhoScEn 94*
Wingate, Richard Anthony 1937- *WhoAmP 93*
Wingate, Robert Bray 1925- *WhoAmA 93*
Wingate, Rosalee Martin 1944- *WhoBlA 94*
Wingblade, Georgie B. 1937- *WhoFI 94*
Winge, Ralph M. 1925- *WhoAmP 93*
Wingenbach, Gregory Charles 1938- *WhoAm 94*
Winger, Debra 1955- *IntMPA 94, IntWW 93, WhoAm 94, WhoHol 92*
Winger, Dennis Lawrence 1947- *WhoAm 94*
Winger, Howard Woodrow 1914- *WhoAm 94*
Winger, Loren *WhoAmP 93*
Winger, Marc Allan 1951- *WhoWest 94*
Winger, Ralph O. 1919- *WhoAm 94*
Wingert, Paul Stover 1900-1974 *WhoAmA 93N*
Wingert, Robert Irvin 1934- *WhoAm 94*
Wingerter, Eugene Joseph 1938- *WhoAm 94*
Wingerter, John Parker 1940- *WhoAmA 93*
Wingerter, John Raymond 1942- *WhoAmL 94*
Winget, Charles Merlin 1925- *WhoWest 94*
Winget, Rodner Reed 1936- *WhoWest 94*
Wingett, Mark *WhoHol 92*
Wingfield *Who 94*
Wingfield, Conway d1948 *WhoHol 92*
Wingfield, Harold Lloyd 1942- *WhoBlA 94*
Wingfield, James Gus 1926- *WhoAmP 93*
Wingfield, John Ernest 1943- *WhoFI 94*
Wingfield, Laura Allison Ross 1954- *WhoMW 93*
Wingfield, Paul 1961- *ConAu 140*
Wingfield, Sheila 1906-1992 *AnObit 1992, WrDr 94N*
Wingfield Digby *Who 94*
Wingfield Digby, Richard Shuttleworth 1911- *Who 94*
Wingfield Digby, Stephen Basil 1910- *Who 94*
Wingler, Lucille Kay Thompson 1941- *WhoMW 93*
Wingo, A. George 1929- *WhoBlA 94*
Wingo, Aurelia d1978 *WhoHol 92*
Wingo, Glenn Max 1913- *WrDr 94*
Wingo, Michael *WhoWest 94*
Wingo, Michael B. 1941- *WhoAmA 93*
Wingo, Paul Gene 1945- *WhoScEn 94*
Wingo, Robert Dean 1949- *WhoWest 94*
Wingrave, Anthony *EncSF 93*
Wingreen, Jason *WhoHol 92*
Wingren, Gustaf Fredrik 1910- *WrDr 94*
Wingrove, David (John) 1954- *EncSF 93, WrDr 94*
Wingrove, James *WhoHol 92*
Wings, Mary *DrAPF 93*
Wingstrand, Hans Anders 1949- *WhoScEn 94*
Wingti, Paias 1951- *IntWW 93*
Winham, Gilbert Rathbone 1938- *WhoAm 94*
Winiarski, Michael Henry 1960- *WhoFI 94*
Winick, Bernyce Alpert 1922- *WhoAmA 93*
Winick, Charles 1922- *WhoAm 94, WrDr 94*
Winick, Herman 1932- *WhoScEn 94*
Winick, Myron 1929- *WhoAm 94*
Winick, Norman M. 1952- *WhoAmP 93*
Winick, Tranquilina Rios 1938- *WhoAsA 94*
Winicker, Steven Ernest 1949- *WhoMW 93*
Winicov, Murray William 1928- *WhoMW 93*
Winik, Jay B. 1957- *WhoAm 94*
Winik, Marion *DrAPF 93*
Winikates, James 1942- *WhoFI 94*
Winiki, Ephriam *EncSF 93*
Winikoff, Robert Lee 1946- *WhoAmL 94*
Winitsky, Alex 1924- *IntMPA 94*
Winitz, Harris 1933- *WhoMW 93, WhoScEn 94*
Wink, Chris 1961- *WhoAmA 93*
Wink, Darlene Jean 1950- *WhoAmP 93*
Wink, Don 1938- *WhoAmA 93*
Wink, John J. 1951- *WhoAmP 93*
Winke, Jeffrey *DrAPF 93*
Winkel, Judy Kay 1947- *WhoAm 94, WhoFI 94*
Winkel, Michael James 1968- *WhoMW 93*
Winkel, Nina 1905-1990 *WhAm 10, WhoAmA 93N*
Winkel, Peter Alexander 1938- *WhoAmP 93*
Winkel, Raymond Norman 1928- *WhoAm 94*
Winkel, Richard J. 1931- *WhoAmP 93*

Winkelhake, Ralph John 1942- *WhoMW 93*
Winkelman, Brent N. *WhoAmP 93*
Winkelman, James Warren 1935- *WhoAm 94*
Winkelman, Joseph William 1941- *Who 94*
Winkelmann, Hermann 1849-1912 *NewGrDO*
Winkin, Justin Philip 1922- *WhoAm 94*
Winkjer, Dean 1923- *WhoAmP 93*
Winkleblack, Jack Dean 1928- *WhoFI 94*
Winkler, Agnieszka M. 1946- *WhoWest 94*
Winkler, Allan Michael 1945- *WhoAm 94, WhoMW 93*
Winkler, Allen Warren 1954- *WhoAmL 94*
Winkler, Anthony C. 1942- *WrDr 94*
Winkler, Carl Gottfried Theodor 1775-1856 *NewGrDO*
Winkler, Charles Howard 1954- *WhoAmL 94*
Winkler, Cheryl *WhoAmP 93*
Winkler, Dana John 1944- *WhoAmL 94*
Winkler, David Arthur 1952- *WhoWest 94*
Winkler, Gunther 1957- *WhoScEn 94*
Winkler, Hans Gunter 1926- *IntWW 93*
Winkler, Henry 1945- *IntMPA 94, WhoHol 92*
Winkler, Henry Franklin 1945- *WhoAm 94*
Winkler, Henry Ralph 1916- *WhoAm 94, WrDr 94*
Winkler, Hermann 1924- *NewGrDO*
Winkler, Howard Leslie 1950- *WhoAm 94, WhoWest 94*
Winkler, Irwin 1931- *IntDcF 2-4 [port], IntMPA 94, WhoAm 94*
Winkler, Joe *WhoAmP 93*
Winkler, John 1935- *WrDr 94*
Winkler, Joseph Conrad 1916- *WhoAm 94*
Winkler, Joseph Mark 1952- *WhoWest 94*
Winkler, Katherine Maurine 1940- *WhoFI 94*
Winkler, Lee B. 1925- *WhoAm 94*
Winkler, Lenny T. *WhoAmP 93*
Winkler, Margo *WhoHol 92*
Winkler, Maria Paula 1945- *WhoAmA 93*
Winkler, Marjorie Everett 1954- *WhoScEn 94, WhoWest 94*
Winkler, Martin Alan 1950- *WhoScEn 94*
Winkler, Michael 1952- *WhoAmA 93*
Winkler, Nancy A. 1952- *WhoFI 94*
Winkler, Peter A. 1946- *WhoAmL 94*
Winkler, Ralph Eugene 1927- *WhoWest 94*
Winkler, Robert *WhoHol 92*
Winkler, Robert Lewis 1943- *WhoAm 94, WhoScEn 94*
Winkler, Robert Norris 1945- *WhoAmL 94*
Winkler, Sheldon 1932- *WhoAm 94*
Winkler, Steven Dale 1954- *WhoMW 93*
Winkler, Steven Robert 1953- *WhoScEn 94*
Winkler, William Ralph 1900- *WhoAmP 93*
Winkles, Dewey Frank 1946- *WhoAmL 94*
Winkless, Jeff *WhoHol 92*
Winkless, Nelson Brock, III 1934- *WhoWest 94*
Winkley, Stephen Charles 1944- *Who 94*
Winks, Robin W(illiam Evert) 1930- *Who 94, WrDr 94*
Winks, Robin William 1930- *WhoAm 94*
Winland, Thomas W. 1949- *WhoAmL 94*
Winmill, Joan *WhoHol 92*
Winn *Who 94*
Winn, Albert Curry 1921- *WhoAm 94*
Winn, Alfred Vernon 1915- *WhoWest 94*
Winn, Allan Kendal 1950- *Who 94*
Winn, Bruce R. 1955- *WhoAmP 93*
Winn, Carol Denise 1962- *WhoBlA 94*
Winn, Colman Byron 1933- *WhoScEn 94*
Winn, Daryl Norman 1941- *WhoWest 94*
Winn, David *DrAPF 93*
Winn, David B. 1937- *WhoAm 94, WhoIns 94, WhoMW 93*
Winn, Delbert Easton 1946- *WhoAmL 94*
Winn, Edward Burton 1920- *WhoAm 94*
Winn, George Michael 1944- *WhoScEn 94*
Winn, Godfrey d1971 *WhoHol 92*
Winn, Harry L., Jr. 1944- *WhoFI 94*
Winn, Herschel Clyde 1931- *WhoAm 94, WhoFI 94*
Winn, Howard *DrAPF 93*
Winn, Hung Nguyen 1953- *WhoMW 93*
Winn, Ira Jay 1929- *WhoWest 94*
Winn, James Julius, Jr. 1941- *WhoAm 94, WhoAmL 94*
Winn, Janet B. *DrAPF 93*
Winn, Jill Kanaga Kline 1944- *WhoMW 93*
Winn, Joan T. 1942- *WhoBlA 94*
Winn, Julie 1956- *WhoAmP 93*
Winn, Kenneth Hugh 1953- *WhoAm 94*
Winn, Kitty 1944- *WhoHol 92*
Winn, Larry, Jr. 1919- *WhoAmP 93*
Winn, Otis Howard 1925- *WhoAm 94*
Winn, Philip Donald 1925- *WhoAmP 93*
Winn, Richard 1750-1818 *WhAmRev*
Winn, Robert Charles 1945- *WhoWest 94*
Winn, Robert Ernest 1938- *WhoAmL 94*
Winn, Stewart Dowse, Jr. 1936- *WhoFI 94*
Winn, Suzanne Barbara 1957- *WhoWest 94*
Winn, Walter Terris, Jr. 1949- *WhoScEn 94*
Winnefeld, James Alexander 1929- *WhoAm 94*
Winnemucca, Sarah 1844-1891 *HisWorL [port]*
Winner, Dennis J. *WhoAmP 93*
Winner, Ellen Plucknett 1943- *WhoAmL 94*
Winner, George H., Jr. 1949- *WhoAmP 93*
Winner, Harold Ivor d1992 *Who 94N*
Winner, Leslie J. *WhoAmP 93*
Winner, Michael 1935- *ConTFT 11, IntMPA 94*
Winner, Michael Robert 1935- *IntWW 93, Who 94, WhoAm 94*
Winner, Stephanie *NewYTBS 93 [port]*
Winner, Thomas Andrew 1931- *WhoAmP 93*
Winner, Thomas G. 1917- *WhoAm 94*
Winnerman, Robert Henry 1921- *WhoAm 94*
Winnerstrand, Olof d1956 *WhoHol 92*
Winnert, Franklin Roy 1932- *WhoAm 94*
Winnet, Nochem Samuel 1898-1990 *WhAm 10*
Winnett, Asa George 1923- *WhoScEn 94*
Winnett, Mark Alan 1957- *WhoFI 94*
Winnick, David Julian 1933- *Who 94*
Winnick, Stephen 1939- *WhoAm 94*
Winnicott, Donald Woods 1896-1971 *DcNaB MP*
Winnie, Alon Palm 1932- *WhoAm 94*
Winnie, Glenna Barbara *WhoScEn 94*
Winnifrith, Charles Boniface 1936- *Who 94*
Winnifrith, (Alfred) John (Digby) d1993 *Who 94N*
Winnifrith, T(homas) J(ohn) 1938- *WrDr 94*
Winning, John Patrick 1952- *WhoAmL 94, WhoFI 94, WhoMW 93*
Winning, Thomas J. *Who 94*
Winning, Thomas Joseph 1925- *IntWW 93*
Winninger, Charles d1969 *WhoHol 92*
Winninger, John J. *WhoAmP 93*
Winningham, Geoff 1943- *WhoAmA 93*
Winningham, Herman S., Jr. 1961- *WhoBlA 94*
Winningham, Leslie 1940- *WhoAmP 93*
Winningham, Mare 1959- *IntMPA 94, WhoHol 92*
Winninghoff, Albert *WhoAm 94, WhoFI 94*
Winninghoff, Mary Ellen 1953- *WhoWest 94*
Winnington, Francis Salwey William 1907- *Who 94*
Winnington-Ingram, Edward John 1926- *Who 94*
Winnington-Ingram, R(eginald) P(epys) 1904-1993 *ConAu 140*
Winnington-Ingram, Reginald Pepys *IntWW 93N*
Winnington-Ingram, Reginald Pepys d1993 *Who 94N*
Winnowski, Thaddeus Richard 1942- *WhoAm 94*
Winograd, Audrey Lesser 1933- *WhoFI 94*
Winograd, Nicholas 1945- *WhoAm 94, WhoScEn 94*
Winograd, Shmuel 1936- *IntWW 93, WhoAm 94, WhoScEn 94*
Winograd, Terry Allen 1946- *WhoScEn 94*
Winogradoff, Anatol d1980 *WhoHol 92*
Winogradsky, Steven 1949- *WhoWest 94*
Winogrand, Garry 1928-1984 *WhoAmA 93N*
Winoker, Diana Lee 1953- *WhoFI 94*
Winokur, George 1925- *WhoAm 94*
Winokur, Herbert Simon, Jr. 1943- *WhoFI 94*
Winokur, James L. 1922- *WhoAmA 93*
Winokur, Jon 1947- *WrDr 94*
Winokur, Neil S. 1945- *WhoAmA 93*
Winokur, Paula Colton 1935- *WhoAmA 93*
Winokur, Robert M. 1924- *WhoAm 94*
Winokur, Robert Mark 1933- *WhoAmA 93*
Winokur, Stephen Charles 1941-1988 *WhAm 10*
Winquist, Thomas Richard 1933- *WhoAmL 94*
Winrich, Lonny Bee 1937- *WhoMW 93*
Winrod, Gerald Burton 1899?-1957 *DcAmReB 2*
Winship, Frederick Moery 1924- *WhoAm 94*
Winship, Henry Dillon, Jr. 1929-1989 *WhAm 10*
Winship, Peter James Joseph 1943- *Who 94*
Winship, Sally Louise 1946- *WhoMW 93*
Winship, Wadleigh Chichester 1940- *WhoAm 94*
Winskill, Archibald (Little) 1917- *Who 94*
Winskill, Robert Wallace 1925- *WhoWest 94*
Winslade, Thomas Edwin 1952- *WhoAmL 94*
Winslett, David c. 1830-1862 *EncNAR*
Winsley, Shirley Joann 1934- *WhoAmP 93*
Winsloe, Christa 1888-1944 *BlmGWL, GayLL*
Winslow, Alfred A. 1923- *WhoBlA 94*
Winslow, Alfred Akers 1923- *WhoMW 93*
Winslow, Anna Green 1759-1779 *BlmGWL*
Winslow, Calvin 1949- *WhoAmP 93*
Winslow, Cleta Meris 1952- *WhoBlA 94*
Winslow, David Allen 1944- *WhoWest 94*
Winslow, Dick d1991 *WhoHol 92*
Winslow, Dick 1915- *WhAm 10*
Winslow, Edward 1595-1655 *WhWE*
Winslow, Edward, Jr. 1745-1815 *WhAmRev*
Winslow, Eugene 1919- *WhoBlA 94*
Winslow, Frances Edwards 1948- *WhoFI 94*
Winslow, George 1946- *WhoHol 92*
Winslow, Helen 1916- *WhoAmA 93*
Winslow, John Franklin 1933- *WhoAmL 94*
Winslow, Joyce *DrAPF 93*
Winslow, Julian Dallas 1914- *WhoAmL 94*
Winslow, Karyl 1949- *WhoAmP 93*
Winslow, Kellen Boswell 1957- *WhoBlA 94*
Winslow, Kenelm Crawford 1921- *WhoWest 94*
Winslow, Kenneth Paul 1949- *WhoBlA 94*
Winslow, Leon Edward 1934- *WhoMW 93*
Winslow, Lillian Ruth 1930- *WhoWest 94*
Winslow, Michael 1958- *WhoHol 92*
Winslow, Norman Eldon 1938- *WhoWest 94*
Winslow, Pauline Glen *ConAu 41NR, WrDr 94*
Winslow, Philip Charles 1924- *WhoWest 94*
Winslow, Ralph E. 1902-1978 *WhoAmA 93N*
Winslow, Reynolds Baker 1933- *WhoBlA 94*
Winslow, Robert Albert 1922- *WhoAm 94*
Winslow, Walter William 1925- *WhoAm 94*
Winslow, Yvonne *WhoHol 92*
Winsor, David John 1947- *WhoWest 94*
Winsor, Frederick Albert 1763-1830 *WorInv*
Winsor, G(eorge) McLeod *EncSF 93*
Winsor, Jackie 1941- *WhoAm 94*
Winsor, Jacque 1941- *WhoAmA 93*
Winsor, Kathleen 1919- *WhoAm 94, WrDr 94*
Winsor, Phil 1938- *ConAu 142*
Winsor, Ralph Everett 1936-1989 *WhAm 10*
Winsor, Travis Walter 1914- *WhoAm 94, WhoScEn 94*
Winstanley, Baron d1993 *Who 94N*
Winstanley, Alan Leslie *Who 94*
Winstanley, John 1919- *Who 94*
Winstanley, John Breyfogle 1874-1947 *WhoAmA 93N*
Winstead, Carol Jackson 1947- *WhoScEn 94*
Winstead, Clint 1956- *WhoFI 94*
Winstead, George Alvis 1916- *WhoAmL 94*
Winstead, Lois McIver 1932- *WhoAmP 93*
Winstead, Nash Nicks 1925- *WhoAm 94*
Winstead, Vernon A., Sr. 1937- *WhoBlA 94*
Winstein, Stewart R. 1914- *WhoAmP 93*
Winsten, Archer 1904- *WhoAm 94*
Winsten, I. W. 1952- *WhoAm 94, WhoAmL 94*
Winston, Barry Thomas 1934- *WhoAmL 94*
Winston, Bonnie Veronica 1957- *WhoBlA 94*
Winston, Bruce d1946 *WhoHol 92*
Winston, Clive Noel 1925- *Who 94*
Winston, Daoma 1922- *WrDr 94*
Winston, Dennis Ray 1946- *WhoBlA 94*
Winston, George 1949- *WhoAm 94*
Winston, George B., III 1943- *WhoBlA 94*
Winston, Gordon Chester 1929- *WhoAm 94*
Winston, Harold Ronald 1932- *WhoAmL 94, WhoMW 93*
Winston, Hattie *WhoHol 92*
Winston, Helene *WhoHol 92*
Winston, Henry 1911- *WhoBlA 94*
Winston, Hubert 1948- *WhoBlA 94*
Winston, Irene d1964 *WhoHol 92*
Winston, Jackie d1971 *WhoHol 92*
Winston, Janet E. 1937- *WhoBlA 94*
Winston, Janet Margaret 1937- *WhoMW 93*
Winston, Jeanne Worley 1941- *WhoBlA 94*
Winston, John B. 1944- *WhoAmL 94*
Winston, John H., Jr. 1928- *WhoBlA 94*
Winston, Joseph 1746-1815 *WhAmRev*
Winston, Joseph Mosby, Jr. 1916- *WhoAmL 94*
Winston, Judith A. *WhoAmP 93*
Winston, Judith Ann 1943- *WhoAm 94, WhoAmL 94*
Winston, Leslie *WhoHol 92*
Winston, Lillie Carolyn 1906- *WhoBlA 94*
Winston, Mark L. 1950- *ConAu 141*
Winston, Michael D. 1942- *WhoIns 94*
Winston, Michael R. 1941- *WhoBlA 94*
Winston, Michael Russell 1941- *WhoAm 94*
Winston, Mike *ConAu 41NR*
Winston, Morton Manuel 1930- *WhoWest 94*
Winston, Phyllis *DrAPF 93*
Winston, Robert *WhoHol 92*
Winston, Robert Maurice Lipson 1940- *Who 94*
Winston, Roland 1936- *WhoAm 94, WhoMW 93*
Winston, Sarah *DrAPF 93*
Winston, Sarah 1912- *WrDr 94*
Winston, Sherry E. 1947- *WhoBlA 94*
Winston, Stan *EncSF 93*
Winstone, Dorothy (Gertrude) 1919- *Who 94*
Winstone, Ray 1958- *WhoHol 92*
Winstone, Reece 1909- *WrDr 94*
Winston-Fox, Ruth 1912- *Who 94*
Wint, Arthur Stanley d1992 *Who 94N*
Wint, Arthur Valentine Noris 1950- *WhoBlA 94*
Wint, Dennis Michael 1943- *WhoAm 94, WhoMW 93*
Winter, Alan 1937- *WhoAm 94*
Winter, Alden Raymond 1897- *WhAm 10*
Winter, Alex *WhoHol 92*
Winter, Alex 1965- *IntMPA 94*
Winter, Allen Ernest 1903- *Who 94*
Winter, Andrew *WhoAm 94*
Winter, Andrew 1892-1958 *WhoAmA 93N*
Winter, Arch Reese 1913- *WhoAm 94*
Winter, Bernadette Grace 1925- *WhoMW 93*
Winter, Bryan Richard 1959- *WhoAmL 94*
Winter, Caryl Elyse 1944- *WhoFI 94, WhoWest 94*
Winter, Charles Milne 1933- *IntWW 93, Who 94*
Winter, Chester Caldwell 1922- *WhoAm 94*
Winter, Dale d1985 *WhoHol 92*
Winter, Daria Portray 1949- *WhoAmP 93, WhoBlA 94, WhoWomW 91*
Winter, David Brian 1929- *Who 94, WrDr 94*
Winter, David Ferdinand 1920- *WhoAm 94*
Winter, David Garrett 1939- *WhoMW 93*
Winter, David Kenneth 1930- *WhoAm 94*
Winter, David L. 1954- *WhoAmA 93*
Winter, David Louis 1930- *WhoScEn 94*
Winter, Dennis Wayne *WhoWest 94*
Winter, Donald Francis 1941- *WhoAm 94*
Winter, Douglas E. 1950- *WhoAm 94, WhoAmL 94*
Winter, Edward *WhoHol 92*
Winter, Elizabeth Ann 1963- *WhoFI 94*
Winter, Ezra 1886-1949 *WhoAmA 93N*
Winter, Frederick Elliot 1922- *WhoAm 94*
Winter, Frederick Thomas 1926- *IntWW 93, Who 94*
Winter, Gerald Bernard 1928- *Who 94*
Winter, Gerald Glen 1936- *WhoAmA 93*
Winter, Gordon 1912-1993 *ConAu 141*
Winter, Gregory Paul 1951- *Who 94*
Winter, H.G. *EncSF 93*
Winter, Harland Steven 1948- *WhoScEn 94*
Winter, Harrison L. 1921-1990 *WhAm 10*
Winter, Harvey John 1915- *WhoAm 94*
Winter, Hope Melamed *WhoAmA 93*
Winter, Horst Henning 1941- *WhoScEn 94*
Winter, Jessie d1971 *WhoHol 92*
Winter, Jimmy Dale 1946- *WhoScEn 94*
Winter, John *WhoAm 94*

Wise, Tom d1928 *WhoHol 92*
Wise, Warren C. 1948- *WhoBlA 94*
Wise, Warren Roberts 1929- *WhoAm 94, WhoAmL 94, WhoFI 94*
Wise, Watson William d1989 *WhAm 10*
Wise, William Allan 1945- *WhoAm 94, WhoFI 94*
Wise, William Clinton, Sr. 1941- *WhoBlA 94*
Wise, William Jerrard 1934- *WhoAm 94*
Wise, William Nesbitt 1959- *WhoWest 94*
Wise, Woodrow Wilson, Jr. 1938- *WhoWest 94*
Wisecarver, Charmaine Francine 1947- *WhoMW 93*
Wisehart, Arthur McKee 1928- *WhoAm 94, WhoAmL 94*
Wiseheart, Malcolm Boyd, Jr. 1942- *WhoAmL 94*
Wisekal, Frank William 1934- *WhoAm 94, WhoFI 94*
Wiseley, Richard Eugene 1945- *WhoAm 94, WhoFI 94*
Wisell, William C. 1939- *WhoAmP 93*
Wise-Love, Karen A. 1946- *WhoBlA 94*
Wiseman, Adele 1928- *BlmGWL, WrDr 94*
Wiseman, Alan 1936- *WrDr 94*
Wiseman, Alan Mitchell 1944- *WhoAm 94, WhoAmL 94*
Wiseman, Arthur Francis, Jr. 1950- *WhoWest 94*
Wiseman, Bernard 1922- *WrDr 94*
Wiseman, Carl Donald 1925- *WhoAm 94*
Wiseman, Charleen Gordon 1942- *WhoAmP 93*
Wiseman, Donald John 1918- *IntWW 93, Who 94, WrDr 94*
Wiseman, Ernest 1925- *Who 94*
Wiseman, Frederick 1930- *IntMPA 94, WhoAm 94*
Wiseman, Jane fl. 1701- *BlmGWL*
Wiseman, Jay Donald 1952- *WhoAm 94, WhoWest 94*
Wiseman, Jeffrey *WhoHol 92*
Wiseman, John William 1957- *Who 94*
Wiseman, Joseph 1918- *IntMPA 94, WhoHol 92*
Wiseman, Laurence Donald 1947- *WhoAm 94*
Wiseman, Randolph Carson 1946- *WhoAmL 94*
Wiseman, Scotty d1981 *WhoHol 92*
Wiseman, Thomas Anderton, Jr. 1930- *WhoAm 94, WhoAmL 94*
Wiseman, Thomas William 1946- *WhoMW 93*
Wiseman, Timothy Peter 1940- *Who 94*
Wiseman, Wesley Lane 1935- *WhoAmP 93*
Wiseman, William Johnston, Jr. 1944- *WhoAmP 93*
Wiseman, William R. 1932- *WhoAmP 93*
Wisenberg, S. L. *DrAPF 93*
Wiser, Betty H. *WhoAmP 93*
Wiser, C. Lawrence 1930- *WhoAmP 93*
Wiser, James Louis 1945- *WhoAm 94*
Wiser, Richard Calvin 1945- *WhoAm 94*
Wiser, William *DrAPF 93*
Wiser, William 1929- *WrDr 94*
Wisgerhof, Jerry G. 1938- *WhoIns 94*
Wish, Jay Barry 1950- *WhoMW 93, WhoScEn 94*
Wisham, Claybron O. 1932- *WhoBlA 94*
Wisham, Lawrence Herman 1918- *WhoAm 94*
Wisham, Mary Ellen 1932- *WhoAmP 93*
Wishard, Della M. 1934- *WhoAmP 93, WhoMW 93*
Wishard, Gordon Davis 1945- *WhoAm 94, WhoAmL 94*
Wishard, Luther DeLoraine 1854-1925 *DcAmReB 2*
Wishart, Harriet Lynn 1948- *WhoAmL 94*
Wishart, Leonard P., III 1934- *CngDr 93*
Wishart, Leonard Plumer, III 1934- *WhoAm 94*
Wishart, Maureen *Who 94*
Wishart, Peter (Charles Arthur) 1921-1984 *NewGrDO*
Wishart, Ronald Sinclair 1925- *WhoAm 94, WhoFI 94*
Wishbow, Gregory J. *WhoFI 94*
Wishek, Michael Bradley 1959- *WhoAmL 94*
Wishman, Thomas Allen 1956- *WhoAmP 93*
Wishner, Julius d1993 *NewYTBS 93*
Wishner, Maynard Ira 1923- *WhoAm 94*
Wishner, Steven R. 1950- *WhoAm 94*
Wishniewsky, Gary 1946- *WhoWest 94*
Wishy, Joseph R. d1993 *NewYTBS 93*
Wiskich, Joseph Tony 1935- *WhoScEn 94*
Wisler, Charles Clifton, Jr. 1926- *WhoAm 94*
Wisler, David Charles 1941- *WhoScEn 94*
Wisler, G(ary) Clifton 1950- *WrDr 94*
Wisler, Willard Eugene 1933- *WhoAm 94*
Wismer, Don(ald Richard) 1946- *EncSF 93*
Wismer, Frank G. 1938- *WhoAm 94*
Wismer, Harry d1967 *WhoHol 92*
Wisner, Cynthia Ficke 1957- *WhoAmL 94*
Wisner, Frank George 1938- *IntWW 93, WhoAmP 93*
Wisner, Henry 1720-1790 *WhAmRev*
Wisner, Michael John 1958- *WhoFI 94*
Wisner, Robert Newell 1939- *WhoMW 93*
Wisner, Roscoe William, Jr. 1926- *WhoFI 94*
Wisneski, Martin Edward 1957- *WhoAmL 94*
Wisneski, Mary Jo Elizabeth 1938- *WhoAm 94*
Wisness, Paul Norman 1946- *WhoAmP 93*
Wisniewski, Andreas *WhoHol 92*
Wisniewski, David 1953- *WrDr 94*
Wisniewski, Felix E. 1924- *WhoAmP 93*
Wisniewski, Henryk Miroslaw 1931- *WhoScEn 94*
Wisniewski, James Allen 1966- *WhoFI 94*
Wisniewski, John William 1932- *WhoAm 94*
Wisniewski, Joseph Michael 1954- *WhoFI 94*
Wisniewski, Paul Michael 1943- *WhoFI 94*
Wisniewski, Richard J. 1950- *WhoIns 94*
Wisniewski, Roland 1929- *WhoScEn 94*
Wisniewski, Roswitha 1926- *WhoWomW 91*
Wisniewski, Stephen Adam 1967- *WhoAm 94, WhoWest 94*
Wisniewski, Thomas Joseph 1926- *WhoAm 94*
Wisnosky, John G. 1940- *WhoAmA 93, WhoWest 94*
Wisoff, Ellen *DrAPF 93*
Wisor, Bernadette Ellen 1936- *WhoMW 93*
Wisotsky, Jerry Joseph 1928- *WhoWest 94*
Wiss, Marcia A. 1947- *WhoAm 94, WhoAmL 94*
Wiss, Marvin J. 1926- *WhoAmP 93*
Wiss, Robert E. 1929- *CngDr 93*
Wissbaum, Donna Cacic 1956- *WhoAmL 94*
Wissemann-Widrig, Nancy *WhoAmA 93*
Wissing, Matthew R. 1958- *WhoAmP 93*
Wissing, Neil Phillip 1931- *WhoFI 94*
Wissler, Eugene Harley 1927- *WhoAm 94*
Wissler, Rudy *WhoHol 92*
Wissler-Thomas, Carrie 1946- *WhoFI 94*
Wissman, Lawrence Yarnell 1947- *WhoWest 94*
Wissman, Matthias 1949- *WhoScEn 94*
Wissmann, Carol Renee 1946- *WhoFI 94*
Wissmann, Hermann Von 1853-1905 *WhWE*
Wissmann, Matthias 1949- *IntWW 93*
Wissmer, Pierre 1915- *NewGrDO*
Wissmeyer, Gunter Gustav 1940- *WhoAmA 93*
Wissner, Seth Ernst 1922- *WhoAm 94*
Wist, Abund Ottokar 1926- *WhoFI 94*
Wist, George Richard 1945- *WhoFI 94*
Wisted, Daniel Jay 1961- *WhoFI 94*
Wister, Sarah 1761-1804 *BlmGWL, WhAmRev*
Wistisen, Martin J. 1938- *WhoAm 94*
Wistrand, Lars Goran 1949- *WhoScEn 94*
Wistrich, Enid Barbara 1928- *Who 94*
Wistrich, Ernest 1923- *Who 94*
Wiswall, Frank Lawrence, Jr. 1939- *WhoAm 94, WhoAmL 94*
Wiswell, James P. 1946- *WhoAmP 93*
Wiszniewski, Zbigniew 1922- *NewGrDO*
Wit, Daniel 1923- *WhoAm 94*
Wit, David Edmund 1962- *WhoFI 94, WhoScEn 94*
Wit, Harold Maurice 1928- *WhoAm 94, WhoFI 94*
Witala, Donald Wayne 1946- *WhoMW 93*
Witcher, Daniel Dougherty 1924- *WhoAm 94, WhoMW 93*
Witcher, Gary Royal 1950- *WhoMW 93*
Witcher, Robert Campbell 1926- *WhoAm 94*
Witcher, Roger Kenneth, Jr. 1952- *WhoAmP 93*
Witcoff, Sheldon William 1925- *WhoAm 94*
Witcombe, R(ick) T(rader) 1943- *WrDr 94*
Witcover, Jules Joseph 1927- *WhoAm 94*
Witek, James Eugene 1932- *WhoAm 94*
Witek, John James 1948- *WhoScEn 94*
Witek, Kate 1954- *WhoAmP 93*
Witemeyer, Hugh Hazen 1939- *WrDr 94*
Witenberg, Earl George 1917- *WhoScEn 94*
Withall, William Nigel James 1928- *Who 94*
Witham, Barry Bates 1939- *WhoAm 94*
Witham, Clyde Lester 1948- *WhoWest 94*
Witham, Robert Rodney 1950- *WhoFI 94*
Witham, Vernon Clint 1925- *WhoAmA 93*
Witham, William L., Jr. 1947- *WhoAmL 94*
Withee, Mabel d1952 *WhoHol 92*
Witheford, Hubert 1921- *WrDr 94*
Withem, Ron 1946- *WhoAmP 93*
Wither, George 1558-1667 *BlmGEL*
Witherbee, Frank S. d1917 *EncABHB 9*
Witherell, Dennis Patrick 1951- *WhoAmL 94*
Witherell, Michael S. 1949- *WhoScEn 94*
Witherings, Thomas c. 1596-1651 *DcNaB MP*
Witherington, Giles Somerville Gwynne 1919- *Who 94*
Witherington, Laura S. 1964- *WhoAmL 94*
Witherite, Richard L. 1940- *WhoIns 94*
Witherow, David Michael Lindley 1937- *Who 94*
Witherow, William Kenneth 1954- *WhoScEn 94*
Withers, Alton Merrill 1926- *WhoFI 94*
Withers, Charles d1947 *WhoHol 92*
Withers, David Alan 1949- *WhoIns 94*
Withers, Googie 1917- *IntMPA 94, Who 94, WhoHol 92*
Withers, Grant d1959 *WhoHol 92*
Withers, Isabel d1968 *WhoHol 92*
Withers, J. Mike 1947- *WhoAmP 93*
Withers, Jane 1926- *WhoHol 92*
Withers, Jane 1927- *IntMPA 94*
Withers, John Keppel Ingold D. *Who 94*
Withers, Josephine 1938- *WhoAmA 93*
Withers, Margaret *WhoHol 92*
Withers, Ramsey Muir 1930- *WhoAm 94*
Withers, Reginald (Greive) 1924- *Who 94*
Withers, Reginald Greive 1924- *IntWW 93*
Withers, Roy Joseph 1924- *Who 94*
Withers, Rupert Alfred 1913- *Who 94*
Withers, W. Russell, Jr. 1936- *WhoAm 94, WhoFI 94*
Withers, W. Wayne 1940- *WhoAm 94, WhoAmL 94, WhoFI 94*
Withers, Welty Kenney 1927- *WhoAm 94*
Witherspoon, Annie C. 1928- *WhoBlA 94*
Witherspoon, Audrey Goodwin 1949- *WhoBlA 94*
Witherspoon, Carolyn Brack 1950- *WhoAm 94*
Witherspoon, Cora d1957 *WhoHol 92*
Witherspoon, Dorothy Karpel 1936- *WhoAmP 93*
Witherspoon, Fredda *WhoBlA 94*
Witherspoon, Fredda Lilly *WhoMW 93*
Witherspoon, Gregory Jay 1946- *WhoWest 94*
Witherspoon, Herbert 1873-1935 *NewGrDO*
Witherspoon, James 1922- *WhoBlA 94*
Witherspoon, James Donald 1933- *WhoAm 94*
Witherspoon, Jere Warthen 1932- *WhoAm 94*
Witherspoon, Jimmy 1923- *WhoHol 92*
Witherspoon, John 1723-1794 *AmSocL, DcAmReB 2, HisWorL, WhAmRev*
Witherspoon, John Knox, Jr. 1928- *WhoAm 94, WhoIns 94*
Witherspoon, John Marshall 1945- *WhoAm 94*
Witherspoon, Mary Elizabeth *DrAPF 93*
Witherspoon, Naomi Long *BlkWr 2*
Witherspoon, R. Carolyn *WhoBlA 94*
Witherspoon, Sharon 1955- *WhoAm 94*
Witherspoon, Walter Pennington, Jr. 1938- *WhoAmP 93*
Witherspoon, William 1909- *WhoAm 94, WhoFI 94, WhoMW 93*
Witherspoon, William David *WhoAmP 93*
Witherspoon, William Roger 1949- *WhoBlA 94*
Witherup, William 1935- *WrDr 94*
Withey, Chester d1939 *WhoHol 92*
Withey, Virginia Philley d1980 *WhoHol 92*
Withington, Frederic B. d1993 *NewYTBS 93*
Withinton, Nancy Kay 1958- *WhoMW 93*
Withrow, Glenn *WhoHol 92*
Withrow, Jackie *WhoAmP 93*
Withrow, Lucille Monnot 1923- *WhoFI 94, WhoScEn 94*
Withrow, Mary Ellen 1930- *WhoAm 94, WhoAmP 93, WhoFI 94, WhoMW 93*
Withrow, Sheila Kay 1959- *WhoMW 93*
Withrow, William *WhoAmP 93*
Withrow, William J. 1926- *WhoAmA 93*
Withrow, William N., Jr. 1954- *WhoAmL 94*
Withrow-Gallanter, Sherrie Anne 1960- *WhoFI 94*
Withuhn, William Lawrence 1941- *WhoFI 94*
Withy, George 1924- *Who 94*
Witiak, Donald Theodore 1935- *WhoAm 94*
Witkacy *EncSF 93, IntDcT 2*
Witke, David Rodney 1937- *WhoAm 94*
Witke, Roxane 1938- *WrDr 94*
Witkiewicz, Stanislaw (Ignacy) 1885-1939 *IntDcT 2*
Witkiewicz, Stanislaw Ignacy 1885-1939 *EncSF 93*
Witkin, Eric Douglas 1948- *WhoAmL 94*
Witkin, Evelyn Maisel 1921- *WhoAm 94*
Witkin, Isaac 1936- *WhoAmA 93*
Witkin, Jerome 1939- *WhoAmA 93*
Witkin, Joel-Peter 1939- *WhoAm 94, WhoAmA 93, WhoWest 94*
Witkin, Mildred Hope Fisher *WhoScEn 94*
Witkin, Susan Beth 1959- *WhoWest 94*
Witkop, Bernhard 1917- *IntWW 93, WhoAm 94, WhoScEn 94*
Witkowski, Charles S. d1993 *NewYTBS 93*
Witkowski, Georges(-Martin) 1867-1943 *NewGrDO*
Witkowski, Michael Robert 1964- *WhoFI 94*
Witkowsky, Gizella *WhoAm 94*
Witman, Leonard Joel 1950- *WhoAmL 94*
Witmer, G. Robert 1904- *WhoAm 94, WhoAmL 94*
Witmer, G. Robert, Jr. 1937- *WhoAm 94*
Witmer, Gary William 1951- *WhoScEn 94*
Witmer, George Robert, Jr. 1937- *WhoAm 94, WhoAmL 94*
Witmer, John Albert 1920- *WhoAm 94*
Witmer, John Harper, Jr. 1940- *WhoAm 94*
Witmer, Steven Andrew 1966- *WhoAmL 94*
Witmer, William Kern 1926-1987 *WhAm 10*
Witmeyer, John Douglas 1945- *WhoAmL 94*
Witmeyer, John Jacob, III 1946- *WhoAmL 94, WhoFI 94*
Witmeyer, Stanley Herbert 1913- *WhoAmA 93*
Witnauer, Ericka *WhoAm 94, WhoFI 94*
Witney, Kenneth Percy 1916- *Who 94*
Witney, Michael d1983 *WhoHol 92*
Witney, Thomas fl. 1292-1342 *DcNaB MP*
Witold-K 1932- *WhoAmA 93*
Witort, Janet Lee 1950- *WhoAmL 94*
Witschey, R. Daniel, Jr. 1950- *WhoAmL 94*
Witschey, Walter Robert Thurmond 1941- *WhoAm 94*
Witschy, Carl E. 1952- *WhoAmL 94*
Witt, Alan Michael 1952- *WhoAmL 94*
Witt, August Ferdinand 1931- *WhoScEn 94*
Witt, Carter H. 1937- *WhoAmP 93*
Witt, Charles E. 1917- *WhoAm 94*
Witt, David L. 1951- *WhoAm 94, WhoAmA 93*
Witt, Gary 1965- *WhoAmP 93*
Witt, Gerhardt Meyer 1953- *WhoScEn 94*
Witt, Harold *DrAPF 93*
Witt, Harold Vernon 1923- *WrDr 94*
Witt, Henriette de 1829-1908 *BlmGWL*
Witt, Herbert 1923- *WhoWest 94*
Witt, Howell Arthur John 1920- *Who 94*
Witt, Hugh Ernest 1921- *WhoAm 94*
Witt, James Lee 1944- *WhoAm 94*
Witt, John 1940- *WhoAmA 93*
Witt, Karen *WhoHol 92*
Witt, Kathryn *WhoHol 92*
Witt, Kathryn L. *WhoAmL 94*
Witt, Maureen Reidy 1955- *WhoAmL 94*
Witt, Merle Dean 1944- *WhoMW 93*
Witt, Nancy Camden 1930- *WhoAmA 93*
Witt, Otto *EncSF 93*
Witt, Paul Junger 1941- *WhoAm 94*
Witt, Paul Junger 1943- *IntMPA 94*
Witt, Raymond Buckner, Jr. 1915- *WhoAm 94*
Witt, Richard 1568-1624 *DcNaB MP*
Witt, Robert Charles 1941- *WhoAm 94, WhoFI 94*
Witt, Robert John, Jr. 1951- *WhoFI 94*
Witt, Robert Louis 1940- *WhoFI 94*
Witt, Robert Wayne 1937- *WhoAm 94*
Witt, Ruth Elizabeth 1922- *WhoAm 94*
Witt, Scot Jeffery 1955- *WhoMW 93*
Witt, Stephen S. 1937- *WhoIns 94*
Witt, Thomas Powell 1946- *WhoAm 94, WhoAmL 94*
Witt, Walter Francis, Jr. 1933- *WhoAm 94, WhoAmL 94*
Witt, William G. *WhoAmP 93*
Wittbrodt, Edwin Stanley 1918- *WhoAm 94*
Wittbrodt, Frederick Joseph, Jr. 1955- *WhoMW 93*
Wittcoff, Harold Aaron 1918- *WhoAm 94*
Witte, Ann Dryden 1942- *WhoFI 94*
Witte, Craig Hess 1943- *WhoMW 93*
Witte, Erich 1911- *NewGrDO*
Witte, John *DrAPF 93*

Witte, John Sterling 1953- *WhoScEn 94*
Witte, Lawrence Mark 1945- *WhoAm 94*
Witte, Mary (Grace) Stieglitz *WhoAmA 93*
Witte, Merlin Michael 1926- *WhoAm 94*
Witte, Nancy Marie 1946- *WhoWest 94*
Witte, Owen Neil 1949- *WhoScEn 94*
Witte, Randall Erwyn 1948- *WhoAm 94*
Witte, Sergei 1849-1915 *HisWorL [port]*
Witte, Wreatha Ann 1947- *WhoWest 94*
Wittebort, Robert John, Jr. 1947- *WhoAmL 94*
Wittels, Anne F. *DrAPF 93*
Witteman, Christopher Paul 1953- *WhoAmL 94*
Witten, David Melvin 1926- *WhoAm 94*
Witten, Edward *WhoAm 94, WhoScEn 94*
Witten, Edward 1951- *IntWW 93*
Witten, Louis 1921- *WhoAm 94, WhoScEn 94*
Witten, Mark Lee 1953- *WhoScEn 94*
Witten, Roger Michael 1946- *WhoAmL 94*
Witten, Thomas Jefferson, Jr. 1942- *WhoScEn 94*
Wittenberg, Jon Albert 1939- *WhoFI 94*
Wittenberg, Merle Eugene 1929- *WhoMW 94*
Wittenberg, Phillip 1895- *WhAm 10*
Wittenberg, Rudolph *DrAPF 93*
Witten Born, George 1905-1974 *WhoAmA 93N*
Wittenbrink, Boniface Leo 1914- *WhoMW 93*
Wittenbrink, Jeffrey Scott 1960- *WhoAmL 94*
Wittenburg, Robert Charles *WhoScEn 94*
Wittenmeyer, Charles E. 1903- *WhoAm 94, WhoAmP 93*
Wittenstein, Arthur 1926-1989 *WhAm 10*
Wittenstein, George Juergen 1919- *WhoWest 94*
Wittenwyler, Ronald P. 1947- *WhoIns 94*
Witter, Ray Cowden 1942- *WhoAm 94*
Witter, Richard Lawrence 1936- *WhoAm 94, WhoScEn 94*
Witter, Robert Edward 1948- *WhoFI 94*
Witter, Wendell Winship 1910- *WhoWest 94*
Witteveen, Hendrikus Johannes 1921- *IntWW 93*
Witteveen, (Hendrikus) Johannes 1921- *Who 93*
Wittfoht, Hans Heinrich Hermann 1924- *WhoFI 94*
Wittgenstein, Herta *DrAPF 93*
Wittgenstein, Ludwig (Josef Johann) 1889-1951 *EncHB*
Wittgraf, George William 1945- *WhoAmP 93*
Witthoefft, Charles Frederick 1946- *WhoAmL 94*
Witthuhn, Burton Orrin 1934- *WhoAm 94*
Witthuhn, Wilfried E. 1946- *WhoAmL 94*
Wittich, John David 1921- *WhoAm 94*
Wittich, Marie 1868-1931 *NewGrDO*
Wittich, William Vincent 1941- *WhoWest 94*
Wittig, Curt *WhoScEn 94*
Wittig, Erland Paul 1955- *WhoWest 94*
Wittig, Georg d1987 *NobelP 91N*
Wittig, Judith *DrAPF 93*
Wittig, Monique *BlmGWL [port]*
Wittig, Monique 1935- *ConWorW 93, EncSF 93, GayLL*
Wittig, Raymond Shaffer 1944- *WhoAmL 94*
Witting, A. E. d1941 *WhoHol 92*
Witting, Amy 1918- *ConAu 140*
Witting, Mattie d1945 *WhoHol 92*
Witting, William Neil 1951- *WhoAm 94*
Wittler, Shirley Joyce 1927- *WhoAm 94, WhoAmP 93*
Wittlich, Gary Eugene 1934- *WhoAm 94*
Wittlin, Thaddeus (Andrew) 1909- *WrDr 94*
Wittlinger, Cheryl A. 1950- *WhoMW 93*
Wittlinger, Ellen *DrAPF 93*
Wittlinger, Timothy David 1940- *WhoAm 94*
Wittlock, Mary Lenore 1932- *WhoMW 93*
Wittmack, Edgar Franklin 1894-1956 *WhoAmA 93N*
Wittman, Connie Susan 1956- *WhoMW 93*
Wittman, Gordon R. *IntWW 93*
Wittman, Stephen Charles 1953- *WhoWest 94*
Wittmann, Mary Xaveria, Sister 1933- *WhoAm 94*
Wittmann, Otto 1911- *WhoAm 94, WhoAmA 93*
Wittmer, James Frederick 1932- *WhoAm 94*
Wittmeyer, Richard Arthur 1947- *WhoMW 93*
Wittner, Arvilla Marie 1929- *WhoAmP 93*
Wittner, Derek Antonow 1943- *WhoAmL 94*
Wittner, Jacob d1993 *NewYTBS 93*

Wittner, Lawrence Stephen 1941- *WrDr 94*
Wittner, Loren Antonow 1938- *WhoAm 94, WhoAmL 94*
Witton-Davies, Carl(yle) 1913-1993 *ConAu 141*
Witton-Davies, Carlyle d1993 *Who 94N*
Witton-Davies, Carlyle 1913- *WrDr 94*
Wittreich, Joseph Anthony, Jr. 1939- *WhoAm 94*
Wittrisch, Marcel 1901-1955 *NewGrDO*
Wittrock, Merlin Carl 1931- *WhoAm 94, WhoScEn 94, WhoWest 94*
Wittrup, Richard Derald 1926- *WhoAm 94*
Wittry, David Beryle 1929- *WhoAm 94, WhoScEn 94*
Wittstein, Edwin Frank 1929- *WhoAm 94, WhoScEn 94*
Witty, (John) David 1924- *Who 94*
Witty, John 1915- *WhoHol 92*
Witty, John Barber 1946- *WhoFI 94*
Witty, Robert Wilks 1941- *WhoFI 94*
Witty, Stanley d1993 *NewYTBS 93*
Witucki, James Charles 1944- *WhoAmP 93*
Witwer, Ronald James 1937- *WhoScEn 94*
Witwer, Samuel Weiler, Sr. 1908- *WhoAm 94, WhoAmP 93*
Witwer, Samuel Weiler, Jr. 1941- *WhoAmL 94*
Witzel, Carla Stone 1948- *WhoAm 94, WhoAmL 94*
Witzel, Lothar Gustav 1939- *WhoScEn 94*
Witzel, William Martin 1953- *WhoScEn 94*
Witzenburger, Edwin Jacob 1920- *WhoAmP 93*
Witzgall, Christoph Johann 1929- *WhoScEn 94*
Witzig, Warren Frank 1921- *WhoAm 94*
Witzthumb, Ignaz *NewGrDO*
Wiviott, Max Davis 1915- *WhoAmP 93*
Wix, Ethel Rose 1921- *Who 94*
Wix, Florence d1956 *WhoHol 92*
Wix, John d1935 *WhoHol 92*
Wix, Mayo 1923- *WhoAmP 93*
Wixell, Ingvar 1931- *NewGrDO*
Wixom, Gary L. 1938- *WhoAmL 94*
Wixom, Robert Llewellyn 1924- *WhoMW 93*
Wixom, William D. 1929- *WhoAmA 93*
Wixom, William David 1929- *WhoAm 94*
Wixon, Rufus 1911- *WhoAm 94*
Wixson, Gerald Ernest 1935- *WhoFI 94*
Wixson, Raymond C. 1935- *WhoAmP 93*
Wixted, Michael-James 1961- *WhoHol 92*
Wixtrom, Donald Joseph 1928- *WhoMW 93*
Wizan, Joe 1935- *IntMPA 94*
Wizard, Brian 1949- *WhoWest 94*
Wizen, Sarabeth Margolis 1950- *WhoFI 94*
Wizmur, Judith H. 1949- *WhoAm 94, WhoAmL 94*
Wizon, Tod 1952- *WhoAmA 93*
Wleugel, John Peter 1929- *WhoAm 94*
Wlodkowski, Raymond John 1943- *WhoWest 94*
Wludyka, Peter *EncSF 93*
Wnek, Richard S. 1954- *WhoIns 94*
Wnuk, Michael Peter 1936- *WhoMW 93*
Wobbekind, Richard Louis 1953- *WhoWest 94*
Wobeser, Wilhelmine Karoline 1769-1807 *BlmGWL*
Wobig, Ellen 1911- *EncSF 93*
Wobst, Frank Georg 1933- *WhoAm 94, WhoFI 94*
Wobus, Reinhard Arthur 1941- *WhoAm 94*
Wochele, Carl Dale 1952- *WhoMW 93*
Wochner, Raymond Dean 1936- *WhoFI 94*
Wochok, Thomas Michael 1949- *WhoAmL 94*
Wochok, Zachary Stephen 1942- *WhoWest 94*
Wodarczyk, Francis John 1944- *WhoScEn 94*
Woddburn, James d1948 *WhoHol 92*
Wodehouse, John *Who 94*
Wodehouse, Lord 1951- *Who 94*
Wodehouse, Lawrence 1934- *ConAu 41NR*
Wodehouse, P(elham) G(renville) 1881-1975 *EncSF 93, RfGShF*
Wodell, Geoffrey Robert 1949- *WhoWest 94*
Wodhams, Jack 1931- *EncSF 93, WrDr 94*
Wodlinger, Eric W. *WhoAm 94, WhoAmL 94*
Wodlinger, Mark Louis 1922- *WhoAm 94*
Wodoslawsky, Theodore Steven 1957- *WhoFI 94, WhoMW 93*
Wodziwob c. 1844-c. 1873 *EncNAR*
Woedtke, Frederick William, Baron von 1740-1776 *WhAmRev*

Woegerer, Otto d1966 *WhoHol 92*
Woehrle, Jeff William 1959- *WhoFI 94*
Woehrlen, Arthur Edward, Jr. 1947- *WhoMW 93*
Woelfel, James Warren 1937- *WhoAm 94*
Woelfel, Lois Jane 1934- *WhoAmP 93*
Woelfel, Stacey William 1959- *WhoMW 93*
Woelffer, Elmer August 1897- *WhoAm 94*
Woelffer, Emerson 1914- *WhoAmA 93*
Woelffer, Emerson Seville 1914- *WhoAm 94*
Woelffer, Neill Carl 1935- *WhoMW 93*
Woelfle, Arthur W. 1920- *IntWW 93*
Woelflein, Kevin Gerard 1933- *WhoAm 94*
Woelkerling, William J. *WhoScEn 94*
Woellmer, Ralph 1958- *WhoWest 94*
Woeltz, Roberta Couch 1956- *WhoAmL 94*
Woerdehoff, Valorie Breyfogle *DrAPF 93*
Woerner, Alfred Ira 1935- *WhoScEn 94*
Woerner, Fred F., Jr. 1933-1990 *WhAm 10*
Woerner, Geldard Harry 1925- *WhoScEn 94*
Woerner, Robert Lester 1925- *WhoAm 94*
Woessner, Frederick T. 1935- *WhoWest 94*
Woessner, Hank *WhoHol 92*
Woessner, Mark Matthias 1938- *IntWW 93, WhoAm 94*
Woessner, Warren *DrAPF 93*
Woeste, John Theodore 1934- *WhoAm 94*
Woeste, William Franklin 1920- *WhoIns 94*
Woestendiek, John, Jr. 1953- *WhoAm 94*
Woetzel, Damian Abdo 1967- *WhoAm 94*
Woffinden, Bob 1948- *WrDr 94*
Woffington, Margaret 1714?-1760 *BlmGEL*
Wofford, Alphonso 1958- *WhoBlA 94*
Wofford, Harris 1926- *CngDr 93*
Wofford, Harris, Jr. *WhoAmP 93*
Wofford, Harris Llewellyn 1926- *IntWW 93, WhoAm 94*
Wofford, Marion *WhoAmP 93*
Wofford, Philip 1935- *WhoAmA 93*
Wofford, Ruth Ann 1935- *WhoFI 94*
Wofford, Sandra Smith 1952- *WhoAmP 93*
Wofsy, David 1946- *WhoWest 94*
Wogaman, George Elsworth 1937- *WhoMW 93*
Wogaman, J(ohn) Philip 1932- *WrDr 94*
Wogan, Chris R. 1950- *WhoAmP 93*
Wogan, Gerald Norman 1930- *IntWW 93, WhoAm 94*
Wogan, Michael Terence 1938- *IntWW 93, Who 94*
Wogan, Patrick Francis Michael *Who 94*
Wogan, Robert 1925- *WhoAm 94*
Wogan, Terri Kay 1953- *WhoWest 94*
Wogen, Warren Ronald 1943- *WhoAm 94*
Woglom, Eric Cooke 1943- *WhoAm 94, WhoAmL 94*
Wogsland, Dan *WhoMW 93*
Wogsland, Daniel K. 1956- *WhoAmP 93*
Wogsland, James Willard 1931- *WhoAm 94, WhoFI 94*
Wogstad, James Everet 1939- *WhoAmA 93*
Wohl, Armand Jeffrey 1946- *WhoScEn 94, WhoWest 94*
Wohl, David *WhoHol 92*
Wohl, David 1950- *WhoAm 94*
Wohl, Joseph Gene 1927-1989 *WhAm 10*
Wohl, Knut Getz 1915-1988 *WhAm 10*
Wohl, Max d1979 *WhoHol 92*
Wohl, Patricia Jeanne 1959- *WhoAmL 94*
Wohl, Pearl d1980 *WhoHol 92*
Wohl, Robert Allen 1931- *WhoAm 94*
Wohl, Ronald Gene 1934- *WhoAm 94*
Wohl, Steven N. 1945- *WhoAmL 94*
Wohleber, Robert Michael 1951- *WhoAm 94, WhoFI 94*
Wohlenhaus, Grace Forcier 1919- *WhoAmA 93*
Wohler, Friedrich 1800-1882 *WorScD [port]*
Wohler, Jeffery Wilson 1947- *WhoWest 94*
Wohlert, Earl Ross 1963- *WhoFI 94*
Wohletz, Kenneth Harold 1952- *WhoWest 94*
Wohletz, Leonard Ralph 1909- *WhoScEn 94, WhoWest 94*
Wohlforth, Carl Curti 1956- *WhoWest 94*
Wohlforth, Eric Evans 1932- *WhoAmL 94*
Wohlgelernter, Beth 1956- *WhoAm 94*
Wohlgelernter, Maurice 1921- *WrDr 94*
Wohlgenant, Michael Kurt 1950- *WhoFI 94*
Wohlgenant, Richard Glen 1930- *WhoAm 94, WhoAmL 94*
Wohlin, John Fredrik 1962- *WhoAmL 94*
Wohlin, Lars Magnus 1933- *IntWW 93*

Wohlmut, Thomas Arthur 1953- *WhoFI 94*
Wohlreich, Jack Jay 1946- *WhoAmL 94*
Wohlschlag, Donald Eugene 1918- *WhoAm 94*
Wohlstetter, Charles 1910- *WhoAm 94, WhoFI 94*
Wohlwend, Clarence 1912- *WhoAmP 93*
Wohmann, Gabriele 1932- *BlmGWL [port], ConWorW 93*
Woide, Robert E. 1927- *WhoAmA 93*
Woirol, Paul C. 1949- *WhoIns 94*
Woiski, Max d1981 *WhoHol 92*
Woit, Bonnie Ford 1931- *WhoAmA 93*
Woit, Erik Peter 1931- *WhoAm 94*
Woitach, Richard 1935- *WhoAm 94*
Woitena, Ben S. 1942- *WhoAmA 93*
Woiwode, Larry *DrAPF 93*
Woiwode, Larry (Alfred) 1941- *WrDr 94*
Woizikowsky, Leon 1899-1975 *IntDcB [port]*
Wojahn, David *DrAPF 93*
Wojahn, David (Charles) 1953- *WrDr 94*
Wojahn, R. Lorraine *WhoAmP 93, WhoWest 94*
Wojcicki, Andrew Adalbert 1935- *WhoAm 94, WhoMW 93*
Wojcicki, Stanley George 1937- *WhoAm 94*
Wojciechowicz, Alex *ProFbHF*
Wojciechowska, Maia *DrAPF 93*
Wojciechowska, Maia (Teresa) 1927- *ConAu 41NR, TwCYAW, WrDr 94*
Wojciechowski, Paul Edward 1955- *WhoMW 93*
Wojcik, Anthony Stephen 1945- *WhoAm 94*
Wojcik, Cass 1920- *WhoFI 94*
Wojcik, Kathleen L. 1936- *WhoAmP 93*
Wojcik, Kathleen Louise 1936- *WhoMW 93*
Wojcik, Lawrence A. 1951- *WhoAm 94, WhoAmL 94*
Wojcik, Mark Edmund 1961- *WhoAmL 94*
Wojcik, Martin Henry 1948- *WhoAm 94*
Wojcik, Mike *WhoAmP 93*
Wojcik, Richard Frank 1936- *WhoFI 94, WhoWest 94*
Wojewodzki, Catherine Willis 1948- *WhoAmP 93*
Wojktkun, James 1958- *WhoMW 93*
Wojnarowicz, David 1954-1992 *AnObit 1992, WhoAmA 93N*
Wojnilower, Albert Martin 1930- *WhoAm 94*
Wojnowski, Edward Joseph 1954- *WhoAmP 93*
Wojtanek, Guy Andrew 1954- *WhoMW 93, WhoScEn 94*
Wojtanowski, Dennis Lee 1950- *WhoAmP 93*
Wojtkowski, Thomas Casmere 1926- *WhoAmP 93*
Wojtyla, Andrzej 1955- *IntWW 93*
Wojtyla, Haase (Walter Joseph) 1933- *WhoAmA 93*
Wojtyla, Karol *IntWW 93*
Wojtyla, Karol Jozef 1920- *WhoAm 94*
Wokral, Larry Stephen 1951- *WhoFI 94*
Wolanek, Anton *NewGrDO*
Wolaner, Robin Peggy 1954- *WhoAm 94, WhoWest 94*
Wolanic, Susan Seseske 1947- *WhoAmA 93*
Wolanin, Barbara A. 1943- *WhoAmA 93*
Wolanin, Barbara Ann Boese 1943- *WhoAm 94*
Wolanin, Sophie Mae 1915- *WhoAm 94, WhoFI 94, WhoMW 93*
Wolansky, Raymond 1926- *NewGrDO*
Wolanskyj, Lidia Alexandra 1950- *WhoMW 93*
Wolas, Herbert 1933- *WhoAm 94, WhoAmL 94, WhoWest 94*
Wolbach, William Wellington, Sr. 1915- *WhoAm 94*
Wolbarsht, James Lester 1947- *WhoFI 94*
Wolber, Paul J. 1935- *WhoAmA 93*
Wolber, William George 1927- *WhoMW 93*
Wolberg, Gary R. 1947- *WhoAmL 94*
Wolbers, Harry Lawrence 1926- *WhoWest 94*
Wolbert, Dorothea d1958 *WhoHol 92*
Wolbert, William d1918 *WhoHol 92*
Wolbrink, Donald Henry 1911- *WhoAm 94*
Wolbrink, James Francis 1942- *WhoAm 94*
Wolck, Wolfgang Hans-Joachim 1932- *WhoAm 94*
Wolcott, John 1738-1819 *BlmGEL*
Wolcott, Craig Stephen 1953- *WhoAmL 94*
Wolcott, Erastus 1722-1793 *WhAmRev*
Wolcott, John J. 1940- *WhoIns 94*

Wolff, Hugh MacPherson 1953- WhoAm 94
Wolff, Ivan Lawrence 1944- WhoAm 94
Wolff, Jesse David 1913- WhoAm 94
Wolff, Kaspar Friedrich 1734-1794 WorScD
Wolff, Kurt H. 1912- WrDr 94
Wolff, Kurt Jakob 1936- WhoAmL 94
Wolff, Lester Bruce 1945- WhoAm 94
Wolff, Lester Lionel 1919- WhoAmP 93
Wolff, Louis Arthur 1933- WhoWest 94
Wolff, Manfred Ernst 1930- WhoAm 94
Wolff, Martha Anne Wood 1949- WhoAm 94
Wolff, Michael 1933- Who 94
Wolff, Nels Christian 1936- WhoWest 94
Wolff, Nelson W. 1940- WhoAm 94, WhoAmP 93
Wolff, Otto Herbert 1920- IntWW 93, Who 94
Wolff, Paul Martin 1941- WhoAm 94, WhoAmL 94
Wolff, Peter Adalbert 1923- WhoAm 94
Wolff, Philippe 1913- IntWW 93
Wolff, Ralph Gerald 1935- WhoScEn 94
Wolff, Richard A. 1933- WhoIns 94
Wolff, Robert Jay 1905-1978 WhoAmA 93N
Wolff, Robert John 1952- WhoMW 93, WhoScEn 94
Wolff, Robert Michael 1955- WhoAmL 94
Wolff, Robert P(aul) 1933- WrDr 94
Wolff, Robert Paul 1933- WhoAm 94
Wolff, Robert W., Jr. 1947- WhoAmA 93
Wolff, Rosemary Langley 1926- Who 94
Wolff, Sanford Irving 1915- WhoAm 94
Wolff, Sarah R. 1952- WhoAmL 94
Wolff, Scott Seanor 1953- WhoMW 93
Wolff, Sheldon 1928- WhoAm 94, WhoScEn 94
Wolff, Sheldon Malcolm 1930- WhoAm 94
Wolff, Sidney Carne 1941- WhoAm 94, WhoScEn 94, WhoWest 94
Wolff, Sonia 1934- WrDr 94
Wolff, Stanley B. 1919- WhoFI 94
Wolff, Steven Alexander 1957- WhoAm 94, WhoFI 94
Wolff, Thomas J. 1928- WhoIns 94
Wolff, Tobias DrAPF 93
Wolff, Tobias 1945- DcLB 130 [port], WhoAm 94
Wolff, Tobias (Jonathan Ansell) 1945- WrDr 94
Wolff, Tobias J. A. 1945- IntWW 93
Wolff, Torben 1919- IntWW 93
Wolff, Victoria 1908- BlmGWL
Wolff, Virginia Euwer 1937- TwCYAW
Wolff, William F., III 1945- WhoAm 94, WhoFI 94
Wolff, William H. 1906-1991 WhoAmA 93N
Wolff, William Steward 1946- WhoFI 94
Wolffe, Alan Paul 1959- WhoScEn 94
Wolf-Ferrari, Ermanno 1876-1948 NewGrDO
Wolff Von Amerongen, Otto 1918- IntWW 93
Wolfgang, Bonnie Arlene 1944- WhoAm 94, WhoWest 94
Wolfgang, Jerald Ira 1938- WhoAmP 93
Wolfgang, Marvin Eugene 1924- WhoAm 94
Wolfgram, Eunice DrAPF 93
Wolfgram, Robert Thomas 1943- WhoFI 94
Wolfinger, Barbara Kaye WhoWest 94
Wolfinger, Bernd Emil 1951- WhoScEn 94
Wolfinger, Raymond Edwin 1931- WhoAm 94
Wolfington, Iggie 1920- WhoHol 92
Wolfit, Donald d1968 WhoHol 92
Wolfl, Joseph 1773-1812 NewGrDO
Wolfle, Dael 1906- WrDr 94
Wolfle, Dael Lee 1906- WhoAm 94, WhoWest 94
Wolfley, Alan 1923- WhoAm 94
Wolfley, Clyde E. 1921- WhoAmP 93
Wolfley, Vern Alvin 1912- WhoWest 94
Wolfman, Arnold B. 1937- WhoFI 94
Wolfman, Bernard 1924- WhoAm 94
Wolfman, Brunetta Reid WhoBlA 94
Wolfman, Earl Frank, Jr. 1926- WhoAm 94
Wolfman, Ira Joel 1950- WhoAm 94
Wolfman, Marv EncSF 93
Wolfman, Toni G. 1942- WhoAmL 94
Wolfman Jack 1938- WhoAm 94, WhoHol 92
Wolford, Dennis Arthur 1946- WhoAm 94
Wolford, Dennis Franklin 1951- WhoAmL 94
Wolford, Matthew Lyons 1961- WhoAmL 94
Wolford, Michael R. 1941- WhoAmL 94
Wolford, Roy, Jr. 1946- WhoFI 94
Wolfowitz, Paul 1943- WhoAmP 93
Wolfowitz, Paul Dundes 1943- IntWW 93
Wolfram, Bradley Allen 1964- WhoFI 94
Wolfram, Charles William 1937- WhoAm 94
Wolfram, Herwig 1934- IntWW 93
Wolfram, Stephen 1959- WhoAm 94
Wolfram, Thomas 1936- WhoAm 94
Wolfram von Eschenbach c. 1170-1220? DcLB 138
Wolfrum, William Harvey 1926- WhoAm 94
Wolfsberg, Max 1928- WhoAm 94, WhoWest 94
Wolfsen, Franklin G. WhoAmP 93
Wolfsheimer, Abbe 1938- WhoAmP 93
Wolfsheimer, Ronald Milton 1952- WhoFI 94
Wolfskill, William 1798-1866 WhWE
Wolfson Who 94
Wolfson, Baron 1927- IntWW 93, Who 94
Wolfson, Brian (Gordon) 1935- Who 94
Wolfson, Dirk Jacob 1933- IntWW 93
Wolfson, Harvey Martin 1933- WhoFI 94
Wolfson, Isaac 1897- WhAm 10
Wolfson, Larry M. 1947- WhoAm 94, WhoAmL 94
Wolfson, Lawrence Aaron 1941- WhoFI 94, WhoScEn 94
Wolfson, Mark Who 94
Wolfson, (Geoffrey) Mark 1934- Who 94
Wolfson, Mark Alan 1952- WhoAm 94
Wolfson, Marsha 1944- WhoWest 94
Wolfson, Martin d1973 WhoHol 92
Wolfson, Martin Henry 1944- WhoMW 93
Wolfson, Michael George 1938- WhoAm 94
Wolfson, Murray 1927- WhoWest 94
Wolfson, Nicholas 1932- WhoAmL 94
Wolfson, Richard 1923- IntMPA 94
Wolfson, Richard Frederick 1923- WhoAm 94, WhoFI 94
Wolfson, Sidney 1911-1973 WhoAmA 93N
Wolfson, Steven Nathan 1944- WhoFI 94
Wolfson, Warren David 1949- WhoAm 94
Wolfson Of Sunningdale, Baron 1935- Who 94
Wolfstone, Billy d1973 WhoHol 92
Wolfthal, Diane (Bette) 1949- WrDr 94
Wolgin, David Lewis 1945- WhoAm 94
Wolheim, Louis d1931 WhoHol 92
Wolicki, Eligius Anthony 1927- WhoAm 94
Wolin, Alfred M. 1932- WhoAm 94, WhoAmL 94
Wolin, Jeffrey Alan 1951- WhoAmA 93
Wolin, Merle Linda 1948- WhoWest 94
Wolins, Joseph 1915- WhoAm 94, WhoAmA 93
Wolinsky, David WhoFI 94
Wolinsky, Emanuel 1917- WhoAm 94
Wolinsky, Steven Mark 1953- WhoScEn 94
Wolintz, Arthur Harry 1937- WhoAm 94
Wolis, Kenneth Arnold 1931- WhoAmL 94
Wolitarsky, James William 1946- WhoAm 94, WhoFI 94
Wolitzer, Hilma DrAPF 93
Wolitzer, Hilma 1930- TwCYAW, WhoAm 94, WrDr 94
Wolitzer, Meg DrAPF 93
Wolitzer, Steven Barry 1953- WhoAm 94
Woliver, Robert 1947- WhoWest 94
Wolk, Bruce Alan 1946- WhoAm 94
Wolk, David S. 1953- WhoAmP 93
Wolk, Emil WhoHol 92
Wolk, Jeffrey S. 1947- WhoAmL 94
Wolk, Joel M.Y. DrAPF 93
Wolk, Martin 1930- WhoScEn 94, WhoWest 94
Wolk, Stuart Rodney 1938- WhoAmL 94
Wolken, Jerome Jay 1917- WhoAm 94
Wolken, Mark William 1957- WhoAmP 93
Wolkers, Jan (Hendrik) 1925- ConWorW 93
Wolkin, Paul Alexander 1917- WhoAm 94, WhoAmL 94
Wolkind, Jack 1920- Who 94
Wolkins, David Alan 1943- WhoAmP 93
Wolkoff, Eugene Arnold 1932- WhoAm 94
Wolkstein, Diane DrAPF 93
Woll, Edward, Jr. 1943- WhoAmL 94
Woll, Harry J. 1920- WhoAm 94
Woll, Michael G. 1944- WhoIns 94
Woll, Peter 1933- WrDr 94
Wollack, Steven Edward 1942- WhoAmL 94
Wollangk, Sandra Jeanne 1949- WhoAmL 94
Wollank, (Johann Ernst) Friedrich 1781-1831 NewGrDO
Wollard, Leslie Ann 1946- WhoFI 94
Wollaston, Nicholas 1926- WrDr 94
Wollaston, William 1660-1724 EncEth
Wollaston, William Hyde 1766-1828 WorScD
Wolle, Charles Robert 1935- WhoAm 94, WhoAmL 94, WhoAmP 93, WhoMW 93
Wolle, Eduardo 1954- WhoHisp 94
Wolle, Gertrud d1952 WhoHol 92
Wolle, June Rose Bush 1941- WhoAm 94
Wolle, Muriel Sibell 1898-1977 WhoAmA 93N
Wolle, William Down 1928- WhoAm 94, WhoAmP 93
Wollen, W. Foster 1936- WhoAm 94
Wollenberg, Bruce Frederick 1942- WhoAm 94
Wollenberg, David Arthur 1947- WhoWest 94
Wollenberg, J. Roger 1919- WhoAm 94
Wollenberg, Richard Peter 1915- WhoAm 94, WhoFI 94, WhoWest 94
Wollenberg, William Louis 1932- WhoAmP 93
Wollenberger, Vera Cornelia 1952- IntWW 93
Woller, James Alan 1946- WhoAmL 94
Wollert, Gerald Dale 1935- WhoAm 94, WhoWest 94
Wollet, Robert James 1927-1990 WhAm 10
Wolley, Hannah 1621?-1676? BlmGWL
Wollheim, Donald A(llen) 1914-1990 EncSF 93
Wollheim, Richard Arthur 1923- IntWW 93, Who 94
Wollheim, Robert 1948- WhoAmL 94
Wollins, David H. 1952- WhoAmL 94
Wollman, Arthur Lee 1943- WhoWest 94
Wollman, Eric 1951- WhoAmP 93
Wollman, Harry 1932- WhoAm 94
Wollman, Leo 1914- WhoAm 94
Wollman, Nathaniel 1915- WhoAm 94
Wollman, Roger L. 1934- WhoAmP 93
Wollman, Roger Leland 1934- WhoAm 94, WhoAmL 94, WhoMW 93
Wollmer, Richard Dietrich 1938- WhoWest 94
Wollner, Thomas Edward 1936- WhoAm 94
Wollny, Lieselotte 1926- WhoWomW 91
Wollstadt, Paul 1910-1987 WhAm 10
Wollstonecraft (Godwin), Mary 1759-1797 EncEth
Wollstonecraft, Mary 1759-1797 BlmGEL, BlmGWL
Wollum, Arthur George, II 1937- WhoAm 94
Wollum, Owen Lee 1959- WhoFI 94, WhoWest 94
Wolman, Abel 1892-1989 EnvEnc [port]
Wolman, Benjamin B 1908- WrDr 94
Wolman, J. Martin 1919- WhoAm 94
Wolman, M. Gordon 1924- WhoAm 94
Wolman, Martin 1937- WhoAm 94, WhoAmL 94
Wolman, Stephen Robert 1943- WhoFI 94
Wolman, William WhoAm 94, WhoFI 94
Wolmer, Viscount 1971- Who 94
Wolner, Rena Meryl 1945- WhoAm 94
Wolnitzek, Stephen Dale 1949- WhoAmL 94
Woloch, Isser 1937- WrDr 94
Woloshansky, Linda Mosora 1950- WhoMW 93
Woloshen, Jeffery Lawrence 1949- WhoMW 93
Woloszyn, John Joseph, Jr. 1944- WhoAm 94, WhoAmL 94
Wolovnick, Jared Hal 1950- WhoAmL 94
Wolowitz, Steven 1952- WhoAm 94, WhoAmL 94
Wolpe, David J. 1958- ConAu 140
Wolpe, Howard Eliot 1939- WhoAmP 93
Wolpe, Joseph 1915- WrDr 94
Wolpe, Stefan 1902-1972 NewGrDO
Wolper, Allan L. WhoAm 94
Wolper, David L. 1928- IntMPA 94
Wolper, David Lloyd 1928- IntWW 93, WhoAm 94
Wolper, Marshall 1922- WhoAm 94, WhoFI 94
Wolper, Robert W. 1959- WhoAmL 94
Wolpers, Emily Kinder 1944- WhoMW 93
Wolpert, Edward Alan 1930- WhoAm 94
Wolpert, Etta WhoAmA 93
Wolpert, Franz Alphons 1917-1978 NewGrDO
Wolpert, Julian 1932- IntWW 93, WhoAm 94
Wolpert, Lewis 1929- IntWW 93, Who 94
Wolpert, Stanley Albert 1927- WrDr 94
Wolrich, Peter M. 1946- WhoAm 94
Wolrige Gordon, Anne 1936- WrDr 94
Wolrige-Gordon, Patrick 1935- Who 94
Wolseley, Charles Garnet Richard Mark 1944- Who 94
Wolseley, Garnet d1991 Who 94N
Wolseley, James Douglas 1937- Who 94
Wolseley, Roland E. 1904- WrDr 94
Wolsey, Thomas 1471-1530 HisWorL [port]
Wolsey, Thomas 1475?-1530 BlmGEL
Wolsiffer, Patricia Rae 1933- WhoAm 94
Wolski, Patrick Edward 1939- WhoAm 94
Wolsky, Albert ConTFT 11
Wolsky, Dave WhoAmP 93
Wolsky, Jack 1930- WhoAmA 93
Wolsky, Murray 1931- WhoAm 94
Wolson, Craig Alan 1949- WhoAm 94, WhoAmL 94, WhoFI 94
Wolstein, Benjamin 1922- WrDr 94
Wolstein, Scott Alan 1952- WhoAm 94
Wolstencroft, Alan 1914- Who 94
Wolstenholme, Gordon (Ethelbert Ward) 1913- Who 94
Wolstenholme, Roy 1936- Who 94
Wolstenholme-Elmy, Elizabeth 1834-1913 BlmGWL
Wolt, Jeffrey Duaine 1951- WhoMW 93
Wolter, Anne Margaret 1937- WhoMW 93
Wolter, Duane Roland 1948- WhoAm 94, WhoFI 94
Wolter, Frank 1943- IntWW 93
Wolter, Fred William, Jr. 1954- WhoMW 93
Wolter, John Amadeus 1925- WhoAm 94
Wolter, Kirk Marcus 1948- WhoMW 93
Wolter, Sherilyn WhoHol 92
Woltering, Denise M. 1958- WhoMW 93
Woltering, Margaret Mae 1913- WhoMW 93
Woltering, Michael J. 1949- WhoFI 94
Wolterink, Lester Floyd 1915- WhoAm 94
Wolters, Curt Cornelis Frederik 1938- WhoAm 94
Wolters, Gale Leon 1939- WhoWest 94
Wolters, Gwyneth Eleanor Mary 1918- Who 94
Wolters, Jackie Margaret 1935- WhoMW 93
Wolters, Oliver William 1915- WhoAm 94, WrDr 94
Wolters, Raymond 1938- WhoAm 94, WrDr 94
Wolters, Richard A 1920- WrDr 94
Wolterstorff, Larry Raymond 1942- WhoFI 94
Wolterstorff, Nicholas (Paul) 1932- WrDr 94
Wolting, Robert Roy 1928- WhoAm 94
Woltkamp, David Bernard 1958- WhoMW 93
Wolton, Harry 1938- Who 94
Woltz, Alan Edward 1932- Who 94
Woltz, Howard Osler, Jr. 1925- WhoAm 94
Woltz, Kenneth Allen 1943- WhoAm 94
Woltz, Mary Lynn Monaco 1951- WhoFI 94, WhoMW 93
Wolverhampton, Bishop Suffragan of 1941- Who 94
Wolverson Cope, F(rederick) Who 94
Wolverton, Baron 1938- Who 94
Wolverton, Dave 1957- EncSF 93
Wolverton, James Newton, Jr. 1943- WhoWest 94
Wolverton, Mary Katherine 1948- WhoAmL 94
Wolverton, Robert E. 1925- WrDr 94
Wolverton, Robert Earl 1925- WhoAm 94
Wolverton, William Thomas, Jr. 1937- WhoAm 94
Wolynes, Peter Guy 1953- WhoAm 94, WhoScEn 94
Wolynic, Edward Thomas 1948- WhoAm 94, WhoScEn 94
Wolz, Henry George 1905- WhoAm 94
Wolzenski, Ben H. 1949- WhoFI 94
Wolzogen, Friederike Sophie Karoline Auguste von 1763-1847 BlmGWL
Wolzogen, Hans (Paul) 1848-1938 NewGrDO
Womach, Emily Hitch 1927- WhoAm 94
Womack, Andy 1945- WhoAmP 93
Womack, Bobby Dwayne 1944- WhoBlA 94
Womack, Carter Devon 1951- WhoBlA 94
Womack, Clay d1948 WhoHol 92
Womack, Doug C. 1950- WhoMW 93
Womack, Edgar Allen, Jr. 1942- WhoAm 94
Womack, Henry Cornelius 1938- WhoBlA 94
Womack, Jack 1956- ConAu 141, EncSF 93
Womack, James Errol 1940- WhoFI 94, WhoWest 94
Womack, Joe Neal, Jr. 1950- WhoBlA 94
Womack, John H. 1944- WhoBlA 94
Womack, Mack 1952- WrDr 94
Womack, Mary Pauline 1942- WhoAmL 94
Womack, Pamela M. WhoAmP 93
Womack, Robert W., Sr. 1916- WhoBlA 94
Womack, Stanley H. 1930- WhoBlA 94
Womack, Steven (James) 1952- WrDr 94

Womack, Terry Dean 1953- *WhoScEn 94*
Womack, Thomas Houston 1940- *WhoWest 94*
Womack, V. Cheryl 1950- *WhoFI 94*
Womack, William Martin 1936- *WhoBlA 94*
Womble, Harlin Clyde, Jr. 1952- *WhoAmL 94*
Womble, Jeffery Maurice 1964- *WhoBlA 94*
Womble, Larry W. 1941- *WhoAmP 93, WhoBlA 94*
Womble, Robert Byron 1954- *WhoAmL 94*
Womble, William F., Jr. 1942- *WhoAmL 94*
Womble, William Fletcher 1916- *WhoAm 94*
Wombwell, George (Philip Frederick) 1949- *Who 94*
Womeldorff, Porter John 1933- *WhoAm 94*
Womer, Charles Berry 1926- *WhoAm 94*
Womersley, Keith *Who 94*
Womersley, (Denis) Keith 1920- *Who 94*
Womersley, Peter (John Walter) 1941- *Who 94*
Womersley, William John 1962- *WhoScEn 94*
Wommack, William Walton 1922- *WhoAm 94*
Wompa, Urmas Jaan 1952- *WhoFI 94*
Won, Ihn-Jae 1943- *WhoScEn 94*
Won, Ko *DrAPF 93*
Won, Kyung-Soo 1928- *WhoWest 94*
Wonacott, Edna May 1932- *WhoHol 92*
Wonder, Betty d1979 *WhoHol 92*
Wonder, John Paul 1921- *WhoWest 94*
Wonder, Stevie 1950- *AfrAmAl 6 [port], IntWW 93, WhoAm 94, WhoBlA 94*
Wonder, Tommy *WhoHol 92*
Wonder, Tommy d1993 *NewYTBS 93*
Wonders, William Clare 1924- *WhoAm 94, WhoWest 94*
Wondra, Janet *DrAPF 93*
Wonfor, Andrea Jean 1944- *Who 94*
Wong, Alan S. 1954- *WhoAsA 94*
Wong, Albert 1938- *WhoAsA 94*
Wong, Albert Y. 1947- *WhoAsA 94*
Wong, Alexius Yu-Ming 1965- *WhoAsA 94*
Wong, Alfred 1919- *WhoAsA 94*
Wong, Aline K. 1941- *WhoWomW 91*
Wong, Alvin C. P. 1950- *WhoAsA 94*
Wong, Amy An Mei *DrAPF 93*
Wong, Andres Ruben 1958- *WhoWest 94*
Wong, Angela Ma 1947- *WhoAsA 94*
Wong, Anna Clara 1959- *WhoAsA 94*
Wong, Anna May d1961 *WhoHol 92*
Wong, Anthony Joseph 1928- *WhoAsA 94*
Wong, Astria Wor 1949- *WhoWest 94*
Wong, B. D. 1962- *WhoAsA 94, WhoHol 92*
Wong, Backman 1927- *WhoAsA 94*
Wong, Barry 1954- *WhoAsA 94*
Wong, Beal d1962 *WhoHol 92*
Wong, Benedict Ding Chung 1955- *WhoAsA 94*
Wong, Benson D. 1952- *WhoAsA 94*
Wong, Bernard P. 1941- *WhoAsA 94, WhoWest 94*
Wong, Bing K. 1938- *WhoAsA 94*
Wong, Bob *WhoAmP 93*
Wong, Bonnie Lee 1957- *WhoWest 94*
Wong, Bradley D. 1949- *WhoAsA 94*
Wong, Bruce d1953 *WhoHol 92*
Wong, Bryan Allen 1958- *WhoAsA 94*
Wong, Buck W. 1933- *WhoAsA 94*
Wong, Byron F. 1948- *WhoAsA 94*
Wong, Chak-Kuen 1938- *WhoAm 94*
Wong, Charles Foo, Jr. 1922- *WhoAsA 94*
Wong, Cheuk-Yin 1941- *WhoScEn 94*
Wong, Chi-Huey 1948- *WhoScEn 94*
Wong, Chi-Shing 1934- *WhoScEn 94*
Wong, Chin Siong 1962- *WhoAsA 94*
Wong, Ching-Ping 1947- *WhoAm 94, WhoScEn 94*
Wong, Chun Wa 1938- *WhoWest 94*
Wong, Clark Chiu-Yuen 1937- *WhoAsA 94*
Wong, Clifford S. 1939- *WhoAsA 94*
Wong, Daniel On-Cheong 1959- *WhoFI 94*
Wong, Daniel W. 1953- *WhoAsA 94*
Wong, David Chungyao 1941- *WhoScEn 94*
Wong, David Craig 1966- *WhoAsA 94*
Wong, David Peter 1960- *WhoFI 94*
Wong, David T. 1935- *WhoMW 93, WhoScEn 94*
Wong, David Tai Wai 1954- *WhoAsA 94*
Wong, David Taiwai 1935- *WhoAsA 94*
Wong, David Y. 1956- *WhoFI 94*
Wong, David Yue 1934- *WhoAm 94, WhoAsA 94*
Wong, Deborah Anne 1959- *WhoAsA 94*
Wong, Dennis Ka-Cheong 1954- *WhoScEn 94*
Wong, Desmond C. 1950- *WhoAsA 94*
Wong, Dolores 1921- *WhoAsA 94*
Wong, Donald Guy 1934- *WhoWest 94*
Wong, Doris Ning 1940- *WhoAsA 94*
Wong, Dorothy 1952- *WhoAsA 94*
Wong, Dorothy Pan *WhoAsA 94*
Wong, Earl Gar, Jr. 1963- *WhoAsA 94*
Wong, Edward J., Jr. 1942- *WhoAmL 94*
Wong, Elizabeth 1937- *WhoWomW 91*
Wong, Eugene 1934- *WhoAsA 94*
Wong, Eugene G. C. 1940- *WhoAsA 94*
Wong, Eugene Hanlai 1964- *WhoAsA 94*
Wong, Evelyn *WhoAsA 94*
Wong, Francis Alvin 1936- *WhoAmP 93*
Wong, Frank F. 1935- *WhoAsA 94*
Wong, Frank Van 1939- *WhoAsA 94*
Wong, Frederick 1929- *WhoAmA 93, WhoAsA 94*
Wong, George 1955- *WhoAsA 94*
Wong, Gregory Dean 1957- *WhoAsA 94*
Wong, Gregory Sterling 1946- *WhoAsA 94*
Wong, Harold H. 1958- *WhoAsA 94*
Wong, Harry Chow 1933- *WhoWest 94*
Wong, Harry Yuen Chee 1916- *WhoAsA 94*
Wong, Henry H. 1951- *WhoAsA 94*
Wong, Henry L. 1940- *WhoAsA 94*
Wong, Henry Li-Nan 1940- *WhoAm 94, WhoFI 94, WhoWest 94*
Wong, Henry Sik-Yin 1942- *WhoAsA 94*
Wong, Iris d1989 *WhoHol 92*
Wong, Jack C. *WhoAmL 94*
Wong, Jacqueline Jeanne 1951- *WhoAsA 94*
Wong, Jade Snow 1919- *BlmGWL*
Wong, Jade Snow 1922- *WhoAsA 94*
Wong, James Bok 1922- *WhoFI 94, WhoScEn 94, WhoWest 94*
Wong, James H. 1964- *WhoAsA 94*
Wong, Jan H. 1953- *WhoWest 94*
Wong, Janet Gaye 1938- *WhoMW 93*
Wong, Janet S. 1958- *WhoAsA 94*
Wong, Janine Mei-Chiao 1956- *WhoAsA 94*
Wong, Jason 1934- *WhoAmA 93*
Wong, Jeffrey Joseph 1943- *WhoAmL 94*
Wong, Jimmy K. 1943- *WhoAmP 93*
Wong, Joe d1978 *WhoHol 92*
Wong, John A. 1948- *WhoAsA 94*
Wong, John Bullitt 1959- *WhoAsA 94*
Wong, John D. 1962- *WhoAsA 94*
Wong, John L. 1951- *WhoAm 94*
Wong, John Lap 1951- *WhoAsA 94*
Wong, Johnny S. 1954- *WhoAsA 94*
Wong, Juan, Jr. *WhoHisp 94*
Wong, K. C. 1954- *WhoAsA 94*
Wong, Kar-yiu 1950- *WhoAsA 94*
Wong, Karl 1967- *WhoAsA 94*
Wong, Kau Fui 1949- *WhoAsA 94*
Wong, Kellogg H. 1928- *WhoAm 94*
Wong, Kenneth K. 1955- *WhoAsA 94, WhoMW 93*
Wong, Kenneth Lee 1947- *WhoScEn 94, WhoWest 94*
Wong, Kenneth P. 1956- *WhoAsA 94*
Wong, Kent Douglas 1956- *WhoAsA 94*
Wong, Kin Fai 1944- *WhoAsA 94*
Wong, Kin-Ping 1941- *WhoAsA 94, WhoWest 94*
Wong, King-Lap 1946- *WhoAsA 94*
Wong, Kuang Chung 1936- *WhoAm 94, WhoAsA 94*
Wong, Kwan P. 1962- *WhoAsA 94*
Wong, Kwan S. 1934- *WhoAm 94*
Wong, Kwee Chang *WhoScEn 94*
Wong, Kwok-Fai Matthew 1961- *WhoAsA 94*
Wong, Liliane R. 1959- *WhoAsA 94*
Wong, Linda *WhoHol 92*
Wong, Linda J. 1949- *WhoAsA 94*
Wong, Margaret Wai 1950- *WhoAmL 94*
Wong, Martha 1939?- *WhoAsA 94*
Wong, Martin Ding-Fat 1956- *WhoAsA 94*
Wong, Mary d1940 *WhoHol 92*
Wong, Maywood 1949- *WhoAsA 94*
Wong, Mel 1938- *WhoAsA 94*
Wong, Morton Min-Fong 1924- *WhoAsA 94*
Wong, Nancy L. 1943- *WhoWest 94*
Wong, Nanying Stella *DrAPF 93*
Wong, Nellie *BlmGWL, DrAPF 93*
Wong, Nellie 1934- *WhoAsA 94*
Wong, Nicole Anna 1968- *WhoAsA 94*
Wong, Norma 1956- *WhoAmP 93*
Wong, Norman Zaw 1941- *WhoAsA 94*
Wong, Otto 1947- *WhoWest 94*
Wong, Ovid K. 1946- *WhoAsA 94*
Wong, Pablo Jose 1956- *WhoAsA 94*
Wong, Pamela Lynn 1947- *WhoWest 94*
Wong, Pat Chung 1956- *WhoAsA 94*
Wong, Patrick Tin-Choi 1942- *WhoScEn 94*
Wong, Paul 1944- *WhoAsA 94*
Wong, Paul K. 1951- *WhoAsA 94*
Wong, Paul Kan 1951- *WhoAmA 93*
Wong, Paul Wing Kon 1932- *WhoAsA 94*
Wong, Peter Alexander 1941- *WhoAsA 94*
Wong, Peter K. 1952- *WhoWest 94*
Wong, Peter M. C. 1953- *WhoAsA 94*
Wong, Peter P. 1941- *WhoAsA 94*
Wong, Philip *WhoAsA 94*
Wong, Philip T. 1953- *WhoAsA 94*
Wong, Po Kee 1934- *WhoAsA 94*
Wong, Pui Kei 1935- *WhoAsA 94, WhoMW 93*
Wong, Raphael Chakching 1948- *WhoScEn 94*
Wong, Ray G. L. 1950- *WhoAsA 94*
Wong, Raymond Y. 1938- *WhoAsA 94*
Wong, Richard Gene 1939- *WhoAsA 94*
Wong, Richard S. H. 1933- *WhoAmP 93*
Wong, Rita F. *WhoAsA 94*
Wong, Robert Eugene 1955- *WhoFI 94*
Wong, Roberta Jean 1957- *WhoWest 94*
Wong, Roger Frederickson 1945- *WhoAmA 93*
Wong, Rosalia Ping 1962- *WhoWest 94*
Wong, Russell 1963- *WhoHol 92*
Wong, Samuel T. 1962- *WhoAsA 94*
Wong, Shawn H. *DrAPF 93*
Wong, Shawn Hsu 1949- *WhoAsA 94*
Wong, Siu G. 1947- *WhoAsA 94*
Wong, Sophie Chao 1927- *WhoAsA 94*
Wong, Steven Dale 1949- *WhoAsA 94*
Wong, Steven W. 1946- *WhoAsA 94*
Wong, Steven Wymann 1946- *WhoFI 94*
Wong, Sue Siu-Wan 1959- *WhoScEn 94, WhoWest 94*
Wong, Suk Yee 1968- *WhoAsA 94*
Wong, Terry Chen Yi 1938- *WhoAsA 94*
Wong, Theodore Yau Sing 1940- *WhoFI 94, WhoWest 94*
Wong, Thomas Tang Yum 1952- *WhoMW 93, WhoScEn 94*
Wong, Tom 1928- *WhoAsA 94*
Wong, Tuck Chuen 1946- *WhoScEn 94*
Wong, Vernon D. B. 1937- *WhoAsA 94*
Wong, Victor *WhoHol 92*
Wong, Victor d1972 *WhoHol 92*
Wong, Victor Kenneth 1938- *WhoAm 94, WhoAsA 94*
Wong, W. M. Peter 1959- *WhoFI 94*
Wong, Wallace 1941- *WhoFI 94, WhoScEn 94, WhoWest 94*
Wong, Walter Foo 1930- *WhoWest 94*
Wong, Wayne D. 1950- *WhoFI 94, WhoWest 94*
Wong, Wendell P. 1953- *WhoAsA 94*
Wong, William 1941- *WhoAsA 94*
Wong, William 1957- *WhoFI 94*
Wong, William G. 1941- *WhoIns 94*
Wong, William K. C. 1941- *WhoAsA 94*
Wong, William Sheh *WhoWest 94*
Wong, William Wai-Lun 1948- *WhoAsA 94*
Wong, William Wai-Lun 1955- *WhoAsA 94*
Wong, Willie 1948- *WhoAmP 93, WhoAsA 94*
Wong, Wing Keung 1933- *WhoFI 94*
Wong, Wing Y. 1941- *WhoAsA 94*
Wong, Ying Wood 1950- *WhoFI 94, WhoWest 94*
Wongananda, Boondharm 1935- *WhoAsA 94*
Wong-Chong, George Michael 1940- *WhoScEn 94*
Wong-Diaz, Francisco Raimundo 1944- *WhoAmL 94, WhoWest 94*
Wong Kan Seng 1946- *IntWW 93*
Wong Kin Chow, Michael 1936- *Who 94*
Wong May *BlmGWL*
Wonham, Frederick Stapley 1931- *WhoAm 94*
Wonham, Walter Murray 1934- *WhoAm 94*
Wonnacott, Elizabeth Sagona 1951- *WhoWest 94*
Wonnacott, James Brian 1945- *WhoScEn 94*
Wonnacott, Paul 1933- *WhoAm 94, WrDr 94*
Wonnacott, Ronald Johnston 1930- *WhoAm 94, WrDr 94*
Wonner, Paul (John) 1920- *WhoAmA 93*
Wonser, Michael Dean 1940- *WhoAm 94*
Wonson-Liukkonen, Barbara Boyce 1953- *WhoMW 93*
Wontner, Arthur d1960 *WhoHol 92*
Wontner, Arthur 1875-1960 *DcNaB MP*
Wontner, Hugh 1908-1992 *AnObit 1992*
Wontner, Hugh Walter Kingwell d1992 *IntWW 93N, Who 94N*
Won Yong-duk 1907-1968 *HisDcKW*
Woo, Benson K. 1954- *WhoAsA 94*
Woo, Buck Hong 1956- *WhoScEn 94*
Woo, Celeste Kimberlee 1956- *WhoAsA 94*
Woo, Christopher Allen 1963- *WhoWest 94*
Woo, Chung S. H. 1962- *WhoAsA 94*
Woo, Dah-Cheng 1921- *WhoScEn 94*
Woo, David Sonny 1954- *WhoWest 94*
Woo, Edward D. *WhoAsA 94*
Woo, Henry 1964- *WhoAsA 94*
Woo, Jacky 1965- *WhoScEn 94*
Woo, James T. K. 1938- *WhoAsA 94*
Woo, John c. 1945- *News 94-2 [port]*
Woo, John 1948- *IntMPA 94*
Woo, Jongsik 1957- *WhoScEn 94*
Woo, Katy 1943- *WhoAmP 93*
Woo, Lecon 1945- *WhoAsA 94*
Woo, Leo (Joseph) 1952- *Who 94*
Woo, Michael *WhoAmP 93*
Woo, Michael K. 1951- *WhoAsA 94*
Woo, Michael T. *WhoAsA 94*
Woo, Ming-Ko 1941- *WhoScEn 94*
Woo, P. T. *WhoAsA 94*
Woo, Peng-Yung 1949- *WhoMW 93*
Woo, Robert Ken, Jr. 1967- *WhoAsA 94*
Woo, S. B. *WhoAmP 93*
Woo, S. B. 1937- *WhoAm 94, WhoAsA 94*
Woo, Savio Lau-Ching 1944- *WhoAsA 94*
Woo, Savio Lau-Yuen 1942- *WhoAm 94, WhoScEn 94*
Woo, Steven Edward 1967- *WhoScEn 94*
Woo, Vernon Ying-Tsai 1942- *WhoAmL 94, WhoAsA 94, WhoWest 94*
Woo, Walter 1948- *WhoScEn 94*
Woo, Wilbert Yuk Cheong 1942- *WhoWest 94*
Woo, William Franklin 1936- *WhoAm 94, WhoAsA 94*
Wood *Who 94*
Wood, Abraham 1608-1673? *WhWE*
Wood, Adrian John Bickersteth 1946- *IntWW 93*
Wood, Alan *EncABHB 9*
Wood, Alan 1935- *WhoAmA 93*
Wood, Alan John 1925- *Who 94*
Wood, Alan Keith 1956- *WhoWest 94*
Wood, Alan Marshall M. *Who 94*
Wood, Albert Elmer 1910- *WhoScEn 94*
Wood, Alfred Ardon 1926- *Who 94*
Wood, Allen d1947 *WhoHol 92*
Wood, Allen George 1950- *WhoMW 93*
Wood, Allen John 1925- *WhoAm 94*
Wood, Allison Lorraine 1962- *WhoAmL 94*
Wood, Andrew Marley 1940- *Who 94*
Wood, Andrew W. 1919- *WhoBlA 94*
Wood, Andy *WhoHol 92*
Wood, Anthony John P. *Who 94*
Wood, Anthony Richard 1932- *Who 94*
Wood, Anton Vernon 1949- *WhoBlA 94*
Wood, Arnold 1918- *Who 94*
Wood, Arthur M. 1913- *IntWW 93*
Wood, Arthur MacDougall 1913- *WhoAm 94*
Wood, Arthur Skevington 1916- *WrDr 94*
Wood, Barbara (Lewandowski) 1947- *WrDr 94*
Wood, Barbara Champion 1924- *WhoAmP 93*
Wood, Barry David 1943- *WhoFI 94*
Wood, Beatrice *WhoAmA 93*
Wood, Betty A. 1943- *WhoAm 94*
Wood, Bobby G. 1935- *WhoAmP 93*
Wood, Bobby Gaines 1931- *WhoAmP 93*
Wood, Brenda Blackmon 1955- *WhoBlA 94*
Wood, Brison Robert 1931- *WhoFI 94*
Wood, Britt d1965 *WhoHol 92*
Wood, Buneva Ann 1948- *WhoFI 94*
Wood, Carol Mae 1927- *WhoMW 93*
Wood, Cecil Gordon 1942- *WhoMW 93*
Wood, Charles 1866-1926 *NewGrDO*
Wood, Charles 1950- *Who 94*
Wood, Charles (Gerald) 1932- *ConDr 93, IntDcT 2*
Wood, Charles (Gerald) 1933- *WrDr 94*
Wood, Charles Cresson 1955- *WhoWest 94*
Wood, Charles Edward 1938- *WhoAmL 94*
Wood, Charles Gerald 1932- *IntWW 93, Who 94*
Wood, Charles Martin, III 1943- *WhoFI 94*
Wood, Charles Norman 1938- *WhoAm 94*
Wood, Charles Richard 1933- *WhoMW 93*
Wood, Charles Ross 1941- *WhoMW 93*
Wood, Charles Tuttle 1933- *WhoAm 94, WrDr 94*
Wood, Christie Ann 1955- *WhoFI 94*
Wood, Christopher (Hovelle) 1935- *ConAu 43NR*
Wood, Christopher L. J. 1947- *WhoAm 94*
Wood, Christopher Lainson 1936- *Who 94*
Wood, Chuck d1978 *WhoHol 92*
Wood, Cindi d1983 *WhoHol 92*
Wood, Clive *WhoHol 92*
Wood, Clyde Maurice 1936- *Who 94*
Wood, Curtis A. 1942- *WhoBlA 94*
Wood, Cynthia d1993 *NewYTBS 93*
Wood, Daniel G. 1941- *WhoAm 94*
Wood, Darrell Eugene 1929- *WhoWest 94*
Wood, David 1944- *Who 94, WhoHol 92, WrDr 94*
Wood, David Bruce 1954- *WhoWest 94*
Wood, David Charles 1943- *WhoAm 94, WhoFI 94*
Wood, David (Basil) H. *Who 94*

Wood, David Kennedy Cornell 1925- *WhoAm 94*
Wood, David Walter 1940- *WhoMW 93*
Wood, Deborah Bedard 1951- *WhoAmP 93*
Wood, Denys Broomfield 1923- *Who 94*
Wood, Derek Alexander 1937- *Who 94*
Wood, Derek Harold 1930- *WrDr 94*
Wood, Derek Rawlins 1921- *Who 94*
Wood, Diana Irene 1947- *WhoFI 94*
Wood, Diane Pamela 1950- *WhoAm 94, WhoAmL 94*
Wood, Dirk Gregory 1953- *WhoMW 93*
Wood, Don 1945- *WrDr 94*
Wood, Donald Craig 1937- *WhoAm 94*
Wood, Donald Euriah 1935- *WhoAm 94*
Wood, Donald F. 1944- *WhoAmL 94*
Wood, Donald Frank 1935- *WhoAm 94, WhoWest 94*
Wood, Donald W. 1925- *WhoFI 94*
Wood, Donna d1947 *WhoHol 92*
Wood, Donna (Marie) 1949- *ConAu 41NR*
Wood, Dorothy Mertis 1928- *WhoAmP 93*
Wood, Doug 1942- *WhoAmP 93*
Wood, Douglas d1966 *WhoHol 92*
Wood, Douglas 1951- *WhoAm 94*
Wood, Dudley Ernest 1930- *Who 94*
Wood, Edgar James 1934- *WhoAmP 93*
Wood, Edward B. 1952- *WhoAmL 94*
Wood, Edward D., Jr. d1978 *WhoHol 92*
Wood, Edward D., Jr. 1924-1978 *HorFD [port]*
Wood, Edward James d1993 *Who 94N*
Wood, Edward John 1931- *ConAu 141*
Wood, Edward Newton 1928- *WhoWest 94*
Wood, Elijah 1981- *IntMPA 94*
Wood, Elizabeth d1993 *NewYTBS 93*
Wood, Ellen 1814-1887 *BlmGEL*
Wood, Elwood Steven, III 1934- *WhoAm 94*
Wood, Emma Lou 1935- *WhAm 10*
Wood, Eric 1931- *Who 94*
Wood, Eric Franklin 1947- *WhoAm 94*
Wood, Ernest d1942 *WhoHol 92*
Wood, Erskine Biddle 1911- *WhoAm 94*
Wood, Eugene d1971 *WhoHol 92*
Wood, Evelyn Nielsen 1909- *WhoAm 94*
Wood, F. Russell 1947- *WhoWest 94*
Wood, Fay S. *WhoFI 94*
Wood, Fergus James 1917- *WhoAm 94, WhoScEn 94, WhoWest 94, WrDr 94*
Wood, Forrest *WhoHol 92*
Wood, Francis Gordon 1924- *Who 94*
Wood, Frank 1929- *Who 94*
Wood, Frank Bradshaw 1915- *WhoAm 94, WhoScEn 94*
Wood, Frank P. 1949- *WhoAmP 93*
Wood, Frank Preuit 1916- *WhoAm 94*
Wood, Franker d1931 *WhoHol 92*
Wood, Frederick (Ambrose Stuart) 1926- *Who 94*
Wood, Freeman d1956 *WhoHol 92*
Wood, G. *WhoHol 92*
Wood, Garland E. 1943- *WhoBlA 94*
Wood, Gary *WhoHol 92*
Wood, George d1977 *WhoHol 92*
Wood, George d1990 *WhoHol 92*
Wood, George Douglas 1919- *WhoWest 94*
Wood, George H. 1946- *WhoAm 94*
Wood, George Marshall 1933- *WhoScEn 94*
Wood, Gerald Lloyd 1938- *WhoMW 93*
Wood, Gerard Edward 1938- *WhoFI 94*
Wood, Gillian *Who 94*
Wood, Gladys Blanche 1921- *WhoWest 94*
Wood, Gloria *WhoHol 92*
Wood, Gordon D. d1954 *WhoHol 92*
Wood, Gordon Harvey *WhoScEn 94*
Wood, Gordon S(tewart) 1933- *WrDr 94*
Wood, Gordon Stewart 1933- *WhoAm 94*
Wood, Grace d1952 *WhoHol 92*
Wood, Gregory Burton, Jr. 1943- *WhoFI 94*
Wood, Harland Goff 1907-1991 *WhAm 10*
Wood, Harleston Read 1913- *EncABHB 9 [port], WhoAm 94*
Wood, Harlington, Jr. *WhoAmP 93*
Wood, Harlington, Jr. 1920- *WhoAm 94, WhoAmL 94, WhoMW 93*
Wood, Harold Leroy 1919- *WhoBlA 94*
Wood, Harold Samuel 1913- *WhoWest 94*
Wood, Harris Spencer, Jr. 1963- *WhoAmL 94*
Wood, Harry Emsley, Jr. 1910- *WhoAmA 93*
Wood, Harry George 1915- *WhoWest 94*
Wood, Harry Stewart 1913- *Who 94*
Wood, Hayes Giering 1959- *WhoAmL 94*
Wood, Helen d1988 *WhoHol 92*
Wood, Henry, Mrs. 1814-1887 *BlmGWL*
Wood, Henry (Peart) 1908- *Who 94*
Wood, Henry J(oseph) 1869-1944 *NewGrDO*
Wood, Hickory d1913 *WhoHol 92*
Wood, Horace Walter, Jr. 1894- *WhAm 10*
Wood, Howard Graham 1910- *WhoAm 94*
Wood, Howard John, III 1938- *WhoScEn 94*
Wood, Hugh Bernard 1909- *WhoWest 94*
Wood, Hugh Bradshaw 1932- *Who 94*
Wood, Humphrey *Who 94*
Wood, (John) Humphrey (Askey) 1932- *Who 94*
Wood, Ian Clark 1942- *Who 94*
Wood, Ira *DrAPF 93*
Wood, (David) Ira 1950- *ConAu 142*
Wood, Ivan, Jr. 1947- *WhoAm 94, WhoAmL 94*
Wood, J.A. *EncSF 93*
Wood, J. Frank 1908-1989 *WhAm 10*
Wood, J. Kenneth, Jr. 1935- *WhoIns 94*
Wood, J(ohn) Laurence 1911- *Who 94*
Wood, Jacalyn Kay 1949- *WhoMW 93*
Wood, Jack Calvin 1933- *WhoAm 94*
Wood, Jacques Martin 1944- *WhoAmL 94*
Wood, James c. 1750-1813 *WhAmRev*
Wood, James 1927- *WhoAm 94*
Wood, James 1930- *WhoAm 94, WhoFI 94*
Wood, James Allen 1906- *WhoAm 94*
Wood, James Arthur 1927- *WhoAmA 93*
Wood, James Clarence 1923- *WhoAm 94*
Wood, James David 1953- *WhoScEn 94*
Wood, James E., Jr. 1922- *WhoAm 94*
Wood, James F. 1949- *WhoAmL 94*
Wood, James Jerry 1940- *WhoAmL 94*
Wood, James Leslie 1941- *WhoWest 94*
Wood, James Michael 1948- *WhoAm 94, WhoAmL 94*
Wood, James Nowell 1941- *WhoAm 94, WhoAmA 93, WhoMW 93*
Wood, Jane Semple 1940- *WhoMW 93*
Wood, Janet *WhoHol 92*
Wood, Jeanne Clarke 1916- *WhoAm 94*
Wood, Jeannette 1932- *WhoAmP 93*
Wood, Jeffrey Bullard 1948- *WhoWest 94*
Wood, Jeffrey L. 1955- *WhoAmL 94*
Wood, Jeffrey S. 1941- *WhoAmL 94*
Wood, Jeremy Scott 1941- *WhoFI 94, WhoScEn 94*
Wood, Jerome H., Jr. 1941- *WhoBlA 94*
Wood, Jerry M. 1937- *WhoAmP 93*
Wood, Joan E. 1934- *WhoAmP 93*
Wood, Joe T. 1922- *WhoAmP 93*
Wood, John *Who 94, WhoHol 92*
Wood, John 1930- *WhoHol 92*
Wood, John 1931- *Who 94*
Wood, John 1947- *WrDr 94*
Wood, John (Kember) 1922- *Who 94*
Wood, John Armstead 1932- *WhoAm 94*
Wood, John Busey 1950- *WhoAmL 94*
Wood, John C(unningham) 1952- *WrDr 94*
Wood, John Denison 1931- *WhoAm 94, WhoWest 94*
Wood, John Edwin 1928- *Who 94*
Wood, John F., Jr. 1936- *WhoAmP 93*
Wood, John M. 1964- *WhoAmL 94*
Wood, John Martin 1944- *WhoAm 94*
Wood, John Mortimer 1934- *WhoFI 94, WhoScEn 94, WhoWest 94*
Wood, John Peter 1925- *Who 94*
Wood, John Thurston 1928- *WhoScEn 94*
Wood, John Turtle 1821-1890 *DcNaB MP*
Wood, Jon C. 1942- *WhoAmL 94*
Wood, Joseph 1712-1791 *WhAmRev*
Wood, Joseph A. 1954- *WhoAmA 93*
Wood, Joseph George 1928- *WhoAm 94*
Wood, Joseph Neville 1916- *Who 94*
Wood, Joshua Warren, III 1941- *WhoAm 94*
Wood, Juanita Wallace 1928- *WhoBlA 94*
Wood, Judith 1906- *WhoHol 92*
Wood, Karen Sue 1950- *WhoAm 94*
Wood, Kathleen Oliver 1921- *WhoMW 93*
Wood, Keith N. 1951- *WhoAmP 93*
Wood, Kenneth Arthur 1926- *WhoAm 94, WhoWest 94*
Wood, Kenneth Maynard 1916- *Who 94*
Wood, Kerry 1907- *WrDr 94*
Wood, Kimba M. 1944- *WhoAm 94, WhoAmL 94*
Wood, Lana 1946- *WhoHol 92*
Wood, Larry *WhoAm 94, WhoFI 94, WhoWest 94*
Wood, Larry Albert 1944- *WhoAmP 93*
Wood, Larry C. 1949- *WhoAmL 94*
Wood, Laura Newbold 1911- *WrDr 94*
Wood, Lawrence Alvin 1949- *WhoBlA 94*
Wood, Leonard C. 1923- *WrDr 94*
Wood, Leonard Earle, III 1942- *WhoMW 93*
Wood, Leonard George *Who 94*
Wood, Leonard George 1923- *WhoMW 93*
Wood, Leslie Ann 1957- *WhoMW 93*
Wood, Leslie Walter 1920- *Who 94*
Wood, Lincoln Jackson 1947- *WhoWest 94*
Wood, Linda May 1942- *WhoAm 94, WhoWest 94*
Wood, Linda Susan 1959- *WhoMW 93*
Wood, Loren Edwin 1927- *WhoScEn 94*
Wood, Lynn *WhoHol 92*
Wood, Marcia Joan 1933- *WhoAmA 93*
Wood, Marcus 1947- *WhoAmL 94*
Wood, Margaret (Lucy Elizabeth) 1910- *ConAu 42NR*
Wood, Margaret A. 1962- *WhoMW 93*
Wood, Margaret Beatrice *WhoBlA 94*
Wood, Marguerite N. *WrDr 94*
Wood, Marian Starr 1938- *WhoAm 94*
Wood, Marjorie d1955 *WhoHol 92*
Wood, Marjorie Ellen 1961- *WhoMW 93*
Wood, Mark *Who 94*
Wood, (Stanley) Mark 1919- *Who 94*
Wood, Mark William 1952- *Who 94*
Wood, Martha S. *WhoAmP 93*
Wood, Martin (Francis) 1927- *IntWW 93, Who 94*
Wood, Mary Anne 1802-1864 *NewGrDO*
Wood, Mary Anne Quinn 1945- *WhoAmL 94*
Wood, Mary Laura *WhoHol 92*
Wood, Mary Marie 1928- *WhoMW 93*
Wood, Maurice 1922- *IntWW 93, WhoAm 94*
Wood, Maurice Arthur Ponsonby 1916- *IntWW 93, Who 94, WrDr 94*
Wood, Maxine d1993 *NewYTBS 93*
Wood, Mccrystle 1947- *WhoAmA 93*
Wood, Michael *WhoHol 92*
Wood, Michael 1936- *WrDr 94*
Wood, Michael Allen 1956- *WhoFI 94, WhoMW 93*
Wood, Michael H. 1942- *WhoBlA 94*
Wood, Michael Neall 1956- *WhoWest 94*
Wood, Mickey d1963 *WhoHol 92*
Wood, Monica 1953- *ConAu 141*
Wood, Montgomery *WhoHol 92*
Wood, Nancy Elizabeth *WhoAm 94*
Wood, Natalie d1981 *WhoHol 92*
Wood, Nathaniel Fay 1919- *WhoWest 94*
Wood, Neal 1922- *WrDr 94*
Wood, Neil Roderick 1931- *WhoAm 94, WhoFI 94*
Wood, Nicholas 1795-1865 *DcNaB MP*
Wood, Nicholas Wheeler 1946- *WhoAmA 93*
Wood, Norman 1905- *Who 94*
Wood, Oliver Gillan, Jr. 1937- *WhoFI 94*
Wood, Orin Lew 1936- *WhoScEn 94*
Wood, Paul F. 1935- *WhoAm 94*
Wood, Peggy d1978 *WhoHol 92*
Wood, Peter *EncSF 93*
Wood, Peter (Lawrence) 1928- *IntWW 93, Who 94*
Wood, Peter Anthony 1943- *Who 94*
Wood, Peter Edric 1929- *Who 94*
Wood, Phil Arnold 1957- *WhoFI 94*
Wood, Philip d1940 *WhoHol 92*
Wood, Philip 1946- *Who 94*
Wood, Phyllis Anderson 1923- *ConAu 43NR, WrDr 94*
Wood, Presnall Hansel 1932- *WhoAm 94*
Wood, Quentin Eugene 1923- *WhoAm 94, WhoFI 94*
Wood, R(obert) W(illiam) 1868-1955 *EncSF 93*
Wood, Raymund Francis 1911- *WhoWest 94*
Wood, Reba Maxine 1919- *WhoMW 93*
Wood, Richard Dean 1953- *WhoMW 93*
Wood, Richard Donald 1926- *WhoAm 94, WhoFI 94*
Wood, Richard Fletcher 1961- *WhoFI 94*
Wood, Richard Frederick *IntWW 93*
Wood, Richard Frederick Marshall 1943- *Who 94*
Wood, Richard J. *WhoAm 94, WhoMW 93*
Wood, Richard James 1920- *Who 94*
Wood, Richard R. 1950- *WhoIns 94*
Wood, Robert (Coldwell) 1923- *WrDr 94*
Wood, Robert B. 1918- *WhoAmP 93*
Wood, Robert C. *WhoIns 94*
Wood, Robert Charles 1956- *WhoAmL 94, WhoFI 94*
Wood, Robert Coldwell 1923- *ConAu 43NR, WhoAm 94*
Wood, Robert Craig 1951- *WhoAmL 94*
Wood, Robert E. 1926- *WhoAmA 93*
Wood, Robert Edward 1941- *WhoAm 94*
Wood, Robert Elkington, II 1938- *WhoFI 94*
Wood, Robert Eric 1909- *Who 94*
Wood, Robert H., Jr. 1931- *WhoAmP 93*
Wood, Robert Henry 1936- *Who 94*
Wood, Robert Noel 1934- *Who 94*
Wood, Robert Warren 1955- *WhoAmL 94, WhoWest 94*
Wood, Robert William, III 1958- *WhoAmL 94*
Wood, Robin 1931- *WrDr 94*
Wood, Roderic Lionel James 1951- *Who 94*
Wood, Roger F. 1947- *WhoAmL 94*
Wood, Roger Holmes 1920- *WhoFI 94, WhoWest 94*
Wood, Roger S. 1927- *WhoAmP 93*
Wood, Roland d1967 *WhoHol 92*
Wood, Roland Arthur *Who 94*
Wood, Ronald 1947- *WhoAm 94*
Wood, Ronald Karslake Starr *Who 94*
Wood, Ronald Karslake Starr 1919- *IntWW 93*
Wood, Roy 1940- *Who 94*
Wood, Royal James 1922- *WhoAmP 93*
Wood, Ruby Fern 1922- *WhoMW 93*
Wood, Russell (Dillon) 1922- *Who 94*
Wood, Ruth Lundgren Williamson *WhoFI 94*
Wood, Ruzena (Alenka Valda) 1937- *WrDr 94*
Wood, Sam d1949 *WhoHol 92*
Wood, Samuel Andrew 1890- *EncSF 93*
Wood, Samuel Eugene 1934- *WhoMW 93*
Wood, Sarah Sayward Barrell Keating 1759-1855 *BlmGWL*
Wood, Sharon 1957- *WhoAm 94*
Wood, Sidney 1911- *BuCMET*
Wood, Silviana 1940- *WhoHisp 94*
Wood, Stephen Wray 1948- *WhoAmP 93*
Wood, Steven Grant 1943- *WhoAmL 94*
Wood, Stuart Kee 1925- *WhoWest 94*
Wood, Susan (Joan) 1948-1980 *EncSF 93*
Wood, Susan Elliott 1951- *WhoMW 93*
Wood, Susan Macduff 1941- *WrDr 94*
Wood, Susan Renee 1965- *WhoFI 94*
Wood, Susanne Griffiths 1933- *WhoMW 93, WhoScEn 94*
Wood, Ted *ConAu 141*
Wood, Terence Courtney 1936- *Who 94*
Wood, Teri Wilford 1950- *WhoAmL 94*
Wood, Thomas c. 1711-1778 *EncNAR*
Wood, Thomas E. 1939- *WhoAm 94*
Wood, Thomas Kemble 1919- *WhoAm 94*
Wood, Thomas Willard 1939- *WhoFI 94*
Wood, Timothy *WhoHol 92*
Wood, Timothy John Rogerson 1940- *Who 94*
Wood, Timothy McDonald 1947- *WhoAm 94*
Wood, Tony *WhoHol 92*
Wood, Ursula 1911- *WrDr 94*
Wood, Victor *Who 94*
Wood, Victor d1958 *WhoHol 92*
Wood, (Rene) Victor 1925- *Who 94*
Wood, Victor Louie 1913- *WhAm 10*
Wood, Victoria 1953- *Who 94*
Wood, Virginia *WhoHol 92*
Wood, Virginia Ann 1936- *WhoMW 93*
Wood, W(illiam) J. 1917- *WrDr 94*
Wood, Wally 1927-1981 *EncSF 93*
Wood, Walter 1914- *Who 94*
Wood, Walter A. d1993 *NewYTBS 93 [port]*
Wood, Warren Wilbur 1937- *WhoScEn 94*
Wood, Wayne W. 1930- *WhoAmP 93*
Wood, Wellington Gibson, III 1945- *WhoMW 93, WhoScEn 94*
Wood, Wendy *DrAPF 93*
Wood, Wendy Deborah 1940- *WhoAm 94, WhoFI 94*
Wood, Wilfred Denniston *Who 94*
Wood, Willard Elloworth 1921- *WhoAmP 93*
Wood, Willard Mark 1942- *WhoAmL 94*
Wood, William (Alan) 1916- *Who 94*
Wood, William B. 1947- *WhoAmL 94*
Wood, William B., III 1938- *IntWW 93*
Wood, William Barry, III 1938- *WhoScEn 94*
Wood, William Clarke 1952- *WhoFI 94*
Wood, William Copeland 1945- *WhoAmL 94*
Wood, William Jerome 1928- *WhoAm 94, WhoAmL 94, WhoFI 94*
Wood, William L., Jr. 1940- *WhoBlA 94*
Wood, William McBrayer 1942- *WhoAmL 94, WhoFI 94*
Wood, William P(reston) 1951- *ConAu 42NR*
Wood, William Philler 1927- *WhoAm 94*
Wood, William Ransom 1907- *WhoAm 94*
Wood, William S. 1926- *WhoBlA 94*
Wood, William Vernell, Sr. 1936- *WhoBlA 94*
Wood, Willie *ProFbHF [port]*
Wood, Willis Bowne, Jr. 1934- *WhoAm 94, WhoFI 94, WhoWest 94*
Woodall, Alec 1918- *Who 94*
Woodall, Ellis O., Sr. 1927- *WhoBlA 94*
Woodall, J. Dan 1924- *WhoAmP 93*
Woodall, Jack David 1936- *WhoAm 94*
Woodall, James Barry 1945- *WhoScEn 94, WhoWest 94*
Woodall, James Daniel, V 1952- *WhoMW 93*
Woodall, John 1940- *WhoAmA 93*
Woodall, John Wesley 1941- *WhoBlA 94*
Woodall, Larry Wayne 1959- *WhoScEn 94*
Woodall, Lowery A. 1929- *WhoAm 94*
Woodall, Norman Eugene 1916- *WhoAm 94*
Woodall, S. Roy, Jr. 1936- *WhoIns 94*
Woodall, Samuel Roy, Jr. 1936- *WhoAm 94*
Woodall, Thomas Edward 1921- *WhoAmP 93*

Woodall, Walter Thomas 1945- *WhoAmP 93*
Woodall, William Leon 1923- *WhoAm 94, WhoFI 94*
Woodard, A. Newton 1936- *WhoBlA 94*
Woodard, Alfre *WhoBlA 94*
Woodard, Alfre 1953- *IntMPA 94, WhoAm 94, WhoHol 92*
Woodard, Alva Abe 1928- *WhoFI 94, WhoWest 94*
Woodard, Barney Paul *WhoAmP 93*
Woodard, Carl Jubal 1924- *WhoAmP 93*
Woodard, Carol Jane 1929- *WhoAm 94*
Woodard, Charlaine *WhoHol 92*
Woodard, Charles D. 1948- *WhoAmP 93*
Woodard, Charles James 1945- *WhoBlA 94*
Woodard, Clarence James 1923- *WhoAm 94*
Woodard, Dorothy Marie 1932- *WhoFI 94, WhoWest 94*
Woodard, Fredrick 1939- *WhoBlA 94*
Woodard, George Sawyer, Jr. 1924- *WhoAm 94*
Woodard, Harold Raymond 1911- *WhoAm 94*
Woodard, Helen Quincy d1993 *NewYTBS 93*
Woodard, John Roger 1932- *WhoAm 94*
Woodard, Joseph Lamar 1937- *WhoAmL 94*
Woodard, Kenneth Emil 1960- *WhoBlA 94*
Woodard, L. Duane 1938- *WhoAmP 93*
Woodard, Larry L. 1936- *WhoWest 94*
Woodard, Lois Marie *WhoBlA 94*
Woodard, Loretta Faye 1943- *WhoAmP 93*
Woodard, Luther T. 1920- *WhoAmP 93*
Woodard, Lynette 1959- *BasBi*
Woodard, Mark Davis 1949- *WhoAmL 94*
Woodard, Nina Elizabeth 1947- *WhoFI 94*
Woodard, Robert Nathaniel 1939- *Who 94*
Woodard, Samuel L. 1930- *WhoBlA 94*
Woodard, Scott Alan 1951- *WhoWest 94*
Woodard, Wilma C. 1934- *WhoAmP 93*
Woodbeck, Frank Raymond 1947- *WhoBlA 94*
Woodberry, Lesley Ellen *WhoAmL 94*
Woodbine Parish, David (Elmer) 1911- *Who 94*
Woodbridge, George d1973 *WhoHol 92*
Woodbridge, Henry Sewall 1906- *WhoAm 94*
Woodbridge, Hensley Charles 1923- *WhoAm 94, WhoMW 93*
Woodbridge, John Marshall 1929- *WhoAm 94*
Woodbridge, John Sylvester 1897- *WhAm 10*
Woodbridge, Linda 1945- *WhoAm 94*
Woodbridge, Norma *DrAPF 93*
Woodburn, Eric *WhoHol 92*
Woodburn, Jeffrey Robert 1965- *WhoAmP 93*
Woodburn, Mary Stuart 1941- *WhoAm 94*
Woodburn, Ralph Robert, Jr. 1946- *WhoAm 94, WhoAmL 94*
Woodburn, Todd Alan 1959- *WhoMW 93*
Woodbury, Alan Tenney 1943- *WhoAm 94*
Woodbury, Charles Putnam 1919- *WhoIns 94*
Woodbury, David Henry 1930- *WhoBlA 94*
Woodbury, David O(akes) 1896-1981 *EncSF 93*
Woodbury, Dixon John 1956- *WhoMW 93, WhoScEn 94*
Woodbury, Doreen d1957 *WhoHol 92*
Woodbury, Franklin Bennett Wessler 1937- *WhoScEn 94*
Woodbury, George Wallis, Jr. 1937- *WhoAm 94*
Woodbury, Joan d1989 *WhoHol 92*
Woodbury, Joyce Carol 1950- *WhoMW 93*
Woodbury, Lael Jay 1927- *WhoAm 94, WhoWest 94*
Woodbury, Louie E., Jr. 1914- *WhoIns 94*
Woodbury, Margaret Clayton 1937- *WhoBlA 94*
Woodbury, Marie Spencer 1951- *WhoAmL 94*
Woodbury, Marion A. 1923- *WhoAm 94*
Woodbury, Max Atkin 1917- *WhoAm 94*
Woodbury, Richard Benjamin 1917- *WhoAm 94, WhoScEn 94*
Woodbury, Richard Coumal 1931- *WhoWest 94*
Woodbury, Robert Charles 1929- *WhoAm 94*
Woodbury, Robert Louis 1938- *WhoAm 94*
Woodbury, Rollin Edwin 1913- *WhoAm 94*
Woodbury, Sara Jorgenson *DrAPF 93*
Woodbury, Stephen Abbott 1952- *WhoMW 93*

Woodbury, Thomas Bowring, II 1937- *WhoAm 94, WhoAmL 94, WhoFI 94*
Woodbury, Verl Angus 1953- *WhoWest 94*
Woodbury-Fariña, Michael A. *WhoHisp 94*
Woodcock, Barbara Louise 1948- *WhoAmL 94*
Woodcock, George 1912- *IntWW 93, Who 94, WhoAm 94, WhoWest 94, WrDr 94*
Woodcock, George Washington 1930- *WhoAmP 93*
Woodcock, Gordon *Who 94*
Woodcock, John 1932- *Who 94*
Woodcock, John Alden 1950- *WhoAmL 94*
Woodcock, John Charles 1926- *Who 94*
Woodcock, John J., III 1946- *WhoAmP 93*
Woodcock, Leonard 1911- *IntWW 93, WhoAm 94, WhoAmP 93*
Woodcock, Michael 1943- *Who 94*
Woodcock, Richard Wesley 1928- *WhoWest 94*
Woodcock, Sharon Lee 1943- *WhoMW 93*
Woodcock, Thomas 1951- *Who 94*
Woodcott, Keith *EncSF 93*
Woodcott, Keith 1934- *WrDr 94*
Woode, Moses Kwamena 1947- *WhoScEn 94*
Woodell, Anne 1936- *WhoAmP 93*
Woodell, Barbara 1918- *WhoHol 92*
Woodell, Pat 1944- *WhoHol 92*
Wooden, Howard Edmund 1919- *WhoAm 94, WhoAmA 93*
Wooden, John 1910- *BasBi [port]*
Wooden, John Robert 1910- *WhoAm 94, WhoWest 94*
Wooden, Ralph L. 1915- *WhoBlA 94*
Wooden, Reba Faye Boyd 1940- *WhoMW 93*
Wooden, Ruth A. 1946- *WhoAm 94*
Wooden Lance c. 1860-1931 *EncNAR*
Woodenlegs, John, Sr. 1912-1981 *EncNAR*
Wood-Felton, Dorothy 1929- *WhoWomW 91*
Woodfield, Clyde V. 1933- *WhoAmP 93*
Woodfield, Denis Buchanan 1933- *WhoFI 94*
Woodfield, Philip (John) 1923- *Who 94*
Woodfolk, Joseph O. 1933- *WhoBlA 94*
Woodford, Anthony Arthur George 1939- *Who 94*
Woodford, Bruce P. *DrAPF 93*
Woodford, Colin Godwin Patrick 1934- *Who 94*
Woodford, David Milner 1930- *Who 94*
Woodford, Don 1941- *WhoAmA 93*
Woodford, Duane Hugh 1939- *WhoFI 94*
Woodford, Hackley Elbridge 1914- *WhoBlA 94*
Woodford, James Elmer, Jr. 1950- *WhoAmP 93*
Woodford, John d1927 *WhoHol 92*
Woodford, John Niles 1941- *WhoBlA 94*
Woodford, Peggy 1937- *WrDr 94*
Woodford, (Frederick) Peter 1930- *Who 94*
Woodford, William 1734-1780 *AmRev, WhAmRev*
Woodforde, James 1740-1803 *DcNaB MP*
Woodforde, John (Edward) Ffooks 1925- *WrDr 94*
Woodfork, Carolyn Amelia 1957- *WhoBlA 94*
Woodgate, Joan Mary 1912- *Who 94*
Woodger, Walter James, Jr. 1913- *WhoFI 94*
Woodhall, David Massey 1934- *Who 94*
Wood Hall, Ellen *WhoAm 94*
Woodhall, John Alexander, Jr. 1929- *WhoFI 94, WhoHol 92*
Woodhall, William Fulton 1944- *WhoWest 94*
Woodham, Derrick James 1940- *WhoAmA 93*
Woodham, Jean *WhoAmA 93*
Woodham, Ronald Ernest 1912- *Who 94*
Woodhead, Christopher Anthony 1946- *Who 94*
Woodhead, David James 1943- *Who 94*
Woodhead, (Susan) Jane d1993 *Who 94N*
Woodhead, Peter *Who 94*
Woodhead, (Anthony) Peter 1939- *Who 94*
Woodhead, Robert Kenneth 1925- *WhoAm 94*
Woodhouse *Who 94*
Woodhouse, Andrew Henry 1923- *Who 94*
Woodhouse, Bernard Lawrence 1936- *WhoAm 94*
Woodhouse, David *Who 94*
Woodhouse, (Charles) David (Stewart) 1934- *Who 94*
Woodhouse, Derrick Fergus 1927- *WhoScEn 94*
Woodhouse, Edward James, Jr. 1953- *WhoAmP 93*

Woodhouse, Emma 1948- *WrDr 94*
Woodhouse, Enoch O'Dell, II 1927- *WhoBlA 94*
Woodhouse, Frank 1943- *Who 94*
Woodhouse, James Stephen 1933- *Who 94*
Woodhouse, John Frederick 1930- *WhoAm 94, WhoFI 94*
Woodhouse, John Henry 1949- *Who 94*
Woodhouse, John Robert 1937- *Who 94*
Woodhouse, Johnny Boyd 1945- *WhoBlA 94*
Woodhouse, Martin (Charlton) 1932- *WrDr 94*
Woodhouse, Michael *Who 94*
Woodhouse, (Ronald) Michael 1927- *Who 94*
Woodhouse, Montague *Who 94*
Woodhouse, (Christopher) Montague 1917- *IntWW 93, Who 94, WrDr 94*
Woodhouse, Owen *Who 94*
Woodhouse, (Arthur) Owen 1916- *IntWW 93, Who 94*
Woodhouse, Rossalind Yvonne 1940- *WhoBlA 94*
Woodhouse, Samuel Mostyn Forbes 1912- *Who 94*
Woodhouse, Stephen Kent 1940- *WhoWest 94*
Woodhouse, Thomas Edwin 1940- *WhoAmL 94, WhoWest 94*
Woodhull, Abraham c. 1750-1826 *WhAmRev*
Woodhull, James Morris, II 1955- *WhoMW 93*
Woodhull, Nancy Jane 1945- *WhoAm 94, WhoFI 94*
Woodhull, Nathaniel 1723-1776 *WhAmRev*
Woodhull, Victoria Claflin 1838-1927 *AmSocL*
Woodie, Henry L. 1940- *WhoBlA 94*
Woodies, Richard 1921- *WhoFI 94*
Woodin, Kerry Jay 1952- *WhoMW 93*
Woodin, Martin Dwight 1915- *WhoAm 94*
Wooding, David Joshua 1959- *WhoBlA 94*
Wooding, Norman (Samuel) 1927- *Who 94*
Wooding, Peter Holden 1940- *WhoAm 94*
Wooding, Sharon L(ouise) 1943- *WrDr 94*
Wooding, Walter Harrison 1910- *WhoWest 94*
Woodiwiss, Kathleen E *WrDr 94*
Woodiwiss, Kathleen E(rin) 1939- *ConAu 41NR*
Woodke, Robert Allen 1950- *WhoAmL 94*
Woodland, Irwin Francis 1922- *WhoAmL 94, WhoWest 94*
Woodland, N. Joseph 1921- *WhoScEn 94*
Woodland, Steven Dee 1951- *WhoAmL 94, WhoWest 94*
Woodlawn, Holly 1947- *WhoHol 92*
Woodley, Arto, Jr. 1965- *WhoMW 93*
Woodley, Chris *WhoHol 92*
Woodley, Edmund Etchison *WhoAmP 93*
Woodley, John Paul, Jr. 1953- *WhoAmP 93*
Woodley, Keith Spencer 1939- *Who 94*
Woodley, Ronald John 1925- *Who 94*
Woodlock, Douglas Preston 1947- *WhoAm 94, WhoAmL 94*
Woodlock, Ethelyn Hurd 1907- *WhoAmA 93*
Woodlock, Jack Terence 1919- *Who 94*
Woodman, Allen *DrAPF 93*
Woodman, Allen 1954- *SmATA 76 [port]*
Woodman, Betty 1930- *WhoAmA 93*
Woodman, David C(harles) 1956- *ConAu 141*
Woodman, G. Roger 1953- *WhoFI 94*
Woodman, Grey Musgrave 1922- *WhoMW 93*
Woodman, Harold David 1928- *WhoAm 94, WrDr 94*
Woodman, Harry Andrews 1928- *WhoAm 94*
Woodman, Timothy 1952- *WhoAm 94, WhoAmA 93*
Woodman, William E. *WhoAm 94*
Woodmansee, Gerald Louis 1930- *WhoAmP 93*
Woodmansey, Kent Robert 1963- *WhoFI 94*
Woodnutt, Thomas Lloyd 1943- *WhoWest 94*
Wood Prince, William Norman 1942- *WhoFI 94*
Woodrell, Frederick Dale 1954- *WhoAm 94*
Woodress, James (Leslie, Jr.) 1916- *WrDr 94*
Woodress, James Leslie, Jr. 1916- *WhoAm 94*
Woodridge, Wilson Jack, Jr. 1950- *WhoBlA 94*
Woodring, Carl 1919- *WrDr 94*

Woodring, DeWayne Stanley 1931- *WhoAm 94*
Woodring, James H. 1942- *WhoAm 94, WhoAmL 94*
Woodring, Paul 1907- *WrDr 94*
Woodroe, Stephen Clark 1940- *WhoAmL 94*
Woodroffe, George Cuthbert Manning 1918- *Who 94*
Woodroffe, Jean Frances 1923- *Who 94*
Woodroffe, Juan F. 1948- *WhoHisp 94*
Woodroofe, Ernest (George) 1912- *Who 94*
Woodroofe, Ernest George 1912- *IntWW 93*
Woodrow, Bill 1948- *IntWW 93*
Woodrow, David 1920- *Who 94*
Woodrow, Gayford William 1922- *Who 94*
Woodrow, James 1828-1907 *DcAmReB 2*
Woodrow, James Irvin 1953- *WhoWest 94*
Woodrow, Kenneth M. 1942- *WhoFI 94, WhoWest 94*
Woodrow, Randall Mark 1956- *WhoAmL 94*
Woodrow-Lafield, Karen Ann 1950- *WhoScEn 94*
Woodruff, Alan Waller d1992 *Who 94N*
Woodruff, Alan Walter d1992 *IntWW 93N*
Woodruff, Bert d1934 *WhoHol 92*
Woodruff, Bruce Emery 1930- *WhoAm 94, WhoAmL 94*
Woodruff, Charles Norman 1941- *WhoAmL 94*
Woodruff, Clyde *EncSF 93*
Woodruff, Constance Oneida 1921- *WhoAmP 93, WhoBlA 94*
Woodruff, Diane d1993 *NewYTBS 93*
Woodruff, Diane Bailey 1940- *WhoAmA 93*
Woodruff, Eleanor d1980 *WhoHol 92*
Woodruff, Eunice d1921 *WhoHol 92*
Woodruff, Fay 1944- *WhoWest 94*
Woodruff, Fred M., Jr. 1944- *WhoAmL 94*
Woodruff, Gene Lowry 1934- *WhoAm 94*
Woodruff, Hale 1900-1979 *AfrAmAl 6*
Woodruff, Hale A. 1900-1980 *WhoAmA 93N*
Woodruff, Harry Wells 1912- *Who 94*
Woodruff, Henry d1916 *WhoHol 92*
Woodruff, James W. *WhoBlA 94*
Woodruff, Jane 1945- *WhoMW 93*
Woodruff, Jeffrey Robert 1943- *WhoBlA 94*
Woodruff, John Douglas 1944- *WhoWest 94*
Woodruff, Judson Sage 1925- *WhoAm 94*
Woodruff, Judy Carline 1946- *IntWW 93, WhoAm 94*
Woodruff, June Yvonne 1930- *WhAm 10*
Woodruff, Laurie *WhoAm 94, WhoFI 94*
Woodruff, Margaret Smith *WhoAm 94, WhoAmL 94*
Woodruff, Michael (Francis Addison) 1911- *Who 94, WrDr 94*
Woodruff, Michael Francis Addison 1911- *IntWW 93*
Woodruff, Michael Shane 1969- *WhoFI 94*
Woodruff, Neil Parker 1919- *WhoAm 94, WhoScEn 94*
Woodruff, Patricia 1945- *WhoAm 94*
Woodruff, Paul A. 1960- *WhoAmP 93*
Woodruff, Paul Harrison 1937- *WhoAm 94*
Woodruff, Philip *IntWW 93, Who 94*
Woodruff, Philip 1906- *WrDr 94*
Woodruff, Randall Lee 1954- *WhoAmL 94*
Woodruff, T. M. 1943- *WhoAmP 93*
Woodruff, Teresa K. 1963- *WhoScEn 94*
Woodruff, Thomas Ellis 1921- *WhoAm 94*
Woodruff, Tom *WhoAmP 93*
Woodruff, Tom, Jr. 1959- *WhoAm 94*
Woodruff, Truman Owen 1925- *WhoAm 94*
Woodruff, Virginia *WhoAm 94*
Woodruff, Wilford 1807-1898 *DcAmReB 2*
Woodruff, William Charles 1921- *Who 94*
Woodrum, Clifton Alexander, III 1938- *WhoAmP 93*
Woodrum, Patricia Ann 1941- *WhoAm 94*
Woodrum, Robert Lee 1945- *WhoAm 94, WhoFI 94*
Woods, Adelaide d1917 *WhoHol 92*
Woods, Al d1946 *WhoHol 92*
Woods, Allie, Jr. *WhoBlA 94*
Woods, Almita 1914- *WhoBlA 94*
Woods, Andre Vincent 1947- *WhoBlA 94*
Woods, Ann Margaret 1967- *WhoFI 94*
Woods, Arleigh Maddox 1929- *WhoBlA 94*
Woods, Arnold Martin 1954- *WhoScEn 94*
Woods, Aubrey 1928- *WhoHol 92*
Woods, Barbara McAlpin 1945- *WhoBlA 94*
Woods, Barry Alan 1942- *WhoFI 94*
Woods, Beatrice 1925- *WhoAmP 93*
Woods, Bernice 1924- *WhoBlA 94*

Woods, Bert Russell 1946- *WhoWest 94*
Woods, Bobby Joe 1935- *WhoWest 94*
Woods, Brian 1928- *Who 94*
Woods, Bruce Walter 1947- *WhoAm 94*
Woods, Charles Laurence, III 1947- *WhoAmL 94*
Woods, Charles Lessly 1915- *WhoAmP 93*
Woods, Charles William 1917- *Who 94*
Woods, Charlotte Ann 1932- *WhoBlA 94*
Woods, Christopher Matthew 1923- *Who 94*
Woods, Clifford Curtis 1898- *WhAm 10*
Woods, Colin (Philip Joseph) 1920- *Who 94*
Woods, Curtis Eugene 1950- *WhoAmL 94*
Woods, Daniel James 1952- *WhoAm 94*
Woods, Darnell 1961- *WhoBlA 94*
Woods, David Fitzwilliam 1936- *WhoFI 94*
Woods, David Lyndon *WhoFI 94*
Woods, Deborah L. 1955- *WhoAmP 93*
Woods, Delbert Leon 1913- *WhoBlA 94*
Woods, Dennis Lynn 1951- *WhoAmL 94*
Woods, Donald 1906- *IntMPA 94*
Woods, Donald 1909- *WhoHol 92*
Woods, Donald DeWayne 1942- *WhoMW 93*
Woods, Donald F., Jr. 1946- *WhoAmL 94*
Woods, Donald Peter 1911- *WhoWest 94*
Woods, Edward d1989 *WhoHol 92*
Woods, Edward V. *WhoAm 94*
Woods, Eldrick 1975- *WhoBlA 94*
Woods, Elisa R. 1959- *WhoBlA 94*
Woods, Elisabeth Ann 1940- *Who 94*
Woods, Forest Arin 1940- *WhoAmP 93*
Woods, Frances Jerome 1913-1992 *WrDr 94N*
Woods, Frank d1992 *IntWW 93N, Who 94N*
Woods, Frederick 1932- *WrDr 94*
Woods, Geneva Halloway 1930- *WhoBlA 94*
Woods, George E. 1923- *WhoAm 94, WhoAmL 94, WhoMW 93*
Woods, George Washington 1916- *WhoBlA 94*
Woods, Gerald Marion Irwin 1947- *WhoAmL 94*
Woods, Gerald T. 1949- *WhoAmL 94*
Woods, Gerald Wayne 1946- *WhoAm 94*
Woods, Geraldine Pittman *WhoAm 94, WhoBlA 94*
Woods, Gerard 1914- *WrDr 94*
Woods, Grant *WhoAm 94, WhoAmL 94, WhoAmP 93, WhoWest 94*
Woods, Grant d1968 *WhoHol 92*
Woods, Granville T. 1856-1910 *AfrAmAl 6, ConBlB 5 [port], WorInv*
Woods, Gurdon 1915- *WhoAmA 93*
Woods, Gurdon Grant 1915- *WhoAm 94, WhoWest 94*
Woods, Harriett 1927- *WhoAmP 93*
Woods, Harriett Ruth 1927- *WhoAm 94*
Woods, Harry d1968 *WhoHol 92*
Woods, Harry Arthur, Jr. 1941- *WhoAmL 94*
Woods, Henry 1918- *WhoAm 94, WhoAmL 94*
Woods, Henry, Jr. 1954- *WhoBlA 94*
Woods, Henry Gabriel 1924- *Who 94*
Woods, Hortense E. 1926- *WhoBlA 94*
Woods, Howard James, Jr. 1955- *WhoFI 94*
Woods, Ickey 1966- *WhoBlA 94*
Woods, Ivan *Who 94*
Woods, (William) Ivan *Who 94*
Woods, J. P. 1950- *WhoFI 94*
Woods, Jack E. *WhoAmP 93*
Woods, Jacqueline Edwards 1947- *WhoBlA 94*
Woods, James 1947- *IntMPA 94, IntWW 93, WhoHol 92*
Woods, James Dudley 1931- *WhoAm 94, WhoFI 94*
Woods, James Howard 1947- *WhoAm 94*
Woods, James Robert 1947- *WhoAm 94*
Woods, James Watson, Jr. 1918- *WhoAm 94*
Woods, Jane Gamble 1928- *WhoBlA 94*
Woods, Jane Haycock 1946- *WhoAm 94*
Woods, Jeff Chandler 1954- *WhoAmL 94*
Woods, Jessie Anderson 1914- *WhoBlA 94*
Woods, Joe Eldon 1933- *WhoWest 94*
Woods, Joel Grant 1954- *WhoAm 94*
Woods, John *DrAPF 93*
Woods, John (Warren) 1926- *WrDr 94*
Woods, John Cahal 1955- *WhoFI 94*
Woods, John David 1939- *Who 94*
Woods, John Elmer 1935- *WhoAm 94*
Woods, John LaRue 1937- *WhoAm 94*
Woods, John Lucius 1912- *WhoAm 94*
Woods, John Mawhinney 1919- *Who 94*
Woods, John Merle 1943- *WhoScEn 94*
Woods, John William 1912- *WhoAm 94*
Woods, John William 1943- *WhoAm 94*
Woods, John Witherspoon 1931- *WhoAm 94, WhoFI 94*

Woods, Karen Marguerite 1945- *WhoScEn 94*
Woods, Kevin Daniel 1961- *WhoFI 94*
Woods, Kristina Margaret 1956- *WhoAmL 94*
Woods, L(eslie) C(olin) 1922- *WrDr 94*
Woods, Lawrence *EncSF 93*
Woods, Lawrence Alan 1939- *WhoMW 93*
Woods, Lawrence Milton 1932- *WhoAm 94, WhoWest 94*
Woods, Leonard 1774-1854 *DcAmReB 2*
Woods, Leslie Colin 1922- *Who 94*
Woods, Leslie Victor 1925- *WhAm 10*
Woods, Lucius Earle 1921- *WhoAmL 94*
Woods, Madelyne I. 1965- *WhoBlA 94*
Woods, Manuel T. 1939- *WhoBlA 94*
Woods, Marvin 1960- *WhoMW 93*
Woods, Maurice Eric 1933- *Who 94*
Woods, Melanie Ann 1957- *WhoWest 94*
Woods, Melvin LeRoy 1938- *WhoBlA 94*
Woods, Michael *WhoHol 92*
Woods, Michael 1935- *IntWW 93*
Woods, Michael Douglas 1947- *WhoFI 94*
Woods, Michael Patrick 1959- *WhoMW 93*
Woods, Nan *WhoHol 92*
Woods, P. F. *ConAu 43NR, EncSF 93*
Woods, Paul Harlow 1906-1989 *WhAm 10*
Woods, Pauline Harper 1930- *WhoAmP 93*
Woods, Philip Wells 1931- *IntWW 93, WhoAm 94, WhoHol 92*
Woods, Ramona Lee 1945- *WhoHisp 94*
Woods, Randi Ellen 1963- *WhoMW 93*
Woods, Randy 1970- *WhoBlA 94*
Woods, Raymond Duval 1960- *WhoWest 94*
Woods, Reginald Foster 1939- *WhoAm 94*
Woods, Ren *WhoHol 92*
Woods, Richard (John Francis) 1941- *WrDr 94*
Woods, Richard Dale 1950- *WhoAm 94, WhoAmL 94*
Woods, Richard Glenn 1933- *WhoAmP 93*
Woods, Richard Irvin 1932- *WhoWest 94*
Woods, Richard James 1939- *WhoAm 94*
Woods, Richard Seavey 1919- *WhoAm 94*
Woods, Rip 1933- *WhoAmA 93*
Woods, Robert A. *WhoAm 94, WhoFI 94*
Woods, Robert Archer 1920- *WhoAm 94*
Woods, Robert Edward 1952- *WhoAm 94, WhoAmL 94*
Woods, Robert Evans, Jr. 1947- *WhoFI 94*
Woods, Robert Joseph 1946- *WhoAm 94*
Woods, Robert Louis 1947- *WhoBlA 94*
Woods, Robert S. 1950- *WhoHol 92*
Woods, Robert Wilmer 1914- *Who 94*
Woods, Roberta Everett 1949- *WhoAmL 94*
Woods, Rodney Ian 1941- *WhoAm 94*
Woods, Ronald Earl 1938- *Who 94*
Woods, Roosevelt, Jr. 1933- *WhoBlA 94*
Woods, Rose Mary 1917- *WhoAm 94*
Woods, Samuel Moses James 1867-1931 *DcNaB MP*
Woods, Sarah Ladd 1895-1980 *WhoAmA 93N*
Woods, Stephanie Elise 1962- *WhoScEn 94*
Woods, Stockton 1932- *WrDr 94*
Woods, Stuart 1938- *WrDr 94*
Woods, Susan *WhoHol 92*
Woods, Susanne 1943- *WhoAm 94*
Woods, Sylvania Webb, Sr. 1927- *WhoBlA 94*
Woods, Sylvania Webb, Jr. 1954- *WhoAmP 93, WhoBlA 94*
Woods, Terry Ray 1957- *WhoAmP 93*
Woods, Thomas d1932 *WhoHol 92*
Woods, Thomas Brian 1938- *WhoScEn 94*
Woods, Thomas Cochrane, Jr. 1920-1989 *WhAm 10*
Woods, Thomas Fabian 1956- *WhoScEn 94*
Woods, Thomas Lamar 1933- *WhoAmP 93*
Woods, Timothy L. *WhoBlA 94*
Woods, Timothy Phillips 1943- *Who 94*
Woods, Tony 1965- *WhoBlA 94*
Woods, Tony 1966- *WhoBlA 94*
Woods, Victoria Patricia Ann 1947- *Who 94*
Woods, Walter Earl 1944- *WhoFI 94, WhoScEn 94*
Woods, Walter Ralph 1931- *WhoAm 94, WhoScEn 94*
Woods, Ward Wilson, Jr. 1942- *WhoAm 94*
Woods, Warren Chip 1948- *WhoMW 93*
Woods, Wilbourne F. 1916- *ConAu 43NR*
Woods, William 1916- *ConAu 43NR*
Woods, William Ellis 1917- *WhoAm 94*
Woods, William Everett 1949- *WhoWest 94*
Woods, Willie G. *WhoBlA 94*
Woods, Willis Franklin 1920-1988 *WhoAmA 93N*

Woodside, Bertram John 1946- *WhoScEn 94*
Woodside, Edmund Rector 1921- *WhAm 10*
Woodside, Frank C., III 1944- *WhoAmL 94*
Woodside, Gordon William *WhoAmA 93*
Woodside, Robert Elmer 1904- *WhoAm 94*
Woodside, William Stewart 1922- *IntWW 93, WhoAm 94, WhoFI 94*
Woodson, Aileen R. 1927- *WhoBlA 94*
Woodson, Alfred F. 1952- *WhoBlA 94*
Woodson, Benjamin N. 1908- *WhoIns 94*
Woodson, Benjamin Nelson, III 1908- *WhoAm 94*
Woodson, Carter G. 1875-1950 *AfrAmAl 6 [port]*
Woodson, Carter G(odwin) 1875-1950 *BlkWr 2, ConAu 141*
Woodson, Carter Godwin 1875-1950 *AmSocL*
Woodson, Charles R. 1942- *WhoBlA 94*
Woodson, Cleveland Coleman, III 1946- *WhoAm 94*
Woodson, Doris 1929- *WhoAmA 93*
Woodson, Ernest Lyle 1937- *WhoHisp 94*
Woodson, Herbert Horace 1925- *WhoAm 94, WhoScEn 94*
Woodson, Jacqueline *DrAPF 93*
Woodson, Jeffrey Anthony 1955- *WhoBlA 94*
Woodson, Mark Winter 1953- *WhoWest 94*
Woodson, Mike 1958- *WhoBlA 94*
Woodson, Richard Peyton, III 1923- *WhoAm 94*
Woodson, Robert L. 1937- *WhoAm 94*
Woodson, Rod 1965- *WhoBlA 94*
Woodson, Roderic L. 1947- *WhoBlA 94*
Woodson, Roderick Kevin 1965- *WhoAm 94*
Woodson, S. Howard, Jr. 1916- *WhoAmP 93*
Woodson, Shawn Harold 1960- *WhoMW 93*
Woodson, Shirley A. 1936- *WhoBlA 94*
Woodson, Shirley Ann 1936- *WhoAmA 93*
Woodson, Stephen William 1950- *WhoFI 94*
Woodson, Thelma L. 1920- *WhoBlA 94*
Woodson, Tracy Todd 1960- *WhoBlA 94*
Woodson, Verna May 1929- *WhoMW 93*
Woodson, William *WhoHol 92*
Woodson, William D. 1909- *WhoBlA 94*
Woodson-Howard, Marlene Erdley 1937- *WhoAmP 93*
Woodstock, Viscount 1953- *Who 94*
Woods Walker, Victoria Patricia Ann *Who 94*
Woodsworth, Anne 1941- *WhoAm 94*
Woodthorpe, Georgia d1927 *WhoHol 92*
Woodthorpe, Peter 1931- *WhoHol 92*
Wood-Trost, Lucille Marie 1938- *WhoWest 94*
Woodville, Catherine 1943- *WhoHol 92*
Woodvine, John 1929- *WhoHol 92*
Woodward, Aaron Alphonso, III *WhoBlA 94*
Woodward, Aaron Alphonso, III 1947- *WhoFI 94*
Woodward, Albert Bruce, Jr. 1941- *WhoFI 94, WhoWest 94*
Woodward, Alison *WhoHol 92*
Woodward, Almon 1932- *WhoAmP 93*
Woodward, Barry *Who 94*
Woodward, Bob 1943- *WrDr 94*
Woodward, C. Vann 1908- *Who 94, WhoAm 94*
Woodward, C(omer) Vann 1908- *IntWW 93, WhoAm 94*
Woodward, Charles Namby Wynn 1924- *WhAm 10*
Woodward, Clinton Benjamin, Jr. 1943- *WhoFI 94*
Woodward, Comer Vann 1908- *AmSocL*
Woodward, Daniel Holt 1931- *WhoAm 94*
Woodward, David Luther 1942- *WhoAmL 94*
Woodward, David Robert 1947- *WhoAm 94*
Woodward, Dorothy Francine 1907- *WhoAmP 93*
Woodward, Douglas P. 1954- *WrDr 94*
Woodward, Douglas R. 1911- *WhoAmP 93*
Woodward, Edward *Who 94*
Woodward, Edward 1930- *IntMPA 94, IntWW 93, Who 94, WhoHol 92*
Woodward, (Albert) Edward 1928- *Who 94*
Woodward, Eugenie d1947 *WhoHol 92*
Woodward, Francis H. 1939- *WhoAmP 93*
Woodward, Frederick Miller 1943- *WhoAm 94*
Woodward, Garry Dale 1926- *WhoAmL 94*

Woodward, Geoffrey Frederick 1924- *Who 94*
Woodward, George Frederick, III 1955- *WhoWest 94*
Woodward, Greta Charmaine 1930- *WhoAm 94*
Woodward, Guy d1919 *WhoHol 92*
Woodward, Halbert Owen 1918- *WhoAmL 94*
Woodward, Isaiah Alfonso 1912- *WhoBlA 94*
Woodward, James Hall 1948- *WhoFI 94*
Woodward, James Hoyt 1939- *WhoAm 94*
Woodward, Joanne 1930- *IntMPA 94, WhoHol 92*
Woodward, Joanne Gignilliat 1930- *IntWW 93, WhoAm 94*
Woodward, John 1945- *WrDr 94*
Woodward, John (Forster) 1932- *Who 94*
Woodward, John Forster 1932- *IntWW 93*
Woodward, John Russell 1951- *WhoWest 94*
Woodward, John Taylor, III 1940- *WhoAm 94*
Woodward, Kenneth Emerson 1927- *WhoScEn 94*
Woodward, Kenneth L. 1935- *ConAu 141*
Woodward, Kesler Edward 1951- *WhoAmA 93*
Woodward, Kirsten 1959- *IntWW 93*
Woodward, Lester Ray 1932- *WhoAm 94*
Woodward, M. Cabell, Jr. 1929- *WhoAm 94, WhoFI 94*
Woodward, Madison Truman, Jr. 1908- *WhoAm 94, WhoAmL 94*
Woodward, Max Wakerley 1908- *Who 94*
Woodward, Morgan *WhoHol 92*
Woodward, Neila Patricia 1954- *WhoAmP 93*
Woodward, Paul Ralph 1946- *WhoMW 93, WhoScEn 94*
Woodward, Philip Timothy, Sr. 1949- *WhoMW 93*
Woodward, Price Purvis 1962- *WhoFI 94*
Woodward, Ralph Lee, Jr. 1934- *WhoAm 94, WrDr 94*
Woodward, Richard G. 1945- *WhoAmL 94*
Woodward, Richard Hollis, Jr. 1947- *WhoFI 94*
Woodward, Richard Joseph, Jr. 1907- *WhoAm 94*
Woodward, Robert d1972 *WhoHol 92*
Woodward, Robert Burns 1917-1979 *WorScD*
Woodward, Robert Forbes 1908- *WhoAm 94*
Woodward, Robert G. 1949- *WhoAmL 94*
Woodward, Robert H 1925- *WrDr 94*
Woodward, Robert Simpson, IV 1943- *WhoFI 94, WhoMW 93*
Woodward, Robert Strong 1885-1957 *WhoAmA 93N*
Woodward, Robert Upshur 1943- *WhoAm 94*
Woodward, Roger Robert 1942- *IntWW 93*
Woodward, Shaun Anthony 1958- *Who 94*
Woodward, Stanley 1890-1970 *WhoAmA 93N*
Woodward, Stephen Mark 1961- *WhoMW 93*
Woodward, Stephen Richard 1953- *WhoWest 94*
Woodward, Steven P. 1953- *WhoAmA 93*
Woodward, Susan Ellen 1949- *WhoAm 94, WhoFI 94*
Woodward, Suzann McDowell 1955- *WhoFI 94*
Woodward, Theodore Englar 1914- *WhoAm 94*
Woodward, Thomas Aiken 1933- *WhoAm 94, WhoAmL 94*
Woodward, Thomas Morgan 1925- *WhoAm 94*
Woodward, Tim 1953- *WhoHol 92*
Woodward, William 1935- *WhoAmA 93*
Woodward, William Charles 1940- *Who 94*
Woodward, William Edward 1954- *WhoWest 94*
Woodward, William Herbert 1941- *WhoWest 94*
Woodward, William Lee 1926- *WhoFI 94*
Woodward, William Walter 1943- *WhoWest 94*
Woodwell, George M. 1928- *ConAu 142, EnvEnc*
Woodwell, George Masters 1928- *WhoAm 94, WhoScEn 94*
Woodworth, Donald Duryea 1935- *WhoFI 94*
Woodworth, Fred Lowe 1940- *WhoAm 94*
Woodworth, Glenn Murray 1937- *WhoAmL 94*
Woodworth, James Vickers 1921- *WhoWest 94*
Woodworth, Marjorie 1923- *WhoHol 92*

Woodworth, Mary Esther *WhoMW 93*
Woodworth, Ramsey Lloyd 1941- *WhoAmL 94*
Woodworth, Scott Allen 1952- *WhoFI 94*
Woodworth, Stephen Davis 1945- *WhoWest 94*
Woodworth, Steven E(dward) 1961- *WrDr 94*
Woodworth-Etter, Maria Beulah Underwood 1844-1924 *DcAmReB 2*
Woody, A-Young Moon 1934- *WhoAsA 94*
Woody, Brenda R. 1951- *WhoMW 93*
Woody, Carol Clayman 1949- *WhoFI 94*
Woody, Clyde Woodrow 1920- *WhoAmL 94*
Woody, Donald Eugene 1948- *WhoAmL 94*
Woody, (Thomas) Howard 1935- *WhoAmA 93*
Woody, Jack *EncNAR*
Woody, Jack d1969 *WhoHol 92*
Woody, Jacqueline Brown 1949- *WhoBlA 94*
Woody, John Frederick 1941- *WhoMW 93*
Woody, Kathleen Joanna 1949- *WhoFI 94*
Woody, Robert Henley 1936- *WhoAmL 94*
Woodyard, George William 1934- *WhoMW 93*
Woodyard, Harry 1930- *WhoAmP 93*
Woodyshek, J. Daniel 1948- *WhoAmL 94*
Woof, Maija Gegeris Zack *WhoAmA 93*
Woof, Robert Edward 1911- *Who 94*
Woof, Robert Samuel 1931- *Who 94*
Woofter, R. D. 1923- *WhoFI 94*
Wool, Christoper *WhoAmA 93*
Wool, Ira Goodwin 1925- *WhoMW 93*
Wool, Rosemary Jane *Who 94*
Woolam, Gerald Lynn 1937- *WhoAm 94*
Wooland, Norman d1989 *WhoHol 92*
Woolard, Edgar S., Jr. 1934- *WhoAm 94, WhoFI 94*
Woolard, Edgar Smith 1934- *Who 94*
Woolard, Edgar Smith, Jr. 1934- *IntWW 93*
Woolard, Henry Waldo 1917- *WhoScEn 94, WhoWest 94*
Woolard, Larry D. 1941- *WhoAmP 93*
Woolard, William Leon 1931- *WhoAm 94*
Woolbert, Maybelle Siegele *WhoAmP 93*
Woolcock, Ozeil Fryer 1910- *WhoBlA 94*
Woolcott, Richard 1928- *IntWW 93*
Wooldredge, William Dunbar 1937- *WhoAm 94, WhoFI 94*
Wooldridge, David 1931- *WhoBlA 94*
Wooldridge, Dean E. 1913- *IntWW 93*
Wooldridge, Dean Everett 1913- *WhoAm 94*
Wooldridge, Ian Edmund 1932- *Who 94*
Wooldridge, Scott Robert 1960- *WhoScEn 94*
Wooldridge, Sherri 1959- *WhoAmP 93*
Wooldridge, Susan *IntMPA 94, WhoHol 92*
Wooldridge, Tim 1960- *WhoAmP 93*
Wooldridge, William Charles 1943- *WhoAmL 94*
Woolery, Ben B. 1939- *WhoFI 94*
Woolery, Chuck *WhoHol 92*
Woolery, Pete (Clarence W.) d1978 *WhoHol 92*
Woolery, Robert Harvey, Sr. 1934- *WhoFI 94*
Woolever, Naomi Louise 1922- *WhoAm 94*
Wooley, Andrew 1943- *WhoAmL 94*
Wooley, Bruce Allen 1943- *WhoAm 94*
Wooley, Donald Alan 1926- *WhoAm 94*
Wooley, James *WhoHol 92*
Wooley, Sheb 1921- *WhoHol 92*
Woolf *Who 94*
Woolf, Baron 1933- *Who 94*
Woolf, Barney d1972 *WhoHol 92*
Woolf, Bob d1993 *NewYTBS 93 [port]*
Woolf, Charles *WhoHol 92*
Woolf, Douglas 1922-1992 *WrDr 94N*
Woolf, Eric Joel 1960- *WhoScEn 94*
Woolf, Geoffrey 1944- *Who 94*
Woolf, Harry 1923- *Who 94, WhoAm 94, WrDr 94*
Woolf, Henry *WhoHol 92*
Woolf, John *Who 94*
Woolf, John 1913- *IntMPA 94*
Woolf, John Moss 1918- *Who 94*
Woolf, John Paul 1943- *WhoAmL 94*
Woolf, Lawrence Donald 1953- *WhoWest 94*
Woolf, Leslie *WhoHol 92*
Woolf, Michael E. 1949- *WhoAm 94, WhoAmL 94*
Woolf, Nancy Jean 1954- *WhoScEn 94*
Woolf, Robert Gary 1928- *WhoAmL 94*
Woolf, Robert Hansen 1945- *WhoWest 94*
Woolf, Samuel J. 1880-1948 *WhoAmA 93N*
Woolf, Steven Michael 1946- *WhoMW 93*
Woolf, Stuart Joseph 1936- *WrDr 94*
Woolf, Virginia 1882-1941 *BlmGEL [port], BlmGWL [port], EncSF 93*
Woolf, (Adeline) Virginia 1882-1941 *GayLL, RfGShF*
Woolf, William Blauvelt 1932- *WhoAm 94*
Woolf, X. F. 1931- *WrDr 94*
Woolfalk, Harold B. 1949- *WhoAmL 94*
Woolfenden, Milton, Jr. 1925- *WhoAm 94*
Woolfenden, William Edward 1918- *WhoAm 94, WhoAmA 93*
Woolfolk, E. Oscar 1912- *WhoBlA 94*
Woolfolk, George Ruble 1915- *WhoBlA 94*
Woolford, Harry Russell Halkerston 1905- *IntWW 93, Who 94*
Woolf-Scott, Helene Lyda 1938- *WhoWest 94*
Woolfson, Mark 1911- *Who 94*
Woolfson, Michael Mark 1927- *IntWW 93, Who 94*
Woolgar, Jack d1978 *WhoHol 92*
Woolhiser, David Arthur 1932- *WhoAm 94*
Woolhouse, Harold William 1932- *Who 94*
Woolhouse, John George 1931- *Who 94*
Woollacott, Angela Mary 1955- *WhoMW 93*
Woollam, John Arthur 1939- *WhoScEn 94*
Woollam, John Victor 1927- *Who 94*
Woollam, Kenneth (Geoffrey) 1937- *NewGrDO*
Woollaston, (Mountford) Tosswill 1910- *Who 94*
Woollcombe, Kenneth John 1924- *IntWW 93, Who 94*
Woollcombe, Robert 1922- *WrDr 94*
Woollcott, Alexander d1943 *WhoHol 92*
Woollen, Evans 1927- *WhoAm 94*
Woollen, Geoff 1945- *ConAu 142*
Woollen, Kenneth Lee 1967- *WhoScEn 94*
Woollett, John Castle 1915- *Who 94*
Woolley, Bryan *DrAPF 93*
Woolley, Bryan 1937- *WrDr 94*
Woolley, Catherine 1904- *WhoAm 94*
Woolley, David Rorie 1939- *Who 94*
Woolley, Gail Suzanne 1965- *WhoScEn 94*
Woolley, George Walter 1904- *WhoAm 94, WhoScEn 94*
Woolley, John C. 1936- *WhoAmL 94*
Woolley, John Edward 1935- *WhoFI 94*
Woolley, John Maxwell 1917- *Who 94*
Woolley, Jonathan Michael 1958- *WhoWest 94*
Woolley, Kenneth Frank 1933- *IntWW 93*
Woolley, Lee James 1962- *WhoFI 94*
Woolley, Mary Elizabeth 1947- *WhoAm 94*
Woolley, (John) Moger 1935- *Who 94*
Woolley, Monty d1963 *WhoHol 92*
Woolley, Roy Gilbert 1922- *Who 94*
Woolley, Russell *Who 94*
Woolliams, Keith Richard 1940- *WhoAm 94, WhoWest 94*
Woolls, Esther Blanche 1935- *WhoAm 94, WhoFI 94*
Woollums, Mark Allen 1961- *WhoAmL 94*
Woolman, Bruce Alan 1955- *WhoWest 94*
Woolman, Claude *WhoHol 92*
Woolman, John 1720-1772 *DcAmReB 2*
Woolman, (Joseph) Roger 1937- *Who 94*
Woolmer, Kenneth John 1940- *Who 94*
Woolpert, Phil 1914- *BasBi*
Woolrich, Cornell 1903-1968 *ConLC 77 [port]*
Woolridge, Doris d1921 *WhoHol 92*
Woolridge, Orlando Vernada 1959- *WhoBlA 94*
Woolrych, Austin (Herbert) 1918- *ConAu 42NR*
Woolrych, Austin Herbert 1918- *Who 94, WrDr 94*
Woolschlager, Laura Totten 1932- *WhoAmA 93*
Woolsey, Clinton Nathan d1993 *IntWW 93N, NewYTBS 93*
Woolsey, David Arthur 1941- *WhoAm 94*
Woolsey, Frederick William 1919- *WhoAm 94*
Woolsey, Gary Frederick 1942- *Who 94*
Woolsey, Jim *NewYTBS 93 [port]*
Woolsey, John Munro, Jr. 1916- *WhoAm 94*
Woolsey, Lynn *WhoAm 94, WhoWest 94*
Woolsey, Lynn 1937- *CngDr 93*
Woolsey, Lynn C. 1937- *WhoAmP 93*
Woolsey, R. James 1941- *IntWW 93, WhoAmP 93*
Woolsey, R. James, Jr. 1941- *WhoAm 94*
Woolsey, Robert d1938 *WhoHol 92*
Woolsey, Robert 1889-1938 *See* Wheeler and Woolsey *WhoCom*
Woolsey, Robert Eugene Donald 1936- *WhoAm 94*
Woolsey, Roy Blakeney 1945- *WhoWest 94*
Woolsey, Thomas 1818-1894 *EncNAR*
Woolsey, Thomas R. 1949- *WhoAmL 94*
Woolson, Charles Edward 1953- *WhoAmL 94*
Woolson, Constance Fenimore 1840-1894 *BlmGWL*
Woolson, Kenneth Hazen 1897- *WhAm 10*
Woolton, Earl of 1958- *Who 94*
Woolverton, Christopher Jude 1960- *WhoScEn 94*
Woolverton, Kenneth Arthur 1926- *Who 94*
Woolverton, William Henderson, III 1951- *WhoAmL 94*
Woolwich, Area Bishop of 1930- *Who 94*
Woolwich, Madlyn-Ann C. 1937- *WhoAmA 93*
Woolwine, Sharon Eileen 1944- *WhoMW 93*
Woon, Peter William 1931- *Who 94*
Woosley, Patrick Glenn 1938- *WhoFI 94, WhoWest 94*
Woosley, Stanford Earl 1944- *WhoScEn 94*
Woosley, W. Golden 1900- *WhoAmP 93*
Woosnam, Charles Richard 1925- *Who 94*
Woosnam, Ian Harold 1958- *IntWW 93, Who 94, WhoAm 94*
Woosnam, Richard Edward 1942- *WhoAmL 94, WhoFI 94*
Wooster, Ann-Sargent 1946- *WhoAmA 93*
Wooster, Clive Edward Dore 1913- *Who 94*
Wooster, David 1710-1777 *AmRev*
Wooster, David 1711-1777 *WhAmRev [port]*
Wooster, James Thompson 1940- *WhoMW 93*
Wooster, Kelly C. 1942- *WhoAmL 94*
Wooster, Robert 1956- *WhoAm 94*
Wooster, Warren Scriver 1921- *WhoAm 94*
Wootan, Gerald Don 1944- *WhoScEn 94*
Wootan, Guy 1938- *WhoAmL 94*
Wooten, Carl Kenneth 1947- *WhoBlA 94*
Wooten, Cecil Aaron 1924- *WhoAm 94*
Wooten, Chuck 1927- *WhoAmP 93*
Wooten, Cynthia 1946- *WhoAmP 93*
Wooten, Don 1929- *WhoAmP 93*
Wooten, Frank Thomas 1935- *WhoAm 94, WhoFI 94, WhoScEn 94*
Wooten, Frederick Oliver 1928- *WhoAm 94, WhoScEn 94, WhoWest 94*
Wooten, Hollis Darwin 1939- *WhoFI 94*
Wooten, Priscilla A. 1936- *WhoAmP 93, WhoBlA 94*
Wooton, John David 1950- *WhoAmP 93*
Wooton, William Robert 1944- *WhoAmP 93*
Wootters, John (Henry, Jr.) 1928- *ConAu 43NR*
Wootton, Barbara 1897-1988 *EncSF 93*
Wootton, Bob G. *WhoAmP 93*
Wootton, Charles Greenwood 1924- *IntWW 93*
Wootton, Godfrey *Who 94*
Wootton, (Norman) Godfrey 1926- *Who 94*
Wootton, (John) Graham (George) 1917- *WrDr 94*
Wootton, Ian David Phimester 1921- *Who 94*
Wootton, Joel Lorimer 1954- *WhoScEn 94*
Wootton, Mack Edward 1937- *WhoAm 94*
Wootton, Richens Lacy 1816-1893 *WhWE*
Wootton, Ronald William 1931- *Who 94*
Woozley, Anthony Douglas 1912- *Who 94*
Wopat, Tom 1951- *IntMPA 94*
Worboys, Anne *WrDr 94*
Worcester, Archdeacon of *Who 94*
Worcester, Bishop of 1929- *Who 94*
Worcester, Dean of *Who 94*
Worcester, Marquess of 1952- *Who 94*
Worcester, Donald E. 1915- *WrDr 94*
Worcester, Donald Emmet 1915- *WhoAm 94*
Worcester, Eva 1892-1970 *WhoAmA 93N*
Worcester, Harris Eugene 1950- *WhoAmP 93*
Worcester, Peggy Jean 1950- *WhoMW 93*
Worcester, Robert M. 1933- *WrDr 94*
Worcester, Robert Milton 1933- *IntWW 93, Who 94*
Worcester, Samuel Austin 1798-1859 *EncNAR*
Worcester, Thomas Kinney 1929- *WhoWest 94*
Word, Carl Oliver 1947- *WhoBlA 94*
Word, Fletcher Henry, Jr. 1919- *WhoBlA 94*
Word, Parker Howell 1921- *WhoBlA 94*
Word, Thomas S., Jr. 1938- *WhoAm 94*
Wordell, Edwin Howland 1927- *WhoAmA 93, WhoWest 94*
Worden, Alfred Merrill 1932- *WhoAm 94*
Worden, Donald Rodney 1955- *WhoMW 93*
Worden, Hank *WhoHol 92*
Worden, Louise d1977 *WhoHol 92*
Worden, Richard L., Sr. *WhoAmP 93*
Worden, William Michael 1942- *WhoMW 93*
Wordie, John (Stewart) 1924- *Who 94*
Wordlaw, Clarence, Jr. 1937- *WhoBlA 94*
Wordley, Ronald William 1928- *Who 94*
Words, Sil *WhoHol 92*
Wordsworth, Barry 1948- *Who 94*
Wordsworth, Dorothy 1771-1855 *BlmGWL, DcNaB MP*
Wordsworth, Richard 1915- *WhoHol 92*
Wordsworth, William 1770-1850 *BlmGEL*
Worek, William Martin 1954- *WhoScEn 94*
Worell, Judith P. *WhoAm 94*
Worenklein, Jacob Joshua 1948- *WhoAm 94, WhoAmL 94*
Worford, Carolyn Kennedy 1949- *WhoBlA 94*
Worgul, Basil Vladimir 1947- *WhoScEn 94*
Worishoffer, Sophie 1838-1890 *BlmGWL*
Work, Bruce Van Syoc 1942- *WhoAm 94*
Work, Charles Robert 1940- *WhoAm 94*
Work, Henry Harcus 1911- *WhoAm 94*
Work, John c. 1792-1861 *WhWE*
Work, Mitchell Robert 1947- *WhoMW 93*
Work, Stephen Walter 1944- *WhoWest 94*
Work, William 1923- *WhoAm 94*
Worke, Gary D. 1949- *WhoAmP 93*
Workman, Aurora Felice Antonette 1962- *WhoBlA 94*
Workman, Betty Gowland 1924- *WhoAmP 93*
Workman, Charles Joseph 1920- *Who 94*
Workman, Chuck *IntMPA 94*
Workman, Fanny Bullock 1859-1925 *WhWE [port]*
Workman, George Henry 1939- *WhoScEn 94*
Workman, Haywoode W. 1966- *WhoBlA 94*
Workman, Jerome James, Jr. 1952- *WhoScEn 94*
Workman, John Mitchell 1949- *WhoMW 93, WhoScEn 94*
Workman, Margaret L. *WhoAmP 93*
Workman, Margaret Lee 1947- *WhoAm 94, WhoAmL 94*
Workman, Paul C. 1954- *WhoAmL 94*
Workman, Robert Little 1914- *Who 94*
Workman, Robert P. 1961- *WhoAmA 93*
Workman, Roger *WhoWest 94*
Workman, Thomas Eldon 1944- *WhoAmL 94, WhoMW 93*
Workman, Timothy 1943- *Who 94*
Workman, Tom 1959- *WhoAmP 93*
Workman, William D(ouglas), Jr. 1914-1990 *WrDr 94N*
Workman, William Douglas, Jr. 1914- *WhAm 10*
Workman, William Douglas, III 1940- *WhoAmP 93*
Workman, William Glenn 1947- *WhoWest 94*
Works, John *DrAPF 93*
Works, John Hamilton, Jr. 1954- *WhoAmL 94*
Works, Madden Travis, Jr. 1943- *WhoScEn 94*
Worley, Alicia Anne 1965- *WhoMW 93*
Worley, Bland Wallace 1917- *WhoAm 94*
Worley, David Allan 1962- *WhoScEn 94*
Worley, Gordon Roger 1919- *WhoAm 94*
Worley, Harold Gene 1949- *WhoAmP 93*
Worley, Jeff *DrAPF 93*
Worley, Jimmy Weldon 1944- *WhoScEn 94*
Worley, Jo Anne 1937- *WhoHol 92*
Worley, Kathryn Ann 1960- *WhoWest 94*
Worley, Marvin George, Jr. 1934- *WhoMW 93, WhoScEn 94*
Worley, Michael Preston 1950- *WhoMW 93*
Worley, Robert William, Jr. 1935- *WhoAmL 94*
Worley, Stella *DrAPF 93*
Worley Katz, Joyce Marie 1939- *WhoWest 94*
Worlock, Derek (John Harford) 1920- *WrDr 94*
Worlock, Derek John Harford *Who 94*
Worlock, Derek John Harford 1920- *IntWW 93*
Worlock, Frederick d1973 *WhoHol 92*
Wormald, Brian Harvey Goodwin 1912- *Who 94*
Wormald, Derrick Bruce 1916- *Who 94*
Wormald, Ethel May d1993 *Who 94N*
Wormald, (Charles) Patrick 1947- *WrDr 94*
Wormald, Peter John 1936- *Who 94*
Worman, Marna Jo 1932- *WhoAmP 93*

Worman, Richard W. 1933- WhoAmP 93, WhoMW 93
Wormhoudt, Arthur Louis 1917- WhoMW 93
Wormhoudt, Pearl Shinn 1915- WhoMW 93
Wormley, Cynthia L. 1953- WhoBlA 94
Wormley, Diane-Louise Lambert 1948- WhoBlA 94
Wormley, Stanton Lawrence 1909-1993 ConAu 142
Worms, Bob d1985 WhoHol 92
Worms, Gerard Etienne 1936- IntWW 93
Wormser, Baron DrAPF 93
Wormser, Edward Carl 1940- WhoFI 94
Wormser, Richard (Edward) 1908-1977 EncSF 93
Wormwood, Richard Naughton 1936- WhoScEn 94
Worne, Duke d1933 WhoHol 92
Worne, Howard Edward 1914- WhoScEn 94
Worner, Hans EncSF 93
Worner, Howard Knox 1913- IntWW 93
Worner, Jennifer Kathryn 1967- WhoMW 93
Worner, Lloyd Edson 1918- WhoAm 94
Worner, Manfred 1934- IntWW 93, Who 94
Worner, Philip (Arthur Incledon) 1910- WrDr 94
Worner, Ruby Kathryn 1900- WhoMW 93
Worobec, Bruce William 1963- WhoWest 94
Woroniak, Alexander 1922- WhoAm 94
Woronoff, Israel 1926- WhoMW 93, WhoScEn 94
Woronov, Mary 1946- IntMPA 94, WhoHol 92
Woronov, Naomi 1938- WrDr 94
Worrall, Anna Maureen Who 94
Worrall, Denis John 1935- IntWW 93, Who 94
Worrall, Ralph Lyndal 1903- WrDr 94
Worrell, Albert Cadwallader 1913- WhoAm 94
Worrell, Anne Everette Rowell 1920- WhoAm 94
Worrell, Arthur R. WhoBlA 94
Worrell, Audrey Martiny 1935- WhoBlA 94
Worrell, Bernie c. 1945- ConMus 11 [port]
Worrell, Cynthia Lee 1957- WhoFI 94
Worrell, David Charles 1951- WhoAm 94, WhoAmL 94
Worrell, Jimmie D. 1950- WhoWest 94
Worrell, Judy S. 1949- WhoMW 93
Worrell, Kaye Sydnell 1952- WhoBlA 94
Worrell, Lee Anthony 1907- WhoAmL 94
Worrell, Richard Vernon 1931- WhoAm 94, WhoBlA 94, WhoScEn 94, WhoWest 94
Worrill, Conrad W. 1941- WhoBlA 94
Worrilow, Richard Charles 1944- WhoWest 94
Worseck, Raymond Adams 1937- WhoAm 94, WhoFI 94, WhoMW 93
Worsfold, Reginald Lewis 1925- Who 94
Worsham, Ernest Lee 1946- WhoAm 94
Worsham, Fabian DrAPF 93
Worsham, Jackson Davis, Jr. 1940- WhoAmP 93
Worsham, James E. 1932- WhoBlA 94
Worsham, Jerry Doyle, II 1956- WhoAmL 94
Worsham, Tommy Dale 1923- WhoAmP 93
Worskett, Roy 1932- Who 94
Worsley, Lord 1990- Who 94
Worsley, Alice F. DrAPF 93
Worsley, Benjamin c. 1617-1677 DcNaB MP
Worsley, Bruce d1980 WhoHol 92
Worsley, Dale DrAPF 93
Worsley, Francis Edward 1941- Who 94
Worsley, Geoffrey Nicolas Ernest T. C. Who 94
Worsley, George Ira, Jr. 1927- WhoBlA 94
Worsley, Jock Who 94
Worsley, John Clayton 1919- WhoAm 94
Worsley, Marcus Who 94
Worsley, (William) Marcus (John) 1925- Who 94
Worsley, Michael Dominic Laurence 1926- Who 94
Worsley, Nicholas Jarvis 1943- Who 94
Worsley, Paul Frederick 1947- Who 94
Worsley, Richard (Edward) 1923- Who 94
Worsley, Thomas Raymond 1942- WhoMW 93
Worsley, Wallace d1944 WhoHol 92
Worster, Donald E(ugene) 1941- ConAu 42NR
Worster, Donald Eugene 1941- WhoMW 93
Worster, Kenneth Berkley 1937- WhAm 10
Worsthorne, Peregrine (Gerard) 1923- Who 94
Worsthorne, Peregrine Gerard 1923- IntWW 93
Worswick, Clark 1940- ConAu 43NR
Worswick, (George) David (Norman) 1916- IntWW 93, Who 94
Worswick, G(eorge) D(avid) N(orman) 1916- ConAu 142
Worswick, Richard David 1946- Who 94
Worth, Brian d1978 WhoHol 92
Worth, Catherine Anne 1952- WhoWest 94
Worth, Charles Joseph 1948- WhoBlA 94
Worth, Constance d1963 WhoHol 92
Worth, Douglas DrAPF 93
Worth, Edgar Randal 1944- WhoAmL 94
Worth, Gary James 1940- WhoAm 94
Worth, George Arthur 1907- Who 94
Worth, George John 1929- WhoAm 94
Worth, Helen 1913- WrDr 94
Worth, Irene 1916- IntMPA 94, IntWW 93, Who 94, WhoAm 94, WhoHol 92
Worth, James Gallagher 1922- WhoFI 94
Worth, Janice Lorraine 1938- WhoBlA 94
Worth, Karen 1924- WhoAmA 93
Worth, Katharine Joyce 1922- Who 94
Worth, Marvin IntMPA 94
Worth, Nicholas WhoHol 92
Worth, Peggy d1956 WhoHol 92
Worth, Peter EncSF 93
Worth, Peter John 1917- WhoAmA 93
Worth, Stefanie Patrice 1962- WhoBlA 94
Worth, Susan Oliver 1934- WhoAmL 94
Worth, Thomas B. 1950- WhoAmL 94
Wortham, Harold 1909-1974 WhoAmA 93N
Wortham, Jacob James WhoBlA 94
Wortham, James Calvin 1928- WhoMW 93
Wortham, James Mason 1954- WhoFI 94
Wortham, Thomas Richard 1943- WhoAm 94
Worthen, Amy Namowitz 1946- WhoAmA 93
Worthen, Harold M., Jr. 1914- WhoAmP 93
Worthen, James Thomas 1954- WhoAmL 94
Worthen, John Edward 1933- WhoAm 94, WhoMW 93
Worthen, Naz Onea 1966- WhoBlA 94
Worthen, Robert D. 1947- WhoAmP 93
Worthey, Carol 1943- WhoWest 94
Worthey, Richard E. 1934- WhoBlA 94
Worthing, Carol Marie 1934- WhoMW 93
Worthing, Helen Lee d1948 WhoHol 92
Worthington, Allan Douglas 1954- WhoAm 94
Worthington, Anthony 1941- Who 94
Worthington, Carol WhoHol 92
Worthington, Charles Roy 1925- WhoAm 94, WhoScEn 94
Worthington, Edgar Barton 1905 IntWW 93, Who 94, WrDr 94
Worthington, Elliott Robert 1937- WhoWest 94
Worthington, George Noel 1923- Who 94
Worthington, George Rhodes 1937- WhoAm 94
Worthington, Janet Evans 1942- WhoAm 94
Worthington, John 1719-1800 WhAmRev
Worthington, John Rice 1930- WhoAmL 94, WhoFI 94
Worthington, Kathy A. 1953- WhoFI 94
Worthington, Leslie Berry 1902- EncABHB 9 [port]
Worthington, Lorne R. 1938- WhoAmP 93
Worthington, Lorne Raymond 1938- WhoFI 94
Worthington, Meg 1956- WhoAmP 93
Worthington, Melvin Leroy 1937- WhoAm 94
Worthington, Pete 1940- WhoAmP 93
Worthington, Robert Melvin 1922- WhoAmP 93
Worthington, William d1941 WhoHol 92
Worthington, William Bowman 1911- WhAm 10
Worthington, William D. 1947- WhoIns 94
Worthy, Barbara Ann 1942- WhoBlA 94
Worthy, James 1961- BasBi, WhoAm 94, WhoBlA 94, WhoWest 94
Worthy, James Carson 1910- WhoAm 94
Worthy, Kenneth Martin 1920- WhoAm 94, WhoAmL 94, WhoAmP 93
Worthy, Larry Elliott 1953- WhoBlA 94
Worthy, Patricia Morris 1944- WhoAm 94
Worthy, William, Jr. 1921- WhoBlA 94
Wortis, Avi 1937- ConAu 42NR, WhoAm 94
Wortley, Alfred Charles, Jr. 1920- WhoAmL 94
Wortley, George C. 1926- WhoAmP 93
Wortley, George Cornelius 1926- WhoAm 94
Wortman, Bret Dean 1965- WhoMW 93
Wortman, Denys 1886-1958 WhoAmA 93N
Wortman, Don d1981 WhoHol 92
Wortman, Don Irvin 1927- WhoAmP 93
Wortman, Joseph John 1940- WhoIns 94
Wortman, Richard M. 1959- WhoAmL 94
Wortman, Richard S. 1938- WhoAm 94
Worton, Ronald Gibert 1942- WhoAm 94
Wortz, Melinda Farris 1940- WhoAmA 93
Wortzel, Adrianne 1941- WhoAmA 93
Wortzel, Lawrence Herbert 1932- WhoAm 94, WhoFI 94
Worzel, John Lamar 1919- WhoAm 94
Wos, Carol Elaine 1957- WhoMW 93, WhoScEn 94
Wos, Joanna H. DrAPF 93
Woskow, Robert Marshall 1951- WhoWest 94
Wosniewski, Thomas Michael 1950- WhoMW 93
Wossner, Mark Matthias Who 94
Wostrel, Nancy J. WhoAmA 93
Woszczyk, Wieslaw Richard 1951- WhoScEn 94
Woteki, Catherine Ellen 1947- WhoAm 94, WhoScEn 94
Wotiz, John Henry 1919- WhoAm 94
Wotkyns, Steele 1960- WhoFI 94
Wotman, Stephen 1931- WhoAm 94
Wott, John Arthur 1939- WhoAm 94, WhoWest 94
Wotton, Robert, Jr. 1963- WhoAmP 93
Wou, Leo S. 1927- WhoAm 94
Wouch, Gerald 1939- WhoScEn 94
Wouczyna, James Michael 1946- WhoAmL 94
Woudenberg, Paul Richard 1927- WhoWest 94
Wouk, Herman 1915- EncSF 93, IntWW 93, Who 94, WhoAm 94, WrDr 94
Woundy, Douglas Stanley 1939- WhoFI 94
Wourms, Mark Kenneth WhoAm 94
Woutat, Paul Gustav 1937- WhoAmL 94
Wouts, Bernard Francois Emile 1940- IntWW 93
Wovoka 1856?-1932 DcAmReB 2, EncNAR [port]
Wovsaniker, Alan 1953- WhoAm 94, WhoAmL 94
Wowchuk, Harry N. 1948- IntMPA 94
Wowchuk, Nicholas IntMPA 94
Wowk, Victor 1948- WhoWest 94
Woxholt, Greta WhoHol 92
Woyach, Robert Bruce 1949- WhoMW 93
Woychik, Eric Charles 1953- WhoWest 94
Woyczynski, Wojbor Andrzej 1943- WhoAm 94, WhoScEn 94
Woydziak, Ida Faye 1955- WhoMW 93
Woyner, Lynn Lamb 1951- WhoIns 94
Woyrsch, Felix 1860-1944 NewGrDO
Woyski, Margaret Skillman 1921- WhoAm 94, WhoWest 94
Woytek, Andrew Joseph 1936- WhoScEn 94
Woytek, Steve Edward 1949- WhoWest 94
Woythal, Constance Lee 1954- WhoMW 93
Woytowicz-Rudnicka, Stefania 1922- IntWW 93
Woytowitz, Donald Vincent 1961- WhoScEn 94
Wozniak, Chester WhoAmP 93
Wozniak, Debra Gail 1954- WhoAmL 94, WhoMW 93
Wozniak, Edward Joseph 1955- WhoFI 94
Wozniak, John N. 1956- WhoAmP 93
Wozniak, Joyce Marie 1955- WhoFI 94, WhoWest 94
Wozniak, Richard Michael, Sr. 1928- WhoMW 93
Wozniak, Steve 1950- WorInv
Wozniak, Teresa WhoWomW 91
Wozniak, Thomas Paul 1953- WhoFI 94
Wozniak, Wayne Theodore 1945- WhoMW 93
Wraase, Dennis Richard 1944- WhoAm 94
Wrabec, Paul Joseph 1956- WhoAmP 93
Wrage, Karol Rae 1958- WhoMW 93
Wragg, David W(illiam) 1946- WrDr 94
Wragg, Edward Conrad 1938- Who 94, WrDr 94
Wragg, John 1937- Who 94
Wragg, Laishley Palmer, Jr. 1933- WhoAm 94, WhoAmL 94, WhoFI 94
Wragg, Laurence Edward 1921- WhoWest 94
Wraight, John (Richard) 1916- Who 94
Wralstad, Phillip Evans 1932- WhoWest 94
Wran, Neville Kenneth Who 94
Wran, Neville Kenneth 1976- IntWW 93
Wrangham, Richard Walter 1948- WhoAm 94
Wranglen, Karl Gustaf Gosta 1923- WhoScEn 94
Wranitzky, Paul 1756-1808 NewGrDO
Wrape, Eric Wayne 1959- WhoFI 94
Wrappe, Thomas Keith 1956- WhoScEn 94
Wraps His Tail d1887 EncNAR
Wrasman, Cynthia Christine 1961- WhoMW 93
Wrather, John Deveraux, Jr. 1918- WhAm 10
Wratislaw, A(lbert) C(harles) 1862- EncSF 93
Wratten, Donald Peter 1925- Who 94
Wratten, William (John) 1939- Who 94
Wraxall, Baron 1928- Who 94
Wraxall, Charles (Frederick Lascelles) 1961- Who 94
Wray, Aloha d1968 WhoHol 92
Wray, Cecil, Jr. 1934- WhoAm 94
Wray, Charles Allen 1954- WhoMW 93
Wray, Charles Kadel 1944- WhoAmL 94
Wray, Charles Williamson, Jr. 1933-1992 WhAm 10
Wray, David Lynn 1947- WhoMW 93
Wray, Dick 1933- WhoAmA 93
Wray, Elizabeth DrAPF 93
Wray, Fay 1907- IntMPA 94, WhoHol 92
Wray, Frank Junior 1921-1992 WhAm 10
Wray, Gordon Richard 1928- IntWW 93, Who 94
Wray, James 1938- Who 94
Wray, John d1940 WhoHol 92
Wray, Karl 1913- WhoWest 94
Wray, Larry Randall 1953- WhoWest 94
Wray, Marc Frederick WhoAm 94, WhoFI 94
Wray, Margaret Masle d1988 WhoAmA 93N
Wray, Mark S. 1953- WhoIns 94
Wray, (Karen) Prudence Patricia Who 94
Wray, Reginald EncSF 93
Wray, Richard Bengt 1947- WhoScEn 94
Wray, Richard K. 1949- WhoAmL 94
Wray, Robert Oakley, Jr. 1957- WhoFI 94
Wray, Thomas Jefferson 1949- WhoAm 94, WhoAmL 94
Wray, Tom C. 1949- WhoAmP 93
Wray, Tom Charles 1949- WhoWest 94
Wray, Wendell Leonard 1926- WhoBlA 94
Wrba, Heinrich 1922- WhoScEn 94
Wrebiak, Andrzej 1954- WhoScEn 94
Wrede, Patricia C(ollins) 1953- TwCYAW, WrDr 94
Wrede, Patricia Collins 1953- WhoMW 93
Wrede, Robert Kendrick 1939- WhoAm 94, WhoAmL 94
Wrede, Stuart Henrik 1944- WhoAm 94
Wreden, William Paul 1910- WhoWest 94
Wreford, David Mathews 1943- WhoAm 94
Wren, Christopher 1632-1723 BlmGEL [port]
Wren, Christopher G(ove) 1950- WrDr 94
Wren, Clara WhoHol 92
Wren, Donald G. 1947- WhoAmP 93
Wren, Harold Gwyn 1921- WhoAm 94
Wren, Jill Robinson 1954- WrDr 94
Wren, Percival Christopher 1875-1941 DcNaB MP
Wren, Robert James 1935- WhoScEn 94
Wren, Sam d1962 WhoHol 92
Wren, Thomas EncSF 93
Wrenbury, Baron 1927- Who 94
Wrench, William Buchanan 1928- WhoFI 94
Wrenn, Bob 1873-1925 BuCMET
Wrenn, Diane Marie 1955- WhoMW 93
Wrenn, James Joseph 1926- WhoAm 94
Wrenn, John Henry 1841-1911 DcLB 140 [port]
Wrenn, Michael Richard 1953- WhoAmL 94
Wrenn, Thomas H., III 1942- WhoBlA 94
Wrenn, Walter Bruce 1950- WhoFI 94, WhoMW 93
Wrexham, Bishop of 1928- Who 94
Wrey, Benjamin Harold Bourchier 1940- Who 94
Wrey, (George Richard) Bourchier 1948- Who 94
Wrice, David 1937- WhoBlA 94
Wrice, Vincent J. 1963- WhoBlA 94
Wriggins, William Howard 1918- WhoAmP 93
Wrigglesworth, Ian (William) 1939- Who 94
Wright, Mrs. fl. 1727-1750 NewGrDO
Wright, A. J. DrAPF 93
Wright, A(mos) J(asper) 1952- WrDr 94
Wright, Alan John 1925- Who 94
Wright, Albert Walter, Jr. 1925- WhoBlA 94
Wright, Alden Halbert 1942- WhoWest 94
Wright, Alec Michael John 1912- Who 94
Wright, Alex 1967- WhoBlA 94

Wright, Alfred 1788-1853 *EncNAR*
Wright, Alfred George James 1916- *WhoAm 94*
Wright, Alison Elizabeth 1945- *Who 94*
Wright, Allan Frederick 1929- *Who 94*
Wright, Allen 1825-1885 *EncNAR*
Wright, Almroth Edward 1861-1947 *WorScD*
Wright, Alonzo Gordon 1930- *WhoBlA 94*
Wright, Alonzo Harold 1947- *WhoMW 93*
Wright, Amy 1950- *IntMPA 94, WhoHol 92*
Wright, Andrew 1923- *WhoAm 94*
Wright, Andrew Scott 1952- *WhoAmP 93*
Wright, Ann Elizabeth 1922- *WhoAm 94*
Wright, Anne Margaret 1946- *Who 94*
Wright, Anthony 1949- *Who 94*
Wright, Anthony Wayland 1948- *Who 94*
Wright, Armand d1965 *WhoHol 92*
Wright, Arnold, Jr. 1938- *WhoAmL 94*
Wright, Arthur Francis Stevenson 1918- *Who 94*
Wright, Arthur Franklin 1950- *WhoFI 94, WhoMW 93*
Wright, Arthur McIntosh 1930- *WhoAmL 94, WhoFI 94*
Wright, Arthur W. *WhoIns 94*
Wright, Asher 1803-1875 *EncNAR*
Wright, Austin *DrAPF 93*
Wright, Austin M 1922- *WrDr 94*
Wright, Austin Tappan 1883-1931 *EncSF 93*
Wright, Barbara 1935- *IntWW 93*
Wright, Barbara W. 1933- *WhoAmP 93*
Wright, Barton Allen 1920- *WhoAmA 93, WhoWest 94*
Wright, Beals 1879-1961 *BuCMET*
Wright, Beatrice Frederika *Who 94*
Wright, Ben d1989 *WhoHol 92*
Wright, Benjamen 1942- *Who 94*
Wright, Benjamin Drake 1926- *WhoAm 94*
Wright, Benjamin Hickman 1923- *WhoBlA 94*
Wright, Bernard 1938- *WhoAmA 93, WhoWest 94*
Wright, Berry Franklin 1945- *WhoScEn 94*
Wright, Betsey *WhoAmP 93*
Wright, Bill 1947- *WhoAmP 93*
Wright, Billy *Who 94*
Wright, Billy Beryl 1926- *WhoAmP 93*
Wright, Blandin James 1947- *WhoAmL 94*
Wright, Brad 1949- *WhoAmP 93*
Wright, Bradley Dean 1963- *WhoScEn 94*
Wright, Brian *Who 94*
Wright, (George) Brian 1939- *Who 94*
Wright, Bruce McM. 1918- *WhoBlA 94*
Wright, C. D. *DrAPF 93*
Wright, C(arolyn) D. 1949- *ConAu 142*
Wright, C. T. Enus 1942- *WhoBlA 94*
Wright, Caleb Merrill 1908- *WhoAm 94, WhoAmL 94*
Wright, Carl Jeffrey 1954- *WhoBlA 94*
Wright, Carol Ann 1956- *WhoMW 93*
Wright, Carole Yvonne 1932- *WhoWest 94*
Wright, Carolyn Elaine 1951- *WhoBlA 94*
Wright, Carolyn Marshall 1960- *WhoFI 94*
Wright, Carolyne *DrAPF 93*
Wright, Carroll Davidson 1840-1909 *AmSocL*
Wright, Catharine Morris 1899-1988 *WhoAmA 93N*
Wright, Cathie 1929- *WhoAmP 93*
Wright, Celeste Turner 1906- *WrDr 94*
Wright, Charles *DrAPF 93*
Wright, Charles 1918- *WhoBlA 94*
Wright, Charles (Penzel, Jr.) 1935- *WrDr 94*
Wright, Charles Alan 1927- *WhoAm 94, WhoAmL 94*
Wright, Charles Christopher 1938- *Who 94*
Wright, Charles E. 1946- *WhoBlA 94*
Wright, Charles Edward 1906- *WhoAm 94, WhoAmL 94*
Wright, Charles H. 1918- *WhoBlA 94*
Wright, Charles John 1958- *WhoMW 93*
Wright, Charles Lee 1949- *WhoWest 94*
Wright, Charles Leslie 1945- *WhoScEn 94*
Wright, Charles P. 1945- *WhoScEn 94*
Wright, Charles Penzel, Jr. 1935- *WhoAm 94*
Wright, Charles Richard 1941- *WhoAm 94*
Wright, Charles S. *DrAPF 93*
Wright, Charles Spaulding, II 1955- *WhoMW 93*
Wright, Charles Stevenson 1932- *WhoBlA 94*
Wright, Charles Ted 1931- *WhoAmP 93*
Wright, Charleye Taze 1937- *WhoWest 94*
Wright, Chatt Grandison 1941- *WhoAm 94, WhoWest 94*
Wright, Christopher 1924- *WrDr 94*
Wright, Christopher 1926-1989 *WhAm 10*
Wright, Christopher Pearce 1939- *WhoMW 93*
Wright, Clarence Johnnie, Sr. 1953- *WhoBlA 94*
Wright, Clark Phillips 1942- *WhoScEn 94*
Wright, Claud William 1917- *Who 94*
Wright, Cliff 1963- *SmATA 76 [port]*
Wright, (Charles) Clifford 1919- *WhoAmA 93*
Wright, Clinton L. A. 1951- *WhoBlA 94*
Wright, Cobina, Sr. d1970 *WhoHol 92*
Wright, Cobina, Jr. 1921- *WhoHol 92*
Wright, (Charles) Conrad 1917- *WrDr 94*
Wright, Cowley d1923 *WhoHol 92*
Wright, Craig 1929- *WhoAm 94*
Wright, Creighton Bolter 1939- *WhoMW 93*
Wright, Crispin James Garth 1942- *Who 94*
Wright, Cynthia Challed 1953- *ConAu 41NR*
Wright, Dana Jace 1952- *WhoFI 94*
Wright, Daniel Godwin 1945- *WhoScEn 94*
Wright, David (John Murray) 1920- *WrDr 94*
Wright, David Austin 1955- *WhoAmP 93*
Wright, David Burton 1933- *WhoAm 94*
Wright, David C. 1946- *WhoAmL 94*
Wright, David George 1931- *WhoAm 94*
Wright, David John 1944- *Who 94*
Wright, David L. 1949- *WhoAm 94*
Wright, David Lee 1946- *WhoWest 94*
Wright, David Lee 1962- *WhoAmP 93*
Wright, David R. 1935- *WhoAmP 93*
Wright, David Stephen 1935- *Who 94*
Wright, David Thomas 1947- *WhoAmA 93*
Wright, Dawin Lyron 1951- *WhoBlA 94*
Wright, Deil Spencer 1930- *WhoAm 94*
Wright, Delivee Loraine 1937- *WhoMW 93*
Wright, Delores C. *WhoAmP 93*
Wright, Denis (Arthur Hepworth) 1911- *Who 94*
Wright, Denise Yvonne 1964- *WhoMW 93*
Wright, Desmond Garforth 1923- *Who 94*
Wright, Dianne Brown 1952- *WhoMW 93*
Wright, Dianne Chandler 1944- *WhoAm 94*
Wright, Dianne Marie 1946- *WhoAmL 94*
Wright, Dmitri 1948- *WhoBlA 94*
Wright, Don 1939- *WhoAmP 93*
Wright, Don C. 1934- *WhoAm 94*
Wright, Donald *Who 94*
Wright, (Arthur Robert) Donald 1923- *Who 94*
Wright, Donald Eugene 1930- *WhoAm 94*
Wright, Donald Franklin 1934- *WhoAm 94, WhoFI 94, WhoWest 94*
Wright, Donald Lee 1937- *WhoScEn 94*
Wright, Dorothy Winslow *DrAPF 93*
Wright, Dorsey 1957- *WhoHol 92*
Wright, Douglas S. *WhoAmP 93*
Wright, Douglas Tyndall 1927- *IntWW 93, WhoAm 94, WhoScEn 94*
Wright, Douglass Brownell 1912- *WhoAm 94*
Wright, Earl Lee 1941- *WhoBlA 94*
Wright, Earl W. 1902-1988 *WhoBlA 94N*
Wright, Ebony *WhoHol 92*
Wright, Ed d1975 *WhoHol 92*
Wright, Edmund Gordon, Mrs. *Who 94*
Wright, Edward (Maitland) 1906- *Who 94*
Wright, Edward G. 1948- *WhoIns 94*
Wright, Edward Lucius 1925- *WhoBlA 94*
Wright, Edward Scott 1950- *WhoMW 93*
Wright, Ellsworth d1988 *WhoHol 92*
Wright, Eric 1929- *WrDr 94*
Wright, Eric 1933- *Who 94*
Wright, Eric 1959- *WhoBlA 94*
Wright, Eric David 1917- *Who 94*
Wright, Erik Olin 1947- *WhoAm 94*
Wright, Ernest Marshall 1940- *WhoAm 94, WhoWest 94*
Wright, Esmond 1915- *Who 94, WrDr 94*
Wright, Eugene Allen 1913- *WhoAm 94, WhoAmL 94, WhoWest 94*
Wright, Faith-Dorian 1934- *WhoAmA 93*
Wright, Fanny d1954 *WhoHol 92*
Wright, Farnsworth 1888-1940 *EncSF 93*
Wright, Felix E. 1935- *WhoAm 94, WhoFI 94*
Wright, Flavel Allen 1913- *WhoAm 94*
Wright, Flonzie B. 1942- *WhoBlA 94*
Wright, Frances *WhoHol 92*
Wright, Frances 1795-1852 *AmSocL [port]*
Wright, Frances Jane 1943- *WhoWest 94*
Wright, Francis 1806-1873 *DcNaB MP*
Wright, Francis X. 1945- *WhoAmL 94*
Wright, Frank 1932- *WhoAmA 93*
Wright, Frank Gardner 1931- *WhoAm 94*
Wright, Frank Hall 1860-1922 *EncNAR*
Wright, Frank Lloyd 1867-1959 *AmCulL*
Wright, Franklin Leatherbury, Jr. 1945- *WhoAm 94, WhoFI 94*
Wright, Fred d1928 *WhoHol 92*
Wright, Fred W., Jr. *DrAPF 93*
Wright, Frederick Bennie 1950- *WhoBlA 94*
Wright, Frederick Douglass 1946- *WhoBlA 94*
Wright, Frederick Fenning 1934- *WhoWest 94*
Wright, Frederick Hamilton 1912- *WhoWest 94*
Wright, Frederick Herman Greene, II 1952- *WhoWest 94*
Wright, Frederick Lewis, II 1951- *WhoAmL 94*
Wright, G. Alan 1927- *WhoAmA 93N*
Wright, Garland 1946- *WhoAm 94, WhoMW 93*
Wright, Gary Albert 1948- *WhoWest 94*
Wright, Gary Donald 1944- *WhoAmP 93, WhoWest 94*
Wright, Gary Henry 1949- *WhoFI 94*
Wright, Gene Arthur 1957- *WhoFI 94*
Wright, Gene Elliot 1925- *WhoMW 93*
Wright, Georg Henrik von 1916- *IntWW 93, Who 94*
Wright, George C., Jr. 1932- *WhoBlA 94*
Wright, George Cullen 1923- *WhoFI 94*
Wright, George Dewitt 1958- *WhoBlA 94*
Wright, George Frederick 1838-1921 *DcAmReB 2*
Wright, George Hand 1872-1951 *WhoAmA 93N*
Wright, George Henry 1935- *Who 94*
Wright, George Paul 1919- *Who 94*
Wright, George Searcy 1925- *WhoAmL 94*
Wright, George T. *DrAPF 93*
Wright, George Thaddeus 1925- *WrDr 94*
Wright, George W. 1923- *WhoAmP 93*
Wright, Gerald Ged 1942- *WhoAmP 93*
Wright, Gerard 1929- *Who 94*
Wright, Gladys Stone 1925- *WhoAm 94*
Wright, Gordon Brooks 1934- *WhoAm 94, WhoWest 94*
Wright, Gordon Pribyl 1938- *WhoAm 94*
Wright, Graeme Alexander 1943- *Who 94*
Wright, Grover Cleveland 1916- *WhoBlA 94*
Wright, Gwen Sloas 1960- *WhoMW 93*
Wright, Gwendolyn 1946- *WhoAm 94*
Wright, H. Humberstone 1885- *WhoHol 92*
Wright, H(enry) Myles 1908- *Who 94*
Wright, Haidee d1943 *WhoHol 92*
Wright, Harold d1993 *NewYTBS 93*
Wright, Harold Bell 1872-1944 *EncSF 93*
Wright, Harold Dale 1935- *WhAm 10*
Wright, Harold David 1942- *WhoAmA 93*
Wright, Harold Stanley 1918- *WhoAmL 94*
Wright, Harriette Simon 1915- *WhoBlA 94*
Wright, Harrison Morris 1928- *WhoAm 94*
Wright, Harry, III 1925- *WhoAm 94*
Wright, Harry Forrest, Jr. 1931- *WhoAm 94*
Wright, Hastings Kemper 1928- *WhoAm 94*
Wright, Haviland 1948- *WhoWest 94*
Wright, Heather *WhoHol 92*
Wright, Helen Kennedy 1927- *WhoFI 94, WhoMW 93*
Wright, Helen L(ouise) 1932- *WrDr 94*
Wright, Helen Patton 1919- *WhoAm 94*
Wright, Helen S. *EncSF 93*
Wright, Helene Segal 1955- *WhoWest 94*
Wright, Herbert Edgar, Jr. 1917- *WhoAm 94, WhoScEn 94*
Wright, Howard *WhoBlA 94*
Wright, Howard d1990 *WhoHol 92*
Wright, Hugh E. d1940 *WhoHol 92*
Wright, Hugh Elliott, Jr. 1937- *WhoAm 94*
Wright, Hugh Raymond 1938- *Who 94*
Wright, Huntley d1941 *WhoHol 92*
Wright, Irving Sherwood 1901- *WhoAm 94*
Wright, Isaiah Israel, Jr. 1954- *WhoMW 93*
Wright, J. Anthony 1952- *WhoMW 93*
Wright, J. B. *SmATA 77*
Wright, J. Craig 1929- *WhoAmL 94, WhoAmP 93, WhoMW 93*
Wright, Jack Clifford 1933- *Who 94*
Wright, Jackson Thomas, Jr. 1944- *WhoBlA 94*
Wright, Jacqueline Stucker 1933- *WhoAmL 94*
Wright, James (the Elder) 1714-1785 *WhAmRev*
Wright, James (the Younger) d1816 *WhAmRev*
Wright, James A. 1937- *WhoBlA 94*
Wright, James Bryan 1955- *WhoAmL 94, WhoWest 94*
Wright, James C. 1938- *WhoAmL 94*
Wright, James C., Jr. 1922- *WhoAmP 93*
Wright, James Christopher 1918- *WhoBlA 94*
Wright, James Claude 1922- *Who 94*
Wright, James Claude, Jr. 1922- *IntWW 93*
Wright, James Corwin 1959- *WhoAm 94*
Wright, James David 1947- *WhoAm 94*
Wright, James Dorsey 1944- *WhoAm 94, WhoAmL 94*
Wright, James E., III 1952- *WhoAmL 94*
Wright, James Edward 1921- *WhoAm 94*
Wright, James L., Jr. 1925- *WhoAmP 93*
Wright, James Lashua 1934- *WhoAmP 93*
Wright, James Lawrence 1943- *WhoAmL 94*
Wright, James Leroy 1947- *WhoAmP 93*
Wright, James R. 1941- *WhoBlA 94*
Wright, James Richard 1921- *WhoBlA 94*
Wright, James Robertson Graeme 1939- *IntWW 93, Who 94*
Wright, James Roscoe 1922- *WhoAm 94*
Wright, James Scott 1959- *WhoFI 94*
Wright, James W. 1949- *WhoAmP 93*
Wright, Jane C. 1919- *WhoBlA 94*
Wright, Jane Cooke 1919- *WhoAm 94*
Wright, Janet Scritsmier 1960- *WhoWest 94*
Wright, Jay 1935- *BlkWr 2*
Wright, Jay Kelly 1943- *WhoAmL 94*
Wright, Jean Sutton 1922- *WhoWest 94*
Wright, Jeanette Tornow 1927- *WhoAm 94*
Wright, Jeanne Elizabeth Jason 1934- *WhoAm 94*
Wright, Jeanne Jason 1934- *WhoBlA 94*
Wright, Jefferson W. 1935- *WhoBlA 94*
Wright, Jeffrey Cyphers *DrAPF 93*
Wright, Jeffrey Joseph 1951- *WhoFI 94*
Wright, Jeffrey L. 1945- *WhoAmP 93*
Wright, Jenny 1962- *WhoHol 92*
Wright, Jenny Lee *WhoHol 92*
Wright, Jerauld 1898- *WhAm 10, Who 94*
Wright, Jeremiah A., Jr. 1941- *WhoBlA 94*
Wright, Jerry Smith 1942- *WhoAmL 94*
Wright, Jesse Graham, Jr. 1939- *WhoAmA 93*
Wright, Jim *WhoAmP 93*
Wright, Jim 1946- *WhoAmP 93*
Wright, Jim Lee 1952- *WhoFI 94*
Wright, Joe 1940- *WhoAmP 93*
Wright, Joe Booth 1920- *Who 94*
Wright, John d1987 *WhoHol 92*
Wright, John 1921- *Who 94*
Wright, John 1941- *WhoAm 94*
Wright, John 1942- *WhoHol 92*
Wright, John Aaron 1939- *WhoBlA 94*
Wright, John Bacon 1920- *WhAm 10*
Wright, John Charles Young 1925- *WhoAm 94*
Wright, John Collins 1927- *WhoAm 94*
Wright, John Curtis 1943- *WhoScEn 94*
Wright, John Emerson 1937- *WhoAm 94*
Wright, John George, Jr. 1947- *WhoWest 94*
Wright, John Hurrell C. *Who 94*
Wright, John Keith 1928- *Who 94*
Wright, John King 1947- *WhoIns 94*
Wright, John L. 1937- *WrDr 94*
Wright, John MacNair, Jr. 1916- *WhoAm 94, WhoWest 94*
Wright, John Pardee 1957- *WhoFI 94*
Wright, John Patrick 1968- *WhoWest 94*
Wright, John Peale 1924- *WhoAm 94*
Wright, John Robert 1935- *WhoAm 94*
Wright, John Stewart 1923- *WhoAm 94*
Wright, John Winfred 1949- *WhoAmL 94*
Wright, Jonathan Clifford 1949- *WhoIns 94*
Wright, Joseph 1756-1793 *WhAmRev*
Wright, Joseph 1917- *Who 94*
Wright, Joseph H., Jr. 1954- *WhoBlA 94*
Wright, Joseph Malcolm 1944- *WhoBlA 94*
Wright, Joseph Robert, Jr. 1938- *WhoAm 94, WhoFI 94*
Wright, Joyce C. 1951- *WhoBlA 94*
Wright, Judith 1915- *BlmGWL, Who 94*
Wright, Judith Arundell 1915- *IntWW 93, WrDr 94*
Wright, Judith Rae 1929- *WhoMW 93*
Wright, Judy Lynne 1958- *WhoMW 93*
Wright, Julie Adesina 1957- *WhoBlA 94*
Wright, Julius Arnette, III 1951- *WhoAmP 93*
Wright, K. C. *DrAPF 93*
Wright, Kara-Lyn Annette 1963- *WhoScEn 94*
Wright, Kathryn Michele 1959- *WhoWest 94*
Wright, Katie Harper 1923- *WhoBlA 94, WhoMW 93*
Wright, Keith 1963- *WrDr 94*
Wright, Keith Derek, Sr. 1953- *WhoBlA 94*
Wright, Keith L. *WhoAmP 93*
Wright, Ken *WhoHol 92*

Wright, Kenneth *ConAu 141, EncSF 93, SmATA 76*
Wright, Kenneth 1915- *WrDr 94*
Wright, Kenneth Brooks 1934- *WhoAm 94*
Wright, Kenneth Campbell 1932- *Who 94*
Wright, Kenneth Dale 1950- *WhoAmP 93*
Wright, Kenneth E. 1941- *WhoAmP 93*
Wright, Kenneth Osborne 1911- *WhoAm 94*
Wright, Kenneth W. 1948- *WhoAmL 94*
Wright, Kieth Carter 1933- *WhoAm 94*
Wright, Kit 1944- *WrDr 94*
Wright, L. R. 1939- *BlmGWL*
Wright, Lacy, Jr. 1946- *WhoAmP 93*
Wright, Lacy Arnold, Jr. 1940- *WhoAm 94*
Wright, Lan 1923- *EncSF 93*
Wright, Lance Armitage 1915- *Who 94*
Wright, Larry 1940- *ConAu 140*
Wright, Larry Donald 1949- *WhoMW 93*
Wright, Larry L. 1953- *WhoBlA 94*
Wright, Laura Maria Sheldon 1809-1886 *EncNAR*
Wright, Laurali R. 1939- *WhoAm 94*
Wright, Lawrence A. 1927- *CngDr 93, WhoAm 94, WhoAmL 94, WhoFI 94*
Wright, Lennon C. 1952- *WhoAmL 94*
Wright, Lester Paul 1946- *Who 94*
Wright, Lin Mary 1933- *WhoWest 94*
Wright, Linda Jean 1949- *WhoFI 94*
Wright, Linwood Clinton 1919- *WhoBlA 94*
Wright, Lisa Ann 1965- *WhoAmL 94, WhoMW 93*
Wright, Lloyd 1890-1978 *WhoAmA 93N*
Wright, Lorin Roderick 1948- *WhoWest 94*
Wright, Louis Donnel 1953- *WhoBlA 94*
Wright, Louis Tompkins 1891-1952 *WorScD*
Wright, Loyce Pierce 1943- *WhoBlA 94*
Wright, M(aureen) R(osemary) *WrDr 94*
Wright, Mack V. d1965 *WhoHol 92*
Wright, Maggie *WhoHol 92*
Wright, Margaret 1931- *Who 94*
Wright, Margaret S. *Who 94*
Wright, Margaret Taylor 1949- *WhoFI 94*
Wright, Marie d1949 *WhoHol 92*
Wright, Marie Anne 1953- *WhoFI 94*
Wright, Marshall 1926- *WhoAm 94*
Wright, Martin 1930- *Who 94*
Wright, Marvin 1917- *WhoBlA 94*
Wright, Mary H. 1916- *WhoBlA 94*
Wright, Mary Lou 1933- *WhoAmP 93*
Wright, Mary Lynn 1958- *WhoFI 94*
Wright, Mary McKenzie 1945- *WhoFI 94*
Wright, Matthew N. 1959- *WhoAmP 93*
Wright, Maureen Smith 1962- *WhoScEn 94*
Wright, Maurice (Willis) 1949- *NewGrDO*
Wright, Max 1943- *WhoHol 92*
Wright, Mehetabel Wesley 1697-1750 *DcNaB MP*
Wright, Michael *Who 94, WhoHol 92*
Wright, (John) Michael 1932- *Who 94*
Wright, Michael George 1939- *WhoScEn 94*
Wright, Michael Thomas 1936- *Who 94*
Wright, Michael Thomas 1947- *Who 94*
Wright, Michael William 1938- *WhoAm 94, WhoFI 94, WhoMW 93*
Wright, Milton 1920- *WhoAmA 93*
Wright, Minturn Tatum, III 1925- *WhoAm 94*
Wright, Mira Renee 1957- *WhoMW 93*
Wright, Muriel Deason 1919- *WhoAm 94*
Wright, Myron Arnold 1911- *WhAm 10*
Wright, Nancy Means *DrAPF 93*
Wright, Nathan Alan 1957- *WhoMW 93*
Wright, Ned d1981 *WhoHol 92*
Wright, Neil Richard 1946- *WhoFI 94*
Wright, Nell Higgins 1912- *WhoAmP 93*
Wright, Nicholas 1940- *ConDr 93, WrDr 94*
Wright, Nicholas Alcwyn 1943- *Who 94*
Wright, Norman Harold 1947- *WhoAm 94, WhoAmL 94*
Wright, Norris P. 1945- *WhoAmL 94*
Wright, Nory *WhoHol 92*
Wright, Oliver *IntWW 93, Who 94*
Wright, Oliver 1921- *WhoAm 94*
Wright, (John) Oliver 1921- *IntWW 93, Who 94*
Wright, Orville 1871-1948 *WorInv [port]*
Wright, Otho *WhoHol 92*
Wright, P. Bruce 1946- *WhoAm 94*
Wright, Patience Lovell 1725-1786 *WhAmRev*
Wright, Patricia 1931- *WhoAmP 93*
Wright, (Mary) Patricia 1932- *WrDr 94*
Wright, Patricia Donovan 1952- *WhoAm 94*
Wright, Patrick *WhoHol 92*
Wright, Patrick (Richard Henry) 1931- *IntWW 93, Who 94*
Wright, Paul, Jr. 1911- *WhoAm 94*
Wright, Paul (Herve Giraud) 1915- *Who 94*
Wright, Paul Bruce 1946- *WhoAmL 94*
Wright, Paul Nathan 1950- *WhoMW 93*
Wright, Paul W. d1993 *NewYTBS 93*
Wright, Paul William 1944- *WhoAmL 94*
Wright, Peggy Ann 1947- *WhoMW 93*
Wright, Penelope Ann *Who 94*
Wright, Peter 1926- *IntDcB [port]*
Wright, Peter 1929- *Who 94*
Wright, Peter 1932- *Who 94*
Wright, Peter (Robert) 1926- *Who 94*
Wright, Peter Meldrim 1946- *WhoAm 94, WhoAmL 94*
Wright, Peter Michael 1954- *Who 94*
Wright, Peter Murrell 1932- *WhoScEn 94*
Wright, Philip A., Jr. 1954- *WhoAmP 93*
Wright, Philip Lincoln 1914- *WhoScEn 94*
Wright, Princa McManus 1931- *WhoAmL 94*
Wright, R(onald W. V.) Selby 1908- *WrDr 94*
Wright, Rachel Ray 1935- *WhoAmP 93*
Wright, Ralph Edward 1950- *WhoBlA 94*
Wright, Ralph G. 1935- *WhoAmP 93*
Wright, Randolph Earle 1920- *WhoAm 94*
Wright, Randolph Milton 1946- *WhoMW 93*
Wright, Raymond LeRoy, Jr. 1950- *WhoBlA 94*
Wright, Raymond Stanford 1949- *WhoBlA 94*
Wright, Rebecca *DrAPF 93*
Wright, Richard d1960 *WhoHol 92*
Wright, Richard 1908-1960 *AfrAmAl 6, ConBlB 5 [port]*
Wright, Richard 1944- *WhoAmP 93*
Wright, Richard (Nathaniel) 1908-1960 *RfGShF, TwCYAW*
Wright, Richard (Michael) C. *Who 94*
Wright, Richard Donald 1936- *WhoFI 94*
Wright, Richard Eustace John G. *Who 94*
Wright, Richard Harrell 1950- *WhoAmP 93*
Wright, Richard John 1951- *WhoAm 94*
Wright, Richard Nathaniel 1908-1960 *AmCulL [port]*
Wright, Richard Newport, III 1932- *WhoAm 94, WhoScEn 94*
Wright, Richard O. 1942- *WhoAmP 93*
Wright, Rickey 1958- *WhoBlA 94*
Wright, Robert 1752-1826 *WhAmRev*
Wright, Robert A. 1900-1958 *WhoAmA 93N*
Wright, Robert A. 1919- *WhoBlA 94*
Wright, Robert Anthony Kent 1922- *Who 94*
Wright, Robert Burroughs 1916- *WhoAm 94*
Wright, Robert C. 1943- *IntMPA 94, WhoAm 94, WhoFI 94*
Wright, Robert Courtlandt 1944- *WhoAmP 93, WhoBlA 94*
Wright, Robert E. Lee 1953- *WhoAmL 94*
Wright, Robert F. *WhoAm 94, WhoFI 94*
Wright, Robert George, II 1951- *WhoAmL 94*
Wright, Robert James 1918- *WhoFI 94*
Wright, Robert James 1935- *WhoFI 94*
Wright, Robert John 1953- *WhoMW 93*
Wright, Robert Joseph 1949- *WhoAm 94, WhoAmL 94*
Wright, Robert L. 1917- *WhoBlA 94*
Wright, Robert Lee 1920- *WrDr 94*
Wright, Robert Michael 1957- *WhoScEn 94*
Wright, Robert Morley 1939- *WhoAmL 94*
Wright, Robert Payton 1951- *WhoAm 94, WhoAmL 94*
Wright, Robert Richard 1915- *WhoAmP 93*
Wright, Robert Thomas, Jr. 1946- *WhoAmL 94*
Wright, Roberta V. Hughes *WhoBlA 94*
Wright, Robin 1966- *WhoHol 92*
Wright, Robin B 1948- *WrDr 94*
Wright, Roderick *Who 94*
Wright, Rodney H. 1931- *WhoAm 94*
Wright, Ronald Selby 1908- *IntWW 93*
Wright, Ronald (William Vernon) Selby 1908- *Who 94*
Wright, Roosevelt R., Jr. 1943- *WhoBlA 94*
Wright, Rosalie Muller 1942- *WhoAm 94, WhoWest 94*
Wright, Rosalind *DrAPF 93*
Wright, Roy Kilner 1926- *Who 94*
Wright, Roy W. 1914- *IntWW 93*
Wright, Roy William 1914- *Who 94*
Wright, Royston Clifford 1922- *Who 94*
Wright, Russel 1904-1976 *WhoAmA 93N*
Wright, Ruth Caldwell 1898- *WhAm 10*
Wright, Ruth M. 1928- *WhoAmP 93*
Wright, Ruth Margaret *Who 94*
Wright, S(ydney) Fowler 1874-1965 *EncSF 93*
Wright, Sam W. 1926- *WhoAmP 93*
Wright, Samuel E. *WhoHol 92*
Wright, Samuel Lamar 1953- *WhoBlA 94*
Wright, Sara E(lizabeth) 1928?- *BlkWr 2*
Wright, Sarah E. 1928- *WhoBlA 94*
Wright, Sarah Elizabeth *DrAPF 93*
Wright, Scott Olin 1923- *WhoAm 94, WhoAmL 94, WhoMW 93*
Wright, Shannon 1956- *WhoMW 93*
Wright, Sheila Angstadt 1937- *WhoAmP 93*
Wright, Sheila Rosemary Rivers 1925- *Who 94*
Wright, Sheryl Ann 1958- *WhoMW 93*
Wright, Shirley A. 1935- *WhoAmP 93*
Wright, Shirley Edwin McEwan 1915- *Who 94*
Wright, Stanley Allen 1926- *WhoAmP 93*
Wright, Stanley Harris 1930- *Who 94*
Wright, Stanley Marc 1911- *WhoAmA 93*
Wright, Stanley V. 1921- *WhoBlA 94*
Wright, Stephen *DrAPF 93, Who 94, WhoHol 92*
Wright, Stephen d1780 *DcNaB MP*
Wright, Stephen 1922- *WrDr 94*
Wright, Stephen 1946- *EncSF 93*
Wright, (John) Stephen 1946- *Who 94*
Wright, Stephen Caldwell *DrAPF 93*
Wright, Stephen Caldwell 1946- *BlkWr 2, ConAu 142*
Wright, Stephen Charles 1951- *WhoFI 94*
Wright, Stephen Gailord 1943- *WhoAm 94, WhoScEn 94*
Wright, Stephen John Leadbetter 1946- *Who 94*
Wright, Stephen Junius, Jr. 1910- *WhoBlA 94*
Wright, Steven 1955- *WhoCom [port]*
Wright, Steven 1956- *WhoHol 92*
Wright, Steven Jay 1949- *WhoScEn 94*
Wright, Susan Webber 1948- *WhoAm 94, WhoAmL 94*
Wright, Sylvester M. 1927- *WhoBlA 94*
Wright, Tamela Jean 1962- *WhoAm 94*
Wright, Tenny d1971 *WhoHol 92*
Wright, Terence Jerome 1954- *WhoMW 93*
Wright, Terence Richard *WhoScEn 94*
Wright, Teresa 1918- *IntMPA 94, WhoHol 92*
Wright, Terry *DrAPF 93*
Wright, Theodore Otis 1921- *WhoScEn 94, WhoWest 94*
Wright, Theodore Paul, Jr. 1926- *WhoAm 94, WrDr 94*
Wright, Theodore Robert Fairbank 1928- *WhoAm 94*
Wright, Thomas *Who 94*
Wright, (Nicholas) Thomas 1948- *Who 94*
Wright, Thomas David 1937- *WhoAm 94*
Wright, Thomas E. *WhoAmP 93*
Wright, Thomas E. 1936- *WhoAmP 93*
Wright, Thomas Henry 1904- *WhoAm 94*
Wright, Thomas Joe 1946- *WhoAm 94*
Wright, Thomas Llewellyn 1935- *WhoWest 94*
Wright, Thomas R. 1942- *WhoAmL 94*
Wright, Thomas William Dunstan 1919- *WhoAm 94*
Wright, Thomas Wilson 1933- *WhoScEn 94*
Wright, Tim Eugene 1943- *WhoWest 94*
Wright, Tom *WhoHol 92*
Wright, Tony d1986 *WhoHol 92*
Wright, Turbutt 1741-1783 *WhAmRev*
Wright, Verlyn LaGlen 1963- *WhoBlA 94*
Wright, Verna 1928- *IntWW 93, Who 94*
Wright, Vernon H. C. 1942- *WhoAm 94*
Wright, Vernon Orville 1920- *WhoAm 94*
Wright, Vicki C. 1956- *WhoAmA 93*
Wright, Virginia L. 1912- *WhoAmP 93*
Wright, Wadell 1944- *WhoWest 94*
Wright, Wallace Mathias 1928- *WhoAm 94*
Wright, Wally 1937- *WhoAmP 93*
Wright, Warren Keith 1954- *WhoMW 93*
Wright, Wayne Keith 1938- *WhoMW 93*
Wright, Weaver *EncSF 93*
Wright, Wen d1954 *WhoHol 92*
Wright, Wilbur 1867-1912 *WorInv [port]*
Wright, Wiley Reed, Jr. 1932- *WhoAm 94*
Wright, Will d1962 *WhoHol 92*
Wright, Willard Jurey 1914- *WhoAm 94, WhoAmL 94*
Wright, William d1949 *WhoHol 92*
Wright, William 1924- *WorESoc*
Wright, William A. 1936- *WhoBlA 94*
Wright, William A. 1959- *WhoAmP 93*
Wright, William Ambrose 1924- *Who 94*
Wright, William Bigelow 1924- *WhoAm 94*
Wright, William David 1906- *Who 94, WrDr 94*
Wright, William Edward 1926- *WrDr 94*
Wright, William Everard, Jr. 1949- *WhoAmL 94*
Wright, William Gaillard 1933- *WhoBlA 94*
Wright, William Howard 1945- *WhoAmP 93*
Wright, William James 1948- *WhoMW 93*
Wright, William Marshall 1926- *WhoAmP 93*
Wright, William Michael 1955- *WhoFI 94*
Wright, Wilson, Jr. 1948- *WhoBlA 94*
Wright, Wilson Walker 1930- *WhoAmL 94, WhoFI 94*
Wright, Wm Robert 1935- *WhoAmP 93*
Wright, Yvonne Febres Cordero De *WhoHisp 94*
Wright-Botchwey, Roberta Yvonne 1946- *WhoBlA 94*
Wrighten, Mary Ann c. 1751-1796 *NewGrDO*
Wright-Gonos, Kelly Lynn 1965- *WhoMW 93*
Wrightman, Eric d1968 *WhoHol 92*
Wright-Miller, Elizabeth Gill 1952- *WhoMW 93*
Wrighton, Mark Stephen 1949- *WhoAm 94*
Wright-Quastler, Reba 1946- *WhoWest 94*
Wrightson, Earl d1993 *NewYTBS 93 [port]*
Wrightson, (Charles) Mark (Garmondsway) 1951- *Who 94*
Wrightson, Patricia 1921- *BlmGWL*
Wrightson, (Alice) Patricia 1921- *TwCYAW, WrDr 94*
Wrigley, Colin Walter 1937- *WhoScEn 94*
Wrigley, Edward Anthony 1931- *IntWW 93, Who 94*
Wrigley, Elizabeth Springer 1915- *WhoAm 94, WhoWest 94*
Wrigley, Gordon 1923- *WrDr 94*
Wrigley, Henry Bertram 1909- *Who 94*
Wrigley, Jack 1923- *Who 94*
Wrigley, Michael Harold 1924- *Who 94*
Wrigley, Rick 1955- *WhoAmA 93*
Wrigley, Robert *DrAPF 93*
Wrigley, Robert Elder 1951- *WhoAmP 93*
Wrigley, Robert Ernest 1943- *WhoMW 93*
Wrigley, Tony *Who 94*
Wrigley, William 1933- *WhoAm 94, WhoFI 94, WhoMW 93*
Wrinkle, John Newton 1929- *WhoAm 94*
Wrintmore, Eric George 1928- *Who 94*
Wriothesley, Henry *BlmGEL*
Wrisley, Albert L., Jr. 1928- *WhoMW 93*
Wrist, Peter Ellis 1927- *WhoAm 94, WhoScEn 94*
Wriston, Barbara 1917- *WhoAmA 93*
Wriston, Walter Bigelow 1919- *WhoAm 94*
Wrixon, Maris *WhoHol 92*
Wrixon-Becher, William F. *Who 94*
Wroath, John Herbert 1932- *Who 94*
Wrobel, Elizabeth Anne 1965- *WhoMW 93*
Wrobel, Robert Franklin 1944- *WhoAm 94*
Wroble, Arthur G. 1948- *WhoAmL 94*
Wrobleski, Jeanne Pauline 1942- *WhoAmL 94*
Wroblewski, Celeste Judine *WhoAm 94*
Wroblewski, Kenneth Andrew 1945- *WhoWest 94*
Wroblewski, Michael Paul 1960- *WhoMW 93*
Wroblewski, Ronald John 1956- *WhoScEn 94*
Wroblewski, Timothy Raymond 1966- *WhoFI 94, WhoMW 93*
Wrobley, Ralph Gene 1935- *WhoAm 94, WhoAmL 94*
Wroe, David Charles Lynn 1942- *Who 94*
Wrona, Leonard Mathhew 1958- *WhoScEn 94*
Wrona, Peter Alexander 1955- *WhoWest 94*
Wrona, Thomas James 1930- *WhoMW 93*
Wrong, Dennis Hume 1923- *WhoAm 94*
Wrong, Henry Lewellys Barker 1930- *Who 94*
Wrong, Hume 1894-1954 *HisDcKW*
Wronski, Stanley Paul 1919- *WhoMW 93*
Wroth, James Melvin 1929- *WhoAm 94*
Wroth, Lawrence Kinvin 1932- *WhoAm 94, WhoAmL 94*
Wroth, Mary 1586?-1652? *BlmGEL*
Wroth, Mary 1587?-1651? *BlmGWL*
Wrottesley, Baron 1968- *Who 94*
Wroughton, John Presbury 1934- *WrDr 94*
Wroughton, Philip Lavallin 1933- *Who 94*
Wruble, Bernhardt Karp 1942- *WhoAm 94, WhoAmL 94*
Wruble, Brian Frederick 1943- *WhoAm 94, WhoFI 94*
Wrves, Orestes G. 1951- *WhoHisp 94*
Wrye, Richard Fred 1944- *WhoWest 94*
Wrzesinski, Elizabeth Jane 1938- *WhoMW 93*
Wrzesinski, John T. *WhoAmP 93*

Wu Xiangbi 1926- IntWW 93,
WhoPRCh 91
Wu Xianhan WhoPRCh 91
Wu Xianzhong 1925- WhoPRCh 91 [port]
Wu Xiaobang 1906- WhoPRCh 91 [port]
Wu Xiaochang 1940- WhoPRCh 91 [port]
Wu Xiaoda WhoPRCh 91
Wu Xiaolan WhoPRCh 91
Wu Xiaoxuan 1958- WhoPRCh 91 [port]
Wu Xihai WhoPRCh 91
Wu Xijun 1933- WhoPRCh 91 [port]
Wu Xin'an WhoPRCh 91
Wu Xiuping 1927- WhoPRCh 91 [port]
Wu Xiuquan 1908- WhoPRCh 91 [port]
Wu Xiuquan 1909- IntWW 93
Wu Xueqian 1921- IntWW 93,
WhoPRCh 91 [port]
Wu Yi WhoWomW 91
Wu Yi 1934- WhoPRCh 91
Wu Yi 1938- IntWW 93,
WhoPRCh 91 [port]
Wu Yigong WhoPRCh 91 [port]
Wu Yigong 1938- IntWW 93
Wu Yikang WhoPRCh 91 [port]
Wu Yingfu WhoPRCh 91 [port]
Wu Yinxian 1900- WhoPRCh 91
Wu Yixia WhoPRCh 91
Wu Yongshi WhoPRCh 91
Wu Youheng WhoPRCh 91 [port]
Wu Yuanjin WhoPRCh 91
Wu Yufang WhoPRCh 91 [port]
Wu Yunchang 1936- WhoPRCh 91 [port]
Wu Ze-tian 624-705 HisWorL [port]
Wu Zhankui WhoPRCh 91
Wu Zhen 1922- IntWW 93,
WhoPRCh 91 [port]
Wu Zhengkai WhoPRCh 91
Wu Zhengyi 1916- WhoPRCh 91 [port]
Wu Zhichao 1914- WhoPRCh 91 [port]
Wu Zhichuan 1921- WhoPRCh 91 [port]
Wu Zhifei WhoPRCh 91
Wu Zhijian WhoPRCh 91
Wu Zhizhong WhoPRCh 91 [port]
Wu Zhonghua IntWW 93N
Wu Zhonghua 1917- WhoPRCh 91 [port]
Wu Zhonglun WhoPRCh 91 [port]
Wu Zhongyuan WhoPRCh 91 [port]
Wu Zhouqun WhoPRCh 91
Wu Ziniu 1953- WhoPRCh 91 [port]
Wu Zuguang 1917- WhoPRCh 91 [port]
Wu Zuoren 1908- IntWW 93,
WhoPRCh 91 [port]
Wu Zuqiang 1927- IntWW 93,
WhoPRCh 91 [port]
Wu Zuxiang 1908- WhoPRCh 91 [port]
Wyand, Keith Allen 1955- WhoMW 93
Wyand, Martin Judd 1931- WhoAm 94
Wyand, Robert Rice, II 1938-1991
WhAm 10
Wyant, Corbin A. WhoAm 94
Wyant, James Clair 1943- WhoAm 94,
WhoScEn 94, WhoWest 94
Wyant, Joseph Andrew 1949- WhoFI 94
Wyant, Maria Sophia 1959- WhoAmP 93
Wyant, Theodore 1954- WhoWest 94
Wyard, Vicki Shaw 1945- WhoFI 94
Wyatt Who 94
Wyatt, Addie L. 1924- WhoBlA 94
Wyatt, Al WhoHol 92
Wyatt, Arthur Hope 1929- Who 94
Wyatt, B.D. EncSF 93
Wyatt, Beatrice E. WhoBlA 94
Wyatt, Charles DrAPF 93
Wyatt, Christopher Terrel 1927-
IntWW 93
Wyatt, Clarence R. 1956- ConAu 142
Wyatt, Claude Stell, Jr. 1921- WhoBlA 94
Wyatt, David Joseph 1931- WhoAm 94
Wyatt, David Kent 1937- WhoAm 94
Wyatt, David M. 1948- WrDr 94
Wyatt, Derrick Arthur 1948- Who 94
Wyatt, Diana E. 1947- WhoAmP 93
Wyatt, Edith Elizabeth 1914- WhoWest 94
Wyatt, Eustace d1944 WhoHol 92
Wyatt, Forest Kent 1934- WhoAm 94
Wyatt, Gavin Edward 1914- Who 94
Wyatt, George W., III 1945- WhoFI 94
Wyatt, Gerard Robert 1925- WhoAm 94
Wyatt, Greg Alan 1949- WhoAmA 93
Wyatt, James Collip 1952- WhoAmL 94
Wyatt, James Frank, Jr. 1922- WhoAm 94
Wyatt, James Franklin 1934- WhoAm 94
Wyatt, James J. 1944- WhoAmP 93
Wyatt, James Luther 1924- WhoAm 94
Wyatt, Jane 1910- IntMPA 94
Wyatt, Jane 1911- WhoHol 92
Wyatt, Janice Barber 1947- WhoAm 94
Wyatt, Joe Billy 1935- WhoAm 94
Wyatt, John Wayne 1950- WhoAmL 94
Wyatt, Joseph Lucian, Jr. 1924-
WhoAm 94, WhoWest 94
Wyatt, Joseph Peyton, Jr. 1941-
WhoAmP 93
Wyatt, Lewis William 1777-1853
DcNaB MP
Wyatt, Marta Villalpando 1940-
WhoHisp 94

Wyatt, Oscar Sherman, Jr. 1924-
WhoAm 94, WhoFI 94
Wyatt, Patrick EncSF 93
Wyatt, Philip Richard 1951- WhoScEn 94
Wyatt, Rachel 1929- BlmGWL
Wyatt, Richard Jed 1939- WhoScEn 94
Wyatt, Robert Odell 1946- WhoAm 94
Wyatt, Rose Marie 1937- WhoAm 94
Wyatt, S. Martin, III 1941- WhoBlA 94
Wyatt, Samuel 1737-1807 DcNaB MP
Wyatt, Sharon WhoHol 92
Wyatt, Spencer 1921- WhoAmP 93
Wyatt, Terrel Who 94
Wyatt, (Christopher) Terrel 1927- Who 94
Wyatt, Tessa 1948- WhoHol 92
Wyatt, Thomas 1503-1542 BlmGEL,
DcLB 132 [port]
Wyatt, Thomas C. 1952- WhoAmL 94
Wyatt, Walter d1986 WhoHol 92
Wyatt, Wendy Who 94
Wyatt, Will Who 94
Wyatt, (Alan) Will 1942- IntWW 93,
Who 94
Wyatt, William Frank, Jr. 1932-
WhoAm 94
Wyatt, William N. 1953- WhoBlA 94
Wyatt, Wilson Watkins 1905- WhoAm 94
Wyatt, Wilson Watkins, Sr. 1905-
WhoAmP 93
Wyatt, Wilson Watkins, Jr. 1943-
WhoAm 94, WhoFI 94
Wyatt, Wyatt DrAPF 93
Wyatt, Zach WrDr 94
Wyatt-Brown, Bertram 1932- WhoAm 94
Wyatt Cummings, Thelma LaVerne 1945-
WhoBlA 94
Wyatt Of Weeford, Baron 1918- Who 94
Wyatt Of Weeford, Baron 1987-
IntWW 93
Wyatt, of Weeford, Lord 1918- WrDr 94
Wybel, Terry Scott 1937- WhoMW 93
Wybourne, Brian Garner 1935- WrDr 94
Wyche, Bradford Wheeler 1950-
WhoAmL 94
Wyche, Lennon Douglas, Jr. 1946-
WhoBlA 94
Wyche, Madison Baker, III 1947-
WhoAmL 94
Wyche, Melville Q., Jr. 1938- WhoBlA 94
Wyche, Paul H., Jr. 1946- WhoBlA 94
Wyche, Samuel David 1945- WhoAm 94
Wyche, Vera Rowena 1923- WhoBlA 94
Wycherley, William 1640-1716 BlmGEL
Wycherley, William 1641-1715
IntDcT 2 [port]
Wycherly, Margaret d1956 WhoHol 92
Wyckoff, Alexander 1898- WhoMW 93
Wyckoff, Edward Lisk, Jr. 1934-
WhoAm 94, WhoAmL 94
Wyckoff, James Donald 1959- WhoFI 94
Wyckoff, Linda S. 1948- WhoAmL 94
Wyckoff, Lorna Matheson 1949-
WhoFI 94
Wyckoff, Margo Gail 1941- WhoAm 94,
WhoWest 94
Wyckoff, Michael d1988 WhoHol 92
Wyckoff, Ralph Walter Graystone 1897-
IntWW 93
Wyckoff, Russell Leroy 1925-
WhoAmP 93
Wyckoff, Sylvia Spencer 1915-
WhoAmA 93
Wycliff, Noel Don 1946- WhoAm 94
Wycliffe, John 1320?-1384 BlmGEL [port],
HisWorL [port]
Wycoff, Charles Coleman 1918-
WhoScEn 94, WhoWest 94
Wycoff, Joseph Ralph 1945- WhoMW 93
Wycoff, Robert E. 1930- WhoAm 94,
WhoFI 94, WhoWest 94
Wycoff, William Mortimer 1941-
WhoAmL 94
Wyczalkowski, Marcin Roman 1910-
WhoFI 94
Wyczalkowski, Wojciech Roman 1946-
WhoScEn 94
Wyden, Ron 1949- CngDr 93
Wyden, Ronald Lee 1949- WhoAm 94,
WhoAmP 93, WhoWest 94
Wydick, Richard Crews 1937- WhoAm 94
Wydler, Hans Ulrich 1923- WhoAmL 94
Wydra, Frank Thomas 1939- WhoMW 93
Wyenn, Than 1919- WhoHol 92
Wyer, James Ingersoll 1923- WhoAm 94
Wyer, William Clarke 1946- WhoAm 94
Wyers, Mary Jane Frances 1914-
WhoAmP 93
Wyes, William d1903 WhoHol 92
Wyeth, Andrew 1917- WhoAm 94
Wyeth, Andrew N. 1917- IntWW 93
Wyeth, Andrew Newell 1917- AmCulL,
Who 94, WhoAmA 93
Wyeth, Henriette 1907- WhoAmA 93
Wyeth, James Browning 1946-
WhoAm 94, WhoAmA 93
Wyeth, Katya WhoHol 92
Wyeth, Mark Thomas 1963- WhoFI 94
Wyeth, Nathaniel 1911-1990 WorInv

Wyeth, Nathaniel Jarvis 1802-1856
WhWE
Wyeth, Sandy Brown WhoHol 92
Wyfold, Baron 1915- Who 94
Wygant, Foster Laurance 1920-
WhoAm 94
Wygant, James Peter 1926- WhoFI 94
Wygle, Peggy Orine 1929- WhoMW 93
Wygle, Ralph William 1926- WhoMW 93
Wygnanski, Israel Jerzy 1935- WhoAm 94
Wygod, Martin J. WhoFI 94
Wyke, Joseph Henry 1928- WhoBlA 94
Wyke, Robert James 1933- WhoIns 94
Wykeham, Peter 1915- Who 94, WrDr 94
Wykes, Alan 1914- EncSF 93, WrDr 94
Wykes, Alan 1914-1993 ConAu 141
Wykes, Edmund Harold 1928-
WhoAm 94
Wykes, James Cochrane d1992 Who 94N
Wykes, Paul David 1959- WhoFI 94
Wykle, May Louise Hinton 1934-
WhoBlA 94
Wykoff, Frank Champion 1942-
WhoAm 94
Wyld, Martin Hugh 1944- Who 94
Wyld, Robert L. 1951- WhoAmL 94
Wyldbore-Smith, (Francis) Brian 1913-
Who 94
Wylde, Thomas 1946- EncSF 93
Wyldeck, Martin d1988 WhoHol 92
Wyle, Ewart Herbert 1904- WhoWest 94
Wyle, Frederick S. 1928- WhoAm 94,
WhoWest 94
Wyle, Michael WhoHol 92
Wyler, Gretchen 1922- WhoHol 92
Wyler, Kathryn Kishpaugh 1937-
WhoAm 93
Wyler, Richard WhoHol 92
Wyler, Susan WhoHol 92
Wyler, William Straus 1946- WhoAmL 94
Wylie, Rt. Hon. Lord 1923- Who 94
Wylie, Alexander Featherstonhaugh
1951- Who 94
Wylie, Calvin Richard 1956- WhoFI 94
Wylie, Campbell d1992 Who 94N
Wylie, Campbell 1905- IntWW 93
Wylie, Chalmers Pangburn 1920-
WhoAmP 93
Wylie, Christopher Craig 1945- WhoAm 94
Wylie, Clarence Raymond, Jr. 1911-
WhoAm 94, WhoScEn 94
Wylie, Derek Who 94
Wylie, (William) Derek 1918- Who 94
Wylie, Dirk EncSF 93
Wylie, Edith d1971 WhoHol 92
Wylie, Elinor 1885-1928 BlmGWL
Wylie, Evan Benjamin 1931- WhoAm 94
Wylie, Frank WhoHol 92
Wylie, J. Kenneth 1927- WhoIns 94
Wylie, J. Michael 1941- WhoAmL 94
Wylie, Judith Babcock 1943- WhoWest 94
Wylie, Laura 1927- WrDr 94
Wylie, Norman Russell Who 94
Wylie, Paul WhoAm 94
Wylie, Paul Richter, Jr. 1936-
WhoAmL 94
Wylie, Philip (Gordon) 1902-1971
EncSF 93
Wylie, Quineta G. Beagle 1948-
WhoAmP 93
Wylie, Sharon 1949- WhoAmP 93
Wylie, Sian Meryl Who 94
Wyller, Egil A. 1925- IntWW 93
Wyllie, Daniel G. 1944- WhoAmL 94
Wyllie, Hugh Rutherford 1934- Who 94
Wyllie, John Cook 1908-1968
DcLB 140 [port]
Wyllie, Loring A., Jr. 1938- WhoAm 94,
WhoWest 94
Wyllie, Meg WhoHol 92
Wyllie, Peter J(ohn) 1930- WrDr 94
Wyllie, Peter John 1930- IntWW 93,
Who 94, WhoAm 94, WhoWest 94
Wyllie, Robert Lyon 1897- Who 94
Wyllie, William Robert Alexander 1932-
Who 94
Wylly, Barbara Bentley 1924- WhoAm 94
Wyllys, Ronald Eugene 1930- WhoAm 94
Wyly, Charles Joseph, Jr. 1933-
WhoAm 94
Wyman, Andrea ConAu 142,
SmATA 75 [port]
Wyman, Bostwick Frampton 1941-
WhoM W 93
Wyman, David Sword 1929- WhoAm 94
Wyman, Franklin, Jr. 1921- WhoFI 94
Wyman, Henry Walter 1919- WhoAm 94
Wyman, James Thomas 1920- WhoAm 94
Wyman, James Vernon 1923- WhoAm 94
Wyman, Jane 1914- IntWW 93,
WhoAm 94, WhoHol 92
Wyman, Jane 1917- IntMPA 94
Wyman, John Bernard 1916- Who 94
Wyman, Linda 1937- WhoMW 93
Wyman, Louis C. 1917- WhoAmP 93
Wyman, Louis Crosby 1917- WhoAm 94
Wyman, Max 1939- ConAu 140
Wyman, Nancy Carol WhoAmP 93

Wyman, Phillip D. 1945- WhoAmP 93
Wyman, Ralph Mark 1926- WhoAm 94
Wyman, Richard Vaughn 1927-
WhoAm 94, WhoWest 94
Wyman, Robert Thomas 1964-
WhoAmL 94
Wyman, Rosalind 1930- WhoAmP 93
Wyman, Stanley Moore 1913- WhoAm 94
Wyman, Thomas H. 1931- IntMPA 94
Wyman, William 1922-1980
WhoAmA 93N
Wyman, William George 1941-
IntWW 93, WhoAm 94
Wymark, Olwen (Margaret) WrDr 94
Wymark, Olwen (Margaret) 1932-
ConDr 93
Wymark, Patrick d1970 WhoHol 92
Wymbs, Norman E. 1923- WhoAmP 93
Wymelenberg, Suzanne 1929- ConAu 140
Wymer, Dennis Paul 1961- WhoFI 94
Wymer, Nancy Elaine 1948- WhoWest 94
Wymore, Bill D. 1940- WhoIns 94
Wymore, Patrice 1926- IntMPA 94,
WhoHol 92
Wynant, H. M. WhoHol 92
Wynant, Patricia d1977 WhoHol 92
Wynar, Bohdan Stephen 1926-
WhoAm 94, WhoWest 94
Wynblatt, Paul Pinhas 1935- WhoAm 94
Wynd, Oswald 1913- WrDr 94
Wynder, Ernst Ludwig 1922- WhoAm 94,
WhoScEn 94
Wynder, William W. 1948- WhoAmL 94
Wyndham Who 94
Wyndham, Charles d1919 WhoHol 92
Wyndham, Dennis 1887- WhoHol 92
Wyndham, Eric Leslie 1946- WhoAmP 93
Wyndham, Esther 1908- Who 94
Wyndham, Francis (Guy Percy) 1924-
WrDr 94
Wyndham, Harald DrAPF 93
Wyndham, Joan 1911- WhoHol 92
Wyndham, John 1903-1969 EncSF 93
Wyndham, Poppy d1928 WhoHol 92
Wyndham-Quin Who 94
Wyndle, Waunda-Mae 1921- WhoMW 93
Wyndrum, Ralph W., Jr. 1937-
WhoAm 94
Wyner, Aaron Daniel 1939- WhoAm 94
Wyner, George WhoHol 92
Wyner, Yehudi 1929- WhoAm 94
Wynes, Charles E. 1929- WrDr 94
Wyness, James Alexander Davidson
1937- Who 94
Wynette, Tammy 1942- IntWW 93,
WhoAm 94, WhoHol 92
Wynford, Baron 1917- Who 94
Wynford, William fl. 1360-1405
DcNaB MP
Wyngaard, Susan Elizabeth WhoAmA 93
Wyngaarden, James Barnes 1924-
Who 94, WhoAm 94, WhoAmP 93
Wyngarde, Peter WhoHol 92
Wynia, Ann Jobe 1943- WhoAmP 93
Wynia, Gary W. 1942- WrDr 94
Wynia, James Paul 1946- WhoWest 94
Wyn-Jones, Alun 1946- WhoScEn 94
Wynkoop, Christopher WhoHol 92
Wynkoop, Donal Brooke 1945- WhoFI 94,
WhoWest 94
Wynkoop, Henry 1737-1816 WhAmRev
Wynkyn de Worde d1534 BlmGEL
Wynn Who 94
Wynn, Albert 1951- WhoBlA 94
Wynn, Albert R. 1951- CngDr 93,
WhoAm 94
Wynn, Albert Russell 1951- WhoAmP 93
Wynn, Arthur Henry Ashford 1910-
Who 94
Wynn, Barry WhoAmP 93
Wynn, Charles Milton 1953- WhoAmL 94
Wynn, Cordell WhoBlA 94
Wynn, Coy Wilton 1920- WhoAm 94
Wynn, D(ale) Richard 1918- ConAu 43NR
Wynn, Dale Richard 1918- WrDr 94
Wynn, Daniel Webster 1919- WhoBlA 94
Wynn, Deborah B. 1947- WhoBlA 94
Wynn, Donald James 1942- WhoAmA 93
Wynn, Doris d1925 WhoHol 92
Wynn, Ed d1966 WhoHol 92
Wynn, Ed 1886-1966 WhoCom
Wynn, Francis J. WhoIns 94
Wynn, Gladys 1926- WhoBlA 94
Wynn, J(ohn) C(harles) 1920- WrDr 94
Wynn, John Charles 1920- WhoAm 94
Wynn, John Patrick 1951- WhoFI 94
Wynn, Keenan d1986 WhoHol 92
Wynn, Kenneth Richard 1952-
WhoAm 94
Wynn, Malcolm 1940- WhoBlA 94
Wynn, May 1930- WhoHol 92
Wynn, Nan d1971 WhoHol 92
Wynn, Ned 1942- WhoHol 92
Wynn, Prathia Hall 1940- WhoBlA 94
Wynn, Robert L., Jr. 1929- WhoBlA 94
Wynn, Robert Louis, II 1954-
WhoMW 93

Wynn, Robert Raymond 1929-
    WhoScEn 94, WhoWest 94
Wynn, Stanford Alan 1950- *WhoAmL 94*
Wynn, Stephen A. 1941- *WhoAm 94,
    WhoFI 94, WhoWest 94*
Wynn, Sylvia J. 1941- *WhoBlA 94*
Wynn, Terence 1946- *Who 94*
Wynn, Terence Bryan 1928- *Who 94*
Wynn, Thomas Harold, Sr. 1931-
    WhoBlA 94
Wynn, Thomas Joseph 1918- *WhoAm 94*
Wynn, Thomas Joseph 1940-
    WhoAmL 94
Wynn, Tom 1902- *WhoHol 92*
Wynn, Tracy Keenan 1945- *IntMPA 94,
    WhoHol 92*
Wynn, (David) Watkin W. *Who 94*
Wynn, William Austin, Jr. 1937-
    WhoBlA 94
Wynn, William Harrison 1931-
    WhoAm 94, WhoFI 94
Wynne, Albert Givens 1922- *WhoAmA 93*
Wynne, Bert d1971 *WhoHol 92*
Wynne, Brian 1939- *WrDr 94*
Wynne, Brian James 1950- *WhoAm 94*
Wynne, Charles Gorrie 1911- *IntWW 93,
    Who 94*
Wynne, David 1900-1983 *NewGrDO*
Wynne, David 1926- *Who 94*
Wynne, Edward A. 1928- *WrDr 94*
Wynne, Frank 1939- *WrDr 94*
Wynne, George C. 1949- *WhoIns 94*
Wynne, J. F. W. *Who 94*
Wynne, James Earl 1950- *WhoAm 94*
Wynne, John *WhoAmP 93*
Wynne, John Benedict 1930- *WhoAm 94*
Wynne, John Oliver 1945- *WhoAm 94*
Wynne, Lyman Carroll 1923- *WhoAm 94*
Wynne, Marvell 1959- *WhoBlA 94*
Wynne, Michael Walter 1944- *WhoAm 94*
Wynne, Robert J. 1942- *WhoAmL 94*
Wynne, Robin *WhoAmP 93*
Wynne, Ronald D(avid) 1934-
    ConAu 42NR
Wynne, Steven E. 1952- *WhoAmL 94*
Wynne, William Joseph 1927-
    WhoAmL 94
Wynne-Davies, Marion 1958- *WrDr 94*
Wynne-Edwards, Hugh Robert 1934-
    WhoAm 94
Wynne-Edwards, Vero Copner 1906-
    IntWW 93, Who 94
Wynne-Jones, Diana *EncSF 93*
Wynne Mason, Walter d1992 *Who 94N*
Wynne-Morgan, David 1931- *IntWW 93*
Wynne-Tyson, Esme *EncSF 93*
Wynns, Corrie 1958- *WhoBlA 94*
Wynns, Theresia 1947- *WhoMW 93*
Wynn-Williams, George d1993 *Who 94N*
Wynnyckyj, Leo George 1931- *WhoFI 94*
Wynonna 1964- *ConMus 11 [port],
    News 93-3 [port]*
Wynorski, Jim 1950- *HorFD*
Wynstra, Nancy Ann 1941- *WhoAmL 94,
    WhoFI 94*
Wynter, Dana 1927- *WhoHol 92*
Wynter, Dana 1931- *IntMPA 94*
Wynter, Hector Lincoln 1926- *IntWW 93*
Wynter, Leon E. 1953- *WhoBlA 94*
Wynter, Mark 1943- *WhoHol 92*
Wynter, Sylvia 1928- *BlkWr 2, BlmGWL*
Wynters, Charlotte d1991 *WhoHol 92*
Wynyard, Diana d1964 *WhoHol 92*
Wyplosz, Charles 1947- *IntWW 93*
Wyre, Stanley Marcel 1953- *WhoBlA 94*
Wyrick, Charles Lloyd, Jr. 1939-
    WhoAm 94, WhoAmA 93
Wyrick, David Alan 1957- *WhoScEn 94*
Wyrick, Floyd I. 1932- *WhoBlA 94*
Wyrick, Phil 1949- *WhoAmP 93*
Wyrick, Rex R. 1923- *WhoAmP 93*
Wyrsch, James Robert 1942-
    WhoAmL 94, WhoMW 93
Wyrtki, Klaus 1925- *WhoAm 94,
    WhoScEn 94*
Wyrwicka, Wanda 1912- *WhoWest 94*
Wyse, Bonita Wensink 1945-
    WhoWest 94
Wyse, Donald L. *WhoScEn 94*
Wyse, Heather Lea 1966- *WhoWest 94*
Wyse, Joseph Edward 1927- *WhoAm 94*
Wyse, Lois *WhoAm 94*
Wyse, Marc A. *WhoAm 94*
Wyse, William Walker 1919- *WhoAm 94,
    WhoAmL 94, WhoWest 94*
Wyser-Pratte, John Michael 1936-
    WhoAm 94
Wyshak, Lillian Worthing 1928-
    WhoAmL 94
Wyslotsky, Ihor 1930- *WhoAm 94,
    WhoFI 94, WhoMW 93, WhoScEn 94*
Wysocki, Charles Joseph 1947-
    WhoScEn 94
Wysocki, Felix Michael 1947- *WhoAm 94,
    WhoAmL 94*
Wysocki, Jacek A. 1944- *WhoAmL 94*
Wysocki, Matthew Serge 1960-
    WhoWest 94

Wysocki, Theodore Joseph, Jr. 1949-
    WhoMW 93
Wysong, Christopher Alan 1965-
    WhoFI 94
Wysong, Margaret Ann 1955- *WhoFI 94*
Wysor, Bettie *DrAPF 93*
Wysor, Rufus J. 1885-1967
    EncABHB 9 [port]
Wyspianski, Stanislaw (Mateusz Ignacy)
    1869-1907 *IntDcT 2*
Wyss, Amanda *WhoHol 92*
Wyss, David Alen 1944- *WhoAm 94,
    WhoFI 94*
Wyss, Johan Rudolf 1781-1830 *EncSF 93*
Wyss, John Benedict 1947- *WhoAm 94*
Wyss, Orville 1912- *WhoAm 94*
Wyss, Thomas J. 1942- *WhoAmP 93*
Wyss, Thomas John 1942- *WhoMW 93*
Wyss, Walther Erwin 1909-1990
    WhAm 10
Wythe, George 1726-1806 *WhAmRev*
Wyton, Alec 1921- *WhoAm 94*
Wytrwal, Joseph A 1924- *WrDr 94*
Wyum, David LeRoy 1954- *WhoMW 93*
Wyzanski, Charles Max 1944-
    WhoAmL 94
Wyzner, Eugeniusz 1931- *IntWW 93*

X-Y

Yang, Dongpyo 1944- WhoAsA 94
Yang, Edward S. 1937- WhoAm 94
Yang, Emiko 1927- WhoAsA 94
Yang, Eugene L. 1935- WhoScEn 94
Yang, Han-Jiang 1956- WhoAsA 94
Yang, Hee K. 1955- WhoAsA 94
Yang, Henry Tsu Yow 1940- WhoAm 94, WhoMW 93, WhoScEn 94
Yang, Henry Tzu-yow 1940- WhoAsA 94
Yang, Hong-Qing 1961- WhoScEn 94
Yang, Hsin-Ming 1952- WhoScEn 94, WhoWest 94
Yang, Hua 1961- WhoFI 94
Yang, In Che 1934- WhoAsA 94
Yang, Jane Jan-Jan 1939- WhoScEn 94
Yang, Jeffrey Chih-Ho 1968- WhoAsA 94
Yang, Jen Tsi 1922- WhoAsA 94
Yang, Jiann-Shiou 1954- WhoAsA 94
Yang, John Eric 1958- WhoAsA 94
Yang, Joseph Chi-Houng 1955- WhoAsA 94
Yang, Julie Chi-Sun 1928- WhoAsA 94
Yang, Julie Lee 1952- WhoWest 94
Yang, Kai 1956- WhoAsA 94
Yang, Karl L. 1958- WhoAsA 94
Yang, Kichoon 1955- WhoAsA 94
Yang, Lang 1968- WhoAsA 94
Yang, Mildred Sze-ming 1950- WhoScEn 94
Yang, Nien-chu C. 1928- WhoAsA 94
Yang, Ping-Yi 1938- WhoScEn 94
Yang, Qing 1957- WhoAsA 94
Yang, Ralph Tzu-Bow 1942- WhoAsA 94
Yang, Ruey-Jen 1954- WhoScEn 94
Yang, Run Sheng 1942- WhoScEn 94
Yang, Samuel Chia-Lin 1969- WhoScEn 94
Yang, Schuman Chuo 1924- WhoAsA 94
Yang, Sen 1960- WhoScEn 94
Yang, Shang Fa 1932- WhoAm 94, WhoAsA 94, WhoScEn 94
Yang, Shi-tien 1946- WhoAsA 94
Yang, Song 1961- WhoAsA 94
Yang, Song-Yu 1938- WhoAsA 94
Yang, Sun Hye 1966- WhoAsA 94
Yang, Susan Y. 1955- WhoAsA 94
Yang, Sze Cheng 1946- WhoAsA 94
Yang, Tah-teh 1927- WhoAsA 94
Yang, Ti Liang 1929- IntWW 93, Who 94
Yang, Timothy C. 1965- WhoAsA 94
Yang, Tony Tien Sheng 1928- WhoAm 94
Yang, Tsu-Ju 1932- WhoAsA 94
Yang, Tuen-Ping 1945- WhoAsA 94
Yang, Victor Chi-Min 1949- WhoAsA 94, WhoScEn 94
Yang, Weitao 1961- WhoAsA 94
Yang, Wen-Ching 1939- WhoAsA 94
Yang, Wen-Jei 1931- WhoAsA 94, WhoFI 94
Yang, William C. T. 1922- WhoAsA 94
Yang, Winston L. 1933- WhoAsA 94
Yang, Xiaowei 1954- WhoAsA 94, WhoScEn 94
Yang, Yenting 1933- WhoWest 94
Yang, Yih-Ming 1947- WhoAsA 94
Yang, Yisong 1958- WhoAsA 94
Yang, Zeren 1958- WhoScEn 94, WhoWest 94
Yang, Zhanbo 1958- WhoAsA 94
Yang Baibing WhoPRCh 91
Yang Baibing 1920- WhoPRCh 91 [port]
Yang Baibing, Gen. 1920- IntWW 93
Yang Bin 1931- WhoPRCh 91 [port]
Yang Bingsun WhoPRCh 91
Yang Bingxun WhoPRCh 91
Yang Bo 1920- IntWW 93
Yang Bo 1921- WhoPRCh 91 [port]
Yang Bozhen WhoPRCh 91
Yang Changqi WhoPRCh 91
Yang Changye ConWorW 93
Yang Chao 1911- WhoPRCh 91
Yang Chengwu 1914- WhoPRCh 91 [port]
Yang Chengwu, Col.-Gen. 1914- IntWW 93
Yang Cheng-Zhi 1938- IntWW 93
Yang Chen Ning 1922- IntWW 93
Yang Chuanwei WhoPRCh 91
Yang Chugui WhoPRCh 91 [port]
Yang Chun WhoPRCh 91
Yang Dengyan WhoPRCh 91
Yang Dezhi 1910- WhoPRCh 91 [port]
Yang Dezhong 1923- WhoPRCh 91 [port]
Yang Dezhong, Lieut.-Gen. 1923- IntWW 93
Yang Di 1923- WhoPRCh 91 [port]
Yang Di 1924- IntWW 93
Yang Enbo WhoPRCh 91
Yang Fangzhi 1906- WhoPRCh 91
Yang Faxun 1928- WhoPRCh 91 [port]
Yang Feng 1921- WhoPRCh 91
Yang Fuchang WhoPRCh 91
Yang Fuxing 1929- WhoPRCh 91 [port]
Yang Gang 1946- WhoPRCh 91
Yang Gaojian, Michael 1931- WhoPRCh 91
Yang Guangjun WhoPRCh 91
Yang Guangqi WhoPRCh 91
Yang Guangyuan WhoPRCh 91 [port]
Yang Guirong WhoPRCh 91
Yang Guizhen 1923- WhoPRCh 91
Yang Guoliang 1938- WhoPRCh 91 [port]
Yang Haibo 1923- WhoPRCh 91 [port]
Yang Hansheng 1902- WhoPRCh 91 [port]
Yang Huan 1927- WhoPRCh 91 [port]
Yang Huiqiu WhoPRCh 91
Yang Huiyun 1932- WhoPRCh 91 [port]
Yang Jianbai 1909- WhoPRCh 91 [port]
Yang Jiang 1911- BlmGWL
Yang Jianhou 1910- WhoPRCh 91 [port]
Yang Jie c. 1930- WhoPRCh 91 [port]
Yang Jike 1921- IntWW 93, WhoPRCh 91 [port]
Yang Jingren 1918- IntWW 93, WhoPRCh 91 [port]
Yang Jiwan 1917- WhoPRCh 91 [port]
Yang Jun 1922- WhoPRCh 91 [port]
Yang-Kang Lin 1927- IntWW 93
Yang Kecheng 1910- WhoPRCh 91 [port]
Yang Keng 1920- WhoPRCh 91 [port]
Yang Ko, Lillian Yang 1944- WhoScEn 94
Yang Le 1940- WhoPRCh 91 [port]
Yang Li 1928- WhoPRCh 91 [port]
Yang Lian 1955- ConWorW 93
Yang Lieyu 1918- WhoPRCh 91 [port]
Yang Ligong 1919- WhoPRCh 91 [port]
Yang Liming WhoPRCh 91
Yangling Doje 1931- WhoPRCh 91 [port]
Yangling Duoji 1931- IntWW 93
Yang Liping c. 1960- WhoPRCh 91 [port]
Yang Maojia 1932- WhoPRCh 91 [port]
Yang Ming 1919- WhoPRCh 91 [port]
Yang Mingyi 1943- WhoPRCh 91 [port]
Yang Minzhi 1933- WhoPRCh 91 [port]
Yang Mo 1914- ConWorW 93, WhoPRCh 91 [port]
Yang Mu 1944- WhoPRCh 91
Yang Muo 1914- BlmGWL
Yang Peijin 1935- WhoPRCh 91
Yang Qi WhoPRCh 91 [port]
Yang Rudai 1924- IntWW 93
Yang Rudai 1926- WhoPRCh 91 [port]
Yang Ruifer 1950- WhoPRCh 91 [port]
Yang Shan 1924- WhoPRCh 91 [port]
Yang Shangkun 1907- IntWW 93, Who 94, WhoPRCh 91 [port]
Yang Shijie WhoPRCh 91
Yang Shiqin WhoPRCh 91
Yang Shiren WhoPRCh 91
Yang Shouzheng WhoPRCh 91
Yang Side 1921- WhoPRCh 91 [port]
Yang Taifang 1927- IntWW 93, WhoPRCh 91 [port]
Yang Tianquan WhoPRCh 91 [port]
Yang Tianshou 1899- WhoPRCh 91 [port]
Yanguas, Lourdes M. 1965- WhoHisp 94
Yan Guosen WhoPRCh 91
Yang Weiguang WhoPRCh 91
Yang Weiqun WhoPRCh 91
Yang Wenchang WhoPRCh 91
Yang Wengui 1929- WhoPRCh 91 [port]
Yang Wenhe WhoPRCh 91
Yang Wenjin 1927- WhoPRCh 91 [port]
Yang Wenyi 1972- WhoPRCh 91 [port]
Yang Xianhui 1946- WhoPRCh 91 [port]
Yang Xianyi 1914- WhoPRCh 91 [port]
Yang Xilan 1962- WhoPRCh 91 [port]
Yang Xingfu 1936- WhoPRCh 91 [port]
Yang Xiongli WhoPRCh 91
Yang Xiushan 1914- WhoPRCh 91 [port]
Yang Xizong 1928- IntWW 93, WhoPRCh 91 [port]
Yang Xuqiang WhoPRCh 91
Yang Yang 1964- WhoPRCh 91 [port]
Yang Yanping 1934- WhoPRCh 91 [port]
Yang Yanwen 1939- WhoPRCh 91 [port]
Yang Yanyin WhoPRCh 91 [port]
Yang Yi WhoPRCh 91
Yang Yichen 1914- WhoPRCh 91 [port]
Yang Yihuai WhoPRCh 91
Yang Yingqun WhoPRCh 91
Yang Yitang 1930- WhoPRCh 91 [port]
Yang Yongliang 1944- WhoPRCh 91 [port]
Yang Yongyi 1941- WhoPRCh 91 [port]
Yang You 1917- WhoPRCh 91 [port]
Yang You Chan 1897-1975 HisDcKW
Yang Zengye WhoPRCh 91
Yang Zhengmin 1909- WhoPRCh 91 [port]
Yang Zhengquan WhoPRCh 91
Yang Zhengwu 1941- WhoPRCh 91
Yang Zhenhuai 1928- IntWW 93, WhoPRCh 91 [port]
Yang Zhenya WhoPRCh 91
Yang Zhenyan WhoPRCh 91
Yang Zhiguang 1930- IntWW 93
Yang Zhiguang 1931- WhoPRCh 91
Yang Zhilin 1907- WhoPRCh 91
Yang Zhiyuan WhoPRCh 91
Yang Zhongshu 1928- WhoPRCh 91 [port]
Yang Ziyuan 1928- WhoPRCh 91 [port]
Yan Haiping 1955- WhoPRCh 91 [port]
Yan Haiwang 1939- WhoPRCh 91 [port]
Yan Han 1916- WhoPRCh 91 [port]
Yan Hong 1965- WhoPRCh 91 [port]
Yan Hongmo 1932- WhoPRCh 91 [port]
Yanish, Elizabeth WhoAmA 93
Yanish, Michael John 1953- WhoWest 94
Yanitelli, Victor d1993 NewYTBS 93 [port]
Yaniz, Henry Alexander 1917- WhoHisp 94
Yan Jiale WhoPRCh 91
Yan Jiaqi 1942- WhoPRCh 91
Yan Jici 1900- IntWW 93, WhoPRCh 91 [port]
Yan Jinsheng WhoPRCh 91 [port]
Yank, Ronald 1942- WhoAmL 94
Yankelovich, Daniel 1924- WhoAm 94
Yanker, Scott William 1960- WhoFI 94
Yankilevsky, Vladimir Borisovich 1938- IntWW 93
Yankov, Alexander 1924- Who 94
Yankovic, Judith E. 1947- WhoAm 94
Yankovic, Weird Al 1959- WhoCom
Yankovic, "Weird" Al 1961- WhoHol 92
Yankovsky, Oleg Ivanovich 1944- IntWW 93
Yankowitz, Susan DrAPF 93, WrDr 94
Yankowitz, Susan 1941- ConDr 93
Yankwich, Peter Ewald 1923- WhoAm 94
Yan Liangkun 1923- WhoPRCh 91 [port]
Yan Longan WhoPRCh 91
Yan Ming 1969- WhoPRCh 91 [port]
Yan Mingfu 1931- WhoPRCh 91 [port]
Yannariello-Brown, Judith I. 1958- WhoScEn 94
Yannas, Ioannis Vassilios 1935- WhoAm 94, WhoScEn 94
Yanne, Jean 1933- WhoHol 92
Yanner, Joseph d1949 WhoHol 92
Yanni 1954- ConMus 11 [port]
Yanni, Rossanna WhoHol 92
Yan Ning 1953- WhoPRCh 91 [port]
Yannone, Mark Joseph 1949- WhoWest 94
Yannucci, Thomas David 1950- WhoAm 94
Yannuzzi, William Anthony 1934- WhoAm 94
Yano, Fleur B. 1934- WhoAsA 94
Yano, Jun'ya 1932- IntWW 93
Yano, Ronald Makoto 1945- WhoAsA 94
Yano, Tadashi 1939- WhoScEn 94
Yanoff, Arthur (Samuel) 1939- WhoAmA 93
Yanoff, Myron 1936- WhoAm 94
Yanofsky, Charles 1925- IntWW 93, WhoAm 94, WhoScEn 94
Yanoshak, Sharyn 1945- WhoWest 94
Yanosko, Raymond Anthony 1929- WhoMW 93
Yanovski, Susan Zelitch 1952- WhoScEn 94
Yanovs'ky, Borys Karlovych 1875-1933 NewGrDO
Yanow, Rhoda Mae WhoAmA 93
Yanowitch, Michael H. 1949- WhoAm 94
Yan Qingqing 1925- WhoPRCh 91 [port]
Yan Renying WhoPRCh 91 [port]
Yan Renying 1913- IntWW 93
Yan Ruizhen WhoPRCh 91
Yanshin, Mikhail d1976 WhoHol 92
Yant, Martin 1949- WrDr 94
Yantis, Fanny d1929 WhoHol 92
Yantis, Phillip Alexander 1928- WhoAm 94
Yantis, Richard Perry 1932- WhoMW 93
Yantis, Richard William 1923- WhoAm 94
Yan Tongmao 1922- WhoPRCh 91 [port]
Yanuck, Martin 1936-1988 WhAm 10
Yan Wanrong WhoPRCh 91
Yan Wenjing 1915- IntWW 93, WhoPRCh 91 [port]
Yan Wenliang 1893- WhoPRCh 91 [port]
Yan Wuhong 1925- WhoPRCh 91 [port]
Yan Yi 1927- WhoPRCh 91 [port]
Yan Ying 1928- WhoPRCh 91 [port]
Yan Youmin 1918- WhoPRCh 91
Yan Zheng WhoPRCh 91
Yan Zhuo WhoPRCh 91
Yao, David D. 1950- WhoAsA 94
Yao, Dennis Alden 1953- WhoAm 94, WhoAmP 93, WhoAsA 94, WhoFI 94
Yao, Dorcas C. WhoAsA 94
Yao, Hilda Maria Hsiang 1956- WhoFI 94
Yao, James Tsu-Ping 1933- WhoScEn 94
Yao, Lun-Shin 1943- WhoAsA 94
Yao, Shi Chune 1946- WhoAsA 94
Yao, Xiang Yu 1961- WhoScEn 94
Yao Guang 1921- WhoPRCh 91 [port]
Yao Jinzhong 1938- WhoPRCh 91 [port]
Yao Jun 1925- WhoPRCh 91 [port]
Yao Minxue 1938- WhoPRCh 91 [port]
Yao Shun 1919- IntWW 93
Yao Shuren WhoPRCh 91
Yao Wenxu 1926- WhoPRCh 91 [port]
Yao Wenyuan 1924- IntWW 93
Yao Xin 1915- WhoPRCh 91
Yao Xin 1925- IntWW 93
Yao Xueyin 1910- WhoPRCh 91 [port]
Yao Yilin 1917- IntWW 93, WhoPRCh 91 [port]
Yao Yongmao 1936- WhoPRCh 91
Yao Youduo 1937- WhoPRCh 91 [port]
Yao Yun WhoPRCh 91
Yao Zhenyan WhoPRCh 91
Yao Zhonghua 1939- IntWW 93, WhoPRCh 91
Yao Zhongming 1912- WhoPRCh 91
Yap, Kie-Han 1925- WhoFI 94, WhoScEn 94
Yap, Stacey G. H. 1955- WhoAsA 94
Yaple, Henry Mack 1940- WhoAm 94
Yapoujian, Nerses Nick 1950- WhoMW 93
Yapp, Malcolm E(dward) 1931- WrDr 94
Yapp, Stanley Graham Who 94
Yaqut Al-Rumi, Shihab Al-Din Abu Abd-Allah 1179-1229 WhWE
Yar'Adua, Shehu 1943- IntWW 93
Yarar, Baki 1941- WhoScEn 94
Yarber, Robert 1948- WhoAmA 93
Yarboro, Theodore Leon 1932- WhoBlA 94
Yarborough, Earl of 1963- Who 94
Yarborough, Barton d1951 WhoHol 92
Yarborough, Camille DrAPF 93
Yarborough, Christine Troutman 1925- WhoAmA 93
Yarborough, Dowd Julius, Jr. 1938- WhoBlA 94
Yarborough, N. Patricia 1936- WhoAm 94
Yarborough, Ralph Webster 1903- WhoAmP 93
Yarborough, Richard A. 1951- WhoBlA 94
Yarborough, Richard Felix, Jr. 1952- WhoAmL 94
Yarborough, Richard W. 1931- WhoAmP 93
Yarborough, William Caleb 1939- WhoAm 94
Yarborough, William Pelham 1912- WhoAm 94
Yarbro, Alan David 1941- WhoAm 94
Yarbro, Chelsea Quinn 1942- EncSF 93, WrDr 94
Yarbro, James Wesley 1920- WhoAm 94
Yarbrough, Camille WhoHol 92
Yarbrough, Camille 1938- BlkWr 2
Yarbrough, Delano 1936- WhoBlA 94
Yarbrough, Earnest 1923- WhoBlA 94
Yarbrough, Edward Meacham 1943- WhoAmL 94
Yarbrough, Emma Joe 1921- WhoAmP 93
Yarbrough, George Malone 1916- WhoAmP 93
Yarbrough, Herbert A. Trey, III 1952- WhoAmL 94
Yarbrough, Jean 1900- HorFD [port]
Yarbrough, Jim David 1946- WhoFI 94
Yarbrough, John Calvin 1962- WhoMW 93
Yarbrough, K. Patrick 1961- WhoMW 93
Yarbrough, Karen Marguerite 1938- WhoScEn 94
Yarbrough, Kenneth Wayne 1937- WhoAmP 93
Yarbrough, Leila Kepert 1932- WhoAmA 93
Yarbrough, Mamie Luella 1941- WhoBlA 94
Yarbrough, Marilyn Virginia 1945- WhoAm 94, WhoBlA 94
Yarbrough, Robert Elzy 1929- WhoBlA 94
Yarbrough, Roosevelt 1946- WhoBlA 94
Yarburgh-Bateson Who 94
Yarchoan, Robert 1950- WhoScEn 94
Yarchun, Hyman Joshua 1946- WhoFI 94, WhoWest 94
Yard, John 1944- Who 94
Yard, Rix Nelson 1917- WhoAm 94
Yard, Sally Elizabeth 1951- WhoAmA 93, WhoWest 94
Yard, Theresa Irene 1962- WhoAmL 94
Yardan, Shana 1942- BlmGWL
Yardbirds, The ConMus 10 [port]
Yarde, Margaret d1944 WhoHol 92
Yarde, Richard 1939- AfrAmAl 6
Yarde, Richard Foster 1939- WhoBlA 94
Yarde-Buller Who 94
Yardis, Pamela Hintz 1944- WhoAm 94
Yardley, Dan 1928- WhoAmP 93
Yardley, David Charles Miller 1929- Who 94
Yardley, George 1928- BasBi
Yardley, James Fredrick 1921- WhoAmP 93
Yardley, John Finley 1925- WhoAm 94, WhoMW 93, WhoScEn 94
Yardley, Jonathan 1939- WhoAm 94
Yardley, Richard Quincy 1903-1979 WhoAmA 93N
Yarger, James Gregory 1951- WhoMW 93, WhoScEn 94
Yarger, Rodney Rowland 1957- WhoMW 93
Yarger, Sam Jacob 1937- WhoAm 94
Yarger, Sylvia Marian 1921- WhoMW 93
Yarian, Stephan Bishop 1946- WhoWest 94

Yarin, Veniamin Aleksandrovich 1940- *IntWW 93*
Yarington, Charles Thomas, Jr. 1934- *WhoAm 94*
Yaris, Christine E. 1957- *WhoAmL 94*
Yariv, Amnon 1930- *WhoAm 94, WhoScEn 94, WhoWest 94*
Yarkony, Gary Michael 1953- *WhoAm 94, WhoMW 93*
Yarlagadda, Rambabu Venkata 1959- *WhoFI 94*
Yarlow, Loretta 1948- *WhoAm 94*
Yarmal, Ann *DrAPF 93*
Yarmey, Richard Andrew 1948- *WhoAmL 94*
Yarmolinsky, Adam 1922- *IntWW 93, WhoAm 94, WhoAmP 93, WrDr 94*
Yarmon, Betty *WhoAm 94*
Yarmouth, Earl of 1958- *Who 94*
Yarmus, James J. 1941- *WhoHisp 94*
Yarnall, Celeste 1946- *WhoHol 92*
Yarnall, D. Robert, Jr. 1925- *WhoAm 94*
Yarnall, Sophia *ConAu 141*
Yarnell, Bruce d1973 *WhoHol 92*
Yarnell, Carolyn Ann 1944- *WhoAmP 93*
Yarnell, Gwen d1987 *WhoHol 92*
Yarnell, Jeffrey Alan 1941- *WhoMW 93*
Yarnell, Lorene 1950- *WhoHol 92*
Yarnell, Michael Allan 1944- *WhoAm 94*
Yarnell, Richard Asa 1929- *WhoAm 94*
Yarnevic, Phyllis N. 1925- *WhoAmP 93*
Yarnold, Edward John 1926- *Who 94*
Yarnold, Patrick 1937- *Who 94*
Yaros, Constance G. *WhoAmA 93*
Yaros, Gerald David 1946- *WhoAmL 94*
Yarosewick, Stanley J. 1939- *WhoAm 94*
Yaroshinskaya, Alla Aleksandrovna 1953- *LngBDD*
Yaroslavsky, Zev 1948- *WhoAmP 93*
Yarotsky, Lori 1955- *WhoAmA 93*
Yarov, Yuri Fedorovich 1942- *IntWW 93*
Yarov, Yury Fedorovich 1942- *LngBDD*
Yarranton, Peter (George) 1924- *Who 94*
Yarrigle, Charlene Sandra Shuey 1940- *WhoFI 94*
Yarris, Steve 1951- *WhoScEn 94*
Yarrow, Alfred 1924- *Who 94*
Yarrow, Eric Grant 1920- *IntWW 93, Who 94*
Yarrow, Peter 1938- *WhoAm 94, WhoHol 92*
Yarrow, Philip John 1917- *WrDr 94*
Yarshater, Ehsan (Ollah) 1920- *WrDr 94*
Yarter, Clynton Paul 1948- *WhoWest 94*
Yarus, Buddy *WhoHol 92*
Yarusso, Lowell Charles 1946- *WhoMW 93*
Yarwood, Dean Lesley 1935- *WhoAm 94*
Yarwood, Doreen 1918- *WrDr 94*
Yarwood, Michael Edward 1941- *Who 94*
Yaryura-Tobias, Jose *DrAPF 93*
Yaryura-Tobias, Jose A. 1934- *WhoHisp 94*
Yasami, Masoud 1949- *WhoWest 94*
Yasbeck, Amy 1962- *WhoHol 92*
Yaseen, Leonard Clayton 1912-1989 *WhAm 10*
Yasenka, Debra Ann 1950- *WhoMW 93*
Yashima, Taro 1908- *WrDr 94*
Yashin, Lev 1929-1990 *WorESoc [port]*
Yashiro, James Takashi 1931- *IntWW 93*
Yashon, David 1935- *WhoAm 94*
Yasinsky, John Bernard 1939- *WhoAm 94, WhoFI 94*
Yasko, Caryl A(nne) 1941- *WhoAmA 93*
Yasnyi, Allan David 1942- *WhoFI 94, WhoWest 94*
Yass, Irving 1935- *Who 94*
Yassin, Ali Mohamed Osman 1943- *Who 94*
Yassin, Mahmoud *WhoHol 92*
Yassin, Rihab R. 1954- *WhoScEn 94*
Yassin, Robert Alan 1941- *WhoAm 94, WhoAmA 93*
Yassine, Ismali d1972 *WhoHol 92*
Yassky, Harold 1930-1992 *WhAm 10*
Yassky, Lester 1941- *WhoAm 94, WhoAmL 94*
Yassukovich, Stanislas Michael 1935- *IntWW 93, Who 94*
Yast, Charles Joseph 1952- *WhoAmL 94*
Yastrow, Shelby 1935- *WhoAmL 94*
Yastrzemski, Carl Michael 1939- *WhoAm 94*
Yasuda, Hirotsugu Koge 1930- *WhoAm 94*
Yasuda, Mac 1949- *WhoWest 94*
Yasuda, Mineo 1937- *WhoScEn 94*
Yasuda, Robert 1940- *WhoAmA 93*
Yasue, Kunio 1951- *WhoScEn 94*
Yasui, Byron Kiyoshi 1940- *WhoWest 94*
Yasui, Kaoru 1907- *IntWW 93*
Yasumoto, Kyoden 1934- *WhoScEn 94*
Yasumoto, Takeshi 1935- *WhoScEn 94*
Yasumura, Seiichi 1932- *WhoAsA 94*
Yasuoka Shotaro 1920- *ConWorW 93*
Yatabe, Jon Mikio 1937- *WhoScEn 94*
Yatch, Lawrence Joseph 1945- *WhoAmP 93*
Yatchak, Michael Gerard 1951- *WhoWest 94*
Yater, George David 1910- *WhoAmA 93*
Yates, Abby Harris 1952- *WhoWest 94*
Yates, Abraham 1724-1796 *WhAmRev*
Yates, Alan G(eoffrey) 1923-1985 *EncSF 93*
Yates, Albert Carl 1941- *WhoAm 94, WhoWest 94*
Yates, Alden Perry 1928-1989 *WhAm 10*
Yates, Alfred 1917- *Who 94, WrDr 94*
Yates, Alfred Glenn, Jr. 1946- *WhoAmL 94*
Yates, Anne *Who 94*
Yates, (Edith) Anne 1912- *Who 94*
Yates, Anthony J. 1937- *WhoBlA 94*
Yates, Aubrey James 1925- *WrDr 94*
Yates, Barbara 1950- *WhoAmL 94*
Yates, Barrie John 1936- *WhoScEn 94*
Yates, Brock W. 1933- *WhoAm 94*
Yates, Cassie 1951- *WhoHol 92*
Yates, Charles Arthur 1947- *WhoAmP 93*
Yates, Charles Richardson 1913- *WhoAm 94*
Yates, David Floyd 1944- *WhoAm 94, WhoAmL 94*
Yates, David John C. 1927- *WhoAm 94, WhoWest 94*
Yates, Edgar *Who 94*
Yates, (William) Edgar 1938- *Who 94*
Yates, Elizabeth 1905- *TwCYAW, WrDr 94*
Yates, Elizabeth Black 1916- *WhoAmP 93*
Yates, Ella Gaines 1927- *WhoAm 94, WhoBlA 94*
Yates, Elton G. 1935- *WhoAm 94, WhoFI 94*
Yates, Frances 1899-1981 *BlmGWL*
Yates, Frank 1902- *IntWW 93, Who 94, WrDr 94*
Yates, Hollye E. 1965- *WhoAmA 93*
Yates, Ian Humphrey Nelson 1931- *Who 94*
Yates, Ivan R. 1929- *Who 94*
Yates, J. Michael 1938- *WrDr 94*
Yates, James d1993 *NewYTBS 93*
Yates, James Bernard 1929- *WhoAmP 93*
Yates, Janelle K(aye) 1957- *SmATA 77*
Yates, Jeffrey M. 1948- *WhoIns 94*
Yates, Jeffrey McKee 1948- *WhoAm 94, WhoFI 94*
Yates, Jere Eugene 1941- *WhoAm 94*
Yates, Joe Elton 1938- *WhoAmP 93*
Yates, John 1925- *Who 94*
Yates, John 1939- *SmATA 74 [port]*
Yates, John Melvin 1939- *WhoAm 94, WhoAmP 93*
Yates, John P. 1921- *WhoAmP 93*
Yates, John Sellers 1923- *WhAm 10*
Yates, John Thomas, Jr. 1935- *WhoAm 94*
Yates, Joseph Walker, III 1944- *WhoAmL 94*
Yates, Kathleen Barrett 1954- *WhoAm 94*
Yates, Keith 1928- *WhoScEn 94*
Yates, Keith Lamar 1927- *WhoWest 94*
Yates, Leighton Delevan, Jr. 1946- *WhoAmL 94*
Yates, LeRoy Louis 1929- *WhoBlA 94*
Yates, Margaret Marlene 1942- *WhoWest 94*
Yates, Marjorie 1941- *WhoHol 92*
Yates, Marvin Clarence 1943- *WhoAmA 93*
Yates, Mary Mitchell 1950- *WhoAm 94, WhoAmL 94*
Yates, Michael Zane *WhoAmP 93*
Yates, Michael Zane 1959- *WhoMW 93*
Yates, Pauline *WhoHol 92*
Yates, Peter 1747-1826 *WhAmRev*
Yates, Peter 1929- *IntMPA 94, IntWW 93, WhoAm 94*
Yates, Peter (James) 1929- *Who 94*
Yates, Renee Harris 1950- *WhoScEn 94*
Yates, Richard *DrAPF 93*
Yates, Richard 1926-1992 *ConAu 43NR*
Yates, Robert Doyle 1931- *WhoAm 94*
Yates, Robert Duane 1946- *WhoAm 94*
Yates, Robert Lynn 1947- *WhoFI 94*
Yates, Ronald Wilburn 1938- *WhoAm 94*
Yates, Sidney R. 1909- *CngDr 93, CurBio 93 [port], WhoAmP 93*
Yates, Sidney Richard 1909- *WhoAm 94, WhoMW 93*
Yates, Sonja L. *WhoWest 94*
Yates, Steven A. *WhoAmA 93*
Yates, Thomas Eugene 1942- *WhoWest 94*
Yates, William 1921- *Who 94*
Yates, William Hugh 1935- *Who 94*
Yates-Carter, Lynne 1950- *WhoAmL 94*
Yatim, Dato Rais 1942- *IntWW 93*
Yatim, Rais 1942- *Who 94*
Yatir, Nisan d1982 *WhoHol 92*
Yatron, Gus 1927- *WhoAmP 93*
Yatskov, Anatoly d1993 *NewYTBS 93*
Yatsu, Kiyoshi 1939- *WhoScEn 94*
Yau, Cheuk Chung 1950- *WhoAsA 94*
Yau, Edward Tintai 1944- *WhoScEn 94*
Yau, John *DrAPF 93*
Yau, John 1950- *WhoAmA 93*
Yau, King-Wai 1948- *WhoAsA 94*
Yau, Shing-Tung 1949- *WhoAm 94, WhoScEn 94*
Yau, Stephen Shing-Toung 1952- *WhoAsA 94*
Yau, Stephen Sik-sang 1935- *WhoAm 94, WhoScEn 94*
Yau, Te-Lin 1945- *WhoScEn 94*
Yau, Timothy S. 1946- *WhoWest 94*
Yauger, Douglas Paul 1955- *WhoAmP 93*
Yaushev, Karim Karamovich 1948- *LngBDD*
Yavas, Ugur 1947- *WhoAm 94*
Yavis, John Constantine, Jr. 1936- *WhoAmL 94*
Yavitz, Boris 1923- *WhoAm 94*
Yavlinsky, Grigory Alekseevich 1952- *IntWW 93, LngBDD*
Yavorivsky, Volodymyr Oleksandrovych 1942- *LngBDD*
Yavornitzki, Mark Leon 1948- *WhoAmP 93*
Yavuz, Tahir 1950- *WhoScEn 94*
Yavuzturk, Zeki 1935- *IntWW 93*
Yaw, Ellen Beach 1869-1947 *NewGrDO*
Yaw, Robert Horton 1921- *WhoWest 94*
Yawkey, Jean 1909-1992 *AnObit 1992*
Yawkey, Jean R. 1909-1992 *WhAm 10*
Yaworski, Alex F(rancis) 1907- *WhoAmA 93*
Yaxley, John Francis 1936- *Who 94*
Yazaki, Toyu 1954- *WhoAsA 94*
Yazawa, Eikichi 1950- *WhoHol 92*
Yazdani, Jamshed Iqbal 1959- *WhoScEn 94*
Yazdi, Ibrahim 1933- *IntWW 93*
Yazel, Eugene Allen 1924- *WhAm 10*
Yazel, Homer Allen 1944- *WhoMW 93*
Yazhe, Herbert 1938- *WhoWest 94*
Yazov, Dmitri Timofeevich 1923- *IntWW 93*
Yazov, Dmitry Timofeevich 1923- *LngBDD*
Ybanez, John P. 1946- *WhoHisp 94*
Ybanez, Luis 1933- *WhoHisp 94*
Ybarra, Albert, Jr. 1959- *WhoHisp 94*
Ybarra, Gloria *WhoHisp 94*
Ybarra, Michael D. 1950- *WhoMW 93*
Ybarra, Renalee Tellez 1962- *WhoWest 94*
Ybarra, Robert Michael 1950- *WhoHisp 94*
Ybarra, Ventura d1965 *WhoHol 92*
Ybarra-Frausto, Tomás *WhoHisp 94*
Ybarra y Churruca, Emilio de 1936- *IntWW 93*
Ybarrondo, Larry J. *WhoHisp 94*
Ye, Jose 1934- *WhoAsA 94*
Yeager, Andrea Wheaton 1951- *WhoAm 94*
Yeager, Anson Anders 1919- *WhoMW 93*
Yeager, Biff *WhoHol 92*
Yeager, Bob *WhoHol 92*
Yeager, Caroline Hale 1946- *WhoWest 94*
Yeager, Charles Elwood 1923- *WhoAm 94, WhoScEn 94, WhoWest 94*
Yeager, Charles V. 1939- *WhoFI 94*
Yeager, Cheryl Lynn 1958- *WhoAm 94*
Yeager, Chuck 1923- *WhoHol 92*
Yeager, Dennis Randall 1941- *WhoAmL 94*
Yeager, E. Kurt 1953- *WhoAmL 94*
Yeager, Ernest Bill 1924- *WhoAm 94*
Yeager, Frederick John 1941- *WhoWest 94*
Yeager, George Michael 1934- *WhoFI 94*
Yeager, Hal K. 1959- *WhoScEn 94*
Yeager, Jacques Stalder, Sr. 1921- *WhoAm 94, WhoFI 94*
Yeager, Jancie Skinner 1945- *WhoMW 93*
Yeager, Jeffrey Benjamin 1955- *WhoFI 94*
Yeager, John Spencer 1940-1992 *WhAm 10*
Yeager, Joseph Heizer, Jr. 1957- *WhoAmL 94*
yeager, larry lee 1948- *WhoScEn 94*
Yeager, Leland E. 1896- *WhAm 10*
Yeager, Mark L. 1950- *WhoAm 94, WhoAmL 94*
Yeager, Peter C(leary) 1949- *WrDr 94*
Yeager, Phillip Charles 1927- *WhoMW 93*
Yeager, Randolph O. 1912- *WrDr 94*
Yeager, Randy 1950- *WhoWest 94*
Yeager, Ruth *WhoAmL 94*
Yeager, Thomas M. 1936- *WhoAmP 93*
Yeager, Thomas Stephen 1942- *WhoBlA 94*
Yeager, Todd Douglas 1968- *WhoMW 93*
Yeager, Weldon O. 1922- *WhoAmP 93*
Yeagley, J. Walter 1909-1990 *WhAm 10*
Yeagley, Joan *DrAPF 93*
Yeakel, Earl L., III 1945- *WhoAmL 94*
Yeakel, Joseph Hughes 1928- *WhoAm 94*
Yeakel, Steven Craig 1956- *WhoAmP 93*
Yeamans, George Thomas 1929- *WhoMW 93*
Yeargin, Charles W. *WhoAmP 93*
Yeargin, Robert 1948- *WhoAmL 94*
Yeargin, Robert Harper 1926- *WhoAm 94*
Yearley, Douglas Cain 1936- *WhoAm 94, WhoFI 94, WhoWest 94*
Yearns, W(ilfred) Buck 1918- *WrDr 94*
Yearsley, Ann 1752-1806 *BlmGWL*
Yearsley, Ralph d1928 *WhoHol 92*
Yearwood, Arem Irene *WhoBlA 94*
Yearwood, David Monroe, Jr. 1945- *WhoBlA 94*
Yearwood, Donald Robert 1939- *WhoAm 94*
Yearwood, Emerson Graham 1955- *WhoAmL 94*
Yearwood, Trisha 1964- *ConMus 10 [port], WhoAm 94*
Yeary, James E., Sr. 1917- *WhoBlA 94*
Yeary, Lee *WhoHol 92*
Yeary, Ruth Ann 1944- *WhoMW 93*
Yeates, Jasper 1745-1817 *WhAmRev*
Yeates, Kenneth W. 1942- *WhoAmL 94*
Yeates, W(illiam) Keith d1992 *IntWW 93N*
Yeates, Zeno Lanier 1915- *WhoAm 94*
Yeatman, Harry Clay 1916- *WhoAm 94*
Yeatman, Hoyt *WhoAm 94*
Yeatman, James Erwin 1818-1901 *DcAmReB 2*
Yeaton, Charles B. 1926- *WhoAmP 93*
Yeats, Murray d1975 *WhoHol 92*
Yeats, Robert Sheppard 1931- *WhoAm 94, WhoWest 94*
Yeats, W. B. 1865-1939 *BlmGEL [port]*
Yeats, W(illiam) B(utler) 1865-1939 *IntDcT 2 [port]*
Yeatts, Dorothy Elizabeth Freeman 1925- *WhoScEn 94*
Yeazel, Barbara Ellen 1947- *WhoMW 93*
Yeazel, Keith Arthur 1956- *WhoAmL 94*
Ye Bochu *WhoPRCh 91*
Ye Chumei *WhoPRCh 91*
Ye Di *WhoPRCh 91*
Ye Disheng 1937- *WhoPRCh 91 [port]*
Yedlicka, William George 1922- *WhoWest 94*
Ye Duyi 1912- *WhoPRCh 91 [port]*
Ye Duzheng 1916- *WhoPRCh 91 [port]*
Yee, Albert Hoy 1929- *WhoAm 94*
Yee, Alfred Alphonse 1925- *WhoAm 94, WhoAsA 94*
Yee, Allen Y. 1958- *WhoAsA 94*
Yee, Angelina Chun-chu 1949- *WhoAsA 94*
Yee, Barbara W. K. 1952- *WhoAsA 94*
Yee, Ben 1946- *WhoWest 94*
Yee, Betty Ting 1957- *WhoWest 94*
Yee, Bruce James 1950- *WhoWest 94*
Yee, Carlton S. 1941- *WhoAsA 94*
Yee, Chiang 1903-1977 *WhoAmA 93N*
Yee, Darlene 1958- *WhoAsA 94*
Yee, Donald H. 1953- *WhoAsA 94*
Yee, Donald Poy 1941- *WhoAsA 94*
Yee, Edmond 1938- *WhoAsA 94*
Yee, Franklin 1942- *WhoAsA 94*
Yee, George Dennis 1957- *WhoWest 94*
Yee, Herman Terence 1959- *WhoScEn 94*
Yee, James *WhoAsA 94*
Yee, Jimmie N. 1960- *WhoAsA 94*
Yee, Joanne *WhoAsA 94*
Yee, John David 1961- *WhoAsA 94*
Yee, Lawrence K. 1948- *WhoAsA 94*
Yee, Leland *WhoAsA 94*
Yee, Lester Wey-Ming 1964- *WhoScEn 94*
Yee, Melinda C. 1963?- *WhoAsA 94*
Yee, Nancy J. 1952- *WhoAsA 94*
Yee, Paul (R.) 1956- *WrDr 94*
Yee, Peter Ben-On 1960- *WhoScEn 94*
Yee, Peter Lung 1949- *WhoMW 93*
Yee, Raymond Kim 1956- *WhoScEn 94*
Yee, Raymond Koon Siu 1926- *WhoWest 94*
Yee, Robert Donald 1945- *WhoAsA 94*
Yee, Shirley J. 1959- *ConAu 141*
Yee, Shirley Jo-Ann 1959- *WhoAsA 94*
Yee, Stanley C. 1939- *WhoAsA 94*
Yee, Virginia Bow Sue 1938- *WhoAsA 94*
Yee, Walter 1955- *WhoAsA 94*
Yee, Wilfred Wee Bin 1949- *WhoAsA 94*
Yee, Wong Herbert 1953- *WhoAsA 94*
Yeend, Frances 1918- *NewGrDO*
Yeend, Geoffrey (John) 1927- *Who 94*
Yeend, Geoffrey John 1927- *IntWW 93*
Yeend, Nancy Neal 1943- *WhoAmL 94*
Yeend, Warren Ernest 1936- *WhoWest 94*
Ye Fei 1914- *WhoPRCh 91 [port]*
Yefimov, Aleksandr Nikolayevich 1923- *IntWW 93*
Yefremov, Ivan (Antonovich) 1907-1972 *EncSF 93*
Yefremov, Oleg Nikolayevich 1927- *IntWW 93*
Ye Ganyun *WhoPRCh 91*
Yegge, Robert Bernard 1934- *WhoAm 94, WhoWest 94*

Yeggy-Davis, Geraldine Marie 1922- *WhoMW 93*
Yegian, Richard 1962- *WhoFI 94*
Ye Gongqi 1929- *WhoPRCh 91 [port]*
Ye Gongqi 1930- *IntWW 93*
Ye Gongshao 1908- *WhoPRCh 91 [port]*
Yegros, Lina d1978 *WhoHol 92*
Yegul, Fikret Kutlu 1941- *WhoAmA 93*
Yeh, Billy Kuo-Jiun 1937- *WhoAsA 94*
Yeh, Carol 1938- *WhoAmA 93*
Yeh, Chai 1911- *WhoAm 94, WhoAsA 94*
Yeh, Chien Jo 1930- *WhoAsA 94*
Yeh, Edward H. Y. 1930- *WhoAsA 94*
Yeh, Gregory S. Y. 1933- *WhoAsA 94*
Yeh, Gregory Soh-Yu 1933- *WhoMW 93*
Yeh, Hen-Geul 1957- *WhoAsA 94*
Yeh, Henry 1958- *WhoAsA 94*
Yeh, Hsi-Han 1935- *WhoAsA 94*
Yeh, Hsien-Yang 1947- *WhoAsA 94, WhoScEn 94*
Yeh, Ida Shuyen Chiang 1912- *WhoAsA 94*
Yeh, James Tehcheng 1933- *WhoAsA 94, WhoScEn 94*
Yeh, Joy 1955- *WhoFI 94*
Yeh, Kung Chie 1930- *WhoAm 94*
Yeh, Lee-Chuan Caroline 1954- *WhoAsA 94*
Yeh, Michelle M. 1955- *WhoAsA 94*
Yeh, Noel K. 1937- *WhoScEn 94*
Yeh, Patrick Jen-Hwa 1961- *WhoWest 94*
Yeh, Paul Pao 1927- *WhoScEn 94*
Yeh, Pu-Sen 1935- *WhoAsA 94*
Yeh, Raymond Wei-Hwa 1942- *WhoAm 94*
Yeh, Susan S. Wang 1961- *WhoAsA 94*
Yeh, Thomas Y. 1936- *WhoAsA 94*
Yeh, Timothy S. 1950- *WhoAsA 94*
Yeh, Walter Huai-Teh 1911- *WhAm 10*
Yeh, William Wen-Gong 1938- *WhoAm 94*
Yeh Chun-Chan *ConWorW 93*
Yehle, Lawrence C. 1938- *WhoWest 94*
Yehoshua, A(braham) B. 1936- *ConAu 43NR, ConWorW 93, RfGShF*
Yehoshua, Abraham B. 1936- *IntWW 93*
Yein, Frederick Shu-Chung 1942- *WhoWest 94*
Yeiser, Charles William 1925- *WhoAmA 93*
Yeiser, Patti 1954- *WhoAmP 93*
Ye Jiayin 1924- *BlmGWL*
Ye Junjian 1914- *ConWorW 93*
Ye Junjian 1915- *WhoPRCh 91*
Ye Junjian (Chun-Chan Yeh) 1915- *IntWW 93*
Ye Juquan 1896- *WhoPRCh 91 [port]*
Yekaterina, II *NewGrDO*
Yektai, Manoucher 1922- *WhoAmA 93*
Yeldandi, Veerainder Antiah 1929- *WhoScEn 94*
Yeldell, Joseph P. 1932- *WhoBlA 94*
Yelding, Eric Girard 1965- *WhoBlA 94*
Yelenosky, Pat 1941- *WhoWest 94*
Ye Liansong 1935- *IntWW 93, WhoPRCh 91 [port]*
Ye Lin 1912- *WhoPRCh 91*
Yelity, Stephen C. 1949- *WhoBlA 94*
Yelland, Mary Virginia 1916- *WhoMW 93*
Yelle, Richard Wilfred 1951- *WhoAm 94*
Yellen, Jack 1892-1991 *WhAm 10*
Yellen, Linda 1949- *IntMPA 94*
Yellen, Linda Beverly *WhoAm 94*
Yellen, Pamela Gay 1952- *WhoWest 94*
Yellin, Herbert 1935- *WhoScEn 94*
Yellin, Judith *WhoScEn 94*
Yellin, Thomas Gilmer 1953- *WhoAm 94*
Yellin, Victor (Fell) 1924- *NewGrDO*
Yellin, Victor Fell 1924- *WhoAm 94*
Yellow Hand c. 1760- *EncNAR*
Yellowlees, Henry 1919- *Who 94*
Yellowtail, Thomas 1903- *EncNAR*
Yellowtail, Tom d1993 *NewYTBS 93*
Yellowtail, William P., Jr. 1948- *WhoAmP 93*
Yelnick, Claude *EncSF 93*
Yelon, William B. 1944- *WhoMW 93*
Ye Longfei *WhoPRCh 91*
Yelton, Ralph 1926- *WhoAmP 93*
Yelton, Steven John 1957- *WhoMW 93*
Yeltsin, Boris (Nikolayevich) 1931- *ConAu 140*
Yeltsin, Boris Nikolaevich 1931- *LngBDD*
Yeltsin, Boris Nikolayevich 1931- *IntWW 93, Who 94*
Yemelyanov, Stanislav Vasilevich 1929- *IntWW 93*
Yemen, Former King of *IntWW 93*
Yemm, Edmund William 1909- *Who 94*
Yen, Alfred Chueh-Chin 1958- *WhoAsA 94*
Yen, Anthony 1962- *WhoScEn 94*
Yen, Ben Chie 1935- *WhoAsA 94*
Yen, Chen-wan L. 1932- *WhoAsA 94*
Yen, Chi-Chung David 1953- *WhoAsA 94*
Yen, Ching-hwang 1937- *WrDr 94*
Yen, David Chi-Chung 1953- *WhoMW 93*
Yen, Duen Hsi 1949- *WhoFI 94, WhoWest 94*
Yen, Henry Chin-Yuan 1958- *WhoFI 94*
Yen, I-Kuen 1930- *WhoAsA 94, WhoWest 94*
Yen, Joan Jue 1930- *WhoAsA 94*
Yen, John 1958- *WhoAsA 94*
Yen, Kang Kenneth 1952- *WhoAsA 94*
Yen, Matthew Ming-Shih 1950- *WhoAsA 94*
Yen, Nai-Chyuan 1936- *WhoAsA 94*
Yen, Peter T. 1937- *WhoAsA 94*
Yen, Sherman M. Y. 1934- *WhoAsA 94*
Yen, Steven T. 1954- *WhoAsA 94*
Yen, Teh Fu 1927- *WhoAm 94, WhoAsA 94, WhoWest 94*
Yen, Tien-Sze Benedict 1953- *WhoAsA 94, WhoWest 94*
Yen, Wen-Hsiung 1934- *WhoAsA 94*
Yen, William Mao-Shung 1935- *WhoAsA 94*
Yen, Yang 1952- *WhoAsA 94*
Ye Nan 1930- *WhoPRCh 91 [port]*
Yenawine, Philip 1942- *WhoAmA 93*
Yen Chen-Hsing 1912- *IntWW 93*
Yen Chia-Kan 1905- *IntWW 93*
Yendler, Boris Semenovich 1946- *WhoFI 94*
Yendo, Masayoshi 1920- *IntWW 93*
Yener, Muzaffer 1947- *WhoWest 94*
Yeni, Leo 1920- *WhoAm 94*
Yenice, Mehmet Fikri 1960- *WhoScEn 94*
Yenkin, Bernard Kalman 1930- *WhoMW 93*
Yen-Koo, Helen Chiang-ying 1925- *WhoAsA 94*
Yennaco, Carol A. 1942- *WhoAmP 93*
Yennimatas, Georgios 1939- *IntWW 93*
Yenson, Evelyn Phoebe 1944- *WhoAsA 94*
Yentes, Rex 1943- *WhoAm 94*
Yentob, Alan 1947- *IntWW 93, Who 94*
Yeo, Diane Helen 1945- *Who 94*
Yeo, Douglas 1925- *Who 94*
Yeo, Edwin Harley, III 1934- *WhoAm 94*
Yeo, Kok Cheang 1903- *Who 94*
Yeo, Ron 1933- *WhoAm 94*
Yeo, Ronald Frederick 1923- *WhoAm 94*
Yeo, Timothy Stephen Kenneth 1945- *Who 94*
Yeo, Yung Kee 1938- *WhoAsA 94*
Yeo Cheow Tong 1947- *IntWW 93*
Yeoh, Rosemary 1958- *WhoAmL 94*
Yeoman, Alan 1933- *Who 94*
Yeoman, Michael Magson 1931- *Who 94*
Yeoman, Philip Metcalfe 1923- *Who 94*
Yeoman, Thomas 1708?-1781 *DcNaB MP*
Yeomans, Donald Keith 1942- *WhoWest 94*
Yeomans, Donald Ralph 1925- *WhoAm 94*
Yeomans, Richard Douglas 1952- *WhoWest 94*
Yeomans, Richard Millett 1932- *Who 94*
Yeomans, Russell Allen 1944- *WhoAmL 94*
Yeo Ning Hong 1943- *IntWW 93*
Yeosock, John John 1937- *WhoAm 94*
Yeovil, Jack *EncSF 93*
Yep, Laurence (Michael) 1948- *EncSF 93, TwCYAW, WrDr 94*
Yep, Laurence Michael 1948- *WhoAm 94, WhoWest 94*
Yep, Lawrence Michael 1948- *WhoAsA 94*
Yep, Ralph Lee 1957- *WhoAsA 94*
Yep, Wallen Lai 1943- *WhoAm 94*
Ye Peida *WhoPRCh 91*
Ye Peiying *WhoPRCh 91 [port]*
Ye Qianyu 1907- *WhoPRCh 91 [port]*
Ye Qing 1933- *WhoPRCh 91 [port]*
Yera, Evelio Jesus 1962- *WhoAmL 94*
Yerant, Gene S. 1947- *WhoIns 94*
Yerburgh *Who 94*
Yerburgh, John Maurice Armstrong 1923- *Who 94*
Yerby, Frank 1916-1991 *AnObit 1992, WhAm 10*
Yerby, Frank (Garvin) 1916-1991 *WrDr 94N*
Yerby, Frank Garvin 1916-1991 *WhoBlA 94N*
Yerby, Joel Talbert 1957- *WhoScEn 94*
Yerbysmith, Ernest Alfred d1952 *WhoAmA 93N*
Yeremin, Yuri Ivanovich 1944- *IntWW 93*
Ye Renshou 1921- *WhoPRCh 91 [port]*
Yergan, Eric *WhoBlA 94*
Yerger, Amos G. 1914- *WhoBlA 94*
Yerger, Ben 1931- *WhoBlA 94*
Yerger, William Swan 1932- *WhoAmL 94, WhoAmP 93*
Yergin, Daniel Howard 1947- *WhoAm 94*
Yergler, Jon C. 1954- *WhoAmL 94*
Yerian, Patrick William 1956- *WhoFI 94*
Yerion, Michael Ross 1955- *WhoScEn 94*
Yerkes, David Norton 1911- *WhoAm 94*
Yerkes, Richard Wilfred 1951- *WhoMW 93*
Yermak d1584 *WhWE*
Yermakov, Nicholas 1951- *WrDr 94*
Yermakov, Nicholas (Valentin) 1951- *EncSF 93*
Yerman, Fredric W. 1943- *WhoAm 94*
Yerman, Fredric Warren 1943- *WhoAmL 94*
Yerman, Robert Neil 1940- *WhoFI 94*
Yermolaev, Aleksei 1910-1975 *IntDcB*
Yermolenko-Yuzhina, Nataliya (Stepanovna) 1881-c. 1924 *NewGrDO*
Yerovsek, Deborah Lee *WhoFI 94*
Yerrill, Victor Malcolm 1941- *WhoIns 94*
Yershov, Ivan Vasil'yevich 1867-1943 *NewGrDO*
Yerushalmi, Yosef Hayim 1932- *WhoAm 94*
Ye Rutang 1940- *IntWW 93, WhoPRCh 91*
Yerxa, Bo 1948- *WhoAmP 93*
Yerxa, Frances *EncSF 93*
Yerxa, Leroy 1915-1946 *EncSF 93*
Yes, Phyllis A. 1941- *WhoAmA 93*
Yes, Phyllis Ann 1941- *WhoWest 94*
Yesawich, Paul J., III 1949- *WhoAmL 94*
Yesawich, Peter Charles 1950- *WhoAm 94*
Ye Shuhua 1927- *WhoPRCh 91 [port]*
Ye Shuifu *WhoPRCh 91*
Yesilada, Birol Ali 1956- *WhoMW 93*
Yeske, David Brent 1957- *WhoFI 94, WhoWest 94*
Yeske, Ronald A. 1946- *WhoScEn 94*
Yestadt, Jim d1993 *NewYTBS 93*
Yeston, Maury 1945- *WhoAm 94*
Yetka, Lawrence Robert 1924- *WhoAmL 94, WhoMW 93*
Yetka, Lawrence Rorbert *WhoAmP 93*
Yetman, Norman Roger 1938- *WhoMW 93*
Yetter, Frank Leon 1953- *WhoFI 94*
Yetter, Karolyn Kaye 1943- *WhoMW 93*
Yetter, Richard 1929- *WhoAmL 94*
Yetto, John Henry 1928- *WhoWest 94*
Yeung, Chun W. 1949- *WhoAsA 94*
Yeung, Edward Szeshing 1948- *WhoAm 94, WhoScEn 94*
Yeung, Kai-Yin 1941- *Who 94*
Yeung, Ronald Wai-Chun 1945- *WhoAsA 94*
Yeung, Tin-Chuen 1952- *WhoScEn 94*
Yeutter, Clayton K. 1930- *IntWW 93*
Yeutter, Clayton Keith 1930- *WhoAmP 93*
Yevoli, Lewis J. 1939- *WhoAmP 93*
Yevstigneyev, Yevgeny Aleksandrovich d1992 *IntWW 93N*
Yevtushenko, Yevgeniy Aleksandrovich 1933- *IntWW 93*
Yevtushenko, Yevgeny *ConWorW 93*
Yevtushenko, Yevgeny 1933- *WhoHol 92*
Yevtushenko, Yevgeny Aleksandrovich 1933- *Who 94*
Yewaisis, Joseph Stephen 1939- *WhoFI 94*
Yewcic, Thomas F. *WhoAmP 93*
Ye Weilin 1935- *IntWW 93, WhoPRCh 91 [port]*
Ye Wenling 1942- *BlmGWL, WhoPRCh 91 [port]*
Ye Xiaogang 1955- *IntWW 93, WhoPRCh 91 [port]*
Ye Xuanping 1924- *IntWW 93, WhoPRCh 91 [port]*
Ye Yonglie *EncSF 93*
Ye Yuange *WhoPRCh 91*
Ye Yushan *WhoPRCh 91 [port]*
Yezbick, David Gerard, Sr. 1952- *WhoFI 94*
Yezerski, Howard J. 1941- *WhoAmA 93*
Ye Zhengda 1927- *WhoPRCh 91 [port]*
Ye Zhishan 1918- *WhoPRCh 91 [port]*
Yezhov, Valentin Ivanovich 1921- *IntWW 93*
Yezierska, Anzia 1885-1970 *BlmGWL*
Yff, David Robert 1955- *WhoScEn 94*
Yglesias, Helen *DrAPF 93*
Yglesias, Helen 1915- *WrDr 94*
Yglesias, Helen Bassine 1915- *WhoAm 94*
Yglesias, Jose *DrAPF 93, WhoHisp 94*
Yglesias, José 1919- *WhoHisp 94, WrDr 94*
Yglesias, Rafael *DrAPF 93*
Yglesias, Rafael 1954- *WhoHisp 94, WrDr 94*
Yguado, Alex Rocco 1939- *WhoFI 94, WhoWest 94*
Yhap, Laetitia 1941- *IntWW 93*
Yhombi-Opango, Joachim 1939- *IntWW 93*
Yhouse, Paul A. 1949- *WhoFI 94*
Yi, Gang 1958- *WhoAsA 94*
Yi, Xiaoxiong 1953- *WhoAsA 94*
Yiannakou, Marietta *WhoWomW 91*
Yiannopoulos, A(thanassios) N. 1928- *WrDr 94*
Yiannopoulos, Athanassios Nicholas 1928- *WhoAm 94*
Yiannopoulos, Evangelos 1918- *IntWW 93*
Yielding, K. Lemone 1931- *WhoAm 94*
Yien, Jean May 1952- *WhoAsA 94*
Yiesla, Sharon A. 1960- *ConAu 142*
Yi Fei 1946- *WhoPRCh 91 [port]*
Yih, Chia-Shun 1918- *WhoAm 94, WhoAsA 94, WhoMW 93*
Yih, Mae Dunn 1928- *WhoAmP 93, WhoWest 94*
Yih, Roy Yangming 1931- *WhoAsA 94*
Yih, Yuehwern 1962- *WhoAsA 94*
Yilek, John A. 1949- *WhoAmL 94*
Yi Lirong 1898- *WhoPRCh 91 [port]*
Yilmaz, A. Mesut 1947- *IntWW 93*
Yim, Chi-Kin Bennett 1961- *WhoAsA 94*
Yim, Louise 1899-1977 *HisDcKW*
Yim, Randall Anthony 1952- *WhoAmL 94*
Yim, Solomon C. S. 1952- *WhoAsA 94*
Yim, Soo Jung 1966- *WhoAsA 94*
Yi Meihou 1910- *WhoPRCh 91 [port]*
Yin, Gang George 1954- *WhoAsA 94*
Yin, George Kuo-Ming 1949- *WhoAsA 94*
Yin, Gerald Zheyao 1944- *WhoWest 94*
Yin, John 1960- *WhoScEn 94*
Yin, Jun-jie 1944- *WhoMW 93, WhoScEn 94*
Yin, Lo I. 1930- *WhoAsA 94*
Yin, Mark Y. Q. 1930- *WhoAsA 94*
Yin, Pak d1987 *WhoHol 92*
Yin, Raymond Wah 1938- *WhoMW 93, WhoScEn 94*
Yin, Ronald L. 1947- *WhoAsA 94*
Yin, Xiao-huang 1954- *WhoAsA 94*
Yin, Zenong 1960- *WhoAsA 94*
Yin Changmin 1923- *IntWW 93, WhoPRCh 91 [port], WhoWomW 91*
Yin Fatang 1922- *WhoPRCh 91 [port]*
Ying, John L. 1948- *WhoFI 94, WhoMW 93*
Ying, Lloyd 1926- *WhoMW 93*
Yingling, Adrienne Elizabeth 1959- *WhoFI 94*
Yingling, Robert Granville, Jr. 1940- *WhoWest 94*
Yingling, William E., III 1944- *WhoWest 94*
Yingqian, Qian *WhoScEn 94*
Ying Ruocheng 1929- *IntWW 93, WhoPRCh 91 [port]*
Ying Tung Fok, Henry *WhoPRCh 91*
Ying Yeping 1910- *WhoPRCh 91 [port]*
Ying Yiquan 1922- *WhoPRCh 91 [port]*
Yin Jieyan *WhoPRCh 91*
Yin Jun 1932- *IntWW 93, WhoPRCh 91 [port]*
Yin Junhua *WhoPRCh 91*
Yin Kesheng 1932- *IntWW 93, WhoPRCh 91 [port]*
Yin Shoushi 1919- *WhoPRCh 91 [port]*
Yip, Cecil Cheung-Ching 1937- *WhoAm 94, WhoScEn 94*
Yip, David *WhoHol 92*
Yip, William d1968 *WhoHol 92*
Yi Pom-sok 1900-1972 *HisDcKW*
Yi Sung-Yop 1905-1953 *HisDcKW*
Yiu, Eric *WhoAsA 94*
Yiu, Pao On *WhoAsA 94*
Yizar, James Horace, Jr. 1957- *WhoBlA 94*
Yliniemi, Hazel Alice 1941- *WhoMW 93*
Ylisela, James Paul, Jr. 1956- *WhoMW 93*
Ylitalo, Caroline Melkonian 1964- *WhoScEn 94*
Ylvisaker, James William 1938- *WhoFI 94*
Ylvisaker, Paul Norman 1921-1992 *WhAm 10*
Ynclan, Nery 1959- *WhoHisp 94*
Ynda, Mary Lou 1936- *WhoWest 94*
Yniguez, Richard *WhoHol 92*
Ynostroza, Carlos G. *WhoHisp 94*
Yoakam, Dwight 1956- *WhoAm 94*
Yoakam, Marvin C. 1948- *WhoMW 93*
Yob, Charles Walter 1937- *WhoAmP 93*
Yob, Iris Mae 1944- *WhoMW 93*
Yocam, Delbert Wayne 1943- *WhoAm 94, WhoWest 94*
Yochelson, Bonnie Ellen 1952- *WhoAm 94*
Yochelson, Ellis Leon 1928- *WhoAm 94, WhoScEn 94*
Yochelson, John 1944- *WhoAm 94*
Yochem, Barbara June 1945- *WhoFI 94, WhoWest 94*
Yoches, Edward Robert 1953- *WhoAmL 94*
Yochim, Louise Dunn 1909- *WhoAmA 93*
Yochim, Marie Hirst *WhoAm 94*
Yochmowitz, Michael George 1948- *WhoFI 94*
Yochum, Philip Theodore 1924- *WhoAm 94*
Yochum, Sharon Kay 1950- *WhoMW 93*
Yock, Robert J. 1938- *CngDr 93*
Yock, Robert John 1938- *WhoAm 94, WhoAmL 94*
Yockel, Dorothy d1978 *WhoHol 92*
Yockim, James C. 1953- *WhoMW 93*
Yockim, James Craig 1953- *WhoAmP 93*
Yocklunn, John (Soong Chung) 1933- *Who 94*

Young, Andrew 1932- AfrAmAl 6 [port], IntWW 93, Who 94, WhoAm 94, WhoAmP 93, WhoBlA 94
Young, Andrew 1962- WhoAmA 93
Young, Andrew Brodbeck 1907- WhoAm 94
Young, Andrew Buchanan 1937- Who 94
Young, Andrew J. 1933- WhoBlA 94
Young, Aner Ruth 1933- WhoBlA 94
Young, Annette 1952- WhoAmP 93
Young, Anthony L. 1948- WhoAmP 93
Young, Anthony Wayne 1966- WhoBlA 94
Young, Archie R., II 1928- WhoBlA 94
Young, Ardell Moody 1911- WhoAm 94, WhoAmL 94
Young, Arlene H. WhoBlA 94
Young, Arthur d1959 WhoHol 92
Young, Arthur Howland 1882-1964 EncABHB 9 [port]
Young, Arthur Price 1940- WhoAm 94
Young, Arthur William 1945- WhoWest 94
Young, Audrey WhoHol 92
Young, Austin Prentiss, III 1940- WhoFI 94
Young, Axel 1950- WrDr 94
Young, B. Ashley WhoBlA 94
Young, Barbara 1920- WhoAm 94, WhoAmA 93
Young, Barbara 1952- ConAu 141
Young, Barbara J. 1937- WhoBlA 94
Young, Barbara Neil 1943- WhoAmA 93
Young, Barbara Scott 1948- Who 94
Young, Barney Thornton 1934- WhoAm 94, WhoAmL 94, WhoFI 94
Young, Bertram Alfred 1912- Who 94
Young, Bing-Lin 1937- WhoAsA 94
Young, Bless Stritar 1947- WhoAm 94, WhoAmL 94
Young, Bracebridge Hemyng 1956- WhoAm 94
Young, Brad 1953- WhoAmP 93
Young, Brian (Walter Mark) 1922- IntWW 93, Who 94
Young, Brigham 1801-1877 AmSocL, DcAmReB 2, HisWorL [port], WhWE [port]
Young, Bruce A. WhoHol 92
Young, Bruce Peter WhoHol 92
Young, Bryant Llewellyn 1948- WhoAm 94
Young, Buck WhoHol 92
Young, "Bull" d1913 WhoHol 92
Young, Burt 1940- IntMPA 94, WhoAm 94, WhoHol 92
Young, C. B. Fehrler 1908- WhoFI 94
Young, C. Clifton 1922- WhoAm 94, WhoAmL 94, WhoAmP 93, WhoWest 94
Young, C. W. 1930- WhoAm 94
Young, C. W. Bill 1930- CngDr 93, WhoAmP 93
Young, Caprice Yvonne 1965- WhoWest 94
Young, Carlene Herb WhoBlA 94
Young, Carleton WhoHol 92
Young, Carleton d1971 WhoHol 92
Young, Carol K. 1953- WhoAmL 94
Young, Carrie ConAu 41NR
Young, Carroll IntMPA 94
Young, Carter Travis 1924- WrDr 94
Young, Cathy 1963- WrDr 94
Young, Cecilia 1712-1789 NewGrDO
See Also Young family NewGrDO
Young, Cedric Jan-Yee 1942- WhoWest 94
Young, Charles, Jr. 1934- WhoBlA 94
Young, Charles Alexander 1930- WhoAmA 93, WhoBlA 94
Young, Charles Edward 1931- WhoAm 94, WhoWest 94
Young, Charles L. 1931- WhoAmP 93
Young, Charles Lemuel, Sr. 1931- WhoBlA 94
Young, Charlie, Jr. 1928- WhoBlA 94
Young, Charlotte d1977 WhoHol 92
Young, Cheryl Lynn 1960- WhoAmL 94
Young, Chesley Virginia (Barnes) 1919- WrDr 94
Young, Chic 1901-1973 WhoAmA 93N
Young, Chris 1971- IntMPA 94, WhoHol 92
Young, Christine Dorothea 1952- WhoMW 93
Young, Christine H. 1948- WhoAm 94
Young, Christopher Godfrey 1932- Who 94
Young, Christopher Michael 1961- WhoWest 94
Young, Clara Kimball d1960 WhoHol 92
Young, Clarence, III 1942- WhoBlA 94
Young, Cliff 1905-1985 WhoAmA 93N
Young, Clifton d1951 WhoHol 92
Young, Clint WhoHol 92
Young, Clive 1948- Who 94
Young, Coleman A. 1918- AfrAmAl 6 [port], WhoAmP 93, WhoBlA 94
Young, Coleman Alexander 1918- WhoAm 94, WhoMW 93
Young, Coleman Milton, III 1930- WhoBlA 94
Young, Colin 1927- Who 94
Young, Connie Sue WhoWest 94
Young, Cornelius Bryant, Jr. 1926- WhoScEn 94
Young, Craig Alan 1954- WhoMW 93
Young, Craig Steven 1965- WhoScEn 94
Young, D. Michael 1944- WhoAmL 94
Young, Dale L. 1928- WhoAmP 93
Young, Dale Lee 1928- WhoAm 94
Young, Dan WhoAm 94
Young, Dan 1951- WhoAmP 93
Young, Dan Robert 1947- WhoAmL 94
Young, Daniel David 1944- WhoMW 93
Young, Daniel Lee 1962- WhoScEn 94
Young, Danny 1962- WhoBlA 94
Young, David DrAPF 93, WhoHol 92
Young, David (Pollock) 1936- WrDr 94
Young, David (Tod) 1926- Who 94
Young, David A. 1963- WhoAmP 93
Young, David Carter 1959- WhoWest 94
Young, David Edward Michael 1940- Who 94
Young, David Elwyn 1915-1987 WhAm 10
Young, David Haywood 1943- WhoAmL 94
Young, David Lincoln 1929-1991 WhAm 10
Young, David Michael 1935- WhoAm 94
Young, David Nigel de Lorentz Who 94
Young, David Pollock 1936- WhoAm 94
Young, David Tyrrell 1938- Who 94
Young, David William 1942- WhoAm 94, WhoFI 94
Young, David Wright Who 94
Young, De De WhoHol 92
Young, Dean (Wayne) 1938- WrDr 94
Young, Dean A. WhoAmP 93
Young, Deborah Schwind 1955- WhoAmL 94
Young, Dennis Eugene 1943- WhoAm 94
Young, Dennis Lee 1944- WhoWest 94
Young, Dennis R. 1945- WhoAmP 93
Young, Desmond d1966 WhoHol 92
Young, Dey 1955- WhoHol 92
Young, Doc 1924- WhoBlA 94
Young, Don 1933- CngDr 93
Young, Don J. 1910- WhoAm 94, WhoAmL 94, WhoMW 93
Young, Dona Davis Gagliano 1954- WhoAmL 94
Young, Donald 1933- WrDr 94
Young, Donald Alan 1939- WhoAm 94
Young, Donald Allen 1931- WhoWest 94
Young, Donald Anthony 1933- Who 94
Young, Donald E. 1933- WhoAm 94, WhoAmP 93, WhoWest 94
Young, Donald Fredrick 1928- WhoAm 94
Young, Donald Roy 1935- WhoScEn 94
Young, Donald Soutar 1936- WhoAm 94
Young, Donald Stirling 1933- WhoScEn 94
Young, Douglas Howard 1948- WhoAmL 94
Young, Douglas Rea 1948- WhoAmL 94
Young, Douglas Ryan 1945- WhoFI 94
Young, Doyle Clyde 1947- WhoMW 93
Young, Dw 1929- WhoIns 94
Young, Dwight Wayne 1925- WhoAm 94
Young, Ed (Tse-chun) 1931- SmATA 74, WrDr 94
Young, Edith Mae 1932- WhoBlA 94
Young, Edna E. 1936- WhoAmA 93
Young, Edna Elizabeth 1936- WhoWest 94
Young, Edward 1683-1765 BlmGEL
Young, Edward Graver 1945- WhoAm 94
Young, Edward Hiram, Jr. 1950- WhoBlA 94
Young, Edward Medhard, Jr. 1954- WhoWest 94
Young, Edward Preston 1913- Who 94
Young, Edwin Allen 1930- WhoWest 94
Young, Edwin Harold 1918- WhoAm 94, WhoMW 93, WhoScEn 94
Young, Edwin S. W. 1943- WhoWest 94
Young, Egerton Ryerson 1840-1909 EncNAR
Young, Elizabeth WrDr 94
Young, Elizabeth fl. 1558- BlmGWL
Young, Elizabeth 1773- NewGrDO
See Also Young family NewGrDO
Young, Elizabeth Bell 1929- WhoBlA 94
Young, Elmer, Jr. 1924- WhoBlA 94
Young, Elroy 1923- WhoBlA 94
Young, Eric WhoHol 92
Young, Eric 1924- Who 94
Young, Eric Tynan WhoHol 92
Young, Eric William 1915- WrDr 94
Young, Esther 1717-1795 NewGrDO
See Also Young family NewGrDO
Young, Everett J. 1913- WhoFI 94
Young, Ewing c. 1792-1841 WhWE
Young, F. Camille 1928- WhoBlA 94
Young, Faron 1932- WhoHol 92
Young, Felix K. C. 1960- WhoWest 94
Young, Florence Nelson 1921- WhoWest 94
Young, Francis A(lfred) 1907- WrDr 94
Young, Francis Allan 1918- WhoAm 94
Young, Francis Arthur 1948- WhoAmP 93
Young, Frank Edward 1931- WhoAm 94
Young, Frank Hood 1939- WhoMW 93
Young, Frank Nelson, Jr. 1915- WhoAm 94
Young, Franklin 1928- WhoAsA 94
Young, Fred Richard 1937- WhoFI 94
Young, Freddie 1902- IntDcF 2-4 [port], IntMPA 94, IntWW 93
Young, Frederic Hisgin 1936- WhoFI 94, WhoMW 93, WhoScEn 94
Young, Frederick Nevin 1932- WhoAmP 93
Young, Frieda Margaret 1913- Who 94
Young, Gary DrAPF 93
Young, Gavin David 1928- Who 94
Young, Gavin Neil B. Who 94
Young, Genevieve Leman 1930- WhoAm 94
Young, Geoffrey P. 1950- WhoAmL 94
Young, George, Jr. 1933- WhoBlA 94
Young, George (Samuel Knatchbull) 1941- Who 94
Young, George Bell 1924- Who 94
Young, George Berkeley 1913-1988 WhAm 10
Young, George Bernard, Jr. 1930- WhoAm 94
Young, George Cressler 1916- WhoAm 94, WhoAmL 94
Young, George Hansen 1962- WhoScEn 94
Young, Georgiana 1922- WhoHol 92
Young, Gerald Anthony 1964- WhoBlA 94
Young, Gerard Francis 1910- Who 94
Young, Gig d1978 WhoHol 92
Young, Gladys d1976 WhoHol 92
Young, Gordon 1919- Who 94
Young, Gordon Douglas 1949- WhoFI 94, WhoWest 94
Young, Gordon Ellsworth 1919- WhoAm 94
Young, Grant
See Soul Asylum ConMus 10
Young, Gregory P. WhoAmP 93
Young, Gwynne A. 1950- WhoAmL 94
Young, H. Dewey, Jr. 1934- WhoFI 94
Young, Hannah Sexton 1956- WhoIns 94
Young, Harold d1959 WhoHol 92
Young, Harold (William) 1923- Who 94
Young, Harold A. 1940- WhoAmL 94
Young, Harrison Hurst, III 1944- WhoAm 94
Young, Heather WhoHol 92
Young, Heidi Rebecca WhoAmL 94
Young, Helen Jamieson 1955- WhoScEn 94
Young, Henry Ben 1913- WhoAm 94
Young, Herman A. 1929- WhoBlA 94
Young, Herrick Black 1904-1990 WhAm 10
Young, Hillyer McD. 1941- WhoAmL 94
Young, Hoa Pham 1941- WhoAsA 94
Young, Howard d1993 NewYTBS 93
Young, Howard 1932- WhoIns 94
Young, Howard Seth 1924- WhoAm 94
Young, Howard Thomas 1926- WhoAm 94
Young, Hubert Howell, Jr. 1945- WhoAmL 94, WhoAmP 93
Young, Hugh David 1930- WhoAm 94
Young, Hugo 1938- WrDr 94
Young, Hugo John Smelter 1938- IntWW 93, Who 94
Young, Ian DrAPF 93
Young, Ian 1945- WrDr 94
Young, Ian Musgrave 1941- WhoFI 94
Young, Ian Robert 1932- Who 94
Young, Ira Mason 1929- WhoBlA 94
Young, Irwin IntMPA 94
Young, Isabella d1795 NewGrDO
See Also Young family NewGrDO
Young, Isabella 1791- NewGrDO
See Also Young family NewGrDO
Young, J. Anthony WhoAm 94
Young, J. Arthur d1943 WhoHol 92
Young, J. Lowell 1925- WhoAm 94, WhoWest 94
Young, J. Talbot, Jr. 1948- WhoAmL 94
Young, J(ohn) Z(achary) 1907- WrDr 94
Young, Jack d1966 WhoHol 92
Young, Jack Allison 1931- WhoFI 94, WhoMW 93
Young, Jacqueline Eurn Hai 1934- WhoAmP 93, WhoAsA 94
Young, James d1985 WhoHol 92
Young, James 1878- WhoHol 92
Young, James Allen 1932- WhAm 10
Young, James Arthur, III 1945- WhoBlA 94
Young, James B. 1943- WhoAmL 94
Young, James E. 1926- WhoBlA 94
Young, James E. 1941- WhoMW 93
Young, James E., Jr. 1931- WhoBlA 94
Young, James Earl 1922- WhoAm 94
Young, James Edward 1946- WhoAm 94, WhoAmL 94
Young, James Edward D. Who 94
Young, James Fred 1934- WhoAm 94
Young, James H., II 1947- WhoAmL 94
Young, James Harry 1936- WhoAm 94
Young, James Harvey 1915- WhoAm 94
Young, James Herbert 1941- WhoScEn 94
Young, James Julius 1926- WhoAm 94
Young, James M., II 1946- WhoBlA 94
Young, James Morningstar 1929- WhoAm 94
Young, James S(terling) 1927- WrDr 94
Young, Jan 1919- WrDr 94
Young, Janet d1940 WhoHol 92
Young, Janet Randall 1919- WrDr 94
Young, Janie Chester 1949- WhoAmA 93
Young, Jay Alan 1943- WhoWest 94
Young, Jean Childs 1933- WhoBlA 94
Young, Jeffery Avery 1962- WhoFI 94
Young, Jeffrey William 1947- WhoWest 94
Young, Jere Arnold 1936- WhoAm 94
Young, Jeremy 1934- WhoHol 92
Young, Jerry Wayne 1938- WhoAm 94
Young, Jerry Wesley 1934- WhoScEn 94
Young, Jess R. 1928- WhoAm 94
Young, Jess Wollett 1926- WhoAmL 94
Young, Jim DrAPF 93
Young, Jimmy Who 94
Young, Joan d1984 WhoHol 92
Young, Joan Crawford 1931- WhoFI 94, WhoWest 94
Young, Joanne Wheeler 1949- WhoAm 94
Young, Jock 1942- WrDr 94
Young, John 1585-1654 DcNaB MP
Young, John 1916- WhoAmP 93
Young, John 1934- WrDr 94
Young, John 1956- WhoAsA 94
Young, John (Kenyon Roe) 1947- Who 94
Young, John (McIntosh) 1919- IntWW 93, Who 94
Young, John Adrian Emile 1934- Who 94
Young, John Alan 1932- WhoAm 94, WhoFI 94, WhoScEn 94, WhoWest 94
Young, John Allen 1921- Who 94
Young, John Andrew 1916- WhoAmL 94
Young, John Atherton IntWW 93
Young, John B. 1929- WhoAmP 93
Young, John Edward 1933- WhoMW 93, WhoScEn 94
Young, John Edward 1935- WhoAm 94
Young, John Hardin 1948- WhoAm 94, WhoAmL 94
Young, John Hendricks 1912- WhoAm 94, WhoAmL 94
Young, John Henry 1955- WhoFI 94
Young, John Jacob, Jr. 1962- WhoScEn 94
Young, John K(arl) 1951- WrDr 94
Young, John Kline 1911- WhoAmL 94
Young, John Mark 1950- WhoAmL 94
Young, John Michael 1944- WhoAm 94
Young, John Morgan 1941- WhoAm 94
Young, John Richard Dendy 1907- Who 94
Young, John Robert Chester 1937- Who 94
Young, John Robertson 1945- Who 94
Young, John T. 1954- WhoAmA 93
Young, John Thomas 1954- WhoWest 94
Young, John W. 1927- WhoBlA 94
Young, John Wallace 1923- WhoAmP 93
Young, John Watts 1930- WhoAm 94, WhoScEn 94
Young, John Wesley 1951- WhoMW 93
Young, John Zachary 1907- IntWW 93, Who 94
Young, Johnny 1940- WhoAmP 93
Young, Johnny Wayne 1949- WhoFI 94
Young, Jon Nathan 1938- WhoWest 94
Young, Jones 1957- WhoBlA 94
Young, Josef A. 1941- WhoBlA 94
Young, Joseph E. 1939- WhoAmA 93
Young, Joseph Earnest 1939- WhoWest 94
Young, Joseph Floyd, Sr. 1927-1993 WhoBlA 94N
Young, Joseph Floyd, Jr. 1950- WhoAmP 93
Young, Joseph H. 1922- WhoAm 94, WhoAmL 94
Young, Joseph Laurie 1924- WhoAm 94
Young, Joseph Louis 1919- WhoAm 94, WhoAmA 93
Young, Joseph Rutledge, Jr. 1943- WhoAmL 94
Young, Joseph Samuel 1898- WhAm 10
Young, Joyce Henry 1930- WhoWest 94
Young, Joyce Howell 1934- WhoBlA 94
Young, Joyce Jean 1936- Who 94
Young, Junor Who 94
Young, (David) Junor 1934- IntWW 93, Who 94
Young, Karen 1958- IntMPA 94
Young, Karen 1959- WhoHol 92
Young, Karl DrAPF 93
Young, Katherine Curtin 1939- WhoFI 94
Young, Kathleen 1961- WhoScEn 94

Yurko, Joseph Andrew 1955-
　WhoScEn 94
Yurko, Richard John 1953- *WhoAmL 94*
Yurkon, John Edward 1949- *WhoMW 93*
Yurman, Rich *DrAPF 93*
Yuro, Robert *WhoHol 92*
Yurow, John Jesse 1931- *WhoAm 94,*
　WhoAmL 94
Yursky, Sergei Yurievich 1935-
　IntWW 93
Yu Ru *BlmGWL*
Yu Ruihuang 1906- *WhoPRCh 91 [port]*
Yu Runyang *WhoPRCh 91*
Yurur, Sukru 1944- *IntWW 93*
Yushchenko, Viktor Andriiovych 1954-
　LngBDD
Yu Shengwu *WhoPRCh 91*
Yu Shizhi 1927- *WhoPRCh 91 [port]*
Yu Shutong *WhoPRCh 91*
Yusko, Theodore 1918- *WhoAmP 93*
Yuspa, Stuart H. 1941- *WhoScEn 94*
Yuspeh, Alan Ralph 1949- *WhoAm 94,*
　WhoAmL 94
Yuspeh, Sonia Elizabeth 1928-1990
　WhAm 10
Yussof, Mohammed 1917- *IntWW 93*
Yussouff, Mohammed 1942- *WhoScEn 94*
Yust, David E. 1939- *WhoAmA 93*
Yusuf, Abul Faiz Mohammad 1926-
　Who 94
Yusuf, Siaka Ojo 1960- *WhoScEn 94*
Yusufu Aisha *WhoPRCh 91*
Yusufu Muhanmode 1933-
　WhoPRCh 91 [port]
Yutang, Lin *EncSF 93*
Yuvarajan, Subbaraya 1941- *WhoAsA 94*
Yu Weichao *WhoPRCh 91*
Yu Wen *IntWW 93*
Yu Wen 1918- *WhoPRCh 91 [port]*
Yuwiler, Arthur 1927- *WhoWest 94*
Yu Xiaoping 1955- *WhoPRCh 91 [port]*
Yu Xiling *WhoPRCh 91*
Yu Xingde *WhoPRCh 91*
Yu Xingzhi *WhoPRCh 91*
Yu Xining 1913- *WhoPRCh 91 [port]*
Yu Yongbo 1931- *WhoPRCh 91 [port]*
Yu Yongbo, Lieut.-Gen. 1931- *IntWW 93*
Yu Youxian 1937- *WhoPRCh 91 [port]*
Yuzeitis, James Richard 1942- *WhoFl 94*
Yu Zemin 1932- *WhoPRCh 91 [port]*
Yu Zhan 1921- *IntWW 93,*
　WhoPRCh 91 [port]
Yu Zhen 1936- *IntWW 93,*
　WhoPRCh 91 [port]
Yu Zhenfei 1901- *WhoPRCh 91 [port]*
Yu Zhenwu 1931- *WhoPRCh 91 [port]*
Yu Zhenxin *WhoPRCh 91*
Yu Zhixue 1935- *WhoPRCh 91*
Yu Zhizhen 1915- *IntWW 93,*
　WhoPRCh 91 [port]
Yu Zhongjia *WhoPRCh 91 [port]*
Yu Zhuoyun 1918- *WrDr 94*
Yuzkov, Leonid Petrovych 1938- *LngBDD*
Yu Zonghuan *WhoPRCh 91*
Yu Zuyao *WhoPRCh 91*
Yvonne *DrAPF 93*
Yzaguirre, Raul 1939- *WhoHisp 94*
Yzaguirre, Ruben Antonio 1947-
　WhoHisp 94
Yzerman, Steve 1965- *WhoAm 94,*
　WhoMW 93

Z

Z' 1941- *WhoAmA 93*

Zaander, Mark C. 1951- *WhoAm 94, WhoAmL 94*

Zabala, J. Luis, Sr. *WhoHisp 94*

Zabala Más, Armando 1953- *WhoHisp 94*

Zabaleta, Nicanor d1993 *IntWW 93N*

Zaban, Erwin 1921- *WhoAm 94, WhoFI 94*

Zabanal, Eduardo Olegario 1952- *WhoAmI. 94*

Zabarsky, Melvin Joel 1932- *WhoAmA 93*

Zabel, Edward 1927- *WhoAm 94, WhoFI 94*

Zabel, Sheldon Alter 1941- *WhoAm 94, WhoAmL 94*

Zabel, Walter L. *WhoAmP 93*

Zabel, William David 1936- *WhoAm 94, WhoAmL 94*

Zabela (-Vrubel), Nadeshda 1868-1913 *NewGrDO*

Zabell, Sandy Lew 1947- *WhoMW 93*

Zabelle, Flora d1968 *WhoHol 92*

Zabin, Burton Allen 1936- *WhoScEn 94*

Zabinsky, Zelda Barbara 1955- *WhoScEn 94, WhoWest 94*

Zabka, William *WhoHol 92*

Zable, Jeffrey A. Z. *DrAPF 93*

Zable, Norman Arnold 1934- *WhoAmA 94*

Zabolotsky, Nikolai 1903-1958 *TwCLC 52 [port]*

Zaboroski, Robert B. 1936- *WhoAmL 94*

Zaborowski, Dennis J. 1943- *WhoAmA 93*

Zaborowski, Roy Allan 1946- *WhoWest 94*

Zaborsky, Daniel John 1945- *WhoIns 94*

Zabotkina, Olga *WhoHol 92*

Zabou *WhoHol 92*

Zabrana, Jan *ConWorW 93*

Zabriski, Steven Warren 1953- *WhoMW 93*

Zabriskie, Grace *WhoHol 92*

Zabriskie, Virginia M. *WhoAm 94, WhoAmA 93*

Zabrocki, Carl J. *WhoAmP 93*

Zabronsky, Daniel 1962- *WhoFI 94*

Zabrosky, Alex Walter 1953- *WhoAm 94*

Zabsky, John Mitchell 1933- *WhoWest 94*

Zacarias, Fernando 1944- *WhoHisp 94*

Zacarias, Ruben 1929- *WhoHisp 94*

Zaccagnino, Joseph Anthony 1946- *WhoAm 94*

Zaccardi, Larry Bryan 1966- *WhoScEn 94*

Zaccaria, Nicola (Angelo) 1923- *NewGrDO*

Zacchini, Eddie d1989 *WhoHol 92*

Zacchini, Hugo *WhoHol 92*

Zaccone, Suzanne Maria 1957- *WhoFI 94, WhoMW 93*

Zacconi, Ermete d1948 *WhoHol 92*

Zacek, Joseph Frederick 1930- *WhoAm 94, WrDr 94*

Zach, Debra Jean 1958- *WhoMW 93*

Zach, Nathan 1930- *ConWorW 93*

Zacha, Jac *WhoHol 92*

Zacha, William 1920- *WhoAmA 93*

Zacharatos, Jerry Frank 1928- *WhoWest 94*

Zachariah, Bobby Verghese 1942- *WhoFI 94*

Zachariah, Joyce Margaret 1932- *Who 94*

Zacharias, Athos 1927- *WhoAmA 93*

Zacharias, Donald Wayne 1935- *WhoAm 94*

Zacharias, James Scott 1965- *WhoFI 94*

Zacharias, Lee *DrAPF 93*

Zacharias, Steffen *WhoHol 92*

Zacharias, Thomas Elling 1954- *WhoFI 94*

Zacharias, William F. 1905- *WhoAmL 94*

Zacharius, Martin Philip 1928- *WhoScEn 94*

Zacharius, Walter 1923- *IntWW 93, WhoAm 94*

Zacharov, Vasilii 1931- *Who 94*

Zacharski, Dennis Edward 1951- *WhoAmL 94*

Zachary, Elizabeth 1928- *WrDr 94*

Zachary, Hubert M. 1936- *WhoBlA 94*

Zachary, Hugh *EncSF 93*

Zachary, Hugh 1928- *WrDr 94*

Zachary, Louis George 1927- *WhoFI 94, WhoMW 93, WhoScEn 94*

Zachary, Ronald F. 1938- *WhoAm 94*

Zachary, Steven W. 1958- *WhoBlA 94*

Zachary-Pike, Annie R. 1931- *WhoBlA 94*

Zachau, Hans G. 1930- *IntWW 93*

Zachem, Harry M. 1944- *WhoFI 94*

Zachert, Martha Jane 1920- *WhoAm 94*

Zachert, Virginia 1920- *WhoAm 94, WhoScEn 94*

Zachery-Hopkins, Donna S. 1952- *WhoMW 93*

Zachman, John Arthur 1934- *WhoWest 94*

Zachos, Cosmas K. 1951- *WhoMW 93*

Zachos, Kimon Stephen 1930- *WhoAm 94*

Zachos, Victoria 1929- *WhoAmP 93*

Zachry, Henry Bartell, Jr. 1933- *WhoFI 94*

Zack, Arnold M(arshall) 1931- *ConAu 42NR*

Zack, Arnold Marshall 1931- *WhoAm 94*

Zack, Badanna Bernice *WhoAmA 93*

Zack, Bill 1956- *ConAu 141*

Zack, Eugene C. 1922- *WhoAmP 93*

Zack, James Gordon, Jr. 1946- *WhoWest 94*

Zack, Neil Richard 1947- *WhoWest 94*

Zack, Richard Stanley, Jr. 1952- *WhoWest 94*

Zackheim, Adrian Walter 1951- *WhoAm 94*

Zackrison, Edwin Harry *WhoWest 94*

Zacks, Arthur 1926- *WhoWest 94*

Zacks, Samuel Jacob 1904-1970 *WhoAmA 93N*

Zacks, Shelemyahu 1932- *ConAu 141*

Zacks, Sumner Irwin 1929- *WhoAm 94*

Zade, Hans Peter 1907- *WrDr 94*

Zadeck, Donald Julian 1927- *WhoFI 94*

Zadeh, Lotfi A. 1921- *WhoAm 94*

Zadek, Hilde 1917- *NewGrDO*

Zadek, Peter 1926- *IntWW 93*

Zader, John Patrick 1961- *WhoFI 94*

Zadok, Haim J. 1913- *IntWW 93*

Zador, Deszo 1873-1931 *NewGrDO*

Zador, Eugene 1894-1977 *NewGrDO*

Zadora, Pia 1954- *WhoHol 92*

Zadvinskis, Ivars 1944- *WhoMW 93*

Zaenglein, Irvin Allen 1940- *WhoFI 94*

Zaenglein, Norman Daniel 1951- *WhoMW 93*

Zaenglein, William George, Jr. 1929- *WhoAm 94*

Zaentz, Saul *IntMPA 94, WhoAm 94*

Zafar, Naeem 1957- *WhoWest 94*

Zaffaroni, Alejandro C. 1923- *WhoAm 94*

Zaffirini, Judith 1946- *WhoAmP 93, WhoHisp 94*

Zaffke, Maurice 1948- *WhoAmP 93*

Zafran, Eric Myles 1946- *WhoAmA 93*

Zafred, Mario 1922-1987 *NewGrDO*

Zafren, Herbert Cecil 1925- *WhoAm 94, WhoMW 93*

Zafris, Nancy *DrAPF 93*

Zagami, Anthony James 1952- *WhoAmL 94*

Zagara, Maurizio 1946- *WhoScEn 94*

Zagarino, Frank *WhoHol 92*

Zagaris, Bruce 1947- *WhoAmL 94, WhoFI 94*

Zagat, Arthur Leo 1895-1949 *EncSF 93*

Zagel, James Block 1941- *WhoAm 94, WhoAmL 94*

Zager, Ronald I. 1934- *WhoScEn 94*

Zager, Steven Mark 1958- *WhoAmL 94*

Zagladin, Vadim Valentinovich 1927- *IntWW 93*

Zago, Tino (Agostino C.) 1937- *WhoAmA 93*

Zagon, Marty *WhoHol 92*

Zagoren, Allen Jeffrey 1947- *WhoMW 93*

Zagoren, Joy Carroll 1933- *WhoFI 94, WhoScEn 94*

Zagoren, Marc Alan 1940- *WrDr 94*

Zagoria, Sam David 1919- *WhoAm 94*

Zagorin, Perez 1920- *WhoAm 94*

Zagorka 1873-1957 *BlmGWL*

Zagotta, Anthony James 1966- *WhoAmP 93*

Zagrosek, Lothar 1942- *NewGrDO*

Zah, Chung-En 1955- *WhoScEn 94*

Zah, Peterson 1937- *WhoAm 94*

Zahalak, George Ireneus 1939- *WhoAm 94, WhoMW 93*

Zaharako, Lew Daleure 1947- *WhoAmL 94*

Zaharchuk, Peter J., Jr. 1947- *WhoAmP 93*

Zaharchuk, Walter Steven 1954- *WhoFI 94*

Zaharia, Eric Stafford 1948- *WhoAm 94*

Zahariev, George Kostadinov 1941- *WhoScEn 94*

Zaharoff, Basil 1849-1936 *DcNaB MP*

Zahary, William 1935- *WhoWest 94*

Zahedi, Ardeshir 1928- *IntWW 93, Who 94*

Zahid, Anwar 1938- *IntWW 93*

Zahid, Khan Hasan 1953- *WhoFI 94*

Zahir, Abdul 1910- *IntWW 93*

Zahir Shah *IntWW 93*

Zahiruddin bin Syed Hassan, Syed 1918- *Who 94*

Zahler, Leah *DrAPF 93*

Zahler, Leonard 1937- *WhoFI 94*

Zahm, John Augustine 1851-1921 *DcAmReB 2*

Zahn, Andrew Joseph 1963- *WhoMW 93*

Zahn, Carl Frederick 1928- *WhoAm 94, WhoAmA 94*

Zahn, Curtis *DrAPF 93*

Zahn, Donald Jack 1941- *WhoAm 94, WhoAmL 94*

Zahn, George Henry 1959- *WhoMW 93*

Zahn, Gordon C(harles) 1918- *WrDr 94*

Zahn, Joachim 1914- *IntWW 93*

Zahn, Johannes 1907- *IntWW 93*

Zahn, Paula *WhoAm 94*

Zahn, Robert Fred 1963- *WhoFI 94*

Zahn, Rudolf Karl 1920- *IntWW 93*

Zahn, Timothy 1951- *EncSF 93, WhoAm 94, WrDr 94*

Zahnd, Hugo 1902- *WhoScEn 94*

Zahnd, Richard Hugo 1946- *WhoAm 94, WhoAmL 94*

Zahner, Kenyon Benedict, Jr. 1930- *WhoAmP 93*

Zahner, Mary Anne 1938- *WhoMW 93*

Zahniser, Ed *DrAPF 93*

Zahniser, Richard Allen 1935- *WhoWest 94*

Zahorowski, Jeffrey John 1966- *WhoWest 94*

Zahorski, Kenneth J. *EncSF 93*

Zahorski, Kenneth James 1939- *WhoMW 93*

Zahortsev, Volodymyr Mykolayovych 1944- *NewGrDO*

Zahourek, Jon Gail 1940- *WhoAmA 93*

Zahreddine, Ziad Nassib 1952- *WhoScEn 94*

Zahrt, William Dietrich, II 1944- *WhoAmL 94*

Zahs, David Karl 1957- *WhoMW 93*

Zaia, John Anthony 1942- *WhoScEn 94*

Zaidi, Iqbal Mehdi 1957- *WhoScEn 94, WhoWest 94*

Zaidi, Mahmood A. 1930- *WhoAm 94*

Zaidins, Clyde Stewart 1939- *WhoWest 94*

Zaiets, Ivan Oleksandrovych 1952- *LngBDD*

Zaikine, Zak (Victor Eugene) 1941- *WhoAmA 93*

Zail Singh, Giani *IntWW 93*

Zaim, Semih 1926- *WhoFI 94*

Zaima, Stephen Gyo 1947- *WhoAmA 93*

Zaiman, Joel Hirsh 1938- *WhoAm 94*

Zaiman, K. Robert 1944- *WhoMW 93*

Zain Azraai, Datuk 1936- *IntWW 93*

Zainuddin, Daim 1938- *IntWW 93*

Zainyeh, George A. 1962- *WhoAmP 93*

Zais, Bernard H. 1916- *WhoIns 94*

Zaiser, Kent Amos 1945 *WhoAm 94*

Zaiser, Sally Solemma Vann 1917- *WhoFI 94, WhoWest 94*

Zaiss, Conrad Penfield 1953- *WhoFI 94, WhoWest 94*

Zaiter, Jose J. 1956- *WhoHisp 94*

Zaitsev, Vitaly Vasilevich 1932- *LngBDD*

Zaitsev, Vladimir Vasilevich 1951- *LngBDD*

Zaitsev, Vyacheslav Mikhailovich 1937- *IntWW 93*

Zaitsev, Yury Vladimirovich 1933- *LngBDD*

Zaitzeff, Roger Michael 1940- *WhoAmL 94*

Zajac, Carol Susan 1947- *WhoMW 93*

Zajac, Jack 1929- *WhoAm 94, WhoAmA 93*

Zajac, John 1946- *WhoWest 94*

Zajac, John J., Jr. *WhoWest 94*

Zajc, Ivan 1832-1914 *NewGrDO*

Zajicek, Jeronym 1926- *WhoAm 94*

Zajicek, Lynn Engelbrecht 1950- *WhoMW 93*

Zak, Josephine Mary 1932- *WhoAmP 93*

Zak, Michele Wender 1940- *WhoWest 94*

Zak, R. Joseph 1946- *WhoAmL 94*

Zak, Robert James 1961- *WhoMW 93*

Zak, Sheldon Jerry 1955- *WhoScEn 94*
Zakaib, Paul, Jr. 1932- *WhoAmP 93*
Zakanitch, Robert Rahway 1935- *WhoAm 94*
Zakanitch, Robert S. 1935- *WhoAmA 93*
Zakarauskas, Pierre 1958- *WhoScEn 94*
Zakaria, Haji Mohamed Ali 1929- *IntWW 93*
Zakarian, Albert 1940- *WhoAm 94*
Zakarin, Keith 1958- *WhoAmL 94*
Zakas, Joseph Conrad 1950- *WhoAmP 93*
Zakharov, Mark Anatolevich 1933- *LngBDD*
Zakharov, Mark Anatolievich 1933- *IntWW 93*
Zakharov, Mikhail Lvovich 1946- *LngBDD*
Zakharov, Olive 1929- *WhoWomW 91*
Zakharov, Rostislav 1907-1975 *IntDcB*
Zakhary, Melissa Trytten 1961- *WhoMW 93*
Zakheim, Barbara Jane 1953- *WhoFI 94*
Zakheim, Dov Solomon 1948- *WhoAm 94*
Zakheim, Irving Lee 1948- *WhoFI 94*
Zakhem, Sam Hanna 1935- *WhoAm 94*
Zakhem, Sam Hanna 1937- *WhoAmP 93*
Zaki, Abdelmoneim Emam 1933- *WhoAm 94*
Zakim, David 1935- *WhoAm 94, WhoScEn 94*
Zakin, Jacques Louis 1927- *WhoAm 94*
Zakin, Kenneth Lee 1947- *WhoFI 94*
Zakin, Mikhail *WhoAmA 93*
Zakis, Eugene 1940- *WhoMW 93*
Zakis, Juris 1936- *IntWW 93*
Zakis, Michael William 1947- *WhoWest 94*
Zakkai, Jamil *WhoHol 92*
Zakkai, Jamil
  See Zale, Alexander & Zakkai, Jamil *WhoHol 92*
Zakkay, Victor 1927- *WhoAm 94*
Zaklinsky, Konstantin 1955- *IntDcB [port]*
Zakrzewski, Sigmund F. 1919- *ConAu 142*
Zakrzewski, Vladimir 1946- *WhoAmA 93*
Zakson, Laurence Scott *WhoAmL 94*
Zal, Roxana 1970- *WhoHol 92*
Zalaznick, David Wayne 1954- *WhoFI 94*
Zalaznick, Sheldon 1928- *WhoAm 94*
Zalben, Jane Breskin *DrAPF 93, WrDr 94*
Zalben, Jane Breskin 1950- *TwCYAW*
Zald, Mayer Nathan 1931- *WrDr 94*
Zaldastani, Othar 1922- *WhoScEn 94*
Zaldivar, Gilberto 1934- *WhoHisp 94*
Zaldivar, Richard L. 1952- *WhoAmP 93*
Zaldívar, Silvia 1928- *WhoHisp 94*
Zaldivar Larrain, Andres 1936- *IntWW 93*
Zaldo, Bruno 1946- *WhoHisp 94*
Zale, Alexander & Zakkai, Jamil *WhoHol 92*
Zalecki, Paul Henry 1931- *WhoAm 94*
Zaleha Bt Ismail, Datin Paduka Hajjah 1936 *WhoWomW 91*
Zaleski, Alan J. *WhoAmP 93*
Zaleski, Alan Joseph 1942- *WhoMW 93*
Zaleski, Brian William 1962- *WhoWest 94*
Zaleski, Jean *WhoAmA 93*
Zaleski, Marek Bohdan 1936- *WhoAm 94, WhoScEn 94*
Zaleski, Michael Louis 1941- *WhoAm 94*
Zaleski, Ronald Joseph 1954- *WhoFI 94, WhoIns 94*
Zaleski, Terence M. 1953- *WhoAmP 93*
Zaleski, Thaddeus B. 1947- *WhoFI 94*
Zalewski, Michelle Susan 1965- *WhoMW 93*
Zaleznik, Abraham 1924- *WhoAm 94, WhoFI 94*
Zalinski, Edmund Louis Gray 1915- *WhoAm 94*
Zaliouk, Yuval Nathan 1939- *WhoAm 94*
Zalisko, Edward John 1958- *WhoScEn 94*
Zalite, Walter M. 1923- *WhoFI 94*
Zalk, Robert H. 1944- *WhoAm 94, WhoAmL 94*
Zalkind, Alan L. 1947- *WhoFI 94*
Zalkind, Norman 1914-1990 *WhAm 10*
Zalkow, Leon H. 1929- *WhoScEn 94*
Zall, Paul M. 1922- *WrDr 94*
Zall, Paul Maxwell 1922- *WhoAm 94*
Zall, Robert Rouben 1925- *WhoAm 94*
Zalle, Paul Martin 1945- *WhoFI 94, WhoWest 94*
Zallen, Dennis Michael 1943- *WhoWest 94*
Zallen, Harold 1926- *WhoAm 94*
Zaller, Robert *DrAPF 93*
Zallinger, Jean Day 1918- *WhoAmA 93*
Zallinger, Peter (Franz) 1943- *WrDr 94*
Zallinger, Rudolph Franz 1919- *WhoAmA 93*
Zaloga, Robert Edwin 1962- *WhoScEn 94*
Zalokar, Julia Ballantine 1926- *WhoWest 94*
Zalokar, Robert H. 1927- *WhoAm 94, WhoFI 94*
Zaloom, Victor Anthony 1944- *WhoScEn 94*
Zaloudek, Duane 1931- *WhoAmA 93*
Zalta, Edward 1930- *WhoAm 94, WhoScEn 94, WhoWest 94*
Zalucha, Peggy Flora 1948- *WhoAmA 93*
Zalucky, Alex David 1960- *WhoWest 94*
Zaluski, Joseph J. *WhoAm 94*
Zalutsky, Morton Herman 1935- *WhoAm 94, WhoAmL 94, WhoWest 94*
Zalygin, Sergey Pavlovich 1913- *IntWW 93*
Zamagni, Stefano 1943- *IntWW 93*
Zaman, Musharraf 1952- *WhoScEn 94*
Zamarripa, Robert S. 1955- *WhoHisp 94*
Zambaras, Vassilis *DrAPF 93*
Zambardino, Rodolfo Alfredo 1930- *WhoScEn 94*
Zambelli, Carlotta 1875-1968 *IntDcB [port]*
Zambello, Francesca 1956- *NewGrDO*
Zambetti, Denis Egan 1953- *WhoWest 94*
Zambie, Allan John 1935- *WhoAm 94*
Zamboni, Gioseffo *NewGrDO*
Zamboni, Luigi 1767-1837 *NewGrDO*
Zamboni, Maria 1895-1976 *NewGrDO*
Zamboni, Richard Frederick Charles 1930- *Who 94*
Zambrana, Rafael 1931- *WhoBlA 94, WhoHisp 94*
Zambrano, Maria 1904-1991 *BlmGWL*
Zambrano, Myrna M. 1958- *WhoHisp 94*
Zambreno, Mary Frances 1954- *ConAu 142, SmATA 75 [port]*
Zamecnik, Evzen 1939- *NewGrDO*
Zamecnik, Paul Charles 1912- *IntWW 93, WhoAm 94, WhoScEn 94*
Zames, George David 1934- *WhoAm 94*
Zamfir, Gheorghe 1941- *IntWW 93*
Zamiatin, Evgenii (Ivanovich) 1884-1937 *RfGShF*
Zamiatin, Yevgeny (Ivanovich) 1884-1937 *EncSF 93*
Zammit, John P. 1942- *WhoMW 93*
Zammit, Joseph Paul 1948- *WhoAmL 94*
Zammitt, Norman 1931- *WhoAm 94, WhoAmA 93*
Zamora, Anthony 1948- *WhoHisp 94*
Zamora, Bernice 1938- *HispLC*
Zamora, Brian Jonathan 1952- *WhoHisp 94*
Zamora, Emilio 1946- *WhoHisp 94*
Zamora, Gloria LuJean Rodriguez 1935- *WhoHisp 94*
Zamora, Juan B. 1931- *WhoHisp 94*
Zamora, Mario Dimarucut 1935- *WhoAm 94, WhoAsA 94*
Zamora, Nassry G. 1950- *WhoHisp 94*
Zamora, S. Robert *WhoHisp 94*
Zamora-Cope, Rosie 1935- *WhoHisp 94*
Zamora Martinez, Ricardo 1901-1978 *WorESoc [port]*
Zamora-Muñoz, Jorge Mario 1945- *WhoHisp 94*
Zamora Rivas, Ruben Ignacio 1942- *IntWW 93*
Zampano, Robert Carmine 1929- *WhoAm 94, WhoAmL 94*
Zamparelli, John F. 1922- *WhoAmP 93*
Zamparelli, Mario Armond *WhoWest 94*
Zampelas, Michael Herodotou 1937- *WhoFI 94*
Zampese, Alan d1984 *WhoHol 92*
Zampi, Mario d1963 *WhoHol 92*
Zampiello, Richard Sidney 1933- *WhoAm 94, WhoFI 94*
Zampieri, Giuseppe d1981 *WhoHol 92*
Zampieri, John James 1941- *WhoAmP 93*
Zampieri, Mara 1941- *NewGrDO*
Zamponi, Gioseffo 1610?-1662 *NewGrDO*
Zamrini, Edward Youssef 1958- *WhoScEn 94*
Zamudio, Adela 1854-1928 *BlmGWL*
Zamvil, Stella *DrAPF 93*
Zamyatin, Leonid Mitrofanovich 1922- *IntWW 93, Who 94*
Zana, Donald Dominick 1942- *WhoScEn 94*
Zanakis, Steve H. 1940- *WhoAm 94*
Zanardelli, John Joseph 1950- *WhoAm 94*
Zanardi, Carlo Antonio 1657-1704 *NewGrDO*
Zanardi, Nicolo *NewGrDO*
Zanbak, Caner 1949- *WhoScEn 94*
Zancanaro, Giorgio 1939- *NewGrDO*
Zand, Charlene Rooth 1930- *WhoMW 93*
Zand, Dale Ezra 1926- *WhoAm 94*
Zande, Michael Dominic 1960- *WhoScEn 94*
Zander, Alvin Frederick 1913- *WhoAm 94*
Zander, Gaillienne Glashow 1932- *WhoMW 93*
Zander, Janet Adele 1950- *WhoMW 93*
Zander, Jessie Mae 1932- *WhoBlA 94*
Zander, Johan David 1753-1796 *NewGrDO*
Zander, Josef 1918- *WhoScEn 94*
Zander, Michael 1932- *Who 94*
Zanders, Alton Wendell 1943- *WhoBlA 94*
Zandin, Kjell Bertil 1937- *WhoAm 94*
Zandman, Felix 1928- *WhoAm 94, WhoFI 94*
Zandonai, Riccardo 1883-1944 *NewGrDO*
Zandt, Marie van *NewGrDO*
Zandvakali, Sourushe 1956- *WhoMW 93*
Zane, Billy 1965- *WhoHol 92*
Zane, Ebenezer 1747-1812 *WhAmRev*
Zane, Elizabeth *WhAmRev*
Zane, Elizabeth c. 1766-c. 1831 *AmRev*
Zane, Lisa 1964- *WhoHol 92*
Zane, Phillip Craig 1961- *WhoAmL 94*
Zane, Raymond John 1939- *WhoAmP 93*
Zanella, (Castore) Amilcare 1873-1949 *NewGrDO*
Zanella, John Anthony, Jr. 1943- *WhoMW 93*
Zanelli (Morales), Renato 1892-1935 *NewGrDO*
Zanercik, Gary Denis 1950- *WhoAm 94*
Zanetta, Joseph Michael 1953- *WhoWest 94*
Zanette, Guy d1962 *WhoHol 92*
Zanetti, Antonio Maria 1706-1778 *NewGrDO*
Zanetti, Francesco *NewGrDO*
Zanetti, John 1955- *WhoAmP 93*
Zanetti, Joseph Maurice, Jr. 1928- *WhoAm 94*
Zang, William Louis 1953- *WhoFI 94*
Zangari, James 1929- *WhoAmP 93*
Zangarini, Carlo 1874-1943 *NewGrDO*
Zang Boping *WhoPRCh 91*
Zangeneh, Fereydoun 1937- *WhoScEn 94*
Zangeneh, Hamid 1945- *ConAu 141*
Zanger, Joseph Anthony 1927- *WhoAmP 93*
Zangerle, John A. 1942- *WhoAm 94, WhoAmL 94*
Zangger, Russell George 1922- *WhoMW 93*
Zang Kejia 1905- *WhoPRCh 91 [port]*
Zangrandi, Giovanna 1910-1988 *BlmGWL*
Zang Shixiong *WhoPRCh 91*
Zangwill, Israel 1864-1926 *DcLB 135 [port]*
Zani, Giselda 1909-1975 *BlmGWL*
Zaniboni, Antonio d1767 *NewGrDO*
Zaniewski, Christine Florence 1943- *WhoAmL 94*
Zaniewski, Michael F. 1961- *WhoAmP 93*
Zank, Neal Steven 1953- *WhoFI 94*
Zanker, Paul 1937- *IntWW 93*
Zankowski, Doreen M. 1959- *WhoAmL 94*
Zannetti, Francesco 1737-1788 *NewGrDO*
Zannettini, Antonio *NewGrDO*
Zanni, Michael A. 1956- *WhoAmP 93*
Zanni, Vilma Ann 1931- *WhoAmP 93*
Zannieri, Nina 1955- *WhoAm 94*
Zannoni, Angelo Maria fl. 1713-1732 *NewGrDO*
Zanone, Valerio 1936- *IntWW 93*
Zanoni, Michael McNeal 1948- *WhoScEn 94*
Zanot, Craig Allen 1955- *WhoAmL 94, WhoFI 94, WhoMW 93*
Zanotti, Marie Louise 1954- *WhoAm 94*
Zant, Robert Franklin 1943- *WhoAm 94*
Zanten, Cornelie van 1855-1946 *NewGrDO*
Zantman, J. B. 1919- *WhoAmA 93*
Zants, Emily 1937- *WrDr 94*
Zanuck, Darryl F. d1979 *WhoHol 92*
Zanuck, Darryl F. 1902-1979 *IntDcF 2-4 [port]*
Zanuck, Lili Fini 1954- *IntMPA 94, News 94-2 [port]*
Zanuck, Richard Darryl 1934- *IntMPA 94, IntWW 93, WhoAm 94*
Zanuck, Susan d1980 *WhoHol 92*
Zanuso, Marco 1916- *IntWW 93*
Zanussi, Krzysztof 1939- *IntWW 93*
Zanville, Bernard *WhoHol 92*
Zany, Bob *WhoHol 92*
Zany, King d1939 *WhoHol 92*
Zanzibar And Tanga, Bishop of *Who 94*
Zanzotto, Andrea 1921- *ConWorW 93*
Zapanta, Al *WhoHisp 94*
Zapapas, James Richard 1926- *WhoAm 94*
Zaparackas, Algis 1940- *WhoAmP 93*
Zapata, Ariel F. 1958- *WhoHisp 94*
Zapata, Candelario 1956- *WhoHisp 94*
Zapata, Carlos Eduardo 1961- *WhoHisp 94*
Zapata, Carmen *WhoHol 92*
Zapata, Carmen Margarita 1927- *WhoHisp 94*
Zapata, Eino 1947- *WhoHisp 94*
Zapata, Emiliano 1879-1919 *HisWorL [port]*
Zapata, Felix Arturo 1956- *WhoHisp 94*
Zapata, Fernando, Jr. 1951- *WhoHisp 94*
Zapata, Joe *WhoHol 92*
Zapata, Jose Angel, Jr. 1958- *WhoHisp 94*
Zapata, Louis J., Sr. 1934- *WhoHisp 94*
Zapata, M. Nelson, Jr. 1950- *WhoHisp 94*
Zapata, Sabas, III 1945- *WhoHisp 94*
Zapatero Gomez, Virgilio 1946- *IntWW 93*
Zapel, Arthur L. 1921- *WhoAm 94, WhoWest 94*
Zapf, Hermann 1918- *WhoAm 94*
Zapfe, Guillermo 1933- *WhoAmA 93*
Zapfe, Helmuth 1913- *IntWW 93*
Zaphiriou, George Aristotle 1919- *WhoAmL 94*
Zapiain, Norman Gerard 1962- *WhoHisp 94*
Zapien, Danny *WhoHol 92*
Zapkus, Kes 1938- *WhoAmA 93*
Zapletal, Clay Michael 1961- *WhoMW 93*
Zaplitny, Andrew Roman 1968- *WhoFI 94*
Zapoleon, Marguerite Wykoff 1907- *WrDr 94*
Zapor, John Randolph 1944- *WhoWest 94*
Zapp, David Edwin 1950- *WhoMW 93*
Zapp, Herbert 1928- *IntWW 93*
Zapp, Robert Louis 1946- *WhoMW 93*
Zappa, Dweezil 1969- *WhoHol 92*
Zappa, Francis Vincent 1940- *AmCulL [port]*
Zappa, Frank 1940- *IntWW 93, WhoAm 94, WhoHol 92*
Zappa, Frank 1940-1993 *NewYTBS 93 [port], News 94-2*
Zappa, William *WhoHol 92*
Zappala, Joseph 1933- *WhoAmP 93*
Zappala, Stephen A. 1932- *WhoAm 94, WhoAmL 94, WhoAmP 93*
Zappe, John Paul 1952- *WhoWest 94*
Zappia, Charles Anthony 1947- *WhoWest 94*
Zappoli, Bernand 1951- *WhoScEn 94*
Zaprianoff, Boris Nichola 1963- *WhoWest 94*
Zar, Jerrold Howard 1941- *WhoAm 94*
Zara, Louis 1910- *WhoAm 94*
Zarafonetis, Chris John Dimiter 1914- *WhoAm 94*
Zaragoza, Al *WhoHisp 94*
Zaragoza, Blanca *WhoHisp 94*
Zaragoza, Federico *WhoHisp 94*
Zaragoza, Federico Mayor 1934- *WhoScEn 94*
Zaragoza, Ronald 1956- *WhoHisp 94*
Zarand, Julius John 1913- *WhoAmA 93*
Zarandona, Joseph L. 1953- *WhoIns 94*
Zaranka, William *DrAPF 93*
Zaranka, William F. 1944- *WhoAm 94*
Zarate, Aminta C. 1918- *WhoHisp 94*
Zárate, Armando E. 1931- *WhoHisp 94*
Zarate, Julian 1913- *WhoHisp 94*
Zarate, Manuela M. 1956- *WhoHisp 94*
Zárate, Narcisa 1925- *WhoHisp 94*
Zarate, Yolanda 1940- *WhoHisp 94*
Zaratzian, Michael Charles 1949- *WhoFI 94*
Zarazik, Danuta *WhoHol 92*
Zarb, Frank G. 1935- *WhoAmP 93*
Zarb, Frank Gustav 1935- *IntWW 93*
Zarb, Frank Gustave 1935- *WhoAm 94, WhoFI 94*
Zarcone, Donna F. 1957- *WhoFI 94*
Zarda, Lilli Ann 1956- *WhoMW 93*
Zardenetta, Antonio *WhoHisp 94*
Zare, Richard Neil 1939- *IntWW 93, WhoAm 94, WhoScEn 94, WhoWest 94*
Zarefsky, David Harris 1946- *WhoAm 94, WhoMW 93*
Zarefsky, Ralph 1950- *WhoAm 94*
Zarek, Richard Paul 1950- *WhoMW 93*
Zarem, Abe Mordecai 1917- *WhoAm 94*
Zarem, Lewis *EncSF 93*
Zaremba, Carolyn Weis 1953- *WhoFI 94*
Zaremba, Eve 1930- *WrDr 94*
Zaremba, Hubert Bernard 1923- *WhoWest 94*
Zaremba, John d1986 *WhoHol 92*
Zarembka, Paul 1942- *WhoAm 94*
Zaremski, Miles Jay 1948- *WhoAm 94, WhoAmL 94*
Zaret, Barry Lewis 1940- *WhoAm 94*
Zaret, Efrem Herbert 1941- *WhoScEn 94*
Zaretski, Ann Pikaart 1954- *WhoMW 93*
Zarian, Larry *WhoAmP 93*
Zarif, Mohammad Farouk 1951- *IntWW 93*
Zarins, Bertram 1942- *WhoAm 94*
Zarins, Christopher Kristaps 1943- *WhoAm 94*
Zarins, Joyce Audy 1949- *WrDr 94*
Zarins, Margers 1910- *NewGrDO*
Zarkhy, Aleksandr Grigoriyevich 1908- *IntWW 93*
Zarkovic, Vidoje 1927- *IntWW 93*
Zarky, Karen Jane 1948- *WhoMW 93*
Zarlenga, Dante Sam 1925- *WhoFI 94*
Zarlenga, Dante Sam, Jr. 1953- *WhoScEn 94*

Zelezny, William Francis 1918- *WhoScEn 94, WhoWest 94*
Zeliff, Bill *WhoAmP 93*
Zeliff, Bill, Jr. 1936- *CngDr 93*
Zeliff, Seymour d1953 *WhoHol 92*
Zeliff, William 1936- *WhoAm 94*
Zeligman, Sergio 1949- *WhoHisp 94*
Zelikoff, Herbert Alfred 1952- *WhoMW 93*
Zelikow, Howard Monroe 1934- *WhoAm 94*
Zelin, Elaine 1931- *WhoAmA 93*
Zelin, Jerome 1930- *WhoAm 94, WhoFI 94*
Zelinger, Geza 1911- *WrDr 94*
Zelinka, Jan Evangelista 1893-1969 *NewGrDO*
Zelinova, Hana 1914- *BlmGWL*
Zelinski, Joseph John 1922- *WhoScEn 94*
Zelinsky, Paul O. 1953- *WhoAm 94*
Zelinsky, Wilbur 1921- *WrDr 94*
Zelis, Karen Dee 1953- *WhoBlA 94*
Zelis, Robert Felix 1939- *WhoAm 94*
Zelitch, David S. 1924- *WhoIns 94*
Zelka, Jeffrey 1952- *WhoFI 94*
Zell, Blair Paul 1942- *WhoMW 93*
Zell, Donald David 1928- *WhoFI 94*
Zell, F. 1829-1895 *NewGrDO*
Zell, Katharina 1497?-1562 *BlmGWL*
Zell, Samuel 1941- *WhoAm 94, WhoFI 94*
Zellars, Anne Yusavage *DrAPF 93*
Zellbell, Ferdinand 1719-1780 *NewGrDO*
Zelle, Joseph Frank 1912- *WhoMW 93*
Zeller, Barbara Ann 1945- *WhoMW 93*
Zeller, Ben *WhoHol 92*
Zeller, Carl (Johann Adam) 1842-1898 *NewGrDO*
Zeller, Claude 1940- *WhoScEn 94*
Zeller, Edward Jacob 1925- *WhoAm 94*
Zeller, Eva 1923- *BlmGWL*
Zeller, Francis Joseph 1943- *WhoMW 93*
Zeller, Frederic 1924- *WhoAmA 93, WrDr 94*
Zeller, George Charles 1949- *WhoMW 93*
Zeller, Heinrich 1856-1934 *NewGrDO*
Zeller, Marilynn Kay 1940- *WhoAm 94*
Zeller, Michael Edward 1939- *WhoAm 94*
Zeller, Michael James 1939- *WhoScEn 94*
Zeller, Ronald John 1940- *WhoAmL 94*
Zellerbach, Harold L. 1895-1978 *WhoAmA 93N*
Zellerbach, Merla *DrAPF 93*
Zellerbach, William Joseph 1920- *IntWW 93, WhoAm 94*
Zellerman, Robert Allen 1952- *WhoMW 93*
Zellers, Carl Fredrick, Jr. 1932- *WhoAm 94*
Zellers, Robert Charles 1943- *WhoFI 94, WhoScEn 94*
Zellick, Graham John 1948- *Who 94*
Zellick, Jennifer *Who 94*
Zellinsky, Paul, Sr. *WhoAmP 93*
Zelliot, Eleanor Mae 1926- *WhoMW 93*
Zellman, Ande 1952- *WhoAm 94*
Zellmer, Arlene 1920- *WhoWest 94*
Zellner, Arnold 1927- *WhoFI 94, WrDr 94*
Zelman, Anita *DrAPF 93*
Zelmanowitz, Julius Martin 1941- *WhoAm 94*
Zelmer, Amy Elliott 1935- *WhoAm 94*
Zelmon, David Norman 1945- *WhoMW 93*
Zelnick, Carl Robert 1940- *WhoAm 94*
Zelnick, Strauss 1957- *IntMPA 94, WhoAm 94*
Zelniker, Michael *WhoHol 92*
Zelon, Laurie Dee 1952- *WhoAm 94, WhoAmL 94*
Zelt, Martha 1930- *WhoAmA 93*
Zelt, Siegfried Werner 1960- *WhoFI 94*
Zelterman, Daniel 1954- *WhoFI 94*
Zeltner, Paul E. *WhoAmP 93*
Zeltzer, Joel *DrAPF 93*
Zelver, Patricia *DrAPF 93*
Zelvin, Elizabeth *DrAPF 93*
Zemach, Margot 1931-1989 *WhAm 10*
Zemaitis, Thomas Edward 1951- *WhoAmL 94*
Zeman, Ivo 1931-1991 *WhAm 10*
Zeman, Jacklyn *WhoHol 92*
Zeman, Jarold Knox 1926- *WhoAm 94*
Zeman, John Robert 1940- *WhoAm 94*
Zeman, Karel 1910-1989 *IntDcF 2-4*
Zeman, Zbynek Anthony Bohuslav 1928- *IntWW 93, Who 94*
Zemanek, Heinz 1920- *IntWW 93*
Zemanian, Armen Humpartsoum 1925- *WhoAm 94*
Zemans, Frances Kahn 1943- *WhoAm 94, WhoAmL 94*
Zemans, Joyce L. 1940- *WhoAmA 93*
Zemans, Joyce Pearl 1940- *WhoAm 94*
Zemansky, Gilbert Marek 1944- *WhoScEn 94*
Zembsch, Kimberley Cypher 1962- *WhoAmL 94*
Zemeckis, Robert 1952- *IntMPA 94*
Zemeckis, Robert L. 1952- *WhoAm 94*
Zemek, Melville Mason 1919- *WhAm 10*
Zemel, Jay Norman 1928- *WhoAm 94*
Zemelman, James Louis 1931- *WhoWest 94*
Zemke, Joseph *WhoAm 94, WhoFI 94, WhoWest 94*
Zemke, Robert Lowell 1935- *WhoMW 93*
Zemke, William A. 1938- *WhoMW 93*
Zemlinsky, Alexander (von) 1871-1942 *NewGrDO*
Zemm, Sandra Phyllis 1947- *WhoAm 94*
Zemmer, Joseph Lawrence, Jr. 1922- *WhoAm 94*
Zemo-Israel, Nina Vera 1947- *WhoWest 94*
Zemp, Lucy Woodruff 1962- *WhoFI 94*
Zemplenyi, Tibor Karol 1916- *WhoAm 94*
Zemprelli, Edward Phillip 1925- *WhoAmP 93*
Zemtsov, Alexander 1959- *WhoScEn 94*
Zen, E-An 1928- *IntWW 93, WhoAm 94, WhoAsA 94, WhoScEn 94*
Zenatello, Giovanni 1876-1949 *NewGrDO*
Zenawi, Meles *IntWW 93*
Zendejas, Esperanza 1952- *WhoHisp 94*
Zendejas, Luis 1961- *WhoHisp 94*
Zendejas, Tony 1960- *WhoHisp 94*
Zender, Hans 1936- *IntWW 93, NewGrDO*
Zender-Boykin, Angelina Elizabeth 1933- *WhoMW 93*
Zendle, Howard Mark 1949- *WhoFI 94, WhoScEn 94*
Zenelaj, Shpresa *WhoWomW 91*
Zener, Clarence Melvin d1993 *NewYTBS 93*
Zenev, Irene Louise 1948- *WhoWest 94*
Zeng Chengkui 1909- *WhoPRCh 91 [port]*
Zeng Delin *WhoPRCh 91*
Zeng Dingshi 1920- *WhoPRCh 91 [port]*
Zenger, John Hancock 1931- *WhoWest 94*
Zenger, John Peter c. 1697-1746 *AmSocL*
Zeng Jianhui 1928- *WhoPRCh 91 [port]*
Zeng Jinyi 1920- *WhoPRCh 91*
Zeng Maochao *WhoPRCh 91*
Zeng Peiyan 1938- *WhoPRCh 91 [port]*
Zeng Qingcun 1935- *WhoPRCh 91*
Zeng Qinghong 1939- *WhoPRCh 91 [port]*
Zeng Shanqing 1932- *WhoPRCh 91 [port]*
Zeng Sheng 1910- *WhoPRCh 91 [port]*
Zeng Tao 1914- *IntWW 93, WhoPRCh 91 [port]*
Zeng Xianlin 1929- *IntWW 93, WhoPRCh 91 [port]*
Zeng Yi 1929- *IntWW 93*
Zeng Zhaoke 1925- *WhoPRCh 91 [port]*
Zeng Zhi *WhoPRCh 91 [port]*
Zenieris, Petros Efstratios 1955- *WhoScEn 94*
Zenined, Abdesselam 1934- *Who 94*
Zenner, Hans Peter 1947- *WhoScEn 94*
Zenner, Sheldon Toby 1953- *WhoAm 94*
Zeno, Apostolo 1668-1750 *NewGrDO*
Zeno, Jo Ann 1952- *WhoMW 93*
Zeno, John Richard 1954- *WhAm 10*
Zeno, Melvin Collins 1945- *WhoBlA 94*
Zeno, Phyllis Wolfe *WhoAm 94*
Zeno, Willie D. 1942- *WhoBlA 94*
Zenobia 3rd cent.- *HisWorL [port]*
Zenone, John Mark 1958- *WhoScEn 94*
Zenor, Michael 1949- *WhoAmP 93*
Zenor, Suzanne *WhoHol 92*
Zenovich, George N. 1922- *WhoAmP 93*
Zenowich, Christopher 1954- *WrDr 94*
Zenowitz, Allan Ralph 1928- *WhoAm 94*
Zens, Will 1920- *IntMPA 94*
Zentar, Mehdi M'rani 1929- *IntWW 93*
Zentmyer, George Aubrey 1913- *WhoAm 94, WhoScEn 94, WhoWest 94*
Zentmyer, George Aubrey, Jr. 1913- *IntWW 93*
Zentmyer, Robert Kenneth 1935- *WhoAm 94*
Zentner, Peter 1932- *WrDr 94*
Zentout, Delphine 1972- *WhoHol 92*
Zentz, John Robert 1938- *WhoAmP 93*
Zentz, Patrick J. *WhoAmA 93*
Zeo, Frank James 1910- *WhoAm 94*
Zepeda, Barbara Joyce 1935- *WhoAmP 93*
Zepeda, Lydia 1959- *WhoHisp 94*
Zepeda, Maria Angelica 1952- *WhoHisp 94*
Zepeda, Paula 1948- *WhoHisp 94*
Zepeda, Rafael *DrAPF 93*
Zepeda, Rafael Joseph 1940- *WhoHisp 94*
Zepeda, Susan Ghozeil 1946- *WhoWest 94*
Zepf, Thomas Herman 1935- *WhoAm 94, WhoScEn 94*
Zepos, Constantine 1931- *IntWW 93*
Zepp, Alison Fielding 1957- *WhoMW 93*
Zepp, Ira G(ilbert), Jr. 1929- *WrDr 94*
Zepp, Lawrence Peter 1952- *WhoScEn 94*
Zeppa, Robert d1993 *NewYTBS 93*
Zeppelin, Ferdinand von 1838-1917 *WorInv [port]*
Zeppili, Alice 1885-1920? *NewGrDO*
Zerbe, Anthony *WhoAm 94, WhoHol 92*
Zerbe, Anthony 1936- *IntMPA 94*
Zerbe, Arnette Jens *WhoHol 92*
Zerbe, Brian Paul 1962- *WhoAmL 94*
Zerbe, Charles James 1951- *WhoWest 94*
Zerbe, John Irwin 1926- *WhoMW 93*
Zerbe, Karl 1903-1972 *WhoAmA 93N*
Zerbini, Euryclides de Jesus d1993 *NewYTBS 93*
Zerbo, Saye 1932- *IntWW 93*
Zerega, Patricia Ann 1952- *WhoMW 93*
Zerella, Joseph T. 1941- *WhoAm 94*
Zeretzke, Frederick Frank H. 1919- *WhoWest 94*
Zerfas, Janice *DrAPF 93*
Zerin, Steven David 1953- *WhoAm 94, WhoAmL 94*
Zerlaut, Gene Arlis 1930- *WhoWest 94*
Zerman, Melvyn Bernard 1930- *WhoFI 94*
Zermatten, Maurice 1910- *IntWW 93*
Zermeno, Alexander Sanchez 1937- *WhoHisp 94*
Zerne, Winnie *DrAPF 93*
Zerner, Henri Thomas 1939- *WhoAmA 93*
Zernow, Louis 1916- *WhoWest 94*
Zeroug, Smaine 1962- *WhoScEn 94*
Zerr, Anna 1822-1881 *NewGrDO*
Zerr, Dean A. 1947- *WhoMW 93*
Zerr, Frank Michael 1949- *WhoMW 93*
Zertuche, Antonio *WhoHisp 94*
Zervas, Nicholas Themistocles 1929- *WhoAm 94, WhoScEn 94*
Zerweck, Richard, Jr. 1932- *WhoFI 94*
Zerwekh, Robert Paul 1939- *WhoAm 94*
Zerwick, Chloe 1923- *EncSF 93*
Zerzan, Charles Joseph, Jr. 1921- *WhoWest 94*
Zesch-Ballot, Hans d1972 *WhoHol 92*
Zesiger, Ann Elizabeth 1949- *WhoMW 93*
Zeta-Jones, Catherine *WhoHol 92*
Zetford, Tully *EncSF 93*
Zetina, Guillermo Gutierrez d1970 *WhoHol 92*
Zetkin, Clara 1857-1933 *BlmGWL*
Zetland, Marquess of 1937- *Who 94*
Zetlin, Lev 1918-1992 *WhAm 10*
Zettel, Richard J. 1948- *WhoAmL 94*
Zetter, Paul Isaac 1923- *Who 94*
Zetterberg, Christer 1941- *IntWW 93, Who 94*
Zetterberg, Stephen Ingersoll 1916- *WhoAmP 93*
Zetterling, Mai 1925- *IntMPA 94, WhoHol 92*
Zetterling, Mai (Elisabeth) 1925- *WrDr 94*
Zetterling, Mai Elisabeth 1925- *IntWW 93*
Zetterling, Mai Elizabeth 1925- *Who 94*
Zetterlund, Yoko Karin 1969- *WhoAsA 94*
Zetterman, Rowen Kent 1944- *WhoMW 93*
Zettick, Elaine Petuch 1934- *WhoAmP 93*
Zettlemoyer, Albert Charles 1915-1991 *WhAm 10*
Zetzel, Louis d1993 *NewYTBS 93*
Zetzer, Roger S. 1930- *WhoIns 94*
Zeug, Mark Edward 1943- *WhoFI 94*
Zeugner, John Finn 1938- *WhoAm 94*
Zeuner, Raymond Alfred 1937- *WhoScEn 94*
Zeuschner, Erwin Arnold 1935- *WhoAm 94*
Zeuske, Cathy Susan 1958- *WhoAmP 93*
Zeveloff, Samuel I. 1950- *ConAu 140*
Zevi, Bruno 1918- *IntWW 93*
Zevnik, Paul A. 1950- *WhoAm 94*
Zevon, Irene 1918- *WhoAmA 93*
Zewail, Ahmed Hassan 1946- *WhoAm 94, WhoScEn 94, WhoWest 94*
Zewiey, Mark Anthony 1961- *WhoFI 94*
Zeybek, Namik Kemal 1944- *IntWW 93*
Zeyen, Richard John 1943- *WhoMW 93*
Zeyen, Richard Leo, III 1957- *WhoScEn 94*
Zeyher, Mark Lewis 1953- *WhoFI 94*
Zezza, Myrna Mazzola 1938- *WhoWest 94*
Zgoda, Larry 1950- *WhoAmA 93*
Zgonc, Janice Ann 1956- *WhoScEn 94*
Zgonc, Robert Joseph 1931- *WhoWest 94*
Zgorski, Robert Francis 1952- *WhoIns 94*
Zgrabik, Michael James 1957- *WhoMW 93*
Zguriska, Zuska 1900-1984 *BlmGWL*
Zhadovskaia, Iuliia Valerianovna 1824-1883 *BlmGWL*
Zhai Yongbo *WhoPRCh 91*
Zhang, Binglin 1937- *WhoScEn 94*
Zhang, Chen-Zhi 1957- *WhoScEn 94*
Zhang, Cheng-Yue 1945- *WhoScEn 94*
Zhang, Fu-Xue 1939- *WhoScEn 94*
Zhang, Guo He 1953- *WhoScEn 94*
Zhang, Hong Tu 1932- *WhoScEn 94*
Zhang, Huilian 1946- *WhoMW 93*
Zhang, Jianhong 1958- *WhoScEn 94*
Zhang, Jiping 1954- *WhoScEn 94*
Zhang, John Z. H. 1961- *WhoAsA 94*
Zhang, Jun Yi 1929- *WhoScEn 94*
Zhang, Li-Xing 1934- *WhoScEn 94*
Zhang, Lixia 1951- *WhoWest 94*
Zhang, Longxi 1947- *WhoAsA 94*
Zhang, Naiqian 1946- *WhoScEn 94*
Zhang, Ping 1937- *WhoScEn 94*
Zhang, Tao 1942- *WhoScEn 94*
Zhang, Theodore Tian-ze 1920- *WhoScEn 94*
Zhang, Tianyou 1938- *WhoScEn 94*
Zhang, Wenxian 1963- *WhoAsA 94*
Zhang, Xiao-Feng 1951- *WhoMW 93*
Zhang, Xiaonan 1957- *WhoFI 94*
Zhang, Yong-Hang 1959- *WhoScEn 94*
Zhang Ailing 1920- *BlmGWL, ConWorW 93, RfGShF*
Zhang Aiping 1910- *WhoPRCh 91 [port]*
Zhang Aiping, Col.-Gen. 1910- *IntWW 93*
Zhang Aizhen *WhoPRCh 91*
Zhang Anzhi 1911- *WhoPRCh 91 [port]*
Zhang Baifa 1933- *WhoPRCh 91 [port]*
Zhang Bangying 1907- *WhoPRCh 91*
Zhang Baoming *WhoPRCh 91*
Zhang Baoshun 1950- *WhoPRCh 91 [port]*
Zhang Bilai 1914- *WhoPRCh 91 [port]*
Zhang Bin 1931- *WhoPRCh 91 [port]*
Zhang Bingduo *WhoPRCh 91*
Zhang Bingxi *WhoPRCh 91*
Zhang Boquan 1913- *WhoPRCh 91 [port]*
Zhang Borong *WhoPRCh 91*
Zhang Boxiang 1918- *WhoPRCh 91 [port]*
Zhang Boxing 1930- *IntWW 93, WhoPRCh 91 [port]*
Zhang Bu 1934- *WhoPRCh 91 [port]*
Zhang Caiqian 1912- *WhoPRCh 91 [port]*
Zhang Caizhen 1930- *WhoPRCh 91 [port]*
Zhang Cangong 1929- *WhoPRCh 91 [port]*
Zhang Ce c. 1919- *WhoPRCh 91*
Zhang Changhai *WhoPRCh 91*
Zhang Changshou *WhoPRCh 91*
Zhang Changshun *WhoPRCh 91*
Zhang Chen 1918- *WhoPRCh 91 [port]*
Zhang Chengxian 1915- *WhoPRCh 91 [port]*
Zhang Chengzhi 1948- *IntWW 93, WhoPRCh 91 [port]*
Zhang Chuanshi *WhoPRCh 91*
Zhang Chukun 1912- *WhoPRCh 91 [port]*
Zhang Chunnan 1941- *WhoPRCh 91 [port]*
Zhang Chunnian *WhoPRCh 91*
Zhang Chunqiao 1917- *WhoPRCh 91 [port]*
Zhang Chunyuan 1938- *WhoPRCh 91 [port]*
Zhang Cunen *WhoPRCh 91*
Zhang Cunhao *WhoPRCh 91*
Zhang Dainian *WhoPRCh 91 [port]*
Zhang Dake *WhoPRCh 91*
Zhang Dazhi 1911- *WhoPRCh 91 [port]*
Zhang Dazhong *WhoPRCh 91*
Zhang Dedi 1933- *WhoPRCh 91 [port]*
Zhang Defu 1928- *WhoPRCh 91 [port]*
Zhang Dehua 1931- *WhoPRCh 91 [port]*
Zhang Dejiang 1946- *WhoPRCh 91 [port]*
Zhang Deliang *WhoPRCh 91*
Zhang Delin *WhoPRCh 91*
Zhang Deqin *WhoPRCh 91*
Zhang Dewei *WhoPRCh 91*
Zhang Dexin 1905- *WhoPRCh 91 [port]*
Zhang Deyi 1947- *WhoPRCh 91*
Zhang Ding 1917- *WhoPRCh 91 [port]*
Zhang Dinghong 1927- *WhoPRCh 91 [port]*
Zhang Dinghua *WhoPRCh 91*
Zhang Dinghua 1933- *WhoPRCh 91 [port]*
Zhang Enshu *WhoPRCh 91 [port]*
Zhang Fengjiao *WhoPRCh 91*
Zhang Fengyu 1934- *WhoPRCh 91*
Zhang Fuyou *WhoPRCh 91*
Zhang Gaoli 1947- *WhoPRCh 91 [port]*
Zhang Ge *WhoPRCh 91*
Zhang Geng *WhoPRCh 91*
Zhang Gensheng 1923- *IntWW 93, WhoPRCh 91 [port]*
Zhang Gong 1935- *WhoPRCh 91 [port]*
Zhang Gong, Maj.-Gen. 1935- *IntWW 93*
Zhang Guangdou 1912- *WhoPRCh 91 [port]*
Zhang Guangnian 1913- *WhoPRCh 91 [port]*
Zhang Guoguang *WhoPRCh 91*
Zhang Guoji 1894- *WhoPRCh 91 [port]*
Zhang Guosheng 1912- *WhoPRCh 91 [port]*
Zhang Guoying 1935- *IntWW 93, WhoPRCh 91 [port], WhoWomW 91*
Zhang Haiyun 1929- *WhoPRCh 91 [port]*
Zhang Hanfu 1930- *WhoPRCh 91 [port]*
Zhang Hanqing *WhoPRCh 91*
Zhang Haoruo 1932- *WhoPRCh 91 [port]*
Zhang Heng *WorInv*
Zhang Hong *WhoPRCh 91*
Zhang Hongnian 1949- *WhoPRCh 91*
Zhang Hongren 1934- *WhoPRCh 91 [port]*
Zhang Hongtu 1943- *WhoPRCh 91*
Zhang Huainian 1933- *WhoPRCh 91 [port]*
Zhang Huijuan 1946- *WhoPRCh 91 [port]*
Zhang Huilan 1896- *WhoPRCh 91 [port]*

Zinn, Keith Marshall 1940- WhoAm 94
Zinn, Michael Wallace 1962- WhoScEn 94
Zinn, Terry Leigh 1951- WhoAmL 94
Zinn, Thomas Roger 1949- WhoFI 94
Zinn, William 1924- WhoAm 94
Zinnemann, Fred 1907- IntMPA 94, IntWW 93, Who 94, WhoAm 94
Zinnemann, Tim IntMPA 94
Zinnen, Robert Oliver 1929- WhoAm 94
Zinner, Hedda 1905- BlmGWL
Zinner, Lea Barbieri 1945- WhoScEn 94
Zinnes, Harriet DrAPF 93, WrDr 94
Zinober, Peter Wolfson 1943- WhoAmL 94
Zinola, Maria WhoHisp 94
Zinov'eva-Annibal, Lidiia Dmitrievna 1866-1907 BlmGWL
Zinoviev, Aleksandr Aleksandrovich 1922- IntWW 93
Zinoviev, Alexander 1922- EncSF 93
Zins, Martha Lee 1945- WhoMW 93
Zins, Sidney d1986 WhoHol 92
Zinser, Elisabeth Ann 1940- WhoAm 94, WhoWest 94
Zinsou, Emile Derlin 1918- IntWW 93
Zinsser, Carl A. WhoAmP 93
Zinsser, Caroline 1930- ConAu 141
Zinsser, Hans 1878-1940 WorScD
Zinsser, William Knowlton 1922- WhoAm 94
Zintel, Harold A. d1993 NewYTBS 93
Zinza, Nonyaniso DrAPF 93
Zinzendorf, Nikolaus Ludvig 1700-1760 EncNAR
Zinzendorf, Nikolaus Ludwig 1700-1760 DcAmReB 2
Zinzow, Lee Alan 1947- WhoFI 94
Ziock, Klaus Otto Heinrich 1925- WhoAm 94
Ziolkowska, Wieslswa WhoWomW 91
Ziolkowski, Heidi M. DrAPF 93
Ziolkowski, Korczak 1908-1982 WhoAmA 93N
Ziolkowski, Theodore 1932- WrDr 94
Ziolkowski, Theodore Joseph 1932- WhoAm 94
Ziomek, Jonathan S. 1947- WhoMW 93
Ziomek, Thomas John 1946- WhoAm 94
Zion, Lettie Backus 1910- WhAm 10
Zion, Madge Barbara 1942- WhoMW 93
Zion, Roger H. 1921- WhoAm 94, WhoAmP 93
Zion-Shelton, Olga-Jean 1957- WhoWest 94
Ziontz, Mel 1942- WhoAmL 94
Ziperski, James Richard 1932- WhoAm 94
Zipes, Douglas Peter 1939- WhoAm 94
Zipf, William Byron 1946- WhoMW 93, WhoScEn 94
Zipfinger, Frank Peter 1953- WhoAmL 94
Zipkin, Sheldon Lee 1951- WhoAmL 94
Zipp, Arden Peter 1938- WhoAm 94
Zipp, Joel Frederick 1948- WhoAm 94, WhoAmL 94
Zipp, Ronald Duane 1946- WhoAmL 94
Zipp, William WhoHol 92
Zippelius, Reinhold 1928- IntWW 93
Zipper, Herbert 1904- WhoAm 94
Zipper, Stuart Charles 1946- WhoWest 94
Zippin, Calvin 1926- WhoAm 94
Zippin, Lawrence M. 1942- WhoIns 94
Zipporah, Zena DrAPF 93
Zipprodt, Patricia WhoAm 94
Zipprodt-Zonka, Constance WhoMW 93
Zipser, Howard Alan 1940- WhoAmL 94
Zipser, Stanley 1923- WhoAmL 94
Zipursky, Morley 1925- WhoFI 94
Zirbes, Mary Kenneth 1926- WhoMW 93
Zirimu, Elvania Namukwaya 1938- BlmGWL
Zirin, Harold 1929- WhoAm 94, WhoScEn 94, WhoWest 94
Zirin, James David 1940- WhoAm 94
Zirin, Nola 1943- WhoAmA 93
Zirinsky, Bruce R. 1947- WhoAmL 94
Zirkel, Gene 1931- WhoAm 94
Zirker, Joseph 1924- WhoAmA 93
Zirkind, Ralph 1918- WhoAm 94, WhoScEn 94
Zirkle, Lewis Greer 1940- WhoAm 94, WhoWest 94
Zirlin, Larry DrAPF 93
Zirnkilton, Stephen Morgan 1958- WhoAmP 93
Ziroli, Angelo Gerardo 1899-1948 WhoAmA 93N
Zirpoli, Alfonso Joseph 1905- WhoAmL 94, WhoWest 94
Zirps, Fotena Anatolia 1958- WhoScEn 94
Zirra, Alexandru 1883-1946 NewGrDO
Zirschky, Stephen Lee 1949- WhoAmL 94
Zirvi, Karimullah Abd 1940- WhoScEn 94
Zis, Peter J. 1959- WhoAmP 93
Zisa, David Anthony 1959- WhoScEn 94
Zischke, Douglas Arthur 1929- WhoAm 94
Zischke, James Braden 1923- WhoWest 94
Zischke, Michael Herman 1954- WhoAmL 94, WhoWest 94
Zisk, Stanley Harris 1931- WhoWest 94
Ziskin, Harriet DrAPF 93
Ziskin, Jay Hersell 1920- WhoScEn 94
Ziskin, Laura IntMPA 94
Zisla, Harold 1925- WhoAmA 93
Zislis, Paul Martin 1948- WhoScEn 94, WhoWest 94
Zisman, Barry Stuart 1937- WhoAmL 94
Zissman, Lorin 1930- WhoFI 94
Zisson, James Stern 1952- WhoFI 94
Zistel, Era ConAu 41NR
Zisu, Mihai IntWW 93
Zitek, Vilem 1890-1956 NewGrDO
Zitney, Stephen Edward 1961- WhoMW 93
Zitnick, John Henry 1950- WhoMW 93
Zitny, Russell James 1956- WhoMW 93
Zito, Greg 1953- WhoAmP 93
Zito, James Anthony 1931- WhoAm 94
Zito, James Prosper 1948- WhoMW 93
Zito, John Francis 1963- WhoFI 94
Zito, Joseph 1949- IntMPA 94
Zito, Joseph (Phillip) 1957- WhoAmA 93
Zito, Michael Anthony 1957- WhoFI 94, WhoWest 94
Zitrin, Arthur 1918- WhoAm 94
Zitterkopf, Irvin Leroy 1933- WhoAm 94
Zitto, Richard Joseph 1945- WhoMW 93
Zittouni, Messaoud 1940- IntWW 93
Zitz, Jon Theodore 1914- WhoWest 94
Zitz, Kathinka 1801-1877 BlmGWL
Zitzer, Catherine Ann 1954- WhoWest 94
Zitzewitz, Paul William 1942- WhoMW 93
Zitzman, Jack Pearson 1937- WhoMW 93
Zitzmann, Frank Richard 1933- WhoFI 94
Zivancevic, Nina DrAPF 93
Ziv-Av, Itzhak 1907- IntWW 93
Zive, Gregg William 1945- WhoAmL 94
Zivic, William Thomas 1930- WhoAmA 93
Zivich, Norma Gase 1947- WhoMW 93
Zivin, Norman H. 1944- WhoAmL 94
Zivitz, Stephen Charles 1943- WhoAm 94, WhoAmL 94
Zivkovic, Zoran 1948- EncSF 93
Zivley, Walter Perry 1931- WhoAm 94, WhoAmL 94
Ziyadah, May 1886-1941 BlmGWL
Zi Yaohua 1900- WhoPRCh 91 [port]
Zi Zhongjun WhoPRCh 91
Zizik, David Walter 1954- WhoAmL 94
Zizmor, Judah d1993 NewYTBS 93 [port]
Zizza, Salvatore J. 1945- WhoFI 94
Zizza, Tony DrAPF 93
Zizzo, Alicia 1945- WhoAm 94
Zizzo, Joyce A. 1956- WhoAmL 94
Zlaket, Thomas WhoAmL 94, WhoWest 94
Zlaket, Thomas A. 1941- WhoAmP 93
Zlatic, Thomas David 1947- WhoMW 93
Zlatkis, Albert 1924- WhoAm 94, WhoScEn 94
Zlatoff-Mirsky, Everett Igor 1937- WhoAm 94, WhoMW 93
Zlatoper, Ronald Joseph 1942- WhoAm 94
Zleh, Noiram DrAPF 93
Zlenko, Anatolii Maksymovych 1938- LngBDD
Zlenko, Anatoly Maksimovich 1938- IntWW 93
Zlobin, Konstantin Sergeevich 1946- LngBDD
Zloch, William J. 1944- WhoAm 94, WhoAmL 94
Zlotnick, Norman Lee 1947- WhoAmL 94
Zlotnick, Peter Bruce 1963- WhoAmL 94
Zlotnik, Albert 1954- WhoScEn 94
Zlowe, Florence M. WhoAmA 93
Zlowe, Florence Markowitz WhoAm 94
Zmed, Adrian 1954- WhoHol 92
Zmeu, Bogdan 1956- WhoScEn 94
Zmuda, Sharon Louise 1942- WhoAm 94, WhoMW 93
Zmudzka, Barbara Zofia 1934- WhoScEn 94
Znamierowski, Donald J. 1934- WhoIns 94
Zobel, Donald Bruce 1942- WhoAm 94
Zobel, Enrique J. 1927- WhoIns 94
Zobel, Hiller Bellin 1932- WhoAm 94
Zobel, Louise Purwin 1922- WhoAm 94
Zobel, Richard WhoHol 92
Zobel, Robert Leonard 1935- WhoMW 93
Zobel, Rya W. 1931- WhoAm 94, WhoAmL 94
Zobel de Ayala, Jaime 1934- Who 94
ZoBell, Bonnie DrAPF 93
ZoBell, Karl 1932- WhoAm 94, WhoWest 94
Zoberi, Nadim Bin-Asad 1951- WhoFI 94, WhoMW 93, WhoScEn 94
Zobrist, Benedict Karl 1921- WhoAm 94, WhoMW 93
Zobrist, Duane Herman 1940- WhoAm 94, WhoAmL 94
Zobrist, George Winston 1934- WhoAm 94
Zobrist, Karl 1949- WhoAmL 94
Zocchi, Donald Anthony 1951- WhoWest 94
Zocchi, Louis Joseph 1935- WhoFI 94
Zochert, Donald (Paul, Jr.) 1938- WrDr 94
Zocholl, Stanley Ernest 1929- WhoAm 94
Zock, Richard 1934- WhoAm 94
Zodhiates, Spiros George 1922- WhoAm 94
Zodl, Joseph Arthur 1948- WhoFI 94, WhoWest 94
Zodrow, George Roy 1950- WhoAm 94
Zody, Artis Alvin 1917- WhoAmP 93
Zoeller, David Louis 1949- WhoAmL 94
Zoeller, Donald J. 1930- WhoAm 94
Zoeller, Fuzzy 1952- WhoAm 94
Zoeller, Jack Carl 1949- WhoAm 94
Zoellick, Robert Bruce 1953- WhoAm 94
Zoellner, Robert William 1956- WhoAm 94, WhoWest 94
Zoellner, Sandra Ann 1964- WhoFI 94
Zoerb, Karen S. 1949- WhoAmP 93
Zoff, Dino 1942- WorESoc [port]
Zoffer, David B. 1947- WhoIns 94
Zoffer, H. Jerome 1930- WhoAm 94, WhoFI 94
Zoffinger, George Richard 1948- WhoAmP 93
Zofnass, Paul Jesse 1947- WhoAm 94
Zogbaum, Wilfrid d1965 WhoAmA 93N
Zogg, Chris John 1929- WhoAmL 94
Zoghbi, Sami Spiridon 1948- WhoScEn 94
Zoghby, Guy Anthony 1934- WhoAmL 94
Zoghby, Linda 1949- NewGrDO
Zoghby, Mary S. WhoAmP 93
Zographou, Lili BlmGWL
Zoh, Young Jae 1949- WhoFI 94
Zohar, Israel 1945- IntWW 93
Zohn, Harry 1923- WhoAm 94, WrDr 94
Zohn, Martin Steven 1947- WhoAm 94, WhoAmL 94
Zohner, Steven K. 1953- WhoWest 94
Zohourian Mashmoul, Mohammad Jalal-od-din 1965- WhoScEn 94
Zoidis, Ann Margaret 1962- WhoScEn 94
Zois, Constantine Nicholas Athanasios 1938- WhoScEn 94
Zoitakis, George 1910- IntWW 93
Zokosky, Peter L. 1957- WhoAmA 93
Zola, Emile 1840-1902 IntDcT 2, NewGrDO
Zola, Emile (Edouard Charles Antoine) 1840-1902 EncSF 93
Zola, Emile Edouard Charles Antoine 1840-1902 BlmGEL
Zola, Jean-Pierre d1979 WhoHol 92
Zola, Michael S. 1942- WhoAmL 94
Zola, Nkenge 1954- WhoBlA 94
Zolberg, Aristide Rodolphe 1931- WhoAm 94
Zolch-Palmer, Elisabeth 1951- WhoWomW 91
Zoleveke, Gideon (Asatori Pitabose) 1922- Who 94
Zolezzi, Samuel Maurice 1949- WhoWest 94
Zoline, Pamela 1941- EncSF 93
Zolkower, Daniel 1933- WhoIns 94
Zoll, Clifford Alexander 1905- WhoMW 93
Zoll, Paul Maurice 1911- WhoAm 94
Zollar, Carolyn Catherine 1947- WhoAmL 94
Zollar, Doris L. 1932- WhoBlA 94
Zollar, Jawole Willa Jo 1951?- ConTFT 11
Zollar, Nikki Michele 1956- WhoBlA 94
Zoller, James A. DrAPF 93
Zoller, Michael 1947- WhoScEn 94
Zoller, Richard Bernard 1929- WhoAm 94
Zollinger, Heinrich Fritz 1919- IntWW 93
Zollinger, Norman 1921- WrDr 94
Zollinger, Thomas Tennant WhoAmP 93
Zollner, Heinrich 1854-1941 NewGrDO
Zollo, Peter F. 1954- WhoMW 93
Zollweg, Aileen Boules WhoAmA 93
Zolno, Mark S. WhoAm 94
Zolo, Danilo 1936- ConAu 141
Zolotas, Xenophon 1904- IntWW 93
Zolotov, Yurii Alexander 1932- WhoScEn 94
Zolotow, Charlotte 1915- WrDr 94
Zolotow, Charlotte Shapiro 1915- WhoAm 94
Zolotow, Maurice 1913- WrDr 94
Zolotow, Maurice 1913-1991 WhAm 10
Zolotow, Sam d1993 NewYTBS 93 [port]
Zoltan, Imre 1909- IntWW 93
Zoltick, Brad J. 1957- WhoScEn 94
Zoltok-Seltzer, Harriet DrAPF 93
Zolynas, Al DrAPF 93
Zomick, David Alan 1941- WhoAm 94
Zommick, Lawrence Raymond 1950- WhoFI 94
Zomorrodian, Asghar 1941- WhoFI 94
Zona, Louis A. 1944- WhoAmA 93
Zona, Louis Albert 1944- WhoMW 93
Zonca, Giovanni Battista 1728-1809 NewGrDO
Zonca, Giuseppe 1715-1772 NewGrDO
Zondervan, Peter John d1993 NewYTBS 93
Zong Bo WhoPRCh 91
Zong Huaide, Joseph 1917- WhoPRCh 91 [port]
Zongolowicz, Helen Michaeline 1936- WhoWest 94
Zong Pu 1928- BlmGWL, IntWW 93, WhoPRCh 91 [port]
Zong Shunliu 1941- WhoPRCh 91 [port]
Zonia, Carolynn L. 1956- WhoMW 93
Zonia, Dhimitri 1921- WhoAmA 93
Zonis, Marvin 1936- WhoAm 94
Zontal, Jorge WhoAmA 93
Zoogman, Nicholas Jay 1947- WhoAm 94, WhoAmL 94
Zook, Bill 1946- WhoAmL 94
Zook, Dianna Lee 1955- WhoMW 93
Zook, Donovan Quay 1918- WhoAm 94
Zook, Elvin Glenn 1937- WhoAm 94
Zook, Ethel M. 1923- WhoAmP 93
Zook, Martha Frances Harris 1921- WhoMW 93, WhoScEn 94
Zook, Merlin Wayne 1937- WhoScEn 94
Zook, Ronald Z. WhoWest 94
Zook, Tom 1932- WhoAmP 93
Zook, Tracy Lynn 1969- WhoWest 94
Zook, Wayne Bowman 1927- WhoWest 94
Zool, M.H. EncSF 93
Zoole, Mark Hanson 1963- WhoFI 94
Zoom, Billy c. 1949- See X ConMus 11
Zoon, Kathryn Egloff 1948- WhoAm 94, WhoScEn 94
Zoon, William K. 1943- WhoFI 94
Zopf, Paul Edward 1931- WhoAm 94
Zopff, Hermann 1826-1883 NewGrDO
Zopp, Andrea Lynne 1957- WhoAmL 94
Zoppelli, Lia d1988 WhoHol 92
Zorach, Marguerite T. 1887-1968 WhoAmA 93N
Zorach, William 1887-1966 WhoAmA 93N
Zoraqi, Nikolla 1929-1991 NewGrDO
Zord, Joseph V., Jr. 1910- WhoAmP 93
Zordell, Jack Warren 1925- WhoFI 94
Zore, Edward John 1945- WhoAm 94
Zorek, Michael WhoHol 92
Zoretich, George Stephen 1918- WhoAmA 93
Zorich, Louis WhoHol 92
Zorie, Stephanie Marie 1951- WhoAmL 94
Zorig, Sanjaasurengiin 1962- IntWW 93
Zorin, Dementy Alexeyevich c. 1755-1777 NewGrDO
Zorin, Valerian A. 1902-1986 HisDcKW
Zorina, Vera 1917- IntDcB [port], WhoHol 92
Zorio, John William 1946- WhoAm 94
Zor'kin, Valery Dmitrievich 1943- IntWW 93, LngBDD
Zorko, Mark A. 1952- WhoFI 94
Zorlutuna, Halide Nusret 1901- BlmGWL
Zorn, Eric 1958- WrDr 94
Zorn, Eric J. 1958- WhoAm 94
Zorn, Eric Stuart 1948- WhoFI 94
Zorn, Max August d1993 NewYTBS 93
Zorn, Robert Lynn 1938- WhoMW 93
Zornes, Milford 1908- WhoAm 94, WhoWest 94
Zornow, David M. 1955- WhoAmL 94
Zornow, William Frank 1920- WhoAm 94, WhoFI 94, WhoMW 93, WrDr 94
Zoroaster 6th cent.BC- BlmGEL
Zoroaster c. 588BC-c. 511BC HisWorL [port]
Zorowski, Carl Frank 1930- WhoAm 94, WhoScEn 94
Zorrilla, Carlos Hugo 1940- WhoHisp 94
Zorrilla, China 1922- IntWW 93
Zorrilla, Monica Salinas 1942- WhoHisp 94
Zorthian, Barry 1920- WhoAm 94
Zorz, Raymond Barry 1955- WhoWest 94
Zorzisto, Luigi NewGrDO
Zoser HisWorL
Zoshchenko, Mikhail (Mikhailovich) 1895-1958 RfGShF
Zoss, Abraham Oscar 1917- WhoFI 94
Zoss, Dean L. 1939- WhoIns 94
Zoss, Joel 1944- ConAu 142
Zotin, Vladislav Maksimovich 1942- LngBDD
Zottmayr, Georg 1869-1941 NewGrDO
Zottmayr, Ludwig 1828-1899 NewGrDO
Zou, Yun 1962- WhoScEn 94
Zoub, Burton Irving 1926- WhoAmL 94
Zoubareff, Olga Vladimir WhoMW 93

Zweifel, Richard George 1926-
  WhoAm 94
Zweifel, Terry L. 1942- WhoScEn 94
Zweig, David 1950- ConAu 140
Zweig, Ellen DrAPF 93
Zweig, George WorScD
Zweig, George 1937- WhoAm 94
Zweig, Howard Paul 1954- WhoAmL 94
Zweig, Michael P. 1952- WhoAm 94
Zweig, Michael Philip 1952- WhoAmL 94
Zweig, Stefan 1881-1942 NewGrDO
Zweigert, Konrad Erdmann 1911-
  IntWW 93
Zweiman, Burton 1931- WhoAm 94,
  WhoScEn 94
Zweizig, John Roderick 1923-
  WhoScEn 94
Zwerdling, Alex 1932- WhoAm 94
Zwerenz, Gerhard 1925- IntWW 93
Zwerenz, Mizzi 1876-1947 NewGrDO
Zwerling, Darrell WhoHol 92
Zwerling, Gary Leslie 1949- WhoAm 94
Zwerling, Israel d1993 NewYTBS 93
Zwerling, Yetta d1982 WhoHol 92
Zwerneman, Farrel Jon 1954-
  WhoScEn 94
Zwi, Rose 1928- BlmGWL
Zwick, Barry Stanley 1942- WhoWest 94
Zwick, Charles John 1926- IntWW 93
Zwick, Christian Robert 1961-
  WhoMW 93
Zwick, Edward 1952- IntMPA 94
Zwick, Jill 1944- WhoAmP 93
Zwick, Joel 1942- IntMPA 94
Zwick, Keith Roger 1943- WhoWest 94
Zwick, Leander Peter, Jr. 1921- WhAm 10
Zwick, Peter Ronald 1942- WhoWest 94
Zwick, Rosemary G. 1925- WhoAmA 93
Zwick, Shelly Crittendon 1941-
  WhoAmL 94
Zwick, Thomas Theodore 1937-
  WhoAm 94
Zwicke, Dianne Lynn 1952- WhoMW 93
Zwicker, Ralph Wise 1903-1991
  WhAm 10
Zwickey, Wayne Roger 1929- WhoMW 93
Zwicknagl, Gertrud WhoScEn 94
Zwicky, Fay 1933- BlmGWL
Zwicky, Fritz 1898-1974 WorScD
Zwiener, James Milton 1942-
  WhoScEn 94
Zwiep, Donald Nelson 1924- WhoAm 94
Zwietnig-Rotterdam, Paul WhoAmA 93
Zwigard, Bruce Albert 1948- WhoFI 94
Zwikiewicz, Wiktor EncSF 93
Zwilgmeyer, Alexander Guillermo 1945-
  WhoMW 93
Zwilich, Ellen Taaffe 1939- WhoAm 94
Zwinge, Randall James Hamilton 1928-
  WhoAm 94
Zwinger, Ann Haymond 1925- WrDr 94
Zwingle, James L. 1906-1990 WhAm 10
Zwingli, Huldrych 1484-1531
  HisWorL [port]
Zwipp, George Kazmer 1925- WhAm 10
Zwiren, Jan Marie 1944- WhoAm 94
Zwirn, Robert 1948- WhoAm 94
Zwisler, Robert John, III 1956-
  WhoMW 93
Zwislocki, Jozef John 1922- WhoAm 94
Zworykin, Vladimir Kosma 1889-1982
  WorInv
Zwoyer, Eugene Milton 1926- WhoAm 94,
  WhoScEn 94, WhoWest 94
Zych, Marilyn 1949- WhoFI 94
Zychick, Joel David 1954- WhoAmL 94
Zychowicz, Ralph Charles 1948-
  WhoAmL 94
Zygas, Kestutis Paul 1942- WhoWest 94
Zygelman, Bernard 1952- WhoWest 94
Zygmund, Antoni d1992 IntWW 93N
Zygmund, Antoni 1900-1992 WhAm 10
Zygmunt, Zielinski 1939- WhoScEn 94
Zygmunt Augustus, II 1520-1572
  HisWorL [port]
Zygulski, Kazimierz 1919- IntWW 93
Zykina, Lyudmila Georgiyevna 1929-
  IntWW 93
Zylberberg, Abraham Lieb 1947-
  WhoAm 94, WhoAmL 94
Zylinski, Faustyn 1796-1867 NewGrDO
Zylis-Gara, Teresa 1935- IntWW 93,
  NewGrDO
Zylis-Gara, Teresa Gerarda 1935-
  WhoAm 94
Zylka, Thaddeus Casimer, II 1958-
  WhoAmP 93
Zylstra, Stanley James 1943- WhoAm 94,
  WhoFI 94
Zylstra, Steven Glenn 1954- WhoWest 94
Zynsky, Toots 1951- WhoAmA 93
Zypman-Niechonski, Fredy Ruben 1960-
  WhoScEn 94
Zyroff, Ellen Slotoroff 1946- WhoScEn 94,
  WhoWest 94
Zysman, Andrew S. d1993 NewYTBS 93
Zytkow, Jan Mikolaj 1944- WhoAm 94

Zyuganov, Gennady Andreevich 1944-
  LngBDD
Zywicki, Robert Albert 1930- WhoAm 94
Zyznewsky, Wladimir A. 1948-
  WhoScEn 94

BGMI 95

ISBN 0-8103-8599-6
90000

9 780810 385993